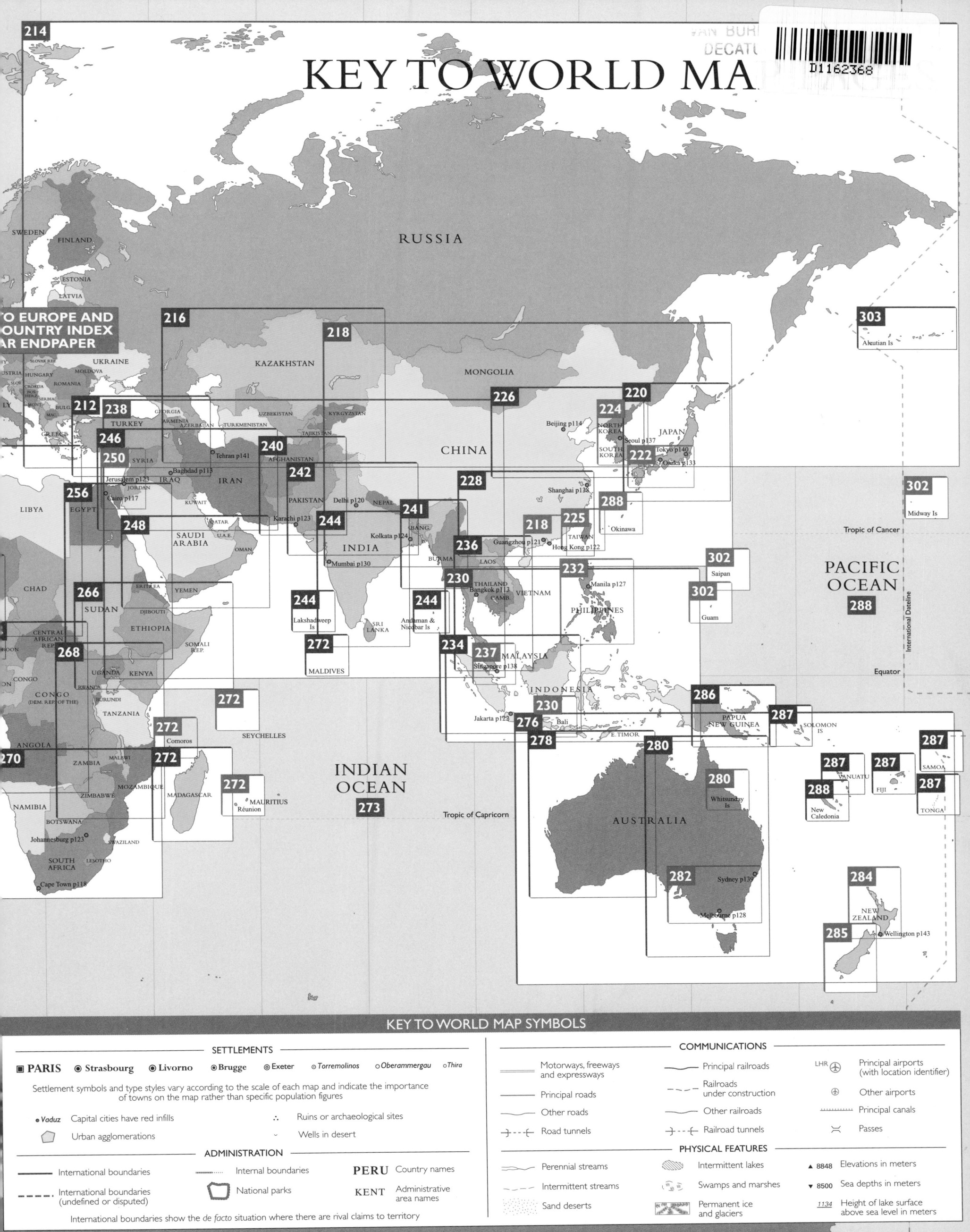

KEY TO WORLD MA...

KEY TO WORLD MAP SYMBOLS

SETTLEMENTS

■ **PARIS** ◉ **Strasbourg** ◉ **Livorno** ● **Brugge** ⊙ **Exeter** ○ *Torremolinos* ○ *Oberammergau* ○ *Thira*

Settlement symbols and type styles vary according to the scale of each map and indicate the importance of towns on the map rather than specific population figures

• *Vaduz* Capital cities have red infills
⬠ Urban agglomerations

∴ Ruins or archaeological sites
✧ Wells in desert

ADMINISTRATION

International boundaries
International boundaries (undefined or disputed)

Internal boundaries
National parks

PERU Country names
KENT Administrative area names

International boundaries show the *de facto* situation where there are rival claims to territory

COMMUNICATIONS

Motorways, freeways and expressways
Principal roads
Other roads
Road tunnels

Principal railroads
Railroads under construction
Other railroads
Railroad tunnels

LHR ⊕ Principal airports (with location identifier)
⊕ Other airports
Principal canals
⋈ Passes

PHYSICAL FEATURES

Perennial streams
Intermittent streams
Sand deserts

Intermittent lakes
Swamps and marshes
Permanent ice and glaciers

▲ 8848 Elevations in meters
▼ 8500 Sea depths in meters
1134 Height of lake surface above sea level in meters

OXFORD
ATLAS
OF THE
WORLD

FIFTEENTH EDITION

THE EDITORS would like to thank **Richard Chiles** and the staff at **NPA Group**, Edenbridge, Kent, UK (www.satmaps.com) for their invaluable assistance in sourcing and processing the satellite imagery that appears in the atlas.

GAZETTEER OF NATIONS
TEXT Keith Lye

PHOTOGRAPHIC ACKNOWLEDGEMENTS
Corbis /*William Caram* 103, /*Nigel J. Dennis/Gallo Images* 84, /*Jay Dickman* 109 (bottom left), /*Yang Liu* 89, /*Gideon Mendel* 94 (left), /*Royalty-Free* 94 (right), 97, /*Liba Taylor* 104, /*David Turnley* 109 (bottom right)
© Crown copyright 2007. Published by the Met Office, UK 80
Galaxy /*Robin Scagell* 69
www.istockphoto.com 101
Javier Méndez (ING)/Nik Szymanek (Univ. Herts) 64
NASA/GSFC 73, 81 (top and bottom), 98, /*Jacques Descloitres, MODIS Rapid Response Team* 79
NPA Group 10–27, 28–29, 62–63, 75, 82, 110–111, 144–145, 156–157, 208–209, 252–253, 274–275, 290–291, 324–325 /*Image provided by the USGS EROS Data Center Satellite Systems Branch* 85

STAR CHARTS (PAGE 65)
Wil Tirion

CARTOGRAPHY BY PHILIP'S

WORLD CITIES
PAGE 120, DUBLIN: The town plan of Dublin is based on Ordnance Survey Ireland by permission of the Government Permit Number 8408. © Ordnance Survey Ireland and Government of Ireland.

PAGE 121, EDINBURGH, and PAGE 125, LONDON:
This product includes mapping data licensed from Ordnance Survey® with the permission of the Controller of Her Majesty's Stationery Office. © Crown copyright 2008. All rights reserved. Licence number 100011710.

VECTOR DATA: Courtesy of Gräfe and Unser Verlag GmbH, München, Germany (city-center maps of Bangkok, Beijing, Cape Town, Jerusalem, Mexico City, Moscow, Singapore, Sydney, Tokyo, and Washington).

The following city maps utilize base data supplied courtesy of MapQuest.com, Inc. (© MapQuest): Las Vegas, New Orleans, Orlando

FOREWORD

AN AUTHORITATIVE AND SERIOUS REFERENCE WORK, the Oxford *Atlas of the World* is one of the finest atlases available anywhere in the world. The atlas incorporates computer-derived maps which have been produced using the very latest in digital cartographic techniques.

The Oxford *Atlas of the World* has been devised with the help of a panel of specialist geography consultants from the United Kingdom and the United States, whose specialties range from the history of cartography, urban and social geography, epidemiology, and the European Union to biogeography and applied geomorphology. The result of their valuable input can be seen in the wealth of maps and data contained in the "*World Geography*" section of this atlas.

Country names are shown in conventional English form and are those that are in common usage. They are the forms used by publications such as *Newsweek* and *The Washington Post,* and by the BBC and the British Foreign Office. Alternative country names appear in parentheses on the maps where space permits – for example, Burma (Myanmar) – and are cross-referenced in the index, for example, Côte d'Ivoire = Ivory Coast.

HOW TO USE THE ATLAS
The atlas is divided into a number of sections which are explained below.

WORLD STATISTICS AND IMAGES OF EARTH
World statistics on topics such as area and population for every country in the world, and physical dimensions – including the largest islands, lakes and seas, the highest mountains and the longest rivers, by continent. Also included in this section is a listing of the world's largest cities by population, arranged in country alphabetical order. This section is followed by a beautifully illustrated satellite section showing 16 of the world's major regions and cities in the Americas, Europe, Africa, Asia, and Australasia.

GAZETTEER OF NATIONS
A comprehensive A–Z reference providing concise profiles of every country's geography, climate, history, politics, and economy, together with ready-reference tables, and illustrated with flags and locator maps.

WORLD GEOGRAPHY
A richly informative section comprising 48 pages of maps, charts, graphs, and diagrams that explain key themes about the world in which we live. The topics covered include the Solar System, oceans, climate, the natural world, energy, and trade. Explanatory text on each spread describes the patterns shown by the data.

CITY MAPS
A detailed selection of maps for 69 urban areas around the world. These are useful for planning trips abroad as well as for comparative studies of cities worldwide.

WORLD MAPS
An outstanding collection of 179 pages of distinctive Philip's cartography. The highly acclaimed physical world maps combine relief shading with layer-colored contours to give a striking visual picture of the Earth's surface. Roads, railroads, canals, and airports are accurately depicted on the maps, and towns and cities are clearly marked. More information on the key features employed in the construction and presentation of the maps is given on the facing page.

GEOGRAPHICAL GLOSSARY AND INDEX
The 84,000-name index to the world maps includes geographical features as well as towns and cities, with both latitude/longitude and letter/figure grid references. Preceding the index is a list of geographical terms from various foreign languages that may be found in the place names on the maps and also in the index, together with their meanings.

SPECIALIST GEOGRAPHY CONSULTANTS

THE EDITORS are grateful to the following for acting as specialist geography consultants on the '*World Geography*' front section:
Professor D. Brunsden Kings College, University of London, UK
Dr C. Clarke Oxford University, UK
Professor P. Haggett University of Bristol, UK
Professor M-L. Hsu University of Minnesota, Minnesota, USA
Professor K. McLachlan School of Oriental and African Studies, University of London, UK
Professor M. Monmonier Syracuse University, New York, USA

Professor M. J. Tooley University of St Andrews, UK
Dr T. Unwin Royal Holloway, University of London, UK

THE EDITORS would also like to thank
Dr Dibyesh Anand
John Burden
Peter Grego
Keith Lye
Garrett Nagle
Ross Reynolds
Robin Scagell
John Woodruff

USER GUIDE

The reference maps which form the main body of this atlas have been prepared in accordance with the highest standards of international cartography to provide an accurate and detailed representation of the Earth. The scales and projections used have been carefully chosen to give balanced coverage of the world, while emphasizing the most densely populated and economically significant regions. A hallmark of Philip's mapping is the use of hill shading and relief coloring to create a graphic impression of landforms: this makes the maps exceptionally easy to read. However, knowledge of the key features employed in the construction and presentation of the maps will enable the reader to derive the fullest benefit from the atlas.

MAP SEQUENCE

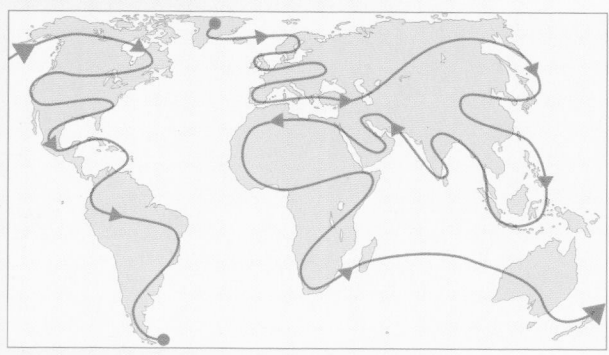

The atlas covers the Earth continent by continent: first Europe; then its land neighbor Asia (mapped north before south, in a clockwise sequence), then Africa, Australia and Oceania, North America, and South America. This is the classic arrangement adopted by most cartographers since the 16th century. For each continent, there are maps at a variety of scales. First, physical relief and political maps of the whole continent; then a series of larger-scale maps of the regions within the continent, each followed, where required, by still larger-scale maps of the most important or densely populated areas. The governing principle is that by turning the pages of the atlas, the reader moves steadily from north to south through each continent, with each map overlapping its neighbors.

MAP PRESENTATION

With very few exceptions (for example, for the Arctic and Antarctic), the maps are drawn with north at the top, regardless of whether they are presented upright or sideways on the page. In the borders will be found the map title; a locator diagram showing the area covered; continuation arrows showing the page numbers for maps of adjacent areas; the scale; the projection used; the degrees of latitude and longitude; and the letters and figures used in the index for locating place names and geographical features. Physical relief maps also have a height reference panel identifying the colors used for each layer of contouring.

MAP SYMBOLS

Each map contains a vast amount of detail which can only be conveyed clearly and accurately by the use of symbols. Points and circles of varying sizes locate and identify the relative importance of towns and cities; different styles of type are employed for administrative, geographical and regional place names to aid identification. A variety of pictorial symbols denote landforms such as glaciers, marshes and coral reefs, and man-made structures including roads, railroads, airports, and canals. International borders are shown by red lines. Where neighboring countries are in dispute, for example in parts of the Middle East, the maps show the *de facto* boundary between nations, regardless of the legal or historical situation.

The symbols are explained on the front endpapers of the atlas.

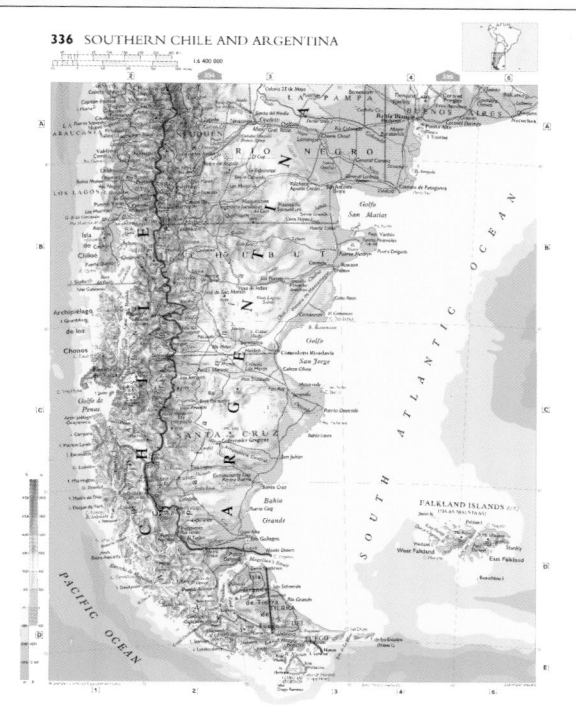

MAP SCALES

1:16 000 000
1 inch = 252 statute miles

The scale of each map is given in the numerical form known as the "representative fraction." The first figure is always one, signifying one unit of distance on the map; the second figure, usually in millions, is the number by which the map unit must be multiplied to give the equivalent distance on the Earth's surface. Calculations can easily be made in centimeters and kilometers, by dividing the Earth units figure by 100 000 (i.e. deleting the last five 0s). Thus 1:1 000 000 means 1 cm = 10 km. The calculation for inches and miles is more laborious, but 1 000 000 divided by 63 360 (the number of inches in a mile) shows that 1:1 000 000 means approximately 1 inch = 16 miles. The table below provides distance equivalents for scales down to 1:50 000 000.

LARGE SCALE		
1:1 000 000	1 cm = 10 km	1 inch = 16 miles
1:2 500 000	1 cm = 25 km	1 inch = 39.5 miles
1:5 000 000	1 cm = 50 km	1 inch = 79 miles
1:6 000 000	1 cm = 60 km	1 inch = 95 miles
1:8 000 000	1 cm = 80 km	1 inch = 126 miles
1:10 000 000	1 cm = 100 km	1 inch = 158 miles
1:15 000 000	1 cm = 150 km	1 inch = 237 miles
1:20 000 000	1 cm = 200 km	1 inch = 316 miles
1:50 000 000	1 cm = 500 km	1 inch = 790 miles
SMALL SCALE		

MEASURING DISTANCES

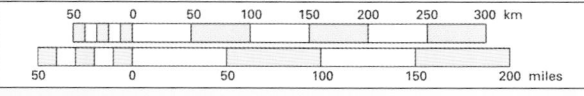

Although each map is accompanied by a scale bar, distances cannot always be measured with confidence because of the distortions involved in portraying the curved surface of the Earth on a flat page. As a general rule, the larger the map scale, the more accurate and reliable will be the distance measured. On small-scale maps such as those of the world and of entire continents, measurement may only be accurate along the "standard parallels," or central axes, and should not be attempted without considering the map projection.

MAP PROJECTIONS

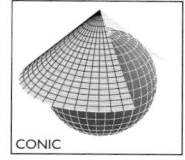 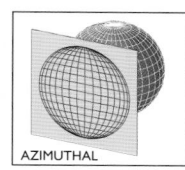 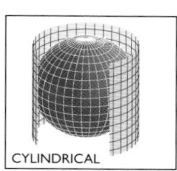

Unlike a globe, no flat map can give a true scale representation of the world in terms of area, shape, and position of every region. Each of the numerous systems that have been devised for projecting the curved surface of the Earth on to a flat page involves the sacrifice of accuracy in one or more of these elements. The variations in shape and position of land masses such as Alaska, Greenland and Australia, for example, can be quite dramatic when different projections are compared.

For this atlas, the guiding principle has been to select projections that involve the least distortion of size and distance. The projection used for each map is noted in the border. Most fall into one of three categories – conic, azimuthal, or cylindrical – whose basic concepts are shown above. Each involves plotting the forms of the Earth's surface on a grid of latitude and longitude lines, which may be shown as parallels, curves, or radiating spokes.

LATITUDE AND LONGITUDE

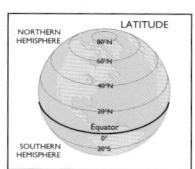 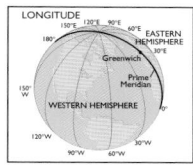 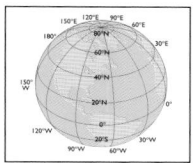

Accurate positioning of individual points on the Earth's surface is made possible by reference to the geometrical system of latitude and longitude. Latitude *parallels* are drawn west–east around the Earth and numbered by degrees north and south of the Equator, which is designated 0° of latitude. Longitude *meridians* are drawn north–south and numbered by degrees east and west of the *prime meridian*, 0° of longitude, which passes through Greenwich in England. By referring to these coordinates and their subdivisions of minutes (1/60th of a degree) and seconds (1/60th of a minute), any place on Earth can be located to within a few hundred meters. Latitude and longitude are indicated by blue lines on the maps; they are straight or curved according to the projection employed. Reference to these lines is the easiest way of determining the relative positions of places on different maps, and for plotting compass directions.

NAME FORMS

For ease of reference, both English and local name forms appear in the atlas. Oceans, seas, and countries are shown in English throughout the atlas; country names may be abbreviated to their commonly accepted form (for example, Germany, not The Federal Republic of Germany). Conventional English forms are also used for place names on the smaller-scale maps of the continents. However, local name forms are used on all large-scale and regional maps, with the English form given in brackets only for important cities – the large-scale map of Russia and Northern Asia thus shows Moskva (Moscow). For countries which do not use a Roman script, place names have been transcribed according to the systems adopted by the British and US Geographic Names Authorities. For China, the Pin Yin system has been used, with some more widely known forms appearing in brackets, as with Beijing (Peking). Both English and local names appear in the index, the English form being cross-referenced to the local form.

CONTENTS

WORLD STATISTICS

COUNTRIES 6
CITIES 7
PHYSICAL DIMENSIONS 8
CLIMATE 9

IMAGES OF EARTH

LONDON, UK 12
VENICE, ITLAY 13
DANUBE DELTA, ROMANIA 14
SHANGHAI, CHINA 15
GLACIERS, BHUTAN 16
UPPER BRAHMAPUTRA, INDIA 17
CAIRO, EGYPT 18
CAPE PENINSULA, SOUTH AFRICA 19
NGORONGORO CRATER, TANZANIA 20
SYDNEY, AUSTRALIA 21
MOUNT TARANAKI, NZ 22
VANCOUVER, CANADA 23
NEW YORK, USA 24
NEW ORLEANS, USA 25
MANAUS, BRAZIL 26
SANTIAGO, CHILE 27

GAZETTEER OF NATIONS

AN A–Z GAZETTEER OF COUNTRIES 30–61

WORLD GEOGRAPHY

THE UNIVERSE 64–65
THE SOLAR SYSTEM 66–67
SEASONS, TIME AND MOTION 68–69
GEOLOGY OF THE EARTH 70–71
LANDFORMS 72–73
OCEANS 74–75
THE ATMOSPHERE 76–77
CLIMATE 78–79
CLIMATE CHANGE AND GLOBAL WARMING 80–81
WATER AND VEGETATION 82–83
BIODIVERSITY AND THE NATURAL WORLD 84–85
POPULATION 86–87
CITIES 88–89
THE HUMAN FAMILY 90–91
CONFLICT AND COOPERATION 92–93
FOOD PRODUCTION 94–95
ENERGY 96–97
MINERALS 98–99
EMPLOYMENT AND INDUSTRY 100–101
TRADE 102–103
HEALTH 104–105
WEALTH 106–107
STANDARDS OF LIVING 108–109

WORLD CITIES

AMSTERDAM 112
ATHENS 112
ATLANTA 113
BAGHDAD 113
BANGKOK 113
BARCELONA 114
BEIJING 114
BERLIN 115
BOSTON 116
BRUSSELS 116
BUDAPEST 117
BUENOS AIRES 117
CAIRO 117
CAPE TOWN 118
COPENHAGEN 118
CHICAGO 119
DELHI 120
DUBLIN 120
EDINBURGH 121
GUANGZHOU (CANTON) 121
HELSINKI 121
HONG KONG 122
ISTANBUL 122
JAKARTA 122
JERUSALEM 123
JOHANNESBURG 123
KARACHI 123
KOLKATA (CALCUTTA) 124
LAGOS 124
LAS VEGAS 124
LIMA 124
LONDON 125
LISBON 126
LOS ANGELES 126
MADRID 127
MANILA 127
MELBOURNE 128
MEXICO CITY 128
MIAMI 128
MILAN 129
MOSCOW 129
MONTREAL 130
MUMBAI (BOMBAY) 130
MUNICH 131
NEW ORLEANS 131
NEW YORK 132
ORLANDO 133
OSAKA 133
OSLO 133
PARIS 134
PRAGUE 135
RIO DE JANEIRO 135
ROME 136
SAN FRANCISCO 136
ST PETERSBURG 137
SANTIAGO 137
SÃO PAULO 137
SEOUL 137
SHANGHAI 138
SINGAPORE 138
STOCKHOLM 139
SYDNEY 139
TOKYO 140
TEHRAN 141
TORONTO 141
VIENNA 142
WARSAW 142
WASHINGTON 143
WELLINGTON 143

WORLD MAPS

THE WORLD

MAP SYMBOLS FRONT ENDPAPER
THE WORLD: PHYSICAL 146–147
1:76 000 000
THE WORLD: POLITICAL 148–149
1:76 000 000
ARCTIC OCEAN 150
1:28 000 000
ANTARCTICA 151
1:28 000 000
ATLANTIC OCEAN 152
1:41 000 000
ISLANDS OF THE ATLANTIC 153
BERMUDA 1:400 000
NEW PROVIDENCE ISLAND 1:400 000
MADEIRA 1:800 000
AZORES 1:1 600 000
CANARY ISLANDS 1:1 600 000
FALKLAND ISLANDS 1:6 400 000
ASCENSION ISLAND 1:400 000
ST HELENA 1:400 000
CAPE VERDE ISLANDS 1:8 000 000
GREENLAND 154
1:10 000 000
ICELAND 155
1:2 000 000

EUROPE

EUROPE: PHYSICAL 158
1:16 000 000
EUROPE: POLITICAL 159
1:16 000 000
SCANDINAVIA 160–161
1:4 800 000
ICELAND 1:4 800 000
FÆROE ISLANDS 1:4 800 000
DENMARK AND SOUTHERN SWEDEN 162–163
1:2 000 000
SOUTHERN NORWAY 164
1:2 000 000
BRITISH ISLES 165
1:4 000 000
IRELAND 166
1:1 600 000
SCOTLAND 167
1:1 600 000
ENGLAND AND WALES 168–169
1:1 600 000
NETHERLANDS, BELGIUM AND LUXEMBOURG 170
1:2 000 000
FRANCE 171
1:4 000 000

NORTHERN FRANCE 172–173
1:2 000 000
SOUTHERN FRANCE 174–175
1:2 000 000
CENTRAL EUROPE 176–177
1:4 000 000
GERMANY AND SWITZERLAND 178–179
1:2 000 000
AUSTRIA, CZECH REPUBLIC AND SLOVAK REPUBLIC 180–181
1:2 000 000
HUNGARY, ROMANIA AND THE LOWER DANUBE 182–183
1:2 000 000
POLAND AND THE SOUTHERN BALTIC 184–185
1:2 000 000
EASTERN EUROPE 186–187
1:8 000 000
BALTIC STATES, BELARUS AND UKRAINE 188–189
1:4 000 000
THE VOLGA BASIN AND THE CAUCASUS 190–191
1:4 000 000
SOUTHERN EUROPE 192–193
1:8 000 000
WESTERN SPAIN AND PORTUGAL 194–195
1:2 000 000
EASTERN SPAIN 196–197
1:2 000 000
NORTHERN ITALY, SLOVENIA AND CROATIA 198–199
1:2 000 000
SOUTHERN ITALY 200–201
1:2 000 000
THE BALKANS 202–203
1:2 000 000
SOUTHERN GREECE AND WESTERN TURKEY 204–205
1:2 000 000
MEDITERRANEAN ISLANDS 206–207
IBIZA, MAJORCA, MINORCA 1:800 000
MALTA 1:400 000
CORFU 1:800 000
RHODES 1:800 000
LEVKAS, ZANTE, CEPHALONIA 1:800 000
CRETE 1:1 000 000
CYPRUS 1:1 000 000

ASIA

ASIA: PHYSICAL 210
1:40 000 000
ASIA: POLITICAL 211
1:40 000 000
TURKEY AND TRANSCAUCASIA 212–213
1:4 000 000

CONTENTS

RUSSIA AND
NORTHERN ASIA 214–215
1:16 000 000

KAZAKHSTAN
AND CENTRAL ASIA 216–127
1:8 000 000

CHINA
AND THE FAR EAST 218–219
1:12 000 000
HONG KONG AND MACAU 1:800 000

JAPAN 220–221
1:4 000 000
RYUKYU ISLANDS 1:4 000 000

SOUTHERN JAPAN 222–223
1:2 000 000

KOREA 224
1:3 100 000

TAIWAN 225
1:1 400 000

NORTHERN CHINA
AND KOREA 226–227
1:4 800 000

SOUTHERN CHINA 228–229
1:4 800 000

SOUTHEAST ASIA 230–231
1:10 000 000
JAVA AND MADURA 1:6 000 000
BALI 1:1 600 000

PHILIPPINES 232–233
1:3 200 000

WESTERN INDONESIA 234–235
1:5 600 000

MAINLAND
SOUTHEAST ASIA 236–237
1:4 800 000
KO PHUKET 1:800 000
KO SAMUI 1:800 000
PINANG 1:800 000
SINGAPORE 1:800 000

SOUTHERN ASIA AND
THE MIDDLE EAST 238–239
1:14 000 000

AFGHANISTAN
AND PAKISTAN 240
1:5 600 000

BANGLADESH,
NORTHEASTERN INDIA
AND BURMA 241
1:4 800 000

NORTHERN INDIA,
PAKISTAN AND
NEPAL 242–243
1:4 800 000

SOUTHERN INDIA AND
SRI LANKA 244–245
1:4 800 000
LAKSHADWEEP ISLANDS 1:4 800 000
ANDAMAN AND
NICOBAR ISLANDS 1:4 800 000

THE MIDDLE EAST 246–247
1:5 600 000

SOUTHERN ARABIAN
PENINSULA 248–249
1:5 600 000

EASTERN
MEDITERRANEAN 250–251
1:2 000 000

AFRICA

AFRICA: PHYSICAL 254
1:33 600 000

AFRICA: POLITICAL 255
1:33 600 000

THE NILE VALLEY 256–257
1:6 400 000
THE NILE DELTA 1:3 200 000

CENTRAL NORTH
AFRICA 258–259
1:6 400 000

NORTHWEST AFRICA 260–261
1:6 400 000

WEST AFRICA 262–263
1:6 400 000

CENTRAL AFRICA 264–265
1:6 400 000
SÃO TOMÉ AND PRÍNCIPE 1:6 400 000

ETHIOPIA AND THE
HORN OF AFRICA 266–267
1:6 400 000

EAST AFRICA 268–269
1:6 400 000

SOUTHERN AFRICA 270–271
1:6 400 000

MADAGASCAR 272
1:6 400 000
COMOROS 1:2 000 000
MAYOTTE 1:800 000
SEYCHELLES 1:2 000 000
RÉUNION 1:800 000
MAURITIUS 1:800 000
MALDIVES 1:6 400 000

INDIAN OCEAN 273
1:40 000 000

AUSTRALIA
AND OCEANIA

AUSTRALIA AND OCEANIA:
PHYSICAL
AND POLITICAL 276–277
1:16 000 000

WESTERN AUSTRALIA 278–279
1:6 400 000

EASTERN AUSTRALIA 280–281
1:6 400 000
WHITSUNDAY GROUP 1:2 000 000
TASMANIA 1:6 400 000
TORRES STRAIT 1:6 400 000

SOUTHEAST
AUSTRALIA 282–283
1:3 200 000

NEW ZEALAND –
NORTH ISLAND 284
1:2 800 000

NEW ZEALAND –
SOUTH ISLAND 285
1:2 800 000
CHATHAM ISLANDS 1:2 800 000

PAPUA NEW GUINEA 286
1:5 200 000

ISLANDS OF THE
SOUTHWEST PACIFIC 287
FIJI 1:4 000 000
VANUATU 1:4 000 000
SOLOMON ISLANDS 1:4 000 000
TONGA 1:4 000 000
YAP 1:830 000
CHUUK 1:830 000
SAMOAN ISLANDS 1:4 000 000

PACIFIC OCEAN 288–289
1:43 200 000
OKINAWA 1:1 550 000
IWO JIMA 1:200 000
PALAU 1:1 550 000
NEW CALEDONIA 1:5 750 000
TAHITI 1:1 150 000
FRENCH POLYNESIA 1:26 000 000
NIUE 1:830 000
RAROTONGA 1:415 000

NORTH
AMERICA

NORTH AMERICA:
PHYSICAL 292
1:28 000 000

NORTH AMERICA:
POLITICAL 293
1:28 000 000

CANADA 294–295
1:12 000 000

WESTERN CANADA 296–297
1:5 600 000

EASTERN CANADA 298–299
1:5 600 000

UNITED STATES 300–301
1:12 000 000
ALASKA 1:12 000 000
HAWAI'I 1:12 000 000

HAWAI'I 302
1:2 500 000
OAHU 1:500 000
NORTHERN MARIANAS 1:12 800 000
WAKE ISLAND 1:200 000
MIDWAY ISLANDS 1:200 000
GUAM 1:800 000
SAIPAN AND TINIAN 1:800 000
TUTUILA 1:640 000
MANUA ISLANDS 1:640 000

ALASKA 303
1:8 000 000

UNITED STATES –
WEST 304–305
1:5 360 000

CENTRAL AND SOUTHERN
CALIFORNIA AND WESTERN
WASHINGTON 306–307
1:2 000 000

UNITED STATES – MIDWEST
AND NORTHEAST 308–309
1:5 360 000

CHICAGO AND
THE MIDWEST 310–311
1:2 000 000

NORTHEASTERN
UNITED STATES 312–313
1:2 000 000

UNITED STATES –
SOUTH 314–315
1:5 360 000

SOUTHEASTERN
UNITED STATES 316–317
1:2 000 000

MEXICO 318–319
1:6 400 000

CENTRAL AMERICA AND
THE WEST INDIES 320–321
1:6 400 000
PUERTO RICO AND THE
VIRGIN ISLANDS 1:1 600 000
JAMAICA 1:1 600 000
PANAMA CANAL 1:800 000

LESSER ANTILLES 322–323
NORTHERN LEEWARDS 1:600 000
ANTIGUA AND BARBUDA 1:600 000
ST KITTS AND NEVIS 1:600 000
GUADELOUPE 1:600 000
ARUBA 1:600 000
NETHERLANDS ANTILLES 1:600 000
MARTINIQUE 1:600 000
DOMINICA 1:600 000
ST LUCIA 1:600 000
ST VINCENT AND
THE GRENADINES 1:600 000
MONTSERRAT 1:600 000
GRENADA 1:600 000
BARBADOS 1:600 000
TRINIDAD AND TOBAGO 1:600 000

SOUTH
AMERICA

SOUTH AMERICA:
PHYSICAL 326
1:28 000 000

SOUTH AMERICA:
POLITICAL 327
1:28 000 000

SOUTH AMERICA –
NORTHWEST 328–329
1:6 400 000

SOUTH AMERICA –
WEST 330–331
1:6 400 000
GALAPAGOS ISLANDS 1:3 200 000
EASTER ISLAND 1:400 000
ROBINSON CRUSOE ISLAND 1:400 000

EASTERN BRAZIL 332–333
1:6 400 000

CENTRAL
SOUTH AMERICA 334–335
1:6 400 000

SOUTHERN CHILE AND
ARGENTINA 336
1:6 400 000

GEOGRAPHICAL
GLOSSARY 337–338

INDEX TO
WORLD MAPS 339–448

WORLD STATISTICS: COUNTRIES

This alphabetical list includes the principal countries and territories of the world. If a territory is not completely independent, the country it is associated with is named. The area figures give the total area of land, inland water, and ice. The population figures are 2007 estimates where available. The annual income is the Gross Domestic Product per capita in US dollars. The figures are the latest available, usually 2007 estimates.

Country/Territory	**Area** km^2 *Thousands*	**Area** miles^2 *Thousands*	**Population** *Thousands*	**Capital**	**Annual Income** US $
Afghanistan	652	252	31,890	Kabul	800
Albania	28.7	11.1	3,601	Tirana	5,500
Algeria	2,382	920	33,333	Algiers	8,100
American Samoa (US)	0.20	0.08	58	Pago Pago	5,800
Andorra	0.47	0.18	72	Andorra La Vella	38,800
Angola	1,247	481	12,264	Luanda	6,500
Anguilla (UK)	0.10	0.04	14	The Valley	8,800
Antigua & Barbuda	0.44	0.17	69	St John's	10,900
Argentina	2,780	1,074	40,302	Buenos Aires	13,000
Armenia	29.8	11.5	2,972	Yerevan	5,700
Aruba (Netherlands)	0.19	0.07	100	Oranjestad	21,800
Australia	7,741	2,989	20,434	Canberra	37,500
Austria	83.9	32.4	8,200	Vienna	39,000
Azerbaijan	86.6	33.4	8,120	Baku	9,000
Azores (Portugal)	2.2	0.86	236	Ponta Delgada	15,000
Bahamas	13.9	5.4	306	Nassau	22,700
Bahrain	0.69	0.27	709	Manama	34,700
Bangladesh	144	55.6	150,448	Dhaka	1,400
Barbados	0.43	0.17	281	Bridgetown	19,700
Belarus	208	80.2	9,725	Minsk	10,200
Belgium	30.5	11.8	10,392	Brussels	36,500
Belize	23.0	8.9	294	Belmopan	7,800
Benin	113	43.5	9,078	Porto-Novo	1,500
Bermuda (UK)	0.05	0.02	66	Hamilton	69,900
Bhutan	47.0	18.1	2,328	Thimphu	1,400
Bolivia	1,099	424	9,119	La Paz/Sucre	4,400
Bosnia-Herzegovina	51.2	19.8	4,552	Sarajevo	6,600
Botswana	582	225	1,816	Gaborone	14,700
Brazil	8,514	3,287	190,011	Brasília	9,700
Brunei	5.8	2.2	375	Bandar Seri Begawan	25,600
Bulgaria	111	42.8	7,323	Sofia	11,800
Burkina Faso	274	106	14,326	Ouagadougou	1,200
Burma (=Myanmar)	677	261	47,374	Rangoon/Naypyidaw	1,900
Burundi	27.8	10.7	8,391	Bujumbura	800
Cambodia	181	69.9	13,996	Phnom Penh	1,800
Cameroon	475	184	18,060	Yaoundé	2,300
Canada	9,971	3,850	33,390	Ottawa	38,200
Canary Is. (Spain)	7.2	2.8	1,682	Las Palmas/Santa Cruz	19,900
Cape Verde Is.	4.0	1.6	424	Praia	7,000
Cayman Is. (UK)	0.26	0.10	47	George Town	43,800
Central African Republic	623	241	4,369	Bangui	700
Chad	1,284	496	9,886	Ndjaména	1,600
Chile	757	292	16,285	Santiago	14,400
China	9,597	3,705	1,321,852	Beijing	5,300
Colombia	1,139	440	44,380	Bogotá	7,200
Comoros	2.2	0.86	711	Moroni	600
Congo	342	132	3,801	Brazzaville	3,700
Congo (Dem. Rep. of the)	2,345	905	65,752	Kinshasa	300
Cook Is. (NZ)	0.24	0.09	22	Avarua	9,100
Costa Rica	51.1	19.7	4,134	San José	13,500
Croatia	56.5	21.8	4,493	Zagreb	15,500
Cuba	111	42.8	11,394	Havana	4,500
Cyprus	9.3	3.6	788	Nicosia	24,600
Czech Republic	78.9	30.5	10,229	Prague	24,400
Denmark	43.1	16.6	5,468	Copenhagen	37,400
Djibouti	23.2	9.0	496	Djibouti	1,000
Dominica	0.75	0.29	72	Roseau	3,800
Dominican Republic	48.5	18.7	9,366	Santo Domingo	9,200
East Timor	14.9	5.7	1,085	Dili	800
Ecuador	284	109	13,756	Quito	7,100
Egypt	1,001	387	80,335	Cairo	5,400
El Salvador	21.0	8.1	6,948	San Salvador	5,200
Equatorial Guinea	28.1	10.8	551	Malabo	4,100
Eritrea	118	45.4	4,907	Asmara	1,000
Estonia	45.1	17.4	1,316	Tallinn	21,800
Ethiopia	1,104	426	76,512	Addis Ababa	700
Faroe Is. (Denmark)	1.4	0.54	48	Tórshavn	31,000
Fiji	18.3	7.1	919	Suva	4,100
Finland	338	131	5,238	Helsinki	35,500
France	552	213	60,876	Paris	33,800
French Guiana (France)	90.0	34.7	200	Cayenne	8,300
French Polynesia (France)	4.0	1.5	279	Papeete	17,500
Gabon	268	103	1,455	Libreville	13,800
Gambia, The	11.3	4.4	1,688	Banjul	800
Gaza Strip (OPT)*	0.36	0.14	1,482	–	1,100
Georgia	69.7	26.9	4,646	Tbilisi	4,200
Germany	357	138	82,401	Berlin	34,400
Ghana	239	92.1	22,931	Accra	1,400
Gibraltar (UK)	0.006	0.002	28	Gibraltar Town	38,200
Greece	132	50.9	10,706	Athens	30,500
Greenland (Denmark)	2,176	840	56	Nuuk	20,000
Grenada	0.34	0.13	90	St George's	3,900
Guadeloupe (France)	1.7	0.66	453	Basse-Terre	7,900
Guam (US)	0.55	0.21	173	Agana	15,000
Guatemala	109	42.0	12,728	Guatemala City	5,400
Guinea	246	94.9	9,948	Conakry	1,000
Guinea-Bissau	36.1	13.9	1,473	Bissau	600
Guyana	215	83.0	769	Georgetown	5,300
Haiti	27.8	10.7	8,706	Port-au-Prince	1,900
Honduras	112	43.3	7,484	Tegucigalpa	3,300
Hungary	93.0	35.9	9,956	Budapest	19,500
Iceland	103	39.8	302	Reykjavik	39,400
India	3,287	1,269	1,129,866	New Delhi	2,700
Indonesia	1,905	735	234,694	Jakarta	3,400
Iran	1,648	636	65,398	Tehran	12,300
Iraq	438	169	27,500	Baghdad	3,600
Ireland	70.3	27.1	4,109	Dublin	45,600
Israel	20.6	8.0	6,427	Jerusalem	28,800
Italy	301	116	58,148	Rome	31,000
Ivory Coast (=Côte d'Ivoire)	322	125	18,013	Yamoussoukro	1,800
Jamaica	11.0	4.2	2,780	Kingston	4,800
Japan	378	146	127,433	Tokyo	33,800
Jordan	89.3	34.5	6,053	Amman	4,700
Kazakhstan	2,725	1,052	15,285	Astana	11,100
Kenya	580	224	36,914	Nairobi	1,600
Kiribati	0.73	0.28	108	Tarawa	1,800
Korea, North	121	46.5	23,302	Pyŏngyang	1,900
Korea, South	99.3	38.3	49,045	Seoul	24,600
Kosovo	10.9	4.2	2,127	Pristina	1,800
Kuwait	17.8	6.9	2,506	Kuwait City	55,300
Kyrgyzstan	200	77.2	5,284	Bishkek	2,000
Laos	237	91.4	6,522	Vientiane	1,900
Latvia	64.6	24.9	2,260	Riga	17,700
Lebanon	10.4	4.0	3,926	Beirut	10,400
Lesotho	30.4	11.7	2,125	Maseru	1,500
Liberia	111	43.0	3,196	Monrovia	500
Libya	1,760	679	6,037	Tripoli	13,100
Liechtenstein	0.16	0.06	34	Vaduz	25,000
Lithuania	65.2	25.2	3,575	Vilnius	16,700
Luxembourg	2.6	1.0	480	Luxembourg	80,800
Macedonia (FYROM)	25.7	9.9	2,056	Skopje	8,400
Madagascar	587	227	19,449	Antananarivo	1,000
Madeira (Portugal)	0.78	0.30	241	Funchal	22,700
Malawi	118	45.7	13,603	Lilongwe	800
Malaysia	330	127	24,821	Kuala Lumpur/Putrajaya	14,400
Maldives	0.30	0.12	369	Malé	3,900
Mali	1,240	479	11,995	Bamako	1,200
Malta	0.32	0.12	402	Valletta	23,700
Marshall Is.	0.18	0.07	62	Majuro	2,900
Martinique (France)	1.1	0.43	436	Fort-de-France	14,400
Mauritania	1,026	396	3,270	Nouakchott	1,800
Mauritius	2.0	0.79	1,251	Port Louis	11,900
Mayotte (France)	0.37	0.14	209	Mamoudzou	4,900
Mexico	1,958	756	108,701	Mexico City	12,500
Micronesia, Fed. States of	0.70	0.27	108	Palikir	2,300
Moldova	33.9	13.1	4,320	Chişinău	2,200
Monaco	0.001	0.0004	33	Monaco	30,000
Mongolia	1,567	605	2,952	Ulan Bator	2,900
Montenegro	14.0	5.4	685	Podgorica	3,800
Morocco	447	172	33,757	Rabat	3,800
Mozambique	802	309	20,906	Maputo	900
Namibia	824	318	2,055	Windhoek	5,200
Nauru	0.02	0.008	14	Yaren District	5,000
Nepal	147	56.8	28,902	Katmandu	1,100
Netherlands	41.5	16.0	16,571	Amsterdam/The Hague	38,600
Netherlands Antilles (Neths)	0.80	0.31	224	Willemstad	16,000
New Caledonia (France)	18.6	7.2	222	Nouméa	15,000
New Zealand	271	104	4,116	Wellington	27,300
Nicaragua	130	50.2	5,675	Managua	3,200
Niger	1,267	489	12,895	Niamey	700
Nigeria	924	357	135,031	Abuja	2,200
Northern Mariana Is. (US)	0.46	0.18	85	Saipan	12,500
Norway	324	125	4,628	Oslo	55,600
Oman	310	119	3,205	Muscat	19,100
Pakistan	796	307	164,742	Islamabad	2,600
Palau	0.46	0.18	21	Melekeok	7,600
Panama	75.5	29.2	3,242	Panamá	9,000
Papua New Guinea	463	179	5,796	Port Moresby	2,900
Paraguay	407	157	6,669	Asunción	4,000
Peru	1,285	496	28,675	Lima	7,600
Philippines	300	116	91,077	Manila	3,300
Poland	323	125	38,518	Warsaw	16,200
Portugal	88.8	34.3	10,643	Lisbon	21,800
Puerto Rico (US)	8.9	3.4	3,944	San Juan	19,600
Qatar	11.0	4.2	907	Doha	29,400
Réunion (France)	2.5	0.97	788	St-Denis	6,200
Romania	238	92.0	22,276	Bucharest	11,100
Russia	17,075	6,593	141,378	Moscow	14,600
Rwanda	26.3	10.2	9,908	Kigali	1,000
St Kitts & Nevis	0.26	0.10	39	Basseterre	8,200
St Lucia	0.54	0.21	171	Castries	4,800
St Vincent & Grenadines	0.39	0.15	118	Kingstown	3,600
Samoa	2.8	1.1	214	Apia	2,100
San Marino	0.06	0.02	30	San Marino	34,100
São Tomé & Príncipe	0.96	0.37	200	São Tomé	1,200
Saudi Arabia	2,150	830	27,601	Riyadh	20,700
Senegal	197	76.0	12,522	Dakar	1,700
Serbia	77.5	29.9	8,024	Belgrade	7,700
Seychelles	0.46	0.18	82	Victoria	18,400
Sierra Leone	71.7	27.7	6,145	Freetown	800
Singapore	0.68	0.26	4,553	Singapore City	48,900
Slovak Republic	49.0	18.9	5,448	Bratislava	19,800
Slovenia	20.3	7.8	2,009	Ljubljana	27,300
Solomon Is.	28.9	11.2	567	Honiara	600
Somalia	638	246	9,119	Mogadishu	600
South Africa	1,221	471	43,998	Cape Town/Pretoria	10,600
Spain	498	192	40,448	Madrid	33,700
Sri Lanka	65.6	25.3	20,926	Colombo	4,100
Sudan	2,506	967	39,379	Khartoum	2,500
Suriname	163	63.0	471	Paramaribo	7,800
Swaziland	17.4	6.7	1,133	Mbabane	4,800
Sweden	450	174	9,031	Stockholm	36,900
Switzerland	41.3	15.9	7,555	Bern	39,800
Syria	185	71.5	19,315	Damascus	4,500
Taiwan	36.0	13.9	22,859	Taipei	29,800
Tajikistan	143	55.3	7,077	Dushanbe	1,600
Tanzania	945	365	39,384	Dodoma	1,100
Thailand	513	198	65,068	Bangkok	8,000
Togo	56.8	21.9	5,702	Lomé	900
Tonga	0.65	0.25	117	Nuku'alofa	2,200
Trinidad & Tobago	5.1	2.0	1,057	Port of Spain	21,700
Tunisia	164	63.2	10,276	Tunis	7,500
Turkey	775	299	71,159	Ankara	9,400
Turkmenistan	488	188	5,097	Ashkhabad	9,200
Turks & Caicos Is. (UK)	0.43	0.17	22	Cockburn Town	11,500
Tuvalu	0.03	0.01	12	Fongafale	1,600
Uganda	241	93.1	30,263	Kampala	1,100
Ukraine	604	233	46,300	Kiev	6,900
United Arab Emirates	83.6	32.3	4,444	Abu Dhabi	55,200
United Kingdom	242	93.4	60,776	London	35,300
United States of America	9,629	3,718	301,140	Washington, DC	46,000
Uruguay	175	67.6	3,461	Montevideo	10,700
Uzbekistan	447	173	27,780	Tashkent	2,200
Vanuatu	12.2	4.7	212	Port-Vila	2,900
Venezuela	912	352	26,024	Caracas	12,800
Vietnam	332	128	85,262	Hanoi	2,600
Virgin Is. (UK)	0.15	0.06	24	Road Town	38,500
Virgin Is. (US)	0.35	0.13	108	Charlotte Amalie	14,500
Wallis & Futuna Is. (France)	0.20	0.08	16	Mata-Utu	3,800
West Bank (OPT)*	5.9	2.3	2,536	–	1,100
Western Sahara	266	103	383	El Aaiún	N/A
Yemen	528	204	22,231	Sana'	2,400
Zambia	753	291	11,477	Lusaka	1,400
Zimbabwe	391	151	12,311	Harare	500

*OPT = Occupied Palestinian Territory   N/A = Not available

This list shows the principal cities with more than 750,000 inhabitants. The figures are taken from the most recent census or estimate available, usually 2007, and as far as possible are the population of the metropolitan area or urban agglomeration (for example, greater New York, Mexico, or Paris). All the figures are in thousands. Local name forms have been used for the smaller cities (for example, Thessaloniki).

AFGHANISTAN
Kabul 3,288
ALGERIA
Algiers 3,260
ANGOLA
Luanda 2,839
ARGENTINA
Buenos Aires 13,349
Córdoba 1,592
Rosario 1,312
Mendoza 1,072
San Miguel de
Tucumán 837
ARMENIA
Yerevan 1,103
AUSTRALIA
Sydney 4,388
Melbourne 3,663
Brisbane 1,769
Perth 1,484
Adelaide 1,137
AUSTRIA
Vienna 2,260
AZERBAIJAN
Baku 1,856
BANGLADESH
Dhaka 12,560
Chittagong 4,171
Khulna 1,497
Rajshahi 1,035
BELARUS
Minsk 1,778
BELGIUM
Brussels 1,012
BOLIVIA
La Paz 1,533
Santa Cruz 1,352
Cochabamba 797
BRAZIL
São Paulo 18,333
Rio de Janeiro 11,469
Belo Horizonte 5,304
Pôrto Alegre 3,795
Recife 3,527
Brasília 3,341
Salvador 3,331
Fortaleza 3,261
Curitiba 2,871
Campinas 2,640
Belém 2,097
Goiânia 1,878
Manaus 1,673
Santos 1,634
Vitória 1,602
Maceió 1,137
Natal 1,049
São Luís 982
São José dos
Campos 972
João Pessoa 931
Teresina 895
Campo Grande 821
BULGARIA
Sofia 1,093
BURKINA FASO
Ouagadougou 870
BURMA (MYANMAR)
Rangoon 4,107
Mandalay 927
CAMBODIA
Phnom Penh 1,364
CAMEROON
Douala 1,980
Yaoundé 1,727
CANADA
Toronto 5,312
Montréal 3,640
Vancouver 2,188
Ottawa 1,156
Calgary 1,058
Edmonton 1,015
CHILE
Santiago 5,683
CHINA
Shanghai 14,503
Beijing 10,717
Guangzhou 8,425
Shenzhen 7,233
Wuhan 7,093
Hong Kong 7,041
Tianjin 7,040
Chongqing 6,363
Shenyang 4,720
Dongguan 4,320
Chengdu 4,065
Xi'an 3,926

Harbin 3,695
Nanjing 3,621
Guiyang 3,447
Dalian 3,073
Changchun 3,046
Zibo 2,982
Kunming 2,837
Hangzhou 2,831
Qingdao 2,817
Taiyuan 2,794
Jinan 2,743
Zhengzhou 2,590
Fuzhou 2,453
Changsha 2,451
Lanzhou 2,411
Xiamen 2,371
Shijiazhuang 2,275
Jinxi 2,268
Jilin 2,255
Wenzhou 2,212
Nanchang 2,188
Zaozhuang 2,096
Nanchong 2,046
Nanning 2,040
Linyi 2,035
Ürümqi 2,025
Yantai 1,991
Wanxian 1,963
Xuzhou 1,960
Baotou 1,920
Hefei 1,916
Suzhou 1,849
Nanyang 1,830
Tangshan 1,825
Ningbo 1,810
Datong 1,763
Yancheng 1,678
Tianmen 1,676
Shangqui 1,650
Lu'an 1,647
Wuxi 1,646
Luoyang 1,644
Hohhot 1,644
Anshan 1,611
Qiqihar 1,607
Tai'an 1,598
Daqing 1,594
Xinghua 1,587
Pingxiang 1,562
Handan 1,535
Xiantao 1,528
Zhanjiang 1,514
Weifang 1,498
Shantou 1,495
Fushun 1,456
Xianyang 1,450
Luzhou 1,447
Neijiang 1,441
Changde 1,429
Huainan 1,420
Liuzhou 1,409
Suining, Sichuan 1,401
Quanzhou 1,377
Xintai 1,334
Mianyang 1,322
Heze 1,318
Yiyang 1,318
Yueyang 1,286
Suqian 1,258
Changzhou 1,249
Huaian 1,243
Chifeng 1,238
Jingmen 1,228
Yuzhou 1,226
Zaoyang 1,210
Huzhou 1,203
Tianshui 1,199
Yongzhou 1,182
Mudanjiang 1,171
Liupanshui 1,149
Leshan 1,143
Jining, Shandong 1,143
Xiaoshan 1,130
Yixing 1,129
Zigong 1,087
Xianyang 1,072
Fuyu 1,068
Yulin 1,060
Baoding 1,042
Xinyi, Jiangsu 1,022
Zhuzhou 1,016
Jixi 1,012
Linqing 1,009
Jiamusi 1,006
Xiangfan 1,006
Zhangjiakou 1,001
Benxi 967

Xiangxiang 936
Zhangjiagang 936
Xinyu 932
Yichun, Heilongjiang 916
Yichun, Jiangxi 890
Jinzhou 888
Zhaotong 879
Yuyao 876
Anshun 864
Hengyang 853
Xuanzhou 851
Tongliao 847
Huaibei 830
Jiaxing 817
Kaifeng 810
Fuxin 807
Hunjiang 798
COLOMBIA
Bogotá 7,594
Medellín 3,236
Cali 2,583
Barranquilla 1,918
Bucaramanga 1,069
Cartagena 1,002
Cúcuta 883
CONGO
Brazzaville 1,173
CONGO
(DEM. REP.)
Kinshasa 6,049
Kolwezi 1,207
Lubumbashi 1,179
Mbuji-Mayi 1,024
COSTA RICA
San José 1,217
CROATIA
Zagreb 1,067
CUBA
Havana 2,192
CZECH REPUBLIC
Prague 1,171
DENMARK
Copenhagen 1,091
DOMINICAN
REPUBLIC
Santo Domingo 2,563
Santiago de los
Caballeros 804
ECUADOR
Guayaquil 2,387
Quito 1,514
EGYPT
Cairo 11,146
Alexandria 3,760
Shubrâ el Kheima 937
EL SALVADOR
San Salvador 1,517
ETHIOPIA
Addis Ababa 2,899
FINLAND
Helsinki 1,091
FRANCE
Paris 9,820
Lyons 1,403
Marseilles 1,382
Lille 1,029
Nice 889
Toulouse 761
Bordeaux 754
GEORGIA
Tbilisi 1,406
GERMANY
Berlin 3,389
Hamburg 1,740
Munich 1,263
Cologne 963
GHANA
Accra 1,981
Kumasi 1,517
GREECE
Athens 3,238
Thessaloniki 824
GUATEMALA
Guatemala City 3,242
GUINEA
Conakry 1,465
HAITI
Port-au-Prince 2,129
HONDURAS
Tegucigalpa 1,061
HUNGARY
Budapest 1,693
INDIA
Mumbai 18,336
Delhi 15,334
Kolkata 14,299
Chennai 6,915

Bangalore 6,532
Hyderabad 6,145
Ahmedabad 5,171
Pune 4,485
Surat 3,671
Kanpur 3,040
Jaipur 2,796
Lucknow 2,589
Nagpur 2,359
Patna 2,066
Indore 1,941
Vadodara 1,686
Bhopal 1,656
Coimbatore 1,628
Ludhiana 1,583
Agra 1,526
Visakhapatnam 1,468
Cochin 1,461
Nashik 1,408
Meerut 1,340
Faridabad 1,330
Varanasi 1,300
Ghaziabad 1,277
Asansol 1,272
Jamshedpur 1,246
Madurai 1,245
Jabalpur 1,234
Rajkot 1,205
Dhanbad 1,195
Amritsar 1,162
Allahabad 1,153
Vijayawada 1,093
Srinagar 1,093
Aurangabad 1,065
Bhilainagar-Durg 1,051
Solapur 1,012
Ranchi 999
Jodhpur 954
Guwahati 941
Gwalior 939
Trivandrum 918
Calicut 917
Tiruchchirapalli 913
Chandigarh 896
Hubli-Dharwad 854
Mysore 851
INDONESIA
Jakarta 13,215
Bandung 4,126
Surabaya 2,992
Medan 2,287
Palembang 1,733
Ujung Pandang 1,284
Bandar Lampung 915
Malang 898
Tegal 898
Semarang 816
Bogor 761
IRAN
Tehran 7,352
Mashhad 2,147
Esfahan 1,547
Tabriz 1,396
Karaj 1,235
Shiraz 1,230
Qom 1,045
Ahvaz 967
Bakhtaran 771
IRAQ
Baghdad 5,910
Mosul 1,236
Basra 1,187
Irbil 840
IRELAND
Dublin 1,037
ISRAEL
Tel Aviv-Yafo 3,025
Haifa 948
ITALY
Rome 3,348
Milan 2,953
Naples 2,245
Turin 1,660
Genoa 803
IVORY COAST
(CÔTE D'IVOIRE)
Abidjan 3,516
JAPAN
Tokyo 12,064
Yokohama 6,427
Osaka 2,599
Nagoya 2,172
Sapporo 1,922
Kobe 1,493
Kyoto 1,468
Fukuoka 1,341
Kawasaki 1,250

Hiroshima 1,126
Kitakyushu 1,011
Sendai 1,008
Chiba 887
Sakai 792
JORDAN
Amman 1,292
KAZAKHSTAN
Almaty 1,156
KENYA
Nairobi 2,818
KOREA, NORTH
Pyŏngyang 3,351
N'ampo 1,102
Hamhung 821
KOREA, SOUTH
Seoul 9,888
Busan 3,830
Incheon 2,884
Daegu 2,675
Daejeon 1,522
Gwangju 1,379
Seognam 1,353
Ulsan 1,340
Ansan 984
Pucheon 900
Suwon 876
Pohang 790
KUWAIT
Kuwait City 1,810
KYRGYZSTAN
Bishkek 828
LATVIA
Riga 719
LEBANON
Beirut 2,070
LIBYA
Tripoli 2,098
Benghazi 1,114
MADAGASCAR
Antananarivo 1,808
MALAYSIA
Kuala Lumpur 1,405
MALI
Bamako 1,379
MEXICO
Mexico City 19,013
Guadalajara 3,905
Monterrey 3,517
Toluca 1,987
Puebla 1,880
Tijuana 1,570
Ciudad Juárez 1,469
León 1,438
Torreón 1,057
San Luis Potosí 927
Mérida 919
Querétaro 913
Mexicali 840
Culiacán 799
MONGOLIA
Ulan Bator 842
MOROCCO
Casablanca 3,743
Rabat 1,859
Fès 1,032
Marrakesh 951
MOZAMBIQUE
Maputo 1,316
NEPAL
Katmandu 1,176
NETHERLANDS
Amsterdam 1,157
Rotterdam 1,112
NEW ZEALAND
Auckland 1,152
NICARAGUA
Managua 1,165
NIGER
Niamey 997
NIGERIA
Lagos 11,135
Kano 2,884
Ibadan 2,375
Kaduna 1,329
Benin City 1,022
Ogbomosho 959
Port Harcourt 942
NORWAY
Oslo 808
PAKISTAN
Karachi 11,819
Lahore 6,373
Faisalabad 2,533
Rawalpindi 1,794
Gujranwala 1,466
Multan 1,459

Hyderabad 1,392
Peshawar 1,255
Islamabad 791
PANAMA
Panamá 1,216
PARAGUAY
Asunción 1,858
PERU
Lima 8,180
PHILIPPINES
Manila 10,677
Davao 1,326
POLAND
Warsaw 1,680
Lódz 815
PORTUGAL
Lisbon 2,761
Porto 1,309
PUERTO RICO
San Juan 2,604
ROMANIA
Bucharest 1,934
RUSSIA
Moscow 10,672
Saint Petersburg 5,315
Novosibirsk 1,425
Nizhniy Novgorod 1,288
Yekaterinburg 1,281
Samara 1,140
Omsk 1,132
Kazan 1,108
Rostov 1,081
Chelyabinsk 1,067
Ufa 1,035
Volgograd 1,016
Perm 1,014
Voronezh 918
Saratov 881
Simbirsk 864
Krasnoyarsk 840
Togliatti 771
SAUDI ARABIA
Riyadh 5,514
Jedda 3,807
Mecca 1,529
Medina 1,044
Dammam 920
SENEGAL
Dakar 2,313
SERBIA
Belgrade 1,116
SIERRA LEONE
Freetown 1,007
SINGAPORE
Singapore City 4,372
SOMALIA
Mogadishu 1,320
SOUTH AFRICA
Johannesburg 3,254
Cape Town 3,083
Durban 2,631
Pretoria 1,271
Vereeniging 1,027
Port Elizabeth 1,006
SPAIN
Madrid 5,608
Barcelona 4,795
SUDAN
Khartoum 4,518
SWEDEN
Stockholm 1,729
Gothenburg 829
SWITZERLAND
Zürich 1,144
SYRIA
Aleppo 2,505
Damascus 2,317
Homs 915
TAIWAN
Taipei 2,606
Kaohsiung 1,515
T'aichung 1,033
TANZANIA
Dar es Salaam 2,683
THAILAND
Bangkok 6,604
TOGO
Lomé 1,337
TUNISIA
Tunis 2,063
TURKEY
Istanbul 9,712
Ankara 3,573
Izmir 2,487
Bursa 1,414
Adana 1,245
Gaziantep 862

Konya 761
UGANDA
Kampala 1,345
UKRAINE
Kiev 2,621
Kharkov 1,521
Dnepropetrovsk 1,122
Donetsk 1,065
Odessa 1,027
Zaporozhye 863
Lvov 794
UNITED ARAB
EMIRATES
Dubai 1,330
Abu Dhabi 928
UNITED KINGDOM
London 8,505
Birmingham 2,280
Manchester 2,228
Liverpool 1,519
Glasgow 1,159
UNITED STATES OF
AMERICA
New York 18,718
Los Angeles 12,298
Chicago 8,814
Miami 5,434
Philadelphia 5,392
Dallas–
Fort Worth 4,655
Boston 4,361
Houston 4,320
Atlanta 4,304
Washington 4,238
Detroit 4,034
Phoenix–Mesa 3,416
San Francisco 3,385
Seattle 2,989
San Diego 2,852
Minneapolis–
St Paul 2,556
Tampa–
St Petersburg 2,252
Denver 2,239
Baltimore 2,205
St Louis 2,159
Cleveland 1,855
Portland 1,810
Pittsburgh 1,806
Las Vegas 1,720
San Bernardino 1,690
San Jose 1,631
Cincinnati 1,599
Sacramento 1,555
Norfolk–
Virginia Beach 1,460
Kansas City 1,437
San Antonio 1,436
Indianapolis 1,387
Milwaukee 1,316
Orlando 1,306
Providence 1,248
Columbus 1,236
Austin 1,107
Memphis 1,053
New Orleans 1,010
Buffalo 977
Stamford 889
Salt Lake City 888
Jacksonville 882
Louisville 864
Hartford 852
Richmond 819
Charlotte 759
URUGUAY
Montevideo 1,353
UZBEKISTAN
Tashkent 2,181
VENEZUELA
Caracas 3,276
Valencia 2,330
Maracaibo 2,182
Maracay 1,138
Ciudad Guayana 966
Barquisimeto 923
VIETNAM
Ho Chi Minh City 5,065
Hanoi 4,164
Haiphong 1,873
YEMEN
Sana' 1,801
ZAMBIA
Lusaka 1,450
ZIMBABWE
Harare 1,527
Bulawayo 824

WORLD STATISTICS: PHYSICAL DIMENSIONS

Each topic list is divided into continents and within a continent the items are listed in order of size. The bottom part of many of the lists is selective in order to give examples from as many different countries as possible. The order of the continents is the same as in the atlas, beginning with Europe and ending with South America. The figures are rounded as appropriate.

World, Continents, Oceans

	km²	miles²	%
The World	509,450,000	196,672,000	–
Land	149,450,000	57,688,000	29.3
Water	360,000,000	138,984,000	70.7
Asia	44,500,000	17,177,000	29.8
Africa	30,302,000	11,697,000	20.3
North America	24,241,000	9,357,000	16.2
South America	17,793,000	6,868,000	11.9
Antarctica	14,100,000	5,443,000	9.4
Europe	9,957,000	3,843,000	6.7
Australia & Oceania	8,557,000	3,303,000	5.7
Pacific Ocean	155,557,000	60,061,000	46.4
Atlantic Ocean	76,762,000	29,638,000	22.9
Indian Ocean	68,556,000	26,470,000	20.4
Southern Ocean	20,327,000	7,848,000	6.1
Arctic Ocean	14,056,000	5,427,000	4.2

Ocean Depths

	m	ft
Atlantic Ocean	m	ft
Puerto Rico (Milwaukee) Deep	8,605	28,232
Cayman Trench	7,680	25,197
Gulf of Mexico	5,203	17,070
Mediterranean Sea	5,121	16,801
Black Sea	2,211	7,254
North Sea	660	2,165
Indian Ocean	m	ft
Java Trench	7,450	24,442
Red Sea	2,635	8,454
Pacific Ocean	m	ft
Mariana Trench	11,022	36,161
Tonga Trench	10,882	35,702
Japan Trench	10,554	34,626
Kuril Trench	10,542	34,587
Arctic Ocean	m	ft
Molloy Deep	5,608	18,399
Southern Ocean	m	ft
South Sandwich Trench	7,235	23,737

Mountains

		m	ft
Europe		m	ft
Elbrus	*Russia*	5,642	18,510
Dykh-Tau	*Russia*	5,205	17,076
Shkhara	*Russia/Georgia*	5,201	17,064
Koshtan-Tau	*Russia*	5,152	16,903
Kazbek	*Russia/Georgia*	5,047	16,558
Pushkin	*Russia/Georgia*	5,033	16,512
Katyn-Tau	*Russia/Georgia*	4,979	16,335
Shota Rustaveli	*Russia/Georgia*	4,860	15,945
Mont Blanc	*France/Italy*	4,808	15,774
Monte Rosa	*Italy/Switzerland*	4,634	15,203
Dom	*Switzerland*	4,545	14,911
Liskamm	*Switzerland*	4,527	14,852
Weisshorn	*Switzerland*	4,505	14,780
Taschorn	*Switzerland*	4,490	14,730
Matterhorn/Cervino	*Italy/Switzerland*	4,478	14,691
Grossglockner	*Austria*	3,797	12,457
Mulhacén	*Spain*	3,478	11,411
Zugspitze	*Germany*	2,962	9,718
Olympus	*Greece*	2,917	9,570
Galdhøpiggen	*Norway*	2,469	8,100
Kebnekaise	*Sweden*	2,117	6,946
Ben Nevis	*UK*	1,342	4,403
Asia		m	ft
Everest	*China/Nepal*	8,850	29,035
K2 (Godwin Austen)	*China/Kashmir*	8,611	28,251
Kanchenjunga	*India/Nepal*	8,598	28,208
Lhotse	*China/Nepal*	8,516	27,939
Makalu	*China/Nepal*	8,481	27,824
Cho Oyu	*China/Nepal*	8,201	26,906
Dhaulagiri	*Nepal*	8,172	26,811
Manaslu	*Nepal*	8,156	26,758
Nanga Parbat	*Kashmir*	8,126	26,660
Annapurna	*Nepal*	8,078	26,502
Gasherbrum	*China/Kashmir*	8,068	26,469
Xixabangma	*China*	8,012	26,286
Kangbachen	*Nepal*	7,858	25,781
Trivor	*Pakistan*	7,720	25,328
Pik Imeni Ismail Samani	*Tajikistan*	7,495	24,590
Demavend	*Iran*	5,604	18,386
Ararat	*Turkey*	5,165	16,945
Gunong Kinabalu	*Malaysia (Borneo)*	4,101	13,455
Fuji-San	*Japan*	3,776	12,388
Africa		m	ft
Kilimanjaro	*Tanzania*	5,895	19,340
Mt Kenya	*Kenya*	5,199	17,057
Ruwenzori (Margherita)	*Ug./Congo (D.R.)*	5,109	16,762
Meru	*Tanzania*	4,565	14,977
Ras Dashen	*Ethiopia*	4,533	14,872
Karisimbi	*Rwanda/Congo (D.R.)*	4,507	14,787
Mt Elgon	*Kenya/Uganda*	4,321	14,176
Batu	*Ethiopia*	4,307	14,130
Toubkal	*Morocco*	4,165	13,665
Mt Cameroun	*Cameroon*	4,070	13,353
Oceania		m	ft
Puncak Jaya	*Indonesia*	5,029	16,499
Puncak Trikora	*Indonesia*	4,730	15,518
Puncak Mandala	*Indonesia*	4,702	15,427
Mt Wilhelm	*Papua New Guinea*	4,508	14,790
Mauna Kea	*USA (Hawai'i)*	4,205	13,796
Mauna Loa	*USA (Hawai'i)*	4,169	13,681
Aoraki Mt Cook	*New Zealand*	3,753	12,313
Mt Kosciuszko	*Australia*	2,228	7,310
North America		m	ft
Mt McKinley (Denali)	*USA (Alaska)*	6,194	20,321
Mt Logan	*Canada*	5,959	19,551
Pico de Orizaba	*Mexico*	5,610	18,405
Mt St Elias	*USA/Canada*	5,489	18,008
Popocatépetl	*Mexico*	5,452	17,887
Mt Foraker	*USA (Alaska)*	5,304	17,401
Iztaccihuatl	*Mexico*	5,286	17,342
Mt Lucania	*Canada*	5,226	17,146
Mt Steele	*Canada*	5,073	16,644
Mt Bona	*USA (Alaska)*	5,005	16,420
Mt Whitney	*USA*	4,418	14,495
Tajumulco	*Guatemala*	4,220	13,845
Chirripó Grande	*Costa Rica*	3,837	12,589
Pico Duarte	*Dominican Rep.*	3,175	10,417
South America		m	ft
Aconcagua	*Argentina*	6,962	22,841
Bonete	*Argentina*	6,872	22,546
Ojos del Salado	*Argentina/Chile*	6,863	22,516
Pissis	*Argentina*	6,779	22,241
Mercedario	*Argentina/Chile*	6,770	22,211
Huascarán	*Peru*	6,768	22,204
Llullaillaco	*Argentina/Chile*	6,723	22,057
Nevado de Cachi	*Argentina*	6,720	22,047
Yerupaja	*Peru*	6,632	21,758
Sajama	*Bolivia*	6,520	21,391
Chimborazo	*Ecuador*	6,267	20,561
Pico Cristóbal Colón	*Colombia*	5,800	19,029
Pico Bolivar	*Venezuela*	5,007	16,427
Antarctica		m	ft
Vinson Massif		4,897	16,066
Mt Kirkpatrick		4,528	14,855

Rivers

		km	miles
Europe		km	miles
Volga	*Caspian Sea*	3,700	2,300
Danube	*Black Sea*	2,850	1,770
Ural	*Caspian Sea*	2,535	1,575
Dnepr (Dnipro)	*Black Sea*	2,285	1,420
Kama	*Volga*	2,030	1,260
Don	*Black Sea*	1,990	1,240
Petchora	*Arctic Ocean*	1,790	1,110
Oka	*Volga*	1,480	920
Dnister (Dniester)	*Black Sea*	1,400	870
Vyatka	*Kama*	1,370	850
Rhine	*North Sea*	1,320	820
N. Dvina	*Arctic Ocean*	1,290	800
Elbe	*North Sea*	1,145	710
Asia		km	miles
Yangtze	*Pacific Ocean*	6,380	3,960
Yenisey–Angara	*Arctic Ocean*	5,550	3,445
Huang He	*Pacific Ocean*	5,464	3,395
Ob–Irtysh	*Arctic Ocean*	5,410	3,360
Mekong	*Pacific Ocean*	4,500	2,795
Amur	*Pacific Ocean*	4,442	2,760
Lena	*Arctic Ocean*	4,402	2,735
Irtysh	*Ob*	4,250	2,640
Yenisey	*Arctic Ocean*	4,090	2,540
Ob	*Arctic Ocean*	3,680	2,285
Indus	*Indian Ocean*	3,100	1,925
Brahmaputra	*Indian Ocean*	2,900	1,800
Syrdarya	*Aral Sea*	2,860	1,775
Salween	*Indian Ocean*	2,800	1,740
Euphrates	*Indian Ocean*	2,700	1,675
Amudarya	*Aral Sea*	2,540	1,575
Africa		km	miles
Nile	*Mediterranean*	6,695	4,160
Congo	*Atlantic Ocean*	4,670	2,900
Niger	*Atlantic Ocean*	4,180	2,595
Zambezi	*Indian Ocean*	3,540	2,200
Oubangi/Uele	*Congo (D.R.)*	2,250	1,400
Kasai	*Congo (D.R.)*	1,950	1,210
Shaballe	*Indian Ocean*	1,930	1,200
Orange	*Atlantic Ocean*	1,860	1,155
Cubango	*Okavango Delta*	1,800	1,120
Limpopo	*Indian Ocean*	1,770	1,100
Senegal	*Atlantic Ocean*	1,640	1,020
Australia		km	miles
Murray–Darling	*Southern Ocean*	3,750	2,330
Darling	*Murray*	3,070	1,905
Murray	*Southern Ocean*	2,575	1,600
Murrumbidgee	*Murray*	1,690	1,050
North America		km	miles
Mississippi–Missouri	*Gulf of Mexico*	5,971	3,710
Mackenzie	*Arctic Ocean*	4,240	2,630
Missouri	*Mississippi*	4,088	2,540
Mississippi	*Gulf of Mexico*	3,782	2,350
Yukon	*Pacific Ocean*	3,185	1,980
Rio Grande	*Gulf of Mexico*	3,030	1,880
Arkansas	*Mississippi*	2,340	1,450
Colorado	*Pacific Ocean*	2,330	1,445
Red	*Mississippi*	2,040	1,270
Columbia	*Pacific Ocean*	1,950	1,210
Saskatchewan	*Lake Winnipeg*	1,940	1,205
South America		km	miles
Amazon	*Atlantic Ocean*	6,450	4,010
Paraná–Plate	*Atlantic Ocean*	4,500	2,800
Purus	*Amazon*	3,350	2,080
Madeira	*Amazon*	3,200	1,990
São Francisco	*Atlantic Ocean*	2,900	1,800
Paraná	*Plate*	2,800	1,740
Tocantins	*Atlantic Ocean*	2,750	1,710
Orinoco	*Atlantic Ocean*	2,740	1,700
Paraguay	*Paraná*	2,550	1,580
Pilcomayo	*Paraná*	2,500	1,550
Araguaia	*Tocantins*	2,250	1,400

Lakes

		km²	miles²
Europe		km²	miles²
Lake Ladoga	*Russia*	17,700	6,800
Lake Onega	*Russia*	9,700	3,700
Saimaa system	*Finland*	8,000	3,100
Vänern	*Sweden*	5,500	2,100
Asia		km²	miles²
Caspian Sea	*Asia*	371,000	143,000
Lake Baikal	*Russia*	30,500	11,780
Tonlé Sap	*Cambodia*	20,000	7,700
Lake Balqash	*Kazakhstan*	18,500	7,100
Aral Sea	*Kazakhstan/Uzbekistan*	17,160	6,625
Africa		km²	miles²
Lake Victoria	*East Africa*	68,000	26,300
Lake Tanganyika	*Central Africa*	33,000	13,000
Lake Malawi/Nyasa	*East Africa*	29,600	11,430
Lake Chad	*Central Africa*	25,000	9,700
Lake Bangweulu	*Zambia*	9,840	3,800
Lake Turkana	*Ethiopia/Kenya*	8,500	3,290
Australia		km²	miles²
Lake Eyre	*Australia*	8,900	3,400
Lake Torrens	*Australia*	5,800	2,200
Lake Gairdner	*Australia*	4,800	1,900
North America		km²	miles²
Lake Superior	*Canada/USA*	82,350	31,800
Lake Huron	*Canada/USA*	59,600	23,010
Lake Michigan	*USA*	58,000	22,400
Great Bear Lake	*Canada*	31,800	12,280
Great Slave Lake	*Canada*	28,500	11,000
Lake Erie	*Canada/USA*	25,700	9,900
Lake Winnipeg	*Canada*	24,400	9,400
Lake Ontario	*Canada/USA*	19,500	7,500
Lake Nicaragua	*Nicaragua*	8,200	3,200
South America		km²	miles²
Lake Titicaca	*Bolivia/Peru*	8,300	3,200
Lake Poopo	*Bolivia*	2,800	1,100

Islands

		km²	miles²
Europe		km²	miles²
Great Britain	*UK*	229,880	88,700
Iceland	*Atlantic Ocean*	103,000	39,800
Ireland	*Ireland/UK*	84,400	32,600
Novaya Zemlya (N.)	*Russia*	48,200	18,600
Sicily	*Italy*	25,500	9,800
Corsica	*France*	8,700	3,400
Asia		km²	miles²
Borneo	*Southeast Asia*	744,360	287,400
Sumatra	*Indonesia*	473,600	182,860
Honshu	*Japan*	230,500	88,980
Sulawesi (Celebes)	*Indonesia*	189,000	73,000
Java	*Indonesia*	126,700	48,900
Luzon	*Philippines*	104,700	40,400
Hokkaido	*Japan*	78,400	30,300
Africa		km²	miles²
Madagascar	*Indian Ocean*	587,040	226,660
Socotra	*Indian Ocean*	3,600	1,400
Réunion	*Indian Ocean*	2,500	965
Oceania		km²	miles²
New Guinea	*Indonesia/Papua NG*	821,030	317,000
New Zealand (S.)	*Pacific Ocean*	150,500	58,100
New Zealand (N.)	*Pacific Ocean*	114,700	44,300
Tasmania	*Australia*	67,800	26,200
Hawai'i	*Pacific Ocean*	10,450	4,000
North America		km²	miles²
Greenland	*Atlantic Ocean*	2,175,600	839,800
Baffin Is.	*Canada*	508,000	196,100
Victoria Is.	*Canada*	212,200	81,900
Ellesmere Is.	*Canada*	212,000	81,800
Cuba	*Caribbean Sea*	110,860	42,800
Hispaniola	*Dominican Rep./Haiti*	76,200	29,400
Jamaica	*Caribbean Sea*	11,400	4,400
Puerto Rico	*Atlantic Ocean*	8,900	3,400
South America		km²	miles²
Tierra del Fuego	*Argentina/Chile*	47,000	18,100
Falkland Is. (E.)	*Atlantic Ocean*	6,800	2,600

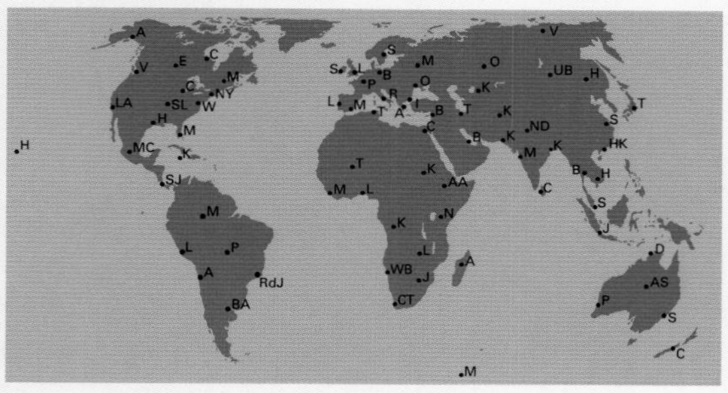

Rainfall and temperature figures are provided for more than 70 cities around the world. As climate is affected by altitude, the height of each city is shown in meters beneath its name. For each location, the top row of figures shows the total rainfall or snow in millimeters, and the bottom row the average temperature in degrees Celsius; the total annual rainfall and average annual temperature are at the end of the rows.

	Jan.	Feb.	Mar.	Apr.	May	June	July	Aug.	Sept.	Oct.	Nov.	Dec.	Year
EUROPE													
Athens, Greece	62	37	37	23	23	14	6	7	15	51	56	71	402
107 m	10	10	12	16	20	25	28	28	24	20	15	11	18
Berlin, Germany	42	33	41	37	54	69	56	58	45	37	44	55	571
55 m	–1	0	4	9	14	17	19	18	15	9	5	1	9
Istanbul, Turkey	87	71	63	45	33	25	24	24	44	71	85	107	655
14 m	5	6	7	11	16	20	23	23	20	16	12	8	14
Lisbon, Portugal	111	110	69	54	44	16	3	4	33	62	93	103	702
77 m	11	12	14	16	17	20	22	23	21	18	14	12	17
London, UK	54	40	37	37	46	45	57	59	49	57	64	48	593
5 m	4	5	7	9	12	16	18	17	15	11	8	5	11
Málaga, Spain	61	51	62	46	26	5	1	3	29	64	64	62	474
33 m	12	13	16	17	19	29	25	26	23	20	16	13	18
Moscow, Russia	39	38	36	37	53	58	88	71	58	45	47	54	624
156 m	–13	–10	–4	6	13	16	18	17	12	6	–1	–7	4
Odesa, Ukraine	57	62	30	21	34	34	42	37	37	13	35	71	473
64 m	–3	–1	2	9	15	20	22	22	18	12	9	1	10
Paris, France	56	46	35	42	57	54	59	64	55	50	51	50	619
75 m	3	4	8	11	15	18	20	19	17	12	7	4	12
Rome, Italy	71	62	57	51	46	37	15	21	63	99	129	93	744
17 m	8	9	11	14	18	22	25	25	22	17	13	10	16
Shannon, Irish Republic	94	67	56	53	61	57	77	79	86	86	96	117	929
2 m	5	5	7	9	12	14	16	16	14	11	8	6	10
Stockholm, Sweden	43	30	25	31	34	45	61	76	60	48	53	48	554
44 m	–3	–3	–1	5	10	15	18	17	12	7	3	0	7
ASIA													
Bahrain	8	18	13	8	3	0	0	0	0	0	18	18	81
5 m	17	18	21	25	29	32	33	34	31	28	24	19	26
Bangkok, Thailand	8	20	36	58	198	160	160	175	305	206	66	5	1,397
2 m	26	28	29	30	29	29	28	28	28	28	26	25	28
Beirut, Lebanon	191	158	94	53	18	3	3	3	5	51	132	185	892
34 m	14	14	16	18	22	24	27	28	26	24	19	16	21
Colombo, Sri Lanka	89	69	147	231	371	224	135	109	160	348	315	147	2,365
7 m	26	26	27	28	28	27	27	27	27	27	26	26	27
Harbin, China	6	5	10	23	43	94	112	104	46	33	8	5	488
160 m	–18	–15	–5	6	13	19	22	21	14	4	–6	–16	3
Ho Chi Minh, Vietnam	15	3	13	43	221	330	315	269	335	269	114	56	1,984
9 m	26	27	29	30	29	28	28	28	27	27	27	26	28
Hong Kong, China	33	46	74	137	292	394	381	361	257	114	43	31	2,162
33 m	16	15	18	22	26	28	28	28	27	25	21	18	23
Jakarta, Indonesia	300	300	211	147	114	97	64	43	66	112	142	203	1,798
8 m	26	26	27	27	27	27	27	27	27	27	27	26	27
Kabul, Afghanistan	34	60	68	72	23	1	6	2	2	4	19	22	313
1,815 m	–3	–1	6	13	18	22	25	24	20	14	7	3	12
Karachi, Pakistan	13	10	8	3	3	18	81	41	13	3	3	5	196
4 m	19	20	24	28	30	31	30	29	28	28	24	20	26
Kazalinsk, Kazakhstan	10	10	13	13	15	5	5	8	8	10	13	15	125
63 m	–12	–11	–3	6	18	23	25	23	16	8	–1	–7	7
Kolkata, India	10	31	36	43	140	297	325	328	252	114	20	5	1,600
6 m	20	22	27	30	30	30	29	29	29	28	23	19	26
Mumbai, India	3	3	3	3	18	485	617	340	264	64	13	3	1,809
11 m	24	24	26	28	30	29	27	27	27	28	27	26	27
New Delhi, India	23	18	13	8	13	74	180	172	117	10	3	10	640
218 m	14	17	23	28	33	34	31	30	29	26	20	15	25
Omsk, Russia	15	8	8	13	31	51	51	51	28	25	18	20	318
85 m	–22	–19	–12	–1	10	16	18	16	10	1	–11	–18	–1
Shanghai, China	48	58	84	94	94	180	147	142	130	71	51	36	1,135
7 m	4	5	9	14	20	24	28	28	23	19	12	7	16
Singapore	252	173	193	188	173	173	170	196	178	208	254	257	2,413
10 m	26	27	28	28	28	28	28	27	27	27	27	27	27
Tehran, Iran	46	38	46	36	13	3	3	3	3	8	20	31	246
1,220 m	2	5	9	16	21	26	30	29	25	18	12	6	17
Tokyo, Japan	48	74	107	135	147	165	142	152	234	208	97	56	1,565
6 m	3	4	7	13	17	21	25	26	23	17	11	6	14
Ulan Bator, Mongolia	3	3	3	5	10	28	76	51	23	5	5	3	208
1,325 m	–26	–21	–13	–1	6	14	16	14	8	–1	–13	–22	–3
Verkhoyansk, Russia	5	5	3	5	8	23	28	25	13	8	8	5	134
100 m	–50	–45	–32	–15	0	12	14	9	2	–15	–38	–48	–17
AFRICA													
Addis Ababa, Ethiopia	3	3	25	135	213	201	206	239	102	28	3	0	1,151
2,450 m	19	20	20	20	19	18	18	19	21	22	21	20	20
Antananarivo, Madagas.	300	279	178	53	18	8	8	10	18	61	135	287	1,356
1,372 m	21	21	21	19	18	15	14	15	17	19	21	21	19
Cairo, Egypt	5	4	4	1	1	0	0	0	0	1	4	6	26
116 m	13	15	18	21	25	28	28	28	26	24	20	15	22
Cape Town, S. Africa	15	8	18	48	79	84	89	66	43	31	18	10	508
17 m	21	21	20	17	14	13	12	13	14	16	18	19	17
Johannesburg, S. Africa	114	109	89	38	25	8	8	8	23	56	107	125	709
1,665 m	20	20	18	16	13	10	11	13	16	18	19	20	16

	Jan.	Feb.	Mar.	Apr.	May	June	July	Aug.	Sept.	Oct.	Nov.	Dec.	Year
Khartoum, Sudan	3	3	3	3	3	8	53	71	18	5	3	0	158
390 m	24	25	28	31	33	34	32	31	32	32	28	25	29
Kinshasa, Congo (D.R.)	135	145	196	196	158	8	3	3	31	119	221	142	1,354
325 m	26	26	27	27	26	24	23	24	25	26	26	26	25
Lagos, Nigeria	28	46	102	150	269	460	279	64	140	206	69	25	1,836
3 m	27	28	29	28	28	26	26	25	26	26	28	28	27
Lusaka, Zambia	231	191	142	18	3	3	3	0	3	10	91	150	836
1,277 m	21	22	21	21	19	16	16	18	22	24	23	22	21
Monrovia, Liberia	31	56	97	216	516	973	996	373	744	772	236	130	5,138
23 m	26	26	27	27	26	25	24	25	25	25	26	26	26
Nairobi, Kenya	38	64	125	211	158	46	15	23	31	53	109	86	958
1,820 m	19	19	19	19	18	16	16	16	18	19	18	18	18
Timbuktu, Mali	1	0	0	1	4	16	54	74	29	4	0	0	183
301 m	22	24	28	32	34	35	32	30	32	31	28	23	29
Tunis, Tunisia	64	51	41	36	18	8	3	8	33	51	48	61	419
66 m	10	11	13	16	19	23	26	27	25	20	16	11	18
Walvis Bay, Namibia	3	5	8	3	3	3	3	3	3	3	3	3	23
7 m	19	19	19	18	17	16	15	14	14	15	17	18	18
AUSTRALIA, NEW ZEALAND AND ANTARCTICA													
Alice Springs, Australia	43	33	28	10	15	13	8	8	8	18	31	38	252
579 m	29	28	25	20	15	12	12	14	18	23	26	28	21
Christchurch, N. Zealand	56	43	48	48	66	66	69	48	46	43	48	56	638
10 m	16	16	14	12	9	6	6	7	9	12	14	16	11
Darwin, Australia	386	312	254	97	15	3	3	3	13	51	119	239	1,491
30 m	29	29	29	29	28	26	25	26	28	29	30	29	28
Mawson, Antarctica	11	30	20	10	44	180	4	40	3	20	0	0	362
14 m	0	–5	–10	–14	–15	–16	–18	–18	–19	–13	–5	–1	–11
Perth, Australia	8	10	20	43	130	180	170	149	86	56	20	13	881
60 m	23	23	22	19	16	14	13	13	15	16	19	22	18
Sydney, Australia	89	102	127	135	127	117	117	76	73	71	73	73	1,181
42 m	22	22	21	18	15	13	12	13	15	18	19	21	17
NORTH AMERICA													
Anchorage, Alaska, USA	20	18	15	10	13	18	41	66	66	56	25	23	371
40 m	–11	–8	–5	2	7	12	14	13	9	2	–5	–11	2
Chicago, Illinois, USA	51	51	66	71	86	89	84	81	79	66	61	51	836
251 m	–4	–3	2	9	14	20	23	22	19	12	5	–1	10
Churchill, Man., Canada	15	13	18	23	32	44	46	58	51	43	39	21	402
13 m	–28	–26	–20	–10	–2	6	12	11	5	–2	–12	–22	–7
Edmonton, Alta., Canada	25	19	19	22	43	77	89	78	39	17	16	25	466
676 m	–15	–10	–5	4	11	15	17	16	11	6	–4	–10	3
Honolulu, Hawai'i, USA	104	66	79	48	25	18	23	28	36	48	64	104	643
12 m	23	18	19	20	22	24	25	26	26	24	22	19	22
Houston, Texas, USA	89	76	84	91	119	117	99	99	104	94	89	109	1,171
12 m	12	13	17	21	24	27	28	29	26	22	16	12	21
Kingston, Jamaica	23	15	23	31	102	89	38	91	99	180	74	36	800
34 m	25	25	25	26	26	28	28	28	27	27	26	26	26
Los Angeles, Calif., USA	79	76	71	25	10	3	3	3	5	15	31	66	381
95 m	13	14	14	16	17	19	21	22	21	18	16	14	17
Mexico City, Mexico	13	5	10	20	53	119	170	152	130	51	18	8	747
2,309 m	12	13	16	18	19	19	17	18	18	16	14	13	16
Miami, Florida, USA	71	53	64	81	173	178	155	160	203	234	71	51	1,516
8 m	20	20	22	23	25	27	28	28	27	25	22	21	24
Montréal, Que., Canada	72	65	74	74	66	82	90	92	88	76	81	87	946
57 m	–10	–9	–3	–6	13	18	21	20	15	9	2	–7	6
New York City, NY, USA	94	97	91	81	81	84	107	109	86	89	76	91	1,092
96 m	–1	–1	3	10	16	20	23	23	21	15	7	2	11
St Louis, Mo., USA	58	64	89	97	114	114	89	86	81	74	71	64	1,001
173 m	0	1	7	13	19	24	26	26	22	15	8	2	14
San José, Costa Rica	15	5	20	46	229	241	211	241	305	300	145	41	1,798
1,146 m	19	19	21	21	22	21	21	21	21	20	20	19	20
Vancouver, BC, Canada	154	115	101	60	52	45	32	41	67	114	150	182	1,113
14 m	3	5	6	9	12	15	17	17	14	10	6	4	10
Washington, DC, USA	86	76	91	84	94	99	112	109	94	74	66	79	1,064
22 m	1	2	7	12	18	23	25	24	20	14	8	3	13
SOUTH AMERICA													
Antofagasta, Chile	0	0	0	3	3	3	5	3	3	3	3	0	13
94 m	21	21	20	18	16	15	14	14	15	16	18	19	17
Buenos Aires, Argentina	122	123	154	107	92	50	53	63	78	139	131	103	1,215
27 m	23	23	21	17	13	9	10	11	13	15	19	22	16
Lima, Peru	3	3	3	3	5	5	8	8	8	3	3	3	41
120 m	23	24	24	22	19	17	17	16	17	18	19	21	20
Manaus, Brazil	249	231	262	221	170	84	58	38	46	107	142	203	1,811
44 m	28	28	28	27	28	28	28	28	29	29	29	28	28
Paraná, Brazil	287	236	239	102	13	3	3	5	28	127	231	310	1,582
260 m	23	23	23	23	23	21	21	22	24	24	24	23	23
Rio de Janeiro, Brazil	125	122	130	107	79	53	41	43	66	79	104	137	1,082
61 m	26	26	25	24	22	21	21	21	21	22	23	25	23

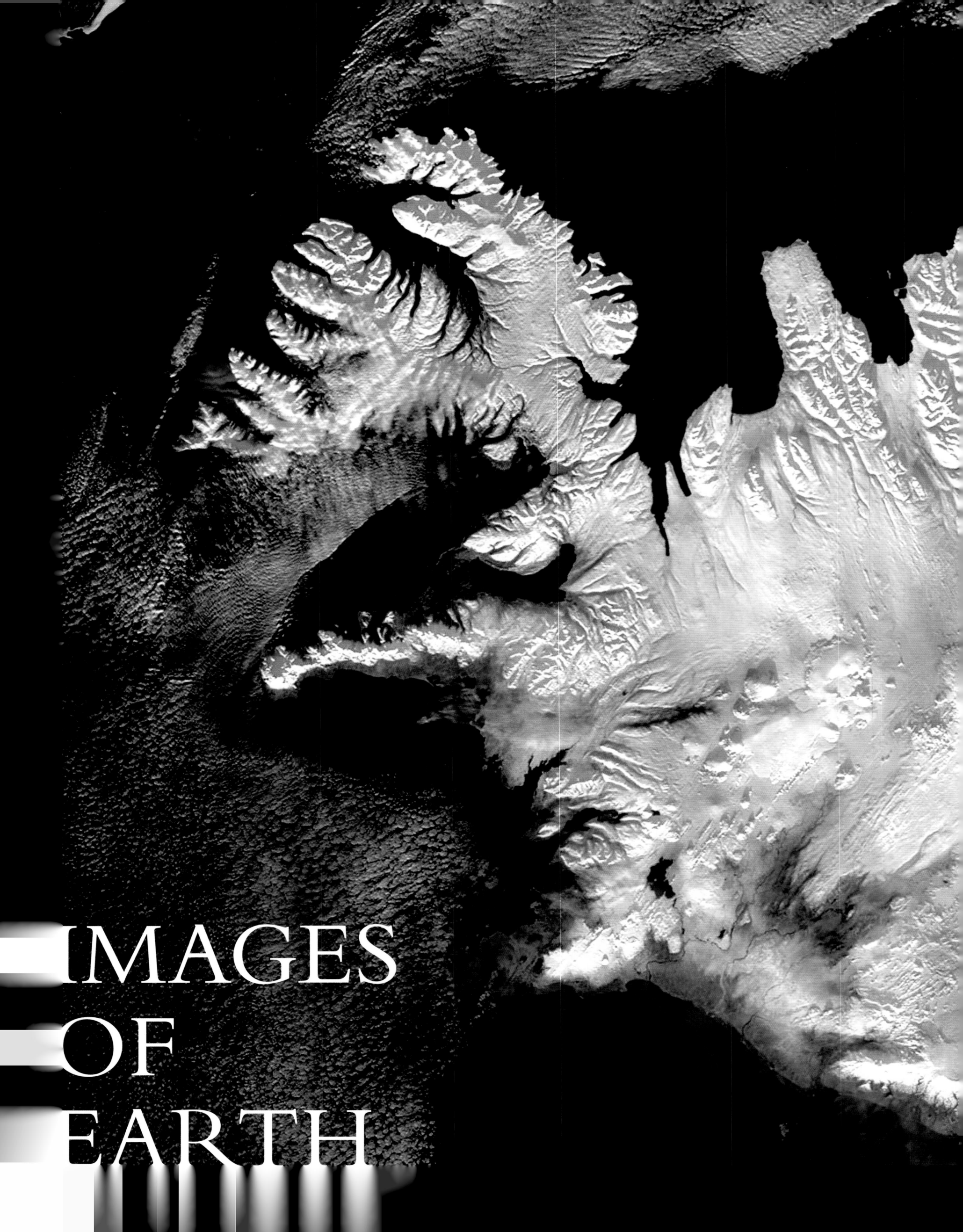

IMAGES
OF
EARTH

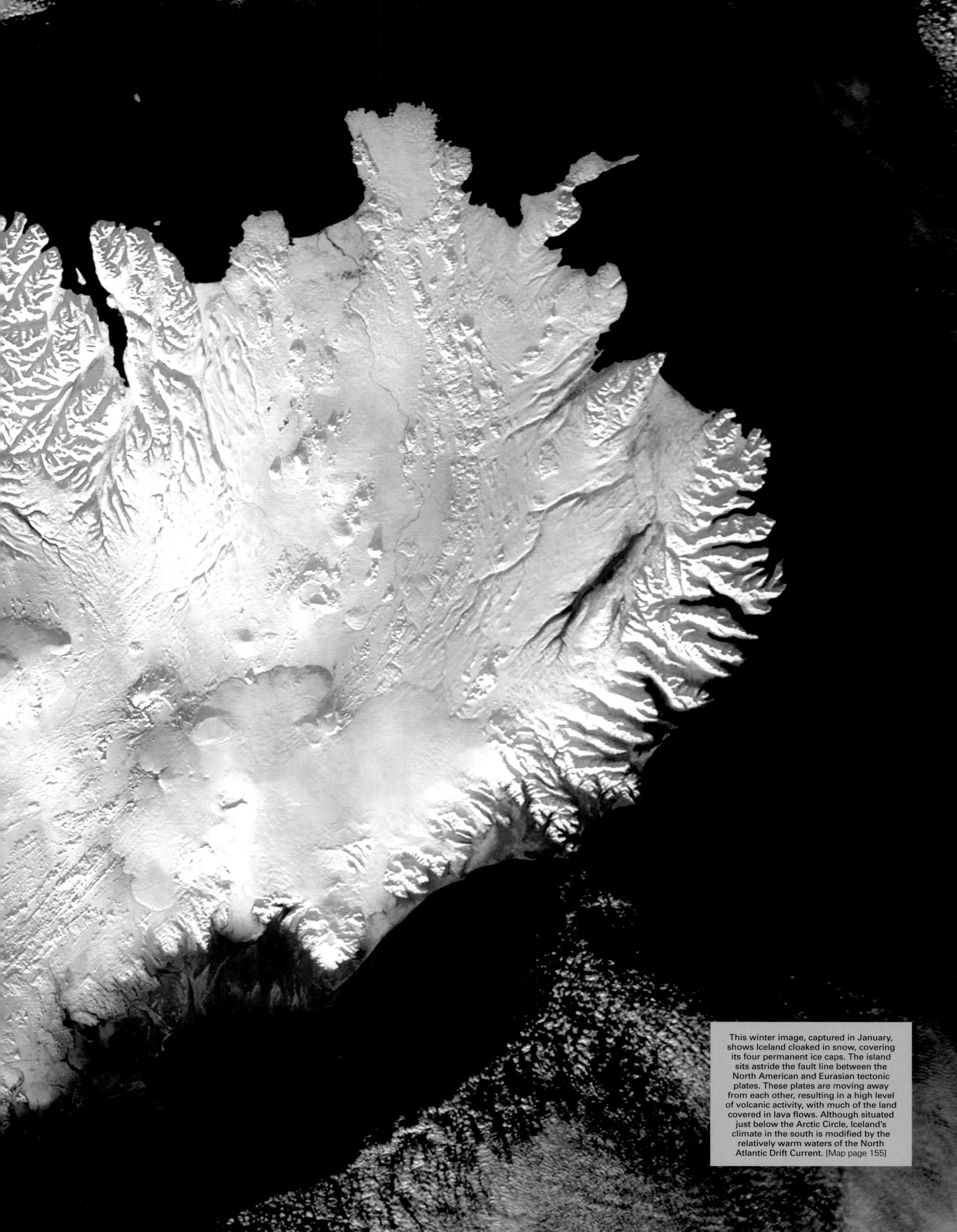

This winter image, captured in January, shows Iceland cloaked in snow, covering its four permanent ice caps. The island sits astride the fault line between the North American and Eurasian tectonic plates. These plates are moving away from each other, resulting in a high level of volcanic activity, with much of the land covered in lava flows. Although situated just below the Arctic Circle, Iceland's climate in the south is modified by the relatively warm waters of the North Atlantic Drift Current. [Map page 155]

The River Thames, flowing from west to east, stands out in this image, as do the former London docks and the extensive reservoirs in the River Lea valley to the northeast. The settlement developed over 1,900 years ago at the river's lowest bridging point, on the main Roman supply route to and from the south coast. Despite having a population in excess of 8 million people, there are still many parks and open spaces around the city center. Some, such as Regents, Hyde, and St James's Parks, are over 300 years old, having previously been royal hunting grounds. [Map page 169]

Built on over 100 small islands in a shallow lagoon, this image shows the largest island on which the main city is built, with the islands of San Michele and Murano to the north. The sinuous Grand Canal connects the train station in the northwest to St Mark's Square in the south, with a network of smaller canals on either side. Since the beginning of the last century the city has been slowly sinking into the mud, due to water extraction on the mainland combined with tidal action. The former has now been stopped and there are plans for a barrage to control tidal surges in the lagoon. *(Satellite image courtesy of Space Imaging)* [Map page 199]

The River Danube discharges into the northwest Black Sea, its flow slowing as a result and thus releasing the sediment it carries. This material accumulates to extend the delta at a rate of up to 98 ft [30 m] a year, forming Europe's largest delta, within which the world's largest reed bed is situated. It hosts over 1,200 plant species, 330 species of birds and 45 species of freshwater fish. The main area was designated a UNESCO World Natural Heritage Site in 1991 and has been identified by the World Wide Fund for Nature (WWF) as one of the 200 most important sites in the world for biodiversity conservation. [Map page 183]

This image shows Shanghai (center) in its setting on the south bank of the mouth of the Chang Jiang (Yangtse) river. Since it sits at the gateway to one of China's richest regions and the river is navigable for ocean-going vessels up to Hankou, a further 600 miles [1,000 km] inland, it has developed to become the world's largest cargo port. It has grown rapidly to become the largest city in China, with over 14 million people, and is the country's major commercial and financial center. [Map page 219]

This image shows glaciers flowing from the snow-covered Himalayas on the northern Bhutan border. Glaciers are an important indicator of temperature change. By comparing imagery, researchers have found a strong correlation between increasing temperatures and glacial retreat, as well as volumes of melt water and the size and number of lakes forming on the surface of the glaciers. About 70% of the world's fresh water is frozen in glaciers and the largest concentration of these outside the polar regions is in the Himalayas. It is believed that 67% of these glaciers are retreating. [Map page 241]

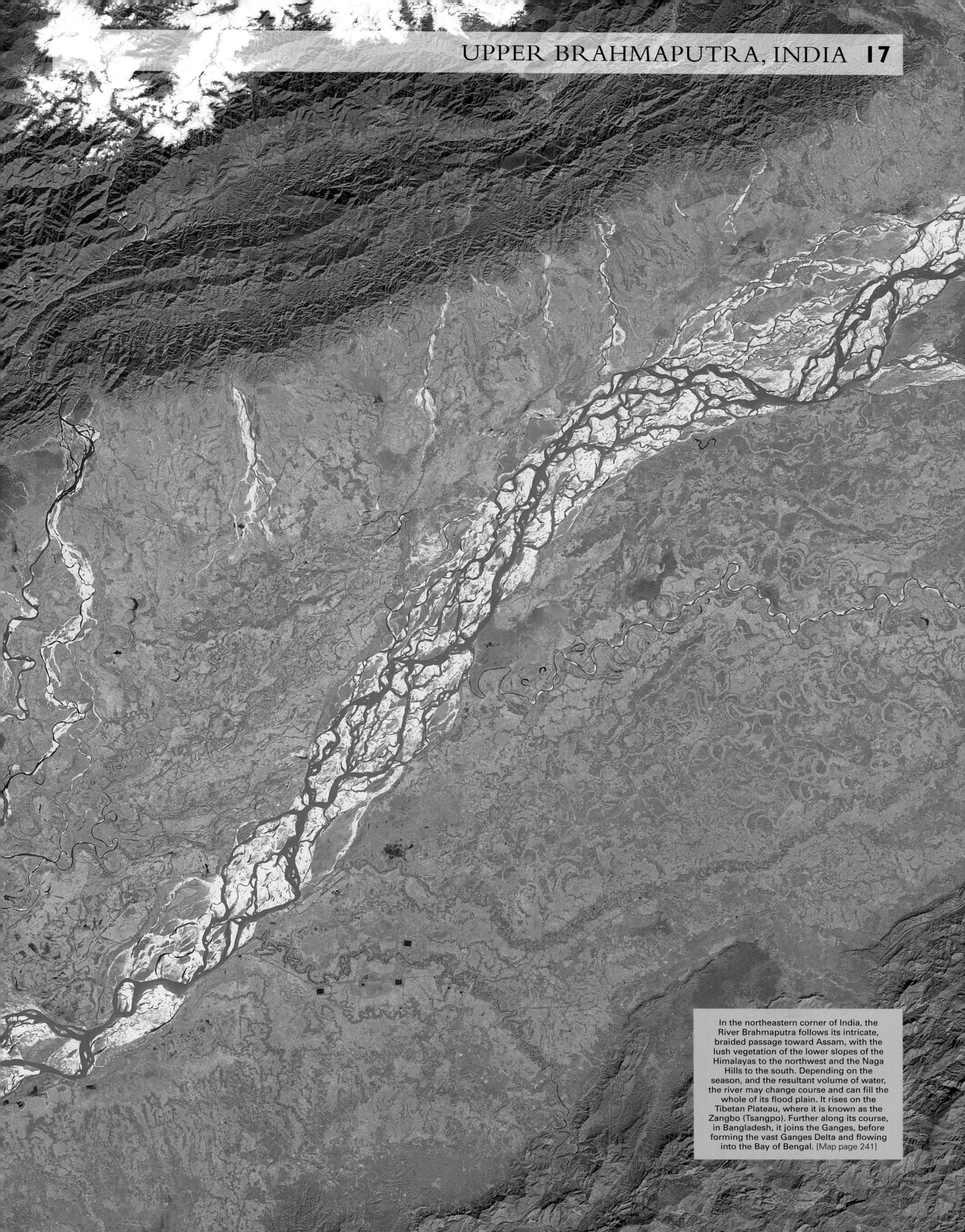

In the northeastern corner of India, the River Brahmaputra follows its intricate, braided passage toward Assam, with the lush vegetation of the lower slopes of the Himalayas to the northwest and the Naga Hills to the south. Depending on the season, and the resultant volume of water, the river may change course and can fill the whole of its flood plain. It rises on the Tibetan Plateau, where it is known as the Zangbo (Tsangpo). Further along its course, in Bangladesh, it joins the Ganges, before forming the vast Ganges Delta and flowing into the Bay of Bengal. [Map page 241]

The largest city in Africa, with over 11 million inhabitants, Cairo evolved on the eastern bank of the River Nile, near its delta. This image clearly shows the differences between the arid desert areas to the southeast and southwest, the fertile lands of the Nile flood plain, and the urban area itself. The shadows of the Pyramids on the Giza Plateau can be seen on the left-hand edge of the cultivated area, below where the road, approaching from the bottom left-hand side, crosses it.

[Map page 256]

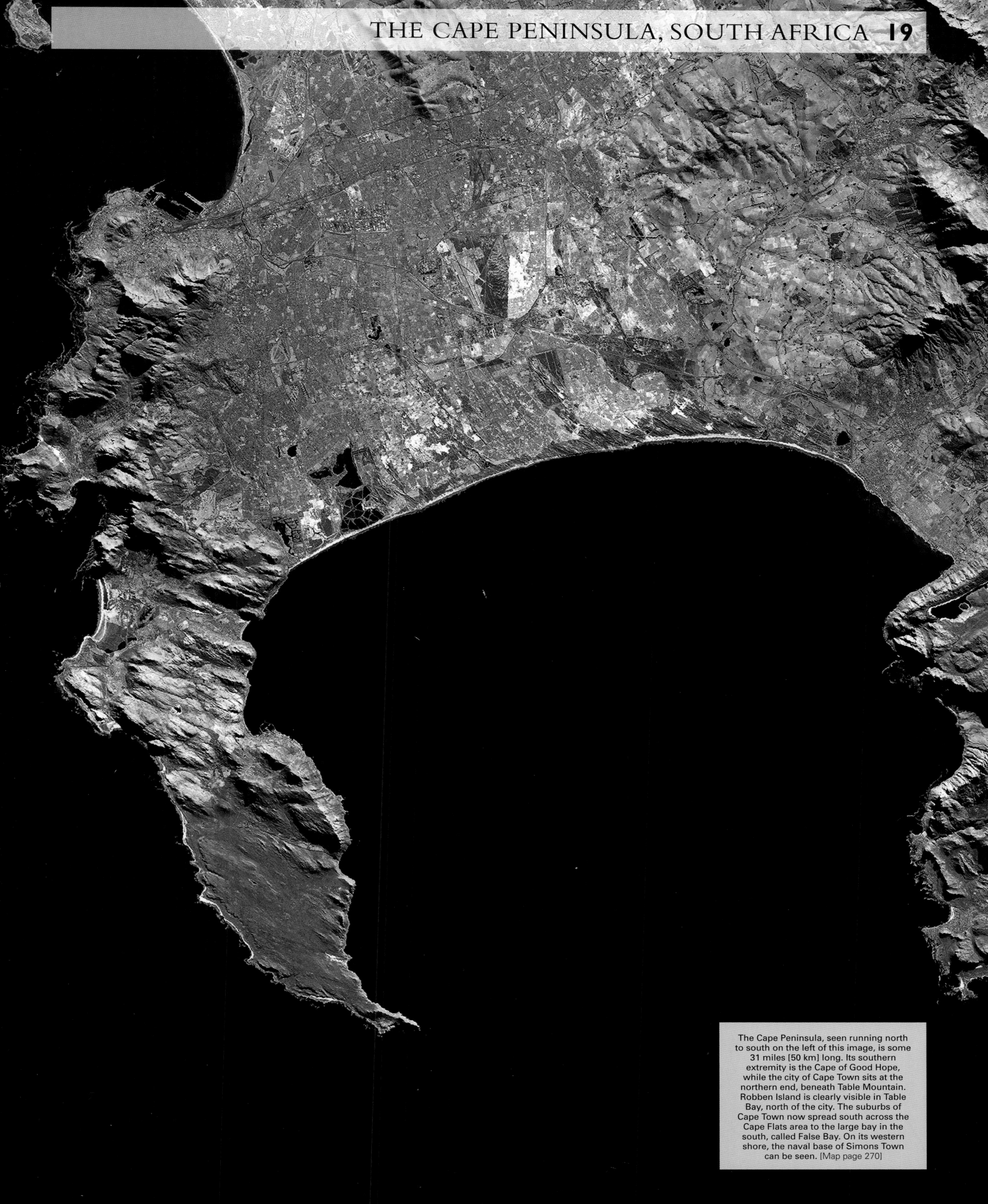

The Cape Peninsula, seen running north to south on the left of this image, is some 31 miles [50 km] long. Its southern extremity is the Cape of Good Hope, while the city of Cape Town sits at the northern end, beneath Table Mountain. Robben Island is clearly visible in Table Bay, north of the city. The suburbs of Cape Town now spread south across the Cape Flats area to the large bay in the south, called False Bay. On its western shore, the naval base of Simons Town can be seen. [Map page 270]

Situated within the Great Rift Valley in northern Tanzania, the crater is the largest complete collapsed volcanic cone, or caldera, in the world. The whole area was one of intense geological activity, as can be seen from the surrounding craters, but currently only one, in the northeast, is active. Ngorongoro is the crater in the south of the image, with Lake Magadi within it. The steep sides of the crater limit normal animal migration, and within it there is a unique ecosystem supporting a wide range of birds and animals. The two lakes in the south are Lake Eyasi (to the west) and Lake Manyara (to the east). [Map page 268]

The largest city in Australia, Sydney was founded at the end of the 18th century on the north shore of Botany Bay. It has since spread inland along the valley of the Parramatta River, but is constrained by the Blue Mountains National Park in the west (the green area in this image). Within this area the reservoir Lake Burragong can be seen, which supplies 80% of the city's water. The runways of Australia's busiest airport are also visible, projecting from the north shore of Botany Bay. [Map page 283]

The lush forests of Egmont National Park, on New Zealand's North Island, contrast with the pasturelands outside the circular park boundaries in this image. The unique shape of the park results from its creation in 1881, which specified that a forest reserve would extend in a radius of 6 miles [9.6 km] from the summit of Mount Taranaki (the volcano originally named Mount Egmont by Captain Cook in 1770). The park covers about 83,000 acres [33,500 hectares], and the volcano, which last erupted in 1755, stands at 8,261 ft [2,518 m]. A series of montane habitats occur up the flanks of the volcano, ranging from rain forest, to shrubs and alpine, and finally snow cover. [Map page 284]

The city of Vancouver grew up around its fine, natural harbor on the north side of the Fraser River delta, developing as the western railhead of the Canadian Pacific Railroad. Just to the south of the delta runs the 49th parallel, the boundary between Canada and the USA. To the north of the city lie the snow-capped Coast Mountains, and to the southwest, across the Strait of Georgia, part of Vancouver Island with the town of Victoria, the capital of British Columbia, can be seen. [Map page 296]

This image covers the largest urban area in the USA, which has a population of over 18 million people. Flowing from the north, the Hudson River divides the two cities of New York (to the east) and New Jersey (to the west). Toward its mouth on the east bank lies Manhattan Island, with Central Park. Below this is Long Island, with its distinctive offshore spits. At its western end lie the urban areas of Brooklyn and Queens, but further southeast are resorts such as Long Beach and the Fire Islands National Seashore.

[Map page 312]

Sometimes called "The Crescent City," the settlement is situated between the south bank of Lake Pontchartrain (the largest in this view) and the Mississippi River. The latter can be seen meandering to the south of the city on its way to the delta, which lies to the southeast. In August 2005 the flood-control system, which was constructed in the early 20th century, failed in the face of the category 5 Hurricane Katrina, which breached two dams and flooded and destroyed parts of the city, making many homeless. The wetlands to the south are themselves being eroded, since less silt is being deposited at the mouth to reinforce the delta. [Map page 315]

The town, with a population of almost 1.7 million, is the light area to the north of the confluence of the Rio Negro, or Black River (to the north), with the Amazon (to the south), some 1,000 miles [1,600 km] from its mouth. The main branch of the river to the south, sometimes also called the Solimões, is carrying a heavy load of sediment from the Andes, hence the marked color difference. For all of its length across Brazil the river is over 100 ft [30 m] deep and ocean-going vessels can navigate this far upstream, and indeed continue a further 1,300 miles [2,100 km] up the Amazon to Iquitos, in northern Peru.
[Map page 329]

Santiago, the capital city of Chile, lies in a fertile valley at the foot of the Andes, some 37 miles [60 km] southeast of the main port of Valparaíso. To the east the mountains rise to over 20,000 ft [6,000 m]. At top right of the image, the boundary with Argentina runs along the watershed. The city expanded rapidly to its current population of over 5 million inhabitants and this resulted in air pollution problems in the 1980s, though measures have since been taken to deal with this.

[Map page 334]

GAZETTEER
OF
NATIONS

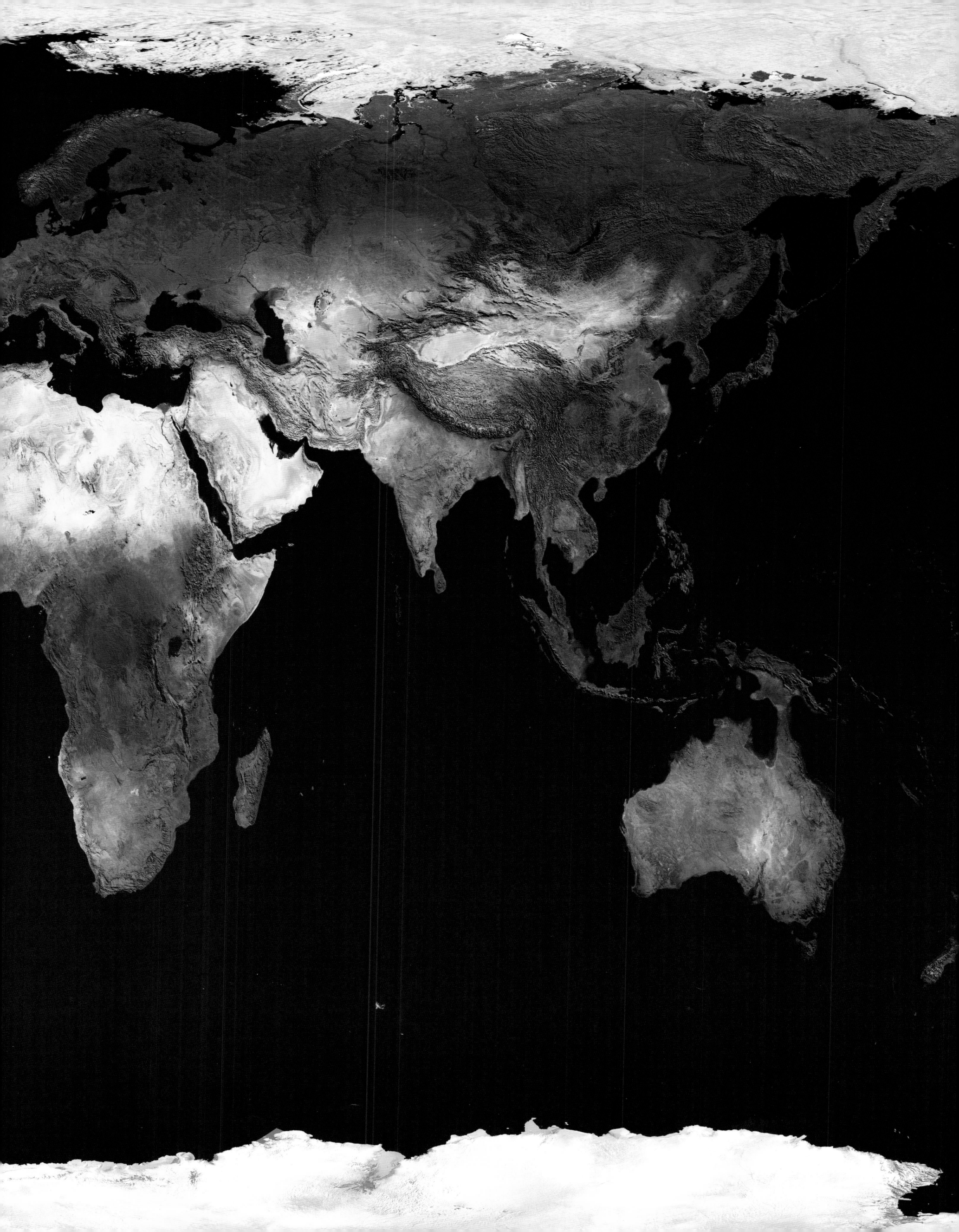

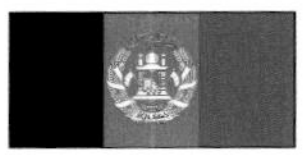
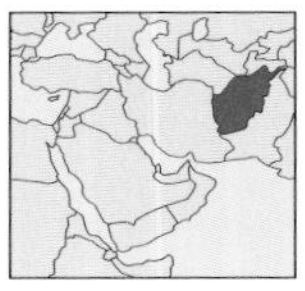

AFGHANISTAN

GEOGRAPHY The Republic of Afghanistan is a landlocked, mountainous country in southern Asia. The central highlands reach a height of more than 22,966 ft [7,000 m] in the east and make up nearly three-quarters of Afghanistan. The main range is the Hindu Kush, which is cut by deep, fertile valleys.

In winter, northerly winds bring cold, snowy weather to the mountains, but summers are hot and dry.

POLITICS & ECONOMY The modern history of Afghanistan began in 1747, when the various tribes in the area united for the first time. In the 19th century, Russia and Britain struggled for control of the country. Following Britain's withdrawal in 1919, Afghanistan became fully independent. Soviet troops invaded in 1979 to support a socialist regime in Kabul, but they withdrew in 1989. By 2001, a group called the Taliban ("Islamic students") controlled 90% of the country. In 2001, following the refusal of the Taliban to hand over the terrorist leader Osama bin Laden, an international force invaded Afghanistan. In 2002, a coalition government was set up under Hamid Karzai, who was elected president in 2004. Parliamentary elections were held in 2005, but fighting continued into 2008.

Afghanistan is a poor country and more then 60% of its people are farmers or nomadic herders. Natural gas is produced, together with some coal, copper, gold, precious stones, and salt.

AREA 251,772 sq mi [652,090 sq km]
POPULATION 31,890,000 **CAPITAL** Kabul
GOVERNMENT Transitional **ETHNIC GROUPS** Pashtun (Pathan) 44%, Tajik 25%, Hazara 10%, Uzbek 8%, others 13%
LANGUAGES Pashtu, Dari/Persian (both official), Uzbek
RELIGIONS Islam (Sunni Muslim 84%, Shi'ite Muslim 15%), others 1%
CURRENCY Afghani = 100 puls

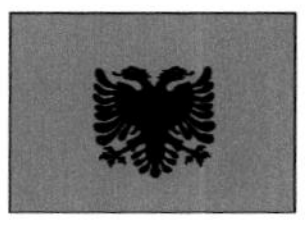
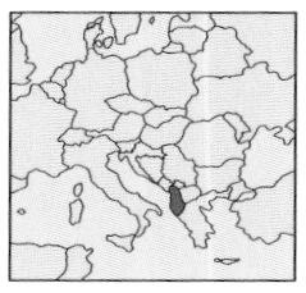

ALBANIA

GEOGRAPHY The Republic of Albania lies in the Balkan peninsula, facing the Adriatic Sea. About 70% of the land is mountainous, but most Albanians live in the west on the coastal lowlands.

The coastal areas of Albania experience a typical Mediterranean climate, with fairly dry, sunny summers and cool, moist winters. The mountains have a severe climate, with heavy winter snowfalls.

POLITICS & ECONOMY Albania is one of Europe's poorest nations. A former Communist country, Albania adopted a multiparty system in the early 1990s. The change proved difficult. But after elections in 1997, a socialist government committed to a market system took office. The transition to democracy has been difficult. The 2005 elections, when the center-right Democratic Party defeated the Socialists, were considered to fall short of international standards.

In 2005, agriculture employed about 50% of the people. Since 1991, private ownership of land has been encouraged, replacing the former state farm and collective system. Albania has some minerals. Chromite, copper, and nickel are exported.

AREA 11,100 sq mi [28,748 sq km] **POPULATION** 3,601,000
CAPITAL Tirana **GOVERNMENT** Multiparty republic
ETHNIC GROUPS Albanian 95%, Greek 3%, Macedonian, Vlachs, Gypsy **LANGUAGES** Albanian (official) **RELIGIONS** Many people say they are non-believers; of the believers, 70% follow Islam and 30% follow Christianity (Orthodox 20%, Roman Catholic 10%)
CURRENCY Lek = 100 qindars

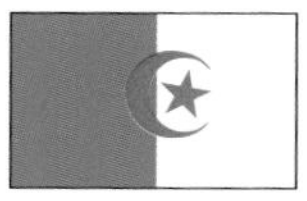
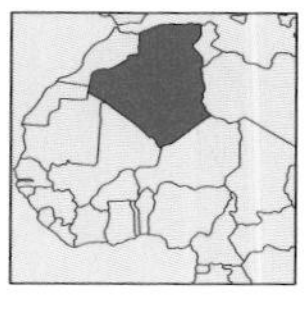

ALGERIA

GEOGRAPHY The People's Democratic Republic of Algeria is Africa's second largest country after Sudan. Most Algerians live in the north, on the fertile coastal plains and hill country bordering the Mediterranean Sea. Four-fifths of Algeria is in the Sahara. The coast has a Mediterranean climate, but the arid Sahara is hot by day and cool at night.

POLITICS & ECONOMY France ruled Algeria from 1830 until 1962, when the socialist FLN (National Liberation Front) formed a one-party government. Following the recognition of opposition parties in 1989, a Muslim group, the FIS (Islamic Salvation Front), won an election in 1991. The FLN canceled the elections and civil conflict broke out. About 100,000 people were killed in the 1990s. In 1999, Abdelaziz Bouteflika was elected president. The scale of violence was reduced. In 2005, the government made concessions to the Berber minority and, in 2006, it began releasing Islamic militants. But violence returned when suicide bombings occurred in 2007 and 2008.

Algeria is a developing country, whose chief resources are oil and natural gas, which were discovered in the Sahara in 1956. The natural gas reserves are among the world's largest, and gas and oil account for 90% of Algeria's exports. Cement, iron and steel, textiles, and vehicles are manufactured. Barley, citrus fruits, dates, potatoes, and wheat are the major crops.

AREA 919,590 sq mi [2,381,741 sq km]
POPULATION 33,333,000 **CAPITAL** Algiers
GOVERNMENT Socialist republic **ETHNIC GROUPS** Arab-Berber 99%
LANGUAGES Arabic and Berber (official), French **RELIGIONS** Sunni Muslim 99% **CURRENCY** Algerian dinar = 100 centimes

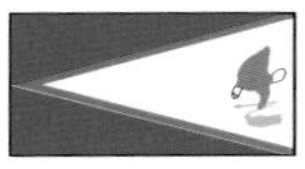
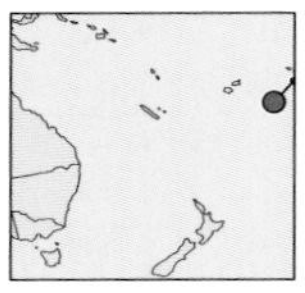

AMERICAN SAMOA

An "unincorporated territory" of the United States, American Samoa lies in the south-central Pacific Ocean.

AREA 77 sq mi [199 sq km]
POPULATION 58,000 **CAPITAL** Pago Pago

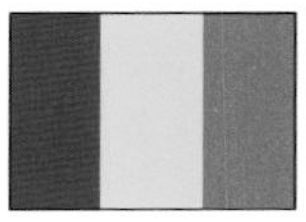
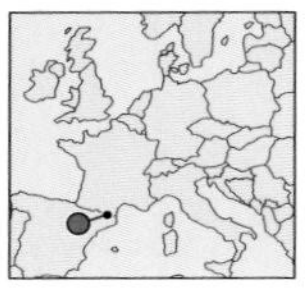

ANDORRA

A mini-state situated in the Pyrenees Mountains, Andorra is a coprincipality whose main activity is tourism. Most Andorrans live in the six valleys (the Valls) that drain into the River Valira.

AREA 181 sq mi [468 sq km]
POPULATION 72,000 **CAPITAL** Andorra La Vella

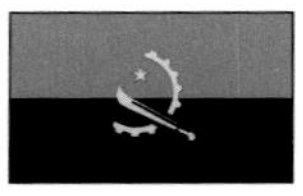
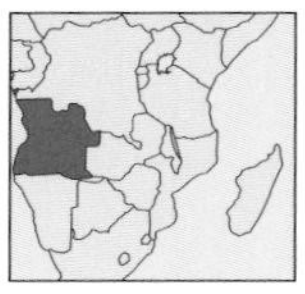

ANGOLA

GEOGRAPHY The Republic of Angola is a large country in southwestern Africa. Much of the country is part of the plateau that forms most of southern Africa, with a narrow coastal plain in the west.

Angola has a tropical climate, with temperatures of over 68°F [20°C] throughout the year, though the highest areas are cooler. The coast is dry, but the rainfall increases to the north and east.

POLITICS & ECONOMY Bantu-speaking people settled in Angola in the 13th century and later founded large kingdoms, such as the Kongo and Mbundu. Portugal controlled the coastal slave trade from the 17th century and extended their control inland in the 19th century. Angola became independent from Portugal in 1975, after which rival nationalist groups struggled for power. Despite a ceasefire in the mid-1990s, conflict finally ended in 2002, when the rebel leader, Jonas Savimbi, was killed. Since the war, Angola has faced severe economic problems, despite its mineral wealth.

Angola is a developing country, where 70% of the people are poor farmers. The main food crops are cassava and maize. Coffee is exported. Angola has important oil reserves and oil is exported. Angola also produces diamonds and has reserves of copper, manganese, and phosphates.

AREA 481,351 sq mi [1,246,700 sq km]
POPULATION 12,264,000 **CAPITAL** Luanda
GOVERNMENT Multiparty republic
ETHNIC GROUPS Ovimbundu 37%, Kimbundu 25%, Bakongo 13%, others 25% **LANGUAGES** Portuguese (official), many others
RELIGIONS Traditional beliefs 47%, Roman Catholic 38%, Protestant 15%
CURRENCY Kwanza = 100 lwei

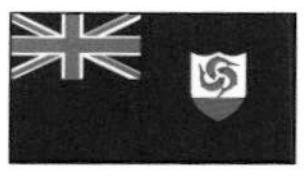
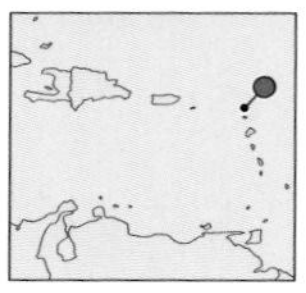

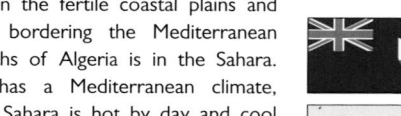

ANGUILLA

Formerly part of St Kitts and Nevis, Anguilla, the most northerly of the Leeward Islands, became a British dependency (now a British overseas territory) in 1980. The main source of revenue is now tourism, although lobster still accounts for half the island's exports.

AREA 37 sq mi [96 sq km]
POPULATION 14,000 **CAPITAL** The Valley

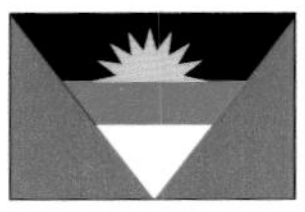
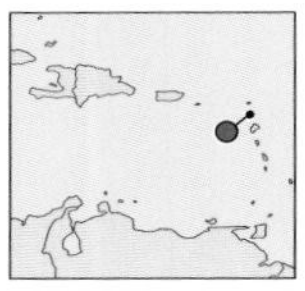

ANTIGUA & BARBUDA

A former British dependency in the Caribbean, Antigua and Barbuda became independent in 1981. Tourism is the main industry, though sugar is an important product.

AREA 171 sq mi [442 sq km]
POPULATION 69,000 **CAPITAL** St John's

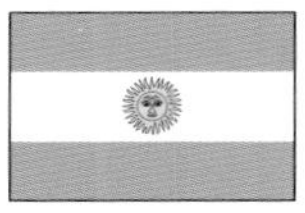
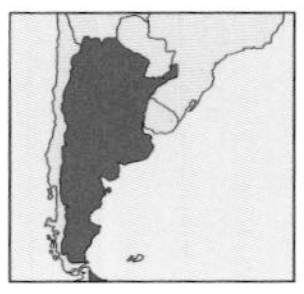

ARGENTINA

GEOGRAPHY The Argentine Republic is South America's second largest and the world's eighth largest country. The high Andes range in the west contains Mount Aconcagua, the highest peak in the Americas. In southern Argentina, the Andes Mountains overlook Patagonia, a plateau region. In east-central Argentina lies a fertile plain called the pampas.

The climate varies from subtropical in the north to temperate in the south. Rainfall is abundant in the north-east but lower to the west and south. Patagonia is largely desert.

POLITICS & ECONOMY The earliest people were American Indians, but 86% of the people are now of European ancestry. Spain took control in the 16th century and ruled until 1816. Argentina later suffered from instability and periods of military rule. In 1982, Argentina's military regime invaded the Falkland (Malvinas) Islands, but Britain regained the islands later that year. Argentina restored civilian rule in 1983. In 2007, Christina Fernández de Kirchner was elected president, succeeding her husband, Néstor Carlos Kirchner, who had served as president from 2003. She was the first woman to be the directly elected president of Argentina.

The World Bank classifies Argentina as an "upper-middle-income" developing country. About 90% of the people live in urban areas. Manufactures include food products, cars, electrical equipment, and textiles. Oil is the chief natural resource and the chief farm products are beef, maize, and wheat. Oil is exported, together with meat, wheat, maize, vegetable oils, hides and skins, and wool. In 1991, Argentina, Brazil, Paraguay and Uruguay set up an alliance, Mercosur, aimed at creating a common market. In the early 2000s, Argentina suffered a severe economic crisis, but by 2008 it appeared to have largely recovered.

AREA 1,073,512 sq mi [2,780,400 sq km]
POPULATION 40,302,000 **CAPITAL** Buenos Aires
GOVERNMENT Federal republic **ETHNIC GROUPS** European 97%, Mestizo, Amerindian **LANGUAGES** Spanish (official)
RELIGIONS Roman Catholic 92%, Protestant 2%, Jewish 2%, others **CURRENCY** Argentine peso = 10,000 australs

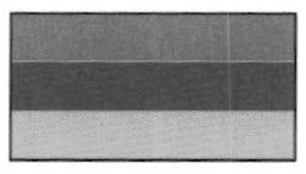
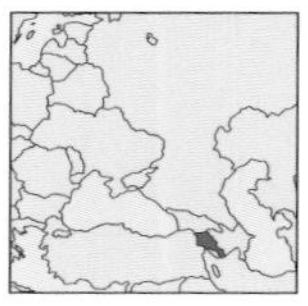

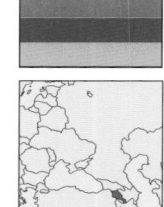

ARMENIA

GEOGRAPHY The Republic of Armenia is a landlocked country in southwestern Asia. Most of Armenia consists of a rugged plateau, crisscrossed by long faults (cracks). Movements along the faults cause earthquakes. The highest point is Mount Aragats, at 13,419 ft [4,090 m] above sea level.

The height of the land, which averages 4,920 ft [1,500 m] above sea level gives rise to severe winters and cool summers. The highest peaks are snow-capped, but the total yearly rainfall is generally low.

POLITICS & ECONOMY In 1920, Armenia became a Communist republic and, in 1922, it became, with Azerbaijan and Georgia, part of the Transcaucasian Republic within the Soviet Union. But the three territories became separate Soviet Socialist Republics in 1936. After the breakup of the Soviet Union in 1991, Armenia became an independent republic. Fighting broke out over Nagorno-Karabakh, an area enclosed by Azerbaijan where most people are Armenians. In 1992, Armenia occupied the land between it and Nagorno-Karabakh. A ceasefire in 1994 left Armenia in control of about 20% of Azerbaijan's land area. Periodic talks with Azerbaijan have ended in failure.

Armenia has a "lower-middle-income" economy. The government has encouraged free enterprise, selling farmland and state-owned businesses.

AREA 11,506 sq mi [29,800 sq km]
POPULATION 2,972,000 **CAPITAL** Yerevan
GOVERNMENT Multiparty republic **ETHNIC GROUPS** Armenian 93%, Russian 2%, Azeri 1%, others (mostly Kurds) 4%
LANGUAGES Armenian (official) **RELIGIONS** Armenian Apostolic 94%
CURRENCY Dram = 100 couma

NOTE: This alphabetical list includes the principal countries and territories of the world. The area figures give the total area of land, inland water, and ice. The population figures are 2007 estimates where available.

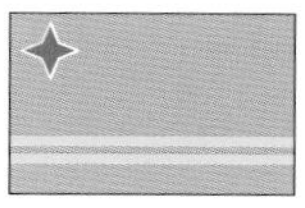
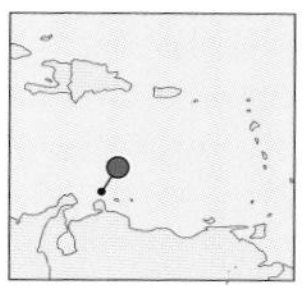

ARUBA

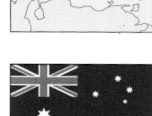

Formerly part of the Netherlands Antilles, Aruba (the most western of the Lesser Antilles) became a separate self-governing Dutch territory in 1986.

AREA 75 sq mi [193 sq km]
POPULATION 100,000 **CAPITAL** Oranjestad

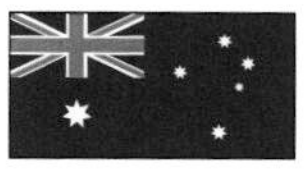
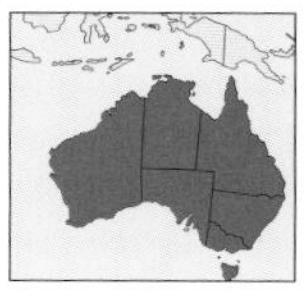

AUSTRALIA

GEOGRAPHY The Commonwealth of Australia, the world's sixth largest country, is also a continent. Australia is the flattest of the continents and the main highland area is in the east. Here the Great Dividing Range separates the eastern coastal plains from the Central Plains. This range extends from the Cape York Peninsula to Victoria in the far south. The longest rivers, the Murray and Darling, drain the south-eastern part of the Central Plains. The Western Plateau makes up two-thirds of Australia. A few mountain ranges break the monotony of the generally flat landscape. Only 10% of Australia, notably the tropical north, the northeast coast and the southeast, has an average annual rainfall of more than 39 inches [1,000 mm]. But, in 2001–7, the Murray–Darling basin in the southeast, which produces about 40% of Australia's farm produce, suffered severe and prolonged drought.

POLITICS & ECONOMY The Aboriginal people of Australia entered the continent from Southeast Asia more than 50,000 years ago. The first European explorers were Dutch in the 17th century, but they did not settle. In 1770, the British Captain Cook explored the east coast and, in 1788, the first British settlement was established for convicts on the site of what is now Sydney. Australia has strong ties with the British Isles. But in the last 50 years, people from other parts of Europe and, most recently, from Asia have settled in Australia. Ties with Britain were also weakened by Britain's membership of the European Union. Many Australians believe that they should become more involved with the nations of eastern Asia and the Americas rather than with Europe. In 1999, a majority of Australians voted to retain the country's status as a monarchy. In 2003, Australian troops joined the coalition forces in invading Iraq. The Labor Party won the 2007 general elections and Kevin Rudd replaced John Howard as prime minister.

Australia is a prosperous country. Crops can be grown on only 6% of the land, but dry pasture covers another 58%. Yet the country remains a major producer and exporter of farm products, particularly cattle, wheat, and wool. Grapes grown for wine-making are also important. The country is a major producer of minerals, including bauxite, coal, copper, diamonds, gold, iron ore, manganese, nickel, silver, tin, tungsten, and zinc. Australia also produces oil and natural gas. Metals, minerals, and farm products account for the bulk of exports. Australia's imports are mostly manufactured goods, especially machinery, though industry is now important, especially the manufacture of consumer goods.

AREA 2,988,885 sq mi [7,741,220 sq km] **POPULATION** 20,434,000
CAPITAL Canberra **GOVERNMENT** Federal constitutional monarchy
ETHNIC GROUPS Caucasian 92%, Asian 7%, Aboriginal 1%
LANGUAGES English (official) **RELIGIONS** Roman Catholic 26%, Anglican 26%, other Christian 24%, non-Christian 24%
CURRENCY Australian dollar = 100 cents

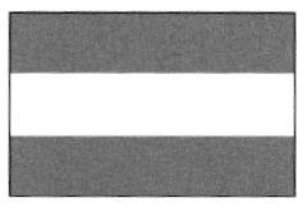
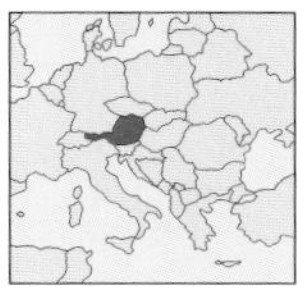

AUSTRIA

GEOGRAPHY Austria is a landlocked country in Europe. Northern Austria contains the valley of the River Danube, which flows from Germany to the Black Sea, and the Vienna basin. Southern Austria contains ranges of the Alps, their highest point at Grossglockner, 12,457 ft [3,797 m] above sea level.

The climate is influenced by westerly and easterly winds. Moist westerly winds bring rain and snow, and moderate temperatures. Dry easterly winds bring cold weather in winter and hot weather in summer.

POLITICS & ECONOMY Formerly part of the monarchy of Austria–Hungary, which collapsed in 1918, Austria was annexed by Germany in 1938. After World War II, the Allies partitioned and occupied the country. In 1955, Austria became a neutral federal republic. It joined the European Union in 1995. In 2000, a coalition government was formed by the right-wing People's Party and the extreme right-wing Freedom Party, which lost much of its support in 2002. In 2007, the Social Democratic Party formed a coalition with the People's Party.

Austria has a highly developed economy, with plenty of hydroelectric power and some oil, gas, and coal reserves. The country's leading economic activity is manufacturing metals and metal products. Crops are grown on 18% of the land, and another 24% is pasture. Dairy and livestock farming are the leading activities. Major crops include barley, potatoes, rye, sugar beet, and wheat. Tourism is a major activity in this scenic country.

AREA 32,378 sq mi [83,859 sq km] **POPULATION** 8,200,000
CAPITAL Vienna **GOVERNMENT** Federal republic
ETHNIC GROUPS Austrian 90%, Croatian, Slovene, others
LANGUAGES German (official) **RELIGIONS** Roman Catholic 78%, Protestant 5%, Islam and others 17% **CURRENCY** Euro = 100 cents

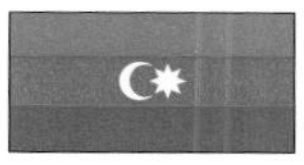
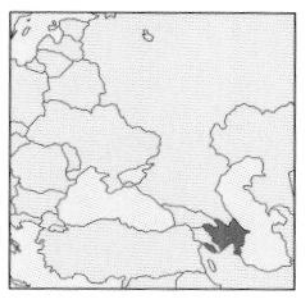

AZERBAIJAN

GEOGRAPHY The Azerbaijani Republic is a country in the southwest of Asia, facing the Caspian Sea to the east. It includes an area called the Naxçivan Autonomous Republic, which is completely cut off from the rest of Azerbaijan by Armenian territory. The Caucasus Mountains border Russia in the north.

Azerbaijan has hot summers and cool winters. The plains are fairly dry, but the mountains are rainy.

POLITICS & ECONOMY After the Russian Revolution of 1917, attempts were made to form a Transcaucasian Federation made up of Armenia, Azerbaijan and Georgia. When this failed, Azerbaijanis set up an independent state. But Russian forces occupied the area in 1920. In 1922, the Communists set up a Transcaucasian Republic consisting of Armenia, Azerbaijan, and Georgia under Russian control. In 1936, the three areas became separate Soviet Socialist Republics within the Soviet Union. In 1991, following the breakup of the Soviet Union, Azerbaijan became an independent nation. After independence, the country's economic progress was slow, partly because of the conflict with Armenia over the enclave of Nagorno-Karabakh, a region in Azerbaijan where the majority of people are Armenians. A ceasefire in 1994 left Armenia in control of about 20% of Azerbaijan's area, including Nagorno-Karabakh. Tension continued and border clashes occurred in 2008.

In the mid-1990s, the World Bank classified Azerbaijan as a "lower-middle-income" economy. But Azerbaijan has huge oil reserves. In 2006, a pipeline, extending from Baku, through Georgia to Turkey, came into operation. Oil extraction and manufacturing, including oil refining and the production of chemicals, machinery, and textiles, are major activities.

AREA 33,436 sq mi [86,600 sq km] **POPULATION** 8,120,000
CAPITAL Baku **GOVERNMENT** Federal multiparty republic
ETHNIC GROUPS Azeri 90%, Dagestani 3%, Russian, Armenian, others **LANGUAGES** Azerbaijani (official), Russian, Armenian
RELIGIONS Islam 93%, Russian Orthodox 2%, Armenian Orthodox 2%
CURRENCY Azerbaijani manat = 100 gopik

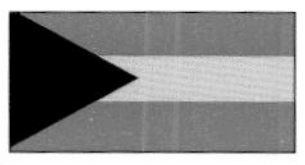
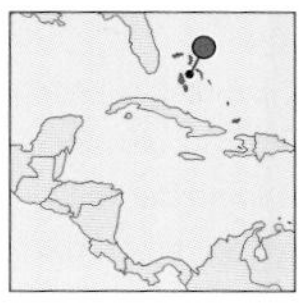

BAHAMAS

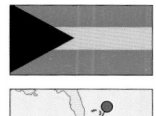

A coral-limestone archipelago off the coast of Florida, the Bahamas became independent from Britain in 1973, and has since developed strong ties with the United States. Tourism and banking are major activities.

AREA 5,358 sq mi [13,878 sq km]
POPULATION 306,000 **CAPITAL** Nassau

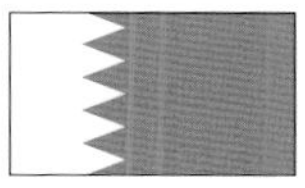
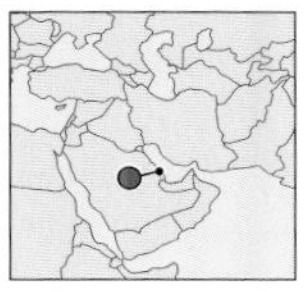

BAHRAIN

The Kingdom of Bahrain, an island nation in the Persian Gulf, became independent from the UK in 1971. Oil accounts for 80% of its exports.

AREA 268 sq mi [694 sq km]
POPULATION 709,000 **CAPITAL** Manama

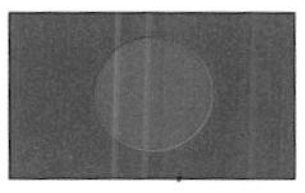
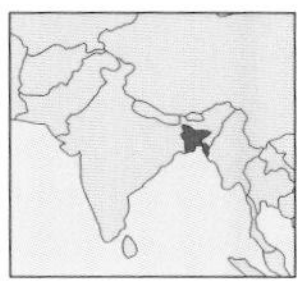

BANGLADESH

GEOGRAPHY The People's Republic of Bangladesh is one of the world's most densely populated countries. Apart from hilly regions in the far northeast and southeast, most of the land is flat and covered by fertile alluvium spread over the land by the Ganges, Brahmaputra and Meghna rivers. These rivers overflow when they are swollen by the annual monsoon rains. Floods also occur along the coast, 357 mi [575 km] long, when cyclones (hurricanes) drive seawater inland. Bangladesh has a tropical monsoon climate. Dry northerly winds blow in winter, but moist southerly winds bring heavy rain in summer.

POLITICS & ECONOMY In 1947, British India was partitioned between the mainly Hindu India and the Muslim Pakistan. Pakistan consisted of two parts, West and East Pakistan, which were separated by about 1,000 mi [1,600 km] of Indian territory. Differences developed between West and East Pakistan. In 1971, the East Pakistanis rebeled. After a nine-month civil war, they declared East Pakistan to be a new nation named Bangladesh. A famine in 1974 and a coup in 1975 were followed by political upheavals. In 2007, following mass protests, elections were postponed. The army took power.

Bangladesh is one of the world's poorest countries. Its economy depends mainly on agriculture, which employs about half the population. Bangladesh is the world's fourth largest producer of rice.

AREA 55,598 sq mi [143,998 sq km]
POPULATION 150,448,000 **CAPITAL** Dhaka
GOVERNMENT Multiparty republic **ETHNIC GROUPS** Bengali 98%, tribal groups **LANGUAGES** Bengali (official), English
RELIGIONS Islam 83%, Hinduism 16% **CURRENCY** Taka = 100 paisas

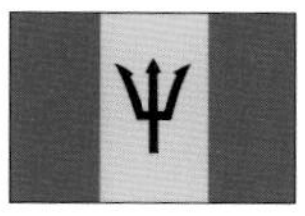
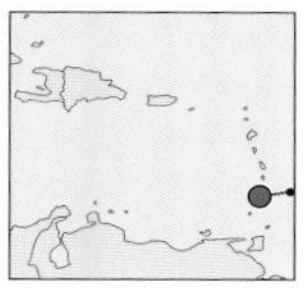

BARBADOS

The most easterly Caribbean country, Barbados became independent from the UK in 1960. A densely populated island, Barbados is prosperous by comparison with most Caribbean countries.

AREA 166 sq mi [430 sq km]
POPULATION 281,000 **CAPITAL** Bridgetown

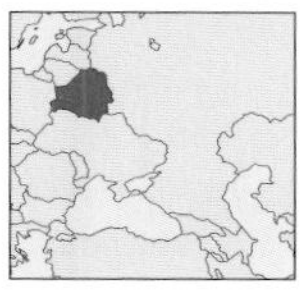

BELARUS

GEOGRAPHY The Republic of Belarus is a landlocked country in Eastern Europe. The land is low-lying and mostly flat. In the south, much of the land is marshy and this area contains Europe's largest marsh and peat bog, the Pripet Marshes. The climate is affected by both the moderating influence of the Baltic Sea and continental conditions to the east. The winters are cold and the summers warm.

POLITICS & ECONOMY In 1918, Belarus (White Russia) became an independent republic, but Russia invaded the country and, in 1919, a Communist state was set up. In 1922, Belarus became a founder republic of the Soviet Union. In 1991, Belarus again became an independent republic, and although Belarus continued to support reunification with Russia, any surrender of sovereignty was not expected. President Alexander Lukashenko, who was elected in flawed elections in 1994, 2001 and 2006, has been criticized for his autocratic rule. His government's poor record on human rights and suppression of freedom of speech has provoked mounting international criticism.

According to the World Bank, Belarus has an "upper-middle-income" economy. Most economic activities remain under government control and, in the 1990s, the economy declined. Mining and manufacturing are the most valuable activities.

AREA 80,154 sq mi [207,600 sq km]
POPULATION 9,725,000 **CAPITAL** Minsk
GOVERNMENT Multiparty republic **ETHNIC GROUPS** Belarusian 81%, Russian 11%, Polish, Ukrainian, others **LANGUAGES** Belarusian, Russian (both official) **RELIGIONS** Eastern Orthodox 80%, others 20% **CURRENCY** Belarusian rouble = 100 kopecks

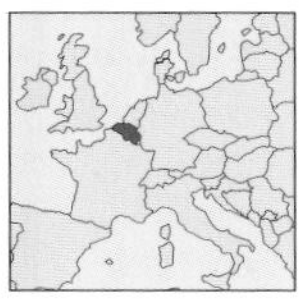

BELGIUM

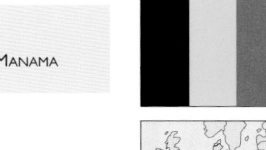

GEOGRAPHY The Kingdom of Belgium is a densely populated country in western Europe. Behind the coastline on the North Sea, which is 39 mi [63 km] long, lie its coastal plains. Central Belgium consists of low plateaux and the only highland region is the Ardennes in the southeast.

Belgium has a cool, temperate climate. Moist winds from the Atlantic Ocean bring fairly heavy rain, especially in the Ardennes. In January and February much snow falls on the Ardennes.

POLITICS & ECONOMY In 1815, Belgium and the Netherlands united as the "low countries," but Belgium became independent in 1830. Belgium's economy was weakened by the two World

Wars, but, from 1945, the country recovered quickly, first through collaboration with the Netherlands and Luxembourg, which formed a customs union called Benelux, and later through its membership of the European Union.

A central political problem in Belgium has been the tension between the Dutch-speaking Flemings and the French-speaking Walloons. In the 1970s, the government divided the country into three economic regions: Dutch-speaking Flanders, French-speaking Wallonia and bilingual Brussels. In 1993, Belgium adopted a federal constitution, giving each region its own parliament. Following national elections in June 2007, the parties failed to agree a coalition and some people believed that Belgium might split apart. But a coalition government was set up in March 2008.

Belgium is a major trading nation with a developed economy, though most materials used in manufacturing must be imported. Major products include chemicals, processed food, and steel. The textile industry has existed since medieval times in the province of Flanders. Agriculture employs less than 2% of the people, but farmers produce most of the food needed by the people. Barley and wheat are the main crops, followed by flax, hops, potatoes, and sugar beet. But the most valuable agricultural activities are dairy farming and livestock rearing.

AREA 11,787 sq mi [30,528 sq km]
POPULATION 10,392,000
CAPITAL Brussels
GOVERNMENT Federal constitutional monarchy
ETHNIC GROUPS Belgian 89% (Fleming 58%, Walloon 31%), others 11% **LANGUAGES** Dutch, French, German (all official)
RELIGIONS Roman Catholic 75%, others 25%
CURRENCY Euro = 100 cents

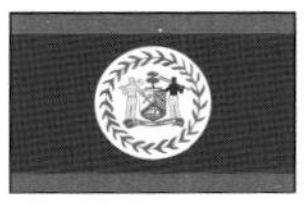
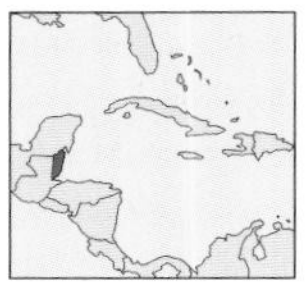

BELIZE

GEOGRAPHY Behind the southern coastal plain, the land rises to the Maya Mountains, which reach 3,674 ft [1,120 m] at Victoria Peak. The north is mostly low-lying and swampy. Temperatures are high all year round, while the average annual rainfall ranges from 51 inches [1,300 mm] in the north to over 150 inches [3,800 mm] in the south. Hurricanes caused much damage in the 1990s and 2000s, but tourist numbers have continued to increase.

POLITICS & ECONOMY From 1862, Belize (then called British Honduras) was a British colony. Full independence was achieved in 1981, but Guatemala, which had claimed the area since the early 19th century, opposed Belize's independence and British troops remained to prevent a possible invasion. In 1983, Guatemala reduced its claim to the southern fifth of Belize. Improved relations in the early 1990s led Guatemala to recognize Belize's independence and, in 1992, Britain agreed to withdraw its troops from the country.

The World Bank classifies Belize as a "lower-middle-income" developing country. Its economy is based on agriculture and sugarcane is the chief commercial crop and export. Other crops include bananas, beans, citrus fruits, maize, and rice. Forestry, fishing, and tourism are other important activities.

AREA 8,867 sq mi [22,966 sq km]
POPULATION 294,000 **CAPITAL** Belmopan
GOVERNMENT Constitutional monarchy **ETHNIC GROUPS** Mestizo 49%, Creole 25%, Mayan Indian 11%, Garifuna 6%, others 9%
LANGUAGES English (official), Spanish, Creole
RELIGIONS Roman Catholic 50%, Protestant 27%, others
CURRENCY Belizean dollar = 100 cents

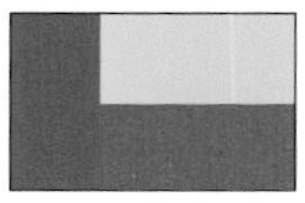
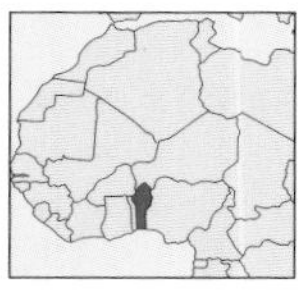

BENIN

GEOGRAPHY The Republic of Benin is one of Africa's smallest countries. It extends north–south for about 390 mi [620 km]. Lagoons line the short coastline, and the country has no natural harbors.

Benin has a hot, wet climate. The average annual temperature on the coast is about 77°F [25°C], and the average rainfall is about 52 inches [1,330 mm]. The inland plains are wetter than the coast.

POLITICS & ECONOMY After slavery was ended in the 19th century, the French began to gain influence in the area. Benin became self-governing in 1958 and fully independent in 1960. After much instability and many changes of government, a military group took over in 1972. The country, renamed Benin in 1975, became a one-party socialist state. Socialism was abandoned in 1989. Former coup leader Mathieu Kérékou served as president until 2006, when a former banker, Yayi Boni, was elected president.

Benin is a poor developing country. About half of the people live by farming, mainly at subsistence level. Exports include cotton, petroleum, and palm products. Cocoa, coffee, groundnuts (peanuts), tobacco, and shea nuts are also grown for export.

AREA 43,483 sq mi [112,622 sq km]
POPULATION 8,078,000 **CAPITAL** Porto-Novo
GOVERNMENT Multiparty republic **ETHNIC GROUPS** Fon, Adja, Bariba, Yoruba, Fulani **LANGUAGES** French (official), Fon, Adja, Yoruba
RELIGIONS Traditional beliefs 50%, Christianity 30%, Islam 20%
CURRENCY CFA franc = 100 centimes

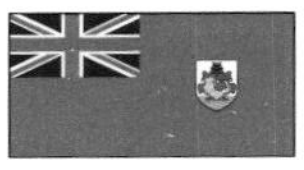
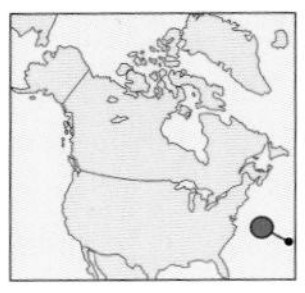

BERMUDA

A group of about 150 small islands situated 570 mi [920 km] east of the USA. Bermuda remains Britain's oldest overseas territory, but it has a long tradition of self-government.

AREA 21 sq mi [53 sq km]
POPULATION 66,000 **CAPITAL** Hamilton

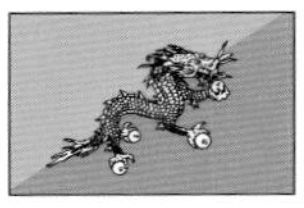
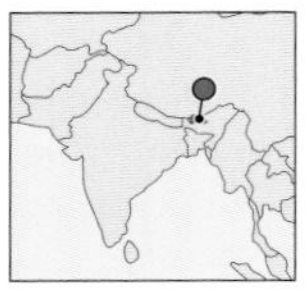

BHUTAN

GEOGRAPHY A mountainous, isolated Himalayan country located between India and Tibet. The climate is similar to that of Nepal, being dependent on altitude and affected by monsoonal winds.

POLITICS & ECONOMY The monarch of Bhutan is head of both state and government, and this predominantly Buddhist country remains, even in the Asian context, both conservative and poor. In 2008, Bhutan held its first ever democratic elections, ending over a century of absolute royal rule and turning Bhutan into a constitutional monarchy.

AREA 18,147 sq mi [47,000 sq km] **POPULATION** 2,328,000
CAPITAL Thimphu **GOVERNMENT** Constitutional monarchy
ETHNIC GROUPS Bhutanese 50%, Nepalese 35%
LANGUAGES Dzongkha (official) **RELIGIONS** Buddhism 75%, Hinduism 25% **CURRENCY** Ngultrum = 100 chetrum

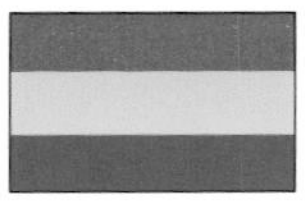
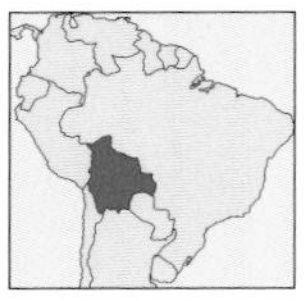

BOLIVIA

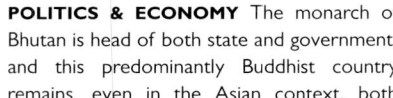

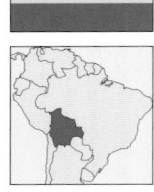

GEOGRAPHY The Republic of Bolivia is a landlocked country which straddles the Andes Mountains in central South America. The Andes rise to a height of 21,391 ft [6,520 m] at Nevado Sajama in the west.

About 40% of Bolivians live on a high plateau called the Altiplano in the Andean region, while the sparsely populated east is essentially a vast lowland plain.

The Bolivian climate is greatly affected by altitude, with the Andean peaks permanently snow-covered, and the eastern plains remaining hot and humid.

POLITICS & ECONOMY American Indians have lived in Bolivia for at least 10,000 years. The main groups today are the Aymara and Quechua people.

In the last 50 years, Bolivia, an independent country since 1825, has been ruled by a succession of civilian and military governments, which violated human rights. Democracy was restored in 1982. Economic problems led a widening of the gap between rich and poor and, in 2005, Evo Morales, a left-wing Aymara farmer, was elected president. In 2006, he nationalized the oil and natural gas industries, and launched a program aimed at redistributing land to poor peasant communities.

Bolivia is one of South America's poorest countries. Its resources include natural gas, silver, tin, and zinc, but the main activity is agriculture which employs more than 40% of the people. Soybeans and soybean products are major exports.

AREA 424,162 sq mi [1,098,581 sq km]
POPULATION 9,119,000 **CAPITAL** La Paz (seat of government); Sucre (legal capital/seat of judiciary)
GOVERNMENT Multiparty republic **ETHNIC GROUPS** Mestizo 30%, Quechua 30%, Aymara 25%, White 15% **LANGUAGES** Spanish, Aymara, Quechua (all official) **RELIGIONS** Roman Catholic 95%
CURRENCY Boliviano = 100 centavos

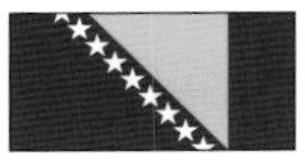
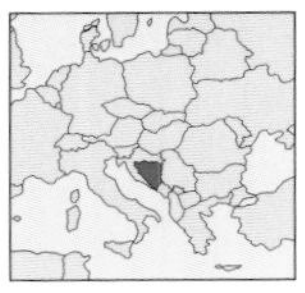

BOSNIA-HERZEGOVINA

GEOGRAPHY The Republic of Bosnia-Herzegovina is one of the five republics to emerge from the former Federal People's Republic of Yugoslavia. Much of the country is mountainous or hilly, with an arid limestone plateau in the southwest. The River Sava, which forms most of the northern border with Croatia, is a tributary of the River Danube. Because of the country's odd shape, the coastline is limited to a short stretch of 13 mi [20 km] on the Adriatic coast.

A Mediterranean climate, with dry, sunny summers and moist, mild winters, prevails only near the coast. Inland, the weather is more severe, with hot, dry summers and bitterly cold, snowy winters.

POLITICS & ECONOMY In 1918, Bosnia-Herzegovina became part of the Kingdom of the Serbs, Croats, and Slovenes, which was renamed Yugoslavia in 1929. Germany occupied the area during World War II (1939–45). From 1945, Communist governments ruled Yugoslavia as a federation containing six republics, one of which was Bosnia-Herzegovina. In the 1980s, the country faced problems as Communist policies proved unsuccessful and differences arose between ethnic groups.

In 1990, free elections were held in Bosnia-Herzegovina and the non-Communists won a majority. A Muslim, Alija Izetbegovic, was elected president. In 1991, Croatia and Slovenia, other parts of the former Yugoslavia, declared themselves independent. In 1992, Bosnia-Herzegovina held a vote on independence. Most Bosnian Serbs boycotted the vote, while the Muslims and Bosnian Croats voted in favor. Many Bosnian Serbs, opposed to independence, started a war against the non-Serbs. They soon occupied more than two-thirds of the land. The Bosnian Serbs were accused of "ethnic cleansing" – that is, the killing or expulsion of other ethnic groups from Serb-occupied areas. The war was later extended when Croat forces seized other parts of the country.

In 1995, the conflict was resolved. Under an agreement, the country's boundaries were maintained, but the territory was divided into two self-governing provinces, one Bosnian-Serb and the other Muslim-Croat, under a central government. Stability was restored with the help of NATO. Following elections in 2006, the EU announced a cut in its peacekeeping force in 2007.

The economy of Bosnia-Herzegovina, the least developed of the six republics of the former Yugoslavia apart from Macedonia, was shattered by the war in the early 1990s. Before the war, manufactures were the main exports, including electrical, machinery and transport equipment, and textiles. Farm products include fruits, maize, tobacco, vegetables, and wheat, but food has to be imported.

AREA 19,767 sq mi [51,197 sq km]
POPULATION 4,552,000 **CAPITAL** Sarajevo
GOVERNMENT Federal republic **ETHNIC GROUPS** Bosnian 48%, Serb 37%, Croat 14% **LANGUAGES** Bosnian, Serbian, Croatian
RELIGIONS Islam 40%, Serbian Orthodox 31%, Roman Catholic 15%, others 14% **CURRENCY** Convertible marka = 100 convertible pfenniga

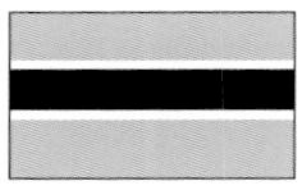
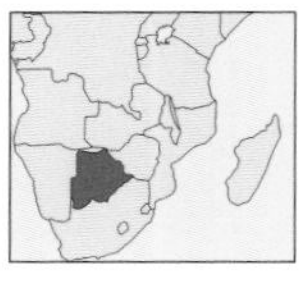

BOTSWANA

GEOGRAPHY The Republic of Botswana is a landlocked country in southern Africa. The Kalahari, a semidesert area covered mostly by grasses and thorn scrub, covers much of the country. Most of the south has no permanent streams. But large depressions in the north are inland drainage basins. In one of them, the Okavango River, which rises in Angola, forms a large, swampy delta.

Temperatures are high in the summer months (October to April), but the winter months are much cooler. In winter, night-time temperatures sometimes drop below freezing point. The average annual rainfall ranges from over 16 inches [400 mm] in the east to less than 8 inches [200 mm] in the southwest.

POLITICS & ECONOMY The earliest inhabitants of the region were the San, who are also called Bushmen. They had a nomadic way of life, hunting wild animals and collecting wild plant foods.

Britain ruled the area as the Bechuanaland Protectorate between 1885 and 1966. When the country became independent, it was renamed Botswana. Since then, the country has been a stable, multiparty democracy. However, a major setback occurred in the early 21st century, when health officials announced that around 25% of the people were infected with HIV/AIDS. In 1966, Botswana was extremely poor, depending on meat and live cattle for its exports. But the discovery of minerals, including coal, cobalt, copper, diamonds, and nickel, has boosted the economy. About 10% of the people now depend on agriculture, raising cattle, and growing crops. Industries include the processing of farm products.

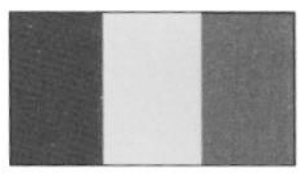

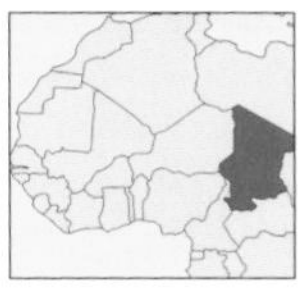

CHAD

GEOGRAPHY The Republic of Chad is a landlocked country in north-central Africa. It is Africa's fifth largest country and is over twice the size of France, the country which once ruled it as a colony.

Ndjamena in central Chad has a hot, tropical climate, with a marked dry season from November to April. The south of the country is wetter, with an average yearly rainfall of around 39 inches [1,000 mm]. The burning-hot desert in the north has an average yearly rainfall of less than 5 inches [130 mm].

POLITICS & ECONOMY Chad straddles two worlds. The north is populated by Muslim Arab and Berber peoples, while black Africans, who follow traditional beliefs or who have converted to Christianity, live in the south. French explorers were active in the area in the late 19th century. France made Chad a colony in 1902.

Chad became independent in 1960, but the 1970s were marked by ethnic conflict that led to civil wars, coups and conflict with Libya, which supported rebel factions. Chad and Libya agreed a truce in 1987 and, in 1994, the International Court of Justice ruled against Libya's claim on the Aozou Strip. From 2004, Chad forces clashed with pro-Sudanese militias as the conflict in Sudan's Darfur province spilled over the border. In 2007–8, rebel forces from the east tried unsuccessfully to overthrow the government.

Chad is one of the world's poorest countries. Farming and fishing employ 83% of the people. Food crops include groundnuts, millet, rice and sorghum, but cotton is the chief export crop. Chad has few manufacturing industries, but its oil reserves hold out hope for development. Oil production began in 2003.

AREA 495,752 sq mi [1,284,000 sq km]
POPULATION 9,886,000 **CAPITAL** Ndjamena
GOVERNMENT Multiparty republic **ETHNIC GROUPS** 200 distinct groups: mostly Muslim in the north and center; mostly Christian or animist in the south **LANGUAGES** French and Arabic (both official), many others **RELIGIONS** Islam 51%, Christianity 35%, animist 7%
CURRENCY CFA franc = 100 centimes

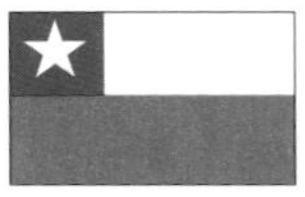

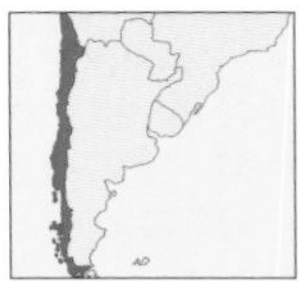

CHILE

GEOGRAPHY The Republic of Chile stretches about 2,650 mi [4,260 km] from north to south, although the maximum east–west distance is only about 267 mi [430 km]. The high Andes Mountains form Chile's eastern borders with Argentina and Bolivia. To the west are basins and valleys, with coastal uplands overlooking the shore. Most people live in the central valley, where Santiago is situated.

Santiago has a Mediterranean climate, with hot, dry summers from November to March and mild, moist winters from April to October. The Atacama Desert in the north is one of the world's driest places, while southern Chile is cold and stormy.

POLITICS & ECONOMY Amerindian people reached the southern tip of South America 8,000 years ago. In 1520, Portuguese navigator Ferdinand Magellan was the first European to sight Chile. The country became a Spanish colony in the 1540s. Chile became independent in 1818. During a war (1879–83), it gained mineral-rich areas from Peru and Bolivia.

In 1970, Salvador Allende became the first Communist leader to be elected democratically. He was overthrown in 1973 by army officers, who were supported by the CIA. General Augusto Pinochet then ruled as a dictator. A new constitution was introduced in 1981. Pinochet remained in power until 1989. Attempts to prosecute Pinochet continued in the 1990s and 2000s, but he died in December 2006 before being brought to trial. In 2006, Michelle Bachelet, a center-left, former torture victim under the Pinochet regime, was elected president of Chile.

According to the World Bank, Chile has a "lower-middle-income" economy. Mining, especially copper, is important and minerals dominate the exports. But manufacturing is the most valuable activity. Products include processed foods, metals, iron and steel, transport equipment and textiles. The chief crop is wheat, while beans, fruits, maize, and livestock products are also important. Chile's fishing industry is one of the world's largest.

AREA 292,133 sq mi [756,626 sq km]
POPULATION 16,285,000 **CAPITAL** Santiago
GOVERNMENT Multiparty republic **ETHNIC GROUPS** Mestizo 95%, Amerindian 3% **LANGUAGES** Spanish (official)
RELIGIONS Roman Catholic 89%, Protestant 11%
CURRENCY Chilean peso = 100 centavos

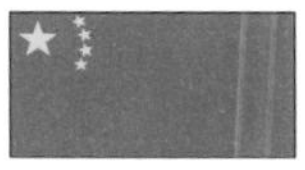

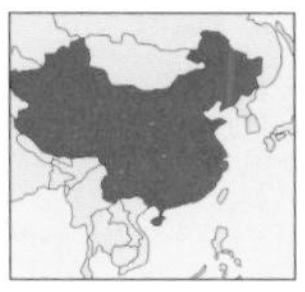

CHINA

GEOGRAPHY The People's Republic of China is the world's third largest country. Most people live in the east – on the coastal plains or in the fertile valleys of the Huang He (Hwang Ho or Yellow River), the Chang Jiang (Yangtze Kiang), which is Asia's longest river at 3,960 mi [6,380 km], and the Xi Jiang (Si Kiang). Western China is thinly populated. It includes the bleak Tibetan plateau which is bounded by the Himalaya, the world's highest mountain range. Deserts include the Gobi Desert along the Mongolian border and the Taklamakan Desert in the far west. Earthquakes are common. In May 2008, a major earthquake in the southwest killed more than 69,000 people and made millions homeless.

Beijing has cold winters and warm summers with moderate rainfall. To the south, Shanghai has milder winters and more rain. The southeast has a wet, subtropical climate, but the west has a severe climate. Lhasa has very cold winters and a low rainfall.

POLITICS & ECONOMY China is one of the world's oldest civilizations, going back 3,500 years. Under the Han dynasty (202 BC to AD 220), the Chinese empire was as large as the Roman empire. Mongols conquered China in the 13th century, but Chinese rule was restored in 1368. The Manchu people of Mongolia ruled the country from 1644 to 1912, when the country became a republic.

War with Japan (1937–45) was followed by civil war between the nationalists and the Communists. The Communists triumphed in 1949, setting up the People's Republic of China. In the 1980s, following the death of the revolutionary leader Mao Zedong (Mao Tse-tung) in 1976, China encouraged formerly forbidden policies, namely private enterprise and foreign investment. But the Communist leaders have not permitted political freedom. Opponents are still harshly treated, while attempts to negotiate some degree of autonomy for Tibet have been rejected.

China's economy has expanded greatly since the 1970s, with many Communist policies being abandoned. Foreign investors have help to set up many new industries in the east. Between 1989 and 2006, the economy grew by an average of more than 9% per year. By 2006, China had the world's fourth largest economy. Only the United States, Japan and Germany had larger GDPs (gross domestic products). China has benefited from the return of Hong Kong in 1997 and its admission to the World Trade Organization in 2001. China would like to regain the island of Taiwan, but this seems unlikely in the near future.

Despite its recent success, China remains a poor country. In 2002, agriculture employed 43% of the work force, although only 10% of the land is farmed. In 2006, plans were announced to help the 800 million people living in the countryside catch up economically with people in the cities.

Farm products include rice, sweet potatoes, tea, and wheat, and many fruits and vegetables. Livestock farming is important, and China has more than a third of the world's pigs. Resources include coal, iron ore, and other metals. Manufactures include cement, chemicals, fertilizers, machinery, telecommunications and recording equipment, and textiles. China is now a major producer of consumer goods, including cameras, computer products, refrigerators, and television sets.

AREA 3,705,387 sq mi [9,596,961 sq km]
POPULATION 1,321,852,000 **CAPITAL** Beijing
GOVERNMENT Single-party Communist republic
ETHNIC GROUPS Han Chinese 92%, many others
LANGUAGES Mandarin Chinese (official) **RELIGIONS** Atheist (official)
CURRENCY Renminbi yuan = 10 jiao = 100 fen

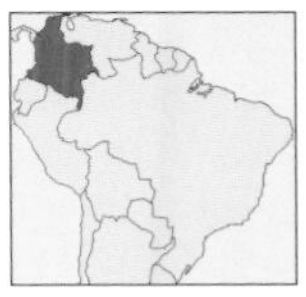

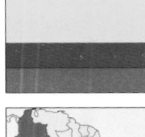

COLOMBIA

GEOGRAPHY The Republic of Colombia, in northeastern South America, is the only country in the continent to have coastlines on both the Pacific and the Caribbean Sea. Colombia also contains the northernmost ranges of the Andes Mountains.

There is a tropical climate in the lowlands, but the altitude greatly affects the climate of the Andes. The capital, Bogotá, which stands on a plateau in the eastern Andes at about 9,200 ft [2,800 m] above sea level, has mild temperatures throughout the year. The rainfall is heavy, especially on the Pacific coast.

POLITICS & ECONOMY Amerindian people have lived in Colombia for thousands of years. But today, only a small proportion of the people are of unmixed Amerindian ancestry. Mestizos (people of mixed white and Amerindian ancestry) form the largest group, followed by whites and mulattos (people of mixed European and African ancestry). Spaniards opened up the area in the early 16th century. They set up a territory known as the Viceroyalty of the New Kingdom of Granada, including Colombia, Ecuador, Panama and Venezuela. In 1819, the area became independent, but Ecuador and Venezuela soon split away, followed by Panama in 1903.

Instability has marked its recent history. Colombia faces economic and security problems, notably combating left-wing guerrillas and right-wing paramilitaries, while controlling the illicit drug industry. Andrés Pastrana, president between 1998 and 2002, tried to end the guerrilla war, but peace talks collapsed in 2002 and conflict resumed. His successor, Alvaro Uribe, elected in 2002 and 2006, pursued a tough line against the rebels.

Colombia has a "lower-middle-income" economy. It exports oil, coffee, and chemicals.

AREA 439,735 sq mi [1,138,914 sq km] **POPULATION** 44,380,000
CAPITAL Bogotá **GOVERNMENT** Multiparty republic
ETHNIC GROUPS Mestizo 58%, White 20%, Mulatto 14%, Black 4%
LANGUAGES Spanish (official) **RELIGIONS** Roman Catholic 90%
CURRENCY Colombian peso = 100 centavos

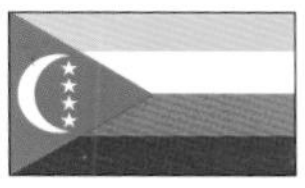

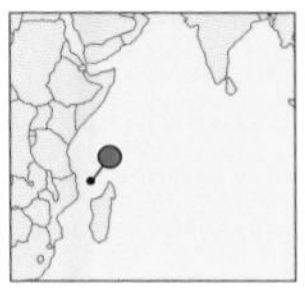

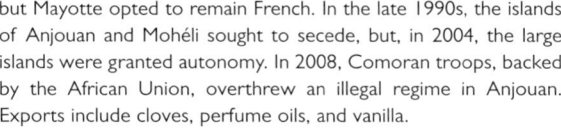

COMOROS

The Union des Isles Comores, as the Comoros is officially called, consists of three large volcanic islands and some smaller ones, lying at the north end of the Mozambique Channel in the Indian Ocean. France took over one of the islands, Mayotte, in 1843, and, in 1886, the other islands came under French protection. The Comoros became independent in 1974, but Mayotte opted to remain French. In the late 1990s, the islands of Anjouan and Mohéli sought to secede, but, in 2004, the large islands were granted autonomy. In 2008, Comoran troops, backed by the African Union, overthrew an illegal regime in Anjouan. Exports include cloves, perfume oils, and vanilla.

AREA 863 sq mi [2,235 sq km] **POPULATION** 711,000 **CAPITAL** Moroni

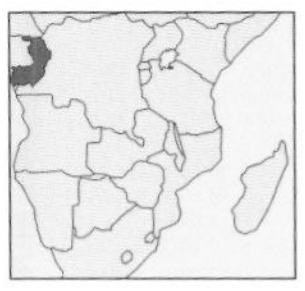

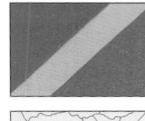

CONGO

GEOGRAPHY The Republic of Congo is a country on the River Congo in west-central Africa. The Equator runs through the center of the country. Congo has a narrow coastal plain on which its main port, Pointe Noire, stands. Behind the plain are uplands through which the River Niari has carved a fertile valley. Central Congo consists of high plains. The north contains large swampy areas in the valleys of the tributaries of the River Congo.

Congo has a hot, wet equatorial climate. Brazzaville has a dry season between June and September. The coast is drier and cooler than the rest of Congo, because of the cold offshore Benguela ocean current.

POLITICS & ECONOMY Part of the huge Kongo kingdom between the 15th and 18th centuries, the coast of the Congo later became a center of the European slave trade. The area came under French protection in 1880. It was later governed as part of a larger region called French Equatorial Africa. The country remained under French control until 1960.

Congo became a one-party state in 1964 and a military group took over the government in 1968. In 1970, Congo declared itself a Communist country, though it continued to seek aid from Western countries. The government officially abandoned its Communist policies in 1990. Multiparty elections were held in 1992, but the elected president, Pascal Lissouba, was overthrown in 1997 by former president Denis Sassou-Nguesso. Civil war again occurred in January 1999, but peace was restored. In 2002, Sassou-Nguesso was elected president.

The World Bank classifies Congo as a "lower-middle-income" developing country. Agriculture is the most important activity, employing about 40% of the people. But many farmers produce little more than they need to feed their families. Major food crops include bananas, cassava, maize, and rice, while the leading cash crops are coffee and cocoa. Congo's main exports are oil (which makes up 90% of the total) and timber. Manufacturing is relatively unimportant at the moment, still hampered by poor transport links, but it is gradually being developed.

AREA 132,046 sq mi [342,000 sq km]
POPULATION 3,801,000 **CAPITAL** Brazzaville
GOVERNMENT Military regime **ETHNIC GROUPS** Kongo 48%, Sangha 20%, Teke 17%, M'bochi 12% **LANGUAGES** French (official), many others **RELIGIONS** Christianity 50%, animist 48%, Islam 2%
CURRENCY CFA franc = 100 centimes

CONGO (DEMOCRATIC REPUBLIC OF THE)

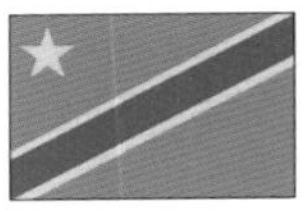

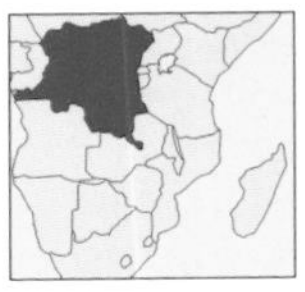

GEOGRAPHY The Democratic Republic of the Congo, formerly known as Zaïre, is the world's 12th largest country. Much of the country lies within the drainage basin of the huge River Congo. The river reaches the sea along the country's coastline, which is 25 mi [40 km] long. Mountains rise in the east, where the country's borders run through lakes Tanganyika, Kivu, Edward, and Albert. The equatorial region has high temperatures and heavy rainfall throughout the year.

POLITICS & ECONOMY Pygmies were the first inhabitants of the region, with Portuguese navigators not reaching the coast until 1482, but the interior was not explored until the late 19th century. In 1885, the country, called Congo Free State, became the personal property of King Léopold II of Belgium. In 1908, the country became a Belgian colony.

The Belgian Congo became independent in 1960 and was renamed Zaïre in 1971. Ethnic rivalries caused instability until 1965, when the country became a one-party state, ruled by President Mobutu. The government allowed the formation of political parties in 1990, but elections were repeatedly postponed. In 1996, fighting broke out in eastern Zaïre, as the Tutsi–Hutu conflict in Burundi and Rwanda spilled over. The rebel leader Laurent Kabila took power in 1997, ousting Mobutu and renaming the country. A rebellion against Kabila broke out in 1998. Rwanda and Uganda supported the rebels, while Angola, Chad, Namibia and Zimbabwe assisted Kabila. A peace treaty was signed in 1999, but fighting continued. Kabila was assassinated in 2001. His son, Major-General Joseph Kabila, became president. Under a new constitution adopted in 2005, Kabila was elected president in 2006. Hopes for stability were high, but sporadic fighting continued in the east.

The World Bank classifies the Democratic Republic of the Congo as a "low-income" developing country, despite its reserves of copper, the main export, and other minerals. Agriculture, mainly at subsistence level, employs 62% of the people.

AREA 905,350 sq mi [2,344,858 sq km]
POPULATION 65,752,000 **CAPITAL** Kinshasa
GOVERNMENT Single-party republic
ETHNIC GROUPS Over 200; the largest are Mongo, Luba, Kongo, Mangbetu-Azande
LANGUAGES French (official), tribal languages
RELIGIONS Roman Catholic 50%, Protestant 20%, Islam 10%, others
CURRENCY Congolese franc = 100 centimes

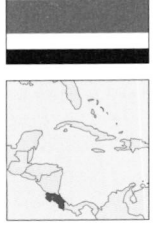

COSTA RICA

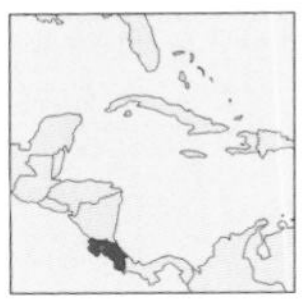

GEOGRAPHY The Republic of Costa Rica in Central America has coastlines on both the Pacific Ocean and also on the Caribbean Sea. Central Costa Rica consists of mountain ranges and plateaux with many volcanoes.

The coolest months are December and January. The northeast trade winds bring heavy rain to the Caribbean coast. There is less rainfall in the highlands and on the Pacific coastlands.

POLITICS & ECONOMY Christopher Columbus reached the Caribbean coast in 1502 and rumors of treasure soon attracted many Spaniards to settle in the country. Spain ruled the country until 1821, when Spain's Central American colonies broke away to join Mexico in 1822. In 1823, the Central American states broke with Mexico and set up the Central American Federation. Later, this large union broke up and Costa Rica became fully independent in 1838.

From the late 19th century, Costa Rica experienced a number of revolutions, with periods of dictatorship and periods of democracy. In 1948, following a revolt, the armed forces were abolished. Since 1948, Costa Rica has enjoyed a long period of stable democracy. In 2006, Nobel Peace Prize winner Oscar Arias was elected president.

Costa Rica is classified by the World Bank as a "lower-middle-income" developing country and one of the most prosperous countries in Central America. There are high educational standards and a high average life expectancy (about 77 years for men and 81 years for women). Agriculture employs 15% of the people. Costa Rica's natural resources include its forests, but it lacks minerals apart from some bauxite and manganese. Manufacturing is increasing. The United States is Costa Rica's main trading partner. Tourism is a fast-growing industry.

AREA 19,730 sq mi [51,100 sq km] **POPULATION** 4,134,000
CAPITAL San José **GOVERNMENT** Multiparty republic
ETHNIC GROUPS White (including Mestizo) 94%, Black 3%, Amerindian 1%, Chinese 1%, others **LANGUAGES** Spanish (official), English **RELIGIONS** Roman Catholic 76%, Evangelical 14%
CURRENCY Costa Rican colón = 100 céntimos

CROATIA

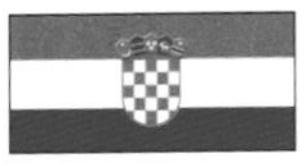

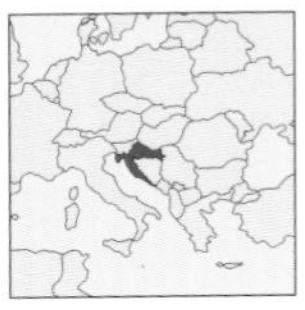

GEOGRAPHY The Republic of Croatia was one of the six republics that made up the former Communist country of Yugoslavia until it became independent in 1991. The region bordering the Adriatic Sea is called Dalmatia. It includes the coastal ranges, which contain large areas of bare limestone. Most of the rest of the country consists of the fertile Pannonian plains.

The coastal area has a typical Mediterranean climate, with hot, dry summers and mild, moist winters. Inland, the climate becomes more continental. Winters are cold, while temperatures often soar to 100°F [38°C] in the summer months.

POLITICS & ECONOMY Slav people settled in the area around 1,400 years ago. In 803, Croatia became part of the Holy Roman empire and the Croats soon adopted Christianity. Croatia was an independent kingdom in the 10th and 11th centuries. In 1102, the king of Hungary also became king of Croatia, creating a union that lasted 800 years. In 1526, part of Croatia came under the Turkish Ottoman empire, while the rest came under the Austrian Habsburgs.

After Austria–Hungary was defeated in World War I (1914–18), Croatia became part of the new Kingdom of the Serbs, Croats, and Slovenes. This kingdom was renamed Yugoslavia in 1929. Germany occupied Yugoslavia during World War II (1939–45). Croatia was proclaimed independent, but it was really ruled by the invaders.

After the war, Communists took power with Josip Broz Tito as the country's leader. Despite ethnic differences between the people, Tito held Yugoslavia together until his death in 1980. In the 1980s, economic and ethnic problems, including a deterioration in relations with Serbia, threatened stability. In the 1990s, Yugoslavia split into five nations, one of which was Croatia, which declared itself independent in 1991.

After Serbia supplied arms to Serbs living in Croatia, war broke out between the two republics, causing great damage. Croatia lost more than 30% of its territory. But in 1992, the United Nations sent a peacekeeping force to Croatia, which effectively ended the war with Serbia.

In 1992, when war broke out in Bosnia-Herzegovina, Bosnian Croats occupied parts of the country. But in 1994, Croatia helped to end Croat–Muslim conflict in Bosnia-Herzegovina and, in 1995, after retaking some areas occupied by Serbs, it helped to draw up the Dayton Peace Accord, ending the civil war. The wars in the early 1990s disrupted the economy. But in the early 21st century, stability, which is so vital to the valuable tourist industry, seemed to be returning. In 2005, the European Union began accession talks with Croatia, though many problems were anticipated. Croatia's main exports are manufactures.

AREA 21,829 sq mi [56,538 sq km] **POPULATION** 4,493,000
CAPITAL Zagreb **GOVERNMENT** Multiparty republic
ETHNIC GROUPS Croat 90%, Serb 5%, others
LANGUAGES Croatian 96% **RELIGIONS** Roman Catholic 88%, Orthodox 4%, Islam 1%, others **CURRENCY** Kuna = 100 lipas

CUBA

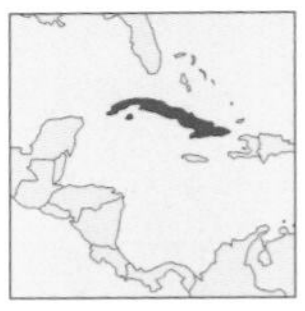

GEOGRAPHY The Republic of Cuba is the largest island country in the Caribbean Sea. It consists of one large island, Cuba, the Isle of Youth (Isla de la Juventud) and about 1,600 small islets. Mountains and hills cover about a quarter of Cuba. The highest mountain range, the Sierra Maestra in the southeast, reaches 6,562 ft [2,000 m] above sea level. The rest of the land consists of gently rolling country or coastal plains, crossed by fertile valleys carved by the short, mostly shallow and narrow rivers.

Cuba lies in the tropics. But sea breezes moderate the temperature, warming the land in winter and cooling it in summer.

POLITICS & ECONOMY Christopher Columbus discovered the island in 1492 and Spaniards began to settle there from 1511. Spanish rule ended in 1898, when the United States defeated Spain in the Spanish–American War. American influence in Cuba remained strong until 1959, when revolutionary forces under Fidel Castro overthrew the dictatorial government of Fulgencio Batista.

The United States opposed Castro's policies, when he turned to the Soviet Union for assistance. In 1961, Cuban exiles attempting an invasion were defeated. In 1962, the US learned that nuclear missile bases armed by the Soviet Union had been established in Cuba. The US ordered the Soviet Union to remove the missiles and bases and, after a few days, when many people feared that a world war might break out, the Soviet Union agreed to the American demands.

Cuba's relations with the Soviet Union remained strong until 1991, when the Soviet Union was broken up. The loss of Soviet aid greatly damaged Cuba's economy, but Castro maintained his left-wing policies. Fidel Castro fell ill in 2007 and his brother Raul took over the reins of government in 2008. He began to introduce some reforms.

The government runs Cuba's economy and owns 70% of the farmland. Agriculture is important and sugar is the chief export, followed by refined nickel ore. Other exports include cigars, citrus fruits, fish, medical products, and rum.

Before 1959, US companies owned most of Cuba's manufacturing industries. But under Fidel Castro, they became government property. After the collapse of Communist governments in the Soviet Union and its allies, Cuba worked to increase its trade with Latin America and China.

AREA 42,803 sq mi [110,861 sq km]
POPULATION 11,394,000 **CAPITAL** Havana
GOVERNMENT Socialist republic
ETHNIC GROUPS Mulatto 51%, White 37%, Black 11%
LANGUAGES Spanish (official) **RELIGIONS** Christianity
CURRENCY Cuban peso = 100 centavos

CYPRUS

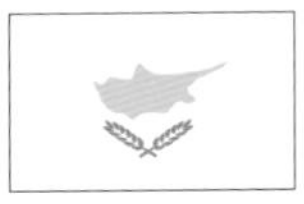

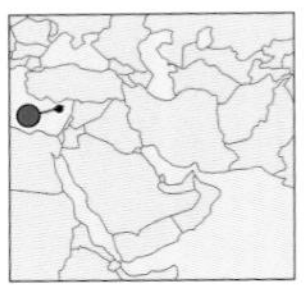

GEOGRAPHY The Republic of Cyprus is an island nation in the northeastern Mediterranean Sea. Geographers regard it as part of Asia, but it resembles southern Europe in many ways. Its scenic mountain ranges include the southern Troodos Mountains, which reach 6,401 ft [1,951 m] at Mount Olympus, and the Kyrenia range in the north. Between them lies the Mesaoria plain. The climate is Mediterranean, with hot, dry summers and mild, moist winters.

POLITICS & ECONOMY Greeks settled on Cyprus around 3,200 years ago. From AD 330, the island was part of the Byzantine empire. In the 1570s, Cyprus became part of the Turkish Ottoman empire. Turkish rule continued until 1878 when Cyprus was leased to Britain. Britain annexed the island in 1914 and proclaimed it a colony in 1925.

In the 1950s, Greek Cypriots, who made up four-fifths of the population, began a campaign for *enosis* (union) with Greece. Their leader was the Greek Orthodox Archbishop Makarios. A secret guerrilla force called EOKA attacked the British, who exiled Makarios. Cyprus became an independent country in 1960, although Britain retained two military bases. Independent Cyprus had a constitution which provided for power-sharing between the Greek and Turkish Cypriots. But the constitution proved unworkable and fighting broke out between the two communities. In 1964, the United Nations sent in a peacekeeping force, but communal clashes recurred in 1967.

In 1974, Cypriot forces led by Greek officers overthrew Makarios. This led Turkey to invade northern Cyprus, a territory occupying about 40% of the island. Many Greek Cypriots fled from the north, which, in 1979, was proclaimed the Turkish Republic of Northern Cyprus. The only country to recognize this state was Turkey. The United Nations regarded Cyprus as a single unit under the Greek-Cypriot government in the south. In 2002, the European Union invited Cyprus to become a member in 2004. In April 2004, the people voted on a UN plan to reunify the island. The Turkish-Cypriots voted in favor, but the Greek-Cypriots voted against. Hence, only the south was admitted to EU membership on May 1, 2004. The election of a Marxist president in 2008 held out hopes of talks that might lead to the reunification of the island.

Cyprus got its name from the Greek word *kypros*, meaning copper. But little copper remains and the chief minerals today are asbestos and chromium. However, the most valuable activity in Cyprus is tourism. Manufactures include cement, clothes, footwear, tiles, and wine.

In the early 1990s, the United Nations reclassified Cyprus as a developed rather than a developing country, reflecting the rapid economic progress in the south. But the north lagged far behind the prosperous Greek-Cypriot south.

AREA 3,572 SQ MI [9,251 SQ KM]
POPULATION 788,000 **CAPITAL** NICOSIA
GOVERNMENT MULTIPARTY REPUBLIC **ETHNIC GROUPS** GREEK CYPRIOT 77%, TURKISH CYPRIOT 18%, OTHERS **LANGUAGES** GREEK AND TURKISH (BOTH OFFICIAL), ENGLISH **RELIGIONS** GREEK ORTHODOX 78%, ISLAM 18%
CURRENCY EURO = 100 CENTS

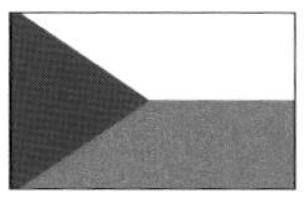

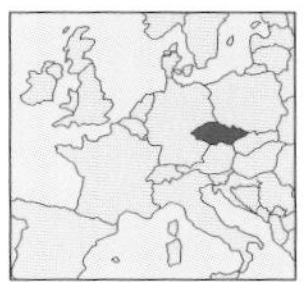

CZECH REPUBLIC

GEOGRAPHY The Czech Republic is the western three-fifths of the former country of Czechoslovakia. It contains two regions: Bohemia in the west and Moravia in the east. Mountains border much of the country in the west. The Bohemian basin in the north-center is a fertile lowland region, with Prague, the capital city, as its main center. Highlands cover much of the center of the country, with lowlands in the southeast.

The climate is influenced by its landlocked position in east-central Europe. Prague has warm, sunny summers and cold winters. The average rainfall is moderate, with 20 inches to 30 inches [500 mm to 750 mm] every year in lowland areas.

POLITICS & ECONOMY After World War I (1914–18), Czechoslovakia was created. Germany seized the country in World War II (1939–45). In 1948, Communist leaders took power and Czechoslovakia was allied to the Soviet Union. When democratic reforms were introduced in the Soviet Union in the late 1980s, the Czechs also demanded reforms. Free elections were held in 1990, but differences between the Czechs and Slovaks led to the partitioning of the country on January 1, 1993. The Czech Republic became a member of NATO in 1999. In 2003, 77% of Czechs voted in favor of their country becoming a member of the European Union. This took place on May 1, 2004.

Under Communist rule the Czech Republic became one of the most industrialized parts of Eastern Europe. The country has deposits of coal, uranium, iron ore, magnesite, tin, and zinc. Manufacturing employs about 25% of the Czech Republic's entire work force. Farming is also important. Under Communism, the government owned the land, but private ownership is now being restored. The country was admitted into the OECD in 1995.

AREA 30,450 SQ MI [78,866 SQ KM]
POPULATION 10,229,000 **CAPITAL** PRAGUE
GOVERNMENT MULTIPARTY REPUBLIC **ETHNIC GROUPS** CZECH 81%, MORAVIAN 13%, SLOVAK 3%, POLISH, GERMAN, SILESIAN, GYPSY, HUNGARIAN, UKRAINIAN **LANGUAGES** CZECH (OFFICIAL) **RELIGIONS** ATHEIST 40%, ROMAN CATHOLIC 39%, PROTESTANT 4%, ORTHODOX 3%, OTHERS
CURRENCY CZECH KORUNA = 100 HALER

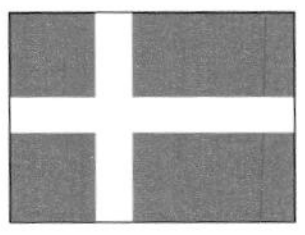

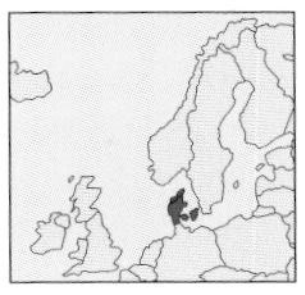

DENMARK

GEOGRAPHY The Kingdom of Denmark is the smallest country in Scandinavia. It consists of a peninsula, called Jutland (or Jylland), which is joined to Germany, and more than 400 islands, 89 of which are inhabited. The land is flat and mostly covered by rocks dropped there by huge ice sheets during the last Ice Age. The highest point in Denmark is on Jutland. It is only 568 ft [173 m] above sea level. Denmark has a mild, moist climate, except during cold spells in winter when The Sound between Sjælland and Sweden may freeze over.

POLITICS & ECONOMY Danish Vikings terrorized much of Western Europe for about 300 years after AD 800. In the late 14th century, Denmark formed a union with Norway and Sweden (which included Finland). Sweden broke away in 1523, while Denmark lost Norway to Sweden in 1814. After 1945, Denmark became a member of the North Atlantic Treaty Organization. It joined the European Union in 1973, though it did not adopt the euro in 2000. The Danes enjoy a high standard of living, but the country's welfare programs are extremely costly.

Denmark has some oil and gas and the economy is highly developed. Manufacturing employs about 15% of the people. Products include furniture, processed food, machinery, television sets, and textiles. Farms cover about three-quarters of the land. Farming employs only 3% of the people, but it is highly scientific. Meat and dairy farming are the chief activities.

AREA 16,639 SQ MI [43,094 SQ KM] **POPULATION** 5,468,000
CAPITAL COPENHAGEN **GOVERNMENT** PARLIAMENTARY MONARCHY
ETHNIC GROUPS SCANDINAVIAN, INUIT, FÆROESE **LANGUAGES** DANISH (OFFICIAL), ENGLISH, FÆROESE **RELIGIONS** EVANGELICAL LUTHERAN 95%
CURRENCY DANISH KRONE = 100 ØRE

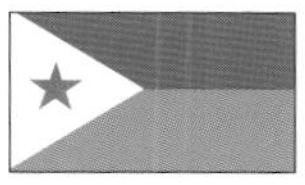

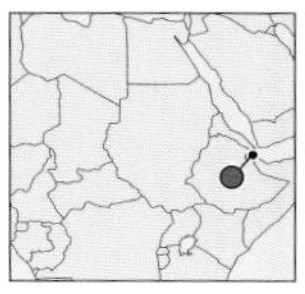

DJIBOUTI

GEOGRAPHY The Republic of Djibouti in eastern Africa occupies a strategic position where the Red Sea meets the Gulf of Aden. Djibouti has one of the world's hottest and driest climates.

POLITICS & ECONOMY France set up a territory called French Somaliland in 1888. Its capital, Djibouti, became important when a railroad was built to Addis Ababa and Djibouti became the main outlet for Ethiopian trade. In 1967, France renamed the dependency the French Territory of the Afars and Issas, but it was renamed Djibouti on independence in 1977. It became a one-party state in 1981, but a new constitution (1992) permitted four parties which had to maintain a balance between the country's ethnic groups. In the 2000s, the United States used Djibouti as a military base to counter terrorism in the region.

Djibouti is a poor country. Its economy is based largely on the revenue it gets from its port and the railroad to Addis Ababa.

AREA 8,958 SQ MI [23,200 SQ KM] **POPULATION** 496,000
CAPITAL DJIBOUTI **GOVERNMENT** MULTIPARTY REPUBLIC
ETHNIC GROUPS SOMALI 60%, AFAR 35% **LANGUAGES** ARABIC AND FRENCH (BOTH OFFICIAL) **RELIGIONS** ISLAM 94%, CHRISTIANITY 6%
CURRENCY DJIBOUTIAN FRANC = 100 CENTIMES

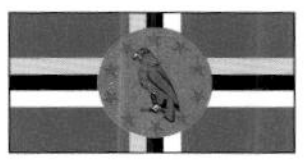

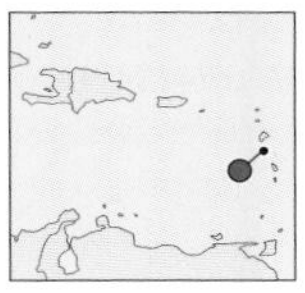

DOMINICA

The Commonwealth of Dominica, a former British colony, became independent in 1978. The island has a mountainous spine and less than 10% of the land is cultivated. But agriculture employs 18% of the people. The manufacture of coconut-based soap is important, while tourism and mining are other economic activities.

AREA 290 SQ MI [751 SQ KM] **POPULATION** 72,000 **CAPITAL** ROSEAU

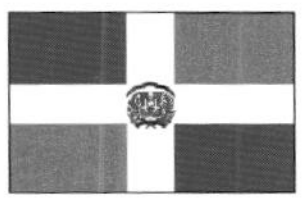

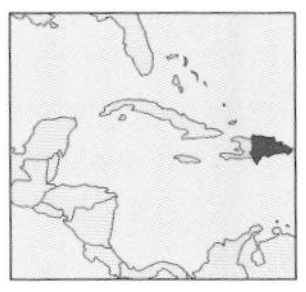

DOMINICAN REPUBLIC

GEOGRAPHY Second largest of the Caribbean nations in both area and population, the Dominican Republic shares the island of Hispaniola with Haiti, with the Dominican Republic occupying the eastern two-thirds. The country is mountainous, and the generally hot and humid climate eases with altitude.

POLITICS & ECONOMY In 1492, Christopher Columbus landed on Hispaniola and Spaniards soon settled the island, followed by the French who occupied the western third of the island (which is now Haiti). The island was held by Haitians from 1822 until 1844, when the Dominican Republic was established. Civil war broke out in 1966 but US intervention ended the conflict. Since 1966, the young democracy has survived violent elections under the watchful eye of the United States.

The Dominican Republic is a developing country and agriculture is the chief activity. Sugarcane, rice, bananas, and cocoa are leading crops. Food processing is also important and some ferronickel is produced.

AREA 18,730 SQ MI [48,511 SQ KM] **POPULATION** 9,366,000
CAPITAL SANTO DOMINGO **GOVERNMENT** MULTIPARTY REPUBLIC
ETHNIC GROUPS MULATTO 73%, WHITE 16%, BLACK 11%
LANGUAGES SPANISH (OFFICIAL) **RELIGIONS** ROMAN CATHOLIC 95%
CURRENCY DOMINICAN PESO = 100 CENTAVOS

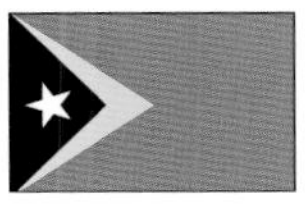

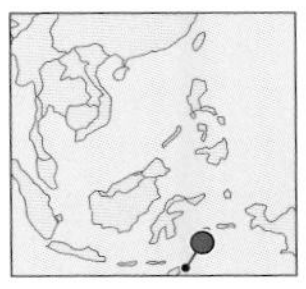

EAST TIMOR

The Republic of East Timor became fully independent and the world's newest country on May 20, 2002. The land is mainly rugged. Temperatures are generally high and the rainfall is moderate. Portugal ruled the area from the late 19th century, when it was called Portuguese Timor. Portugal withdrew in 1975 and Indonesia seized the area. Guerrilla activity mounted under Indonesian rule and, in 1999, the people voted for independence. Agriculture is the main activity and East Timor is the poorest country in Southeast Asia. But, in 2006, East Timor and Australia signed a deal to share the revenue from the oil and natural gas deposits under the Timor Sea.

AREA 5,743 SQ MI [14,874 SQ KM] **POPULATION** 1,085,000 **CAPITAL** DILI

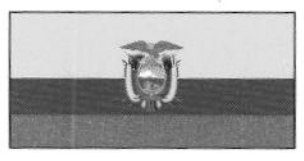

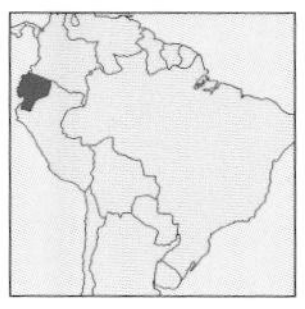

ECUADOR

GEOGRAPHY The Republic of Ecuador straddles the Equator on the west coast of South America. Three ranges of the high Andes Mountains form the backbone of the country. Between the towering, snow-capped peaks of the mountains, some of which are volcanoes, lie a series of high plateaux, or basins. Nearly half of Ecuador's population lives on these plateaux. The coast has a warm tropical climate, despite the cold offshore Peruvian Current. Inland, the altitude gives the plateaux spring-like weather throughout the year.

POLITICS & ECONOMY The Inca people of Peru conquered much of what is now Ecuador in the late 15th century. They introduced their language, Quechua, which is widely spoken today. Spanish forces defeated the Incas in 1533 and took control of Ecuador. The country became independent in 1822, following the defeat of a Spanish force in a battle near Quito.

In the 19th and 20th centuries, Ecuador suffered from political instability, while successive governments failed to tackle the country's social and economic problems. A war with Peru in 1941 led to a loss of territory. Disputes continued until 1995, but a border agreement was signed in January 1998. Economic crises in the early 21st century led to the adoption of the US dollar as the official currency. Political instability marred progress. A coup in 2000 was led by Colonel Lucio Gutiérrez, who was elected president in 2002. He was overthrown in 2005. In 2006, the leftist Rafael Correa was elected president and, in 2007, the people voted in favor of overhauling the political system.

The World Bank classifies Ecuador as a "lower-middle-income" developing country. Agriculture employs 8% of the people and bananas, cocoa, and coffee are all important crops. Fishing, forestry, mining, and manufacturing are other activities.

AREA 109,483 SQ MI [283,561 SQ KM]
POPULATION 13,756,000 **CAPITAL** QUITO
GOVERNMENT MULTIPARTY REPUBLIC
ETHNIC GROUPS MESTIZO (MIXED WHITE/AMERINDIAN) 65%, AMERINDIAN 25%, WHITE 7%, BLACK 3%
LANGUAGES SPANISH (OFFICIAL), QUECHUA
RELIGIONS ROMAN CATHOLIC 95%
CURRENCY US DOLLAR = 100 CENTS

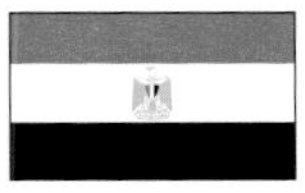

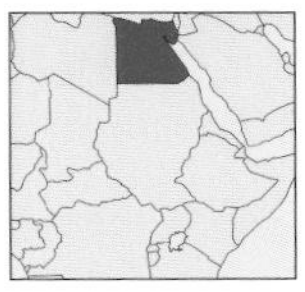

EGYPT

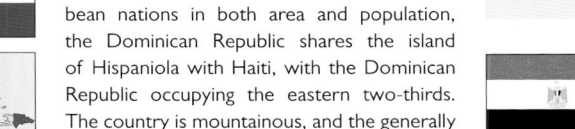

GEOGRAPHY The Arab Republic of Egypt is Africa's second largest country by population after Nigeria, though it ranks 13th in area. Most of Egypt is desert. Almost all the people live either in the Nile Valley and its fertile delta or along the Suez Canal, the artificial waterway between the Mediterranean and Red seas. This canal shortens the sea journey between the United Kingdom and India by 6,027 mi [9,700 km]. Recent attempts have been made to irrigate parts of the western desert and thus redistribute the rapidly growing Egyptian population into previously uninhabited regions.

Apart from the Nile Valley, Egypt has three other main regions. The Western and Eastern deserts are parts of the Sahara. The Sinai peninsula (Es Sina), to the east of the Suez Canal, is a mountainous desert region, geographically within Asia. It contains Egypt's highest peak, Gebel Katherina (8,650 ft [2,637 m]); few people live in this area.

Egypt is a dry country. The low rainfall occurs, if at all, in winter and the country is one of the sunniest places on Earth.

POLITICS & ECONOMY Ancient Egypt, which was founded about 5,000 years ago, was one of the great early civilizations. Throughout the country, pyramids, temples and richly decorated tombs are memorials to its great achievements.

After Ancient Egypt declined, the country came under successive foreign rulers. Arabs occupied Egypt in AD 639–42. They introduced the Arabic language and Islam. Their influence was so great that most Egyptians now regard themselves as Arabs.

Egypt came under British rule in 1882, but it gained partial independence in 1922, becoming a monarchy. The monarchy was abolished in 1952, when Egypt became a republic. The creation of Israel in 1948 led Egypt into a series of wars in 1948–9, 1956, 1967 and 1973. Since the late 1970s, Egypt has sought for peace. In 1979, Egypt signed a peace treaty with Israel and regained the Sinai region which it had lost in a war in 1967. Extremists opposed contacts with Israel and, in 1981, President Sadat, who had signed the treaty, was assassinated.

While Egypt plays a major part in Arab affairs, most of its people are poor. Some Islamic fundamentalists, who dislike Western influences on their way of life, have resorted to violence. In the

1990s, attacks on foreign visitors caused a decline in the valuable tourist industry, as also did the events of September 11, 2001, and the subsequent "war against terrorism." Hosni Mubarak, president since 1981, was re-elected in 2005, though supporters of the banned Muslim Brotherhood made gains in parliamentary elections.

Egypt is Africa's second most industrialized country after South Africa, but most people are poor. Oil and textiles are the country's main exports. In 2007, the government announced plans to build several nuclear power stations to generate electricity.

AREA 386,659 SQ MI [1,001,449 SQ KM]
POPULATION 80,335,000 **CAPITAL** CAIRO
GOVERNMENT REPUBLIC
ETHNIC GROUPS EGYPTIANS/BEDOUINS/BERBERS 99%
LANGUAGES ARABIC (OFFICIAL), FRENCH, ENGLISH
RELIGIONS ISLAM (MAINLY SUNNI MUSLIM) 94%, CHRISTIANITY (MAINLY COPTIC CHRISTIAN) AND OTHERS 6%
CURRENCY EGYPTIAN POUND = 100 PIASTRES

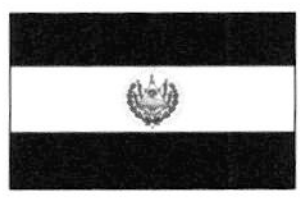
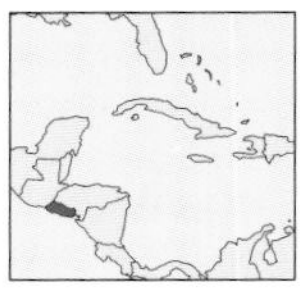

EL SALVADOR

GEOGRAPHY The Republic of El Salvador is the only country in Central America which does not have a coast on the Caribbean Sea. El Salvador has a narrow coastal plain along the Pacific Ocean. Behind the coastal plain, the coastal range is a zone of rugged mountains, including volcanoes, which overlooks a densely populated inland plateau. Beyond the plateau, the land rises to the sparsely populated interior highlands. The coast has a hot, tropical climate. Inland the climate is moderated by the altitude. Rain falls on practically every afternoon between May and October.

POLITICS & ECONOMY Amerindians have lived in El Salvador for thousands of years. The ruins of Mayan pyramids built between AD 100 and 1000 are still found in the western part of the country. Spanish soldiers conquered the area in 1524 and 1525, and Spain ruled until 1821. In 1823, all the Central American countries, except for Panama, set up a Central American Federation. But El Salvador withdrew in 1840 and declared its independence in 1841. El Salvador suffered from instability throughout the 19th century. The 20th century saw a more stable government, but from 1931 military dictatorships alternated with elected governments.

The country remained poor. In the 1970s, protesters demanded that the government introduce reforms to help the poor. Kidnappings and murders committed by left- and right-wing groups caused instability. A civil war broke out in 1979 between the US-backed government forces and left-wing guerrillas. In 12 years, more than 750,000 people died and many were made homeless. A ceasefire was agreed in 1992 and democratic elections were held in 1993, 1999, 2003 and 2006.

The World Bank classifies El Salvador as a "lower-middle-income" economy. About three-quarters of the country is farmed. Coffee, grown in the highlands, is the main export, followed by sugar and cotton, which grow on the coastal lowlands. Fishing for lobsters and shrimps is important, but manufacturing is on a small scale.

AREA 8,124 SQ MI [21,041 SQ KM]
POPULATION 6,948,000 **CAPITAL** SAN SALVADOR
GOVERNMENT REPUBLIC **ETHNIC GROUPS** MESTIZO (MIXED WHITE AND AMERINDIAN) 90%, WHITE 9%, AMERINDIAN 1%
LANGUAGES SPANISH (OFFICIAL) **RELIGIONS** ROMAN CATHOLIC 83%
CURRENCY US DOLLAR = 100 CENTS

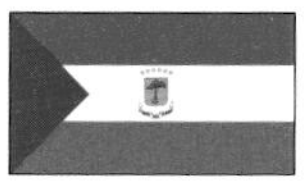
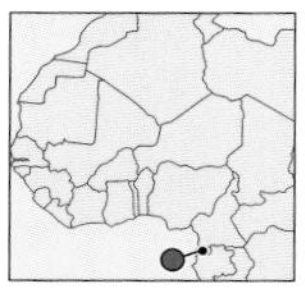

EQUATORIAL GUINEA

GEOGRAPHY The Republic of Equatorial Guinea is a small republic in west-central Africa. It consists of a mainland territory which makes up 90% of the land area, called Rio Muni, between Cameroon and Gabon, and five offshore islands in the Bight of Bonny, the largest of which is Bioko. The island of Annobon lies 350 mi [560 km] southwest of Rio Muni. Rio Muni consists mainly of hills and plateaux behind the coastal plains.

The climate is hot and humid. Bioko is mountainous, with the land rising to 9,869 ft [3,008 m], and hence it is particularly rainy. However, there is a marked dry season between the months of December and February. Mainland Rio Muni has a similar climate, though the rainfall diminishes inland.

POLITICS & ECONOMY Portuguese navigators reached the area in 1471. In 1778, Portugal granted Bioko, together with rights over Rio Muni, to Spain.

In 1959, Spain made Bioko and Rio Muni provinces of overseas Spain and, in 1963, it gave the provinces a degree of self-government. Equatorial Guinea became independent in 1968.

The first president of Equatorial Guinea, Francisco Macias Nguema, proved to be a tyrant. He was overthrown in 1979 and a group of officers, led by Lieutenant-Colonel Teodoro Obiang Nguema Mbasogo, set up a Supreme Military Council to rule the country. In 1991, the people voted to set up a multiparty democracy. Elections were held, but accusations of human rights abuses continued. In 2004, a coup attempt by mercenaries was foiled and its leaders were arrested.

Agriculture employs two-thirds of the people. The most valuable crop is coffee. Oil, which has been produced since 1966, accounts for most of the export revenue.

AREA 10,830 SQ MI [28,051 SQ KM] **POPULATION** 551,000
CAPITAL MALABO **GOVERNMENT** MULTIPARTY REPUBLIC (TRANSITIONAL)
ETHNIC GROUPS BUBI (ON BIOKO), FANG (IN RIO MUNI)
LANGUAGES SPANISH AND FRENCH (BOTH OFFICIAL)
RELIGIONS CHRISTIANITY **CURRENCY** CFA FRANC = 100 CENTIMES

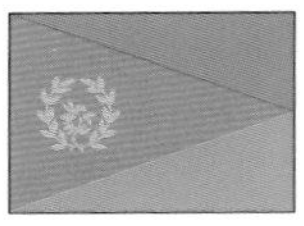
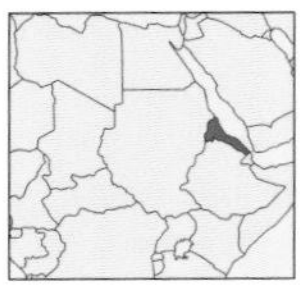

ERITREA

GEOGRAPHY The State of Eritrea consists of a hot, dry coastal plain facing the Red Sea, with a fairly mountainous area in the center. Most people live in the cooler highland area.

POLITICS & ECONOMY From the 1st century AD, Eritrea was part of the ancient Kingdom of Axum, which adopted Christianity in the 4th century AD. It began to decline in the 7th century. The Ottoman Turks took over the area in the 16th century and it became an Italian colony in the 1880s. The Italians were driven out in 1941 and, in 1952, it became part of Ethiopia.

A guerrilla struggle launched in 1961 ended in 1993, when Eritrea became independent. Economic recovery was hampered by conflict with Yemen over three islands in the Red Sea. In 1988–9, clashes occurred along the border with Ethiopia. A peace agreement was signed in 2000, but problems continued. In 2007–8, Eritrea was accused of supporting Islamist forces in Somalia – possibly as a reaction to Ethiopia's military support for Somalia's interim government.

The main economic activities are farming and livestock rearing. The few manufacturing industries are based mainly in Asmara.

AREA 45,405 SQ MI [117,600 SQ KM] **POPULATION** 4,907,000
CAPITAL ASMARA **GOVERNMENT** TRANSITIONAL GOVERNMENT
ETHNIC GROUPS TIGRINYA 50%, TIGRE AND KUNAMA 40%, AFAR 4%, SAHO 3%, OTHERS **LANGUAGES** AFAR, ARABIC, TIGRE AND KUNAMA, TIGRINYA **RELIGIONS** ISLAM, COPTIC CHRISTIAN, ROMAN CATHOLIC
CURRENCY NAKFA = 100 CENTS

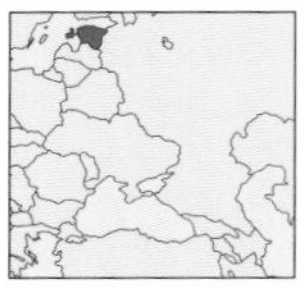

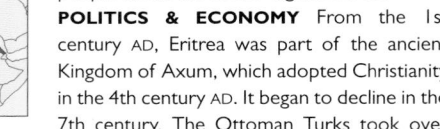

ESTONIA

GEOGRAPHY The Republic of Estonia is the smallest of the three states on the Baltic Sea, which were formerly part of the Soviet Union, but which became independent in the early 1990s. Estonia consists of a generally flat plain which was covered by ice sheets during the Ice Age. The land is strewn with moraine (rocks deposited by the ice).

The country is dotted with more than 1,500 small lakes. The large Lake Peipus (Chudskoye Ozero) and the River Narva together make up much of Estonia's eastern border with Russia. The largest of the islands is Saaremaa (Sarema). The climate is fairly mild because of the moderating effects of the sea.

POLITICS & ECONOMY The ancestors of the Estonians, who are related to the Finns, settled in the area several thousand years ago. German crusaders, known as the Teutonic Knights, introduced Christianity in the early 13th century. By the 16th century, German noblemen owned much of the land in Estonia. In 1561, Sweden took the northern part of the country and Poland the south. From 1625, Sweden controlled the entire country until Sweden handed it over to Russia in 1721.

Estonian nationalists campaigned for their independence from around the mid-19th century. Finally, Estonia was proclaimed independent in 1918. In 1919, the government began to break up the large estates and distribute land among the peasants.

In 1939, Germany and the Soviet Union agreed to take over parts of Eastern Europe. In 1940, Soviet forces occupied Estonia, but they were driven out by the Germans in 1941. Soviet troops returned in 1944 and Estonia became one of the 15 Soviet Socialist Republics of the Soviet Union. The Estonians strongly opposed Soviet rule. Many of them were deported to Siberia.

Political changes in the Soviet Union in the late 1980s led to renewed demands for freedom. In 1990, the Estonian government declared the country independent and, finally, the Soviet Union recognized this act in September 1991, shortly before the Soviet Union was dissolved. Estonia adopted a new constitution in 1992, when multiparty elections were held for a new national assembly. In 1993, Estonia negotiated an agreement with Russia to withdraw its troops.

Under Soviet rule, Estonia was the most prosperous of the three Baltic states. Since 1988, Estonia has worked to restructure its economy. Turning increasingly to the West, it became a member of both the North Atlantic Treaty Organization and the European Union in 2004. Estonia's resources include oil shale and its forests. Industries produce fertilizers, processed food, machinery, petrochemical products, wood products, and textiles. Agriculture and fishing are also important activities.

AREA 17,413 SQ MI [45,100 SQ KM] **POPULATION** 1,316,000
CAPITAL TALLINN **GOVERNMENT** MULTIPARTY REPUBLIC
ETHNIC GROUPS ESTONIAN 65%, RUSSIAN 28%, UKRAINIAN 3%, BELARUSIAN 2%, FINNISH 1% **LANGUAGES** ESTONIAN (OFFICIAL), RUSSIAN
RELIGIONS LUTHERAN, RUSSIAN AND ESTONIAN ORTHODOX, METHODIST, BAPTIST, ROMAN CATHOLIC **CURRENCY** ESTONIAN KROON = 100 SENTI

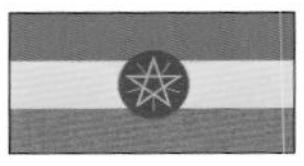
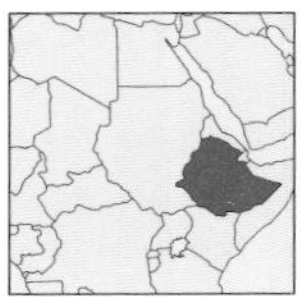

ETHIOPIA

GEOGRAPHY Ethiopia is a landlocked country in northeastern Africa. The land is mainly mountainous, though there are extensive plains in the east, bordering southern Eritrea, and in the south, bordering Somalia. The highlands are divided into two blocks by an arm of the Great Rift Valley which runs throughout eastern Africa. North of the Rift Valley, the land is especially rugged, rising to 15,157 ft [4,620 m] at Ras Dashen. Southeast of Ras Dashen is Lake Tana, source of the River Abay (Blue Nile). The climate is affected by the altitude. The rainfall in the highlands is generally more than 39 inches [1,000 mm]. The lowlands are hot and arid.

POLITICS & ECONOMY Ethiopia was the home of an ancient monarchy, which became Christian in the 4th century. In the 7th century, Muslims gained control of the lowlands, but Christianity survived in the highlands. Ethiopia resisted attempts to colonize it, but Italy invaded the country in 1935. The Italians were driven out in 1941 during World War II.

In 1952, Eritrea, on the Red Sea coast, was federated with Ethiopia. But in 1961, Eritrean nationalists demanded their freedom and began a struggle that ended in their independence in 1993. In 1995, because of Ethiopia's great ethnic diversity, the country was divided into nine provinces, each with its own regional assembly. In 1998, boundary disputes with Eritrea led to conflict. A peace agreement was reached in 2001, but tensions mounted in 2005–6 when Ethiopia failed to accept an international ruling over the border settlement of Badme. In 2006–7, Ethiopian troops intervened on behalf of the provisional government in Somalia, defeating the Islamist Union of Islamic Courts, which had taken control of Mogadishu.

Ethiopia is one of the world's poorest countries and it is heavily dependent on aid. In 2004, a UN report stated that Ethiopia remained on the brink of disaster, with spiraling population growth, slow economic growth and environmental degradation. Agriculture remains the main activity.

AREA 426,370 SQ MI [1,104,300 SQ KM]
POPULATION 76,512,000 **CAPITAL** ADDIS ABABA
GOVERNMENT FEDERATION OF NINE PROVINCES
ETHNIC GROUPS OROMO 40%, AMHARA AND TIGRE 32%, SIDAMO 9%, SHANKELLA 6%, SOMALI 6%, OTHERS **LANGUAGES** AMHARIC (OFFICIAL), MANY OTHERS **RELIGIONS** ISLAM 47%, ETHIOPIAN ORTHODOX 40%, TRADITIONAL BELIEFS 12% **CURRENCY** BIRR = 100 CENTS

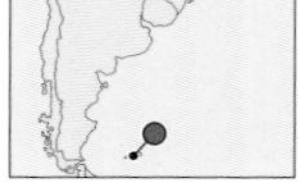
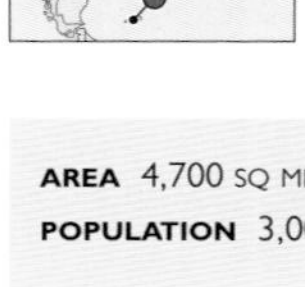

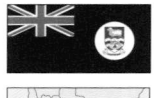

FALKLAND ISLANDS

Comprising two main islands and over 200 small islands, the Falkland Islands (or the Islas Malvinas, as they are called in Argentina) lie 300 mi [480 km] from South America. Sheep farming is the main activity, though the search for oil and diamonds holds out hope for the future of this harsh and virtually treeless environment.

AREA 4,700 SQ MI [12,173 SQ KM]
POPULATION 3,000 **CAPITAL** STANLEY

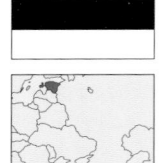

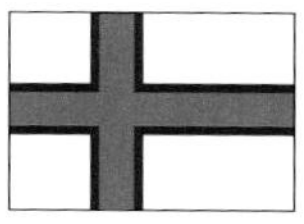
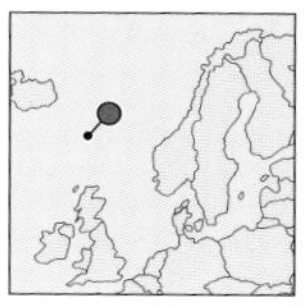

FÆROE ISLANDS

The Færoe Islands are a group of 18 volcanic islands and some reefs in the North Atlantic Ocean. The islands have been Danish since the 1380s, but they became largely self-governing in 1948. In 2001, a referendum on independence was called off after Denmark said that subsidies would end soon after independence.

AREA 540 sq mi [1,399 sq km]
POPULATION 48,000 **CAPITAL** Tórshavn

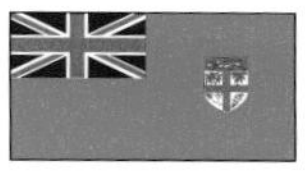
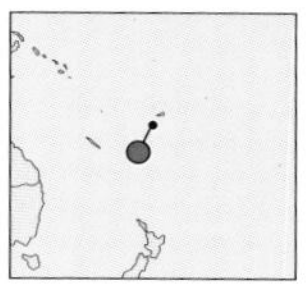

FIJI ISLANDS

The Fiji Islands (the official name of Fiji since 1998) is a republic consisting of more than 800 Melanesian islands, the biggest being Viti Levu and Vanua Levu. The climate is tropical. A former British colony, Fiji became independent in 1970. Its recent history has been marred by efforts by ethnic Fijians to impose their rule, stopping members of the ethnic Indian community from holding senior cabinet posts. Coups have occurred in 1987, 2000, and 2006.

AREA 7,056 sq mi [18,274 sq km] **POPULATION** 919,000 **CAPITAL** Suva

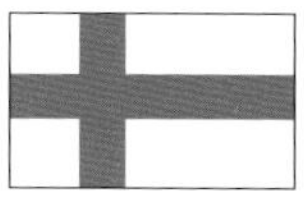
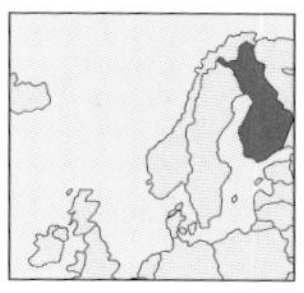

FINLAND

GEOGRAPHY The Republic of Finland is a beautiful country in northern Europe. In the south, behind the coastal lowlands where most Finns live, lies a region of sparkling lakes worn out by ice sheets in the Ice Age. The thinly populated northern uplands cover about two-fifths of the country.

Helsinki, the capital city, has warm summers, but the average temperatures between the months of December and March are below freezing point. Snow covers the land in winter. The north has less precipitation than the south, but it is much colder.

POLITICS & ECONOMY Between 1150 and 1809, Finland was under Swedish rule. The close links between the countries continue today. Swedish remains an official language in Finland and many towns have Swedish as well as Finnish names.

In 1809, Finland became a grand duchy of the Russian empire. It finally declared itself independent in 1917, after the Russian Revolution and the collapse of the Russian empire. But during World War II (1939–45), the Soviet Union declared war on Finland and took part of Finland's territory. Finland allied itself with Germany, but it lost more land to the Soviet Union at the end of the war.

After World War II, Finland became a neutral country and negotiated peace treaties with the Soviet Union. Finland also strengthened its relations with other northern European countries and became an associate member of the European Free Trade Association (EFTA) in 1961. Finland became a full member of EFTA in 1986, but it became a member of the European Union on January 1, 1995. In 2002, Finland adopted the euro as its sole unit of currency. Finland has also discussed joining NATO, but the re-election of the center-left Tarja Halonen in 2006 suggested that NATO membership was unlikely during her six-year term.

Forests are the chief resource and wood, wood products and paper once dominated the economy. They still make up about a quarter of the exports, but, since World War II, Finland has set up many new industries, producing machinery and transport equipment. The economy has expanded quickly and machinery and apparatus now account for more than a third of the exports.

AREA 130,558 sq mi [338,145 sq km]
POPULATION 5,238,000 **CAPITAL** Helsinki
GOVERNMENT Multiparty republic **ETHNIC GROUPS** Finnish 93%, Swedish 6% **LANGUAGES** Finnish and Swedish (both official)
RELIGIONS Evangelical Lutheran 89% **CURRENCY** Euro = 100 cents

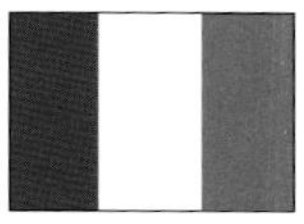
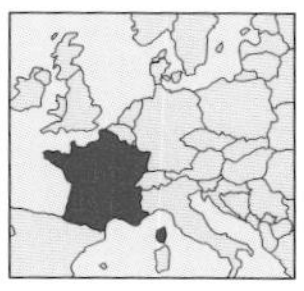

FRANCE

GEOGRAPHY The Republic of France is the largest country in Western Europe. The scenery is extremely varied. The Vosges Mountains overlook the Rhine valley in the northeast, the Jura Mountains and the Alps form the borders with Switzerland and Italy in the southeast, while the Pyrenees straddle France's border with Spain. The only large highland area entirely within France is the Massif Central between the Rhône-Saône valley and the basin of Aquitaine in southern France.

Brittany (Bretagne) and Normandy (Normande) form a scenic hill region. Fertile lowlands cover most of northern France, including the densely populated Paris basin. Another major lowland area, the Aquitanian basin, is in the southwest, while the Rhône-Saône valley and the Mediterranean lowlands are in the southeast.

The climate of France varies from west to east and from north to south. The west comes under the moderating influence of the Atlantic Ocean, giving generally mild weather. To the east, summers are warmer and winters colder. The climate also becomes warmer as one travels from north to south. The Mediterranean Sea coast has hot, dry summers and mild, moist winters. The Alps, Jura, and Pyrenees mountains have snowy winters. Winter sports centers are found in all three areas. Large glaciers occupy high valleys in the Alps.

POLITICS & ECONOMY The Romans conquered France (then called Gaul) in the 50s BC. Roman rule began to decline in the fifth century AD and, in 486, the Frankish realm (as France was called) became independent under a Christian king, Clovis. In 800, Charlemagne, who had been king since 768, became emperor of the Romans. He extended France's boundaries, but, in 843, his empire was divided into three parts and the area of France contracted. After the Norman invasion of England in 1066, large areas of France came under English rule, but this was finally ended in 1453.

France later became a powerful monarchy. But the French Revolution (1789–99) ended absolute rule by French kings. In 1799, Napoleon Bonaparte took power and fought a series of brilliant military campaigns before his final defeat in 1815. The monarchy was restored until 1848, when the Second Republic was founded. In 1852, Napoleon's nephew became Napoleon III, but the Third Republic was established in 1875. France was the scene of much fighting during World War I (1914–18) and World War II (1939–45), causing great loss of life and much damage to the economy.

In 1946, France adopted a new constitution, establishing the Fourth Republic. But political instability and costly colonial wars slowed France's post-war recovery. In 1958, Charles de Gaulle was elected president and he introduced a new constitution, giving the president extra powers and inaugurating the Fifth Republic.

Since the 1960s, France has made rapid economic progress, becoming one of the most prosperous nations in the European Union. But France's government faced a number of problems, including unemployment, pollution, and the growing number of elderly people, who find it difficult to live when inflation rates are high. One social problem concerns the presence in France of large numbers of immigrants from Africa and southern Europe, many of whom live in poor areas.

In 2002, the euro became France's sole unit of currency, replacing the franc. In 2005, the people voted against a proposed constitution for the European Union in a national referendum. In 2005, France was rocked by inter-ethnic violence and, in 2007, the right-wing Nicolas Sarkozy was elected president, defeating his socialist rival, Ségolène Royal.

France is one of the world's most developed countries. Its natural resources include its fertile soil, together with deposits of bauxite, coal, iron ore, oil and natural gas, and potash. France is also one of the world's top manufacturing nations, and it has often innovated in bold and imaginative ways. The TGV and hypermarkets are typical examples. Paris is a world center of fashion industries, but France has many other industrial towns and cities. Major manufactures include aircraft, cars, chemicals, electronic and metal products, machinery, processed food, steel, and textiles.

Agriculture employs about 3% of the people, but France is the largest producer of farm products in Western Europe, producing most of the food it needs. Wheat is the leading crop and livestock farming is of major importance. Fishing and forestry are leading industries, while tourism is a major activity.

AREA 212,934 sq mi [551,500 sq km] **POPULATION** 60,876,000
CAPITAL Paris **GOVERNMENT** Multiparty republic
ETHNIC GROUPS Celtic, Latin, Arab, Teutonic, Slavic
LANGUAGES French (official) **RELIGIONS** Roman Catholic 85%, Islam 8%, others **CURRENCY** Euro = 100 cents

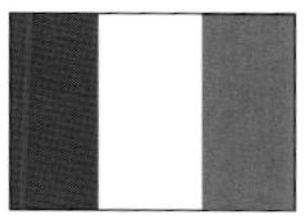
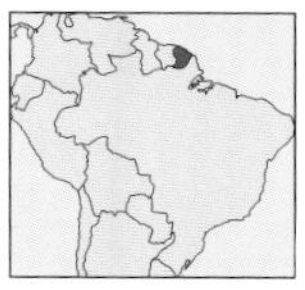

FRENCH GUIANA

GEOGRAPHY French Guiana is the smallest country in mainland South America. The coastal plain is swampy in places, but some dry areas are cultivated. Inland lies a plateau, with the low Tumachumac Mountains in the south. Most of the rivers run north toward the Atlantic Ocean.

French Guiana has a hot, equatorial climate, with high temperatures throughout the year. The rainfall is heavy, especially between December and June, but it is dry between August and October. The northeast trade winds blow constantly across the country.

POLITICS & ECONOMY The first people to live in what is now French Guiana were Amerindians. Today, only a few of them survive in the interior. The first Europeans to explore the coast arrived in 1500, and they were followed by adventurers seeking El Dorado, the mythical city of gold. Cayenne was founded in 1637 by a group of French merchants. The area became a French colony in the late 17th century.

France used the colony as a penal settlement for political prisoners from the times of the French Revolution in the 1790s. From the 1850s to 1945, the country became notorious as a place where prisoners were harshly treated. Many of them died, unable to survive in the tropical conditions.

In 1946, French Guiana became an overseas department of France, and in 1974 it also became an administrative region. An independence movement developed in the 1980s, but most people want to retain their links with France and continue to obtain financial aid to develop their territory.

Although it has rich forest and mineral resources, such as bauxite (aluminum ore), French Guiana is a developing country. It depends greatly on France for money to run its services and the government is the country's biggest employer. Since 1968, Kourou in French Guiana, the European Space Agency's rocket-launching site, has earned money for France by sending communications satellites into space.

AREA 34,749 sq mi [90,000 sq km]
POPULATION 200,000 **CAPITAL** Cayenne
GOVERNMENT Overseas department of France
ETHNIC GROUPS Black or Mulatto 66%, East Indian/Chinese and Amerindian 12%, White 12%, others 10% **LANGUAGES** French (official) **RELIGIONS** Roman Catholic **CURRENCY** Euro = 100 cents

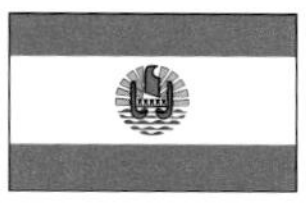
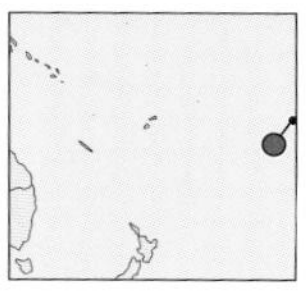

FRENCH POLYNESIA

French Polynesia consists of 130 islands, scattered over 1 million sq mi [2.5 million sq km] of the Pacific Ocean. Tribal chiefs in the area agreed to a French protectorate in 1843. They gained increased autonomy in 1984, but the links with France ensure a high standard of living.

AREA 1,544 sq mi [4,000 sq km]
POPULATION 279,000 **CAPITAL** Papeete

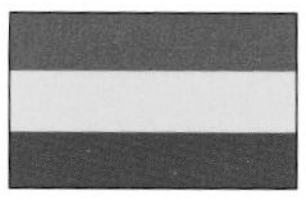
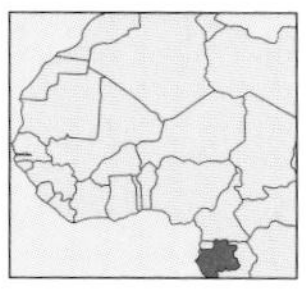

GABON

GEOGRAPHY The Gabonese Republic lies on the Equator in west-central Africa. In area, it is a little larger than the United Kingdom, with a coastline 500 mi [800 km] long. Behind the narrow, partly lagoon-lined coastal plain, the land rises to hills, plateaux and mountains divided by deep valleys carved by the River Ogooué and its tributaries.

Most of Gabon has an equatorial climate, with high temperatures and humidity throughout the year. The rainfall is heavy and the skies are often cloudy.

POLITICS & ECONOMY Gabon became a French colony in the 1880s, but it achieved full independence in 1960. In 1964, an attempted coup was put down when French troops intervened and crushed the revolt. In 1967, Bernard-Albert Bongo, who later renamed himself El Hadj Omar Bongo, became president. He declared Gabon a one-party state in 1968. Opposition parties were legalized in 1991, but Bongo was re-elected president in 1993. In 2003, constitutional changes enabled Bongo to stand again in 2005, when he was re-elected.

Gabon's natural resources include its forests, oil and gas deposits, manganese, and uranium. Its mineral deposits make it one of Africa's better-off countries. But agriculture still employs more than a third of the people and many farmers produce little more than they need to support their families.

AREA 103,347 sq mi [267,668 sq km]
POPULATION 1,455,000 **CAPITAL** Libreville
GOVERNMENT Multiparty republic
ETHNIC GROUPS Four major Bantu tribes: Fang, Bapounou, Nzebi and Obamba **LANGUAGES** French (official), Fang, Myene, Nzebi, Bapounou/Eschira, Bandjabi
RELIGIONS Christianity 75%, animist, Islam
CURRENCY CFA franc = 100 centimes

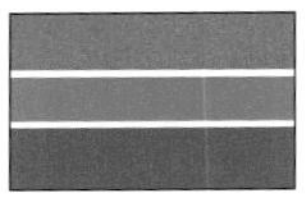

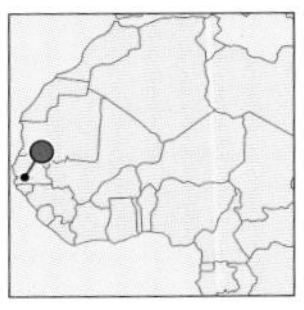

GAMBIA, THE

GEOGRAPHY The Republic of The Gambia is the smallest country in mainland Africa. It consists of a narrow strip of land bordering the River Gambia. The Gambia is almost entirely enclosed by Senegal, except along the short Atlantic coastline.

The Gambia has hot and humid summers, but the winter temperatures (November to May) drop to around 61°F [16°C]. In the summer, moist southwesterlies bring rain, which is heaviest on the coast.

POLITICS & ECONOMY English traders bought rights to trade on the River Gambia in 1588, and in 1664 the English established a settlement on an island in the river estuary. In 1765, the British founded Senegambia, which included parts of The Gambia and Senegal. In 1783, Britain handed this colony over to France. In the 19th century, Britain and France discussed the exchange of The Gambia for some other French territory, but an agreement was reached and Britain made The Gambia a British colony in 1888.

The Gambia achieved independence in 1965 and it became a republic in 1970. Relations between the English-speaking Gambians and the French-speaking Senegalese are a major political issue. In 1981, an attempted coup in The Gambia was put down with the help of Senegalese troops. In 1982, The Gambia and Senegal set up a defense alliance, called the Confederation of Senegambia. But this alliance was dissolved in 1989. In 1994, a military group overthrew the president, Sir Dawda Jawara, who fled into exile. Captain Yahya Jammeh, who took power, was elected president in 1996 and re-elected in 2001 and 2006.

Agriculture is the chief activity. Food crops include cassava, millet, and sorghum, but groundnuts and groundnut products are the main exports. Tourism is growing and, in 2004, the government announced the discovery of offshore oilfields.

AREA 4,361 SQ MI [11,295 SQ KM]
POPULATION 1,688,000 **CAPITAL** BANJUL
GOVERNMENT MILITARY REGIME
ETHNIC GROUPS MANDINKA 42%, FULA 18%, WOLOF 16%, JOLA 10%, SERAHULI 9%, OTHERS
LANGUAGES ENGLISH (OFFICIAL), MANDINKA, WOLOF, FULA
RELIGIONS ISLAM 90%, CHRISTIANITY 9%, TRADITIONAL BELIEFS 1%
CURRENCY DALASI = 100 BUTUT

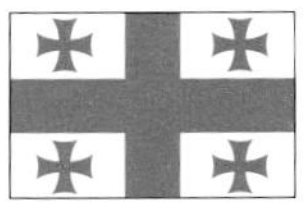

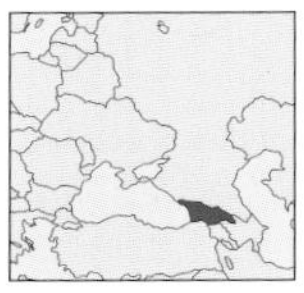

GEORGIA

GEOGRAPHY Georgia is a country on the borders of Europe and Asia, facing the Black Sea. The land is rugged with the Caucasus Mountains forming its northern border. The highest mountain in this range, Mount Elbrus (18,510 ft [5,642 m]), lies over the border in Russia.

The Black Sea plains have hot summers and mild winters. The rainfall is heavy, though inland areas are drier.

POLITICS & ECONOMY The first Georgian state was set up nearly 2,500 years ago. But for much of its history, the area was ruled by various conquerors. Christianity was introduced in AD 330. Georgia freed itself of foreign rule in the 11th and 12th centuries, but Mongol armies attacked in the 13th century. From the 16th to the 18th centuries, Iran and the Turkish Ottoman empire struggled for control of the area, and in the late 18th century Georgia sought the protection of Russia and, by the early 19th century, Georgia was part of the Russian empire. After the Russian Revolution of 1917, Georgia declared its independence, but Russia invaded, making the country part of the Soviet regime. Georgia declared itself independent in 1991. It became a separate country when the Soviet Union was dissolved in December 1991.

Georgia contains three regions containing minority peoples: Abkhazia in the northwest, South Ossetia in north-central Georgia, and Adjaria (also spelled Adzharia) in the southwest. Civil war broke out in South Ossetia in the early 1990s, while fierce fighting continued in Abkhazia until the late 1990s. In 2000, Georgia agreed to recognize Adjaria's autonomy in the country's constitution. In 2002, Russian and Georgian troops attacked Chechen rebels in Pankisi Gorge in northeastern Georgia. In 2003, the pro-Western Mikhail Saakashvili was elected president following the "Rose Revolution." Following Saakashvili's re-election in 2008, relations with Russia deteriorated markedly when Georgia accused Russia of supporting secessionist groups.

Georgia is a developing country. Agriculture, food processing, and perfume-making are important activities. Products include barley, citrus fruits, grapes for wine-making, maize, tea, tobacco, and vegetables. Sheep and cattle are reared.

AREA 26,911 SQ MI [69,700 SQ KM]
POPULATION 4,646,000 **CAPITAL** TBILISI
GOVERNMENT MULTIPARTY REPUBLIC
ETHNIC GROUPS GEORGIAN 70%, ARMENIAN 8%, RUSSIAN 6%, AZERI 6%, OSSETIAN 3%, GREEK 2%, ABKHAZ 2%, OTHERS 3%
LANGUAGES GEORGIAN (OFFICIAL), RUSSIAN
RELIGIONS GEORGIAN ORTHODOX 65%, ISLAM 11%, RUSSIAN ORTHODOX 10%, ARMENIAN APOSTOLIC 8% **CURRENCY** LARI = 100 TETRI

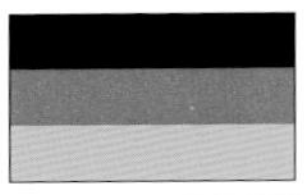

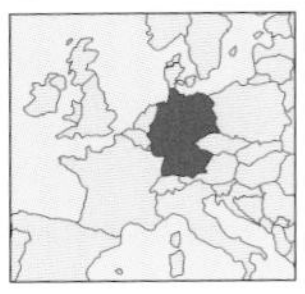

GERMANY

GEOGRAPHY The Federal Republic of Germany is the fourth largest country in Western Europe, after France, Spain and Sweden. The North German plain borders the North Sea in the northwest and the Baltic Sea in the northeast. Major rivers draining the plain include the Weser, Elbe and Oder.

The central highlands include the Harz Mountains, the Thuringian Forest (Thüringer Wald), the Ore Mountains (Erzgebirge), and the Bohemian Forest (Böhmerwald) on the Czech border. The Bavarian Alps in the south contain Germany's highest peak, Zugspitze, at 9,718 ft [2,962 m] above sea level. The Black Forest (Schwarzwald) in the southwest overlooks the River Rhine. Northwestern Germany has a mild climate, but the Baltic coasts are cooler. To the south, the climate becomes more continental, especially in the highlands. The precipitation is greatest on the uplands, with snow in winter.

POLITICS & ECONOMY Germany and its allies were defeated in World War I (1914–18) and the country became a republic. Adolf Hitler came to power in 1933 and ruled as a dictator. His order to invade Poland led to the start of World War II (1939–45), which ended with Germany in ruins.

In 1945, Germany was divided into four military zones. In 1949, the American, British and French zones were amalgamated to form the Federal Republic of Germany (West Germany), while the Soviet zone became the German Democratic Republic (East Germany), a Communist state. Berlin, which had also been partitioned, became a divided city. West Berlin was part of West Germany, while East Berlin became the capital of East Germany. Bonn was the capital of West Germany.

Tension between East and West mounted during the Cold War, but West Germany rebuilt its economy quickly. In East Germany, the recovery was less rapid. In the late 1980s, reforms in the Soviet Union led to unrest in East Germany. Free elections were held in East Germany in 1990 and, on October 3, 1990, Germany was reunited.

The united Germany adopted West Germany's official name, the Federal Republic of Germany. In the 1990s, the government faced many problems, especially those arising from reunification. In 1999, the parliament moved from Bonn to a reconstructed Reichstag building in Berlin. In 2005, Angela Merkel became Germany's first female Chancellor, when she led the Christian Democratic Union to a narrow victory over the Social Democrats.

West Germany's "economic miracle" after World War II was greatly helped by foreign aid. Today, Germany is one of the world's top economic powers. Manufacturing is the mainstay of the economy and manufactured goods are the chief exports. Cars and other vehicles, cement, chemicals, computers, electrical equipment, processed food, machinery, scientific instruments, ships, steel, textiles, and tools are manufactured. Germany has some coal, potash and rock salt deposits, but it imports many industrial raw materials. Germany also imports food. Leading products include fruits, grapes for wine-making, potatoes, sugar beet, and vegetables. Livestock include beef and dairy cattle.

AREA 137,846 SQ MI [357,022 SQ KM]
POPULATION 82,401,000 **CAPITAL** BERLIN
GOVERNMENT FEDERAL MULTIPARTY REPUBLIC
ETHNIC GROUPS GERMAN 92%, TURKISH 3%, SERBO-CROATIAN, ITALIAN, GREEK, POLISH, SPANISH **LANGUAGES** GERMAN (OFFICIAL)
RELIGIONS PROTESTANT (MAINLY LUTHERAN) 34%, ROMAN CATHOLIC 34%, ISLAM 4%, OTHERS **CURRENCY** EURO = 100 CENTS

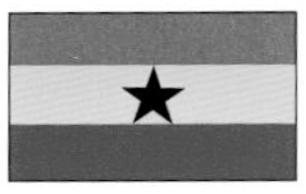

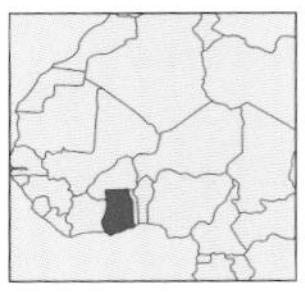

GHANA

GEOGRAPHY The Republic of Ghana faces the Gulf of Guinea in West Africa. This hot country, just north of the Equator, was formerly called the Gold Coast. Behind the thickly populated southern coastal plains, which are lined with lagoons, lies a plateau region in the southwest.

Accra has a hot, tropical climate. Rain occurs all through the year, though Accra is drier than areas inland.

POLITICS & ECONOMY Portuguese explorers reached the area in 1471 and named it the Gold Coast. The area became a center of the slave trade in the 17th century. The slave trade was ended in the 1860s and, gradually, the British took control of the area. After independence in 1957, attempts were made to develop the economy by creating large state-owned manufacturing industries. But debt and corruption, together with falls in the price of cocoa, the chief export, caused economic problems. This led to instability and frequent coups. In 1981, power was invested in a Provisional National Defense Council, led by Flight-Lieutenant Jerry Rawlings.

The government steadied the economy and introduced several new policies, including the relaxation of government controls. In 1992, the government introduced a new constitution, which allowed for multiparty elections. Rawlings was elected president in 1992 and 1996, but he retired in 2002. He was succeeded as president by John Ageykum Kufuor. The World Bank classifies Ghana as a "low-income" developing country. Most people are poor and farming employs 50% of the population.

AREA 92,098 SQ MI [238,533 SQ KM] **POPULATION** 22,931,000
CAPITAL ACCRA **GOVERNMENT** REPUBLIC
ETHNIC GROUPS AKAN 44%, MOSHI-DAGOMBA 16%, EWE 13%, GA 8%, GURMA 3%, YORUBA 1% **LANGUAGES** ENGLISH (OFFICIAL), AKAN, MOSHI-DAGOMBA, EWE, GA **RELIGIONS** CHRISTIANITY 63%, TRADITIONAL BELIEFS 21%, ISLAM 16% **CURRENCY** CEDI = 100 PESEWAS

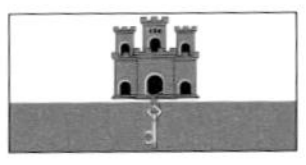

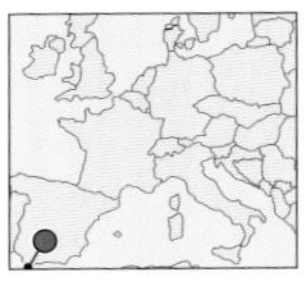

GIBRALTAR

Gibraltar occupies a strategic position on the south coast of Spain where the Mediterranean meets the Atlantic. It was recognized as a British possession in 1713 and, despite Spanish claims, its population has consistently voted to retain its contacts with Britain.

AREA 2.3 SQ MI [6 SQ KM]
POPULATION 28,000 **CAPITAL** GIBRALTAR TOWN

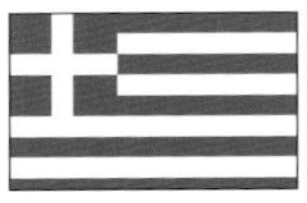

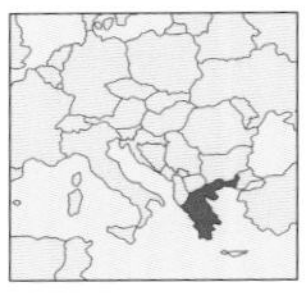

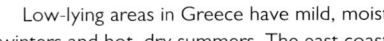

GREECE

GEOGRAPHY The Hellenic Republic, as Greece is officially called, is a rugged country situated at the southern end of the Balkan peninsula. Olympus, at 9,570 ft [2,917 m] is the highest peak. Islands make up about a fifth of the land.

Low-lying areas in Greece have mild, moist winters and hot, dry summers. The east coast has more than 2,700 hours of sunshine a year and only about half of the rainfall of the west. The mountains have a much more severe climate, with snow on the higher slopes in winter.

POLITICS & ECONOMY Around 2,500 years ago, Greece became the birthplace of Western civilization and Ancient Greek ruins and art still attract millions of tourists to the country. The first civilization, the Minoan, was centered on Crete. It flourished between about 3000 and 1400 BC. Following the end of the related Mycaenean period on the mainland (1580–1100 BC), a "dark age" lasted until about 800 BC. But from 750 BC, Greeks became rich traders and the city-state of Athens reached its peak in 461–431 BC. Greece became a Roman province in 146 BC and, in AD 365, it became part of the Byzantine Empire.

The Byzantine empire fell to the Turks in 1453. But Greece became an independent monarchy in 1830. After World War II (1939–45), when Germany ruled Greece, a civil war broke out between Greek Communists and nationalists. It ended in 1949 and a military dictatorship seized power in 1967. The monarchy was abolished in 1973 and democracy was restored in 1974. Greece joined the European Community (now the European Union) in 1981 and, on January 1, 2002, the euro became the sole unit of currency in Greece.

Greece is one of the EU's less economically developed members. Manufactured products include processed food, cement, chemicals, metal products, textiles and tobacco. Greece also mines lignite (brown coal), bauxite, and chromite. Farmland covers about a third of the country and grazing land another 40%. Crops include barley, grapes for wine-making, dried fruits, olives, potatoes, sugar beet, and wheat. Livestock farming is also important. Greece's beaches and ancient ruins make the country a major tourist destination.

AREA 50,949 SQ MI [131,957 SQ KM]
POPULATION 10,706,000 **CAPITAL** ATHENS
GOVERNMENT MULTIPARTY REPUBLIC **ETHNIC GROUPS** GREEK 98%
LANGUAGES GREEK (OFFICIAL) **RELIGIONS** GREEK ORTHODOX 98%
CURRENCY EURO = 100 CENTS

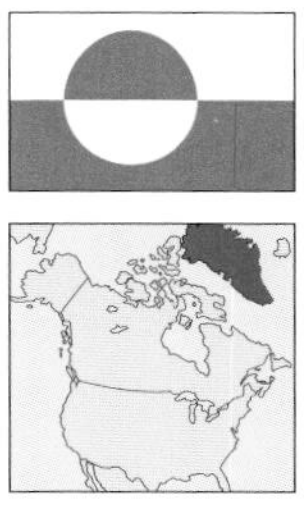

GREENLAND

Greenland is the world's largest island. Settlements are confined to the coast, because an ice sheet covers four-fifths of the land. Greenland became a Danish possession in 1380. Full internal self-government was granted in 1981 and, in 1997, Danish place names were superseded by Inuit forms. However, Greenland remains heavily dependent on Danish subsidies.

AREA 838,999 sq mi [2,175,600 sq km]
POPULATION 56,000 **CAPITAL** Nuuk (Godthåb)

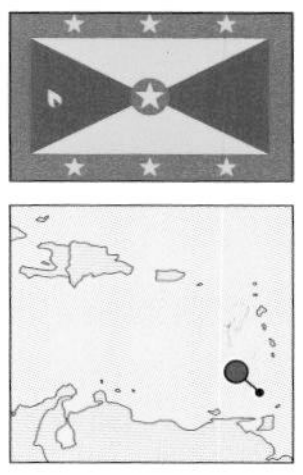

GRENADA

The most southerly of the Windward Islands in the Caribbean Sea, Grenada became independent from the UK in 1974. A military group seized power in 1983, when the prime minister was killed. US troops intervened and restored order and constitutional government.

AREA 133 sq mi [344 sq km]
POPULATION 90,000 **CAPITAL** St George's

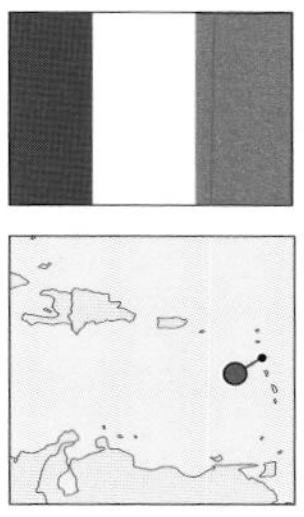

GUADELOUPE

Guadeloupe is a French overseas department which includes seven Caribbean islands, the largest of which is Basse-Terre. French aid has helped to mantain a reasonable standard of living for the people.

AREA 658 sq mi [1,705 sq km]
POPULATION 453,000 **CAPITAL** Basse-Terre

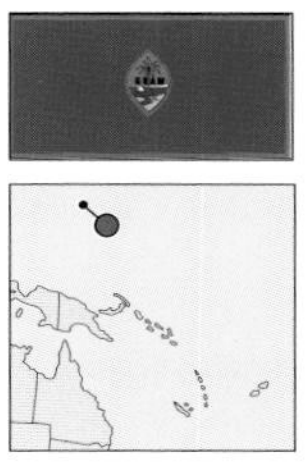

GUAM

Guam, a strategically important "unincorporated territory" of the USA, is the largest of the Mariana Islands in the Pacific Ocean. It is composed of a coralline limestone plateau.

AREA 212 sq mi [549 sq km]
POPULATION 173,000 **CAPITAL** Agana

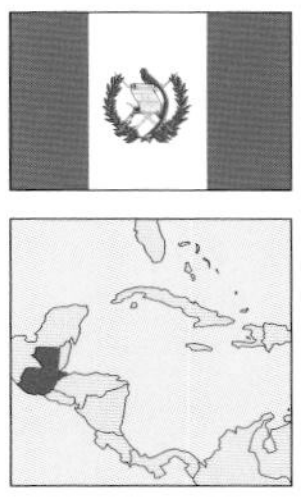

GUATEMALA

GEOGRAPHY The Republic of Guatemala in Central America contains a thickly populated mountain region, with fertile soils. The mountains, which run in an east–west direction, contain many volcanoes, some of which are active. Volcanic eruptions and earthquakes are common in the highlands. South of the mountains lie the thinly populated Pacific coastlands, while a large inland plain occupies the north.

The lowlands of Guatemala are hot and rainy, but the central highlands are cooler and drier. Guatemala City has a pleasant. warm climate with a dry season between November and April.

POLITICS & ECONOMY Much of what is now Guatemala was part of the Maya empire which thrived between AD 300 and 900. Spain ruled the area from the 1520s until 1821. In 1823, Guatemala joined the Central American Federation. But it became fully independent in 1839. Instability and periodic violence have marred its progress. Guatemala has a long-standing claim over Belize, but this was reduced in 1983 to the southern fifth of the country. Between 1960 and 1996, civil war occurred between left-wing groups, including many Amerindians, and government forces. The war claimed perhaps 200,000 lives. In 2004, the government paid US$3.5 million to victims of state-sponsored oppression. In 2007, Alvaro Colom, a center-left politician, became president.

Guatemala is ranked as a "lower-middle-income" economy. Agriculture employs 38% of the population. Coffee, sugar, bananas, and beef are exported, and the spice cardamom and cotton are also important. Maize is the main food crop.

AREA 42,042 sq mi [108,889 sq km]
POPULATION 12,728,000 **CAPITAL** Guatemala City
GOVERNMENT Republic **ETHNIC GROUPS** Ladino (mixed Hispanic and Amerindian) 55%, Amerindian 43%, others 2%
LANGUAGES Spanish (official), Amerindian languages
RELIGIONS Christianity, indigenous Mayan beliefs
CURRENCY US dollar; Quetzal = 100 centavos

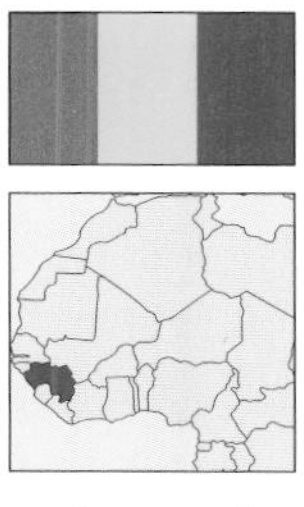

GUINEA

GEOGRAPHY The Republic of Guinea faces the Atlantic Ocean in West Africa. A flat, swampy plain borders the coast. Behind this plain, the land rises to a plateau region called Fouta Djalon. The Upper Niger plains, named after one of Africa's longest rivers, the Niger, which rises there, are in the northeast.

Guinea has a tropical climate and Conakry, on the coast, has heavy rains between May and November. This is also the coolest period in the year. During the dry season, hot, dry harmattan winds blow southwestward from the Sahara Desert.

POLITICS & ECONOMY Guinea came under the influence of several medieval African states, including Ancient Ghana and Ancient Mali. France began to control the area in the late 19th century. Guinea became independent in 1958. Its leaders pursued socialist policies but resorted to repressive measures to hold on to power. A military regime under Lansana Conté took over in 1984, but a multiparty system was restored in 1992. Conté was elected president in 1993 and again in 1998 and 2002. In 2007, his rule was threatened following huge protests by trade unionists and soldiers with grievances over pay and housing.

Guinea is a "low-income" developing country. Its resources include bauxite (aluminum ore), diamonds, gold, iron ore, and uranium. Bauxite and alumina (processed bauxite) account for more than half of the exports. Agriculture employs more than 70% of the people, but most farmers are poor. Manufactures include alumina, processed food, and textiles.

AREA 94,925 sq mi [245,857 sq km]
POPULATION 9,948,000 **CAPITAL** Conakry
GOVERNMENT Multiparty republic
ETHNIC GROUPS Peuhl 40%, Malinke 30%, Soussou 20%, others 10% **LANGUAGES** French (official)
RELIGIONS Islam 85%, Christianity 8%, traditional beliefs 7%
CURRENCY Guinean franc = 100 cauris

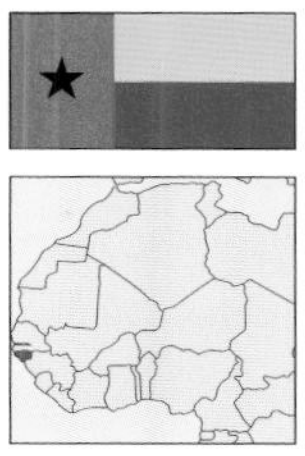

GUINEA-BISSAU

GEOGRAPHY The Republic of Guinea-Bissau, formerly known as Portuguese Guinea, is a small country in West Africa. The land is mostly low-lying, with a broad, swampy coastal plain and many flat offshore islands, including the Bijagós Archipelago.

The country has a tropical climate, with one dry season (December to May) and a rainy season from June to November.

POLITICS & ECONOMY Portuguese explorers reached Guinea-Bissau in 1446 and the area became a center of the slave trade. From 1836, Portugal administered Guinea-Bissau with the Cape Verde Islands but, in 1879, the territories were separated. Guinea-Bissau became a separate colony called Portuguese Guinea. But economic development in the colony was slow.

In 1956, African nationalists in Portuguese Guinea and Cape Verde founded the African Party for the Independence of Guinea and Cape Verde (PAIGC). Because Portugal seemed determined to hang on to its overseas territories, the PAIGC began a guerrilla war in 1963. By 1968, it held two-thirds of the country. In 1972, a rebel National Assembly, elected by the people in the PAIGC-controlled area, voted to make the country independent as Guinea-Bissau.

In 1974, newly independent Guinea-Bissau faced many problems arising from its underdeveloped economy and its lack of trained people to work in the administration. One objective of the leaders of Guinea-Bissau was to unite their country with Cape Verde. But, in 1980, army leaders overthrew Guinea-Bissau's government. The Revolutionary Council, which took over, opposed unification with Cape Verde. Guinea-Bissau ceased to be a one-party state in 1991 and multiparty elections were held in 1994. Civil war broke out in 1998 and a military coup occurred in 1999. Elections were held in 2000. Another coup occurred in 2003, but civilian government was restored in 2004. In 2005, a former military leader, Joao Bernardo Viera, was elected president.

Agriculture, mainly at subsistence level, employs 76% of the people. Crops include coconuts, groundnuts, maize, and rice.

AREA 13,948 sq mi [36,125 sq km]
POPULATION 1,473,000 **CAPITAL** Bissau
GOVERNMENT "Interim" government
ETHNIC GROUPS Balanta 30%, Fula 20%, Manjaca 14%, Mandinga 13%, Papel 7% **LANGUAGES** Portuguese (official), Crioulo
RELIGIONS Traditional beliefs 50%, Islam 45%, Christianity 5%
CURRENCY CFA franc = 100 centimes

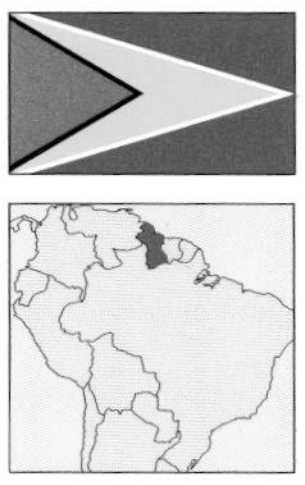

GUYANA

GEOGRAPHY The Cooperative Republic of Guyana is a country facing the Atlantic Ocean in northeastern South America. The coastal plain is flat and much of it is below sea level.

The climate is hot and humid, though the interior highlands are cooler than the coast. The rainfall is heavy, occurring on more than 200 days a year.

POLITICS & ECONOMY Britain gained control of the area in 1814 and ruled British Guiana until it became independent as Guyana in 1966. A black lawyer, Forbes Burnham, was the first prime minister. Under a new constitution adopted in 1980, the president's powers were increased. Burnham became president and served in this post until he died in 1985. He was succeeded by Hugh Desmond Hoyte, who was defeated in 1993 by an ethnic Indian, Cheddi Jagan. Jagan died in 1997 and was succeeded by his wife, Janet. In 1999, Bharrat Jagdeo was elected president. He was re-elected in 2001.

Guyana is a poor country. Its resources include gold, bauxite (aluminum ore) and other minerals, forests, and fertile soils. Sugarcane and rice are leading crops. Guyana has potential for producing hydroelectricity from its many rivers.

AREA 83,000 sq mi [214,969 sq km]
POPULATION 769,000 **CAPITAL** Georgetown
GOVERNMENT Multiparty republic
ETHNIC GROUPS East Indian 50%, Black 36%, Amerindian 7%, others 7% **LANGUAGES** English (official), Creole, Hindi, Urdu
RELIGIONS Christianity 50%, Hinduism 35%, Islam 10%, others 5%
CURRENCY Guyanese dollar = 100 cents

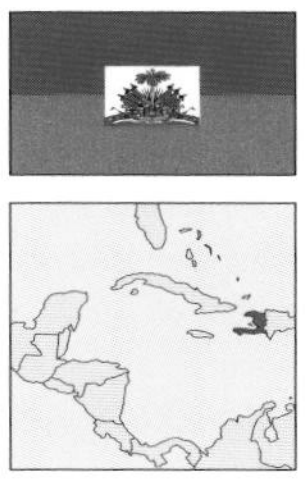

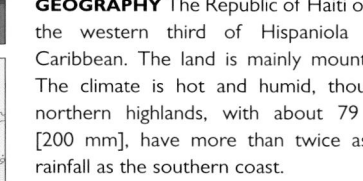

HAITI

GEOGRAPHY The Republic of Haiti occupies the western third of Hispaniola in the Caribbean. The land is mainly mountainous. The climate is hot and humid, though the northern highlands, with about 79 inches [200 mm], have more than twice as much rainfall as the southern coast.

POLITICS & ECONOMY Visited by Christopher Columbus in 1492, Haiti was later developed by the French. The African slaves revolted in 1791 and the country became independent in 1804. Haiti subsequently suffered from instability, violence and dictatorial rule. Elections in 1990 returned Jean-Bertrand Aristide as president, but he was overthrown in 1991. In 1995, René Préval was elected president, but Aristide was again elected president in 2000. In 2004, rebel activity forced Aristide to flee the country. A US-backed government was set up to restore order and, in 2006, René Préval was re-elected president. Soaring food and fuel prices in 2008 led Haiti's Senate to dismiss the prime minister, Jacques-Edouard Alexis.

AREA 10,714 sq mi [27,750 sq km]
POPULATION 8,706,000 **CAPITAL** Port-au-Prince
GOVERNMENT Multiparty republic **ETHNIC GROUPS** Black 95%, Mulatto/White 5% **LANGUAGES** French and Creole (both official)
RELIGIONS Roman Catholic 80%, Voodoo
CURRENCY Gourde = 100 centimes

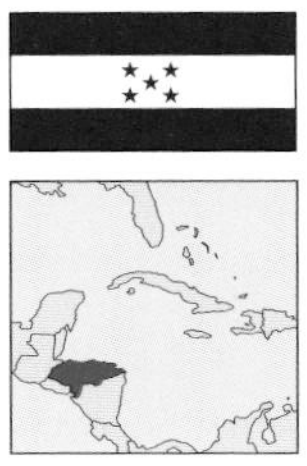

HONDURAS

GEOGRAPHY The Republic of Honduras is the second largest country in Central America. The northern coast on the Caribbean Sea extends more than 373 mi [600 km], but the Pacific coast in the southeast is only about 50 mi [80 km] long. Honduras has a tropical climate, but the highlands are cooler. The rainiest months are between May and November. Hurricanes often hit the north coast. Hurricane Mitch in 1998 caused the worst destruction in modern times.

POLITICS & ECONOMY Western Honduras was part of the Maya empire which flourished between AD 300 and 900. Christopher Columbus claimed the area for Spain in 1502 and Spain ruled from 1625 until 1821. Honduras became part of the Central American Federation but withdrew in 1838.

In the 1890s, American companies developed plantations to grow bananas. They soon became the country's chief source of income and Honduras became known as a "banana republic." But instability slowed economic progress. In 1969, Honduras fought a short "Soccer War" with El Salvador. The war was sparked off by the treatment of fans in a World Cup soccer series, though the real reason was that Salvadoreans in Honduras had been forced to give

up land. Since 1980, civilian governments have ruled Honduras, but the military remain influential.

Honduras is a developing country. Its few resources include silver, lead and zinc. Agriculture is the main activity. Bananas and coffee are exported and maize is the chief food crop. Honduras is one of Central America's least industrialized countries. Products include processed food, textiles and wood products.

AREA 43,277 sq mi [112,088 sq km]
POPULATION 7,484,000 **CAPITAL** Tegucigalpa
GOVERNMENT Republic **ETHNIC GROUPS** Mestizo 90%, Amerindian 7%, Black (including Black Carib) 2%, White 1% **LANGUAGES** Spanish (official), Amerindian dialects **RELIGIONS** Roman Catholic 97%
CURRENCY Honduran lempira = 100 centavos

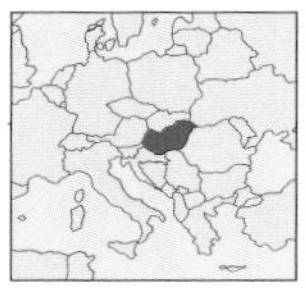

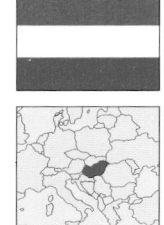

HUNGARY

GEOGRAPHY The Hungarian Republic is a landlocked country in central Europe. The land is mostly low-lying and drained by the Danube (Duna) and its tributary, the Tisza. Most of the land east of the Danube belongs to a region called the Great Plain (Nagyalföld), which covers about half of Hungary.

Hungary lies far from the moderating influence of the sea. As a result, summers are warmer and sunnier, and the winters colder than in Western Europe.

POLITICS & ECONOMY Hungary entered World War II (1939–45) in 1941, as an ally of Germany, but the Germans occupied the country in 1944. The Soviet Union invaded Hungary in 1944 and, in 1946, the country became a republic. The Communists gradually took over the government, taking complete control in 1949. From 1949, Hungary was an ally of the Soviet Union. In 1956, Soviet troops crushed an anti-Communist revolt. But in the 1980s, reforms in the Soviet Union led to the growth of anti-Communist groups in Hungary. In 1989, Hungary adopted a new constitution making it a multiparty state. Elections held in 1990 led to a victory for the non-Communist Democratic Forum. In 2002, the Hungarian Socialist Party, in alliance with the liberal Free Democrats, won a majority in parliament. In 2004, Hungary became a member of both the North Atlantic Treaty Organization and the European Union.

Before World War II, Hungary's economy was based mainly on agriculture. But the Communists set up many manufacturing industries. The new factories were owned by the government, as also was most of the land. However, from the late 1980s, the government has worked to increase private ownership. This change of policy caused many problems, including inflation and high rates of unemployment. Manufacturing is the chief activity. Major products include aluminum, chemicals, and electrical and electronic goods.

AREA 35,920 sq mi [93,032 sq km]
POPULATION 9,956,000 **CAPITAL** Budapest
GOVERNMENT Multiparty republic
ETHNIC GROUPS Magyar 90%, Gypsy, German, Serb, Romanian, Slovak **LANGUAGES** Hungarian (official)
RELIGIONS Roman Catholic 68%, Calvinist 20%, Lutheran 5%, others **CURRENCY** Forint = 100 fillér

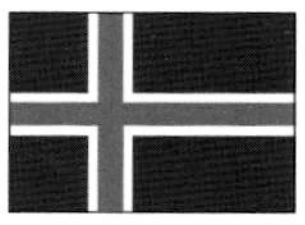
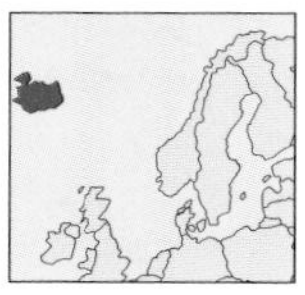

ICELAND

GEOGRAPHY The Republic of Iceland, in the North Atlantic Ocean, is closer to Greenland than Scotland. Iceland sits astride the Mid-Atlantic Ridge. It is slowly getting wider as the ocean is being stretched apart by continental drift.

Iceland has around 200 volcanoes, and eruptions are frequent. An eruption under the Vatnajökull ice cap in 1996 created a subglacial lake which subsequently burst, causing severe flooding. Geysers and hot springs are other common volcanic features. Ice caps and glaciers cover about an eighth of the land. The only habitable regions are the coastal lowlands.

Although it lies far to the north, Iceland's climate is moderated by the warm waters of the Gulf Stream. The port of Reykjavik is ice-free all the year round.

POLITICS & ECONOMY Norwegian Vikings colonized Iceland in AD 874, and in 930 the settlers founded the world's oldest parliament, the Althing.

Iceland united with Norway in 1262. But when Norway united with Denmark in 1380, Iceland came under Danish rule. Iceland became a self-governing kingdom, united with Denmark, in 1918. It became a fully independent republic in 1944, following a referendum in which 97% of the people voted to break their country's ties with Denmark. Iceland has played a leading part in European affairs and is a member of the North Atlantic Treaty Organization. But it has been involved in fishing disputes. In 1992, it left the International Whaling Commission because of its alleged anti-whaling policy. It rejoined in 2002, but, in 2003, it undertook its first whale hunt for 15 years, stating that its aim was to study the impact of whales on fish stocks.

Iceland has few resources besides its fishing grounds. Fishing and fish processing dominate Iceland's overseas trade, but it is one of Europe's richest countries. Barely 1% of the land is used to grow crops, but 23% of the country can be used for grazing sheep and cattle. Vegetables and fruit are grown in greenhouses, heated by water from hot springs.

AREA 39,768 sq mi [103,000 sq km]
POPULATION 302,000 **CAPITAL** Reykjavik
GOVERNMENT Multiparty republic
ETHNIC GROUPS Icelandic 97%, Danish 1%
LANGUAGES Icelandic (official) **RELIGIONS** Evangelical Lutheran 87%, other Protestant 4%, Roman Catholic 2%, others
CURRENCY Icelandic króna = 100 aurar

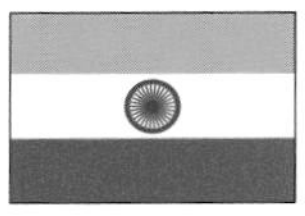
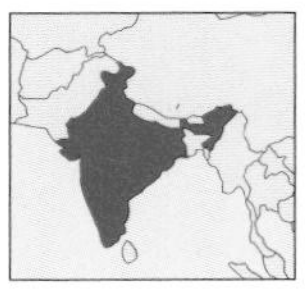

INDIA

GEOGRAPHY The Republic of India is the world's seventh largest country. In population, it ranks second only to China. The north is mountainous, with mountains and foothills of the Himalayan range. Rivers, such as the Brahmaputra and Ganges (Ganga), rise in the Himalaya and flow across the fertile northern plains. Southern India consists of a large plateau, called the Deccan. The Deccan is bordered by two mountain ranges, the Western Ghats and the Eastern Ghats.

India has three main seasons. The cool season runs from October to February. The hot season runs from March to June. The rainy monsoon season starts in the middle of June and continues into September. Delhi has a moderate rainfall, with about 25 inches [640 mm] a year. The southwestern coast and the northeast have far more rain. Darjeeling in the northeast has an average annual rainfall of 120 inches [3,040 mm]. But parts of the Thar Desert in the northwest have only 2 inches [50 mm] of rain per year.

POLITICS & ECONOMY In southern India, most of the people are descendants of the dark-skinned Dravidians, who were among India's earliest people. Most northerners are descendants of lighter-skinned Aryans who arrived around 3,500 years ago.

India was the birthplace of several major religions, including Hinduism, Buddhism and Sikhism. Islam was introduced from about AD 1000. The Muslim Mughal empire was founded in 1526. From the 17th century, Britain began to gain influence. From 1858 to 1947, India was ruled as part of the British empire. An independence movement began after the Sepoy Rebellion (1857–9) and, in 1885, the Indian National Congress was formed. In 1920, Mohandas K. Gandhi became its leader and it soon became a mass movement. When independence was finally achieved in 1947, British India was divided into modern India and Muslim Pakistan. Partition was marred by mass slaughter as Hindus and Sikhs fled from Pakistan, and Indian Muslims poured into Pakistan. In the ensuing disputes, some 1 million people were killed.

Although India has 15 major languages and hundreds of minor ones, together with many religions, the country remains the world's largest democracy. It has faced many problems, especially with Pakistan, over the disputed territory of Jammu and Kashmir. Two wars in 1965 and 1972 failed to alter greatly the 1948 ceasefire lines. In the late 1980s, Kashmiri nationalists in the Indian-controlled area waged a campaign, demanding either integration into Pakistan or independence. India sent in troops and accused Pakistan of intervention. In the 1990s, Pakistani-backed guerrillas fought to break India's hold on the Srinigar valley, Kashmir's most populous region. The tense situation was further aggravated by the testing of nuclear devices by both India and Pakistan in 1998. In 2003–7, India and Pakistan launched a series of peace moves, raising hopes of an agreement, despite continuing intermittent conflict on the ground.

The World Bank classifies India as a "low-income" developing country. To boost the economy, the right-wing coalition government, led by the Hindu Bharatiya Janata Party, introduced free-enterprise policies. However, in 2004, the left-wing United Progressive Alliance was victorious at elections. Manmohan Singh became prime minister.

Agriculture employs 52% of the people. Crops include rice, wheat, millet, sorghum, peas, and beans. India has more cattle than any other country. Milk is produced, but Hindus do not eat beef. Resources include coal, iron ore, and oil. Manufacturing has expanded greatly since 1947. Iron and steel, machinery, refined petroleum, textiles, and transport equipment are major products.

AREA 1,269,212 sq mi [3,287,263 sq km]
POPULATION 1,129,866,000 **CAPITAL** New Delhi
GOVERNMENT Multiparty federal republic
ETHNIC GROUPS Indo-Aryan (Caucasoid) 72%, Dravidian (Aboriginal) 25%, others (mainly Mongoloid) 3%
LANGUAGES Hindi, English, Telugu, Bengali, Marathi, Tamil, Urdu, Gujarati, Malayalam, Kannada, Oriya, Punjabi, Assamese, Kashmiri, Sindhi, and Sanskrit are all official languages
RELIGIONS Hinduism 82%, Islam 12%, Christianity 2%, Sikhism 2%, Buddhism and others **CURRENCY** Indian rupee = 100 paisa

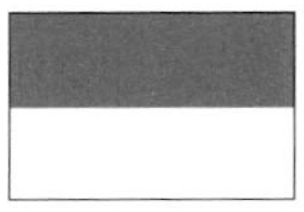
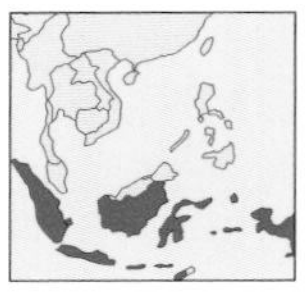

INDONESIA

GEOGRAPHY The Republic of Indonesia is an island nation in Southeast Asia. In all, Indonesia contains about 13,600 islands, less than 6,000 of which are inhabited. Three-quarters of the country is made up of five main areas: the islands of Sumatra, Java and Sulawesi (Celebes), together with Kalimantan (southern Borneo) and Irian Jaya (western New Guinea). The islands are generally mountainous and volcanic. The larger islands have extensive coastal lowlands. The climate is hot and humid, with a high rainfall. Only Java and the Sunda Islands have relatively dry seasons.

POLITICS & ECONOMY Indonesia is the world's most populous Muslim nation, though Islam was introduced as recently as the 15th century. The Dutch became active in the area in the early 17th century and Indonesia became a Dutch colony in 1799. After a long struggle, the Netherlands recognized Indonesia's independence in 1949. The economy has expanded, but ethnic and religious conflict have slowed down economic progress.

In the early 21st century, Indonesia was facing many problems, arising from widespread corruption in the government and the army. Separatists were operating in Aceh province in northern Sumatra and in West Papua (formerly Irian Jaya), Christian-Muslim clashes led to loss of life in the Moluccas, and East (formerly Portuguese) Timor became an independent country. Terrorist incidents occurred in the early 21st century. In December 2004, a tsunami killed more than 100,000 people. Worst hit was Aceh, but the tragedy was followed by the granting of autonomy for Aceh province in 2006. A severe earthquake hit Java in 2006. Indonesia is a developing country with a growing industrial sector. It exports oil and natural gas, and also mines tin and other minerals. Timber, textiles, rubber, coffee, and tea are also exported. Rice is the main food crop.

AREA 735,354 sq mi [1,904,569 sq km]
POPULATION 234,694,000 **CAPITAL** Jakarta
GOVERNMENT Multiparty republic
ETHNIC GROUPS Javanese 45%, Sundanese 14%, Madurese 7%, coastal Malays 7%, approximately 300 others
LANGUAGES Bahasa Indonesian (official), many others
RELIGIONS Islam 88%, Roman Catholic 3%, Hinduism 2%, Buddhism 1%
CURRENCY Indonesian rupiah = 100 sen

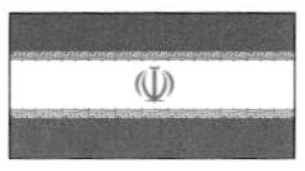
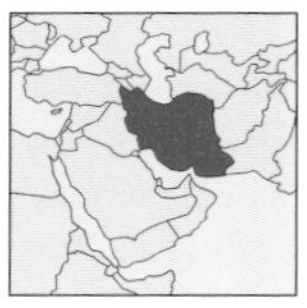

IRAN

GEOGRAPHY The Republic of Iran contains a barren central plateau which covers about half of the country. It includes the Dasht-e-Kavir (Great Salt Desert) and the Dasht-e-Lut (Great Sand Desert). The Elburz Mountains north of the plateau contain Iran's highest peak, Damavand, while narrow lowlands lie between the mountains and the Caspian Sea. West of the plateau are the Zagros Mountains, beyond which the land descends to the plains bordering the Persian Gulf.

Much of Iran has a severe, dry climate, with hot summers and cold winters. In Tehran, rain falls on only about 30 days in the year and the annual temperature range is more than 45°F [25°C]. The climate in the lowlands, however, is generally milder.

POLITICS & ECONOMY Iran was called Persia until 1935. The empire of Ancient Persia flourished between 550 and 350 BC, when it fell to Alexander the Great. Islam was introduced in AD 641.

Britain and Russia competed for influence in the area in the 19th century, and in the early 20th century the British began to develop the country's oil resources. In 1925, the Pahlavi family took power.

Reza Khan became shah (king) and worked to modernize the country. The Pahlavi dynasty was ended in 1979 when a religious leader, Ayatollah Ruhollah Khomeini, made Iran an Islamic republic. In 1980–8, Iran and Iraq fought a war over disputed borders. Khomeini died in 1989, but his fundamentalist views and anti-Western attitudes continued to dominate politics. In 2005, a hardliner, Mahmoud Ahmadinejad, was elected president. His government's support for Iran's nuclear program, which many in the West considered was intended to develop nuclear weapons, led to international sanctions being applied against Iran in 2006–7.

Iran's prosperity is based on its oil production and oil accounts for more than 80% of the country's exports. However, the economy was severely damaged by the Iran–Iraq war in the 1980s. Oil revenues have been used to develop a growing manufacturing sector. Agriculture is important even though farms cover only a tenth of the land. The main crops are wheat and barley. Livestock farming and fishing are other important activities, although Iran has to import much of the food it needs.

AREA 636,368 SQ MI [1,648,195 SQ KM]
POPULATION 65,398,000 **CAPITAL** TEHRAN
GOVERNMENT ISLAMIC REPUBLIC **ETHNIC GROUPS** PERSIAN 51%, AZERI 24%, GILAKI AND MAZANDARANI 8%, KURD 7%, ARAB 3%, LUR 2%, BALUCHI 2%, TURKMEN 2% **LANGUAGES** PERSIAN 58%, TURKIC 26%, KURDISH **RELIGIONS** ISLAM (SHI'ITE MUSLIM 89%)
CURRENCY IRANIAN RIAL = 100 DINARS

IRAQ

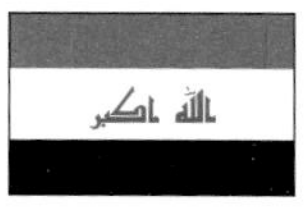

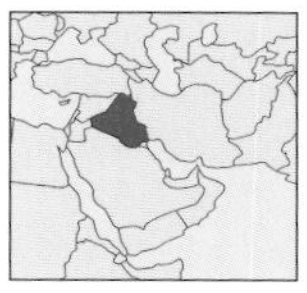

GEOGRAPHY The Republic of Iraq is a southwest Asian country at the head of the Persian Gulf. Rolling deserts cover western and southwestern Iraq, with part of the Zagros Mountains in the northeast, where farming can be practiced without irrigation. The northern plains, across which flow the rivers Euphrates (Nahr al Furat) and Tigris (Nahr Dijlah), are dry. But the southern plains, including Mesopotamia and the delta of the Shatt al Arab, contain irrigated farmland, together with marshland.

The climate of Iraq ranges from temperate in the north to subtropical in the south. Baghdad, in central Iraq, has cool winters, with occasional frosts, and hot summers. The rainfall is generally low.

POLITICS & ECONOMY Mesopotamia was the home of several great civilizations, including Sumer, Babylon and Assyria. It later became part of the Persian empire. Islam was introduced in AD 637 and Baghdad became the brilliant capital of the powerful Arab empire. But Mesopotamia declined after the Mongols invaded it in 1258. From 1534, Mesopotamia became part of the Turkish Ottoman empire. Britain invaded the area in 1916. In 1921, Britain renamed the country Iraq and set up an Arab monarchy. Iraq finally became independent in 1932.

By the 1950s, oil dominated Iraq's economy. In 1952, Iraq agreed to take 50% of the profits of the foreign oil companies. This revenue enabled the government to pay for welfare services and development projects. But many Iraqis felt that they should benefit more from their oil. Since 1958, when army officers killed the king and made Iraq a republic, Iraq has undergone turbulent times. In the 1960s, the Kurds, who live in northern Iraq and also in Iran, Turkey, Syria and Armenia, asked for self-rule. The government rejected their demands and war broke out. A peace treaty was signed in 1975, but conflict has continued.

In 1979, Saddam Hussein became Iraq's president. Under his leadership, Iraq invaded Iran in 1980, starting an eight-year war. Iraqi Kurds supported Iran and the Iraqi government attacked Kurdish villages with poison gas. In 1990, Iraqi troops occupied Kuwait, but an international force drove them out in 1991. Since 1991, Iraqi troops have attacked Shi'ite Marsh Arabs and Kurds. In 1998, Iraq's failure to permit UN inspectors, charged with disposing of Iraq's deadliest weapons, access to suspect sites led to the Western bombardment of Iraqi military sites. Another major offensive occurred in 2001. In 2002–3, pressure mounted on Iraq to dispose of its alleged weapons of mass destruction. In March–April 2003, a coalition force headed by the United States invaded Iraq. It rapidly achieved its objective, but violence continued. Elections were held in 2005, despite a boycott by Sunni Muslims. Nouri al-Maliki became prime minister, but his government was weakened by ethnic and sectarian divisions.

Civil war, war damage in 1991 and 2003, UN sanctions and mismanagement have all contributed to economic chaos. Oil remains Iraq's main resource, but a UN trade embargo in 1990 halted oil exports. Farmland, including pasture, covers about a fifth of the land. Products include barley, cotton, dates, fruit, livestock, wheat, and wool, but Iraq still has to import food. Industries include oil refining and the manufacture of petrochemicals and consumer goods.

AREA 169,234 SQ MI [438,317 SQ KM]
POPULATION 27,500,000 **CAPITAL** BAGHDAD
GOVERNMENT REPUBLIC **ETHNIC GROUPS** ARAB 77%, KURDISH 19%, ASSYRIAN AND OTHERS **LANGUAGES** ARABIC (OFFICIAL), KURDISH (OFFICIAL IN KURDISH AREAS), ASSYRIAN, ARMENIAN **RELIGIONS** ISLAM 97%, CHRISTIANITY AND OTHERS **CURRENCY** NEW IRAQI DINAR

IRELAND

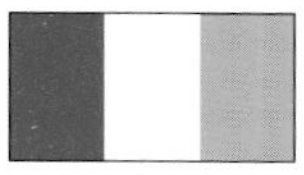

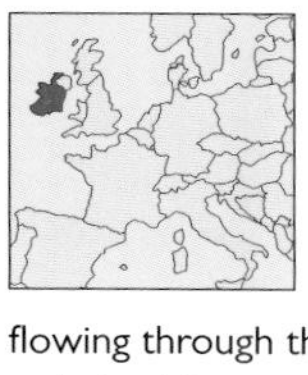

GEOGRAPHY The Republic of Ireland occupies five-sixths of the island of Ireland. The country consists of a large lowland region surrounded by a broken rim of low mountains. The uplands include the Mountains of Kerry where Carrauntoohill, Ireland's highest peak at 3,415 ft [1,041 m], is situated. The River Shannon is the longest in Ireland, flowing through three large lakes, loughs Allen, Ree, and Derg.

Ireland has a mild, rainy climate influenced by the warm Gulf Stream current, whose effects are greatest in the west. However, Dublin in the east is cooler than places on the west coast.

POLITICS & ECONOMY In 1801, the Act of Union created the United Kingdom of Great Britain and Ireland. But Irish discontent intensified in the 1840s when a potato blight caused a famine in which a million people died and nearly a million emigrated. Britain was blamed for not having done enough to help. In 1916, an uprising in Dublin was crushed, but between 1919 and 1922 civil war occurred. In 1922, the Irish Free State was created as a Dominion in the British Commonwealth. But Northern Ireland remained part of the UK.

Ireland became a republic in 1949. In 1973, Ireland became a member of the European Community (now the European Union) and, since then, the country has prospered economically. In 1998, Ireland took part in the negotiations to produce a constitutional settlement in Northern Ireland. Ireland agreed to give up its claim on Northern Ireland and, in 2007, a power-sharing government was set up in the north.

Major farm products in Ireland include barley, cattle and dairy products, pigs, potatoes, poultry, sheep, sugar beet, and wheat, while fishing provides another valuable source of food. Farming is now profitable, aided by European Union grants, but manufacturing is the leading economic sector. Many factories produce food and beverages. Chemicals and pharmaceuticals, electronic equipment, machinery, paper, and textiles are also important.

AREA 27,132 SQ MI [70,273 SQ KM]
POPULATION 4,109,000 **CAPITAL** DUBLIN
GOVERNMENT MULTIPARTY REPUBLIC **ETHNIC GROUPS** IRISH 94%
LANGUAGES IRISH (GAELIC) AND ENGLISH (BOTH OFFICIAL)
RELIGIONS ROMAN CATHOLIC 92%, PROTESTANT 3%
CURRENCY EURO = 100 CENTS

ISRAEL

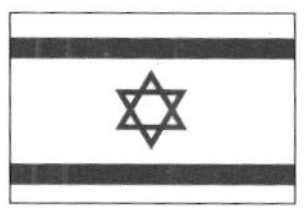

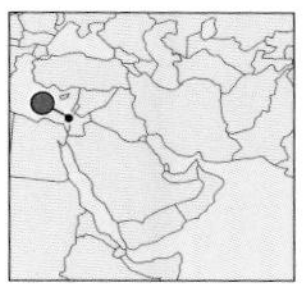

GEOGRAPHY The State of Israel is a small country in the eastern Mediterranean. It includes a fertile coastal plain, where Israel's main industrial cities, Haifa (Hefa) and Tel Aviv-Jaffa are situated. Inland lie the Judaeo-Galilean highlands, which run from northern Israel to the northern tip of the Negev Desert. To the east lies part of the Great Rift Valley which contains the River Jordan, the Sea of Galilee and the Dead Sea. Summers are hot and dry. Winters on the coast are mild and moist, but the rainfall decreases from west to east and from north to south.

POLITICS & ECONOMY Israel is part of a region called Palestine. Some Jews have always lived in the area, though most modern Israelis are descendants of immigrants who began to settle there from the 1880s. Britain ruled Palestine from 1917. Large numbers of Jews escaping Nazi persecution arrived in the 1930s, provoking an Arab uprising against British rule. In 1947, the UN agreed to partition Palestine into an Arab and a Jewish state. Fighting broke out after Arabs rejected the plan. The State of Israel came into being in May 1948, but fighting continued into 1949. Other Arab-Israeli wars in 1956, 1967 and 1973 led to land gains for Israel.

In 1978, Israel signed a treaty with Egypt which led to the return of the occupied Sinai peninsula to Egypt in 1979. But conflict continued between Israel and the PLO (Palestine Liberation Organization). In 1993, the PLO and Israel agreed to establish Palestinian self-rule in two areas: the occupied Gaza Strip, and in the town of Jericho in the occupied West Bank. The agreement was extended in 1995 to include more than 30% of the West Bank. Israel's prime minister, Yitzhak Rabin, was assassinated in 1995. In 1996, Benjamin Netanyahu was elected prime minister. The peace process stalled until Ehud Barak defeated Netanyahu in 1999. After more violence, Barak resigned and, in 2001, Ariel Sharon succeeded him. In 2005, Sharon ordered the withdrawal of Israeli forces and the handing over of the Gaza Strip, which came under the Palestinian Authority. Sharon formed a new political party, Kadima. After he suffered a stroke, Ehud Olmert became its leader. Olmert became prime minister in 2006. In 2006–8, Israeli forces clashed with Palestinians in southern Lebanon and Gaza.

Israel's most valuable activity is manufacturing and the country's products include chemicals, electronic equipment, fertilizers, military equipment, plastics, processed food, scientific instruments, and textiles. Fruits and vegetables are leading exports.

AREA 7,954 SQ MI [20,600 SQ KM] **POPULATION** 6,427,000
CAPITAL JERUSALEM **GOVERNMENT** MULTIPARTY REPUBLIC
ETHNIC GROUPS JEWISH 80%, ARAB AND OTHERS 20%
LANGUAGES HEBREW AND ARABIC (BOTH OFFICIAL)
RELIGIONS JUDAISM 80%, ISLAM (MOSTLY SUNNI) 14%, CHRISTIANITY 2%, DRUZE AND OTHERS 2% **CURRENCY** NEW ISRAELI SHEKEL = 100 AGORAT

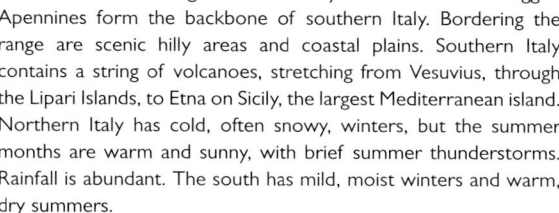

ITALY

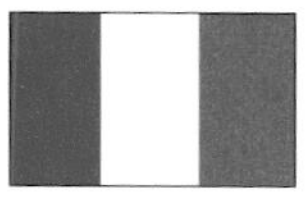

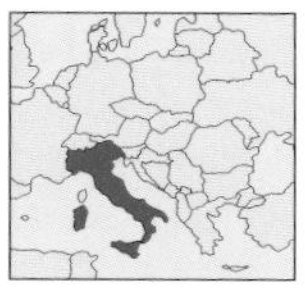

GEOGRAPHY The Republic of Italy is famous for its history and traditions, its art and culture, and its beautiful scenery. Northern Italy is bordered in the north by the high Alps, with their many climbing and skiing resorts. The Alps overlook the northern plains – Italy's most fertile and densely populated region – drained by the River Po. The rugged Apennines form the backbone of southern Italy. Bordering the range are scenic hilly areas and coastal plains. Southern Italy contains a string of volcanoes, stretching from Vesuvius, through the Lipari Islands, to Etna on Sicily, the largest Mediterranean island. Northern Italy has cold, often snowy, winters, but the summer months are warm and sunny, with brief summer thunderstorms. Rainfall is abundant. The south has mild, moist winters and warm, dry summers.

POLITICS & ECONOMY Magnificent ruins throughout Italy testify to the glories of the ancient Roman Empire, which was founded, according to legend, in 753 BC. It reached its peak in the AD 100s. It finally collapsed in the 400s, although the Eastern Roman empire, also called the Byzantine empire, survived for another 1,000 years.

In the Middle Ages, Italy was split into many tiny states. These states made a great contribution to the revival of art and learning, called the Renaissance, in the 14th to 16th centuries. Beautiful cities, such as Florence (Firenze) and Venice (Venézia), testify to the artistic achievements of this period.

Italy finally became a united kingdom in 1861, although the Papal Territories (a large area ruled by the Roman Catholic Church) was not added until 1870. The Pope and his successors disputed the takeover of the Papal Territories. The dispute was finally resolved in 1929, when the Vatican City was set up in Rome as a fully independent state.

Italy fought in World War I (1914–18) alongside the Allies – Britain, France and Russia. In 1922, the dictator Benito Mussolini, leader of the Fascist Party, took power. Under Mussolini, Italy conquered Ethiopia. During World War II (1939–45), Italy at first fought on Germany's side against the Allies. But in late 1943, Italy declared war on Germany. Italy became a republic in 1946. It has played an important part in European affairs. It was a founder member of the North Atlantic Treaty Organization (NATO) in 1949 and also of what has now become the European Union in 1958.

After the setting up of the European Union, Italy's economy developed quickly. But the country faced many problems. For example, much of the economic development was in the north. This forced many people to leave the poor south to find jobs in the north or abroad. Social problems, corruption at high levels of society, and a succession of weak coalition governments all contributed to instability. Elections in 1996 were won by the left-wing Olive Tree Alliance led by Romano Prodi. However, in 2001, a center-right coalition led by media tycoon Silvio Berlusconi was elected. A center-left coalition headed by Romano Prodi took power in 2006, but Berlusconi's right-wing coalition swept back into office following elections in 2008.

Only 50 years ago, Italy was a mainly agricultural society. But today it is a leading industrial power. It lacks mineral resources, and imports most of the raw materials used in industry. Manufactures include textiles and clothing, processed food, machinery, cars and chemicals. The chief industrial region is in the northwest.

Farmland covers around 42% of the land, pasture 17%, and forest and woodland 22%. Major crops include citrus fruits, grapes which are used to make wine, olive oil, sugar beet, and vegetables. Livestock farming is important, though meat is imported.

AREA 116,339 sq mi [301,318 sq km]
POPULATION 58,148,000 **CAPITAL** Rome
GOVERNMENT Multiparty republic **ETHNIC GROUPS** Italian 94%, German, French, Albanian, Slovene, Greek **LANGUAGES** Italian (official), German, French, Slovene **RELIGIONS** Predominantly Roman Catholic **CURRENCY** Euro = 100 cents

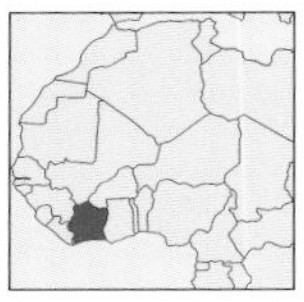

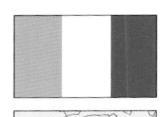

IVORY COAST

GEOGRAPHY The Republic of the Ivory Coast, in West Africa, is officially known as Côte d'Ivoire. The southeast coast is bordered by sand bars that enclose lagoons. The southwest coast is lined by rocky cliffs.

Ivory Coast has a hot and humid tropical climate, with high temperatures all year. The south has two rainy seasons: between May and July, and from October to November. Inland, the rainfall decreases and the north has one dry and one rainy season.

POLITICS & ECONOMY From 1895, Ivory Coast was governed as part of French West Africa, which also included what are now Benin, Burkina Faso, Guinea, Mali, Mauritania, Niger, and Senegal. In 1946, Ivory Coast became a territory in the French Union.

Ivory Coast became fully independent in 1960. Its first president, Félix Houphouët-Boigny, became the longest serving head of state in Africa with an uninterrupted period in office which ended with his death in 1993. Houphouët-Boigny, a pro-Western leader, made Ivory Coast a one-party state. In 1983, the National Assembly voted to make Yamoussoukro, the president's birthplace, the new capital. In 1999, a military coup occurred, but civilian rule was restored in 2000, when Laurent Gbagbo was elected president. An army rebellion began in 2002. By 2004, the government held the south, while mainly Muslim rebels held the north. In 2007, the government agreed a peace deal, holding out hopes of a settlement.

Agriculture employs about 45% of the people, and farm products make up nearly half the value of the exports. Manufacturing has grown in importance since 1960; products include fertilizers, processed food, refined oil, textiles, and timber.

AREA 124,503 sq mi [322,463 sq km]
POPULATION 18,013,000 **CAPITAL** Yamoussoukro
GOVERNMENT Multiparty republic **ETHNIC GROUPS** Akan 42%, Voltaiques 18%, Northern Mandes 16%, Krous 11%, Southern Mandes 10% **LANGUAGES** French (official), many native dialects
RELIGIONS Islam 40%, Christianity 30%, traditional beliefs 30%
CURRENCY CFA franc = 100 centimes

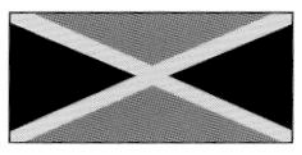

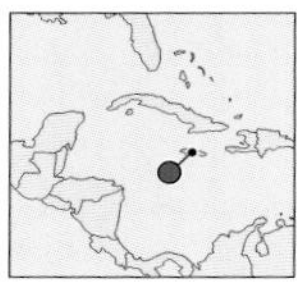

JAMAICA

GEOGRAPHY Third largest of the Caribbean islands, half of Jamaica lies above 1,000 ft [300 m] and moist southeast trade winds bring rain to the central mountain range.

The "cockpit country" in the northwest of the island is an inaccessible limestone area of steep broken ridges and isolated basins.

POLITICS & ECONOMY Britain took Jamaica from Spain in the 17th century, and the island did not gain its independence until 1962. Power has alternated between the People's National Party (PNP) and Jamaica Labor Party. In 2006, Portia Simpson Miller succeeded Percival Patterson as prime minister, but she was defeated in elections in 2007. Tourism and farming are important. Sugarcane is the main crop, but alumina and bauxite make up 60% of the exports.

AREA 4,244 sq mi [10,991 sq km]
POPULATION 2,780,000 **CAPITAL** Kingston
GOVERNMENT Constitutional monarchy
ETHNIC GROUPS Black 91%, Mixed 7%, East Indian 1%
LANGUAGES English (official), patois English
RELIGIONS Protestant 61%, Roman Catholic 4%
CURRENCY Jamaican dollar = 100 cents

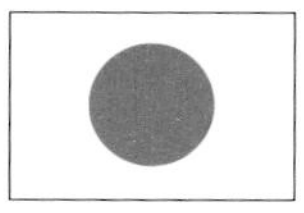

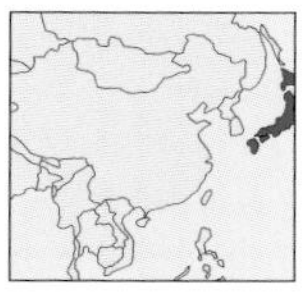

JAPAN

GEOGRAPHY Japan's four largest islands – Honshu, Hokkaido, Kyushu, and Shikoku – make up 98% of the country. But Japan contains thousands of small islands. The four largest islands are mainly mountainous, while many of the small islands are the tips of volcanoes. Japan has more than 150 volcanoes, about 60 of which are active. Volcanic eruptions, earthquakes and tsunamis (destructive sea waves triggered by underwater earthquakes and eruptions) are common because the islands lie in an unstable part of our planet, where continental plates are always on the move. One powerful recent earthquake killed more than 5,000 people in Kobe in 1995.

The climate of Japan varies greatly from north to south. Hokkaido in the north has cold, snowy winters. At Sapporo, temperatures below 4°F [–20°C] have been recorded between December and March. But summers are warm, with temperatures sometimes exceeding 86°F [30°C]. Rain falls throughout the year, though Hokkaido is one of the driest parts of Japan. Tokyo has higher rainfall and temperatures, while the southern islands of Shikoku and Kyushu have warm temperate climates. Summers are long and hot. Winters are cold.

POLITICS & ECONOMY In the late 19th century, Japan began a program of modernization. Under its new imperial leaders, it began to look for lands to conquer. In 1894–5, it fought a war with China and, in 1904–5, it defeated Russia. Soon its overseas empire included Korea and Taiwan. In 1930, Japan invaded Manchuria (northeast China) and, in 1937, it began a war against China. In 1941, Japan launched an attack on the US base at Pearl Harbor in Hawai'i. This drew both Japan and the United States into World War II.

Japan surrendered in 1945 when the Americans dropped atomic bombs on two cities, Hiroshima and Nagasaki. The United States occupied Japan until 1952. During this period, Japan adopted a democratic constitution. The emperor, who had previously been regarded as a god, became a constitutional monarch. Power was vested in the prime minister and cabinet, who are chosen from the Diet (elected parliament).

From the 1960s, Japan experienced many changes as the country rapidly built up new industries. By the early 1990s, Japan had become the world's second richest economic power after the US. But economic success has brought problems. For example, the rapid growth of cities has led to housing shortages and pollution. Another problem is that the proportion of people over 65 years of age is steadily increasing.

Japan has the world's second highest gross domestic product (GDP) after the United States. [The GDP is the total value of all goods and services produced in a country in one year.] The most important sector of the economy is industry. Yet Japan has to import most of the raw materials and fuels it needs for its industries. Its success is based on its use of the latest technology, its skilled and hard-working labor force, its vigorous export policies and its comparatively small government spending on defense. Manufactures dominate its exports, which include machinery, electrical and electronic equipment, vehicles and transport equipment, iron and steel, chemicals, textiles, and ships. Japan experienced an economic slowdown in the 1990s, which developed into a recession. Signs of recovery appeared in 2005–8.

Japan is one of the world's top fishing nations and fish is an important source of protein. Because the land is so rugged, only 15% of the country can be farmed. Yet Japan produces about 70% of the food it needs. Rice is the chief crop, taking up about half of the total farmland. Other major products include fruits, sugar beet, tea, and vegetables. Livestock farming has increased since the 1950s.

AREA 145,880 sq mi [377,829 sq km]
POPULATION 127,433,000 **CAPITAL** Tokyo
GOVERNMENT Constitutional monarchy
ETHNIC GROUPS Japanese 99%, Chinese, Korean, Brazilian and others
LANGUAGES Japanese (official) **RELIGIONS** Shintoism and Buddhism 84% (most Japanese consider themselves to be both Shinto and Buddhist), others **CURRENCY** Yen = 100 sen

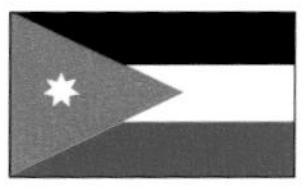

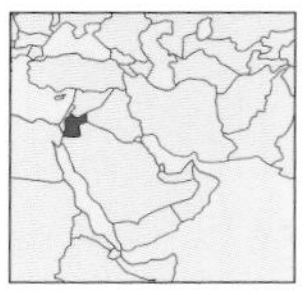

JORDAN

GEOGRAPHY The Hashemite Kingdom of Jordan is an Arab country in southwestern Asia. The Great Rift Valley in the west contains the River Jordan and the Dead Sea, which Jordan shares with Israel. East of the Rift Valley is the Transjordan plateau, where most Jordanians live. To the east and south lie vast areas of desert.

Amman has a much lower rainfall and longer dry season than the Mediterranean lands to the west. The Transjordan plateau, on which Amman stands, is a transition zone between the Mediterranean climate zone and the desert climate to the east.

POLITICS & ECONOMY In 1921, Britain created a territory called Transjordan east of the River Jordan. In 1923, Transjordan became self-governing, but Britain retained control of its defenses, finances, and foreign affairs. This territory became fully independent as Jordan in 1946. Jordan has suffered from instability arising from the Arab–Israeli conflict since the creation of the State of Israel in 1948. After the first Arab–Israeli War in 1948–9, Jordan acquired East Jerusalem and a fertile area called the West Bank. In 1967, Israel occupied this area. In Jordan, the presence of Palestinian refugees led to civil war in 1970–1.

In 1974, Arab leaders declared that the PLO (Palestine Liberation Organization) was the sole representative of the Palestinian people. In 1988, King Hussein of Jordan renounced Jordan's claims to the West Bank and passed responsibility for it to the PLO. Opposition parties were legalized in 1991 and elections were held in 1993. In October 1994, Jordan and Israel signed a peace treaty, ending a state of war that had lasted more than 40 years. Jordan's King Hussein commanded respect for his role in Middle Eastern affairs until his death in 1999. He was succeeded by his eldest son, who became Abdullah II. Jordan supported the US-led war on terrorism. But its reputation as one of the safest countries in the Middle East was damaged in 2005 by suicide bombings on hotels in Amman. National elections in 2007 were considered to be part of Jordan's transition to democracy.

Jordan has a "lower-middle-income" economy. It lacks natural resources, apart from phosphates and potash, and depends on substantial aid. Less than 6% of the land is farmed or used as pasture. Jordan has an oil refinery and manufactures include cement, pharmaceuticals, processed food, fertilizers, and textiles.

AREA 34,495 sq mi [89,342 sq km]
POPULATION 6,053,000 **CAPITAL** Amman
GOVERNMENT Constitutional monarchy **ETHNIC GROUPS** Arab 98%, of which Palestinians make up roughly half **LANGUAGES** Arabic (official) **RELIGIONS** Islam (mostly Sunni) 94%, Christianity (mostly Greek Orthodox) 6% **CURRENCY** Jordanian dinar = 1,000 fils

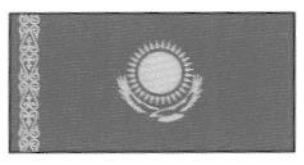

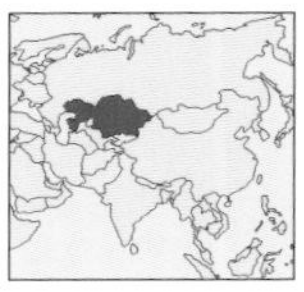

KAZAKHSTAN

GEOGRAPHY Kazakhstan is a large country in west-central Asia. In the west, the Caspian Sea lowlands include the Karagiye depression, which reaches 433 ft [132 m] below sea level. The lowlands extend eastward through the Aral Sea area. The north contains high plains, but the highest land is along the eastern and southern borders. These areas include parts of the Altai and Tian Shan mountain ranges. Eastern Kazakhstan contains several freshwater lakes, the largest of which is Lake Balkhash. The water in the rivers has been used for irrigation, causing ecological problems. For example, the Aral Sea, deprived of water, shrank from 25,830 sq mi [66,900 sq km] in 1960 to 12,989 sq mi [33,642 sq km] in 1993. Large areas are now barren desert.

Kazakhstan lies far from the moderating influence of the oceans and it has an extreme climate. Winters are cold and snow covers the land for about 100 days at Almaty. The rainfall is generally low.

POLITICS & ECONOMY After the Russian Revolution of 1917, many Kazakhs wanted to make their country independent. But the Communists prevailed and in 1936 Kazakhstan became a republic of the Soviet Union, called the Kazakh Soviet Socialist Republic. During World War II and also after the war, the Soviet government moved many people from the west into Kazakhstan. From the 1950s, people were encouraged to work on a "Virgin Lands" project, which involved bringing large areas of grassland under cultivation.

Reforms in the Soviet Union in the 1980s led to its breakup in December 1991. Kazakhstan maintained contacts with Russia through the Commonwealth of Independent States (CIS). In 1997, the government moved its capital from Almaty to Aqmola (later renamed Astana), a town in the north. By the mid-2000s, the economy was in better shape than the other ex-Soviet republics in Central Asia. But President Nursultan Nazarbaev was criticized for his authoritarian rule, and the elections in 2004, won by his party, were described as flawed. In 2007, the governing party won all the seats in parliament, taking 88% of the vote.

The World Bank classifies Kazakhstan as a "lower-middle-income" developing country. Livestock farming, especially sheep and cattle, is an important activity, and major crops include barley, cotton, rice, and wheat. The country is rich in mineral resources, including coal and oil reserves, together with bauxite, copper, lead, tungsten, and zinc. Manufactures include chemicals, food products, machinery, and textiles. Oil is exported via a pipeline through Russia; however, to reduce dependence on Russia, Kazakhstan signed an agreement in 1997 to build a new pipeline to China. Other exports include metals, chemicals, grain, wool and meat.

AREA 1,052,084 sq mi [2,724,900 sq km] **POPULATION** 15,285,000
CAPITAL Astana **GOVERNMENT** Multiparty republic
ETHNIC GROUPS Kazakh 53%, Russian 30%, Ukrainian 4%, German 2%, Uzbek 2% **LANGUAGES** Kazakh (official); Russian, the former official language, is widely spoken **RELIGIONS** Islam 47%, Russian Orthodox 44% **CURRENCY** Tenge = 100 tiyn

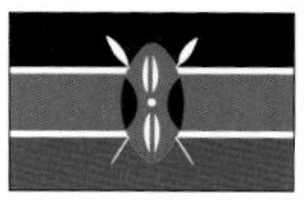
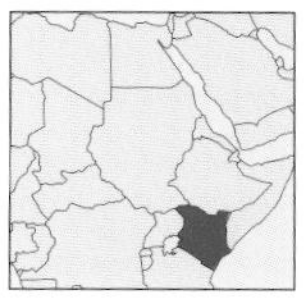

KENYA

GEOGRAPHY The Republic of Kenya is a country in East Africa which straddles the Equator. Behind the narrow coastal plain on the Indian Ocean, the land rises to high plains and highlands, broken by volcanic mountains, including Mount Kenya, the country's highest peak at 17,057 ft [5,199 m]. Crossing the country is an arm of the Great Rift Valley, on the floor of which are several lakes, including Baringo, Magadi, Naivasha, Nakuru and, on the northern frontier, Lake Turkana (formerly Lake Rudolf).

The climate is moderated by the terrain. Nairobi, in the southwestern highlands, has summer temperatures which are 18°F [10°C] lower than humid Mombasa. Nairobi's main rainy season is from April to May, but only about 15% of Kenya has a reliable annual rainfall of 31 inches [800 mm].

POLITICS & ECONOMY The Kenyan coast has been a trading center for more than 2,000 years. Britain took over the coast in 1895 and soon extended its influence inland. In the 1950s, a secret movement, called Mau Mau, launched an armed struggle against British rule. Although Mau Mau was eventually defeated, Kenya became independent in 1963.

Kenya was a one-party state for much of the time after 1963. Democracy was restored in 1992. But elections in December 2007 sparked off inter-ethnic violence when the opposition refused to accept the declared results. In 2008, a power-sharing deal agreed by President Mwai Kibaki and opposition leader Raila Odinga, who became prime minister, restored peace.

Kenya remains a "low-income" developing country. Many Kenyans are subsistence farmers. The chief food crop is maize. The main cash crops and the leading exports are coffee and tea. Manufactures include chemicals, leather and footwear, processed food, petroleum products, and textiles.

AREA 224,080 sq mi [580,367 sq km]
POPULATION 36,914,000 **CAPITAL** Nairobi
GOVERNMENT Multiparty republic **ETHNIC GROUPS** Kikuyu 22%, Luhya 14%, Luo 13%, Kalenjin 12%, Kamba 11%, others
LANGUAGES Kiswahili and English (both official)
RELIGIONS Protestant 45%, Roman Catholic 33%, traditional beliefs 10%, Islam 10% **CURRENCY** Kenyan shilling = 100 cents

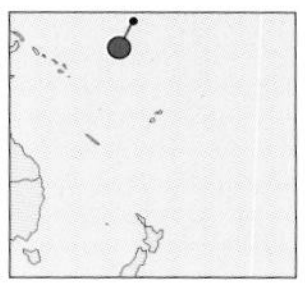

KIRIBATI

The Republic of Kiribati comprises three groups of coral atolls scattered over about 2 million sq mi [5 million sq km]. Kiribati straddles the equator and temperatures are high and the rainfall is abundant.

Formerly part of the British Gilbert and Ellice Islands, Kiribati became independent in 1979. The main export is copra and the country depends heavily on foreign aid.

AREA 280 sq mi [726 sq km] **POPULATION** 108,000 **CAPITAL** Tarawa

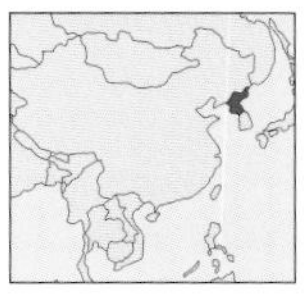

KOREA, NORTH

GEOGRAPHY The Democratic People's Republic of Korea occupies the northern part of the Korean peninsula which extends south from northeastern China. Mountains form the heart of the country, with the highest peak, Paektu-san, reaching 9,003 ft [2,744 m] on the northern border.

North Korea has a fairly severe climate, with cold, snowy winters. In summer, moist winds from the oceans bring rain.

POLITICS & ECONOMY North Korea was created in 1945, when the peninsula, which had been a Japanese colony since 1910, was divided into two parts. Soviet forces occupied the north, with US forces in the south. Soviet occupation led to a Communist government being established in 1948 under the leadership of Kim Il Sung, who effectively became a dictator.

The Korean War began in June 1950 when North Korean troops invaded the south. North Korea, aided by China and the Soviet Union, fought with South Korea, which was supported by troops from the United States and other UN members. The war ended in July 1953. An armistice was signed but no permanent peace treaty was agreed. The end of the Cold War in the late 1990s eased the situation. North and South Korea joined the United Nations in 1991, although North Korea remained isolated from most other countries. In 1993, North Korea withdrew from the Nuclear Non-Proliferation Treaty, arousing suspicions that it was developing nuclear weapons. Kim Il Sung died in 1994 and was succeeded by his son, Kim Jong Il. From 2003, the United States accused North Korea of developing nuclear weapons and, in 2006, the country conducted its first nuclear test. However, North Korea agreed to a nuclear freeze in 2007 in return for foreign aid.

North Korea's resources include coal, copper, iron ore, lead, tin, tungsten, and zinc. Under Communism, the country developed heavy, state-owned industries. Manufactures include chemicals, iron and steel, machinery, processed food and textiles. Agriculture employs 27% of the people. Rice is the chief food crop, but food shortages have occurred in recent years.

AREA 46,540 sq mi [120,538 sq km]
POPULATION 23,302,000 **CAPITAL** Pyŏngyang
GOVERNMENT Single-party people's republic
ETHNIC GROUPS Korean 99%
LANGUAGES Korean (official)
RELIGIONS Buddhism and Confucianism
CURRENCY North Korean won = 100 chon

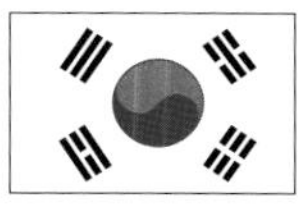
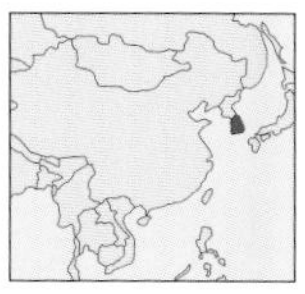

KOREA, SOUTH

GEOGRAPHY The Republic of Korea, as South Korea is officially known, occupies the southern part of the Korean peninsula. Mountains cover much of the country. The southern and western coasts are major farming regions. Many islands are found along the west and south coasts. The largest of these is Cheju-do, which contains South Korea's highest peak, Halla-San, which rises to 6,398 ft [1,950 m].

Like North Korea, South Korea is chilled in winter by cold, dry winds from central Asia. Summers are hot and wet, especially in July and August.

POLITICS & ECONOMY After Japan's defeat in World War II (1939–45), North Korea was occupied by troops from the Soviet Union, while South Korea was occupied by United States forces. A National Assembly elected in 1948 in South Korea created the Republic of Korea, while North Korea became a Communist state. North Korea invaded the South in June 1950, sparking off the Korean War (1950–3). Despite the destruction caused by the war, South Korea under a series of rather authoritarian governments began to industrialize the economy between the 1960s and 1980s. In 1987, a new constitution permitted the election of presidents every five years. In the 2000s, South Korea worked to engage the North in closer relations.

In recent years, South Korea has been one of the world's fastest growing industrial economies. Its resources include coal and tungsten, and its main manufactures are processed food and textiles. Heavy industries produce chemicals, fertilizers, iron and steel, and ships. The country also produces such consumer products as computers, cars and television sets.

Farming remains important in South Korea. Rice is the chief crop, together with fruits, grains and vegetables, while fishing provides a major source of protein.

AREA 38,327 sq mi [99,268 sq km]
POPULATION 49,045,000 **CAPITAL** Seoul
GOVERNMENT Multiparty republic **ETHNIC GROUPS** Korean 99%
LANGUAGES Korean (official) **RELIGIONS** No affiliation 46%, Christianity 26%, Buddhism 26%, Confucianism 1%
CURRENCY South Korean won = 100 chon

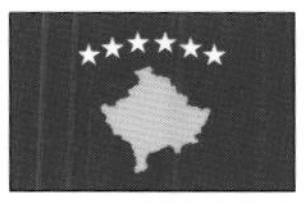
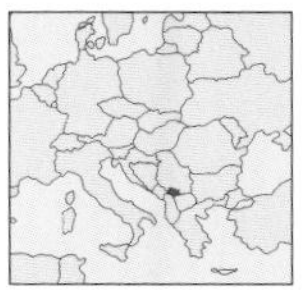

KOSOVO

GEOGRAPHY The Republic of Kosovo, formerly part of Serbia and, before 2003, part of Yugoslavia, declared its independence in February 2008. Its independence was recognized by the United States and major EU countries. But Serbia and its ally Russia refused recognition. It is a landlocked country, consisting of a river basin bounded by uplands in the north and southwest. It has cold, snowy winters and hot, dry summers.

POLITICS & ECONOMY Most people are Albanian-speakers who are Muslims, but there is an important Christian Serb minority. In the early 13th century, Kosovo was part of the Serbian empire but, after 1389, it came under Muslim Turkish Ottoman rule. Serbia regained control of Kosovo in 1912 and, in 1918, it became part of the Kingdom of Serbia. In 1946, it became part of the Socialist Federal Republic of Yugoslavia, becoming an autonomous province within the Republic of Serbia. In 1989, Serbia curtailed Kosovo's autonomy, while Albanian speakers declared their province independent. In 1995, the Albanian speakers set up the Kosovo Liberation Army, which launched an uprising against Serbia. In 1998, Serbia began repressive measures against Kosovo resulting in massacres and ethnic cleansing of Albanian-speaking Kosovars. In 1999, NATO forces bombed Serbia and placed Kosovo under a temporary administration, pending agreement on Kosovo's future status. Finally, the Kosovo Assembly declared its independence on February 17, 2008.

Kosovo is a poor country, with the lowest per capita income in Europe. Many people are subsistence farmers and its industries have declined because of lack of investment. The economy is highly dependent on international aid.

AREA 4,203 sq mi [10,887 sq km]
POPULATION 2,127,000 **CAPITAL** Pristina
GOVERNMENT Republic
ETHNIC GROUPS Albanian 88%, Serb 7%, others 5%
LANGUAGES Albanian and Serbian (both official), Turkish
RELIGIONS Islam, Serbian Orthodox, Roman Catholic
CURRENCY Euro = 100 cents

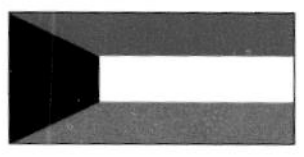
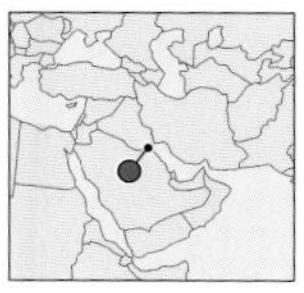

KUWAIT

GEOGRAPHY The State of Kuwait at the north end of the Persian Gulf is an emirate (ruled by an emir or amir). The land is low-lying and largely desert. Summer temperatures are high but winters are cooler. The rainfall is low.

POLITICS & ECONOMY British influence began in 1775 and, in 1899, the local ruler concluded a treaty with Britain, agreeing to support British interests in return for British protection. Kuwait became independent in 1961. Its revenue from its oil exports made it highly prosperous. Iraq invaded Kuwait in 1990 and much damage was inflicted in 1991 when Kuwait was liberated by a coalition force. In 2004, the government announced draft legislation for women to vote and stand for parliament.

AREA 6,880 sq mi [17,818 sq km]
POPULATION 2,506,000 **CAPITAL** Kuwait City

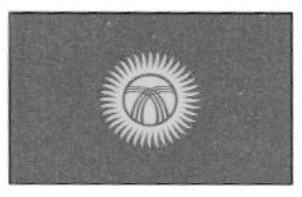
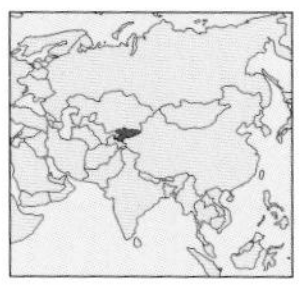

KYRGYZSTAN

GEOGRAPHY The Republic of Kyrgyzstan is a landlocked country between China, Tajikistan, Uzbekistan and Kazakhstan. The country is mountainous, with spectacular scenery. The highest mountain, Pik Pobedy in the Tian Shan range, reaches 24,406 ft [7,439 m] in the east. The lowlands have warm summers and cold winters. But January temperatures in the mountains plummet to –18°F [–28°C]. Kyrgyzstan has a low annual rainfall.

POLITICS & ECONOMY In 1876, Kyrgyzstan became a province of Russia and Russian settlement in the area began. In 1916, Russia crushed a rebellion among the Kyrgyz, and many subsequently fled to China. In 1922, the area became an autonomous oblast (self-governing region) of the newly formed Soviet Union but, in 1936, it became one of the Soviet Socialist Republics. Under Communist rule, local customs and religious worship were suppressed, but education and health services were greatly improved.

In 1991, Kyrgyzstan became an independent country following the breakup of the Soviet Union. The Communist Party was dissolved, but the country maintained ties with Russia through an organization called the Commonwealth of Independent States. Elections were held under a new constitution adopted in 1994. Massive protests followed elections in 2005. President Askar Akayev fled the country. His successor, Kurmanbek Bakiyev, introduced a new constitution, which was approved in a referendum in 2007. In the 1990s, Kyrgyzstan sought to reform its Soviet-style economy. It is now classified as a "lower-middle-income" developing country. Agriculture is the leading activity. The chief products include cotton, eggs, fruits, grain, tobacco, vegetables, and wool. But food is imported. Most industries are concentrated around the capital Bishkek.

AREA 77,181 sq mi [199,900 sq km]
POPULATION 5,284,000 **CAPITAL** Bishkek
GOVERNMENT Multiparty republic
ETHNIC GROUPS Kyrgyz 65%, Russian 13%, Uzbek 13%
LANGUAGES Kyrgyz and Russian (both official)
RELIGIONS Islam 75%, Russian Orthodox 20%
CURRENCY Kyrgyzstani som = 100 tyiyn

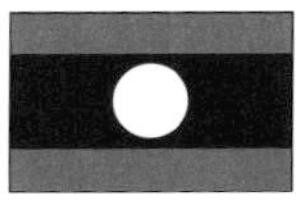
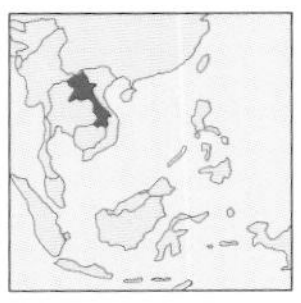

LAOS

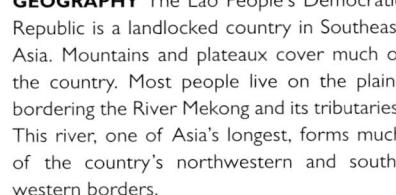

GEOGRAPHY The Lao People's Democratic Republic is a landlocked country in Southeast Asia. Mountains and plateaux cover much of the country. Most people live on the plains bordering the River Mekong and its tributaries. This river, one of Asia's longest, forms much of the country's northwestern and southwestern borders.

Laos has a tropical monsoon climate. Winters are dry and sunny, with winds blowing in from the northeast. The temperatures rise until April, when the wind directions are reversed and moist southwesterly winds reach Laos, heralding the start of the wet monsoon season.

POLITICS & ECONOMY France made Laos a protectorate in the late 19th century and ruled it, with Cambodia and Vietnam, as part of French Indochina. Laos became an independent kingdom in 1954. After independence, a power struggle between royalist government forces and a pro-Communist group called Pathet Lao caused instability. A civil war broke out and continued into the 1970s. The Pathet Lao took control in 1975 and the king abdicated. Laos then came under the influence of Communist Vietnam, which had used Laos as a supply base during the Vietnam War (1957–75).

Laos is one of the world's poorest countries. Agriculture employs about 35% of the population and accounts for 29% of the gross domestic product. Rice is the main crop. Timber and coffee are exported. But the most valuable export is electricity, which is produced at hydroelectric power stations on the River Mekong and is exported to Thailand. Laos also produces opium.

AREA 91,428 sq mi [236,800 sq km]
POPULATION 6,522,000 **CAPITAL** Vientiane
GOVERNMENT Single-party republic
ETHNIC GROUPS Lao Loum 68%, Lao Theung 22%, Lao Soung 9%
LANGUAGES Lao (official), French, English **RELIGIONS** Buddhism 60%, traditional beliefs and others 40% **CURRENCY** Kip = 100 at

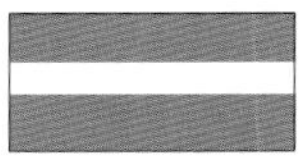
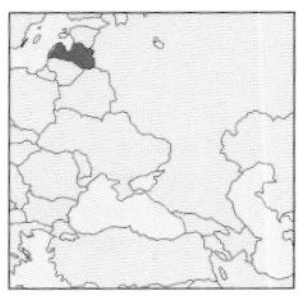

LATVIA

GEOGRAPHY The Republic of Latvia is one of three states on the southeastern corner of the Baltic Sea which were ruled as parts of the Soviet Union between 1940 and 1991. Latvia consists mainly of flat plains separated by low hills, composed of moraine (ice-worn rocks).

Riga has warm summers, but the winter months are subzero. The rainfall is moderate.

POLITICS & ECONOMY In 1800, Russia was in control of Latvia, but Latvians declared their independence after World War I. In 1940, under a German-Soviet pact, Soviet troops occupied Latvia, but they were driven out by the Germans in 1941. Soviet troops returned in 1944 and Latvia became part of the Soviet Union. Under Soviet rule, many Russian immigrants settled in Latvia and many Latvians feared that the Russians would become the dominant ethnic group.

In the late 1980s, when reforms were being introduced in the Soviet Union, Latvia's government ended absolute Communist rule and made Latvian the official language. In 1990, it declared the country to be independent, an act which was finally recognized by the Soviet Union in September 1991.

Latvia held its first free elections to its parliament (the Saeima) in 1993. Voting was limited only to citizens of Latvia on June 17, 1940, and their descendants. This meant that about 34% of Latvian residents were unable to vote. In 1994, Latvia restricted the naturalization of non-Latvians, including many Russian settlers, who were not allowed to vote or own land. However, in 1998, the government agreed that all children born since independence should have automatic citizenship. Its cultivation of closer ties to the West was realized in 2004 when Latvia was admitted to membership of both the North Atlantic Treaty Organization and the European Union.

The World Bank classifies Latvia as a "lower-middle-income" country and, in the 1990s, it faced many problems in turning its economy into a free-market system. Products include electronic goods, farm machinery, fertilizers, processed food, plastics, radios, and vehicles. Latvia produces only about a tenth of the electricity it needs. It imports the rest from Belarus, Russia, and Ukraine.

AREA 24,942 sq mi [64,600 sq km]
POPULATION 2,260,000 **CAPITAL** Riga
GOVERNMENT Multiparty republic
ETHNIC GROUPS Latvian 58%, Russian 30%, Belarusian, Ukrainian, Polish, Lithuanian **LANGUAGES** Latvian (official), Lithuanian, Russian **RELIGIONS** Lutheran, Roman Catholic, Russian Orthodox
CURRENCY Latvian lat = 10 santimi

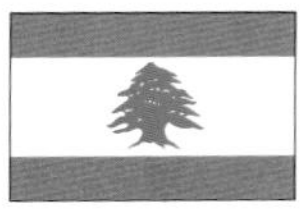
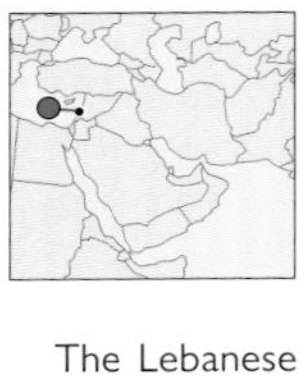

LEBANON

GEOGRAPHY The Republic of Lebanon is a country on the eastern shores of the Mediterranean Sea. Behind the coastal plain are the rugged Lebanon Mountains (Jabal Lubnan), which rise to 10,131 ft [3,088 m]. Another range, the Anti-Lebanon Mountains (Al Jabal Ash Sharqi), form the eastern border with Syria. Between the two ranges is the Bekaa (Beqaa) Valley, a fertile farming region.

The Lebanese coast has the hot, dry summers and mild, wet winters that are typical of many Mediterranean lands. Inland, onshore winds bring heavy rain to the western slopes of the mountains in the winter months, with snow at the higher altitudes.

POLITICS & ECONOMY Lebanon was ruled by Turkey from 1516 until World War I. France ruled the country from 1923, but Lebanon became independent in 1946. After independence, the Muslims and Christians agreed to share power, and Lebanon made rapid economic progress. But from the late 1950s, development was slowed by periodic conflict between Sunni and Shia Muslims, Druze and Christians. The situation was further complicated by the presence of Palestinian refugees who used bases in Lebanon to attack Israel.

In 1975, civil war broke out as private armies representing the many factions struggled for power. This led to intervention by Israel in the south and Syria in the north. UN peacekeeping forces arrived in 1978, but violence continued in the 1980s. Peace was restored in the 1990s, but, in 2005, the assassination of Rafik Hariri, former prime minister, was blamed on Syria. Under pressure, Syria withdrew its forces from Lebanon. In 2006, a 34-day conflict between Israeli troops and Hezbollah guerrillas caused devastation in southern Lebanon.

Lebanon's civil war almost destroyed valuable trade and financial services that had been Lebanon's chief source of income, together with tourism. Manufacturing, formerly a major activity, was badly hit.

AREA 4,015 sq mi [10,400 sq km]
POPULATION 3,926,000 **CAPITAL** Beirut
GOVERNMENT Multiparty republic **ETHNIC GROUPS** Arab 95%, Armenian 4%, others **LANGUAGES** Arabic (official), French, English, Armenian **RELIGIONS** Islam 70%, Christianity 30%
CURRENCY Lebanese pound = 100 piastres

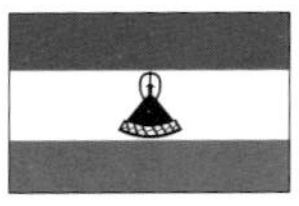
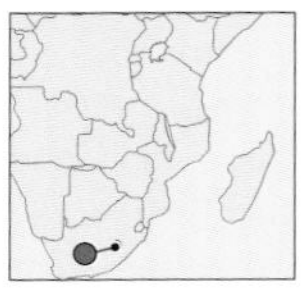

LESOTHO

GEOGRAPHY The Kingdom of Lesotho is a landlocked country, completely enclosed by South Africa. The land is mountainous, rising to 11,424 ft [3,482 m] on the northeastern border. The Drakensberg range covers most of the country.

The climate of Lesotho is greatly affected by the altitude, because most of the country lies above 4,920 ft [1,500 m]. Summers are warm but winters are cold. The rainfall averages about 28 inches [700 mm].

POLITICS & ECONOMY The Basotho nation was founded in the 1820s by King Moshoeshoe I, who united various groups fleeing from tribal wars in southern Africa. Britain made the area a protectorate in 1868 and, in 1871, placed it under the British Cape Colony in South Africa. But in 1884, Basutoland, as the area was called, was reconstituted as a British protectorate, where whites were not allowed to own land.

The country finally became independent in 1966 as the Kingdom of Lesotho, with Moshoeshoe II, great-grandson of Moshoeshoe I, as its king. Since independence, Lesotho has suffered instability. The military seized power in 1986 and stripped Moshoeshoe II of his powers in 1990, installing his son, Letsie III, as monarch. After elections in 1993, Moshoeshoe II was restored to office in 1995. But after his death in a car crash in 1996, Letsie III again became king. In 1998, an army revolt, following an election in which the ruling party won 79 out of the 80 seats, caused much damage to the economy. Lesotho has faced many problems, including drought, while 25% of the people have been infected by the HIV virus. In 2005, the government offered HIV tests to all citizens.

Lesotho lacks natural resources, and the UN has stated that 40% of the people are "ultra-poor." Agriculture employs 18% of the people, mostly at subsistence level. Remittances sent home by Basotho working abroad are important to the economy.

AREA 11,720 sq mi [30,355 sq km]
POPULATION 2,125,000 **CAPITAL** Maseru
GOVERNMENT Constitutional monarchy
ETHNIC GROUPS Sotho 99% **LANGUAGES** Sesotho and English (both official) **RELIGIONS** Christianity 80%, traditional beliefs 20%
CURRENCY Loti = 100 lisente

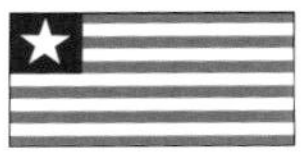
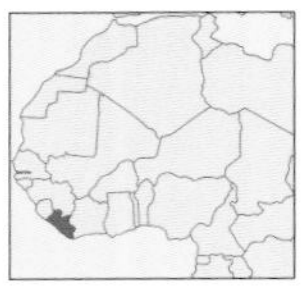

LIBERIA

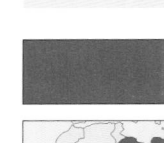

GEOGRAPHY The Republic of Liberia is a country in West Africa. Behind the coastline, 311 mi [500 km] long, lies a narrow coastal plain. Beyond, the land rises to a plateau region, with the highest land along the border with Guinea. Liberia has a tropical climate with high temperatures and high humidity all through the year. The rainfall is abundant all year round, but there is a particularly wet period from June to November. The rainfall generally increases from east to west.

POLITICS & ECONOMY In the late 18th century, some white Americans in the United States wanted to help freed black slaves to return to Africa. In 1816, they set up the American Colonization Society, which bought land in what is now Liberia.

In 1822, the Society landed former slaves at a settlement on the coast which they named Monrovia. In 1847, Liberia became a fully independent republic with a constitution much like that of the United States. For many years, the Americo-Liberians controlled the country's government. US influence remained strong and the American Firestone Company, which ran Liberia's rubber plantations, was especially influential. Foreign companies were also involved in exploiting Liberia's mineral resources, including its huge iron-ore deposits.

In 1980, a military group composed of people from the local population killed the Americo-Liberian president, William R. Tolbert. An army sergeant, Samuel K. Doe, was made president of Liberia. Elections held in 1985 resulted in victory for Doe. From 1989, the country was plunged into civil war between various ethnic groups. Doe was assassinated in 1990 and the struggle with rebel groups continued. West African peacekeeping forces arrived in Liberia and, in 1995, a ceasefire was agreed. A council of state, composed of former warlords, was set up in 1997 and Charles Taylor became president. Taylor fled the country in 2003 and, in 2006, he was extradited and charged with war crimes. Following elections in 2005, Ellen Sirleaf-Johnson was elected president. She became Africa's first woman president.

Liberia's economy was devastated by the civil war. Agriculture is important, but most farmers live at subsistence level. Food crops include cassava, rice, and sugarcane, while rubber, cocoa, and coffee are exported. The most valuable export is rubber.

Liberia also obtains revenue from its "flag of convenience," which is used by about one-sixth of the world's commercial shipping, exploiting low taxes.

AREA 43,000 sq mi [111,369 sq km]
POPULATION 3,196,000 **CAPITAL** Monrovia
GOVERNMENT Multiparty republic **ETHNIC GROUPS** Indigenous African tribes 95% (including Kpelle, Bassa, Grebo, Gio, Kru, Mano)
LANGUAGES English (official), ethnic languages
RELIGIONS Christianity 40%, Islam 20%, traditional beliefs and others 40% **CURRENCY** Liberian dollar = 100 cents

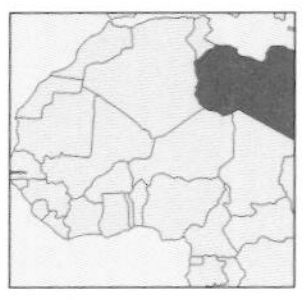

LIBYA

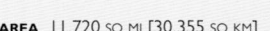

GEOGRAPHY The Socialist People's Libyan Arab Jamahiriya, as Libya is officially called, is a large country in North Africa. Most people live on the coastal plains in the northeast and northwest. The Sahara, the world's largest desert which occupies 95% of Libya, reaches the Mediterranean coast along the Gulf of Sidra (Khalij Surt).

The coastal plains in the northeast and northwest have Mediterranean climates, with hot, dry summers and mild, sometimes wet winters. Inland, the average yearly rainfall drops to 4 inches [100 mm] or less.

POLITICS & ECONOMY Italy took over Libya in 1911, but lost it during World War II. Britain and France jointly ruled Libya until 1951, when the country became an independent kingdom.

In 1969, a military group headed by Colonel Muammar Gaddafi deposed the king and set up a military government. Under Gaddafi, the government took control of the economy and used money from oil exports to finance welfare services and development projects. Gaddafi was criticized for supporting terrorist groups around the world, and Libya became isolated from the mid-1980s. In 1998, he tried to restore Libya's reputation by surrendering for trial two Libyans suspected of planting a bomb on a PanAm plane which exploded over the Scottish town of Lockerbie in 1988. In 2001, one of the Libyans was found guilty and the other acquitted of the bombing. In 2003, Libya announced that it would pay compensation to victims of the bombing. In 2004, relations with the West improved and, in 2006, the United States rescinded its designation of Libya as a state sponsor of terrorism. Full diplomatic relations were restored.

The discovery of oil and natural gas in 1959 led to a transformation of Libya's economy. This formerly poor country soon became Africa's richest in terms of its per capita income. But it remains a developing country, because oil accounts for nearly all its export revenues. Agriculture is important, although Libya imports food. Crops include barley, citrus fruits, dates, olives, potatoes and wheat, while cattle, sheep, and poultry are raised. Libya has oil refineries and petrochemical plants. Other manufactures include cement and steel.

AREA 679,358 SQ MI [1,759,540 SQ KM] **POPULATION** 6,037,000
CAPITAL TRIPOLI **GOVERNMENT** SINGLE-PARTY SOCIALIST STATE
ETHNIC GROUPS LIBYAN ARAB AND BERBER 97%
LANGUAGES ARABIC (OFFICIAL), BERBER **RELIGIONS** ISLAM (SUNNI MUSLIM) 97% **CURRENCY** LIBYAN DINAR = 1,000 DIRHAMS

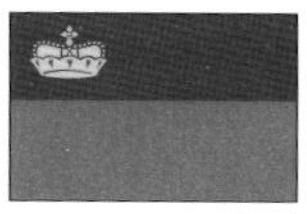
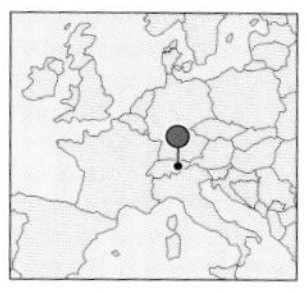

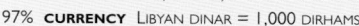

LIECHTENSTEIN

The tiny Principality of Liechtenstein is sandwiched between Switzerland and Austria. The River Rhine flows along its western border, while Alpine peaks rise in the east and south. The climate is relatively mild. Since 1924, Liechtenstein has been in a customs union with Switzerland. Taxation is low and the country is a haven for foreign companies. In 2003, the people voted to give their head of state, Prince Hans Adam II, sovereign powers. However, he later announced his retirement from politics. In 2004, he handed over the running of the country to his son, Prince Alois, although he remained the titular head of state.

AREA 62 SQ MI [160 SQ KM] **POPULATION** 34,000 **CAPITAL** VADUZ

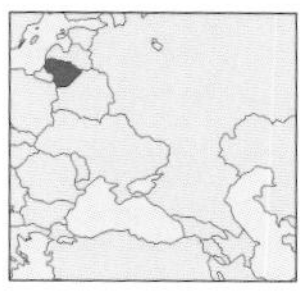

LITHUANIA

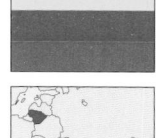

GEOGRAPHY The Republic of Lithuania is the southernmost of the three Baltic states which were ruled as part of the Soviet Union between 1940 and 1991. Much of the land is flat or gently rolling, with the highest land in the southeast.

Winters are cold and summers warm. The annual rainfall in the west is about 25 inches [630 mm]. Eastern areas are drier.

POLITICS & ECONOMY The Lithuanian people were united into a single nation in the 12th century, and later joined a union with Poland. In 1795, Lithuania came under Russian rule. After World War I (1914–18), Lithuania declared itself independent, and in 1920 it signed a peace treaty with the Russians, though Poland held Vilnius until 1939. In 1940, the Soviet Union occupied Lithuania, but the Germans invaded in 1941. Soviet forces returned in 1944, and Lithuania was integrated into the Soviet Union. In 1988, when the Soviet Union was introducing reforms, the Lithuanians demanded independence. Their language is one of the oldest in the world, and the country was always the most homogenous of the Baltic states, staunchly Catholic and resistant of attempts to suppress their culture. Pro-independence groups won the national elections in 1990 and, in 1991, the Soviet Union recognized Lithuania's independence.

Since 1991, Lithuania has sought to reform its economy and introduce a private enterprise system. Lithuania has also drawn closer to the West and, in 2004, it became a member of both the North Atlantic Treaty Organization and the European Union.

The World Bank classifies Lithuania as a "lower-middle-income" developing country. Lithuania lacks natural resources, but manufacturing, based on imported materials, is the most valuable activity.

AREA 25,174 SQ MI [65,200 SQ KM]
POPULATION 3,575,000 **CAPITAL** VILNIUS
GOVERNMENT MULTIPARTY REPUBLIC
ETHNIC GROUPS LITHUANIAN 80%, RUSSIAN 9%, POLISH 7%, BELARUSIAN 2% **LANGUAGES** LITHUANIAN (OFFICIAL), RUSSIAN, POLISH
RELIGIONS MAINLY ROMAN CATHOLIC **CURRENCY** LITAS = 100 CENTAI

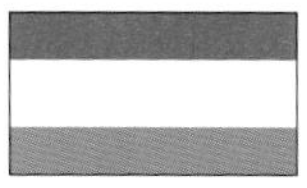
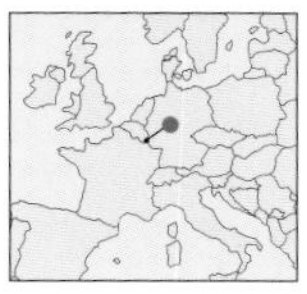

LUXEMBOURG

GEOGRAPHY The Grand Duchy of Luxembourg is one of the smallest and oldest countries in Europe. The north belongs to an upland region which includes the Ardenne in Belgium and Luxembourg, and the Eifel highlands in Germany.

Luxembourg has a temperate climate. The south has warm summers and falls, when grapes ripen in sheltered southeastern valleys. Winters are sometimes severe, especially in upland areas.

POLITICS & ECONOMY Germany occupied Luxembourg in World Wars I and II. In 1944–5, northern Luxembourg was the scene of the famous Battle of the Bulge. In 1948, Luxembourg joined Belgium and the Netherlands in a union called Benelux and, in the 1950s, it was one of the six founders of what is now the European Union. Luxembourg has played a major role in Europe. Its capital contains the headquarters of several international agencies, including the European Coal and Steel Community and the European Court of Justice. The city is also a major financial center.

Luxembourg has iron-ore reserves and is a major steel producer. It also has many high-technology industries, producing electronic goods and computers. Steel and other manufactures, including chemicals, rubber products, glass and aluminum, dominate the country's exports. Other major activities include tourism and financial services.

AREA 998 SQ MI [2,586 SQ KM]
POPULATION 480,000 **CAPITAL** LUXEMBOURG
GOVERNMENT CONSTITUTIONAL MONARCHY (GRAND DUCHY)
ETHNIC GROUPS LUXEMBOURGER 71%, PORTUGUESE, ITALIAN, FRENCH, BELGIAN, SLAVS **LANGUAGES** LUXEMBOURGISH (OFFICIAL), FRENCH, GERMAN **RELIGIONS** ROMAN CATHOLIC 87%, OTHERS 13%
CURRENCY EURO = 100 CENTS

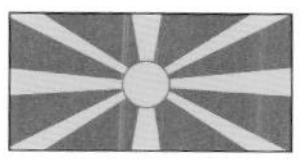
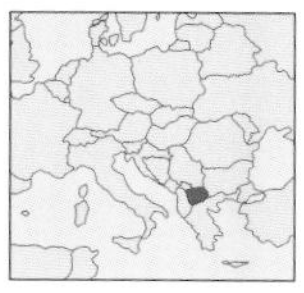

MACEDONIA (FYROM)

GEOGRAPHY The Republic of Macedonia is a country in southeastern Europe, which was once one of the six republics that made up the former Federal People's Republic of Yugoslavia. This landlocked country is largely mountainous or hilly. Macedonia has hot summers, though highland areas are cooler. Winters are cold and snowfalls are often heavy. The climate is fairly continental in character and rain occurs throughout the year.

POLITICS & ECONOMY Until the 20th century, Macedonia's history was closely tied to a larger area, also called Macedonia, which included parts of northern Greece and southwestern Bulgaria. This region reached its peak in power at the time of Philip II (382–336 BC) and his son Alexander the Great (336–323 BC). After Alexander's death, his empire was split up and it gradually declined. The area became a Roman province in the 140s BC and part of the Byzantine Empire from AD 395. In the 6th century, Slavs from eastern Europe settled in the area, followed by the Bulgars from central Asia in the 9th century. The Byzantine Empire regained control in 1018, but Serbia took Macedonia in the early 14th century. In 1371, the Ottoman Turks conquered the area and ruled it for more than 500 years. In 1913, at the end of the Balkan Wars, the area was divided between Serbia, Bulgaria and Greece. At the end of World War I, Serbian Macedonia became part of the Kingdom of the Serbs, Croats, and Slovenes, which was renamed Yugoslavia in 1929. After World War II, Yugoslavia became a Communist country under ex-partisan leader Josip Broz Tito.

Tito died in 1980 and, in the early 1990s, the country broke up into five separate republics. Macedonia declared its independence in September 1991. Greece objected to this territory using the name Macedonia, which it considered to be a Greek name. It also objected to a symbol on Macedonia's flag and a reference in the constitution to the desire to reunite the three parts of the old Macedonia.

Macedonia adopted a new clause in its constitution rejecting any Macedonian claims on Greek territory and, in 1993, the United Nations accepted the new republic as a member under the name of The Former Yugoslav Republic of Macedonia (FYROM). By the end of 1993, all the countries of the EU, except Greece, were establishing diplomatic relations with the FYROM. In 1995, Greece lifted its trade ban, when Macedonia agreed to redesign its flag and remove territorial claims from its constitution. In 2001, fighting along the Kosovo border was attributed to people who wanted to create a Greater Albania. The uprising ended when Macedonia granted its Albanian-speakers increased rights. In 2004, the USA recognized the name Republic of Macedonia instead of FYROM. Despite Greek objections, other nations followed this lead.

The World Bank describes Macedonia as a "lower-middle-income" economy. Manufactures dominate the country's exports. Coal is mined, but oil and natural gas are imported. The country is self-sufficient in its basic food needs.

AREA 9,928 SQ MI [25,713 SQ KM] **POPULATION** 2,056,000
CAPITAL SKOPJE **GOVERNMENT** MULTIPARTY REPUBLIC
ETHNIC GROUPS MACEDONIAN 64%, ALBANIAN 25%, TURKISH 4%, ROMANIAN 3%, SERB 2% **LANGUAGES** MACEDONIAN AND ALBANIAN (OFFICIAL) **RELIGIONS** MACEDONIAN ORTHODOX 70%, ISLAM 29%
CURRENCY MACEDONIAN DENAR = 100 PARAS

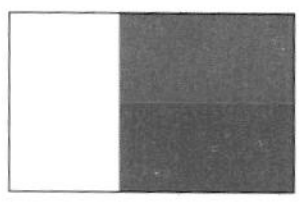
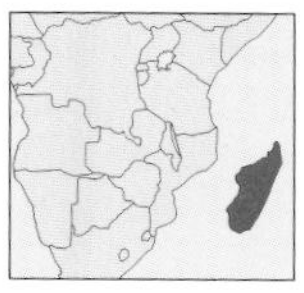

MADAGASCAR

GEOGRAPHY The Democratic Republic of Madagascar, in southeastern Africa, is an island nation, which has a larger area than France. Behind the narrow coastal plains in the east lies a highland zone, mostly between 2,000 ft and 4,000 ft [610 m to 1,220 m] above sea level. Broad plains border the Mozambique Channel in the west.

Temperatures in the highlands are moderated by the altitude. The winters (from April to September) are dry, but heavy rains occur in summer. The eastern coastlands are warm and humid. The west is drier and the south and southwest are hot and dry.

POLITICS & ECONOMY People from Southeast Asia began to settle on Madagascar around 2,000 years ago. Subsequent influxes from Africa and Arabia added to the island's diverse heritage, culture and language.

French troops defeated a Malagasy army in 1895 and Madagascar became a French colony. In 1960, it achieved full independence as the Malagasy Republic. In 1972, army officers seized control and, in 1975, under the leadership of Lieutenant-Commander Didier Ratsiraka, the country was renamed Madagascar. Parliamentary elections were held in 1977, but Ratsiraka remained president of a one-party socialist state. In 2002, the country came close to civil war when Ratsiraka and his opponent, Marc Ravalomanana, both claimed victory in presidential elections. Ravalomanana was finally recognized as president. Re-elected in 2006, he has introduced many economic reforms.

Madagascar is a poor country. Poverty and population growth impose pressure on the dwindling forests and the unique wildlife, as well as causing severe soil erosion. Farming, fishing, and forestry employ more than 70% of the people. Food crops include bananas, cassava, rice, and sweet potatoes. Coffee is exported.

AREA 226,657 SQ MI [587,041 SQ KM]
POPULATION 19,449,000 **CAPITAL** ANTANANARIVO
GOVERNMENT REPUBLIC **ETHNIC GROUPS** MERINA, BETSIMISARAKA, BETSILEO, TSIMIHETY, SAKALAVA AND OTHERS
LANGUAGES MALAGASY AND FRENCH (BOTH OFFICIAL)
RELIGIONS TRADITIONAL BELIEFS 52%, CHRISTIANITY 41%, ISLAM 7%
CURRENCY MALAGASY FRANC = 100 CENTIMES

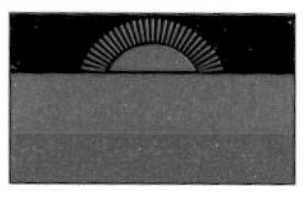
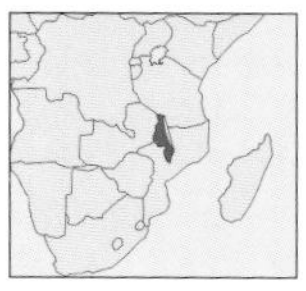

MALAWI

GEOGRAPHY The Republic of Malawi includes part of Lake Malawi, which is drained by the River Shire, a tributary of the River Zambezi. The land is mostly mountainous. The highest peak, Mulanje, reaches 9,843 ft [3,000 m] in the southeast.

While the low-lying areas of Malawi are hot and humid all year round, the uplands have a pleasant climate. Lilongwe, at about 3,609 ft [1,100 m] above sea level, has a warm and sunny climate. Frosts sometimes occur in July and August, in the middle of the long dry season.

POLITICS & ECONOMY Malawi, then called Nyasaland, became a British protectorate in 1891. In 1953, Britain established the Federation of Rhodesia and Nyasaland, which also included what are now Zambia and Zimbabwe. Black African opposition, led in Nyasaland by Dr Hastings Kamuzu Banda, led to the dissolution of the federation in 1963. In 1964, Nyasaland became independent as Malawi, with Banda as prime minister. Banda became president when the country became a republic in 1966 and, in 1971, he was made president for life. Banda was an autocrat, ruling through the only party, the Malawi Congress Party. But a multiparty system was restored in 1993. Bakili Muluzi became president and, in 2004, he was succeeded by Bingu wa Mutharika, leader of the United Democratic Front (UDF). In 2005, he resigned from the UDF and set up a new Democratic Progressive Party.

Malawi is one of the world's poorest countries. More than 80% of the people are farmers, but many grow little more than they need to feed their families.

AREA 45,747 SQ MI [118,484 SQ KM]
POPULATION 13,603,000 **CAPITAL** LILONGWE
GOVERNMENT MULTIPARTY REPUBLIC
ETHNIC GROUPS CHEWA, NYANJA, TONGA, TUMBUKA, LOMWE, YAO, NGONI, AND OTHERS
LANGUAGES CHICHEWA AND ENGLISH (BOTH OFFICIAL)
RELIGIONS PROTESTANT 55%, ROMAN CATHOLIC 20%, ISLAM 20%
CURRENCY MALAWIAN KWACHA = 100 TAMBALA

MALAYSIA

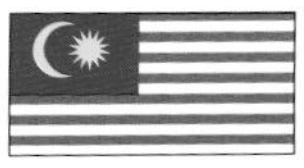

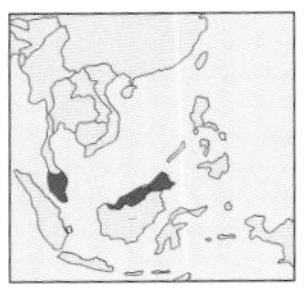

GEOGRAPHY The Federation of Malaysia consists of two main parts. Peninsular Malaysia, which is joined to mainland Asia, contains about 80% of the population. The other main regions, Sabah and Sarawak, are in northern Borneo, an island which Malaysia shares with Indonesia. Behind the coastal lowlands, the interior is mountainous.

Malaysia has a hot equatorial climate. The temperatures are high all through the year, though the mountains are much cooler than the lowland areas. The rainfall is heavy throughout the year.

POLITICS & ECONOMY Around 1,200 years ago, Indian traders introduced Hinduism and Buddhism into the Malay peninsula, while Arabs introduced Islam in the 15th century. Portuguese traders reached Melaka in 1509, but the Dutch took over in 1641. Britain became established in the area in 1786.

Japan occupied the area during World War II (1939–45), but the area reverted to British rule in 1945. In the 1940s and 1950s, Communist guerrillas battled unsuccessfully for power. Malaya (Peninsular Malaysia) became independent in 1957. Malaysia was created in 1963, when Malaya, Singapore, Sabah and Sarawak agreed to unite, but Singapore withdrew in 1965.

From 1981, under the leadership of Dr Mahathir bin Mohamad, Malaysia achieved rapid economic progress. However, together with other countries in eastern Asia, it experienced an economic recession in 1997. In response to the crisis, the government ordered the repatriation of many foreign workers and initiated measures aimed at restoring confidence and avoiding the chronic debt problems affecting some other Asian countries. Mahathir bin Mohamad retired in 2003. Abdullah Ahmad Badawi, who became prime minister, won a landslide election victory in 2004.

The World Bank classifies Malaysia as an "upper-middle-income" developing country. Palm oil, rubber, and tin are major products. Manufactures include cars, chemicals, a wide range of electronic goods, plastics, textiles, rubber, and wood products.

AREA 127,320 sq mi [329,758 sq km] **POPULATION** 24,821,000
CAPITAL Kuala Lumpur; Putrajaya (administrative capital awaiting completion)
GOVERNMENT Federal constitutional monarchy
ETHNIC GROUPS Malay and other indigenous groups 58%, Chinese 24%, Indian 8%, others **LANGUAGES** Malay (official), Chinese, English **RELIGIONS** Islam, Buddhism, Daoism, Hinduism, Christianity, Sikhism **CURRENCY** Ringgit = 100 cents

MALDIVES

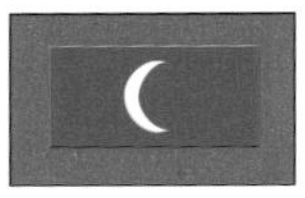

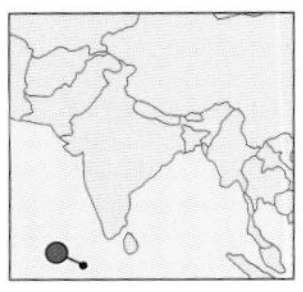

The Republic of the Maldives consists of about 1,200 low-lying coral islands, south of India. The highest point is 79 ft [24 m], but most of the land is only 6 ft [1.8 m] above sea level. The islands became a British territory in 1887 and independence was achieved in 1965. Tourism and fishing are the main industries.

AREA 115 sq mi [298 sq km] **POPULATION** 369,000 **CAPITAL** Malé

MALI

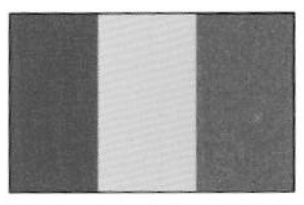

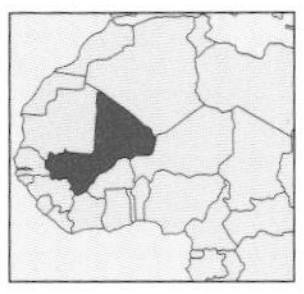

GEOGRAPHY The Republic of Mali is a landlocked country in northern Africa. The land is generally flat, with the highest land in the north. Northern Mali is hot and practically rainless. The south has enough rain for farming.

POLITICS & ECONOMY Between the 4th and 16th centuries, Mali was part of three African empires – ancient Ghana, ancient Mali and Songhay. However, after 1591, when Songhay was defeated by Morocco, the area was divided into small kingdoms. France ruled the area, then known as French Sudan, from 1893 until the country became independent as Mali in 1960.

The first socialist government was overthrown in 1968 by an army group led by Moussa Traoré, but he was ousted in 1991. Multiparty democracy was restored in 1992 and Alpha Oumar Konaré was elected president. Konaré stood down in 2002 and Ahmadou Toure, who had restored democracy in 1992, was elected president. He was re-elected in 2007.

Mali is one of the world's poorest countries and 70% of the land is desert or semidesert. Only about 2% of the land is used for growing crops, while 25% is used for grazing animals. Despite this, agriculture employs nearly 80% of the people, many of whom subsist by nomadic livestock rearing.

AREA 478,838 sq mi [1,240,192 sq km]
POPULATION 11,995,000 **CAPITAL** Bamako
GOVERNMENT Multiparty republic **ETHNIC GROUPS** Mande 50% (Bambara, Malinke, Soninke), Peul 17%, Voltaic 12%, Songhai 6%, Tuareg and Moor 10%, others **LANGUAGES** French (official), many African languages **RELIGIONS** Islam 90%, traditional beliefs 9%, Christianity 1% **CURRENCY** CFA franc = 100 centimes

MALTA

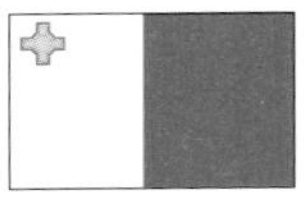

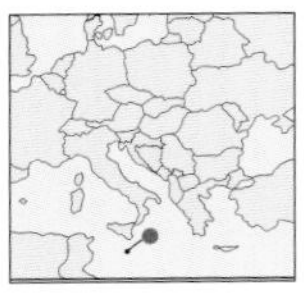

GEOGRAPHY The Republic of Malta consists of two main islands, Malta and Gozo, a third, much smaller island called Comino lying between the two large islands and two islets. The climate is typically Mediterranean, with hot, dry summers and mild, moist winters.

POLITICS & ECONOMY Malta has fascinating Stone and Bronze age remains. The islands later came under Phoenician, Greek, Carthaginian, Roman and Arab rule. In about 1090, Malta came under the Norman kings of Sicily and, from 1530, the Knights Hospitallers (also called the Knights of St John of Jerusalem). France took the islands in 1798, but the British drove them out in 1800. British rule was officially recognized in 1815.

During World War I (1914–18), Malta was an important naval base. In World War II (1939–45), Italian and German aircraft bombed the islands. In recognition of the islanders' bravery, the British King George VI awarded the George Cross to Malta in 1942. In 1953, Malta became a base for NATO (North Atlantic Treaty Organization). Malta became independent in 1964 and a republic in 1974. In 1979, Malta ceased to be a British military base and all British forces withdrew. Malta was declared a neutral country in the 1980s. It became a member of the European Union on May 1, 2004.

The World Bank classifies Malta as an "upper-middle-income" developing country. It lacks natural resources, and most people work in the former naval dockyards, which are now used for commercial shipbuilding and repair, in manufacturing industries and in the tourist industry.

Manufactures include processed food and chemicals. Farming is difficult, because of the rocky soils. Crops include barley, fruits, potatoes, and wheat. Malta also has a small fishing industry.

AREA 122 sq mi [316 sq km] **POPULATION** 402,000
CAPITAL Valletta **GOVERNMENT** Multiparty republic
ETHNIC GROUPS Maltese 96%, British 2% **LANGUAGES** Maltese and English (both official) **RELIGIONS** Roman Catholic 98%
CURRENCY Euro = 100 cents

MARSHALL ISLANDS

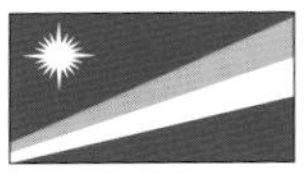

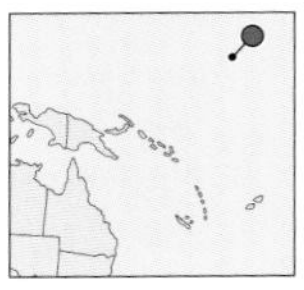

The Republic of the Marshall Islands, a former US territory, became fully independent in 1991. This island nation, lying north of Kiribati in a region known as Micronesia, is heavily dependent on US aid. The main activities are agriculture and tourism.

AREA 70 sq mi [181 sq km]
POPULATION 62,000 **CAPITAL** Majuro

MARTINIQUE

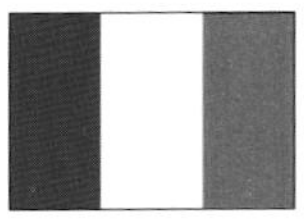

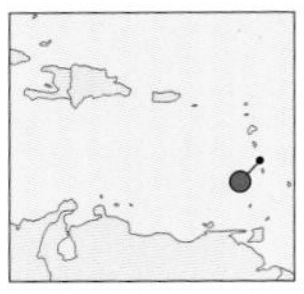

Martinique, a volcanic island nation in the Caribbean, was colonized by France in 1635. It became a French overseas department in 1946. Tourism and agriculture are major activities. About 70% of Martinique's gross domestic product is provided by the French government, allowing for a good standard of living.

AREA 425 sq mi [1,102 sq km]
POPULATION 436,000 **CAPITAL** Fort-de-France

MAURITANIA

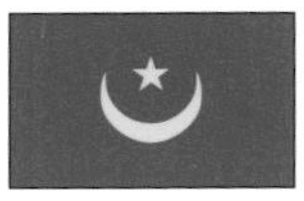

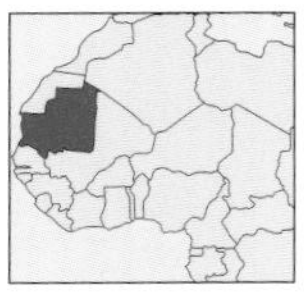

GEOGRAPHY The Islamic Republic of Mauritania in northwestern Africa is nearly twice the size of France. But France has more than 28 times as many people. Part of the world's largest desert, the Sahara, covers northern Mauritania and most Mauritanians live in the southwest. The amount of rainfall and the length of the rainy season increase from north to south. Much of the land is desert, but southwesterly winds bring summer rain to the south.

POLITICS & ECONOMY Originally part of the great African empires of Ghana and Mali, France set up a protectorate in Mauritania in 1903, attempting to exploit the trade in gum arabic. The country became a territory of French West Africa and a French colony in 1920. French West Africa was a huge territory, which included present-day Benin, Burkina Faso, Guinea, Ivory Coast, Mali, Niger and Senegal, as well as Mauritania. In 1958, Mauritania became a self-governing territory in the French Union and it became fully independent in 1960.

In 1976, Spain withdrew from Spanish (now Western) Sahara, a territory bordering Mauritania to the north. Morocco occupied the northern two-thirds of this territory, while Mauritania took the rest. But Saharan guerrillas belonging to POLISARIO (the Popular Front for the Liberation of Saharan Territories) began an armed struggle for independence. In 1979, Mauritania withdrew from the southern part of Western Sahara, which was then occupied by Morocco. Democracy was restored after a new constitution was adopted in 1991. A military group seized power in 2005, but democratic elections were held in 2007. Sidi Ould Sheikh Abdallahi was elected president.

Mauritania is a "low-income" developing country. Nearly half of the people are engaged in agriculture. In 2006, Mauritania became Africa's newest oil producer, when an offshore platform came online for the first time.

AREA 395,953 sq mi [1,025,520 sq km]
POPULATION 3,270,000 **CAPITAL** Nouakchott
GOVERNMENT Multiparty Islamic republic
ETHNIC GROUPS Mixed Moor/Black 40%, Moor 30%, Black 30%
LANGUAGES Arabic and Wolof (both official), French
RELIGIONS Islam
CURRENCY Ouguiya = 5 khoums

MAURITIUS

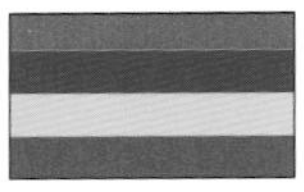

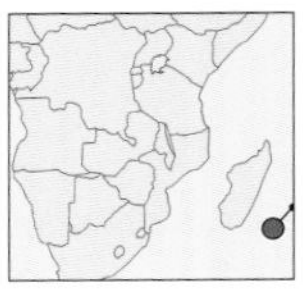

The Republic of Mauritius, an Indian Ocean nation lying east of Madagascar, was previously ruled by France and Britain until it achieved independence in 1968. It became a republic in 1992. Sugar production is in decline but tourism is vital to the economy.

AREA 788 sq mi [2,040 sq km]
POPULATION 1,251,000 **CAPITAL** Port Louis

MEXICO

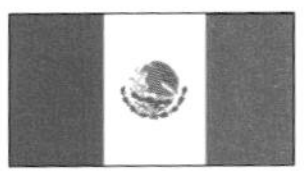

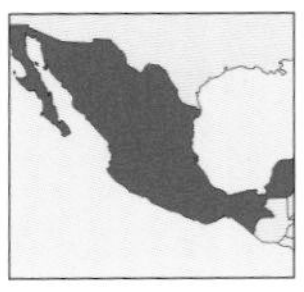

GEOGRAPHY The United Mexican States, as Mexico is officially named, is the world's most populous Spanish-speaking country. Much of the land is mountainous, although most people live on the central plateau. Mexico contains two large peninsulas, Lower (or Baja) California in the northwest and the flat Yucatán peninsula in the southeast.

The climate varies according to the altitude. The resort of Acapulco on the southwest coast has a dry and sunny climate. Mexico City, at about 7,546 ft [2,300 m] above sea level, is much cooler. Most rain occurs between June and September. The rainfall decreases north of Mexico City and northern Mexico is mainly arid.

POLITICS & ECONOMY In the mid-19th century, Mexico lost land to the United States, and between 1910 and 1921 violent revolutions created chaos.

Reforms were introduced in the 1920s and, in 1929, the Institutional Revolutionary Party (PRI) was formed. The PRI ruled Mexico effectively as a one-party state until it was finally defeated in 2001. The new president, Vicente Fox, faced many problems. He was succeeded in 2006 by Felipe Calderón, who won by an extremely narrow margin. Opposition supporters contested the result, but Calderón took up his office in December 2006.

The World Bank classifies Mexico as an "upper-middle-income" developing country. Agriculture is important. Food crops include beans, maize, rice, and wheat, while cash crops include coffee, cotton, fruits, and vegetables. Beef cattle, dairy cattle, and other livestock are raised and fishing is also important.

But oil and oil products are the chief exports, while manufacturing is the most valuable activity. Mexico is the world's leading silver producer, and it also mines copper, gold, lead, zinc, and other minerals. Many factories near the northern border assemble goods, such as car parts and electrical products, for US companies. These factories are called *maquiladoras*. Hope for the future lies in increasing economic cooperation with the USA and Canada

through NAFTA (North American Free Trade Agreement), which came into being on January 1, 1994.

AREA 756,061 sq mi [1,958,201 sq km]
POPULATION 108,701,000 **CAPITAL** Mexico City
GOVERNMENT Federal republic
ETHNIC GROUPS Mestizo 60%, Amerindian 30%, White 9%
LANGUAGES Spanish (official)
RELIGIONS Roman Catholic 90%, Protestant 6%
CURRENCY Mexican peso = 100 centavos

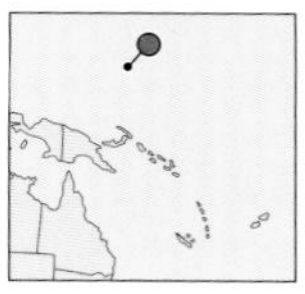

MICRONESIA

The Federated States of Micronesia, a former US territory covering a vast area in the western Pacific Ocean, became fully independent in 1991. The main export is copra. Fishing and tourism are also important.

AREA 271 sq mi [702 sq km]
POPULATION 108,000 **CAPITAL** Palikir

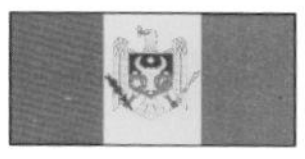
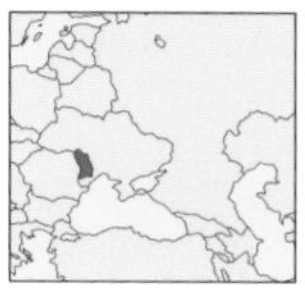

MOLDOVA

GEOGRAPHY The Republic of Moldova is a small country sandwiched between Ukraine and Romania. It was formerly one of the 15 republics that made up the Soviet Union. Much of the land is hilly and the highest areas are near the center of the country.

Moldova has a moderately continental climate, with warm summers and fairly cold winters when temperatures dip below freezing point. Most of the rain comes in the warmer months.

POLITICS & ECONOMY In the 14th century, the Moldavians formed a state called Moldavia. It included part of Romania and Bessarabia (now the modern country of Moldova). The Ottoman Turks took the area in the 16th century, but in 1812 Russia took over Bessarabia. In 1861, Moldavia and Walachia united to form Romania. Russia retook southern Bessarabia in 1878.

After World War I (1914–18), all of Bessarabia was returned to Romania, but the Soviet Union did not recognize this act. From 1944, the Moldovan Soviet Socialist Republic was part of the Soviet Union.

In 1989, the Moldovans asserted their independence and ethnicity by making Romanian the official language and, at the end of 1991, Moldova became an independent nation. But Trans-Dniester, an area east of the River Dniester, has sought autonomy. In 2006, its people voted for independence and union with Russia. This vote was not recognized internationally.

In 2001, Moldovans returned the Communist Party to power in a general election, becoming the first ex-Soviet republic to return the Communist Party to power. It was re-elected in 2005, although, by then, it advocated closer ties with the West – a matter of some concern to Russia.

In terms of its GNP per capita, Moldova is Europe's poorest country. Agriculture is the leading activity and products include fruits, maize, tobacco, and wine. Moldova has few natural resources and it imports materials and fuels for its industries. Light industries, such as food processing and factories making household appliances, are increasing.

AREA 13,070 sq mi [33,851 sq km]
POPULATION 4,320,000 **CAPITAL** Chişinău
GOVERNMENT Multiparty republic
ETHNIC GROUPS Moldovan/Romanian 65%, Ukrainian 14%, Russian 13%, others
LANGUAGES Moldovan/Romanian and Russian (official)
RELIGIONS Eastern Orthodox 98%
CURRENCY Moldovan leu = 100 bani

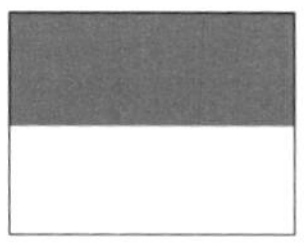
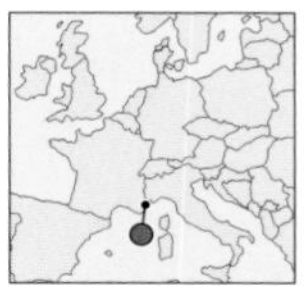

MONACO

The tiny Principality of Monaco consists of a narrow strip of coastline and a rocky peninsula on the French Riviera. Its considerable wealth is derived largely from banking, finance, gambling and tourism. Monaco's citizens do not pay any state tax. The reigning prince is Albert II, son of Prince Rainier III, who died in 2005, and his wife, the American actress Grace Kelly.

AREA 0.4 sq mi [1 sq km] **POPULATION** 33,000 **CAPITAL** Monaco

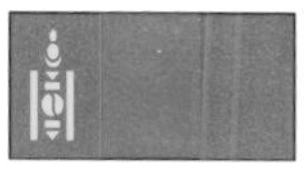
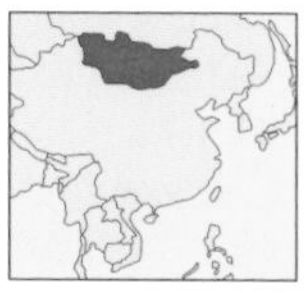

MONGOLIA

GEOGRAPHY The State of Mongolia is the world's largest landlocked country. It consists mainly of high plateaux, with the Gobi Desert in the southeast.

Ulan Bator lies on the northern edge of a desert plateau. It has bitterly cold winters. Summer temperatures are moderated by the altitude.

POLITICS & ECONOMY In the 13th century, Genghis Khan united the Mongolian peoples and built up a great empire. Under his grandson, Kublai Khan, the Mongol empire extended from Korea and China to eastern Europe and present-day Iraq.

The Mongol empire broke up in the late 14th century. In the early 17th century, Inner Mongolia came under Chinese control, and by the late 17th century Outer Mongolia had become a Chinese province. In 1911, the Mongolians drove the Chinese out of Outer Mongolia and made the area a Buddhist kingdom. But in 1924, under Russian influence, the Communist Mongolian People's Republic was set up. From the 1950s, Mongolia supported the Soviet Union in its disputes with China. In 1990, the people demonstrated for more freedom, and free elections in June 1990 were won by the Communist Mongolian People's Revolutionary Party (MPRP). The Democratic Union coalition won power in 1996, but the MPRP regained power in 2000. In 2004, after disputed elections, a coalition government was set up. In 2005, the MPRP candidate, Nambaryn Enkhbayar, became president.

The World Bank classifies Mongolia as a "lower-middle-income" developing country. Most people were once nomads, who moved around with their herds of sheep, cattle, goats, and horses. Under Communist rule, most people were moved into permanent homes on government-owned farms. But livestock and animal products remain leading exports. The Communists also developed industry, especially the mining of coal, copper, gold, molybdenum, tin and tungsten, and manufacturing. Minerals and fuels now account for around half of Mongolia's exports.

AREA 604,826 sq mi [1,566,500 sq km]
POPULATION 2,952,000 **CAPITAL** Ulan Bator
GOVERNMENT Multiparty republic **ETHNIC GROUPS** Khalkha Mongol 85%, Kazakh 6% **LANGUAGES** Khalkha Mongolian (official), Turkic, Russian **RELIGIONS** Tibetan Buddhist Lamaism 96%
CURRENCY Tugrik = 100 möngös

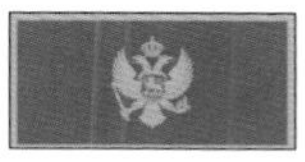
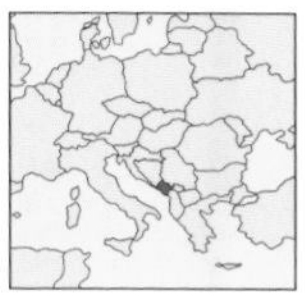

MONTENEGRO

The Republic of Montenegro became a fully independent nation in 2006. It was formerly part of the Union of Serbia and Montenegro and, before 2003, part of Yugoslavia. The coastal region has a Mediterranean climate. However, inland, the Dinaric Alps, which reach a height of 8,274 ft [2,522 m], have a more severe climate.

Serbia fell under Turkish rule in the 14th century, but Montenegro remained Christian. Montenegro was absorbed into Serbia in 1918. It became part of the Kingdom of the Serbs, Croats, and Slovenes, which was renamed Yugoslavia in 1929. After World War II, Montenegro was recognized as one of the six republics in the Federal People's Republic of Yugoslavia.

Manufacturing is the leading activity, and steel and aluminum are major products. But farming remains important. Forests cover more than half of the land.

AREA 5,415 sq mi [14,026 sq km]
POPULATION 685,000 **CAPITAL** Podgorica
GOVERNMENT Republic **ETHNIC GROUPS** Montenegrin 43%, Serb 32%, Bosnian 8%, Albanian 5%, others
LANGUAGES Serbian (official), Bosnian, Albanian, Croatian
RELIGIONS Orthodox, Islam, Roman Catholic
CURRENCY Euro = 100 cents

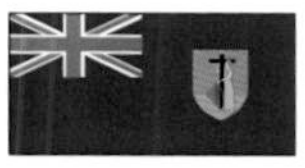
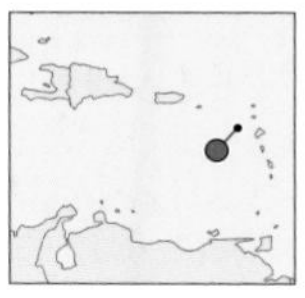

MONTSERRAT

Montserrat is a British overseas territory in the Caribbean Sea. The climate is tropical and hurricanes often cause much damage. Intermittent eruptions of the Soufrière Hills volcano between 1995 and 1998, and again in 2003, led to the emigration of many people and the virtual destruction of Plymouth, the capital. A new airport was opened in 2005.

AREA 39 sq mi [102 sq km] **POPULATION** 10,000 **CAPITAL** Plymouth

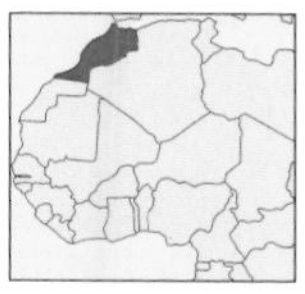

MOROCCO

GEOGRAPHY The Kingdom of Morocco lies in northwestern Africa. Its name comes from the Arabic Maghreb-el-Aksa, meaning "the farthest west." Behind the western coastal plain the land rises to a broad plateau and ranges of the Atlas Mountains. The High (Haut) Atlas contains the highest peak, Djebel Toubkal, at 13,665 ft [4,165 m]. East of the mountains, the land descends to the Sahara. The Canaries Current cools the Atlantic coast. Inland, summers are hot and dry. Winters are mild, with moderate rainfall. Snow often falls on the High Atlas Mountains.

POLITICS & ECONOMY The original people of Morocco were the Berbers. But in the 680s, Arab invaders introduced Islam and the Arabic language. By the early 20th century, France and Spain controlled Morocco, which became an independent kingdom in 1956. Although Morocco is a constitutional monarchy, King Hassan II ruled the country in a generally authoritarian way from the time of his accession to the throne in 1961 to his death in 1999. His successor, Mohamed VI, faced several problems, including that of Western Sahara, which he claimed for Morocco, and the activities of Islamic extremists, including suicide bombings in Casablanca in 2007.

Morocco is classified as a "lower-middle-income" developing country. It is the world's third largest producer of phosphate rock, which is used to make fertilizer. One of the reasons why Morocco wants to keep Western Sahara is that it, too, has large phosphate reserves. Farming employs about 40% of Moroccans. Chief crops include barley, beans, citrus fruits, maize, olives, sugar beet, and wheat. Processed phosphates are exported, but most of Morocco's manufactures are for home consumption. Fishing and tourism are also important.

AREA 172,413 sq mi [446,550 sq km]
POPULATION 33,757,000 **CAPITAL** Rabat
GOVERNMENT Constitutional monarchy
ETHNIC GROUPS Arab-Berber 99%
LANGUAGES Arabic (official), Berber dialects, French
RELIGIONS Islam 99% **CURRENCY** Moroccan dirham = 100 centimes

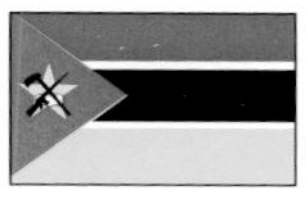
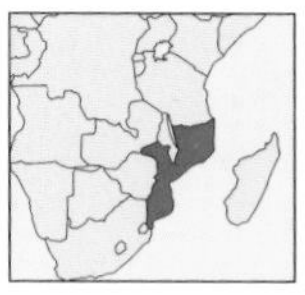

MOZAMBIQUE

GEOGRAPHY The Republic of Mozambique borders the Indian Ocean in southeastern Africa. The coastal plains are narrow in the north but broaden in the south. Inland lie plateaux and hills, which make up another two-fifths of the country. Mozambique has a mostly tropical climate. The capital Maputo, which lies outside the tropics, has hot and humid summers, though the winters are mild and fairly dry.

POLITICS & ECONOMY In 1885, when the European powers divided Africa, Mozambique was recognized as a Portuguese colony. But black African opposition to European rule gradually increased. In 1961, the Front for the Liberation of Mozambique (FRELIMO) was founded to oppose Portuguese rule. In 1964, FRELIMO launched a guerrilla war, which continued for ten years. Mozambique became independent in 1975.

After independence, Mozambique became a one-party state. Its government aided African nationalists in Rhodesia (now Zimbabwe) and South Africa. But the white governments of these countries helped an opposition group, the Mozambique National Resistance Movement (RENAMO) to lead an armed struggle against Mozambique's government. Civil war, combined with droughts, caused much suffering in the 1980s. In 1989, FRELIMO declared that it had dropped its Communist policies and ended one-party rule. The war ended in 1992 and multiparty elections in 1994 heralded more stable conditions. In 1995 Mozambique became the 53rd member of the Commonwealth.

In the early 1990s, the UN rated Mozambique as one of the world's poorest countries. The second half of the 1990s saw the start of renewed economic growth, but floods in 2000–1 and prolonged droughts in the mid-2000s proved to be major setbacks. About 80% of the people are poor farmers. Crops include cassava, cotton, maize, rice, and tea.

AREA 309,494 sq mi [801,590 sq km]
POPULATION 20,906,000 **CAPITAL** Maputo
GOVERNMENT Multiparty republic **ETHNIC GROUPS** Indigenous tribal groups (Shangaan, Chokwe, Manyika, Sena, Makua, others) 99%
LANGUAGES Portuguese (official), many others
RELIGIONS Traditional beliefs 50%, Christianity 30%, Islam 20%
CURRENCY Metical = 100 centavos

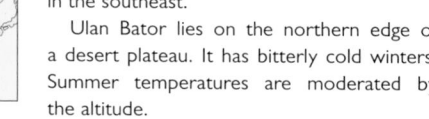

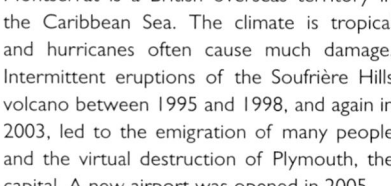

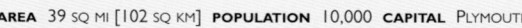

NAMIBIA

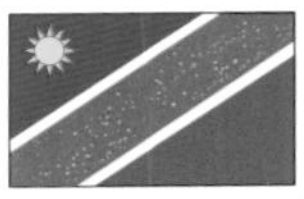

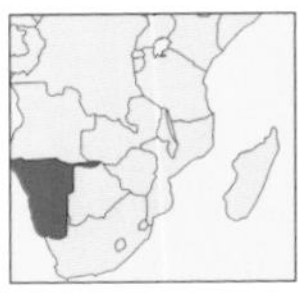

GEOGRAPHY The Republic of Namibia was formerly ruled by South Africa, which called it South West Africa. The country became independent in 1990. The coastal region contains the arid Namib Desert, which is virtually uninhabited. Inland is a central plateau, bordered by a rugged spine of mountains stretching north–south. Eastern Namibia contains part of the Kalahari Desert, a semidesert area which extends into Botswana. Namibia is a warm and arid country. Lying at 5,500 ft [1,700 m] above sea level, Windhoek has an average annual rainfall of about 15 inches [370 mm], often occurring during thunderstorms in the hot summer months.

POLITICS & ECONOMY During World War I, South African troops defeated the Germans who ruled what is now Namibia. After World War II, many people challenged South Africa's right to govern the territory and a civil war began in the 1960s between African guerrillas and South African troops. A ceasefire was agreed in 1989 and Namibia became independent in 1990. In the 1990s, the government pursued a policy of "national reconciliation." An enclave on the coast, called Walvis Bay (Walvisbaai), remained part of South Africa until 1994, when it was transferred to Namibia. In 2004, the nationalist leader, Sam Nujoma, president since 1990, retired and was succeeded by Hifikepunye Pohamba.

Namibia has reserves of diamonds, uranium, zinc, and copper. Minerals make up the bulk of the exports, though agriculture employs 20% of the people. Sea fishing is also important. Namibia has few industries, but tourism is expanding.

AREA 318,259 SQ MI [824,292 SQ KM]
POPULATION 2,055,000 **CAPITAL** WINDHOEK
GOVERNMENT MULTIPARTY REPUBLIC **ETHNIC GROUPS** OVAMBO 50%, KAVANGO 9%, HERERO 7%, DAMARA 7%, WHITE 6%, NAMA 5%
LANGUAGES ENGLISH (OFFICIAL), AFRIKAANS, GERMAN, INDIGENOUS DIALECTS **RELIGIONS** CHRISTIANITY 90% (LUTHERAN 51%)
CURRENCY NAMIBIAN DOLLAR = 100 CENTS

NAURU

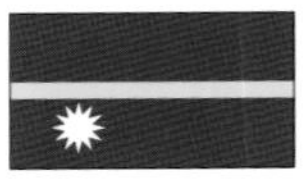

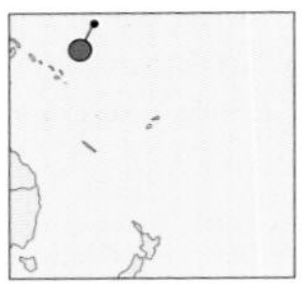

Nauru is the world's smallest republic, located in the western Pacific Ocean, close to the equator. Independent since 1968, Nauru's prosperity is based on phosphate mining, but the reserves are running out.

AREA 8 SQ MI [21 SQ KM]
POPULATION 14,000 **CAPITAL** YAREN

NEPAL

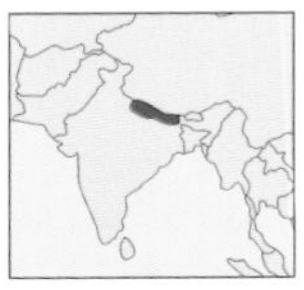

GEOGRAPHY Over three-quarters of Nepal lies in the Himalayan region, culminating in the world's highest peak (Mount Everest, or Chomolongma in Nepali) at 29,035 ft [8,850 m]. As a result, climatic conditions vary widely according to the altitude.

POLITICS & ECONOMY Nepal was united in the late 18th century, although its complex topography has ensured that it remains a diverse patchwork of peoples. From the mid-19th century to 1951, power was held by the royal Rana family. The first democratic elections in 32 years were held in 1991, but, by the early 21st century, Nepal faced many problems, including an uprising of Maoist guerrillas. In 2005, King Gyanendra seized power but failed to stop the conflict. In 2006, the Maoists, who demanded the abolition of the monarchy, joined a provisional coalition government. In elections in April 2008, the Maoists emerged as the largest single party and, in May, the national assembly voted to make Nepal a republic.

Agriculture remains the chief activity in this overwhelmingly rural country and the government is heavily dependent on aid. Tourism, centered around the high Himalaya, grows in importance each year, although Nepal was closed to foreigners until 1951. There are also ambitious plans to exploit the hydroelectric potential offered by the ferocious Himalayan rivers.

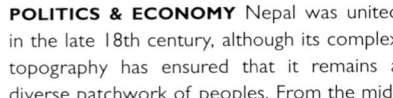

AREA 56,827 SQ MI [147,181 SQ KM] **POPULATION** 28,902,000
CAPITAL KATMANDU **GOVERNMENT** MULTIPARTY REPUBLIC
ETHNIC GROUPS BRAHMAN, CHETRI, NEWAR, GURUNG, MAGAR, TAMANG, SHERPA, AND OTHERS
LANGUAGES NEPALI (OFFICIAL), LOCAL LANGUAGES
RELIGIONS HINDUISM 86%, BUDDHISM 8%, ISLAM 4%
CURRENCY NEPALESE RUPEE = 100 PAISA

NETHERLANDS

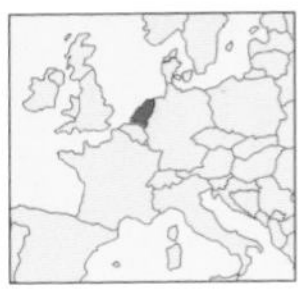

GEOGRAPHY The Netherlands lies at the western end of the North European Plain, which extends to the Ural Mountains in Russia. Except for the far southeastern corner, the Netherlands is flat and about 40% lies below sea level at high tide. To prevent flooding, the Dutch have built dykes (sea walls) to hold back the waves. Large areas which were once under the sea, but which have been reclaimed, are called polders. Because of its position on the North Sea, the Netherlands has a temperate climate, with mild, rainy winters.

POLITICS & ECONOMY Before the 16th century, the area that is now the Netherlands was under a succession of foreign rulers, including the Romans, the Germanic Franks, the French and the Spanish. The Dutch declared their independence from Spain in 1581 and their status was finally recognized by Spain in 1648. In the 17th century, the Dutch built up a great overseas empire, especially in Southeast Asia. But in the early 18th century, the Dutch lost control of the seas to England.

France controlled the Netherlands from 1795 to 1813. In 1815, the Netherlands, then containing Belgium and Luxembourg, became an independent kingdom. Belgium broke away in 1830 and Luxembourg followed in 1890.

The Netherlands was neutral in World War I (1914–18), but was occupied by Germany in World War II (1939–45). After the war, the Netherlands Indies became independent as Indonesia. The Netherlands became active in West European affairs. With Belgium and Luxembourg, it formed a customs union called Benelux in 1948. In 1949, it joined NATO (the North Atlantic Treaty Organization), and the European Coal and Steel Community (ECSC) in 1953. In 1957, it became a founder member of the European Economic Community (now the European Union) and, in 2002, it adopted the euro as its sole unit of currency. In 2002, an anti-immigration group made sweeping gains in national elections. It joined a coalition government, which collapsed later that year. Following elections in 2003, a center-right coalition took office.

The Netherlands is a highly industrialized country and industry and commerce are the most valuable activities. Its resources include natural gas, some oil, salt, and china clay. But the Netherlands imports many of the materials needed by its industries and it is, therefore, a major trading country. Industrial products are wide-ranging, including aircraft, chemicals, electronic equipment, machinery, textiles, and vehicles. Agriculture employs only 3% of the people, but scientific methods are used and yields are high. Dairy farming is the leading farming activity. Major products include barley, flowers and bulbs, potatoes, sugar beet, and wheat.

AREA 16,033 SQ MI [41,526 SQ KM]
POPULATION 16,571,000
CAPITAL AMSTERDAM; THE HAGUE (SEAT OF GOVERNMENT)
GOVERNMENT CONSTITUTIONAL MONARCHY
ETHNIC GROUPS DUTCH 83%, INDONESIAN, TURKISH, MOROCCAN AND OTHERS **LANGUAGES** DUTCH (OFFICIAL), FRISIAN
RELIGIONS ROMAN CATHOLIC 31%, PROTESTANT 21%, ISLAM 4%, OTHERS
CURRENCY EURO = 100 CENTS

NETHERLANDS ANTILLES

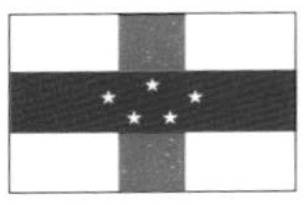

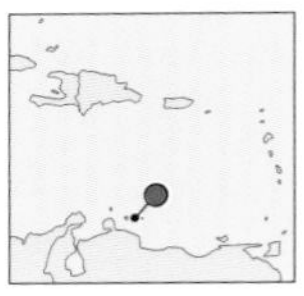

The Netherlands Antilles consists of two different island groups; one off the coast of Venezuela, and the other at the northern end of the Leeward Islands, some 500 mi [800 km] away. In 2006, Curaçao and Saint Maarten voted for autonomy, while the small islands of Bonaire, Saint Eustatius and Saba voted to become a type of Dutch municipality.

AREA 309 SQ MI [800 SQ KM] **POPULATION** 224,000 **CAPITAL** WILLEMSTAD

NEW CALEDONIA

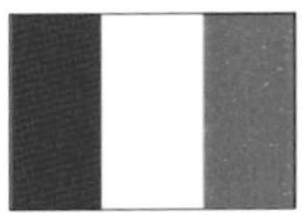

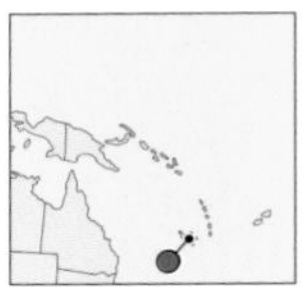

New Caledonia is the most southerly of the Melanesian countries in the Pacific. It has been a French possession since 1853 and an Overseas Territory since 1958. In 1998, France announced an agreement with local Melanesians that a vote on independence would be postponed until 2014. The country is rich in mineral resources, especially nickel.

AREA 7,172 SQ MI [18,575 SQ KM] **POPULATION** 222,000 **CAPITAL** NOUMÉA

NEW ZEALAND

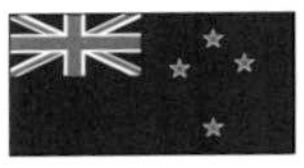

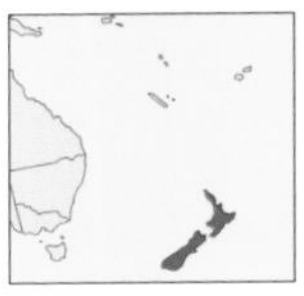

GEOGRAPHY New Zealand lies about 994 mi [1,600 km] southeast of Australia. It consists of two main islands and several other small ones. Much of North Island is volcanic. Active volcanoes include Ngauruhoe and Ruapehu. Hot springs and geysers are common, and steam from the ground is used to produce electricity. The Southern Alps, which contain the country's highest peak, Aoraki Mount Cook, at 12,313 ft [3,753 m], form the backbone of South Island. The island also has some large, fertile plains.

Auckland in the north has a warm, humid climate throughout the year. Wellington has cooler summers, while in Dunedin, in the southeast, temperatures sometimes dip below freezing in winter. The rainfall is heaviest on the western highlands.

POLITICS & ECONOMY Evidence suggests that early Maori settlers arrived in New Zealand more than 1,000 years ago. The Dutch navigator Abel Tasman reached New Zealand in 1642, but his discovery was not followed up. In 1769, the British Captain James Cook rediscovered the islands. In the early 19th century, British settlers arrived and, in 1840, under the Treaty of Waitangi, Britain took possession of the islands. From the 1870s, the Maoris were gradually integrated into colonial society.

In 1907, New Zealand became a self-governing dominion in the British Commonwealth. The country's economy developed quickly and the people became increasingly prosperous. However, after Britain joined the European Economic Community in 1973, New Zealand's exports to Britain shrank and the country had to reassess its economic and defense strategies and seek new markets. The world recession led the government to cut back on welfare spending in the 1990s. The preservation of Maori culture and Maori rights are major issues. The Maoris, a Polynesian people, make up about 13% of the population. Other mainly Polynesian Pacific people make up another 6%. Ties with Britain have been reduced. Helen Clark, leader of the Labor Party and prime minister since 1999, has expressed the view that New Zealand will eventually abolish the monarchy and become a republic. In 2005, the Labor Party won narrowly in national elections and formed a coalition with other parties.

The economy once depended on agriculture, but manufacturing now employs twice as many people as farming. Meat and dairy products are leading commodities. Sheep rearing has declined as the area under cattle, deer, and vines has expanded. Crops include barley, fruits, potatoes and other vegetables, and wheat.

AREA 104,453 SQ MI [270,534 SQ KM]
POPULATION 4,116,000 **CAPITAL** WELLINGTON
GOVERNMENT CONSTITUTIONAL MONARCHY
ETHNIC GROUPS NEW ZEALAND EUROPEAN 74%, NEW ZEALAND MAORI 13%, POLYNESIAN 6% **LANGUAGES** ENGLISH AND MAORI (BOTH OFFICIAL) **RELIGIONS** ANGLICAN 24%, PRESBYTERIAN 18%, ROMAN CATHOLIC 15%, OTHERS
CURRENCY NEW ZEALAND DOLLAR = 100 CENTS

NICARAGUA

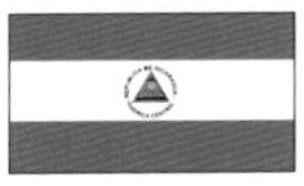

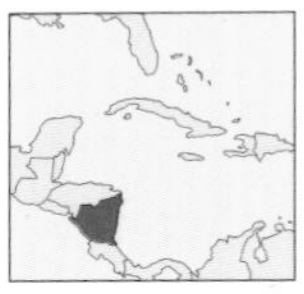

GEOGRAPHY The Republic of Nicaragua is a large country in Central America. In the east is a broad plain bordering the Caribbean Sea. The plain is drained by rivers that flow from the Central Highlands. The fertile western Pacific region contains about 40 volcanoes, many of which are active, and earthquakes are common.

Nicaragua has a tropical climate. Managua is hot throughout the year and there is a marked rainy season from May to October. In October 1998, Hurricane Mitch caused great devastation in Nicaragua. The Central Highlands and Caribbean region are cooler and wetter. The wettest region is the humid Caribbean plain.

POLITICS & ECONOMY In 1502, Christopher Columbus claimed the area for Spain, which ruled Nicaragua until 1821. By the early 20th century, the United States had considerable influence in the country and, in 1912, US forces entered Nicaragua to protect US interests. From 1927 to 1933, rebels under General Augusto César Sandino, tried to drive US forces out of the country. In 1933, US marines set up a Nicaraguan army, the National Guard, to help to defeat the rebels. Its leader, Anastasio Somoza Garcia, had Sandino murdered in 1934 and, from 1937, Somoza ruled as a dictator.

In the mid-1970s, many people began to protest against Somoza's rule. Many joined a guerrilla force, called the Sandinista National Liberation Front, named after General Sandino. The rebels defeated the Somoza regime in 1979. In the 1980s, the US-supported forces, called the "Contras," launched a

campaign against the Sandinista government. The US government opposed the Sandinista regime, under Daniel José Ortega Saavedra, claiming that it was a Communist dictatorship. A coalition, the National Opposition Union, defeated the Sandinistas in 1990. In 2001, the Sandinista candidate, Daniel Ortega, was defeated in presidential elections, but he was re-elected president of Nicaragua in 2006.

In the early 1990s, Nicaragua faced many problems in rebuilding its shattered economy. Agriculture is the main activity, employing more than a third of the population. Coffee, cotton, sugar, and bananas are grown for export, while rice is the main food crop.

AREA 50,193 sq mi [130,000 sq km]
POPULATION 5,675,000 **CAPITAL** Managua
GOVERNMENT Multiparty republic
ETHNIC GROUPS Mestizo 69%, White 17%, Black 9%, Amerindian 5%
LANGUAGES Spanish (official)
RELIGIONS Roman Catholic 85%, Protestant
CURRENCY Córdoba oro (gold córdoba) = 100 centavos

NIGER

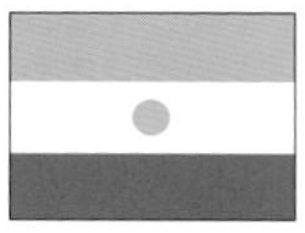

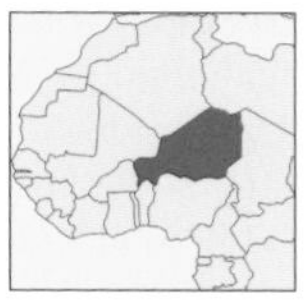

GEOGRAPHY The Republic of Niger is a landlocked nation in north-central Africa. The northern plateaux lie in the Sahara Desert, while Central Niger contains the rugged Aïr Mountains. The most fertile, densely populated region is the Niger valley in the southwest.

Niger has a tropical climate and the south has a rainy season between June and September. The north is practically rainless.

POLITICS & ECONOMY Since independence in 1960, Niger, a French territory from 1900, has suffered severe droughts. Food shortages and the collapse of the traditional nomadic way of life of some of Niger's people have caused political instability. After a period of military rule, a multiparty constitution was adopted in 1992, but the military again seized power in 1996. Later that year, the coup leader, Colonel Ibrahim Barre Mainassara, was elected president. He was assassinated in 1999, but parliamentary rule was rapidly restored and Tandja Mamadou was elected president. He was re-elected in December 2004.

Niger's chief resource is uranium and the country is the fourth largest producer. In 2003, accusations that Niger supplied uranium to Iraq for its nuclear program proved to be baseless. Some tin and tungsten are also mined, though other mineral reserves are largely untouched. Despite its resources, Niger is one of the world's poorest countries. Farming employs 80% of the people, but only 3% of the land can be used for crops and 8% for grazing.

AREA 489,189 sq mi [1,267,000 sq km]
POPULATION 12,895,000 **CAPITAL** Niamey
GOVERNMENT Multiparty republic **ETHNIC GROUPS** Hausa 56%, Djerma 22%, Tuareg 8%, Fula 8%, others **LANGUAGES** French (official), Hausa, Djerma **RELIGIONS** Islam 80%, indigenous beliefs, Christianity **CURRENCY** CFA franc = 100 centimes

NIGERIA

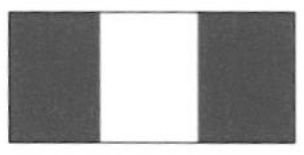

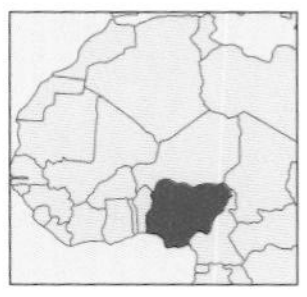

GEOGRAPHY The Federal Republic of Nigeria is the most populous nation in Africa. The country's main rivers are the Niger and Benue, which meet in central Nigeria. North of the two river valleys are high plains and plateaux. The Lake Chad basin is in the northeast, with the Sokoto plains in the northwest. The south contains hilly uplands and plains. The south has a hot, rainy climate. The north is drier and often hotter than the south.

POLITICS & ECONOMY Nigeria has a long artistic tradition. Major cultures include the Nok (500 BC to AD 200), the Ife, a major Yoruba culture which developed about 1,000 years ago, and the Benin (15th to 17th centuries). Britain gradually extended its influence over the area in the second half of the 19th century.

Nigeria became independent in 1960 and a federal republic in 1963. A federal constitution dividing the country into regions was necessary because Nigeria contains more than 250 ethnic and linguistic groups, as well as several religious ones. Local rivalries have long been a threat to national unity, and six new states were created in 1996 in an attempt to overcome this. Civil war occurred between 1967 and 1970, when the people of the southeast attempted unsuccessfully to secede during the Biafran War. Between 1960 and 1998, Nigeria had only nine years of civilian government.

In 1998–9, civilian rule was restored and Olusegun Obasanjo became president. He was re-elected in 2003. Nigeria faced many problems, including violence in the Niger delta region and religious conflict. Presidential elections in 2007 were marked by allegations of vote-rigging and fraud. The victor was Umar Yar-dua, the Muslim governor of the northern state of Katsina.

Nigeria is a developing country with great potential. Its chief natural resource is oil, which accounts for most of its exports. Agriculture employs 59% of the people and the country is a major producer of cocoa, palm oil and palm kernels, groundnuts (peanuts), and rubber. Industry is increasing and manufactures include cement, chemicals, fertilizers, textiles, and timber.

AREA 356,667 sq mi [923,768 sq km]
POPULATION 135,031,000 **CAPITAL** Abuja
GOVERNMENT Federal multiparty republic
ETHNIC GROUPS Hausa and Fulani 29%, Yoruba 21%, Ibo (or Igbo) 18%, Ijaw 10%, Kanuri 4%, many others
LANGUAGES English (official), Hausa, Yoruba, Ibo
RELIGIONS Islam 50%, Christianity 40%, traditional beliefs 10%
CURRENCY Naira = 100 kobo

NORTHERN MARIANA ISLANDS

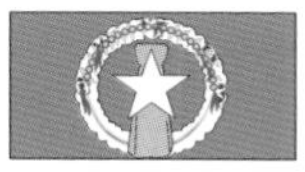

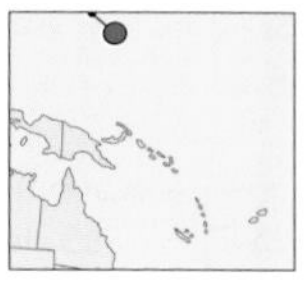

The Commonwealth of the Northern Mariana Islands contains 16 mountainous islands north of Guam in the western Pacific Ocean. In a 1975 plebiscite, the islanders voted for Commonwealth status in union with the United States and, in 1986, they were granted US citizenship.

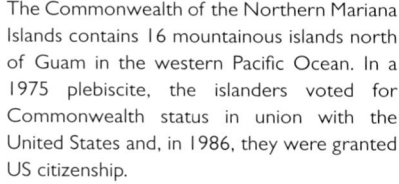

AREA 179 sq mi [464 sq km] **POPULATION** 85,000 **CAPITAL** Saipan

NORWAY

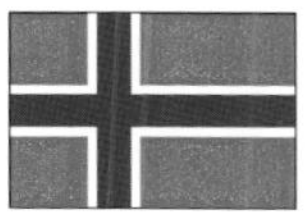

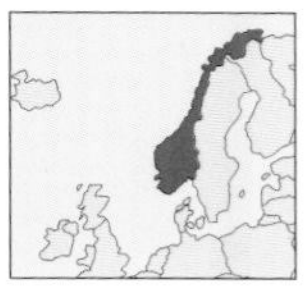

GEOGRAPHY The Kingdom of Norway forms the western part of the rugged Scandinavian peninsula. The deep inlets along the highly indented coastline were worn out by glaciers during the Ice Age. The warm North Atlantic Drift off the coast of Norway moderates the climate, with mild winters and cool summers. Nearly all the ports are ice-free throughout the year. Inland, winters are colder and snow cover lasts for at least three months a year.

POLITICS & ECONOMY Between about AD 800 and 1100, Norwegian Vikings ravaged western Europe. In 1380, Norway was united with Denmark. But in 1814, Denmark handed Norway over to Sweden, though it kept Norway's colonies – Greenland, Iceland and the Færoe Islands. Norway briefly became independent, but Swedish forces defeated the Norwegians and Norway had to accept Sweden's king as its ruler. The union with Sweden ended in 1903. Germany occupied Norway during World War II (1939–45). Norway recovered quickly after the war and it now has one of the world's highest standards of living. In 1960, Norway and six other countries formed the European Free Trade Association (EFTA). But, in 1994, Norway voted against joining the European Union. In the 1990s and 2000s, Norwegian diplomats sought to broker peace deals in Palestine and Sri Lanka.

Norway's chief resources and exports are oil and natural gas which come from wells under the North Sea. Farmland covers only 3% of the land. Dairy farming and meat production are important, but Norway has to import food. Norway has many industries powered by cheap hydroelectricity.

AREA 125,049 sq mi [323,877 sq km]
POPULATION 4,628,000 **CAPITAL** Oslo
GOVERNMENT Constitutional monarchy
ETHNIC GROUPS Norwegian 97%
LANGUAGES Norwegian (official)
RELIGIONS Evangelical Lutheran 86%
CURRENCY Norwegian krone = 100 ore

OMAN

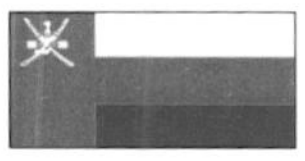

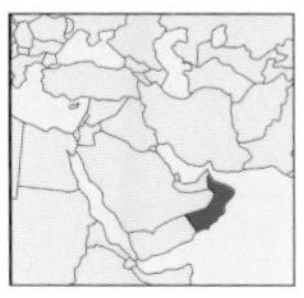

GEOGRAPHY The Sultanate of Oman occupies the southeastern corner of the Arabian peninsula. It also includes the tip of the Musandam peninsula, overlooking the strategic Strait of Hormuz.

Oman has a hot tropical climate. In Muscat, temperatures may reach 117°F [47°C] in the summer months.

POLITICS & ECONOMY British influence in Oman dates back to the end of the 18th century, but the country became fully independent in 1971. Since then, using revenue from oil, which was discovered in 1964, the absolute ruler, Qaboos ibn Said, and his government have sought to modernize Oman. In 2000, Oman held elections to its consultative parliament. In 2004, the Sultan appointed Oman's first woman minister without portfolio. In 2005, 31 Islamists were convicted of trying to overthrow the government, but they were later pardoned.

Oman has an "upper-middle-income" economy. Oil accounts for the bulk of the exports and huge natural gas deposits were discovered in 1991. But agriculture remains important. Crops include alfalfa, bananas, coconuts, dates, limes, tobacco, vegetables, and wheat. Fishing is also important, but Oman imports food.

AREA 119,498 sq mi [309,500 sq km]
POPULATION 3,205,000 **CAPITAL** Muscat
GOVERNMENT Monarchy with consultative council
ETHNIC GROUPS Arab, Baluchi, Indian, Pakistani
LANGUAGES Arabic (official), Baluchi, English
RELIGIONS Islam (mainly Ibadhi), Hinduism
CURRENCY Omani rial = 100 baizas

PAKISTAN

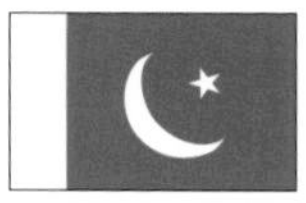

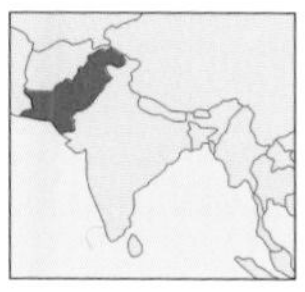

GEOGRAPHY The Islamic Republic of Pakistan contains high mountains, fertile plains and rocky deserts. The Karakoram range, which contains K2, the world's second highest peak, lies in the northern part of Jammu and Kashmir, which is occupied by Pakistan but claimed by India. Other mountains rise in the west. Plains, drained by the River Indus and its tributaries, occupy much of eastern Pakistan. Arid areas include the Thar Desert and the Baluchistan plateau. Most of Pakistan has hot summers and mild winters, though the mountains have cold winters. The rainfall is generally sparse.

POLITICS & ECONOMY Pakistan was the site of the Indus Valley civilization which developed about 4,500 years ago. But Pakistan's modern history dates from 1947, when British India was divided into India and Pakistan. Muslim Pakistan was divided into two parts: East and West Pakistan, but East Pakistan broke away in 1971 to become Bangladesh. In 1948–9, 1965 and 1971, Pakistan and India clashed over Kashmir. In 1998, Pakistan responded in kind to India's nuclear weapons tests, but, in 2003–5, Pakistan and India launched a series of initiatives aimed at achieving peace.

Pakistan has been subject to several periods of military rule, but elections in 1988 led to Benazir Bhutto becoming prime minister. She was removed from office in 1990, but she returned as prime minister between 1993 and 1996. In 1997, Narwaz Sharif was elected prime minister, but a military coup in 1999 brought General Pervez Musharraf to power. Musharraf's powers were increased in 2002 despite international criticism. The security situation deteriorated in 2006–7. In 2007, Musharraf was re-elected president and stood down as army chief. He called for elections in February 2008. During the election campaign, the opposition leader Benazir Bhutto was assassinated. However, the opposition parties heavily defeated Musharraf's party and set up a coalition government.

According to the World Bank, Pakistan is a "low-income" developing country. The economy is based on farming or rearing goats and sheep. Agriculture employs 40% of the people. Major crops include cotton, fruits, rice, sugarcane, and wheat.

AREA 307,372 sq mi [796,095 sq km]
POPULATION 164,742,000 **CAPITAL** Islamabad
GOVERNMENT Military regime **ETHNIC GROUPS** Punjabi, Sindhi, Pashtun (Pathan), Baluchi, Muhajir
LANGUAGES Urdu (official), many others
RELIGIONS Islam 97%, Christianity, Hinduism
CURRENCY Pakistani rupee = 100 paisa

PALAU

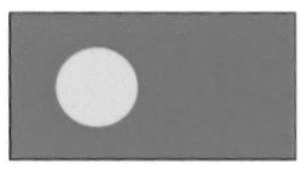

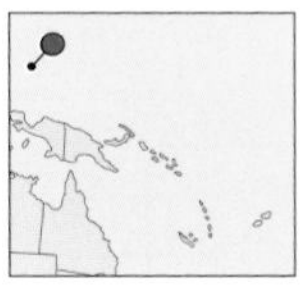

The Republic of Palau became fully independent in 1994, after the USA refused to accede to a 1979 referendum that declared this island nation a nuclear-free zone. In December 1994 Palau joined the United Nations. The economy relies heavily on US aid, tourism, fishing and subsistence agriculture. The main crops include cassava, coconuts, and copra.

AREA 177 sq mi [459 sq km] **POPULATION** 21,000 **CAPITAL** Melekeok

PANAMA

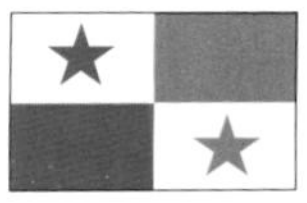

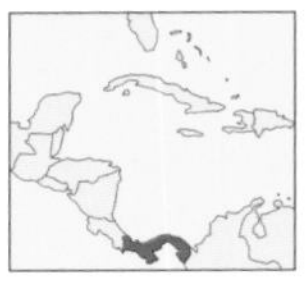

GEOGRAPHY The Republic of Panama forms an isthmus linking Central America to South America. The Panama Canal, which is 50.7 mi [81.6 km] long, cuts across the isthmus. It has made the country a major transport center.

Panama has a tropical climate. Temperatures are high, though the mountains are much cooler than the coastal plains. The main rainy season is between May and December.

POLITICS & ECONOMY Christopher Columbus landed in Panama in 1502 and Spain soon took the area. In 1821, Panama became independent from Spain and a province of Colombia.

In 1903, Colombia refused a request by the United States to build a canal. Panama then revolted against Colombia, and became independent. The United States then began to build the canal, which was opened in 1914. The United States administered the Panama Canal Zone, a strip of land along the canal. But many Panamanians resented US influence and, in 1979, the Canal Zone was returned to Panama. Control of the canal itself was handed over by the USA to Panama on December 31, 1999.

Panama's government has changed many times since independence, and there have been periods of military dictatorships, including that of General Manuel Antonio Noriega in the 1980s. He was finally convicted of drug offences in the United States in 1992. Panama held national elections in 1994. In 1999, Mireya Moscoso became Panama's first woman president. She was succeeded in 2004 by Martin Torrijos, son of a former military dictator.

The World Bank classifies Panama as a "lower-middle-income" developing country. The Panama Canal is an important source of revenue and, in 2006, a plan was announced to widen the canal to take giant container ships. Away from the canal, the main activity is agriculture, which employs 14% of the people.

AREA 29,157 sq mi [75,517 sq km] **POPULATION** 3,242,000
CAPITAL Panamá **GOVERNMENT** Multiparty republic
ETHNIC GROUPS Mestizo 70%, Black and Mulatto 14%, White 10%, Amerindian 6% **LANGUAGES** Spanish (official), English **RELIGIONS** Roman Catholic 85%, Protestant 15%
CURRENCY US dollar; Balboa = 100 centésimos

PAPUA NEW GUINEA

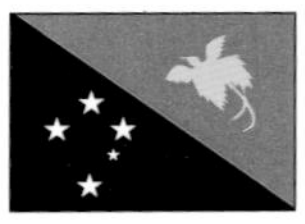

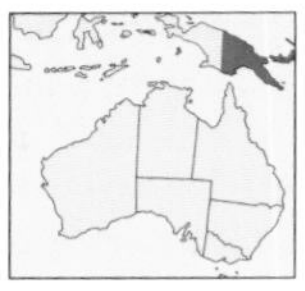

GEOGRAPHY Papua New Guinea is an independent country in the Pacific Ocean, north of Australia. It is part of a Pacific island region called Melanesia. Papua New Guinea includes the eastern part of New Guinea, the Bismarck Archipelago, the northern Solomon Islands, the D'Entrecasteaux Islands and the Louisiade Archipelago. The land is largely mountainous.

Papua New Guinea has a tropical climate, with high temperatures throughout the year. Most of the rain occurs during the monsoon season (from December to April), when the northwesterly winds blow. Winds blow from the southeast during the dry season.

POLITICS & ECONOMY The Dutch took western New Guinea (now part of Indonesia) in 1828, but it was not until 1884 that Germany took northeastern New Guinea and Britain took the southeast. In 1906, Britain handed the southeast over to Australia. It then became known as the Territory of Papua. When World War I broke out in 1914, Australia took German New Guinea and, in 1921, the League of Nations gave Australia a mandate to rule the area, which was named the Territory of New Guinea. Japan invaded New Guinea in 1942, but the Allies reconquered the area in 1944. In 1949, Papua and New Guinea were combined into the Territory of Papua and New Guinea. Papua New Guinea became fully independent in 1975.

Mining is important. An important mine was on Bougainville, where a secessionist group declared the island independent. Under a peace treaty in 2001, Bougainville became autonomous and held elections in 2005. In 2004, Australia sent police to Papua New Guinea to help fight crime. They were withdrawn in 2005, following a Supreme Court ruling that their presence was unconstitutional.

The country has a "lower-middle-income" economy. Agriculture employs 70% of the people, mostly at subsistence level. Petroleum and minerals, notably copper, are major exports.

AREA 178,703 sq mi [462,840 sq km] **POPULATION** 5,796,000
CAPITAL Port Moresby **GOVERNMENT** Constitutional monarchy
ETHNIC GROUPS Papuan, Melanesian, Micronesian **LANGUAGES** English (official), Melanesian Pidgin; more than 700 indigenous languages **RELIGIONS** Traditional beliefs 34%, Roman Catholic 22%, Lutheran 16% **CURRENCY** Kina = 100 toea

PARAGUAY

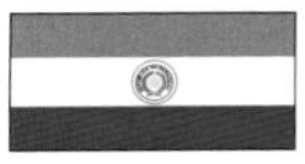

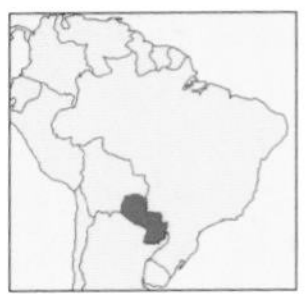

GEOGRAPHY The Republic of Paraguay is a landlocked country and rivers, notably the Paraná, Pilcomayo (Brazo Sur) and Paraguay, form most of its borders. A flat region called the Gran Chaco lies in the northwest, while the southeast contains plains, hills and plateaux. Northern Paraguay lies in the tropics, while the south is subtropical. Most of the country has a warm, humid climate.

POLITICS & ECONOMY In 1776, Paraguay became part of a large colony called the Viceroyalty of La Plata, with Buenos Aires as the capital. Paraguayans opposed this move and the country declared its independence in 1811.

For many years, Paraguay was torn by internal strife and conflict with its neighbors. A war against Brazil, Argentina and Uruguay (1865–70) led to the deaths of more than half of Paraguay's population, and a great loss of territory.

General Alfredo Stroessner took power in 1954 and ruled as a dictator. His government imprisoned many opponents. Stroessner was overthrown in 1989 (he died in exile in Brazil in 2006). However, the return of democracy in the years that followed often seemed precarious, because of rivalries between politicians and army leaders, together with economic problems arising partly from the severe problems experienced in neighboring Argentina and Brazil in 1999. In 2008, a former Roman Catholic bishop, Fernando Lugo, who was regarded as a champion of the poor, was elected president. His victory ended more than six decades of rule by the Colorado Party.

The World Bank classifies Paraguay as a "lower-middle-income" developing country. Agriculture and forestry, employing about a third of the population, are important. Paraguay produces hydroelectricity and exports power to its neighbors.

AREA 157,047 sq mi [406,752 sq km]
POPULATION 6,669,000 **CAPITAL** Asunción
GOVERNMENT Multiparty republic **ETHNIC GROUPS** Mestizo 95%
LANGUAGES Spanish and Guaraní (both official)
RELIGIONS Roman Catholic 90%, Protestant
CURRENCY Guaraní = 100 céntimos

PERU

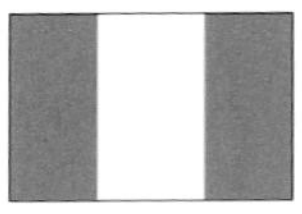

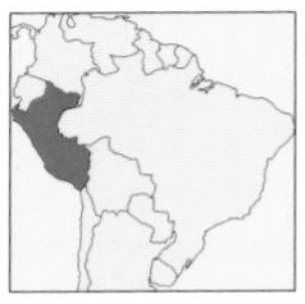

GEOGRAPHY The Republic of Peru lies in the tropics in western South America. A narrow coastal plain borders the Pacific Ocean in the west. Inland are ranges of the Andes Mountains, which rise to 22,205 ft [6,768 m] at Mount Huascarán, an extinct volcano. East of the Andes lies the Amazon basin.

Lima, on the coastal plain, has an arid climate. The coastal region is chilled by the cold, offshore Humboldt Current. The rainfall increases inland and many mountains in the high Andes are snow-capped.

POLITICS & ECONOMY Spanish conquistadors conquered Peru in the 1530s. In 1820, an Argentinian, José de San Martín, led an army into Peru and declared it independent. But Spain still held large areas. In 1823, the Venezuelan Simon Bolívar led another army into Peru and, in 1824, one of his generals defeated the Spaniards at Ayacucho. The Spaniards surrendered in 1826. Peru suffered much instability throughout the 19th century.

Instability continued in the 20th century. In 1980, when civilian rule was restored, a left-wing group called the Sendero Luminoso, or the "Shining Path," began guerrilla warfare against the government. In 1990, Alberto Fujimori, son of Japanese immigrants, became president. In 1992, he suspended the constitution and dismissed the legislature. The guerrilla leader, Abimael Guzmán, was arrested in 1992. Fujimori resigned and left Peru after disputed elections in 2000. Alejandro Toledo became the first Amerindian Peruvian to serve as president (2001–6). In 2006, a state of emergency was declared in six central provinces after suspected "Shining Path" activity. Later that year, Guzmán was found guilty and sentenced to life imprisonment.

The World Bank classifies Peru as a "lower-middle-income" developing country. Major food crops include beans, maize, potatoes, and rice. Fish products are exported, but the most valuable export is copper. Peru also produces lead, silver, zinc, and iron ore.

AREA 496,222 sq mi [1,285,216 sq km]
POPULATION 28,675,000 **CAPITAL** Lima
GOVERNMENT Transitional republic **ETHNIC GROUPS** Amerindian 45%, Mestizo 37%, White 15% **LANGUAGES** Spanish and Quechua (both official), Aymara, other Amazonian languages **RELIGIONS** Roman Catholic 90% **CURRENCY** New sol = 100 centavos

PHILIPPINES

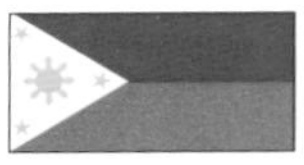

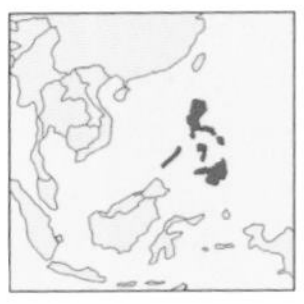

GEOGRAPHY The Republic of the Philippines is an island country in southeastern Asia. It includes about 7,100 islands, of which 2,770 are named and about 1,000 are inhabited. Luzon and Mindanao, the two largest islands, make up more than two-thirds of the country. The land is mainly mountainous.

The country has a hot tropical climate. The dry season runs from December to April. The rest of the year is wet. Much of the rainfall comes from the typhoons which periodically strike the east coast. In November 2006, a powerful typhoon struck Luzon in the Philippines. The typhoon triggered mudslides on the slopes of Mount Mayon, one of the country's many volcanoes. The mudslides destroyed several villages and killed around 1,000 people.

POLITICS & ECONOMY The first European to reach the Philippines was the Portuguese navigator Ferdinand Magellan in 1521. Spanish explorers claimed the region in 1565 when they established a settlement on Cebu. The Spaniards ruled the country until 1898, when the United States took over at the end of the Spanish–American War. Japan invaded the Philippines in 1941, but US forces returned in 1944. The country became fully independent as the Republic of the Philippines in 1946.

Since independence, the country's problems have included armed uprisings by left-wing guerrillas demanding land reform, and Muslim separatist groups, crime, corruption and unemployment. The dominant figure in recent times was Ferdinand Marcos, who ruled in a dictatorial manner from 1965 to 1986. His successors were Corazon Aquino (1986–92), Fidel Ramos (1992–8), and Joseph Estrada, who resigned following accusations of corruption. He was succeeded by Vice-President Gloria Arroyo, who was re-elected president in 2004. Conflict continued in the south and, in 2006, the government declared a state of emergency after the army said that it had prevented a planned coup. Following mass demonstrations, the state of emergency was soon lifted.

The Philippines is a developing country. Agriculture employs around 30% of the people. The main foods are rice and maize, while bananas, cocoa, coffee, sugarcane, and tobacco are grown commercially. Shellfish and sea fishing in coastal waters are also important, while manufacturing plays an increasingly significant part in the economy.

AREA 115,830 sq mi [300,000 sq km]
POPULATION 91,077,000 **CAPITAL** Manila
GOVERNMENT Multiparty republic
ETHNIC GROUPS Christian Malay 92%, Muslim Malay 4%, Chinese and others **LANGUAGES** Filipino (Tagalog) and English (both official), Spanish, many others
RELIGIONS Roman Catholic 83%, Protestant 9%, Islam 5%
CURRENCY Philippine peso = 100 centavos

PITCAIRN

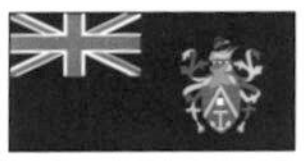

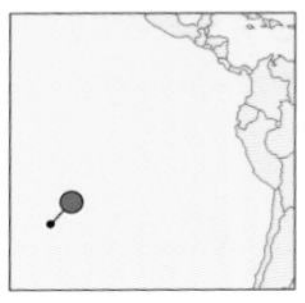

Pitcairn Island is a British overseas territory in the Pacific Ocean. Its inhabitants are descendants of the original settlers – nine mutineers from HMS *Bounty* and 18 Tahitians who arrived in 1790.

AREA 21 sq mi [55 sq km]
POPULATION 48 **CAPITAL** Adamstown

POLAND

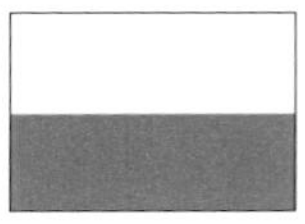

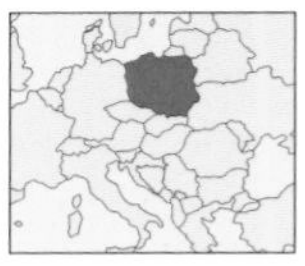

GEOGRAPHY The Republic of Poland faces the Baltic Sea and, behind its lagoon-fringed coast, lies a broad plain. A plateau lies in the southeast, while the Sudeten Highlands straddle part of the border with the Czech Republic. Part of the Carpathian Range (the Tatra) lies in the southeast.

Poland's climate is influenced by its position in Europe. Warm, moist air masses come from the west, while cold air masses come from the north and east. Summers are warm, but winters are cold and snowy.

POLITICS & ECONOMY Poland's boundaries have changed several times in the last 200 years, partly as a result of its geographical location between the powers of Germany and Russia. It disappeared from the map in the late 18th century, when a Polish state called the Grand Duchy of Warsaw was set up. But in 1815, the country was partitioned, between Austria, Prussia and Russia. Poland became independent in 1918, but in 1939 it was divided between Germany and the Soviet Union. The country again became independent in 1945, when it lost land to Russia

but gained some from Germany. Communists took power in 1948, but opposition mounted and eventually became focused through an organization called Solidarity.

Solidarity was led by a trade unionist, Lech Walesa. A coalition government was formed between Solidarity and the Communists in 1989. In 1990, the Communist Party was dissolved and Walesa became president. But Walesa faced many problems in turning Poland toward a market economy, and he was defeated in presidential elections in 1995. But his successor followed westward-looking policies. Poland joined NATO in 1999 and the European Union in 2004. In 2005, a nationalist, Lech Kaczynski, was elected president. Following elections in 2007, Donald Tusk, chairman of the pro-European Civic Platform, replaced Jaroslaw Kaczynski, the president's twin brother, as prime minister.

Poland has large reserves of coal and deposits of various minerals which are used in its factories. Manufactures include chemicals, processed food, machinery, ships, steel, and textiles.

AREA 124,807 SQ MI [323,250 SQ KM]
POPULATION 38,518,000 **CAPITAL** WARSAW
GOVERNMENT MULTIPARTY REPUBLIC
ETHNIC GROUPS POLISH 97%, BELARUSIAN, UKRAINIAN, GERMAN
LANGUAGES POLISH (OFFICIAL) **RELIGIONS** ROMAN CATHOLIC 95%, EASTERN ORTHODOX **CURRENCY** ZLOTY = 100 GROSZY

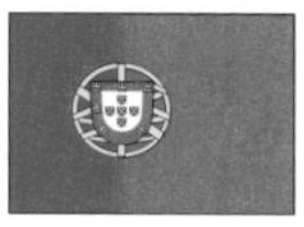

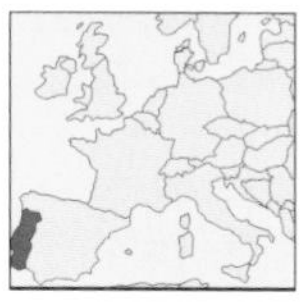

PORTUGAL

GEOGRAPHY The Republic of Portugal is the most westerly of Europe's mainland countries. The land rises from the coastal plains on the Atlantic Ocean to the western edge of the huge plateau, or Meseta, which occupies most of the Iberian peninsula. The climate is moderated by winds blowing from the Atlantic Ocean. Summers are cooler and winters are milder than in other Mediterranean lands. Portugal also contains two autonomous regions, the Azores and Madeira island groups.

POLITICS & ECONOMY Portugal became a separate country, independent of Spain, in 1143. In the 15th century, Portugal led the "Age of European Exploration." This led to the growth of a large Portuguese empire, with colonies in Africa, Asia and, most valuable of all, Brazil in South America. Portuguese power began to decline in the 16th century and, between 1580 and 1640, Portugal was ruled by Spain. Portugal lost Brazil in 1822 and, in 1910, Portugal became a republic. Instability hampered progress and army officers seized power in 1926. In 1928, they chose Antonio de Salazar to be minister of finance.

Salazar became prime minister in 1932 and ruled as a dictator from 1933 until 1968. In 1974, army officers mounted a coup. The new regime made most of Portugal's colonies independent and held free elections in 1978. Portugal joined the European Community (now the European Union) in 1986 and, in 2002, the euro became the sole unit of currency. In 2005, the Socialists, led by a moderate, José Socrates, won a decisive victory in parliamentary elections.

Agriculture and fishing were the mainstays of the economy until the mid-20th century, when manufacturing became the most valuable activity. The timber industry received a major setback in 2003 and again in 2005 when forest fires caused great damage.

AREA 34,285 SQ MI [88,797 SQ KM]
POPULATION 10,643,000 **CAPITAL** LISBON
GOVERNMENT MULTIPARTY REPUBLIC **ETHNIC GROUPS** PORTUGUESE 99%
LANGUAGES PORTUGUESE (OFFICIAL) **RELIGIONS** ROMAN CATHOLIC 94%, PROTESTANT **CURRENCY** EURO = 100 CENTS

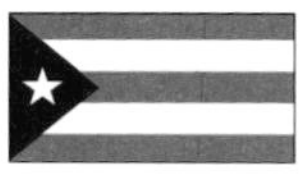

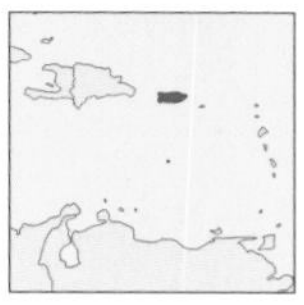

PUERTO RICO

The Commonwealth of Puerto Rico, a mainly mountainous island, is the easternmost of the Greater Antilles chain. The climate is hot and wet. Puerto Rico is a dependent territory of the USA and the people are US citizens. In 1998, 50.2% of the population voted in a referendum on possible statehood to maintain the status quo.

Puerto Rico is the most industrialized country in the Caribbean. Tax exemptions attract US companies to the island and manufacturing is expanding. The chief exports are chemicals and chemical products, machinery, and food.

AREA 3,427 SQ MI [8,875 SQ KM]
POPULATION 3,944,000 **CAPITAL** SAN JUAN

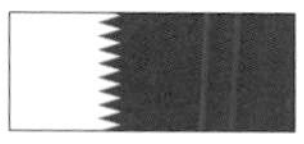

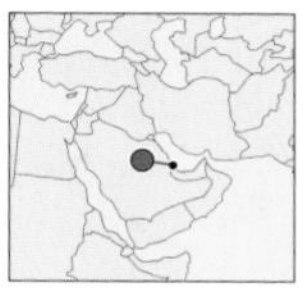

QATAR

The State of Qatar occupies a low, barren peninsula that extends northward from the Arabian peninsula into the Persian Gulf. The climate is hot and dry. Qatar became a British protectorate in 1916, but it became fully independent in 1971. Oil, first discovered in 1939, is the mainstay of the economy of this prosperous nation.

AREA 4,247 SQ MI [11,000 SQ KM] **POPULATION** 907,000 **CAPITAL** DOHA

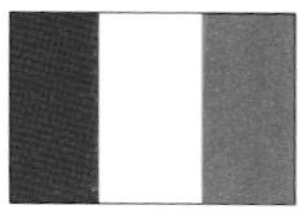

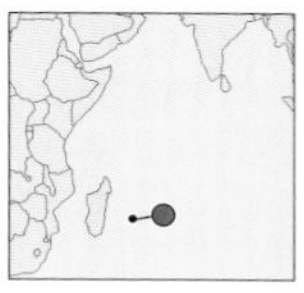

RÉUNION

Réunion is a French overseas department in the Indian Ocean. The land is mainly mountainous, though the lowlands are intensely cultivated. Sugar and sugar products are the main exports, but French aid, given to the island in return for its use as a military base, is important to the economy.

AREA 969 SQ MI [2,510 SQ KM]
POPULATION 788,000 **CAPITAL** ST-DENIS

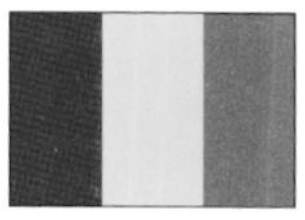

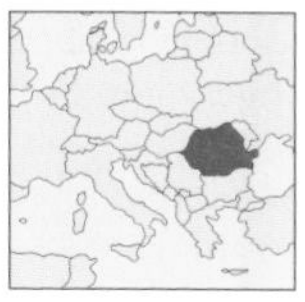

ROMANIA

GEOGRAPHY Romania is a country on the Black Sea in eastern Europe. Eastern and southern Romania form part of the Danube river basin. The delta region, near the mouths of the Danube, where the river flows into the Black Sea, is one of Europe's finest wetlands. The southern part of the coast contains several resorts. The heart of the country is called Transylvania. It is ringed in the east, south and west by scenic mountains which are part of the Carpathian mountain system. Romania has hot summers and cold winters. The rainfall is heaviest in spring and early summer.

POLITICS & ECONOMY From the late 18th century, the Turkish empire began to break up. The modern history of Romania began in 1861 when Walachia and Moldavia united. After World War I (1914–18), Romania, which had fought on the side of the victorious Allies, obtained large areas, including Transylvania, where most people were Romanians. This almost doubled the country's size and population. In 1939, Romania lost territory to Bulgaria, Hungary and the Soviet Union. Romania fought alongside Germany in World War II, and Soviet troops occupied the country in 1944. Hungary returned northern Transylvania to Romania in 1945, but Bulgaria and the Soviet Union kept former Romanian territory. In 1947, Romania officially became a Communist country.

In 1990, Romania held its first free elections since the end of World War II. The National Salvation Front, led by Ion Iliescu and containing many former Communist leaders, won a large majority. A new constitution, approved in 1991, made the country a democratic republic. Elections held under this constitution in 1992 again resulted in victory for Ion Iliescu, whose party was renamed the Party of Social Democracy (PDSR) in 1993. But the government faced many problems. Iliescu was defeated in 1996, but he served again as president between 2000 and 2004, when he stood down. Romania joined NATO in 2004 and became a member of the European Union on January 1, 2007.

Romania has a "lower-middle-income" economy. Under Communist rule, industry, including mining and manufacturing, became more important than farming.

AREA 92,043 SQ MI [238,391 SQ KM]
POPULATION 22,276,000 **CAPITAL** BUCHAREST
GOVERNMENT MULTIPARTY REPUBLIC
ETHNIC GROUPS ROMANIAN 89%, HUNGARIAN 7%, ROMA 2%, UKRAINIAN **LANGUAGES** ROMANIAN (OFFICIAL), HUNGARIAN, GERMAN **RELIGIONS** EASTERN ORTHODOX 87%, PROTESTANT 7%, ROMAN CATHOLIC 5% **CURRENCY** LEU = 100 BANI

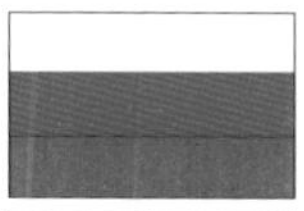

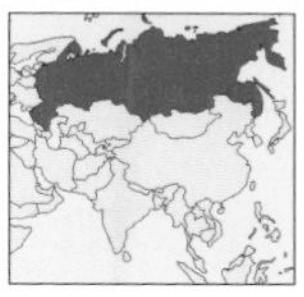

RUSSIA

GEOGRAPHY Russia is the world's largest country. About 25% lies west of the Ural Mountains in European Russia, where 80% of the population lives. It is mostly flat or undulating, but the land rises to the Caucasus Mountains in the south, where Russia's highest peak, Elbrus, at 18,481 ft [5,633 m], is found. Asian Russia, or Siberia, contains vast plains and plateaux, with mountains in the east and south. The Kamchatka peninsula in the far east has many active volcanoes. Russia contains many of the world's longest rivers, including the Yenisey-Angara and the Ob-Irtysh. It also includes part of the world's largest inland body of water, the Caspian Sea, and Lake Baikal, the world's deepest lake.

Moscow has a continental climate with cold and snowy winters and warm summers. Siberia has a harsher, drier climate.

POLITICS & ECONOMY In the 9th century AD, a state called Kievan Rus was formed by a group of people called the East Slavs. Kiev, now capital of Ukraine, became a major trading center, but, in 1237, Mongol armies conquered Russia and destroyed Kiev. Russia was part of the Mongol empire until the late 15th century. Under Mongol rule, Moscow became the leading Russian city.

In the 16th century, Moscow's grand prince was retitled "tsar." The first tsar, Ivan the Terrible, expanded Russian territory. In 1613, after a period of civil war, Michael Romanov became tsar, founding a dynasty which ruled until 1917. In the early 18th century, Tsar Peter the Great began to westernize Russia and, by 1812, when Napoleon failed to conquer the country, Russia was a major European power. But during the 19th century, many Russians demanded reforms and discontent was widespread.

In World War I (1914–18), the Russian people suffered great hardships and, in 1917, Tsar Nicholas II was forced to abdicate. In November 1917, the Bolsheviks seized power under Vladimir Lenin. In 1922, the Bolsheviks set up a new nation, the Union of Soviet Socialist Republics (also called the USSR or the Soviet Union).

From 1924, Joseph Stalin introduced a socialist economic program, suppressing all opposition. In 1939, the Soviet Union and Germany signed a non-aggression pact, but Germany invaded the Soviet Union in 1941. Soviet forces pushed the Germans back, occupying eastern Europe. They reached Berlin in May 1945. From the late 1940s, tension between the Soviet Union and its allies and Western nations developed into a "Cold War." This continued until 1991, when the Soviet Union was dissolved.

The Soviet Union collapsed because of the failure of its economic policies. From 1991, President Boris Yeltsin introduced democratic and economic reforms. Yeltsin retired in 1999 and, in 2000, was succeeded by Vladimir Putin. Putin, who was re-elected in 2004, has sought to develop contacts with the West. He supported the US-declared "war on terrorism," though he opposed the invasion of Iraq in 2003. The secessionist conflict in Chechenia, including the occupation of a school by Muslim extremists in 2004, causing more than 330 deaths, provoked outrage. In 2005, violent incidents in the republics of Dagestan, Ingushetia and Kabardino-Balkaria further confirmed that Russia's size and diversity make national unity hard to achieve. From 2006, relations with the West appeared to deteriorate, with Russia criticizing the expansion of NATO in Eastern Europe. In 2008, Putin, having served two terms as president, was replaced by his ally Dmitry Medvedev. But Putin took the key post of prime minister.

Russia's economy was thrown into disarray after the collapse of the Soviet Union, and in the early 1990s the World Bank described Russia as a "lower-middle-income" economy. Russia was admitted to the Council of Europe in 1997 and was also invited to attend the G7 summit in 1997, and it appeared that it would now take its place among the world's most powerful economies. Industry is Russia's most valuable activity, though, under Communist rule, manufacturing was less efficient than in the West. Today, the production of consumer goods has become more important. Russia's abundant resources include oil and natural gas, coal, timber, metal ores, and hydroelectric power.

Russia is a major producer of farm products, though it imports grains. Major crops include barley, flax, fruits, oats, rye, potatoes, sugar beet, sunflower seeds, vegetables, and wheat.

AREA 6,592,812 SQ MI [17,075,400 SQ KM]
POPULATION 141,378,000 **CAPITAL** MOSCOW
GOVERNMENT FEDERAL MULTIPARTY REPUBLIC
ETHNIC GROUPS RUSSIAN 82%, TATAR 4%, UKRAINIAN 3%, CHUVASH 1%, MORE THAN 100 OTHERS **LANGUAGES** RUSSIAN (OFFICIAL), MANY OTHERS
RELIGIONS MAINLY RUSSIAN ORTHODOX, ISLAM, JUDAISM
CURRENCY RUSSIAN RUBLE = 100 KOPEKS

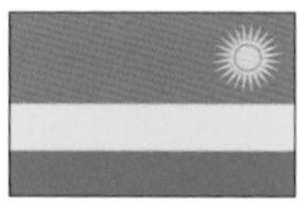

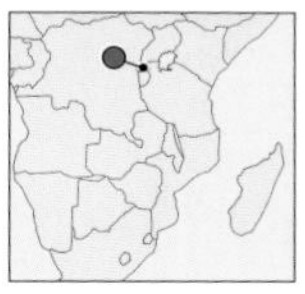

RWANDA

GEOGRAPHY The Republic of Rwanda is a small, landlocked country in east-central Africa. Lake Kivu and the River Ruzizi in the Great African Rift Valley form the country's western border.

Kigali stands on the central plateau of Rwanda. Here, temperatures are moderated by the altitude. The rainfall is abundant, but much

heavier rain falls on the western uplands, while the Rift Valley floor is drier and warmer than the rest of Rwanda.

POLITICS & ECONOMY Germany conquered the area, called Ruanda-Urundi, in the 1890s. However, Belgium occupied the region during World War I (1914–18) and ruled it until 1961, when the people of Ruanda voted for their country to become a republic, called Rwanda. This decision followed a rebellion by the majority Hutu people against the Tutsi monarchy. About 150,000 deaths resulted from this conflict. Many Tutsis fled to Uganda, where they formed a rebel army. Relations between Hutus and Tutsis deteriorated and, in 1994, between 500,000 and 800,000 people were massacred in Rwanda. After the Tutsis had restored order, Hutu rebels fled into the Democratic Republic of the Congo (then Zaïre). Rwanda intervened in the Congo in 1996–2002. In the 2000s, Paul Kagame, Rwanda's leader since 1994, worked to create unity and restore stability.

According to the World Bank, Rwanda is a "low-income" developing country. Most people are poor farmers. Food crops include bananas, beans, cassava, and sorghum. Some cattle are raised.

AREA 10,169 SQ MI [26,338 SQ KM]
POPULATION 9,908,000 **CAPITAL** KIGALI
GOVERNMENT REPUBLIC **ETHNIC GROUPS** HUTU 84%, TUTSI 15%, TWA 1% **LANGUAGES** FRENCH, ENGLISH AND KINYARWANDA (ALL OFFICIAL) **RELIGIONS** ROMAN CATHOLIC 57%, PROTESTANT 26%, ADVENTIST 11%, ISLAM 5% **CURRENCY** RWANDAN FRANC = 100 CENTIMES

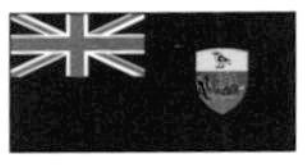
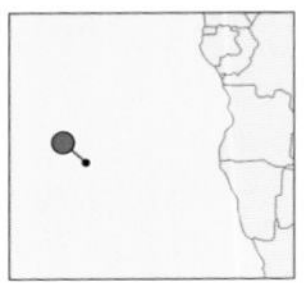

ST HELENA

St Helena, which became a British colony in 1834, is an isolated volcanic island in the south Atlantic Ocean. Now a British overseas territory, it is also the administrative center of Ascension and Tristan da Cunha.

AREA 47 SQ MI [122 SQ KM]
POPULATION 8,000 **CAPITAL** JAMESTOWN

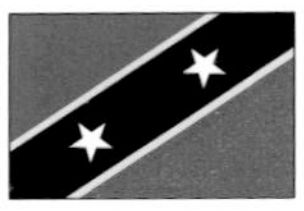
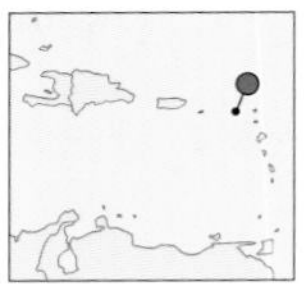

ST KITTS AND NEVIS

The Federation of St Kitts and Nevis comprises two well-watered volcanic islands, with mountains rising to around 3,300 ft [1,000 m]. The islands were the first in the Caribbean to be colonized by Britain (in 1623 and 1628), and they became an independent country in 1983. In 1998, a vote for the secession of Nevis fell short of the two-thirds majority required. Tourism has replaced sugar as the principal earner.

AREA 101 SQ MI [261 SQ KM]
POPULATION 39,000 **CAPITAL** BASSETERRE

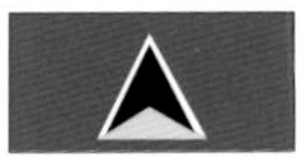
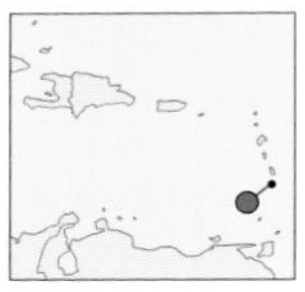

ST LUCIA

St Lucia, which became independent from Britain in 1979, is a mountainous, forested island of extinct volcanoes. It exports bananas and coconuts, and now attracts many tourists.

AREA 208 SQ MI [539 SQ KM]
POPULATION 171,000 **CAPITAL** CASTRIES

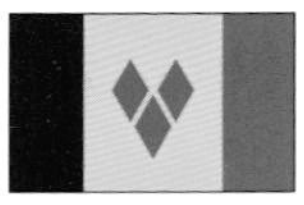
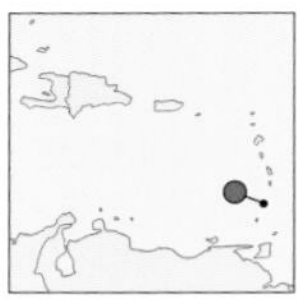

ST VINCENT AND THE GRENADINES

St Vincent and the Grenadines achieved its independence from Britain in 1979. Tourism is growing, but the territory is less prosperous than its neighbors.

AREA 150 SQ MI [388 SQ KM]
POPULATION 118,000 **CAPITAL** KINGSTOWN

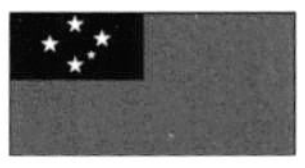
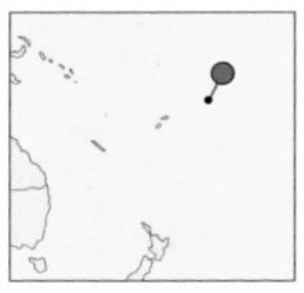

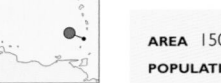

SAMOA

The Independent State of Samoa (formerly Western Samoa) comprises two islands in the South Pacific Ocean. Governed by New Zealand from 1920, the territory became independent in 1962. Exports include coconut cream and beer.

AREA 1,093 SQ MI [2,831 SQ KM]
POPULATION 214,000 **CAPITAL** APIA

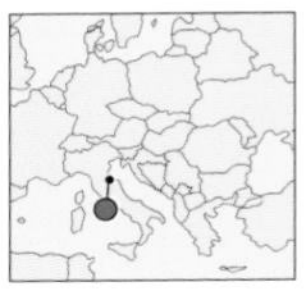

SAN MARINO

San Marino in northern Italy has been independent since 885 and a republic since the 14th century. It is the world's oldest republic. It has a friendship and cooperation treaty with Italy dating back to 1862. The state is governed by an elected council and has its own legal system. It has no armed forces and the police are "hired" from the Italian constabulary. The chief occupations are tourism, limestone quarrying, textiles, and wine-making.

AREA 24 SQ MI [61 SQ KM] **POPULATION** 30,000 **CAPITAL** SAN MARINO

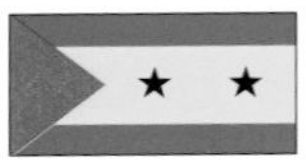
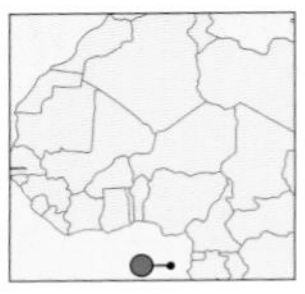

SÃO TOMÉ AND PRÍNCIPE

The Democratic Republic of São Tomé and Príncipe, a mountainous island territory west of Gabon, became a Portuguese colony in 1522. Following independence in 1975, the islands became a one-party Marxist state, but multiparty elections were held in 1991.

AREA 372 SQ MI [964 SQ KM] **POPULATION** 200,000 **CAPITAL** SÃO TOMÉ

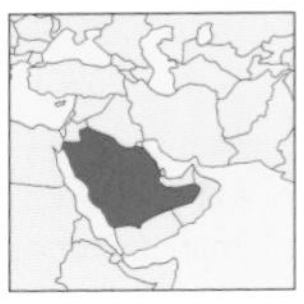

SAUDI ARABIA

GEOGRAPHY The Kingdom of Saudi Arabia occupies about three-quarters of the Arabian peninsula in southwest Asia. Deserts cover most of the land. Mountains border the Red Sea plains in the west. In the north is the sandy Nafud Desert (An Nafud). In the south is the Rub' al Khali (the "Empty Quarter"), one of the world's bleakest deserts.

Saudi Arabia has a hot, dry climate. In the summer months, the temperatures in Riyadh often exceed 104°F [40°C], though the nights are cool.

POLITICS & ECONOMY Saudi Arabia contains the two holiest places in Islam – Mecca (or Makka), the birthplace of the Prophet Muhammad in AD 570, and Medina (Al Madinah) where Muhammad went in 622. These places are visited by many pilgrims.

Saudi Arabia was poor until the oil industry began to operate on the eastern plains in 1933. Oil revenues have been used to develop the country and Saudi Arabia has given aid to poorer Arab nations. The monarch has supreme authority and Saudi Arabia has no formal constitution. Saudi Arabia supported Iraq against Iran in 1980–8. But when Iraq invaded Kuwait in 1990, it joined the alliance against Iraq. Many of the alleged terrorists involved in the terrorist attacks on the US on September 11, 2001, were Saudi nationals. Saudi Arabia condemned the violence and, from 2003, Islamists launched attacks in Saudi Arabia. In 2007, the government arrested 172 people accused of planning air suicide attacks on oil installations and army bases.

Saudi Arabia has about 25% of the world's known oil reserves and oil products make up about 90% of its exports. Agriculture remains important. Irrigation and desalination schemes have increased crop production.

AREA 829,995 SQ MI [2,149,690 SQ KM]
POPULATION 27,601,000 **CAPITAL** RIYADH
GOVERNMENT ABSOLUTE MONARCHY WITH CONSULTATIVE ASSEMBLY
ETHNIC GROUPS ARAB 90%, AFRO-ASIAN 10%
LANGUAGES ARABIC (OFFICIAL)
RELIGIONS ISLAM 100%
CURRENCY SAUDI RIYAL = 100 HALALAS

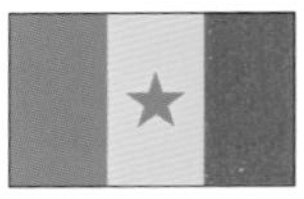
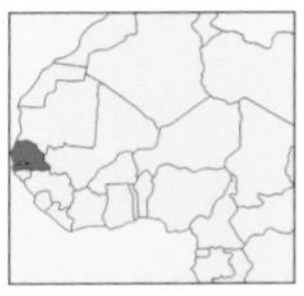

SENEGAL

GEOGRAPHY The Republic of Senegal is on the northwest coast of Africa. The volcanic Cape Verde (Cap Vert), on which Dakar stands, is the most westerly point in Africa. Plains cover most of Senegal, though the land rises gently in the southeast.

Dakar has a tropical climate, with a short rainy season between July and October.

POLITICS & ECONOMY In 1882, Senegal became a French colony, and from 1895 it was ruled as part of French West Africa, the capital of which, Dakar, developed as a major port and city.

In 1959, Senegal joined French Sudan (now Mali) to form the Federation of Mali. But Senegal withdrew in 1960 and became the separate Republic of Senegal. Its first president, Léopold Sédar Senghor, served until 1981, when he was succeeded by Abdou Diouf. However, in 2000, Diouf was defeated in elections by Abdoulaye Wade. In 2001, the government signed a peace treaty with separatist rebels in the southern Casamance province, but sporadic unrest continued into the mid-2000s.

In the past, Senegal has usually enjoyed close relations with The Gambia, despite their differing traditions. In 1981, Senegalese troops put down an attempted coup in The Gambia and, in 1982, the countries set up a defense alliance, called the Confederation of Senegambia. But this alliance was dissolved in 1989.

According to the World Bank, Senegal is a "lower-middle-income" developing country. It was badly hit in the 1960s and 1970s by droughts, which caused starvation. Agriculture still employs 65% of the population, though many farmers produce little more than they need to feed their families. Food crops include groundnuts, millet, and rice. Phosphates are the country's chief resource, but Senegal also refines oil which it imports from Gabon and Nigeria. Dakar is a busy port and has many industries.

AREA 75,954 SQ MI [196,722 SQ KM]
POPULATION 12,522,000 **CAPITAL** DAKAR
GOVERNMENT MULTIPARTY REPUBLIC
ETHNIC GROUPS WOLOF 44%, PULAR 24%, SERER 15%
LANGUAGES FRENCH (OFFICIAL), TRIBAL LANGUAGES
RELIGIONS ISLAM 94%, CHRISTIANITY (MAINLY ROMAN CATHOLIC) 5%, TRADITIONAL BELIEFS 1%
CURRENCY CFA FRANC = 100 CENTIMES

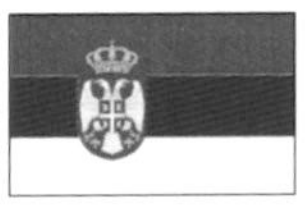
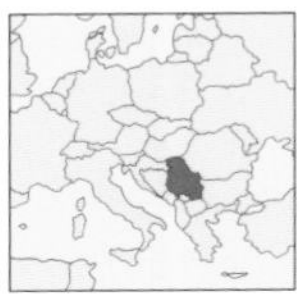

SERBIA

GEOGRAPHY The Republic of Serbia lies in the central Balkan peninsula. A landlocked country, it contains large, fertile lowlands drained by the River Danube and its tributaries, with uplands in the south. Most of Serbia has a continental climate, with cold, snowy winters and hot, dry summers. Heavy rains fall in spring and fall.

POLITICS & ECONOMY Around 1,500 years ago, South Slavs moved into the Balkan peninsula, and each group founded its own state. Serbia came under the Turkish Ottoman Empire in the 15th century. In the 19th century, many Slavs worked for independence and Slavic unity. In 1914, Austria–Hungary declared war on Serbia, blaming it for the assassination of Archduke Franz Ferdinand of Austria–Hungary. In 1918, the South Slavs united in the Kingdom of the Serbs, Croats, and Slovenes, which was renamed Yugoslavia in 1929. Germany invaded in 1941, but Communist partisans, led by Josip Broz (Tito), took power in 1945.

From 1945, the country became the Federal People's Republic of Yugoslavia. In 1991–2, the country split apart, with Bosnia-Herzegovina, Croatia, Macedonia, and Slovenia proclaiming their independence. The remaining republics, Serbia and Montenegro, retained the name Yugoslavia. In 2003, these two republics agreed to form the loose Union of Serbia and Montenegro. In 2006, the Montenegrins voted for full independence, and Serbia and Montenegro became separate republics. In 2008, the province of Kosovo, which had been under a NATO administration since 1999, declared itself independent. Its new status was recognized by the United States and several leading EU countries, but it was not accepted by Serbia and its ally Russia.

Serbia's resources include bauxite, coal, copper and other metals, together with oil and natural gas. Manufactured products include aluminum, machinery, plastics, steel, textiles, and vehicles. Crops include fruits, maize, potatoes, tobacco, and wheat. Livestock include cattle, pigs, and sheep.

AREA 29,913 SQ MI [77,474 SQ KM]
POPULATION 8,024,000 **CAPITAL** BELGRADE
GOVERNMENT REPUBLIC
ETHNIC GROUPS SERB 83%, HUNGARIAN 4%, OTHERS
LANGUAGES SERBIAN (OFFICIAL), HUNGARIAN
RELIGIONS SERBIAN ORTHODOX, ROMAN CATHOLIC, ISLAM, PROTESTANT
CURRENCY NEW DINAR = 100 PARAS

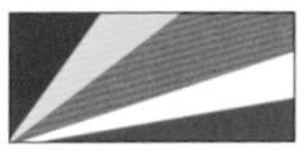
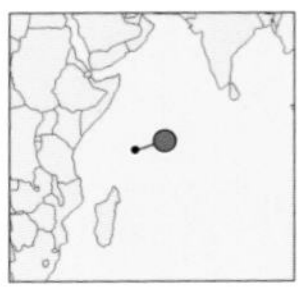

SEYCHELLES

The Republic of Seychelles in the western Indian Ocean achieved independence from Britain in 1976. Coconuts are the main cash crop, and fishing and tourism are important to the country's economy.

AREA 176 SQ MI [455 SQ KM]
POPULATION 82,000 **CAPITAL** VICTORIA

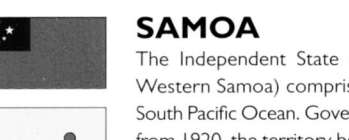

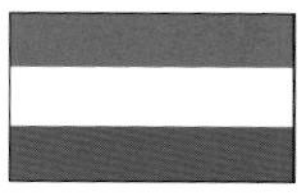

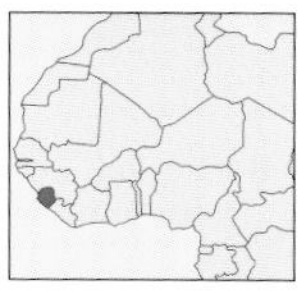

SIERRA LEONE

GEOGRAPHY The Republic of Sierra Leone in West Africa is about the same size as the Republic of Ireland. The coast contains several deep estuaries in the north, with lagoons in the south. The most prominent feature is the mountainous Freetown (or Sierra Leone) peninsula.

Sierra Leone has a tropical climate, with heavy rainfall between April and November.

POLITICS & ECONOMY A former British territory, Sierra Leone became independent in 1961 and a republic in 1971. It became a one-party state in 1978, but, in 1991, the people voted for the restoration of democracy. The military seized power in 1992 and a civil war caused much destruction in 1994–5. Elections in 1996 were followed by another military coup. In 1998, the West African Peace Force restored the deposed President Ahmed Tejan Kabbah. In 1999, a peace agreement followed further conflict. As part of this agreement, Foday Sankoh, one of the rebel leaders, became vice-president. However, he was arrested in 2000 and charged with war crimes. Conflict resumed, but another ceasefire was agreed. In 2004, President Kabbah declared a successful end to the disarmament process. The last of the UN forces left the country in 2005 and national elections were held in 2007.

Sierra Leone has a "low-income" economy. About 60% of the people live by farming, mainly at subsistence level. The leading exports are minerals, including diamonds, bauxite, and rutile (titanium ore). The country has few manufacturing industries.

AREA 27,699 sq mi [71,740 sq km]
POPULATION 6,145,000 **CAPITAL** Freetown
GOVERNMENT Single-party republic **ETHNIC GROUPS** Native African tribes 90% **LANGUAGES** English (official), Mende, Temne, Krio
RELIGIONS Islam 60%, traditional beliefs 30%, Christianity 10%
CURRENCY Leone = 100 cents

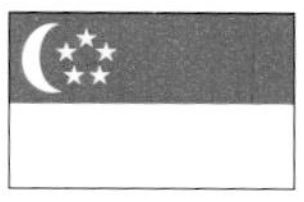

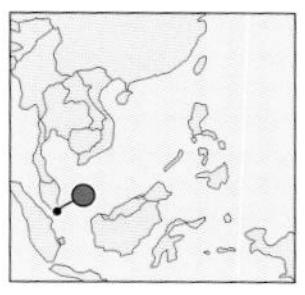

SINGAPORE

GEOGRAPHY The Republic of Singapore is an island country at the southern tip of the Malay peninsula. It consists of the large Singapore Island and 58 small islands, 20 of which are inhabited. The climate is hot and humid. Temperatures are high and rainfall is heavy throughout the year.

POLITICS & ECONOMY In 1819, Sir Thomas Stamford Raffles (1781–1826), agent of the British East India Company, made a treaty with the Sultan of Johor allowing the British to build a settlement on Singapore Island. Singapore soon became the leading British trading center in South-east Asia and it later became a naval base. Japanese forces seized the island in 1942, but British rule was restored in 1945.

In 1963, Singapore became part of the Federation of Malaysia, which also included Malaya and the territories of Sabah and Sarawak on Borneo. In 1965, Singapore broke away and became independent.

The People's Action Party (PAP) has ruled Singapore since 1959. Its leader, Lee Kuan Yew, served as prime minister from 1959 until 1990, when he resigned and was succeeded by Goh Chok Tong. In 2004, Lee Hsien Loong, eldest son of Lee Kuan Yew, succeeded Goh Chok Tong as prime minister. His ruling People's Action Party won 82 out of 84 seats in parliament in 2006.

The World Bank classifies Singapore as a "high-income" economy. A skilled work force has created a fast-growing economy, but the recession in 1997–8 was a setback. Trade and finance are leading activities. Manufactures include electronic products, machinery, scientific instruments, textiles, and ships. Singapore has a large oil refinery. Petroleum products and manufactures are the main exports.

AREA 264 sq mi [683 sq km]
POPULATION 4,553,000 **CAPITAL** Singapore City
GOVERNMENT Multiparty republic
ETHNIC GROUPS Chinese 77%, Malay 14%, Indian 8%
LANGUAGES Chinese, Malay, Tamil and English (all official)
RELIGIONS Buddhism, Islam, Christianity, Hinduism
CURRENCY Singapore dollar = 100 cents

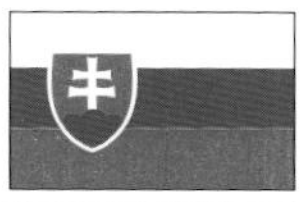

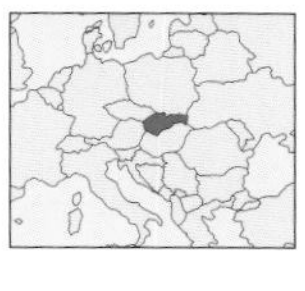

SLOVAK REPUBLIC

GEOGRAPHY The Slovak Republic is a predominantly mountainous country, consisting of part of the Carpathian range. The highest peak is Gerlachovsky in the Tatra Mountains, which reaches 8,711 ft [2,655 m]. The south is a fertile lowland. The Slovak Republic has cold winters and warm summers. Kosice, in the east, has average temperatures ranging from 27°F [–3°C] in January to 68°F [20°C] in July. The highland areas are much colder. Snow or rain falls throughout the year. Kosice has an average annual rainfall of 24 inches [600 mm], the wettest months being July and August.

POLITICS & ECONOMY Slavic peoples settled in the region in the 5th century AD. They were subsequently conquered by Hungary, beginning a millennium of Hungarian rule and suppression of Slovak culture.

In 1867, Hungary and Austria united to form Austria–Hungary, of which the present-day Slovak Republic was a part. Austria–Hungary collapsed at the end of World War I (1914–18). The Czech and Slovak people then united to form a new nation, Czechoslovakia. But Czech domination led to resentment by many Slovaks. In 1939, the Slovak Republic declared itself independent, but Germany occupied the country. At the end of World War II, the Slovak Republic again became part of Czechoslovakia.

The Communist Party took control in 1948. In the 1960s, many people sought reform, but they were crushed by the Russians. In the late 1980s, demands for democracy mounted and a non-Communist government took office in 1990. Elections in 1992 led to victory for the Movement for a Democratic Slovakia headed by a former Communist and nationalist, Vladimir Meciar, and the independent Slovak Republic came into existence on January 1, 1993.

Independence raised national aspirations among Slovakia's Magyar-speaking community, but relations with Hungary deteriorated when the Magyars felt that administrative changes under-represented them politically. The government also made Slovak the only official language. The government's autocratic rule and human rights record provoked international criticism. But the government continued to strengthen its ties with the West, gaining membership of NATO and the European Union in 2004. After elections in 2006, Robert Fico, leader of the opposition party Smer, became prime minister.

Before 1948, the Slovak Republic's economy was based on farming, but Communist governments developed manufacturing industries, producing such things as chemicals, machinery, steel, and weapons. Since the late 1980s, many state-run businesses have been handed over to private owners.

AREA 18,924 sq mi [49,012 sq km]
POPULATION 5,448,000 **CAPITAL** Bratislava
GOVERNMENT Multiparty republic
ETHNIC GROUPS Slovak 86%, Hungarian 11%
LANGUAGES Slovak (official), Hungarian
RELIGIONS Roman Catholic 60%, Protestant 8%, Orthodox 4%, others **CURRENCY** Slovak koruna = 100 halierov

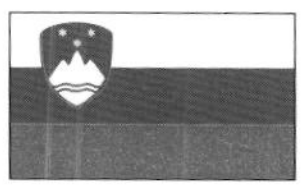

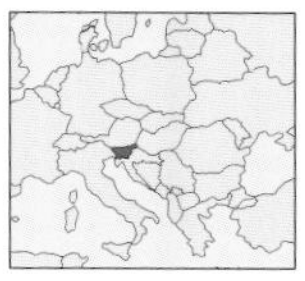

SLOVENIA

GEOGRAPHY The Republic of Slovenia was one of the six republics which made up the former Yugoslavia. Much of the land is mountainous, rising to 9,393 ft [2,863 m] at Mount Triglav in the Julian Alps (Julijske Alpe) in the northwest. Central Slovenia contains the limestone Karst region. The Postojna caves near Ljubljana are among the largest in Europe.

The coast has a mild Mediterranean climate, but inland the climate is more continental. The mountains are snow-capped in winter.

POLITICS & ECONOMY In the last 2,000 years, the Slovene people have been independent as a nation for less than 50 years. The Austrian Habsburgs ruled over the region from the 13th century until World War I. Slovenia became part of the Kingdom of the Serbs, Croats, and Slovenes (later called Yugoslavia) in 1918. During World War II, Slovenia was invaded and partitioned between Italy, Germany and Hungary, but, after the war, Slovenia again became part of Yugoslavia.

From the late 1960s, some Slovenes demanded independence, but the central government opposed the breakup of the country. In 1990, when Communist governments had collapsed throughout Eastern Europe, elections were held and a non-Communist coalition government was set up. Slovenia then declared itself independent. This led to fighting between Slovenes and the federal army, but Slovenia did not become a battlefield. Slovenia's independence was recognized in 1992 and a coalition led by the Liberal Democrats was elected in 1992, 1996, and 2000. In 2004, Slovenia became a member of the North Atlantic Treaty Organization and the European Union. In 2007, Slovenia became the 13th country in the European Union to adopt the euro as its official currency.

The reform of the formerly state-run economy caused problems for Slovenia. However, it has enjoyed considerable economic progress, with one of Europe's fastest growing economies. In 1992, the World Bank classified Slovenia's economy as "upper-middle-income."

Manufacturing is the leading activity and manufactures are the main exports. Manufactures include chemicals, machinery and transport equipment, metal goods, and textiles. Slovenia mines some iron ore, lead, lignite, and mercury. Agriculture and forestry employ 8% of the people. Fruits, maize, potatoes and wheat are major crops, and many farmers raise animals.

AREA 7,821 sq mi [20,256 sq km]
POPULATION 2,009,000 **CAPITAL** Ljubljana
GOVERNMENT Multiparty republic
ETHNIC GROUPS Slovene 92%, Croat 1%, Serb, Hungarian, Bosniak
LANGUAGES Slovenian (official), Serbo-Croatian
RELIGIONS Mainly Roman Catholic
CURRENCY Euro = 100 cents

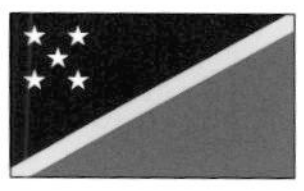

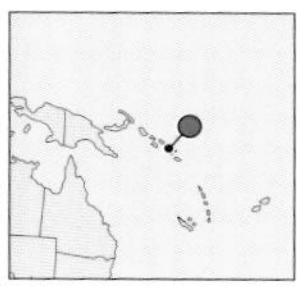

SOLOMON ISLANDS

The Solomon Islands, a chain of mainly volcanic islands in the Pacific Ocean, were a British territory between 1893 and 1978. The chain extends for some 1,400 mi [2,250 km]. They were the scene of fierce fighting during World War II. Most people are Melanesians, and the islands have a young population profile, with half the people aged under 20. Fish, coconuts, and cocoa are leading products, though development is hampered by mountainous, forested terrain.

AREA 11,157 sq mi [28,896 sq km]
POPULATION 567,000 **CAPITAL** Honiara

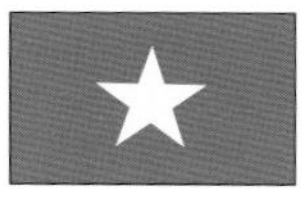

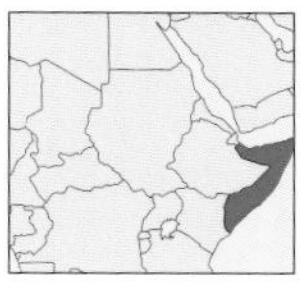

SOMALIA

GEOGRAPHY The Somali Democratic Republic, or Somalia, is in a region known as the "Horn of Africa." It is more than twice the size of Italy, the country which once ruled the southern part of Somalia. The most mountainous part of the country is in the north, behind the narrow coastal plains that border the Gulf of Aden.

Rainfall is light throughout Somalia. The wettest regions are the south and the northern mountains, but droughts often occur. Temperatures are high on the low plateaux and plains.

POLITICS & ECONOMY European powers became interested in the Horn of Africa in the 19th century. In 1884, Britain made the northern part of what is now Somalia a protectorate, while Italy took the south in 1905. The new boundaries divided the Somalis into five areas: the two Somalilands, Djibouti (which was taken by France in the 1880s), Ethiopia and Kenya. Since then, many Somalis have wanted to create a Greater Somalia. Italy invaded British Somaliland in 1940, but was defeated in 1941. Britain ruled both Somalilands until 1950, when the United Nations asked Italy to take over the former Italian Somaliland for ten years. In 1960, the two Somalilands united to become Somalia.

Somalia has faced many problems. Economic difficulties led a military group to seize power in 1969. In the 1970s, Somalia supported an uprising of Somali-speaking people in the Ogaden region of Ethiopia. But, in 1988, Somalia and Ethiopia signed a peace treaty. In the 1990s, Somalia gradually broke apart. In 1991, the people in what was once British Somaliland set up the "Somaliland Republic," but it failed to get international recognition. The northeast, called Puntland, also seceded, while the south was riven by clan warfare. In 2004–5, a Somali parliament was set up in Kenya. In 2006, it moved to Baidoa, in Somalia (Mogadishu was regarded as unsafe). In 2006, Mogadishu was taken over by the Islamist Union of Islamic Courts, but government forces backed by Ethiopian troops defeated the Islamists. In 2007, the transitional government sought to replace Ethiopian troops with an African Union force, but most of the promised soldiers failed to arrive.

Somalia's economy has been shattered by war, droughts, and periodic floods. Many Somalis are nomads, who raise livestock. Live animals, meat, and hides and skins are exported. Crops include bananas, citrus fruits, cotton, maize, and sugarcane. Mining and manufacturing are relatively unimportant.

AREA 246,199 sq mi [637,657 sq km] **POPULATION** 9,119,000
CAPITAL Mogadishu **GOVERNMENT** Single-party republic, military dominated **ETHNIC GROUPS** Somali 85%, Bantu, Arab
LANGUAGES Somali (official), Arabic **RELIGIONS** Islam (Sunni Muslim)
CURRENCY Somali shilling = 100 cents

SOUTH AFRICA

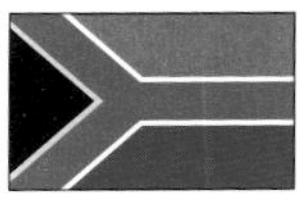

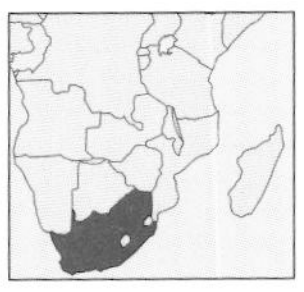

GEOGRAPHY The Republic of South Africa is made up largely of the southern part of the huge plateau which makes up most of southern Africa. The highest peaks are in the Drakensberg range, which is formed by the uplifted rim of the plateau. The coastal plains include part of the Namib Desert in the northwest. Most of South Africa has a mild, sunny climate. Much of the coastal strip, including Cape Town, has warm, dry summers and mild, rainy winters. Inland, large areas are arid.

POLITICS & ECONOMY Early inhabitants in South Africa were the Khoisan. In the last 2,000 years, Bantu-speaking people moved into the area. Their descendants include the Zulu, Xhosa, Sotho and Tswana. The Dutch founded a settlement at the Cape in 1652, but Britain took over in the early 19th century, making the area a colony. The Dutch, called Boers or Afrikaners, resented British rule and moved inland. Rivalry between the groups led to Anglo-Boer Wars in 1880–1 and 1899–1902.

In 1910, the country was united as the Union of South Africa. In 1948, the National Party won power and introduced a policy known as apartheid, under which non-whites had no votes and their human rights were strictly limited. In 1990, Nelson Mandela, leader of the African National Congress (ANC), was released from prison. Multiracial elections were held in 1994 and Mandela became president. After Mandela's retirement in 1999, his successor, Thabo Mbeki, led the ANC to victory in national elections. In 2004, the ANC won again by a landslide. Taking almost 70% of the vote, it was far ahead of its nearest rival, the Democratic Alliance, which polled only 13%. However, the government faced massive problems of poverty and underdevelopment, and maintaining national unity. South Africa also faces a health crisis because it has more people infected with the HIV virus than any other country. In 2007, Jacob Zuma was elected president of the ANC, making him the likely ANC presidential candidate in the 2009 elections.

South Africa is Africa's most developed country. However, most of the black people are poor, with low standards of living. Natural resources include diamonds, gold and many other metals. Mining and manufacturing are the most valuable activities.

AREA 471,442 SQ MI [1,221,037 SQ KM] **POPULATION** 43,998,000
CAPITAL CAPE TOWN (LEGISLATIVE); PRETORIA/TSHWANE (ADMINISTRATIVE); BLOEMFONTEIN (JUDICIARY) **GOVERNMENT** MULTIPARTY REPUBLIC
ETHNIC GROUPS BLACK 76%, WHITE 13%, COLORED 9%, ASIAN 2%
LANGUAGES AFRIKAANS, ENGLISH, NDEBELE, PEDI, SOTHO, SWAZI, TSONGA, TSWANA, VENDA, XHOSA, AND ZULU (ALL OFFICIAL)
RELIGIONS CHRISTIANITY 68%, ISLAM 2%, HINDUISM 1%
CURRENCY RAND = 100 CENTS

SPAIN

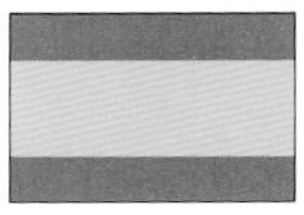

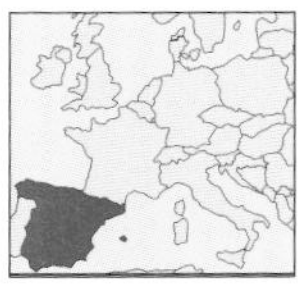

GEOGRAPHY The Kingdom of Spain is the second largest country in Western Europe after France. It shares the Iberian peninsula with Portugal. A large plateau, called the Meseta, covers most of Spain. Much of the Meseta is flat, but it is crossed by several mountain ranges, called sierras.

The northern highlands include the Cantabrian Mountains (Cordillera Cantabrica) and the high Pyrenees, which form Spain's border with France. But Mulhacén, the highest peak on the Spanish mainland, is in the Sierra Nevada in the southeast. Spain also contains fertile coastal plains. Other major lowlands are the Ebro river basin in the northeast and the Guadalquivir river basin in the southwest. Spain also includes the Balearic Islands in the Mediterranean Sea and the Canary Islands off the northwest coast of Africa.

The Meseta has a continental climate, with hot summers and cold winters, when temperatures often fall below freezing point. Snow frequently covers the mountain ranges on the Meseta. The Mediterranean coasts have hot, dry summers and mild winters.

POLITICS & ECONOMY In the 16th century, Spain became a world power. At its peak, it controlled much of Central and South America, parts of Africa and the Philippines in Asia. Spain began to decline in the late 16th century. Its sea power was destroyed by a British fleet in the Battle of Trafalgar (1805). By the 20th century, it was a poor country.

Spain became a republic in 1931, but the republicans were defeated in the Spanish Civil War (1936–9). General Francisco Franco (1892–1975) became the country's dictator, though, technically, it was a monarchy. When Franco died, the monarchy was restored. Prince Juan Carlos became king.

Spain has several groups with their own languages and cultures. Some of these people want to run their own regional affairs. In the northern Basque region, some nationalists have waged a terrorist campaign. A truce in 1998 was ended in 1999 when talks failed to produce results. In 2003, Spain's Supreme Court voted to ban Batasuna, the Basque separatist party.

Since the 1970s, regional parliaments with a considerable degree of autonomy have been set up in the Basque Country (called Euskadi in the indigenous language and Pais Vasco in Spanish), in Catalonia in the northeast, and in Galicia in the northwest. From the 1960s, Eta, a Basque terrorist group, waged a violent campaign for the secesssion of the Basque Country and, in 2003, Batasuna, the Basque separatist party, was banned. In March 2004, bombings attributed to al Qaida terrorists killed about 200 people in Madrid. The opposition socialists won the parliamentary elections that followed. In 2005, the government rejected proposals to make the Basque Country a "free state" associated with Spain. In 2006, ETA declared a permanent ceasefire, but this ended in 2007 and the government's campaign against ETA was intensified.

In the last 50 years, Spain has changed from one of Europe's poorest countries into a prosperous nation and major holiday destination. Agriculture employs 4% of the people, as compared with 15% in mining and manufacturing. Farmland makes up two-thirds of Spain, with forests covering most of the rest. Crops include barley, citrus fruits, grapes for wine-making, olives, potatoes, and wheat. Spain lacks natural resources apart from some high-grade iron ore in the north. Manufactures include cars, chemicals, electronic goods, food, metal goods, and textiles.

AREA 192,103 SQ MI [497,548 SQ KM]
POPULATION 40,448,000 **CAPITAL** MADRID
GOVERNMENT CONSTITUTIONAL MONARCHY
ETHNIC GROUPS COMPOSITE OF MEDITERRANEAN AND NORDIC TYPES
LANGUAGES CASTILIAN SPANISH (OFFICIAL) 74%, CATALAN 17%, GALICIAN 7%, BASQUE 2%
RELIGIONS ROMAN CATHOLIC 94%, OTHERS
CURRENCY EURO = 100 CENTS

SRI LANKA

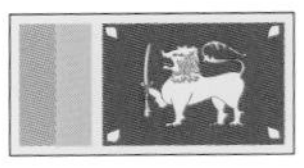

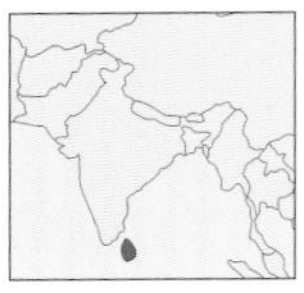

GEOGRAPHY The Democratic Socialist Republic of Sri Lanka is an island nation, separated from the southeast coast of India by the Palk Strait. The land is mostly low-lying, but a mountain region dominates the south-central part of the country.

The western part of Sri Lanka has a wet equatorial climate. Temperatures are high and the rainfall is heavy. Eastern Sri Lanka is drier than the west of the country.

POLITICS & ECONOMY From the early 16th century, Ceylon (as Sri Lanka was then known) was ruled successively by the Portuguese, Dutch and British. Independence was achieved in 1948 and the country was renamed Sri Lanka in 1972.

After independence, rivalries between the two main ethnic groups, the Sinhalese and Tamils, marred progress. In the 1950s, the government made Sinhala the official language. Following protests, the prime minister made provisions for Tamil to be used in some areas. In 1959, the prime minister was assassinated by a Sinhalese extremist and he was succeeded by Sirimavo Bandanaraike, the world's first woman prime minister.

Conflict between Tamils and Sinhalese continued in the 1970s and 1980s. In 1987, India helped to engineer a ceasefire. Indian troops arrived to enforce the agreement, but withdrew in 1990 after failing to subdue the main guerrilla group, the Tamil Tigers, who wanted to set up an independent Tamil homeland in northern Sri Lanka. In 1993, the country's president was assassinated by a suspected Tamil separatist. Offensives against the Tamil Tigers continued until hopes of peace were raised in 2002, with the signing of a ceasefire. In late 2004, a tsunami, caused by a sudden movement of the plates underlying the eastern Indian Ocean, struck parts of the coast of Sri Lanka, killing more than 30,000 people. Some hoped that the tragedy might lead to a reconciliation, but despite attempts to start peace talks, fighting intensified in 2006–8.

Sri Lanka is classed as a "low-income" economy. Agriculture employs about 28% of the people. Coconuts, rubber, and tea are exported, but rice is the main food crop. Factories process farm products and manufacture textiles.

AREA 25,332 SQ MI [65,610 SQ KM]
POPULATION 20,926,000 **CAPITAL** COLOMBO
GOVERNMENT MULTIPARTY REPUBLIC
ETHNIC GROUPS SINHALESE 74%, TAMIL 18%, MOOR 7%
LANGUAGES SINHALA AND TAMIL (BOTH OFFICIAL)
RELIGIONS BUDDHISM 70%, HINDUISM 15%, CHRISTIANITY 8%, ISLAM 7%
CURRENCY SRI LANKAN RUPEE = 100 CENTS

SUDAN

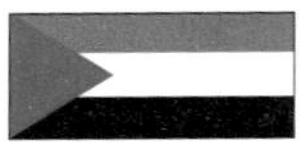

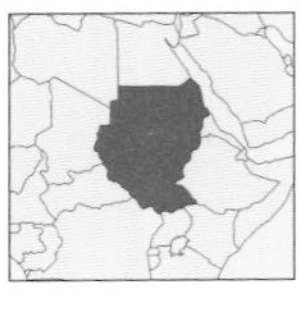

GEOGRAPHY The Republic of Sudan is the largest country in Africa. From north to south, it spans a vast area extending from the arid Sahara in the north to the wet equatorial region in the south. The land is mostly flat, with the highest mountains in the far south. The main physical feature is the River Nile. The north is virtually rainless, while the south has a wet equatorial climate.

POLITICS & ECONOMY In the 19th century, Egypt gradually took over Sudan. In 1881, a Muslim religious teacher, the Mahdi ("divinely appointed guide"), led an uprising. Britain and Egypt put the rebellion down in 1898. In 1899, they agreed to rule Sudan jointly as a condominium. After independence in 1952, the black Africans in the south, who were either Christians or followers of traditional religions, feared domination by the Muslim north. They objected to Arabic becoming the sole official language and, in 1964, civil war broke out. The war ended in 1972, when the south was granted regional self-government.

In 1983, the announcement that Islamic law would apply throughout Sudan sparked off further resistance from the rebel Sudan People's Liberation Army (SPLA) in the south. In 1998, Sudan's government announced that it accepted the idea of a referendum in the south. In 2005, a peace agreement was signed, bringing peace to the south. Since 2003, another conflict has raged in the western province of Darfur, where government-backed militias have attacked the population in an operation described as genocide and ethnic cleansing. Thousands of refugees fled into Chad and fighting spilled over the border.

Agriculture employs 57% of the people and cotton is the chief crop. Cotton, gum arabic, and sesame seeds are exported, but the most valuable exports are oil and oil products. Manufacturing industries produce items mainly for home consumption.

AREA 967,494 SQ MI [2,505,813 SQ KM]
POPULATION 39,379,000 **CAPITAL** KHARTOUM
GOVERNMENT MILITARY REGIME **ETHNIC GROUPS** BLACK 52%, ARAB 39%, BEJA 6%, OTHERS **LANGUAGES** ARABIC (OFFICIAL), NUBIAN, TA BEDAWIE **RELIGIONS** ISLAM 70%, TRADITIONAL BELIEFS 25%
CURRENCY SUDANESE DINAR = 10 SUDANESE POUNDS

SURINAME

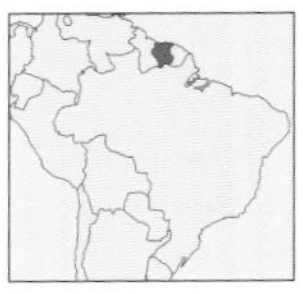

GEOGRAPHY The Republic of Suriname is sandwiched between French Guiana and Guyana in northeastern South America. The narrow coastal plain was once swampy, but it has been drained and now consists mainly of farmland. Inland lie hills and low mountains, which rise to 4,199 ft [1,280 m].

Suriname has a hot, wet and humid climate. Temperatures are high throughout the year.

POLITICS & ECONOMY In 1667, the British handed Suriname to the Dutch in return for New Amsterdam, an area that is now the state of New York. Slave revolts and Dutch neglect hampered development. In the early 19th century, Britain and the Netherlands disputed the ownership of the area. The British gave up their claims in 1813. Slavery was abolished in 1863 and, soon afterward, Indian and Indonesian laborers were introduced to work on the plantations. Suriname became fully independent in 1975, but the economy was weakened when thousands of skilled people emigrated from Suriname to the Netherlands. Following a coup in 1980, Suriname was ruled by a military dictator, Dési Bouterse. The adoption of a new constitution led to the restoration of democracy in 1988, though another military coup occurred in 1990. Ronald Venetiaan was elected president in 2000 and his government replaced the guilder with the Surinamese dollar in 2004. Venetiaan was re-elected in 2005, when his New Front coalition won a narrow majority in elections. Severe flooding in lowland areas in 2006 left more than 20,000 people homeless.

The World Bank classifies Suriname as an "upper-middle-income" developing country. Its economy is based on mining and metal processing. Suriname is a leading producer of bauxite, from which the metal aluminum is made.

AREA 63,037 SQ MI [163,265 SQ KM]
POPULATION 471,000 **CAPITAL** PARAMARIBO
GOVERNMENT MULTIPARTY REPUBLIC
ETHNIC GROUPS HINDUSTANI/EAST INDIAN 37%, CREOLE (MIXED WHITE AND BLACK) 31%, JAVANESE 15%, BLACK 10%, AMERINDIAN 2%, CHINESE 2%, OTHERS **LANGUAGES** DUTCH (OFFICIAL), SRANANG TONGA
RELIGIONS HINDUISM 27%, PROTESTANT 25%, ROMAN CATHOLIC 23%, ISLAM 20% **CURRENCY** SURINAMESE DOLLAR= 100 CENTS

SWAZILAND

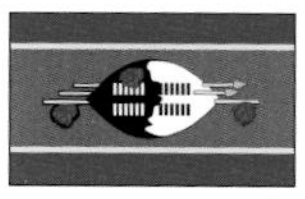

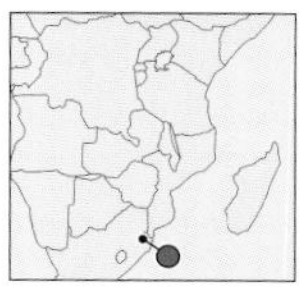

GEOGRAPHY The Kingdom of Swaziland is a small, landlocked country in southern Africa. The country has four regions which run north–south. In the west, the Highveld, with an average height of 3,950 ft [1,200 m], makes up 30% of Swaziland. The Middleveld, between 1,150 ft and 3,280 ft [350 m to 1,000 m], covers 28% of the country. The Lowveld, with an average height of 886 ft [270 m], covers another 33%. Finally, the Lebombo Mountains reach 2,600 ft [800 m] along the eastern border. The Lowveld is almost tropical, with average temperatures of 72°F [22°C] and low rainfall. The altitude moderates the climate in the west.

POLITICS & ECONOMY In 1894, Britain and the Boers of South Africa agreed to put Swaziland under the control of the South African Republic (the Transvaal). But at the end of the Anglo–Boer War (1899–1902), Britain took control of the country. In 1968, when Swaziland became fully independent as a constitutional monarchy, the head of state was King Sobhuza II. Sobhuza died in 1982 and was succeeded by his son, who, in 1986, became King Mswati III. Political parties were banned in elections in 1993 and 1998. Mswati ruled by decree. In 2005, Mswati signed a new constitution, combining traditional and modern values, though political parties remain banned.

The World Bank classifies Swaziland as a "lower-middle-income" developing country. Agriculture employs 50% of the people, and farm products and processed foods, including soft drink concentrates, sugar, wood pulp, citrus fruits, and canned fruit, are the leading exports. Many farmers live at subsistence level. Swaziland is heavily dependent on South Africa and the two countries are linked through a customs union. Swaziland shares two major problems with South Africa – the widespread poverty and the high incidence of HIV/AIDS. Experts have reported that Swaziland has the world's highest HIV infection rate of 42.6%.

AREA 6,704 sq mi [17,364 sq km]
POPULATION 1,133,000 **CAPITAL** Mbabane
GOVERNMENT Monarchy **ETHNIC GROUPS** African 97%, European 3% **LANGUAGES** Siswati and English (both official)
RELIGIONS Zionist (a mix of Christianity and traditional beliefs) 40%, Roman Catholic 20%, Islam 10% **CURRENCY** Lilangeni = 100 cents

SWEDEN

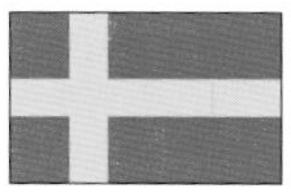

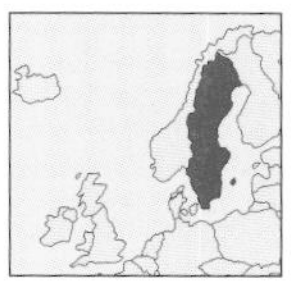

GEOGRAPHY The Kingdom of Sweden is the largest of the countries of Scandinavia in both area and population. It shares the Scandinavian peninsula with Norway. The western part of the country, along the border with Norway, is mountainous. The highest point is Kebnekaise, which reaches 6,946 ft [2,117 m] in the northwest.

The climate of Sweden becomes more severe from south to north. Stockholm has cold winters and cool summers. The far south is much milder.

POLITICS & ECONOMY Swedish Vikings plundered areas to the south and east between the 9th and 11th centuries. Sweden, Denmark and Norway were united in 1397, but Sweden regained its independence in 1523. In 1809, Sweden lost Finland to Russia, but, in 1814, it gained Norway from Denmark. The union between Sweden and Norway was dissolved in 1905. Sweden was neutral in World Wars I and II. Since 1945, Sweden has become a prosperous country. In 1995, it joined the European Union. However, many people were sceptical about the advantages of EU membership and Sweden did not adopt the euro, the single EU currency, in 1999.

Sweden has wide-ranging welfare services. But many people are concerned about the high cost of these services and the high taxes they must pay. In a general election in 2006, a center-right alliance won 178 out of the 349 seats in parliament, defeating the Social Democrats, who had ruled Sweden for 65 of the past 74 years and introduced most of the welfare services. Fredrick Reinfeldt replaced Göran Persson as prime minister.

Sweden is a highly developed industrial country. Major products include steel and steel goods. Steel is used in the engineering industry to manufacture aircraft, cars, machinery, and ships. Sweden has some of the world's richest iron ore deposits. They are located near Kiruna in the far north. But most of this ore is exported, and Sweden imports most of the materials needed by its industries. Sweden also has a major forestry industry. Development of hydroelectricity has made up for the lack of oil and coal. In 1996, a decision was taken to decommission all of Sweden's nuclear power stations. The first reactor closed in 1999, followed by a second in 2005. Another ten reactors remain to be decommissioned.

AREA 173,731 sq mi [449,964 sq km]
POPULATION 9,031,000 **CAPITAL** Stockholm
GOVERNMENT Constitutional monarchy **ETHNIC GROUPS** Swedish 91%, Finnish, Sami **LANGUAGES** Swedish (official), Finnish, Sami
RELIGIONS Lutheran 87%, Roman Catholic, Orthodox
CURRENCY Swedish krona = 100 öre

SWITZERLAND

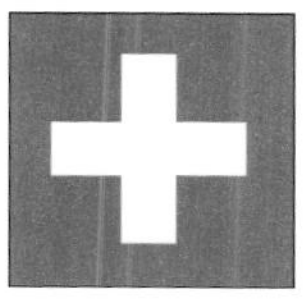

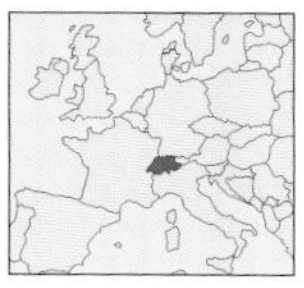

GEOGRAPHY The Swiss Confederation is a landlocked country in Western Europe. Much of the land is mountainous. The Jura Mountains lie along Switzerland's western border with France, while the Swiss Alps make up about 60% of the country in the south and east. Four-fifths of the people of Switzerland live on the fertile Swiss plateau, which contains most of Switzerland's large cities.

The climate of Switzerland varies greatly according to the height of the land. The plateau region has a central European climate with warm summers, but cold and snowy winters. Rain occurs all through the year. The rainiest months are in summer.

POLITICS & ECONOMY In 1291, three small cantons (states) united to defend their freedom against the Habsburg rulers of the Holy Roman Empire. They were Schwyz, Uri, and Unterwalden, and they called the confederation they formed "Switzerland." Switzerland expanded and, in the 14th century, defeated Austria in three wars of independence. After a defeat by the French in 1515, the Swiss adopted a policy of neutrality, which they still follow. In 1815, the Congress of Vienna expanded Switzerland to 22 cantons and guaranteed its neutrality. Switzerland's 23rd canton, Jura, was created in 1979 from part of Bern. Neutrality combined with the vigor and independence of its people have made Switzerland prosperous. The Swiss have voted against joining the European Union, although, in 2002, the country joined the United Nations. In 2005, it also joined the Schengen group, a European passport-free zone.

Although lacking in natural resources, Switzerland is a wealthy, industrialized country. Many workers are highly skilled. Major products include chemicals, electrical equipment, machinery and machine tools, precision instruments, processed food, watches, and textiles. Farmers produce about three-fifths of the country's food – the rest is imported. Livestock raising, especially dairy farming, is the chief agricultural activity. Crops include fruits, potatoes, and wheat. Tourism and banking are also important. Swiss banks attract investors from all over the world.

AREA 15,940 sq mi [41,284 sq km] **POPULATION** 7,555,000
CAPITAL Bern **GOVERNMENT** Federal republic
ETHNIC GROUPS German 65%, French 18%, Italian 10%, Romansch 1%, others **LANGUAGES** French, German, Italian, and Romansch (all official) **RELIGIONS** Roman Catholic 46%, Protestant 40% **CURRENCY** Swiss franc = 100 centimes

SYRIA

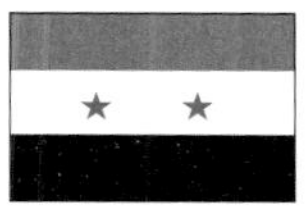

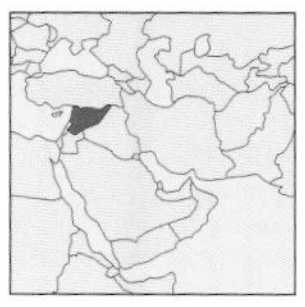

GEOGRAPHY The Syrian Arab Republic is a country in southwestern Asia. The narrow coastal plain is overlooked by a low mountain range which runs north–south. Another range, the Jabal ash Sharqi, runs along the border with Lebanon. South of this range is the Golan Heights, which Israel has occupied since 1967.

The coast has a Mediterranean climate, with dry, warm summers and wet, mild winters. The low mountains cut off Damascus from the sea. It has less rainfall than the coastal areas. To the east, the land becomes drier.

POLITICS & ECONOMY After the collapse of the Turkish Ottoman empire in World War I, Syria was ruled by France. Since independence in 1946, Syria has been involved in the Arab–Israeli wars and, in 1967, it lost a strategic border area, the Golan Heights, to Israel. In 1970, Lieutenant-General Hafez al-Assad took power, establishing a stable but repressive regime. Syria sent troops into Lebanon in 1976 in an effort to halt the civil war there, but, in 2005, following demonstrations, Syria withdrew its troops. Hafez al-Assad died in 2000 and was succeeded by his son, Bashar al-Assad. In 2007, Israel launched an air strike on an alleged nuclear installation in Syria.

The World Bank classifies Syria as a "lower-middle-income" developing country. But it has great potential for development. Its main resources are oil, hydroelectricity from the dam at Lake Assad, and fertile land. Oil is the main export; farm products, textiles and phosphates are also important. Agriculture employs about 23% of the work force.

AREA 71,498 sq mi [185,180 sq km]
POPULATION 19,315,000 **CAPITAL** Damascus
GOVERNMENT Multiparty republic **ETHNIC GROUPS** Arab 90%, Kurdish, Armenian, others **LANGUAGES** Arabic (official), Kurdish, Armenian **RELIGIONS** Sunni Muslim 74%, other Islam 16%
CURRENCY Syrian pound = 100 piastres

TAIWAN

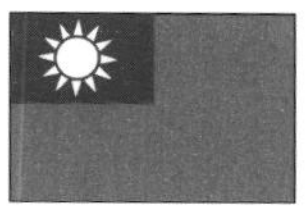

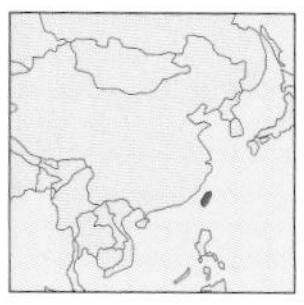

GEOGRAPHY High mountain ranges run down the length of the island, with dense forest in many areas. The climate is warm, moist and suitable for agriculture.

POLITICS & ECONOMY Chinese settlers occupied Taiwan from the 7th century. In 1895, Japan seized the territory from the Portuguese, who had named it Isla Formosa, or "beautiful island." China regained the island after World War II. In 1949, it became the refuge of the Nationalists who had been driven out of China by the Communists. They set up the Republic of China, which, with US help, began to expand its economy. Today, it produces a wide range of manufactured goods.

In the early 21st century, the Taiwanese declared full nationhood for Taiwan. But the government of mainland China threatened to attack the territory if it did not accept the fact that it was a self-governing province of China. But reunification seemed a remote prospect.

AREA 13,900 sq mi [36,000 sq km]
POPULATION 22,859,000 **CAPITAL** Taipei
GOVERNMENT Unitary multiparty republic
ETHNIC GROUPS Taiwanese 84%, mainland Chinese 14%
LANGUAGES Mandarin Chinese (official), Min, Hakka
RELIGIONS Buddhism, Taoism, Confucianism
CURRENCY New Taiwan dollar = 100 cents

TAJIKISTAN

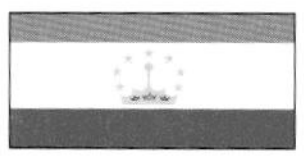

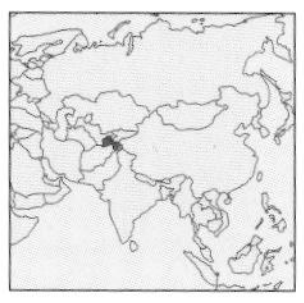

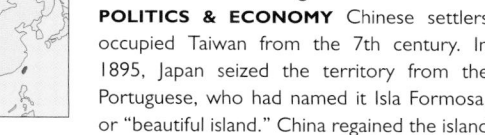

GEOGRAPHY The Republic of Tajikistan is one of the five central Asian republics that formed part of the former Soviet Union. Only 7% of the land is below 3,280 ft [1,000 m], while almost all of eastern Tajikistan is above 9,840 ft [3,000 m]. The highest point is Pik Imeni Ismail Samani (formerly known as Communism Peak or Pik Kommunizma), which reaches 24,590 ft [7,495 m]. The main ranges are the westward extension of the Tian Shan Range in the north and the snow-capped Pamirs in the southeast. Earthquakes are common throughout the country. The climate is continental, with hot, dry summers in the lower valleys and bitterly cold winters, especially in the mountains.

POLITICS & ECONOMY Russia conquered parts of Tajikistan in the late 19th century and, by 1920, Russia took complete control. In 1924, Tajikistan became part of the Uzbek Soviet Socialist Republic, but, in 1929, it was expanded, taking in some areas populated by Uzbeks, becoming the Tajik Soviet Socialist Republic.

While the Soviet Union began to introduce reforms during the 1980s, many Tajiks demanded freedom. In 1989, the Tajik government made Tajik the official language instead of Russian and, in 1990, it stated that its local laws overruled Soviet laws. Tajikistan became fully independent in 1991, following the breakup of the Soviet Union. In 1992, civil war broke out between the government, which was run by former Communists, and an alliance of democrats and Islamic forces. A ceasefire was agreed in 1996 and, in 1997, opposition leaders were brought into the government. In 2003, changes to the constitution enabled President Emomali Rakhmanov, president since 1994, to serve two more seven-year terms after elections in 2006, when he was re-elected with 79.3% of the vote.

The World Bank classifies Tajikistan as a "low-income" developing country. Agriculture, mainly on irrigated land, is the main activity and cotton is the chief product. Other crops include fruits, grains, and vegetables. The country has large hydroelectric power resources and it produces aluminum.

AREA 55,521 sq mi [143,100 sq km]
POPULATION 7,077,000 **CAPITAL** Dushanbe
GOVERNMENT Transitional democracy
ETHNIC GROUPS Tajik 65%, Uzbek 25%, Russian
LANGUAGES Tajik (official), Russian
RELIGIONS Islam (Sunni Muslim 85%)
CURRENCY Somoni = 100 dirams

TANZANIA

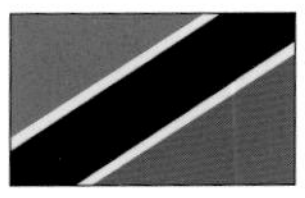
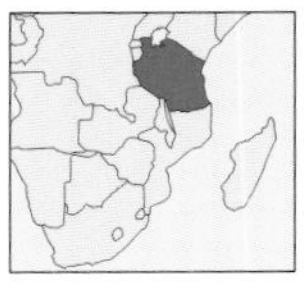

GEOGRAPHY The United Republic of Tanzania consists of the former mainland country of Tanganyika and the island nation of Zanzibar, which also includes the island of Pemba. Behind a narrow coastal plain, most of Tanzania is a plateau, which is broken by arms of the Great African Rift Valley. In the west, this valley contains lakes Nyasa and Tanganyika. The highest peak is Kilimanjaro, Africa's tallest mountain.

The coast has a hot and humid climate, with the greatest rainfall in April and May. The inland plateaux and mountains are cooler and less humid.

POLITICS & ECONOMY Mainland Tanganyika became a German territory in the 1880s, while Zanzibar and Pemba became a British protectorate in 1890. Following Germany's defeat in World War I, Britain took over Tanganyika, which remained a British territory until its independence in 1961. In 1964, Tanganyika and Zanzibar united to form the United Republic of Tanzania. The country's president, Julius Nyerere, pursued socialist policies of self-help (*ujamaa*) and egalitarianism. Many of its social reforms were successful, though the country failed to make economic progress. Nyerere resigned as president in 1985. His successors, Ali Hassan Mwinyi and Benjamin Mkapa (1995–2006), followed more liberal economic policies. In 2006, Jakaya Kikwete, leader of the ruling party, Chama Cha Mapinduzi, was elected president.

Tanzania is a poor country. Crops are grown on only 4.2% of the land, yet agriculture employs nearly 80% of the people. Food crops include bananas, cassava, maize, millet, and rice. Minerals, including gold, as well as cashews, tobacco, coffee, and tea are exported.

AREA 364,899 sq mi [945,090 sq km]
POPULATION 39,384,000 **CAPITAL** Dodoma
GOVERNMENT Multiparty republic
ETHNIC GROUPS Native African 99% (of whch 95% are Bantu consisting of more than 130 tribes)
LANGUAGES Swahili (Kiswahili) and English (both official)
RELIGIONS Islam 35% (99% in Zanzibar), traditional beliefs 35%, Christianity 30%
CURRENCY Tanzanian shilling = 100 cents

THAILAND

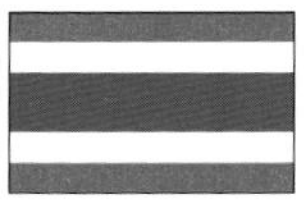
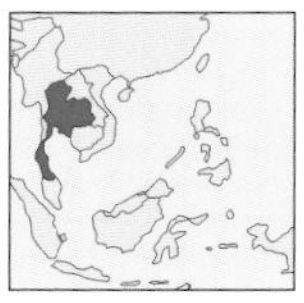

GEOGRAPHY The Kingdom of Thailand is one of the ten countries in Southeast Asia. The highest land is in the north, where Doi Inthanon, the highest peak, reaches 8,415 ft [2,565 m]. The Khorat plateau, in the northeast, makes up about 30% of the country and is the most heavily populated part of Thailand. In the south, Thailand shares the finger-like Malay peninsula with Burma and Malaysia.

Thailand has a tropical climate. Monsoon winds from the southwest bring heavy rains in May to October. Mountains shelter the central plains from the rain-bearing winds.

POLITICS & ECONOMY The first Thai state was set up in the 13th century. By 1350, it included most of what is now Thailand. European contact began in the early 16th century. But, in the late 17th century, the Thais, fearing interference in their affairs, forced all Europeans to leave. This policy continued for 150 years. In 1782, a Thai General, Chao Phraya Chakkri, became king, founding a dynasty which continues today. The country became known as Siam, and Bangkok became its capital. From the mid-19th century, contacts with the West were restored. In World War I, Siam supported the Allies against Germany and Austria–Hungary. But in 1941, the country was conquered by Japan and became its ally. After 1945, it became an ally of the United States.

After 1967, when Thailand became a member of ASEAN (Association of Southeast Asian Nations), its economy expanded rapidly, especially in manufacturing and service industries. In 1997, with other eastern Asian economies, it suffered an economic recession. Thailand has also faced conflict in southern Thailand, where the government has clashed with Muslim groups who feel that the government discriminates against them. In 2001, Thaksin Shinawatra, a businessman, became prime minister. In 2006, his party won a majority, the result of a boycott of opposition parties. Following mass protests, a military *junta* took power. Civilian rule was restored in 2008 when an ally of Thaksin, Samak Sundaravej, was elected prime minister.

Agriculture employs 41% of the people and rice is the chief crop. Cassava, cotton, maize, rubber, sugarcane, and tobacco are also grown. Tin is mined, but the chief exports are manufactures and food products. Tourism is important, but the devastating tsunami in December 2004 cast a shadow over its future growth.

AREA 198,114 sq mi [513,115 sq km]
POPULATION 65,068,000 **CAPITAL** Bangkok
GOVERNMENT Constitutional monarchy
ETHNIC GROUPS Thai 75%, Chinese 14%, others 11%
LANGUAGES Thai (official), English, ethnic and regional dialects
RELIGIONS Buddhism 95%, Islam, Christianity
CURRENCY Baht = 100 satang

TOGO

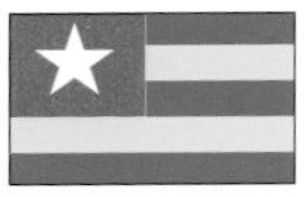
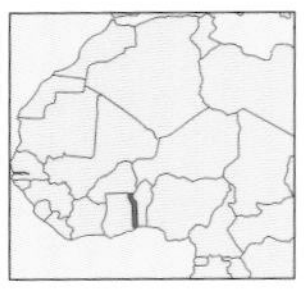

GEOGRAPHY The Republic of Togo is a long, narrow country in West Africa. From north to south, it extends about 311 mi [500 km]. Its coastline on the Gulf of Guinea is only 40 mi [64 km] long and it is only 90 mi [145 km] at its widest point.

Togo has high temperatures all through the year. The main wet season is from March to July, with a minor wet season in October and November.

POLITICS & ECONOMY Togo became a German protectorate in 1884 but, in 1919, Britain took over the western third of the territory, while France took over the eastern two-thirds. In 1956, the people of British Togoland voted to join Ghana, while French Togoland became an independent republic in 1960.

A military regime took power in 1963. In 1967, General Gnassingbé Eyadéma became head of state and suspended the constitution. Under a new constitution adopted in 1992, multiparty elections were held in 1994. However, in 1998, the count in the presidential elections was stopped when it became clear that Eyadéma had been defeated. The opposition boycotted subsequent elections. Eyadéma died in 2005. His son, Faure, took over as president, but international pressure forced him to step down. However, Faure was elected president in April 2005.

Togo is a poor, developing country dependent on agriculture. Major food crops include cassava, maize, millet, and yams. Phosphate rock is the leading export.

AREA 21,925 sq mi [56,785 sq km]
POPULATION 5,702,000 **CAPITAL** Lomé
GOVERNMENT Multiparty republic **ETHNIC GROUPS** Native African 99% (largest tribes are Ewe, Mina and Kabre) **LANGUAGES** French (official), African languages **RELIGIONS** Traditional beliefs 51%, Christianity 29%, Islam 20% **CURRENCY** CFA franc = 100 centimes

TONGA

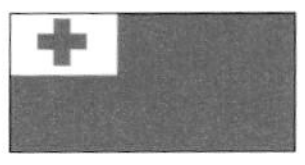
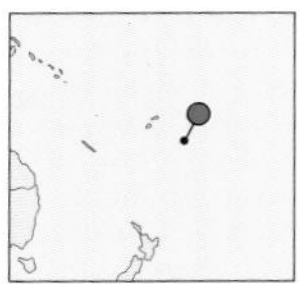

The Kingdom of Tonga, a former British protectorate, became independent in 1970. Situated in the South Pacific Ocean, it contains more than 170 islands, 36 of which are inhabited. Agriculture is the main activity; coconuts, copra, fruits, and fish are leading products.

AREA 251 sq mi [650 sq km] **POPULATION** 117,000 **CAPITAL** Nuku'alofa

TRINIDAD AND TOBAGO

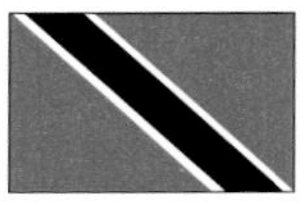
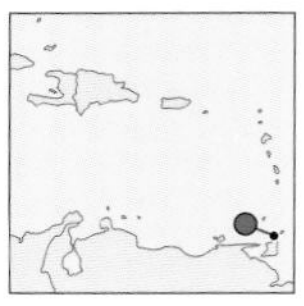

The Republic of Trinidad and Tobago became independent from Britain in 1962. These tropical islands, populated by people of African, Asian (mainly Indian) and European origin, are hilly and forested, though there are some fertile plains. Oil production is the mainstay of the economy.

AREA 1,981 sq mi [5,130 sq km]
POPULATION 1,057,000 **CAPITAL** Port of Spain

TUNISIA

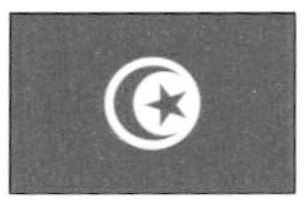
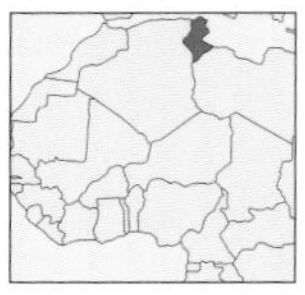

GEOGRAPHY The Republic of Tunisia is the smallest country in North Africa. The mountains in the north are an eastward and comparatively low extension of the Atlas Mountains. To the north and east of the mountains lie fertile plains, especially between Sfax, Tunis and Bizerte. In the south, low-lying regions contain a vast salt pan, called the Chott Djerid, and part of the Sahara Desert.

Northern Tunisia has a Mediterranean climate, with dry, sunny summers, and mild winters with a moderate rainfall. The average yearly rainfall decreases toward the south.

POLITICS & ECONOMY In 1881, France established a protectorate over Tunisia and ruled the country until 1956. The new parliament abolished the monarchy and declared Tunisia to be a republic in 1957, with the nationalist leader, Habib Bourguiba, as president. His government introduced many reforms, including votes for women, but various problems arose, including unemployment among the middle class and fears that Western values introduced by tourists might undermine Muslim values. In 1987, the prime minister, Zine el Abidine Ben Ali, removed Bourguiba, and succeeded him as president. Tunisia's government was widely criticized internationally for its poor human rights record in the 2000s.

The World Bank classifies Tunisia as a "middle-income" developing country. The main resources and chief exports are phosphates and oil. Most industries are concerned with food processing. Agriculture employs 16% of the people, and barley, dates, grapes, olives, and wheat are major crops. Fishing is important, as is tourism.

AREA 63,170 sq mi [163,610 sq km] **POPULATION** 10,276,000
CAPITAL Tunis **GOVERNMENT** Multiparty republic
ETHNIC GROUPS Arab 98%, European 1% **LANGUAGES** Arabic (official), French **RELIGIONS** Islam 98%, Christianity 1%, others
CURRENCY Tunisian dinar = 1,000 millimes

TURKEY

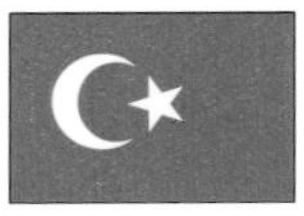
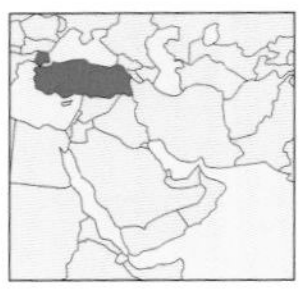

GEOGRAPHY The Republic of Turkey lies in two continents. European Turkey, also called Thrace, lies west of a waterway linking the Mediterranean and Black seas. Most of Asian Turkey consists of plateaux and mountains, which rise to 16,945 ft [5,165 m] at Mount Ararat (Agri Dagi) near the border with Armenia. Earthquakes are common. Central Turkey has a dry climate, with hot, sunny summers and cold winters. The west has a Mediterranean climate, but the Black Sea coast has cooler summers.

POLITICS & ECONOMY In AD 330, the Roman empire moved its capital to Byzantium, which it renamed Constantinople. Constantinople became capital of the East Roman (or Byzantine) empire in 395. Muslim Seljuk Turks from central Asia invaded Anatolia in the 11th century. In the 14th century, another group of Turks, the Ottomans, conquered the area. In 1453, the Ottoman Turks took Constantinople, which they called Istanbul. The Ottomans built up a vast empire which finally collapsed during World War I (1914–18). Turkey became a republic in 1923. Its leader, Mustafa Kemal, or Atatürk ("father of the Turks") began to modernize and secularize the country.

Since the 1940s, Turkey has sought to strengthen its ties with Western powers. It joined NATO (North Atlantic Treaty Organization) in 1951 and it applied to join the European Economic Community in 1987. But Turkey's conflict with Greece, together with its invasion of northern Cyprus in 1974, have led many Europeans to treat Turkey's aspirations with caution. Political instability, military coups, conflict with Kurdish nationalists in eastern Turkey and concern about the country's record on human rights are other problems. Turkey has enjoyed democracy since 1983, though, in 1998, the government banned the Islamist Welfare Party, which it accused of violating secular principles. In 1999, the Muslim Virtue Party (successor to Islamist Welfare Party) lost ground. The largest numbers of parliamentary seats were won by the ruling Democratic Left Party and the far-right National Action Party. However, in the elections in 2002, the moderate Islamic Justice and Development Party (AKP) won 362 of the 500 seats in parliament. Despite its Islamist roots, the AKP was re-elected in 2007, vowing to keep Turkey a secular state. In 2007–8, the activities of separatist Kurdish Workers' Party (PKK) guerrillas led Turkey to launch bombing raids in northern (Kurdish) Iraq, where it claimed the guerrillas had bases.

The World Bank classifies Turkey as a "lower-middle-income" developing country. Agriculture employs 25% of the people, and barley, cotton, fruits, maize, tobacco, and wheat are major crops. Livestock farming is important and wool is a leading product. Turkey produces chromium, but manufacturing is the chief activity. Manufactures include processed farm products and textiles, cars, fertilizers, iron and steel, machinery, metal products, and paper products.

AREA 299,156 sq mi [774,815 sq km]
POPULATION 71,159,000 **CAPITAL** Ankara
GOVERNMENT Multiparty republic **ETHNIC GROUPS** Turkish 80%, Kurdish 20% **LANGUAGES** Turkish (official), Kurdish, Arabic
RELIGIONS Islam (mainly Sunni Muslim) 99%
CURRENCY New Turkish lira = 100 kurus

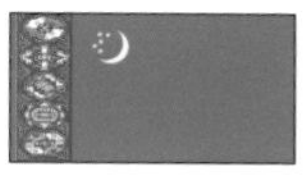
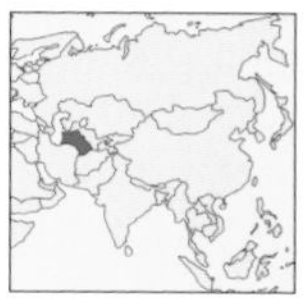

TURKMENISTAN

GEOGRAPHY The Republic of Turkmenistan is one of the five central Asian republics which once formed part of the former Soviet Union. Most of the land is low-lying, with mountains lying on the southern and southwestern borders. In the west lies the salty Caspian Sea. Most of Turkmenistan is arid and the Garagum, Asia's largest sand desert, covers about 80% of the country. Turkmenistan has a continental climate, with average annual rainfall varying from 3 inches [80 mm] in the desert to 12 inches [300 mm] in the mountains. Summer months are hot, but winter temperatures drop well below freezing point.

POLITICS & ECONOMY Just over 1,000 years ago, Turkic people settled in the lands east of the Caspian Sea and the name "Turkmen" comes from this time. Mongol armies conquered the area in the 13th century and Islam was introduced in the 14th century. Russia took over the area in the 1870s and 1880s. After the Russian Revolution of 1917, the area came under Communist rule and, in 1924, it became the Turkmen Soviet Socialist Republic. The Communists strictly controlled all aspects of life and discouraged religion. But they improved such services as education, health, housing, and transport.

In the 1980s, when the Soviet Union began to introduce reforms, the Turkmen began to demand more freedom. In 1990, the Turkmen government stated that its laws overruled Soviet laws. In 1991, Turkmenistan became fully independent after the breakup of the Soviet Union. But the country kept ties with Russia through the Commonwealth of Independent States (CIS).

In 1992, Turkmenistan adopted a new constitution, allowing for the setting up of political parties, providing that they were not ethnic or religious in character. But, effectively, Turkmenistan remained a one-party state and, in 1992, Saparmurad Niyazov, the former Communist and now Democratic Party leader, was the only candidate. In 1999, parliament declared Niyazov president for life. Niyazov died in 2006 and was succeeded by Gurbanguly Berdymukhammedov. He was formally elected (no opposition candidates were allowed to stand) and was sworn in as president in 2007.

Faced with many economic problems, Turkmenistan began to look south rather than to the CIS for support. As part of this policy, it joined the Economic Cooperation Organization, which had been set up in 1985 by Iran, Pakistan and Turkey. In 1996, the completion of a rail link from Turkmenistan to the Iranian coast was an important step in the development of Central Asia. Oil and natural gas are Turkmenistan's chief resources, but agriculture is the main activity. Cotton, grown on irrigated land, is the main crop. Manufactures include cement, glass, petrochemicals, and textiles.

AREA 188,455 SQ MI [488,100 SQ KM] **POPULATION** 5,097,000
CAPITAL ASHKHABAD **GOVERNMENT** SINGLE-PARTY REPUBLIC
ETHNIC GROUPS TURKMEN 85%, UZBEK 5%, RUSSIAN 4%
LANGUAGES TURKMEN (OFFICIAL), RUSSIAN, UZBEK **RELIGIONS** ISLAM 89%, EASTERN ORTHODOX 9% **CURRENCY** TURKMEN MANAT = 100 TENESI

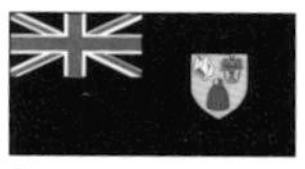
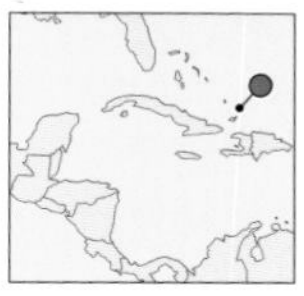

TURKS AND CAICOS ISLANDS

The Turks and Caicos Islands, a British territory in the Caribbean since 1776, are a group of about 30 islands. Fishing and tourism are major activities.

AREA 166 SQ MI [430 SQ KM]
POPULATION 22,000 **CAPITAL** COCKBURN TOWN

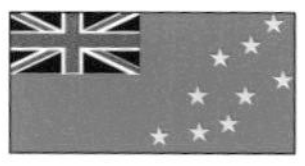
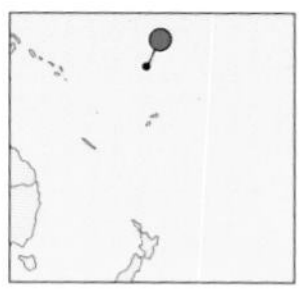

TUVALU

Tuvalu, formerly called the Ellice Islands, was a British territory from the 1890s until it became independent in 1978. It consists of nine low-lying coral atolls in the southern Pacific Ocean. Copra is the chief export.

AREA 10 SQ MI [26 SQ KM]
POPULATION 12,000 **CAPITAL** FONGAFALE

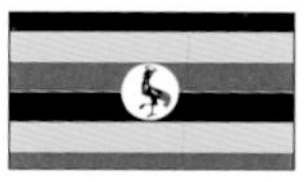
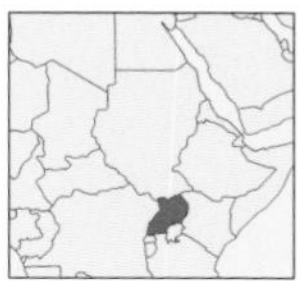

UGANDA

GEOGRAPHY The Republic of Uganda is a landlocked country on the East African plateau. It contains part of Lake Victoria, Africa's largest lake and a source of the River Nile, which occupies a shallow depression in the plateau.

The equator runs through Uganda and the country is warm throughout the year, though the high altitude moderates the temperature. The wettest regions are the lands to the north of Lake Victoria, where Kampala is situated, and the western mountains, especially the high Ruwenzori range.

POLITICS & ECONOMY Little is known of the early history of Uganda. When Europeans first reached the area in the 19th century, many of the people were organized in kingdoms, the most powerful of which was Buganda, the home of the Baganda people. Britain took over the country between 1894 and 1914, and ruled it until independence in 1962.

In 1967, Uganda became a republic and Buganda's Kabaka (king), Sir Edward Mutesa II, was made president. But tensions between the Kabaka and the prime minister, Apollo Milton Obote, led to the dismissal of the Kabaka in 1966. Obote also abolished the traditional kingdoms, including Buganda. Obote was overthrown in 1971 by an army group led by General Idi Amin Dada. Amin ruled as a dictator. He forced most of the Asians who lived in Uganda to leave the country and had many of his opponents killed.

In 1978, a border dispute between Uganda and Tanzania led Tanzanian troops to enter Uganda. With help from Ugandan opponents of Amin, they overthrew Amin's government. In 1980, Obote led his party to victory in national elections. But after charges of fraud, Obote's opponents began guerrilla warfare. A military group overthrew Obote in 1985, though strife continued until 1986, when Yoweri Museveni's National Resistance Movement seized power. In 1993, Museveni restored the traditional kingdoms. Elections were held in 1994, but political parties were forbidden. Museveni was elected in 1996, 2001 and again in 2006, when political parties were permitted. In recent years, Uganda has suffered from a conflict with a rebel force in the north, known as the Lord's Resistance Army. A truce was agreed in 2006, but a peace settlement has proved difficult to achieve.

Internal strife since the 1960s has greatly damaged the economy, but conditions improved during the relative stability of the 1990s and 2000s. Agriculture dominates the economy, employing 76% of the people. The chief export is coffee.

AREA 93,065 SQ MI [241,038 SQ KM]
POPULATION 30,263,000 **CAPITAL** KAMPALA
GOVERNMENT REPUBLIC IN TRANSITION
ETHNIC GROUPS BAGANDA 17%, ANKOLE 8%, BASOGO 8%, ITESO 8%, BAKIGA 7%, LANGI 6%, RWANDA 6%, BAGISU 5%, ACHOLI 4%, LUGBARA 4% AND OTHERS
LANGUAGES ENGLISH AND SWAHILI (BOTH OFFICIAL), GANDA
RELIGIONS ROMAN CATHOLIC 33%, PROTESTANT 33%, TRADITIONAL BELIEFS 18%, ISLAM 16%
CURRENCY UGANDAN SHILLING = 100 CENTS

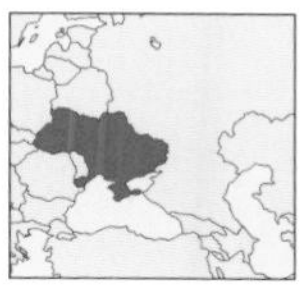

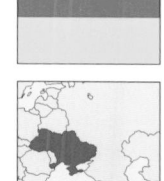

UKRAINE

GEOGRAPHY Ukraine is the second largest country in Europe after Russia. It was formerly part of the Soviet Union, which split apart in 1991. This mostly flat country faces the Black Sea in the south. The Crimean peninsula includes a highland region overlooking Yalta. Ukraine has warm summers, but the winters are cold, becoming more severe from west to east. In the summer, the east of the country is often warmer than the west. The heaviest rainfall occurs in the summer.

POLITICS & ECONOMY Kiev was the original capital of the early Slavic civilization known as Kievan Rus. In the 17th and 18th centuries, parts of Ukraine came under Polish and Russian rule. But Russia gained most of Ukraine in the late 18th century. In 1918, Ukraine became independent, but in 1922 it became part of the Soviet Union. Millions of people died in the 1930s as a result of Soviet policies, while millions more died during the Nazi occupation (1941–4).

In the 1980s, Ukrainian people demanded more say over their affairs. The country became independent in 1991. Leonid Kuchma, who became president in 1994, came under fire in the early 2000s for maladministration and for his alleged involvement in the murder of a journalist. In 2005, the pro-Western leader Victor Yuschenko was elected president. Economic problems and political infighting led to a Russian-leaning party, led by Viktor Yanukovich, winning most seats in parliament in 2006. Yuschenko became prime minister, but an election in 2007 resulted in a pro-Western coalition government, supported by the president's party, and led by a former prime minister, Yulia Tymoshenko.

The World Bank classifies Ukraine as a "lower-middle-income" economy. Agriculture is important. Wheat and sugar are exported. Barley, maize, potatoes, sunflowers, and tobacco are also grown. Livestock rearing and fishing are also important.

Manufacturing is the chief economic activity. Major manufactures include iron and steel, machinery and vehicles. Ukraine has large coalfields. The country imports oil and natural gas, but it has hydroelectric and nuclear power stations.

AREA 233,089 SQ MI [603,700 SQ KM]
POPULATION 46,300,000 **CAPITAL** KIEV
GOVERNMENT MULTIPARTY REPUBLIC
ETHNIC GROUPS UKRAINIAN 78%, RUSSIAN 17%, BELARUSIAN, MOLDOVAN, BULGARIAN, HUNGARIAN, POLISH
LANGUAGES UKRAINIAN (OFFICIAL), RUSSIAN
RELIGIONS MOSTLY UKRAINIAN ORTHODOX
CURRENCY HRYVNIA = 100 KOPIYKAS

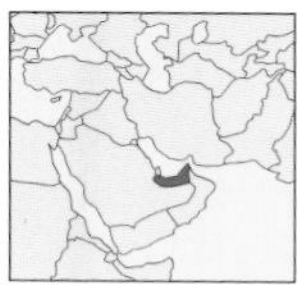

UNITED ARAB EMIRATES

The United Arab Emirates were formed in 1971 when the seven Trucial States of the Persian Gulf (Abu Dhabi, Dubai, Sharjah, Ajman, Umm al Qawayn, Ra's al Khaymah and Al Fujayrah) opted to join together and form an independent country. The economy of this hot and dry country depends on oil production, and oil revenues give the United Arab Emirates one of the highest per capita GNPs in Asia.

AREA 32,278 SQ MI [83,600 SQ KM]
POPULATION 4,444,000 **CAPITAL** ABU DHABI

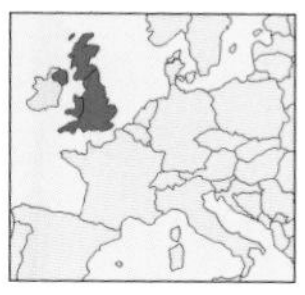

UNITED KINGDOM

GEOGRAPHY The United Kingdom (or UK) is a union of four countries. Three of them – England, Scotland, and Wales – make up Great Britain. The fourth country is Northern Ireland. The Isle of Man and the Channel Islands, including Jersey and Guernsey, are not part of the UK. They are self-governing British dependencies.

The land is highly varied. Much of Scotland and Wales is mountainous, and the highest peak is Scotland's Ben Nevis at 4,404 ft [1,342 m]. England has some highland areas, including the Cumbrian Mountains (or Lake District) and the Pennine range in the north. But England also has large areas of fertile lowland. Northern Ireland is also a mixture of lowlands and uplands. It contains the UK's largest lake, Lough Neagh.

The UK has a mild climate, influenced by the warm Gulf Stream which flows across the Atlantic from the Gulf of Mexico, then past the British Isles. Moist winds from the southwest bring rain, but the rainfall decreases from west to east. Winds from the east and north bring cold weather in winter.

POLITICS & ECONOMY In ancient times, Britain was invaded by many peoples, including Iberians, Celts, Romans, Angles, Saxons, Jutes, Norsemen, Danes, and Normans, who arrived in 1066. The evolution of the United Kingdom spanned hundreds of years. The Normans finally overcame Welsh resistance in 1282, when King Edward I annexed Wales and united it with England. Union with Scotland was achieved by the Act of Union of 1707. This created a country known as the United Kingdom of Great Britain.

Ireland came under Norman rule in the 11th century, and much of its later history was concerned with a struggle against English domination. In 1801, Ireland became part of the United Kingdom of Great Britain and Ireland. But in 1921, southern Ireland broke away to become the Irish Free State. Most of the people in the Irish Free State were Roman Catholics. In Northern Ireland, where the majority of the people were Protestants, most people wanted to remain citizens of the United Kingdom. As a result, the country's official name changed to the United Kingdom of Great Britain and Northern Ireland.

The modern history of the UK began in the 18th century when the British empire began to develop, despite the loss in 1783 of its 13 North American colonies which became the core of the modern United States. The other major event occurred in the late 18th century, when the UK became the first country to industrialize its economy.

The British empire broke up after World War II (1939–45), though the UK still administers many small, mainly island, territories around the world. The empire was transformed into the Commonwealth of Nations, a free association of independent countries which numbered 53 in 2006.

The UK has retained an important world role. For example, in 2001, it played a prominent role in creating a broad alliance to counter international terrorism following the attacks on the United

States. It was also a prominent member of the coalition force which invaded Iraq in 2003. However, the UK has recognized that its economic future lies within Europe. It became a member of the European Economic Community (now the European Union) in 1973. Membership of the EU has been important to the British economy, but some people fear a loss of British identity should the EU ever evolve into a political union. Another matter of public concern is large-scale immigration, both from the EU and outside.

The UK is a major industrial and trading nation. It lacks natural resources apart from coal, iron ore, oil, and natural gas, and has to import most of the materials it needs for its industries. The UK also has to import food, because it produces only about two-thirds of the food it needs. In the first half of the 20th century, Britain was a major exporter of cars, ships, steel, and textiles. But many industries have suffered from competition from other countries, with lower labor costs. Today, industries have to use high-technology in order to compete on the world market.

The UK is one of the world's most urbanized countries, and agriculture employs only 1% of the people. Production is high because of the use of scientific methods and modern machinery. However, in the early 21st century, especially following the outbreak of foot-and-mouth disease in 2001, questions were raised about the future of rural industries. Major crops include barley, potatoes, sugar beet, and wheat. Sheep are the leading livestock, but beef and dairy cattle, pigs, and poultry are also important. Fishing is another major activity and the UK is one of the largest fishing countries in the EU. Important catches include cod, haddock, plaice, and mackerel.

Service industries play a major part in the UK's economy. Financial and insurance services bring in much-needed foreign exchange, while tourism has become a major earner.

AREA 93,381 sq mi [241,857 sq km]
POPULATION 60,776,000 **CAPITAL** London
GOVERNMENT Constitutional monarchy
ETHNIC GROUPS English 82%, Scottish 10%, Irish 2%, Welsh 2%, Ulster 2%, West Indian, Indian, Pakistani, and others **LANGUAGES** English (official), Welsh, Gaelic
RELIGIONS Christianity (Anglican, Roman Catholic, Presbyterian, Methodist), Islam, Sikhism, Hinduism, Judaism
CURRENCY Pound sterling = 100 pence

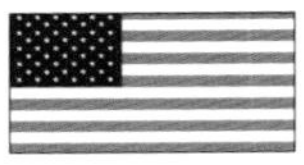
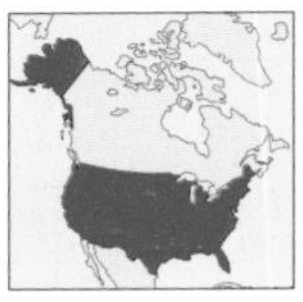

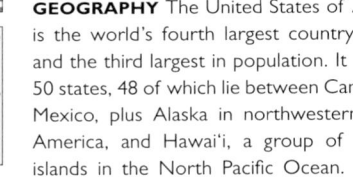

UNITED STATES OF AMERICA

GEOGRAPHY The United States of America is the world's fourth largest country in area and the third largest in population. It contains 50 states, 48 of which lie between Canada and Mexico, plus Alaska in northwestern North America, and Hawai'i, a group of volcanic islands in the North Pacific Ocean. Densely populated coastal plains lie to the east and south of the Appalachian Mountains. The central lowlands drained by the Mississippi–Missouri rivers stretch from the Appalachians to the Rocky Mountains in the west. The Pacific region contains fertile valleys, separated by mountain ranges.

The climate varies greatly, ranging from the Arctic cold of Alaska to the intense heat of Death Valley, a bleak desert in California. Of the 48 states between Canada and Mexico, winters are cold and snowy in the north, but mild in the south, a region which is often called the "Sun Belt."

POLITICS & ECONOMY The first people in North America, the ancestors of the Native Americans (or American Indians) arrived perhaps 40,000 years ago from Asia. Although Vikings probably reached North America 1,000 years ago, European exploration proper did not begin until the late 15th century.

The first Europeans to settle in large numbers were the British, who founded settlements on the eastern coast in the early 17th century. British rule ended in the War of Independence (1775–83). The country expanded in 1803 when a vast territory in the south and west was acquired through the Louisiana Purchase, while the border with Mexico was fixed in the mid-19th century. The Civil War (1861–5) ended slavery and the serious threat that the nation might split into two parts. In the late 19th century, the West was opened up, while immigrants flooded in from Europe and elsewhere.

During the late 19th and early 20th centuries, industrialization led to the United States becoming the world's leading economic superpower and a pioneer in science and technology. It took on the mantle of the champion of Western democracy and, following the breakup of the former Soviet Union, it became the world's only superpower. But the attacks on the country on September 11, 2001, revealed its vulnerability to terrorists and rogue states. The response was vigorous. In 2001, it attacked the Taliban government in Afghanistan, which was protecting al Qaida terrorists. Then, in 2003, it led a coalition force to invade Iraq and overthrow Saddam Hussein. President George W. Bush was re-elected in 2004. However, in 2006, in national elections, the Republican Party lost control of both houses of Congress to the Democratic Party, which had criticized the government for its handling of the Iraq war.

The United States has the world's largest economy in terms of the total value of its production. Although agriculture employs only about 1.5% of the people, farming is highly mechanized and scientific, and the United States leads the world in farm production. Major products include beef and dairy cattle, together with such crops as cotton, fruits, groundnuts, maize, potatoes, soybeans, tobacco, and wheat.

Natural resources include oil, natural gas, coal, a wide range of metal ores, and timber, especially from the Pacific northwest. Manufacturing is the single most valuable activity, employing 10.9% of the people. Major products include vehicles, food products, chemicals, machinery, printed goods, metal products, and scientific instruments. California, with its high-tech electronics industries, is the top manufacturing state. Many southern states, petroleum-rich and climatically favored, have also become highly prosperous in recent years.

AREA 3,717,792 sq mi [9,629,091 sq km]
POPULATION 301,140,000 **CAPITAL** Washington, DC
GOVERNMENT Federal republic
ETHNIC GROUPS White 77%, African American 13%, Asian 4%, Amerindian 2%, others **LANGUAGES** English (official), Spanish, more than 30 others **RELIGIONS** Protestant 56%, Roman Catholic 28%, Islam 2%, Judaism 2%
CURRENCY US dollar = 100 cents

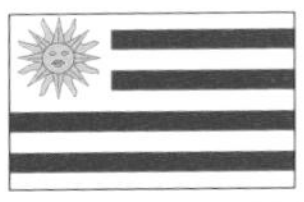
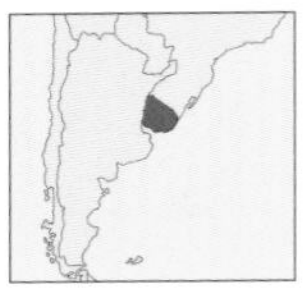

URUGUAY

GEOGRAPHY Uruguay is South America's second smallest independent country after Suriname. The land consists mainly of flat plains and hills. The River Uruguay, which forms the country's western border, flows into the Río de la Plata, a large estuary which leads into the South Atlantic Ocean.

Uruguay has a mild climate, with rain in every month, though droughts sometimes occur. Summers are pleasantly warm, especially near the coast. The weather remains relatively mild throughout the winter.

POLITICS & ECONOMY In 1726, Spanish settlers founded Montevideo in order to halt the Portuguese gaining influence in the area. By the late 18th century, Spaniards had settled in most of the country. Uruguay became part of a colony called the Viceroyalty of La Plata, which also included Argentina, Paraguay, and parts of Bolivia, Brazil, and Chile. In 1820 Brazil annexed Uruguay, ending Spanish rule. In 1825, Uruguayans, supported by Argentina, began a struggle for independence. Finally, in 1828, Brazil and Argentina recognized Uruguay as an independent republic. Social and economic developments were slow, but, from 1903, Uruguay became stable and democratic.

From the 1950s, economic problems caused unrest. Terrorist groups, notably the Tupumaros, carried out murders and kidnappings. The army crushed the Tupumaros in 1972, but the army took over the government in 1973. Military rule continued until 1984 when elections were held. In the early 21st century, Uruguay faced many economic problems, many of which were the result of the economic crisis in its neighbor, Argentina, and its imposition of banking controls in 2004. In 2005, Uruguay's first leftist president, Tabare Vasquez, was sworn in. He restored ties with Cuba and introduced measures to combat poverty.

The World Bank classifies Uruguay as an "upper-middle-income" developing country. Agriculture employs 10% of the people, but farm products, notably hides and leather goods, beef, and wool, are the main exports, while many manufacturing industries process farm products. Crops include maize, potatoes, wheat, and sugar beet. Uruguay depends largely on hydroelectric power for energy; it exports electricity to Argentina.

AREA 67,574 sq mi [175,016 sq km]
POPULATION 3,461,000 **CAPITAL** Montevideo
GOVERNMENT Multiparty republic
ETHNIC GROUPS White 88%, Mestizo 8%, Mulatto or Black 4%
LANGUAGES Spanish (official)
RELIGIONS Roman Catholic 66%, Protestant 2%, Judaism 1%
CURRENCY Uruguayan peso = 100 centésimos

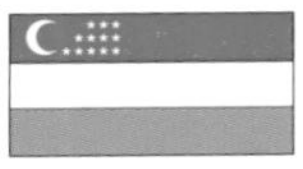
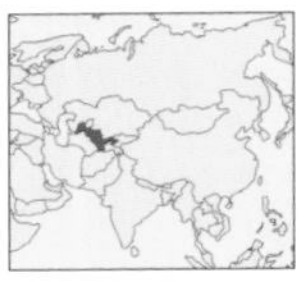

UZBEKISTAN

GEOGRAPHY The Republic of Uzbekistan is one of the five republics in Central Asia which were once part of the Soviet Union. Plains cover most of western Uzbekistan, with highlands in the east. The main rivers, the Amu (or Amu Darya) and Syr (or Syr Darya), drain into the Aral Sea. So much water has been taken from these rivers to irrigate the land that the Aral Sea has now shrunk to about a quarter of its size in 1960. The dried-up lake area has become desert, like much of the rest of the country. Uzbekistan has a continental climate with cold winters and hot summers. The west is extremely arid, with an average annual rainfall of about 8 inches [200 mm].

POLITICS & ECONOMY Russia took the area in the 19th century. After the Russian Revolution of 1917, the Communists took over and, in 1924, they set up the Uzbek Soviet Socialist Republic. Under Communism, all aspects of Uzbek life were controlled and religious worship was discouraged. But education, health, housing, and transport were improved. In the late 1980s, the people demanded more freedom and, in 1990, the government stated that its laws overruled those of the Soviet Union. Uzbekistan became independent in 1991 when the Soviet Union broke up, but it retained links with Russia through the Commonwealth of Independent States. Islam Karimov, leader of the People's Democratic Party (formerly the Communist Party), was elected president in December 1991. In 1992–3, many opposition leaders were arrested because the government said that they threatened national stability. In 1994–5, the PDP was victorious in national elections and, in 1995, a referendum extended Karimov's term in office until 2000. He was re-elected in 2001 and 2007. Uzbekistan allowed the United States to use bases in Uzbekistan for its military campaign in Afghanistan, but it demanded that US forces leave in 2005. International groups continued to criticize Uzbekistan's poor record on human rights.

The World Bank classifies Uzbekistan as a "lower-middle-income" developing country and the government still controls most economic activity. The country produces coal, copper, gold, oil, and natural gas.

AREA 172,741 sq mi [447,400 sq km]
POPULATION 27,780,000 **CAPITAL** Tashkent
GOVERNMENT Socialist republic **ETHNIC GROUPS** Uzbek 80%, Russian 5%, Tajik 5%, Kazakh 3%, Tatar 2%, Kara-Kalpak 2%
LANGUAGES Uzbek (official), Russian **RELIGIONS** Islam 88%, Eastern Orthodox 9% **CURRENCY** Uzbekistani sum = 100 tiyin

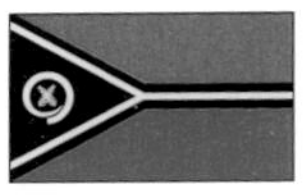
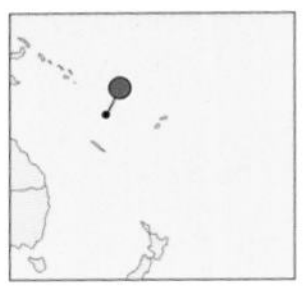

VANUATU

The Republic of Vanuatu, formerly the Anglo-French Condominium of the New Hebrides, became independent in 1980. It consists of a chain of 80 islands in the South Pacific Ocean. Its economy is based on agriculture and it exports copra, beef and veal, timber and cocoa.

AREA 4,706 sq mi [12,189 sq km]
POPULATION 212,000 **CAPITAL** Port-Vila

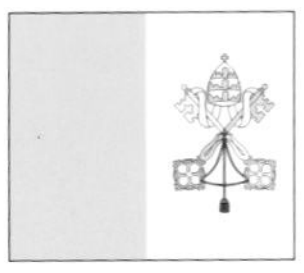
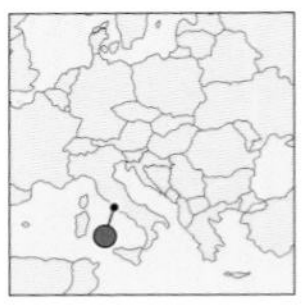

VATICAN CITY

Vatican City State, the world's smallest independent nation, is an enclave on the west bank of the River Tiber in Rome. It forms an independent base for the Holy See, the governing body of the Roman Catholic Church.

AREA 0.17 sq mi [0.44 sq km]
POPULATION 1,000

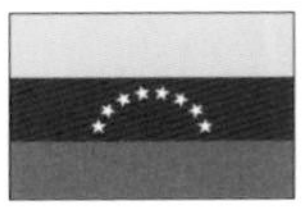
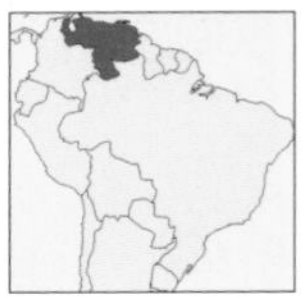

VENEZUELA

GEOGRAPHY The Bolivarian Republic of Venezuela, in northern South America, contains the Maracaibo lowlands around the oil-rich Lake Maracaibo in the west. Andean ranges enclose the lowlands and extend across most of northern Venezuela. The Orinoco river basin, containing tropical grasslands called *llanos*, lies between the northern highlands and the Guiana Highlands in the southeast. The Orinoco is Venezuela's longest river.

Venezuela has a tropical climate. Temperatures are high

throughout the year on the lowlands, though the mountains are much cooler. The rainfall is heaviest in the mountains. But much of the country has a marked dry season between December and April.

POLITICS & ECONOMY In the early 19th century, Venezuelans, such as Simón Bolívar and Francisco de Miranda, began a struggle against Spanish rule. Venezuela declared its independence in 1811. But it only became truly independent in 1821, when the Spanish were defeated in a battle near Valencia.

The development of Venezuela in the 19th and the first half of the 20th centuries was marred by instability, violence and periods of harsh dictatorial rule. But Venezuela has had elected governments since 1958. The country has greatly benefited from its oil resources which were first exploited in 1917. In 1960, Venezuela helped to form OPEC (the Organization of Petroleum Exporting Countries) and, in 1976, the government of Venezuela took control of the entire oil industry. In 1999, Hugo Chavez, who had staged an unsuccessful coup in 1992, was elected president. Chavez survived an attempted coup in 2002 and, in 2004, he won a majority in a referendum that had been intended by the opposition to remove him from office. He was re-elected in 2006, and his left-wing policies and support for other leftist regimes in Latin America continued to arouse US hostility.

With oil accounting for about 90% of its exports, Venezuela has an "upper-middle-income" economy. Other exports include bauxite and aluminum, iron ore, and farm products. Beef cattle, dairy cattle, and poultry are raised. Crops include bananas, cassava, citrus fruits, coffee, and rice. The main industry is petroleum refining. Cement, steel, and textiles are also produced.

AREA 352,143 SQ MI [912,050 SQ KM] **POPULATION** 26,024,000
CAPITAL CARACAS **GOVERNMENT** FEDERAL REPUBLIC
ETHNIC GROUPS SPANISH, ITALIAN, PORTUGUESE, ARAB, GERMAN, AFRICAN, INDIGENOUS PEOPLE **LANGUAGES** SPANISH (OFFICIAL), INDIGENOUS DIALECTS **RELIGIONS** ROMAN CATHOLIC 96%
CURRENCY BOLÍVAR = 100 CÉNTIMOS

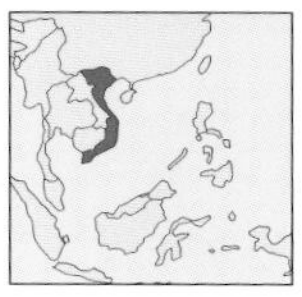

VIETNAM

GEOGRAPHY The Socialist Republic of Vietnam occupies an S-shaped strip of land facing the South China Sea in Southeast Asia. The coastal plains include two densely populated, fertile delta regions: the Red (Hong) delta facing the Gulf of Tonkin in the north, and the Mekong delta in the south.

Vietnam has a tropical climate, though the driest months of January to March are a little cooler than the wet, hot summer months, when monsoon winds blow from the southwest. Typhoons (cyclones or hurricanes) sometimes hit the coast, causing extensive flooding and much damage.

POLITICS & ECONOMY China dominated Vietnam for a thousand years before AD 939, when a Vietnamese state was founded. The French took over the area between the 1850s and 1880s. They ruled Vietnam as part of French Indochina, which also included Cambodia and Laos.

Japan conquered Vietnam during World War II (1939–45). In 1946, war broke out between a nationalist group, called the Vietminh, and the French colonial government. France withdrew in 1954 and Vietnam was divided into a Communist North Vietnam, led by the Vietminh leader, Ho Chi Minh, and a non-Communist South.

A force called the Viet Cong rebeled against South Vietnam's government in 1957 and a war began, which gradually increased in intensity. The United States aided the South, but after it withdrew in 1975, South Vietnam surrendered. In 1976, the united Vietnam became a Socialist Republic.

Vietnamese troops intervened in Cambodia in 1978 to defeat the Communist Khmer Rouge government, but it withdrew its troops in 1989. In the 1990s, Vietnam began to introduce reforms. In 1995, the United States opened an embassy in Hanoi and, in 2002, trade relations with the US were normalized. In 2007, Vietnam became the 150th member of the World Trade Organization. In recent years, the economy has expanded quickly, although agriculture remains the main activity. Rice is the chief food crop. Vietnam produces chromium, tin and phosphates.

AREA 128,065 SQ MI [331,689 SQ KM]
POPULATION 85,262,000 **CAPITAL** HANOI
GOVERNMENT SOCIALIST REPUBLIC
ETHNIC GROUPS VIETNAMESE 87%, CHINESE, HMONG, THAI, KHMER, CHAM, MOUNTAIN GROUPS **LANGUAGES** VIETNAMESE (OFFICIAL), ENGLISH, CHINESE **RELIGIONS** BUDDHISM, CHRISTIANITY, INDIGENOUS BELIEFS
CURRENCY DONG = 10 HAO = 100 XU

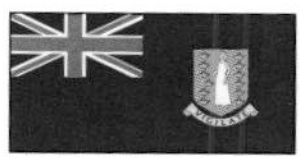
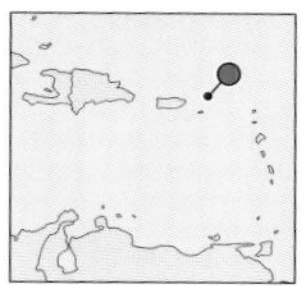

VIRGIN ISLANDS, BRITISH

The British Virgin Islands, the most northerly of the Lesser Antilles, are a British overseas territory, with a substantial measure of self-government.

AREA 58 SQ MI [151 SQ KM]
POPULATION 24,000 **CAPITAL** ROAD TOWN

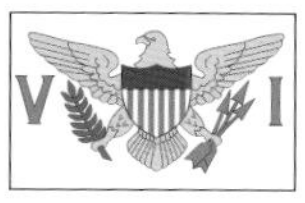
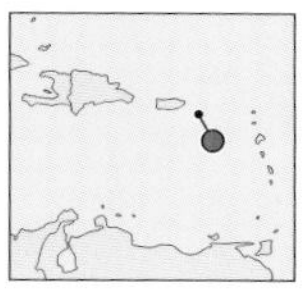

VIRGIN ISLANDS, US

The Virgin Islands of the United States, a group of three islands and 65 small islets, are a self-governing US territory. Purchased from Denmark in 1917, its residents are US citizens and they elect a non-voting delegate to the US House of Representatives.

AREA 134 SQ MI [347 SQ KM]
POPULATION 108,000 **CAPITAL** CHARLOTTE AMALIE

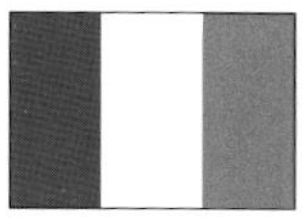
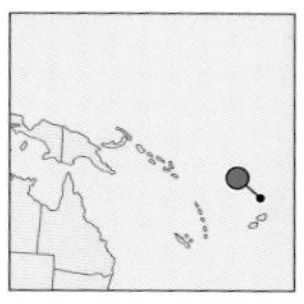

WALLIS AND FUTUNA

Wallis and Futuna, in the South Pacific Ocean, is the smallest and the poorest of France's overseas territories. French aid remains vital to an economy based on subsistence agriculture.

AREA 77 SQ MI [200 SQ KM]
POPULATION 16,000 **CAPITAL** MATA-UTU

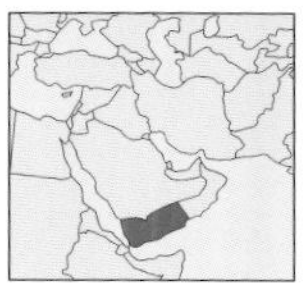

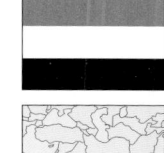

YEMEN

GEOGRAPHY The Republic of Yemen faces the Red Sea and the Gulf of Aden in the southwestern corner of the Arabian peninsula. Behind the narrow coastal plain along the Red Sea, the land rises to a mountain region called High Yemen. The climate ranges from hot and often humid conditions on the coast to the cooler highlands. Most of the country is arid. The south coasts are particularly hot and humid.

POLITICS & ECONOMY After World War I, northern Yemen, which had been ruled by Turkey, began to evolve into a separate state from the south, where Britain was in control. Britain withdrew in 1967 and a left-wing government took power in the south. In North Yemen, the monarchy was abolished in 1962 and the country became a republic.

Clashes occurred between the traditionalist Yemen Arab Republic in the north and the formerly British Marxist People's Democratic Republic of Yemen but, in 1990, the two Yemens merged to form a single country. Further conflict occurred in 1994, when southern secessionist forces were defeated. In 1998 and 1999, militants in the Aden-Abyan Islamic army sought to destabilize the country. In 2000, suicide bombers, thought to be part of the al Qaida network, steered a craft into a US destroyer in Aden harbor, killing 17 sailors. Bombings, often attributed by the government to al Qaida and often involving tourists, have caused serious security problems in recent years.

Yemen is a developing country and agriculture employs about half of the people. Sheep are reared and such crops as barley, fruits, wheat, and vegetables are grown in highland valleys and around oases. Cash crops include coffee and cotton.

Imported oil is refined at Aden and petroleum extraction began in the northwest in the 1980s. Handicrafts, leather goods, and textiles are manufactured. Remittances from Yemenis abroad are a major source of revenue.

AREA 203,848 SQ MI [527,968 SQ KM] **POPULATION** 22,231,000
CAPITAL SANA' **GOVERNMENT** MULTIPARTY REPUBLIC
ETHNIC GROUPS PREDOMINANTLY ARAB **LANGUAGES** ARABIC (OFFICIAL)
RELIGIONS ISLAM **CURRENCY** YEMENI RIAL = 100 FILS

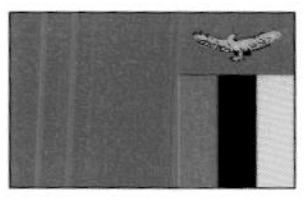
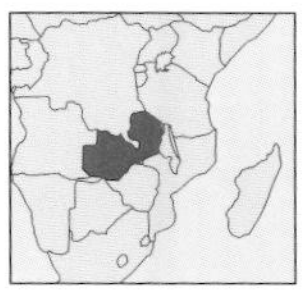

ZAMBIA

GEOGRAPHY The Republic of Zambia is a landlocked country in southern Africa. Zambia lies on the plateau that makes up most of southern Africa. Much of the land is between 2,950 ft to 4,920 ft [900 m and 1,500 m] above sea level. The Muchinga Mountains in the northeast rise above this flat land. Lakes include Bangweulu, which is entirely within Zambia, together with parts of lakes Mweru and Tanganyika in the north. Zambia lies in the tropics, but temperatures are moderated by the altitude.

POLITICS & ECONOMY European contact with Zambia began in the 19th century, when the explorer David Livingstone crossed the River Zambezi. In the 1890s, the British South Africa Company, set up by Cecil Rhodes (1853–1902), the British financier and statesman, made treaties with local chiefs and gradually took over the area. In 1911, the Company named the area Northern Rhodesia. In 1924, Britain took over the government of the country.

In 1953, Britain formed a federation of Northern Rhodesia, Southern Rhodesia (now Zimbabwe), and Nyasaland (now Malawi). Because of African opposition, the federation was dissolved in 1963 and Northern Rhodesia became independent as Zambia in 1964. Kenneth Kaunda became president and one-party rule was introduced in 1972. Under a new constitution, Frederick Chiluba was elected president in 1996. He stood down in 2001 and Levy Mwanawasa became president. In 2005, the Supreme Court rejected a challenge to Mwanawasa's election, but stated that the 2001 ballot had been flawed.

Copper, the main resource, accounted for 50% of the exports in 2002. Zambia also produces cobalt, lead, zinc, and gemstones. Agriculture employs 62% of the people, as compared with 4% in industry and mining. Food crops include cassava, fruits and vegetables, maize, millet, and sorghum, while cash crops include coffee, sugarcane, and tobacco.

AREA 290,586 SQ MI [752,618 SQ KM]
POPULATION 11,477,000 **CAPITAL** LUSAKA
GOVERNMENT MULTIPARTY REPUBLIC **ETHNIC GROUPS** NATIVE AFRICAN (BEMBA, TONGA, MARAVI/NYANJA) **LANGUAGES** ENGLISH (OFFICIAL), BEMBA, KAONDA, NYANJA, AND ABOUT 70 OTHERS **RELIGIONS** CHRISTIANITY 70%, ISLAM, HINDUISM **CURRENCY** ZAMBIAN KWACHA = 100 NGWEE

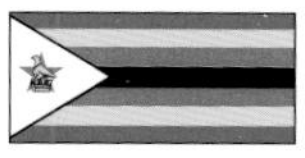
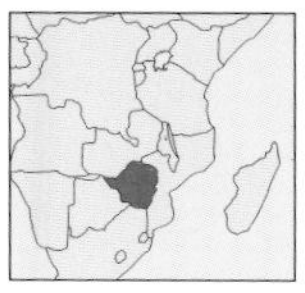

ZIMBABWE

GEOGRAPHY The Republic of Zimbabwe is a landlocked country in southern Africa. Most of the country lies on a high plateau between the Zambezi and Limpopo rivers between 2,950 ft and 4,920 ft [900 m to 1,500 m] above sea level. From October to March, the weather is hot and wet, but in the winter, daily temperatures can vary greatly.

POLITICS & ECONOMY The Shona people became dominant in the region about 1,000 years ago. The British South Africa Company, under the statesman Cecil Rhodes (1853–1902), occupied the area in the 1890s, after obtaining mineral rights from local chiefs. The area was named Rhodesia and later Southern Rhodesia. It became a self-governing British colony in 1923. Between 1953 and 1963, Southern and Northern Rhodesia (now Zambia) were joined to Nyasaland (Malawi) in the Central African Federation.

In 1965, the European government of Southern Rhodesia (then called Rhodesia) declared their country independent but Britain refused to accept this. Finally, after a civil war, the country became legally independent in 1980, though rivalries between the Shona and Ndebele people threatened stability. Order was restored when the Shona prime minister, Robert Mugabe, brought his Ndebele rivals into his government. In 1987, Mugabe became the country's executive president and, in 1991, the government renounced its Marxist ideology. Mugabe was re-elected president in 1990 and 1996.

From the late 1990s, Mugabe's government seized white-owned farms and landless "war veterans" began to occupy them. In 2002, Mugabe was re-elected amid accusations of electoral irregularities. The Commonwealth suspended Zimbabwe's membership and, in 2004, the European Union renewed sanctions against the country. In parliamentary elections in 2008, Mugabe's party was defeated, while Mugabe lost to Morgan Tsvangirai in the presidential election. A run-off was ordered, but brutal intimidation of opposition supporters led Tsvangirai to withdraw his candidacy. Amid international condemnation, Mugabe was re-elected unopposed.

In the 2000s, the economy collapsed and many people faced starvation. Zimbabwe has valuable mineral reserves and minerals are important exports. Agriculture employs 56% of the people. Maize is the chief food crop. Cash crops include cotton, sugar, and tobacco. Cattle ranching is also important.

AREA 150,871 SQ MI [390,757 SQ KM]
POPULATION 12,311,000 **CAPITAL** HARARE
GOVERNMENT MULTIPARTY REPUBLIC **ETHNIC GROUPS** SHONA 82%, NDEBELE 14%, OTHER AFRICAN GROUPS 2%, MIXED AND ASIAN 1%
LANGUAGES ENGLISH (OFFICIAL), SHONA, NDEBELE
RELIGIONS CHRISTIANITY, TRADITIONAL BELIEFS
CURRENCY ZIMBABWEAN DOLLAR = 100 CENTS

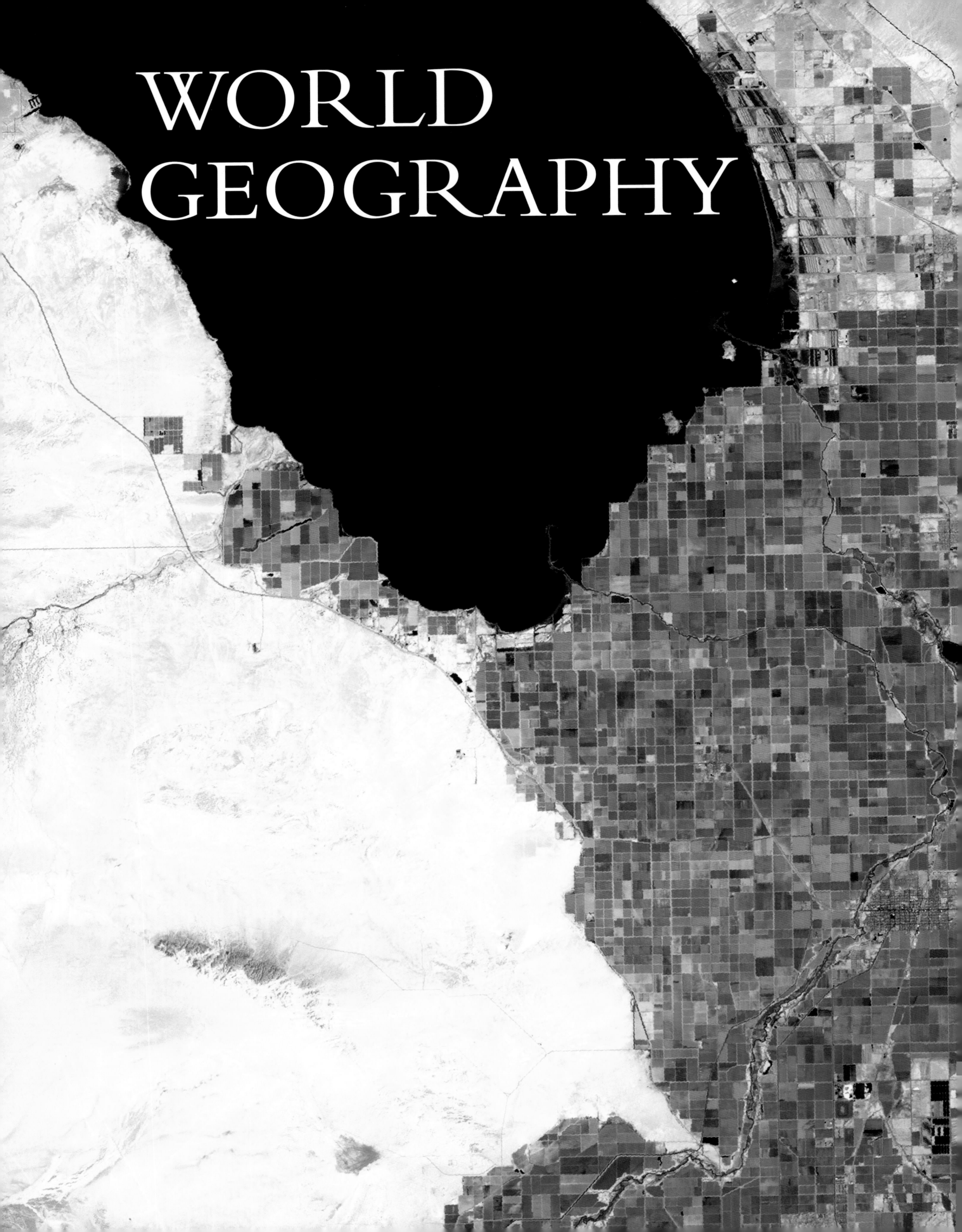

WORLD GEOGRAPHY

– IMPERIAL VALLEY, USA/MEXICO –
The dark area at top left of this false-color image is the Salton Sea. It is the largest lake in California but was created inadvertently in 1905 during an attempt to divert the flow of the Colorado River for irrigation. The resultant floodwaters filled part of the Imperial Valley. It lies 236 ft [72 m] below sea level and is very saline. To the south is a large area of productive land, which uses irrigated water from the river. The vegetation appears bright red on this image. [Map page 307]

For more information:
66 Orbits of the planets
Planetary data

About 13.7 billion years ago, time and space began with the most colossal explosion in cosmic history: the so-called Big Bang that is believed to have initiated the Universe. According to current theory, in the first millionth of a second of its existence it expanded from a dimensionless point of infinite mass and density into a fireball about the size of our present Solar System – and it has been expanding ever since.

It took about 300,000 years for the primal fireball to cool enough for atoms to form. They were mostly hydrogen which is still the most abundant material in the Universe. The radiation from this era still pervades the Universe, though its subsequent expansion means that we see it at about 3° above absolute zero instead of its original 3,000° C. Observations of this faint background glow reveal slight fluctuations. It is these which appear to have become, over the next billion years or so, the large-scale structures in the present Universe. As well as the matter which we can see, there is evidence of a much greater quantity of dark matter whose nature remains unknown. Within knots of this dark matter, the first stars and galaxies formed, probably within the first billion years of the life of the Universe. Our own galaxy was among them.

There were several generations of stars, each feeding on the wreckage of its extinct predecessors as well as the original galactic gas swirls. With each new generation, progressively larger atoms were forged in stellar furnaces, and the galaxy's range of elements, once restricted to hydrogen and helium, grew larger. About 9 billion years after the Big Bang, a star formed on the outskirts of our galaxy with enough matter left over to create a retinue of planets. Nearly 5 billion years after that, human beings evolved.

The Sun is one of more than 100 billion stars in the home galaxy alone. Our galaxy, in turn, forms part of a local group consisting of approximately 30 similar structures, mostly small "dwarf" galaxies but a few large ones, and one – the Andromeda Galaxy – larger than our own. There are at least 100 billion galaxies in the Universe, many of which are members of huge galaxy clusters.

LIFE OF A STAR

For most of its existence, a star produces energy by the nuclear fusion of hydrogen into helium at its core. The duration of this hydrogen-burning period – known as the *main sequence* – depends on the star's mass; the greater the mass, the higher the core temperatures and the sooner the star's supply of hydrogen is exhausted. Dim, dwarf stars consume their hydrogen slowly, eking it out over billions of years. The Sun, like other stars of its mass, should spend about 10 billion years on the main sequence; since it was formed less than 5 billion years ago, it still has half its life left.

Once all of a star's core hydrogen has been fused into helium, nuclear activity moves outward into layers of unconsumed hydrogen. For a time, energy production sharply increases: the star grows hotter and expands enormously, turning into a so-called red giant. Its energy output will increase a thousandfold, and it will swell to a hundred times its former diameter.

After a few hundred million years, helium in the core will become sufficiently compressed to initiate a new cycle of nuclear fusion: from helium to carbon. The star will contract somewhat, before beginning its last expansion, in the Sun's case engulfing the Earth and perhaps Mars. In this bloated condition, the Sun's outer layers will break off into space, leaving a tiny inner core, mainly of carbon, that shrinks progressively under its own gravity. The white dwarf star thus formed can attain a density more than 10,000 times that of normal matter, with crushing surface gravity to match. Gradually, the nuclear fires will die down, and the Sun will reach its terminal stage: a black dwarf, emitting insignificant amounts of energy.

Black holes

However, stars more massive than the Sun may undergo a different transformation. The additional mass allows gravitational collapse to continue indefinitely: eventually, all the star's remaining matter shrinks to a point, and its density approaches infinity – a state that will not permit even subatomic structures to survive.

The star has become a *black hole*: an anomalous "singularity" in the fabric of space and time. Although vast coruscations of radiation will be emitted by any matter falling into its grasp, the singularity itself has an escape velocity that exceeds the speed of light, and nothing can ever be released from it. Within the boundaries of the black hole, the laws of physics are suspended.

GALACTIC STRUCTURES

Many of the Universe's 100 billion galaxies show clear structural patterns, originally classified by the American astronomer Edwin Hubble in 1925. Spiral galaxies like our own have a central, almost spherical bulge and a surrounding disk composed of spiral arms. Barred spirals have a central bar of stars across the nucleus, with spiral arms trailing from the ends of the bar. Elliptical galaxies have a more uniform appearance, ranging from a flattened disk to a near sphere.

▲ M51, the Whirlpool Nebula, comprises the large spiral galaxy NGC 5194 and its smaller, barred companion NGC 5195. M51 was the first astronomical object in which a spiral structure was identified, in 1845. Although smaller and less massive than our own Galaxy, M51 is much brighter, due to recent star formation.

Most galaxies, however, have no obvious structure at all. Galaxies also vary enormously in size, from dwarf galaxies only 2,000 light-years across to great assemblies of stars 80 or more times larger.

THE HOME GALAXY

The Sun and its planets are located in one of the spiral arms of the Galaxy, about 26,000 light-years from the galactic center and orbiting around it in a period of about 220 million years. The center is invisible from the Earth, masked by vast, light-absorbing clouds of interstellar dust.

The Galaxy is probably around 12 billion years old and, like other spiral galaxies, has three distinct regions. The central bulge is about 30,000 light-years in diameter. The disk in which the Sun is located is not much more than 1,000 light-years thick, but approximately 100,000 light-years from end to end. Around the Galaxy is the halo, a spherical zone 300,000 light-years across, studded with globular star clusters and sprinkled with individual suns.

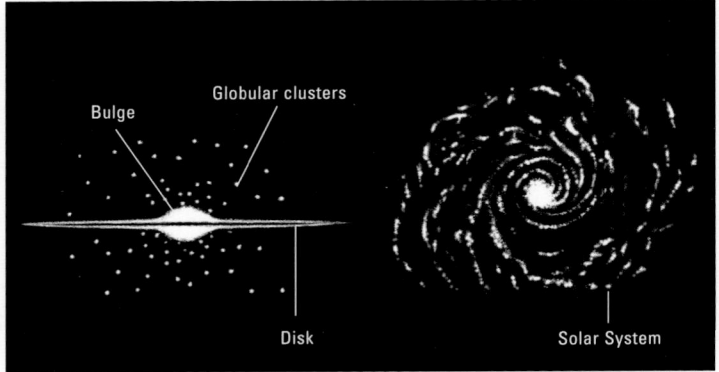

Bulge

Globular clusters

Disk

Solar System

THE END OF THE UNIVERSE

The likely fate of the Universe is disputed. According to one theory (*top of diagram, below*), the expansion begun at the time of the Big Bang will continue "indefinitely," with aging galaxies moving further and further apart in an immense, dark graveyard.

Alternatively, gravity may overcome the expansion (*bottom of diagram*). Galaxies will fall back together until everything is again concentrated at a single point, followed by a new Big Bang and a new expansion, in an endlessly repeated cycle.

The first theory is supported by the amount of visible matter in the Universe; the second theory assumes that there is enough dark material in the Universe to bring about the gravitational collapse.

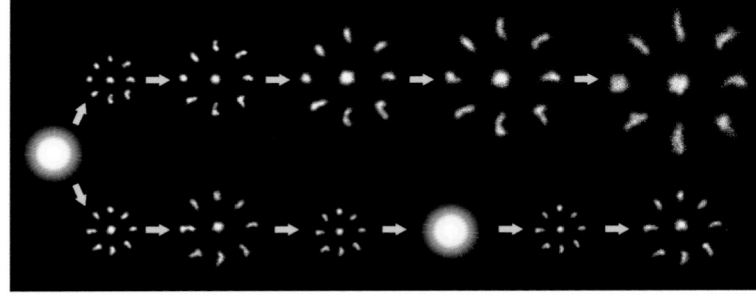

THE NEAREST STARS

The 22 nearest stars, excluding the Sun, with their distance from Earth in light-years*

Proxima Centauri	4.2	UV Ceti A	8.7	61 Cygni A	11.4
Alpha Centauri A	4.4	UV Ceti B	8.7	Procyon A	11.4
Alpha Centauri B	4.4	Ross 154	9.7	Procyon B	11.4
Barnard's Star	5.9	Ross 248	10.3	61 Cygni B	11.4
Wolf 359	7.8	Epsilon Eridani	10.5	HD 173740	11.5
Lalande 21185	8.3	HD 217987	10.7	HD 173739	11.7
Sirius A	8.6	Ross 128	10.9	* A light-year is about 5,900	
Sirius B	8.6	L789-6	11.2	billion miles [9,500 billion km]	

Many of the nearest stars, like Alpha Centauri A and B, are double stars, orbiting about their common center of gravity and to all intents and purposes equidistant from Earth. Many of them are dim objects, with no name other than the designation given to them by the astronomers who first investigated them.

However, they include Sirius, the brightest star in the sky, and Procyon, the seventh brightest. Both are larger than the Sun; of the nearest stars, only Epsilon Eridani is similar in size and luminosity. Most of the other bright stars in the sky are within 500 light-years of the Sun – a small fraction of the diameter of our galaxy.

STAR CHARTS

NORTHERN HEMISPHERE SKY

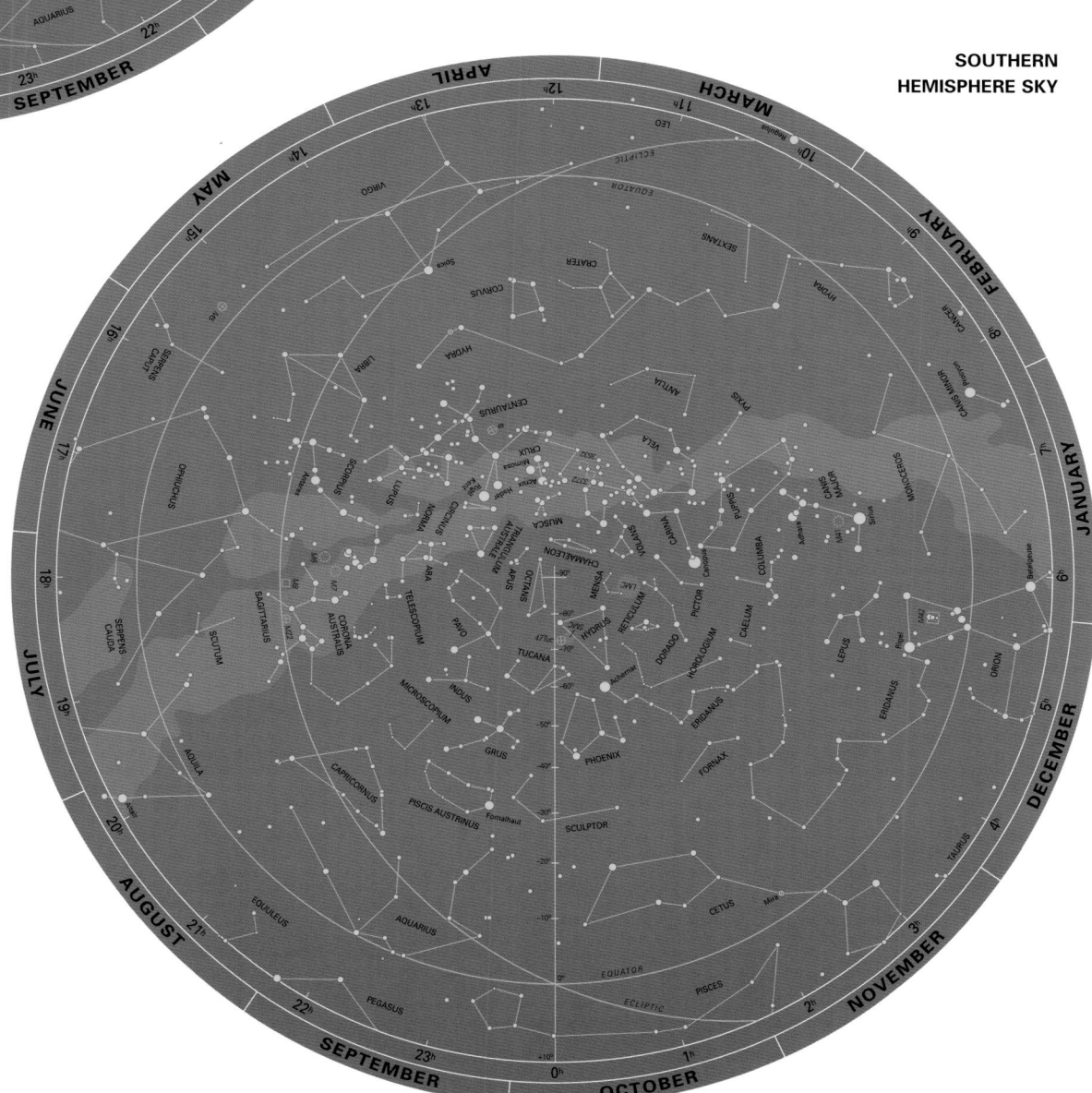

THE CONSTELLATIONS
The constellations and their English names

Andromeda	Andromeda	Lacerta	Lizard
Antlia	Air Pump	Leo	Lion
Apus	Bird of Paradise	Leo Minor	Little Lion
Aquarius	Water Carrier	Lepus	Hare
Aquila	Eagle	Libra	Scales
Ara	Altar	Lupus	Wolf
Aries	Ram	Lynx	Lynx
Auriga	Charioteer	Lyra	Lyre
Boötes	Herdsman	Mensa	Table Mountain
Caelum	Chisel	Microscopium	Microscope
Camelopardalis	Giraffe	Monoceros	Unicorn
Cancer	Crab	Musca	Fly
Canes Venatici	Hunting Dogs	Norma	Level
Canis Major	Great Dog	Octans	Octant
Canis Minor	Little Dog	Ophiuchus	Serpent Bearer
Capricornus	Sea Goat	Orion	Orion
Carina	Ship's Keel	Pavo	Peacock
Cassiopeia	Cassiopeia	Pegasus	Winged Horse
Centaurus	Centaur	Perseus	Perseus
Cepheus	Cepheus	Phoenix	Phoenix
Cetus	Whale	Pictor	Easel
Chamaeleon	Chameleon	Pisces	Fishes
Circinus	Compasses	Piscis Austrinus	Southern Fish
Columba	Dove	Puppis	Ship's Stern
Coma Berenices	Berenice's Hair	Pyxis	Mariner's Compass
Corona Australis	Southern Crown	Reticulum	Net
Corona Borealis	Northern Crown	Sagitta	Arrow
Corvus	Crow	Sagittarius	Archer
Crater	Cup	Scorpius	Scorpion
Crux	Southern Cross	Sculptor	Sculptor
Cygnus	Swan	Scutum	Shield
Delphinus	Dolphin	Serpens	Serpent
Dorado	Swordfish	Sextans	Sextant
Draco	Dragon	Taurus	Bull
Equuleus	Little Horse	Telescopium	Telescope
Eridanus	River Eridanus	Triangulum	Triangle
Fornax	Furnace	Triangulum Australe	Southern Triangle
Gemini	Twins	Tucana	Toucan
Grus	Crane	Ursa Major	Great Bear
Hercules	Hercules	Ursa Minor	Little Bear
Horologium	Clock	Vela	Ship's Sails
Hydra	Water Snake	Virgo	Virgin
Hydrus	Sea Serpent	Volans	Flying Fish
Indus	Indian	Vulpecula	Fox

The charts on this page show the entire heavens divided into northern and southern hemispheres, with 10° of overlap between them around the perimeter of each one. However, the view from any particular location on Earth will be different, and will change both hourly as the Earth turns, and throughout the year as the Earth goes around the Sun.

The Sun's annual path through the heavens is known as the "ecliptic," and is shown here by an orange line. When the Sun is in the sky its light drowns out our view of the stars, so only that part of the heavens opposite the Sun is visible at a particular time. The sky's equivalent of longitude is known as "right ascension." As the stars appear to rotate around the Earth once every 24 hours, right ascension is measured eastward in hours and minutes and is marked around the edge of the maps. The equivalent of latitude is "declination," measured in degrees north or south of the celestial equator, and shown by the vertical line on each chart.

Using the charts

At any place and time you can see half of the whole sky, assuming a flat horizon. If you were at one of the poles your view would be shown as a circle centered on the middle of the map for the appropriate hemisphere, with the horizon marked by the celestial equator. From all other locations the center of your view (your overhead point) will be at some other point on the map whose location changes with time. The closer you are to Earth's equator, the closer the center will be to the edge of the map and more stars in the opposite hemisphere will be visible.

So first choose the appropriate chart for your hemisphere and hold it with the month at the bottom. At 11 p.m., not allowing for daylight saving time (Summer Time), your overhead point will be at the same declination as your geographical latitude and stars lower on the map will be due south (or north in the southern hemisphere). From latitude 50° in mid August, for example, your overhead point will be close to the star Deneb in the constellation of Cygnus. Stars on the opposite side of the map will be below your northern horizon, while stars below Deneb will be due south.

SOUTHERN HEMISPHERE SKY

STAR MAGNITUDES
Apparent visual magnitudes

The magnitude scale of star brightnesses is developed from the system used by the Ancient Greeks in which the brightest stars were first magnitude and the faintest visible to the naked eye were sixth. Today the scale has a mathematical basis and extends, at the brightest end, through to negative magnitudes.

The Milky Way is shown in light blue on these charts.

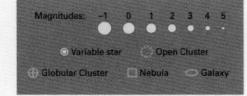

Magnitudes: -1 0 1 2 3 4 5
● Variable star   ○ Open Cluster
⊕ Globular Cluster   ▢ Nebula   ◇ Galaxy

For more information:
64 The Home Galaxy
68 The seasons
   Day and night
69 The Moon

Lying about halfway from the center of one of billions of galaxies that populate the observable Universe, our Solar System contains eight planets and their moons, three dwarf planets, innumerable asteroids, comets and other icy bodies, and a miscellany of dust and gas, all tethered by the immense gravitational field of the Sun, the star whose thermonuclear furnaces provide them all with heat and light.

The Solar System was formed about 5 billion years ago, when a spinning cloud of gas, mostly hydrogen but seeded with other heavier elements, condensed enough to ignite a nuclear reaction and create a star. The Sun still accounts for almost 99.9% of the system's total mass.

By composition as well as distance, the planetary array divides quite neatly in two: an inner system of four small, solid planets, including the Earth, and an outer system, from Jupiter to Neptune, of four much larger planets composed of lighter materials, such as gas, liquid and ice. Lying mostly between the two groups is a scattering of rocky asteroids, numbering perhaps a million or more. They may be debris left over from the formation of the inner Solar System. In 2006, Pluto was demoted from its former status as a planet and is now regarded as a member of the Kuiper Belt of icy bodies at the fringes of the Solar System.

Much of the early history of science is the story of people trying to make sense of the wandering points of light that were all they knew of the planets. Now, men have themselves stood on the Earth's Moon, space probes have landed on Mars and Venus, and distant landscapes have been mapped with astonishing accuracy, transforming our knowledge of our celestial environment.

In the 1980s, the Voyager space probes skimmed all four major planets of the outer Solar System, bringing new revelations with each close approach. The Magellan (Venus), Galileo (Jupiter) and Cassini–Huygens (Saturn) missions have transformed our knowledge of those planets and the giants' moons, and a host of orbiters and landers have shown us Mars in a new light. A spacecraft is also on its way to visit Pluto.

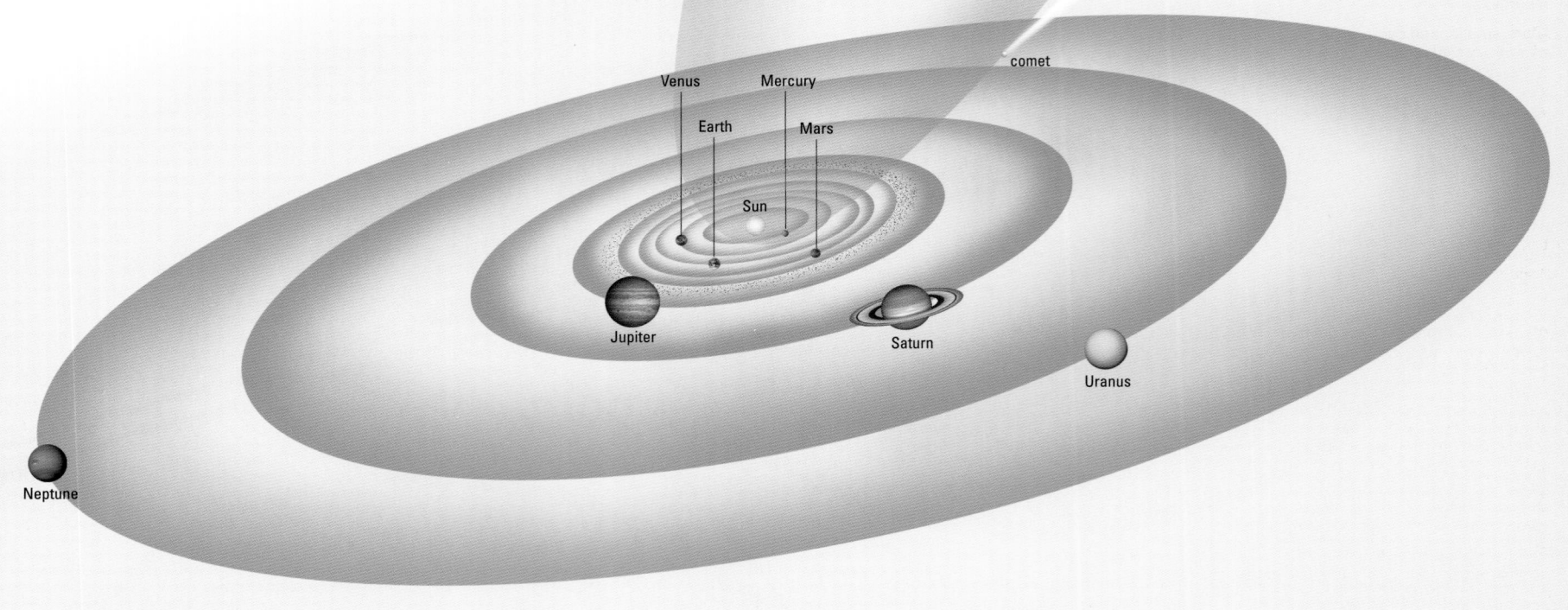

Diagram not drawn to scale

ORBITS OF THE PLANETS

The diagram above shows the Solar System as it might appear to an observer a few light-hours away in the direction of the constellation Hercules. Seen from such a position, above the plane of the ecliptic, all the planets revolve about the Sun in a counterclockwise direction. The perspective view exaggerates the elliptical form of all the planetary orbits: only Mercury follows a path that deviates noticeably from circularity. The diagram also shows the main swarm of asteroids between Mars and Jupiter, and the orbit of a comet. Comets reside in a vast spherical halo beyond the Solar System, and are occasionally diverted toward the Sun on highly elliptical orbits which may take many thousands of years to complete. Most, therefore, still await discovery, though there are a number of shorter-period comets which return regularly, such as Halley's Comet.

PLANETARY DATA

	Mean distance from Sun (million miles)	Mass (Earth = 1)	Period of orbit (Earth days/years)	Period of rotation (Earth days)	Equatorial diameter (miles)	Average density (water = 1)	Surface gravity (Earth = 1)	Number of known satellites*
Sun	–	332,946	–	25.38	865,000	1.41	27.9	–
Mercury	36.0	0.06	87.97d	58.65	3,032	5.43	0.38	0
Venus	67.2	0.82	224.7d	243.02	7,521	5.24	0.91	0
Earth	93.0	1.00	365.3d	1.00	7,926	5.52	1.00	1
Mars	141.6	0.11	687.0d	1.029	4,220	3.94	0.38	2
Jupiter	483.7	317.8	11.86y	0.411	88,848	1.33	2.36	63
Saturn	886.6	95.2	29.45y	0.428	74,900	0.69	0.91	60
Uranus	1,784.0	14.5	84.02y	0.720	31,764	1.27	0.89	27
Neptune	2,295.2	17.2	164.8y	0.673	30,776	1.64	1.13	13

Planetary days are given in sidereal days – that is, with respect to the stars rather than the Sun. The difference is caused by the movement of the planet in its orbit, so the interval between successive noons is slightly different from that between the rising of a particular star. The Earth's own sidereal day is 23h 56m in solar time. The equatorial diameters of most planets differ from their polar diameters as a consequence of their rotation, which is most marked in the case of Jupiter and Saturn, which are very noticeably flattened at the poles. Strictly speaking, the figures for surface gravity apply to the four inner planets only, as the outer planets have no solid surfaces. In their case, the figure is given for an arbitrary point in the atmosphere where the pressure is 1 bar.

* Number of known satellites at mid-2008

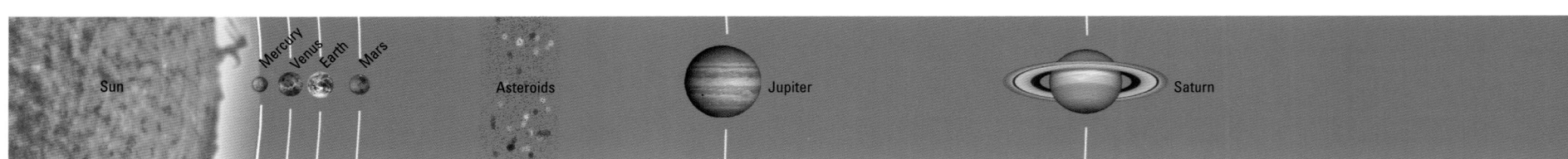

THE PLANETS

Mercury is the closest planet to the Sun and hence the fastest-moving. It is very hot, with a cratered, wrinkled surface very similar to that of Earth's Moon. It is small and has low gravity, so there is no significant atmosphere.

Venus has much the same physical dimensions as Earth. Its dense atmosphere is composed of 97% carbon dioxide resulting in a runaway greenhouse effect that makes the surface, at 890°F, the hottest of all the planets in the Solar System. Radar mapping revealed a terrain consisting of highland regions and vast, rolling plains crossed by volcanic flows and dotted with craters. Discharges from volcanic regions could explain the sulfuric-acid rain detected by spacecraft. Soft-landers last less than an hour in Venus's fierce climate.

Earth seen from space is easily the most beautiful of the inner planets; it is also, and more objectively, the largest, as well as the only known home of life. Living things are the main reason why the Earth is able to retain a substantial proportion of reactive oxygen in its atmosphere; the oxygen in turn supports the life that constantly regenerates it. The Earth's natural satellite, the Moon, is believed to have been created when an asteroid struck our planet in its infancy.

Mars, smaller and cooler than the Earth, is nevertheless the most likely planet other than Earth where life may have formed. The planet was until recently (in astronomical terms) a geologically active world with water on its surface: rivers, lakes, and even an ocean. Liquid water may well exist today, but trapped beneath its dusty, boulder-strewn surface. The Martian landscape features huge extinct volcanoes, a giant canyon system, craters, and sand dunes. Its thin atmosphere is mostly carbon dioxide, and its polar caps are of frozen carbon dioxide and water ice. It has two tiny moons, probably captured asteroids.

Jupiter has about three times the mass of all the other planets combined. The planet is mostly gas, under intense pressure in the lower atmosphere above a core of fiercely compressed hydrogen and helium. The upper layers form strikingly colored rotating belts, the outward sign of the intense storms created by Jupiter's rapid rotation. The Great Red Spot is a storm feature that has persisted for at least 170 years. Jupiter has at least 63 moons. Most are very small, but the four largest – Io, Europa, Ganymede, and Callisto – are fascinating worlds in their own right. Io is the most volcanically active world known, and Europa possesses an ocean deep below its icy surface. The planet also has a system of rings, though nowhere near as prominent as Saturn's.

Saturn is structurally similar to Jupiter, rotating fast enough to produce an obvious bulge at its equator. It is composed of 89% hydrogen and 11% helium, and has wind velocities in the outer atmosphere of 1,600 ft/sec. Ever since the invention of the telescope, Saturn's rings have been the feature that has most attracted observers. The rings consist of thousands of individual ringlets, composed of icy particles ranging in size from 30 feet down to microscopic. Titan, the largest of Saturn's 60 known moons, has a dense atmosphere.

Uranus was unknown to the ancients. Although it is faintly visible to the naked eye, it was not established as a planet until 1781. In its interior is probably a rocky core surrounded by frozen methane, water, and ammonia; the atmosphere is of hydrogen, helium, and some methane, which gives the planet its greenish-blue color. There is a system of thin, dark rings and a retinue of 27 moons, all but five of which are small.

Neptune is always more than 2.5 billion miles from Earth, and despite its diameter of over 31,000 miles, it can only be seen by telescope. Its discovery in 1846 was the result of mathematical predictions by astronomers seeking to explain irregularities in the orbit of Uranus. Like Uranus, it has a ring system; recent observations have revealed a total of 13 moons.

In 2006, following an increasing number of discoveries of objects orbiting the Sun of similar size to Pluto but at a greater distance, the International Astronomical Union issued for the first time a definition of a planet. A planet is defined as "a body orbiting the Sun, which is essentially round as a consequence of its gravity, and which does not share its orbital neighborhood with similar bodies." On this definition, Pluto is no longer classified as a planet, but is instead a member of a new category of "dwarf planet," which relaxes the last criterion but excludes bodies in orbit around another one.

Mean distance from the Sun in millions of miles

Planet	Distance
Mercury	36.0 Mercury
Venus	67.2 Venus
Earth	93.0 Earth
Mars	141.6 Mars
Jupiter	483.7 Jupiter
Saturn	886.6 Saturn
Uranus	1,784.0 Uranus
Neptune	2,795.2 Neptune

Diagrams not drawn to scale

Uranus

Neptune

For more information:

66 Orbits of the planets

75 Ocean currents

76 Circulation of the air

78 Climate

The basic units of time measurement are the day and the year. The day is one rotation of the Earth on its axis. Our present calendar is based on the solar year of 365.24 days, the time taken by the Earth to orbit the Sun. Calendars based on the movements of the Sun and Moon have been used since ancient times. The length of the year, reckoned by the Julian Calendar introduced by Julius Caesar, was about 11 minutes too long. The cumulative error was rectified in 1582 by the Gregorian Calendar, when Pope Gregory XIII decreed that the day following October 4 was October 15, and that century years did not count as leap years unless they were divisible by 400. England finally adopted the reformed calendar in 1752, when it was 11 days behind the European mainland.

The rotation of the Earth on its axis causes day and night. The Earth rotates through 360° every 24 hours, and the world is divided into 24 time zones centered on lines of longitude at 15° intervals.

The tilt of the Earth's axis, which is also called the "obliquity of the ecliptic," accounts for the seasons which are so familiar in the middle latitudes. However, geological evidence shows that, over long periods of time, climates change, and the advances and retreats of the ice during the Pleistocene Ice Age may have been caused by regular variations in the Earth's tilt, its orbit around the Sun, and changes in the season when it is closest to the Sun (perihelion).

THE SEASONS

Seasons occur because the Earth's axis is tilted at an angle of approximately 23½°. When the northern hemisphere is tilted to a maximum extent toward the Sun, on June 21, the Sun is overhead at the Tropic of Cancer (latitude 23½° North). This is midsummer, or the summer solstice, in the northern hemisphere.

On September 22 or 23, the Sun is overhead at the equator, and day and night are of equal length throughout the world. This is the autumnal equinox in the northern hemisphere.

On December 21 or 22, the Sun is overhead at the Tropic of Capricorn (23½° South), the winter solstice in the northern hemisphere. The overhead Sun then tracks north until, on March 21, it is overhead at the equator. This is the spring (vernal) equinox in the northern hemisphere.

In the southern hemisphere, the seasons are the reverse of those in the north.

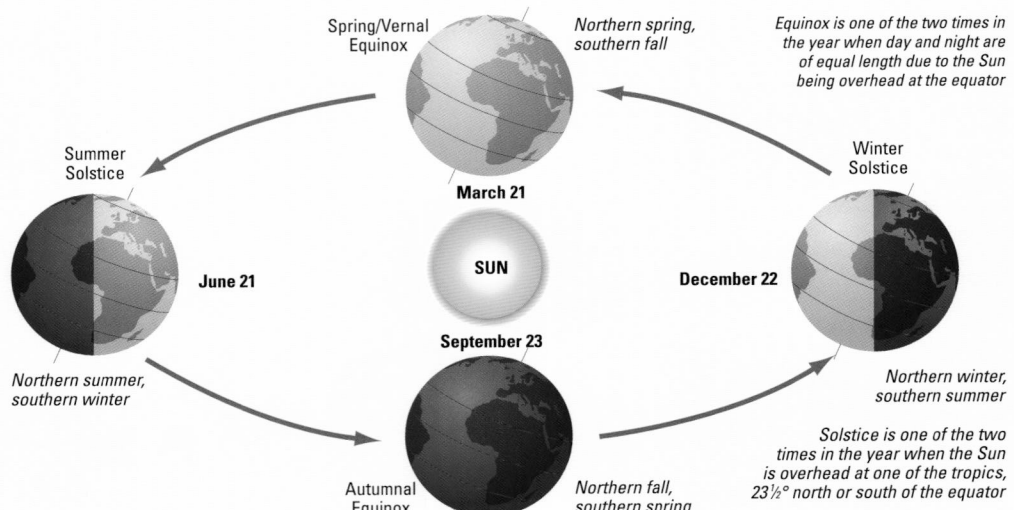

DAY AND NIGHT

The Sun appears to rise in the east, reach its highest point at noon, and then set in the west, to be followed by night. In reality, it is not the Sun that is moving but the Earth rotating from west to east. The moment when the Sun's upper limb first appears above the horizon is termed sunrise; the moment when the Sun's upper limb disappears below the horizon is sunset.

At the summer solstice in the northern hemisphere (June 21), the Arctic has total daylight and the Antarctic total darkness. The opposite occurs at the winter solstice (December 21 or 22). At the equator, the length of day and night are almost equal all year.

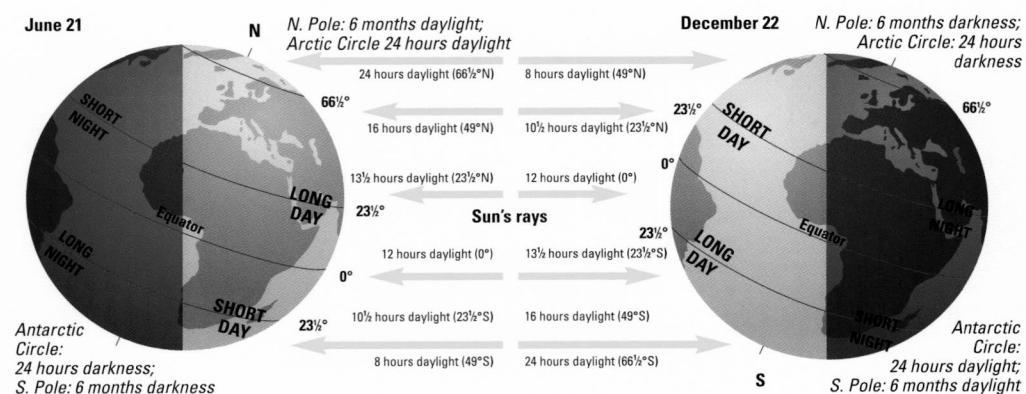

EARTH DATA

Aphelion (maximum distance from Sun):	94,508,166 miles	Length of year:	365 days, 5 hours, 48 minutes, 46 seconds of mean solar time	Polar circumference:	24,860 miles
Perihelion (minimum distance from Sun):	91,403,477 miles			Equatorial diameter:	7,926 miles
		Superficial area:	197,000,000 sq miles	Polar diameter:	7,900 miles
Angle of tilt (obliquity of the ecliptic):	23° 27′ 08″	Land surface:	57,500,000 sq miles (29.2%)	Equatorial radius:	3,963 miles
				Polar radius:	3,950 miles
Length of year – solar tropical (equinox to equinox):	365.24 days	Water surface:	139,500,000 sq miles (70.8%)	Volume of the Earth:	$259,880 \times 10^{6}$ cu miles
		Equatorial circumference:	24,901 miles	Mass of the Earth:	5.97×10^{24} kg

SUNRISE AND SUNSET

The term "equinox" comes from the Latin for "equal night." At the spring and autumnal equinoxes, the Sun is vertically overhead at midday at the equator and all places on Earth have 12 hours of darkness and 12 hours of daylight. The graphs of sunrise and sunset show that these occasions occur on March 21 and on September 22 or 23. The graphs also show that, because the Sun remains high in the sky at the equator throughout the year, the length of day and night there remains roughly the same throughout the year, with sunrise around 6 a.m. and sunset around 6 p.m.

The further north or south one travels, the greater the difference between the number of hours of daylight and darkness. For example, the graph (*right*) shows that at latitude 60°N sunrise varies from just after 9 a.m. in midwinter (on December 22 or 23) to about 2.30 a.m. in midsummer (around the summer solstice on June 21). By contrast, the second graph (*far right*) shows that sunset at latitude 60°N occurs at about 2.45 p.m. in midwinter and 9.20 p.m. in midsummer.

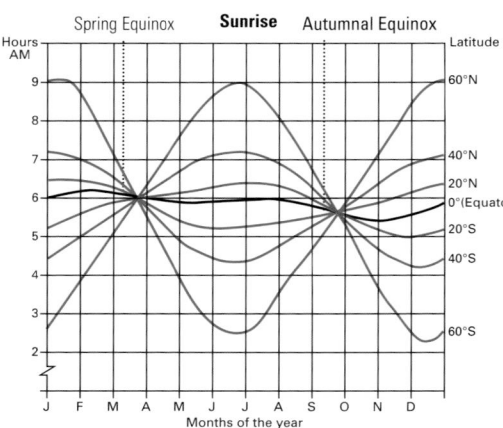

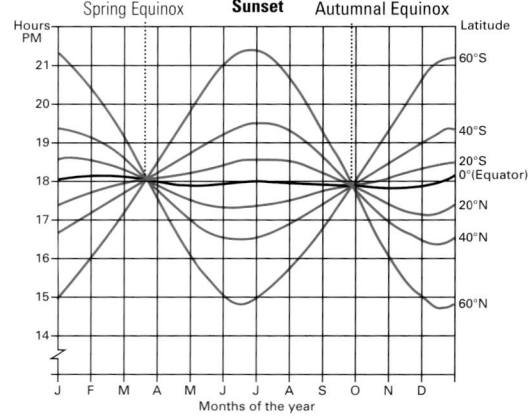

THE MOON

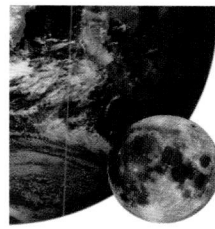

The Moon rotates more slowly than the Earth, taking just over 27 days to make one complete rotation on its axis. This corresponds to the Moon's orbital period around the Earth, and therefore the Moon always presents the same hemisphere toward us; some 41% of the Moon's far side is never visible from the Earth. The interval between one New Moon and the next is 29½ days – this is called a lunation, or lunar month. The Moon shines only by reflected sunlight, and emits no light of its own. During each lunation the Moon displays a complete cycle of phases, caused by the changing angle of illumination from the Sun.

PHASES OF THE MOON

Mean distance from Earth: 238,856 miles; Mean diameter: 2,159 miles;
Mass: approximately 1/80 that of Earth; Surface gravity: one-sixth of Earth's;
Daily range of temperature at lunar equator: 504°F; Average orbital speed: 2,287 mph

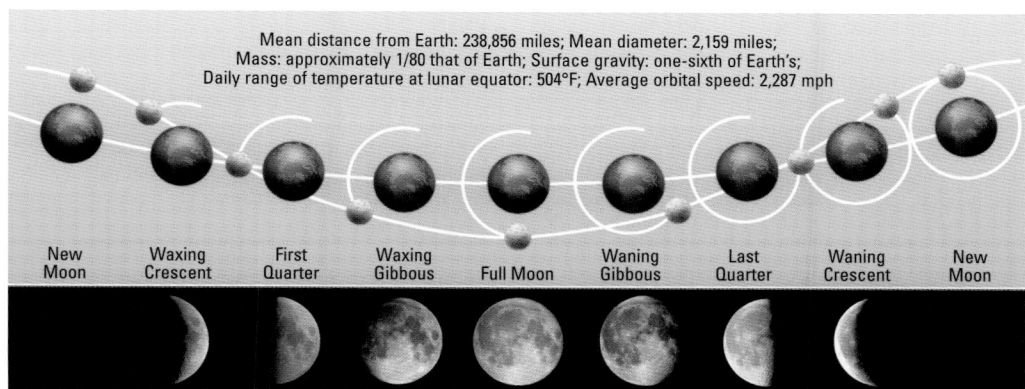

New Moon | Waxing Crescent | First Quarter | Waxing Gibbous | Full Moon | Waning Gibbous | Last Quarter | Waning Crescent | New Moon

MOON DATA

Distance from Earth

The Moon orbits at a mean distance of 238,856 miles, at an average speed of 2,287 mph in relation to the Earth.

Size and mass

The average diameter of the Moon is 2,159 miles. It is 400 times smaller than the Sun but is about 400 times closer to the Earth, so we see them as the same size. The Moon has a mass of 7.35×10^{22} kg, with a density 3.344 times that of water.

Visibility

Only 59% of the Moon's surface is visible from the Earth over time. Sunlight reflected from the Moon takes 1.3 seconds to reach the Earth (the Sun itself is around 8½ light-minutes away).

Temperature

With the Sun overhead, the temperature on the lunar equator can reach 243°F [117°C]. At night it can sink to −261°F [−163°C].

ECLIPSES

When the Moon passes between the Sun and the Earth, the Sun becomes partially eclipsed (1). A partial eclipse becomes a total eclipse if the Moon proceeds to cover the Sun completely (2) and the dark central part of the lunar shadow touches the Earth. The broad geographical zone covered by the Moon's outer shadow (P), has only a very small central area (often less than 62 miles wide) that experiences totality. Totality can never last for more than 7½ minutes at maximum, but is usually much briefer than this. Lunar eclipses take place when the Moon moves through the shadow of the Earth, and can be partial or total. Any single location on Earth can experience a maximum of four solar and three lunar eclipses in any single year, while a total solar eclipse occurs an average of once every 360 years for any given location.

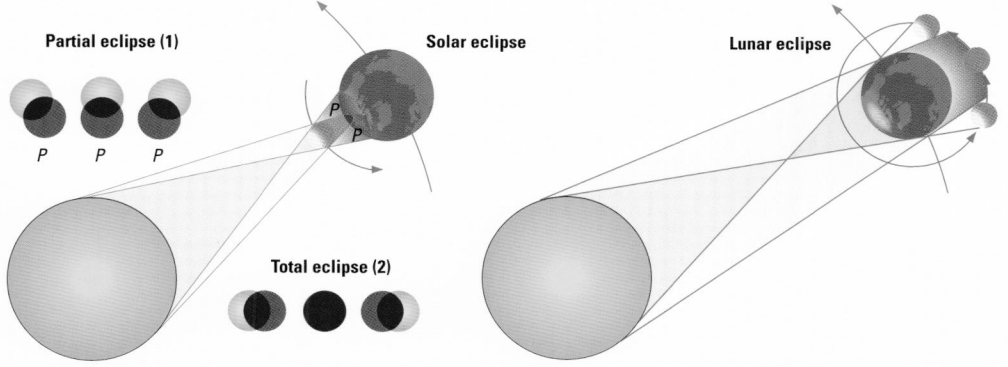

Partial eclipse (1)

Solar eclipse

Lunar eclipse

Total eclipse (2)

TIDES

The daily rise and fall of the ocean's tides are the result of the gravitational pull of the Moon and that of the Sun, though the effect of the latter is not as strong as that of the Moon. This effect is greatest on the hemisphere facing the Moon and causes a tidal "bulge." Spring tides occur when the Sun, Earth, and Moon are aligned; high tides are at their highest, and low tides fall to their lowest. When the Moon and Sun are furthest out of line (near the Moon's First and Last Quarters), neap tides occur, producing the smallest range between high and low tides.

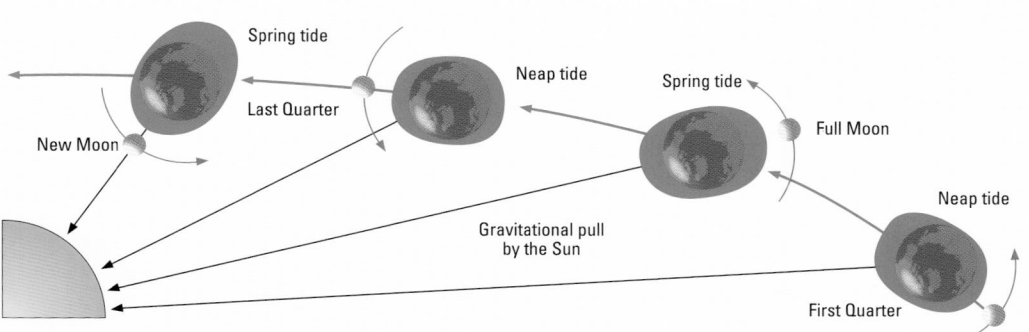

Spring tide
Neap tide
Spring tide
Last Quarter
New Moon
Full Moon
Neap tide
Gravitational pull by the Sun
First Quarter

TIME ZONES

The Earth rotates through 360° in 24 hours, and so moves 15° every hour. The world is divided into 24 standard time zones, each centered on lines of longitude at 15° intervals. At the center of the first zone is the prime meridian, or Greenwich meridian. All places to the west of Greenwich are one hour behind for every 15° of longitude; places to the east are ahead by one hour for every 15°.

International Date Line

When it is 12 noon on the Greenwich meridian, 180° east it is midnight of the same day – while 180° west the day is just beginning. To overcome this, the International Date Line was established, approximately following the 180° meridian. Thus, if you were to travel eastward from Japan (140°E) to Samoa (170°W), you would pass from Sunday night into Sunday morning.

10   Hours behind or ahead of UT or Coordinated Universal Time

Zones using UT (GMT)

Zones behind UT (GMT)

International boundaries

Zones ahead of UT (GMT)

Half-hour zones

Time-zone boundaries

International Date Line

Actual solar time when time at Greenwich is 12:00 (noon)

Note: Some of the above time zones are affected by the incidence of daylight saving time in countries where it is adopted.

Projection: Mercator

For more information:

72 Types of rock
   Mountain building
73 Surface processes
98 Minerals

Every year, earthquakes and volcanic eruptions cause much destruction throughout the world. Such phenomena were once thought to be unconnected, but since the late 1960s, scientists have understood that these events are surface manifestations of the tremendous forces operating in the Earth's interior that are slowly but constantly changing the face of our planet.

The Earth is divided into three zones. The crust, a brittle, low-density zone, overlies the dense mantle. Separating the crust from the mantle is a distinct boundary called the Mohorovičić (or Moho) discontinuity. Enclosed by the mantle is the Earth's core, which consists mainly of iron and nickel.

Temperatures inside the Earth range from about 1,600°F in the upper mantle to perhaps 9,000°F in the core. Heat creates convection currents in a semimolten part of the mantle called the asthenosphere. Above the asthenosphere is the lithosphere, a solid layer about 40 miles thick, consisting of the crust and part of the mantle. The lithosphere is divided into rigid plates, moved around by the currents in the asthenosphere, a process named plate tectonics.

The Earth was formed around 4.6 billion years ago. Lighter elements floated toward the surface, where they formed crustal rocks. The oldest rocks so far discovered are about 4 billion years old, while the oldest fossils occur in rocks formed around 3.5 billion years ago. An explosion of life occurred at the start of the Cambrian period, 570 million years ago. The fossil record since the start of the Cambrian has enabled scientists to piece together the story of life on Earth.

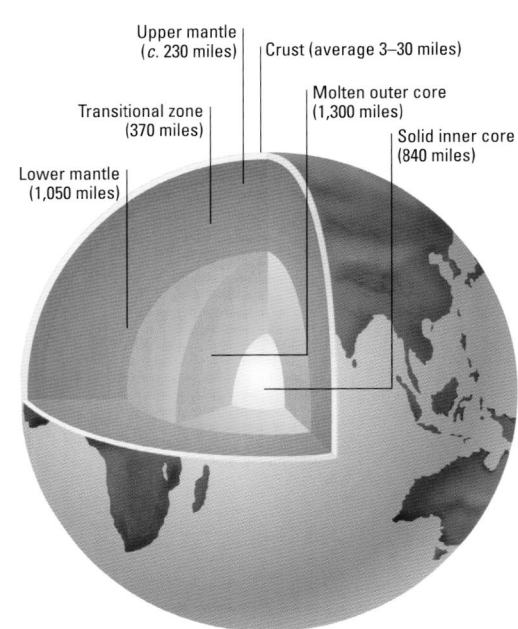

Upper mantle (c. 230 miles)
Crust (average 3–30 miles)
Molten outer core (1,300 miles)
Transitional zone (370 miles)
Solid inner core (840 miles)
Lower mantle (1,050 miles)

CONTINENTAL DRIFT

——— Trench
——— Rift
▨ New ocean floor
——— Zones of slippage

In 1915, Alfred Wegener produced a series of world maps proposing that, around 200 million years ago, the continents had been joined together in a supercontinent that he called Pangaea. This land mass started to break up about 180 million years ago and the parts drifted to their present positions. In the 1950s and 1960s, evidence from studies of the ocean floor suggested that the low-density continents rest on huge slow-moving plates. The arrows on the present-day world map (*below*) show that the continents are still on the move.

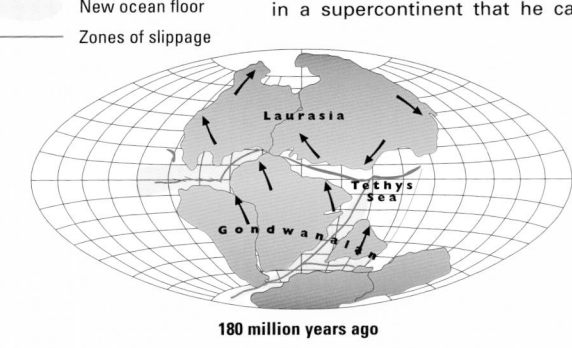

180 million years ago

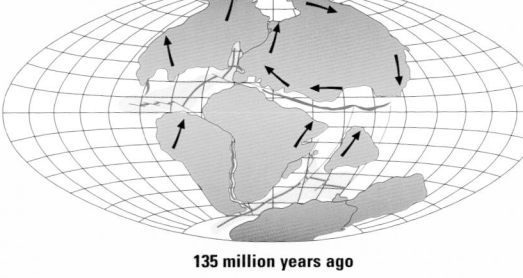

135 million years ago

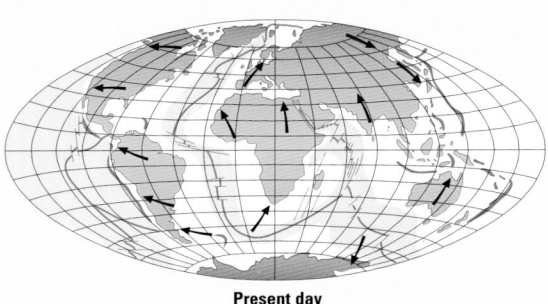

Present day

DISTRIBUTION OF VOLCANOES

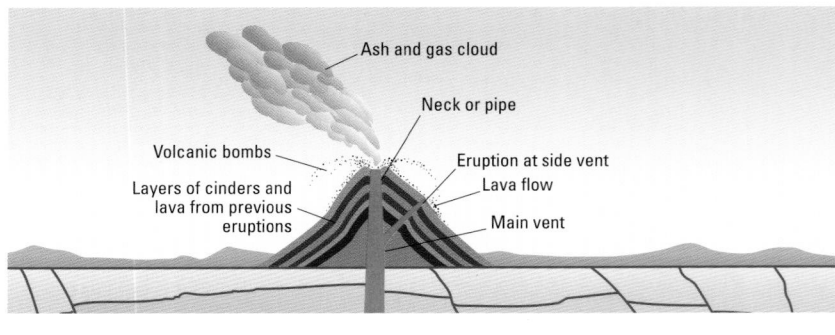

Ash and gas cloud
Neck or pipe
Volcanic bombs
Eruption at side vent
Lava flow
Layers of cinders and lava from previous eruptions
Main vent

Volcanoes occur when hot liquefied rock beneath the Earth's crust is pushed up by pressure to the surface as molten lava. There are some 550 known active volcanoes, around 20 of which are erupting at any one time.

○ Submarine volcanoes

▲ Land volcanoes active since 1700

— Boundaries of tectonic plates

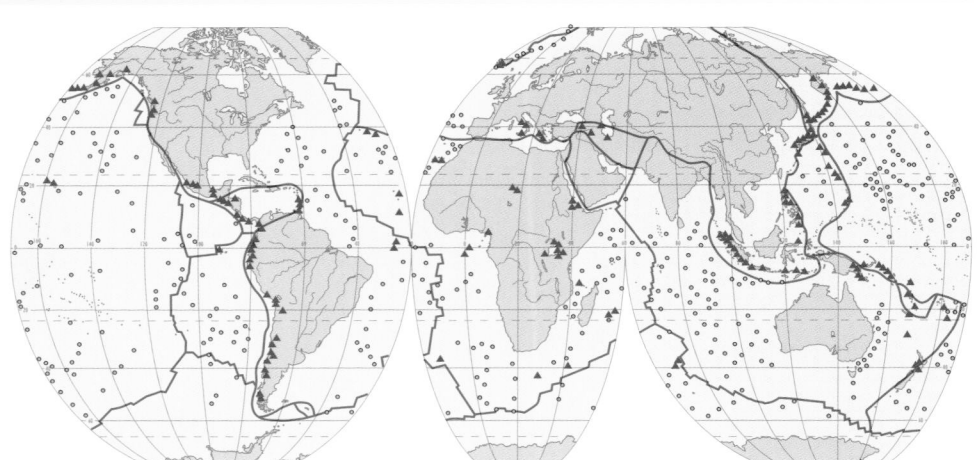

PLATE TECTONICS

The huge ridges that run through the oceans represent boundaries between plates. Here plates are diverging and molten magma from the mantle rises along a central rift valley to form new crustal rock. These ocean ridges, which are active zones where earthquakes and volcanic eruptions are common, are called constructive plate margins. Destructive plate margins, which occur when two contrasting plates converge, are marked by deep-ocean trenches as one plate is forced under the other. The descending plate is melted to produce the magma that fuels volcanoes alongside the trenches. Movements of descending plates are often sudden, triggering earthquakes in overlying continental areas.

Sea-floor spreading in the Atlantic Ocean and plate collision

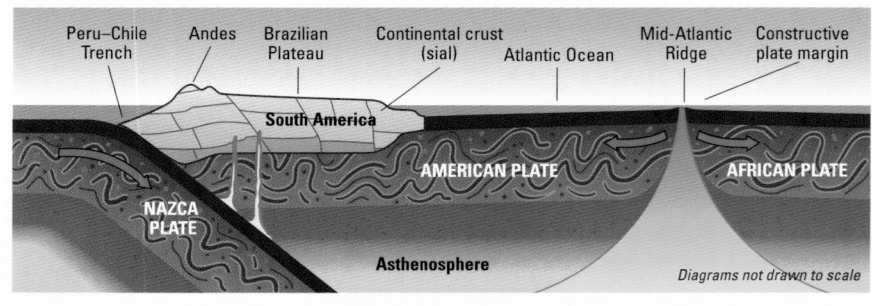

Peru–Chile Trench
Andes
Brazilian Plateau
Continental crust (sial)
Atlantic Ocean
Mid-Atlantic Ridge
Constructive plate margin
South America
AMERICAN PLATE
AFRICAN PLATE
NAZCA PLATE
Asthenosphere
Diagrams not drawn to scale

Sea-floor spreading in the Indian Ocean and continental plate collision

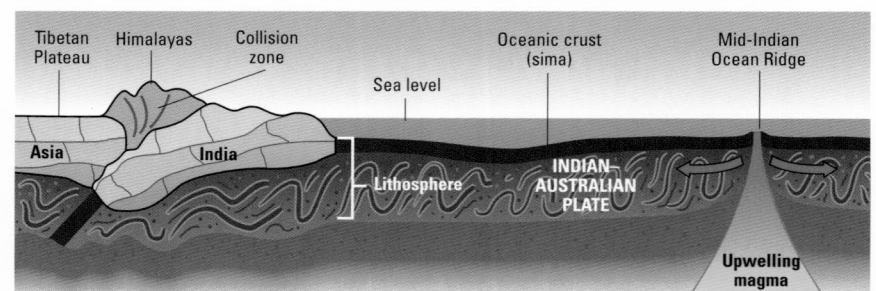

Tibetan Plateau
Himalayas
Collision zone
Sea level
Oceanic crust (sima)
Mid-Indian Ocean Ridge
Asia
India
Lithosphere
INDIAN–AUSTRALIAN PLATE
Upwelling magma

GEOLOGICAL TIME

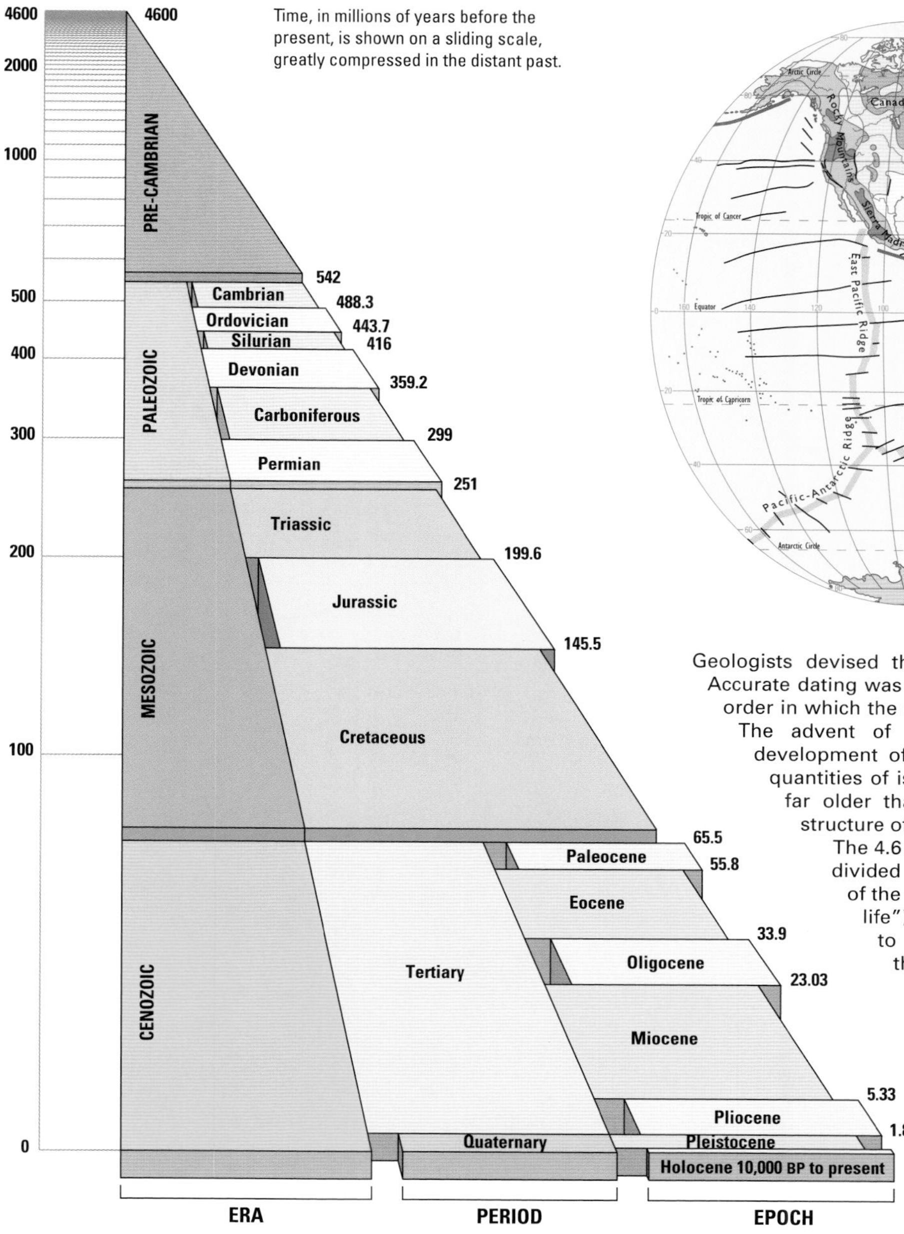

Time, in millions of years before the present, is shown on a sliding scale, greatly compressed in the distant past.

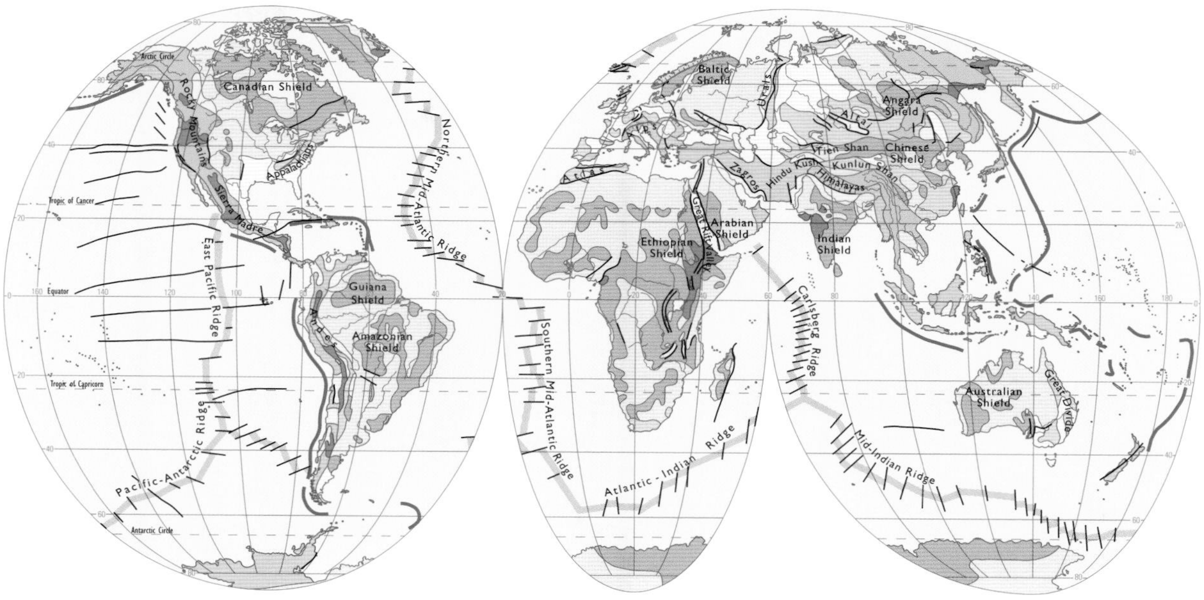

Geological time chart (left):

4600 — 4600

PRE-CAMBRIAN

PALEOZOIC
- Cambrian — 542
- Ordovician — 488.3
- Silurian — 443.7
- Devonian — 416
- Carboniferous — 359.2
- Permian — 299

MESOZOIC
- Triassic — 251
- Jurassic — 199.6
- Cretaceous — 145.5

CENOZOIC
- Tertiary — 65.5
  - Paleocene — 55.8
  - Eocene — 33.9
  - Oligocene — 23.03
  - Miocene
  - Pliocene — 5.33
- Quaternary — 1.81
  - Pleistocene
  - Holocene 10,000 BP to present

ERA | PERIOD | EPOCH

Geologists devised their timescale on the basis of relative, not calendar, ages. Accurate dating was impossible and estimates were often bitterly disputed, but the order in which the rocks were formed could be deduced from careful observation. The advent of radioactive dating – culminating in the 1950s with the development of a mass spectrometer capable of accurately measuring tiny quantities of isotopes – appears to have settled the arguments. The Earth is far older than geologists first imagined, but their painstakingly-created structure of geological time has withstood the advent of high technology.

The 4.6 billion (4,600 million) years since the formation of the Earth are divided into four great eras, further split into periods and, in the case of the most recent era, epochs. The present era is the Cenozoic ("new life"), extending backward through "middle life" and "ancient life" to the Pre-Cambrian, named after the Latin word for Wales, the location of some of the earliest known fossils. Most of the Earth's geological history is encompassed by the Pre-Cambrian: though traces of ancient life have since been found, it was largely the proliferation of fossils from the beginning of the Paleozoic era onward, some 570 million years ago, which first allowed precise subdivisions to be made.

Like the Cambrian, most are named after regions exemplifying a period's geology. Others – such as the Carboniferous ("coal-bearing") or the Cretaceous ("chalk-bearing") – are more directly descriptive.

Map legend:
- Pre-Cambrian shields
- Sedimentary cover on Pre-Cambrian shields
- Paleozoic (Caledonian and Hercynian) folding
- Sedimentary cover on Paleozoic folding
- Mesozoic folding
- Sedimentary cover on Mesozoic folding
- Cenozoic (Alpine) folding
- Sedimentary cover on Cenozoic folding
- Intensive Mesozoic and Cenozoic vulcanism
- Principal faults
- Oceanic marginal troughs
- Mid-oceanic ridges
- Overthrust faults

EARTHQUAKES

Earthquake magnitude is usually rated according to either the Richter or the Modified Mercalli scale, both devised by seismologists in the 1930s. The Richter scale measures absolute earthquake power with mathematical precision: each step upward represents a tenfold increase in the amplitude of the shockwave. Theoretically, there is no upper limit, but most of the largest earthquakes measured have been rated at between 8.8 and 8.9. The 12-point Mercalli scale, based on observed effects, is often more meaningful, ranging from I (earthquakes noticed only by seismographs) to XII (total destruction); intermediate points include V (people awakened at night; unstable objects overturned), VII (collapse of ordinary buildings; chimneys and monuments fall), and IX (conspicuous cracks in ground; serious damage to reservoirs).

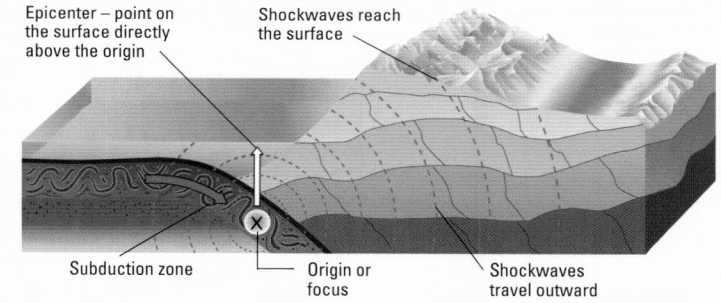

Epicenter – point on the surface directly above the origin

Shockwaves reach the surface

Subduction zone

Origin or focus

Shockwaves travel outward

Map legend:
- Mobile land areas
- Submarine zones of mobile land areas
- Stable land platforms
- Submarine extensions of land platforms
- Mid-oceanic volcanic ridges
- Oceanic platforms

1976 ○ Principal earthquakes and dates (since 1900)

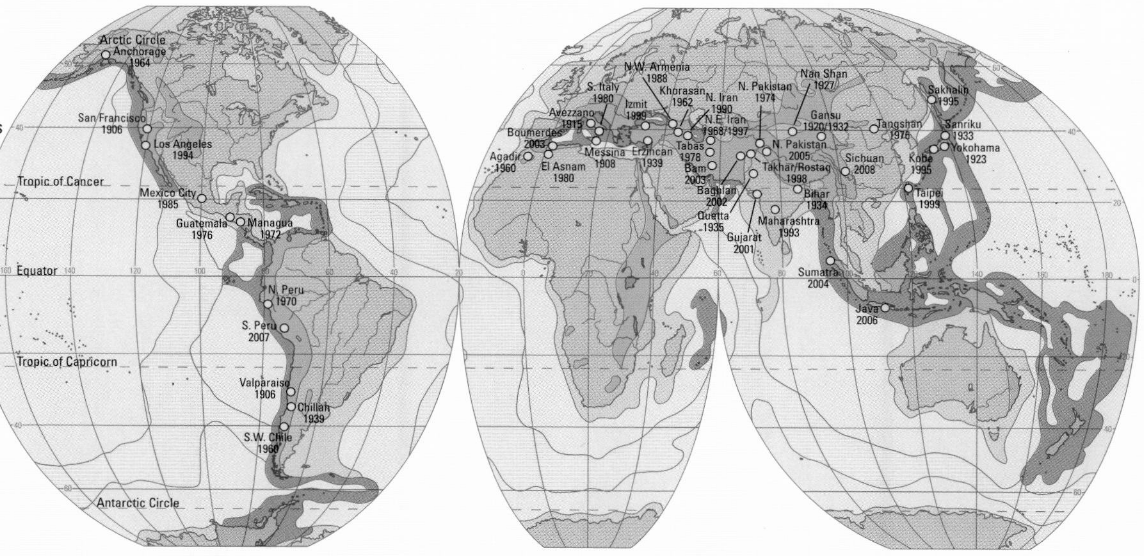

Earthquakes are a series of rapid vibrations originating from the slipping or faulting of parts of the Earth's crust when stresses within build up to breaking point. They usually happen at depths varying from 5 to 20 miles. Severe earthquakes cause extensive damage when they take place in populated areas, destroying structures and severing communications. Most initial loss of life occurs due to secondary causes such as falling masonry, fires, and flooding.

Notable Earthquakes Since 1900

Year	Location	Mag.	Deaths
1906	San Francisco, USA	8.3	3,000
1906	Valparaiso, Chile	8.6	22,000
1908	Messina, Italy	7.5	83,000
1915	Avezzano, Italy	7.5	30,000
1920	Gansu (Kansu), China	8.6	180,000
1923	Yokohama, Japan	8.3	143,000
1927	Nan Shan, China	8.3	200,000
1932	Gansu (Kansu), China	7.6	70,000
1933	Sanriku, Japan	8.9	2,990
1934	Bihar, India/Nepal	8.4	10,700
1935	Quetta, India*	7.5	60,000
1939	Chillan, Chile	8.3	28,000
1939	Erzincan, Turkey	7.9	30,000
1960	S. W. Chile	9.5	2,200
1960	Agadir, Morocco	5.8	12,000
1962	Khorasan, Iran	7.1	12,230
1964	Anchorage, USA	9.2	125
1968	N. E. Iran	7.4	12,000
1970	N. Peru	7.8	70,000
1972	Managua, Nicaragua	6.2	5,000
1974	N. Pakistan	6.3	5,200
1976	Guatemala	7.5	22,500
1976	Tangshan, China	8.2	255,000
1978	Tabas, Iran	7.7	25,000
1980	El Asnam, Algeria	7.3	20,000
1980	S. Italy	7.2	4,800
1985	Mexico City, Mexico	8.1	4,200
1988	N.W. Armenia	6.8	55,000
1990	N. Iran	7.7	36,000
1993	Maharashtra, India	6.4	30,000
1994	Los Angeles, USA	6.6	51
1995	Kobe, Japan	7.2	5,000
1995	Sakhalin Is., Russia	7.5	2,000
1997	N. E. Iran	7.1	2,400
1998	Takhar, Afghanistan	6.1	4,200
1998	Rostag, Afghanistan	7.0	5,000
1999	Izmit, Turkey	7.4	15,000
1999	Taipei, Taiwan	7.6	1,700
2001	Gujarat, India	7.7	14,000
2002	Baghlan, Afghanistan	6.1	1,000
2003	Boumerdes, Algeria	6.8	2,200
2003	Bam, Iran	6.6	30,000
2004	Sumatra, Indonesia	9.0	250,000
2005	N. Pakistan	7.6	74,000
2006	Java, Indonesia	6.4	6,200
2007	S. Peru	8.0	600
2008	Sichuan, China	7.9	70,000

An earthquake off the coast of Sumatra on December 26, 2004, triggered a deadly tsunami that swept across the Indian Ocean, causing devastation in many countries, in particular Sri Lanka, India, Thailand, and Indonesia, where the loss of life was greatest.

* now Pakistan

For more information:
70 The Earth's structure
   Plate tectonics
   Volcanoes
71 Geological time
74 Oceans
82 Hydrological cycle
99 Structural regions

The theory of plate tectonics has offered new insights into how the Earth works, elucidating mysteries concerning continental drift, volcanic eruptions, and earthquakes. It has also contributed to our understanding of how collisions between plates can squeeze up layers of sediments on seabeds, forming fold mountain ranges, such as the Himalayas.

Yet even as mountains rise, natural forces are wearing them away. In hot, dry climates, mechanical weathering (a result of rapid temperature changes) causes the outer layers of rocks to peel away, while, in cold mountain regions, boulders are prised apart when water freezes in cracks in rocks. Chemical weathering is responsible for hollowing out limestone caves and decomposing granites.

Climatic conditions have a great bearing on the principal agent of erosion in any particular area. Running water is most important in moist temperate regions. In cold regions, ice is the major agent of erosion, and in many mountain ranges, U-shaped valleys are evidence of the erosive power of valley glaciers.

Ice sheets molded much of the Earth's surface during the Ice Ages, the most recent of which, in the northern hemisphere, ended only 10,000 years ago. Polar climates also shape the scenery of the periglacial areas that border bodies of ice. Such areas are subject to constant freeze-thaw action, which creates such features as pingos (domed mounds).

Climatic change has also affected many of the landforms in hot deserts, which were shaped by running water at a time when the deserts enjoyed much wetter climates. However, the major agent of erosion in deserts today is wind-blown sand, which erodes rock strata to form caves and mushroom-shaped rocks.

The surface of the Earth is under constant assault from tectonic processes and the agents of erosion. The products of erosion, fragments of rock such as sand, are deposited to form sedimentary rocks. Metamorphic rocks are created when igneous or sedimentary rocks are buried and metamorphosed by heat and pressure. Eventually the rocks are recycled to form magma, which rises upward to start the rock cycle all over again.

THE ROCK CYCLE

James Hutton first proposed the rock cycle in the late 1700s after he observed the slow but steady effects of erosion.

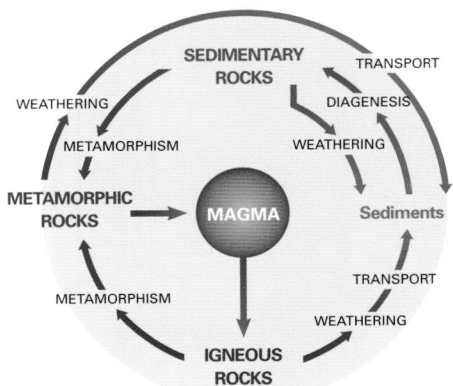

Rocks are divided into three types, according to the way in which they are formed:

Igneous rocks, including granite and basalt, are formed when magma cools inside the Earth's crust or on the surface.

Metamorphic rocks, such as slate, marble, and quartzite, are formed below the Earth's surface by the compression or baking of existing rocks.

Sedimentary rocks, like sandstone and limestone, are formed on the surface of the Earth from the remains of living organisms and eroded fragments of older rocks.

MOUNTAIN BUILDING

Mountains are formed when pressures on the Earth's crust caused by continental drift become so intense that the surface buckles or cracks. This happens where oceanic crust is subducted by continental crust or, more dramatically, where two continental plates collide: the Rockies, Andes, Alps, Urals, and Himalayas resulted from such impacts. These are known as fold mountains because they were formed by the compression of the rocks. The Himalayas were formed from the folded former sediments of the Tethys Sea, which was trapped in the collision zone between the Indian–Australian and Eurasian plates.

The other main mountain-building processes occur when the crust fractures to create faults, allowing rock to be forced upward in large blocks, or when the pressure of magma within the crust forces the surface to bulge into a dome, or erupts to form a volcano.

Large mountain ranges may reveal a combination of these features. The Alps, for example, have been compressed so violently that the folds are fragmented by numerous faults and intrusions of molten igneous rock.

Over millions of years, even the greatest mountain ranges can be reduced by the agents of erosion (especially rivers) to a low, rugged landscape known as a peneplain.

Types of faults: Faults occur where the crust is being stretched or compressed so violently that the rock strata break in a horizontal or vertical movement. They are classified by the direction in which the blocks of rock have moved. A normal fault results when a vertical movement causes the surface to break apart; compression causes a reverse fault. Horizontal movement causes shearing, known as a strike-slip fault. When the rock breaks in two places, the central block may be pushed up in a horst fault, or sink (creating a rift valley) in a graben fault.

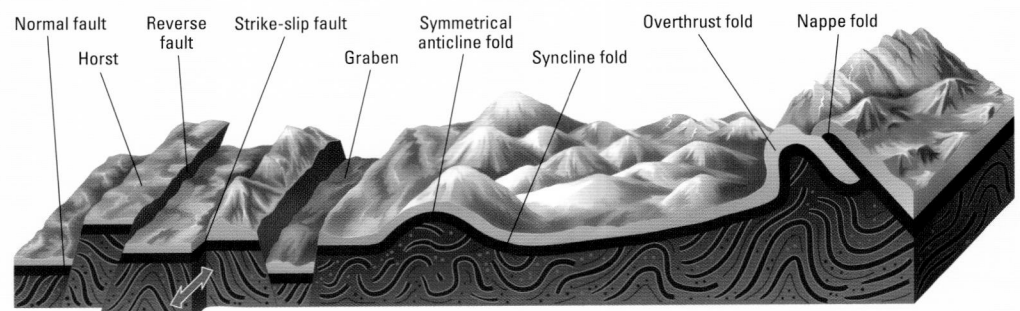

Normal fault · Reverse fault · Strike-slip fault · Symmetrical anticline fold · Overthrust fold · Nappe fold · Horst · Graben · Syncline fold

Types of fold: Folds occur when rock strata are squeezed and compressed. They are common, therefore, at destructive plate margins and where plates have collided, forcing the rocks to buckle into mountain ranges. Geographers give different names to the degrees of fold that result from continuing pressure on the rock. A simple fold may be symmetric, with even slopes on either side, but as the pressure builds up, one slope becomes steeper and the fold becomes asymmetric. Later, the ridge or "anticline" at the top of the fold may slide over the lower ground or "syncline" to form a recumbent fold. Eventually, the rock strata may break under the pressure to form an overthrust and finally a nappe fold.

CONTINENTAL GLACIATION

Many landforms in the northern hemisphere were shaped by ice sheets and meltwater during the Pleistocene Ice Age, which began about 2 million years ago. During the Ice Age, the ice sheets periodically advanced and retreated. The first map (*below left*) shows the ice cover at its greatest extent about 200,000 years BP (before the present), when it covered about 30% of the land surface, as compared with 10% today. About 18,000 years BP, the ice covered most of Canada and extended as far south as the Bristol Channel in England. Around the ice sheets, land areas experienced periglacial conditions.

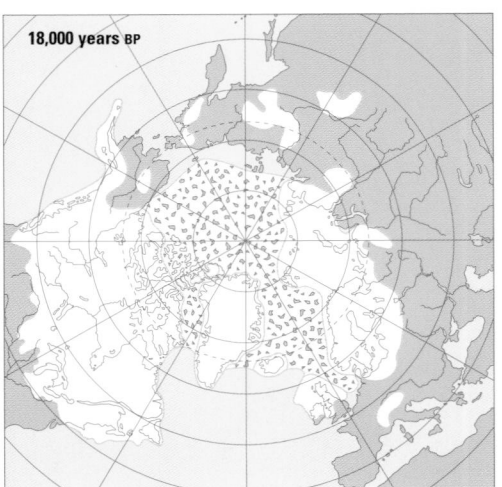

200,000 years BP

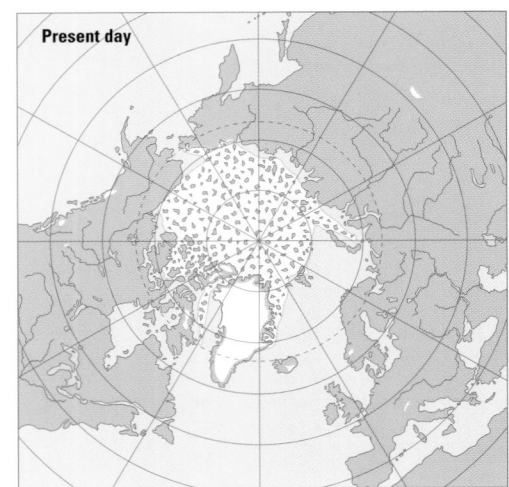

18,000 years BP

Present day

NATURAL LANDFORMS

Natural landforms reflect the influence of plate tectonics, through mountain-building and the generation of new rocks from the Earth's interior, together with the agents of erosion – running water, ice, winds, and coastal waves. Over millions of years, mountains are gradually eroded, with the eroded material redistributed, usually at lower levels. The resultant landforms reflect the major forces that have been at work, as well as the underlying geology, the climatic conditions, which often vary over time, and the vegetation cover. The study of these processes and the landforms they create is called geomorphology. The stylized diagram (*below*) shows some major natural landforms found in the mid-latitudes.

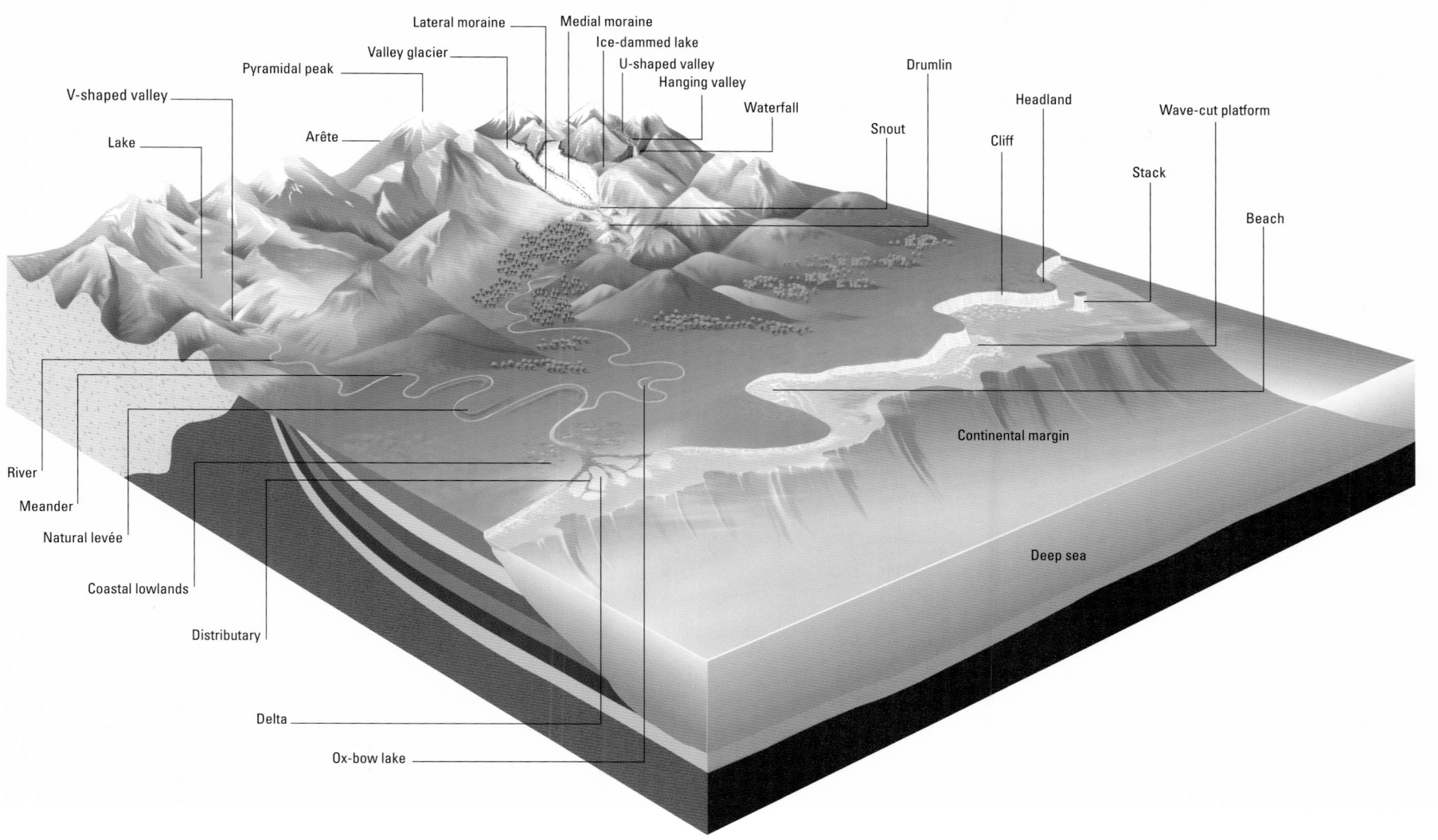

SURFACE PROCESSES

Catastrophic changes to landforms are caused periodically by such phenomena as avalanches, landslides and volcanic eruptions, but most of the processes that shape the Earth's surface operate extremely slowly in human terms.

Chemical weathering is at its greatest in warm, humid regions, while mechanical weathering (the physical breakup of rocks) predominates in cold mountain or hot desert regions. The most familiar type of chemical weathering is caused by the reaction of rainwater containing dissolved carbon dioxide on limestone; this leads to the creation of labyrinthine cave networks dissolved by groundwater. Mechanical weathering includes frost action, while in hot deserts, rapid temperature changes cause the outer layers of rocks to expand and contract until they crack and peel away, a process called exfoliation.

Running water is probably the world's leading agent of erosion and transportation. The energy of a river depends on several factors, including its velocity and volume, and its erosive power is at its peak when it is in full flood, sweeping soil, pebbles, and even boulders along its course, cutting downward into the bedrock or widening its valley.

Sea waves also exert tremendous erosive power during storms, when they hurl pebbles and large rocks against the shore, undercutting cliffs and hollowing out caves. Headlands are often attacked on both sides, forming caves, then a natural arch and eventually an isolated stack.

Glacier ice forms in mountain hollows, called cirques, and spills out to form valley glaciers, which transport rocks shattered by frost action. As a glacier moves, rocks embedded in the base and sides scrape away bedrock, eroding steep-sided, flat-bottomed, U-shaped valleys. Evidence of past glaciation in mountain regions includes cirques, knife-edged ridges, or arêtes, and pyramidal peaks, or horns.

DESERT LANDFORMS

Deserts are defined as places with an average annual precipitation of 10 inches [250 mm] per year, though places with a higher rainfall and a high evaporation rate may also qualify as deserts.

The three types of desert landforms are known by their Arabic names, a reflection of the fact that the Sahara in North Africa is the world's largest desert. Sand desert, called *erg*, covers about one-fifth of the world's deserts. The rest is divided between *hammada* (areas of bare rock) and *reg* (broad plains covered by loose gravel or pebbles).

The shapes of dunes in sand deserts reflect the character of local winds. Where winds are constant in direction, the sand often piles up in crescent-shaped dunes, called *barchans*. Barchans are constantly on the move and their forward march, unless halted by vegetation, may overwhelm settlements at oases. *Seif* dunes, named after the Arabic word for "sword," are long ridges of sand that lie parallel to the direction of the wind, but where winds are variable, the sand sheets are often featureless.

Wind-blown sand is an effective agent of erosion, but because of the weight of sand grains, this type of erosion is confined to within approximately 7 feet [2 meters] of the land surface, creating caves and mushroom-shaped rocks.

In assessing desert landforms, it is important to remember that other processes were at work in the past when the climate was very different from today. For example, cave paintings suggest that the Sahara had a much wetter climate after the end of the Ice Age and only began to dry up after about 5000 BC. However, human action, including overgrazing and the cutting down of trees for firewood, can turn a grassland region into desert – a process known as desertification.

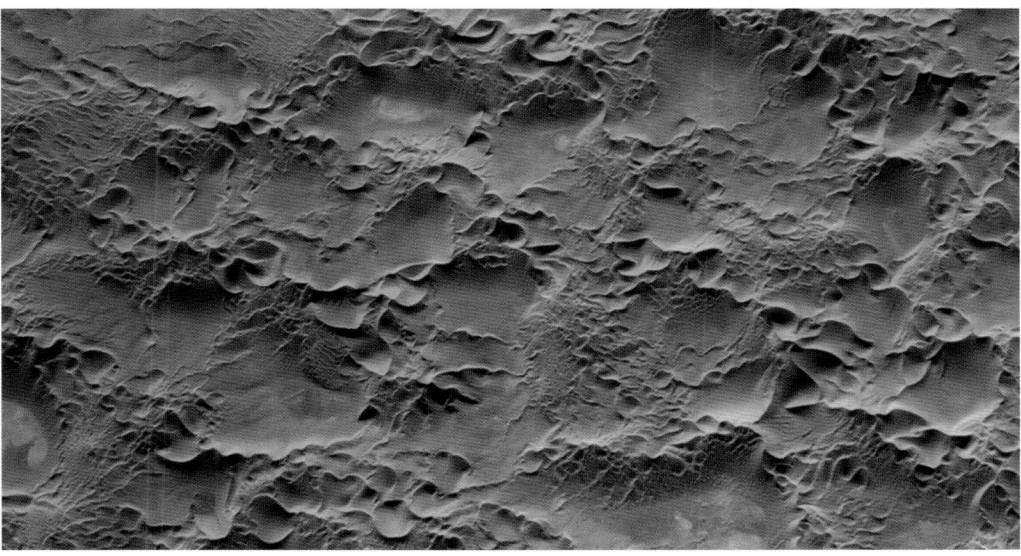

◄ The Erg (meaning "sand sea") Issaouane is located in eastern Algeria. Considered to be part of the Sahara Desert, it covers approximately 14,700 sq miles [38,000 sq km]. The active nature of this portion of the Erg is well illustrated by this image – smaller dunes form and migrate along the flanks of the larger dunes and sand ridges. Occasional precipitation fills basins formed by the dunes; as the water evaporates, salt deposits are left behind which appear as bluish-white areas.

For more information:
69   Tides
70   Plate tectonics
76   Atmosphere
81   Rising sea levels
82   Hydrological cycle
     Water distribution
83   Watersheds
85   Water pollution
103 World shipping

The last 40 years have been described as the "Space Age," but another exciting and perhaps even more important area of discovery, proceeding at the same time, has been the exploration of the oceans which cover more than 70% of our planet. Studies of the ocean floor and oceanic islands have revealed features that help to explain how continents move, and how the movements are related to earthquakes and volcanic activity.

Manned submersibles have established that life exists even in the deepest trenches, where the pressure reaches 1,000 atmospheres, the equivalent of the force of six and a half tons bearing down on every square inch. Further exploration in the pitch-black environment of the ocean ridges has revealed strange forms of marine life around scalding hot vents. The creatures include giant tubeworms, blind shrimps, and bacteria, some of which are genetically very different from any other known life forms. In 1996, an analysis of one micro-organism revealed that at least half of its 1,700 or so genes were hitherto unknown. This environment, which is based on chemicals, not sunlight, may resemble the places where life on Earth first began.

Another vital area of contemporary research concerns the interactions between the oceans and the atmosphere, as exemplified in the El Niño–Southern Oscillation (ENSO) cycle, and the bearing that these have on climatic change (*see below*).

Most geographers divide the world's ocean waters into five areas: the Pacific, Atlantic, Indian, Southern, and Arctic oceans. The most active zone in the oceans is the sunlit upper layer, where the water is moved around by wind-blown currents. It is the home of most sea life and acts as a membrane through which the ocean breathes,

ATOLL BUILDING

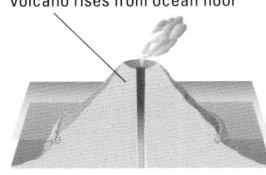

Volcano rises from ocean floor

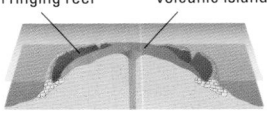

Fringing reef   Extinct, eroding volcanic island

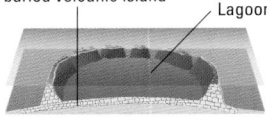

After subsidence, reef covers buried volcanic island   Lagoon

A coral atoll usually begins existence as a bare volcanic peak, thrusting above the surface of the ocean. A colony of coral – organisms with calcium carbonate skeletons – forms itself in the shallow water around the peak. The volcano is eroded and slowly sinks, leaving the coral forming a ring of hard limestone around its remnant. In time, the barrier reef of an atoll is all that remains.

LIFE IN THE OCEANS

An imaginary profile of the typical coastal and oceanic zones is shown, with a selection of the life forms that might occur in the waters off the Pacific Coast of Central America. The animals illustrated are not drawn to scale as the range of sizes is too great. Most marine life is confined to the first 650 feet, the upper sunlit (photic) zone, where sunlight can still penetrate. Plant and animal plankton, the basis of life in the oceans, occur in great quantities in all zones.

In the pelagic environment (open sea), vertical gradients, including those of light, temperature, and salinity, determine the distribution of organisms. From the tidal zone at the coastline, the continental shelf, geologically still part of the continental land mass, drops gently to about 650 feet – the sunlit zone. At the end of the shelf, the seabed falls away in the steeper angle of the continental slope. The subsequent descent to the deep-ocean floor, known as the continental rise, is more gentle, with gradients between 1 in 100 and 1 in 700 until the abyssal plains and hills between 8,000 and 19,500 feet below the surface.

The deep-sea floor contains seamounts, some of which are capped by coral reefs, ocean ridges – the longest mountain chains on Earth – and deep-ocean trenches, especially in the Pacific Ocean where six trenches reach depths of more than 33,000 feet, including the Mariana Trench at 36,161 feet deep .

Each of these zones contains a distinctive community of species adapted to the different conditions of salinity, temperature, and light intensity. Indeed, a few organisms have been found even in the abyssal darkness of the great ocean trenches.

absorbing great quantities of carbon dioxide and partly exchanging it for oxygen.

As the depth increases, so light fades and temperatures fall until just before 3,000 feet where there is a marked temperature change at the thermocline, the boundary between the warm surface zone and the cold deep zone. Below the thermocline, slow currents are caused by density differences between bodies of water with varying temperatures and salinity.

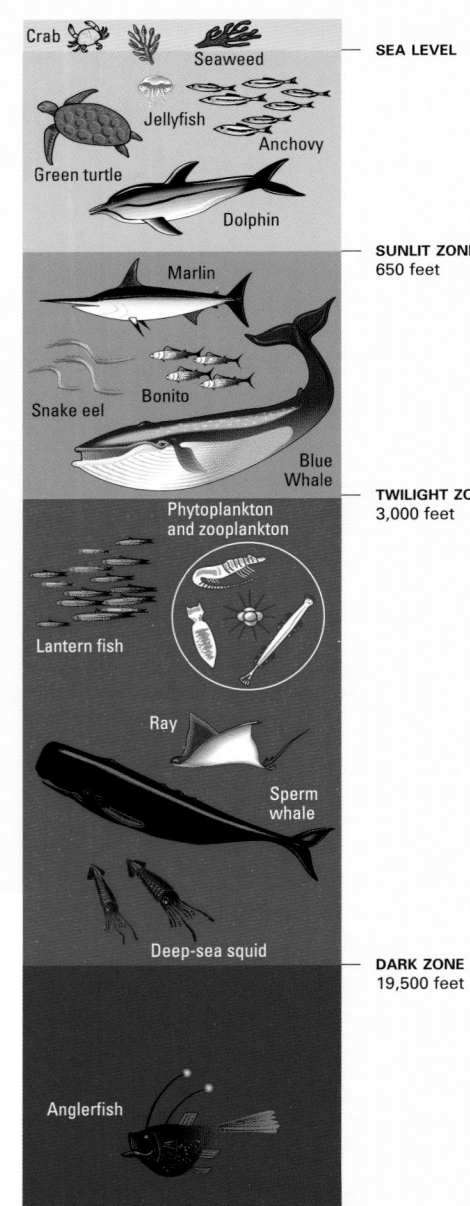

Crab   Seaweed   SEA LEVEL
          Jellyfish
                              Anchovy
Green turtle
                    Dolphin

                                          SUNLIT ZONE
                                          650 feet
              Marlin

Snake eel   Bonito
                              Blue
                              Whale
                                          TWILIGHT ZONE
                                          3,000 feet
          Phytoplankton
          and zooplankton

Lantern fish

              Ray

                    Sperm
                    whale

Deep-sea squid   DARK ZONE
                                          19,500 feet

Anglerfish

              Halosaur
Sea cucumber
              Sponge

                                          TRENCH ZONE
                                          33,000 feet
          Isopod

EL NIÑO PHENOMENON

Typical air and sea circulation pattern

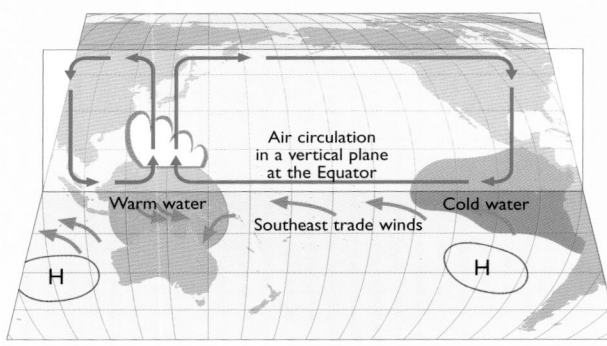

Air circulation in a vertical plane at the Equator

Warm water   Cold water
Southeast trade winds

H   H

El Niño air and sea circulation pattern

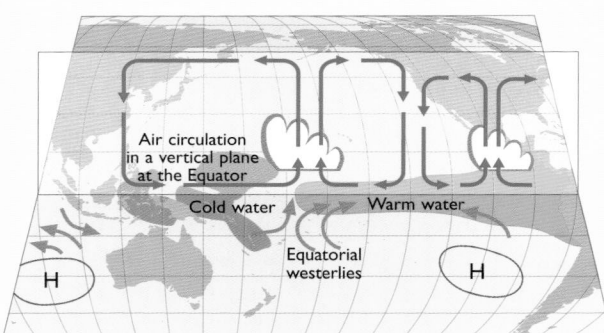

Air circulation in a vertical plane at the Equator

Cold water   Warm water
          Equatorial westerlies

H   H

The importance of the ocean–atmosphere interaction is nowhere more dramatically demonstrated than in the El Niño phenomenon of the southern Pacific Ocean. Under normal conditions, called La Niña, cold, nutrient-rich water rises to the surface off South America and spreads westward. In the western Pacific, sea surface temperatures reach 82°F or more and warm air rises, creating a low-pressure air system and causing heavy rains. The rising air spreads out and some of it descends over South America and the eastern Pacific, creating a high-pressure air system from which winds blow westward.

An El Niño event is characterized by a

reversal of currents. The upwelling of cold water is greatly reduced and surface water temperatures rise, causing a drastic reduction in fish life. The heaviest rainfall is over the eastern Pacific, while Southeast Asia is drier than usual. However, each El Niño event is unique in terms of its strength as well as its impact.

During an intense El Niño, the effects of the current and wind reversals affect the weather around the world. In the 1997 El Niño event there was a very suppressed hurricane season in the Caribbean but numerous super typhoons in the Pacific. Whilst South America and East Africa were much wetter than average, West Africa and parts of

Indonesia were much drier than normal. Algal blooms occurred in Australia's drought–stricken rivers and there were numerous super bush fires in Indonesia.

Scientists have found evidence that the frequency of the El Niño event, which normally occurs every three to seven years, and lasts between 12–18 months, may have increased in recent years.

We do not fully understand the causes of the El Niño event, though some researchers are currently investigating possible connections between major volcanic eruptions in the tropical Pacific region, the El Niño Southern Oscillation (ENSO) cycle, and atmospheric circulation.

OCEAN CURRENTS

JANUARY CURRENTS
(Northern Hemisphere: winter)

Cold	Warm	Speed (knots)
← - -	- - ←	Less than 0.5
←	←	0.5 – 1.0
◄	◄	Over 1.0

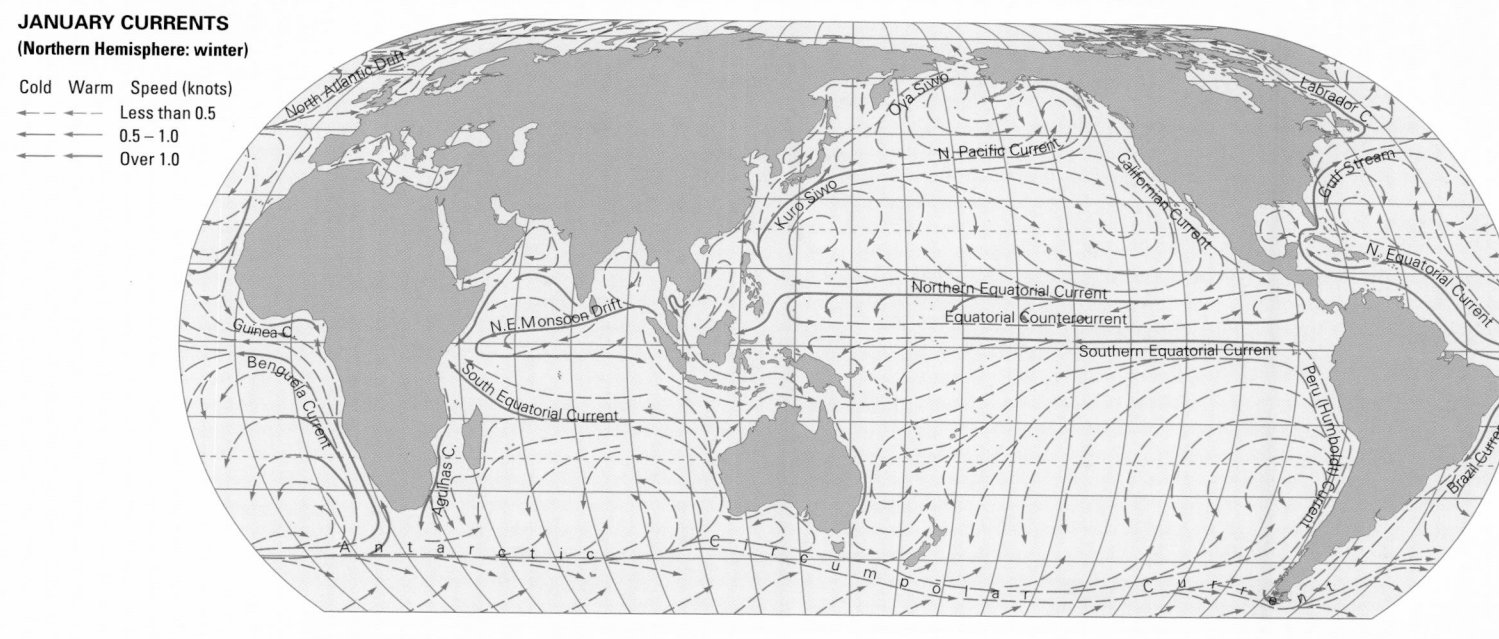

JULY CURRENTS
(Northern Hemisphere: summer)

Cold	Warm	Speed (knots)
← - -	- - ←	Less than 0.5
←	←	0.5 – 1.0
◄	◄	Over 1.0

Moving immense quantities of energy as well as billions of tons of water every hour, the ocean currents are a vital part of the great heat engine that drives the Earth's climate. They themselves are produced by a twofold mechanism. At the surface, winds push huge masses of water before them; in the deep ocean below, an abrupt temperature gradient separates the churning surface waters from the still depths (see the ocean conveyor belt diagram, below left).

Coriolis effect
The pattern of circulation of the great surface currents is determined by the displacement known as the Coriolis effect. As the Earth turns, the vast mass of ocean water is deflected to one side. The deflection is most obvious near the equator, where the Earth's surface is spinning eastward at 1,000 mph; currents moving poleward are curved clockwise in the northern hemisphere and counterclockwise in the southern hemisphere.

Ocean currents
The result is a system of spinning circles known as "gyres." Warm currents move constantly from the equator toward the poles, while cold water moves in the reverse direction. In this way, ocean currents act like a thermostat, helping to regulate temperatures around the world.
Depending on the annual movements of the prevailing wind belts, some currents on or near the equator may reverse their direction in the course of the year, a variation on which Asia's monsoon rains depend and whose occasional failure has brought disaster to millions of people.

THE OCEAN CONVEYOR BELT

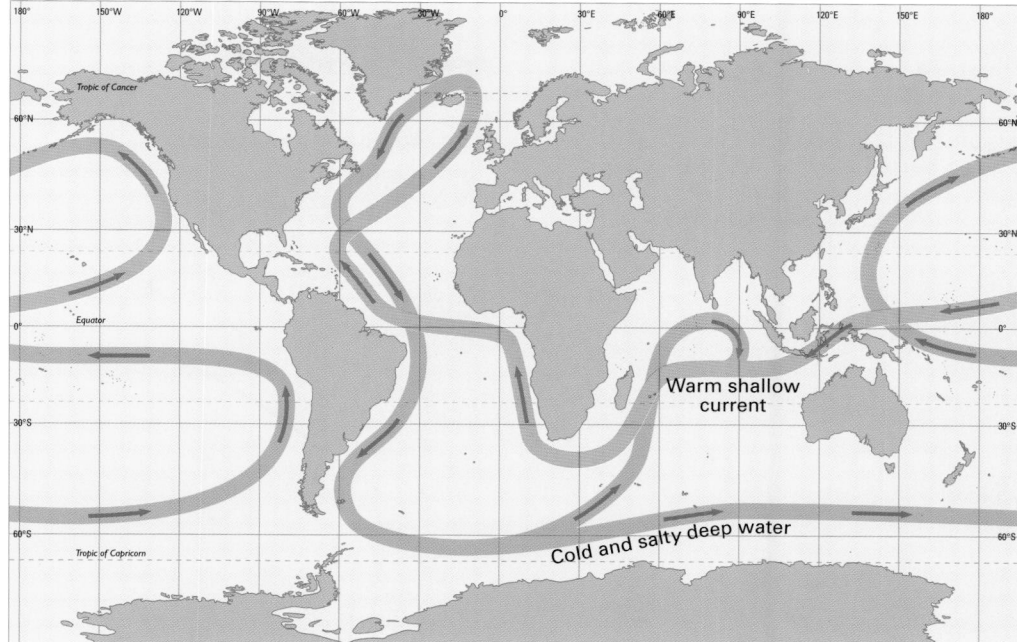

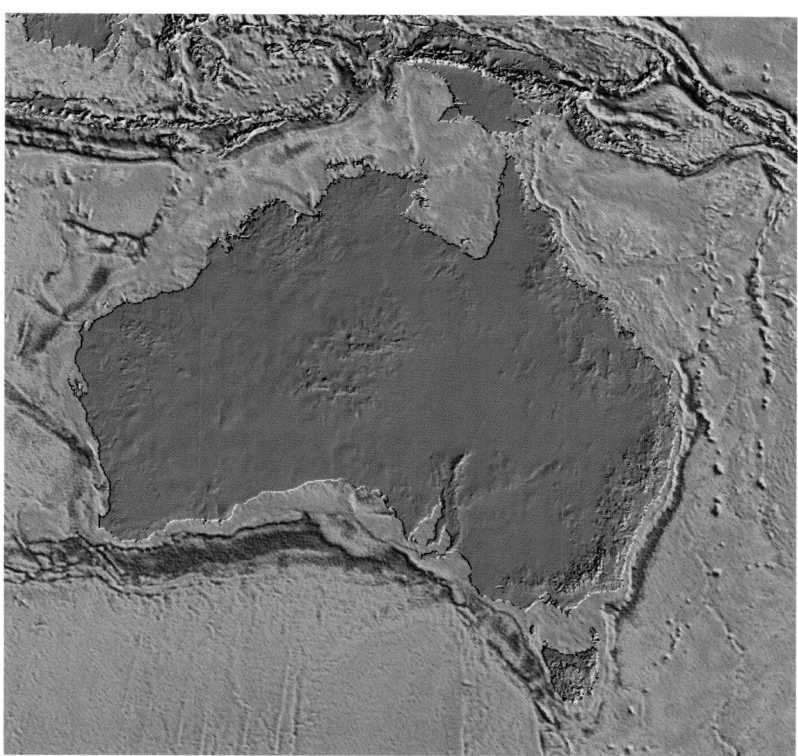

Thermohaline circulation, or the ocean conveyor belt, refers to the global, density-driven circulation of the oceans. The name comes from "thermo," for temperature, and "haline," for salt, which together determine the density of sea water.
The cycle starts near the equator in the Pacific Ocean, where surface currents drive the water westward. This water is warm and not very salty, making it lightweight, so it travels along the surface of the ocean.

As the water progresses west it eventually works its way into the North Atlantic where it cools, increases in salinity, and sinks. It slowly circulates southward then eastward towards the Antarctic where it splits into two routes: one to the Indian Ocean and one into the Pacific.
As the water recycles, it once again becomes warmer, less salty, lighter, and upwells in the Pacific to start the cycle all over again.

▲ In the image above, land areas are shown in gray, with shaded relief. The colors represent sea depths, with red representing the shallowest areas, through yellow and green to dark blue (the deepest). The data for the sea topography are from the Seasat radar satellite. The deep blue area in the upper left is the Java Trench, which forms the boundary between the Indian–Australian plate and the Eurasian plate. In the top right, the New Guinea trench, which has a maximum depth of 29,865 feet, forms the border of the Indian–Australian and Pacific plates. Alongside the trenches are volcanic islands formed from magma, created as the edge of the Indian–Australian plate is subducted and melted.

For more information:
75 Ocean currents
79 Beaufort wind scale
   Monsoon
80 Climate change
   Global warming

The atmosphere is a meteor shield, a radiation deflector, a thermal blanket, and a source of chemical energy for the Earth's diverse life forms. Five-sixths of its mass is in the lowest layer, the troposphere, which ranges in thickness from 11–6 miles between the equator and the poles. Powered by the Sun, the air is always on the move, flowing generally from high- to low-pressure areas. The troposphere is the layer where virtually all weather phenomena, including clouds, precipitation, and winds, occur. Above the troposphere is the stratosphere, which contains the important ozone layer and extends to about 30 miles above the Earth's surface. Beyond 60 miles, atmospheric density is lower than most laboratory vacuums.

STRUCTURE OF THE ATMOSPHERE

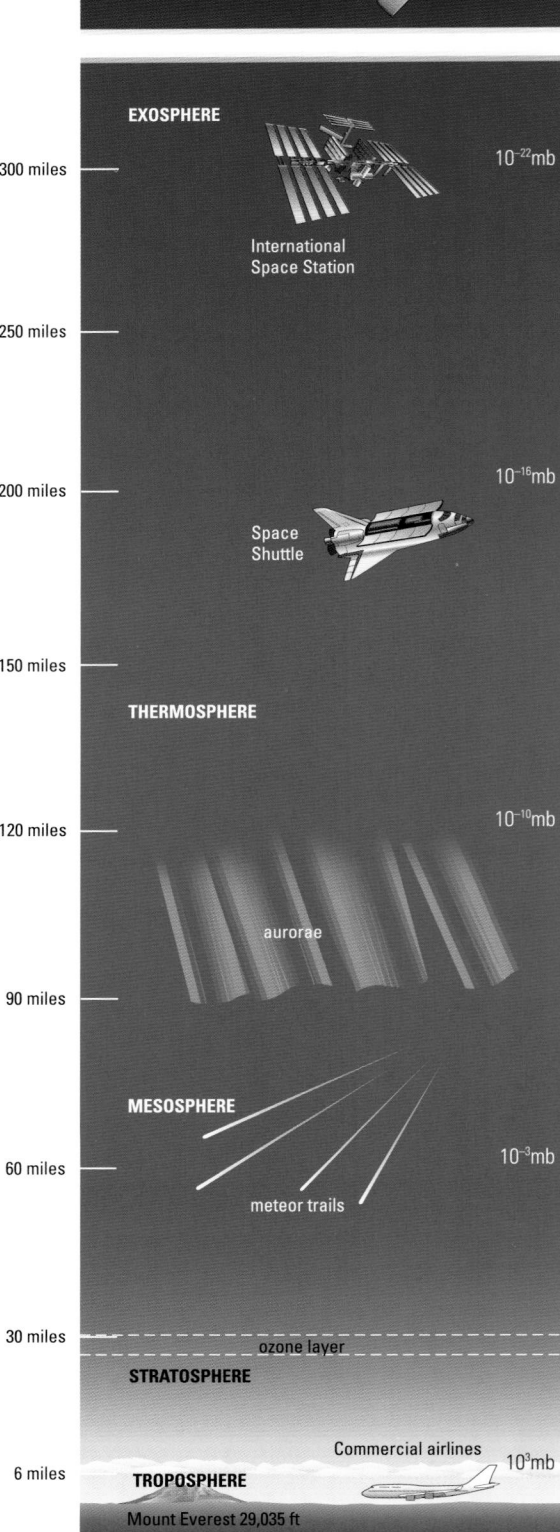

400 miles — Hubble Space Telescope — pressure 10^{-35}mb

EXOSPHERE

300 miles — International Space Station — 10^{-22}mb

250 miles

THERMOSPHERE

200 miles — Space Shuttle — 10^{-16}mb

150 miles

120 miles — 10^{-10}mb

aurorae

90 miles

MESOSPHERE

60 miles — meteor trails — 10^{-3}mb

30 miles — ozone layer

STRATOSPHERE

6 miles — Commercial airlines — 10^{3}mb

TROPOSPHERE

Mount Everest 29,035 ft

CIRCULATION OF THE AIR

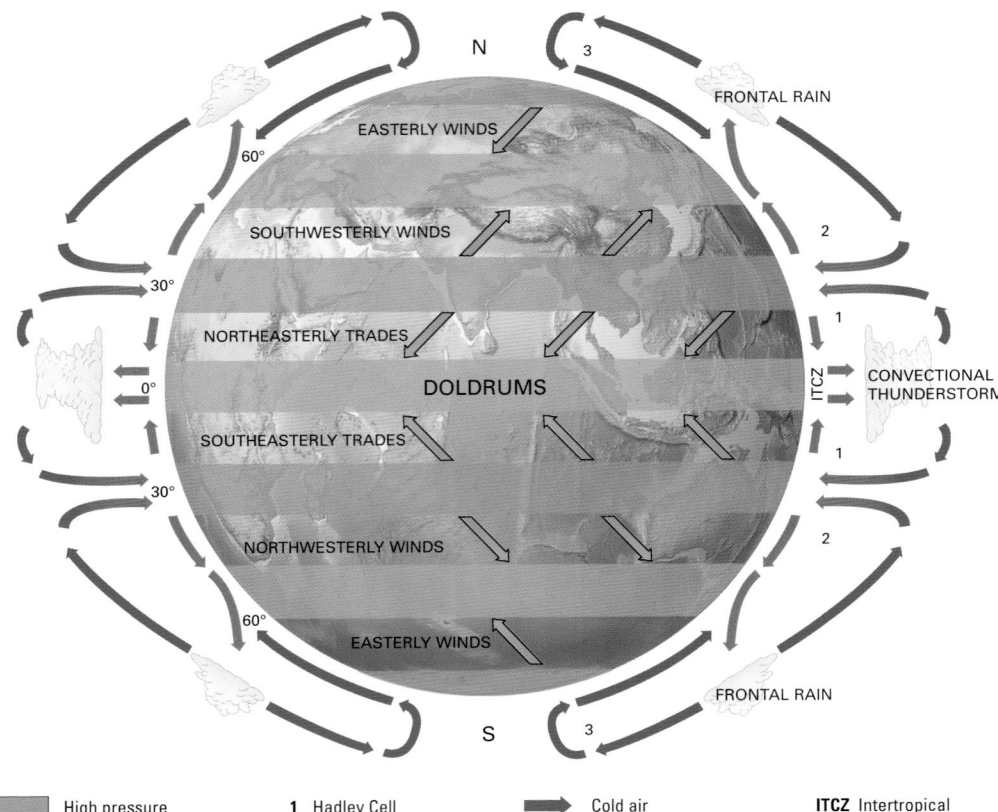

N
3
FRONTAL RAIN
EASTERLY WINDS
60°
SOUTHWESTERLY WINDS
2
30°
NORTHEASTERLY TRADES
1
0°
DOLDRUMS
ITCZ
CONVECTIONAL THUNDERSTORM
SOUTHEASTERLY TRADES
1
30°
NORTHWESTERLY WINDS
2
60°
EASTERLY WINDS
FRONTAL RAIN
S
3

	High pressure		**1** Hadley Cell		Cold air		**ITCZ** Intertropical Convergence Zone
	Low pressure		**2** Ferrel Cell		Surface winds		
	Warm air		**3** Polar Cell		Clouds		

FRONTAL SYSTEMS

Depressions, also known as cyclones or lows, form on the polar front where relatively cold and dry polar air flows alongside warmer, moister subtropical air. They occur when the flow high above the polar front generates a surface inward swirling circulation that moves along the polar front as a wave.

The warm front is the leading edge of the subtropical air that glides up and over the cooler air ahead of it. This gently ascending flow produces a characteristic sequence of clouds ahead of the warm front and a band of precipitation a few hundred miles wide immediately in advance it. Conditions within the warm sector are often overcast with layer cloud and generally light rain or drizzle. The cloud sometimes breaks up downwind of hills.

Another band of precipitation often occurs just ahead of the cold front that is the leading edge of the cooler polar air. Cumulus clouds tend to occur in the air behind the cold front, producing scattered showers. The changes of temperature, wind direction, and cloud, etc, are illustrated by the diagram below.

CHEMICAL COMPOSITION

Gaseous composition of the principal atmospheric layers

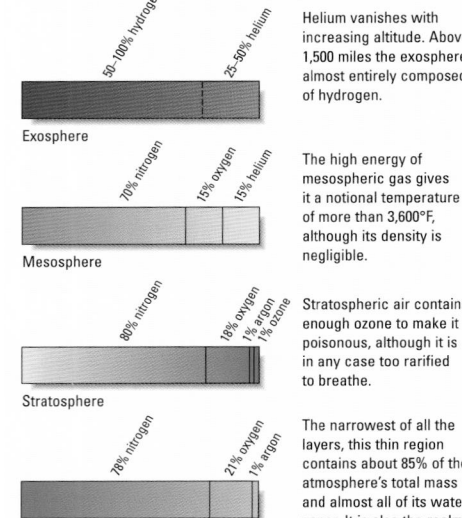

50–100% hydrogen | 25–50% helium
Exosphere

70% nitrogen | 15% oxygen | 15% helium
Mesosphere

80% nitrogen | 18% oxygen | 1% argon | 1% ozone
Stratosphere

78% nitrogen | 21% oxygen | 1% argon
Troposphere

Helium vanishes with increasing altitude. Above 1,500 miles the exosphere is almost entirely composed of hydrogen.

The high energy of mesospheric gas gives it a notional temperature of more than 3,600°F, although its density is negligible.

Stratospheric air contains enough ozone to make it poisonous, although it is in any case too rarified to breathe.

The narrowest of all the layers, this thin region contains about 85% of the atmosphere's total mass and almost all of its water vapor. It is also the realm of the Earth's weather.

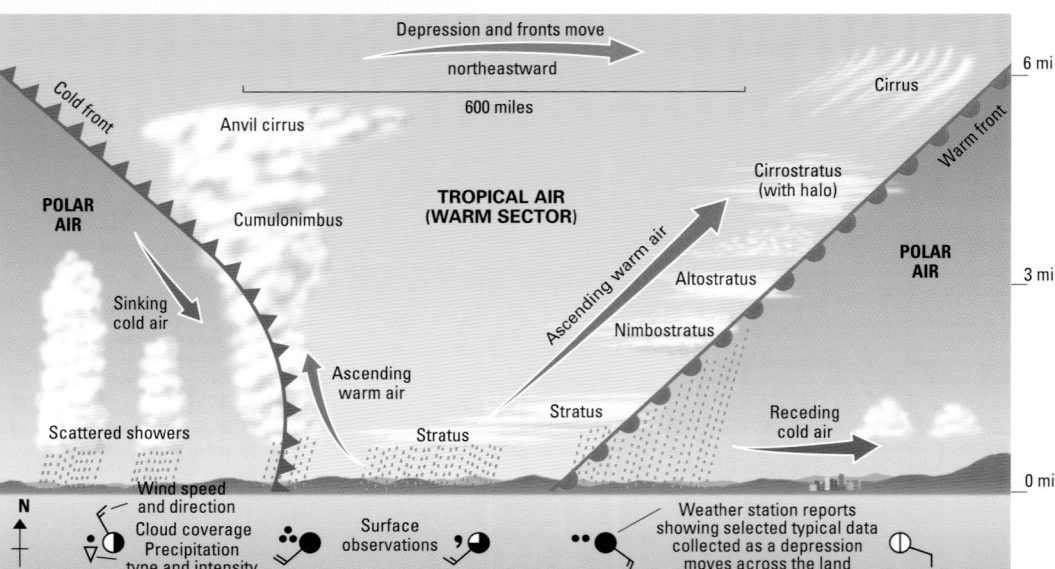

Depression and fronts move northeastward
600 miles
Cold front
Anvil cirrus
Cirrus
6 mi
POLAR AIR
Cumulonimbus
TROPICAL AIR (WARM SECTOR)
Cirrostratus (with halo)
Warm front
Ascending warm air
Altostratus
POLAR AIR
Sinking cold air
Nimbostratus
3 mi
Ascending warm air
Stratus
Scattered showers
Stratus
Receiving cold air
Receding cold air
0 mi
N
Wind speed and direction
Cloud coverage
Precipitation type and intensity
Surface observations
Weather station reports showing selected typical data collected as a depression moves across the land

AIR MASSES

Air masses are extensive regions of air, typically a few thousand miles across, that have horizontally gently varying temperature and humidity characteristics produced by the underlying continental or maritime surfaces over which they occur. They can, for example, be warm and moist air or cold and dry air that spiral slowly out from their "source regions." These are the highs marked on the world maps below.

A particular location's weather associated with an air mass depends on the air's source region (for example, the North Atlantic subtropical high), the track it has taken (for example, long maritime or continental track), and the time of year (for example, across a cold or strongly heated continent). The polar front and its frontal cyclones is a gently sloping, troposphere-deep surface that separates two air masses – the North Atlantic subtropical high and the North American wintertime anticyclone. The warmer, damper subtropical air rides up and over the cooler, drier polar air to produce widespread frontal cloud and precipitation.

Air masses are classified as, amongst others, "polar continental," "polar maritime" or "tropical maritime." The massive Asian high in January is a source of polar continental, very cold, very dry air, while in contrast the extensive North Pacific and North Atlantic highs are sources of warm and very moist air throughout the year.

CLASSIFICATION OF CLOUDS

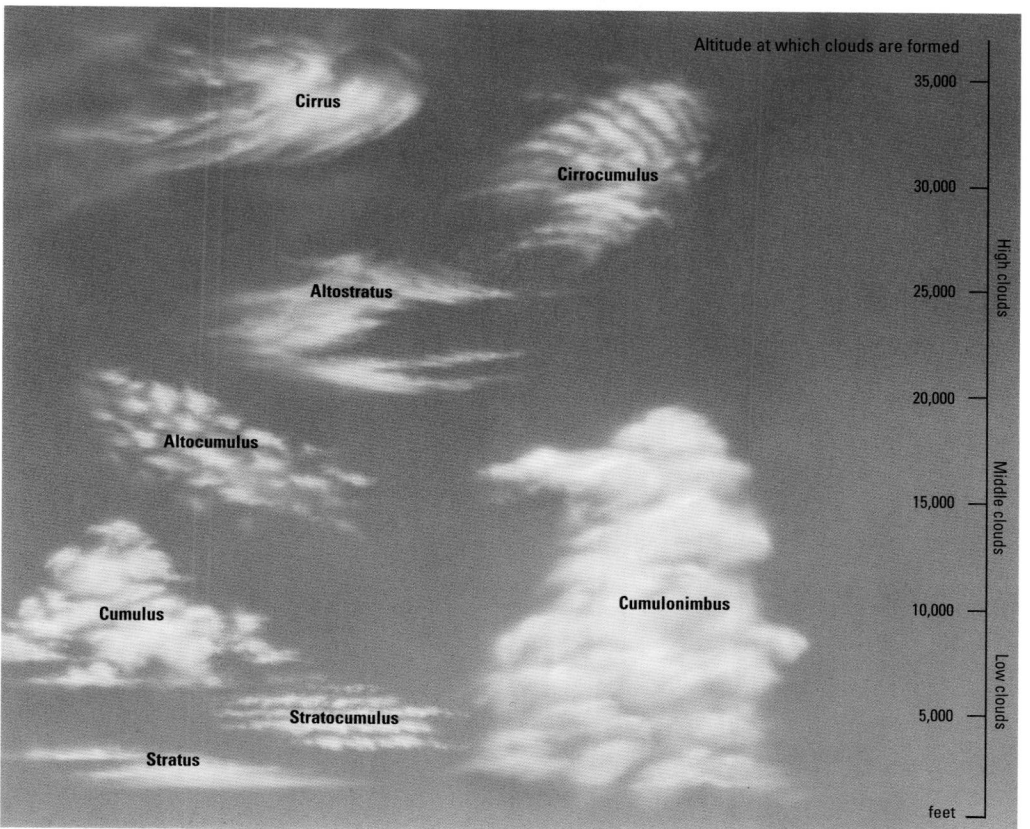

Clouds form when damp, usually rising, air is cooled. Thus they form when a wind rises to cross hills or mountains; when a mass of air rises over, or is pushed up by, another mass of denser air; or when local heating of the ground causes convection currents.

The first classification of clouds was developed by a London chemist, Luke Howard, in 1803, and it was later modified by the World Meteorological Organization. The types of clouds are classified according to altitude as high, middle, or low. The high ones, composed of ice crystals, are cirrus, cirrostratus, and cirrocumulus.

The middle clouds are altostratus – a gray or bluish striated, fibrous or uniform sheet producing light drizzle – and altocumulus, a thicker and fluffier version of cirrocumulus.

Low clouds include nimbostratus, a dark gray layer that brings rain or snow; cumulus, a detached heap, dark at the base; stratus, which forms dull, overcast skies at low levels; and stratocumulus, which consists of fluffy grayish-white layers.

Cumulonimbus, associated with storms and rains, heavy and dense with a flat base and a high, fluffy outline, can be tall enough to occupy middle as well as low altitudes.

PRESSURE AND SURFACE WINDS

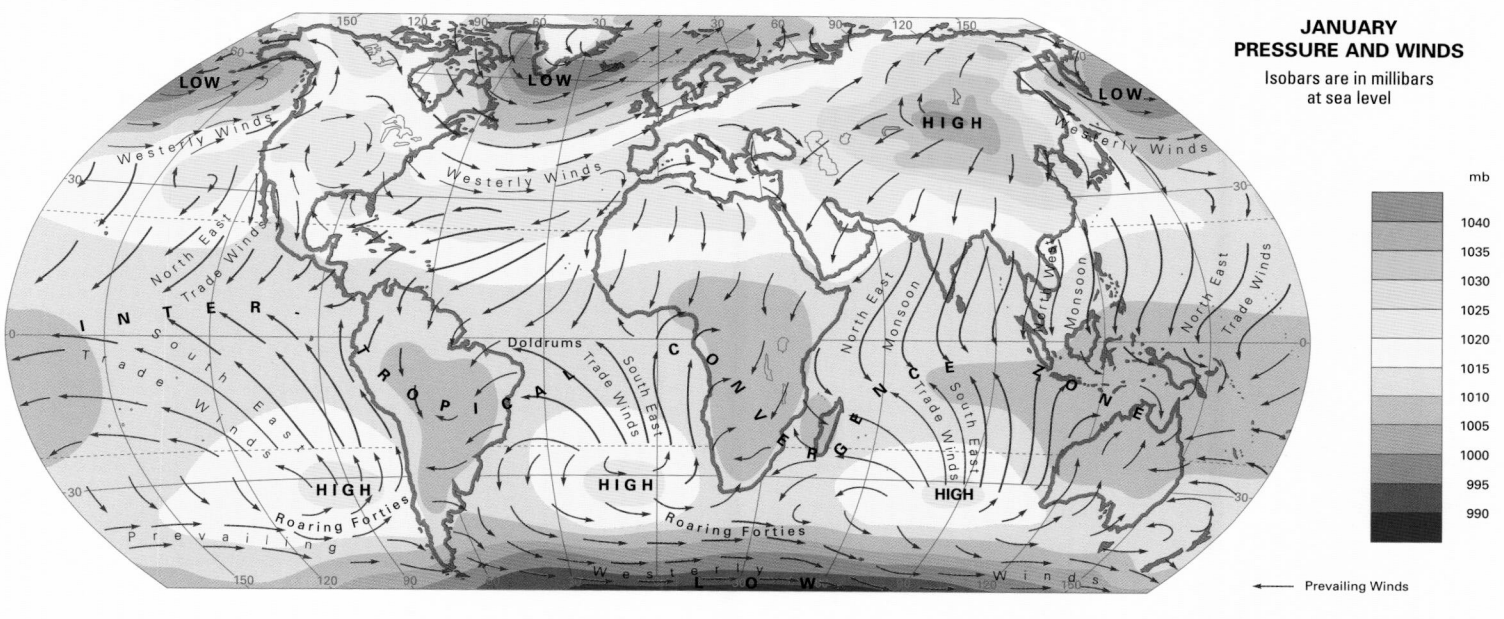

JANUARY PRESSURE AND WINDS
Isobars are in millibars at sea level

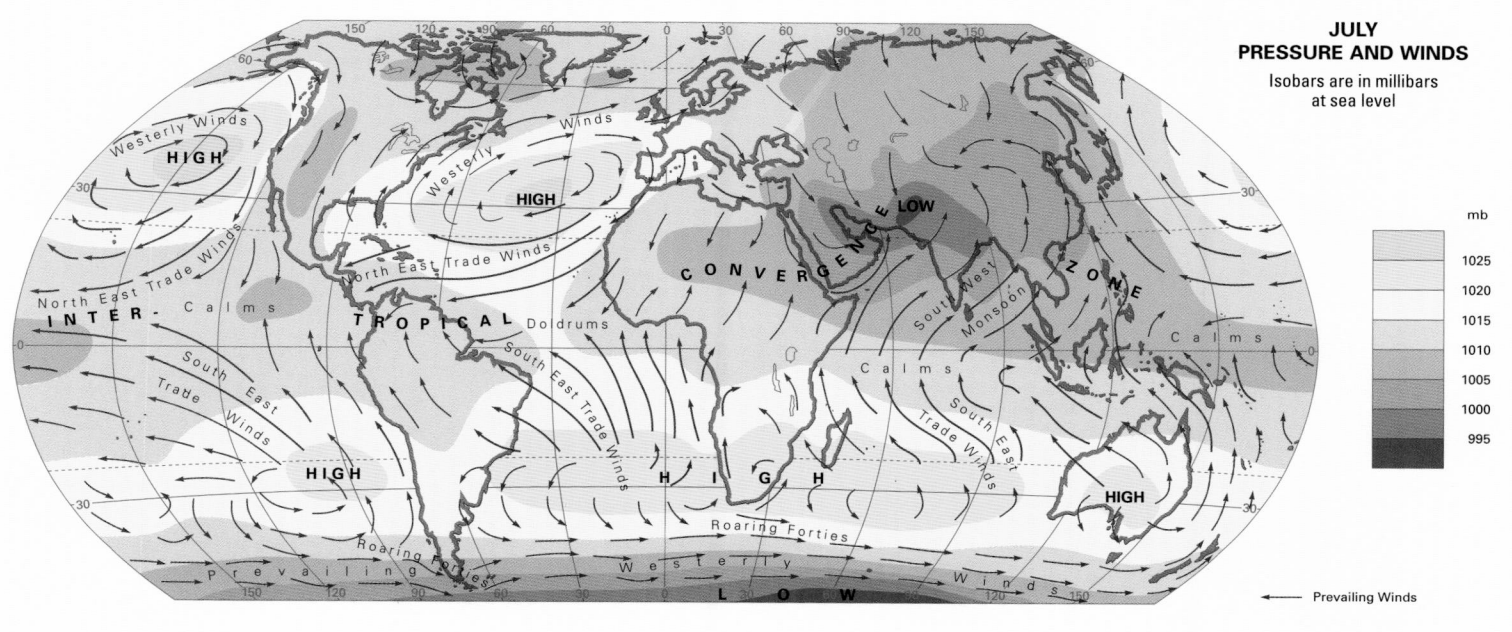

JULY PRESSURE AND WINDS
Isobars are in millibars at sea level

WEATHER RECORDS

Pressure and winds

Highest barometric pressure:
Agata, Siberia, 1,083.8 mb at altitude 862 ft [262 m], December 31, 1968.

Lowest barometric pressure:
Typhoon Tip, 300 miles [480 km] west of Guam, Pacific Ocean, 870 mb, October 12, 1979.

Highest recorded wind speed:
Bridge Creek, Oklahoma, USA, 318 mph [512 km/h], May 3, 1999. Measured by Doppler radar monitoring a tornado.

Windiest place:
Port Martin, Antarctica, where winds of more than 40 mph [64 km/h] occur for not less than 100 days a year.

Worst recorded storm:
Bangladesh (then East Pakistan) cyclone, November 13, 1970 – over 300,000 dead or missing. The 1991 cyclone, Bangladesh's and the world's second worst in terms of loss of life, killed an estimated 138,000 people.

Worst recorded tornado:
Tri-state tornado – Missouri/Illinois/Indiana, USA, March 18, 1925 – 695 deaths, lasted 3 hours with 219 mi [352 km] path length. A suspected tornado in Bangladesh on April 26, 1989, killed approximately 1,300 people.

For more information:
75 Ocean currents
76 Circulation of the air
77 Classification of clouds
Pressure and winds
80 Greenhouse effect
Global warming
82 Hydrological cycle
83 Natural vegetation

Weather is the day-to-day or hour-to-hour condition of the air, while climate is weather in the long term – the seasonal pattern of hot and cold, wet and dry, averaged over a long period.

Most classifications of climate are based on a system developed in the early 19th century by Vladimir Köppen, a Russian meteorologist. Using a code based on letters and a classification centered on two main features, temperature and precipitation, he identified five main climatic types: tropical (A), dry (B), warm temperate (C), cold temperate (D), and polar (E). A highland mountain climate (H) was added later to account for the variety of altitudinal climatic zones on high mountains. Each

of these main regions was then further subdivided.

Latitude is a major factor in determining climate, but other factors add to the complexity. These include the differential heating of land and sea, the distance from the sea, the effect of mountains on winds, and the influence of ocean currents. For example, New York City, Naples, and the Gobi Desert share almost the same latitude, but their climates are very different.

During the last Ice Age, the Earth underwent alternating cold periods, called glacials, separated by warm interglacials. The Milankovich theory suggests such cycles may be caused by variations in the Earth's path around the Sun, changing

from almost circular to elliptical every 95,000 years, and variations in the Earth's tilt from 21.5° to 24.5° every 42,000 years. Another factor is that the Earth is now closest to the Sun in the middle of winter in the northern hemisphere and furthest away in summer. But 12,000 years ago, at the height of the last glacial period, the northern winter fell with the Sun at its most distant.

Studies of these cycles suggest that we are now in an interglacial with a new glacial period on the way. However, scientists believe that global warming, largely a result of burning fossil fuels and deforestation, may be occurring much faster than the great, slow cycles of the Solar System.

Tropical rainy climates
All mean monthly temperatures above 64°F.

Af	Rain forest climate
Am	Monsoon climate
Aw	Savanna climate

Dry climates
Low rainfall combined with a wide range of temperatures

| BS | Steppe climate |
| BW | Desert climate |

Warm temperate rainy climates
The mean temperature is below 64°F but above 26°F and that of the warmest month is over 50°F.

Cw	Dry winter climate
Cs	Dry summer climate
Cf	Climate with no dry season

Cold temperate rainy climates
The mean temperature of the coldest month is below 26°F but that of the warmest month is still over 50°F.

| Dw | Dry winter climate |
| Df | Climate with no dry season |

Polar climates
The mean temperature of the warmest month is below 50°F, giving permanently frozen subsoil.

| ET | Tundra climate |

The mean temperature of the warmest month is below 32°F, giving permanent ice and snow.

| EF | Polar climate |

CLIMATE REGIONS

Vladimir Köppen divided the world's land areas into five main climatic regions, designated **A, B, C, D,** and **E,** which correspond broadly to the five vegetation types. Each of the five climatic regions is further subdivided using other letter codes. For example, dry climates are subdivided into deserts (**W**) and dry, semiarid steppe (**S**), while polar climates contain areas permanently covered by ice sheets and ice caps (**F**), and tundra areas (**T**).

Other letters cover particular features of precipitation, namely **f** for places with precipitation throughout the year; **m** for tropical areas with a marked monsoon season; **s** for places with a dry summer season; and **w** for places with a dry winter.

Another group of letters is concerned primarily with temperature, namely **a** for places with a hot summer; **b** for places with a warm summer; **c** for places with a cool, short summer; **d** for places with a cool, short summer and a cold winter; **h** for a hot, dry climate; and **k** for a cool, dry climate.

The classification **H** is sometimes used for mountain climates, which may, in the tropics, range from **Af** or **Aw** at the base, with **ET** and **EF** climates at the top.

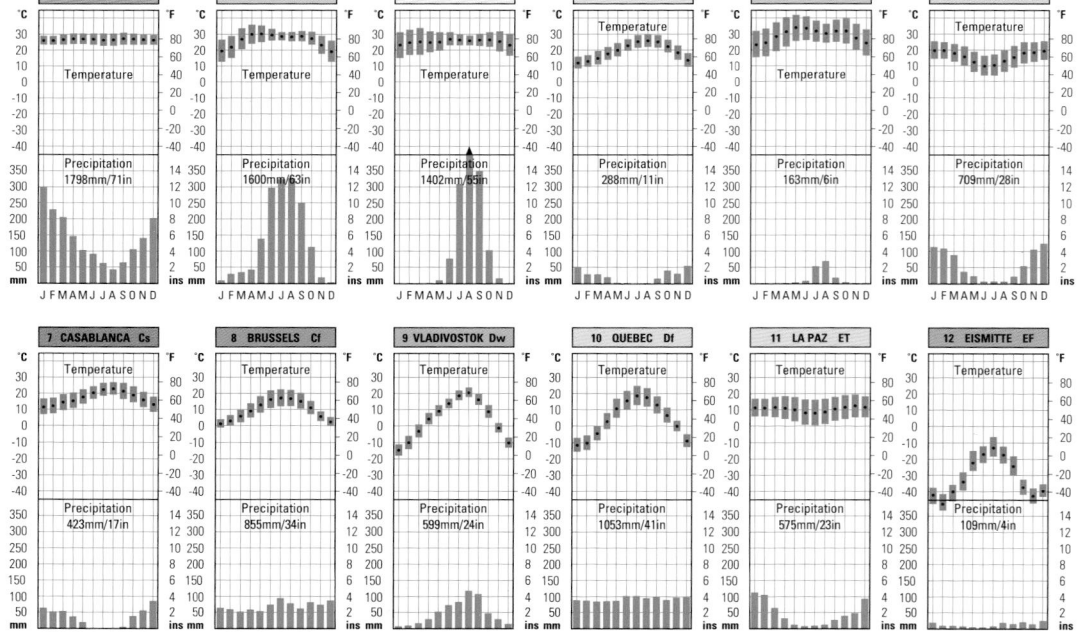

CLIMATE AND WEATHER TERMS

Anticyclone: area of high pressure with light winds and generally quiet weather.
Absolute humidity: mass of water vapor contained in a given volume of air.
Cloud cover: amount of cloud in the sky; measured in oktas (from 0–9), with 0 clear, and 9 "sky obscured."
Condensation: the conversion of water vapor into liquid.
Cyclone: violent storm resulting from counterclockwise rotation of winds in the northern hemisphere and clockwise in the southern: called hurricane in North America, typhoon in the Far East.
Depression: large area of low barometric pressure, a few thousand miles across.
Dew: deposition of small water droplets on the Earth's surface by direct condensation of water vapor.
Dew point: the temperature at which air becomes saturated by cooling at constant barometric pressure and absolute humidity
Drizzle: precipitation drops between 0.01–0.02 inches [0.2 and 0.5 mm] in diameter.
Evaporation: conversion of water from liquid into vapor or moisture in the air.
Front: the dividing line between two air masses.
Frost: the surface deposition of water vapor as minute ice crystals, when temperature reaches the frost point.

Hail: variably-sized pieces of ice that fall in downdrafts from cumulonimbus clouds.
Humidity: amount of water vapor in the air.
Isobar: line joining places with the same barometric pressure.
Isotherm: line connecting places of equal temperature.
Lightning: massive electrical discharge released in thunderstorm from cloud to cloud or cloud to ground, the result of the top becoming positively charged and the bottom negatively charged.
Precipitation: measurable rain, snow, sleet, or hail.
Prevailing wind: most common direction of wind at a given location.
Rain: precipitation of liquid particles with diameter larger than 0.02 inches [0.5 mm].
Relative humidity: observed quantity of water vapor in a mass of air over the saturation value at a given temperature (as a percentage).
Snow: flake-like coagulations of ice crystals that fall from clouds in subzero temperatures.
Thunder: sound produced by the rapid expansion of air heated by lightning.
Tornado: rapidly-rotating funnel-shaped cloud or debris column that must reach the surface and be attached to a parent cumulonimbus cloud.

BEAUFORT WIND SCALE

Named after Admiral Sir Francis Beaufort, the 19th-century British naval officer who devised it, the Beaufort Scale assesses wind speed according to its effects. It was originally designed as an aid for sailors, but has since been adapted for use on the land. It is used internationally.

Scale	Wind speed mph	km/h	Effect
0	0–1	0–1	**Calm** Smoke rises vertically
1	1–3	1–5	**Light air** Wind direction shown only by smoke drift
2	4–7	6–11	**Light breeze** Wind felt on face; leaves rustle; vanes moved by wind
3	8–12	12–19	**Gentle breeze** Leaves and small twigs in constant motion; wind extends small flag
4	13–18	20–28	**Moderate** Raises dust and loose paper; small branches move
5	19–24	29–38	**Fresh** Small trees in leaf sway; crested wavelets on inland waters
6	25–31	39–49	**Strong** Large branches move; difficult to use umbrellas; overhead wires whistle
7	32–38	50–61	**Near gale** Whole trees in motion; difficult to walk against wind
8	39–46	62–74	**Gale** Twigs break from trees; walking very difficult
9	47–54	75–88	**Strong gale** Slight structural damage
10	55–63	89–102	**Storm** Trees uprooted; serious structural damage
11	64–72	103–117	**Violent storm** Widespread damage
12	73+	118+	**Hurricane**

▲ On September 14, 2003, Hurricane Isabel was located over the Atlantic Ocean, 400 miles [640 km] north of Puerto Rico. It moved in a northwestward direction with maximum winds of 155 mph [250 km/h], making it a Category 5 hurricane.

THE MONSOON

Monsoon is the term given to the seasonal reversal of wind direction, most noticeably in Southeast Asia. It results from a combination of factors: the extreme heating and cooling of large land masses in relation to the less marked changes in temperature of the adjacent seas; the northward movement of the Intertropical Convergence Zone (ITCZ); and the effect of the Himalayas on the circulation of the air.

In March, winds blow outward from the mainland. But as the Sun and the ITCZ move northward, the land is intensely heated, and a low-pressure system develops. The southeast trade winds change direction and are sucked into the interior to become southwesterlies, bringing heavy rain. By November, the Sun and the ITCZ have again moved south and the wind directions are again reversed. Cool winds blow from the Asian interior to the sea, losing any moisture on the Himalayas before descending to the coast.

TEMPERATURE

Average temperature in January

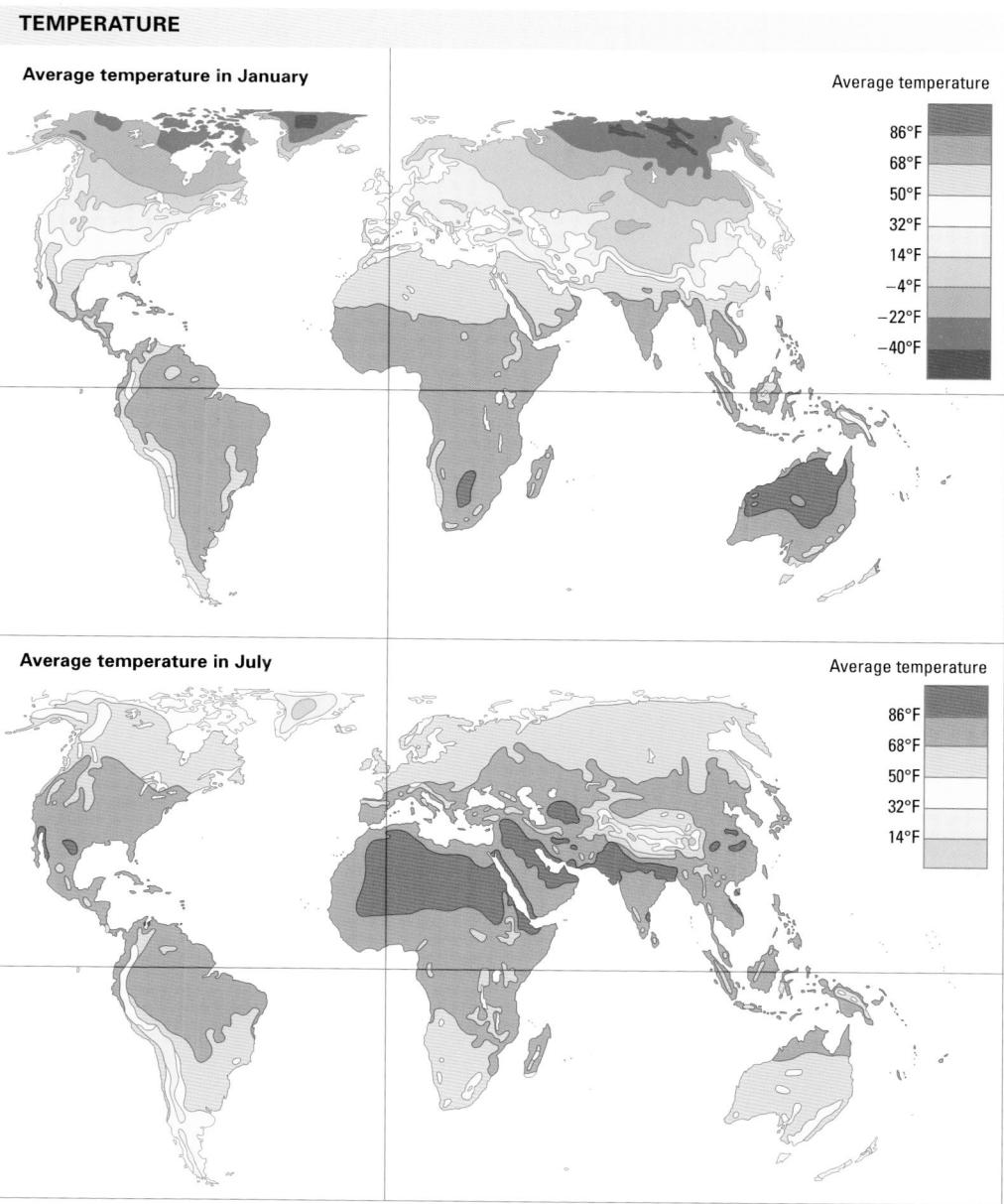

Average temperature
86°F
68°F
50°F
32°F
14°F
−4°F
−22°F
−40°F

Average temperature in July

Average temperature
86°F
68°F
50°F
32°F
14°F

PRECIPITATION (RAINFALL AND SNOW)

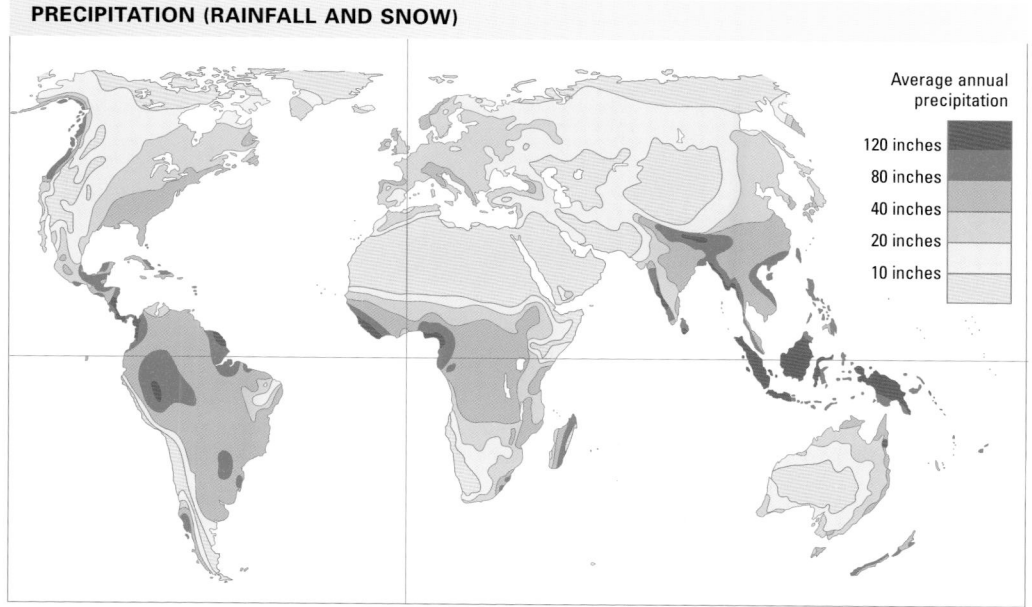

Average annual precipitation
120 inches
80 inches
40 inches
20 inches
10 inches

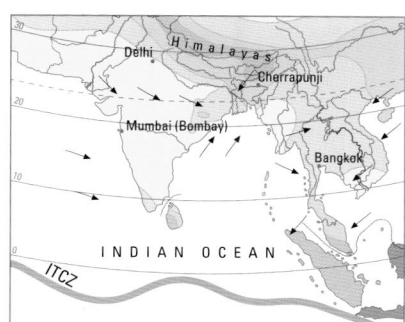

March – Start of the hot, dry season. The ITCZ is over the southern Indian Ocean.

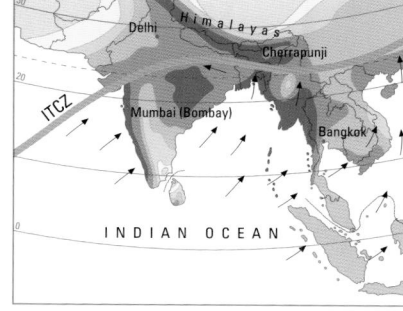

July – The rainy season. The ITCZ has migrated northward; winds blow onshore.

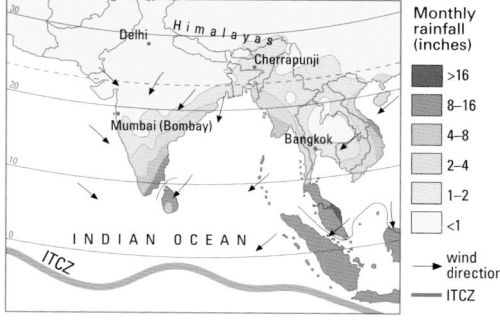

November – The ITCZ has returned south. The offshore winds are cool and dry.

Monthly rainfall (inches)
>16
8–16
4–8
2–4
1–2
<1
→ wind direction
— ITCZ

CLIMATE RECORDS

TEMPERATURE

Highest recorded temperature:
Al Aziziyah, Libya, 135.9°F [57.7°C], September 13, 1922.

Highest mean annual temperature:
Dallol, Ethiopia, 94°F [34.4°C], 1960–6.

Longest heatwave:
Marble Bar, W. Australia, 162 days over 100°F [38°C], October 23, 1923, to April 7, 1924.

Lowest recorded temperature (outside poles):
Verkhoyansk, Siberia, −93.6°F [−69.8°C], February 7, 1982. Verkhoyansk also registered the greatest annual range of temperature: −90°F to 98°F [−68°C to 37°C].

Lowest mean annual temperature:
Polus Nedostupnosti, Pole of Cold, Antarctica, −72°F [−57.8°C].

PRECIPITATION

Driest place:
Quillagua, N. Chile, Mean annual rainfall 0.02 inches [0.5 mm], 1964–2001

Wettest place (average):
Mt Wai'ale'ale, Hawai'i, USA, mean annual rainfall 459.8 inches [11,680 mm].

Wettest place (12 months):
Cherrapunji, Meghalaya, N.E. India, 1,042 inches [26,461 mm], August 1860 to August 1861. Cherrapunji also holds the record for rainfall in one month: 115 inches [2,930 mm], July 1861. (*See Monsoon maps below.*)

Wettest place (24 hours):
Fac Fac, Réunion, Indian Ocean, 71.9 inches [1,825 mm], March 15–16, 1952.

Heaviest hailstones:
Gopalganj, Bangladesh, up to 2.25 lb [1.02 kg], April 14, 1986 (killed 92 people).

Heaviest snowfall (continuous):
Bessans, Savoie, France, 68 inches [1,730 mm] in 19 hours, April 5–6, 1969.

Heaviest snowfall (season/year):
Mt Baker, Washington, USA, 1,140 inches [28,956 mm], June 1998 to June 1999.

For more information:
75 Ocean currents
76 Atmosphere
78 Climate

Ever since the Industrial Revolution began, the amount of carbon dioxide in the atmosphere has steadily increased. It is the result of burning fossil fuels – coal, oil, and natural gas, and also the destruction of forests which absorb carbon dioxide. In the late 18th century, carbon dioxide made up about 280 parts per million by volume (ppmv). Since 1958, regular measurements have been made at the Mauna Kea Observatory, Hawai'i, to avoid local pollution. It has since risen from316 ppmv to 387 ppmv in 2008.

Carbon dioxide is one of the "greenhouse gases," which also include CFCs, which also cause ozone depletion in the upper atmosphere, methane, and nitrous oxides. Water vapor is another greenhouse gas. The volume of vapor in the atmosphere is not changing significantly, though it may increase if the atmosphere warms up, causing an increase in the evaporation of surface waters.

Greenhouse gases are so-called because they slow the escape of heat which is reradiated from the Earth's surface, much like the glass walls and roof of a greenhouse block the escape of heat. The greenhouse effect is essential for life on Earth. Without it, our planet would be some 54°F [30°C] colder than it is. But the increase in the volume of carbon dioxide in particular has caused global temperatures to rise. These changes were detailed by the Inter-governmental Panel on Climate Change (IPCC) report in 2007. While computer projections are difficult to make, the IPCC report concluded that a rise in temperatures of 7°F [4°C] was likely by 2100. Global warming will almost certainly alter weather patterns, causing extreme food and water shortages in vulnerable parts of the world, massive floods, and a rise in sea levels between 7 and 23 inches [18–59 cm].

While a partial international ban has been imposed on some greenhouse gases, their residence time in the atmosphere has long-lasting consequences

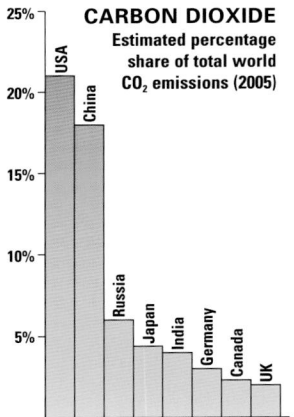

CARBON DIOXIDE
Estimated percentage share of total world CO_2 emissions (2005)

In June 2007, it was estimated that China was building two coal-fired power stations every week to support its economic boom. If this is the case, it will soon overtake the USA and become the world's biggest producer of carbon dioxide.

GLOBAL WARMING

High atmospheric concentrations of heat-absorbing gases appear to be causing a rise in average temperatures worldwide – up by approximately 3°F [1.5°C] by the year 2020, according to some estimates. Global warming is also likely to bring about a rise in sea levels that may flood some of the world's densely populated coastal areas.

Evidence of global warming is attributed mainly to the "greenhouse effect," caused by the emission of certain gases, notably carbon dioxide, into the atmosphere. Despite some international action to control emissions of some greenhouse gases, carbon dioxide levels are still rising.

Carbon dioxide emissions in tons per capita (2005)

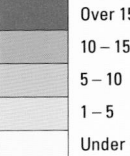

Over 15
10 – 15
5 – 10
1 – 5
Under 1

▲ Over 75% increase in total carbon dioxide emissions 2000 – 2005

CLIMATE CHANGE

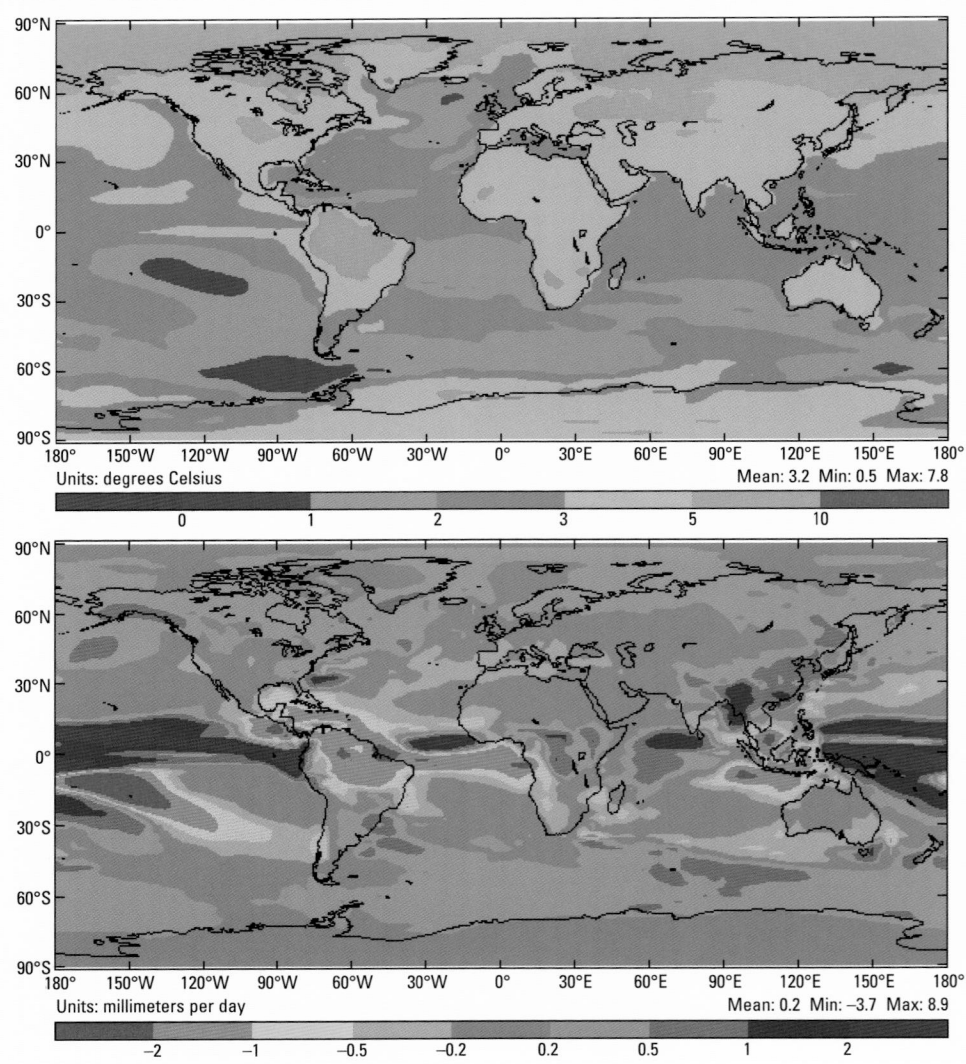

Units: degrees Celsius
Mean: 3.2 Min: 0.5 Max: 7.8

0 1 2 3 5 10

Units: millimeters per day
Mean: 0.2 Min: –3.7 Max: 8.9

–2 –1 –0.5 –0.2 0.2 0.5 1 2

Annual average surface air temperature

The map summarizes the change in long-term mean values between the predicted average for the period from 2070 to 2100, and the observed average for 1960 to 1990. The predictions are from a long-term "run" of a "coupled" atmosphere-ocean computer model that represents the complex processes in the Earth's climate system. It assumes that the atmospheric concentration of carbon dioxide will increase more than twofold during the 21st century, assuming "medium growth" of the global economy, and that no measures to combat the emission of greenhouse gases are taken. Note that the predicted increase in average surface temperature suggests a warming across Britain and Ireland of between 3.6°F [2°C] in the north and west to possibly 7.2°F [4°C] in the southeast. Very broadly, the oceans and some adjacent continental areas are likely to see the smaller increases.

Annual average precipitation

Predictions from climate models always involve some degree of uncertainty. This is because our understanding of the climate system and its complex workings are imperfect, as are the model representations of the physical system. Additionally, we are unsure quite how the world will evolve economically and politically over the coming decades – although different scenarios are used in this regard. The map of predicted precipitation change indicates broadly, for example, an increase across Britain and Ireland. The largest increases of some 0.01–0.02 inches [0.2–0.5 mm] a day are anticipated to be over northern and western areas. This equates to some 3–7 inches [75–180 mm] a year.

It should be noted that both these maps mask quite significant seasonal detail, which is also predicted by the models.

ANTARCTICA

▶ Between January and March 2002, the 1,255 sq mi [3,250 sq km] Larsen B ice shelf on the Antarctic Peninsula collapsed. The left-hand image shows its area (in blue) in December 2001 before the collapse, while the right-hand image shows the area fragmented in December 2002 after the collapse. The 656 ft [200 m] thick ice sheet had been retreating before this date, but over 500 billion tons of ice collapsed in under a month. This was due to rising temperatures of 0.9°F [0.5°C] per year in this part of Antarctica.

 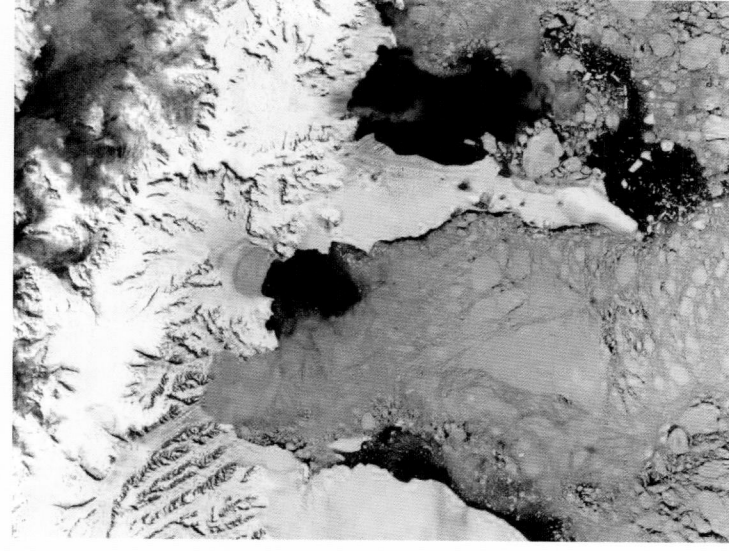

TEMPERATURE CHANGE

Climate modelers have produced simulations of global and continental surface temperature changes over the last century. This is done using only "natural forcing" by modeling the impact on atmospheric temperatures from known solar variability and volcanic eruptions. In addition, the same period of time is simulated by adding to natural forcing the impact of anthropogenic (human) influence due to measured changes in the concentration of greenhouse gases, particulate matter, etc.

The separate model "runs" are then compared with the observed temperature changes to illustrate which of the simulations matches the observations best.

This is a powerful means of verifying the relative roles of natural and human induced changes in atmospheric composition, and known solar output fluctuations on climate change.

▶ Climate model simulations for 1906 to 2005 using natural forcings only (blue bands) and natural plus anthropogenic forcings (pink bands). Regional decadal averages of observed temperature (black lines) are plotted as anomalies with respect to the 1901 to 1950 average. Blue and pink bands define the 5% to 95% range of possibilities for 19 runs produced by five models (natural forcing) and 58 simulations from 14 models (natural plus anthropogenic forcing).

▬ Models using only natural forcings

▬ Models using both natural and anthropogenic forcings

▬ Observations
(dashed when spatial coverage is less than 50%)

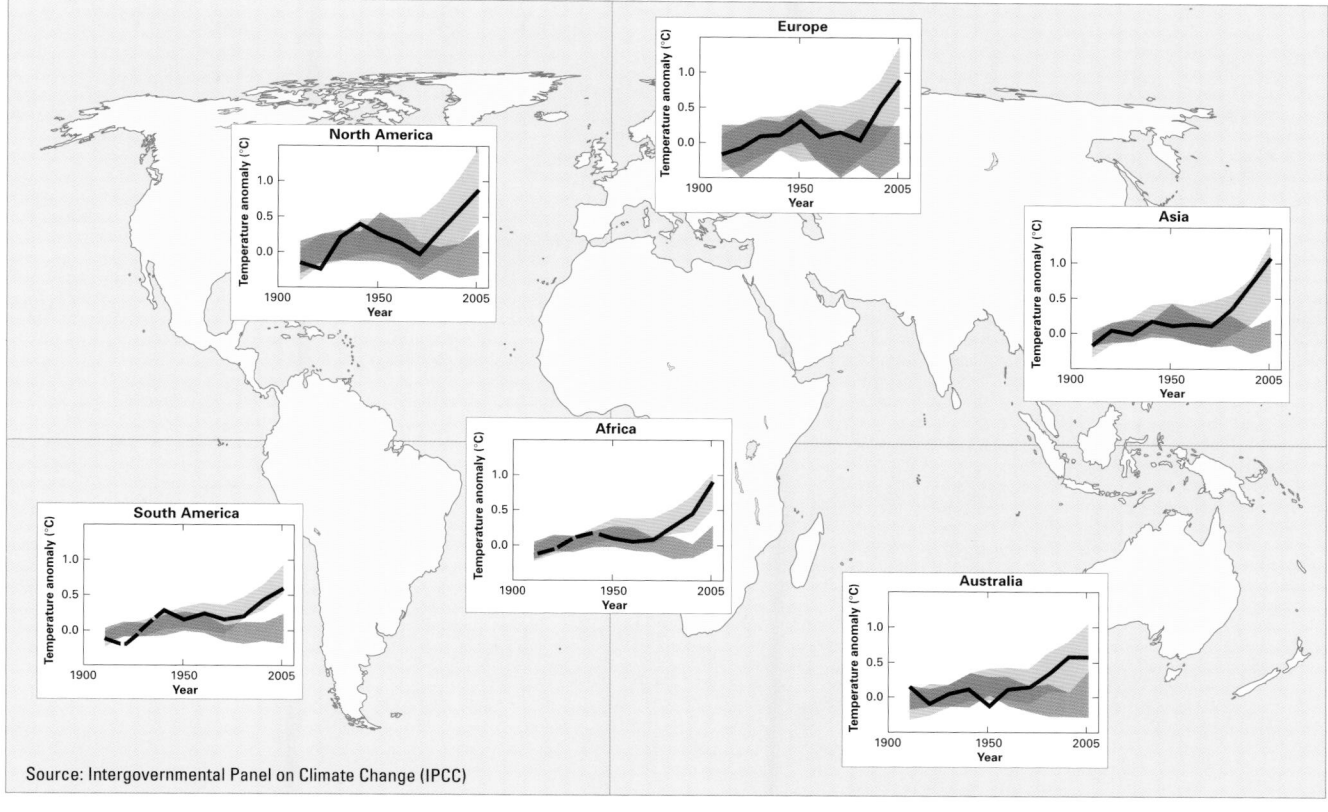

Source: Intergovernmental Panel on Climate Change (IPCC)

PROJECTED CHANGE IN GLOBAL WARMING

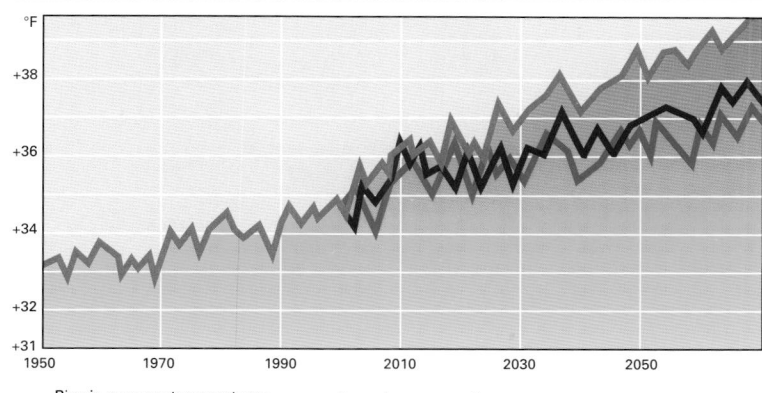

⋀ Rise in average temperatures assuming present trends in CO_2 emissions continue

⋀ Assuming some cuts are made in emissions

⋀ Assuming drastic cuts are made in emissions

Climate models are used to provide the best scientifically-based estimates of the future global climate. A typical method is to run the models for some decades ahead and then to compare the predicted average with a past 30-year period. A range of climate models are used, run with different scenarios that express the breadth of possibilities of, for example, industrial development and the degree of atmospheric pollution "clean-up" by industrial nations.

The diagram above shows global observed and predicted surface mean temperature change from 1950 to 2080 with three prediction scenarios for this century. The first (red) assumes rapid economic growth and continued population increases. The second (blue) assumes some attempts are made to cut greenhouse gas emissions, while the green line involves the greater use of cleaner technologies, with global population peaking mid-century then declining.

THE THINNING OZONE LAYER

Total atmospheric ozone concentration in the southern and northern hemispheres (Dobson Units, 2000)
In 1985, scientists working in Antarctica discovered a thinning of the ozone layer, commonly known as an "ozone hole." This caused immediate alarm because the ozone layer absorbs most of the Sun's dangerous ultraviolet radiation, which is believed to cause an increase in skin cancer, cataracts, and damage to the immune system.

Since 1985, ozone depletion has increased and, by 2002, the ozone hole over the South Pole was estimated to be three times as large as the USA. The false-color images (*below*) show the total atmospheric ozone concentration in the southern hemisphere (in September 2000) and the northern hemisphere (in March 2000), with the ozone hole clearly identifiable in blue at the center. The data is from the Tiros weather satellite. The colors represent the ozone concentration in Dobson Units (DU).

Scientists agree that ozone depletion is caused by CFCs, a group of manufactured chemicals used in air-conditioning systems and refrigerators. In a 1987 treaty, most industrial nations agreed to phase out CFCs, and a complete ban on most CFCs was agreed after the end of 1995. However, scientists believe that the chemicals will remain in the atmosphere for 50 to 100 years. As a result, ozone depletion will continue for many years.

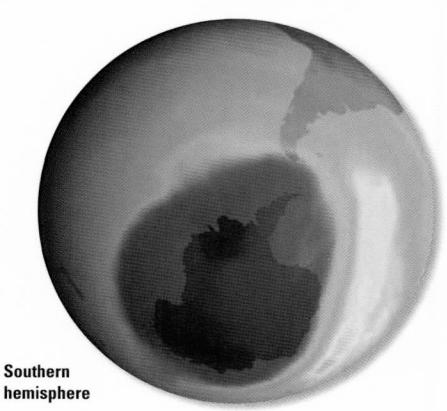

Southern hemisphere

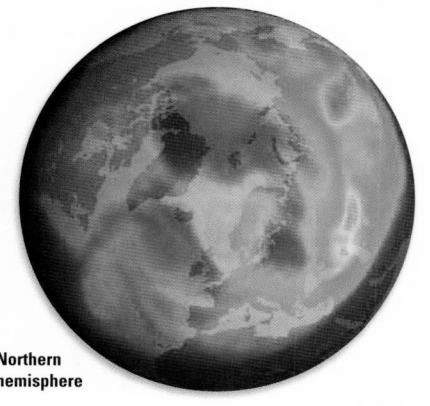

Northern hemisphere

For more information:
78 Climate regions
79 Precipitation
84 Biodiversity

Without the hydrological cycle, by which water is constantly recycled between the oceans, the atmosphere and the land, the continents would be barren. Precipitation enables plants to grow and soils to form, creating the world's natural vegetation regions and the ecosystems that support animal life.

Running water also plays a major role in shaping landforms. Yet in many parts of the world, people do not have safe water to drink and suffer from diseases caused by water-borne organisms and pollution. In 2005, an estimated 1.1 billion people lacked access to safe water and 2.6 billion people lacked basic sanitation.

Experts argue that world demand for water is increasing at about twice the rate of population growth. It is predicted that, by 2025, half the world's population will face water shortages. This could lead to conflict and even boundary wars – 300 major rivers cross national frontiers and access to their water is likely to be disputed.

THE HYDROLOGICAL CYCLE

The world's water balance is regulated by the constant recycling of water between the oceans, the atmosphere and the land. The movement of water between these three reservoirs is known as the *hydrological cycle*. The oceans play a vital role in the hydrological cycle: 74% of the total precipitation falls over the oceans and 84% of the total evaporation comes from the oceans. Water vapor in the atmosphere circulates around the planet, transporting energy as well as the water itself. When the vapor cools, it falls as rain or snow. The whole cycle is driven by the Sun.

WATER DISTRIBUTION

The distribution of planetary water, by percentage. Oceans and ice caps together account for more than 99% of the total; the breakdown of the remainder is estimated.

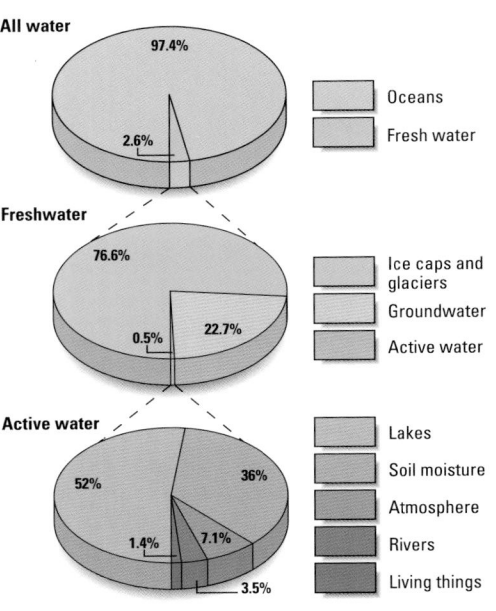

Almost all the world's water is 3,000 million years old, and all of it cycles endlessly through the hydrosphere, though at different rates. Water vapor circulates over days, even hours; deep-ocean water circulates over millennia; and ice-cap water remains solid for millions of years.

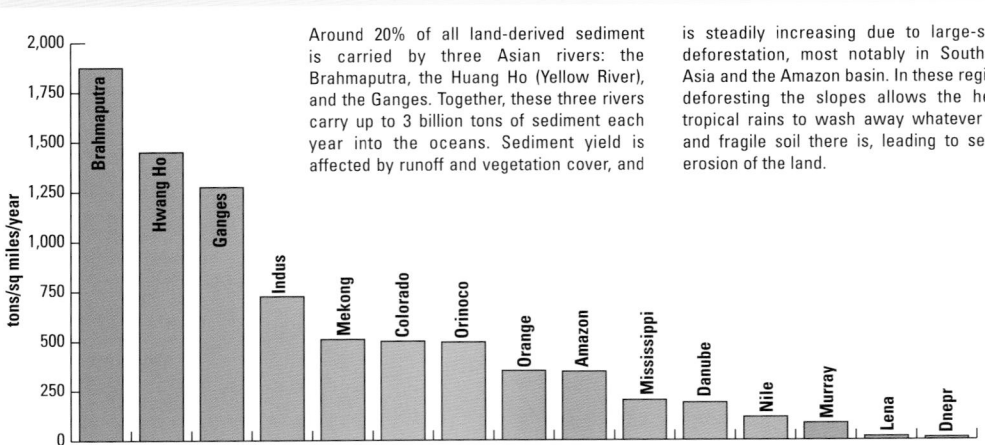

ANNUAL SEDIMENT YIELD

Around 20% of all land-derived sediment is carried by three Asian rivers: the Brahmaputra, the Huang Ho (Yellow River), and the Ganges. Together, these three rivers carry up to 3 billion tons of sediment each year into the oceans. Sediment yield is affected by runoff and vegetation cover, and is steadily increasing due to large-scale deforestation, most notably in Southeast Asia and the Amazon basin. In these regions, deforesting the slopes allows the heavy tropical rains to wash away whatever thin and fragile soil there is, leading to severe erosion of the land.

WATER RUNOFF

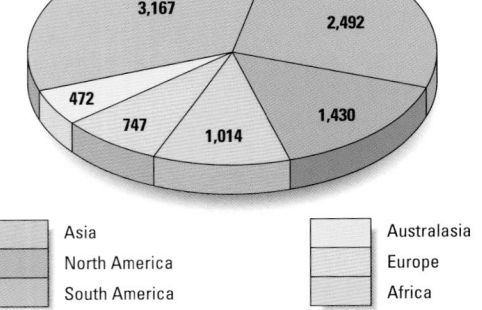

▶ The River Amazon is the world's second-longest river (after the River Nile), draining the vast rain forest basin of northern South America. The Amazon carries by far the greatest volume of water of any river in the world: the average rate of discharge is approximately 3,355,000 cu ft [95,000 cu m] per second, nearly three times as much as its nearest rival, the Congo. The flow is so great that its silt discolors the water up to 125 miles [200 km] into the Atlantic. At approximately 2.7 million sq miles [7 million sq km], the Amazon basin comprises nearly 40% of the whole of South America. Nevertheless, in 2005 large parts of the Amazon rain forest were at their driest in living memory, partly related to the severe hurricane season off the US Gulf coast. Rainfall was significantly below average, causing water levels to drop to record lows. At Tabatinga, 600 miles [970 km] west of Manaus, rainfall was almost 70% down from 2004. Rivers and lakes began to dry up, revealing huge sandbanks and making navigation difficult for boats.

COPYRIGHT PHILIP'S

WATERSHEDS

The map below shows the world's major rivers, with the ranking of the 20 longest rivers shown in square brackets after their name, led by the Nile [1] and the Amazon [2].

The map shows the direction of freshwater flow on a continental scale, whereas the water runoff chart on the facing page indicates the quantities involved annually.

The rate of runoff varies seasonally and is affected by the surface vegetation and climate. Most of the world's major rivers discharge into the Atlantic Ocean.

Where the rivers run

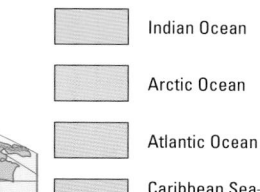

Pacific Ocean

Indian Ocean

Arctic Ocean

Atlantic Ocean

Caribbean Sea– Gulf of Mexico

Mediterranean Sea

Inland basins, ice caps and deserts

NATURAL VEGETATION

The map below illustrates the natural "climax vegetation" of a region, as dictated by its climate and topography. In most cases, human agricultural activity has drastically altered the pattern of the vegetation. The various vegetation regions support different kinds of animals and wildlife, and, in an undisturbed state, they are highly developed biological communities, or "biomes."

The blue line on the map represents the northern limit of tree growth, and the red lines indicate the northern and southern limits of palm growth. The majority of the numerous species are tropical or subtropical. Some, such as the coconut, date, sago, and oil palms, are important economically.

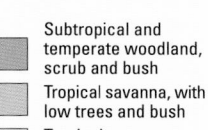

Tropical rain forest

Subtropical and temperate rain forest

Monsoon woodland and open jungle

Subtropical and temperate woodland, scrub and bush

Tropical savanna, with low trees and bush

Tropical savanna and grasslands

Dry semidesert, with shrub and grass

Desert shrub

Desert

Dry steppe and shrub

Temperate grasslands, prairie and steppe

Mediterranean hard-wood forest and scrub

Temperate deciduous forest and meadow

Temperate deciduous and coniferous forest

Northern coniferous forest (taïga)

Mountainous forest, mainly coniferous

High plateau steppe and tundra

Arctic tundra

Polar and mountain-ous ice desert

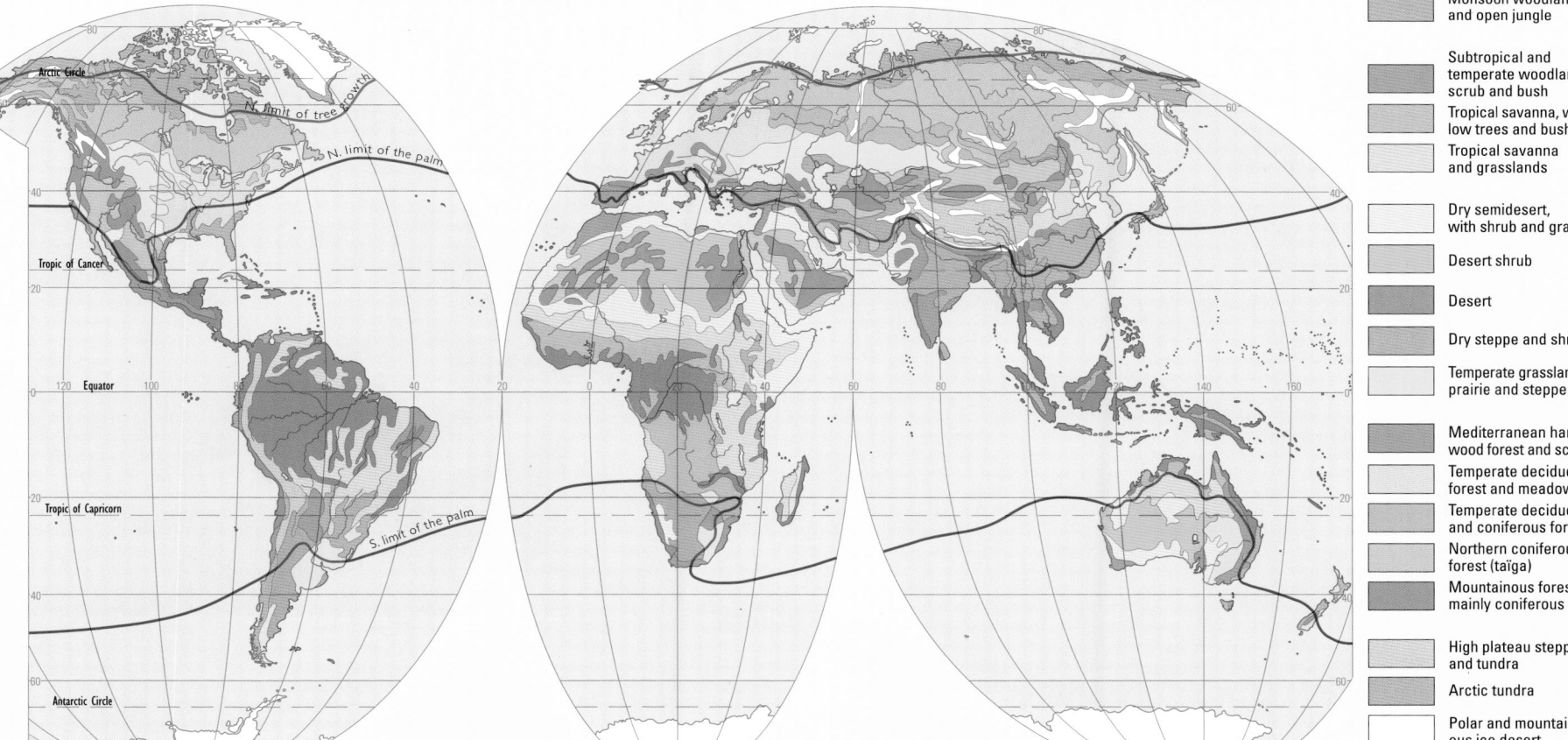

For more information:
74 Life in the oceans
78 Climate
80 Climate change
   Global warming
83 Natural vegetation
94 Agriculture

Levels of Endemism
Known endemic species per
100 sq miles (2004), selected countries

USA
Congo (Dem. Rep.)
Kenya
Ethiopia
India
Burma (Myanmar)
China
Australia
Italy
Bulgaria
Turkey
Peru
Greece
Japan
Mexico
Venezuela
Indonesia
Malaysia
Madagascar
Colombia
Ecuador
Costa Rica   0.9

0.2   0.4   0.6

Biodiversity refers to the variety of living material. It includes the variety of species, the variety within the same species, and the variety of ecosystems within which species operate. Estimates of the number of species in the world vary from between 7 million and 80 million. The currently accepted total is about 14 million, yet only 2 million species have been formally identified.

Biodiversity is vital for human survival. It remains the basis for our food and most of our medicine. In less economically developed countries (LEDCs), over 20% of the food consumed is gathered from natural sources. At a global level, over 15% of animal protein consumed is from sea fish caught in the wild. More than 60% of the world's population rely on traditional medicines for their health care. In Mexico, the Popoluca Indians "farm" over 250 species of plant. Many medicines come from natural sources. Aspirin, for example, comes from an acid taken from the bark of willow trees. The anti-cancer drug "taxol" originates from the wild Pacific yew tree. It is estimated that the

pharmaceuticals industry gains US $32 billion per year in profits from traditional remedies.

However, the loss of biodiversity is increasing at an accelerating rate. Up to 27,000 species a year may be lost, and the United Nations Environment Program (UNEP) suggests that the current rate of extinction is 50–100 times greater than "normal," and believes that up to 25% of all the world's species may be lost by 2025. The main reasons for the decline are the introduction of alien species and habitat destruction. Human impact on biodiversity has brought about more extinctions than any other single factor since the extinction of the dinosaurs (65 million years ago).

Since 1600, 39% of animal extinctions have been due to the introduction of alien species, 36% from habitat destruction, and 23% from hunting or deliberate extermination. The introduction of rats, cats and other species has led to the extinction of many flight-less birds in Polynesia. Plantation crops, such as rubber, often thrive best when taken away from their natural homes, since in the new lands

there may not be the pests to control them. One noted example of extinction was that caused by the introduction of the Nile perch into Lake Victoria, East Africa. Introduced in the 1960s, it led to the extinction of some 50 species of cichlid fish within 20 years.

In 2007, a report by the International Union for the Conservation of Nature listed 16,306 organisms facing extinction. Up to 46% of primates are said to be at risk of extinction. Overall, some 25% of mammals are endangered – including "charismatic" species such as the tiger and the panda, but equally less recognizable species of bats, rodents, and marsupials. Up to one-fifth of reptiles, one-third of amphibians, and one-third of bird species are at risk of extinction. The most threatened group are fish (one-third are at risk), largely as a result of overfishing. The World Conservation Union reported that 8% of mammals were threatened in the US compared with 32% in the Philippines and 44% in Madagascar, two countries where habitat destruction has been proceeding on a large scale.

THREATENED MAMMAL SPECIES

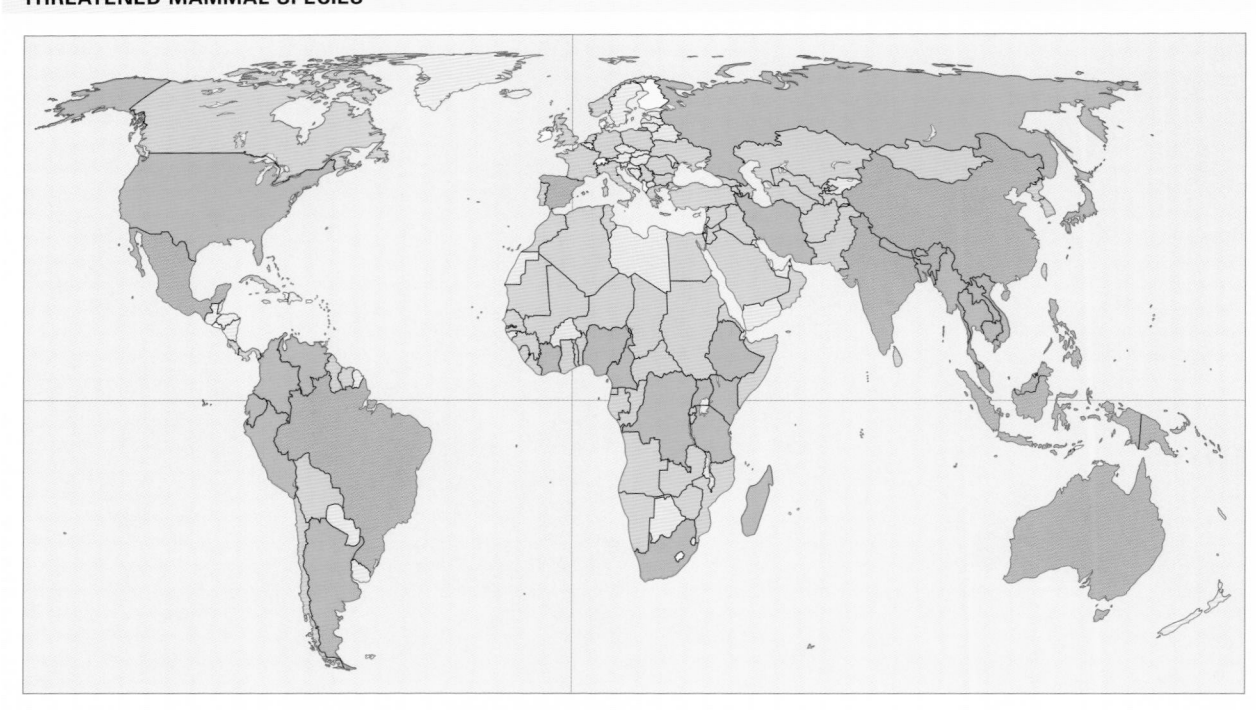

Mammal species threatened with extinction (2006)

Over 50
25 – 50
10 – 25
5 – 10
Under 5

Countries with the highest number of mammal species threatened with extinction (2006)

Indonesia	146
India	89
China	84
Mexico	74
Brazil	73
Australia	64
Papua New Guinea	58
Malaysia	51
Philippines	51
Spain	50

NATIVE ("ENDEMIC") SPECIES AS A PROPORTION OF TOTAL SPECIES (SELECTED COUNTRIES)

Country	Mammals (2004) Total	Mammals (2004) Endemic	Birds (2004) Total	Birds (2004) Endemic	Higher Plants (2004) Total	Higher Plants (2004) Endemic
Australia	376	225	851	387	15,638	14,074
Brazil	578	131	1,712	207	56,215	18,000
Burma (Myanmar)	288	4	1,047	24	7,000	1,071
China	502	78	1,221	92	32,200	18,000
Colombia	467	43	1,821	84	51,220	15,000
Congo (Dem. Rep.)	430	26	1,148	24	11,007	1,100
Ecuador	341	26	1,515	56	19,362	4,000
Ethiopia	288	34	839	24	6,603	1,000
India	422	44	1,180	70	18,664	5,000
Indonesia	667	216	1,604	443	29,375	17,500
Japan	171	43	592	55	5,565	2,000
Madagascar	165	102	262	111	9,505	6,500
Malaysia	337	35	746	26	15,500	3,600
Mexico	544	155	1,026	125	26,071	12,500
Peru	441	48	1,781	125	17,144	5,356
Philippines	222	106	590	205	8,931	3,500
South Africa	320	33	829	27	23,420	8,200
Turkey	145	4	436	3	8,650	2,675
USA	468	104	888	122	19,473	4,036
Venezuela	353	18	1,392	46	21,073	8,000

▲ Madagascar has developed in isolation since it split from Africa 150 million years ago. As a result of this isolation, a unique range of plants and animals have evolved, adapted to its own specific conditions. Over 95% of Madagascar's mammals, 90% of its reptiles, over 66% of its plants, and over 40% of its breeding birds do not exist anywhere else.

Madagascar is home to all of the world's lemurs (all of which are endangered, such as the aye-aye pictured above) and two-thirds of the world's chameleons. Its plant species include pitcher plants, orchids, and the Madagascan rosy periwinkle (the most effective known treatment for childhood leukemia). However, large-scale deforestation since the 1970s has reduced Madagascar's cover of rain forest to less than 10% of the island's original forest cover.

ENVIRONMENTAL HOTSPOTS

Up to 75% of the world's most threatened mammals, birds, and amphibians live in an area covering just 2.3% of the Earth's surface, and roughly half of all flowering plant species and 42% of land-based vertebrates exist in 34 biological hotspots.

Scientists argue that, with limited financial resources, governments and conservationists should prioritize by protecting the small total land areas that account for a very high percentage of global biodiversity. In 1999, scientists identified 25 such areas, mostly in the tropics, which were the center of global biodiversity.

By 2005, the number of hotspots had risen to 34. These include the mountains of central Asia, the whole of Japan, the Horn of Africa including the Ethiopian highlands, and the Himalayas region. The hotspots once covered 15.7% of the Earth's surface, an area roughly the size of Russia and Australia combined – now they cover only 2.3% of the Earth's surface, an area slightly larger than India.

Over 70% of all mammals, 86% of all birds, and 92% of all amphibians are crammed into this small area of the world's total land mass. Madagascar and the Indian Ocean Islands hotspot was found to have very high concentrations of plant and vertebrate families that are found nowhere else on the globe.

Global warming could have a devastating effect on biodiversity hotspots such as the Amazonian and Indonesian rain forests. By 2100, between 12% and 39% of the land surface of the Earth will have a new climate. There are numerous species which will be unable to move in order to stay within their preferred climate range. These species will either have to evolve rapidly or die out.

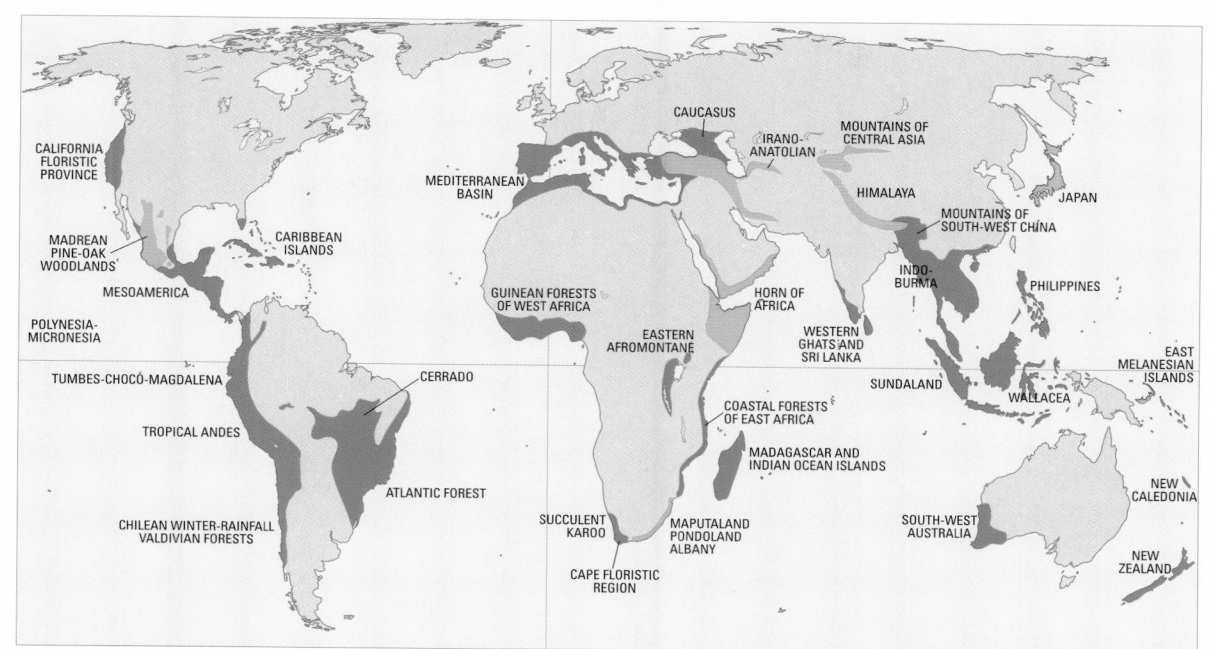

New hotspots

Recognized environmental areas

AUSTRALIA'S INTRODUCED SPECIES

Australia's native plants and animals adapted to life on an isolated continent over millions of years. Since European settlement in the 18th century they have had to compete with a range of species introduced by the settlers, which impact on the native species by predation, competition for food and shelter, destroying habitat, and by spreading diseases. Introduced species typically have few predators or fatal diseases and some have very high reproductive rates.

Management and the prevention of the introduction of new invasive species are key environmental and agricultural policy issues for the Australian federal and state governments.

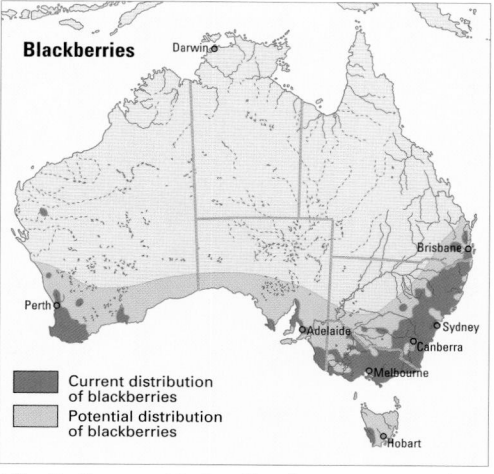

Rabbits

Distribution of feral rabbits

Rabbit Proof Fence No.1 (built in 1907, 3,250km, but failed to protect WA's pastoral areas)

▲ Rabbits were introduced to Australia from England in 1859 for hunting, and quickly spread throughout the country. They are one of the most destructive introduced species in Australia, competing with native wildlife, damaging vegetation and degrading the land.

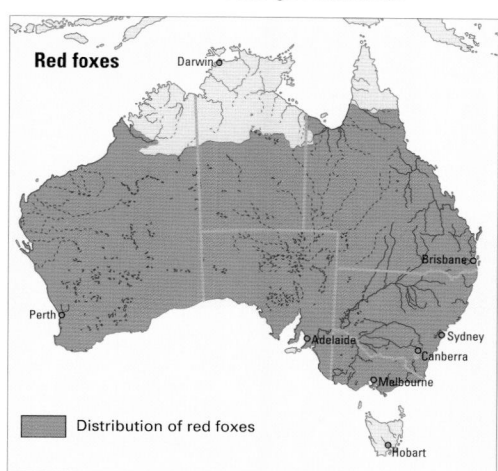

Red foxes

Distribution of red foxes

▲ The red fox was introduced from Europe for recreational hunting in 1855 and populations became established in the wild within 15 years. They prey on newborn lambs and have also been responsible for the decline of a number of native species.

Blackberries

Current distribution of blackberries

Potential distribution of blackberries

▲ The blackberry was introduced from Europe as a source of fresh fruit. It is now regarded as one of the worst weeds in Australia because of its invasiveness, spreading through farmland, forests, and scrub. It out-competes many native plants, prevents light reaching the ground below, and provides food and shelter for pests.

Cane toads

Distribution of cane toads

▲ Cane toads were introduced in 1935 to control beetles which were threatening the sugar-cane industry. However, this was a failure and both the toad and the beetle are still thriving. They adapted well to the Australian environment and with no natural predators they quickly spread. They eat small native wildlife and poison any predators.

ESTIMATED VALUE OF WILD RESOURCES IN LESS ECONOMICALLY DEVELOPED COUNTRIES

Tropical non-coniferous forest product exports	US $11 billion per year
Fruit/latex harvesting, Peru	US $6,330 per hectare
Sustainable timber harvesting, Peru	US $490 per hectare
Buffalo range ranching, Zimbabwe	US $3.5–4.5 per hectare
Wetlands fish and fuelwood, Nigeria	US $38–59 per hectare
Viewing value of elephants, Kenya	US $25 million per year
Ecotourism, Costa Rica	US $1,250 per hectare
Tourism, Thailand	US $385,000–860,000 per year
Research/education, Thailand	US $38,000–77,000 per year
Tourism, Cameroon	US $10 per hectare
Genetic value, Cameroon	US $7 per hectare
Pharmaceutical prospecting, Costa Rica	US $4,981 million per product

▲ Bolivia has over 100,000 sq miles [250,000 sq km] of dry tropical forest, home to animals such as jaguars and ocelots. It is, however, being cleared at a rate of over 2% per annum. This false-color image shows an area that has been almost completely cleared. The darkest areas are remnants of the original forest, some of which have been retained as wind breaks between newly created arable fields. The radial patterns are fields with new villages at their centers, part of a government resettlement scheme.

For more information:

88 Urbanization of the Earth

Urban population

89 Largest cities

95 Food and population

106 Wealth and population

In 8000 BC, following the development of agriculture, the world had an estimated population of 8 million and by AD 1000 it was about 300 million. The onset of the Industrial Revolution in the late 18th century led to a population explosion. The 1,000 million mark was passed by 1850, it doubled by the 1920s, and doubled again to 4,000 million by 1975.

In the 1990s, demographers estimated that the world's population, which passed the 6 billion mark in 1999, would reach 9.3 billion by 2050 and only level out in 2200, at a peak of around 11 billion. However, in the early 21st century, after the rate of population growth had shown signs of decline, the Institute for Applied Systems Analysis suggested that the world's population might peak at about 9 billion in 2070. Whatever the global projections, everyone agreed that the greatest population growth would be in the developing countries.

The developing world includes what the World Bank (2006) describes as low-income economies (average per capita GNI of US $584), lower-middle-income economies (average per capita GNI of US $1,778) and upper-middle-income economies (average per capita GNI of US $5,053). Most developing countries are in Africa, Asia, and Latin America. The developed world, made up of high-income, industrialized economies (average per capita GNI of US $34,962), contains Australasia, most of Europe and North America, and Japan.

In developing countries, a high proportion of the population is young and so these countries face high expenditure on health and education. In developed countries, the population pyramids are becoming top-heavy, with increasingly aging populations.

LARGEST NATIONS

The world's most populous nations, in millions (2007 est.)

1.	China	1,322
2.	India	1,130
3.	USA	301
4.	Indonesia	235
5.	Brazil	190
6.	Pakistan	165
7.	Bangladesh	150
8.	Russia	141
9.	Nigeria	135
10.	Japan	127
11.	Mexico	109
12.	Philippines	91
13.	Vietnam	85
14.	Germany	82
15.	Egypt	80
16.	Ethiopia	77
17.	Turkey	71
18.	Congo (Dem.Rep.)	66
19.	Iran	65
20.	Thailand	65
21.	France	61
22.	UK	61
23.	Italy	58
24.	South Korea	49
25.	Burma (Myanmar)	47

MOST CROWDED NATIONS

Population per square mile (2007 est.)

1.	Monaco	81,678
2.	Singapore	17,512
3.	Gaza Strip	10,589
4.	Malta	3,349
5.	Maldives	3,076
6.	Bahrain	2,624
7.	Bangladesh	2,505
8.	Barbados	1,652
9.	Nauru	1,649
10.	Taiwan	1,644

LEAST CROWDED NATIONS

Population per square mile (2007 est.)

1.	Western Sahara	3.7
2.	Mongolia	4.9
3.	Namibia	6.5
4.	Australia	6.8
5.	Suriname	7.5
6.	Iceland	7.6
7.	Botswana	8.1
8.	Mauritania	8.3
9.	Canada	8.7
10.	Libya	8.8

POPULATION DENSITY

The places marked on the map reflect the size of the urban agglomerations and conurbations, rather than the actual city limits. San Francisco itself, for example, has an official population of less than a million people.

Inhabitants per square mile

- Over 500
- 250 – 500
- 125 – 250
- 65 – 125
- 15 – 65
- 8 – 15
- 3 – 8
- Under 3

Urban population

- ■ Over 10,000,000
- ● 5,000,000 – 10,000,000
- • 1,000,000 – 5,000,000

POPULATION CHANGE

The projected population change for the years 2004–2050

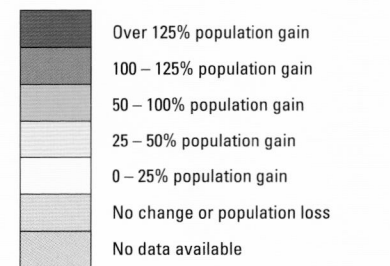

- Over 125% population gain
- 100 – 125% population gain
- 50 – 100% population gain
- 25 – 50% population gain
- 0 – 25% population gain
- No change or population loss
- No data available

Based on estimates for the year 2050, below are listed the ten most populous nations in the world, in millions:

1.	India	1,628	6.	Pakistan	295
2.	China	1,437	7.	Bangladesh	280
3.	USA	420	8.	Brazil	221
4.	Indonesia	308	9.	Congo (Dem. Rep.)	181
5.	Nigeria	307	10.	Ethiopia	173

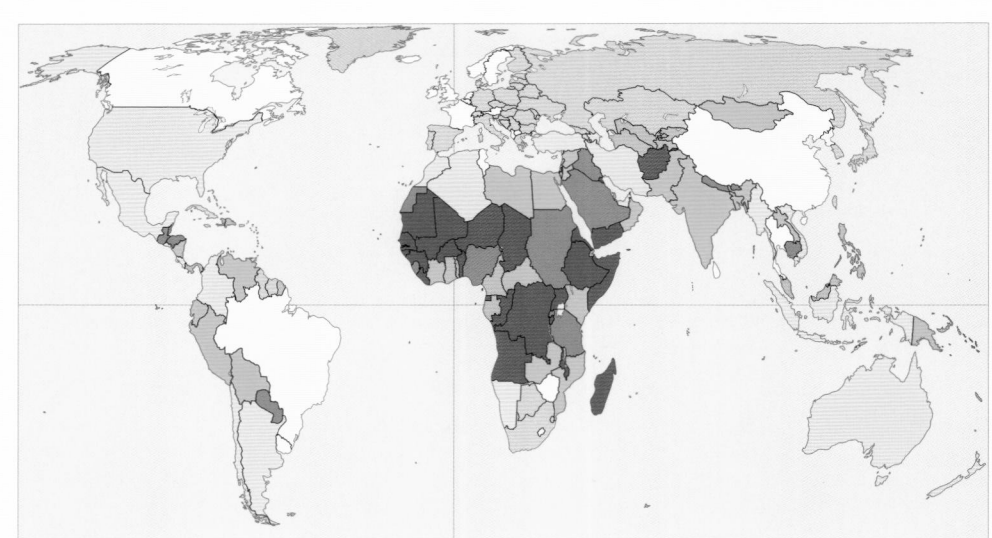

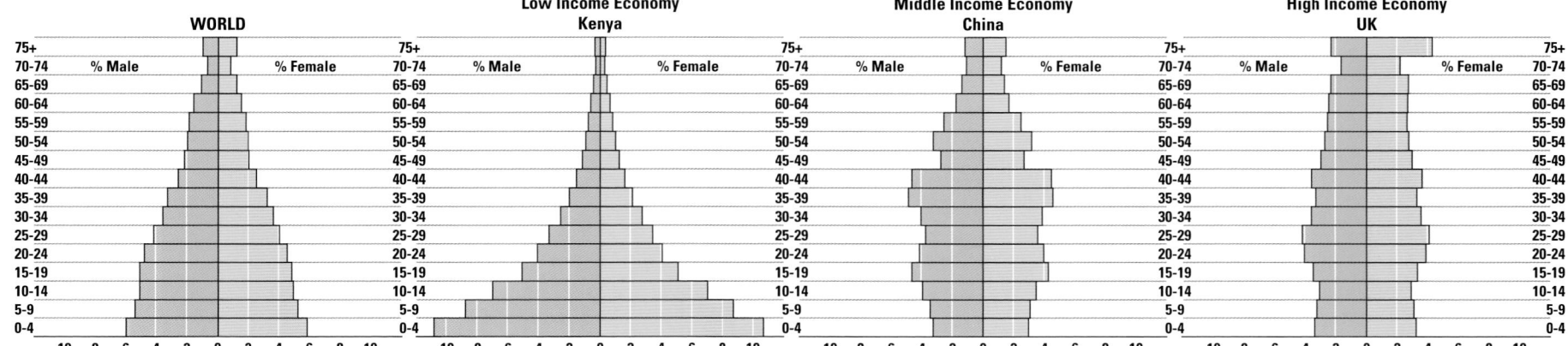

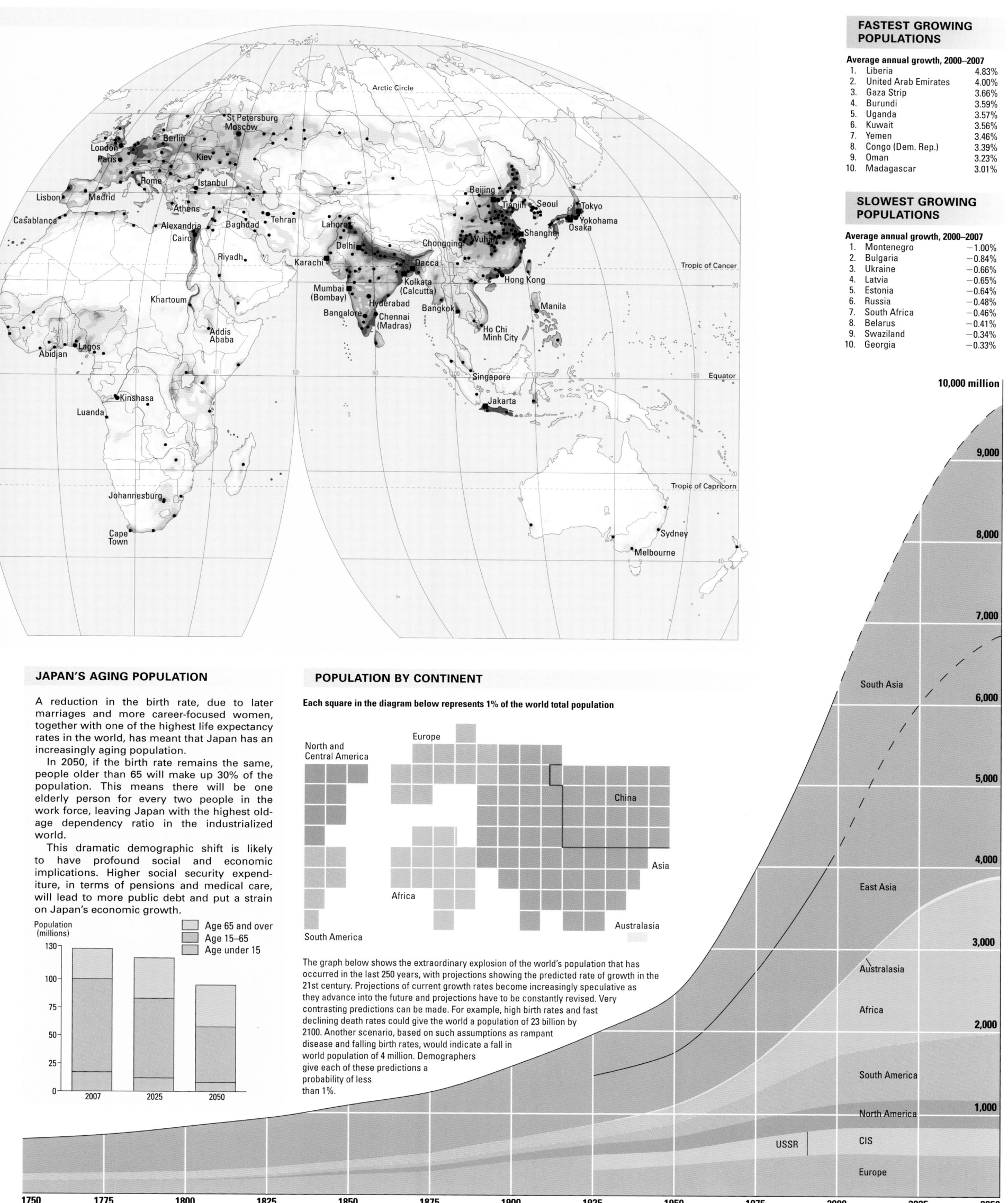

FASTEST GROWING POPULATIONS

Average annual growth, 2000–2007

1.	Liberia	4.83%
2.	United Arab Emirates	4.00%
3.	Gaza Strip	3.66%
4.	Burundi	3.59%
5.	Uganda	3.57%
6.	Kuwait	3.56%
7.	Yemen	3.46%
8.	Congo (Dem. Rep.)	3.39%
9.	Oman	3.23%
10.	Madagascar	3.01%

SLOWEST GROWING POPULATIONS

Average annual growth, 2000–2007

1.	Montenegro	−1.00%
2.	Bulgaria	−0.84%
3.	Ukraine	−0.66%
4.	Latvia	−0.65%
5.	Estonia	−0.64%
6.	Russia	−0.48%
7.	South Africa	−0.46%
8.	Belarus	−0.41%
9.	Swaziland	−0.34%
10.	Georgia	−0.33%

JAPAN'S AGING POPULATION

A reduction in the birth rate, due to later marriages and more career-focused women, together with one of the highest life expectancy rates in the world, has meant that Japan has an increasingly aging population.

In 2050, if the birth rate remains the same, people older than 65 will make up 30% of the population. This means there will be one elderly person for every two people in the work force, leaving Japan with the highest old-age dependency ratio in the industrialized world.

This dramatic demographic shift is likely to have profound social and economic implications. Higher social security expenditure, in terms of pensions and medical care, will lead to more public debt and put a strain on Japan's economic growth.

POPULATION BY CONTINENT

Each square in the diagram below represents 1% of the world total population

The graph below shows the extraordinary explosion of the world's population that has occurred in the last 250 years, with projections showing the predicted rate of growth in the 21st century. Projections of current growth rates become increasingly speculative as they advance into the future and projections have to be constantly revised. Very contrasting predictions can be made. For example, high birth rates and fast declining death rates could give the world a population of 23 billion by 2100. Another scenario, based on such assumptions as rampant disease and falling birth rates, would indicate a fall in world population of 4 million. Demographers give each of these predictions a probability of less than 1%.

For more information:

82 Water distribution
83 Population density
103 The world's ports

Following the development of agriculture more than 10,000 years ago, people began to live in farming villages. Around 5,500 years ago, the world's first cities appeared in the lower Tigris and Euphrates valleys in Mesopotamia. Cities were founded in Ancient Egypt around 5,000 years ago and in China around 3,600 years ago. By contrast with the villages, most people in the early cities were not engaged in farming. Instead, they worked in craft industries, in government services, in religion and in trade. The cities became centers of early civilizations and, through trade, their influence spread far and wide. However, they were dependent on the surrounding farming communities for their food and other materials.

In 1750, prior to the start of the Industrial Revolution, barely 3% of the world's population lived in urban areas. By 1850, London and Paris had more than a million people, and, by 1900, 14% of the world's population lived in cities. By 1950, the world had 83 cities with more than a million people, and

by 1996 there were 280; by 2015, experts predict there will be more than 500. New York City was the only city with a population in excess of 10 million in 1950; by 2015, experts predict there will be 27 such cities worldwide, the majority located in the developing world.

However, predictions have to be constantly revised in light of new data. For example, in the late 1990s, demographers calculated that urban areas then accounted for 50% of the world's population. But after much lower census figures emerged for many cities in the early 21st century, the estimated date by which half of the world's population would be living in cities was pushed back to 2007.

Urbanization is greatest in industrialized countries. For example, in 2004, 81% of the people in the United States lived in urban areas. However, in low-income countries, which contained nearly 40% of the world's population in the early 21st century, only 31% lived in urban areas.

The rapid rate of urbanization has created

many social problems, especially in cities that have been unable to provide enough jobs and services for the new arrivals. Many of the new city dwellers come from rural areas and take time to adjust to urban life and employment possibilities.

A typical city in a developing country contains millions of people living, often illegally, in shanty towns (or "informal settlements"), while thousands live on the streets. Yet many of these shanty towns are healthier than the industrial cities of 19th-century Europe and North America. Indeed, surveys have shown that migrants to cities in developing countries are less likely to face poverty than they are in rural areas, while benefiting from greater access to healthcare services and education.

Modern cities face many problems today, including pollution, crime, and unemployment. Yet, given competent central and local government, they are capable of generating the wealth they need to solve them, as well as making a major contribution to the nation's economy.

URBAN POPULATION

Percentage of total population living in towns and cities (2004)

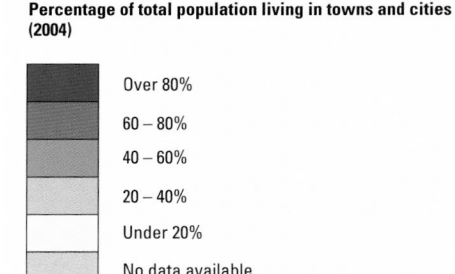

- Over 80%
- 60 – 80%
- 40 – 60%
- 20 – 40%
- Under 20%
- No data available

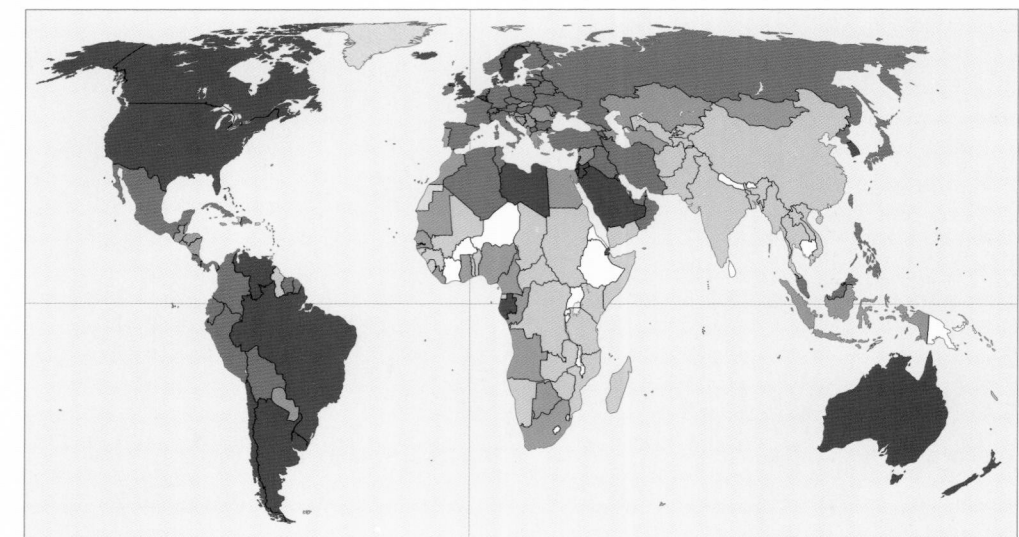

Most urbanized		Least urbanized	
Singapore	100%	Burundi	10%
Kuwait	98%	Bhutan	11%
Belgium	97%	Trinidad & Tobago	12%
Bahrain	96%	Uganda	13%
Qatar	95%	Papua New Guinea	13%

THE URBANIZATION OF THE EARTH

City-building, 1900–2005; each white spot represents a city of at least 1 million inhabitants

1900

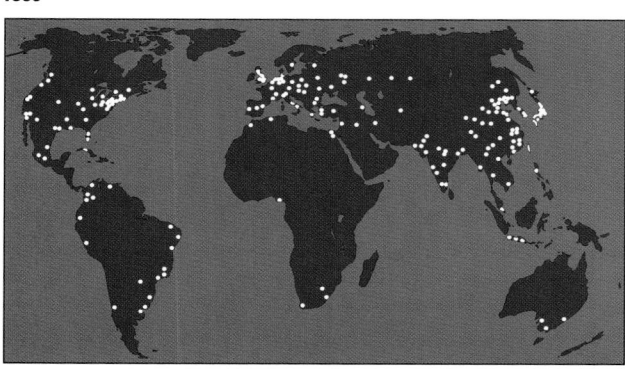

1975

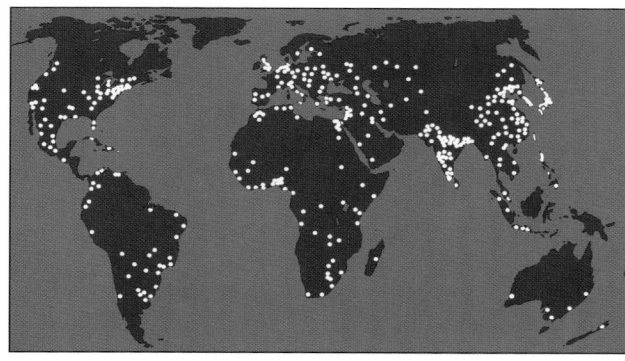

1950

2005

URBANIZATION

The urban population of 3.3 billion people in 2008 is larger than the entire global population in 1947, 61 years earlier. Cities and urban areas are gaining an estimated 60 million people per year – over 1 million every week.

Urbanization rates vary across the world; the UK and US have far lower rates of urbanization compared to less developed countries. This is because a high proportion of their populations already live in cities. The largest percentage increases in the urban population in the next decade will be in Africa and Asia. Dhaka in Bangladesh, for example, nearly doubled in population between 1990 and 2000.

Rapid urban growth reflects three factors:
1. Migration to cities from rural areas
2. Natural population increases (births minus deaths)
3. Reclassification of previously rural areas as urban as they become built up and engulfed by urban sprawl.

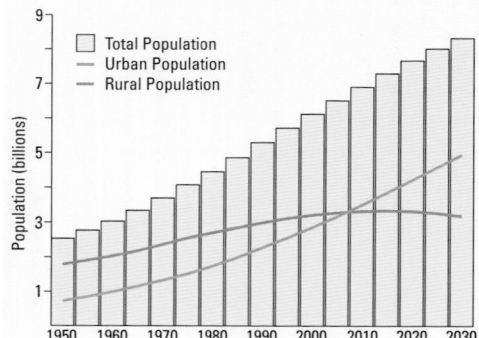

SLUM CITIES

The total number of slum dwellers in the world reached 1 billion in 2007. One in every three city residents live in inadequate housing, with no or few basic services.

Urbanization in most developing countries has been proceeding so rapidly that local governments have been unable to provide the necessary services and housing to meet demand.

In some cities, many people make their homes in squatter settlements, or slums, which are frequently without basic services such as power, water, and sanitation. They are often on hazardous, dangerous, or polluted land and the building structures are inadequate and sometimes unsafe. Slum dwellers have limited access to credit and formal job markets due to stigmatization, discrimination, and geographical isolation.

Slums have a high concentration of poverty and social and economic deprivation, which may include broken families, unemployment and economic, physical, and social exclusion. Yet these communities are often a dynamic part of the city's economy, keeping the wheels of the city turning in many different ways. Their inhabitants often take the initiative in setting up their own local government and self-help associations.

Some of the world's richest cities also have a homeless underclass, although calculating the numbers of people involved is problematic. Yet it is the case that homelessness and unemployment are currently affecting an increasing number of people in the developed world.

The locus of poverty is moving from the countryside to cities, in a process now recognized as the "urbanization of poverty."

Efforts to improve the living conditions of slum dwellers peaked during the 1980s. However, renewed concern about poverty has recently led governments to adopt specific targets on slums in the United Nations Millennium Declaration, which aims to improve the lives of at least 100 million slum dwellers by the year 2020.

CITIES IN DANGER

In mid-2002, a "brown haze," stretching 2 miles [3 km] high, covered much of southern Asia. Caused mainly by the burning of coal and biomass, it caused respiratory diseases and many deaths. Alarm concerning urban air pollution had been expressed much earlier, but controls since the 1980s had proved difficult to enforce and expensive to introduce.

Those cities taking part in the United Nation's Global Environment Monitoring System frequently show dangerous levels of pollutants, ranging from soot to sulfur dioxide and photochemical smog. Air in the majority of cities without such sampling equipment is likely to be at least as bad. Traffic, a major source of air pollution worldwide, loses Thailand's work force 44 working days each year. It has been a major cause for concern in the run-up to the 2008 Beijing Olympic Games.

URBAN ADVANTAGES

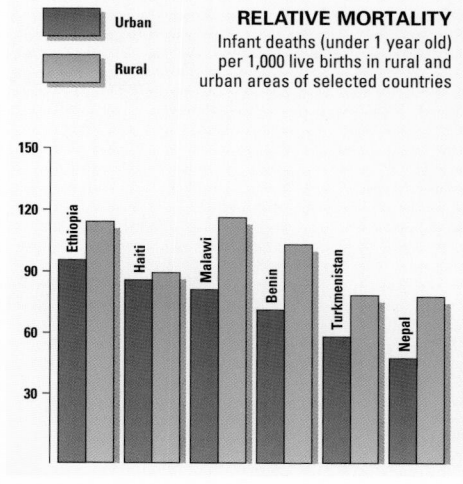

RELATIVE MORTALITY
Infant deaths (under 1 year old) per 1,000 live births in rural and urban areas of selected countries

Urban
Rural

SLUM FACTBOX

● 78% of the urban population in developing countries live in slums.

● The total number of slum dwellers in the world increased by about 36% during the 1990s.

● More than 41% of Kolkata's slum households have lived there for more than 30 years.

● In most African cities between 40% and 70% of the city's population live in slums or squatter settlements.

● Slum populations in some parts of the world (for example, Pune in India and Ibadan in Nigeria) quite often include university lecturers, students, civil servants and formal private sector employees.

● All slum households in Bangkok have a color television.

● Singapore is one of the few countries that successfully practices comprehensive public sector housing development.

LARGEST CITIES

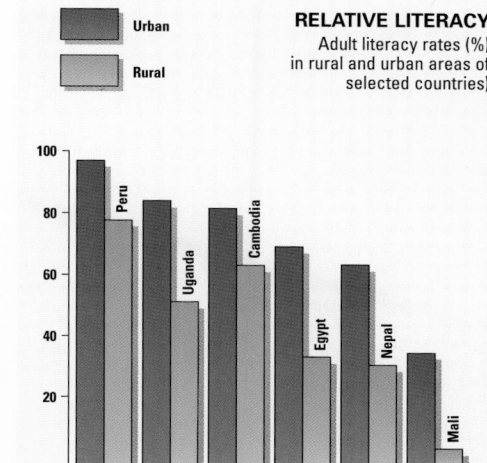

RELATIVE LITERACY
Adult literacy rates (%) in rural and urban areas of selected countries

Urban
Rural

Despite overcrowding and poor housing, living standards in the developing world's cities are almost invariably better than in the surrounding countryside. Resources – financial, material, and administrative – are concentrated in the towns, which are usually also the centers of political activity and pressure. Governments – frequently unstable, and rarely established on a solid democratic base – are usually more responsive to urban discontent than to rural misery.

In many developing countries, especially in Africa, food prices are kept artificially low, thus appeasing the underemployed urban masses at the expense of agricultural development.

This imbalance encourages further cityward migration, helping to account for the astonishing rate of post-1950 urbanization and putting great strain on the ability of many nations to provide even modest improvements for their people.

CITY GROWTH

The growth of some of the world's largest cities in millions, 1950–2015
Comparisons of city populations over time are problematic due to changes in the definition of the city limits. These figures attempt to take such changes into consideration.

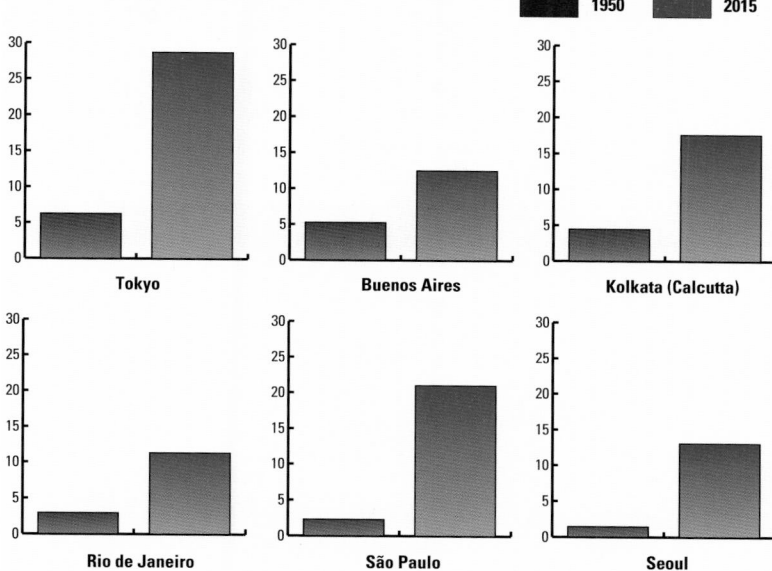

■ 1950   ■ 2015

Tokyo   Buenos Aires   Kolkata (Calcutta)
Rio de Janeiro   São Paulo   Seoul

◄ Originally a fishing village, Shanghai's skyscrapers and modern lifestyle are often seen as representing China's recent economic development. It is now the sixth largest city in the world and home to many of Asia's tallest buildings, including the Jinmao Tower on the right of this image.

In 2007, for the first time in history, the majority of the world's population will live in cities. Below is a list of all the cities with more than 10 million inhabitants, based on estimates for the year 2015.

1.	Tokyo–Yokohama	28.7
2.	Mumbai (Bombay)	27.4
3.	Lagos	24.1
4.	Shanghai	23.2
5.	Jakarta	21.5
6.	São Paulo	21.0
7.	Karachi	20.6
8.	Beijing	19.6
9.	Dhaka	19.2
10.	Mexico City	19.1
11.	Kolkata (Calcutta)	17.6
12.	Delhi	17.5
13.	New York City	17.4
14.	Tianjin	17.1
15.	Manila	14.9
16.	Cairo	14.7
17.	Los Angeles	14.5
18.	Seoul	13.1
19.	Buenos Aires	12.5
20.	Istanbul	12.1
21.	Rio de Janeiro	11.3
22.	Lahore	10.9
23.	Hyderabad	10.6
24.	Bangkok	10.4
25.	Osaka	10.2
26.	Lima	10.1
27.	Tehran	10.0

The city populations above are based on urban agglomerations rather than legal city limits. In some cases, where two adjacent cities have merged into one concentration, such as Tokyo–Yokohama, they have been regarded as a single unit.

For more information:
86 Population density
92 The world's refugees
    War since 1945
93 United Nations
    International
    organizations

Racial, language, and religious differences have led to appalling acts of inhumanity throughout history. Yet, strictly speaking, all human beings belong to one species, *Homo sapiens*, which has no subspecies. The differences between the three racial types which most people identify – Caucasoid, Mongoloid, and Negroid – reflect not so much evolutionary differences as long periods of separation.

Migration has recently mingled the various groups to an unprecedented extent, and most nations now have some degree of racial mixing. For example, the USA has often been called a melting pot, because of the large numbers of people from various geographical locations which make up the population. The country has no official language but, until recently, English was spoken by the vast majority of the people. But in recent years, some of the immigrants from Mexico, Cuba, and other parts of Latin America have not learned English and speak only Spanish. This development disturbs those Americans who believe that the use of English binds the nation together, and several states have passed laws stating that English is their only official language.

Language is fundamental to human culture. Because definitions of languages vary, estimates of the total number range from 3,000 to 6,000, although most are spoken by only a few people. Chinese is spoken by more people as a first language than any other, while English ranks second, but English is the leading international language, because so many people speak it as their second tongue.

Like language, religion encourages cohesion in single human groups and it satisfies a deep human need by assigning people a place in a divinely ordered world. Religion is a way in which a culture can express its individuality. For example, the rise of Islamic fundamentalism in the late 20th century was partly an expression of resentment that secular Western values were being imposed on Muslims.

WORLD MIGRATION

The greatest voluntary migration was the colonization of North America by 30–35 million European settlers during the 19th century. The greatest forced migration involved 9–11 million Africans taken as slaves to America between 1550 and 1860. The migrations shown on the map below are mostly international, as population movements within borders are not usually recorded. Many of the statistics are necessarily estimates as so many refugees and migrant workers enter countries illegally and unrecorded. Emigrants may have a variety of motives for leaving, thus making it difficult to distinguish between voluntary and involuntary migrations.

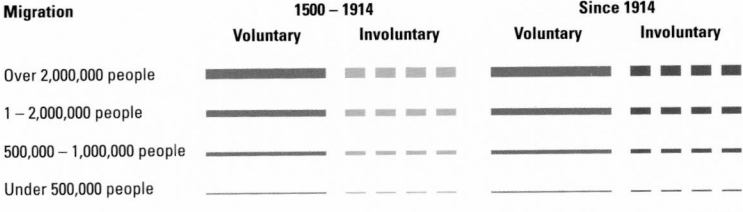

Foreign born, as a % of total population (2005)
- More than 20%
- 10 – 20%
- 5 – 10%
- 2 – 5%
- Less than 2%
- No available data

Migration
- Over 2,000,000 people
- 1 – 2,000,000 people
- 500,000 – 1,000,000 people
- Under 500,000 people

	1500 – 1914		Since 1914	
	Voluntary	Involuntary	Voluntary	Involuntary

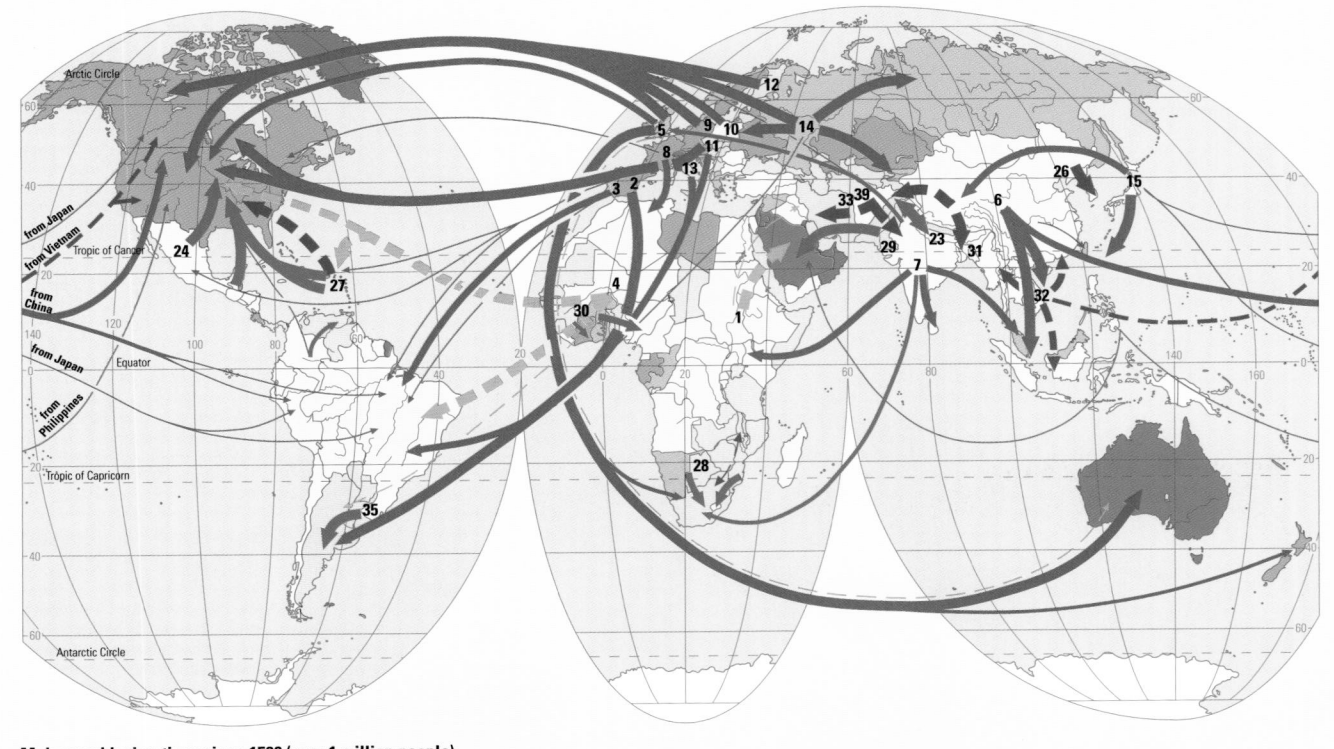

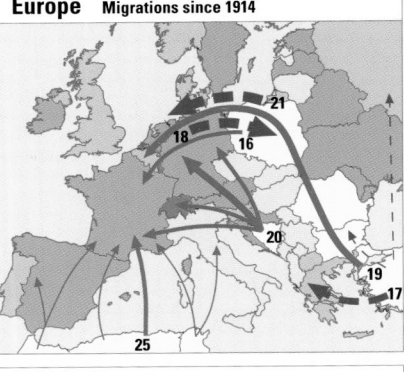

Europe Migrations since 1914

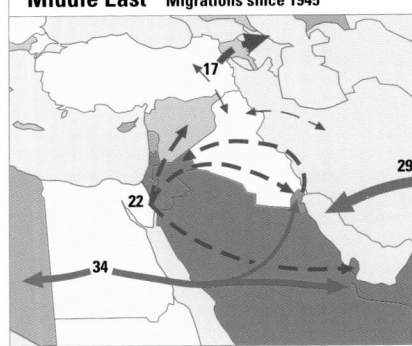

Middle East Migrations since 1945

Major world migrations since 1500 (over 1 million people)

1. North and East African slaves to Arabia (4.3m) 1500–1900
2. Spanish to South and Central America (2.3m) 1530–1914
3. Portuguese to Brazil (1.4m) 1530–1914
4. West African slaves to South America (4.6m) 1550–1860
    to Caribbean (4m) 1580–1860
    to North/Central America (1m) 1650–1820
5. British and Irish to North America (13.5m) 1620–1914
    to Australasia and South Africa (3m) 1790–1914
6. Chinese to Southeast Asia (22m) 1820–1914
    to North America (1m) 1880–1914
7. Indian migrant workers (3m) 1850–1914
8. French to North Africa (1.5m) 1850–1914
9. Germans to North America (5m) 1850–1914
10. Poles to North America (3.6m) 1850–1914
11. Austro-Hungarians to North America (3.2m) 1850–1914
    to Western Europe (3.4m) 1850–1914
    to South America (1.8m) 1850–1914

12. Scandinavians to North America (2.7m) 1850–1914
13. Italians to North America (5m) 1860–1914
    to South America (3.7m) 1860–1914
14. Russians to North America (2.2m) 1880–1914
    to Western Europe (2.2m) 1880–1914
    to Siberia (6m) 1880–1914
    to Central Asia (4m) 1880–1914
15. Japanese to Eastern Asia, Southeast Asia and America (8m) 1900–1914
16. Poles to Western Europe (1m) 1920–1940
17. Greeks and Armenians from Turkey (1.6m) 1922–1923
18. European Jews to extermination camps (5m) 1940–1944
19. Turks to Western Europe (1.9m) 1940–
20. Yugoslavs to Western Europe (2m) 1940–
21. Germans to Western Europe (9.8m) 1945–1947
22. Palestinian refugees (2m) 1947–
23. Indian and Pakistani refugees (15m) 1947
24. Mexicans to North America (9m) 1950–

25. North Africans to Western Europe (1.1m) 1950–
26. Korean refugees (5m) 1950–1954
27. Latin Americans and West Indians to North America (4.7m) 1960–
28. Migrant workers to South Africa (1.5m) 1960–
29. Indians and Pakistanis to the Persian Gulf (2.4m) 1970–
30. Migrant workers to Nigeria and Ivory Coast (3m) 1970–
31. Bangladeshi and Pakistani refugees (2m) 1972
32. Vietnamese and Cambodian refugees (1.5m) 1975–
33. Afghan refugees (6.1m) 1979–
34. Egyptians to the Persian Gulf and Libya (2.9m) 1980–
35. Migrant workers to Argentina (2m) 1980–
36. Mozambique refugees (1.7m) 1985–
37. Yugoslav/Balkan refugees (1.7m) 1992–
38. Rwanda/Burundi refugees (2.6m) 1994–
39. Afghan refugees (2.1m) 2001–

BUILDING THE USA

US Immigration, 1920 and 2006

For decades the USA was the magnet that attracted millions of immigrants, notably from Central and Eastern Europe, the flow peaking in the early years of the 20th century. By the mid-1990s the proportion of immigrants had increased again to pre-World War II rates, reaching over 12% by 2006. However, the balance of origin had swung from Europe to Latin America and Asia, as the graphs indicate.

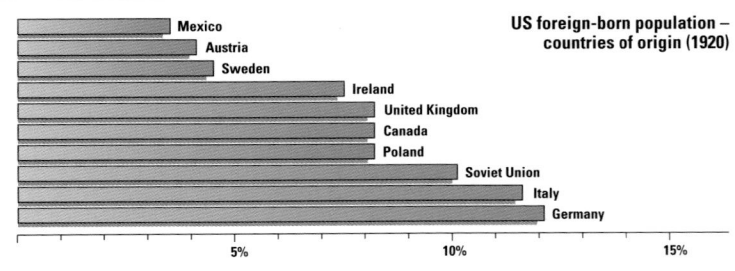

US foreign-born population – countries of origin (1920)

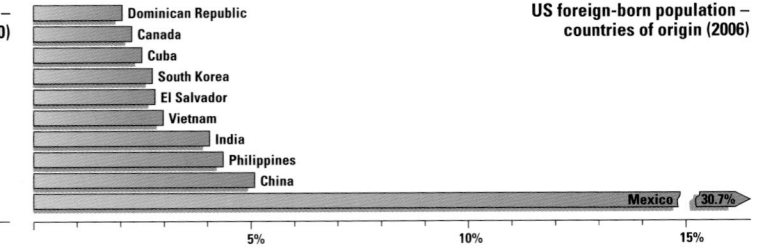

US foreign-born population – countries of origin (2006)

PREDOMINANT LANGUAGES

INDO-EUROPEAN FAMILY
1. Balto-Slavic group (incl. Russian, Ukrainian)
2. Germanic group (incl. English, German)
3. Celtic group
4. Greek
5. Albanian
6. Iranian group
7. Armenian
8. Romance group (incl. Spanish, Portuguese, French, Italian)
9. Indo-Aryan group (incl. Hindi, Bengali, Urdu, Punjabi, Marathi)

10. **CAUCASIAN FAMILY**

AFRO-ASIATIC FAMILY
11. Semitic group (incl. Arabic)
12. Kushitic group
13. Berber group

14. **KHOISAN FAMILY**

15. **NIGER-CONGO FAMILY**

16. **NILO-SAHARAN FAMILY**

17. **URALIC FAMILY**

ALTAIC FAMILY
18. Turkic group (incl. Turkish)
19. Mongolian group
20. Tungus-Manchu group
21. Japanese and Korean

SINO-TIBETAN FAMILY
22. Sinitic (Chinese) languages (incl. Mandarin, Wu, Yue)
23. Tibetic-Burmic languages

24. **TAI FAMILY**

AUSTRO-ASIATIC FAMILY
25. Mon-Khmer group
26. Munda group
27. Vietnamese

28. **DRAVIDIAN FAMILY** (incl. Telugu, Tamil)

29. **AUSTRONESIAN FAMILY** (incl. Malay-Indonesian, Javanese)

30. **OTHER LANGUAGES**

First-language speakers, in millions (2005)

Mandarin Chinese	873m
Spanish	322m
English	309m
Portuguese	230m
Arabic	206m
Hindi	181m
Bengali	171m
Russian	145m
Japanese	122m
German	95m
Wu Chinese	77m
Javanese	75m
Telugu	70m
Marathi	68m
Vietnamese	67m
Korean	67m
Tamil	66m
French	65m
Italian	62m
Punjabi	60m

Languages form a kind of tree of development, splitting from a few ancient proto-tongues into branches that have grown apart and further divided with the passage of time. English and Hindi, for example, both belong to the great Indo-European family, although the relationship is only apparent after much analysis and comparison with non-Indo-European languages such as Chinese or Arabic. Hindi is part of the Indo-Aryan subgroup, whereas English is a member of Indo-European's Germanic branch. French, another Indo-European tongue, traces its descent through the Latin, or Romance, branch. A few languages – Basque is one example – have no apparent links with any other, living or dead. Most modern languages, of course, have acquired enormous quantities of vocabulary from each other.

DISTRIBUTION OF LIVING LANGUAGES

The figures refer to the number of languages currently in use in the regions shown

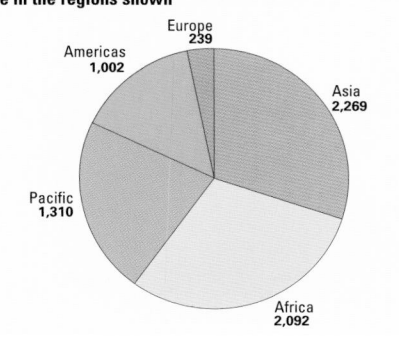

Europe 239
Americas 1,002
Asia 2,269
Pacific 1,310
Africa 2,092

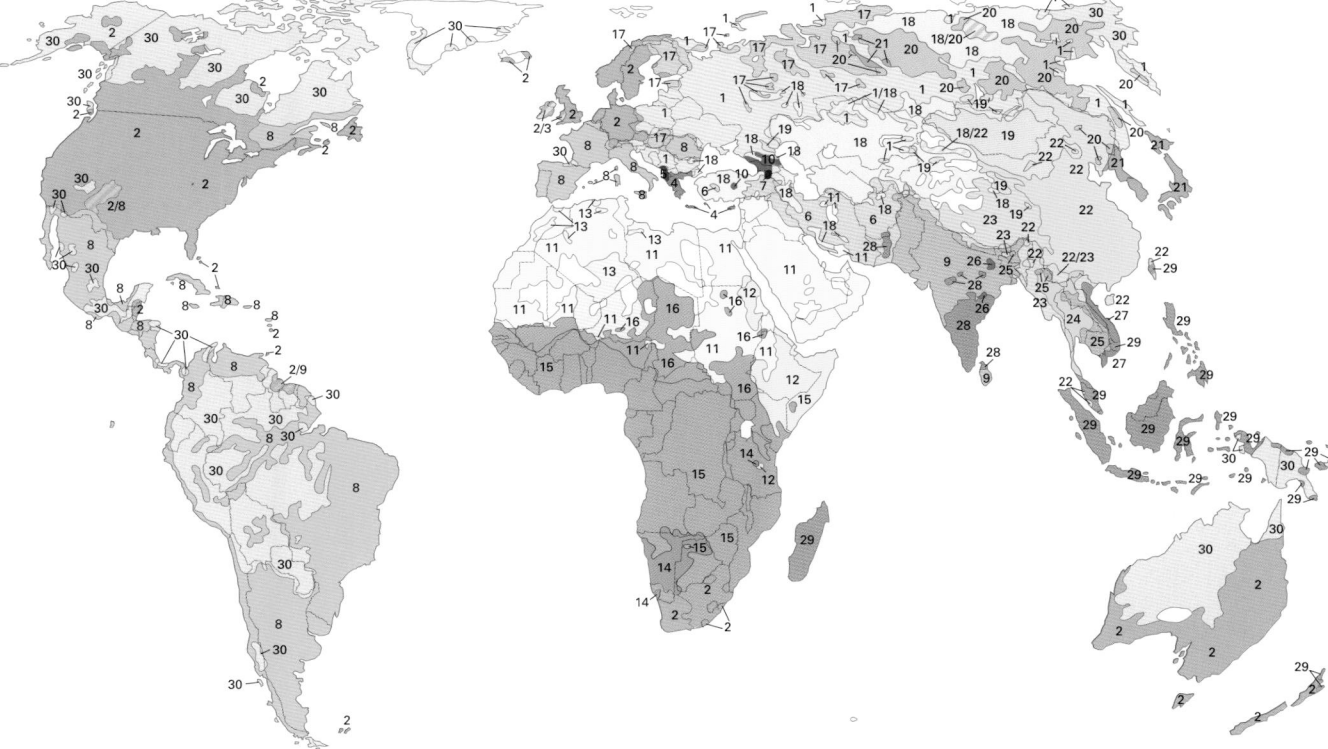

PREDOMINANT RELIGIONS

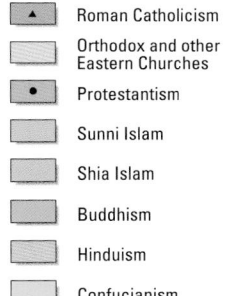

- ▲ Roman Catholicism
- Orthodox and other Eastern Churches
- • Protestantism
- Sunni Islam
- Shia Islam
- Buddhism
- Hinduism
- Confucianism
- ✦ Judaism
- Shintoism
- Tribal Religions

Religions are not as easily mapped as the physical contours of the land. Divisions are often blurred and frequently overlapping: most nations include people of many different faiths – or no faith at all. Some religions, like Islam and Christianity, have proselytes worldwide; others, like Hinduism and Confucianism, are restricted to a particular area, though modern migrations have taken some Indians and Chinese very far from their cultural origins. It is also difficult to show the degree to which religion controls daily life: Christian Western Europe, for example, is now far less dominated by its religion than are the Islamic nations of the Middle East. Similarly, figures for the major faiths' adherents make no distinction between nominal believers enrolled at birth and those for whom religion is a vital part of their existence.

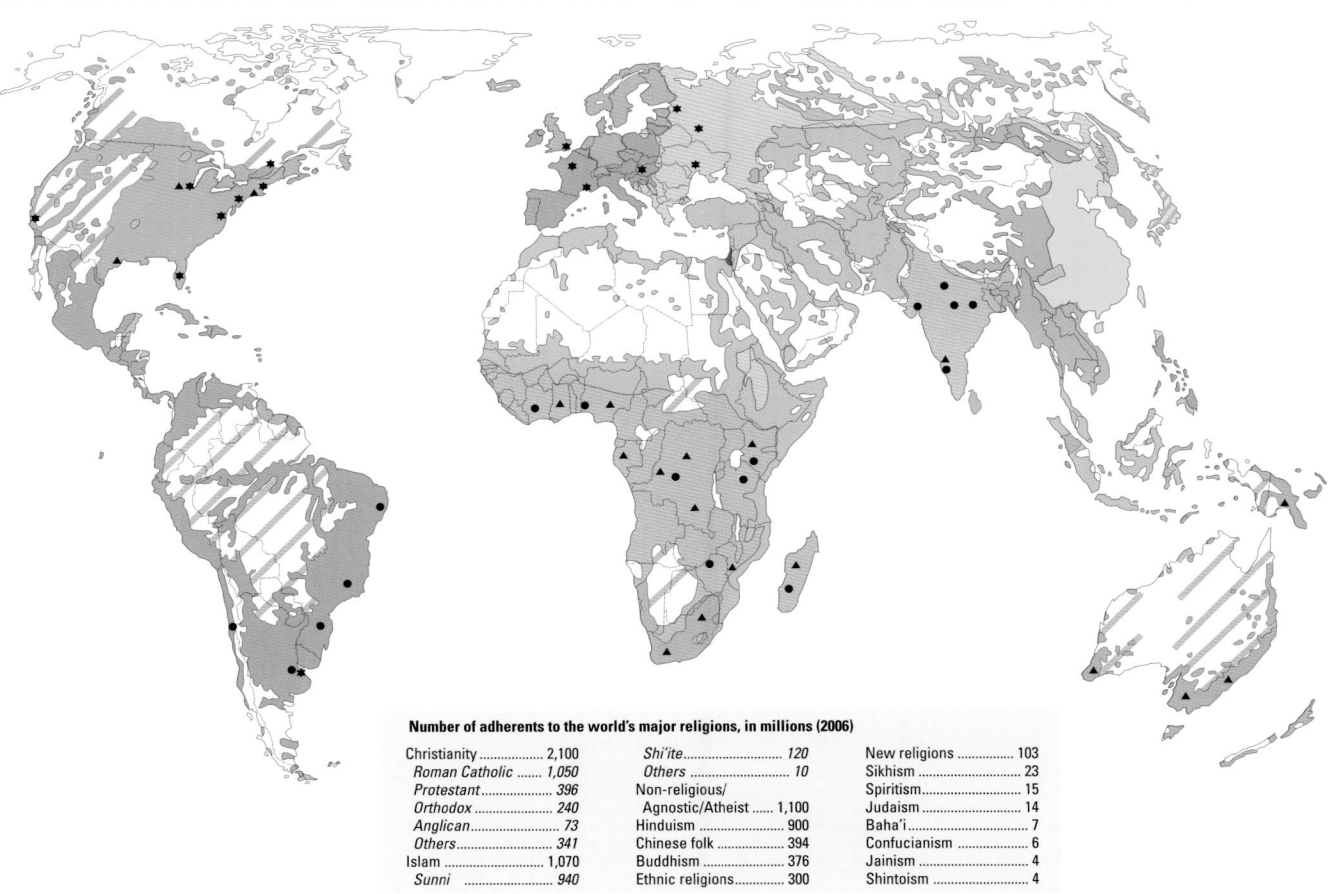

Number of adherents to the world's major religions, in millions (2006)

Christianity	2,100	Shi'ite	120	New religions	103
Roman Catholic	1,050	Others	10	Sikhism	23
Protestant	396	Non-religious/		Spiritism	15
Orthodox	240	Agnostic/Atheist	1,100	Judaism	14
Anglican	73	Hinduism	900	Baha'i	7
Others	341	Chinese folk	394	Confucianism	6
Islam	1,070	Buddhism	376	Jainism	4
Sunni	940	Ethnic religions	300	Shintoism	4

For more information:
90 Migration
91 Religion

The 20th century witnessed two world wars, followed by a Cold War which several times threatened to erupt into a third world war, fought with nuclear weapons. The Cold War was marked by a great number of conflicts. Some were colonial wars, as the empires of the first half of the century fell apart, some were border wars, and some were civil wars. All the wars have caused great suffering among civilians, many of whom were forced to join the ranks of the world's refugees.

In the late 1980s, many people hoped that the end of the Cold War, following the collapse of Communist regimes in the former Soviet Union and Eastern Europe, would herald a new era of international stability. Instead, old ethnic and religious antagonisms surfaced in many areas, leading to civil war in such places as Chechenia, in Russia, and the former Yugoslavia. Nationalist rivalries, suppressed under Communist rule, replaced ideological factors as the major cause of conflict.

War is a very human activity, with no real equivalent in any other species. Yet humans also function well when they cooperate. Evolution has made this so. Hunter-gatherers in cooperative bands were far more effective than animals that prowled. Agriculture, urbanization and industrialization all depend on the ability of humans to cooperate.

The creation of the United Nations in 1945 held out hope that the world's nations, tired of war, would have the means to control humanity's aggressive instincts. Although the UN lacks the power to halt conflicts, it has often helped to achieve negotiation. Economic pressures have led to another kind of cooperation, resulting in the creation of common markets and economic unions, such as ASEAN in Southeast Asia, the European Union, and NAFTA in North America.

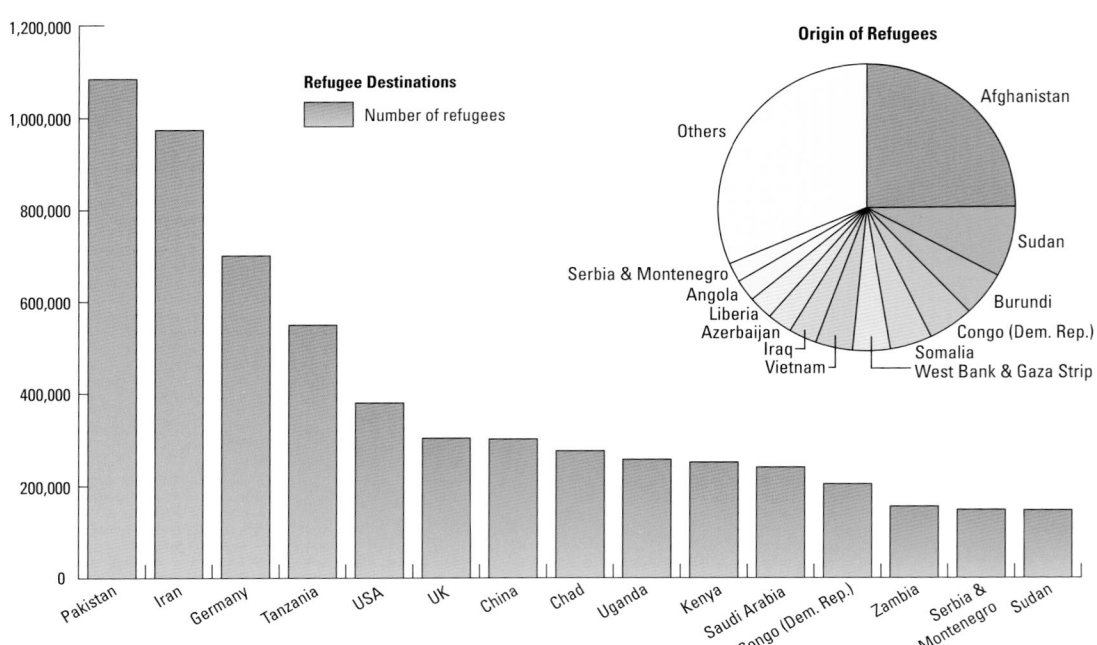

THE WORLD'S REFUGEES

Refugees by host nation (bar-chart, left) and by nation of origin (pie-chart, left) (2005). The source is the United Nations High Commission for Refugees (UNHCR).

The pie-chart shows the origins of the world's refugees, while the bar-chart below shows their destinations. According to the United Nations High Commission for Refugees (UNHCR) in 2005 there were 8.7 million refugees. However, the UNHCR definition of a refugee, "a person who has left or remains outside their own country because they have a well-founded fear of persecution, or because their safety is threatened by events seriously disturbing public order," does not include people who are in a refugee-like situation but who have not been formally recognized. In 2005, there were a further 6.6 million people who were internally displaced, and a total "population of concern" of 21 million people, worldwide.

All but a few who cross international boundaries seek asylum in neighboring countries, which are often the least equipped to deal with them. Lacking any rights or power, they frequently become an unwelcome burden to their hosts. Usually, the best any refugee can hope for is rudimentary food and shelter in temporary camps. Many Palestinians have been forced to live in camps since 1948.

WAR SINCE 1945

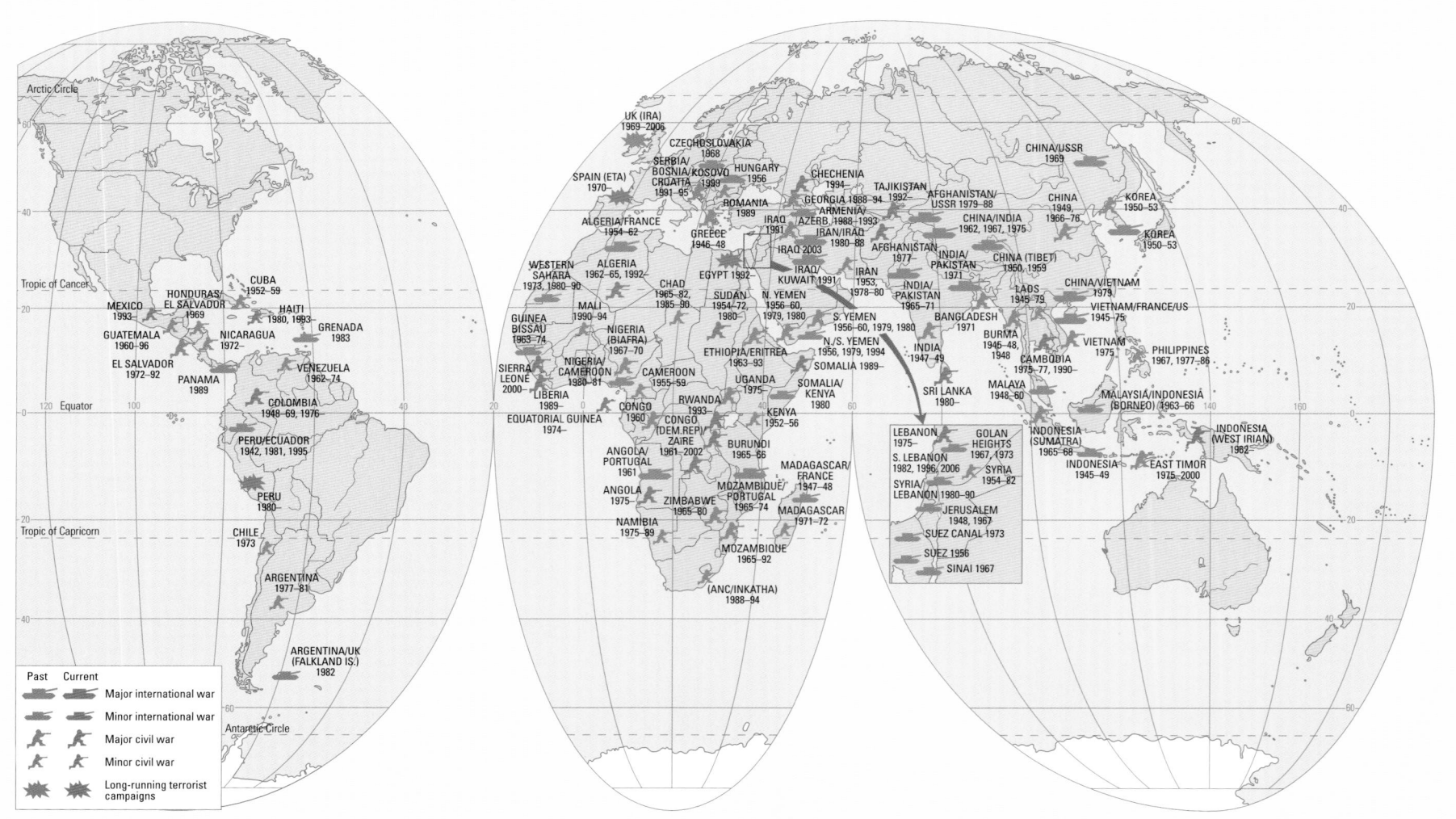

INTERNATIONAL ORGANIZATIONS

OAS Organization of American States (formed in 1948). It aims to promote social and economic cooperation between countries in the developed North America and developing Latin America.
EU European Union (evolved from the European Community in 1993). Cyprus, the Czech Republic, Estonia, Hungary, Latvia, Lithuania, Malta, Poland, the Slovak Republic, and Slovenia joined the EU in May 2004, Bulgaria and Romania joined in 2007. The other 15 members of the EU are Austria, Belgium, Denmark, Finland, France, Germany, Greece, Ireland, Italy, Luxembourg, Netherlands, Portugal, Spain, Sweden and the UK – together they aim to integrate economies, co-ordinate social developments and bring about political union.
AU The African Union was set up in 2002, taking over from the Organization of African Unity (1963). It has 53 members. Working languages are Arabic, English, French, and Portuguese.
COLOMBO PLAN (formed in 1951) Its 25 members aim to promote economic and social development in Asia and the Pacific.

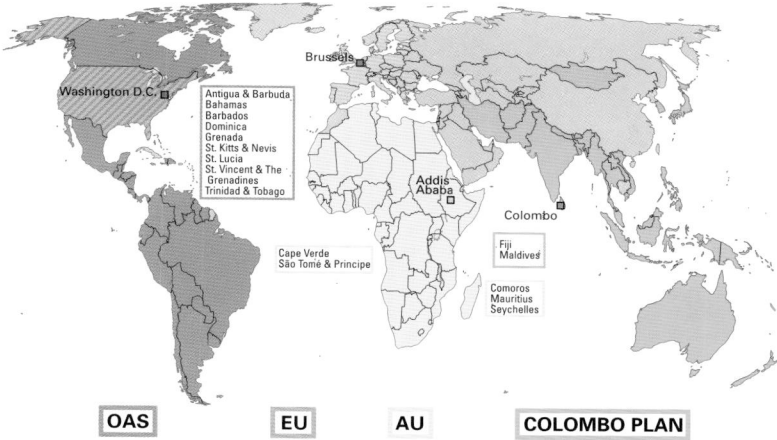

| OAS | EU | AU | COLOMBO PLAN |

G8 Group of eight leading industrialized nations, comprising Canada, France, Germany, Italy, Japan, Russia, the UK and the USA. Periodic meetings are held to discuss major world issues, such as world recessions.
APEC Asia-Pacific Economic Cooperation (formed in 1989). It aims to enhance economic growth and prosperity for the region and to strengthen the Asia-Pacific community. APEC is the only intergovernmental grouping in the world operating on the basis of non-binding commitments, open dialogue, and equal respect for the views of all participants. There are 21 member economies.
OECD Organization for Economic Cooperation and Development (formed in 1961). It comprises 30 major free-market economies. The "G8" is its "inner group" of leading industrial nations, comprising Canada, France, Germany, Italy, Japan, Russia, the UK, and the USA.
ACP African-Caribbean-Pacific (formed in 1963). Members enjoy economic ties with the EU.
OPEC Organization of Petroleum Exporting Countries (formed in 1960). It controls about three-quarters of the world's oil supply. Gabon formally withdrew from OPEC in August 1996.

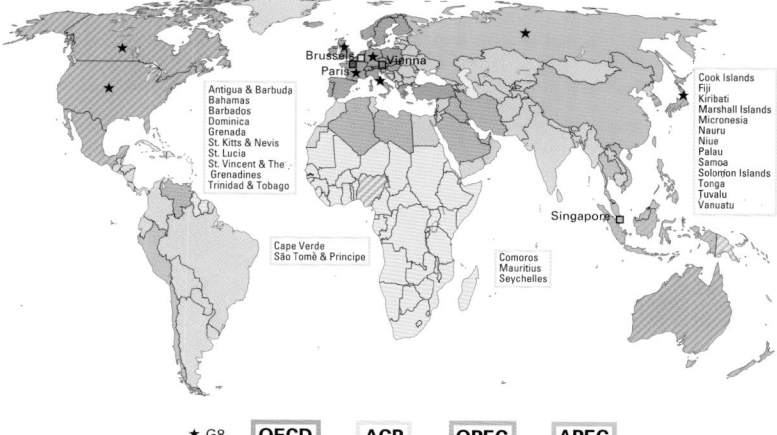

| ★ G8 | OECD | ACP | OPEC | APEC |

NATO North Atlantic Treaty Organization (formed in 1949). It continues despite the winding up of the Warsaw Pact in 1991. Bulgaria, Estonia, Latvia, Lithuania, Romania, the Slovak Republic, and Slovenia became members in 2004.
LAIA The Latin American Integration Association (formed in 1980) superceded the Latin American Free Trade Association formed in 1961. Its aim is to promote freer regional trade.
ARAB LEAGUE (1945) Aims to promote economic, social, political, and military cooperation. There are 22 member nations.
COMMONWEALTH The Commonwealth of Nations evolved from the British Empire. Pakistan was suspended in 1999, but reinstated in 2004. Zimbabwe was suspended in 2002 and, in response to its continued suspension, Zimbabwe left the Commonwealth in December 2003. Fiji Islands was suspended in December 2006 following a military coup. It now comprises 16 Queen's realms, 31 republics, and 6 indigenous monarchies, giving a total of 53 member states.
ASEAN Association of Southeast Asian Nations (formed in 1967). Cambodia joined in 1999.

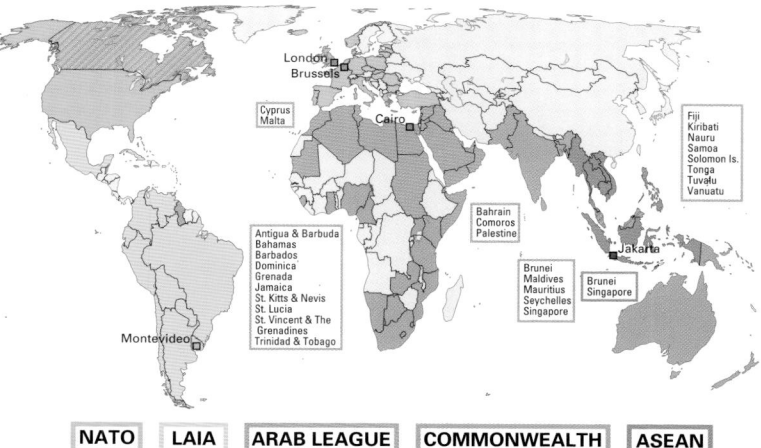

| NATO | LAIA | ARAB LEAGUE | COMMONWEALTH | ASEAN |

UNITED NATIONS

The United Nations Organization was born as World War II drew to its conclusion. Six years of strife had strengthened the world's desire for peace, but an effective international organization was needed to help achieve it. That body would replace the League of Nations which, since its inception in 1920, had failed to curb the aggression of at least some of its member nations. At the United Nations Conference on International Organization held in San Francisco, the United Nations Charter was drawn up. Ratified by the Security Council and signed by the 51 original members, it came into effect on October 24, 1945.

The Charter set out the aims of the organization: to maintain peace and security, and develop friendly relations between nations; to achieve international cooperation in solving economic, social, cultural, and humanitarian problems; to promote respect for human rights and fundamental freedoms; and to harmonize the activities of nations in order to achieve these common goals.

The United Nations has five principal organs:

The General Assembly The forum at which member nations discuss moral and political issues affecting world development, peace, and security meets annually in September, under a newly-elected President whose tenure lasts one year. Any member can bring business to the agenda, and each member nation has one vote.

The Security Council A legislative and executive body, the Security Council is the primary instrument for establishing and maintaining international peace by attempting to settle disputes between nations. It has the power to dispatch UN forces, and member nations undertake to provide armed forces, assistance, and facilities. The Security Council has ten temporary members elected by the General Assembly for two-year terms, and five permanent members – China, France, Russia, the UK, and the USA.

The Economic and Social Council By far the largest United Nations executive, the Council operates as a conduit between the General Assembly and the many United Nations agencies it instructs to implement Assembly decisions, and whose work it coordinates. The Council also commissions studies on economic conditions, collects data, and makes recommendations to the Assembly.

The Secretariat This is the staff of the United Nations, and its task is to administer the policies and programs of the UN and its organs, and assist and advise the Head of the Secretariat, the Secretary-General – a full-time, non-political appointment made by the General Assembly.

The Trusteeship Council This no longer administers any of the original 11 trust territories as they are all now independent.

The International Court of Justice (the World Court) The World Court is the judicial organ of the United Nations. It deals only with United Nations disputes and all members are subject to its jurisdiction. There are 15 judges, elected for nine-year terms by the General Assembly and the Security Council.

The social and humanitarian operations of the UN include:

United Nations Development Program (UNDP) Plans and funds projects to help developing countries make better use of their resources.
United Nations International Childrens' Fund (UNICEF) Created at the General Assembly's first session in 1945 to help children in the aftermath of World War II, it now provides basic health care and aid worldwide.
Food and Agriculture Organization (FAO) Aims to raise living standards and nutrition levels in rural areas by improving food production and distribution.
United Nations Educational, Scientific and Cultural Organization (UNESCO) Promotes international cooperation through broader and better education.
World Health Organization (WHO) Promotes and provides for better health care, public and environmental health, and medical research.

United Nations agencies are involved in many aspects of international trade, safety and security:

International Maritime Organization (IMO) Promotes unity amongst merchant shipping, especially in regard to safety, marine pollution, and standardization.
International Labor Organization (ILO) Seeks to improve labor conditions and promote productive employment to raise living standards.
World Meteorological Organization (WMO) Promotes cooperation in weather observation, reporting and forecasting.
World Trade Organization (WTO) On January 1, 1995, the WTO replaced GATT. It advocates a common code of conduct and its aim is the liberalization of world trade.
Disarmament Commission Considers and makes recommendations to the General Assembly on disarmament issues.
International Atomic Energy Agency (IAEA) Fosters development of peaceful uses for nuclear energy and establishes safety standards.

The World Bank comprises three United Nations agencies:

International Monetary Fund (IMF) Cultivates international monetary cooperation and the expansion of trade.
International Bank for Reconstruction and Development (IBRD) Provides funds and technical assistance to developing countries.
International Finance Corporation (IFC) Encourages the growth of productive private enterprise in less developed countries.

Membership There are two independent states which are not members of the UN – Taiwan and Vatican City. Official languages are Chinese, English, French, Russian, Spanish, and Arabic.

Funding The UN regular budget for 2007 was US$2.1 billion. Contributions are assessed by the members' ability to pay, with the maximum 24% of the total (USA's share), the minimum 0.01%. The EU pays over 37% of the budget.

Peacekeeping The UN has been involved in 65 peacekeeping operations worldwide since 1948.

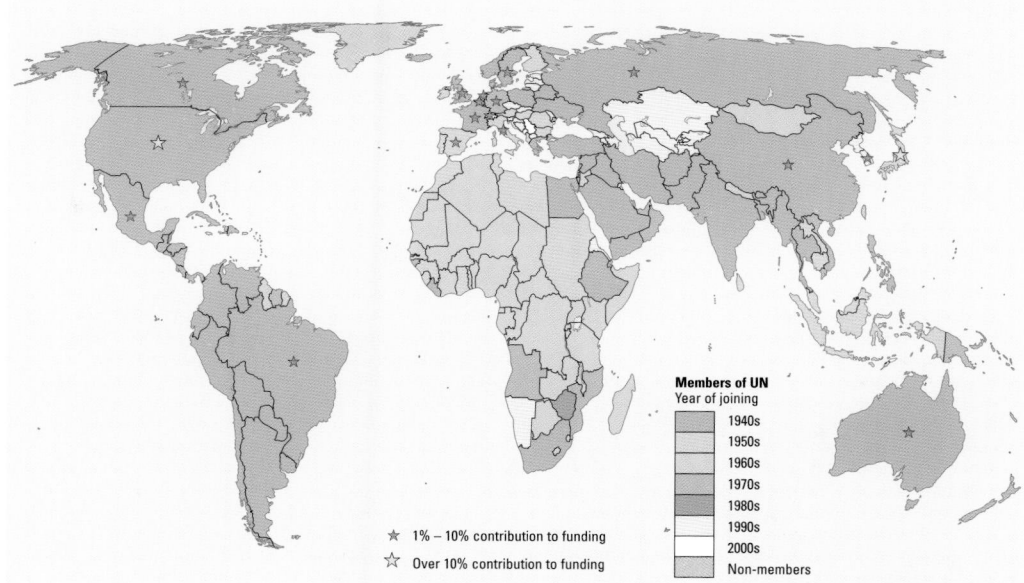

Members of UN
Year of joining
1940s
1950s
1960s
1970s
1980s
1990s
2000s
Non-members

★ 1% – 10% contribution to funding
☆ Over 10% contribution to funding

For more information:

78 Climate regions

79 Temperature and precipitation

82 Water distribution

83 Natural vegetation

100 Division of employment

▼ These two images illustrate the opposite sides of world agriculture. The farmers with the plow in southern Africa (*below*) are engaged in subsistence agriculture, in which they can only produce enough food to feed themselves. There is, therefore, no surplus to sell and no money to spend on equipment to make the farm more productive. The second photograph (*right*) is of a commercial grain farm in North America, where fertilizers and pesticides are used. This, combined with huge field sizes that enable large machinery to be used for sowing and harvesting the crops, results in very high crop yields per person employed. The crops are then all sold on the open market.

The world's population continues to increase quickly. From around 6.5 billion, UN demographers predicted in 2005 that it would rise to 9.1 billion by 2050. Most of the growth will occur in the developing world, while the populations of the developed countries will, overall, remain static at around 1.2 billion.

Predictions of population growth raise concerns about food supply, especially the problem of how to feed the people of the developing world, where much of the agriculture is at subsistence level. Crops in the developing world are grown mainly for consumption. Relatively little of the harvest enters the commercial sector, whereas agriculture is scientific and highly mechanized in the developed world.

This contrast is reflected in the proportions of people who work on the land. While agriculture employs less than 1% of the work force in the United States, it accounts for around two-thirds of the population in sub-Saharan Africa.

The production of new crop varieties, the use of irrigation, fertilizers, and pesticides transformed world agriculture during the Green Revolution which began in the 1950s.

Then, in the early 2000s, many people thought that genetically-modified (GM) crops would lead to another revolution. Despite opposition to GM crops by environmental activists in Western Europe, they have been widely used in the United States and also in developing countries, notably Argentina and Brazil, without any of the predicted environmental and health problems.

But from 2006, food prices for basic food crops began to rise rapidly, reversing decades of falling prices. This new trend is particularly disturbing in developing countries where a high proportion of a family's income goes on food.

Several factors have affected price rises. Poor harvests have long caused falls in food production and price rises. For example, in 2007 wheat stocks were at their lowest for nearly 60 years, the result of a long drought in Australia and increased demand.

Some people are concerned that the apparently increasing number of extreme weather events will make crop failures increasingly common. Extreme weather events, such as the hurricanes which cause devastation in tropical and sub-tropical regions, are often attributed to global warming. Global warming will inevitably cause serious problems in food production, especially if large areas of now productive land are reduced to desert, as computer models suggest.

An immediate effect of global warming has been the recent emphasis on the production of biofuels, which are seen as a means of reducing carbon dioxide emissions and so a weapon in the battle against radical climate change. Yet the planting of crops to produce ethanol, which command high prices, has inevitably reduced the area of land under food production.

Many fear that food production will fall in developing countries, reducing their net food exports. As a result, agricultural production must rise considerably if these countries are to feed their fast-increasing populations.

However, the developing countries face many great challenges, many of which are likely to be caused by climate change, including desertification in already marginal farming areas and consequent soil erosion. Any large rise in food production will inevitably increase the pressure on already fragile environments.

LAND USE

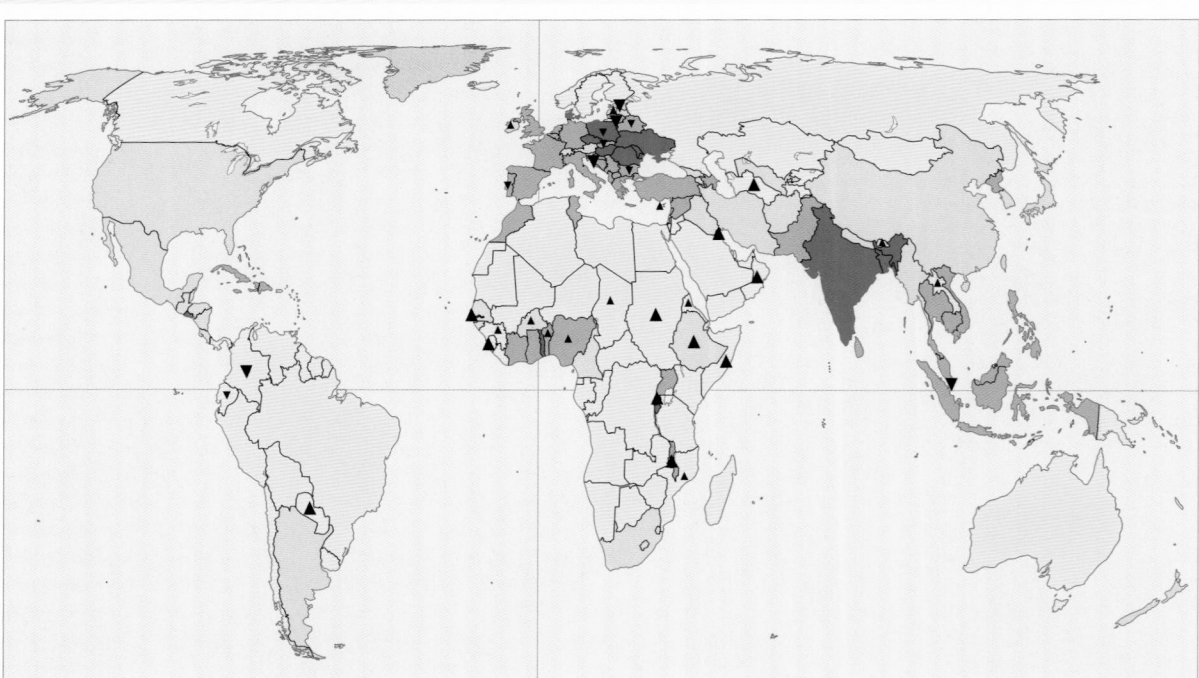

Arable and permanent crops as a percentage of total land area (2005)

- Over 40%
- 20 – 40%
- 10 – 20%
- Under 10%
- No data available

Percentage change in area of arable and permanent crops (2000 – 2005)

- ▲ Over 20% increase
- ▲ 10 – 20% increase
- ▼ Over 20 % decrease
- ▼ 10 – 20% decrease

Arable land is land that is plowed to produce crops, which are often rotated every year and sometimes left fallow. Permanent crops, such as orchards or vineyards, are sown or planted once and then occupy the land for several years.

Total area of arable and permanent crops (2005)

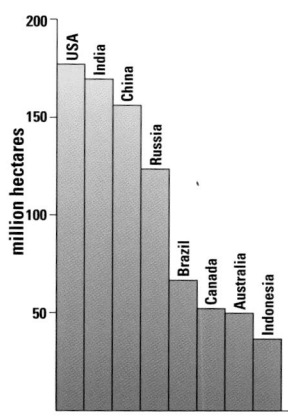

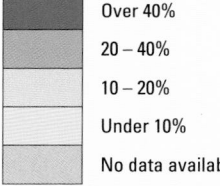

million hectares

USA, India, China, Russia, Brazil, Canada, Australia, Indonesia

PRODUCTION OF MAJOR FOOD COMMODITIES

Wheat: Grown in a range of climates, with most varieties – including the highest-quality bread wheats – requiring temperate conditions. Mainly used in baking, it is also used for pasta and breakfast cereals.

Maize: Originating in the New World and still an important human food in Africa and Latin America, in the developed world it is processed into breakfast cereals, oil, starches, and adhesives. Maize is used in the production of the fuel additive ethanol. It is also used for animal feed.

Beef and Veal: Most beef and veal is reared for home markets, and the top five producers are also the biggest consumers. The United States produces nearly a fifth of the world's beef and eats even more.

World total (2006): 605,946,000 tons

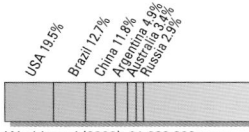

World total (2006): 695,228,000 tons

World total (2006): 61,033,000 tons

Rice: Thrives on the high humidity and temperatures of the Far East, where it is the traditional staple food of half the human race. Usually grown standing in water, rice responds well to continuous cultivation, with three or four crops annually.

Soya: Beans from soya bushes (soybeans) are very high (30–40%) in protein. Most are processed into oil and proprietary protein foods. Consumption since 1950 has tripled, mainly due to the health-conscious developed world.

Milk: Many human groups, including most Asians, find raw milk indigestible after infancy, and it is often only the starting point for other dairy products, such as butter, cheese and yoghurt. Most world production comes from cows, but sheep's milk and goats' milk are also important.

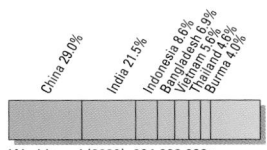

World total (2006): 634,606,000 tons

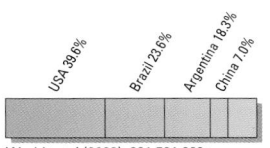

World total (2006): 221,501,000 tons

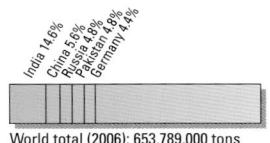

World total (2006): 653,789,000 tons

WORLD FISHING AREAS

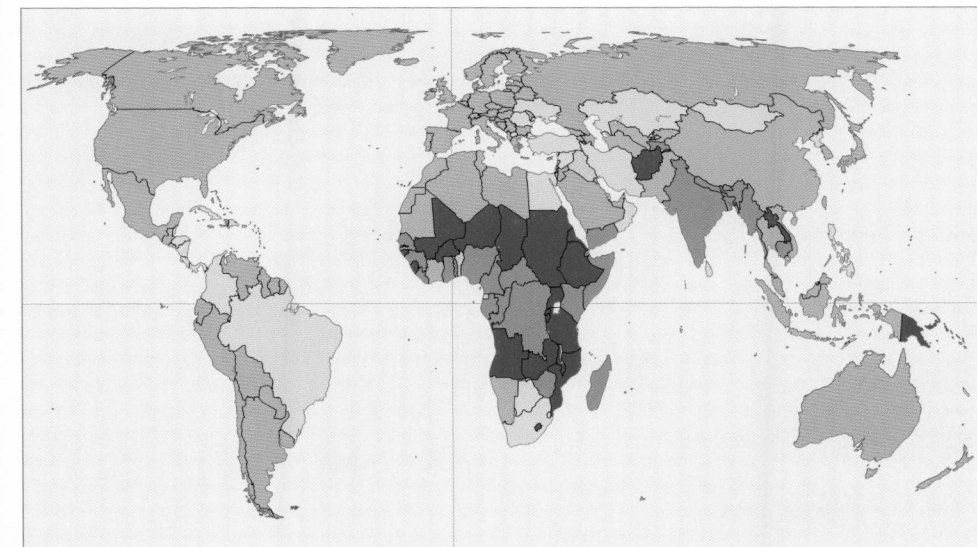

Total world fish catch in metric tons (2005) (inland and marine fishing)

- Over 5 million
- 1 million – 5 million
- 500,000 – 1 million
- 10,000 – 500,000
- Under 10,000
- No data available

Leading fishing nations

World total (2004): 95,000,000 tons

With many marine stocks now fully exploited or over-exploited, future fish supplies are likely to be constrained by resource limits.

AGRICULTURAL WORK FORCE

Percentage of the total work force dependent on agriculture for their livelihood (2006)

- Over 80% dependent
- 60 – 80% dependent
- 40 – 60% dependent
- 20 – 40% dependent
- Under 20% dependent
- No data available

Top 5 countries		Bottom 5 countries	
Burundi	94%	USA	0.7%
Burkina Faso	90%	Singapore	1.0%
Malawi	90%	Luxembourg	1.0%
Niger	90%	Kuwait	1.0%
Rwanda	90%	Bahrain	1.0%

FOOD & POPULATION

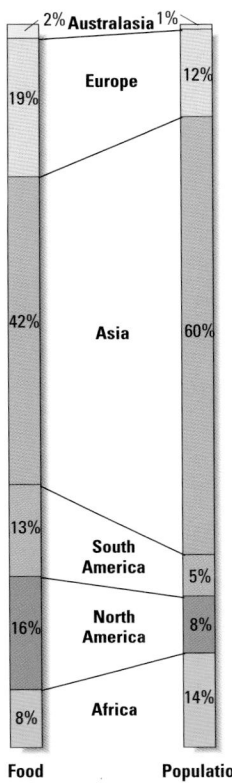

Comparison of food production and population by continent

The left column indicates the proportion of world food production and the right shows population in proportion.

As world population increases so demand for food increases. Developing countries will become increasingly dependent on imports of cereals. Traditional exporters such as North America, Western Europe, and Australia will have to increase their net exports to fill the demand.

Crop production will also have to increase in the developing world. Most of this increase will have to be achieved by intensifying production through higher yields, multiple cropping, and shorter fallow periods. Irrigation is also expected to play an important role.

RISING FOOD PRICES

After decades of falling food prices, the price of staples such as corn, wheat, and maize nearly doubled between 2006 and 2007. Soya prices increased by 87% and wheat by 130%. Several factors have contributed to these rises: low levels of world stocks following below-average harvests, and crop failures in 2006–7 are partly to blame. The growing world population is also a factor – it is expected to reach 8.3 billion by 2030 and 9.1 billion by 2050. This increase in the number of mouths to feed puts pressure on resources.

Another significant factor is the economic boom driving emerging economies such as those in China and India. Economic growth has generated a new tier of middle-class consumers able to buy more meat and processed foods, which were previously viewed as luxuries. Meat consumption in many countries has

soared. China, for example, consumed 44 lb [20 kg] of meat per capita in 1980. By 2007 this had increased to 110 lb [50 kg] per capita.

Climate change and global warming also play a significant role in rising food prices. Desertification is accelerating in China and sub-Saharan Africa, while more frequent flooding and changing patterns of rainfall are having an impact on agricultural production. This curtails the amount of land available for food crops and pushes up the price of wheat and maize on international commodity markets.

All of this has a disastrous effect on the poorest economies of the world where a high percentage of a family's income is spent on food. For example, in Bangladesh about 40% of income is spent on food compared with 13% in the US.

Food prices (2000-2007) 1998-2000 average = 100

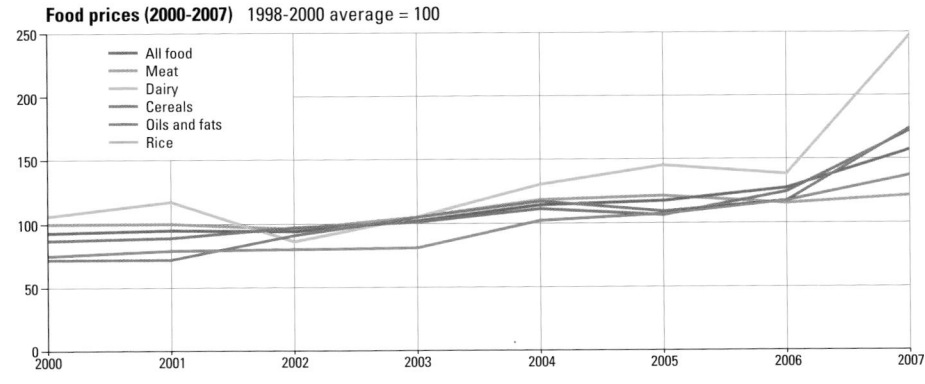

- All food
- Meat
- Dairy
- Cereals
- Oils and fats
- Rice

BIOFUELS

The possibility of a food crisis is exacerbated by fears over energy security, with some countries opting to plant biofuel crops in place of traditional crops. In 2008, 18% of US grain production will be converted into biofuels such as ethanol.

There are two main methods of production. The first takes crops producing sugar or starch, such as maize or wheat, and ferments these to create ethanol (industrial alcohol). The second uses oil-producing plants such as palm or soybean and converts them to biodiesel.

To achieve this, in the US 8 million hectares, which once provided animal feed and food, have been taken out of food production. Large areas of Brazil, Argentina, Canada, and Eastern Europe are also diverting sugarcane, palmoil and soybean crops to biofuel production.

Production is due to continue to increase dramatically in the next 15 years. The US plans to produce 30 billion gallons [136 billion liters] by 2022, which means trebling maize production. The EU aims to make 5.75% of transport fuels from biofuels by 2010.

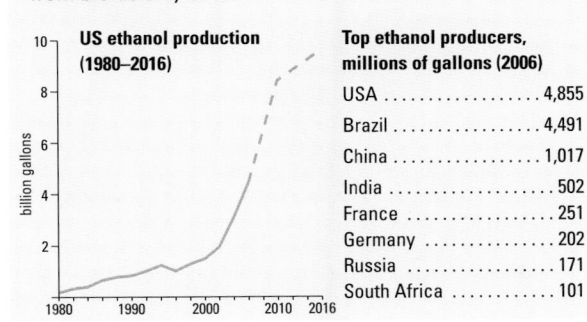

US ethanol production (1980–2016)

Top ethanol producers, millions of gallons (2006)

USA	4,855
Brazil	4,491
China	1,017
India	502
France	251
Germany	202
Russia	171
South Africa	101

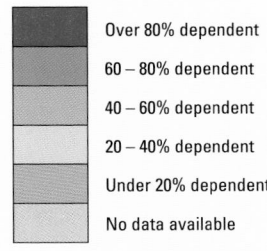

For more information:
80 Global warming
    Carbon dioxide
98 Minerals
103 World shipping

Every year, the world's energy consumption is about the equivalent of what would come from burning 10,000 million tons of oil (10,000 MtOe) – a 20-fold increase since 1850. Two-fifths of this total actually comes from burning oil and most of the rest comes from coal and natural gas.

The oil crises in the 1970s precipitated concern over dependence on finite fossil fuels as the primary source of energy, and growing environmental awareness has added impetus to the search for alternative energy resources. Fossil fuel combustion damages the environment through the release of gases and particulate matter, but two other major sources of energy, hydroelectricity and nuclear power, are also controversial. Hydroelectricity production involves flooding large areas to create reservoirs, while nuclear power stations generate dangerous radioactive wastes and can cause major disasters. Nuclear power is now a growing source of energy. In 2006, over 16% of the world's electricity was produced by nuclear plants, compared with 3.3% in 1973.

Alternative energy resources may soon provide a much larger proportion of the world's energy consumption. Solar and wind energy may become important in such countries as China and India, while tidal, wave, and geothermal energy all have potential in appropriate areas. Experts calculate that solar power could, in theory, supply between five and ten times the present electricity supply of developing countries.

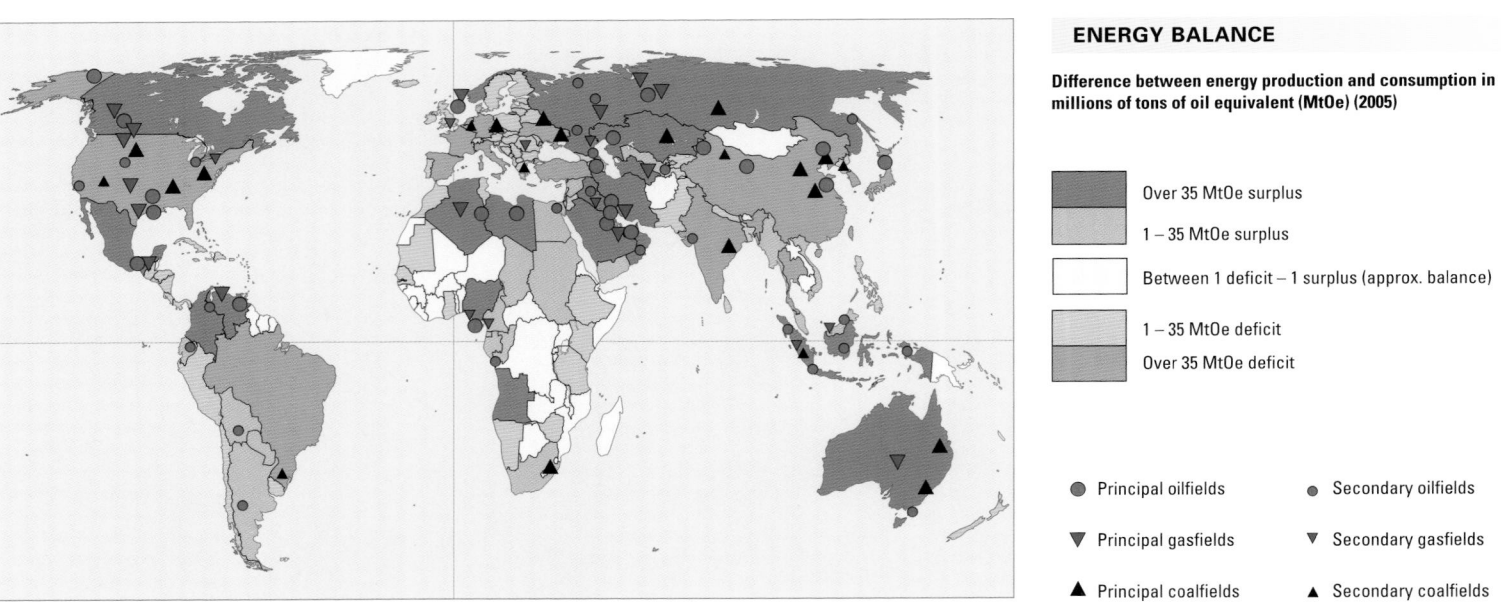

ENERGY BALANCE

Difference between energy production and consumption in millions of tons of oil equivalent (MtOe) (2005)

- Over 35 MtOe surplus
- 1 – 35 MtOe surplus
- Between 1 deficit – 1 surplus (approx. balance)
- 1 – 35 MtOe deficit
- Over 35 MtOe deficit

- ● Principal oilfields   ● Secondary oilfields
- ▼ Principal gasfields   ▼ Secondary gasfields
- ▲ Principal coalfields   ▲ Secondary coalfields

ENERGY CONSUMPTION

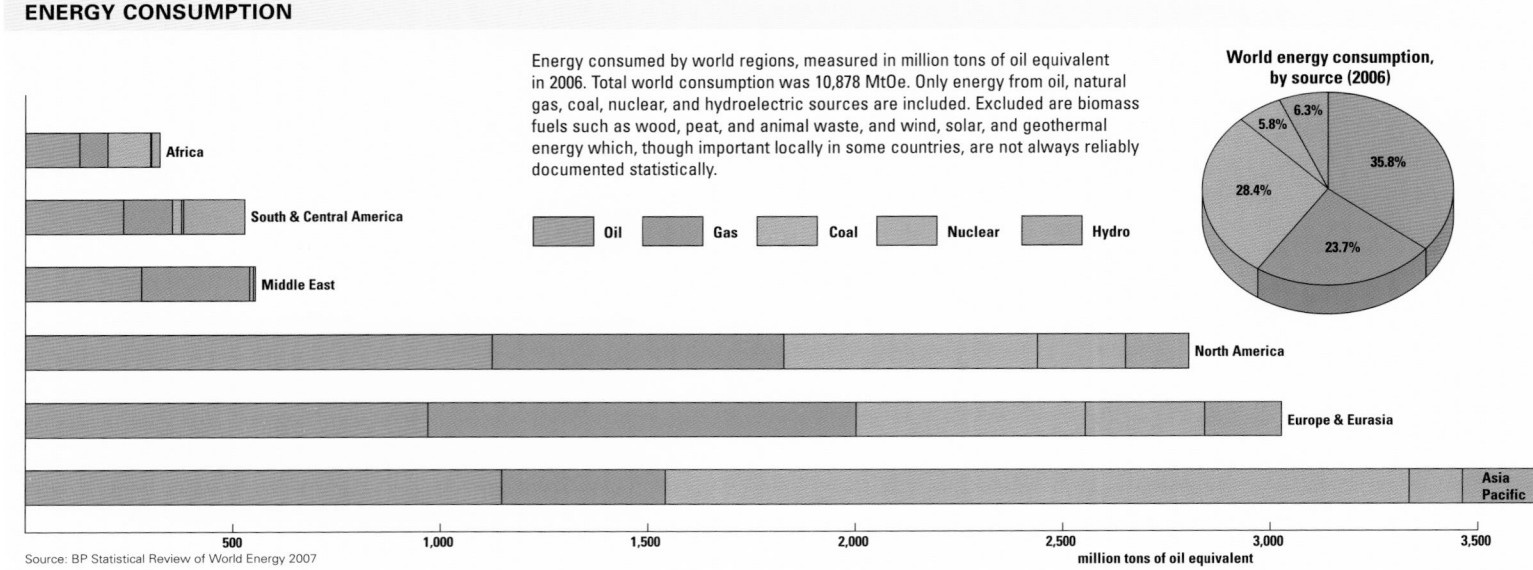

Energy consumed by world regions, measured in million tons of oil equivalent in 2006. Total world consumption was 10,878 MtOe. Only energy from oil, natural gas, coal, nuclear, and hydroelectric sources are included. Excluded are biomass fuels such as wood, peat, and animal waste, and wind, solar, and geothermal energy which, though important locally in some countries, are not always reliably documented statistically.

Oil   Gas   Coal   Nuclear   Hydro

World energy consumption, by source (2006)

6.3%
5.8%
35.8%
28.4%
23.7%

Africa
South & Central America
Middle East
North America
Europe & Eurasia
Asia Pacific

500   1,000   1,500   2,000   2,500   3,000   3,500

million tons of oil equivalent

Source: BP Statistical Review of World Energy 2007

ENERGY PRODUCTION

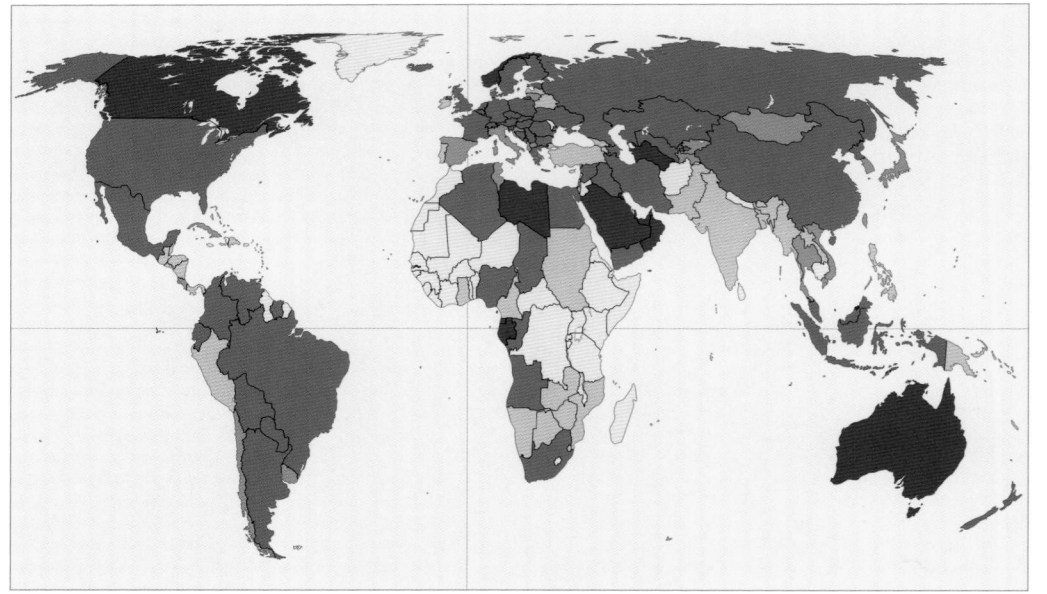

Energy production in tons of oil equivalent per capita (2005)

- Over 10
- 1 – 10
- 0.5 – 1
- 0.1 – 0.5
- Under 0.1
- No data available

Highest energy producers, tons of oil equivalent per capita

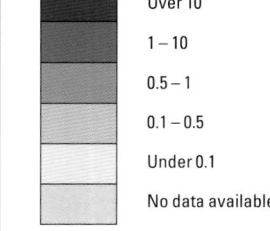

Qatar	111.1
United Arab Emirates	74.1
Kuwait	65.4
Brunei	58.9
Norway	58.0

OIL MOVEMENTS

Major world movements of oil in millions of tons (2006)

1.	Middle East to Asia (not China or Japan)	390.8
2.	Former Soviet Union to Europe	290.8
3.	Middle East to Japan	209.1
4.	Middle East to Europe	159.3
5.	South and Central America to USA	133.1
6.	Canada to USA	113.6
7.	Middle East to USA	113.2
8.	North Africa to Europe	96.4
9.	West Africa to USA	95.2
10.	Mexico to USA	84.4
11.	Middle East to China	73.9
Total world imports		**2,590.4 million tons**

In 1990, China consumed 120 million tons of oil, leaving a surplus for export. In 2007 it consumed 350 million tons, of which it had to import around half. It is predicted that by 2030 China will be consuming over 800 million tons of oil, importing around three quarters.

The majority of China's imported oil comes from the Middle East and Africa and has to pass through the narrow and crowded Singaport Strait. The Chinese government is pushing for alternative routes, such as a pipeline from Kazakhstan and a transit route from the Indian Ocean through Burma to Southern China.

◄ With many of the world's onshore oilfields reaching their maturity, exploration and production in ever-deeper ocean waters is taking place to try to satisfy demand. The current deepest production well is 7 miles [11 km] offshore of Sakhalin in eastern Russia, with a depth of 39,222 ft [11,680 m].

ENERGY RESERVES

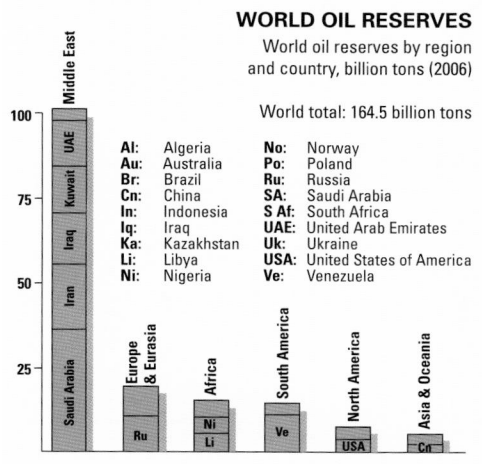

WORLD OIL RESERVES
World oil reserves by region and country, billion tons (2006)

World total: 164.5 billion tons

Al:	Algeria	No:	Norway
Au:	Australia	Po:	Poland
Br:	Brazil	Ru:	Russia
Cn:	China	SA:	Saudi Arabia
In:	Indonesia	S Af:	South Africa
Iq:	Iraq	UAE:	United Arab Emirates
Ka:	Kazakhstan	Uk:	Ukraine
Li:	Libya	USA:	United States of America
Ni:	Nigeria	Ve:	Venezuela

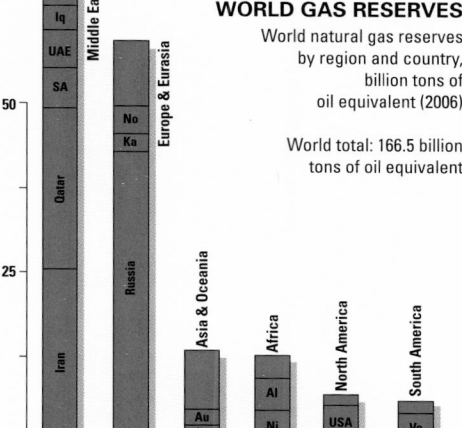

WORLD GAS RESERVES
World natural gas reserves by region and country, billion tons of oil equivalent (2006)

World total: 166.5 billion tons of oil equivalent

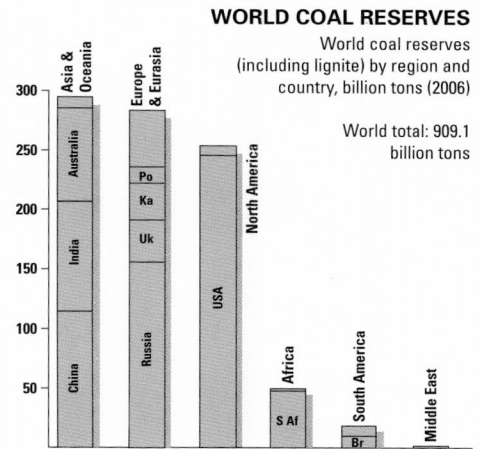

WORLD COAL RESERVES
World coal reserves (including lignite) by region and country, billion tons (2006)

World total: 909.1 billion tons

NUCLEAR POWER

Major producers by percentage of world total and by percentage of domestic electricity generation (2006)

Country	% of world total production	Country	% of nuclear as proportion of domestic electricity
1. USA	29.6%	1. France	78.7%
2. France	16.1%	2. Lithuania	64.2%
3. Japan	10.9%	3. Slovak Rep.	57.3%
4. Germany	6.0%	4. Belgium	54.7%
5. Russia	5.4%	5. Ukraine	48.4%
6. South Korea	5.3%	6. Switzerland	47.1%
7. Canada	3.4%	7. Bulgaria	43.4%
8. Ukraine	3.2%	8. Sweden	41.5%
9. UK	2.6%	9. Armenia	40.5%
10. Sweden	2.4%	10. South Korea	38.6%

Although the 1980s were a bad time for the nuclear power industry (fears of long-term environmental damage were heavily reinforced by the 1986 disaster at Chernobyl), the industry picked up in the early 1990s. Sixteen countries currently rely on nuclear power to supply over 25% of their total electricity requirements. There are over 400 operating nuclear power stations worldwide, with over 100 more planned or under construction.

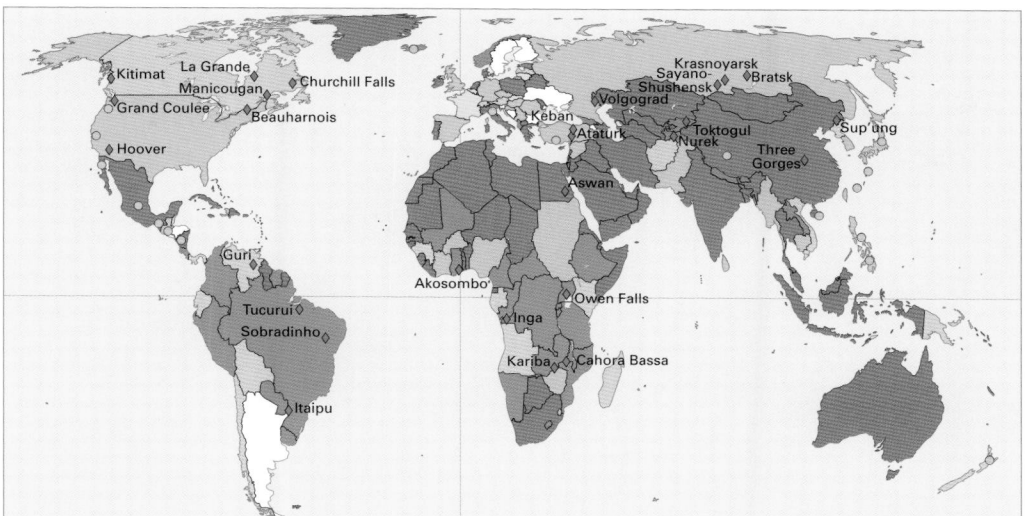

ELECTRICITY PRODUCTION

Percentage of electricity generated by source (2005)

- Over 75% from thermal
- 50 – 75% from thermal
- Over 75% from hydro
- 50 – 75% from hydro
- Over 50% from nuclear
- Other (no dominant source)
- No data available

○ Selected geothermal plants

◆ Selected hydroelectric plants

HYDROELECTRICITY

Major producers by percentage of world total and by percentage of domestic electricity generation (2006)

Country	% of world total production	Country	% of hydroelectric as proportion of domestic electricity
1. China	13.7%	1. Bhutan	100%
2. Canada	12.4%	= Paraguay	100%
3. Brazil	11.5%	= Lesotho	100%
4. USA	9.3%	4. Uganda	99.8%
5. Russia	6.0%	= Nepal	99.8%
6. Norway	4.6%	6. Congo (Rep. Dem.)	99.7%
7. India	3.4%	= Congo	99.7%
8. Japan	2.7%	= Mozambique	99.7%
9. Venezuela	2.6%	9. Zambia	99.4%
10. Sweden	2.5%	10. Norway	99.0%

Countries heavily reliant on hydroelectricity are usually small and non-industrial: a high proportion of hydroelectric power more often reflects a modest energy budget than vast hydroelectric resources. The USA, for instance, produces only 6.7% of its power requirements from hydroelectricity; yet that 6.7% amounts to almost half the hydropower generated by the whole of Africa.

ALTERNATIVE ENERGY RESOURCES

Solar: Each year the Sun bestows upon the Earth almost a million times as much energy as is locked up in all the planet's oil reserves, but only an insignificant fraction is trapped and used commercially. In a few installations around the world, mirrors focus the Sun's rays on to boilers, whose steam generates electricity by spinning turbines.

Wind: Caused by uneven heating of the Earth, winds are themselves a form of solar energy. Windmills have been long used for wind power; recent models, often arranged in banks on wind-swept high ground or off coastlines, usually generate electricity. Wind-power figures are given in the table (*right*). Although it currently produces less than 1% of the world's electricity, it contributes 19% of all electricity generated in Denmark.

Tidal: The energy from tides is potentially enormous, although only a few installations have so far been built to exploit it. In theory, at least, waves and currents could also provide almost unimaginable power, and the thermal differences in the ocean depths are another huge well

of potential energy. But work on extracting it is still at the experimental stage.

Geothermal: The Earth's temperature rises by 1°F for every 50 feet descent, with much steeper temperature gradients in geologically active areas. El Salvador, for example, produces 25% of its electricity from geothermal power stations, whilst the USA is the world's leading producer. Some of the oldest and most successful applications are in Iceland, where 86% of all households are heated by geothermal energy.

Biomass: The oldest of human fuels ranges from animal dung, still burned in cooking fires in much of North Africa and elsewhere, to sugarcane plantations feeding high-technology distilleries to produce ethanol for motor-vehicle engines. In Brazil and South Africa, plant ethanol provides up to 25% of motor fuel. Throughout the developing world, most biomass energy comes from firewood: although accurate figures are impossible to obtain, it may yield as much as 10% of the world's total energy consumption.

WIND POWER

World wind energy generating capacity, in megawatts

1980	10
1982	90
1984	600
1986	1,270
1988	1,580
1990	1,930
1992	2,510
1994	3,710
1996	6,115
1998	9,600
1999	11,700
2000	17,800
2001	23,300
2002	31,000
2003	39,300
2004	47,671
2005	58,982
2006	59,300
2007	74,300

For more information:
70 Geology
101 Patterns of production
103 World shipping

The use of metals played a vital part in the evolving technologies of early peoples. Copper first came into use around 10,000 years ago, bronze about 5,000 years ago, and iron 3,300 years ago. In the early stages of the Industrial Revolution, the location of coal, iron ore, and water power usually determined the location of new industries. But due to continuing improvements in transport, including oil pipelines, industries can now be located almost anywhere.

Minerals are distributed unevenly and some industrial countries, lacking their own mineral resources, import most of the raw materials they need. Some imports come from mineral-rich countries, such as Australia, but others come from developing countries, especially in Africa and South America. Most developing countries export unprocessed ores, losing out on the higher revenues gained from exporting metals.

Most minerals come from land deposits, because undersea deposits, with the exception of oil reserves under the continental shelves, have been inaccessible. But shortages of terrestrial minerals may one day encourage exploitation of the ocean floor.

▶ Bingham Canyon Mine in Utah, USA, is one of the largest open-pit mines in the world. It measures over 2.5 miles [4 km] wide and 3,900 ft [1,200 m] deep. Copper-containing rocks are excavated from the surface downward in terraces. These terraces are 50–80 ft [15–25 m] high and provide access for equipment to work the rock face whilst maintaining stability of the sloping pit walls.

Today's copper market is booming due to global demands from construction, telecommunications, and electronics companies. Over 17 million tons of copper have been mined from Bingham Canyon Mine to date.

URANIUM

Uranium was first discovered by the German chemist Martin Klaproth in 1789. In its pure state, uranium is an immensely heavy, white metal. Its main use is as a fuel in nuclear reactors and in nuclear weaponry, although depleted uranium is employed as a projectile in anti-missile cannons, where its mass ensures a lethal punch.

Uranium is very scarce: the main source is the rare ore pitchblende, which itself contains only 0.2% uranium oxide. This blackish, lustrous ore occurs in quartz veins. Only a minute fraction of that is the radioactive U^{235} isotope, though so-called breeder reactors can transmute the more common U^{238} into highly radioactive plutonium.

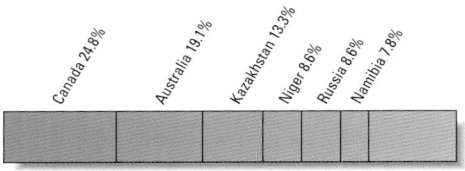

Canada 24.8% | Australia 19.1% | Kazakhstan 13.5% | Niger 8.6% | Russia 8.6% | Namibia 7.8%

World total (2006): 39,700 tons

DIAMOND

Most of the world's diamond is found in kimberlite, or "blue ground," a basic peridotite rock; erosion may wash the diamond from its kimberlite matrix and deposit it with sand or gravel on river beds. Only a small proportion of the world's diamond, the most flawless, is cut into gemstones – "diamonds"; most are used in industry, where the material's remarkable hardness and abrasion resistance finds a use in cutting tools, drills, and dies. The world's major producers are Australia (29.4%), Democratic Republic of the Congo (28.2%), Russia (17.6%), South Africa (10.6%) and Botswana (9.4%). Natural diamonds now account for less than 10% of all industrial diamond output. Synthetic diamond production in centers such as Ireland, Japan, Russia, and the USA far exceeds it.

METALS

Figures refer to ore production unless otherwise specified after the world total figure.

The world's leading producers of aluminum ore (bauxite) in 2006 were as follows:

1. Australia 34.7%
2. Brazil 11.9%
3. China 11.3%
4. Guinea 8.6%
5. Jamaica 8.4%
6. India 7.3%
7. Russia 4.1%
8. Venezuela 3.4%
9. Kazakhstan 2.8%
10. Suriname 2.7%

The figures shown above are in stark contrast to the figures showing aluminum production (*see above right*). Australia, for example, produces 34.7% of the world's bauxite but only 5.7% of aluminum. Guinea and Jamaica account for almost 17% of the bauxite mined but have no smelters and export virtually all of it to countries like the USA and Canada.

Aluminum: Produced mainly from its oxide, bauxite, which yields 25% of its weight in aluminum. The cost of refining and production is often too high for producer-countries to bear, so bauxite is largely exported. Lightweight and corrosion resistant, aluminum alloys are widely used in aircraft, vehicles, cans and packaging.

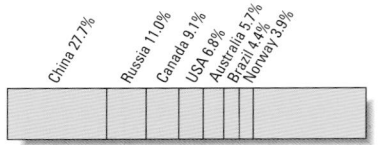

China 27.7% | Russia 11.0% | Canada 9.1% | USA 6.0% | Australia 5.7% | Brazil 4.4% | Norway 3.9%

World total (2006): 33,700,000 tons

Lead: A soft metal, obtained mainly from galena (lead sulfide), which occurs in veins associated with iron, zinc and silver sulfides. Its use in vehicle batteries accounts for the USA's prime consumer status; lead is also made into sheeting and piping. Its use as an additive to paints and petrol is decreasing.

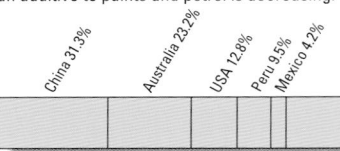

China 31.3% | Australia 23.2% | USA 12.8% | Peru 9.5% | Mexico 4.2%

World total (2006): 3,360,000 tons

Tin: Soft, pliable, and non-toxic, used to coat "tin" (tin-plated steel) cans, in the manufacture of foils and in alloys. The principal tin-bearing mineral is cassiterite (SnO_2), found in ore formed from molten rock. Producers and refiners were hit by a price collapse in 1991.

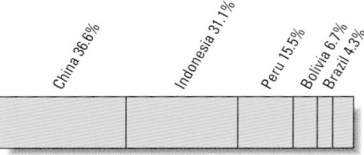

China 38.6% | Indonesia 31.1% | Peru 15.5% | Bolivia 6.7% | Brazil 4.3%

World total (2006): 273,000 tons

Gold: Regarded for centuries as the most valuable metal in the world and used to make coins, gold is still recognized as the monetary standard. A soft metal, it is alloyed to make jewelry; the electronics industry values its corrosion resistance and conductivity.

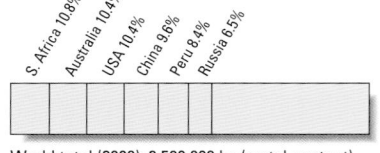

S. Africa 10.9% | Australia 10.4% | USA 10.4% | China 9.6% | Peru 8.4% | Russia 6.5%

World total (2006): 2,500,000 kg (metal content)

Copper: Derived from low-yielding sulfide ores, copper is an important export for several developing countries. An excellent conductor of heat and electricity, it forms part of most electrical items, and is used in the manufacture of brass and bronze. Major importers include Japan and Germany.

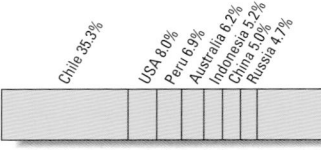

Chile 35.3% | USA 8.0% | Peru 6.9% | Australia 6.2% | Indonesia 5.2% | China 5.0% | Russia 4.7%

World total (2006): 15,300,000 tons

Mercury: The only metal that is liquid at normal temperatures, most is derived from its sulfide, cinnabar, found only in small quantities in volcanic areas. Apart from its value in thermometers and other instruments, most mercury production is used in anti-fungal and anti-fouling preparations, and to make detonators.

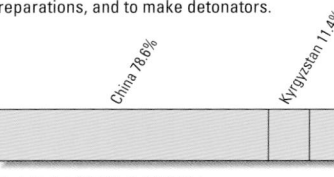

China 78.6% | Kyrgyzstan 11.4%

World total (2006): 1,400,000 kg

Zinc: Often found in association with lead ores, zinc is highly resistant to corrosion, and about 40% of the refined metal is used to plate sheet steel, particularly vehicle bodies – a process known as galvanizing. Zinc is also used in dry batteries, paints, and dyes.

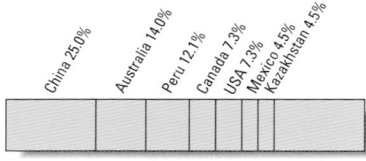

China 25.0% | Australia 14.0% | Peru 12.1% | Canada 7.3% | USA 7.3% | Mexico 5.5% | Kazakhstan 4.5%

World total (2006): 10,000,000 tons

Silver: Most silver comes from ores mined and processed for other metals (including lead and copper). Pure or alloyed with harder metals, it is used for jewelry and ornaments. Industrial use includes dentistry, electronics, photography, and as a chemical catalyst.

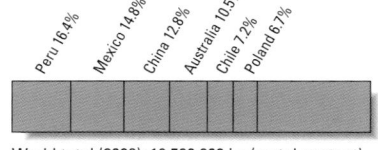

Peru 16.4% | Mexico 14.8% | China 12.8% | Australia 10.5% | Chile 7.2% | Poland 6.7%

World total (2006): 19,500,000 kg (metal content)

DISTRIBUTION OF MINERALS

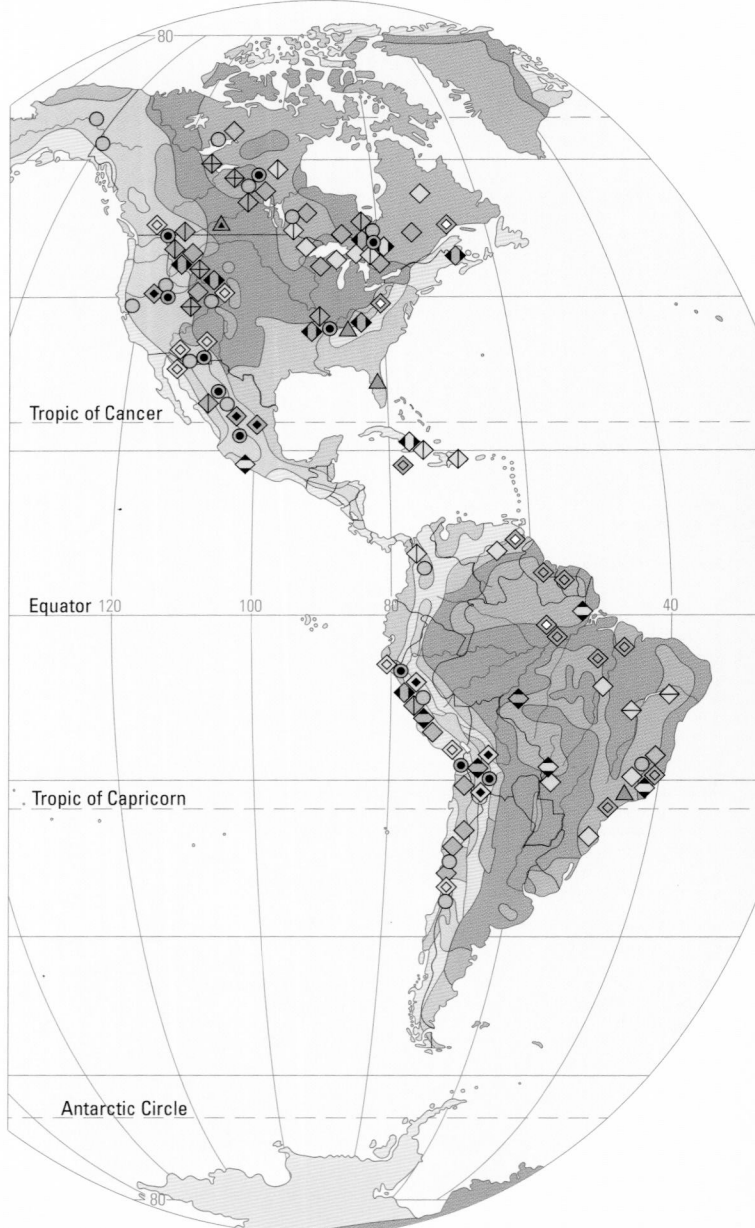

Tropic of Cancer

Equator

Tropic of Capricorn

Antarctic Circle

IRON ORE

Ever since the art of high-temperature smelting was discovered, some time in the second millennium BC, iron has been by far the most important metal known to man. The earliest iron plows transformed primitive agriculture and led to the first human population explosion, while iron weapons – or the lack of them – ensured the rise or fall of entire cultures.

Widely distributed around the world, iron ores usually contain 25–60% iron; blast furnaces process the raw product into pig-iron, which is then alloyed with carbon and other minerals to produce steels of various qualities. From the time of the Industrial Revolution, steel has been almost literally the backbone of modern civilization, the prime structural material on which all else is built.

Iron smelting usually developed close to the sources of ore and, later, to the coalfields that fueled the furnaces. Today, most ore comes from a few richly-endowed locations where large-scale mining is possible.

Iron and steel plants are generally built at coastal sites so that giant ore carriers, which account for a sizable proportion of the world's merchant fleet, can easily discharge their cargoes.

World production of pig-iron (2006)

**Total world production:
837 million tons**

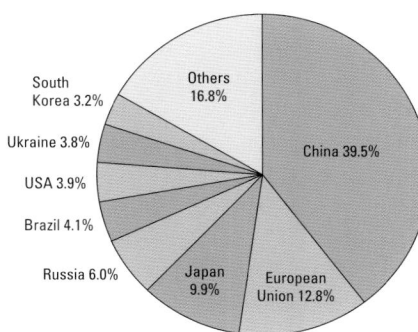

South Korea 3.2%
Others 16.8%
Ukraine 3.8%
China 39.5%
USA 3.9%
Brazil 4.1%
Russia 6.0%
Japan 9.9%
European Union 12.8%

Chromium: Most of the world's chromium production is alloyed with iron and other metals to produce steels with various different properties. Combined with iron, nickel, cobalt, and tungsten, chromium produces an exceptionally hard steel, resistant to heat; chrome steels are used for many household items where utility must be matched with appearance – cutlery, for example. Chromium is also used in the production of refractory bricks, and its salts for tanning and dyeing leather and cloth.

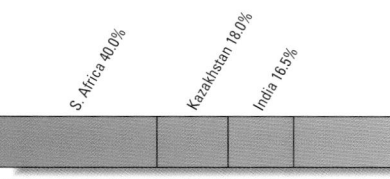

S. Africa 40.0%   Kazakhstan 18.0%   India 16.5%

World total (2006): 20,000,000 tons

Manganese: In its pure state, manganese is a hard, brittle metal. Alloyed with chromium, iron, and nickel, it produces abrasion-resistant steels; manganese-aluminum alloys are light but tough. Found in batteries and inks, manganese is also used in glass production. Manganese ores are frequently found in the same location as sedimentary iron ores. Pyrolusite (MnO_2) and psilomelane are the main economically-exploitable sources.

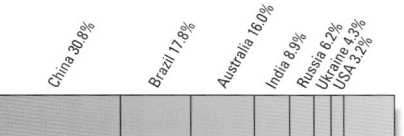

China 30.8%   Brazil 17.8%   Australia 16.0%   India 8.9%   Russia 6.2%   Ukraine 4.4%   USA 3.2%

World total production of iron ore (2006):
1,690,000,000 tons

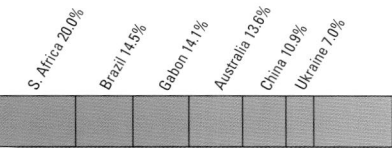

S. Africa 20.0%   Brazil 14.5%   Gabon 14.1%   Australia 13.6%   China 10.9%   Ukraine 7.0%

World total (2006): 11,000,000 tons

Nickel: Combined with chromium and iron, nickel produces stainless and high-strength steels; similar alloys go to make magnets and electrical heating elements. Nickel combined with copper is widely used to make coins; cupro-nickel alloy is very resistant to corrosion. Its ores yield only modest quantities of nickel – 0.5% to 3% – but also contain copper, iron, and small amounts of precious metals. Japan, USA, UK, Germany, and France are the principal importers.

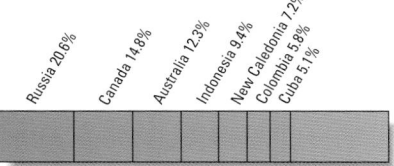

Russia 20.6%   Canada 14.8%   Australia 12.3%   Indonesia 9.4%   New Caledonia 7.2%   Colombia 5.8%   Cuba 5.1%

World total (2006): 1,550,000 tons (metal content)

SCRAP METAL

Scrap metal has been an important source material for the manufacturing industry in domestic markets for decades, its value fluctuating according to the state of the local economy. Recently, however, with growing concern for the global environment and the rapid development of the economies in the Far East, the industry has become far more globalized. Container loads of processed-metal scrap from time-expired machinery in the Western world are now being exported to the Far East to be recycled. Processed-steel scrap accounts for almost half of the requirements for "furnace feed" for the world's steelmakers, and 40% of the world's copper requirements are derived from scrap.

Two major advantages of using scrap rather than refining mined ore are the energy and raw material savings that can be made. If 1 ton of steel scrap is recycled, it saves 120 lb [54 kg] of limestone, 2,500 lb [1,130 kg] of iron ore, and 1,400 lb [635 kg] of coal, with a consequent 86% reduction in air pollution, 40% saving in water use, and 76% reduction in water pollution. Huge energy savings, with consequent cuts in greenhouse-gas emissions, can also be made by using scrap.

As well as bulk minerals, such as those quoted above, alloys using nickel, chromium, tungsten, molybdenum, cobalt, and titanium, which are often only available in limited supplies and are expensive to produce, can also be recycled. The techniques involved to do this work are often very sophisticated, involving X-ray spectrometry and other computer-controlled methods, in order to recover high-value but low-volume metals from devices such as computers and televisions.

With companies having to take increased responsibility for their products, from manufacturing to sale and thence to their ultimate disposal at the end of their useful life, recycling scrap metals will become a much more important method of conserving the world's raw materials and preserving the environment in the future.

STRUCTURAL REGIONS

- Pre-Cambrian shields
- Sedimentary cover on Pre-Cambrian shields
- Paleozoic (Caledonian and Hercynian) folding
- Sedimentary cover on Paleozoic folding
- Mesozoic folding
- Sedimentary cover on Mesozoic folding
- Cenozoic (Alpine) folding
- Sedimentary cover on Cenozoic folding
- Intensive Mesozoic and Cenozoic vulcanism

DISTRIBUTION
Iron and ferro-alloys

- Chromium
- Cobalt
- Iron ore
- Manganese
- Molybdenum
- Nickel ore
- Tungsten

Non-ferrous metals

- Bauxite   (Aluminum)
- Copper
- Lead
- Mercury
- Tin
- Zinc
- Uranium

Precious metals and stones

- Diamonds
- Gold
- Silver

Fertilizers

- Phosphates
- Potash

For more information:

82 Water distribution
94 Land use
98 Minerals
99 Iron and ferro-alloys
102 Major exports
      Traded products

The Industrial Revolution, which began in Britain in the late 18th century, represented a major technological advance in the evolution of human society. It enabled a group of countries to become prosperous by replacing expensive human labor with increasingly sophisticated machinery. In economic terms, manufacturing is the transformation of raw materials, energy, labor and machines into finished goods, which have a higher value than the various elements used in production.

The economies of countries can be compared by reference to their per capita Gross Domestic Products (GDPs), namely, the total value of goods and services produced within a country in a year, divided by the population. The industrialized, or developed, countries accounted for 16% of the world's population in 2007 with an average per capita GDP of more than US $32,000. On the other hand, low-income developing countries, with small industrial sectors, accounted for 37% of the world's population. Their per capita GDPs are less than $2,000, with some as low as $500.

Kenya, with its low-income economy, had a per capita GDP in 2007 of US $1,600. Agriculture employs 75% of the people, while industry together with services employs 25%. The main industries are the processing of agricultural imports and import substitution (making such necessities as cement, footwear, and textiles). Heavy industry plays only a small part. By contrast, Germany had a per capita GDP in 2007 of $34,400. Agriculture employs only 3% of the population, with 33% in industry and 64% in services. Germany's industrial sector differs greatly from Kenya's, with its emphasis on vehicles, machinery, chemicals, and electronics.

Since the 1970s, some former developing countries in eastern Asia achieved rapid economic growth through industrialization. Despite setbacks in the late 1990s, they demonstrated that a developing industrial sector can transform an economy, which starts off with certain advantages, such as low labor costs. But economic success also depends on such factors as education to provide skills, and regulations that attract foreign investors. China, whose economy grew by more than 9% per year between 2001 and 2005, satisfies many of these criteria, though its record on human rights leaves much to be desired.

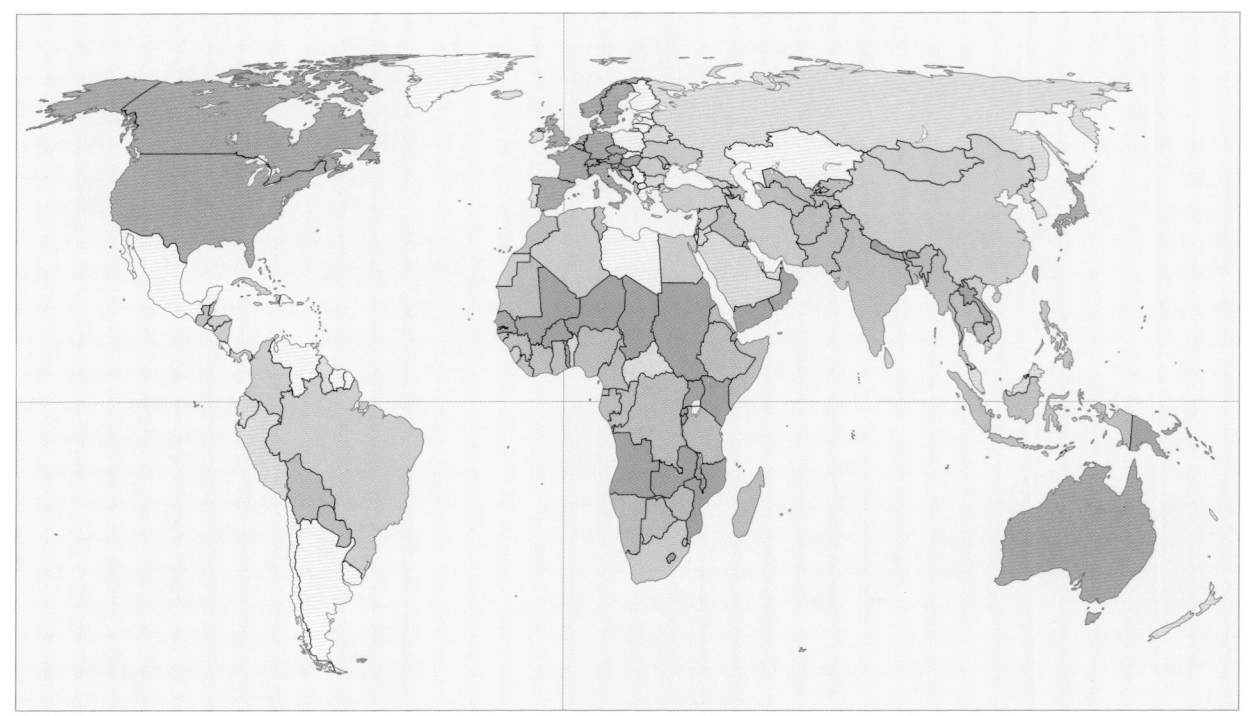

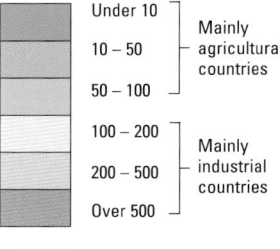

EMPLOYMENT

The number of workers employed in manufacturing for every 100 workers engaged in agriculture (2006)

Under 10	Mainly agricultural countries
10 – 50	
50 – 100	
100 – 200	Mainly industrial countries
200 – 500	
Over 500	
	No data available

Countries with the highest number of workers employed in manufacturing per 100 workers in agriculture (2006)

Bahrain	7,900
San Marino	4,200
USA	3,271
Liechtenstein	2,350
Brunei	2,107
Andorra	2,000
Belgium	1,884
Luxembourg	1,380
UK	1,300
Croatia	1,215

DIVISION OF EMPLOYMENT

Distribution of workers between agriculture, industry, and services, selected countries (2006)

The six countries selected illustrate the usual stages of economic development, from dependence on agriculture through industrial growth to the expansion of the service sector.

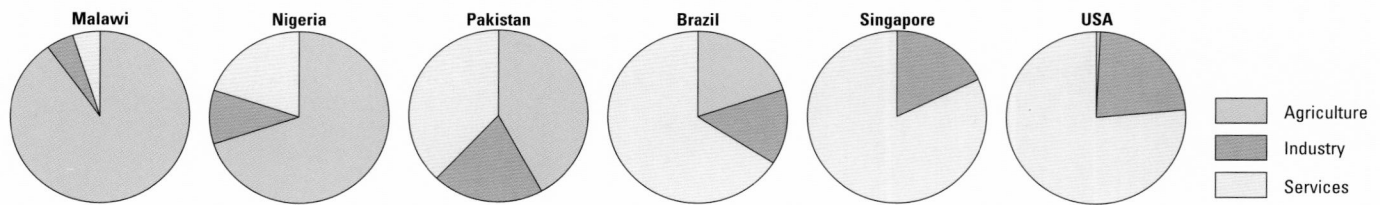

Malawi Nigeria Pakistan Brazil Singapore USA

Agriculture
Industry
Services

THE WORK FORCE

Percentages of men and women between 15 and 64 in employment (selected countries)

The figures include employees and the self-employed, who in developing countries are often subsistence farmers. People in full-time education are excluded. Because of the population age structure in developing countries, the employed population has to support a far larger number of non-workers than its industrial equivalent. For example, more than 52% of Kenya's people are under 15, an age group that makes up less than a tenth of the UK population.

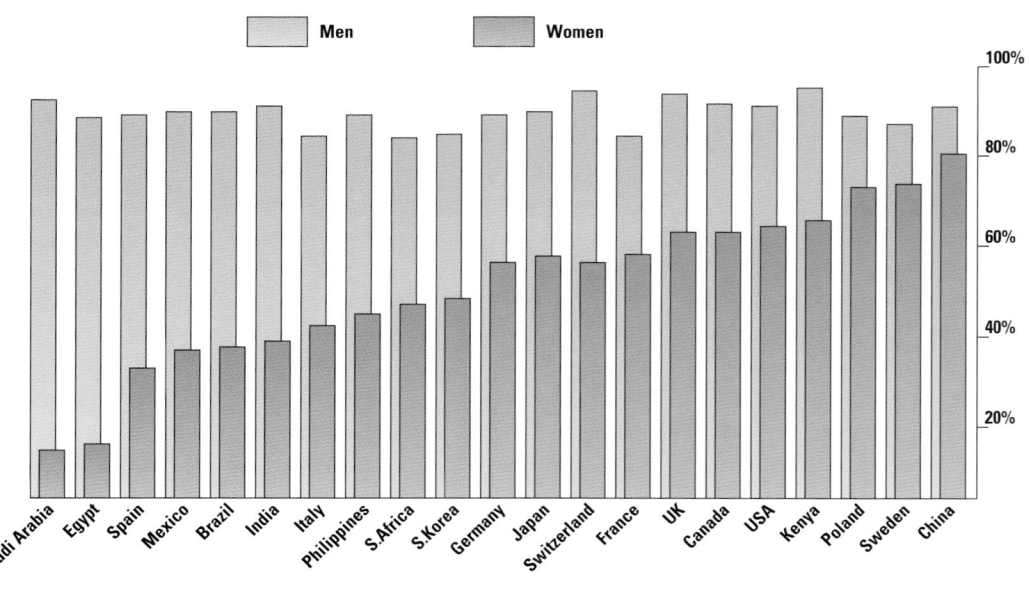

Men Women

Saudi Arabia, Egypt, Spain, Mexico, Brazil, India, Italy, Philippines, S.Africa, S.Korea, Germany, Japan, Switzerland, France, UK, Canada, USA, Kenya, Poland, Sweden, China

WEALTH CREATION

The Gross National Income (GNI) of the world's largest economies, US $ million (2006)

1.	USA	13,386,900	21.	Saudi Arabia	331,000
2.	Japan	4,934,700	22.	Austria	329,200
3.	Germany	3,032,600	23.	Norway	318,900
4.	China	2,621,000	24.	Indonesia	315,800
5.	UK	2,455,700	25.	Poland	313,000
6.	France	2,306,700	26.	Greece	305,300
7.	Italy	1,882,500	27.	Denmark	283,300
8.	Spain	1,206,200	28.	South Africa	255,400
9.	Canada	1,196,600	29.	Finland	217,800
10.	India	909,100	30.	Iran	205,000
11.	Brazil	892,600	31.	Argentina	201,300
12.	South Korea	856,600	32.	Hong Kong	199,100
13.	Russia	822,300	33.	Thailand	193,700
14.	Mexico	815,700	34.	Ireland	191,300
15.	Australia	742,300	35.	Portugal	189,000
16.	Netherlands	703,500	36.	Venezuela	164,000
17.	Switzerland	434,800	37.	Malaysia	146,800
18.	Belgium	405,400	38.	Israel	142,200
19.	Sweden	395,400	39.	Colombia	142,000
20.	Turkey	393,900	40.	Czech Rep	131,400

INDUSTRIAL OUTPUT

Largest industrial output (mining, manufacturing, construction, energy and water production), US $ billion (2004)

1.	USA	2,271	22. Austria	81
2.	Japan	1,308	23. Belgium	80
3.	China	893	24. Switzerland	76
4.	Germany	721	25. Thailand	70
5.	UK	496	26. Poland	69
6.	Italy	417	27. Iran	67
7.	France	399	28. South Africa	61
8.	Canada	285	29. Malaysia	60
9.	Spain	274	30. UAE	57
10.	South Korea	247	31. Ireland	56
11.	Brazil	211	= Turkey	56
12.	Russia	182	33. Denmark	51
13.	India	171	34. Finland	50
14.	Mexico	162	= Argentina	50
15.	Saudi Arabia	147	36. Algeria	44
16.	Netherlands	132	37. Greece	42
17.	Australia	124	38. Venezuela	41
18.	Indonesia	113	39. Nigeria	40
19.	Taiwan	90	40. Portugal	39
20.	Sweden	87	41. Chile	38
=	Norway	87	42. Czech Rep.	37

INDUSTRY AND TRADE

Manufactured goods (including machinery and transport) as a percentage of total exports (2006)

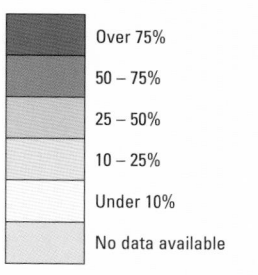

Over 75%
50 – 75%
25 – 50%
10 – 25%
Under 10%
No data available

Countries most dependent on the export of manufactured goods

Israel	94%
Japan	93%
Switzerland	93%
South Korea	92%
China	92%
Bangladesh	90%

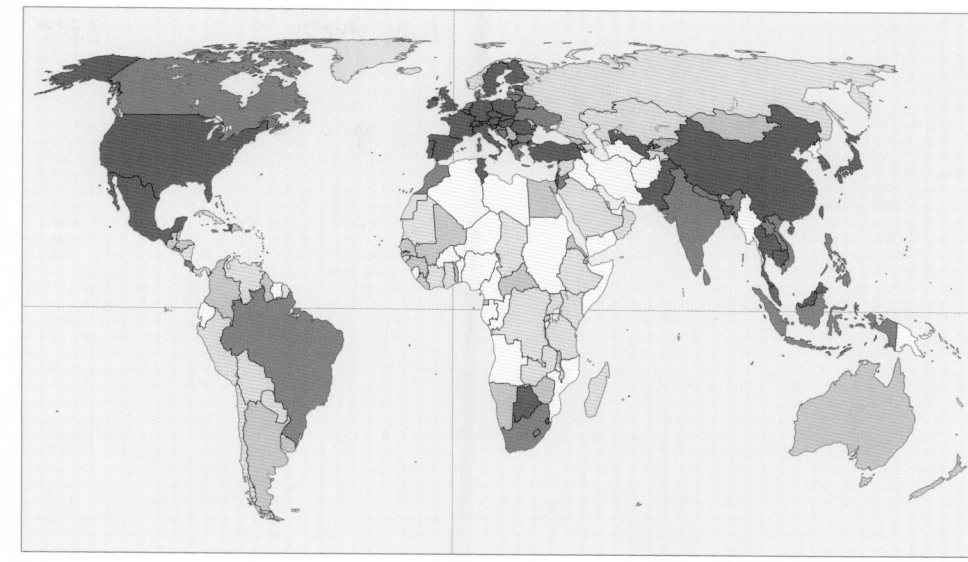

UNEMPLOYMENT

Highest rates of unemployment, percentage of the labor force (2004)

1.	Macedonia	37.2%
2.	Namibia	33.8%
3.	South Africa	27.1%
4.	West Bank and Gaza	26.7%
5.	Guadeloupe	24.7%
6.	Ethiopia	22.9%
7.	Martinique	22.4%
8.	Botswana	19.4%
9.	Poland	19.0%
10.	Dominican Republic	18.4%
11.	Slovakia	18.1%
12.	Algeria	17.7%
13.	Uruguay	16.9%
14.	Venezuela	15.8%
15.	Argentina	15.6%
16.	Albania	15.2%
=	Serbia & Montenegro	15.2%
18.	Tunisia	14.3%
19.	Burundi	14.0%
=	Suriname	14.0%

◄ This photograph shows a cement-manufacturing plant in Vác, Hungary. Cement production figures are often an indicator of the relative prosperity of a country, since they show the construction of roads, dams, and other infrastructure projects (*see the graph below*). However, cement manufacture emits high levels of carbon dioxide into the atmosphere.

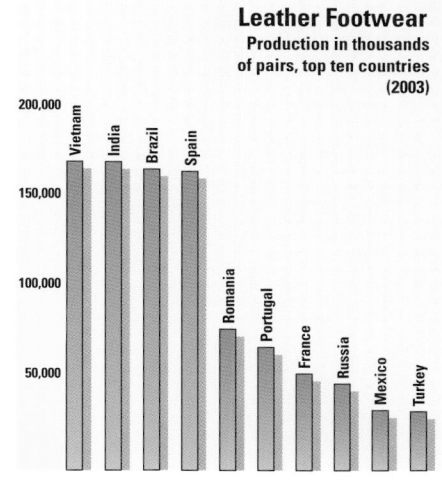

Leather Footwear
Production in thousands of pairs, top ten countries (2003)

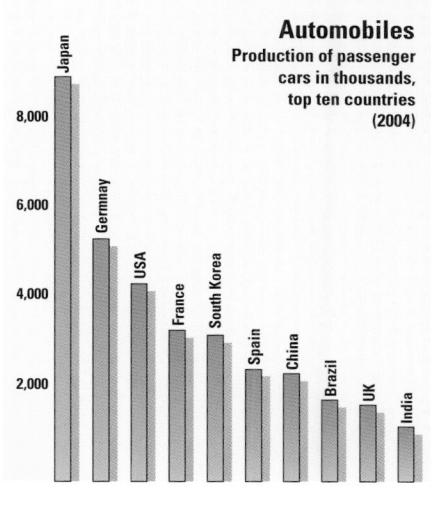

Automobiles
Production of passenger cars in thousands, top ten countries (2004)

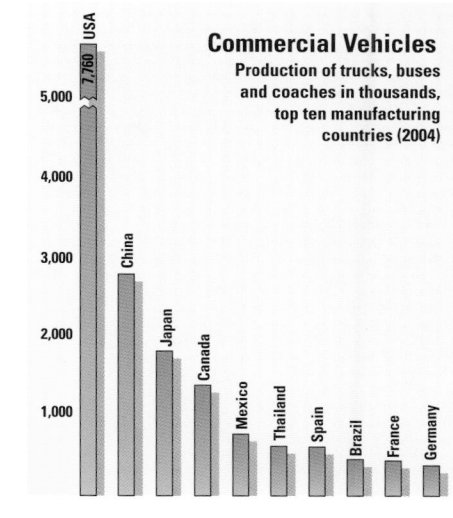

Commercial Vehicles
Production of trucks, buses and coaches in thousands, top ten manufacturing countries (2004)

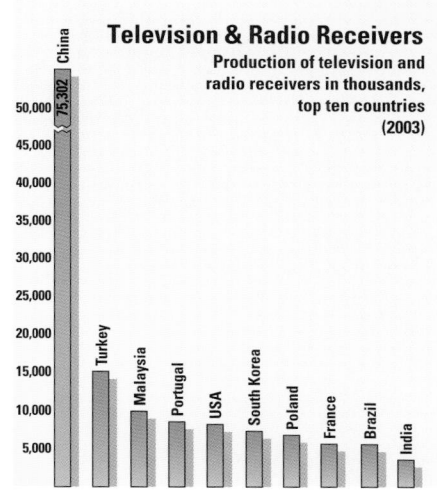

Television & Radio Receivers
Production of television and radio receivers in thousands, top ten countries (2003)

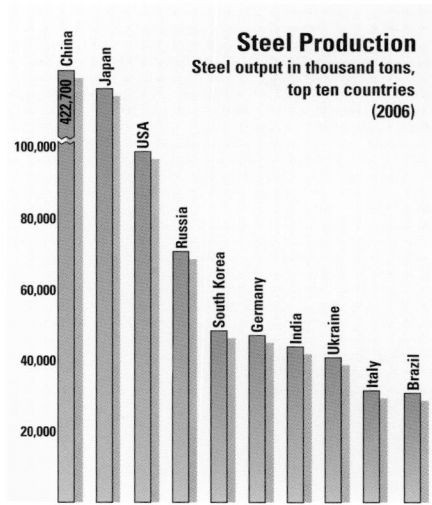

Steel Production
Steel output in thousand tons, top ten countries (2006)

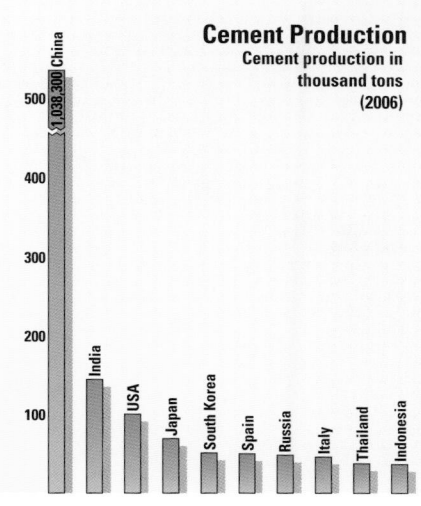

Cement Production
Cement production in thousand tons (2006)

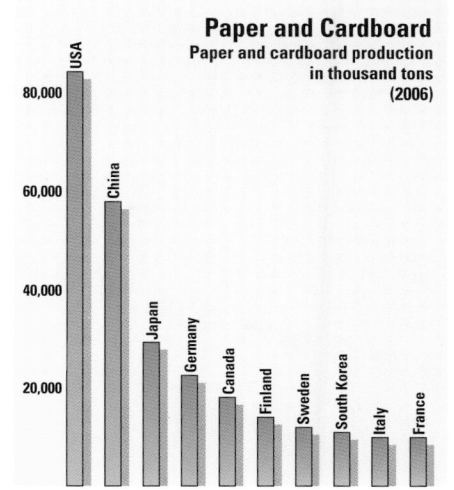

Paper and Cardboard
Paper and cardboard production in thousand tons (2006)

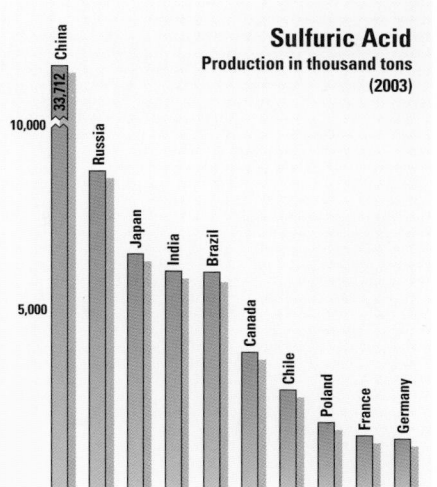

Sulfuric Acid
Production in thousand tons (2003)

For more information:

93 International organizations
97 Movements of oil
98 Minerals
100 Wealth creation
101 Industry and trade
107 Air travel and tourism
    Inflation

Trade played a vital role in the growth of early civilizations and it was later a spur to European exploration and colonization. The colonial powers grew rich by exporting cheap manufactures, such as clothing and footwear, while obtaining primary products from their colonies.

From the late 19th century to the early 1950s, as transport technology improved, primary products, especially oil in the later stages of this period, dominated world

trade. However, since that time, manufactures have become the chief commodities in world trade, which is dominated by the industrialized countries. Nearly half of all world trade flows between the developed market economies of the European Union, the United States, and Japan, although a number of Asian economies, notably China, Malaysia, Singapore, South Korea, Taiwan, and Thailand, increased their share since the 1990s.

China's remarkable growth means that it has rapidly overtaken countries such as Japan, Mexico, and Germany, to become the second biggest exporter to the United States. China's low production costs, especially its cheap labor, were estimated to be one-twentieth of those of Japan, making its high-quality exports highly competitive in price. Growth in world trade is regarded as a sign of economic health, as is a favorable balance of trade (or trade surplus) in any country.

WORLD TRADE

Percentage share of total world exports by value (2007)

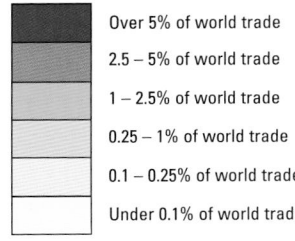

- Over 5% of world trade
- 2.5 – 5% of world trade
- 1 – 2.5% of world trade
- 0.25 – 1% of world trade
- 0.1 – 0.25% of world trade
- Under 0.1% of world trade

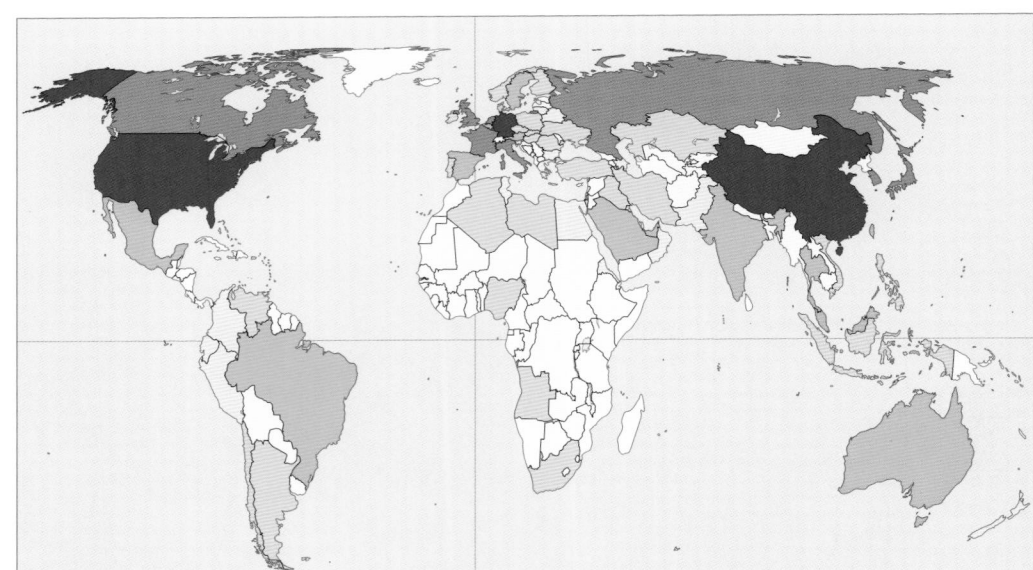

International trade is dominated by a handful of powerful maritime nations. The members of "G8" (Canada, France, Germany, Italy, Japan, Russia, the United Kingdom, and the United States) account for more than one third of the total. The majority of nations contribute less than a quarter of 1% to the worldwide total of exports.

DEPENDENCE ON TRADE

Exports as a percentage of GDP (2007)

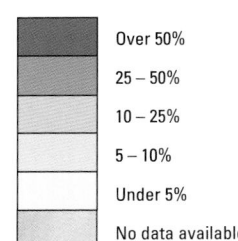

- Over 50%
- 25 – 50%
- 10 – 25%
- 5 – 10%
- Under 5%
- No data available

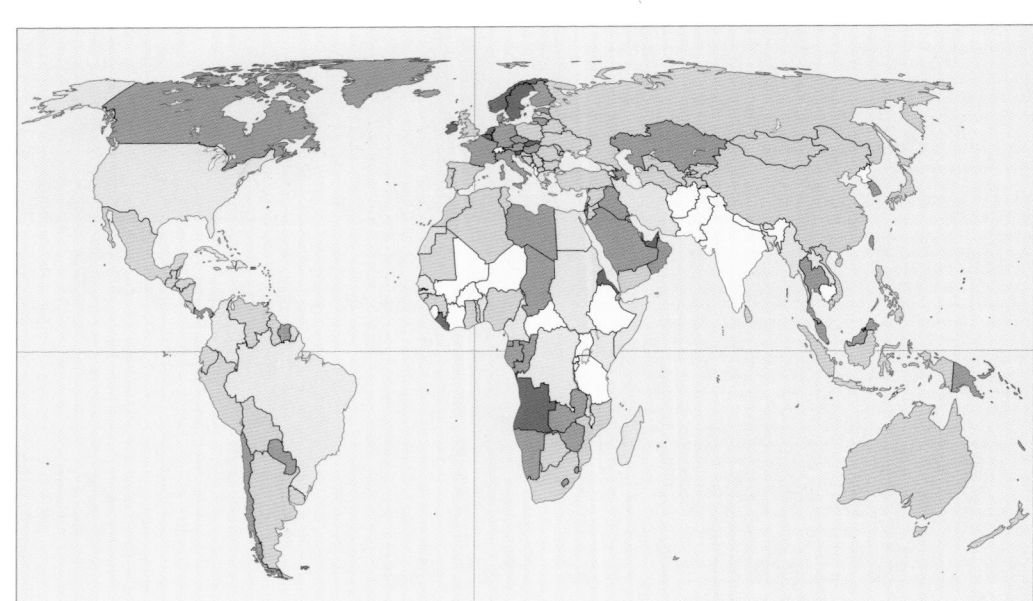

The character of world trade has changed a great deal in the last 50 years or so. While many developing countries still remain heavily dependent on exporting mineral ores, fossil fuels or farm products, such as coffee or cocoa, world trade is now dominated by manufactured goods. Since the 1980s, high-tech products, such as computer equipment, telecommunications gear, and transistors, have become increasingly important.

TRADED PRODUCTS

World merchandise exports by product, percentage of total value (2007)

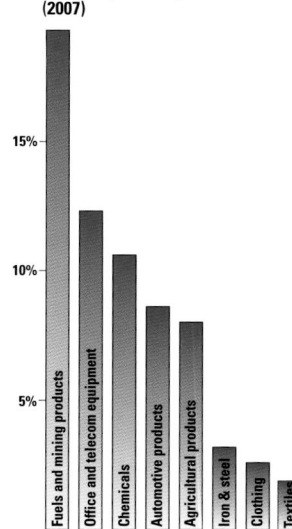

MAJOR EXPORTS

Leading manufactured items and their exporters (2007)

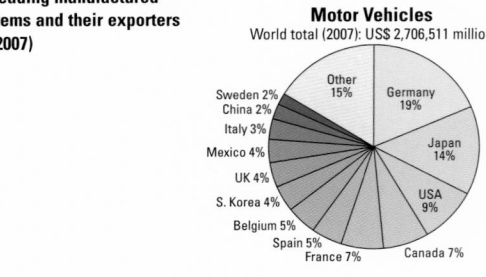

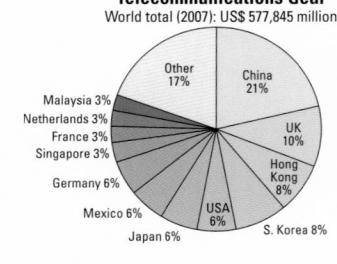

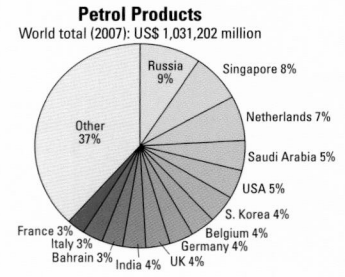

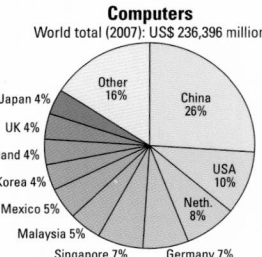

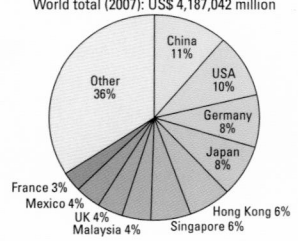

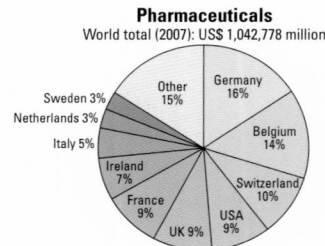

WORLD SHIPPING

While ocean passenger traffic is relatively modest nowadays, sea transport still carries most of the world's trade. Oil and bulk carriers make up the majority of the world fleet, although the general cargo category is the fastest growing. Two innovations have revolutionized sea transport. The first is the development of the roll-on/roll-off (Ro-Ro) method where trucks or even trains loaded with freight are driven straight on to the ship, thus saving time. The second is containerization in which goods are packed into containers (the dimensions of which are fixed) at the factory, driven to the port, and loaded on board by specialist machinery.

Almost 30% of world shipping today sails under a "flag of convenience," whereby owners take advantage of low taxes by registering their vessels in a foreign country the ships will never see, notably Panama and Liberia.

MERCHANT FLEETS

Merchant fleets in thousand gross registered tonnage (2006). Although a large number of vessels are registered in Liberia and Panama, they are not part of the national fleet

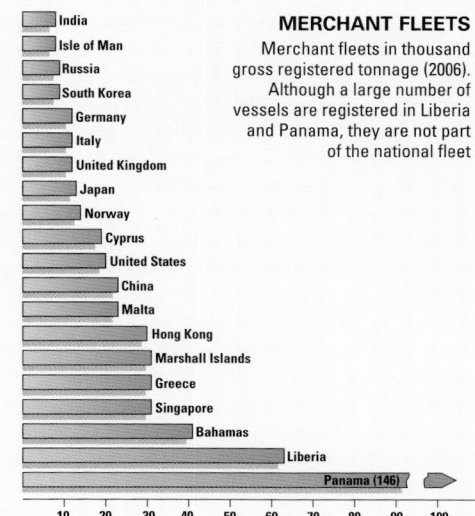

TYPES OF VESSELS

World merchant fleet by type of vessel and deadweight tonnage (2006)

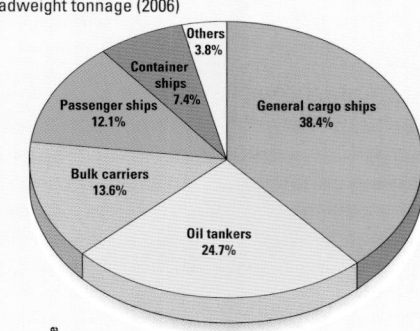

- Others 3.8%
- Container ships 7.4%
- Passenger ships 12.1%
- General cargo ships 38.4%
- Bulk carriers 13.6%
- Oil tankers 24.7%

TOP TEN PORTS

Total container traffic, in million TEU (2006)

("TEU" stands for Twenty-foot Equivalent Unit, the equivalent of a standard container)

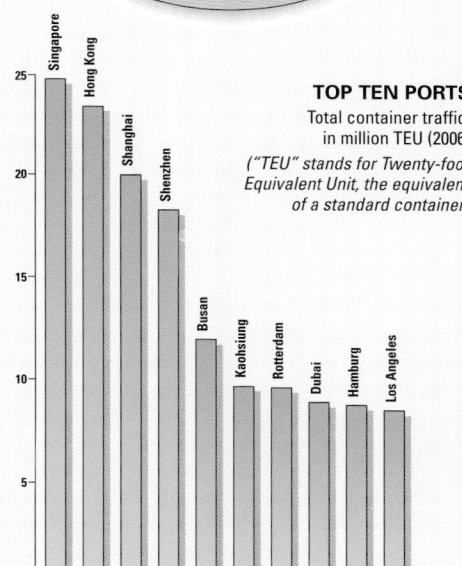

▲ A container ship being unloaded in the port of Melbourne, Australia. World trade depends on transport. Containerization, introduced in the 1950s, reduced the risk of damage to cargo and cut the time and cost of loading and unloading.

TRADE IN PRIMARY EXPORTS

Primary exports as a percentage of total export value (2005)

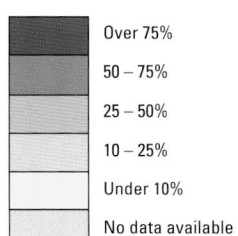

- Over 75%
- 50 – 75%
- 25 – 50%
- 10 – 25%
- Under 10%
- No data available

Primary exports are raw materials or partly processed products that form the basis for manufacturing. They are the necessary requirements of industries and include agricultural products, minerals, fuels, and timber, as well as many semimanufactured goods such as cotton, which has been spun but not woven, wood pulp or flour. Many developed countries have few natural resources and rely on imports for the majority of their primary products. The countries of Southeast Asia export hardwoods to the rest of the world, while many South American countries are heavily dependent on coffee exports.

BALANCE OF TRADE

Value of exports in proportion to the value of imports (2007)

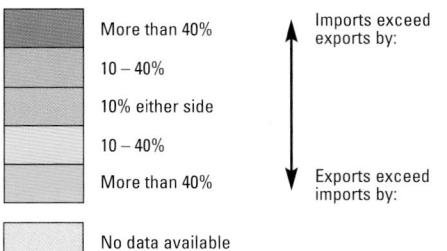

- More than 40% — Imports exceed exports by:
- 10 – 40%
- 10% either side
- 10 – 40%
- More than 40% — Exports exceed imports by:
- No data available

The total world trade balance should amount to zero, since exports must equal imports on a global scale. In practice, though, at least US $100 billion in exports go unrecorded, leaving the world with an apparent deficit and many countries in a better position than public accounting reveals. However, a favorable trade balance is not necessarily a sign of prosperity: many poorer countries must maintain a high surplus in order to service debts, and do so by restricting imports below the levels needed to sustain successful economies.

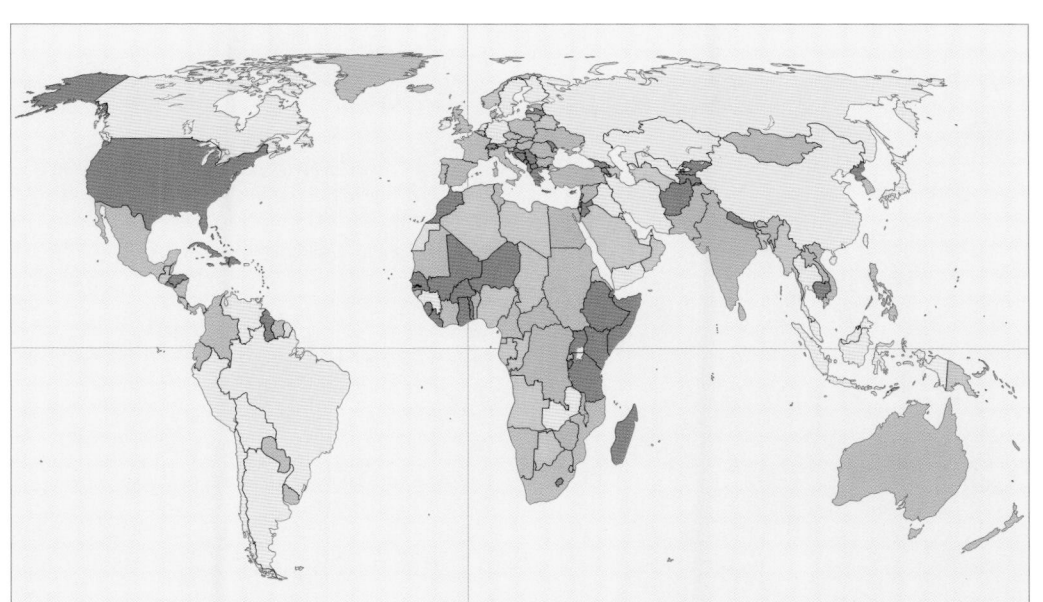

For more information:
82 Water distribution
89 Urban pollution
   Urban advantages
95 Crisis in Africa
   Food and
   population
109 Distribution of
   spending

Until the late 1990s, when the full extent of the AIDS crisis emerged, average life expectancies at birth were rising almost everywhere. By 2005, they ranged from 78 years in high-income economies to 46 in sub-Saharan Africa. These figures represented an enormous advance on the situation in 1880, when citizens of Berlin had an estimated life expectancy of 30 years.

The ravages of AIDS have been greatest in southern Africa. One of the worst affected countries is Swaziland, where over 33% of the adult population were thought to be infected in 2006. Life expectancies have fallen to 31 years in 2007, instead of an original estimate of 57 years and 16,000 people died in 2006. However, in much of the world, average life expectancies are still increasing. The rises are attributed to improvements in agriculture and, hence, nutrition, as well as health education, improved sanitation and the quality of drinking water, together with advances in medicine.

Besides AIDS, the people of the developing world are subject to another affliction – malnutrition. The map below shows that in most of Africa, Asia, and Latin America, the average daily calorie supply per person is so low as to cause malnutrition. Malnutrition is a serious condition – among pregnant women it causes high rates of child mortality.

Deficiency diseases occur when people do not have a balanced diet. Protein deficiency causes stunting and kwashiorkor, which can be fatal, especially among young children, while vitamin deficiencies cause such illnesses as beri beri, pellagra, scurvy, and rickets. Iron deficiency causes anemia, while a lack of iodine causes mental retardation.

Infectious diseases, in association with deficient diets, continue to affect people in developing countries. Around the turn of the century, a WHO report stated that infectious diseases cause over 16 million deaths a year. Most of the victims are young and otherwise fit people in developing countries. The major killers are AIDS, cholera, dysentery, malaria, measles, pneumonia, respiratory infections, tuberculosis, and typhoid.

Infectious diseases are much less important as causes of death in developed countries, where cancer and circulatory diseases, such as atherosclerosis and hypertension, which cause strokes and heart attacks, are the most common causes of fatality. Because these diseases tend to kill older people, they are relatively less important in the developing countries where people have shorter lifespans.

Harmful habits are also generally practiced more by the rich than the poor. For example, smoking is an important cause of death in developed countries, while poor diet and high alcohol consumption can badly affect health.

▲ Almost 25% of the world's population does not have access to safe water (the diagram at the bottom left-hand corner of this page shows how this breaks down by continent). This places a huge strain on the millions of mainly women and children who have to walk, collect, and carry drinkable water in order to survive. UNICEF is dedicated to help improve this situation and to react swiftly in the case of emergencies such as civil war, as with the case of this man in Liberia.

FOOD CONSUMPTION

Average daily food intake in calories per person (2003)

- Over 3,500 calories
- 3,000 – 3,500 calories
- 2,500 – 3,000 calories
- 2,000 – 2,500 calories
- Under 2,000 calories
- No data available

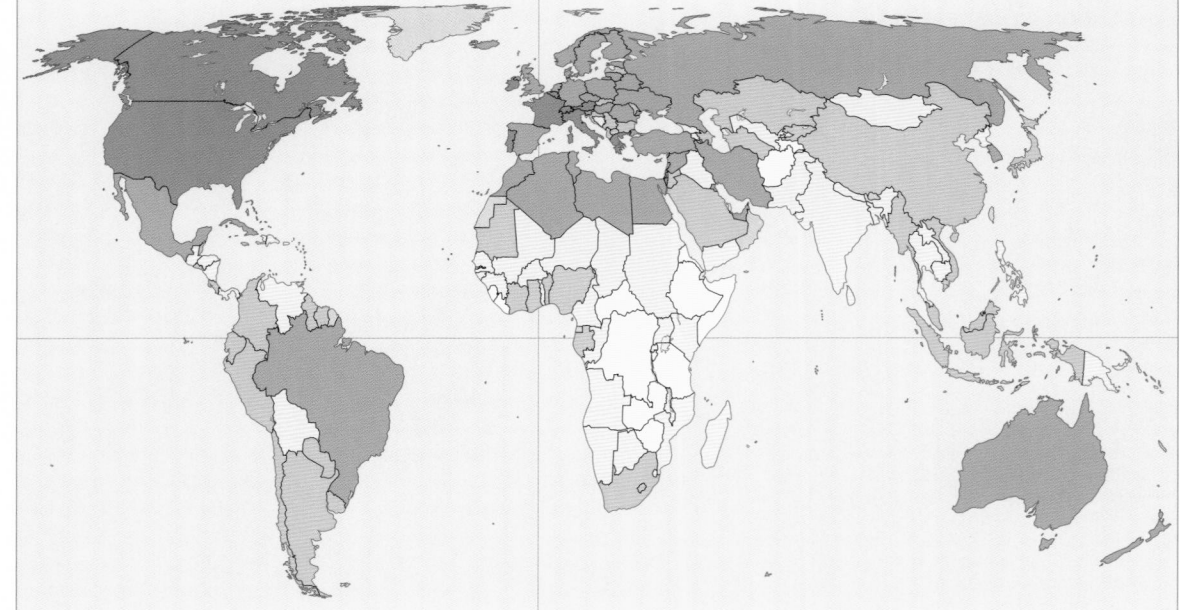

The daily food intake rated adequate by the World Health Organization is between 2,300 and 2,500 calories per day. Approximately 6 million children under the age of 5 years die of starvation each year, the vast majority in Africa. In 2006, the FAO estimated that 854 million people were undernourished, contrasting sharply with the overconsumption of food in some Western cultures.

ACCESS TO SAFE WATER

- Urban
- Rural

Proportion of urban and rural population with access to safe water, by region (2004)

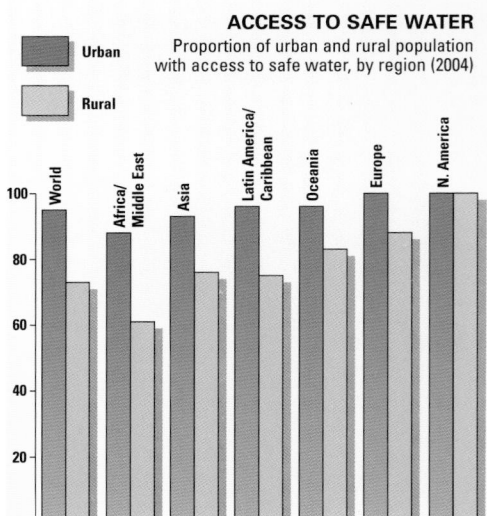

TOBACCO

1.3 billion people smoke worldwide (1 billion men and 0.3 billion women). According to the World Health Organization, tobacco claims 4.9 million lives each year. At the end of 2007, 29 countries had introduced smoking bans in public places.

Percentage of the population who smoke

	Men	Women
Africa	29%	4%
North America	35%	22%
Eastern Mediterranean	35%	4%
Europe	46%	26%
Southeast Asia	44%	4%
Western Pacific	60%	8%

Countries with the highest annual consumption of cigarettes per person

1. Greece	4,313	5. South Korea	2,918
2. Hungary	3,265	6. Slovenia	2,917
3. Kuwait	3,062	7. Spain	2,779
4. Japan	3,023	8. Switzerland	2,720

ALCOHOL

The average Western European and North American drinks over a third more alcohol than the average person living in any other region. Globally, alcohol consumption has increased in recent decades, with all of that increase being found in developing countries. Alcohol consumption has health and social consequences and is responsible for 1.8 millions deaths per year.

Liters of alcohol consumed per person per year

	1980	1990	2000	2007
Developed countries	11.1	9.5	8.9	8.7
Developing countries	2.0	2.4	2.9	3.1

Countries with the highest annual consumption of alcohol per person (liters)

1. Luxembourg	15.6	6. Croatia	12.3
2. Ireland	13.7	7. Germany	12.0
3. Hungary	13.6	8. UK	11.8
4. Moldova	13.2	9. Denmark	11.7
5. Czech Republic	13.0	= Spain	11.7

INFANT MORTALITY

Number of babies who died under the age of one, per 1,000 live births (2007)

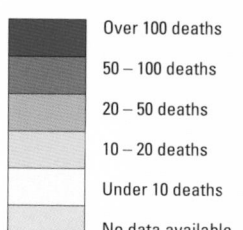

Over 100 deaths
50 – 100 deaths
20 – 50 deaths
10 – 20 deaths
Under 10 deaths
No data available

Highest infant mortality
Angola ....185 deaths
Sierra Leone ....158 deaths
Afghanistan ....157 deaths

Lowest infant mortality
Singapore .... 2 deaths
Sweden .... 3 deaths
Japan .... 3 deaths

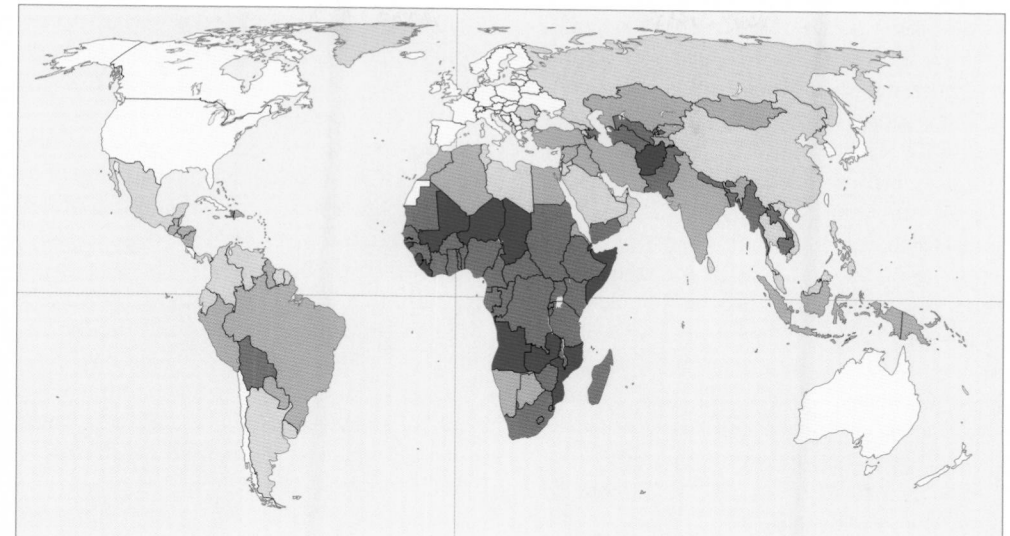

THE AIDS CRISIS

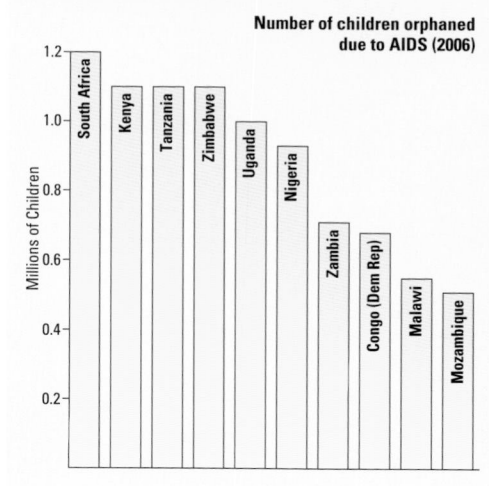

Number of children orphaned due to AIDS (2006)

(bar chart, Millions of Children: South Africa, Kenya, Tanzania, Zimbabwe, Uganda, Nigeria, Zambia, Congo (Dem Rep), Malawi, Mozambique)

Percentage of the population infected with HIV/AIDS (2006)

Over 10 %
5 – 10 %
2.5 – 5 %
1 – 2.5 %
0 – 1 %
No data available

Countries with the highest total number of adults and children living with HIV/AIDS
India 5,700,000
South Africa 5,500,000
Nigeria 2,900,000
Mozambique 1,800,000
Zimbabwe 1,700,000
Ethiopia 1,500,000
Tanzania 1,400,000

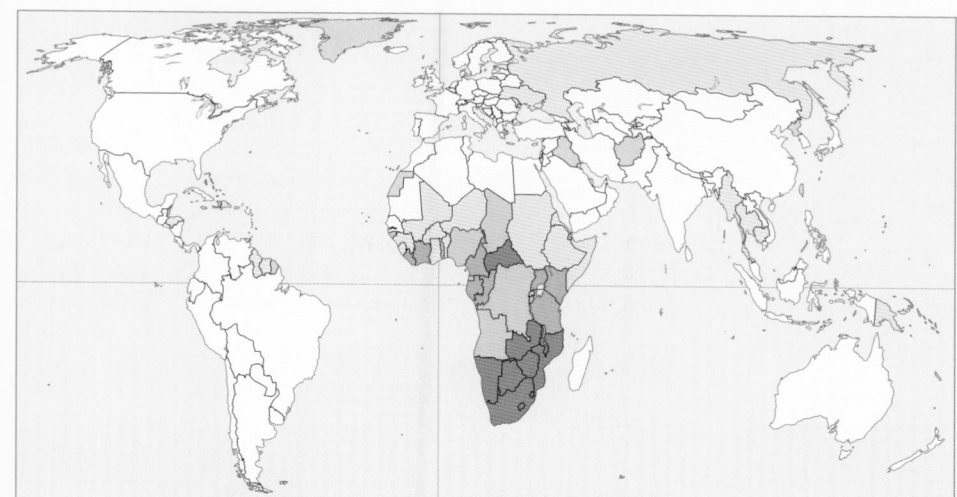

EXPENDITURE ON HEALTH

Public health expenditure per capita, in US $ (2004)

Countries with the highest spending		Countries with the lowest spending	
USA	$6,096	Congo (Dem. Rep.)	$15
Luxembourg	$5,178	Burundi	$16
Norway	$4,080	Ethiopia	$21
Switzerland	$4,011	Comoros	$25
Austria	$3,418	Niger	$26
Iceland	$3,294	Eritrea	$27
Canada	$3,173	Guinea-Bissau	$28
Germany	$3,171	Madagascar	$29
Belgium	$3,133	Tanzania	$29
Australia	$3,123	Congo	$30

The allocation of limited funds for health care in developing countries is rarely evenly spread – for example, the quality of treatment can vary enormously from place to place within the same country. Urban dwellers tend to have much better access to health provisions than those living in rural areas.

CAUSES OF DEATH

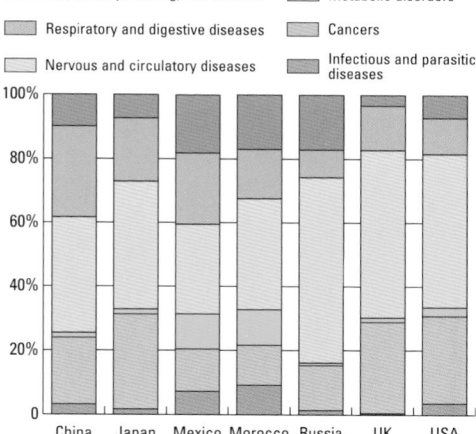

Accidents, poisoning, and violence
Respiratory and digestive diseases
Nervous and circulatory diseases
Metabolic disorders
Cancers
Infectious and parasitic diseases

(stacked bar chart: China, Japan, Mexico, Morocco, Russia, UK, USA)

MEDICAL PROVISION

Doctors per 100,000 population, selected countries (2006)

Although the ratio of people to doctors gives a good approximation of a country's health provision, it is not an absolute indicator. Raw numbers may mask inefficiency and other weaknesses. The definition of a doctor also varies from nation to nation.

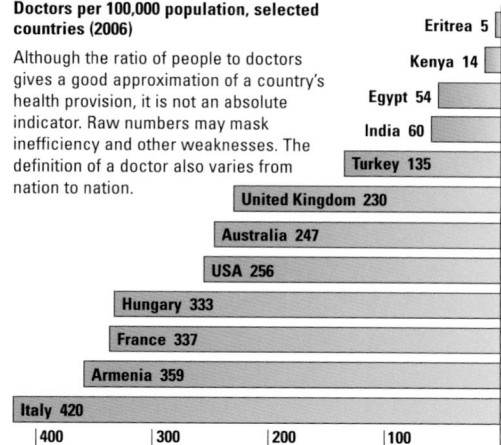

Eritrea 5
Kenya 14
Egypt 54
India 60
Turkey 135
United Kingdom 230
Australia 247
USA 256
Hungary 333
France 337
Armenia 359
Italy 420

(scale: 400 300 200 100)

OBESITY IN EUROPE

The percentage of adults who are obese (2005)

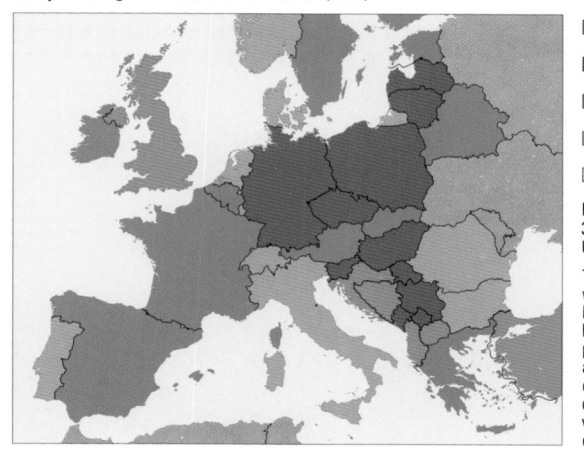

Over 20%
15 – 20%
10 – 15%
Under 10%
No data available

By comparison, over 32% of people in the USA are obese.

The global epidemic of overweight and obesity is rapidly becoming a major public health problem in many parts of the world. It is associated with diet-related chronic diseases such as diabetes, strokes, cardio-vascular disease, and certain cancers.

SANITATION

Percentage of population with access to sanitation services, selected countries (2004)

Urban
Rural

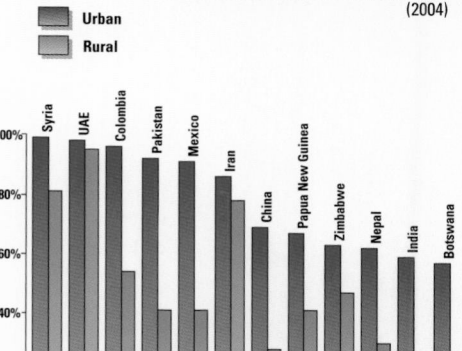

(bar chart: Syria, UAE, Colombia, Pakistan, Mexico, Iran, China, Papua New Guinea, Zimbabwe, Nepal, India, Botswana)

MALARIA

Cases of malaria per 100,000 people exposed to malaria-infected environments (2003)

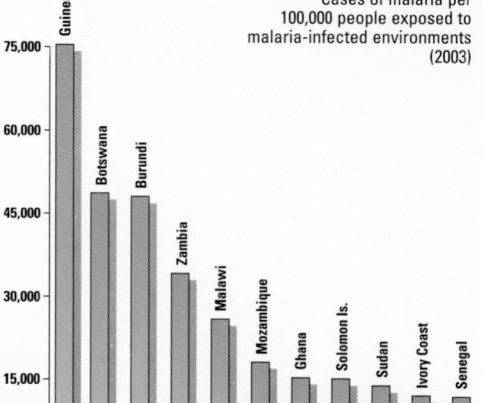

(bar chart: Guinea, Botswana, Burundi, Zambia, Malawi, Mozambique, Ghana, Solomon Is., Sudan, Ivory Coast, Senegal)

For more information:
100 Wealth creation
101 Industrial output
102 World trade
    Major exports
103 Balance of trade
109 Distribution of spending

Perhaps the most glaring differences in the world today are those between the rich and the poor. The World Bank divides countries into three main groups based on average economic production expressed in terms of per capita GNI (Gross National Income). They are the low-income economies (most African countries and much of Asia), the middle-income economies (most of Latin America and most of the former USSR), and the high-income economies of Canada, the United States, Western Europe, Japan, and Australia.

Per capita GNIs are a measure of the total goods and services produced by a country divided by the population, and then converted into US dollars at official exchange rates. They are useful indicators of a country's prosperity, though, like all statistics, they must be treated with care. For example, the prices for goods and services in China are far cheaper than they are in the United States. China's per capita GNI in 2006 was $2,000 (as compared with $44,710 in the US), but the PPP (Purchasing Power Parity – which adjusts the figure for cost-of-living differences) estimate of China's per capita GNI was considerably higher at $4,660. Another problem with per capita GNIs is that they are averages, which often conceal wide internal variations.

The pattern of poverty varies from region to region. In Latin America, much progress has been made through industrialization, though startling inequalities still exist between rich and poor. China and other countries in eastern Asia, including South Korea and Taiwan, have followed Japan's example in pursuing export-led industrial policies. The success of China's Special Economic Zones, where foreign investment is encouraged, has led to a huge rise in China's per capita GNI.

In contrast to the dynamism of Asia, Africa lags behind as an impoverished continent. Corrupt governments, wasteful expenditures, civil wars, natural disasters, faulty national and international policy environments, high population growth, and the failure to break away from the neo-colonial trading patterns – all these contribute to keeping the majority of Africans impoverished. An initiative in some African countries has been to improve the infrastructure and develop tourism, creating employment and providing much-needed foreign currency. But the social and environmental cost of mass tourism needs to be taken seriously too.

The International Monetary Fund and the World Bank argue that real economic progress in Africa will be achieved only when African countries create market-friendly economies that encourage trade through export-led manufacturing, while at the same time strictly controlling public spending.

CONTINENTAL SHARES

Shares of population and of wealth (GNI) by continent

These generalized continental figures show the startling difference between rich and poor, but mask the successes or failures of individual countries. Japan, for example, with less than 4% of Asia's population, produces almost 40% of the continent's output. Within countries, the difference between rich and poor can also be startling. In Brazil, for example, the richest 20% of the population own 60% of the wealth.

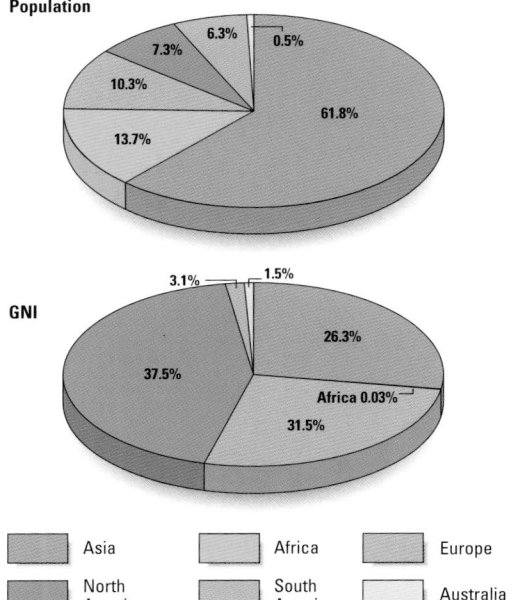

Population

GNI

Asia | Africa | Europe
North America | South America | Australia

LEVELS OF INCOME

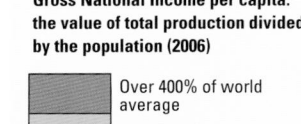

Gross National Income per capita: the value of total production divided by the population (2006)

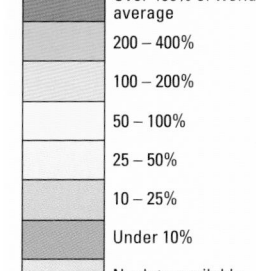

Over 400% of world average
200 – 400%
100 – 200%
50 – 100%
25 – 50%
10 – 25%
Under 10%
No data available

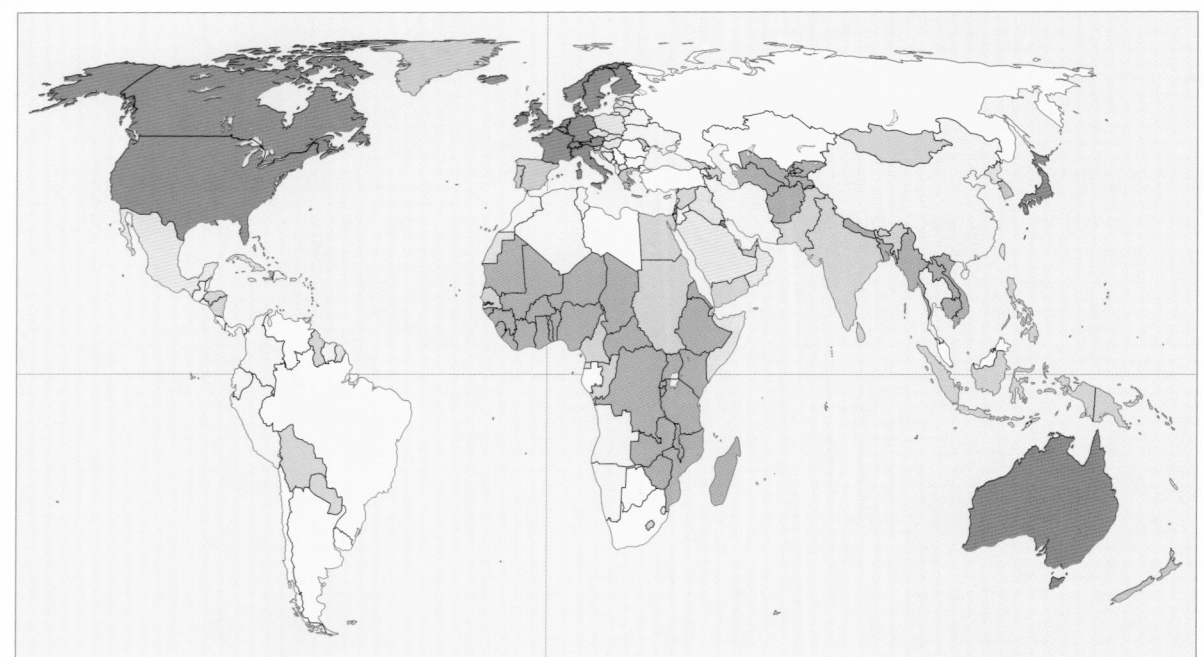

Top 5 countries
Luxembourg	$71,240
Norway	$68,440
Switzerland	$58,050
Denmark	$52,110
Iceland	$49,960

Bottom 5 countries
Burundi	$100
Congo (Dem. Rep.)	$130
Liberia	$130
Ethiopia	$170
Eritrea	$190

INDICATORS

The gap between the world's rich and poor is now so great that it is difficult to illustrate on a single graph. Within each income group (as defined by the World Bank), however, comparisons have some meaning. The wealth gap in many developing countries, though, is wide, with a small, rich class and a large, impoverished majority, while many high-income countries contain an underclass of unemployed and homeless people.

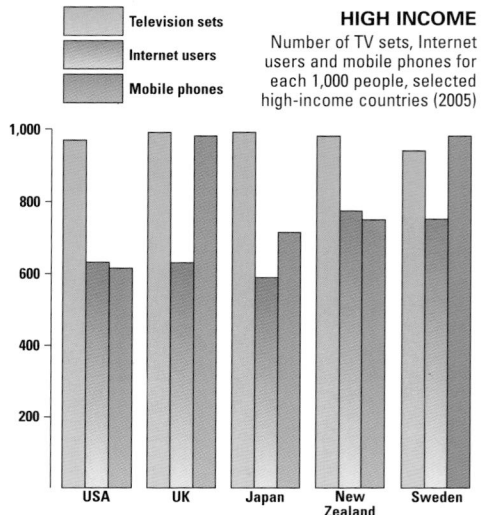

Television sets
Internet users
Mobile phones

HIGH INCOME
Number of TV sets, Internet users and mobile phones for each 1,000 people, selected high-income countries (2005)

USA | UK | Japan | New Zealand | Sweden

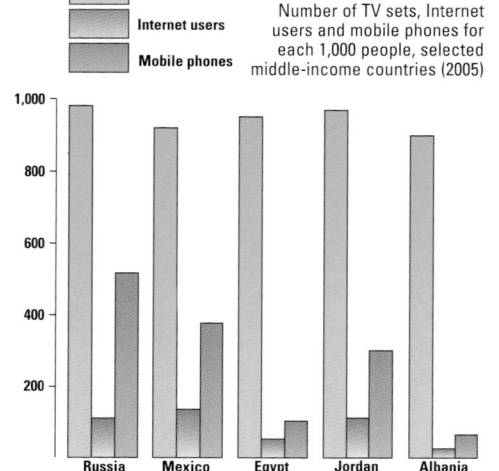

Television sets
Internet users
Mobile phones

MIDDLE INCOME
Number of TV sets, Internet users and mobile phones for each 1,000 people, selected middle-income countries (2005)

Russia | Mexico | Egypt | Jordan | Albania

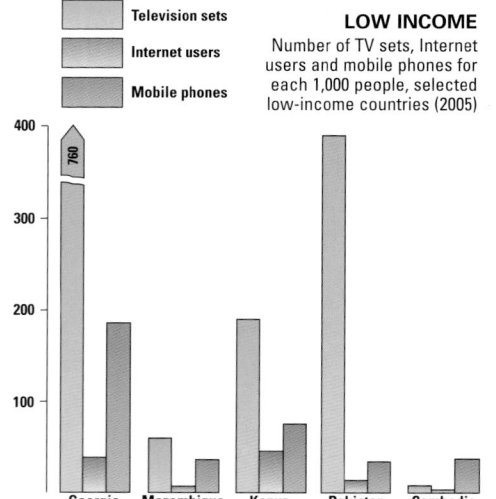

Television sets
Internet users
Mobile phones

LOW INCOME
Number of TV sets, Internet users and mobile phones for each 1,000 people, selected low-income countries (2005)

Georgia | Mozambique | Kenya | Pakistan | Cambodia

STATE FINANCE

Inflation rates (*shown on the map, right*) are an indication of a country's financial stability and, usually, of its prosperity. Annual inflation rates above 20% are usually marked by slow or even negative growth of the GNI. Above 50%, it becomes hyperinflation and an economy is left reeling.

In the late 1980s and early 1990s, many high-income countries had to contend with annual inflation rates of 10% or more, while Japan, the growth leader, had an average inflation rate of just 1.3% between 1985 and 1994.

Market-friendly policies, including low taxes and state spending, liberal trade policies, and a warm welcome for foreign investors, are major factors in countries that have enjoyed rapid economic growth in the decades since 1980. For example, the setting up of Special Economic Zones in eastern China has led to a spectacular rise in that country's per capita GNI. However, an effective state remains a crucial factor in economic growth in most countries.

Other successful countries include South Korea and Singapore, although an Asian market crash in 1997 temporarily halted the dramatic economic expansion of these countries.

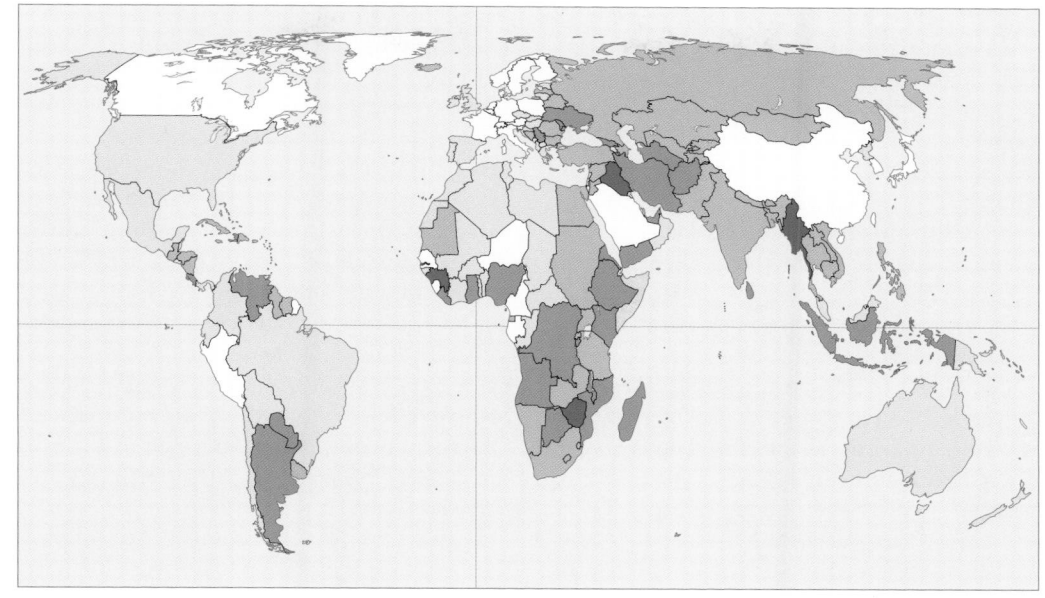

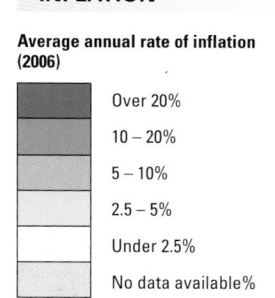

INFLATION

Average annual rate of inflation (2006)

	Over 20%
	10 – 20%
	5 – 10%
	2.5 – 5%
	Under 2.5%
	No data available%

Highest average inflation

Zimbabwe	976.4%
Iraq	64.8%
Guinea	29.0%

Lowest average inflation

Nauru	–3.6%
Vanuatu	–1.6%
San Marino	–1.5%

GROWTH IN GNI

GNI per capita annual growth rate (1999–2005)

	Over 12%
	8 – 12%
	4 – 8%
	0 – 4%
	Under 0%
	No data available

Countries with highest growth rates

Angola	38.0%
Bhutan	27.7%
Albania	27.5%
Latvia	27.2%
Estonia	26.0%

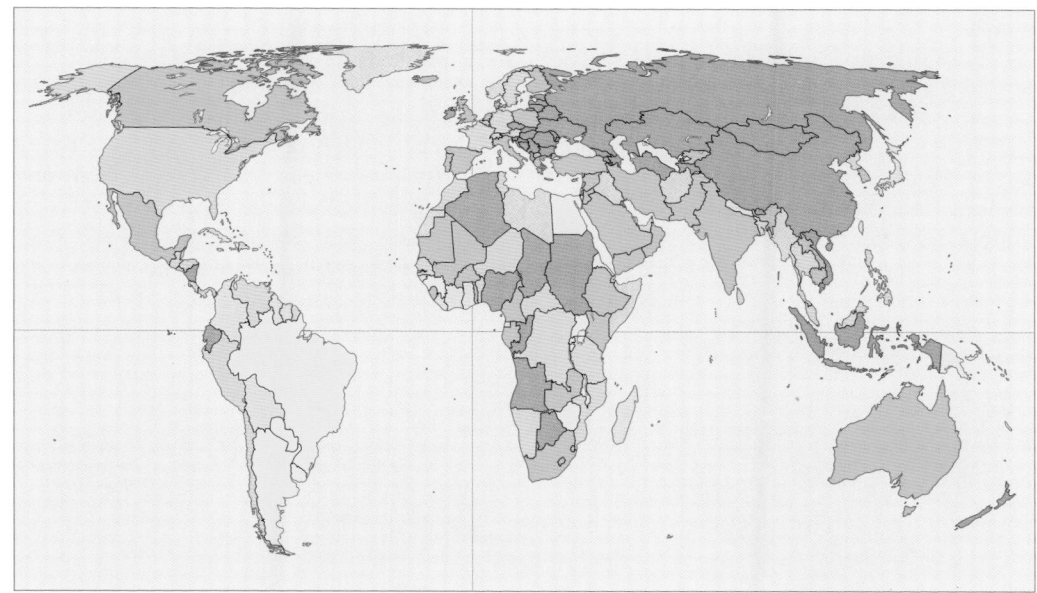

WORLD AIR TRAVEL

Leisure and tourism is the world's second largest industry in terms of revenue generated. Small economies in attractive areas are often completely dominated by tourism: in some Caribbean islands, for example, tourist spending provides over 90% of the total income and is the biggest foreign-exchange earner.

In cash terms, the United States is the world leader: its 2006 earnings exceeded US $85 billion, although that sum amounted to approximately 0.6% of its total GNI. Of the 46 million visitors to the US, 29% came from Canada and 20% came from Mexico. Germany spends the most on overseas tourism; this amounts to nearly US $75,000 million. The next biggest spenders are the US, the UK, and France.

The world's travel and tourist industry was predicted to generate 74 million jobs in 2006. If the broader travel and tourist economy is considered, this total would increase to 215 million.

Major airports
Number of passengers (international and domestic) per year

● Over 25 million
· 15 – 25 million
· 10 – 15 million

Major air routes
Number of international flights per year

⟷ Over 50 million
⟶ 10 – 50 million
→ 5 – 10 million

Total world air passenger traffic (2006)

Africa 3%
Middle East 2%
Latin America & Caribbean 6%
North America 37%
Asia Pacific 21%
Europe 31%

WORLD'S BUSIEST AIRPORTS

Total passengers in millions (2006)

1.	Atlanta Hartsfield Intl. (ATL)	84.8
2.	Chicago O'Hare Intl. (ORD)	77.0
3.	London Heathrow (LHR)	67.5
4.	Tokyo Haneda (HND)	65.8
5.	Los Angeles Intl. (LAX)	61.0
6.	Dallas/Fort Worth Intl. (DFW)	60.2
7.	Paris Charles de Gaulle (CDG)	56.8
8.	Frankfurt Intl. (FRA)	52.8
9.	Beijing Capital Intl. (PEK)	48.7
10.	Denver Intl. (DEN)	47.3

For more information:
82   Water supply
86   Population density
88   Urban population
89   Urban advantages
92   World's refugees
      War since 1945
100 Employment
      The work force
105 Infant mortality
106 Wealth

Wealth is a basic factor in determining standards of living. Everywhere, the rich have more of everything, including higher average life expectancies, while the poor have to spend most of their income on basic human needs, such as food and clothing. Yet poverty and wealth are relative terms: slum dwellers living on social security in an industrial society feel their poverty acutely, but have far more resources than an average African living in a rural area.

IIn 1990 the United Nations Development Program published its first Human Development Index (HDI), an attempt to construct a comparative scale by which a simplified form of well-being might be measured. The HDI, expressed as a value between 0 and 0.999, combines figures for life expectancy and literacy with a wealth scale, based on Purchasing Power Parity.

The world's countries are divided into three groups, those with a high HDI (0.8 and above); those with a medium HDI (0.5 to 0.799); and those with a low HDI (below 0.5). In 2005, Norway and Iceland were top in the world rankings and Sierra Leone was bottom. In fact, all of the 22 countries with a low HDI were from Africa. Besides having low per capita GNIs, the average life

expectancy in these countries was 48 years, while the adult literacy rate was 56%. By comparison, the average life expectancy at birth in countries in the high HDI group was 76 years, while the literacy rate was 96%.

Comparisons between countries with similar per capita GNIs reveal the effects of government actions. For example, the World Bank classifies both India and China as low-income economies, but India's HDI at 0.619 is much lower than that of China, at 0.777. This reflects not only China's economic progress in the 1980s and 1990s, but also differences in average life expectancies (68 years in India and 72 years in China), and adult literacy rates (61% in India and 91% in China).

Disparities in standards of living exist not only between countries but also between individuals, groups, and regions within countries. For example, income distribution figures for 2005 show that, in the United States, the poorest 20% of households received less than 3% of the income.

Other contrasts exist in developing countries between rural communities, where incomes are low and basic services are often in short supply, and urban areas, where even those living in slums are

generally better off than their rural neighbors. Other striking differences exist between men and women. For example, while adult literacy rates for men and women living in developed countries are more or less the same, large differences exist in many developing countries. In 2004, in countries in the lowest HDI category, only 64% of women were literate, as compared with 73% of men.

Female education is a factor in population control, especially as women's fertility rates appear to fall in direct proportion to the amount of secondary education they receive. This point was acknowledged in 2004 by the UN Population Fund, which defined four main objectives relating to women and population control: the reduction of maternal, infant, and child mortality; better education, especially for girls; universal access to reproductive health services; and gender equality.

Statistical analysis presents many problems of interpretation, especially when trying to define such intangible factors as a sense of well-being. For example, education helps create wealth; but are rich countries wealthy because their people are well educated, or are they well educated because they are rich?

HUMAN DEVELOPMENT INDEX

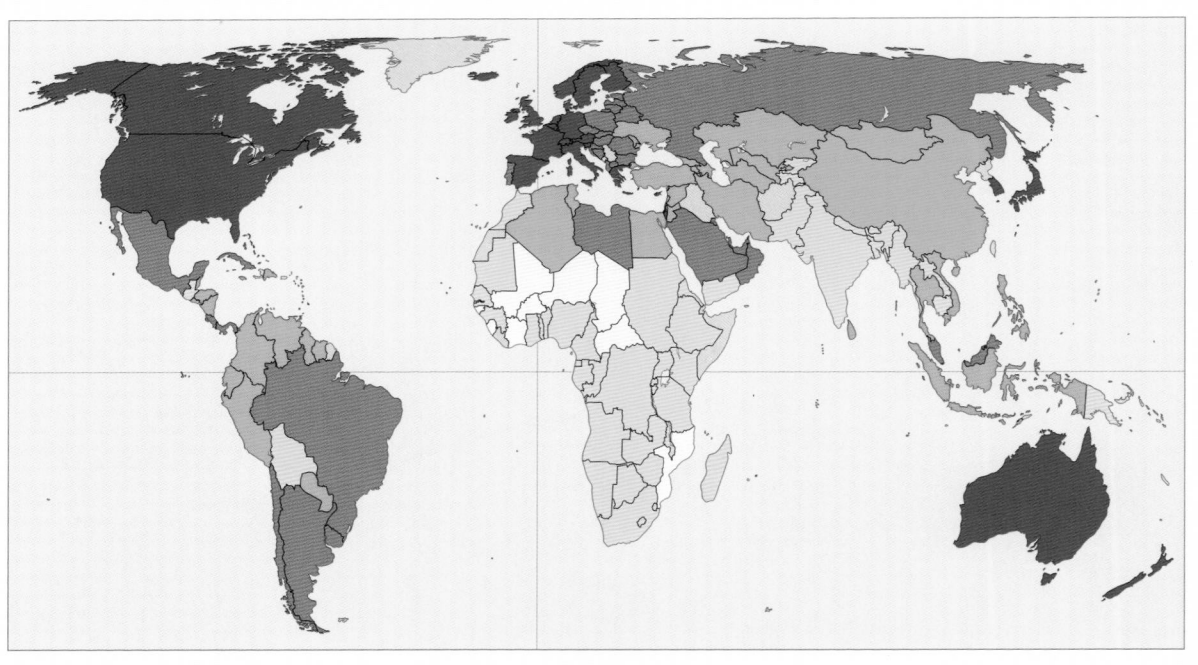

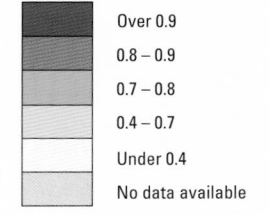

The Human Development Index (HDI), calculated by the UN Development Program (UNDP), gives a value to countries using indicators of life expectancy, education, and standards of living in 2005. Higher values show more developed countries.

- Over 0.9
- 0.8 – 0.9
- 0.7 – 0.8
- 0.4 – 0.7
- Under 0.4
- No data available

Highest values
Norway 0.968
Iceland 0.968
Australia 0.962
Canada 0.961
Ireland 0.959

Lowest values
Sierra Leone 0.336
Burkina Faso 0.370
Niger 0.374
Guinea-Bissau 0.374
Mali 0.380

EDUCATION

The developing countries made great efforts in the 1970s and 1980s to bring at least a basic education to their people. In all but the poorest nations, primary school enrolments rose above 60%. However, figures often include teenagers or young adults, and there are still 300 million children worldwide who receive no schooling at all. A lack of resources has restricted the development of secondary and higher education. Most primary school education is free in the poorer countries, but fees are often paid for secondary and higher education, thus heightening the differences between rich and poor.

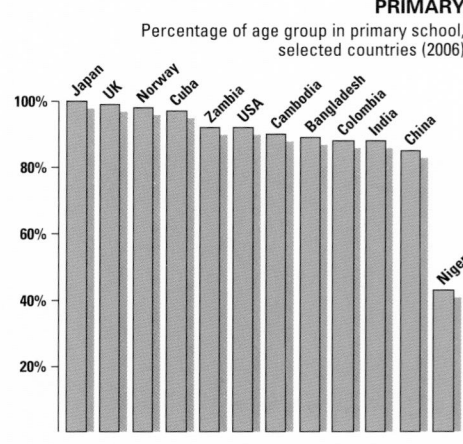

PRIMARY
Percentage of age group in primary school, selected countries (2006)

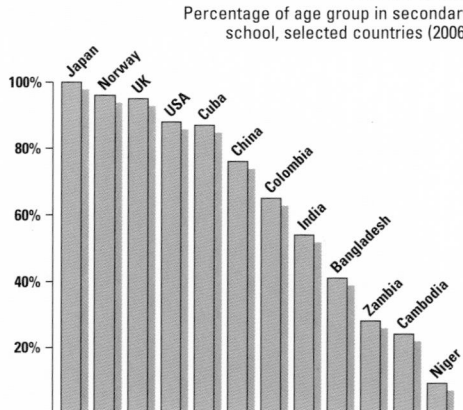

SECONDARY
Percentage of age group in secondary school, selected countries (2006)

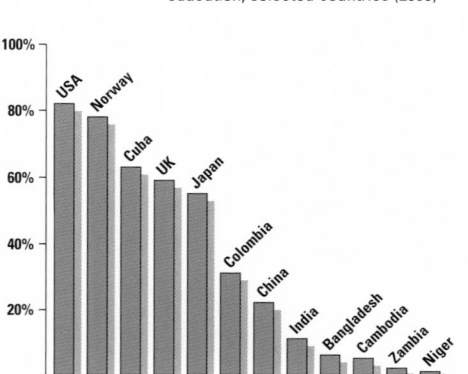

HIGHER
Percentage of age group in higher education, selected countries (2006)

DISTRIBUTION OF SPENDING

Percentage share of household spending

A high proportion of the average income of households in developing nations is spent on basic needs such as food and clothing. In most Western countries food and clothing account for less than 25% of expenditure.

- Food
- Clothing
- Energy & Housing
- Medicine & Education
- Transport
- Other

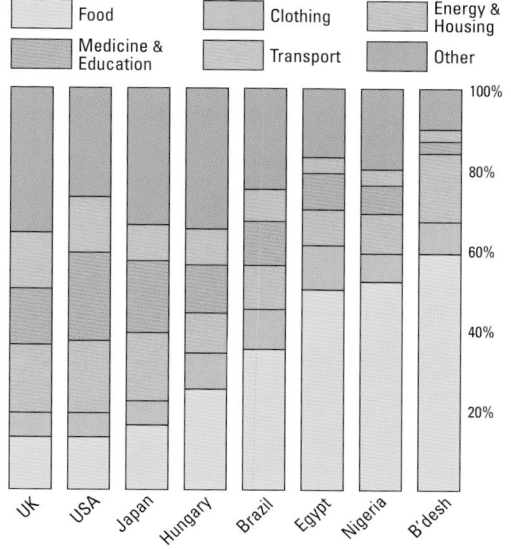

UK USA Japan Hungary Brazil Egypt Nigeria B'desh

STANDARDS OF LIVING IN THE USA BY RACE, AGE AND REGION

A comparison of measures of income and education, by selected characteristics (2005)

Median income per household (US $), by age and region

15–24 years	28,770
25–34 years	47,379
35–44 years	58,084
45–54 years	63,581
55–64 years	52,260
65 years and over	26,036
Northeast	50,882
Midwest	45,950
South	42,138
West	50,002

Per capita income (US $), by race and Hispanic origin of householder

ALL RACES	24,672
White	26,005
Black	16,224
Asian and Pacific Is.	27,334
Hispanic (any race)	14,101

The poorest 20% of households received just 2.4% of the income, whereas the richest 20% received 55.4%.

Percentage of persons aged 25 and over who have completed High School, by race or origin

ALL RACES	1975	62.5
	2005	85.5
White	1975	64.5
	2005	86.1
Black	1975	42.5
	2005	80.7
Hispanic	1975	37.9
	2005	59.3

FERTILITY AND EDUCATION

Fertility rates compared with female education, selected countries (2000–2005)

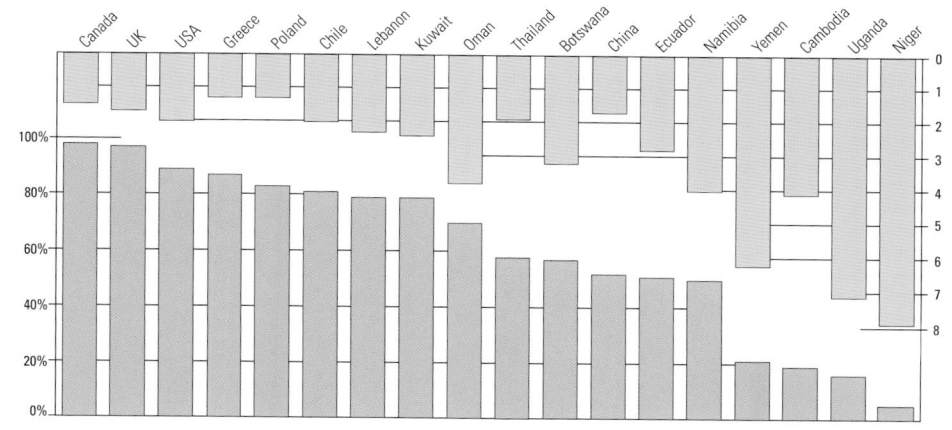

Canada UK USA Greece Poland Chile Lebanon Kuwait Oman Thailand Botswana China Ecuador Namibia Yemen Cambodia Uganda Niger

There seems to be a strong link between access to secondary education and the fertility rate. In developed countries, young girls have a high access to education and a low fertility rate. In contrast, in many developing countries women have a high fertility rate but lack access to education. This can be for a complex mix of social, economic, and cultural reasons. Despite a few high-profile examples of female politicians in different parts of the world, all evidence points to the continuing marginalization of women from the political and economic processes of decision-making. Female wages are, on average, only two thirds of those of men.

- Fertility rate: average number of children borne per woman
- Percentage of females aged 12–17 in secondary education

GENDER DEVELOPMENT INDEX

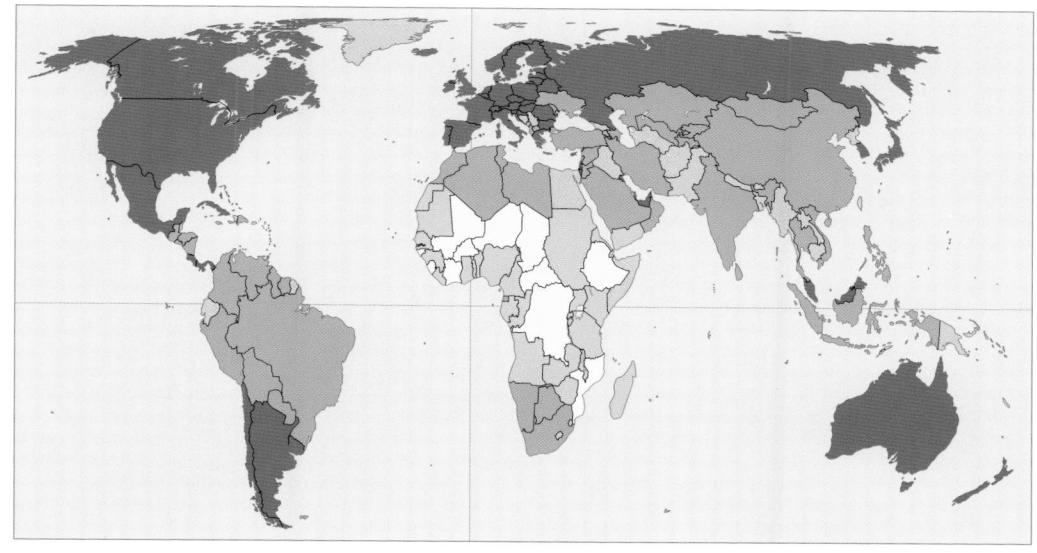
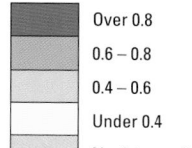

The **Gender Development Index (GDI)** shows economic and social differences between men and women by using various UNDP indicators (2005). Countries with higher values of GDI have more equality between men and women.

- Over 0.8
- 0.6 – 0.8
- 0.4 – 0.6
- Under 0.4
- No data available

Highest values

Iceland	0.962
Australia	0.960
Norway	0.957
Canada	0.956

Lowest values

Sierra Leone	0.320
Niger	0.355
Guinea-Bissau	0.355
Burkina Faso	0.354

REGIONAL INEQUALITY IN ITALY

The southern part of Italy, known as the *Mezzogiorno*, has been described as one of the poorest parts of the European Union. It is identifiable on the map (*right*) as all the regions with a GDP per capita of less than US $25,000 (including the two islands of Sicily and Sardinia).

The *Mezzogiorno* region suffers from a lack of energy resources, minerals, industry, commerce, services, and skilled labor. As a result, standards of living in the region are well below the rest of Italy. Employment is predominantly agricultural and small-scale.

The north of Italy accounts for 60% of the population but 80% of the GDP, whereas the *Mezzogiorno* accounts for 40% of the population and only 20% of the GDP. Manpower surpluses in the south led to emigration to other parts of Europe and the Americas.

It has also led, especially in the last 50 years, to inter-regional migration from the islands and the southern mainland to the north. The main regions attracting migrants are the northwest (the prosperous Liguria–Piedmont–Lombardy triangle, with its great industrial cities of Genoa, Milan, and Turin) and the Venetia region in the northeast.

As a result, the north has experienced much higher population growth rates than the rest of Italy.

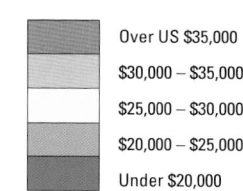

Gross Domestic Product (GDP) per capita in Italy, by region (2004)

- Over US $35,000
- $30,000 – $35,000
- $25,000 – $30,000
- $20,000 – $25,000
- Under $20,000

The average GDP per capita for Italy is US $31,000. By comparison, the GDP for the UK is $35,300; for the USA $46,000; and for the EU $32,900.

The number of inhabitants per doctor, another social indicator, varies from less than 600 in the northwest of Italy to nearly 800 in the far south (the *Mezzogiorno*), with a national average of 628.

◄ These two images illustrate the reality of suburban life for people at either end of the economic scale. On the far left is part of a huge area of "tract housing" in California, where large houses of a similar design are laid out by a developer, complete with gardens, drives, and swimming pools. On the right is a much more haphazard arrangement of home-built, rudimentary shelters, many without sanitation and most with no electricity, in Crossroads Township, outside Cape Town in South Africa.

WORLD CITIES

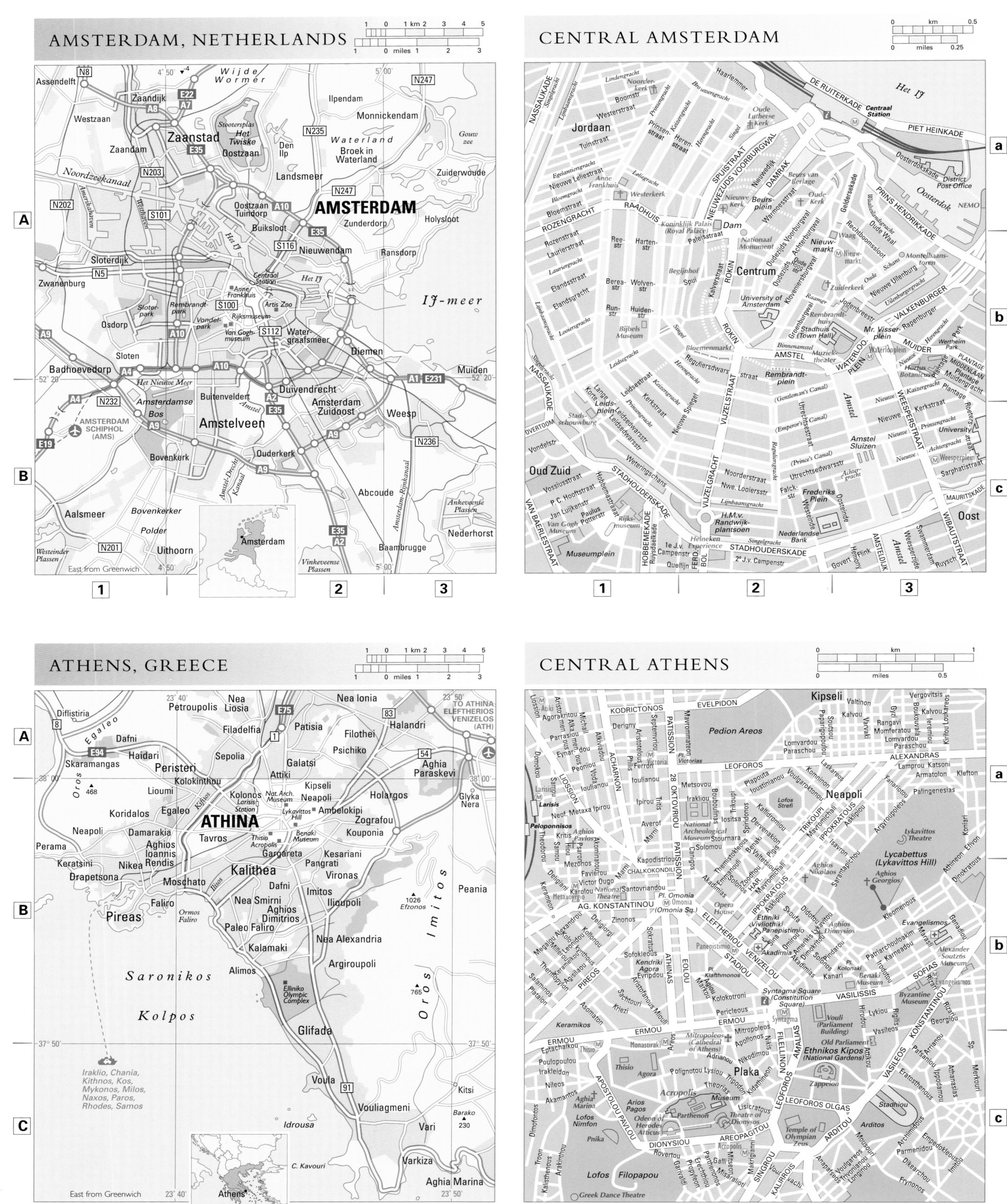

AMSTERDAM, NETHERLANDS

CENTRAL AMSTERDAM

ATHENS, GREECE

CENTRAL ATHENS

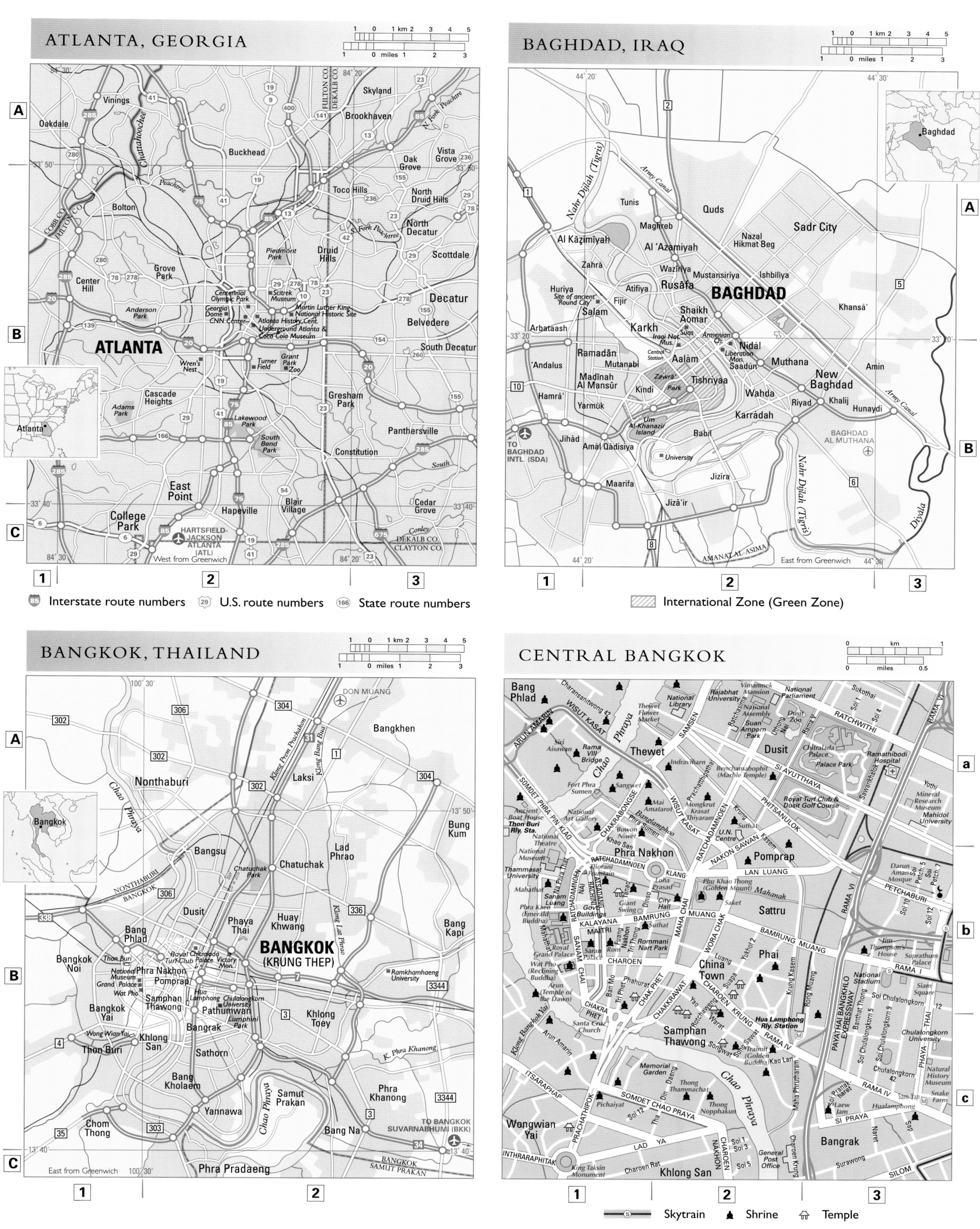

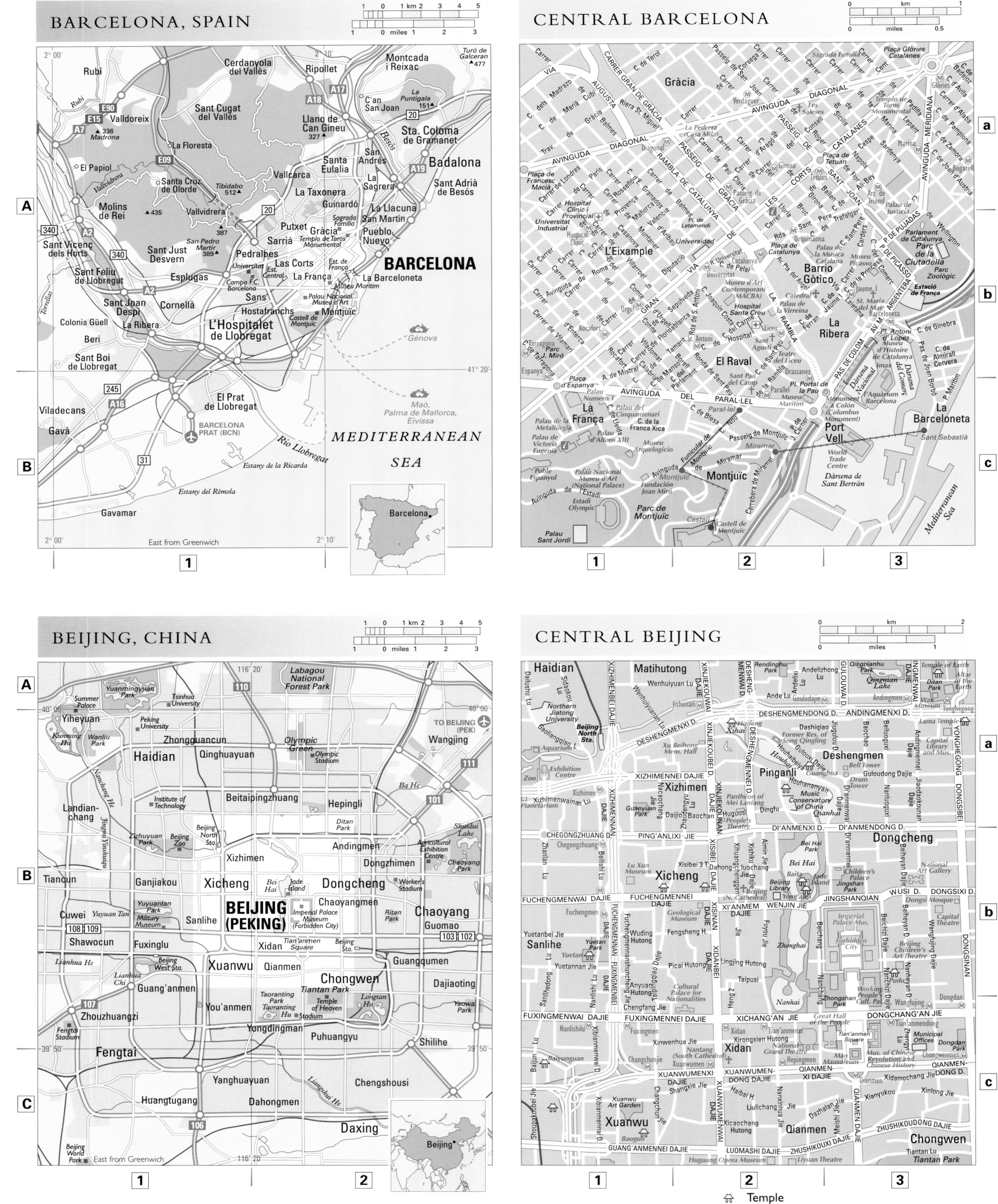

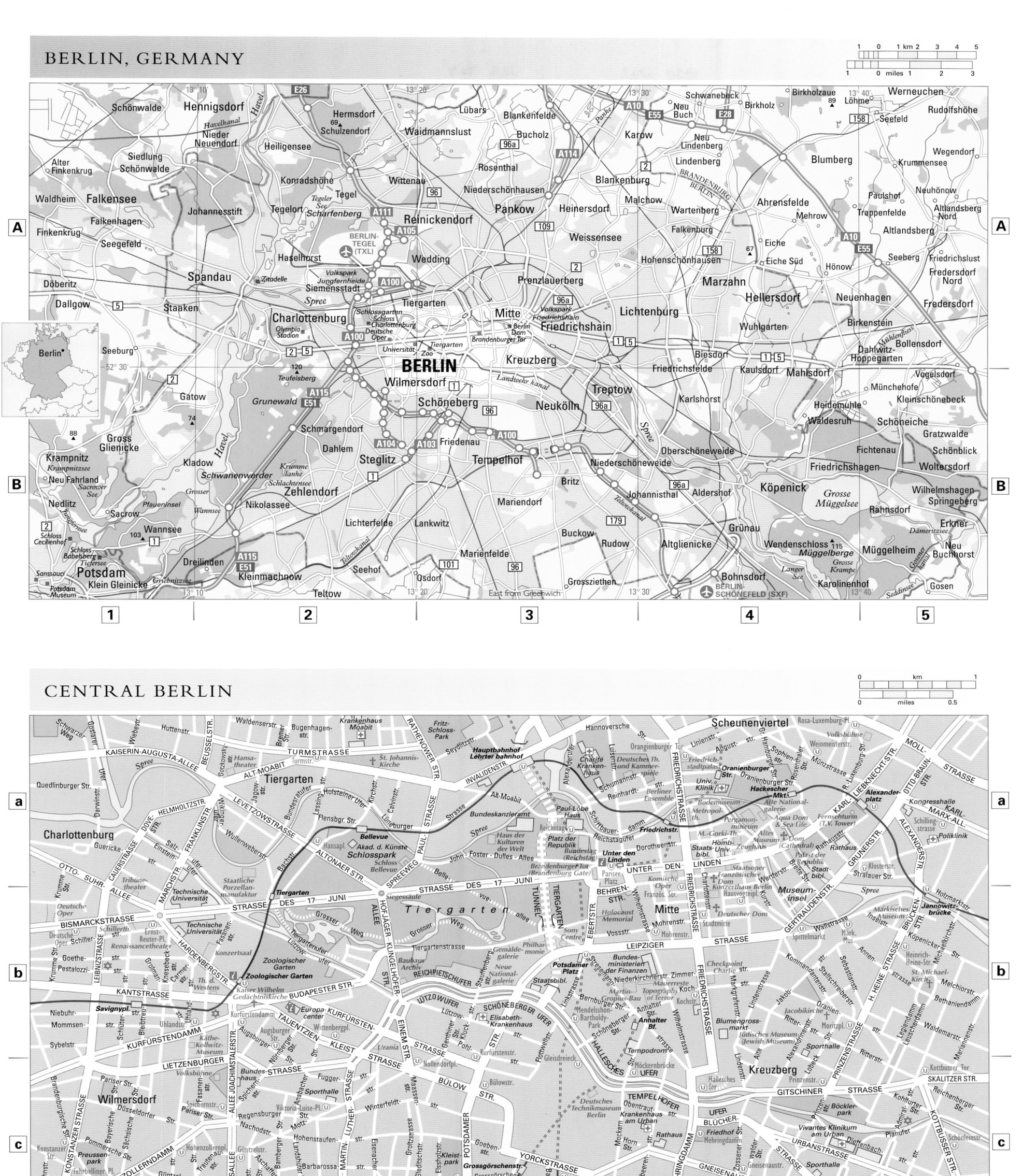

BERLIN, GERMANY

CENTRAL BERLIN

COPYRIGHT PHILIP'S

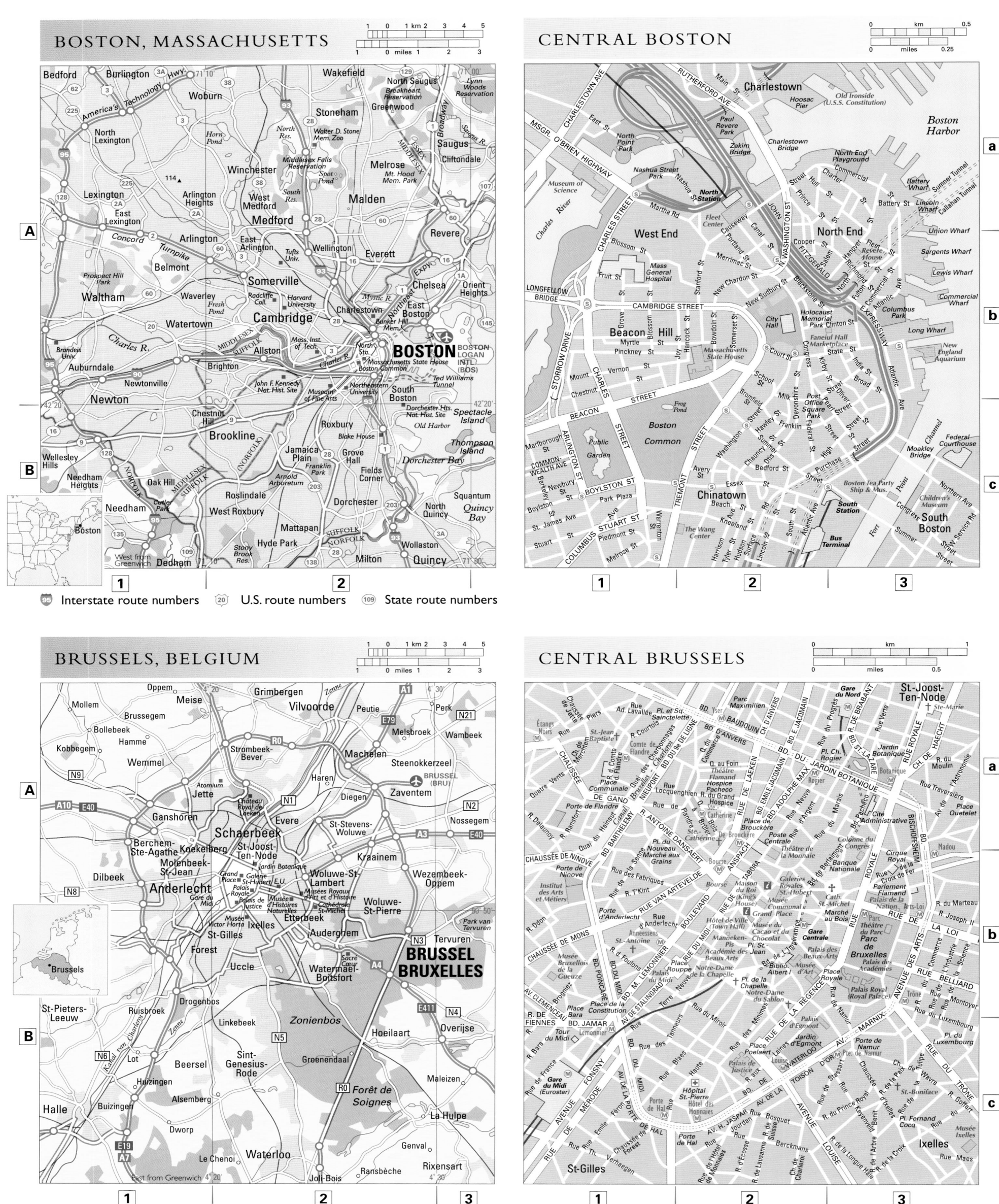

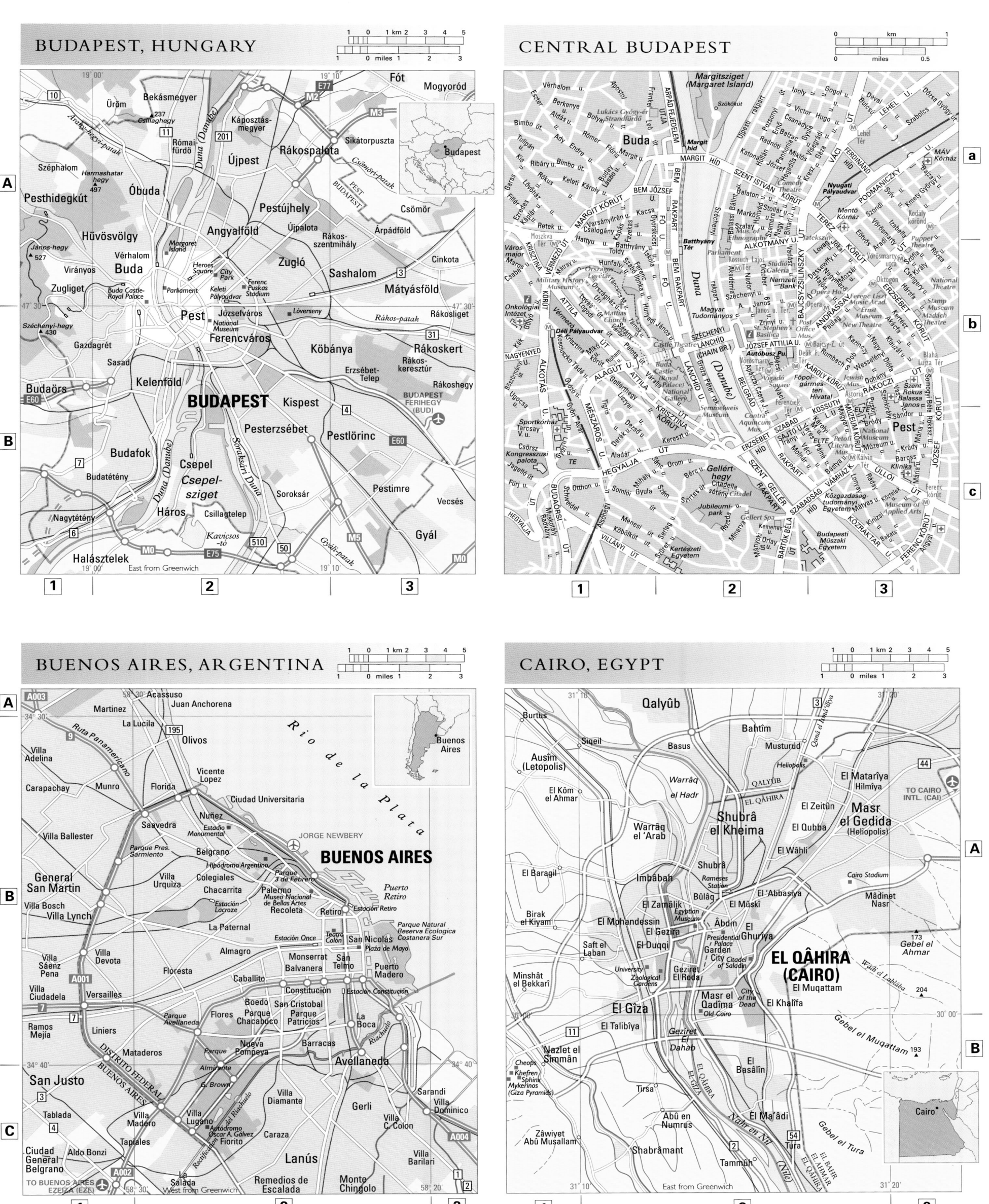

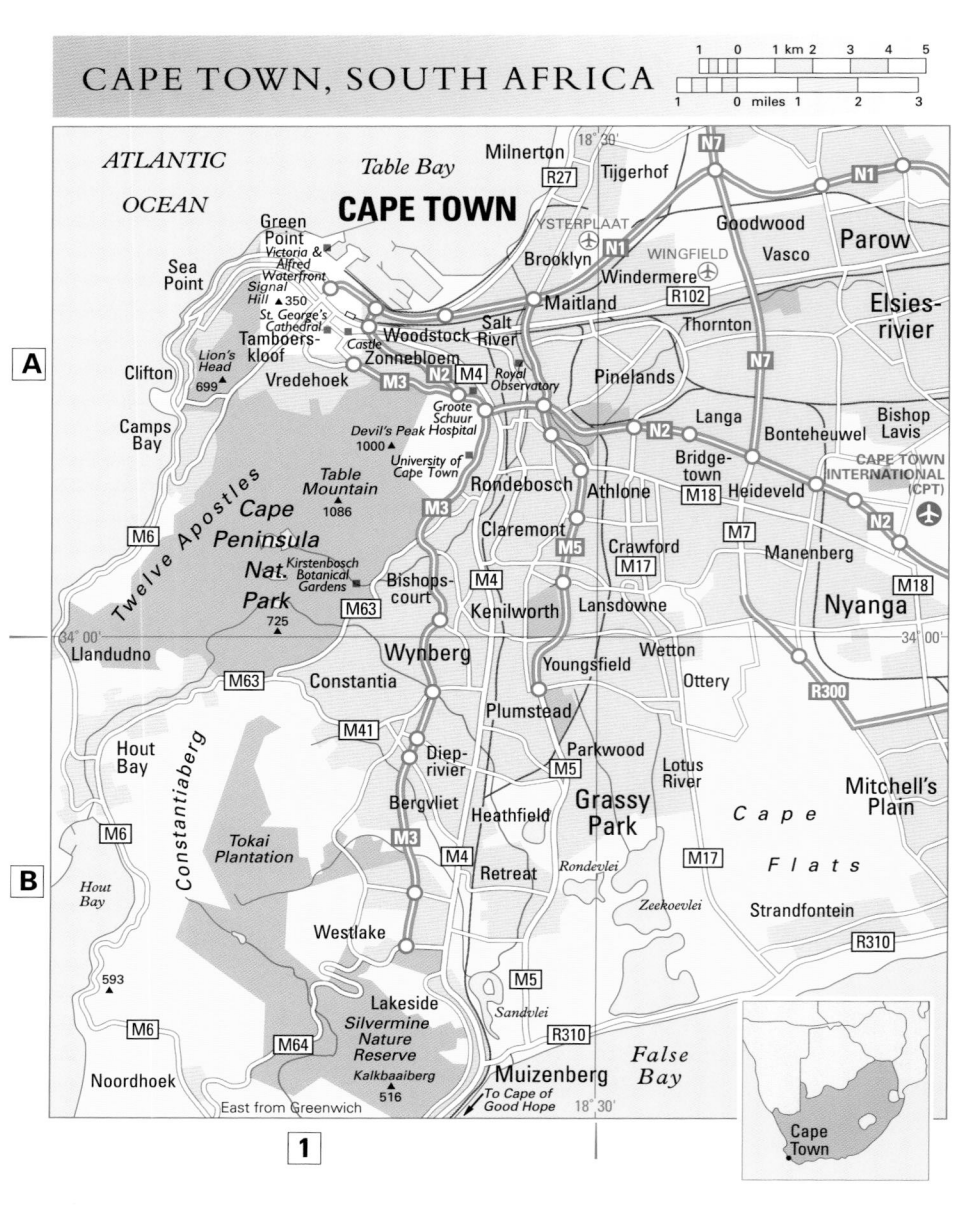

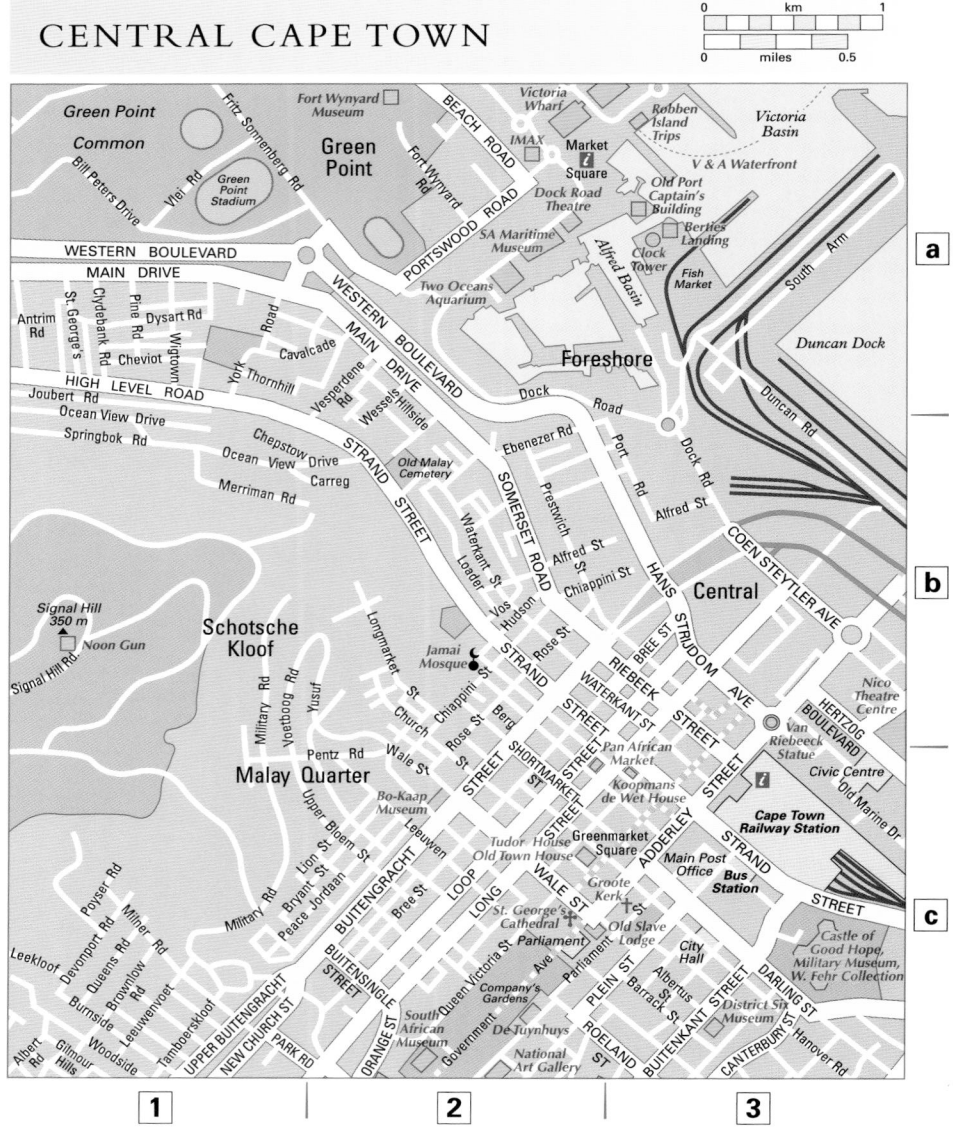

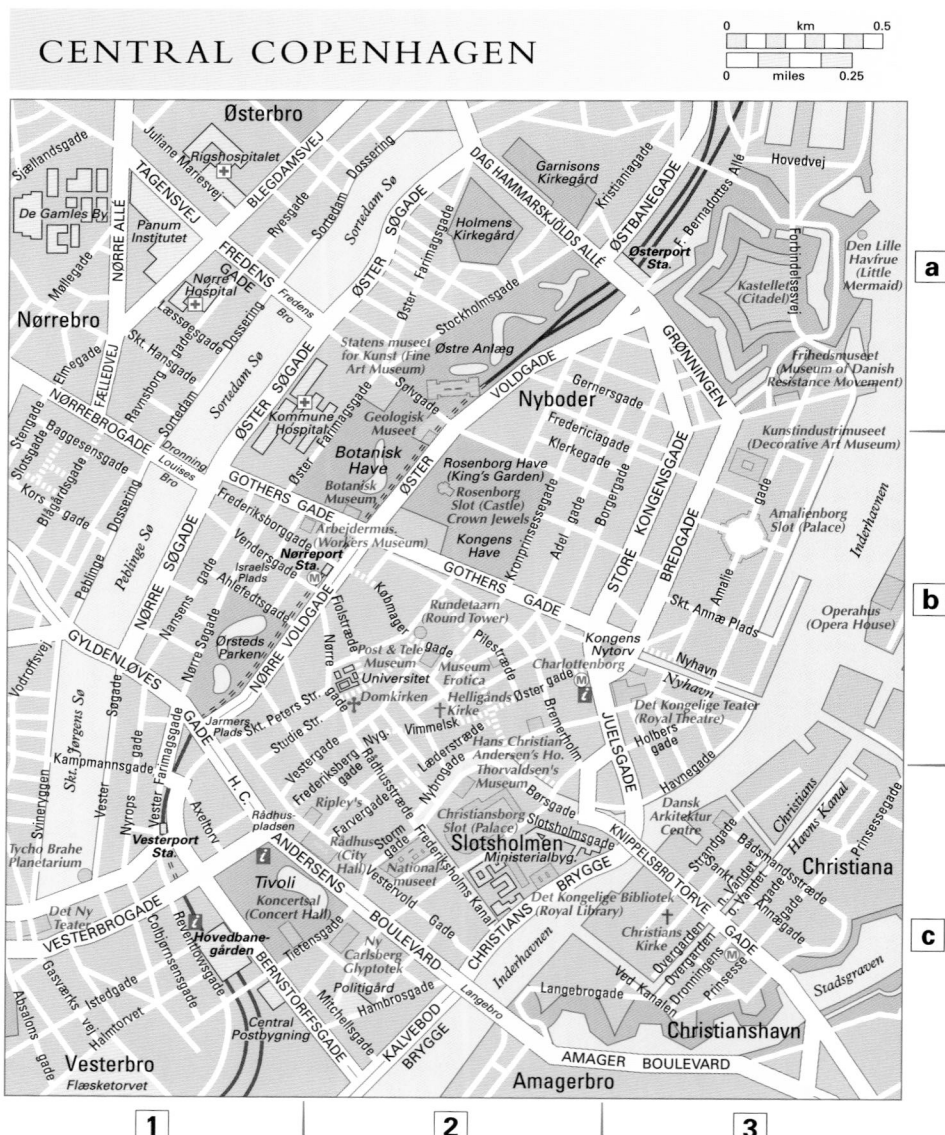

CHICAGO, ILLINOIS

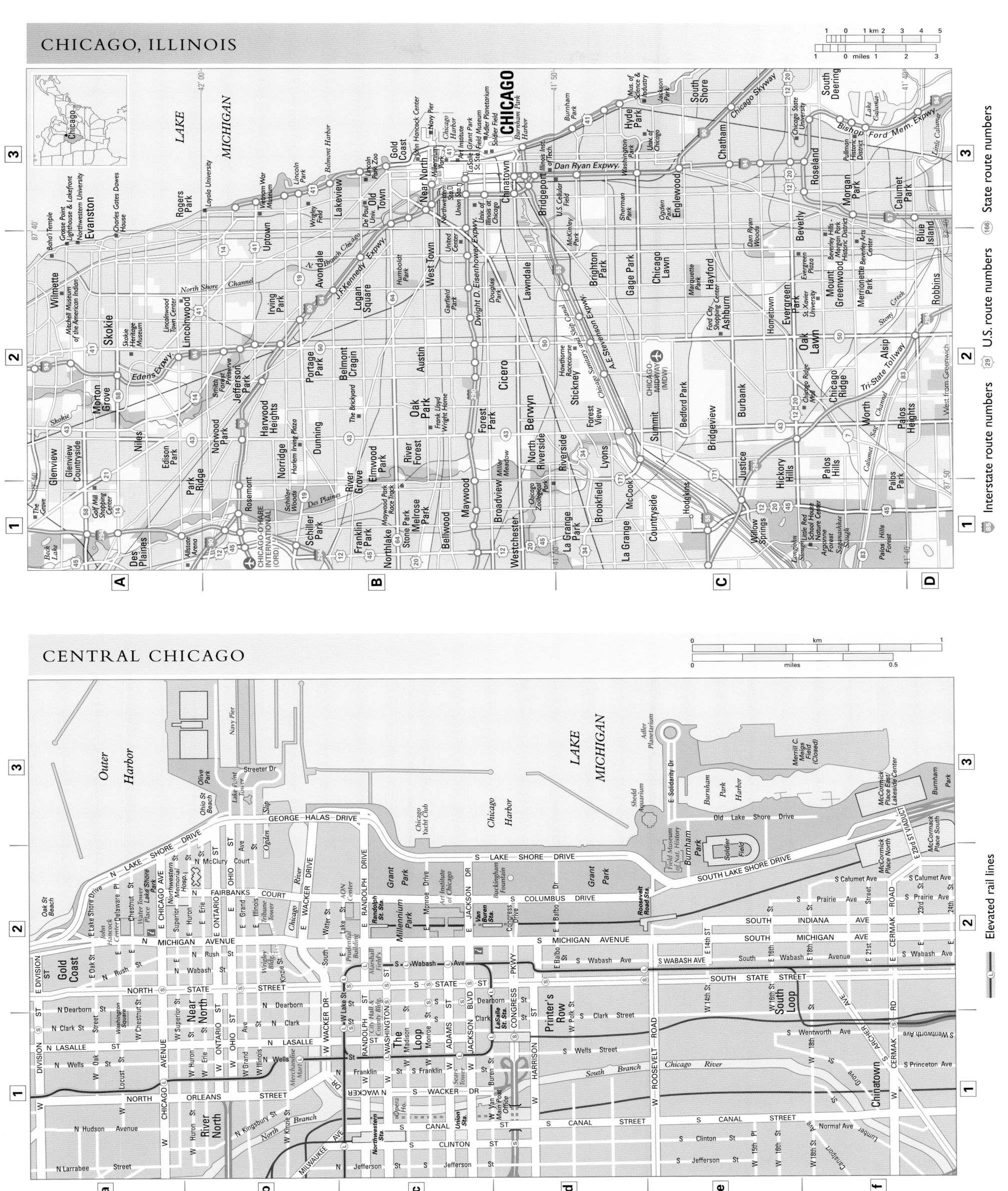

CENTRAL CHICAGO

State route numbers
U.S. route numbers
Interstate route numbers
Elevated rail lines

COPYRIGHT PHILIP'S

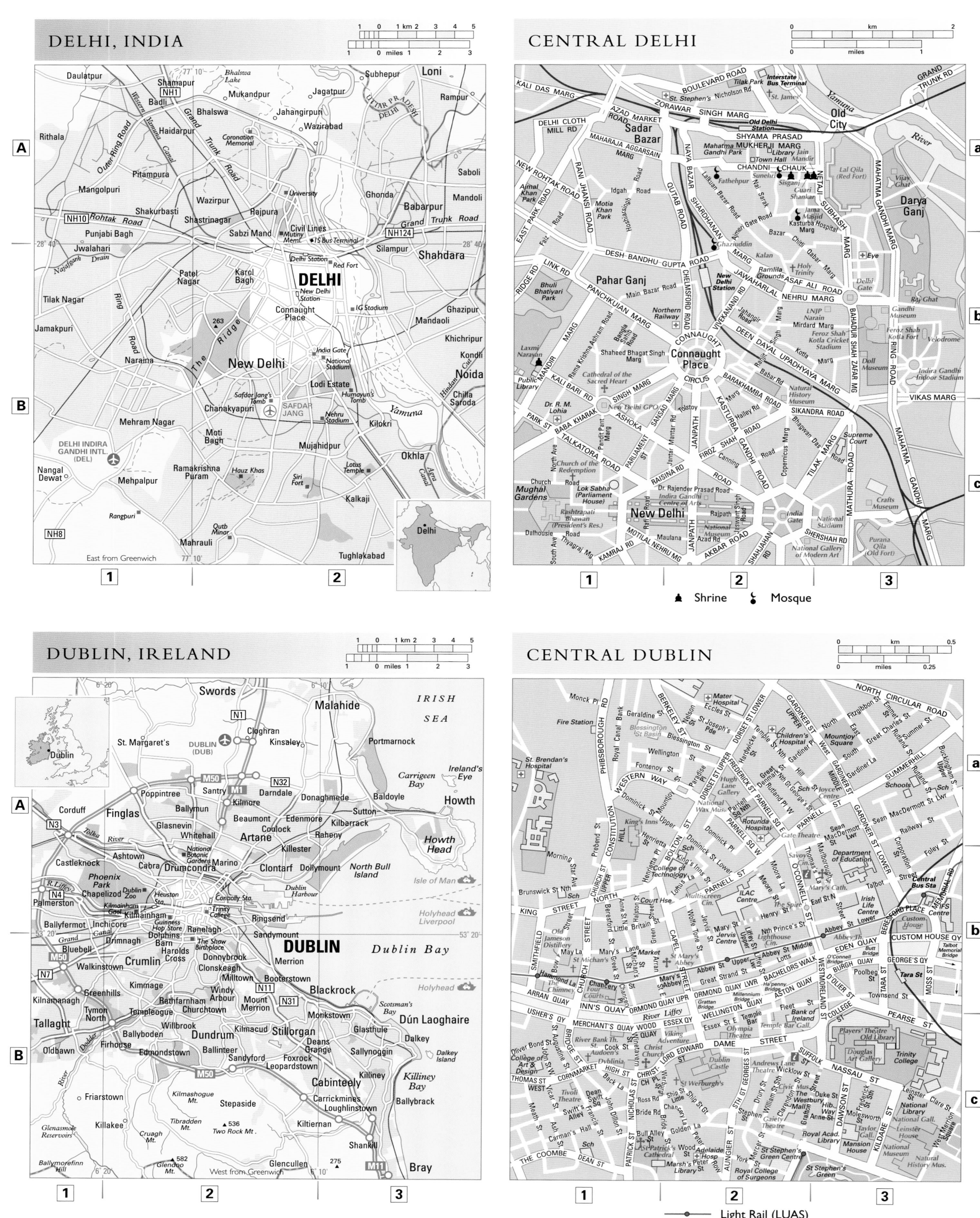

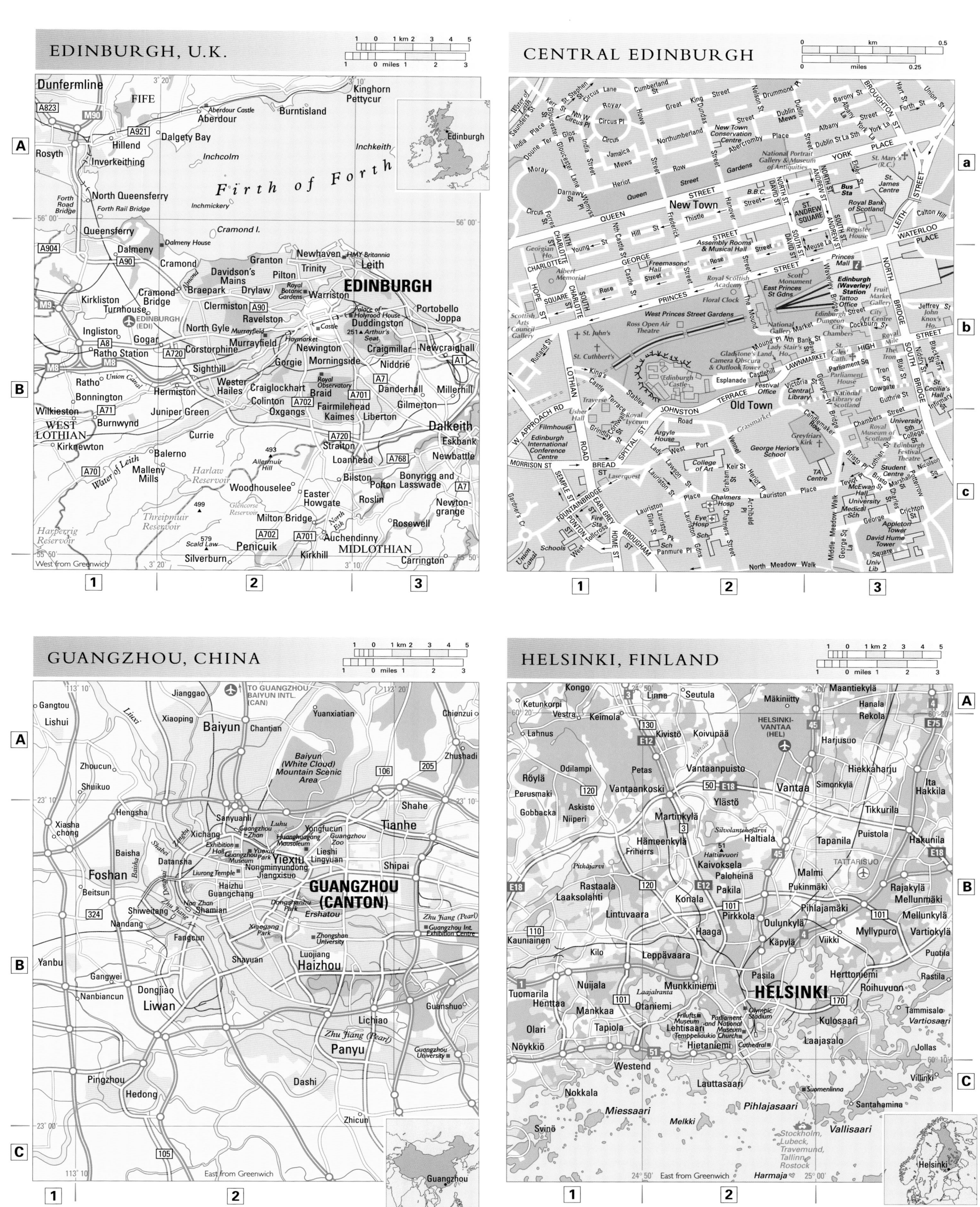

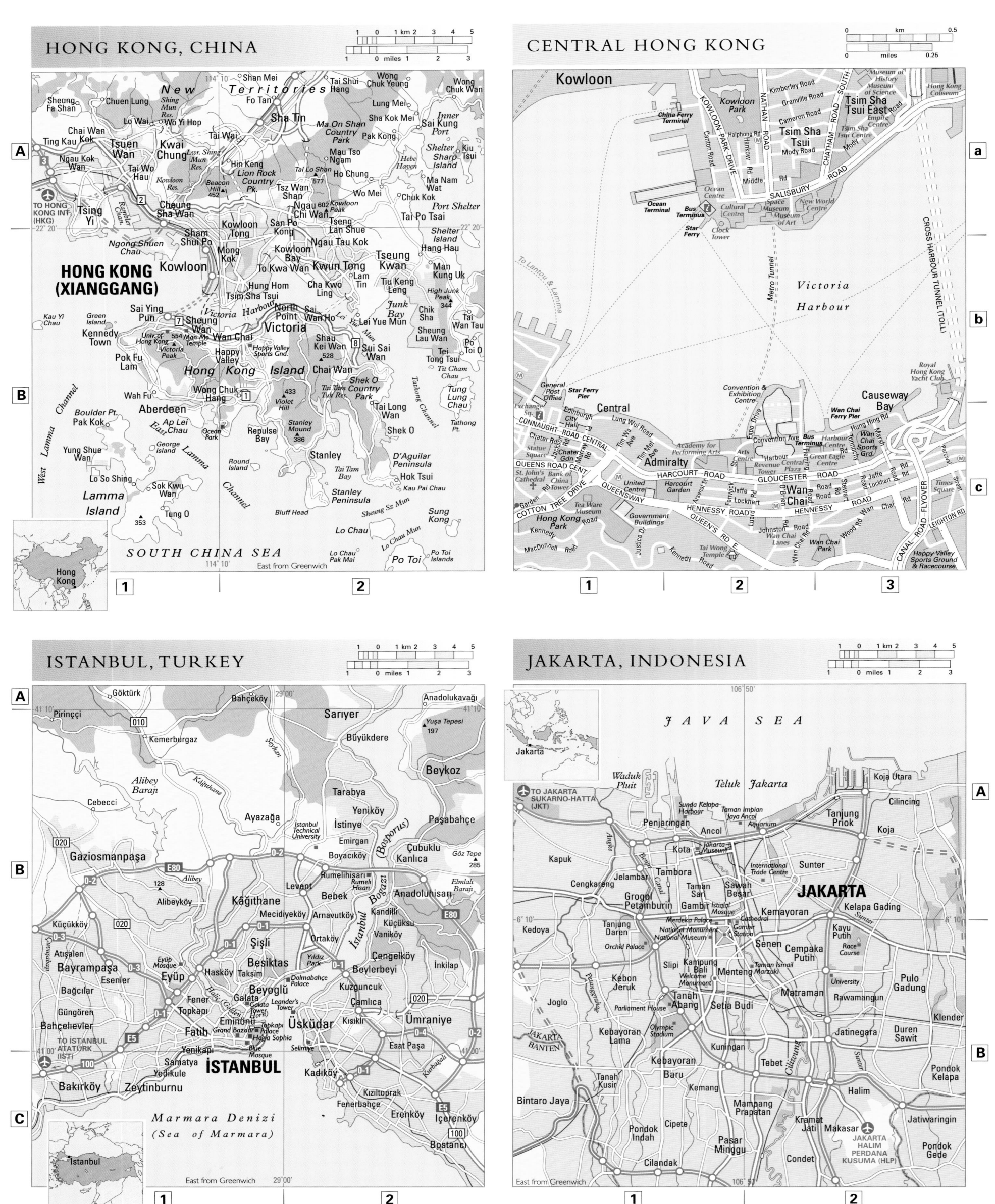

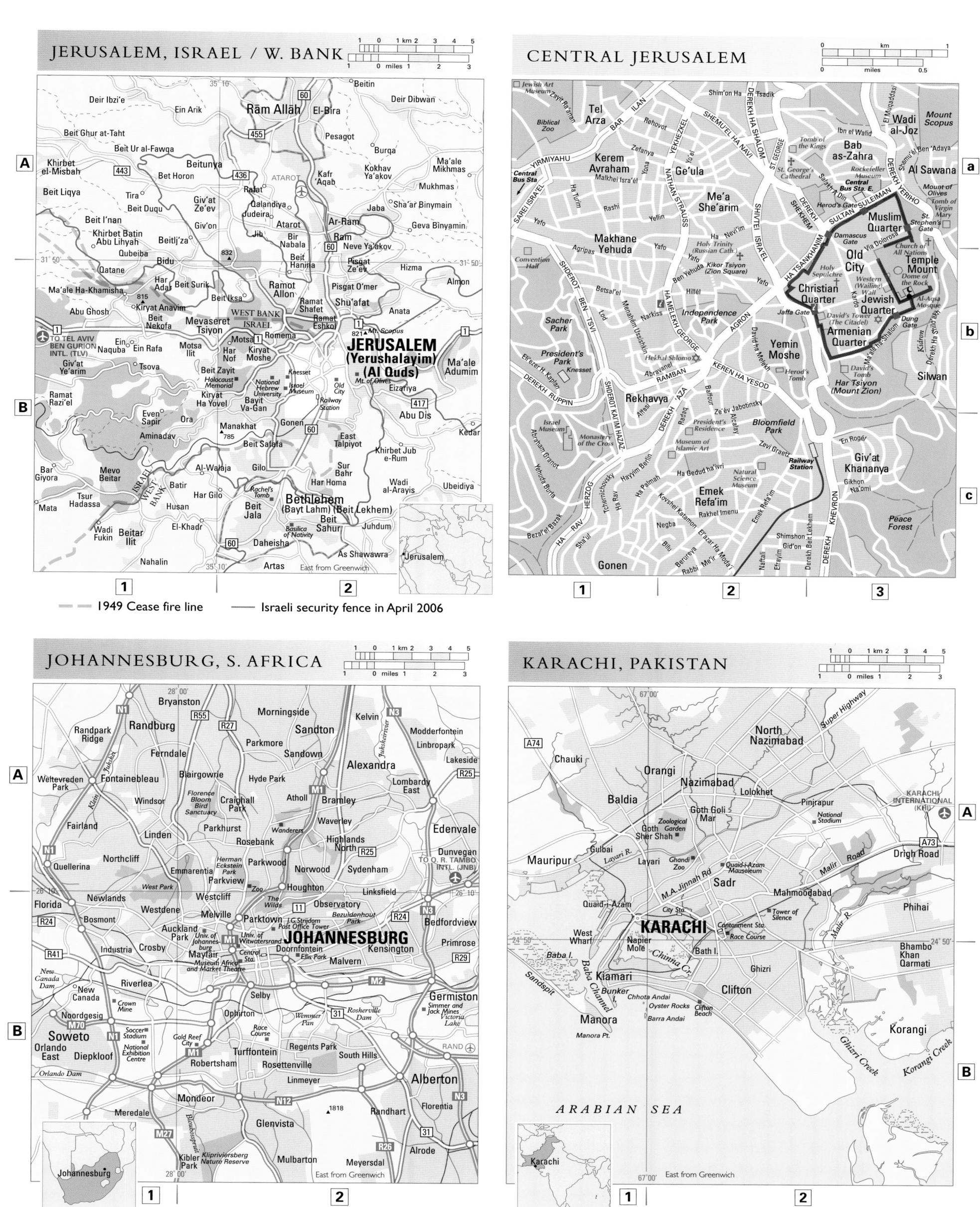

KOLKATA, INDIA

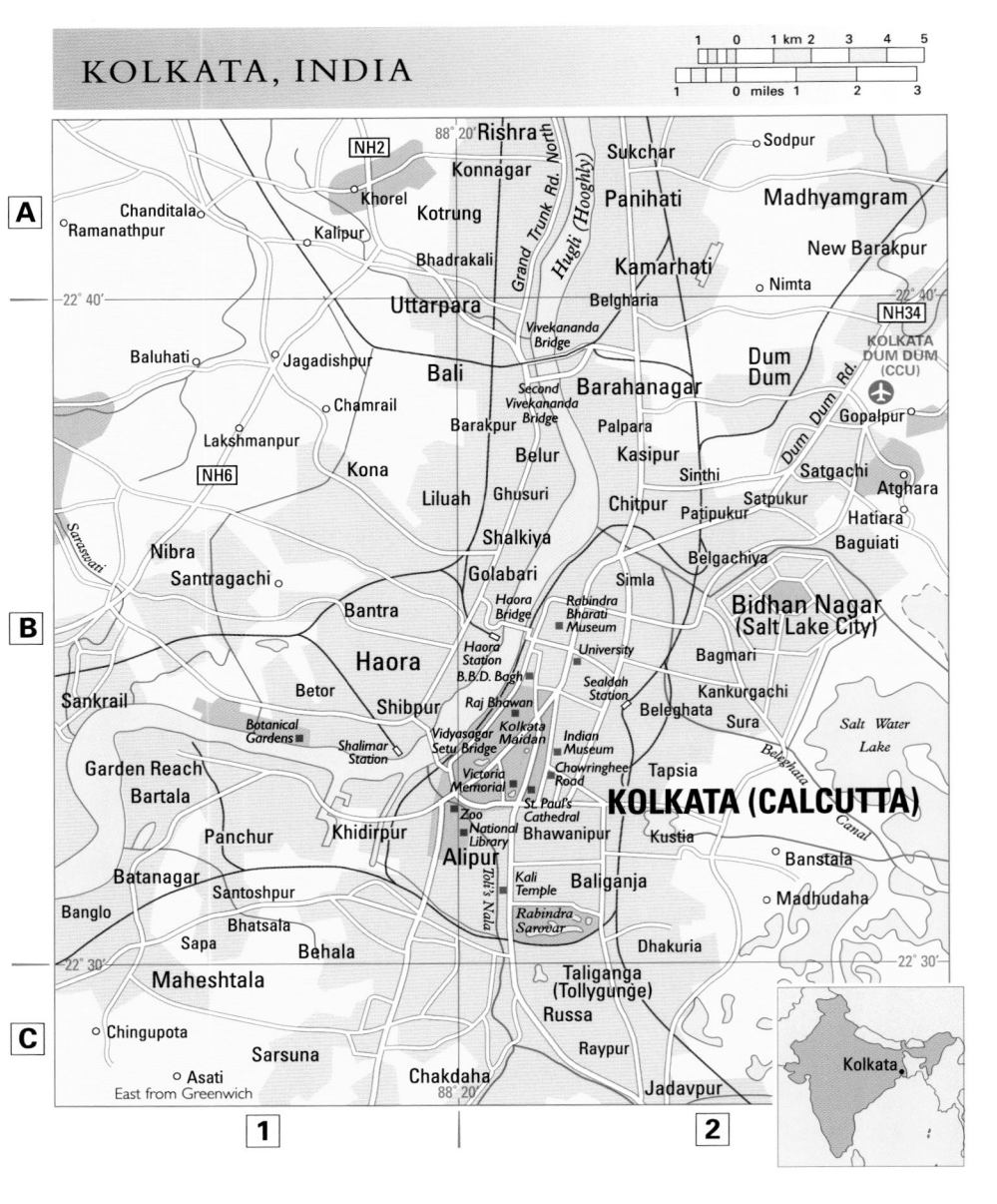

LAGOS, NIGERIA

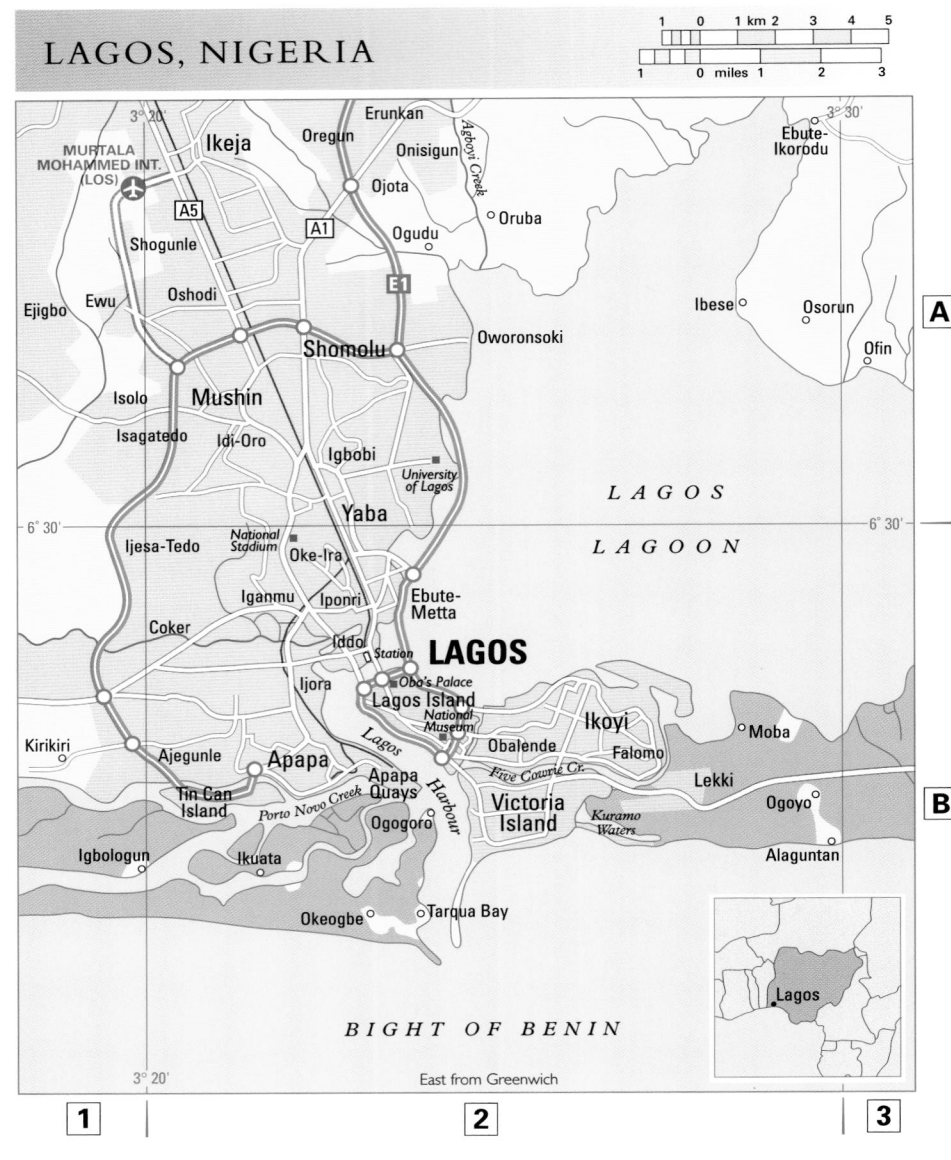

LAS VEGAS, NEVADA

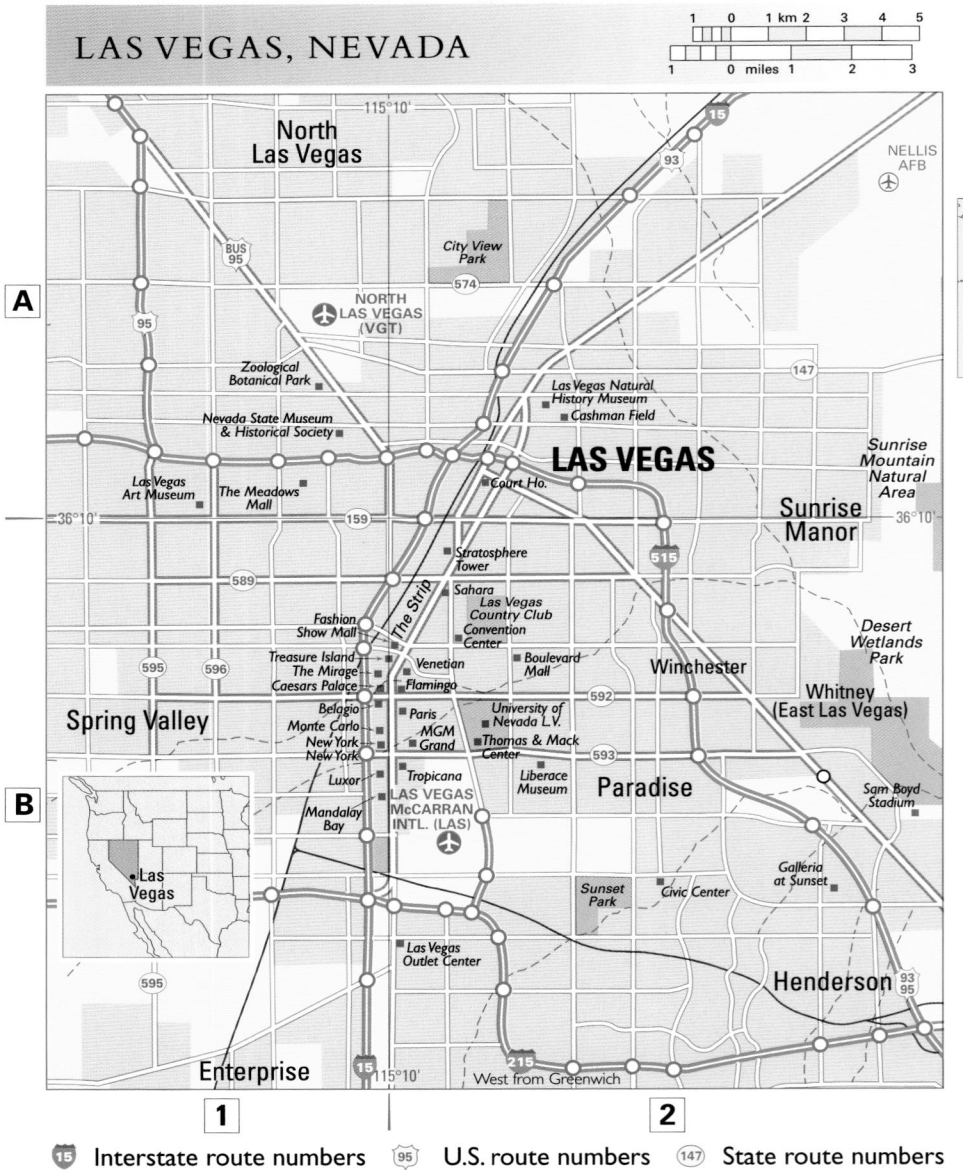

LIMA, PERU

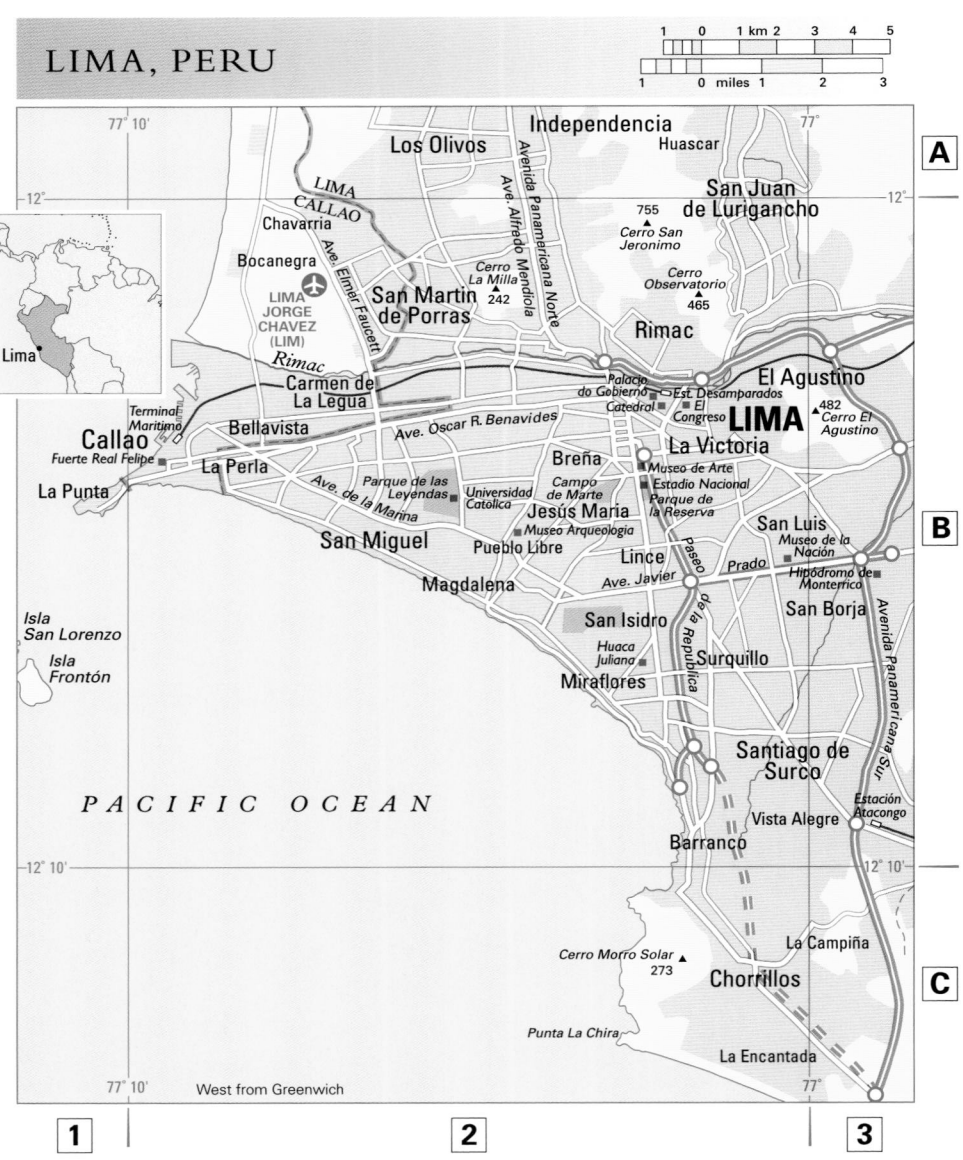

15 Interstate route numbers   95 U.S. route numbers   147 State route numbers

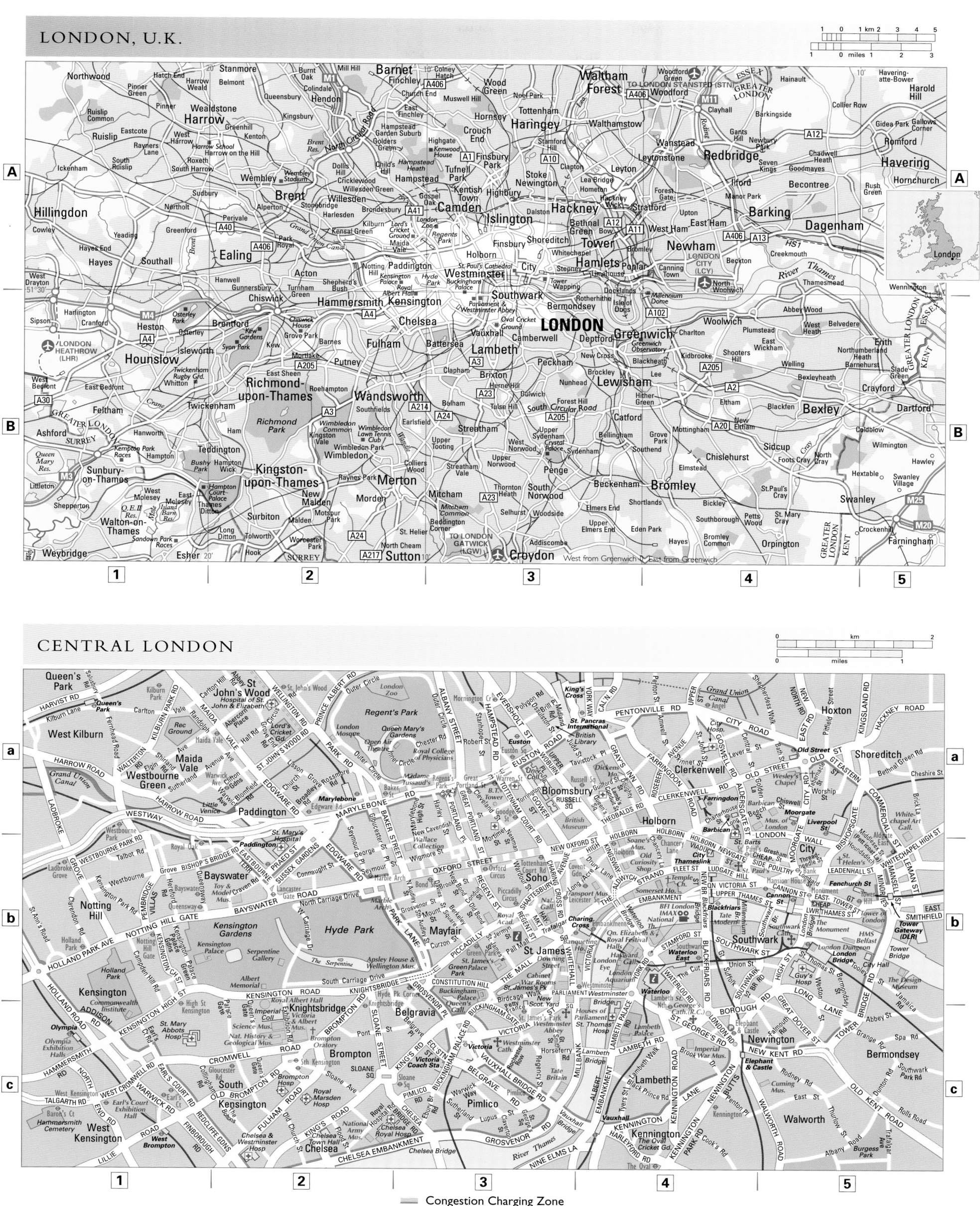

LONDON, U.K.

CENTRAL LONDON

Congestion Charging Zone

COPYRIGHT PHILIP'S

LISBON, PORTUGAL

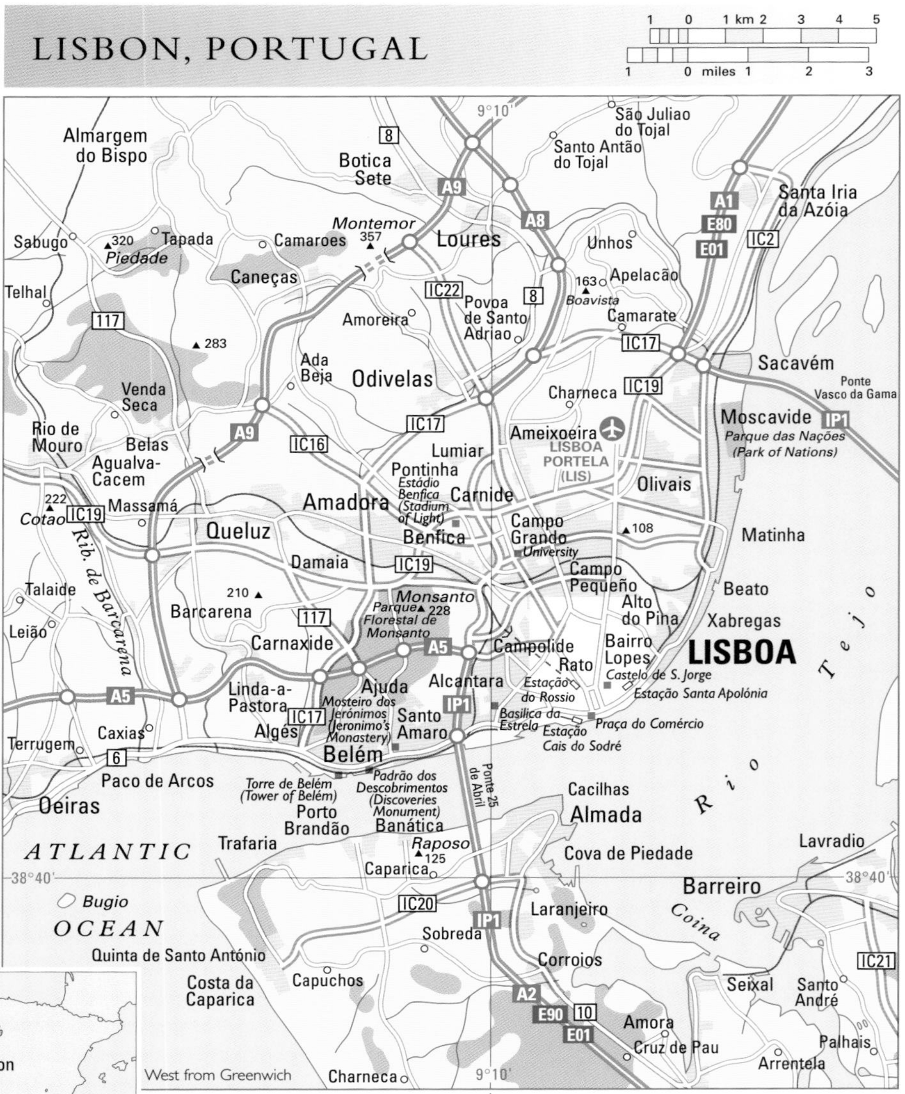

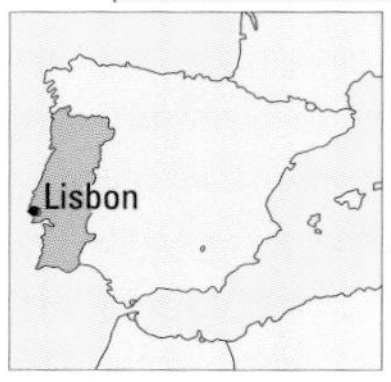

CENTRAL LISBON

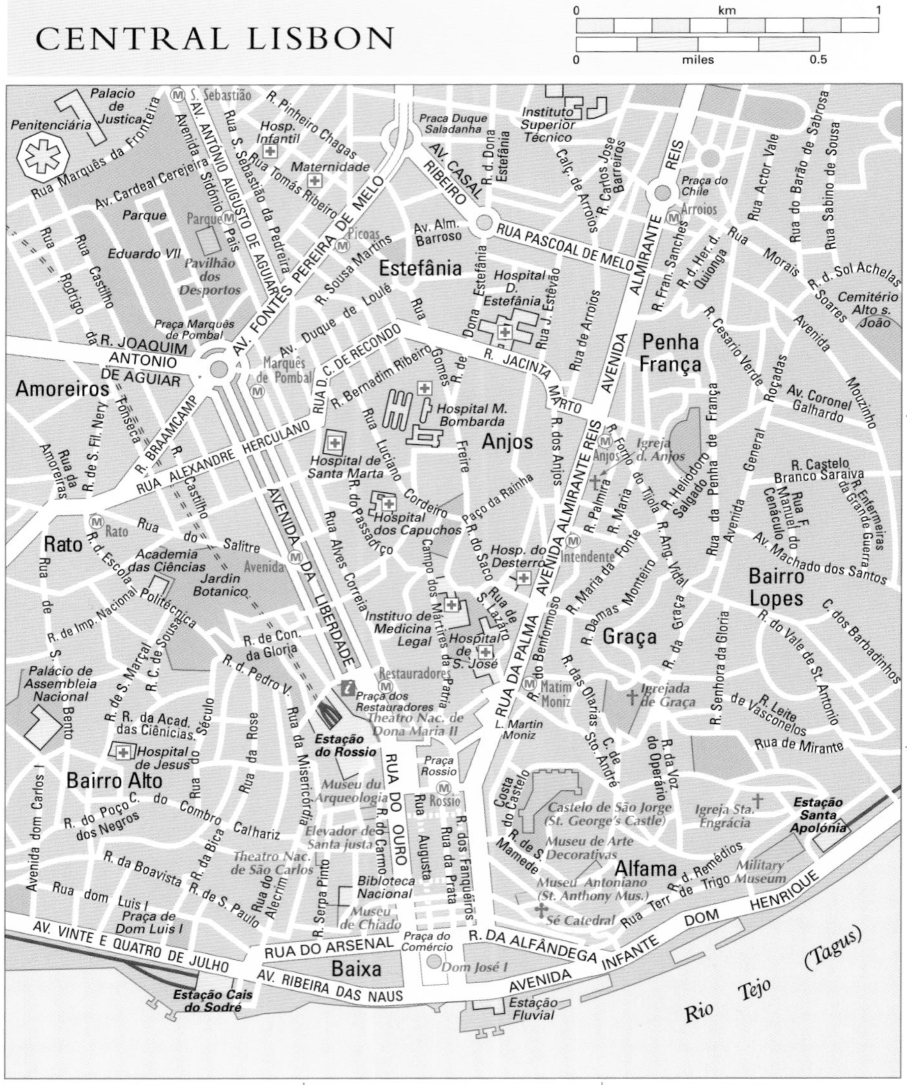

LOS ANGELES, CALIFORNIA

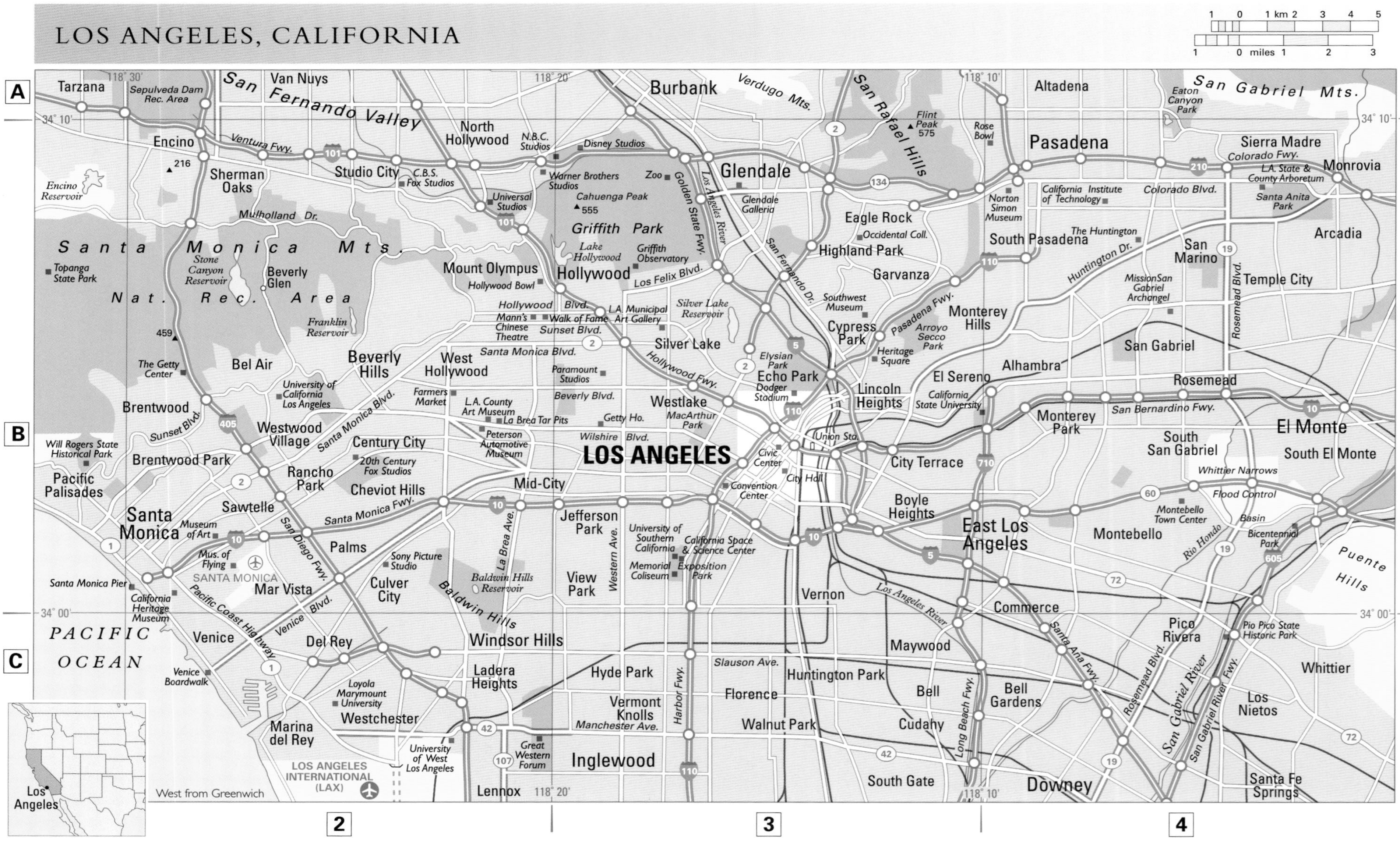

Lisbon, Portugal (left map)

Almargem do Bispo · Botica Sete · São Julião do Tojal · Santo Antão do Tojal · Santa Iria da Azóia · Sabugo · Tapada · Piedade · Montemor · Camaroes · Loures · Unhos · Apelação · Telhal · Caneças · Amoreira · Póvoa de Santo Adrião · Camarate · Boavista · Ada Beja · Odivelas · Charneca · Sacavém · Venda Seca · Belas · Aguala-Cacem · Massamá · Lumiar · Pontinha · Estádio Benfica (Stadium) (of Light) · Carnide · Ameixoeira · LISBOA PORTELA (LIS) · Moscavide · Parque das Nações (Park of Nations) · Olivais · Rio de Mouro · Amadora · Queluz · Campo Grande · University · Matinha · Cotaol · Damaia · Benfica · Campo Pequeno · Beato · Talaide · Barcarena · Parque Florestal de Monsanto · Alto do Pina · Xabregas · Leião · Campolide · Rato · Bairro Lopes · Castelo de S. Jorge · LISBOA · Carnaxide · Ajuda · Alcântara · Estação do Rossio · Estação Santa Apolónia · Caxias · Linda-a-Pastora · Algés · Mosteiro dos Jerónimos (Jeronimo's Monastery) · Santo Amaro · Basílica da Estrela · Estação Cais do Sodré · Praça do Comércio · Terrugem · Paco de Arcos · Belém · Torre de Belém (Tower of Belém) · Porto Brandão · Banática · Cacilhas · Oeiras · Padrão dos Descobrimentos (Discoveries Monument) · Raposo · Almada · Lavradio · Trafaria · Caparica · Cova de Piedade · ATLANTIC · Bugio · OCEAN · Barreiro · Quinta de Santo António · Costa da Caparica · Sobreda · Laranjeiro · Coina · Capuchos · Corroios · Amora · Seixal · Santo André · Cruz de Pau · Palhais · Arrentela · Charneca

West from Greenwich

Lisbon (inset)

Central Lisbon

Palácio de Justiça · Penitenciária · S. Sebastião · Praça Duque Saladanha · Instituto Superior Técnico · Praça de Chile · Rua Marquês da Fronteira · Hosp. Infantil · Maternidade · Parque Eduardo VII · Pavilhão dos Desportos · Estefânia · Amoreiros · Marquês de Pombal · Penha França · Rato · Anjos · Hospital de Santa Marta · Hospital M. Bombarda · Bairro Lopes · Academia das Ciências · Jardim Botânico · Hosp. dos Capuchos · Graça · Instituto de Medicina Legal · Hospital de S. José · Igreja de Graça · Palácio de Assembleia Nacional · Hospital de Jesus · Praça dos Restauradores · Teatro Nac. de Dona Maria II · Estação do Rossio · Alfama · Bairro Alto · Elevador de Santa Justa · Castelo de São Jorge (St. George's Castle) · Museu de Arte Decorativas · Igreja Sta. Engrácia · Estação Santa Apolónia · Museu do Arqueologia · Museu Nac. de São Carlos · Biblioteca Nacional · Museu do Chiado · Sé Catedral · Praça de Chiado · Baixa · RUA DO ARSENAL · Praça do Comércio · Dom José I · Estação Cais do Sodré · AV. RIBEIRA DAS NAUS · Estação Fluvial · Rio Tejo (Tagus)

Los Angeles, California

Tarzana · Sepulveda Dam Rec. Area · Van Nuys · San Fernando Valley · Burbank · Verdugo Mts. · Altadena · Eaton Canyon Park · San Gabriel Mts. · Encino · Ventura Fwy. · North Hollywood · N.B.C. Studios · Disney Studios · Flint Peak · Rose Bowl · Pasadena · Sierra Madre · Colorado Fwy. · Monrovia · Encino Reservoir · Sherman Oaks · Studio City · C.B.S. Fox Studios · Warner Brothers Studios · Zoo · Cahuenga Peak · Glendale · Glendale Galleria · Norton Simon Museum · California Institute of Technology · Colorado Blvd. · Santa Anita Park · Arcadia · Santa Monica Mts. · Mulholland Dr. · Universal Studios · Griffith Park · Lake Hollywood · Griffith Observatory · Eagle Rock · Occidental Coll. · Highland Park · South Pasadena · The Huntington · San Marino · Mission San Gabriel Archangel · Temple City · Topanga State Park · Stone Canyon Reservoir · Beverly Glen · Mount Olympus · Hollywood Bowl · Hollywood · Los Feliz Blvd. · Garvanza · Huntington Dr. · Nat. Rec. Area · Franklin Reservoir · Hollywood Blvd. · L.A. Municipal Art Gallery · Silver Lake Reservoir · Southwest Museum · Monterey Hills · San Gabriel · The Getty Center · Mann's Chinese Theatre · Sunset Blvd. · Silver Lake · Cypress Park · Heritage Square · Alhambra · Rosemead · Bel Air · Beverly Hills · West Hollywood · Santa Monica Blvd. · Paramount Studios · Hollywood Fwy. · Echo Park · Lincoln Heights · El Sereno · Monterey Park · San Bernardino Fwy. · Brentwood · University of California Los Angeles · Farmers Market · L.A. County Art Museum · Beverly Blvd. · Getty Ho. · Westlake · MacArthur Park · Dodger Stadium · California State University · El Monte · Will Rogers State Historical Park · Westwood Village · Century City · 20th Century Fox Studios · Cheviot Hills · Peterson Automotive Museum · Wilshire Blvd. · LOS ANGELES · Civic Center · City Terrace · South San Gabriel · South El Monte · Pacific Palisades · Brentwood Park · Rancho Park · Sawtelle · Palms · Mid-City · Convention Center · City Hall · Boyle Heights · East Los Angeles · Montebello · Montebello Town Center · Whittier Narrows · Flood Control Basin · Santa Monica · Museum of Art · Mus. of Flying · SANTA MONICA · Mar Vista · Culver City · Sony Picture Studio · Jefferson Park · University of Southern California · California Space & Science Center · Memorial Coliseum · Vernon · Commerce · Pico Rivera · Pio Pico State Historic Park · Puente Hills · Santa Monica Pier · California Heritage Museum · Baldwin Hills · View Park · Exposition Park · Los Angeles River · Maywood · Bicentennial Park · PACIFIC OCEAN · Venice · Venice Boardwalk · Del Rey · Windsor Hills · Baldwin Hills Reservoir · Hyde Park · Slauson Ave. · Huntington Park · Bell · Bell Gardens · Whittier · Los Nietos · Marina del Rey · Loyola Marymount University · Westchester · Ladera Heights · Vermont Knolls · Manchester Ave. · Florence · Walnut Park · Cudahy · Santa Fe Springs · LOS ANGELES INTERNATIONAL (LAX) · University of West Los Angeles · Great Western Forum · Inglewood · Lennox · South Gate · Downey

West from Greenwich

Los Angeles (inset)

🛡 85 Interstate route numbers   ⬡ 166 State route numbers

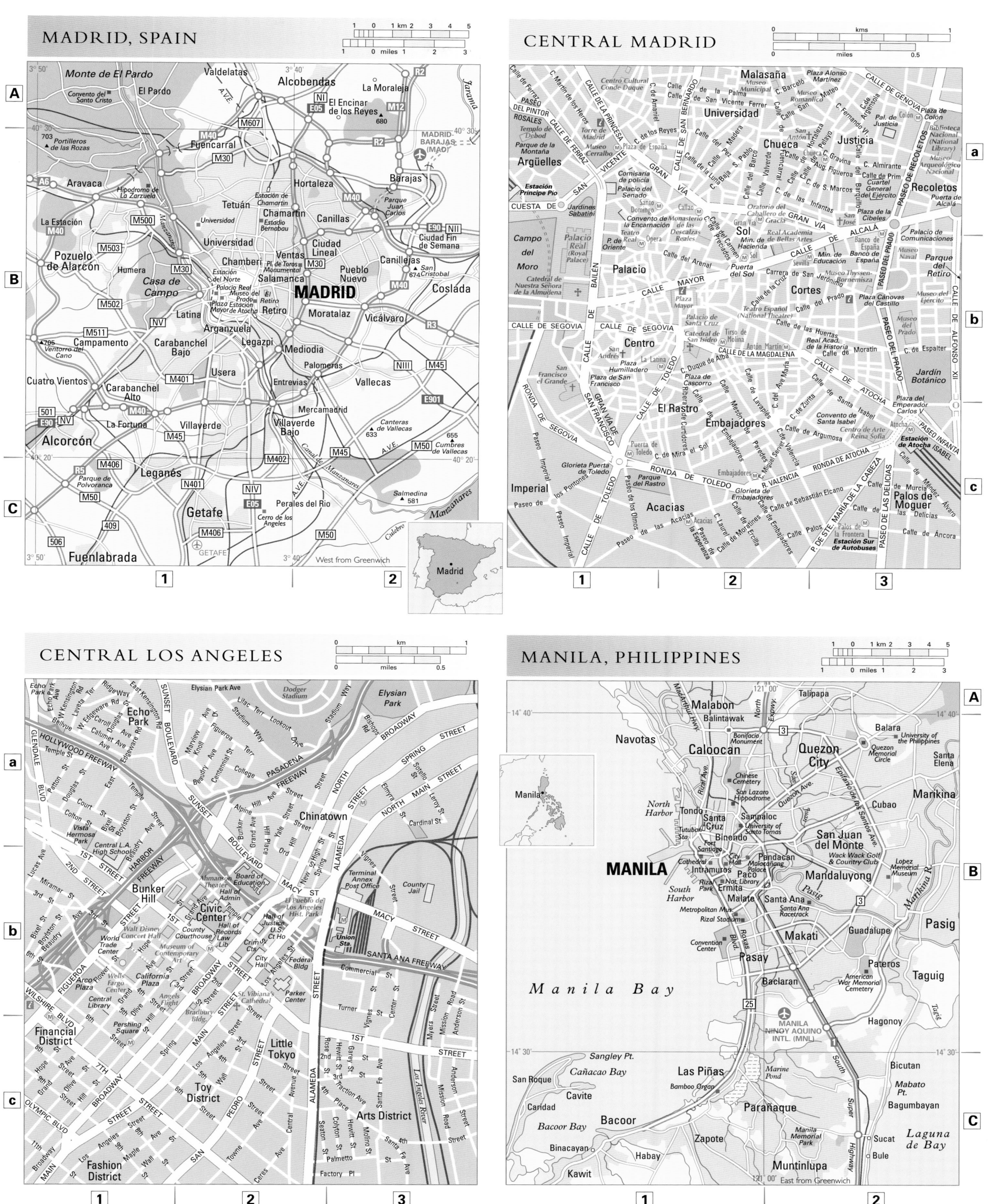

MADRID, SPAIN

Monte de El Pardo
Valdelatas
Alcobendas
La Moraleja
El Encinar de los Reyes
Convento del Santo Cristo
El Pardo
680
Portilleros de las Rozas
703
Fuencarral
M607
MADRID-BARAJAS (MAD)
Aravaca
Hipodromo de La Zarzuela
Hortaleza
Barajas
La Estación
Tetuán
Chamartín
Estadio Bernabeu
Canillas
Estación de Chamartín
Ciudad Fin de Semana
Pozuelo de Alarcón
Humera
Universidad
Ventas
Ciudad Lineal
Canillejas
San Cristobal
674
Casa de Campo
Chamberí
Pl. de Toros Monumental
Salamanca
MADRID
Estación del Norte
Palacio Real
Museo del Prado
El Retiro
Plaza Estación Mayor de Atocha
Pueblo Nuevo
Coslada
Campamento
Ventorro del Cano
795
Latina
Retiro
Moratalaz
Vicálvaro
Carabanchel Bajo
Arganzuela
Legazpi
Cuatro Vientos
Carabanchel Alto
Usera
Mediodia
Palomeras
Entrevias
Vallecas
La Fortuna
Villaverde
Mercamadrid
Villaverde Bajo
Canteras de Vallecas
633
Alcorcón
Parque de Polvoranca
Leganés
Canal de Manzanares
Cumbres de Vallecas
655
Salmedina
581
Getafe
Cerro de los Angeles
Perales del Rio
Fuenlabrada
GETAFE
West from Greenwich

Madrid

CENTRAL MADRID

Malasaña
Plaza Alonso Martínez
Centro Cultural Conde Duque
Universidad
Chueca
Justicia
Argüelles
Torre de Madrid
Parque de la Montaña
Plaza de España
Estación Príncipe Pío
Palacio del Senado
GRAN VIA
Callao
Sol
Palacio Real (Royal Palace)
Opera
Palacio
Catedral de Nuestra Señora de la Almudena
Puerta del Sol
Cortes
CALLE DE SEGOVIA
Plaza Mayor
Palacio de Santa Cruz
Teatro Español (National Theatre)
Centro
San Francisco el Grande
El Rastro
Embajadores
Acacias
Imperial
Palos de Moguer

CENTRAL LOS ANGELES

Echo Park
Dodger Stadium
Elysian Park
HOLLYWOOD FREEWAY
SUNSET BOULEVARD
PASADENA FREEWAY
Chinatown
BROADWAY
SPRING STREET
Bunker Hill
Civic Center
Walt Disney Concert Hall
Museum of Contemporary Art
Union Sta.
SANTA ANA FREEWAY
Financial District
Little Tokyo
Toy District
Arts District
Fashion District
OLYMPIC BLVD

MANILA, PHILIPPINES

Talipapa
Malabon
Balintawak
Balara
University of the Philippines
Navotas
Caloocan
Quezon City
Quezon Memorial Circle
Santa Elena
Bonifacio Monument
Marikina
Chinese Cemetery
San Lazaro Hippodrome
Cubao
North Harbor
Tondo
Santa Cruz
Sampaloc
University of Santo Tomas
San Juan del Monte
Wack Wack Golf & Country Club
Lopez Memorial Museum
MANILA
Binondo
Fort Santiago
Intramuros
Cathedral
City Hall
Pandacan
Malacañang Palace
Mandaluyong
Pasig
South Harbor
Ermita
Paco
Nat. Library
Rizal Park
Malate
Santa Ana
Santa Ana Racetrack
Metropolitan Mus.
Rizal Stadium
Makati
Guadalupe
Pasig
Convention Center
Pasay
Pateros
Taguig
Manila Bay
Baclaran
American War Memorial Cemetery
Hagonoy
MANILA NINOY AQUINO INTL. (MNL)
Sangley Pt.
Las Piñas
Marine Pond
Bicutan
San Roque
Cañacao Bay
Bamboo Organ
Mabato Pt.
Cavite
Caridad
Parañaque
Bagumbayan
Bacoor Bay
Bacoor
Manila Memorial Park
Sucat
Laguna de Bay
Binacayan
Habay
Zapote
Kawit
Muntinlupa
Bule
East from Greenwich

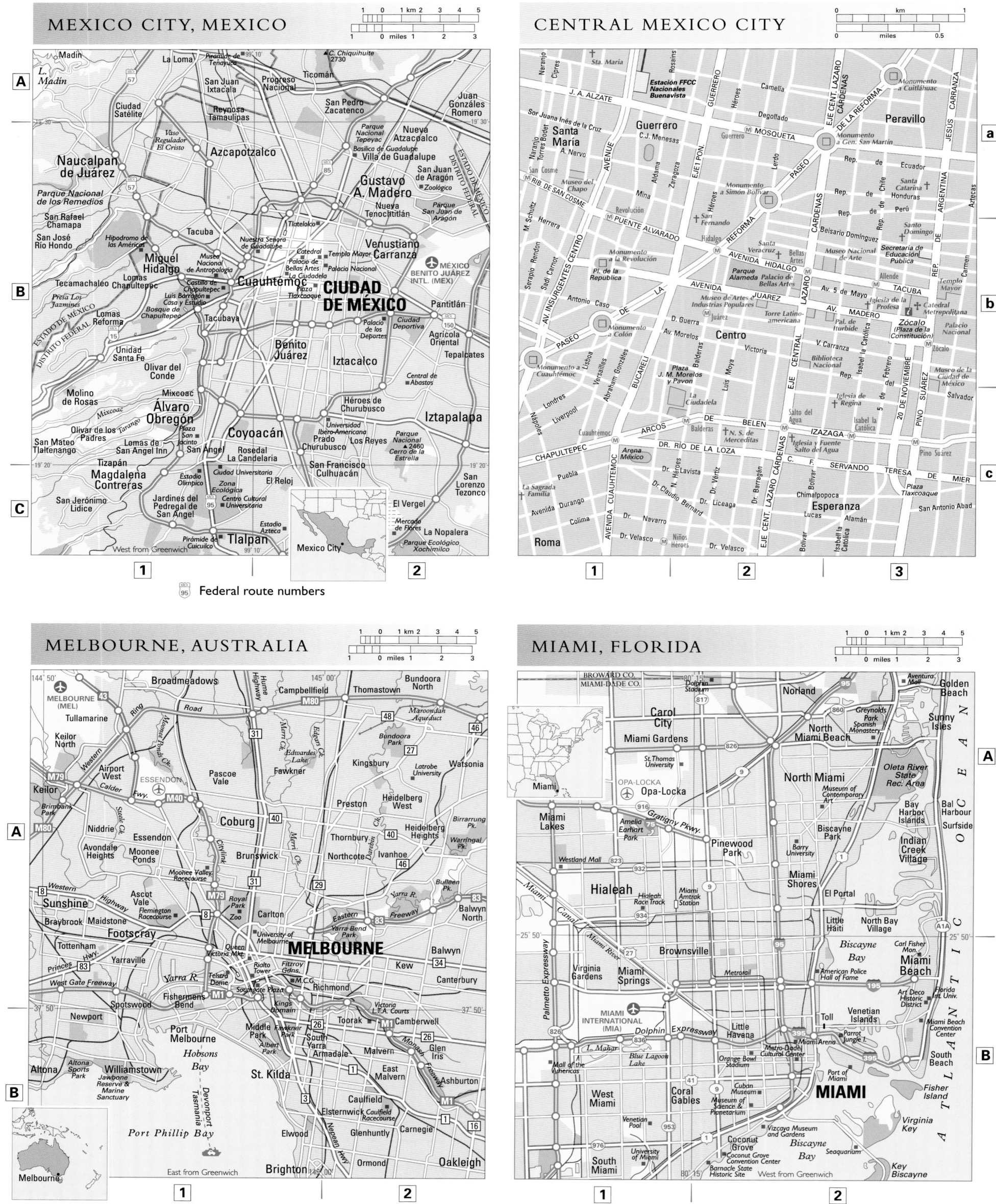

MEXICO CITY, MEXICO

CENTRAL MEXICO CITY

MELBOURNE, AUSTRALIA

MIAMI, FLORIDA

Federal route numbers

Interstate route numbers   U.S. route numbers   State route numbers

COPYRIGHT PHILIP'S

MILAN, ITALY

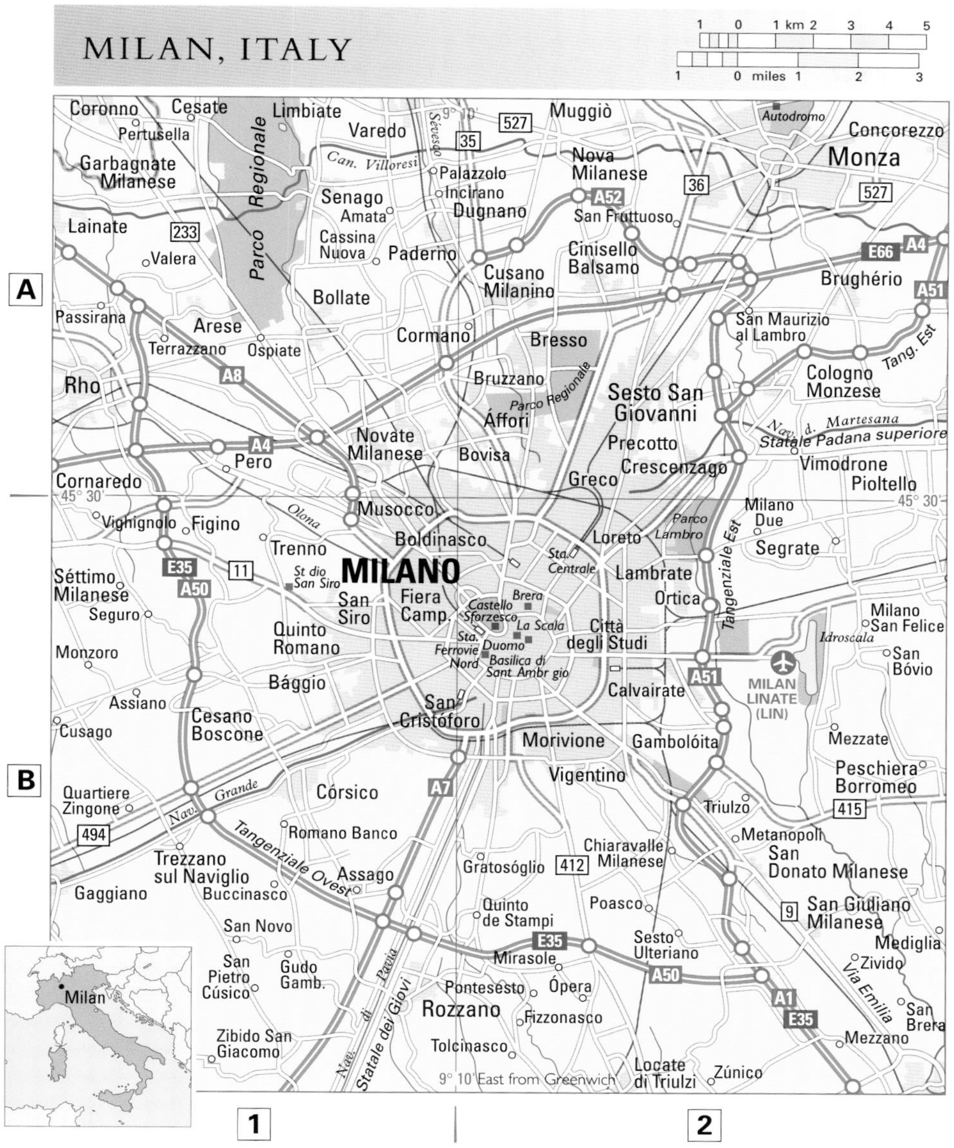

1 0 1 km 2 3 4 5
1 0 miles 1 2 3

Coronno
Cesate
Pertusella
Limbiate
Garbagnate
Milanese
Varedo
Muggiò
Autodromo
Concorezzo
Monza
527
35
Senago
Palazzolo
Incirano
Nova
Milanese
Lainate
233
Amata
Dugnano
San Fruttuoso
36
527
Cassina
Nuova
A52
Passirana
Arese
Terrazzano
Ospiate
Paderno
Cusano
Milanino
Cinisello
Balsamo
E66 A4
Brughério
A51
Valera
Bollate
Cormano
San Maurizio
al Lambro
Cologno
Monzese
Rho
A8
Pero
A4
Bruzzano
Affori
Bresso
Sesto San
Giovanni
Precotto
Tang. Est
Crescenzago
Vimodrone
Pioltello
Cornaredo
E35
A50
11
Vighignolo
Figino
Novàte
Milanese
Bovisa
Musocco
Loreto
Martesana
Greco
Milano
Due
Séttimo
Milanese
Trenno
Boldinasco
MILANO
San
Siro
Fiera
Camp.
Brera
La Scala
Duomo
Loreto
Parco
Lambro
Segrate
Seguro
Quinto
Romano
Città
degli Studi
Lambrate
Ortica
Milano
San Felice
Monzoro
Bággio
San
Cristoforo
Calvairate
A51
MILAN LINATE
(LIN)
San
Bóvio
Assiano
Cesano
Boscone
Morivione
Gambolóita
Mezzate
Cusago
Córsico
Vigentino
Triulzo
Peschiera
Borromeo
415
Quartiere
Zingone
494
Romano Banco
Trezzano
sul Naviglio
Assago
Buccinasco
Gratosóglio
Chiaravalle
Milanese
Metanopoli
San
Donato Milanese
412
Gaggiano
San Novo
Quinto
de' Stampi
Poasco
9
Zivido
San Giuliano
Milanese
Mediglia
San
Pietro
Cúsico
Gudo
Gamb.
Mirasole
Ópera
Fizzonasco
A50
A1
E35
Zibido San
Giacomo
Rozzano
Pontesesto
Tolcinasco
Locate
di Triulzi
Zúnico
Mezzano
San
Brera
9° 10° East from Greenwich

A B 1 2

CENTRAL MOSCOW

0 km 1
0 miles 0.5

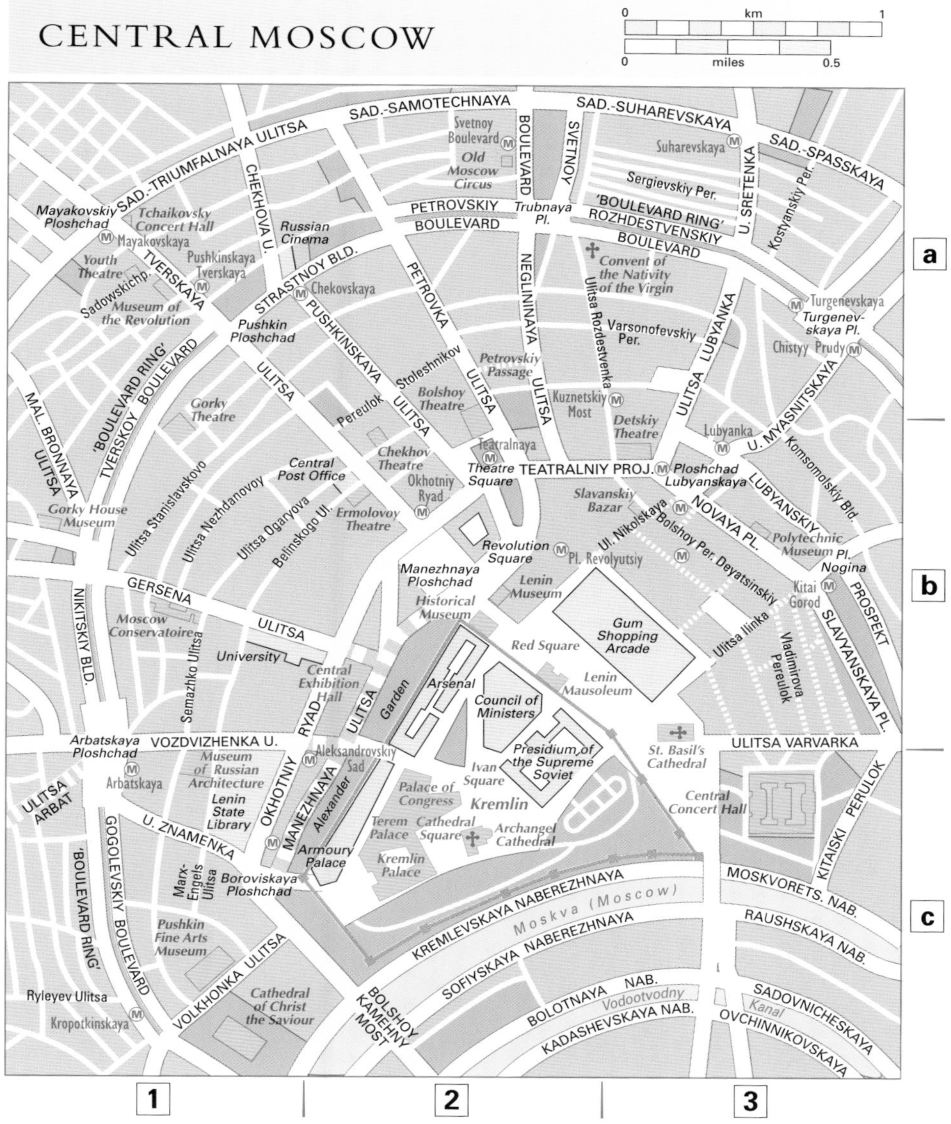

SAD.-SAMOTECHNAYA
SAD.-SUHAREVSKAYA
SAD.-SPASSKAYA
SAD.-TRIUMFALNAYA ULITSA
CHEKHOVA U.
Svetnoy
Boulevard
BOULEVARD
Svetnoy
'BOULEVARD RING'
ROZHDESTVENSKIY
BOULEVARD
Mayakovskiy
Ploshchad
Tchaikovsky
Concert Hall
Mayakovskaya
PETROVSKIY
BOULEVARD
Trubnaya
Pl.
U. SRETENKA
Youth
Theatre
Pushkinskaya
Tverskaya
Russian
Cinema
Sergievskiy Per.
Convent of
the Nativity
of the Virgin
Turgenevskaya
Turgenev-
skaya Pl.
Chistyy Prudy
Museum of
the Revolution
Pushkin
Ploshchad
PUSHKINSKAYA
PETROVKA
NEGLINNAYA
Varsonofevskiy
Per.
U. LUBYANKA
ULITSA
Gorky
Theatre
Stoleshnikov
Petrovskiy
Passage
Bolshoy
Theatre
Kuznetskiy
Most
Detskiy
Theatre
U. MYASNITSKAYA
Gorky
House
Museum
Ulitsa Stanislavskovo
ULITSA
TEATRALNIY PROJ.
Teatralnaya
Lubyanka
NOVAYA PL.
Komsomolskiy Blvd
Chekhov
Theatre
Okhotnyy
Ryad
Slavyanskiy
Bazar
LUBYANSKIY
Polytechnic
Museum
Nogina
Gorky House
Museum
Ulitsa Nechayanov
Ulitsa Ogaryova
Belinskogo U.
Ermolovoy
Theatre
Theatre
Square
Ploshchad
Lubyanskaya
Vladimirova
Pereulok
SLAVYANSKAYA PL.
PROSPEKT
Manezhnaya
Ploshchad
Revolution
Square
Pl.
Revolyutsiy
UI. Nikolskaya
Ulitsa Ilinka
Kitai
Gorod
NIKITSKIY BLD
GERSENA
ULITSA
Central
Exhibition
Hall
Historical
Museum
Lenin
Museum
Gum
Shopping
Arcade
University
Moscow
Conservatoire
Arbatskaya
Ploshchad
VOZDVIZHENKA U.
RYAD
ULITSA
Red Square
Lenin
Mausoleum
Arbatskaya
Museum of
Russian
Architecture
OKHOTNYY
Alexandrovskiy
Sad
Arsenal
Council of
Ministers
Ivan
Square
Presidium of
the Supreme
Soviet
St. Basil's
Cathedral
ULITSA VARVARKA
ULITSA
ARBAT
U. ZNAMENKA
Lenin State
Library
Palace of
Congress
Kremlin
Terem
Palace
Cathedral
Square
Armoury
Palace
Kremlin
Palace
Archangel
Cathedral
Central
Concert Hall
KITAISKI PERULOK
MOSKVORETS. NAB.
Pushkin
Fine Arts
Museum
Mark-
Engels
Ulitsa
Borovitskaya
Ploshchad
RAUSHSKAYA NAB.
GOGOLEVSKIY BOULEVARD
KREMLEVSKAYA NABEREZHNAYA
Moskva (Moscow)
BOULEVARD RING
VOLKHONKA ULITSA
SOFIYSKAYA NABEREZHNAYA
SADOVNICHESKAYA
Ryleyev Ulitsa
Cathedral
of Christ
the Saviour
BOLSHOY
KAMENYY
MOST
BOLOTNAYA NAB.
Vodootvodnyy
Kanal
OVCHINNIKOVSKAYA
Kropotkinskaya
KADASHEVSKAYA NAB.

a b c 1 2 3

MOSCOW, RUSSIA

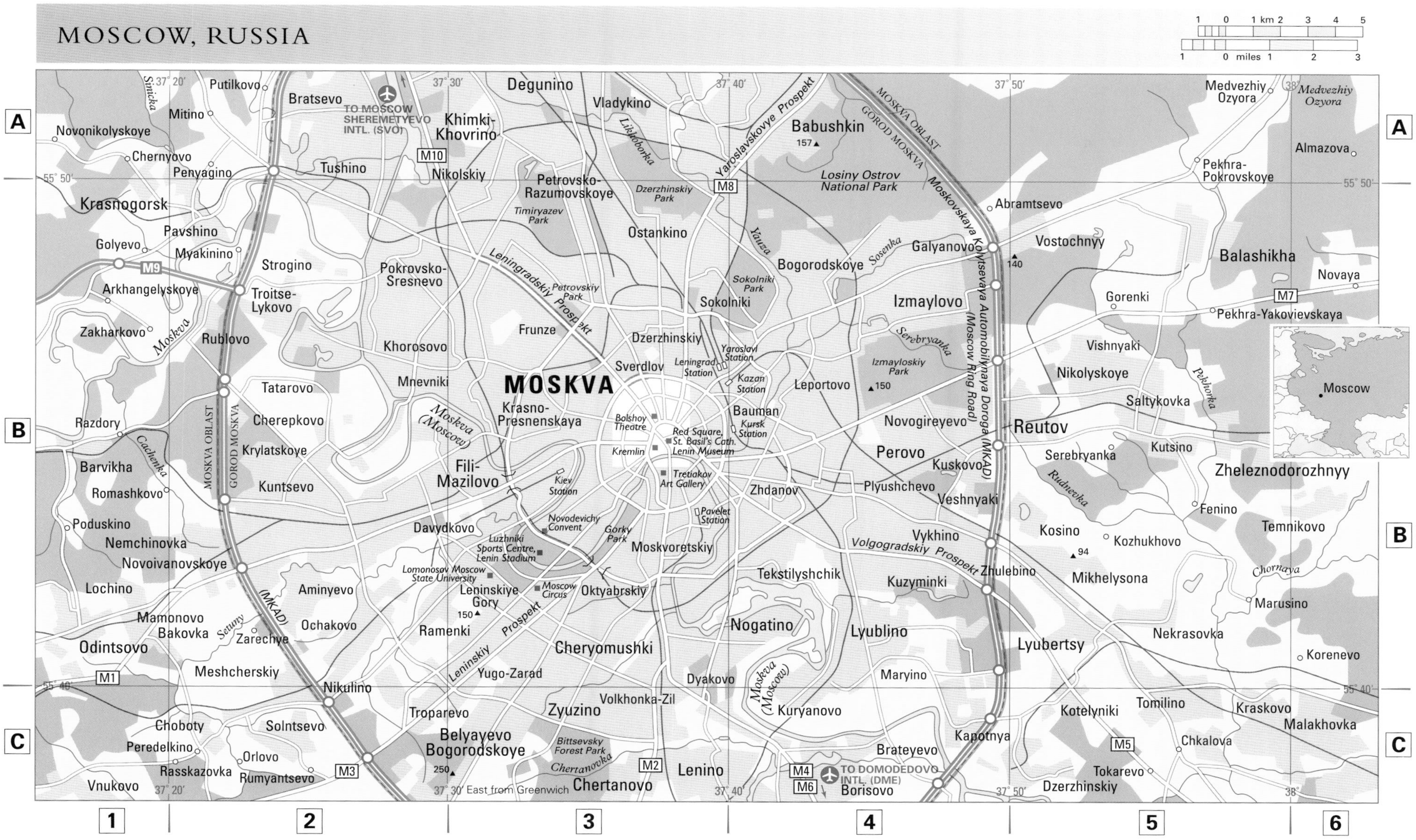

1 0 1 km 2 3 4 5
1 0 miles 1 2 3

37° 20'
37° 30'
37° 40'
37° 50'
38°
Sinicka
Putilkovo
Bratsevo
Degunino
TO MOSCOW
SHEREMETYEVO
INTL. (SVO)
Vladykino
Moskovskaya
Medvezhiy
Ozyora
Medvezhiy
Ozyora
Novonikolyskoye
Mitino
Khimki-
Khovrino
Babushkin
157
GOROD MOSKVA
Chernyovo
Penyagino
Tushino
Nikolskiy
M10
Petrovsko-
Razumovskoye
Dzerzhinskiy
Park
M8
Losiny Ostrov
National Park
Abramtsevo
Pekhra-
Pokrovskoye
Almazova
Krasnogorsk
55° 50'
Pavshino
Myakinino
Strogino
Timiryazev
Park
Ostankino
Viuza
Sosenka
Galyanovo
Vostochnyy
140
Balashikha
55° 50'
Golyево
M9
Pokrovsko-
Sresnevo
Leningradskiy Prospkt
Petrovskiy
Park
Bogorodskoye
Izmaylovo
Moskva Oblast
Novaya
Arkhangelskoye
Zakharkovo
Rublovo
Moskva
Troitse-
Lykovo
Khorosovo
Frunze
Sokolniki
Park
Sokolniki
Serebryanka
Izmayloskiy
Park
Gorenki
Pekhra-Yakovievskaya
M7
Razdory
Tatarovo
Mnevniki
Dzerzhinskiy
Sverdlov
MOSKVA
Leningrad
Station
Yaroslavl
Station
Kazan
Station
Leportovo
150
Moscow Ring Road
Vishnyaki
Nikolyskoye
Saltykovka
Barvikha
Cherepkovo
Krylatskoye
Moskva
(Moscow)
Krasno-
Presnenskaya
Bolshoy
Theatre
Kremlin
Red Square,
St. Basil's Cath.,
Lenin Museum
Bauman
Kursk
Station
Novogireyevo
Reutov
Serebryanka
Kutsino
Zheleznodorozhnyy
Romashkovo
Kuntsevo
Fili-
Mazilovo
Kiev
Station
Perovo
Kuskovo
Rudnevka
Poduskino
Nemchinovka
Novoivanovskoye
Davydkovo
Luzhniki
Sports Centre,
Lenin Stadium
Novodevichy
Convent
Gorky
Park
Pavelet
Station
Tretiakov
Art Gallery
Moskvoretskiy
Zhdanov
Plyushchevo
Veshnyaki
Vykhino
Zhulebino
Fenino
Temnikovo
Lochino
M1
Aminyevo
Ochakovo
Leninskiye
Gory
Moscow
Circus
Oktyabrskiy
Tekstilyshchik
Kuzyminki
Kosino
Kozhukhovo
Mikhelysona
Marusino
55° 40'
Mamonovo
Bakovka
Zarechye
Ramenki
Yugo-Zarad
Volgogradskiy Prospekt
Moskva
(Moscow)
Chornaya
Odintsovo
Meshcherskiy
Nikulino
Cheryomushki
Nogatino
Lyublino
Lyubertsy
55° 40'
Zyuzino
Dyakovo
Maryino
Nekrasovka
Korenevo
Choboty
Solntsevo
Belyayevo
Bogorodskoye
Volkhonka-Zil
Kuryanovo
Kotelniki
Tomilino
Kraskovo
Peredelkino
Orlovo
250
Bittsevsky
Forest Park
Troparevo
Kapotnya
Chkalova
Malakhovka
Vnukovo
Rasskazovka
Rumyantsevo
M3
Chernavka
M2
Chertanovo
Lenin
Borisovo
Brateyevo
M5
Dzerzhinskiy
M4
M6
TO DOMODEDOVO
INTL. (DME)
Tokarevo
37° 20'
37° 30' East from Greenwich
37° 40'
37° 50'
38°

A B C 1 2 3 4 5 6

Moscow

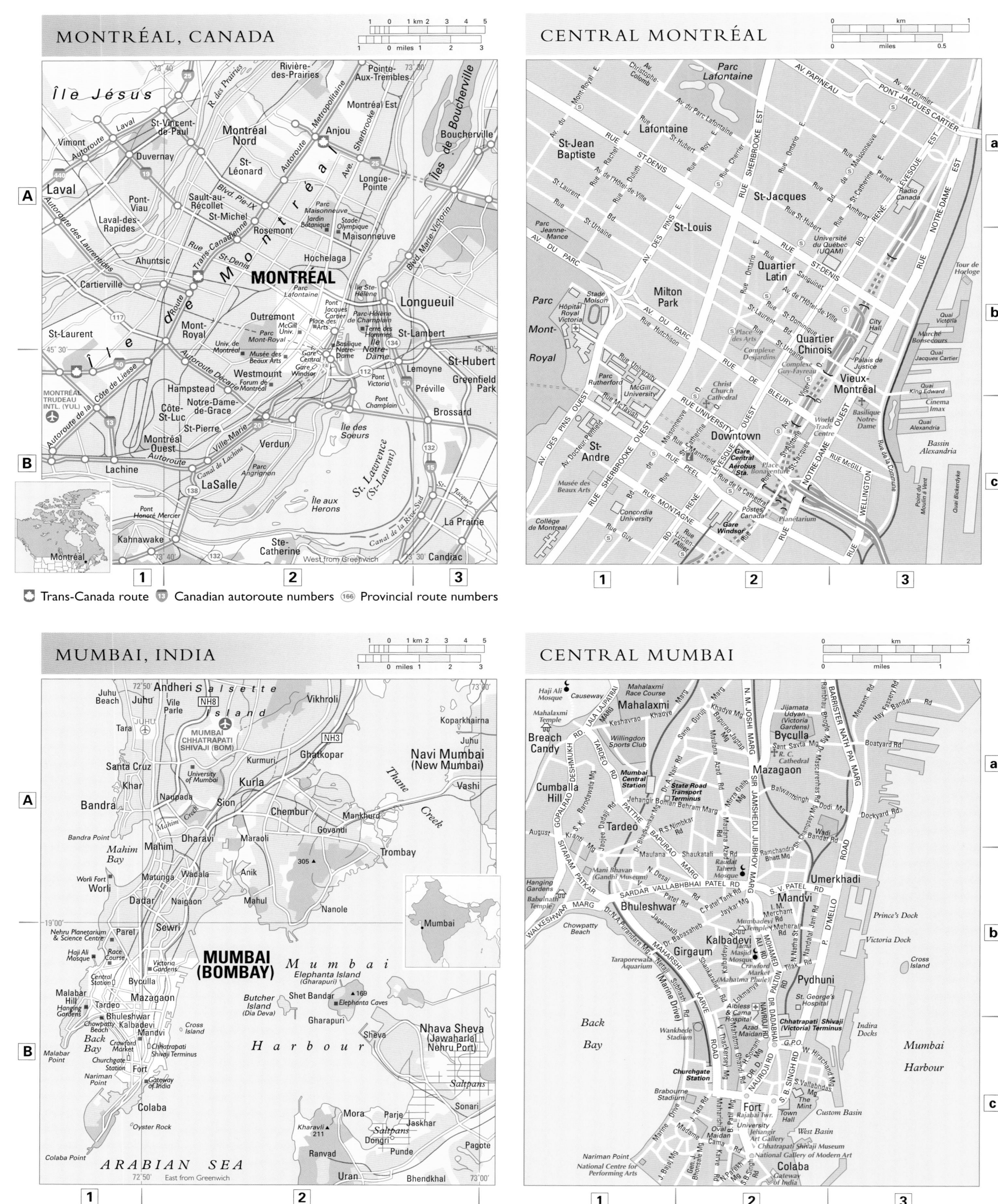

MONTRÉAL, CANADA

Île Jésus
Rivière-des-Prairies
Pointe-Aux-Trembles
St-Vincent-de-Paul
Vimont
Laval
Montréal Est
Montréal Nord
Anjou
Duvernay
St-Léonard
Longue-Pointe
Laval
Pont-Viau
Sault-au-Récollet
St-Michel
Laval-des-Rapides
Rosemont
Parc Maisonneuve
Jardin Botanique
Stade Olympique
Maisonneuve
Ahuntsic
Cartierville
Parc Lafontaine
Île Ste-Hélène
MONTRÉAL
Hochelaga
Longueuil
St-Laurent
Outremont
Mont-Royal
McGill Univ.
Parc Mont-Royal
Univ. de Montréal
Musée des Beaux Arts
Place des Arts
Parc-Hélène de Champlain
Île Notre-Dame
St-Lambert
Basilique Notre-Dame
Gare Central
St-Hubert
Westmount
Gare Windsor
Lemoyne
Greenfield Park
Hampstead
Forum de Montréal
Côte-St-Luc
Notre-Dame-de-Grace
St-Pierre
Ville Marie
Montréal Ouest
Verdun
Brossard
Lachine
Canal de Lachine
LaSalle
Parc Angrignon
Île des Soeurs
St. Laurence (St-Laurent)
Île aux Herons
La Prairie
Pont Honoré Mercier
Kahnawake
Ste-Catherine
West from Greenwich
Candiac
MONTRÉAL TRUDEAU INTL. (YUL)
Montréal

Trans-Canada route · Canadian autoroute numbers · Provincial route numbers

CENTRAL MONTRÉAL

Parc Lafontaine
St-Jean Baptiste
Lafontaine
St-Jacques
St-Louis
Parc Jeanne-Mance
Milton Park
Quartier Latin
Université du Québec (UQAM)
Parc Mont-Royal
Stade Molson
Hôpital Royal Victoria
McGill University
Quartier Chinois
Tour de l'Horloge
Parc Rutherford
Christ Church Cathedral
Place des Arts
Complexe Desjardins
Vieux-Montréal
Marché Bonsecours
Quai Jacques Cartier
Palais de Justice
Downtown
World Trade Centre
Quai King Edward
Cinema Imax
St-Andre
Gare Central Aerobus Sta.
Basilique Notre-Dame
Quai Alexandria
Musée des Beaux Arts
Bassin Alexandria
Collège de Montréal
Concordia University
Gare Windsor
Postes Canada
Planétarium
Point du Moulin à Vent
Quai Bickerdyke

MUMBAI, INDIA

Andheri
Salsette Island
Juhu Beach
Juhu
Vile Parle
Vikhroli
Tara
MUMBAI CHHATRAPATI SHIVAJI (BOM)
Ghatkopar
Koparkhairna
Juhu
Santa Cruz
University of Mumbai
Kurmuri
Navi Mumbai (New Mumbai)
Khar
Nagpada
Kurla
Vashi
Bandra
Sion
Chembur
Mankhurd
Thane Creek
Govandi
Bandra Point
Mahim
Dharavi
Maraoli
Mahim Bay
Matunga
Anik
Trombay
Wadala
Worli Fort
Worli
Dadar
Naigaon
Mahul
305
Nanole
Nehru Planetarium & Science Centre
Parel
Sewri
Mumbai
Haji Ali Mosque
Race Course
MUMBAI (BOMBAY)
Elephanta Island (Gharapuri)
Central Station
Victoria Gardens
Byculla
Malabar Hill
Mazagaon
Hanging Gardens
Tardeo
Butcher Island (Dia Deva)
Shet Bandar
Elephanta Caves
169
Bhuleshwar
Kalbadevi
Mandvi
Cross Island
Chowpatty Beach
Crawford Market
Chhatrapati Shivaji Terminus
Gharapuri
Sheva
Nhava Sheva (Jawaharlal Nehru Port)
Malabar Point
Back Bay
Churchgate Station
Fort
Harbour
Nariman Point
Gateway of India
Colaba
Colaba Point
ARABIAN SEA
East from Greenwich
Mora
Parje
Jaskhar
Saltpans
Kharavli 211
Sonari
Dongri
Saltpans
Punde
Pagote
Ranvad
Uran
Bhendkhal

CENTRAL MUMBAI

Haji Ali Mosque
Causeway
Mahalaxmi Race Course
Jijamata Udyan (Victoria Gardens)
Mahalaxmi
Mahalaxmi Temple
Keshavrao
Khadye
Byculla
Breach Candy
Willingdon Sports Club
Mazagaon
Cumballa Hill
Mumbai Central Station
State Road Transport Terminus
R. C. Cathedral
Tardeo
Jehangir Boman
Behram Marg
Umerkhadi
Mani Bhavan (Gandhi Museum)
Randal Tahera Mosque
Mandvi
Hanging Gardens
Bhuleshwar
I.M. Merchant
Prince's Dock
Babulnath Temple
Chowpatty Beach
Girgaum
Mumbadevi Temple
Kalbadevi
Jama Masjid Mosque
Victoria Dock
Taraporewala Aquarium
Back Bay
Crawford Market
Pydhuni
Cross Island
St. George's Hospital
Albless & Cama Hospital
Azad Maidan
Chhatrapati Shivaji (Victoria) Terminus
Indira Docks
Wankhede Stadium
G.P.O.
Churchgate Station
Mumbai Harbour
Brabourne Stadium
Fort
The Mint
Rajabai Twr.
Town Hall
Custom Basin
University
Jehangir Art Gallery
West Basin
Nariman Point
Oval Maidan
Chhatrapati Shivaji Museum
National Gallery of Modern Art
National Centre for Performing Arts
Colaba
Gateway of India

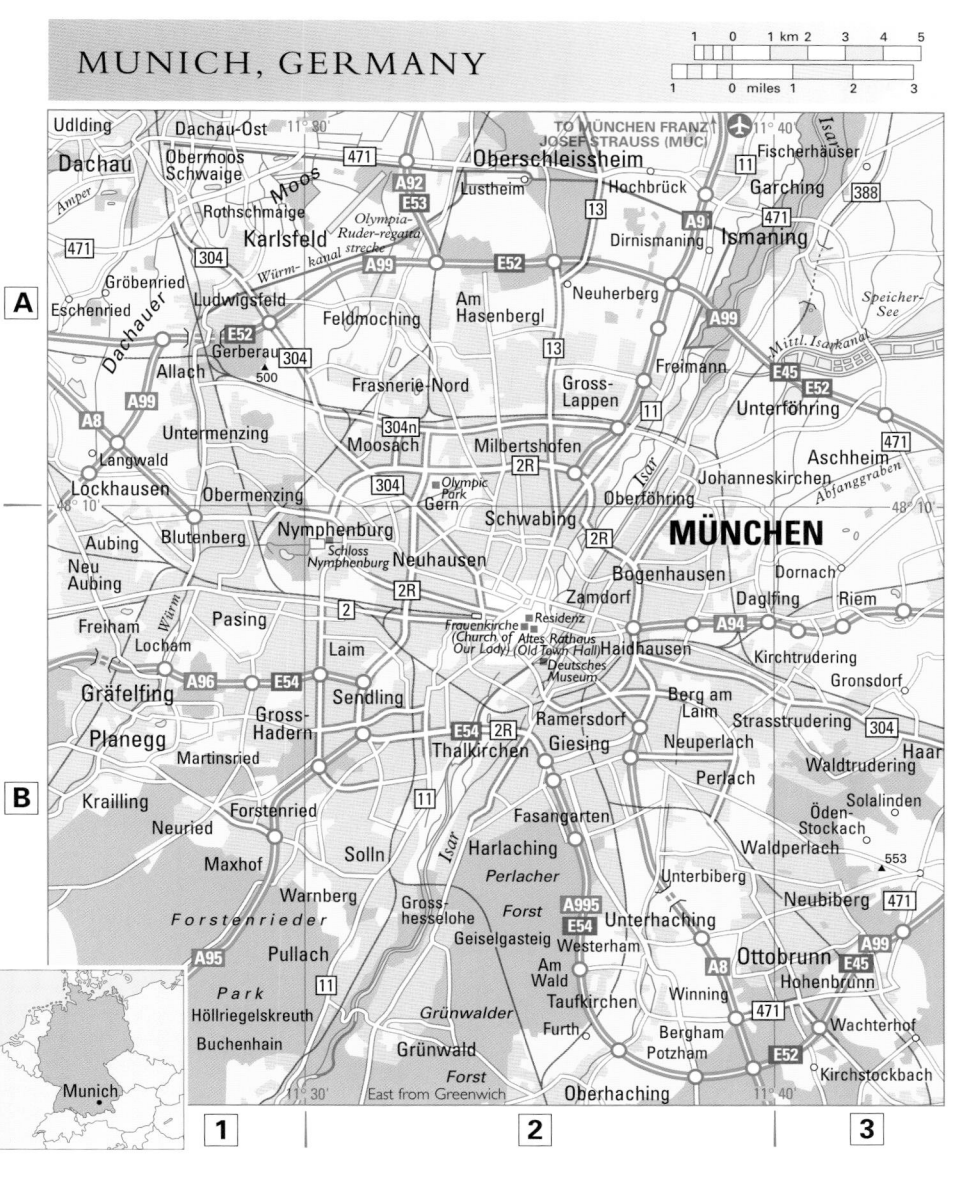

MUNICH, GERMANY

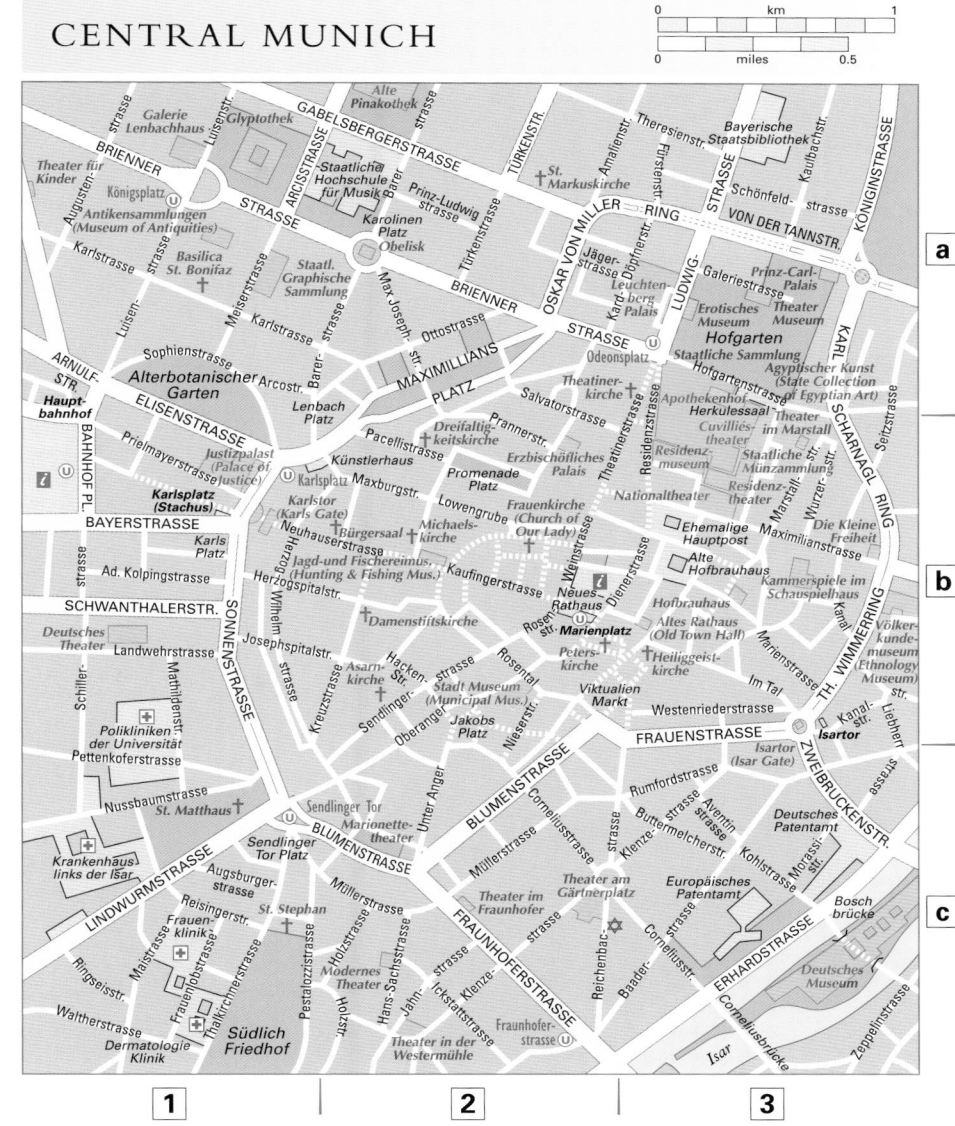

CENTRAL MUNICH

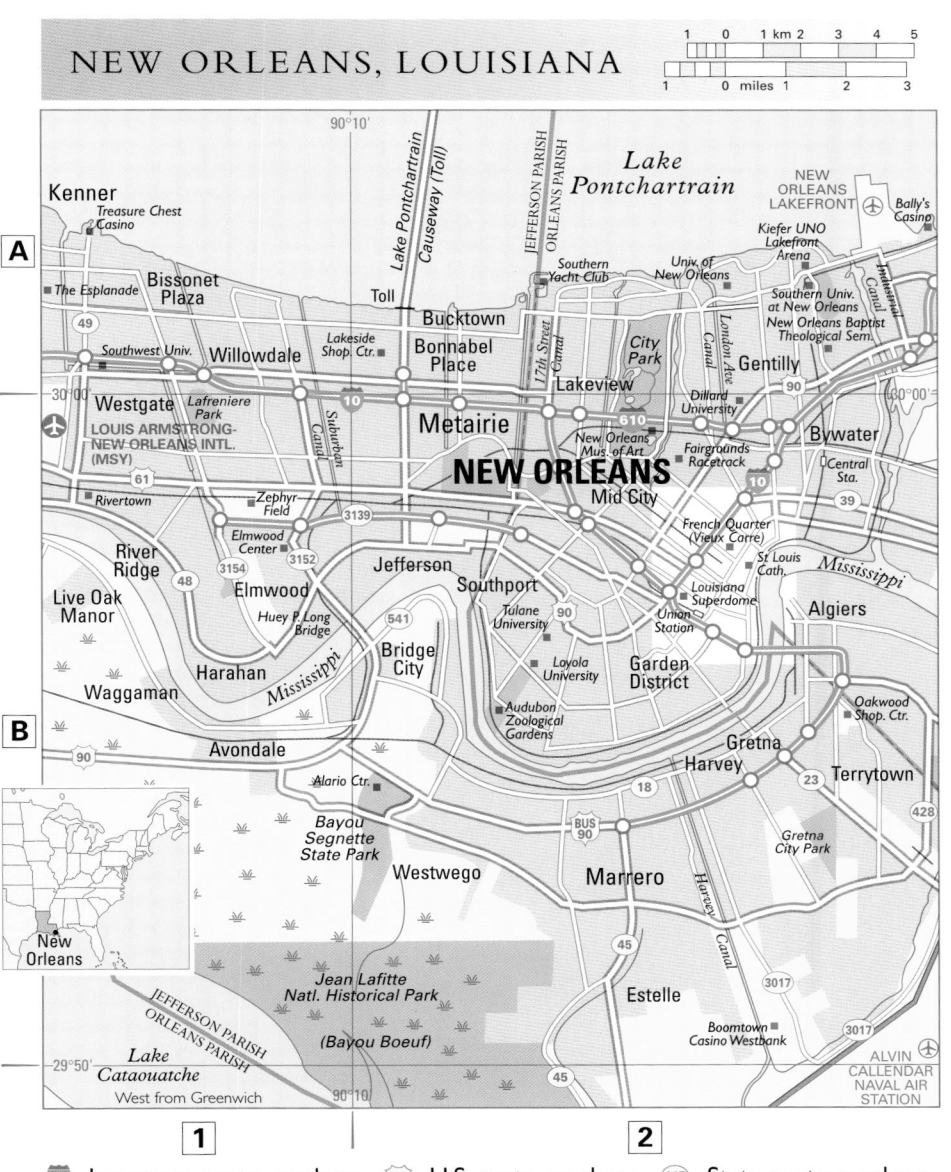

NEW ORLEANS, LOUISIANA

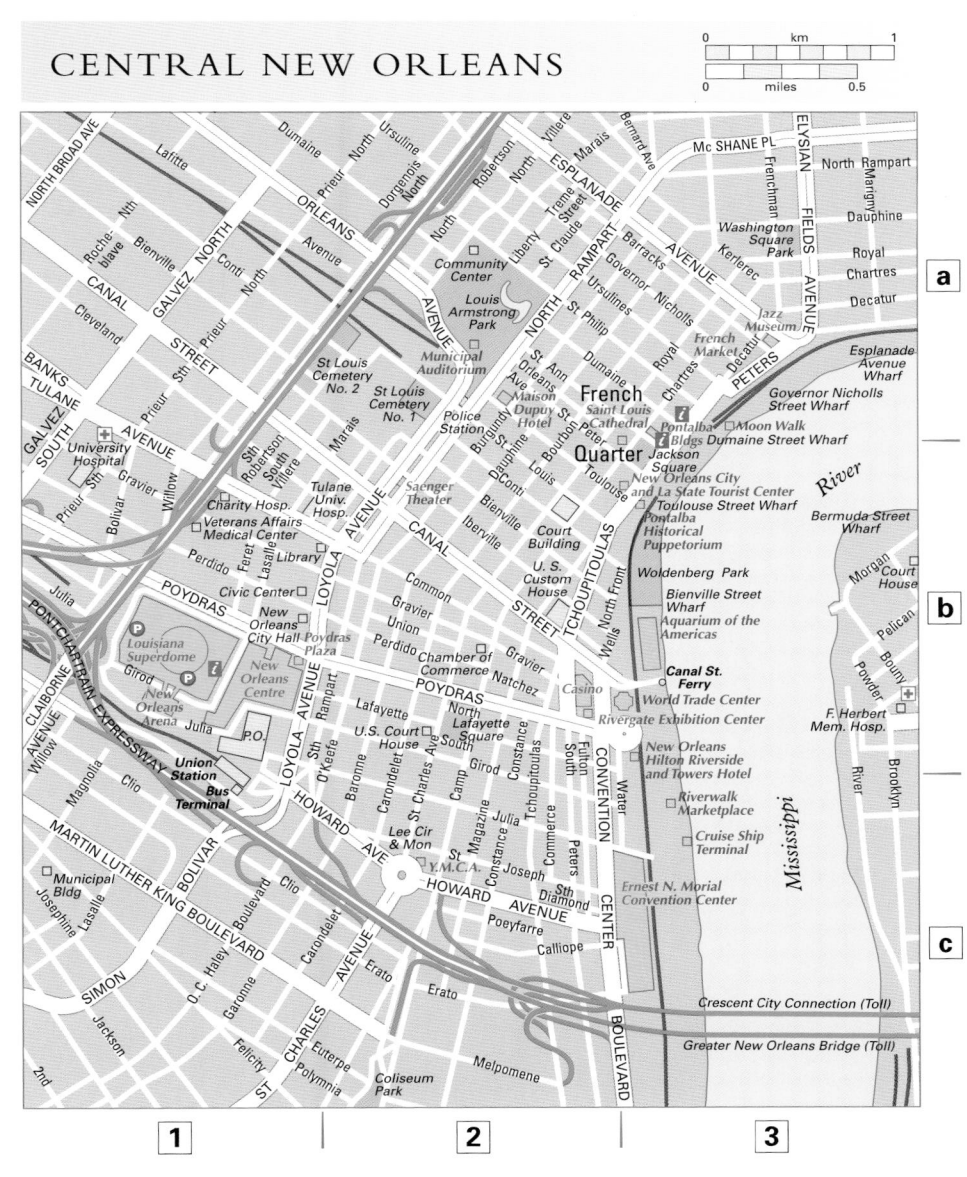

CENTRAL NEW ORLEANS

Interstate route numbers   U.S. route numbers   State route numbers

COPYRIGHT PHILIP'S

NEW YORK, NEW YORK

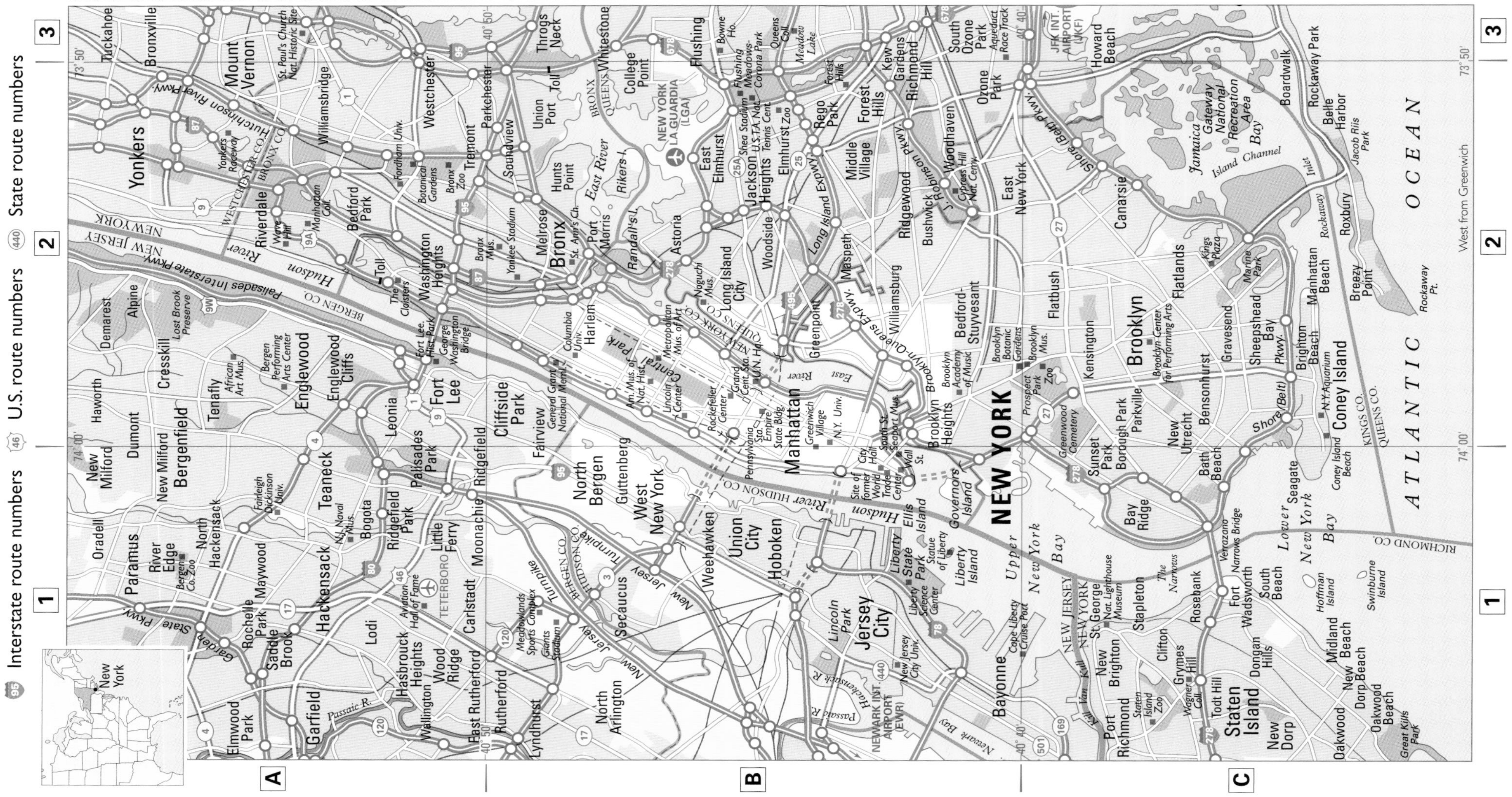

CENTRAL NEW YORK

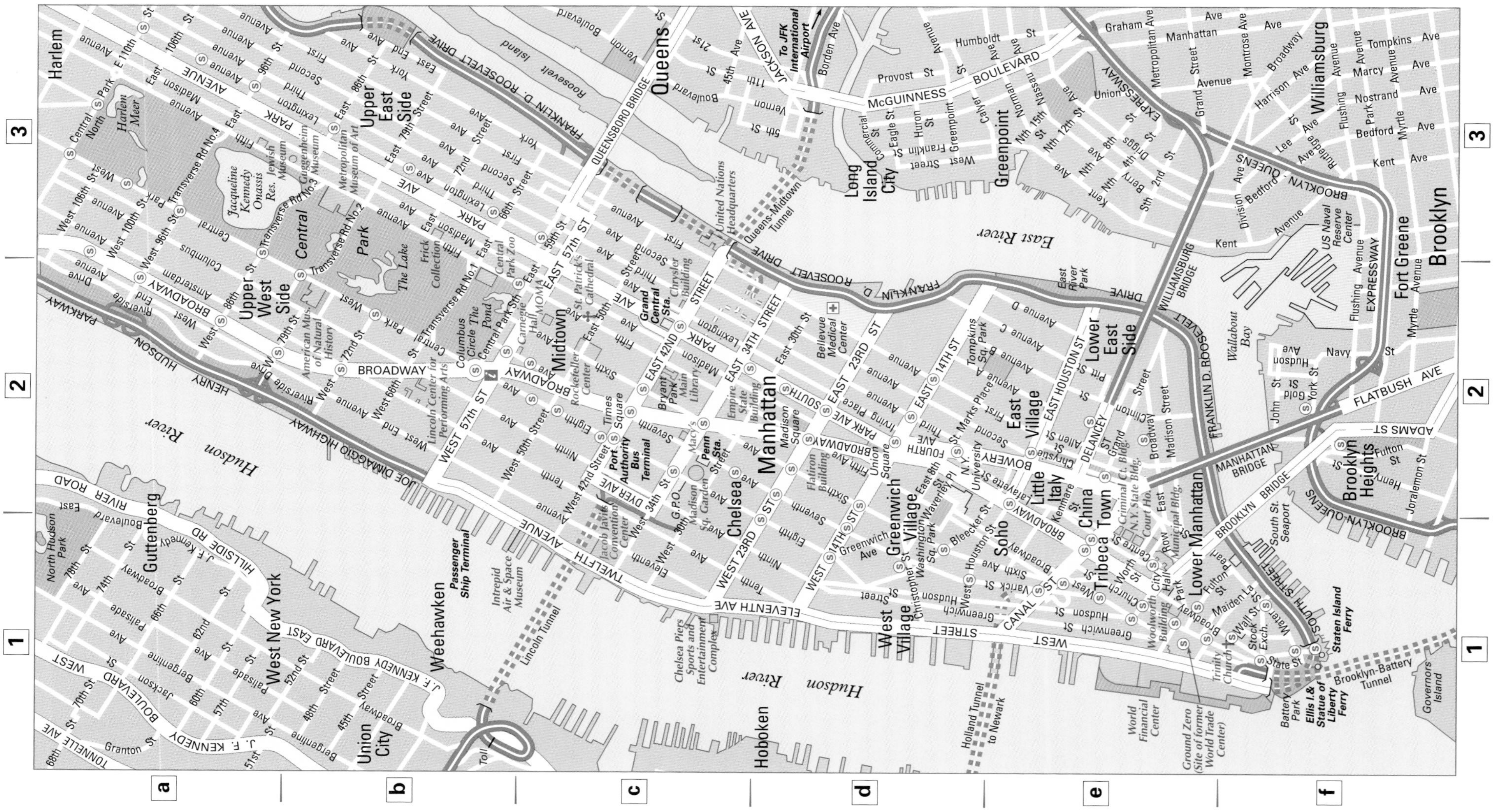

Interstate route numbers

U.S. route numbers

State route numbers

COPYRIGHT PHILIP'S

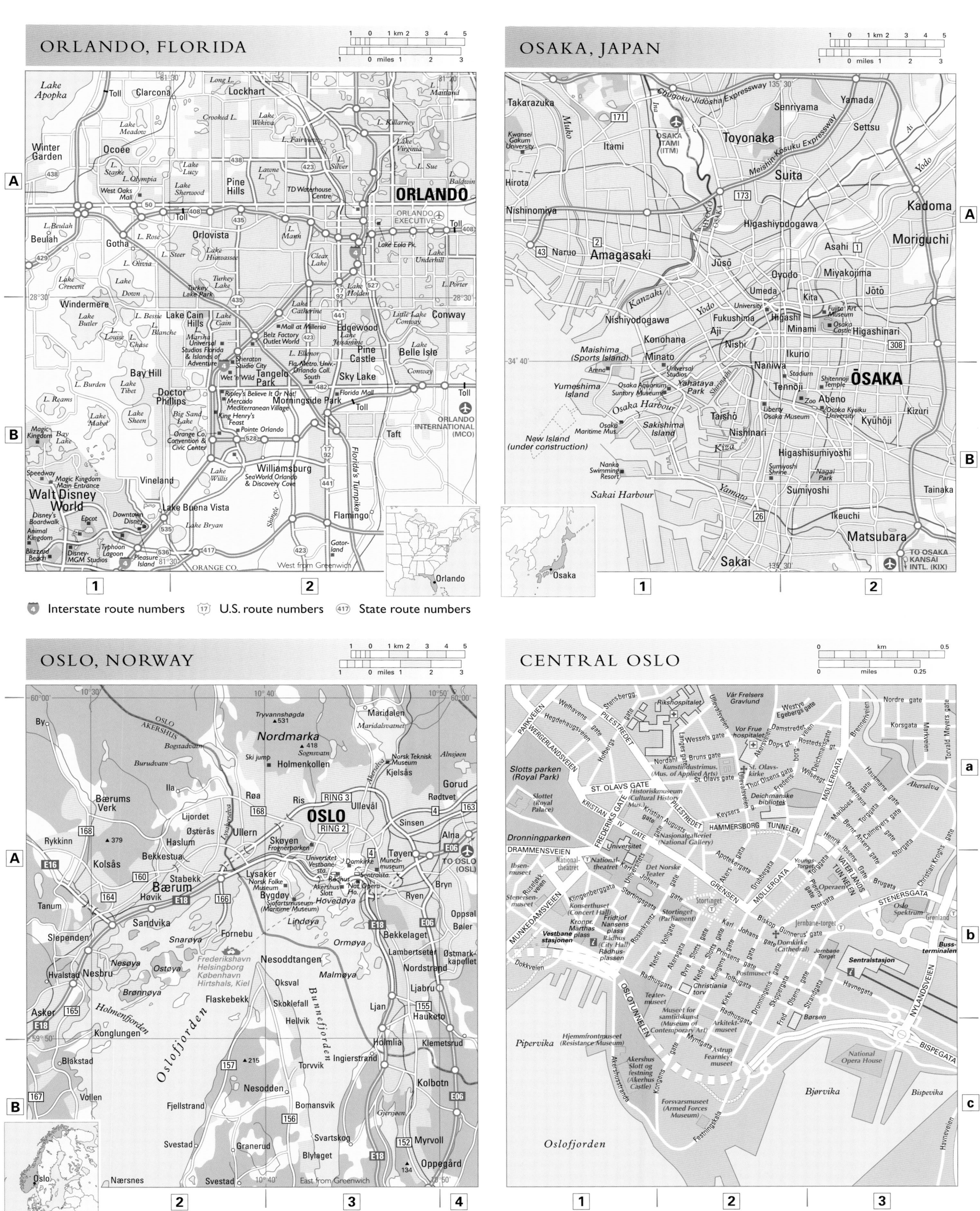

PARIS, FRANCE

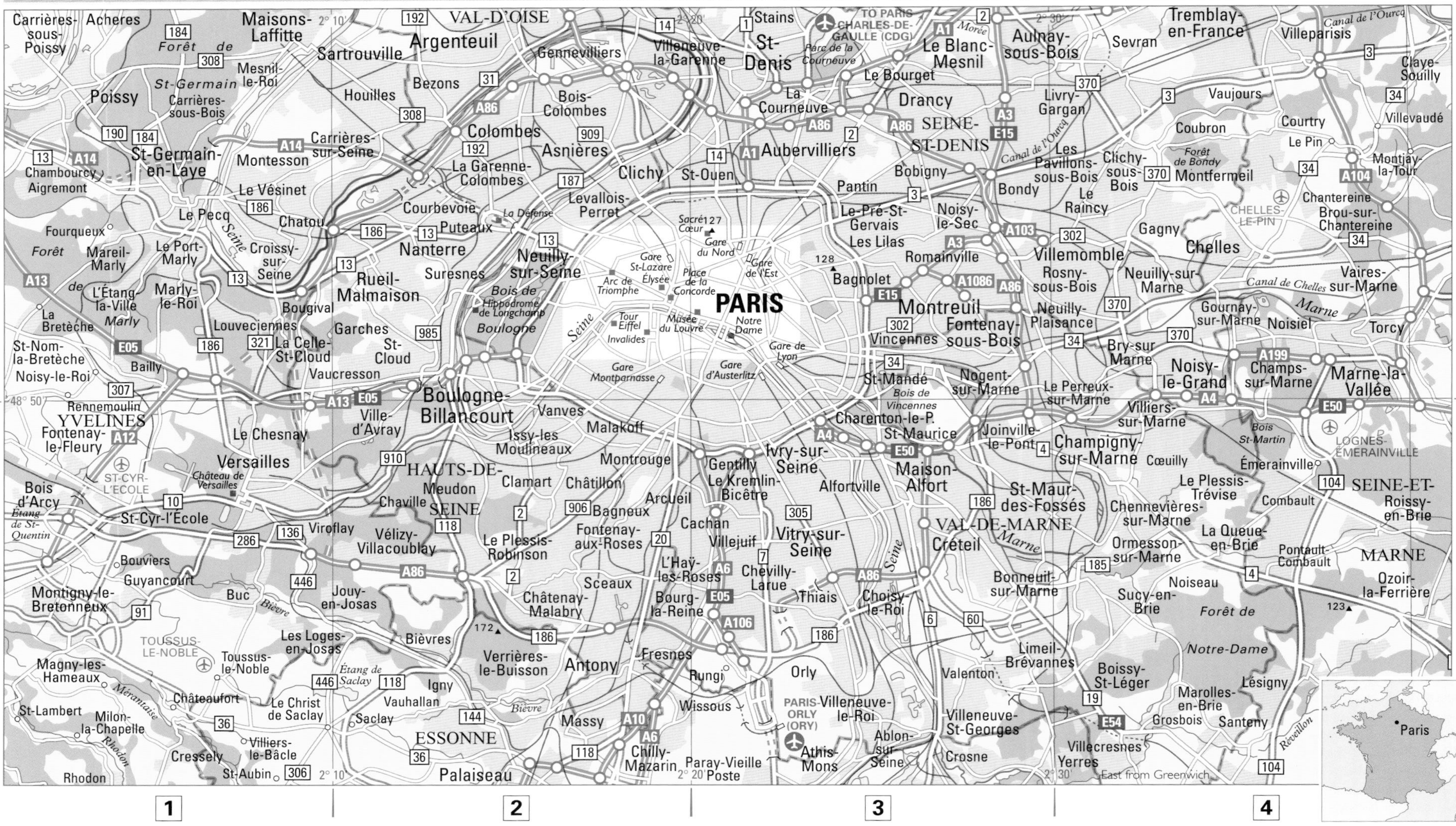

1 0 1 km 2 3 4 5
1 0 miles 1 2 3

48° 50'

A

B

Carrières-sous-Poissy · Achères · Maisons-Laffitte · VAL-D'OISE · Stains · St-Denis · TO PARIS CHARLES-DE-GAULLE (CDG) · Le Blanc-Mesnil · Aulnay-sous-Bois · Sevran · Tremblay-en-France · Villeparisis · Claye-Souilly · Villevaudé

Poissy · Forêt de St-Germain · Mesnil-le-Roi · Sartrouville · Argenteuil · Gennevilliers · Villeneuve-la-Garenne · La Courneuve · Le Bourget · Drancy · Livry-Gargan · Vaujours · Coubron · Courtry · Le Pin · Montjay-la-Tour

Carrières-sous-Bois · Houilles · Bezons · Colombes · Bois-Colombes · Aubervilliers · Bobigny · SEINE-ST-DENIS · Les Pavillons-sous-Bois · Clichy-sous-Bois · Forêt de Bondy · Montfermeil · Chantereine · Brou-sur-Chantereine

St-Germain-en-Laye · Chambourcy · Aigremont · Montesson · La Garenne-Colombes · Asnières · Clichy · St-Ouen · Pantin · Le Pré-St-Gervais · Les Lilas · Romainville · Noisy-le-Sec · Villemomble · Gagny · Chelles · CHELLES-LE-PIN · Vaires-sur-Marne

Fourqueux · Le Pecq · Croissy-sur-Seine · Courbevoie · Puteaux · La Défense · Neuilly-sur-Seine · Gare St-Lazare · Gare du Nord · Gare de l'Est · Bagnolet · Montreuil · Rosny-sous-Bois · Neuilly-sur-Marne · Gournay-sur-Marne · Noisiel · Torcy

Mareil-Marly · Le Vésinet · Chatou · Nanterre · Suresnes · Rueil-Malmaison · Arc de Triomphe · **PARIS** · Notre Dame · Vincennes · Neuilly-Plaisance · Bry-sur-Marne · Marne

Le Port-Marly · Bougival · Louveciennes · Garches · St-Cloud · Bois de Boulogne · Tour Eiffel · Invalides · Musée du Louvre · Gare de Lyon · St-Mandé · Bois de Vincennes · Nogent-sur-Marne · Le Perreux-sur-Marne · Noisy-le-Grand · Champs-sur-Marne · Marne-la-Vallée · LOGNES EMERAINVILLE

Marly-le-Roi · La Celle-St-Cloud · Vaucresson · Boulogne-Billancourt · Gare Montparnasse · Gare d'Austerlitz · Charenton-le-P. · St-Maurice · Joinville-le-Pont · Champigny-sur-Marne · Villiers-sur-Marne · Bois St-Martin

La Bretèche · St-Nom-la-Bretèche · Bailly · Le Chesnay · Ville-d'Avray · Vanves · Issy-les-Moulineaux · Malakoff · Montrouge · Gentilly · Ivry-sur-Seine · Maisons-Alfort · Créteil · VAL-DE-MARNE · St-Maur-des-Fossés · Chennevières-sur-Marne · Le Plessis-Trévise · Combault · SEINE-ET-ROISSY-EN-BRIE

YVELINES · Fontenay-le-Fleury · Versailles · Château de Versailles · Meudon · HAUTS-DE-SEINE · Clamart · Châtillon · Arcueil · Le Kremlin-Bicêtre · Alfortville · Ormesson-sur-Marne · La Queue-en-Brie · Pontault-Combault · MARNE

Bois d'Arcy · ST-CYR-L'ÉCOLE · Chaville · Vélizy-Villacoublay · Bagneux · Cachan · Vitry-sur-Seine · Choisy-le-Roi · Sucy-en-Brie · Forêt de Notre-Dame · Ozoir-la-Ferrière

Montigny-le-Bretonneux · St-Cyr-l'École · Viroflay · Le Plessis-Robinson · Fontenay-aux-Roses · Villejuif · L'Haÿ-les-Roses · Chevilly-Larue · Thiais · Bonneuil-sur-Marne · Noiseau · Boissy-St-Léger · Lésigny

Guyancourt · Buc · Jouy-en-Josas · Châtenay-Malabry · Sceaux · Bourg-la-Reine · Rungis · Orly · Valenton · Villecresnes · Marolles-en-Brie · Grosbois · Santeny

Magny-les-Hameaux · Toussus-le-Noble · Les Loges-en-Josas · Bièvres · Verrières-le-Buisson · Antony · Fresnes · PARIS ORLY (ORY) · Villeneuve-le-Roi · Ablon-sur-Seine · Villeneuve-St-Georges · Boissy-St-Léger · Yerres · Réveillon

St-Lambert · Milon-la-Chapelle · Châteaufort · Le Christ de Saclay · Saclay · ESSONNE · Igny · Vauhallan · Massy · Wissous · Chilly-Mazarin · Paray-Vieille-Poste · Athis-Mons · Crosne

Cressely · St-Aubin · Palaiseau · Rhodon

East from Greenwich

Paris

1 **2** **3** **4**

CENTRAL PARIS

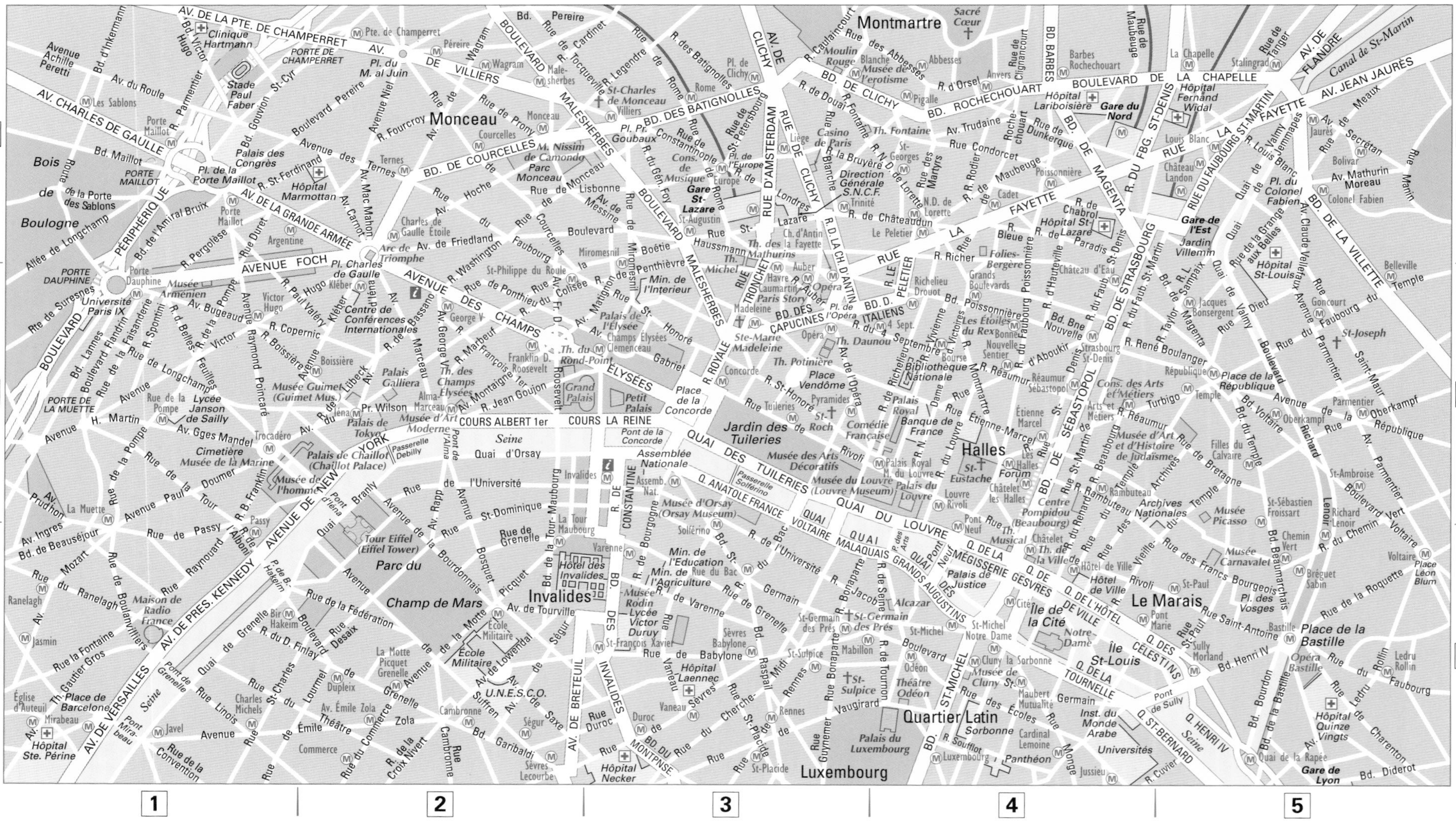

0 km 1
0 miles 0.5

a

b

c

Montmartre · Sacré Cœur · AV. DE LA PTE. DE CHAMPERRET · Pte. de Champerret · PORTE DE CHAMPERRET · Monceau · Gare St-Lazare · Gare du Nord · Gare de l'Est · AV. JEAN JAURÈS · Canal de St-Martin

Bois de Boulogne · PORTE MAILLOT · Arc de Triomphe · Pl. Charles de Gaulle · AVENUE FOCH · PORTE DAUPHINE · Musée Guimet (Guimet Mus.) · Opéra · BD. DE STRASBOURG · Belleville

Palais de Chaillot (Chaillot Palace) · Tour Eiffel (Eiffel Tower) · Parc du Champ de Mars · Invalides · Jardin des Tuileries · Musée du Louvre (Louvre Museum) · Musée d'Orsay (Orsay Museum) · Halles · Centre Pompidou (Beaubourg) · Le Marais · Musée Picasso · Place de la République

AV. DE VERSAILLES · Quartier Latin · Palais du Luxembourg · Luxembourg · Panthéon · Île de la Cité · Notre Dame · Île St-Louis · Place de la Bastille · Gare de Lyon

1 **2** **3** **4** **5**

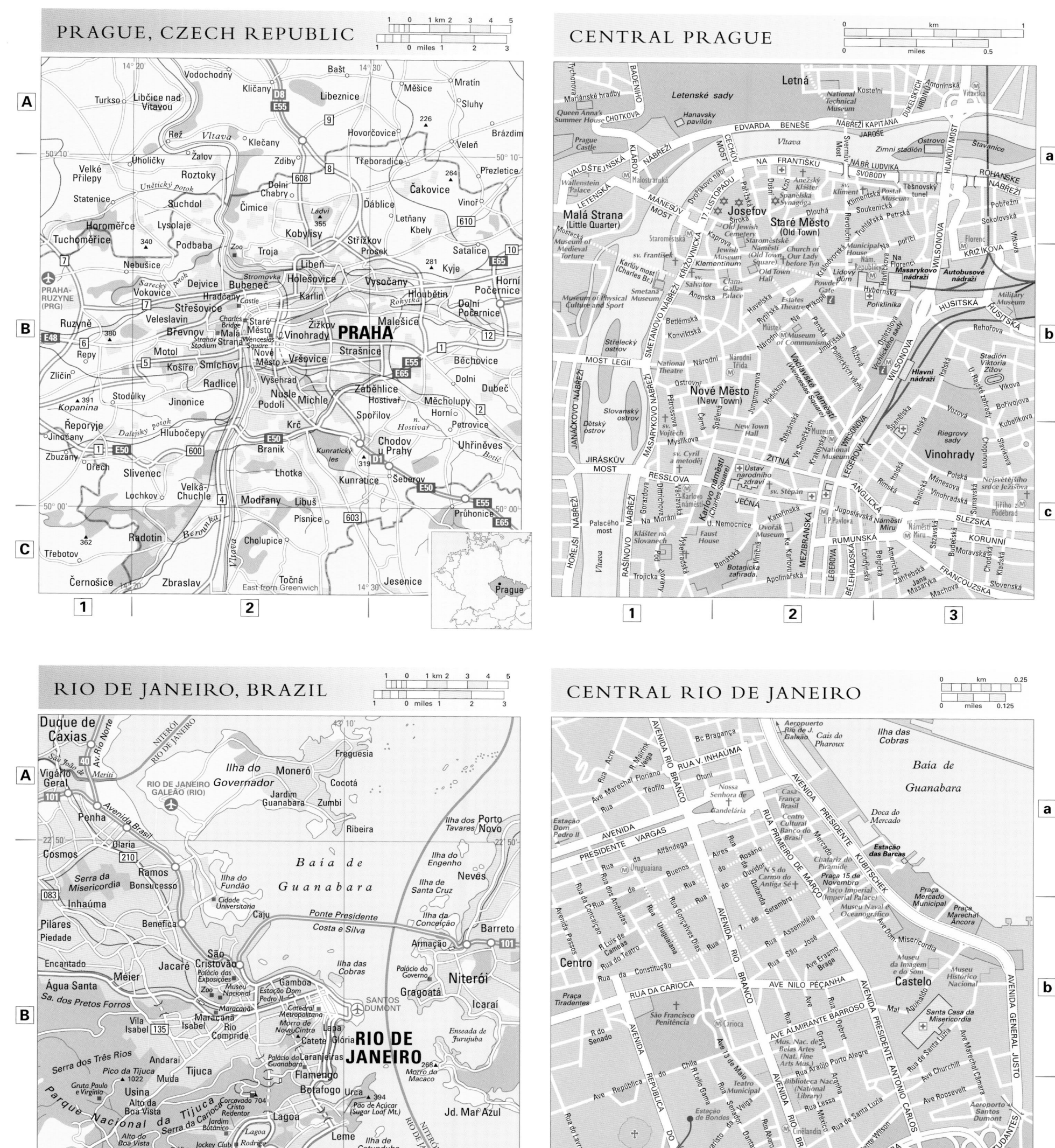

PRAGUE, CZECH REPUBLIC

CENTRAL PRAGUE

RIO DE JANEIRO, BRAZIL

CENTRAL RIO DE JANEIRO

ROME, ITALY

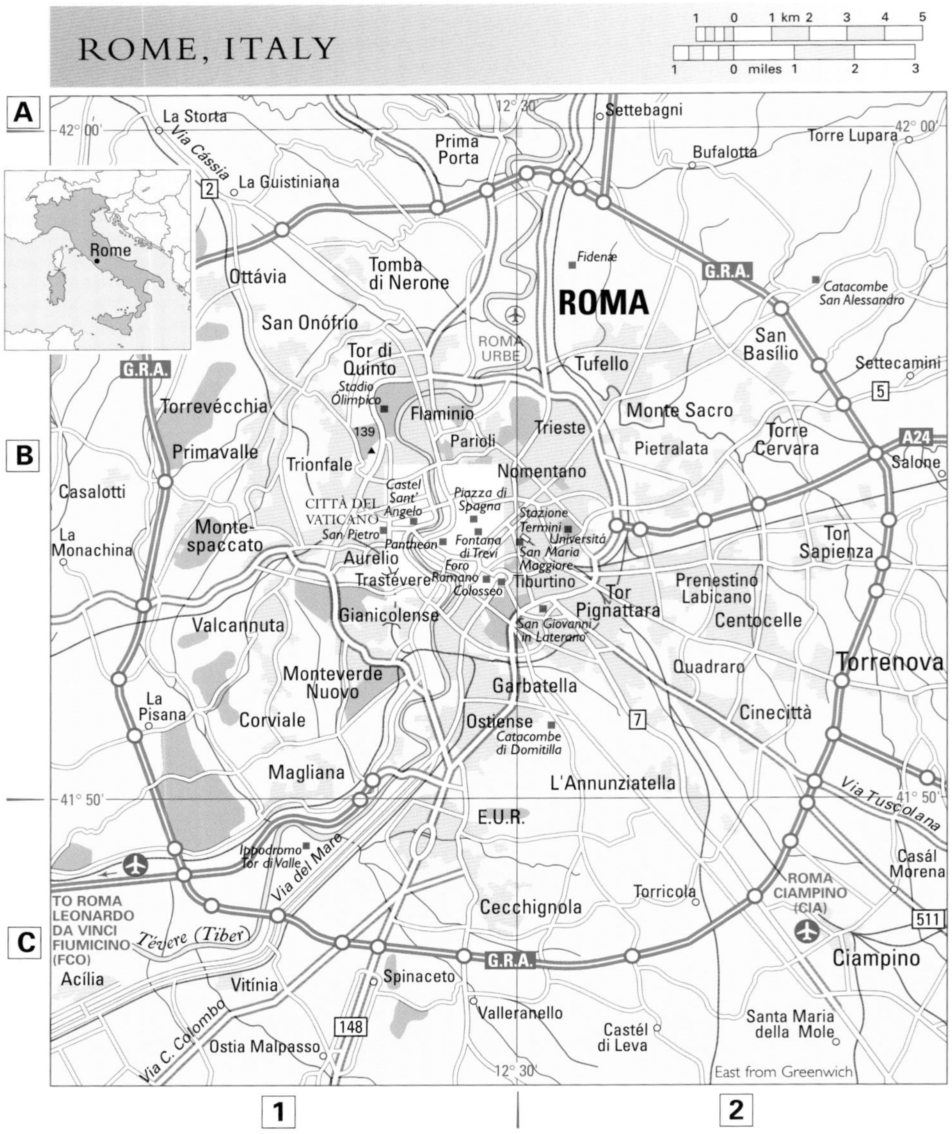

1 0 1 km 2 3 4 5
1 0 miles 1 2 3

A
42° 00' 12° 30' Settebagni 42° 00'
La Storta
Prima Porta Bufalotta
La Giustiniana
Torre Lupara
Ottávia Tomba di Nerone Fidene Catacombe San Alessandro
San Onófrio ROMA
ROMA URBE San Basílio Settecamini
Tor di Quinto G.R.A.
G.R.A. Stadio Olimpico 139 Flaminio Tufello 5
Torrevécchia Monte Sacro A24
Primavalle Trionfale Parioli Torre Cervara Salone
Nomentano Pietralata
Casalotti Monte-spaccato CITTÀ DEL VATICANO Trieste
La Monachina Aurélio San Pietro Piazza di Spagna Stazione Termini Tor Sapienza
Pantheon Università Fontana di Trevi San Maria Maggiore
Trastévere Foro Romano Tiburtino
Valcannuta Gianicolense Colosseo Tor Pignattara Prenestino Labicano Torrenova
San Giovanni in Laterano Centocelle
Monteverde Nuovo Garbatella Quadraro
La Pisana Corviale Ostiense Cinecittà 7
Catacombe di Domitilla
Magliana
41° 50' L'Annunziatella 41° 50'
E.U.R. Via Tuscolana
TO ROMA LEONARDO DA VINCI FIUMICINO (FCO) Ippodromo Tor di Valle Casál Morena 511
Acília Térevé (Tiber) ROMA CIAMPINO (CIA)
Cecchignola Torricola Ciampino
Vitínia G.R.A.
Spinaceto
148 Valleranello
Ostia Malpasso Castél di Leva Santa Maria della Mole
East from Greenwich

1   2

CENTRAL ROME

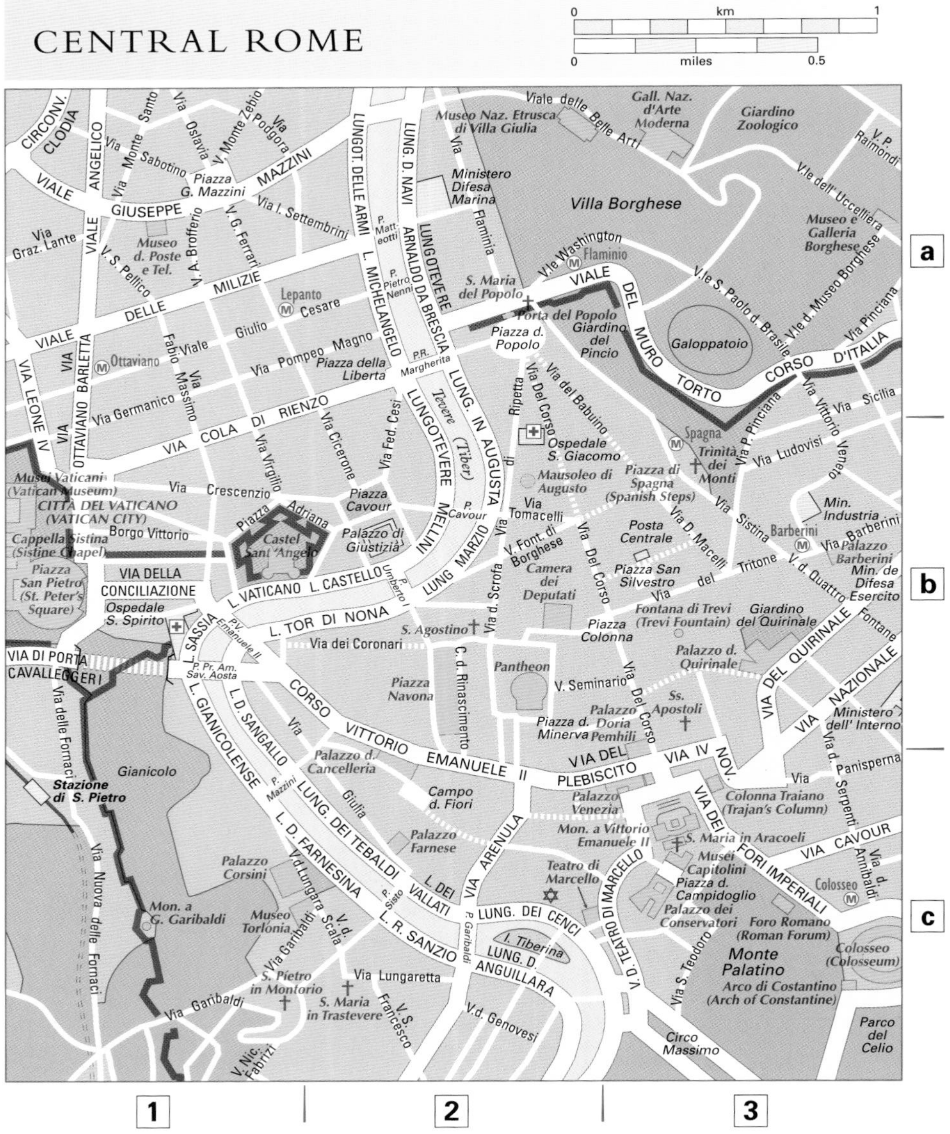

0 km 1
0 miles 0.5

a
CIRCONV. CLODIA Gall. Naz. d'Arte Moderna Giardino Zoologico
Museo Naz. Etrusca di Villa Giulia Villa Borghese Museo e Galleria Borghese
VIALE GIUSEPPE Museo d. Poste e Tel. Galoppatoio
Piazza d. Popolo Giardino del Pincio CORSO D'ITALIA
b
Musei Vaticani (Vatican Museum) Ospedale S. Giacomo Mausoleo di Augusto Piazza di Spagna (Spanish Steps) Trinità dei Monti Min. Industria
CITTÀ DEL VATICANO (VATICAN CITY) Posta Centrale Barberini
Cappella Sistina (Sistine Chapel) Borgo Vittorio Camera dei Deputati Piazza San Silvestro Palazzo Barberini Min. de Esercito
Castel Sant'Angelo Palazzo di Giustizia Fontana di Trevi (Trevi Fountain) Giardino del Quirinale
VIA DELLA CONCILIAZIONE Piazza San Pietro (St. Peter's Square) Ospedale S. Spirito Piazza Navona Pantheon Palazzo del Quirinale VIA NAZIONALE
VIA DI PORTA CAVALLEGGERI Piazza Colonna Ministero dell'Interno
Stazione di S. Pietro CORSO VITTORIO EMANUELE II Palazzo Venezia Colonna Traiano (Trajan's Column)
Gianicolo Campo d. Fiori Mon. a Vittorio Emanuele II S. Maria in Aracoeli VIA CAVOUR
c
Mon. a G. Garibaldi Museo Torlonia Teatro di Marcello Campidoglio Foro Romano (Roman Forum) Colosseo (Colosseum)
S. Pietro in Montorio S. Maria in Trastevere Monte Palatino Arco di Costantino (Arch of Constantine) Parco del Celio
Circo Massimo

1   2   3

SAN FRANCISCO, CALIF.

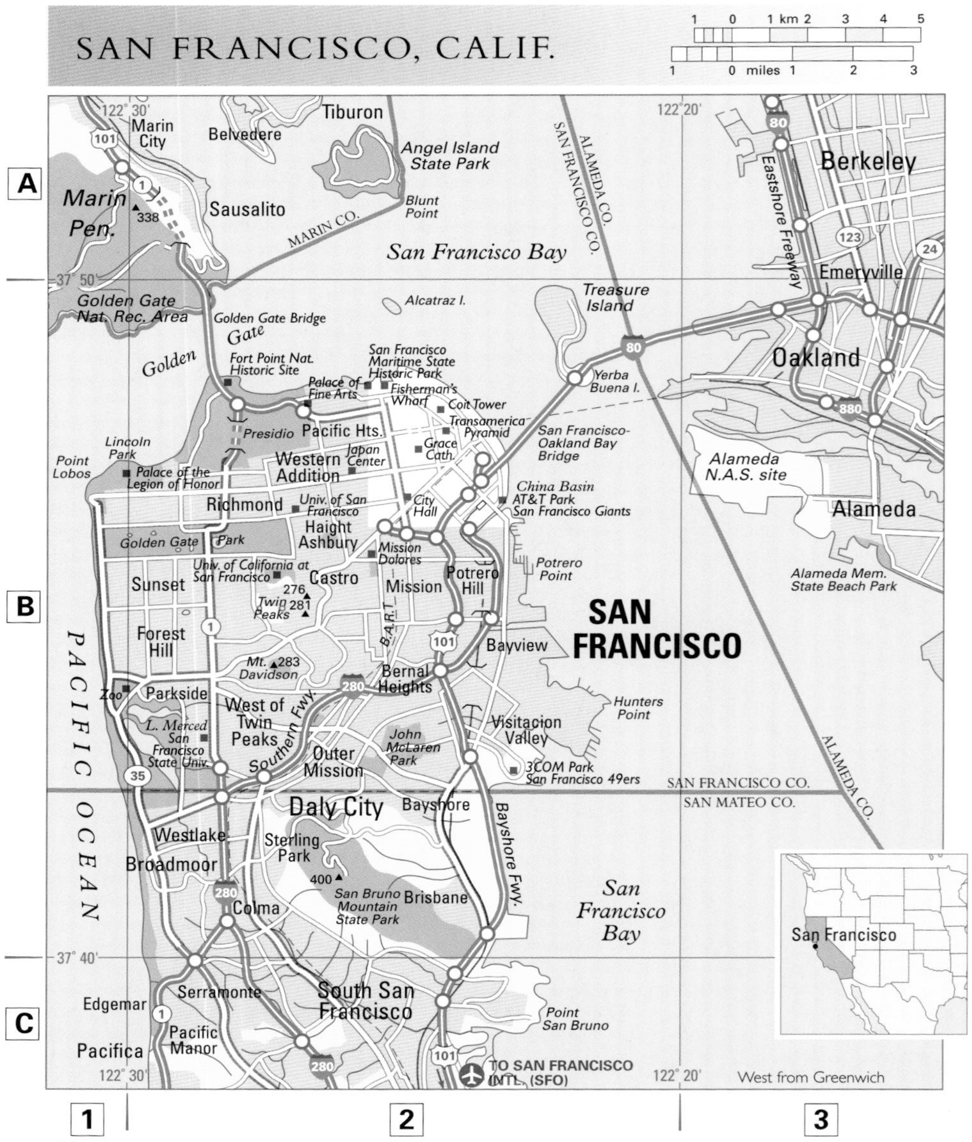

1 0 1 km 2 3 4 5
1 0 miles 1 2 3

A
122° 30' Tiburon 122° 20'
Marin City Belvedere Angel Island State Park Berkeley
101 Eastshore Freeway
Marin Pen. 338 Sausalito MARIN CO. San Francisco Bay 123 24
37° 50' Emeryville
Golden Gate Nat. Rec. Area Alcatraz I. Treasure Island 80
Golden Gate Bridge Gate Fort Point Nat. Historic Site Yerba Buena I. Oakland 880
Palace of the Fine Arts San Francisco Maritime State Historic Park
Lincoln Park Coit Tower Fisherman's Wharf San Francisco-Oakland Bay Bridge Alameda N.A.S. site
Point Lobos Palace of the Legion of Honor Presidio Pacific Hts. Transamerica Pyramid
Western Addition Japan Center Grace Cath. China Basin AT&T Park Alameda
Richmond Univ. of San Francisco City Hall San Francisco Giants Alameda Mem. State Beach Park
B
Golden Gate Park Haight Ashbury Mission Dolores Potrero Hill SAN FRANCISCO
Sunset Univ. of California at San Francisco 276 Castro Mission Potrero Point Bayview 101
Forest Hill 281 Twin Peaks Bernal Heights Hunters Point
Parkside Mt. 283 Davidson Visitacion Valley
West of Twin Peaks John McLaren Park 3COM Park San Francisco 49ers SAN FRANCISCO CO.
L. Merced San Francisco State Univ. Outer Mission SAN MATEO CO. ALAMEDA CO.
Zoo Southern Fwy. 280
Westlake Daly City Bayshore San Francisco Bay
Broadmoor 400 San Bruno Mountain State Park Brisbane
280 Sterling Park San Francisco
37° 40' Colma
Edgemar Serramonte South San Francisco Point San Bruno
Pacifica Pacific Manor 280 101 TO SAN FRANCISCO INTL. (SFO)
122° 30' 122° 20' West from Greenwich
PACIFIC OCEAN

San Francisco (inset)

1   2   3

CENTRAL SAN FRANCISCO

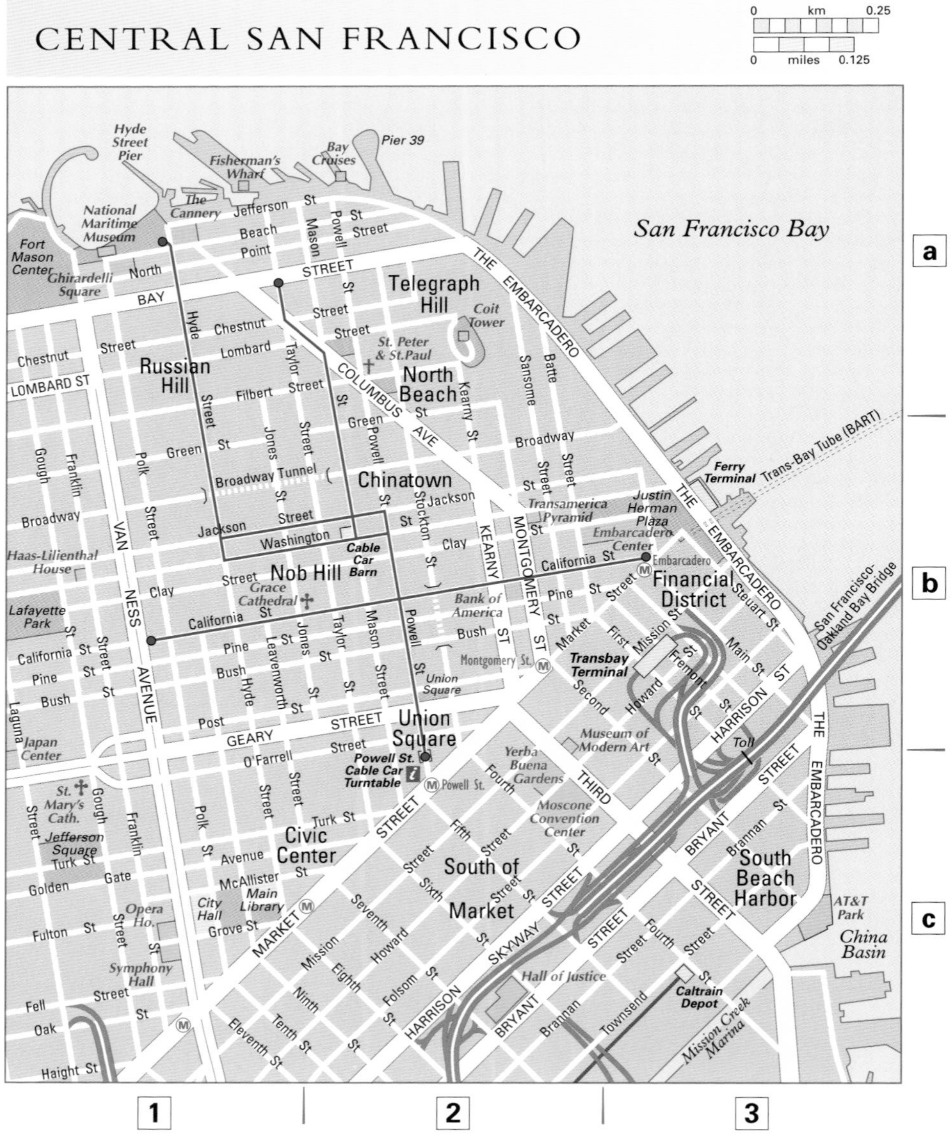

0 km 0.25
0 miles 0.125

a
Hyde Street Pier Bay Cruises Pier 39
National Maritime Museum The Cannery Fisherman's Wharf
Fort Mason Center Ghirardelli Square Jefferson St THE EMBARCADERO San Francisco Bay
Telegraph Hill Coit Tower
St. Peter & St.Paul North Beach
Russian Hill Chinatown Broadway Ferry Terminal Trans-Bay Tube (BART)
LOMBARD ST Broadway Tunnel Justin Herman Plaza Embarcadero Center
b
Transamerica Pyramid Financial District
Haas-Lilienthal House Nob Hill Cable Car Barn Grace Cathedral Bank of America San Francisco-Oakland Bay Bridge
Lafayette Park Transbay Terminal Museum of Modern Art
Japan Center Union Square Yerba Buena Gardens Toll
VAN NESS AVENUE GEARY Powell St. Cable Car Turntable THE EMBARCADERO
St. Mary's Cath. Moscone Convention Center HARRISON
c
Civic Center South of Market South Beach Harbor
Jefferson Square Park McAllister AT&T Park China Basin
Opera Ho. City Hall Main Library SKYWAY
Symphony Hall MARKET Hall of Justice Caltrain Depot Mission Creek Marina

1   2   3

(30) Interstate route numbers (101) U.S. route numbers (124) State route numbers

— Cable Car route

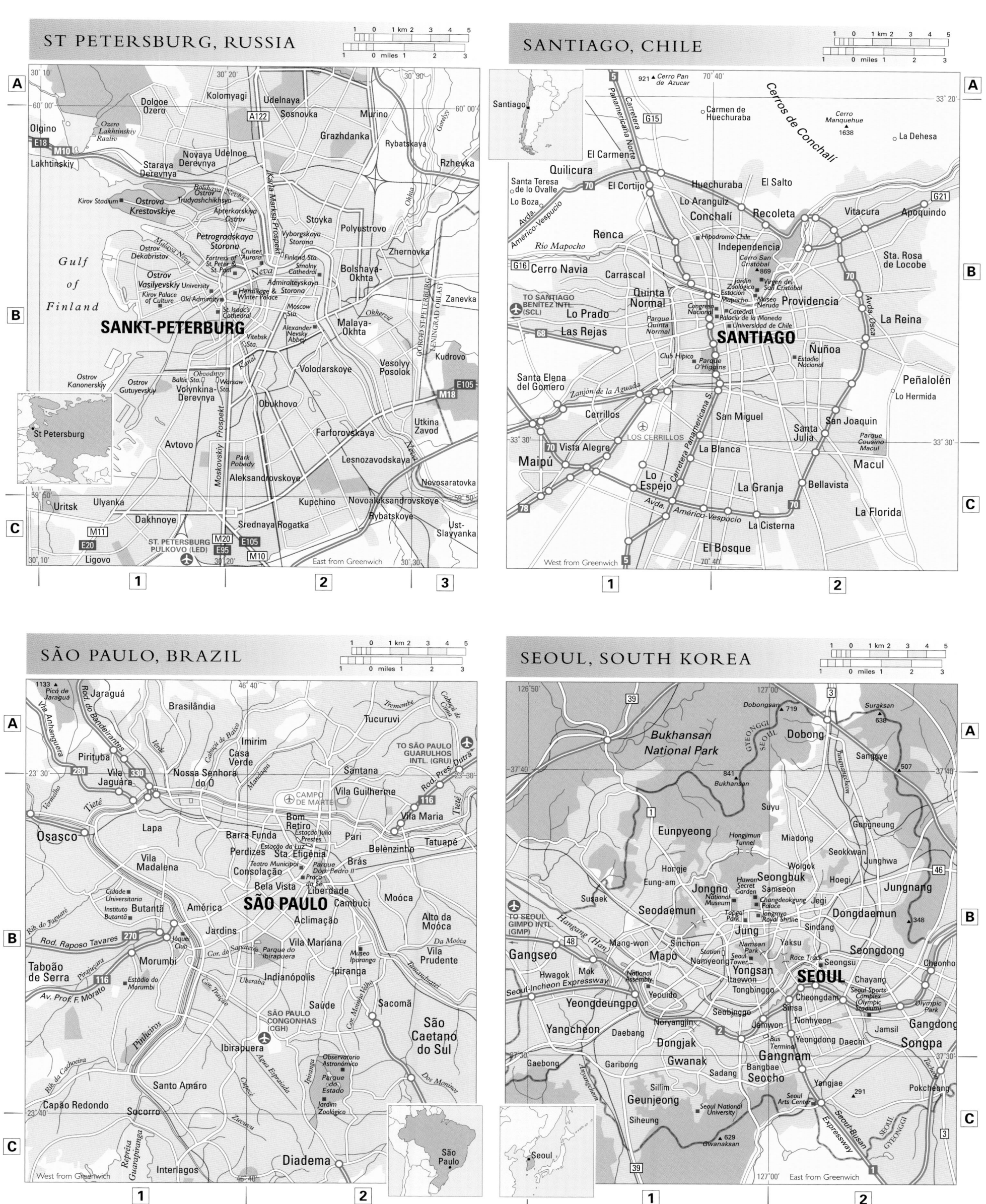

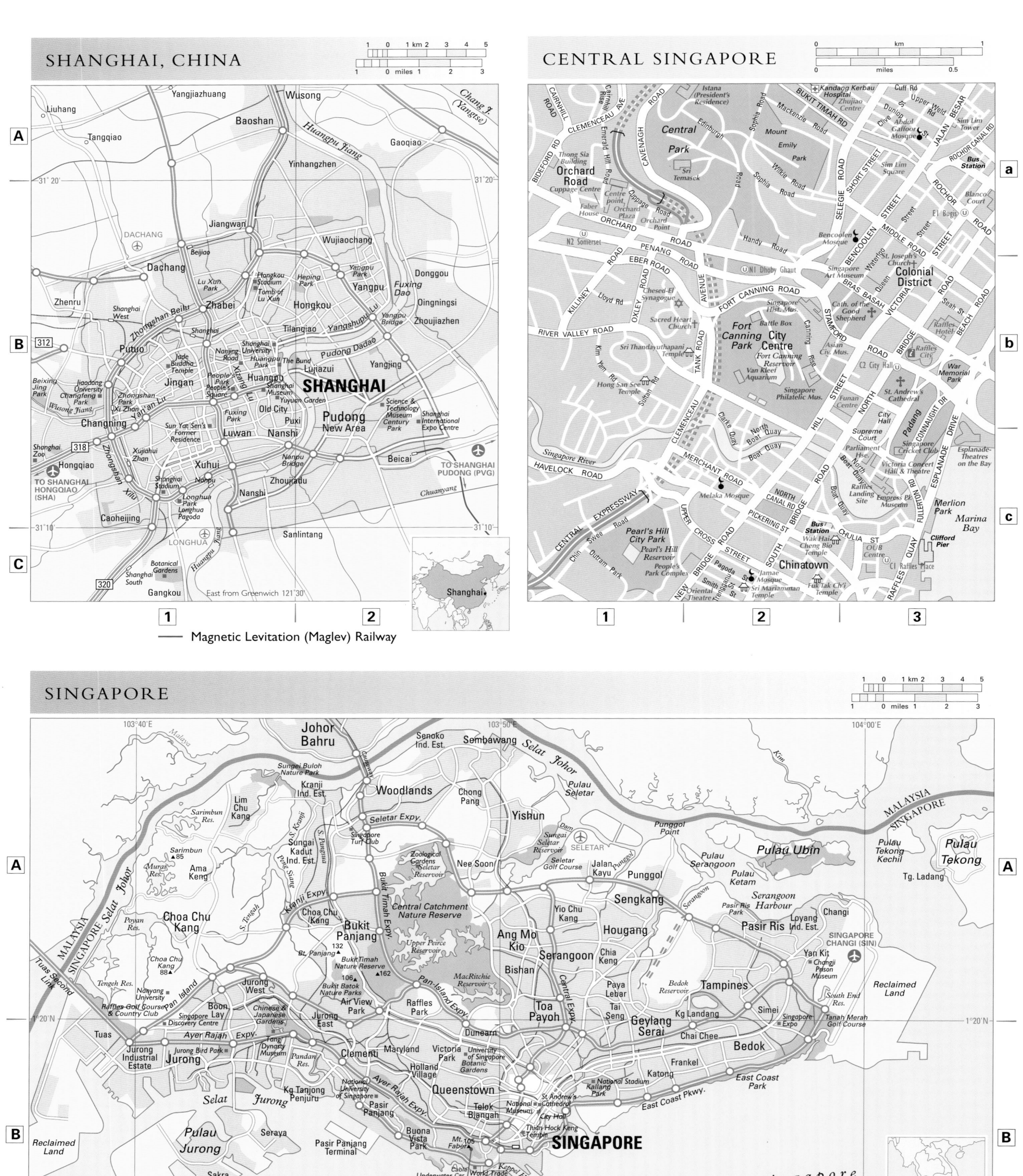

SHANGHAI, CHINA

1 0 1 km 2 3 4 5
1 0 miles 1 2 3

A

Liuhang
Tangqiao
Yangjiazhuang
Baoshan
Wusong
Chang J. (Yangtse)
Yinhangzhen
Gaoqiao
Huangpu Jiang
31° 20′
Jiangwan
DACHANG
Wujiaochang
Donggou
31°20′
Beijiao
Dachang
Lu Xun Park
Hongkou Stadium
Tomb of Lu Xun
Heping Park
Yangpu Park
Yangpu
Fuxing Dao
Qingningsi
Zhoujiazhen
Zhenru
Zhongshan Beilu
Zhabei
Tilanqiao
Yangshupu Lu
Yangpu Bridge
Yangjing
Zhoujiazhen
312
Putuo
Jade Buddha Temple
Shanghai
Nanjing University
The Bund
Huangpu Park
Pudong Dadao
Lujiazui
Shanghai West
Jingan
People's Park
People's Square
Huangpu
Shanghai Museum
Yuyuan Garden
SHANGHAI
Beixing Jing Park
Jiaodong University
Changfeng Park
Xi Zhan
Zhongshan Park
Yan'an Lu
Fuxing Park
Old City
Puxi
Pudong New Area
Science & Technology Museum
Century Park
Shanghai International Expo Centre
Changning
Zhongshan Xilu
Xujiahui Zhan
Luwan
Nanshi
Nanpu Bridge
Beicai
Shanghai Zoo
318
Hongqiao
Sun Yat-Sen's Former Residence
Xuhui
Nanpu
Zhoujiadu
TO SHANGHAI PUDONG (PVG)
TO SHANGHAI HONGQIAO (SHA)
Shanghai Stadium
Longhua Park
Longhua Pagoda
Nanshi
Chuanyang
31°10′
Caoheijing
31°10′
LONGHUA
Sanlintang
C
320
Botanical Gardens
Shanghai South
Huangpu Jiang
Gangkou
East from Greenwich 121°30′

Shanghai

1   2

— Magnetic Levitation (Maglev) Railway

CENTRAL SINGAPORE

0 km 1
0 miles 0.5

a

CAIRNHILL ROAD
CAIRNHILL RISE
CLEMENCEAU AVE
ROAD
Istana (President's Residence)
BUKIT TIMAH RD
Kandang Kerbau Hospital
Zhujiao Centre
Cuff Rd
Upper Weld
Dunlop
Clive
Abdul Gaffoor Mosque
Sim Lim Tower
Central Park
Edinburgh
Emerald Hill Rd
Sophia Road
Mackenzie Rd
Wilkie Road
SELEGIE ROAD
SHORT STREET
Sim Lim Square
ROCHOR
JALAN BESAR
ROCHOR CANAL ROAD
BIDEFORD RD
Thong Sia Building
Orchard Road
Cuppage Centre
Faber House
Centre point
Orchard Plaza
Orchard Road
Orchard Point
Mount Emily Park
Sophia Road
Bencoolen Mosque
BENCOOLEN
MIDDLE ROAD
STREET
Blanco Court
El Bogis
ROAD
a
ORCHARD
ROAD
N2 Somerset
Handy Road
N1 Dhoby Ghaut
PENANG ROAD
EBER ROAD
Chesed-El Synagogue
FORT CANNING ROAD
Singapore Art Museum
Waterloo
St. Joseph's Church
Colonial District
b
KILLINEY ROAD
OXLEY ROAD
Lloyd Rd
Sacred Heart Church
AVENUE
Singapore Hist. Mus.
Cath. of the Good Shepherd
Queen
VICTORIA
Seah St
Raffles Hotel
BEACH RD
RIVER VALLEY ROAD
Kim
Yan
Rd
Sri Thandayuthapani Temple
TANK ROAD
Fort Canning Park
STAMFORD
City Centre
Battle Box
Fort Canning Reservoir
Van Kleef Aquarium
Canning Rise
HILL STREET
C2 City Hall
BRIDGE
Raffles City
War Memorial Park
b
Hong San See Temple
Sutton Quay
Singapore Philatelic Mus.
NORTH
Funan Centre
St. Andrew's Cathedral
City Hall
Padang
CONNAUGHT DR
River Valley
CLEMENCEAU
Clarke Quay
North Quay
Boat Quay
North Boat Quay
ROAD
Supreme Court
Parliament
Empress Pl. Museum
Raffles Landing Site
Victoria Concert Hall & Theatre
ESPLANADE
Esplanade-Theatres on the Bay
c
Singapore River
HAVELOCK ROAD
MERCHANT ROAD
Boat Quay
Beach Rd
Singapore Cricket Club
Melaka Mosque
UPPER CROSS
PICKERING ST
Bus Station
FULLERTON RD
Merlion Park
Marina Bay
c
CENTRAL EXPRESSWAY
Chin Swee Road
Pearl's Hill City Park
Pearl's Hill Reservoir
People's Park Complex
NEW BRIDGE ROAD
Pagoda St
Smith St
Oriental Theatre
Trengganu St
SOUTH BRIDGE ROAD
Jamae Mosque
Sri Mariamman Temple
Wak Hai Cheng Bio Temple
Chinatown
CHULIA ST
Fuk Tak Ch'i Temple
OUB Centre
C1 Raffles Place
RAFFLES QUAY
Clifford Pier

1   2   3

SINGAPORE

1 0 1 km 2 3 4 5
1 0 miles 1 2 3

A

Malaysia
Johor Bahru
Causeway
Senoko Ind. Est.
Sembawang
Selat Johor
103°50′E
103°40′E
104°00′E
Sungei Buloh Nature Park
Kranji Ind. Est.
Woodlands
Chong Pang
Pulau Seletar
Lim Chu Kang
Sarimbun Res.
Seletar Expy.
Yishun
Singapore Turf Club
Sungai Seletar Reservoir
SELETAR
Punggol Point
MALAYSIA SINGAPORE
Sarimbun 85
Sungai Kadut Ind. Est.
Zoological Gardens
Seletar Reservoir
Nee Soon
Seletar Golf Course
Jalan Kayu
Pulau Seletar
Punggol
Pulau Serangoon
Pulau Ketam
Pulau Ubin
Pulau Tekong Kechil
Pulau Tekong
A
Murai Res.
Ama Keng
Bukit Timah Expy.
Central Catchment Nature Reserve
Yio Chu Kang
Sengkang
Serangoon
Pasir Ris Park
Serangoon Harbour
Tg. Ladang
Choa Chu Kang
S. Tengah
Choa Chu Kang
Kranji Expy.
Bukit Panjang
132
Upper Peirce Reservoir
Ang Mo Kio
Hougang
Chia Keng
Changi
Loyang Ind. Est.
Poyan Res.
Choa Chu Kang 88▲
Bukit Timah Nature Reserve
106
162▲
Bukit Batok Nature Parks
MacRitchie Reservoir
Pan-Island Expy.
Serangoon
Bishan
Paya Lebar
Bedok Reservoir
Tampines
Yan Kit
Changi Prison Museum
SINGAPORE CHANGI (SIN)
Tengeh Res.
Nanyang University
Jurong West
Air View Park
Raffles Park
Toa Payoh
Tai Seng
1°20′N
Geylang Serai
Simei
Singapore Expo
Tanah Merah Golf Course
Reclaimed Land
1°20′N
Boon Lay
Raffles Golf Course & Country Club
Singapore Discovery Centre
Chinese & Japanese Gardens
Tang Dynasty Village
Jurong East
Dunearn
Chai Chee
Bedok
East Coast Park
Jurong Industrial Estate
Jurong
Jurong Bird Park
Ayer Rajah Expy.
Pandan Res.
Clementi
Maryland
Holland Village
Victoria Park
University of Singapore Botanic Gardens
National Stadium
Kallang Park
Frankel
Katong
East Coast Pkwy.
Pulau Jurong
Seraya
National University of Singapore
Pasir Panjang
Queenstown
Telok Blangah
National Museum
St Andrew's Cathedral
City Hall
Thian Hock Keng Temple
SINGAPORE
Reclaimed Land
Sakra
Selat Jurong
Pasir Panjang Terminal
Buona Vista Park
Mt. 105 Faber
Keppel Harbour
Straits of Singapore
B
Reclaimed Land
Selat Pandan
Pulau Busing
Pulau Bukum
Underwater World
Cable Car
World Trade Centre P. Brani
Sentosa Gardens
Sentosa
Tanjong Golf Course
East from Greenwich
Singapore

1   2   3   4

STOCKHOLM, SWEDEN

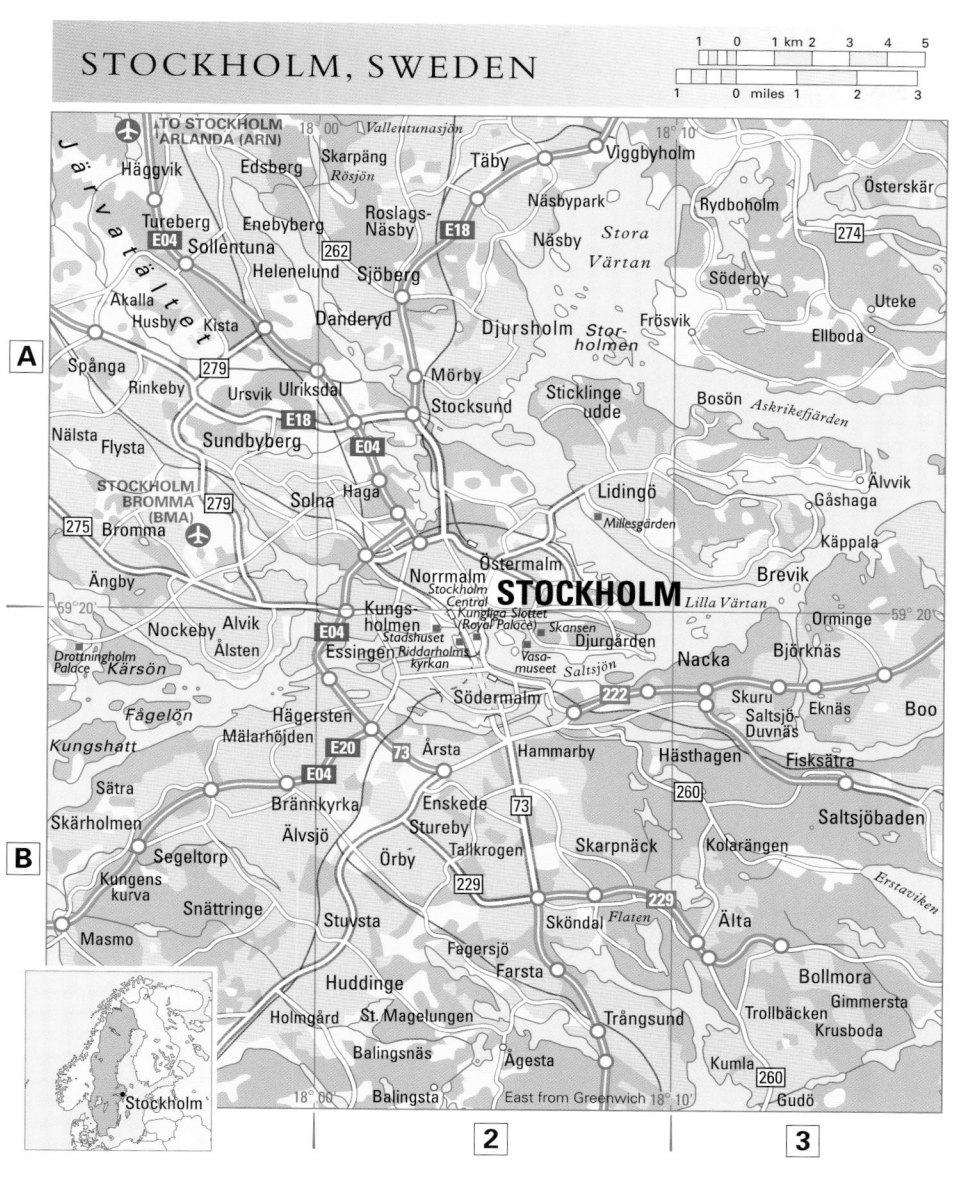

CENTRAL STOCKHOLM

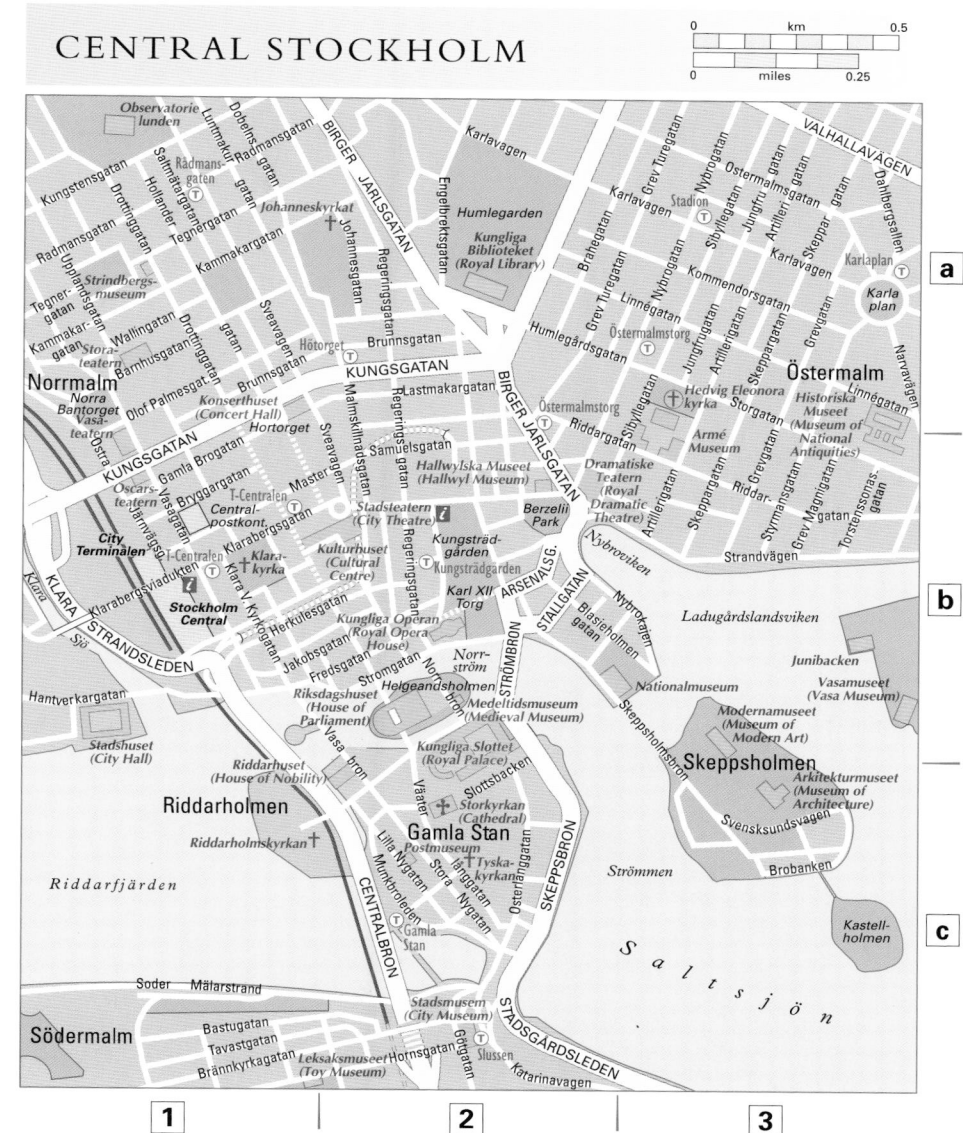

SYDNEY, AUSTRALIA

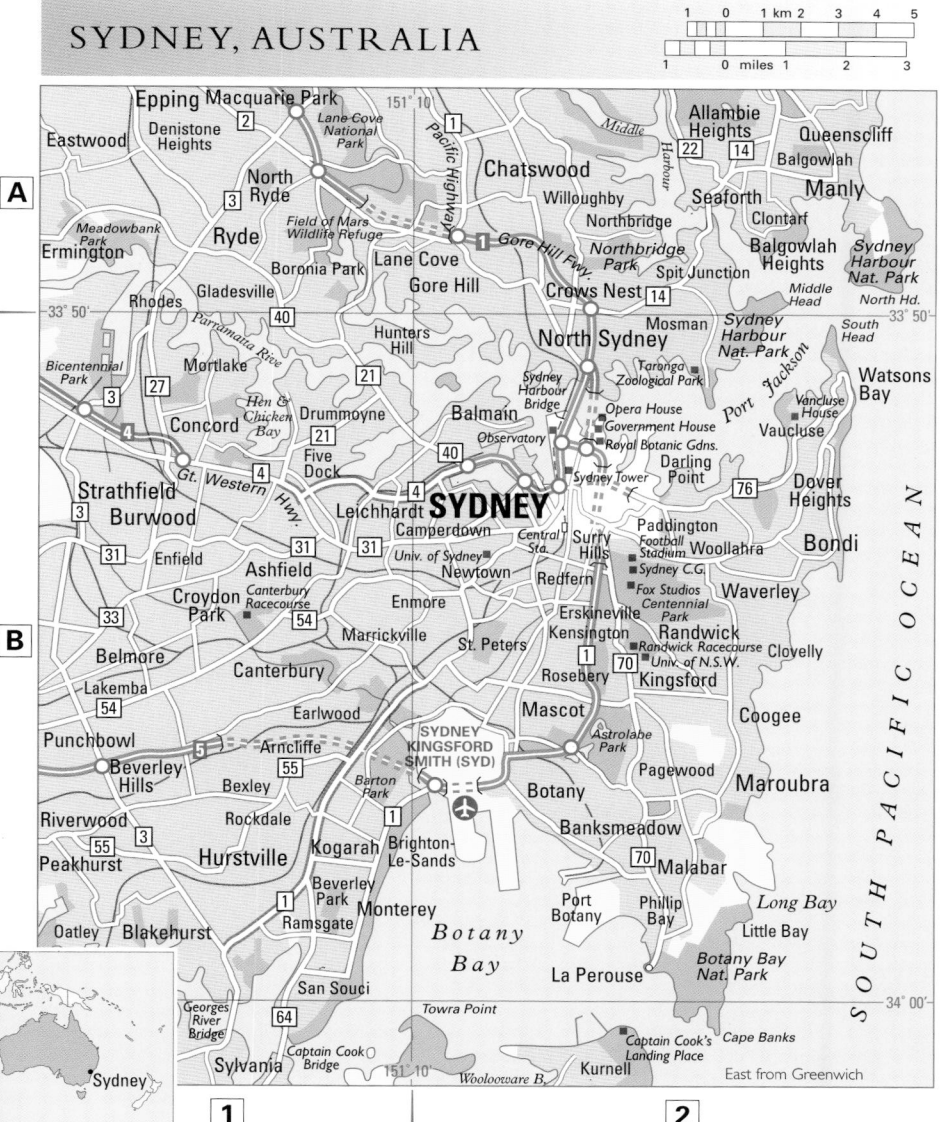

CENTRAL SYDNEY

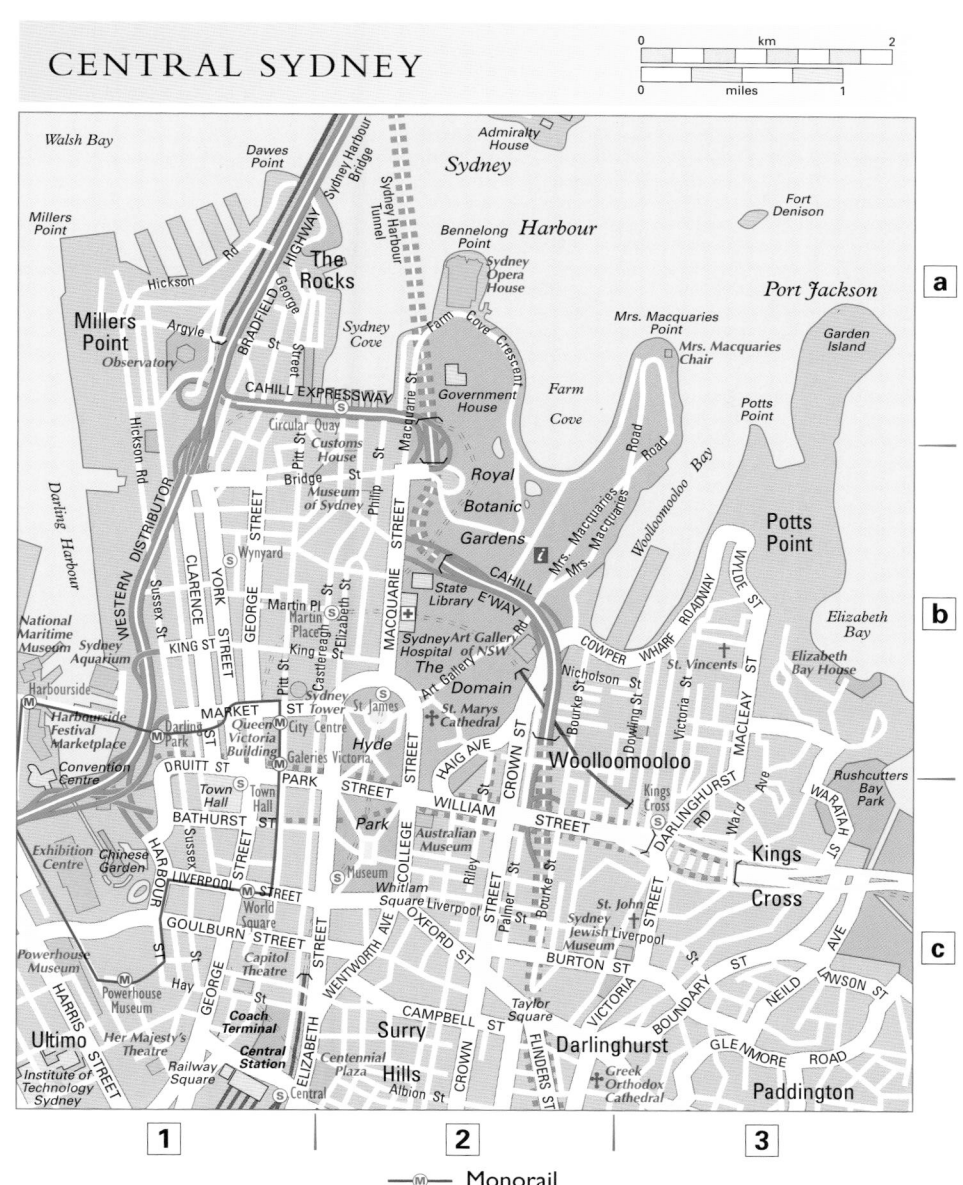

Ⓜ Monorail

COPYRIGHT PHILIP'S

TOKYO, JAPAN

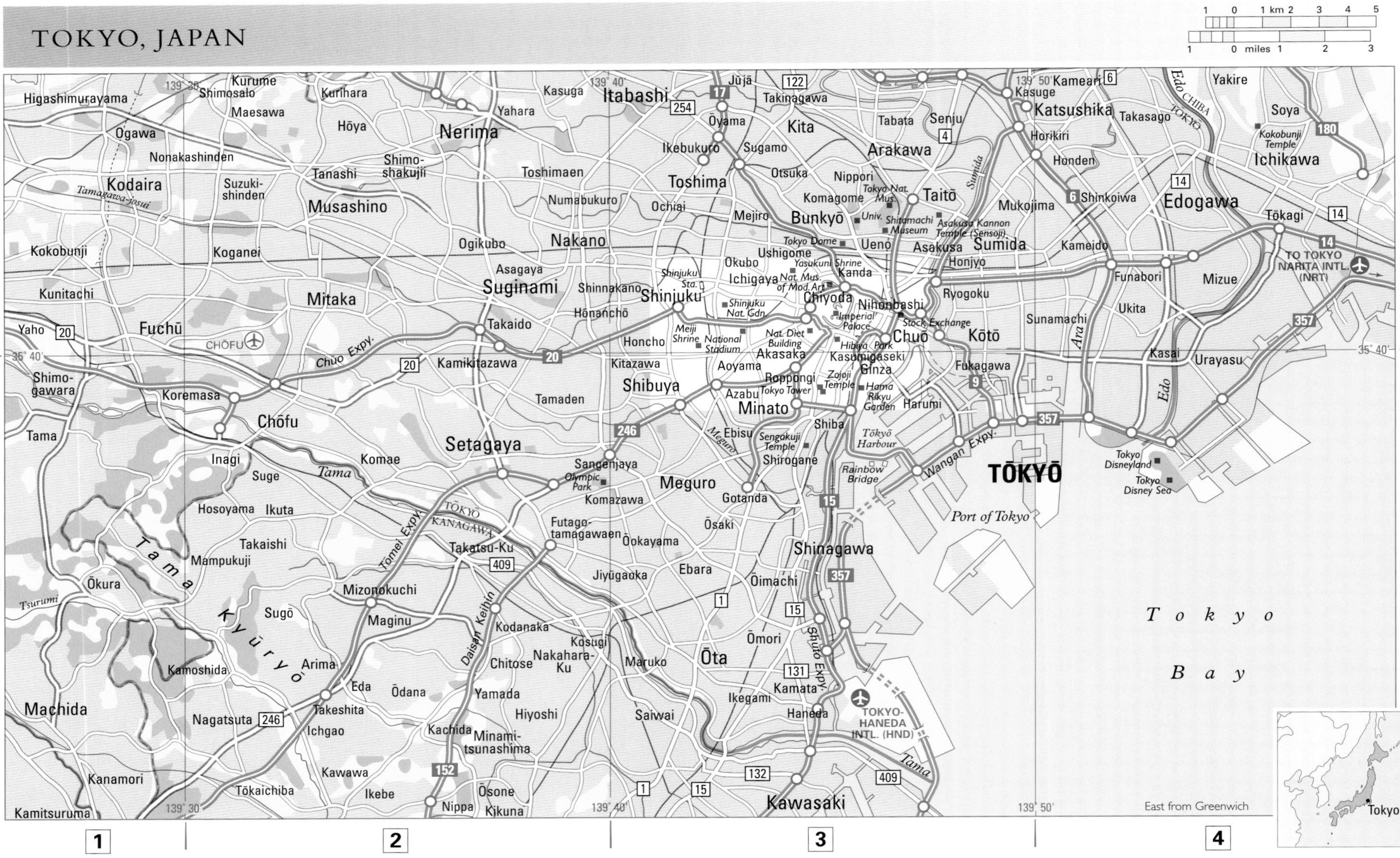

1 0 1 km 2 3 4 5
1 0 miles 1 2 3

Higashimurayama, Kurume, Shimosato, Kurihara, Kasuga, Itabashi, Jūjō, Takinagawa, Kameari, Katsushika, Takasago, Yakire, Soya

Ogawa, Shimo-shakuji, Hōya, Yahara, Kita, Tabata, Senju, Horikiri, Honden, Kokubunji Temple, Ichikawa

Kodaira, Suzuki-shinden, Tanashi, Toshimaen, Ikebukuro, Sugamo, Otsuka, Nippori, Arakawa, Mukojima, Shinkoiwa, Edogawa

Kokubunji, Koganei, Ogikubo, Asagaya, Numabukuro, Ochiai, Mejiro, Komagome, Tokyo Nat. Mus., Taitō, Asakusa, Sumida, Honjyo, Tōkagi

Kunitachi, Musashino, Nakano, Toshima, Bunkyō, Ueno, Asakusa Kannon Temple (Sensoji), Kamejdo, Funabori, Mizue

Yaho, Fuchū, Mitaka, Suginami, Shinnakano, Honanchō, Shinjuku, Okubo, Yasukuni Shrine, Nat. Mus. of Mod. Art, Kanda, Chiyoda, Nihonbashi, Stock Exchange, Ryogoku, Sunamachi, Ukita, Kasai, Urayasu

Shimo-gawara, Koremasa, Chōfu, Takaido, Kamikitazawa, Honcho, Kitazawa, Meiji Shrine, National Stadium, Nat. Diet Building, Akasaka, Aoyama, Roppongi, Kasumigaseki, Ginza, Chūō, Kōtō, Fukagawa

Tama, Inagi, Suge, Komae, Tamaden, Shibuya, Azabu, Minato, Tokyo Tower, Shiba, Hama Rikyu Garden, Harumi, TŌKYŌ

Hosoyama, Ikuta, Setagaya, Sangenjaya, Olympic Park, Komazawa, Meguro, Ebisu, Sengakuji Temple, Shirogane, Shirokane, Zojoji Temple, Rainbow Bridge, Port of Tokyo, Tokyo Disneyland, Tokyo Disney Sea

Takaishi, Mampukuji, Mizonokuchi, Maginu, Takatsu-Ku, Futago-tamagawaen, Ōokayama, Jiyūgaoka, Ebara, Ōimachi, Shinagawa, Tokyo Bay

Ōkura, Sugō, Arima, Eda, Ōdana, Kodanaka, Nakahara-Ku, Kosugi, Maruko, Ōsaki, Ōmori, Ōta

Machida, Kamoshida, Nagatsuta, Takeshita, Ichigao, Chitose, Yamada, Hiyoshi, Saiwai, Ikegami, Kamata, Haneda, TOKYO-HANEDA INTL. (HND)

Kanamori, Nagatsuta, Kachida, Minami-tsunashima, Kawawa, Ōsone, Kawasaki

Kamitsuruma, Tōkaichiba, Ikebe, Nippa, Kikuna

Tsurumi, Kyūryō, Tama, Machida, Kanagawa

CENTRAL TOKYO

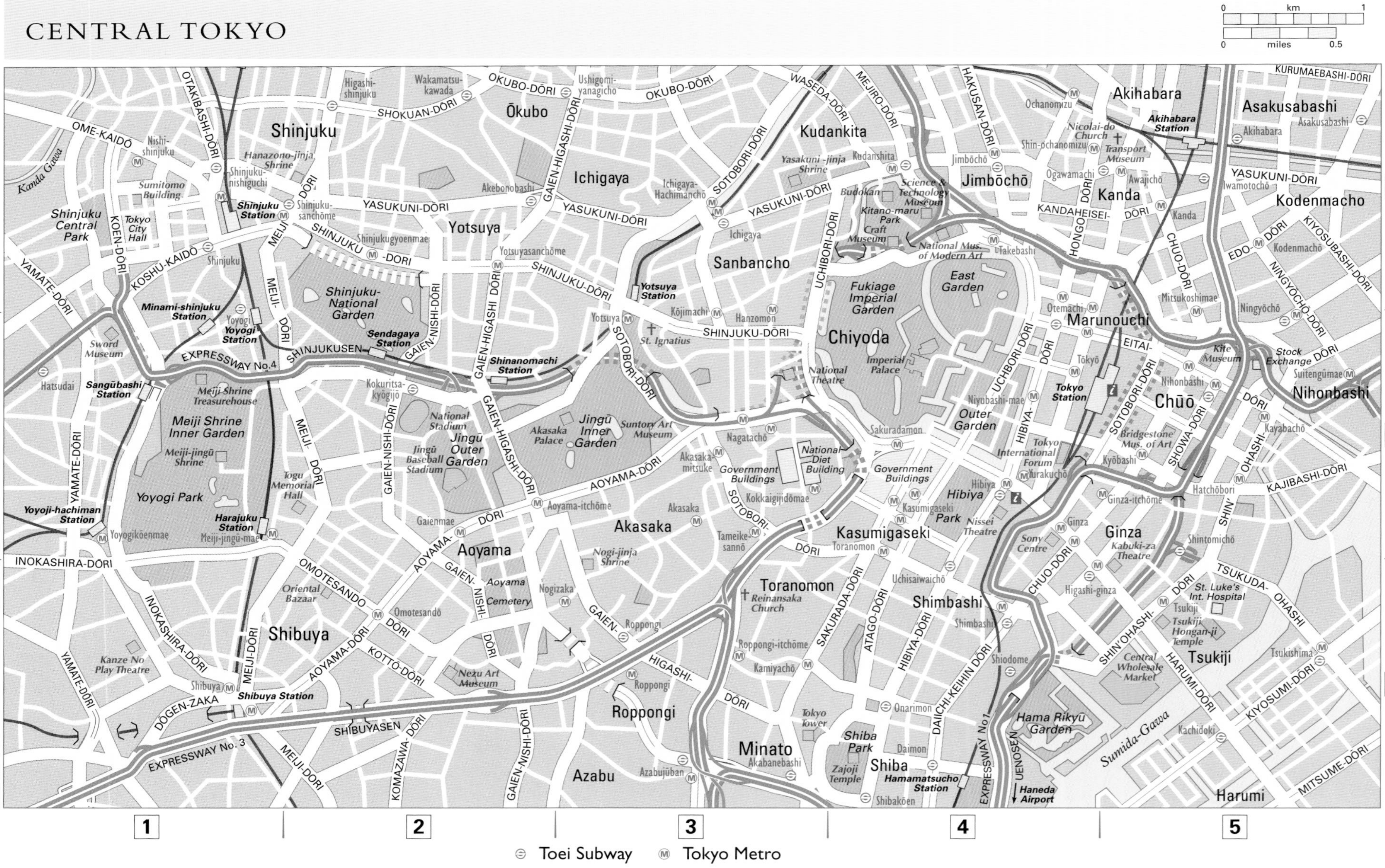

0 km 1
0 miles 0.5

Shinjuku, Ōkubo, Kudankita, Akihabara, Asakusabashi, Ichigaya, Yotsuya, Sanbancho, Jimbōchō, Kanda, Kodenmacho, Chiyoda, Marunouchi, Nihonbashi, Chūō, Yoyogi Park, Meiji Shrine Inner Garden, Harajuku Station, Shibuya, Aoyama, Akasaka, Kasumigaseki, Hibiya, Ginza, Toranomon, Shimbashi, Tsukiji, Roppongi, Minato, Shiba, Harumi

Toei Subway · Tokyo Metro

TEHRAN, IRAN

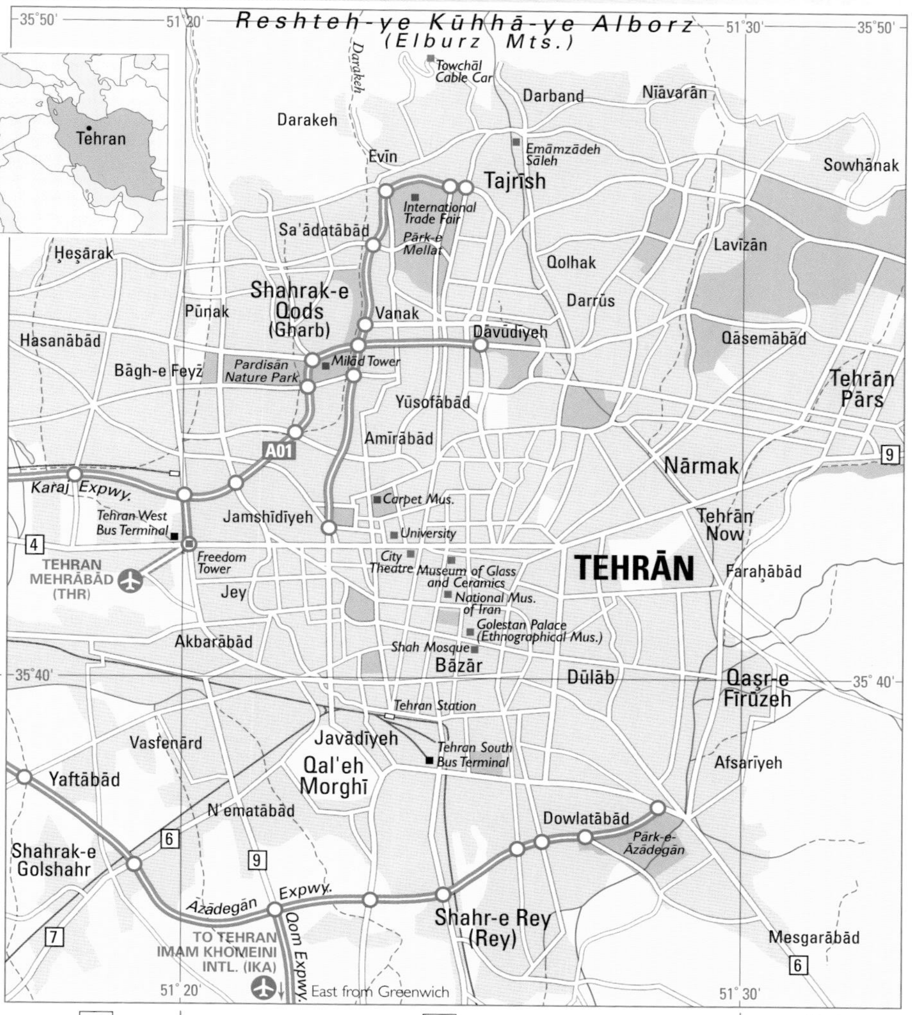

Scale: 1 0 1 km 2 3 4 5 / 1 0 miles 1 2 3

Reshteh-ye Kūhhā-ye Alborz (Elburz Mts.)

Tehran

35°50' 51°20' 51°30' 35°50'

Darakeh, Darband, Darakeh, Nīāvarān, Evin, Towchāl Cable Car, Emāmzādeh Sāleh, Tajrīsh, Sowhānak, Sa'ādatābād, Qolhak, Lavīzān, Vanak, Darrūs, Qāsemābād, Dāvūdīyeh, Tehrān Pārs, Amīrābād, Nārmak, Yūsofābād, Tehrān Now, Jamshīdīyeh, Farahābād, City Theatre, Museum of Glass and Ceramics, National Mus. of Iran, Golestan Palace (Ethnographical Mus.), Shah Mosque, Bāzār, Dūlāb, Qaṣr-e Fīrūzeh, Tehran Station, Vasfenārd, Javādīyeh, Qal'eh Morghī, Tehran South Bus Terminal, Afsarīyeh, N'ematābād, Dowlatābād, Pārk-e Āzādegān, Shahrak-e Golshahr, Āzādegān Expwy., Shahr-e Rey (Rey), Mesgārābād

Shahrak-e Qods (Gharb), Pardisan Nature Park, Mīlād Tower, Heṣārak, Hasanābād, Bāgh-e Feyż, Pūnak, Punak, Karaj Expwy., Tehran West Bus Terminal, TEHRAN MEHRĀBĀD (THR), Freedom Tower, Jey, Akbarābād, Yaftābād, TO TEHRAN IMAM KHOMEINI INTL. (IKA), Qom Expwy., East from Greenwich

A01, Corpet Mus., University, TEHRĀN, Park-e Mellat, International Trade Fair

CENTRAL TORONTO

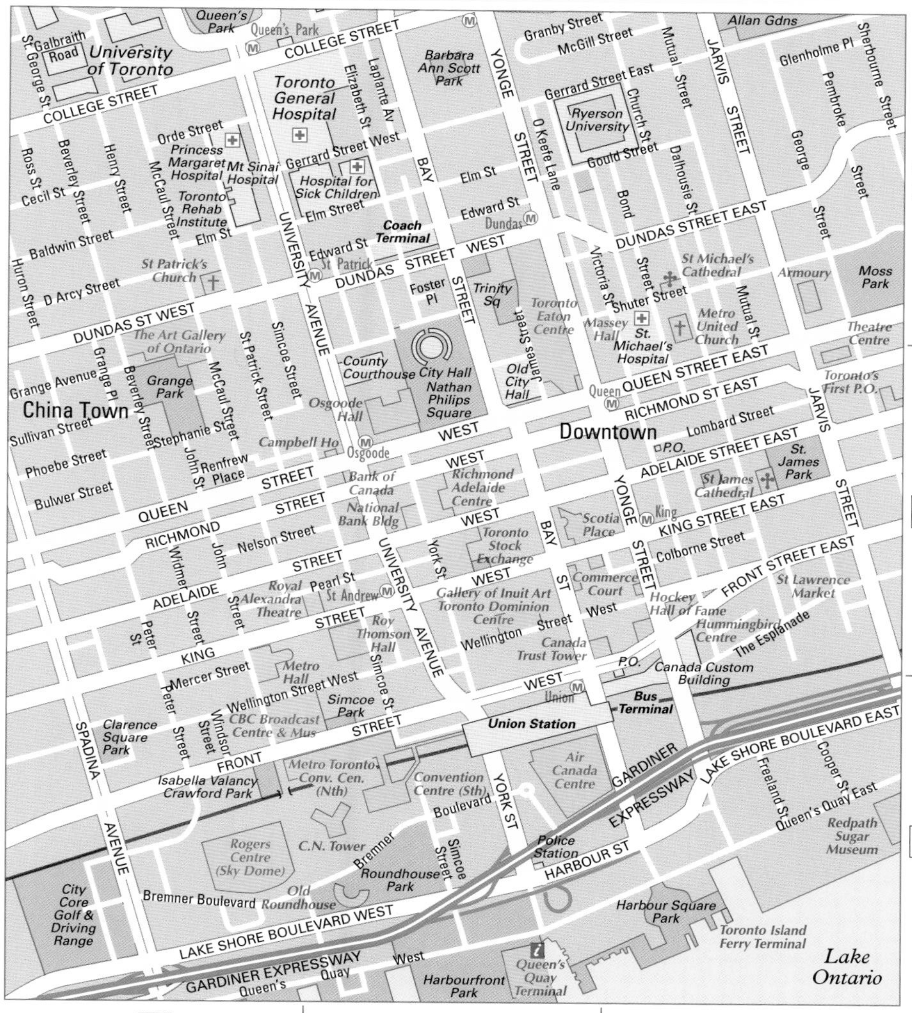

Scale: 0 km 0.5 / 0 miles 0.25

Queen's Park, University of Toronto, College Street, Granby Street, McGill Street, Allan Gdns, Glenholme Rd, Sherbourne Street, Galbraith Road, Gerrard Street East, Barbara Ann Scott Park, Yonge Street, Jarvis Street, George Street, Toronto General Hospital, Orde Street, Princess Margaret Hospital, Mt Sinai Hospital, Hospital for Sick Children, Ryerson University, Gould Street, Gerrard Street West, Elm St, Edward St, Dundas Street East, Toronto Rehab Institute, Coach Terminal, St Michael's Cathedral, Armoury, Moss Park, St Patrick's Church, The Art Gallery of Ontario, Dundas Street West, Foster Pl, Trinity Sq, Toronto Eaton Centre, Massey Hall, St Michael's Hospital, Metro United Church, Theatre Centre, Grange Avenue, Grange Park, County Courthouse, City Hall, Nathan Phillips Square, Old City Hall, Queen Street East, Toronto's First P.O., China Town, Osgoode Hall, Downtown, Lombard Street, Richmond St East, Phoebe Street, Osgoode, Campbell Ho, Richmond Adelaide Centre, Bank of Canada, National Bank Bldg, Scotia Place, Adelaide Street East, St James Park, Bulwer Street, Queen Street, Richmond Street, Nelson Street, Toronto Stock Exchange, St James Cathedral, King Street East, Adelaide Street, Royal Alexandra Theatre, St Andrew, Gallery of Inuit Art, Toronto Dominion Centre, Commerce Court, Colborne Street, King Street, Mercer Street, Metro Hall, Roy Thomson Hall, Canada Trust Tower, Hockey Hall of Fame, Hummingbird Centre, St Lawrence Market, Wellington Street West, Canada Custom Building, The Esplanade, Spadina Avenue, Clarence Square Park, Windsor Street, Front Street, Union Station, Bus Terminal, Gardiner Expressway, Lake Shore Boulevard East, Isabella Valancy Crawford Park, Metro Toronto Conv. Cen. (Nth), Convention Centre (Sth), Air Canada Centre, Queen's Quay East, Redpath Sugar Museum, Rogers Centre (Sky Dome), C.N. Tower, Bremner Park, Roundhouse Park, Police Station, Harbour St, City Core Golf & Driving Range, Bremner Boulevard, Roundhouse, Lake Shore Boulevard West, Gardiner Expressway, Harbourfront Park, Queen's Quay Terminal, Harbour Square Park, Toronto Island Ferry Terminal, Lake Ontario

TORONTO, CANADA

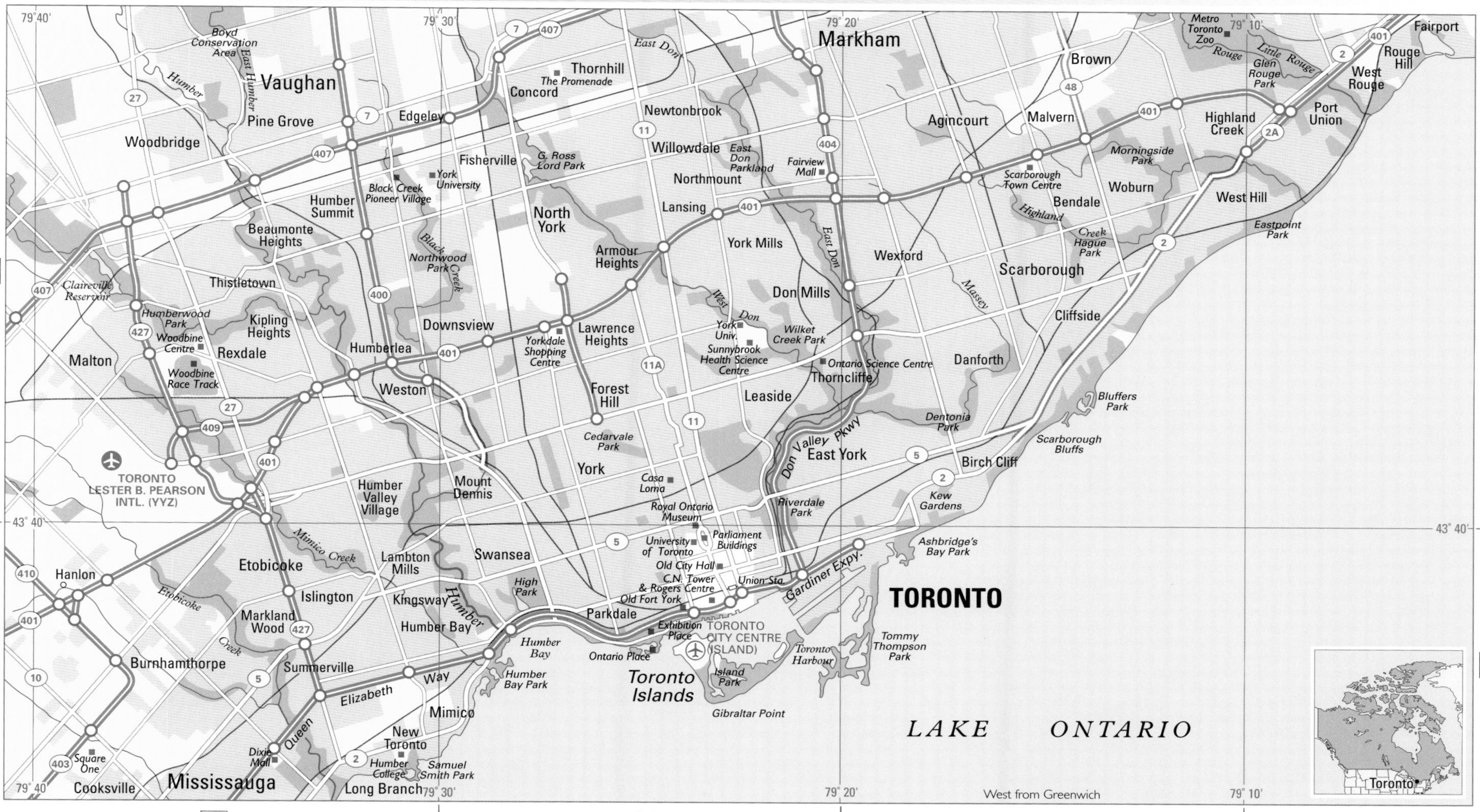

Scale: 1 0 1 km 2 3 4 5 / 1 0 miles 1 2 3

79°40' 79°30' 79°20' 79°10'

Boyd Conservation Area, Vaughan, Thornhill, Markham, Brown, Metro Toronto Zoo, Fairport, Rouge Hill, West Rouge, Port Union, Woodbridge, Pine Grove, Edgeley, Concord, The Promenade, East Don, Newtonbrook, Agincourt, Malvern, Highland Creek, Fisherville, G. Ross Lord Park, Willowdale, East Don Parkland, Fairview Mall, Scarborough Town Centre, Morningside Park, York University, Black Creek Pioneer Village, North York, Northmount, Lansing, Woburn, Bendale, West Hill, Eastpoint Park, Humber Summit, Beaumonte Heights, Black Creek, Northwood Park, Armour Heights, York Mills, Wexford, Scarborough, Cliffside, Don Mills, Humberwood Park, Clairville Reservoir, Kipling Heights, Rexdale, Humberlea, Downsview, Lawrence Heights, Yorkdale Shopping Centre, York Univ., Wilket Creek Park, Sunnybrook Health Science Centre, Ontario Science Centre, Thorncliffe, Danforth, Malton, Woodbine Centre, Weston, Forest Hill, Leaside, Dentonia Park, Scarborough Bluffs, Bluffers Park, TORONTO LESTER B. PEARSON INTL. (YYZ), Cedarvale Park, York, Casa Loma, Royal Ontario Museum, East York, Don Valley Pkwy, Birch Cliff, Kew Gardens, Humber Valley Village, Mount Dennis, Riverdale Park, Humber, Lambton Mills, Swansea, High Park, University of Toronto, Parliament Buildings, Old City Hall, C.N. Tower & Rogers Centre, Old Fort York, Ashbridge's Bay Park, Hanlon, Etobicoke, Islington, Kingsway, Parkdale, Union Sta, Gardiner Expy., TORONTO, Markland Wood, Humber Bay, Exhibition Place, TORONTO CITY CENTRE (ISLAND), Toronto Harbour, Tommy Thompson Park, Burnhamthorpe, Summerville, Way, Humber Bay Park, Ontario Place, Island Park, Elizabeth, Mimico, New Toronto, Dixie, Square One, Humber College, Samuel Smith Park, Long Branch, Toronto Islands, Gibraltar Point, Cooksville, Mississauga

LAKE ONTARIO

Toronto

427 Provincial route numbers

COPYRIGHT PHILIP'S

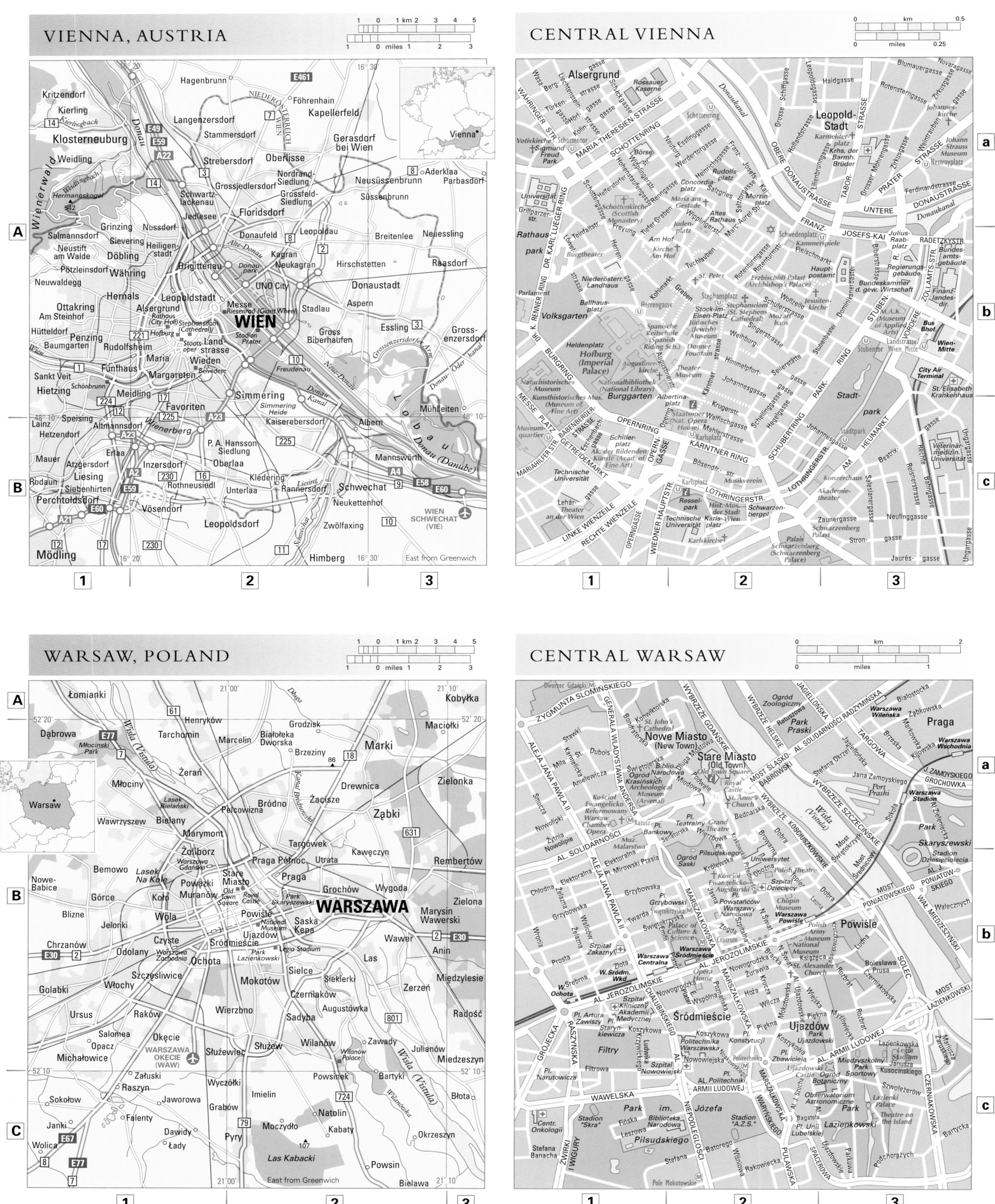

WASHINGTON D.C.

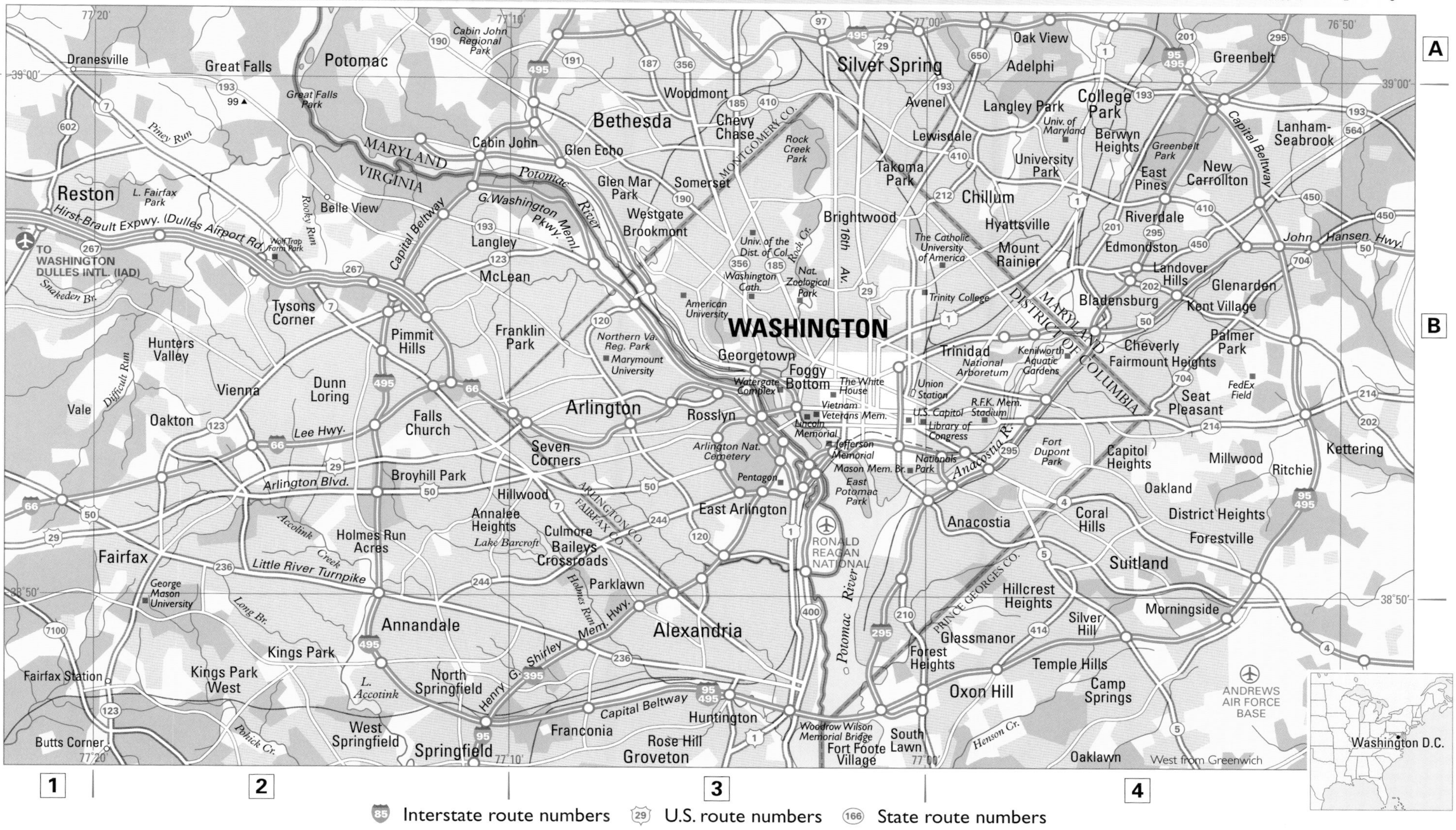

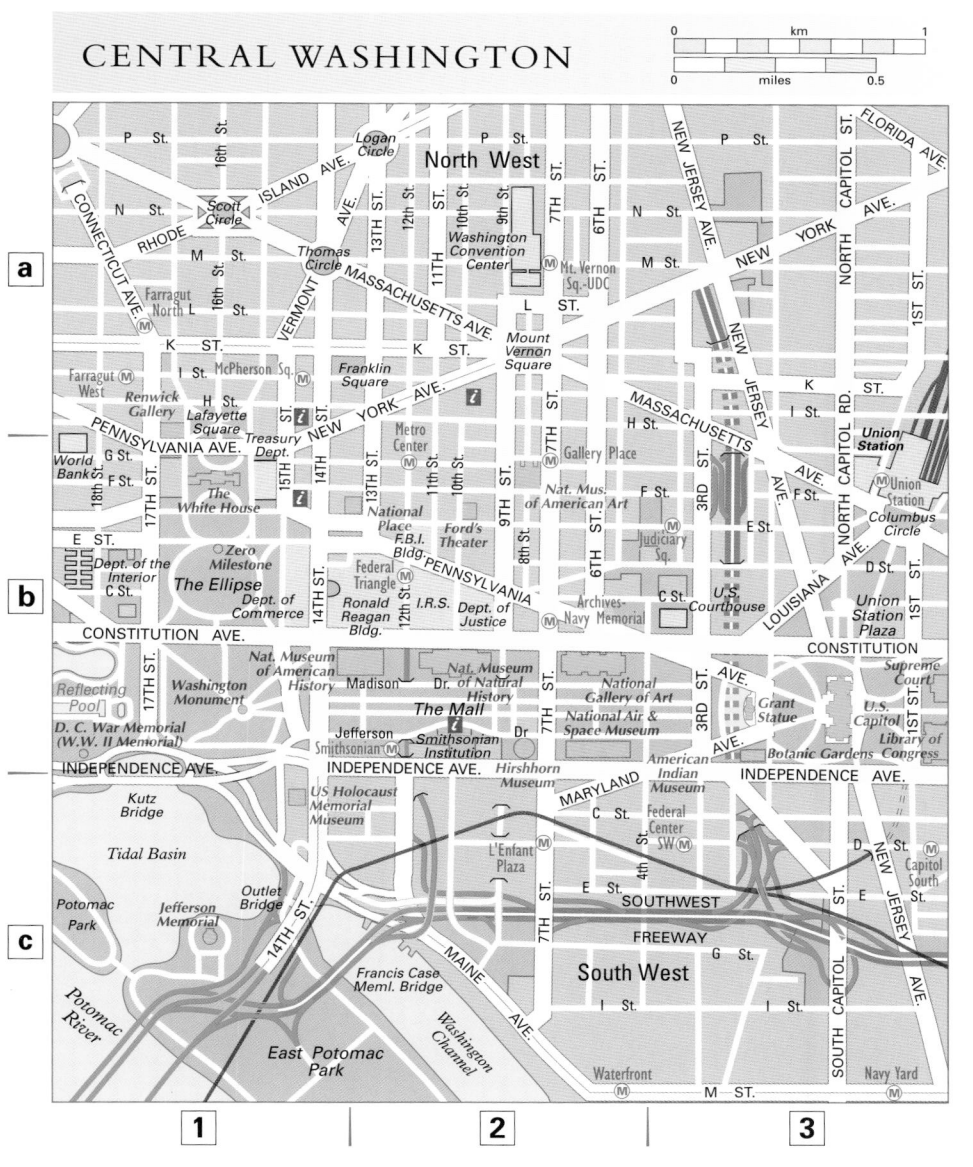

CENTRAL WASHINGTON

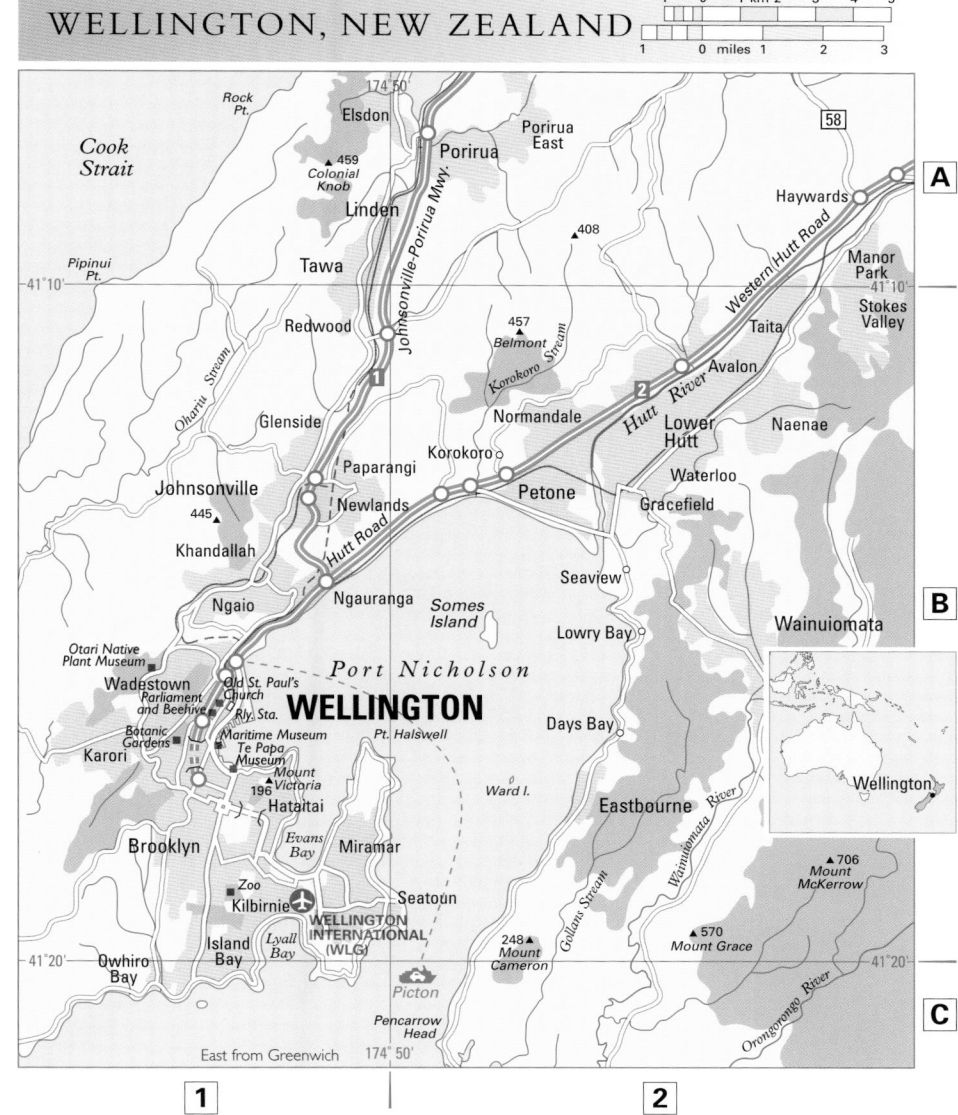

WELLINGTON, NEW ZEALAND

85 Interstate route numbers   29 U.S. route numbers   166 State route numbers

WORLD
MAPS

1 2 3 4 5 6 7 8 9 10

A B C D E F G H

Beaufort Sea Pt. Barrow Banks I. Parry Is. Queen Elizabeth Islands Ellesmere I. Greenland Greenland Sea North Magnetic Pole

Alaska Yukon Mt. McKinley 6194 (Denali) Bering Str. Bering Sea 60 Gulf of Alaska Kodiak I. Aleutian Is. Queen Charlotte Is. Vancouver I.

Victoria I. Gr. Bear L. Gr. Slave L. Mackenzie Baffin Island Hudson Str. Devon I. Davis Str. Jan Mayen Norwegian Sea

Arctic Circle 3360 Denmark Str. Iceland 2119 Faroe Is. 2469

Coast Mts. North America L. Winnipeg Nelson Hudson Bay Labrador Labrador Sea Newfoundland C. Farewell British Isles 1342 North Sea

A 40

Great Plains Rocky Mountains Great Lakes Laurentian Plateau G. of St. Lawrence St. Lawrence Nova Scotia C. Race B. of Biscay Mt. Blanc 4809 Pic d'Aneto 3404 Iberian Pen. Med

C. Mendocino Sierra Nevada Columbia R. Snake R. Mt. Elbert 4399 Arkansas Ohio Missouri Appalachian Mts. Mt. Mitchell 2037 C. Cod NORTH Azores Med

Mt. Whitney 4418 Death Valley 86 Colorado Rio Grande Mississippi Florida C. Hatteras Bermuda ATLANTIC Madeira Canary Is. 3718 Atlas Mts. Toubkal 4165 Maghreb Hogg

Great Basin Lower California Sierra Madre Gulf of Mexico Florida Str. Bahamas Sargasso Sea OCEAN Tropic of Cancer Sah a

Hawaiian Is. Mauna Kea 4205 C. San Lucas Revilla Gigedo Is. Popocatepetl 5610 Pico de Orizaba 6462 Cuba Hispaniola 3175 Milwaukee Deep 9200 C. Verde Is. C. Verde Af

20 Yucatan Greater Antilles Jamaica Puerto Rico Lesser Antilles Gu

PACIFIC 4093 Central America Caribbean Sea Trinidad 5778 1752 G Mt. Cameroon 4095 C. Palmas

Isthmus of Panama Llanos Orinoco Mt. Roraima 2810 Guiana Highlands Equator Gulf of Guinee

Galapagos Is. 3014 Negro Japurá Amazon South C. de São Roque Ascension

OCEAN Chimborazo 6267 Marañón Purus Madeira Tapajós America Selvas Tocantins São Francisco Plateau of Mato Grosso SOUTH St. Helena

Line Is. Kiritimati 0 Marquesas Is. 6788 Andes Bolivian Plateau L. Titicaca 8425 Brazilian Highlands 2890 Trindade Tropic of Capricorn

Polynesia Society Is. Tuamotu Is. Tahiti Cook Is. Tubuai Is. 20 Pitcairn I. Easter I. Chile Trench 8050 Cerro Ojos del Salado 6863 Gran Chaco Paraná C. Frio ATLANTIC

Arch. de Juan Fernández Cerro Aconcagua 6960 Pampas R. de la Plata Tristan da Cunha OCEAN

40 Patagonia -40 4058 Falkland Is. 2937 S. Georgia Bouvet

Magellan's Str. C. Horn Tierra del Fuego Scotia Sea South Sandwich Is. South Orkney Is. Antarctic Circle

Drake Passage South Shetland Is. Antarctic Peninsula Weddell Sea Queen

Bellingshausen Sea Alexander I. Palmer Land Caird Coast

Amundsen Sea Thurston I. Ellsworth Land Vinson Massif 4897 Ronne Ice Shelf Berkner I. Coats Land

Marie Byrd Land Roosevelt I. 80 Ross Sea

Projection: Winkel III

West from Greenwich

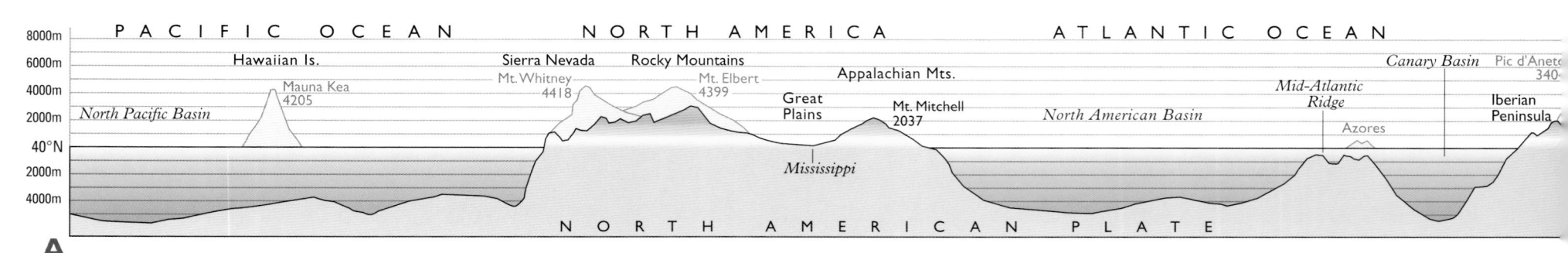

8000m PACIFIC OCEAN NORTH AMERICA ATLANTIC OCEAN
6000m Hawaiian Is. Sierra Nevada Rocky Mountains Appalachian Mts. Canary Basin Pic d'Aneto
4000m Mauna Kea 4205 Mt. Whitney 4418 Mt. Elbert 4399 Mid-Atlantic Ridge 340
2000m North Pacific Basin Great Plains Mt. Mitchell 2037 North American Basin Azores Iberian Peninsula
40°N
2000m Mississippi
4000m NORTH AMERICAN PLATE

A

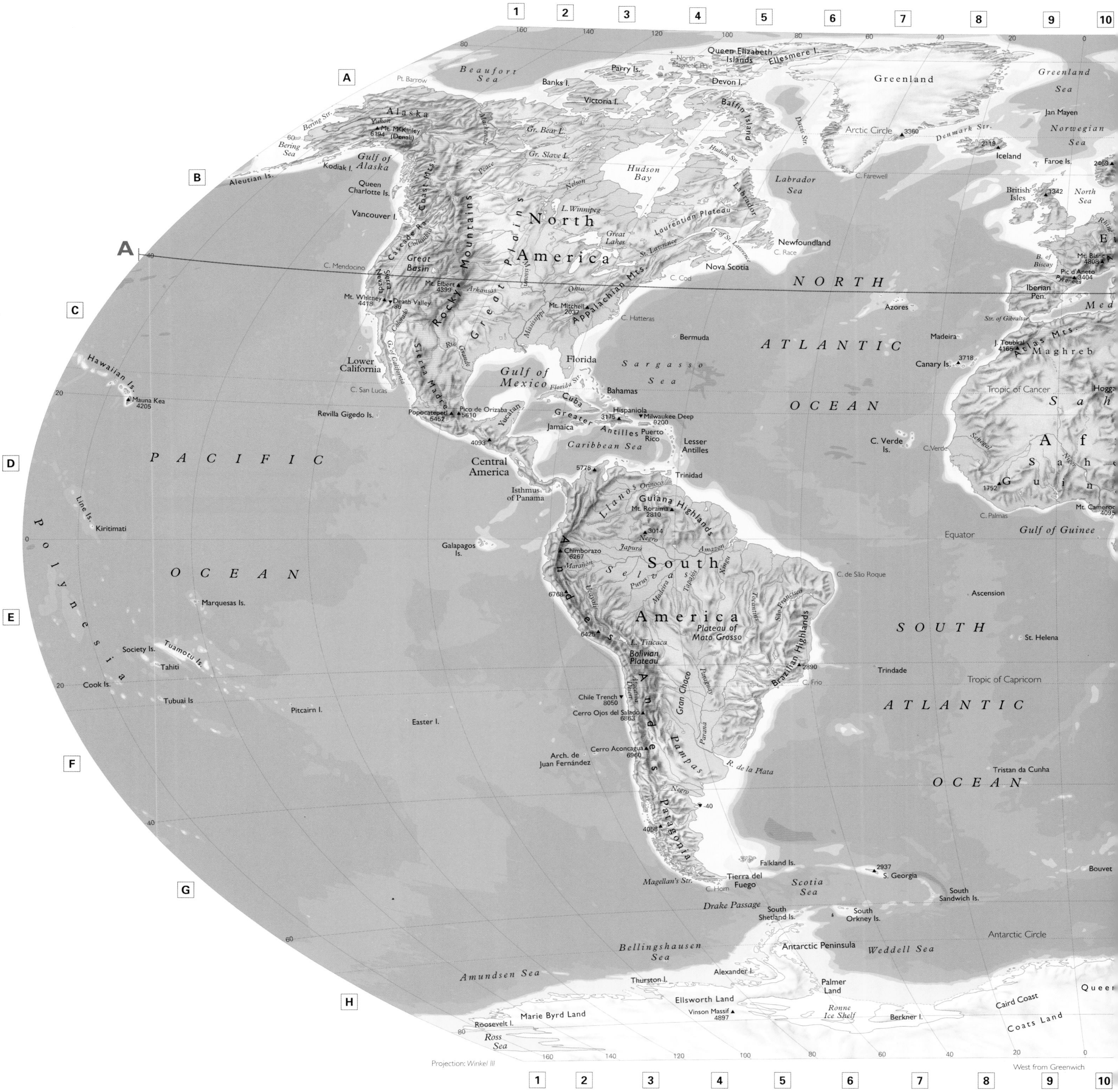

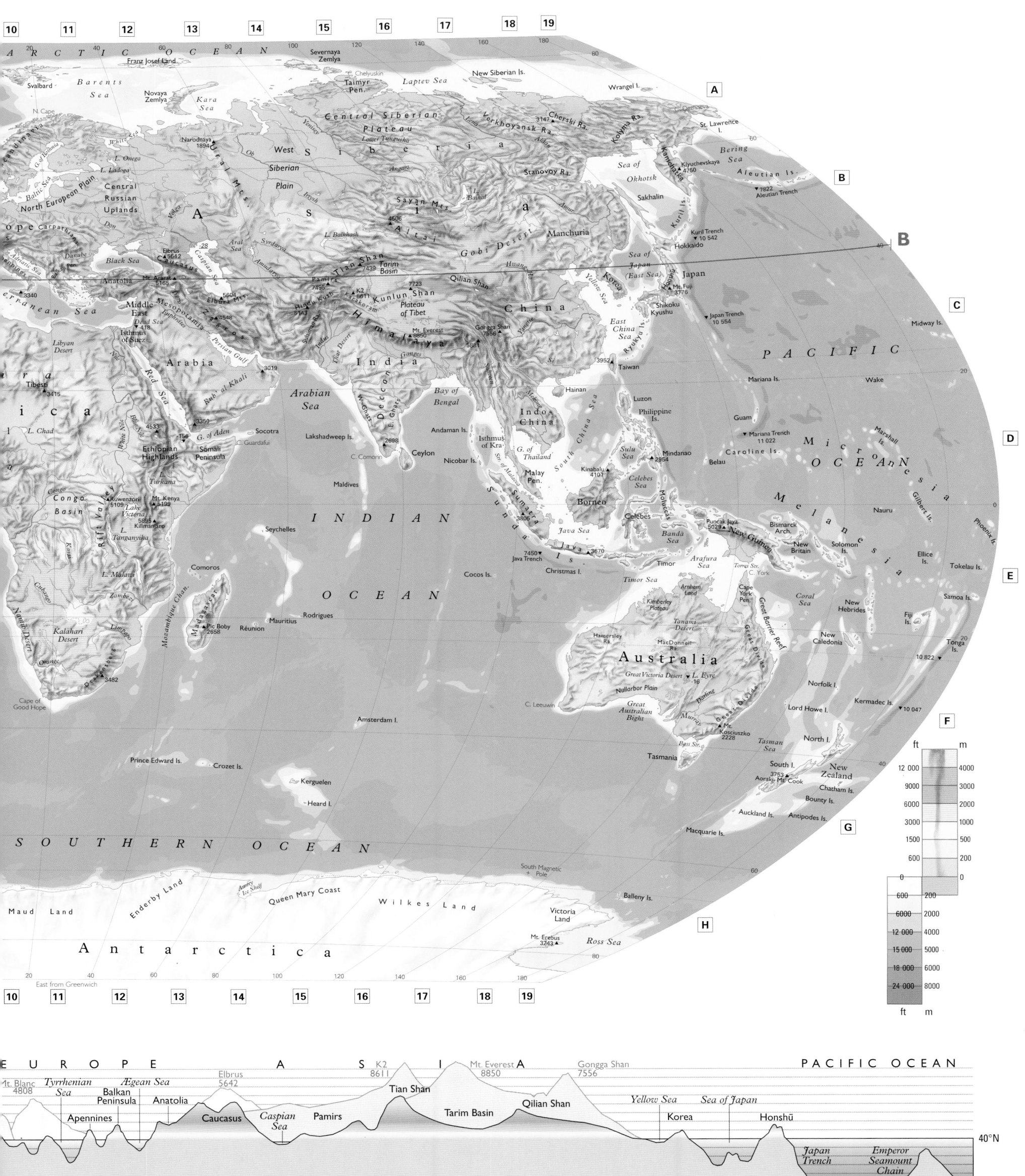

ft	m
12 000	4000
9000	3000
6000	2000
3000	1000
1500	500
600	200
0	0
600	200
6000	2000
12 000	4000
15 000	5000
18 000	6000
24 000	8000

ft   m

COPYRIGHT PHILIP'S

Equatorial Scale 1·76 000 000

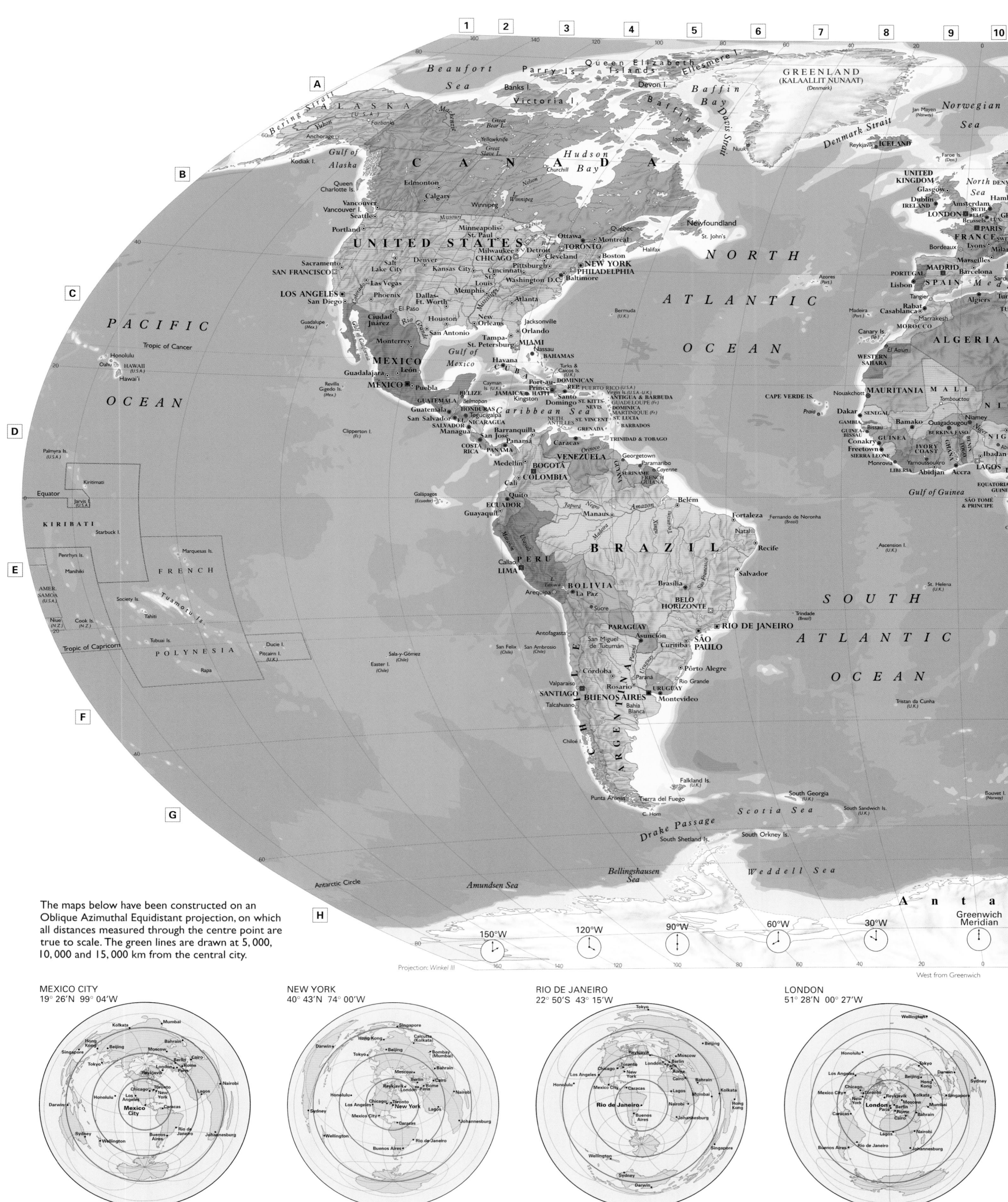

The maps below have been constructed on an Oblique Azimuthal Equidistant projection, on which all distances measured through the centre point are true to scale. The green lines are drawn at 5,000, 10,000 and 15,000 km from the central city.

Projection: Winkel III

West from Greenwich

MEXICO CITY
19° 26'N 99° 04'W

NEW YORK
40° 43'N 74° 00'W

RIO DE JANEIRO
22° 50'S 43° 15'W

LONDON
51° 28'N 00° 27'W

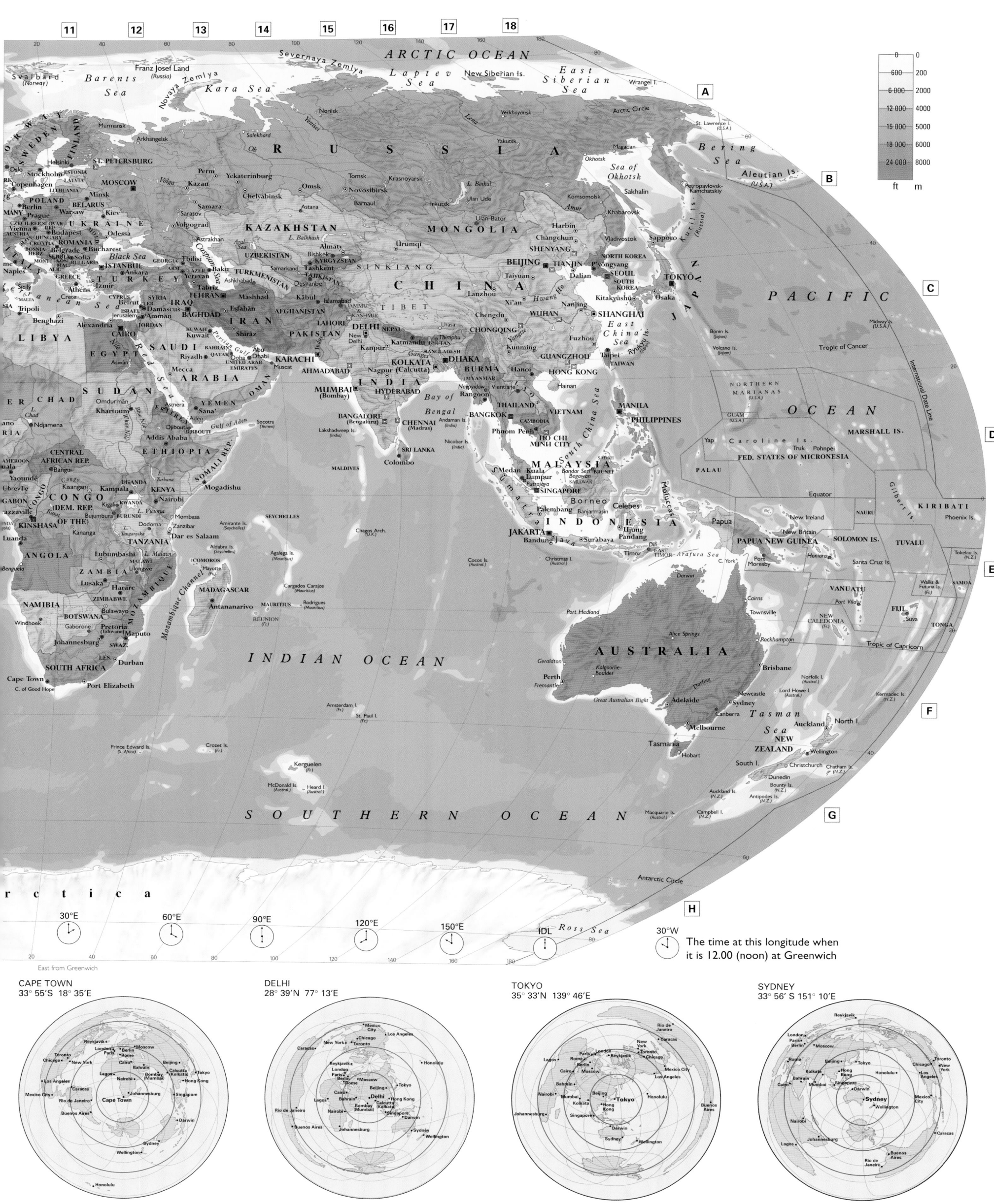

The time at this longitude when it is 12.00 (noon) at Greenwich

CAPE TOWN
33° 55'S 18° 35'E

DELHI
28° 39'N 77° 13'E

TOKYO
35° 33'N 139° 46'E

SYDNEY
33° 56' S 151° 10'E

COPYRIGHT PHILIP'S

100 0 200 400 600 800 1000 1200 1400 km

100 0 200 400 600 800 1000 miles

1:28 000 000

Maximum extent of sea ice

Minimum extent of sea ice (September 2007)

Ice caps and permanent ice shelf

Projection : Zenithal Equidistant

West from Greenwich   East from Greenwich

COPYRIGHT PHILIP'S

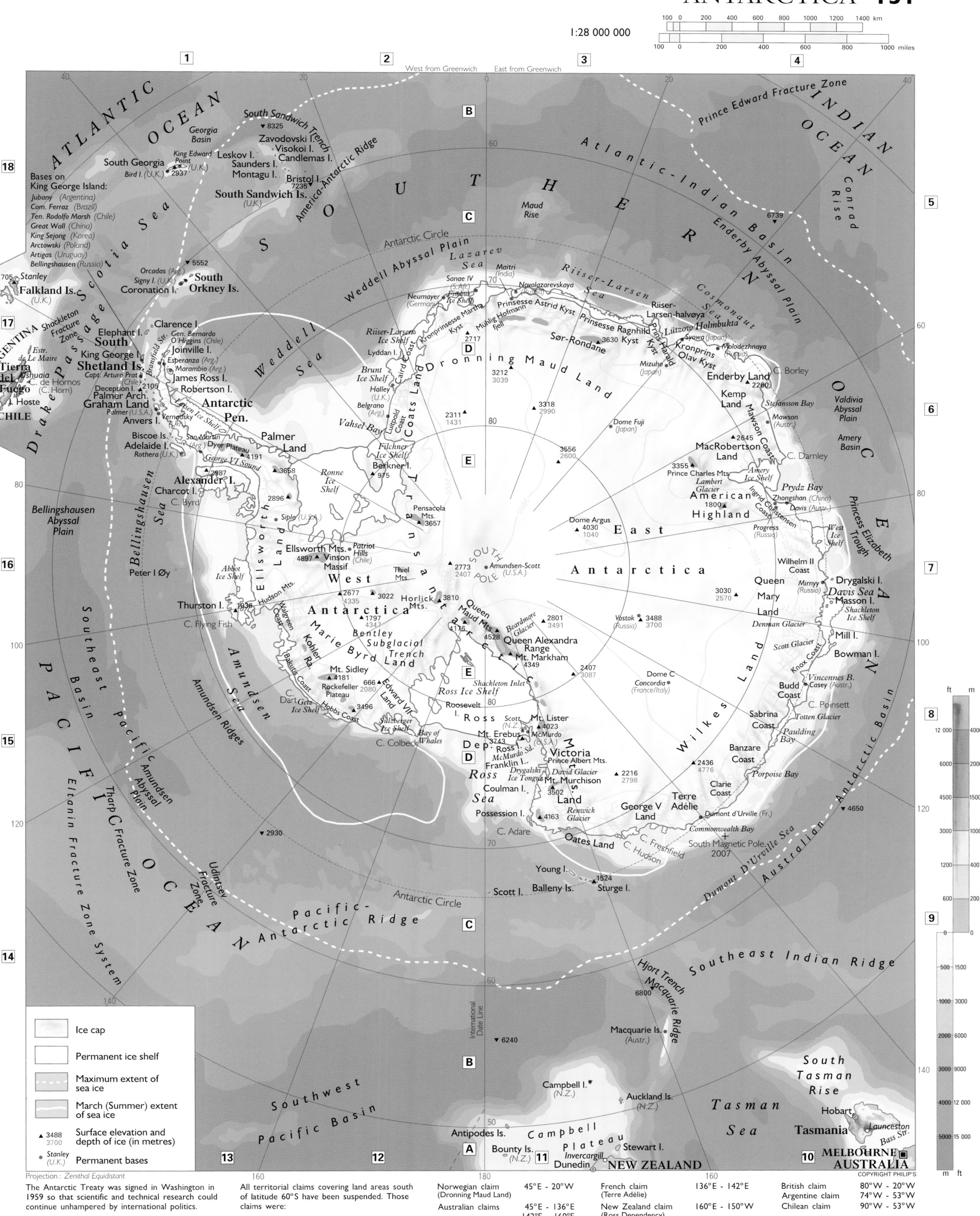

1:28 000 000

Bases on King George Island:
Jubany (Argentina)
Com. Ferraz (Brazil)
Ten. Rodolfo Marsh (Chile)
Great Wall (China)
King Sejong (Korea)
Arctowski (Poland)
Artigas (Uruguay)
Bellingshausen (Russia)

Legend

	Ice cap
	Permanent ice shelf
	Maximum extent of sea ice
	March (Summer) extent of sea ice
▲ 3488 / 3700	Surface elevation and depth of ice (in metres)
● Stanley	Permanent bases

Projection: Zenithal Equidistant

The Antarctic Treaty was signed in Washington in 1959 so that scientific and technical research could continue unhampered by international politics.

All territorial claims covering land areas south of latitude 60°S have been suspended. Those claims were:

Norwegian claim (Dronning Maud Land)	45°E – 20°W	French claim (Terre Adélie)	136°E – 142°E
Australian claims	45°E – 136°E / 142°E – 160°E	New Zealand claim (Ross Dependency)	160°E – 150°W
British claim	80°W – 20°W		
Argentine claim	74°W – 53°W		
Chilean claim	90°W – 53°W		

COPYRIGHT PHILIP'S

Equatorial Scale 1:41 000 000

GREENLAND (Denmark)
Nuuk
Tasiilaq
ICELAND
Öræfajökull 2119
Reykjavik
Denmark Strait
Norwegian Sea
Norwegian Basin
Tórshavn
Føroyar (Den.)
NORWAY
Trondheim
Bergen
Oslo
Stockholm
Göteborg
DENMARK
Malmö
København
Hamburg
Berlin
GERMANY
POLAND
Warszawa
Baltic Sea
Gdańsk
CZECH REP.
SLOVAK REP.
AUSTRIA
HUNGARY
Wien
München
Milano
CROATIA
BOS. H.
Zagreb
Adriatic Sea
Sicilia
Roma
Nápoli
ITALY
Corse
Sardegna

Hudson Bay
Churchill
Belcher Is.
C. Henrietta Maria
James Bay
CANADA
Nelson
L. Winnipeg
Regina
Winnipeg
Minneapolis
Ottawa
Montréal
Toronto
Québec
St. Lawrence
Gulf of St. Lawrence
Cape Breton I.
St. John's
C. Race
Newfoundland
Halifax
Grand Banks of Newfoundland
Flemish Cap
Labrador Sea
Hudson Str.
C. Chidley
Nunap Isua (K. Farvell)
Hudson Strait
Hamilton Inlet
Str. of Belle Isle
Northwest Atlantic Mid-Ocean Canyon
Davis Strait
Charlie Gibbs Fracture Zone
Reykjanes Ridge
Rockall (U.K.)
Rockall Trough
King's Trough
Azores-Biscay Rise
Porcupine Abyssal Plain
Biscay Abyssal Plain
Bay of Biscay
Celtic Sea
North Sea
UNITED KINGDOM
Glasgow
Liverpool
Dublin
IRELAND
London
Amsterdam
NETH.
Brussel
Le Havre
Paris
Bern
SWITZ.
FRANCE
Mt. Blanc 4808
Bordeaux
Marseille
A Coruña
C. Fisterra
Vigo
Porto
Douro
PORTUGAL
Lisboa
Madrid
SPAIN
Barcelona
Is. Baleares
Alger
TUNISIA
MALTA
Tunis
Mediterranean Sea
Tarābulus
Str. of Gibraltar
Tanger
Rabat
Casablanca
MOROCCO
Marrakech
Funchal
Madeira (Port.)
C. de São Vicente
Açores (Port.)
Ponta Delgada
2351

Minneapolis
Chicago
Detroit
Omaha
L. Michigan
L. Huron
L. Erie
L. Ontario
Pittsburgh
St. Louis
Ohio
Missouri
UNITED STATES
New York
Philadelphia
Baltimore
Washington D.C.
Boston
C. Cod
Chesapeake Bay
New England Seamounts
Atlanta
Alabama
Tennessee
Arkansas
Red
Mississippi
Appalachian Mts.
Charleston
Jacksonville
C. Hatteras
Hamilton
Bermuda (U.K.)
Bermuda Rise
Sohm 6028 Abyssal Plain
Corner Seamounts
NORTH ATLANTIC OCEAN
Sargasso Sea
Hatteras Abyssal Plain
Houston
Galveston
New Orleans
Gulf of Mexico
Sigsbee 3504
Deep Canal de Yucatan
Tampico
G. de Campeche
Veracruz
MEXICO
BELIZE
GUATEMALA
Guatemala
HONDURAS
EL SALVADOR
NICARAGUA
L. de Nicaragua
COSTA RICA
Panamá
PANAMA
G. de Panamá
G. del Darién
Miami
Nassau
BAHAMAS
Tropic of Cancer
Florida Strait
CUBA
La Habana
Santiago de Cuba
JAMAICA
Kingston
HAITI
DOM. REP.
Santo Domingo
PUERTO RICO (USA)
San Juan
Milwaukee Deep 9200
Puerto Rico Trench
West Indies
Nares Abyssal Plain
ANTIGUA
ST. KITTS
GUADELOUPE (Fr.)
Leeward Is.
DOMINICA
MARTINIQUE (Fr.)
ST. LUCIA
ST. VINCENT
BARBADOS
GRENADA
Windward Is.
Coyman Trench
Cayman Is.
Colombian Basin
G. de Venezuela
Curaçao
Caribbean Sea
Barranquilla
Santa Marta
Sierra Nevada de Santa Marta
Caracas
TRINIDAD & TOBAGO
Port of Spain
VENEZUELA
Bogotá
Cali
COLOMBIA
Orinoco
Meta
Mt. Roraima
GUYANA
Georgetown
Paramaribo
SURINAM
Cayenne
FRENCH GUIANA
C. Orange
Sierra Pacaraima
Demerara Abyssal Plain
Ceara Rise
Ceara Abyssal Plain
C. de San Francisco
Quito
ECUADOR
Cotopaxi 5897
Chimborazo 6267
Guayaquil
G. de Guayaquil
Pta. Pariñas
Negro
Japurá
Putumayo
Branco
Amazonas
Iquitos
Santarém
Manaus
Belém
São Luís
BRAZIL
Madeira
Tapajós
Purus
Uçayali
Marañón
Trujillo
Lima
PERU
Equator
Fernando de Noronha
C. de São Roque
Natal
Fortaleza
Recife
Maceió
Pernambuco Abyssal Plain
São Pedro & São Paulo (Brazil)
Sierra Leone Rise
Sierra Leone Basin
CAPE VERDE IS.
Cape Verde Abyssal Plain
Cape Verde Plateau
Ras Nouâdhibou
Dakar
C. Vert
Praia
St-Louis
SENEGAL
GAMBIA
Banjul
GUINEA-BISSAU
GUINEA
Conakry
Freetown
SIERRA LEONE
LIBERIA
Monrovia
IVORY COAST
Abidjan
GHANA
Accra
Sekondi-Takoradi
TOGO
BENIN
Lagos
NIGERIA
Niger
Benue
CAMEROON
Douala
Port Harcourt
Bioko
EQUATORIAL GUINEA
São Tomé & Príncipe
Libreville
GABON
C. Lopez
Ogooué
Annobón
Gulf of Guinea
Guinea Basin
MAURITANIA
Nouakchott
Saharan Seamounts
Is. Canarias (Sp.)
Las Palmas
El Aaiún
WESTERN SAHARA
Sahara
ALGERIA
Chott Djerid
NIGER
Kano
MALI
Senegal
Kayes
Bamako
Ouagadougou
BURKINA FASO
Tombouctou
5638
7292
2829
37185

BRAZIL
Brasília
Goiânia
Belo Horizonte
São Paulo
Rio de Janeiro
Santos
Curitiba
Porto Alegre
São Francisco
Sierra da Mantiqueira
C. de São Tomé
C. Frio
Nevado Ancohuma 6559
La Paz
BOLIVIA
L. Titicaca
L. de Poopó
Arica
Iquique
Antofagasta
8064
PARAGUAY
Asunción
CHILE
San Miguel de Tucumán
Ojos del Salado 6863
Córdoba
Santa Fe
Rosario
URUGUAY
Montevideo
Buenos Aires
ARGENTINA
Aconcagua 6962
Valparaíso
Santiago
Concepción
Bahía Blanca
Rio de la Plata
L. dos Patos
Paraná
Uruguay
Salado
Colorado
Pampas
Gran Chaco
Pilcomayo
Brazil Basin
Ascension I. (U.K.)
Hotspur Seamount
Banco Abrolhos
Vitória Seamount
Martin Vaz Trindade (Brazil)
Mid-Atlantic Ridge
St. Helena (U.K.)
SOUTH ATLANTIC OCEAN
Tropic of Capricorn
Angola Basin
Luanda
Lobito
Benguela
Namibe
ANGOLA
Angola Abyssal Plain
Pointe Noire
C. Fria
NAMIBIA
Walvis Ridge
Walvis Bay
Lüderitz
Nambia Abyssal Plain
Port Nolloth
SOUTH AFRICA
Cape Town
C. of Good Hope
Cape Basin
Agulhas Ridge
Discovery Seamount
Gough I. (U.K.)
Tristan da Cunha (U.K.) 2062
6537
2890
638
887
5457
5656
7758
411
5704

PACIFIC OCEAN
Nazca Ridge
Peru-Chile Trench
Chile Basin
Arch. de Juan Fernández (Chile)
San Ambrosio (Chile)
Chile Rise
Valparaíso
Puerto Montt
I. de Chiloé
Arch. de los Chonos
Pen. de Taitao
G. de Penas
Patagonia
Est. de Magallanes (Magellan Str.)
Punta Arenas
I. Santa Inés
Tierra del Fuego
C. de Hornos
Chubut
G. San Matías
Pen. Valdés
Golfo San Jorge
Bahía Blanca
102
Argentine Basin
Argentine Abyssal Plain
Falkland Is. (U.K.)
Stanley
Falkland Plateau
Falkland Ridge
Burdwood Bank
Shag Rocks
South Georgia (U.K.)
Georgia Basin
Grytviken 8325
Mt. Paget 2934
South Sandwich Trench
Bouvetøya (Norw.)
Rio Grande Rise

ft m
12000 4000
9000 3000
6000 2000
3000 1000
1500 500
600 200
0 0
200 600
1000 3000
2000 6000
4000 12000
6000 18000
8000 24000
m ft

West from Greenwich
Projection: Mollweide
COPYRIGHT PHILIP'S

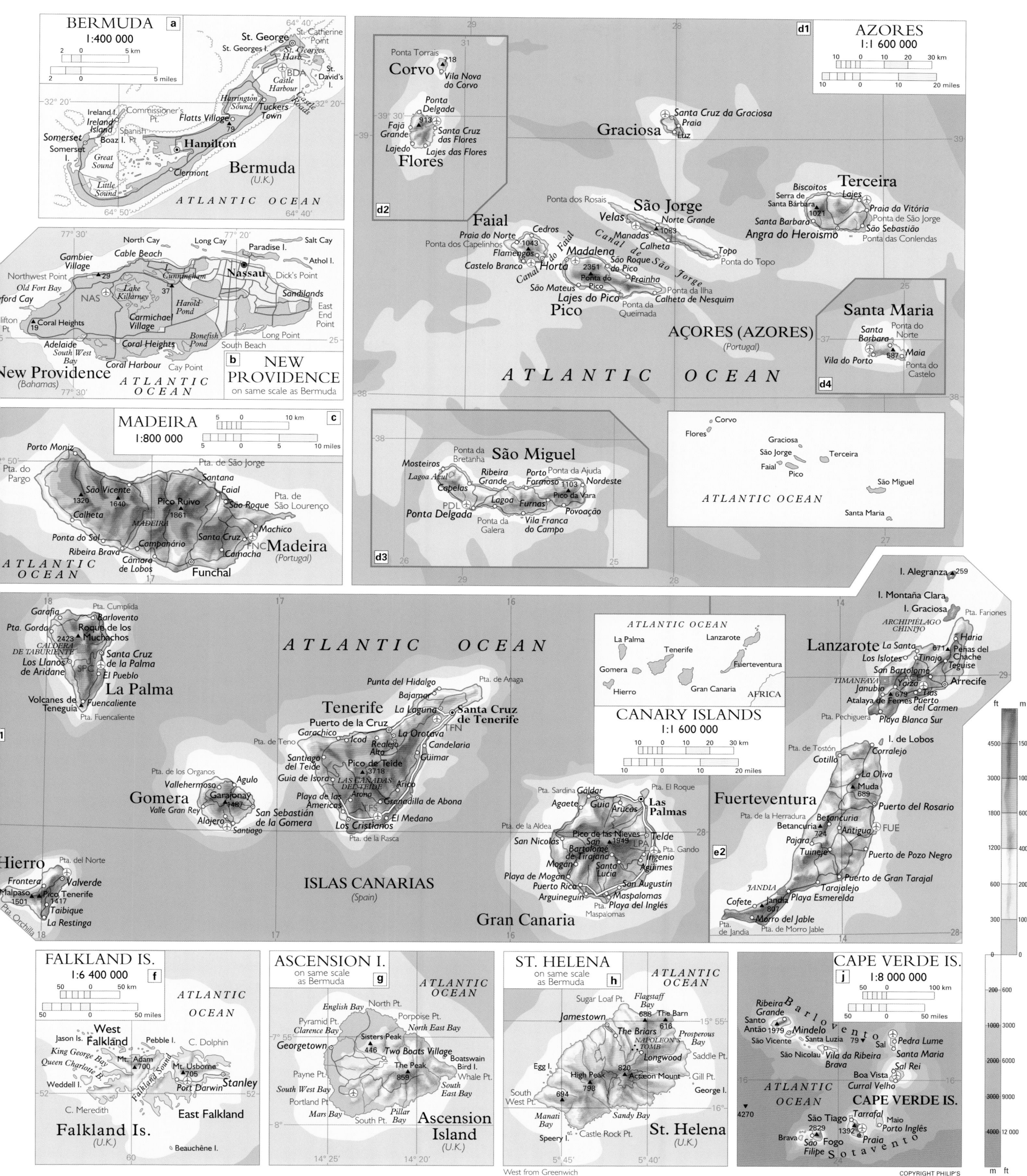

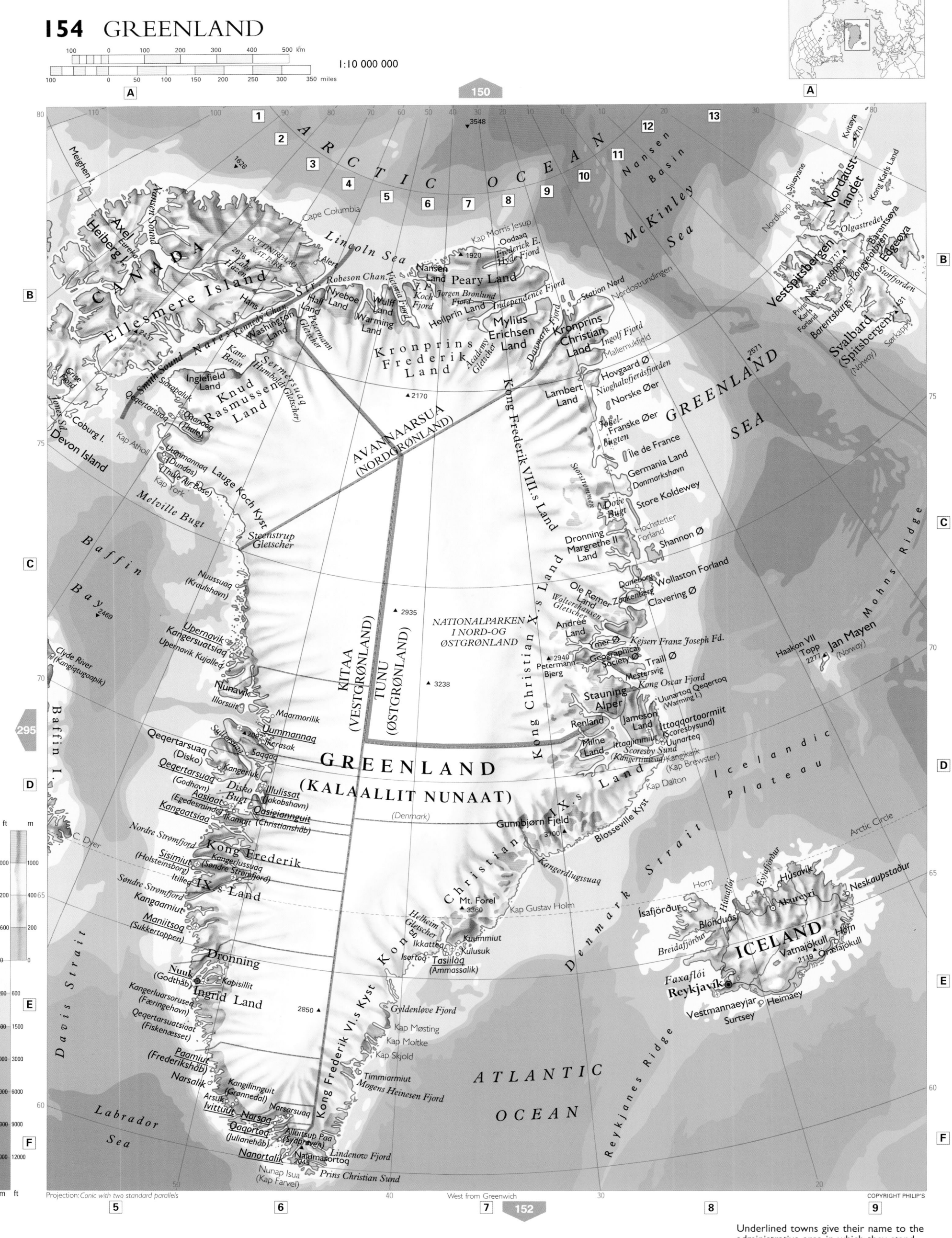

1:10 000 000

Projection: Conic with two standard parallels

West from Greenwich

COPYRIGHT PHILIP'S

Underlined towns give their name to the
administrative area in which they stand.

1:2 000 000

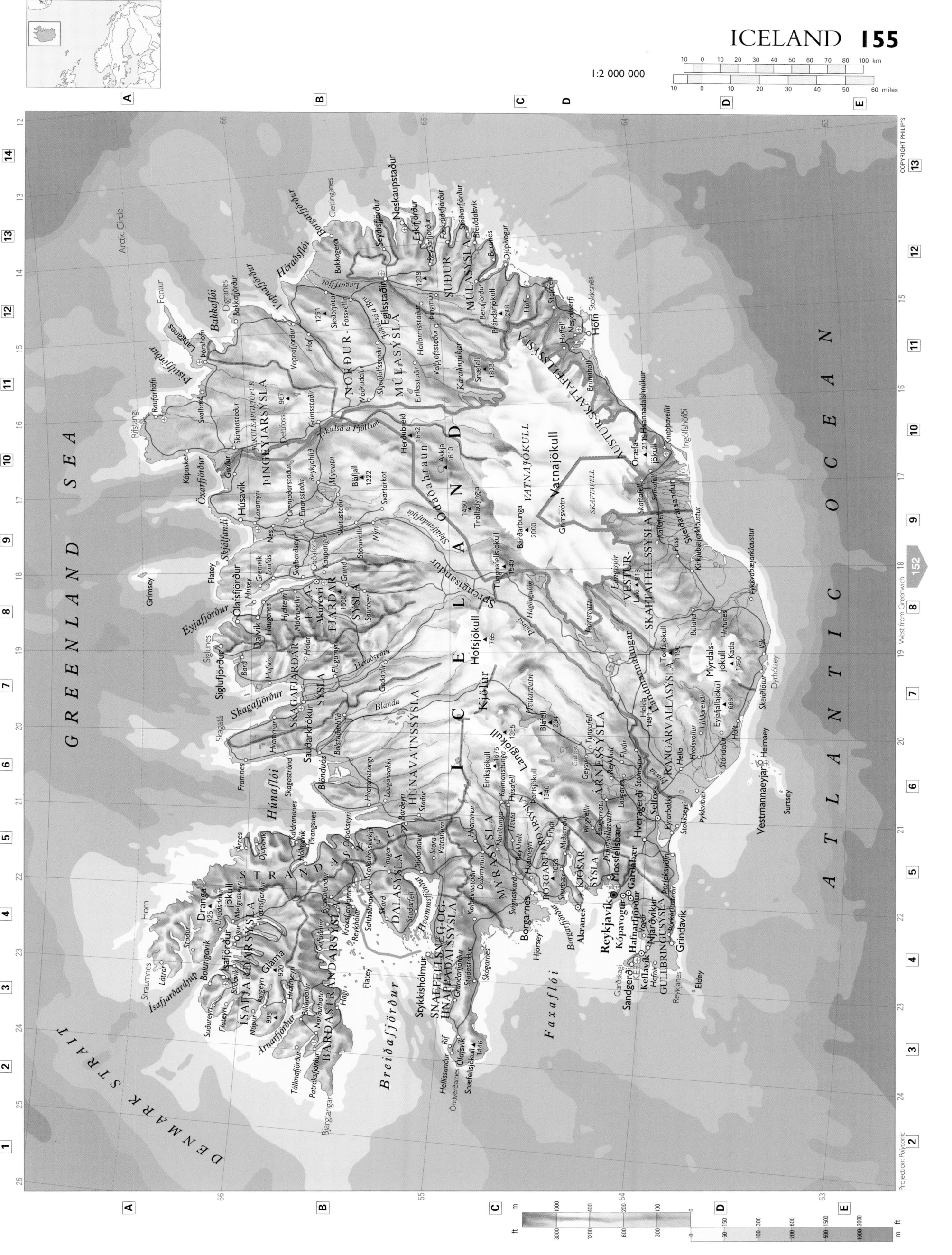

GREENLAND SEA

ATLANTIC OCEAN

DENMARK STRAIT

Arctic Circle

ICELAND

Reykjavík

Vatnajökull

Hofsjökull

Langjökull

Mýrdals-jökull

Myvatn

Akureyri

Egilsstaðir

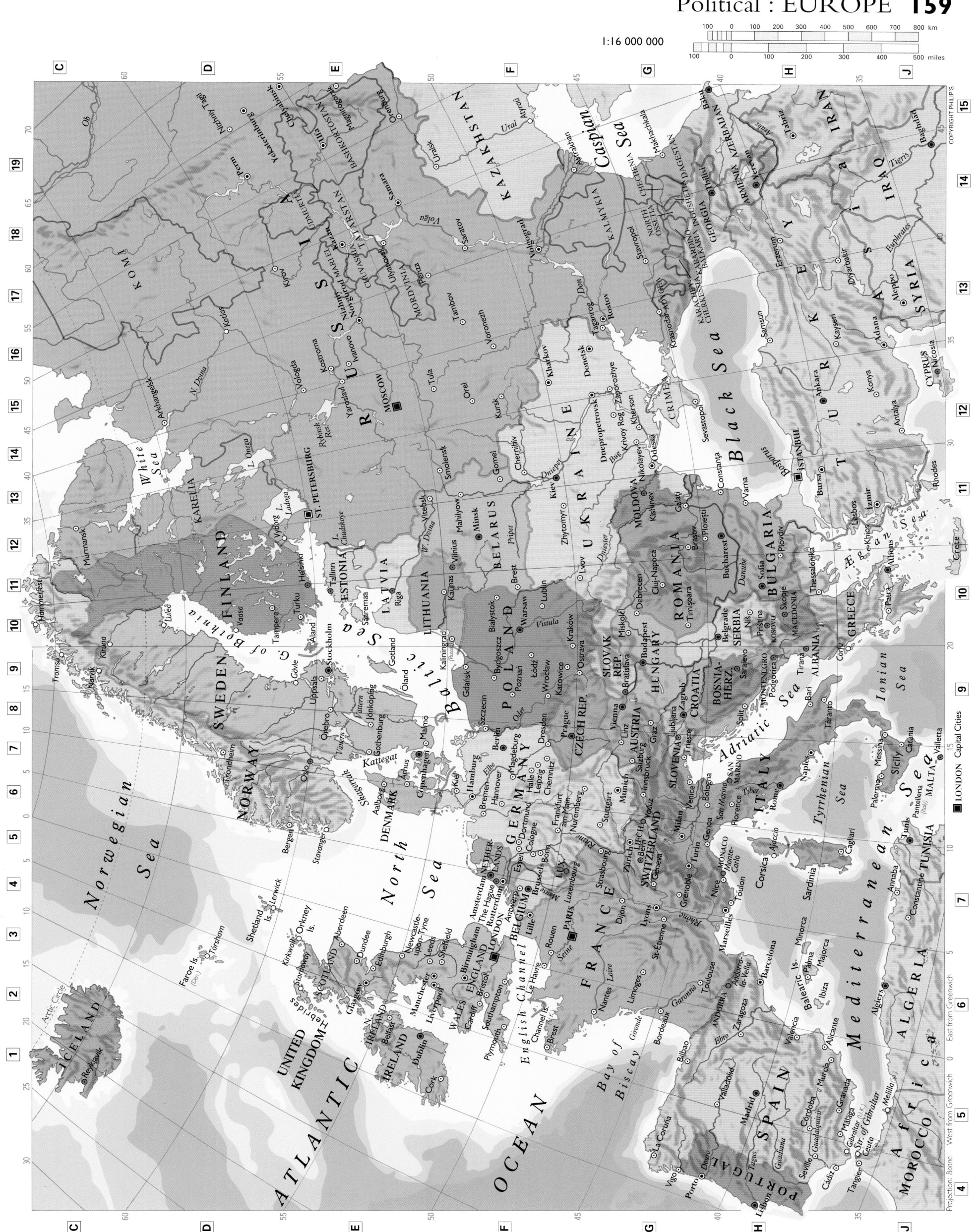

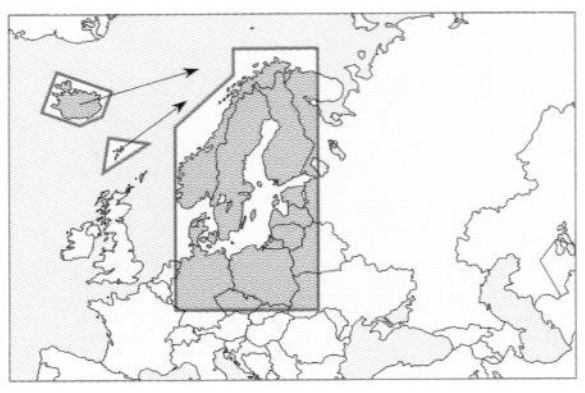

1:4 800 000

km 50 0 25 50 75 100 125 150 175 km
miles 50 0 25 50 75 100 125 miles

BARENTS SEA

RUSSIA

KARELIA

FINLAND

NORWAY

SWEDEN

Sverige

Lappland

Finnmark

ATLANTIC OCEAN

NORWEGIAN SEA

Gulf of Bothnia

ICELAND
on same scale

FÆROE ISLANDS
on same scale
Føroyar (Færoe Is.)

Murmansk
Reykjavik
Oulu
Tampere
Trondheim
Narvik
Kiruna
Rovaniemi
Tornio
Kemi
Luleå
Skellefteå
Umeå
Sundsvall
Östersund
Bodø
Mo i Rana
Namsos
Ålesund
Molde
Vardø
Kirkenes
Hammerfest
Tromsø
Harstad
Bergen

Arctic Circle

West from Greenwich

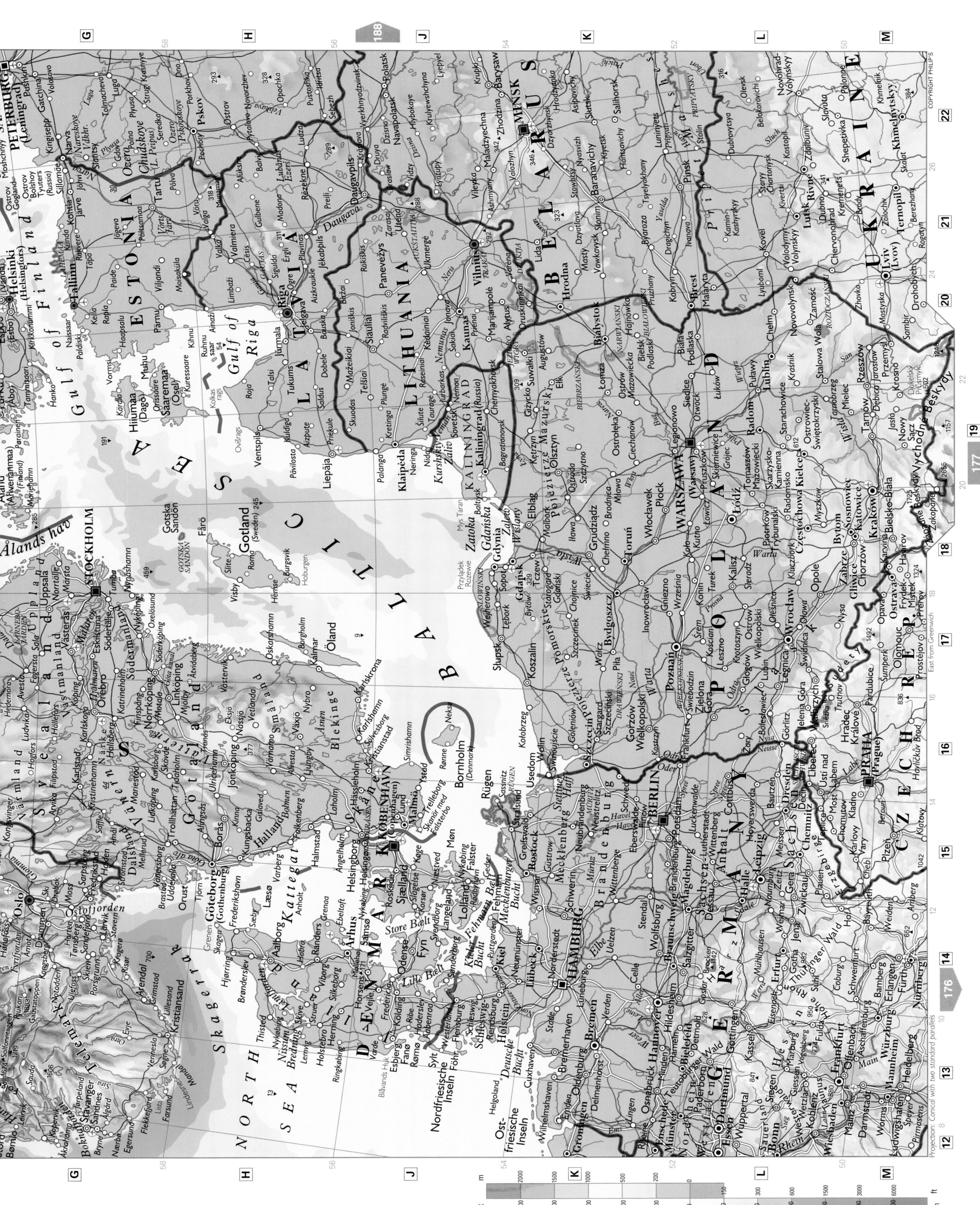

Projection: Conical with two standard parallels

East from Greenwich

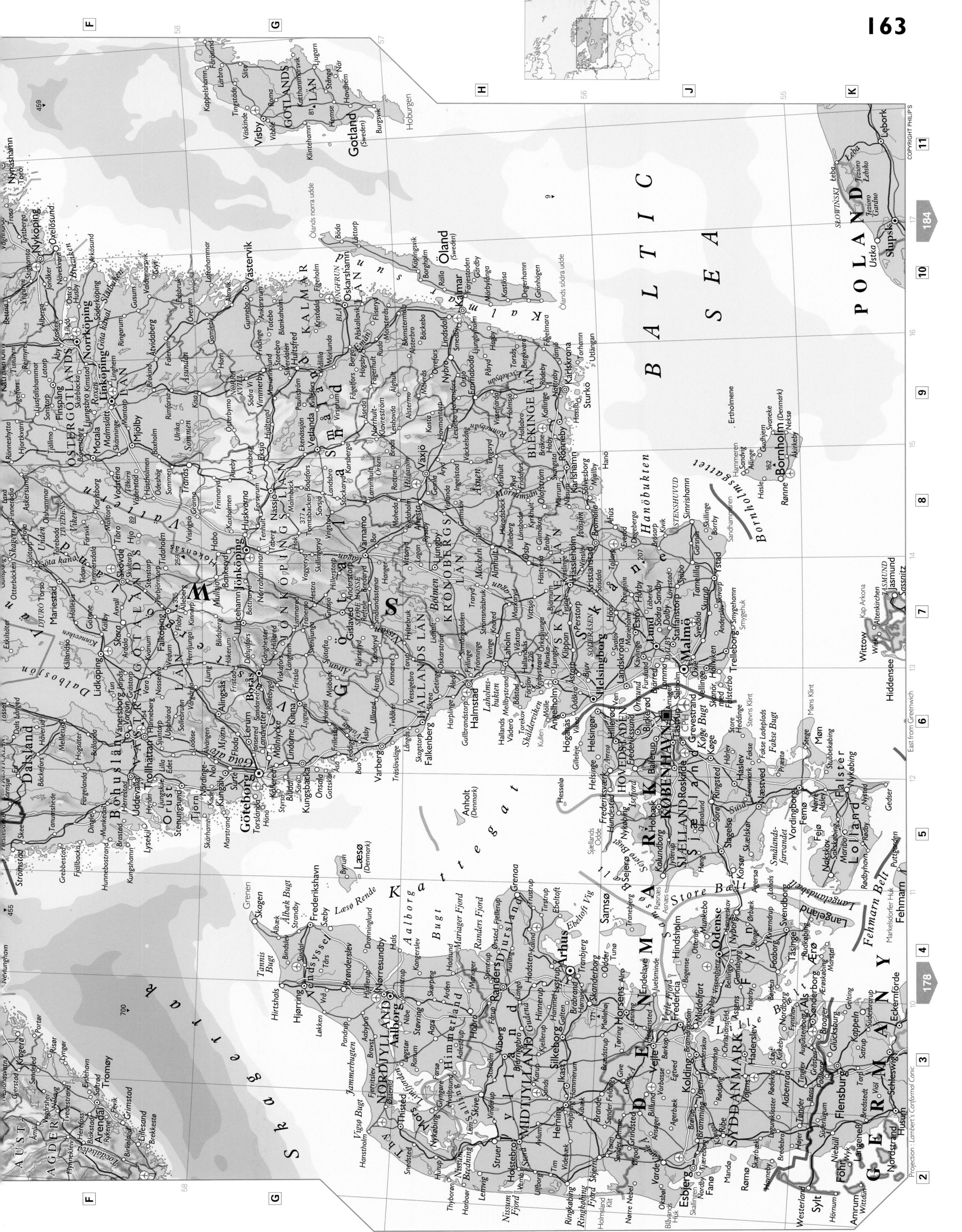

Projection : Lambert's Conformal Conic

East from Greenwich

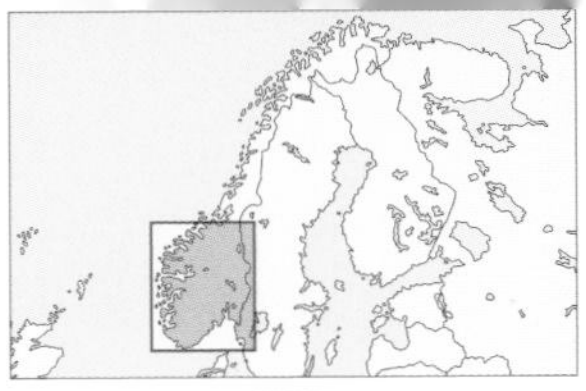

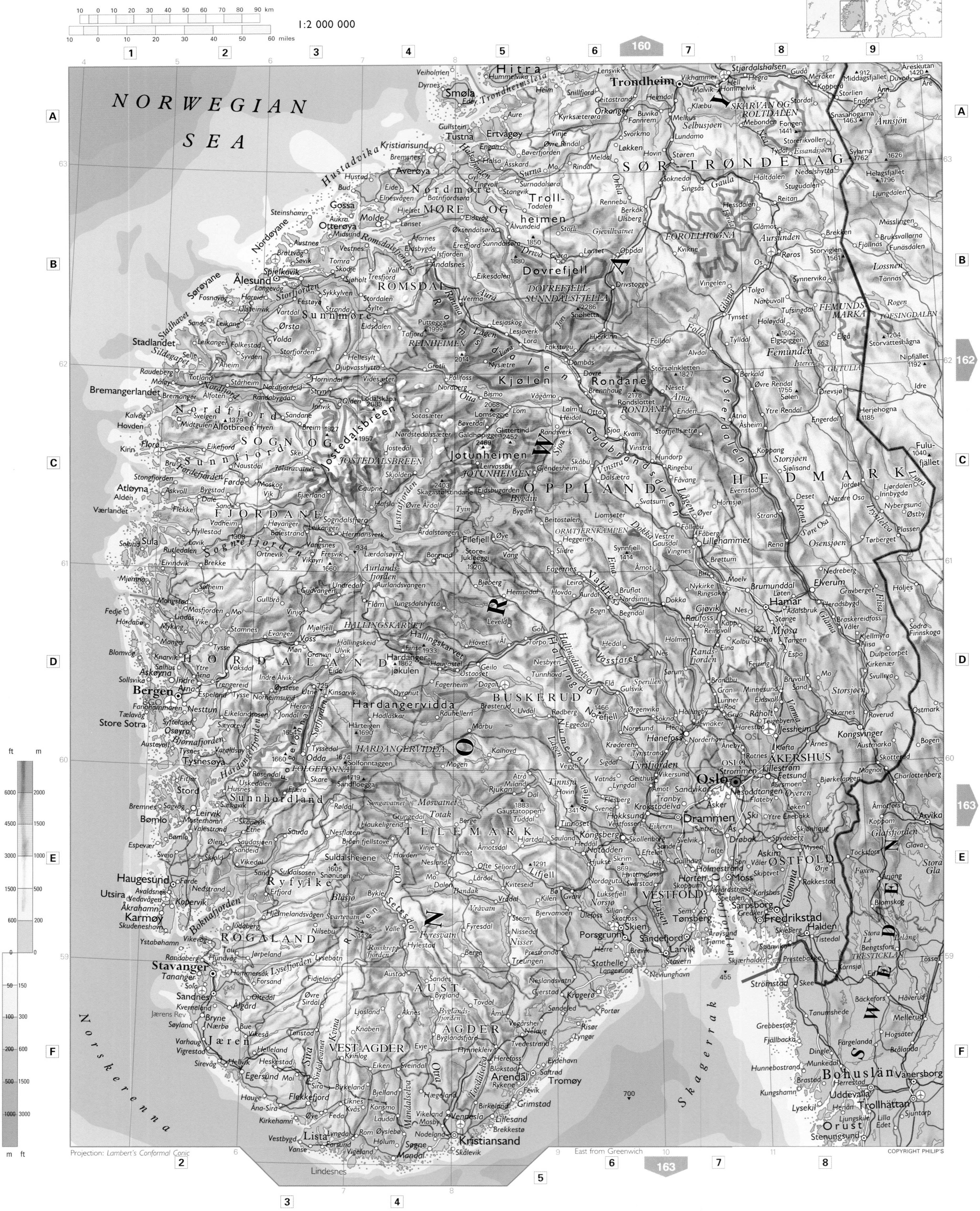
1:2 000 000
km
miles
NORWEGIAN SEA
Norskerenna
Skagerrak
SØR-TRØNDELAG
MØRE OG ROMSDAL
SOGN OG FJORDANE
HORDALAND
ROGALAND
VEST-AGDER
AUST-AGDER
TELEMARK
BUSKERUD
VESTFOLD
ØSTFOLD
AKERSHUS
OPPLAND
HEDMARK
NORWAY
SWEDEN
Trondheim
Kristiansund
Molde
Ålesund
Bergen
Stavanger
Haugesund
Kristiansand
Oslo
Drammen
Lillehammer
Hamar
Fredrikstad
Arendal
Jotunheimen
Hardangervidda
Dovrefjell
Rondane
Jostedalsbreen
Sognefjorden
Hardangerfjorden
Femunden
Mjøsa
Lindesnes
Projection: Lambert's Conformal Conic
East from Greenwich
COPYRIGHT PHILIP'S
160
162
163
A
B
C
D
E
F

1:4 000 000

50   0   25 50 75 100 125 150 175 km
50   0   25   50   75   100   125 miles

ATLANTIC OCEAN

NORTH SEA

IRISH SEA

CELTIC SEA

English Channel

St. George's Channel

Bristol Channel

NORWAY

Shetland Is. (U.K.)
Yell
Unst
Fetlar
Foula
Mainland
Lerwick
Fair Isle

Bergen
Askøyna
Stord
Leitvik
Bømlo
Haugesund
Kopervik
Åkrahamn
Stavanger
Sandnes
Bryne
Nærbø
Boknafjorden
Osøyro

Orkney Is.
Westray
Sanday
Stronsay
Mainland
Kirkwall
Hoy
South Ronaldsay
Pentland Firth
C. Wrath
Thurso
Wick
Helmsdale

SCOTLAND
Outer Hebrides
Lewis
Stornoway
Harris
St. Kilda (U.K.)
North Uist
Benbecula
South Uist
Barra
Inner Hebrides
Sea of the Hebrides
North Minch
North West Highlands
Ullapool
Lairg
Golspie
Tain
Dingwall
Invergordon
Nairn
Inverness
Elgin
Buckie
Banff
Fraserburgh
Peterhead
Huntly
Inverurie
Aberdeen
CAIRNGORMS Mts.
Glen More
Aviemore
Ben Nevis
Fort William
Mallaig
Rhum
Eigg
Coll
Skye
Portree
Tobermory
Mull
Oban
Tiree
Colonsay
Jura
Islay
Arran
Campbeltown
GRAMPIAN Mts.
L. Ness
L. LOMOND & TROSSACHS
L. Awe
L. Lomond
Perth
Dundee
St. Andrews
Glenrothes
Kirkcaldy
Dunbar
Montrose
Arbroath
Forfar
Ballater
Stonehaven
Stirling
Dunfermline
GLASGOW
Paisley
Greenock
Dumbarton
Motherwell
Hamilton
East Kilbride
Irvine
Kilmarnock
Ayr
Girvan
Edinburgh
Berwick-upon-Tweed
Galashiels
Jedburgh
Hawick
Cheviot Hills
Alnwick
Southern Uplands
Dumfries
Annan
Carlisle
Hexham
NORTHUMBERLAND
Newcastle-upon-Tyne
South Shields
Sunderland
Gateshead
Durham
Hartlepool
Redcar
Darlington
Middlesbrough
Stockton-on-Tees
Stranraer
Kirkcudbright
Workington
Whitehaven
Cumbrian Mts.
LAKE DISTRICT
Barrow-in-Furness
Pennines
N. YORK MOORS
Scarborough
YORKSHIRE DALES
Bridlington

IRELAND
NORTHERN IRELAND
Ulster
Londonderry
Coleraine
Ballymena
Antrim
Larne
Bangor
Belfast
Lisburn
Lurgan
Portadown
Armagh
Newry
Lough Neagh
Buncrana
Letterkenny
Lifford
Omagh
Enniskillen
Clones
Cavan
GLENVEAGH
Donegal
Bundoran
Sligo
Leitrim
Ballina
Achill I.
L. Conn
Castlebar
Westport
Lough Mask
Connemara
Galway B.
Galway
Aran Is.
BURREN
Ennis
Lough Corrib
Roscommon
Longford
Athlone
Ballinasloe
Lough Ree
Mullingar
Ceanannus Mor
Dundalk
Drogheda
Boyne
DUBLIN
Dun Laoghaire
Bray
Birr
Tullamore
Port Laoise
Athy
Carlow
Kilkenny
Arklow
Wicklow Mts.
Wexford
Rosslare
Kilrush
Shannon
Listowel
Tralee
Dingle
Carrantoohill
Killarney
Macgillycuddy's Reeks
Kilrush
Limerick
Nenagh
Thurles
Tipperary
Clonmel
Carrick-on-Suir
Waterford
Dungarvan
Youghal
Cork
Cobh
Bandon
Kinsale
Bantry
C. Clear
Valencia
Mallow
Blackwater
Munster
Malin Hd.
North Channel
Firth of Clyde
Mull of Galloway
Douglas
I. of Man

UNITED KINGDOM

ENGLAND
Blackpool
Preston
Blackburn
Burnley
Keighley
Bradford
Leeds
York
Beverley
Kingston upon Hull
Halifax
Huddersfield
Barnsley
Doncaster
Rotherham
Sheffield
Scunthorpe
Grimsby
Humber
Lincoln
Louth
Skegness
Boston
The Wash
King's Lynn
Cromer
THE BROADS
Great Yarmouth
Lowestoft
MANCHESTER
LIVERPOOL
Bolton
Oldham
Stockport
Warrington
Chester
Crewe
PEAK DISTRICT
Chesterfield
Mansfield
Derby
Nottingham
Grantham
Stoke on Trent
Stafford
Telford
Shrewsbury
Welshpool
Leicester
Nuneaton
Peterborough
Corby
Thetford
Norwich
BIRMINGHAM
Wolverhampton
Coventry
Rugby
Northampton
Bedford
Ely
Bury St. Edmunds
Ipswich
Cambridge
Harwich
Felixstowe
Colchester
Redditch
Worcester
Hereford
Royal Leamington Spa
Milton Keynes
Stevenage
Cotswold Hills
Gloucester
Cheltenham
Oxford
High Wycombe
Hemel Hempstead
Luton
Harlow
Chelmsford
Southend-on-Sea
Basildon
LONDON
Slough
Reading
Newbury
Swindon
Bath
Bristol
Watford
Maidstone
Chatham
Canterbury
Margate
Dover
Folkestone
Ashford
Reigate
Crawley
Guildford
Basingstoke
Winchester
Salisbury
Southampton
Portsmouth
Fareham
Havant
Worthing
Brighton
Eastbourne
Hastings
Str. of Dover
New Forest
Isle of Wight
Newport
Weymouth
Poole
Bournemouth
Yeovil
Taunton
Exeter
Exmouth
Torbay
Exmoor
Barnstaple
Bude
Newquay
Truro
St. Austell
Plymouth
Falmouth
Penzance
Land's End
Isles of Scilly
DARTMOOR
Weston-super-Mare

WALES
Holyhead
Anglesey
Bangor
Colwyn Bay
Wrexham
Pwllheli
Snowdon
SNOWDONIA
Cambrian Mts.
Aberystwyth
Cardigan Bay
Cardigan
Carmarthen
BRECON BEACONS
Brecon
Merthyr Tydfil
Neath
Rhondda
Cwmbran
Newport
Cardiff
Barry
Swansea
Llanelli
Port Talbot
PEMBROKESHIRE COAST
Milford Haven
Pembroke
Haverfordwest
Fishguard
EXMOOR

NETHERLANDS
Texel
Den Helder
Alkmaar
Haarlem
's-Gravenhage (Den Haag)
Hoek van Holland
ROTTERDAM
Dordrecht

BELGIUM
BRUSSEL (Bruxelles)
Antwerpen
Gent
Brugge
Mechelen
Oostende
Zeebrugge
Vlissingen
LILLE
Roubaix
Tournai
Valenciennes
Cambrai

FRANCE
Dunkerque
Calais
Gris Nez
Boulogne-sur-Mer
Le Touquet-Paris-Plage
Béthune
Lens
Bruay-la-Buissière
St-Omer
Abbeville
Le Tréport
Dieppe
Fécamp
Le Havre
C. de la Hague
Pte. de Barfleur
Cherbourg
Valognes
Trouville-sur-Mer
Bayeux
Caen
Lisieux
Elbeuf
Rouen
Pays de Caux
Seine
Amiens
Laon
St-Quentin
Picardie
Bolbec

Guernsey
St. Peter Port
Sark
Jersey
St. Helier
Alderney
Channel Is. (U.K.)
Cotentin

Projection: Conical with two standard parallels
West from Greenwich
East from Greenwich
COPYRIGHT PHILIP'S

1224
316
789
1182
1311
1214
973
840
816
893
238
636
1085
886
978
618
926
1041
953
99
16
36
33

161
176
171

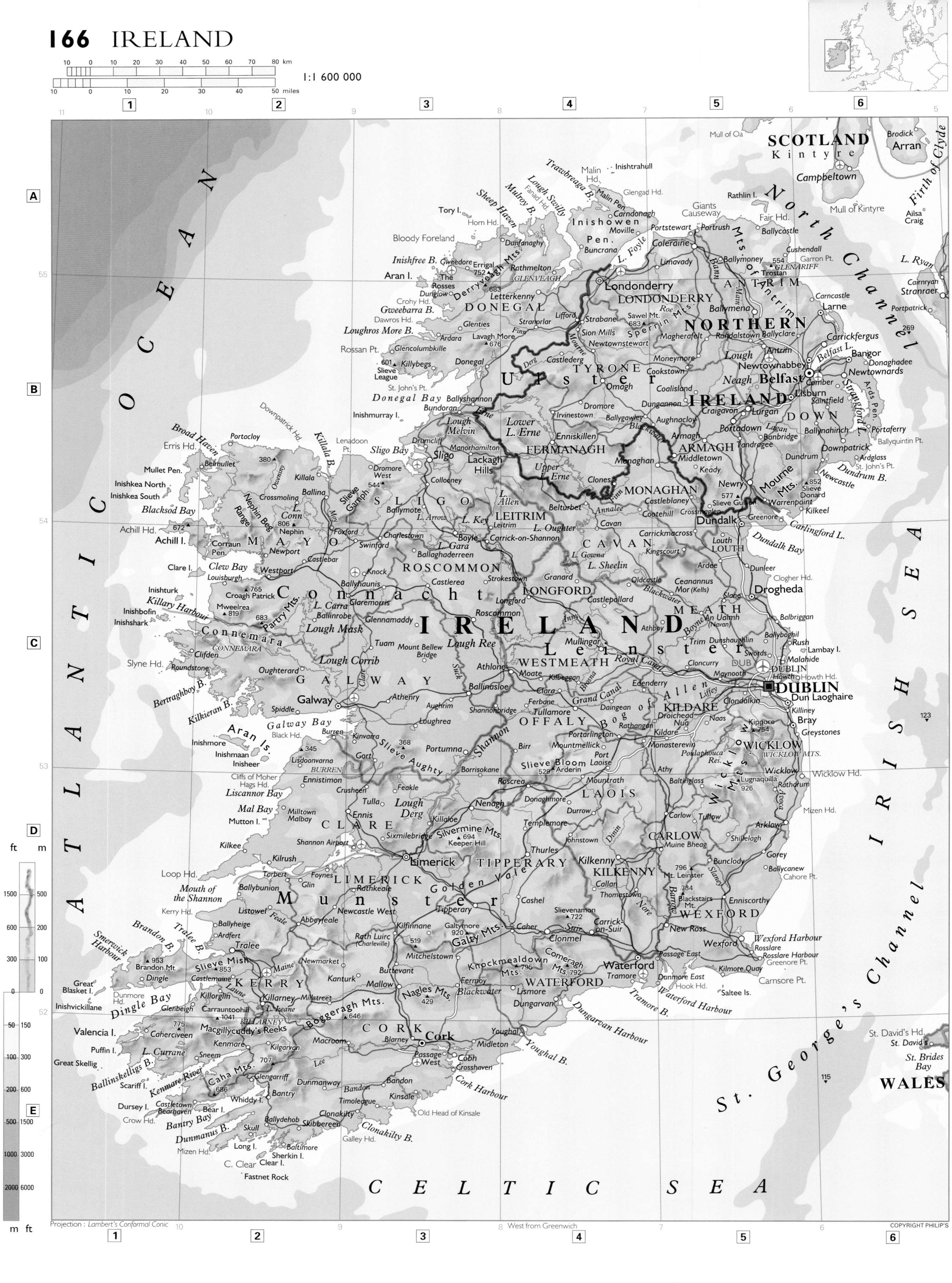

1:1 600 000

Projection: Lambert's Conformal Conic

West from Greenwich

COPYRIGHT PHILIP'S

ATLANTIC OCEAN

NORTHERN IRELAND

IRELAND

CELTIC SEA

IRISH SEA

St. George's Channel

North Channel

Firth of Clyde

SCOTLAND Kintyre

WALES

Ulster

Connacht

Leinster

Munster

DONEGAL
LONDONDERRY
TYRONE
FERMANAGH
ANTRIM
DOWN
ARMAGH
MONAGHAN
CAVAN
LEITRIM
SLIGO
MAYO
ROSCOMMON
LONGFORD
WESTMEATH
MEATH
LOUTH
GALWAY
OFFALY
KILDARE
DUBLIN
WICKLOW
LAOIS
CLARE
TIPPERARY
LIMERICK
KERRY
CORK
WATERFORD
KILKENNY
CARLOW
WEXFORD

Londonderry
Belfast
Dublin
Cork
Limerick
Galway
Sligo
Waterford
Dundalk
Drogheda
Dun Laoghaire
Wexford
Kilkenny
Tralee
Killarney
Ennis
Athlone
Mullingar
Naas
Bray
Greystones
Arklow
Carlow
Clonmel
Tipperary
Cashel
Thurles
Nenagh
Roscrea
Birr
Tullamore
Portlaoise
Carlow

Giants Causeway
Rathlin I.
Malin Hd.
Mull of Oa
Mull of Kintyre
Campbeltown
Ailsa Craig
Brodick
Arran
Stranraer
Cairnryan
L. Ryan
Portpatrick

Lough Neagh
Lough Erne
Lower L. Erne
Upper L. Erne
Lough Corrib
Lough Mask
Lough Ree
Lough Derg
Lough Allen
L. Key
L. Gara
L. Arrow
L. Conn
L. Carra
L. Oughter
L. Sheelin
L. Gowna
L. Ennell
Killala B.
Blacksod Bay
Clew Bay
Galway Bay
Donegal Bay
Dingle Bay
Bantry Bay
Kenmare River
Cork Harbour
Youghal B.
Dundalk Bay
Dundrum B.
Carlingford L.
Strangford L.
Belfast L.
Wexford Harbour
Waterford Harbour
Tramore B.

Macgillycuddy's Reeks
Carrauntoohil 1041
Slieve Bloom
Wicklow Mts.
Lugnaquilla 926
Mt. Leinster 796
Galty Mts.
Galtymore 920
Knockmealdown Mts. 792
Comeragh Mts. 796
Nephin 806
Croagh Patrick 765
Mweelrea 819
Errigal 752
Slieve Donard 852
Sawel Mt. 683
Trostan 554
Slieve Gullion 577
Keeper Hill 694
Silvermine Mts.
Slieve Bloom 529

Aran Is.
Achill I.
Clare I.
Inishbofin
Inishturk
Valencia I.
Great Blasket I.
Great Skellig
Cape Clear
Fastnet Rock

m ft

ft m
1500
600
300
0
1500 500
600 200
300 100
0 0
50 150
100 300
200 600
500 1500
1000 3000
2000 6000

10 0 10 20 30 40 50 60 70 80 km
10 0 10 20 30 40 50 miles

1:1 600 000

10   0   10   20   30   40   50   60   70   80 km
10   0   10   20   30   40   50 miles

Key to Scottish unitary authorities on map
1 CITY OF ABERDEEN
2 DUNDEE CITY
3 WEST DUNBARTONSHIRE
4 EAST DUNBARTONSHIRE
5 CITY OF GLASGOW
6 INVERCLYDE
7 RENFREWSHIRE
8 EAST RENFREWSHIRE
9 NORTH LANARKSHIRE
10 FALKIRK
11 CLACKMANNANSHIRE
12 WEST LOTHIAN
13 CITY OF EDINBURGH
14 MIDLOTHIAN

ORKNEY IS.
on same scale

ORKNEY

North Ronaldsay
Papa Westray
Westray
Eday
Sanday
Rousay
Stronsay
Brough Hd.
Mainland
Shapinsay
Stromness
Kirkwall
Hoy
Scapa Flow
St. Mary's
Burray
Burwick
South Ronaldsay
Dunnet Hd.
Stroma
Duncansby Head
John o' Groats
Pentland Firth
Sinclair's Bay
Thurso

SHETLAND IS.
on same scale

Muckle Flugga
Unst
Haroldswick
Fetlar
Yell
Out Skerries
Whalsay
Esha Ness
Ulsta
St. Magnus Bay
Sullom Voe
Papa Stour
Voe
Foula
Walls
Scalloway
Lerwick
Bressay
West Burra
Boddam
Sumburgh Hd.
SHETLAND

WESTERN ISLES
Flannan Is.
Butt of Lewis
Stornoway
Broad Bay
Eye Peninsula
Gallan Hd.
Scarp
Lewis
Taransay
Clisham 799
Tarbert
L. Seaforth
Harris
Toe Hd.
Pabbay
Berneray
Sound of Harris
North Uist
Lochmaddy
Baleshare
Grimsay
Benbecula
Ardivachar Pt.
South Uist
Ben Mhor 620
Lochboisdale
Eriskay
Barra
Castlebay
Vatersay
Sandray
Barra Hd. 268
Rhum (Rùm)
Eigg
Muck
Canna

ATLANTIC OCEAN

The Hebrides
Sea of the Hebrides
Inner Hebrides
Coll
Tiree
Passage of Tiree
Staffa
Iona
Ulva
Mull
Ben More 966
Kerrera
Colonsay
Oronsay
Scarba
Lochgilphead
Islay
Bowmore
Port Ellen
Rhinns Pt.
Gigha
Jura
Sd. of Jura
Mull of Oa
Rubh a' Mhail
Ardnave Pt.

C. Wrath
Durness
L. Eriboll
Strathy Pt.
Dounreay
Dunnet Hd.
Stroma
John o' Groats
Pentland Firth
Hoy 481
Scapa Flow
Burwick
Thurso
Halkirk
Reay Forest
Handa
Tongue
Naver
Caithness
Sinclair's Bay
Noss Hd.
Wick
Lybster
Ben Hope 927
961
Eddrachillis B.
Pt. of Stoer
L. Laxford
Sutherland
Helmsdale 705
Ord of Caithness
Helmsdale
Brora
Golspie
Rubha Coigeach
Enard B.
Lochinver
Ben More Assynt 998
L. Assynt
Oykel
Lairg
L. Shin
Brora
Greenstone Pt.
L. Ewe
Ullapool
L. Broom
Gruinard B.
Carron
Bonar Bridge
Dornoch
Dornoch Firth
Tarbat Ness
Tain
Moray Firth
Lossiemouth
Portknockie
Portsoy
Rosehearty
Kinnairds Hd.
Fraserburgh
Rattray Hd.
Peterhead
Buchan Ness
Cruden Bay
Ellon
Oldmeldrum
Inverurie
Dyce
Aberdeen
Girdle Ness
Peterculter
Stonehaven
Inverbervie
Laurencekirk
Brechin
Montrose
Arbroath
Carnoustie
Monifieth
Firth of Tay
Taysort
Dundee
Perth
Scone
St. Andrews
Fife Ness
Anstruther
Crail
Leven
Buckhaven
Kirkcaldy
North Berwick
Dunbar
St. Abb's Head
Eyemouth
Berwick-upon-Tweed
Holy I.
Farne Is.
Bamburgh
Wooler
Alnwick
Alnmouth
Amble
Morpeth
Newcastle-upon-Tyne
Blaydon
Gateshead
Stanley
Consett
Crook
Bishop Auckland
Barnard Castle

NORTH WEST HIGHLANDS
North Minch
Little Minch
Sound of Raasay
Inner Sound
Rona
Raasay
Skye
Portree
Uig
Dunvegan
Cuillin Hills
Cuillin Sound
Sd. of Sleat
Kyle of Lochalsh
Kyleakin
Scalpay
Dornie
Stromeferry
L. Carron
L. Torridon
Gairloch
L. Maree 1053
L. Gairloch
Rubha Hunish
Wiay

HIGHLAND
Ben Wyvis 1045
Alness
Invergordon
Cromarty
Burghead
Elgin
Forres
Nairn
MORAY
Buckie
Cullen
Banff
Macduff
Fochabers
Keith
Huntly
Turriff
Aberchirder
Rothes
Dufftown
Charlestown of Aberlour
BUCHAN
Deveron
Yihan
Dingwall
Strathpeffer
Muir of Ord
Beauly
Beauly
Inverness
Loch Ness
Glen Affric
Glen Moriston
Fort Augustus
Carn Eige 1182
992
1068
Drumnadrochit
MONADHLIATH MTS.
Aviemore
Grantown-on-Spey
Strath Spey
Tomintoul
Alford
ABERDEENSHIRE
Westhill
Kintore
Don
Inverurie
Aboyne
Banchory
Ballater
Braemar
Ben Macdhui 1309
CAIRNGORMS
CAIRNGORM MTS.
Kingussie
Newtonmore
Cairn Gorm 1245
941
Glen More
Lochnagar 1154
N. Esk
ANGUS
Kirriemuir
Forfar
Strathmore
Alyth
Blairgowrie
Glen Garry
GLEN
Loch Lochy 1128
Loch Spean
Glen Spean
Spean
Glen Roy
1342
Fort William
Ben Nevis 1344
Kinlochleven
L. Arkaig
L. Lochy
LOCHABER
L. Morar
Arisaig
Mallaig
L. Shiel
L. Eil
L. Sunart
L. Moidart
Ardnamurchan
Tobermory
Morvern
Sound of Mull
Lismore
Loch Etive
Oban
LORN
Loch Awe
ARGYLL AND BUTE
Ben Cruachan 1126
Crianlarich
Ben More 1174
983
Ben Lawers 1214
Ben Vorlich 985
Killin
LOCH LOMOND & THE TROSSACHS
Ben Lomond 973
Loch Katrine
Inveraray
Loch Fyne
Loch Lomond
Tarbert
QUEEN ELIZABETH
Loch Long
Aberfoyle
Callander
Crieff
Auchterarder
PERTH AND KINROSS
Aberfeldy
Pitlochry
Blair Atholl 1121
Forest of Atholl
Blairgowrie
Dunkeld
L. Rannoch
Rannoch Moor
Loch Leven
Kinross
Ochil Hills 720
Dollar
Dunblane
STIRLING
Stirling
Bannockburn
Alloa
Clackmannan
Grangemouth
Bo'ness
Falkirk
Denny
Helensburgh
Alexandria
Dumbarton
Clydebank
Greenock
Gourock
Port Glasgow
Dunoon
Rothesay
Bute
Kirkintilloch
Cumbernauld
Coatbridge
Airdrie
Motherwell
GLASGOW
Paisley
Hamilton
East Kilbride
Wishaw
Carluke
Lanark
Strathaven
Biggar
Peebles
Livingston
Bathgate
Bonnyrigg
Penicuik
PENTLAND HILLS 535
MOORFOOT HILLS 651
EDINBURGH
Musselburgh
Dalkeith
Haddington
EAST LOTHIAN
Lammermuir Hills
Duns
Coldstream
Kelso
Galashiels
Melrose
Selkirk
SCOTTISH BORDERS
Jedburgh
Hawick
Broad Law 840
The Cheviot 816
Cheviot Hills
NORTHUMBERLAND
Kielder Water

SCOTLAND

NORTH SEA

Firth of Clyde
Kintyre
Kilbrannan Sd.
Goat Fell 874
Arran
Brodick
Campbeltown
Mull of Kintyre
Ardrossan
Saltcoats
Irvine
Troon
Prestwick
Ayr
Kilwinning
Dalry
Kilmarnock
NORTH AYRSHIRE
EAST AYRSHIRE
Cumnock
Sanquhar
Maybole
Girvan
Ailsa Craig
SOUTH AYRSHIRE
Dalmellington
Dalrymple
New Galloway
Merrick 844
GALLOWAY
SOUTHERN UPLANDS
Moffat
Lockerbie
Langholm
Lochmaben
Lochmaben
DUMFRIES & GALLOWAY
Dumfries
Annan
Gretna
Dalbeattie
Castle Douglas
Kirkcudbright
Gatehouse of Fleet
Newton Stewart
Wigtown
Whithorn
Burrow Hd.
Mull of Galloway
Luce Bay
Wigtown B.
Glenluce
Stranraer
Cairnryan
Portpatrick
L. Ryan
Solway Firth
Carlisle
Brampton
Haltwhistle
Hexham
Silloth
Aspatria
Maryport
Workington
Whitehaven
St. Bees Hd.
Cockermouth
Wigton
Penrith
Appleby-in-Westmorland
CUMBRIA
Keswick
Skiddaw 931
Helvellyn 950
Derwent Water
Ullswater
Cross Fell 893
NORTHUMBERLAND
DURHAM

NORTHERN IRELAND
Larne
Carrickfergus
Belfast L.
Belfast
Bangor
Donaghadee
Newtownards
Cushendall
Garron Pt.
269
North Channel

ENGLAND

ft   m
3000   1000
1500   500
600   200
300   100
0   0
50   150
100   300
200   600
500   1500
1000   3000
m   ft

Projection : Lambert's Conformal Conic
West from Greenwich
COPYRIGHT PHILIP'S

166   168

10 0 10 20 30 40 50 60 70 80 km
10 0 10 20 30 40 50 miles

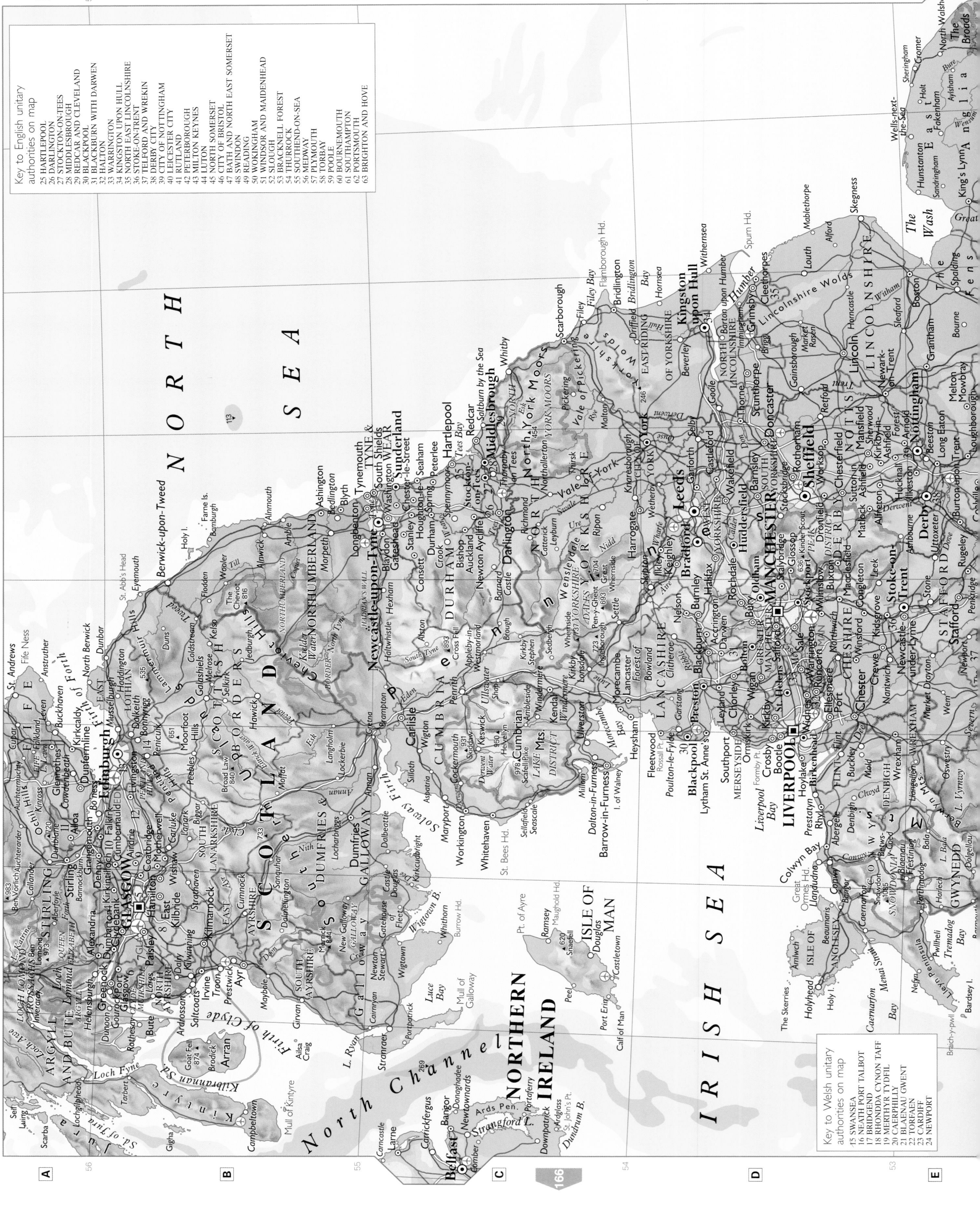

1:1 600 000

Key to English unitary authorities on map

25 HARTLEPOOL
26 DARLINGTON
27 STOCKTON-ON-TEES
28 MIDDLESBROUGH
29 REDCAR AND CLEVELAND
30 BLACKPOOL
31 BLACKBURN WITH DARWEN
32 HALTON
33 WARRINGTON
34 KINGSTON UPON HULL
35 NORTH EAST LINCOLNSHIRE
36 STOKE-ON-TRENT
37 TELFORD AND WREKIN
38 DERBY CITY
39 CITY OF NOTTINGHAM
40 LEICESTER CITY
41 RUTLAND
42 PETERBOROUGH
43 MILTON KEYNES
44 LUTON
45 NORTH SOMERSET
46 CITY OF BRISTOL
47 BATH AND NORTH EAST SOMERSET
48 SWINDON
49 READING
50 WOKINGHAM
51 WINDSOR AND MAIDENHEAD
52 SLOUGH
53 BRACKNELL FOREST
54 THURROCK
55 SOUTHEND-ON-SEA
56 MEDWAY
57 PLYMOUTH
58 TORBAY
59 POOLE
60 BOURNEMOUTH
61 SOUTHAMPTON
62 PORTSMOUTH
63 BRIGHTON AND HOVE

Key to Welsh unitary authorities on map

15 SWANSEA
16 NEATH PORT TALBOT
17 BRIDGEND
18 RHONDDA CYNON TAFF
19 MERTHYR TYDFIL
20 CAERPHILLY
21 BLAENAU GWENT
22 TORFAEN
23 CARDIFF
24 NEWPORT

NORTH SEA

IRISH SEA

North Channel

NORTHERN IRELAND

ISLE OF MAN

SCOTLAND

NORTHUMBERLAND

CUMBRIA

LAKE DISTRICT

DURHAM

NORTH YORKSHIRE

NORTH YORK MOORS

LANCASHIRE

EAST RIDING OF YORKSHIRE

LINCOLNSHIRE

The Wash

The Broads

EAST ANGLIA

Edinburgh
Glasgow
Belfast
Newcastle-upon-Tyne
Sunderland
Middlesbrough
Leeds
Bradford
MANCHESTER
Liverpool
Sheffield
Chester
Stoke-on-Trent
Derby
Nottingham
Lincoln
Kingston upon Hull

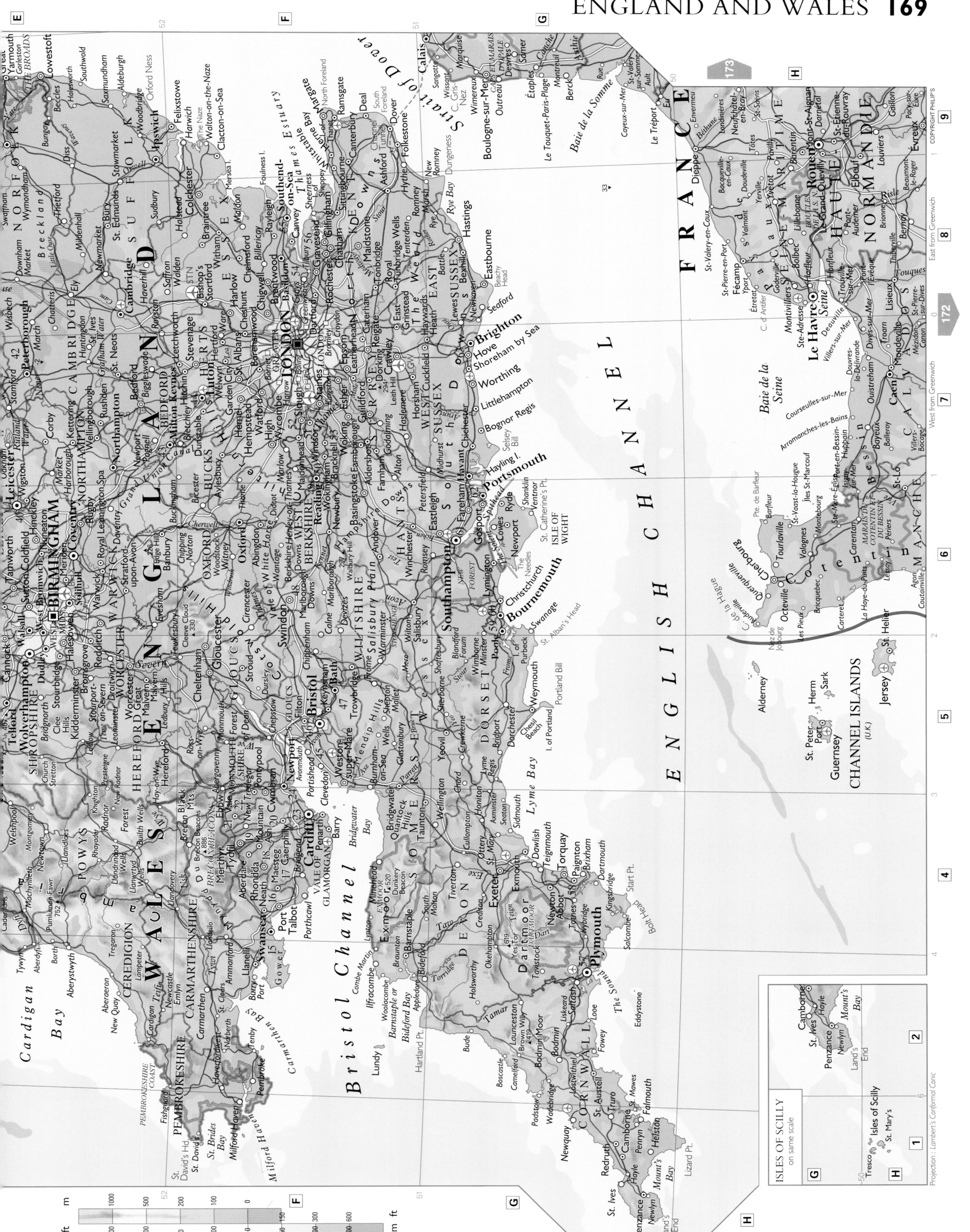

Projection : Lambert's Conformal Conic

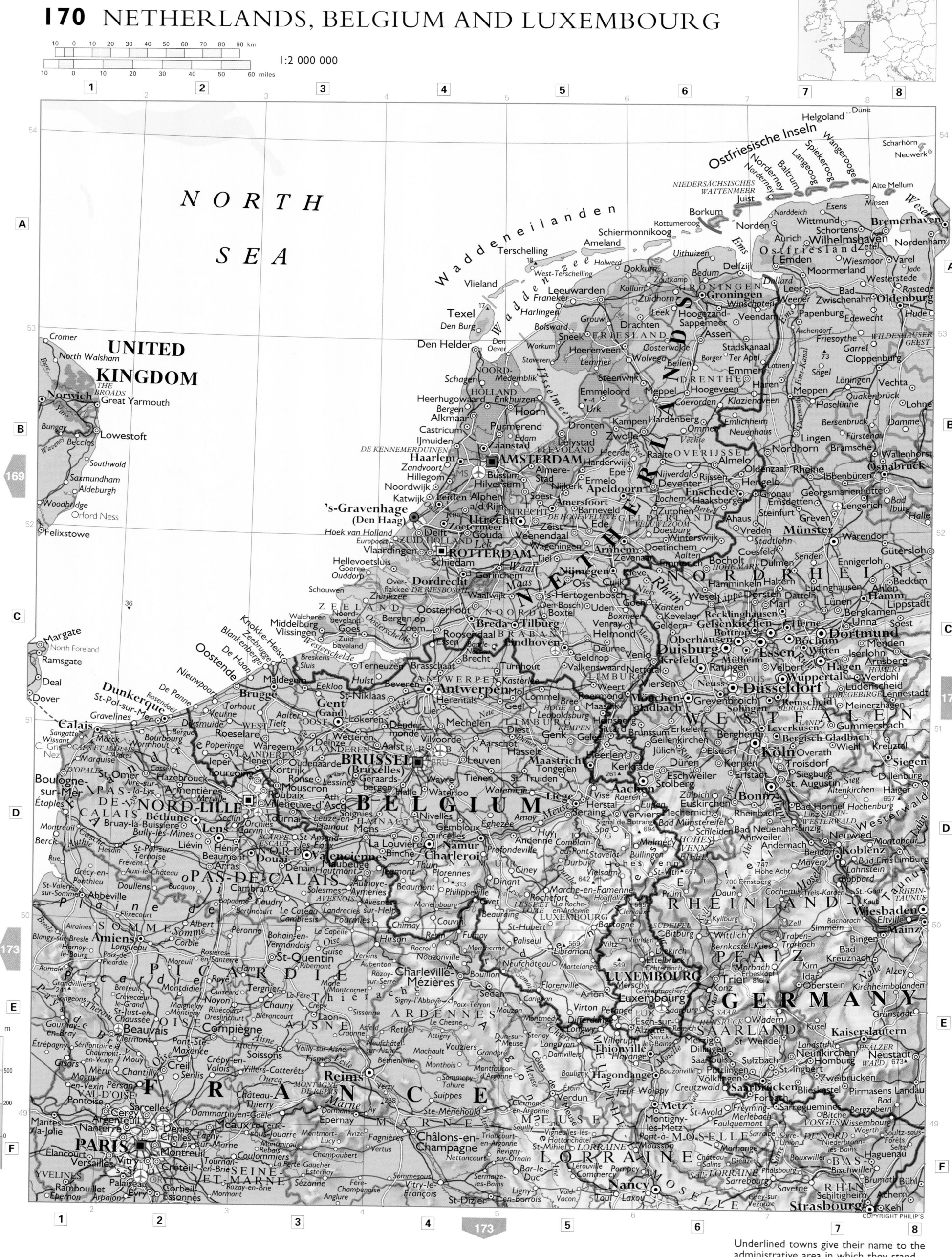

1:2 000 000

Underlined towns give their name to the administrative area in which they stand.

COPYRIGHT PHILIP'S

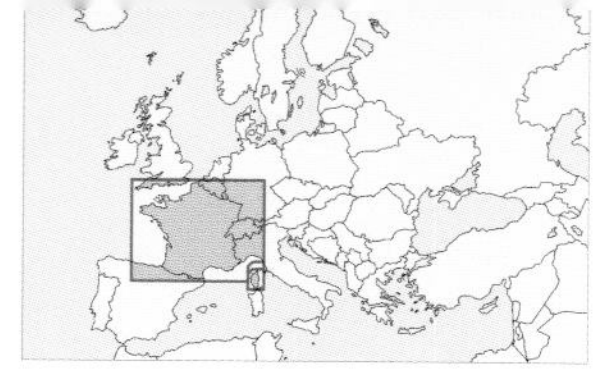

1:4 000 000

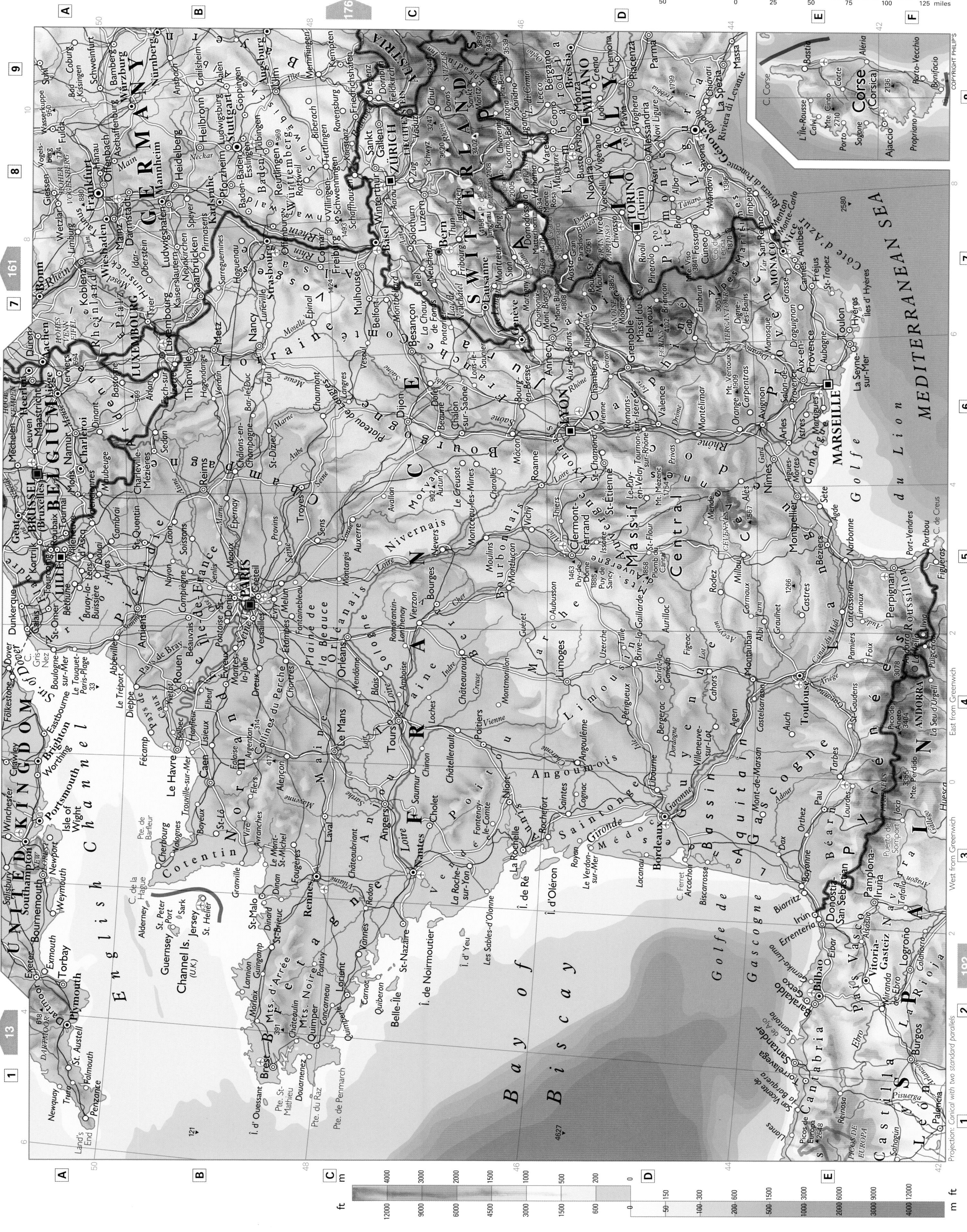

50 25 0 25 50 75 100 125 150 175 km
50 25 0 25 50 75 100 125 miles

COPYRIGHT PHILIP'S

GERMANY

BELGIUM

LUXEMBOURG

SWITZERLAND

AUSTRIA

ITALY

UNITED KINGDOM

ANDORRA

SPAIN

Corse (Corsica)

MEDITERRANEAN SEA

Bay of Biscay

English Channel

FRANCE

PARIS

Projection: Conical with two standard parallels

East from Greenwich
West from Greenwich

ft m
12000 4000
9000 3000
6000 2000
4500 1500
3000 1000
1500 500
600 200
0 0
-150 -50
-300 -100
-600 -200
1500 500
3000 1000
6000 2000
9000 3000
12000 4000
m ft

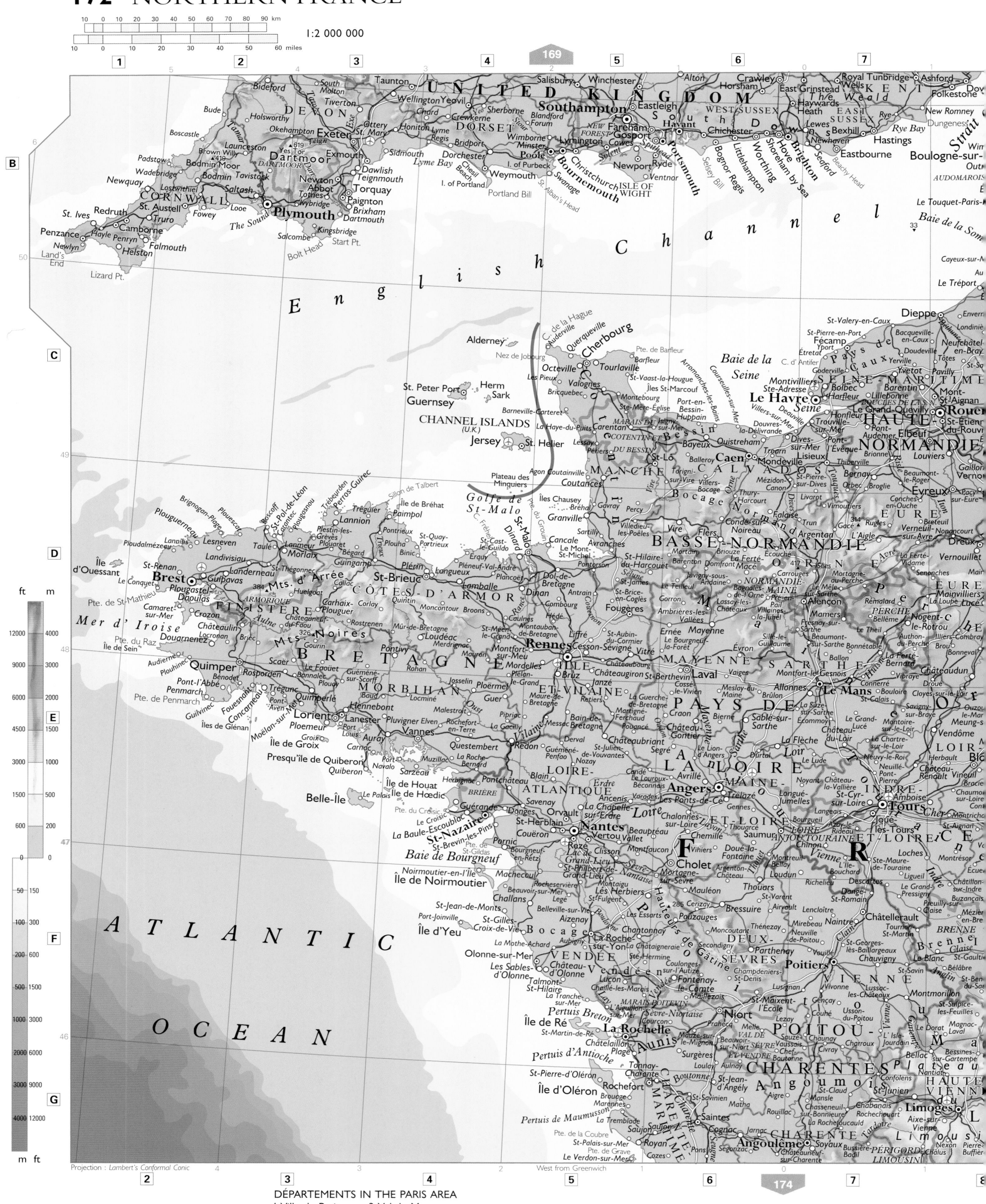

1:2 000 000

DÉPARTEMENTS IN THE PARIS AREA
1 Ville de Paris 3 Val-de-Marne
2 Seine-St-Denis 4 Hauts-de-Seine

Projection : Lambert's Conformal Conic

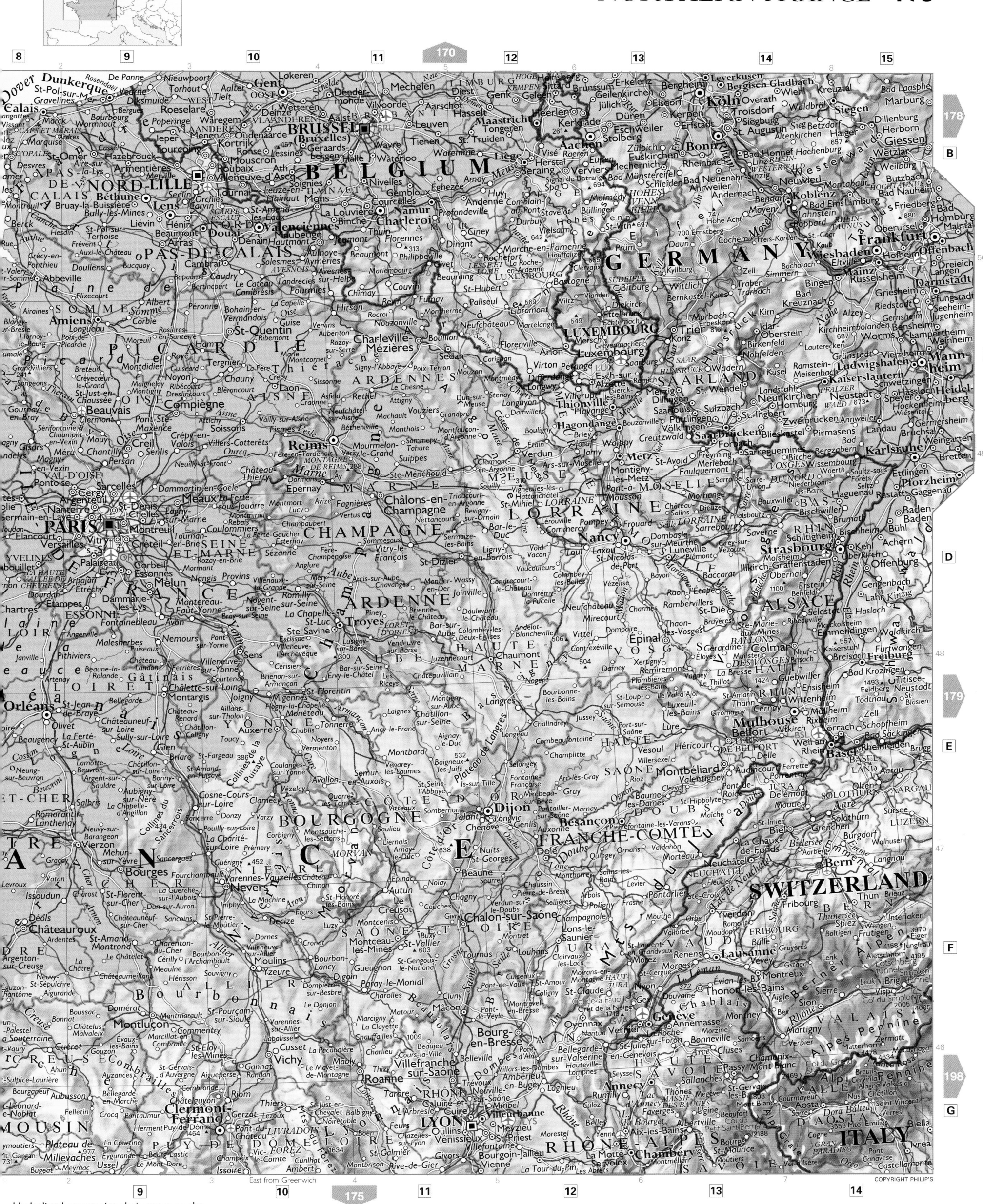

Underlined towns give their name to the
administrative area in which they stand.

COPYRIGHT PHILIP'S

1:2 000 000

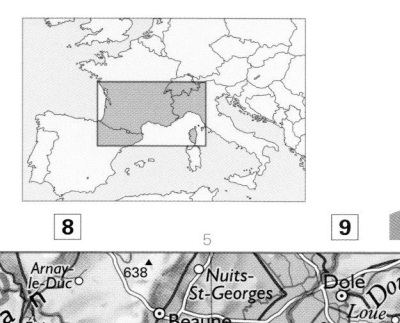

1:4 000 000

50 · 0 · 25 · 50 · 75 · 100 · 150 · 175 km
50 · 0 · 25 · 50 · 75 · 100 · 125 miles

Projection: Conical with two standard parallels

NORTH SEA

BALTIC SEA

ADRIATIC SEA

DENMARK

UNITED KINGDOM

NETHERLANDS

BELGIUM

LUXEMBOURG

GERMANY

FRANCE

SWITZERLAND

ITALY

AUSTRIA

CZECH

SLOVENIA

Major cities and towns:

HAMBURG · BREMEN · BERLIN · AMSTERDAM · ROTTERDAM · BRUSSEL (Bruxelles) · LILLE · PARIS · HANNOVER · Magdeburg · Potsdam · Leipzig · Dresden · Köln (Cologne) · Düsseldorf · Dortmund · Essen · Frankfurt · Mannheim · Stuttgart · Nürnberg · München (Munich) · Augsburg · Strasbourg · ZÜRICH · Bern · Genève · Lyon · MILANO · TORINO (Turin) · Genova · MARSEILLE · PRAHA (Prague) · Plzeň · Wien · Linz · Salzburg · Innsbruck · Graz · Ljubljana · ZAGREB · Trieste · Venézia (Venice) · Szczecin · Gorzów Wielkopolski · Zielona Góra · Rügen · Kiel · Lübeck · Rostock · Schwerin

ft · m
12000 · 4000
9000 · 3000
6000 · 2000
4500 · 1500
3000 · 1000
1500 · 500
600 · 200
0 · 0
150
300
600
3000
6000
m · ft

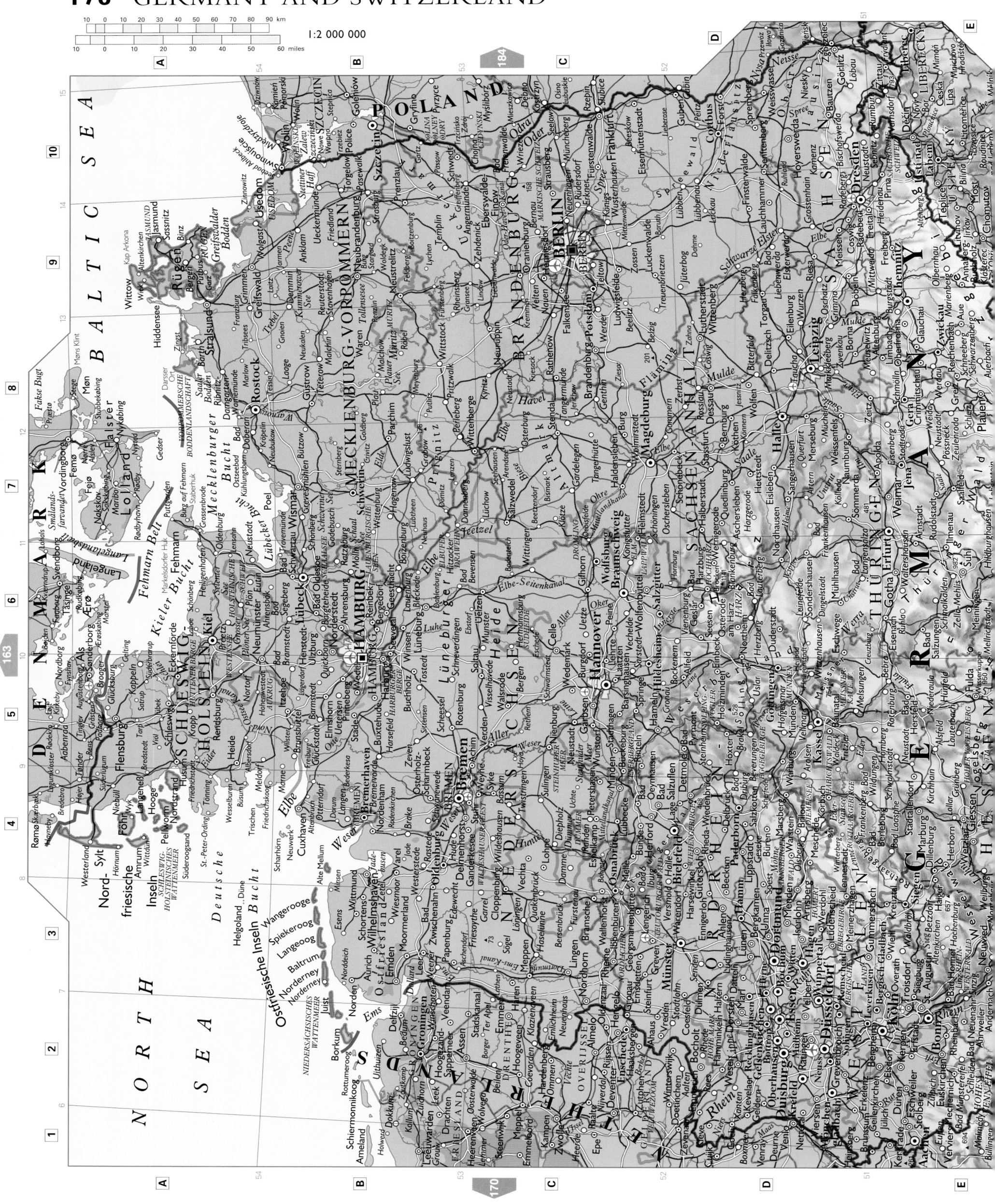

Underlined towns give their name to the administrative area in which they stand.

1:2 000 000

Projection : Lambert's Conformal Conic

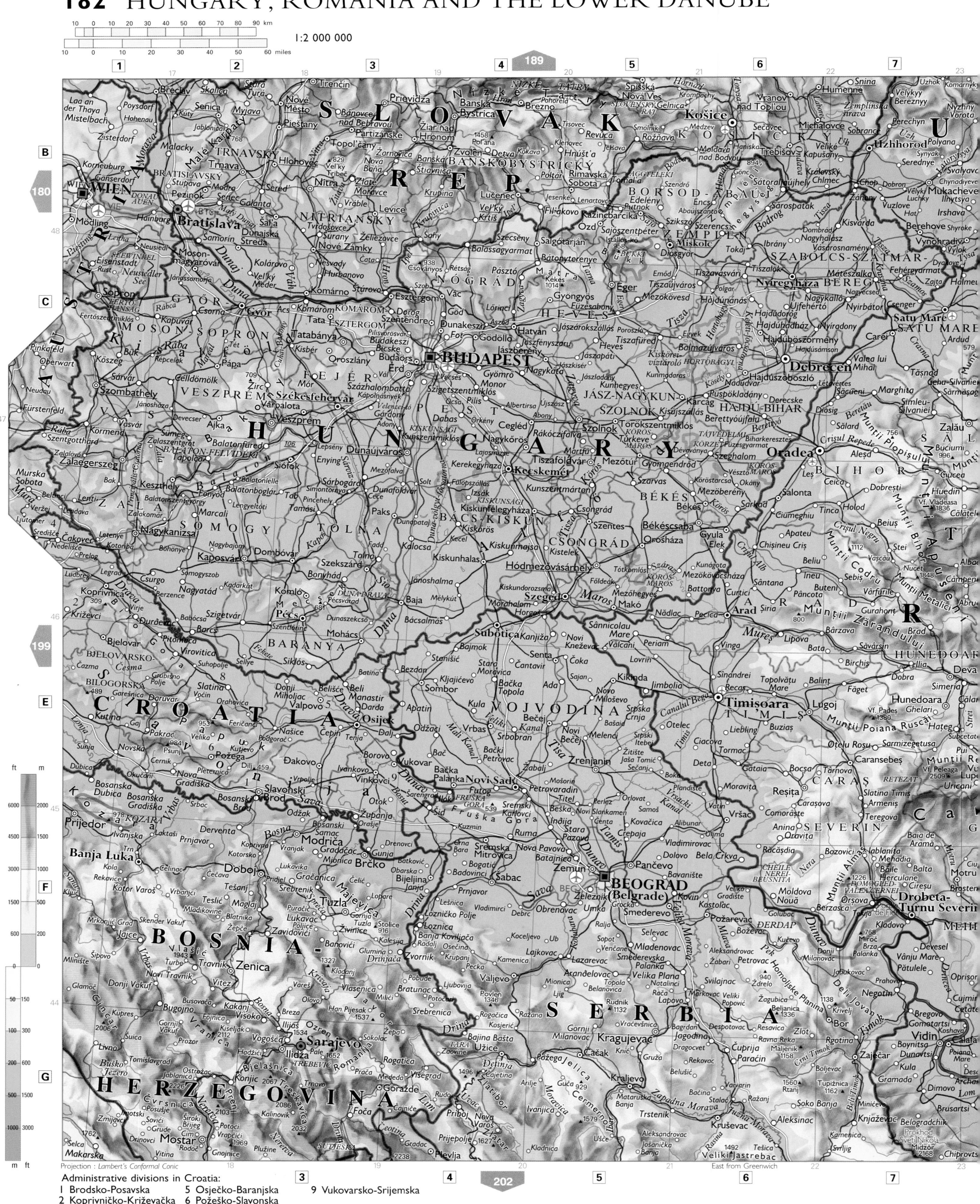

1:2 000 000

Administrative divisions in Croatia:
1 Brodsko-Posavska   5 Osječko-Baranjska   9 Vukovarsko-Srijemska
2 Koprivničko-Križevačka 6 Požeško-Slavonska
4 Medimurska   8 Virovitičko-Podravska

Projection : Lambert's Conformal Conic

East from Greenwich

Underlined towns give their name to the
administrative area in which they stand.

10 0 10 20 30 40 50 60 70 80 90 km

10 0 10 20 30 40 50 60 miles

1:2 000 000

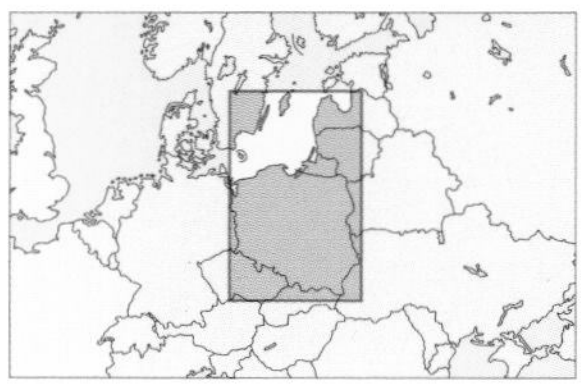

Major labels

SWEDEN

LATVIA

LITHUANIA

KALININGRAD (Russia)

BALTIC SEA

Gulf of Riga

Gotland (Sweden)

Öland (Sweden)

Bornholm (Denmark)

WARMIŃSKO-MAZURSKIE

POMORSKIE

ZACHODNIO-POMORSKIE

KUJAWSKO-

Hanöbukten

Selected place names

Riga, Jūrmala, Jelgava, Dobele, Tukums, Talsi, Ventspils, Liepāja, Šiauliai, Telšiai, Klaipėda, Palanga, Kaunas, Marijampolė, Suwałki, Kaliningrad, Gusev, Chernyakhovsk, Sovetsk, Neman, Gdańsk, Gdynia, Sopot, Elbląg, Malbork, Olsztyn, Ełk, Koszalin, Słupsk, Ustka, Darłowo, Kołobrzeg, Szczecin, Świnoujście, Hrodna, Białystok, Augustów

Jönköping, Kalmar, Karlskrona, Västervik, Visby, Ronneby, Växjö

Gulf of Riga, Zalew Wiślany, Zalew Kuroński (Kurshskaya Kosa)

Neman / Nemunas

Underlined towns give their name to the
administrative area in which they stand.

1:8 000 000

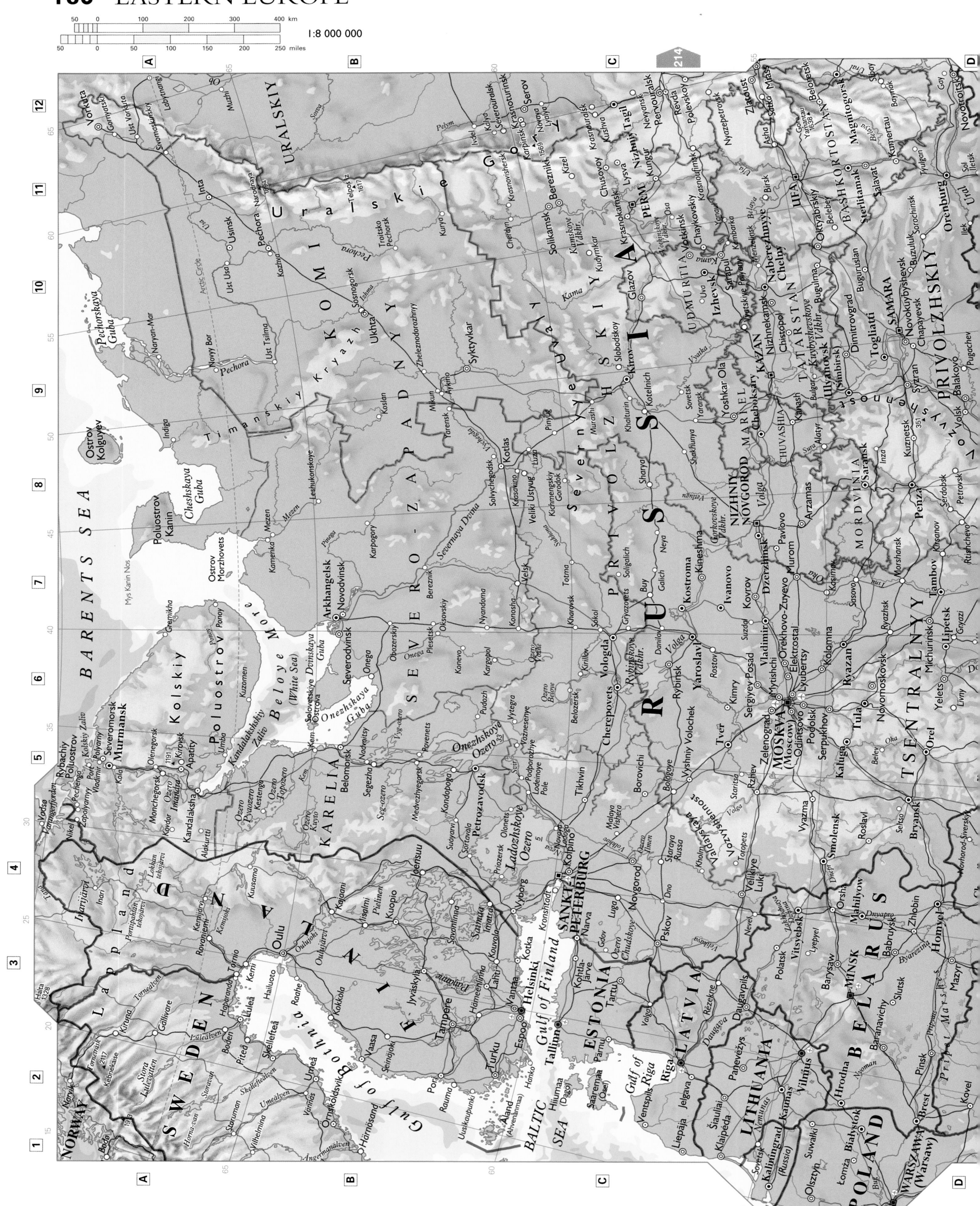

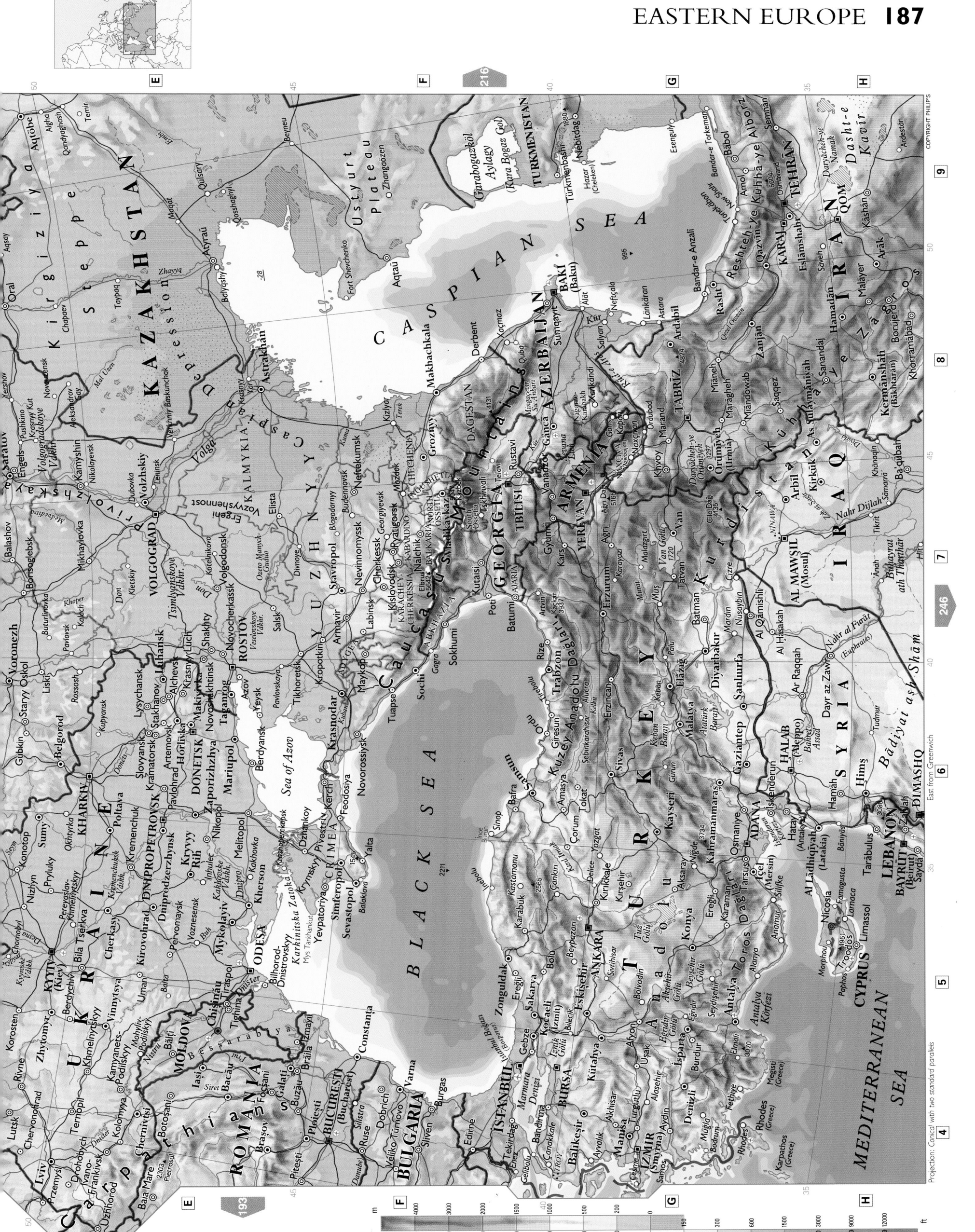

Projection: Conical with two standard parallels

East from Greenwich

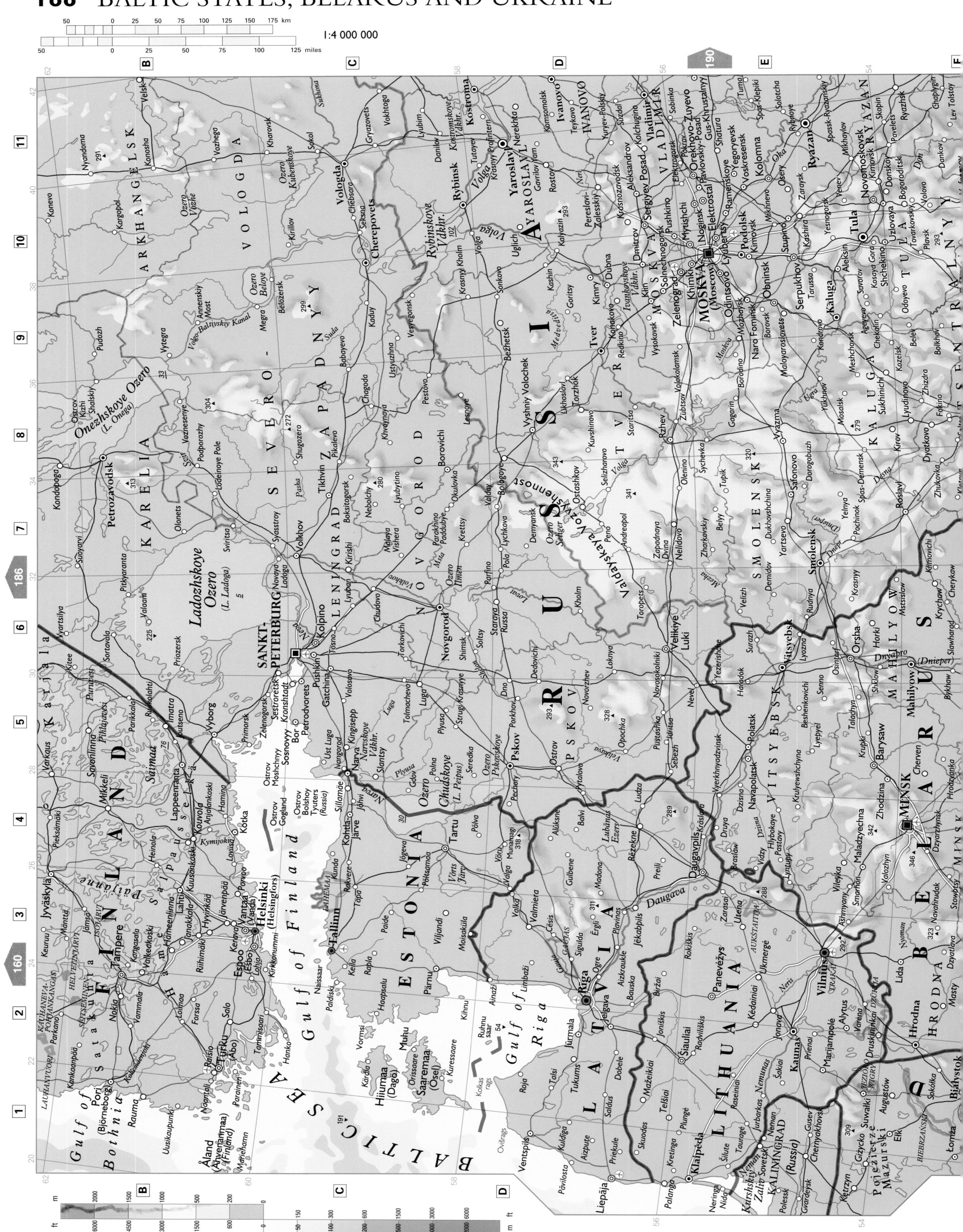

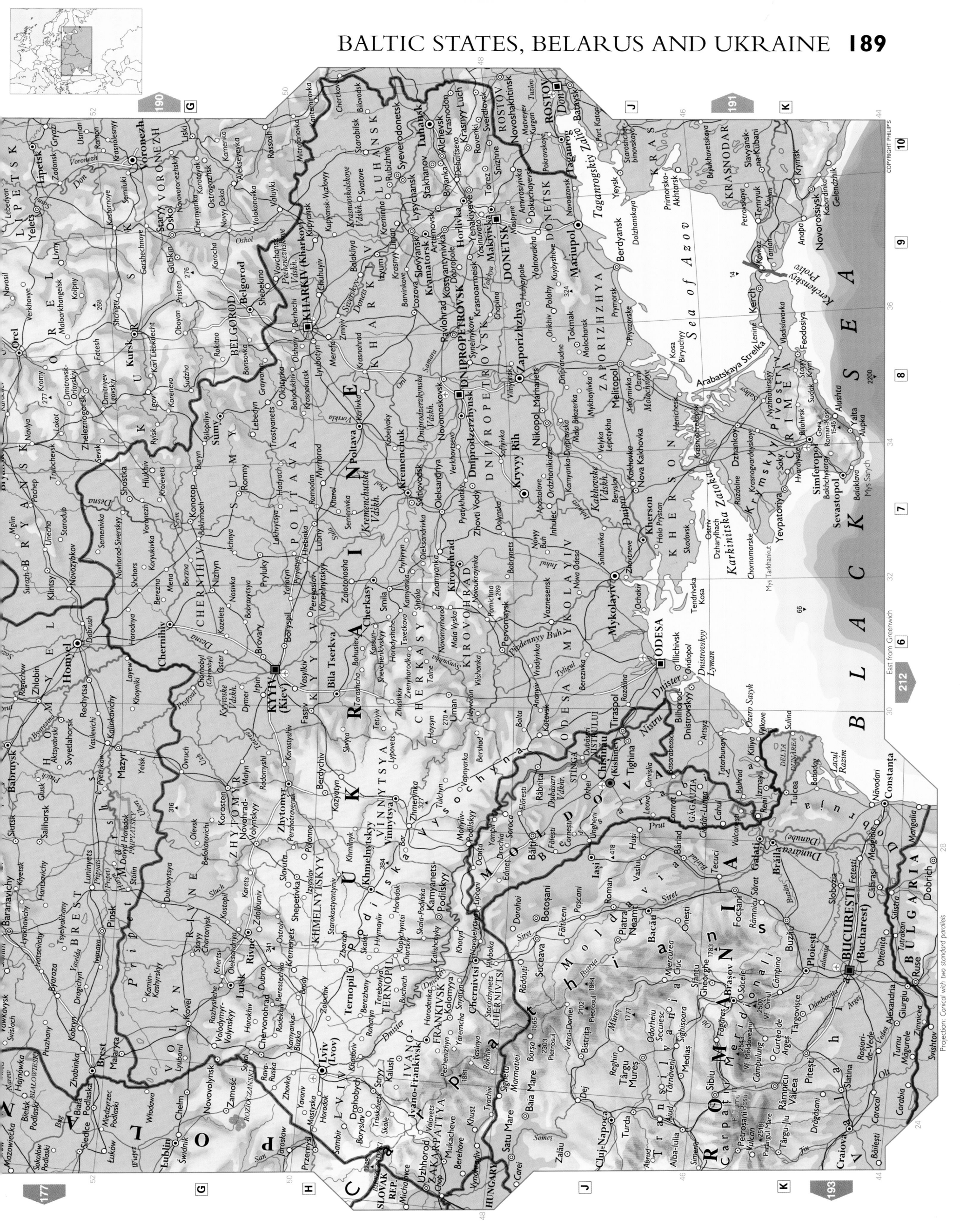

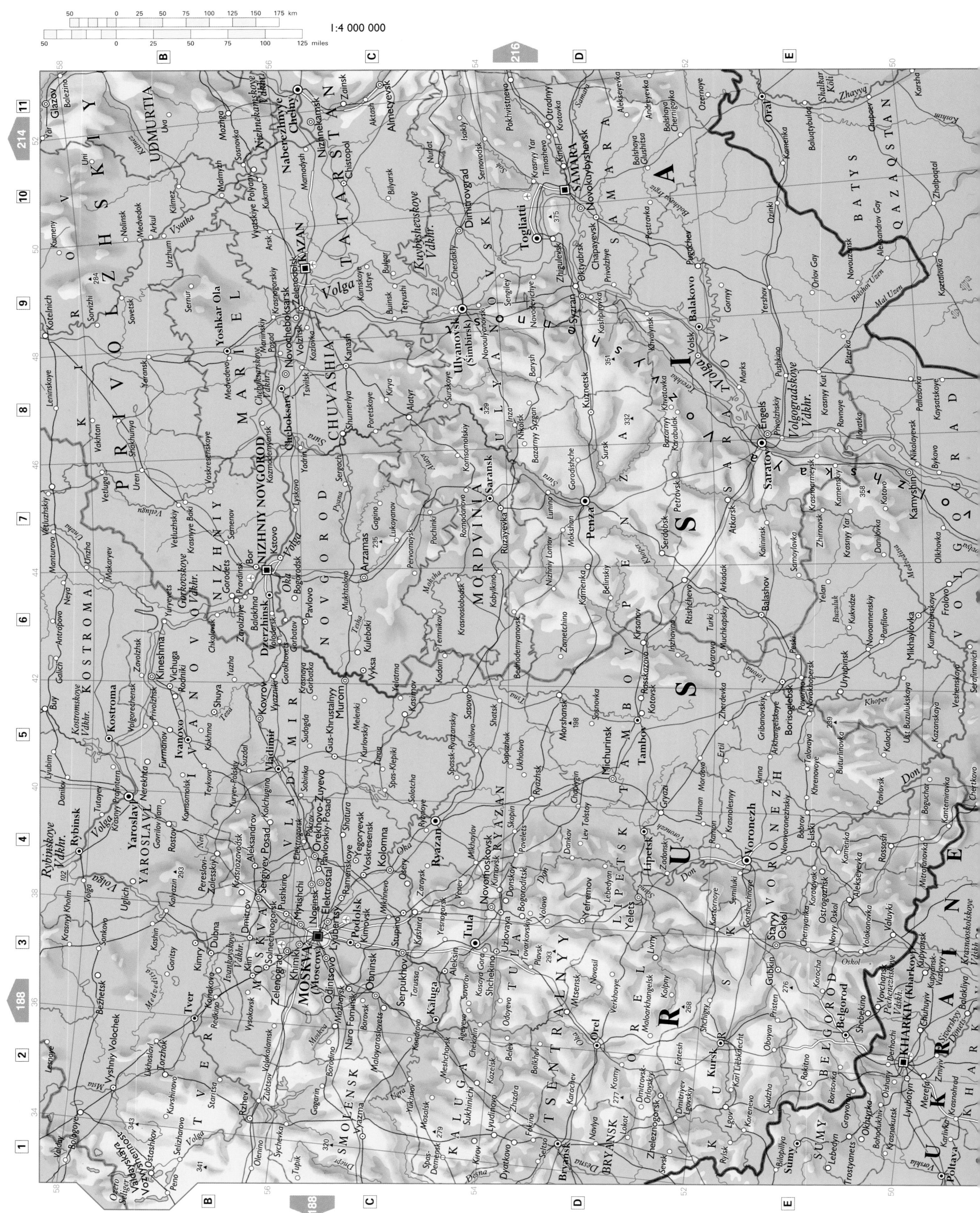

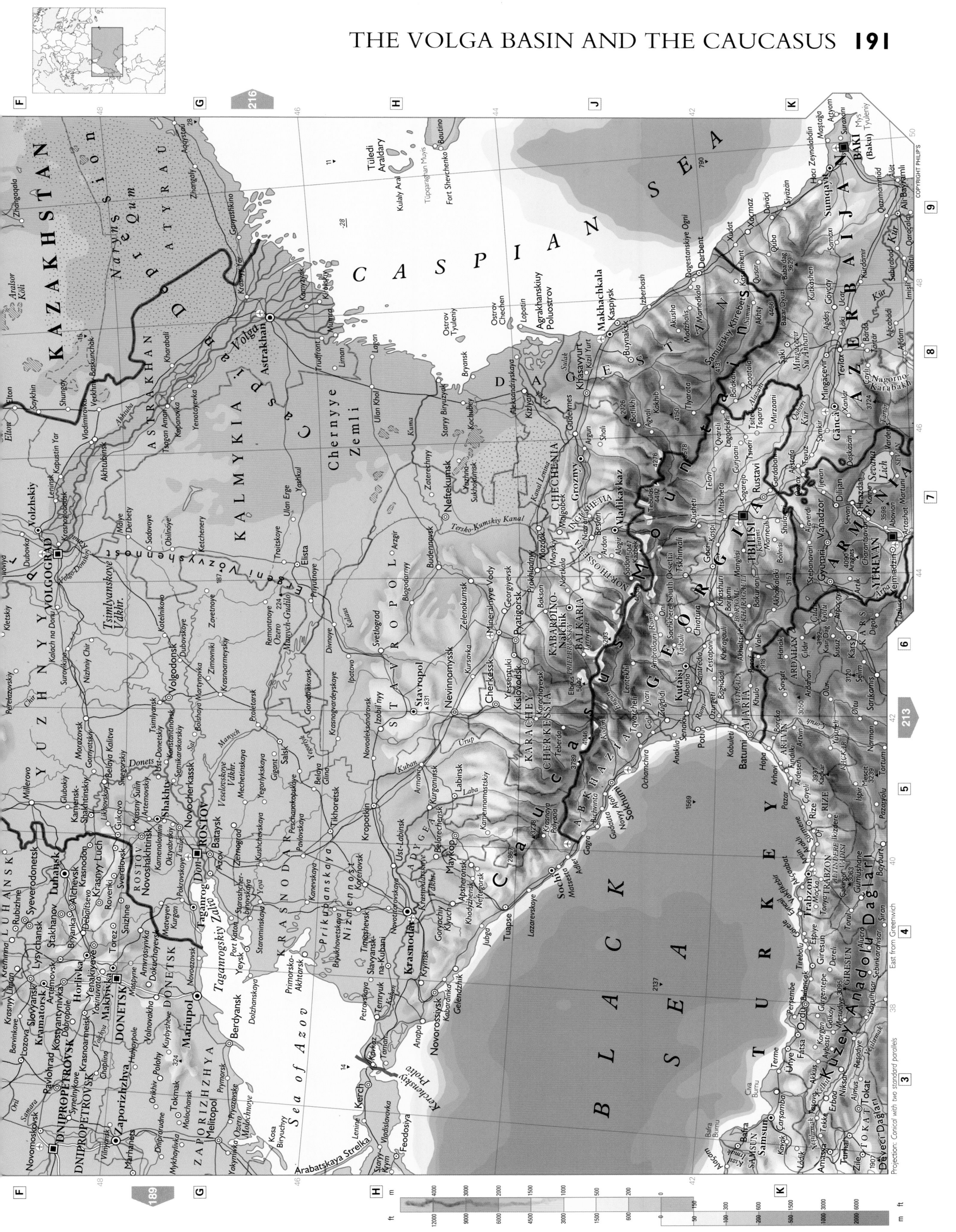

Projection: Conical with two standard parallels

East from Greenwich

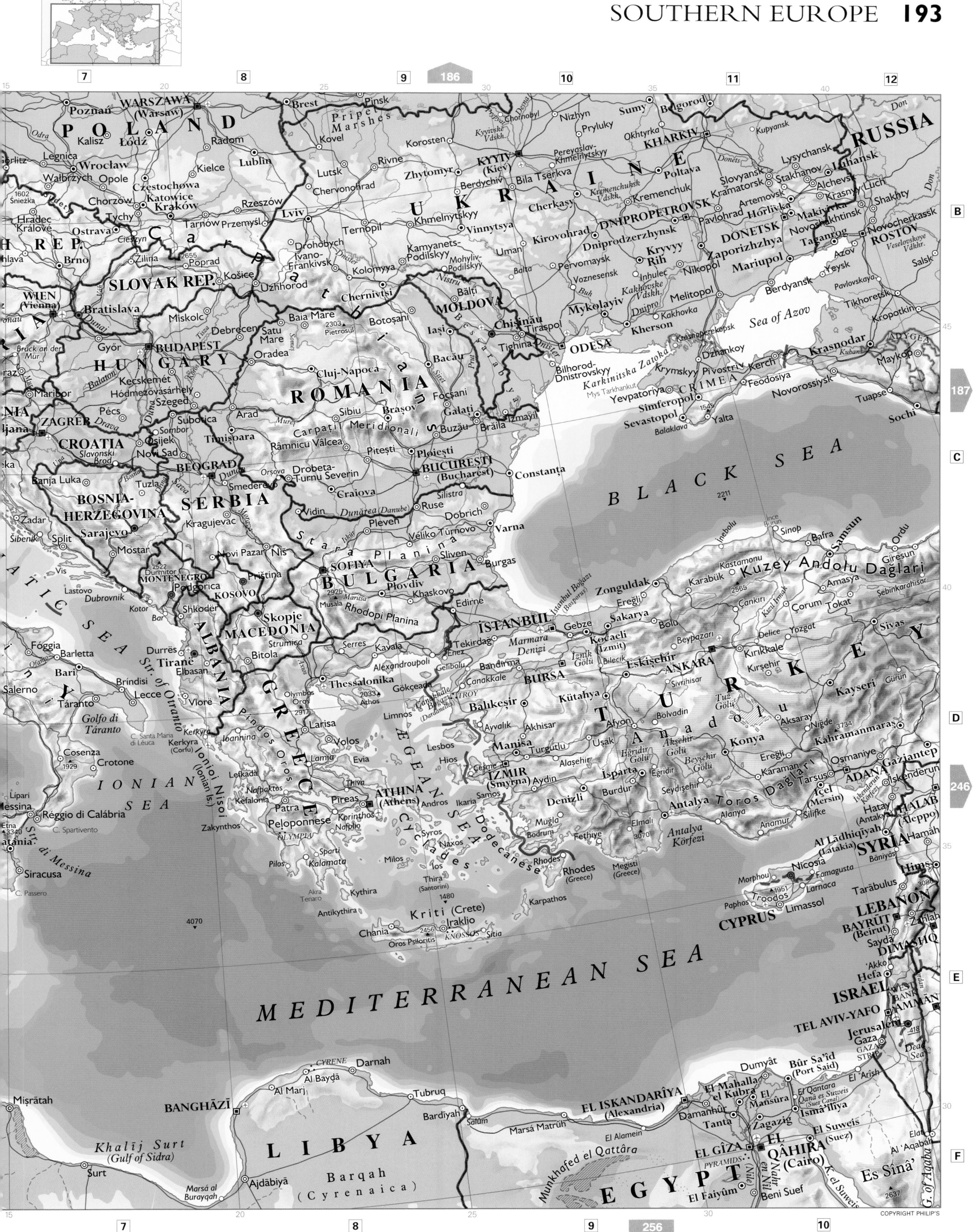

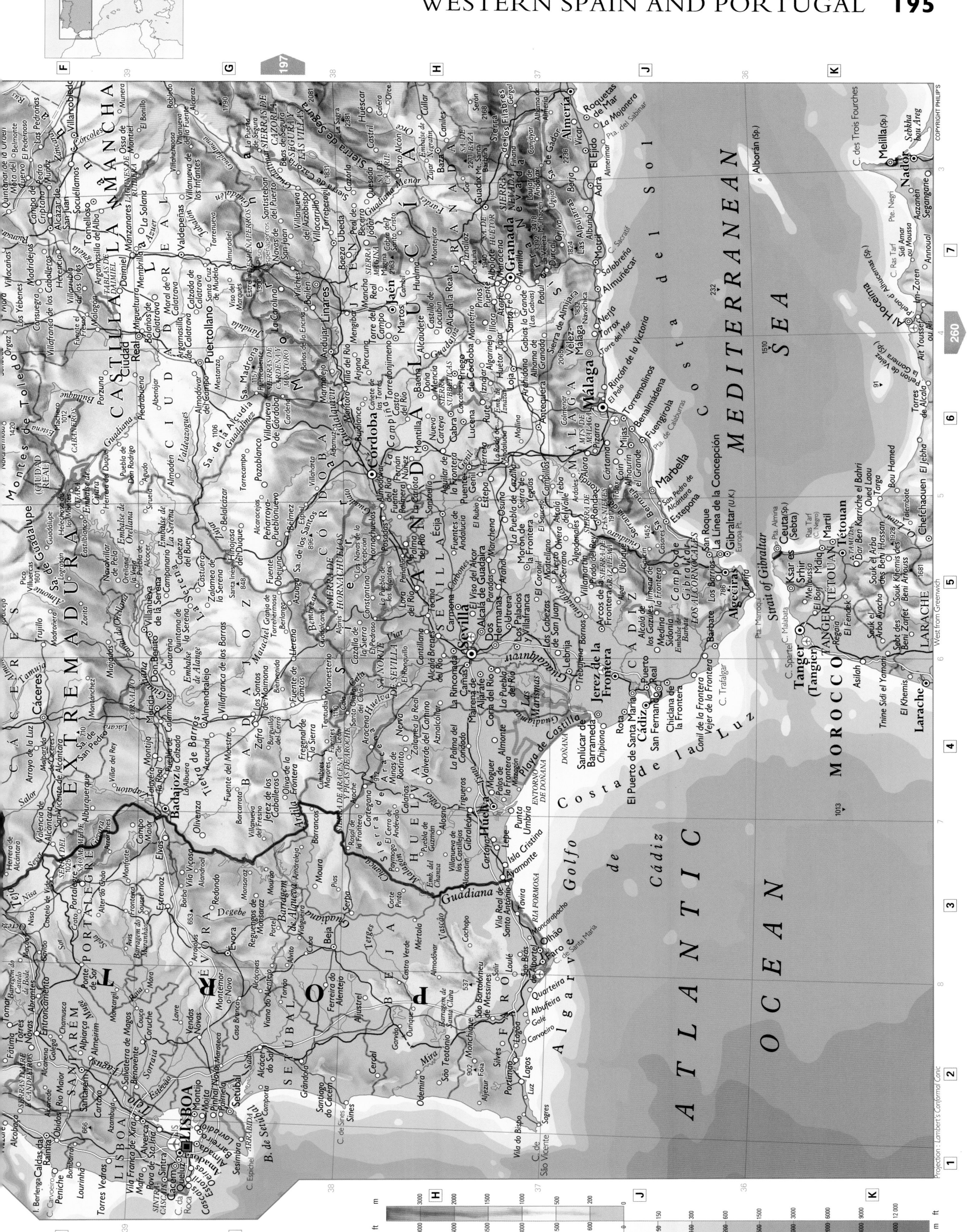

1:2 000 000

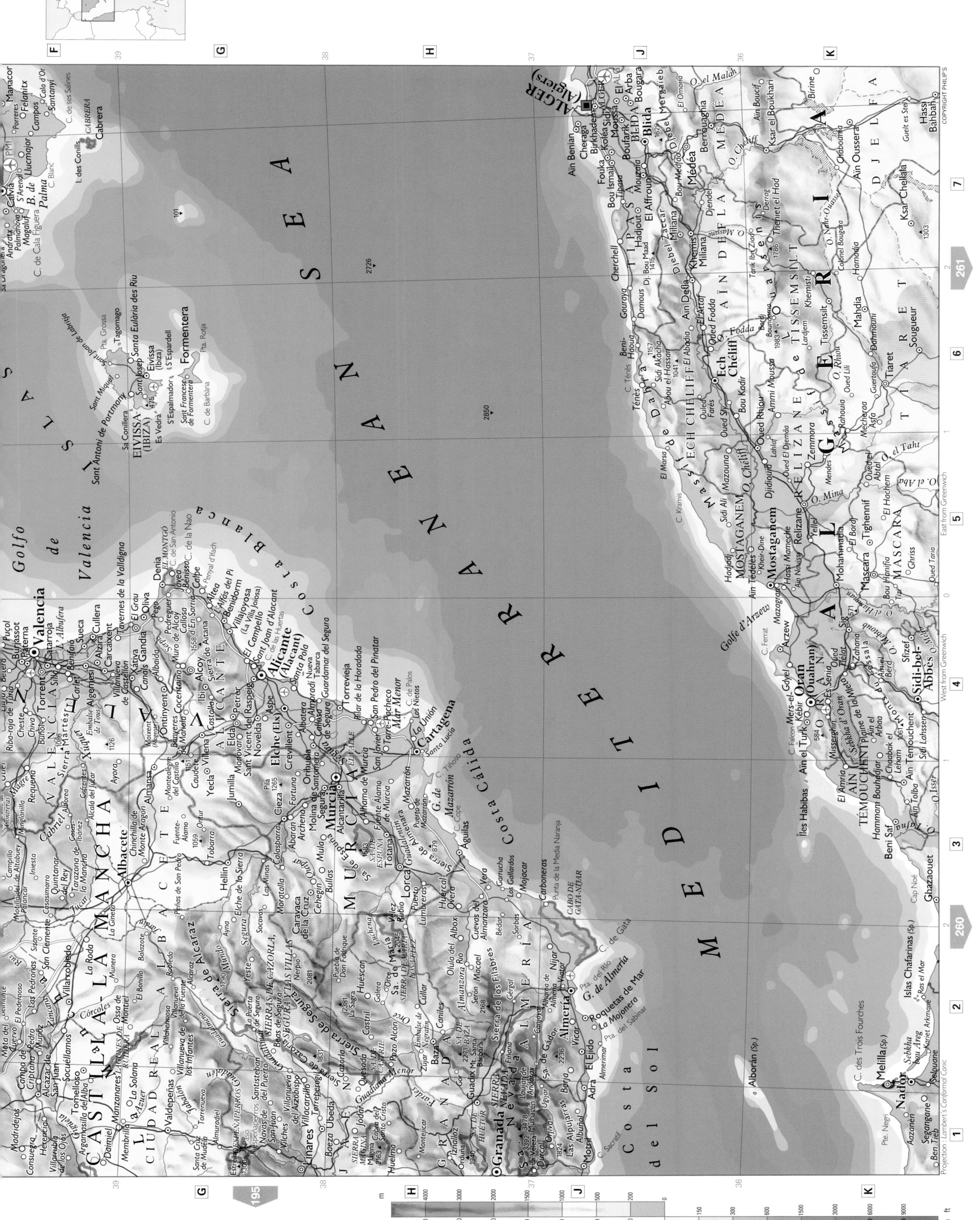

1:2 000 000

Administrative divisions in Croatia:

Brodsko-Posavska	4 Medimurska	8 Virovitičko-Podravska
Koprivničko-Križevačka	6 Požeško-Slavonska	10 Zagreba čka
Krapinsko-Zagorska	7 Varaždinska	

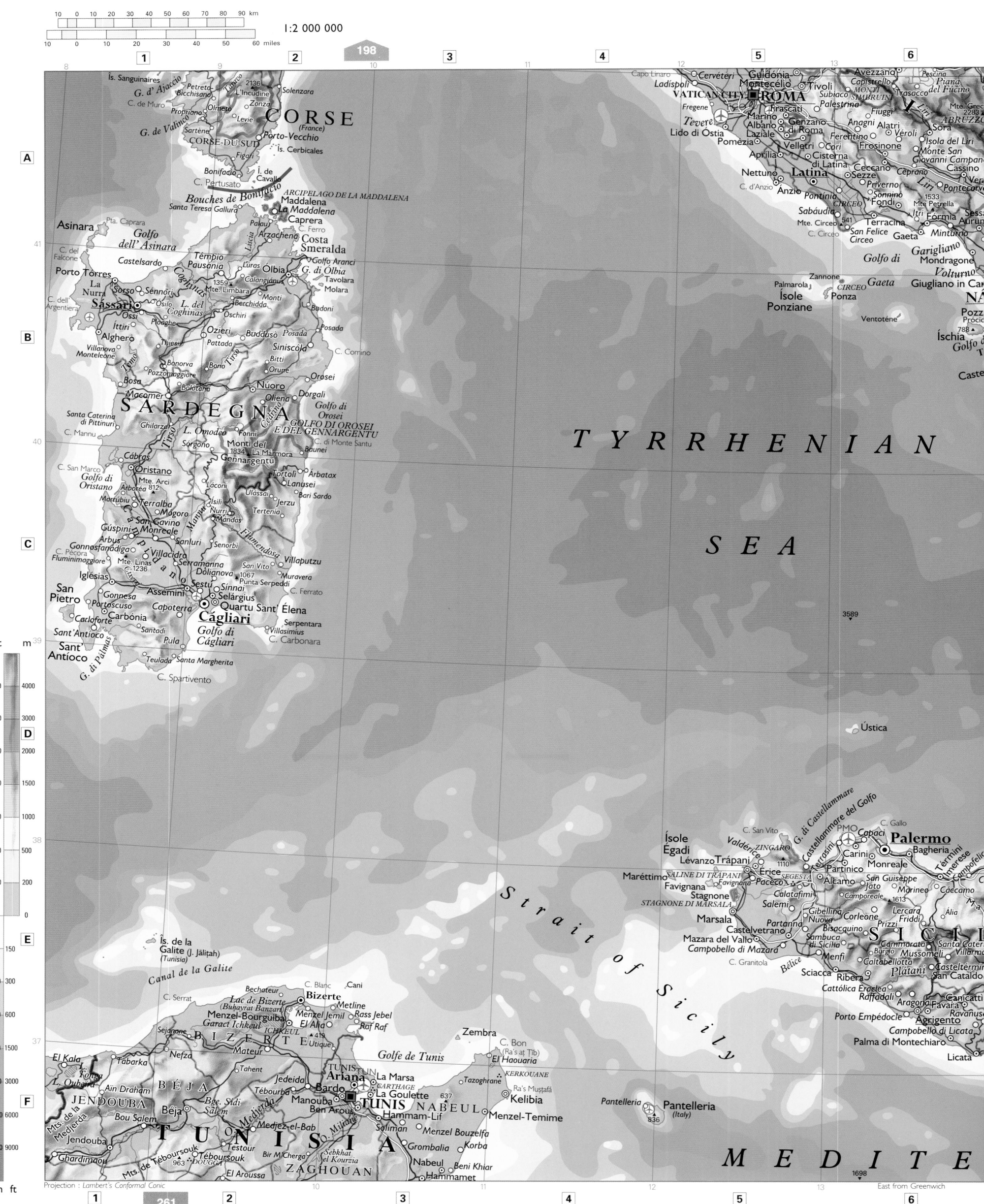

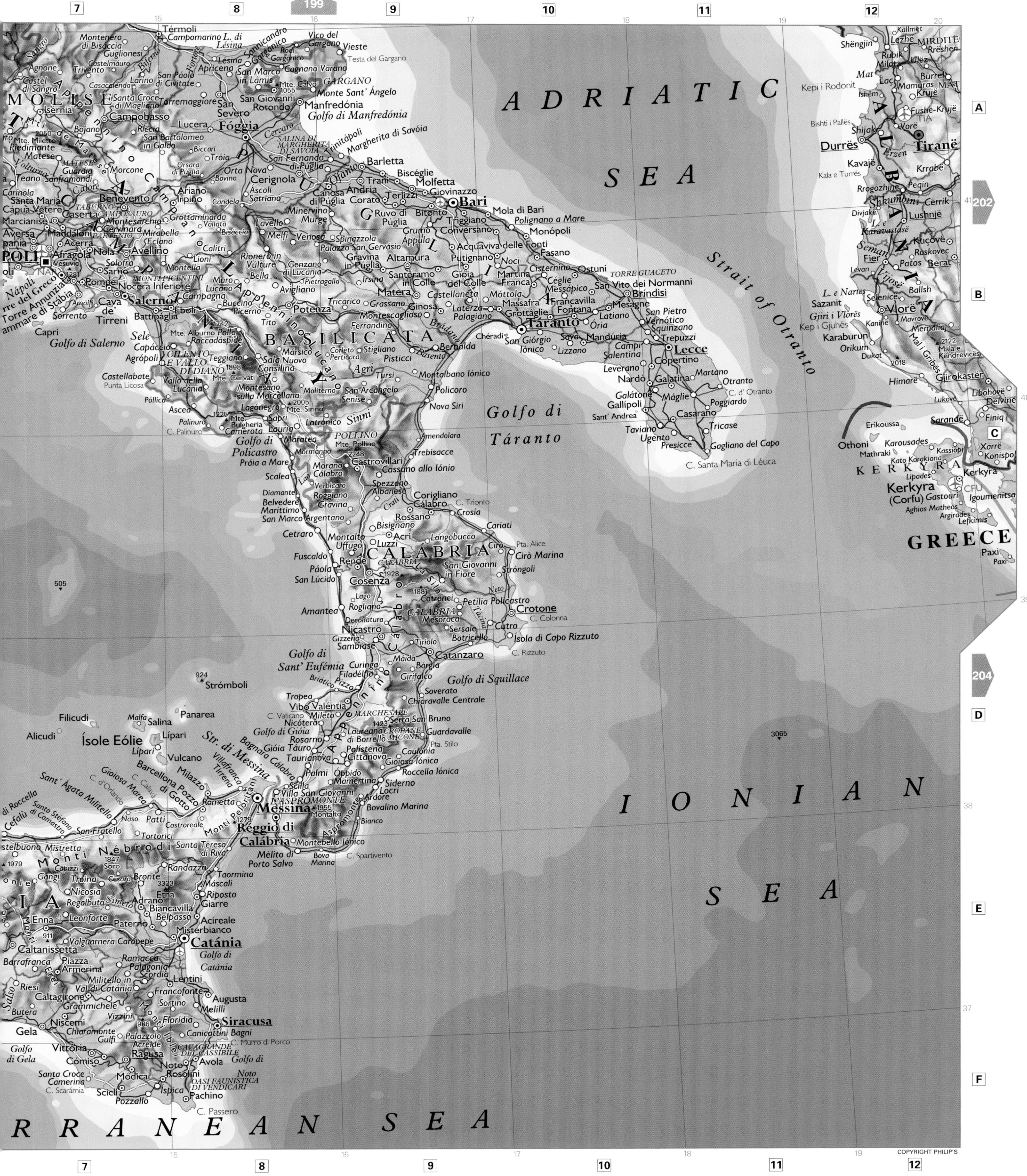

Underlined towns give their name to the
administrative area in which they stand.

COPYRIGHT PHILIP'S

10 0 10 20 30 40 50 60 70 80 90 km

10 0 10 20 30 40 50 60 miles

1:2 000 000

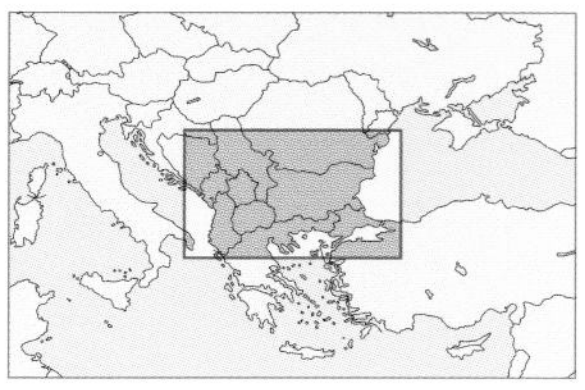

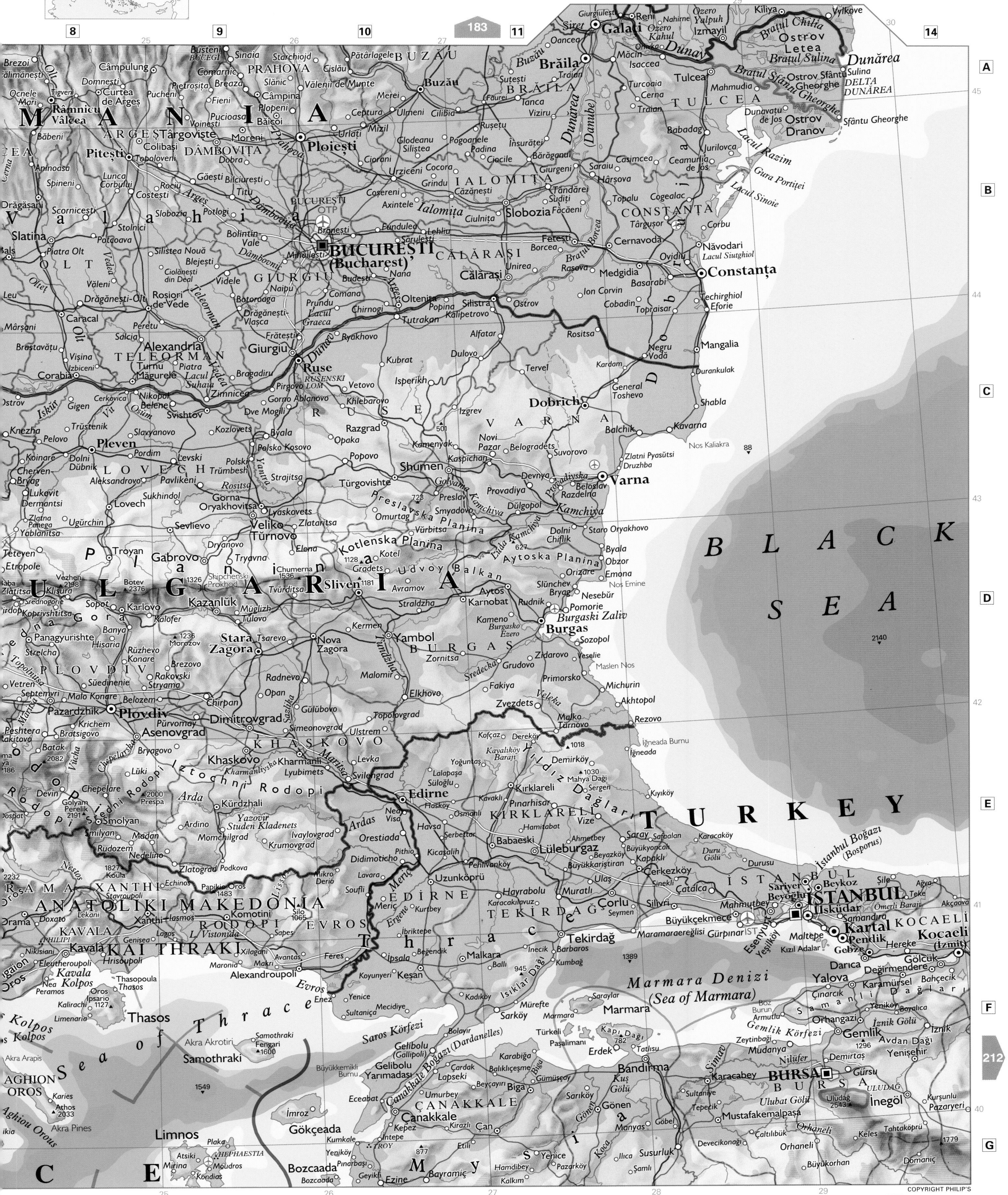

BLACK SEA

Underlined towns give their name to the
administrative area in which they stand.

COPYRIGHT PHILIP'S

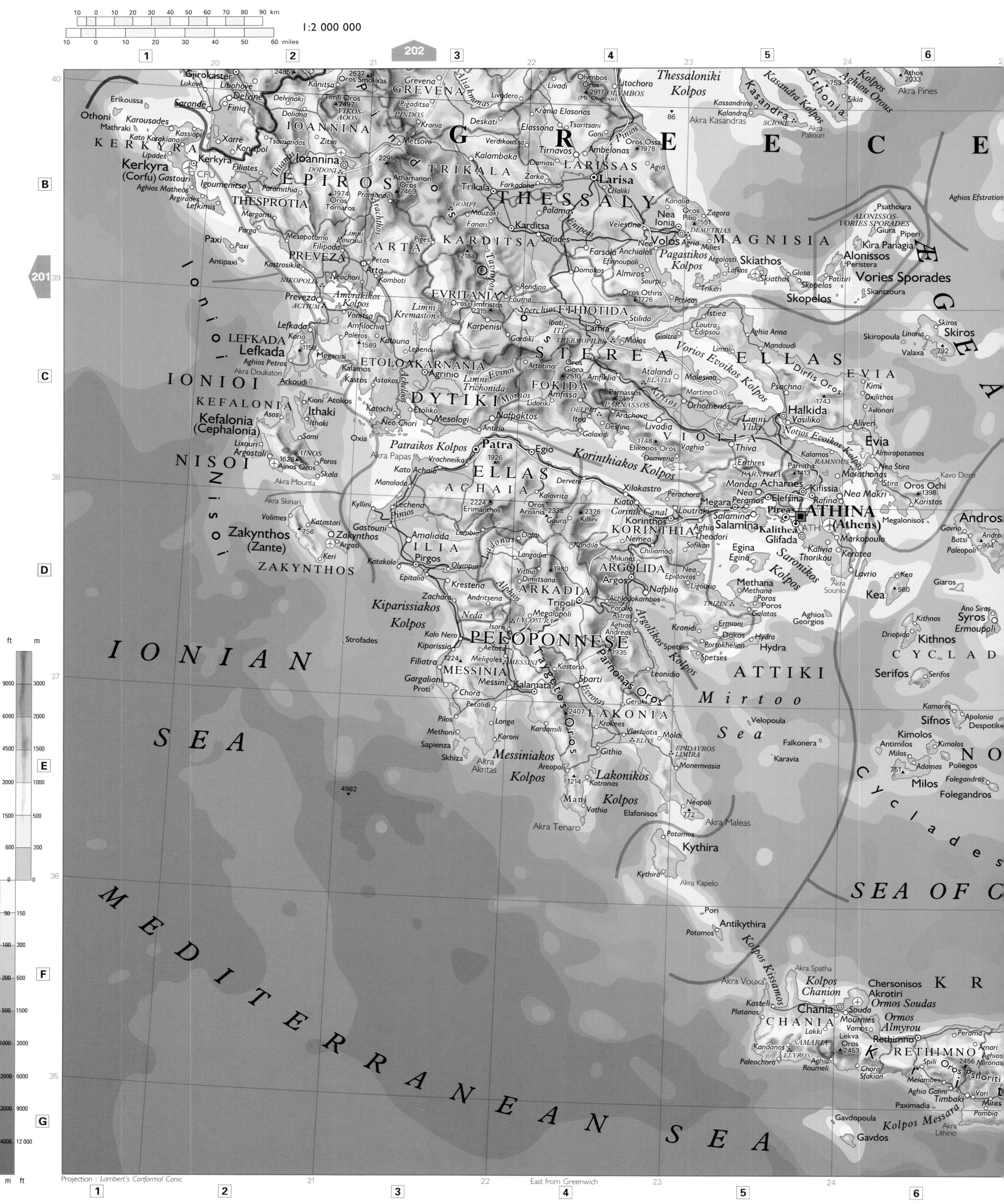

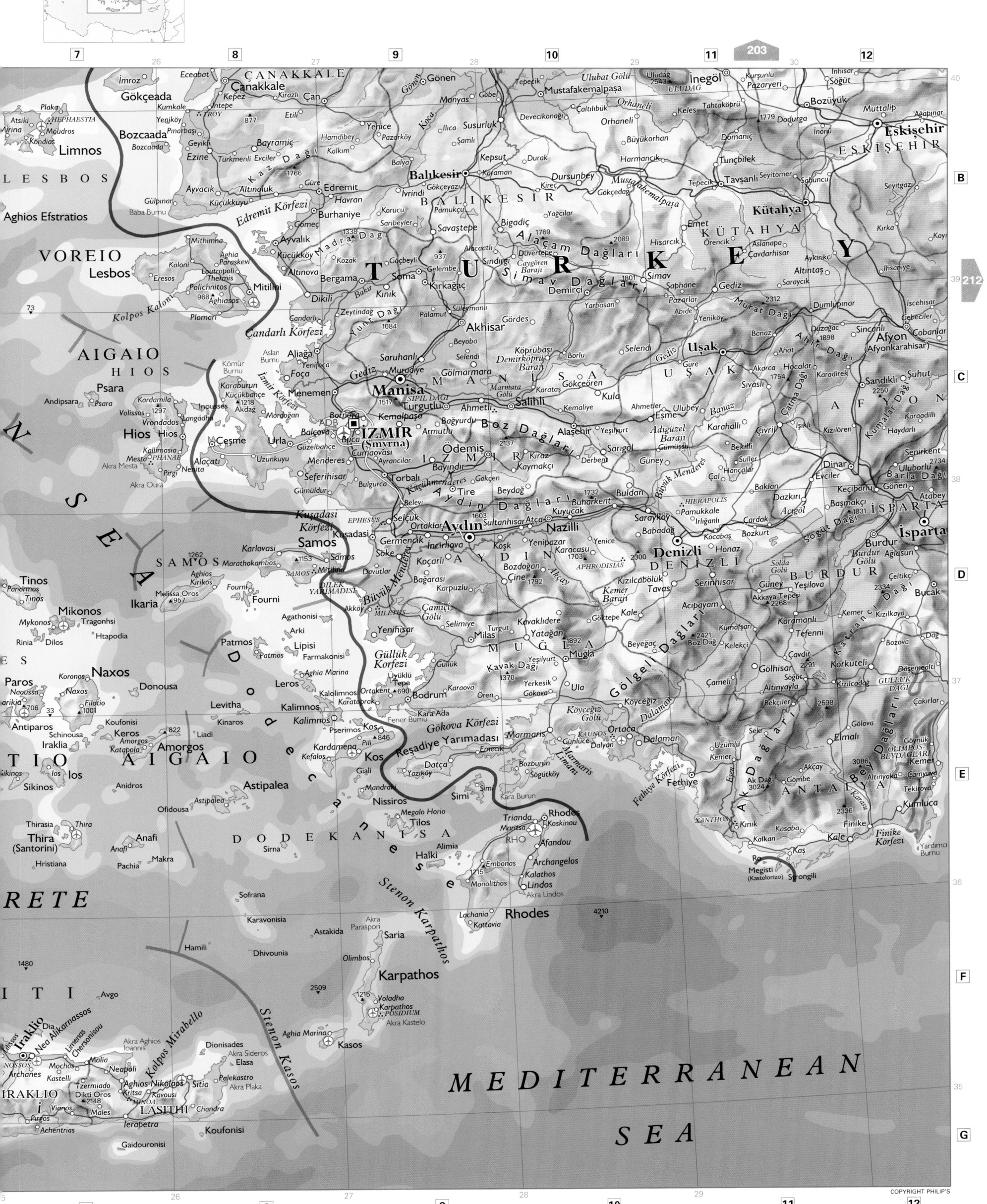

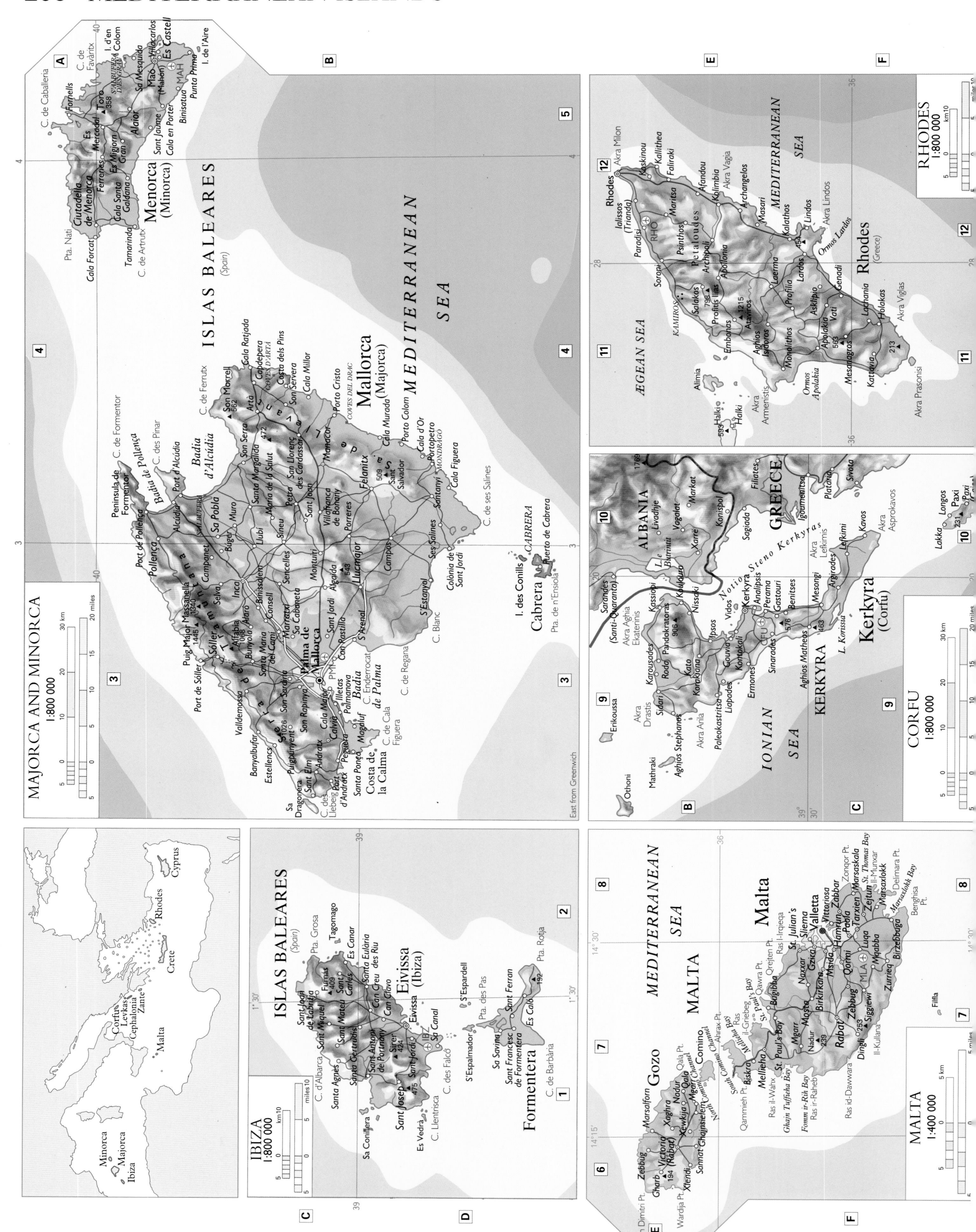

MAJORCA AND MINORCA
1:800 000

Menorca (Minorca)

C. de Caballeria
Fornells
Pta. Nati
Ciutadella de Menorca
Es Mercadal
Ferreries
Cala Santa Galdana
Cala Forcat
Tamarinda
C. de Artrutx

Toro 358
Alaior
Sant Jaume
Cala en Porter
Binisatua
Binisaida
Maó (Mahon)
Es Migjorn Gran
Sant Lluís
MAH
Es Castell
I. d'en Colom
Illacarlos
I. de l'Aire
C. de Favàritx
Punta Prima

ISLAS BALEARES
(Spain)

MEDITERRANEAN SEA

Mallorca (Majorca)

C. de Ferrutx
Cala Ratjada
Capdepera
Costa dels Pins
COVES D'ARTÀ
Son Morrell 562
Artà
Son Serra
Son Servera
Cala Millor
Porto Cristo
Cala Murada
Manacor
Porto Colom
Cala d'Or
Portopetro
MONDRAGÓ
Cala Figuera
C. de Salines
C. de ses Salines

Peninsula de Formentor
C. de Formentor
C. des Pinar
Badia de Pollença
Port d'Alcúdia
Badia d'Alcúdia

Pto. de Pollença
Pollença
Port de Sóller
Puig Major Massanella 1445 1340
Sóller
Valldemossa
Banyalbufar
Estellencs
Sa Dragonera
C. des Llebeg
Port d'Andratx
Andratx
Sant Elm
Peguera
Santa Ponça
Magaluf
Palmanova
Costa de la Calma
C. de Cala Figuera

Alcúdia
Sa Pobla
Muro
Campanet
Selva
Inca
Binissalem
Consell
Santa Maria del Camí
Bunyola
Marratxí
Sa Cabaneta
Santa Maria
Son Sardina
Palma de Mallorca
PMI
Badia de Palma
Illetas
Cala Major
Calvià
1026

Sa Pobla
Búger
Llubí
Sineu
Petra
Sant Joan
Vilafranca de Bonany
Porreres
Felanitx
Sant Salvador 509
Santanyí
Cala Santanyí

Muro
Santa Margalida
San Llorenç des Cardassar 472
Son Carrió
Sant Llorenç

Sencelles
Algaida
Montuïri
Lloret
Llucmajor 543
Campos
Ses Salines
Colònia de Sant Jordi
C. Blanc

Marratxí
Sant Jordi
Can Pastilla
S'Arenal
S'Estanyol
C. de Regana

East from Greenwich

I. des Conills
I. des Conills
CABRERA
Cabrera
Puerto de Cabrera
Pta. de n'Ensiola

IBIZA
1:800 000

ISLAS BALEARES
(Spain)

Eivissa (Ibiza)

Sant Joan de Labritja
Portinatx
Pta. Grosa
Tagomago
Es Canar
Santa Eulària des Riu
Can Creu des Riu

Sant Miquel 409
Santa Agnès
Sant Mateu
Sant Carles
Sant Antoni de Portmany
Sant Rafel 424
Sant Josep 475
Sant Jordi
Eivissa
IBZ
Santa Gertrudis
Can Clavo

Sa Conillera
Es Vedra
C. Llentrisca
C. des Falcó

S'Espalmador
S'Espardell
Sa Savina
Sant Francesc de Formentera
Pta. des Pas
Es Caló 192
Sant Ferran
Pta. Roija
Formentera
C. de Barbaria

MEDITERRANEAN SEA

Corfu
Corfù
Levkas
Cephalonia
Zante
Crete
Rhodes
Cyprus
Minorca
Majorca
Ibiza
Malta

ALBANIA
1769
Livadhje
Vagalat
Xarrë
Markat
Konispol
Butrinti
Sarandes (Santi-Quaranta)
Akra Aghia Ekaterinis

GREECE
Filiates
Igoumenitsa
Platória
Sivota
Akra Lefkimis
Lefkimi
Kavos
Akra Asprokavos

Kerkyra (Corfu)

Erikoussa
Mathraki
Othoni
Akra Drastis
Sidari
Roda
Kassiopi
Kouloura
Karousades
Pandokratoras 906
Kato
Korakiana
Gouvia
Kontokali
CFU
Kerkyra
Vidos
Ipsos
Liapades
Ermones
Pelekas
Sinarades
Benitses
Gastouri
Perama
Analipsis
576
Aghios Matheos
Paleokastritsa
Akra Arila
Aghios Stephanos
L. Korissia
Mesongi
Argirades
Notiza Steno Kerkyras

IONIAN SEA

CORFU
1:800 000

RHODES
1:800 000

Akra Milon
Rhodes
Ialissos (Trianda)
Paradisi
RHO
Kritika
Kaskinou
Kallithea
Faliraki
Afandou
Kolimbia
Archangelos
Marisa
Masari
Kalathos
Akra Vagia
Psinthos
Petaloudes
Archipoli
Apollona
Salakos 798
Profitis Ilias 1215
Embonas
Laerma
Lardos
Akra Lindos
Lindos
Ormos Lardos
Aghios Isidoros
Monolithos
Profilia
Askläpio
Genadi
Vati 563
Apolakia
Mesanagros
Lachania
Holakas
213
Katavia
Akra Viglas
Akra Prasonisi
Rhodes (Greece)

MEDITERRANEAN SEA

AEGEAN SEA

Alimia
Akra Armenistis
Halki
Ormos Apolakia

MEDITERRANEAN SEA

Gozo
San Dimitri Pt.
Zebbug
Gharb
Victoria (Rabat) 194
Xaghra
Nadur
Xewkija
Qala
Marsalforn
Somnet Ghajnsielem
Qala Pt.
Ghasri
Comino
South Comino Channel
North Comino Channel

MALTA
Mellieha
Qammieh Pt.
Ras il-Wahx
Ghajn Tuffieha Bay
Ras il-Raheb
Il-Kullana
Rabat
Dingli
253
Mdina
Siggiewi
Mgarr
Mosta
Naxxar
Birkirkara
Zebbug
Qormi
Zejtun
Luqa
MLA
Paola
Tarxien
Marsaskala
Marsaxlokk
Birzebbuga
Valletta
Sliema
St. Julian's
Vittoriosa
Hamrun
Zabbar
Gudja
Zurrieq
St. Thomas Bay
St. Paul's Bay
Bugibba
Qawra Pt.
Salina Bay
Delimara Pt.
Marsaxlokk Bay
Benghisa Pt.
Filfla

MALTA
1:400 000

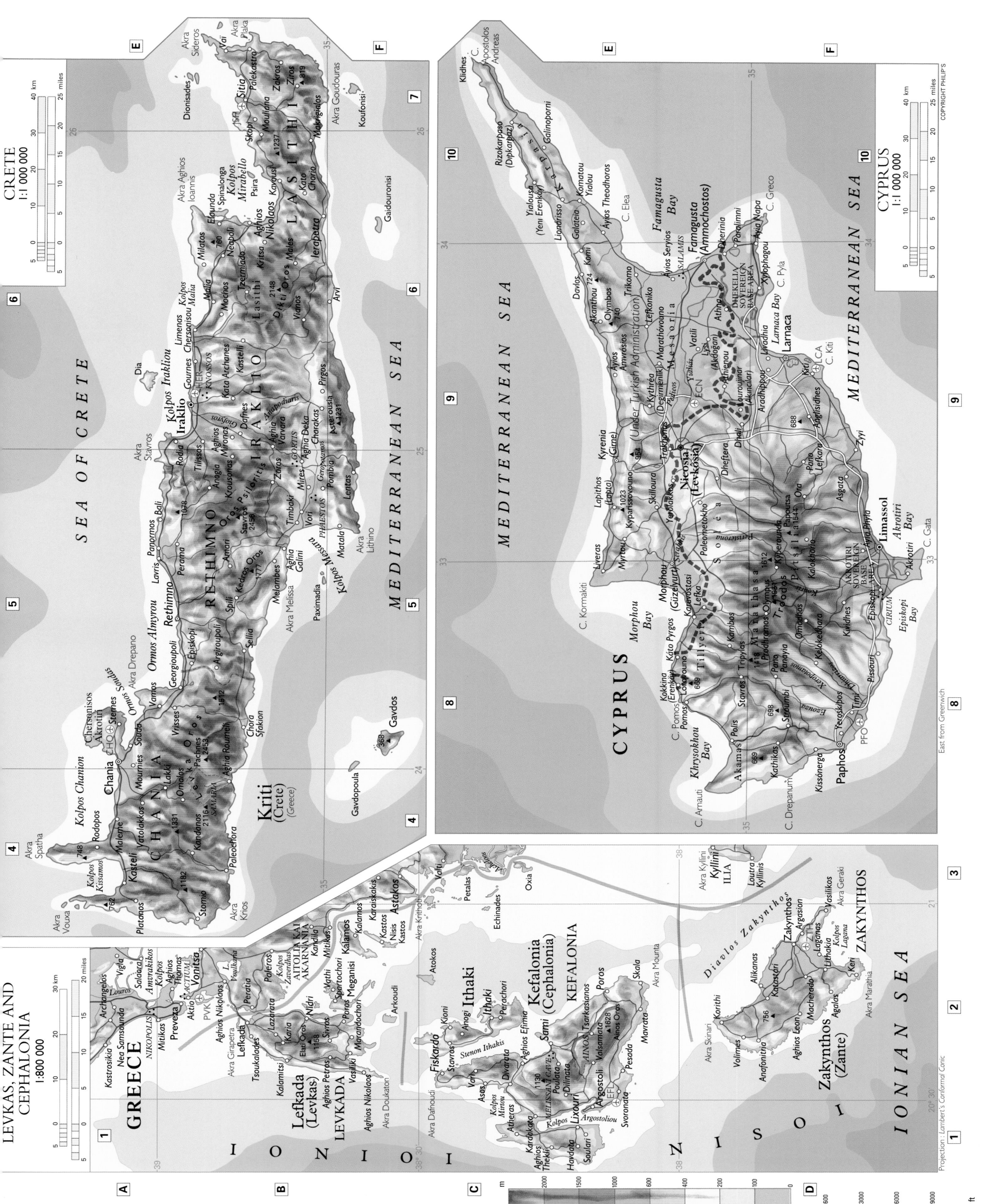

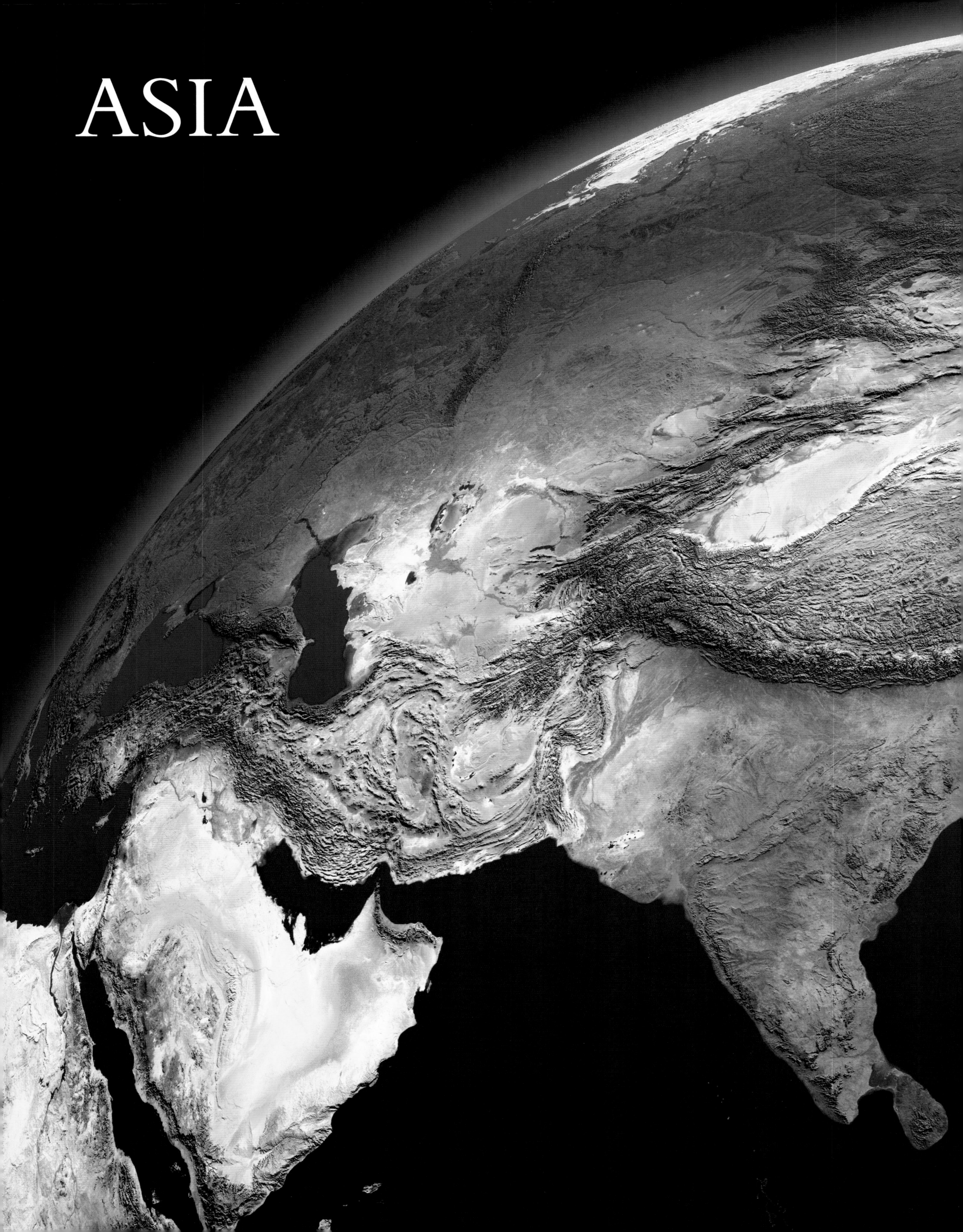

ASIA

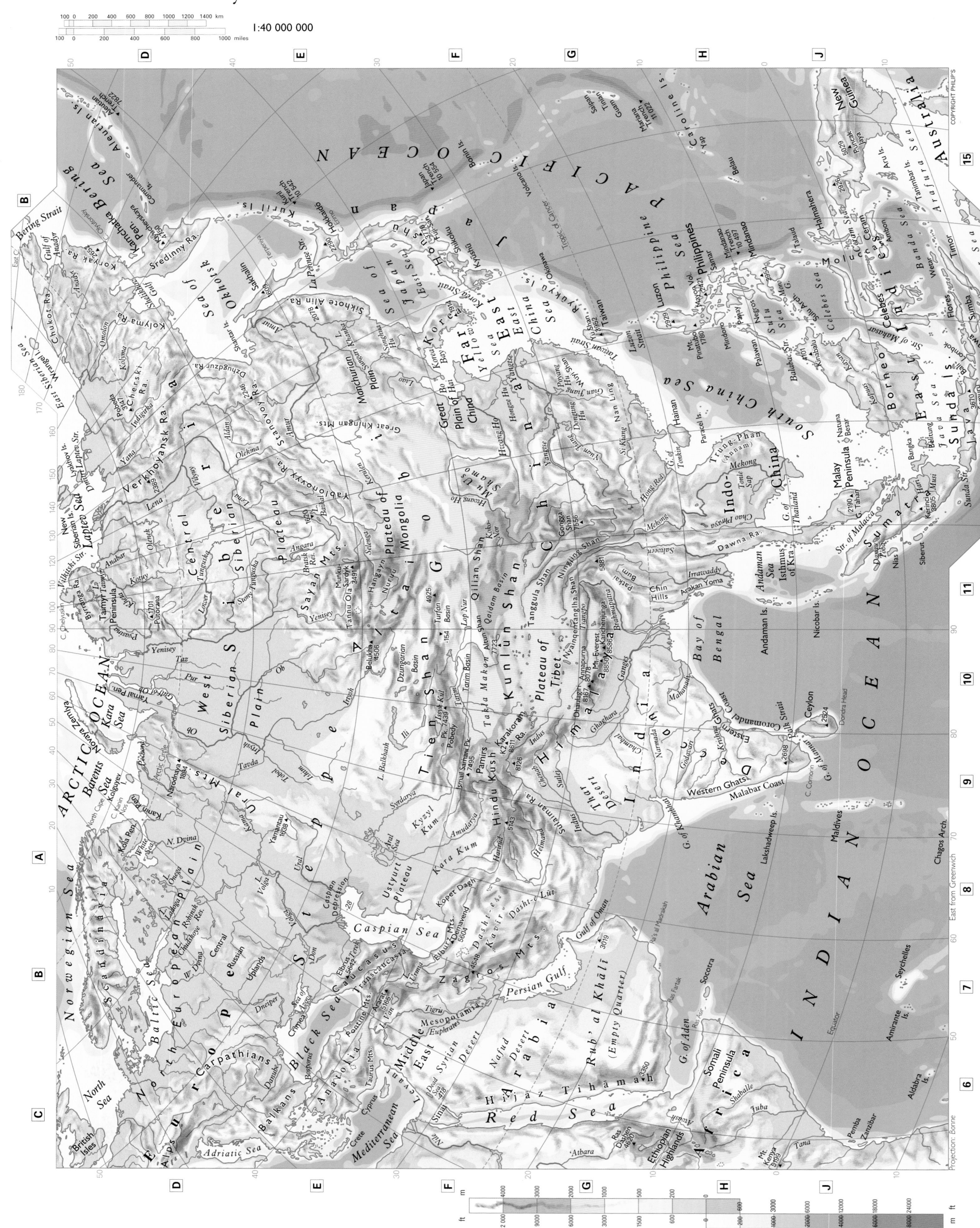

1:40 000 000

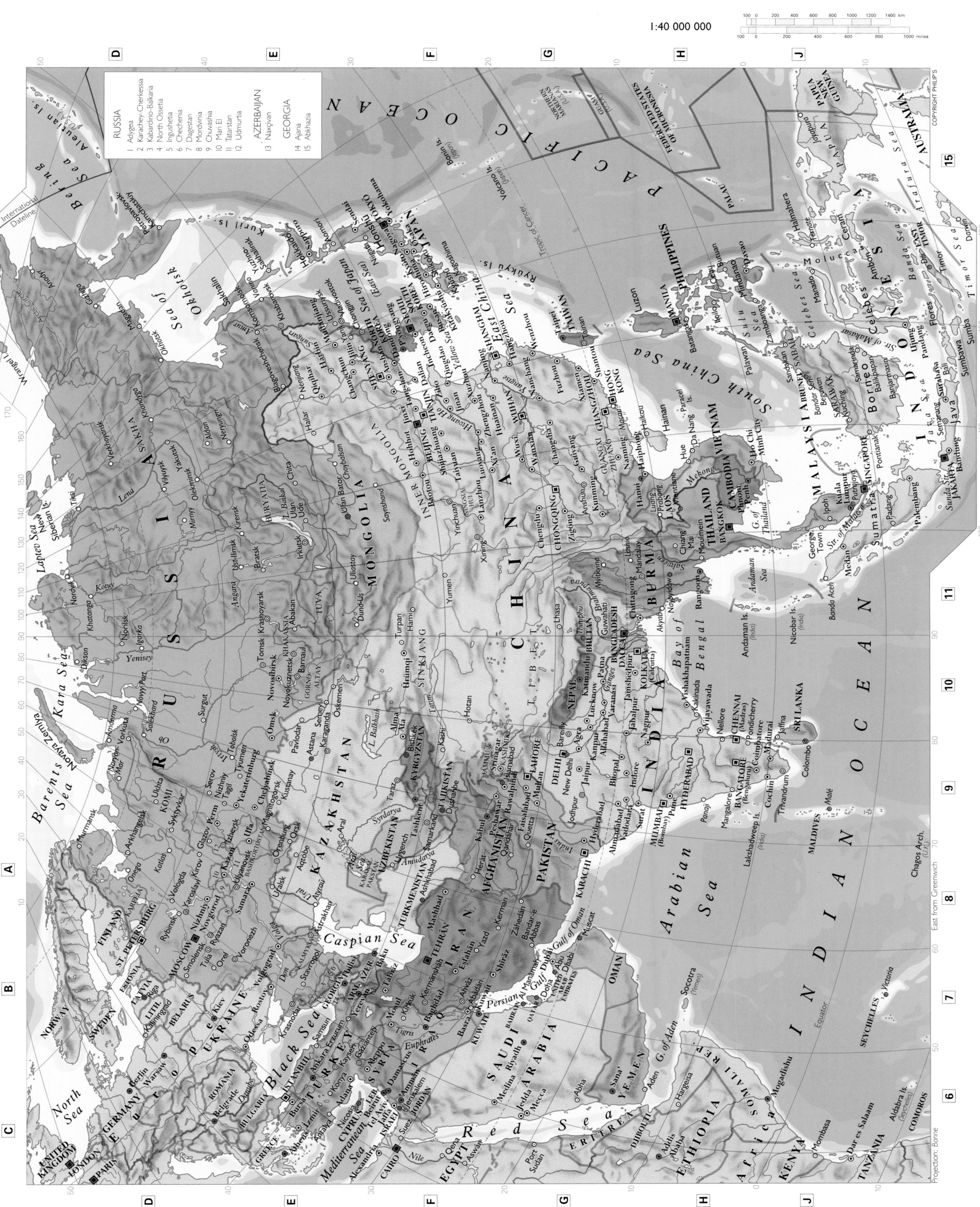

50 25 0 25 50 75 100 150 175 km
1 : 4 000 000
50 25 0 25 50 75 100 125 miles

1 26 **2** 28 **3** 30 **4** 32 **189** **5** 34 **6** 36 **7**

A

BULGARIA

B L A C K   S E A

203

Stara Zagora
Yambol
Aytos
Burgas
Nos Emine
1830
2206

B

Elkhovo
Michurin
Kırklareli
Edirne
Pınarhisar
Igneada
Demirköy
İgneada Burnu
1018
Yıldız Dağları
Orestiada
Babaeski
Lüleburgaz
Vize
Saray
Çerkezköy
İstanbul Boğazı (Bosporus)
Kerempe Burnu
İnebolu
Çatalzeytin
İnce Burun
SINOP
Sinop
Erfelek
Ayancık
Kilimli
Bartın
Devrekâni
Kastamonu
Küre Dağları
Kargı
SAMSUN
Samsun
Terme
Uzunköprü
Hayrabolu
Muratlı
Çorlu
Çatalca
Tekirdağ
ISTANBUL
Kartal Kocaeli Sakarya (İzmit) (Adapazarı)
Zonguldak
Kozlu
Çaycuma
Ereğli
Devrek
Karabük
Safranbolu
Araç
İlgaz Dağları
Tosya
Osmancık
Merzifon
Vezirköprü
Altınkaya
Havza
Kavak
Çarşamba
Ünye
Fatsa
Ordu
Gürgentepe

C

Thrace
Evros
Enez
Keşan
Malkara
Saros Körfezi
Gelibolu
GALLIPOLI YARIMADASI
Marmara Denizi (Sea of Marmara)
Büyükçekmece
Gebze
Darıca
Körfez
Yalova
Gölcük
Sapanca
Akyazı
Hendek
Cumaova
Bolu
Gerede
Çerkeş
Kurşunlu
Çankırı
Kızılcahamam
Çubuk
Çorum
Mecitözü
Amasya
Turhal
Erbaa
Niksar
Reşadiye
KUZEY

Samothraki
Gökçeada
Bozcaada
Çanakkale Boğazı (Dardanelles)
Lapseki
Biga
Karabiga
Bandırma
Gemlik
Mudanya
İznik
İznik Gölü
Geyve
Göynük
Seben
Mudurnu
ÇANKIRI
Kızılırmak
İskilip
Kızılırmak
Günüşhacıköy
Ladik
Tekke
Akkuş
Aybastı
Mesu

TROY
Ezine
Ayvacık
Baba Burnu
Bayramiç
Balya
Susurluk
Karacabey
Mustafakemalpaşa
BURSA
Uludağ Gölü
Orhangazi
Yenişehir
Bilecik
Söğüt
Sakarya
Nallıhan
Beypazarı
Ayaş
Sincan
ANKARA
Kalecik
Delice
Sungurlu
Alaca
Boğazkale
Zile
TOKAT
Tokat
Almus
Devecı Dağları
Yeşilırmak
Artova
Çırçır

Edremit Körfezi
Edremit
Burhaniye
Balıkesir
Bigadiç
Dursunbey
Domaniç
BURSA
Bozüyük
Eskişehir
Alpu
Mihalıççık
Sivrihisar
Polatlı
Gölbaşı
ANKARA
Bala
Keskin
Yerköy
Yozgat
Sorgun
YOZGAT
Akdağmadeni
Sefaatli
Yıldızeli
SİVAS
Sivas
Hafik
Ak Dağları
Tecer Dağı

D

GREECE

Lesbos
Hios
Mitilini
Foça
Karaburun
Menemen
Manisa
İZMİR (Smyrna)
Çeşme
Urla
İZMİR
Seferihisar
Torbalı
MANİSA
Akhisar
Soma
Bergama
Kırkağaç
Demirci
Simav
Gediz
Kütahya
KÜTAHYA
Tavşanlı
Emet
Uşak
Banaz
Murat Dağı
Afyon (Afyonkarahisar)
AFYON
Bolvadin
Eber Gölü
Akşehir Gölü
Sultan Dağları
Ilgın
Kadınhanı
Kulu
Tuz Gölü
Şereflikoçhisar
Ortaköy
AKSARAY
Aksaray
NEVŞEHİR
GÖREME
Ürgüp
İncesu
KAYSERİ
Kayseri
Talas
Pınarbaşı
Tomarza
Develi
Gürün
Darende
Afşin
Elbistan
Doğanşehir

Hios
Samos
Ikaria
Kuşadası
EPHESUS
Selçuk
Aydın
Tire
Nazilli
Ödemiş
Sarıgöl
Alaşehir
Eşme
Ulubey
Sandıklı
Şuhut
Çivril
Güney
Dinar
Çal
Senirkent
Yalvaç
Gelendost
Eğridir Gölü
Sarayönü
KONYA
Konya
Obruk
Dinek
Obruk Ovası
Nevşehir
Hacılar
Yeşilhisar
Bakırdağ
Sarız
TURKEY

Samos
Fourni
Patmos
DİLEK YARIMADASI
Söke
İncirliova
Karacasu
Çine
Bozdoğan
MUĞLA
DENİZLİ
Denizli
Sarayköy
Buldan
Honaz Dağı
Acıgöl
Burdur Gölü
Eğridir
Isparta
ISPARTA
Beyşehir Gölü
Beyşehir
KONYA
Çumra
Karapınar
Ereğli
Ulukışla
Pozantı
NIGDE
Niğde
Çamardı
Feke
Kozan
Kadirli
İmamoğlu
ADANA
Kahramanmaraş
KAHRAMAN-MARAŞ
Göksun
Pazarcık
Araban
Besni
Gölbaşı

MİLETUS
Milas
Yatağan
Kale
Tavas
Kızılhisar
Çameli
Tefenni
Bucak
Ağlasun
Sütçüler
Bozkır
Hadim
Karaman
KARAMAN
Göksu
Mut
Ermenek
Gülnar
Silifke
Erdemli
İçel (Mersin)
Tarsus
Adana
Ceyhan
Osmaniye
İslâhiye
Gaziantep
Nizip
Oğuzeli

Kalimnos
Kos
Güllük
MUĞLA
Ula
Göcek Dağları
Marmaris
Ortaca
Dalaman
Fethiye
Göcek Körfezi
Datça
Bozburun
Tilos
Simi
Rhodes (Rhodes)

E

Dodecanese
Astipalea
Karpathos
Kasos

204

GREECE

Rhodes
Lindos

LYCIA
XANTHOS
Kalkan
Kaş
Kale
Finike
Megiste
BEYDAĞLARI OLİMPOS
Kemer
Kumluca
Antalya
Manavgat
Side
Serik
ASPENDOS
PAMPHYLIA
Alanya
Gazipaşa
Anamur
Anamur Burnu
Bozyazı
İncekum Burnu
Silifke
Karataş
Yumurtalık
İskenderun
İskenderun Körfezi
Dörtyol
Payas
HATAY
Kırıkhan
Kilis
Manbij
Afrin

C. Apostolos Andreas
Rizokarpaso
Kyrenia
Morphou
Polis
Paphos
Episkopi
Akrotiri
Limassol
Troodos
Olympus 1951
Nicosia
Famagusta
Larnaca
HALAB
HALAB (Aleppo)
As Safirah
Ma'arrat an Nu'man
İdlib
IDLIB
Khan Shaykhun

CYPRUS

F

M E D I T E R R A N E A N   S E A

Al Lādhiqīyah (Latakia)
Jablah
Bāniyās
TARTŪS
Tartūs
Al Hamidiyah
Şāfītā
Tall Kalakh
Hamāh
HAMĀH
As Salamiyah
Maşyaf
Himş (Homs)
HIMŞ
Shinshār
Furqlus
Al Qaryatayn
Tarābulus (Tripoli) Al Batrūn
Zgharta
3088
Bsharri
Al Qusayr
Jubayl
An Nabk
Yabrūd
Jayrūd
Sab' Ābar

LEBANON
BAYRŪT (Beirut)
Jūniyah
Zahlah
Ba'labakk
Şaydā
Sūr
Qatana
Az Zabdani
Yabrūd
DIMASHQ (Damascus)
Jaramānah
Dūmā
An Nabk

G

2775

ISRAEL
Hadera
Netanya
TEL AVIV-YAFO
Rehovot
Ashdod
Ashqelon
Qiryat Shemona
Nahariyya
'Akko
Zefat
Hefa (Haifa)
HA KARMEL
Teverya
Nazerat
Nābulus
WEST BANK
Ramla
El 'Arīḥā
Jerusalem
AMMĀN
Dar'ā
Irbid
Al-Mafraq
Az Zarqā'
As Salt
Salkhad
As Suwaydā'
AS SUWAYDĀ'
Shahbā
JORDAN
SYRIA
Al Qunayṭirah
Yarmūk

Projection: Conical with two standard parallels

256 **3** 30 **4** 32 **5** 34 36

Division between Greeks and Turks
in Cyprus; Turks to the North.

6

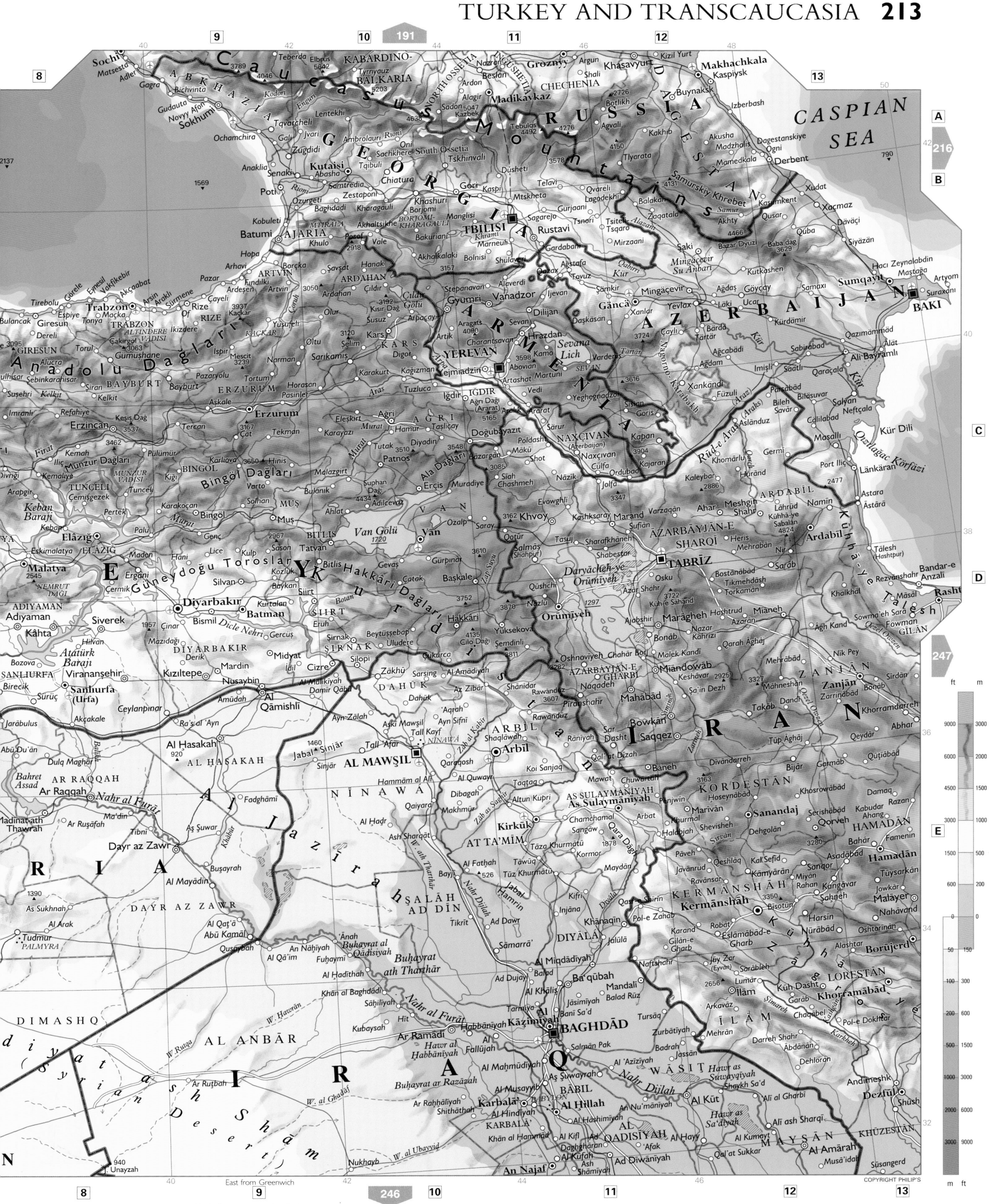

COPYRIGHT PHILIP'S

1:16 000 000

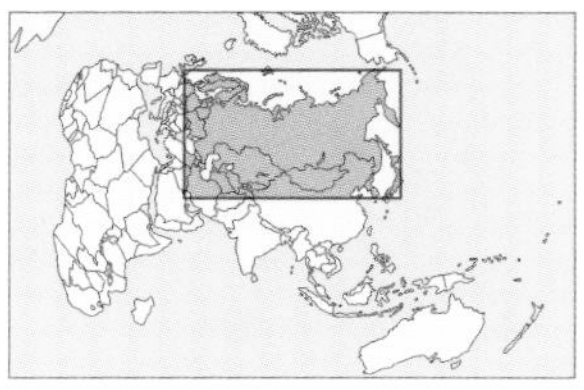

OCEAN

East Siberian Sea

Chukchi Sea

Bering Strait

Bering Sea

Laptev Sea

Severnaya Zemlya

Poluostrov Gory Byrranga Taymyr

Sea of Okhotsk

Sakhalin

Kamchatka Poluostrov

Kurilskiye Ostrova

R U S S I A

Arctic Circle

Verkhoyanskiy Khrebet

Khrebet Cherskogo

Stanovoy Khrebet

Yablonovyy Khrebet

Sikhote Alin

Khrebet Dzhugdzur

HOKKAIDO

SAPPORO

Hakodate

Sea of Japan (East Sea)

Honshū

Norilsk

Krasnoyarsk

Bratsk

Irkutsk

Ulan Ude

Yakutsk

Magadan

Petropavlovsk-Kamchatskiy

Yuzhno-Sakhalinsk

Khabarovsk

Komsomolsk-na-Amur

Vladivostok

Nakhodka

M O N G O L I A

(Aerhtai Shan)

Hangayn Nuruu

Hentiyn Nuruu

Ulaanbaatar

Gobi

C H I N A

D o n g b e i (Manchuria)

HARBIN

QIQIHAR

DAQING

CHANGCHUN

JILIN

MUDANJIANG

JIAMUSI

JIXI

HEGANG

YICHUN

SHENYANG

FUSHUN

ANSHAN

CHIFENG

HOHHOT

BAOTOU

ZHANGJIAKOU

BEIJING

TANGSHAN

DALIAN

NORTH KOREA

PYONGYANG

NAMP'O

Hamhüng

Kimch'aek

Ch'ŏngjin

SOUTH KOREA

SEOUL

INCHEON

DAEJEON

DAEGU

BUSAN

GWANGJU

JAPAN

KYOTO

KOBE

OSAKA

COPYRIGHT PHILIP'S

Underlined towns give their name to the
administrative area in which they stand.

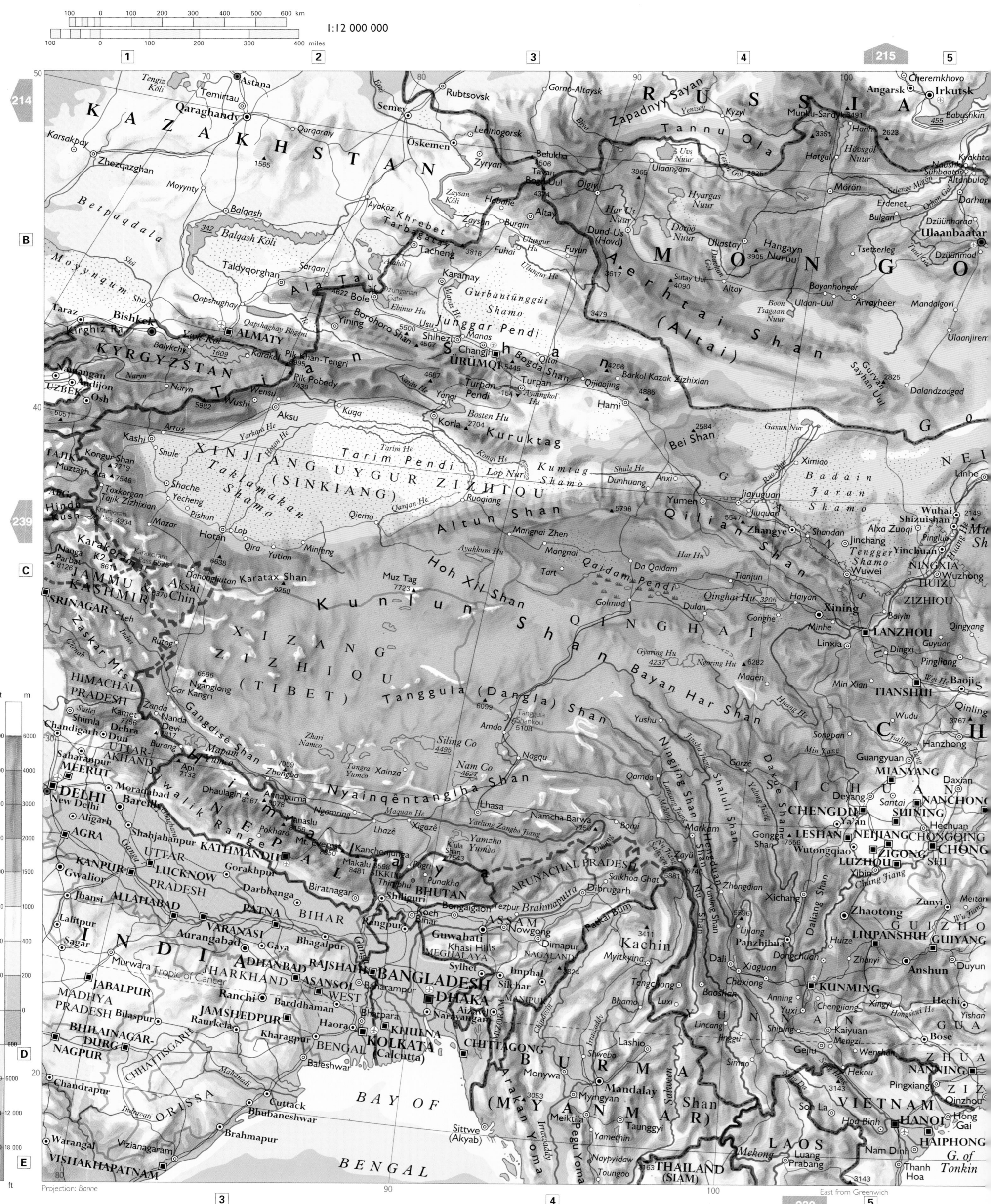

1:12 000 000

Projection: Bonne

East from Greenwich

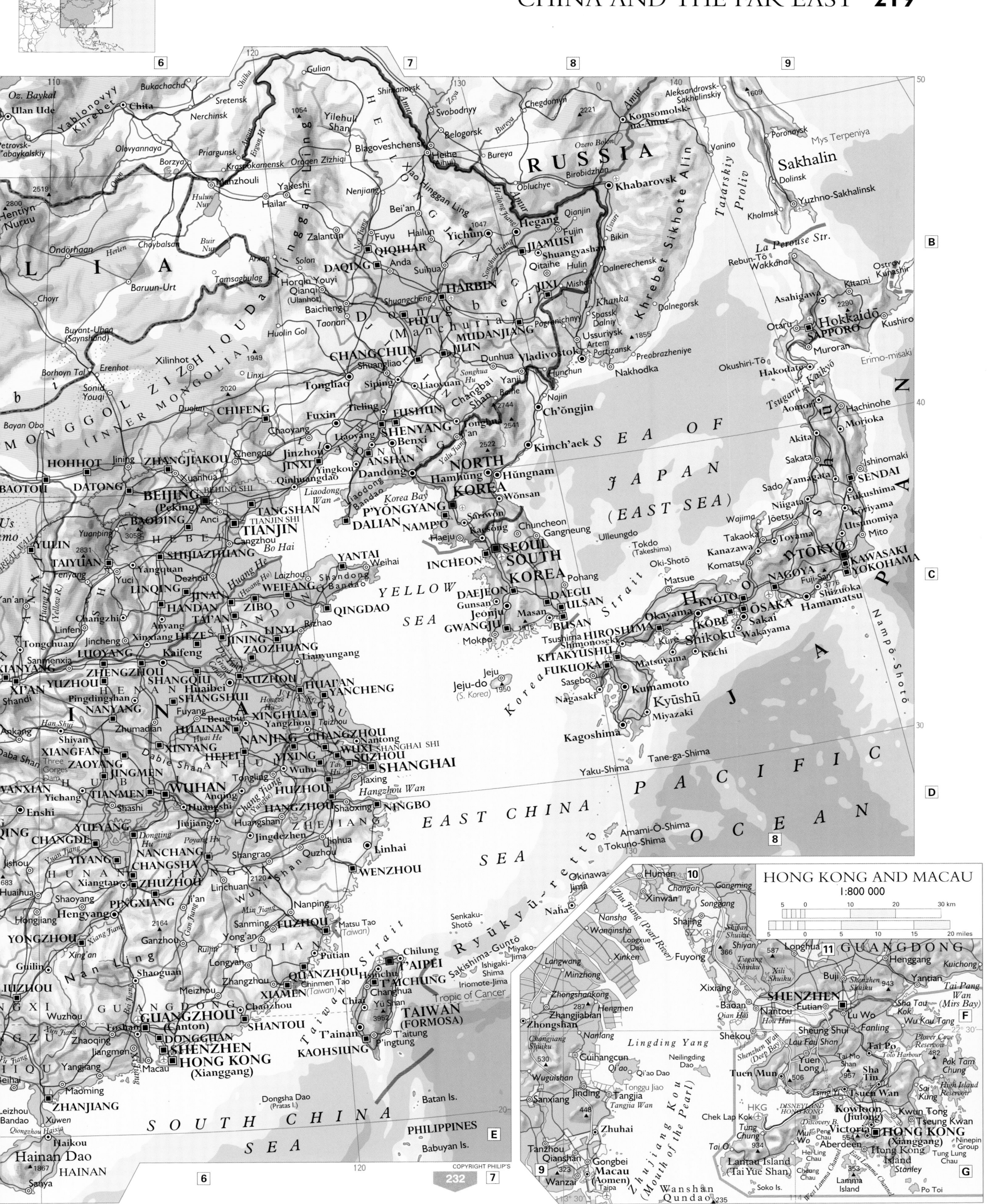

HONG KONG AND MACAU
1:800 000

COPYRIGHT PHILIP'S

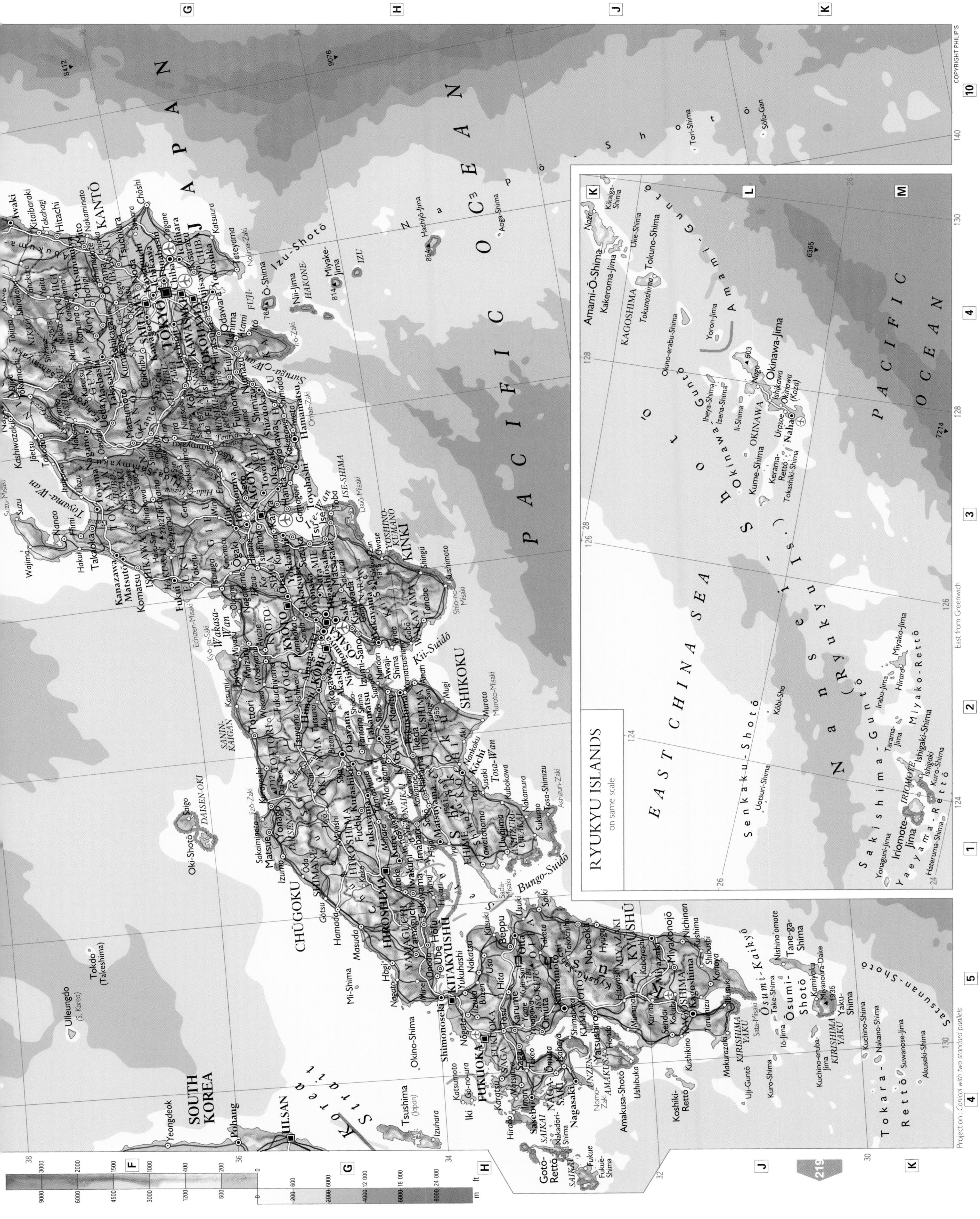

RYUKYU ISLANDS
on same scale

Projection: Conical with two standard parallels

East from Greenwich

1:2 000 000

SEA OF JAPAN
(EAST SEA)

SOUTH KOREA

CHŪGOKU-DISTRICT

Korea Strait

Tsushima

Shikoku
SHIKOKU-DISTRICT

Kyūshū
KYŪSHŪ-DISTRICT

Shinkansen line

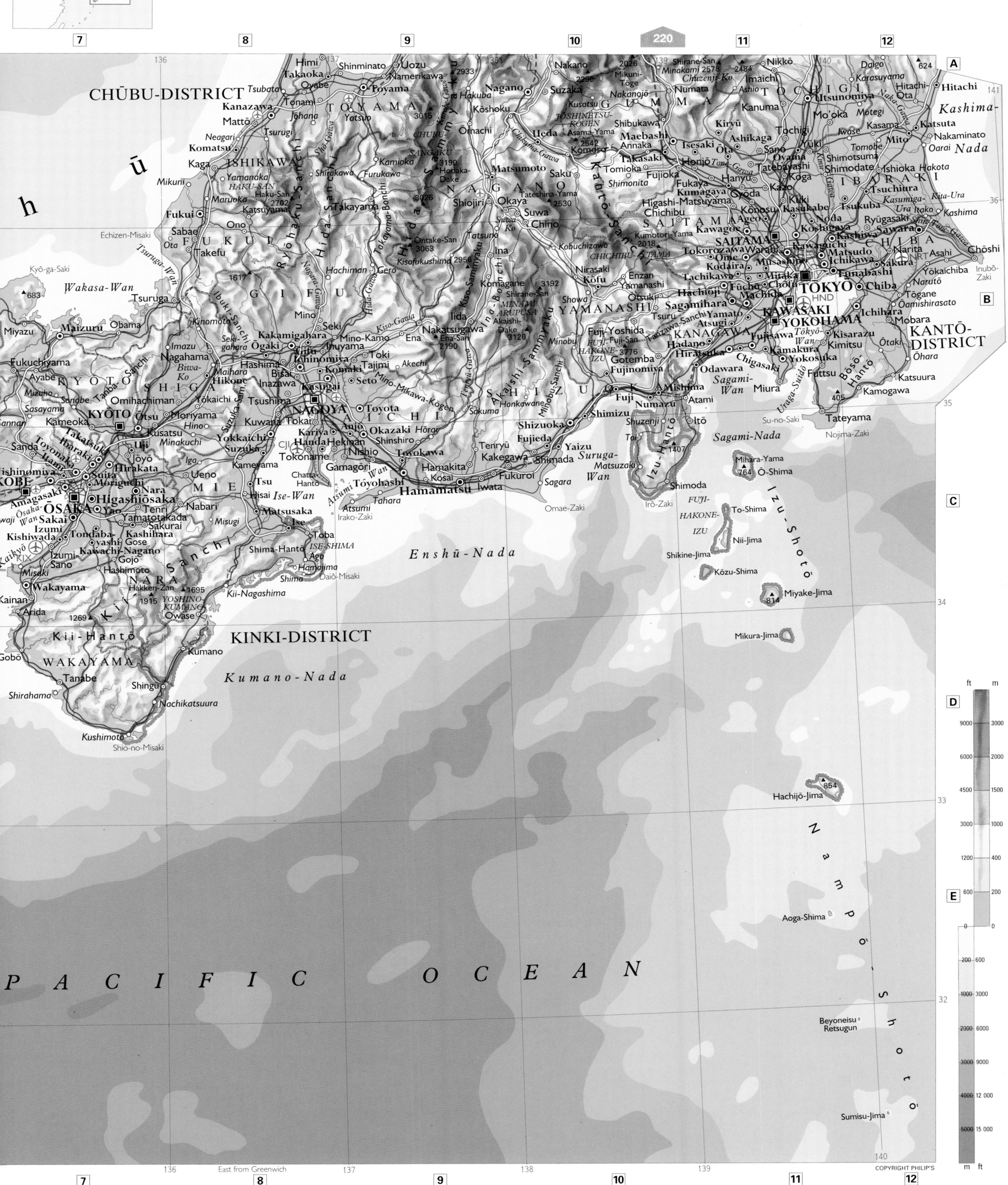

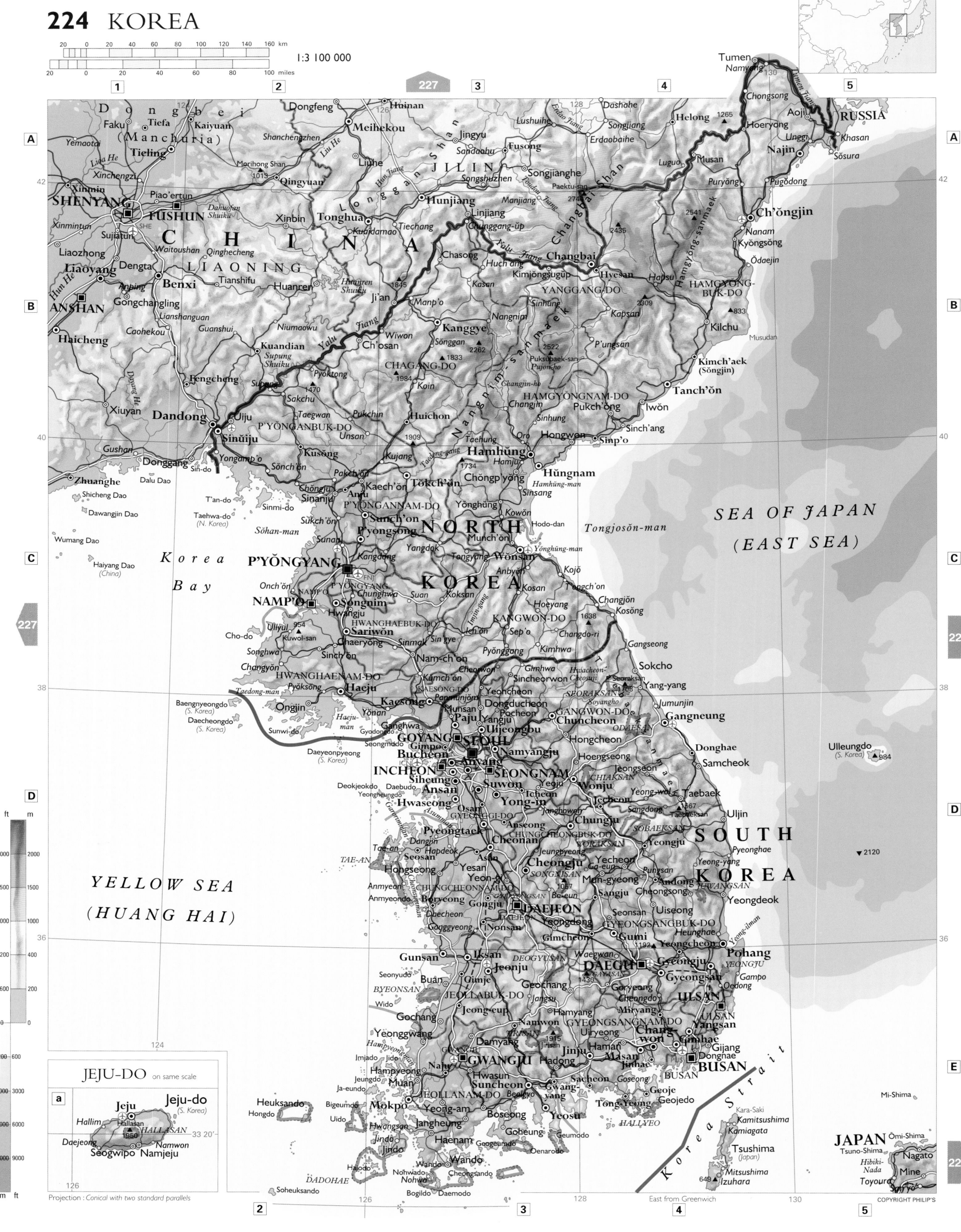

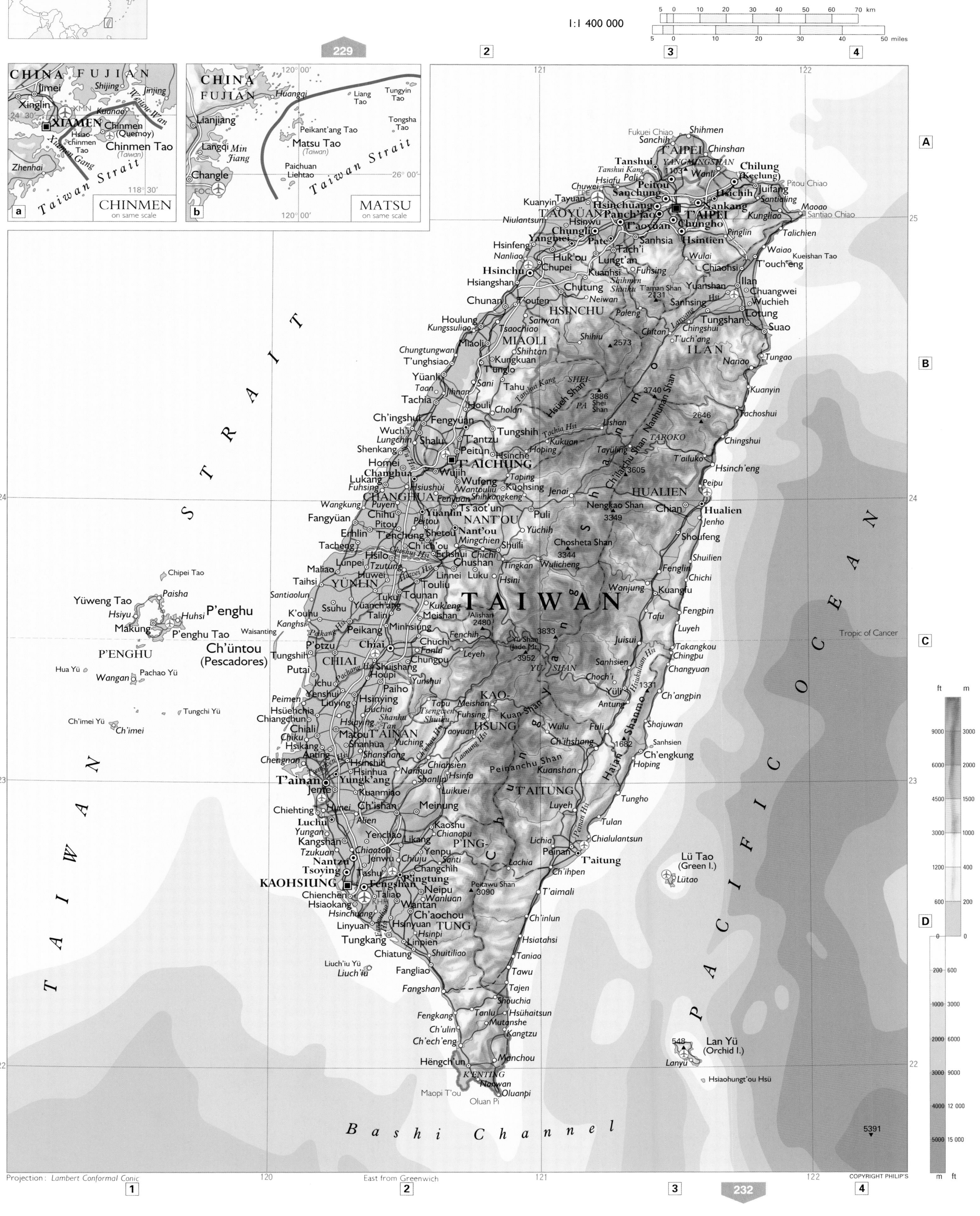

1:1 400 000

5 0 10 20 30 40 50 60 70 km
5 0 10 20 30 40 50 miles

CHINA FUJIAN
Jimei
Xinglin
Shijing
Jinjing
KMN
Xiamen
Kuanao
Hsiao-chinmen Tao
Chinmen (Quemoy)
Xiamen Gang
Chinmen Tao
Zhenhai
Taiwan Strait
CHINMEN on same scale **a**

CHINA FUJIAN
Huangqi
Liang Tao
Tungyin Tao
Lianjiang
Peikant'ang Tao
Tongsha Tao
Langqi *Min Jiang*
Matsu Tao (Taiwan)
Change
Paichuan
Liehtao
Taiwan Strait
MATSU on same scale **b**

229

TAIWAN

T A I W A N   S T R A I T

Fukuei Chiao
Shihmen
Chinshan
Tanshui
T'AIPEI
YANGMINGSHAN
Chilung (Keelung)
Tanshui Kang
Hsiafu Pali
1103
Wanli
Juifang
Pitou Chiao
Chuwei
Peitou
Haichih
Nankang
Santiaoling
Kuanyin
Tayuan
Sanchung
T'AIPEI
Kungliao
Maoao
Niulantsun
TAOYUAN
Panch'iao
Chungho
Pinglin
Santiao Chiao
Hsinchuang
Taoyuan
Hsintien
Talichien
Chungli
Pate
Tach'i
Wulai
Waiao
Kueishan Tao
Hsinfeng
Nanliao
Kuanhsi
Fuhsing
Chiaohsi
T'ouch'eng
Huk'ou
Chupei
Shihmen Shihku
Yuanshan
Chuangwei
Hsinchu
T'aman Shan 2131
Ilan
Wuchieh
Hsiangshan
Chutung
Neiwan
Sanhsing
Lotung
Chunan
T'oufen
Tsaochiao
Paleng
Hsi
Chingshui
Suao
Houlung
Miaoli
Shihtan
Chiftan
T'uch'ang
Kungssuliao
MIAOLI
Shihiu
2573
ILAN
T'unghsiao
Kungkuan
Nanao
Chungtungwan
T'unglo
SHEI-
PA
3740
Kuanyin
Yuanli
Taan
Tahu
Tungshan
Tachoshui
Sani
Tsanshui Kang
3886
Shei Shan
Tachia
Houli
Hsueh Shan
Ushan
2646
Ch'ingshui
Fengyüan
Cholan
Tachia Hsi
TAROKO
Wuch'i
Tungshih
Kukuan
Tayuling
Chingshui
Lungching
Shalu
Hoping
T'ailuko
Hsinch'eng
Shenkang
Peitun
Hsinche
Chiakuhsi Shan 3605
Homei
T'AICHUNG
Peipu
Changhua
Wujih
Taping
HUALIEN
Lukang
Wufeng
Kuohsing
Jenai
Chian
Hualien
Fuhsing
CHANGHUA
Fenyuan
Shihkangkeng
Nengkao Shan
Jenho
Wangkung
Puyen
Yüanlin
NANTOU
Puli
3349
Fangyüan
Chihu
Peitou
Nant'ou
Yüchih
Shoufeng
Erhlin
T'enchung
Mingchien
Choshul Shan
Fenglin
Tacheng
Ch'ich'iou
Shetou
Shuili
3344
Chichi
Hsilo
Lunpei
Erhshui
Chushan
Tingkan
Wulicheng
Wanjung
Kuangfu
Maliao
Tzutung
Linnei
Luku
Hsini
Taihsi
YÜNLIN
Touliu
Chichi
Santiaolun
Tuku
Tounan
TAIWAN
Tafu
Fengpin
K'ouhu
Yuanch'ang
Talin
Meishan
Alishan 2480
Fenchih
Chishui
Peikang
Minhsiung
Luyeh
Waisanting
Peikang
Chai
Chuchi
Fanlu
Yü Shan (Jade Mtn.) 3833
Juisui
Takangkou
Chingpu
Tropic of Cancer
P'otzu
CHIAI
Chai
Leyeh
3952
YÜ SHAN
Sanhsien
Changyuan
Putai
Chungpu
Choch'i
Ichu
Shuishang
Yunshui
Yüli
Ch'angpin
Peimen
Yenshui
Houpi
Antung
1331
Hsüehchia
Liuying
Paiho
Tabu Meishan
Fuhsing
Kuan Shan
Ch'ihshang
Chiangchun
Shanhua
Luchia
Shanlun
Tsengwen
Taoyuan
KAO-
Wulu
Sanhsien
Chiali
Matou T'AINAN
Shanhua
Yuching
Fuli
Ch'engkung
Chiku
Hsikang
Shanshang
Chiahsien
HSUNG
Ch'ihshang
Hoping
Chengnan
Hsinshih
Namhua
Peinanchu Shan
Kuanshan
Anting
Hsinhua
Shanlin
Hsinfa
T'ainan
Yungk'ang
Luikuei
T'aitung
Tungho
Jente
Kuanmiao
Meinung
Luyeh
Chiehting
Hunei
Ch'ishan
Lichia
Tulan
Luchu
Kaoshu
Chianpu
Peinan
Yungan
Yenchao
Likang
P'ING-
Chialulantsun
Kangshan
Yenpu
Changchih
T'aitung
Tzukuan
Chigatou
Santi
Lachia
Nantzu
Tashu
Chruju
T'ung
Ch'ihpen
KAOHSIUNG
Fengshan
Peitawu Shan 3090
Tsoying
Neipu
Chienchen
Taliao
Wanluan
T'aimali
Hsiaokang
Wantan
Ch'inlun
Hsinchuang
Ch'aochou
TUNG
Linyuan
Hsinyuan
Linpien
Hsiatahsi
Tungkang
Hsinpi
Taniao
Chiatung
Tawu
Liuch'iu Yü
Fangliao
Tajen
Shouchia
Liuch'iu
Fangshan
Tanlu
Hsühaitsun
Fengkang
Mutanshe
Ch'ulin
Kangtzu
Ch'ech'eng
548 Lan Yü (Orchid I.)
Hengch'un
Manchou
Lanyu
Hsiaohungt'ou Hsü
Maopi T'ou
K'ENTING
Nanwan
Oluanpi
Oluan Pi

Lü Tao (Green I.)
Lütao

P A C I F I C   O C E A N

Yüweng Tao
Hsiyu
Paisha
Huhsi
P'enghu
Chipei Tao
Makung
P'enghu Tao
Ch'üntou (Pescadores)
Hua Yü
Wangan
Pachao Yü
P'ENGHU
Ch'imei Yü
Tungchi Yü
Ch'imei

T A I W A N
S T R A I T

B a s h i   C h a n n e l

5391

ft m
9000 3000
6000 2000
4500 1500
3000 1000
1200 400
600 200
0 0
200 600
1000 3000
2000 6000
3000 9000
4000 12 000
5000 15 000
m ft

Projection: Lambert Conformal Conic

East from Greenwich

COPYRIGHT PHILIP'S

232

1:4 800 000

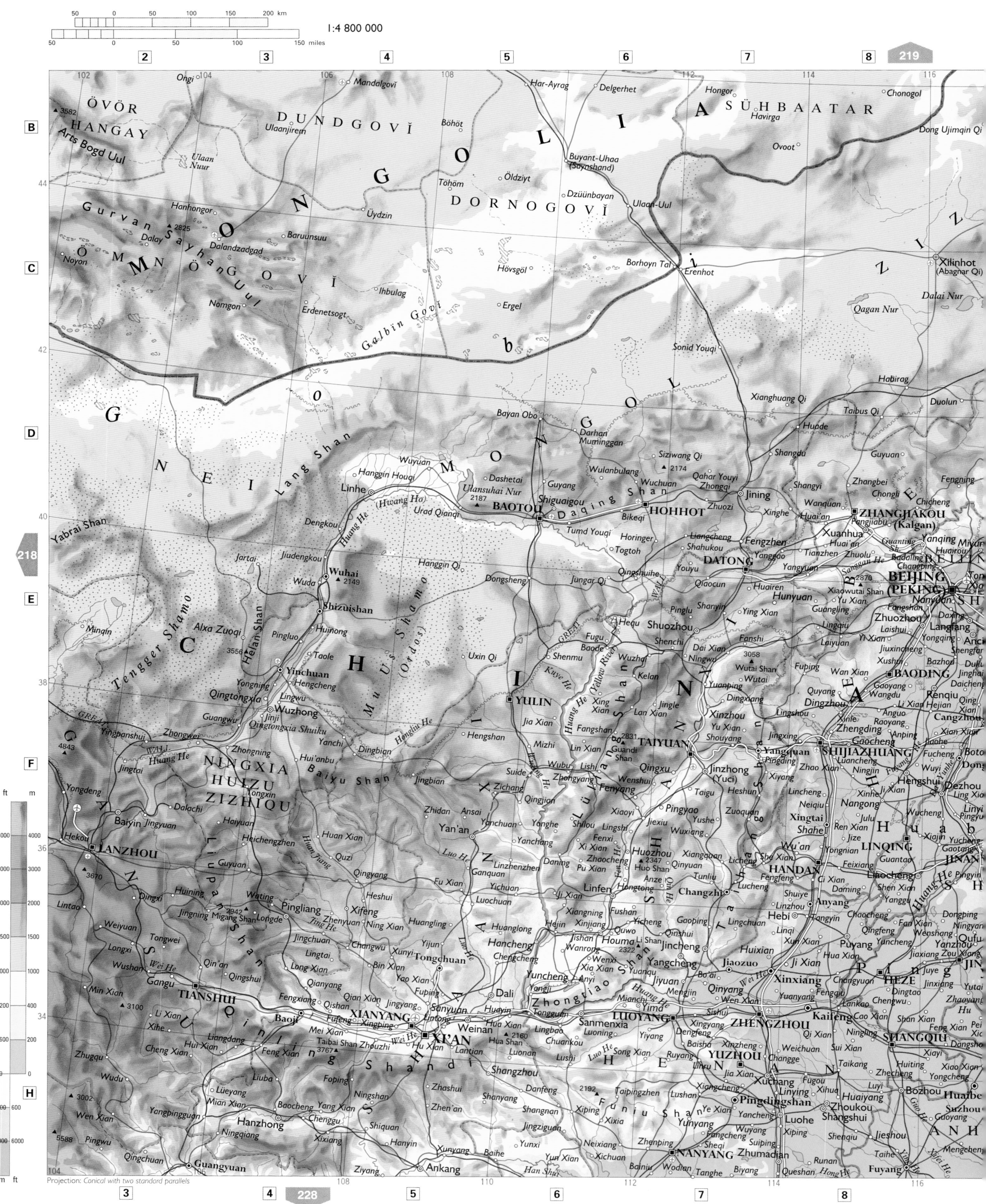

Projection: Conical with two standard parallels

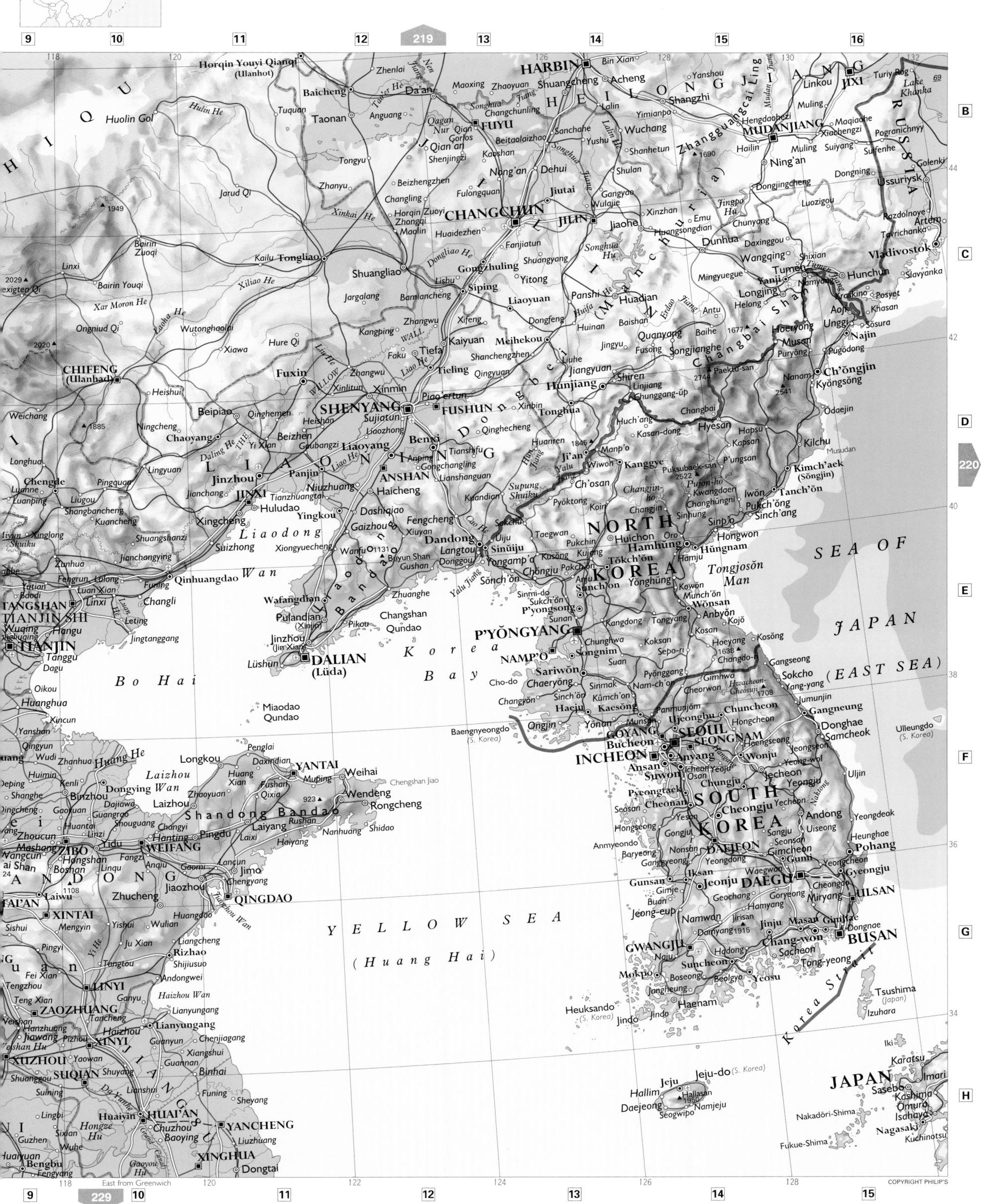

B

C

D

220

E

F

G

H

RUSSIA

HARBIN
MUDANJIANG
Vladivostok
Ussuriysk

HEILONGJIANG

CHANGCHUN
JILIN

Changbai Shan

NORTH
KOREA
P'YŎNGYANG
NAMP'O

SHENYANG
FUSHUN

LIAONING

DALIAN
(Lüda)

Bo Hai

Korea
Bay

SEA OF
JAPAN

(EAST SEA)

SEOUL
INCHEON
SEONGNAM

SOUTH
KOREA
DAEJEON

DAEGU
ULSAN
BUSAN

GWANGJU

YELLOW SEA

(Huang Hai)

Korea Strait

JAPAN

Jeju-do (S. Korea)

Nagasaki

TIANJIN SHI
TIANJIN

QINGDAO
WEIFANG
ZIBO
XINTAI
LINYI
ZAOZHUANG
XUZHOU
SUQIAN
HUAI'AN
YANCHENG
XINGHUA

1:4 800 000

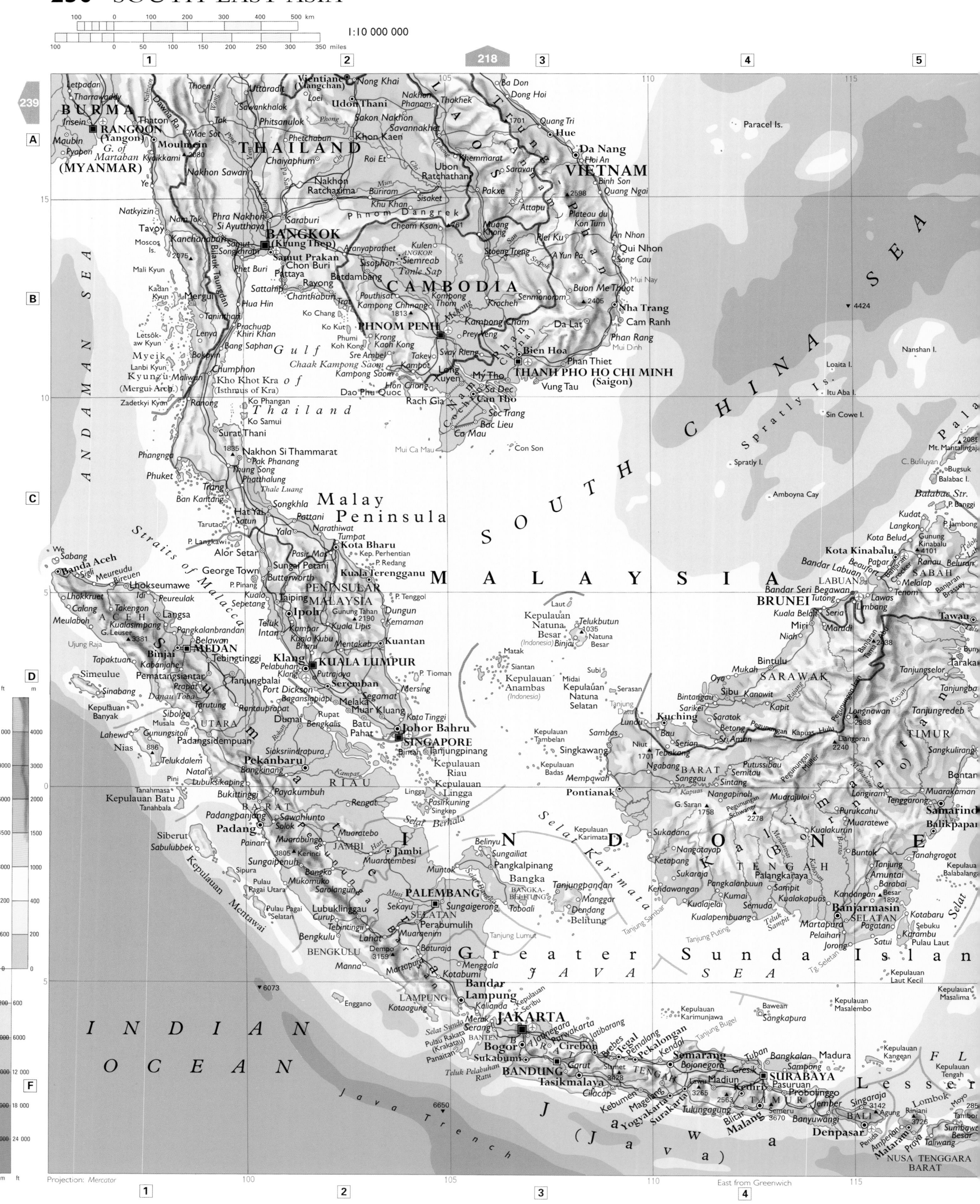

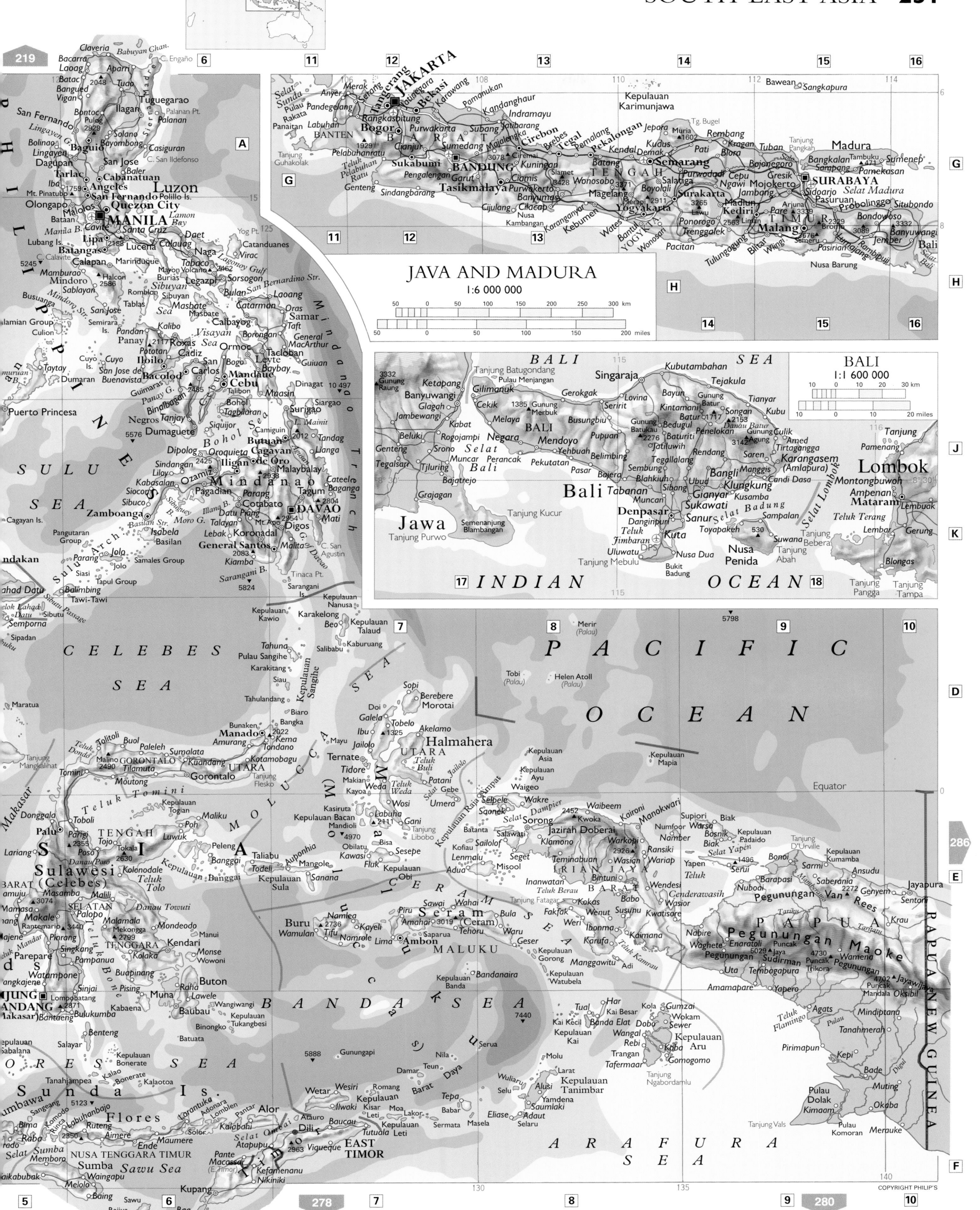

1:3 200 000

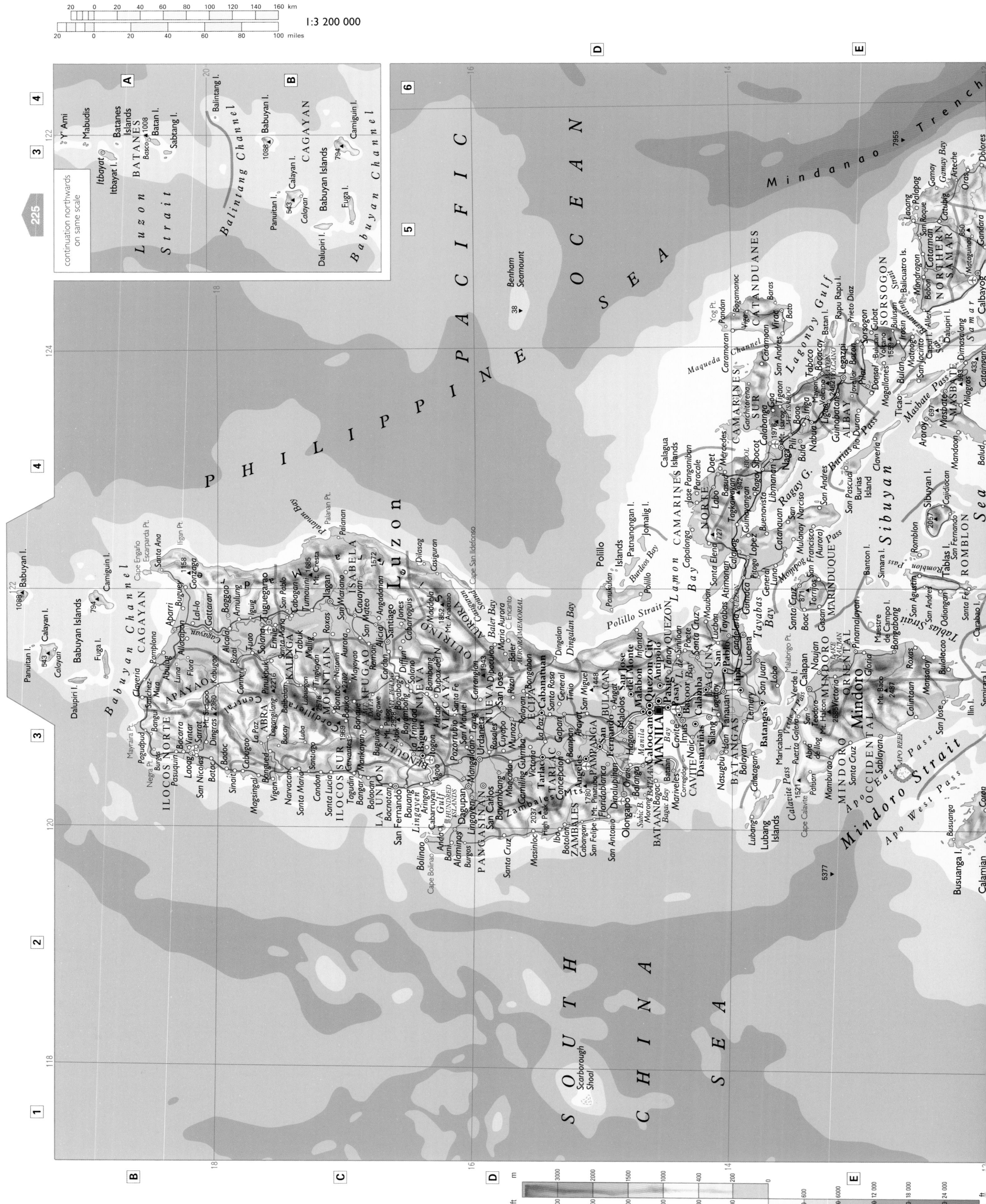

continuation northwards
on same scale

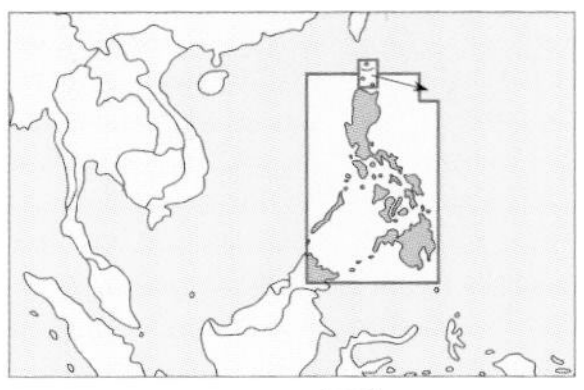

SULU SEA
CELEBES SEA
Mindanao
Palawan
Negros
Panay
Bohol Sea
Moro Gulf
Davao Gulf
Leyte Gulf
Illana Bay
PALAWAN Passage
Cuyo West Pass
Cuyo East Pass
Basilan Strait
Sulu Archipelago
MALAYSIA
SABAH
Borneo
Zamboanga
DAVAO
Cebu
Iloilo
Bacolod
Puerto Princesa
Cagayan de Oro
Iligan
General Santos
Cotabato
Tacloban
Dumaguete
Sandakan
Jolo
TUBBATAHA REEFS
Cagayan Is.
Turtle Islands
Sibutu Passage
Projection: Lambert Conformal Conic
East from Greenwich
COPYRIGHT PHILIP'S

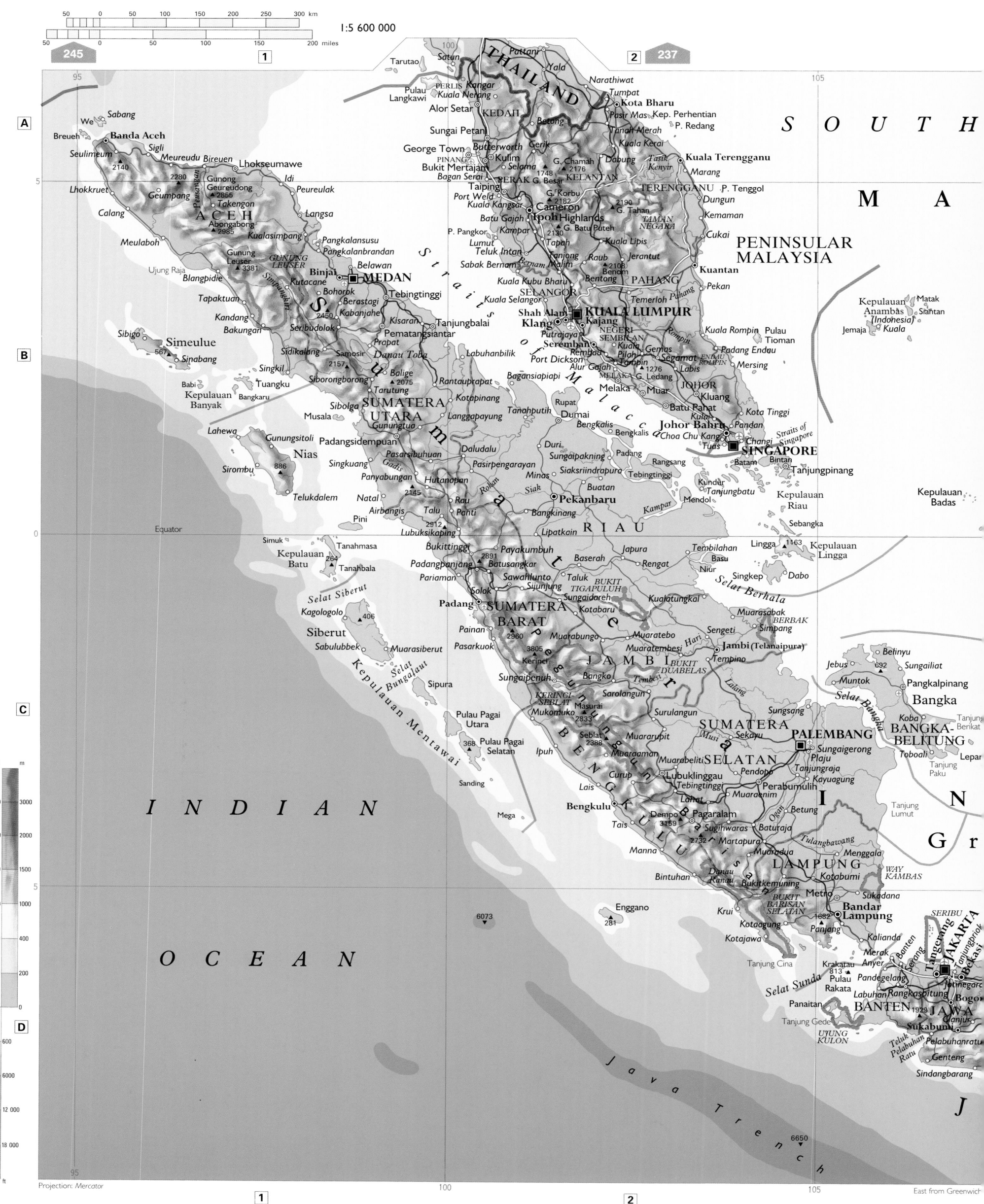

1:5 600 000

Projection: Mercator

East from Greenwich

3 **4** **5** 233

C H I N A   S E A

M A L A Y S I A

Laut

Kepulauan Natuna Besar *(Indonesia)* 1035 Natuna Besar Ranai Binjai
Midai Subi Serasan
Kepulauan Natuna Selatan *(Indonesia)*

Kepulauan Tambelan *(Indonesia)*

P. Balambangan
Tg. Sempang Mengayou P. Banggi 572
Kudat P. Malawali
Langkon Senaja P. Jambongan
KINABALU Datong Turtle Islands
Mt. Palin Tanjong Pisau
Kota Belud 2579 1216
Tuaran G. Tambuyukon 4101 Klagon Beluran SULU SEA
Kota Kinabalu Ranau 2000 Mt. Sandakan
Penampang G. Kinabalu Meutapok
Papar CROCKER RANGE Tambunan G. Trus Madi 2649
LABUAN Pulau Labuan Beaufort 1966 SABAH Batu Puteh Litang
Bandar Labuan Keningau Banjaran Witti Lamag Tungku
Sipitang 1667 Banjaran Maitland Kuamut Lahad Datu
BRUNEI Tenom Telok Lahad Datu Tanjong
Bandar Seri Begawan Lawas Persiangan Alang Sibuko Labian
Kuala Belait Limbang Lumaku Sapulot Kalabakan Sebatik Semporna
Lutong Bangar Lumbis Kunak 1310 **Tawau**
Miri Marudi 850 Atap Sipadan
LAMBIR HILLS GUNUNG MULU 2376 Longberang Sesayap **PHILIPPINES**
Niah G. Mulu Bunyu
SIMILAJAU NIAH HILLS Long Akah **Tarakan**
Tanjong Kidurong LOAGAN BUNUT KAYAN MENTARANG 1450 Tanjungselor
Bintulu 1064 Bukit Kalulong Nameh Longbia
Tubau 1641 Longjelai Berau Tanjungbatu
Oya Mukah Tatau Longagung Telukbayur (Berau) Maratua
Dalat Beraga Bukit Batu Bora Datadian Kongkemul Tanjungredeb Rantaupanjang
Sibu 987 1429 2012 2053 Muarawahau
Kanowit Bukit Batu Longnawan KALIMANTAN Sangkulirang
Sarikei Kapit 2988 Menyapa 2000 TIMUR Batuputih 510
Tanjong Datu *TANJUNG DATU* Tanjong Sipang Betong Hulu Baleh Kubumesaai Sepasu Tanjung Mangkalihat
Sematan 1650 Tanjong Po Tanjong Saratok 1390
Paloh *GUNUNG GADING* Lundu BAKO Debak Liangpran Tabang
Singkawang Bau KUBAH **Kuching** MALUDAM 2240 BalKlampo
Sambas 996 Simunjan BATANG AI Nahabuan *KUTAI* Bontang
Bengkayang 1701 Serian Sri Aman BENTUANG 1730 Equator
Niut Tebakang (Simanggang) Engkilili KARIMUN Murung Tenggarong **Samarinda** Donggala 2100
Mempawah Balaikarangan Danau Luar Putussibau Muarakaman Santan
Ngabang Danau Sentarum Nangamentebah Tabang Muarakaman Palu
Jungkat Balaisabut Semitau 1396 Sangasangadalam 3127
Pontianak Sintang 1744 Danau Jempang Sungaitiram
Sungaidurian Tayan Sekadau Nangamau Menate 1770 Muarajuloi Longiram Muarabenangin Samboja Lariang
Padangtikar KALIMANTAN Nangapinoh Melawi Purukcahu 1230 **Balikpapan** Karosa
BARAT Gunung Saran 1758 Seipinang Muaratewe Tewah Sebakung
510 Telukbatang BUKIT BAKA BUKIT RAYA Kualakurun Sulawesi
Maya Sukadana Kotabaru Pegunungan Schwaner 2278 Tahahgrogot (Celebes)
Nangatayap Sandai *GUNUNG PALUNG* Rantaupanjang KALIMANTAN Tanjung 1380 SULAWESI Mamuju
Ketapang Marau Tumbangsamba TENGAH Pujon Tamianglayang BARAT
Kepulauan Karimata Padang Riam Mendawai Bawan Palangkaraya Amuntai Jangeru 3074 Mamasa
Kualapesaguan Panopah Kasongan Buntok Barabai Kepulauan Balabalangan Malunda Makale
Tanjungpandan 510 Sukaraja Rantaupulut Sampit Kotabesi Pulangpisau Kandangan Tanjungbatu Onang Polewali
Manggar Sukamara Katawaringin Sampit Kualakapuas Marabahan Besar Majene Enrekang
Gantung Belitung Kualajelai Kumai Semuda Pangkoh 1892 Meratus 725 Parepare Pinrang
Membalong Dendang TANJUNG PUTING Kualapembuang **Banjarmasin** Banjarbaru Rantau Kotabaru Watansoppeng Rapang
Tanjung Sambar Teluk Sampit KALIMANTAN Sebuku Sumpangbinangae
I N D O N E S I A Tanjung Puting Martapura SELATAN Karambu Pangkajene Maros

eater S u n d a   I s l a n d s
Pelaihari Pagatan Pulau Laut Pangkajene
Batakan Kintap **UJUNG PANDANG** (Makasar)
Tanjung Selatan Jorong Sungguminasa 2871
Satui Patalasang Bantaeng
J A V A   S E A
Kepulauan Laut Kecil Bontosunggu
Kepulauan Masalembo
Bawean 645 Sangkapura Kepulauan Masalima
Kepulauan Karimunjawa *F L O R E S*
Tanjung Bugel Kepulauan Kangean Kepulauan Sabalana
Karawang Pamanukan Jepara Muria Kepulauan *S E A*
Purwokerto Subang Indramayu Rembang Kragan Tuban Tanjung Pangkah Sumenep Sabalana
Jatibarang Pemalang Kudus 1602 Bojonegoro Lamongan Sampang Kepulauan
Cirebon Brebes Pekalongan Batang Demak Pati Blora Gresik Madura Pamekasan Puteran Tengah
BANDUNG Majalengka Tegal Semarang Purwodadi Ngawi Mojokerto Bangkalan Sapudi
Garut Kuningan Slamet JAWA TENGAH Salatiga Sragen **SURABAYA** Pasuruan Sepanjang Kepulauan
Ciamis 3428 Wonosobo 3371 Madiun Sidoarjo Probolinggo Panarukan Tengah
Banjar Magelang Merapi Klaten Wilis Kertosono Pasuruan *L E S S E R   S u n d a   I s l a n d s*
Cilacap 2911 Sleman Yogyakarta Lawu 2563 Kediri Malang 3676 Lumajang Jember Bondowoso BALURAN
Nusa Kambangan Kebumen Wates YOGYAKARTA Ponorogo Madiun 3265 JAWA TIMUR Semeru Panarukan Bali Singaraja Moyo
Karanganyar Pacitan Trenggalek Tulungagung Blitar Wlingi Krangkasem Agung Sumbawa Tambora Sangeang
a w a Surakarta 3089 Rambipuji RINJANI 3142 Tanjung 2821 Dompu Raba Labuanbajo
(J a v a) MERU BETIRI Banyuwangi BALI BARAT Rinjani 3728 Alas Besar KOMODO
Nusa Barung Denpasar Mataram Praya Selong Taliwang Sumbawa Plampang Tente Sape Rinca
NUSA TENGGARA BARAT Lombok 1167 Sumbawa Flores
COPYRIGHT PHILIP'S

3 **4** **5**
110 115

1:4 800 000

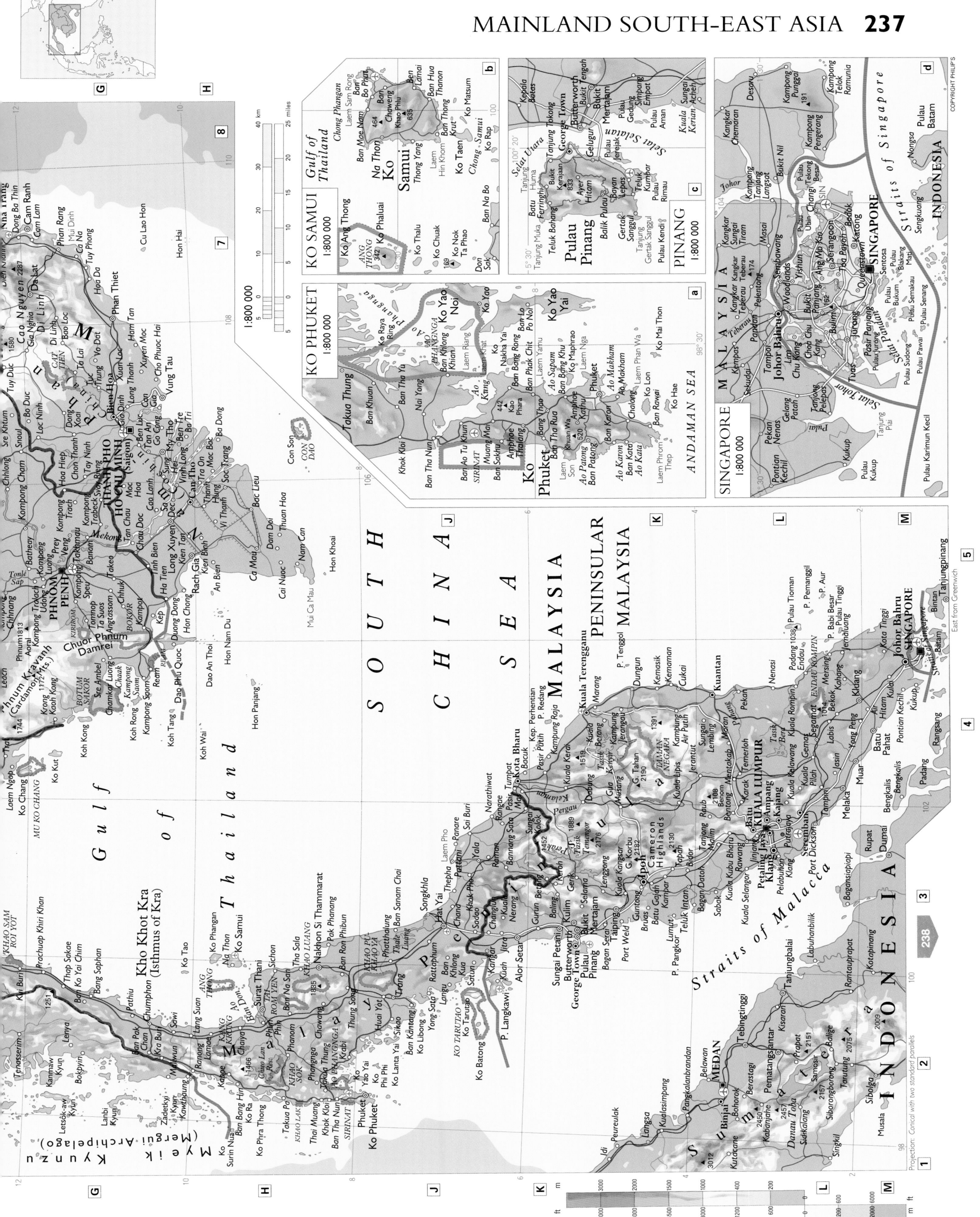

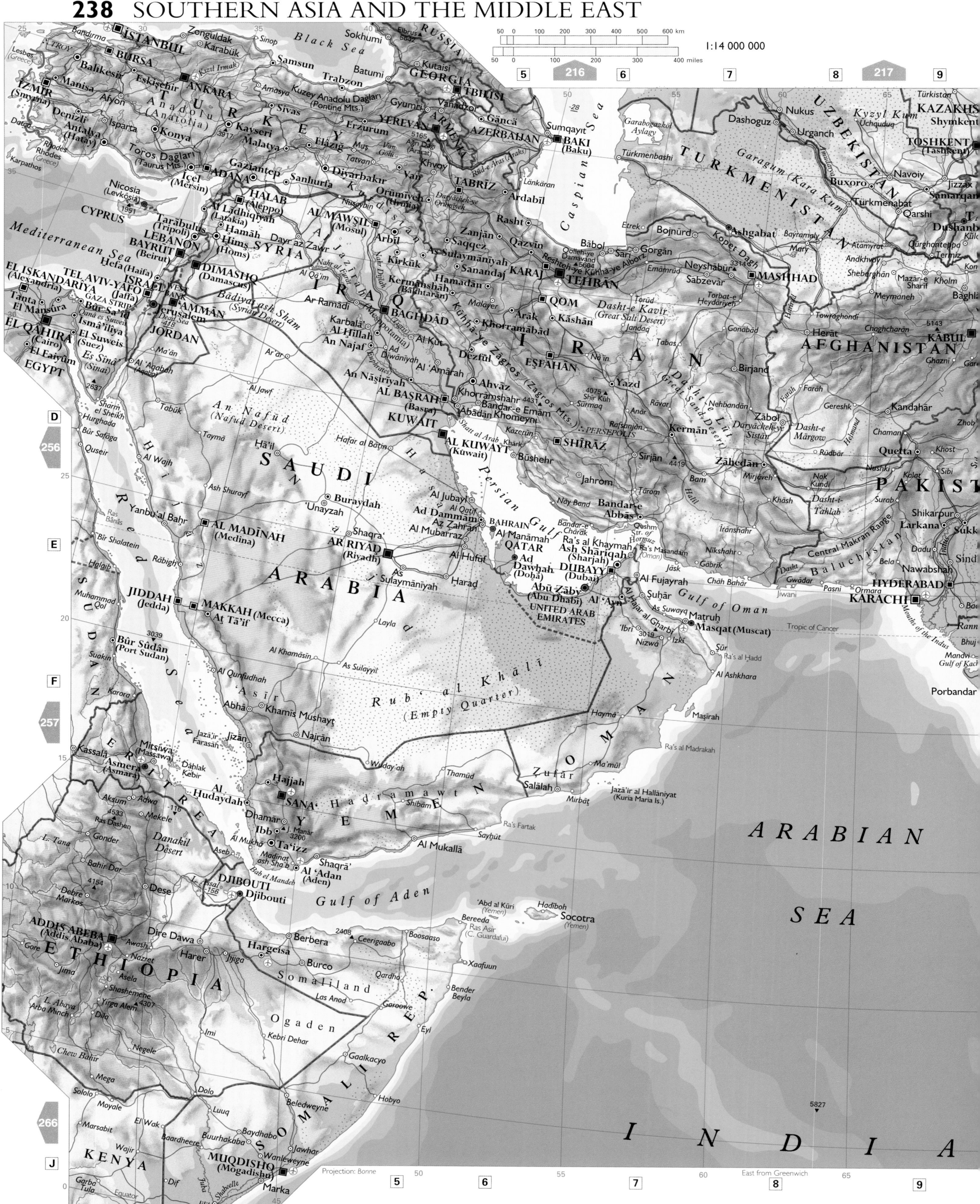

1:14 000 000

Projection: Bonne

East from Greenwich

50 0 50 100 150 200 250 300 km

1:5 600 000

50 0 50 100 150 200 miles

TURKMENISTAN

Garagum (Kara Kum)

UZBEKISTAN

TAJIKISTAN

CHINA

IRAN

AFGHANISTAN

Hindu Kush

PAKISTAN

INDIA

ARABIAN SEA

Tropic of Cancer

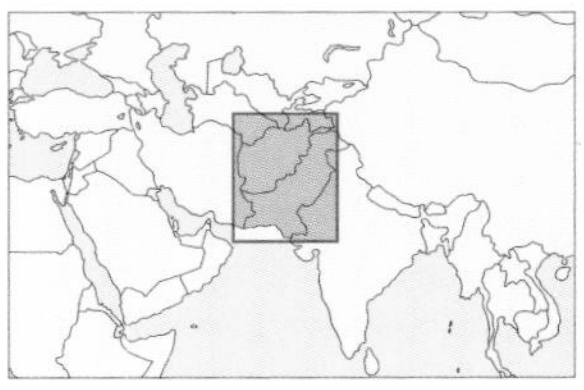

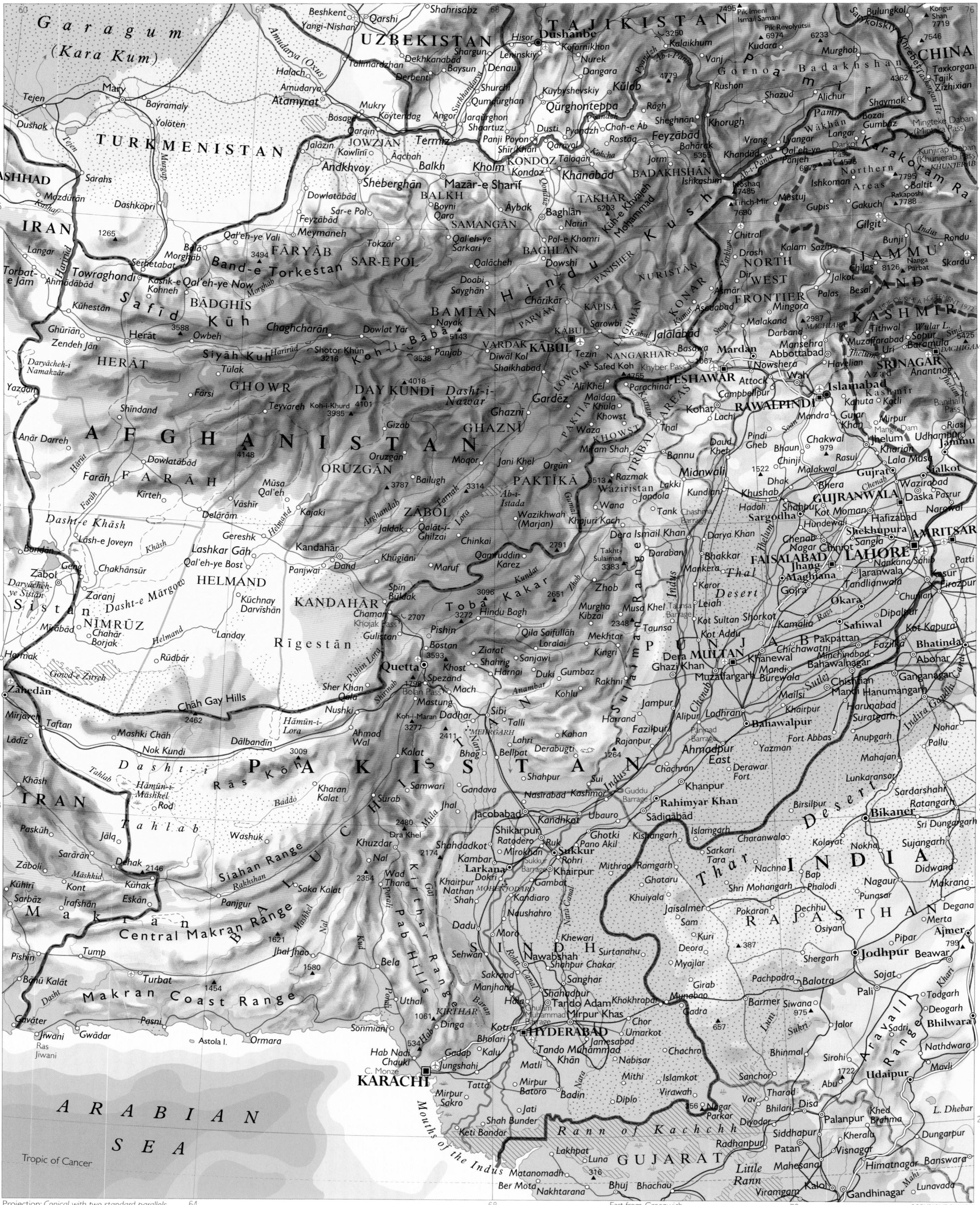

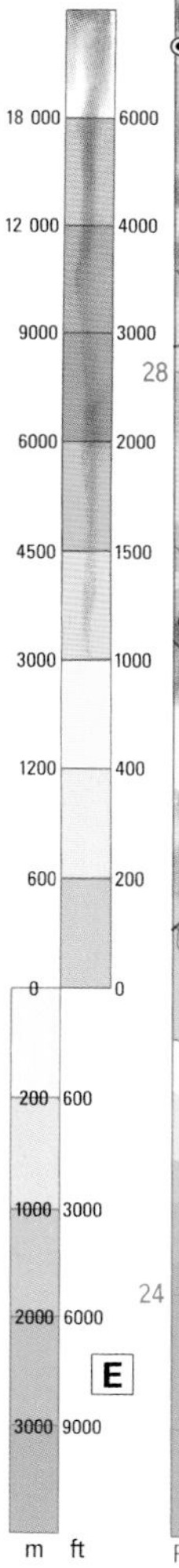

Projection: Conical with two standard parallels

East from Greenwich

COPYRIGHT PHILIP'S

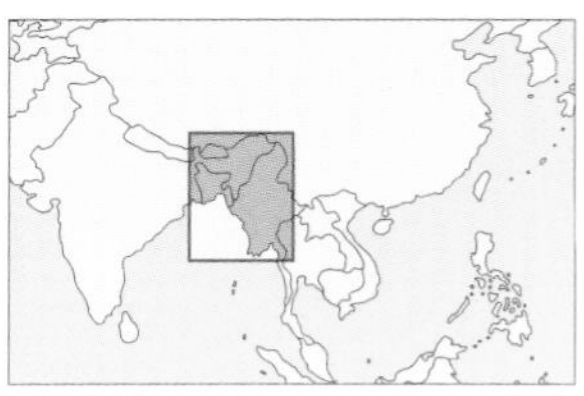

1:4 800 000

50 0 50 100 150 200 km
50 0 50 100 150 miles

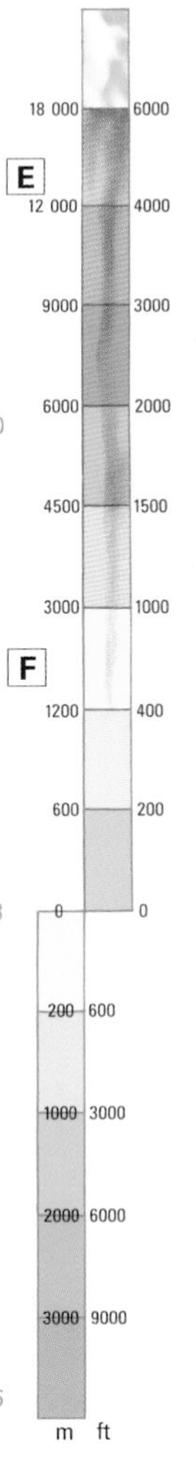

CHINA

XIZANG ZIZHIQU (TIBET)

NEPAL

BHUTAN

INDIA

ARUNACHAL PRADESH

Mishmi Hills

Abor Hills

ASSAM

NAGALAND

MEGHALAYA

Garo Hills   Khasi Hills

MANIPUR

SIKKIM

WEST BENGAL

BANGLADESH

TRIPURA

MIZORAM

SAGAING

KACHIN

YUNNAN

CHINA

DHAKA

RAJSHAHI

KHULNA

KOLKATA

CHITTAGONG

Tropic of Cancer

CHIN

BURMA (MYANMAR)

SHAN

MAGWE

PEGU

KAYAH

THAILAND

MON

Mandalay

RANGOON (YANGON)

Moulmein

BAY OF BENGAL

INDIAN OCEAN

Mouths of the Ganges

The Sandheads

Arakan Coast

Mouths of the Irrawaddy

G. of Martaban

Projection: Conical with two standard parallels

East from Greenwich

COPYRIGHT PHILIP'S

ft m
18 000 6000
12 000 4000
9000 3000
6000 2000
4500 1500
3000 1000
1200 400
600 200
0 0
200 600
1000 3000
2000 6000
3000 9000
m ft

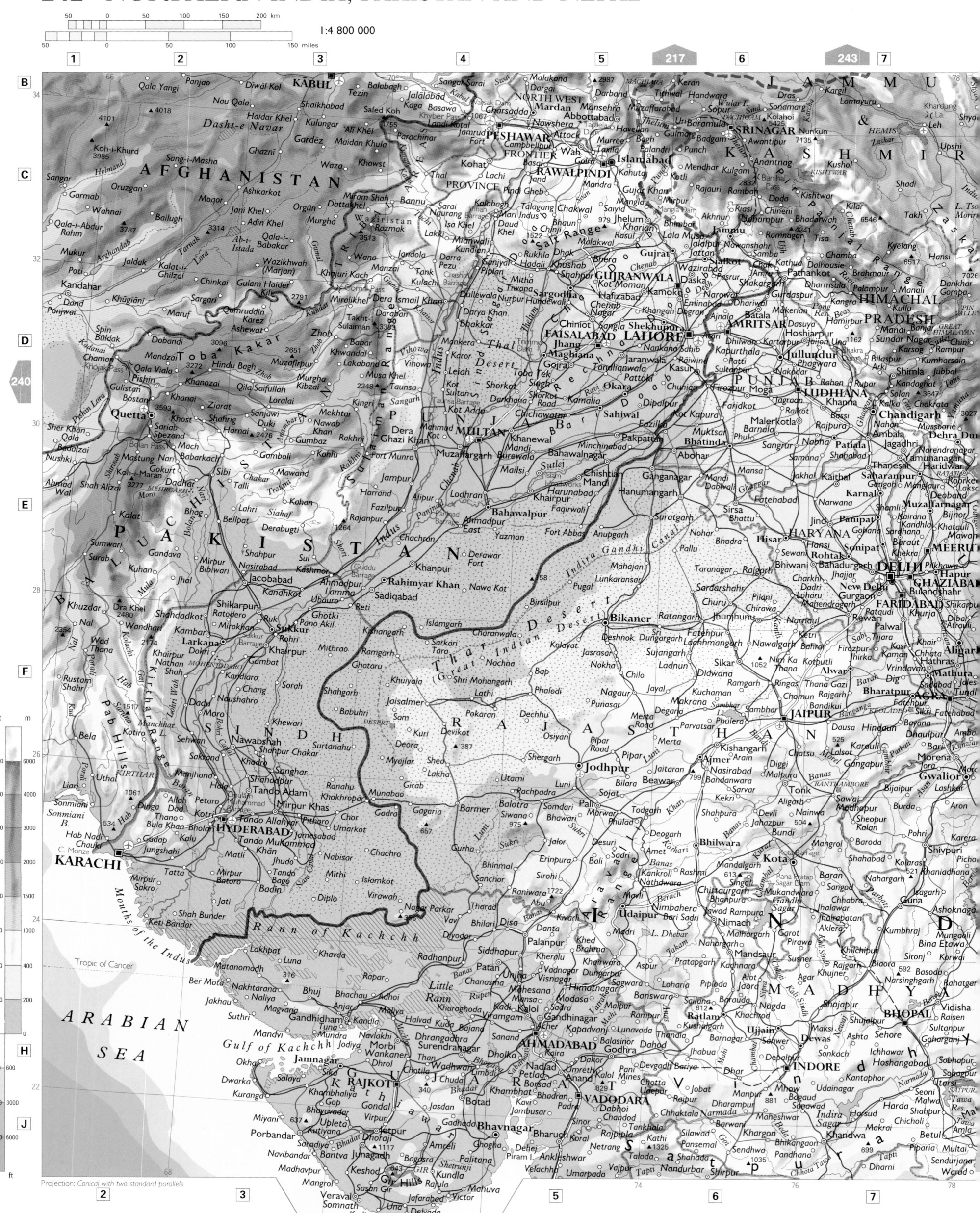

1:4 800 000

Projection: Conical with two standard parallels

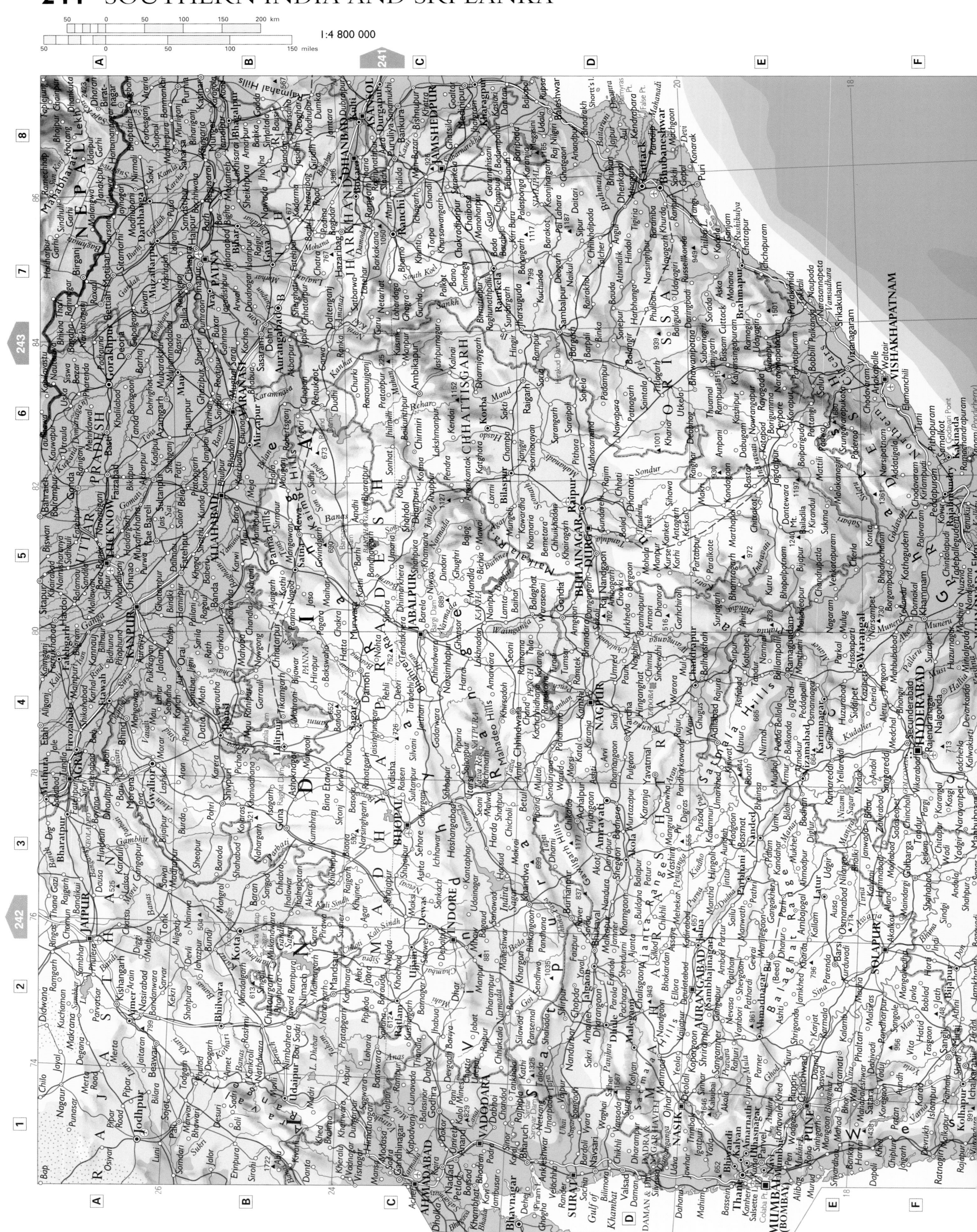

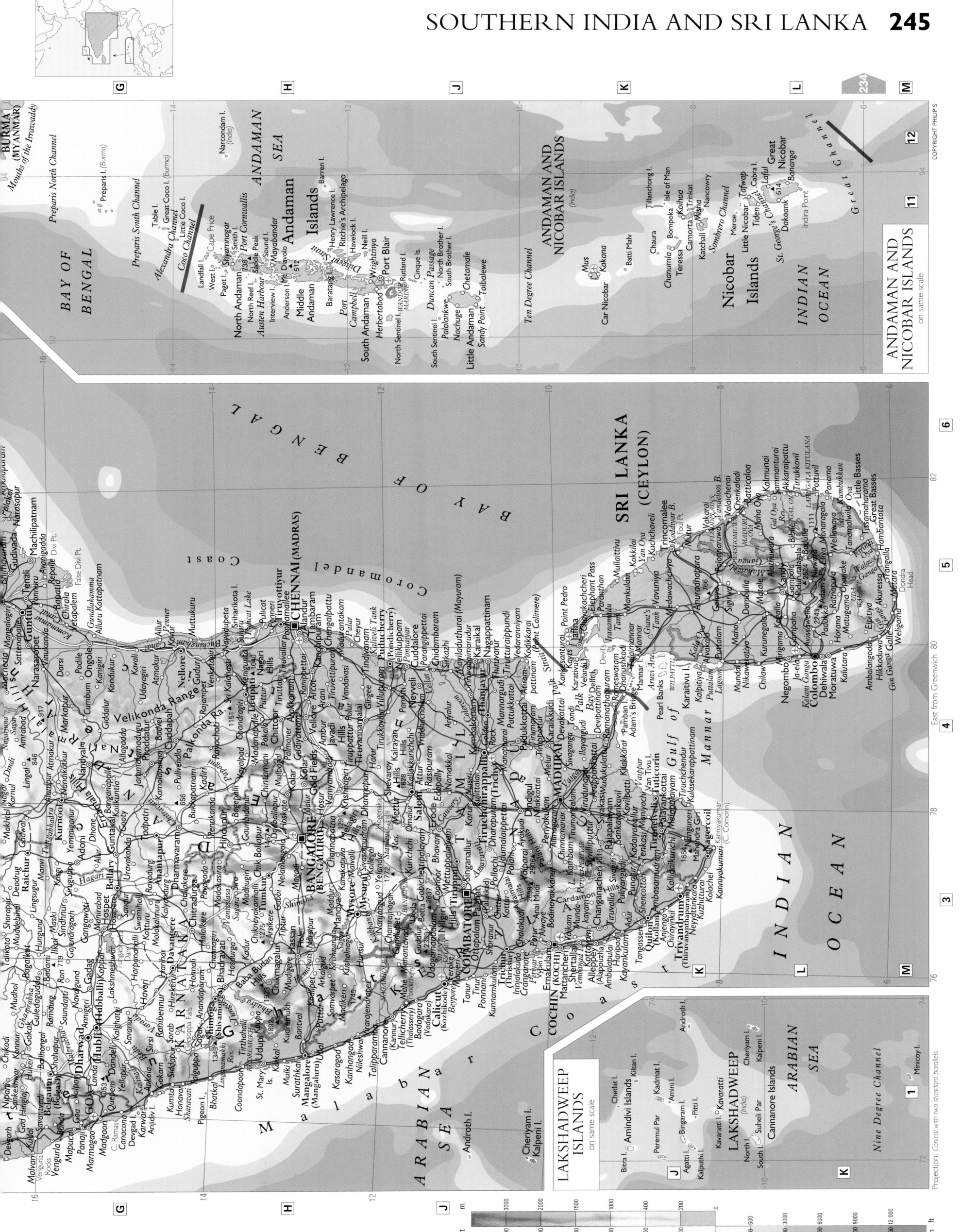

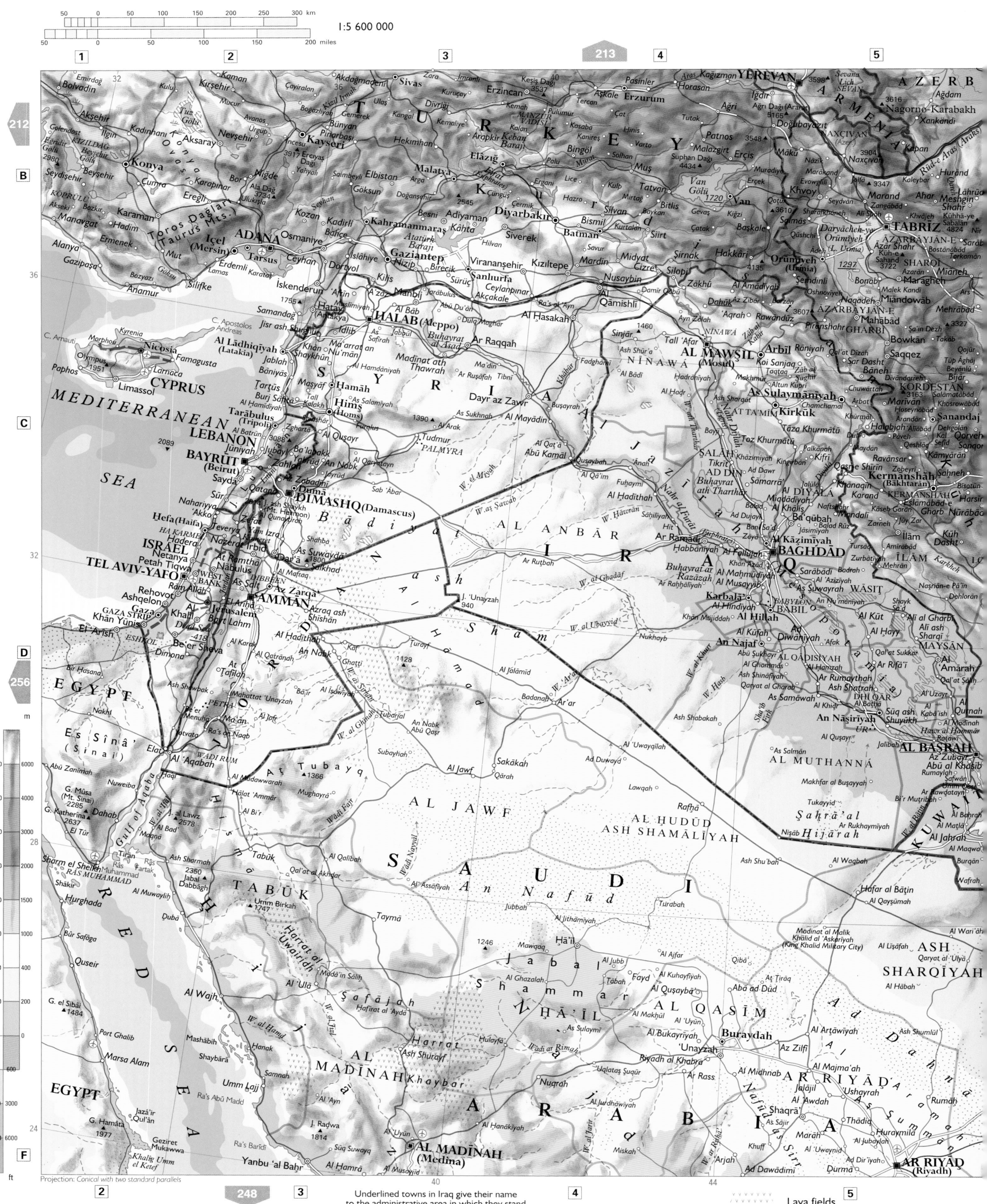

1:5 600 000

Projection: Conical with two standard parallels

Underlined towns in Iraq give their name
to the administrative area in which they stand

Lava fields

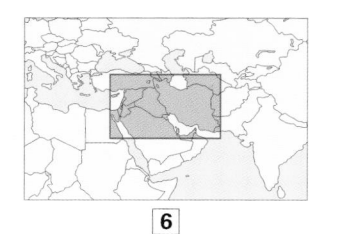

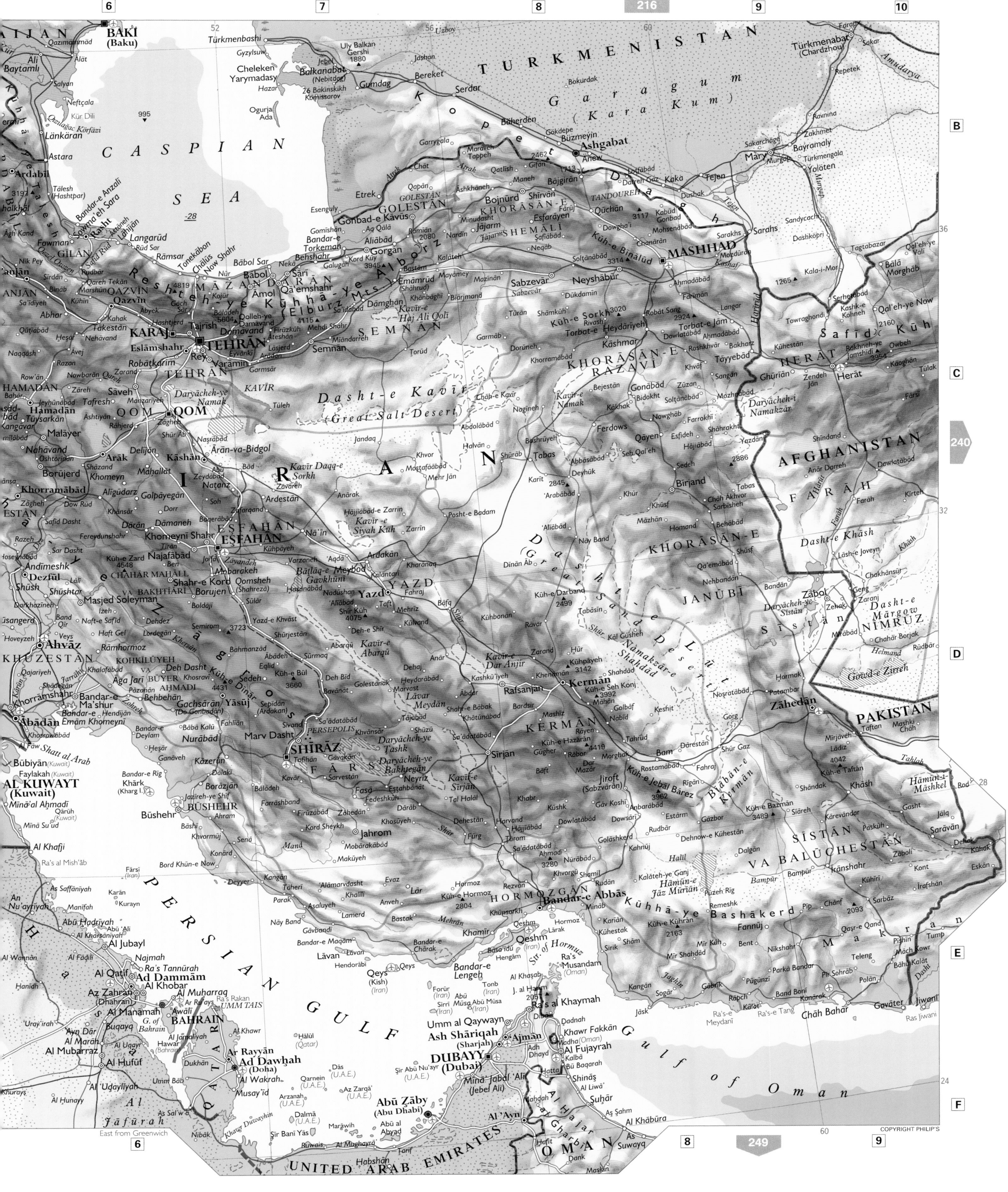

1:5 600 000

Projection: Conical with two standard parallels

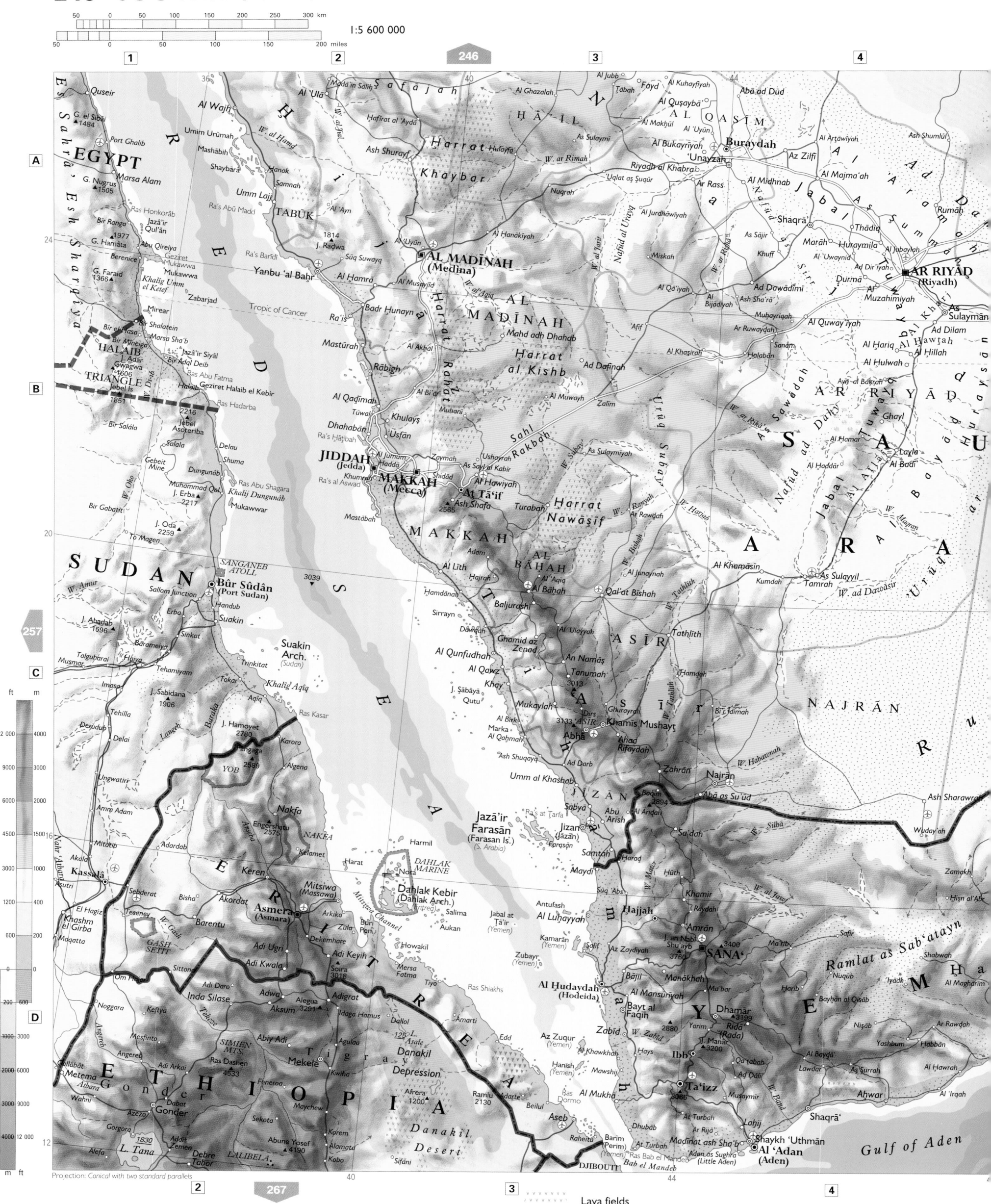

Lava fields

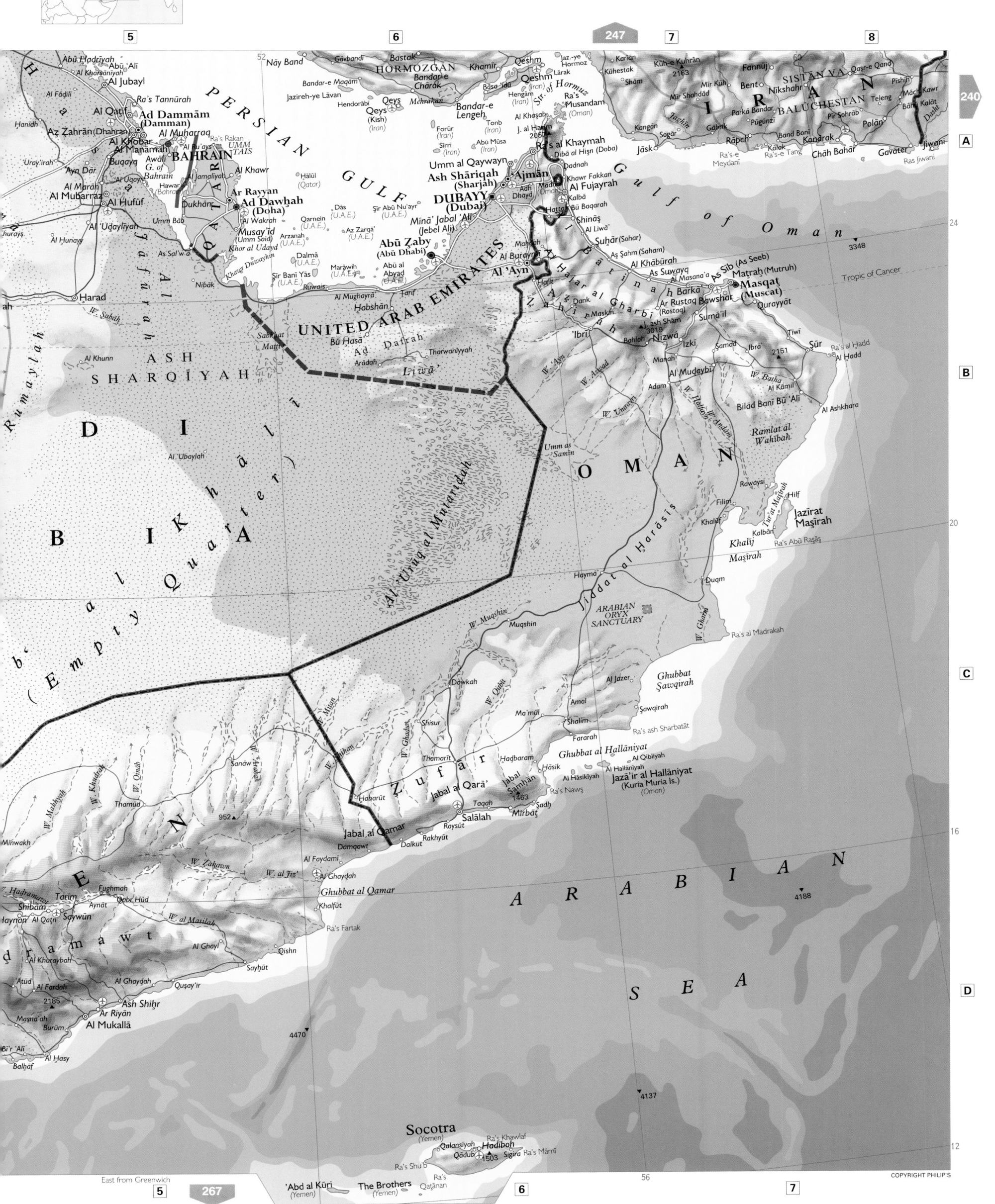

1:2 000 000

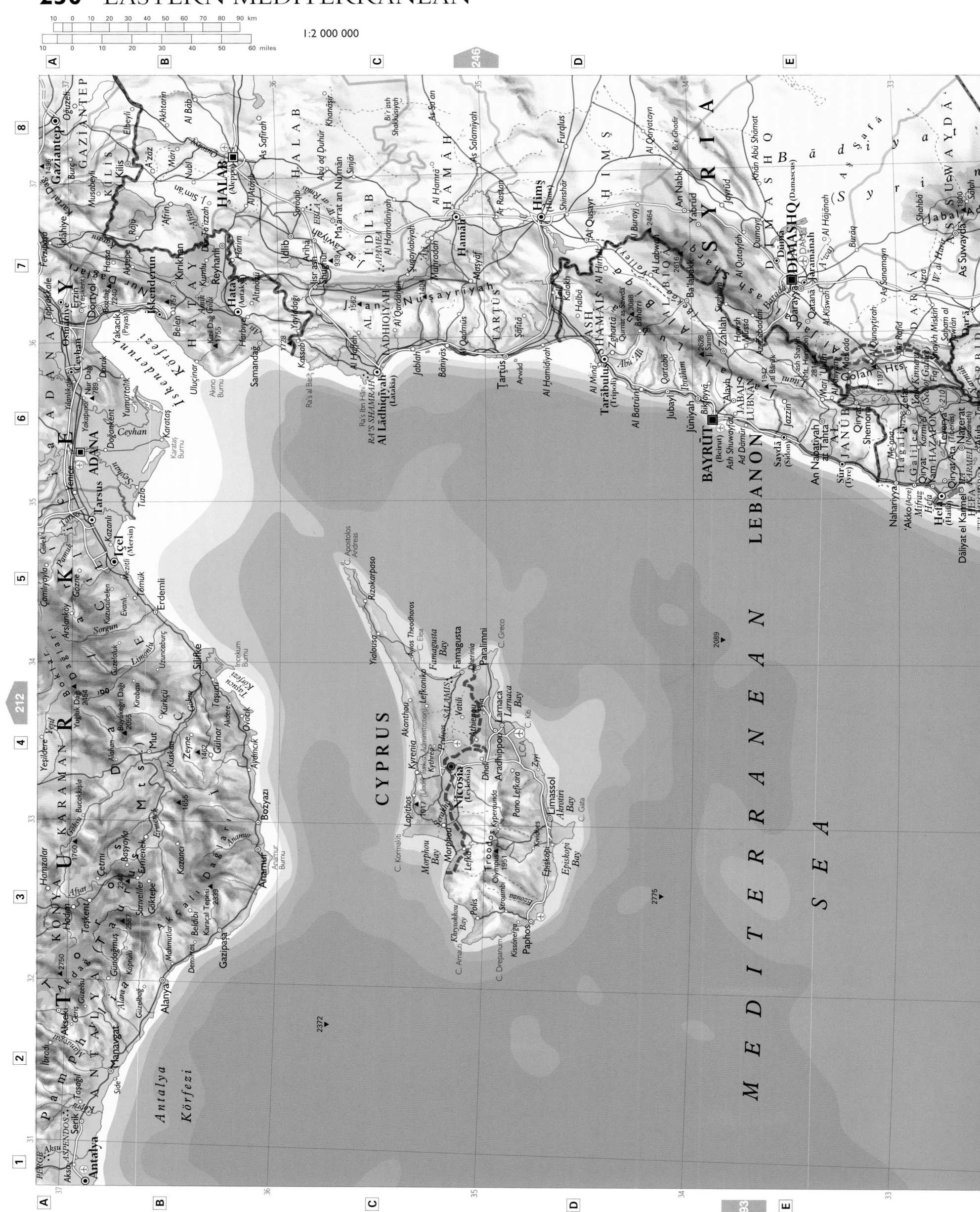

MEDITERRANEAN SEA

CYPRUS

SYRIA

LEBANON

TURKEY

HALAB (Aleppo)

Hịmṣ (Homs)

Hamāh

DIMASHQ (Damascus)

BAYRŪT (Beirut)

Nicosia (Lefkosia)

ANTALYA

Antalya Körfezi

İskenderun Körfezi

ADANA

Tarsus

İçel (Mersin)

Al Lādhiqīyah (Latakia)

Ṭarābulus (Tripoli)

Famagusta

Larnaca Bay

Limassol

Paphos

Gaziantep

=== 1974 Cease Fire Lines

AFRICA

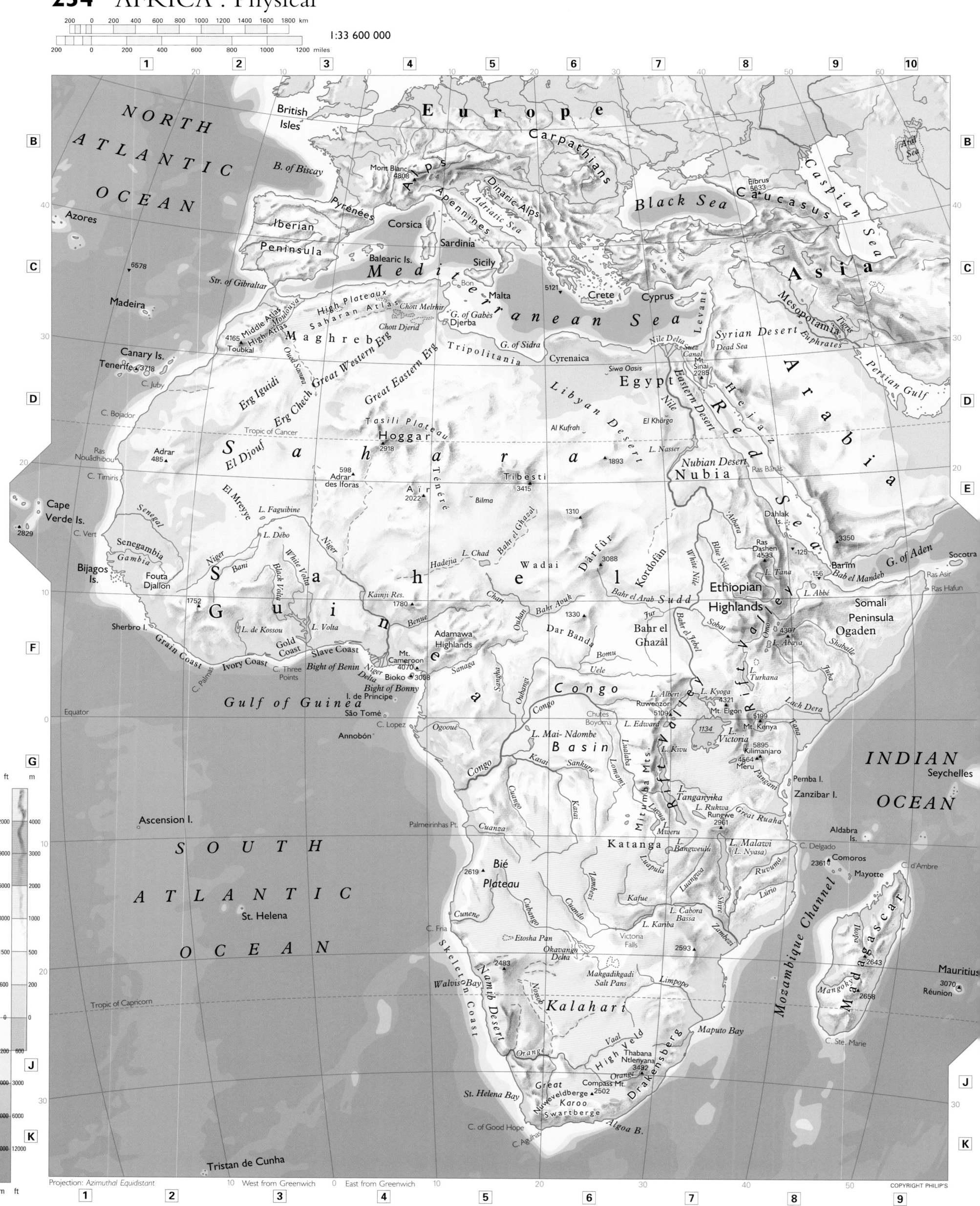

1:33 600 000

Projection: Azimuthal Equidistant

COPYRIGHT PHILIP'S

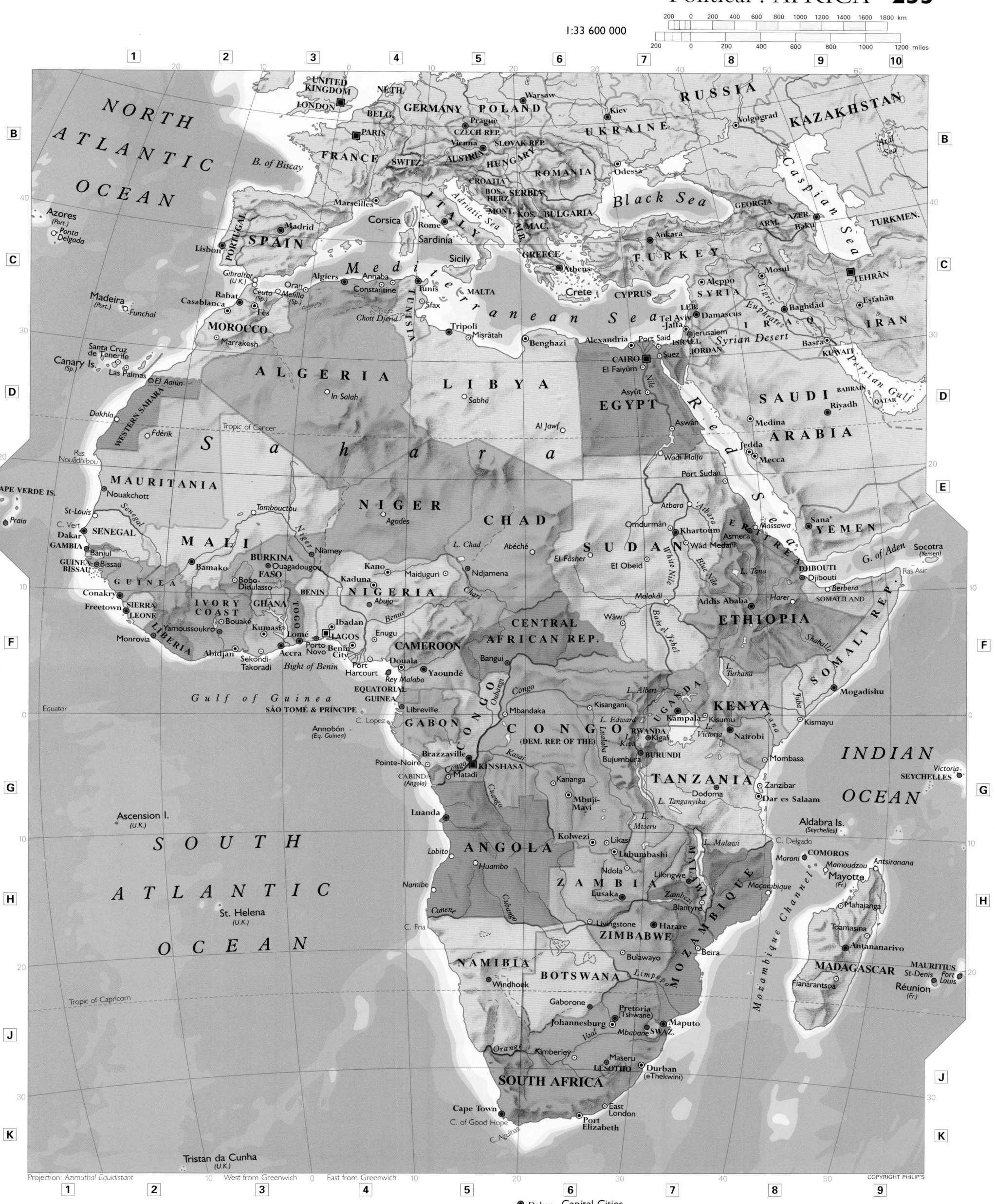

1:33 600 000

200 0 200 400 600 800 1000 1200 1400 1600 1800 km

200 0 200 400 600 800 1000 1200 miles

1 | **2** | **3** | **4** | **5** | **6** | **7** | **8** | **9** | **10**

NORTH

ATLANTIC

OCEAN

B. of Biscay

UNITED KINGDOM
LONDON
NETH.
BELG.
FRANCE
SWITZ.
GERMANY
POLAND
Warsaw
Prague
CZECH REP.
Vienna
SLOVAK REP.
AUSTRIA
HUNGARY
CROATIA
BOS.-HERZ.
MONT.
KOS.
MAC.
SERBIA
BULGARIA
ROMANIA
Odessa
UKRAINE
Kiev
RUSSIA
Volgograd
KAZAKHSTAN
Aral Sea

Paris
Marseilles
Corsica
ITALY
Rome
Sardinia
Adriatic Sea
Black Sea
GEORGIA
ARM.
AZER.
Baku
Caspian Sea
TURKMEN.

PORTUGAL
SPAIN
Madrid
Lisbon
Gibraltar (U.K.)
Sicily
GREECE
Athens
Crete
CYPRUS
Ankara
TURKEY
Aleppo
Mosul
SYRIA
Tehrān
Eṣfahān
IRAN

Madeira (Port.)
Funchal
Santa Cruz de Tenerife
Canary Is. (Sp.)
Las Palmas
Rabat
Casablanca
Fès
Marrakesh
MOROCCO
Oran
Melilla (Sp.)
Ceuta (Sp.)
Algiers
Annaba
Constantine
Mediterranean Sea
Tunis
TUNISIA
MALTA
Sfax
Tripoli
Miṣrātah
Benghazi
Alexandria
Port Said
Damascus
LEB.
Tel Aviv -Jaffa
ISRAEL
Jerusalem
JORDAN
Baghdād
Euphrates
Tigris
Basra
KUWAIT
Persian Gulf
BAHRAIN
QATAR

Dakhla
Ras Nouâdhibou
WESTERN SAHARA
El Aaiún
Fdérik
Tropic of Cancer
ALGERIA
In Salah
Sabhā
LIBYA
Al Jawf
EGYPT
Asyût
Aswân
Cairo
El Faiyûm
Suez
Nile
Red Sea
Medina
Jedda
Mecca
SAUDI
ARABIA
Riyadh

CAPE VERDE IS.
Praia
C. Vert
Dakar
GAMBIA
Banjul
GUINEA-BISSAU
Bissau
SENEGAL
Nouakchott
St-Louis
Senegal
MAURITANIA
Tombouctou
MALI
Bamako
Niger
Agadès
NIGER
Niamey
L. Chad
CHAD
Abéché
Ndjamena
El Fâsher
SUDAN
Omdurmân
Khartoum
Wâd Medani
El Obeid
Atbara
Atbara
Port Sudan
Wadi Halfa
Massawa
Asmera
ERITREA
Sana'
YEMEN
G. of Aden
Socotra (Yemen)
Ras Asir

Conakry
Freetown
SIERRA LEONE
Monrovia
LIBERIA
GUINEA
BURKINA FASO
Ouagadougou
Bobo-Dioulasso
IVORY COAST
Yamoussoukro
Bouaké
Abidjan
Sekondi-Takoradi
GHANA
Kumasi
Accra
TOGO
Lomé
Porto Novo
BENIN
Benin City
Lagos
Ibadan
Kaduna
Kano
Maiduguri
NIGERIA
Abuja
Enugu
Benue
CAMEROON
Douala
Yaoundé
Rey Malabo
Bangui
CENTRAL AFRICAN REP.
Chari
L. Tana
DJIBOUTI
Djibouti
Berbera
SOMALILAND
Addis Ababa
Harer
ETHIOPIA
Blue Nile
White Nile
Wâw
Malakâl
Bahr el Jebel
Shabeelle
SOMALI REP.
Mogadishu

Gulf of Guinea
Bight of Benin
Port Harcourt
EQUATORIAL GUINEA
SÃO TOMÉ & PRÍNCIPE
Libreville
C. Lopez
GABON
Annobón (Eq. Guinea)
Equator
CONGO
Brazzaville
Pointe-Noire
KINSHASA
Matadi
CABINDA (Angola)
CONGO (DEM. REP. OF THE)
Mbandaka
Ubangi
Congo
Kasai
Kananga
Mbuji-Mayi
Kisangani
L. Albert
L. Edward
UGANDA
Kampala
RWANDA
Kigali
BURUNDI
Bujumbura
L. Kivu
Lualaba
Kisumu
L. Victoria
Nairobi
KENYA
Turkana
L. Turkana
Juba
Kismayu
INDIAN
OCEAN
Victoria
SEYCHELLES
Mombasa

Ascension I. (U.K.)
SOUTH
ATLANTIC
OCEAN
St. Helena (U.K.)
Luanda
ANGOLA
Lobito
Huambo
Namibe
Cuanza
Kwango
Kasai
Cuango
TANZANIA
Dodoma
Dar es Salaam
Zanzibar
L. Tanganyika
L. Mweru
Kolwezi
Likasi
Lubumbashi
Ndola
L. Malawi
C. Delgado
Aldabra Is. (Seychelles)
COMOROS
Moroni
Mamoudzou
Mayotte (Fr.)
Antsiranana

ZAMBIA
Lusaka
Lilongwe
MALAWI
Blantyre
Zambezi
Moçambique
MOZAMBIQUE
Mahajanga
Tropic of Capricorn

Cubango
Cunene
C. Fria
Livingstone
Harare
ZIMBABWE
Bulawayo
Beira
Mozambique Channel
Toamasina
MADAGASCAR
Antananarivo
MAURITIUS
St-Denis
Port Louis
Réunion (Fr.)
Fianarantsoa

NAMIBIA
Windhoek
BOTSWANA
Gaborone
Limpopo
Pretoria (Tshwane)
Maputo
Johannesburg
Vaal
Mbabane SWAZ.
Kimberley
Orange
Maseru
LESOTHO
Durban (eThekwini)
SOUTH AFRICA

Cape Town
C. of Good Hope
C. Agulhas
Port Elizabeth
East London

Tristan da Cunha (U.K.)

Projection: Azimuthal Equidistant

10 West from Greenwich 0 East from Greenwich 10

1 | **2** | **3** | **4** | **5** | **6** | **7** | **8** | **9**

● Dakar Capital Cities

COPYRIGHT PHILIP'S

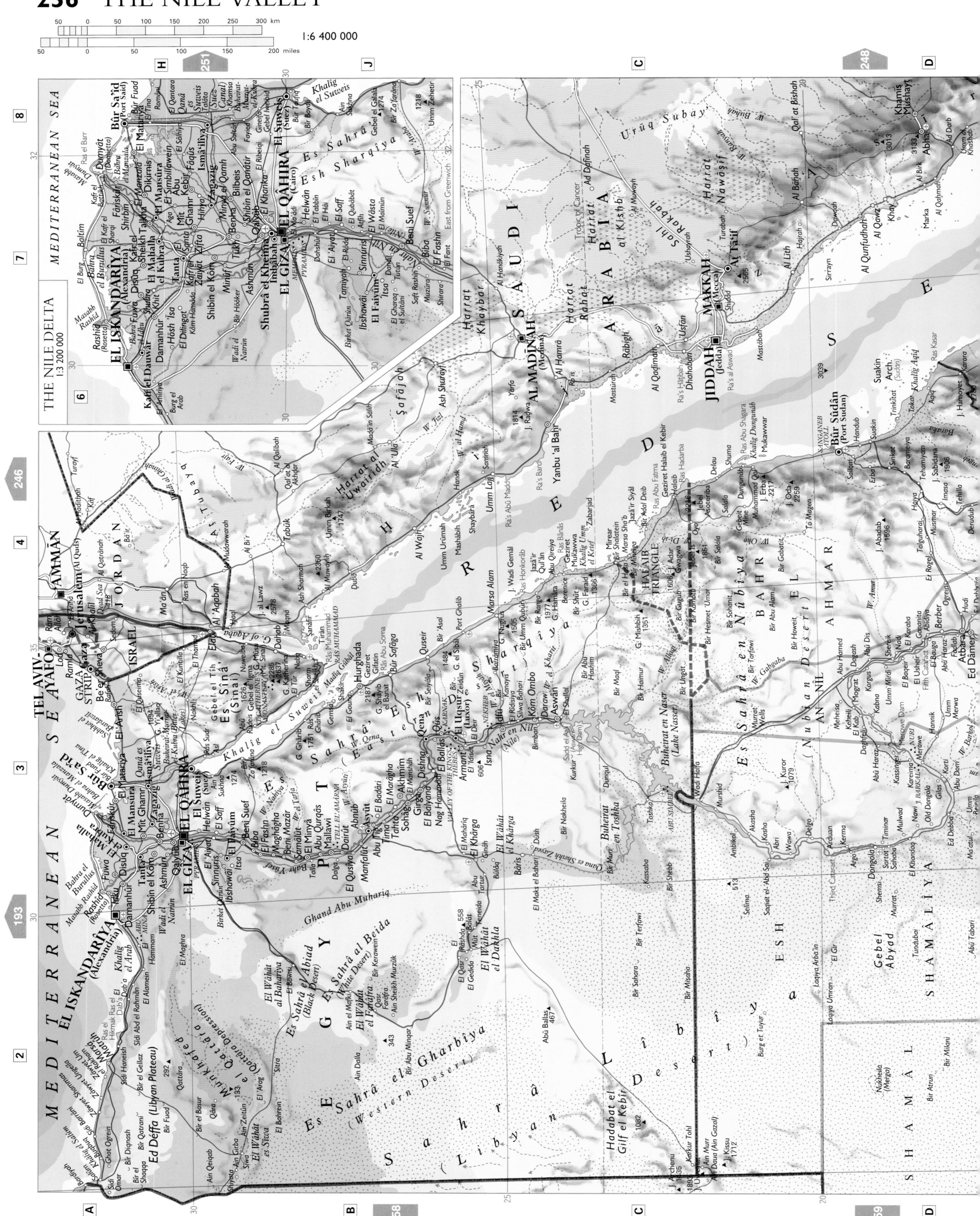

1:6 400 000

THE NILE DELTA
1:3 200 000

MEDITERRANEAN SEA

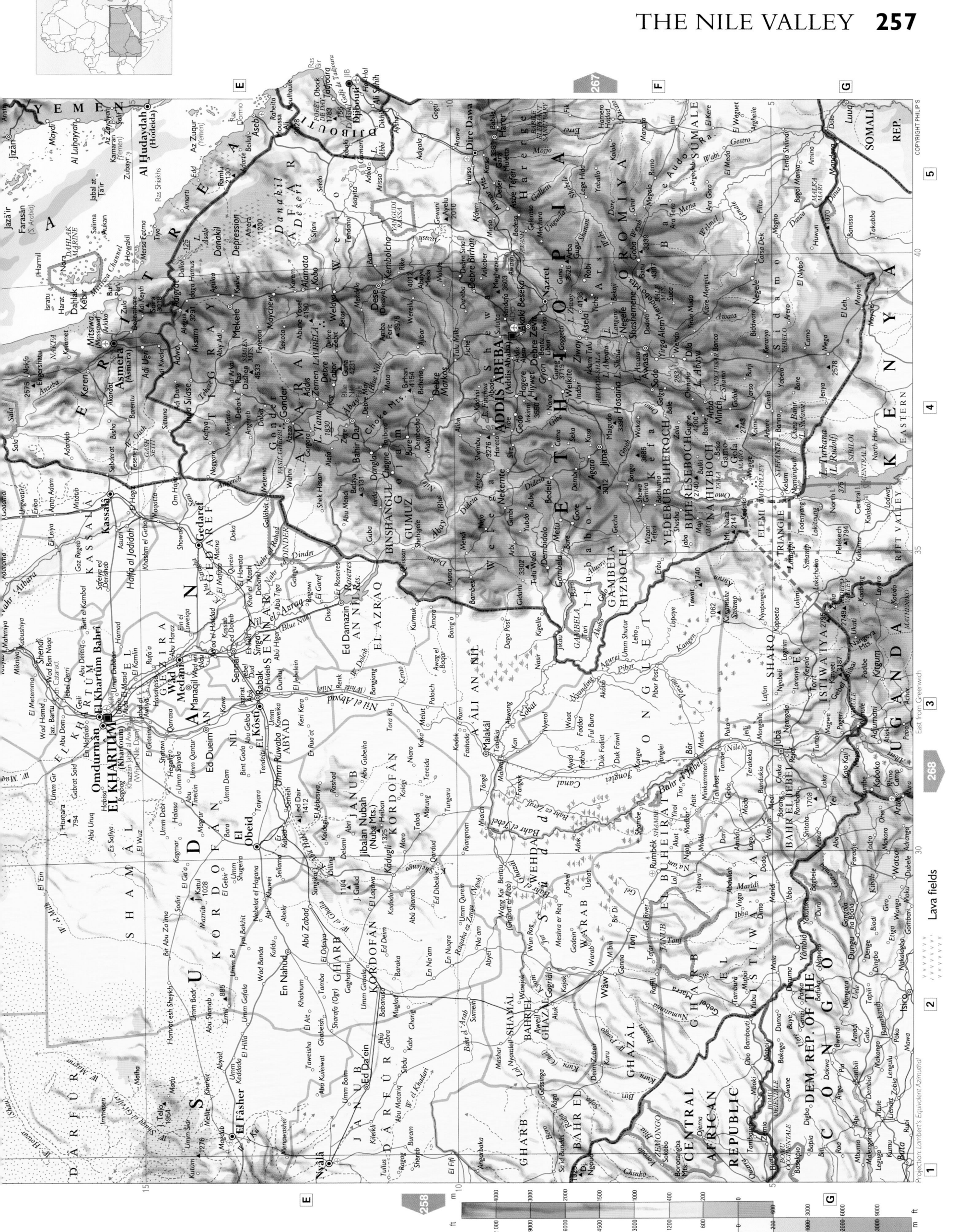

50 0 50 100 150 200 250 300 km

1:6 400 000

50 0 50 100 150 200 miles

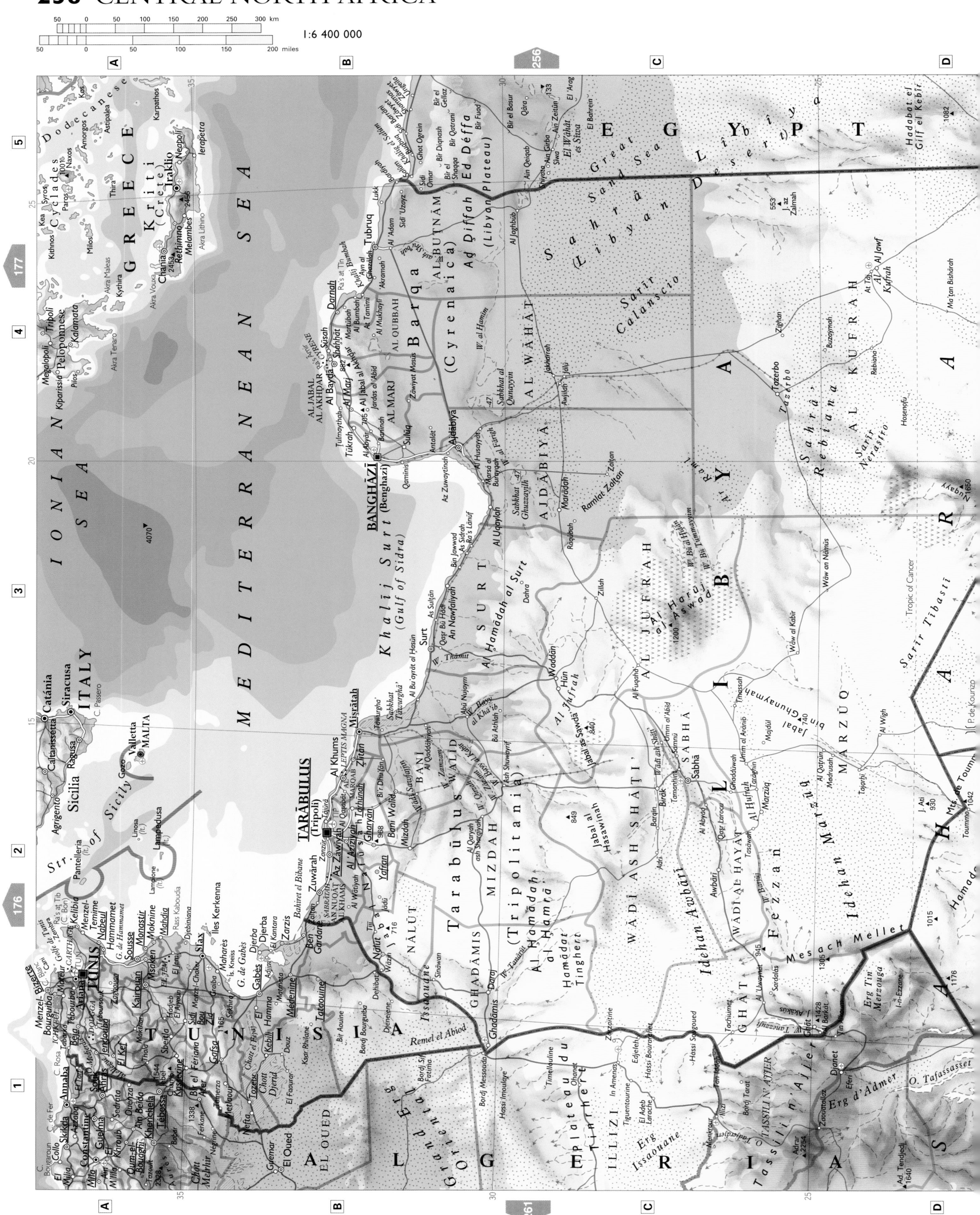

GREECE

Dodecanese

Kriti (Crete)
Iraklio

Cyclades

Peloponnese

IONIAN SEA

MEDITERRANEAN SEA

ITALY

Sicilia (Sicily)

Str. of Sicily

MALTA

TUNIS

TUNISIA

ALGERIA

BANGHĀZĪ (Benghazi)

Khalīj Surt (Gulf of Sidra)

TARĀBULUS (Tripoli)

Tarābulus (Tripolitania)

Darrnah

Barqa (Cyrenaica)

AL JABAL AL AKHDAR

AL QUBBAH

AL MARJ

AJDĀBIYĀ

SURT

AL WĀHĀT

Sahrā' Lībiyā (Libyan Desert)

EGYPT

Sarir Calanscio

Great Sand Sea

Ed Déffa (Libyan Plateau)

AL BUTNĀM

Tubruq

AL KUFRAH

Al Kufrah

LIBYA

Sarir Rebiana

Sarir Nerastro

Sarir Tibasti

Tropic of Cancer

MIZDAH

BANI WALĪD

GHADĀMIS

NALŪT

AL JUFRAH

WĀDĪ ASH SHĀTI'

SABHĀ

WADĪ AL HAYĀT

Fezzan

MARZŪQ

GHĀT

Idehan Awbārī

Idehan Marzūq

Mesach Mellet

TASSILI N'AJJER

Erg d'Admer

Erg Issaouane

Plateau du Tinrhert

ILLIZI

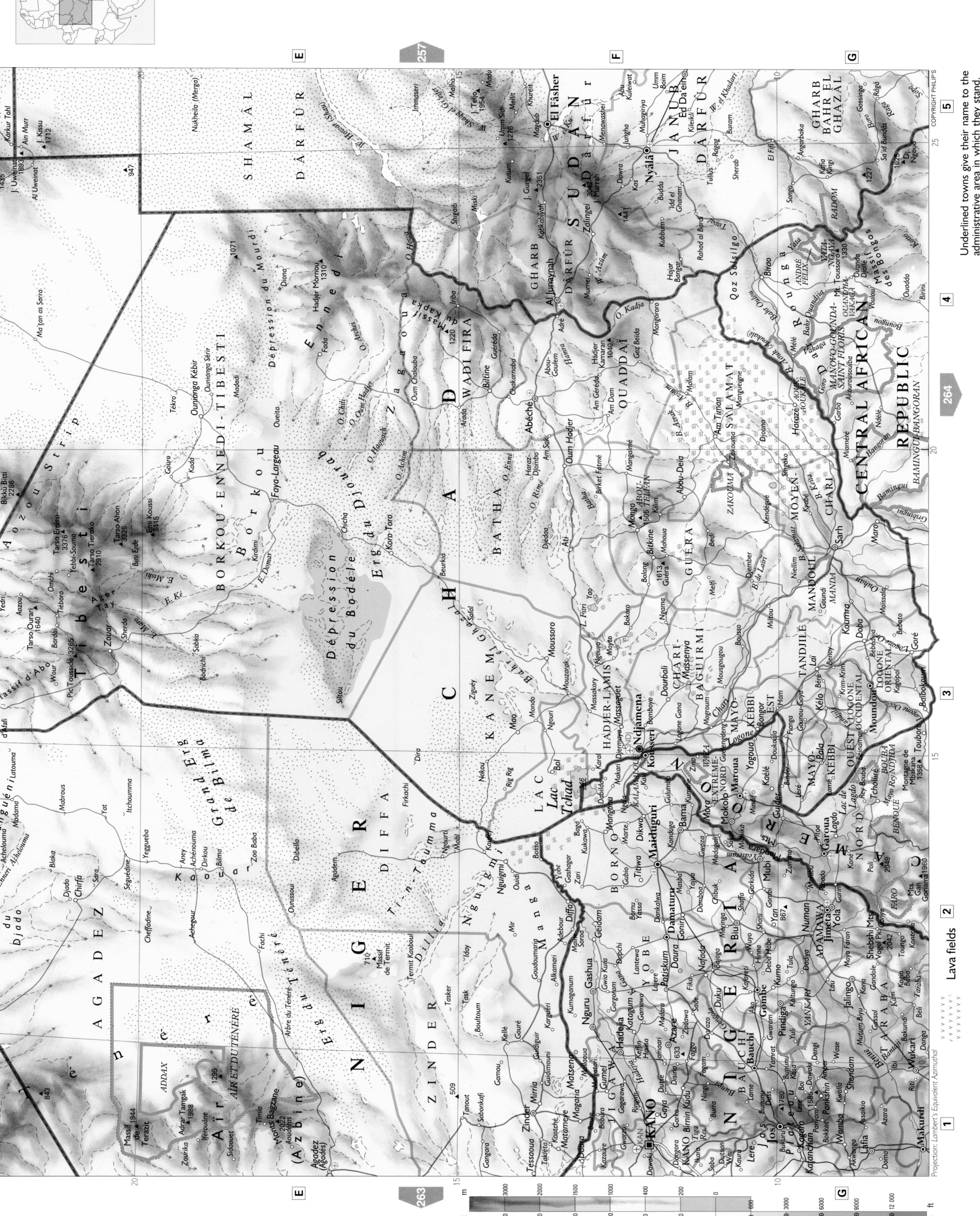

Underlined towns give their name to the administrative area in which they stand.

Lava fields

Projection: Lambert's Equivalent Azimuthal

COPYRIGHT PHILIP'S

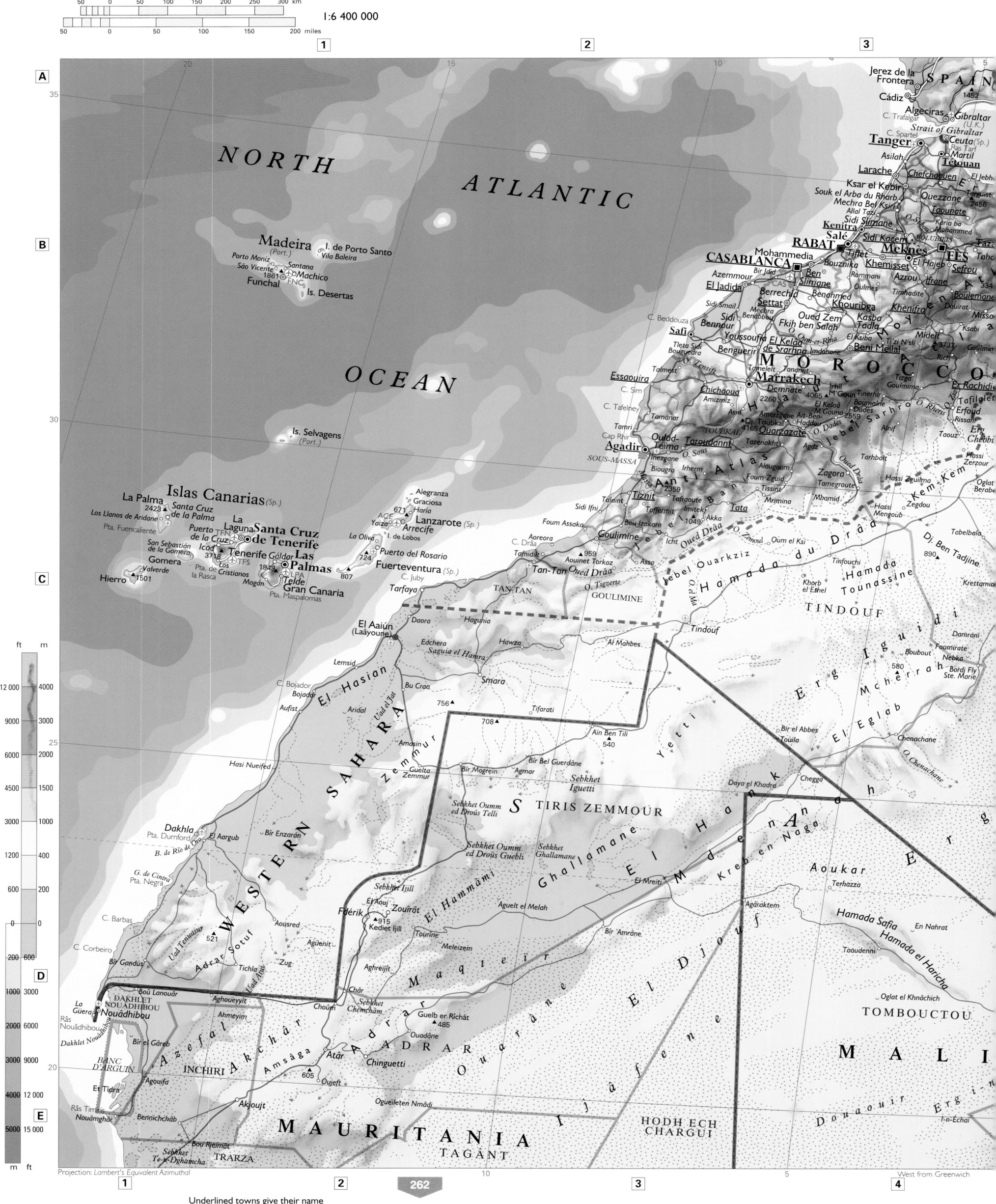

1:6 400 000

Projection: Lambert's Equivalent Azimuthal

Underlined towns give their name
to the administrative area in which they stand

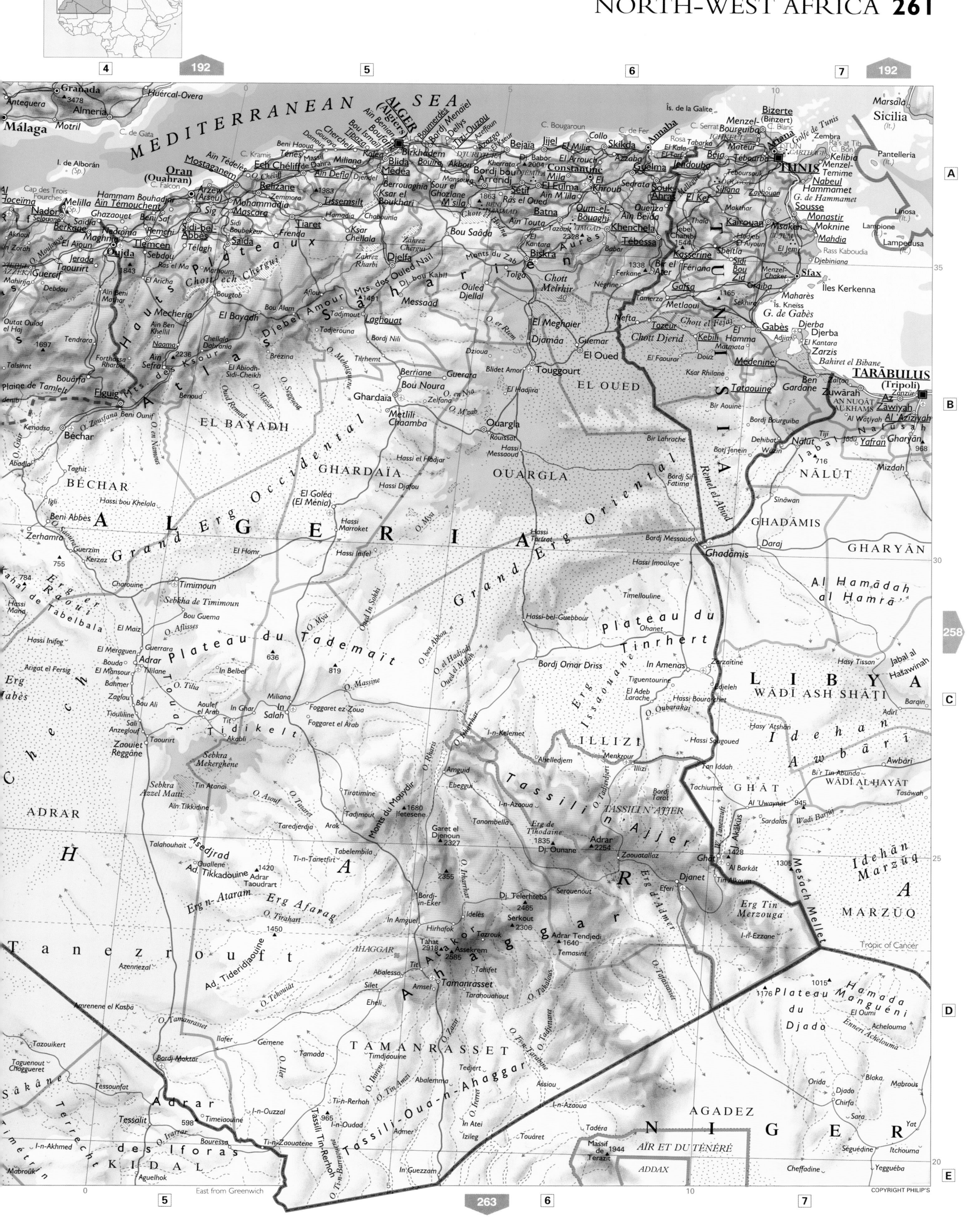

MEDITERRANEAN SEA

Málaga
Antequera
Almería
Motril
I. de Alborán (Sp.)
Huércal-Overa
C. de Gata
Granada
3478
Oran (Quahran)
Mostaganem
C. Falcon
Arzew (Arseu)
Mohammadia
Sig
Mascara
Relizane
Tiaret
Frenda
Chellala
Ksar Chellala
Aïn Defla
Miliana
Blida
Médéa
ALGER (Algiers)
Birkhadem
Boumerdès
Bordj Menaïel
Dellys
Tizi-Ouzou
Azeffoun
Bejaïa
Jijel
El Milia
Skikda
Collo
Annaba
Bizerte (Binzert)
Menzel-Bourguiba
TUNIS
Sicilia (It.)
Marsalà
Pantelleria (It.)

MEDITERRANEAN

ALGERIA

LIBYA

TUNISIA

NIGER

Tropic of Cancer

East from Greenwich

COPYRIGHT PHILIP'S

258

A

B

C

D

E

Projection : Lambert's Equivalent Azimuthal

Underlined towns give their name to the
administrative area in which they stand.

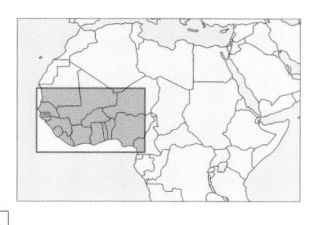

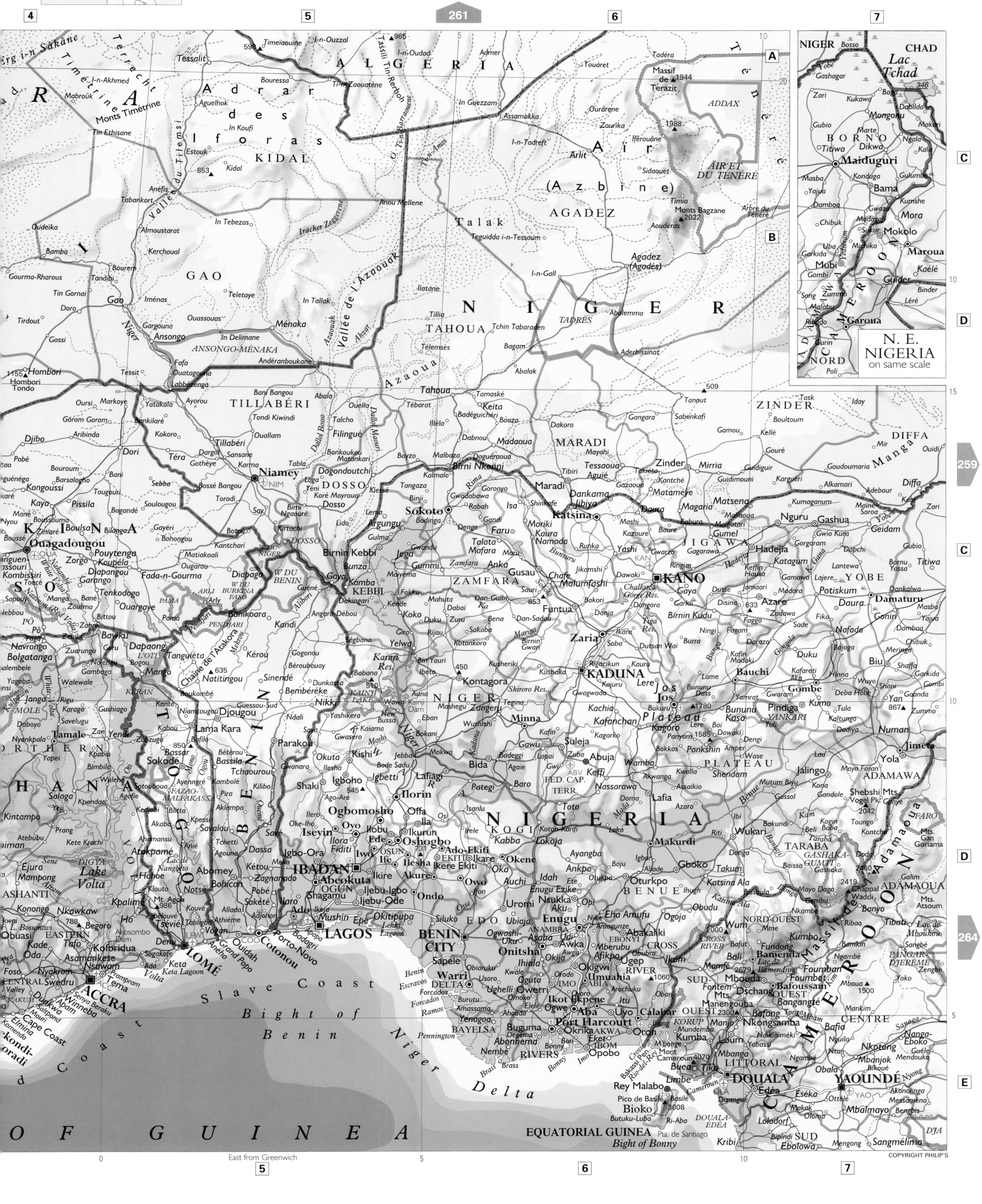

1:6 400 000

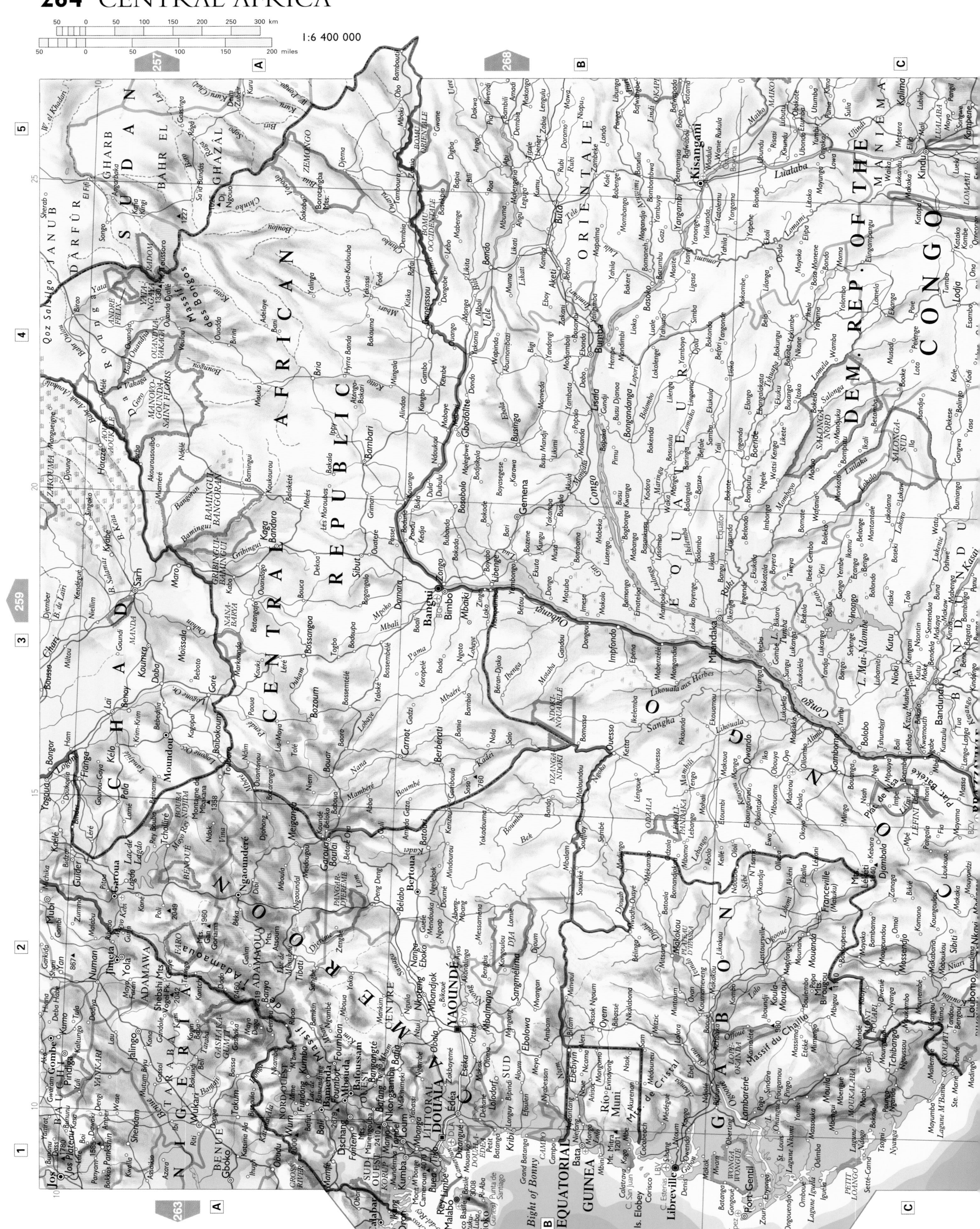

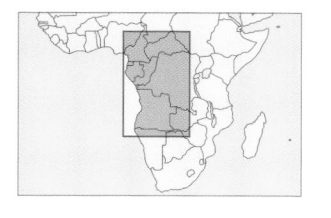

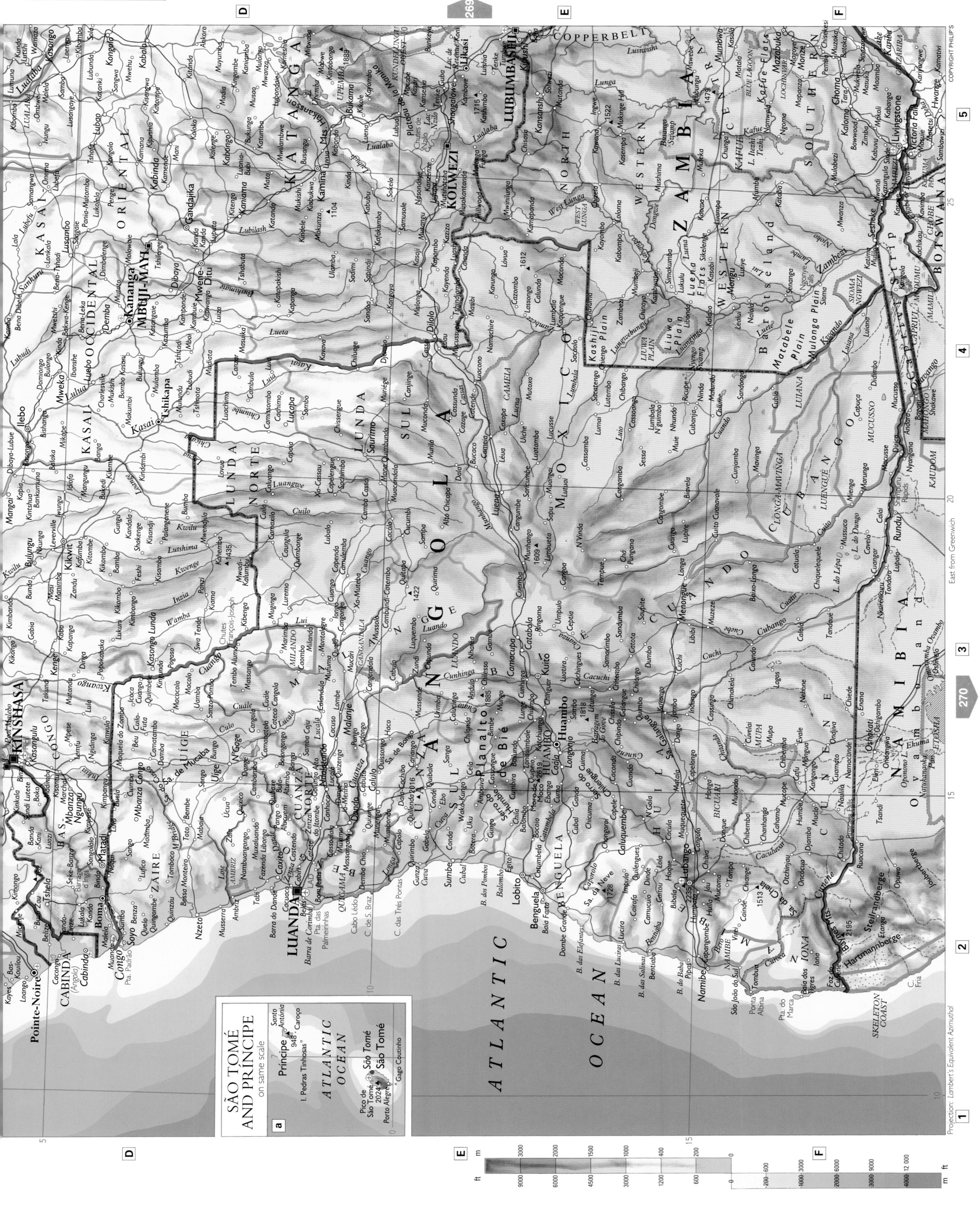

COPYRIGHT PHILIP'S

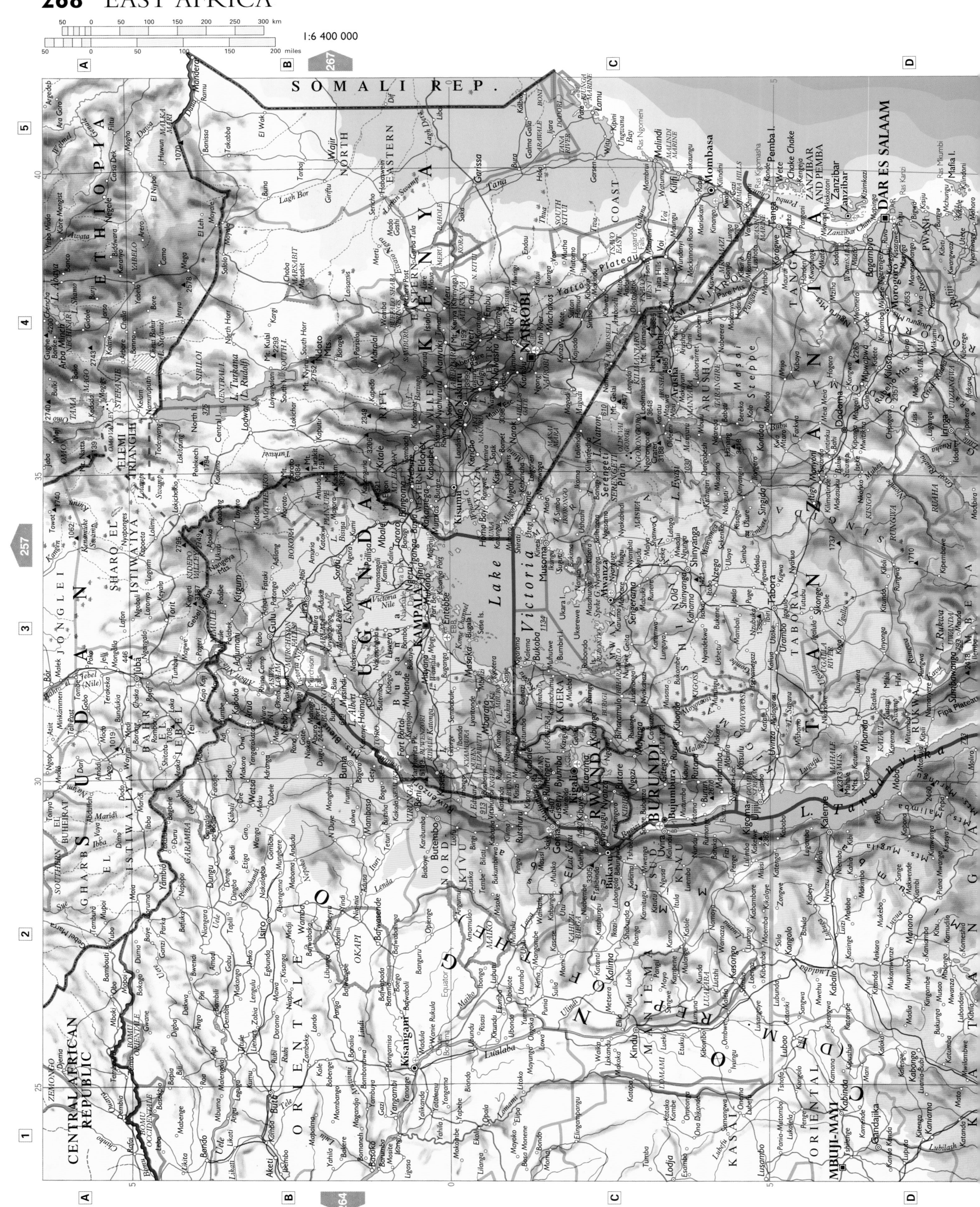

1:6 400 000

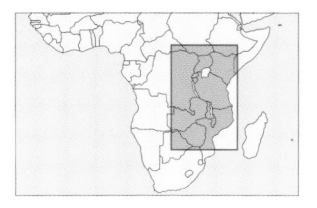

50 0 50 100 150 200 250 300 km

1:6 400 000

50 0 50 100 150 200 miles

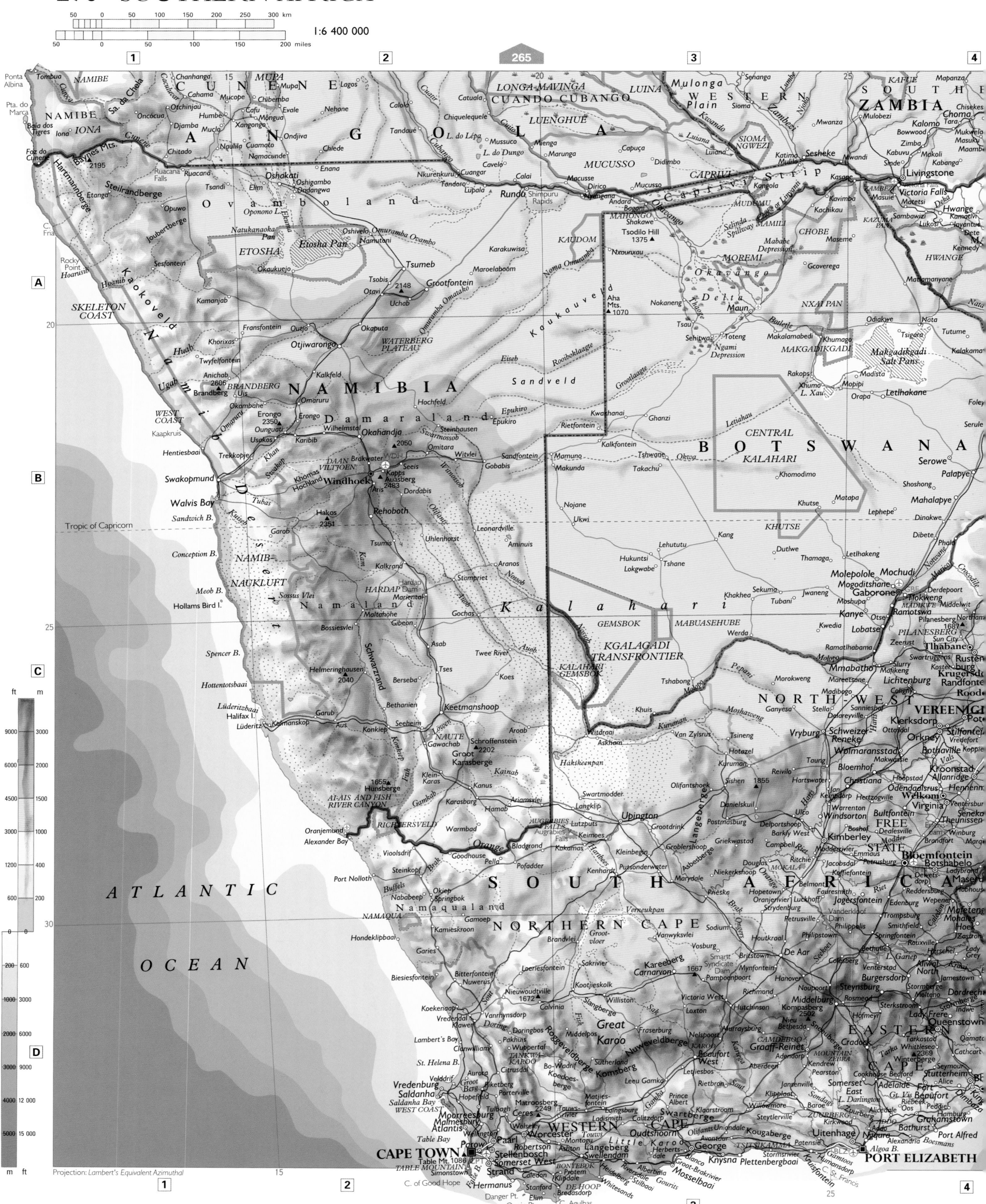

MOZAMBIQUE

CHANNEL

Bassas da India
(Fr.)

Île Europa
(Fr.)

Tropic of Capricorn

INDIAN

OCEAN

ZIMBABWE

HARARE
Chitungwiza

Bulawayo

LIMPOPO

PRETORIA
(Tshwane)

JOHANNESBURG

MPUMALANGA

SWAZILAND

MAPUTO

LESOTHO

KWAZULU

NATAL

EASTERN
CAPE

Pietermaritzburg

DURBAN

Richards Bay

Beira

Quelimane

Mocuba

MALAWI

ZAMBEZIA

Île de
Júan de Nova
(Fr.)

I. Angoche
Angoche

Tropic of Capricorn

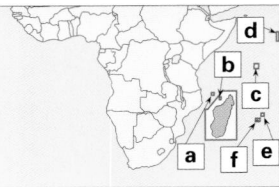

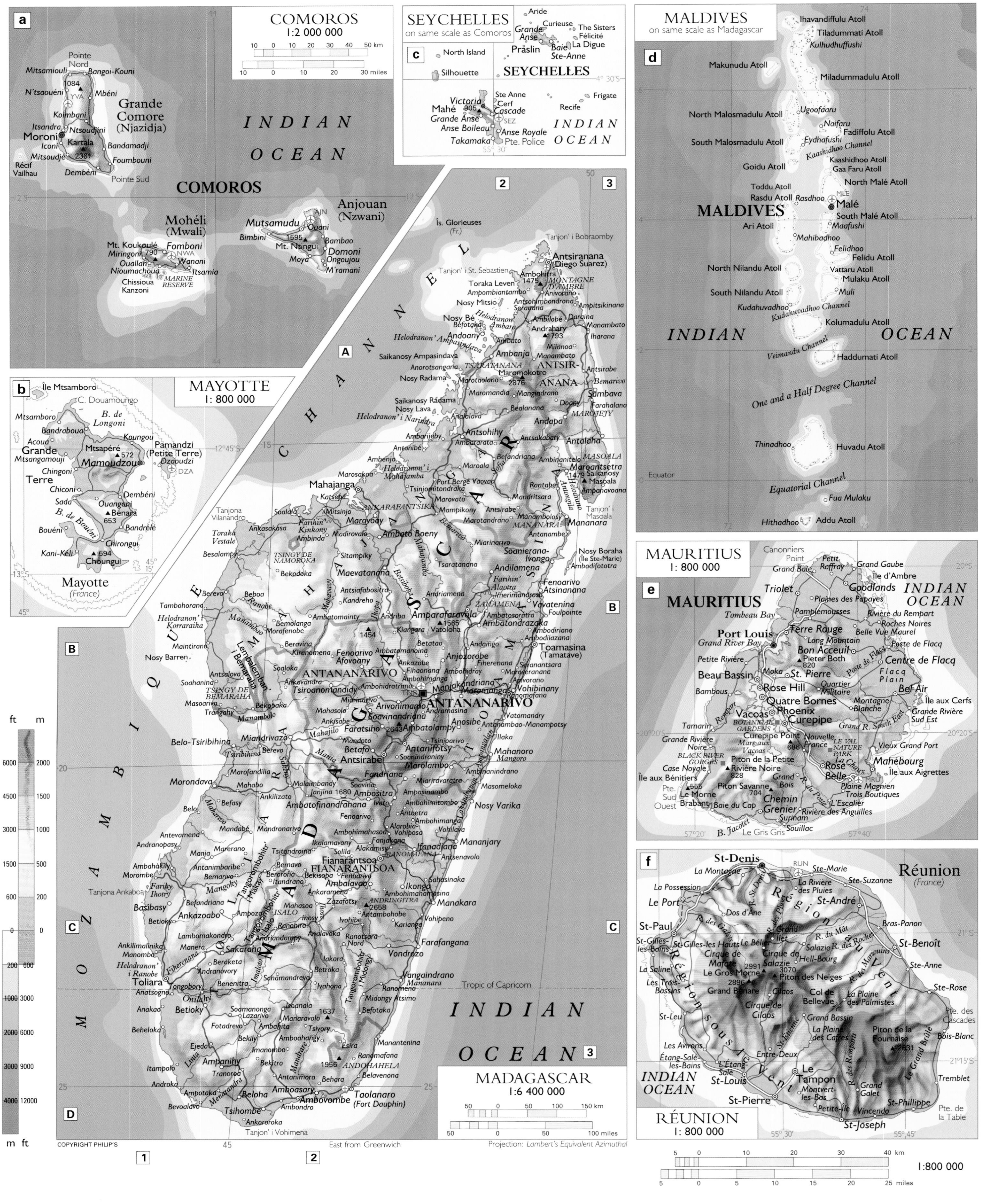

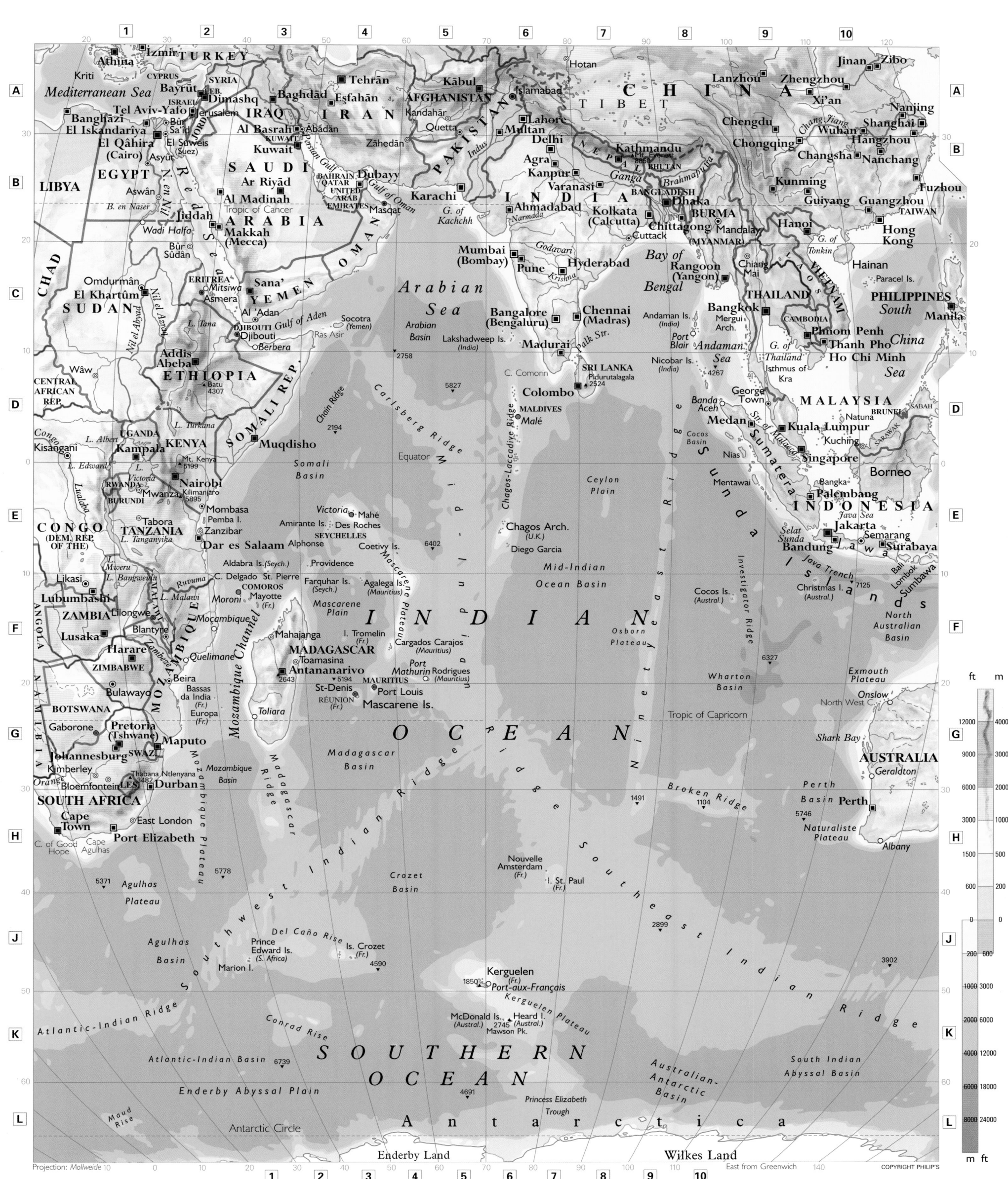

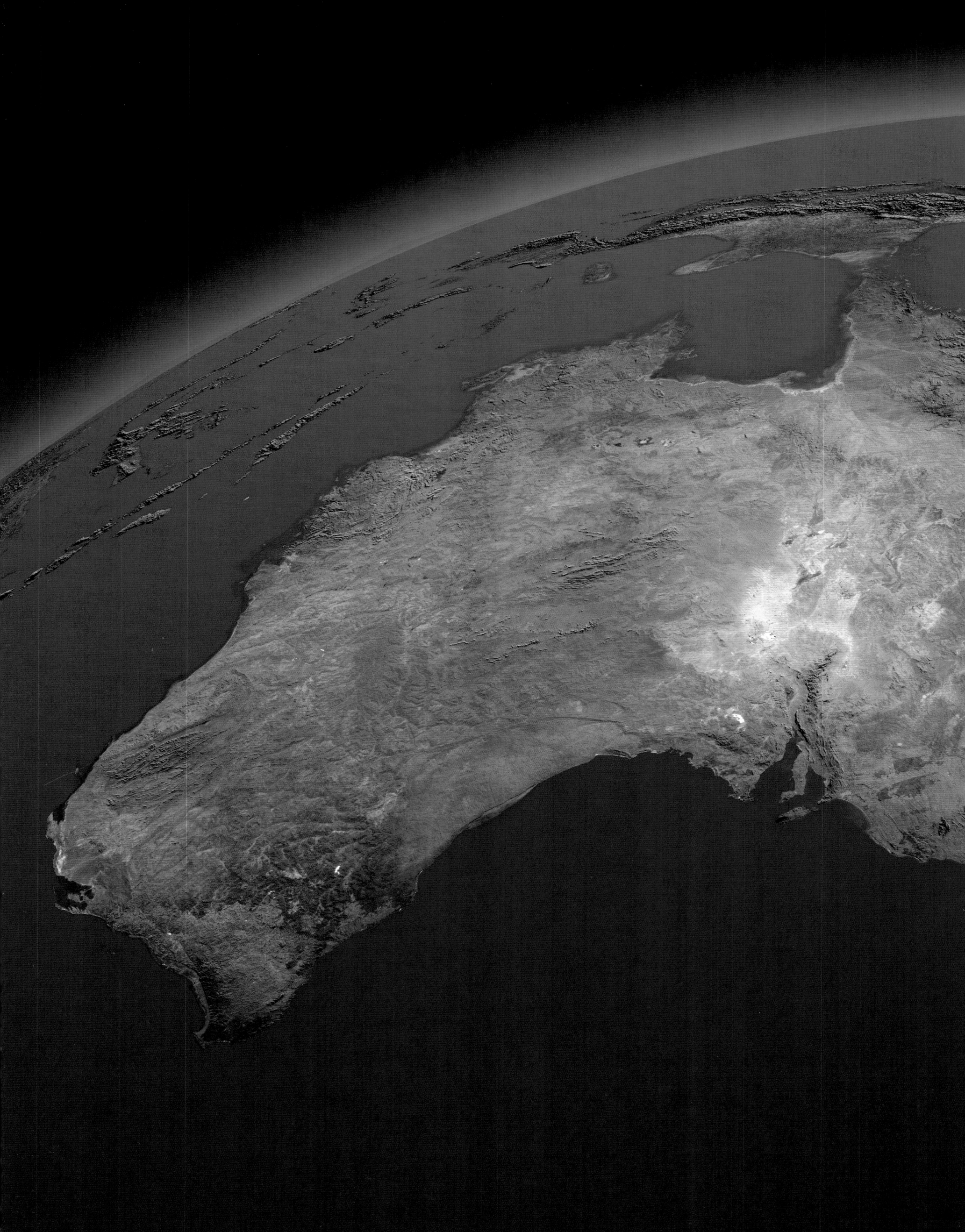

AUSTRALIA
AND
OCEANIA

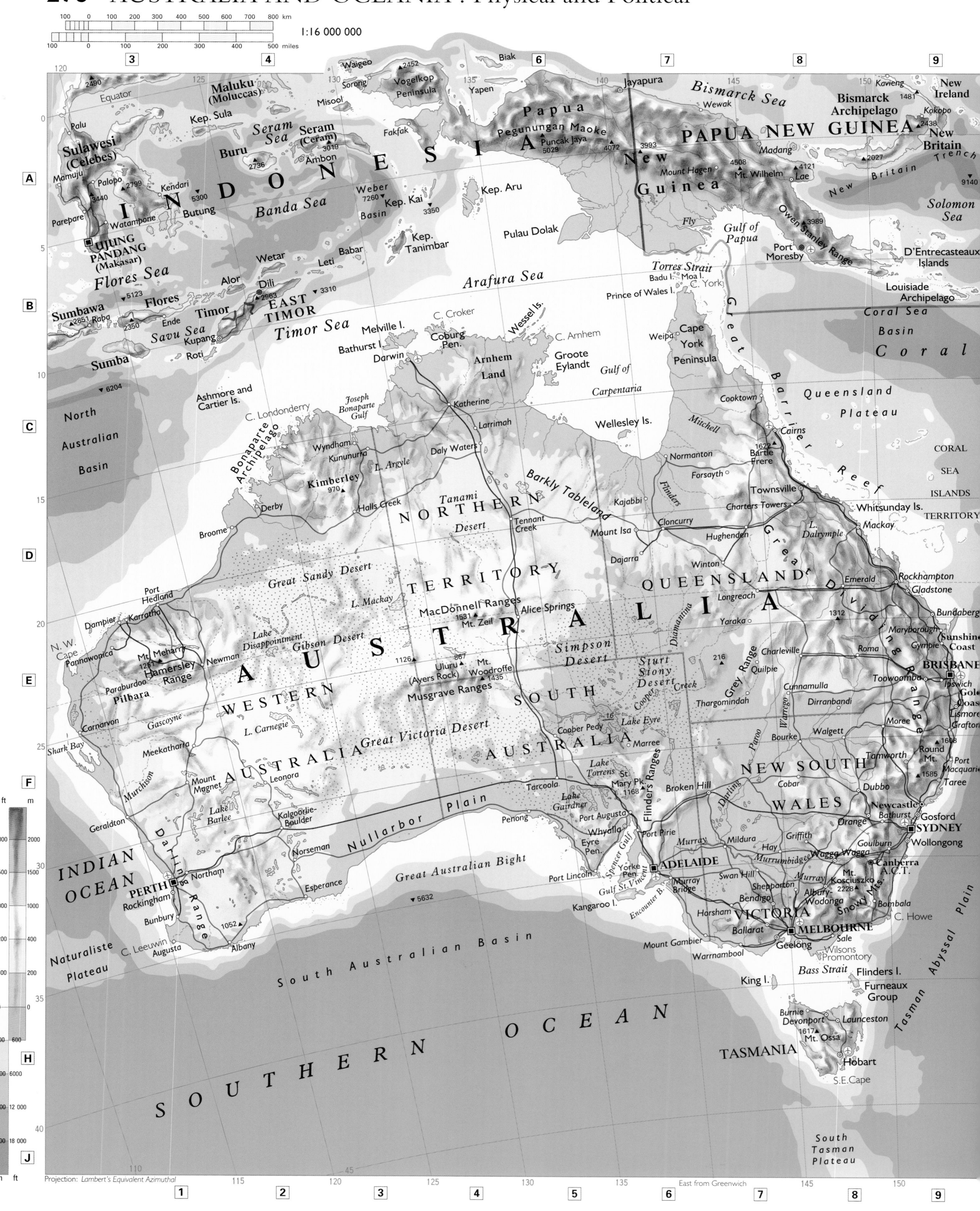

1:16 000 000

Projection: *Lambert's Equivalent Azimuthal*

East from Greenwich

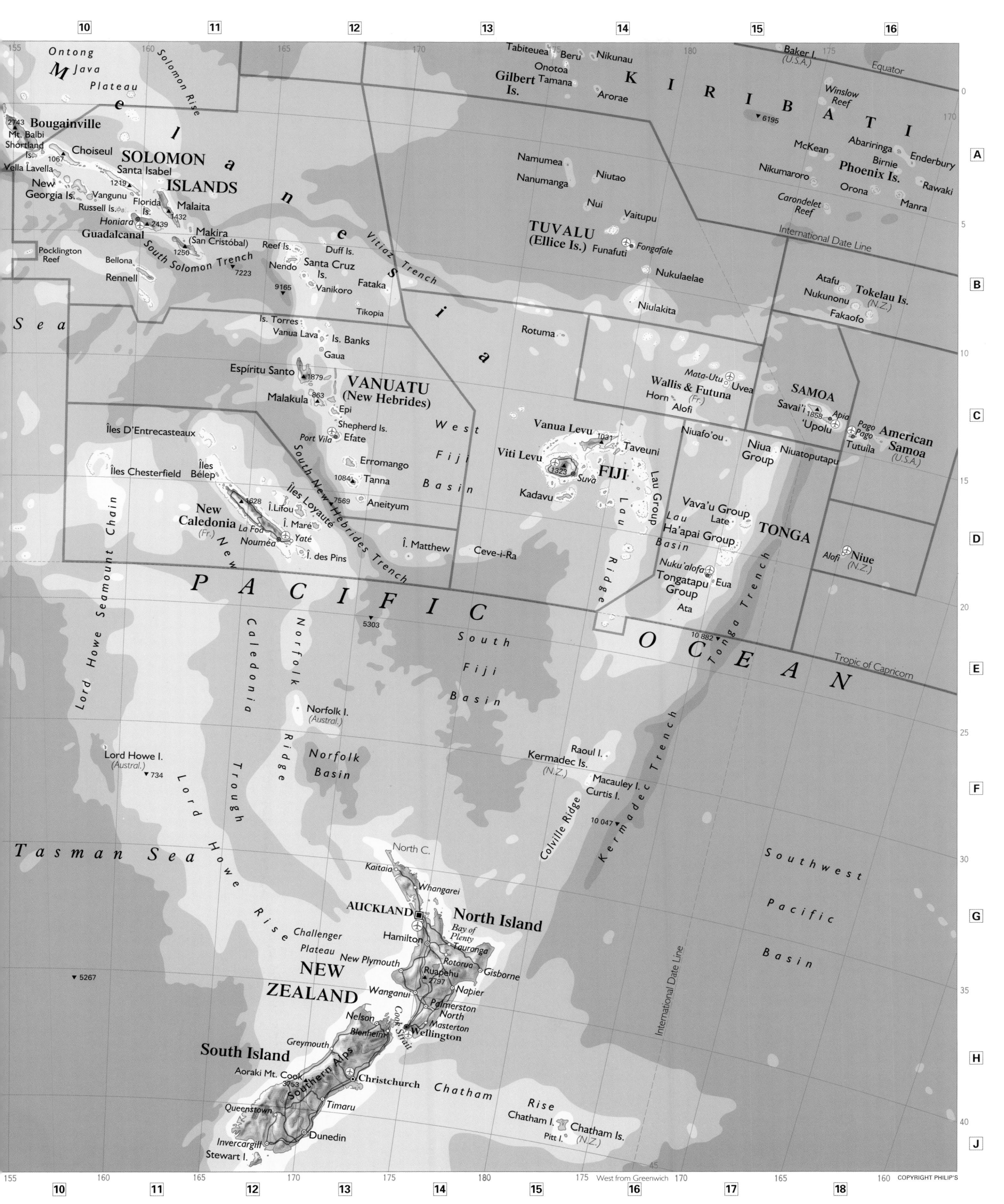

Ontong
Java
Plateau

Solomon Rise

K I R I B A T I

Tabiteuea Beru Nikunau
Onotoa
Gilbert Tamana
Is.
Arorae

Winslow
Reef

Baker I.
(U.S.A.)

Equator

▼6195

McKean

Abariringa Enderbury
Birnie
Phoenix Is. Rawaki
Nikumaroro
Orona Manra

2743 ▲ Bougainville
Mt. Balbi
Shortland
Is.
Vella Lavella 1067
New
Georgia Is. 1219
Vanunu
Russell Is.
Honiara ▲2439
Guadalcanal
Bellona
Rennell

Choiseul
Santa Isabel
SOLOMON
ISLANDS
Florida
Is. Malaita
▲1432
Makira
(San Cristóbal)
1250

Pocklington
Reef

South Solomon Trench

Namumea
Nanumanga

Niutao

TUVALU
(Ellice Is.) Funafuti

Nui
Vaitupu

Fongafale

Nukulaelae

Niulakita

Atafu
Nukunonu Tokelau Is.
(N.Z.)
Fakaofo

Rotuma

M e l a n e s i a

Vitiaz Trench

Reef Is.
Duff Is.
Nendo Santa Cruz
7223 Is.
9165 Vanikoro
Fataka
Tikopia

Is. Torres
Vanua Lava
Gaua Is. Banks

Espíritu Santo ▲1879
VANUATU
Malakula (New Hebrides)
▲863
Epi
Shepherd Is.
Port Vila Efate
Erromango
1084 Tanna
7569 Aneityum

S e a

Mata-Utu ✈ Uvea
Wallis & Futuna
Horn (Fr.)
Alofi

Niuafo'ou

SAMOA
Savai'i 1858 Apia
Upolu Pago American
Pago Samoa
Tutuila (U.S.A.)

West
Fiji
Basin

Vanua Levu
1031
Viti Levu Taveuni
▲1323
Suva
FIJI
Kadavu

Niua
Group Niuatoputapu

Lau Group

Vava'u Group
Lau Late
Ha'apai Group TONGA
Basin
Nuku'alofa Eua
Tongatapu
Group
Ata

Alofi Niue
(N.Z.)

Îles D'Entrecasteaux
Îles Chesterfield Îles
Bélep
New ▲1628 Î.Lifou
Caledonia Î. Maré
(Fr.) La Foa
Nouméa Yaté
Î. des Pins

South New Hebrides Trench

Î. Matthew

Ceve-i-Ra

5303

Lau
Ridge

10 882 ▼

Tonga Trench

Tropic of Capricorn

P A C I F I C

New
Caledonia

Norfolk Ridge

South
Fiji
Basin

O C E A N

Lord Howe Seamount Chain

Caledonia Trough

Norfolk I.
(Austral.)

Lord Howe I.
(Austral.) ▼734

Lord Howe Rise

Norfolk
Basin

Raoul I.
Kermadec Is.
(N.Z.)
Macauley I.
Curtis I.
10 047 ▼

Colville Ridge

Kermadec Trench

Southwest

Pacific

Basin

International Date Line

Tasman Sea

North C.
Kaitaia
Whangarei
AUCKLAND
Hamilton
Challenger Bay of
Plenty Tauranga
Plateau New Plymouth
Rotorua Gisborne
NEW Ruapehu
▲2797
Wanganui Napier
ZEALAND Palmerston
North
Nelson Masterton
Blenheim Wellington
South Island Greymouth

North Island

Cook Strait

Chatham

Rise

Chatham I. Chatham Is.
Pitt I. (N.Z.)

▼5267

Aoraki Mt. Cook
3753 Southern Alps Christchurch
Queenstown Timaru
Invercargill Dunedin
Stewart I.

West from Greenwich

COPYRIGHT PHILIP'S

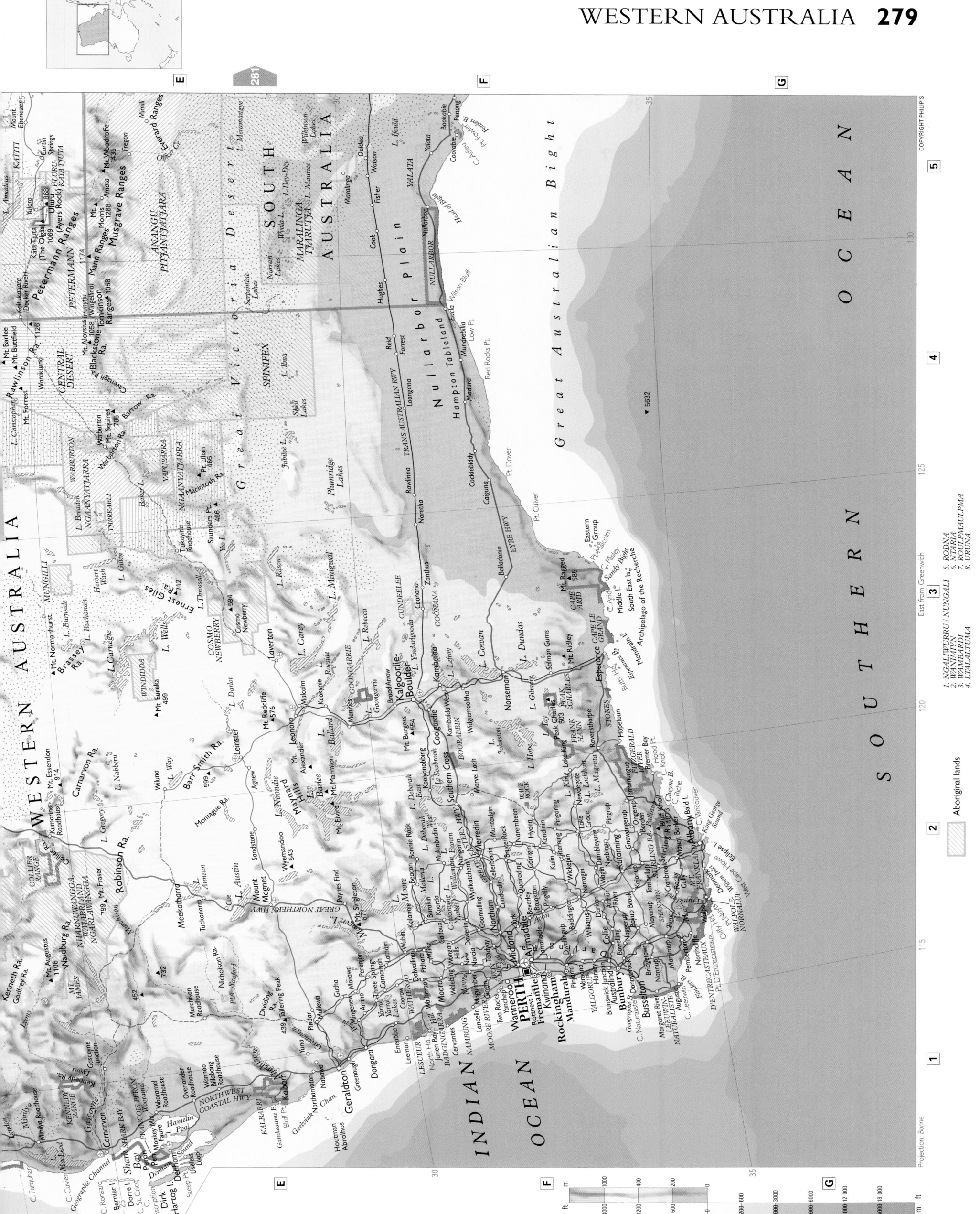

WESTERN AUSTRALIA

SOUTH AUSTRALIA

INDIAN OCEAN

OCEAN

SOUTHERN

Great Australian Bight

PERTH

Fremantle

Kalgoorlie-Boulder

Geraldton

Bunbury

Albany

Esperance

Nullarbor Plain

Hampton Tableland

Great Victoria Desert

SPINIFEX

Petermann Ranges

Musgrave Ranges

ANANGU PITJANTJATJARA

MARALINGA TJARUTJA

Uluru (Ayers Rock) KATA TJUTA

Kata Tjuta (The Olgas)

Aboriginal lands

1. NGALIIVIIRRU/NUNGALI
2. WANMIYN
3. WAMBARDI
4. LHALALTUMA
5. RODNA
6. NTARIA
7. ROULPMAULPMA
8. URUNA

East from Greenwich

Projection: Bonne

Scale:
m ft
6000 18 000
4000 12 000
2000 6000
1000 3000
600 2000
400 1200
200 600
0 0
200 - 600

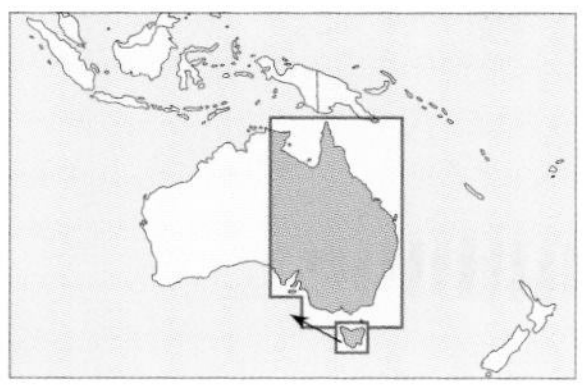

TASMAN SEA

QUEENSLAND

NEW SOUTH WALES

SOUTH AUSTRALIA

VICTORIA

TASMANIA

BRISBANE

SYDNEY

Newcastle

Canberra

MELBOURNE

ADELAIDE

Wollongong

Great Dividing Range

Darling Range

Flinders Ranges

Lake Eyre

Lake Torrens

Lake Gairdner

Bass Strait

Great Australian Bight

Murray R.

Darling R.

Gulf St Vincent

Spencer Gulf

Eyre Peninsula

Yorke Peninsula

Kangaroo I.

King Island

Flinders Island

Furneaux Group

Cape Barren I.

Hobart

Launceston

Devonport

Aboriginal lands

COPYRIGHT PHILIP'S

East from Greenwich

Projection: Bonne

1:3 200 000

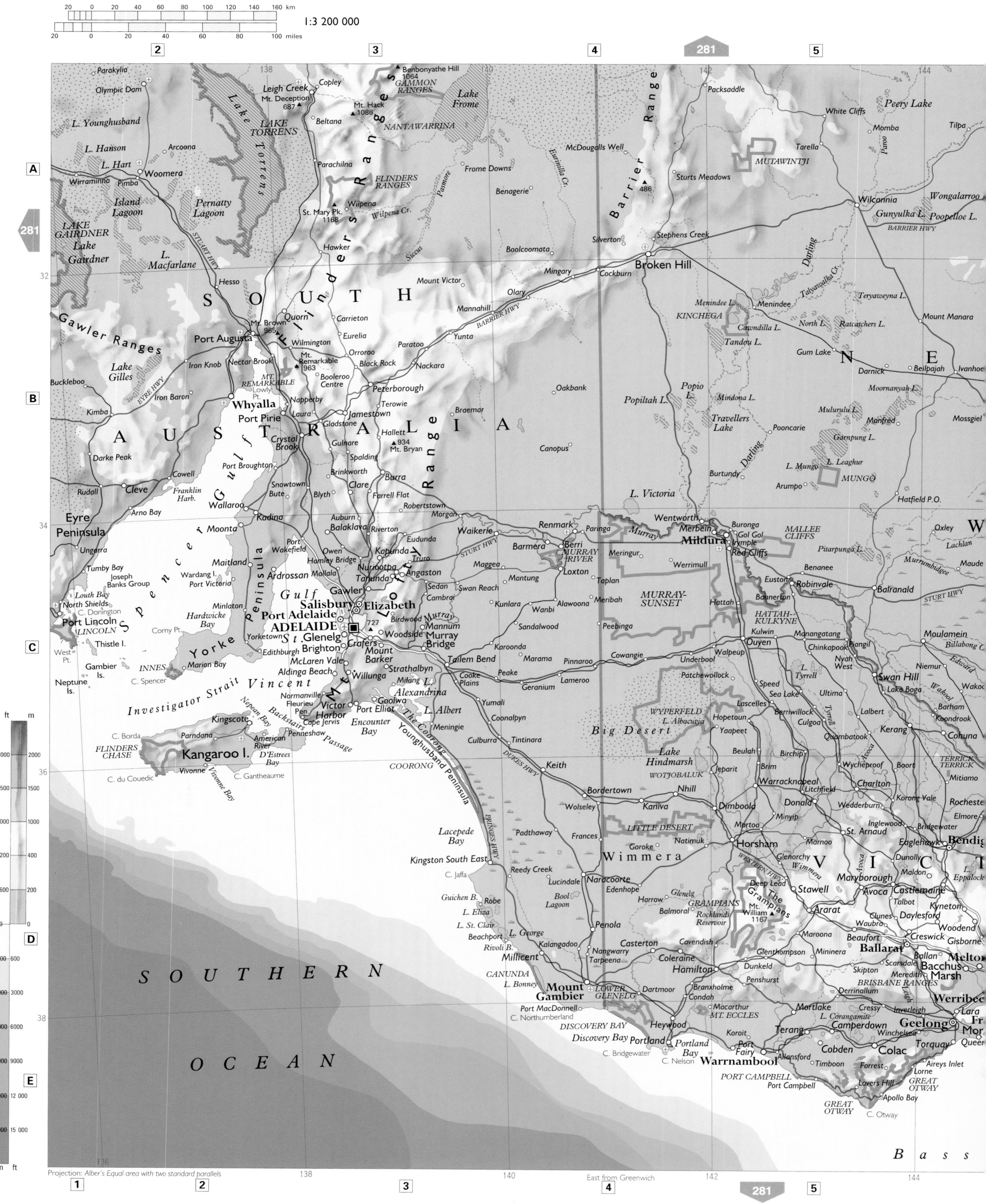

SOUTHERN

OCEAN

SOUTH AUSTRALIA

NEW SOUTH WALES

VICTORIA

ADELAIDE

FLINDERS RANGES

Gawler Ranges

Eyre Peninsula

Yorke Peninsula

Spencer Gulf

Gulf St Vincent

Investigator Strait

Kangaroo I.

Lake Torrens

Lake Gairdner

Lake Frome

Barrier Range

Big Desert

Wimmera

The Grampians

Broken Hill

Mildura

Port Augusta

Whyalla

Port Lincoln

Mount Gambier

Ballarat

Geelong

Warrnambool

Aboriginal lands

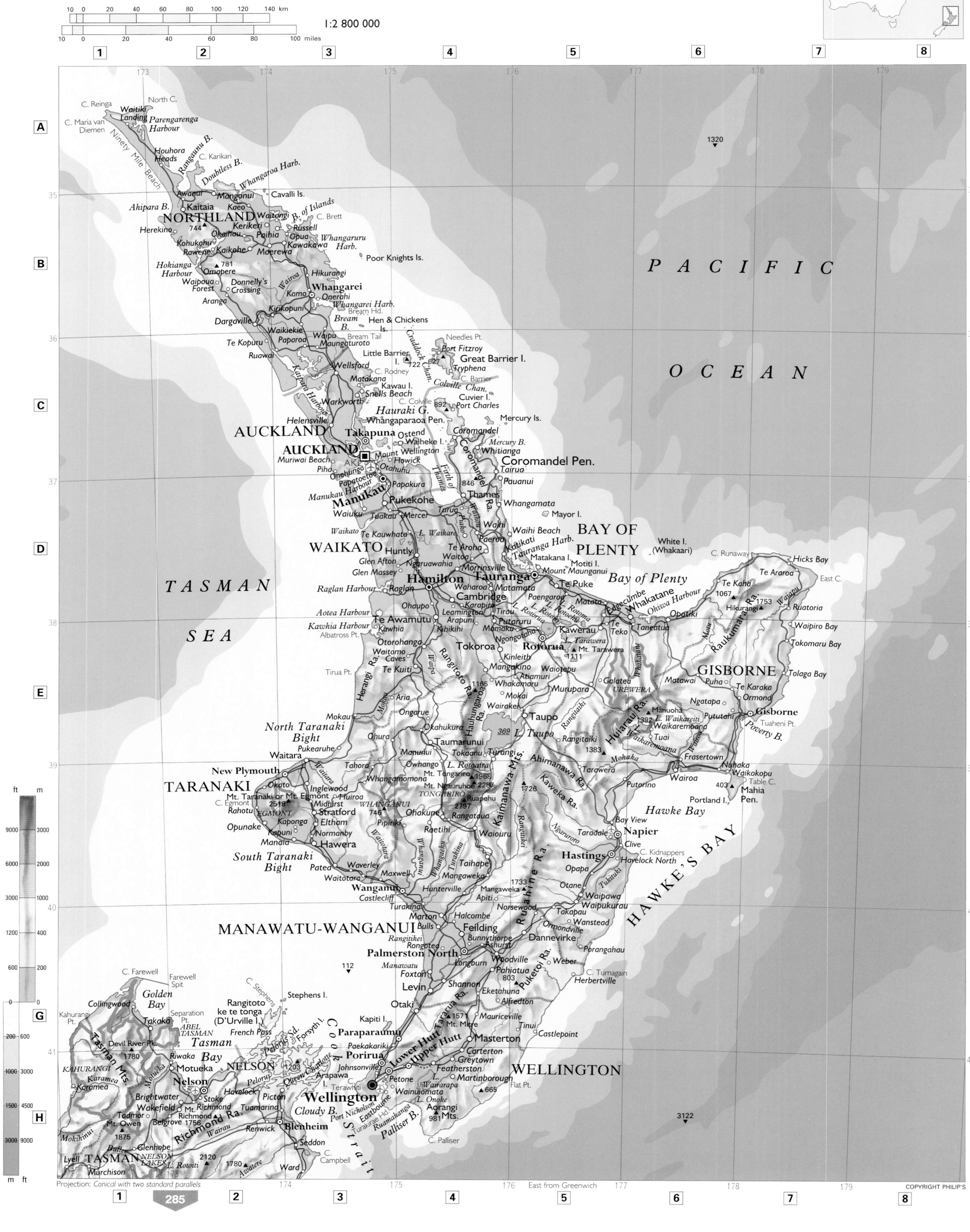

10 0   20   40   60   80   100 120 140 km
10 0   20   40   60   80   100 miles

1:2 800 000

| 1 | 2 | 3 | 4 | 5 | 6 | 7 | 8 |

PACIFIC

OCEAN

TASMAN

SEA

C. Reinga
North C.
Waitiki Landing
C. Maria van Diemen
Parengarenga Harbour
Houhora Heads
Rangaunu B.
Ninety Mile Beach
Awanui
Mongonui
C. Karikari
Cavalli Is.
Ahipara B.
Kaitaia
Kaeo
Doubless B.
Whangaroa Harb.
744
Herekino
Kohukohu
Rawene
Kerikeri
Okaihau
Paihia
Opua
Kawakawa
Russell
Waitangi
C. Brett
B. of Islands
Whangaruru Harb.
NORTHLAND
Kaikohe
Moerewa
Hikurangi
Hokianga Harbour
781
Omapere
Waipoua Forest
Donnelly's Crossing
Aranga
Wairoa
Kamo
Onerahi
Whangarei
Whangarei Harb.
Poor Knights Is.
Kirikopuni
Bream Hd.
Dargaville
Bream B.
Hen & Chickens Is.
Te Kopuru
Paparoa
Waipu
Bream Tail
Waikiekie
Maungaturoto
Ruawai
Wellsford
722 627
Little Barrier I.
Port Fitzroy
Great Barrier I.
Tryphena
Matakana
C. Rodney
Kawau I.
Cuvier I.
Port Charles
Warkworth
Snells Beach
892
C. Barrier
Colville Chan.
Mercury Is.
Cruddock Chan.
Needles Pt.
Helensville
Hauraki G.
Whangaparaoa Pen.
Coromandel
Mercury B.
AUCKLAND
Takapuna
Ostend
Waiheke I.
Whitianga
AUCKLAND
Mount Wellington
Coromandel Pen.
Muriwai Beach
Howick
AKL
Piha
Onehunga
Otahuhu
Tairua
Pauanui
Papatoetoe
846
Manukau
Papakura
Firth of Thames
Whangamata
Coromandel Ra.
Pukekohe
Thames
Mayor I.
Waiuku
Tuakau
Mercer
Waihi
Manukau Harbour
Waitoa
Paeroa
Waihi Beach
BAY OF
Waikato
Te Kauwhata
L. Waikare
Katikati
Tauranga Harb.
PLENTY
WAIKATO
Huntly
Te Aroha
Matakana I.
White I.
(Whakaari)
Glen Afton
Ngaruawahia
Morrinsville
Mount Maunganui
C. Runaway
Hicks Bay
Glen Massey
Matamata
Tauranga
Te Kaha
Te Araroa
Raglan Harbour
Waharoa
Te Puke
Matata
Paengaroa
Bay of Plenty
East C.
Hamilton
Cambridge
1067
Raglan
Karapiro
Kawerau
Whakatane
Hikurangi
1753
Ruatoria
Aotea Harbour
Leamington
Tirau
L. Rotorua
Ohiwa Harbour
Raukumara Ra.
Te Awamutu
Kihikihi
Putaruru
Kaweroa
Te Teko
Opotiki
Waipiro Bay
Kawhia
Arapuni
Momoko
L. Rotoiti
Taneatua
Tokomaru Bay
Kawhia Harbour
Otorohanga
Tokoroa
Rotorua
Albatross Pt.
Waitomo Caves
1185
Whakamaru
Mt. Tarawera
GISBORNE
Tolaga Bay
Tirua Pt.
Te Kuiti
Kinleith
Mangakino
1111
Matawai
Puha
Te Karaka
Aria
Atiamuri
Waiotapu
UREWERA
Ormond
Mokau
Ongarue
Mokai
Murupara
Galatea
Ngatapa
Gisborne
North Taranaki Bight
Ohura
Okahukura
Wairakei
Manuoha
Tuai
Poverty B.
Pukearuhe
Taumarunui
Taupo
L. Waikaremoana
Tuaheni Pt.
Waitara
Tahora
Owhango
L. Rotoaira
369
L. Taupo
1392
Waikaremoana
Pututahi
New Plymouth
Whangamomona
Mt. Tangariro 1968
Rangitaiki
1383
Okato
Inglewood
Mt. Ngauruhoe 2290
Hauhungaroa Ra.
Mohaka
Fraserton
Nuhaka
C. Egmont
Midhirst
TONGARIRO
Turangi
Ahimanawa Ra.
Tarawera
Putorino
Wairoa
Waikokopu
TARANAKI
Mt. Taranaki or Mt. Egmont
2518
Huiroa
WHANGANUI
Ahimanawa Ra.
Tarawera
403 Table C.
Rahotu
EGMONT
Stratford
746
Ohakune
Ruapehu 2797
Kaweka Ra.
Mahia Pen.
Opunake
Kaponga
Eltham
Pipiriki
1728
Bay View
Portland I.
Manaia
Kapuni
Normanby
Raetihi
Rangataua
Waiouru
Ngaruroro
Napier
Hawke Bay
Hawera
South Taranaki Bight
Taihape
Kaimanawa Mts.
Taradale
Clive
Patea
Mangaweka
Hastings
C. Kidnappers
Waverley
Maxwell
Mangaweka
Waipawa
Havelock North
Waitotara
Turakina
1733
Apiti
Norsewood
HAWKE'S
Wanganui
Hunterville
Takapau
Castlecliff
Marton
Ormondville
BAY
Bulls
Feilding
Dannevirke
Pohangahau
MANAWATU-WANGANUI
Halcombe
Bunnythorpe
Ashhurst
Weber
Rangitikei
Rongotea
Woodville
C. Turnagain
Palmerston North
Manawatu
Pahiatua
803
Herbertville
112
Foxton
Longburn
Shannon
Pahiatua
Levin
Eketahuna
Alfredton
Otaki
Mauriceville
Kapiti I.
157
Tinui
Castlepoint
Paraparaumu
Mt. Mitre
Paekakariki
Masterton
C. Farewell
Farewell Spit
Porirua
Carterton
C. Stephens
Rangitoto ke te tonga (D'Urville I.)
Upper Hutt
Greytown
Stephens I.
Lower Hutt
Featherston
WELLINGTON
Collingwood
Golden Bay
French Pass
Petone
Martinborough
Takaka
Separation Pt.
Pelorus Sd.
Johnsonville
Wainuiomata
Flat Pt.
Kahurangi Pt.
ABEL TASMAN
Forsyth I.
Terawhiti
Wellington
L. Onoke
1780
Devil River Pk.
Riwaka
Motueka
Queen Charlotte Sd.
665
Wairarapa
Tasman Bay
Havelock
Picton
Palliser B.
KAHURANGI MTS.
Karamea
NELSON
1203
Arapawa I.
Wairau
Port Nicholson
Aorangi Mts.
981
Karamea
Brightwater
Nelson
Eastbourne
Tuamarino
Palliser Mts.
C. Palliser
Mokihinui
Wakefield
Stoke
Richmond
Cook Strait
Mt. Richmond
Tadmor
Belgrove
1756
Renwick
3122
Lyell
Glenhope
Richmond Ra.
Blenheim
Murchison
1875
NELSON
2120
1780
Seddon
TASMAN
NELSON LAKES
L. Rotoiti
Awatere
Ward
Campbell

ft	m
9000	3000
6000	2000
3000	1000
1200	400
600	200
0	0

m	ft
200	600
1500	3000
1500	4500
3000	9000

Projection: Conical with two standard parallels

1320

East from Greenwich

COPYRIGHT PHILIP'S

1:2 800 000

10 20 40 60 80 100 120 140 km
10 0 20 40 60 80 100 miles

284

1 2 3 4 5 6 7 8 9

167 168 169 170 171 172 173 174

A

C. Farewell
Farewell Spit
Collingwood *Golden Bay* Takaka
C. Stephens
Stephens I.
Rangitoto ke te tonga (D'Urville I.)
Kahurangi Pt. Separation Pt. French Pass
ABEL TASMAN Forsyth I.
Riwaka *Tasman* Jackson
Devil River Pk ▲ 1780 Motueka *Bay* Petone Sd.
KAHURANGI Moutere French Pass
Tasman Mts Brightwater **NELSON** Queen Charlotte Sd.
Karamea ▲ Mt Owen ▲ 1875 Richmond Arapawa I.
Karamea Bight Wakefield Stoke Havelock ▲ 1203
Waimarie Tadmor *Richmond Ra.* Picton
Seddonville Glenhope Mt Richmond 1756 Cloudy B.
Granity Millerton *TASMAN* Renwick Tuamarina
Waimangaroa Lyell Buller Belgrove Wairau **Blenheim**
Westport Gorge Murchison Renwick C. Campbell
C. Foulwind Buller L. *MARLBOROUGH* Seddon
Inangahua Mt Travers ▲ 2337 Ward
PAPAROA Reefton Rotoroa Molesworth Wharanui
Punakaiki Victoria Mt Franklin ▲ 2340 *Inland Kaikoura Ra.* ▲ 2885
Paparoa Ra. Grey *Ra.* *NELSON LAKES* Tapuaeoenuku ▲ Tenuku
Ikamatua Marua Lewis Clarence *Seaward Kaikoura Ra.* ▲ 2608
Blackball Ahaura Springs Pass Hanmer Springs Manakau ▲
Runanga Lewis Pass ▲ 1747 Kaikoura
Greymouth L. Sumner ▲ 1615 Waiau Kaikoura Pen.
Taramakau Kaimata *ARTHUR'S* Parnassus
Hokitika Brunner *PASS* Mt Ajax ▲ 1834 Waiau Hurunui
Kumara Waikari Domett
Jacksons Otira Mt Crossley ▲ 1980 Culverden Seargill
Ross Otira Arthur's Pass 926 Hurunui *Pegasus Bay*
Kaniere Gorge Waikari Amberley
Wanganui Harihari Mt Marchison ▲ 2408 Ashley Sefton
About Hd. Whataroa Coleridge *Ra.* Oxford Rangiora
Whitcombe Pass Lake Springfield Kaiapoi
Okarito ▲ 2650 Coleridge Sheffield Belfast
Gillespies Pt. Mt Taylor ▲ 2333 Whitecliffs New Brighton
L. Mapourika *WESTLAND* Darfield Riccarton **Christchurch**
Franz Josef Glacier Arrowsmith ▲ 2781 Highbank Rolleston Sumner
Bruce B. Fox Glacier South Branch Hornby Lyttelton
MT COOK Methven Leeston Little River ▲ 919 *Banks Pen.*
Tititira Hd. Mt Tasman ▲ 3497 *Two Thumbs Ra.* Lincoln Akaroa
Aoraki Mount Cook ▲ 3753 ▲ 2251 Mount Somers L. Ellesmere
Tasman Gl. Mount Cook Rakaia Southbridge
Jackson Glentanner L. Tekapo Tinwald *Akaroa Harbour*
Jackson Hd. B. Haast Ben Ohau Ra. ▲ 2590 Lake Tekapo Ashburton
Okuru *Barrier Ra.* L. Pukaki Geraldine
Cascade Pt. Haast L. Ohau *Mackenzie Plains* Hinds Ashburton
Awarua Pt. *MOUNT ASPIRING* 1894 Fairlie *CANTERBURY*
Awarua B. Mt Aspiring ▲ 3033 *Waitaki Plains* Winchester *Canterbury Bight*
Olivine Ra. L. Wanaka Temuka
Yates Pt. *Darran Mts* ▲ 2723 Benmore Pk. ▲ Pleasant Point
Milford Sd. Mt Tutoko Hawea Kirkliston Ra. *The Hunter Hills* **Timaru**
Mitre Peak ▲ 1683 Mt Earnslaw ▲ 2819 L. Hawea L. Aviemore Waitaki St Andrews
Milford Sound Harris Mts Hawea Flat Mt St. Bathan's ▲ 2087 Hunter
Sutherland Falls *Pisa Ra.* Hakataramea Studholme
George Sound Glenorchy Wanaka ▲ 1936 St. Bathans Kurow Waimate
Caswell Sound Richardson Mts *Dunstan Mts* Duntroon Waihao
Charles Sound Stuart Mts Arrowtown Tokarahi Morven
Thompson Sd. Murchison Mts ▲ 1610 *The Remarkables* ▲ 2319 Ngapara Glenavy
Secretary I. Mts Queenstown Double Cone Naseby *Kakanui Mts* Windsor
Doubtful Sd. Te Anau Cromwell Clyde Maheno
Dagg Sd. Mt Lyall ▲ 1892 *OTAGO* Rough Ridge Ranfurly Pukeuri
FIORDLAND Kepler Mts L. Te Anau Garvie Mts ▲ 2022 Hyde **Oamaru**
Breaksea Sd. Hunter Mts Alexandra Dunback
Resolution I. Heath Mts *Eyre Mts* Jane Pk. ▲ 1449 *Waikouaiti Downs* Shag Pt.
Dusky Sd. Kaherekoau Mts L. Manapouri Roxburgh Middlemarch Palmerston
Cameron Mts ▲ 1704 Manapouri *Umbrella Mts* Sutton Waikouaiti
C. Providence Caroline Pk. Mossburn Miller's Flat Waikouaiti Port Chalmers
Chalky Inlet Lumsden Edievale Beaumont Warrington *Otago Harbour*
Preservation Inlet Coal *SOUTHLAND* Waikaia Lawrence C. Saunders
Puysegur Pt. Poteriteri Birchwood *Waimea Plain* Tapanui **Dunedin**
Te Waewae B. Monowai Dipton Kelso Mosgiel St Kilda
L. Hauroko Ohai Nightcaps Waikaka Clutha Taieri
Tuatapere Orawia Winton Riversdale Waipahi Clinton Allanton Waihola
Pahia Pt. Clifden **Gore** Clinton Milton L. Waihola
Orepuki Te Waewae Mataura Stirling
Riverton Thornbury Hedgehope Waipahi Kaitangata
Wallacetown Makarewa Edendale Balclutha
Centre I. Glenham Wyndham Owaka
South Invercargill **Invercargill** Tahakopa Nugget Pt.
Bluff Fortrose Catlins
Solander I. Toetoes Waipapa Pt. Chaslands Mistake
Bluff Harbour Long Pt.
Mt Anglem ▲ 980 *Foveaux Str.*
Codfish I. Ruapuke I.
Mason B. Halfmoon Bay Paterson Inlet
Doughboy B. *RAKIURA*
South West C. Port Pegasus **Stewart I. (Rakiura)**

TASMAN SEA

Westland Bight

SOUTHERN ALPS

CANTERBURY PLAINS

PACIFIC OCEAN

▲ 4870

CHATHAM ISLANDS on same scale

a

178 177 176

PACIFIC OCEAN

The Sisters

C. Young Munning Pt.
Western Reef Te One Chatham I. (Rekohu)
Waitangi The Forty Fours
The Horns Owenga C. Fournier
Mangere I. Star Keys
Pitt Strait Pitt I.
The Pyramid Rangatira I.

Chatham Islands (Wharekauri)

West from Greenwich

ft m
9000 3000
6000 2000
3000 1000
1200 400
600 200
0 0
200 600
1000 3000
1500 4500
3000 9000
4000 12 000
m ft

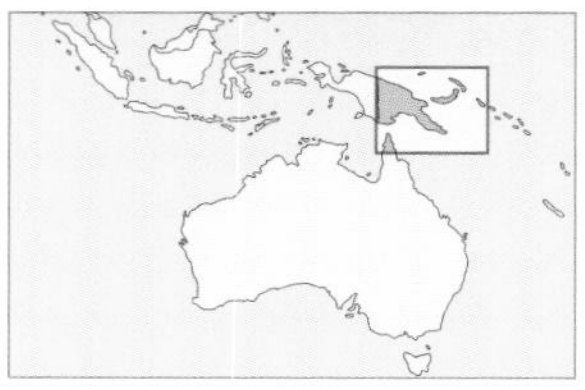

50 0 50 100 150 200 km
1:5 200 000
50 0 50 100 150 miles

COPYRIGHT PHILIP'S

East from Greenwich

Projection: Lambert Conformal Conic

PACIFIC OCEAN

NORTH SOLOMONS

Solomon Islands

Solomon Sea

Bismarck Sea

NEW IRELAND

NEW HANOVER

St. Matthias Group

Admiralty Islands

MANUS

Bismarck Archipelago

NEW BRITAIN

EAST NEW BRITAIN

WEST NEW BRITAIN

PAPUA NEW GUINEA

WEST SEPIK

EAST SEPIK

MADANG

MOROBE

ENGA

WESTERN HIGHLANDS

SOUTHERN HIGHLANDS

EASTERN HIGHLANDS

CHIMBU

CENTRAL

NORTHERN

MILNE BAY

GULF

WESTERN

Gulf of Papua

Coral Sea

Great Barrier Reef

Torres Strait

AUSTRALIA

QUEENSLAND

Cape York Peninsula

INDONESIA

PAPUA

Port Moresby

Owen Stanley Range

Louisiade Archipelago

D'Entrecasteaux Islands

Trobriand Is.

Woodlark I.

Bougainville I.

Buka I.

Kieta

Mt. Balbi 2715

Bougainville Trench 9140

New Ireland

Kavieng

Rabaul

Gazelle Peninsula

Kimbe Bay

Huon Gulf

Huon Peninsula

Lae

Madang

Wewak

Mt. Wilhelm 4508

Mt. Giluwe 4368

Mt. Victoria 4035

Finisterre Ra.

Bismarck Range

Central Range

Torricelli Mts.

Fly

Sepik River

Ramu

Markham

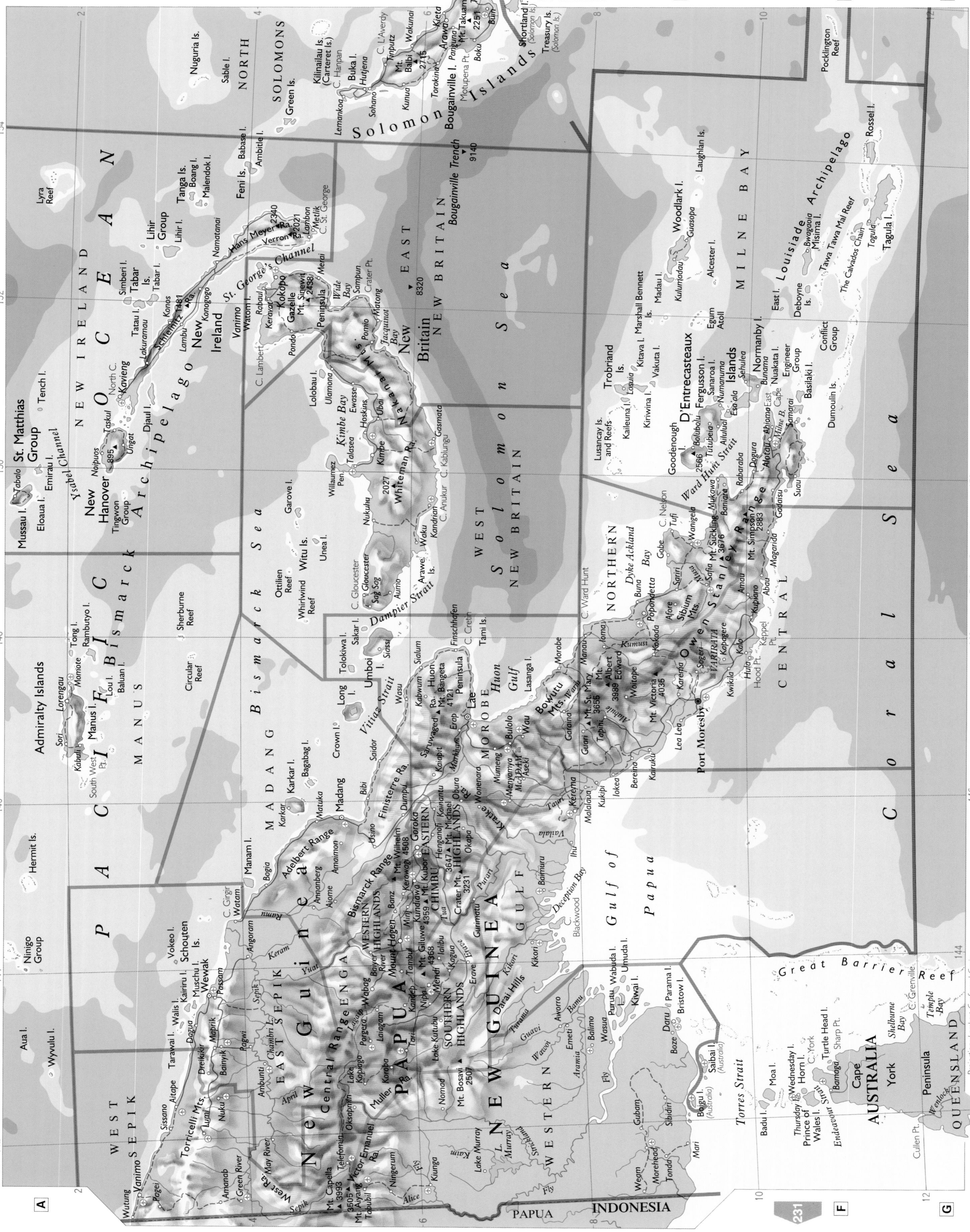

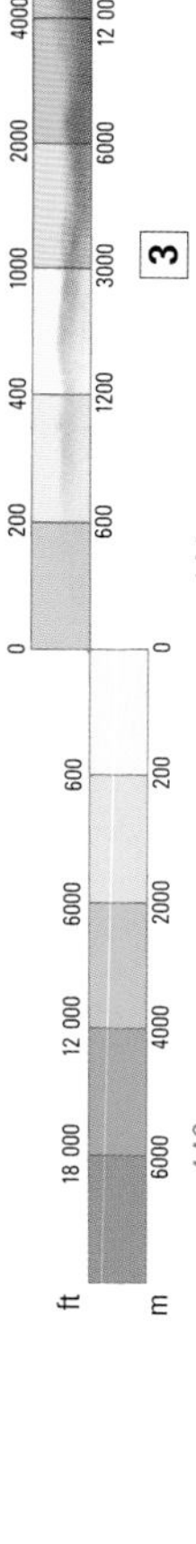

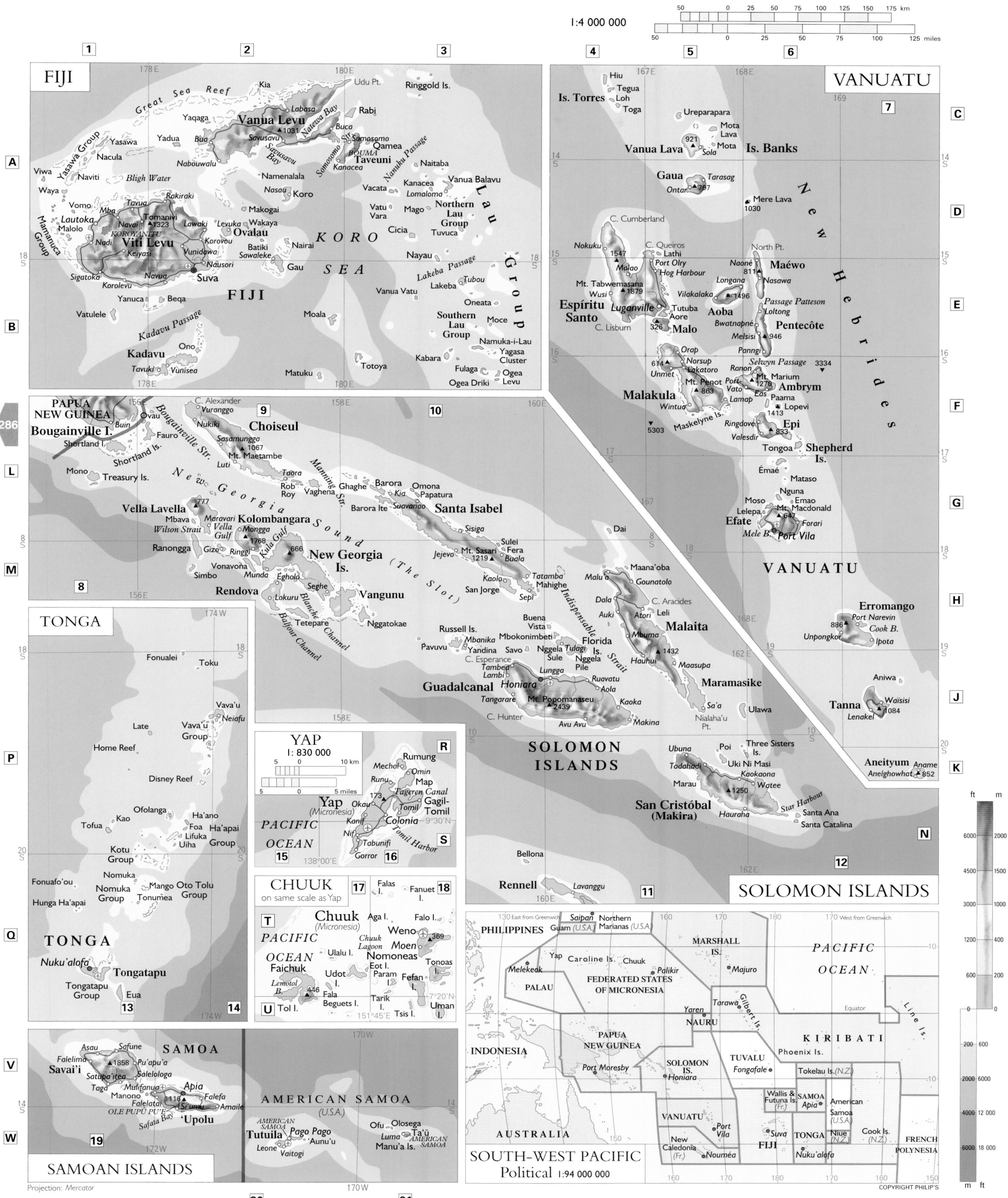

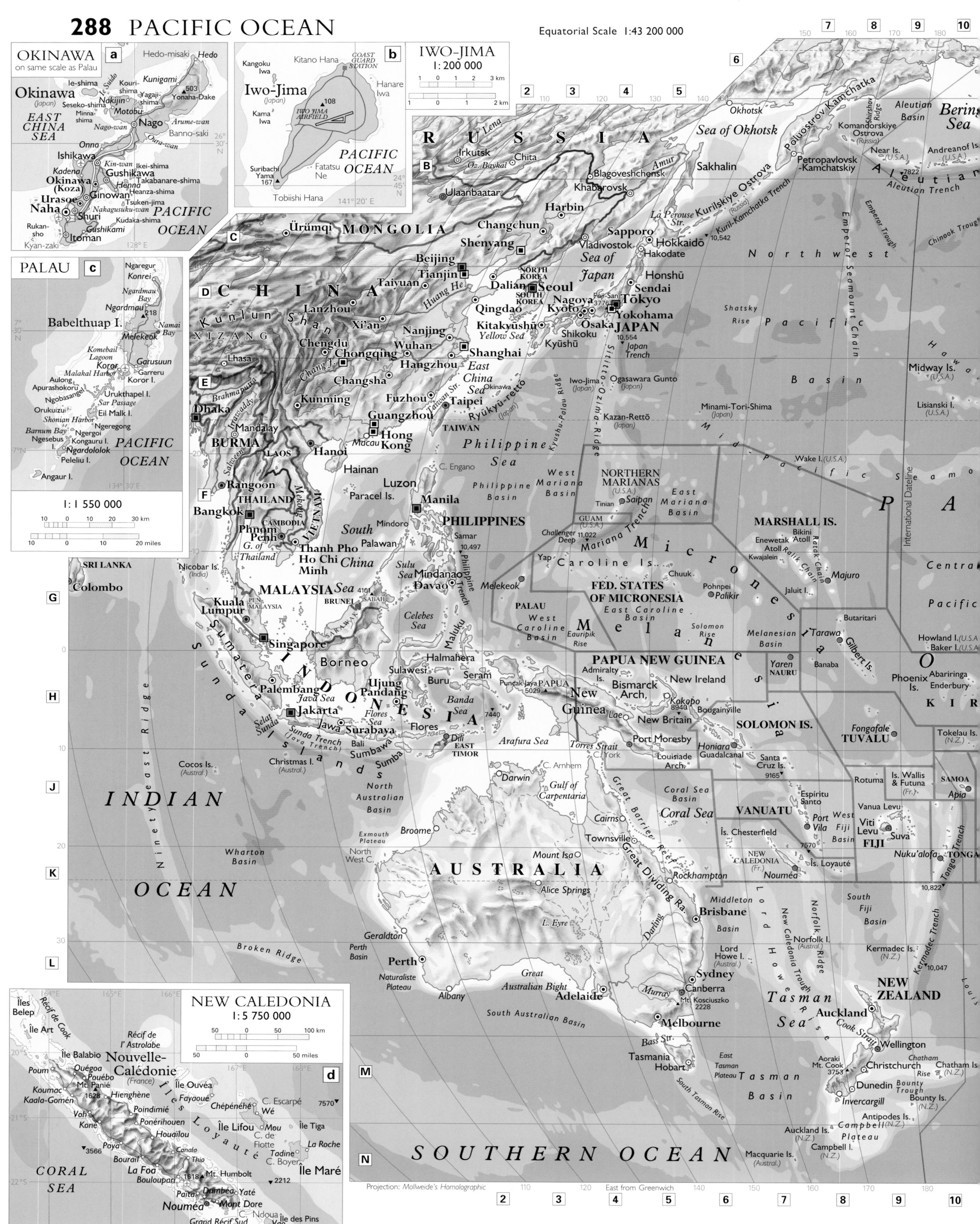

Main Map

Arctic Circle

ALASKA (U.S.A.)
Anchorage
Bristol Bay
Gulf of Alaska
Juneau
CANADA
Prince of Wales I. (U.S.A.)
Prince Rupert
Queen Charlotte Is. (Canada)
Edmonton
Calgary
Vancouver
Vancouver I.
Victoria
Seattle
Portland
ROCKY Mts
Tufts Abyssal Plain
Northeast
Mendocino Fracture Zone   C. Mendocino
Boise
Snake
Salt Lake City
Denver
Sacramento
San Francisco
Murray Fracture Zone
Los Angeles
San Diego
Phoenix
Colorado
UNITED STATES
Oklahoma City
Memphis
Atlanta
Dallas
Pacific
Molokai Fracture Zone
Guadalupe (Mex.)
Baja California
Houston
San Antonio
New Orleans
Jacksonville
Mississippi
Miami
BAHAMAS
Tropic of Cancer
Ciudad Juárez
Gulf of Mexico
Monterrey
3504
Sigsbee Deep
Florida Str.
CUBA
La Habana
Canal de Yucatán
HAITI
Honolulu
O'ahu   HAWAI'I (U.S.A.)
4205
Hawai'i
Basin
Johnston I. (U.S.A.)
Clarion Fracture Zone
Is. de Revillagigedo (Mex.)
Guadalajara
Mexico   5610
Puebla
Acapulco
Mérida
7680
JAMAICA
Kingston
PACIFIC
Middle America Trench
GUATEMALA
Guatemala
Guatemala Basin
Caribbean Sea
BELIZE
HONDURAS
San Salvador
EL SALVADOR
NICARAGUA
Managua
Barranquilla
San José
COSTA RICA
Colón   Panamá
PANAMA
Cocos Ridge
Panama Basin
I. del Coco (Costa Rica)
I. de Malpelo (Colombia)
Medellín
Cali
COLOMBIA
Palmyra Is. (U.S.A.)
North West Christmas I. Ridge
Cooper Ridge
Teraina
Tabuaeran
Kiritimati
Jarvis I. (U.S.A.)
Line Islands
KIRIBATI
Equator
Clipperton Fracture Zone
Î. Clipperton (Fr.)
Clipperton Fracture Zone
East Pacific Rise
Galapagos Fracture Zone
Galápagos (Ecuador)
Carnegie Ridge
Quito
ECUADOR
Guayaquil
C. Pariñas
Phoenix Is.
Malden I.
Starbuck I.
Penrhyn (Tongareva)
Caroline I. (Millennium I.)
Nuku Hiva
Îs. Marquises
Hiva Oa
Marquesas Fracture Zone
Manihiki
Pukapuka
Manihiki
Plateau
MER. SAMOA (U.S.A.)
Suwarrow Is.
Vostok I.
Flint I.
Îs. de la Société
Bora Bora
Huahine
Raiatea   Tahiti
Papeete
Rangiroa
Îs. Tuamotu
Mururoa
Îs. Gambier
Tuamotu
Cook Is. (N.Z.)
Aitutaki
Atiu
Rarotonga
Mangaia
Niue (N.Z.)
Austral seamount Chain
FRENCH POLYNESIA
Îs. Tubuaï
Yupanqui Basin
Mendaña Fracture Zone
Peru Basin
Nazca Ridge
PERU
6369
Lima
Cuzco
L. Titicaca
Arequipa
Nevado Ancohuma 6550
6866
Peru-Chile
Arica
La Paz
BOLIVIA
Iquique
Chile
Antofagasta
Chile Basin
8064
Trench
San Félix (Chile)
San Ambrosio (Chile)
Tropic of Capricorn
Easter Fracture Zone
Sala-y-Gómez (Chile)
Sala y Gómez Ridge
I. de Pascua (Chile)
Easter Fracture Zone
Oeno I.
Henderson I.
Ducie I.
Pitcairn I. (U.K.)
Rapa
Roggeveen Basin
Arch. de Juan Fernández (Chile)
Aconcagua 6962
Valparaíso
Santiago
Concepción
Córdoba
Rosario
Buenos Aires
URUGUAY
Montevideo
Río de la Plata
PARAGUAY
Asunción
San Miguel de Tucumán
Pôrto Alegre
ARGENTINA
Argentine Basin
SOUTH ATLANTIC OCEAN
Southwest Pacific Basin
Nemo Point (furthest point from any land)
East Pacific Rise
Pacific-Antarctic Ridge
114
Challenger Fracture Zone
Chile Rise
Menard Fracture Zone
Southeast Pacific Basin
Punta Arenas
Est. de Magallanes
C. de Hornos
Tierra del Fuego
Drake Passage
4402
South Georgia Ridge
Falkland Plateau
Falkland Is. (U.K.)
6212
Georgia Basin
South Georgia (U.K.)

Inset e — TAHITI 1:1 150 000

Pte. Aroa
B. de Matavai
Pte. Vénus
Mahina
Papetoai
Papeari
Poopao
Papenoo
Mt. Tohiea 1207
Afareaitu
Pirae
Papeete
Aruo
Tiarei
Hitiaa
Tahiti (France)
Moorea
Haapiti
Faaa
Faaone
Mt. Aorai 2060
Mt. Orohena 2241
Punaauia
Mt. Tetufera 1798
Lac Vaihiria
Paea
Taravao
Maraa
Papara
Pueu
Tautira
Atimaono
Mataiea
Vairao
Mt. Rooniu 1332
PACIFIC OCEAN
Teahupoo
Presqu'île de Taiarapu
Isthme de Taravao
Pte. Afaahiti
Tatatua
1:1 150 000

Inset f — FRENCH POLYNESIA 1:26 000 000

Hatutu
Eiao
Îles Marquises
Nuku Hiva
Ua Huka
Ua Pu
Hiva Oa
Tahuata
Motané
4884
Flint I. (Kiribati)
6513
Îles Tuamotu
Îles du Désappointement
Manihi
Ahé
Takaroa
Tikahau
Rangiroa
Apataki
Tikei
Puka Puka
Matahiva
Arutua
Kauehi
Raroia
Fangatau
Makemo
Tatakoto
Bora Bora   Îles du Vent
Île Palliser
Maupiti
Raiatea
Huahine
Fakarava
Île Raeuki
Tekokota
Moorea   Tahiti
Anaa   Hikueru
Marokau
Amanu
Puka Ruha
Maupihaa
Haraiki
Papeete   Méhétia
Ravahere
Hao
Paraoa
Vahitahi
Réao
Hérehérétué
Nengonengo
Ahunui
Îles du Duc-de-Gloucester
Vanavana
Tureia
Vairaatea
Îles Maria
Rurutu
Tematagi
Mururoa
Actéon
Fangataufa
Rimatara
Raivavae
Tropic of Capricorn
Moraně
Îles Gambier
Tubuaï
Récif Portland
Îles de la Société
Îles Sous-le-Vent
Rapa
Îots de Bass
Récif Neilson
Îles Tubuaï (Îles Australes)
Récif Président-Thiers
PACIFIC OCEAN

Inset g — NIUE 1:830 000

Hikutavake
Mutalau
Namukulu
Toi
Tuapa
Makefu   Lakepa
Alofi Bay
Alofi
Liku
Niue (N.Z.)
Halangingie Pt.
Fonuakula
Tamakautogo
Avatele
Vaiea   Hakupu
Tepa Pt.
PACIFIC OCEAN

Inset h — RAROTONGA 1:415 000

Rarotonga (N.Z.)
Avarua Harbour
Pue
Nikao
Avatiu
Avarua
Matavera
Arorangi
509
Te Manga
Ngatangiia
Maungaroa
588   653
Motu Tapu
222   Te Kou
Oneroa
Maungatangalti   329
Muri
Koromiri
Taakoka
Taroume
Titikaveka
PACIFIC OCEAN
159°45'W

Depth/Elevation Scale

ft   m
12 000   4000
9000   3000
6000   2000
3000   1000
1500   600
600   200
0   0
200   600
1000   3000
2000   6000
4000   12 000
6000   18 000
8000   24 000
m   ft

West from Greenwich

NORTH
AMERICA

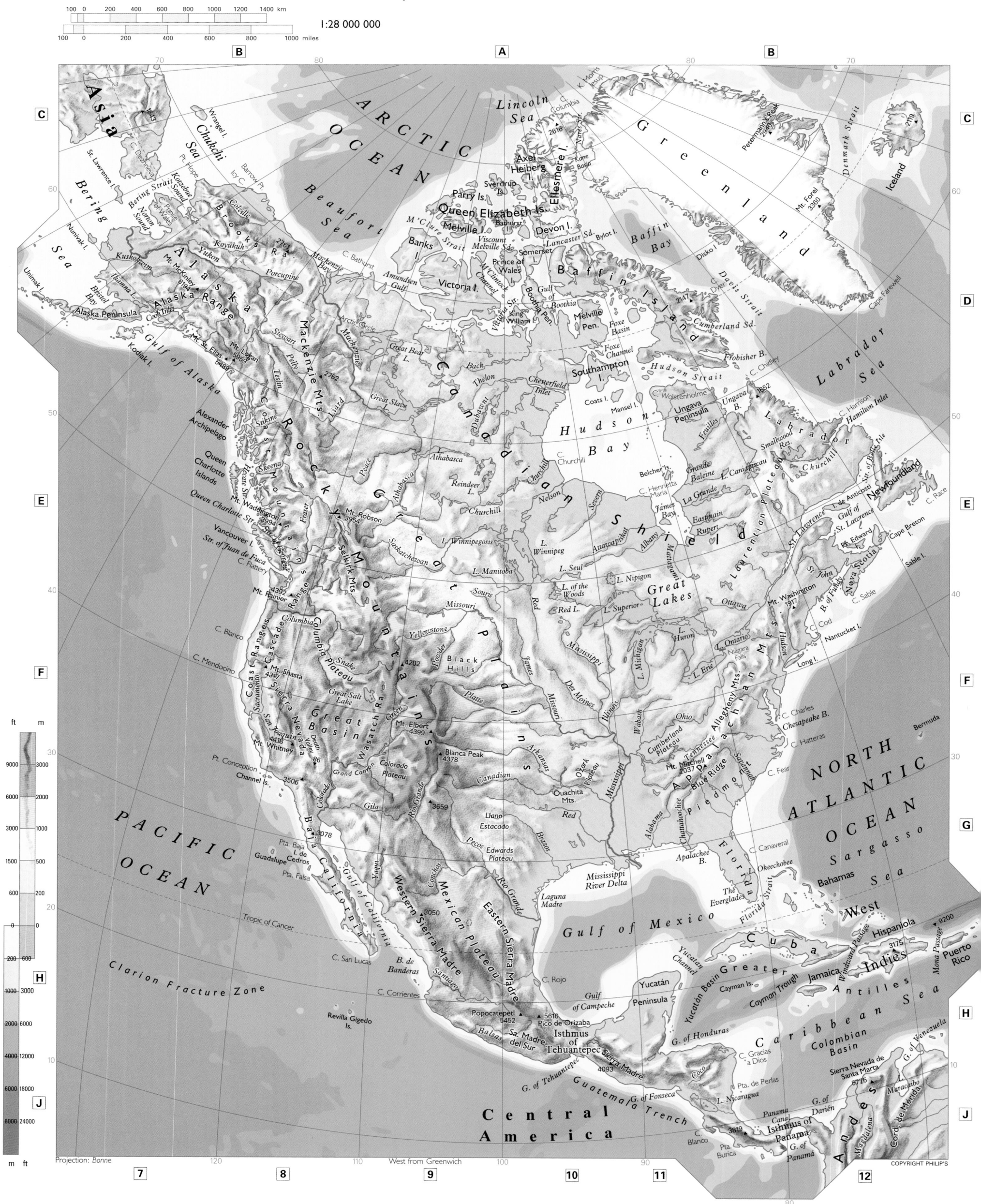

1:28 000 000

Projection: *Bonne*

West from Greenwich

COPYRIGHT PHILIP'S

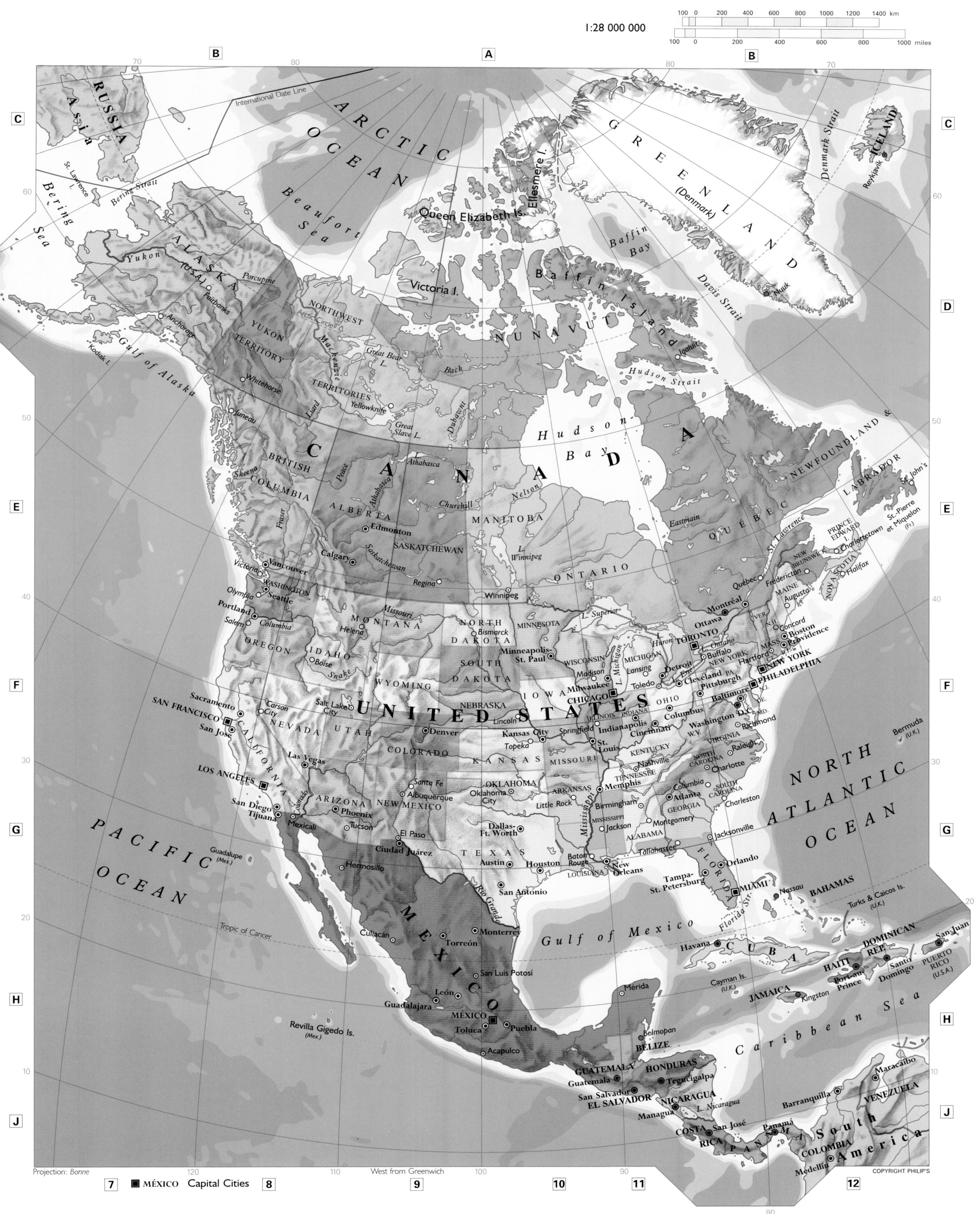

1:28 000 000

100 0 200 400 600 800 1000 1200 1400 km

100 0 200 400 600 800 1000 miles

C

RUSSIA

Asia

St. Lawrence I.

Bering Strait

Bering Sea

ARCTIC OCEAN

Beaufort Sea

International Date Line

Queen Elizabeth Is.

Ellesmere I.

GREENLAND (Denmark)

Denmark Strait

ICELAND

Reykjavik

C

Yukon

ALASKA (U.S.A.)

Porcupine

Anchorage

Fairbanks

Kodiak I.

Gulf of Alaska

Victoria I.

Baffin Bay

Baffin Island

Davis Strait

Nuuk

D

NORTHWEST

Arctic Circle

YUKON TERRITORY

Whitehorse

Juneau

Mackenzie

Great Bear L.

NUNAVUT

Back

Hudson Strait

Iqaluit

D

BRITISH COLUMBIA

Skeena

Fraser

Peace

Liard

TERRITORIES

Yellowknife

Great Slave L.

Athabasca

Dubawnt

Hudson Bay

E

Victoria

Vancouver

Calgary

ALBERTA

Edmonton

SASKATCHEWAN

Saskatchewan

Regina

CANADA

Athabasca

Churchill

Nelson

L. Winnipeg

MANITOBA

Eastmain

QUÉBEC

St. Lawrence

NEWFOUNDLAND & LABRADOR

St. John's

St-Pierre et Miquelon (Fr.)

E

WASHINGTON

Olympia

Seattle

OREGON

Portland

Salem

Columbia

Snake

IDAHO

Boise

MONTANA

Helena

Missouri

Winnipeg

ONTARIO

L. Superior

Ottawa

TORONTO

L. Huron

Québec

Montréal

Fredericton

NEW BRUNSWICK

MAINE

Augusta

PRINCE EDWARD I.

Charlottetown

NOVA SCOTIA

Halifax

F

Sacramento

SAN FRANCISCO

San Jose

CALIFORNIA

Carson City

Salt Lake City

NEVADA

UTAH

WYOMING

NORTH DAKOTA

Bismarck

SOUTH DAKOTA

MINNESOTA

Minneapolis

St. Paul

WISCONSIN

Madison

L. Michigan

Milwaukee

MICHIGAN

Lansing

Detroit

L. Erie

L. Ontario

Buffalo

Erie

PA

Cleveland

Pittsburgh

NEW YORK

Hartford

New York

PHILADELPHIA

Boston

Providence

MASS

Concord

N.Y.

CHICAGO

IOWA

ILLINOIS

INDIANA

OHIO

Columbus

Cincinnati

Toledo

W.V.

Baltimore

Washington D.C.

MD.

Richmond

DE.

N.J.

F

San Diego

Tijuana

Los Angeles

Las Vegas

UNITED STATES

COLORADO

Denver

NEBRASKA

Lincoln

KANSAS

Topeka

Kansas City

MISSOURI

St. Louis

Springfield

Indianapolis

KENTUCKY

Nashville

TENNESSEE

Memphis

VIRGINIA

NORTH CAROLINA

Raleigh

Charlotte

Columbia

SOUTH CAROLINA

Charleston

NORTH ATLANTIC OCEAN

Bermuda (U.K.)

G

PACIFIC OCEAN

Guadalupe (Mex.)

ARIZONA

Phoenix

Tucson

Mexicali

NEW MEXICO

Albuquerque

Santa Fe

El Paso

Colorado

OKLAHOMA

Oklahoma City

ARKANSAS

Little Rock

Dallas-Ft. Worth

Mississippi

Birmingham

Jackson

MISSISSIPPI

ALABAMA

Montgomery

GEORGIA

Atlanta

Columbia

Jacksonville

FLORIDA

G

Ciudad Juárez

Hermosillo

Río Grande

TEXAS

Austin

Houston

San Antonio

LOUISIANA

Baton Rouge

New Orleans

Tallahassee

Orlando

Tampa-St. Petersburg

MIAMI

Nassau

BAHAMAS

Florida Str.

Turks & Caicos Is. (U.K.)

H

Tropic of Cancer

Culiacán

Torreón

Monterrey

MEXICO

San Luis Potosí

León

Guadalajara

Revilla Gigedo Is. (Mex.)

Gulf of Mexico

Havana

CUBA

Cayman Is. (U.K.)

JAMAICA

Kingston

HAITI

Port-au-Prince

DOMINICAN REP.

Santo Domingo

PUERTO RICO (U.S.A.)

San Juan

Caribbean Sea

H

Mérida

MÉXICO

Toluca

Puebla

Acapulco

Belmopan

BELIZE

GUATEMALA

Guatemala

HONDURAS

Tegucigalpa

San Salvador

EL SALVADOR

NICARAGUA

Managua

L. Nicaragua

Barranquilla

Maracaibo

VENEZUELA

J

COSTA RICA

San José

PANAMA

Panamá

COLOMBIA

Medellín

South America

J

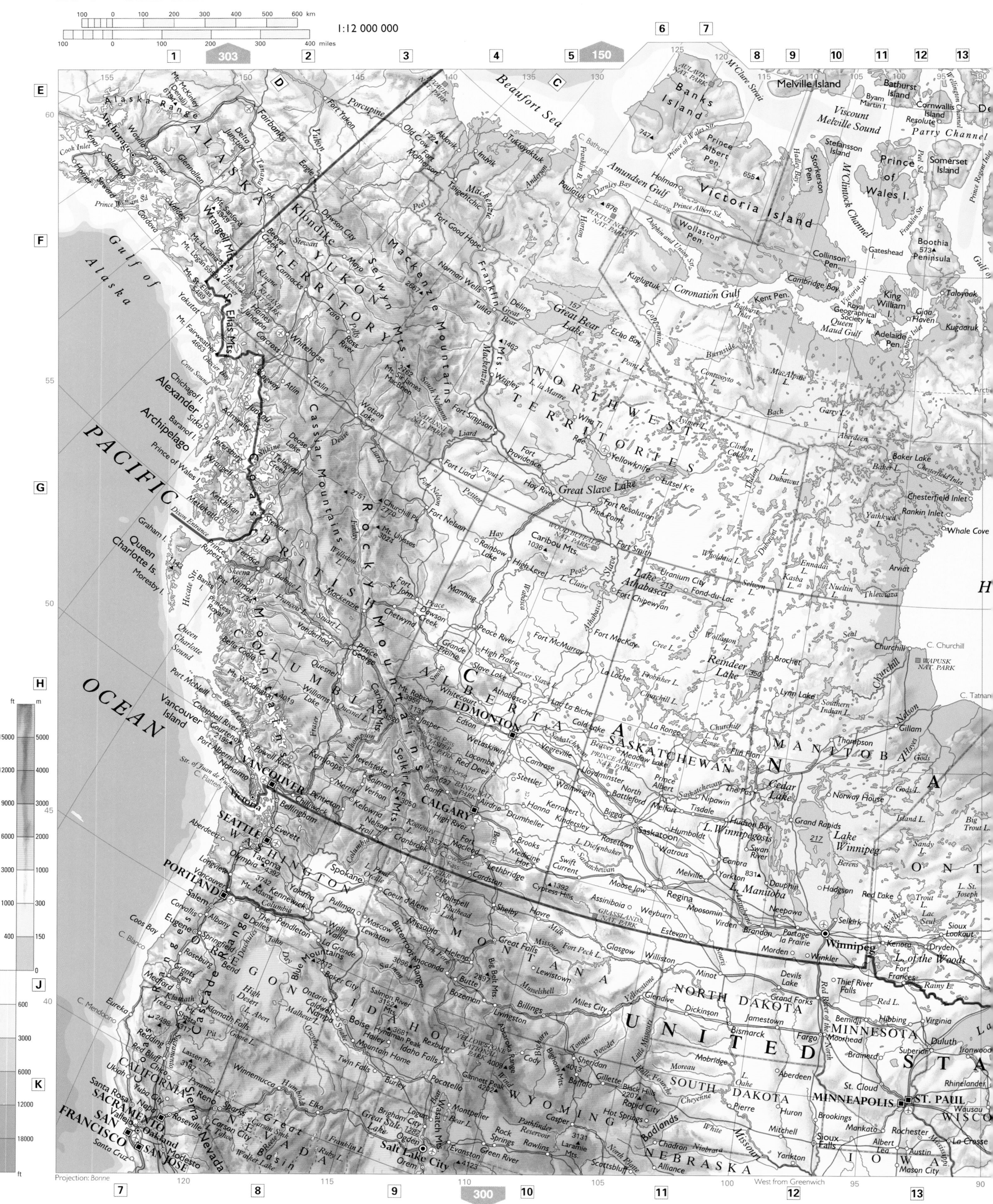

Projection: Bonne

1:12 000 000

West from Greenwich

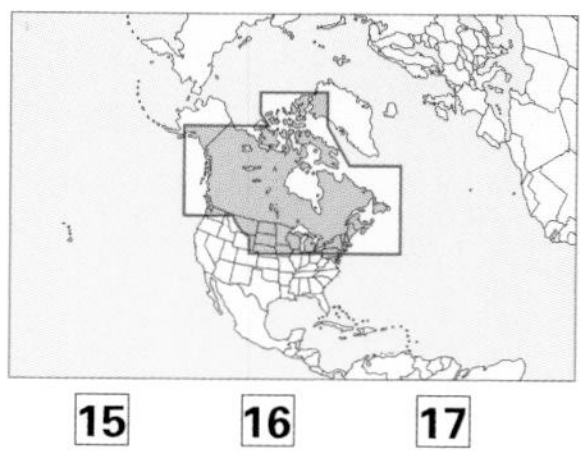

NORTHERN CANADA
continuation northwards on same scale as main map

Main map labels

Jones Sound
von Island
1951
Lancaster Sound
Baffin Bay
Nunavik
Brodeur Peninsula
Admiralty Inlet
Nanisivik
Arctic Bay
Borden Pen.
Bylot I.
Eclipse Sd.
Pond Inlet
Clyde River
C. Adair
C. Raper
SIRMILIK NAT. PARK
2469
Davis Strait
Boothia
Fury and Hecla Str.
Steensby Inlet
Home B.
AUYUITTUQ NAT. PARK
Cumberland Peninsula
C. Dyer
Simpson Pen.
Igloolik
Rowley
Hall Beach
Prince Charles I.
Air Force I.
Spicer Is.
Taverner Bay
2147
Pangnirtung
Hoare B.
Melville Peninsula
Foxe Basin
Nettilling L.
Cumberland Sd.
C. Mercy
Wales
Rae Isthmus
Circle
Repulse Bay
NUNAVUT
Vansittart I.
C. Dorchester
Amadjuak L.
Hall Peninsula
Frobisher Bay
Koukdjuak
Meta Incognita Peninsula
Resolution I.
Roes Welcome Sd.
Southampton I.
Foxe Channel
Mill I.
Kinngait
Iqaluit
Salisbury I.
Kimmirut
C. Chidley
Coral Harbour
Bell Pen.
Nottingham I.
Charles I.
Salluit
Hudson Strait
Coats I.
Digges Is.
Ivujivik
Quaqtaq
Akpatok I.
Mansel I.
Kangiqsujuaq
Cratère du Nouveau-Québec
642
657
Torngat Mts.
Smith I.
Péninsule d'Ungava
Kangirsuk
Arnaud
Ungava Bay
1652
Mt. d'Iberville
Caubvick
Hebron
Ottawa Is.
Puvirnituq
L. Payne
Fatilles
Kangiqsualujjuaq
Kuujjuaq
George
Nain
257
Inukjuak
L. Minto
Melèzes
Koksoak
Hopedale
Hudson Bay
Sleeper Is.
King George Is.
Bakers Dozen Is.
L. à l'Eau Claire
C. Harrison
Rigolet
Cartwright
NEWFOUNDLAND & LABRADOR
Port Hope Simpson
Sanikiluaq
Belcher Is.
C. Henrietta Maria
Kuujjuarapik
Grande Baleine
L. Bienville
Petitsikapau L.
Esker
Churchill Falls
Smallwood Res.
North West River
Happy Valley-Goose Bay
Churchill
St. Anthony
Grey Is.
Belle Isle
St. of Belle Isle
C. Bauld
Peawanuck
Winisk
Kanaaupscow
La Grande
Caniapiscau
Schefferville
Labrador
Labrador City
Fermont
L. Ashuanipi
St-Augustin
Baie Verte
Notre Dame B.
Lewisporte
Gander
Bonavista
Chisasibi
Twin Is.
Akimiski I.
Wemindji
Eastmain
Mts. Otish
1135
Gagnon
Moisie
Natashquan
Deer Lake
Corner Brook
815
Grand Falls
Windsor
Newfoundland
St. John's
Carbonear
Attawapiskat
Fort Albany
Albany
Rupert
Waskaganish
L. Mistassini
L. Albanel
Mts. Groulx
1104
Havre-St-Pierre
Grandes-Bergeronnes
Baie-Comeau
Port-Cartier
Sept-Îles
Dét. de Jacques-Cartier
Î. d'Anticosti
Channel-Port aux Basques
Placentia B.
Avalon Pen.
C. Race
Moosonee
Eastmain
Rés. Manicouagan
Manicouagan
Gulf of St. Lawrence
320
Marystown
St-Pierre et Miquelon (Fr.)
Placentia
Nakina
Kenogami
Opinaca
Chibougamau
Dolbeau-Mistassini
Alma
Roberval
St-Laurent (St-Laurent)
Pén. de la Gaspésie
Gaspé
C. Ray
Cabot Strait
Cape Breton I.
Glace Bay
Sydney
Port Hawkesbury
Greenstone
Hearst
Matagami
Rés. Gouin
St-Jean
Chicoutimi
Jonquière
1172
Rimouski
Matane
Chaleur B.
PRINCE EDWARD I.
Summerside
Charlottetown
Antigonish
New Glasgow
Thunder Bay
L. Nipigon
Kapuskasing
Abitibi
Val-d'Or
La Tuque
Rés. Cabonga
Saguenay
Rivière-du-Loup
Campbellton
NEW BRUNSWICK
Miramichi
Bathurst
NOVA SCOTIA
Amherst
Truro
Dartmouth
Halifax
Nipigon
Marathon
Oba
Timmins
Kirkland Lake
Rouyn-Noranda
Shawinigan
Trois-Rivières
Edmundston
Grand Falls
Woodstock
Fredericton
Moncton
Kentville
Bridgewater
Liverpool
Sable I. (Nova Scotia)
6309
Wawa
Chapleau
New Liskeard
QUÉBEC
Québec
Lévis
St-Georges
MAINE
Saint John
Digby
B. of Fundy
Yarmouth
C. Sable
Houghton
183
Sault Ste. Marie
Elliot Lake
Sudbury
North Bay
Pembroke
Hull
OTTAWA
Cornwall
MONTRÉAL
St-Hyacinthe
Sherbrooke
Drummondville
Thetford Mines
Augusta
Bangor
Portland
Marquette
Escanaba
Menominee
Manistique
Manitoulin I.
Georgian Bay
Parry Sound
Huntsville
Orillia
Brockville
Kingston
1629
Lewiston
VERMONT
NEW HAMPSHIRE
Montpelier
Concord
Manchester
Lowell
BOSTON
C. Cod
Green Bay
Appleton
Sheboygan
Traverse City
Cadillac
Petoskey
Lake Huron
Owen Sound
Barrie
Peterborough
Burlington
Adirondack Mts.
Albany
Springfield
MASS
CONN
R.I.
Hartford
Providence
New Haven
MILWAUKEE
Madison
L. Michigan
Saginaw
Flint
Grand Rapids
TORONTO
Kitchener
Hamilton
Niagara
Oshawa
L. Ontario
Rochester
Syracuse
Elmira
NEW YORK
Binghamton
DETROIT
Windsor
L. Erie
Sarnia
London
Toledo
CLEVELAND
PENNSYLVANIA
Lansing
Jamestown
174

Northern Canada inset labels

ARCTIC OCEAN
North Magnetic Pole 2007
1626
C. Columbia
2170
Lincoln Sea
Kronprins Frederik Land
GREENLAND (KALAALLIT NUNAAT)
Alert
Nyeboe Land
Petermann Gletscher
QUTTINIRPAAQ NAT. PARK
2616
Lake Hazon
Barbeau Pk.
Agassiz Icecap
Sermersuaq (Humboldt Gletscher)
C. Thomas Hubbard
Meighen I.
Nansen Sd.
Greely Fiord
Eureka
Kane Basin
Knud Rasmussen Land
C. Isachsen
Borden Island
Prince of Wales Icefield
Brock I.
Axel Heiberg Island
2210
Qaanaaq (Thule)
Prince Patrick Island
Mackenzie King I.
Ellef Ringnes Island
Amund Ringnes
Norwegian Bay
Graham I.
Grise Fiord
Qeqertarsuaq
Lauge Koch Kyst
Uummannaq (Dundas)
Eglinton I.
Emerald I.
Lougheed I.
N.W.T.
Queen Elizabeth Islands
Cornwall I.
Grinnell Pen.
Jones Sound
Coburg I.
Kap York
Melville Bugt
776
Parry Islands
NUNAVUT
Bathurst Island
Wellington Channel
1951
M'Clure Strait
Melville Island
Byam Martin I.
Cornwallis Island
Devon Island
2469
Viscount Melville Sound
Lowther I.
Resolute
Parry Channel
Lancaster Sound
Stefansson Island
Prince of Wales I.
Somerset Island
SIRMILIK NAT. PARK
1951
Nanisivik
Borden Pen.
Bylot I.
Eclipse Sd.
Pond Inlet
Arctic Bay
Brodeur Pen.
Baffin Bay

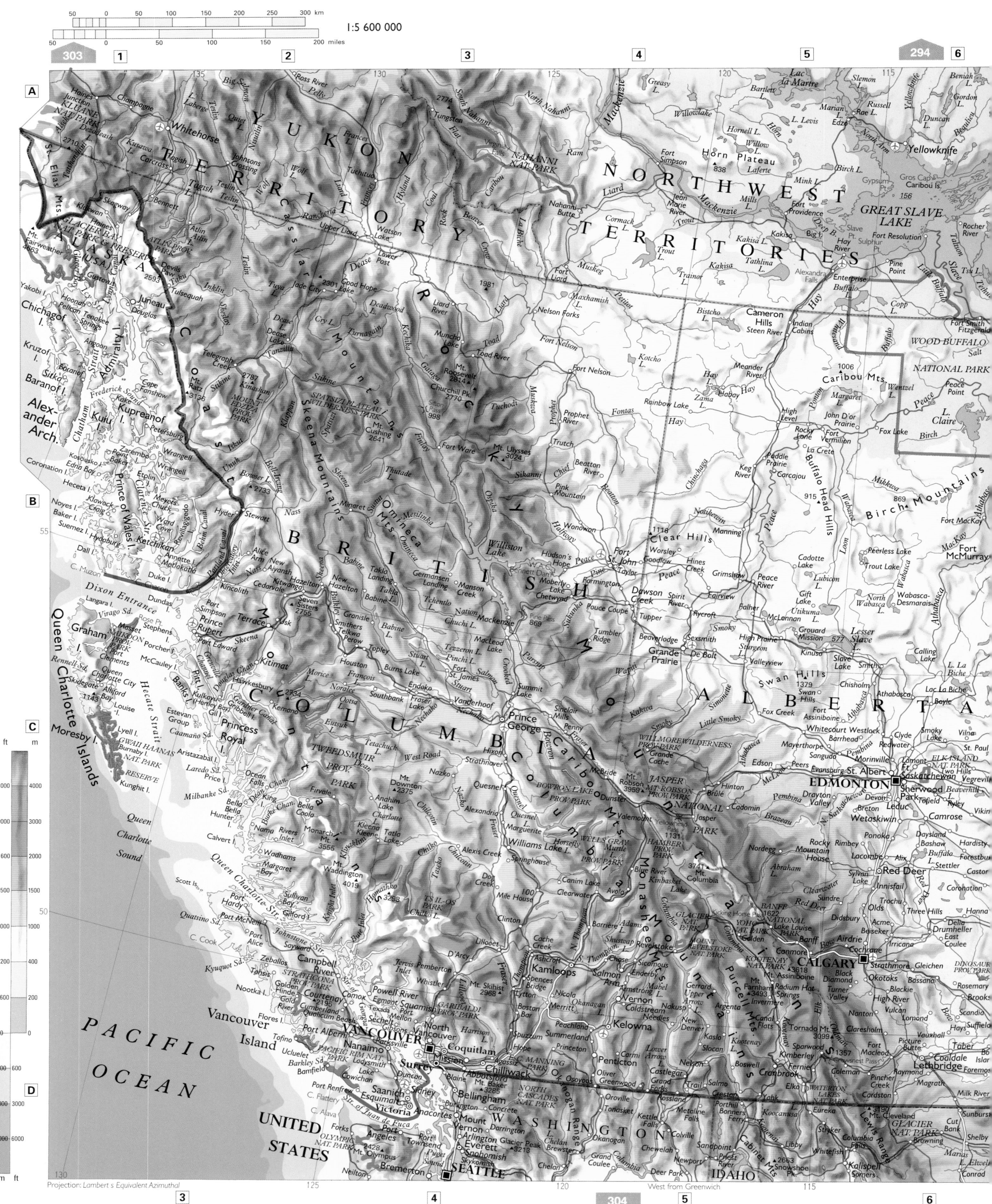

Projection: Lambert's Equivalent Azimuthal

West from Greenwich

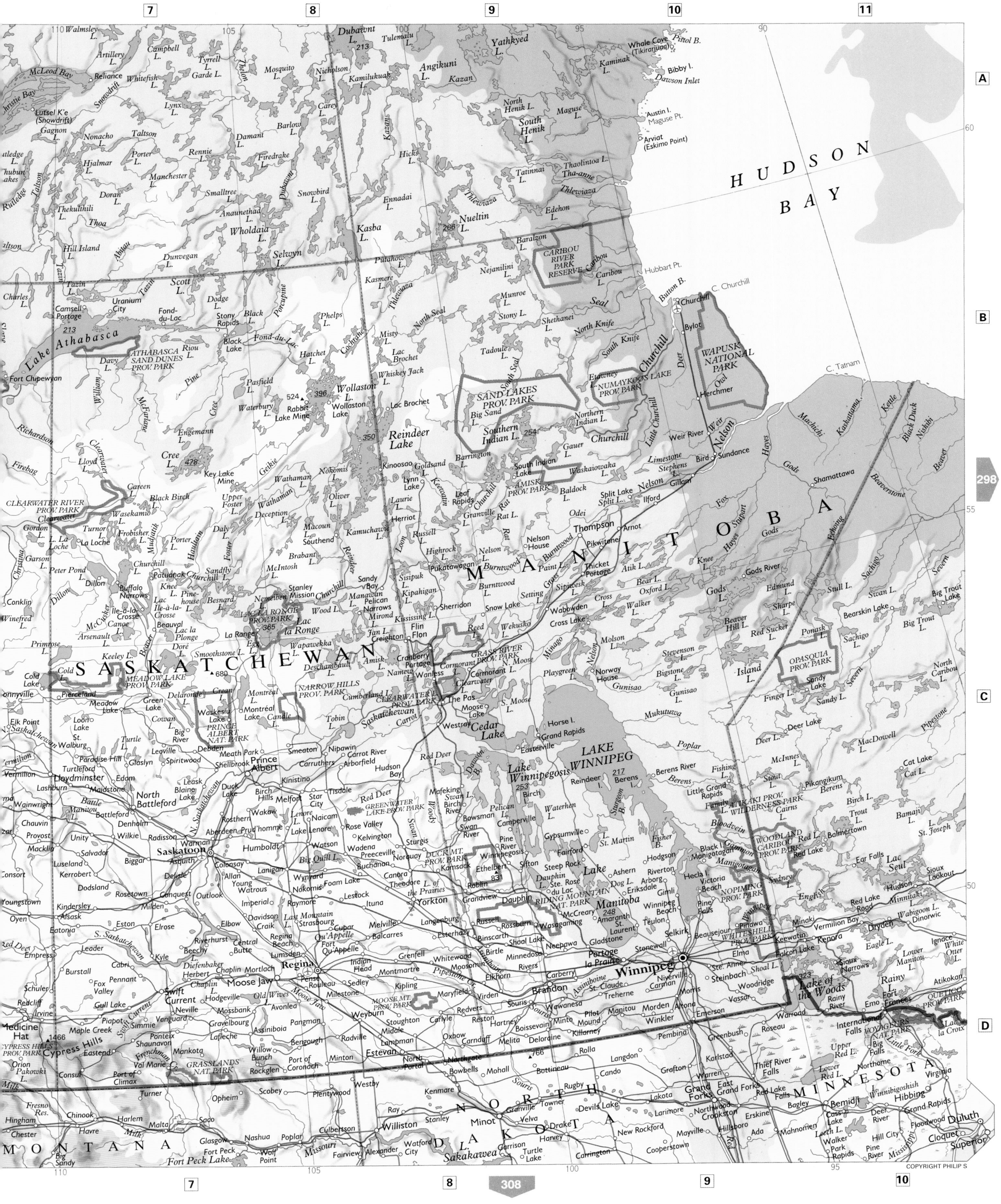

1:5 600 000

Projection: Lambert's Equivalent Azimuthal

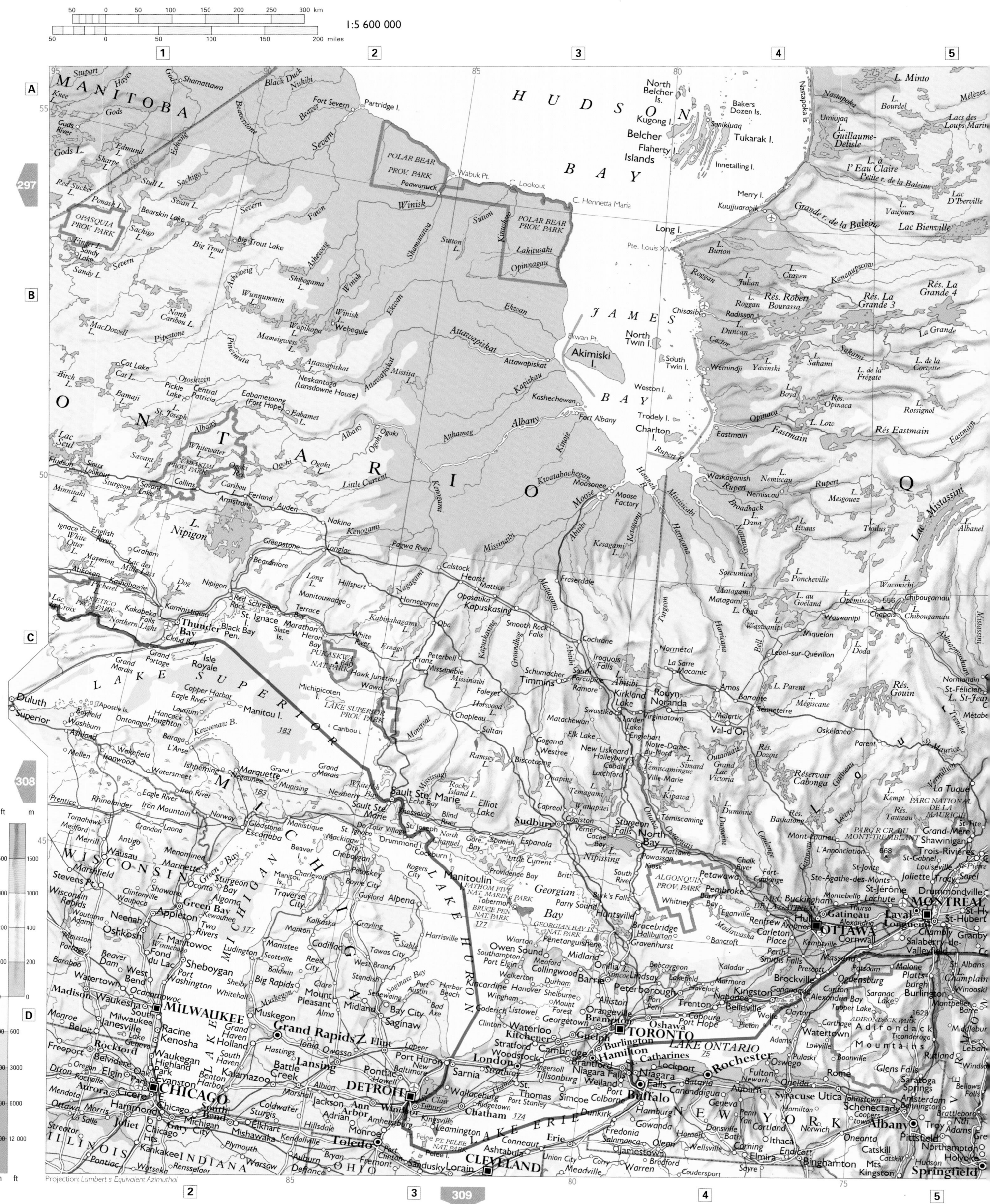

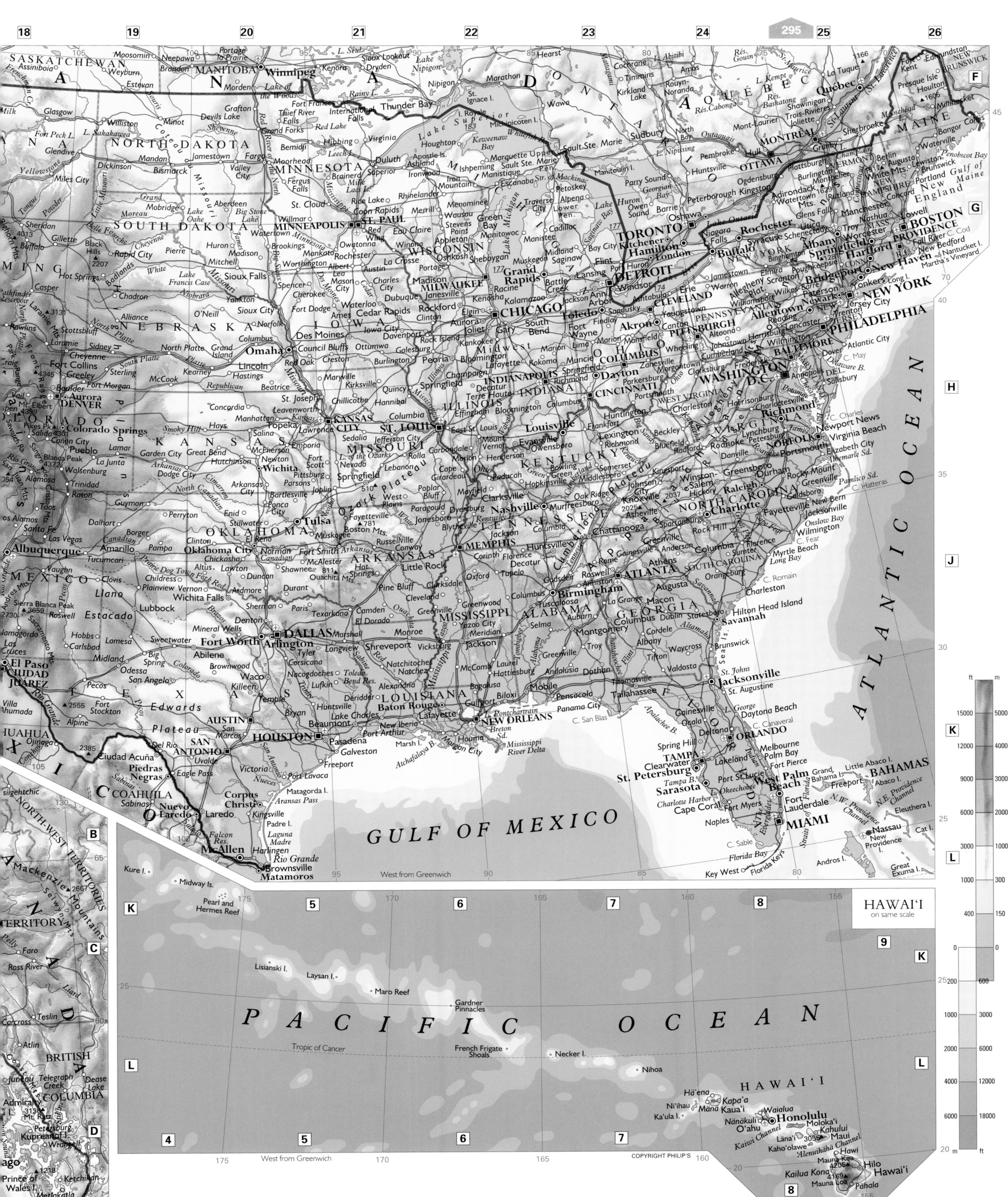

GULF OF MEXICO

ATLANTIC OCEAN

PACIFIC OCEAN

HAWAI'I on same scale

West from Greenwich

COPYRIGHT PHILIP'S

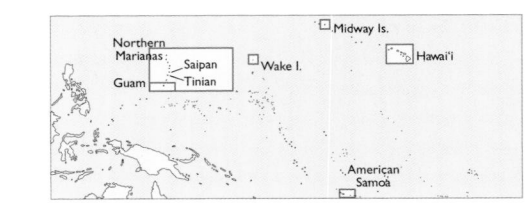

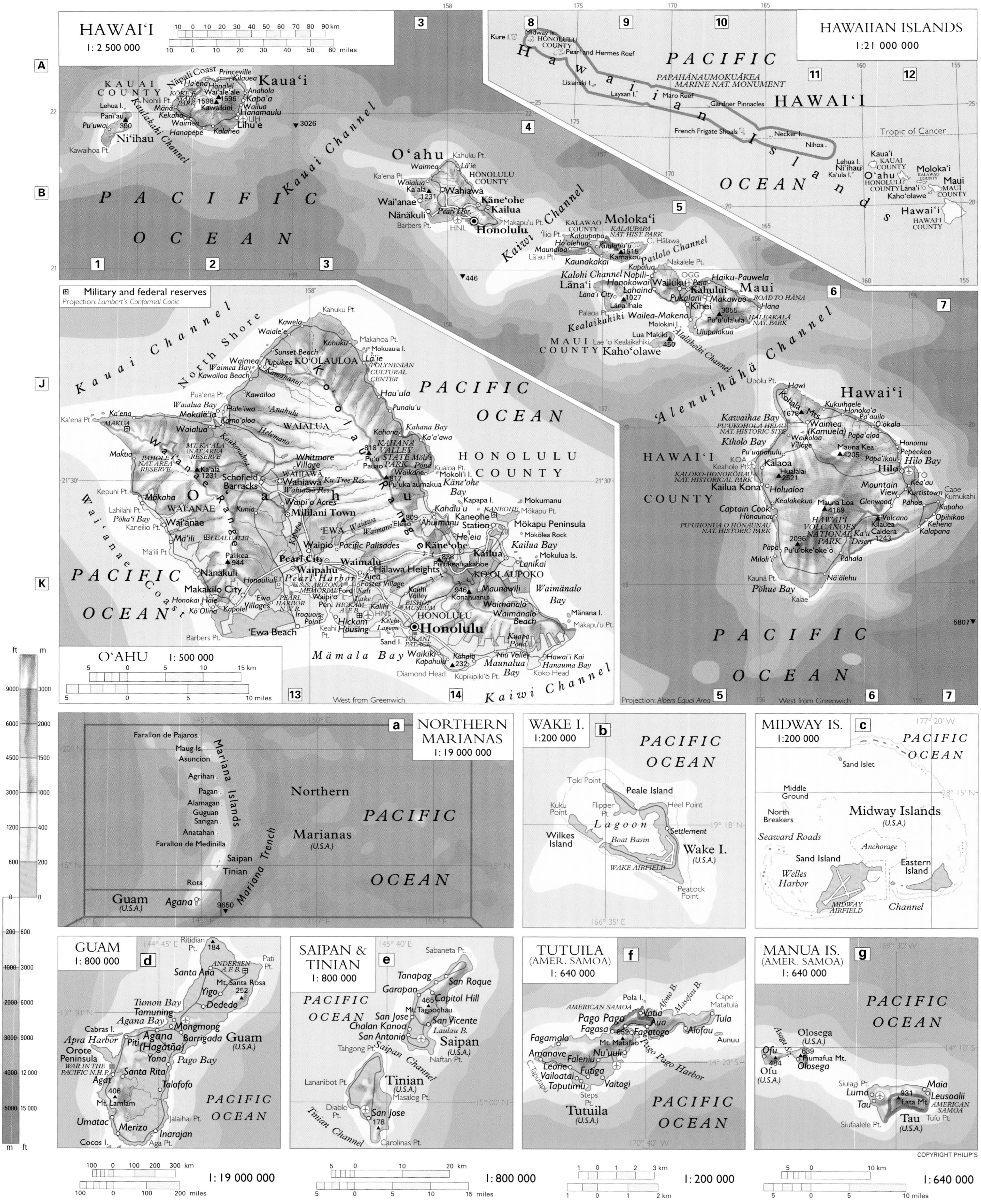

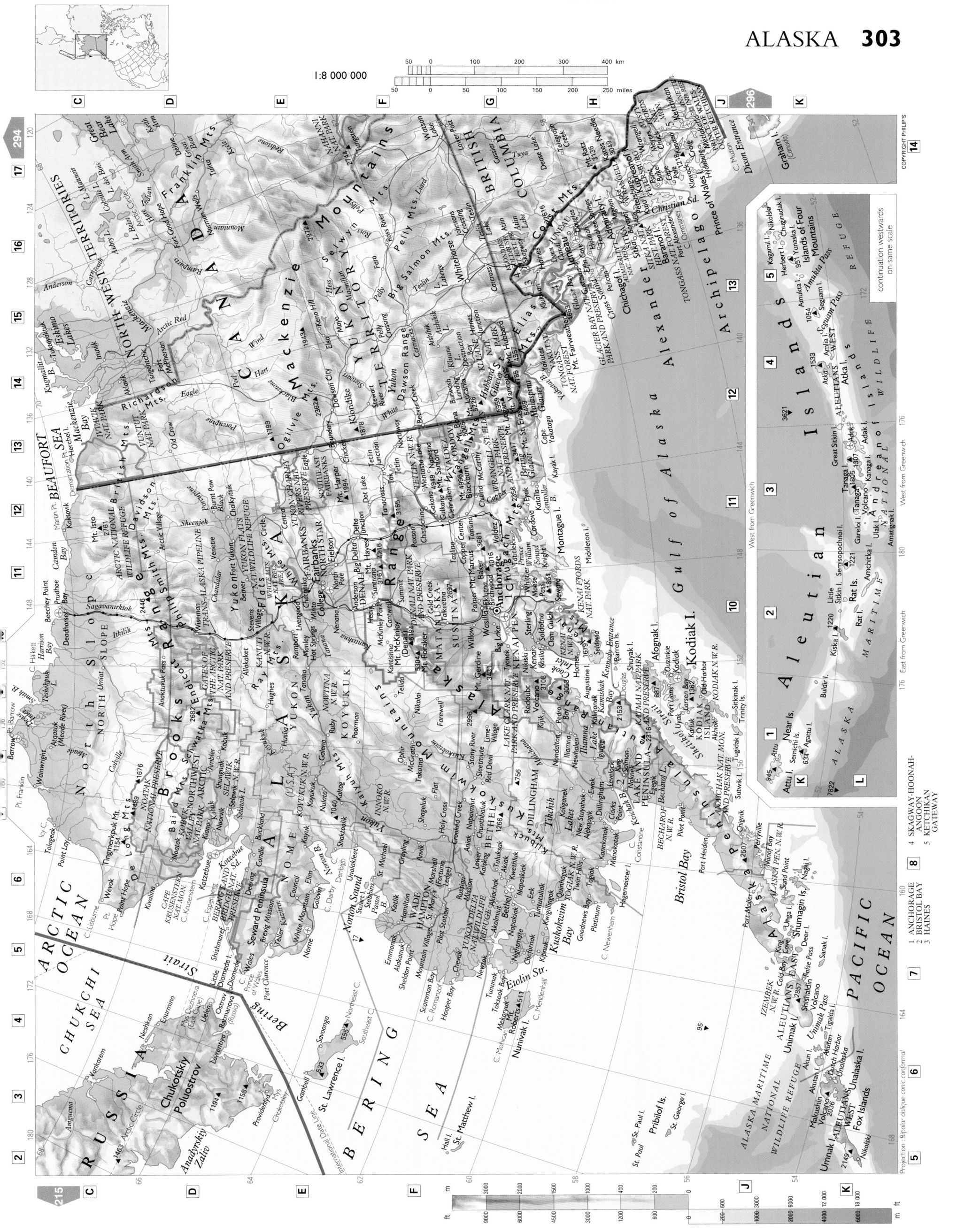

1:5 360 000

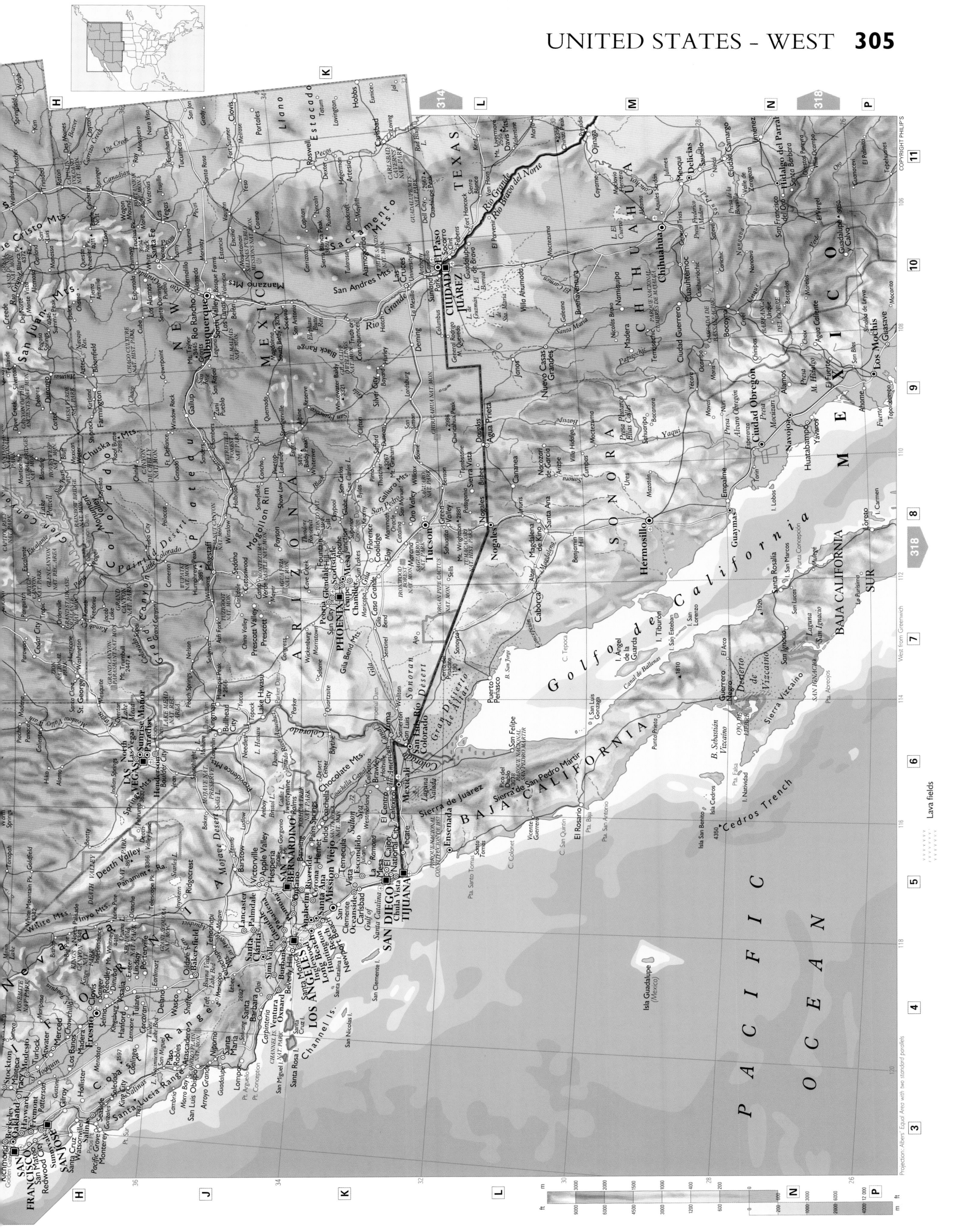

1:2 000 000

km scale: 10 0 10 20 30 40 50 60 70 80 90 km
miles scale: 10 0 10 20 30 40 50 60 miles

WESTERN WASHINGTON REGION on same scale

PACIFIC OCEAN

BRITISH COLUMBIA

CANADA

Vancouver Island

Strait of Georgia

Strait of Juan de Fuca

WASHINGTON

OREGON

OLYMPIC Mountains
OLYMPIC NATIONAL PARK

Mt Olympus 2428

VANCOUVER
New Westminster
Victoria
SEATTLE
Bellevue
Everett
Tacoma
Olympia
Centralia
Chehalis
PORTLAND
Vancouver
Gresham

MT RAINIER NATIONAL PARK
Mt. Rainier 4392

MT ST HELENS NATIONAL VOLCANIC MONUMENT
Mt St. Helens 2550
Mt. Adams 3742

CASCADE RANGE

Pahute Mesa

White Mts. 4006

Inyo Mts.
Owens

SIERRA NEVADA

YOSEMITE NATIONAL PARK
Mt. Dana 3975
Half Dome 2695
El Capitan 2307
Mt. Lyell 3997

KINGS CANYON NATIONAL PARK
Mt. Whitney 4418
Mt. Williamson 4383
North Palisade 4341

SEQUOIA NATIONAL PARK

DEVILS POSTPILE NATIONAL MONUMENT

Mono Lake

Lake Tahoe 1899

Reno
Sparks
Carson City
Minden

Sacramento Valley

SACRAMENTO
Chico
Oroville
Yuba City
Marysville
Roseville
Woodland
Davis
Davis
Fairfield
Vacaville
Napa
Santa Rosa

SAN FRANCISCO
Oakland
Berkeley
Richmond
San Rafael
Daly City
San Mateo
Redwood City
Palo Alto
Mountain View
Sunnyvale
SAN JOSE
Santa Clara
Fremont
Hayward
Livermore
Pleasanton
Concord
Walnut Creek
Stockton
Modesto
Turlock
Merced
Madera
FRESNO
Clovis
Visalia
Tulare
Hanford
Porterville

San Joaquin Valley

Diablo Range

Santa Lucia Range

Salinas Valley
Salinas
Monterey
Monterey Bay
Santa Cruz
Paso Robles

MONTEREY BAY NATIONAL MARINE SANCTUARY

PINNACLES NATIONAL MONUMENT

POINT REYES NATIONAL SEASHORE

Lava fields

West from Greenwich

Projection: Bonne

1:5 360 000

Projection: Albers' Equal Area with two standard parallels

West from Greenwich

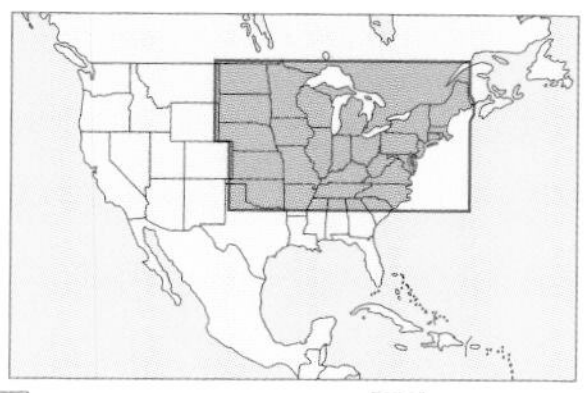

ONTARIO

QUÉBEC

MAINE

NEW BRUNS.

NEW HAMPSHIRE

VERMONT

MASSACHUSETTS

NEW YORK

PENNSYLVANIA

OHIO

WEST VIRGINIA

VIRGINIA

MARYLAND

DELAWARE

NEW JERSEY

NORTH CAROLINA

SOUTH CAROLINA

GEORGIA

KENTUCKY

LAKE SUPERIOR

LAKE HURON

LAKE ERIE

LAKE ONTARIO

GULF OF MAINE

ATLANTIC OCEAN

CHESAPEAKE BAY

DELAWARE BAY

Montréal · Ottawa · Québec · Toronto · DETROIT · CLEVELAND · PITTSBURGH · COLUMBUS · CINCINNATI · PHILADELPHIA · WASHINGTON D.C. · BALTIMORE · NEW YORK · BOSTON · PROVIDENCE · NORFOLK · Richmond · Charlotte · Raleigh · ATLANTA · Buffalo · Rochester · Albany · Grand Rapids

1:2 000 000

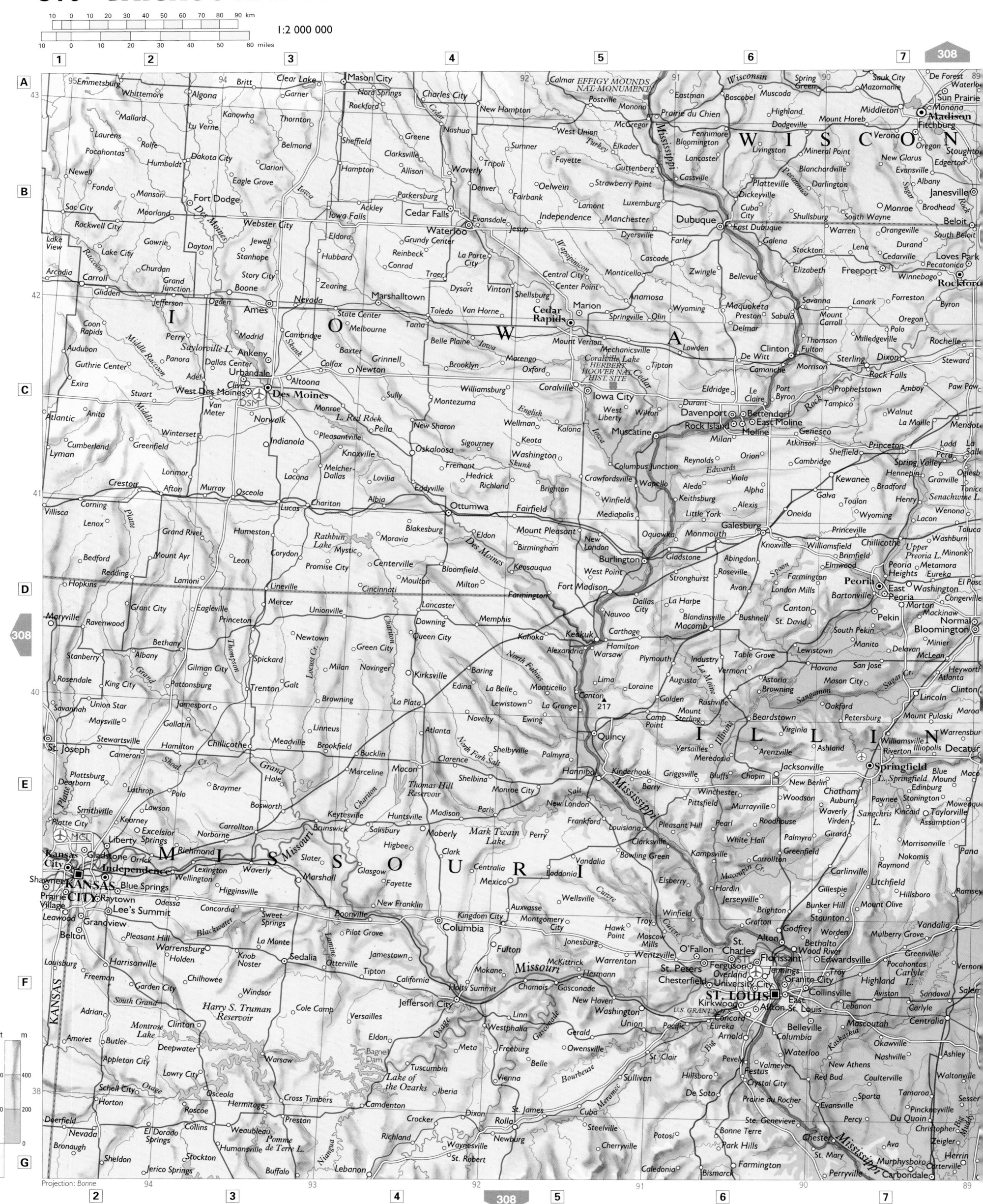

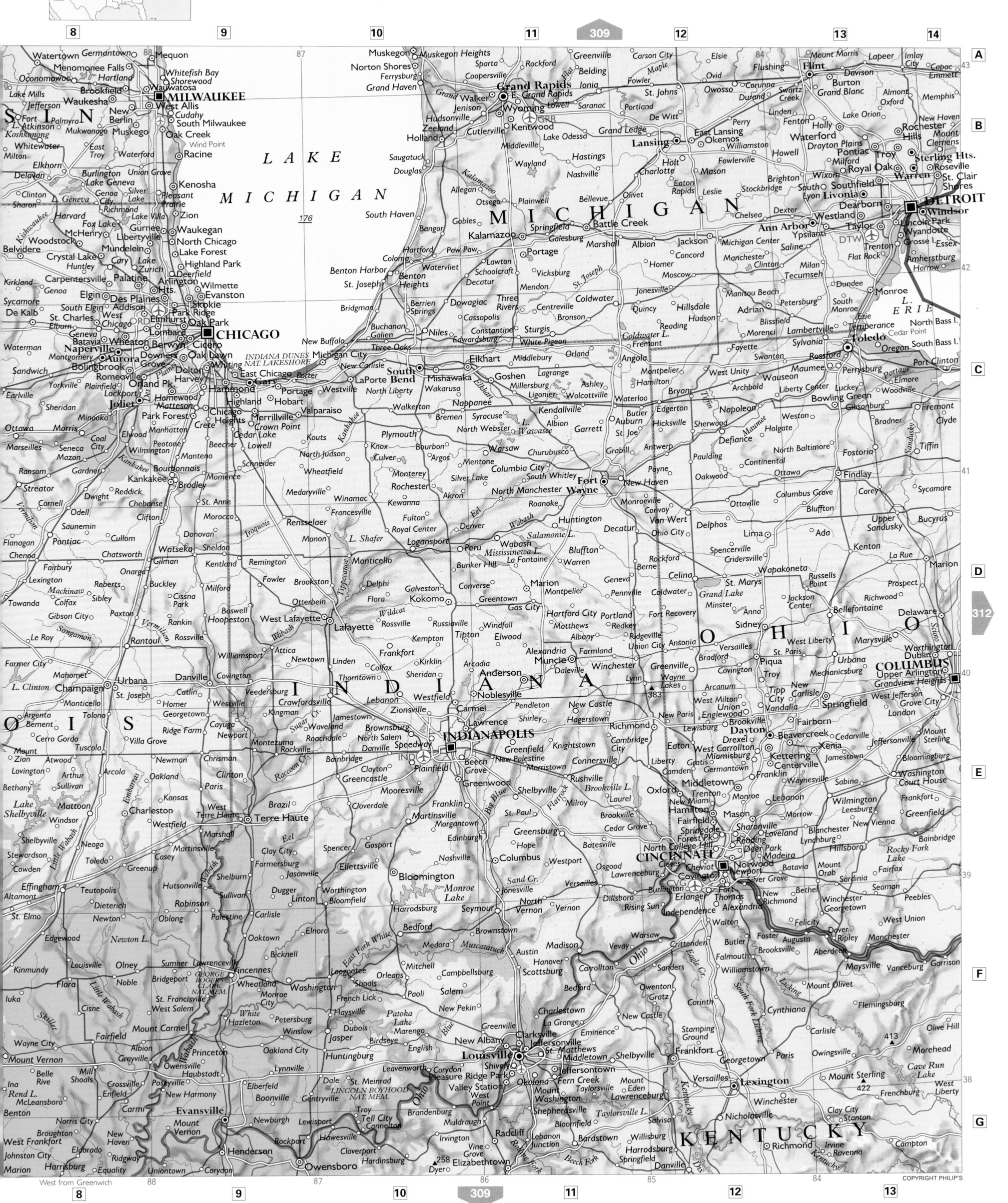

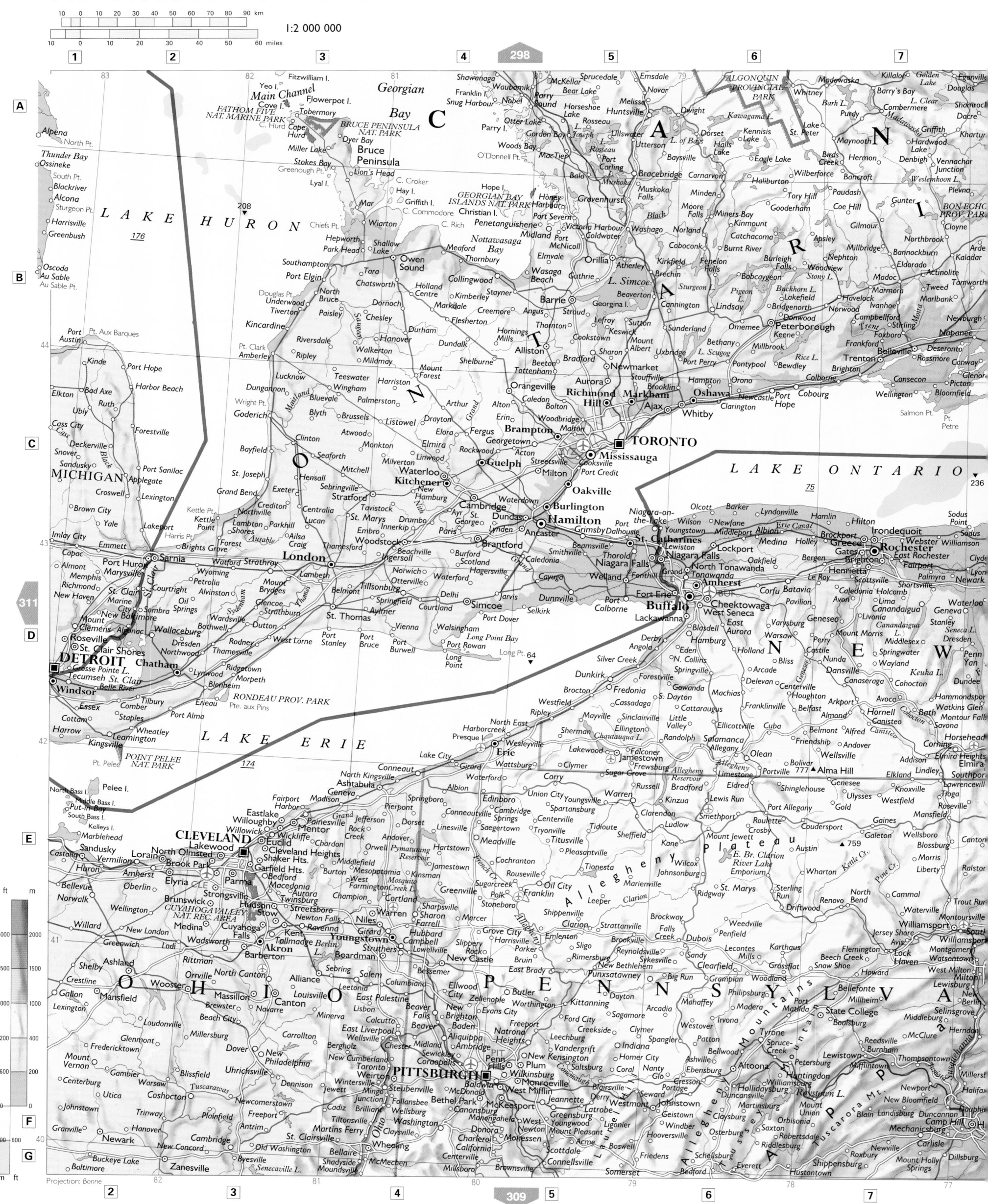

1:2 000 000

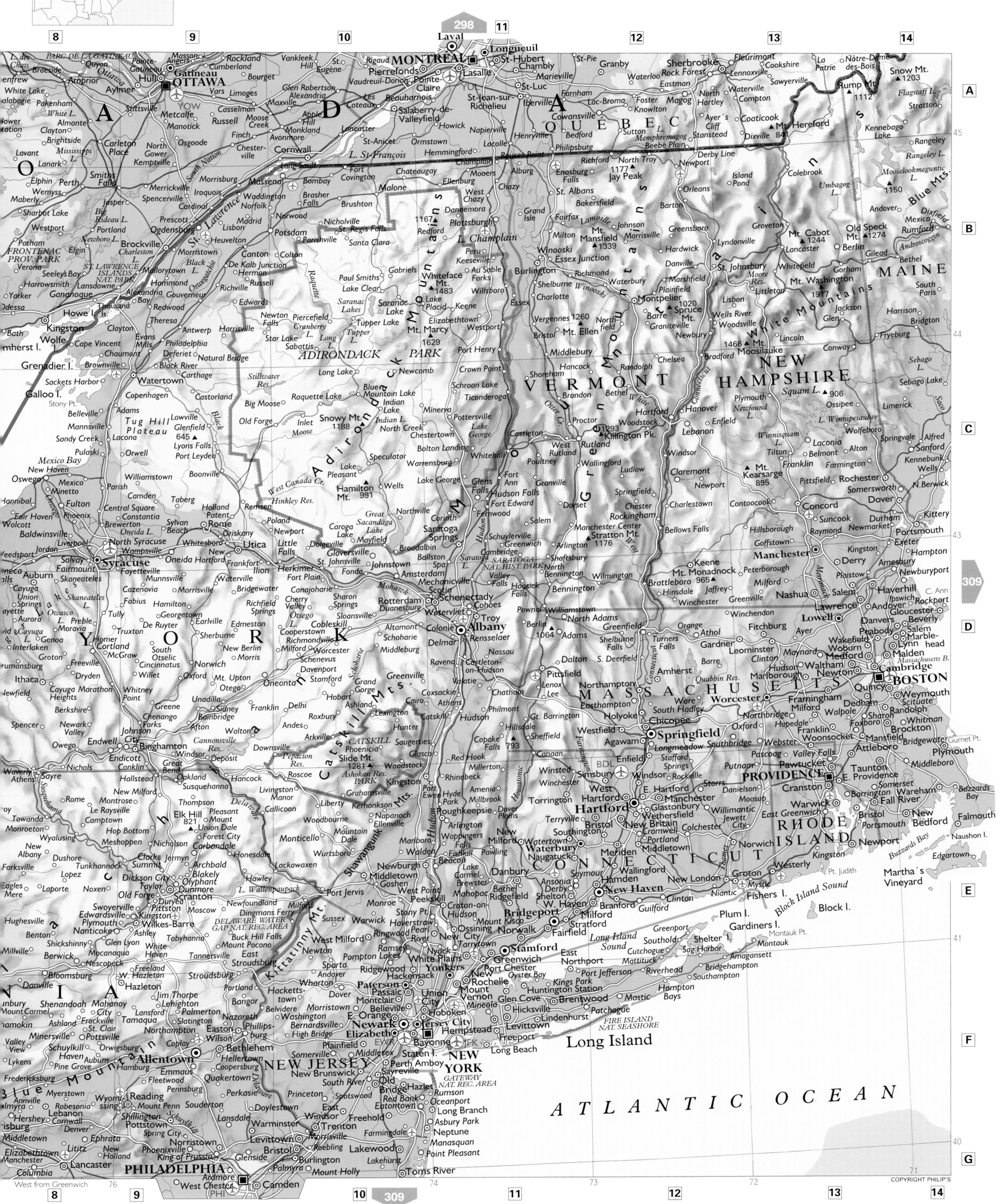

1:5 360 000

Projection: Albers' Equal Area with two standard parallels

West from Greenwich

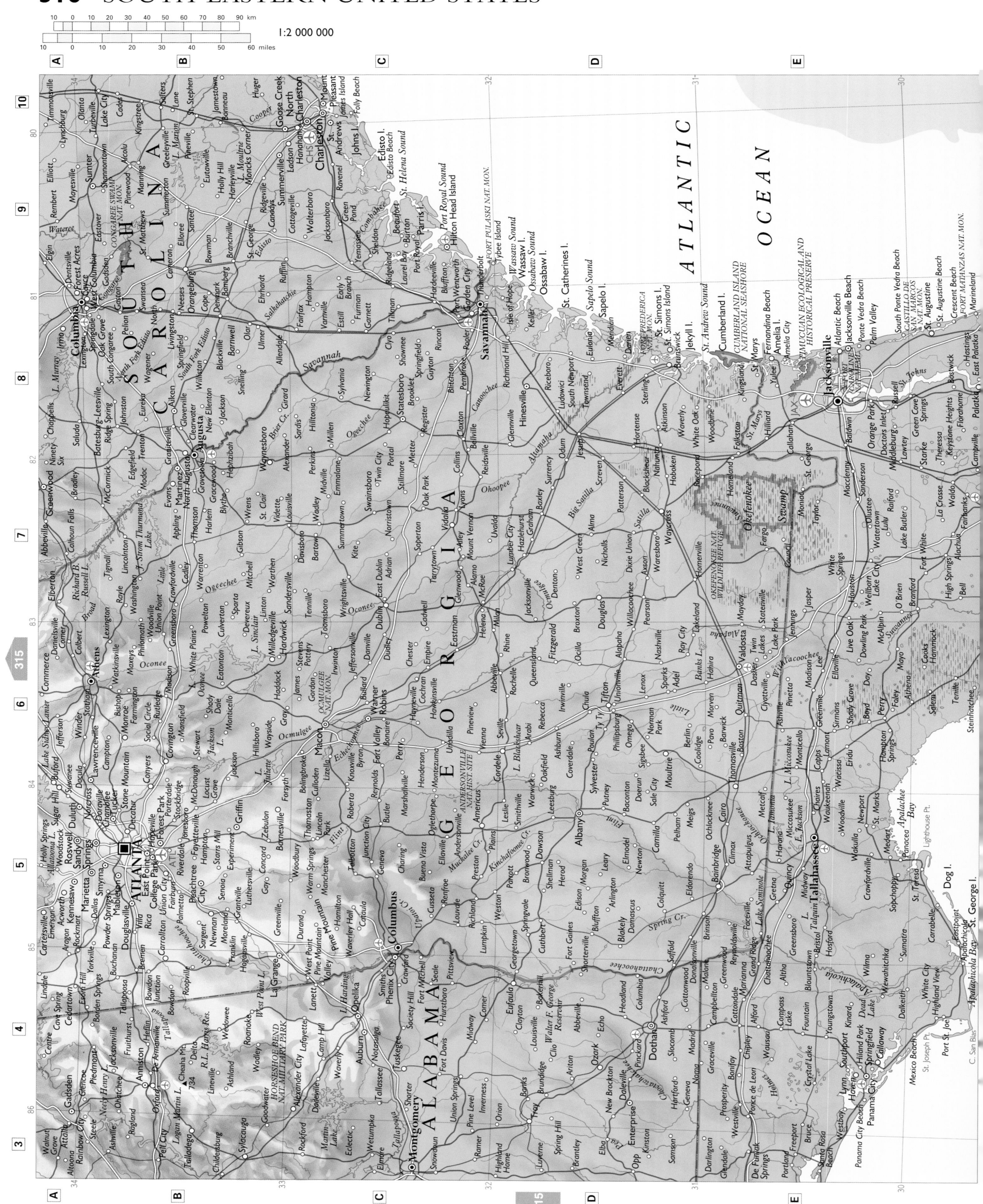

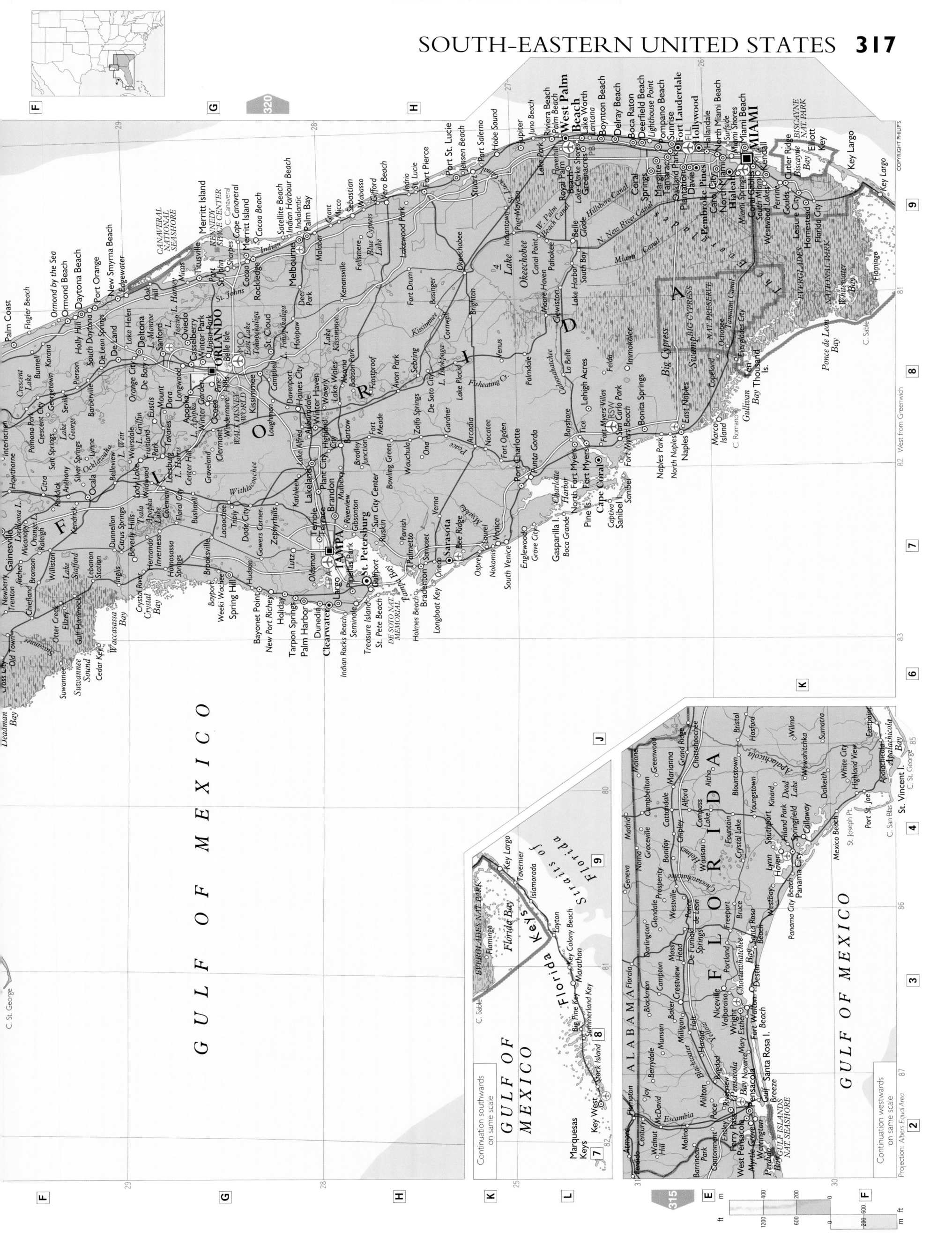

50   0   50   100   150   200   250   300 km
50   0   50   100   150   200 miles

1:6 400 000

1   **2**   305   **3**   314   **4**

Projection: Bi-polar oblique Conical Orthomorphic

State names in Central Mexico

1 DISTRITO FEDERAL   3 GUANAJUATO   5 MÉXICO   7 QUERÉTARO
2 AGUASCALIENTES   4 HIDALGO   6 MORELOS   8 TLAXCALA

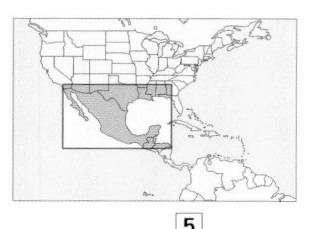

5

PUERTO RICO AND THE VIRGIN IS.
b   1:1 600 000

10 0 10 20 30 40 50 70 km
10 0 10 20 30 40 50 miles

ATLANTIC OCEAN

The Settlement
Ruffling Pt.
Anegada
East Pt.

VIRGIN ISLANDS (U.K.)

Jost Van Dyke I.   Great Camanoe
Hans Lollik I.   Guana I.   Virgin Gorda
Tortola   521   Beef I.
Cruz Bay   Road Town   Spanish Town
Charlotte Amalie   St. John I.   Peter I.
St. Thomas I.   VIRGIN IS. NAT. PARK

VIRGIN ISLANDS (U.S.A.)

Pta. Agujereada
Quebradillas   Camuy   Hatillo
Isabela   Arecibo
Aguadilla   Barceloneta   Vega Baja   Levittown   SAN JUAN
Pta. Higuero   Moca   Manati   Vega Alta   SJU   Carolina
Rincon   Aguada   PARQUE DE LAS CAVERNAS DEL RIO CAMUY   OBSERVATORIO DE ARECIBO   Rio Grande
San Sebastian   Florida   Ciales   Trujillo Alto   Luquillo   Fajardo
Añasco   Lares   Utuado   PUERTO RICO   Corozo   Gurabo   Sierra de Luquillo   EL YUNQUE   Ceiba
Mayagüez   Maricao   Adjuntas   Cordillera Central   Comerio   Caguas   Naguabo
Hormigueros   1338   Cerro de Punta   Villalba   Cayey   Juncos   Humacao
Cabo Rojo   San German   Mts. de Uroyan   Juana Dias   Coamo   Las Piedras
Sabana Grande   Yauco   Ponce   Salinas   Guayama   Yabucoa   Pta. Arenas   Isabel Segunda
Parguera   Guanica   Guayanilla   Patillas   Maunabo   Esperanza   Vieques
Santa Isabel   I. Caja de Muertos   Pta. Puerca

Dewey   Culebra

CARIBBEAN SEA

Frederiksted   353 ▲ Mt. Eagle   Christiansted   East Pt.
Southwest Pt.   St. Croix I. (U.S.A.)

West from Greenwich

AMAS   **BAMAS**

rthur's Town
New Bight
Cat I.
San Salvador I.
Conception I.
Rum Cay
Long I.
Clarence Town   Samana Cay
Cay   Crooked I. Passage   Plana Cays
Albert Town   Snug Corner
Cay Verde   Acklins I.
Mira por vos Cay

Tropic of Cancer

Caicos Passage
Turks & Caicos Is. (U.K.)
Caicos Is.
Turks Island Passage
Cockburn Town
Turks Is.

Hogsty Reef
Cay Santo Domingo
Little Inagua I.
Lake Rose   Great Inagua I.
INAGUA   Matthew Town
Mouchoir Bank
Silver Bank Passage   Silver Bank
Navidad Bank

ATLANTIC OCEAN

Puerto Rico Trench

C. Lucrecia
ntilla   Moa
ayari   Baracoa
Guantánamo   Pta. de Maisi
GUANTANAMO BAY (U.S.A.)   Î. de la Tortue
Paso de los Vientos (Windward Passage)   Cap-Haïtien   Monte Cristi   LA ISABELA
Jean Rabel   Port-de-Paix   Fort Liberté   Santiago de los Caballeros   San Francisco de Macoris   Milwaukee Deep 9200
Cap-à-Foux   G. de la Gonâve   Gonaïves   Cara   La Vega   Nagua   Samana
St-Marc   Hinche   Pico Duarte   Sanchez   Sabana de la Mar   Samana
HAITI   DOMINICAN REP.   Hato Mayor   C. Engaño   Aguadilla   Arecibo   Bayamón   SAN JUAN   Anegada   Virgin Is. (U.K.)
Jérémie   Î. de la Gonâve   PORT-AU-PRINCE   San Pedro de Macoris   Higüey   1338   Carolina   St. Thomas   Tortola   Virgin Gorda   Sombrero (U.K.)
Jamaica   Dame Marie   Les Cayes   Aquin   2680   SANTO DOMINGO   La Romana   ESTE   Mayagüez   Ponce   Fajardo   Road Town   Anguilla (U.K.)
Massif de la Hotte   Petit Goâve   Jacmel   SIERRA DE BAHORUCO   San Cristóbal   Bani   B. de Yuma   Mona Passage   PUERTO RICO (U.S.A.)   Caguas   Charlotte Amalie   St.-Martin (Fr.)
Pointe-à-Gravois   Î. à Vache   Pedernales   Barahona   Compostela   Isla Mona   Guayama   Vieques   Virgin Is. (U.S.A.)   St.-Barthélemy (Fr.)
Carcasse   I. Beata   C. Beata   Christiansted   St. Maarten (Neth.)   Saba (Neth.)   Barbuda
HISPANIOLA   Antilles   Frederiksted   St. Croix   St. Eustatius (Neth.)   Mt. Liamuiga 1156   ST. KITTS & NEVIS   St. John's   ANTIGUA & BARBUDA
Redonda   Nevis   Antigua
Soufriere   Montserrat (U.K.)   914   Hills   Guadeloupe Passage
Beata Ridge   Ste -Rose   Le Moule   La Désirade
GUADELOUPE (Fr.)   1467   Pointe-à-Pitre
Basse-Terre   Marie-Galante (Fr.)   Grand-Bourg
I. des Saintes (Fr.)
Dominica Passage
Portsmouth   1447   DOMINICA
Morne Diablotin   MORNE TROIS PITONS
Roseau   Martinique Passage
Venezuelan   SEA   I. de Aves (Venezuela)   Mt. Pelée   Ste -Marie
Basin   1397   Le François
Fort-de-France   Rivière-Pilote
MARTINIQUE
St. Lucia Channel (Fr.)
Castries   950   ST. LUCIA
Soufrière
St. Vincent Passage
Soufrière 1234   St. Vincent   Speightstown   340
Kingstown   BARBADOS
Bequia   Bridgetown
B   E   A   N   SEA   ABC   Lesser   Antilles   Canouan   ST. VINCENT & THE GRENADINES
ombian   Basin   Islands   Aruba (Neth.)   Curaçao   Bonaire   Carriacou   The Grenadines
Oranjestad   Willemstad   NETH. ANTILLES   St. George's   GRENADA
Pta. Gallinas   Pen. de la Guajira   Punta Cardón   Paraguaná   ARC. LOS ROQUES   I. Blanquilla (Ven.)   Is. Los Hermanos (Ven.)
Ríohacha   Uribia   Punto Fijo   Is. Las Aves (Ven.)   I. Orchila (Ven.)   NUEVA ESPARTA   Is. Los Testigos (Ven.)   Tobago
Santa Marta   GUAJIRA   C. San Román   MEDANOS DE CORO   Is. Los Roques (Ven.)   I. de Margarita   Scarborough
ARRAN-QUILLA   TAYRONA   ISLA DE SALAMANCA   Golfo de Venezuela   Coro   La Vela   NUEVA   La Asunción   Galera Point
Ciénaga   SA. NEVADA DE STA. MARTA   Pta. Espada   CUEVA DE LA QUEBRADA DEL TORO   Porlamar   Port of Spain   940
Baranoa   Sierra Nevada de Santa Marta   5775   MARACAIBO   Altagracia   FALCÓN   Maiquetía   CARACAS   La Guaira   I. La Tortuga (Ven.)
TLANTICO   Soledad   Sabanalarga   La Concepción   Santa Rita   Mene de Mauroa   HENRI PITTIER   Vargas   Trinidad   Arima
MAGDALENA   Fundación   Ciudad Ojeda   Cabimas   Baragua   San Felipe   MARACAY   Pen. de Paria   Güiria   Río Claro
Calamar   Plato   Valledupar   CÉSAR   Machiques   Lago de Maracaibo   LARA   YARACUY   Villa de Cura   MIRANDA   Cumaná   Puerto La Cruz   SUCRE   TRINIDAD & TOBAGO
El Carmen   Zambrano   Agustín Codazzi   Mene Grande   Carora   BARQUISIMETO   VALENCIA   Los Teques   Río Chico   G. de Paria   San Fernando
ince-lejo   COLOMBIA   Mompós   ZULIA   PERIJA   Trujillo   Acarigua   El Tocuyo   San Juan de los Morros   Carúpano   Cariaco   Serpent's Mouth
Corozal   San Carlos del Zulia   Valera   COJEDES   Aragua de Barcelona   Barcelona   Caripito   MONAGAS
Sincé   El Banco   NORTE DE   MÉRIDA   Betijoque   San Carlos   El Sombrero   Anaco   MARIUSA
n Marcos   Planeta Rica   SANTANDER   Ocaña   MÉRIDA 5002   Barinas   GUÁRICO   Valle de la Pascua   Cantaura   El Tigre   DELTA
oro   Magangué   BOLÍVAR   OCAÑA   SA. NEVADA   Ciudad Bolivia   PORTUGUESA   Calabozo   ANZOÁTEGUI   Tucupita
Caucasia   Cúcuta   TÁCHIRA   San Cristóbal   Guanare   Santa María de Ipire   Maturín   AMACURO
OBA   Ayapel   Simiti   Barbara   LIBERTAD   BARINAS   Los Barrancos
Bruzual   San Fernando de Apure   Soledad   Ciudad Guayana
VENEZUELA   Achaguas   Apure   Orinoco   Ciudad Bolívar   El Pao   Sierra Imataca
Mapire   El Callao
Guanipa   Tumeremo
Embalse de Guri   Guasipati   Upata

West from Greenwich

COPYRIGHT PHILIP'S

ft   m

328

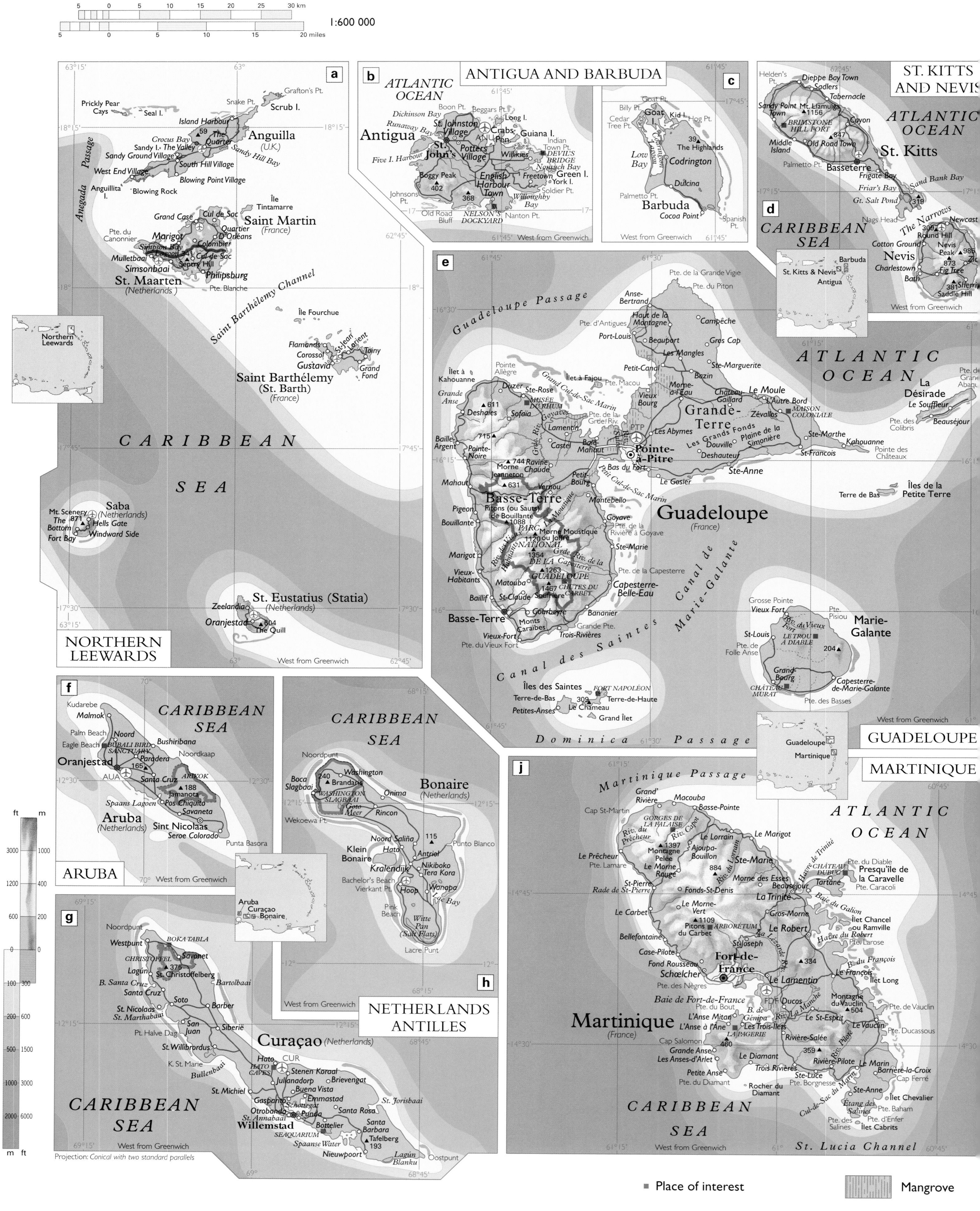

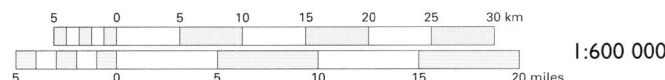

5 0 5 10 15 20 25 30 km
1:600 000
5 0 5 10 15 20 miles

a

63°15' 63° 18°15'

Prickly Pear Cays
Seal I.
Snake Pt.
Grafton's Pt.
Scrub I.
Island Harbour
59 The Quarter
Crocus Bay
Sandy I. The Valley
Anguilla (U.K.)
Sandy Ground Village
South Hill Village
West End Village
Sandy Hill Bay
Blowing Point Village
Anguillita I.
Blowing Rock
Île Tintamarre

Anegada Passage

Pte. du Canonnier
Grand Case
Cul-de-Sac
Île Tintamarre
Quartier D'Orleans
Saint Martin (France)
Marigot
Colombier
Simpson Bay
Cul de Sac
Mulletbaai
Sentry Hill
Simsonbaai
Philipsburg
St. Maarten (Netherlands)
Pte. Blanche

Saint Barthélemy Channel

18°

Île Fourchue

Flamands
Corossol
Gustavia
St-Jean
Lorient
Toiny
Grand Fond
Saint Barthélemy (St. Barth) (France)

Northern Leewards

CARIBBEAN

17°45'

SEA

Mt. Scenery
Saba (Netherlands)
871
The Bottom
Hells Gate
Windward Side
Fort Bay

17°30'
63°15'

Zeelandia
St. Eustatius (Statia) (Netherlands)
Oranjestad
604
The Quill

NORTHERN LEEWARDS

West from Greenwich 62°45'

b

ATLANTIC OCEAN

ANTIGUA AND BARBUDA

61°45'

Dickinson Bay
Boon Pt.
Beggars Pt.
Long I.
St. Johnston Village
Crabs Pen
Guiana I.
Indian Town Pt.
Antigua
Runaway Bay
ANU
St. John's
Potters Village
Willikies
39 DEVIL'S BRIDGE
Nonuch Bay
Five I. Harbour
Green I.
York I.
Boggy Peak 402
English Harbour Town
Freetown
Soldier Pt.
Johnsons Pt.
368
Willoughby Bay
Old Road Bluff
NELSON'S DOCKYARD
Nanton Pt.
17°

West from Greenwich 61°45'

c

Billy Pt.
Goat Pt.
Cedar Tree Pt.
Goat I.
Kid I. Hog Pt.
Low Bay
The Highlands
Codrington
Palmetto Pt.
Dulcina
Barbuda
Cocoa Point
Spanish Pt.
West from Greenwich 61°30'

ST. KITTS AND NEVIS

Helden's Pt.
Dieppe Bay Town
Sadlers
Tabernacle
Sandy Point Town
Mt. Liamuiga 1156
Cayon
BRIMSTONE HILL FORT
847
Middle Island
Old Road Town
St. Kitts
Palmetto Pt.
Basseterre
Frigate Bay
ATLANTIC OCEAN
Friar's Bay
Gt. Salt Pond
Sand Bank Bay
319
17°15'

CARIBBEAN SEA

Nags Head
The Narrows
305
Newcastle
Round Hill
Cotton Ground
Nevis 985
Nevis Peak
873 Fig Tree
Charlestown
Bath
381 Sheriff
Saddle Hill

d

St. Kitts & Nevis
Barbuda
Antigua

West from Greenwich

e

61°45' 61°30'

Pte. de la Grande Vigie

Guadeloupe Passage

16°30'

Anse-Bertrand
Pte. du Piton
Haut de la Montagne
Campêche
Port-Louis
Beauport
Gros Cap
Pte. d'Antigues
Ste-Marguerite
Petit-Canal
Les Mangles
Bazin
Pointe Allègre
Îlet à Fajou
Morne-à-l'Eau
Château Gaillard
Le Moule
L'Autre Bord
Îlet à Kahouanne
Ste-Rose
Grande Anse
611
Deshaies
MUSÉE DU RHUM
Sofaia
Lamentin
Grande-Terre
Zévallos
MAISON COLONIALE
16°15'
Baie-Mahault
Les Grands Fonds
Douville
Plaine de la Simonière
St-Marthe
Kahouanne
Baille-Argent
715
Castel
Pte. des Colibris
Pointe-Noire
PTP
Les Abymes
Pointe-à-Pitre
Ste-Anne
St-François
Pte. des Châteaux
La Désirade
Le Souffleur
Beauséjour
744 Ravine Chaude
Morne Jeanneton
Bas du Fort
Le Gosier
Mahaut
631
Vernou
Petit-Bourg
Terre de Bas
Îles de la Petite Terre
Pigeon
Basse-Terre
Pitons (ou Sauts) de Bouillante
1088
Mantebello
Goyave
Pte. de la Rivière à Goyave
Bouillante
PARC
Morne Moustique
mou Jolfre
NATIONAL
1354
DE LA
GUADELOUPE
1263
Ste-Marie
Guadeloupe (France)
Grosse Pointe
Vieux Fort
Marigot
La Capesterre
Rio. du Vieux
Pte. Pisiou
17°
Vieux-Habitants
Matouba
1467 CHUTES DU CARBET
Capesterre-Belle-Eau
St-Louis
Marie-Galante
204
Baillif
St-Claude
Soufrière
Bananier
LE TROU À DIABLE
Pte. de Folle Anse
Basse-Terre
Monts Caraïbes
Grande Pte.
Trois-Rivières
Vieux-Fort
Pte. du Vieux Fort
Grand-Bourg
CHÂTEAU MURAT
Capesterre-de-Marie-Galante
Pte. des Basses

Canal des Saintes

Canal de Marie-Galante

Îles des Saintes
FORT NAPOLÉON
Terre-de-Bas
309
Terre-de-Haute
Petites-Anses
Le Chameau
Grand Îlet

West from Greenwich

Dominica Passage 61°30'

Guadeloupe
Martinique

GUADELOUPE

f

CARIBBEAN SEA

Kudarebe
Malmok
Palm Beach
Noord
Bushiribana
Eagle Beach
BUBALI BIRD SANCTUARY
Noordkaap
Oranjestad
Paradera
165
AUA
Santa Cruz
ARIKOK
12°30'
Jamanota
188
Spaans Lagoen
Pos Chiquito
Savaneta
Aruba (Netherlands)
Sint Nicolaas
Seroe Colorado
Punta Basora

ARUBA

70° West from Greenwich

g

69°15'

Noordpunt
Westpunt
BOKA TABLA
CHRISTOFFEL
Savonet
Lagún
375 St. Christoffelberg
Bartolbaai
B. Santa Cruz
Santa Cruz
St. Nicolaas
Soto
Barber
St. Marthabaai
San Juan
Siberie
Pt. Halve Dag
K. St. Marie
St. Willibrordus
Hato
CUR
Bullenbaai
HATO CAVES
Stenen Koraal
St. Michiel
Julianadorp
Brievengat
12°
Buena Vista
Gasparito
Emmastad
Santa Rosa
Otrobanda
Punda
Santa Barbara
St. Annabaai
Botttelier
SEAQUARIUM
Willemstad
Tafelberg 193
Spaanse Water
Lagún Blanku
Nieuwpoort
Oostpunt

CARIBBEAN SEA

Curaçao (Netherlands)

69°15' West from Greenwich 69°

Projection: Conical with two standard parallels

h

68°45'

Noordpunt
Boca Slagbaai
240
Washington
Brandaris
Onima
Bonaire (Netherlands)
WASHINGTON SLAGBAAI
Gote Meer
Rincon
Wekoewa Pt.
Noord Saliña
12°15'
Klein Bonaire
Hato
115
Antriol
Punto Blanco
Nikiboko
Tera Kora
Kralendijk
Wanapa
Bachelor's Beach
Vierkant Pt.
Hoop
Life Bay
Pink Beach
Witte Pan (Salt Flats)
12°
Lacre Punt

West from Greenwich 68°15'

Aruba
Curaçao
Bonaire

NETHERLANDS ANTILLES

j

61°15' 61°

Martinique Passage

Cap St-Martin
Grand' Rivière
Macouba
Basse-Pointe
GORGES DE LA FALAISE
Riv. du Prêcheur
1397
Le Lorrain
Le Marigot
Le Prêcheur
Montagne Pelée
Ajoupa-Bouillon
Pte. du Diable
14°45'
St-Pierre
884
Morne des Esses
Ste-Marie
CHÂTEAU DUBUC
Presqu'île de la Caravelle
Rade de St-Pierre
Fonds-St-Denis
Beauséjour
Tartane
Pte. Caracoli
Le Carbet
La Trinité
1109
Pitons du Carbet
ARBORETUM
Gros-Morne
Îlet Chancel ou Ramville
Bellefontaine
Le Morne-Vert
Le Robert
Pte. Larose
ATLANTIC OCEAN
St-Joseph
Case-Pilote
Fond Rousseau
334
Le François
Îlet Long
Schoelcher
Fort-de-France
Le Lamentin
Montagne du Vauclin
Pte. des Nègres
FDF
Ducos
504
Pte. de Vauclin
Baie de Fort-de-France
L'Anse Mitan
B. de Génipa
Le St-Esprit
Le Vauclin
L'Anse à l'Âne
LA PAGERIE
Rivière-Salée
Cap Salomon
Les Trois-Îlets
460
14°30'
Grande Anse
359
Rivière-Pilote
Le Marin
Les Anses-d'Arlet
Le Diamant
Barrière-la-Croix
Petite Anse
Trois Rivières
Ste-Luce
Cap Ferré
Pte. du Diamant
Ste-Anne
Îlet Chevalier
Rocher du Diamant
Étang des Salines
Pte. Baham
Cul-de-Sac du Marin
Pte. d'Enfer
Pte. des Salines
Îlet Cabrits
St. Lucia Channel

CARIBBEAN SEA

Martinique (France)

West from Greenwich 61° 60°45'

MARTINIQUE

ft m
3000 1000
1200 400
600 200
0 0
100 300
200 600
500 1500
1000 3000
2000 6000
m ft

■ Place of interest

▦ Mangrove

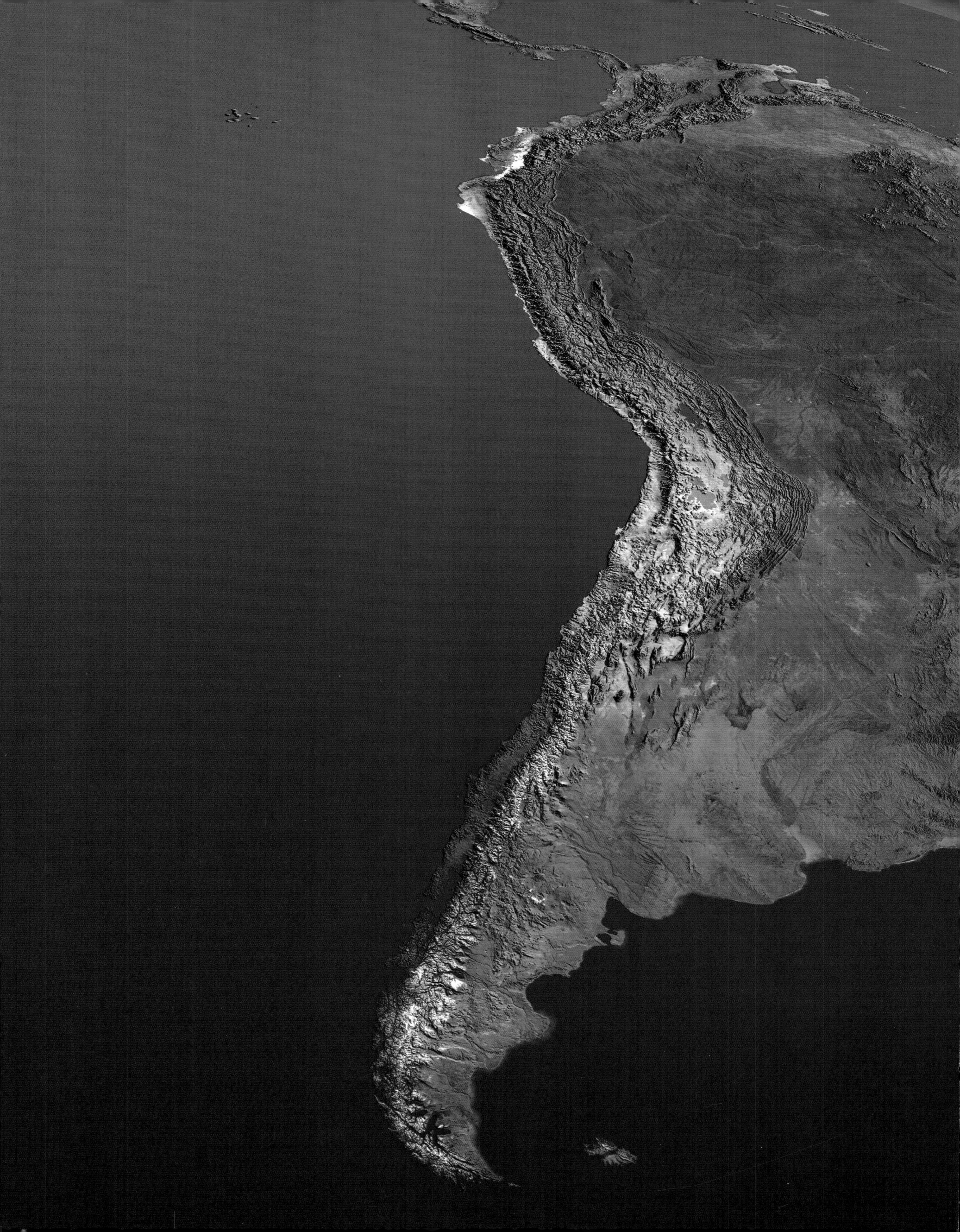

SOUTH
AMERICA

1:28 000 000

Projection: Lambert's Azimuthal Equal Area

COPYRIGHT PHILIP'S

1:28 000 000

NORTH

ATLANTIC

OCEAN

Tropic of Cancer

Havana
BAHAMAS
C U B A
Turks & Caicos Is.
(U.K.)
Cayman Is.
(U.K.)
HAITI
DOMINICAN
REP.
San Juan
Virgin Is. (U.S.A.–U.K.)
Anguilla (U.K.)
St. Martin (Fr.–Neth.)
ANTIGUA &
BARBUDA
MEXICO
BELIZE
JAMAICA
Kingston
Port-au-
Prince
Santo
Domingo
PUERTO
RICO
(U.S.A.)
ST. KITTS
& NEVIS
Basse-Terre
GUADELOUPE
(Fr.)
GUATEMALA
Guatemala
HONDURAS
Tegucigalpa
DOMINICA
Fort-de-France
MARTINIQUE
(Fr.)
San Salvador
EL SALVADOR
NICARAGUA
Managua
Castries
ST. VINCENT
ST. LUCIA
Aruba
(Neth.)
NETH.
ANTILLES
BARBADOS
Bridgetown
COSTA
RICA
San José
Oranjestad
Willemstad
Kingstown
GRENADA
St. George's

Caribbean Sea

Panamá
P A N A M A
Barranquilla
Cartagena
G. of
Darién
Maracaibo
Caracas
Port of
Spain
TRINIDAD &
TOBAGO
I. del Coco
(Costa Rica)
Gulf of Panama
Cúcuta
San Cristóbal
Barquisimeto
Valencia
Medellín
Bucaramanga
VENEZUELA
Orinoco
Ciudad Guayana
Georgetown
Paramaribo
I. de Malpelo
(Colombia)
Cali
BOGOTÁ
GUYANA
SURINAME
Cayenne
C. Orange
COLOMBIA
RORAIMA
FRENCH
GUIANA
Branco
Essequibo
AMAPÁ
Equator
Galapagos Is.
(Ecuador)
Quito
ECUADOR
Putumayo
Japurá
Amazon
Marajó
I.
Belém
Guayaquil
Napo
Manaus
Santarém
São Luís
G. of Guayaquil
Iquitos
Marañón
AMAZONAS
Amazon
PARÁ
Tocantins
Fortaleza
Chiclayo
Ucayali
Juruá
Madeira
MARANHÃO
Teresina
CEARÁ
RIO G.
DO NORTE
Natal
Trujillo
Purus
ACRE
Pôrto Velho
Tapajós
Xingu
PIAUÍ
Parnaíba
PARAÍBA
Campina Grande
Chimbote
RONDÔNIA
PERNAMBUCO
Recife
Callao
LIMA
PERU
Maure de Dios
BRAZIL
MATO GROSSO
Araguaia
TOCANTINS
ALAGOAS
SERGIPE
Maceió
Aracaju
Cuzco
Mamoré
Cuiabá
GOIÁS
São Francisco
BAHÍA
Salvador
L. Titicaca
Arequipa
La Paz
BOLIVIA
Cochabamba
Santa Cruz
Paraguay
DIS. FED
Brasília
Goiânia
Iquique
Sucre
MATO GROSSO
DO SUL
MINAS GERAIS
Ribeirão
Prêto
Belo
Horizonte
Vitória
ESPÍRITO
SANTO
Campos
Tropic of Capricorn
Antofagasta
Salta
PARAGUAY
Paraná
Pilcomayo
Asunción
PARANÁ
SÃO PAULO
Campinas
Santos
SÃO
PAULO
R. DE J.
RIO DE
JANEIRO
Niterói
San Miguel
de Tucumán
Curitiba
San Félix
(Chile)
San Ambrosio
(Chile)
Resistencia
Corrientes
SANTA CATARINA
Uruguay
RIO GRANDE
DO SUL
Pôrto Alegre
Córdoba
San Juan
Santa Fé
Paraná
Rosario
Pelotas
Viña del Mar
Valparaíso
SANTIAGO
Mendoza
BUENOS AIRES
URUGUAY
Montevideo
Arch. de Juan Fernández
(Chile)
Robinson
Crusoe
Talca
La Plata
Río de la Plata
Concepción
Bahía
Blanca
Mar del Plata
Valdivia
Colorado
Negro
Viedma
Puerto Montt
Comodoro Rivadavia
Gulf of San Jorge
Chubut
Gulf of Penas
West Falkland
FALKLAND IS.
(U.K.)
Stanley
East Falkland
Punta Arenas
Magellan's Str.
Tierra del Fuego
C. Horn
South Georgia
(U.K.)

PACIFIC

OCEAN

C H I L E

A R G E N T I N A

SOUTH

ATLANTIC

OCEAN

Projection: Lambert's Azimuthal Equal Area

West from Greenwich

COPYRIGHT PHILIP'S

■ LIMA Capital Cities

1:6 400 000

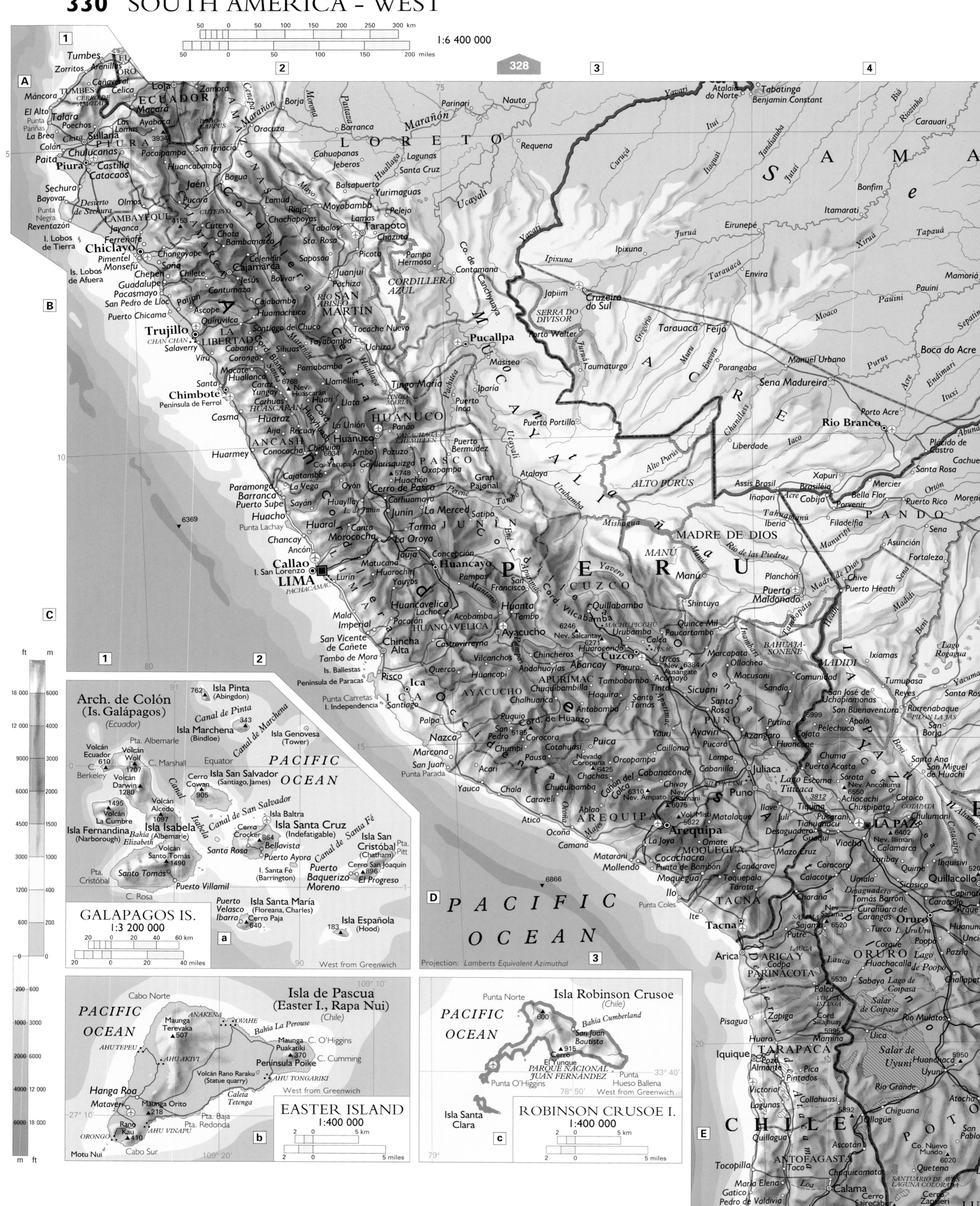

50   0   50   100   150   200   250   300 km

50   0   50   100   150   200 miles

1:6 400 000

328

Arch. de Colón
(Is. Galápagos)
(Ecuador)

GALAPAGOS IS.
1:3 200 000

20   0   20   40   60 km

20   0   20   40 miles

a

PACIFIC
OCEAN

Isla de Pascua
(Easter I., Rapa Nui)
(Chile)

EASTER ISLAND
1:400 000

2   0   5 miles

b

Isla Robinson Crusoe
(Chile)

PACIFIC
OCEAN

PARQUE NACIONAL
JUAN FERNANDEZ

Isla Santa
Clara

ROBINSON CRUSOE I.
1:400 000

2   0   5 km

2   0   5 miles

c

Projection: Lamberts Equivalent Azimuthal

PACIFIC

OCEAN

PACIFIC OCEAN

LORETO

ECUADOR

PERU

CHILE

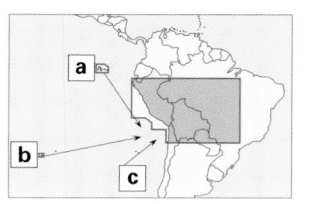

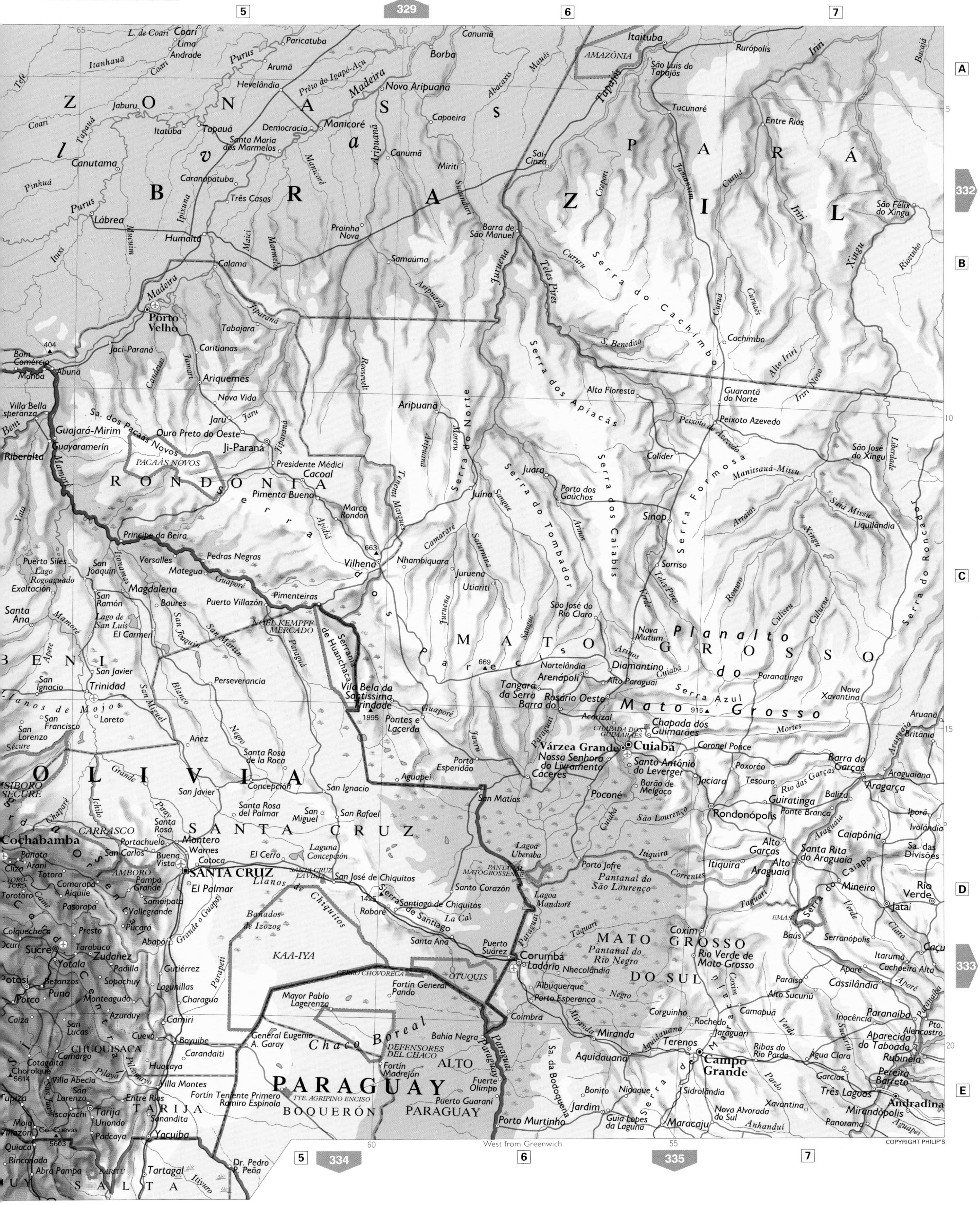

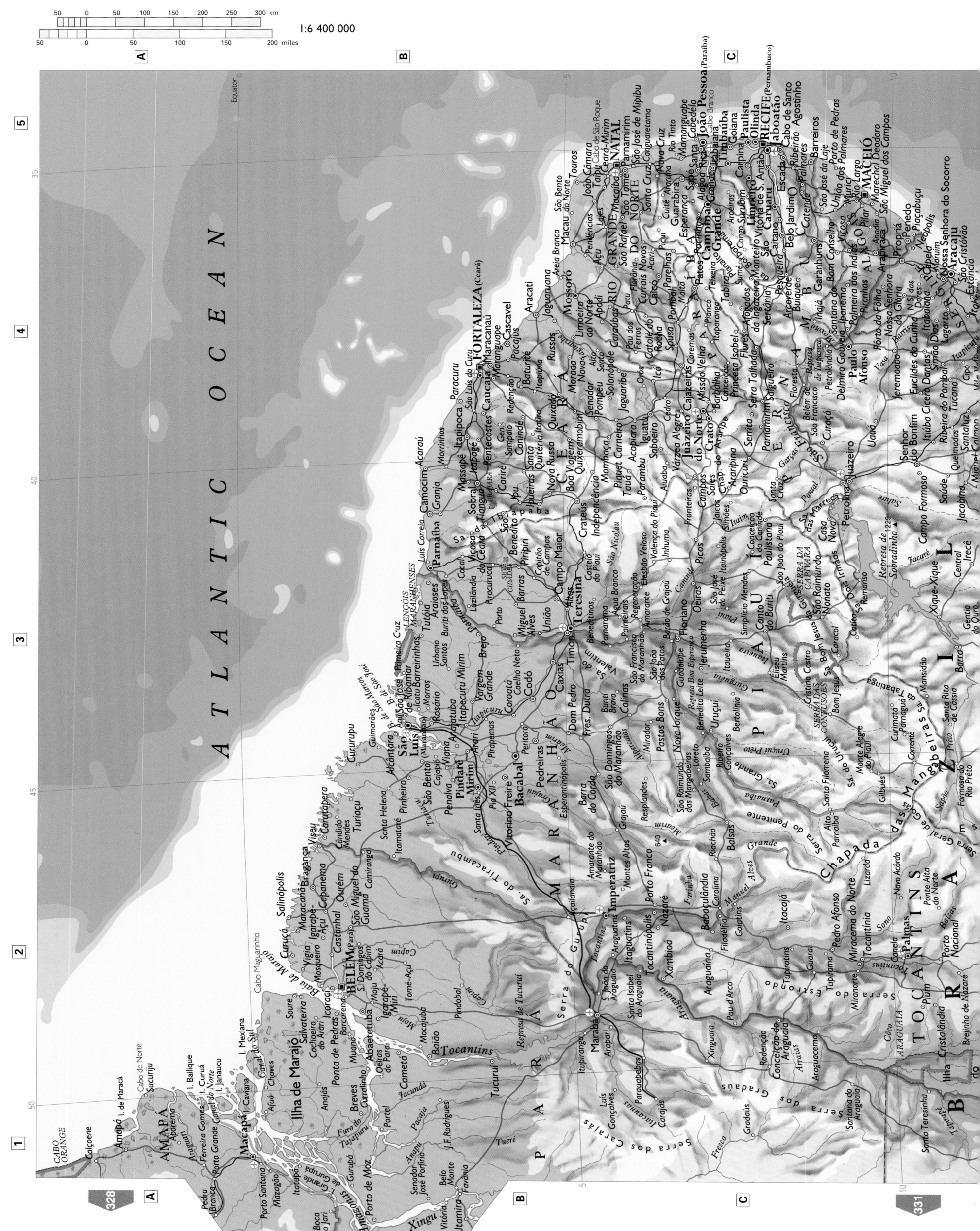

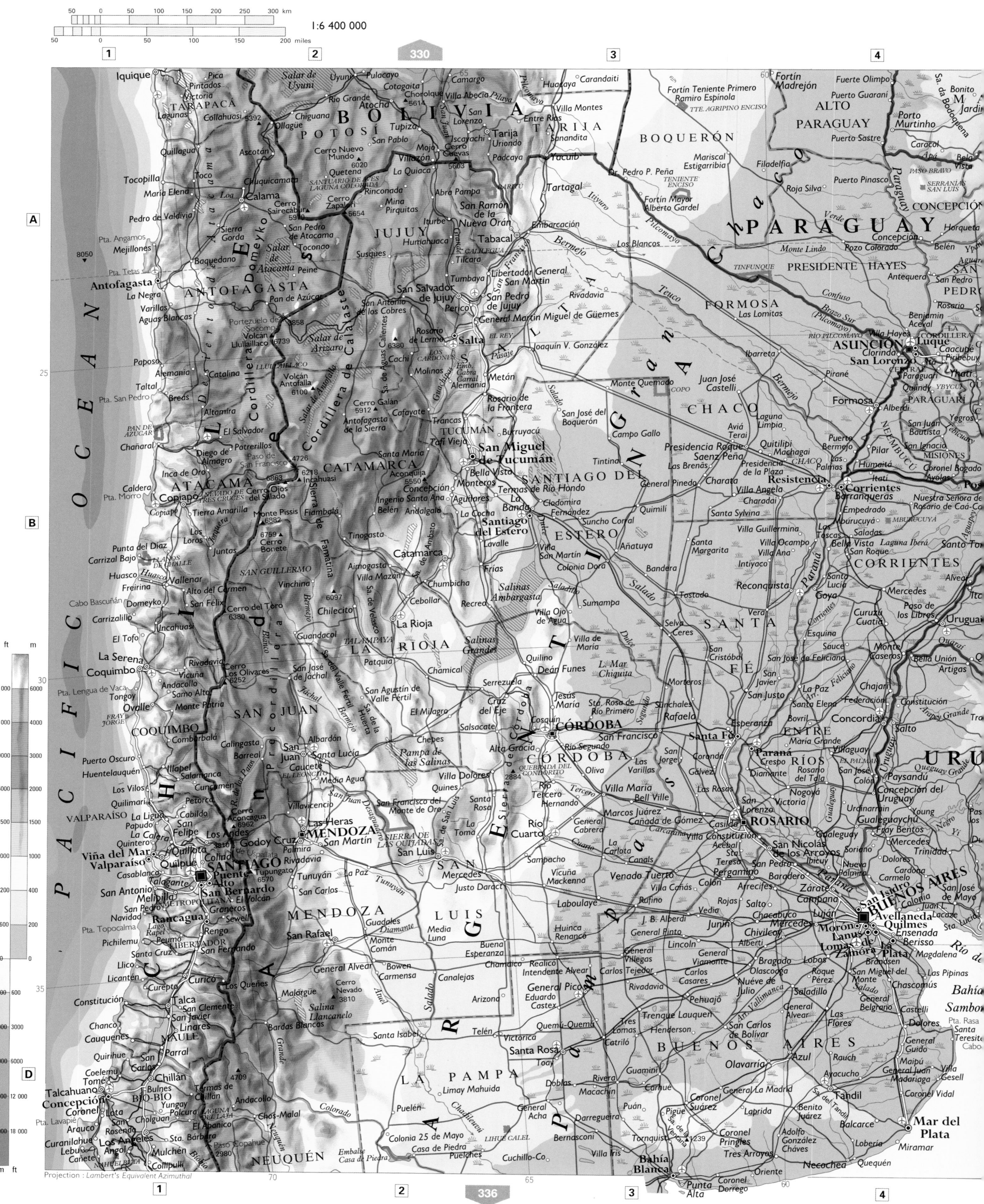

331 5   6   333   7

A

B

C

D

Tropic of Capricorn

25

30

35

BELO HORIZONTE
Betim · Contagem · Itabirito
Congonhas
Conselheiro Lafaiete
Ouro Prêto
Ponte Nova
CAPARAÓ Pico da Bandeira 2890
VITÓRIA
Vila Velha
Guarapari

Oliveira
Campo Belo · São João del Rei
Lavras
Barbacena
Ubá · Muriaé
Cataguases
Leopoldina
Carangola
Alegre
Castelo
Cachoeiro de Itapemirim
Itapemirim

Passos
Batatais
São Sebastião do Paraíso
Guaxupé
Alfenas
Varginha
Poços de Caldas
Três Corações
Juiz de Fora
Três Rios
Além Paraíba
Campos
Cabo de São Tomé
São João da Barra
RESTINGA DE JURUBATIBA

Olímpia
São José do Rio Prêto
Ribeirão Prêto
Jaboticabal
Mococa
Casa Branca
São João da Boa Vista
Pinhal · Santo Antônio
Pouso Alegre
Itajubá
São Lourenço
Guaratinguetá
Taubaté
Macaé
Nova Friburgo
Petrópolis
RIO DE JANEIRO
Niterói
São Gonçalo
Duque de Caxias
Nova Iguaçu
São João de Meriti
Cabo Frio
L. de Araruama

Andradina
Mirassol
São José do Rio Prêto
Araçatuba
Catanduva
Taquaritinga
Penápolis
Lins
Araraquara
São Carlos
Rio Claro
Limeira
Americana
Sumaré
CAMPINAS
Jundiaí
São Paulo
Mogi Guaçu
Mogi das Cruzes
Santos
Guarujá
Praia Grande
Itanhaém
Angra dos Reis
Ilha Grande
Bahia da Ilha Grande
Pta. da Juatinga

Três Lagoas
Xavantina
Panorama
Nova Alvorada do Sul
Presidente Epitácio
Adamantina
Santo Anastácio
SÃO PAULO
Tupã
Bauru
Bariri
Jaú
Piracicaba
Botucatu
Avaré
Tatuí
Sorocaba
Osasco
Santo André
São Bernardo do Campo
São Vicente
Itapetininga

TO · GROSSO
DO · SUL
Sidrolândia
Nioaque
Maracaju
Dourados
Ponta Porã
Pedro Juan Caballero
Amambai
Presidente Prudente
Martinópolis
Marília
Garça
Itaporanga

BRAZIL
PARANÁ
Londrina
Maringá
Cianorte
Apucarana
Campo Mourão
Guarapuava
CURITIBA
Ponta Grossa
Antonina
Paranaguá
Guaratuba
Ilha do Cardoso
SUPERAGÜI
Ilha Comprida
Registro
Iguape

Umuarama
Cascavel
Toledo
Foz do Iguaçu
Ciudad del Este
Medianeira
IGUAÇU
Prudentópolis
Pato Branco
Palmas
Porto União
Mafra
Joinville
São Francisco do Sul
Itajaí
Blumenau
Brusque
São José
Ilha de Santa Catarina
Florianópolis

SANTA CATARINA
Chapecó
Concórdia
Joaçaba
Campos Novos
Lages
Rio do Sul
Santa Cecília
Curitibanos

RIO · GRANDE
DO · SUL
Santa Maria
Santa Cruz do Sul
Cruz Alta
Passo Fundo
Carazinho
Vacaria
Caxias do Sul
Bento Gonçalves
Novo Hamburgo
Taquara
São Leopoldo
Canoas
PORTO ALEGRE
Viamão
Osório

APARADOS DA SERRA
Torres
Araranguá
Criciúma
Tubarão
Laguna
Cabo Santa Marta Grande

URUGUAY
Tacuarembó
Rivera
Santana do Livramento
São Gabriel
Dom Pedrito
Bagé
Pinheiro Machado
Pelotas
Rio Grande
São José do Norte
LAGOA DOS PATOS
LAGOA DO PEIXE
Mostardas
Tapes
São Lourenço do Sul
Camaquã

Melo
Jaguarão
Rio Branco
Vergara
L. Mirim
Treinta y Tres
Lagoa Mangueira
Santa Vitória do Palmar
Chuy
Lascano
SANTA TERESA
Castillos
Rocha
Maldonado
Pta. del Este
MONTEVIDEO
Río de la Plata

ATLANTIC

OCEAN

5304

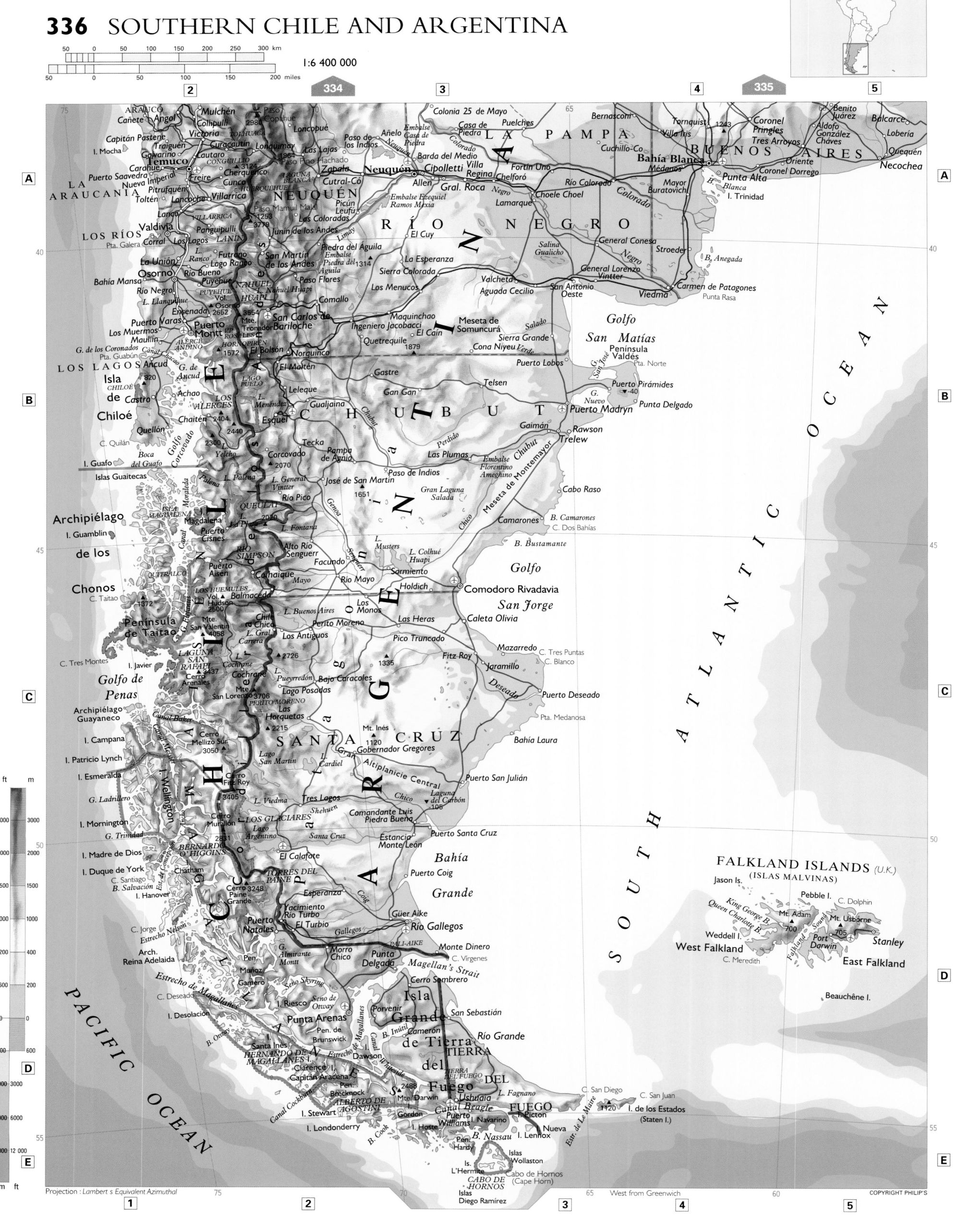

1:6 400 000

Projection : Lambert's Equivalent Azimuthal

West from Greenwich

COPYRIGHT PHILIP'S

GEOGRAPHICAL GLOSSARY

This is a list of the geographical terms from various foreign languages that are found in the place names on the maps and in the index. Each is followed by the language and its English meaning.

Afr. Afrikaans
Alb. Albanian
Amh. Amharic
Ar. Arabic
Belo. Belorussian
Berb. Berber
Bulg. Bulgarian
Burm. Burmese
Cam. Cambodian
Cat. Catalan
Chin. Chinese
Czec. Czech
Dan. Danish
Dut. Dutch
Est. Estonian
Fin. Finnish
Fr. French
Gae. Gaelic
Ger. German
Gr. Greek
Heb. Hebrew
Hin. Hindi
Hung. Hungarian
I.-C. Indo-Chinese
Ice. Icelandic
It. Italian
Indo. Indonesian
Jap. Japanese
Kaz. Kazakh
Kor. Korean
Kyrg. Kyrgyz
Lapp. Lapp (Sami)
Lat. Latvian
Lith. Lithuanian
Malag. Malagasy
Mong. Mongolian
Nor. Norway
Pash. Pashto
Per. Persian
Pol. Polish
Port. Portuguese
Rom. Romanian
Russ. Russian
Sin. Sinhalese
Ser.-Cr. Serbo-Croat
Slov. Slovene
Som. Somali
Span. Spanish
Swe. Swedish
Tib. Tibetan
Turk. Turkish
Ukr. Ukrainian
Viet. Vietnamese

-á *Ice.* river
-å *Dan., Nor., Swe.* stream
-abad *Farsi, Russ.* town
Abyad *Ar.* white mountain
Ada, Adasi *Turk.* island
Addis *Amh.* new
Adrar *Ar., Berb.* mountains
Aiguille *Fr.* peak
Aïn, Aîn (A.) *Ar.* spring
Ákra *Gr.* cape, point
Akrotíri *Gr.* cape, point
Alb *Ger.* mountains
Albufera *Span.* lagoon
-ålen *Nor.* islands
Alpen *Ger.* mountain ranges
Alpes *Fr.* mountains
Alpi *It.* mountains
Alt *Ger.* old
Alta, Alto *Port.* high, upper
Altos *Span.* mountains
-älv, -älven *Swe.* stream, river
Amtskommune (Amt.) *Dan.* first-order administrative division
-ån *Swe.* river
Anse *Fr.* bay
Ao *Thai* bay
Appennino *It.* mountain range
Archipel *Fr.* archipelago
Archipiélago (Arch.) *Span.* archipelago
Arcipélago *It.* archipelago
Arquipélago (Arq.) *Port.* archipelago
Arrecife *Span.* reef
Arroyo (Arr.) *Span.* stream
-ås, -åsen *Nor., Swe.* hill
Ayios *Gr.* island
Ayn *Ar.* well, waterhole

Baai, -baai *Afr., Dut.* bay
Bāb *Ar.* gate, strait
Bäck, -bäcken *Swe.* stream
Back, -backen, *Swe.* hill
Bad, -baden *Ger.* spa
Badia *Cat.* bay
Bādiyah, Bādiyat *Ar.* desert
Bæk *Dan.* stream
Bælt *Dan.* strait
Baharu *Malay* new
Bahía (B.) *Span.* bay
Bahiret *Ar.* lagoon
Bahr *Ar.* sea, lake, river
Bahra Bahrat *Ar.* lake
Baia (B.) *Port.* bay
Baie (B.) *Fr.* bay
Baixa, Baixo *Port.* lower
Baja, Bajo *Span.* lower
Bakke *Nor.* hill
Bala *Farsi* upper
Ballon *Fr.* dome
Baltă *Rom.* marsh, lake
Ban *Lao, Thai* village
-Bana *Jap.* cape
Banc *Fr.* bank
Banco *Span.* bank
Bandao *Chin.* peninsula
Bandar *Ar., Malay* port, harbour
Bandar *Farsi* bay
Banja *Ser.-Cr.* spa, resort
Banjaran *Malay* mountain range
Baraji *Turk.* dam
Barat *Indo., Malay* western
Barrage (Barr.) *Fr.* dam
Barragem (Barr.) *Port.* dam, reservoir
Bas, basse *Fr.* lower
Bassin *Fr.* basin
-batang *Indo.* river
Baṭlaq *Farsi* marsh
Batu *Malay* mountain
Bayt *Heb.* house, village
Bazar *Hin.* market, bazaar
-beek *Afr., Dut.* river
Be'er *Heb.* well
Bei *Chin.* north, northern
Beinn, Ben *Gae.* mountain
Beit *Heb.* village
Belaya, Belo, Beloye, Belyy *Russ.* white
Belogorye *Russ.* hills, mountain range
Bender *Som.* harbour
Berg(e), -berg(e) *Afr., Ger.* mountain(s)
-berg, -en, -et *Nor., Swe.* hill, mountain, rock
Besar *Indo., Malay* big
Bet *Heb.* house, village
Bir, Bîr, Bi'r *Ar.* well
Birkat, Birket *Ar.* lake, marsh, well
Bishti *Alb.* cape
-bjerg *Dan.* hill, point
Blaenau *Welsh* upland
-bo *Chin.* lake
Boca *Port., Span.* river mouth, inlet
Bodden *Ger.* bay, inlet
Bogaz, Boğazı *Turk.* channel, strait
Bogd *Mong.* mountain range
Bois *Fr.* woods
Boka *Ser.-Cr.* gulf, inlet
Bolshoi, Bolshaya, Bolshoye (Bol.) *Russ.* great, large
Bordj (Bj.) *Ar.* fort
-borg *Dan., Nor., Swe.* castle, fort
Bory *Pol.* woods
Bosque *Span.* woods
-botn *Nor.* valley floor
Bouche(s) *Fr.* mouth(s)
Braţul *Rom.* distributary stream, branch
-bre, -breen *Nor.* glacier
Bredning *Dan.* bay
Brücke *Ger.* bridge
-brug *Dut.* bridge
-brunn *Swe.* well, spring
Bucht *Ger.* bay
Bugt *Dan.* bay
-bugten *Dan.* bay
Buheirat *Ar.* lake, reservoir
Bukit *Malay* hill
-bukt, -a *Nor.* bay
-bukten *Swe.* bay
-bulag *Mong.* spring
Bulag *Chin.* lake
Bulu *Malay* mountain
Bum *Burm.* mountain
Bûr *Ar.* port
Burg. *Ar.* fort
Burg, -burg *Ger.* castle
Burnu, Burun *Turk.* cape
Butt *Gae.* promontory
Büyük *Turk.* big
-by *Dan., Nor., Swe.* town
-byen *Nor., Swe.* town

Cabeza *Span.* peak, hill
Cabo (C.) *Port., Span.* headland, cape
Cachoeira *Port.* waterfall
Cala Cat. *It.* bay
Camp Port. *Span.* land, field
Câmpia *Rom.* plain
Campo *It., Port., Span.* plain
Campos *Span.* upland
Canal (Can.) *Fr., Port., Span.* canal, channel
Canale (Can.) *It.* channel
Canalul (Can.) *Ser.-Cr.* canal
Cao Nguyen *Thai* plateau, tableland
Cap (C.) *Cat., Fr.* cape
Capo (C) *It.* cape
Carn *Gae.* hill
Carse *Gae.* valley
Catarata *Port., Span.* cataract
Cauce *Span.* intermittent stream
Causse *Fr.* limestone plateau
Cay, Cayi, -cay, -cayi *Turk.* river
Cayo(s) *Span.* rock(s), islet(s)
Cefn *Welsh* hill
Cerro *Span.* hill, peak
Česká, Český, České *Czec.* Czech
Chaco *Span.* jungle
Chaîne(s) *Fr.* mountain range(s)
Chang *Chin.* mountain
Chapa *Span.* hills, upland
Chapada *Port.* hills, upland
Chaung *Burm.* stream, river
Chi *Chin.* small lake
-ch'ŏn *Kor.* river
-chŏsuji *Kor.* reservoir
Chott *Ar.* salt lake, depression
Chu *Tib.* river
Chute *Fr.* waterfall
Città *It.* city
Ciudad *Span.* city
Co *Tib.* lake
Cochilla (Coch.) *Port.* hills
Col *Fr., It.* pass
Colina(s) *Span.* hill(s)
Colle *It.* pass
Colline(s) *Fr.* hill(s)
Conca *It.* plain, basin
Cordillera (Cord.) *Span.* mountain range
Costa *It., Port., Span.* coast
Côte *Fr.* coast, slope, hill
Coteaux *Fr.* hills
Cuchilla *Span.* hills
Cuenca *Span.* river basin
Cu-Lao *Viet.* island

Da *Chin.* big
Da *Viet.* river
Daban *Mong.* pass
Dağ(ı) *Turk.* mountain(s)
Dāgh *Farsi* mountain
Dağları *Turk.* mountain range
-dai, -daichi *Jap.* plateau
-Dake *Jap.* mountain
-dal, -e *Dan., Swe.* valley
-dal, -en *Swe., Nor.* valley, stream
Dalay Mong. large lake
-dalir, -dalur *Ice.* valley
-damm, -en *Swe.* lake
Danau *Malay* lake
Dao *Chin., Viet.* island
Dar *Ar.* region
Darya *Russ.* river
Daryācheh *Farsi* marshy lake, lake
Dasht *Farsi* desert, steppe
Daung *Burm.* mountain, hill
Dayr *Ar.* monastery
Debre *Amh.* hill
Deli *Ser.-Cr.* mountain
Deniz, -i *Turk.* sea
Département (Dépt.) *Fr.* first-order administrative division
Dere *Turk.* stream
Desierto (Des.) *Span.* desert
Détroit *Fr.* strait
Dhar *Ar.* region, mountain range
Diep *Dut.* channel
Dijk *Dut.* dyke
Ding *Chin.* mountain
Dingzi *Chin.* hill, mountain
Djebel (Dj.) *Ar.* mountain
-djúp *Ice.* fjord
-djupet *Swe.* channel, sound
-Do *Jap., Kor.* island
Dolina *Russ.* valley
Dolna, Dolni *Bulg.* lower
Dolna, Dolne, Dolny *Russ.* lower
Dolní *Czec.* lower
Dolok (D.) *Malay* mountain
-dong *Kor.* village, town
Dong *Chin.* east, eastern
Donja, Donji *Ser.-Cr.* lower
-dorf *Ger.* village
-dorp *Afr.* village
-drif *Afr.* ford
-dybet *Dan.* marine channel
Dzong *Tib.* town, settlement
Dzüün *Mong.* east, eastern

-egga *Nor.* peak
-eiland, -en (eil.) *Afr., Dut.* island(s)
Eilean *Gae.* island
-elv, -a *Nor.* river
Embalse *Span.* reservoir
'Emeq *Heb.* plain, valley
Ensenada *Span.* bay
Erg *Ar.* sand desert
Estero *Span.* estuary
Estrada *Span.* bay
Estrecho *Span.* strait
Estuaire *Fr.* estuary
Estuario *Span.* estuary
Étang *Fr.* lagoon, lake
-ey, -jar *Ice.* island(s)
-ežeras *Lith.* lake
-ezers *Lat.* lake

Falaise *Fr.* cliff
-fallet *Swe.* waterfall
Farihy *Malag.* lake
Faro *Span.* lighthouse
-feld *Ger.* field
-fell *Ice.* mountain, hill
Feng *Chin.* mountain range
Fiume (F.) *It.* river
-fjäll, -en, -et *Swe.* hill(s), mountain(s), ridge
-fjärden *Swe.* fjord
Fjeld *Dan.* mountain
-fjell, -et *Nor.* mountain range
-fjord, -en *Dan., Nor., Swe.* fjord
-fjorður *Ice.* fjord, bay, inlet
Fleuve (Fl.) *Fr.* river
-flói *Ice.* bay, marshy country
Fluss (F.) *Ger.* river
Foce, Foci *It.* mouth(s)
Folyó (F.) *Hung.* river
-fonn *Nor.* glacier
-fontein *Afr.* fountain, spring
Forêt *Fr.* forest
-fors, -en *Swe.* waterfall, rapids
-foss, -en *Ice., Nor.* waterfall
Forst *Ger.* forest
Foum *Ar.* pass
Fuente *Span.* source
-furt *Ger.* ford
Fylke *Nor.* first-order administrative division

-gang *Chin.* bay, harbour
-gang *Kor.* river
Ganga *Hin., Sin.* river
Gangri *Tib.* mountain
Gaoyuan *Chin.* plateau
-gat *Dan.* sound
-Gata *Jap.* lake
-gau *Ger.* district
-Gawa *Jap.* river
Gebel (G.) *Ar.* mountain
Gebirge (Geb.) *Ger.* hills, mountains
Gezirat, Geziret *Ar.* island
Ghat *Hin.* range of hills
Ghiol *Rom.* lake
Ghubbat *Ar.* bay, inlet
Gjiri *Alb.* bay
Gjol *Alb.* lagoon, lake
Glava (Gl.) *Ser.-Cr.* mountain, peak
Glen *Gae.* valley
Gletscher (Gl.) *Ger.* glacier
Gobi *Mong.* desert
Gol *Mong.* river
Göl *Azeri, Turk.* lake
Golfe (G.) *Fr.* gulf
Golfo (G.) *It., Span.* gulf
Gölü *Turk.* lake
Gomba *Tib.* settlement
Gora, Góra *Bulg., Russ., Ser.-Cr., Pol.* mountain
Gorje *Ser.-Cr.* hills, mountains
Gorno *Russ.* mountainous
-gorod *Russ.* small town
Gory, Góry *Pol., Russ.* mountain
-grad *Bulg. Russ., Ser.-Cr.* town, city
-grada *Russ.* ridge
Gran *It., Span.* big, great
Grand, -e *Fr.* big, great
Groot (Gt.) *Afr., Dut.* big, great
Gross, -e, -en, -er *Ger.* big, great(er)
Grupo *Span.* group
Gruppo *It.* group
Guan *Chin.* pass
Guba (G.) *Russ.* bay
-Guntō *Jap.* island group
Gunong, Gunung (G.) *Indo., Malay* mountain
Gură *Rom.* passage

Hadabat *Ar.* plateau
Hadjer *Ar.* mountain
-hafen *Ger.* harbour, port
Haff *Ger.* bay, lagoon
Hai *Chin.* lake, sea
Haixia *Chin.* channel, strait
Halbinsel *Ger.* peninsula
Halvø *Dan.* peninsula
Halvøya *Nor.* peninsula
Hāmad, Hamada, Hammādah, Hammādat *Ar.* stony desert, plateau
-hamn *Swe., Nor.* harbour, anchorage
Hāmūn *Farsi* marsh, lake
-Hantō *Jap.* peninsula
Har(e) *Heb.* hill(s), mountain(s)
Hassi (Hi.) *Ar.* well
-haug *Nor.* hill
Hav, Havet *Nor., Swe.* sea
-havn *Dan., Nor.* bay, harbour
Havre *Fr.* harbour
Hawd *Ar.* oasis
Hawr *Ar.* lake, marsh
He *Chin.* river
-hegység *Hung.* hills, forest
Heide *Ger.* heath, moor
Helodranon' *Malag.* bay
Higashi *Jap.* east, eastern
-ho *Kor.* lake
-hø *Nor.* peak
Hoch *Ger.* high
Hochland *Afr.* highland
Hoek, -hoek *Afr., Dut.* cape, point
-höfn *Ice.* harbour, port
-hög, -en, -högar, -högarna *Swe.* hill(s), peak, mountain
Höhe *Ger.* height
Hohen *Ger.* high, upper
-hoi *Chin.* bay
-høj, -e *Dan.* hills
-holm, -holme, -holmen *Dan., Nor., Swe.* island
Hon *Viet.* island
Hoog *Dut.* high
Hora *Czec., Ukr.* mountain
-horn *Ger.* peak
Hory *Czec.* mountains, hills
-hot *Mong.* town
-hoved *Dan.* point, headland, peninsula
-hrad *Czec.* town
Hráun *Ice.* lava
-hsi *Chin.* river
-hsia *Chin.* gorge, strait
-hsien *Chin.* district
Hu *Chin.* lake, reservoir
Huk *Dan., Ger.* cape
-huk *Swe.* cape
Huken *Nor.* cape

Idd *Ar.* well
Idehan *Ar., Berb.* sandy plain, dunes
-ike *Jap.* lake
Île(s) (I(s).) *Fr.* island(s)
Ilha(s) (I(s).) *Port.* island(s)
imeni *Russ.* 'in the name of'
Inish *Gae.* island
Insel(n) (I.) *Ger.* island(s)
Irmak *Turk.* river
'Irq *Ar.* dunes
Isla(s) (I(s).) *Span.* island(s)
Iso *Fin.* big, great
Isol, -a, -e (I.) *It.* island(s)
Isthme *Fr.* isthmus
Istmo *Span.* isthmus
-iwa *Jap.* island

Jabal *Ar.* mountain range
Järv *Est.* lake
järvi *Fin.* lake, bay, pond
-jaur, -javre *Lapp.* lake
Jazā'ir *Ar.* islands
Jazīra, jazīrat *Ar.* island
Jazireh *Farsi* island
Jebel *Ar.* mountain
Jezero *Ser.-Cr.* lake
Jezioro *Pol.* lake
Jiang *Chin.* river
Jiao *Chin.* cape
-Jima *Jap.* island
Jøkulen *Nor.* glacier, ice cap
-joki *Fin.* river
-jökull *Ice.* glacier, ice cap
Jūras Līcis *Lat.* bay, gulf

Kaap (K.) *Afr.* cape
-kai *Jap.* bay, channel, sea
-kaikyō *Jap.* strait
-kaise *Lapp.* mountain
kalnas *Lith.* hill
Kamennyy *Russ.* stony
Kampong *Cam.* village
Kampung *Malay* village
-kanaal *Dut.* canal
Kanal *Dan.* channel, gulf
Kanal *Ger., Swe.* canal
-kanal *Ser.-Cr.* channel, canal
Kanava *Fin.* canal
Kang *Kor.* river, bay
Kap (K.) *Dan., Ger.* cape, point
-kapp *Nor.* cape, point
-kaupstaður *Ice.* market town
-kaupunki *Fin.* town
Kavīr *Farsi* salt desert
Kébir *Ar.* great
Kecil *Malay* lesser, little
Kefar *Heb.* village, hamlet
-Ken *Jap.* first-order administrative division
Kep, -i (K.) *Alb.* cape
Kepulauan (Kep.) *Indo., Malay* archipelago
Keski- *Fin.* middle, central
Khalīg, Khalīj *Ar.* gulf
-khamba *Tib.* source, spring
Khawr *Ar.* bay, channel, wadi
Khlong *Thai* river
Kho Khot *Thai* isthmus
Khōr *Farsi* bay, estuary
Khrebet *Russ.* mountain range
Kita- *Jap.* north
Klein,-e, -er *Ger.* small
-klint *Dan.* cliff
Klintar *Swe.* hills
-kloof *Afr.* gorge, pass
Knude *Dan.* point
-Ko *Jap.* lake
Ko *Thai* island
-kōchi *Jap.* mountainous region
-kōgen *Jap.* plateau
Kohi *Pash.* mountains
Kol *Kaz., Kyrg.* lake
Kólpos *Gr., Turk.* gulf, bay
Kolymskoye *Russ.* mountain range
Kompong *Malay* landing place
-kop *Afr.* hill
-kopf *Ger.* hill
-köping *Swe.* market town
Körfäzi *Azeri* gulf
Körfezi *Turk.* gulf
Kosa *Russ., Ukr.* spit
-koski *Fin.* rapids
-kraal *Afr.* native village
-kraj *Czec., Pol., Ser.-Cr.* region
Krasnyy *Russ.* red
Kryazh *Russ.* ridge, hills
Kuala *Malay* bay
-kuan *Chin.* pass
Kūh(ha) *Farsi* mountain(s)
Kul *Russ.* lake
-kulle *Swe.* hill
Kum *Russ.* sandy desert
Kumpu *Fin.* hill
Kwe *Burm.* bay, gulf
-kylä *Fin.* village
Kyst, -en *Dan., Nor.* coast
Kyun(zu) *Burm.* island(s)

La *Tib.* pass
-laagte *Afr.* watercourse

Lääni *Fin.* first-order administrative division
Lac (L.) *Fr.* lake
Lacul (L.) *Rom.* lake, lagoon
Lago (L.) *It., Port., Span.* lake, lagoon
Lagoa (L.) *Port.* lagoon
Lagos *Port., Span.* lakes
Laguna (L.) *It., Span.* lagoon, lake
Lagune (L.) *Fr.* lake
-laht *Est.* bay
Lahti *Fin.* bay, gulf, cove
Lakhti *Russ.* bay, gulf
Lam *Thai* river
Lampi *Fin.* lake
Län *Swe.* first-order administrative division
Land *Ger.* first-order administrative division
-land *Dan.* region
-land *Afr., Nor.* land, province
Lande *Fr.* heath
Laut *Indo.* sea
Law *Gae.* hill, mountain
Līcis *Lat.* gulf
Lido *It.* beach, shore
Liedao *Chin.* islands
Lilla *Swe.* small
Lille *Dan., Nor.* small
Liman *Russ.* bay, gulf
Límni (L.) *Gr.* lake
Ling *Chin.* mountain range
-linna *Fin.* fort
Llano *Span.* prairie, plain
Llyn *Welsh* lake
Loch (L.) *Gae.* lake, inlet
Lough (L.) *Gae.* lake, inlet
Lum *Alb.* river
Lund *Dan.* forest
-lund, -en *Swe.* wood(s)
-luoto *Fin.* island

-maa *Est.* island
Madīnat *Ar.* town, city
Madiq *Ar.* strait
Maja *Alb.* mountains
-mäki *Fin.* hill, hillside
Mal *Alb.* mountain
Maloye, Malyy, Malyya *Russ.* little, small
Mala, Mali, Malo *Ser.-Cr.* little, small
Malaya *Belo.* small
Malé *Czec., Slovak* small
Mali *Alb.* mountain
-man *Kor.* bay
Mar *Span.* lagoon, sea
Marais *Fr.* marsh
Mare *It.* sea
Mare *Rom.* great
Marisma *Span.* marsh
-mark *Dan., Nor.* land
Marsâ *Ar.* anchorage, bay, inlet
Masabb *Ar.* river mouth, estuary
Massif *Fr.* upland, mountains
Mato *Port.* forest
Mazar *Farsi* shrine, tomb
Meer, -meer *Afr., Dut., Ger.* lake, sea
-men *Chin.* bay, gorge, channel
Mesto *Ser.-Cr., Czec.* town
Mezzo *It.* middle
Midbar *Heb.* wilderness
Mierzeja *Pol.* spit
Mifraz *Heb.* bay
Mina *Ar.* port
Minami *Jap.* south, southern
-misaki *Jap.* cape, point
Mittel *Ger.* central, middle
-mo *Nor., Swe.* heath, island
-mon *Swe.* heath
Mong *Burm.* town
Mont(s) (Mt(s).) *Fr.* hill(s), mountain(s)
Montagna (Mt.) *It.* mountain
Montagne(s) (Mt(s).) *Fr.* hill(s), mountain(s)
Montaña(s) (Mt(s).) *Span.* mountain(s)
Montanyes *Cat.* mountains
Monte(s) (Mte(s).) *It., Port., Span.* mountain(s)
Monti (Mti.) *It.* mountains
More *Russ.* sea
Mörön *Mong.* river
Moyen *Fr.* central, middle
Muang *Malay* town
Mui *Viet.* cape
Mull *Gae.* promontory
Mund, -mund *Afr.* mouth
Munkhafed *Ar.* depression
Munte (Mte.) *Rom.* mount
Munţi(i) (Mti.) *Rom.* mountain(s)
Muong *Malay* village
Myit *Burm.* river
Myitwanya *Burm.* mouths of river
Mynydd *Welsh* mountain
-myr *Nor., Swe.* swamp
-mýri *Ice.* swamp
Mys (M.) *Russ.* cape

-Nada *Jap.* bay, gulf
-næs *Dan.* point, cape
Nafūd *Ar.* sandy desert
Nagorye *Russ.* hills, mountains
Nagy *Hung.* big
Nahal (N.) *Heb.* river
Nahr (N.) *Ar.* river, stream
Najd *Ar.* plateau, pass
Nakhon *Thai* town
Nam *Kor., Viet.* river
-nam *Kor.* south
Namakzār *Per.* salt flat
Nan *Chin.* south, southern
-nao *Chin.* lake
-näs *Swe.* cape
Neder *Dut.* lower
Nedre *Nor.* lower
Nei *Chin.* inner
Nek *Afr.* pass
-nes *Ice., Nor.* cape
Ness, -ness *Gae.* promontory, cape
Nevada, Nevado *Span.* snow-capped mountain
Nez *Fr.* cape
Nieder *Ger.* lower
-niemi *Fin.* cape, point, peninsula, island
Nieuw, -e *Dut.* new
Nishi *Jap.* west, western
Nisos, Nisoi *Gr.* island(s)
Nizhneye, Nizhniy *Russ.* lower
Nizina *Belo., Pol.* lowland
Nizmennost *Russ.* plain, lowland
Nízní *Czec.* lower
Noord *Dut.* north, northern
Nord *Fr.* north, northern
Norra *Swe.* north, northern
Nørre *Dan.* north, northern
Norte *Port., Span.* north, northern
Nos *Bulg., Russ.* cape, point
Nosy *Malag.* island
Nouveau, Nouvelle *Fr.* new
Nova, Novi *Bulg., Port., Serb.-Cr.* new
Novaya, Novo, Novoye, Novyy *Russ.* new
Nové, Novy *Czec., Slovak* new
Novo *Port.* new
Nowa, Nowe, Nowy *Pol.* new
Nudo *Span.* mountain
Nueva, Nuevo *Span.* new
Nur *Chin.* lake
Nur *Tib.* peak
Nuruu *Mong.* mountain range
Nusa *Indo.* island
Nuur *Mong.* lake
Ny *Dan., Nor., Swe.* new

-ø *Dan., Nor.* island
-ö *Swe.* island,
-öar, -na *Swe.* islands
Ober *Ger., Ukr.* upper
Oblast *Russ.* administrative division
Öbor *Mong.* inner
Occidental *Fr., Span.* western
-odde *Dan., Nor.* point, peninsula, cape
Oeste *Span.* west, western
Oglat *Ar.* well
Oji *Alb.* bay
Ojo *Span.* spring
-Oki *Jap.* bay
-ön *Swe.* island
Ondör *Mong.* upper
Oost(er) *Dut.* east(ern)
Oraşu *Rom.* city
Ord *Gae.* point
Óri *Gr.* mountains
Oriental, -e *Fr., Span.* east, eastern
Órmos *Gr.* bay
Óros *Gr.* mountain(s)
Ort *Ger.* point, cape
Ost *Ger.* east
Øst(er) *Den., Nor.* east(ern)
Öst(ra) *Swe.* east(ern)
Ostriv *Ukr.* island
Ostrov(a) *Russ.* island(s)
Otok(i) *Ser.-Cr.* island(s)
Ouabi, Ouadi (O.) *Ar.* dry watercourse, wadi
Oud, -e *Dut.* old
Oued, -i (O.) *Ar.* watercourse
Ouest *Fr.* west, western
Ouzan *Farsi* river
Ova, -si *Turk.* plains, lowlands
Over- *Dan., Dut.* upper
Över-, Övre *Nor., Swe.* upper
-øy, -a *Nor.* island(s)
Oya *Hin.* point
Oya *Sin.* river
Ozero, Ozera (Oz.) *Russ., Ukr.* lake(s)

-pää *Fin.* hill(s), mountain
Pahta *Lapp.* hill
Pampa(s) *Span.* plain(s)
Pantanal *Port.* marsh
Pantano *Span.* reservoir
Pantao *Chin.* peninsula
Parbat *Urdu* mountain
Pas *Fr.* strait
Paso (P.) *Span.* pass
Passage *Fr.* channel
Passe *Fr.* channel
Passo (P.) *It.* pass
Pasul (P.) *Rom.* pass
Patam *Hin.* small village
Patna, -patnam *Hin.* small village
Pegunungan *Indo., Malay* mountain range
Pei, -pei *Chin.* north
Pélagos *Gr.* sea
Pen *Welsh* hill
Peña *Span.* rock, peak
Pendi *Chin.* basin, depression
Péninsule *Fr.* peninsula
Penisola (Pen.) *It.* peninsula
Pereval (Per.) *Russ.* pass
Pervo-, Pervyy- *Russ.* first
Pertuis *Fr.* channel, strait
Peski *Russ.* sand desert
Petit, -e *Fr.* small
Phanom *Thai* mountain
Phnum *Cam.* mountain
Phou *Lao.* mountain
Phu *Thai, Viet.* mountain
Piano *It.* plain
Pic *Cat., Fr.* peak
Pico(s) *Span.* peak(s)
-piggen *Dan.* peak
Pik *Russ.* peak
Pingyuan *Chin.* plain
Pique *Fr.* peak
Piton *Fr.* peak
Pivostriv *Ukr.* peninsula
Piz, Pizzo *It.* peak
Plage *Fr.* beach
Plaine *Fr.* plain
Planalto *Port.* plateau
Planina (Pl.) *Bulg., Ser.-Cr.* mountain range
Plato *Russ., Bulg.* plateau
Playa *Span.* beach
-po *Chin.* lake, wetland
Pointe (Pte.) *Fr.* point, cape
Pojezierze *Pol.* lakes
Polder *Dut.* reclaimed farmland
-pólis *Gr.* city, town
Poluostrov (Pov.) *Russ.* peninsula
Półwysep *Pol.* peninsula
Pont *Fr.* bridge
Ponta (Pta.) *Port.* point, cape
Ponte *Port.* bridge
Poort *Afr.* passage, gate
-poort *Dut.* port
Porta *Port.* pass
Porţile *Rom.* gate
Portillo *Span.* pass
Porto *It., Port., Span.* port
Potámi, Potamós *Gr.* river
Pradesh *Hin.* state
Praia *Port.* beach, shore
Presa *Span.* reservoir
Presqu'île *Fr.* peninsula
Prokhod *Bulg.* pass
Proliv *Russ.* strait
Promontorio *Span.* promontory
Průsmyk (Pr.) *Czec.* pass
Pueblo *Span.* village
Puerto (Pto.) *Span.* port
Puig *Cat.* peak
Pulau (P.) *Indo., Malay* island
Puna *Span.* desert plateau
Puncak *Indo.* peak
Punta (Pta.) *It., Span.* point, peak
Puy *Fr.* peak

Qal'at *Ar.* fort
Qanat *Ar.* canal
Qasr *Ar.* fort
Qiryat *Heb.* town
Qiuling *Chin.* plateau
Qolleh *Farsi* mountain
-qundao *Chin.* islands

Rach *Viet.* river
Rags *Lat.* cape
Rambla *Cat.* river
Ramlat *Ar.* sandy desert
Rão (R.) *Port.* river
Rann *Hin.* swampy region
Rao *I.-C.* river
Ras *Amh., Ar., Farsi* cape, point
Récif(s) *Fr.* reef(s)
Recife(s) *Port.* reef(s)
Reka *Bulg.* river
Repede *Rom.* rapids
Reprêsa *Port.* reservoir
Reshteh *Farsi* mountain range
-rettō *Jap.* group of islands, chain
Ria *Port., Span.* estuary, bay
Ribeirão (R.) *Port.* river
Ribera (R.) *Span.* river bank
Rijeka *Ser.-Cr.* river
Rio (R.) *Port., Span.* river
Rivier (R.) *Afr., Dut.* river
Riviera *It.* coastal plain, coast
Rivière (R.) *Fr.* river
Roca *Span.* rock
Rocca *It.* rock, peak
Roche *Fr.* rock
Rt *Ser.-Cr.* cape, point
Rubh', Rubha *Gae.* cape, point
-rück *Ger.* ridge
Rūd *Farsi* stream, river
Rudohorie *Slovak* mountains
Rzeka (R.) *Pol.* river

-saar *Est.* island
-saari *Fin.* island
Sabkhat, Sabkhet *Ar.* salt flats
Sadd *Ar.* dam
Sagar,-a *Hin., Urdu* lake
Sahrâ *Ar.* desert
-Saki *Jap.* cape, point
Salar *Span.* salt flat
Salina(s) *Span.* salt marsh(es)
-salmi *Fin.* strait, sound, lake, channel
Saltsjöbad *Swe.* resort
-Sammyaku *Jap.* mountain range
Samut *Thai* gulf
San (S.) *It., Port., Span.* saint
-San *Jap., Kor.* hill, mountain
-Sanchi *Jap.* mountain range
Sankt (St.) *Ger., Russ.* saint
-sanmaek *Kor.* mountain range
-sanmyaku *Jap.* mountain range
Santa (Sta.) *It., Port., Span.* saint
Santo (Sto.) *It. Port., Span.* saint
São (S.) *Port.* saint
Sarīr *Ar.* desert
Sasso *It.* mountain
Satu *Rom.* village
Saurums *Lat.* strait
Sebkha, Sebkhet *Ar.* salt flat
See, -see *Ger.* lake
-şehir *Turk.* town
Selat *Indo., Malay* strait
Selatan *Indo.* southern
-selkä *Fin.* bay, lake, ridge, hills
Selo *Ser.-Cr., Russ.* village
Selva *Port., Span.* forest, wood
Seno *Span.* bay, sound
Serir *Ar.* stony desert
Serra (Sa.) *Cat., Port.* range of hills
Serrania *Span.* mountain ridge
Severo, Severnaya, Severnoye, Severnyy (Sev.) *Russ.* north, northern
Sfântu *Rom.* saint
Shahr, -shahr *Farsi* city, town
Shamo *Chin.* desert
Shan *Chin.* hills, mountains
Shankou *Chin.* pass
Shanmo *Chin.* mountain range
Sharm *Ar.* bay
Shatt *Ar.* river mouth, estuary
-Shima *Jap.* island
Shimāli *Ar.* northern
-Shotō *Jap.* group of islands
-shui *Chin.* river
-shuiku *Chin.* reservoir
Sierra (Sa.) *Span.* mountain range
-sjö, -sjön, -sjø *Swe., Nor.* lake
-sjøen *Dan.* sea
-sjór *Ice.* lake
-sker *Ice.* island
-skär *Swe.* island, rock, cape
-skog, -skogen *Nor., Swe.* wood(s)
-skov *Dan.* forest
Slieve *Gae.* hill, mountain
Sø *Dan., Nor.* lake
Söder, Södra *Swe.* south, southern
Sør *Nor.* south, southern
Solonchak *Russ.* salt lake, marsh
Sønder, Søndra *Dan.* south, southern
Song *Viet.* river
Souk *Ar.* market
-spitze *Ger.* peak, mountain
-spruit *Afr.* stream
Sredna, Sredno *Bulg.* middle, central
Sredne, Sredneye *Russ.* middle, central
Srednja *Ser.-Cr.* middle, central
-stad *Afr., Nor., Swe.* town
-stadt *Ger.* town
-staður *Ice.* town
Stara, Stari *Ser.-Cr.* old
Stará, Staré, Stary *Czec.* old
Staraya, Staroye, Staryy *Russ.* old
Stare, Staro, Stary *Ukr.* old
Stausee *Ger.* reservoir
Stenón *Gr.* strait, pass
Step *Russ.* steppe
Stor, -a *Swe.* big
Store *Dan.* big
-strand *Dan., Ger., Nor., Swe.* beach
-strede *Nor.* straits
Strelka *Russ.* spit
-strete *Nor.* straits
Stretto (Str.) *It.* strait
Strædet (Str.) *Dan.* strait
-ström, -strömmen *Swe.* stream(s)
-stroom *Afr.* large river
Sud *Fr.* south, southern
Süd, -er *Ger.* south, southern
Suid *Afr.* south, southern
-Suidō *Jap.* strait, channel
Sul *Port.* south, southern
Sûn *Burm.* cape
-sund, -et *Swe., Nor.* sound, estuary, inlet
Sungai *Indo., Malay* river
Sur *Span.* south, southern
Sveti *Bulg.* saint
Syd *Dan., Swe.* south, southern
Sýsla *Ice.* first-order administrative division

-tag *Uighur* mountain
Tai -tai *Chin.* tower
-Take *Jap.* mountain
Tal *Mong.* plain, steppe
-tal *Ger.* valley
Tall *Ar.* hills
Tanjona *Malag.* cape, point
Tanjung, Tanjong (Tg.) *Indo., Malay.* cape, point
Tao *Chin.* island
Tasik *Malay* lake
Tassili *Ar.* rocky plateau
Tau *Russ.* mountain range
Taung *Burm.* mountain
Taungdan. *Burm.* mountain range
Taunggya *Burm.* pass
-tekojärvi *Fin.* reservoir
Teluk *Indo., Malay* bay, gulf
Ténéré *Berb.* desert
Tengah *Indo.* middle, central
-thal *Ger.* valley
Thok *Tib.* town
Tien *Chin.* lake, marsh
Tierra *Span.* land, country
Timur *Indo.* eastern
-tind *Nor.* peak
-ting *Chin.* mountain
Tjärn, -en, -et *Swe.* lake
-Tō *Jap.* island
Tong *Kor.* village, town
Tong *Burm., Thai, Kor.* mountain range
Tonlé *Cam.* lake
Top *Dut.* peak
-topp, -en *Nor.* peak
-träsk *Swe.* lake, swamp
Tsangpo *Tib.* large river
Tso *Tib.* lake
Tsu *Jap.* entrance, bay
Tsui *Chin.* cape, point
Tulur *Ar.* hill
-tunturi *Fin.* hill(s), mountain(s), ridge

Uad *Ar.* dry watercourse, wadi
Über *Ger.* upper
-udde, -udden *Swe.* point, cape
Uebi *Som.* river
Ujung *Indo., Malay* cape
Unter- *Ger.* lower
Us *Mong.* water
Ust, Ustye *Russ.* river mouth
Utara *Indo.* north, northern
Uttar *Hin.* north, northern
Uul *Mong., Russ.* mountain range

-vaara *Fin.* hill, mountain ridge, peak
Vaart *Dut.* canal
-våg *Nor.* bay
Val *Fr., Port., Span.* valley
Valea *Rom.* valley
-vall, -en *Swe.* mountain
Valle *It., Span.* valley
Vallée *Fr.* valley
Valli *It.* lake, lagoon
-város *Hung.* town
-varre *Nor.* mountain
Väst, Västra *Swe.* west, western
-vatn *Ice., Nor.* lake
-vatnet *Nor.* lake
-vatten, vattnet *Swe.* lake
-vecchio *It.* old
Vechi *Rom.* old
-ved, -veden *Swe.* hills
Veld, -veld *Afr.* field
Velha, Velho *Port.* old
Velika, Velike, Veliki, Veliko *Ser.-Cr., Slov.* big, large
Velikaya, Velikiy *Russ.* big, large
Velká, Velké, Velký *Czec.* big, large
Verkhne, Verkhniy *Russ.* upper
-vesi *Fin.* water, lake, bay, sound, strait
Vest, Vester, Vestre *Dan., Nor.* west, western
-vidda *Nor.* plateau
Vieille, Vieux *Fr.* old
Vieja, Vejo *Span.* old
Vig *Dan.* bay, inlet, cove, lagoon, lake
-vik *Ice.* bay
-vik, -a, -en *Nor., Swe.* bay, gulf, inlet, lake
Vila *Port.* small town
Villa *Span.* town
Ville *Fr.* town
Vinh *Viet.* bay
Vîrful (Vf.) *Rom.* peak, mountain
-viz *Hung.* river
-víztároló *Hung.* reservoir
-vlei *Afr.* lake, salt pan
-vliet *Dut.* canal
-vloer *Afr.* salt pan
Vodokhranilishche (Vdkhr.) *Russ.* reservoir
Vodoskovyshche (Vdskh.) *Ukr.* reservoir
Volcán (Vol.) *Span.* volcano, mountain
Vorota *Russ.* pass, channel, strait
Vostochno, Vostochnyy *Russ.* east, eastern
-vötn *Ice.* lakes
Vozvyshennost *Russ.* heights, uplands
Vozyera *Belo.* lake
Vrata *Bulg.* gate, pass
Vrchovina *Czec.* mountainous country
Vrch(y) *Czec.* mountain (range)
Vung *Viet.* bay, gulf
-vuori *Fin.* mountain, hill
Vychodné *Slovak* east, eastern
Vysochyna *Ukr.* upland

-waard *Dut.* polder
Wadi (W.) *Ar.* dry watercourse
Wâhât *Ar.* oasis
Wald *Ger.* forest, mountains
-Wan *Chin., Jap.* bay, harbour
Wāw *Ar.* well
Webi *Amh.* river
Wes *Afr.* west, western
Wielka, Wielki, Wielko *Pol.* big, large
Woestyn *Afr.* desert
Wysoka, Wysoki *Pol.* upper
Wyżyna *Pol.* plateau

Xi *Chin.* river
Xia *Chin.* gorge, strait
Xiao *Chin.* small

Yam *Heb.* sea
-Yama *Jap.* mountain
-yan *Chin.* gorge, island
Yang *Chin.* bay, sea, sound
Yangi *Russ.* new
Yazovir *Bulg.* reservoir
Yeni *Turk.* new
Yli *Fin.* upper
Ynys *Welsh* island
Yoma *Burm.* mountain range
Ytre-, Ytter- *Nor., Swe.* outer
-yuan *Chin.* stream
Yugo- *Ser.-Cr.* south, southern
Yunhe *Chin.* canal
Yuzhni, Yuzhno *Russ.* south, southern

-Zaki *Jap.* point
Zalew *Pol.* lagoon, swamp
Zaliv *Russ.* bay, gulf
-Zan *Jap.* mountain
Zangbo *Tib.* stream, river
Zapadnaya, Zapadno, Zapadnyi (Zap.) *Russ.* west, western
Zatoka *Pol., Ukr.* bay, gulf
-zee *Dut.* lake, sea
Zemlya *Russ.* land, island(s)
Zhang *Chin.* mountain
-zhou *Chin.* island
Zhong *Chin.* middle, central
Zhou *Chin.* island
Zizhiqu *Chin.* autonomous region
Zuid, Zuider *Dut.* south, southern

INDEX TO WORLD MAPS

HOW TO USE THE INDEX

The index contains the names of all the principal places and features shown on the World and City Maps. Each name is followed by an additional entry in italics giving the country or region within which it is located. The alphabetical order of names composed of two or more words is governed primarily by the first word, then by the second, and then by the country or region name that follows. This is an example of the rule:

Mir *Niger*	14°5N 11°59E	**259** F2
Mīr Kūh *Iran*	26°22N 58°55E	**247** E8
Mīr Shahdād *Iran*	26°15N 58°29E	**247** E8
Mira *Italy*	45°26N 12°8E	**199** C9

Physical features composed of a proper name (Erie) and a description (Lake) are positioned alphabetically by the proper name. The description is positioned after the proper name and is usually abbreviated:

Erie, L. *N. Amer.*	42°15N 81°0W	**312** D4

Where a description forms part of a settlement or administrative name, however, it is always written in full and put in its true alphabetical position:

Mount Olive *U.S.A.*	39°4N 89°44W	**310** E7

Names beginning with M' and Mc are indexed as if they were spelled Mac. Names beginning St. are alphabetized under Saint, but Sankt, Sint, Sant', Santa and San are all spelt in full and are alphabetized accordingly. If the same place name occurs two or more times in the index and all are in the same country, each is followed by the name of the administrative subdivision in which it is located.

The geographical co-ordinates which follow each name in the index give the latitude and longitude of each place. The first co-ordinate indicates latitude – the distance north or south of the Equator. The second co-ordinate indicates longitude – the distance east or west of the Greenwich Meridian. Both latitude and longitude are measured in degrees and minutes (there are 60 minutes in a degree). Latitude and longitude references are not used on the Central Area City Maps.

The latitude is followed by N(orth) or S(outh) and the longitude by E(ast) or W(est).

The number in bold type which follows the geographical co-ordinates refers to the number of the map page where that feature or place will be found. This is usually the largest scale at which the place or feature appears.

The letter and figure that are immediately after the page number give the grid square on the map page, within which the feature is situated. The letter represents the latitude and the figure the longitude. A lower-case letter immediately after the page number refers to an inset map on that page.

In some cases the feature itself may fall within the specified square, while the name is outside. This is usually the case only with features that are larger than a grid square.

Rivers are indexed to their mouths or confluences, and carry the symbol → after their names. The following symbols are also used in the index: ■ country, ▨ overseas territory or dependency, □ first-order administrative area, ☆ U.S. county, △ national park, ⌓ other park (provincial park, nature reserve or game reserve), ✪ Australian aboriginal land, ▲ U.S. Indian reservation ✈ (LHR) principal airport (and location identifier).

HOW TO PRONOUNCE PLACE NAMES

English-speaking people usually have no difficulty in reading and pronouncing correctly English place names. However, foreign place name pronunciations may present many problems. Such problems can be minimized by following some simple rules. However, these rules cannot be applied to all situations, and there will be many exceptions.

1. In general, stress each syllable equally, unless your experience suggests otherwise.
2. Pronounce the letter 'a' as a broad 'a' as in 'arm'.
3. Pronounce the letter 'e' as a short 'e' as in 'elm'.
4. Pronounce the letter 'i' as a cross between a short 'i' and long 'e', as the two 'i's in 'California'.
5. Pronounce the letter 'o' as an intermediate 'o' as in 'soft'.
6. Pronounce the letter 'u' as an intermediate 'u' as in 'sure'.
7. Pronounce consonants hard, except in the Romance-language areas where 'g's are likely to be pronounced softly like 'j' in 'jam'; 'j' itself may be pronounced as 'y'; and 'x's may be pronounced as 'h'.
8. For names in mainland China, pronounce 'q' like the 'ch' in 'chin', 'x' like the 'sh' in 'she', 'zh' like the 'j' in 'jam', and 'z' as if it were spelled 'dz'. In general, pronounce 'a' as in 'father', 'e' as in 'but', 'i' as in 'keep', 'o' as in 'or', and 'u' as in 'rule'.

Moreover, English has no diacritical marks (accent and pronunciation signs), although some languages do. The following is a brief and general guide to the pronunciation of those most frequently used in the principal Western European languages.

		Pronunciation as in
French	é	day and shows that the 'e' is to be pronounced; e.g. Orléans.
	è	mare
	î	used over any vowel and does not affect pronunciation; shows contraction of the name, usually omission of 's' following a vowel.
	ç	's' before 'a', 'o' and 'u'.
	ë, ï, ü	over 'e', 'i' and 'u' when they are used with another vowel and shows that each is to be pronounced.
German	ä	fate
	ö	fur
	ü	no English equivalent; like French 'tu'.
Italian	à, é	over vowels and indicates stress.
Portuguese	ã, õ	vowels pronounced nasally.
	ç	boss
	á	shows stress.
	ô	shows that a vowel has an 'i' or 'u' sound combined with it.
Spanish	ñ	canyon
	ü	pronounced as 'w' and separately from adjoining vowels.
	á	usually indicates that this is a stressed vowel.

ABBREVIATIONS

A.C.T. – Australian Capital Territory
A.R. – Autonomous Region
Afghan. – Afghanistan
Afr. – Africa
Ala. – Alabama
Alta. – Alberta
Amer. – America(n)
Ant. – Antilles
Arch. – Archipelago
Ariz. – Arizona
Ark. – Arkansas
Atl. Oc. – Atlantic Ocean
B. – Baie, Bahía, Bay, Bucht, Bugt
B.C. – British Columbia
Bangla. – Bangladesh
Barr. – Barrage
Bos.-H. – Bosnia-Herzegovina
C. – Cabo, Cap, Cape, Coast
C.A.R. – Central African Republic
C. Prov. – Cape Province
Calif. – California
Cat. – Catarata
Cent. – Central
Chan. – Channel
Colo. – Colorado
Conn. – Connecticut
Cord. – Cordillera
Cr. – Creek
Czech. – Czech Republic
D.C. – District of Columbia
Del. – Delaware
Dem. – Democratic
Dep. – Dependency
Des. – Desert
Dét. – Détroit
Dist. – District
Dj. – Djebel
Dom. Rep. – Dominican Republic
E. – East
El Salv. – El Salvador
Eq. Guin. – Equatorial Guinea
Est. – Estrecho
Falk. Is. – Falkland Is.
Fd. – Fjord
Fla. – Florida
Fr. – French
G. – Golfe, Golfo, Gulf, Guba, Gebel
Ga. – Georgia
Gt. – Great, Greater
Guinea-Biss. – Guinea-Bissau
H.K. – Hong Kong
H.P. – Himachal Pradesh
Hants. – Hampshire
Harb. – Harbor, Harbour
Hd. – Head
Hts. – Heights
I.(s). – Île, Ilha, Insel, Isla, Island, Isle
Ill. – Illinois
Ind. – Indiana
Ind. Oc. – Indian Ocean
Ivory C. – Ivory Coast
J. – Jabal, Jebel
Jaz. – Jazīrah
Junc. – Junction
K. – Kap, Kapp
Kans. – Kansas
Kep. – Kepulauan
Ky. – Kentucky
L. – Lac, Lacul, Lago, Lagoa, Lake, Limni, Loch, Lough
La. – Louisiana
Ld. – Land
Liech. – Liechtenstein
Lux. – Luxembourg
Mad. P. – Madhya Pradesh
Madag. – Madagascar
Man. – Manitoba
Mass. – Massachusetts
Md. – Maryland
Me. – Maine
Medit. S. – Mediterranean Sea
Mich. – Michigan
Minn. – Minnesota
Miss. – Mississippi
Mo. – Missouri
Mont. – Montana
Mozam. – Mozambique
Mt.(s) – Mont, Montaña, Mountain
Mte. – Monte
Mti. – Monti
N. – Nord, Norte, North, Northern, Nouveau, Nahal, Nahr
N.B. – New Brunswick
N.C. – North Carolina
N. Cal. – New Caledonia
N. Dak. – North Dakota
N.H. – New Hampshire
N.I. – North Island
N.J. – New Jersey
N. Mex. – New Mexico
N.S. – Nova Scotia
N.S.W. – New South Wales
N.W.T. – North West Territory
N.Y. – New York
N.Z. – New Zealand
Nac. – Nacional
Nat. – National
Nebr. – Nebraska
Neths. – Netherlands
Nev. – Nevada
Nfld & L.. – Newfoundland and Labrador
Nic. – Nicaragua
O. – Oued, Ouadi
Occ. – Occidentale
Okla. – Oklahoma
Ont. – Ontario
Or. – Orientale
Oreg. – Oregon
Os. – Ostrov
Oz. – Ozero
P. – Pass, Passo, Pasul, Pulau
P.E.I. – Prince Edward Island
Pa. – Pennsylvania
Pac. Oc. – Pacific Ocean
Papua N.G. – Papua New Guinea
Pass. – Passage
Peg. – Pegunungan
Pen. – Peninsula, Péninsule
Phil. – Philippines
Pk. – Peak
Plat. – Plateau
Prov. – Province, Provincial
Pt. – Point
Pta. – Ponta, Punta
Pte. – Pointe
Qué. – Québec
Queens. – Queensland
R. – Rio, River
R.I. – Rhode Island
Ra. – Range
Raj. – Rajasthan
Recr. – Recreational, Récréatif
Reg. – Region
Rep. – Republic
Res. – Reserve, Reservoir
Rhld-Pfz. – Rheinland-Pfalz
S. – South, Southern, Sur
Si. Arabia – Saudi Arabia
S.C. – South Carolina
S. Dak. – South Dakota
S.I. – South Island
S. Leone – Sierra Leone
Sa. – Serra, Sierra
Sask. – Saskatchewan
Scot. – Scotland
Sd. – Sound
Sev. – Severnaya
Sib. – Siberia
Sprs. – Springs
St. – Saint
Sta. – Santa
Ste. – Sainte
Sto. – Santo
Str. – Strait, Stretto
Switz. – Switzerland
Tas. – Tasmania
Tenn. – Tennessee
Terr. – Territory, Territoire
Tex. – Texas
Tg. – Tanjung
Trin. & Tob. – Trinidad & Tobago
U.A.E. – United Arab Emirates
U.K. – United Kingdom
U.S.A. – United States of America
Univ. – University, Université, Universidad
Ut. P. – Uttar Pradesh
Va. – Virginia
Vdkhr. – Vodokhranilishche
Vdskh. – Vodoskhovyshche
Vf. – Vírful
Vic. – Victoria
Vol. – Volcano
Vt. – Vermont
W. – Wadi, West
W. Va. – West Virginia
Wall. & F. Is. – Wallis and Futuna Is.
Wash. – Washington
Wis. – Wisconsin
Wlkp. – Wielkopolski
Wyo. – Wyoming
Yorks. – Yorkshire

340 A 'Âli an Nîl INDEX

A

A 'Âli an Nîl □ Sudan 9°30N 33°0E 257 F3
A Baña Spain 42°58N 8°46W 194 C2
A Cañiza Spain 42°13N 8°16W 194 C2
A Coruña Spain 43°20N 8°25W 194 B2
A Coruña □ Spain 43°10N 8°30W 194 B2
A Cruz do Incio Spain 42°39N 7°21W 194 C3
A Estrada Spain 42°43N 8°27W 194 C2
A Fonsagrada Spain 43°8N 7°4W 194 B3
A Guarda Spain 41°56N 8°52W 194 D2
A Gudiña Spain 42°4N 7°8W 194 C3
A Pobre Spain 42°58N 7°3W 194 C3
A Ramallosa Spain 42°45N 8°30W 194 C2
A Rúa Spain 42°24N 7°6W 194 C3
A Serra de Outes Spain 42°52N 8°55W 194 C2
Aabenraa Denmark 55°3N 9°25E 163 J3
Aabybro Denmark 57°10N 9°44E 163 G3
Aachen Germany 50°45N 6°6E 178 E2
Aalām Iraq 33°19N 44°23E 113 B2
Aalborg Denmark 57°2N 9°54E 163 G3
Aalborg Bugt Denmark 56°50N 10°35E 163 H4
Aalen Germany 48°51N 10°6E 179 G6
Aalestrup Denmark 56°42N 9°29E 163 H3
Aalsmeer Neths. 52°16N 4°46E 112 B1
Aalst Belgium 50°56N 4°2E 170 D4
Aalten Neths. 51°56N 6°35E 170 C6
Aalter Belgium 51°5N 3°28E 170 C3
Äänekoski Finland 62°36N 25°44E 160 E21
Aarau Switz. 47°23N 8°4E 179 H4
Aarberg Switz. 47°2N 7°16E 179 H3
Aare → Switz. 47°33N 8°14E 179 H4
Aargau □ Switz. 47°26N 8°10E 179 H4
Aarhus = Århus Denmark 56°8N 10°11E 163 H4
Aarlen = Arlon Belgium 49°42N 5°49E 170 E5
Aars Denmark 56°48N 9°30E 163 H3
Aarschot Belgium 50°59N 4°49E 170 D4
Aasiaat Greenland 68°43N 52°56W 154 D5
Ab-i-Istada Afghan. 32°29N 67°55E 240 B3
Ab-i-Panja = Pyandzh → Asia 37°6N 68°20E 240 A2
Aba Sichuan, China 32°59N 101°42E 228 A3
Aba Dem. Rep. of the Congo 3°58N 30°17E 268 B3
Aba Nigeria 5°10N 7°19E 263 D6
Âbâ, Jazîrat Sudan 13°30N 32°31E 257 E3
Abacaxis → Brazil 3°54S 58°47W 329 D6
Abaco I. Bahamas 26°25N 77°10W 320 A4
Abadab, J. Sudan 18°54N 35°56E 256 D4
Ābādān Iran 30°22N 48°20E 247 D6
Abade Ethiopia 9°22N 38°3E 257 F4
Ābādeh Iran 31°8N 52°40E 247 D7
Abadín Spain 43°21N 7°29W 194 B3
Abadla Algeria 31°2N 2°45W 261 B4
Abaeté Brazil 19°9S 45°27W 333 E2
Abaeté → Brazil 18°2S 45°12W 333 E2
Abaetetuba Brazil 1°40S 48°50W 332 B2
Abagnar Qi = Xilinhot China 43°52N 116°2E 226 C9
Abah, Tanjung Indonesia 8°46S 115°38E 231 K18
Abai Paraguay 25°58S 55°54W 335 B4
Abak Nigeria 4°58N 7°50E 263 E6
Abakaliki Nigeria 6°22N 8°2E 263 D6
Abakan Russia 53°40N 91°10E 217 B12
Abala Congo 1°17S 15°35E 264 C3
Abala Niger 14°56N 3°22E 263 C5
Abalak Niger 15°22N 6°21E 263 B6
Abalemma Algeria 20°51N 5°59E 261 D6
Abalemma Niger 16°12N 7°50E 263 B6
Abalessa Algeria 22°58N 4°47E 261 D5
Abana Turkey 41°59N 34°1E 212 B6
Abancay Peru 13°35S 72°55W 330 C3
Abanga → Gabon 0°20S 10°30E 264 C2
Abano Terme Italy 45°22N 11°46E 199 C8
Abapó Bolivia 18°48S 63°25W 331 D5
Abarán Spain 38°12N 1°23W 197 G3
Abariringa Kiribati 2°50S 171°40W 277 A16
Abarqū Iran 31°10N 53°20E 247 D7
Abasha Georgia 42°11N 42°13E 191 J6
Abashiri Japan 44°0N 144°15E 220 B12
Abashiri-Wan Japan 44°0N 144°30E 220 C12
Abau Papua N. G. 10°11S 148°46E 286 F5
Abaújszántó Hungary 48°16N 21°12E 182 B6
Abava → Latvia 57°6N 21°54E 184 A8
Ābay = Nîl el Azraq → Sudan 15°38N 32°31E 257 D3
Abay Kazakhstan 49°38N 72°53E 217 C8
Abaya, L. Ethiopia 6°30N 37°50E 257 F4
Abaza Russia 52°39N 90°6E 217 B12
Abba C.A.R. 5°20N 15°11E 264 A3
Abbadia di Fiastra ⌂ Italy 43°12N 13°24E 199 E10
Abbadia San Salvatore Italy 42°53N 11°41E 199 F8
'Abbāsābād Iran 33°34N 58°23E 247 C8
Abbay = Nîl el Azraq → Sudan 15°38N 32°31E 257 D3
Abbaye, Pt. U.S.A. 46°58N 88°8W 308 B9
Abbazia = Opatija Croatia 45°21N 14°17E 199 C11
Abbé, L. Ethiopia 11°8N 41°47E 257 E5
Abbeville Somme, France 50°6N 1°49E 173 B8
Abbeville Ala., U.S.A. 31°34N 85°15W 316 D4
Abbeville Ga., U.S.A. 31°59N 83°18W 316 D6
Abbeville La., U.S.A. 29°58N 92°8W 314 G8
Abbeville S.C., U.S.A. 34°11N 82°23W 316 A7
Abbey Wood U.K. 51°29N 0°7E 125 B4
Abbeyfeale Ireland 52°23N 9°18W 166 D2
Abbiategrasso Italy 45°24N 8°54E 198 C5
Abbot Ice Shelf Antarctica 73°0S 92°0W 151 D16
Abbotsford Canada 49°5N 122°20W 296 D4
Abbottabad Pakistan 34°10N 73°15E 242 B5
Abbou, O. ben → Algeria 28°32N 5°14E 261 C5
ABC Islands = Netherlands Antilles ☒ W. Indies 12°15N 69°0W 328 A4
Abcoude Neths. 52°17N 4°59E 112 B2
Abd al Kūrī Yemen 12°5N 52°20E 249 D6
Ābdānān Iran 32°56N 47°28E 213 F12
Ābdar Iran 30°16N 55°19E 247 D7
Âbdin Egypt 30°2N 31°14E 117 A2
'Abdolābād Iran 34°12N 56°30E 247 C8
Abdulino Russia 53°42N 53°40E 216 B4
Abdulpur Bangla. 24°15N 88°59E 241 C2
Abéché Chad 13°50N 20°35E 259 F4
Abejar Spain 41°48N 2°47W 196 D2
Abekr Sudan 12°45N 28°50E 257 E2
Abel Tasman △ N.Z. 40°59S 173°3E 285 A8
Abengourou Ivory C. 6°42N 3°27W 262 D4
Abeno Japan 34°38N 135°31E 133 B2
Abenójar Spain 38°53N 4°21W 195 G6
Åbenrå = Aabenraa Denmark 55°3N 9°25E 163 J3
Abensberg Germany 48°48N 11°51E 179 G7
Abeokuta Nigeria 7°3N 3°19E 263 D5
Aberaeron U.K. 52°15N 4°15W 169 E3
Aberayron = Aberaeron U.K. 52°15N 4°15W 169 E3
Aberchirder U.K. 57°34N 2°37W 167 D6
Abercorn = Mbala Zambia 8°46S 31°24E 269 D3
Abercorn Australia 25°12S 151°5E 281 D5
Abercrombie River △ Australia 34°5S 149°40E 283 C8
Aberdare U.K. 51°43N 3°27W 169 F4
Aberdare △ Kenya 0°22S 36°44E 268 C4
Aberdare Ra. Kenya 0°15S 36°50E 268 C4
Aberdeen N.S.W., Australia 32°9S 150°56E 283 B9
Aberdeen Sask., Canada 52°20N 106°8W 297 C7
Aberdeen Hong Kong, China 22°14N 114°8E 122 B1
Aberdeen Eastern Cape, S. Africa 32°28S 24°2E 270 D3
Aberdeen C. of Aberd., U.K. 57°9N 2°5W 167 D6
Aberdeen Idaho, U.S.A. 42°57N 112°50W 304 E7
Aberdeen Md., U.S.A. 39°31N 76°10W 309 F15
Aberdeen Miss., U.S.A. 33°49N 88°33W 315 E10
Aberdeen Ohio, U.S.A. 38°39N 83°46W 311 F13
Aberdeen S. Dak., U.S.A. 45°28N 98°29W 308 C4
Aberdeen Wash., U.S.A. 46°59N 123°50W 306 D3
Aberdeen, City of □ U.K. 57°10N 2°10W 167 D6
Aberdeen L. Canada 64°30N 99°0W 294 E12
Aberdeenshire □ U.K. 57°17N 2°36W 167 D6
Aberdour U.K. 56°3N 3°18W 121 A2
Aberdour Castle U.K. 56°3N 3°18W 121 A2
Aberdovey = Aberdyfi U.K. 52°33N 4°3W 169 E3
Aberdyfi U.K. 52°33N 4°3W 169 E3
Aberfeldy U.K. 56°37N 3°51W 167 E5
Aberfoyle U.K. 56°11N 4°23W 167 E4
Abergavenny U.K. 51°49N 3°1W 169 F4
Abergele U.K. 53°17N 3°35W 168 D4
Abernathy U.S.A. 33°50N 101°51W 314 E4
Abert, L. U.S.A. 42°38N 120°14W 304 E3
Aberystwyth U.K. 52°25N 4°5W 169 E3
Abfanggraben → Germany 48°10N 11°41E 131 A3
Abhā Si. Arabia 18°0N 42°34E 248 C3
Abhar Iran 36°9N 49°13E 213 D13
Abhayapuri India 26°24N 90°38E 241 B3
Abia □ Nigeria 5°30N 7°35E 263 D6
Abide Turkey 38°55N 29°20E 205 C11
Abidiya Sudan 18°18N 34°3E 256 D3
Abidjan Ivory C. 5°26N 3°58W 262 D4
Abilene Kans., U.S.A. 38°55N 97°13W 308 F5
Abilene Tex., U.S.A. 32°28N 99°43W 314 E5
Abingdon Oxon., U.K. 51°40N 1°17W 169 F6
Abingdon Ill., U.S.A. 40°48N 90°24W 310 D6
Abingdon Va., U.S.A. 36°43N 81°59W 309 G13
Abingdon, I. = Pinta, I. Ecuador 0°35N 90°44W 330 a
Abington Reef Australia 18°0S 149°35E 280 B4
Abiod, Remel el Tunisia 31°45N 9°35E 261 B6
Abitau → Canada 59°53N 109°3W 297 B7
Abitibi → Canada 51°3N 80°55W 298 B3
Abitibi, L. Canada 48°40N 79°40W 298 C4
Abiy Adi Ethiopia 13°39N 39°3E 257 E4
Abiyata, L. Ethiopia 7°37N 38°36E 266 C4
Abiyata-Shala △ Ethiopia 7°40N 38°37E 257 F4
Abkhaz Republic = Abkhazia □ Georgia 43°12N 41°5E 191 J5
Abkhazia □ Georgia 43°12N 41°5E 191 J5
Ablon-sur-Seine France 48°43N 2°25E 134 B3
Abminga Australia 26°8S 134°51E 281 D1
Abnûb Egypt 27°18N 31°4E 256 B3
Åbo = Turku Finland 60°30N 22°19E 188 B2
Abo, Massif d' Chad 21°41N 16°8E 259 D3
Abohar India 30°10N 74°10E 242 D6
Aboisso Ivory C. 5°30N 3°5W 262 D4
Abolo Congo 0°8N 14°16E 264 B2
Abomey Benin 7°10N 2°5E 263 D5
Abong-Mbang Cameroon 4°0N 13°8E 264 B2
Abongabong Indonesia 4°15N 96°48E 234 B1
Abonnema Nigeria 4°41N 6°49E 263 E6
Abony Hungary 47°12N 20°3E 182 C5
Abor Hills India 28°25N 94°46E 241 A5
Aborlan Phil. 9°26N 118°33E 233 G2
Aboso Ghana 5°23N 1°57W 262 D4
Abou-Deïa Chad 11°20N 19°20E 259 F3
Abou-Goulem Chad 13°37N 21°38E 259 F4
Abou-Telfan ⌂ Chad 12°2N 18°58E 259 F3
Abovian Armenia 40°16N 44°37E 191 K7
Aboyne U.K. 57°4N 2°47W 167 D6
Abra □ Phil. 17°35N 120°45E 232 C3
Abra de Ilog Phil. 13°27N 120°44E 232 E3
Abra Pampa Argentina 22°43S 65°42W 334 A2
Abraham L. Canada 52°15N 116°35W 296 C5
Abramtsevo Russia 55°49N 37°49E 129 B4
Abrantes Portugal 39°24N 8°7W 195 F2
Abreojos, Pta. Mexico 26°50N 113°40W 318 B2
Abri Esh Shamâliya, Sudan 20°50N 30°27E 256 C3
Abri Janub Kordofân, Sudan 11°40N 30°21E 257 E3
Abrolhos, Banco dos Brazil 18°0S 38°0W 333 E4
Abrud Romania 46°19N 23°5E 182 D8
Abruzzo □ Italy 42°15N 14°0E 199 F10
Absaroka Range U.S.A. 44°45N 109°50W 304 D9
Abtenau Austria 47°33N 13°21E 180 D6
Abu India 24°41N 72°50E 242 G5
Abū aḍ Ḍuhūr Syria 35°44N 37°2E 250 C8
Abū al Abyad U.A.E. 24°11N 53°50E 247 E7
Abū al Khaṣīb Iraq 30°25N 48°0E 246 D5
Abū 'Alī Si. Arabia 27°20N 49°27E 247 E6
Abū 'Alī → Lebanon 34°25N 35°50E 250 D6
Abū 'Arīsh Si. Arabia 16°53N 42°48E 248 C3
Abu 'Aweigîla Egypt 30°50N 34°7E 251 H5
Abu Ballas Egypt 24°26N 27°36E 256 C2
Abu Deleiq Sudan 15°57N 33°48E 257 D3
Abu Dhabi = Abū Ẓāby U.A.E. 24°28N 54°22E 247 E7
Abu Dis Sudan 19°12N 33°38E 256 D3
Abu Dis West Bank 31°46N 35°16E 123 B2
Abu Dom Sudan 16°18N 32°25E 257 D3
Abū Du'ān Syria 36°25N 38°15E 213 D8
Abu el Gaīn, W. → Egypt 29°35N 33°30E 251 J4
Abû en Numrus Egypt 29°57N 31°12E 117 B2
Abu Fatma, Ras Sudan 22°25N 36°25E 256 C4
Abû Gabra Sudan 11°2N 26°50E 257 E2
Abu Ga'da, W. → Egypt 29°15N 32°53E 251 J3
Abu Gelba Sudan 13°11N 31°52E 257 E3
Abu Ghosh Israel 31°48N 35°6E 123 B1
Abu Gubeiha Sudan 11°30N 31°15E 257 E3
Abu Habl, Khawr → Sudan 12°37N 31°0E 257 E3
Abū Ḥadrīyah Si. Arabia 27°20N 48°58E 247 E6
Abu Hamed Sudan 19°32N 33°13E 256 D3
Abu Haraz An Nîl el Azraq, Sudan 18°1N 33°58E 256 D3
Abu Haraz El Gezira, Sudan 14°35N 33°30E 257 E3
Abu Haraz Esh Shamâliya, Sudan 19°8N 32°18E 256 D3
Abû Higar Sudan 12°50N 33°59E 257 E3
Abū Kamāl Syria 34°30N 41°0E 213 E9
Abu Kebîr Egypt 30°43N 31°40E 251 H2
Abu Kuleiwat Sudan 12°20N 26°0E 257 E2
Abū Madd, Ra's Si. Arabia 24°50N 37°7E 246 E3
Abu Matariq Sudan 10°59N 26°9E 257 E2
Abu Mendi Ethiopia 11°48N 35°42E 257 E4
Abū Mūsā U.A.E. 25°52N 55°3E 247 E7
Abū Qaṣr Si. Arabia 30°21N 38°34E 246 D3
Abu Qireiya Egypt 24°5N 35°28E 256 C4
Abu Qurqâs Egypt 28°1N 30°44E 256 B3
Abū Raṣāṣ, Ra's Oman 20°10N 58°38E 249 B7
Abu Rudeis Egypt 28°54N 33°11E 251 K4
Abu Shagara, Ras Sudan 21°4N 37°19E 256 C4
Abû Shanab Janub Kordofân, Sudan 10°47N 29°32E 266 B2
Abû Shanab Shamâl Kordofân, Sudan 13°58N 27°49E 257 E2
Abu Simbel Egypt 22°18N 31°40E 256 C3
Abū Şukhayr Iraq 31°54N 44°30E 213 G11
Abu Sultân Egypt 30°24N 32°21E 256 H8
Abu Tabari Sudan 17°32N 28°32E 256 D2
Abu Tig Egypt 27°4N 31°15E 256 B3
Abu Tiga Sudan 12°47N 34°12E 257 E3
Abu Tineitin Sudan 14°24N 31°1E 257 E3
Abû Uruq Sudan 15°52N 30°25E 257 D3
Abû Zabad Sudan 12°25N 29°10E 257 E2
Abū Ẓāby U.A.E. 24°28N 54°22E 247 E7
Abū Zeydābād Iran 33°54N 51°45E 247 C6
Abufari Brazil 5°25S 62°59W 331 B5
Abuja Nigeria 9°5N 7°32E 263 D6
Abukuma-Gawa → Japan 38°6N 140°52E 220 E10
Abukuma-Sammyaku Japan 37°30N 140°45E 220 F10
Abulug Phil. 18°27N 121°27E 232 B3
Abumombazi Dem. Rep. of the Congo 3°42N 22°10E 264 B4
Abunã Brazil 9°40S 65°20W 331 B4
Abunã → Brazil 9°41S 65°20W 331 B4
Abune Yosef Ethiopia 12°5N 39°12E 257 E4
Aburatsu Japan 31°34N 131°24E 222 F3
Aburo Dem. Rep. of the Congo 2°4N 30°53E 268 B3
Abut Hd. N.Z. 43°7S 170°15E 285 D5
Abuye Meda Ethiopia 10°30N 39°49E 257 E4
Abuyog Phil. 10°45N 125°0E 233 F5
Abwong Sudan 9°2N 32°14E 257 F3
Åby Sweden 58°40N 16°10E 163 F10
Aby, Lagune Ivory C. 5°15N 3°14W 262 D4
Abyad Sudan 13°47N 26°24E 257 E2
Abyei Sudan 9°36N 28°26E 257 F2
Ābyek Iran 36°4N 50°33E 247 B6
Acacías Colombia 3°59N 73°46W 328 C3
Acacias Madrid, Spain 127 c2
Academy Gletscher Greenland 82°2N 34°0W 154 A7
Acadia △ U.S.A. 44°20N 68°13W 309 C19
Açailandia Brazil 5°0S 47°30W 332 C2
Acajutla El Salv. 13°36N 89°50W 320 D2
Acámbaro Mexico 20°2N 100°44W 318 D4
Acandí Colombia 8°32N 77°14W 328 B2
Acanthus Greece 40°27N 23°47E 202 F7
Acaponeta Mexico 22°30N 105°22W 318 C3
Acapulco Mexico 16°51N 99°55W 319 D5
Acapulco Trench Pac. Oc. 12°0N 88°0W 320 D2
Acará Brazil 1°57S 48°11W 332 B2
Acaraí, Serra Brazil 1°50N 57°50W 329 C6
Acaraú Brazil 2°53S 40°7W 332 B3
Acari Brazil 6°31S 36°38W 332 C4
Acarí Peru 15°25S 74°36W 330 D3
Acarigua Venezuela 9°33N 69°12W 328 B4
Acassuso Argentina 34°29S 58°30W 117 A2
Acatlán Mexico 18°12N 98°3W 319 D5
Acayucán Mexico 17°57N 94°55W 319 D6
Accéglio Italy 44°28N 7°0E 198 D4
Accomac U.S.A. 37°43N 75°40W 309 G16
Accotink, L. U.S.A. 38°47N 77°13W 143 C2
Accotink Cr. → U.S.A. 38°51N 77°15W 143 B2
Accous France 43°0N 0°36W 174 E3
Accra Ghana 5°35N 0°6W 263 D4
Accrington U.K. 53°45N 2°22W 168 D5
Acebal Argentina 33°20S 60°50W 334 C3
Aceh □ Indonesia 4°15N 97°30E 234 B1
Acerra Italy 40°57N 14°22E 201 B7
Aceuchal Spain 38°39N 6°30W 195 G4
Achacachi Bolivia 16°3S 68°43W 330 D4
Achaguas Venezuela 7°46N 68°14W 328 B4
Achaia □ Greece 38°5N 21°45E 204 C3
Achalpur India 21°22N 77°32E 244 D3
Achao Chile 42°28S 73°30W 336 B2
Acharnes Greece 38°5N 23°44E 204 C5
Achegour Niger 19°10N 11°54E 259 E2
Acheloos → Greece 38°19N 21°7E 204 C3
Achelouma Niger 22°12N 12°50E 259 D2
Achelouma, E. → Niger 21°55N 13°35E 259 D2
Acheng China 45°30N 126°58E 227 B14
Achenkirch Austria 47°32N 11°45E 180 D4
Achénouma Niger 19°7N 12°55E 259 E2
Achensee Austria 47°26N 11°45E 180 D4
Achentrias Greece 34°59N 25°13E 205 G7
Acher India 23°10N 72°32E 242 H5
Achères France 48°57N 2°3E 134 A1
Achern Germany 48°37N 8°4E 179 G4
Acheron → N.Z. 42°16S 173°4E 285 C8
Achill Hd. Ireland 53°58N 10°15W 166 C1
Achill I. Ireland 53°58N 10°1W 166 C1
Achim Germany 53°1N 9°3E 178 B5
Achinsk Russia 56°20N 90°20E 215 D10
Achladokambos Greece 37°31N 22°35E 204 D4
Achouka Gabon 0°52S 9°45E 264 C2
Acıgöl Turkey 37°50N 29°50E 205 D11
Acília Italy 41°47N 12°21E 136 C1
Acıpayam Turkey 37°26N 29°22E 205 D11
Acireale Italy 37°37N 15°10E 201 E8
Ackerman U.S.A. 33°19N 89°11W 315 E10
Ackley U.S.A. 42°33N 93°3W 310 B3
Acklins I. Bahamas 22°30N 74°0W 321 B5
Aclimação Brazil 23°34S 46°37W 137 B2
Acme Alta., Canada 51°33N 113°30W 296 C6
Acme Pa., U.S.A. 40°8N 79°26W 312 F5
Acobamba Peru 12°52S 74°35W 330 C3
Acomayo Peru 13°55S 71°38W 330 C3
Aconcagua, Cerro Argentina 32°39S 70°0W 334 C2
Aconquija, Mt. Argentina 27°0S 66°0W 334 B2
Acopiara Brazil 6°6S 39°27W 332 C4
Açores, Is. dos Atl. Oc. 38°0N 27°0W 153 d1
Acorizal Brazil 15°12S 56°22W 331 D6
Acornhoek S. Africa 24°37S 31°2E 271 B5
Acoua Mayotte 12°43S 45°4E 272 b
Acquapendente Italy 42°44N 11°52E 199 F8
Acquasanta Terme Italy 42°46N 13°24E 199 F10
Acquasparta Italy 42°41N 12°33E 199 F9
Acquaviva delle Fonti Italy 40°54N 16°50E 201 B9
Ácqui Terme Italy 44°41N 8°28E 198 D5
Acraman, L. Australia 32°2S 135°23E 281 E2
Acre = 'Akko Israel 32°55N 35°4E 250 F6
Acre □ Brazil 9°1S 71°0W 330 B3
Acre → Brazil 8°45S 67°22W 330 B4
Acri Italy 39°29N 16°23E 201 C9
Acropolis Athens, Greece 112 c2
Acs Hungary 47°42N 18°2E 182 C3
Actæon Mt. St. Helena 15°58S 5°42W 153 h
Actéon, Groupe French Polynesia 21°20S 136°30W 289 f
Actinolite Canada 44°32N 77°19W 312 B7
Actium Greece 38°57N 20°45E 207 B2
Acton Ont., Canada 43°38N 80°3W 312 C4
Acton London, U.K. 51°30N 0°16W 125 A2
Açu Brazil 5°34S 36°54W 332 C4
Açúcar, Pão de Brazil 22°56S 43°9W 135 B2
Acul = Vidin Bulgaria 43°59N 22°50E 202 C6
Acworth U.S.A. 34°4N 84°41W 316 A5
Ad Dafinah Si. Arabia 23°18N 41°58E 248 B3
Aḍ Ḍafrah U.A.E. 23°30N 54°30E 249 B6
Ad Daghghāran Iraq 32°8N 44°55E 213 G11
Ad Dahnā Si. Arabia 24°30N 48°10E 249 A5
Aḍ Ḍāli' Yemen 13°42N 44°44E 248 D4
Ad Dammām Si. Arabia 26°20N 50°5E 247 E6
Ad Dāmūr Lebanon 33°43N 35°27E 250 E6
Ad Darb Si. Arabia 18°2N 43°7E 248 C3
Ad Dawādimī Si. Arabia 24°35N 44°15E 246 E5
Ad Dawḥah Qatar 25°15N 51°35E 247 E6
Ad Dawr Iraq 34°27N 43°47E 213 E10
Aḍ Ḍiffah Libya 30°30N 24°30E 258 B4
Ad Dilam Si. Arabia 23°55N 47°10E 248 B4
Ad Dir'īyah Si. Arabia 24°44N 46°35E 246 E5
Ad Dīwānīyah Iraq 32°0N 45°0E 213 F11
Ad Dujayl Iraq 33°51N 44°14E 213 F11
Ad Duwayd Si. Arabia 30°15N 42°17E 246 D4
Ada Ghana 5°44N 0°40E 263 D5
Ada Serbia 45°49N 20°9E 182 E5
Ada Minn., U.S.A. 47°18N 96°31W 308 B5
Ada Ohio, U.S.A. 40°46N 83°49W 311 D13
Ada Okla., U.S.A. 34°46N 96°41W 314 D6
Ada Beja Portugal 38°47N 9°13W 126 A1
Adad Somali Rep. 9°27N 46°49E 267 C6
Adado, Ras Somali Rep. 11°19N 48°39E 267 B6
Adair, C. Canada 71°30N 71°34W 295 C17
Adaja → Spain 41°32N 4°52W 194 D6
Adak U.S.A. 51°45N 176°45W 303 L3
Adak I. U.S.A. 51°45N 176°45W 303 L3
Ådalsbruk Norway 60°43N 11°19E 164 D8
Adam Oman 22°15N 57°28E 249 B7
Adam, Mt. Falk. Is. 51°34S 60°4W 153 f
Adamantina Brazil 21°42S 51°4W 333 F1
Adamaoua □ Cameroon 6°30N 13°30E 263 D7
Adamaoua, Massif de l' Cameroon 7°20N 12°20E 263 D7
Adamawa □ Nigeria 9°20N 12°30E 263 D7
Adamawa Highlands = Adamaoua, Massif de l' Cameroon 7°20N 12°20E 263 D7
Adamello, Mte. Italy 46°9N 10°30E 198 B7
Adamello ⌂ Italy 46°4N 10°28E 198 B7
Adami Tulu Ethiopia 7°53N 38°41E 257 F4
Adaminaby Australia 36°0S 148°45E 283 D8
Adams Mass., U.S.A. 42°38N 73°7W 313 D11
Adams N.Y., U.S.A. 43°49N 76°1W 313 C8
Adams Wis., U.S.A. 43°57N 89°49W 308 D9
Adams, Mt. U.S.A. 46°12N 121°30W 306 D5
Adam's Bridge Sri Lanka 9°15N 79°40E 245 K4
Adams L. Canada 51°10N 119°40W 296 C5
Adams Park U.S.A. 33°43N 84°27W 113 B2
Adam's Peak Sri Lanka 6°48N 80°30E 245 L5
Adamuz Spain 38°2N 4°32W 195 G6
Adana Turkey 37°0N 35°16E 250 B6
Adana □ Turkey 37°0N 35°30E 250 B6
Adanero Spain 40°56N 4°36W 194 E6
Adapazarı = Sakarya Turkey 40°48N 30°25E 212 B4
Adar Gwagwa, J. Sudan 22°15N 35°20E 256 C4
Adarama Sudan 17°10N 34°52E 257 D3
Adare, C. Antarctica 71°0S 171°0E 151 D11
Adarte Eritrea 13°18N 42°8E 257 E5
Adaut Indonesia 8°8S 131°7E 231 F8
Adavale Australia 25°52S 144°32E 281 D3
Adda → Italy 45°8N 9°53E 198 C6
Addatigala India 17°31N 82°3E 244 F6
Addax ⌂ Niger 19°17N 9°22E 259 E1
Addis Ababa = Addis Abeba Ethiopia 9°2N 38°42E 257 F4
Addis Abeba Ethiopia 9°2N 38°42E 257 F4
Addis Alem Ethiopia 9°0N 38°17E 257 F4
Addis Zemen Ethiopia 12°7N 37°47E 257 E4
Addiscombe U.K. 51°22N 0°4W 125 B3
Addison Ill., U.S.A. 41°55N 88°0W 311 C8
Addison N.Y., U.S.A. 42°1N 77°14W 312 D7
Addo S. Africa 33°32S 25°45E 270 D4
Addo △ S. Africa 33°30S 25°50E 270 D4
Addu Atoll Maldives 0°38S 73°10E 272 d
Adebour Niger 13°17N 11°50E 259 F2
Ādeh Iran 37°42N 45°11E 246 B5
Adel Ga., U.S.A. 31°8N 83°25W 316 D6
Adel Iowa, U.S.A. 41°37N 94°1W 310 C2
Adel Bagrou Mauritania 15°29N 6°57W 262 B3
Adelaide S. Austral., Australia 34°52S 138°30E 282 C3
Adelaide Eastern Cape, S. Africa 32°42S 26°20E 270 D4
Adelaide I. Antarctica 67°15S 68°30W 151 C17
Adelaide Pen. Canada 68°15N 97°30W 294 D12
Adelaide River Australia 13°15S 131°7E 278 B5
Adelaide Village Bahamas 25°0N 77°31W 153 b
Adelanto U.S.A. 34°35N 117°22W 307 L9
Adelaye C.A.R. 7°7N 22°49E 264 A4
Adele I. Australia 15°32S 123°9E 278 C3
Adélie, Terre Antarctica 68°0S 140°0E 151 C10
Adelie Land = Adélie, Terre Antarctica 68°0S 140°0E 151 C10
Adelong Australia 35°16S 148°4E 283 C8
Adelphi U.S.A. 39°0N 76°58W 143 A4
Adelsk Belarus 53°24N 23°47E 184 E10
Ademuz Spain 40°5N 1°13W 196 E3
Aden = Al 'Adan Yemen 12°45N 45°0E 248 D4
Aden, G. of Ind. Oc. 12°30N 47°30E 267 B6
Adendorp S. Africa 32°15S 24°30E 270 D3
Aderbissinat Niger 15°34N 7°54E 263 B6
Aderklaa Austria 48°17N 16°32E 142 A3
Adh Dhayd U.A.E. 25°17N 55°53E 247 E7
Adhoi India 23°26N 70°32E 242 H4
Adi Indonesia 4°15S 133°30E 231 E8
Adi Arkai Ethiopia 13°35N 37°57E 257 E4
Adi Daro Ethiopia 14°20N 38°14E 257 E4
Adi Keyih Eritrea 14°51N 39°22E 257 E4
Adi Kwala Eritrea 14°38N 38°48E 257 E4
Adi Ugri Eritrea 14°58N 38°48E 257 E4
Adieu, C. Australia 32°0S 132°10E 279 F5
Adieu Pt. Australia 15°14S 124°35E 278 C3
Adigala Ethiopia 10°24N 42°15E 257 E5
Adige → Italy 45°9N 12°20E 199 C9
Adigrat Ethiopia 14°20N 39°26E 257 E4
Adıgüzel Barajı Turkey 38°13N 29°14E 205 C11
Adilabad India 19°33N 78°20E 244 E4
Adilcevaz Turkey 38°47N 42°43E 213 C10
Adīrī Libya 27°32N 13°2E 258 C2
Adirondack ⌂ U.S.A. 44°0N 74°20W 313 C10
Adirondack Mts. U.S.A. 44°0N 74°0W 313 C10
Adis Abeba = Addis Abeba Ethiopia 9°2N 38°42E 257 F4
Adıyaman Turkey 37°45N 38°16E 213 D8
Adıyaman □ Turkey 37°30N 38°10E 213 D8
Adjim Tunisia 33°47N 10°50E 258 B2
Adjohon Benin 6°41N 2°32E 263 D5
Adjud Romania 46°7N 27°10E 183 D12
Adjumani Uganda 3°20N 31°50E 268 B3
Adjuntas Puerto Rico 18°10N 66°43W 321 b
Adlavik Is. Canada 55°0N 58°40W 299 B8
Adler Russia 43°28N 39°52E 191 J4
Adler Planetarium Chicago, U.S.A. 119 e3
Admer Algeria 20°21N 5°27E 261 D6
Admer, Erg d' Algeria 24°0N 9°5E 261 D6
Admiralteyskaya Storona Russia 59°56N 30°20E 137 B2
Admiralty G. Australia 14°20S 125°55E 278 B4
Admiralty Gulf ⚙ Australia 14°16S 125°52E 278 B4
Admiralty I. U.S.A. 57°30N 134°30W 296 B2
Admiralty Inlet Canada 72°30N 86°0W 295 C14
Admiralty Is. Papua N. G. 2°0S 147°0E 286 B4
Admiralty Island ⌂ U.S.A. 57°40N 134°10W 303 H14
Adnan Menderes, İzmir ✈ (ADB) Turkey 38°23N 27°6E 205 C9
Ado Nigeria 6°36N 2°56E 263 D5
Ado-Ekiti Nigeria 7°38N 5°12E 263 D6
Adok Sudan 8°10N 30°20E 257 F3
Adola Ethiopia 11°14N 41°44E 257 E5
Adolfo González Chaves Argentina 38°2S 60°5W 334 D3
Adolfo Ruiz Cortines, Presa Mexico 27°15N 109°6W 318 B3
Adonara Indonesia 8°15S 123°5E 231 F6
Adoni India 15°33N 77°18E 245 G3
Adony Hungary 47°6N 18°52E 182 C3
Adour → France 43°32N 1°32W 174 E2
Adra India 23°30N 86°42E 243 H12
Adra Spain 36°43N 3°3W 195 J7
Adrano Italy 37°40N 14°50E 201 E7
Adrar Algeria 27°51N 0°11E 261 C4
Adrar □ Algeria 25°45N 1°0E 261 C5
Adrar □ Mauritania 21°0N 10°0W 260 D3
Adrar des Iforas Africa 19°40N 1°40E 261 D5
Adré Chad 13°40N 22°20E 259 F4
Ádria Italy 45°3N 12°3E 199 C9
Adrian Ga., U.S.A. 32°33N 82°35W 316 C7
Adrian Mich., U.S.A. 41°54N 84°2W 311 C12
Adrian Mo., U.S.A. 38°24N 94°21W 310 F2
Adrian Tex., U.S.A. 35°16N 102°40W 314 D3
Adrianople = Edirne Turkey 41°40N 26°34E 203 E10
Adriatic Sea Medit. S. 43°0N 16°0E 193 C7
Adua Indonesia 1°45S 129°50E 231 E7
Adung Long Burma 28°7N 97°42E 241 A6
Adur India 9°8N 76°40E 245 K3
Adwa Ethiopia 14°15N 38°52E 257 E4
Adygea □ Russia 45°0N 40°0E 191 H5
Adzhar Republic = Ajaria □ Georgia 41°30N 42°0E 191 K6
Adzhibakul = Qazımämmäd Azerbaijan 40°3N 49°0E 191 K9
Adzopé Ivory C. 6°7N 3°49W 262 D4
Ægean Sea Medit. S. 38°30N 25°0E 205 C7
Aerhtai Shan Mongolia 46°40N 92°45E 217 C12
Ærø Denmark 54°52N 10°25E 163 K4
Ærøskøbing Denmark 54°53N 10°24E 163 K4
Aetos Greece 37°15N 21°50E 204 D3
Afaahiti Tahiti 17°45S 149°17W 289 e
Afafi, Massif d' Niger 22°11N 15°10E 259 D3
'Afak Iraq 32°4N 45°15E 213 F11
Afandou Greece 36°18N 28°12E 206 E12
Afar □ Ethiopia 12°0N 41°0E 257 E5
Afarag, Erg Algeria 23°50N 2°47E 261 D5
Afareaitu Moorea 17°33S 149°47W 289 e
Åfarnes Norway 62°40N 7°32E 164 B4
Afdega Ethiopia 6°4N 43°30E 267 C5
Afdem Ethiopia 9°28N 41°0E 267 C5
Áffori Italy 45°31N 9°10E 129 A2
Affton U.S.A. 38°33N 90°20W 310 F6
Afghanistan ■ Asia 33°0N 65°0E 240 B2
Afgooye Somali Rep. 2°7N 44°59E 267 D5
'Afif Si. Arabia 23°53N 42°56E 248 B3
Afikpo Nigeria 5°53N 7°54E 263 D6
Aflandshage Denmark 55°33N 12°35E 118 B3
Aflisses, O. → Algeria 28°40N 0°50E 261 C5
Aflou Algeria 34°7N 2°3E 261 B5
Afmadow Somali Rep. 0°31N 42°4E 267 D5
Afogados da Ingàzeira Brazil 7°45S 37°39W 332 C4
Afognak I. U.S.A. 58°15N 152°30W 303 G9
Afono B. Amer. Samoa 14°15S 170°38W 302 f
Afore Papua N. G. 9°9S 148°23E 286 E5
Afragóla Italy 40°55N 14°18E 201 B7
Afram → Ghana 7°0N 0°52W 263 D4
Afrera Ethiopia 13°16N 41°5E 257 E5
Africa 10°0N 20°0E 254 E6
'Afrīn Syria 36°32N 36°50E 250 B7
'Afrīn → Syria 36°20N 36°35E 250 B7
Afşar → Turkey 37°2N 32°35E 250 A3
Afsarīyeh Iran 35°39N 51°30E 141 B2
Afşin Turkey 38°14N 36°55E 212 C7
Afton Iowa, U.S.A. 41°2N 94°12W 310 C2
Afton N.Y., U.S.A. 42°14N 75°32W 313 D9
Afton Wyo., U.S.A. 42°44N 110°56W 304 E8
Afuá Brazil 0°15S 50°20W 329 D7
'Afula Israel 32°37N 35°17E 250 F6
Afumba Zambia 15°38S 24°56E 265 F4
Afyon Turkey 38°45N 30°33E 205 C12
Afyon □ Turkey 38°25N 30°30E 205 C12
Afyonkarahisar = Afyon Turkey 38°45N 30°33E 205 C12
Aga Egypt 30°55N 31°10E 256 H7
Aga I. Micronesia 7°29N 151°43E 287 T18
Āgā Jarī Iran 30°42N 49°50E 247 D6
Agadem Niger 16°50N 13°11E 259 E2
Agadés = Agadez Niger 16°58N 7°59E 259 E1
Agadez Niger 16°58N 7°59E 259 E1
Agadir Morocco 30°28N 9°55W 260 B3
Agadir □ Morocco 30°42N 9°0W 260 B3
Agaete Canary Is. 28°6N 15°43W 153 e1
Agaie Nigeria 9°1N 6°18E 263 D6
Agalas Greece 37°43N 20°47E 207 D2
Agalega Is. Mauritius 11°0S 57°0E 273 F4
Agana Guam 13°28N 144°45E 302 d
Agana B. Guam 13°29N 144°45E 302 d
Ağapınar Turkey 39°48N 30°47E 205 B12
Agar India 23°40N 76°2E 242 H7
Agar → India 21°0N 82°57E 244 D6
Agâraktem Mali 23°8N 6°22W 260 D3
Agaro Ethiopia 7°50N 36°38E 257 F4
Agartala India 23°50N 91°23E 241 D3
Agăş Romania 46°28N 26°15E 183 D11
Agassiz Canada 49°14N 121°46W 296 D4
Agassiz Icecap Canada 80°15N 76°0W 295 A16
Agat Guam 13°25N 144°40E 302 d
Agats Indonesia 5°33S 138°0E 231 F9
Agatti I. India 10°50N 72°12E 245 J1
Agattu I. U.S.A. 52°25N 173°35E 303 K1
Agawam U.S.A. 42°5N 72°37W 313 D12
Agbélouvé Togo 6°35N 1°14E 263 D5
Agboville Ivory C. 5°55N 4°15W 262 D4
Agboyi Cr. → Nigeria 6°33N 3°24E 124 A2
Ağcabädi Azerbaijan 40°5N 47°27E 191 K8
Ağdam Azerbaijan 40°0N 46°58E 191 L8
Ağdaş Azerbaijan 40°44N 47°22E 191 K8
Agde France 43°19N 3°28E 174 E7
Agde, C. d' France 43°16N 3°28E 174 E7
Agdz Morocco 30°47N 6°30W 260 B3
Agdzhabedi = Ağcabädi Azerbaijan 40°5N 47°27E 191 K8
Agen France 44°12N 0°38E 174 D4
Ageo Japan 35°58N 139°36E 223 B11
Ager Tay Chad 20°0N 17°41E 259 E3
Agerbæk Denmark 55°36N 8°48E 163 J2
Agersø Denmark 55°13N 11°12E 163 J5
Ågerup Denmark 55°43N 12°19E 118 A1
Ågesta Sweden 59°12N 18°6E 139 B2
Ageyevo Russia 54°10N 36°27E 188 E9
Aggteleki △ Hungary 48°27N 20°36E 182 B5
Āgh Kand Iran 37°15N 48°4E 213 D13
Aghathonisi Greece 37°28N 27°0E 205 D8
Aghia Anna Greece 38°52N 23°24E 204 C5
Aghia Deka Greece 35°3N 24°58E 207 E5
Aghia Ekaterinis, Akra Greece 39°50N 19°50E 206 B9
Aghia Galini Greece 35°6N 24°41E 207 E5
Aghia Marina Athina, Greece 37°48N 23°51E 112 C3
Aghia Marina Kasos, Greece 35°27N 26°53E 205 F8
Aghia Marina Leros, Greece 37°11N 26°48E 205 D8
Aghia Paraskevi Athina, Greece 38°1N 23°49E 112 A2
Aghia Paraskevi Voreio Aigaio, Greece 39°14N 26°21E 205 B8
Aghia Roumeli Greece 35°14N 23°58E 207 E4
Aghia Varvara Greece 35°8N 25°1E 207 E6
Aghiasos Greece 39°5N 26°23E 205 B8
Aghio Theodori Greece 37°55N 23°9E 204 D5
Aghion Oros □ Greece 40°25N 24°6E 203 F8
Aghios Andreas Greece 37°21N 22°45E 204 D4
Aghios Dimitrios Greece 37°53N 23°44E 112 B2
Aghios Efimia Greece 38°18N 20°36E 207 C2
Aghios Efstratios Greece 39°34N 24°58E 204 B6
Aghios Georgios Greece 37°28N 23°57E 204 D5
Aghios Ioannis, Akra Greece 35°20N 25°40E 207 E6
Aghios Ioannis Rendis Greece 37°57N 23°39E 112 B1
Aghios Isidoros Greece 36°9N 27°51E 206 E11
Aghios Kirikos Greece 37°34N 26°17E 205 D8
Aghios Leon Greece 37°47N 20°43E 207 D2
Aghios Matheos Greece 39°30N 19°47E 206 C9
Aghios Mironas Greece 35°15N 25°1E 207 E6
Aghios Nikolaos Etoloakarnania, Greece 38°52N 20°48E 207 B2
Aghios Nikolaos Kriti, Greece 35°11N 25°41E 207 E6
Aghios Nikolaos Lefkada, Greece 38°36N 20°34E 207 B2
Aghios Oros = Athos Greece 40°9N 24°22E 203 F8
Aghios Petros Greece 38°40N 20°36E 207 B2
Aghios Stephanos Greece 39°46N 19°39E 206 B9
Aghios Thekli Greece 38°15N 20°23E 207 C1
Aghios Thomas Greece 38°58N 20°47E 207 B2
Aghiou Orous, Kolpos Greece 40°6N 24°0E 202 F7
Aghireşu Romania 46°53N 23°15E 183 D8
Aghoueyyît Mauritania 21°10N 15°6W 260 D1
Aghreïjît Mauritania 21°58N 12°11W 260 D2
Agia Greece 39°43N 22°45E 204 B4
Agincourt Canada 43°47N 79°16W 141 A3
Aginskoye Russia 51°6N 114°32E 215 D12
Agjert Mauritania 16°23N 9°17W 262 B3
Ağlasun Turkey 37°39N 30°31E 205 D12
Agly → France 42°46N 3°3E 174 F7
Agmar Mauritania 25°18N 10°50W 260 C2
Agnew Australia 28°1S 120°31E 279 E3
Agnibilékrou Ivory C. 7°10N 3°11W 262 D4
Agnita Romania 45°59N 24°40E 183 E9
Agnone Italy 41°48N 14°22E 199 G11
Ago Japan 34°20N 136°51E 223 C8
Ago-Are Nigeria 8°30N 3°25E 263 D5
Agofie Ghana 8°27N 0°15E 263 D5
Agogna → Italy 45°4N 8°54E 198 C5
Agoitz = Aoiz Spain 42°46N 1°22W 196 C3
Agön Sweden 61°34N 17°23E 162 C11
Agon Coutainville France 49°2N 1°34W 172 C5
Agoo Phil. 16°20N 120°22E 232 C3
Agora Athens, Greece 112 c1
Ágordo Italy 46°18N 12°2E 199 B9
Agori India 24°33N 82°57E 243 G10
Agouifa Mauritania 19°57N 16°10W 260 E1
Agouna Benin 7°39N 1°47E 263 D5
Agout → France 43°47N 1°41E 174 E5
Agra India 27°17N 77°58E 242 F7
Agra Canal India 28°33N 77°17E 120 B2
Agrakhanskiuy Poluostrov Russia 43°42N 47°36E 191 J8
Agram = Zagreb Croatia 45°50N 15°58E 199 C12
Agramunt Spain 41°48N 1°6E 196 D6
Ágreda Spain 41°51N 1°55W 196 D3
Ağri Turkey 39°44N 43°3E 213 C10
Ağri □ Turkey 39°45N 43°5E 213 C10
Agri → Italy 40°13N 16°44E 201 B9
Ağrı Dağı Turkey 39°50N 44°15E 213 C11
Ağri Karakose = Ağri Turkey 39°44N 43°3E 213 C10
Agria Greece 39°20N 23°1E 204 B5
Agricola Oriental Mexico 19°23N 99°4W 128 B2
Agrigento Italy 37°19N 13°34E 200 E6
Agrihan N. Marianas 18°46N 145°40E 302 a
Agrinio Greece 38°37N 21°27E 204 C3
Agrópoli Italy 40°21N 14°59E 201 B7
Ağstafa Azerbaijan 41°7N 45°27E 191 K7
Água Branca Brazil 5°50S 42°40W 332 C3
Agua Caliente Mexico 32°29N 116°59W 307 N10
Agua Caliente Springs U.S.A. 32°56N 116°19W 307 N10
Água Clara Brazil 20°25S 52°45W 331 E7
Água Espraiada → Brazil 23°36S 46°41W 137 B2
Agua Fria ⌂ U.S.A. 34°14N 112°0W 305 J8
Agua Hechicera Mexico 32°28N 116°15W 307 N10
Água Preta → Brazil 1°41S 63°48W 329 D5
Agua Prieta Mexico 31°18N 109°34W 318 A3
Aguachica Colombia 8°19N 73°38W 328 B3
Aguada Puerto Rico 18°23N 67°11W 321 b
Aguada Cecilio Argentina 40°51S 65°51W 336 B3
Aguadas Colombia 5°40N 75°38W 328 B2
Aguadilla Puerto Rico 18°26N 67°10W 321 C6
Aguadulce Panama 8°15N 80°32W 320 E3
Agualva-Cacem Portugal 38°46N 9°15W 126 A1
Aguanga U.S.A. 33°27N 116°51W 307 M10
Aguanish Canada 50°14N 62°2W 299 B7
Aguanish → Canada 50°13N 62°5W 299 B7
Aguapeí Brazil 16°12S 59°43W 331 D6
Aguapeí → Brazil 21°0S 51°0W 333 F1
Aguapey → Argentina 29°7S 56°36W 334 B4
Aguaray Guazú → Paraguay 24°47S 57°19W 334 A4
Aguarico → Ecuador 0°59S 75°11W 328 D2
Aguaro-Guariquito △ Venezuela 8°20N 66°35W 328 B4
Aguas → Spain 41°20N 0°30W 196 D4
Aguas Blancas Chile 24°15S 69°55W 334 A2
Aguas Calientes, Sierra de Argentina 25°26S 66°40W 334 B2
Águas Formosas Brazil 17°5S 40°57W 333 E3
Aguascalientes Mexico 21°53N 102°18W 318 C4
Aguascalientes □ Mexico 22°0N 102°20W 318 C4
Agudo Spain 38°59N 4°52W 195 G6
Águeda Portugal 40°34N 8°27W 194 E2
Agueda → Spain 41°2N 6°56W 194 D4
Aguelhok Mali 19°29N 0°52E 261 E5
Aguelt el Melah Mauritania 23°3N 10°40W 260 D2
Agüenit W. Sahara 22°11N 13°8W 260 D2
Aguié Niger 13°31N 7°46E 263 C6
Aguila, Punta Puerto Rico 17°57N 67°13W 321 b
Aguilafuente Spain 41°13N 4°7W 194 D6
Aguilar de Campóo Spain 42°47N 4°15W 194 C6
Aguilar de la Frontera Spain 37°31N 4°40W 195 H6
Aguilares Argentina 27°26S 65°35W 334 B2
Águilas Spain 37°23N 1°35W 197 H3
Agüimes Canary Is. 27°58N 15°27W 153 e1
Aguja, C. de la Colombia 11°18N 74°12W 328 A3
Agujereada, Pta. Puerto Rico 18°30N 67°8W 321 b
Agulaa Ethiopia 13°40N 39°40E 257 E4
Agulhas, C. S. Africa 34°52S 20°0E 270 D3
Agulhas Ridge Atl. Oc. 42°0S 15°0E 152 L13
Agulo Canary Is. 28°11N 17°12W 153 e1
Agung, Gunung Indonesia 8°20S 115°28E 231 J18
Agur Uganda 2°28N 32°55E 268 B3
Agusan → Phil. 9°0N 125°30E 233 G5
Agusan del Norte □ Phil. 9°20N 125°10E 233 G5
Agusan del Sur □ Phil. 8°30N 125°30E 233 G5

Agustín Codazzi Colombia 10°2N 73°14W 328 A3
Agutaya I. Phil. 11°9N 120°58E 233 F3
Ağva Turkey 41°8N 29°51E 203 E13
Agvali Russia 42°36N 46°8E 191 J8
Aha Mts. Botswana 19°45S 21°0E 270 A3
Ahad Rifaydah Si. Arabia 17°50N 42°50E 248 C3
Ahaggar Algeria 23°0N 6°30E 261 D6
Ahaggar △ Algeria 23°0N 4°50E 261 D5
Ahal □ Turkmenistan 37°0N 57°0E 216 E5
Ahamansu Ghana 7°38N 0°35E 263 D5
Ahar Iran 38°35N 47°0E 213 C12
Ahat Turkey 38°39N 29°47E 205 C11
Ahaura → N.Z. 42°21S 171°34E 285 C6
Ahaus Germany 52°4N 7°0E 178 C2
Ahé French Polynesia 14°30S 146°18W 289 f
Åheim Norway 62°2N 5°13E 164 B2
Ahelledjem Algeria 26°37N 6°58E 261 C6
Ahimanawa Ra. N.Z. 39°3S 176°30E 284 F5
Ahioma Papua N. G. 10°20S 150°33E 286 F6
Ahipara B. N.Z. 35°5S 173°5E 284 B2
Ahir Dağı Turkey 38°45N 30°10E 205 C12
Ahiri India 19°30N 80°0E 244 E5
Ahlat Turkey 38°45N 42°29E 213 C10
Ahlen Germany 51°45N 7°53E 178 D3
Ahmad Wal Pakistan 29°18N 65°58E 242 E1
Ahmadabad India 23°0N 72°40E 242 H5
Aḩmadābād Khorāsān, Iran 35°3N 60°50E 247 C9
Aḩmadābād Khorāsān, Iran 35°49N 59°42E 247 C8
Aḩmadī Iran 27°56N 56°42E 247 E8
Ahmadnagar India 19°7N 74°46E 244 E2
Ahmadpur India 18°40N 76°57E 244 E3
Ahmadpur East Pakistan 29°12N 71°10E 242 E4
Ahmadpur Lamma Pakistan 28°19N 70°3E 242 E4
Ahmanson Theater Los Angeles, U.S.A. 127 b2
Ahmar, Mts. Ethiopia 9°20N 41°15E 257 F5
Ahmedabad = Ahmadabad India 23°0N 72°40E 242 H5
Ahmednagar = Ahmadnagar India 19°7N 74°46E 244 E2
Ahmetbey Turkey 41°26N 27°34E 203 E11
Ahmetler Turkey 38°28N 29°5E 205 C11
Ahmetli Turkey 38°32N 27°57E 205 C9
Ahmeyim Mauritania 20°51N 14°25W 260 D2
Ahoada Nigeria 5°8N 6°36E 263 D6
Ahome Mexico 25°55N 109°11W 318 B3
Ahon, Tarso Chad 20°23N 18°18E 259 D3
Ahoskie U.S.A. 36°17N 76°59W 315 C16
Ahr → Germany 50°32N 7°16E 178 E3
Ahram Iran 28°52N 51°16E 247 D6
Ahrax Pt. Malta 36°0N 14°22E 206 F7
Ahrensbök Germany 54°2N 10°35E 178 A6
Ahrensburg Germany 53°40N 10°13E 178 B6
Ahrensfelde Germany 52°34N 13°34E 115 A4
Ahu Akivi Chile 27°7S 109°24W 330 b
Ahu Tepeu Chile 27°6S 109°25W 330 b
Ahu Tongariki Chile 27°8S 109°17W 330 b
Ahu Vinapu Chile 27°10S 109°25W 330 b
Ahuachapán El Salv. 13°54N 89°52W 320 D2
'Āhuimanu U.S.A. 21°26N 157°50W 302 K14
Ahun France 46°4N 2°5E 173 F9
Ahuntsic Canada 45°32N 73°41W 130 A1
Ahunui French Polynesia 19°39S 140°25W 289 f
Ahuriri → N.Z. 44°31S 170°12E 285 E5
Åhus Sweden 55°56N 14°18E 163 J8
Ahvāz Iran 31°20N 48°40E 247 D6
Ahvenanmaa = Åland Finland 60°15N 20°0E 161 F19
Aḩwar Yemen 13°30N 46°40E 248 D4
Ahzar → Mali 15°30N 3°20E 263 B5
Ai → India 26°26N 90°44E 241 B3
Ai → Ōsaka, Japan 34°46N 135°35E 133 A2
Ai-Ais Namibia 27°54S 17°59E 270 C2
Ai-Ais and Fish River Canyon △ Namibia 24°45S 17°15E 270 B2
Aiari → Brazil 1°22N 68°36W 328 C4
Aichach Germany 48°27N 11°8E 179 G7
Aichi □ Japan 35°0N 137°15E 223 C9
'Aiea U.S.A. 21°23N 157°56W 302 K14
Aigle Switz. 46°18N 6°58E 179 J2
Aignay-le-Duc France 47°40N 4°43E 173 E11
Aigoual, Mt. France 44°8N 3°35E 174 D7
Aigre France 45°54N 0°1E 174 C4
Aigremont France 48°54N 2°1E 134 A1
Aigrettes, Île aux Mauritius 20°25S 57°43E 272 e
Aiguá Uruguay 34°13S 54°46W 335 C5
Aigueperse France 46°3N 3°13E 173 F10
Aigues → France 44°7N 4°43E 175 D8
Aigues-Mortes France 43°35N 4°12E 175 E8
Aigues-Mortes, G. d' France 43°31N 4°3E 175 E8
Aigües-Tortes i Estany de St. Maurici △ Spain 42°38N 0°31E 196 C4
Aiguilles France 44°47N 6°51E 175 D10
Aiguillon France 44°18N 0°21E 174 D4
Aigurande France 46°27N 1°49E 173 F8
Aihui = Heihe China 50°10N 127°30E 219 A7
Aija Peru 9°50S 77°45W 330 B2
Aikawa Japan 38°2N 138°15E 220 E9
Aiken U.S.A. 33°34N 81°43W 316 B8
Ailao Shan China 24°0N 101°20E 228 F3
Aileron Australia 22°39S 133°20E 280 C1
Ailey U.S.A. 32°11N 82°34W 316 C7
Ailigandi Panama 9°14N 78°1W 328 B2
Aillant-sur-Tholon France 47°52N 3°20E 173 E10
Aillik Canada 55°11N 59°18W 299 A8
Ailsa Craig Ont., Canada 43°8N 81°33W 312 C3
Ailsa Craig S. Ayrs., U.K. 55°15N 5°6W 167 F3
Ailulual Papua N. G. 9°38S 150°35E 286 E6
Aim Russia 59°0N 133°55E 215 D14
Aimere Indonesia 8°45S 121°3E 231 F6
Aimogasta Argentina 28°33S 66°50W 334 B2
Aimorés Brazil 19°30S 41°4W 333 E3
Ain □ France 46°5N 5°20E 173 F12
Ain → France 45°45N 5°11E 175 C9
Aïn Beïda Algeria 35°50N 7°29E 261 A6
Aïn Ben Khellil Algeria 33°15N 0°49W 261 B4
Aïn Ben Tili Mauritania 25°59N 9°27W 260 C3
Aïn Beni Mathar Morocco 34°1N 2°0W 261 B4
Aïn Benian Algeria 36°48N 2°55E 261 A5
Ain Dalla Egypt 27°20N 27°23E 256 B2
Ain Defla Algeria 36°16N 1°58E 261 A5
Ain Defla □ Algeria 36°10N 2°10E 261 A5
Ain el Akhḑar Egypt 28°50N 33°55E 251 K4
Ain el Mafki Egypt 27°30N 28°15E 256 B2
Ain Girba Egypt 29°20N 25°14E 256 B2
Aïn M'lila Algeria 36°2N 6°35E 261 A6
Ain Murr Sudan 21°50N 25°9E 256 C2
Ain Qeiqab Egypt 29°42N 24°55E 256 B1
Aïn Salah = In Salah Algeria 27°10N 2°32E 261 C5
Aïn-Sefra Algeria 32°47N 0°37W 261 B4
Ain Sheikh Murzûk Egypt 26°47N 27°45E 256 B2
Ain Sudr Egypt 29°50N 33°6E 251 J4
Ain Sukhna Egypt 29°32N 32°20E 256 J8
Aïn Tédelès Algeria 36°0N 0°21E 261 A5
Aïn Témouchent Algeria 35°16N 1°8W 261 A4
Aïn Témouchent □ Algeria 35°20N 1°5W 261 A4
Aïn Tikkidine Algeria 25°33N 1°24E 261 C5
Aïn Touta Algeria 35°26N 5°54E 261 A6
Ain Zeitûn Egypt 29°10N 25°48E 256 B2
Aïn Zorah Morocco 34°37N 3°32W 261 B4
Ainaži Latvia 57°50N 24°24E 188 D3
Ainos Oros Greece 38°9N 20°40E 207 C2
Ainsworth U.S.A. 42°33N 99°52W 308 D4
Aintab = Gaziantep Turkey 37°6N 37°23E 250 A8
Aioi Japan 34°48N 134°28E 222 C6
Aiome Papua N. G. 5°8S 144°44E 286 C3
Aipe Colombia 3°13N 75°15W 328 C2
Aiquile Bolivia 18°10S 65°10W 331 D4
Aïr Niger 18°30N 8°0E 259 E1
Air Canada Centre Toronto, Canada 141 c2
Aïr et du Ténéré ⌓ Niger 18°12N 9°56E 263 B6
Air Force I. Canada 67°58N 74°5W 295 D17
Air Hitam Malaysia 1°55N 103°11E 237 M4
Air View Park Singapore 1°20N 103°46E 138 A2
Aira Japan 31°43N 130°43E 222 F2
Airaines France 49°58N 1°55E 173 C8
Airão Brazil 1°56S 61°22W 329 D5
Airdrie Alta., Canada 51°18N 114°2W 296 C6
Airdrie N. Lanarks., U.K. 55°52N 3°57W 167 F5
Aire → Meuse, France 49°18N 4°49E 173 C11
Aire → N. Yorks., U.K. 53°43N 0°55W 168 D7
Aire, I. de l' Spain 39°48N 4°16E 206 B5
Aire-sur-la-Lys France 50°37N 2°22E 173 B9
Aire-sur-l'Adour France 43°42N 0°15W 174 E3
Aireys Inlet Australia 38°29S 144°5E 282 E6
Airlie Beach Australia 20°16S 148°43E 280 b
Airport West Australia 37°42S 144°52E 128 A1
Airvault France 46°50N 0°8W 172 F6
Aisch → Germany 49°49N 10°58E 179 F6
Aisen □ Chile 46°30S 73°0W 336 C2
Aisne □ France 49°42N 3°40E 173 C10
Aisne → France 49°26N 2°50E 173 C9
Ait India 25°54N 79°14E 243 G8
Ait Ben Haddou Morocco 31°3N 7°7W 260 B3
Aitana, Sierra de Spain 38°35N 0°24W 197 G4
Aitape Papua N. G. 3°11S 142°22E 286 B2
Aitkin U.S.A. 46°32N 93°42W 308 B7
Aitutaki Cook Is. 18°52S 159°45W 289 J12
Aiuaba Brazil 6°38S 40°7W 332 C3
Aiud Romania 46°19N 23°44E 183 D8
Aix-en-Provence France 43°32N 5°27E 175 E9
Aix-la-Chapelle = Aachen Germany 50°45N 6°6E 178 E2
Aix-les-Bains France 45°41N 5°53E 175 C9
Aixe-sur-Vienne France 45°47N 1°9E 174 C5
Aiyang, Mt. Papua N. G. 5°10S 141°20E 286 C1
Aíyina = Egina Greece 37°45N 23°26E 204 D5
Aizawl India 23°40N 92°44E 241 D4
Aizenay France 46°44N 1°38W 172 F5
Aizkraukle Latvia 56°36N 25°11E 188 D3
Aizpute Latvia 56°43N 21°40E 184 B8
Aizuwakamatsu Japan 37°30N 139°56E 220 F9
Ajabshir Iran 37°28N 45°54E 213 D11
Ajaccio France 41°55N 8°40E 175 G12
Ajaccio, G. d' France 41°52N 8°40E 175 G12
Ajai ⌓ Uganda 2°52N 31°16E 268 B3
Ajaigarh India 24°52N 80°16E 243 G9
Ajajú → Colombia 0°59N 72°20W 328 C3
Ajalpan Mexico 18°22N 97°15W 319 D5
Ajanta India 20°30N 75°48E 244 D2
Ajanta Ra. India 20°28N 75°50E 244 D2
Ajari Rep. = Ajaria □ Georgia 41°30N 42°0E 191 K6
Ajaria □ Georgia 41°30N 42°0E 191 K6
Ajax Canada 43°50N 79°1W 312 C5
Ajax, Mt. N.Z. 42°35S 172°5E 285 C7
Ajdābiyā Libya 30°54N 20°4E 258 B4
Ajdābiyā □ Libya 29°0N 20°0E 258 C4
Ajdovščina Slovenia 45°54N 13°54E 199 C10
Ajegunle Nigeria 6°26N 3°20E 124 B2
Aji Japan 34°40N 135°27E 133 A1
Ajibar Ethiopia 10°35N 38°36E 257 E4
Ajka Hungary 47°4N 17°31E 182 C2
'Ajlūn Jordan 32°18N 35°47E 251 F6
'Ajmān U.A.E. 25°25N 55°30E 247 E7
Ajmer India 26°28N 74°37E 242 F6
Ajnala India 31°50N 74°48E 242 D6
Ajo U.S.A. 32°22N 112°52W 305 K7
Ajo, C. de Spain 43°31N 3°35W 194 B7
Ajoupa-Bouillon Martinique 14°49N 61°7W 322 j
Ajuda Portugal 38°42N 9°12W 126 A1
Ajuda, Pta. da Azores 37°52N 25°19W 153 d3
Ajuy Phil. 11°10N 123°1E 233 F4
Ak Dağ Turkey 36°30N 29°32E 205 E11
Ak Dağlar Turkey 39°32N 36°12E 212 C7
Ak Dağları Turkey 36°30N 29°30E 205 E11
Ak-Dovurak Russia 51°11N 90°36E 217 B12
Ak-Mechet = Qyzylorda Kazakhstan 44°48N 65°28E 217 D7
Ak-Mednet = Chornomorske Ukraine 45°31N 32°40E 189 K7
Ak-Sheikh = Razdolnoye Ukraine 45°46N 33°29E 189 K7
Akaba Togo 8°10N 1°2E 263 D5
Akabira Japan 43°33N 142°5E 220 C11
Akabli Algeria 26°49N 1°31E 261 C5
Akademika Obrucheva, Khrebet Russia 51°50N 96°0E 217 B13
Akagera △ Rwanda 1°31S 30°33E 268 C3
Akaishi-Dake Japan 35°27N 138°9E 223 B10
Akaishi-Sammyaku Japan 35°25N 138°10E 223 B10
Akaki Beseka Ethiopia 8°55N 38°45E 257 F4
Akākūs, J. Libya 25°20N 10°30E 258 C2
Akalkot India 17°32N 76°13E 244 F3
Akalla Sweden 59°24N 17°55E 139 A1
Akamas Cyprus 35°3N 32°18E 207 E8
Akan △ Japan 43°20N 144°20E 220 C12
Akanthou Cyprus 35°22N 33°45E 207 E9
Akarca Turkey 38°35N 29°35E 205 C11
Akaroa N.Z. 43°49S 172°59E 285 D7
Akaroa Harbour N.Z. 43°50S 172°55E 285 D7
Akasaka Tokyo, Japan 140 b3
Akasha Sudan 21°10N 30°32E 256 C3
Akashi Japan 34°45N 134°58E 222 C6
Akbarābād Iran 35°40N 51°20E 141 A2
Akbarpur Bihar, India 24°39N 83°58E 243 G10
Akbarpur Ut. P., India 26°25N 82°32E 243 F10
Akbou Algeria 36°31N 4°31E 261 A5
Akbulak Russia 51°1N 55°37E 216 B5
Akçaabat Turkey 41°1N 39°34E 213 B8
Akçadağ Turkey 38°27N 37°43E 212 C7
Akçakale Turkey 36°41N 38°56E 213 D8
Akçakoca Turkey 41°5N 31°8E 212 B4
Akçalı Dağları Turkey 36°18N 33°21E 250 B4
Akçaova Turkey 41°3N 29°57E 203 E13
Akçay Turkey 36°36N 29°45E 205 E11
Akçay → Turkey 37°50N 28°15E 205 D10
Akchâr Mauritania 20°20N 14°28W 260 D2
Akchi-Karasu = Toktogul Kyrgyzstan 41°50N 72°50E 217 D8
Akdağ Antalya, Turkey 37°0N 32°0E 250 B3
Akdağ İzmir, Turkey 38°33N 26°30E 205 C8
Akdağmadeni Turkey 39°39N 35°53E 212 C6
Akdere Turkey 36°14N 33°46E 250 B4
Akdoğan = Lysi Cyprus 35°6N 33°41E 207 E9
Akechi Japan 35°18N 137°23E 223 B9
Akelamo Indonesia 1°35N 129°40E 231 D7
Åkernes = Åknes Norway 58°45N 7°30E 164 F4
Åkers styckebruk Sweden 59°15N 17°5E 162 E11
Åkersberga Sweden 59°29N 18°18E 162 E12
Akershus □ Norway 60°0N 11°10E 164 D8
Akershus Slott Oslo, Norway 133 c1
Akeru → India 17°25N 80°5E 244 F5
Aketi Dem. Rep. of the Congo 2°38N 23°47E 264 B4
Akhalkalaki Georgia 41°27N 43°25E 191 K6
Akhaltsikhe Georgia 41°40N 43°0E 191 K6
Akhḑar, W. al → Si. Arabia 28°36N 36°36E 251 K7
Akhiok U.S.A. 56°57N 154°10W 303 H9
Akhisar Turkey 38°56N 27°48E 205 C9
Akhmîm Egypt 26°31N 31°47E 256 B3
Akhnur India 32°52N 74°45E 243 C6
Akhtarīn Syria 36°31N 37°20E 250 B8
Akhtopol Bulgaria 42°6N 27°56E 203 D11
Akhtuba → Russia 47°41N 46°55E 191 G8
Akhtubinsk Russia 48°13N 46°7E 191 F8
Akhty Russia 41°30N 47°45E 191 K8
Akhtyrka = Okhtyrka Ukraine 50°25N 35°0E 189 G8
Aki Japan 33°30N 133°54E 222 D5
Aki-Nada Japan 34°5N 132°40E 222 C4
Akiachak U.S.A. 60°55N 161°26W 303 F7
Akiak U.S.A. 60°55N 161°13W 303 F7
Akiéni Gabon 1°11S 13°53E 264 C2
Akihabara Tokyo, Japan 140 a5
Akimiski I. Canada 52°50N 81°30W 298 B3
Akimovka Ukraine 46°44N 35°0E 189 J8
Akıncı Burnu Turkey 36°19N 35°46E 250 B6
Akincilar = Louroujina Cyprus 35°0N 33°28E 207 F9
Åkirkeby Denmark 55°4N 14°55E 163 J8
Akita Japan 39°45N 140°7E 220 E10
Akita □ Japan 39°40N 140°30E 220 E10
Akjoujt Mauritania 19°45N 14°15W 262 B2
Akka Mali 15°24N 4°11W 262 B4
Akka Morocco 29°22N 8°9W 260 C3
Akkaraipattu Sri Lanka 7°13N 81°51E 245 L5
Akkaya Tepesi Turkey 37°25N 29°38E 205 D11
Akkerman = Bilhorod-Dnistrovskyy Ukraine 46°11N 30°23E 189 J6
Akkeshi Japan 43°2N 144°51E 220 C12
'Akko Israel 32°55N 35°4E 250 F6
Akköy Turkey 37°29N 27°15E 205 D9
Akkuş Turkey 40°47N 37°0E 212 B7
Aklampa Benin 8°15N 2°10E 263 D5
Aklan □ Phil. 11°50N 122°30E 233 F4
Aklavik Canada 68°12N 135°0W 294 D4
Aklera India 24°26N 76°32E 242 G7
Akmenė Lithuania 56°15N 22°45E 184 B9
Akmenrags Latvia 56°50N 21°4E 184 B8
Akmolinsk = Astana Kazakhstan 51°10N 71°30E 217 B8
Akmonte = Almonte Spain 37°13N 6°38W 195 H4
Åknes Norway 58°45N 7°30E 164 F4
Aknoul Morocco 34°40N 3°55W 261 B4
Akō Japan 34°45N 134°24E 222 C6
Ako Nigeria 10°19N 10°48E 263 C7
Akôbô Sudan 7°47N 33°1E 257 F3
Akobo → Ethiopia 7°48N 33°3E 257 F3
Akola Maharashtra, India 20°42N 77°2E 244 D3
Akola Maharashtra, India 19°32N 74°3E 244 E2
Akolmiut U.S.A. 60°55N 162°20W 303 F7
Akonolinga Cameroon 3°50N 12°18E 263 E7
Akor Mali 14°59N 6°58W 262 C3
Akordat Eritrea 15°30N 37°40E 257 D4
Akosombo Dam Ghana 6°20N 0°5E 263 D5
Akot India 21°10N 77°10E 244 D3
Akot Sudan 6°31N 30°9E 257 F3
Akoupé Ivory C. 6°23N 3°54W 262 D4
Akourousoulba C.A.R. 8°58N 20°46E 264 A4
Akpatok I. Canada 60°25N 68°8W 295 E18
Åkrahamn Norway 59°15N 5°10E 164 E2
'Akramah Libya 32°2N 23°41E 258 B4
Akranes Iceland 64°19N 22°5W 155 C4
Akreïjit Mauritania 18°19N 9°11W 262 B3
Akritas, Akra Greece 36°43N 21°54E 204 E3
Akron Colo., U.S.A. 40°10N 103°13W 304 F12
Akron Ind., U.S.A. 41°2N 86°1W 311 C10
Akron Ohio, U.S.A. 41°5N 81°31W 312 E3
Akrotiri Cyprus 34°36N 32°57E 207 F8
Akrotiri, Akra Greece 40°26N 25°27E 203 F9
Akrotiri Bay Cyprus 34°35N 33°10E 207 F9
Aksai Chin China 35°15N 79°55E 243 B8
Aksaray Turkey 38°25N 34°2E 212 C6
Aksaray □ Turkey 38°20N 33°45E 212 C5
Aksay = Aqsay Kazakhstan 51°11N 53°0E 187 D9
Akşehir Turkey 38°18N 31°30E 212 C4
Akşehir Gölü Turkey 38°30N 31°25E 212 C4
Akseki Turkey 37°2N 31°47E 250 A2
Akstafa = Ağstafa Azerbaijan 41°7N 45°27E 191 K7
Aksu Xinjiang Uygur, China 41°5N 80°10E 217 D10
Aksu Turkey 36°57N 30°50E 250 B1
Aksu → Turkey 36°52N 30°57E 250 B1
Aksu He → China 40°26N 80°59E 217 D10
Aksum Ethiopia 14°5N 38°40E 257 E4
Aktash Russia 55°2N 52°3E 190 C11
Aktepe Turkey 36°42N 36°27E 250 B7
Aktio Greece 38°57N 20°46E 207 B2
Akto China 39°5N 75°59E 217 E9
Aktsyabrski Belarus 52°38N 28°53E 177 B15
Aktyubinsk = Aqtöbe Kazakhstan 50°17N 57°10E 187 D10
Aku Nigeria 6°40N 7°18E 263 D6
Akula Dem. Rep. of the Congo 2°22N 20°12E 264 B4
Akun I. U.S.A. 54°11N 165°32W 303 J6
Akune Japan 32°1N 130°12E 222 E2
Akure Nigeria 7°15N 5°5E 263 D6
Akurenan Eq. Guin. 1°2N 10°40E 264 B2
Akuressa Sri Lanka 6°5N 80°29E 245 L5
Akureyri Iceland 65°40N 18°6W 155 B8
Akuseki-Shima Japan 29°27N 129°37E 221 K4
Akusha Russia 42°18N 47°30E 191 J8
Akutan U.S.A. 54°8N 165°46W 303 J6
Akutan I. U.S.A. 54°7N 165°55W 303 J6
Akwa-Ibom □ Nigeria 4°30N 7°30E 263 E6
Akwanga Nigeria 8°55N 8°23E 263 D6
Akyab = Sittwe Burma 20°18N 92°45E 241 E4
Akyazı Turkey 40°40N 30°38E 212 B4
Ål Norway 60°38N 8°33E 164 D5
Al Abyaḑ Libya 26°49N 14°1E 258 C2
Al Abyār Libya 32°9N 20°29E 258 B4
Al 'Adam Libya 31°51N 23°55E 258 B4
Al 'Adan Yemen 12°45N 45°0E 248 D4
Al Aḩsā = Hasa Si. Arabia 25°50N 49°0E 247 E6
Al Ajfar Si. Arabia 27°26N 43°0E 246 E4
Al Amādīyah Iraq 37°5N 43°30E 213 D10
Al 'Amārah Iraq 31°55N 47°15E 213 G12
Al Anbār □ Iraq 33°25N 42°0E 246 C4
Al 'Aqabah Jordan 29°31N 35°0E 251 J6
Al 'Aqabah □ Jordan 29°30N 35°0E 251 J6
Al 'Aqīq Si. Arabia 20°39N 41°25E 248 B3
Al Arak Syria 34°38N 38°35E 213 E8
Al 'Aramah Si. Arabia 25°30N 46°0E 246 E5
Al 'Ariḑah Si. Arabia 17°3N 43°5E 248 C3
Al 'Arţāwīyah Si. Arabia 26°31N 45°20E 246 E5
Al Ashkhara Oman 21°50N 59°30E 249 B7
Al 'Āşimah = 'Ammān □ Jordan 31°40N 36°30E 251 G7
Al 'Assāfīyah Si. Arabia 28°17N 38°59E 246 D3
Al Atārib Syria 36°9N 36°49E 250 B7
Al 'Awdah Si. Arabia 25°32N 45°41E 246 E5
Al 'Ayn Si. Arabia 25°4N 38°6E 246 E3
Al 'Ayn U.A.E. 24°15N 55°45E 247 E7
Al 'Azamīyah Iraq 33°22N 44°22E 113 A2
Al 'Azīzīyah Iraq 32°54N 45°4E 213 F11
Al 'Azīzīyah Libya 32°30N 13°1E 258 B2
Al 'Azīzīyah □ Libya 32°31N 13°1E 261 B7
Al Bāb Syria 36°23N 37°29E 250 B8
Al Bad' Si. Arabia 28°28N 35°1E 246 D2
Al Bādī Iraq 35°56N 41°32E 246 C4
Al Badī' Si. Arabia 22°0N 46°35E 248 B4
Al Bāḩah Si. Arabia 20°1N 41°28E 256 C5
Al Bāḩah □ Si. Arabia 20°30N 41°30E 248 B3
Al Baḩrah Kuwait 29°40N 47°52E 246 D5
Al Baḩral Mayyit = Dead Sea Asia 31°30N 35°30E 251 G6
Al Balqā' □ Jordan 32°5N 35°45E 251 F6
Al Barkāt Libya 24°56N 10°14E 258 D2
Al Bārūk, J. Lebanon 33°39N 35°40E 250 E6
Al Bāşah Si. Arabia 20°1N 41°28E 256 C5
Al Başrah Iraq 30°30N 47°50E 246 D5
Al Baţḩā Iraq 31°6N 45°53E 246 D5
Al Batinah Oman 24°10N 56°50E 249 A7
Al Batrūn Lebanon 34°15N 35°40E 250 D6
Al Bayāḑ Si. Arabia 22°0N 47°0E 248 B4
Al Bayḑā Libya 32°50N 21°44E 258 B4
Al Bayḑā' Yemen 14°5N 45°42E 248 D4
Al Bi'ār Si. Arabia 22°39N 39°40E 248 B2
Al Biqā Lebanon 34°10N 36°10E 250 D7
Al Biqā □ Lebanon 34°0N 36°5E 250 E7
Al Bi'r Si. Arabia 28°51N 36°16E 251 K7
Al Birk Si. Arabia 18°13N 41°33E 248 C3
Al Bu'ayrāt al Ḩasūn Libya 31°24N 15°44E 258 B3
Al Bukayrīyah Si. Arabia 26°9N 43°40E 246 E4
Al Bumbah Libya 32°24N 23°8E 258 B4
Al Burayj Syria 34°15N 36°46E 250 D7
Al Buţnām □ Libya 30°0N 24°0E 258 B4
Al Buţnān □ Libya 31°40N 24°30E 258 B4
Al Faḑilī Si. Arabia 26°58N 49°10E 247 E6
Al Fallūjah Iraq 33°20N 43°55E 213 F10
Al Fatḩah Iraq 35°3N 43°33E 213 E10
Al Fāw Iraq 30°0N 48°30E 247 D6
Al Faydamī Yemen 16°25N 52°26E 249 C6
Al Fujayrah U.A.E. 25°7N 56°18E 247 E8
Al Ghadaf, W. → Jordan 31°26N 36°43E 251 G7
Al Ghammās Iraq 31°45N 44°37E 246 D5
Al Gharīb Libya 32°35N 21°11E 258 B4
Al Ghayḑah Ḩaḑramaut, Yemen 14°55N 50°0E 249 D5
Al Ghayḑah Qamar, Yemen 16°13N 52°11E 249 C6
Al Ghayl Yemen 15°30N 50°54E 249 D5
Al Ghazālah Si. Arabia 26°48N 41°19E 246 E4
Al Ḩadd Oman 22°32N 59°48E 249 B7
Al Ḩaddār Si. Arabia 21°58N 45°57E 248 B4
Al Ḩadīthah Iraq 34°0N 41°13E 213 E10
Al Ḩadīthah Si. Arabia 31°28N 37°8E 246 D3
Al Ḩaḑr Iraq 35°35N 42°44E 213 E10
Al Ḩaffah Syria 35°36N 36°1E 250 C7
Al Hājānah Syria 33°20N 36°33E 250 E7
Al Ḩajar al Gharbī Oman 24°10N 56°15E 247 E8
Al Hallānīyah Oman 17°30N 56°1E 249 C7
Al Hāmad Si. Arabia 31°30N 39°30E 246 D3
Al Ḩamādah al Ḩamrā' Libya 29°30N 12°0E 258 C2
Al Ḩamar Si. Arabia 22°26N 46°12E 248 B4
Al Ḩamdānīyah Syria 35°25N 36°50E 250 C7
Al Ḩamīdīyah Syria 34°42N 35°57E 250 D6
Al Ḩammār Iraq 30°57N 46°51E 246 D5
Al Ḩamrā' Si. Arabia 24°2N 38°55E 246 E3
Al Ḩamrā' Syria 35°19N 37°5E 250 C8
Al Ḩamzah Iraq 31°43N 44°58E 246 D5
Al Ḩanākīyah Si. Arabia 24°51N 40°31E 246 E4
Al Ḩarīq Si. Arabia 23°29N 46°27E 248 B4
Al Harūj al Aswad Libya 27°0N 17°10E 258 C3
Al Ḩasakah Syria 36°35N 40°45E 213 D9
Al Ḩasakah □ Syria 36°40N 40°50E 213 D9
Al Hāshimīyah Iraq 32°22N 44°39E 213 G11
Al Hāsikīyah Oman 17°28N 55°36E 249 C6
Al Ḩasy Yemen 14°3N 48°40E 249 D5
Al Hawīyah Ash Sharqīyah, Si. Arabia 24°45N 49°6E 249 A5
Al Hawīyah Makkah, Si. Arabia 21°26N 40°30E 248 B3
Al Ḩawrah Yemen 13°50N 47°35E 248 D4
Al Hawtah = Laḩij Yemen 13°4N 44°53E 248 D4
Al Ḩawţah Si. Arabia 23°30N 47°0E 248 B4
Al Ḩayy Iraq 32°5N 46°5E 213 F12
Al Ḩijarah Asia 30°0N 44°0E 246 D4
Al Ḩillah Iraq 32°30N 44°25E 213 F11
Al Ḩillah Si. Arabia 23°35N 46°50E 248 B4
Al Hindīyah Iraq 32°30N 44°10E 213 F11
Al Hirmil Lebanon 34°26N 36°24E 250 D7
Al Hoceïma Morocco 35°8N 3°58W 261 A4
Al Ḩudaydah Yemen 14°50N 43°0E 248 D3
Al Ḩudūd ash Shamālīyah □ Si. Arabia 29°10N 42°30E 246 D4
Al Ḩufrah Libya 25°32N 14°1E 258 C2
Al Hufūf Si. Arabia 25°25N 49°45E 247 E6
Al Ḩulwah Si. Arabia 23°24N 46°48E 248 B4
Al Ḩumayḑah Si. Arabia 29°14N 34°56E 251 J5
Al Ḩunayy Si. Arabia 25°58N 48°45E 247 E6
Al Husayyāt Libya 30°24N 20°37E 258 B4
Al 'Irqah Yemen 13°39N 47°22E 248 D4
Al Īsāwīyah Si. Arabia 30°43N 37°59E 246 D3
Al Ittihad = Madīnat ash Sha'b Yemen 12°50N 45°0E 248 D4
Al Jabal al Akhḑar Libya 32°30N 21°30E 258 B4
Al Jabal al Akhḑar □ Libya 32°30N 21°41E 258 B4
Al Jafr Jordan 30°18N 36°14E 251 H7
Al Jāfūrah Si. Arabia 25°0N 50°15E 247 E7
Al Jaghbūb Libya 29°42N 24°38E 258 C4
Al Jahrah Kuwait 29°25N 47°40E 246 D5
Al Jalāmīd Si. Arabia 31°20N 40°6E 246 D3
Al Jamalīyah Qatar 25°37N 51°5E 247 E6
Al Janūb □ Lebanon 33°20N 35°20E 250 E6
Al Jawf Libya 24°10N 23°24E 258 D4
Al Jawf Si. Arabia 29°55N 39°40E 246 D3
Al Jawf □ Si. Arabia 29°30N 39°30E 246 D3
Al Jazair = Algeria ■ Africa 28°30N 2°0E 261 C5
Al Jazirah Iraq 33°30N 44°0E 213 E10
Al Jithāmīyah Si. Arabia 27°41N 41°43E 246 E4
Al Jubayl Si. Arabia 27°0N 49°50E 247 E6
Al Jubaylah Si. Arabia 24°55N 46°25E 246 E5
Al Jubb Si. Arabia 27°11N 42°17E 246 E4
Al Jufrah Libya 29°10N 16°0E 258 C3
Al Jufrah □ Libya 27°30N 17°30E 258 C3
Al Jumūm Si. Arabia 21°37N 39°42E 248 B2
Al Junaynah Sudan 13°27N 22°45E 259 F4
Al Kabā'ish Iraq 30°58N 47°0E 246 D5
Al Kāmil Oman 22°13N 59°12E 249 B7
Al Karak Jordan 31°11N 35°42E 251 G6
Al Karak □ Jordan 31°0N 36°0E 251 H7
Al Kāẓimīyah Iraq 33°22N 44°18E 213 F11
Al Khābūrah Oman 23°57N 57°5E 247 F8
Al Khafji Si. Arabia 28°24N 48°29E 247 E6
Al Khalīl West Bank 31°32N 35°6E 251 G6
Al Khāliş Iraq 33°49N 44°32E 213 F11
Al Khamāsīn Si. Arabia 20°29N 44°46E 248 B4
Al Kharj Si. Arabia 24°0N 47°0E 248 B4
Al Kharsānīyah Si. Arabia 27°13N 49°18E 247 E6
Al Khaşab Oman 26°14N 56°15E 247 E8
Al Khāşirah Si. Arabia 23°30N 43°47E 248 B3
Al Khawr Qatar 25°41N 51°30E 247 E6
Al Khiḑr Iraq 31°12N 45°33E 246 D5
Al Khiyām Lebanon 33°20N 35°36E 250 E6
Al Khobar Si. Arabia 26°17N 50°12E 247 E6
Al Khums Libya 32°40N 14°17E 258 B2
Al Kifl Iraq 32°13N 44°22E 213 G11
Al Kiswah Syria 33°23N 36°14E 250 E7
Al Kūfah Iraq 32°2N 44°24E 213 F11
Al Kufrah Libya 24°17N 23°15E 258 D4
Al Kuhayfīyah Si. Arabia 27°12N 43°3E 246 E4
Al Kumayt Iraq 32°2N 46°52E 213 G12
Al Kūt Iraq 32°30N 46°0E 213 F11
Al Kuwayt Kuwait 29°30N 48°0E 246 D5
Al Labwah Lebanon 34°11N 36°20E 250 D7
Al Lādhiqīyah Syria 35°30N 35°45E 250 C6
Al Lādhiqīyah □ Syria 35°45N 36°0E 250 C7
Al Līth Si. Arabia 20°9N 40°15E 248 B3
Al Liwā' Oman 24°31N 56°36E 247 E8
Al Luḩayyah Yemen 15°45N 42°40E 248 D3
Al Madīnah Iraq 30°57N 47°16E 246 D5
Al Madīnah Si. Arabia 24°35N 39°52E 246 E3
Al Madīnah □ Si. Arabia 23°50N 40°30E 248 B3
Al Mafraq Jordan 32°17N 36°14E 251 F7
Al Mafraq □ Jordan 32°17N 36°15E 251 F7
Al Maghārīm Yemen 15°1N 47°49E 248 D4
Al Maghreb = Morocco ■ N. Afr. 32°0N 5°50W 260 B3
Al Mahbes W. Sahara 27°10N 9°50W 260 C3
Al Maḩmūdīyah Iraq 33°3N 44°21E 213 F11
Al Majma'ah Si. Arabia 25°57N 45°22E 246 E5
Al Makhruq, W. → Jordan 31°28N 37°0E 251 G8
Al Makḩūl Si. Arabia 26°37N 42°39E 246 E4
Al Mālikīyah Syria 37°10N 42°8E 213 D10
Al Manāmah Bahrain 26°10N 50°30E 247 E6
Al Maqwa' Kuwait 29°10N 47°59E 246 D5
Al Marāḩ Si. Arabia 25°35N 49°35E 247 E6
Al Marj Libya 32°25N 20°30E 258 B4
Al Marj □ Libya 32°0N 21°0E 258 B4
Al Marqab □ Libya 32°32N 14°35E 258 B2
Al Maţlā Kuwait 29°24N 47°40E 246 D5
Al Mawşil Iraq 36°15N 43°5E 213 D10
Al Mayādin Syria 35°1N 40°27E 213 E9
Al Mazār Jordan 31°4N 35°41E 251 G6
Al Midhnab Si. Arabia 25°50N 44°18E 246 E5
Al Minā' Lebanon 34°24N 35°49E 250 D6
Al Miqdādīyah Iraq 34°0N 45°0E 213 E11
Al Mubarraz Si. Arabia 25°30N 49°40E 247 E6
Al Mudawwarah Jordan 29°19N 36°0E 251 J7
Al Muḑaybī Oman 22°34N 58°7E 249 B7
Al Mughayrā' U.A.E. 24°5N 53°32E 247 E7
Al Muḩarraq Bahrain 26°15N 50°40E 247 E6
Al Mukallā Yemen 14°33N 49°2E 249 D5
Al Mukhā Yemen 13°18N 43°15E 248 D3
Al Mukhaylī Libya 32°10N 22°17E 258 B4
Al Musayjīd Si. Arabia 24°5N 39°5E 246 E3
Al Musayyib Iraq 32°49N 44°20E 213 F11
Al Muthanná □ Iraq 30°30N 45°15E 246 D5
Al Muwayh Si. Arabia 22°41N 41°37E 256 C5
Al Muwayliḩ Si. Arabia 27°40N 35°30E 246 E2
Al Muzāḩimīyah Si. Arabia 24°29N 46°18E 248 A4
Al Owuho = Otukpa Nigeria 7°9N 7°41E 263 D6
Al Qaddāḩīyah Libya 31°15N 15°9E 258 B3
Al Qaḑīmah Si. Arabia 22°20N 39°13E 248 B2
Al Qādisīyah □ Iraq 32°0N 45°0E 246 D5
Al Qadmūs Syria 35°5N 36°10E 250 C7
Al Qaḩmah Si. Arabia 18°0N 41°41E 248 C3
Al Qā'im Iraq 34°21N 41°7E 213 E9
Al Qā'iyah Si. Arabia 24°33N 43°15E 248 A3
Al Qalībah Si. Arabia 28°24N 37°42E 246 D3
Al Qāmishlī Syria 37°2N 41°14E 213 D9
Al Qardāḩah Syria 35°27N 36°3E 250 C7
Al Qaryah ash Sharqīyah Libya 30°28N 13°40E 258 B2
Al Qaryatayn Syria 34°12N 37°13E 250 D8
Al Qaşabāt Libya 32°39N 14°1E 258 B2
Al Qaşīm □ Si. Arabia 26°0N 43°0E 246 E4
Al Qaţ'ā Syria 34°40N 40°48E 213 E9
Al Qaţīf Si. Arabia 26°35N 50°0E 247 E6
Al Qaţn Yemen 15°51N 48°26E 249 D5
Al Qatrānah Jordan 31°12N 36°6E 251 G7
Al Qaţrūn Libya 24°56N 15°3E 258 D3
Al Qawz Si. Arabia 18°58N 41°26E 248 C3
Al Qayşūmah Si. Arabia 28°20N 46°7E 246 D5
Al Qiblīyah Oman 17°30N 56°20E 249 C7
Al Qubbah □ Libya 31°0N 23°40E 258 B4
Al Quds = Jerusalem Israel/West Bank 31°47N 35°10E 123 B2
Al Qunayţirah Syria 32°55N 35°45E 250 F6
Al Qunfudhah Si. Arabia 19°3N 41°4E 248 C3
Al Qurayyāt Oman 23°17N 58°53E 249 B7
Al Qurḩ Yemen 16°44N 51°29E 249 C5
Al Qurnah Iraq 31°1N 47°25E 246 D5
Al Quşayr Iraq 30°39N 45°50E 246 D5
Al Quşayr Syria 34°31N 36°34E 250 D7
Al Qutayfah Syria 33°44N 36°36E 250 E7
Al Quway'īyah Si. Arabia 24°3N 45°15E 248 A4
Al Quwayr Iraq 36°2N 43°29E 213 D10
Al 'Ubaylah Si. Arabia 21°59N 50°57E 249 B5
Al 'Uḑaylīyah Si. Arabia 25°8N 49°18E 247 E6
Al 'Ulā Si. Arabia 26°35N 38°0E 246 E3
Al 'Ulayyah Si. Arabia 19°39N 41°54E 248 C3
Al Uqaylah ash Sharqīgah Libya 30°12N 19°10E 258 B3
Al 'Uqayr Si. Arabia 25°40N 50°15E 247 E6
Al 'Urūq al Mutariḑah Si. Arabia 21°0N 53°30E 249 B6
Al 'Uwaynāt Libya 25°47N 10°33E 261 C7
Al 'Uwaynid Si. Arabia 24°50N 46°0E 246 E5
Al 'Uwayqīlah Si. Arabia 30°30N 42°10E 246 D4
Al Uweinat Libya 21°34N 24°50E 259 D4
Al 'Uyūn Ḩijāz, Si. Arabia 24°33N 39°35E 246 E3
Al 'Uyūn Najd, Si. Arabia 26°30N 43°50E 246 E4
Al 'Uzayr Iraq 31°19N 47°25E 246 D5
Al Wāḩāt □ Libya 29°0N 22°0E 258 C4
Al Wajh Si. Arabia 26°10N 36°30E 246 E3
Al Wakrah Qatar 25°10N 51°40E 247 E6
Al-Walaja West Bank 31°44N 35°9E 123 B1
Al Waqbah Si. Arabia 28°48N 45°33E 246 D5
Al Wari'āh Si. Arabia 27°51N 47°25E 246 E5
Al Wāţīyah Libya 32°28N 11°57E 258 B2
Al Wīgh Libya 24°16N 14°58E 258 D2
Al Yaman = Yemen ■ Asia 15°0N 44°0E 248 D4
Ala Italy 45°45N 11°0E 198 C8
Ala Dağ Turkey 37°44N 35°9E 246 B2
Ala Dağları Turkey 39°15N 43°33E 213 C10
Ala Tau Asia 45°30N 80°40E 217 C10
Ala Tau Shankou = Dzungarian Gate Asia 45°10N 82°0E 217 C10
Alabama □ U.S.A. 33°0N 87°0W 315 E11
Alabama → U.S.A. 31°8N 87°57W 315 F11
Alabaster U.S.A. 33°15N 86°49W 315 E11
Alabat I. Phil. 14°7N 122°3E 232 D4
Alabel Phil. 6°4N 125°16E 233 H5
Alabule → Papua N. G. 8°31S 146°56E 286 E4
Alaca Turkey 40°10N 34°51E 212 B6
Alacaatlı Turkey 39°15N 28°3E 205 B10
Alaçam Turkey 41°36N 35°36E 212 B6
Alaçam Dağları Turkey 39°18N 28°49E 205 B10
Alacant = Alicante Spain 38°23N 0°30W 197 G4
Alaçatı Turkey 38°15N 26°22E 205 C8
Alachua U.S.A. 29°47N 82°30W 316 F7
Alaejos Spain 41°18N 5°13W 194 D5
Alagir Russia 43°3N 44°14E 191 J7
Alagna Valsésia Italy 45°51N 7°56E 198 C4
Alagoa de Baixo = Sertânia Brazil 8°5S 37°20W 332 C4
Alagoa Grande Brazil 7°3S 35°35W 332 C4
Alagoas = Marechal Deodoro Brazil 9°43S 35°54W 332 C4
Alagoas □ Brazil 9°0S 36°0W 332 C4
Alagoinhas Brazil 12°7S 38°20W 333 D4
Alagón Spain 41°46N 1°12W 196 D3
Alagón → Spain 39°44N 6°53W 194 F4
Alaguntan Nigeria 6°25N 3°29E 124 B2
Alagyoz = Aragats Armenia 40°30N 44°15E 191 K7
Alahan Turkey 36°46N 33°19E 250 B4
Alai Range Asia 39°45N 72°0E 217 E8
Alaior Spain 39°57N 4°8E 206 B5
Alajero Canary Is. 28°3N 17°13W 153 e1
Alajuela Costa Rica 10°2N 84°8W 320 D3
Alajuela, L. Panama 9°14N 79°34W 320 c
Alakamisy Madag. 21°19S 47°14E 272 C2
Alakanuk U.S.A. 62°41N 164°37W 303 E6
Alaknanda → India 30°8N 78°36E 243 D8
Alaköl Kazakhstan 46°0N 81°5E 217 C10
Alakurtti Russia 66°58N 30°25E 160 C24
'Alaläkeiki Channel U.S.A. 20°30N 156°30W 302 C5
Alalapura Suriname 2°20N 56°25W 329 C6
Alalaú → Brazil 0°30S 61°9W 329 D5
Alamagan N. Marianas 17°36N 145°50E 302 a
Alamarvdasht Iran 27°37N 52°59E 247 E7
Alamata Ethiopia 12°25N 39°33E 257 E4
Alameda Calif., U.S.A. 37°46N 122°15W 136 B3
Alameda N. Mex., U.S.A. 35°11N 106°37W 305 J10
Alameda, Parque Mexico City, Mexico 128 b2
Alameda Memorial State Beach Park U.S.A. 37°45N 122°16W 136 B3
Alaminos Phil. 16°10N 119°59E 232 C2
Alamo Ga., U.S.A. 32°9N 82°47W 316 C7
Alamo Nev., U.S.A. 37°22N 115°10W 307 H11
Alamogordo U.S.A. 32°54N 105°57W 305 K11
Alamos Mexico 27°1N 108°56W 318 B3
Alamosa U.S.A. 37°28N 105°52W 305 H11
Alampur India 15°55N 78°6E 245 G4
Åland Finland 60°15N 20°0E 161 F19
Aland India 17°36N 76°35E 244 F3
Alandroal Portugal 38°41N 7°24W 195 G3
Ålands hav Europe 60°0N 19°30E 161 G18
Alandur India 13°0N 80°15E 245 H5
Alange, Embalse d' Spain 38°45N 6°18W 195 G4
Alania = North Ossetia □ Russia 43°30N 44°30E 191 J7
Alanís Spain 38°3N 5°43W 195 G5
Alanya Turkey 36°38N 32°0E 250 B3
Alaotra, Farihin' Madag. 17°30S 48°30E 272 B2
Alapaha U.S.A. 31°23N 83°13W 316 D6
Alapayevsk Russia 57°52N 61°42E 214 D7
Alappuzha = Alleppey India 9°30N 76°28E 245 K3
'Alāqán Si. Arabia 29°10N 35°21E 251 J6
Alar del Rey Spain 42°38N 4°20W 194 C6
Alara → Turkey 36°38N 31°39E 250 B2
Alaraz Spain 40°45N 5°17W 194 E5
Alarcón, Embalse de Spain 39°36N 2°10W 196 F2
Alaró Spain 39°42N 2°47E 206 B3
Alarobia-Vohiposa Madag. 20°59S 47°9E 272 C2
Alaşehir Turkey 38°23N 28°30E 205 C10
Alashtar Iran 33°51N 48°15E 213 F13
Alaska □ U.S.A. 64°0N 154°0W 303 D9
Alaska, G. of Pac. Oc. 58°0N 145°0W 303 G11
Alaska Maritime Nat. Wildlife Refuge ⌓ U.S.A. 52°0N 174°0W 303 L4
Alaska Peninsula U.S.A. 56°0N 159°0W 303 H8
Alaska Peninsula Nat. Wildlife Refuge ⌓ U.S.A. 56°0N 159°0W 303 J8
Alaska Range U.S.A. 62°50N 151°0W 303 E10
Alássio Italy 44°0N 8°10E 198 E5
Älät Azerbaijan 39°58N 49°25E 191 L9
Alatau Shan = Ala Tau Asia 45°30N 80°40E 217 C10
Alatri Italy 41°43N 13°21E 199 G10
Alatyr Russia 54°55N 46°35E 190 C8
Alatyr → Russia 54°52N 46°36E 190 C8
Alaungdaw Kathapa △ Burma 22°30N 94°30E 241 D5
Alausi Ecuador 2°0S 78°50W 328 D2
Álava □ Spain 42°48N 2°28W 196 C2
Alava, C. U.S.A. 48°10N 124°44W 304 B1
Alaverdi Armenia 41°15N 44°37E 191 K7
Alavo = Alavus Finland 62°35N 23°36E 160 E20
Alavus Finland 62°35N 23°36E 160 E20
Alawa ✪ Australia 15°42S 134°39E 280 B1
Alawoona Australia 34°45S 140°30E 282 C4
Alayawarra ✪ Australia 22°0S 134°30E 280 C1
'Alayh Lebanon 33°46N 35°33E 250 E6
Alazani → Azerbaijan 41°5N 46°40E 191 K8
Alba Italy 44°42N 8°2E 198 D5
Alba □ Romania 46°10N 23°30E 183 D8
Alba Adriática Italy 42°50N 13°56E 199 F10
Alba de Tormes Spain 40°50N 5°30W 194 E5
Alba-Iulia Romania 46°8N 23°39E 183 D8
Albac Romania 46°28N 22°58E 182 D7
Albacete Spain 39°0N 1°50W 197 F3
Albacete □ Spain 38°50N 2°0W 197 G3
Albacutya, L. Australia 35°45S 141°58E 282 C4
Ålbæk Denmark 57°36N 10°25E 163 G4
Ålbæk Bugt Denmark 57°35N 10°40E 163 G4
Albaida Spain 38°51N 0°31W 197 G4
Albalate de las Nogueras Spain 40°22N 2°18W 196 E2
Albalate del Arzobispo Spain 41°6N 0°31W 196 D4
Alban France 43°53N 2°28E 174 E6
Albanel, L. Canada 50°55N 73°12W 298 B5
Albania ■ Europe 41°0N 20°0E 202 E4
Albano Laziale Italy 41°44N 12°39E 199 G9
Albany W. Austral., Australia 35°1S 117°58E 279 G2
Albany Ga., U.S.A. 31°35N 84°10W 316 D5
Albany Ind., U.S.A. 40°18N 85°14W 311 D11
Albany Mo., U.S.A. 40°15N 94°20W 310 D2
Albany N.Y., U.S.A. 42°39N 73°45W 313 D11
Albany Oreg., U.S.A. 44°38N 123°6W 304 D2
Albany Tex., U.S.A. 32°44N 99°18W 314 E5
Albany Wis., U.S.A. 42°42N 89°26W 310 B7
Albany → Canada 52°17N 81°31W 298 B3
Albarca, C. d' Spain 39°4N 1°22E 206 C1
Albardón Argentina 31°20S 68°30W 334 C2
Albarracín Spain 40°25N 1°26W 196 E3
Albarracín, Sierra de Spain 40°30N 1°30W 196 E3
Albatera Spain 38°11N 0°52W 197 G4
Albatross B. Australia 12°45S 141°30E 280 A3
Albatross Pt. N.Z. 38°7S 174°44E 284 E3
Albay □ Phil. 13°13N 123°33E 232 E4
Albegna → Italy 42°30N 11°11E 199 F8
Albemarle U.S.A. 35°21N 80°12W 315 D14
Albemarle, I. = Isabela, I. Ecuador 0°30S 91°4W 330 a
Albemarle, Pta. Ecuador 0°11N 91°21W 330 a
Albemarle Sd. U.S.A. 36°5N 76°0W 315 C16
Albenga Italy 44°3N 8°13E 198 D5
Alberche → Spain 39°58N 4°46W 194 F6
Alberdi Paraguay 26°14S 58°20W 334 B4
Albères, Mts. France 42°28N 2°56E 174 F6
Ålberga Sweden 58°44N 16°35E 163 F10
Alberga → Australia 27°6S 135°33E 281 D2
Albern Austria 48°9N 16°29E 142 B2
Albersdorf Germany 54°8N 9°17E 178 A5
Albert France 50°0N 2°38E 173 C9
Albert, L. Africa 1°30N 31°0E 268 B3

Albert, L. S. Austral.,
  Australia 35°30S 139°10E **282** C3
Albert Edward, Mt.
  Papua N. G. 8°20S 147°24E **286** E4
Albert Edward Ra.
  Australia 18°17S 127°57E **278** C4
Albert Lea U.S.A. 43°39N 93°22W **308** D7
Albert Nat. Park = Virunga △
  Dem. Rep. of the Congo 0°5N 29°38E **268** B2
Albert Nile → Uganda 3°36N 32°2E **268** B3
Albert Park Australia 37°51S 144°58E **128** B1
Albert Town Bahamas 22°37N 74°33W **321** B5
Albert Town Jamaica 18°17N 77°33W **320** a
Alberta □ Canada 54°40N 115°0W **296** C6
Albertina Argentina 35°1S 60°16W **334** D3
Albertinia S. Africa 34°11S 21°34E **270** D3
Albertirsa Hungary 47°14N 19°37E **182** C4
Alberto de Agostini △
  Chile 54°38S 71°37W **336** D2
Alberton P.E.I., Canada 46°50N 64°0W **299** C7
Alberton Gauteng, S. Africa 26°15S 28°7E **123** B2
Albertslund Denmark 55°39N 12°21E **118** B2
Albertville = Kalemie
  Dem. Rep. of the Congo 5°55S 29°9E **268** D2
Albertville Savoie, France 45°40N 6°22E **175** C10
Albertville Ala., U.S.A. 34°16N 86°13W **315** D11
Albi France 43°56N 2°9E **174** E6
Albia U.S.A. 41°2N 92°48W **310** C4
Albina Suriname 5°37N 54°15W **329** B7
Albina, Ponta Angola 15°52S 11°44E **265** F2
Albino Italy 45°46N 9°47E **198** C6
Albion U.S.A. 38°23N 88°4W **311** F8
Albion Ind., U.S.A. 41°24N 85°25W **311** C11
Albion Mich., U.S.A. 42°15N 84°45W **311** B12
Albion Nebr., U.S.A. 41°42N 98°0W **308** E4
Albion Pa., U.S.A. 41°53N 80°22W **312** E4
Albocàsser Spain 40°21N 0°1E **196** E5
Albolote Spain 37°14N 3°39W **195** H7
Alborán Medit. S. 35°57N 3°0W **195** K7
Alborea Spain 39°17N 1°24W **197** F3
Ålborg = Aalborg Denmark 57°2N 9°54E **163** G3
Ålborg Bugt = Aalborg Bugt
  Denmark 56°50N 10°35E **163** H4
Alborz, Reshteh-ye Kūhhā-ye
  Iran 36°0N 52°0E **247** C7
Albox Spain 37°23N 2°8W **197** H2
Albuera Spain 10°55N 124°42E **233** F5
Albufeira Portugal 37°5N 8°15W **195** H2
Albula → Switz. 46°38N 9°28E **179** C5
Albuñol Spain 36°48N 3°11W **195** J7
Albuquerque Brazil 15°25S 57°26W **331** D6
Albuquerque N. Mex.,
  U.S.A. 35°5N 106°39W **305** J10
Albuquerque, Cayos de
  Caribbean 12°10N 81°50W **320** D3
Alburg U.S.A. 44°59N 73°18W **313** B11
Alburno, Mte. Italy 40°33N 15°17E **201** B8
Albury Australia 36°3S 146°56E **283** C7
Albury U.S.A. 36°3S 146°56E **283** C7
Alcácer do Sal Portugal 38°22N 8°33W **195** G2
Alcaçovas Portugal 38°23N 8°9W **195** G2
Alcala Phil. 17°54N 121°39E **232** C3
Alcalá de Guadaira Spain 37°20N 5°50W **195** H5
Alcalá de Henares Spain 40°28N 3°22W **194** E7
Alcalá de Xivert Spain 40°19N 0°13E **196** E5
Alcalá del Júcar Spain 39°12N 1°26W **197** F3
Alcalá del Río Spain 37°31N 5°59W **195** H5
Alcalá la Real Spain 37°27N 3°57W **195** H7
Álcamo Italy 37°59N 12°55E **200** E5
Alcanadre → Spain 42°24N 2°7W **196** C2
Alcanadre → Spain 41°43N 0°12W **196** D4
Alcanar Spain 40°33N 0°28E **196** E5
Alcanede Portugal 39°25N 8°49W **195** F2
Alcanena Portugal 39°25N 8°40W **195** F2
Alcañices Spain 41°41N 6°21W **194** D4
Alcañiz Spain 41°2N 0°8W **196** D4
Alcântara Brazil 2°20S 44°30W **332** B3
Alcántara Lisboa, Portugal 38°43N 9°10W **126** A1
Alcántara Spain 39°41N 6°57W **194** F4
Alcántara, Embalse de
  Spain 39°44N 6°50W **194** F4
Alcantarilla Spain 37°59N 1°12W **197** H3
Alcaracejos Spain 38°24N 4°58W **195** G6
Alcaraz Spain 38°40N 2°29W **197** G2
Alcaraz, Sierra de Spain 38°40N 2°20W **197** G2
Alcatraz I. U.S.A. 37°49N 122°25W **306** H4
Alcaudete Spain 37°35N 4°5W **195** H6
Alcázar de San Juan
  Spain 39°24N 3°12W **195** F7
Alcazarquivir = Ksar el Kebir
  Morocco 35°0N 6°0W **260** B3
Alcedo, Volcán Ecuador 0°24S 91°6W **330** a
Alchevsk Ukraine 48°30N 38°45E **189** H10
Alcira = Alzira Spain 39°9N 0°30W **197** F4
Alcobaça = Tucuruí
  Brazil 3°42S 49°44W **332** B2
Alcobaça Portugal 39°32N 8°58W **195** F2
Alcobendas Spain 40°32N 3°38W **127** A2
Alcolea del Pinar Spain 41°2N 2°28W **196** D2
Alcoma U.S.A. 27°54N 81°29W **317** M8
Alcorcón Spain 40°20N 3°48W **127** B1
Alcoutim Portugal 37°25N 7°28W **195** H3
Alcova U.S.A. 42°34N 106°43W **304** C10
Alcoy Spain 38°43N 0°30W **197** G4
Alcubierre, Sierra de
  Spain 41°45N 0°22W **196** D4
Alcublas Spain 39°48N 0°43W **196** F4
Alcúdia Spain 39°51N 3°7E **206** B4
Alcúdia, B. d' Spain 39°47N 3°15E **206** B4
Alcúdia, Sierra de la
  Spain 38°34N 4°30W **195** G6
Aldabra Is. Seychelles 9°22S 46°28E **255** G8
Aldama Mexico 22°55N 98°4W **319** C5
Aldan Russia 58°40N 125°30E **215** D13
Aldan → Russia 63°28N 129°35E **215** C13
Aldea, Pta. de la
  Canary Is. 28°0N 15°50W **153** e1
Aldeburgh U.K. 52°10N 1°37E **169** E9
Alden Norway 61°19N 4°45E **164** C1
Alder Pk. U.S.A. 35°53N 121°22W **306** K5
Alderney U.K. 49°42N 2°11W **169** H5
Aldershof Germany 52°27N 13°32E **134** A4
Aldershot U.K. 51°15N 0°44W **169** F7
Aldinga Beach Australia 35°17S 138°27E **282** C1
Aldo Bonzi Argentina 34°42S 58°31W **117** C1
Åled Sweden 56°44N 12°57E **163** H6
Aledo U.S.A. 41°12N 90°45W **310** C6
Alefa Ethiopia 11°55N 36°55E **257** E4
Aleg Mauritania 17°3N 13°55W **262** B2
Alegranza Canary Is. 29°23N 13°32W **260** B2
Alegranza, I. Canary Is. 29°23N 13°32W **153** e2
Alegre Brazil 20°50S 41°30W **333** F3
Alegrete Brazil 29°40S 56°0W **335** B4
Aleknagik U.S.A. 59°17N 158°36W **303** G8
Aleksandriya = Oleksandriya
  Kirovohrad, Ukraine 48°42N 33°3E **189** H7
Aleksandriya = Oleksandriya Rivne,
  Ukraine 50°37N 26°19E **187** C14
Aleksandriyskaya Russia 43°59N 47°14E **191** J8
Aleksandropol = Gyumri
  Armenia 40°47N 43°50E **191** K6
Aleksandrov Russia 56°23N 38°44E **188** D10
Aleksandrov Gay Russia 50°9N 48°34E **190** E9

Aleksandrovac Serbia 43°28N 21°3E **202** C5
Aleksandrovac Serbia 44°28N 21°13E **202** B5
Aleksandrovka = Oleksandrivka
  Ukraine 48°25N 32°20E **189** H7
Aleksandrovka = Ordzhonīkīdze
  Ukraine 47°39N 34°3E **189** J8
Aleksandrovo Bulgaria 43°14N 24°51E **203** C8
Aleksandrovsk = Belogorsk
  Russia 51°0N 128°20E **215** D13
Aleksandrovsk = Polyarny
  Russia 69°8N 33°20E **160** B25
Aleksandrovsk = Zaporizhzhya
  Ukraine 47°50N 35°10E **189** J8
Aleksandrovsk-Grushevsky =
  Shakhty Russia 47°40N 40°16E **191** G5
Aleksandrovsk-Sakhalinskiy
  Russia 50°50N 142°20E **215** D15
Aleksandrovskoye
  Russia 59°51N 30°20E **137** B2
Aleksandrovskoye
  Russia 50°43N 38°40E **189** G10
Alekseyevka Samara,
  Russia 52°35N 51°17E **190** D10
Alekseyevka Voronezh,
  Russia 50°43N 38°40E **189** G10
Alekseyevsk = Svobodny
  Russia 51°20N 128°0E **215** D13
Alekseyevskoye = Qazyghurt
  Kazakhstan 41°45N 69°23E **217** D7
Aleksin Russia 54°31N 37°9E **188** E9
Aleksinac Serbia 43°31N 21°42E **202** C5
Além Paraíba Brazil 21°52S 42°41W **333** F3
Alemania Argentina 25°40S 65°30W **334** B2
Alemania Chile 25°10S 69°55W **334** B2
Alen Eq. Guin. 1°30N 11°19E **264** B2
Alençon France 48°27N 0°4E **172** D7
'Alenuihāhā Channel
  U.S.A. 20°30N 156°0W **302** C5
Aleppo = Ḥalab Syria 36°10N 37°15E **250** B8
Aleria France 42°5N 9°26E **175** F13
Alert Canada 83°2N 60°0W **295** A20
Aleru India 17°39N 79°3E **244** F4
Alès France 44°9N 4°5E **175** D8
Aleşd Romania 47°3N 22°22E **182** C7
Alessándria Italy 44°54N 8°37E **198** D5
Ålesund Norway 62°28N 6°12E **164** B3
Alet-les-Bains France 42°59N 2°14E **174** F6
Aletschhorn Switz. 46°28N 8°0E **179** J4
Aleutian Basin Pac. Oc. 57°0N 177°0E **288** B9
Aleutian Is. Pac. Oc. 52°0N 175°0W **303** K3
Aleutian Range U.S.A. 60°0N 154°0W **303** G9
Aleutian Trench Pac. Oc. 48°0N 180°0E **150** D17
Alexander U.S.A. 47°51N 103°39W **308** B2
Alexander, C. Solomon Is. 6°34S 156°32E **287** L9
Alexander, Mt. Australia 26°3S 135°10E **279** E3
Alexander Arch. U.S.A. 56°0N 136°0W **303** J14
Alexander Bay S. Africa 28°40S 16°30E **270** C2
Alexander City U.S.A. 32°56N 85°58W **316** C4
Alexander I. Antarctica 69°0S 70°0W **151** C17
Alexander Nevsky Abbey
  Russia 59°54N 30°23E **137** B2
Alexander Soutzos Museum
  Athens, Greece 112 b3
Alexandra Vic., Australia 37°8S 145°40E **283** D6
Alexandra N.Z. 45°14S 169°25E **285** F4
Alexandra Singapore 1°17N 103°49E **138** B2
Alexandra Gauteng, S. Africa 26°6S 28°5E **123** A2
Alexandra Channel
  Burma 14°7N 93°13E **245** G11
Alexandra Falls Canada 60°29N 116°18W **296** A5
Alexandretta = İskenderun
  Turkey 36°32N 36°10E **250** B7
Alexandria = El Iskandarîya
  Egypt 31°13N 29°58E **256** H7
Alexandria B.C., Canada 52°35N 122°27W **296** C4
Alexandria Ont., Canada 45°19N 74°38W **313** A10
Alexandria Romania 43°57N 25°24E **183** G10
Alexandria Eastern Cape,
  S. Africa 33°38S 26°28E **270** D4
Alexandria W. Dunb., U.K. 55°59N 4°35W **167** F4
Alexandria Ind., U.S.A. 40°16N 85°41W **311** D11
Alexandria Ky., U.S.A. 38°58N 84°23W **311** F12
Alexandria La., U.S.A. 31°18N 92°27W **314** F8
Alexandria Minn., U.S.A. 45°53N 95°22W **308** C6
Alexandria Mo., U.S.A. 40°27N 91°28W **310** D6
Alexandria S. Dak.,
  U.S.A. 43°39N 97°47W **308** D5
Alexandria Va., U.S.A. 38°48N 77°3W **312** F7
Alexandria Bay U.S.A. 44°20N 75°55W **313** B9
Alexandrina, L.
  Australia 35°25S 139°10E **282** C2
Alexandroúpoli Greece 40°50N 25°54E **203** F9
Alexis → U.S.A. 41°4N 90°3W **310** C6
Alexis Creek Canada 52°10N 123°20W **296** C4
Aley → Russia 52°51N 83°36E **217** B10
Aleysk Russia 52°40N 83°0E **217** B10
Alfabia Spain 39°44N 2°44E **206** B3
Alfama Lisbon, Portugal 126 c3
Alfambra Spain 40°33N 1°5W **196** E3
Alfândega da Fé Portugal 41°20N 6°59W **194** D4
Alfaro Spain 42°10N 1°50W **196** C3
Alfatar Bulgaria 43°59N 27°13E **203** C11
Alfeld Germany 51°59N 9°50E **178** D5
Alfenas Brazil 21°20S 46°10W **335** A6
Alföld Hungary 46°30N 20°0E **182** D5
Alfonsine Italy 44°30N 12°3E **199** D9
Alford Aberds., U.K. 57°14N 2°41W **167** D6
Alford Lincs., U.K. 53°15N 0°10E **168** D8
Alfortville France 48°48N 2°24E **134** B3
Alfotbreen Norway 61°45N 5°39E **164** D2
Alföten Norway 61°51N 5°41E **164** C2
Alfred Maine, U.S.A. 43°29N 70°43W **313** C14
Alfred N.Y., U.S.A. 42°16N 77°48W **312** D7
Alfred N.Z. 40°41S 175°54E **284** G4
Alfreton U.K. 53°6N 1°24W **168** D6
Alfta Sweden 61°21N 16°4E **162** C10
Algaida Spain 39°33N 2°53E **206** B3
Algård Norway 58°46N 5°53E **164** F2
Algarinejo Spain 37°19N 4°9W **195** H6
Algarve Portugal 36°58N 8°20W **195** J2
Algeciras Spain 36°9N 5°28W **195** J5
Algemesí Spain 39°11N 0°27W **197** F4
Alger Algeria 36°42N 3°8E **261** A6
Alger U.S.A. 40°39N 83°51W **311** E12
Alger ✈ (ALG) Algeria 36°43N 3°13E **197** a
Algeria ■ Algeria 28°30N 2°0E **261** C5
Alghabas Kazakhstan 49°53N 57°20E **187** E17
Alghero Italy 40°33N 8°19E **200** B1
Alghult Sweden 57°0N 15°33E **163** H9
Algiers = Alger Algeria 36°42N 3°8E **261** A6
Algiers U.S.A. 29°56N 90°2W **131** B2
Algoa B. S. Africa 33°50S 25°45E **270** D4
Algodonales Spain 36°54N 5°24W **195** J5

Algodor → Spain 39°55N 3°53W **194** F7
Algoma U.S.A. 44°36N 87°26W **308** C10
Algona U.S.A. 43°4N 94°14W **310** A2
Algonac U.S.A. 42°37N 82°32W **312** D2
Algonquin △ Canada 45°50N 78°30W **298** C4
Alhama de Almería Spain 36°57N 2°34W **195** J8
Alhama de Aragón Spain 41°18N 1°54W **196** D3
Alhama de Granada Spain 37°0N 3°59W **195** H7
Alhambra U.S.A. 34°5N 118°8W **307** K8
Alhaurín el Grande Spain 36°39N 4°41W **195** J6
Alhucemas = Al Hoceïma
  Morocco 35°8N 3°58W **261** A4
'Alī al Gharbī Iraq 32°30N 46°45E **213** F12
'Alī ash Sharqī Iraq 32°7N 46°44E **213** F12
'Alī Bayramlı Azerbaijan 39°59N 48°52E **191** L9
Ali Sahīh Djibouti 11°10N 42°44E **257** E5
Alī Shāh Iran 38°9N 45°50E **246** B5
Ália Italy 37°47N 13°43E **200** E6
'Alīābād Golestān, Iran 36°40N 54°33E **247** B7
'Alīābād Khorāsān, Iran 32°30N 57°30E **247** C8
'Alīābād Kordestān, Iran 35°4N 46°58E **246** C5
'Alīābād Yazd, Iran 31°41N 53°49E **247** D7
Aliade Nigeria 7°18N 8°29E **263** D6
Aliaga Turkey 40°40N 0°42W **196** E4
Aliağa Turkey 38°47N 26°59E **205** C8
Aliakmonas → Greece 40°30N 22°36E **204** E4
Alibag India 18°38N 72°56E **244** E1
Alibey → Turkey 41°3N 28°56E **122** B1
Alibey Baraji Turkey 41°4N 28°53E **122** B1
Alibeyköy Turkey 41°4N 28°56E **122** B1
Alibo Ethiopia 9°52N 37°5E **257** F4
Alibori → Benin 11°56N 3°17E **263** C5
Alibunar Serbia 45°5N 20°57E **182** E5
Alicante Spain 38°23N 0°30W **197** G4
Alicante □ Spain 38°30N 0°37W **197** G4
Alicante ✈ (ALC) Spain 38°14N 0°36W **197** G4
Alice S. Africa
  Eastern Cape,
  S. Africa 32°48S 26°55E **270** D4
Alice Tex., U.S.A. 27°45N 98°5W **314** H5
Alice → Queens.,
  Australia 24°2S 144°50E **280** C3
Alice → Queens.,
  Australia 15°35S 142°20E **280** B3
Alice, Punta Italy 39°24N 17°9E **201** C10
Alice Arm Canada 55°29N 129°31W **296** B3
Alice Springs Australia 23°40S 133°50E **280** C1
Alicedale S. Africa 33°15S 26°4E **270** D4
Aliceville U.S.A. 33°8N 88°9W **315** E10
Alicia Bohol, Phil. 9°54N 124°26E **233** G5
Alicia Isabela, Phil. 16°46N 121°42E **232** C3
Alicudi Italy 38°33N 14°20E **201** D7
Alien Taiwan 22°52N 120°19E **225** D2
Aliganj India 27°30N 79°10E **243** F8
Aligarh Raj., India 25°55N 76°15E **242** F7
Aligarh Ut. P., India 27°55N 78°10E **242** F6
Alīgūdarz Iran 33°25N 49°45E **247** C6
Alijó Portugal 41°16N 7°27W **194** D3
Alikanas Greece 37°51N 20°47E **207** D2
Alima → Congo 1°35S 16°37E **264** C3
Alimia Greece 36°16N 27°43E **206** E11
Alimodian Phil. 10°49N 122°26E **233** F4
Alimos Greece 37°52N 23°43E **112** B2
Alindao C.A.R. 5°2N 21°13E **264** A4
Alingsås Sweden 57°56N 12°31E **163** G6
Alipur W. Bengal, India 22°43N 88°12E **124** B1
Alipur Pakistan 29°25N 70°55E **242** E4
Alipur Duar India 26°30N 89°35E **241** B2
Aliquippa U.S.A. 40°37N 80°15W **312** F4
Alishan Taiwan 23°31N 120°48E **225** C2
Aliste → Spain 41°34N 5°58W **194** D5
Alitus = Alytus Lithuania 54°24N 24°3E **188** E3
Aliveri Greece 38°24N 24°2E **204** C6
Aliwal North S. Africa 30°45S 26°45E **270** D4
Alix Canada 52°24N 113°11W **296** C6
Aljezur Portugal 37°18N 8°49W **195** H2
Aljustrel Portugal 37°55N 8°10W **195** H2
Alkamari Niger 13°27N 11°10E **263** C7
Alkmaar Neths. 52°37N 4°45E **170** B4
All American Canal
  U.S.A. 32°45N 115°15W **305** K6
Allacapan Phil. 18°15N 121°35E **232** B3
Allach Germany 48°11N 11°27E **131** A1
Allada Benin 6°41N 2°9E **263** D5
Allagadda India 15°8N 78°30E **245** G4
Allagash → U.S.A. 47°5N 69°3W **309** B19
Allah Dad Pakistan 25°38N 67°34E **242** G2
Allahabad India 25°25N 81°58E **243** G9
Allakaket U.S.A. 66°34N 152°39W **303** C9
Allal Tazi Morocco 34°30N 6°20W **260** B3
Allambie Heights
  Australia 33°46S 151°15E **139** A2
Allan Canada 51°53N 106°4W **297** C7
Allanche France 45°14N 2°57E **174** C6
Allanmyo Burma 19°30N 95°17E **241** F5
Allanridge S. Africa 27°45S 26°40E **270** C4
Allansford Australia 38°26S 142°39E **282** C5
Allanton N.Z. 45°55S 170°17E **285** F4
Allaqi, Wadi → Egypt 22°7N 32°47E **256** C3
Allariz Spain 42°11N 7°50W **194** C3
Allassac France 45°15N 1°29E **174** C5
Allatoona L., U.S.A. 34°10N 84°44E **316** A3
Ålleberg Sweden 58°8N 13°36E **163** F7
Allegan U.S.A. 42°32N 85°51W **311** B11
Allegany U.S.A. 42°6N 78°30W **312** D6
Alleghe Italy 46°25N 12°0E **199** B8
Allegheny → U.S.A. 40°27N 80°1W **312** F5
Allegheny Mts. U.S.A. 38°15N 80°10W **309** F13
Allegheny Plateau
  U.S.A. 41°30N 78°30W **309** E14
Allegheny Res. U.S.A. 41°50N 78°30W **312** E6
Allègre France 45°12N 3°41E **174** C7
Allègre, Pte. Guadeloupe 16°22N 61°46W **322** a
Allen Argentina 38°58S 67°50W **334** D3
Allen Queens., Australia 23°39S 146°37E **280** C4
Allen, Bog of Ireland 53°15N 7°0W **166** C5
Allen, L. Ireland 54°8N 8°4W **166** B3
Allendale U.S.A. 33°1N 81°18W **316** B8
Allende Mexico 28°20N 100°51W **318** B4
Allenstein = Olsztyn
  Poland 53°48N 20°29E **184** E7
Allentown U.S.A. 40°37N 75°29W **313** F9
Allentsteig Austria 48°41N 15°20E **142** A8
Alleppey India 9°30N 76°28E **245** K3
Allepuz Spain 40°29N 0°44W **196** E4
Aller → Germany 52°56N 9°12E **178** C5
Allermuir Hill U.K. 55°53N 3°14W **126** B2
Alleur Suriname 5°20N 54°42W **329** B7
Alleynes B. Barbados 13°13N 59°39W **323** g
Allgäu Alpen Germany 47°30N 10°20E **179** E6
Alliance Suriname 5°53N 54°45W **329** B7
Alliance Nebr., U.S.A. 42°6N 102°52W **308** E2
Alliance Ohio, U.S.A. 40°55N 81°6W **312** F3
Allier → France 46°57N 3°4E **174** B7
Allier □ France 46°25N 3°0E **174** B7
Alliford Bay Canada 53°12N 131°58W **296** C2
Alligator Pond Jamaica 17°52N 77°34W **320** a
Allinagaram India 10°2N 77°30E **245** J3
Allinge Denmark 55°17N 14°50E **163** J8
Allison U.S.A. 42°45N 92°48W **310** B4
Alliston Canada 44°9N 79°52W **312** B5
Alloa U.K. 56°7N 3°47W **167** E5
Allones France 48°20N 1°40E **172** D8
Allora Australia 28°2S 152°0E **281** D5
Allos France 44°15N 6°38E **175** D10
Alloue France 44°15N 6°38E **175** D10
Allstate Arena U.S.A. 42°1N 87°54W **119** A1
Alluitsup Paa Greenland 60°30N 45°35W **154** C6

Allur India 14°40N 80°4E **245** G5
Alluru Kottapatnam India 15°24N 80°7E **245** G5
Alma Qué., Canada 48°35N 71°40W **299** C5
Alma Ga., U.S.A. 31°33N 82°28W **316** D7
Alma Kans., U.S.A. 39°1N 96°17W **308** F5
Alma Mich., U.S.A. 43°23N 84°39W **309** D11
Alma Nebr., U.S.A. 40°6N 99°22W **308** E4
Alma Wis., U.S.A. 44°20N 91°55W **308** C8
Alma Ata = Almaty
  Kazakhstan 43°15N 76°57E **217** D9
Alma Hill U.S.A. 42°2N 78°0W **312** D7
Almacelles Spain 41°43N 0°27E **196** D5
Almada Portugal 38°41N 9°8W **126** A2
Almadén Spain 38°49N 4°52E **195** G6
Almaden Australia 17°22S 144°40E **280** B4
Almagro Argentina 34°38S 58°24W **117** B2
Almagro Spain 38°50N 3°45W **195** G7
Almansa Spain 38°51N 1°5W **197** G3
Almanor, L. U.S.A. 40°14N 121°9W **304** F3
Almansa Spain 38°51N 1°5W **197** G3
Almanzor, Pico Spain 40°15N 5°18W **194** E5
Almanzora → Spain 37°14N 1°46W **197** H3
Almaty Kazakhstan 43°15N 76°57E **217** D9
Almaty □ Kazakhstan 44°30N 78°0E **217** D9
Almazán Spain 41°30N 2°30W **196** D2
Almazora Russia 55°50N 38°3E **129** A4
Almeirim Brazil 1°30S 52°34W **329** D7
Almeirim Portugal 39°12N 8°37W **195** F2
Almelo Neths. 52°22N 6°42E **170** B6
Almenar Spain 41°43N 2°12W **196** D2
Almenar de Soria Spain 41°43N 2°12W **196** D2
Almenara Brazil 16°11S 40°42W **333** E3
Almenara Spain 39°46N 0°14W **196** F4
Almenara, Sierra de
  Spain 37°34N 1°32W **197** H3
Almendra, Embalse de
  Spain 41°10N 6°5W **194** D4
Almendralejo Spain 38°41N 6°26W **195** G4
Almere-Stad Neths. 52°20N 5°15E **170** B5
Almería Spain 36°52N 2°27W **195** J8
Almería □ Spain 37°20N 2°20W **197** H2
Almería, G. de Spain 36°41N 2°28W **197** J2
Almetyevsk Russia 54°53N 52°20E **190** C11
Älmhult Sweden 56°33N 14°8E **163** H8
Almirante Panama 9°10N 82°30W **320** E3
Almirante G. Brown, Parque
  Argentina 34°40S 58°28W **117** C2
Almirante Montt, G.
  Chile 51°52S 72°50W **336** D2
Almirópotamos Greece 38°16N 24°11E **204** C6
Almiros Greece 39°11N 22°45E **204** B4
Almodôvar Portugal 37°31N 8°2W **195** H2
Almodóvar del Campo
  Spain 38°43N 4°10W **195** G6
Almodóvar del Río Spain 37°48N 5°11W **195** H5
Almon West Bank 31°49N 35°17E **123** B2
Almond → U.S.A. 42°19N 77°44W **312** D7
Almond → U.K. 55°58N 3°18W **126** B1
Almont U.S.A. 42°55N 83°3W **312** D1
Almonte Ont., Canada 45°14N 76°12W **313** A8
Almora India 29°38N 79°40E **243** E8
Almoradi Spain 38°7N 0°46W **197** G4
Almorox Spain 40°14N 4°24W **194** E6
Almoustarat Mali 17°35N 0°8E **263** B5
Almyrou, Ormos Greece 35°23N 24°20E **207** D5
Alness U.K. 57°41N 4°16W **167** D4
Alness → U.K. 57°44N 4°16W **167** D4
Alnif Morocco 31°10N 5°8W **260** B3
Alnmouth U.K. 55°24N 1°37W **168** B6
Alnsjøen Norway 59°57N 10°51E **133** A4
Alnwick U.K. 55°24N 1°42W **168** B6
Alofau Amer. Samoa 14°16S 170°36W **302** f
Alofi Niue 19°1S 169°55W **289** g
Alofi, I. Wall. & F. Is. 14°22S 178°5W **277** C15
Alofi B. Niue 19°1S 169°55W **289** g
Aloi Uganda 2°16N 33°10E **268** B3
Alon Burma 22°12N 95°5E **241** D5
Along India 28°20N 94°46E **241** A5
Alonissos Greece 39°12N 23°50E **204** B5
Alonissos-Northern Sporades △
  Greece 39°15N 24°5E **204** B6
Alor Indonesia 8°15S 124°30E **231** F6
Alor Setar Malaysia 6°7N 100°22E **237** J3
Ålora Spain 36°49N 4°46W **195** J6
Alosno Spain 37°33N 7°7W **195** H3
Alost = Aalst Belgium 50°56N 4°2E **170** D4
Alot India 23°56N 75°40E **242** H6
Alotau Papua N. G. 10°16S 150°30E **286** F6
Alougoum Morocco 30°17N 6°56W **260** B3
Aloum Cameroon 2°16N 10°34E **264** B2
Aloysius, Mt. Australia 26°0S 128°38E **279** E4
Alpaugh U.S.A. 35°53N 119°29W **306** K7
Alpe Apuane □ Italy 44°4N 10°15E **198** D7
Alpedrinha Portugal 40°6N 7°27W **194** E3
Alpena U.S.A. 45°4N 83°27W **309** C12
Alpercatas → Brazil 6°2S 44°19W **332** D3
Alpes-de-Haute-Provence □
  France 44°8N 6°10E **175** D10
Alpes-Maritimes □
  France 43°55N 7°10E **175** E11
Alpha Queens., Australia 23°39S 146°37E **280** C4
Alpha Ill., U.S.A. 41°19N 90°23W **310** C6
Alpha Ridge Arctic 84°10N 118°0W **151** A2
Alphen aan den Rijn Neths. 52°7N 4°40E **170** B4
Alphios → Greece 37°40N 21°33E **204** D3
Alphonse Seychelles 7°0S 52°45E **273** E4
Alpiarça Portugal 39°15N 8°35W **195** F2
Alpine Ariz., U.S.A. 33°51N 109°9W **305** K9
Alpine Calif., U.S.A. 32°50N 116°46W **307** N10
Alpine N.J., U.S.A. 40°57N 73°56W **119** B5
Alpine Tex., U.S.A. 30°22N 103°40W **313** A7
Alpine △ Australia 36°56S 148°10E **283** C7
Alps Europe 46°30N 9°30E **179** C5
Alpu Turkey 39°46N 30°58E **205** B6
Alpurrulam Australia 20°59S 137°50E **280** C2
Alqueta, Barragem do 38°20N 7°25W **195** G3
Alrø Denmark 55°52N 10°5E **163** J4
Alrode S. Africa 26°17S 28°7E **123** B2
Als Denmark 54°59N 9°55E **163** K3
Alsace □ France 48°15N 7°25E **173** D14
Alsask Canada 51°21N 109°59W **297** C7
Alsasua Spain 42°54N 2°10W **196** C2
Alsek → U.S.A. 59°10N 138°12W **303** G12
Alsemberg Belgium 50°44N 4°20E **133** E4
Alsergrund Austria 48°13N 16°21E **129** E2
Asfeld Germany 50°45N 9°16E **178** E5
Alsh, L. U.K. 57°15N 5°35W **167** D3
Alsip U.S.A. 41°40N 87°44W **119** C2
Alsó → Sweden 65°58N 12°40E **160** D15
Alston U.K. 54°49N 2°25W **168** C5

Alta Finnmark, Norway 69°57N 23°10E **160** B20
Älta Sweden 59°15N 18°11E **139** B3
Alta, Sierra Spain 40°31N 1°30W **196** E3
Alta Floresta Brazil 9°57S 55°58W **331** B6
Alta Gracia Argentina 31°40S 64°30W **334** C3
Alta Sierra U.S.A. 35°42N 118°33W **307** K8
Altadena U.S.A. 34°11N 118°8W **126** A4
Altaelva → Norway 69°54N 23°17E **160** B20
Altafjorden Norway 70°5N 23°5E **160** A20
Altagracia Venezuela 10°45N 71°30W **328** A3
Altagracia de Orituco
  Venezuela 9°52N 66°23W **328** B4
Altai = Aerhtai Shan
  Mongolia 46°40N 92°45E **217** C12
Altai = Gorno-Altay □
  Russia 51°0N 86°0E **217** B11
Altamachi → Bolivia 16°8S 66°50W **330** D4
Altamaha → U.S.A. 31°20N 81°20E **308** D4
Altamira Brazil 3°12S 52°10W **329** D7
Altamira Chile 25°47S 69°51W **334** B2
Altamira Colombia 2°3N 75°47W **328** C2
Altamira Tamaulipas,
  Mexico 22°24N 97°55W **319** C5
Altamira, Cuevas de Spain 43°20N 4°4W **194** B6
Altamont N.Y., U.S.A. 42°42N 74°2W **313** D10
Altamont Oreg., U.S.A. 42°12N 121°44W **304** E3
Altamura Italy 40°49N 16°33E **201** B9
Altanbulag Mongolia 50°16N 106°30E **218** A5
Altar Mexico 30°43N 111°44W **318** A2
Altar, Gran Desierto de
  Mexico 31°50N 114°10W **318** B2
Altata Mexico 24°40N 107°55E **318** C3
Altavas Phil. 11°32N 122°29E **233** F4
Altavista U.S.A. 37°6N 79°17W **309** G13
Altay China 47°48N 88°10E **217** C11
Altdorf Switz. 46°52N 8°36E **179** J4
Alte Mellum □ Germany 53°43N 8°10E **178** B4
Altea Spain 38°38N 0°2W **197** G4
Altenberg Germany 50°45N 13°45E **178** E9
Altenbruch Germany 53°49N 8°46E **178** B4
Altenburg Germany 50°59N 12°25E **178** E8
Altenkirchen
  Mecklenburg-Vorpommern,
  Germany 54°38N 13°22E **178** A9
Altenkirchen Rhld-Pfz.,
  Germany 50°41N 7°39E **178** E3
Alter do Chão Brazil 2°31S 54°57W **329** D6
Alter do Chão Portugal 39°12N 7°40W **195** F3
Alter Finkenkrug
  Germany 52°35N 13°3E **115** A1
Altes Rathaus Munich, Germany 131 b3
Altglienicke Germany 52°25N 13°32E **115** B4
Altha U.S.A. 30°34N 85°8W **316** D4
Altınkaya Barajı Turkey 41°18N 35°30E **212** B6
Altınoluk → Turkey 39°34N 26°45E **205** B8
Altınova Turkey 39°12N 26°47E **205** B8
Altıntaş Turkey 39°4N 30°7E **205** B12
Altınyaka Turkey 36°33N 30°20E **205** D11
Altınyayla Turkey 37°0N 29°33E **205** D11
Altiplano Bolivia 17°0S 68°0W **330** D4
Altkirch France 47°37N 7°15E **173** E14
Altlandsberg Germany 52°33N 13°43E **115** A5
Altlandsberg Nord
  Germany 52°34N 13°43E **115** A5
Altmannsdorf Austria 48°9N 16°18E **142** B1
Altmark Germany 52°45N 11°58E **178** C7
Altmühl → Germany 48°54N 11°52E **179** G7
Altmühltal □ Germany 48°55N 11°15E **179** G7
Altmünster Austria 47°55N 13°45E **180** D6
Alto Adige = Trentino-Alto
  Adige □ Italy 46°30N 11°0E **199** B8
Alto Alegre Brazil 2°50N 61°20W **329** D5
Alto Araguaia Brazil 17°15S 53°20W **331** D7
Alto Chicapa Angola 10°52S 19°17E **265** E3
Alto Cuchumatanes =
  Cuchumatanes, Sierra de los
  Guatemala 15°35N 91°25W **320** C1
Alto Cuito → Angola 13°27S 18°49E **265** E3
Alto da Boa Vista Brazil 22°57S 43°16W **135** B1
Alto da Mooca Brazil 23°34S 46°33W **137** B2
Alto del Carmen Chile 28°46S 70°30W **334** B1
Alto do Pina Portugal 38°44N 9°7W **126** A2
Alto Garças Brazil 16°56S 53°30W **331** D7
Alto Irirí → Brazil 7°30S 55°0W **329** D6
Alto Ligonha Mozam. 15°30S 38°11E **269** F4
Alto Molocue Mozam. 15°50S 37°35E **269** F4
Alto Paraguai Brazil 14°30S 56°31W **331** D6
Alto Paraguay □
  Paraguay 21°0S 58°30W **334** A4
Alto Paraná □ Paraguay 25°30S 54°50W **335** B5
Alto Parnaíba Brazil 9°6S 45°57W **332** D2
Alto Purús → Peru 9°12S 70°28W **330** B3
Alto Río Senguerr
  Argentina 45°30S 70°50W **336** C2
Alto Santo Brazil 5°31S 38°15W **332** C4
Alto Sucuriú Brazil 19°15S 52°47W **331** E7
Alton Hants., U.K. 51°9N 0°59W **169** F7
Alton Ill., U.S.A. 38°53N 90°11W **310** F6
Alton N.H., U.S.A. 43°27N 71°13W **313** C13
Altona Vic., Australia 37°51S 144°49E **128** B1
Altona Man., Canada 49°6N 97°33W **297** D9
Altoona Iowa, U.S.A. 41°39N 93°28W **310** C3
Altoona Pa., U.S.A. 40°31N 78°24W **312** F6
Altos Brazil 5°3S 42°28W **332** C3
Altötting Germany 48°12N 12°39E **179** G8
Altstätten Switz. 47°22N 9°33E **179** H5
Altun Kupri Iraq 35°45N 44°9E **213** C11
Altun Shan China 38°30N 88°0E **217** C11
Alturas U.S.A. 41°29N 120°32W **304** F3
Altus U.S.A. 34°38N 99°20W **314** D5
Alubijid Phil. 8°35N 124°42E **233** G6
Alucra Turkey 40°22N 38°47E **212** B7
Aluk South Sudan 8°25N 27°36E **257** G2
Alūksne Latvia 57°24N 27°3E **188** D5
Alunda Sweden 60°4N 18°5E **162** D12
Alunite U.S.A. 35°59N 114°55W **307** K12
Aluoro → Ethiopia 6°40N 35°45E **257** F4
Alupka Ukraine 44°23N 34°2E **189** K8
Alur Gajah Malaysia 2°23N 102°13E **234** B2
Alushta Ukraine 44°40N 34°25E **189** K8
Alusi Indonesia 7°35S 131°40E **231** F8
Alustante Spain 40°36N 1°40W **196** E3
Alutgama Sri Lanka 6°26N 79°59E **245** L4
Alutnuwara Sri Lanka 7°19N 80°45E **245** L5
Aluva = Alwaye India 10°8N 76°24E **245** J3
Alva U.S.A. 36°48N 98°40W **314** C5
Alva → Portugal 40°20N 8°20W **194** E2
Alvaiázere Portugal 39°49N 8°23W **194** F2
Älvängen Sweden 57°57N 12°8E **163** G6
Alvão □ Portugal 41°20N 7°47W **194** D3
Alvarado Mexico 18°46N 95°46W **319** D5
Alvarado U.S.A. 32°24N 97°13W **314** E6
Alvaro Obregón, Presa
  Mexico 27°52N 109°52W **318** B3

Alvdal Norway 62°6N 10°37E **164** B7
Älvdalen Sweden 61°13N 14°4E **162** C7
Alvear Argentina 29°5S 56°30W **334** B4
Alverca Portugal 38°56N 9°1W **195** G1
Alvesta Sweden 56°54N 14°35E **163** H8
Alvik Sweden 59°19N 17°58E **139** B3
Alvin U.S.A. 29°26N 95°15W **314** G7
Alvin Callendar Naval Air Station
  U.S.A. 29°50N 90°1W **131** B2
Alvinston Canada 42°49N 81°52W **312** D3
Alvito Portugal 38°15N 7°58W **195** G3
Älvkarleby Sweden 60°34N 17°26E **162** D11
Alvorada Brazil 12°28S 49°6W **333** D2
Alvord Desert U.S.A. 42°30N 118°25W **304** E4
Alvros Sweden 62°3N 14°38E **162** B8
Älvsbyn Sweden 65°40N 21°0E **160** D18
Alwar India 27°38N 76°34E **242** F7
Alway India 10°8N 76°24E **245** J3
Alwaye India 10°8N 76°24E **245** J3
Alxa Zuoqi China 38°50N 105°40E **226** D3
Alyangula Australia 13°55S 136°30E **280** A2
Alyata = Älät Azerbaijan 39°58N 49°25E **191** L9
Alyth U.K. 56°38N 3°13W **167** E5
Alytus Lithuania 54°24N 24°3E **188** E3
Alzada U.S.A. 45°2N 104°25W **304** D11
Alzamay Russia 55°33N 98°39E **215** D10
Alzey Germany 49°45N 8°7E **179** F4
Alzira Spain 39°9N 0°30W **197** F4
Am Dam Chad 12°40N 20°35E **259** F4
Am Géréda Chad 12°53N 21°14E **259** F4
Am Hasenbergl Germany 48°12N 11°33E **131** A2
Am Sak Chad 13°39N 20°8E **259** F4
Am Steinhof Austria 48°12N 16°17E **142** A1
Am Timan Chad 11°0N 20°10E **259** F4
Am Wald Germany 48°3N 11°36E **131** B2
Ama Keng Singapore 1°23N 103°41E **138** A1
Amacayacu △ Colombia 3°21S 70°8W **328** D4
Amada Gaza C.A.R. 4°46N 15°9E **264** B3
Amadeus, L. Australia 24°54S 131°0E **279** D5
Amadi
  Dem. Rep. of the Congo 3°40N 26°40E **268** B2
Amādi Sudan 5°10N 30°22E **257** G2
Amadjuak L. Canada 65°0N 71°8W **295** E17
Amadora Portugal 38°45N 9°13W **126** A1
Amagansett U.S.A. 40°59N 72°9W **313** F12
Amagasaki Japan 34°42N 135°23E **133** A1
Amager Denmark 55°36N 12°35E **118** B3
Amagi Japan 33°25N 130°39E **222** D2
Amagunze Nigeria 6°20N 7°40E **263** D6
Amahai Indonesia 3°20S 128°55E **231** E7
Amaile Samoa 13°59S 171°22W **287** V20
Amaimon Papua N. G. 5°12S 145°30E **286** C3
Amaiun-Maia Spain 43°12N 1°29W **196** C3
Amakusa-Nada Japan 32°35N 130°5E **222** E2
Amakusa-Shotō Japan 32°15N 130°10E **222** E2
Amal Oman 18°21N 55°39E **249** C6
Āmāl Sweden 59°3N 12°42E **163** G6
Amal Qādisiya Iraq 33°16N 44°20E **113** B2
Amalapuram India 16°35N 81°55E **245** E5
Amalfi Colombia 6°55N 75°4W **328** B2
Amalfi Italy 40°38N 14°36E **201** B7
Amaliada Greece 37°47N 21°22E **204** D3
Amalias = Amaliada
  Greece 37°47N 21°22E **204** D3
Amalner India 21°5N 75°5E **244** D2
Amambaí Brazil 23°5S 55°13W **335** A4
Amambaí → Paraguay 23°22S 53°56W **335** A5
Amambay □ Paraguay 23°0S 56°0W **335** A4
Amambay, Cordillera de
  S. Amer. 23°0S 55°45W **335** A4
Amami-Guntō Japan 27°16N 129°21E **221** L4
Amami-Ō-Shima Japan 28°16N 129°21E **221** L4
Amana → Venezuela 9°36N 62°42W **328** B6
Amaná, L. Brazil 2°35S 64°40W **329** D5
Amanab Papua N. G. 3°40S 141°14E **286** B1
Amanat → India 24°7N 84°4E **243** G11
Amandave Amer. Samoa 14°20S 170°50W **302** f
Amanda Park U.S.A. 47°28N 123°55W **306** C3
Amankeldi Kazakhstan 50°10N 65°10E **217** B7
Amantea Italy 39°8N 16°4E **201** C9
Amanu French Polynesia 17°48S 140°46W **289** f
Amapá Brazil 2°5N 50°50W **329** D7
Amapá □ Brazil 1°40N 52°0W **329** D7
Amapari = Ferreira Gomes
  Brazil 0°48N 51°8W **329** D7
Amapari Brazil 0°51N 51°39W **329** D7
Amara Sudan 10°25N 34°10E **257** E3
Amara → Ethiopia 12°30N 37°30E **257** E4
Amaração = Luís Correia
  Brazil 3°0S 41°35W **332** B3
Amarante Brazil 6°14S 42°50W **332** D3
Amarante Portugal 41°16N 8°5W **194** D2
Amarante do Maranhão
  Brazil 5°36S 46°45W **332** D2
Amaranth Canada 50°36N 98°43W **297** C9
Amarapura Burma 21°54N 96°3E **241** E6
Amaravati → India 11°0N 78°15E **245** J3
Amareleja Portugal 38°12N 7°13W **195** G3
Amargosa Brazil 13°2S 39°36W **333** D4
Amargosa → U.S.A. 36°14N 116°51W **307** J10
Amargosa Desert
  U.S.A. 36°40N 116°40W **307** J10
Amargosa Range
  U.S.A. 36°20N 116°45W **307** J10
Amári Greece 35°13N 24°40E **207** D5
Amarillo U.S.A. 35°13N 101°50W **314** D4
Amarkantak India 22°40N 81°45E **243** H9
Amârna, Tell el' Egypt 27°38N 30°52E **256** F8
Amarnath India 19°12N 73°22E **244** E1
Amaro, Mte. Italy 42°5N 14°5E **199** F11
Amarpur Bihar, India 25°5N 87°0E **243** G12
Amarpur Tripura, India 23°31N 91°39E **243** H14
Amarti Eritrea 14°17N 41°6E **257** E5
Amarwara India 22°18N 79°10E **243** H8
Amasin W. Sahara 25°45N 13°20W **260** C2
Amasra Turkey 41°45N 32°23E **212** B5
Amassama Nigeria 5°1N 6°2E **263** D6
Amasya Turkey 40°40N 35°50E **212** B6
Amasya □ Turkey 40°40N 35°50E **212** B6
Amata S. Austral., Australia 26°9S 131°9E **279** E5
Amatikulu S. Africa 29°3S 31°33E **271** B5
Amatitlán Guatemala 14°29N 90°38W **320** D1
Amatrice Italy 42°38N 13°17E **199** F10
Amau Papua N. G. 10°2S 148°34E **286** F5
Amay Belgium 50°33N 5°19E **170** D5
Amazon = Amazonas →
  S. Amer. 0°5S 50°0W **329** D8
Amazonas □ Brazil 5°0S 65°0W **329** E5
Amazonas □ Colombia 1°0S 72°0W **328** D4
Amazonas □ Peru 5°0S 78°0W **330** B2
Amazonas □ Venezuela 3°30N 66°0W **328** C5
Amazonas → S. Amer. 0°5S 50°0W **329** D8
Amba Ferit Ethiopia 10°55N 38°50E **257** E4
Ambad India 19°38N 75°50E **244** E2
Ambagarh Chowki India 20°47N 80°43E **244** D4
Ambah India 26°43N 78°13E **242** F8
Ambahakily Madag. 21°36S 43°41E **272** C1
Ambahita Madag. 24°1S 45°16E **272** C2
Ambajogai India 18°43N 76°56E **244** E3
Ambala India 30°23N 76°56E **242** D7
Ambalangoda Sri Lanka 6°15N 80°5E **245** L5

Ambalapulai India 9°25N 76°25E 245 K3
Ambalavao Madag. 21°50S 46°56E 272 C2
Ambam Cameroon 2°20N 11°15E 264 B2
Ambanja Madag. 13°40S 48°27E 272 A2
Ambararata Madag. 15°3S 48°33E 272 B2
Ambarchik Russia 69°40N 162°20E 215 C17
Ambarijeby Madag. 14°56S 47°41E 272 A2
Ambaro, Helodranon' Madag. 13°23S 48°38E 272 A2
Ambasamudram India 8°43N 77°25E 245 K3
Ambato Ecuador 1°5S 78°42W 328 D2
Ambato Madag. 13°24S 48°29E 272 A2
Ambato, Sierra de Argentina 28°25S 66°10W 334 B2
Ambato Boeny Madag. 16°28S 46°43E 272 B2
Ambatofinandrahana Madag. 20°33S 46°48E 272 C2
Ambatolampy Madag. 19°20S 47°35E 272 B2
Ambatomainty Madag. 17°41S 45°40E 272 B2
Ambatomanoina Madag. 18°18S 47°37E 272 B2
Ambatondrazaka Madag. 17°55S 48°28E 272 B2
Ambatosoratra Madag. 17°37S 48°31E 272 B2
Ambelokipi Greece 37°58N 23°47E 112 B2
Ambelonas Greece 39°45N 22°22E 204 B4
Ambenja Madag. 15°17S 46°58E 272 B2
Amberg Germany 49°26N 11°52E 179 F7
Ambergris Cay Belize 18°0N 87°55W 320 C2
Ambérieu-en-Bugey France 45°57N 5°20E 175 C9
Amberley Ont., Canada 44°2N 81°42W 312 B3
Amberley N.Z. 43°9S 172°44E 285 D7
Ambert France 45°33N 3°44E 174 C7
Ambidédi Mali 14°35N 11°47W 262 C2
Ambikapur India 23°15N 83°15E 243 H10
Ambikol Sudan 21°20N 30°50E 256 C3
Ambilobé Madag. 13°10S 49°3E 272 A2
Ambinanindrano Madag. 20°5S 48°23E 272 C2
Ambinanitelo Madag. 15°21S 49°35E 272 B2
Ambinda Madag. 16°25S 45°52E 272 B2
Ambitle I. Papua N. G. 4°5S 153°37E 286 C7
Amble U.K. 55°20N 1°36W 168 B6
Ambler U.S.A. 67°5N 157°52W 303 C8
Ambleside U.K. 54°26N 2°58W 168 C5
Ambo Peru 10°5S 76°10W 330 C2
Amboahangy Madag. 24°15S 46°22E 272 C2
Amboasary Madag. 25°1S 46°45E 272 D2
Ambodifototra Madag. 16°59S 49°52E 272 B2
Ambodilazana Madag. 18°6S 49°10E 272 B2
Ambodiriana Madag. 17°55S 49°18E 272 B2
Ambohidratrimo Madag. 18°50S 47°26E 272 B2
Ambohidray Madag. 18°36S 48°18E 272 B2
Ambohimahamasina Madag. 21°56S 47°11E 272 C2
Ambohimahasoa Madag. 21°7S 47°13E 272 C2
Ambohimanga Madag. 20°52S 47°36E 272 C2
Ambohimitombo Madag. 20°43S 47°26E 272 C2
Ambohitra Madag. 12°30S 49°10E 272 A2
Amboise France 47°24N 1°2E 172 E8
Amboiva Angola 11°33S 14°43E 265 E2
Ambon Indonesia 3°43S 128°12E 231 E7
Ambondro Madag. 25°13S 45°44E 272 D2
Amboró △ Bolivia 17°39S 64°3W 331 D5
Amboseli, L. Kenya 2°40S 37°10E 268 C4
Amboseli △ Kenya 2°37S 37°13E 268 C4
Ambositra Madag. 20°31S 47°25E 272 C2
Ambovombe Madag. 25°11S 46°5E 272 D2
Amboy Calif., U.S.A. 34°33N 115°45W 307 L11
Amboy Ill., U.S.A. 41°44N 89°20W 310 C7
Amboyna Cay S. China Sea 7°50N 112°50E 230 C4
Ambre, Île d' Mauritius 20°2S 57°41E 272 e
Ambridge U.S.A. 40°36N 80°14W 312 F4
Ambriz Angola 7°48S 13°8E 265 D2
Ambriz ⌓ Angola 7°56S 10°27E 265 D2
Ambrolauri Georgia 42°31N 43°9E 213 A10
Ambrym Vanuatu 16°15S 168°10E 287 F6
Ambunti Papua N. G. 4°13S 142°52E 286 C2
Ambur India 12°48N 78°43E 245 H4
Amchitka I. U.S.A. 51°32N 179°0E 303 L2
Amderma Russia 69°45N 61°30E 214 C7
Amdhi India 23°51N 81°27E 243 H9
Ameca Mexico 20°33N 104°2W 318 C4
Ameca → Mexico 20°41N 105°18W 318 C3
Amecameca de Juárez Mexico 19°8N 98°46W 319 D5
Ameixoeira Portugal 38°46N 9°8W 126 A2
Ameland Neths. 53°27N 5°45E 170 A5
Amélia Italy 42°33N 12°25E 199 F9
Amelia City U.S.A. 30°35N 81°28W 316 E8
Amelia I. U.S.A. 30°40N 81°25W 316 E8
Amendolara Italy 39°57N 16°35E 201 C9
Amenia U.S.A. 41°51N 73°33W 313 E11
América Brazil 23°35S 46°41W 137 B1
America-Antarctica Ridge S. Ocean 59°0S 16°0W 151 B2
American Falls U.S.A. 42°47N 112°51W 304 E7
American Falls Res. U.S.A. 42°47N 112°52W 304 E7
American Fork U.S.A. 40°23N 111°48W 304 F8
American Highland Antarctica 73°0S 75°0E 151 D6
American Indian Museum Washington, D.C., U.S.A. 143 b3
American Museum of Natural History New York, U.S.A. 132 b2
American Police Hall of Fame U.S.A. 25°49N 80°11W 128 B2
American River Australia 35°47S 137°46E 282 C2
American Samoa ⊠ Pac. Oc. 14°20S 170°0W 302 f
American Samoa △ Amer. Samoa 14°15S 170°28W 302 g
American Univ. U.S.A. 38°56N 77°15W 143 B3
Americana Brazil 22°45S 47°20W 335 A6
Americus U.S.A. 32°4N 84°14W 316 C5
Amerigo Vespucci, Firenze ✈ (FLR) Italy 43°49N 11°13E 199 E8
Amerika = Nakhodka Russia 42°53N 132°54E 220 C6
Amersfoort Neths. 52°9N 5°23E 170 B5
Amersfoort Mpumalanga, S. Africa 26°59S 29°53E 271 C4
Amery Basin S. Ocean 68°15S 74°30E 151 C6
Amery Ice Shelf Antarctica 69°30S 72°0E 151 C6
Amerzgane Morocco 31°4N 7°14W 260 B3
Ames = Bertamirans Spain 42°54N 8°38W 194 C2
Ames U.S.A. 42°2N 93°37W 310 C3
Amesbury U.S.A. 42°51N 70°56W 313 D14
Amet India 25°18N 73°56E 242 G5
Amfiklia Greece 38°38N 22°35E 204 C4
Amfilochia Greece 38°52N 21°9E 204 C3
Amfipoli Greece 40°48N 23°52E 202 F7
Amfissa Greece 38°32N 22°22E 204 C4
Amga Russia 60°50N 132°0E 215 C14
Amga → Russia 62°38N 134°32E 215 C14
Amgaon India 21°22N 80°22E 244 D5
Amgu Russia 45°45N 137°15E 220 B8
Amguid Algeria 26°26N 5°22E 261 C6
Amgun → Russia 52°56N 139°38E 215 D14
Amherst = Kyaikkami Burma 16°4N 97°34E 241 G6
Amherst N.S., Canada 45°48N 64°8W 299 C7
Amherst Mass., U.S.A. 42°23N 72°31W 313 D12
Amherst N.Y., U.S.A. 42°59N 78°48W 312 D6
Amherst Ohio, U.S.A. 41°24N 82°14W 312 E2
Amherst I. Canada 44°8N 76°43W 313 B8
Amherstburg Canada 42°6N 83°6W 311 B13
Amiata, Mte. Italy 42°53N 11°37E 199 F8
Amidon U.S.A. 46°29N 103°19W 308 B2
Amiens France 49°54N 2°16E 173 C9
Amik Gölü Turkey 36°22N 36°17E 250 B7
Amili India 28°25N 95°52E 241 A5
Amin Iraq 33°19N 44°29E 113 B2
Aminadav Israel 31°45N 35°8E 123 B1
Amindeo Greece 40°42N 21°42E 202 F5
Amindivi Is. India 11°23N 72°23E 245 J1
Amingaon India 26°11N 91°40E 241 B3
Amini I. India 11°6N 72°45E 245 J1
Åminne Sweden 57°7N 14°0E 163 G7
Amino Ethiopia 4°25N 41°52E 257 G5
Aminuis Namibia 23°43S 19°21E 270 B2
Aminyevo Russia 55°41N 37°25E 129 B2
Āmir, Ra's Libya 32°57N 21°43E 258 B4
Amīrābād Īlām, Iran 33°20N 46°16E 246 C5
Amīrābād Tehrān, Iran 35°43N 51°24E 141 A2
Amirante Is. Seychelles 6°0S 53°0E 210 J7
Amisk ⌓ Canada 56°43N 98°0W 297 B9
Amisk L. Canada 54°35N 102°15W 297 C8
Amistad, Presa de la Mexico 29°26N 101°3W 318 B4
Amistad ⌓ U.S.A. 29°32N 101°12W 314 G4
Amite U.S.A. 30°44N 90°30W 315 F9
Amizmiz Morocco 31°12N 8°15W 260 B3
Amla India 21°56N 78°7E 242 J8
Amlapura = Karangasem Indonesia 8°27S 115°37E 231 J18
Åmli Norway 58°45N 8°32E 164 F5
Amlia I. U.S.A. 52°4N 173°30W 303 K4
Amlwch U.K. 53°24N 4°20W 168 D3
Amm Adam Sudan 16°20N 36°1E 257 D4
'Ammān Jordan 31°57N 35°52E 251 G6
'Ammān □ Jordan 31°40N 36°30E 251 G7
Ammanford U.K. 51°48N 3°59W 169 F4
Ammassalik = Tasiilaq Greenland 65°40N 37°20W 154 D7
Ammerån → Sweden 63°9N 16°13E 162 A10
Ammersee Germany 48°0N 11°7E 179 G7
Ammochostos = Famagusta Cyprus 35°8N 33°55E 207 E9
Ammon U.S.A. 43°28N 111°58W 304 E8
Amnat Charoen Thailand 15°51N 104°38E 236 E5
Amnura Bangla. 24°37N 88°25E 243 G13
Amo Jiang → China 23°0N 101°50E 228 F3
Āmol Iran 36°23N 52°20E 247 B7
Amora Portugal 38°37N 9°6W 126 B2
Amoreira Portugal 38°48N 9°11W 126 A1
Amoret U.S.A. 38°15N 94°35W 310 F2
Amorgos Greece 36°50N 25°57E 205 E7
Amory U.S.A. 33°59N 88°29W 315 E10
Amos Canada 48°35N 78°5W 298 C4
Åmot Buskerud, Norway 59°57N 9°54E 164 E6
Åmot Oppland, Norway 61°0N 10°2E 164 D7
Åmot Telemark, Norway 59°34N 8°0E 164 E5
Åmotfors Sweden 59°47N 12°22E 162 E6
Åmotsdal Norway 59°37N 8°26E 164 E5
Amour, Djebel Algeria 33°42N 1°37E 261 B5
Amoy = Xiamen China 24°25N 118°4E 229 E12
Ampanavoana Madag. 15°41S 50°22E 272 B3
Ampang Malaysia 3°8N 101°45E 237 L3
Ampangalana, Lakandranon' Madag. 22°48S 47°50E 272 C2
Ampani India 19°35N 82°38E 244 E6
Ampanihy Madag. 24°40S 44°45E 272 C1
Amparafaravola Madag. 17°35S 48°13E 272 B2
Ampasinambo Madag. 20°31S 48°0E 272 C2
Ampasindava, Helodranon' Madag. 13°40S 48°15E 272 A2
Ampasindava, Saikanosy Madag. 13°42S 47°55E 272 A2
Ampato, Nevado Peru 15°40S 71°56W 330 D3
Ampenan Indonesia 8°34S 116°4E 231 K18
Amper Nigeria 9°25N 9°40E 263 D6
Amper → Bayern, Germany 48°29N 11°55E 179 G7
Amper → Oberbayern, Germany 48°14N 11°25E 131 A1
Ampezzo Italy 46°25N 12°48E 199 B9
Amphoe Kathu Thailand 7°55N 98°21E 237 a
Amphoe Thalang Thailand 8°1N 98°20E 237 a
Ampitsikinana Madag. 12°57S 49°49E 272 A2
Ampombiantambo Madag. 12°42S 48°57E 272 A2
Amposta Spain 40°43N 0°34E 196 E5
Ampotaka Madag. 25°3S 44°41E 272 D1
Ampoza Madag. 22°20S 44°44E 272 C1
Amqui Canada 48°28N 67°27W 299 C6
Amrabad India 16°23N 78°50E 245 F4
'Amrān Yemen 15°41N 43°55E 248 D3
Amraoti = Amravati India 20°55N 77°45E 244 D3
Amravati India 20°55N 77°45E 244 D3
Amreli India 21°35N 71°17E 242 J4
Amrenene el Kasba Algeria 22°10N 0°30E 261 D5
Amritsar India 31°35N 74°57E 242 D6
Amroha India 28°53N 78°30E 243 E8
Amrum Germany 54°38N 8°22E 178 A4
Amsâga Mauritania 20°7N 14°10W 260 D2
Amsel Algeria 22°47N 5°29E 261 D6
Amstel Amsterdam, Neths. 112 b2
Amstel → Amsterdam, Neths. 112 b3
Amstel-Drecht-Kanaal Neths. 52°18N 4°54E 112 B2
Amstelveen Neths. 52°18N 4°51E 112 B2
Amsterdam Neths. 52°23N 4°54E 112 A2
Amsterdam N.Y., U.S.A. 42°56N 74°11W 313 D10
Amsterdam ✈ (AMS) Neths. 52°18N 4°45E 112 B1
Amsterdam, I. = Nouvelle Amsterdam, Î. Ind. Oc. 38°30S 77°30E 273 H6
Amsterdam-Rijnkanaal Neths. 51°53N 5°28E 112 B3
Amsterdam Zuidoost Neths. 52°18N 4°58E 112 B2
Amsterdamse Bos Neths. 52°19N 4°50E 112 B1
Amstetten Austria 48°7N 14°51E 180 C7
'Amūdah Syria 37°6N 40°55E 213 D9
Amudarya Turkmenistan 37°53N 65°15E 216 E7
Amudarya → Uzbekistan 43°58N 59°34E 216 D5
Amukta I. U.S.A. 52°30N 171°16W 303 K5
Amukta Pass U.S.A. 52°0N 171°0W 303 K5
Amulung Phil. 17°50N 121°43E 232 C3
Amund Ringnes I. Canada 78°20N 96°25W 295 B12
Amundsen Abyssal Plain S. Ocean 65°0S 125°0W 151 C14
Amundsen Basin Arctic 87°30N 80°0E 150 A
Amundsen Gulf Canada 71°0N 124°0W 294 C7
Amundsen Ridges S. Ocean 69°15S 123°0W 151 C14
Amundsen-Scott Antarctica 90°0S 166°0E 151 E
Amundsen Sea Antarctica 72°0S 115°0W 151 D15
Amungen Sweden 61°10N 15°40E 162 C9
Amuntai Indonesia 2°28S 115°25E 235 C5
Amur → Russia 52°56N 141°10E 215 D15
Amur, W. → Sudan 18°56N 33°34E 256 D3
Amurang Indonesia 1°5N 124°40E 231 D6
Amurrio Spain 43°3N 3°0W 196 B1
Amursk Russia 50°14N 136°54E 215 D14
Amusco Spain 42°10N 4°28W 194 C6
Amvrakikos Kolpos Greece 39°0N 20°55E 204 C2
Amvrosiyivka Ukraine 47°43N 38°30E 189 J10
Amyderya = Amudarya → Uzbekistan 43°58N 59°34E 216 D5
An Burma 19°48N 94°0E 241 F5
An Bien Vietnam 9°45N 105°0E 237 H5
An Cabhán = Cavan Ireland 54°0N 7°22W 166 B4
An Cóbh = Cóbh Ireland 51°51N 8°17W 166 E3
An Daingean = Dingle Ireland 52°9N 10°17W 166 D1
An Hoa Vietnam 15°40N 108°5E 236 E7
An Longfort = Longford Ireland 53°43N 7°49W 166 C4
An Muileann gCearr = Mullingar Ireland 53°31N 7°21W 166 C4
An Nabatīyah at Tahta Lebanon 33°23N 35°27E 250 E6
An Nabk Si. Arabia 31°20N 37°20E 246 D3
An Nabk Syria 34°2N 36°44E 250 D7
An Nafūd Si. Arabia 28°15N 41°0E 246 D4
An Nāḩīyah Iraq 34°26N 41°33E 213 E9
An Najaf Iraq 32°3N 44°15E 213 G11
An Namāş Si. Arabia 19°7N 42°8E 248 C3
An Nás = Naas Ireland 53°12N 6°40W 166 C5
An Nāşirīyah Iraq 31°0N 46°15E 246 D5
An Nawfaliyah Libya 30°54N 17°58E 258 B3
An Nhon Vietnam 13°55N 109°7E 236 F7
An Nîl □ Sudan 19°30N 33°0E 256 D3
An Nîl el Abyad □ Sudan 14°0N 32°15E 257 E3
An Nîl el Azraq □ Sudan 11°30N 34°30E 257 E3
An Nu'ayrīyah Si. Arabia 27°30N 48°30E 247 E6
An Nu'mānīyah Iraq 32°32N 45°25E 213 F11
An Nuqat Alkhams □ Libya 32°42N 11°57E 261 B7
An Ros = Rush Ireland 53°31N 6°6W 166 C5
An tAonach = Nenagh Ireland 52°52N 8°11W 166 D3
An Thoi, Dao Vietnam 9°58N 104°0E 237 H5
An tInbhear Mór = Arklow Ireland 52°48N 6°10W 166 D5
An Uaimh Ireland 53°39N 6°41W 166 C5
Åna-Sira Norway 58°17N 6°25E 164 F3
Anaa French Polynesia 17°25S 145°30W 289 f
Anabar → Russia 73°8N 113°36E 215 B12
Anaco Venezuela 9°27N 64°28W 329 B5
Anaconda U.S.A. 46°8N 112°57W 304 C7
Anacortes U.S.A. 48°30N 122°37W 306 B4
Anacosta → U.S.A. 38°52N 77°1W 143 B4
Anacostia U.S.A. 38°51N 76°59W 143 B4
Anacuao, Mt. Phil. 16°16N 121°53E 232 C3
Anadarko U.S.A. 35°4N 98°15W 314 D5
Anadia Brazil 9°42S 36°18W 332 C4
Anadia Portugal 40°26N 8°27W 194 E2
Anadolu Turkey 39°0N 30°0E 212 C5
Anadoluhisarı Turkey 41°4N 29°3E 122 B2
Anadolukavağı Turkey 41°10N 29°7E 122 A2
Anadyr Russia 64°35N 177°20E 215 C18
Anadyr → Russia 64°55N 176°5E 215 C18
Anadyrskiy Zaliv Russia 64°0N 180°0E 215 C19
Anafi Greece 36°22N 25°48E 205 E7
Anafonitria Greece 37°51N 20°39E 207 D2
Anaga, Pta. de Canary Is. 28°34N 16°9W 153 e1
Anagni Italy 41°44N 13°9E 199 G10
'Ānah Iraq 34°25N 42°0E 213 E10
Anaheim U.S.A. 33°50N 117°55W 307 M9
Anahim Lake Canada 52°28N 125°18W 296 C3
Anahola U.S.A. 22°9N 159°19W 302 A2
'Anahulu → U.S.A. 21°37N 158°6W 302 J13
Anai Mudi India 10°12N 77°4E 245 J3
Anaichak ⌓ U.S.A. 56°50N 158°15W 303 H8
Anaimalai Hills India 10°20N 76°40E 245 J3
Anajás Brazil 0°59S 49°57W 332 B2
Anajatuba Brazil 3°16S 44°37W 332 B3
Anakao Madag. 23°40S 43°39E 272 C1
Anakapalle India 17°42N 83°6E 244 F6
Anakena Chile 27°5S 109°20W 330 b
Anakie Australia 23°32S 147°45E 280 C4
Anaklia Georgia 42°22N 41°35E 191 J5
Anaktuvuk Pass U.S.A. 68°8N 151°45W 303 B10
Analalava Madag. 14°35S 48°0E 272 A2
Analavoka Madag. 22°23S 46°30E 272 C2
Analipsis Greece 39°36N 19°55E 206 B9
Anamã Brazil 3°35S 61°22W 329 D5
Anambar → Pakistan 30°15N 68°50E 242 D3
Anambas, Kepulauan Indonesia 3°20N 106°30E 234 B3
Anambas Is. = Anambas, Kepulauan Indonesia 3°20N 106°30E 234 B3
Anambra □ Nigeria 6°20N 7°0E 263 D6
Aname Vanuatu 20°8S 169°47E 287 K7
Anamosa U.S.A. 42°7N 91°17W 310 B5
Anamur Turkey 36°8N 32°58E 250 B3
Anamur → Turkey 36°5N 32°53E 250 B3
Anamur Burnu Turkey 36°2N 32°47E 250 B3
Anan Japan 33°54N 134°40E 222 D6
Anand India 22°32N 72°59E 242 H5
Anandapuram India 14°5N 75°12E 245 G2
Anandpur India 21°16N 86°13E 244 D8
Ananes Greece 36°33N 24°9E 204 E6
Anangu Pitjantjatjara ☼ Australia 27°0S 132°0E 279 E5
Anantapur India 14°39N 77°42E 245 G3
Anantnag India 33°45N 75°10E 243 C6
Ananyiv Ukraine 47°44N 29°58E 183 C14
Anapa Russia 44°55N 37°25E 189 K9
Anapodiaris → Greece 34°59N 25°20E 207 F6
Anápolis = Simão Dias Brazil 10°44S 37°49W 332 D4
Anápolis Brazil 16°15S 48°50W 333 E2
Anapu → Brazil 1°53S 50°53W 329 D7
Anār Iran 30°55N 55°13E 247 D7
Anār Darreh Afghan. 32°46N 61°39E 240 B1
Anārak Iran 33°25N 53°40E 247 C7
Anarisfjällen Sweden 63°6N 13°10E 162 A7
Anas → India 23°26N 74°0E 242 H5
Añasco Puerto Rico 18°17N 67°8W 321 b
Anata West Bank 31°49N 35°16E 123 B2
Anatahan N. Marianas 16°21N 145°40E 302 a
Anatolia = Anadolu Turkey 39°0N 30°0E 212 C5
Anatsogno Madag. 23°33S 43°46E 272 C1
Añatuya Argentina 28°20S 62°50W 334 B3
Anatye ☼ Australia 22°29S 137°3E 280 C2
Anauá → Brazil 0°58N 61°21W 329 C5
Anaunethad L. Canada 60°55N 104°25W 297 A8
Anavilhanas, Arquipélago das Brazil 2°42S 60°45W 329 D5
Anbyŏn N. Korea 39°1N 127°35E 224 C3
Ancares, Sierra dos Spain 42°51N 6°52W 194 C4
Ancares ⌓ Spain 42°50N 6°40W 194 C4
Ancash □ Peru 9°30S 77°45W 330 B2
Ancaster Canada 43°13N 79°59W 312 C5
Ancenis France 47°21N 1°10W 172 E5
Anchieta = Piatã Brazil 13°9S 41°48W 333 D3
Anch'ing = Anqing China 30°30N 117°3E 229 B11
Ancho, Canal Chile 50°0S 74°20W 336 D2
Anchor Bay U.S.A. 38°48N 123°34W 306 G3
Anchorage U.S.A. 61°13N 149°54W 303 F10
Anchorage ✈ (ANC) U.S.A. 61°10N 150°0W 303 F10
Anci China 39°20N 116°40E 226 E9
Ancohuma, Nevado Bolivia 16°0S 68°50W 330 D4
Ancol Indonesia 6°7S 106°49E 122 A1
Ancón Peru 11°50S 77°10W 330 C2
Ancona Italy 43°38N 13°30E 199 E10
Ancud Chile 42°0S 73°50W 336 B2
Ancud, G. de Chile 42°0S 73°0W 336 B2
Ancy-le-Franc France 47°46N 4°10E 173 E11
Anda Heilongjiang, China 46°24N 125°19E 219 B7
Anda Phil. 16°17N 119°57E 232 C2
Andacollo Argentina 37°10S 70°42W 334 D1
Andacollo Chile 30°14S 71°6W 334 C1
Andahuaylas Peru 13°40S 73°25W 330 C3
Andaingo Madag. 18°12S 48°17E 272 B2
Andalgalá Argentina 27°40S 66°30W 334 B2
Åndalsnes Norway 62°35N 7°43E 164 B4
Andalucía □ Spain 37°35N 5°0W 195 H6
'Andalus Iraq 33°19N 44°18E 113 B1
Andalusia = Andalucía □ Spain 37°35N 5°0W 195 H6
Andalusia U.S.A. 31°18N 86°29W 315 F11
Andaman & Nicobar Is. □ India 10°0N 93°0E 245 K11
Andaman Is. Ind. Oc. 12°30N 92°45E 245 H11
Andaman Sea Ind. Oc. 13°0N 96°0E 230 B1
Andamooka Australia 30°27S 137°9E 281 E2
Andapa Madag. 14°39S 49°39E 272 A2
Andara Namibia 18°2S 21°9E 270 A3
Andaraí Bahia, Brazil 12°48S 41°20W 333 D3
Andaraí Rio de J., Brazil 22°56S 43°14W 135 B1
Andelot-Blancheville France 48°15N 5°18E 173 D12
Andenes Norway 69°19N 16°18E 160 B17
Andenne Belgium 50°28N 5°5E 170 D5
Andéranboukane Mali 15°26N 3°2E 263 B5
Anderlecht Belgium 50°50N 4°19E 116 A1
Andermatt Switz. 46°38N 8°35E 179 J4
Andernach Germany 50°26N 7°24E 178 E3
Andernos-les-Bains France 44°44N 1°6W 174 D2
Andersen Air Force Base Guam 13°35N 144°55E 302 d
Anderslöv Sweden 55°26N 13°19E 163 J7
Anderson Vic., Australia 38°31S 145°26E 283 E6
Anderson Alaska, U.S.A. 64°25N 149°15W 303 D10
Anderson Calif., U.S.A. 40°27N 122°18W 304 F2
Anderson Ind., U.S.A. 40°10N 85°41W 311 D11
Anderson Mo., U.S.A. 36°39N 94°27W 308 G6
Anderson S.C., U.S.A. 34°31N 82°39W 315 D13
Anderson → Canada 69°42N 129°0W 294 D6
Anderson I. India 12°46N 92°43E 245 H11
Anderson Park U.S.A. 33°45N 84°27W 113 B2
Andersonville U.S.A. 32°12N 84°9W 316 C5
Andersonville ⌓ U.S.A. 32°12N 84°1W 316 C5
Anderstorp Sweden 57°19N 13°39E 163 G7
Andes Colombia 5°39N 75°54W 328 B2
Andes N.Y., U.S.A. 42°12N 74°47W 313 D10
Andes, Cord. de los S. Amer. 20°0S 68°0W 330 E4
Andfjorden Norway 69°10N 16°20E 160 B17
Andhra, L. India 18°54N 73°32E 244 E1
Andhra Pradesh □ India 18°0N 79°0E 244 F4
Andijon Uzbekistan 41°10N 72°15E 217 D8
Andijon □ Uzbekistan 40°45N 72°20E 217 D8
Andikíthira = Antikythira Greece 35°52N 23°15E 204 F5
Andilamena Madag. 17°1S 48°35E 272 B2
Andīmeshk Iran 32°27N 48°21E 213 F13
Andímilos = Antimilos Greece 36°47N 24°12E 204 E6
Andingmen China 39°55N 116°23E 114 B2
Andíparos = Antiparos Greece 37°0N 25°3E 205 D7
Andípaxoi = Antipaxi Greece 39°9N 20°13E 204 B2
Andipsara Greece 38°30N 25°29E 205 C7
Andizhan = Andijon Uzbekistan 41°10N 72°15E 217 D8
Andkhvoy Afghan. 36°52N 65°8E 240 A2
Andoain Spain 43°13N 2°1W 196 B2
Andoany Madag. 13°25S 48°16E 272 A2
Andoas Peru 2°55S 76°25W 328 D2
Andohahela ⌓ Madag. 24°4S 46°44E 272 C2
Andol India 17°51N 78°4E 244 F4
Andola India 16°57N 76°50E 244 F3
Andong S. Korea 36°40N 128°43E 224 D4
Andongwei China 35°6N 119°20E 227 G10
Andorra Spain 40°59N 0°28W 196 E4
Andorra ■ Europe 42°30N 1°30E 174 F5
Andorra La Vella Andorra 42°31N 1°32E 174 F5
Andover Hants., U.K. 51°12N 1°29W 169 F6
Andover Maine, U.S.A. 44°38N 70°45W 313 B14
Andover Mass., U.S.A. 42°40N 71°8W 313 D13
Andover N.J., U.S.A. 40°59N 74°45W 313 F10
Andover N.Y., U.S.A. 42°10N 77°48W 312 D7
Andover Ohio, U.S.A. 41°36N 80°34W 312 E4
Andøya Norway 69°10N 15°50E 160 B16
Andrade Brazil 4°40S 63°45W 329 D5
Andradina Brazil 20°54S 51°23W 333 F1
Andrahary Madag. 13°37S 49°17E 272 A2
Andramasina Madag. 19°11S 47°35E 272 B2
Andranopasy Madag. 21°17S 43°44E 272 C1
Andranovory Madag. 23°8S 44°10E 272 C1
Andratx Spain 39°39N 2°25E 206 B3
André Félix △ C.A.R. 9°29N 23°18E 264 A4
Andreanof Is. U.S.A. 51°30N 176°0W 303 L4
Andreapol Russia 56°40N 32°17E 188 D7
Andrée Land Greenland 73°40N 26°0W 154 C8
Andrews S.C., U.S.A. 33°27N 79°34W 315 E15
Andrews Tex., U.S.A. 32°19N 102°33W 314 E3
Andreyev = Jędrzejów Poland 50°35N 20°15E 185 H7
Andreyevka Russia 52°19N 51°55E 190 D10
Ándria Italy 41°13N 16°17E 201 A9
Andriamena Madag. 17°26S 47°30E 272 B2
Andriandampy Madag. 22°45S 45°41E 272 C2
Andriba Madag. 17°30S 46°58E 272 B2
Andrijevica Montenegro 42°45N 19°48E 202 D3
Andringitra ⌓ Madag. 22°13S 46°5E 272 C2
Andritsena Greece 37°29N 21°52E 204 D3
Androka Madag. 24°58S 44°2E 272 C1
Andropov = Rybinsk Russia 58°5N 38°50E 188 C10
Andros Greece 37°50N 24°57E 204 D6
Andros I. Bahamas 24°30N 78°0W 320 B4
Andros Town Bahamas 24°43N 77°47W 320 B4
Androscoggin → U.S.A. 43°58N 69°52W 313 C14
Androth I. India 10°50N 73°41E 245 J1
Andrychów Poland 49°51N 19°18E 185 J6
Andselv Norway 69°4N 18°34E 160 B18
Andújar Spain 38°3N 4°5W 195 G6
Andulo Angola 11°25S 16°45E 265 E3
Åneby Akershus, Norway 60°5N 10°51E 164 D7
Aneby Sweden 57°48N 14°49E 163 G8
Anéfis Mali 18°2N 0°36E 263 B5
Anegada Br. Virgin Is. 18°45N 64°20W 321 C7
Anegada, B. Argentina 40°20S 62°20W 336 B4
Anegada Passage W. Indies 18°15N 63°45W 321 C7
Aného Togo 6°12N 1°34E 263 D5
Aneityum Vanuatu 20°12S 169°45E 287 K7
Anelghowhat Vanuatu 20°19S 169°43E 287 K7
Añelo Argentina 38°20S 68°45W 336 A3
Anenni-Noi Moldova 46°53N 29°15E 183 D14
Aneto, Pico de Spain 42°37N 0°40E 196 C5
Änew Turkmenistan 37°52N 58°31E 216 E5
Aney Niger 19°15N 12°50E 259 E2
Añez Bolivia 15°40S 63°10W 331 D5
Anfu China 27°21N 114°40E 229 D10
Ang Mo Kio Singapore 1°23N 103°50E 138 A3
Ang Thong Thailand 14°35N 100°31E 236 E3
Ang Thong, Ko Thailand 9°37N 99°41E 237 b
Ang Thong △ Thailand 9°40N 99°43E 237 H2
Angadanan Phil. 16°45N 121°45E 232 C3
Angamos, Punta Chile 23°1S 70°32W 334 A1
Angara → Russia 58°5N 94°20E 215 D10
Angara-Débou Benin 11°19N 3°3E 263 C5
Angarbaka Sudan 9°44N 24°44E 257 F1
Angarsk Russia 52°30N 104°0E 215 D11
Angas Hills Australia 23°0S 127°50E 278 D4
Angaston Australia 34°30S 139°8E 282 C3
Angat Phil. 14°56N 121°2E 232 D3
Angaur I. Palau 6°54N 134°9E 288 c
Ängby Sweden 59°20N 17°53E 139 A1
Ånge Sweden 62°31N 15°35E 162 B9
Ángel, Salto = Angel Falls Venezuela 5°57N 62°30W 329 B5
Ángel de la Guarda, I. Mexico 29°20N 113°25W 318 B2
Angel Falls Venezuela 5°57N 62°30W 329 B5
Angel I. U.S.A. 37°52N 122°25W 136 A2
Angel Island State Park ⌓ U.S.A. 37°52N 122°25W 136 A2
Angeles Phil. 15°9N 120°33E 232 D3
Ängelholm Sweden 56°15N 12°58E 163 H6
Angels Camp U.S.A. 38°4N 120°32W 306 G6
Ängelsberg Sweden 59°58N 16°0E 162 E10
Anger → Ethiopia 9°37N 36°6E 257 F4
Angerburg = Węgorzewo Poland 54°13N 21°43E 184 D8
Angereb Ethiopia 13°11N 37°7E 257 E4
Angereb → Ethiopia 13°45N 36°40E 257 E4
Ångermanälven → Sweden 64°0N 17°20E 162 A11
Ångermanland Sweden 63°36N 17°45E 160 E17
Angermünde Germany 53°0N 14°0E 178 B9
Angers Qué., Canada 45°31N 75°29W 313 A9
Angers Maine-et-Loire, France 47°30N 0°35W 172 E6
Angerville France 48°19N 2°0E 173 D9
Ängesån → Sweden 66°16N 22°47E 160 C20
Angical Brazil 12°0S 44°42W 333 D3
Angikuni L. Canada 62°12N 99°59W 297 A9
Angke, Kali → Indonesia 6°6S 106°46E 122 A1
Angkor Cambodia 13°22N 103°50E 236 F4
Angledool Australia 29°5S 147°55E 281 D4
Anglem, Mt. N.Z. 46°45S 167°53E 285 G2
Anglès Spain 41°57N 2°38E 196 D7
Anglesey U.K. 53°17N 4°20W 168 D3
Anglesey, Isle of □ U.K. 53°16N 4°18W 168 D3
Anglet France 43°29N 1°31W 174 E2
Angleton U.S.A. 29°10N 95°26W 314 G7
Anglin → France 46°42N 0°52E 174 B4
Anglisidhes Cyprus 34°51N 33°27E 207 F9
Anglure France 48°35N 3°50E 173 D10
Angmagssalik = Tasiilaq Greenland 65°40N 37°20W 154 D7
Ango Dem. Rep. of the Congo 4°10N 26°5E 268 B2
Angoche Mozam. 16°8S 39°55E 269 F4
Angoche, I. Mozam. 16°20S 39°50E 269 F4
Angol Chile 37°56S 72°45W 334 D1
Angola Ind., U.S.A. 41°38N 85°0W 311 C12
Angola N.Y., U.S.A. 42°38N 79°2W 312 D5
Angola ■ Africa 12°0S 18°0E 265 E3
Angola Abyssal Plain Atl. Oc. 15°0S 2°0E 152 H12
Angola Basin Atl. Oc. 15°0S 3°0E 152 H12
Angoon U.S.A. 57°30N 134°35W 303 H14
Angora = Ankara Turkey 39°57N 32°54E 212 C5
Angoram Papua N. G. 4°4S 144°4E 286 C3
Angoulême France 45°39N 0°10E 174 C4
Angoumois France 45°50N 0°25E 174 C4
Angra do Heroismo Azores 38°39N 27°13W 153 d1
Angra dos Reis Brazil 23°0S 44°10W 335 A7
Angrapa → Russia 54°37N 21°54E 184 D8
Angren Uzbekistan 41°1N 70°12E 217 D8
Angtassom Cambodia 11°1N 104°41E 237 G5
Angu Dem. Rep. of the Congo 3°23N 24°30E 264 B4
Anguang China 45°15N 123°45E 227 B12
Anguilla ⊠ W. Indies 18°14N 63°5W 322 a
Anguillita I. Anguilla 18°9N 63°11W 322 a
Angul India 20°51N 85°6E 244 D7
Anguo China 38°28N 115°15E 226 E8
Angurugu Australia 14°0S 136°25E 280 A2
Angus Canada 44°19N 79°53W 312 B5
Angus □ U.K. 56°46N 2°56W 167 E6
Angwa → Zimbabwe 16°0S 30°23E 271 A5
Angyalföld Hungary 47°32N 19°5E 117 A2
Anhanduí → Brazil 21°46S 52°9W 335 A5
Anholt Denmark 56°42N 11°33E 163 H5
Anhua China 28°23N 111°12E 229 C8
Anhui □ China 32°0N 117°0E 229 B11
Anhwei = Anhui □ China 32°0N 117°0E 229 B11
Aniak U.S.A. 61°35N 159°32W 303 F8
Anichab Namibia 21°0S 14°46E 270 B1
Anicuns Brazil 16°28S 49°58W 333 E2
Anidros Greece 36°38N 25°43E 205 E7
Anié Togo 7°42N 1°8E 263 D5
Anik India 19°1N 72°53E 130 A2
Anil Brazil 2°32S 44°14W 332 B3
Animas → U.S.A. 36°43N 108°13W 305 H9
Anin Poland 52°13N 21°9E 142 B2
Anina Romania 45°6N 21°51E 182 E6
Anini-y Phil. 10°25N 121°55E 233 F3
Aninoasa Romania 44°47N 24°10E 183 F9
Añisoc Eq. Guin. 1°51N 10°46E 264 B2
Anita U.S.A. 41°27N 94°46W 310 C2
Anivorano Antsiranana, Madag. 12°44S 49°14E 272 A2
Anivorano Toamasina, Madag. 18°44S 48°58E 272 B2
Aniwa Vanuatu 19°17S 169°35E 287 J7
Anjalankoski Finland 60°45N 26°51E 188 B4
Anjangaon India 21°10N 77°20E 244 D3
Anjar India 23°6N 70°10E 242 H4
Anjengo India 8°40N 76°46E 245 K3
Anji China 30°46N 119°40E 229 B12
Anjidiv I. India 14°40N 74°10E 245 G2
Anjō Japan 34°57N 137°5E 223 C9
Anjou Qué., Canada 45°36N 73°33W 130 A2
Anjou Maine-et-Loire, France 47°20N 0°15W 172 E6
Anjouan Comoros Is. 12°15S 44°20E 272 a
Anjouan ✈ (AJN) Comoros Is. 12°9S 44°26E 272 a
Anjozorobe Madag. 18°22S 47°52E 272 B2
Anju N. Korea 39°36N 125°40E 224 C2
Anka Nigeria 12°13N 5°58E 263 C6
Ankaboa, Tanjona Madag. 21°58S 43°20E 272 C1
Ankang China 32°40N 109°1E 226 H5
Ankara Turkey 39°57N 32°54E 212 C5
Ankara □ Turkey 39°55N 32°50E 212 C5
Ankarafantsika ⌓ Madag. 16°8S 47°5E 272 B2
Ankaramena Madag. 21°57S 46°39E 272 C2
Ankarsrum Sweden 57°41N 16°20E 163 G10
Ankasakasa Madag. 16°21S 44°52E 272 B1
Ankavandra Madag. 18°46S 45°18E 272 B2
Ankazoabo Madag. 22°18S 44°31E 272 C1
Ankazobe Madag. 18°20S 47°10E 272 B2
Ankeny U.S.A. 41°44N 93°36W 310 C3
Ankhialo = Pomorie Bulgaria 42°32N 27°41E 203 D11
Ankilimalinika Madag. 22°58S 43°45E 272 C1
Ankilizato Madag. 20°25S 45°1E 272 C2
Anking = Anqing China 30°30N 117°3E 229 B11
Ankisabe Madag. 19°17S 46°29E 272 B2
Anklam Germany 53°51N 13°41E 178 B9
Ankleshwar India 21°38N 73°3E 244 D1
Ankober Ethiopia 9°35N 39°40E 257 F4
Ankola India 14°40N 74°18E 245 G2
Ankoro Dem. Rep. of the Congo 6°45S 26°55E 268 D2
Ankororoka Madag. 25°30S 45°11E 272 D2
Ankpa Nigeria 7°22N 7°38E 263 D6
Anlong China 25°2N 105°27E 228 E5
Anlong Veng Cambodia 14°14N 104°5E 236 E5
Anlu China 31°15N 113°45E 229 B9
Anmyeondo S. Korea 36°25N 126°25E 224 D3
Ånn Sweden 63°19N 12°33E 162 A6
Ann, C. U.S.A. 42°38N 70°35W 313 D14
Ann Arbor U.S.A. 42°17N 83°45W 311 B13
Anna Russia 51°28N 40°23E 190 E5
Anna Ill., U.S.A. 37°28N 89°15W 308 G9
Anna Ohio, U.S.A. 40°24N 84°11W 311 D12
Anna Regina Guyana 7°10N 58°30W 329 B6
Annaba Algeria 36°50N 7°46E 261 A6
Annaba □ Algeria 36°12N 7°45E 261 A6
Annaberg-Buchholz Germany 50°34N 13°0E 178 E9
Annai Guyana 3°57N 59°8W 329 C6
Annaka Japan 36°19N 138°54E 223 A10
Annalee → Ireland 54°2N 7°24W 166 B4
Annalee Heights U.S.A. 38°51N 77°10W 143 B2
Annam Vietnam 16°0N 108°0E 236 E7
Annamitique, Chaîne Asia 17°0N 106°0E 236 D6
Annan U.K. 54°59N 3°16W 167 G5
Annan → U.K. 54°58N 3°16W 167 G5
Annanberg Papua N. G. 4°52S 144°42E 286 C3
Annandale U.S.A. 38°50N 77°11W 143 C2
Annapolis U.S.A. 38°59N 76°30W 309 F15
Annapolis Royal Canada 44°44N 65°32W 299 D6
Annapurna Nepal 28°34N 83°50E 243 E10
Anne Frankhuis Amsterdam, Neths. 112 a1
Annean, L. Australia 26°54S 118°14E 279 E2
Anneberg Sweden 57°44N 14°49E 163 G8
Annecy France 45°55N 6°8E 175 C10
Annecy, Lac d' France 45°52N 6°10E 175 C10
Annemasse France 46°12N 6°16E 173 F13
Annenfeld = Şämkir Azerbaijan 40°50N 46°0E 191 K8
Annenskiy Most Russia 60°45N 37°10E 188 B9
Annette I. U.S.A. 55°9N 131°28W 296 B2
Annette Island ▲ U.S.A. 55°9N 131°28W 303 J15
Annigeri India 15°26N 75°26E 245 G2
Anning China 24°55N 102°26E 228 E4
Anniston U.S.A. 33°39N 85°50W 316 B4
Annobón Atl. Oc. 1°25S 5°36E 255 G4
Annonay France 45°15N 4°40E 175 C8
Annot France 43°58N 6°38E 175 E10
Annotto B. Jamaica 18°17N 76°45W 320 a
Annotto Bay Jamaica 18°16N 76°47W 320 a
Ånnsjön Sweden 63°19N 12°34E 162 A6
Annville U.S.A. 40°20N 76°31W 313 F8
Annweiler Germany 49°12N 7°57E 179 F3
Ano Poroia Greece 41°17N 23°2E 202 E7
Ano Siros Greece 37°29N 24°56E 204 D6
Anogi Greece 38°25N 20°40E 207 C2
Anogia Greece 35°16N 24°52E 207 E5
Anorotsangana Madag. 13°56S 47°55E 272 A2
Anosibe Madag. 19°26S 48°13E 272 B2
Anou Mellene Mali 17°29N 0°33E 263 B5
Anoumaba Ivory C. 6°23N 4°38W 262 D4
Anping Hebei, China 38°15N 115°30E 226 E8
Anping Liaoning, China 41°5N 123°30E 224 B1
Anpu Gang China 21°25N 109°50E 228 G7
Anqing China 30°30N 117°3E 229 B11
Anqiu China 36°25N 119°10E 227 F10
Anren China 26°43N 113°18E 229 D9
Ansager Denmark 55°43N 8°45E 163 J2
Ansai China 36°50N 109°20E 226 F5
Ansan S. Korea 37°21N 126°52E 224 D3
Ansbach Germany 49°28N 10°34E 179 F6
Anse-Bertrand Guadeloupe 16°28N 61°32W 322 e
Anse Boileau Seychelles 4°43S 55°29E 272 c
Anse Royale Seychelles 4°44S 55°31E 272 c
Anseba → Eritrea 16°0N 38°30E 257 D4
Anseong S. Korea 37°0N 127°16E 224 D3
Anserma Colombia 5°13N 75°48W 328 B2
Ansfelden Austria 48°12N 14°17E 180 C7
Anshan China 41°5N 122°58E 224 B1
Anshun China 26°18N 105°57E 228 D5
Ansião Portugal 39°56N 8°27W 194 F2
Ansley U.S.A. 41°18N 99°23W 308 E4
Ansó Spain 42°51N 0°48W 196 C4
Ansoáin Spain 42°50N 1°38W 196 C3
Anson U.S.A. 32°45N 99°54W 314 E5
Anson B. Australia 13°20S 130°6E 278 B5
Ansongo Mali 15°25N 0°35E 263 B5
Ansongo-Ménaka ⌓ Mali 15°3N 1°37E 263 B5
Ansonia Conn., U.S.A. 41°21N 73°5W 313 E11
Ansonia Ohio, U.S.A. 40°13N 84°38W 311 D12
Anstruther U.K. 56°14N 2°41W 167 E6
Ansudu Indonesia 2°11S 139°22E 231 E9
Antabamba Peru 14°40S 73°0W 330 C3
Antagarh India 20°6N 81°9E 244 D5
Antakya = Hatay Turkey 36°14N 36°10E 250 B7
Antalaha Madag. 14°57S 50°20E 272 A3
Antalāt Libya 31°8N 20°42E 258 B4
Antalya Turkey 36°52N 30°45E 250 B1
Antalya □ Turkey 36°50N 30°45E 205 E12
Antalya Körfezi Turkey 36°15N 31°30E 250 B2
Antambohobe Madag. 22°20S 46°47E 272 C2
Antanambao-Manampotsy Madag. 19°29S 48°34E 272 B2
Antanambe Madag. 16°26S 49°52E 272 B2
Antananarivo Madag. 18°55S 47°31E 272 B2
Antananarivo □ Madag. 19°0S 47°0E 272 B2
Antanifotsy Madag. 19°39S 47°19E 272 B2
Antanimbaribe Madag. 21°30S 44°48E 272 C1
Antanimora Madag. 24°49S 45°40E 272 C2
Antarctic Pen. Antarctica 67°0S 60°0W 151 C18
Antarctica 90°0S 0°0 151 E3
Antécume Pata Fr. Guiana 3°17N 54°4W 329 C7
Antelope Zimbabwe 21°2S 28°31E 269 G2
Antequera Paraguay 24°8S 57°7W 334 A4
Antequera Spain 37°5N 4°33W 195 H6
Antero, Mt. U.S.A. 38°41N 106°15W 304 G10
Antevamena Madag. 21°2S 44°8E 272 C1
Anthony Fla., U.S.A. 29°18N 82°7W 317 F7
Anthony Kans., U.S.A. 37°9N 98°2W 308 G4
Anthony N. Mex., U.S.A. 32°0N 106°36W 305 K10
Anti Atlas Morocco 30°0N 8°30W 260 C3
Anti-Lebanon = Sharqi, Al Jabal ash Lebanon 33°40N 36°10E 250 E7
Antibes France 43°34N 7°6E 175 E11
Antibes, C. d' France 43°31N 7°7E 175 E11
Anticosti, Î. d' Canada 49°30N 63°0W 299 C7
Antifer, C. d' France 49°41N 0°10E 172 C7
Antigo U.S.A. 45°9N 89°9W 308 C9
Antigonish Canada 45°38N 61°58W 299 C7
Antigua Canary Is. 28°24N 14°1W 153 e2

Antigua Guatemala 14°34N 90°41W 320 D1
Antigua W. Indies 17°0N 61°50W 322 b
Antigua & Barbuda ■ W. Indies 17°20N 61°48W 322 b
Antigua Int. ✈ (ANU) Antigua & B. 17°8N 61°47W 322 b
Antigues, Pte. d' Guadeloupe 16°26N 61°32W 322 e
Antikythira Greece 35°52N 23°15E 204 F5
Antilla Cuba 20°40N 75°50W 320 B4
Antilles = West Indies Cent. Amer. 15°0N 65°0W 321 D7
Antimilos Greece 36°47N 24°12E 204 E6
Anting Taiwan 23°7N 120°14E 225 C2
Antioch = Hatay Turkey 36°14N 36°10E 250 B7
Antioch U.S.A. 38°1N 121°48W 306 G5
Antioche, Pertuis d' France 46°6N 1°20W 174 B2
Antioquia Colombia 6°40N 75°55W 328 B2
Antioquia □ Colombia 7°0N 75°30W 328 B2
Antiparos Greece 37°0N 25°3E 205 D7
Antipaxi Greece 39°9N 20°13E 204 B2
Antipodes Is. Pac. Oc. 49°45S 178°40E 288 M9
Antipolo Phil. 14°35N 121°10E 232 D3
Antique □ Phil. 11°10N 122°5E 233 F4
Antirio Greece 38°20N 21°46E 204 C3
Antlers U.S.A. 34°14N 95°37W 314 D7
Antoetra Madag. 20°46S 47°20E 272 C2
Antofagasta Chile 23°50S 70°30W 334 A1
Antofagasta □ Chile 24°0S 69°0W 334 A2
Antofagasta de la Sierra Argentina 26°5S 67°20W 334 B2
Antofalla Argentina 25°30S 68°5W 334 B2
Antofalla, Salar de Argentina 25°40S 67°45W 334 B2
Antoine, L. Grenada 12°11N 61°36W 323 q
Anton U.S.A. 33°49N 102°10W 314 E3
Antongila, Helodrano Madag. 15°30S 49°50E 272 B2
Antonibé Madag. 15°7S 47°24E 272 B2
Antonina Brazil 25°26S 48°42W 335 B6
Antonio B. Won Pat Int. ✈ (GUM) Guam 13°29N 144°48E 302 d
António Enes = Angoche Mozam. 16°8S 39°55E 269 F4
Antony France 48°44N 2°17E 134 B2
Antrain France 48°28N 1°30W 172 D5
Antrim Antrim, U.K. 54°43N 6°14W 166 B5
Antrim Ohio, U.S.A. 40°7N 81°21W 312 F3
Antrim □ U.K. 54°56N 6°25W 166 B5
Antrim, Mts. of U.K. 55°3N 6°14W 166 A5
Antrim Plateau Australia 18°8S 128°20E 278 C4
Antriol Neth. Ant. 12°12N 68°16W 322 h
Antrodoco Italy 42°25N 13°5E 199 F10
Antropovo Russia 58°24N 43°6E 190 A6
Antsakabary Madag. 15°3S 48°56E 272 B2
Antsalova Madag. 18°40S 44°37E 272 B1
Antsenavolo Madag. 21°24S 48°3E 272 C2
Antsiafabositra Madag. 17°18S 46°57E 272 B2
Antsirabe Antananarivo, Madag. 19°55S 47°2E 272 B2
Antsirabe Antsiranana, Madag. 14°0S 49°59E 272 A2
Antsirabe Mahajanga, Madag. 15°57S 48°58E 272 B2
Antsiranana Madag. 12°25S 49°20E 272 A2
Antsiranana □ Madag. 12°16S 49°17E 272 A2
Antsohihy Madag. 14°50S 47°59E 272 A2
Antsohimbondrona Seranana Madag. 13°7S 48°48E 272 A2
Antu China 42°30N 128°20E 227 C15
Antufash Yemen 15°42N 42°25E 248 D3
Antung Taiwan 23°18N 121°20E 225 C3
Antwerp = Antwerpen Belgium 51°13N 4°25E 170 C4
Antwerp N.Y., U.S.A. 44°12N 75°37W 313 B9
Antwerp Ohio, U.S.A. 41°11N 84°45W 311 C12
Antwerpen Belgium 51°13N 4°25E 170 C4
Antwerpen □ Belgium 51°15N 4°40E 170 C4
Anukur, C. Papua N. G. 6°18S 149°37E 286 D5
Anupgarh India 29°10N 73°10E 242 E5
Anuppur India 23°6N 81°41E 243 H9
Anuradhapura Sri Lanka 8°22N 80°28E 245 K5
Anurrete ☼ Australia 20°50S 135°38E 280 C2
Anveh Iran 27°23N 54°11E 247 E7
Anvers = Antwerpen Belgium 51°13N 4°25E 170 C4
Anvers I. Antarctica 64°30S 63°40W 151 C17
Anvik U.S.A. 62°39N 160°13W 303 E7
Anwen China 29°4N 120°26E 229 C13
Anxi Fujian, China 25°2N 118°12E 229 E12
Anxi Gansu, China 40°30N 95°43E 218 B4
Anxian China 31°40N 104°25E 228 B5
Anxiang China 29°27N 112°11E 229 C9
Anxious B. Australia 33°24S 134°45E 281 E1
Anyama Ivory C. 5°30N 4°3W 262 D4
Anyang Henan, China 36°5N 114°21E 226 F8
Anyang S. Korea 37°23N 126°55E 224 D3
Anyer Indonesia 6°4S 105°53E 234 D3
Anyi Jiangxi, China 28°49N 115°25E 229 C10
Anyi Shanxi, China 35°2N 111°2E 226 G6
Anyuan China 25°9N 115°21E 229 E10
Anyue China 30°9N 105°50E 228 B5
Anza U.S.A. 33°35N 116°39W 307 M10
Anze China 36°10N 112°12E 226 F7
Anzeglouf Algeria 26°50N 0°1E 261 C5
Anzhero-Sudzhensk Russia 56°10N 86°0E 214 D9
Ánzio Italy 41°27N 12°37E 200 A5
Anzoátegui □ Venezuela 9°0N 64°30W 329 B5
Ao Makham Thailand 7°50N 98°24E 237 a
Ao Phangnga △ Thailand 8°10N 98°32E 237 a
Aoba Vanuatu 15°25S 167°50E 287 E5
Aoga-Shima Japan 32°28N 139°46E 223 E11
Aoiz Spain 42°46N 1°22W 196 C3
Aoji N. Korea 42°31N 130°23E 224 A5
Aola Solomon Is. 9°30S 160°30E 287 M11
Aomen = Macau China 22°12N 113°33E 219 G10
Aomori Japan 40°45N 140°45E 220 D10
Aomori □ Japan 40°45N 140°40E 220 D10
AON Center Chicago, U.S.A. 119 b2
Aonla India 28°16N 79°11E 243 E8
Aono-Yama Japan 34°28N 131°48E 222 C3
Aorai, Mt. Tahiti 17°34S 149°30W 289 e
Aoraki Mount Cook N.Z. 43°36S 170°9E 285 D5
Aoral, Phnum Cambodia 12°0N 104°15E 237 G5
Aorangi Ra. N.Z. 41°28S 175°22E 284 H4
Aore Vanuatu 15°35S 167°10E 287 E5
Aoreora Morocco 28°51N 10°53W 260 C2
Aosta Italy 45°45N 7°20E 198 C4
Aotea Harbour N.Z. 38°0S 174°50E 284 E3
Aotearoa = New Zealand ■ Oceania 40°0S 176°0E 284 G5
Aoudéras Niger 17°45N 8°20E 259 E1
Aouinet Torkoz Morocco 28°31N 9°46W 260 C3
Aouk, Bahr → Africa 8°51N 18°53E 259 G3
Aouk-Aoukalé ⌓ C.A.R. 9°52N 21°25E 264 A4
Aoukar Mali 23°50N 2°45W 260 D4
Aoukâr Mauritania 17°40N 10°0W 262 B3
Aoulef el Arab Algeria 26°55N 1°2E 261 C5
Aousred W. Sahara 22°32N 14°17W 260 D2
Aoyama Tokyo, Japan 140 b2
Aozou Chad 21°45N 17°28E 259 D3
Aozou Strip Chad 22°0N 19°0E 259 D3
Ap Lei Chau China 22°14N 114°9E 122 B1
Apá → S. Amer. 22°6S 58°2W 334 A4
Apache U.S.A. 34°54N 98°22W 314 D5
Apache Junction U.S.A. 33°25N 111°33W 305 K8
Apalachee B. U.S.A. 30°0N 84°0W 316 E5
Apalachicola U.S.A. 29°43N 84°59W 316 F5
Apalachicola → U.S.A. 29°43N 84°58W 316 F5
Apalachicola B. U.S.A. 29°40N 85°0W 316 F3
Apam Ghana 5°19N 0°42W 263 D4
Apamea Syria 35°31N 36°28E 250 C7
Apapa Nigeria 6°26N 3°21E 124 B2
Apapa Quays Nigeria 6°26N 3°23E 124 B2
Apaporis → Colombia 1°23S 69°25W 328 D4
Aparados da Serra △ Brazil 29°10S 50°8W 335 B5
Aparecida = Bertolínia Brazil 7°38S 43°57W 332 C3
Aparecida de Goiânia Brazil 16°45S 49°16W 333 E2
Aparecida do Taboado Brazil 20°5S 51°5W 333 F1
Aparri Phil. 18°22N 121°38E 232 B3
Aparurén Venezuela 5°6N 62°8W 329 B5
Apataki French Polynesia 15°26S 146°20W 289 f
Apateu Romania 46°36N 21°47E 182 D6
Apatin Serbia 45°40N 19°0E 182 E4
Apatity Russia 67°34N 33°22E 160 C25
Apatou Fr. Guiana 5°9N 54°20W 329 B7
Apatula = Finke Australia 25°34S 134°35E 280 D1
Apatzingán Mexico 19°5N 102°21W 318 D4
Apayao □ Phil. 18°10N 121°10E 232 B3
Apelacão Portugal 38°48N 9°7W 126 A2
Apeldoorn Neths. 52°13N 5°57E 170 B5
Apen Germany 53°13N 7°48E 178 B3
Apennines = Appennini Italy 44°30N 10°0E 198 D7
Apenrade = Aabenraa Denmark 55°3N 9°25E 163 J3
Apere → Bolivia 13°44S 65°18W 331 C4
Aphrodisias Turkey 37°42N 28°46E 205 D10
Api Nepal 30°0N 80°57E 218 C3
Apia Samoa 13°50S 171°50W 287 V20
Apiacás, Serra dos Brazil 9°50S 57°0W 331 B6
Apiaí Brazil 24°31S 48°50W 333 F2
Apiaú → Brazil 2°39N 61°12W 329 C5
Apiaú, Serra do Brazil 2°30N 62°0W 329 C5
Apidiá → Brazil 11°39S 61°11W 331 C5
Apies → S. Africa 25°15S 28°8E 271 C4
Apinajé Brazil 11°31S 48°18W 333 D2
Apiti N.Z. 39°58S 175°54E 284 F4
Apizaco Mexico 19°25N 98°8W 319 D5
Aplao Peru 16°0S 72°40W 330 D3
Apo, Mt. Phil. 6°53N 125°14E 233 H5
Apo East Pass Phil. 12°40N 120°40E 232 E3
Apo Reef △ Phil. 12°50N 120°50E 232 E3
Apo West Pass Phil. 12°31N 120°22E 232 E3
Apodi Brazil 5°39S 37°48W 332 C4
Apoera Suriname 5°12N 57°10W 329 B6
Apolakia Greece 36°5N 27°48E 206 E11
Apolakia, Ormos Greece 36°5N 27°45E 206 E11
Apolda Germany 51°2N 11°32E 178 D7
Apollo Bay Australia 38°45S 143°40E 282 E5
Apollonia = Sūsah Libya 32°52N 21°59E 258 B4
Apollonia Greece 36°15N 27°58E 206 E11
Apolo Bolivia 14°30S 68°30W 330 C4
Apolonia Greece 36°58N 24°43E 204 E6
Apónguao → Venezuela 4°48N 61°36W 329 C5
Apopa El Salv. 13°48N 89°10W 320 D2
Apopka U.S.A. 28°40N 81°31W 317 G8
Apopka, L. U.S.A. 28°37N 81°37W 133 A1
Apoquindo Chile 33°24S 70°32W 137 B2
Aporé Brazil 18°58S 52°1W 331 D7
Aporé → Brazil 19°27S 50°57W 333 E1
Aporema Brazil 1°14N 50°49W 332 A1
Apostle Is. U.S.A. 47°0N 90°40W 308 B8
Apostle Islands ⌓ U.S.A. 46°55N 91°0W 308 B8
Apóstoles Argentina 28°0S 56°0W 335 B4
Apostolos Andreas, C. Cyprus 35°42N 34°35E 207 E10
Apostolovo Ukraine 47°39N 33°39E 189 J7
Apoteri Guyana 4°2N 58°32W 329 C6
Appalachian Mts. U.S.A. 38°0N 80°0W 309 G14
Äppelbo Sweden 60°29N 14°1E 162 D8
Appennini Italy 44°30N 10°0E 198 D7
Appennino Ligure Italy 44°30N 9°0E 198 D6
Appenzell-Ausser Rhoden □ Switz. 47°23N 9°23E 179 H5
Appenzell-Inner Rhoden □ Switz. 47°20N 9°25E 179 H5
Appiano Italy 46°28N 11°15E 199 B8
Apple Hill Canada 45°13N 74°46W 313 A10
Apple Valley U.S.A. 34°32N 117°14W 307 L9
Appleby-in-Westmorland U.K. 54°35N 2°29W 168 C5
Appledore U.K. 51°3N 4°13W 169 F3
Appleton U.S.A. 44°16N 88°25W 308 C9
Appleton City U.S.A. 38°11N 94°2W 310 F2
Appleton Rum Distillery Jamaica 18°10N 77°44W 320 a
Appling U.S.A. 33°33N 82°19W 316 B7
Approuague Fr. Guiana 4°20N 52°0W 329 C7
Apra Harbor Guam 13°26N 144°40E 302 d
Apricena Italy 41°47N 15°27E 199 G12
April → Papua N. G. 4°18S 142°26E 286 C2
Aprília Italy 41°36N 12°39E 200 A5
Apsheronsk Russia 44°28N 39°42E 191 H4
Apsley Canada 44°45N 78°6W 312 B6
Apt France 43°53N 5°24E 175 E9
Apterkarskiy Ostrov Russia 59°57N 30°20E 137 B2
Apuane, Alpi Italy 44°7N 10°14E 198 D7
Apuaú Brazil 2°25S 60°53W 329 D5
Apucarana Brazil 23°55S 51°33W 335 A5
Apulia = Púglia □ Italy 41°15N 16°15E 201 A9
Apurashokoru Palau 7°16N 134°17E 288 c
Apurauan Phil. 9°35N 118°20E 233 G2
Apure □ Venezuela 7°10N 68°50W 328 B4
Apure → Venezuela 7°37N 66°25W 328 B4
Apurímac □ Peru 14°0S 73°0W 330 C3
Apurimac → Peru 12°17S 73°56W 330 C3
Apuseni, Munţii Romania 46°30N 22°45E 182 D7
Āq Qālā Iran 37°10N 54°30E 247 B7
Aqaba = Al 'Aqabah Jordan 29°31N 35°0E 251 J6
Aqaba, G. of Red Sea 29°0N 34°40E 251 K5
'Aqabah, Khalīj al = Aqaba, G. of Red Sea 29°0N 34°40E 251 K5
Aqadyr Kazakhstan 48°17N 74°50E 217 C8
Āqchah Afghan. 36°56N 66°11E 240 A2
'Aqdā Iran 32°26N 53°37E 247 C7
Aqîq Sudan 18°14N 38°12E 256 D4
Aqîq, Khalîg Sudan 18°20N 38°10E 256 D4
'Aqīq, W. al → Si. Arabia 20°16N 41°40E 248 B3
Aqköl Kazakhstan 51°59N 70°56E 217 B8
Aqmola = Astana Kazakhstan 51°10N 71°30E 217 B8
Aqmola □ Kazakhstan 51°30N 70°0E 217 B8
'Aqrah Iraq 36°46N 43°45E 213 D10
Aqsay Kazakhstan 51°11N 53°0E 187 D9
Aqshataū Kazakhstan 47°59N 74°3E 217 C8
Aqsū Ongtüstik Qazaqstan, Kazakhstan 42°25N 69°50E 217 D7
Aqsū Pavlodar, Kazakhstan 52°2N 76°55E 217 B9
Aqsügek Kazakhstan 44°37N 74°30E 217 D8
Aqtaū Mangghystaū, Kazakhstan 43°39N 51°12E 187 F9
Aqtaū Qaraghandy, Kazakhstan 50°14N 73°3E 217 B8
Aqtöbe Kazakhstan 50°17N 57°10E 187 D10
Aqtoghay Kazakhstan 46°57N 79°40E 217 C9
Aquarium of the Americas New Orleans, U.S.A. 131 b3
Aquidauana Brazil 20°30S 55°50W 331 E6
Aquidauana → Brazil 19°44S 56°50W 331 D6
Aquila Mexico 18°36N 103°30W 318 D4
Aquiles Serdán Mexico 28°36N 105°53W 318 B3
Aquin Haiti 18°16N 73°24W 321 C5
Aquitain, Bassin France 44°0N 0°30W 171 D3
Aquitaine □ France 44°25N 0°30W 174 D3
Ar Kazimiyah Iraq 33°22N 44°20E 113 B1
Ar Rafīd Syria 32°57N 35°52E 250 F6
Ar Raḩḩālīyah Iraq 32°44N 43°23E 213 F10
Ar Ram West Bank 31°51N 35°15E 123 A2
Ar Ramādī Iraq 33°25N 43°20E 213 F10
Ar Raml Libya 26°45N 19°40E 258 C3
Ar Ramthā Jordan 32°34N 36°0E 251 F7
Ar Raqqah Syria 35°59N 39°8E 213 E8
Ar Raqqah □ Syria 36°20N 39°10E 213 D8
Ar Rashidiya = Er Rachidia Morocco 31°58N 4°20W 260 B4
Ar Rass Si. Arabia 25°50N 43°40E 246 E4
Ar Rastan Syria 34°55N 36°43E 250 D7
Ar Rawḑah Si. Arabia 21°16N 42°50E 248 B3
Ar Rawḑah Yemen 14°28N 47°17E 248 D4
Ar Rayyan Qatar 25°17N 51°25E 247 E6
Ar Rifā'ī Iraq 31°50N 46°10E 246 D5
Ar Rijā' Yemen 13°1N 44°35E 248 D4
Ar Riyāḑ Si. Arabia 24°41N 46°42E 246 E5
Ar Riyāḑ □ Si. Arabia 23°0N 45°50E 248 B4
Ar Riyān Yemen 14°39N 49°19E 267 B6
Ar Rmās, W. → Syria 35°47N 36°50E 250 C7
Ar Ru'ays Qatar 26°8N 51°12E 247 E6
Ar Rukhaymīyah Iraq 29°22N 45°38E 246 D5
Ar Rumaythah Iraq 31°31N 45°12E 246 D5
Ar Ruşāfah Syria 35°45N 38°49E 213 E8
Ar Ruţbah Iraq 33°0N 40°15E 213 F9
Ar Ruwayḑah Si. Arabia 23°40N 44°40E 248 B4
Ara India 25°35N 84°32E 243 G11
Ara → Japan 35°41N 139°50E 140 A4
Ara Goro Ethiopia 5°48N 41°18E 257 F5
Ara Tera Ethiopia 6°38N 40°57E 257 F5
Arab U.S.A. 34°19N 86°30W 315 D11
'Arab, Bahr el → Sudan 9°0N 29°30E 257 F2
Arab, Khalîg el Egypt 30°55N 29°0E 256 A2
Arab, Shatt al → Asia 29°57N 48°34E 247 D6
'Araba, W. → Egypt 28°19N 33°31E 256 J8
'Arabābād Iran 33°2N 57°41E 247 C8
'Arabah, W. → Yemen 18°5N 51°26E 249 C5
Araban Turkey 37°28N 37°44E 212 D7
Arabatskaya Strelka Ukraine 45°40N 35°0E 189 K8
Arabba Italy 46°30N 11°52E 199 B8
Arabelo Venezuela 4°55N 64°13W 329 C5
Arabi U.S.A. 31°50N 83°44W 316 D6
Arabia Asia 25°0N 45°0E 210 F6
Arabian Basin Ind. Oc. 11°30N 65°0E 273 C5
Arabian Desert = Es Sahrâ' Esh Sharqîya Egypt 27°30N 32°30E 256 B3
Arabian Gulf = Persian Gulf Asia 27°0N 50°0E 247 E6
Arabian Sea Ind. Oc. 16°0N 65°0E 238 F9
Arabistan = Khūzestān □ Iran 31°0N 49°0E 247 D6
Araç Turkey 41°15N 33°21E 212 B5
Aracaju Brazil 10°55S 37°4W 332 D4
Aracataca Colombia 10°38N 74°9W 328 A3
Aracati Brazil 4°30S 37°44W 332 B4
Araçatuba Brazil 21°10S 50°30W 335 A5
Araceli Phil. 10°33N 119°59E 233 F2
Aracena Spain 37°53N 6°38W 195 H4
Aracena, Sierra de Spain 37°50N 6°50W 195 H4
Arachova Greece 38°28N 22°35E 204 C4
Arachthos → Greece 39°20N 21°4E 204 B3
Aracides, C. Solomon Is. 8°21S 161°0E 287 M11
Aračinovo Macedonia 42°1N 21°34E 202 D5
Araçuaí Brazil 16°52S 42°4W 333 E3
Araçuaí → Brazil 16°46S 42°2W 333 E3
'Arad Israel 31°15N 35°12E 251 G6
Arad Romania 46°10N 21°20E 182 D6
Arad □ Romania 46°20N 22°0E 182 D6
Arada Chad 15°0N 20°20E 259 F4
Arādān Iran 35°21N 52°30E 247 C7
Aradhippou Cyprus 34°57N 33°36E 207 F9
Arafura Sea E. Indies 9°0S 135°0E 288 H5
Aragarças Brazil 15°55S 52°15W 331 D7
Aragats Armenia 40°30N 44°15E 191 K7
Aragon U.S.A. 34°2N 85°3W 316 A4
Aragón □ Spain 41°25N 0°40W 196 D4
Aragón → Spain 42°13N 1°44W 196 C3
Aragona Italy 37°24N 13°27E 200 E6
Aragua □ Venezuela 10°0N 67°10W 328 B4
Aragua de Barcelona Venezuela 9°28N 64°49W 329 B5
Araguacema Brazil 8°50S 49°20W 332 C2
Araguaçu = Paraguaçu Paulista Brazil 22°22S 50°35W 335 A5
Araguaçu Brazil 12°49S 49°51W 333 D2
Araguaia → Brazil 5°21S 48°41W 332 C2
Araguaia △ Brazil 10°30S 50°0W 332 D2
Araguaiana Brazil 15°43S 51°51W 331 D7
Araguaína Brazil 7°12S 48°12W 332 C2
Araguari Brazil 18°38S 48°11W 333 E2
Araguari → Brazil 1°15N 49°55W 329 C8
Araguatins Brazil 5°38S 48°7W 332 C2
Arahal Spain 37°15N 5°33W 195 H5
Arain India 26°27N 75°2E 242 F6
Araioses Brazil 2°53S 41°55W 332 B3
Arak Algeria 25°20N 3°45E 261 C5
Arāk Iran 34°0N 49°40E 247 C6
Araka Sudan 4°20N 30°23E 257 G3
Arakan □ Burma 19°0N 94°15E 241 F5
Arakan Coast Burma 19°0N 94°0E 241 F4
Arakan Yoma Burma 20°0N 94°40E 241 F5
Arakawa Japan 35°44N 139°48E 140 A3
Arakkonam India 13°7N 79°43E 245 H4
Araklı Turkey 41°6N 40°2E 213 B9
Araks = Aras, Rūd-e → Asia 40°5N 48°29E 191 K9
Araks → Iran 39°10N 47°10E 216 E3
Aral Kazakhstan 46°41N 61°45E 216 C6
Aral Mangy Qaraqumy Kazakhstan 46°50N 63°10E 216 C6
Aral Sea Asia 44°30N 60°0E 216 C5
Aral Tengizi = Aral Sea Asia 44°30N 60°0E 216 C5
Aralık Turkey 39°52N 44°31E 213 C11
Aralqum Asia 44°30N 60°35E 216 D6
Aralsk = Aral Kazakhstan 46°41N 61°45E 216 C6
Aralskoye More = Aral Sea Asia 44°30N 60°0E 216 C5
Aralsor, Ozero = Aralsor Köli Kazakhstan 49°5N 48°12E 191 F9
Aralsor Köli Kazakhstan 49°5N 48°12E 191 F9
Aramac Australia 22°58S 145°14E 280 C4
Aramia → Papua N. G. 7°55S 143°22E 286 D2
Aran → India 19°55N 78°12E 244 E4
Aran Areh Ethiopia 9°2N 43°54E 267 C5
Aran I. Ireland 55°0N 8°30W 166 A3
Aran Is. Ireland 53°6N 9°38W 166 C2
Aranda de Duero Spain 41°39N 3°42W 194 D7
Arandān Iran 35°23N 46°55E 246 C5
Aranđelovac Serbia 44°18N 20°34E 202 B4
Aranga N.Z. 35°44S 173°40E 284 B2
Arani Bolivia 17°34S 65°46W 331 D4
Arani India 12°43N 79°19E 245 H4
Aranjuez Spain 40°1N 3°40W 194 E7
Aranos Namibia 24°9S 19°7E 270 B2
Aransas Pass U.S.A. 27°55N 97°9W 314 H6
Arany-hegyi-patak → Hungary 47°34N 19°4E 117 A2
Aranyaprathet Thailand 13°41N 102°30E 236 F4
Arao Japan 32°59N 130°25E 222 E2
Araouane Mali 18°55N 3°30W 262 B4
Arapahoe U.S.A. 40°18N 99°54W 308 E4
Arapari Brazil 5°34S 49°15W 332 C2
Arapawa I. N.Z. 41°11S 174°17E 285 B9
Arapey Grande → Uruguay 30°55S 57°49W 334 C4
Arapgir Turkey 39°5N 38°30E 213 C8
Arapiraca Brazil 9°45S 36°39W 332 C4
Arapis, Akra Greece 40°27N 24°0E 203 F8
Arapongas Brazil 23°29S 51°28W 335 A5
Arapuni N.Z. 38°4S 175°39E 284 E4
Ar'ar Si. Arabia 30°59N 41°2E 246 D4
Araracuara Colombia 0°24S 72°17W 328 D3
Araranguá Brazil 29°0S 49°30W 335 B6
Araraquara Brazil 21°50S 48°0W 333 F2
Araras Brazil 22°22S 47°23W 333 F2
Ararás, Serra das Brazil 25°0S 53°10W 335 B5
Ararat Armenia 39°48N 44°50E 213 C11
Ararat Vic., Australia 37°16S 142°58E 282 D5
Ararat, Mt. = Ağrı Dağı Turkey 39°50N 44°15E 213 C11
Arari Brazil 3°28S 44°47W 332 B3
Araria India 26°9N 87°33E 243 F12
Araripe, Chapada do Brazil 7°20S 40°0W 332 C4
Araripina Brazil 7°33S 40°34W 332 C3
Araruama, L. de Brazil 22°53S 42°12W 333 F3
Araruna Brazil 6°52S 35°44W 332 C4
Aras = Aras, Rūd-e → Asia 40°5N 48°29E 191 K9
Aras, Rūd-e → Asia 40°5N 48°29E 191 K9
Aratãne Mauritania 18°24N 8°32W 262 B3
Araticu = Oeiras do Para Brazil 1°58S 49°51W 329 D8
Arauca Colombia 7°0N 70°40W 328 B3
Arauca □ Colombia 6°40N 71°0W 328 B3
Arauca → Venezuela 7°24N 66°35W 328 B4
Arauco Chile 37°16S 73°25W 334 D1
Araújos Brazil 19°56S 45°14W 333 E2
Arauquita Colombia 7°2N 71°25W 328 B3
Araure Venezuela 9°34N 69°13W 328 B4
Aravaca Spain 40°27N 3°47W 127 B1
Aravalli Range India 25°0N 73°30E 242 G5
Arawa Ethiopia 9°57N 41°58E 257 F5
Arawale ⌓ Kenya 1°24S 40°9E 268 C5
Arawe Is. Papua N. G. 6°6S 149°0E 286 D5
Arawhata → N.Z. 44°0S 168°40E 285 E3
Araxá Brazil 19°35S 46°55W 333 E2
Araxes = Aras, Rūd-e → Asia 40°5N 48°29E 191 K9
Araya, Pen. de Venezuela 10°40N 64°0W 329 A5
Arayat Phil. 15°10N 120°46E 232 D3
Araz = Aras, Rūd-e → Asia 40°5N 48°29E 191 K9
Arba Gugu Ethiopia 8°40N 40°15E 257 F5
Arba Minch Ethiopia 6°0N 37°30E 257 F4
Arbat Iraq 35°25N 45°35E 213 E11
Arbataash Iraq 33°20N 44°19E 113 A1
Árbatax Italy 39°56N 9°42E 200 C2
Arbi Ethiopia 9°4N 35°7E 257 F4
Arbīl Iraq 36°15N 44°5E 213 D11
Arbīl □ Iraq 36°20N 44°20E 213 D11
Arboga Sweden 59°24N 15°52E 162 E9
Arbois France 46°55N 5°46E 173 F12
Arboletes Colombia 8°51N 76°26W 328 B2
Arbore Ethiopia 5°3N 36°50E 257 F4
Arboréa Italy 39°46N 8°35E 200 C1
Arborfield Canada 53°6N 103°39W 297 C8
Arborg Canada 50°54N 97°13W 297 C9
Arbre du Ténéré Niger 17°50N 10°4E 259 E2
Arbroath U.K. 56°34N 2°35W 167 E6
Arbuckle U.S.A. 39°1N 122°3W 306 F4
Arbus Italy 39°30N 8°33E 200 C1
Arc → France 45°34N 6°12E 175 C10
Arc de Triomphe Paris, France 134 a2
Arc-lès-Gray France 47°28N 5°34E 173 E12
Arcachon France 44°40N 1°10W 174 D2
Arcachon, Bassin d' France 44°42N 1°10W 174 D2
Arcade U.S.A. 42°32N 78°25W 312 D6
Arcadia Calif., U.S.A. 34°7N 118°1W 126 B4
Arcadia Fla., U.S.A. 27°13N 81°52W 317 H8
Arcadia Ind., U.S.A. 40°11N 86°1W 311 D10
Arcadia Iowa, U.S.A. 42°5N 95°3W 310 B1
Arcadia La., U.S.A. 32°33N 92°55W 314 E8
Arcadia Pa., U.S.A. 40°47N 78°51W 312 F6
Arcanum U.S.A. 39°59N 84°33W 311 E12
Arcata U.S.A. 40°52N 124°5W 304 F1
Arcévia Italy 43°30N 12°56E 199 E9
Archanes Greece 35°16N 25°11E 205 F7
Archangel = Arkhangelsk Russia 64°38N 40°36E 186 B7
Archangelos Preveza, Greece 39°6N 20°42E 207 A2
Archangelos Rhodes, Greece 36°13N 28°7E 206 E12
Archar Bulgaria 43°50N 22°54E 202 C6
Archbald U.S.A. 41°30N 75°32W 313 E9
Archbold U.S.A. 41°31N 84°18W 311 C12
Archena Spain 38°9N 1°16W 197 G3
Archenu, J. Libya 22°15N 24°45E 259 D4
Archer U.S.A. 29°32N 82°32W 317 F7
Archer → Australia 13°28S 141°41E 280 A3
Archer B. Australia 13°20S 141°30E 280 A3
Archer Bend = Mungkan Kandju △ Australia 13°35S 142°52E 280 A3
Archers Post Kenya 0°35N 37°35E 268 B4
Arches △ U.S.A. 38°45N 109°25W 304 G9
Archidona Spain 37°6N 4°22W 195 H6
Archipel-de-Mingan △ Canada 50°13N 63°10W 299 B7
Archipiélago Chinijo △ Canary Is. 29°20N 13°30W 153 e2
Archipiélago Los Roques △ Venezuela 11°50N 66°44W 321 D6
Archives Navy Memorial Washington, D.C., U.S.A. 143 b2
Arci, Mte. Italy 39°47N 8°45E 200 C1
Arcidosso Italy 42°52N 11°33E 199 F8
Arcila = Asilah Morocco 35°29N 6°0W 260 A3
Arcipelago de la Maddalena △ Italy 41°14N 9°24E 200 A2
Arcipelago Toscano △ Italy 42°45N 10°15E 198 F7
Arcis-sur-Aube France 48°32N 4°10E 173 D11
Arckaringa Cr. → Australia 28°10S 135°22E 281 D2
Arco Italy 45°55N 10°53E 198 C7
Arco Idaho, U.S.A. 43°38N 113°18W 304 E7
Arco Plaza Los Angeles, U.S.A. 127 b1
Arcola U.S.A. 39°41N 88°19W 311 E8
Arcoona Australia 31°2S 137°1E 282 A2
Arcos de Jalón Spain 41°12N 2°16W 196 D2
Arcos de la Frontera Spain 36°45N 5°49W 195 J5
Arcos de Valdevez Portugal 41°55N 8°22W 194 D2
Arcot India 12°53N 79°20E 245 H4
Arcoverde Brazil 8°25S 37°4W 332 C4
Arcozelo Portugal 40°32N 7°47W 194 E3
Arctic Bay Canada 73°1N 85°7W 295 C14
Arctic Mid-Ocean Ridge Arctic 87°0N 90°0E 150 A
Arctic Ocean Arctic 78°0N 160°0W 150 B18
Arctic Red River = Tsiigehtchic Canada 67°15N 134°0W 294 D5
Arctic Village U.S.A. 68°8N 145°32W 303 B11
Arctowski Antarctica 62°30S 58°0W 151 C18
Arcueil France 48°48N 2°19E 134 B2
Arda → Bulgaria 41°40N 26°30E 203 E10
Arda → Italy 45°2N 10°2E 198 C7
Ardabīl Iran 38°15N 48°18E 213 C13
Ardabīl □ Iran 38°15N 48°20E 247 B6
Ardahan Turkey 41°7N 42°41E 213 B10
Ardahan □ Turkey 41°10N 42°50E 213 B10
Ardakān = Sepīdān Iran 30°20N 52°5E 247 D7
Ardakān Iran 32°19N 53°59E 247 C7
Ardala Sweden 58°22N 13°19E 163 F7
Ardales Spain 36°53N 4°51W 195 J6
Årdalstangen Norway 61°14N 7°43E 164 C4
Ardara Ireland 54°46N 8°25W 166 B3
Ardas → Greece 41°40N 26°30E 203 E10
Ardèche □ France 44°42N 4°16E 175 D8
Ardèche → France 44°16N 4°39E 175 D8
Ardee Ireland 53°52N 6°33W 166 C5
Arden Ont., Canada 44°43N 76°56W 312 B8
Arden Denmark 56°46N 9°52E 163 H3
Arden Calif., U.S.A. 38°36N 121°33W 306 G5
Arden Nev., U.S.A. 36°1N 115°14W 307 J11
Ardenne Belgium 49°50N 5°5E 170 E5
Ardennes = Ardenne Belgium 49°50N 5°5E 170 E5
Ardennes □ France 49°35N 4°40E 173 C11
Ardentes France 46°45N 1°50E 173 F8
Arderin Ireland 53°2N 7°39W 166 C4
Ardeşen Turkey 41°12N 41°2E 213 B9
Ardestān Iran 33°20N 52°25E 247 C7
Ardfert Ireland 52°20N 9°47W 166 D2
Ardglass U.K. 54°17N 5°36W 166 B6
Ardhéa = Aridea Greece 40°58N 22°3E 202 F6
Ardila → Portugal 38°12N 7°28W 195 G3
Ardino Bulgaria 41°34N 25°9E 203 E9
Ardivachar Pt. U.K. 57°23N 7°26W 167 D1
Ardlethan Australia 34°22S 146°53E 283 C7
Ardmore Okla., U.S.A. 34°10N 97°8W 314 D6
Ardmore Pa., U.S.A. 40°2N 75°17W 313 F9
Ardnamurchan, Pt. of U.K. 56°43N 6°14W 167 E2
Ardnave Pt. U.K. 55°53N 6°20W 167 F2
Ardon Russia 43°10N 44°18E 191 J7
Ardore Italy 38°11N 16°10E 201 D9
Ardres France 50°50N 1°59E 173 B8
Ardrossan S. Austral., Australia 34°26S 137°53E 282 C2
Ardrossan N. Ayrs., U.K. 55°39N 4°49W 167 F4
Ards Pen. U.K. 54°33N 5°34W 166 B6
Arduan Sudan 19°54N 30°20E 256 D3
Ardud Romania 47°37N 22°52E 182 C7
Åre Sweden 63°22N 13°15E 162 A7
Arecibo Puerto Rico 18°29N 66°43W 321 C6
Areia Branca Brazil 5°0S 37°0W 332 C4
Arena, Pt. U.S.A. 38°57N 123°44W 306 G3
Arenal Honduras 15°21N 86°50W 320 C2
Arenales, Cerro Chile 47°5S 73°40W 336 C2
Arenápolis Brazil 14°26S 56°49W 331 C6
Arenas = Las Arenas Spain 43°17N 4°50W 194 B6
Arenas, Pta. Venezuela 10°31N 64°14W 329 A5
Arenas de San Pedro Spain 40°12N 5°5W 194 E5
Arendal Norway 58°28N 8°46E 164 F5
Arendsee Germany 52°52N 11°27E 178 C7
Arenillas Ecuador 3°33S 80°10W 328 D1
Arensburg = Kuressaare Estonia 58°15N 22°30E 188 C2
Arenys de Mar Spain 41°35N 2°33E 196 D7
Arenzano Italy 44°24N 8°41E 198 D5
Arenzville U.S.A. 39°53N 90°22W 310 E6
Areopoli Greece 36°40N 22°22E 204 E4
Arequipa Peru 16°20S 71°30W 330 D3
Arequipa □ Peru 16°0S 72°50W 330 D3
Arere Brazil 0°16S 53°52W 329 D7
Arero Ethiopia 4°41N 38°50E 257 G4
Arès France 44°47N 1°8W 174 D2
Arese Italy 45°32N 9°4E 129 A1
Arévalo Spain 41°3N 4°43W 194 D6
Arezzo Italy 43°25N 11°53E 199 E8
Arga Turkey 38°21N 37°59E 246 B3
Arga → Spain 42°18N 1°47W 196 C3
Argalasti Greece 39°13N 23°13E 204 B5
Argamakmur Indonesia 3°35S 102°0E 234 C2
Argamasilla de Alba Spain 39°8N 3°5W 195 F7
Argamasilla de Calatrava Spain 38°44N 4°4W 195 G6
Arganda del Rey Spain 40°19N 3°26W 194 E7
Arganil Portugal 40°13N 8°3W 194 E2
Arganzuela Spain 40°23N 3°42W 127 B1
Argao Phil. 9°52N 123°36E 233 G4
Argarapa ☼ Australia 22°20S 134°58E 280 C1
Argasi Greece 37°45N 20°56E 207 D2
Argedeb Ethiopia 6°11N 41°13E 257 F5
Argelès-Gazost France 43°0N 0°6W 174 E3
Argelès-sur-Mer France 42°34N 3°1E 174 F7
Argens → France 43°24N 6°44E 175 E10
Argent-sur-Sauldre France 47°33N 2°25E 173 E9
Argenta = North Little Rock U.S.A. 34°45N 92°16W 314 D8
Argenta B.C., Canada 50°11N 116°56W 296 C5
Argenta Italy 44°37N 11°50E 199 D8
Argenta Ill., U.S.A. 39°59N 88°49W 311 E8
Argentan France 48°45N 0°1W 172 D6
Argentário, Mte. Italy 42°24N 11°9E 199 F8
Argentat France 45°6N 1°56E 174 C5
Argentera Italy 44°12N 7°5E 198 D4
Argenteuil France 48°56N 2°15E 134 A2
Argentia Canada 47°18N 53°58W 299 C9
Argentiera, C. dell' Italy 40°44N 8°8E 200 B1
Argentina ■ S. Amer. 35°0S 66°0W 327 G4
Argentine Abyssal Plain Atl. Oc. 46°0S 52°0W 152 L6
Argentine Basin Atl. Oc. 45°0S 45°0W 152 L7
Argentino, L. Argentina 50°10S 73°0W 336 D2
Argenton-Château France 46°59N 0°27W 172 F6
Argenton-sur-Creuse France 46°36N 1°30E 173 F8
Argeş □ Romania 45°0N 24°45E 183 F9
Argeş → Romania 44°5N 26°38E 183 F11
Arghandab → Afghan. 31°30N 64°15E 242 D1
Argheile Ethiopia 5°19N 42°4E 257 F5
Argirades Greece 39°27N 19°58E 206 C9
Argiroupoli Athina, Greece 37°52N 23°44E 112 B2
Argiroupoli Kriti, Greece 35°17N 24°20E 207 E5
Argo Sudan 19°28N 30°30E 256 D3
Argolida □ Greece 37°38N 22°50E 204 D4
Argolikos Kolpos Greece 37°20N 22°52E 204 D4
Argonne France 49°10N 5°0E 173 C12
Argonne Forest U.S.A. 41°42N 87°53W 119 C1
Argos Greece 37°40N 22°43E 204 D4
Argos Ind., U.S.A. 41°14N 86°15W 311 C10
Argos Orestiko Greece 40°27N 21°18E 202 F5
Argostoli Greece 38°11N 20°29E 207 C2
Argostoliou, Kolpos Greece 38°10N 20°27E 207 C1
Arguedas Spain 42°11N 1°36W 196 C3
Argüelles Madrid, Spain 127 a1
Arguello, Pt. U.S.A. 34°35N 120°39W 307 L6
Arguineguín Canary Is. 27°46N 15°41W 153 e1
Argun Russia 43°18N 45°52E 191 J7
Argun → Russia 53°20N 121°28E 215 D13
Argungu Nigeria 12°40N 4°31E 263 C5
Argus Pk. U.S.A. 35°52N 117°26W 307 K9
Argyle, L. Australia 16°20S 128°40E 278 C4
Argyle Waterfalls Trin. & Tob. 11°15N 60°35W 323 s
Argyll ⌓ U.K. 56°6N 5°0W 167 E4
Argyll & Bute □ U.K. 56°13N 5°28W 167 E3
Arhavi Turkey 41°21N 41°18E 213 B9
Århus Denmark 56°8N 10°11E 163 H4
Ari Atoll Maldives 3°53N 72°50E 272 d
Aria N.Z. 38°33S 175°0E 284 E4
Ariadnoye Russia 45°8N 134°25E 220 B7
Ariamsvlei Namibia 28°9S 19°51E 270 C2
Ariana Tunisia 36°52N 10°12E 258 A2
Ariana □ Tunisia 36°50N 9°52E 261 A6
Ariano Irpino Italy 41°9N 15°5E 201 A8
Ariari → Colombia 2°35N 72°47W 328 C3
Aribinda Burkina Faso 14°17N 0°52W 263 C4
Arica Chile 18°32S 70°20W 330 D3
Arica Colombia 2°0S 71°50W 328 D3
Arica y Parinacota □ Chile 17°40S 69°50W 330 D4
Arico Canary Is. 28°9N 16°29W 153 e1
Arid, C. Australia 34°1S 123°10E 279 F3
Arida Japan 34°5N 135°8E 223 C7
Aridal W. Sahara 25°59N 13°54W 260 C2
Aride Seychelles 4°13S 55°40E 272 c
Aridea Greece 40°58N 22°3E 202 F6
Ariège □ France 42°56N 1°30E 174 F5
Ariège → France 43°30N 1°25E 174 E5
Arieş → Romania 46°24N 23°20E 183 D8
Arigat el Fersig Algeria 27°35N 2°7W 261 C4
Arihā Israel 31°51N 35°27E 256 A4
Arīḩā Syria 35°49N 36°35E 250 C7
Arikok △ Aruba 12°31N 69°56W 322 f
Arila, Akra Greece 39°43N 19°39E 206 B9
Arilje Serbia 43°44N 20°7E 202 C4
Arima Kanagawa, Japan 35°33N 139°33E 140 B2
Arima Trin. & Tob. 10°38N 61°17W 323 t
Arima → Trin. & Tob. 10°35N 61°16W 323 t
Aringay Phil. 16°26N 120°21E 232 C3
Arinos → Brazil 10°25S 58°20W 331 C6
Ario de Rosales Mexico 19°12N 101°43W 318 D4
Ariogala Lithuania 55°16N 23°28E 184 C10
Arios Pagos Athens, Greece 112 c1
Aripo → Trin. & Tob. 10°35N 61°14W 323 t
Aripo, Mt. Trin. & Tob. 10°45N 61°15W 323 t
Aripo Caves Trin. & Tob. 10°43N 61°14W 323 t
Aripuanã Brazil 9°25S 60°30W 331 B5
Aripuanã → Brazil 5°7S 60°25W 331 B5
Ariquemes Brazil 9°55S 63°6W 331 B5
Arisaig U.K. 56°55N 5°51W 167 E3
Arîsh, W. el → Egypt 31°9N 33°49E 256 A3
Arissa Ethiopia 11°10N 41°35E 257 E5
Aristazabal I. Canada 52°40N 129°10W 296 C3
Arita Japan 33°11N 129°54E 222 D1
Aritao Phil. 16°18N 121°2E 232 C3
Ariton U.S.A. 31°36N 85°43W 316 D4
Arivonimamo Madag. 19°1S 47°11E 272 B2
Ariyalur India 11°8N 79°8E 245 J4
Ariza Spain 41°19N 2°3W 196 D2
Arizaro, Salar de Argentina 24°40S 67°50W 334 A2
Arizona Argentina 35°45S 65°25W 334 D2
Arizona □ U.S.A. 34°0N 112°0W 305 J8
Arizpe Mexico 30°20N 110°10W 318 A2
'Arjah Si. Arabia 24°43N 44°17E 246 E5
Årjäng Sweden 59°24N 12°8E 162 E6
Arjeplog Sweden 66°3N 17°54E 160 C17
Arjepluovve = Arjeplog Sweden 66°3N 17°54E 160 C17
Arjona Colombia 10°14N 75°22W 328 A2
Arjona Spain 37°56N 4°4W 195 H6
Arjuna Indonesia 7°49S 112°34E 235 D4
Arka Russia 60°15N 142°0E 215 C15
Arkadak Russia 51°58N 43°30E 190 E6
Arkadelphia U.S.A. 34°7N 93°4W 314 D8
Arkadia □ Greece 37°30N 22°20E 204 D4
Arkaig, L. U.K. 56°59N 5°10W 167 E3
Arkalgud India 12°46N 76°3E 245 H3
Arkalyk = Arqalyk Kazakhstan 50°13N 66°50E 217 B7
Arkansas □ U.S.A. 35°0N 92°30W 314 D8
Arkansas → U.S.A. 33°47N 91°4W 314 E9
Arkansas City U.S.A. 37°4N 97°2W 308 G5
Arkaroola Australia 30°20S 139°22E 281 E2
Arkavāz Iran 33°22N 46°35E 213 F12
Arkhangelsk Russia 64°38N 40°36E 186 B7
Arkhangelskoye Russia 51°32N 40°58E 190 E5
Arkhangelyskoye Russia 55°47N 37°17E 129 B1
Arki Greece 37°24N 26°44E 205 D8
Arki India 31°9N 76°58E 242 D7
Arkiko Eritrea 15°33N 39°30E 257 D4
Arklow Ireland 52°48N 6°10W 166 D5
Arkona, Kap Germany 54°42N 13°26E 178 A9
Arkösund Sweden 58°29N 16°56E 163 F10
Arkoudi Greece 38°33N 20°43E 207 B2
Arkport U.S.A. 42°24N 77°42W 312 D7
Arkticheskiy, Mys Russia 81°10N 95°0E 215 A10
Arkul Russia 57°17N 50°3E 190 B10
Arkville U.S.A. 42°9N 74°37W 313 D10
Årla Sweden 59°17N 16°40E 162 E10
Arlanda, Stockholm ✈ (ARN) Sweden 59°41N 17°56E 139 A1
Arlanza → Spain 42°6N 4°9W 194 C6
Arlanzón → Spain 42°3N 4°17W 194 C6
Arlbergpass Austria 47°9N 10°12E 180 D3
Arlbergtunnel Austria 47°9N 10°12E 180 D3
Arles France 43°41N 4°40E 175 E8
Arli Burkina Faso 11°35N 1°28E 263 C5
Arli △ Burkina Faso 11°35N 1°28E 263 C5
Arlington Free State, S. Africa 28°1S 27°53E 271 C4
Arlington Ga., U.S.A. 31°26N 84°44W 316 D5
Arlington Mass., U.S.A. 42°24N 71°10W 116 A1
Arlington N.Y., U.S.A. 41°42N 73°54W 313 E11
Arlington Oreg., U.S.A. 45°43N 120°12W 304 D3
Arlington S. Dak., U.S.A. 44°22N 97°8W 308 C5
Arlington Tex., U.S.A. 32°44N 97°6W 314 E6
Arlington Va., U.S.A. 38°53N 77°7W 143 B3
Arlington Vt., U.S.A. 43°5N 73°9W 313 C11
Arlington Wash., U.S.A. 48°12N 122°8W 306 B4
Arlington Heights Ill., U.S.A. 42°5N 87°59W 311 B9
Arlington Heights Mass., U.S.A. 42°25N 71°10W 116 A1
Arlington Nat. Cemetery U.S.A. 38°52N 77°4W 143 B3
Arlon Belgium 49°42N 5°49E 170 E5
Arlparra Australia 22°11S 134°30E 280 C1
Arltunga Australia 23°26S 134°41E 280 C1
Armação Brazil 22°52S 43°6W 135 B2
Armadale Vic., Australia 37°51S 145°0E 128 B2
Armadale W. Austral., Australia 32°9S 116°0E 279 F2
Armagh U.K. 54°21N 6°39W 166 B5
Armagh □ U.K. 54°18N 6°37W 166 B5
Armagnac France 43°50N 0°10E 174 E4
Armançon → France 47°59N 3°30E 173 E10
Armando Bermudez △ Dom. Rep. 19°3N 71°0W 321 C5

Armant *Egypt* 25°37N 32°32E **256** B3
Armatree *Australia* 31°26S 148°28E **283** A8
Armavir *Russia* 45°2N 41°7E **191** H5
Armenia *Colombia* 4°35N 75°45W **328** C2
Armenia ■ *Asia* 40°20N 45°0E **191** K7
Armenian Quarter *Jerusalem* **123** b3
Armeniş *Romania* 45°13N 22°17E **182** E7
Armenistis, Akra *Greece* 36°8N 27°42E **206** E11
Armentières *France* 50°40N 2°50E **173** B9
Armero *Colombia* 4°58N 74°54W **328** C3
Armidale *Australia* 30°30S 151°40E **283** A9
Armilla *Spain* 37°9N 3°37W **195** H7
Armori *India* 20°28N 79°59E **244** D4
Armorique ⌂ *France* 48°22N 3°50W **172** D3
Armour *U.S.A.* 43°19N 98°21W **308** D4
Armour Heights *Canada* 43°45N 79°25W **141** A2
Armstrong *B.C., Canada* 50°25N 119°10W **296** C5
Armstrong *Ont., Canada* 50°18N 89°4W **298** B2
Armur *India* 18°48N 78°16E **244** E4
Armutlu *Bursa, Turkey* 40°31N 28°50E **203** F12
Armutlu *İzmir, Turkey* 38°24N 27°34E **205** C9
Arnarfjörður *Iceland* 65°48N 23°40W **155** B3
Arnaud ➔ *Canada* 59°59N 69°46W **295** F18
Arnauti, C. *Cyprus* 35°6N 32°17E **207** E8
Arnay-le-Duc *France* 47°10N 4°27E **173** E11
Arncliffe *Australia* 33°56S 151°8E **139** B1
Arnea *Greece* 40°30N 23°38E **202** F7
Arnedillo *Spain* 42°13N 2°14W **196** C2
Arnedo *Spain* 42°12N 2°5W **196** C2
Árnes *Iceland* 66°1N 21°31W **155** A5
Årnes *Akershus, Norway* 60°7N 11°28E **164** D8
Árnessýsla ☐ *Iceland* 64°15N 20°30W **155** C6
Arnett *U.S.A.* 36°8N 99°46W **314** C5
Arnhem *Neths.* 51°58N 5°55E **170** C5
Arnhem, C. *Australia* 12°20S 137°30E **280** A2
Arnhem B. *Australia* 12°20S 136°10E **280** A2
Arnhem Land *Australia* 13°10S 134°30E **280** A1
Arnhem Land ☼
Australia 12°50S 134°50E **280** A1
Arnissa *Greece* 40°47N 21°49E **202** F5
Arno ➔ *Italy* 43°41N 10°17E **198** E7
Arno Bay *Australia* 33°54S 136°34E **282** B2
Arnold *Notts., U.K.* 53°1N 1°7W **168** D6
Arnold *Calif., U.S.A.* 38°15N 120°21W **306** G6
Arnold *Mo., U.S.A.* 38°26N 90°23W **310** F6
Arnold Arboretum *U.S.A.* 42°18N 71°8W **116** B2
Arnoldstein *Austria* 46°33N 13°43E **180** E6
Arnon ➔ *France* 47°13N 2°1E **173** E9
Arnos Vale *Trin. & Tob.* 11°13N 60°45W **323** e
Arnot *Canada* 55°56N 96°41W **297** B9
Arnøya *Norway* 70°9N 20°40E **160** A19
Arnprior *Canada* 45°26N 76°21W **313** A8
Arnsberg *Germany* 51°24N 8°5E **178** D4
Arnsberger Wald ⌂
Germany 51°25N 8°20E **178** D4
Arnstadt *Germany* 50°50N 10°56E **178** E6
Arnswalde = Choszczno
Poland 53°7N 15°25E **185** E2
Aro ➔ *Venezuela* 8°1N 64°11W **329** B5
Aroa, Pte. *Moorea* 17°28S 149°46W **289** e
Aroab *Namibia* 26°41S 19°39E **270** C2
Aroania Oros *Greece* 37°56N 22°12E **204** D4
Aroche *Spain* 37°56N 6°57W **195** H4
Arochuku *Nigeria* 5°21N 7°54E **263** D6
Aroeiras *Brazil* 7°31S 35°41W **332** C4
Arolsen *Germany* 51°23N 9°2E **178** D5
Aron *India* 25°57N 77°56E **242** G6
Aron ➔ *France* 46°50N 3°28E **173** F10
Arona *Canary Is.* 28°6N 16°40W **153** e1
Arona *Italy* 45°46N 8°34E **198** C5
Arorae *Kiribati* 2°38S 176°49E **277** A14
Arorangi *Cook Is.* 21°13S 159°49W **289** h
Aroroy *Phil.* 12°31N 123°24E **232** E4
Aros ➔ *Mexico* 29°9N 107°57W **318** B3
Arouca *Trin. & Tob.* 10°38N 61°20W **323** f
Arousa, Ría de ➔ *Spain* 42°28N 8°57W **194** C2
Årøysund *Norway* 59°10N 10°27E **164** E7
Arpa ➔ *Asia* 39°28N 44°56E **213** C11
Arpaçay *Turkey* 40°50N 43°19E **213** B10
Árpádföld *Hungary* 47°32N 19°8E **117** A3
Arpajon *France* 48°36N 2°15E **173** D9
Arpajon-sur-Cère *France* 44°53N 2°28E **174** D6
Arpaşu de Jos *Romania* 45°47N 24°37E **183** E9
Arqalyk *Kazakhstan* 50°13N 66°50E **217** B7
Arque *Bolivia* 17°48S 66°23W **330** D4
Arrah = Ara *India* 25°35N 84°32E **243** G11
Arrah *Ivory C.* 6°40N 3°58W **262** D4
Arraias *Brazil* 12°56S 46°57W **333** D2
Arraias ➔ *Mato Grosso,*
Brazil 11°10S 53°35W **331** C7
Arraias ➔ *Pará, Brazil* 7°30S 49°20W **332** C2
Arraijan *Panama* 8°56N 79°36W **320** c
Arraiolos *Portugal* 38°44N 7°59W **195** G3
Arran *U.K.* 55°34N 5°12W **167** F3
Arras *France* 50°17N 2°46E **173** B9
Arrasate *Spain* 43°4N 2°30W **196** B2
Arrats ➔ *France* 44°6N 0°52E **174** E4
Arreau *France* 42°54N 0°22E **174** F4
Arrecife *Canary Is.* 28°57N 13°37W **153** e2
Arrecifes *Argentina* 34°6S 60°9W **334** C3
Arrée, Mts. d' *France* 48°26N 3°55W **172** D3
Arrentela *Portugal* 38°37N 9°6W **126** B2
Arresø *Denmark* 55°58N 12°6E **163** J6
Arriaga *Mexico* 16°14N 93°54W **319** D6
Arribes del Duero ⌂
Spain 41°11N 6°39W **194** D4
Arrilalah *Australia* 23°43S 143°54E **280** C3
Arrino *Australia* 29°30S 115°40E **279** E2
Arriondas *Spain* 43°23N 5°11W **194** B5
Arrojado ➔ *Brazil* 13°24S 44°20W **333** D3
Arromanches-les-Bains
France 49°20N 0°38W **172** C6
Arronches *Portugal* 39°8N 7°16W **195** F3
Arros ➔ *France* 43°40N 0°2W **174** E3
Arrow, L. *Ireland* 54°3N 8°19W **166** B3
Arrowsmith, Mt. *N.Z.* 43°20S 170°55E **285** D5
Arrowtown *N.Z.* 44°57S 168°50E **285** E3
Arroyo de la Luz *Spain* 39°30N 6°38W **195** F4
Arroyo del Puerco = Arroyo de la
Luz *Spain* 39°30N 6°38W **195** F4
Arroyo Grande *U.S.A.* 35°7N 120°35W **307** K6
Arroyo Seco Park *U.S.A.* 34°6N 118°11W **126** B3
Ars *Iran* 37°9N 47°46E **246** B5
Ars-sur-Moselle *France* 49°5N 6°4E **173** C13
Arsenault L. *Canada* 55°6N 108°32W **297** B7
Arsenev *Russia* 44°10N 133°15E **220** B6
Arsi *Ethiopia* 7°45N 39°0E **257** F4
Arsiero *Italy* 45°48N 11°21E **199** C8
Arsikere *India* 13°15N 76°15E **245** H3
Arsin *Turkey* 41°8N 39°55E **213** B8
Arsk *Russia* 56°10N 49°50E **190** B9
Arslanköy *Turkey* 37°0N 34°17E **250** B5
Årsta *Sweden* 59°17N 18°3E **139** B2
Årsunda *Sweden* 60°31N 16°45E **162** D10
Art, Î. *N. Cal.* 19°43S 163°38E **288** d
Arta *Greece* 39°8N 21°2E **204** B3
Artà *Spain* 39°41N 3°21E **206** B4
Arta ☐ *Greece* 39°15N 21°5E **204** B3
Artà, Coves d *Spain* 39°40N 3°24E **206** B4
Artane *Ireland* 53°22N 6°12W **120** A2
Artas *West Bank* 31°41N 35°11E **123** B2
Artashat *Armenia* 40°0N 44°35E **213** B11
Arteaga *Mexico* 18°28N 102°25W **318** D4
Arteche *Phil.* 12°17N 125°22E **232** E5
Arteijo = Arteixo *Spain* 43°19N 8°29W **194** B2
Arteixo *Spain* 43°19N 8°29W **194** B2
Artem = Artyom
Azerbaijan 40°28N 50°20E **191** K10
Artem *Russia* 43°22N 132°13E **220** C6
Artemovsk *Sib., Russia* 54°45N 93°35E **215** D10
Artemovsk *Ukraine* 48°35N 38°0E **189** H9
Artemovskiy *Russia* 47°45N 40°16E **191** G5
Artenay *France* 48°5N 1°50E **173** D8
Artern *Germany* 51°22N 11°18E **178** D7
Artesa de Segre *Spain* 41°54N 1°3E **196** D6
Artesia = Mosomane
Botswana 24°2S 26°19E **270** B4
Artesia *U.S.A.* 32°51N 104°24W **305** K11
Arthington *Liberia* 6°35N 10°45W **262** D2
Arthur *Ont., Canada* 43°50N 80°32W **312** C4
Arthur *Ill., U.S.A.* 39°43N 88°28W **311** E8
Arthur ➔ *Australia* 41°2S 144°40E **281** G3
Arthur Cr. ➔ *Australia* 22°30S 136°25E **280** C2
Arthur Pt. *Australia* 22°7S 150°3E **280** C5
Arthur River *Australia* 33°20S 117°2E **279** F2
Arthur's Pass *N.Z.* 42°54S 171°35E **285** C6
Arthur's Pass △ *N.Z.* 42°53S 171°42E **285** C6
Arthur's Seat *U.K.* 55°56N 3°9W **121** B3
Arthur's Town *Bahamas* 24°38N 75°42W **321** B4
Artigas = Río Branco
Uruguay 32°40S 53°40W **335** C5
Artigas *Antarctica* 62°30S 58°0W **151** C18
Artigas *Uruguay* 30°20S 56°30W **334** C4
Artik *Armenia* 40°38N 43°58E **191** K6
Artillery L. *Canada* 63°9N 107°52W **297** A7
Artois *France* 50°20N 2°30E **173** B9
Artotina *Greece* 38°42N 22°2E **204** C4
Artova *Turkey* 40°5N 36°28E **212** B7
Artrutx, C. de *Spain* 39°55N 3°49E **206** B4
Arts, Place des *Montréal, Canada* **130** b2
Artsyz *Ukraine* 46°4N 29°26E **183** D14
Artux *China* 39°40N 76°10E **217** E9
Artvin *Turkey* 41°14N 41°44E **213** B9
Artvin ☐ *Turkey* 41°10N 41°50E **213** B9
Artyk *Russia* 64°12N 145°6E **215** C15
Artyom *Azerbaijan* 40°28N 50°20E **191** K10
Aru, Kepulauan *Indonesia* 6°0S 134°30E **231** F8
Aru Is. = Aru, Kepulauan
Indonesia 6°0S 134°30E **231** F8
Arua *Uganda* 3°1N 30°58E **268** B3
Aruanã *Brazil* 14°54S 51°10W **333** D1
Aruba ☒ *W. Indies* 12°30N 70°0W **322** f
Arudy *France* 43°7N 0°28W **174** E3
Arué *Tahiti* 17°31S 149°30W **289** e
Arumã *Brazil* 4°44S 62°8W **329** D5
Arume-wan *Japan* 26°35N 128°8E **288** a
Arumpo *Australia* 33°48S 142°55E **282** B5
Arun *Bangkok, Thailand* **113** b1
Arun ➔ *Nepal* 26°55N 87°10E **243** F12
Arun ➔ *W. Susx., U.K.* 50°49N 0°33W **169** G7
Arunachal Pradesh ☐
India 28°0N 95°0E **241** B5
Aruppukkottai *India* 9°31N 78°8E **245** K4
Arusha *Tanzania* 3°20S 36°40E **268** C4
Arusha ☐ *Tanzania* 4°0S 36°30E **268** C4
Arusha △ *Tanzania* 3°16S 36°47E **268** C4
Arusha Chini *Tanzania* 3°32S 37°20E **268** C4
Arut ➔ *Indonesia* 2°42S 111°34E **235** C4
Aruvi ➔ *Sri Lanka* 8°48N 79°53E **245** K4
Aruwimi ➔
Dem. Rep. of the Congo 1°13N 23°36E **264** B4
Arvada *Colo., U.S.A.* 39°48N 105°5W **304** G11
Arvada *Wyo., U.S.A.* 44°39N 106°8W **304** D10
Arvakalu *Sri Lanka* 8°20N 79°58E **245** K4
Arvayheer *Mongolia* 46°15N 102°48E **218** B5
Arve ➔ *France* 46°11N 6°8E **173** F13
Arvi *Kriti, Greece* 34°59N 25°28E **207** F6
Arvi *India* 20°59N 78°16E **244** D4
Arviat *Canada* 61°6N 93°59W **297** A10
Arvidsjaur *Sweden* 65°35N 19°10E **160** D18
Arvika *Sweden* 59°40N 12°36E **162** E6
Arvin *U.S.A.* 35°12N 118°50W **307** K8
Arwad *Syria* 34°51N 35°51E **250** D6
Arwal *India* 25°15N 84°41E **243** G11
Arxan *China* 47°11N 119°57E **219** B6
Åryd *Sweden* 56°49N 14°59E **163** H8
Arys *Kazakhstan* 42°26N 68°48E **217** D7
Arzachena *Italy* 41°5N 9°23E **200** A2
Arzamas *Russia* 55°27N 43°55E **190** C6
Arzanah *U.A.E.* 24°47N 52°34E **247** E7
Arzew *Algeria* 35°50N 0°23W **261** A4
Arzgir *Russia* 45°18N 44°23E **191** H7
Arzignano *Italy* 45°31N 11°20E **199** C8
Arzúa *Spain* 42°56N 8°9W **194** C2
Aš *Czech Rep.* 50°13N 12°12E **180** A5
Ås *Akershus, Norway* 59°40N 10°48E **164** E7
Ås *Sweden* 63°15N 14°34E **162** A8
As Pontes de García Rodríguez
Spain 43°27N 7°51W **194** B3
As Sa'an *Syria* 35°16N 37°22E **250** C8
Aş Şafā *Syria* 33°10N 37°0E **250** E8
Aş Şaffānīyah *Si. Arabia* 27°55N 48°50E **247** E6
Aş Şafīrah *Syria* 36°5N 37°21E **250** B8
Aş Şahm *Oman* 24°10N 56°53E **247** E8
Aş Şājir *Si. Arabia* 25°11N 44°36E **246** E5
As Salamīyah *Syria* 35°1N 37°2E **250** C8
As Salmān *Iraq* 30°30N 44°32E **246** D5
As Salţ *Jordan* 32°2N 35°43E **251** F6
As Sal'w'a *Qatar* 24°23N 50°50E **247** E6
As Samāwah *Iraq* 31°15N 45°15E **246** D5
As Sanamayn *Syria* 33°3N 36°10E **250** E7
As Sawādah *Si. Arabia* 22°24N 44°28E **248** B4
As Sayl al Kabīr
Si. Arabia 21°38N 40°25E **248** B3
As Shawawra *West Bank* 31°41N 35°15E **123** B2
As Sohar = Şuḩār *Oman* 24°20N 56°40E **247** E8
As Sukhnah *Syria* 34°52N 38°52E **213** E8
As Sulaymānīyah *Iraq* 35°35N 45°29E **213** E11
As Sulaymānīyah
Si. Arabia 24°9N 47°18E **248** A4
As Sulaymānīyah ☐
Iraq 35°50N 45°30E **213** E11
As Sulaymī *Si. Arabia* 26°17N 41°21E **246** E4
As Sulayyil *Si. Arabia* 20°27N 45°34E **248** B4
As Sulţān *Libya* 31°4N 17°8E **258** B3
As Summān *Si. Arabia* 25°0N 47°0E **246** E5
Aş Şurrah *Yemen* 13°57N 46°14E **248** D4
Aş Şuwar *Syria* 35°30N 40°38E **213** E9
As Suwaydā' *Syria* 32°40N 36°30E **250** F7
As Suwaydā' ☐ *Syria* 32°45N 36°45E **250** F7
As Suwayq *Oman* 23°51N 57°26E **247** F8
Aş Şuwayrah *Iraq* 32°55N 45°0E **213** F11
Åsa *Sweden* 57°21N 12°8E **163** G6
Asa Wright Nature Centre
Trin. & Tob. 10°43N 61°17W **323** f
Asab *Namibia* 25°30S 18°0E **270** C2
Asaba *Nigeria* 6°12N 6°38E **263** D6
Asad, Buḩayrat al *Syria* 36°0N 38°15E **213** E8
Asadābād *Iran* 34°47N 48°7E **213** E13
Asafo *Ghana* 6°20N 2°40W **262** D4
Asaga Str. *Amer. Samoa* 14°10S 169°37W **302** g
Asagaya *Japan* 35°41N 139°38E **140** A2
Asahi *Chiba, Japan* 35°43N 140°39E **223** B12
Asahi *Ōsaka, Japan* 34°43N 135°31E **133** A2
Asahi-Gawa ➔ *Japan* 34°36N 133°58E **222** C5
Asahigawa *Japan* 43°46N 142°22E **220** C11
Asakusa *Japan* 35°42N 139°47E **140** A3
Asakusabashi *Tokyo, Japan* **140** a5
Asale, L. *Ethiopia* 14°0N 40°20E **257** E5
Asaluyeh *Iran* 27°29N 52°37E **247** E7
Asama-Yama *Japan* 36°24N 138°31E **223** A10
Asamankese *Ghana* 5°50N 0°40W **263** D4
Asan *S. Korea* 36°48N 127°1E **224** D3
Asan ➔ *India* 26°37N 78°24E **243** F8
Asansol *India* 23°40N 87°1E **243** H12
Åsarna *Sweden* 62°39N 14°22E **162** B8
Asati *India* 22°28N 88°15E **124** C1
Asau *Samoa* 13°27S 172°33W **287** V19
Asayita *Ethiopia* 11°35N 41°23E **257** E5
Asba Littoria = Asbe Teferi
Ethiopia 9°4N 40°49E **257** F5
Asbe Teferi *Ethiopia* 9°4N 40°49E **257** F5
Asbesberge *S. Africa* 29°0S 23°0E **270** C3
Asbestos *Canada* 45°47N 71°58W **299** C5
Asbury Park *U.S.A.* 40°13N 74°1W **313** F10
Ascea *Italy* 40°8N 15°11E **201** B8
Ascensión *Mexico* 31°6N 107°59W **318** A3
Ascensión, B. de la
Mexico 19°40N 87°30W **319** D7
Ascension I. *Atl. Oc.* 7°57S 14°23W **153** g
Aschach an der Donau
Austria 48°22N 14°2E **180** C7
Aschaffenburg *Germany* 49°58N 9°6E **179** F5
Aschendorf *Germany* 53°3N 7°19E **178** B3
Aschersleben *Germany* 51°45N 11°29E **178** D7
Aschheim *Germany* 48°10N 11°42E **131** A3
Asciano *Italy* 43°14N 11°33E **199** E8
Ascoli Piceno *Italy* 42°51N 13°34E **199** F10
Ascoli Satriano *Italy* 41°11N 15°32E **201** A8
Ascope *Peru* 7°46S 79°8W **330** B2
Ascot Vale *Australia* 37°46S 144°53E **128** A1
Ascotán *Chile* 21°45S 68°17W **334** A2
Ascuncion *Phil.* 7°35N 125°45E **233** H5
Aseb *Eritrea* 13°0N 42°40E **257** E5
Åseda *Sweden* 57°10N 15°20E **163** G9
Asedjrad *Algeria* 24°51N 1°29E **261** D5
Aseki *Papua N. G.* 7°21S 146°12E **286** D4
Asela *Ethiopia* 8°0N 39°0E **257** F4
Åsen *Sweden* 61°17N 13°50E **162** C7
Asenovgrad *Bulgaria* 42°1N 24°51E **203** D8
Aseral *Norway* 58°37N 7°25E **164** E4
Asfeld *France* 49°27N 4°5E **173** C11
Asfûn el Matâ'na *Egypt* 25°26N 32°30E **256** B3
Asgabat = Ashgabat
Turkmenistan 38°0N 57°50E **247** B8
Åsgårdstrand *Norway* 59°22N 10°27E **164** E7
Asgata *Cyprus* 34°46N 33°15E **207** F9
Ash Fork *U.S.A.* 35°13N 112°29W **305** J7
Ash Grove *U.S.A.* 37°19N 93°35W **308** G7
Ash Shabakah *Iraq* 30°49N 43°39E **246** D4
Ash Shafa *Si. Arabia* 21°27N 39°49E **248** B2
Ash Shamāl ☐ *Lebanon* 34°25N 36°0E **250** D7
Ash Shāmīyah *Iraq* 31°55N 44°35E **213** G11
Ash Sha'rā' *Si. Arabia* 24°16N 44°11E **248** A4
Ash Shāriqah *U.A.E.* 25°23N 55°26E **247** E7
Ash Sharmah *Si. Arabia* 28°1N 35°16E **251** K6
Ash Sharqāt *Iraq* 35°27N 43°16E **213** E10
Ash Sharqīyah ☐
Si. Arabia 23°0N 50°30E **249** B6
Ash Shāţi *Libya* 27°30N 12°30E **258** C2
Ash Shaţrah *Iraq* 31°30N 46°10E **246** D5
Ash Shawbak *Jordan* 30°32N 35°34E **246** D2
Ash Shaykh Ḩumayd
Si. Arabia 28°6N 34°33E **251** K5
Ash Shifā' *Si. Arabia* 28°30N 35°30E **251** K6
Ash Shiḩr *Yemen* 14°45N 49°36E **249** D5
Ash Shināfiyah *Iraq* 31°35N 44°39E **246** D5
Ash Shu'bah *Si. Arabia* 28°54N 44°44E **246** D5
Ash Shumlūl *Si. Arabia* 26°31N 47°20E **246** E5
Ash Shuqayq *Si. Arabia* 17°44N 42°1E **248** C3
Ash Shūr'a *Iraq* 35°58N 43°13E **246** C4
Ash Shurayf *Si. Arabia* 25°43N 39°14E **246** E3
Ash Shuwayfāt *Lebanon* 33°45N 35°30E **250** E6
Ash Shuwayrif *Libya* 29°59N 14°16E **258** C2
Asha *Russia* 55°0N 57°16E **186** D10
Ashanti ☐ *Ghana* 7°30N 1°30W **263** D4
Ashau *Vietnam* 16°6N 107°22E **236** D6
Ashbourne *U.K.* 53°2N 1°43W **168** D6
Ashbridge's Bay Park
Canada 43°40N 79°18W **141** B3
Ashburn *Ga., U.S.A.* 31°43N 83°39W **316** D6
Ashburn *Ill., U.S.A.* 41°45N 87°43W **119** C2
Ashburton *Vic., Australia* 37°51S 145°4E **128** B2
Ashburton *N.Z.* 43°53S 171°48E **285** D6
Ashburton ➔ *Australia* 21°40S 114°56E **278** D1
Ashburton, North Branch ➔
N.Z. 43°54S 171°44E **285** D6
Ashburton, South Branch ➔
N.Z. 43°54S 171°44E **285** D6
Ashcroft *Canada* 50°40N 121°20W **296** C4
Ashdod *Israel* 31°49N 34°35E **251** G5
Ashdown *U.S.A.* 33°40N 94°8W **314** E7
Asheboro *U.S.A.* 35°43N 79°49W **315** D15
Ashern *Canada* 51°11N 98°21W **297** C9
Asherton *U.S.A.* 28°27N 99°46W **314** G5
Asheville *U.S.A.* 35°36N 82°33W **315** D13
Ashewat *Pakistan* 31°22N 68°32E **242** D3
Asheweig ➔ *Canada* 54°17N 87°12W **298** B2
Ashfield *Australia* 33°53S 151°7E **139** B1
Ashford *N.S.W., Australia* 29°15S 151°3E **281** D5
Ashford *Kent, U.K.* 51°8N 0°53E **169** F8
Ashford *Surrey, U.K.* 51°25N 0°26W **125** B1
Ashford *Ala., U.S.A.* 31°11N 85°14W **316** D4
Ashgabat *Turkmenistan* 38°0N 57°50E **247** B8
Ashhurst *N.Z.* 40°16S 175°45E **284** G4
Ashibetsu *Japan* 43°31N 142°11E **220** C11
Ashikaga *Japan* 36°28N 139°29E **223** A11
Ashington *U.K.* 55°11N 1°33W **168** B6
Ashio *Japan* 36°38N 139°27E **223** A11
Ashizuri-Uwakai △
Japan 32°56N 132°32E **222** E4
Ashizuri-Zaki *Japan* 32°44N 133°0E **222** E5
Ashkarkot *Afghan.* 33°3N 67°58E **242** C2
Ashkhabad = Ashgabat
Turkmenistan 38°0N 57°50E **247** B8
Āshkhāneh *Iran* 37°26N 56°55E **247** B8
Ashland *Ala., U.S.A.* 33°16N 85°50W **316** B4
Ashland *Ill., U.S.A.* 39°53N 90°1W **310** E7
Ashland *Kans., U.S.A.* 37°11N 99°46W **308** G4
Ashland *Ky., U.S.A.* 38°28N 82°38W **309** F12
Ashland *Maine, U.S.A.* 46°38N 68°24W **309** B19
Ashland *Mont., U.S.A.* 45°36N 106°16W **304** D10
Ashland *Ohio, U.S.A.* 40°52N 82°19W **312** F2
Ashland *Oreg., U.S.A.* 42°12N 122°43W **304** E2
Ashland *Pa., U.S.A.* 40°45N 76°22W **313** F8
Ashland *Va., U.S.A.* 37°46N 77°29W **309** G15
Ashland *Wis., U.S.A.* 46°35N 90°53W **308** B8
Ashley *Ill., U.S.A.* 38°20N 89°11W **310** F7
Ashley *Ind., U.S.A.* 41°32N 85°4W **311** C11
Ashley *N. Dak., U.S.A.* 46°2N 99°22W **308** B4
Ashley *Pa., U.S.A.* 41°12N 75°55W **313** E9
Ashley ➔ *N.Z.* 43°17S 172°44E **285** D7
Ashmore and Cartier Is.
Ind. Oc. 12°15S 123°0E **278** B3
Ashmore Reef *Australia* 12°14S 123°5E **278** B3
Ashmûn *Egypt* 30°18N 30°58E **255** H1
Ashmyany *Belarus* 54°26N 25°52E **177** A13
Ashokan Res. *U.S.A.* 41°56N 74°13W **313** E10
Ashoknagar *India* 24°34N 77°43E **244** B3
Ashqelon *Israel* 31°42N 34°35E **251** G5
Ashraf = Behshahr *Iran* 36°45N 53°35E **247** B7
Ashta *India* 23°1N 76°43E **242** H7
Ashtabula *U.S.A.* 41°52N 80°47W **312** E4
Ashti *Maharashtra, India* 21°12N 78°11E **244** D4
Ashti *Maharashtra, India* 18°50N 75°15E **244** E2
Āshtīyān *Iran* 34°31N 50°0E **247** C6
Ashton *Western Cape,*
S. Africa 33°50S 20°5E **270** D3
Ashton *Idaho, U.S.A.* 44°4N 111°27W **304** D8
Ashtown *Ireland* 53°22N 6°19W **120** A2
Ashuanipi, L. *Canada* 52°45N 66°15W **299** B6
Ashuapmushuan ➔
Canada 48°37N 72°20W **298** C5
Ashville *Ala., U.S.A.* 33°50N 86°15W **316** B3
Ashville *Fla., U.S.A.* 30°37N 83°39W **316** E6
Ashville *Pa., U.S.A.* 40°34N 78°33W **312** F6
'Āşī ➔ *Asia* 36°1N 35°59E **250** B6
Asia 45°0N 75°0E **210** E9
Asia, Kepulauan *Indonesia* 1°0N 131°13E **231** D8
Asiago *Italy* 45°52N 11°30E **199** C8
Asidonhoppo *Suriname* 3°50N 55°30W **329** C6
Asifabad *India* 19°20N 79°24E **244** E4
Asilah *Morocco* 35°29N 6°0W **260** A3
Asinara *Italy* 41°4N 8°16E **200** A1
Asinara, G. dell' *Italy* 41°0N 8°30E **200** A1
Asino *Russia* 57°0N 86°0E **214** D9
Asipovichy *Belarus* 53°19N 28°33E **177** B15
'Asīr *Si. Arabia* 18°40N 42°30E **248** C3
Asir, Ras *Somali Rep.* 11°55N 51°10E **267** B7
Aska *India* 19°2N 84°42E **244** E7
Aşkale *Turkey* 39°55N 40°41E **213** C9
Asker *Norway* 59°50N 10°29E **164** E7
Askersund *Sweden* 58°53N 14°55E **163** F8
Askham *S. Africa* 26°59S 20°47E **270** C3
Askī Mawşil *Iraq* 36°30N 42°44E **213** D10
Askim *Norway* 59°35N 11°10E **164** E8
Askio, Oros *Greece* 40°25N 21°35E **202** F5
Askola *Finland* 60°16N 24°47E **121** B1
Askja *Iceland* 65°3N 16°48W **155** B10
Asklipio *Greece* 36°4N 27°56E **206** E11
Askøyna *Norway* 60°29N 5°10E **164** D2
Askrikefjärden *Sweden* 59°22N 18°13E **139** A3
Askvoll *Norway* 61°21N 5°4E **164** C2
Asl *Egypt* 29°33N 32°44E **256** B3
Aslan Burnu *Turkey* 38°44N 26°45E **205** C8
Aslanapa *Turkey* 39°13N 29°52E **205** B11
Aslānduz *Iran* 39°26N 47°24E **213** C12
Asmār *Afghan.* 35°10N 71°27E **240** B3
Asmara = Asmera
Eritrea 15°19N 38°55E **257** D4
Asmera *Eritrea* 15°19N 38°55E **257** D4
Asnæs *Denmark* 55°40N 11°0E **163** J4
Åsnen *Sweden* 56°37N 14°45E **163** H8
Asni *Morocco* 31°17N 7°58W **260** B3
Asnières *France* 48°54N 2°16E **134** A2
Aso *Japan* 32°55N 131°5E **222** E3
Aso Kuju △ *Japan* 32°53N 131°6E **222** E3
Aso-Zan *Japan* 32°53N 131°6E **222** E3
Asola *Italy* 45°13N 10°24E **198** C7
Asos *Greece* 38°22N 20°33E **207** C2
Asosa *Ethiopia* 10°3N 34°32E **257** E3
Asoteriba, Jebel *Sudan* 21°51N 36°30E **256** C4
Asouf, O. ➔ *Algeria* 25°40N 2°8E **261** C5
Aspatria *U.K.* 54°47N 3°19W **168** C4
Aspe *Spain* 38°20N 0°40W **197** G4
Aspen *U.S.A.* 39°11N 106°49W **304** G10
Aspendos *Turkey* 36°54N 31°7E **250** B2
Aspermont *U.S.A.* 33°8N 100°14W **314** E4
Aspern *Austria* 48°13N 16°29E **142** A2
Aspet *France* 43°1N 0°48E **174** E4
Aspiring, Mt. *N.Z.* 44°23S 168°46E **285** E3
Aspres-sur-Buëch *France* 44°32N 5°44E **175** D9
Asprokavos, Akra *Greece* 39°21N 20°6E **206** C10
Aspromonte △ *Italy* 38°9N 15°58E **201** D8
Aspur *India* 23°58N 74°7E **242** H6
Asquith *Canada* 52°8N 107°13W **297** C7
Assa *Morocco* 28°35N 9°6W **260** C3
Assab = Aseb *Eritrea* 13°0N 42°40E **257** E5
Assâba ☐ *Mauritania* 16°40N 11°40W **262** B2
Assâba, Massif de l'
Mauritania 16°10N 11°45W **262** B2
Assagny △ *Ivory C.* 5°10N 4°48W **262** D4
Assago *Italy* 45°24N 9°7E **129** B1
Assaikio *Nigeria* 8°34N 8°55E **263** D6
Assal, L. *Djibouti* 11°40N 42°26E **257** E5
Assam ☐ *India* 26°0N 93°0E **241** C4
Assamakka *Niger* 19°21N 5°38E **263** B6
Assateague Island ⌂
U.S.A. 38°15N 75°10W **309** F16
Assaye *India* 20°15N 75°53E **244** D2
Asse *Belgium* 50°24N 4°10E **170** D4
Assekrem *Algeria* 23°16N 5°49E **261** D6
Assémini *Italy* 39°17N 9°0E **200** C1
Assen *Neths.* 53°0N 6°35E **170** A6
Assendelft *Neths.* 52°28N 4°45E **112** A1
Assens *Denmark* 55°16N 9°55E **163** J3
Assiano *Italy* 45°27N 9°3E **129** B1
Assini *Ivory C.* 5°9N 3°17W **262** D4
Assiniboia *Canada* 49°40N 105°59W **297** D7
Assiniboine ➔ *Canada* 49°53N 97°8W **297** D9
Assiniboine, Mt.
Canada 50°52N 115°39W **296** C5
Assiou *Algeria* 21°7N 7°36E **261** D6
Assis *Brazil* 22°40S 50°20W **335** A5
Assis Brasil *Brazil* 10°55S 69°32W **330** C4
Assisi *Italy* 43°4N 12°37E **199** E9
Asskard *Norway* 63°1N 8°30E **164** A5
Assok Ngoum *Gabon* 1°45N 11°39E **264** B2
Assumption *U.S.A.* 39°31N 89°3W **310** E7
Assynt, L. *U.K.* 58°10N 5°3W **167** C3
Astaffort *France* 44°4N 0°40E **174** D4
Astakida *Greece* 35°53N 26°50E **205** F8
Astakos *Greece* 38°32N 21°5E **207** B3
Astana *Kazakhstan* 51°10N 71°30E **217** B8
Āstāneh *Iran* 37°17N 49°59E **247** B6
Astapovo = Lev Tolstoy
Russia 53°13N 39°29E **188** F10
Astara *Azerbaijan* 38°30N 48°50E **213** C13
Āstārā *Iran* 38°42N 48°52E **213** C13
Astarabad = Gorgān *Iran* 36°55N 54°30E **247** B7
Astoranca *Greece* 34°59N 25°3E **207** F6
Asti *Italy* 44°54N 8°12E **198** D5
Astipalea *Greece* 36°32N 26°22E **205** E8
Astola I. *Pakistan* 25°7N 63°51E **240** D1
Aston *Davao del S., Phil.* 6°54N 125°27E **233** H5
Astorga *Spain* 42°29N 6°8W **194** C4
Astoria *Ill., U.S.A.* 40°14N 90°21W **310** D6
Astoria *N.Y., U.S.A.* 40°46N 73°55W **132** B2
Astoria *Oreg., U.S.A.* 46°11N 123°50W **306** D3
Åstorp *Sweden* 56°6N 12°55E **163** H6
Astrakhan *Russia* 46°25N 48°5E **191** G9
Astrakhan ☐ *Russia* 47°45N 46°20E **191** G8
Astrebla Downs
Australia 24°12S 140°34E **280** C3
Astrolabe, Récifs de l'
N. Cal. 19°48S 165°37E **288** d
Astrolabe Park *Australia* 33°57S 151°12E **139** B2
Astudillo *Spain* 42°12N 4°22W **194** C6
Asturias ☐ *Spain* 43°15N 6°0W **194** B4
Asturias ✕ **(OVD)** *Spain* 43°33N 6°3W **194** B4
Asumman *S. Korea* 37°4N 126°40E **224** D3
Asunción *Bolivia* 11°46S 67°50W **330** C4
Asuncion *N. Marianas* 19°40N 145°24E **302** a
Asunción *Paraguay* 25°10S 57°30W **334** B4
Asunción Nochixtlán
Mexico 17°28N 97°14W **319** D5
Åsunden *Sweden* 58°0N 15°51E **163** F9
Asutri *Sudan* 15°25N 35°45E **257** D4
Aswa ➔ *Uganda* 3°43N 31°55E **268** B3
Aswa-Lolim ⌂ *Uganda* 2°43N 31°35E **268** B3
Aswad, Ra's al *Si. Arabia* 21°20N 39°0E **248** B2
Aswân *Egypt* 24°4N 32°57E **256** C3
Aswan High Dam = Sadd el Aali
Egypt 23°54N 32°54E **256** C3
Asyût *Egypt* 27°11N 31°4E **256** B3
Asyûti, Wadi ➔ *Egypt* 27°11N 31°16E **256** B3
Aszód *Hungary* 47°39N 19°28E **182** C4
At-Bashy *Kyrgyzstan* 41°10N 75°48E **217** D9
Aţ Ţafīlah *Jordan* 30°45N 35°30E **251** H6
Aţ Ţafīlah ☐ *Jordan* 30°45N 35°30E **251** H6
Aţ Tā'if *Si. Arabia* 21°5N 40°27E **248** B3
Aţ Tāj *Libya* 24°13N 23°18E **258** D4
At Ta'mīm ☐ *Iraq* 35°30N 44°20E **246** C5
At Tamīmī *Libya* 32°20N 23°4E **258** B4
Aţ Ţirāq *Si. Arabia* 27°19N 44°33E **246** E5
Aţ Tubayq *Si. Arabia* 29°30N 37°0E **251** J8
Aţ Ţunayb *Jordan* 31°48N 35°57E **251** G6
At Turbah *Lahij, Yemen* 12°40N 43°30E **248** D3
At Turbah *Ta'izz, Yemen* 13°13N 44°7E **248** D4
Atabey *Turkey* 37°57N 30°39E **205** D12
Atacama ☐ *Chile* 27°30S 70°0W **334** B2
Atacama, Desierto de
Chile 24°0S 69°20W **334** A2
Atacama, Salar de *Chile* 23°30S 68°20W **334** A2
Ataco *Colombia* 3°35N 75°23W **328** C2
Atafu *Pac. Oc.* 8°32S 172°31W **277** B16
Atakeye ☼ *Australia* 22°30S 133°45E **278** D5
Atakor *Algeria* 23°27N 5°31E **261** D6
Atakpamé *Togo* 7°31N 1°13E **263** D5
Atalaia do Norte *Brazil* 4°20S 70°12W **328** D3
Atalandi *Greece* 38°39N 22°58E **204** C4
Atalaya *Peru* 10°45S 73°50W **330** C3
Atalaya de Femes
Canary Is. 28°56N 13°47W **153** e2
Ataléia *Brazil* 18°3S 41°6W **333** E3
Atami *Japan* 35°5N 139°4E **223** B11
Atamyrat *Turkmenistan* 37°50N 65°12E **217** E7
Atankawng *Burma* 25°50N 97°47E **241** C6
Atapupu *Indonesia* 9°0S 124°51E **231** F6
Atâr *Mauritania* 20°30N 13°5W **260** D2
Ataram, Erg n- *Algeria* 23°57N 2°0E **261** D5
Atarfe *Spain* 37°13N 3°40W **195** H7
Atari *Pakistan* 30°56N 74°2E **242** D6
Atarot *West Bank* 31°52N 35°13E **123** A2
Atarot ✕ **(JRS)** *West Bank* 31°52N 35°14E **123** A2
Atascadero *U.S.A.* 35°29N 120°40W **306** K6
Atasū *Kazakhstan* 48°30N 71°0E **217** C8
Atatürk, İstanbul ✕ **(IST)**
Turkey 40°59N 28°49E **203** F12
Atatürk Barajı *Turkey* 37°28N 38°30E **213** D8
Atauro *E. Timor* 8°10S 125°30E **231** F7
Ataviros *Greece* 36°12N 27°50E **206** E11
'Atbara *Sudan* 17°42N 33°59E **256** D3
'Atbara, Nahr ➔ *Sudan* 17°40N 33°56E **256** D3
Atbasar *Kazakhstan* 51°48N 68°20E **217** B7
Atbashi = At-Bashy
Kyrgyzstan 41°10N 75°48E **217** D9
Atça *Turkey* 37°53N 28°13E **205** D10
Atchafalaya B. *U.S.A.* 29°25N 91°25W **314** G9
Atchison *U.S.A.* 39°34N 95°7W **308** F6
Atebubu *Ghana* 7°47N 1°0W **263** D4
Ateca *Spain* 41°20N 1°49W **196** D3
Aterno ➔ *Italy* 42°11N 13°51E **199** F10
Āteshān *Iran* 35°35N 52°37E **247** C7
Atesine, Alpi *Italy* 46°55N 11°30E **199** B8
Atessa *Italy* 42°4N 14°27E **199** F11
Atfîh *Egypt* 29°25N 31°15E **256** J7
Atghara *India* 22°37N 88°26E **124** B2
Ath *Belgium* 50°38N 3°47E **170** D3
Athabasca *Canada* 54°45N 113°20W **296** C6
Athabasca ➔ *Canada* 58°40N 110°50W **297** B6
Athabasca, L. *Canada* 59°15N 109°15W **297** B7
Athabasca Sand Dunes ⌂
Canada 59°4N 108°43W **297** B7
Athagarh *India* 20°32N 85°37E **244** D7
Athamanon Oros *Greece* 39°30N 21°26E **204** B3
Athboy *Ireland* 53°37N 6°56W **166** C5
Athena *U.S.A.* 29°59N 83°30W **316** F6
Athenry *Ireland* 53°18N 8°44W **166** C3
Athens = Athina *Greece* 37°58N 23°43E **112** B2
Athens *Ala., U.S.A.* 34°48N 86°58W **315** D11
Athens *Ga., U.S.A.* 33°57N 83°23W **316** B6
Athens *N.Y., U.S.A.* 42°16N 73°49W **313** D11
Athens *Ohio, U.S.A.* 39°20N 82°6W **309** F12
Athens *Pa., U.S.A.* 41°57N 76°31W **313** E8
Athens *Tenn., U.S.A.* 35°27N 84°36W **315** D12
Athens *Tex., U.S.A.* 32°12N 95°51W **314** E7
Atheras *Greece* 38°19N 20°25E **207** C1
Atherley *Canada* 44°37N 79°20W **312** B5
Atherton *Australia* 17°17S 145°30E **280** B4
Athi River *Kenya* 1°28S 36°58E **268** C4
Athiéme *Benin* 6°37N 1°40E **263** D5
Athienou *Cyprus* 35°3N 33°32E **207** E9
Athina *Greece* 37°58N 23°43E **112** B2
Athina ✕ **(ATH)** *Greece* 37°56N 23°56E **112** A3
Athinai = Athina *Greece* 37°58N 23°43E **112** B2
Athis-Mons *France* 48°42N 2°23E **134** B3
Athlone *Westmeath,*
Ireland 53°25N 7°56W **166** C4
Athlone *Western Cape,*
S. Africa 33°57S 18°30E **118** A2
Athmalik *India* 20°43N 84°32E **244** D7
Athna *Cyprus* 35°3N 33°47E **207** E9
Athni *India* 16°44N 75°6E **244** F2
Athol *N.Z.* 45°30S 168°35E **285** F3
Athol *Mass., U.S.A.* 42°36N 72°14W **313** D12
Athol I. *Bahamas* 25°5N 77°15W **153** b
Athol *S. Africa* 26°7S 28°3E **123** A2
Atholl, Forest of *U.K.* 56°51N 3°50W **167** E5
Atholl, Kap *Greenland* 76°25N 69°30W **154** B4
Atholville *Canada* 47°59N 66°43W **299** C6
Athos *Greece* 40°9N 24°22E **203** F8
Athy *Ireland* 53°0N 7°0W **166** C5
Ati *Chad* 13°13N 18°20E **259** F3
Ati *Sudan* 13°5N 29°2E **257** E2
Ati, J. *Libya* 23°24N 14°21E **258** D2
Atiak *Uganda* 3°12N 32°2E **268** B3
Atiamuri *N.Z.* 38°24S 176°5E **284** E5
Atico *Peru* 16°14S 73°40W **330** D3
Atienza *Spain* 41°12N 2°52W **196** D2
Atīfiya *Iraq* 33°23N 44°12E **113** A2
Atiit *Sudan* 6°10N 30°35E **257** F3
Atik L. *Canada* 55°15N 96°0W **297** B9
Atikaki ⌂ *Canada* 51°30N 95°31W **297** C9
Atikameg ➔ *Canada* 52°30N 82°46W **298** B3
Atikokan *Canada* 48°45N 91°37W **298** C1
Atikonak L. *Canada* 52°40N 64°32W **299** B7
Atimaono *Tahiti* 17°46S 149°28W **289** e
Atimonan *Phil.* 14°0N 121°55E **232** D3
'Ātinah, W. ➔ *Oman* 18°23N 53°28E **249** C6
Atirampattinam *India* 10°28N 79°20E **245** J4
Atişalen *Turkey* 41°3N 28°52E **122** B1
Atitlán △ *Cent. Amer.* 14°38N 91°10W **320** D1
Atiu *Cook Is.* 20°0S 158°10W **289** J12
Atka *Russia* 60°50N 151°48E **215** C16
Atka *Alaska, U.S.A.* 52°12N 174°12W **303** K4
Atka I. *U.S.A.* 52°7N 174°30W **303** K4
Atkarsk *Russia* 51°55N 45°2E **190** E7
Atkinson *Ga., U.S.A.* 31°13N 81°47W **316** D8
Atkinson *Ill., U.S.A.* 41°25N 90°1W **310** C6
Atkinson *Nebr., U.S.A.* 42°32N 98°59W **308** D4
Atlanta *Ga., U.S.A.* 33°45N 84°23W **313** B5
Atlanta *Ill., U.S.A.* 40°16N 89°14W **310** D7
Atlanta *Mo., U.S.A.* 39°54N 92°29W **310** E4
Atlanta *Tex., U.S.A.* 33°7N 94°10W **314** E7
Atlanta Hartsfield Int. ✕ **(ATL)**
U.S.A. 33°38N 84°26W **113** C2
Atlanta Zoo *U.S.A.* 33°44N 84°22W **113** B2
Atlantic *U.S.A.* 41°24N 95°1W **310** C2
Atlantic Beach *U.S.A.* 30°20N 81°24W **316** E8
Atlantic City *U.S.A.* 39°21N 74°27W **309** F16
Atlantic-Indian Basin
Antarctica 60°0S 30°0E **151** B4
Atlantic Ocean 0°0 20°0W **152** F8
Atlántico ☐ *Colombia* 10°45N 75°0W **328** A3
Atlantis *S. Africa* 33°34S 18°29E **270** D2
Atlas Mts. = Haut Atlas
Morocco 32°30N 5°0W **260** B4
Atlin *Canada* 59°31N 133°41W **296** B2
Atlin, L. *Canada* 59°26N 133°45W **296** B2
Atlin ⌂ *Canada* 59°10N 134°30W **296** B2
Atløyna *Norway* 61°21N 4°58E **164** C1
Atmakur *Andhra Pradesh,*
India 18°45N 78°39E **244** E4
Atmakur *Andhra Pradesh,*
India 14°37N 79°40E **245** G4
Atmakur *Andhra Pradesh,*
India 15°53N 78°35E **245** G4
Atmore *U.S.A.* 31°2N 87°29W **315** F11
Atna *Norway* 61°44N 10°49E **164** C7
Atna ➔ *Norway* 61°44N 10°49E **164** C7
Atō *Japan* 34°25N 131°40E **222** C3
Atocha *Bolivia* 20°56S 66°14W **330** E4
Atok *Phil.* 16°35N 120°41E **232** C3
Atoka *U.S.A.* 34°23N 96°8W **314** D6
Atokos *Greece* 38°28N 20°49E **207** C2
Atolia *U.S.A.* 35°19N 117°37W **307** K9
Atomium *Belgium* 50°54N 4°20E **116** A2
Atongo-Bakari *C.A.R.* 5°49N 21°35E **264** A4
Atori *Solomon Is.* 8°42S 160°59E **287** M11
Atqasuk *U.S.A.* 70°28N 157°24W **303** A8
Atqasuk ➔ *U.S.A.* 70°52N 155°55W **303** A9
Atrå *Norway* 59°59N 8°45E **164** E5
Atrai ➔ *Bangla.* 24°7N 89°22E **241** C2
Atrak = Atrek ➔
Turkmenistan 37°35N 53°58E **247** B8
Ätran *Sweden* 57°7N 12°57E **163** G6
Ätran ➔ *Sweden* 56°53N 12°30E **163** H6
Atrato ➔ *Colombia* 8°17N 76°58W **328** B2
Atrauli *India* 28°2N 78°20E **242** E8
Atrek ➔ *Turkmenistan* 37°35N 53°58E **247** B8
Atri *Italy* 42°35N 13°58E **199** F10
Atsiki *Greece* 39°56N 25°13E **205** B7
Atsoum, Mts. *Cameroon* 6°41N 12°57E **263** D7
Atsugi *Japan* 35°25N 139°21E **223** B11
Atsumi *Japan* 34°35N 137°4E **223** C9
Atsumi-Wan *Japan* 34°44N 137°13E **223** C9
Atsuta *Japan* 43°24N 141°26E **220** C10
Attalla *U.S.A.* 34°1N 86°6W **316** A3
Attapu *Laos* 14°48N 106°50E **236** E6
Attapulgus *U.S.A.* 30°45N 84°29W **316** E5
Attawapiskat *Canada* 52°56N 82°24W **298** B3
Attawapiskat ➔ *Canada* 52°57N 82°18W **298** B3
Attawapiskat L. *Canada* 52°18N 87°54W **298** B2
Attersee *Austria* 47°55N 13°32E **180** D6
Attica *Ind., U.S.A.* 40°18N 87°15W **311** D9
Attica *Ohio, U.S.A.* 41°4N 82°53W **312** E2
Attichy *France* 49°25N 3°3E **173** C10
Attigny *France* 49°28N 4°35E **173** C11
Attika = Attiki ☐ *Greece* 37°10N 23°40E **204** D5
Attikamagen L. *Canada* 55°0N 66°30W **299** B6
Attiki *Greece* 38°0N 23°43E **112** A2
Attiki ☐ *Greece* 37°10N 23°40E **204** D5
Attleboro *U.S.A.* 41°57N 71°17W **313** E13
Attock *Pakistan* 33°52N 72°20E **242** C5
Attopeu = Attapu *Laos* 14°48N 106°50E **236** E6
Attu *U.S.A.* 52°56N 173°15E **303** K1
Attu I. *U.S.A.* 52°55N 172°55E **303** K1
Attunga *Australia* 30°55S 150°50E **283** A9
Attur *India* 11°35N 78°30E **245** J4
'Atūd *Yemen* 14°53N 48°10E **249** D5
Atuel ➔ *Argentina* 36°17S 66°50W **334** D2
Atura *Uganda* 2°7N 32°20E **268** B3
Åtvidaberg *Sweden* 58°12N 16°0E **163** F10
Atwater *U.S.A.* 37°21N 120°37W **306** H6
Atwood *Ont., Canada* 43°40N 81°1W **312** C3
Atwood *Ill., U.S.A.* 39°48N 88°28W **311** E8
Atwood *Kans., U.S.A.* 39°48N 101°3W **308** F3
Atyraū *Kazakhstan* 47°5N 52°0E **187** E9
Atzgersdorf *Austria* 48°8N 16°18E **142** B1
Au Sable *U.S.A.* 44°25N 83°20W **312** B1
Au Sable ➔ *U.S.A.* 44°25N 83°20W **309** C12
Au Sable Forks *U.S.A.* 44°27N 73°41W **313** B11
Au Sable Pt. *U.S.A.* 44°20N 83°20W **312** B1
Au Vent, Région *Réunion* 21°0S 55°35E **272** f
Aua *Amer. Samoa* 14°17S 170°40W **302** f
Auas *Honduras* 15°29N 84°20W **320** C3
Auasberg *Namibia* 22°37S 17°13E **270** B2
Aubagne *France* 43°17N 5°37E **175** E9
Aube ☐ *France* 48°15N 4°10E **173** D11
Aube ➔ *France* 48°34N 3°43E **173** D10
Aubenas *France* 44°37N 4°24E **175** D8
Aubenton *France* 49°50N 4°12E **173** C11
Auberry *U.S.A.* 37°7N 119°29W **306** H7
Aubervilliers *France* 48°54N 2°22E **134** A3
Aubigny-sur-Nère *France* 47°30N 2°24E **173** E9
Aubin *France* 44°33N 2°15E **174** D6
Aubing *Germany* 48°9N 11°25E **131** B1
Aubrac, Mts. d' *France* 44°40N 3°2E **174** D7
Auburn *S. Austral.,*
Australia 34°1S 138°42E **282** C3
Auburn *Ala., U.S.A.* 32°36N 85°29W **316** C4
Auburn *Calif., U.S.A.* 38°54N 121°4W **306** G5
Auburn *Ill., U.S.A.* 39°36N 89°45W **310** E7
Auburn *Ind., U.S.A.* 41°22N 85°4W **311** C11
Auburn *Maine, U.S.A.* 44°6N 70°14W **309** C18
Auburn *N.Y., U.S.A.* 42°56N 76°34W **313** D8
Auburn *Nebr., U.S.A.* 40°23N 95°51W **308** E6
Auburn *Pa., U.S.A.* 40°36N 76°6W **313** F8
Auburn *Wash., U.S.A.* 47°18N 122°14W **306** C4
Auburn Ra. *Australia* 25°15S 150°30E **281** D5
Auburndale *Fla., U.S.A.* 28°4N 81°48W **317** G8
Auburndale *Mass.,*
U.S.A. 42°20N 71°14W **116** A1
Aubusson *France* 45°57N 2°11E **174** C6
Auce *Latvia* 56°28N 22°53E **184** B9
Auch *France* 43°39N 0°36E **174** E4
Auchendinny *U.K.* 55°51N 3°11W **121** B2
Auchi *Nigeria* 7°6N 6°13E **263** D6
Auchterarder *U.K.* 56°18N 3°41W **167** E5
Auchtermuchty *U.K.* 56°18N 3°13W **167** E5
Auckland *N.Z.* 36°52S 174°46E **284** C3
Auckland ☐ *N.Z.* 36°50S 175°0E **284** C3
Auckland Is. *Pac. Oc.* 50°40S 166°5E **288** N8
Auckland Park *S. Africa* 26°11S 28°0E **123** B2
Aude ☐ *France* 43°8N 2°28E **174** E6
Aude ➔ *France* 43°13N 3°14E **174** E7
Auden *Canada* 50°14N 87°53W **298** B2
Auderghem *Belgium* 50°49N 4°26E **116** B2
Auderville *France* 49°43N 1°57W **172** C5
Audierne *France* 48°1N 4°34W **172** D2
Audincourt *France* 47°30N 6°50E **173** E13
Audo Ra. *Ethiopia* 6°20N 41°50E **257** F5
Audubon *U.S.A.* 41°43N 94°56W **310** C2
Aue *Germany* 50°35N 12°41E **178** E8
Auerbach *Germany* 50°30N 12°24E **178** E8
Aufist *W. Sahara* 25°44N 14°39W **260** C2
Augathella *Australia* 25°48S 146°35E **281** D4
Aughnacloy *U.K.* 54°25N 6°59W **166** B5
Aughrim *Ireland* 53°18N 8°19W **166** C3
Augrabies Falls *S. Africa* 28°35S 20°20E **270** C3
Augrabies Falls △
S. Africa 28°40S 20°22E **270** C3
Augsburg *Germany* 48°25N 10°52E **179** G6
Augsburg-Westliche Wälder ⌂
Germany 48°22N 10°40E **179** G6

August Town Jamaica 17°59N 76°44W 320 a
Augusta W. Austral., Australia 34°19S 115°9E 279 F2
Augusta Italy 37°13N 15°13E 201 E8
Augusta Ark., U.S.A. 35°17N 91°22W 314 D9
Augusta Ga., U.S.A. 33°28N 81°58W 316 B8
Augusta Ill., U.S.A. 40°14N 90°57W 310 D6
Augusta Kans., U.S.A. 37°41N 96°59W 308 G5
Augusta Ky., U.S.A. 38°47N 84°0W 311 F12
Augusta Maine, U.S.A. 44°19N 69°47W 309 C19
Augusta Mont., U.S.A. 47°30N 112°24W 304 C7
Augusta, Mausoleo di Rome, Italy 136 b2
Augustenborg Denmark 54°57N 9°53E 163 K3
Augustine I. U.S.A. 59°22N 153°26W 303 G9
Augusto Cardosa = Metangula Mozam. 12°40S 34°50E 269 E3
Augustów Poland 53°51N 23°0E 184 E9
Augustówka Poland 52°11N 21°5E 142 B2
Augustus, Mt. Australia 24°20S 116°50E 279 D2
Augustus I. Australia 15°20S 124°30E 278 C3
Aujuittuq = Grise Fiord Canada 76°25N 82°57W 295 B15
Aukan Eritrea 15°29N 40°50E 257 D5
Auki Solomon Is. 8°45S 160°42E 287 M11
Aukra Norway 62°47N 6°55E 164 B3
Aukštaitija △ Lithuania 55°15N 26°0E 161 J22
Aukum U.S.A. 38°34N 120°43W 306 G6
Aul India 20°41N 86°39E 244 D8
Aulavik △ Canada 73°42N 119°55W 294 C8
Auld, L. Australia 22°25S 123°50E 278 D3
Āūlīeköl Kazakhstan 52°32N 62°45E 216 B6
Auliefeltet Norway 60°30N 11°21E 162 D5
Auliye-Ata = Taraz Kazakhstan 42°54N 71°22E 217 D8
Aulla Italy 44°12N 9°58E 198 D6
Aulnay France 46°2N 0°22W 174 B3
Aulnay-sous-Bois France 48°56N 2°29E 134 A3
Aulne → France 48°17N 4°16W 172 D2
Aulnoye-Aymeries France 50°12N 3°50E 173 B10
Aulong Palau 7°16N 134°17E 288 c
Ault Somme, France 50°8N 1°26E 172 B8
Ault Colo., U.S.A. 40°35N 104°44W 304 F11
Aulus-les-Bains France 42°49N 1°19E 174 F5
Aumale = Sour el Ghozlane Algeria 36°10N 3°45E 261 A5
Aumale France 49°46N 1°46E 173 C8
Aumo Papua N. G. 5°44S 148°30E 286 C5
Aumont-Aubrac France 44°43N 3°17E 174 D7
Auna Nigeria 10°9N 4°42E 263 C5
Aundah India 19°32N 77°3E 244 E3
Aundh India 17°33N 74°23E 244 F2
Auning Denmark 56°26N 10°22E 163 H4
Aunis France 46°5N 0°50W 174 B3
Aunu'u Amer. Samoa 14°20S 170°31W 302 f
Auponhia Indonesia 1°58S 125°27E 231 E7
Aups France 43°37N 6°15E 175 E10
Aur, Pulau Malaysia 2°35N 104°10E 237 L5
Aura Burma 26°59N 97°57E 241 B6
Auraiya India 26°28N 79°33E 243 F8
Aurangabad Bihar, India 24°45N 84°18E 243 G11
Aurangabad Maharashtra, India 19°50N 75°23E 244 E2
Auray France 47°40N 2°59W 172 E4
Aurdal Norway 60°55N 9°26E 164 D6
Aure Norway 63°16N 8°33E 164 A5
Aurelio Italy 41°54N 12°26E 136 B1
Aurès Algeria 35°8N 6°30E 261 A6
Aurich Germany 53°28N 7°28E 178 B3
Aurilândia Brazil 16°44S 50°28W 333 E1
Aurillac France 44°55N 2°26E 174 D6
Aurlandsfjorden Norway 61°3N 7°1E 164 C4
Aurlandsvangen Norway 60°55N 7°12E 164 D4
Auronzo di Cadore Italy 46°33N 12°26E 199 B9
Aurora = Maéwo Vanuatu 15°10S 168°10E 287 E6
Aurora = San Francisco Phil. 13°21N 122°31E 232 E4
Aurora Ont., Canada 44°0N 79°28W 312 C5
Aurora Isabela, Phil. 16°59N 121°38E 232 C3
Aurora Zamboanga del S., Phil. 7°57N 123°36E 233 H4
Aurora Western Cape, S. Africa 32°40S 18°29E 270 D2
Aurora Colo., U.S.A. 39°43N 104°49W 304 G11
Aurora Ill., U.S.A. 41°45N 88°19W 311 C8
Aurora Mo., U.S.A. 36°58N 93°43W 308 G7
Aurora N.Y., U.S.A. 42°45N 76°42W 313 D8
Aurora Nebr., U.S.A. 40°52N 98°0W 308 E5
Aurora Ohio, U.S.A. 41°21N 81°20W 312 E3
Aurora □ Phil. 15°30N 121°30E 232 D3
Aurora △ Phil. 15°40N 121°20E 232 D3
Aursmoen Norway 59°55N 11°26E 164 E8
Aursunden Norway 62°40N 11°40E 164 B8
Aurukun Australia 13°20S 141°45E 280 A3
Aurukun ⊙ Australia 13°36S 141°48E 280 A3
Aus Namibia 26°35S 16°12E 270 C2
Ausa India 18°15N 76°30E 244 E3
Ausable → Canada 43°19N 81°46W 312 C3
Auschwitz = Oświęcim Poland 50°2N 19°11E 185 H6
Ausīm Egypt 30°7N 31°8E 117 A1
Auski Roadhouse Australia 22°22S 118°41E 278 D2
Auspitz = Hustopeče Czech Rep. 48°57N 16°43E 181 C9
Aussig = Ústí nad Labem Czech Rep. 50°41N 14°3E 180 A7
Aust-Agder □ Norway 58°45N 8°0E 164 F4
Austad Norway 58°58N 7°37E 164 F4
Austen Harbour India 12°55N 92°45E 245 H11
Austerlitz = Slavkov u Brna Czech Rep. 49°10N 16°52E 181 B9
Austerlitz, Gare d' France 48°50N 2°22E 134 A3
Austevoll Norway 60°5N 5°13E 164 D2
Austin Ill., U.S.A. 41°53N 87°45W 119 B2
Austin Ind., U.S.A. 38°45N 85°49W 311 F11
Austin Minn., U.S.A. 43°40N 92°58W 308 D7
Austin Nev., U.S.A. 39°30N 117°4W 304 G5
Austin Pa., U.S.A. 41°38N 78°6W 312 E6
Austin Tex., U.S.A. 30°17N 97°45W 316 F6
Austin, L. Australia 27°40S 118°0E 279 E2
Austin I. Canada 61°10N 94°0W 297 A10
Austmarka Norway 60°6N 12°21E 164 D9
Austnes Norway 62°33N 6°16E 164 B3
Austra Norway 65°8N 11°55E 160 D14
Austral Is. = Tubuaï, Îs. French Polynesia 25°0S 150°0W 289 f
Austral Seamount Chain Pac. Oc. 24°0S 150°0W 289 K13
Australia ■ Oceania 23°0S 135°0E 276 E3
Australian-Antarctic Basin S. Ocean 60°0S 120°0E 151 C9
Australian Capital Territory □ Australia 35°30S 149°0E 283 C8
Australind Australia 33°17S 115°42E 279 F2
Austria ■ Europe 47°0N 14°0E 180 E7
Austur-Skaftafellssýsla □ Iceland 64°15N 16°0W 155 C10
Austvågøya Norway 68°20N 14°40E 160 B16
Autazes Brazil 3°35S 59°8W 329 D6
Auterive France 43°21N 1°29E 174 E5
Authie → France 50°22N 1°38E 173 B8
Authon-du-Perche France 48°12N 0°54E 172 D7
Autlán de Navarro Mexico 19°46N 104°22W 318 D4
Autun France 46°58N 4°17E 173 F11
Auvergne □ France 45°20N 3°15E 174 C7
Auvergne, Mts. d' France 45°20N 2°55E 174 C6
Auvézère → France 45°12N 0°50E 174 C4
Auxerre France 47°48N 3°32E 173 E10
Auxi-le-Château France 50°15N 2°8E 173 B9
Auxonne France 47°10N 5°20E 173 E12
Auxvasse U.S.A. 39°1N 91°54W 310 E5
Auyuittuq △ Canada 67°30N 66°0W 295 D18
Auzances France 46°2N 2°30E 173 F9
Auzangate, Nevado Peru 13°47S 71°13W 330 C3
Av-Dovurak Russia 51°17N 91°35E 215 D10
Ava Ill., U.S.A. 37°53N 89°30W 310 G7
Ava Mo., U.S.A. 36°57N 92°40W 308 G7
Avaldsnes Norway 59°21N 5°20E 164 E2
Avallon France 47°30N 3°53E 173 E10
Avalon N.Z. 41°12S 174°56E 143 B2
Avalon Calif., U.S.A. 33°21N 118°20W 307 M8
Avalon Pen. Canada 47°30N 53°20W 299 C9
Avana → Cook Is. 21°14S 159°43W 289 h
Avanavero Suriname 4°51N 57°22W 329 C6
Avanigadda India 16°0N 80°56E 245 G5
Avannaarsua □ Greenland 80°0N 55°0W 154 B5
Avanos Turkey 38°43N 34°51E 212 C6
Avantas Greece 40°57N 25°56E 203 F9
Avaré Brazil 23°4S 48°58W 335 A6
Avarua Cook Is. 21°12S 159°46W 289 h
Avarua Harb. Cook Is. 21°12S 159°46W 289 h
Avatele Cook Is. 19°6S 169°55W 289 g
Avatiu Cook Is. 21°12S 159°47W 289 h
Avawatz Mts. U.S.A. 35°40N 116°30W 307 K10
Avdan Dağı Turkey 40°23N 29°46E 203 F13
Avedøre Denmark 55°37N 12°27E 118 B2
Aveiro Brazil 3°10S 55°5W 329 D6
Aveiro Portugal 40°37N 8°38W 194 E2
Aveiro □ Portugal 40°40N 8°35W 194 E2
Āvej Iran 35°40N 49°15E 247 C6
Avellaneda Argentina 34°40S 58°22W 117 C2
Avellino Italy 40°54N 14°47E 201 B7
Avenal U.S.A. 36°0N 120°8W 306 K6
Avenel U.S.A. 38°59N 76°59W 143 B4
Averøya Norway 63°0N 7°35E 164 A4
Aversa Italy 40°58N 14°12E 201 B7
Avery U.S.A. 47°15N 115°49W 304 C6
Aves, I. de W. Indies 15°45N 63°55W 321 C7
Aves, Is. las Venezuela 12°0N 67°30W 321 D6
Aves Laguna Colorada, Santuario de △ Bolivia 22°30S 67°30W 330 E4
Aves Ridge W. Indies 14°0N 63°30W 321 D7
Avesnes-sur-Helpe France 50°8N 3°55E 173 B10
Avesnois △ France 50°10N 3°45E 173 B10
Avesta Sweden 60°9N 16°10E 162 D10
Aveyron □ France 44°22N 2°45E 174 D6
Aveyron → France 44°5N 1°16E 174 D5
Avezzano Italy 42°2N 13°25E 199 F10
Avgo Greece 35°33N 25°37E 205 F7
Aviá Terai Argentina 26°45S 60°50W 334 B3
Aviano Italy 46°4N 12°36E 199 B9
Aviatu → Cook Is. 21°12S 159°49W 289 h
Aviemore U.K. 57°12N 3°50W 167 D5
Aviemore, L. N.Z. 44°37S 170°18E 285 E5
Avigliana Italy 45°5N 7°23E 198 C4
Avigliano Italy 40°44N 15°43E 201 B8
Avignon France 43°57N 4°50E 175 E8
Ávila Spain 40°39N 4°43W 194 E6
Ávila □ Spain 40°30N 5°0W 194 E6
Ávila, Sierra de Spain 40°40N 5°15W 194 E5
Avila Beach U.S.A. 35°11N 120°44W 307 K6
Avilés Spain 43°35N 5°57W 194 B5
Avintes Portugal 41°7N 8°33W 194 D2
Avis Portugal 39°4N 7°53W 195 F3
Avis Pa., U.S.A. 41°11N 77°19W 312 E7
Avísio → Italy 46°7N 11°5E 198 B8
Avissawella Sri Lanka 6°56N 80°11E 245 L5
Aviston U.S.A. 38°36N 89°36W 310 F7
Aviz = Avis Portugal 39°4N 7°53W 195 F3
Avize France 48°59N 4°1E 173 D11
Avlona = Vlorë Albania 40°32N 19°28E 202 F3
Avlonari Greece 38°31N 24°8E 204 C6
Avlum Denmark 56°16N 8°47E 163 H2
Avoca Vic., Australia 37°5S 143°26E 282 D5
Avoca N.Y., U.S.A. 42°25N 77°25W 312 D7
Avoca → Vic., Australia 35°40S 143°43E 282 C5
Avoca → Wicklow, Ireland 52°48N 6°10W 166 D5
Avola B.C., Canada 51°45N 119°19W 296 C5
Avola Italy 36°56N 15°7E 201 F8
Avon Ill., U.S.A. 40°40N 90°26W 310 D6
Avon N.Y., U.S.A. 42°55N 77°45W 312 D7
Avon → W. Austral., Australia 31°40S 116°7E 279 F2
Avon → Bristol, U.K. 51°29N 2°41W 169 F5
Avon → Dorset, U.K. 50°44N 1°46W 169 G6
Avon → Warks., U.K. 52°0N 2°8W 169 E5
Avon Park U.S.A. 27°36N 81°31W 317 H8
Avondale Ill., U.S.A. 41°56N 87°41W 119 B2
Avondale La., U.S.A. 29°54N 90°12W 131 B1
Avondale Zimbabwe 17°43S 30°58E 269 F3
Avondale Heights Australia 37°45S 144°52E 128 A1
Avonlea Canada 50°0N 105°0W 297 D8
Avonmore Canada 45°10N 74°58W 313 A10
Avonmouth U.K. 51°30N 2°42W 169 F5
Avramov Bulgaria 42°45N 26°38E 203 D10
Avranches France 48°40N 1°20W 172 D5
Avre → France 48°47N 1°22E 172 D8
Avrig Romania 45°43N 24°21E 183 E9
Avrillé France 47°30N 0°35W 172 E6
Avtovac Bos.-H. 43°9N 18°35E 202 C2
Avtovo Russia 59°51N 30°16E 137 B1
Avu Avu Solomon Is. 9°50S 160°22E 287 M11
Awa-Shima Japan 38°27N 139°14E 220 E9
Awag el Baqar Sudan 10°10N 33°10E 257 E3
A'waj → Syria 33°23N 36°20E 250 E7
Awaji Japan 34°32N 135°1E 223 C7
Awaji-Shima Japan 34°30N 134°50E 222 C6
'Awālī Bahrain 26°0N 50°30E 247 E6
Awantipur India 33°55N 75°3E 243 C6
Awanui N.Z. 35°4S 173°17E 284 B2
Aware Ethiopia 8°16N 44°9E 267 C5
Awarja → India 17°5N 76°15E 244 F3
Awarua B. N.Z. 44°28S 168°4E 285 E3
Awarua Pt. N.Z. 44°15S 168°5E 285 E3
Awasa Ethiopia 7°2N 38°28E 257 F4
Awasa, L. Ethiopia 7°0N 38°30E 257 F4
Awash Ethiopia 9°1N 40°10E 257 F5
Awash → Ethiopia 11°45N 41°5E 257 E5
Awash △ Ethiopia 9°8N 40°0E 257 F5
Awaso Ghana 6°15N 2°22W 262 D4
Awat China 40°35N 80°24E 217 D10
Awatere → N.Z. 41°37S 174°10E 285 B9
Awbārī Libya 26°46N 12°57E 258 C2
Awbārī, Idehan Libya 27°10N 11°30E 258 C2
Awdal □ Somali Rep. 10°30N 43°30E 267 B5
Awdheegle Somali Rep. 1°59N 44°50E 267 D5
Awe, L. U.K. 56°17N 5°16W 167 E3
Aweil Sudan 8°42N 27°20E 257 F2
Awgu Nigeria 6°4N 7°24E 263 D6
Awjilah Libya 29°8N 21°7E 258 C4
Awka Nigeria 6°12N 7°5E 263 D6
Aworro Papua N. G. 7°43S 143°11E 286 D2
Awsard Mauritania 22°37N 14°22W 260 D2
Ax-les-Thermes France 42°44N 1°50E 174 F5
Axat France 42°48N 2°13E 174 F6
Axe → U.K. 50°42N 3°4W 169 F5
Axel Heiberg I. Canada 80°0N 90°0W 295 B14
Axim Ghana 4°51N 2°15W 262 E4
Axinim Brazil 4°2S 59°22W 329 D6
Axintele Romania 44°37N 26°47E 183 F11
Axioma Brazil 6°45S 64°31W 331 B5
Axios → Greece 40°57N 22°35E 202 F6
Axminster U.K. 50°46N 3°0W 169 G4
Axson U.S.A. 31°17N 82°44W 316 D7
Axvall Sweden 58°23N 13°34E 163 F7
Ay France 49°3N 4°1E 173 C11
Ayaantang Eq. Guin. 1°58N 10°24E 264 B2
Ayabaca Peru 4°40S 79°53W 330 A2
Ayabe Japan 35°20N 135°20E 223 B7
Ayacucho Argentina 37°5S 58°20W 334 D4
Ayacucho Peru 13°0S 74°0W 330 C3
Ayacucho □ Peru 14°0S 74°0W 330 C3
Ayaguz = Ayaköz Kazakhstan 48°10N 80°10E 217 C10
Ayakkum Hu China 37°30N 89°20E 217 E11
Ayaköz Kazakhstan 48°10N 80°10E 217 C10
Ayaköz → Kazakhstan 46°40N 79°14E 217 C9
Ayakudi India 10°28N 77°56E 245 J3
Ayala Phil. 6°57N 121°57E 233 H3
Ayamé Ivory C. 5°35N 3°9W 262 D4
Ayamonte Spain 37°12N 7°24W 195 H3
Ayan Russia 56°30N 138°16E 215 D14
Ayancık Turkey 41°57N 34°35E 212 B6
Ayangba Nigeria 7°31N 7°8E 263 D6
Ayapel Colombia 8°19N 75°9W 328 B2
Ayas Turkey 40°2N 32°21E 212 B5
Ayaviri Peru 14°50S 70°35W 330 C3
Ayazağa Turkey 41°6N 28°59E 122 B1
Āybak Afghan. 36°15N 68°5E 240 A3
Aybastı Turkey 40°41N 37°23E 212 B7
Aydarkŭl Uzbekistan 40°50N 67°10E 217 D7
Aydın Turkey 37°51N 27°51E 212 D2
Aydın □ Turkey 37°50N 28°0E 205 D9
Aydin Dağları Turkey 38°0N 28°0E 205 D10
Aydıncık Turkey 36°9N 33°21E 250 B4
Aydingkol Hu China 42°40N 89°15E 217 D11
Ayelu Ethiopia 10°5N 40°42E 257 E5
Ayenngré Togo 8°40N 1°1E 263 D5
Ayer U.S.A. 42°34N 71°35W 313 D13
Ayer Chawan, Pulau Singapore 1°16N 103°41E 138 B2
Ayer Hitam Malaysia 5°24N 100°16E 237 c
Ayer Merbau, Pulau Singapore 1°16N 103°42E 138 B2
Ayerbe Spain 42°17N 0°41W 196 C4
Ayer's Cliff Canada 45°10N 72°3W 313 A12
Ayers Rock = Uluru Australia 25°23S 131°5E 279 E5
Ayeyarwady = Irrawaddy → Burma 15°50N 95°6E 241 G5
Áyia Napa Cyprus 34°59N 34°0E 207 F10
Áyia Phyla Cyprus 34°43N 33°1E 207 F9
Áyios Amvrósios Cyprus 35°20N 33°35E 207 D12
Áyios Seryios Cyprus 35°12N 33°53E 207 D12
Áyios Theodhoros Cyprus 35°22N 34°1E 207 D13
Áyios Yeóryios = Aghios Georgios Greece 37°28N 23°57E 204 D5
Aykhal Russia 66°0N 111°30E 215 C12
Aykino Russia 62°15N 49°56E 186 B8
Aykirikçi Turkey 39°8N 30°9E 205 B12
Aylesbury U.K. 51°49N 0°49W 169 F7
Aylmer Canada 42°46N 80°59W 312 D4
Aylmer, L. Canada 64°5N 108°30W 294 E10
'Ayn, Wādī al Oman 22°15N 55°28E 247 F7
'Ayn al Ghazālah Libya 32°10N 23°20E 258 B4
Ayn Dār Si. Arabia 25°55N 49°10E 247 E7
Ayn Sifnī Iraq 36°41N 43°20E 213 D10
Ayn Zālah Iraq 36°45N 42°35E 213 D10
Ayna Spain 38°34N 2°3W 197 G2
Aynāt Yemen 16°4N 49°9E 249 D5
'Aynūnah Si. Arabia 28°5N 35°8E 251 K6
Ayod Sudan 8°7N 31°26E 257 F3
Ayolas Paraguay 27°10S 56°59W 334 B4
Ayon, Ostrov Russia 69°50N 169°0E 215 C17
Ayora Spain 39°3N 1°3W 197 F3
Ayorou Niger 14°53N 1°0E 263 C5
Ayos Cameroon 3°53N 12°31E 264 B2
'Ayoûn el 'Atroûs Mauritania 16°38N 9°37W 262 B3
Ayr Queens., Australia 19°35S 147°25E 280 B4
Ayr Ont., Canada 43°17N 80°27W 312 C4
Ayr S. Ayrs., U.K. 55°28N 4°38W 167 F4
Ayr → U.K. 55°28N 4°38W 167 F4
Ayrancı Turkey 37°21N 33°41E 212 D5
Ayrancılar Turkey 38°15N 27°18E 205 C9
Ayre, Pt. of I. of Man 54°25N 4°21W 168 C3
Ayribaba Turkmenistan 37°50N 66°34E 217 E7
Aysha Ethiopia 10°50N 42°23E 257 E5
Ayton Australia 15°56S 145°22E 280 B4
Aytos Bulgaria 42°42N 27°16E 203 D11
Aytoska Planina Bulgaria 42°45N 27°30E 203 D11
Ayu, Kepulauan Indonesia 0°35N 131°5E 231 D8
Ayutla Guatemala 14°40N 92°10W 320 D1
Ayutla de los Libres Mexico 16°54N 99°13W 319 D5
Ayvacık Turkey 39°36N 26°24E 212 C2
Ayvalık Turkey 39°20N 26°46E 205 B8
Az Zabadānī Syria 33°43N 36°5E 250 E7
Az Ẓāhirah Asia 23°30N 56°10E 249 B7
Az Ẓāhirīyah West Bank 31°25N 34°58E 251 G5
Az Ẓahrān Si. Arabia 26°10N 50°7E 247 E6
Az Zarqā Jordan 32°5N 36°4E 251 F7
Az Zarqā' U.A.E. 24°53N 53°4E 247 E7
Az Zāwiyah Libya 32°52N 12°56E 258 B2
Az Zāwiyah □ Libya 32°44N 12°43E 261 B7
Az Zaydīyah Yemen 15°20N 43°1E 248 D3
Az Zībār Iraq 36°52N 44°4E 213 D11
Az Zilfī Si. Arabia 26°12N 44°52E 246 E5
Az Zubayr Iraq 30°26N 47°40E 246 D5
Az Zuqur Yemen 14°0N 42°45E 248 D3
Az Zuwaytīnah Libya 30°58N 20°7E 258 B4
Azabu Tokyo, Japan 140 c3
Azad Kashmir □ Pakistan 33°50N 73°50E 243 C5
Azambuja Portugal 39°4N 8°51W 195 F2
Azamgarh India 26°5N 83°13E 243 F10
Azangaro Peru 14°55S 70°13W 330 C3
Azaoua Niger 15°50N 4°0E 263 B5
Azaouad Mali 19°0N 3°0W 262 B4
Azaouak → Mali 15°30N 3°18E 263 B5
Azaouak, Vallée de l' Mali 15°50N 3°20E 263 B5
Āzār Shahr Iran 37°45N 45°59E 213 D11
Azara Nigeria 8°22N 9°12E 263 D6
Azarān Iran 37°25N 47°16E 213 D12
Azärbayjan = Azerbaijan ■ Asia 40°20N 48°0E 191 K9
Āzarbāyjān-e Gharbī □ Iran 37°0N 44°30E 246 B5
Āzarbāyjān-e Sharqī □ Iran 37°20N 47°0E 246 B5
Azare Nigeria 11°55N 10°10E 263 C7
Azay-le-Rideau France 47°16N 0°30E 172 E7
A'zāz Syria 36°36N 37°4E 250 B8
Azazga Algeria 36°48N 4°22E 261 A5
Azbine = Aïr Niger 18°30N 8°0E 259 E1
Azcapotzalco Mexico 19°28N 99°10W 128 B1
Azefal Mauritania 21°0N 14°45W 260 D2
Azeffoun Algeria 36°51N 4°26E 261 A5
Azemmour Morocco 33°20N 9°20W 260 B3
Azennezal Algeria 22°58N 0°43E 261 D5
Azerbaijan ■ Asia 40°20N 48°0E 191 K9
Azezo Ethiopia 12°28N 37°15E 257 E4
Azimganj India 24°14N 88°16E 243 G13
Aznalcóllar Spain 37°32N 6°17W 195 H4
Azogues Ecuador 2°35S 78°0W 328 D2
Azores = Açores, Is. dos Atl. Oc. 38°0N 27°0W 153 d1
Azores-Biscay Rise Atl. Oc. 42°0N 20°0W 152 B9
Azoum, B. → Chad 10°53N 20°15E 259 F4
Azov Russia 47°3N 39°25E 191 G4
Azov, Sea of Europe 46°0N 36°30E 189 J9
Azovskoye More = Azov, Sea of Europe 46°0N 36°30E 189 J9
Azpeitia Spain 43°12N 2°19W 196 B2
Azrak, B. → Chad 10°52N 20°35E 259 F4
Azraq ash Shīshān Jordan 31°50N 36°49E 251 G7
Azrou Morocco 33°28N 5°19W 260 B3
Aztec U.S.A. 36°49N 107°59W 305 H10
Azteca, Estadia Mexico 19°19N 99°9W 128 C2
Azúa de Compostela Dom. Rep. 18°25N 70°44W 321 C5
Azuaga Spain 38°16N 5°39W 195 G5
Azuara Spain 41°15N 0°53W 196 D4
Azuay □ Ecuador 2°55S 79°0W 328 D2
Azucar, Cerro Pan de Chile 33°19S 70°41W 137 A1
Azuer → Spain 39°8N 3°36W 195 F7
Azuero, Pen. de Panama 7°30N 80°30W 320 E3
Azuga Romania 45°27N 25°33E 183 E10
Azul Argentina 36°42S 59°43W 334 D4
Azul, Lagoa Azores 37°52N 25°47W 153 d3
Azul, Serra Brazil 14°50S 54°50W 331 C7
Azurduy Bolivia 19°59S 64°29W 331 D5
Azusa U.S.A. 34°8N 117°52W 307 L9
Azzaba Algeria 36°48N 7°6E 261 A6
Azzano Décimo Italy 45°52N 12°56E 199 C9
Azzel Matti, Sebkra Algeria 26°10N 0°43E 261 C5

B

Ba Be △ Vietnam 22°25N 105°37E 236 A5
Ba Don Vietnam 17°45N 106°26E 236 D6
Ba Dong Vietnam 9°40N 106°33E 237 H6
Ba Ngoi = Cam Lam Vietnam 11°54N 109°10E 237 G7
Ba Tri Vietnam 10°2N 106°36E 237 G6
Ba Vi △ Vietnam 21°1N 105°22E 236 B5
Ba Xian = Bazhou China 39°8N 116°22E 226 E9
Baa Indonesia 10°50S 123°0E 278 B3
Baambrugge Neths. 52°15N 4°59E 112 B2
Baamonde Spain 43°7N 7°44W 194 B3
Baao Phil. 13°27N 123°22E 232 E4
Baardheere Somali Rep. 2°20N 42°27E 267 D5
Baarle-Nassau Belgium 51°27N 4°56E 170 C4
Bab el Mandeb Red Sea 12°35N 43°25E 248 D3
Baba Bulgaria 42°44N 23°59E 202 D7
Baba, B. do Angola 14°50S 12°14E 265 E2
Bābā, Koh-i- Afghan. 34°30N 67°0E 240 B2
Baba Budan Hills India 13°30N 75°44E 245 H2
Baba Burnu Turkey 39°29N 26°2E 205 B8
Baba Channel Pakistan 24°48N 66°58E 123 B1
Baba dag Azerbaijan 41°0N 48°19E 191 K9
Baba I. Pakistan 24°49N 66°57E 123 B1
Bābā Kalū Iran 30°7N 50°49E 247 D6
Babaçulândia Brazil 7°13S 47°46W 332 C2
Babadag Romania 44°53N 28°44E 183 F13
Babadağ Turkey 37°49N 28°52E 205 D10
Babaeski Turkey 41°26N 27°6E 203 E11
Babahoyo Ecuador 1°40S 79°30W 328 D2
Babai = Sarju → India 27°21N 81°23E 243 F9
Babak Phil. 7°8N 125°41E 233 H5
Babana Nigeria 10°31N 3°46E 263 C5
Babanusa Sudan 11°20N 27°48E 257 E2
Babar Algeria 35°10N 7°6E 261 A6
Babar Indonesia 8°0S 129°30E 231 F7
Babar Pakistan 31°7N 69°32E 242 D3
Babarkach Pakistan 29°45N 68°0E 242 E3
Babarpur India 28°41N 77°16E 120 A2
Babase I. Papua N. G. 4°0S 153°42E 286 B7
Babayevo Russia 59°24N 35°55E 188 C8
Babb U.S.A. 48°51N 113°27W 304 B7
Babelthuap Palau 7°30N 134°30E 288 c
Babenhausen Germany 49°57N 8°57E 179 F4
Băbeni Romania 44°59N 24°11E 183 F9
Baberu India 25°33N 80°43E 243 G9
Babi Indonesia 2°5N 96°39E 234 B1
Babi Besar, Pulau Malaysia 2°25N 103°59E 237 L4
Babia Gora Europe 49°38N 19°38E 185 J6
Babian Jiang → China 22°55N 101°47E 228 F3
Bābil □ Iraq 32°30N 44°30E 246 C5
Babile Ethiopia 9°16N 42°11E 257 F5
Babile △ Ethiopia 8°45N 42°20E 267 C5
Babimost Poland 52°10N 15°49E 184 F2
Babinda Australia 17°20S 145°56E 280 B4
Babine Canada 55°22N 126°37W 296 B3
Babine → Canada 55°45N 127°44W 296 B3
Babine L. Canada 54°48N 126°0W 296 C3
Babiogórski △ Poland 49°38N 19°39E 185 J6
Babo Indonesia 2°30S 133°30E 231 E8
Babócsa Hungary 46°2N 17°21E 182 D2
Bābol Iran 36°40N 52°50E 247 B7
Bābol Sar Iran 36°45N 52°45E 247 B7
Babor, Dj. Algeria 36°31N 5°25E 261 A6
Baborów Poland 50°7N 18°1E 185 H5
Baboua C.A.R. 5°49N 14°58E 264 A2
Babruysk Belarus 53°10N 29°15E 177 B15
Babson Park U.S.A. 27°49N 81°32W 317 H8
Babuhri India 26°49N 69°43E 242 F3
Babuna Macedonia 41°30N 21°40E 202 E5
Babura Nigeria 12°51N 8°59E 263 C6
Babusar Pass Pakistan 35°12N 73°59E 243 B5
Babushkin Russia 55°51N 37°42E 129 A4
Babušnica Serbia 43°7N 22°27E 202 C6
Babuyan Phil. 10°0N 118°54E 233 F2
Babuyan Chan. Phil. 18°40N 121°30E 232 B3
Babuyan I. Phil. 19°32N 121°57E 232 B3
Babuyan Is. Phil. 19°10N 121°40E 232 B3
Babylon Iraq 32°34N 44°22E 213 F11
Bač Serbia 45°29N 19°17E 182 E4
Bâc → Moldova 46°55N 29°26E 183 D14
Bac Can Vietnam 22°8N 105°49E 228 F5
Bac Giang Vietnam 21°16N 106°11E 228 G6
Bac Lieu Vietnam 9°17N 105°43E 237 H5
Bac Ninh Vietnam 21°13N 106°4E 228 G6
Bac Phan Vietnam 22°0N 105°0E 228 G5
Bac Quang Vietnam 22°30N 104°48E 228 F5
Bacaadweyn Somali Rep. 7°15N 47°40E 267 C6
Bacabal Brazil 4°15S 44°45W 332 B3
Bacacay Phil. 13°18N 123°47E 232 E4
Bacajá → Brazil 3°25S 51°50W 329 D7
Bacalar Mexico 18°43N 88°27W 319 D7
Bacan, Kepulauan Indonesia 0°35S 127°30E 231 E7
Bacarra Phil. 18°15N 120°37E 232 B3
Bacău Romania 46°35N 26°55E 183 D11
Bacău □ Romania 46°30N 26°45E 183 D11
Baccarat France 48°28N 6°42E 173 D13
Bacchus Marsh Australia 37°43S 144°27E 282 D6
Bacerac Mexico 30°18N 108°50W 318 A3
Băceşti Romania 46°50N 27°11E 183 D12
Bach Long Vi, Dao Vietnam 20°10N 107°40E 236 B6
Bach Ma △ Vietnam 16°11N 107°49E 236 D6
Bachaquero Venezuela 9°56N 71°8W 328 B3
Bacharach Germany 50°3N 7°44E 179 E3
Bachelor's Beach Neth. Ant. 12°11N 68°18W 322 h
Bachhwara India 25°35N 85°54E 243 G11
Bachu China 39°46N 78°34E 217 E9
Bachuma Ethiopia 6°48N 35°53E 257 F4
Bačina Serbia 43°42N 21°23E 202 C5
Back → Canada 65°10N 104°0W 294 D11
Back B. India 18°56N 72°48E 130 B1
Bačka Palanka Serbia 45°17N 19°27E 182 E4
Bačka Topola Serbia 45°49N 19°39E 182 E4
Bäckebo Sweden 56°53N 16°4E 163 H10
Bäckefors Sweden 58°48N 12°9E 163 F6
Bäckhammar Sweden 59°10N 14°11E 162 E8
Bački Petrovac Serbia 45°29N 19°32E 182 E4
Backnang Germany 48°56N 9°26E 179 G5
Backstairs Passage Australia 35°40S 138°5E 282 C3
Baclaran Phil. 14°31N 121°0E 127 B2
Baco, Mt. Phil. 12°49N 121°10E 232 E3
Bacolod Phil. 10°40N 122°57E 233 F4
Bacon Phil. 13°3N 124°3E 232 E5
Baconton U.S.A. 31°23N 84°10W 316 D5
Bacoor Phil. 14°27N 120°56E 127 C1
Bacoor B. Phil. 14°27N 120°54E 127 C1
Bacqueville-en-Caux France 49°47N 1°0E 172 C8
Bács-Kiskun □ Hungary 46°43N 19°30E 182 D4
Bácsalmás Hungary 46°8N 19°17E 182 D4
Bacuag = Placer Phil. 9°36N 125°38E 233 G5
Bacuit = El Nido Phil. 11°10N 119°25E 233 F2
Bacuk Malaysia 6°4N 102°25E 237 J4
Bácum Mexico 27°33N 110°5W 318 B2
Bād Iran 33°41N 52°1E 247 C7
Bad → U.S.A. 44°21N 100°22W 308 C3
Bad Aussee Austria 47°43N 13°45E 180 D6
Bad Axe U.S.A. 43°48N 83°0W 312 C2
Bad Bergzabern Germany 49°6N 7°59E 179 F3
Bad Berleburg Germany 51°2N 8°26E 178 D4
Bad Bevensen Germany 53°5N 10°35E 178 B6
Bad Bramstedt Germany 53°55N 9°53E 178 B5
Bad Brückenau Germany 50°18N 9°47E 179 E5
Bad Doberan Germany 54°6N 11°53E 178 A7
Bad Driburg Germany 51°43N 9°1E 178 D5
Bad Ems Germany 50°20N 7°43E 179 E3
Bad Frankenhausen Germany 51°21N 11°5E 178 D7
Bad Freienwalde Germany 52°46N 14°1E 178 C10
Bad Goisern Austria 47°38N 13°38E 180 D6
Bad Harzburg Germany 51°52N 10°34E 178 D6
Bad Hersfeld Germany 50°52N 9°42E 178 E5
Bad Hofgastein Austria 47°17N 13°6E 180 D6
Bad Homburg Germany 50°13N 8°38E 179 E4
Bad Honnef Germany 50°38N 7°13E 178 E3
Bad Iburg Germany 52°10N 8°3E 178 C4
Bad Ischl Austria 47°44N 13°38E 180 D6
Bad Kissingen Germany 50°11N 10°4E 179 E6
Bad Königshofen Germany 50°17N 10°28E 179 E6
Bad Kreuznach Germany 49°50N 7°51E 179 F3
Bad Krozingen Germany 47°54N 7°42E 179 H3
Bad Kudowa = Kudowa-Zdrój Poland 50°27N 16°15E 185 H3
Bad Laasphe Germany 50°56N 8°25E 178 E4
Bad Landeck = Lądek-Zdrój Poland 50°21N 16°53E 185 H3
Bad Langensalza Germany 51°5N 10°38E 178 D6
Bad Lauterberg Germany 51°38N 10°28E 178 D6
Bad Leonfelden Austria 48°31N 14°18E 180 C7
Bad Liebenwerda Germany 51°31N 13°24E 178 D9
Bad Mergentheim Germany 49°28N 9°42E 179 F5
Bad Münstereifel Germany 50°33N 6°46E 178 E2
Bad Nauheim Germany 50°21N 8°43E 179 E4
Bad Neuenahr-Ahrweiler Germany 50°32N 7°5E 178 E3
Bad Neustadt Germany 50°18N 10°13E 179 E6
Bad Oeynhausen Germany 52°12N 8°46E 178 C4
Bad Oldesloe Germany 53°48N 10°22E 178 B6
Bad Orb Germany 50°12N 9°22E 179 E5
Bad Polzin = Polanica-Zdrój Poland 50°24N 16°32E 185 H3
Bad Pyrmont Germany 51°59N 9°16E 178 D5
Bad Reichenhall Germany 47°43N 12°54E 179 H8
Bad Reinerz = Duszniki-Zdrój Poland 50°24N 16°24E 185 H3
Bad Säckingen Germany 47°33N 7°56E 179 H3
Bad St. Leonhard Austria 46°58N 14°47E 180 E7
Bad Salzuflen Germany 52°5N 8°45E 178 C4
Bad Salzungen Germany 50°48N 10°14E 178 E6
Bad Schönfliess = Trzcińsko Zdrój Poland 52°58N 14°35E 185 F1
Bad Schwartau Germany 53°55N 10°41E 178 B6
Bad Segeberg Germany 53°56N 10°17E 178 B6
Bad Tölz Germany 47°45N 11°34E 179 H7
Bad Urach Germany 48°29N 9°23E 179 G5
Bad Vöslau Austria 47°58N 16°12E 181 D9
Bad Waldsee Germany 47°55N 9°45E 179 H5
Bad Wildungen Germany 51°6N 9°7E 178 D5
Bad Wimpfen Germany 49°13N 9°11E 179 F5
Bad Windsheim Germany 49°36N 10°25E 179 F6
Bad Zwischenahn Germany 53°12N 8°1E 178 B4
Bada Barabil India 22°7N 85°24E 243 H11
Badagara India 11°35N 75°40E 245 J2
Badagri Nigeria 6°25N 2°55E 263 D5
Badain Jaran Shamo China 40°23N 102°0E 218 B5
Badajós, L. Brazil 3°15S 62°50W 329 D5
Badajoz Spain 38°50N 6°59W 195 G4
Badajoz □ Spain 38°40N 6°30W 195 G4
Badakhshān □ Afghan. 36°30N 71°0E 240 A3
Badaling China 40°21N 116°0E 219 B6
Badalona Spain 41°26N 2°15E 114 A2
Badalzai Afghan. 29°50N 65°35E 242 E1
Badami India 15°55N 75°41E 245 G2
Badampahar India 22°10N 86°10E 244 C8
Badanah Si. Arabia 30°58N 41°30E 246 D4
Badarinath India 30°45N 79°30E 243 D8
Badarpur India 24°54N 92°36E 241 C4
Badas, Kepulauan Indonesia 0°45N 107°5E 234 B3
Baddo → Pakistan 28°0N 64°20E 240 D2
Bade Indonesia 7°10S 139°35E 231 F9
Badeggi Nigeria 9°1N 6°8E 263 D6
Badéguichéri Niger 14°30N 5°22E 263 C6
Baden Austria 48°1N 16°13E 181 C9
Baden Switz. 47°28N 8°18E 179 H4
Baden Pa., U.S.A. 40°38N 80°14W 312 F4
Baden-Baden Germany 48°44N 8°13E 179 G4
Baden-Württemberg □ Germany 48°20N 8°40E 179 G4
Badgam India 34°1N 74°45E 243 B6
Badgastein Austria 47°7N 13°9E 180 D6
Badger Nfld. & L., Canada 49°0N 56°4W 299 C8
Badger Calif., U.S.A. 36°38N 119°1W 306 J7
Bādghīs □ Afghan. 35°0N 63°0E 240 B1
Badgingarra △ Australia 30°23S 115°22E 279 F2
Badhoevedorp Neths. 52°20N 4°47E 112 A1
Badia Polésine Italy 45°5N 11°29E 199 C8
Badian Phil. 9°55N 123°24E 233 G4
Badiar △ Guinea 13°37N 13°11W 262 C2
Badin Pakistan 24°38N 68°54E 242 G3
Badinka ⌓ Mali 13°31N 9°28W 262 C3
Badjokola Dem. Rep. of the Congo 3°54N 20°17E 264 B4
Badlands U.S.A. 43°55N 102°30W 308 D2
Badlands △ U.S.A. 43°38N 102°56W 308 D2
Badli India 28°44N 77°8E 120 A1
Badnera India 20°48N 77°44E 244 D3
Badoc Phil. 17°56N 120°28E 232 C3
Badogo Mali 11°2N 8°13W 262 C3
Badoumbé Mali 13°42N 10°15W 262 C2
Badr Ḥunayn Si. Arabia 23°44N 38°46E 248 B2
Badrah Iraq 33°6N 45°58E 213 F11
Badrinath India 30°44N 79°29E 243 D8
Badu Australia 10°7S 142°11E 280 a
Badulla Sri Lanka 7°1N 81°7E 245 L5
Badung, Selat Indonesia 8°40S 115°22E 231 K18
Badupi Burma 21°36N 93°27E 241 E4
Badvel India 14°45N 79°3E 245 G4
Baena Spain 37°37N 4°20W 195 H6
Baengnyeongdo S. Korea 37°57N 124°40E 224 D2
Baerami Australia 32°27S 150°27E 283 B9
Bærum Norway 59°54N 10°36E 133 A2
Baetov Kyrgyzstan 41°13N 74°54E 217 D8
Baeza Ecuador 0°25S 77°53W 328 D2
Baeza Spain 37°57N 3°25W 195 H7
Bafang Cameroon 5°9N 10°11E 263 D7
Bafatá Guinea-Biss. 12°8N 14°40W 262 C2
Baffin B. N. Amer. 72°0N 64°0W 295 C19
Baffin I. Canada 68°0N 75°0W 295 D17
Bafia Cameroon 4°40N 11°10E 263 E7
Bafilo Togo 9°22N 1°22E 263 D5
Bafing → Mali 13°49N 10°50W 262 C2
Bafing △ Mali 12°38N 10°28W 262 C2
Bafliyūn Syria 36°37N 36°59E 246 B3
Bafoulabé Mali 13°50N 10°55W 262 C2
Bafoussam Cameroon 5°28N 10°25E 263 D7
Bāfq Iran 31°40N 55°25E 247 D7
Bafra Turkey 41°34N 35°54E 212 B6
Bafra Burnu Turkey 41°45N 36°2E 212 B7
Bāft Iran 29°15N 56°38E 247 D8
Bafut Cameroon 6°6N 10°2E 263 D7
Bafwasende Dem. Rep. of the Congo 1°3N 27°5E 268 B2
Bagabag Phil. 16°30N 121°15E 232 C3
Bagabag I. Papua N. G. 4°48S 146°14E 286 C4
Bagac Phil. 14°36N 120°23E 232 D3
Bagac Bay Phil. 14°36N 120°20E 232 D3
Bagaha India 27°6N 84°5E 244 A7
Bagalkot India 16°10N 75°40E 245 F2
Bagam Niger 15°43N 6°35E 263 B6
Bagamanoc Phil. 13°57N 124°17E 232 E5
Bagamoyo Tanzania 6°28S 38°55E 268 D4
Bagan = Pagan Burma 21°10N 94°52E 241 E5
Bagan Datoh Malaysia 3°59N 100°47E 237 L3
Bagan Serai Malaysia 5°1N 100°32E 237 K3
Baganga Phil. 7°34N 126°33E 233 H6
Bagani Namibia 18°7S 21°41E 270 A3
Bagansiapiapi Indonesia 2°12N 100°50E 234 B2
Bagasra India 21°30N 71°0E 242 J4
Bagata Dem. Rep. of the Congo 3°44S 17°57E 264 C3
Bagaud India 22°19N 75°53E 242 H6
Bagawi Sudan 12°20N 34°18E 257 E3
Bagbag Sudan 15°23N 31°30E 257 D3
Bağcılar Turkey 41°2N 28°49E 122 B1
Bagdad Calif., U.S.A. 34°35N 115°53W 307 L11
Bagdad Fla., U.S.A. 30°36N 87°2W 317 E2
Bagdarin Russia 54°26N 113°36E 215 D12
Bagé Brazil 31°20S 54°15W 335 C5
Bagenalstown = Muine Bheag Ireland 52°42N 6°58W 166 D5
Bagepalli India 13°47N 77°47E 245 H3
Bagevadi India 16°35N 75°58E 244 F2
Baggao Phil. 17°56N 121°46E 232 C3
Bággio Italy 45°27N 9°6E 129 B1
Baggs U.S.A. 41°2N 107°39W 304 F10
Bagh Pakistan 33°59N 73°45E 243 C5
Bāgh-e-Feyz Iran 35°44N 51°19E 141 A1
Baghain → India 25°32N 81°1E 243 G9
Baghdād Iraq 33°20N 44°23E 113 A2
Baghdād al Muthana ✕ (BGW) Iraq 33°17N 44°30E 113 B2
Baghdad Int. ✕ (SDA) Iraq 33°15N 44°14E 113 B1
Baghdadi Georgia 42°5N 42°49E 213 A10
Bagherhat Bangla. 22°40N 89°47E 241 D2
Bagheria Italy 38°5N 13°30E 200 D6
Baghlān Afghan. 32°12N 68°46E 240 A3
Baghlān □ Afghan. 36°0N 68°30E 240 B3
Bagley U.S.A. 47°32N 95°24W 308 B6
Bagmari India 22°34N 88°23E 124 B2
Bagn Norway 60°49N 9°34E 164 D6
Bagnara Cálabra Italy 38°17N 15°48E 201 D8
Bagnasco Italy 44°18N 8°2E 198 D5
Bagnell Dam U.S.A. 38°14N 92°36W 310 F4
Bagnères-de-Bigorre France 43°5N 0°9E 174 E4
Bagnères-de-Luchon France 42°47N 0°38E 174 F4
Bagneux France 48°47N 2°18E 134 B2
Bagni di Lucca Italy 44°1N 10°35E 198 D7
Bagno di Romagna Italy 43°50N 11°57E 199 E8
Bagnoles-de-l'Orne France 48°32N 0°25W 172 D6
Bagnolet France 48°52N 2°25E 134 A3
Bagnols-sur-Cèze France 44°10N 4°36E 175 D8
Bagnorea = Bagnorégio Italy 42°37N 12°5E 199 F9
Bagnorégio Italy 42°37N 12°5E 199 F9
Bago = Pegu Burma 17°20N 96°29E 241 G6
Bago Phil. 10°32N 122°50E 233 F4
Bagodar India 24°5N 85°52E 243 G11
Bagrationovsk Russia 54°23N 20°39E 184 D7
Bagrdan Serbia 44°5N 21°11E 202 B5
Bagsværd Denmark 55°45N 12°27E 118 A2
Bagsværd Sø Denmark 55°46N 12°28E 118 A2
Bagua Peru 5°35S 78°22W 330 B2
Baguiati India 22°36N 88°25E 124 B2
Baguio Phil. 16°26N 120°34E 232 C3
Bagumbayan Phil. 14°28N 121°3E 127 C2
Bağyurdu Turkey 38°25N 27°41E 205 C9
Bagzane, Monts Niger 17°43N 8°45E 259 E1
Bah India 26°53N 78°36E 243 F8
Bahabón de Esgueva Spain 41°52N 3°43W 194 D7
Bahadurabad Ghat Bangla. 25°11N 89°44E 241 C2
Bahadurganj India 26°16N 87°49E 243 F12
Bahadurgarh India 28°40N 76°57E 242 E7
Baha'i Temple U.S.A. 42°4N 87°41W 119 A2
Bahaja Somali Rep. 11°16N 49°50E 267 B6
Baham, Pte. Martinique 14°24N 60°50W 322 j
Bahama, Canal Viejo de W. Indies 22°10N 77°30W 320 B4
Bahamas ■ N. Amer. 24°0N 75°0W 321 B5
Bahār Iran 34°54N 48°26E 213 E13
Bahārak Afghan. 37°0N 70°53E 240 A3
Baharampur India 24°2N 88°27E 243 G13
Baharîya, El Wâhât al Egypt 28°0N 28°50E 256 B2
Baharu Pandan = Pandan Malaysia 1°32N 103°46E 237 d
Bahawalnagar Pakistan 30°0N 73°15E 242 E5
Bahawalpur Pakistan 29°24N 71°40E 242 E4
Bahçe Turkey 37°13N 36°34E 212 D7
Bahçecik Turkey 40°41N 29°44E 203 F13

Bahçeköy *Turkey* 41°10N 28°59E **122** A1
Bahçelievler *Turkey* 41°0N 28°50E **122** B1
Baheli *Phil.* 10°0N 118°47E **233** F2
Bäherden *Turkmenistan* 38°25N 57°26E **247** B8
Baheri *India* 28°45N 79°34E **243** E8
Bahgul → *India* 27°45N 79°36E **243** F8
Bahi *Tanzania* 5°58S 35°21E **268** D4
Bahi Swamp *Tanzania* 6°10S 35°0E **268** D4
Bahía = Salvador *Brazil* 13°0S 38°30W **333** D4
Bahia □ *Brazil* 12°0S 42°0W **333** D3
Bahía, Is. de la *Honduras* 16°45N 86°15W **320** C2
Bahía Blanca *Argentina* 38°35S 62°13W **334** D3
Bahía de Caráquez *Ecuador* 0°40S 80°27W **328** D1
Bahía Kino *Mexico* 28°47N 111°58W **318** B2
Bahía Laura *Argentina* 48°10S 66°30W **336** C3
Bahía Mansa *Chile* 40°33S 73°46W **336** B2
Bahía Negra *Paraguay* 20°5S 58°5W **331** E6
Bahía Solano *Colombia* 6°14N 77°25W **328** B2
Bahir Dar *Ethiopia* 11°37N 37°10E **257** E4
Bahlah *Oman* 22°58N 57°18E **249** B7
Bahmanzād *Iran* 31°15N 51°47E **247** D6
Bahmer *Algeria* 27°32N 0°10W **261** C4
Bahr el Ahmar □ *Egypt* 28°40N 31°30E **251** K2
Bahr el Ahmar □ *Sudan* 20°0N 35°0E **256** D4
Bahr el Jabal □ *Sudan* 4°0N 31°0E **257** G3
Bahraich *India* 27°38N 81°37E **243** F9
Bahrain ■ *Asia* 26°0N 50°35E **247** E6
Bahror *India* 27°51N 76°20E **242** F7
Bahtîm *Egypt* 30°8N 31°15E **117** A2
Bāhū Kalāt *Iran* 25°43N 61°25E **247** E9
Bai *Mali* 13°35N 3°28W **262** C4
Bai Bung, Mui = Ca Mau, Mui *Vietnam* 8°38N 104°44E **237** H5
Bai Duc *Vietnam* 18°3N 105°49E **236** C5
Bai Thuong *Vietnam* 19°54N 105°23E **236** C5
Baia de Aramă *Romania* 45°0N 22°50E **182** E7
Baía dos Tigres *Angola* 16°40S 11°47E **265** F2
Baía Farta *Angola* 12°40S 13°11E **265** E2
Baia Mare *Romania* 47°40N 23°35E **183** C8
Baia-Sprie *Romania* 47°41N 23°43E **183** C8
Baião *Brazil* 2°40S 49°40W **332** B2
Baïbokoum *Chad* 7°46N 15°43E **259** G3
Baicheng *Jilin, China* 45°38N 122°42E **227** B12
Baicheng *Xinjiang Uygur, China* 41°46N 81°52E **217** D10
Băicoi *Romania* 45°3N 25°52E **183** E10
Baidoa = Baydhabo *Somali Rep.* 3°8N 43°30E **267** D5
Baie-Comeau *Canada* 49°12N 68°10W **299** C6
Baie du Cap *Mauritius* 20°29S 57°22E **272** d
Baie-Mahault *Guadeloupe* 16°16N 61°35W **322** e
Baie-St-Paul *Canada* 47°28N 70°32W **299** C5
Baie Ste-Anne *Seychelles* 4°18S 55°45E **272** c
Baie-Trinité *Canada* 49°25N 67°20W **299** C6
Baie Verte *Canada* 49°55N 56°12W **299** C8
Baignes-Ste-Radegonde *France* 45°23N 0°25W **174** C3
Baigneux-les-Juifs *France* 47°31N 4°39E **173** E11
Baihar *India* 22°6N 80°33E **243** H9
Baihe *China* 32°50N 110°5E **226** H6
Ba'ījī *Iraq* 35°0N 43°30E **213** E10
Baijnath *India* 29°55N 79°37E **243** E8
Baikal, L. = Baykal, Oz. *Russia* 53°0N 108°0E **215** D11
Baikonur = Bayqongyr *Kazakhstan* 45°40N 63°20E **216** C6
Baikunthpur *India* 23°15N 82°33E **243** H10
Bailadila, Mt. *India* 18°43N 81°15E **244** E5
Baile Átha Cliath = Dublin *Ireland* 53°21N 6°15W **120** A2
Baile Átha Fhirdhia = Ardee *Ireland* 53°52N 6°33W **166** C5
Baile Átha I = Athy *Ireland* 53°0N 7°0W **166** C5
Baile Átha Luain = Athlone *Ireland* 53°25N 7°56W **166** C4
Baile Átha Troim = Trim *Ireland* 53°33N 6°48W **166** C5
Baile Brigín = Balbriggan *Ireland* 53°37N 6°11W **166** C5
Băile Govora *Romania* 45°5N 24°11E **183** E9
Băile Herculane *Romania* 44°53N 22°26E **182** F7
Băile Olăneşti *Romania* 45°12N 24°14E **183** E9
Băile Tuşnad *Romania* 46°9N 25°51E **183** D10
Bailén *Spain* 38°8N 3°48W **195** G7
Băileşti *Romania* 44°1N 23°20E **183** F8
Baileys Crossroads *U.S.A.* 38°50N 77°6W **143** B3
Bailhongal *India* 15°55N 74°53E **245** G2
Bailique, Ilha *Brazil* 1°2N 49°58W **332** A2
Baille-Argent *Guadeloupe* 16°15N 61°48W **322** e
Baillif *Guadeloupe* 16°1N 61°44W **322** e
Bailly *France* 48°50N 2°4E **134** A1
Bailugh *Afghan.* 32°40N 66°47E **240** B2
Bailundo = Luau *Angola* 10°40S 22°10E **265** E4
Bailundo *Angola* 12°10S 15°50E **265** E3
Baima *China* 33°0N 100°26E **228** A3
Baimuru *Papua N. G.* 7°35S 144°51E **286** D3
Bain-de-Bretagne *France* 47°50N 1°40W **172** E5
Bainbridge *Ga., U.S.A.* 30°55N 84°35W **316** E5
Bainbridge *Ind., U.S.A.* 39°46N 86°49W **311** E10
Bainbridge *N.Y., U.S.A.* 42°18N 75°29W **313** D9
Bainbridge *Ohio, U.S.A.* 39°14N 83°16W **311** E13
Bainbridge Island *U.S.A.* 47°38N 122°32W **306** C4
Baing *Indonesia* 10°14S 120°34E **231** F6
Bainiu *China* 32°50N 112°15E **226** H7
Bainyik *Papua N. G.* 3°40S 143°4E **286** B2
Baiona *Spain* 42°6N 8°52W **194** C2
Bā'ir *Jordan* 30°45N 36°55E **251** H7
Bā'ir, W. → *Jordan* 30°59N 37°24E **251** H8
Baird Mts. *U.S.A.* 67°0N 160°0W **303** C7
Bairiki = Tarawa *Kiribati* 1°30N 173°0E **288** G9
Bairin Youqi *China* 43°30N 118°35E **227** C10
Bairin Zuoqi *China* 43°58N 119°15E **227** C10
Bairnsdale *Australia* 37°48S 147°36E **283** D7
Bairro Alto *Lisbon, Portugal* **126** c1
Bairro Lopes *Lisbon, Portugal* **126** b3
Bais *Phil.* 9°35N 123°7E **233** G4
Baisha *Guangdong, China* 23°8N 113°11E **121** B2
Baisha *Henan, China* 34°20N 112°32E **226** G7
Baissa *Nigeria* 7°14N 10°38E **263** D7
Baitadi *Nepal* 29°35N 80°25E **243** E9
Baitarani → *India* 20°45N 86°48E **244** D8
Baixa *Lisbon, Portugal* **126** c2
Baixa Grande *Brazil* 11°57S 40°11W **333** D3
Baixa Limia-Sierra do Xurés ⌂ *Spain* 41°59N 8°2W **194** D2
Baixo-Longa *Angola* 15°41S 18°45E **265** F3
Baiyer River *Papua N. G.* 5°32S 144°9E **286** C3
Baiyin *China* 36°45N 104°14E **226** F3
Baiyü *China* 31°16N 98°50E **228** B2
Baiyu Shan *China* 37°15N 107°30E **226** F4
Baiyuda *Sudan* 17°35N 32°7E **256** D3
Baiyun *China* 23°11N 113°16E **121** A2
Baiyun Hill *China* 23°8N 113°15E **121** B2
Baiyun Mountain Scenic Area *China* 23°11N 113°17E **121** A2
Baj Baj *India* 22°30N 88°5E **243** H13
Baja *Hungary* 46°12N 18°59E **182** D3
Baja, Pta. *Easter I., Chile* 27°10S 109°22W **330** b
Baja, Pta. *Baja Calif., Mexico* 29°58N 115°49W **318** B1
Baja California *Mexico* 31°10N 115°12W **318** A1
Baja California □ *Mexico* 30°0N 115°0W **318** B2
Baja California Sur □ *Mexico* 25°50N 111°50W **318** B2
Bajag *India* 22°40N 81°21E **243** H9
Bajamar *Canary Is.* 28°33N 16°20W **153** e1
Bajana *India* 23°7N 71°49E **242** H4
Bajatrejo *Indonesia* 8°29S 114°19E **231** J17
Bajera *Indonesia* 8°31S 115°2E **231** J18
Bājgīrān *Iran* 37°36N 58°24E **247** B8
Bājil *Yemen* 15°4N 43°17E **248** D3
Bajimba, Mt. *Australia* 29°17S 152°6E **281** D5
Bajina Bašta *Serbia* 43°58N 19°35E **202** C3
Bajmok *Serbia* 45°57N 19°24E **182** E4
Bajo Boquete *Panama* 8°46N 82°27W **320** E3
Bajo Caracoles *Argentina* 47°27S 70°56W **336** C2
Bajo Nuevo *Caribbean* 15°40N 78°50W **320** C4
Bajoga *Nigeria* 10°57N 11°20E **263** C7
Bajool *Australia* 23°40S 150°35E **280** C5
Bak *Hungary* 46°43N 16°51E **182** D1
Bakala *C.A.R.* 6°15N 20°20E **264** A4
Bakar *Croatia* 45°18N 14°32E **199** C11
Bakassi Pen. *Cameroon* 4°42N 8°20E **263** E6
Bakel *Senegal* 14°56N 12°20W **262** C2
Baker *Calif., U.S.A.* 35°16N 116°4W **307** K10
Baker *Fla., U.S.A.* 30°48N 86°41W **317** E3
Baker *Mont., U.S.A.* 46°22N 104°17W **304** C11
Baker, Canal *Chile* 47°45S 74°45W **336** C2
Baker, L. *Canada* 64°0N 96°0W **294** E12
Baker, Mt. *U.S.A.* 48°50N 121°49W **304** B3
Baker City *U.S.A.* 44°47N 117°50W **304** D5
Baker I. *Pac. Oc.* 0°10N 176°35W **277** A15
Baker I. *Alaska, U.S.A.* 55°20N 133°40W **296** B2
Baker L. *Australia* 26°54S 126°5E **279** E4
Baker Lake *Canada* 64°20N 96°3W **294** E12
Bakere *Dem. Rep. of the Congo* 1°36N 23°50E **264** B4
Bakerhill *U.S.A.* 31°47N 85°18W **316** D4
Bakers Creek *Australia* 21°13S 149°7E **280** C4
Bakers Dozen Is. *Canada* 56°45N 78°45W **298** A4
Bakersfield *Calif., U.S.A.* 35°23N 119°1W **307** K8
Bakersfield *Vt., U.S.A.* 44°45N 72°48W **313** B12
Bakharden = Bäherden *Turkmenistan* 38°25N 57°26E **247** B8
Bakhchysaray *Ukraine* 44°40N 33°45E **189** K7
Bakhmach *Ukraine* 51°10N 32°45E **189** G7
Bakhmut = Artemovsk *Ukraine* 48°35N 38°0E **189** H9
Bākhtarān = Kermānshāh *Iran* 34°23N 47°0E **213** E12
Bākhtarān = Kermānshāh □ *Iran* 34°0N 46°30E **246** C5
Baki = Krasnyye Baki *Russia* 57°8N 45°10E **190** B7
Bakı *Azerbaijan* 40°29N 49°56E **191** K9
Baki *Somali Rep.* 10°30N 43°8E **267** B5
Bakır → *Turkey* 38°55N 27°0E **205** C9
Bakırdağı *Turkey* 38°13N 35°46E **212** C6
Bakırköy *Turkey* 40°58N 28°52E **122** C1
Bakkafjörður *Iceland* 66°2N 14°48W **155** A12
Bakkaflói *Iceland* 66°10N 14°45W **155** A12
Bakkagerði *Iceland* 65°31N 13°49W **155** B13
Baklan *Turkey* 38°0N 29°36E **205** C11
Bako *Ethiopia* 5°51N 36°23E **257** F4
Bako *Ivory C.* 9°8N 7°40W **262** D3
Bako △ *Malaysia* 1°43N 110°28E **235** B4
Bakony *Hungary* 47°10N 17°30E **182** C2
Bakony Forest = Bakony *Hungary* 47°10N 17°30E **182** C2
Bakool □ *Somali Rep.* 4°0N 44°0E **267** D5
Bakori *Nigeria* 11°34N 7°25E **263** C6
Bakouma *C.A.R.* 5°40N 22°56E **264** A4
Bakovka *Russia* 55°40N 37°19E **129** B2
Baksan *Russia* 43°42N 43°32E **191** J6
Bakswaho *India* 24°15N 79°18E **243** G8
Baku = Bakı *Azerbaijan* 40°29N 49°56E **191** K9
Bakundi *Nigeria* 8°2N 10°45E **263** D7
Bakuriani *Georgia* 41°44N 43°31E **213** B10
Bakutis Coast *Antarctica* 74°0S 120°0W **151** D15
Bakwa-Kenge *Dem. Rep. of the Congo* 4°51S 22°4E **265** C4
Bakwanga = Mbuji-Mayi *Dem. Rep. of the Congo* 6°9S 23°40E **265** D4
Baky = Bakı *Azerbaijan* 40°29N 49°56E **191** K9
Bal Harbor *U.S.A.* 25°53N 80°7W **128** A2
Bala *Ont., Canada* 45°1N 79°37W **312** A5
Bala *Senegal* 14°1N 13°8W **262** C2
Balâ *Turkey* 39°32N 33°6E **212** C5
Bala *Gwynedd, U.K.* 52°54N 3°36W **168** E4
Bala, L. *U.K.* 52°53N 3°37W **168** E4
Bālā Morghāb *Afghan.* 35°35N 63°20E **240** B1
Balabac *Phil.* 7°59N 117°4E **233** H1
Balabac I. *Phil.* 8°0N 117°0E **233** G1
Balabac Str. *E. Indies* 7°53N 117°5E **230** C5
Balabagh *Afghan.* 34°25N 70°12E **242** B4
Ba'labakk *Lebanon* 34°0N 36°10E **250** E7
Balabalangan, Kepulauan *Indonesia* 2°20S 117°30E **235** C5
Balabio, Î. *N. Cal.* 20°7S 164°11E **288** d
Bălăciţa *Romania* 44°23N 23°8E **183** F8
Balad *Iraq* 34°0N 44°9E **213** F11
Balad Rūz *Iraq* 33°42N 45°5E **213** F11
Bālādeh *Fārs, Iran* 29°17N 51°56E **247** D6
Bālādeh *Māzandaran, Iran* 36°12N 51°48E **247** B6
Balaghat *India* 21°49N 80°12E **244** D5
Balaghat Ra. *India* 18°50N 76°30E **244** E3
Balaguer *Spain* 41°50N 0°50E **196** D5
Balaka *Dem. Rep. of the Congo* 4°52S 19°57E **265** C3
Balakän *Azerbaijan* 41°43N 46°24E **213** B12
Balakété *C.A.R.* 6°56N 19°54E **264** A3
Balakhna *Russia* 56°25N 43°32E **190** B6
Balaklava *S. Austral., Australia* 34°7S 138°22E **282** C3
Balaklava *Ukraine* 44°30N 33°30E **189** K7
Balakliya *Ukraine* 49°28N 36°55E **189** H9
Balakovo *Russia* 52°4N 47°55E **190** D8
Balamau *India* 27°10N 80°21E **243** F9
Balamban *Phil.* 10°30N 123°43E **233** F4
Balambangan *Malaysia* 7°17N 116°55E **235** A5
Bălan *Romania* 46°39N 25°48E **183** D10
Balancán *Mexico* 17°48N 91°32W **319** D6
Balanda = Kalininsk *Russia* 51°30N 44°40E **190** E7
Balandra B. *Trin. & Tob.* 10°42N 61°0W **323** t
Balanga *Phil.* 14°41N 120°32E **232** D3
Balangala *Dem. Rep. of the Congo* 0°30N 19°56E **264** B3
Balangiga *Phil.* 11°7N 125°23E **233** F5
Balangir *India* 20°43N 83°35E **244** D6
Balanivka *Ukraine* 48°24N 29°24E **183** B14
Balaoan *Phil.* 16°49N 120°24E **232** C3
Balapur *India* 20°40N 76°45E **244** D3
Balara *Phil.* 14°39N 121°3E **127** B2
Balashikha *Russia* 55°48N 37°58E **129** B5
Balashov *Russia* 51°30N 43°10E **190** E6
Balasinor *India* 22°57N 73°23E **242** H5
Balasore = Baleshwar *India* 21°35N 87°3E **244** D8
Balassagyarmat *Hungary* 48°4N 19°15E **182** B4
Balât *Egypt* 25°36N 29°19E **256** B2
Balaton *Hungary* 46°50N 17°40E **182** D2
Balaton-Felvidéki △ *Hungary* 46°52N 17°30E **182** D2
Balatonboglár *Hungary* 46°46N 17°40E **182** D2
Balatonfüred *Hungary* 46°58N 17°54E **182** D2
Balatonszentgyörgy *Hungary* 46°41N 17°19E **182** D2
Balayan *Phil.* 13°57N 120°44E **232** E3
Balazote *Spain* 38°54N 2°9W **197** G2
Balbalan *Phil.* 17°27N 121°12E **232** C3
Balbi, Mt. *Papua N. G.* 5°55S 154°58E **286** C8
Balbieriškis *Lithuania* 54°32N 23°53E **184** D10
Balbigny *France* 45°49N 4°11E **175** C8
Balbina *Brazil* 1°58S 59°29W **329** D6
Balbina, Represa de *Brazil* 2°0S 59°30W **329** D6
Balboa *Panama* 8°57N 79°34W **320** c
Balbriggan *Ireland* 53°37N 6°11W **166** C5
Balcarce *Argentina* 38°0S 58°10W **334** D4
Balcarres *Canada* 50°50N 103°35W **297** C8
Bălceşti *Romania* 44°37N 23°57E **183** F8
Balchik *Bulgaria* 43°28N 28°11E **203** C12
Balclutha *N.Z.* 46°15S 169°45E **285** G4
Balcones Escarpment *U.S.A.* 29°30N 99°15W **314** G5
Balçova *Turkey* 38°22N 27°4E **205** C9
Bald I. *Australia* 34°57S 118°27E **279** F2
Bald Knob *U.S.A.* 35°19N 91°34W **314** D9
Baldenburg = Biały Bór *Poland* 53°53N 16°51E **184** E3
Baldia *Pakistan* 24°54N 66°58E **123** A1
Baldock L. *Canada* 56°33N 97°57W **297** B9
Baldoyle *Ireland* 53°24N 6°8W **120** A3
Baldwin *Fla., U.S.A.* 30°18N 81°59W **316** E8
Baldwin *Mich., U.S.A.* 43°54N 85°51W **309** D11
Baldwin *Pa., U.S.A.* 40°21N 79°58W **312** F5
Baldwin, L. *U.S.A.* 28°34N 81°19W **133** A3
Baldwin Hills *U.S.A.* 34°0N 118°21W **126** B2
Baldwin Hills Res. *U.S.A.* 34°0N 118°21W **126** B2
Baldwinsville *U.S.A.* 43°10N 76°20W **313** C8
Baldy Peak *U.S.A.* 33°54N 109°34W **305** K9
Bale *Croatia* 45°4N 13°46E **199** C10
Bale *Oromiya, Ethiopia* 6°57N 40°8E **257** F5
Bale *Oromiya, Ethiopia* 6°20N 41°30E **257** F5
Bale Mts. △ *Ethiopia* 6°59N 39°52E **257** F4
Baleares, Is. *Spain* 39°30N 3°0E **206** B4
Balearic Is. = Baleares, Is. *Spain* 39°30N 3°0E **206** B4
Baleia, Pta. da *Brazil* 17°40S 39°7W **333** E4
Baleine → *Canada* 58°15N 67°40W **299** A6
Baleine, Petite R. de la → *Canada* 56°0N 76°45W **298** A4
Băleni *Romania* 45°48N 27°51E **183** E12
Baler *Phil.* 15°46N 121°34E **232** D3
Baler Bay *Phil.* 15°50N 121°35E **232** D3
Baleshare *U.K.* 57°31N 7°22W **167** D1
Baleshwar *India* 21°35N 87°3E **244** D8
Balestrand *Norway* 61°11N 6°31E **164** C3
Baley *Russia* 51°36N 116°37E **215** D12
Balezino *Russia* 58°2N 53°6E **190** B11
Balfate *Honduras* 15°48N 86°25W **320** C2
Balfour Channel *Solomon Is.* 8°43S 157°27E **287** M9
Balgo *Australia* 20°9S 127°58E **278** D4
Balgowlah *Australia* 33°47S 151°16E **139** A2
Balgowlah Heights *Australia* 33°48S 151°16E **139** A2
Balham *U.K.* 51°26N 0°8W **125** B3
Balharshah *India* 19°50N 79°23E **244** E4
Bali *Cameroon* 5°54N 10°0E **263** D7
Bali *Dem. Rep. of the Congo* 2°50S 16°12E **264** C3
Bali *Kriti, Greece* 35°25N 24°47E **207** E5
Bali *Raj., India* 25°11N 73°17E **242** G5
Bali *W. Bengal, India* 22°39N 88°20E **124** B1
Bali *Indonesia* 8°20S 115°0E **231** J18
Bali □ *Indonesia* 8°20S 115°0E **231** J18
Bali, Selat *Indonesia* 8°18S 114°25E **231** J17
Bali Barat △ *Indonesia* 8°12S 114°35E **235** D4
Bali Sea *Indonesia* 8°0S 115°0E **231** J17
Balia *S. Leone* 9°22N 11°1W **262** D2
Baliapal *India* 21°40N 87°17E **243** J12
Baliceaux *St. Vincent* 12°57N 61°8W **323** n
Balicuatro Is. *Phil.* 12°39N 124°24E **232** E5
Baliganja *India* 22°31N 88°22E **124** B2
Balige *Indonesia* 2°14N 99°7E **237** L2
Baligród *Poland* 49°20N 22°17E **185** J9
Baliguda *India* 20°12N 83°55E **244** D6
Balik Pulau *Malaysia* 5°21N 100°14E **237** c
Balıkeşir *Turkey* 39°39N 27°53E **205** B9
Balıkeşir □ *Turkey* 39°45N 28°0E **205** B9
Balīkh → *Syria* 35°52N 39°12E **213** E8
Balıkçeşme *Turkey* 40°18N 27°5E **203** F11
Balikpapan *Indonesia* 1°10S 116°55E **235** C5
Balimbing *Phil.* 5°5N 119°58E **233** J2
Balimo *Papua N. G.* 8°6S 142°57E **286** E2
Baling *Malaysia* 5°41N 100°55E **237** K3
Balingasag *Phil.* 8°45N 124°47E **233** G5
Balingen *Germany* 48°16N 8°51E **179** G4
Balingsnäs *Sweden* 59°13N 18°0E **139** B2
Balingsta *Sweden* 59°12N 18°3E **139** B2
Balinţ *Romania* 45°48N 21°54E **182** E6
Balintang Channel *Phil.* 19°49N 121°40E **232** B3
Balintang I. *Phil.* 19°58N 122°9E **232** B3
Balintawak *Phil.* 14°39N 120°59E **127** B1
Baliza *Brazil* 16°0S 52°20W **331** D7
Baljurashī *Si. Arabia* 19°51N 41°33E **248** C3
Balkan □ *Turkmenistan* 40°0N 54°30E **216** D5
Balkan Mts. = Stara Planina *Bulgaria* 43°15N 23°0E **202** C7
Balkanabat *Turkmenistan* 39°30N 54°22E **247** B7
Balkh *Afghan.* 36°44N 66°47E **217** E7
Balkh □ *Afghan.* 36°50N 67°0E **240** A2
Balkhash = Balqash *Kazakhstan* 46°50N 74°50E **214** E8
Balkhash, Ozero = Balqash Köli *Kazakhstan* 46°0N 74°50E **217** C8
Balkonda *India* 18°52N 78°21E **244** E4
Ballachulish *U.K.* 56°41N 5°8W **167** E3
Balladonia *Australia* 32°27S 123°51E **279** F3
Ballaghaderreen *Ireland* 53°55N 8°34W **166** C3
Ballan *Australia* 37°35S 144°13E **282** D6
Ballarat *Australia* 37°33S 143°50E **282** D5
Ballard, L. *Australia* 29°20S 120°40E **279** E3
Ballater *U.K.* 57°3N 3°3W **167** D5
Ballé *Mali* 15°18N 8°33W **262** B3
Ballenas, Canal de *Mexico* 29°10N 113°29W **318** B2
Balleny Is. *Antarctica* 66°30S 163°0E **151** C11
Balleroy *France* 49°11N 0°50W **172** C6
Ballerup *Denmark* 55°43N 12°21E **118** A2
Ballestas, Is. *Peru* 13°44S 76°25W **330** C2
Ballı *Turkey* 40°50N 27°3E **203** F11
Ballia *India* 25°46N 84°12E **243** G11
Ballina *N.S.W., Australia* 28°50S 153°31E **281** D5
Ballina *Mayo, Ireland* 54°7N 9°9W **166** B2
Ballinasloe *Ireland* 53°20N 8°13W **166** C3
Ballinger *U.S.A.* 31°45N 99°57W **314** F5
Ballinrobe *Ireland* 53°38N 9°13W **166** C2
Ballinskelligs B. *Ireland* 51°48N 10°13W **166** E1
Ballinteer *Ireland* 53°17N 6°15W **120** B2
Ballon *France* 48°10N 0°14E **172** D7
Ballons des Vosges ⌂ *France* 48°0N 7°0E **173** E14
Ballsh *Albania* 40°36N 19°44E **202** F3
Ballston Spa *U.S.A.* 43°0N 73°51W **313** D11
Ballyboden *Ireland* 53°17N 6°18W **120** B2
Ballyboghil *Ireland* 53°32N 6°16W **166** C5
Ballybrack *Ireland* 53°15N 6°7W **120** B3
Ballybunion *Ireland* 52°31N 9°40W **166** D2
Ballycanew *Ireland* 52°37N 6°19W **166** D5
Ballycastle *U.K.* 55°12N 6°15W **166** A5
Ballyclare *U.K.* 54°46N 6°0W **166** B5
Ballydehob *Ireland* 51°34N 9°28W **166** E2
Ballyfermot *Ireland* 53°20N 6°21W **120** A1
Ballygawley *U.K.* 54°27N 7°2W **166** B4
Ballyhaunis *Ireland* 53°46N 8°46W **166** C3
Ballyheige *Ireland* 52°23N 9°49W **166** D2
Ballymena *U.K.* 54°52N 6°17W **166** B5
Ballymoney *U.K.* 55°5N 6°31W **166** A5
Ballymorefinn Hill *Ireland* 53°14N 6°22W **120** B1
Ballymote *Ireland* 54°5N 8°31W **166** B3
Ballymun *Ireland* 53°23N 6°16W **120** A2
Ballynahinch *U.K.* 54°24N 5°54W **166** B6
Ballyquintin Pt. *U.K.* 54°20N 5°30W **166** B6
Ballyshannon *Ireland* 54°30N 8°11W **166** B3
Balmaceda *Chile* 46°0S 71°50W **336** C2
Balmain *Australia* 33°51S 151°11E **139** B2
Balmaseda *Spain* 43°11N 3°12W **196** B1
Balmazújváros *Hungary* 47°37N 21°21E **182** C6
Balmertown *Canada* 51°4N 93°41W **297** C10
Balmoral *Australia* 37°15S 141°48E **282** D4
Balmorhea *U.S.A.* 30°59N 103°45W **314** F3
Balochistan = Baluchistan □ *Pakistan* 27°30N 65°0E **240** D2
Balod *India* 20°44N 81°13E **244** D5
Balombo *Angola* 12°21S 14°46E **265** E2
Balombo → *Angola* 11°57S 13°46E **265** E2
Balonne → *Australia* 28°47S 147°56E **281** D4
Balotra *India* 25°50N 72°14E **242** G5
Balpyq Bī *Kazakhstan* 44°52N 78°12E **217** D9
Balqash *Kazakhstan* 46°50N 74°50E **214** E8
Balqash Köli *Kazakhstan* 46°0N 74°50E **217** C8
Balrampur *India* 27°30N 82°20E **243** F10
Balranald *Australia* 34°38S 143°33E **282** C5
Balş *Romania* 44°22N 24°5E **183** F9
Balsapuerto *Peru* 5°48S 76°33W **330** B2
Balsas → *Maranhão, Brazil* 7°15S 44°35W **332** C3
Balsas → *Tocantins, Brazil* 9°58S 47°52W **332** C2
Balsas → *Michoacan, Mexico* 17°55N 102°10W **318** D4
Balsas del Norte *Mexico* 18°0N 99°46W **319** D5
Bålsta *Sweden* 59°35N 17°30E **162** E11
Balta *Romania* 44°54N 22°38E **182** F7
Balta *Ukraine* 48°2N 29°45E **183** B14
Baltakōl *Kazakhstan* 43°7N 67°46E **217** D7
Baltanás *Spain* 41°56N 4°15W **194** D6
Bălţi *Moldova* 47°48N 27°58E **183** C12
Baltic Sea *Europe* 57°0N 19°0E **161** H18
Baltîm *Egypt* 31°35N 31°10E **256** H7
Baltimore *Cork, Ireland* 51°29N 9°22W **166** E2
Baltimore *Md., U.S.A.* 39°17N 76°36W **309** F15
Baltimore *Ohio, U.S.A.* 39°51N 82°36W **312** G2
Baltinglass *Ireland* 52°56N 6°43W **166** D5
Baltit *Pakistan* 36°15N 74°40E **243** A6
Baltiysk *Russia* 54°41N 19°58E **184** D6
Baltiyskiy = Paldiski *Estonia* 59°23N 24°9E **188** C3
Baltra, I. *Ecuador* 0°26S 90°16W **330** a
Baltrum *Germany* 53°43N 7°24E **178** B3
Baluan I. *Papua N. G.* 2°33S 147°17E **286** B4
Baluchistan □ *Pakistan* 27°30N 65°0E **240** D2
Balud *Phil.* 12°2N 123°12E **232** E4
Baluhati *India* 22°39N 88°15E **124** B1
Baluqtybulaq *Kazakhstan* 50°51N 51°8E **190** E10
Baluran △ *Indonesia* 7°50S 114°23E **235** D4
Balurghat *India* 25°15N 88°44E **241** C2
Balvanera *Argentina* 34°37S 58°23W **117** B2
Balvi *Latvia* 57°8N 27°15E **188** D4
Balwyn *Australia* 37°48S 145°4E **128** A2
Balwyn North *Australia* 37°47S 145°4E **128** A2
Balya *Turkey* 39°44N 27°35E **205** B9
Balykchy *Kyrgyzstan* 42°26N 76°12E **217** D9
Balyqshy *Kazakhstan* 47°4N 51°52E **187** E9
Balzar *Ecuador* 2°2S 79°54W **328** D2
Bam *Iran* 29°7N 58°14E **247** D8
Bama *Guangxi Zhuangzu, China* 24°8N 107°12E **228** E6
Bama *Nigeria* 11°33N 13°41E **263** C7
Bamaga *Australia* 10°50S 142°25E **280** A3
Bamaji L. *Canada* 51°9N 91°25W **298** B1
Bamako *Mali* 12°34N 7°55W **262** C3
Bamba *Dem. Rep. of the Congo* 5°45S 18°23E **265** D3
Bamba *Mali* 17°5N 1°24W **263** B4
Bambama *Congo* 2°32S 13°32E **264** C2
Bambamarca *Peru* 6°36S 78°32W **330** B2
Bambang *Phil.* 16°23N 121°6E **232** C3
Bambannan I. *Phil.* 5°37N 120°17E **233** J3
Bambara *Comoros Is.* 12°11S 44°31E **272** a
Bambara Maoundé *Mali* 13°26N 4°3W **262** B4
Bambari *C.A.R.* 5°40N 20°35E **264** A4
Bambaroo *Australia* 18°50S 146°10E **280** B4
Bambaya *Guinea* 10°55N 13°38W **262** C2
Bamberg *Bayern, Germany* 49°54N 10°54E **179** F6
Bamberg *S.C., U.S.A.* 33°18N 81°2W **316** B8
Bambesi *Ethiopia* 9°45N 34°40E **257** F3
Bambey *Senegal* 14°42N 16°28W **262** C1
Bambili *Dem. Rep. of the Congo* 3°40N 26°0E **268** B2
Bambinga *Dem. Rep. of the Congo* 3°43S 18°53E **264** C3
Bambio *C.A.R.* 3°55N 16°57E **264** B3
Bamboi *Ghana* 8°13N 2°1W **262** D4
Bamboo Avenue *Jamaica* 18°6N 77°47W **320** a
Bambous *Mauritius* 20°15S 57°24E **272** e
Bambouti *C.A.R.* 5°24N 27°12E **264** A5
Bambuí *Brazil* 20°1S 45°58W **333** F2
Bamburgh *U.K.* 55°37N 1°43W **168** B6
Bamenda *Cameroon* 5°57N 10°11E **263** D7
Bamendjing, L. de *Cameroon* 5°50N 10°30E **263** D7
Bamfield *Canada* 48°45N 125°10W **296** D3
Bāmīān *Afghan.* 34°49N 67°49E **217** F7
Bāmīān □ *Afghan.* 35°0N 67°0E **240** B2
Bamiancheng *China* 43°15N 124°2E **227** C13
Bamingui *C.A.R.* 7°34N 20°11E **264** A4
Bamingui → *C.A.R.* 8°33N 19°5E **264** A3
Bamingui-Bangoran △ *C.A.R.* 8°30N 19°46E **264** A3
Bamkin *Cameroon* 6°3N 11°27E **263** D7
Bampan *Phil.* 15°40N 120°20E **232** D3
Bampūr *Iran* 27°15N 60°21E **247** E9
Bampūr → *Iran* 27°24N 59°0E **247** E8
Bamu → *Papua N. G.* 8°1S 143°33E **286** E2
Ban *Burkina Faso* 14°5N 2°27W **262** C4
Ban Ao Tu Khun *Thailand* 8°9N 98°20E **237** a
Ban Ban *Laos* 19°31N 103°30E **236** C4
Ban Bang Hin *Thailand* 9°32N 98°35E **237** H2
Ban Bang Khu *Thailand* 7°57N 98°23E **237** a
Ban Bang Rong *Thailand* 8°3N 98°25E **237** a
Ban Bo Phut *Thailand* 9°33N 100°2E **237** b
Ban Chaweng *Thailand* 9°32N 100°3E **237** b
Ban Chiang Klang *Thailand* 19°25N 100°55E **236** C3
Ban Choho *Thailand* 15°2N 102°9E **236** E4
Ban Dan Lan Hoi *Thailand* 17°0N 99°35E **236** D2
Ban Don = Surat Thani *Thailand* 9°6N 99°20E **237** H2
Ban Don *Vietnam* 12°53N 107°48E **236** F6
Ban Don, Ao → *Thailand* 9°20N 99°25E **237** H2
Ban Dong *Thailand* 19°30N 100°59E **236** C3
Ban Hong *Thailand* 18°18N 98°50E **236** C2
Ban Hua Thanon *Thailand* 9°26N 100°1E **237** b
Ban Kantang *Thailand* 7°25N 99°31E **237** J2
Ban Karon *Thailand* 7°51N 98°18E **237** a
Ban Kata *Thailand* 7°50N 98°18E **237** a
Ban Keun *Laos* 18°22N 102°35E **236** C4
Ban Khai *Thailand* 12°46N 101°18E **236** F3
Ban Kheun *Laos* 20°13N 101°7E **236** B3
Ban Khlong Khian *Thailand* 8°10N 98°26E **237** a
Ban Khlong Kua *Thailand* 6°57N 100°8E **237** J3
Ban Khuan *Thailand* 8°20N 98°25E **237** a
Ban Khuan Mao *Thailand* 7°50N 99°37E **237** J2
Ban Ko Yai Chim *Thailand* 11°17N 99°26E **237** G2
Ban Laem *Thailand* 13°13N 99°59E **236** F2
Ban Lamai *Thailand* 9°28N 100°3E **237** b
Ban Lao Ngam *Laos* 15°28N 106°10E **236** E6
Ban Le Kathe *Thailand* 15°49N 98°53E **236** E2
Ban Lo Po Noi *Thailand* 8°1N 98°34E **237** a
Ban Mae Chedi *Thailand* 19°11N 99°31E **236** C2
Ban Mae Nam *Thailand* 9°34N 100°0E **237** b
Ban Mae Sariang *Thailand* 18°10N 97°56E **236** C1
Ban Mê Thuôt = Buon Ma Thuot *Vietnam* 12°40N 108°3E **236** F7
Ban Mi *Thailand* 15°3N 100°32E **236** E3
Ban Muong Mo *Laos* 19°4N 103°58E **236** C4
Ban Na Bo *Thailand* 9°19N 99°41E **237** b
Ban Na Mo *Laos* 17°7N 105°40E **236** D5
Ban Na San *Thailand* 8°53N 99°52E **237** H2
Ban Na Tong *Laos* 20°56N 101°47E **236** B3
Ban Nam Bac *Laos* 20°38N 102°20E **236** B4
Ban Nam Ma *Laos* 22°2N 101°37E **236** A3
Ban Ngang *Laos* 15°59N 106°11E **236** E6
Ban Nong Bok *Laos* 17°5N 104°48E **236** D5
Ban Nong Boua *Laos* 15°40N 106°33E **236** E6
Ban Nong Pling *Thailand* 15°40N 100°10E **236** E3
Ban Pak Chan *Thailand* 10°32N 98°51E **237** G2
Ban Patong *Thailand* 7°54N 98°18E **237** a
Ban Phai *Thailand* 16°4N 102°44E **236** D4
Ban Phak Chit *Thailand* 8°0N 98°24E **237** a
Ban Pong *Thailand* 13°50N 99°55E **236** F2
Ban Rawai *Thailand* 7°47N 98°20E **237** a
Ban Ron Phibun *Thailand* 8°9N 99°51E **237** H2
Ban Sakhu *Thailand* 8°4N 98°18E **237** a
Ban Sanam Chai *Thailand* 7°33N 100°25E **237** J3
Ban Sangkha *Thailand* 14°37N 103°52E **236** E4
Ban Tak *Thailand* 17°2N 99°4E **236** D2
Ban Tako *Thailand* 14°5N 102°40E **236** E4
Ban Tha Dua *Thailand* 17°59N 98°39E **236** D2
Ban Tha Nun *Thailand* 8°12N 98°18E **237** a
Ban Tha Rua *Thailand* 7°59N 98°22E **237** a
Ban Tha Yu *Thailand* 8°17N 98°22E **237** a
Ban Thahine *Laos* 14°12N 105°33E **236** E5
Ban Thong Krut *Thailand* 9°25N 99°57E **237** b
Ban Xien Kok *Laos* 20°54N 100°39E **236** B3
Ban Yen Nhan *Vietnam* 20°57N 106°2E **236** B6
Banā, W. → *Yemen* 13°3N 45°24E **248** D4
Banaadir □ *Somali Rep.* 2°7N 45°24E **267** D6
Banaba *Kiribati* 0°45S 169°50E **288** H8
Banalia *Dem. Rep. of the Congo* 1°32N 25°5E **268** B2
Banam *Cambodia* 11°20N 105°17E **237** G5
Banamba *Mali* 13°29N 7°22W **262** C3
Banana Is. *S. Leone* 8°7N 13°15W **262** D2
Bananal, I. do *Brazil* 11°30S 50°30W **333** D1
Bananga *India* 6°57N 93°54E **245** L11
Bananier *Guadeloupe* 16°0N 61°36W **322** e
Banaras = Varanasi *India* 25°22N 83°0E **243** G10
Banas → *Gujarat, India* 23°45N 71°25E **242** H4
Banas → *Mad. P., India* 24°15N 81°30E **243** G9
Bânâs, Ras *Egypt* 23°57N 35°59E **256** C4
Banática *Portugal* 38°40N 9°11W **126** A1
Banaue *Phil.* 16°55N 121°4E **232** C3
Banaz *Turkey* 38°46N 29°46E **205** C11
Banaz → *Turkey* 38°12N 29°14E **205** C11
Banbridge *U.K.* 54°22N 6°16W **166** B5
Banbury *U.K.* 52°4N 1°20W **169** E6
Banc d'Arguin △ *Mauritania* 20°10N 16°20W **260** D1
Banchory *U.K.* 57°3N 2°29W **167** D6
Banco *Ethiopia* 6°12N 38°13E **257** F4
Banco do Brasil, Centro Cultural *Rio de J., Brazil* **135** a2
Bancoran *Phil.* 7°45N 118°30E **233** H2
Bancroft = Chililabombwe *Zambia* 12°18S 27°43E **269** E2
Bancroft *Canada* 45°3N 77°51W **312** A7
Band *Romania* 46°30N 24°25E **183** D9
Band Bonī *Iran* 25°30N 59°33E **247** E8
Band-e Torkestan *Afghan.* 35°30N 64°0E **240** B2
Band Qīr *Iran* 31°39N 48°53E **247** D6
Banda *Cameroon* 3°58N 14°32E **264** B2
Banda *Mad. P., India* 24°3N 78°57E **243** G8
Banda *Maharashtra, India* 15°49N 73°52E **245** G1
Banda *Ut. P., India* 25°30N 80°26E **243** G9
Banda, Kepulauan *Indonesia* 4°37S 129°50E **231** E7
Banda Aceh *Indonesia* 5°35N 95°20E **234** A1
Banda Banda, Mt. *Australia* 31°10S 152°28E **283** A10
Banda Elat *Indonesia* 5°40S 133°5E **231** F8
Banda Is. = Banda, Kepulauan *Indonesia* 4°37S 129°50E **231** E7
Banda Kani *Dem. Rep. of the Congo* 4°48S 13°52E **265** C2
Banda Sea *Indonesia* 6°0S 130°0E **231** F8
Bandai-Asahi △ *Japan* 37°38N 140°5E **220** F10
Bandai-San *Japan* 37°36N 140°4E **220** F10
Bandak *Norway* 59°23N 8°29E **164** E5
Bandama → *Ivory C.* 6°32N 4°30W **262** D3
Bandama Blanc → *Ivory C.* 6°55N 5°30W **262** D3
Bandama Rouge → *Ivory C.* 6°55N 5°30W **262** D4
Bandamadji *Comoros Is.* 11°47S 43°26E **272** a
Bandān *Iran* 31°23N 60°44E **247** D9
Bandanaira *Indonesia* 4°32S 129°54E **231** E7
Bandanwara *India* 26°9N 74°38E **242** F6
Bandar = Machilipatnam *India* 16°12N 81°8E **245** F5
Bandar-e Abbās *Iran* 27°15N 56°15E **247** E8
Bandar-e Anzalī *Iran* 37°30N 49°30E **213** D13
Bandar-e Bushehr = Būshehr *Iran* 28°55N 50°55E **247** D6
Bandar-e Chārak *Iran* 26°45N 54°20E **247** E7
Bandar-e Deylam *Iran* 30°5N 50°10E **247** D6
Bandar-e Emām Khomeynī *Iran* 30°30N 49°5E **247** D6
Bandar-e Lengeh *Iran* 26°35N 54°58E **247** E7
Bandar-e Maqām *Iran* 26°56N 53°29E **247** E7
Bandar-e Ma'shur *Iran* 30°35N 49°10E **247** D6
Bandar-e Rīg *Iran* 29°29N 50°38E **247** D6
Bandar-e Torkeman *Iran* 37°0N 54°10E **247** B7
Bandar Lampung *Indonesia* 5°20S 105°10E **234** D3
Bandar Maharani = Muar *Malaysia* 2°3N 102°34E **237** L4
Bandar Penggaram = Batu Pahat *Malaysia* 1°50N 102°56E **237** M4
Bandar Seri Begawan *Brunei* 4°52N 115°0E **235** B4
Bandar Sri Aman = Sri Aman *Malaysia* 1°15N 111°32E **235** B4
Bandawe *Malawi* 11°58S 34°5E **269** E3
Bande *Spain* 42°3N 7°58W **194** C3
Bandeira, Pico da *Brazil* 20°26S 41°47W **333** F3
Bandeirante *Brazil* 13°41S 50°48W **333** D1
Bandera *Argentina* 28°55S 62°20W **334** B3
Banderas, B. de *Mexico* 20°40N 105°25W **318** C3
Bandhavgarh *India* 23°40N 81°2E **243** H9
Bandhavgarh △ *India* 23°45N 81°10E **244** C5
Bandi → *India* 26°12N 75°47E **242** F6
Bandia → *India* 19°2N 80°28E **244** E5
Bandiagara *Mali* 14°12N 3°29W **262** C4
Bandikui *India* 27°3N 76°34E **242** F7
Bandipur △ *India* 11°45N 76°30E **245** J3
Bandırma *Turkey* 40°20N 28°0E **203** F11
Bandjarmasin = Banjarmasin *Indonesia* 3°20S 114°35E **235** C4
Bandol *France* 43°8N 5°46E **175** E9
Bandon *Ireland* 51°44N 8°44W **166** E3
Bandon → *Ireland* 51°43N 8°37W **166** E3
Bandra *India* 19°3N 72°49E **130** A1
Bandra Pt. *India* 19°2N 72°49E **130** A1
Bandraboua *Mayotte* 12°42S 45°8E **272** b
Bandrélé *Mayotte* 12°55S 45°11E **272** b
Bandula *Mozam.* 19°0S 33°7E **269** F3
Bandundu *Dem. Rep. of the Congo* 3°15S 17°22E **264** C3
Bandundu □ *Dem. Rep. of the Congo* 4°0S 17°30E **264** C3
Bandung *Indonesia* 6°54S 107°36E **235** D3
Bané *Burkina Faso* 11°42N 0°15W **263** C4
Băneasa *Romania* 45°56N 27°55E **183** E12
Baneh *Iran* 35°59N 45°53E **213** E11
Banes *Cuba* 21°0N 75°42W **320** B4
Banff *Alta., Canada* 51°10N 115°34W **296** C5
Banff *Aberds., U.K.* 57°40N 2°33W **167** D6
Banff △ *Canada* 51°30N 116°15W **296** C5
Banfora *Burkina Faso* 10°40N 4°40W **262** C4
Bang Fai → *Laos* 16°57N 104°45E **236** D5
Bang Hieng → *Laos* 16°10N 105°10E **236** D5
Bang Kapi *Thailand* 13°45N 100°38E **113** B2
Bang Krathum *Thailand* 16°34N 100°18E **236** D3
Bang Lamung *Thailand* 13°3N 100°56E **236** F3
Bang Mun Nak *Thailand* 16°2N 100°23E **236** D3
Bang Na *Thailand* 13°40N 100°36E **113** B2
Bang Pa In *Thailand* 14°14N 100°35E **236** E3
Bang Phlad *Bangkok, Thailand* **113** a1
Bang Rakam *Thailand* 16°45N 100°7E **236** D3
Bang Saphan *Thailand* 11°14N 99°28E **237** G2
Bang Thao *Thailand* 7°59N 98°18E **237** a
Banga *Angola* 8°43S 15°13E **265** D3
Banga *Dem. Rep. of the Congo* 5°25S 20°28E **265** D4
Banga *Aklan, Phil.* 11°38N 122°20E **233** F4
Banga *S. Cotabato, Phil.* 6°21N 124°47E **233** H5
Bangaduni I. *India* 21°34N 88°52E **241** E2
Bangala Dam *Zimbabwe* 21°7S 31°25E **269** G3
Bangalore *India* 12°59N 77°40E **245** H3
Banganapalle *India* 15°19N 78°14E **245** G4
Banganga → *India* 27°6N 77°25E **242** F6
Bangangté *Cameroon* 5°8N 10°32E **263** D7
Bangaon *India* 23°0N 88°47E **243** H13
Bangar *Phil.* 16°54N 120°25E **232** C3
Bangassou *C.A.R.* 4°55N 23°7E **264** B4
Bangbae *S. Korea* 37°29N 126°59E **137** C1
Bangeta, Mt. *Papua N. G.* 6°21S 147°3E **286** D4
Banggai *Indonesia* 1°34S 123°30E **231** E6
Banggai, Kepulauan *Indonesia* 1°40S 123°30E **231** E6
Banggai Arch. = Banggai, Kepulauan *Indonesia* 1°40S 123°30E **231** E6
Banggi, Pulau *Malaysia* 7°17N 117°12E **235** A5
Banghāzī *Libya* 32°11N 20°3E **258** B4
Banghāzī □ *Libya* 32°7N 20°4E **258** B4
Bangil *Indonesia* 7°36S 112°50E **235** D4
Bangjang *Sudan* 11°23N 32°41E **257** E3
Bangka *Sulawesi, Indonesia* 1°50N 125°5E **231** D7
Bangka *Sumatera, Indonesia* 2°0S 105°50E **234** C3
Bangka, Selat *Indonesia* 2°30S 105°30E **234** C3
Bangka-Belitung □ *Indonesia* 2°30S 107°0E **234** C3
Bangkalan *Indonesia* 7°2S 112°46E **235** D4
Bangkaru *Indonesia* 2°4N 97°7E **234** B1
Bangkhen *Thailand* 13°52N 100°36E **113** A2
Bangkinang *Indonesia* 0°18N 101°5E **234** B2
Bangko *Indonesia* 2°5S 102°9E **234** C2
Bangkok *Thailand* 13°45N 100°35E **113** B2
Bangkok Don Muang Int. ✈ (BKK) *Thailand* 13°53N 100°36E **113** A2
Bangkok Noi *Thailand* 13°45N 100°29E **113** B1
Bangkok Yai *Thailand* 13°43N 100°29E **113** B1
Bangla = West Bengal □ *India* 23°0N 88°0E **243** H13
Bangladesh ■ *Asia* 24°0N 90°0E **241** D3
Bangli *Indonesia* 8°27S 115°21E **231** J18
Banglo *India* 22°33N 88°14E **124** B1
Bangoi-Kouni *Comoros Is.* 11°22S 43°21E **272** a
Bangolo *Ivory C.* 7°1N 7°29W **262** D3
Bangong Co *China* 33°45N 78°43E **243** C8
Bangor *Down, U.K.* 54°40N 5°40W **166** B6
Bangor *Gwynedd, U.K.* 53°14N 4°8W **168** D3
Bangor *Maine, U.S.A.* 44°48N 68°46W **309** C19
Bangor *Mich., U.S.A.* 42°18N 86°7W **311** B10
Bangor *Pa., U.S.A.* 40°52N 75°13W **313** F9
Bangoran → *C.A.R.* 8°42N 19°6E **264** A3
Bangrak *Thailand* 13°43N 100°31E **113** B2
Bangsue *Thailand* 13°49N 100°31E **113** B2
Bangu *Dem. Rep. of the Congo* 0°3N 19°12E **264** C3
Bangued *Phil.* 17°40N 120°37E **232** C3
Bangui *C.A.R.* 4°23N 18°35E **264** B3
Bangui *Phil.* 18°32N 120°46E **232** B3
Banguru *Dem. Rep. of the Congo* 0°30N 27°10E **268** B2
Bangweulu, L. *Zambia* 11°0S 30°0E **269** E3
Bangweulu Swamp *Zambia* 11°20S 30°15E **269** E3
Banhine △ *Mozam.* 22°49S 32°55E **271** B5
Bani *Burkina Faso* 13°43N 0°10W **263** C4
Bani *C.A.R.* 7°6N 22°50E **264** A4
Bani *Dom. Rep.* 18°16N 70°22W **321** C5
Bani *Phil.* 16°11N 119°52E **232** C2
Bani → *Mali* 14°30N 4°12W **262** C4
Bani, Jebel *Morocco* 29°16N 8°0W **260** C3
Bani Bangou *Niger* 15°3N 2°42E **263** B5
Banī Sa'd *Iraq* 33°34N 44°32E **213** F11
Banī Walīd *Libya* 31°49N 14°0E **258** B2
Banī Walīd □ *Libya* 31°46N 13°59E **258** B2
Bania *C.A.R.* 4°1N 16°7E **264** B3
Bania *Ivory C.* 9°4N 3°6W **262** D4
Baniara *Papua N. G.* 9°44S 149°54E **286** E5
Banihal Pass *India* 33°30N 75°12E **243** C6
Banikoara *Benin* 11°18N 2°26E **263** C5
Banīnah *Libya* 32°0N 20°12E **258** B4
Banissa *Kenya* 3°55N 40°19E **257** G5
Bāniyās *Syria* 35°10N 36°0E **250** C7
Banja Luka *Bos.-H.* 44°49N 17°11E **182** F2
Banjar *India* 31°38N 77°21E **242** D7
Banjar *Indonesia* 7°24S 108°30E **235** D3
Banjar → *India* 22°36N 80°22E **243** H9
Banjarmasin *Indonesia* 3°20S 114°35E **235** C4
Banjarnegara *Indonesia* 7°24S 109°42E **235** D3
Banjul *Gambia* 13°28N 16°40W **262** C1
Bank *London, U.K.* **125** b5
Bank of America *San Francisco, U.S.A.* **136** b2
Bank of China Tower *Hong Kong, China* **122** c1
Banka *India* 24°53N 86°55E **243** G12
Bankas *Mali* 14°4N 3°31W **262** C4
Bankeryd *Sweden* 57°53N 14°6E **163** G8
Banket *Zimbabwe* 17°27S 30°19E **269** F3
Bankilaré *Niger* 14°35N 0°44E **263** C5
Bankot *India* 17°58N 73°2E **244** F1
Banks *U.S.A.* 31°49N 85°51W **316** D4
Banks, C. *Australia* 34°0S 151°16E **139** C2
Banks I. = Moa *Australia* 10°11S 142°16E **280** a
Banks I. *B.C., Canada* 53°20N 130°0W **296** C3
Banks I. *N.W.T., Canada* 73°15N 121°30W **294** C7
Banks Is. *Vanuatu* 13°50S 167°30E **287** C5

Banks L. *U.S.A.* 31°2N 83°6W **316** D6
Banks Pen. *N.Z.* 43°45S 173°15E **285** D8
Banks Str. *Australia* 40°40S 148°10E **281** G4
Banksmeadow *Australia* 33°57S 151°12E **139** B2
Bankumuna *Dem. Rep. of the Congo* 4°28S 19°57E **265** C3
Bankura *India* 23°11N 87°18E **243** H12
Bankya *Bulgaria* 42°43N 23°8E **202** D7
Banmankhi *India* 25°53N 87°11E **243** G12
Banmauk *Burma* 24°24N 95°51E **241** C5
Bann → *Armagh, U.K.* 54°30N 6°31W **166** B5
Bann → *L'derry., U.K.* 55°8N 6°41W **166** A5
Bannaanka Saraar *Somali Rep.* 9°25N 46°17E **267** C6
Bannalec *France* 47°57N 3°42W **172** E3
Bannang Sata *Thailand* 6°16N 101°16E **237** J3
Bannerton *Australia* 34°42S 142°47E **282** C5
Banning *U.S.A.* 33°56N 116°53W **307** M10
Banningville = Bandundu *Dem. Rep. of the Congo* 3°15S 17°22E **264** C3
Banno *Ethiopia* 4°51N 37°24E **257** G4
Banno-saki *Japan* 26°33N 128°8E **288** a
Bannockburn *Ont., Canada* 44°39N 77°33W **312** B7
Bannockburn *Stirling, U.K.* 56°5N 3°55W **167** E5
Bannockburn *Zimbabwe* 20°17S 29°48E **269** G2
Bannu *Pakistan* 33°0N 70°18E **240** B3
Bano *India* 22°40N 84°55E **243** H11
Bañolas = Banyoles *Spain* 42°16N 2°44E **196** C7
Banon *France* 44°2N 5°38E **175** D9
Baños de la Encina *Spain* 38°10N 3°46W **195** G7
Baños de Molgas *Spain* 42°15N 7°40W **194** C3
Bánovce nad Bebravou *Slovak Rep.* 48°44N 18°16E **181** C11
Banovići *Bos.-H.* 44°25N 18°32E **182** F3
Bansagar Dam *India* 24°11N 81°17E **244** B5
Bansalan *Phil.* 6°55N 125°13E **233** H5
Bansgaon *India* 26°33N 83°21E **243** F10
Banská Bystrica *Slovak Rep.* 48°46N 19°14E **181** C12
Banská Štiavnica *Slovak Rep.* 48°25N 18°55E **181** C11
Bansko *Bulgaria* 41°52N 23°28E **202** E7
Banskobystrický □ *Slovak Rep.* 48°20N 19°0E **181** C12
Banstala *India* 22°31N 88°24E **124** B2
Banswara *India* 23°32N 74°24E **242** H6
Bantaeng *Indonesia* 5°32S 119°56E **231** F5
Bantaji *Nigeria* 8°6N 10°5E **263** D7
Bantayan *Phil.* 11°10N 123°43E **233** F4
Bantayan I. *Phil.* 11°13N 123°44E **233** F4
Banten *Indonesia* 6°5S 106°8E **234** D3
Banten □ *Indonesia* 6°30S 106°0E **231** G11
Banton I. *Phil.* 12°56N 122°4E **232** E4
Bantra *India* 22°35N 88°18E **124** B1
Bantry *Ireland* 51°41N 9°27W **166** E2
Bantry B. *Ireland* 51°37N 9°44W **166** E2
Bantul *Indonesia* 7°55S 110°19E **235** D4
Bantva *India* 21°29N 70°12E **242** J4
Bantval *India* 12°55N 75°0E **245** H2
Banya *Bulgaria* 42°33N 24°50E **203** D8
Banyak, Kepulauan *Indonesia* 2°10N 97°10E **234** B1
Banyalbufar *Spain* 39°42N 2°31E **206** B3
Banyeres de Mariola *Spain* 38°44N 0°38W **197** G4
Banyo *Cameroon* 6°52N 11°45E **263** D7
Banyoles *Spain* 42°16N 2°44E **196** C7
Banyuls-sur-Mer *France* 42°28N 3°8E **174** F7
Banyumas *Indonesia* 7°32S 109°18E **235** D3
Banyuwangi *Indonesia* 8°13S 114°21E **231** J17
Banz *Papua N. G.* 5°47S 144°37E **286** C3
Banza *Dem. Rep. of the Congo* 0°28N 20°10E **264** B4
Banzare Coast *Antarctica* 68°0S 125°0E **151** C9
Banzyville = Mobayi *Dem. Rep. of the Congo* 4°15N 21°8E **264** B4
Bao Ha *Vietnam* 22°11N 104°21E **228** F5
Bao Lac *Vietnam* 22°57N 105°40E **236** A5
Bao Loc *Vietnam* 11°32N 107°48E **237** G6
Bao'an = Shenzhen *China* 22°32N 114°5E **219** F10
Baocheng *China* 33°12N 106°56E **226** H4
Baode *China* 39°1N 111°5E **226** E6
Baodi *China* 39°38N 117°20E **227** E9
Baoding *China* 38°50N 115°28E **226** E8
Baoji *China* 34°20N 107°5E **226** G4
Baojing *China* 28°45N 109°41E **228** C7
Baokang *China* 31°54N 111°12E **229** B8
Baoro *C.A.R.* 5°40N 15°58E **264** A3
Baoshan *Shanghai, China* 31°24N 121°28E **138** A1
Baoshan *Yunnan, China* 25°10N 99°5E **228** E2
Baotou *China* 40°32N 110°2E **226** D6
Baotow = Baotou *China* 40°32N 110°2E **226** D6
Baoulé → *Mali* 12°36N 9°45W **262** C3
Baoxing *China* 30°24N 102°50E **228** B4
Baoying *China* 33°17N 119°20E **227** H10
Baoyou = Ledong *China* 18°41N 109°5E **236** C7
Bap *India* 27°23N 72°18E **242** F5
Bapatla *India* 15°55N 80°30E **245** G5
Bapaume *France* 50°7N 2°50E **173** B9
Baqar, Bahr el → *Egypt* 31°7N 32°6E **251** G3
Bāqerābād *Iran* 33°2N 51°58E **247** C6
Ba'qūbah *Iraq* 33°45N 44°50E **213** F11
Baquedano *Chile* 23°20S 69°52W **334** A2
Bar *Montenegro* 42°8N 19°6E **202** D3
Bar *Ukraine* 49°4N 27°40E **177** D14
Bar Bigha *India* 25°21N 85°47E **243** G11
Bar Giyora *Israel* 31°45N 35°5E **123** B1
Bar Harbor *U.S.A.* 44°23N 68°13W **309** C19
Bar-le-Duc *France* 48°47N 5°10E **173** D12
Bar-sur-Aube *France* 48°14N 4°40E **173** D11
Bar-sur-Seine *France* 48°7N 4°20E **173** D11
Bara *India* 25°16N 81°43E **243** G9
Bâra *Romania* 47°2N 27°3E **183** C12
Bara *Sudan* 13°42N 30°22E **266** B3
Bara Banki *India* 26°55N 81°12E **243** F9
Baraawe *Somali Rep.* 1°20N 44°8E **267** D5
Barabai *Indonesia* 2°32S 115°34E **235** C5
Baraboo *U.S.A.* 43°28N 89°45W **308** D9
Baracoa *Cuba* 20°20N 74°30W **321** B5
Baradā → *Syria* 33°33N 36°34E **250** E7
Baradero *Argentina* 33°52S 59°29W **334** C4
Baradine *Australia* 30°56S 149°4E **283** A8
Baraga *U.S.A.* 46°47N 88°30W **308** B9
Bărăganul *Romania* 44°49N 27°31E **183** F12
Baragoi *Kenya* 1°47N 36°47E **268** B4
Barah → *India* 27°42N 77°5E **242** F6
Barahanagar *India* 22°39N 88°22E **124** B2
Barahona *Dom. Rep.* 18°13N 71°7W **321** C5
Barail Range *India* 25°15N 93°20E **241** C4
Barajas *Spain* 40°28N 3°34W **127** B2
Barajas, Madrid ✕ (MAD) *Spain* 40°26N 3°34W **127** B2
Barak → *India* 24°52N 92°20E **241** C4
Baraka *Sudan* 10°59N 27°59E **257** E2
Baraka → *Sudan* 18°13N 37°35E **256** D4
Barakaldo *Spain* 43°18N 2°59W **196** B2
Barakar → *India* 24°7N 86°14E **243** G12
Barakee △ *Australia* 31°37S 151°53E **283** A9
Barakot *India* 21°33N 84°59E **243** J11
Barakpur *India* 22°47N 88°21E **124** A2
Baralaba *Australia* 24°13S 149°50E **280** C4
Baralla *Spain* 42°53N 7°15W **194** C3
Baralzon L. *Canada* 60°0N 98°3W **297** B9
Baram → *Malaysia* 4°35N 113°58E **235** B4
Baramati *India* 18°11N 74°33E **244** E2
Baramba *India* 20°25N 85°23E **244** D7
Barameiya *Sudan* 18°32N 36°38E **256** D4
Baramula *India* 34°15N 74°20E **243** B6
Baran *India* 25°9N 76°40E **242** G7
Baran → *Pakistan* 25°13N 68°17E **242** G3
Barañain *Spain* 42°48N 1°40W **196** C3
Baranavichy *Belarus* 53°10N 26°0E **177** B14
Barani *Burkina Faso* 13°9N 3°51W **262** C4
Baranoa *Colombia* 10°48N 74°55W **328** A3
Baranof *U.S.A.* 57°5N 134°50W **296** B2
Baranof I. *U.S.A.* 57°0N 135°0W **303** H14
Baranów Sandomierski *Poland* 50°29N 21°30E **185** H8
Baranowicze = Baranavichy *Belarus* 53°10N 26°0E **177** B14
Baranya □ *Hungary* 46°0N 18°15E **182** E3
Barão de Cocais *Brazil* 19°56S 43°28W **333** E3
Barão de Grajaú *Brazil* 6°45S 43°1W **332** C3
Barão de Melgaço *Mato Grosso, Brazil* 16°14S 55°52W **331** D6
Barão de Melgaço *Rondônia, Brazil* 11°50S 60°45W **331** C5
Baraolt *Romania* 46°5N 25°34E **183** D10
Baraona *Spain* 41°17N 2°39W **196** D2
Barapasi *Indonesia* 2°15S 137°5E **231** E9
Barapina = Panguna *Papua N. G.* 6°21S 155°25E **286** D8
Baras *Phil.* 13°40N 124°22E **232** E5
Barasat *India* 22°46N 88°31E **243** H13
Barat Daya, Kepulauan *Indonesia* 7°30S 128°0E **231** F7
Baratang I. *India* 12°13N 92°45E **245** H11
Barataria B. *U.S.A.* 29°20N 89°55W **315** G10
Barauda *India* 23°33N 75°15E **242** H6
Baraut *India* 29°13N 77°7E **242** E7
Baraya *Colombia* 3°10N 75°4W **328** C2
Barbacan = Roxas *Phil.* 10°20N 119°21E **233** F2
Barbacena *Brazil* 21°15S 43°56W **333** F3
Barbacoas *Colombia* 1°45N 78°0W **328** C2
Barbados ■ *W. Indies* 13°10N 59°30W **323** r
Barbalha *Brazil* 7°19S 39°17W **332** C4
Barban *Croatia* 45°5N 14°2E **199** C11
Barbària, C. de *Spain* 38°39N 1°24E **206** D1
Barbaros *Turkey* 40°54N 27°27E **203** F11
Barbas, C. *W. Sahara* 22°20N 16°42W **260** D1
Barbastro *Spain* 42°2N 0°5E **196** C5
Barbate *Spain* 36°13N 5°56W **195** J5
Barbaza *Phil.* 11°12N 122°2E **233** F4
Barbeau Pk. *Canada* 81°54N 75°1W **295** A16
Barber *Neth. Ant.* 12°17N 69°4W **322** g
Barberini, Palazzo *Rome, Italy* **136** b3
Barberino di Mugello *Italy* 44°0N 11°15E **199** E8
Barbers Pt. *U.S.A.* 21°18N 158°7W **302** K13
Barberton *Mpumalanga, S. Africa* 25°42S 31°2E **271** C5
Barberton *Ohio, U.S.A.* 41°1N 81°39W **312** E3
Barberville *U.S.A.* 29°11N 81°26W **317** F8
Barbezieux-St-Hilaire *France* 45°28N 0°9W **174** C3
Barbican *London, U.K.* **125** a4
Barbosa *Colombia* 5°57N 73°37W **328** B3
Barbourville *U.S.A.* 36°52N 83°53W **309** G12
Barbuda *W. Indies* 17°30N 61°40W **322** c
Bârca *Romania* 43°59N 23°36E **183** G8
Barcaldine *Australia* 23°43S 145°6E **280** C4
Barcarena *Brazil* 1°30S 48°40W **332** B2
Barcarena *Lisboa, Portugal* 38°43N 9°16W **126** A1
Barcarena, Rib. de → *Portugal* 38°41N 9°16W **126** A1
Barcarrota *Spain* 38°31N 6°51W **195** G4
Barce = Al Marj *Libya* 32°25N 20°30E **258** B4
Barcellona Pozzo di Gotto *Italy* 38°9N 15°13E **201** D8
Barcelona *Spain* 41°22N 2°10E **114** A2
Barcelona *Venezuela* 10°10N 64°40W **329** A5
Barcelona □ *Spain* 41°30N 2°0E **196** D7
Barcelona-Prat ✕ (BCN) *Spain* 41°18N 2°5E **114** B1
Barceloneta *Puerto Rico* 18°27N 66°32W **321** b
Barcelonette *France* 44°23N 6°40E **175** D10
Barcelos *Brazil* 1°0S 63°0W **329** D5
Barcin *Poland* 52°52N 17°55E **185** F4
Barclayville *Liberia* 4°48N 8°10W **262** E3
Barcoo → *Australia* 25°30S 142°50E **280** D3
Barcroft, L. *U.S.A.* 38°52N 77°9W **143** B3
Barcs *Hungary* 45°58N 17°28E **182** E2
Barczewo *Poland* 53°50N 20°42E **184** E7
Bärdä *Azerbaijan* 40°25N 47°10E **191** K8
Barda del Medio *Argentina* 38°45S 68°11W **336** A3
Bardaï *Chad* 21°25N 17°0E **259** D3
Bardas Blancas *Argentina* 35°49S 69°45W **334** D2
Bardawîl, Sabkhet el *Egypt* 31°10N 33°15E **251** G4
Barddhaman *India* 23°14N 87°39E **243** H12
Bardejov *Slovak Rep.* 49°18N 21°15E **181** B14
Bardera = Baardheere *Somali Rep.* 2°20N 42°27E **267** D5
Barð *Iceland* 66°3N 19°8W **155** A7
Bárðarbunga *Iceland* 64°38N 17°32W **155** C9
Barðastrandarsýsla □ *Iceland* 65°40N 23°0W **155** B3
Bardi *Italy* 44°38N 9°44E **198** D6
Bardīyah *Libya* 31°45N 25°5E **258** B5
Bardoli *India* 21°12N 73°5E **244** D1
Bardolino *Italy* 45°33N 10°43E **198** C7
Bardonécchia *Italy* 45°5N 6°42E **198** C3
Bardsey I. *U.K.* 52°45N 4°47W **168** E3
Bardstown *U.S.A.* 37°49N 85°28W **311** G11
Bare *Ethiopia* 4°37N 42°43E **267** D5
Bareilly *India* 28°22N 79°27E **243** E8
Barela *India* 23°6N 80°3E **243** H9
Barellan *Australia* 34°16S 146°24E **283** C7
Barentin *France* 49°33N 0°58E **172** C7
Barenton *France* 48°38N 0°50W **172** D6
Barents Sea *Arctic* 73°0N 39°0E **150** B9
Barentsøya *Svalbard* 78°25N 21°20E **154** B13
Barentu *Eritrea* 15°2N 37°35E **257** D4
Barfleur *France* 49°40N 1°17W **172** C5
Barfleur, Pte. de *France* 49°42N 1°16W **172** C5
Barfurush = Bābol *Iran* 36°40N 52°50E **247** B7
Barga *Italy* 44°4N 10°29E **198** D7
Bargaal *Somali Rep.* 11°25N 51°0E **267** B7
Bargara *Australia* 24°50S 152°25E **280** C5
Bargas *Spain* 39°56N 4°3W **194** F6
Bărgăului Bistrița *Romania* 47°13N 24°46E **183** C9
Barge *Italy* 44°43N 7°20E **198** D4
Bargi Dam *India* 22°59N 80°0E **244** C5
Bargo *Australia* 34°18S 150°35E **283** C9
Bargteheide *Germany* 53°44N 10°14E **178** B6
Barguzin *Russia* 53°37N 109°37E **215** D11
Barh *India* 25°29N 85°46E **243** G11
Barhaj *India* 26°18N 83°44E **243** F10
Barham *Australia* 35°36S 144°8E **282** C6
Barharwa *India* 24°52N 87°47E **243** G12
Barhi *India* 24°15N 85°25E **243** G11
Bari *Dem. Rep. of the Congo* 3°20N 19°25E **264** B3
Bari *India* 26°39N 77°39E **242** F7
Bari *Italy* 41°8N 16°51E **201** A9
Bari □ *Somali Rep.* 10°0N 50°0E **267** B6
Bari Doab *Pakistan* 30°20N 73°0E **242** D5
Bari Sadri *India* 24°28N 74°30E **242** G6
Bari Sardo *Italy* 39°50N 9°38E **200** C2
Barīdī, Ra's *Si. Arabia* 24°17N 37°31E **246** E3
Barīm *Yemen* 12°39N 43°25E **248** D3
Barima → *Guyana* 8°33N 60°25W **329** B5
Barinas *Venezuela* 8°36N 70°15W **328** B3
Barinas □ *Venezuela* 8°10N 69°50W **328** B4
Baring *U.S.A.* 40°15N 92°12W **310** D4
Baring, C. *Canada* 70°0N 117°30W **294** D8
Baringa *Dem. Rep. of the Congo* 0°45N 20°52E **264** B4
Baringo *Kenya* 0°38N 36°16E **266** D4
Baringo, L. *Kenya* 0°47N 36°16E **268** B4
Barinitas *Venezuela* 8°45N 70°25W **328** B3
Baripada *India* 21°57N 86°45E **244** D8
Bariri *Brazil* 22°4S 48°44W **333** F2
Bârîs *Egypt* 24°42N 30°31E **256** C3
Barisal *Bangla.* 22°45N 90°20E **241** D3
Barisal □ *Bangla.* 22°45N 90°20E **241** D3
Barisan, Pegunungan *Indonesia* 3°30S 102°15E **234** C2
Barito → *Indonesia* 4°0S 114°50E **235** C4
Baritú △ *Argentina* 23°43S 64°40W **334** A3
Barjac *France* 44°20N 4°22E **175** D8
Barjols *France* 43°34N 6°2E **175** E10
Barjūj, Wadi → *Libya* 25°26N 12°12E **258** C2
Bark L. *Canada* 45°27N 77°51W **312** A7
Barka = Baraka → *Sudan* 18°13N 37°35E **256** D4
Barkā' *Oman* 23°40N 58°0E **249** B7
Barkakana *India* 23°37N 85°29E **243** H11
Barkal, J. *Sudan* 18°32N 31°50E **256** D3
Barkald *Norway* 61°59N 10°53E **164** C7
Barkam *China* 31°51N 102°28E **228** B4
Barker *U.S.A.* 43°20N 78°33W **312** C6
Barking *U.K.* 51°32N 0°5E **125** A4
Barkingside *U.K.* 51°35N 0°4E **125** A4
Barkley, L. *U.S.A.* 37°1N 88°14W **315** C10
Barkley Sound *Canada* 48°50N 125°10W **296** D3
Barkly East *S. Africa* 30°58S 27°33E **270** D4
Barkly Homestead *Australia* 19°52S 135°50E **280** B2
Barkly Tableland *Australia* 17°50S 136°40E **280** B2
Barkly West *S. Africa* 28°5S 24°31E **270** C3
Barkol, Wadi → *Sudan* 17°40N 32°0E **256** D3
Barkol Kazak Zizhixian *China* 43°37N 93°2E **218** B4
Barla Dağı *Turkey* 38°5N 30°40E **205** C12
Bârlad *Romania* 46°15N 27°38E **183** D12
Bârlad → *Romania* 45°38N 27°32E **183** E12
Barlee, L. *Australia* 29°15S 119°30E **279** E2
Barlee, Mt. *Australia* 24°38S 128°13E **279** D4
Barletta *Italy* 41°19N 16°17E **201** A9
Barlinek *Poland* 53°0N 15°15E **185** F2
Barlovento *Canary Is.* 28°48N 17°48W **153** e1
Barlovento *C. Verde Is.* 17°0N 25°0W **153** j
Barlow L. *Canada* 62°0N 103°0W **297** A8
Barmedman *Australia* 34°9S 147°21E **283** C7
Barmer *India* 25°45N 71°20E **242** G4
Barmera *Australia* 34°15S 140°28E **282** C4
Barmouth *U.K.* 52°44N 4°4W **168** E3
Barmstedt *Germany* 53°47N 9°46E **178** B5
Barn, The *St. Helena* 15°55S 5°40W **153** h
Barna → *India* 25°21N 83°3E **243** G10
Barnagar *India* 23°7N 75°19E **242** H6
Barnala *India* 30°23N 75°33E **242** D6
Barnard → *Australia* 31°34S 151°25E **283** A9
Barnard Castle *U.K.* 54°33N 1°55W **168** C6
Barnato *Australia* 31°38S 145°0E **283** A6
Barnaul *Russia* 53°20N 83°40E **217** B10
Barnes *N.S.W., Australia* 36°2S 144°49E **282** D6
Barnes *London, U.K.* 51°28N 0°14W **125** B2
Barnesville *Ga., U.S.A.* 33°3N 84°9W **316** B5
Barnesville *Minn., U.S.A.* 46°43N 96°28W **308** B5
Barnet *U.K.* 51°39N 0°11W **125** A2
Barnet □ *U.K.* 51°38N 0°9W **169** F7
Barneveld *Neths.* 52°7N 5°36E **170** B5
Barneville-Cartevert *France* 49°23N 1°46W **172** C5
Barnhart *U.S.A.* 31°8N 101°10W **314** F4
Barnsley *U.K.* 53°34N 1°27W **168** D6
Barnstable *U.S.A.* 41°42N 70°18W **309** E18
Barnstaple *U.K.* 51°5N 4°4W **169** F3
Barnstaple Bay = Bideford Bay *U.K.* 51°5N 4°20W **169** F3
Barnum B. *Palau* 7°6N 134°15E **288** c
Barnwell *U.S.A.* 33°15N 81°23W **316** B8
Baro *Nigeria* 8°35N 6°18E **263** D6
Baro → *Ethiopia* 8°26N 33°13E **257** F3
Barobo *Phil.* 8°33N 126°7E **233** G6
Baroda = Vadodara *India* 22°20N 73°10E **242** H5
Baroda *India* 25°29N 76°35E **242** G7
Baroe *S. Africa* 33°13S 24°33E **270** D3
Baron Ra. *Australia* 23°30S 127°45E **278** D4
Barong *China* 31°3N 99°20E **228** B2
Barora *Solomon Is.* 7°30S 158°20E **287** L10
Barora Ite *Solomon Is.* 7°36S 158°24E **287** L10
Barotse = Western □ *Zambia* 15°0S 24°4E **265** F4
Barotseland *Zambia* 15°0S 24°0E **265** F4
Barouéli *Mali* 13°4N 6°50W **262** C3
Barpali *India* 21°11N 83°35E **244** D6
Barpathar *India* 26°17N 93°53E **241** B4
Barpeta *India* 26°20N 91°10E **241** B3
Barqa *Libya* 27°0N 23°0E **258** C4
Barqin *Libya* 27°33N 13°34E **258** C2
Barques, Pt. Aux *U.S.A.* 44°4N 82°58W **312** B2
Barquisimeto *Venezuela* 10°4N 69°19W **328** A4
Barr, Ras el *Egypt* 31°32N 31°50E **256** A3
Barr Smith Range *Australia* 27°4S 120°20E **279** E3
Barra *Brazil* 11°5S 43°10W **332** D3
Barra *Gambia* 13°28N 16°32W **262** C1
Barra *W. Isles, U.K.* 57°0N 7°29W **167** E1
Barra, Sd. of *U.K.* 57°4N 7°25W **167** D1
Barra Andai *Pakistan* 24°47N 66°59E **123** B2
Barra Bonita = Ibaiti *Brazil* 23°50S 50°10W **333** F1
Barra da Estiva *Brazil* 13°38S 41°19W **333** D3
Barra de Navidad *Mexico* 19°12N 104°41W **318** D4
Barra de São Manuel *Brazil* 7°19S 58°5W **331** B6
Barra do Bugres *Brazil* 15°0S 57°11W **331** D6
Barra do Corda *Brazil* 5°30S 45°10W **332** C2
Barra do Dande *Angola* 8°28S 13°22E **265** D2
Barra do Garças *Brazil* 15°54S 52°16W **331** D7
Barra do Mendes *Brazil* 11°43S 42°4W **333** D3
Barra do Piraí *Brazil* 22°30S 43°50W **333** F3
Barra Falsa, Pta. da *Mozam.* 22°58S 35°37E **271** B6
Barra Funda *Brazil* 23°31S 46°39W **137** B2
Barra Hd. *U.K.* 56°47N 7°40W **167** E1
Barra Mansa *Brazil* 22°35S 44°12W **333** F3
Barraba *Australia* 30°21S 150°35E **283** A9
Barracão do Barreto *Brazil* 8°48S 58°24W **331** B6
Barracas *Argentina* 34°40S 58°22W **117** B2
Barracas al Sur = Avellaneda *Argentina* 34°40S 58°22W **117** C2
Barrackpur = Barakpur *India* 22°47N 88°21E **124** A2
Barrafranca *Italy* 37°22N 14°12E **201** E7
Barraigh = Barra *U.K.* 57°0N 7°29W **167** E1
Barrāmīya *Egypt* 25°4N 33°47E **256** B3
Barranca *Lima, Peru* 10°45S 77°50W **330** C2
Barranca *Loreto, Peru* 4°50S 76°50W **328** D2
Barranca del Cobre ⌂ *Mexico* 27°18N 107°40W **318** B3
Barrancabermeja *Colombia* 7°0N 73°50W **328** B3
Barrancas *Colombia* 10°57N 72°50W **328** A3
Barrancas *Venezuela* 8°55N 62°5W **329** B5
Barranco *Peru* 12°9S 77°2W **124** B2
Barrancones Pt. *Trin. & Tob.* 10°31N 61°28W **323** t
Barrancos *Portugal* 38°10N 6°58W **195** G4
Barranqueras *Argentina* 27°30S 59°0W **334** B4
Barranquilla *Colombia* 11°0N 74°50W **328** A3
Barranquitas *Puerto Rico* 18°11N 66°19W **321** b
Barras *Brazil* 4°15S 42°18W **332** B3
Barras *Colombia* 1°45S 73°13W **328** D3
Barraute *Canada* 48°26N 77°38W **298** C4
Barre *Mass., U.S.A.* 42°25N 72°6W **313** D12
Barre *Vt., U.S.A.* 44°12N 72°30W **313** B12
Barre de L'Isle Ridge *St. Lucia* 13°55N 60°58W **323** m
Barreal *Argentina* 31°33S 69°28W **334** C2
Barrei *Ethiopia* 6°10N 42°49E **267** C5
Barreiras *Brazil* 12°8S 45°0W **333** D3
Barreirinha *Brazil* 2°47S 57°3W **329** D6
Barreirinhas *Brazil* 2°30S 42°50W **332** B3
Barreiro *Portugal* 38°39N 9°5W **126** B2
Barreiros *Brazil* 8°49S 35°12W **332** C4
Barrême *France* 43°57N 6°23E **175** E10
Barren I. *India* 12°16N 93°51E **245** H11
Barren Is. *U.S.A.* 58°55N 152°15W **303** G9
Barreto *Brazil* 22°50S 43°5W **135** B2
Barretos *Brazil* 20°30S 48°35W **333** F2
Barrhead *Canada* 54°10N 114°24W **296** C6
Barrie *Canada* 44°24N 79°40W **312** B5
Barrier, C. *N.Z.* 36°25S 175°32E **284** C4
Barrier Ra. *N.S.W., Australia* 31°0S 141°30E **282** A4
Barrier Ra. *Otago, N.Z.* 44°15S 169°32E **285** E4
Barrier Ra. *W. Coast, N.Z.* 44°30S 168°30E **285** E3
Barrier Reef *Belize* 17°9N 88°3W **319** D7
Barrière *Canada* 51°12N 120°7W **296** C4
Barrière-la-Croix *Martinique* 14°27N 60°51W **322** j
Barrigada *Guam* 13°28N 144°48E **302** d
Barrineau Park *U.S.A.* 30°42N 87°26W **317** E2
Barrington *U.S.A.* 41°44N 71°18W **313** E13
Barrington, I. = Santa Fé, I. *Ecuador* 0°49S 90°5W **330** a
Barrington L. *Canada* 56°55N 100°15W **297** B8
Barrington Tops *Australia* 32°6S 151°28E **283** B9
Barrington Tops △ *Australia* 32°4S 151°25E **283** B9
Barringun *Australia* 29°1S 145°41E **281** D4
Barrit-Luluno = Luba *Phil.* 17°19N 120°42E **232** C3
Barron *U.S.A.* 45°24N 91°51W **308** C8
Barrouallie *St. Vincent* 13°14N 61°17W **323** n
Barrow *U.S.A.* 71°18N 156°47W **303** A8
Barrow → *Ireland* 52°25N 6°58W **166** D5
Barrow, Pt. *U.S.A.* 71°23N 156°29W **303** A8
Barrow Creek *Australia* 21°30S 133°55E **280** C1
Barrow I. *Australia* 20°45S 115°20E **278** D2
Barrow-in-Furness *U.K.* 54°7N 3°14W **168** C4
Barrow Pt. *Australia* 14°20S 144°40E **280** A3
Barrow Ra. *Australia* 26°0S 127°40E **279** E4
Barrow Str. *Canada* 74°20N 95°0W **150** B3
Barruecopardo *Spain* 41°4N 6°40W **194** D4
Barruelo de Santullán *Spain* 42°54N 4°17W **194** C6
Barry *V. of Glam., U.K.* 51°24N 3°16W **169** F4
Barry *Ill., U.S.A.* 39°42N 91°2W **310** E5
Barry's Bay *Canada* 45°29N 77°41W **312** A7
Barsalogho *Burkina Faso* 13°25N 1°3W **263** C4
Barsat *Pakistan* 36°10N 72°45E **243** A5
Barsham *Syria* 35°21N 40°33E **213** E9
Barsi *India* 18°10N 75°50E **244** E2
Barsinghausen *Germany* 52°18N 9°28E **178** C5
Barsoi *India* 25°48N 87°57E **241** C1
Barstow *U.S.A.* 34°54N 117°1W **307** L9
Barta *India* 22°32N 88°15E **124** B1
Bartenstein = Bartoszyce *Poland* 54°15N 20°55E **184** D7
Bartfeld = Bardejov *Slovak Rep.* 49°18N 21°15E **181** B14
Barth *Germany* 54°22N 12°42E **178** A8
Barthélemy, Col *Vietnam* 19°26N 104°6E **236** C5
Bartica *Guyana* 6°25N 58°40W **329** B6
Bartın *Turkey* 41°38N 32°21E **212** B5
Bartle Frere *Australia* 17°27S 145°50E **280** B4
Bartlesville *U.S.A.* 36°45N 95°59W **314** C7
Bartlett *Calif., U.S.A.* 36°29N 118°2W **306** J8
Bartlett *Tenn., U.S.A.* 35°12N 89°52W **315** D10
Bartlett, L. *Canada* 63°5N 118°20W **296** A5
Bartolbaai *Neth. Ant.* 12°20N 69°2W **322** g
Bartolo = Betanzos *Bolivia* 19°34S 65°27W **331** D4
Bartolomeu Dias *Mozam.* 21°10S 35°8E **269** G4
Barton *Phil.* 10°24N 119°8E **233** F2
Barton *Vt., U.S.A.* 44°45N 72°11W **313** B12
Barton Park *Australia* 33°56S 151°9E **139** B1
Barton upon Humber *U.K.* 53°41N 0°25W **168** D7
Bartonville *U.S.A.* 40°39N 89°39W **310** D7
Bartoszyce *Poland* 54°15N 20°55E **184** D7
Bartow *Fla., U.S.A.* 27°54N 81°50W **317** H8
Bartow *Ga., U.S.A.* 32°53N 82°29W **316** C7
Bartyki *Poland* 52°10N 21°6E **142** C2
Barú, I. de *Colombia* 10°15N 75°35W **328** A2
Barú, Volcan *Panama* 8°55N 82°35W **320** E3
Barumba *Dem. Rep. of the Congo* 1°3N 23°37E **268** B1
Barumbu *Dem. Rep. of the Congo* 1°14N 23°31E **264** B4
Baruth *Germany* 52°4N 13°30E **178** C9
Baruun Urt *Mongolia* 46°46N 113°15E **215** E12
Baruunsuu *Mongolia* 43°43N 105°35E **226** C3
Barvikha *Russia* 55°44N 37°16E **129** B1
Barvinkove *Ukraine* 48°57N 37°0E **189** H9
Bärwalde = Barwice *Poland* 53°44N 16°21E **184** E3
Barwani *India* 22°2N 74°57E **242** H6
Barwice *Poland* 53°44N 16°21E **184** E3
Barwick *U.S.A.* 30°54N 83°44W **316** E6
Barycz → *Poland* 51°42N 16°15E **185** G3
Barysaw *Belarus* 54°17N 28°28E **177** A15
Barysh *Russia* 53°39N 47°8E **190** D8
Barzān *Iraq* 36°55N 44°3E **246** B5
Bârzava *Romania* 46°7N 21°59E **182** D6
Bas-Congo □ *Dem. Rep. of the Congo* 5°0S 15°0E **265** D2
Bas du Fort *Guadeloupe* 16°13N 61°30W **322** e
Bas-Kouilou *Congo* 4°28S 11°42E **265** C2
Bas-Rhin □ *France* 48°40N 7°30E **173** D14
Basaid *Serbia* 45°38N 20°25E **182** E5
Bāsa'idū *Iran* 26°35N 55°20E **247** E7
Basal *Pakistan* 33°33N 72°13E **242** C5
Basankusa *Dem. Rep. of the Congo* 1°5N 19°50E **264** B3
Basarabeasca *Moldova* 46°21N 28°58E **183** D13
Basarabi *Romania* 44°10N 28°26E **183** F13
Basarabiya = Bessarabiya *Moldova* 47°0N 28°10E **177** E15
Basauri *Spain* 43°13N 2°53W **196** B2
Basawa *Afghan.* 34°15N 70°50E **242** B4
Basco *Phil.* 20°27N 121°58E **232** A3
Bascuñán, C. *Chile* 28°52S 71°35W **334** B1
Basekpio *Dem. Rep. of the Congo* 4°43N 24°36E **264** B4
Basel *Switz.* 47°35N 7°35E **179** H3
Basel, Euroairport ✕ (BSL) *Europe* 47°36N 7°33E **173** E14
Basel-Landschaft □ *Switz.* 47°26N 7°45E **179** H3
Basento → *Italy* 40°20N 16°49E **201** B9
Basey *Phil.* 11°17N 125°4E **233** F5
Bashākerd, Kūhhā-ye *Iran* 26°42N 58°35E **247** E8
Bashanta = Gorodovikovsk *Russia* 46°8N 41°58E **191** G5
Bashaw *Canada* 52°35N 112°58W **296** C6
Bāshī *Iran* 28°41N 51°4E **247** D6
Bashi Channel *Asia* 21°25N 121°30E **225** E2
Bashkir Republic = Bashkortostan □ *Russia* 54°0N 57°0E **186** D10
Bashkortostan □ *Russia* 54°0N 57°0E **186** D10
Bashtanivka *Ukraine* 45°46N 29°29E **183** E14
Basibasy *Madag.* 22°10S 43°40E **272** C1
Basilaki I. *Papua N. G.* 10°35S 151°0E **286** F6
Basilan *Phil.* 6°35N 122°0E **233** H4
Basilan □ *Phil.* 6°33N 122°4E **233** H4
Basilan Str. *Phil.* 6°50N 122°0E **233** H4
Basildon *U.K.* 51°34N 0°28E **169** F8
Basilé *Eq. Guin.* 3°42N 8°48E **263** E6
Basilé, Pico de *Eq. Guin.* 3°36N 8°49E **263** E6
Basilicata □ *Italy* 40°30N 16°30E **201** B9
Basim = Washim *India* 20°3N 77°0E **244** D3
Basin *U.S.A.* 44°23N 108°2W **304** D9
Basinger *U.S.A.* 27°23N 81°2W **317** H8
Basingstoke *U.K.* 51°15N 1°5W **169** F6
Basirhat *Bangla.* 22°40N 88°54E **241** D2
Basīţ, Ra's al *Syria* 35°51N 35°48E **250** C6
Baška *Croatia* 44°58N 14°45E **199** D11
Başkale *Turkey* 38°2N 43°59E **213** C10
Baskatong, Rés. *Canada* 46°46N 75°50W **298** C4
Basle = Basel *Switz.* 47°35N 7°35E **179** H3
Başmakçı *Turkey* 37°54N 30°1E **205** D12
Basmat *India* 19°15N 77°12E **244** E3
Basoda *India* 23°52N 77°54E **242** H7
Basoko *Dem. Rep. of the Congo* 1°16N 23°40E **264** B4
Basongo *Dem. Rep. of the Congo* 4°15S 20°20E **265** C4
Basora, Pta. *Aruba* 12°25N 69°51W **322** f
Basque, Pays *France* 43°15N 1°20W **174** E2
Basque Provinces = País Vasco □ *Spain* 42°50N 2°45W **196** C2
Basra = Al Başrah *Iraq* 30°30N 47°50E **246** D5
Bass, Îs. de *French Polynesia* 27°55S 143°26W **289** f
Bass Str. *Australia* 39°15S 146°30E **281** F4
Bassano *Canada* 50°48N 112°20W **296** C6
Bassano del Grappa *Italy* 45°46N 11°44E **199** C8
Bassar *Togo* 9°19N 0°57E **263** D5
Bassas da India *Ind. Oc.* 22°0S 39°0E **269** G4
Basse-Normandie □ *France* 48°45N 0°30W **172** D6
Basse-Pointe *Martinique* 14°52N 61°8W **322** j
Basse Santa-Su *Gambia* 13°13N 14°15W **262** C2
Basse-Terre *Guadeloupe* 16°0N 61°44W **322** e
Basse Terre *Trin. & Tob.* 10°7N 61°19W **323** t
Bassein *Burma* 16°45N 94°30E **241** G5
Bassein *India* 19°26N 72°48E **244** E1
Basses, Pte. des *Guadeloupe* 15°52N 61°17W **322** e
Basses-Alpes = Alpes-de-Haute-Provence □ *France* 44°8N 6°10E **175** D10
Basses-Pyrénées = Pyrénées-Atlantiques □ *France* 43°10N 0°50W **174** E3
Basseterre *St. Kitts & Nevis* 17°17N 62°43W **322** d
Bassett *U.S.A.* 42°35N 99°32W **308** D4
Bassi *India* 30°44N 76°21E **242** D7
Bassigny *France* 48°0N 5°30E **173** E12
Bassikounou *Mauritania* 15°55N 6°1W **262** B3
Bassila *Benin* 9°1N 1°46E **263** D5
Bassum *Germany* 52°50N 8°40E **178** C4
Båstad *Sweden* 56°25N 12°51E **163** H6
Bastak *Iran* 27°15N 54°25E **247** E7
Baştām *Iran* 36°29N 55°4E **247** B7
Bastar *India* 19°15N 81°40E **244** E5
Bastelica *France* 42°1N 9°3E **175** F13
Basti *India* 26°52N 82°55E **243** F10
Bastia *France* 42°40N 9°30E **175** F13
Bastille, Place de la *Paris, France* **134** c5
Bastogne *Belgium* 50°1N 5°43E **170** D5
Bastrop *La., U.S.A.* 32°47N 91°55W **314** E9
Bastrop *Tex., U.S.A.* 30°7N 97°19W **314** F6
Basu *Indonesia* 0°18S 103°35E **234** C2
Basud *Phil.* 14°4N 122°58E **232** D4
Basuo = Dongfang *China* 18°50N 108°33E **236** C7
Basus *Egypt* 30°7N 31°12E **117** A2
Basutoland = Lesotho ■ *Africa* 29°40S 28°0E **271** C4
Başyayla *Turkey* 36°45N 32°40E **250** B3
Bat Yam *Israel* 32°2N 34°44E **251** F5
Bata *Eq. Guin.* 1°57N 9°50E **264** B1
Bata *Romania* 46°1N 22°4E **182** D7
Bataan □ *Phil.* 14°40N 120°25E **232** D3
Bataan △ *Phil.* 14°45N 120°27E **232** D3
Batabanó *Cuba* 22°41N 82°18W **320** B3
Batabanó, G. de *Cuba* 22°30N 82°30W **320** B3
Batac *Phil.* 18°3N 120°34E **232** B3
Batagai *Russia* 67°38N 134°38E **215** C14
Batajnica *Serbia* 44°54N 20°17E **202** B4
Batak *Bulgaria* 41°57N 24°12E **203** E8
Batala *India* 31°48N 75°12E **242** D6
Batalha *Portugal* 39°40N 8°50W **194** F2
Batalpashinsk = Cherkessk *Russia* 44°15N 42°5E **191** H6
Batam *Indonesia* 1°5N 104°3E **234** B2
Batama *Dem. Rep. of the Congo* 0°58N 26°33E **268** B2
Batamay *Russia* 63°30N 129°15E **215** C13
Batan I. *Albay, Phil.* 13°15N 124°0E **232** E4
Batan I. *Batanes, Phil.* 20°26N 121°58E **232** A3
Batanagar *India* 22°31N 88°15E **124** B1
Batanes □ *Phil.* 20°40N 121°55E **232** A3
Batanes Is. *Phil.* 20°30N 122°0E **232** A3
Batang *Sichuan, China* 30°1N 99°0E **228** B2
Batang *Indonesia* 6°55S 109°45E **235** D3
Batang Ai △ *Malaysia* 1°32N 112°2E **235** B4
Batanga *Gabon* 0°21S 9°18E **264** C1
Batangafo *C.A.R.* 7°25N 18°20E **264** A3
Batangas *Phil.* 13°35N 121°10E **232** D3
Batangas □ *Phil.* 13°40N 121°5E **232** E3
Batanghari *Indonesia* 1°36S 103°37E **234** C2
Batanta *Indonesia* 0°55S 130°40E **231** E8
Bataraza *Phil.* 8°40N 117°37E **233** G1
Batas I. *Phil.* 11°10N 119°36E **233** F2
Batatais *Brazil* 20°54S 47°37W **335** A6
Batavia = Jakarta *Indonesia* 6°9S 106°52E **122** A2
Batavia *Ill., U.S.A.* 41°51N 88°19W **311** C8
Batavia *N.Y., U.S.A.* 43°0N 78°11W **312** D6
Batavia *Ohio, U.S.A.* 39°5N 84°11W **311** E12
Bataysk *Russia* 47°3N 39°45E **189** J10
Batbakara = Amankeldi *Kazakhstan* 50°10N 65°10E **217** B7
Batchelor *Australia* 13°4S 131°1E **278** B5
Batdambang *Cambodia* 13°7N 103°12E **236** F4
Batéké, Plateau *Congo* 3°30S 15°45E **264** C3
Batemans B. *Australia* 35°40S 150°12E **283** C9
Batemans Bay *Australia* 35°44S 150°11E **283** C9
Batesburg-Leesville *U.S.A.* 33°54N 81°33W **316** B8
Batesville *Ark., U.S.A.* 35°46N 91°39W **314** D9
Batesville *Ind., U.S.A.* 39°18N 85°13W **311** E11
Batesville *Miss., U.S.A.* 34°19N 89°57W **315** D10
Batesville *Tex., U.S.A.* 28°58N 99°37W **314** G5
Bath *Ont., Canada* 44°11N 76°47W **313** B8
Bath *St. Kitts & Nevis* 17°8N 62°37W **322** d
Bath *Bath & N.E. Somerset, U.K.* 51°23N 2°22W **169** F5
Bath *Maine, U.S.A.* 43°55N 69°49W **309** D19
Bath *N.Y., U.S.A.* 42°20N 77°19W **312** D7
Bath & North East Somerset □ *U.K.* 51°21N 2°27W **169** F5
Bath Beach *U.S.A.* 40°36N 74°0W **132** C1
Bath I. *Pakistan* 24°49N 67°1E **123** B2
Batha □ *Chad* 14°0N 19°0E **259** F3
Batha → *Chad* 12°47N 17°34E **259** F3
Batheay *Cambodia* 11°59N 104°57E **237** G5
Bathsheba *Barbados* 13°13N 59°32W **323** r
Bathurst = Banjul *Gambia* 13°28N 16°40W **262** C1
Bathurst *N.S.W., Australia* 33°25S 149°31E **283** B8
Bathurst *N.B., Canada* 47°37N 65°43W **299** C6
Bathurst *Eastern Cape, S. Africa* 33°30S 26°50E **270** D4
Bathurst, C. *Canada* 70°34N 128°0W **294** C6
Bathurst B. *Australia* 14°16S 144°25E **280** A3
Bathurst Harb. *Australia* 43°15S 146°10E **281** G4
Bathurst I. *N. Terr., Australia* 11°30S 130°10E **278** B5
Bathurst I. *Nunavut, Canada* 76°0N 100°30W **295** B11
Bathurst Inlet *Canada* 66°50N 108°1W **294** D10
Bati *Ethiopia* 11°10N 40°0E **257** E5
Batie *Burkina Faso* 9°53N 2°53W **262** D4
Batiki *Fiji* 17°48S 179°10E **287** A2
Batir *West Bank* 31°43N 35°8E **123** B1
Batken *Kyrgyzstan* 40°3N 70°50E **217** D8
Batken □ *Kyrgyzstan* 39°50N 71°0E **217** E8
Batlow *Australia* 35°31S 148°9E **283** C8
Batman *Turkey* 37°55N 41°5E **213** D9
Baţn al Ghūl *Jordan* 29°36N 35°56E **251** J6
Batna *Algeria* 35°34N 6°15E **261** A6
Batna □ *Algeria* 35°30N 5°55E **261** A6
Batnfjordsøra *Norway* 62°53N 7°42E **164** B4
Bato *Catanduanes, Phil.* 13°36N 124°18E **232** E5
Bato *Leyte, Phil.* 10°13N 124°48E **233** F5
Bato Bato *Phil.* 5°6N 119°49E **233** J2
Batoala *Gabon* 0°48N 13°27E **264** B2
Batobato = San Isidro *Phil.* 6°50N 126°5E **233** H6
Batočina *Serbia* 44°7N 21°5E **202** B5
Batok, Bukit *Singapore* 1°21N 103°46E **138** A2
Batoka *Zambia* 16°45S 27°15E **269** F2
Baton Rouge *U.S.A.* 30°27N 91°11W **314** F9
Batong, Ko *Thailand* 6°32N 99°12E **237** J2
Bátonyterenye *Hungary* 47°59N 19°50E **182** C4
Batopilas *Mexico* 27°1N 107°44W **318** B3
Batouri *Cameroon* 4°30N 14°25E **264** B2
Batovany = Partizánske *Slovak Rep.* 48°38N 18°23E **181** C11
Båtsfjord *Norway* 70°38N 29°39E **160** A23
Batsi *Greece* 37°52N 24°47E **204** D6
Battambang = Batdambang *Cambodia* 13°7N 103°12E **236** F4
Battersea *U.K.* 51°28N 0°9W **125** B3
Battery Park *New York, U.S.A.* **132** f1
Batti Malv *India* 8°50N 92°51E **245** K11
Batticaloa *Sri Lanka* 7°43N 81°45E **245** L5
Battipáglia *Italy* 40°37N 14°58E **201** B7
Battle *U.K.* 50°55N 0°30E **169** G8
Battle → *Canada* 52°43N 108°15W **297** C7
Battle Creek *U.S.A.* 42°19N 85°11W **311** B11
Battle Ground *U.S.A.* 45°47N 122°32W **306** E4
Battle Harbour *Canada* 52°16N 55°35W **299** B8
Battle Lake *U.S.A.* 46°17N 95°43W **308** B6
Battle Mountain *U.S.A.* 40°38N 116°56W **304** F5
Battlefields *Zimbabwe* 18°37S 29°47E **269** F2
Battleford *Canada* 52°45N 108°15W **297** C7
Battonya *Hungary* 46°16N 21°3E **182** D6
Batu *Ethiopia* 6°55N 39°45E **257** F4
Batu *Malaysia* 3°15N 101°40E **237** L3
Batu, Bukit *Malaysia* 2°16N 113°43E **235** B4
Batu, Kepulauan *Indonesia* 0°30S 98°25E **234** C1
Batu Bora, Bukit *Malaysia* 2°43N 114°43E **235** B4
Batu Ferringhi *Malaysia* 5°28N 100°15E **237** c
Batu Gajah *Malaysia* 4°28N 101°3E **237** K3
Batu Is. = Batu, Kepulauan *Indonesia* 0°30S 98°25E **234** C1
Batu Pahat *Malaysia* 1°50N 102°56E **237** M4
Batu Puteh, Gunung *Malaysia* 4°15N 101°31E **234** B2
Batuata *Indonesia* 6°12S 122°42E **231** F6
Batugondang, Tanjung *Indonesia* 8°6S 114°29E **231** J17
Batukau, Gunung *Indonesia* 8°20S 115°5E **231** J18
Batulaki *Phil.* 5°34N 125°19E **233** J5
Batuli = San Isidro *Phil.* 6°50N 126°5E **233** H6
Batumi *Georgia* 41°39N 41°44E **191** K5
Batur *Indonesia* 8°15S 115°20E **231** J18
Batur, Danau *Indonesia* 8°15S 115°24E **231** J18
Batur, Gunung *Indonesia* 8°14S 115°23E **231** J18
Batura Sar *Pakistan* 36°30N 74°31E **243** A6
Baturaja *Indonesia* 4°11S 104°15E **234** C2
Baturité *Brazil* 4°28S 38°45W **332** B4
Baturiti *Indonesia* 8°19S 115°11E **231** J18
Batusangkar *Indonesia* 0°27S 100°35E **234** C2
Batys Qazaqstan □ *Kazakhstan* 50°0N 50°0E **216** C3
Bau *Malaysia* 1°25N 110°9E **235** B4
Bauang *Phil.* 16°31N 120°20E **232** C3
Baubau *Indonesia* 5°25S 122°38E **231** F6
Baucau *E. Timor* 8°27S 126°27E **231** F7
Bauchi *Nigeria* 10°22N 9°48E **263** C6
Bauchi □ *Nigeria* 10°30N 10°0E **263** C7
Baud *France* 47°52N 3°1W **172** E3
Bauda *India* 20°50N 84°25E **244** D7
Baudette *U.S.A.* 48°43N 94°36W **308** A6
Bauer, C. *Australia* 32°44S 134°4E **281** E1
Bauerwitz = Baborów *Poland* 50°7N 18°1E **185** H5
Bauguen = Salcedo *Phil.* 11°9N 125°40E **233** F5
Bauhinia *Australia* 24°35S 149°18E **280** C4
Baukau = Baucau *E. Timor* 8°27S 126°27E **231** F7
Bauko *Phil.* 17°0N 120°52E **232** C3
Baulai → *Bangla.* 24°22N 91°1E **241** C3
Bauld, C. *Canada* 51°38N 55°26W **295** G20
Bauman *Russia* 55°45N 37°40E **129** B4
Baume-les-Dames *France* 47°22N 6°22E **173** E13
Baumgarten *Austria* 48°12N 16°17E **142** A1
Baunatal *Germany* 51°14N 9°24E **178** D5
Baunei *Italy* 40°2N 9°40E **200** B2
Baure *Nigeria* 12°52N 8°50E **263** C6
Baures *Bolivia* 13°35S 63°35W **331** C5
Bauru *Brazil* 22°10S 49°0W **335** A6
Baús *Brazil* 18°22S 52°47W **331** D7
Bausi *India* 24°48N 87°1E **243** G12
Bauska *Latvia* 56°24N 24°15E **184** B11

Bautino Kazakhstan 44°35N 50°14E 191 H10
Bautzen Germany 51°10N 14°26E 178 D10
Bauya S. Leone 8°12N 12°38W 262 D2
Bavānāt Iran 30°28N 53°27E 247 D7
Bavanište Serbia 44°49N 20°55E 182 F5
Bavaria = Bayern □ Germany 48°50N 12°0E 179 G7
Båven Sweden 59°0N 16°56E 162 E10
Bavispe → Mexico 29°15N 109°11W 318 B3
Baw Baw △ Australia 37°50S 146°17E 283 D7
Bawdwin Burma 23°5N 97°20E 241 D6
Bawean Indonesia 5°46S 112°35E 235 D4
Bawku Ghana 11°3N 0°19W 263 C4
Bawlake Burma 19°11N 97°21E 241 F6
Bawolung China 28°50N 101°16E 228 C3
Baxley U.S.A. 31°47N 82°21W 316 D7
Baxoi China 30°1N 96°50E 228 B1
Baxter Iowa, U.S.A. 41°49N 93°9W 310 C3
Baxter Minn., U.S.A. 46°21N 94°17W 308 B6
Baxter Springs U.S.A. 37°2N 94°44W 308 G6
Baxter State ⌂ U.S.A. 46°5N 68°57W 309 B19
Bay □ Somali Rep. 3°0N 43°30E 267 D5
Bay, L. U.S.A. 28°25N 81°34W 133 A2
Bay, L. de Phil. 14°20N 121°11E 232 D3
Bay City Mich., U.S.A. 43°36N 83°54W 309 D12
Bay City Tex., U.S.A. 28°59N 95°58W 314 G7
Bay Harbor Islands U.S.A. 25°53N 80°7W 128 A2
Bay Hill U.S.A. 28°28N 81°30W 133 B1
Bay Minette U.S.A. 30°53N 87°46W 315 F11
Bay of Plenty □ N.Z. 38°0S 177°0E 284 D5
Bay Ridge U.S.A. 40°37N 74°1W 132 C1
Bay Roberts Canada 47°36N 53°16W 299 C9
Bay St. Louis U.S.A. 30°19N 89°20W 315 F10
Bay Springs U.S.A. 31°59N 89°17W 315 F10
Bay View N.Z. 39°25S 176°50E 284 F5
Baya Dem. Rep. of the Congo 11°53S 27°25E 269 E2
Bayambang Phil. 15°49N 120°27E 232 D3
Bayamo Cuba 20°20N 76°40W 320 B4
Bayamón Puerto Rico 18°24N 66°9W 321 C6
Bayan Har Shan China 34°0N 98°0E 218 C4
Bayan Hot = Alxa Zuoqi China 38°50N 105°40E 226 E3
Bayan Lepas Malaysia 5°17N 100°16E 237 c
Bayan Obo China 41°52N 109°59E 226 D5
Bayan-Ovoo = Erdenetsogt Mongolia 42°55N 106°5E 226 C4
Bayan-Tumen = Choybalsan Mongolia 48°4N 114°30E 219 B6
Bayana India 26°55N 77°18E 242 F7
Bayanaūyl Kazakhstan 50°45N 75°45E 217 B9
Bayandalay Mongolia 43°30N 103°29E 226 C2
Bayanhongor Mongolia 46°8N 102°43E 218 B5
Bayard N. Mex., U.S.A. 32°46N 108°8W 305 K9
Bayard Nebr., U.S.A. 41°45N 103°20W 308 E2
Bayawan Phil. 9°46N 122°45E 233 G4
Baybay Phil. 10°40N 124°55E 233 F5
Bayburt Turkey 40°15N 40°20E 213 B9
Bayburt □ Turkey 40°35N 39°25E 213 B8
Baydaratskaya Guba Russia 69°0N 67°30E 214 C7
Baydhabo Somali Rep. 3°8N 43°30E 267 D5
Bayelsa □ Nigeria 4°30N 6°0E 263 E6
Bayerische Alpen Germany 47°35N 11°30E 179 H7
Bayerische Rhön ⌂ Germany 50°15N 10°5E 179 E6
Bayerischer Spessart ⌂ Germany 49°59N 10°15E 179 F6
Bayerischer Wald Germany 48°56N 12°50E 179 G8
Bayern □ Germany 48°50N 12°0E 179 G7
Bayeux France 49°17N 0°42W 172 C6
Bayfield Ont., Canada 43°34N 81°42W 312 C3
Bayfield Wis., U.S.A. 46°49N 90°49W 308 B8
Bayḥān al Qiṣāb Yemen 15°48N 45°44E 248 D4
Bayındır Turkey 38°13N 27°39E 205 C9
Baykal, Oz. Russia 53°0N 108°0E 215 D11
Baykan Turkey 38°7N 41°44E 213 C9
Baymak Russia 52°36N 58°19E 186 D10
Baynes Mts. Namibia 17°15S 13°0E 270 A1
Bayombong Phil. 16°30N 121°10E 232 C3
Bayon France 48°30N 6°20E 173 D13
Bayona = Baiona Spain 42°6N 8°52W 194 C2
Bayonet Point U.S.A. 28°20N 82°41W 317 G7
Bayonne Pyrénées-Atlantiques, France 43°30N 1°28W 174 E2
Bayonne N.J., U.S.A. 40°40N 74°6W 132 B1
Bayou Boeuf U.S.A. 29°50N 90°10W 131 B1
Bayou Segnette State Park ⌂ U.S.A. 29°53N 90°10W 131 B2
Bayovar Peru 5°50S 81°0W 330 B1
Bayport U.S.A. 28°32N 82°39W 317 G7
Bayqongyr Kazakhstan 45°40N 63°20E 216 C6
Bayram-Ali = Bayramaly Turkmenistan 37°37N 62°10E 247 B9
Bayramaly Turkmenistan 37°37N 62°10E 247 B9
Bayramiç Turkey 39°48N 26°36E 205 B8
Bayrampaşa Turkey 41°1N 28°56E 122 B1
Bayreuth Germany 49°56N 11°35E 179 F7
Bayrischzell Germany 47°41N 12°0E 179 H8
Bayrūt Lebanon 33°53N 35°31E 250 E6
Bays, L. of Canada 45°15N 79°4W 312 A5
Bayshore Calif., U.S.A. 37°42N 122°24W 136 B2
Bayshore Fla., U.S.A. 26°43N 81°50W 317 J8
Baysville Canada 45°9N 79°7W 312 A5
Bayswater London, U.K. 125 b2
Bayt al Faqīh Yemen 14°31N 43°19E 248 D3
Bayt Lahm West Bank 31°43N 35°12E 123 B2
Baytik Shan China 45°15N 90°50E 217 C12
Baytown U.S.A. 29°43N 94°59W 314 G7
Bayugan Phil. 8°43N 125°42E 233 G5
Bayun Indonesia 8°11S 115°16E 231 J18
Bayview U.S.A. 37°44N 122°23W 136 B2
Bayville = Kirkwood S. Africa 33°22S 25°15E 270 D4
Bayy al Kabir, W. Libya 31°10N 15°53E 258 B3
Bayy al Khā'ib, Wādī → Libya 30°55N 15°29E 258 B3
Bazo Niger 13°52N 4°35E 263 C5
Baza Spain 37°30N 2°47W 195 H8
Bāzār Iran 35°40N 51°25E 141 A2
Bazar Dyuzi Russia 41°12N 47°50E 191 K8
Bazardüzü = Bazar Dyuzi Russia 41°12N 47°50E 191 K8
Bāzargān Iran 39°22N 44°26E 213 C11
Bazargic = Dobrich Bulgaria 43°37N 27°49E 203 C11
Bazarny Karabulak Russia 52°20N 46°29E 190 D8
Bazarnyy Syzgan Russia 53°45N 46°40E 190 D8
Bazaruto, I. do Mozam. 21°40S 35°28E 271 B6
Bazaruto △ Mozam. 21°42S 35°26E 271 B6
Bazas France 44°27N 0°13W 174 D3
Bazhong China 31°52N 106°46E 228 B6
Bazhou China 39°8N 116°22E 226 E9
Bazin Guadeloupe 16°22N 61°26W 322 e
Bazmān, Kūh-e Iran 28°4N 60°1E 247 D9
Baztan = Elizondo Spain 43°12N 1°30W 196 B3
Beach U.S.A. 46°58N 104°0W 308 B2
Beach City U.S.A. 40°39N 81°35W 312 F3
Beachport Australia 37°29S 140°0E 282 D4
Beachville Canada 43°5N 80°49W 312 C4
Beachy Hd. U.K. 50°44N 0°15E 169 G8
Beacon W. Austral., Australia 30°26S 117°52E 279 F2
Beacon N.Y., U.S.A. 41°30N 73°58W 313 E11
Beacon Hill Hong Kong, China 22°21N 114°10E 122 A2
Beacon Hill Boston, U.S.A. 116 b1
Beaconsfield Australia 41°11S 146°48E 281 G4
Beagle, Canal S. Amer. 55°0S 68°30W 336 E3
Beagle Bay Australia 16°58S 122°40E 278 C3
Beagle Bay ✪ Australia 16°53S 122°40E 278 C3
Beagle G. Australia 12°15S 130°25E 278 B5
Béal an Átha = Ballina Ireland 54°7N 9°9W 166 B2
Béal Átha na Sluaighe = Ballinasloe Ireland 53°20N 8°13W 166 C3
Bealanana Madag. 14°33S 48°44E 272 A2
Beals Cr. → U.S.A. 32°10N 100°51W 314 E4
Beamsville Canada 43°12N 79°28W 312 C5
Bear → Calif., U.S.A. 38°56N 121°36W 306 G5
Bear → Utah, U.S.A. 41°30N 112°8W 300 G17
Béar, C. France 42°31N 3°8E 174 F7
Bear I. Ireland 51°38N 9°50W 166 E2
Bear I. Man., Canada 55°8N 96°0W 297 B9
Bear L. Utah, U.S.A. 41°59N 111°21W 304 F8
Bear Lake Canada 45°27N 79°35W 312 A5
Beardmore Canada 49°36N 87°57W 298 C2
Beardmore Glacier Antarctica 84°30S 170°0E 151 E11
Beardstown U.S.A. 40°1N 90°26W 310 E6
Bearma → India 24°20N 79°51E 243 G8
Béarn France 43°20N 0°30W 174 E3
Bearpaw Mts. U.S.A. 48°12N 109°30W 304 B9
Bearskin Lake Canada 53°58N 91°2W 298 B1
Beas → India 31°10N 74°59E 242 D6
Beas de Segura Spain 38°15N 2°53W 195 G8
Beasain Spain 43°3N 2°11W 196 B2
Beata, C. Dom. Rep. 17°40N 71°30W 321 C5
Beata, I. Dom. Rep. 17°34N 71°31W 321 C5
Beata Ridge W. Indies 16°0N 72°30W 321 C5
Beato Portugal 38°44N 9°5W 126 A2
Beatrice Nebr., U.S.A. 40°16N 96°45W 308 E5
Beatrice Zimbabwe 18°15S 30°55E 269 F3
Beatrice, C. Australia 14°20S 136°55E 280 A2
Beatton → Canada 56°15N 120°45W 296 B4
Beatton River Canada 57°26N 121°20W 296 B4
Beatty U.S.A. 36°54N 116°46W 306 J10
Beau Bassin Mauritius 20°13S 57°27E 272 e
Beauaraba = Pittsworth Australia 27°41S 151°37E 281 D5
Beaucaire France 43°48N 4°39E 175 E8
Beauce, Plaine de la France 48°10N 1°45E 173 D8
Beauceville Canada 46°13N 70°46W 299 C5
Beauchêne, I. Falk. Is. 52°55S 59°15W 153 f
Beaudesert Australia 27°59S 153°0E 281 D5
Beaufort Vic., Australia 37°25S 143°25E 282 D5
Beaufort Savoie, France 45°44N 6°34E 175 C10
Beaufort Malaysia 5°30N 115°40E 235 A5
Beaufort N.C., U.S.A. 34°43N 76°40W 315 D16
Beaufort S.C., U.S.A. 32°26N 80°40W 316 C9
Beaufort Sea Arctic 72°0N 140°0W 292 B5
Beaufort West S. Africa 32°18S 22°36E 270 D3
Beaugency France 47°47N 1°38E 173 E8
Beauharnois Canada 45°20N 73°52W 313 A11
Beaujeu France 46°10N 4°35E 173 F11
Beaujolais France 46°0N 4°22E 173 F11
Beaulieu → Canada 62°3N 113°11W 296 A6
Beaulieu-sur-Dordogne France 44°58N 1°50E 174 D5
Beaulieu-sur-Mer France 43°42N 7°20E 175 E11
Beauly U.K. 57°30N 4°28W 167 D4
Beauly → U.K. 57°29N 4°27W 167 D4
Beaumaris U.K. 53°16N 4°6W 168 D3
Beaumont Belgium 50°15N 4°14E 170 D4
Beaumont Dordogne, France 44°45N 0°46E 174 D4
Beaumont Dublin, Ireland 53°23N 6°13W 120 A2
Beaumont N.Z. 45°50S 169°33E 285 F4
Beaumont Tex., U.S.A. 30°5N 94°6W 314 F7
Beaumont-de-Lomagne France 43°53N 1°0E 174 E5
Beaumont-le-Roger France 49°4N 0°47E 172 C7
Beaumont-sur-Sarthe France 48°13N 0°8E 172 D7
Beaumonte Heights Canada 43°45N 79°34W 141 A1
Beaune France 47°2N 4°50E 173 E11
Beaune-la-Rolande France 48°4N 2°25E 173 D9
Beauport Guadeloupe 16°25N 61°30W 322 e
Beaupré Canada 47°3N 70°54W 299 C5
Beaupréau France 47°12N 1°0W 172 E6
Beauraing Belgium 50°7N 4°57E 170 D4
Beaurepaire France 45°22N 5°1E 175 C9
Beausejour Man., Canada 50°5N 96°35W 297 C9
Beauséjour Guadeloupe 16°18N 61°4W 322 e
Beauséjour Martinique 14°44N 60°57W 322 j
Beauvais France 49°25N 2°8E 173 C9
Beauval Canada 55°9N 107°37W 297 B7
Beauvoir-sur-Mer France 46°55N 2°2W 172 F4
Beauvoir-sur-Niort France 46°12N 0°30W 174 B3
Beaver Alaska, U.S.A. 66°22N 147°24W 303 C11
Beaver Okla., U.S.A. 36°49N 100°31W 314 C4
Beaver Pa., U.S.A. 40°42N 80°19W 312 F4
Beaver Utah, U.S.A. 38°17N 112°38W 304 G7
Beaver → B.C., Canada 59°52N 124°20W 296 B4
Beaver → Ont., Canada 55°55N 87°48W 298 A2
Beaver → Sask., Canada 55°26N 107°45W 297 B7
Beaver → Okla., U.S.A. 36°35N 99°30W 314 C5
Beaver City U.S.A. 40°8N 99°50W 308 E4
Beaver Creek Canada 63°0N 141°0W 294 E3
Beaver Dam U.S.A. 43°28N 88°50W 308 D9
Beaver Falls U.S.A. 40°46N 80°20W 312 F4
Beaver Hill L. Canada 54°5N 94°50W 297 C10
Beaver I. U.S.A. 45°40N 85°33W 309 C11
Beavercreek U.S.A. 39°43N 84°11W 311 E12
Beaverhill L. Canada 53°27N 112°32W 296 C6
Beaverlodge Canada 55°11N 119°29W 296 B5
Beaverstone → Canada 54°59N 89°25W 298 B2
Beaverton Ont., Canada 44°26N 79°9W 312 B5
Beaverton Oreg., U.S.A. 45°29N 122°48W 306 E4
Beawar India 26°3N 74°18E 242 F6
Bebedouro Brazil 21°0S 48°25W 335 A6
Bebek Turkey 41°4N 29°2E 122 B2
Bebera, Tanjung Indonesia 8°44S 115°51E 231 K18
Beboa Madag. 17°22S 44°33E 272 B1
Beboto Chad 8°16N 16°56E 259 G3
Bebra Germany 50°58N 9°48E 178 E5
Becán Mexico 18°34N 89°31W 319 D7
Bécancour Canada 46°20N 72°26W 299 C5
Beccles U.K. 52°27N 1°35E 169 E9
Bečej Serbia 45°36N 20°3E 182 E5
Beceni Romania 45°23N 26°48E 183 E11
Becerreá Spain 42°51N 7°10W 194 C3
Béchar Algeria 31°38N 2°18W 261 B4
Béchar □ Algeria 30°15N 3°5E 261 B5
Becharof L. U.S.A. 57°56N 156°23W 303 H8
Becharof Nat. Wildlife Refuge ⌂ U.S.A. 58°0N 156°15W 303 H8
Běchovice Czech Rep. 50°4N 14°36E 135 B3
Bechuanaland = Botswana ■ Africa 22°0S 24°0E 270 B3
Bechyně Czech Rep. 49°17N 14°29E 180 B7
Beck L. U.S.A. 42°4N 87°52W 119 A1
Beckenham U.K. 51°24N 0°1W 125 B3
Bečkerek = Zrenjanin Serbia 45°22N 20°23E 182 E5
Beckley U.S.A. 37°47N 81°11W 309 G13
Beckton U.K. 51°30N 0°4E 125 A4
Beckum Germany 51°45N 8°3E 178 D4
Beclean Romania 47°11N 24°11E 183 C9
Becontree U.K. 51°33N 0°7E 125 A4
Bečov nad Teplou Czech Rep. 50°5N 12°49E 180 A5
Bečva → Czech Rep. 49°31N 17°20E 181 B10
Bédar Spain 37°11N 1°59W 197 H3
Bédarieux France 43°37N 3°10E 174 E7
Beddington Corner U.K. 51°23N 0°9W 125 B3
Beddouza, C. Morocco 32°33N 9°9W 260 B3
Bedeau = Ras el Ma Algeria 34°26N 0°50W 261 B4
Bedele Ethiopia 8°31N 36°23E 257 F4
Bederkesa Germany 53°37N 8°50E 178 B4
Bederwanak Somali Rep. 9°34N 44°23E 267 C5
Bedeso Ethiopia 9°58N 40°52E 257 F5
Bedford Qué., Canada 45°7N 72°59W 313 A12
Bedford Eastern Cape, S. Africa 32°40S 26°10E 270 D4
Bedford Beds., U.K. 52°8N 0°28W 169 E7
Bedford Ind., U.S.A. 38°52N 86°29W 311 F10
Bedford Iowa, U.S.A. 40°40N 94°44W 310 D2
Bedford Ky., U.S.A. 38°36N 85°19W 311 F11
Bedford Mass., U.S.A. 42°27N 71°15W 116 A1
Bedford Ohio, U.S.A. 41°23N 81°32W 312 E3
Bedford Pa., U.S.A. 40°1N 78°30W 312 F6
Bedford Va., U.S.A. 37°20N 79°31W 309 G14
Bedford, C. Australia 15°14S 145°21E 280 B4
Bedford Park Ill., U.S.A. 41°46N 87°46W 119 C2
Bedford Park N.Y., U.S.A. 40°52N 73°52W 132 A2
Bedford Stuyvesant U.S.A. 40°41N 73°56W 132 B2
Bedford View S. Africa 26°10S 28°7E 123 B2
Bedfordshire □ U.K. 52°4N 0°28W 169 E7
Bedi Chad 11°6N 18°33E 259 F3
Będków Poland 51°36N 19°44E 185 G6
Bednja → Croatia 46°20N 16°52E 199 B13
Bednodemyanovsk Russia 53°55N 43°15E 190 D6
Bedok Singapore 1°19N 103°56E 138 B3
Bedok, Res. Singapore 1°20N 103°56E 138 A3
Bedónia Italy 44°30N 9°38E 198 D6
Bedourie Australia 24°30S 139°30E 280 C2
Bedti → India 14°50N 74°44E 245 G2
Bedum Neths. 53°18N 6°36E 170 A6
Będzin Poland 50°19N 19°7E 185 H6
Bee Ridge U.S.A. 27°17N 82°29W 317 H7
Beebe Plain Canada 45°1N 72°9W 313 A12
Beech Creek U.S.A. 41°5N 77°36W 312 E7
Beech Fork → U.S.A. 37°46N 85°41W 311 G11
Beech Grove U.S.A. 39°43N 86°5W 311 E10
Beecher U.S.A. 41°21N 87°38W 311 C9
Beechey Point U.S.A. 70°29N 149°9W 303 A10
Beechworth Australia 36°22S 146°43E 283 D7
Beechy Canada 50°53N 107°24W 297 C7
Beed = Bir India 19°4N 75°46E 244 E2
Beef I. Br. Virgin Is. 18°26N 64°30W 321 b
Beelitz Germany 52°14N 12°58E 178 C8
Beenleigh Australia 27°43S 153°10E 281 D5
Be'er Menuḥa Israel 30°19N 35°8E 246 D2
Be'er Sheva Israel 31°15N 34°48E 251 G5
Beersel Belgium 50°46N 4°18E 116 B1
Beersheba = Be'er Sheva Israel 31°15N 34°48E 251 G5
Beeskow Germany 52°10N 14°15E 178 C10
Beestekraal S. Africa 25°23S 27°38E 271 C4
Beeston U.K. 52°56N 1°14W 168 E6
Beeton Canada 44°5N 79°47W 312 B5
Beetzendorf Germany 52°42N 11°6E 178 C7
Beeville U.S.A. 28°24N 97°45W 314 G6
Befale Dem. Rep. of the Congo 0°25N 20°45E 264 B4
Befandriana Mahajanga, Madag. 15°16S 48°32E 272 B2
Befandriana Toliara, Madag. 21°55S 44°0E 272 C1
Befasy Madag. 20°33S 44°23E 272 C1
Befori Dem. Rep. of the Congo 0°8N 22°22E 264 B4
Befotaka Antsiranana, Madag. 13°15S 48°16E 272 A2
Befotaka Fianarantsoa, Madag. 23°49S 47°0E 272 C2
Bega Australia 36°41S 149°51E 283 D8
Bega, Canalul Romania 45°37N 20°46E 182 E5
Bégard France 48°38N 3°18W 172 D3
Beğendik Turkey 40°55N 26°34E 203 F10
Beggars Pt. Antigua & B. 17°10N 61°48W 322 b
Begndal Norway 60°49N 9°46E 164 D6
Begoro Ghana 6°23N 0°23W 263 D4
Begusarai India 25°24N 86°9E 243 G12
Behābād Iran 32°24N 59°47E 247 C8
Behala India 22°30N 88°18E 124 B1
Behara Madag. 24°55S 46°20E 272 C2
Behbehān Iran 30°30N 50°15E 247 D6
Beheloka Madag. 23°54S 43°40E 272 C1
Behm Canal U.S.A. 55°10N 131°0W 296 B2
Behshahr Iran 36°45N 53°35E 247 B7
Bei Hai Beijing, China 114 b2
Bei Hai Park Beijing, China 114 b2
Bei Jiang → China 23°2N 112°58E 229 F9
Bei Shan China 41°30N 96°0E 218 B4
Bei'an China 48°10N 126°20E 219 B7
Beibei China 29°47N 106°22E 228 C6
Beicai China 31°11N 121°32E 138 B2
Beichuan China 31°55N 104°39E 228 B5
Beihai China 21°28N 109°6E 228 G7
Beijing China 39°53N 116°21E 114 B1
Beijing □ China 39°55N 116°20E 226 E9
Beijing Zoo Beijing, China 114 a1
Beilau = Pilawa Poland 51°57N 21°32E 185 G8
Beilen Neths. 52°52N 6°27E 170 B6
Beiliu China 22°41N 110°21E 229 F8
Beilngries Germany 49°2N 11°28E 179 F7
Beilpajah Australia 32°54S 143°52E 282 B5
Beilul Eritrea 13°2N 42°20E 257 E5
Béinamar Chad 8°40N 15°23E 259 G3
Beinn na Faoghla = Benbecula U.K. 57°26N 7°21W 167 D1
Beipan Jiang China 25°7N 106°1E 228 E5
Beipiao China 41°52N 120°32E 227 D11
Beira Mozam. 19°50S 34°52E 269 F3
Beirut = Bayrūt Lebanon 33°53N 35°31E 250 E6
Beiseker Canada 51°23N 113°32W 296 C6
Beit Duqu West Bank 31°51N 35°6E 123 A1
Beit Ghur at-Taht West Bank 31°54N 35°5E 123 A1
Beit Ghur el-Fawqa West Bank 31°53N 35°5E 123 A1
Beit Hanina West Bank 31°50N 35°12E 123 B2
Beit Ij'za West Bank 31°51N 35°9E 123 A1
Beit Iksa West Bank 31°49N 35°11E 123 B2
Beit I'nan West Bank 31°51N 35°7E 123 A1
Beit Jala West Bank 31°43N 35°11E 123 B2
Beit Lekhem = Bayt Lahm West Bank 31°43N 35°12E 123 B2
Beit Liqya West Bank 31°52N 35°4E 123 A1
Beit Nekofa Israel 31°49N 35°7E 123 B1
Beit Sahur West Bank 31°42N 35°13E 123 B2
Beit Sofafa West Bank 31°45N 35°12E 123 B2
Beit Surik West Bank 31°50N 35°9E 123 B1
Beit Ur al-Fawqa West Bank 31°53N 35°7E 123 A1
Beit Zayit Israel 31°47N 35°9E 123 B1
Beitaipingzhuan China 39°57N 116°21E 114 B1
Beitaolaizhao China 44°58N 125°58E 227 B13
Beitar Illit West Bank 31°42N 35°7E 123 B1
Beitbridge Zimbabwe 22°12S 30°0E 269 G3
Beitin West Bank 31°56N 35°14E 123 A2
Beitsun China 23°7N 113°10E 121 B2
Beitunya West Bank 31°53N 35°10E 123 A2
Beiuş Romania 46°40N 22°21E 182 D7
Beixing Jing Park China 31°14N 121°21E 138 B1
Beizhen = Binzhou China 37°20N 118°2E 227 F10
Beizhen China 41°38N 121°54E 227 D11
Beizhengzhen China 44°31N 123°30E 227 B12
Beja Portugal 38°2N 7°53W 195 G3
Béja Tunisia 36°43N 9°12E 258 A1
Beja □ Portugal 37°55N 7°55W 195 H3
Béja □ Tunisia 36°40N 9°29E 261 A6
Bejaïa Algeria 36°42N 5°2E 261 A6
Bejaïa □ Algeria 36°40N 4°55E 261 A5
Béjar Spain 40°23N 5°46W 194 E5
Bejestān Iran 34°30N 58°5E 247 C8
Bek-Budi = Qarshi Uzbekistan 38°53N 65°48E 217 E7
Bekaa Valley = Al Biqā Lebanon 34°10N 36°10E 250 D7
Bekasi Indonesia 6°14S 106°59E 234 D3
Békásmegyer Hungary 47°35N 19°3E 117 A2
Bekçiler Turkey 36°56N 29°44E 205 E11
Bekdash Turkmenistan 41°34N 52°32E 216 D4
Békés Hungary 46°47N 21°9E 182 D6
Békés □ Hungary 46°45N 21°0E 182 D6
Békéscsaba Hungary 46°40N 21°5E 182 D6
Bekilli Turkey 38°17N 29°27E 205 C11
Bekily Madag. 24°13S 45°19E 272 C2
Bekisopa Madag. 21°40S 45°54E 272 C2
Bekitro Madag. 24°33S 45°18E 272 C2
Bekkelaget Norway 59°53N 10°47E 133 A3
Bekkestua Norway 59°55N 10°35E 133 A2
Bekodoka Madag. 16°58S 45°7E 272 B2
Bekoji Ethiopia 7°40N 39°17E 257 F4
Bekok Malaysia 2°20N 103°7E 237 L4
Bekopaka Madag. 19°9S 44°48E 272 B1
Bekuli Indonesia 8°22S 114°13E 231 J17
Bekwai Ghana 6°30N 1°34W 263 D4
Bel Air Mauritius 20°15S 57°44E 272 e
Bel Air Calif., U.S.A. 34°4N 118°27W 126 B2
Bela India 25°50N 82°0E 243 G10
Bela Pakistan 26°12N 66°20E 242 F2
Bela Aliança = Rio do Sul Brazil 27°13S 49°37W 335 B6
Bela Bela S. Africa 24°51S 28°19E 271 B4
Bela Crkva Serbia 44°55N 21°27E 182 F6
Bela Palanka Serbia 43°13N 22°17E 202 C6
Bela Vista Mato Grosso do Sul, Brazil 22°12S 56°20W 334 A4
Bela Vista São Paulo, Brazil 23°33S 46°38W 137 B2
Bela Vista Mozam. 26°10S 32°44E 271 C5
Bélabo Cameroon 4°56N 13°18E 264 B2
Bélâbre France 46°34N 1°8E 174 B5
Belaga Malaysia 2°42N 113°47E 235 B4
Belalcázar Spain 38°35N 5°10W 195 G5
Belan → India 24°2N 81°45E 243 G9
Bélanger Canada 45°35N 73°42W 130 A1
Belanovica Serbia 44°15N 20°23E 202 B4
Belarus ■ Europe 53°30N 27°0E 177 B14
Belas Angola 8°55S 13°9E 265 D2
Belas Lisboa, Portugal 38°46N 9°17W 126 A1
Belau = Palau ■ Palau 7°30N 134°30E 288 c
Belavenona Madag. 24°50S 47°4E 272 C2
Belawan Indonesia 3°33N 98°32E 234 B1
Belaya Ethiopia 11°25N 36°8E 257 E4
Belaya → Russia 54°40N 56°0E 186 C9
Belaya Glina Russia 46°5N 40°48E 191 G5
Belaya Kalitva Russia 48°13N 40°50E 191 F5
Belaya Tserkov = Bila Tserkva Ukraine 49°45N 30°10E 177 D16
Belaya Zemlya, Ostrova Russia 81°36N 62°18E 214 A7
Belayan → Indonesia 0°14S 116°36E 235 C5
Belceşti Romania 47°19N 27°7E 183 C12
Bełchatów Poland 51°21N 19°22E 185 G6
Belcher Is. Canada 56°15N 78°45W 298 A3
Belchite Spain 41°18N 0°43W 196 D4
Belden U.S.A. 40°2N 121°17W 306 E5
Beldibi Turkey 36°25N 32°26E 250 B3
Belding U.S.A. 43°6N 85°14W 311 A11
Belebey Russia 54°7N 54°7E 186 D9
Beledweyne Somali Rep. 4°30N 45°5E 267 D6
Beleghata India 22°33N 88°22E 124 B2
Belém = Palmeirais Brazil 6°0S 43°0W 332 C3
Belém Brazil 1°20S 48°30W 332 B2
Belém Lisboa, Portugal 38°41N 9°12W 126 A1
Belém, Torre de Portugal 38°41N 9°12W 126 A1
Belém de São Francisco Brazil 8°46S 38°58W 332 C4
Belén Argentina 27°40S 67°5W 334 B2
Belén Colombia 1°26N 75°56W 328 C2
Belén Paraguay 23°30S 57°6W 334 A4
Belen Turkey 36°31N 36°10E 250 B7
Belen N. Mex., U.S.A. 34°40N 106°46W 305 J10
Belene Bulgaria 43°39N 25°10E 203 C9
Belènzinho Brazil 23°32S 46°34W 137 B2
Belep, Îs. N. Cal. 19°45S 163°40E 288 d
Bélesta France 42°55N 1°56E 174 F5
Belet Uen = Beledweyne Somali Rep. 4°30N 45°5E 267 D6
Belev Russia 53°50N 36°5E 188 F9
Belevi Turkey 38°0N 27°28E 205 C9
Belfair U.S.A. 47°27N 122°50W 306 C4
Belfast N.Z. 43°27S 172°39E 285 D7
Belfast Mpumalanga, S. Africa 25°42S 30°2E 271 C5
Belfast Antrim, U.K. 54°37N 5°56W 166 B6
Belfast Maine, U.S.A. 44°26N 69°1W 309 C19
Belfast N.Y., U.S.A. 42°21N 78°7W 312 D6
Belfast L. U.K. 54°40N 5°50W 166 B6
Belfield U.S.A. 46°53N 103°12W 308 B2
Belfort France 47°38N 6°50E 173 E13
Belfort, Territoire de □ France 47°40N 6°55E 173 E13
Belfry U.S.A. 45°9N 109°1W 304 D9
Belgachiya India 22°36N 88°23E 124 B2
Belgard = Białogard Poland 54°2N 15°58E 184 D2
Belgaum India 15°55N 74°35E 245 G2
Belgavi = Belgaum India 15°55N 74°35E 245 G2
Belgharia India 22°39N 88°22E 124 B2
Belgian Congo = Congo, Dem. Rep. of the ■ Africa 3°0S 23°0E 265 C4
Belgioioso Italy 45°10N 9°19E 198 C6
Belgium ■ Europe 50°30N 5°0E 170 D4
Belgodère France 42°35N 9°1E 175 F13
Belgorod Russia 50°35N 36°35E 189 G9
Belgorod □ Russia 50°45N 36°45E 189 G9
Belgorod-Dnestrovskiy = Bilhorod-Dnistrovskyy Ukraine 46°11N 30°23E 189 J6
Belgrade = Beograd Serbia 44°50N 20°37E 202 B4
Belgrade U.S.A. 45°47N 111°11W 304 D8
Belgrano Antarctica 77°52S 34°37W 151 D1
Belgrano B. Aires, Argentina 34°33S 58°27W 117 B2
Belgravia London, U.K. 125 c3
Belgrove N.Z. 41°27S 172°59E 285 B7
Belhaven U.S.A. 35°33N 76°37W 315 D16
Béli Guinea-Biss. 11°51N 13°56W 262 C2
Beli Nigeria 7°52N 10°55E 263 D7
Beli Drim → Europe 42°6N 20°25E 202 D4
Beli Manastir Croatia 45°45N 18°36E 182 E3
Beli Timok → Serbia 43°53N 22°14E 202 C6
Bélice → Italy 37°35N 12°55E 200 E5
Belimbing Indonesia 8°24S 115°2E 231 J18
Bélinga Gabon 1°10N 13°2E 264 B2
Belinskiy Russia 53°0N 43°25E 190 D6
Belinyu Indonesia 1°35S 105°50E 234 C3
Beliton Is. = Belitung Indonesia 3°10S 107°50E 235 C3
Belitung Indonesia 3°10S 107°50E 235 C3
Beliu Romania 46°30N 22°0E 182 D6
Belize ■ Cent. Amer. 17°0N 88°30W 320 C2
Belize City Belize 17°25N 88°10W 320 C2
Beljakovci Macedonia 42°6N 21°59E 202 D5
Beljanica Serbia 44°8N 21°43E 202 B5
Belkovskiy, Ostrov Russia 75°32N 135°44E 215 B14
Bell Calif., U.S.A. 33°58N 118°11W 126 C3
Bell Fla., U.S.A. 29°45N 82°52W 316 F7
Bell → Canada 49°48N 77°38W 298 C4
Bell Gardens U.S.A. 33°58N 118°9W 126 C4
Bell I. Canada 50°46N 55°35W 299 B8
Bell-Irving → Canada 56°12N 129°5W 296 B3
Bell Peninsula Canada 63°50N 82°0W 295 E15
Bell Tower Beijing, China 114 a3
Bell Ville Argentina 32°40S 62°40W 334 C3
Bella Italy 40°45N 15°32E 201 B8
Bella Bella Canada 52°10N 128°10W 296 C3
Bella Coola Canada 52°25N 126°40W 296 C3
Bella Flor Bolivia 11°9S 67°49W 330 C4
Bella Unión Uruguay 30°15S 57°40W 334 C4
Bella Vista Corrientes, Argentina 28°33S 59°0W 334 B4
Bella Vista Tucuman, Argentina 27°10S 65°25W 334 B2
Bellac France 46°7N 1°3E 174 B5
Bellágio Italy 45°59N 9°15E 198 C6
Bellaire U.S.A. 40°1N 80°45W 312 F4
Bellária Italy 44°9N 12°28E 199 D9
Bellary India 15°10N 76°56E 245 G3
Bellata Australia 29°53S 149°46E 281 D4
Bellavista Santiago, Chile 33°31S 70°35W 137 C2
Bellavista Galápagos Is., Ecuador 0°41S 90°18W 330 a
Bellavista Lima, Peru 12°4S 77°8W 124 B2
Belle U.S.A. 38°17N 91°43W 310 F5
Belle → Trin. & Tob. 11°14N 60°37W 323 s
Belle Fille → Dominica 15°25N 61°16W 323 k
Belle Fourche U.S.A. 44°40N 103°51W 308 C2
Belle Fourche → U.S.A. 44°26N 102°18W 301 G19
Belle Glade U.S.A. 26°41N 80°40W 317 J9
Belle Harbor U.S.A. 40°34N 73°51W 132 C2
Belle-Île France 47°20N 3°10W 172 E3
Belle Isle Nfld. & L., Canada 51°57N 55°25W 299 B8
Belle Isle Fla., U.S.A. 28°27N 81°12W 133 B2
Belle Isle, Str. of Canada 51°30N 56°30W 299 B8
Belle Plaine U.S.A. 41°54N 92°17W 310 C4
Belle Rive U.S.A. 38°14N 88°45W 311 F8
Belle River Canada 42°18N 82°43W 312 D2
Belle View U.S.A. 38°57N 77°14W 143 B2
Belle Vue Maurel Mauritius 20°7S 57°39E 272 e
Belle Yella Liberia 7°24N 10°0W 262 D3
Belledonne France 45°20N 6°10E 175 C10
Bellefontaine Martinique 14°39N 61°10W 322 j
Bellefontaine Ohio, U.S.A. 40°22N 83°46W 311 D13
Bellefonte U.S.A. 40°55N 77°47W 312 F7
Bellegarde France 47°59N 2°26E 173 E9
Bellegarde-en-Marche France 45°59N 2°18E 174 C6
Bellegarde-sur-Valserine France 46°4N 5°50E 173 F12
Bellême France 48°22N 0°34E 172 D7
Belleoram Canada 47°31N 55°25W 299 C8
Belleplaine Barbados 13°15N 59°34W 323 r
Belleview U.S.A. 29°4N 82°3W 317 F7
Belleville Ont., Canada 44°10N 77°23W 312 B7
Belleville Rhône, France 46°7N 4°45E 173 F11
Belleville Ill., U.S.A. 38°31N 89°59W 310 F7
Belleville Kans., U.S.A. 39°50N 97°38W 308 F5
Belleville N.J., U.S.A. 40°47N 74°9W 313 F10
Belleville N.Y., U.S.A. 43°46N 76°10W 313 C8
Belleville-sur-Vie France 46°46N 1°25W 172 F5
Bellevue Idaho, U.S.A. 43°28N 114°16W 304 E6
Bellevue Iowa, U.S.A. 42°16N 90°26W 310 B6
Bellevue Mich., U.S.A. 42°27N 85°1W 311 B11
Bellevue Nebr., U.S.A. 41°9N 95°54W 308 E6
Bellevue Ohio, U.S.A. 41°17N 82°51W 312 E2
Bellevue Wash., U.S.A. 47°37N 122°12W 306 C4
Bellevue, Col de Réunion 21°9S 55°36E 272 f
Bellevue, Schloss Berlin, Germany 115 a2
Belley France 45°46N 5°41E 175 C9
Bellin = Kangirsuk Canada 60°0N 70°0W 295 F18
Bellinge Denmark 55°20N 10°20E 163 J4
Bellingen Australia 30°25S 152°50E 283 A10
Bellingham London, U.K. 51°25N 0°1W 125 B3
Bellingham Wash., U.S.A. 48°46N 122°29W 306 B4
Bellingshausen Abyssal Plain S. Ocean 64°0S 90°0W 151 C16
Bellingshausen Sea Antarctica 66°0S 80°0W 151 C17
Bellinzona Switz. 46°11N 9°1E 179 J5
Bello Colombia 6°20N 75°33W 328 B2
Bellona Solomon Is. 11°17S 159°47E 287 N10
Bellows Falls U.S.A. 43°8N 72°27W 313 C12
Bellpat Pakistan 29°0N 68°5E 242 E3
Bellpuig Spain 41°37N 1°1E 196 D6
Bells Dominica 15°25N 61°21W 323 k
Belluno Italy 46°9N 12°13E 199 B9
Bellville U.S.A. 32°9N 81°59W 316 C8
Bellwood Ill., U.S.A. 41°52N 87°53W 119 B1
Bellwood Pa., U.S.A. 40°36N 78°20W 312 F6
Belmanier Dominica 15°35N 61°24W 323 k
Bélmez Spain 38°17N 5°17W 195 G5
Belmond U.S.A. 42°51N 93°37W 310 B3
Belmont N.S.W., Australia 33°4S 151°42E 283 B9
Belmont Ont., Canada 42°53N 81°5W 312 D3
Belmont Grenada 12°2N 61°45W 323 q
Belmont Northern Cape, S. Africa 29°28S 24°22E 270 C3
Belmont London, U.K. 51°36N 0°18W 125 A2
Belmont Mass., U.S.A. 42°23N 71°10W 116 A1
Belmont N.Y., U.S.A. 42°14N 78°2W 312 D6
Belmont, Mt. N.Z. 41°11S 174°53E 143 B2
Belmont Cragin U.S.A. 41°55N 87°45W 119 B2
Belmont Harbor U.S.A. 41°56N 87°38W 119 B3
Belmonte Brazil 16°0S 39°0W 333 E4
Belmonte Portugal 40°21N 7°20W 194 E3
Belmonte Spain 39°34N 2°43W 197 F2
Belmopan Belize 17°18N 88°30W 320 C2
Belmore Australia 33°55S 151°5E 139 B1
Belmullet Ireland 54°14N 9°58W 166 B2
Belo Dem. Rep. of the Congo 0°32S 23°13E 264 C4
Belo Madag. 20°44S 44°0E 272 C1
Belo Horizonte Brazil 19°55S 43°56W 333 E3
Belo Jardim Brazil 8°20S 36°26W 332 C4
Belo Monte Brazil 3°5S 51°46W 329 D7
Belo-Tsiribihina Madag. 19°40S 44°30E 272 B1
Belogorsk = Bilohirsk Ukraine 45°3N 34°35E 189 K8
Belogorsk Russia 51°0N 128°20E 215 D13
Belogradchik Bulgaria 43°53N 22°42E 202 C6
Belogradets Bulgaria 43°22N 27°18E 203 C11
Beloha Madag. 25°10S 45°3E 272 D2
Beloit Kans., U.S.A. 39°28N 98°6W 308 F4
Beloit Wis., U.S.A. 42°31N 89°2W 310 B7
Belokalitvenskaya = Belaya Kalitva Russia 48°13N 40°50E 191 F5
Belokorovichi Ukraine 51°7N 28°2E 177 C15
Belomorsk Russia 64°35N 34°54E 186 B5
Belondo Dem. Rep. of the Congo 0°19S 19°31E 264 C3
Belonge Dem. Rep. of the Congo 2°7S 19°33E 264 C3
Belonia India 23°15N 91°30E 241 D3
Belopolye = Bilopillya Ukraine 51°14N 34°20E 189 G8
Belorechensk Russia 44°46N 39°52E 191 H4
Beloretsk Russia 53°58N 58°24E 186 D10
Belorussia = Belarus ■ Europe 53°30N 27°0E 177 B14
Beloshchelye = Naryan-Mar Russia 67°42N 53°12E 186 A9
Beloslav Bulgaria 43°11N 27°42E 203 C11
Belotsarsk = Kyzyl Russia 51°50N 94°30E 217 B12
Beloūsovka Kazakhstan 50°8N 82°31E 217 B10
Belovo Bulgaria 42°13N 24°1E 203 D8
Belovo Russia 54°30N 86°0E 217 B11
Belovodsk Ukraine 49°13N 39°36E 189 H10
Beloyarskiy Russia 63°42N 66°40E 214 C7
Beloye, Ozero Russia 60°10N 37°35E 188 B9
Beloye More Russia 66°30N 38°0E 160 C25
Belozem Bulgaria 42°12N 25°2E 203 D9
Belozersk Russia 60°1N 37°45E 188 B9
Belpasso Italy 37°35N 14°58E 201 E7
Belpre U.S.A. 39°17N 81°34W 309 F13
Belrain India 28°23N 80°55E 243 E9
Belt U.S.A. 47°23N 110°55W 304 C8
Beltana Australia 30°48S 138°25E 282 A3
Belterra Brazil 2°45S 55°0W 329 D7
Beltinci Slovenia 46°37N 16°20E 199 B13
Belton Mo., U.S.A. 38°49N 94°32W 310 F2
Belton Tex., U.S.A. 31°3N 97°28W 314 F6
Belton L. U.S.A. 31°6N 97°28W 314 F6
Beltsy = Bălţi Moldova 47°48N 27°58E 183 C12
Belturbet Ireland 54°6N 7°26W 166 B4
Belukha Russia 49°50N 86°50E 217 C11
Belur India 22°37N 88°21E 124 B2
Beluran Malaysia 5°48N 117°35E 235 A5
Beluša Slovak Rep. 49°5N 18°17E 181 B11
Belushya Guba Russia 71°32N 52°19E 214 B6
Belušić Serbia 43°50N 21°10E 202 C5
Belvedere St. Vincent 13°8N 61°11W 323 n
Belvedere London, U.K. 51°29N 0°9E 125 B4
Belvedere Calif., U.S.A. 37°52N 122°27W 136 A2
Belvedere Georgia, U.S.A. 33°45N 84°16W 113 B3
Belvedere Marittimo Italy 39°37N 15°52E 201 C8
Belvès France 44°46N 1°0E 174 D5
Belvidere Ill., U.S.A. 42°15N 88°50W 311 B8
Belvidere N.J., U.S.A. 40°50N 75°5W 313 F9
Belvis de la Jara Spain 39°45N 4°57W 194 F6
Bely Bychek = Chagoda Russia 59°10N 35°15E 188 C8
Belyando → Australia 21°38S 146°50E 280 C4
Belyando Crossing Australia 21°32S 146°51E 280 C4
Belyayevo Bogorodskoye Russia 55°39N 37°31E 129 C3
Belyuen Australia 12°34S 130°42E 278 B5
Belyy Russia 55°49N 33°3E 188 E7
Belyy, Ostrov Russia 73°30N 71°0E 214 B8
Belyy Yar Russia 58°26N 84°39E 214 D9
Belyye Vody = Aqsū Kazakhstan 42°25N 69°50E 217 D7
Belz Ukraine 50°23N 24°1E 185 H11
Bełżec Poland 50°23N 23°26E 185 H10
Belzig Germany 52°8N 12°35E 178 C8
Belzoni U.S.A. 33°11N 90°29W 315 E9
Bełżyce Poland 51°11N 22°17E 185 G9
Bemaraha, Lembalemban' i Madag. 18°40S 44°45E 272 B1
Bemarivo Madag. 21°45S 44°45E 272 C1
Bemarivo → Antsiranana, Madag. 14°9S 50°9E 272 A3
Bemarivo → Mahajanga, Madag. 15°27S 47°40E 272 B2
Bemavo Madag. 21°33S 45°25E 272 C2
Bembe Angola 7°3S 14°25E 265 D2
Bembéréke Benin 10°11N 2°43E 263 C5
Bembesi Zimbabwe 20°0S 28°58E 269 G2
Bembesi → Zimbabwe 18°57S 27°47E 269 F2
Bembézar → Spain 37°45N 5°13W 195 H5
Bembibre Spain 42°37N 6°25W 194 C4
Bemboka △ Australia 36°35S 149°41E 283 D8
Bement U.S.A. 39°55N 88°34W 311 E8
Bemetara India 21°42N 81°32E 243 J9
Bemidji U.S.A. 47°28N 94°53W 308 B6
Bemolanga Madag. 17°44S 45°6E 272 B2
Bemowo Poland 52°15N 20°53E 142 B1
Ben Iran 32°32N 50°45E 247 C6
Ben Boyd △ Australia 37°0S 149°55E 283 D8
Ben Cruachan U.K. 56°26N 5°8W 167 E3
Ben Dearg U.K. 57°47N 4°56W 167 D4
Ben En △ Vietnam 19°37N 105°30E 236 C5
Ben Gardane Tunisia 33°11N 11°11E 258 B2
Ben Halls Gap △ Australia 31°37S 151°1E 283 A9
Ben Hope U.K. 58°25N 4°36W 167 C4
Ben Lawers U.K. 56°32N 4°14W 167 E4
Ben Lomond N.S.W., Australia 30°1S 151°43E 281 E5
Ben Lomond Tas., Australia 41°38S 147°42E 281 G4
Ben Lomond Stirling, U.K. 56°11N 4°38W 167 E4
Ben Lomond △ Australia 41°33S 147°39E 281 G4
Ben Luc Vietnam 10°39N 106°29E 237 G6
Ben Macdhui U.K. 57°4N 3°40W 167 D5
Ben Mhor U.K. 57°15N 7°18W 167 D1
Ben More Argyll & Bute, U.K. 56°26N 6°1W 167 E2
Ben More Stirling, U.K. 56°23N 4°32W 167 E4
Ben More Assynt U.K. 58°8N 4°52W 167 C4
Ben Nevis U.K. 56°48N 5°1W 167 E3
Ben Ohau Ra. N.Z. 44°1S 170°4E 285 E5
Ben Quang Vietnam 17°3N 106°55E 236 D6
Ben Slimane Morocco 33°38N 7°7W 260 B3
Ben Slimane □ Morocco 33°30N 7°10W 260 B3
Ben Tadjine, Djebel Algeria 29°0N 3°30W 260 C4
Ben Tre Vietnam 10°14N 106°23E 237 G6
Ben Vorlich U.K. 56°21N 4°14W 167 E4
Ben Wyvis U.K. 57°40N 4°35W 167 D4
Bena Nigeria 11°20N 5°50E 263 C6
Bena-Dibele Dem. Rep. of the Congo 4°4S 22°50E 265 C4
Bena-Leka Dem. Rep. of the Congo 5°8S 22°10E 265 D4
Bena-Tshadi Dem. Rep. of the Congo 4°40S 22°49E 265 C4
Benagerie Australia 31°25S 140°22E 282 A4
Benahmed Morocco 33°4N 7°9W 260 B3
Benaki Museum Athens, Greece 112 b3

Benalla Australia 36°30S 146°0E 283 D7
Benalmádena Spain 36°36N 4°34W 195 J6
Benambra, Mt. Australia 36°31S 147°34E 283 D7
Benanee Australia 34°31S 142°52E 282 C5
Bénara Mayotte 12°53S 45°9E 272 b
Benares = Varanasi India 25°22N 83°0E 243 G10
Bénat, C. France 43°5N 6°22E 175 E10
Benavente Portugal 38°59N 8°49W 195 G2
Benavente Spain 42°2N 5°43W 194 C5
Benavides U.S.A. 27°36N 98°25W 314 H5
Benavides de Órbigo
Spain 42°30N 5°54W 194 C5
Benbecula U.K. 57°26N 7°21W 167 D1
Benbonyathe Hill
Australia 30°25S 139°11E 282 A3
Bend U.S.A. 44°4N 121°19W 304 D3
Bendale Canada 43°45N 79°13W 141 A3
Bendela
Dem. Rep. of the Congo 3°18S 17°36E 264 C3
Bendemeer Australia 30°53S 151°8E 283 A9
Bender Beyla Somali Rep. 9°30N 50°48E 267 C7
Bendery = Tighina
Moldova 46°50N 29°30E 183 D14
Bendigo Australia 36°40S 144°15E 282 D6
Bendin = Będzin Poland 50°19N 19°7E 185 H6
Bendorf Germany 50°25N 7°35E 178 E3
Bendsburg = Będzin
Poland 50°19N 19°7E 185 H6
Benē Beraq Israel 32°6N 34°51E 251 F5
Beneditinos Brazil 5°27S 42°22W 332 C3
Benedito Leite Brazil 7°13S 44°34W 332 C3
Benefica Brazil 22°52S 43°14W 135 B1
Bénéna Mali 13°9N 4°17W 262 C4
Benenitra Madag. 23°27S 45°5E 272 C2
Benešov Czech Rep. 49°46N 14°41E 180 B7
Benevento Italy 41°8N 14°45E 201 A7
Benfeld France 48°22N 7°34E 173 D14
Benfica Portugal 38°45N 9°11W 126 A1
Benga Mozam. 16°11S 33°40E 269 F3
Bengal = West Bengal □
India 23°0N 88°0E 243 H13
Bengal, Bay of Ind. Oc. 15°0N 90°0E 239 F14
Bengaluru = Bangalore
India 12°59N 77°40E 245 H3
Bengbis Cameroon 3°27N 12°36E 263 E7
Bengbu China 32°58N 117°20E 227 H9
Benghazi = Banghāzī
Libya 32°11N 20°3E 258 B4
Benghisa Point Malta 35°49N 14°33E 206 F8
Bengkalis Indonesia 1°30N 102°10E 237 M4
Bengkulu Indonesia 3°50S 102°12E 234 C2
Bengkulu □ Indonesia 3°48S 102°16E 234 C2
Bengo Dem. Rep. of the Congo 2°11S 19°5E 264 C3
Bengo □ Angola 9°0S 13°10E 265 D2
Bengough Canada 49°25N 105°10W 297 D7
Bengtsfors Sweden 59°2N 12°14E 162 E6
Benguela Angola 12°37S 13°25E 265 E2
Benguela □ Angola 13°0S 13°30E 265 E2
Benguerir Morocco 32°16N 7°56W 260 B3
Benguérua, I. Mozam. 21°58S 35°28E 271 B6
Benguet □ Phil. 16°30N 120°40E 232 C3
Benha Egypt 30°26N 31°8E 256 H7
Benham Seamount
Pac. Oc. 15°40N 124°30E 232 D5
Beni Dem. Rep. of the Congo 0°30N 29°27E 268 B2
Beni □ Bolivia 14°0S 65°0W 331 C5
Beni → Bolivia 10°23S 65°24W 331 C4
Beni Abbès Algeria 30°5N 2°5W 261 B4
Beni Hammad Algeria 35°49N 4°47E 261 A5
Beni Haoua Algeria 36°30N 1°30E 261 A5
Beni Mazâr Egypt 28°32N 30°44E 256 B3
Beni Mellal Morocco 32°21N 6°21W 260 B3
Beni Mellal □ Morocco 32°0N 6°30W 260 B3
Beni Ounif Algeria 32°0N 1°10W 261 B4
Beni Saf Algeria 35°17N 1°15W 261 A4
Beni Suef Egypt 29°5N 31°6E 256 J7
Beniah L. Canada 63°23N 112°17W 296 A6
Benicarló Spain 40°23N 0°23E 196 E5
Benicássim Spain 40°3N 0°4E 196 E5
Benidorm Spain 38°33N 0°9W 197 G4
Benin ■ Africa 10°0N 2°0E 263 D5
Benin → Nigeria 5°45N 5°4E 263 D6
Benin, Bight of W. Afr. 5°0N 3°0E 263 E5
Benin City Nigeria 6°20N 5°31E 263 D6
Benissa Spain 38°43N 0°3E 197 G5
Benitez Int. ✈ (SCL)
Chile 33°33S 70°42W 137 B1
Bénitiers, Île aux Mauritius 20°24S 57°20E 272 e
Benito Juárez Argentina 37°40S 59°43W 334 D4
Benito Juárez, Int. ✈ (MEX)
Mexico 19°25N 99°5W 128 B2
Benitses Greece 39°32N 19°55E 206 B9
Benjamin Aceval
Paraguay 24°58S 57°34W 334 A4
Benjamin Constant Brazil 4°40S 70°15W 328 D3
Benjamin Hill Mexico 30°9N 111°7W 318 A2
Benkelman U.S.A. 40°3N 101°32W 308 E3
Benkovac Croatia 44°2N 15°37E 199 D12
Benmore Pk. N.Z. 44°25S 170°8E 285 E5
Bennett Canada 59°51N 135°0W 296 B2
Bennett, L. Australia 22°50S 131°2E 278 D5
Bennetta, Ostrov
Russia 76°21N 148°56E 215 B15
Bennettsville U.S.A. 34°37N 79°41W 315 D15
Bennichchãb Mauritania 19°32N 15°12W 262 B1
Bennington N.H., U.S.A. 43°0N 71°55W 313 D11
Bennington Vt., U.S.A. 42°53N 73°12W 313 D11
Beno Dem. Rep. of the Congo 3°41S 17°49E 264 C3
Bénodet France 47°53N 4°7W 172 E2
Benom Malaysia 3°50N 102°6E 237 L4
Benoni S. Africa 26°11S 28°18E 271 C4
Benoud Algeria 32°20N 0°16E 261 B5
Bénoué △ Cameroon 8°30N 13°55E 264 A2
Benoy Chad 8°59N 16°19E 259 G3
Benque Viejo Belize 17°5N 89°8W 320 C2
Bense Dominica 15°35N 61°22W 323 k
Bensheim Germany 49°40N 8°38E 179 F4
Benson Ariz., U.S.A. 31°58N 110°18W 305 L8
Benson Minn., U.S.A. 45°19N 95°36W 308 C6
Bensonhurst U.S.A. 40°35N 73°59W 132 C2
Bent Iran 26°20N 59°31E 247 E8
Benteng Indonesia 6°10S 120°30E 231 F6
Bentiaba Angola 14°15S 12°21E 265 E2
Bentinck I. Australia 17°3S 139°35E 280 B2
Bentiu Sudan 9°10N 29°55E 257 F2
Bentley Subglacial Trench
Antarctica 80°0S 115°0W 151 E15
Bento Gonçalves Brazil 29°10S 51°31W 335 B5
Benton Ark., U.S.A. 34°34N 92°35W 314 D8
Benton Calif., U.S.A. 37°48N 118°32W 306 H8
Benton Ill., U.S.A. 38°0N 88°55W 310 G8
Benton Pa., U.S.A. 41°12N 76°23W 313 E8
Benton Harbor U.S.A. 42°6N 86°27W 311 D10
Benton Heights U.S.A. 42°7N 86°24W 311 D10
Bentong Malaysia 3°31N 101°55E 237 L3
Bentonville U.S.A. 36°22N 94°13W 314 C7
Bentu Liben Ethiopia 8°32N 38°21E 257 F4
Bentuang Karimun △
Indonesia 1°11N 113°38E 235 B4
Benue □ Nigeria 7°20N 8°45E 263 D6
Benue → Nigeria 7°48N 6°46E 263 D6
Benxi China 41°20N 123°48E 224 B1
Benza
Dem. Rep. of the Congo 4°49S 13°17E 265 D2
Benzdorp Suriname 3°44N 54°5W 329 C7
Beo Indonesia 4°25N 126°50E 231 D7
Beograd Serbia 44°50N 20°37E 202 B4
Beograd ✈ (BEG) Serbia 43°49N 20°17E 202 C4
Beolgyo S. Korea 34°51N 127°21E 224 E3
Beoumi Ivory C. 7°45N 5°23W 262 D3
Bepan Jiang → China 24°55N 106°5E 228 E6
Beppu Japan 33°15N 131°30E 222 D3
Beppu-Wan Japan 33°18N 131°34E 222 D3
Beqa Fiji 18°23S 178°8E 287 B2
Beqaa Valley = Al Biqā
Lebanon 34°10N 36°10E 250 D7
Bequia St. Vincent 13°0N 61°15W 323 n
Ber Mota India 23°27N 68°34E 242 H3
Bera Bangla. 24°5N 89°37E 241 C2
Bera, Tasik Malaysia 3°5N 102°38E 237 L4
Berach → India 25°15N 75°2E 242 G6
Beraketa Madag. 23°7S 44°25E 272 C1
Béran-Djoko Congo 3°15N 17°0E 264 B3
Berane Montenegro 42°51N 19°52E 202 D3
Berastagi Indonesia 3°11N 98°31E 237 L2
Berat Albania 40°43N 19°59E 202 F3
Berau = Tanjungredeb
Indonesia 2°9N 117°29E 235 B5
Berau → Indonesia 2°10N 117°42E 235 B5
Berau, Teluk Indonesia 2°30S 132°30E 231 E8
Beravina Madag. 18°10S 45°14E 272 B2
Berbak △ Indonesia 1°27S 104°19E 234 C2
Berber Sudan 18°0N 34°0E 256 D3
Berbera Somali Rep. 10°30N 45°2E 267 B6
Berbérati C.A.R. 4°15N 15°40E 264 B3
Berbice → Guyana 6°20N 57°32W 329 B6
Berceto Italy 44°31N 9°51E 198 D6
Berchem-Ste-Agathe
Belgium 50°52N 4°17E 116 A1
Berchidda Italy 40°47N 9°10E 200 B2
Berchtesgaden Germany 47°38N 13°0E 179 H8
Berchtesgaden △
Germany 47°34N 12°55E 179 H8
Berck France 50°25N 1°36E 173 B8
Berdaale Somali Rep. 3°14N 43°11E 267 D5
Berdale Somali Rep. 7°4N 47°51E 267 C6
Berdichev = Berdychiv
Ukraine 49°57N 28°30E 177 D15
Berdsk Russia 54°47N 83°2E 217 B10
Berdyansk Ukraine 46°45N 36°50E 189 J9
Berdychiv Ukraine 49°57N 28°30E 177 D15
Béré Chad 9°20N 16°9E 259 G3
Berea U.S.A. 37°34N 84°17W 309 G11
Berebere Indonesia 2°25N 128°45E 231 D7
Bereda Somali Rep. 11°45N 51°0E 267 B7
Berehomet Ukraine 48°10N 25°19E 183 B10
Berehove Ukraine 48°15N 22°35E 182 B7
Bereina Papua N. G. 8°39S 146°30E 286 E4
Bereket Turkmenistan 39°16N 55°32E 247 B7
Berekua Dominica 15°14N 61°20W 323 k
Berekum Ghana 7°29N 2°34W 262 D4
Berenice Egypt 24°2N 35°25E 256 C4
Berens → Canada 52°25N 97°2W 297 C9
Berens I. Canada 52°18N 97°18W 297 C9
Berens River Canada 52°25N 97°0W 297 C9
Beresfield Australia 32°50S 151°40E 283 B9
Beresford U.S.A. 43°5N 96°47W 308 D5
Berestechko Ukraine 50°22N 25°5E 177 C13
Bereşti Romania 46°6N 27°50E 183 D12
Beretău → Romania 47°10N 21°50E 182 C6
Berettyó → Hungary 46°59N 21°7E 182 D6
Berettyóújfalu Hungary 47°13N 21°33E 182 C6
Berevo Mahajanga, Madag. 17°14S 44°17E 272 B1
Berevo Toliara, Madag. 19°44S 44°58E 272 B1
Bereza = Byaroza Belarus 52°31N 24°51E 189 F3
Berezhany Ukraine 49°26N 24°58E 177 D13
Berezina = Byarezina →
Belarus 52°33N 30°14E 177 B16
Berezivka Ukraine 47°14N 30°55E 189 J6
Berezna Ukraine 51°35N 31°46E 189 G6
Bereznik Russia 62°51N 42°40E 186 B7
Berezniki Russia 59°24N 56°46E 186 C10
Berezovo Russia 64°0N 65°0E 214 C7
Berezyne Ukraine 46°14N 29°12E 183 D14
Berg am Laim Germany 48°7N 11°38E 131 B2
Berga Spain 42°6N 1°48E 196 C6
Berga Kalmar, Sweden 57°14N 16°3E 163 G10
Bergama Turkey 39°8N 27°11E 205 B9
Bérgamo Italy 45°41N 9°43E 198 C6
Bergaon India 20°41N 80°27E 244 D5
Bergara Spain 43°9N 2°28W 196 B2
Bergby Sweden 60°57N 17°2E 162 D11
Berge Norway 59°34N 8°10E 162 E2
Bergedorf Germany 53°28N 10°6E 178 B6
Bergeforsen Sweden 62°32N 17°23E 162 B11
Bergen Mecklenburg-Vorpommern,
Germany 54°25N 13°25E 178 A9
Bergen Niedersachsen,
Germany 52°49N 9°57E 178 C5
Bergen Neths. 52°40N 4°43E 170 B4
Bergen Hordaland, Norway 60°20N 5°20E 164 D2
Bergen N.Y., U.S.A. 43°5N 77°57W 312 C7
Bergen ✈ (BGO) Norway 60°17N 5°19E 164 D2
Bergen op Zoom Neths. 51°28N 4°18E 170 C4
Bergenfield U.S.A. 40°55N 73°59W 132 A2
Bergerac France 44°51N 0°30E 174 D4
Bergham Germany 48°2N 11°37E 131 B2
Bergheim Germany 50°57N 6°38E 178 E2
Bergholz U.S.A. 40°31N 80°53W 312 F4
Bergisch Gladbach
Germany 50°59N 7°8E 170 D7
Bergisches Land △
Germany 51°0N 7°30E 178 E3
Bergkamen Germany 51°37N 7°38E 178 D3
Bergkvara Sweden 56°23N 16°5E 163 H10
Bergshamra Sweden 59°38N 18°37E 162 E12
Bergsjö Sweden 61°59N 17°3E 162 C11
Bergstadt = Leśnica
Poland 50°26N 18°11E 185 H5
Bergstrasse-Odenwald △
Germany 49°45N 5°55E 179 F1
Bergues France 50°58N 2°24E 173 B9
Bergviken Sweden 61°15N 16°40E 162 C10
Bergville S. Africa 28°52S 29°18E 271 C4
Bergvliet S. Africa 34°2S 18°25E 118 B1
Berhala, Selat Indonesia 1°0S 104°15E 234 C2
Berhampore = Baharampur
India 24°2N 88°27E 243 G13
Berhampur = Brahmapur
India 19°15N 84°54E 244 E7
Berheci → Romania 45°58N 27°28E 183 E12
Beri Spain 41°20N 2°1E 114 A1
Bering Glacier U.S.A. 60°20N 143°30W 303 F12
Bering Land Bridge △
U.S.A. 66°20N 165°0W 303 C6
Bering Sea Pac. Oc. 58°0N 171°0W 292 D2
Bering Strait Pac. Oc. 65°30N 169°0W 303 D5
Beringovskiy Russia 63°3N 179°19E 215 C18
Berisso Argentina 34°56S 57°50W 334 C4
Berja Spain 36°50N 2°56W 195 J8
Berkåk Norway 62°50N 10°0E 164 B6
Berkane Morocco 34°52N 2°20W 261 B4
Berkeley U.S.A. 37°51N 122°16W 136 A3
Berkeley, C. Ecuador 0°1N 91°35W 330 a
Berkner I. Antarctica 79°30S 50°0W 151 D18
Berkovitsa Bulgaria 43°16N 23°8E 202 C7
Berkshire U.S.A. 42°19N 76°11W 313 D8
Berkshire Downs U.K. 51°33N 1°29W 169 F6
Berlanga Spain 38°17N 5°50W 195 G5
Berlenga, I. Portugal 39°25N 9°30W 195 F1
Berlengas = Valença do Piauí
Brazil 6°20S 41°45W 332 C3
Berlin = Kitchener
Canada 43°27N 80°29W 312 C4
Berlin Berlin, Germany 52°31N 13°23E 115 A3
Berlin Ga., U.S.A. 31°4N 83°37W 316 D6
Berlin Md., U.S.A. 38°20N 75°13W 309 F16
Berlin N.H., U.S.A. 44°28N 71°11W 313 B13
Berlin N.Y., U.S.A. 42°42N 73°23W 313 D11
Berlin Wis., U.S.A. 43°58N 88°57W 308 D9
Berlin □ Germany 52°30N 13°20E 178 C9
Berlin Dom Germany 52°31N 13°24E 115 A3
Berlin L. U.S.A. 41°3N 81°0W 312 E4
Berlin Tegel ✈ (TXL)
Germany 52°35N 13°14E 115 A2
Berlinchen = Barlinek
Poland 53°0N 15°15E 185 F2
Bermagui Australia 36°25S 150°4E 283 D9
Bermeja, Sierra Spain 36°30N 5°11W 195 J5
Bermejo → Formosa,
Argentina 26°51S 58°23W 334 B4
Bermejo → San Juan,
Argentina 32°30S 67°30W 334 C2
Bermejo, Paso = Uspallata, P. de
Argentina 32°37S 69°22W 334 C2
Bermen, L. Canada 53°35N 68°55W 299 B6
Bermeo Spain 43°25N 2°47W 196 B2
Bermillo de Sayago Spain 41°22N 6°8W 194 D4
Bermondsey U.K. 51°29N 0°3W 125 B3
Bermuda ☑ Atl. Oc. 32°18N 64°45W 153 a
Bermuda Int. ✈ (BDA)
Bermuda 32°22N 64°41W 153 a
Bermuda Rise Atl. Oc. 32°30N 65°0W 152 C5
Bern Switz. 46°57N 7°28E 179 J3
Bern □ Switz. 46°45N 7°40E 179 J3
Bernabeu, Estadio Spain 40°27N 3°41W 127 B1
Bernal Heights U.S.A. 37°44N 122°24W 136 B2
Bernalda Italy 40°24N 16°41E 201 B9
Bernalillo U.S.A. 35°18N 106°33W 305 J10
Bernam → Malaysia 3°45N 101°5E 234 B2
Bernardo de Irigoyen
Argentina 26°15S 53°40W 335 B5
Bernardo O'Higgins △
Chile 48°50S 75°36W 336 C1
Bernardsville U.S.A. 40°43N 74°34W 313 F10
Bernasconi Argentina 37°55S 63°44W 334 D3
Bernau Bayern, Germany 47°47N 12°22E 179 H8
Bernau Brandenburg,
Germany 52°40N 13°35E 178 C9
Bernay France 49°5N 0°35E 172 C7
Bernburg Germany 51°47N 11°44E 178 D7
Berndorf Austria 47°59N 16°1E 180 D9
Berne = Bern Switz. 46°57N 7°28E 179 J3
Berne = Bern □ Switz. 46°45N 7°40E 179 J3
Berne U.S.A. 40°39N 84°57W 311 D12
Berner Alpen Switz. 46°27N 7°35E 179 J3
Berneray U.K. 57°43N 7°11W 167 D1
Bernier I. Australia 24°50S 113°12E 279 D1
Bernina, Piz Switz. 46°20N 9°54E 179 J5
Bernkastel-Kues Germany 49°55N 7°3E 179 F3
Bernstadt = Bierutów
Poland 51°7N 17°32E 185 G4
Bernstein = Pełczyce
Poland 53°3N 15°16E 185 E2
Bero → Angola 15°10S 12°9E 265 F2
Beroroha Madag. 21°40S 45°10E 272 C2
Béroubouay Benin 10°34N 2°46E 263 C5
Beroun Czech Rep. 49°57N 14°5E 180 B7
Berounka → Czech Rep. 50°0N 14°22E 180 B7
Berovo Macedonia 41°38N 22°51E 202 E6
Berre, Étang de France 43°27N 5°5E 175 E9
Berre-l'Étang France 43°27N 5°10E 175 E9
Berrechid Morocco 33°18N 7°36W 260 B3
Berri Australia 34°14S 140°35E 282 C4
Berriane Algeria 32°50N 3°46E 261 B5
Berridale Australia 36°22S 148°48E 283 D8
Berrien Springs U.S.A. 41°57N 86°20W 311 C10
Berrigan Australia 35°38S 145°49E 283 C6
Berriwillock Australia 35°36S 142°59E 282 C5
Berrouaghia Algeria 36°10N 2°53E 261 A5
Berry N.S.W., Australia 34°46S 150°43E 283 C9
Berry Indre, France 46°50N 2°0E 173 F8
Berry Is. Bahamas 25°40N 77°50W 320 A4
Berrydale U.S.A. 30°53N 87°3W 317 E2
Berryessa, L. U.S.A. 38°31N 122°6W 306 G4
Berryville U.S.A. 36°22N 93°34W 314 C8
Berseba Namibia 26°0S 17°46E 270 C2
Bersenbrück Germany 52°34N 7°56E 178 C3
Bershad Ukraine 48°22N 29°31E 183 B14
Bertamirans Spain 42°54N 8°38W 194 C2
Berthold U.S.A. 48°19N 101°44W 308 A3
Berthoud U.S.A. 40°19N 105°5W 304 F11
Bertincourt France 50°5N 2°58E 173 B9
Bertolínia Brazil 7°38S 43°57W 332 C3
Bertoua Cameroon 4°30N 13°45E 264 B2
Bertraghboy B. Ireland 53°22N 9°54W 166 C2
Bertys = Balqash
Kazakhstan 46°50N 74°50E 214 E8
Beru Kiribati 1°20S 176°0E 277 A14
Berufjörður Iceland 64°48N 14°29W 155 C12
Berunes Iceland 64°42N 14°16W 155 C12
Beruni Uzbekistan 41°41N 60°45E 216 D6
Beruri Brazil 3°54S 61°22W 329 D5
Berwick U.S.A. 41°3N 76°14W 313 E8
Berwick-upon-Tweed
U.K. 55°46N 2°0W 168 B6
Berwyn U.S.A. 41°50N 87°47W 119 B2
Berwyn Heights U.S.A. 38°59N 76°55W 143 B4
Berwyn Mts. U.K. 52°54N 3°26W 168 E4
Beryslav Ukraine 46°50N 33°30E 189 J7
Berzasca Romania 44°39N 21°58E 182 F6
Berzence Hungary 46°12N 17°11E 182 D2
Besal Pakistan 35°4N 73°56E 243 B5
Besalampy Madag. 16°43S 44°29E 272 B1
Besançon France 47°15N 6°2E 173 E13
Besar Indonesia 2°40S 116°0E 235 C5
Besar, Gunong Malaysia 5°10N 101°18E 234 A2
Beshenkovichi Belarus 55°2N 29°29E 188 E5
Beşiktaş Turkey 41°2N 29°0E 122 B2
Beška Serbia 45°8N 20°6E 182 E5
Beslan Russia 43°15N 44°28E 191 J7
Besna Kobila Serbia 42°31N 22°10E 202 D6
Besnard L. Canada 55°25N 106°0W 297 B7
Besni Turkey 37°41N 37°52E 212 D7
Besor, N. → Egypt 31°28N 34°22E 251 G5
Besós → Spain 41°24N 2°13E 114 A2
Bessa Monteiro Angola 7°7S 13°44E 265 D2
Bessarabiya Moldova 47°0N 28°10E 177 E15
Bessarabka = Basarabeasca
Moldova 46°21N 28°58E 183 D13
Bessèges France 44°18N 4°8E 175 D8
Bessemer Ala., U.S.A. 33°24N 86°58W 315 E11
Bessemer Mich., U.S.A. 46°29N 90°3W 308 B8
Bessemer Pa., U.S.A. 40°59N 80°30W 312 F4
Bessie, L. U.S.A. 28°29N 81°31W 133 B1
Bessin France 49°18N 1°0W 172 C6
Bessines-sur-Gartempe
France 46°6N 1°22E 174 B5
Beswick Australia 14°34S 132°53E 278 B5
Beswick © Australia 14°31S 132°51E 278 B5
Bet Horon West Bank 31°52N 35°7E 123 A1
Bet She'an Israel 32°30N 35°30E 251 F6
Bet Shemesh Israel 31°44N 35°0E 251 G6
Betafo Madag. 19°50S 46°51E 272 B2
Betamba
Dem. Rep. of the Congo 2°17S 21°24E 264 C4
Betancuria Canary Is. 28°25N 14°3W 153 e2
Betancuria, Mt. Canary Is. 28°25N 14°6W 153 e2
Betania Colombia 4°22N 72°54W 328 C3
Betanzos Bolivia 19°34S 65°27W 331 D4
Betanzos Spain 43°15N 8°12W 194 B2
Bétaré Oya Cameroon 5°40N 14°5E 264 A2
Betatao Madag. 18°11S 47°52E 272 B2
Bétera Spain 39°35N 0°28W 197 F4
Bétérou Benin 9°12N 2°16E 263 D5
Bethal S. Africa 26°27S 29°28E 271 C4
Bethalto U.S.A. 38°55N 90°2W 310 F6
Bethanien Namibia 26°31S 17°8E 270 C2
Bethany Ont., Canada 44°11N 78°34W 312 B6
Bethany Ill., U.S.A. 39°39N 88°45W 311 E8
Bethany Mo., U.S.A. 40°16N 94°2W 310 D2
Bethany Okla., U.S.A. 35°31N 97°38W 314 D6
Bethel Montserrat 16°44N 62°9W 323 p
Bethel Alaska, U.S.A. 60°48N 161°45W 303 F7
Bethel Conn., U.S.A. 41°22N 73°25W 313 E11
Bethel Maine, U.S.A. 44°25N 70°47W 313 B14
Bethel Ohio, U.S.A. 38°58N 84°5W 311 F12
Bethel Vt., U.S.A. 43°50N 72°38W 313 C12
Bethel Park U.S.A. 40°19N 80°2W 312 F4
Béthenville France 49°18N 4°23E 173 C11
Bethesda U.S.A. 38°59N 77°6W 143 B3
Bethlehem = Bayt Lahm
West Bank 31°43N 35°12E 123 B2
Bethlehem Free State,
S. Africa 28°14S 28°18E 271 C4
Bethlehem Pa., U.S.A. 40°37N 75°23W 313 F9
Bethnal Green U.K. 51°31N 0°2W 125 A3
Bethulie S. Africa 30°30S 25°59E 270 D4
Béthune France 50°30N 2°38E 173 B9
Béthune → France 49°53N 1°9E 172 C8
Bethungra Australia 34°45S 147°51E 283 C7
Betijoque Venezuela 9°23N 70°44W 328 B3
Betim Brazil 19°58S 44°13W 333 E3
Betioky Toliara, Madag. 23°48S 44°20E 272 C1
Betioky Toliara, Madag. 22°27S 43°43E 272 C1
Betong Malaysia 1°24N 111°31E 235 B4
Betong Thailand 5°45N 101°5E 237 K3
Betoota Australia 25°45S 140°42E 280 D3
Betor Ethiopia 11°37N 39°2E 257 E4
Betor W. Bengal, India 22°34N 88°17E 124 B1
Bétou Congo 3°2N 18°32E 264 B3
Betpaqdala Kazakhstan 45°45N 70°30E 217 C8
Betroka Madag. 23°16S 46°0E 272 C2
Betsiamites Canada 48°56N 68°40W 299 C6
Betsiamites → Canada 48°56N 68°38W 299 C6
Betsiboka → Madag. 16°3S 46°36E 272 B2
Bettendorf U.S.A. 41°32N 90°30W 310 C6
Bettiah India 26°48N 84°33E 243 F11
Bettna Sweden 58°55N 16°38E 163 F10
Béttola Italy 44°47N 9°36E 198 D6
Betul India 21°58N 77°59E 244 D3
Betws-y-Coed U.K. 53°5N 3°48W 168 D4
Betxi Spain 39°56N 0°12W 196 F4
Betzdorf Germany 50°46N 7°52E 178 E3
Béu Angola 6°15S 15°32E 265 D3
Beuil France 44°6N 6°59E 175 D10
Beulah Vic., Australia 35°58S 142°29E 282 C5
Beulah Fla., U.S.A. 28°32N 81°34W 133 A1
Beulah Mich., U.S.A. 44°38N 86°6W 308 C10
Beulah N. Dak., U.S.A. 47°16N 101°47W 308 B3
Beulah, L. U.S.A. 28°32N 81°33W 133 A1
Beurkia Chad 15°20N 17°56E 259 E3
Beurs van Berlage Amsterdam, Neths. 112 a2
Beuthen = Bytom Poland 50°25N 18°54E 185 H5
Beuthen an der Oder = Bytom
Odrzański Poland 51°44N 15°48E 185 G2
Beuvron → France 47°29N 1°15E 172 E8
Beveren Belgium 51°12N 4°16E 170 C4
Beverley W. Austral.,
Australia 32°9S 116°56E 279 F2
Beverley E. Riding, U.K. 53°51N 0°26W 168 D7
Beverley Hills Australia 33°56S 151°5E 139 B1
Beverley Park Australia 33°58S 151°8E 139 B1
Beverly Ill., U.S.A. 41°42N 87°39W 119 C3
Beverly Mass., U.S.A. 42°33N 70°53W 313 D14
Beverly Arts Center
U.S.A. 41°41N 87°40W 119 C2
Beverly Glen U.S.A. 34°6N 118°26W 126 B2
Beverly Hills Calif.,
U.S.A. 34°5N 118°24W 126 B2
Beverly Hills Fla., U.S.A. 28°55N 82°28W 317 G7
Beverly Hills -Morgan Park Historic
District U.S.A. 41°41N 87°40W 119 C2
Beverungen Germany 51°39N 9°22E 178 D5
Bevoalavo Madag. 25°13S 45°26E 272 D2
Bewas → India 23°59N 79°21E 243 H8
Bewdley Canada 44°5N 78°19W 312 B6
Bex Switz. 46°15N 7°1E 179 J3
Bexhill U.K. 50°51N 0°29E 169 G8
Bexley Australia 33°56S 151°7E 139 B1
Bexley □ U.K. 51°27N 0°9E 125 B4
Bexleyheath U.K. 51°27N 0°8E 125 B4
Bey Dağları Turkey 36°38N 30°29E 205 E12
Beyānlū Iran 36°0N 47°51E 246 C5
Beyazköy Turkey 41°21N 27°42E 203 E11
Beyçayırı Turkey 40°15N 26°55E 203 F10
Beydağ Turkey 38°5N 28°13E 205 C10
Beyeğaç Turkey 37°14N 28°53E 205 D10
Beyin Ghana 5°1N 2°41W 262 D4
Beykoz Turkey 41°7N 29°7E 122 B2
Beyla Guinea 8°30N 8°38W 262 D3
Beylerbeyi Turkey 41°2N 29°2E 122 B2
Beynat France 45°8N 1°44E 174 C5
Beyneu Kazakhstan 45°18N 55°9E 187 E10
Beyoba Turkey 38°48N 27°47E 205 C9
Beyoğlu Turkey 41°1N 28°58E 122 B1
Beyoneisu Retsugan
Japan 31°55N 139°55E 223 F11
Beypazarı Turkey 40°10N 31°56E 212 B4
Beypore → India 11°10N 75°47E 245 J2
Beyra Somali Rep. 6°57N 47°19E 267 C6
Beyşehir Turkey 37°41N 31°43E 212 D4
Beyşehir Gölü Turkey 37°41N 31°33E 212 D4
Beytüşşebap Turkey 37°35N 43°10E 213 D10
Bezdan Serbia 45°50N 18°57E 182 E3
Bezhetsk Russia 57°47N 36°39E 188 D9
Béziers France 43°20N 3°12E 174 E7
Bezons France 48°56N 2°13E 134 A2
Bezuidenhout Park
S. Africa 26°10S 28°5E 123 B2
Bezwada = Vijayawada
India 16°31N 80°39E 244 F5
Bhabua India 25°3N 83°37E 243 G10
Bhachau India 23°20N 70°16E 242 H4
Bhadar → Gujarat, India 22°17N 72°20E 242 H5
Bhadar → Gujarat, India 21°27N 69°47E 242 J3
Bhadarwah India 32°58N 75°46E 243 C6
Bhadgaon = Bhaktapur
Nepal 27°38N 85°24E 243 F11
Bhadohi India 25°25N 82°34E 243 G10
Bhadra India 29°8N 75°14E 242 E6
Bhadra → India 14°0N 75°20E 245 H2
Bhadrachalam India 17°40N 80°53E 244 F5
Bhadrakali India 22°40N 88°20E 124 A2
Bhadrakh India 21°10N 86°30E 244 D8
Bhadran India 22°19N 72°6E 242 H5
Bhadravati India 13°49N 75°40E 245 H2
Bhag Pakistan 29°2N 67°49E 242 E2
Bhagalpur India 25°10N 87°0E 243 G12
Bhagirathi → Uttarakhand,
India 30°8N 78°35E 243 D8
Bhagirathi → W. Bengal,
India 23°25N 88°23E 243 H13
Bhainsa India 19°10N 77°58E 244 E3
Bhairab → Bangla. 22°51N 89°34E 241 D2
Bhairab Bazar Bangla. 24°4N 90°58E 241 C3
Bhakkar Pakistan 31°40N 71°5E 242 D4
Bhakra Dam India 31°30N 76°45E 242 D7
Bhaktapur Nepal 27°38N 85°24E 243 F11
Bhalki India 18°2N 77°13E 244 E3
Bhalswa India 28°44N 77°10E 120 A2
Bhambo Khan Qarmati
Pakistan 24°49N 67°7E 123 B2
Bhamo Burma 24°15N 97°15E 241 C6
Bhamragarh India 19°30N 80°40E 244 E5
Bhandara India 21°5N 79°42E 244 D4
Bhanpura India 24°31N 75°44E 242 G6
Bhanrer Ra. India 23°40N 79°45E 243 H8
Bhaptiahi India 26°19N 86°44E 243 F12
Bharat = India ■ Asia 20°0N 78°0E 239 F11
Bharatpur Chhattisgarh,
India 23°44N 81°46E 243 H9
Bharatpur Raj., India 27°15N 77°30E 242 F7
Bharatpur Nepal 27°34N 84°10E 243 F11
Bharno India 23°14N 84°53E 243 H11
Bharuch India 21°47N 73°0E 244 D1
Bhatghar L. India 18°10N 73°48E 244 E1
Bhatiapara Ghat Bangla. 23°13N 89°42E 241 D2
Bhatinda India 30°15N 74°57E 242 D6
Bhatkal India 13°58N 74°35E 245 H2
Bhatpara India 22°50N 88°25E 243 H13
Bhatsala India 22°30N 88°16E 124 B1
Bhattu India 29°36N 75°19E 242 E6
Bhaun Pakistan 32°55N 72°40E 242 C5
Bhaunagar = Bhavnagar
India 21°45N 72°10E 244 D1
Bhavani India 11°27N 77°43E 245 J3
Bhavnagar India 21°45N 72°10E 244 D1
Bhawanipatna India 19°55N 83°10E 244 E5
Bhawanipur India 22°32N 88°21E 124 B2
Bhawari India 25°42N 73°4E 242 G5
Bhayavadar India 21°51N 70°15E 242 J4
Bhendkhal India 18°52N 72°59E 130 B2
Bhera Pakistan 32°29N 72°57E 242 C5
Bhikangaon India 21°52N 75°57E 242 J6
Bhilai = Bhilainagar-Durg
India 21°13N 81°26E 244 D5
Bhilainagar-Durg India 21°13N 81°26E 244 D5
Bhilsa = Vidisha India 23°28N 77°53E 242 H7
Bhilwara India 25°25N 74°38E 242 G6
Bhima → India 16°25N 77°17E 244 F3
Bhimavaram India 16°30N 81°30E 245 F5
Bhimbar Pakistan 32°59N 74°3E 243 C6
Bhind India 26°30N 78°46E 243 F8
Bhinga India 27°43N 81°56E 243 F9
Bhinmal India 25°0N 72°15E 242 G5
Bhisho S. Africa 32°50S 27°23E 270 D4
Bhiwandi India 19°20N 73°0E 244 E1
Bhiwani India 28°50N 76°9E 242 E7
Bhogava → India 22°26N 72°20E 242 H5
Bhokardan India 20°16N 75°46E 244 D2
Bhola Bangla. 22°45N 90°35E 241 D3
Bholari Pakistan 25°19N 68°13E 242 G3
Bhongir India 17°30N 78°56E 244 F4
Bhopal India 23°20N 77°30E 242 H7
Bhopalpatnam India 18°52N 80°23E 244 E5
Bhor India 18°12N 73°53E 244 E1
Bhuban India 20°53N 85°50E 244 D7
Bhubaneshwar India 20°15N 85°50E 244 D7
Bhuj India 23°15N 69°49E 242 H3
Bhuleshwar Mumbai, India 130 b2
Bhumiphol Res. Thailand 17°20N 98°40E 236 D2
Bhusawal India 21°3N 75°46E 244 D2
Bhutan ■ Asia 27°25N 90°30E 241 B3
Biá → Brazil 3°28S 67°23W 328 D4
Biafra, B. of = Bonny, Bight of
Africa 3°30N 9°20E 263 E6
Biak Indonesia 1°10S 136°6E 231 E9
Biała Poland 50°24N 17°40E 185 H4
Biała → Poland 50°3N 20°55E 185 H7
Biała Piska Poland 53°37N 22°5E 184 E9
Biała Podlaska Poland 52°4N 23°6E 185 F10
Biała Rawska Poland 51°48N 20°29E 185 G7
Białobrzegi Poland 51°39N 20°57E 185 G7
Białogard Poland 54°2N 15°58E 184 D2
Białołęka Dworska Poland 52°19N 21°1E 142 B2
Białowieski △ Poland 52°43N 23°50E 185 F10
Białowieża Poland 52°41N 23°49E 185 F10
Biały Bór Poland 53°53N 16°51E 184 E3
Białystok Poland 53°10N 23°10E 185 E10
Biancavilla Italy 37°38N 14°52E 201 E7
Bianco Italy 38°5N 16°9E 201 D9
Biankouma Ivory C. 7°50N 7°40W 262 D3
Biaora India 23°56N 76°56E 242 H7
Bīārjmand Iran 36°6N 55°53E 247 B7
Biaro Indonesia 2°5N 125°26E 231 D7
Biarritz France 43°29N 1°33W 174 E2
Bias Indonesia 8°24S 115°36E 231 J18
Biasca Switz. 46°22N 8°58E 179 J4
Biavela Angola 14°43S 19°47E 265 E3
Biba Egypt 28°55N 31°0E 256 J7
Bibai Japan 43°19N 141°52E 220 C10
Bibala Angola 14°44S 13°24E 265 E2
Bibane, Bahiret el Tunisia 33°16N 11°13E 258 B2
Bibassé Gabon 1°27N 11°37E 264 B2
Bibbiena Italy 43°42N 11°49E 199 E8
Bibby I. Canada 61°55N 93°0W 297 A10
Bibei → Spain 42°24N 7°13W 194 C3
Biberach Germany 48°5N 9°47E 179 G5
Bibi Papua N. G. 5°30S 146°2E 286 C4
Bibiani Ghana 6°30N 2°8W 262 D4
Bibile Sri Lanka 7°10N 81°25E 245 L5
Bibungwa
Dem. Rep. of the Congo 2°40S 28°15E 268 C2
Bicaj Albania 41°58N 20°25E 202 E4
Bicaz Romania 46°53N 26°5E 183 D11
Bicazu Ardelean
Romania 46°51N 25°56E 183 D10
Biccari Italy 41°23N 15°12E 201 A8
Bicentennial Park N.S.W.,
Australia 33°51S 151°5E 139 B1
Bicentennial Park Calif.,
U.S.A. 34°1N 118°1W 126 B4
Bicester U.K. 51°54N 1°9W 169 F6
Biche Trin. & Tob. 10°26N 61°8W 323 t
Bichena Ethiopia 10°28N 38°10E 257 E4
Bicheno Australia 41°52S 148°18E 281 G4
Bichia India 22°27N 80°42E 243 H9
Bichvinta Georgia 43°9N 40°21E 191 J5
Bickerton I. Australia 13°45S 136°10E 280 A2
Bickley U.K. 51°23N 0°3E 125 B4
Bicknell U.S.A. 38°47N 87°19W 311 F9
Bicske Hungary 47°29N 18°38E 182 C3
Bicuari △ Angola 15°14S 14°45E 265 F2
Bicutan Phil. 14°30N 121°3E 127 C2
Bid = Bir India 19°4N 75°46E 244 E2
Bida Dem. Rep. of the Congo 4°55N 19°56E 264 B3
Bida Nigeria 9°3N 5°58E 263 D6
Bidar India 17°55N 77°35E 244 F3
Bidde Somali Rep. 0°58N 42°37E 267 D5
Biddeford U.S.A. 43°30N 70°28W 309 D18
Biddwara Ethiopia 5°11N 38°34E 257 F4
Bideford U.K. 51°1N 4°13W 169 F3
Bideford Bay U.K. 51°5N 4°20W 169 F3
Bidhan Nagar India 22°35N 88°25E 124 B2
Bidhuna India 26°49N 79°31E 243 F8
Bīdokht Iran 34°20N 58°46E 247 C8
Bidor Malaysia 4°6N 101°15E 237 K3
Bidu West Bank 31°50N 35°9E 123 B1
Bidyadanga Australia 18°45S 121°43E 278 C3
Bidzar Cameroon 9°54N 14°7E 264 A2
Bie Sweden 59°5N 16°12E 162 E10
Bié □ Angola 12°30S 17°0E 265 E3
Bié, Planalto de Angola 12°0S 16°0E 265 E3
Bieber U.S.A. 41°7N 121°8W 304 F3
Biebrza → Poland 53°13N 22°25E 185 E9
Biebrzański △ Poland 53°36N 22°45E 184 E9
Biecz Poland 49°44N 21°15E 185 J8
Biel Switz. 47°8N 7°14E 179 H3
Bielany Poland 52°17N 20°57E 142 B1
Bielawa Dolnośląskie,
Poland 50°43N 16°37E 185 H3
Bielawa Warszawa, Poland 52°8N 21°9E 142 C2
Bielefeld Germany 52°1N 8°33E 178 C4
Bielersee Switz. 47°6N 7°5E 179 H3
Bielitz = Bielsko-Biała
Poland 49°50N 19°2E 185 J6
Biella Italy 45°34N 8°3E 198 C5
Bielsk Podlaski Poland 52°47N 23°12E 185 F10
Bielsko-Biała Poland 49°50N 19°2E 185 J6
Bien Hoa Vietnam 10°57N 106°49E 237 G6
Bienne = Biel Switz. 47°8N 7°14E 179 H3
Bienvenida Spain 38°18N 6°12W 195 G4
Bienvenue Fr. Guiana 3°0N 52°30W 329 C7
Bienville, L. Canada 55°5N 72°40W 298 A5
Bierné France 47°48N 0°33W 172 E6
Bierun Poland 50°6N 19°6E 185 H6
Bierutów Poland 51°7N 17°32E 185 G4
Biescas Spain 42°37N 0°20W 196 C4
Biesdorf Germany 52°30N 13°33E 115 A4
Biese → Germany 52°53N 11°46E 178 C7
Biesiesfontein S. Africa 30°57S 17°58E 270 D2
Bieszczadzki △ Poland 49°5N 22°43E 185 J9
Bietigheim-Bissingen
Germany 48°58N 9°8E 179 G5
Bièvre → France 48°44N 2°9E 134 B1
Bièvres France 48°45N 2°13E 134 B1
Bieżuń Poland 52°58N 19°55E 185 F6
Biferno → Italy 41°59N 15°2E 199 G12
Bifoum Gabon 0°20S 10°23E 264 C2
Big → Nfld. & L., Canada 54°50N 58°55W 299 B8
Big → Mo., U.S.A. 38°28N 90°37W 310 F6
Big B. = Awarua B. N.Z. 44°28S 168°4E 285 E3
Big B. Canada 55°43N 60°35W 299 A7
Big Bear City U.S.A. 34°16N 116°51W 307 L10
Big Bear Lake U.S.A. 34°15N 116°56W 307 L10
Big Belt Mts. U.S.A. 46°30N 111°25W 304 C8
Big Bend Swaziland 26°50S 31°58E 271 C5
Big Bend △ U.S.A. 29°20N 103°5W 314 G3
Big Black → U.S.A. 32°3N 91°4W 315 E9
Big Blue → Ind., U.S.A. 39°12N 85°56W 311 E11
Big Blue → Kans., U.S.A. 39°35N 96°34W 308 F5
Big Creek U.S.A. 37°11N 119°14W 306 H7
Big Cypress △ U.S.A. 26°0N 81°10W 317 J8
Big Cypress Swamp
U.S.A. 26°15N 81°30W 317 J8
Big Delta U.S.A. 64°10N 145°51W 303 D11
Big Desert Australia 35°45S 141°10E 281 F3
Big Falls U.S.A. 48°12N 93°48W 308 A7
Big Fork → U.S.A. 48°31N 93°43W 308 A7
Big Horn Mts. = Bighorn Mts.
U.S.A. 44°25N 107°0W 304 D10
Big I. Canada 61°7N 116°45W 296 A5
Big Lake Alaska, U.S.A. 61°20N 150°20W 303 F10
Big Lake Tex., U.S.A. 31°12N 101°28W 314 F4
Big Moose U.S.A. 43°49N 74°58W 313 C10
Big Muddy → U.S.A. 37°33N 89°32W 310 G8
Big Muddy Cr. →
U.S.A. 48°8N 104°36W 304 B11
Big Pine U.S.A. 37°10N 118°17W 306 H8
Big Pine Key U.S.A. 24°40N 81°21W 317 L8
Big Piney U.S.A. 42°32N 110°7W 304 E8
Big Quill L. Canada 51°55N 104°30W 297 C8
Big Rapids U.S.A. 43°42N 85°29W 309 D11
Big Rideau L. Canada 44°40N 76°15W 313 B8
Big River Canada 53°50N 107°0W 297 C7
Big Run U.S.A. 40°57N 78°55W 312 F6
Big Sable Pt. U.S.A. 44°3N 86°1W 308 C10
Big Salmon → Canada 61°52N 134°55W 296 A2
Big Sand L. Canada 57°45N 99°45W 297 B9
Big Sand Lake U.S.A. 28°25N 81°29W 133 B2
Big Sandy U.S.A. 48°11N 110°7W 304 B8
Big Sandy → U.S.A. 38°25N 82°36W 309 F12
Big Sandy Cr. = Sandy Cr. →
U.S.A. 41°51N 109°47W 304 F9
Big Sandy Cr. →
U.S.A. 38°7N 102°29W 304 G12
Big Satilla Cr. → U.S.A. 31°27N 82°3W 316 D7
Big Sioux → U.S.A. 42°29N 96°27W 308 D5
Big South Fork △
U.S.A. 36°27N 84°47W 315 C12
Big Spring U.S.A. 32°15N 101°28W 314 E4
Big Stone City U.S.A. 45°18N 96°28W 308 C5
Big Stone Gap U.S.A. 36°52N 82°47W 309 G12
Big Stone L. U.S.A. 45°18N 96°27W 308 C5
Big Sur U.S.A. 36°15N 121°48W 306 J5
Big Timber U.S.A. 45°50N 109°57W 304 D9
Big Trout L. Canada 53°40N 90°0W 298 B2
Big Trout Lake Canada 53°45N 90°0W 298 B2
Biğa Turkey 40°13N 27°14E 203 F11
Biga → Turkey 40°20N 27°14E 203 F11
Bigadiç Turkey 39°22N 28°7E 205 B10
Biganos France 44°39N 0°59W 174 D3
Bigeumdo S. Korea 34°45N 126°56E 224 E3
Biggar Sask., Canada 52°4N 108°0W 297 C7
Biggar S. Lanarks., U.K. 55°38N 3°32W 167 F5
Bigge I. Australia 14°35S 125°10E 278 B4
Biggenden Australia 25°31S 152°4E 281 D5
Biggleswade U.K. 52°5N 0°14W 169 E7
Biggs U.S.A. 39°25N 121°43W 306 F5
Bighorn U.S.A. 46°10N 107°27W 304 C10
Bighorn → U.S.A. 46°10N 107°28W 304 C10
Bighorn Canyon △
U.S.A. 45°10N 108°0W 304 D10
Bighorn L. U.S.A. 44°55N 108°15W 304 D9
Bighorn Mts. U.S.A. 44°25N 107°0W 304 D10
Bigi Dem. Rep. of the Congo 3°2N 22°25E 264 B4
Bignona Senegal 12°52N 16°14W 262 C1
Bigorre France 43°10N 0°5E 174 E4
Bigstone L. Canada 53°42N 95°44W 297 C9
Biguglia, Étang de France 42°36N 9°29E 175 F13
Bigwa Tanzania 7°10S 39°10E 268 D4
Bihać Bos.-H. 44°49N 15°57E 199 D12
Bihar India 25°5N 85°40E 243 G11
Bihar □ India 25°0N 86°0E 243 G12
Biharamulo Tanzania 2°25S 31°25E 268 C3
Biharamulo △ Tanzania 2°24S 31°26E 268 C3
Bihariganj India 25°44N 86°59E 243 G12
Biharkeresztes Hungary 47°8N 21°44E 182 C6
Bihor □ Romania 47°0N 22°10E 182 D7
Bihor, Munții Romania 46°29N 22°47E 182 D7
Bijagós, Arquipélago dos
Guinea-Biss. 11°15N 16°10W 262 C1
Bijaipur India 26°2N 77°20E 242 F7
Bijapur Chhattisgarh, India 18°50N 80°50E 244 E5
Bijapur Karnataka, India 16°50N 75°55E 244 F2
Bījār Iran 35°52N 47°35E 213 E12
Bijawar India 24°38N 79°30E 243 G8
Bijbels Museum Amsterdam, Neths. 112 b1
Bijela Montenegro 42°28N 18°39E 202 D2
Bijeljina Bos.-H. 44°46N 19°14E 182 F4
Bijelo Polje Montenegro 43°1N 19°45E 202 C3
Bijie China 27°20N 105°16E 228 D5
Bijnor India 29°27N 78°11E 242 E8
Bikaner India 28°2N 73°18E 242 E5
Bikapur India 26°30N 82°7E 243 F10

Bikeqi China 40°43N 111°20E 226 D6
Bikfayyā Lebanon 33°55N 35°41E 250 E6
Bikié Congo 3°7S 13°52E 264 C2
Bikin Russia 46°50N 134°20E 220 A7
Bikin → Russia 46°51N 134°2E 220 A7
Bikini Atoll Marshall Is. 12°0N 167°30E 288 F8
Bikita Zimbabwe 20°6S 31°41E 271 B5
Bikkū Bīttī Libya 22°0N 19°12E 259 D3
Bikoro
Dem. Rep. of the Congo 0°48S 18°15E 264 C3
Bikoué Cameroon 3°55N 11°50E 263 E7
Bila Tserkva Ukraine 49°45N 30°10E 177 D16
Bilanga Burkina Faso 12°40N 0°1W 263 C4
Bilara India 26°14N 73°53E 242 F5
Bilasipara India 26°13N 90°14E 241 B3
Bilaspur Chhattisgarh, India 22°2N 82°15E 243 H10
Bilaspur Punjab, India 31°19N 76°50E 242 D7
Biläsuvar Azerbaijan 39°27N 48°32E 213 C13
Bilauk Taungdan Thailand 13°0N 99°0E 236 F2
Bilbao Spain 43°16N 2°56W 196 B2
Bilbao ✈ (BIO) Spain 43°18N 2°57W 196 B2
Bilbeis Egypt 30°25N 31°34E 256 H7
Bilbo = Bilbao Spain 43°16N 2°56W 196 B2
Bilbor Romania 47°6N 25°30E 183 C10
Bilche-Zolote Ukraine 48°47N 25°53E 183 B10
Bilciureşti Romania 44°44N 25°48E 183 F10
Bíldudalur Iceland 65°41N 23°36W 155 B3
Bílé Karpaty Europe 49°5N 18°0E 181 B11
Bileća Bos.-H. 42°53N 18°27E 202 D2
Bilecik Turkey 40°5N 30°5E 212 B4
Bilecik ☐ Turkey 40°0N 30°0E 212 B3
Bilećko Jezero Bos.-H. 42°48N 18°28E 202 D2
Bileh Savār Iran 39°21N 48°21E 213 C13
Biłgoraj Poland 50°33N 22°42E 185 H9
Bilgram India 27°11N 80°2E 243 F9
Bilhaur India 26°51N 80°5E 243 F9
Bilhorod-Dnistrovskyy Ukraine 46°11N 30°23E 189 J6
Bili → Dem. Rep. of the Congo 4°9N 22°29E 264 B4
Bilibino Russia 68°3N 166°20E 215 C17
Bilibiza Mozam. 12°30S 40°20E 269 E5
Bilimora India 20°45N 72°57E 244 D1
Bilin Burma 17°14N 97°15E 241 G6
Biliran ☐ Phil. 11°35N 124°28E 233 F5
Bilisht Albania 40°37N 21°2E 202 F5
Billabong Cr. → Australia 35°5S 144°2E 282 C6
Billdal Sweden 57°35N 11°57E 163 G5
Billiluna Australia 19°37S 127°41E 278 C4
Billings U.S.A. 45°47N 108°30W 304 D9
Billiton Is. = Belitung Indonesia 3°10S 107°50E 235 C3
Billsta Sweden 63°20N 18°28E 162 A12
Billund Denmark 55°44N 9°6E 163 J3
Billy Pt. Antigua & B. 17°4N 61°52W 322 c
Bilma Niger 18°50N 13°30E 259 E2
Bilo Gora Croatia 45°53N 17°15E 182 E2
Biloela Australia 24°24S 150°31E 280 C5
Bilohirsk Ukraine 45°3N 34°35E 189 K8
Biloku Guyana 1°50N 58°25W 329 C6
Biloli India 18°46N 77°44E 244 E3
Bilopillya Ukraine 51°14N 34°20E 189 G8
Biloxi U.S.A. 30°24N 88°53W 315 F10
Bilpa Morea Claypan Australia 25°0S 140°0E 280 D3
Bilqās Qism Awwal Egypt 31°12N 31°21E 251 G2
Bilston U.K. 55°52N 3°10W 121 B2
Biltine Chad 14°40N 20°50E 259 F4
Bilugyun Burma 16°24N 97°32E 241 G6
Bilyarsk Russia 54°58N 50°22E 190 C10
Bima Indonesia 8°22S 118°49E 235 D5
Bimban Egypt 24°24N 32°54E 256 C3
Bimbe Angola 11°50S 15°50E 265 E3
Bimberi Pk. Australia 35°44S 148°51E 283 C8
Bimbila Ghana 8°54N 0°5E 263 D5
Bimbini Comoros Is. 12°11S 44°14E 272 a
Bimbo C.A.R. 4°15N 18°33E 264 B3
Bimini Is. Bahamas 25°42N 79°25W 320 A4
Bin Ghunaymah, Jabal Libya 25°0N 15°30E 258 D3
Bin Jawwād Libya 30°47N 18°4E 258 B3
Bin Xian Heilongjiang, China 45°42N 127°32E 227 B14
Bin Xian Shaanxi, China 35°2N 108°4E 226 G5
Bin Yauri Nigeria 10°46N 4°45E 263 C5
Bina-Etawah India 24°13N 78°14E 242 G8
Binacayan Phil. 14°27N 120°55E 127 C1
Binalbagan Phil. 10°12N 122°50E 233 F4
Binalong Australia 34°40S 148°39E 283 C8
Bīnālūd, Kūh-e Iran 36°30N 58°30E 247 B8
Binangonan de Lampon = Infanta Phil. 14°45N 121°39E 232 D3
Binatang = Bintangau Malaysia 2°10N 111°40E 235 B4
Binche Belgium 50°26N 4°10E 170 D4
Binchuan China 25°42N 100°38E 228 E3
Binda Dem. Rep. of the Congo 5°52S 13°14E 265 D2
Binder Chad 9°56N 14°27E 259 G2
Bindki India 26°2N 80°36E 243 F9
Bindloe, I. = Marchena, I. Ecuador 0°19N 90°29W 330 a
Bindoy Phil. 9°48N 123°5E 233 G4
Bindslev Denmark 57°33N 10°11E 163 G4
Bindura Zimbabwe 17°18S 31°18E 269 F3
Binéfar Spain 41°51N 0°18E 196 D5
Bingara Australia 29°52S 150°36E 281 D5
Bingaram I. India 10°56N 72°17E 245 J1
Bingen Germany 49°57N 7°55E 179 F3
Bingerau = Węgrów Poland 52°24N 22°0E 185 F9
Bingerville Ivory C. 5°18N 3°49W 262 D4
Bingham U.S.A. 45°3N 69°53W 309 C19
Binghamton U.S.A. 42°6N 75°55W 313 D9
Bingo-Ochiai Japan 34°59N 133°8E 222 C4
Bingöl Turkey 38°53N 40°29E 213 C9
Bingöl ☐ Turkey 38°55N 40°30E 213 C9
Bingöl Dağları Turkey 39°16N 41°9E 213 C9
Bingsjö Sweden 61°1N 15°39E 162 C9
Binh Dinh = An Nhon Vietnam 13°55N 109°7E 236 F7
Binh Khe Vietnam 13°57N 108°51E 236 F7
Binh Son Vietnam 15°20N 108°40E 236 E7
Binhai China 34°2N 119°49E 227 G10
Bini Erde Chad 20°6N 18°1E 259 D3
Binic France 48°46N 2°50W 172 D4
Binisatua Spain 39°50N 4°11E 206 B5
Binissalem Spain 39°41N 2°50E 206 B3
Binjai Indonesia 3°20N 98°30E 234 B1
Binji Nigeria 13°10N 4°55E 263 C5
Binka India 21°2N 83°48E 244 D6
Binnah, Ras Somali Rep. 11°9N 51°10E 267 B7
Binnaway Australia 31°28S 149°24E 283 A8
Binondo Phil. 14°36N 120°58E 127 B1
Binongko Indonesia 5°57S 124°2E 231 F6
Binscarth Canada 50°37N 101°17W 297 C8
Binshangul Gumuz ☐ Ethiopia 11°0N 35°30E 257 E4
Bint Goda Sudan 13°17N 31°33E 257 E3
Bintan Indonesia 1°0N 104°0E 234 B2
Bintangau Malaysia 2°10N 111°40E 235 B4
Bintaro Jaya Indonesia 6°16S 106°44E 122 B1
Bintulu Malaysia 3°10N 113°0E 235 B4
Bintuni Indonesia 2°7S 133°32E 231 E8
Binyang China 23°12N 108°47E 228 F7
Binz Germany 54°24N 13°35E 178 A9
Binza Dem. Rep. of the Congo 4°21S 15°14E 265 C3
Binzert = Bizerte Tunisia 37°15N 9°50E 258 A1
Binzhou China 37°20N 118°2E 227 F10
Bío Bío ☐ Chile 37°35S 72°0W 334 D1
Biobío → Chile 36°49S 73°10W 334 D1
Biograd na Moru Croatia 43°56N 15°29E 199 E12
Biogradska Gora △ Montenegro 42°55N 19°40E 202 D3
Bioko Eq. Guin. 3°30N 8°40E 263 E6
Biokovo Croatia 43°23N 17°0E 199 E14
Biougra Morocco 30°15N 9°14W 260 B3
Bipindi Cameroon 3°6N 10°30E 263 E7
Bir India 19°4N 75°46E 244 E2
Bir, Ras Djibouti 12°0N 43°20E 257 E5
Bîr Abu Hashim Egypt 23°42N 34°6E 256 C3
Bîr Abu Minqar Egypt 26°33N 27°33E 256 B2
Bîr Abu Muḥammad Egypt 29°44N 34°14E 251 J5
Bîr Abu Sandûq Egypt 29°24N 32°30E 251 J3
Bîr Adal Deib Sudan 22°35N 36°10E 256 C4
Bi'r al Butayyihāt Jordan 29°47N 35°20E 251 J6
Bi'r al Ḥamḍah Si. Arabia 28°30N 34°55E 251 K5
Bi'r al Mārī Jordan 30°4N 35°33E 251 H6
Bi'r al Musallam Si. Arabia 28°56N 35°38E 251 K6
Bi'r al Qattār Jordan 29°47N 35°32E 251 J6
Bir 'Ali Yemen 14°1N 48°20E 249 D5
Bîr 'Amrâne Mauritania 22°45N 8°39W 260 D3
Bir Aouine Tunisia 32°25N 9°18E 258 B1
Bîr 'Asal Egypt 25°55N 34°20E 256 B3
Bi'r ash Shakkūsīyah Syria 35°23N 37°26E 250 C8
Bir Atrun Sudan 18°15N 26°40E 256 D2
Bîr Beiḍa Egypt 30°25N 34°29E 251 H5
Bîr Bel Guerdâne Mauritania 25°24N 10°31W 260 C2
Bîr Bireida Egypt 29°8N 32°7E 251 J3
Bîr Buerât Egypt 28°59N 32°11E 251 K3
Bi'r Dhu'fān Libya 31°59N 14°32E 258 B2
Bîr Di Sudan 7°34N 28°49E 257 F2
Bîr Diqnash Egypt 31°3N 25°23E 256 A2
Bîr el 'Abbes Algeria 26°7N 6°9W 260 C3
Bîr el 'Abd Egypt 31°2N 33°0E 251 G4
Bîr el 'Agramîya Egypt 29°38N 31°50E 251 J2
Bir el Ater Algeria 34°46N 8°3E 261 B6
Bîr el Basur Egypt 29°51N 25°49E 256 B2
Bîr el Biarât Egypt 29°30N 34°43E 251 J5
Bîr el Dakhal Egypt 28°39N 32°23E 251 K3
Bîr el Duweidar Egypt 30°56N 32°32E 251 H3
Bîr el Garârât Egypt 31°3N 33°34E 251 G4
Bîr el Gâreb Mauritania 20°33N 16°12W 260 D1
Bîr el Gellaz Egypt 30°50N 26°40E 256 A2
Bîr el Ghamr Egypt 28°43N 31°20E 251 K2
Bîr el Heisi Egypt 29°22N 34°36E 251 J5
Bîr el Jafir Egypt 30°50N 32°41E 251 H3
Bîr el Mâlḥi Egypt 30°38N 33°19E 251 H4
Bîr el Manâyif Egypt 30°31N 32°12E 251 H3
Bîr el-Naṣb Egypt 29°3N 33°2E 251 J4
Bîr el Şafra Egypt 28°45N 34°21E 251 K5
Bîr el-Saura Egypt 29°9N 34°30E 251 J5
Bîr el Shaqqa Egypt 30°54N 25°1E 256 A2
Bîr el Thamâda Egypt 30°12N 33°27E 251 H4
Bir Enzarán W. Sahara 23°53N 14°32W 260 D2
Bîr Fuad Egypt 30°35N 26°28E 256 A2
Bîr Gandús W. Sahara 21°36N 16°30W 260 D1
Bîr Gebeil Ḥiṣn Egypt 30°2N 33°18E 251 H4
Bi'r Ghadīr Syria 34°6N 37°3E 250 D8
Bîr Ghalla Egypt 28°23N 32°19E 251 K3
Bi'r Gharr Si. Arabia 28°7N 35°32E 251 K6
Bîr Gindali Egypt 29°55N 31°40E 251 J2
Bîr Haimur Egypt 22°45N 33°40E 256 C3
Bîr Ḥasana Egypt 30°29N 33°46E 251 H4
Bîr Hôôker Egypt 30°22N 30°21E 256 H7
Bi'r Idimah Si. Arabia 18°31N 44°12E 248 C4
Bi'r Jadīd Si. Arabia 28°10N 35°6E 251 J6
Bir Jdid Morocco 33°26N 8°0W 260 B3
Bîr Kanayis Egypt 24°59N 33°15E 256 C3
Bîr Kaseiba Egypt 31°0N 33°17E 251 H4
Bir Kerawein Egypt 27°10N 28°25E 256 B2
Bîr Lahfân Egypt 31°0N 33°51E 251 H4
Bir Lahrache Algeria 32°1N 8°12E 261 B6
Bîr Madkûr Egypt 30°44N 32°33E 251 H3
Bîr Maql Egypt 23°7N 33°40E 256 C3
Bîr Mîneiga Sudan 22°47N 35°12E 256 C4
Bîr Misaha Egypt 22°13N 27°59E 256 C2
Bir Mogreïn Mauritania 25°10N 11°25W 260 C2
Bîr Mureir Egypt 28°25N 31°15E 251 K2
Bîr Murr Egypt 23°28N 30°10E 256 C3
Bi'r Muṭribah Kuwait 29°54N 47°17E 246 D5
Bîr Nabala West Bank 31°51N 35°12E 123 A2
Bîr Nakheila Egypt 24°1N 30°50E 256 C3
Bîr Nakhul Egypt 29°5N 33°16E 251 J4
Bîr Qaṭia Egypt 30°58N 32°45E 251 H3
Bîr Qatrani Egypt 30°55N 26°10E 256 A2
Bîr Ranga Egypt 24°25N 35°15E 256 C4
Bîr Sahara Egypt 22°54N 28°40E 256 C2
Bîr Sa'id Egypt 29°38N 31°24E 251 J2
Bîr Seiyâla Egypt 26°10N 33°50E 256 B3
Bîr Shalatein Egypt 23°5N 35°25E 256 C4
Bîr Shebb Egypt 22°25N 29°40E 256 C2
Bîr Shût Egypt 23°50N 35°15E 256 C4
Bîr Sidri Egypt 28°53N 33°28E 251 K4
Bîr Tâba Egypt 29°29N 34°53E 251 J5
Bîr Terfawi Egypt 22°57N 28°55E 256 C2
Bi'r Tin Abunda Libya 26°28N 12°27E 261 C7
Bîr Umm Qubûr Egypt 24°35N 34°2E 256 C3
Bîr Ungât Egypt 22°8N 33°48E 256 C3
Bîr Wuseit Egypt 29°14N 33°1E 251 J4
Bîr Za'farâna Egypt 29°10N 32°40E 256 J8
Bîr Zeidûn Egypt 25°45N 33°40E 256 B3
Birāk Libya 27°31N 14°20E 258 C2
Birak el Kiyam Egypt 30°2N 31°9E 117 A1
Biramféro Guinea 11°40N 9°10W 262 C3
Birao C.A.R. 10°20N 22°47E 264 A4
Biratnagar Nepal 26°27N 87°17E 243 F12
Birawa Dem. Rep. of the Congo 2°20S 28°48E 268 C2
Birch → Canada 58°28N 112°17W 296 B6
Birch Cliff Canada 43°41N 79°16W 141 A3
Birch Grove Grenada 12°6N 61°40W 323 q
Birch Hills Canada 52°59N 105°25W 297 C7
Birch I. Canada 52°26N 99°54W 297 C9
Birch L. N.W.T., Canada 62°4N 116°33W 296 A5
Birch L. Ont., Canada 51°23N 92°18W 298 B1
Birch Mts. Canada 57°30N 113°10W 296 B6
Birch River Canada 52°24N 101°6W 297 C8
Birchip Australia 35°56S 142°55E 282 C5
Birchiş Romania 45°58N 22°9E 182 E7
Birchwood N.Z. 45°55S 167°53E 285 F2
Birchwood Alaska, U.S.A. 61°24N 149°28W 303 F10
Bird Canada 56°30N 94°13W 297 B10
Bird I. = Aves, I. de W. Indies 15°45N 63°55W 321 C7
Bird I. S. Georgia 54°0S 38°3W 151 B1
Bird Rock Canada 45°6N 77°52W 312 A7
Birdseye U.S.A. 38°19N 86°42W 311 F10
Birdsville Australia 25°51S 139°20E 280 D2
Birdum Cr. → Australia 15°14S 133°0E 278 C5
Birdwood Australia 34°51S 138°58E 282 C3
Birecik Turkey 37°2N 38°0E 213 D8
Bireun Indonesia 5°14N 96°39E 234 A1
Birein Israel 30°50N 34°28E 251 H5
Birgu = Vittoriosa Malta 35°54N 14°31E 206 F8
Birhan Ethiopia 10°45N 38°4E 266 B4
Biri Norway 60°58N 10°35E 164 D7
Biri → Sudan 7°56N 26°33E 257 F2
Birifo Gambia 13°30N 14°0W 262 C2
Birigüi Brazil 21°18S 50°16W 335 A5
Birini C.A.R. 7°51N 22°24E 264 A4
Bīrjand Iran 32°53N 59°13E 247 C8
Birkeland Norway 58°24N 7°12E 164 F4
Birkenfeld Germany 49°38N 7°9E 179 F3
Birkenhead U.K. 53°23N 3°2W 168 D4
Birkenstein Germany 52°31N 13°40E 115 A5
Birkerød Denmark 55°50N 12°25E 163 J6
Birket Fatmé Chad 12°55N 19°7E 259 F3
Birket Qârûn Egypt 29°30N 30°40E 256 J7
Birkfeld Austria 47°21N 15°45E 180 D8
Birkhadem Algeria 36°43N 3°3E 261 A5
Birkholz Germany 52°37N 13°34E 115 A4
Birkholzaue Germany 52°38N 13°36E 115 A4
Birkirkara Malta 35°54N 14°28E 206 F7
Bîrlad = Bârlad Romania 46°15N 27°38E 183 D12
Birmingham W. Mids., U.K. 52°29N 1°52W 169 E6
Birmingham Ala., U.S.A. 33°31N 86°48W 315 E11
Birmingham Iowa, U.S.A. 40°53N 91°57W 310 D5
Birmingham Int. ✈ (BHX) U.K. 52°26N 1°45W 169 E6
Birmitrapur India 22°24N 84°46E 244 C7
Birni Ngaouré Niger 13°5N 2°51E 263 C5
Birni Nkonni Niger 13°55N 5°15E 263 C6
Birnie Kiribati 3°35S 171°31W 277 A16
Birnin Gwari Nigeria 11°0N 6°45E 263 C6
Birnin Kebbi Nigeria 12°32N 4°12E 263 C5
Birnin Kudu Nigeria 11°30N 9°29E 263 C6
Birobidzhan Russia 48°50N 132°50E 215 E14
Birougou, Mts. Gabon 1°51S 12°20E 264 C2
Birr Ireland 53°6N 7°54W 166 C4
Birrarrung Park Australia 37°45S 145°4E 128 A2
Birrie → Australia 29°43S 146°37E 281 D4
Birsilpur India 28°11N 72°15E 242 E5
Birsk Russia 55°25N 55°30E 186 C10
Birštonas Lithuania 54°37N 24°2E 184 D11
Birtle Canada 50°30N 101°5W 297 C8
Biryuchiy Ukraine 46°10N 35°0E 189 J8
Biržai Lithuania 56°11N 24°45E 188 D3
Birzebbugga Malta 35°50N 14°32E 206 F8
Birzhi = Madona Latvia 56°53N 26°5E 188 D4
Birzula = Kotovsk Ukraine 47°45N 29°35E 177 E15
Bisa Indonesia 1°15S 127°28E 231 E7
Bisáccia Italy 41°1N 15°22E 201 A8
Bisacquino Italy 37°42N 13°15E 200 E6
Bisai Japan 35°16N 136°44E 223 B8
Bisalpur India 28°14N 79°48E 243 E8
Bisbee U.S.A. 31°27N 109°55W 305 L9
Biscarrosse France 44°22N 1°20W 174 D2
Biscarrosse et de Parentis, Étang de France 44°21N 1°10W 174 D2
Biscay, B. of Atl. Oc. 45°0N 2°0W 171 D1
Biscay Abyssal Plain Atl. Oc. 45°0N 8°0W 152 B11
Biscayne ⌂ U.S.A. 25°25N 80°12W 317 K9
Biscayne B. U.S.A. 25°40N 80°12W 317 K9
Biscayne Park U.S.A. 25°52N 80°10W 128 A2
Biscéglie Italy 41°14N 16°30E 201 A9
Bischheim France 48°37N 7°46E 173 D14
Bischoflack = Škofja Loka Slovenia 46°9N 14°19E 199 B11
Bischofsburg = Biskupiec Poland 53°53N 20°58E 184 E7
Bischofshofen Austria 47°26N 13°14E 180 D6
Bischofstal = Ujazd Poland 50°23N 18°21E 185 H5
Bischofstein = Bisztynek Poland 54°8N 20°53E 184 D7
Bischofswerda Germany 51°7N 14°10E 178 D10
Bischwiller France 48°46N 7°50E 173 D14
Biscoe Is. Antarctica 66°0S 67°0W 151 C17
Biscoitos Azores 38°47N 27°15W 153 d1
Biscotasing Canada 47°18N 82°9W 298 C3
Biševo Croatia 42°57N 16°3E 199 F13
Bisha Eritrea 15°30N 37°31E 257 D4
Bishah, W. → Si. Arabia 21°24N 43°26E 248 B3
Bishan China 29°33N 106°12E 228 C6
Bishanga Dem. Rep. of the Congo 4°31S 21°2E 265 C4
Bishkek Kyrgyzstan 42°54N 74°46E 214 E8
Bishnath India 26°40N 93°10E 241 B4
Bishnupur India 23°8N 87°20E 243 H12
Bisho = Bhisho S. Africa 32°50S 27°23E 270 D4
Bishop Calif., U.S.A. 37°22N 118°24W 306 H8
Bishop Ga., U.S.A. 33°49N 83°26W 316 B6
Bishop Tex., U.S.A. 27°35N 97°48W 314 H6
Bishop Auckland U.K. 54°39N 1°40W 168 C6
Bishop Lavis S. Africa 33°56S 18°35E 118 A2
Bishop Museum U.S.A. 21°20N 157°52W 302 K14
Bishop's Falls Canada 49°2N 55°30W 299 C8
Bishop's Stortford U.K. 51°52N 0°10E 169 F8
Bishopscourt S. Africa 33°59S 18°27E 118 A1
Bisignano Italy 39°31N 16°17E 201 C9
Bisina, L. Uganda 1°38N 33°56E 268 B3
Biskra Algeria 34°50N 5°44E 261 B6
Biskra Malta 35°58N 14°21E 206 F7
Biskra ☐ Algeria 34°40N 5°25E 261 B6
Biskupiec Poland 53°53N 20°58E 184 E7
Bismarck Mo., U.S.A. 37°46N 90°38W 310 G6
Bismarck N. Dak., U.S.A. 46°48N 100°47W 308 B3
Bismarck Arch. Papua N. G. 2°30S 150°0E 286 B6
Bismarck Ra. Papua N. G. 5°35S 145°0E 286 C3
Bismarck Sea Papua N. G. 4°10S 146°50E 286 C4
Bismarckburg = Kasanga Tanzania 8°30S 31°10E 269 D3
Bismark Germany 52°40N 11°33E 178 C7
Bismil Turkey 37°51N 40°40E 213 D9
Bismo Norway 61°54N 8°15E 164 C5
Biso Uganda 1°44N 31°26E 268 B3
Bison U.S.A. 45°31N 102°28W 308 C2
Bīsotūn Iran 34°23N 47°26E 213 E12
Bispebjerg Denmark 55°42N 12°31E 118 A3
Bispgården Sweden 63°2N 16°40E 162 A10
Bissagos = Bijagós, Arquipélago dos Guinea-Biss. 11°15N 16°10W 262 C1
Bissam Cuttack India 19°31N 83°31E 244 E6
Bissau Guinea-Biss. 11°45N 15°45W 262 C1
Bissaula Nigeria 7°0N 10°27E 263 D7
Bissigh, Lach → Somali Rep. 0°45N 41°33E 267 D5
Bissikrima Guinea 10°50N 10°58W 262 C2
Bissonet Plaza U.S.A. 30°1N 90°13W 131 A1
Bissorã Guinea-Biss. 12°16N 15°35W 262 C1
Bistcho L. Canada 59°45N 118°50W 296 B5
Bistreţ Romania 43°54N 23°23E 183 G8
Bistrica = Ilirska-Bistrica Slovenia 45°34N 14°14E 199 C11
Bistriţa Romania 47°9N 24°35E 183 C9
Bistriţa → Romania 46°30N 26°57E 183 D11
Bistriţa Năsăud ☐ Romania 47°15N 24°30E 183 C9
Bistriţei, Munţii Romania 47°15N 25°40E 183 C10
Biswan India 27°29N 81°2E 243 F9
Bisztynek Poland 54°8N 20°53E 184 D7
Bita → C.A.R. 6°26N 24°43E 264 A4
Bitam Gabon 2°5N 11°25E 264 B2
Bitburg Germany 49°58N 6°31E 179 F2
Bitche France 49°2N 7°25E 173 C14
Bithynia Turkey 40°40N 31°0E 212 B4
Bitkine Chad 11°59N 18°13E 259 F3
Bitlis Turkey 38°20N 42°3E 213 C10
Bitlis ☐ Turkey 38°20N 42°5E 213 C10
Bitola Macedonia 41°1N 21°20E 202 E5
Bitolj = Bitola Macedonia 41°1N 21°20E 202 E5
Bitonto Italy 41°6N 16°41E 201 A9
Bitra I. India 11°33N 72°9E 245 J1
Bitter Creek U.S.A. 41°33N 108°33W 304 F9
Bitter L. = Buheirat-Murrat-el-Kubra Egypt 30°18N 32°26E 256 H8
Bitterfeld Germany 51°37N 12°20E 178 D8
Bitterfontein S. Africa 31°1S 18°32E 270 D2
Bitterroot → U.S.A. 46°52N 114°7W 304 C6
Bitterroot Range U.S.A. 46°0N 114°20W 304 D6
Bitterwater U.S.A. 36°23N 121°0W 306 J6
Bitti Italy 40°29N 9°23E 200 B2
Bittou Burkina Faso 11°17N 0°18W 263 C4
Biu Nigeria 10°40N 12°3E 263 C7
Bivolari Romania 47°31N 27°27E 183 C12
Bivolu, Vf. Romania 47°16N 25°58E 183 C10
Biwa-Ko Japan 35°15N 136°10E 223 B8
Biwabik U.S.A. 47°32N 92°21W 308 B7
Bixad Romania 47°56N 23°28E 183 C8
Bixby U.S.A. 35°57N 95°53W 314 D7
Biya → Russia 52°25N 85°0E 217 B11
Biyala Egypt 31°10N 31°13E 251 G2
Biyang China 32°38N 113°21E 226 H7
Biysk Russia 52°40N 85°0E 217 B11
Bizana S. Africa 30°50S 29°52E 271 D4
Bizen Japan 34°43N 134°8E 222 C6
Bizerte Tunisia 37°15N 9°50E 258 A1
Bizerte ☐ Tunisia 37°5N 9°25E 261 A6
Bjåen fjellstove Norway 59°37N 7°26E 164 E4
Bjargtangar Iceland 65°30N 24°30W 155 B2
Bjarkalundur Iceland 65°33N 22°9W 155 B4
Bjärnum Sweden 56°17N 13°43E 163 H7
Bjästa Sweden 63°12N 18°29E 162 A12
Bjelasica Montenegro 42°50N 19°40E 202 D3
Bjelašnica Bos.-H. 43°43N 18°9E 182 G3
Bjelland Norway 58°23N 7°32E 164 F4
Bjelovar Croatia 45°56N 16°49E 199 C13
Bjerringbro Denmark 56°23N 9°39E 163 H3
Bjervamoen Norway 59°17N 9°5E 164 E6
Bjøberg Norway 60°56N 8°13E 164 D5
Björbo Sweden 60°27N 14°44E 162 D8
Bjørkelangen Norway 59°53N 11°34E 164 E8
Björklinge Sweden 60°2N 17°33E 162 D11
Björknäs Sweden 59°19N 18°12E 139 B3
Bjørnafjorden Norway 60°7N 5°28E 164 D2
Björneborg = Pori Finland 61°29N 21°48E 188 B1
Björneborg Sweden 59°14N 14°16E 162 E8
Bjørnevatn Norway 69°40N 30°0E 160 B24
Bjørnøya Arctic 74°30N 19°0E 150 B8
Björsäs Sweden 60°44N 15°25E 162 D9
Bjuv Sweden 56°5N 12°55E 163 H6
Bla Mali 12°56N 5°47W 262 C3
Blå Jungfrun Sweden 57°16N 16°47E 163 G10
Blace Serbia 43°18N 21°17E 202 C5
Blachownia Poland 50°49N 18°56E 185 H5
Black = Da → Vietnam 21°15N 105°20E 228 G5
Black → Ont., Canada 44°42N 79°19W 312 B5
Black → Alaska, U.S.A. 66°42N 144°42W 303 C11
Black → Ariz., U.S.A. 33°44N 110°13W 305 K8
Black → Ark., U.S.A. 35°38N 91°20W 314 D9
Black → La., U.S.A. 31°16N 91°50W 314 F9
Black → Mich., U.S.A. 42°59N 82°27W 312 D2
Black → N.Y., U.S.A. 43°59N 76°4W 313 C8
Black → Wis., U.S.A. 43°57N 91°22W 308 D8
Black Bay Pen. Canada 48°38N 88°21W 298 C2
Black Birch L. Canada 56°53N 107°45W 297 B7
Black Canyon of the Gunnison ⌂ U.S.A. 38°40N 107°35W 304 G10
Black Cr. → Canada 43°40N 79°30W 141 A2
Black Creek Pioneer Village Canada 43°46N 79°30W 141 A1
Black Diamond = Pittsburg U.S.A. 38°2N 121°53W 306 G5
Black Diamond Canada 50°45N 114°14W 296 C6
Black Duck → Canada 56°51N 89°2W 298 A2
Black Forest = Schwarzwald Germany 48°30N 8°20E 179 G4
Black Forest U.S.A. 39°0N 104°43W 304 G11
Black Hd. Ireland 53°9N 9°16W 166 C2
Black Hills U.S.A. 44°0N 103°45W 308 D2
Black I. Canada 51°12N 96°30W 297 C9
Black L. Sask., Canada 59°12N 105°15W 297 B7
Black L. Mich., U.S.A. 45°28N 84°16W 309 C11
Black L. N.Y., U.S.A. 44°31N 75°36W 313 B9
Black Lake Canada 59°11N 105°20W 297 B7
Black Mesa U.S.A. 36°58N 102°58W 314 C3
Black Mountain Australia 30°18S 151°39E 283 A9
Black Mt. = Mynydd Du U.K. 51°52N 3°50W 169 F4
Black Mt. Bhutan 27°20N 90°25E 241 B3
Black Mts. U.K. 51°55N 3°7W 169 F4
Black Range U.S.A. 33°15N 107°50W 305 K10
Black River Jamaica 18°0N 77°50W 320 a
Black River N.Y., U.S.A. 44°0N 75°47W 313 C9
Black River B. Jamaica 18°0N 77°51W 320 a
Black River Falls U.S.A. 44°18N 90°51W 308 C8
Black River Gorges Mauritius 20°24S 57°25E 272 e
Black Rock S. Austral., Australia 32°50S 138°44E 282 B3
Black Rock Barbados 13°7N 59°37W 323 r
Black Rock Desert U.S.A. 41°10N 118°50W 304 F4
Black Sea Eurasia 43°30N 35°0E 187 F6
Black Tickle Canada 53°28N 55°45W 299 B8
Black Volta → Africa 8°41N 1°33W 262 D4
Black Warrior → U.S.A. 32°32N 87°51W 315 E11
Blackall Australia 24°25S 145°45E 280 C4
Blackball N.Z. 42°22S 171°26E 285 C6
Blackbraes △ Australia 19°10S 144°10E 280 B3
Blackbull Australia 17°55S 141°45E 280 B3
Blackburn U.K. 53°45N 2°29W 168 D5
Blackburn, Mt. U.S.A. 61°44N 143°26W 303 F12
Blackburn with Darwen ☐ U.K. 53°45N 2°29W 168 D5
Blackdown Tableland △ Australia 23°52S 149°8E 280 C4
Blackfen U.K. 51°26N 0°6E 125 B4
Blackfoot U.S.A. 43°11N 112°21W 304 E7
Blackfoot → U.S.A. 46°52N 113°53W 304 C7
Blackfoot Res. U.S.A. 42°55N 111°39W 304 E8
Blackheath U.K. 51°28N 0°0 125 B4
Blackman U.S.A. 30°56N 86°38W 317 E3
Blackpool U.K. 53°49N 3°3W 168 D4
Blackpool ☐ U.K. 53°49N 3°3W 168 D4
Blackriver U.S.A. 44°46N 83°17W 312 B1
Blackrock Ireland 53°18N 6°11W 120 B2
Blacks Harbour Canada 45°3N 66°49W 299 C6
Blacksburg U.S.A. 37°14N 80°25W 309 G13
Blackshear U.S.A. 31°18N 82°14W 316 D7
Blackshear, L. U.S.A. 31°51N 83°56W 316 D6
Blacksod B. Ireland 54°6N 10°0W 166 B1
Blackstairs Mt. Ireland 52°33N 6°48W 166 D5
Blackstone U.S.A. 37°5N 78°0W 309 G14
Blackstone Ra. Australia 26°0S 128°30E 279 E4
Blackville U.S.A. 33°22N 81°16W 316 B8
Blackwater = West Road → Canada 53°18N 122°53W 296 C4
Blackwater Australia 23°35S 148°53E 280 C4
Blackwater → Meath, Ireland 53°39N 6°41W 166 C4
Blackwater → Waterford, Ireland 52°4N 7°52W 166 D4
Blackwater → Armagh, U.K. 54°31N 6°35W 166 B5
Blackwater → Fla., U.S.A. 30°36N 87°2W 317 E2
Blackwater → Mo., U.S.A. 38°56N 92°57W 310 F4
Blackwell U.S.A. 36°48N 97°17W 314 C6
Blackwells Corner U.S.A. 35°37N 119°47W 307 K7
Blackwood, C. Papua N. G. 7°49S 144°31E 286 D3
Bladensburg U.S.A. 38°55N 76°55W 143 B4
Bladensburg △ Australia 22°30S 142°59E 280 C3
Blaenau Ffestiniog U.K. 53°0N 3°56W 168 E4
Blaenau Gwent ☐ U.K. 51°48N 3°12W 169 F4
Bláfell Iceland 64°30N 19°51W 155 C7
Bláfjall Iceland 65°26N 16°50W 155 B10
Blagaj Bos.-H. 43°16N 17°55E 202 C1
Blagnac France 43°37N 1°23E 174 E5
Blagnac, Toulouse ✈ (TLS) France 43°37N 1°22E 174 E5
Blagodarnoye = Blagodarnyy Russia 45°7N 43°37E 191 H6
Blagodarnyy Russia 45°7N 43°37E 191 H6
Blagoevgrad Bulgaria 42°2N 23°5E 202 D7
Blagoveshchensk Russia 50°20N 127°30E 215 D13
Blahkiuh Indonesia 8°31S 115°12E 231 J18
Blain Loire-Atlantique, France 47°29N 1°45W 172 E5
Blain Pa., U.S.A. 40°20N 77°31W 312 F7
Blaine Minn., U.S.A. 45°10N 93°13W 308 C7
Blaine Wash., U.S.A. 48°59N 122°45W 306 B4
Blaine Lake Canada 52°51N 106°52W 297 C7
Blair U.S.A. 41°33N 96°8W 308 E5
Blair Athol Australia 22°42S 147°31E 280 C4
Blair Atholl U.K. 56°46N 3°50W 167 E5
Blair Village U.S.A. 33°40N 84°23W 113 C2
Blairgowrie Gauteng, S. Africa 26°6S 28°0E 123 A2
Blairgowrie Perth & Kinr., U.K. 56°35N 3°21W 167 E5
Blairsden U.S.A. 39°47N 120°37W 306 F6
Blairsville U.S.A. 40°26N 79°16W 312 F5
Blaj Romania 46°10N 23°57E 183 D8
Blaka Niger 21°21N 12°47E 259 D2
Blakang Mati, Pulau Singapore 1°15N 103°50E 237 d
Blake House U.S.A. 42°19N 71°3W 116 B2
Blake Pt. U.S.A. 48°11N 88°25W 308 A9
Blakehurst Australia 33°59S 151°6E 139 B1
Blakely Ga., U.S.A. 31°23N 84°56W 316 D5
Blakely Pa., U.S.A. 41°28N 75°37W 313 E9
Blakeney Australia 40°58N 92°38W 310 D4
Blakstad Akershus, Norway 59°49N 10°28E 133 B1
Blakstad Aust-Agder, Norway 58°30N 8°39E 164 F5
Blâmont France 48°35N 6°50E 173 D13
Blanc, C. Spain 39°21N 2°51E 206 B3
Blanc, C. Tunisia 37°15N 9°56E 258 A1
Blanc, Mont Europe 45°48N 6°50E 175 C10
Blanca, B. Argentina 39°10S 61°30W 336 A4
Blanca Peak U.S.A. 37°35N 105°29W 305 H11
Blanchardville U.S.A. 42°49N 89°52W 310 B7
Blanche, C. Australia 33°1S 134°9E 281 E1
Blanche, L. S. Austral., Australia 29°15S 139°40E 281 D2
Blanche, L. W. Austral., Australia 22°25S 123°17E 278 D3
Blanche, L. Fla., U.S.A. 28°28N 81°30W 133 B1
Blanche, Pte. St. Lucia 13°53N 61°5W 323 m
Blanche, Pte. St.-Maarten 18°0N 63°2W 322 a
Blanche Channel Solomon Is. 8°30S 157°30E 287 M9
Blanchester U.S.A. 39°17N 83°59W 311 E13
Blanchisseuse Trin. & Tob. 10°48N 61°18W 323 t
Blanco Western Cape, S. Africa 33°55S 22°23E 270 D3
Blanco Tex., U.S.A. 30°6N 98°25W 314 F5
Blanco → Argentina 30°20S 68°42W 334 C2
Blanco → Bolivia 12°30S 64°18W 331 C5
Blanco, C. Costa Rica 9°34N 85°8W 320 E2
Blanco, C. Oreg., U.S.A. 42°51N 124°34W 304 E1
Blanco, Pta. Neth. Ant. 12°13N 68°14W 322 h
Blandford Forum U.K. 50°51N 2°9W 169 G5
Blanding U.S.A. 37°37N 109°29W 305 H9
Blandinsville U.S.A. 40°33N 90°52W 310 D6
Blanes Spain 41°40N 2°48E 196 D7
Blangy-sur-Bresle France 49°55N 1°37E 173 C8
Blanice → Czech Rep. 49°10N 14°5E 180 B7
Blankaholm Sweden 57°36N 16°31E 163 G10
Blankenberge Belgium 51°20N 3°9E 170 C3
Blankenburg Berlin, Germany 52°35N 13°27E 115 A3
Blankenburg Sachsen-Anhalt, Germany 51°47N 10°57E 178 D6
Blankenfelde Germany 52°37N 13°23E 115 A3
Blanquefort France 44°55N 0°38W 174 D3
Blanquilla Venezuela 11°51N 64°37W 321 D7
Blanquillo Uruguay 32°53S 55°37W 335 C4
Blansko Czech Rep. 49°22N 16°40E 181 B9
Blantyre Malawi 15°45S 35°0E 269 F4
Blarney Ireland 51°56N 8°33W 166 E3
Blasdell U.S.A. 42°48N 78°50W 312 D6
Blåsjø Norway 59°20N 6°50E 164 E3
Błaszki Poland 51°38N 18°30E 185 G5
Blatná Czech Rep. 49°25N 13°52E 180 B6
Blato Croatia 42°56N 16°48E 199 F13
Blaubeuren Germany 48°24N 9°46E 179 G5
Blaustein Germany 48°25N 9°53E 179 G5
Blåvands Huk Denmark 55°33N 8°4E 163 J2
Blaydon U.K. 54°58N 1°42W 168 C6
Blaye France 45°8N 0°40W 174 C3
Blaye-les-Mines France 44°1N 2°8E 174 D6
Blayney Australia 33°32S 149°14E 283 B8
Blaze, Pt. Australia 12°56S 130°11E 278 B5
Błażowa Poland 49°53N 22°7E 185 J9
Blechhammer = Blachownia Poland 50°49N 18°56E 185 H5
Bleckede Germany 53°17N 10°43E 178 B6
Bled Slovenia 46°27N 14°7E 199 B11
Blefjell Norway 59°48N 9°10E 164 E6
Bleiburg Austria 46°35N 14°49E 180 E7
Blejeşti Romania 44°19N 25°27E 183 F10
Blekinge Sweden 56°25N 15°20E 161 H16
Blekinge län ☐ Sweden 56°20N 15°20E 163 H9
Blenheim Ont., Canada 42°20N 82°0W 312 D3
Blenheim N.Z. 41°38S 173°57E 285 B8
Bléone → France 44°5N 6°0E 175 D10
Blérancourt France 49°31N 3°9E 173 C10
Bletchley U.K. 51°59N 0°44W 169 F7
Bleus, Monts Dem. Rep. of the Congo 1°30N 30°30E 268 B3
Blida Algeria 36°30N 2°49E 261 A5
Blida ☐ Algeria 36°35N 3°0E 261 A5
Blidet Amor Algeria 32°59N 5°58E 261 B6
Blidö Sweden 59°37N 18°53E 162 E12
Blidsberg Sweden 57°56N 13°30E 163 G7
Blieskastel Germany 49°14N 7°12E 179 F3
Bligh Sound N.Z. 44°47S 167°32E 285 E2
Bligh Water Fiji 17°0S 178°0E 287 A2
Blind River Canada 46°10N 82°58W 298 C3
Blinisht Albania 41°52N 19°59E 202 E3
Bliss Idaho, U.S.A. 42°56N 114°57W 304 E6
Bliss N.Y., U.S.A. 42°34N 78°15W 312 D6
Blissfield Mich., U.S.A. 41°50N 83°52W 311 C13
Blissfield Ohio, U.S.A. 40°24N 81°58W 312 F3
Blitar Indonesia 8°5S 112°11E 235 D4
Blitchton U.S.A. 32°12N 81°26W 316 C8
Blitta Togo 8°23N 1°6E 263 D5
Blizne Poland 52°14N 20°52E 142 B1
Block I. U.S.A. 41°11N 71°35W 313 E13
Block Island Sd. U.S.A. 41°15N 71°40W 313 E13
Bloemenmarkt Amsterdam, Neths. 112 b2
Bloemfontein S. Africa 29°6S 26°7E 270 C4
Bloemhof S. Africa 27°38S 25°32E 270 C4
Blois France 47°35N 1°20E 172 E8
Blomskog Sweden 59°16N 12°2E 162 E6
Blomstermåla Sweden 56°59N 16°21E 163 H10
Blomvåg Norway 60°32N 4°50E 164 D1
Blönduós Iceland 65°40N 20°12W 155 B6
Blongas Indonesia 8°53S 116°2E 231 K19
Blonie Poland 52°12N 20°37E 185 F7
Bloodvein → Canada 51°47N 96°43W 297 C9
Bloody B. Trin. & Tob. 11°18N 60°38W 323 s
Bloody Foreland Ireland 55°10N 8°17W 166 A3
Bloom = Chicago Heights U.S.A. 41°30N 87°38W 311 C9
Bloomer U.S.A. 45°6N 91°29W 308 C8
Bloomfield Ont., Canada 43°59N 77°14W 312 C7
Bloomfield Ind., U.S.A. 39°1N 86°57W 311 E10
Bloomfield Iowa, U.S.A. 40°45N 92°25W 310 D4
Bloomfield Ky., U.S.A. 37°55N 85°19W 311 G11
Bloomfield N. Mex., U.S.A. 36°43N 107°59W 305 H10
Bloomfield Nebr., U.S.A. 42°36N 97°39W 308 D5
Bloomingburg U.S.A. 39°36N 83°24W 311 E13
Bloomington Ill., U.S.A. 40°28N 89°0W 310 D8
Bloomington Ind., U.S.A. 39°10N 86°32W 311 E10
Bloomington Minn., U.S.A. 44°50N 93°17W 308 C7
Bloomington Wis., U.S.A. 42°53N 90°55W 310 B6
Bloomsburg U.S.A. 41°0N 76°27W 313 F8
Bloomsbury Australia 20°48S 148°38E 280 b
Bloomsbury London, U.K. 125 a3
Blora Indonesia 6°57S 111°25E 235 D4
Blossburg U.S.A. 41°41N 77°4W 312 E7
Blosseville Kyst Greenland 68°50N 26°30W 154 D8
Blota Poland 52°9N 21°11E 142 C3
Blouberg S. Africa 23°8S 28°59E 271 B4
Blountstown U.S.A. 30°27N 85°3W 316 E4
Blowing Point Village Anguilla 18°11N 63°6W 322 a
Blowing Rock Anguilla 18°9N 63°10W 322 a
Bludenz Austria 47°10N 9°50E 180 D2
Blue → U.S.A. 38°11N 86°19W 311 F10
Blue Cypress L. U.S.A. 27°44N 80°45W 317 H9
Blue Earth U.S.A. 43°38N 94°6W 308 D6
Blue Hole Jamaica 18°10N 76°24W 320 a
Blue Hole △ Belize 17°24N 88°30W 320 C2
Blue Island U.S.A. 41°40N 87°40W 119 D2
Blue Lagoon △ Zambia 15°28S 27°26E 269 F2
Blue Mesa Res. U.S.A. 38°28N 107°20W 304 G10
Blue Mosque = Sultanahme Caml Turkey 41°0N 28°58E 122 B1
Blue Mound U.S.A. 39°42N 89°7W 310 E7
Blue Mountain Lake U.S.A. 43°51N 74°27W 313 C10
Blue Mountain Pk. Jamaica 18°3N 76°36W 320 a
Blue Mountains and John Crow Mountains Nat. Park △ Jamaica 18°5N 76°34W 320 a
Blue Mt. U.S.A. 40°30N 76°30W 313 F8
Blue Mts. N.S.W., Australia 33°40S 150°15E 283 B9
Blue Mts. Jamaica 18°3N 76°36W 320 a
Blue Mts. Maine, U.S.A. 44°50N 70°35W 313 B14
Blue Mts. Oreg., U.S.A. 45°0N 118°20W 304 D4
Blue Mts. △ Australia 34°2S 150°15E 283 C9
Blue Mud B. Australia 13°30S 136°0E 280 A2
Blue Mud Bay ☼ 13°25S 136°2E 280 A2
Blue Nile = Nîl el Azraq → Sudan 15°38N 32°31E 257 D3
Blue Nile Falls Ethiopia 11°25N 37°45E 257 E4
Blue Rapids U.S.A. 39°41N 96°39W 308 F5
Blue Ridge U.S.A. 36°40N 80°50W 309 G13
Blue River Canada 52°6N 119°18W 296 C5
Blue Springs U.S.A. 39°1N 94°17W 310 E2
Bluebell Ireland 53°19N 6°21W 120 B1
Bluefield U.S.A. 37°15N 81°17W 309 G13
Bluefields Nic. 12°20N 83°50W 320 D3
Bluevale Canada 43°51N 81°15W 312 C3
Bluff Queens., Australia 23°35S 149°4E 280 C4
Bluff N.Z. 46°37S 168°20E 285 G3
Bluff Utah, U.S.A. 37°17N 109°33W 305 H9
Bluff Harbour N.Z. 46°36S 168°21E 285 G3
Bluff Hd. China 22°11N 114°12E 122 B2
Bluff Knoll Australia 34°24S 118°15E 279 F2
Bluff Pt. Australia 27°50S 114°5E 279 E1
Bluffers Park Canada 43°43N 79°14W 141 A3
Bluffs U.S.A. 39°45N 90°32W 310 E6
Bluffton Ga., U.S.A. 31°31N 84°52W 316 D5
Bluffton Ind., U.S.A. 40°44N 85°11W 311 D11
Bluffton Ohio, U.S.A. 40°54N 83°54W 311 D13
Bluffton S.C., U.S.A. 32°14N 80°52W 316 C9
Blumberg Germany 52°36N 13°39E 115 A4
Blumenau = Stettler Canada 52°19N 112°40W 296 C6
Blumenau Brazil 27°0S 49°0W 335 B6
Blunt U.S.A. 44°31N 99°59W 308 C4
Blunt Pt. U.S.A. 37°51N 122°25W 136 A2
Blutenberg Germany 48°9N 11°27E 131 B1
Bly U.S.A. 42°24N 121°3W 304 E3
Blyde River Canyon ⌂ S. Africa 24°37S 31°2E 271 B5
Blylaget Norway 59°46N 10°41E 133 B3
Blyth S. Austral., Australia 33°49S 138°28E 282 B3
Blyth Ont., Canada 43°44N 81°26W 312 C3
Blyth Northumberland, U.K. 55°8N 1°31W 168 B6
Blythe Calif., U.S.A. 33°37N 114°36W 307 M12
Blythe Ga., U.S.A. 33°17N 82°12W 316 B7
Blytheville U.S.A. 35°56N 89°55W 315 D10
Bø Telemark, Norway 59°25N 9°3E 164 E6
Bo S. Leone 7°55N 11°50W 262 D2
Bo Duc Vietnam 11°58N 106°50E 237 G6
Bo-eun S. Korea 36°29N 127°43E 224 D3
Bo Hai China 39°0N 119°0E 227 E10
Bo-Kaap Museum Cape Town, S. Africa 118 c2
Bō-no-Misaki Japan 31°15N 130°13E 222 F2
Bo Xian = Bozhou China 33°55N 115°41E 226 H8
Boa Esperança Brazil 3°21N 61°23W 329 C5
Boa Esperança, Represa Brazil 6°50S 43°50W 332 C3
Boa Nova Brazil 14°22S 40°10W 333 D3
Boa Viagem Brazil 5°7S 39°44W 332 C4

Boa Vista = Tocantinópolis
Brazil 6°20S 47°25W **332** C2
Boa Vista *Brazil* 2°48N 60°30W **329** C5
Boa Vista *C. Verde Is.* 16°0N 22°49W **153** j
Boa Vista, Alto do *Brazil* 22°58S 43°16W **135** B1
Boa Vista do Erechim = Erechim
Brazil 27°35S 52°15W **335** B5
Boac *Phil.* 13°27N 121°50E **232** E3
Boaco *Nic.* 12°29N 85°35W **320** D2
Bo'ai *China* 35°10N 113°3E **226** G7
Boal *Spain* 43°25N 6°49W **194** B4
Boali *C.A.R.* 4°48N 18°7E **264** B3
Boalsburg *U.S.A.* 40°47N 77°49W **312** F7
Boane *Mozam.* 26°6S 32°19E **271** C5
Boang I. *Papua N. G.* 3°23S 153°18E **286** B7
Boardman *U.S.A.* 41°2N 80°40W **312** E4
Boardwalk *U.S.A.* 40°34N 73°49W **132** C3
Boath *India* 19°20N 78°20E **244** E4
Boatswain Bird I.
Ascension I. 7°56S 14°18W **153** g
Boavista *Portugal* 38°48N 9°8W **126** A2
Boaz I. *Bermuda* 32°18N 64°51W **153** a
Bob Marley Mausoleum
Jamaica 18°18N 77°18W **320** a
Bobadah *Australia* 32°19S 146°41E **283** B7
Bobai *China* 22°17N 109°59E **228** F7
Bobbili *India* 18°35N 83°30E **244** E6
Bòbbio *Italy* 44°46N 9°23E **198** D6
Bobcaygeon *Canada* 44°33N 78°33W **312** B6
Bobigny *France* 48°54N 2°26E **134** A3
Boblad *India* 17°13N 75°26E **244** F2
Böblingen *Germany* 48°40N 9°1E **179** G5
Bobo-Dioulasso
Burkina Faso 11°8N 4°13W **262** C4
Bobolice *Poland* 53°58N 16°37E **184** E3
Bobon *Phil.* 12°32N 124°34E **232** E5
Bobonaza → *Ecuador* 2°36S 76°38W **328** D2
Bobonong *Botswana* 21°58S 28°20E **271** B4
Boboshevo *Bulgaria* 42°9N 23°0E **202** D7
Bobov Dol *Bulgaria* 42°20N 23°0E **202** D6
Bóbr → *Poland* 52°4N 15°4E **185** F2
Bobraomby, Tanjon' i
Madag. 12°40S 49°10E **272** A2
Bobrinets *Ukraine* 48°4N 32°5E **189** H7
Bobrov *Russia* 51°5N 40°2E **190** E5
Bobrovitsa *Ukraine* 50°45N 31°23E **189** G6
Bobruysk = Babruysk
Belarus 53°10N 29°15E **177** B15
Bobures *Venezuela* 9°15N 71°11W **328** B3
Boca del Río *Mexico* 19°5N 96°4W **319** D5
Boca do Acre *Brazil* 8°50S 67°27W **330** B4
Boca do Jari *Brazil* 1°7S 51°58W **329** D7
Boca Grande *Fla., U.S.A.* 26°45N 82°16W **317** J7
Boca Grande *Venezuela* 8°40N 60°40W **329** B5
Boca Raton *U.S.A.* 26°21N 80°5W **317** J9
Bocaiúva *Brazil* 17°7S 43°49W **333** E3
Bocanda *Ivory C.* 7°5N 4°31W **262** D4
Bocanegra *Peru* 12°1S 77°7W **124** B2
Bocaranga *C.A.R.* 7°0N 15°35E **264** A3
Bocas del Dragón = Dragon's
Mouths *Venezuela* 11°0N 61°50W **323** t
Bocas del Toro *Panama* 9°15N 82°20W **320** E3
Boceguillas *Spain* 41°20N 3°39W **194** D7
Bochkarevo = Belogorsk
Russia 51°0N 128°20E **215** D13
Bochmanivka *Ukraine* 47°40N 29°34E **183** C14
Bochnia *Poland* 49°58N 20°27E **185** J7
Bocholt *Germany* 51°50N 6°36E **178** D2
Bochum = Senwabarana
S. Africa 23°17S 29°7E **271** B4
Bochum *Germany* 51°28N 7°13E **178** D3
Bockenem *Germany* 52°1N 10°8E **178** C6
Boćki *Poland* 52°39N 23°3E **185** F10
Bocognano *France* 42°5N 9°4E **175** F13
Bocoio *Angola* 12°28S 14°10E **265** E2
Boconó *Venezuela* 9°15N 70°16W **328** B3
Boconó → *Venezuela* 8°43N 69°34W **328** B4
Bocoyna *Mexico* 27°52N 107°35W **318** B3
Bocșa *Romania* 45°21N 21°47E **182** E6
Boda *C.A.R.* 4°19N 17°26E **264** B3
Böda *Dalarna, Sweden* 61°1N 15°13E **162** C9
Böda *Kalmar, Sweden* 57°15N 17°3E **163** G11
Boda *Västernorrland,*
Sweden 62°52N 16°39E **162** B10
Bodafors *Sweden* 57°48N 14°23E **163** G8
Bodaybo *Russia* 57°50N 114°0E **215** D12
Boddam *U.K.* 59°56N 1°17W **167** B7
Boddington *Australia* 32°50S 116°30E **279** F2
Bode Sadu *Nigeria* 9°0N 4°47E **263** D5
Bodega Bay *U.S.A.* 38°20N 123°3W **306** G3
Boden *Sweden* 65°50N 21°42E **160** D19
Bodensee *Europe* 47°35N 9°25E **179** H5
Bodenteich *Germany* 52°50N 10°42E **178** C6
Bodhan *India* 18°40N 77°44E **244** E3
Bodinayakkanur *India* 10°2N 77°10E **245** J3
Bodinga *Nigeria* 12°58N 5°10E **263** C6
Bodmin *U.K.* 50°28N 4°43W **169** G3
Bodmin Moor *U.K.* 50°33N 4°36W **169** G3
Bodø *Norway* 67°17N 14°24E **160** C16
Bodoquena, Serra da
Brazil 21°0S 56°50W **331** E6
Bodoupa *C.A.R.* 5°43N 17°36E **264** A3
Bodrichi *Chad* 19°11N 15°54E **259** E3
Bodrog → *Hungary* 48°11N 21°22E **182** B6
Bodrum *Turkey* 37°3N 27°30E **205** D9
Boduna
Dem. Rep. of the Congo 5°5N 19°44E **264** A3
Bódva → *Hungary* 48°19N 20°45E **182** B5
Boedo *Argentina* 34°38S 58°26W **117** B2
Boembé *Congo* 2°54S 15°39E **264** C3
Boën *France* 45°44N 4°1E **175** C8
Boende
Dem. Rep. of the Congo 0°24S 21°12E **264** C4
Boerne *U.S.A.* 29°47N 98°44W **314** G5
Boesmans → *S. Africa* 33°42S 26°39E **270** D4
Boffa *Guinea* 10°16N 14°3W **262** C2
Bog Walk *Jamaica* 18°6N 77°1W **320** a
Bogal, Lagh → *Kenya* 0°41N 40°57E **267** D5
Bogale *Burma* 16°17N 95°24E **241** G5
Bogalusa *U.S.A.* 30°47N 89°52W **315** F10
Bogan → *Australia* 30°20S 146°55E **283** A7
Bogan Gate *Australia* 33°7S 147°49E **283** B7
Bogandé *Burkina Faso* 13°2N 0°8W **263** C4
Bogangolo *C.A.R.* 5°34N 18°15E **264** A3
Bogantungan *Australia* 23°41S 147°17E **280** C4
Bogata *U.S.A.* 33°28N 95°13W **314** E7
Bogatić *Serbia* 44°51N 19°30E **202** B3
Boğazkale *Turkey* 40°2N 34°37E **212** B6
Boğazlıyan *Turkey* 39°11N 35°14E **212** C6
Bogbonga
Dem. Rep. of the Congo 1°36N 19°24E **264** B3
Bogda Shan *China* 43°35N 89°40E **217** D11
Bogen *Sweden* 60°4N 12°32E **162** D6
Bogenhausen *Germany* 48°8N 11°36E **131** B2
Bogense *Denmark* 55°34N 10°5E **163** J4
Bogetići *Montenegro* 42°41N 18°58E **202** D2
Boggabilla *Australia* 28°36S 150°24E **281** D5
Boggabri *Australia* 30°45S 150°5E **283** A9
Boggeragh Mts. *Ireland* 52°2N 8°55W **166** D3
Boggy Peak *Antigua & B.* 17°2N 61°52W **322** b
Boghari = Ksar el Boukhari
Algeria 35°51N 2°52E **261** A5
Bogia *Papua N. G.* 4°9S 145°0E **286** C3
Bogildo *S. Korea* 34°9N 126°32E **224** E3
Boglan = Solhan *Turkey* 38°57N 41°3E **213** C9
Bogles *Grenada* 12°30N 61°26W **323** q
Bognor Regis *U.K.* 50°47N 0°40W **169** G7
Bogo *Phil.* 11°3N 124°0E **233** F4
Bogodukhov = Bohodukhiv
Ukraine 50°9N 35°33E **189** G8
Bogol Manya *Ethiopia* 4°34N 41°29E **257** G5
Bogong, Mt. *Australia* 36°47S 147°17E **283** D7
Bogor *Indonesia* 6°36S 106°48E **234** D3
Bogoroditsk *Russia* 53°47N 38°8E **188** F10
Bogorodsk = Noginsk
Russia 55°50N 38°25E **188** E10
Bogorodsk *Russia* 56°4N 43°30E **190** B6
Bogorodskoye = Kamskoye Ustye
Russia 55°10N 49°20E **190** C9
Bogorodskoye = Leninskoye
Russia 58°23N 47°3E **190** A8
Bogorodskoye *Russia* 55°48N 37°42E **129** B4
Bogoslovsky = Karpinsk
Russia 59°45N 60°1E **186** C11
Bogoso *Ghana* 5°38N 2°3W **262** D4
Bogotá *Colombia* 4°34N 74°0W **328** C3
Bogota *N.J., U.S.A.* 40°52N 74°2W **132** A1
Bogotol *Russia* 56°15N 89°50E **214** D9
Bogou *Togo* 10°40N 0°12E **263** C5
Bogra *Bangla.* 24°51N 89°22E **241** C2
Bogstadvatnet *Norway* 59°58N 10°37E **133** A2
Boguchany *Russia* 58°40N 97°30E **215** D10
Boguchar *Russia* 49°55N 40°32E **190** F5
Bogué *Mauritania* 16°45N 14°10W **262** B2
Boguszów-Gorce *Poland* 50°45N 16°12E **185** H3
Bohain-en-Vermandois
France 49°59N 3°28E **173** C10
Bohdan *Ukraine* 48°2N 24°22E **183** B9
Bohemian Forest = Böhmerwald
Germany 49°8N 13°14E **179** F9
Bohena Cr. → *Australia* 30°17S 149°42E **283** A8
Bohinjska Bistrica
Slovenia 46°17N 14°1E **199** B11
Böhmerwald *Germany* 49°8N 13°14E **179** F9
Böhmisch-Brod = Český Brod
Czech Rep. 50°4N 14°52E **180** A7
Böhmisch-Leipa = Česká Lípa
Czech Rep. 50°45N 14°30E **180** A7
Böhmisch-Trübau = Česká Třebová
Czech Rep. 49°54N 16°27E **181** B9
Bohmte *Germany* 52°22N 8°19E **178** C4
Bohnsdorf *Germany* 52°23N 13°34E **115** B4
Bohodukhiv *Ukraine* 50°9N 35°33E **189** G8
Bohol *Somali Rep.* 5°45N 46°9E **267** C6
Bohol □ *Phil.* 9°50N 124°10E **233** G5
Bohol Sea *Phil.* 9°0N 124°0E **233** G5
Bohol Str. *Phil.* 9°45N 123°40E **233** G4
Bohongou *Burkina Faso* 12°30N 0°40E **263** C5
Böhönye *Hungary* 46°25N 17°28E **182** D2
Bohorodchany *Ukraine* 48°48N 24°32E **183** B9
Bohorok *Indonesia* 3°30N 98°12E **237** L2
Bohu *China* 41°58N 86°37E **217** D11
Bohuslän *Sweden* 58°25N 12°0E **163** F5
Bohuslev *Ukraine* 49°33N 30°56E **189** H6
Boi *Nigeria* 9°35N 9°27E **263** D6
Boi, Pta. do *Brazil* 23°55S 45°15W **335** A6
Boiaçu *Brazil* 0°27S 61°46W **329** D5
Boigu *Australia* 9°16S 142°13E **280** a
Boigu I. *Australia* 9°15S 142°15E **280** a
Boileau, C. *Australia* 17°40S 122°7E **278** C3
Boim *Brazil* 2°49S 55°10W **329** D6
Boing'o *Sudan* 9°58N 33°44E **257** F3
Boipariguda *India* 18°46N 82°26E **244** E6
Boipeba, I. de *Brazil* 13°39S 38°55W **333** D4
Boiro *Spain* 42°39N 8°54W **194** C2
Bois → *Brazil* 18°35S 50°2W **333** E1
Bois-Blanc *Réunion* 21°11S 55°49E **272** f
Bois-Colombes *France* 48°55N 2°16E **134** A2
Bois-d'Arcy *France* 48°48N 2°1E **134** B1
Boise *U.S.A.* 43°37N 116°13W **304** E5
Boise City *U.S.A.* 36°44N 102°31W **314** C3
Boissevain *Canada* 49°15N 100°5W **297** D8
Boissy-St-Léger *France* 48°44N 2°31E **134** B4
Boîte → *Italy* 46°5N 12°5E **199** B9
Boitzenburg *Germany* 53°16N 13°36E **178** B9
Boizenburg *Germany* 53°23N 10°43E **178** B6
Bojador *W. Sahara* 23°56N 15°49W **260** D1
Bojador, C. *W. Sahara* 26°0N 14°30W **260** C2
Bojana → *Albania* 41°52N 19°22E **202** E3
Bojano *Italy* 41°29N 14°29E **201** A7
Bojanowo *Poland* 51°43N 16°42E **185** G3
Bøjden *Denmark* 55°6N 10°7E **163** J4
Bojnūrd *Iran* 37°30N 57°20E **247** B8
Bojonegoro *Indonesia* 7°11S 111°54E **235** D4
Boju *Nigeria* 7°22N 7°55E **263** D6
Boka *Serbia* 45°22N 20°52E **182** E5
Boka Kotorska
Montenegro 42°23N 18°32E **202** D2
Boka Tabla *Neth. Ant.* 12°22N 69°8W **322** g
Bokada
Dem. Rep. of the Congo 4°8N 19°23E **264** B3
Bokala *Dem. Rep. of the Congo* 3°8S 17°4E **264** C3
Bokala *Ivory C.* 8°31N 4°33W **262** D4
Bokani *Nigeria* 9°28N 5°10E **263** D6
Bokaro *India* 23°46N 85°55E **243** H11
Bokatola
Dem. Rep. of the Congo 0°38S 18°46E **264** C3
Boké *Guinea* 10°56N 14°17W **262** C2
Bokela
Dem. Rep. of the Congo 1°10S 21°59E **264** C4
Bokenda
Dem. Rep. of the Congo 1°16N 21°22E **264** B4
Bokhara → *Australia* 29°55S 146°42E **281** D4
Bokkos *Nigeria* 9°17N 9°1E **263** D6
Boklar Dağları *Turkey* 37°5N 33°55E **250** A4
Boknafjorden *Norway* 59°14N 5°40E **164** E2
Boko *Congo* 4°46S 14°36E **265** C2
Bokode
Dem. Rep. of the Congo 3°55N 19°30E **264** B3
Bokolo *Gabon* 2°40S 10°10E **264** C2
Bokondo
Dem. Rep. of the Congo 0°15N 22°32E **264** B4
Bokor △ *Cambodia* 10°50N 104°1E **237** G5
Bokoro *Chad* 12°25N 17°14E **259** F3
Bokota
Dem. Rep. of the Congo 0°56S 22°24E **264** C4
Bokote
Dem. Rep. of the Congo 0°12S 21°8E **264** C4
Bokpyin *Burma* 11°18N 98°42E **237** G2
Boksitogorsk *Russia* 59°22N 33°50E **188** C7
Boku *Papua N. G.* 6°34S 155°21E **286** D8
Bokungu
Dem. Rep. of the Congo 0°35S 22°50E **264** C4
Bol *Chad* 13°30N 14°40E **259** F2
Bol *Croatia* 43°18N 16°38E **199** E13
Bolama *Guinea-Biss.* 11°30N 15°30W **262** C1
Bolan → *Pakistan* 28°38N 67°42E **242** E2
Bolan Pass *Pakistan* 29°50N 67°20E **240** C2
Bolaños → *Mexico* 21°12N 104°5W **318** C4
Bolaños de Calatrava
Spain 38°54N 3°40W **195** G7
Bolayır *Turkey* 40°31N 26°45E **203** F10
Bolbec *France* 49°30N 0°30E **172** C7
Boldājī *Iran* 31°56N 51°3E **247** D6
Boldești-Scăeni *Romania* 45°3N 26°2E **183** E11
Boldinasco *Italy* 45°29N 9°8E **129** B1
Bole *Xinjiang Uygur,*
China 45°11N 81°37E **217** C10
Bole *Ethiopia* 6°36N 37°20E **257** F4
Bole *Ghana* 9°3N 2°23W **262** D4
Bolekhiv *Ukraine* 49°0N 23°57E **177** D12
Boleko
Dem. Rep. of the Congo 1°35S 19°50E **264** C3
Bøler *Norway* 59°53N 10°50E **133** A4
Bolesławiec *Poland* 51°17N 15°37E **185** G2
Bolgatanga *Ghana* 10°44N 0°53W **263** C4
Bolgrad = Bolhrad
Ukraine 45°40N 28°32E **183** E13
Bolhrad *Ukraine* 45°40N 28°32E **183** E13
Bolia *Dem. Rep. of the Congo* 1°36S 18°22E **264** C3
Bolinao *Phil.* 16°23N 119°54E **232** C2
Bolinao, C. *Phil.* 16°23N 119°55E **232** C2
Bolingbroke *U.S.A.* 32°57N 83°48W **316** C6
Bolingbrook *U.S.A.* 41°42N 88°4W **311** C8
Bolingo
Dem. Rep. of the Congo 3°31S 21°43E **264** C4
Bolintin-Vale *Romania* 44°27N 25°46E **183** F10
Bolívar *Antioquia, Colombia* 5°50N 76°1W **328** B2
Bolívar *Cauca, Colombia* 2°0N 77°0W **328** C2
Bolívar *Peru* 7°18S 77°48W **330** B2
Bolivar *Mo., U.S.A.* 37°37N 93°25W **308** G7
Bolivar *N.Y., U.S.A.* 42°4N 78°10W **312** D6
Bolivar *Tenn., U.S.A.* 35°12N 89°0W **315** D10
Bolívar □ *Colombia* 9°0N 74°40W **328** B3
Bolívar □ *Ecuador* 1°15S 79°5W **328** D2
Bolívar □ *Venezuela* 6°20N 63°30W **329** B5
Bolivia ■ *S. Amer.* 17°6S 64°0W **331** D5
Bolivian Plateau = Altiplano
Bolivia 17°0S 68°0W **330** D4
Boljevac *Serbia* 43°51N 21°58E **202** C5
Bolkhov *Russia* 53°25N 36°0E **188** F9
Bolków *Poland* 50°55N 16°6E **185** H3
Bollate *Italy* 45°32N 9°7E **129** A1
Bollebeek *Belgium* 50°55N 4°14E **116** A1
Bollebygd *Sweden* 57°40N 12°35E **163** G6
Bollène *France* 44°18N 4°45E **175** D8
Bollensdorf *Germany* 52°30N 13°42E **115** A5
Bollmora *Sweden* 59°14N 18°14E **139** B3
Bollnäs *Sweden* 61°21N 16°24E **162** C10
Bollon *Australia* 28°2S 147°29E **281** D4
Bollstabruk *Sweden* 62°59N 17°40E **162** B11
Bolmen *Sweden* 56°55N 13°40E **163** H7
Bolnisi *Georgia* 41°26N 44°32E **191** K7
Bolobo *Dem. Rep. of the Congo* 2°6S 16°20E **264** C3
Bologna *Italy* 44°29N 11°20E **199** D8
Bologna ✕ (BLQ) *Italy* 44°34N 11°16E **199** D8
Bologoye *Russia* 57°55N 34°5E **188** D8
Bolomba
Dem. Rep. of the Congo 0°35N 19°0E **264** B3
Bolombo →
Dem. Rep. of the Congo 1°32N 21°14E **264** B4
Bolonchén *Mexico* 20°1N 89°45W **319** D7
Bolondo
Dem. Rep. of the Congo 2°12S 18°42E **264** C3
Bolong *Chad* 12°3N 17°45E **259** F3
Bolong *Phil.* 7°6N 122°14E **233** H4
Bolongongo *Angola* 8°28S 15°16E **265** D3
Bolótana *Italy* 40°20N 8°52E **200** B1
Boloven, Cao Nguyen
Laos 15°10N 106°30E **236** E6
Bolpur *India* 23°40N 87°45E **243** H12
Bolsena *Italy* 42°39N 11°59E **199** F8
Bolsena, L. di *Italy* 42°36N 11°56E **199** F8
Bolshakovo *Russia* 54°53N 21°40E **184** D8
Bolshaya Chernigovka
Russia 52°6N 50°52E **190** D10
Bolshaya Garmanda = Evensk
Russia 62°12N 159°30E **215** C16
Bolshaya Glushitsa
Russia 52°28N 50°30E **190** D10
Bolshaya Martynovka
Russia 47°19N 41°37E **191** G5
Bolshaya Okhta *Russia* 59°56N 30°26E **137** B2
Bolshaya Tsaryovshchina =
Volzhskiy *Russia* 48°56N 44°46E **191** F7
Bolshaya Vradiyevka
Ukraine 47°50N 30°40E **189** J6
Bolshevik, Ostrov
Russia 78°30N 102°0E **215** B11
Bolshoy Anyuy →
Russia 68°30N 160°49E **215** C17
Bolshoy Begichev, Ostrov
Russia 74°20N 112°30E **215** B12
Bolshoy Kamen *Russia* 43°7N 132°19E **220** C6
Bolshoy Kavkas = Caucasus
Mountains *Eurasia* 42°50N 44°0E **191** J7
Bolshoy Lyakhovskiy, Ostrov
Russia 73°35N 142°0E **215** B15
Bolshoy Theatre *Moscow, Russia* **129** b2
Bolshoy Tokmak = Tokmak
Kyrgyzstan 42°49N 75°15E **217** D9
Bolshoy Tyuters, Ostrov
Russia 59°51N 27°13E **188** C4
Bólstaðarhlíð *Iceland* 65°31N 19°49W **155** B7
Bolsward *Neths.* 53°3N 5°32E **170** A5
Bolt Head *U.K.* 50°12N 3°48W **169** G4
Boltaña *Spain* 42°28N 0°4E **196** C5
Boltigen *Switz.* 46°38N 7°24E **179** J3
Bolton *Ont., Canada* 43°54N 79°45W **312** C5
Bolton *Gt. Man., U.K.* 53°35N 2°26W **168** D5
Bolton *Georgia, U.S.A.* 33°48N 84°28W **113** B2
Bolton Landing *U.S.A.* 43°32N 73°35W **313** C11
Bolu *Turkey* 40°45N 31°35E **212** B4
Bolu □ *Turkey* 40°40N 31°30E **212** B4
Bolubolu *Papua N. G.* 9°21S 150°20E **286** E6
Bolungavík *Iceland* 66°9N 23°15W **155** A3
Boluo *China* 23°3N 114°21E **229** F10
Bolvadin *Turkey* 38°45N 31°4E **212** C4
Bolzano *Italy* 46°31N 11°22E **199** B8
Bom Comércio *Brazil* 9°45S 65°54W **331** B4
Bom Conselho *Brazil* 9°10S 36°41W **332** C4
Bom Despacho *Brazil* 19°43S 45°15W **333** E2
Bom Jesus *Angola* 9°11S 13°34E **265** D2
Bom Jesus *Brazil* 9°4S 44°22W **332** C3
Bom Jesus da Gurguéia, Serra
Brazil 9°0S 43°0W **332** C3
Bom Jesus da Lapa
Brazil 13°15S 43°25W **333** D3
Bom Retiro *Brazil* 23°31S 46°38W **137** B2
Boma *Dem. Rep. of the Congo* 5°50S 13°4E **265** D2
Bomaderry *Australia* 34°52S 150°37E **283** C9
Bomandjokou *Congo* 0°34N 14°23E **264** B2
Bomaneh
Dem. Rep. of the Congo 1°18N 23°47E **264** B4
Bomassa *Congo* 2°12N 16°12E **264** B3
Bomate
Dem. Rep. of the Congo 2°14N 25°15E **264** C3
Bombala *Australia* 36°56S 149°15E **283** D8
Bombarral *Portugal* 39°15N 9°9W **195** F1
Bombay = Mumbai *India* 18°56N 72°50E **130** B2
Bombay *U.S.A.* 44°56N 74°34W **313** B10
Bombedor, Pta. *Venezuela* 9°53N 61°37W **329** G9
Bombo Kasani
Dem. Rep. of the Congo 5°51S 21°54E **265** D4
Bomboma
Dem. Rep. of the Congo 2°25N 18°55E **264** B3
Bombombwa
Dem. Rep. of the Congo 1°40N 25°40E **268** B2
Bomboyo *Chad* 12°1N 15°28E **259** F3
Bomdila *India* 27°18N 92°22E **241** B4
Bomdo *India* 28°44N 94°54E **241** A5
Bomet *Kenya* 0°47S 35°21E **266** E4
Bomi Hills *Liberia* 7°1N 10°38W **262** D2
Bomili *Dem. Rep. of the Congo* 1°45N 27°5E **268** B2
Bømlo *Norway* 59°37N 5°13E **164** E2
Bomokandi →
Dem. Rep. of the Congo 3°39N 26°8E **268** B2
Bomongo
Dem. Rep. of the Congo 1°27N 18°21E **264** B3
Bompoka *India* 8°15N 93°13E **245** K11
Bomputu
Dem. Rep. of the Congo 0°23S 20°6E **264** C4
Bomst = Babimost *Poland* 52°10N 15°49E **185** F2
Bomu → *C.A.R.* 4°40N 22°30E **264** B4
Bomu Occidentale ⌂
Dem. Rep. of the Congo 4°48N 24°17E **264** B4
Bomu Orientale ⌂
Dem. Rep. of the Congo 5°0N 25°50E **264** B2
Bon, C. = Ra's aţ Tib
Tunisia 37°1N 11°2E **258** A2
Bon Acceuil *Mauritius* 20°10S 57°39E **272** e
Bon Echo ⌂ *Canada* 44°55N 77°16W **312** B7
Bon Sar Pa *Vietnam* 12°24N 107°35E **236** F6
Bona, Mt. *U.S.A.* 61°23N 141°45W **303** F12
Bonāb *Āzarbājān-e Sharqī,*
Iran 37°20N 46°4E **213** D12
Bonāb *Zanjān, Iran* 36°35N 48°41E **213** D13
Bonaigarh *India* 21°50N 84°57E **243** J11
Bonaire *Neth. Ant.* 12°10N 68°15W **322** h
Bonaire *Ga., U.S.A.* 32°33N 83°36W **316** C6
Bonampak *Mexico* 16°44N 91°5W **319** D6
Bonang *Australia* 37°11S 148°41E **283** D8
Bonanza *Nic.* 13°54N 84°35W **320** D3
Bonaparte Arch.
Australia 14°0S 124°30E **278** B3
Bonaparte Rocks *Grenada* 12°24N 61°30W **323** q
Boñar *Spain* 42°52N 5°19W **194** C5
Bonar Bridge *U.K.* 57°54N 4°20W **167** D4
Bonasse *Trin. & Tob.* 10°5N 61°54W **323** t
Bonaventure *Canada* 48°5N 65°32W **299** C6
Bonaventure, Place *Montréal, Canada* **130** c2
Bonavista *Canada* 48°40N 53°5W **299** C9
Bonavista, C. *Canada* 48°42N 53°5W **299** C9
Bonavista B. *Canada* 48°45N 53°25W **299** C9
Bondeno *Italy* 44°53N 11°25E **199** D8
Bondi *Australia* 33°53S 151°16E **139** B2
Bondo *Équateur,*
Dem. Rep. of the Congo 1°22S 23°54E **264** C4
Bondo *Orientale,*
Dem. Rep. of the Congo 3°55N 23°53E **264** B4
Bondoukou *Ivory C.* 8°2N 2°47W **262** D4
Bondowoso *Indonesia* 7°55S 113°49E **235** D4
Bondy *France* 48°54N 2°28E **134** A3
Bondy, Forêt de *France* 48°54N 2°33E **134** A4
Bône = Annaba *Algeria* 36°50N 7°46E **261** A6
Bone, Teluk *Indonesia* 4°10S 120°50E **231** E6
Bonefish Pond *Bahamas* 25°59N 77°23W **153** b
Bonerate *Indonesia* 7°25S 121°5E **231** F6
Bonerate, Kepulauan
Indonesia 6°30S 121°10E **231** F6
Bo'ness *U.K.* 56°1N 3°37W **167** E5
Bonete, Cerro *Argentina* 27°55S 68°40W **334** B2
Bonfim = Senhor-do-Bonfim
Brazil 10°30S 40°10W **332** D3
Bonfim *Brazil* 3°33N 59°25W **329** C6
Bong Son = Hoai Nhon
Vietnam 14°28N 109°1E **236** E7
Bonga *Ethiopia* 7°15N 36°14E **257** F4
Bongabon *Phil.* 15°38N 121°8E **232** D3
Bongabong *Phil.* 12°45N 121°29E **232** E3
Bongaigaon *India* 26°28N 90°34E **241** B3
Bongandanga
Dem. Rep. of the Congo 1°24N 21°3E **264** B4
Bongao *Phil.* 5°2N 119°46E **233** J2
Bongo
Dem. Rep. of the Congo 1°47S 17°41E **264** C3
Bongo, Sa. de *Angola* 10°3S 15°15E **265** E3
Bongor *Chad* 10°35N 15°20E **259** F3
Bongos, Massif des *C.A.R.* 8°40N 22°25E **264** A4
Bongouanou *Ivory C.* 6°42N 4°15W **262** D4
Bonham *U.S.A.* 33°35N 96°11W **314** E6
Boni *Mali* 15°3N 2°10W **262** B4
Boni ⌂ *Kenya* 1°35S 41°18E **268** C5
Bonifacio *France* 41°24N 9°10E **175** G13
Bonifacio, Bouches de
Medit. S. 41°12N 9°15E **200** A2
Bonifacio Monument
Phil. 14°38N 120°58E **127** B1
Bonifay *U.S.A.* 30°47N 85°41W **316** E4
Bonin Is. = Ogasawara Gunto
Pac. Oc. 27°0N 142°0E **211** F16
Bonita Springs *U.S.A.* 26°21N 81°47W **317** J8
Bonito *Brazil* 21°8S 56°28W **331** E6
Bonke *Ethiopia* 6°5N 37°16E **257** F4
Bonkoukou *Niger* 14°0N 3°15E **263** C5
Bonn *Germany* 50°46N 7°6E **178** E3
Bonnabel Place *U.S.A.* 30°0N 90°8W **131** A2
Bonnat *France* 46°20N 1°54E **173** F8
Bonne Terre *U.S.A.* 37°55N 90°33W **310** G6
Bonneau *U.S.A.* 33°16N 79°58W **316** B10
Bonners Ferry *U.S.A.* 48°42N 116°19W **304** B5
Bonnétable *France* 48°11N 0°25E **172** D7
Bonneuil-sur-Marne
France 48°46N 2°30E **134** B4
Bonneval *France* 45°22N 7°3E **175** C11
Bonneval-sur-Arc *France* 48°11N 1°24E **172** D8
Bonneville *France* 46°4N 6°24E **173** F13
Bonney, L. *Australia* 37°50S 140°20E **282** D4
Bonnie Doon *Australia* 37°2S 145°53E **283** D6
Bonnie Rock *Australia* 30°29S 118°22E **279** F2
Bonnington *U.K.* 55°54N 3°25W **121** B1
Bonny *Nigeria* 4°25N 7°13E **263** E6
Bonny → *Nigeria* 4°20N 7°10E **263** E6
Bonny, Bight of *Africa* 3°30N 9°20E **263** E6
Bonny Hills *Australia* 31°36S 152°51E **283** A10
Bonny-sur-Loire *France* 47°33N 2°50E **173** E9
Bonnyrigg *U.K.* 55°53N 3°6W **167** F5
Bonnyrigg and Lasswade
U.K. 55°52N 3°6W **121** B3
Bonnyville *Canada* 54°20N 110°45W **297** C6
Bono *Italy* 40°25N 9°2E **200** B2
Bonoi *Indonesia* 1°45S 137°41E **231** E9
Bonorva *Italy* 40°25N 8°46E **200** B1
Bonsall *U.S.A.* 33°16N 117°14W **307** M9
Bonsucesso *Brazil* 22°51S 43°15W **135** B1
Bontang *Indonesia* 0°10N 117°30E **235** B5
Bontebok △ *S. Africa* 34°5S 20°28E **270** D3
Bonteheuwel *S. Africa* 33°57S 18°33E **118** A2
Bonthe *S. Leone* 7°30N 12°33W **262** D2
Bontoc *Phil.* 17°7N 120°58E **232** C3
Bonyeri *Ghana* 5°1N 2°46W **262** D4
Bonyhád *Hungary* 46°18N 18°32E **182** D3
Bonython Ra. *Australia* 23°40S 128°45E **278** D4
Boo *Sweden* 59°20N 18°16E **139** A3
Booderee △ *Australia* 35°12S 150°42E **283** C9
Boodjamulla △ *Australia* 18°15S 138°6E **280** B2
Bookabie *Australia* 31°50S 132°41E **279** F5
Booke *Dem. Rep. of the Congo* 2°34S 22°3E **264** C4
Booker *U.S.A.* 36°27N 100°32W **314** C4
Bool Lagoon *Australia* 37°7S 140°40E **282** D4
Boola *Guinea* 8°22N 8°41E **262** D3
Boolcoomata *Australia* 31°57S 140°33E **282** A4
Booleroo Centre
Australia 32°53S 138°21E **282** B3
Booligal *Australia* 33°58S 144°53E **283** B6
Boon Pt. *Antigua & B.* 17°10N 61°50W **322** b
Böön Tsagaan Nuur
Mongolia 45°35N 99°9E **218** B4
Boonah *Australia* 27°58S 152°41E **281** D5
Boone *Iowa, U.S.A.* 42°4N 93°53W **310** B3
Boone *N.C., U.S.A.* 36°13N 81°41W **315** C14
Booneville *Ark., U.S.A.* 35°8N 93°55W **314** D8
Booneville *Miss., U.S.A.* 34°39N 88°34W **315** D10
Boonville *Calif., U.S.A.* 39°1N 123°22W **306** F3
Boonville *Ind., U.S.A.* 38°3N 87°16W **311** F9
Boonville *Mo., U.S.A.* 38°58N 92°44W **310** F4
Boonville *N.Y., U.S.A.* 43°29N 75°20W **313** C9
Boorabbin △ *Australia* 31°30S 120°10E **279** F3
Boorama *Somali Rep.* 9°55N 43°7E **267** C5
Boorindal *Australia* 30°22S 146°11E **281** E4
Boorowa *Australia* 34°28S 148°44E **283** C8
Boort *Australia* 36°7S 143°46E **282** D5
Boosaaso *Somali Rep.* 11°12N 49°18E **267** B6
Booterstown *Ireland* 53°19N 6°12W **120** B2
Boothia, Gulf of *Canada* 71°0N 90°0W **294** C14
Boothia Pen. *Canada* 71°0N 94°0W **294** C13
Bootle *U.K.* 53°28N 3°1W **168** D4
Booué *Gabon* 0°5S 11°55E **264** C2
Bopako
Dem. Rep. of the Congo 1°53N 21°13E **264** B4
Boppard *Germany* 50°13N 7°35E **179** E3
Boquerón □ *Paraguay* 23°0S 60°0W **331** E6
Boquilla, Presa de la
Mexico 27°31N 105°30W **318** B3
Boquillas del Carmen
Mexico 29°11N 102°58W **318** B4
Bor *Czech Rep.* 49°41N 12°45E **180** B5
Bor *Russia* 56°28N 43°59E **190** B7
Bor *Serbia* 44°5N 22°7E **202** B6
Bôr *Sudan* 6°10N 31°40E **257** F3
Bor *Sweden* 57°9N 14°10E **163** G8
Bor *Turkey* 37°54N 34°32E **212** D6
Bor, Lagh → *Kenya* 1°18N 40°40E **267** D5
Bor Mashash *Israel* 31°7N 34°50E **251** G5
Bor u Ceske Lipy = Nový Bor
Czech Rep. 50°46N 14°35E **180** A7
Bora Bora
French Polynesia 16°30S 151°45W **289** f
Borah Peak *U.S.A.* 44°8N 113°47W **304** D7
Borang *Sudan* 4°50N 30°59E **257** G3
Borangapara *India* 25°14N 90°14E **241** C3
Borås *Sweden* 57°43N 12°56E **163** G6
Borāzjān *Iran* 29°22N 51°10E **247** D6
Borba *Brazil* 4°12S 59°34W **329** D6
Borba *Portugal* 38°50N 7°26W **195** G3
Borbon *Phil.* 10°50N 124°2E **233** F5
Borborema, Planalto da
Brazil 7°0S 37°0W **332** C4
Borcea *Romania* 44°20N 27°45E **183** F12
Borchalo = Marneuli
Georgia 41°30N 44°48E **191** K7
Borçka *Turkey* 41°25N 41°41E **213** B9
Bord Khūn-e Now *Iran* 28°3N 51°28E **247** D6
Borda, C. *Australia* 35°45S 136°34E **282** C2
Bordeaux *France* 44°50N 0°36W **174** D3
Bordeaux ✕ (BOD)
France 44°50N 0°35W **174** D3
Borden *Australia* 34°3S 118°12E **279** F2
Borden-Carleton *Canada* 46°18N 63°47W **299** C7
Borden I. *Canada* 78°30N 111°30W **295** B9
Borden Pen. *Canada* 73°0N 83°0W **295** C15
Borden Springs *U.S.A.* 33°56N 85°28W **316** B4
Border Ranges △
Australia 28°24S 152°56E **281** D5
Borders = Scottish Borders □
U.K. 55°35N 2°50W **167** F6
Bordertown *Australia* 36°19S 140°45E **282** D4
Borðeyri *Iceland* 65°12N 21°6W **155** B5
Bordighera *Italy* 43°46N 7°39E **198** E4
Bordj bou Arreridj *Algeria* 36°4N 4°45E **261** A5
Bordj Bourguiba *Tunisia* 32°12N 10°2E **258** B2
Bordj Fly Ste. Marie
Algeria 27°19N 2°32W **260** C4
Bordj-in-Eker *Algeria* 24°9N 5°3E **261** D6
Bordj Menaïel *Algeria* 36°46N 3°43E **261** A5
Bordj Messouda *Algeria* 30°12N 9°25E **261** B6
Bordj Mokhtar *Algeria* 21°20N 0°56E **261** D5
Bordj Nili *Algeria* 33°28N 3°2E **261** B5
Bordj Omar Driss *Algeria* 28°10N 6°40E **261** C6
Bordj Sif Fatima *Algeria* 31°6N 8°41E **261** B6
Bordj Tarat *Algeria* 25°55N 9°3E **261** C6
Borduttighat *India* 26°57N 93°58E **241** B4
Bore *Ethiopia* 4°39N 37°39E **257** G4
Borehamwood *U.K.* 51°40N 0°15W **169** F7
Borek Wielkopolski
Poland 51°54N 17°11E **185** G4
Borensberg *Sweden* 58°34N 15°17E **163** F9
Borgå = Porvoo *Finland* 60°24N 25°40E **188** B3
Borgampad *India* 17°39N 80°52E **244** F5
Borgarfjarðarsýsla □
Iceland 64°30N 21°30W **155** C5
Borgarfjörður *Borgarfjarðarsýsla,*
Iceland 64°30N 22°0W **155** C4
Borgarfjörður *Norður-Múlasýsla,*
Iceland 65°33N 13°47W **155** B13
Borgarnes *Iceland* 64°32N 21°55W **155** C5
Børgefjellet *Norway* 65°20N 13°45E **160** D15
Borger *Neths.* 52°54N 6°44E **170** B6
Borger *Tex., U.S.A.* 35°39N 101°24W **314** D4
Borgholm *Sweden* 56°52N 16°39E **163** H10
Bórgia *Italy* 38°49N 16°30E **201** D9
Borgnesse, Pte. *Martinique* 14°26N 60°54W **322** j
Borgo San Dalmazzo *Italy* 44°20N 7°30E **198** D4
Borgo San Donnino = Fidenza
Italy 44°52N 10°3E **198** D7
Borgo San Lorenzo *Italy* 43°57N 11°23E **199** E8
Borgo Val di Taro *Italy* 44°29N 9°46E **198** D6
Borgo Valsugana *Italy* 46°3N 11°27E **199** B8
Borgomanero *Italy* 45°42N 8°28E **198** C5
Borgorose *Italy* 42°11N 13°13E **199** F10
Borgosésia *Italy* 45°43N 8°16E **198** C5
Borgotaro = Borgo Val di Taro
Italy 44°29N 9°46E **198** D6
Borgund *Norway* 61°3N 7°48E **164** C4
Borhoyn Tal *Mongolia* 43°50N 111°58E **226** C6
Bori *Nigeria* 4°42N 7°21E **263** E6
Borigumma *India* 19°3N 82°33E **244** E6
Borikhane *Laos* 18°33N 103°43E **236** C4
Borisoglebsk *Russia* 51°27N 42°5E **190** E6
Borisov = Barysaw
Belarus 54°17N 28°28E **177** A15
Borisovgrad = Pŭrvomay
Bulgaria 42°8N 25°17E **203** D9
Borisovka *Russia* 50°36N 36°1E **189** G9
Borisovo *Russia* 55°38N 37°44E **129** C4
Borj Jeneïn *Tunisia* 31°45N 10°9E **258** B2
Borja *Peru* 4°20S 77°40W **328** D2
Borja *Spain* 41°48N 1°34W **196** D3
Borjas Blancas = Les Borges
Blanques *Spain* 41°31N 0°52E **196** D5
Borjomi *Georgia* 41°48N 43°28E **191** K6
Børkop *Denmark* 55°39N 9°39E **163** J3
Borkou *Chad* 18°15N 18°50E **259** E3
Borkou-Ennedi-Tibesti □
Chad 18°0N 19°0E **259** E3
Borkum *Germany* 53°34N 6°40E **178** B2
Borlänge *Sweden* 60°29N 15°26E **162** D9
Borle *India* 19°2N 72°54E **130** A2
Borley, C. *Antarctica* 66°15S 52°30E **151** C5
Borlu *Turkey* 38°44N 28°27E **205** C10
Bormida → *Italy* 44°23N 8°13E **198** D5
Bórmio *Italy* 46°28N 10°22E **198** B7
Borna *Germany* 51°7N 12°29E **178** D8
Borne Sulinowo *Poland* 53°32N 16°36E **184** E3
Borneo *E. Indies* 1°0N 115°0E **235** B4
Bornholm *Denmark* 55°10N 15°0E **163** J8
Bornholmsgattet *Europe* 55°15N 14°20E **163** J8
Borno □ *Nigeria* 11°30N 13°0E **263** C7
Bornos *Spain* 36°48N 5°42W **195** J5
Bornova *Turkey* 38°27N 27°14E **205** C9
Bornu Yassa *Nigeria* 12°14N 12°25E **263** C7
Boro → *Sudan* 8°52N 26°11E **257** F2
Borobudur *Indonesia* 7°36S 110°13E **235** D4
Borodino *Russia* 55°31N 35°40E **188** E8
Borodino *Ukraine* 46°18N 29°15E **183** D14
Borogontsy *Russia* 62°42N 131°8E **215** C14
Borohoro Shan *China* 44°6N 83°10E **217** D10
Boromo *Burkina Faso* 11°45N 2°58W **262** C4
Boron *U.S.A.* 35°0N 117°39W **307** L9
Boronga Is. *Burma* 19°58N 93°6E **241** F4
Borongan *Phil.* 11°37N 125°26E **233** F5
Boronia Park *Australia* 33°49S 151°8E **139** A1
Borotangba Mts. *C.A.R.* 6°30N 25°0E **257** F2
Borotou *Ivory C.* 8°46N 7°30W **262** D3
Borovan *Bulgaria* 43°27N 23°45E **202** C7
Borovichi *Russia* 58°25N 33°55E **188** C7
Borovsk *Russia* 55°12N 36°24E **188** E9
Borovskoye *Kazakhstan* 53°48N 64°9E **216** B6
Borrby *Sweden* 55°27N 14°10E **163** J8
Borrego Springs
U.S.A. 33°15N 116°23W **307** M10
Borriol *Spain* 40°4N 0°4W **196** E4
Borrisokane *Ireland* 53°0N 8°7W **166** D3
Borroloola *Australia* 16°4S 136°17E **280** B2
Borșa *Cluj, Romania* 46°56N 23°40E **183** D8
Borșa *Maramureș,*
Romania 47°41N 24°50E **183** C9
Borsad *India* 22°25N 72°54E **242** H5
Borsec *Romania* 46°57N 25°34E **183** D10
Borshchiv *Ukraine* 48°48N 26°3E **183** B11
Borsod-Abaúj-Zemplén □
Hungary 48°20N 21°0E **182** B6
Bort-les-Orgues *France* 45°24N 2°29E **174** C6
Borth *U.K.* 52°29N 4°2W **169** E3
Börtnan *Sweden* 62°45N 13°50E **162** B7
Borūjerd *Iran* 33°55N 48°50E **213** F13
Boryeong *S. Korea* 36°21N 126°36E **224** D3
Borynya *Ukraine* 49°4N 23°0E **185** J10
Boryslav *Ukraine* 49°18N 23°28E **185** J10
Boryspil *Ukraine* 50°21N 30°59E **189** G6
Borzhomi = Borjomi
Georgia 41°48N 43°28E **191** K6
Borzna *Ukraine* 51°18N 32°26E **189** G7
Borzya *Russia* 50°24N 116°31E **215** D12
Bosa *Italy* 40°18N 8°30E **200** B1
Bosa Monene
Dem. Rep. of the Congo 1°16S 23°40E **264** C4
Bosaga *Turkmenistan* 37°33N 65°41E **240** A2
Bosambi
Dem. Rep. of the Congo 2°24N 22°39E **264** B4
Bosanska Dubica
Bos.-H. 45°10N 16°50E **199** C13
Bosanska Gradiška
Bos.-H. 45°10N 17°15E **182** E2
Bosanska Kostajnica
Bos.-H. 45°11N 16°33E **199** C13
Bosanska Krupa
Bos.-H. 44°53N 16°10E **199** D13
Bosanski Brod *Bos.-H.* 45°10N 18°0E **182** E2
Bosanski Novi *Bos.-H.* 45°2N 16°22E **199** C13
Bosanski Petrovac
Bos.-H. 44°35N 16°21E **199** D13
Bosanski Šamac *Bos.-H.* 45°3N 18°29E **182** E3
Bosansko Grahovo
Bos.-H. 44°12N 16°26E **199** D13
Bosavi, Mt. *Papua N. G.* 6°30S 142°49E **286** D2
Boscastle *U.K.* 50°41N 4°42W **169** G3
Boscobel *U.S.A.* 43°8N 90°42W **310** A6
Boscobelle *Barbados* 13°17N 59°35W **323** r
Bose *China* 23°53N 106°35E **228** F6
Boseki
Dem. Rep. of the Congo 2°34S 19°38E **264** C3
Boseong *S. Korea* 34°46N 127°5E **224** E3
Boshan *China* 36°28N 117°49E **227** F9
Boshof *S. Africa* 28°31S 25°13E **270** C4
Boshrūyeh *Iran* 33°50N 57°30E **247** C8
Bosilegrad *Serbia* 42°30N 22°27E **202** D6
Boskovice *Czech Rep.* 49°29N 16°40E **181** B9
Bosmont *S. Africa* 26°10S 27°57E **123** B1
Bosna → *Bos.-H.* 45°4N 18°29E **182** E3
Bosna i Hercegovina = Bosnia-
Herzegovina ■ *Europe* 44°0N 18°0E **182** G2
Bosnia-Herzegovina ■
Europe 44°0N 18°0E **182** G2
Bosnik *Indonesia* 1°5S 136°10E **231** E9
Bōsō-Hantō *Japan* 35°20N 140°20E **223** B12
Bosobolo
Dem. Rep. of the Congo 4°15N 19°50E **264** B3
Bosön *Sweden* 59°22N 18°11E **139** A3
Bosporus = İstanbul Boğazı
Turkey 41°5N 29°3E **122** B2
Bosque Farms *U.S.A.* 35°51N 106°42W **305** J10
Bossangoa *C.A.R.* 6°35N 17°30E **264** A3
Bossé Bangou *Niger* 13°20N 1°18E **263** C5
Bossembélé *C.A.R.* 5°25N 17°40E **264** A3
Bossemtélé *C.A.R.* 5°41N 16°38E **264** A3
Bossier City *U.S.A.* 32°31N 93°44W **314** E8
Bossiesvlei *Namibia* 25°1S 16°44E **270** C2
Bosso *Niger* 13°43N 13°19E **259** F2
Bosso, Dallol → *Niger* 12°25N 2°50E **263** C5
Bostan *Pakistan* 30°26N 67°2E **242** D2
Bostānābād *Iran* 37°50N 46°50E **213** D12
Bostancı *Turkey* 40°57N 29°5E **122** C2
Bosten Hu *China* 41°55N 87°40E **217** D11
Boston *Phil.* 7°52N 126°22E **233** H6
Boston *Lincs., U.K.* 52°59N 0°2W **168** E7
Boston *Ga., U.S.A.* 30°47N 83°47W **316** E6
Boston *Mass., U.S.A.* 42°22N 71°3W **116** A2
Boston Bar *Canada* 49°52N 121°30W **296** D4
Boston Bay *Jamaica* 18°9N 76°22W **320** a
Boston Common *Boston, U.S.A.* **116** c1
Boston Logan Int. ✕ (BOS)
U.S.A. 42°22N 71°1W **116** A2
Boston Mts. *U.S.A.* 35°42N 93°15W **314** D8
Boston Tea Party Ship & Museum
Boston, U.S.A. **116** c3
Bostwick *U.S.A.* 29°46N 81°38W **316** F8
Bosumtwi, L. *Ghana* 6°30N 1°25W **263** D4
Bosusulu
Dem. Rep. of the Congo 0°50N 20°45E **264** B4
Bosut → *Croatia* 45°20N 18°45E **182** E3
Boswell *B.C., Canada* 49°28N 116°45W **296** D5
Boswell *Ind., U.S.A.* 40°31N 87°23W **311** D9
Boswell *Pa., U.S.A.* 40°10N 79°2W **312** F5
Bosworth *U.S.A.* 39°28N 93°20W **310** E3
Botad *India* 22°15N 71°40E **242** H4
Botafogo *Brazil* 22°56S 43°10W **135** B1
Botan → *Turkey* 37°57N 42°2E **213** D10
Botanic Gardens
Washington, D.C., U.S.A. **143** b3
Botanisk Have *Copenhagen, Denmark* **118** b2
Botany *Australia* 33°56S 151°12E **139** B2
Botany B. *Australia* 33°58S 151°11E **139** B2
Botany Bay △ *Australia* 34°0S 151°14E **139** B2
Botene *Laos* 17°35N 101°12E **236** D3
Botera *Angola* 11°37S 14°16E **265** E2
Botev *Bulgaria* 42°44N 24°52E **203** D8
Botevgrad *Bulgaria* 42°55N 23°47E **202** D7
Bothaville *S. Africa* 27°23S 26°34E **270** C4
Bothnia, G. of *Europe* 62°0N 20°0E **160** F19
Bothwell *Tas., Australia* 42°20S 147°1E **281** G4
Bothwell *Ont., Canada* 42°38N 81°52W **312** D3
Botić → *Czech Rep.* 50°4N 14°26E **135** B3
Botica Sete *Portugal* 38°49N 9°10W **126** A1
Boticas *Portugal* 41°41N 7°40W **194** D3

INDEX
Brokind 353

Botletle → *Botswana* 20°10S 23°15E **270** B3
Botlikh *Russia* 42°39N 46°11E **191** J8
Botna → *Moldova* 46°45N 29°34E **183** D14
Botola *Dem. Rep. of the Congo* 1°17S 18°13E **264** C3
Botolan *Phil.* 15°17N 120°1E **232** D3
Botoroaga *Romania* 44°8N 25°32E **183** F10
Botoşani *Romania* 47°42N 26°41E **183** C11
Botoşani □ *Romania* 47°50N 26°50E **183** C11
Botou *Burkina Faso* 12°42N 1°59E **263** C5
Botricello *Italy* 38°56N 16°51E **201** D9
Botro *Ivory C.* 7°51N 5°19W **262** D3
Botshabelo *S. Africa* 29°14S 26°44E **270** C4
Botswana ■ *Africa* 22°0S 24°0E **270** B3
Bottellier *Neth. Ant.* 12°6N 68°54W **322** g
Bottineau *U.S.A.* 48°50N 100°27W **308** A3
Bottnaryd *Sweden* 57°47N 13°50E **163** G7
Bottom, The *Neth. Ant.* 17°38N 63°15W **322** a
Bottopassi *Suriname* 4°14N 55°27W **329** C6
Bottrop *Germany* 51°31N 6°58E **170** C6
Botucatu *Brazil* 22°55S 48°30W **335** A6
Botum Sakor △ *Cambodia* 11°5N 103°15E **237** G4
Botwood *Canada* 49°6N 55°23W **299** C8
Bou Alam *Algeria* 33°50N 1°26E **261** B5
Bou Ali *Algeria* 27°11N 0°4W **261** C4
Bou Djébéha *Mali* 18°25N 2°45W **262** B4
Bou Guema *Algeria* 28°49N 0°19E **261** C5
Bou Ismaïl *Algeria* 36°38N 2°42E **261** A5
Bou Izakarn *Morocco* 29°12N 9°46W **260** C3
Boû Lanouâr *Mauritania* 21°12N 16°34W **260** D1
Bou Naga *Mauritania* 18°49N 13°20W **262** B2
Bou Noura *Algeria* 32°29N 3°43E **261** B5
Boû Rjeïmât *Mauritania* 19°4N 15°3W **262** B1
Bou Saâda *Algeria* 35°11N 4°9E **261** A5
Bou Salem *Tunisia* 36°45N 9°2E **258** A1
Bouaflé *Ivory C.* 7°1N 5°47W **262** D3
Bouaké *Ivory C.* 7°40N 5°2W **262** D3
Bouanga *Congo* 2°7S 16°8E **264** C3
Bouar *C.A.R.* 6°0N 15°40E **264** A3
Bouârfa *Morocco* 32°32N 1°58W **261** B4
Bouba Ndjida △ *Cameroon* 8°50N 14°45E **264** A2
Boubout *Algeria* 27°26N 4°30W **260** C4
Bouca *C.A.R.* 6°45N 18°25E **264** A3
Boucaut B. *Australia* 12°0S 134°25E **280** A1
Boucherville *Canada* 45°36N 73°28W **130** A3
Boucherville, Îs. de *Canada* 45°36N 73°28W **130** A3
Bouches-du-Rhône □ *France* 43°37N 5°2E **175** E9
Boucle de Baoulé △ *Mali* 13°53N 9°0W **262** C3
Boucles de la Seine Normande △ *France* 49°32N 0°35E **172** C7
Bouctouche *Canada* 46°30N 64°45W **299** C7
Bouda *Algeria* 27°50N 0°27W **261** C4
Boudenib *Morocco* 31°59N 3°31W **260** B4
Bouéni *Mayotte* 12°54S 45°4E **272** b
Bouéni, B. de *Mayotte* 12°55S 45°7E **272** b
Boufarik *Algeria* 36°34N 2°58E **261** A5
Bougainville, C. *Australia* 13°57S 126°4E **278** B4
Bougainville I. *Papua N. G.* 6°0S 155°0E **287** L8
Bougainville Reef *Australia* 15°30S 147°5E **280** B4
Bougainville Str. *Solomon Is.* 6°40S 156°10E **287** L9
Bougaroun, C. *Algeria* 37°6N 6°30E **261** A6
Bougie = Bejaïa *Algeria* 36°42N 5°2E **261** A6
Bougival *France* 48°51N 2°8E **134** A1
Bougouni *Mali* 11°30N 7°20W **262** C3
Bougtob *Algeria* 34°2N 0°5E **261** B5
Bouillante *Guadeloupe* 16°8N 61°46W **322** e
Bouillante, Pitons de *Guadeloupe* 16°8N 61°43W **322** e
Bouillon *Belgium* 49°44N 5°3E **170** E5
Bouïra *Algeria* 36°20N 3°59E **261** A5
Bouïra □ *Algeria* 36°15N 3°55E **261** A5
Boukombé *Benin* 10°13N 1°9E **263** C5
Boulal *Mali* 15°8N 8°21W **262** B3
Boulazac *France* 45°10N 0°47E **174** C4
Boulder *Colo., U.S.A.* 40°1N 105°17W **304** F11
Boulder *Mont., U.S.A.* 46°14N 112°7W **304** C7
Boulder City *U.S.A.* 35°58N 114°49W **307** K12
Boulder Creek *U.S.A.* 37°7N 122°7W **306** H4
Boulder Dam = Hoover Dam *U.S.A.* 36°1N 114°44W **307** K12
Boulder Pt. *China* 22°14N 114°6E **122** B1
Boulemane □ *Morocco* 33°10N 4°0W **260** B4
Boulembo *Gabon* 1°26S 12°0E **264** C2
Bouli *Mauritania* 15°17N 12°18W **262** B2
Boulia *Australia* 22°52S 139°51E **280** C2
Bouligny *France* 49°17N 5°45E **173** C12
Boulogne → *France* 47°12N 1°47W **172** E5
Boulogne, Bois de *France* 48°51N 2°14E **134** A2
Boulogne-Billancourt *France* 48°50N 2°14E **134** A2
Boulogne-sur-Gesse *France* 43°18N 0°38E **174** E4
Boulogne-sur-Mer *France* 50°42N 1°36E **173** B8
Bouloire *France* 47°59N 0°45E **172** E7
Boulou → *C.A.R.* 6°45N 24°16E **264** A4
Boulouli *Mali* 15°30N 9°25W **262** B3
Bouloupari *N. Cal.* 21°52S 166°4E **288** d
Boulouposse *Congo* 1°58S 12°40E **264** C2
Boulsa *Burkina Faso* 12°39N 0°34W **263** C4
Boultoum *Niger* 14°45N 10°25E **259** F2
Bouma △ *Fiji* 16°50S 179°52E **287** A2
Boumalne Dadès *Morocco* 31°25N 6°0W **260** B3
Boumba → *Cameroon* 2°2N 15°12E **264** B2
Boumbé → *C.A.R.* 4°4N 15°23E **264** B3
Boûmdeïd *Mauritania* 17°25N 9°50W **262** B2
Boumerdès *Algeria* 36°46N 3°28E **261** A5
Boumerdès □ *Algeria* 36°45N 3°40E **261** A5
Boun Neua *Laos* 21°38N 101°54E **236** B3
Boun Tai *Laos* 21°23N 101°58E **236** B3
Bouna *Ivory C.* 9°10N 3°0W **262** D4
Boundary *U.S.A.* 64°5N 141°1W **303** D12
Boundary Peak *U.S.A.* 37°51N 118°21W **306** H8
Boundiali *Ivory C.* 9°30N 6°20W **262** D3
Boungou → *C.A.R.* 8°21N 23°48E **264** A4
Bountiful *U.S.A.* 40°53N 111°52W **304** F8
Bounty Is. *Pac. Oc.* 48°0S 178°30E **288** M9
Bounty Trough *Pac. Oc.* 46°0S 178°0E **288** M9
Boura *Mali* 12°25N 4°33W **262** C4
Bourail *N. Cal.* 21°34S 165°30E **288** d
Bourbeuse → *U.S.A.* 38°24N 90°53W **310** F6
Bourbon *U.S.A.* 41°18N 86°7W **311** C10
Bourbon-Lancy *France* 46°37N 3°45E **174** B7
Bourbon-l'Archambault *France* 46°36N 3°4E **173** F10
Bourbon Street *New Orleans, U.S.A.* **131** b2
Bourbonnais *Allier, France* 46°28N 3°0E **173** F10
Bourbonnais *Ill., U.S.A.* 41°9N 87°52W **311** C9
Bourbonne-les-Bains *France* 47°54N 5°45E **173** E12
Bourbourg *France* 50°56N 2°12E **173** B9
Bourdel L. *Canada* 56°43N 74°10W **298** A5
Bourem *Mali* 17°0N 0°24W **263** B4
Bouressa *Mali* 20°0N 2°15E **261** E5
Bourg *France* 45°3N 0°34W **174** C3
Bourg-Argental *France* 45°18N 4°32E **175** C8
Bourg-de-Péage *France* 45°2N 5°3E **175** C9
Bourg-en-Bresse *France* 46°13N 5°12E **173** F12
Bourg-la-Reine *France* 48°46N 2°19E **134** B2
Bourg-Lastic *France* 45°39N 2°35E **174** C6
Bourg-Madame *France* 42°26N 1°55E **174** F5
Bourg-St-Andéol *France* 44°23N 4°39E **175** D8
Bourg-St-Maurice *France* 45°35N 6°46E **175** C10
Bourganeuf *France* 45°57N 1°45E **174** C5
Bourgas = Burgas *Bulgaria* 42°33N 27°29E **203** D11
Bourges *France* 47°9N 2°25E **173** E9
Bourget *Canada* 45°26N 75°9W **313** A9
Bourget, Lac du *France* 45°44N 5°52E **175** C9
Bourgneuf, B. de *France* 47°3N 2°10W **172** E4
Bourgneuf-en-Retz *France* 47°2N 1°58W **172** E5
Bourgogne □ *France* 47°0N 4°50E **173** F11
Bourgoin-Jallieu *France* 45°36N 5°17E **175** C9
Bourgueil *France* 47°17N 0°10E **172** E7
Bourke *Australia* 30°8S 145°55E **281** E4
Bourne *U.K.* 52°47N 0°22W **168** E7
Bournemouth *U.K.* 50°43N 1°52W **169** G6
Bournemouth □ *U.K.* 50°43N 1°52W **169** G6
Bouroum *Burkina Faso* 13°37N 0°39W **263** C4
Bouse *U.S.A.* 33°56N 114°0W **307** M13
Boussac *France* 46°22N 2°13E **173** F9
Boussé *Burkina Faso* 12°39N 1°53W **263** C4
Bousso *Chad* 10°34N 16°52E **259** F3
Boussouma *Burkina Faso* 12°52N 1°13W **263** C4
Bout, Pte. du *Martinique* 14°33N 61°34W **322** j
Bout Stable Bay *Dominica* 15°21N 61°15W **323** k
Boutilimit *Mauritania* 17°45N 14°40W **262** B2
Boutonne → *France* 45°54N 0°50W **174** C3
Bouvet I. = Bouvetøya *Antarctica* 54°26S 3°24E **152** M12
Bouvetøya *Antarctica* 54°26S 3°24E **152** M12
Bouviers *France* 48°46N 2°4E **134** B1
Bouxwiller *France* 48°49N 7°27E **173** D14
Bouza *Niger* 14°29N 6°2E **263** C6
Bouznika *Morocco* 33°46N 7°6W **260** B3
Bouzonville *France* 49°17N 6°32E **173** C13
Bova Marina *Italy* 37°56N 15°55E **201** E8
Bovalino Marina *Italy* 38°10N 16°10E **201** D9
Bovec *Slovenia* 46°20N 13°33E **199** B10
Boven Kapuas, Pegunungan *Malaysia* 1°25N 113°15E **235** B4
Bovenkerk *Neths.* 52°18N 4°51E **112** B2
Bovenkerker Polder *Neths.* 52°16N 4°52E **112** B2
Bøverdal *Norway* 61°44N 8°20E **164** C5
Bøverfjorden *Norway* 63°1N 8°32E **164** A5
Bovill *U.S.A.* 46°51N 116°24W **304** C5
Bovino *Italy* 41°15N 15°20E **201** A8
Bovisa *Italy* 45°30N 9°10E **129** A2
Bovril *Argentina* 31°21S 59°26W **334** C4
Bow *U.K.* 51°31N 0°1W **125** A3
Bow → *Canada* 49°57N 111°41W **296** C6
Bow Island *Canada* 49°50N 111°23W **304** B8
Bowbells *U.S.A.* 48°48N 102°15W **308** A2
Bowdle *U.S.A.* 45°27N 99°39W **308** C4
Bowdon *U.S.A.* 33°32N 85°15W **316** B4
Bowdon Junction *U.S.A.* 33°40N 85°9W **316** B4
Bowelling *Australia* 33°25S 116°30E **279** F2
Bowen *Argentina* 35°0S 67°31W **334** D2
Bowen *Queens., Australia* 20°0S 148°16E **280** J6
Bowen Mts. *Australia* 37°0S 147°50E **283** D7
Bowers Basin *Pac. Oc.* 53°45N 176°0E **150** D16
Bowers Ridge *Pac. Oc.* 54°0N 180°0E **150** D17
Bowery *New York, U.S.A.* **132** e2
Bowie *Ariz., U.S.A.* 32°19N 109°29W **305** K9
Bowie *Tex., U.S.A.* 33°34N 97°51W **314** E6
Bowkān *Iran* 36°31N 46°12E **213** D12
Bowland, Forest of *U.K.* 54°0N 2°30W **168** D5
Bowling Green *Fla., U.S.A.* 27°38N 81°50W **317** H8
Bowling Green *Ky., U.S.A.* 36°59N 86°27W **308** G10
Bowling Green *Mo., U.S.A.* 39°21N 91°12W **310** E5
Bowling Green *Ohio, U.S.A.* 41°23N 83°39W **311** C13
Bowling Green, C. *Australia* 19°19S 147°25E **280** B4
Bowling Green Bay △ *Australia* 19°26S 146°57E **280** B4
Bowman *N. Dak., U.S.A.* 46°11N 103°24W **308** B2
Bowman *S.C., U.S.A.* 33°21N 80°41W **316** B9
Bowman I. *Antarctica* 65°0S 104°0E **151** C8
Bowmanville = Clarington *Canada* 43°55N 78°41W **312** C6
Bowmore *U.K.* 55°45N 6°17W **167** F2
Bowral *Australia* 34°26S 150°27E **283** C9
Bowraville *Australia* 30°37S 152°52E **281** E5
Bowron → *Canada* 54°3N 121°50W **296** C4
Bowron Lake ⌂ *Canada* 53°10N 121°5W **296** C4
Bowser L. *Canada* 56°30N 129°30W **296** B3
Bowsman *Canada* 52°14N 101°12W **297** C8
Bowutu Mts. *Papua N. G.* 7°45S 147°10E **286** D4
Bowwood *Zambia* 17°5S 26°20E **269** F2
Box Cr. → *Australia* 34°10S 143°50E **281** E3
Boxholm *Sweden* 58°12N 15°3E **163** F9
Boxmeer *Neths.* 51°38N 5°56E **170** C5
Boxtel *Neths.* 51°36N 5°20E **170** C5
Boyabat *Turkey* 41°28N 34°47E **212** B6
Boyabo *Dem. Rep. of the Congo* 3°43N 18°46E **264** B3
Boyacá □ *Colombia* 5°30N 73°20W **328** B3
Boyacıköy *Turkey* 41°5N 29°2E **122** B2
Boyalıca *Turkey* 40°29N 29°33E **203** F13
Boyang *China* 29°0N 116°38E **229** C11
Boyany *Ukraine* 48°17N 26°8E **183** B11
Boyasegese *Dem. Rep. of the Congo* 3°29N 20°33E **264** B4
Boyce *U.S.A.* 31°23N 92°40W **314** F8
Boyd *U.S.A.* 30°11N 83°37W **316** E6
Boyd Conservation Area *Canada* 43°49N 79°35W **141** A1
Boyd L. *Canada* 52°46N 76°42W **298** B4
Boyenge *Dem. Rep. of the Congo* 0°14N 18°55E **264** B3
Boyer, C. *N. Cal.* 21°37S 168°6E **288** d
Boyera *Dem. Rep. of the Congo* 0°40S 19°23E **264** C3
Boyle *Alta., Canada* 54°35N 112°49W **296** C6
Boyle *Roscommon, Ireland* 53°59N 8°18W **166** C3
Boyle Heights *U.S.A.* 34°1N 118°12W **126** B3
Boyne → *Ireland* 53°43N 6°15W **166** C5
Boyne City *U.S.A.* 45°13N 85°1W **309** C11
Boyni Qara *Afghan.* 36°20N 67°0E **240** A2
Boynitsa *Bulgaria* 43°58N 22°32E **202** C6
Boynton Beach *U.S.A.* 26°32N 80°4W **317** J9
Boyolali *Indonesia* 7°32S 110°35E **235** D4
Boyoma, Chutes *Dem. Rep. of the Congo* 0°35N 25°23E **264** B5
Boysen Res. *U.S.A.* 43°25N 108°11W **304** E9
Boyup Brook *Australia* 33°50S 116°23E **279** F2
Boz Burun *Turkey* 40°32N 28°46E **203** F12
Boz Dağ *Turkey* 37°18N 29°11E **205** D11
Boz Dağları *Turkey* 38°20N 28°0E **205** C10
Bozai Gumbaz *Afghan.* 37°8N 74°0E **240** A6
Bozburun *Turkey* 36°43N 28°4E **205** E10
Bozcaada *Turkey* 39°49N 26°3E **212** C2
Bozdağ *Turkey* 36°50N 36°22E **250** B7
Bozdoğan *Turkey* 37°40N 28°17E **205** D10
Boze *Papua N. G.* 9°3S 143°3E **286** E2
Bozeman *U.S.A.* 45°41N 111°2W **304** D8
Bozen = Bolzano *Italy* 46°31N 11°22E **199** B8
Bozene *Dem. Rep. of the Congo* 2°56N 19°12E **264** B3
Boževac *Serbia* 44°32N 21°24E **202** B5
Bozhou *China* 33°55N 115°41E **226** H8
Bozkır *Turkey* 37°11N 32°14E **212** D5
Bozkurt *Turkey* 37°50N 29°37E **205** D11
Bozouls *France* 44°28N 2°43E **174** D6
Bozoum *C.A.R.* 6°25N 16°35E **264** A3
Bozova *Antalya, Turkey* 37°13N 30°18E **205** D12
Bozova *Sanliurfa, Turkey* 37°21N 38°32E **213** D8
Bozovici *Romania* 44°56N 22°0E **182** F7
Bozüyük *Turkey* 39°54N 30°3E **205** B12
Bozyazı *Turkey* 36°6N 33°0E **250** B4
Bra *Italy* 44°42N 7°51E **198** D4
Braås *Sweden* 57°4N 15°3E **163** G9
Brabant □ *Belgium* 50°46N 4°30E **170** D4
Brabant L. *Canada* 55°58N 103°43W **297** B8
Brabrand *Denmark* 56°9N 10°7E **163** H4
Brač *Croatia* 43°20N 16°40E **199** E13
Bracadale, L. *U.K.* 57°20N 6°30W **167** D2
Bracciano *Italy* 42°6N 12°10E **199** F9
Bracciano, L. di *Italy* 42°7N 12°14E **199** F9
Bracebridge *Canada* 45°2N 79°19W **312** A5
Bracieux *France* 47°30N 1°30E **172** E8
Bräcke *Sweden* 62°45N 15°26E **162** B9
Brackettville *U.S.A.* 29°19N 100°25W **314** G4
Bracki Kanal *Croatia* 43°24N 16°40E **199** E13
Bracknell *U.K.* 51°25N 0°43W **169** F7
Bracknell Forest □ *U.K.* 51°25N 0°44W **169** F7
Brad *Romania* 46°10N 22°50E **182** D7
Brådano → *Italy* 40°23N 16°51E **201** B9
Bradbury Building *Los Angeles, U.S.A.* **127** b2
Bradenton *U.S.A.* 27°30N 82°34W **317** H7
Bradford *Ont., Canada* 44°7N 79°34W **312** B5
Bradford *W. Yorks., U.K.* 53°47N 1°45W **168** D6
Bradford *Ill., U.S.A.* 41°11N 89°39W **310** C7
Bradford *Ohio, U.S.A.* 40°8N 84°27W **311** D12
Bradford *Pa., U.S.A.* 41°58N 78°38W **312** E6
Bradford *Vt., U.S.A.* 43°59N 72°9W **313** C12
Bradley *Ark., U.S.A.* 33°6N 93°39W **314** E8
Bradley *Calif., U.S.A.* 35°52N 120°48W **306** K6
Bradley *Ill., U.S.A.* 41°9N 87°52W **311** C9
Bradley Institute *Zimbabwe* 17°7S 31°25E **269** F3
Bradley Junction *U.S.A.* 27°48N 81°59W **317** H8
Bradner *U.S.A.* 41°20N 83°26W **311** C13
Brady *U.S.A.* 31°9N 99°20W **314** F5
Brædstrup *Denmark* 55°58N 9°37E **163** J3
Braemar *Australia* 33°12S 139°35E **282** B3
Brae Park *U.K.* 55°58N 3°18W **121** B2
Braeside *Canada* 45°28N 76°24W **313** A8
Braeton *Jamaica* 17°57N 76°53W **320** a
Braga *Portugal* 41°35N 8°25W **194** D2
Braga □ *Portugal* 41°30N 8°30W **194** D2
Bragadiru *Romania* 43°46N 25°31E **183** G10
Bragado *Argentina* 35°2S 60°27W **334** D3
Bragança *Brazil* 1°0S 47°2W **332** B2
Bragança *Portugal* 41°48N 6°50W **194** D4
Bragança □ *Portugal* 41°30N 6°45W **194** D4
Bragança Paulista *Brazil* 22°55S 46°32W **335** A6
Bragg's Spur = West Memphis *U.S.A.* 35°8N 90°10W **315** D9
Brahestad = Raahe *Finland* 64°40N 24°28E **160** D21
Brahmakund *India* 27°52N 96°22E **241** B6
Brahmanbaria *Bangla.* 23°58N 91°15E **241** D3
Brahmani → *India* 20°39N 86°46E **244** D8
Brahmapur *India* 19°15N 84°54E **244** E7
Brahmaputra → *Asia* 23°40N 90°35E **241** D3
Braich-y-pwll *U.K.* 52°47N 4°46W **168** E3
Braid *U.K.* 55°55N 3°11W **121** B2
Braidwood *Australia* 35°27S 149°49E **283** C8
Brăila *Romania* 45°19N 27°59E **183** E12
Brăila □ *Romania* 45°5N 27°30E **183** E12
Brainerd *U.S.A.* 46°22N 94°12W **308** B6
Braintree *Essex, U.K.* 51°53N 0°34E **169** F8
Braintree *Mass., U.S.A.* 42°13N 71°0W **313** D14
Brak → *S. Africa* 29°35S 22°55E **270** C3
Brake *Germany* 53°20N 8°28E **178** B4
Brakel *Germany* 51°42N 9°11E **178** D5
Brakna □ *Mauritania* 17°0N 13°20W **262** B2
Bräkne-Hoby *Sweden* 56°14N 15°6E **163** H9
Brakwater *Namibia* 22°28S 17°3E **270** B2
Brålanda *Sweden* 58°34N 12°21E **163** F6
Bramberg *Germany* 50°6N 10°40E **179** E6
Bramdrupdam *Denmark* 55°31N 9°28E **163** J3
Bramhapuri *India* 20°36N 79°52E **244** D4
Bramley *S. Africa* 26°7S 28°4E **123** A2
Bramming *Denmark* 55°28N 8°42E **163** J2
Brämön *Sweden* 62°14N 17°40E **162** B11
Brampton *Ont., Canada* 43°45N 79°45W **312** C5
Brampton *Cumb., U.K.* 54°57N 2°44W **168** C5
Brampton I. *Australia* 20°49S 149°16E **280** b
Bramsche *Germany* 52°24N 7°59E **178** C3
Branchville *U.S.A.* 33°15N 80°49W **316** B9
Branco → *Brazil* 1°20S 61°50W **329** D5
Branco, C. *Brazil* 7°9S 34°47W **332** C5
Brandaris *Neth. Ant.* 12°16N 68°23W **322** h
Brandberg *Namibia* 21°10S 14°33E **270** B1
Brandberg ⌂ *Namibia* 21°10S 14°30E **270** B1
Brandbu *Norway* 60°26N 10°28E **164** D7
Brande *Denmark* 55°57N 9°8E **163** J3
Brandeis Univ. *U.S.A.* 42°21N 71°17W **116** A1
Brandenburg = Neubrandenburg *Germany* 53°33N 13°15E **178** B9
Brandenburg *Brandenburg, Germany* 52°25N 12°33E **178** C8
Brandenburg *Ky., U.S.A.* 38°0N 86°10W **311** G10
Brandenburg □ *Germany* 52°50N 13°0E **178** C9
Brandenburger Tor *Germany* 52°30N 13°21E **115** A3
Brandfort *S. Africa* 28°40S 26°30E **270** C4
Brando *France* 42°47N 9°27E **175** F13
Brandon *Man., Canada* 49°50N 99°57W **297** D9
Brandon *Fla., U.S.A.* 27°56N 82°17W **317** H7
Brandon *Vt., U.S.A.* 43°48N 73°6W **313** C11
Brandon B. *Ireland* 52°17N 10°8W **166** D1
Brandon Mt. *Ireland* 52°15N 10°15W **166** D1
Brandsen *Argentina* 35°10S 58°15W **334** D4
Brandvlei *S. Africa* 30°25S 20°30E **270** D3
Brandýs nad Labem *Czech Rep.* 50°10N 14°40E **180** A7
Brăneşti *Romania* 44°27N 26°20E **183** F11
Branford *Conn., U.S.A.* 41°17N 72°49W **313** E12
Branford *Fla., U.S.A.* 29°58N 82°56W **316** F7
Brani, Pulau *Singapore* 1°15N 103°50E **138** B3
Braniewo *Poland* 54°25N 19°50E **184** D6
Branik *Czech Rep.* 50°1N 14°25E **135** B2
Brännkyrka *Sweden* 59°17N 18°0E **139** B2
Bransfield Str. *Antarctica* 63°0S 59°0W **151** C18
Brańsk *Poland* 52°45N 22°50E **185** F9
Branson *U.S.A.* 36°39N 93°13W **308** G7
Brantford *Canada* 43°10N 80°15W **312** C4
Brantley *U.S.A.* 31°35N 86°16W **316** D3
Brantôme *France* 45°22N 0°39E **174** C4
Branxholme *Australia* 37°52S 141°49E **282** D4
Branxton *Australia* 32°38S 151°21E **283** B9
Branzi *Italy* 46°1N 9°46E **198** B6
Brás *Amazonas, Brazil* 2°5S 58°10W **329** D6
Brás *São Paulo, Brazil* 23°32S 46°36W **137** B2
Bras d'Or L. *Canada* 45°50N 60°50W **299** C7
Bras-Panon *Réunion* 20°59S 55°41E **272** f
Brasher Falls *U.S.A.* 44°49N 74°47W **313** B10
Brasil = Brazil ■ *S. Amer.* 12°0S 50°0W **327** E6
Brasil, Planalto *Brazil* 18°0S 46°30W **326** E6
Brasil Novo *Brazil* 3°19S 52°38W **329** D7
Brasilândia *Brazil* 23°28S 46°42W **137** A1
Brasiléia *Brazil* 11°0S 68°45W **330** C4
Brasília *Distrito Federal, Brazil* 15°47S 47°55W **333** E2
Brasília *Minas Gerais, Brazil* 16°12S 44°26W **333** E3
Brasília △ *Brazil* 15°41S 48°8W **333** E2
Brasília Legal *Brazil* 3°49S 55°36W **329** D6
Braskereidfoss *Norway* 60°44N 11°46E **164** D8
Braslaw *Belarus* 55°38N 27°0E **188** E4
Braslovče *Slovenia* 46°21N 15°3E **199** B12
Braşov *Romania* 45°38N 25°35E **183** E10
Braşov □ *Romania* 45°45N 25°15E **183** E10
Brass *Nigeria* 4°35N 6°14E **263** E6
Brass → *Nigeria* 4°15N 6°13E **263** E6
Brassac-les-Mines *France* 45°24N 3°20E **174** C7
Brasschaat *Belgium* 51°19N 4°27E **170** C4
Brassey, Banjaran *Malaysia* 5°0N 117°15E **235** B5
Brassey Ra. *Australia* 25°8S 122°15E **279** E3
Brasso Seco *Trin. & Tob.* 10°45N 61°16W **323** t
Brasstown Bald *U.S.A.* 34°53N 83°49W **315** D13
Brastad *Sweden* 58°23N 11°30E **163** F5
Brastavăţu *Romania* 43°55N 24°24E **183** G9
Bratan = Morozov *Bulgaria* 42°30N 25°10E **203** D9
Brateş *Romania* 45°50N 26°4E **183** E11
Brateyevo *Russia* 55°39N 37°45E **129** C4
Bratislava *Slovak Rep.* 48°10N 17°7E **181** C10
Bratislava M.R. Stefanik ✕ **(BTS)** *Slovak Rep.* 48°11N 17°9E **181** C10
Bratislavský □ *Slovak Rep.* 48°15N 17°20E **181** C10
Bratsberg = Telemark □ *Norway* 59°25N 8°30E **164** E5
Bratsevo *Russia* 55°51N 37°24E **129** A2
Bratsigovo *Bulgaria* 42°1N 24°22E **203** D8
Bratsk *Russia* 56°10N 101°30E **215** D11
Brattleboro *U.S.A.* 42°51N 72°34W **313** D12
Brattvåg *Norway* 62°37N 6°25E **164** B3
Bratunac *Bos.-H.* 44°13N 19°21E **182** F4
Braunau *Austria* 48°15N 13°3E **180** C6
Braunsberg = Braniewo *Poland* 54°25N 19°50E **184** D6
Braunschweig *Germany* 52°15N 10°31E **178** C6
Braunton *U.K.* 51°7N 4°10W **169** F3
Brava = Baraawe *Somali Rep.* 1°20N 44°8E **267** D5
Brava *C. Verde Is.* 15°0N 24°40W **153** j
Bravicea *Moldova* 47°22N 28°27E **183** C13
Bråviken *Sweden* 58°38N 16°32E **163** F10
Bravo del Norte, Rio = Grande, Rio → *N. Amer.* 25°58N 97°9W **314** J6
Brawley *U.S.A.* 32°59N 115°31W **307** N11
Bray *Ireland* 53°13N 6°7W **166** C5
Bray, Mt. *Australia* 14°0S 134°30E **280** A1
Bray, Pays de *France* 49°46N 1°26E **171** B4
Bray-sur-Seine *France* 48°25N 3°14E **173** D10
Braybrook *Australia* 37°46S 144°51E **128** A1
Braymer *U.S.A.* 39°35N 93°48W **310** E3
Brázdim *Czech Rep.* 50°10N 14°35E **135** A3
Brazeau → *Canada* 52°55N 115°14W **296** C5
Brazil *U.S.A.* 39°32N 87°8W **311** E9
Brazil ■ *S. Amer.* 12°0S 50°0W **327** E6
Brazil Basin *Atl. Oc.* 15°0S 25°0W **152** H9
Brazilian Highlands = Brasil, Planalto *Brazil* 18°0S 46°30W **326** E6
Brazo Sur → *S. Amer.* 25°21S 57°42W **334** B4
Brazos → *U.S.A.* 28°53N 95°23W **314** G7
Brazzaville *Congo* 4°9S 15°12E **265** C3
Brčko *Bos.-H.* 44°54N 18°46E **182** F3
Brda → *Poland* 53°8N 18°8E **185** E5
Brdy *Czech Rep.* 49°43N 13°55E **180** B6
Bré = Bray *Ireland* 53°13N 6°7W **166** C5
Breach Candy *Mumbai, India* **130** a1
Breaden, L. *Australia* 25°51S 125°28E **279** E4
Breakheart Reservation *U.S.A.* 42°28N 71°1W **116** A2
Breaksea Sd. *N.Z.* 45°35S 166°35E **285** F1
Bream B. *N.Z.* 35°56S 174°28E **284** B3
Bream Hd. *N.Z.* 35°51S 174°36E **284** B3
Bream Tail *N.Z.* 36°3S 174°36E **284** C3
Breas *Chile* 25°29S 70°24W **334** B1
Breaza *Romania* 45°11N 25°40E **183** E10
Brebes *Indonesia* 6°52S 109°3E **235** D3
Brechin *Ont., Canada* 44°32N 79°10W **312** B5
Brechin *Angus, U.K.* 56°44N 2°39W **167** E6
Brecht *Belgium* 51°21N 4°38E **170** C4
Breckenridge *Colo., U.S.A.* 39°29N 106°3W **304** G10
Breckenridge *Minn., U.S.A.* 46°16N 96°35W **308** B5
Breckenridge *Tex., U.S.A.* 32°45N 98°54W **314** E5
Breckland *U.K.* 52°30N 0°40E **169** E8
Brecknock, Pen. *Chile* 54°35S 71°30W **336** D2
Břeclav *Czech Rep.* 48°46N 16°53E **181** C9
Brecon *U.K.* 51°57N 3°23W **169** F4
Brecon Beacons *U.K.* 51°53N 3°26W **169** F4
Brecon Beacons △ *U.K.* 51°50N 3°30W **169** F4
Breda *Neths.* 51°35N 4°45E **170** C4
Bredaryd *Sweden* 57°10N 13°45E **163** G7
Bredasdorp *S. Africa* 34°33S 20°2E **270** D3
Bredbo *Australia* 35°58S 149°10E **283** C8
Brede *Denmark* 55°47N 12°30E **118** A3
Bredebro *Denmark* 55°4N 8°50E **163** J2
Bredstedt *Germany* 54°37N 8°55E **178** A4
Bredy *Russia* 52°26N 60°21E **216** B6
Bree *Belgium* 51°8N 5°35E **170** C5
Breezy Point *U.S.A.* 40°33N 73°56W **132** C2
Bregalnica → *Macedonia* 41°43N 22°9E **202** E6
Bregenz *Austria* 47°30N 9°45E **180** D2
Bregovo *Bulgaria* 44°9N 22°39E **202** B6
Bréhal *France* 48°53N 1°30W **172** D5
Bréhat, Î. de *France* 48°51N 3°0W **172** D4
Breiðafjörður *Iceland* 65°15N 23°15W **155** B3
Breiðdalsvík *Iceland* 64°44N 14°0W **155** C13
Breil-sur-Roya *France* 43°56N 7°31E **175** E11
Breim *Norway* 61°44N 6°25E **164** C3
Breisach *Germany* 48°1N 7°36E **179** G3
Breitenlee *Austria* 48°15N 16°30E **142** A3
Brejinho de Nazaré *Brazil* 11°1S 48°34W **332** D2
Brejo *Brazil* 3°41S 42°47W **332** B3
Brekke *Norway* 61°1N 5°26E **164** C2
Brekken *Norway* 62°40N 11°55E **164** B8
Brekkestø *Norway* 58°11N 8°22E **164** F5
Bremanger *Norway* 61°51N 4°58E **164** C1
Bremangerlandet *Norway* 61°51N 5°0E **164** C1
Bremen *Bremen, Germany* 53°4N 8°47E **178** B4
Bremen *Ga., U.S.A.* 33°43N 85°9W **316** B4
Bremen *Ind., U.S.A.* 41°27N 86°9W **311** C10
Bremen □ *Germany* 53°4N 8°50E **178** B4
Bremer Bay *Australia* 34°21S 119°20E **279** F2
Bremer I. *Australia* 12°5S 136°45E **280** A2
Bremerhaven *Germany* 53°33N 8°36E **178** B4
Bremersdorp = Manzini *Swaziland* 26°30S 31°25E **271** C5
Bremerton *U.S.A.* 47°34N 122°37W **306** C4
Bremervörde *Germany* 53°29N 9°8E **178** B5
Bremnes *Norway* 59°47N 5°8E **164** E2
Bremsnes *Norway* 63°6N 7°40E **164** A4
Breña *Peru* 12°3S 77°3W **124** B2
Brenes *Spain* 37°32N 5°54W **195** H5
Brenham *U.S.A.* 30°10N 96°24W **314** F6
Brenne *France* 46°44N 1°14E **174** B5
Brenne △ *France* 46°40N 1°15E **174** B5
Brennerpass *Austria* 47°2N 11°30E **180** D4
Brennhaug *Norway* 61°54N 9°21E **164** C6
Breno *Italy* 45°57N 10°18E **198** C7
Brent *U.S.A.* 32°56N 87°10W **315** E11
Brent □ *U.K.* 51°33N 0°16W **125** A2
Brent Res. *U.K.* 51°34N 0°14W **125** A2
Brenta → *Italy* 45°11N 12°18E **199** C9
Brentford *U.K.* 51°28N 0°18W **125** B2
Brentwood *Essex, U.K.* 51°37N 0°19E **169** F8
Brentwood *Calif., U.S.A.* 34°3N 118°28W **126** B2
Brentwood *Calif., U.S.A.* 37°56N 121°42W **306** H5
Brentwood *N.Y., U.S.A.* 40°47N 73°15W **313** F11
Brentwood Park *U.S.A.* 34°3N 118°29W **126** B2
Brera *Italy* 45°28N 9°11E **129** B2
Brereton *Barbados* 13°7N 59°30W **323** r
Bréscia *Italy* 45°33N 10°15E **198** C7
Breskens *Neths.* 51°23N 3°33E **170** C3
Breslau = Wrocław *Poland* 51°5N 17°5E **185** G4
Bresle → *France* 50°4N 1°22E **172** B8
Bressanone *Italy* 46°43N 11°39E **199** B8
Bressay *U.K.* 60°9N 1°6W **167** A7
Bresse *France* 46°50N 5°10E **173** F12
Bresso *Italy* 45°32N 9°11E **129** A2
Bressuire *France* 46°51N 0°30W **172** F6
Brest *Belarus* 52°10N 23°40E **177** B12
Brest *Finistère, France* 48°24N 4°31W **172** D2
Brest □ *Belarus* 52°30N 26°10E **189** F4
Brest-Litovsk = Brest *Belarus* 52°10N 23°40E **177** B12
Bretagne □ *France* 48°10N 3°0W **172** D3
Bretanha, Pta. da *Azores* 37°54N 25°47W **153** d3
Bretçu *Romania* 46°7N 26°18E **183** D11
Bretenoux *France* 44°54N 1°51E **174** D5
Breteuil *Eure, France* 48°50N 0°57E **172** D7
Breteuil *Oise, France* 49°38N 2°18E **173** C9
Breton *Canada* 53°7N 114°28W **296** C6
Breton, Pertuis *France* 46°17N 1°25W **174** B2
Breton Sd. *U.S.A.* 29°35N 89°15W **315** G10
Brett, C. *N.Z.* 35°10S 174°20E **284** B3
Bretten *Germany* 49°2N 8°42E **179** F4
Breuil-Cervínia *Italy* 45°56N 7°38E **198** C4
Brevard *U.S.A.* 35°14N 82°44W **315** D13
Breves *Brazil* 1°40S 50°29W **332** B1
Brevig Mission *U.S.A.* 65°20N 166°29W **303** D6
Brevik *Telemark, Norway* 59°4N 9°42E **164** E6
Brevik *Stockholm, Sweden* 59°20N 18°12E **139** A3
Břevnov *Czech Rep.* 50°4N 14°22E **135** B2
Brewarrina *Australia* 30°0S 146°51E **281** E4
Brewer *U.S.A.* 44°48N 68°46W **309** C19
Brewer, Mt. *U.S.A.* 36°44N 118°28W **306** J8
Brewerville *Liberia* 6°26N 10°47W **262** D2
Brewster *N.Y., U.S.A.* 41°24N 73°36W **313** E11
Brewster *Ohio, U.S.A.* 40°43N 81°36W **312** F3
Brewster *Wash., U.S.A.* 48°6N 119°47W **304** B4
Brewster, Kap = Kangikajik *Greenland* 70°7N 22°0W **154** C8
Brewton *U.S.A.* 31°7N 87°4W **315** F11
Breyten *S. Africa* 26°16S 30°0E **271** C5
Breza *Bos.-H.* 44°2N 18°16E **182** F3
Brežice *Slovenia* 45°54N 15°35E **199** C12
Brézina *Algeria* 33°4N 1°14E **261** B5
Březnice *Czech Rep.* 49°32N 13°57E **180** B6
Breznik *Bulgaria* 42°44N 22°55E **202** D6
Brezno *Slovak Rep.* 48°50N 19°40E **181** C12
Brezoi *Romania* 45°21N 24°15E **183** E9
Brezovica *Kosovo* 42°15N 21°3E **202** D5
Brezovo *Bulgaria* 42°21N 25°5E **203** D9
Bria *C.A.R.* 6°30N 21°58E **264** A4
Briançon *France* 44°54N 6°39E **175** D10
Briare *France* 47°38N 2°45E **173** E9
Briars, The *St. Helena* 15°56S 5°43W **153** h
Briático *Italy* 38°43N 16°2E **201** D9
Bribie I. *Australia* 27°0S 153°10E **281** D5
Bribri *Costa Rica* 9°38N 82°50W **320** E3
Briceni *Moldova* 48°22N 27°6E **183** B12
Brickyard, The *U.S.A.* 41°55N 87°47W **119** B2
Bricquebec *France* 49°28N 1°38W **172** C5
Bridge City *U.S.A.* 29°55N 90°9W **131** B2
Bridgehampton *U.S.A.* 40°56N 72°19W **313** F12
Bridgend *U.K.* 51°30N 3°34W **169** F4
Bridgend □ *U.K.* 51°36N 3°36W **169** F4
Bridgenorth *Canada* 44°23N 78°23W **312** B6
Bridgeport *Calif., U.S.A.* 38°15N 119°14W **306** G7
Bridgeport *Conn., U.S.A.* 41°11N 73°12W **313** E11
Bridgeport *Ill., U.S.A.* 41°50N 87°38W **119** B3
Bridgeport *Ill., U.S.A.* 38°43N 87°46W **311** F9
Bridgeport *N.Y., U.S.A.* 43°9N 75°58W **313** C9
Bridgeport *Nebr., U.S.A.* 41°40N 103°6W **308** E2
Bridgeport *Tex., U.S.A.* 33°13N 97°45W **314** E6
Bridger *U.S.A.* 45°18N 108°55W **304** D9
Bridgeton *U.S.A.* 39°26N 75°14W **309** F16
Bridgetown *W. Austral., Australia* 33°58S 116°7E **279** F2
Bridgetown *Barbados* 13°6N 59°37W **323** r
Bridgetown *N.S., Canada* 44°55N 65°18W **299** D6
Bridgetown *Western Cape, S. Africa* 33°58S 18°33E **118** A2
Bridgeview *U.S.A.* 41°45N 87°48W **119** C2
Bridgewater *Tas., Australia* 42°44S 147°14E **281** G4
Bridgewater *Vic., Australia* 36°36S 143°59E **282** D5
Bridgewater *N.S., Canada* 44°25N 64°31W **299** D7
Bridgewater *Mass., U.S.A.* 41°59N 70°58W **313** E14
Bridgewater *N.Y., U.S.A.* 42°53N 75°15W **313** D9
Bridgewater, C. *Australia* 38°23S 141°23E **282** E4
Bridgman *U.S.A.* 41°57N 86°33W **311** C10
Bridgnorth *U.K.* 52°32N 2°25W **169** E5
Bridgton *U.S.A.* 44°3N 70°42W **313** B14
Bridgwater *U.K.* 51°8N 2°59W **169** F5
Bridgwater B. *U.K.* 51°15N 3°15W **169** F4
Bridlington *U.K.* 54°5N 0°12W **168** C7
Bridlington B. *U.K.* 54°4N 0°10W **168** C7
Bridport *Tas., Australia* 40°59S 147°23E **281** G4
Bridport *Dorset, U.K.* 50°44N 2°45W **169** G5
Briec *France* 48°6N 4°0W **172** D2
Brieg = Brzeg *Poland* 50°52N 17°30E **185** H4
Brienne-le-Château *France* 48°24N 4°30E **173** D11
Brienon-sur-Armançon *France* 47°59N 3°38E **173** E10
Brienz *Switz.* 46°46N 8°2E **179** J4
Brienzersee *Switz.* 46°44N 7°53E **179** J3
Brier Cr. → *U.S.A.* 32°44N 81°26W **316** C8
Brière ⌂ *France* 47°22N 2°13W **172** E4
Brievengat *Neth. Ant.* 12°9N 68°54W **322** g
Brig *Switz.* 46°18N 7°59E **179** J3
Brigg *U.K.* 53°34N 0°28W **168** D7
Brigham City *U.S.A.* 41°31N 112°1W **304** F7
Bright *Australia* 36°42S 146°56E **283** D7
Brighton *S. Austral., Australia* 35°5S 138°30E **282** C3
Brighton *Vic., Australia* 37°55S 144°59E **128** B1
Brighton *Ont., Canada* 44°2N 77°44W **312** B7
Brighton *Trin. & Tob.* 10°13N 61°39W **323** t
Brighton *Brighton & Hove, U.K.* 50°49N 0°7W **169** G7
Brighton *Fla., U.S.A.* 27°14N 81°6W **317** H8
Brighton *Ill., U.S.A.* 39°2N 90°8W **310** E6
Brighton *Iowa, U.S.A.* 41°10N 91°49W **310** C5
Brighton *Mass., U.S.A.* 42°21N 71°9W **116** A2
Brighton *Mich., U.S.A.* 42°32N 83°47W **311** B13
Brighton *N.Y., U.S.A.* 43°8N 77°34W **312** C7
Brighton Beach *U.S.A.* 40°34N 73°57W **132** C2
Brighton-Le-Sands *Australia* 33°57S 151°9E **139** B1
Brighton Park *U.S.A.* 41°48N 87°41W **119** C2
Brightside *Canada* 45°7N 76°29W **313** A8
Brightwater *N.Z.* 41°22S 173°9E **285** B8
Brightwood *U.S.A.* 38°57N 77°1W **143** B3
Brigittenau *Austria* 48°14N 16°22E **142** A2
Brignogan-Plage *France* 48°40N 4°20W **172** D2
Brignoles *France* 43°25N 6°5E **175** E10
Brihuega *Spain* 40°45N 2°52W **196** E2
Brikama *Gambia* 13°15N 16°45W **262** C1
Brilliant *U.S.A.* 40°15N 80°39W **312** F4
Brilon *Germany* 51°23N 8°35E **178** D4
Brim *Australia* 36°3S 142°27E **282** D5
Brimbank Park *Australia* 37°43S 144°50E **128** A1
Brimfield *U.S.A.* 40°50N 89°53W **310** D7
Brimstone Hill Fort *St. Kitts & Nevis* 17°20N 62°50W **322** d
Brindabella △ *Australia* 35°14S 148°5E **283** C8
Brindisi *Italy* 40°39N 17°55E **201** B10
Brinje *Croatia* 44°59N 15°9E **199** D12
Brinkley *U.S.A.* 34°53N 91°12W **314** D9
Brinkworth *Australia* 33°42S 138°26E **282** B3
Brinnon *U.S.A.* 47°41N 122°54W **306** C4
Brinson *U.S.A.* 30°59N 84°44W **316** E5
Brion, Î. *Canada* 47°46N 61°26W **299** C7
Brionne *France* 49°11N 0°43E **172** C7
Brionski *Croatia* 44°55N 13°45E **199** D10
Brioude *France* 45°18N 3°24E **174** C7
Briouze *France* 48°42N 0°23W **172** D6
Brisay *Canada* 54°26N 70°31W **299** B5
Brisbane *Queens., Australia* 27°25S 153°2E **281** D5
Brisbane *Calif., U.S.A.* 37°40N 122°24W **136** B2
Brisbane → *Australia* 27°24S 153°9E **281** D5
Brisbane Ranges △ *Australia* 37°47S 144°16E **282** D6
Brisbane Water △ *Australia* 33°26S 151°13E **283** B9
Brisighella *Italy* 44°13N 11°46E **199** D8
Bristol *Bristol, U.K.* 51°26N 2°35W **169** F5
Bristol *Conn., U.S.A.* 41°40N 72°57W **313** E12
Bristol *Fla., U.S.A.* 30°26N 84°59W **316** E5
Bristol *Pa., U.S.A.* 40°6N 74°51W **313** F10
Bristol *R.I., U.S.A.* 41°40N 71°16W **313** E13
Bristol *Tenn., U.S.A.* 36°36N 82°11W **315** C13
Bristol *Vt., U.S.A.* 44°8N 73°4W **313** B11
Bristol, City of □ *U.K.* 51°27N 2°36W **169** F5
Bristol B. *U.S.A.* 58°0N 160°0W **303** H8
Bristol Channel *U.K.* 51°18N 4°30W **169** F3
Bristol I. *Antarctica* 58°45S 28°0W **151** B1
Bristol L. *U.S.A.* 34°28N 115°41W **305** J6
Bristow *U.S.A.* 35°50N 96°23W **314** D6
Bristow I. *Papua N. G.* 9°8S 143°14E **286** E2
Britain = Great Britain *Europe* 54°0N 2°15W **158** E5
Britânia *Brazil* 15°14S 51°9W **331** D7
British Central Africa = Malawi ■ *Africa* 11°55S 34°0E **269** E3
British Columbia □ *Canada* 55°0N 125°15W **296** C3
British East Africa = Kenya ■ *Africa* 1°0N 38°0E **268** B4
British Guiana = Guyana ■ *S. Amer.* 5°0N 59°0W **329** C6
British Honduras = Belize ■ *Cent. Amer.* 17°0N 88°30W **320** C2
British Indian Ocean Terr. = Chagos Arch. ☑ *Ind. Oc.* 6°0S 72°0E **211** J9
British Isles *Europe* 54°0N 4°0W **165** D5
British Mts. *N. Amer.* 68°50N 140°0W **300** B12
British Museum *London, U.K.* **125** a3
British Virgin Is. ☑ *W. Indies* 18°30N 64°30W **321** C7
Brits *S. Africa* 25°37S 27°48E **271** C4
Britstown *S. Africa* 30°37S 23°30E **270** D3
Britt *Ont., Canada* 45°46N 80°34W **298** C3
Britt *Iowa, U.S.A.* 43°6N 93°48W **310** A3
Brittany = Bretagne □ *France* 48°10N 3°0W **172** D3
Britton *U.S.A.* 45°48N 97°45W **308** C5
Britz *Germany* 52°26N 13°27E **115** B3
Brive-la-Gaillarde *France* 45°10N 1°32E **174** C5
Briviesca *Spain* 42°32N 3°19W **194** C7
Brixen = Bressanone *Italy* 46°43N 11°39E **199** B8
Brixham *U.K.* 50°23N 3°31W **169** G4
Brixton *U.K.* 51°27N 0°8W **125** B3
Brnaze *Croatia* 43°41N 16°40E **199** E13
Brnenský □ *Czech Rep.* 49°10N 16°40E **181** B9
Brno *Czech Rep.* 49°10N 16°35E **181** B9
Broach = Bharuch *India* 21°47N 73°0E **244** D1
Broad → *Ga., U.S.A.* 33°59N 82°39W **316** B7
Broad → *S.C., U.S.A.* 34°1N 81°4W **315** D14
Broad Arrow *Australia* 30°23S 121°15E **279** F3
Broad B. *U.K.* 58°14N 6°18W **167** C2
Broad Haven *Ireland* 54°20N 9°55W **166** B2
Broad Law *U.K.* 55°30N 3°21W **167** F5
Broad Pk. = Faichan Kangri *India* 35°48N 76°34E **243** B7
Broad Sd. *Australia* 22°0S 149°45E **280** C4
Broadalbin *U.S.A.* 43°4N 74°12W **313** C10
Broadback → *Canada* 51°21N 78°52W **298** B4
Broadford *Australia* 37°14S 145°4E **283** D6
Broadhurst Ra. *Australia* 22°30S 122°30E **278** D3
Broadmeadows *Australia* 37°40S 144°55E **128** A1
Broadmoor *U.S.A.* 37°41N 122°29W **136** B2
Broads, The *U.K.* 52°45N 1°30E **168** E9
Broadus *U.S.A.* 45°27N 105°25W **304** D11
Broadview *U.S.A.* 41°51N 87°52W **119** B1
Broadway *New York, U.S.A.* **132** d2
Broager *Denmark* 54°53N 9°40E **163** K3
Broby *Sweden* 56°15N 14°4E **163** H8
Broćeni *Latvia* 56°42N 22°32E **184** B9
Brochet *Canada* 57°53N 101°40W **297** B8
Brochet, L. *Canada* 58°36N 101°35W **297** B8
Brock I. *Canada* 77°52N 114°19W **295** B9
Brocken *Germany* 51°47N 10°37E **178** D6
Brocklehurst *Australia* 32°9S 148°38E **283** B8
Brocklesby *Australia* 35°48S 146°40E **283** C7
Brockley *U.K.* 51°27N 0°2W **125** B3
Brockport *U.S.A.* 43°13N 77°56W **312** C7
Brockton *U.S.A.* 42°5N 71°1W **313** D13
Brockville *Canada* 44°35N 75°41W **313** B9
Brockway *Mont., U.S.A.* 47°18N 105°45W **304** C11
Brockway *Pa., U.S.A.* 41°15N 78°47W **312** E6
Brocton *U.S.A.* 42°23N 79°26W **312** D5
Brod *Macedonia* 41°32N 21°17E **202** E5
Brodarevo *Serbia* 43°14N 19°44E **202** C3
Brodeur Pen. *Canada* 72°30N 88°10W **295** C14
Brodhead *U.S.A.* 42°37N 89°22W **310** B7
Brodick *U.K.* 55°35N 5°9W **167** F3
Brodnica *Poland* 53°15N 19°25E **185** E6
Bródno *Poland* 52°17N 21°1E **142** B2
Bródnowski, Kanał *Poland* 52°17N 21°3E **142** B2
Brody *Ukraine* 50°5N 25°10E **177** C13
Broek *Neths.* 52°26N 5°0E **112** A2
Brogan *U.S.A.* 44°15N 117°31W **304** D5
Broglie *France* 49°2N 0°30E **172** C7
Brok *Poland* 52°43N 21°52E **185** F8
Broken Arrow *U.S.A.* 36°3N 95°48W **314** C7
Broken Bow *Nebr., U.S.A.* 41°24N 99°38W **308** E4
Broken Bow *Okla., U.S.A.* 34°2N 94°44W **314** D7
Broken Bow Lake *U.S.A.* 34°9N 94°40W **314** D7
Broken Hill = Kabwe *Zambia* 14°30S 28°29E **269** E2
Broken Hill *Australia* 31°58S 141°29E **282** A4
Broken River Ra. *Australia* 21°0S 148°22E **280** b
Brokind *Sweden* 58°13N 15°42E **163** F9

Brokopondo Suriname 5°3N 54°59W 329 B7
Bromberg = Bydgoszcz Poland 53°10N 18°0E 185 E5
Bromley □ U.K. 51°24N 0°2E 125 B4
Bromley Common U.K. 51°22N 0°2E 125 B4
Bromma Sweden 59°21N 17°55E 139 A1
Bromma ✈ (BMA) Sweden 59°21N 17°56E 139 A1
Bromo Indonesia 7°55S 112°55E 231 G15
Bromölla Sweden 56°5N 14°28E 163 H8
Brompton London, U.K. 125 c2
Bromsgrove U.K. 52°21N 2°2W 169 E5
Bronaugh U.S.A. 37°41N 94°28W 310 G2
Brøndby Strand Denmark 55°36N 12°25E 118 B2
Brøndbyøster Denmark 55°39N 12°26E 118 B2
Brøndbyvester Denmark 55°37N 12°23E 118 B2
Brønderslev Denmark 57°16N 9°57E 163 G3
Brondesbury U.K. 51°32N 0°12W 125 A2
Brong-Ahafo □ Ghana 7°50N 2°0W 262 D4
Broni Italy 45°4N 9°16E 198 C6
Bronkhorstspruit S. Africa 25°46S 28°45E 271 C4
Brønnøya Norway 59°51N 10°32E 133 A2
Brønnøysund Norway 65°28N 12°14E 160 D15
Brønshøj Denmark 55°41N 12°29E 118 A2
Bronson Fla., U.S.A. 29°27N 82°39W 317 F7
Bronson Mich., U.S.A. 41°52N 85°12W 311 C11
Bronte Italy 37°47N 14°50E 201 E7
Bronwood U.S.A. 31°50N 84°22W 316 D5
Bronxville U.S.A. 40°56N 73°49W 132 A3
Brook Park U.S.A. 41°23N 81°48W 312 E4
Brooke's Point Phil. 8°47N 117°50E 233 G1
Brookfield Ill., U.S.A. 41°48N 87°50W 119 C1
Brookfield Mo., U.S.A. 39°47N 93°4W 310 E3
Brookfield Wis., U.S.A. 43°4N 88°9W 311 A8
Brookhaven Georgia, U.S.A. 33°52N 84°19W 113 A2
Brookhaven Miss., U.S.A. 31°35N 90°26W 315 F9
Brookings Oreg., U.S.A. 42°3N 124°17W 304 E1
Brookings S. Dak., U.S.A. 44°19N 96°48W 308 C5
Brookland = West Columbia U.S.A. 33°59N 81°4W 316 B8
Brooklet U.S.A. 32°23N 81°40W 316 C8
Brooklin Canada 43°55N 78°55W 312 C6
Brookline U.S.A. 42°19N 71°8W 116 B2
Brooklyn N.Z. 41°18S 174°46E 143 B1
Brooklyn Western Cape, S. Africa 33°54S 18°29E 118 A1
Brooklyn Iowa, U.S.A. 41°44N 92°27W 310 C4
Brooklyn New York, U.S.A. 132 f3
Brooklyn-Battery Tunnel New York, U.S.A. 132 f1
Brooklyn Bridge New York, U.S.A. 132 f2
Brooklyn Heights New York, U.S.A. 132 f2
Brooklyn Park U.S.A. 45°6N 93°23W 308 C7
Brookmont U.S.A. 38°57N 77°7W 143 B3
Brooks Canada 50°35N 111°55W 296 C6
Brooks Range U.S.A. 68°0N 152°0W 303 C9
Brookston U.S.A. 40°36N 86°52W 311 D10
Brooksville Fla., U.S.A. 28°33N 82°23W 317 G7
Brooksville Ky., U.S.A. 38°41N 84°4W 311 F12
Brookton Australia 32°22S 117°0E 279 F2
Brookville Ind., U.S.A. 39°25N 85°1W 311 E12
Brookville Ohio, U.S.A. 39°50N 84°24W 311 E12
Brookville Pa., U.S.A. 41°10N 79°5W 312 E5
Brookville L. U.S.A. 39°28N 85°0W 311 E11
Broom, L. U.K. 57°55N 5°15W 167 D3
Broome Australia 18°0S 122°15E 278 C3
Broons France 48°20N 2°16W 172 D4
Brora U.K. 58°0N 3°52W 167 C5
Brora → U.K. 58°0N 3°51W 167 C5
Brørup Denmark 55°29N 9°1E 163 J2
Brösarp Sweden 55°43N 14°6E 163 J8
Brosna → Ireland 53°14N 7°58W 166 C4
Brossard Canada 45°27N 73°28W 130 B3
Broşteni Mehedinţi, Romania 44°45N 22°59E 182 F7
Broşteni Suceava, Romania 47°14N 25°43E 183 C10
Brøsterud Norway 60°18N 8°34E 164 D5
Brotas de Macaúbas Brazil 12°0S 42°38W 333 D3
Brothers U.S.A. 43°49N 120°36W 304 E3
Brothers, The Yemen 12°8N 53°10E 249 D6
Brøttum Norway 61°2N 10°34E 164 C7
Brou France 48°13N 1°11E 172 D8
Brou-sur-Chantereine France 48°53N 2°37E 134 A4
Brouage France 45°52N 1°4W 174 C2
Brough U.K. 54°32N 2°18W 168 C5
Brough Hd. U.K. 59°8N 3°20W 167 B5
Broughton U.S.A. 37°56N 88°27W 311 G8
Broughton Island = Qikiqtarjuaq Canada 67°33N 63°0W 295 D19
Broumov Czech Rep. 50°35N 16°20E 181 A9
Brovary Ukraine 50°34N 30°48E 189 G6
Brovst Denmark 57°6N 9°31E 163 G3
Brown Canada 43°48N 79°14W 141 A3
Brown, L. Australia 31°5S 118°15E 279 F2
Brown, Mt. Australia 32°30S 138°0E 282 B3
Brown, Pt. Australia 32°32S 133°50E 281 E1
Brown City U.S.A. 43°13N 82°59W 312 C2
Brown Willy U.K. 50°35N 4°37W 169 G3
Brownfield U.S.A. 33°11N 102°17W 314 E3
Browning Ill., U.S.A. 40°8N 90°22W 310 D6
Browning Mo., U.S.A. 40°3N 93°12W 310 D3
Browning Mont., U.S.A. 48°34N 113°1W 304 B7
Browns Town Jamaica 18°24N 77°22W 320 a
Brownsburg U.S.A. 39°51N 86°24W 311 E10
Brownstown U.S.A. 38°53N 86°3W 311 F10
Brownsville Oreg., U.S.A. 44°24N 122°59W 304 D2
Brownsville Pa., U.S.A. 40°1N 79°53W 312 F5
Brownsville Tenn., U.S.A. 35°36N 89°16W 315 D10
Brownsville Tex., U.S.A. 25°54N 97°30W 314 J6
Brownsweg Suriname 5°5N 55°15W 329 B6
Brownville U.S.A. 44°0N 75°59W 313 C9
Brownwood U.S.A. 31°43N 98°59W 314 F5
Browse I. Australia 14°7S 123°33E 278 B3
Broxton U.S.A. 31°38N 82°53W 316 D7
Broyhill Park U.S.A. 38°52N 77°12W 143 B2
Bru Norway 61°32N 5°11E 164 C2
Bruas Malaysia 4°30N 100°47E 237 K3
Bruay-la-Buissière France 50°29N 2°33E 173 B9
Bruce U.S.A. 30°28N 85°58W 316 E4
Bruce, Mt. Australia 22°37S 118°8E 278 D2
Bruce B. N.Z. 43°35S 169°42E 285 D4
Bruce Pen. Canada 45°0N 81°30W 312 B3
Bruce Peninsula △ Canada 45°14N 81°36W 312 A3
Bruce Rock Australia 31°52S 118°8E 279 F2
Bruche → France 48°34N 7°43E 173 D14
Bruchsal Germany 49°7N 8°35E 179 F4
Bruck an der Leitha Austria 48°1N 16°47E 181 C9
Bruck an der Mur Austria 47°24N 15°16E 180 D8
Brue → U.K. 51°13N 2°59W 169 F5
Bruflat Norway 60°53N 9°37E 164 D6
Bruges = Brugge Belgium 51°13N 3°13E 170 C3
Brugg Switz. 47°29N 8°11E 179 H4
Brugge Belgium 51°13N 3°13E 170 C3
Brughério Italy 45°33N 9°17E 129 A2
Bruin U.S.A. 41°3N 79°43W 312 E5
Bruini India 29°10N 96°11E 241 A6
Brûk, W. el → Egypt 30°15N 33°50E 251 H4
Brûlé Canada 53°15N 117°58W 296 C5
Brûlé, L. Canada 53°35N 64°4W 299 B7
Brûlon France 47°58N 0°15W 172 E6
Brumado Brazil 14°14S 41°40W 333 D3
Brumado → Brazil 14°13S 41°40W 333 D3
Brumath France 48°43N 7°40E 173 D14
Brumunddal Norway 60°53N 10°56E 164 D7
Brundidge U.S.A. 31°43N 85°49W 316 D4
Bruneau U.S.A. 42°53N 115°48W 304 E6
Bruneau → U.S.A. 42°56N 115°57W 304 E6
Bruneck = Brunico Italy 46°48N 11°56E 199 B8
Brunei = Bandar Seri Begawan Brunei 4°52N 115°0E 235 B4
Brunei ■ Asia 4°50N 115°0E 235 B4
Brunflo Sweden 63°5N 14°50E 162 A8
Brunico Italy 46°48N 11°56E 199 B8
Brünn = Brno Czech Rep. 49°10N 16°35E 181 B9
Brunnen Switz. 46°59N 8°37E 179 J4
Brunner, L. N.Z. 42°37S 171°27E 285 C6
Brunnhóll Iceland 64°17N 15°26W 155 C11
Brunsbüttel Germany 53°53N 9°6E 178 B5
Brunssum Neths. 50°57N 5°59E 170 D5
Brunswick = Braunschweig Germany 52°15N 10°31E 178 C6
Brunswick Vic., Australia 37°45S 144°57E 128 A1
Brunswick Ga., U.S.A. 31°10N 81°30W 316 D8
Brunswick Maine, U.S.A. 43°55N 69°58W 309 D19
Brunswick Md., U.S.A. 39°19N 77°38W 309 F15
Brunswick Mo., U.S.A. 39°26N 93°8W 310 E3
Brunswick Ohio, U.S.A. 41°14N 81°51W 312 E3
Brunswick, Pen. de Chile 53°30S 71°30W 336 D2
Brunswick B. Australia 15°15S 124°50E 278 C3
Brunswick Junction Australia 33°15S 115°50E 279 F2
Brunt Ice Shelf Antarctica 75°30S 25°0W 151 D2
Bruntál Czech Rep. 49°59N 17°27E 181 B10
Brus Laguna Honduras 15°47N 84°35W 320 C3
Brusa = Bursa Turkey 40°15N 29°5E 203 F13
Brusartsi Bulgaria 43°40N 23°5E 202 C7
Brush U.S.A. 40°15N 103°37W 304 F12
Brushton U.S.A. 44°50N 74°31W 313 B10
Brusio Switz. 46°14N 10°8E 179 J6
Brusque Brazil 27°5S 49°0W 335 B6
Brussegem Belgium 50°56N 4°16E 116 A1
Brussel Belgium 50°51N 4°21E 116 A2
Brussel ✈ (BRU) Belgium 50°54N 4°29E 116 A2
Brussels = Brussel Belgium 50°51N 4°21E 116 A2
Brussels Canada 43°44N 81°15W 312 C3
Brusy Poland 53°53N 17°43E 184 E4
Bruthen Australia 37°42S 147°50E 283 D7
Bruvoll Norway 60°27N 11°29E 164 D8
Bruxelles = Brussel Belgium 50°51N 4°21E 116 A2
Bruyères France 48°10N 6°40E 173 D13
Bruz France 48°1N 1°46W 172 D5
Bruzzano Italy 45°31N 9°10E 129 A2
Brwinów Poland 52°9N 20°40E 185 F7
Bry-sur-Marne France 48°50N 2°32E 134 A4
Bryagovo Bulgaria 41°58N 25°8E 203 E9
Bryan Ohio, U.S.A. 41°28N 84°33W 311 C12
Bryan Tex., U.S.A. 30°40N 96°22W 314 F6
Bryan, L. U.S.A. 28°22N 81°29W 133 B2
Bryan, Mt. Australia 33°30S 139°5E 282 B3
Bryanka Ukraine 48°32N 38°45E 189 H10
Bryansk Bryansk, Russia 53°13N 34°25E 189 F8
Bryansk Dagestan, Russia 44°20N 47°10E 191 H8
Bryansk □ Russia 53°10N 33°10E 189 F7
Bryanskoye = Bryansk Russia 44°20N 47°10E 191 H8
Bryanston S. Africa 26°4S 28°1E 123 A1
Bryant Park New York, U.S.A. 132 c2
Bryce Canyon △ U.S.A. 37°30N 112°10W 305 H7
Bryn Norway 59°55N 10°27E 133 A1
Bryne Norway 58°44N 5°38E 164 F2
Bryson City U.S.A. 35°26N 83°27W 315 D13
Bryukhovetskaya Russia 45°48N 39°0E 189 K10
Brza Palanka Serbia 44°28N 22°27E 202 B6
Brzeg Poland 50°52N 17°30E 185 H4
Brzeg Dolny Poland 51°16N 16°41E 185 G3
Brześć Kujawski Poland 52°36N 18°55E 185 F5
Brzešć nad Bugiem = Brest Belarus 52°10N 23°40E 177 B12
Brzesko Poland 49°59N 20°34E 185 J7
Brzeziny Łódzkie, Poland 51°49N 19°42E 185 G6
Brzeziny Warszawa, Poland 52°19N 21°2E 142 B2
Brzozów Poland 49°41N 22°3E 185 J9
Bsharri Lebanon 34°15N 36°0E 250 D7
Bū al Ḩidān, W. → Libya 27°25N 19°22E 258 C3
Bū Athlah Libya 30°9N 15°39E 258 B3
Bū Baqarah U.A.E. 25°35N 56°25E 247 E8
Bū Craa W. Sahara 26°45N 12°50W 260 C2
Bū Ḩasā U.A.E. 23°30N 53°20E 247 F7
Bū Tummayyim, W. → Libya 26°56N 19°13E 258 C3
Bua Fiji 16°48S 178°37E 287 A2
Bua Sweden 57°14N 12°7E 163 G6
Bua → Malawi 12°45S 34°16E 269 E3
Bua Yai Thailand 15°33N 102°26E 236 E4
Bu'aale Somali Rep. 1°6N 42°35E 267 D5
Buad I. Phil. 11°40N 124°51E 233 F5
Buala Solomon Is. 8°10S 159°35E 287 M10
Buan S. Korea 35°44N 126°44E 224 E3
Buapinang Indonesia 4°40S 121°30E 231 E6
Buayan = General Santos Phil. 6°5N 125°14E 233 H5
Buba Guinea-Biss. 11°40N 14°59W 262 C2
Bubali Bird Sanctuary Aruba 12°33N 70°2W 322 f
Bubanda Dem. Rep. of the Congo 4°14N 19°38E 264 B3
Bubanza Burundi 3°6S 29°23E 268 C2
Bubaque Guinea-Biss. 11°16N 15°51W 262 C1
Bube Ethiopia 8°46N 35°48E 257 F4
Bubeneč Czech Rep. 50°6N 14°24E 135 B2
Bubi → Zimbabwe 22°20S 31°7E 271 B5
Būbiyān Kuwait 29°45N 48°15E 247 D6
Buc France 48°46N 2°7E 134 B1
Buca Fiji 16°38S 179°52E 287 A2
Buca Turkey 38°22N 27°11E 205 C9
Bucaco Angola 11°26S 20°10E 265 E4
Bucak Turkey 37°28N 30°36E 205 D12
Bucakkışla Turkey 36°57N 33°1E 250 B4
Bucaramanga Colombia 7°0N 73°0W 328 B3
Bucas Grande I. Phil. 9°40N 125°57E 233 G5
Bucasia Australia 21°2S 149°10E 280 b
Bucay Phil. 17°32N 120°43E 232 C3
Buccaneer Arch. Australia 16°7S 123°20E 278 C3
Buccino Italy 40°38N 15°22E 201 B8
Buccoo Reef Trin. & Tob. 11°10N 60°51W 323 s
Bucecea Romania 47°47N 26°28E 183 C11
Bucegi △ Romania 45°25N 25°25E 183 E10
Buchach Ukraine 49°5N 25°25E 177 D13
Buchan Vic., Australia 37°30S 148°12E 283 D8
Buchan Aberds., U.K. 57°32N 2°21W 167 D6
Buchan Ness U.K. 57°29N 1°46W 167 D7
Buchanan Sask., Canada 51°40N 102°45W 297 C8
Buchanan Liberia 5°57N 10°2W 262 D2
Buchanan Ga., U.S.A. 33°48N 85°11W 316 B4
Buchanan Mich., U.S.A. 41°50N 86°22W 311 C10
Buchanan, L. Queens., Australia 21°35S 145°52E 280 C4
Buchanan, L. W. Austral., Australia 25°33S 123°2E 279 E3
Buchanan, L. Tex., U.S.A. 30°45N 98°25W 314 F5
Buchanan Cr. → Australia 19°13S 136°33E 280 B2
Buchans Canada 48°50N 56°52W 299 C8
Bucharest = Bucureşti Romania 44°27N 26°10E 183 F11
Buchen Germany 49°32N 9°20E 179 F5
Buchenhain Germany 48°1N 11°29E 131 B1
Bucheon S. Korea 37°28N 126°45E 224 D3
Buchholz Berlin, Germany 52°36N 13°25E 115 A3
Buchholz Niedersachsen, Germany 53°19N 9°52E 178 B5
Buchloe Germany 48°1N 10°44E 179 G6
Buchon, Pt. U.S.A. 35°15N 120°54W 306 K6
Buciumi Romania 47°3N 23°1E 182 C8
Buck Hill Falls U.S.A. 41°11N 75°16W 313 E9
Bückeburg Germany 52°16N 9°2E 178 C5
Buckeye Lake U.S.A. 39°55N 82°29W 312 G2
Buckhannon U.S.A. 39°0N 80°8W 309 F13
Buckhaven U.K. 56°11N 3°3W 167 E5
Buckhead U.S.A. 33°51N 84°24W 113 A2
Buckhorn L. Canada 44°29N 78°23W 312 B6
Buckie U.K. 57°41N 2°58W 167 D6
Buckingham Qué., Canada 45°37N 75°24W 298 C4
Buckingham Bucks., U.K. 51°59N 0°57W 169 F7
Buckingham B. Australia 12°10S 135°40E 280 A2
Buckingham Canal India 14°0N 80°5E 245 H5
Buckingham Fountain Chicago, U.S.A. 119 d2
Buckingham Palace London, U.K. 125 b3
Buckinghamshire □ U.K. 51°53N 0°55W 169 F7
Buckland U.S.A. 65°59N 161°8W 303 D7
Buckle Hd. Australia 14°26S 127°52E 278 B4
Buckleboo Australia 32°54S 136°12E 282 B2
Buckley Flints., U.K. 53°10N 3°5W 168 D4
Buckley Ill., U.S.A. 40°36N 88°2W 311 D8
Buckley → Australia 20°10S 138°49E 280 C2
Bucklin Kans., U.S.A. 37°33N 99°38W 308 G4
Bucklin Mo., U.S.A. 39°47N 92°53W 310 E4
Buckow Germany 52°25N 13°26E 115 B3
Bucks L. U.S.A. 39°54N 121°12W 306 F5
Bucktown U.S.A. 30°1N 90°8W 131 A2
Buco Zau Angola 4°46S 12°33E 265 C2
Bucquoy France 50°9N 2°43E 173 B9
Bucureşti Romania 44°27N 26°10E 183 F11
Bucureşti Otopeni ✈ (OTP) Romania 44°30N 26°11E 183 F11
Bucyrus U.S.A. 40°48N 82°59W 311 D14
Bud Norway 62°55N 6°55E 164 B3
Bud Bud Somali Rep. 4°11N 46°28E 267 D6
Buda Hungary 47°30N 19°2E 117 A2
Buda Castle = Budavári palota Budapest, Hungary 117 b2
Budacu, Vf. Romania 47°7N 25°41E 183 C10
Budafok Hungary 47°25N 19°2E 117 B2
Budalin Burma 22°20N 95°10E 241 D5
Budaörs Hungary 47°27N 18°57E 117 B1
Budapest Hungary 47°29N 19°3E 117 B2
Budapest □ Hungary 47°29N 19°5E 182 C4
Budapest ✈ (BUD) Hungary 47°26N 19°14E 117 B3
Budatétény Hungary 47°25N 19°1E 117 B2
Budaváripalota Budapest, Hungary 117 b2
Budawang △ Australia 35°10S 150°12E 283 C9
Budd Coast Antarctica 68°0S 112°0E 151 C8
Buddenbrock = Brodnica Poland 53°15N 19°25E 185 E6
Budderoo △ Australia 35°40S 150°41E 283 C9
Buddinge Denmark 55°44N 12°30E 118 A3
Budduso Italy 40°35N 9°15E 200 B2
Bude U.K. 50°49N 4°34W 169 G3
Budennovsk Russia 44°50N 44°10E 191 H7
Budeşti Romania 44°13N 26°30E 183 F11
Budeyi Ukraine 48°3N 29°16E 183 B14
Budge Budge = Baj Baj India 22°30N 88°5E 243 H13
Budgewoi Australia 33°13S 151°34E 283 B9
Búðardalur Iceland 65°7N 21°46W 155 B5
Budia Spain 40°38N 2°46W 196 E2
Büdingen Germany 50°16N 9°7E 179 E5
Budjala Dem. Rep. of the Congo 2°50N 19°40E 264 B3
Budokan Tokyo, Japan 140 a4
Budoni Italy 40°40N 9°45E 200 B2
Búdrio Italy 44°32N 11°32E 199 D8
Budszentmihály = Tiszavasvári Hungary 47°58N 21°18E 182 C6
Budva Montenegro 42°17N 18°50E 202 D2
Budweis = České Budějovice Czech Rep. 48°55N 14°25E 180 C7
Budyonnovka = Novoazovsk Ukraine 47°15N 38°4E 189 J10
Budzyń Poland 52°54N 16°59E 185 F3
Bue Norway 58°40N 5°58E 164 F2
Buea Cameroon 4°10N 9°9E 263 E6
Buela Angola 5°54S 14°40E 265 D2
Buellton U.S.A. 34°37N 120°12W 307 L6
Buena Esperanza Argentina 34°45S 65°15W 334 C2
Buena Park U.S.A. 33°52N 117°59W 307 M9
Buena Vista Bolivia 17°27S 63°40W 331 D5
Buena Vista Neth. Ant. 12°8N 68°57W 322 g
Buena Vista Solomon Is. 8°52S 160°3E 287 M11
Buena Vista Colo., U.S.A. 38°51N 106°8W 304 G10
Buena Vista Ga., U.S.A. 32°19N 84°31W 316 C5
Buena Vista Va., U.S.A. 37°44N 79°21W 309 G14
Buena Vista Lake Bed U.S.A. 35°12N 119°18W 307 K7
Buenaventura Colombia 3°53N 77°4W 328 C2
Buenaventura Chihuahua, Mexico 29°51N 107°29W 318 B3
Buenaventura, B. de Colombia 3°48N 77°17W 328 C2
Buenavista Agusan del N., Phil. 8°59N 125°24E 233 G5
Buenavista Quezon, Phil. 13°35N 122°34E 232 E4
Buendía, Embalse de Spain 40°25N 2°43W 196 E2
Buenópolis Brazil 17°54S 44°11W 333 E3
Buenos Aires Argentina 34°36S 58°22W 117 B2
Buenos Aires Colombia 1°36N 73°18W 328 C3
Buenos Aires Costa Rica 9°10N 83°20W 320 E3
Buenos Aires □ Argentina 36°30S 60°0W 334 D4
Buenos Aires, L. Argentina 46°35S 72°30W 336 C2
Buenos Aires Ezeiza ✈ (EZE) Argentina 34°49S 58°32W 117 C1
Buenos Ayres Trin. & Tob. 10°6N 61°41W 323 t
Buesaco Colombia 1°23N 77°9W 328 C2
Bufalotta Italy 41°59N 12°33E 136 B2
Buff Bay Jamaica 18°14N 76°40W 320 a
Buffalo Mo., U.S.A. 37°39N 93°6W 310 G3
Buffalo N.Y., U.S.A. 42°53N 78°53W 312 D6
Buffalo Okla., U.S.A. 36°50N 99°38W 314 C5
Buffalo S. Dak., U.S.A. 45°35N 103°33W 308 C2
Buffalo Wyo., U.S.A. 44°21N 106°42W 304 D10
Buffalo → Alta., Canada 60°5N 115°5W 296 A5
Buffalo → S. Africa 28°43S 30°37E 271 C5
Buffalo ⌓ U.S.A. 36°14N 92°36W 314 C8
Buffalo Head Hills Canada 57°25N 115°55W 296 B5
Buffalo L. Alta., Canada 52°27N 112°54W 296 C6
Buffalo L. N.W.T., Canada 60°12N 115°25W 296 A5
Buffalo Narrows Canada 55°51N 108°29W 297 B7
Buffalo Springs ⌓ Kenya 0°32N 37°35E 268 B4
Buffels → S. Africa 29°36S 17°3E 270 C2
Buford U.S.A. 34°10N 84°0W 315 D12
Bug = Buh → Ukraine 46°59N 31°58E 189 J6
Bug → Poland 52°31N 21°5E 185 F8
Buga Colombia 4°0N 76°15W 328 C2
Bugala I. Uganda 0°40S 32°20E 268 C3
Buganda Uganda 0°0 31°30E 268 C3
Buganga Uganda 0°3S 32°0E 268 C3
Bugasong Phil. 11°3N 122°4E 233 F4
Bugda Acable Somali Rep. 4°4N 45°15E 267 D6
Bugeat France 45°36N 1°55E 174 C5
Bugel, Tanjung Indonesia 6°26S 111°3E 234 D4
Búger Spain 39°45N 2°59E 206 B3
Bugibba Malta 35°57N 14°25E 206 F7
Bugio Portugal 38°39N 9°18W 126 B1
Bugojno Bos.-H. 44°2N 17°25E 182 F2
Bugsuk I. Phil. 8°12N 117°18E 233 G1
Buguey Phil. 18°17N 121°50E 232 B3
Buguias Phil. 16°43N 120°50E 232 C3
Bugulma Russia 54°33N 52°48E 186 D9
Buguma Nigeria 4°42N 6°55E 263 E6
Bugungu △ Uganda 2°17N 31°50E 268 B3
Buguruslan Russia 53°39N 52°26E 186 D9
Buh → Ukraine 46°59N 31°58E 189 J6
Buharkent Turkey 37°58N 28°44E 205 D10
Buheirat-Murrat-el-Kubra Egypt 30°18N 32°26E 256 H8
Buhera Zimbabwe 19°18S 31°29E 271 A5
Bühl Baden-W., Germany 48°40N 8°8E 179 G4
Buhl Idaho, U.S.A. 42°36N 114°46W 304 E6
Buhuşi Romania 46°41N 26°45E 183 D11
Bui △ Ghana 8°21N 2°21W 262 D4
Buiksloot Neths. 52°24N 4°55E 112 A2
Builth Wells U.K. 52°9N 3°25W 169 E4
Buin Papua N. G. 6°48S 155°42E 287 L8
Buinsk Russia 55°0N 48°18E 190 C9
Buique Brazil 8°37S 37°9W 332 C4
Buir Nur Mongolia 47°50N 117°42E 219 B6
Buis-les-Baronnies France 44°17N 5°16E 175 D9
Buitenveldert Neths. 52°20N 4°53E 112 B2
Buitenzorg = Bogor Indonesia 6°36S 106°48E 234 D3
Buitrago del Lozoya Spain 40°58N 3°38W 194 E7
Buizingen Belgium 50°44N 4°15E 116 B1
Bujalance Spain 37°54N 4°23W 195 H6
Bujanovac Serbia 42°28N 21°44E 202 D5
Bujaraloz Spain 41°29N 0°10W 196 D4
Buje Croatia 45°24N 13°39E 199 C10
Buji China 22°37N 114°5E 219 F11
Bujumbura Burundi 3°16S 29°18E 268 C2
Bük Hungary 47°22N 16°45E 182 C1
Buk Poland 52°21N 16°30E 185 F3
Buka I. Papua N. G. 5°10S 154°35E 286 C8
Bukachacha Russia 52°55N 116°50E 215 D12
Bukama Dem. Rep. of the Congo 9°10S 25°50E 269 D2
Bukavu Dem. Rep. of the Congo 2°20S 28°52E 268 C2
Bukene Tanzania 4°15S 32°48E 268 C3
Bukhansan S. Korea 37°38N 126°58E 137 B1
Bukhara = Buxoro Uzbekistan 39°48N 64°25E 216 E6
Bukhoro = Buxoro Uzbekistan 39°48N 64°25E 216 E6
Bukidnon □ Phil. 8°0N 125°0E 233 H5
Bukima Tanzania 1°50S 33°25E 268 C3
Bukit Badung Indonesia 8°49S 115°10E 231 K18
Bukit Baka Bukit Raya △ Indonesia 0°43S 112°40E 235 C4
Bukit Barisan Selatan △ Indonesia 5°8S 104°4E 234 D2
Bukit Duabelas △ Indonesia 2°3S 102°48E 234 C2
Bukit Kerajaan Malaysia 5°25N 100°15E 237 c
Bukit Mertajam Malaysia 5°22N 100°28E 237 c
Bukit Ni Malaysia 1°22N 104°12E 237 d
Bukit Panjang Singapore 1°23N 103°46E 237 d
Bukit Panjang Nature Reserve Singapore 1°22N 103°45E 138 A2
Bukit Tengah Malaysia 5°22N 100°25E 237 c
Bukit Tigapuluh △ Indonesia 1°15S 102°25E 234 C2
Bukit Timah Nature Reserve Singapore 1°20N 103°47E 138 A2
Bukittinggi Indonesia 0°20S 100°20E 234 C2
Bükk Hungary 48°0N 20°30E 182 B5
Bukkapatnam India 14°14N 77°46E 245 G3
Bükki △ Hungary 48°3N 20°30E 182 B5
Bukoba Tanzania 1°20S 31°49E 268 C3
Bukum, Pulau Singapore 1°14N 103°46E 138 B2
Bukuru Nigeria 9°42N 8°48E 263 D6
Bukuya Uganda 0°40N 31°52E 268 B3
Būl, Kuh-e Iran 30°48N 52°45E 247 D7
Bula Guinea-Biss. 12°7N 15°43W 262 C1
Bula Indonesia 3°6S 130°30E 231 E8
Bula Camarines S., Phil. 13°28N 123°16E 232 E4
Bula-Atumba Angola 8°41S 14°52E 265 D2
Bulacan □ Phil. 15°0N 121°5E 232 D3
Bülach Switz. 47°31N 8°32E 179 H4
Bulaevo Kazakhstan 54°54N 70°26E 217 B8
Bulahdelah Australia 32°23S 152°13E 283 B10
Bulalacao Phil. 12°31N 121°26E 232 E3
Bulan Phil. 12°40N 123°52E 232 E4
Bulancak Turkey 40°56N 38°14E 251 B8
Búland Iceland 63°46N 18°30W 155 D8
Bulandshahr India 28°28N 77°51E 242 E7
Bulanık Turkey 39°4N 42°14E 213 C10
Bûlâq El Khârga, Egypt 25°10N 30°38E 256 B3
Bûlâq El Qâhira, Egypt 30°3N 31°14E 117 A2
Bulawayo Zimbabwe 20°7S 28°32E 269 G2
Buldan Turkey 38°2N 28°50E 205 C10
Buldana India 20°30N 76°18E 244 D3
Buldir I. U.S.A. 52°21N 175°56E 303 K1
Buldon Phil. 7°33N 124°25E 233 H5
Bule Phil. 14°26N 121°2E 127 C2
Bulenga Ghana 9°56N 2°12W 262 D4
Bulgan Mongolia 48°45N 103°34E 218 B5
Bulgar Russia 54°57N 49°4E 190 C9
Bulgaria ■ Europe 42°35N 25°30E 203 D9
Bulgheria, Monte Italy 40°4N 15°26E 201 B8
Bulgurca Turkey 38°10N 27°9E 205 C9
Bulhale Somali Rep. 5°20N 46°29E 267 C6
Bulhar Somali Rep. 10°25N 44°30E 257 E5
Buli, Teluk Indonesia 0°48N 128°25E 231 D7
Buliluyan, C. Phil. 8°20N 117°15E 233 G1
Bulim Singapore 1°22N 103°43E 138 A2
Bulki Ethiopia 6°11N 36°31E 257 F4
Bulkley → Canada 55°15N 127°40W 296 B3
Bull Head Jamaica 18°10N 77°15W 320 a
Bull Savanna Jamaica 17°53N 77°35W 320 a
Bull Shoals L. U.S.A. 36°22N 92°35W 314 C8
Bullaque → Spain 38°59N 4°17W 195 G6
Bullara Australia 22°40S 114°3E 278 D1
Bullard U.S.A. 32°38N 83°30W 316 C6
Bullas Spain 38°2N 1°40W 197 G3
Bulle Switz. 46°37N 7°3E 179 J3
Bullen Park Australia 37°46S 145°4E 128 A2
Bullenbaai Neth. Ant. 12°11N 69°2W 322 g
Buller → N.Z. 41°44S 171°36E 285 B6
Buller, Mt. Australia 37°10S 146°28E 283 D7
Buller Gorge N.Z. 41°40S 172°10E 285 B7
Bulleringa △ Australia 17°39S 143°56E 280 B3
Bullhead City U.S.A. 35°8N 114°32W 307 K12
Bulli Australia 34°15S 150°57E 283 C9
Büllingen Belgium 50°25N 6°16E 170 D6
Bullock Creek Australia 17°43S 144°31E 280 B3
Bulloo → Australia 28°43S 142°30E 281 D3
Bulloo L. Australia 28°43S 142°25E 281 D3
Bulls N.Z. 40°10S 175°24E 284 G4
Bully-les-Mines France 50°27N 2°44E 173 B9
Bulman Australia 13°39S 134°20E 280 A1
Bulnes Chile 36°42S 72°19W 334 D1
Bulo Ghedudo Somali Rep. 2°52N 43°1E 267 D5
Bulolo Papua N. G. 7°10S 146°40E 286 D4
Bulongo Dem. Rep. of the Congo 4°45S 21°30E 265 C4
Bulqizë Albania 41°30N 20°21E 202 E4
Bulsar = Valsad India 20°40N 72°58E 244 D1
Bultfontein S. Africa 28°18S 26°10E 270 C4
Buluan Phil. 6°44N 124°47E 233 H5
Buluan, L. Phil. 6°40N 124°49E 233 H5
Bulukumba Indonesia 5°33S 120°11E 231 F6
Bulun Russia 70°37N 127°30E 215 B13
Bulungkol China 38°36N 74°58E 217 E8
Bulungu Bandundu, Dem. Rep. of the Congo 4°33S 18°36E 265 C3
Bulungu Kasai-Occ., Dem. Rep. of the Congo 6°4S 21°54E 265 D4
Bulusan Phil. 12°45N 124°8E 232 E5
Bulusan Vol. Phil. 12°46N 124°3E 232 E5
Bumba Bandundu, Dem. Rep. of the Congo 6°58S 19°19E 265 D3
Bumba Équateur, Dem. Rep. of the Congo 2°13N 22°30E 264 B4
Bumbah, Khalīj Libya 32°20N 23°15E 258 B4
Bumbeşti-Jiu Romania 45°10N 23°24E 183 E8
Bumbiri I. Tanzania 1°40S 31°55E 268 C3
Bumbuna S. Leone 9°2N 11°49W 262 D2
Bumhkang Burma 26°51N 97°40E 241 B6
Bumhpa Bum Burma 26°51N 97°14E 241 B6
Bumi → Zimbabwe 17°0S 28°20E 269 F2
Bumtang → Bhutan 26°56N 90°53E 241 B3
Bumthang = Jakar Dzong Bhutan 27°33N 90°43E 241 B3
Buna Dem. Rep. of the Congo 3°14S 18°59E 264 C3
Buna North Eastern, Kenya 2°58N 39°30E 268 B4
Buna Papua N. G. 8°42S 148°27E 286 E5
Bunaken Indonesia 1°37N 124°46E 231 D6
Bunama Papua N. G. 10°9S 151°9E 286 F6
Bunawan Phil. 8°12N 125°57E 233 G5
Bunazi Tanzania 1°3S 31°23E 268 C3
Bunbury Australia 33°20S 115°35E 279 F2
Bunclody Ireland 52°39N 6°40W 166 D5
Buncrana Ireland 55°8N 7°27W 166 A4
Bund, The China 31°14N 121°30E 138 B1
Bunda Dem. Rep. of the Congo 4°58S 14°29E 265 C3
Bundaberg Australia 24°54S 152°22E 281 C5
Bundanoon Australia 34°40S 150°16E 283 C9
Bünde Germany 52°11N 8°35E 178 C4
Bundestag = Reichstag Berlin, Germany 115 a3
Bundey → Australia 21°46S 135°37E 280 C2
Bundi India 25°30N 75°35E 242 G6
Bundjalung △ Australia 29°16S 153°21E 281 D5
Bundoora North Australia 37°41S 145°2E 128 A2
Bundoora Park Australia 37°42S 145°2E 128 A2
Bundoran Ireland 54°28N 8°16W 166 B3
Bundukia Sudan 5°14N 30°55E 257 F3
Bundure Australia 35°10S 146°1E 283 C7
Bung Kan Thailand 18°23N 103°37E 236 C4
Bunga → Nigeria 11°23N 9°56E 263 C6
Bungalaut, Selat Indonesia 2°0S 99°25E 234 C1
Bungay U.K. 52°27N 1°28E 169 E9
Bungendore Australia 35°14S 149°30E 283 C8
Bungil Cr. → Australia 27°5S 149°5E 281 D4
Bungle Bungle = Purnululu △ Australia 17°20S 128°20E 278 C4
Bungo Angola 7°26S 15°23E 265 D3
Bungo, Gunung Malaysia 1°16N 110°9E 235 B4
Bungo-Suidō Japan 33°0N 132°15E 222 E4
Bungoma Kenya 0°34N 34°34E 268 B3
Bungotakada Japan 33°35N 131°25E 222 D3
Bungu Tanzania 7°35S 39°0E 268 D4
Bunia Dem. Rep. of the Congo 1°35N 30°20E 268 B3
Bunianga Dem. Rep. of the Congo 3°28S 20°11E 264 C4
Bunji Pakistan 35°45N 74°40E 243 B6
Bunker Hill Ill., U.S.A. 39°3N 89°57W 310 E7
Bunker Hill Ind., U.S.A. 40°40N 86°6W 311 D10
Bunker Hill Memorial U.S.A. 42°22N 71°4W 116 A2
Bunker I. Pakistan 24°48N 66°57E 123 B1
Bunkie U.S.A. 30°57N 92°11W 314 F8
Bunkyō Japan 35°42N 139°45E 140 A3
Bunnefjorden Norway 59°50N 10°44E 133 A3
Bunnell U.S.A. 29°28N 81°16W 317 F8
Bunnythorpe N.Z. 40°16S 175°39E 284 G4
Buñol Spain 39°25N 0°47W 197 F4
Bunsuru Nigeria 13°21N 6°23E 263 C5
Buntok Indonesia 1°40S 114°58E 235 C4
Bununu Dass Nigeria 10°5N 9°31E 263 C6
Bununu Kasa Nigeria 9°51N 9°32E 263 D6
Bunya Mts. △ Australia 26°51S 151°34E 281 D5
Bünyan Turkey 38°51N 35°51E 212 C6
Bunyola Spain 39°41N 2°42E 206 B3
Bunyu Indonesia 3°35N 117°50E 235 B5
Bunza Nigeria 12°8N 4°0E 263 C5
Bunzlau = Bolesławiec Poland 51°17N 15°37E 185 G2
Buol Indonesia 1°15N 121°32E 231 D6
Buon Brieng Vietnam 13°9N 108°12E 236 F7
Buon Ma Thuot Vietnam 12°40N 108°3E 236 F7
Buona Vista Park Singapore 1°16N 103°47E 138 B2
Buong Long Cambodia 13°44N 106°59E 236 F6
Buorkhaya, Mys Russia 71°50N 132°40E 215 B14
Buqayq Si. Arabia 26°0N 49°45E 247 E6
Buqbuq Egypt 31°29N 25°29E 256 A2
Bur Acaba = Buurhakaba Somali Rep. 3°12N 44°20E 267 D5
Bûr Fuad Egypt 31°15N 32°20E 256 H8
Bûr Safâga Egypt 26°43N 33°57E 246 E2
Bûr Sa'îd Egypt 31°16N 32°18E 256 H8
Bûr Sûdân Sudan 19°32N 37°9E 256 D4
Bûr Taufiq Egypt 29°54N 32°32E 256 J8
Bura Kenya 1°4S 39°58E 268 C4
Buraan Somali Rep. 10°14N 48°44E 267 B6
Burakin Australia 30°31S 117°10E 279 F2
Buram Sudan 10°51N 25°9E 257 E2
Buran = Buraan Somali Rep. 10°14N 48°44E 267 B6
Burao = Burco Somali Rep. 9°32N 45°32E 267 C6
Burāq Syria 33°11N 36°29E 250 E7
Burauen Phil. 10°58N 124°53E 233 F5
Buraydah Si. Arabia 26°20N 43°59E 246 E4
Burbank Calif., U.S.A. 34°12N 118°18W 126 A3
Burbank Ill., U.S.A. 41°44N 87°46W 119 C2
Burç Turkey 36°59N 37°8E 250 B8
Burcher Australia 33°30S 147°16E 283 B7
Burco Somali Rep. 9°32N 45°32E 267 C6
Burda India 25°50N 77°35E 242 G7
Burdekin → Australia 19°38S 147°25E 280 B4
Burden, L. U.S.A. 28°27N 81°33W 133 B1
Burdeos Bay Phil. 14°44N 122°4E 232 D4
Burdur Turkey 37°45N 30°17E 205 D12
Burdur □ Turkey 37°45N 30°0E 205 D12
Burdur Gölü Turkey 37°44N 30°10E 205 D12
Burdwan = Barddhaman India 23°14N 87°39E 243 H12
Burdwood Bank Atl. Oc. 54°0S 59°0W 152 M6
Bure Gojam, Ethiopia 10°40N 37°4E 257 E4
Bure Ilubabor, Ethiopia 8°19N 35°8E 257 F4
Bure → U.K. 52°38N 1°43E 168 E9
Büren Germany 51°33N 8°35E 178 D4
Bureya → Russia 49°27N 129°30E 215 E13
Burford Canada 43°7N 80°27W 312 C4
Burg Germany 52°16N 11°51E 178 C7
Burg auf Fehmarn Germany 54°28N 11°9E 178 A7
Burg el Arab Egypt 30°54N 29°32E 256 H6
Burg et Tuyur Sudan 20°55N 27°56E 256 C2
Burg Stargard Germany 53°29N 13°18E 178 B9
Burgas Bulgaria 42°33N 27°29E 203 D11
Burgas □ Bulgaria 42°30N 26°50E 203 D10
Burgaski Zaliv Bulgaria 42°30N 27°39E 203 D11
Burgdorf Niedersachsen, Germany 52°27N 10°1E 178 C6
Burgdorf Switz. 47°3N 7°37E 179 H3
Burgenland □ Austria 47°20N 16°20E 181 D9
Burgeo Canada 47°37N 57°38W 299 C8
Burgersdorp S. Africa 31°0S 26°20E 270 D4
Burgess, Mt. Australia 30°50S 121°5E 279 F3
Burghausen Germany 48°9N 12°49E 179 G8
Burghead U.K. 57°43N 3°30W 167 D5
Búrgio Italy 37°36N 13°17E 200 E6
Burglengenfeld Germany 49°12N 12°2E 179 F8
Burgohondo Spain 40°26N 4°47W 194 E6
Burgos Ilocos N., Phil. 18°31N 120°39E 232 B3
Burgos Pangasinan, Phil. 16°4N 119°52E 232 C2
Burgos Spain 42°21N 3°41W 194 C7
Burgos □ Spain 42°21N 3°42W 194 C7
Burgstädt Germany 50°54N 12°49E 178 E8
Burgsvik Sweden 57°3N 18°19E 163 G12
Burguillos del Cerro Spain 38°23N 6°35W 195 G4
Burgundy = Bourgogne □ France 47°0N 4°50E 173 F11
Burhaniye Turkey 39°30N 26°58E 205 B8
Burhanpur India 21°18N 76°14E 244 D3
Burhi Gandak → India 25°20N 86°37E 243 G12
Burhner → India 22°43N 80°31E 243 H9
Buri Pen. Eritrea 15°25N 39°55E 257 D4
Burias I. Phil. 12°55N 123°5E 232 E4
Burias Pass Phil. 13°0N 123°15E 232 E4
Burica, Pta. Costa Rica 8°3N 82°51W 320 E3
Burien U.S.A. 47°28N 122°20W 306 C4
Burigi, L. Tanzania 2°2S 31°22E 268 C3
Burigi △ Tanzania 2°20S 31°6E 268 C3
Burin Canada 47°1N 55°14W 299 C8
Buriram Thailand 15°0N 103°0E 236 E4
Buriti Alegre Brazil 18°9S 49°3W 333 E2
Buriti Bravo Brazil 5°50S 43°50W 332 C3
Buriti dos Lopes Brazil 3°10S 41°52W 332 B3
Burji Ethiopia 5°29N 37°51E 257 F4
Burkburnett U.S.A. 34°6N 98°34W 314 D5
Burke → Australia 23°12S 139°33E 280 C2
Burke Chan. Canada 52°10N 127°30W 296 C3
Burketown Australia 17°45S 139°33E 280 B2
Burkina Faso ■ Africa 12°0N 1°0W 262 C4
Burk's Falls Canada 45°37N 79°24W 298 C4
Burlada Spain 42°49N 1°36W 196 C3
Burleigh Falls Canada 44°33N 78°12W 312 B6
Burley U.S.A. 42°32N 113°48W 304 E7
Burlingame U.S.A. 37°35N 122°21W 306 H4
Burlington Ont., Canada 43°18N 79°45W 312 C5
Burlington Colo., U.S.A. 39°18N 102°16W 304 G12
Burlington Iowa, U.S.A. 40°49N 91°14W 310 D5
Burlington Kans., U.S.A. 38°12N 95°45W 308 F6
Burlington Ky., U.S.A. 39°2N 84°43W 311 E12
Burlington Mass., U.S.A. 42°30N 71°13W 116 A1
Burlington N.C., U.S.A. 36°6N 79°26W 315 C15
Burlington N.J., U.S.A. 40°4N 74°51W 313 F10
Burlington Vt., U.S.A. 44°29N 73°12W 313 B11
Burlington Wash., U.S.A. 48°28N 122°20W 306 B4
Burlington Wis., U.S.A. 42°41N 88°17W 311 B8
Burma ■ Asia 21°0N 96°30E 241 E6
Burnaby I. Canada 52°25N 131°19W 296 C2
Burnet U.S.A. 30°45N 98°14W 314 F5
Burney U.S.A. 40°53N 121°40W 304 F3
Burnham U.S.A. 40°38N 77°34W 312 F7
Burnham-on-Sea U.K. 51°14N 3°0W 169 F5
Burnham Park U.S.A. 41°49N 87°35W 119 C3
Burnham Park Harbor Chicago, U.S.A. 119 e3
Burnhamthorpe Canada 43°37N 79°35W 141 B1
Burnie Australia 41°4S 145°56E 281 G4
Burnley U.K. 53°47N 2°14W 168 D5
Burns U.S.A. 43°35N 119°3W 304 E4
Burns Junction U.S.A. 42°47N 117°51W 304 E5
Burns Lake Canada 54°14N 125°45W 296 C3
Burnside → Canada 66°51N 108°4W 294 D10
Burnside, L. Australia 25°22S 123°0E 279 E3
Burnsville U.S.A. 44°47N 93°17W 308 C7
Burnt Oak U.K. 51°36N 0°15W 125 A2
Burnt Paw U.S.A. 66°54N 143°44W 303 C12
Burnt River Canada 44°41N 78°42W 312 B6
Burntisland U.K. 56°4N 3°13W 121 A2
Burntwood → Canada 56°8N 96°34W 297 B9
Burntwood L. Canada 55°22N 100°26W 297 B8
Burnwynd U.K. 55°54N 3°23W 121 B1
Buronga Australia 34°18S 142°20E 282 C5
Burqa West Bank 31°54N 35°15E 123 A2
Burqān Kuwait 29°0N 47°57E 246 D5
Burqin China 47°43N 87°0E 217 C11
Burra S. Austral., Australia 33°40S 138°55E 282 B3
Burra Nigeria 11°0N 8°56E 263 C6
Burragorang, L. Australia 33°52S 150°37E 283 B9
Burray U.K. 58°51N 2°54W 167 C6
Burrel Albania 41°36N 20°1E 202 E4
Burren Ireland 53°9N 9°5W 166 C2
Burren △ Ireland 53°1N 8°58W 166 C3
Burren Junction Australia 30°7S 148°58E 281 E4
Burrendong, L. Australia 32°45S 149°10E 283 B8
Burriana Spain 39°50N 0°4W 196 F4
Burrinjuck, L. Australia 35°0S 148°36E 283 C8
Burro, Serranías del Mexico 28°56N 102°5W 318 B4
Burrow Hd. U.K. 54°41N 4°24W 167 G4
Burrowa-Pine Mountain △ Australia 36°6S 147°45E 283 D7
Burrum Coast △ Australia 25°13S 152°36E 281 D5
Burruyacú Argentina 26°30S 64°40W 334 B3
Burry Port U.K. 51°41N 4°15W 169 F3
Bursa Turkey 40°15N 29°5E 203 F13
Bursa □ Turkey 40°10N 29°5E 212 B3
Burseryd Sweden 57°12N 13°17E 163 G7
Burstall Canada 50°39N 109°54W 297 C7
Burton Mich., U.S.A. 43°0N 83°40W 311 B13
Burton Ohio, U.S.A. 41°28N 81°8W 312 E3
Burton S.C., U.S.A. 32°26N 80°43W 315 E14
Burton, L. Canada 54°45N 78°20W 298 B4

Burton upon Trent U.K. 52°48N 1°38W 168 E6
Burtundy Australia 33°45S 142°15E 282 B5
Burtus Egypt 30°8N 31°8E 117 A1
Buru Indonesia 3°30S 126°30E 231 E7
Buruanga Phil. 11°51N 121°53E 233 F3
Burudvatn Norway 59°58N 10°35E 133 A2
Burullus, Bahra el Egypt 31°25N 31°0E 256 H7
Burūm Yemen 14°22N 48°59E 249 D5
Burûn, Râs Egypt 31°14N 33°7E 251 G4
Burundi ■ Africa 3°15S 30°0E 268 C3
Burunny = Tsagan Aman Russia 47°34N 46°43E 191 G8
Bururi Burundi 3°57S 29°37E 268 C2
Burutu Nigeria 5°20N 5°29E 263 D6
Burwell U.S.A. 41°47N 99°8W 308 E4
Burwick U.K. 58°45N 2°58W 167 C5
Burwood Australia 33°52S 151°5E 139 B1
Bury U.K. 53°35N 2°17W 168 D5
Bury St. Edmunds U.K. 52°15N 0°43E 169 E8
Buryatia □ Russia 53°0N 110°0E 215 D12
Būrylbaytal Kazakhstan 44°56N 74°0E 217 D8
Buryn Ukraine 51°13N 33°50E 189 G7
Burzenin Poland 51°28N 18°47E 185 G5
Busa, Mt. Phil. 6°8N 124°39E 233 H5
Busalla Italy 44°34N 8°57E 198 D5
Busan S. Korea 35°5N 129°0E 224 E4
Busanga Dem. Rep. of the Congo 0°53S 22°7E 264 C4
Busango Swamp Zambia 14°15S 25°45E 269 E2
Busaso = Boosaaso Somali Rep. 11°12N 49°18E 267 B6
Buşayrah Syria 35°9N 40°26E 213 E9
Busca Italy 44°31N 7°29E 198 D4
Bûsh Egypt 29°9N 31°8E 251 J2
Bushat Albania 41°58N 19°34E 202 E3
Būshehr Iran 28°55N 50°55E 247 D6
Būshehr □ Iran 28°20N 51°45E 247 D6
Bushenyi Uganda 0°35S 30°10E 268 C3
Bushimaie → Dem. Rep. of the Congo 6°2S 23°45E 265 D4
Bushire = Būshehr Iran 28°55N 50°55E 247 D6
Bushiribana Aruba 12°33N 69°58W 322 f
Bushnell Fla., U.S.A. 28°40N 82°7W 317 G7
Bushnell Ill., U.S.A. 40°33N 90°31W 310 D6
Bushtyna Ukraine 48°3N 23°28E 183 B8
Bushwick U.S.A. 40°41N 73°54W 132 B2
Bushy Park U.K. 51°24N 0°20W 125 B1
Busie Ghana 10°29N 2°22W 262 C4
Businga Dem. Rep. of the Congo 3°16N 20°59E 264 B4
Büsingen Germany 47°42N 8°41E 179 H4
Buskerud □ Norway 60°20N 9°0E 164 D5
Busko-Zdrój Poland 50°28N 20°42E 185 H7
Buslei Ethiopia 5°28N 44°25E 267 C5
Busovača Bos.-H. 44°6N 17°53E 182 F2
Buşra ash Shām Syria 32°30N 36°25E 251 F7
Busselton Australia 33°42S 115°15E 279 F2
Busseri → Sudan 7°41N 28°3E 257 F2
Busseto Italy 44°59N 10°2E 198 D7
Bussière-Badil France 45°39N 0°36E 174 C4
Bussolengo Italy 45°28N 10°51E 198 C7
Bussum Neths. 52°16N 5°10E 170 B5
Bustamante, B. Argentina 45°5S 66°18W 336 C3
Buşteni Romania 45°24N 25°32E 183 E10
Busto, C. Spain 43°34N 6°28W 194 B4
Busto Arsízio Italy 45°37N 8°51E 198 C5
Busu Djanoa Dem. Rep. of the Congo 1°43N 21°23E 264 B4
Busu Kwanga Dem. Rep. of the Congo 1°48N 20°21E 264 B4
Busu Mandji Dem. Rep. of the Congo 2°52N 21°14E 264 B4
Busuanga Phil. 12°14N 119°52E 232 E2
Busuanga I. Phil. 12°10N 120°0E 232 E2
Büsum Germany 54°7N 8°51E 178 A4
Busungbiu Indonesia 8°16S 114°58E 231 J17
Busy Corner Trin. & Tob. 10°18N 61°17W 323 t
Buta Dem. Rep. of the Congo 2°50N 24°53E 264 B4
Butantã Brazil 23°34S 46°42W 137 B1
Butare Rwanda 2°31S 29°52E 268 C2
Butaritari Kiribati 3°30N 174°0E 288 G9
Butcher I. India 18°57N 72°53E 130 B2
Bute S. Austral., Australia 33°51S 138°0E 282 B3
Bute Scotland, U.K. 55°48N 5°2W 167 F3
Bute Inlet Canada 50°40N 124°53W 296 C4
Butemba Uganda 1°9N 31°37E 268 B3
Butembo Dem. Rep. of the Congo 0°9N 29°18E 268 B2
Buteni Romania 46°19N 22°7E 182 D7
Butera Italy 37°11N 14°11E 201 E7
Butere Kenya 0°13N 34°30E 268 B3
Butha-Buthe Lesotho 28°47S 28°14E 271 C4
Butha Qi China 48°0N 122°32E 219 B7
Buthidaung Burma 20°52N 92°32E 241 E4
Butiaba Uganda 1°50N 31°20E 268 B3
Butler Ga., U.S.A. 32°33N 84°14W 316 C5
Butler Ind., U.S.A. 41°26N 84°52W 311 C12
Butler Ky., U.S.A. 38°47N 84°22W 311 F12
Butler Mo., U.S.A. 38°16N 94°20W 310 F2
Butler Pa., U.S.A. 40°52N 79°54W 312 F5
Butler, L. U.S.A. 28°29N 81°33W 133 B1
Buton Indonesia 5°0S 122°45E 231 E6
Bütow = Bytów Poland 54°10N 17°30E 184 D4
Butrintit, L. e Albania 39°43N 20°5E 206 B10
Butte Mont., U.S.A. 46°0N 112°32W 304 C7
Butte Nebr., U.S.A. 42°58N 98°51W 308 D4
Butte Creek → U.S.A. 39°12N 121°56W 306 F5
Butterworth = Gcuwa S. Africa 32°20S 28°11E 271 D4
Butterworth Malaysia 5°24N 100°23E 237 c
Buttevant Ireland 52°14N 8°40W 166 D3
Buttfield, Mt. Australia 24°45S 128°9E 279 D4
Button B. Canada 58°45N 94°23W 297 B10
Buttonwillow U.S.A. 35°24N 119°28W 307 K7
Butts Corner U.S.A. 38°46N 77°19W 143 C2
Butty Hd. Australia 33°54S 121°39E 279 F3
Butuan Phil. 8°57N 125°33E 233 G5
Butuku-Luba Eq. Guin. 3°29N 8°33E 263 E6
Butung = Buton Indonesia 5°0S 122°45E 231 E6
Buturlinovka Russia 50°50N 40°35E 190 E5
Butzbach Germany 50°25N 8°40E 179 E4
Bützow Germany 53°50N 11°58E 178 B7
Buuhoodle Somali Rep. 8°20N 46°25E 267 C6
Buulobarde Somali Rep. 3°50N 45°33E 267 D6
Buur Gaabo Somali Rep. 1°13S 41°51E 267 E5
Buurhakaba Somali Rep. 3°12N 44°20E 267 D5
Buvika Norway 63°18N 10°11E 164 A7
Buxa Duar India 27°45N 89°35E 243 F13
Buxar India 25°34N 83°58E 243 G10
Buxoro Uzbekistan 39°48N 64°25E 216 E6
Buxtehude Germany 53°28N 9°39E 178 B5
Buxton U.K. 53°16N 1°54W 168 D6
Buxy France 46°44N 4°40E 173 F11
Buy Russia 58°28N 41°28E 190 A5
Buyant-Uhaa Mongolia 44°55N 110°11E 219 B6
Buynaksk Russia 42°48N 47°7E 191 J8
Buyo Ivory C. 6°21N 7°5W 262 D3
Buyo, L. de Ivory C. 6°16N 7°10W 262 D3
Büyük Menderes → Turkey 37°28N 27°11E 205 D9
Büyükçekmece Turkey 41°2N 28°35E 203 E12
Büyükdere Turkey 41°9N 29°2E 122 B2
Büyükeğri Dağı Turkey 36°45N 33°33E 250 B4
Büyükkarıştiran Turkey 41°18N 27°33E 203 E11
Büyükkemikli Burnu Turkey 40°18N 26°14E 203 F10
Büyükorhan Turkey 39°46N 28°56E 205 B10
Büyükyoncalı Turkey 41°20N 27°55E 203 E11
Buzançais France 46°54N 1°25E 172 F8
Buzău Romania 45°10N 26°50E 183 E11
Buzău □ Romania 45°20N 26°30E 183 E11
Buzău → Romania 45°26N 27°44E 183 E12
Buzău, Pasul Romania 45°35N 26°12E 183 E11
Buzaymah Libya 24°55N 22°2E 258 D4
Buzen Japan 33°35N 131°5E 222 D3
Buzet Croatia 45°24N 13°58E 199 C10
Buzi → Mozam. 19°50S 34°43E 269 F3
Buziaş Romania 45°38N 21°36E 182 E6
Büzmeýin Turkmenistan 38°3N 58°12E 247 B8
Buzuluk Russia 52°48N 52°12E 186 D9
Buzuluk → Russia 50°15N 42°7E 190 E6
Buzzards Bay U.S.A. 41°45N 70°37W 313 E14
Bwagaoia Papua N. G. 10°40S 152°52E 286 F7
Bwana Mkubwa Zambia 13°8S 28°38E 269 E2
Bwasa Dem. Rep. of the Congo 3°55S 18°24E 264 C3
Bwatnapné Vanuatu 15°41S 168°9E 287 E6
Bwindi △ Uganda 1°2S 29°42E 268 C2
Byakar Dzong = Jakar Dzong Bhutan 27°33N 90°43E 241 B3
Byala Ruse, Bulgaria 43°28N 25°44E 203 C9
Byala Varna, Bulgaria 42°53N 27°55E 203 D11
Byala Slatina Bulgaria 43°26N 23°58E 202 C7
Byam Martin I. Canada 75°15N 104°15W 295 B11
Byarezina → Belarus 52°33N 30°14E 177 B16
Byaroza Belarus 52°31N 24°51E 189 F3
Bychawa Poland 51°1N 22°36E 185 G9
Byculla India 18°58N 72°50E 130 B2
Byczyna Poland 51°7N 18°12E 185 G5
Bydgoszcz Poland 53°10N 18°0E 185 E5
Byelorussia = Belarus ■ Europe 53°30N 27°0E 177 B14
Byeonsan △ S. Korea 35°40N 126°30E 224 E3
Byers U.S.A. 39°43N 104°14W 304 G11
Byesville U.S.A. 39°58N 81°32W 312 G3
Byfield △ Australia 22°52S 150°45E 280 C5
Bygdin Norway 61°21N 8°32E 164 C5
Bygdøy Norway 59°54N 10°40E 133 A3
Bygland Norway 58°50N 7°48E 164 F4
Byglandsfjorden Norway 58°44N 7°50E 164 F4
Bygstad Norway 61°23N 5°40E 164 C2
Bykhaw Belarus 53°31N 30°14E 177 B16
Bykhov = Bykhaw Belarus 53°31N 30°14E 177 B16
Bykle Norway 59°20N 7°22E 164 E4
Bykovo Russia 49°50N 45°25E 190 F7
Bylas U.S.A. 33°8N 110°7W 305 K8
Bylot Canada 58°25N 94°8W 297 B10
Bylot I. Canada 73°13N 78°34W 295 C16
Byrd, C. Antarctica 69°38S 76°7W 151 C17
Byrock Australia 30°40S 146°27E 283 A7
Byron Ga., U.S.A. 32°39N 83°46W 316 C6
Byron Ill., U.S.A. 42°8N 89°15W 310 B7
Byron, C. Australia 28°43S 153°38E 281 D5
Byron Bay Australia 28°43S 153°37E 281 D5
Byrranga, Gory Russia 75°0N 100°0E 215 B11
Byrranga Mts. = Byrranga, Gory Russia 75°0N 100°0E 215 B11
Byrum Denmark 57°16N 11°0E 163 G5
Byske Sweden 64°57N 21°11E 160 D19
Byskeälven → Sweden 64°57N 21°13E 160 D19
Bystrytsya Ukraine 48°27N 24°14E 183 B9
Bystrzyca → Dolnośląskie, Poland 51°12N 16°55E 185 G3
Bystrzyca → Lubelskie, Poland 51°21N 22°46E 185 G9
Bystrzyca Kłodzka Poland 50°19N 16°39E 185 H3
Bytča Slovak Rep. 49°13N 18°34E 181 B11
Bytkiv Ukraine 48°38N 24°28E 183 B9
Bytom Poland 50°25N 18°54E 185 H5
Bytom Odrzański Poland 51°44N 15°48E 185 G2
Bytów Poland 54°10N 17°30E 184 D4
Byumba Rwanda 1°35S 30°4E 268 C3
Bywater U.S.A. 29°58N 90°2W 131 B2
Bzenec Czech Rep. 48°58N 17°18E 181 C10
Bzura → Poland 52°25N 20°15E 185 F7

C

C.B.S. Fox Studios U.S.A. 34°9N 118°24W 126 B2
C.N.N. Center U.S.A. 33°45N 84°23W 113 B2
C.N. Tower Toronto, Canada 141 c1
C.W. McConaughy, L. U.S.A. 41°14N 101°40W 308 E3
Ca → Vietnam 18°45N 105°45E 236 C5
Ca Mau Vietnam 9°7N 105°8E 237 H5
Ca Mau, Mui Vietnam 8°38N 104°44E 237 H5
Ca Na Vietnam 11°20N 108°54E 237 G7
Caacupé Paraguay 25°23S 57°5W 334 B4
Caaguazú △ Paraguay 26°5S 55°31W 335 B4
Caála Angola 12°46S 15°30E 265 E3
Caamaño Sd. Canada 52°55N 129°25W 296 C3
Caapiranga Brazil 3°18S 61°13W 329 D5
Caazapá Paraguay 26°8S 56°19W 334 B4
Caazapá □ Paraguay 26°10S 56°0W 335 B4
Cabaad, Ras Somali Rep. 6°18N 49°4E 267 C6
Cabadbaran Phil. 9°10N 125°38E 233 G5
Cabagan Phil. 17°26N 121°46E 232 C3
Cabalian = San Juan Phil. 10°16N 125°10E 233 F5
Caballeria, C. de Spain 40°5N 4°5E 206 A5
Caballito Argentina 34°37S 58°25W 117 B2
Cabana Peru 8°25S 78°5W 330 B2
Cabana de Bergantiños Spain 43°13N 8°54W 194 B2
Cabanaconde Peru 15°38S 71°58W 330 D3
Cabañaquinta Spain 43°10N 5°38W 194 B5
Cabanatuan Phil. 15°30N 120°58E 232 D3
Cabañeros ⌂ Spain 39°18N 4°35W 195 F6
Cabanes Spain 40°9N 0°2E 196 E5
Cabangon Phil. 15°10N 120°3E 232 D3
Cabanilla Peru 15°36S 70°28W 330 D3
Cabano Canada 47°40N 68°56W 299 C6
Čabar Croatia 45°36N 14°39E 199 C11
Cabarroguis Phil. 16°50N 121°30E 232 C3
Cabarruyan I. Phil. 16°18N 119°59E 232 C2
Cabazon U.S.A. 33°55N 116°47W 307 M10
Cabedelo Brazil 7°0S 34°50W 332 C5
Cabeza del Buey Spain 38°44N 5°13W 195 G5
Cabezón de la Sal Spain 43°18N 4°14W 194 B6
Cabildo Chile 32°30S 71°5W 334 C1
Cabimas Venezuela 10°23N 71°25W 328 A3
Cabin John U.S.A. 38°58N 77°10W 143 B2
Cabin John Regional Park ⌂ U.S.A. 39°0N 77°10W 143 A2
Cabinda Angola 5°33S 12°11E 265 D2
Cabinda □ Angola 5°0S 12°30E 265 D2
Cabinet Mts. U.S.A. 48°10N 115°50W 304 B6
Cabinteely Ireland 53°16N 6°9W 120 B3
Cabiri Angola 8°52S 13°39E 265 D2
Cable Beach Bahamas 25°4N 77°24W 153 b
Cabo Blanco Argentina 47°15S 65°47W 336 C3
Cabo de Gata-Níjar ⌂ Spain 36°51N 2°6W 197 J2
Cabo de Hornos △ Chile 55°42S 67°20W 336 E3
Cabo de Santo Agostinho Brazil 8°20S 34°55W 332 C5
Cabo Frio Brazil 22°51S 42°3W 333 F3
Cabo Pantoja Peru 1°0S 75°10W 328 D2
Cabo Raso Argentina 44°20S 65°15W 336 B3
Cabo Rojo Puerto Rico 18°5N 67°9W 321 b
Cabo San Lucas Mexico 22°53N 109°54W 318 C3
Cabo Verde = Cape Verde Is. ■ Atl. Oc. 16°0N 24°0W 153 j
Cabo Yubi = Tarfaya Morocco 27°55N 12°55W 260 C2
Cabonga, Réservoir Canada 47°20N 76°40W 298 C4
Cabool U.S.A. 37°7N 92°6W 308 G7
Caboolture Australia 27°5S 152°58E 281 D5
Cabora Bassa Dam = Cahora Bassa, Lago de Mozam. 15°20S 32°50E 269 F3
Caborca Mexico 30°37N 112°6W 318 A2
Cabot, Mt. U.S.A. 44°30N 71°25W 313 B13
Cabot Hd. Canada 45°14N 81°17W 312 A3
Cabot Str. Canada 47°15N 59°40W 299 C8
Cabra Dublin, Ireland 53°21N 6°18W 120 A2
Cabra Spain 37°30N 4°28W 195 H6
Cabra del Santo Cristo Spain 37°42N 3°16W 195 H7
Cabra I. India 7°18N 93°50E 245 L11
Cábras Italy 39°56N 8°32E 200 C1
Cabras I. Guam 13°27N 144°44E 302 d
Cabrera Spain 39°8N 2°57E 206 B3
Cabrera, Sierra Spain 42°12N 6°40W 194 C4
Cabrera △ Spain 39°13N 2°53E 197 F7
Cabri Canada 50°35N 108°25W 297 C7
Cabriel → Spain 39°14N 1°3W 197 F3
Cabrits, Î. Martinique 14°23N 60°52W 322 j
Cabrits △ Dominica 15°35N 61°26W 323 k
Cabruta Venezuela 7°50N 66°10W 328 B4
Cabucgayan Phil. 11°29N 124°34E 233 F5
Cabuçú de Baixo → Brazil 23°30S 46°40W 137 A1
Cabuçú de Cima → Brazil 23°30S 46°33W 137 A2
Cabugao Phil. 17°48N 120°27E 232 C3
Cabulauan Is. Phil. 11°25N 120°8E 233 F3
Cabulo Angola 10°18S 16°22E 265 E3
Caburan = Jose Abad Santos Phil. 5°55N 125°39E 233 J5
Cabuta Angola 9°48S 14°58E 265 D2
Cabuyaro Colombia 4°18N 72°49W 328 C3
Cacabelos Spain 42°36N 6°44W 194 C4
Caçador Brazil 26°47S 51°0W 335 B5
Čačak Serbia 43°54N 20°20E 202 C4
Cacandee Settlement Trin. & Tob. 10°33N 61°26W 323 t
Cacao Fr. Guiana 4°33N 52°26W 329 C7
Caçapava do Sul Brazil 30°30S 53°30W 335 C5
Cáccamo Italy 37°56N 13°40E 200 E6
Cacém Portugal 38°46N 9°18W 195 G1
Cáceres Brazil 16°5S 57°40W 331 D6
Cáceres Colombia 7°35N 75°20W 328 B2
Cáceres Spain 39°26N 6°23W 195 F4
Cáceres □ Spain 39°45N 6°0W 194 F5
Cachan France 48°47N 2°19E 134 B2
Cache Bay Canada 46°22N 80°0W 298 C4
Cache Cr. → U.S.A. 38°42N 121°42W 306 G5
Cache Creek Canada 50°48N 121°19W 296 C4
Cachenka → Russia 55°46N 37°17E 129 B1
Cacheu Guinea-Biss. 12°14N 16°8W 262 C1
Cachi Argentina 25°5S 66°10W 334 B2
Cachimbo Brazil 8°57S 54°54W 331 B7
Cachimbo, Serra do Brazil 9°30S 55°30W 331 B6
Cachimo Angola 8°21S 21°24E 265 D4
Cachinal de la Sierra Chile 24°58S 69°32W 334 A2
Cachingues Angola 13°5S 16°43E 265 E3
Cachoeira = Solonópole Brazil 5°44S 39°1W 332 C4
Cachoeira Brazil 12°30S 39°0W 333 D4
Cachoeira, Rib. da → Brazil 23°38S 46°43W 137 B1
Cachoeira Alta Brazil 18°48S 50°58W 333 E1
Cachoeira do Sul Brazil 30°3S 52°53W 335 C5
Cachoeiro de Itapemirim Brazil 20°51S 41°7W 333 F3
Cachoeiro do Arari Brazil 1°1S 48°58W 332 B2
Cachopo Portugal 37°20N 7°49W 195 H3
Cachuela Esperanza Bolivia 10°32S 65°38W 331 C4
Cacilhas Portugal 38°41N 9°8W 126 A2
Cacine Guinea-Biss. 11°8N 14°57W 262 C1
Cacoal Brazil 11°32S 61°18W 331 C5
Cacólo Angola 10°9S 19°21E 265 E3
Caconda Angola 13°48S 15°8E 265 E3
Cacongo Angola 5°11S 12°5E 265 D2
Caçu Brazil 18°37S 51°4W 333 E1
Cacuaco Angola 8°47S 13°21E 265 D2
Cacuchi → Angola 14°26S 16°46E 265 E3
Cacula Angola 14°29S 14°10E 265 E2
Caculé Brazil 14°30S 42°13W 333 D3
Caculuvar → Angola 16°47S 14°56E 265 F2
Cacuso Angola 9°25S 15°45E 265 D3
Cadale Somali Rep. 2°45N 46°19E 267 D6
Čadca Slovak Rep. 49°26N 18°45E 181 B11
Caddo U.S.A. 34°7N 96°16W 314 D6
Cader Idris U.K. 52°42N 3°53W 169 E4
Cadereyta de Jiménez Mexico 25°36N 100°0W 318 B5
Cades U.S.A. 33°47N 79°47W 316 B10
Cadí, Sierra del Spain 42°17N 1°42E 196 C6
Cadí-Moixeró ⌂ Spain 42°17N 1°44W 196 C3
Cadibarrawirracanna, L. Australia 28°52S 135°27E 281 D2
Cadillac Gironde, France 44°38N 0°20W 174 D3
Cadillac Mich., U.S.A. 44°15N 85°24W 309 C11
Cadiz Phil. 10°57N 123°15E 233 F4
Cádiz Spain 36°30N 6°20W 195 J4
Cadiz Calif., U.S.A. 34°30N 115°28W 307 L11
Cadiz Ohio, U.S.A. 40°22N 81°0W 312 F4
Cádiz □ Spain 36°36N 5°45W 195 J5
Cádiz, G. de Spain 36°40N 7°0W 195 J3
Cadiz L. U.S.A. 34°18N 115°24W 305 J6
Cadley U.S.A. 33°32N 82°40W 316 B7
Cadney Park Australia 27°55S 134°3E 281 D1
Cadomin Canada 53°2N 117°20W 296 C5
Cadotte Lake Canada 56°26N 116°23W 296 B5
Cadours France 43°44N 1°2E 174 E5
Cadoux Australia 30°46S 117°7E 279 F2
Cadwell U.S.A. 32°20N 83°3W 316 C6
Caen France 49°10N 0°22W 172 C6
Caernarfon U.K. 53°8N 4°16W 168 D3
Caernarfon B. U.K. 53°4N 4°40W 168 D3
Caernarvon = Caernarfon U.K. 53°8N 4°16W 168 D3
Caerphilly U.K. 51°35N 3°13W 169 F4
Caerphilly □ U.K. 51°37N 3°12W 169 F4
Caesarea Israel 32°30N 34°53E 251 F5
Caeté Brazil 19°55S 43°40W 333 E3
Caetité Brazil 13°50S 42°32W 333 D3
Cafayate Argentina 26°2S 66°0W 334 B2
Cafu Angola 16°30S 15°8E 265 F3
Cagayan □ Phil. 18°0N 121°50E 232 C3
Cagayan → Phil. 18°25N 121°42E 232 B3
Cagayan de Oro Phil. 8°30N 124°40E 233 G5
Cagayan Is. Phil. 9°40N 121°16E 233 G3
Cagayan Sulu I. Phil. 7°1N 118°30E 233 H2
Cagli Italy 43°33N 12°39E 199 E9
Cágliari Italy 39°13N 9°7E 200 C2
Cágliari, G. di Italy 39°8N 9°11E 200 C2
Cagnano Varano Italy 41°49N 15°47E 199 G12
Cagnes-sur-Mer France 43°40N 7°9E 175 E11
Caguán → Colombia 0°8S 74°18W 328 D3
Caguas Puerto Rico 18°14N 66°2W 321 C6
Caha Mts. Ireland 51°45N 9°40W 166 E2
Cahama Angola 16°17S 14°19E 265 F2
Caher Ireland 52°22N 7°56W 166 D4
Cahersiveen Ireland 51°56N 10°14W 166 E1
Cahora Bassa, Lago de Mozam. 15°20S 32°50E 269 F3
Cahore Pt. Ireland 52°33N 6°12W 166 D5
Cahors France 44°27N 1°27E 174 D5
Cahuapanas Peru 5°15S 77°0W 330 B2
Cahuenga Park U.S.A. 34°8N 118°19W 126 B3
Cahuinari → Colombia 1°21S 70°44W 328 D3
Cahuinari △ Colombia 1°20S 71°10W 328 D3
Cahul Moldova 45°50N 28°15E 183 E13
Cài Bau, Dao Vietnam 21°10N 107°27E 228 G6
Cai Nuoc Vietnam 8°56N 105°1E 237 H5
Caia Mozam. 17°51S 35°24E 269 F4
Caiabis, Serra dos Brazil 11°30S 56°30W 331 C6
Caianda Angola 11°2S 23°31E 265 E4
Caiapó, Serra do Brazil 17°0S 52°0W 331 D7
Caiapônia Brazil 16°57S 51°49W 331 D7
Caibarién Cuba 22°30N 79°30W 320 B4
Caibiran Phil. 11°34N 124°35E 233 F5
Caiçara = Alvarães Brazil 3°12S 64°50W 329 D5
Caicara Bolívar, Venezuela 7°38N 66°10W 328 B4
Caicara Monagas, Venezuela 9°52N 63°38W 329 B5
Caicó Brazil 6°20S 37°0W 332 C4
Caicos Is. Turks & Caicos 21°40N 71°40W 321 B5
Caicos Passage W. Indies 22°45N 72°45W 321 B5
Caidian China 30°35N 114°2E 229 B10
Caiguna Australia 32°16S 125°29E 279 F4
Caillandre, Morne St. Lucia 13°46N 60°57W 323 m
Caille I. Grenada 12°16N 61°34W 323 q
Cailloma Peru 15°9S 71°45W 330 D3
Cain, L. U.S.A. 28°28N 81°28W 133 B2
Căinari Moldova 46°41N 29°3E 183 D14
Cainde Angola 15°29S 13°24E 265 F2
Caine → Bolivia 18°23S 65°21W 331 D4
Caird Coast Antarctica 75°0S 25°0W 151 D1
Cairn Gorm U.K. 57°7N 3°39W 167 D5
Cairngorm Mts. U.K. 57°6N 3°42W 167 D5
Cairngorms △ U.K. 57°10N 3°50W 167 D5
Cairnryan U.K. 54°59N 5°1W 167 G3
Cairns Australia 16°57S 145°45E 280 B4
Cairns L. Canada 51°42N 94°30W 297 C10
Cairo = El Qâhira Egypt 30°2N 31°13E 117 A2
Cairo Ga., U.S.A. 30°52N 84°13W 316 E5
Cairo Ill., U.S.A. 37°0N 89°11W 308 G9
Cairo N.Y., U.S.A. 42°18N 74°0W 313 D10
Cairo Int. ✈ (CAI) Egypt 30°7N 31°24E 117 A3
Cairo Montenotte Italy 44°23N 8°16E 198 D5
Cairofa Angola 14°3S 12°54E 265 E2
Caiseal = Cashel Ireland 52°30N 7°53W 166 D4
Caisleán an Bharraigh = Castlebar Ireland 53°52N 9°18W 166 C2
Caithness U.K. 58°25N 3°35W 167 C5
Caithness, Ord of U.K. 58°8N 3°36W 167 C5
Caitou Angola 14°28S 13°7E 265 E2
Caiuás = Rio Brilhante Brazil 21°48S 54°33W 335 A5
Caiundo Angola 15°50S 17°28E 265 F3
Caiza Bolivia 20°2S 65°40W 331 E4
Caja de Muertos, I. Puerto Rico 17°54N 66°32W 321 b
Cajabamba Peru 7°38S 78°4W 330 B2
Cajamarca Peru 7°5S 78°28W 330 B2
Cajamarca □ Peru 6°15S 78°50W 330 B2
Cajamarquilla = Bolívar Peru 7°18S 77°48W 330 B2
Cajapió Brazil 2°58S 44°48W 332 B3
Cajarc France 44°29N 1°50E 174 D5
Cajas △ Ecuador 2°48S 79°15W 328 D2
Cajatambo Peru 10°30S 77°2W 330 C2
Cajazeiras Brazil 6°52S 38°30W 332 C4
Čajetina Serbia 43°47N 19°42E 202 C3
Cajidiocan Phil. 12°22N 122°41E 232 E4
Caju Brazil 22°52S 43°12W 135 B1
Çakirgol Turkey 40°33N 39°40E 213 B8
Çakırlar Turkey 36°52N 30°33E 205 E12
Čakovec Croatia 46°23N 16°26E 199 B13
Čakovice Czech Rep. 50°9N 14°31E 135 B3
Çal Turkey 38°4N 29°23E 205 C11
Cala Spain 37°59N 6°21W 195 H4
Cala → Spain 37°38N 6°5W 195 H4
Cala Cadolar, Punta de = Rotja, Pta. Spain 38°38N 1°35E 206 D2
Cala d'Or Spain 39°23N 3°14E 206 B4
Cala en Porter Spain 39°52N 4°8E 206 B5
Cala Figuera Spain 39°20N 3°10E 206 B4
Cala Figuera, C. de Spain 39°27N 2°31E 206 B3
Cala Forcat Spain 40°0N 3°47E 206 B4
Cala Major Spain 39°33N 2°37E 206 B3
Cala Mezquida = Sa Mesquida Spain 39°55N 4°16E 206 B5
Cala Millor Spain 39°35N 3°22E 206 B4
Cala Murada Spain 39°27N 3°17E 206 B4
Cala Ratjada Spain 39°43N 3°27E 206 B4
Cala Santa Galdana Spain 39°56N 3°58E 206 B4
Calabanga Phil. 13°42N 123°17E 232 E4
Calabar Nigeria 4°57N 8°20E 263 E6
Calabogie Canada 45°18N 76°43W 313 A8
Calabozo Venezuela 9°0N 67°28W 328 B4
Calábria □ Italy 39°0N 16°30E 201 C9
Calábria △ Italy 39°6N 16°35E 201 C9
Calaburras, Pta. de Spain 36°30N 4°38W 195 J6
Calaceite Spain 41°1N 0°11E 196 D5
Calacoto Bolivia 17°16S 68°38W 330 D4
Calacuccia France 42°21N 9°1E 175 F13
Calafat Romania 43°58N 22°59E 182 G7
Calafell Spain 41°11N 1°34E 196 D6
Calagua Is. Phil. 14°30N 122°55E 232 D4
Calahorra Spain 42°18N 1°59W 196 C3
Calai Angola 17°47S 19°41E 265 F3
Calais Pas-de-Calais, France 50°57N 1°56E 173 B8
Calais Maine, U.S.A. 45°11N 67°17W 309 C20
Calakmul ⌂ Mexico 18°14N 89°48W 319 D7
Calalaste, Cord. de Argentina 25°0S 67°0W 334 B2
Calama Brazil 8°0S 62°50W 331 B5
Calama Chile 22°30S 68°55W 334 A2
Calamar Bolívar, Colombia 10°15N 74°55W 328 A3
Calamar Vaupés, Colombia 1°58N 72°32W 328 C3
Calamarca Bolivia 16°55S 68°9W 330 D4
Calamba Cavite, Phil. 14°13N 121°10E 232 D3
Calamba Mis. Occ., Phil. 8°35N 123°39E 233 G4
Calamian Group Phil. 11°50N 119°55E 233 F2
Calamocha Spain 40°50N 1°17W 196 E3
Calamonte Spain 38°53N 6°23W 195 G4
Călan Romania 45°44N 22°59E 182 E7
Calañas Spain 37°40N 6°53W 195 H4
Calanda Spain 40°56N 0°15W 196 E4
Calandagan I. Phil. 10°39N 120°15E 233 F3
Calandula Angola 9°6S 15°57E 265 D3
Calang Indonesia 4°37N 95°37E 234 B1
Calangiánus Italy 40°56N 9°11E 200 B2
Calanscio, Sarīr Libya 27°30N 21°30E 258 C4
Calapan Phil. 13°25N 121°7E 232 E3
Călăraşi Moldova 47°16N 28°19E 183 C13
Călăraşi Romania 44°12N 27°20E 183 F12
Călăraşi □ Romania 44°10N 27°0E 183 F12
Calasparra Spain 38°14N 1°41W 197 G3
Calatafimi Italy 37°55N 12°52E 200 E5
Calatagan Phil. 13°50N 120°38E 232 E3
Calatayud Spain 41°20N 1°40W 196 D3
Călăţele Romania 46°46N 23°1E 182 D8
Calato = Kalathos Greece 36°9N 28°8E 206 E12
Calatrava Eq. Guin. 1°6N 9°25E 264 B1
Calauag Phil. 13°55N 122°15E 232 E4
Calavà, C. Italy 38°11N 14°55E 201 D7
Calavite, C. Phil. 13°26N 120°20E 232 E3
Calavite Pass Phil. 13°36N 120°25E 232 E3
Calayan Phil. 19°16N 121°28E 232 B3
Calayan I. Phil. 19°20N 121°27E 232 B3
Calbayog Phil. 12°4N 124°38E 232 E5
Calbiga Phil. 11°38N 125°0E 233 F5
Calca Peru 13°22S 72°0W 330 C3
Calcasieu L. U.S.A. 29°55N 93°18W 314 G8
Calcium U.S.A. 44°1N 75°50W 313 B9
Calcutta = Kolkata India 22°34N 88°21E 124 B2
Calcutta U.S.A. 40°40N 80°34W 312 F4
Caldaro Italy 46°25N 11°14E 199 B8
Caldas □ Colombia 5°15N 75°30W 328 B2
Caldas da Rainha Portugal 39°24N 9°8W 195 F1
Caldas de Reis Spain 42°36N 8°39W 194 C2
Caldas Novas Brazil 17°45S 48°38W 333 E2
Calder → U.K. 53°44N 1°22W 168 D6
Caldera Chile 27°5S 70°55W 334 B1
Caldera de Taburiente △ Canary Is. 28°43N 17°52W 153 e1
Caldwell Idaho, U.S.A. 43°40N 116°41W 304 E5
Caldwell Kans., U.S.A. 37°2N 97°37W 308 G5
Caldwell Tex., U.S.A. 30°32N 96°42W 314 F6
Caledon Ont., Canada 43°51N 79°51W 312 C5
Caledon Western Cape, S. Africa 34°14S 19°26E 270 D2
Caledon → S. Africa 30°31S 26°5E 270 D4
Caledon B. Australia 12°45S 137°0E 280 A2
Caledonia Ont., Canada 43°7N 79°58W 312 C5
Caledonia Mo., U.S.A. 37°45N 90°46W 310 G6
Caledonia N.Y., U.S.A. 42°58N 77°51W 312 D7
Calella Spain 41°37N 2°40E 196 D7
Calemba Angola 16°0S 15°44E 270 A2
Calen Australia 20°56S 148°48E 280 b
Calenzana France 42°31N 8°51E 175 F12
Caleta Olivia Argentina 46°25S 67°25W 336 C3
Caletones Chile 34°6S 70°27W 334 C1
Calexico U.S.A. 32°40N 115°30W 307 N11
Calf of Man I. of Man 54°3N 4°48W 168 C3
Calgary Canada 51°0N 114°10W 296 C6
Calheta Azores 38°36N 28°1W 153 d1
Calheta Madeira 32°44N 17°11W 153 c
Calheta de Nesquim Azores 38°24N 28°5W 153 d1
Calhoun U.S.A. 34°30N 84°57W 315 D12
Calhoun Falls U.S.A. 34°6N 82°36W 316 A7
Cali Colombia 3°25N 76°35W 328 C2
Calibishie Dominica 15°35N 61°21W 323 k
Calicut India 11°15N 75°43E 245 J2
Caliente U.S.A. 37°37N 114°31W 305 H6
California Trin. & Tob. 10°24N 61°28W 323 t
California Mo., U.S.A. 38°38N 92°34W 310 F4
California Pa., U.S.A. 40°4N 79°54W 312 F5
California □ U.S.A. 37°30N 119°30W 306 H7
California, Baja, T.N. = Baja California □ Mexico 30°0N 115°0W 318 B2
California, Baja, T.S. = Baja California Sur □ Mexico 25°50N 111°50W 318 B2
California, G. de Mexico 27°0N 111°0W 318 B2
California City U.S.A. 35°10N 117°55W 307 K9
California Hot Springs U.S.A. 35°51N 118°41W 307 K8
California Inst. of Tech. U.S.A. 34°8N 118°8W 126 B4
California Los Angeles, Univ. of U.S.A. 34°4N 118°27W 126 B2
California Plaza Los Angeles, U.S.A. 127 b1
California State Univ. U.S.A. 34°4N 118°10W 126 B3
Cälilabad Azerbaijan 39°12N 48°29E 213 C13
Calilegua △ Argentina 25°36S 64°50W 334 B3
Călimăneşti Romania 45°14N 24°20E 183 E9
Călimani, Munţii Romania 47°12N 25°0E 183 C10
Calingasta Argentina 31°15S 69°30W 334 C2
Calinog Phil. 11°7N 122°32E 233 F4
Calintaan Phil. 12°35N 120°57E 232 E3
Calipatria U.S.A. 33°8N 115°31W 307 M11
Calistoga U.S.A. 38°35N 122°35W 306 G4
Calitri Italy 40°54N 15°26E 201 B8
Calitzdorp S. Africa 33°33S 21°42E 270 D3
Calivigny I. Grenada 12°0N 61°43W 323 q
Callabonna, L. Australia 29°40S 140°5E 281 D3
Callac France 48°25N 3°27W 172 D3
Callahan U.S.A. 30°34N 81°50W 316 E8
Callahan Tunnel Boston, U.S.A. 116 a3
Callan Ireland 52°32N 7°24W 166 D4
Callander U.K. 56°15N 4°13W 167 E4
Callang = San Manuel Phil. 16°4N 120°40E 232 C3
Callao Peru 12°3S 77°8W 124 B2
Callaway U.S.A. 30°8N 85°36W 316 E4
Calliaqua St. Vincent 13°8N 61°12W 323 n
Callicoon U.S.A. 41°46N 75°3W 313 E9
Calling Lake Canada 55°15N 113°12W 296 B6
Calliope Australia 24°0S 151°16E 280 C5
Callosa de Segura Spain 38°7N 0°53W 197 G4
Callosa d'En Sarrià Spain 38°40N 0°8W 197 G4
Calma, Costa de la Spain 39°28N 2°26E 206 B3
Calmar U.S.A. 43°11N 91°52W 310 A5
Calne U.K. 51°26N 2°0W 169 F6
Calola Angola 16°25S 17°48E 265 F3
Calolbon = San Andres Phil. 13°36N 124°6E 232 E5
Calonge Spain 41°52N 3°5E 196 D8
Caloocan Phil. 14°39N 120°58E 127 B1
Caloosahatchee → U.S.A. 26°31N 82°1W 317 J7
Calore → Italy 41°11N 14°28E 201 A7
Caloundra Australia 26°45S 153°10E 281 D5
Calpe Spain 38°39N 0°3E 197 G5
Calpella U.S.A. 39°14N 123°12W 306 F3
Calpine U.S.A. 39°40N 120°27W 306 F6
Calstock Canada 49°47N 84°9W 298 C3
Caltabellotta Italy 37°34N 13°13E 200 E6
Caltagirone Italy 37°14N 14°31E 201 E7
Caltanissetta Italy 37°29N 14°4E 201 E7
Çaltılıbük Turkey 39°57N 28°36E 203 G12
Caluango Angola 8°20S 19°39E 265 D3
Calubian Phil. 11°27N 124°26E 233 F5
Calucinga Angola 11°18S 16°12E 265 E3
Caluire-et-Cuire France 45°48N 4°52E 173 G11
Calulo Angola 10°1S 14°56E 265 E2
Calumet L. U.S.A. 41°41N 87°35W 119 C3
Calumet Park U.S.A. 41°40N 87°39W 119 C3
Calumet Sag Channel → U.S.A. 41°40N 87°47W 119 C2
Calunda Angola 12°7S 23°36E 265 E4
Caluquembe Angola 13°47S 14°44E 265 E2
Caluso Italy 45°18N 7°53E 198 C4
Caluula Somali Rep. 11°50N 50°45E 267 B7
Caluya I. Phil. 11°55N 121°34E 233 F3
Calvados □ France 49°5N 0°15W 172 C6
Calvados Chain, The Papua N. G. 11°10S 152°45E 286 F7
Calvairate Italy 45°27N 9°13E 129 B2
Calvert → Australia 16°17S 137°44E 280 B2
Calvert I. Canada 51°30N 128°0W 296 C3
Calvert Ra. Australia 24°0S 122°30E 278 D3
Calvi France 42°34N 8°45E 175 F12
Calvià Spain 39°34N 2°31E 206 B3
Calvillo Mexico 21°51N 102°43W 318 C4
Calvinia S. Africa 31°28S 19°45E 270 D2
Calvo, Mte. Italy 41°44N 15°46E 199 G12
Calwa U.S.A. 36°42N 119°46W 306 J7
Calzada Almuradiel = Almuradiel Spain 38°32N 3°28W 195 G7
Calzada de Calatrava Spain 38°42N 3°46W 195 G7
Cam → U.K. 52°21N 0°16E 169 E8
Cam Lam Vietnam 11°54N 109°10E 237 G7
Cam Pha Vietnam 21°7N 107°18E 228 G6
Cam Ranh Vietnam 11°54N 109°12E 237 G7
Cam Xuyen Vietnam 18°15N 106°0E 236 C6
Camabatela Angola 8°20S 15°26E 265 D3
Camacã Brazil 15°24S 39°30W 333 E4
Camaçari Brazil 12°41S 38°18W 333 D4
Camacha Madeira 32°41N 16°49W 153 c
Camacupa Angola 11°58S 17°22E 265 E3
Camaguán Venezuela 8°6N 67°36W 328 B4
Camagüey Cuba 21°20N 77°55W 320 B4
Camagüey, Arch. de Cuba 22°18N 78°0W 320 B4
Camaiore Italy 43°56N 10°18E 198 E7
Camamu Brazil 13°57S 39°7W 333 D4
Camaná Peru 16°30S 72°50W 330 D3
Camanche U.S.A. 41°47N 90°15W 310 C6
Camanche Res. U.S.A. 38°14N 121°1W 306 G6
Camapuã Brazil 19°30S 54°5W 331 D7
Camaquã Brazil 30°51S 51°49W 335 C5
Camaquã → Brazil 31°17S 51°47W 335 C5
Câmara de Lobos Madeira 32°39N 16°59W 153 c
Camararé → Brazil 12°15S 58°55W 331 C6
Camarat, C. France 43°12N 6°41E 175 E10
Camarate Portugal 38°48N 9°7W 126 A2
Çamardı Turkey 37°49N 34°58E 212 D6
Camarès France 43°49N 2°53E 174 E6
Camaret-sur-Mer France 48°16N 4°37W 172 D2
Camargo Bolivia 20°38S 65°15W 331 E4
Camargo Tamaulipas, Mexico 26°19N 98°50W 319 B5
Camargue France 43°34N 4°34E 175 E8
Camargue ⌂ France 43°30N 4°40E 175 E8
Camarillo U.S.A. 34°13N 119°2W 307 L7
Camariñas Spain 43°8N 9°12W 194 B1
Camarines Norte □ Phil. 14°10N 122°45E 232 D4
Camarines Sur □ Phil. 13°40N 123°20E 232 E4
Camaroes Portugal 38°49N 9°14W 126 A1
Camarón, C. Honduras 16°0N 85°5W 320 C2
Camarones Argentina 44°50S 65°40W 336 B3
Camarones, B. Argentina 44°45S 65°35W 336 B3
Camas Spain 37°24N 6°2W 195 H4
Camas Wash., U.S.A. 45°35N 122°24W 306 E4
Camas Valley U.S.A. 43°2N 123°40W 304 E2
Camatambo Angola 6°31S 15°21E 265 D3
Camataquí = Villa Abecia Bolivia 21°0S 68°18W 334 A2
Camaxilo Angola 8°21S 18°56E 265 D3
Camba Cassai Angola 9°47S 19°9E 265 D3
Camballin Australia 17°59S 124°12E 278 C3
Cambamba Angola 8°53S 14°44E 265 D2
Cambará Brazil 23°2S 50°5W 335 A5
Cambay = Khambhat India 22°23N 72°33E 242 H5
Cambay, G. of = Khambhat, G. of India 20°45N 72°30E 239 E10
Camberwell Vic., Australia 37°50S 145°5E 128 B2
Camberwell London, U.K. 51°28N 0°5W 125 B3
Cambil Spain 37°40N 3°33W 195 H7
Cambo Angola 10°55S 20°6E 265 D3
Cambo-les-Bains France 43°22N 1°23W 174 E2
Cambodia ■ Asia 12°15N 105°0E 236 F5
Camborne U.K. 50°12N 5°19W 169 G2
Cambrai S. Austral., Australia 34°40S 139°16E 282 C3
Cambrai Nord, France 50°11N 3°14E 173 B10
Cambre Spain 43°17N 8°20W 194 B2
Cambria U.S.A. 35°34N 121°5W 306 K5
Cambrian Mts. U.K. 52°3N 3°57W 169 E4
Cambridge Ont., Canada 43°23N 80°15W 312 C4
Cambridge Jamaica 18°18N 77°54W 320 a
Cambridge N.Z. 37°54S 175°29E 284 D4
Cambridge Cambs., U.K. 52°12N 0°8E 169 E8
Cambridge Ill., U.S.A. 41°18N 90°12W 310 C6
Cambridge Iowa, U.S.A. 41°54N 93°32W 310 C3
Cambridge Mass., U.S.A. 42°23N 71°7W 116 A2
Cambridge Minn., U.S.A. 45°34N 93°13W 308 C7
Cambridge N.Y., U.S.A. 43°2N 73°22W 313 C11
Cambridge Nebr., U.S.A. 40°17N 100°10W 308 E3
Cambridge Ohio, U.S.A. 40°2N 81°35W 312 F3
Cambridge Bay Canada 69°10N 105°0W 294 D11
Cambridge City U.S.A. 39°49N 85°10W 311 E11
Cambridge G. Australia 14°55S 128°15E 278 B4
Cambridge Springs U.S.A. 41°48N 80°4W 312 E4
Cambridgeshire □ U.K. 52°25N 0°7W 169 E7
Cambrils Spain 41°8N 1°3E 196 D6
Cambuci Rio de J., Brazil 21°35S 41°55W 333 F3
Cambuci São Paulo, Brazil 23°33S 46°47W 137 B2
Cambulo Angola 7°49S 21°15E 265 D4
Cambundi-Catembo Angola 10°10S 17°35E 265 E3
Camdeboo △ S. Africa 32°28S 24°25E 270 D3
Camden N.S.W., Australia 34°1S 150°43E 283 C9
Camden Ala., U.S.A. 31°59N 87°17W 315 F11
Camden Ark., U.S.A. 33°35N 92°50W 314 E8
Camden Maine, U.S.A. 44°13N 69°4W 309 C19
Camden N.J., U.S.A. 39°55N 75°7W 313 G9
Camden N.Y., U.S.A. 43°20N 75°45W 313 C9
Camden Ohio, U.S.A. 39°38N 84°39W 311 E12
Camden S.C., U.S.A. 34°16N 80°36W 315 D14
Camden □ U.K. 51°32N 0°8W 125 A3
Camden Bay U.S.A. 70°10N 145°15W 303 A11
Camden Sd. Australia 15°27S 124°25E 278 C3
Camdenton U.S.A. 38°1N 92°45W 310 F4
Cameia △ Angola 12°5S 21°40E 265 E4
Camelford U.K. 50°37N 4°42W 169 G3
Çameli Turkey 37°5N 29°24E 205 D11
Camenca Moldova 48°3N 28°42E 183 B13
Camerino Italy 43°8N 13°4E 199 E10
Camerón Chile 53°38S 69°39W 336 D3
Cameron Ariz., U.S.A. 35°53N 111°25W 305 J8
Cameron La., U.S.A. 29°48N 93°20W 314 G8
Cameron Mo., U.S.A. 39°44N 94°14W 310 E2
Cameron S.C., U.S.A. 33°34N 80°43W 316 B9
Cameron Tex., U.S.A. 30°51N 96°59W 314 F6
Cameron, Mt. N.Z. 41°20S 174°52E 143 B2
Cameron Highlands Malaysia 4°27N 101°22E 237 K3
Cameron Hills Canada 59°48N 118°0W 296 B5
Cameron Mts. N.Z. 46°1S 167°0E 285 G2
Cameroon ■ Africa 6°0N 12°30E 264 A2
Camerota Italy 40°2N 15°22E 201 B8
Cameroun → Cameroon 4°0N 9°35E 263 E6
Cameroun, Mt. Cameroon 4°13N 9°10E 263 E6
Cametá Brazil 2°12S 49°30W 332 B2
Çamiçi Gölü Turkey 37°29N 27°28E 205 D9
Camiguin □ Phil. 9°11N 124°42E 233 G5
Camiguin I. Phil. 18°56N 121°55E 232 B3
Camiling Phil. 15°42N 120°24E 232 D3
Camilla U.S.A. 31°14N 84°12W 316 D5
Caminha Portugal 41°50N 8°50W 194 D2

Camino *U.S.A.* 38°44N 120°41W **306** G6
Camiranga *Brazil* 1°48S 46°17W **332** B2
Camiri *Bolivia* 20°3S 63°31W **331** E5
Camissombo *Angola* 8°7S 20°38E **265** D4
Çamlıca *Turkey* 41°1N 29°3E **122** B2
Çamlıyayla *Turkey* 37°10N 34°36E **250** A5
Cammal *Italy* 41°24N 77°28W **312** E7
Cammarata *Italy* 37°38N 13°38E **200** E6
Cammin = Kamień Pomorski
  Poland 53°57N 14°43E **184** L1
Camo *Ethiopia* 4°29N 38°24E **266** D4
Camocim *Brazil* 2°55S 40°50W **332** B3
Camooweal *Australia* 19°56S 138°7E **280** B2
Camooweal Caves △
  Australia 20°1S 138°11E **280** C2
Camopi *Fr. Guiana* 3°12N 52°17W **329** C7
Camopi → *Fr. Guiana* 3°12N 52°20W **329** C7
Camorta *India* 8°8N 93°30E **245** K11
Camotes Is. *Phil.* 10°40N 124°24E **233** F5
Camotes Sea *Phil.* 10°30N 124°15E **233** F5
Camp Coulter = Powell
  U.S.A. 44°45N 108°46W **304** D9
Camp Hill *Ala., U.S.A.* 32°48N 85°39W **316** C4
Camp Hill *Pa., U.S.A.* 40°14N 76°55W **312** F8
Camp Nelson *U.S.A.* 36°8N 118°39W **307** J8
Camp Pendleton
  U.S.A. 33°13N 117°24W **307** M9
Camp Point *U.S.A.* 40°3N 91°4W **310** D5
Camp Springs *U.S.A.* 38°48N 96°55W **143** C4
Camp Verde *U.S.A.* 34°34N 111°51W **305** J8
Camp Wood *U.S.A.* 29°40N 100°1W **314** G4
Campagna *Italy* 40°40N 15°6E **201** B8
Campama *Spain* 40°23N 3°46W **127** B1
Campana *Argentina* 34°10S 58°55W **334** C4
Campana, I. *Chile* 48°20S 75°20W **336** C1
Campanário *Madeira* 32°39N 17°2W **153** a
Campanet *Spain* 39°46N 2°58E **206** B3
Campánia □ *Italy* 41°0N 14°30E **201** B7
Campbell *Northern Cape,*
  S. Africa 28°48S 23°44E **270** C3
Campbell *Calif., U.S.A.* 37°17N 121°57W **306** H5
Campbell *Fla., U.S.A.* 28°16N 81°27W **317** G8
Campbell *Ohio, U.S.A.* 41°5N 80°37W **312** E4
Campbell, C. *N.Z.* 41°47S 174°18E **285** B9
Campbell I. *Pac. Oc.* 52°30S 169°0E **288** N8
Campbell L. *Canada* 63°14N 106°55W **297** A7
Campbell Plateau
  S. Ocean 50°0S 170°0E **151** A11
Campbell River *Canada* 50°5N 125°20W **296** D3
Campbellfield *Australia* 37°41S 144°57E **128** A1
Campbellford *Canada* 44°18N 77°48W **312** B7
Campbellpur *Pakistan* 33°46N 72°26E **242** C5
Campbellsburg *U.S.A.* 38°39N 86°16W **311** F10
Campbellsville *U.S.A.* 37°21N 85°20W **309** G11
Campbellton *N.B.,*
  Canada 47°57N 66°43W **299** C6
Campbellton *Fla., U.S.A.* 30°57N 85°24W **316** E4
Campbelltown = Bluff
  N.Z. 46°37S 168°20E **285** G3
Campbelltown *Australia* 34°4S 150°49E **283** C9
Campbeltown *U.K.* 55°26N 5°36W **167** F3
Campeche *Guadeloupe* 16°26N 61°26W **322** e
Campeche *Campeche,*
  Mexico 19°50N 90°32W **319** D6
Campeche □ *Mexico* 19°0N 90°30W **319** D6
Campeche, Banco *Mexico* 22°30N 88°0W **320** B2
Campeche, Golfo de
  Mexico 19°30N 93°0W **319** D6
Câmpeni *Romania* 46°22N 23°3E **182** D8
Camperdown *N.S.W.,*
  Australia 33°53S 151°11E **139** B2
Camperdown *Vic.,*
  Australia 38°14S 143°9E **282** E5
Camperville *Canada* 51°59N 100°9W **297** C8
Campi Salentina *Italy* 40°24N 18°1E **201** B11
Câmpia Turzii *Romania* 46°34N 23°53E **183** D8
Campidano *Italy* 39°30N 8°47E **200** C1
Campidoglio, Piazza de *Rome, Italy* 41°53N 12°29E **e**
Campíglia Maríttima *Italy* 43°4N 10°37E **198** E7
Campillo de Altobuey
  Spain 39°36N 1°49W **197** F3
Campillos *Spain* 37°4N 4°51W **195** H6
Câmpina *Romania* 45°10N 25°45E **183** E10
Campina Grande *Brazil* 7°20S 35°47W **332** C4
Campina Verde *Brazil* 19°31S 49°28W **333** E2
Campinas *Brazil* 22°50S 47°0W **335** A6
Campione *Italy* 45°58N 8°58E **175** C12
Campli *Italy* 42°43N 13°41E **199** F10
Campo = N'tem →
  Cameroon 2°21N 9°49E **264** B2
Campo *Cameroon* 2°22N 9°50E **264** B1
Campo *Spain* 42°25N 0°24E **196** C5
Campo, Casa de *Spain* 40°25N 3°45W **127** B1
Campo → *Cameroon* 2°23N 10°55E **264** B2
Campo Belo *Brazil* 20°52S 45°16W **333** F2
Campo de Criptana *Spain* 39°24N 3°7W **195** F4
Campo de Diauarum
  Brazil 11°12S 53°14W **331** C7
Campo de Gibraltar *Spain* 36°15N 5°25W **195** J5
Campo F.C. Barcelona
  Spain 41°22N 2°7E **114** A1
Campo Florido *Brazil* 19°45S 48°35W **333** E2
Campo Formoso = Campo Florido
  Brazil 19°47S 48°35W **333** E2
Campo Formoso *Brazil* 10°30S 40°20W **332** D3
Campo Grande *Brazil* 20°25S 54°40W **331** E7
Campo Grande *Portugal* 38°45N 9°9W **126** A2
Campo Maior *Brazil* 4°50S 42°12W **332** B3
Campo Maior *Portugal* 39°2N 7°7W **195** F3
Campo Mourão *Brazil* 24°3S 52°22W **335** A5
Campo Pequeno *Portugal* 38°44N 9°9W **126** A2
Campo Túres *Italy* 46°54N 11°55W **199** B8
Campoalegre *Colombia* 2°41N 75°20W **328** C2
Campobasso *Italy* 41°34N 14°39E **201** A7
Campobello di Licata
  Italy 37°15N 13°55E **200** E6
Campobello di Mazara
  Italy 37°38N 12°45E **200** E5
Campofelice di Roccella
  Italy 37°59N 13°53E **200** E6
Campomarino *Italy* 41°57N 15°2E **199** G12
Campomarino *Italy* 37°54N 13°6E **200** E6
Camporrobles *Spain* 39°39N 1°24W **196** F3
Campos *Brazil* 21°50S 41°20W **333** F3
Campos *Spain* 39°26N 3°1E **206** B4
Campos Altos *Brazil* 19°43S 46°10W **333** E2
Campos Belos *Brazil* 13°10S 47°3W **333** D2
Campos del Paraíso = Carrascosa
  del Campo *Spain* 40°2N 2°45W **196** E2
Campos Novos *Brazil* 27°21S 51°50W **335** B5
Campos Sales *Brazil* 7°4S 40°23W **332** D3
Camprodon *Spain* 42°19N 2°23E **196** C7
Camps Bay *S. Africa* 33°57S 18°23E **118** C4
Campton *Fla., U.S.A.* 30°53N 86°31W **317** E3
Campton *Ky., U.S.A.* 37°44N 83°33W **311** G13
Camptonville *U.S.A.* 39°27N 121°3W **306** F5
Camptown *U.S.A.* 41°44N 76°14W **313** E8
Câmpulung *Argeş,*
  Romania 45°17N 25°3E **183** E10
Câmpulung *Suceava,*
  Romania 47°32N 25°53E **183** C10
Câmpuri *Romania* 45°0N 26°50E **183** D11
Campuya → *Peru* 1°40S 73°30W **328** D3

Campville *U.S.A.* 29°40N 82°7W **316** F6
Camrose *Canada* 53°0N 112°50W **296** C6
Camsell Portage *Canada* 59°37N 109°15W **297** B7
Camucuio *Angola* 14°7S 13°15E **265** E2
Camuy *Puerto Rico* 18°29N 66°51W **321** b
Çamyuva *Turkey* 36°30N 30°30E **205** E12
Çan *Turkey* 40°2N 27°3E **203** F11
Can Clavo *Spain* 38°57N 1°27E **206** D1
Can Gio *Vietnam* 10°25N 106°58E **237** G6
Can Pastilla *Spain* 39°32N 2°42E **206** B3
C'an San Joan *Spain* 41°28N 2°11E **114** A2
Can Tho *Vietnam* 10°2N 105°46E **237** G5
Canaan *Trin. & Tob.* 11°9N 60°49W **323** s
Canaan *Conn., U.S.A.* 42°2N 73°20W **313** D11
Canaan *Hill Jamaica* 18°23N 77°14W **320** a
Cañacona *India* 15°1N 74°4E **245** G2
Canada ■ *N. Amer.* 60°0N 100°0W **294** D11
Canada Abyssal Plain
  Arctic 80°0N 140°0W **150** B18
Canada Basin *Arctic* 80°0N 145°0W **150** B18
Canadian *U.S.A.* 35°55N 100°23W **314** D4
Canadian → *U.S.A.* 35°28N 95°3W **314** D7
Canadian Shield *Canada* 53°0N 75°0W **292** D12
Canadys *U.S.A.* 33°3N 80°37W **316** D9
Canajoharie *U.S.A.* 42°54N 74°35W **313** D10
Çanakkale *Turkey* 40°8N 26°24E **203** F10
Çanakkale □ *Turkey* 40°10N 26°25E **203** F10
Çanakkale Boğazı
  Turkey 40°17N 26°32E **203** F10
Canal Flats *Canada* 50°10N 115°48W **296** C5
Canal Point *U.S.A.* 26°52N 80°38W **317** J9
Canal Street *New Orleans, U.S.A.* 131 b2
Canala *N. Cal.* 21°32S 165°57E **288** d
Canalejas *Argentina* 35°15S 66°34W **334** C2
Canals *Argentina* 33°35S 62°53W **334** C3
Canals *Spain* 38°58N 0°35W **197** G4
Canandaigua *U.S.A.* 42°54N 77°17W **312** D7
Canandaigua L. *U.S.A.* 42°47N 77°19W **312** D7
Cananea *Mexico* 31°0N 110°18W **318** A2
Cañar *Ecuador* 2°33S 78°56W **328** D2
Cañar □ *Ecuador* 2°30S 79°0W **328** D2
Canarias, Is. *Atl. Oc.* 28°30N 16°0W **153** e1
Canary Is. = Canarias, Is.
  Atl. Oc. 28°30N 16°0W **153** e1
Canaseraga *U.S.A.* 42°27N 77°45W **312** D7
Canastra, Serra da *Brazil* 20°0S 46°20W **333** F2
Canatlán *Mexico* 24°31N 104°47W **318** C4
Cañaveral *Peru* 3°56S 80°39W **328** D1
Cañaveral, C. *U.S.A.* 28°27N 80°32W **317** G9
Cañaveral *U.S.A.* 28°28N 80°34W **317** G9
Cañaveruelas *Spain* 40°24N 2°38W **196** E2
Canavieiras *Brazil* 15°39S 39°0W **333** E4
Canbelego *Australia* 31°32S 146°18E **283** A7
Canberra *Australia* 35°15S 149°8E **283** C8
Canby *Calif., U.S.A.* 41°27N 120°52W **304** F3
Canby *Minn., U.S.A.* 44°43N 96°16W **308** C5
Canby *Oreg., U.S.A.* 45°16N 122°42W **306** E4
Cancale *France* 48°40N 1°50W **172** D5
Cancellaria, Palazzo dei *Rome, Italy* **e**
Canche → *France* 50°30N 1°39E **173** B8
Canchungo = Teixeira Pinto
  Guinea-Biss. 12°3N 16°0W **262** C1
Canchyuaya, Cordillera de
  Peru 7°30S 74°0W **330** B3
Cancún *Mexico* 21°8N 86°44W **319** C7
Candanchú *Spain* 42°47N 0°32W **196** C4
Çandarlı *Turkey* 17°15S 70°13W **330** D3
Çandarlı Körfezi *Turkey* 38°52N 26°55E **205** C8
Candás *Spain* 43°35N 5°45W **194** B5
Candé *France* 47°34N 1°0W **172** E5
Candeias → *Brazil* 8°39S 63°31W **330** D5
Candela *Italy* 41°8N 15°31E **201** A8
Candelaria *Argentina* 27°29S 55°44W **335** B4
Candelaria *Canary Is.* 28°22N 16°22E **153** e1
Candelario *Spain* 40°27N 5°46W **194** E5
Candeleda *Spain* 40°10N 5°14W **194** E5
Candi Dasa *Indonesia* 8°30S 115°34E **231** J18
Candia = Iraklio *Greece* 35°20N 25°12E **207** E6
Candia, Sea of = Crete, Sea of
  Greece 36°0N 25°0E **205** E7
Candiac *Canada* 45°23N 73°29W **130** B3
Cândido de Abreu *Brazil* 24°35S 51°20W **333** F1
Cândido Mendes *Brazil* 1°27S 45°43W **332** B2
Candle *U.S.A.* 65°55N 161°56W **303** D7
Candle L. *Canada* 53°50N 105°18W **297** C7
Candlemas I. *Antarctica* 57°3S 26°40W **151** B1
Cando *U.S.A.* 48°32N 99°12W **308** A4
Candon *Phil.* 17°12N 120°27E **232** C3
Cane = Chania *Greece* 35°30N 24°4E **207** E5
Caneças *Portugal* 38°48N 9°13W **126** A1
Canefield *Dominica* 15°20N 61°24W **323** k
Canela *Brazil* 10°15S 48°25W **332** D2
Canelles → *St. Lucia* 13°47N 60°55W **323** m
Canelli *Italy* 44°43N 8°17E **198** D5
Canelones *Uruguay* 34°32S 56°17W **335** C4
Canet-Plage *France* 42°41N 3°2E **174** F7
Cañete *Chile* 37°50S 73°30W **334** D1
Cañete *Spain* 40°3N 1°54W **196** E3
Cañete de las Torres
  Spain 37°53N 4°19W **195** H6
Cangamba *Angola* 13°40S 19°54E **265** E3
Cangandala *Angola* 9°45S 16°33E **265** D3
Cangandala △ *Angola* 9°53S 16°42E **265** D3
Cangas *Spain* 42°16N 8°47W **194** C2
Cangas de Onís *Spain* 43°21N 5°8W **194** B5
Cangombe *Angola* 14°24S 19°59E **265** E3
Cangonga *Angola* 9°24S 17°30E **265** D3
Canguaretama *Brazil* 6°20S 35°5W **332** C4
Cangucu *Brazil* 31°22S 52°43W **335** C5
Cangucu, Serra do *Brazil* 13°46S 47°20W **333** E2
Cangumbe *Angola* 11°58S 19°12E **265** E3
Cangwu *China* 23°25N 111°17E **229** F8
Cangxi *China* 31°47N 105°59E **228** B5
Cangyuan *China* 23°12N 99°14E **228** F2
Cangzhou *China* 38°19N 116°52E **226** F9
Canhoca *Angola* 9°15S 14°41E **265** D2
Cani, I. *Tunisia* 36°21N 10°5E **258** A2
Caniapiscau → *Canada* 56°40N 69°30W **299** A6
Caniapiscau, L. *Canada* 54°10N 69°55W **299** B6
Canicatti *Italy* 37°21N 13°51E **200** E6
Canicattini Bagni *Italy* 37°2N 15°4E **201** F8
Canim Lake *Canada* 51°47N 120°54W **296** C4
Canindé → *Brazil* 4°2S 39°11W **332** B4

Canindé → *Brazil* 6°15S 42°52W **332** C3
Canindeyu □ *Paraguay* 24°10S 55°0W **335** A5
Canino *Italy* 42°28N 11°45E **199** F8
Canisteo *U.S.A.* 42°16N 77°36W **312** D7
Canisteo → *U.S.A.* 42°7N 77°8W **312** D7
Cañitas de Felipe Pescador
  Mexico 23°36N 102°43W **318** C4
Cañizal *Spain* 41°12N 5°22W **194** D5
Canjáyar *Spain* 37°1N 2°44W **195** H8
Canjinge *Angola* 10°1S 21°17E **265** E4
Çankırı *Turkey* 40°40N 33°37E **212** B5
Çankırı □ *Turkey* 40°40N 33°37E **212** B5
Cankuzo *Burundi* 3°10S 30°31E **268** C3
Canlaon *Phil.* 10°22N 123°12E **233** F4
Canlaon Volcano *Phil.* 10°25N 123°8E **233** F4
Canmore *Canada* 51°7N 115°18W **296** C5
Cann River *Australia* 37°35S 149°7E **283** D8
Canna *U.K.* 57°3N 6°33W **167** D2
Cannanore *India* 11°53N 75°27E **245** J2
Cannanore Is. *India* 11°30N 72°30E **245** J1
Cannelton *U.S.A.* 37°55N 86°45W **311** G10
Cannery, The *San Francisco, U.S.A.* **c1**
Cannes *France* 43°32N 7°1E **175** E11
Canning Town = Port Canning
  India 22°23N 88°40E **243** H13
Canning Town *U.K.* 51°31N 0°1E **125** A4
Cannington *Canada* 44°20N 79°2W **312** B5
Cannóbio *Italy* 46°4N 8°42E **198** B5
Cannock *U.K.* 52°41N 2°1W **169** E5
Cannonball → *U.S.A.* 46°26N 100°35W **308** B3
Cannonsville Res. *U.S.A.* 42°4N 75°22W **313** D9
Cannonvale *Australia* 20°17S 148°43E **280** b
Caño Colorado *Colombia* 12°8N 68°22W **328** C4
Canoas *Brazil* 29°56S 51°11W **335** B5
Canoe L. *Canada* 55°10N 108°15W **297** B7
Cañon City *U.S.A.* 38°27N 105°14W **304** G11
Cañón de Río Blanco △
  Mexico 18°43N 97°15W **319** D5
Cañón del Río Lobos △
  Spain 41°46N 3°28W **194** D7
Cañón del Sumidero △
  Mexico 19°22N 96°24W **319** D5
Cannonnier, Pte. du
  St.-Martin 18°4N 63°7W **322** a
Canonniers Pt. *Mauritius* 20°2S 57°32E **272** e
Canoochee → *U.S.A.* 31°59N 81°19W **316** D8
Canopus *Australia* 33°29S 140°42E **282** B4
Canora *Canada* 51°40N 102°30W **297** C8
Canosa di Púglia *Italy* 41°13N 16°4E **201** A9
Canourgue *St. Vincent* 12°43N 61°20W **323** n
Canowindra *Australia* 33°35S 148°38E **283** B8
Canso *Canada* 45°20N 61°0W **299** C7
Canta *Peru* 11°29S 76°37W **330** C2
Cantabria □ *Spain* 43°10N 4°0W **194** B7
Cantabria, Sierra de *Spain* 42°40N 2°30W **196** C2
Cantabrian Mts. = Cantábrica,
  Cordillera *Spain* 43°0N 5°10W **194** C5
Cantábrica, Cordillera
  Spain 43°0N 5°10W **194** C5
Cantal □ *France* 45°5N 2°45E **174** D6
Cantal, Plomb du *France* 45°3N 2°45E **174** D6
Cantanhede *Portugal* 40°20N 8°36W **194** E2
Cantaura *Venezuela* 9°19N 64°21W **329** B5
Cantavieja *Spain* 40°31N 0°25W **196** E4
Cantemir *Moldova* 46°17N 28°14E **183** D13
Canteras de Vallecas
  Spain 40°20N 3°37W **127** B2
Canterbury = Invermere
  Canada 50°30N 116°2W **296** C5
Canterbury *N.S.W.,*
  Australia 33°55S 151°7E **139** B1
Canterbury *Queens.,*
  Australia 25°23S 141°53E **280** D3
Canterbury *Vic., Australia* 37°49S 145°4E **128** A2
Canterbury *Kent, U.K.* 51°16N 1°6E **169** F9
Canterbury □ *N.Z.* 43°45N 171°19E **285** D6
Canterbury Bight *N.Z.* 44°16S 171°55E **285** E6
Canterbury Plains *N.Z.* 43°55S 171°22E **285** E6
Cantil *U.S.A.* 35°18N 117°58W **307** K9
Cantilan *Phil.* 9°20N 125°58E **233** G5
Cantillana *Spain* 37°36N 5°50W **195** H5
Canto do Buriti *Brazil* 8°7S 42°58W **332** D3
Canton = Guangzhou
  China 23°6N 113°13E **121** B2
Canton *Ga., U.S.A.* 34°14N 84°29W **315** D12
Canton *Ill., U.S.A.* 40°33N 90°2W **310** D5
Canton *Miss., U.S.A.* 32°37N 90°2W **315** D9
Canton *Mo., U.S.A.* 40°8N 91°32W **310** D5
Canton *N.Y., U.S.A.* 44°36N 75°10W **313** B9
Canton *Ohio, U.S.A.* 40°48N 81°23W **312** F3
Canton *S. Dak., U.S.A.* 43°18N 96°35W **308** D6
Canton *L., U.S.A.* 36°6N 98°35W **314** C5
Cantonment *U.S.A.* 30°37N 87°20W **317** E1
Cantù *Italy* 45°44N 9°8E **198** C6
Cantwell *U.S.A.* 63°24N 148°57W **303** B5
Canudos *Brazil* 7°13S 58°5W **331** B6
Canumã *Amazonas, Brazil* 6°2S 59°4W **329** D6
Canumã *Amazonas, Brazil* 7°8S 60°10W **329** D6
Canumã → *Brazil* 3°55S 59°10W **331** B6
Canunda △ *Australia* 37°42S 140°16E **282** D4
Canutama *Brazil* 6°30S 64°20W **330** C5
Canutillo *U.S.A.* 31°55N 106°36W **314** F1
Canvey *U.K.* 51°31N 0°37E **169** F8
Canyon *U.S.A.* 34°59N 101°55W **314** D4
Canyon De Chelly △
  U.S.A. 36°10N 109°20W **305** H9
Canyonlands △ *U.S.A.* 38°15N 110°0W **305** G9
Canyonville *U.S.A.* 42°56N 123°17W **304** E2
Canzar *Angola* 7°35S 21°34E **265** D4
Cao Bang *Vietnam* 22°40N 106°15E **228** F6
Cao He → *China* 40°10N 124°32E **227** D13
Cao Lanh *Vietnam* 10°27N 105°38E **237** G5
Cao Xian *China* 34°50N 115°35E **226** G8
Caohejing *China* 31°10N 121°25E **138** B1
Caombo *Angola* 8°42S 16°15E **265** D3
Cáorle *Italy* 45°36N 12°51E **199** C9
Cap-aux-Meules *Canada* 47°23N 61°52W **299** C7
Cap-Chat *Canada* 49°6N 66°40W **299** C6
Cap-de-la-Madeleine
  Canada 46°22N 72°31W **298** C5
Cap Pt. *St. Lucia* 14°7N 60°57W **323** m
Cap-Haïtien *Haiti* 19°40N 72°20W **321** C5
Cap St. Lucia 14°7N 60°57W **323** m
Capac *U.S.A.* 43°1N 82°56W **312** D2
Capácci *Italy* 40°25N 15°5E **201** B8
Capaci *Italy* 38°10N 13°14E **200** D6
Capaia *Angola* 8°27S 20°13E **265** D4
Capalonga *Phil.* 14°20N 122°30E **232** D4
Capanaparo → *Venezuela* 7°1N 67°7W **328** B4
Capanema *Brazil* 1°10S 47°0W **332** B2
Capandombe *Angola* 15°6S 13°9E **265** F2
Cápannori *Italy* 43°50N 10°35E **198** E7
Capão Redondo *Brazil* 23°39S 46°45W **137** B1
Capão Redondo *Brazil* 23°39S 46°45W **137** B1
Caparaó △ *Brazil* 20°25S 41°46W **333** F3
Caparica *Portugal* 38°40N 9°13W **126** A1
Caparica, Costa da
  Portugal 38°38N 9°15W **126** B1
Caparo → *Trin. & Tob.* 10°28N 61°17W **323** t
Capatárida *Venezuela* 11°11N 70°37W **328** A3

Capayas *Phil.* 10°28N 119°39E **233** F2
Capbreton *France* 43°39N 1°26W **174** E2
Capdenac *France* 44°34N 2°5E **174** D6
Capdepera *Spain* 39°42N 3°26E **206** B4
Cape → *Australia* 20°59S 146°51E **280** C4
Cape Arid △ *Australia* 33°58S 123°13E **279** F3
Cape Barren I. *Australia* 40°25S 148°15E **281** E4
Cape Basin *Atl. Oc.* 34°0S 7°0W **152** K12
Cape Breton Highlands △
  Canada 46°50N 60°40W **299** C7
Cape Breton I. *Canada* 46°0N 60°30W **299** C7
Cape Canaveral *U.S.A.* 28°24N 80°36W **317** G9
Cape Charles *U.S.A.* 37°16N 76°1W **309** G15
Cape Coast *Ghana* 5°5N 1°15W **263** D4
Cape Cod △ *U.S.A.* 41°56N 70°6W **309** E17
Cape Coral *U.S.A.* 26°33N 81°57W **317** J8
Cape Crawford *Australia* 16°41S 135°43E **280** B2
Cape Dorset = Kinngait
  Canada 64°14N 76°32W **295** E16
Cape Fear → *U.S.A.* 33°53N 78°1W **315** D15
Cape Flats *S. Africa* 34°3S 18°33E **118** B2
Cape Girardeau *U.S.A.* 37°19N 89°32W **308** G9
Cape Hatteras △ *U.S.A.* 35°30N 75°28W **315** D17
Cape Hillsborough △
  Australia 20°54S 149°2E **280** b
Cape Jervis *Australia* 35°40S 138°5E **282** C2
Cape Krusenstern △
  U.S.A. 67°30N 163°30W **303** C7
Cape Le Grand △
  Australia 33°54S 122°26E **279** F3
Cape Lisburne = Wevok
  U.S.A. 68°53N 166°13W **303** B6
Cape Lookout △ *U.S.A.* 35°45N 76°25W **315** D16
Cape May *U.S.A.* 38°56N 74°56W **309** F16
Cape May Point *U.S.A.* 38°56N 74°58W **309** F16
Cape Melville △
  Australia 14°26S 144°28E **280** A3
Cape Mount → *Liberia* 6°44N 11°24W **262** D2
Cape Pole *U.S.A.* 55°58N 133°48W **303** J14
Cape Range △ *Australia* 22°3S 114°0E **278** D1
Cape St. George *Canada* 48°28N 59°14W **299** C8
Cape Tormentine *Canada* 46°8N 63°47W **299** C7
Cape Town *S. Africa* 33°55S 18°22E **118** C3
Cape Town Int. ✈ (CPT)
  S. Africa 33°58S 18°35E **118** A2
Cape Upstart △ *Australia* 19°45S 147°48E **280** B4
Cape Verde Is. ■ *Atl. Oc.* 16°0N 24°0W **153** j
Cape Verde Abyssal Plain
  Atl. Oc. 23°0N 26°0W **152** D7
Cape Verde Plateau
  Atl. Oc. 18°0N 20°0W **152** E10
Cape Vincent *U.S.A.* 44°8N 76°20W **313** B8
Cape Yakataga *U.S.A.* 60°4N 142°26W **303** F12
Cape York Peninsula
  Australia 12°0S 142°30E **280** A3
Capela *Brazil* 10°30S 37°0W **332** D4
Capelas *Azores* 37°50N 25°41W **153** d3
Capelinha *Brazil* 17°42S 42°31W **333** E3
Capella *Australia* 23°2S 148°1E **280** C4
Capella, Mt. *Papua N. G.* 5°4S 141°8E **286** C1
Capelongo *Angola* 14°54S 15°8E **265** E3
Capena *France* 43°11N 2°31E **174** E6
Capendu *France* 43°11N 2°31E **174** E6
Capertree *Australia* 33°8S 149°58E **283** B8
Capestang *France* 43°20N 3°2E **174** E7
Capestrano, Grande Rivière de la →
  Guadeloupe 16°3N 61°33W **322** e
Capesterre, Pte. de la
  Guadeloupe 16°3N 61°33W **322** e
Capesterre-Belle-Eau
  Guadeloupe 16°4N 61°36W **322** e
Capesterre-de-Marie-Galante
  Guadeloupe 15°53N 61°14W **322** e
Capim → *Brazil* 1°40S 47°47W **332** B2
Capinópolis *Brazil* 18°41S 49°35W **333** E2
Capinota *Bolivia* 17°43S 66°14W **330** D4
Capira *Panama* 8°45N 79°53W **328** B2
Capitachouane → *Canada* 47°55N 76°40W **298** C4
Capitan *U.S.A.* 33°35N 105°35W **305** K11
Capitán Arenaca, I.
  Chile 54°10S 71°20W **336** D2
Capitán Arturo Prat
  Antarctica 63°0S 61°0W **151** C17
Capitán Pastene *Chile* 38°13S 73°1W **336** A2
Capitão de Campos *Brazil* 4°30S 41°55W **332** B3
Capitol Heights *U.S.A.* 38°16N 76°54W **143** C4
Capitol Hill *N. Marianas* 15°13N 145°45E **302** e
Capitol Reef △ *U.S.A.* 38°15N 111°10W **305** G8
Capitola *U.S.A.* 36°59N 121°57W **306** J5
Capitolini, Musei *Rome, Italy* **136** c3
Capivara, Serra da *Brazil* 14°35S 45°0W **333** D2
Capiz □ *Phil.* 11°35N 122°30E **233** F4
Capizzi *Italy* 37°51N 14°29E **201** E7
Capoche → *Mozam.* 15°35S 33°0E **269** F3
Capodichino, Nápoli ✈ (NAP)
  Italy 40°53N 14°16E **201** B7
Capoeira *Brazil* 5°7S 59°33W **331** B6
Capolo *Angola* 10°22S 14°7E **265** E2
Caporetto = Kobarid
  Slovenia 46°15N 13°30E **199** B10
Caporolo → *Angola* 12°56S 12°58E **265** E2
Capot → *Martinique* 14°50N 61°5W **322** c
Capoterra *Italy* 39°11N 8°58E **200** C1
Cappadócia *Turkey* 39°0N 35°0E **212** C6
Cappoquin *Ireland* 52°8N 7°51W **167** F3
Capraia *Italy* 43°3N 9°50E **198** E3
Caprara, Pta. *Italy* 41°7N 8°19E **200** A1
Caprarola *Italy* 42°19N 12°14E **199** F9
Capreol *Canada* 46°43N 80°56W **298** C3
Capri *Italy* 40°33N 14°14E **201** B7
Capricorn Coast
  Australia 23°16S 150°49E **280** C5
Capricorn Group
  Australia 23°30S 151°55E **280** C5
Capricorn Ra. *Australia* 23°20S 116°50E **278** D2
Caprino Veronese *Italy* 45°36N 10°47E **198** C7
Caprivi Game △ *Namibia* 17°55S 22°37E **270** A3
Caprivi Strip *Namibia* 18°0S 23°0E **270** A3
Caps et Marais d'Opale △
  France 50°40N 2°0E **173** B9
Captain Cook *U.S.A.* 19°30N 155°55W **302** D6
Captain Cook Bridge
  Australia 34°0S 151°7E **139** C1
Captain Cook Landing Place Park
  Australia 34°1S 151°14E **139** C2
Captains Flat *Australia* 35°35S 149°27E **283** C8
Captieux *France* 44°18N 0°16W **174** D3
Captiva *U.S.A.* 26°31N 82°11W **317** J7
Capuça → *Angola* 12°25S 21°18E **265** E4
Capuchos *Portugal* 38°39N 9°14W **126** A1
Capul I. *Phil.* 12°20N 124°10E **233** E5
Capulin Volcano △
  U.S.A. 36°47N 103°58W **314** C2
Capunda *Angola* 10°41S 17°23E **265** E3
Caquetá □ *Colombia* 1°0N 74°0W **328** C3
Caquetá → *Colombia* 1°15S 69°15W **328** D4
Car Nicobar *India* 9°10N 92°47E **245** K11
Cara-Paraná → *Colombia* 1°45S 73°13W **328** D3
Carabanchel Alto *Spain* 40°22N 3°44W **127** B1

Carabanchel Bajo *Spain* 40°23N 3°44W **127** B1
Caracal *Romania* 44°8N 24°22E **183** F9
Caracas ● *Venezuela* 10°30N 66°55W **328** A4
Caracol *Mato Grosso do Sul,*
  Brazil 22°18S 57°1W **334** A4
Caracol *Piauí, Brazil* 9°15S 43°22W **332** D3
Caracollo *Bolivia* 17°39S 67°10W **330** D4
Caraga *China* 26°26N 126°34E **233** H6
Caragabal *Australia* 33°49S 147°45E **283** B7
Carahue *Chile* 38°43S 73°12W **336** D2
Caraí *Brazil* 17°12S 41°42W **333** E3
Carajás *Brazil* 2°57S 51°22W **332** C1
Carajás, Serra dos *Brazil* 6°0S 51°30W **332** C1
Caramoan *Phil.* 13°46N 123°52E **232** E4
Caramoran *Phil.* 14°0N 124°8E **232** D5
Caranapatuba *Brazil* 6°38S 62°34W **331** B5
Carangola *Brazil* 20°45S 42°5W **333** F3
Caransebeş *Romania* 45°28N 22°18E **182** D7
Carantec *France* 48°40N 3°55W **172** D3
Carapachay *Argentina* 34°4S 58°55W **334** C2
Carapicuíba *Brazil* 23°31S 46°50W **137** A1
Carapo → *Barinas,*
  Venezuela 7°46N 70°23W **328** B3
Carapo → *Bolívar,*
  Venezuela 7°30N 64°0W **329** B5
Carapuse B. *Trin. & Tob.* 11°14N 60°33W **323** s
Caraquet *Canada* 47°48N 64°57W **299** C6
Carás *Peru* 9°3S 77°47W **330** B2
Caraşova *Romania* 45°11N 21°51E **182** E6
Caratasca, L. de
  Honduras 15°20N 83°40W **320** C3
Caratinga *Brazil* 19°50S 42°10W **333** E3
Carauarí *Brazil* 4°52S 66°54W **328** D5
Caraúbas *Brazil* 5°43S 37°33W **332** C4
Caravaca de la Cruz *Spain* 38°8N 1°52W **197** G3
Caravággio *Italy* 45°30N 9°38E **198** C6
Caravelas *Brazil* 17°45S 39°15W **333** E4
Caravelí *Peru* 15°45S 73°25W **330** D3
Caravelle, Presqu'île de la
  Martinique 14°46N 60°48W **322** j
Caraz *Peru* 9°3S 77°47W **330** B2
Caraza *Argentina* 34°41S 58°25W **117** C2
Carazinho *Brazil* 28°16S 52°46W **335** B5
Carballino = O Carballiño
  Spain 42°26N 8°5W **194** C2
Carballo *Spain* 43°13N 8°41W **194** B2
Carberry *Canada* 49°50N 99°25W **297** D9
Carbet, Chutes du
  Guadeloupe 16°2N 61°38W **322** e
Carbet, Pitons du
  Martinique 14°42N 61°7W **322** j
Carbó *Mexico* 29°42N 110°58W **318** B2
Carbón, L. del *Argentina* 49°35S 68°21W **336** C3
Carbonara, C. *Italy* 39°6N 9°31E **200** D2
Carbondale *Colo.,*
  U.S.A. 39°24N 107°13W **304** G10
Carbondale *Ill., U.S.A.* 37°44N 89°13W **310** G7
Carbondale *Pa., U.S.A.* 41°35N 75°30W **313** E9
Carbonear *Canada* 47°42N 53°13W **299** C9
Carboneras *Spain* 36°59N 1°53W **197** J3
Carboneras de Guadazaón
  Spain 39°54N 1°50W **196** F3
Carbónia *Italy* 39°10N 8°30E **200** C1
Carcabuey *Spain* 37°27N 4°17W **195** H6
Carcagente = Carcaixent
  Spain 39°8N 0°28W **197** F4
Carcaixent *Spain* 39°8N 0°28W **197** F4
Carcajou *Canada* 57°47N 117°6W **296** B5
Carcar *Phil.* 10°6N 123°38E **233** F4
Carcarana → *Argentina* 32°27S 60°48W **334** C3
Carcassonne *France* 43°13N 2°20E **174** E6
Carchi □ *Ecuador* 0°45N 78°0W **328** C2
Carcoar *Australia* 33°36S 149°8E **283** B8
Carcross *Canada* 60°13N 134°45W **296** A2
Çardak *Çanakkale, Turkey* 40°22N 26°43E **205** D10
Çardak *Denizli, Turkey* 37°49N 29°39E **205** D11
Çardamon Hills *India* 9°30N 77°15E **245** K3
Cardamon Mts. = Kravanh, Chuor
  Phnum *Cambodia* 12°0N 103°32E **237** G4
Cárdenas *Cuba* 23°0N 81°30W **320** B3
Cárdenas *San Luis Potosí,*
  Mexico 22°0N 99°38W **319** C5
Cárdenas *Tabasco, Mexico* 17°59N 93°22W **319** D6
Cardener → *Spain* 41°41N 1°51E **196** D6
Cardenete *Spain* 39°46N 1°41W **196** F3
Cardiel, L. *Argentina* 48°55S 71°10W **336** C2
Cardiff *U.K.* 51°29N 3°10W **169** F4
Cardiff □ *U.K.* 51°31N 3°12W **169** F4
Cardiff-by-the-Sea
  U.S.A. 33°1N 117°17W **307** M9
Cardigan *U.K.* 52°5N 4°40W **169** E3
Cardigan B. *U.K.* 52°30N 4°30W **169** E3
Cardinal *Canada* 44°47N 75°23W **313** B9
Cardón, Punta *Venezuela* 11°37N 70°14W **328** A3
Cardona *Spain* 41°56N 1°40E **196** D6
Cardona *Uruguay* 33°53S 57°18W **334** C4
Cardoso, Ilha do *Brazil* 25°8S 47°58W **335** B6
Cardston *Canada* 49°15N 113°20W **296** D6
Cardwell *Australia* 18°14S 146°2E **280** B4
Careen L. *Canada* 57°0N 108°11W **297** B7
Carei *Romania* 47°40N 22°29E **182** C7
Careiro *Brazil* 3°12S 59°45W **329** D6
Careme = Ciremay
  Indonesia 6°55S 108°27E **235** D3
Carentan *France* 49°19N 1°15W **172** C5
Carey *Idaho, U.S.A.* 43°19N 113°57W **304** E7
Carey *Ohio, U.S.A.* 40°57N 83°23W **311** D13
Carey, L. *Australia* 29°0S 122°15E **279** E3
Carey L. *Canada* 62°12N 102°55W **297** A8
Careysburg *Liberia* 6°34N 10°30W **262** D2
Cargados Carajos *Ind. Oc.* 17°0S 59°0E **273** F4
Cargèse *France* 42°7N 8°35E **175** F12
Carhaix-Plouguer *France* 48°18N 3°36W **172** D3
Carhuamayo *Peru* 10°51S 76°4W **330** C2
Carhué *Argentina* 37°10S 62°50W **334** D3
Caria *Turkey* 37°20N 28°10E **205** D10
Cariacica *Brazil* 20°16S 40°25W **333** F3
Cariaco *Venezuela* 10°30N 63°33W **329** A5
Cariati *Italy* 39°30N 16°57E **201** C9
Caribbean Sea *W. Indies* 15°0N 75°0W **320** D7
Cariboo Mts. *Canada* 53°0N 121°0W **296** C4
Caribou *U.S.A.* 46°52N 68°1W **309** B20
Caribou → *Man.,*
  Canada 59°20N 94°44W **297** B10
Caribou → *N.W.T.,*
  Canada 61°27N 125°45W **296** A4
Caribou I. *Canada* 47°22N 85°49W **298** C2
Caribou Is. *Canada* 61°55N 113°15W **296** A6
Caribou L. *Man., Canada* 59°21N 96°10W **297** B9
Caribou L. *Ont., Canada* 50°25N 89°5W **298** B2
Caribou Mts. *Canada* 59°12N 115°40W **296** B5
Caribou River △ *Canada* 59°35N 96°35W **297** B9

Caroni Swamp Trin. & Tob. 10°36N 61°27W 323 t
Caronie = Nébrodi, Monti
Italy 37°54N 14°35E 201 E7
Caroona Australia 31°24S 150°26E 283 A9
Carora Venezuela 10°11N 70°5W 328 A3
Carpathians Europe 49°30N 21°0E 177 D11
Carpaţii Meridionali
Romania 45°30N 25°0E 183 E9
Carpentaria, G. of
Australia 14°0S 139°0E 280 A2
Carpentersville U.S.A. 42°6N 88°17W 311 B8
Carpentras France 44°3N 5°2E 175 D9
Carpi Italy 44°47N 10°53E 198 D7
Carpina Brazil 7°56S 35°15W 332 C4
Cărpineni Moldova 46°46N 28°22E 183 D13
Carpinteria U.S.A. 34°24N 119°31W 307 L7
Carpio Spain 41°13N 5°7W 194 D5
Carr Boyd Ra. Australia 16°15S 128°35E 278 C4
Carra, L. Ireland 53°41N 9°14W 166 C2
Carrabelle U.S.A. 29°51N 84°40W 316 F5
Carraig Mhachdire Rois =
Carrickmacross Ireland 53°59N 6°43W 166 C5
Carraig na Siúire = Carrick-on-Suir
Ireland 52°21N 7°24W 166 D4
Carral Spain 43°14N 8°21W 194 B2
Carranglan Phil. 15°58N 121°4E 232 D3
Carranya ⊙ Australia 19°13S 127°46E 278 C4
Carranza, Presa V.
Mexico 27°20N 100°50W 318 B4
Carrara Italy 44°5N 10°6E 198 D7
Carrascal Santiago, Chile 33°25S 70°42W 137 B1
Carrascal Phil. 9°22N 125°56E 233 G5
Carrasco △ Bolivia 17°23S 64°59W 331 D5
Carrascosa del Campo
Spain 40°2N 2°45W 196 E2
Carrauntoohill Ireland 52°0N 9°45W 166 D2
Carretas, Punta Peru 14°12S 76°17W 330 C2
Carriacou Grenada 12°29N 61°26W 323 q
Carrick-on-Shannon
Ireland 53°57N 8°5W 166 C3
Carrick-on-Suir Ireland 52°21N 7°24W 166 D4
Carrickfergus U.K. 54°43N 5°49W 166 B6
Carrickmacross Ireland 53°59N 6°43W 166 C5
Carrickmines Ireland 53°15N 6°10W 120 B3
Carrières-sous-Bois France 48°55N 2°6E 134 A1
Carrières-sous-Poissy
France 48°56N 2°2E 134 A1
Carrieton Australia 32°25S 138°31E 282 B3
Carrigeen B. Ireland 53°24N 6°5W 120 A3
Carrillo Mexico 26°54N 103°55W 318 B4
Carrington U.S.A. 47°27N 99°8W 308 B4
Carrión → Spain 41°53N 4°32W 194 D6
Carrión de los Condes
Spain 42°20N 4°37W 194 C6
Carrizal Bajo Chile 28°5S 71°20W 334 B1
Carrizalillo Chile 29°5S 71°30W 334 B1
Carrizo Cr. → U.S.A. 36°55N 103°55W 305 H12
Carrizo Plain △ U.S.A. 35°11N 119°47W 306 K7
Carrizo Springs U.S.A. 28°31N 99°52W 314 G5
Carrizozo U.S.A. 33°38N 105°53W 305 K11
Carroll U.S.A. 42°4N 94°52W 310 D2
Carrollton Ga., U.S.A. 33°35N 85°5W 316 B3
Carrollton Ill., U.S.A. 39°18N 90°24W 310 E6
Carrollton Ky., U.S.A. 38°41N 85°11W 311 F11
Carrollton Mo., U.S.A. 39°22N 93°30W 310 F3
Carrollton Ohio, U.S.A. 40°34N 81°5W 312 F3
Carron → U.K. 57°53N 4°22W 167 D4
Carron, L. U.K. 57°22N 5°35W 167 D3
Carrot → Canada 53°50N 101°17W 297 C8
Carrot River Canada 53°17N 103°35W 297 C8
Carrouges France 48°34N 0°10W 172 D6
Carrù Italy 44°29N 7°52E 198 D4
Carruthers Canada 52°52N 109°16W 297 C7
Carsa Dek Ethiopia 5°13N 39°50E 257 F4
Carşamba Turkey 41°11N 36°44E 212 B7
Carsóli Italy 42°6N 13°5E 199 F10
Carson Calif., U.S.A. 33°49N 118°16W 307 M8
Carson N. Dak., U.S.A. 46°25N 101°34W 308 B3
Carson → U.S.A. 39°45N 118°40W 306 F8
Carson City Mich.,
U.S.A. 43°11N 84°51W 311 A12
Carson City Nev., U.S.A. 39°10N 119°46W 306 F7
Carson Sink U.S.A. 39°50N 118°25W 304 G4
Carstensz Pyramid = Jaya, Puncak
Indonesia 3°57S 137°17E 231 E9
Cartagena Colombia 10°25N 75°33W 328 A2
Cartagena Spain 37°38N 0°59W 197 H4
Cartago Colombia 4°45N 75°55W 328 C2
Cartago Costa Rica 9°50N 83°55W 320 E3
Cártama Spain 36°43N 4°39W 195 J6
Cartaxo Portugal 39°10N 8°47W 195 F2
Cartaya Spain 37°16N 7°9W 195 H3
Carteret Is. = Kilinailau Is.
Papua N. G. 4°45S 155°20E 286 C8
Carterton N.Z. 41°2S 175°31E 284 H4
Carterton U.K. 51°46N 1°34W 169 D6
Carthage Tunisia 36°52N 10°20E 200 D3
Carthage Ill., U.S.A. 40°25N 91°8W 310 D5
Carthage Mo., U.S.A. 37°11N 94°19W 308 G6
Carthage N.Y., U.S.A. 43°59N 75°37W 309 D16
Carthage Tex., U.S.A. 32°9N 94°20W 314 E7
Cartier I. Australia 12°31S 123°29E 278 B3
Cartierville Canada 45°31N 73°42W 130 A1
Cartwright Canada 53°41N 56°58W 299 B8
Caruaru Brazil 8°15S 35°55W 332 C4
Carúpano Venezuela 10°39N 63°15W 329 A5
Caruray Phil. 10°20N 119°0E 233 F2
Carutapera Brazil 1°13S 46°1W 332 B2
Caruthersville U.S.A. 36°11N 89°39W 308 G9
Carvalho Brazil 2°16S 51°29W 329 D7
Carvin France 50°30N 2°57E 173 B9
Carvoeiro Brazil 1°30S 61°59W 329 D6
Carvoeiro, C. Portugal 39°21N 9°24W 195 F1
Cary Ill., U.S.A. 42°13N 88°14W 311 B8
Cary N.C., U.S.A. 35°47N 78°46W 315 D15
Casa, Pas de la = Envalira, Port d'
Europe 42°33N 1°43E 196 C6
Casa Branca Brazil 21°46S 47°4W 333 F2
Casa Branca Brazil 38°29N 8°12W 195 G2
Casa de Piedra Argentina 38°5S 67°28W 334 D2
Casa de Piedra, Embalse
Argentina 38°5S 67°32W 334 D2
Casa Grande U.S.A. 32°53N 111°45W 305 K8
Casa Nova Brazil 9°25S 41°5W 332 C3
Casa Nova Brazil 9°25S 41°5W 332 C3
Casablanca Chile 33°20S 71°25W 334 C1
Casablanca Morocco 33°36N 7°36W 260 B3
Casablanca 🛪 Morocco 33°38N 7°39W 260 B3
Casacalenda Italy 41°44N 14°51E 199 G11
Casal Morena Italy 41°49N 12°37E 136 C2
Casalbordino Italy 42°10N 14°35E 199 F11
Casale Monferrato Italy 45°8N 8°27E 198 C5
Casalmaggiore Italy 44°59N 10°25E 198 D7
Casalotti Italy 41°54N 12°22E 136 B1
Casalpusterlengo Italy 45°10N 9°40E 198 C6
Casamance → Senegal 12°33N 16°46W 262 C1
Casanare □ Colombia 5°30N 72°30W 328 B4
Casanare → Colombia 6°2N 69°51W 328 B4
Casarano Italy 40°0N 18°10E 201 B11
Casares Spain 36°27N 5°16W 195 J5
Casas Ibáñez Spain 39°17N 1°30W 197 F3
Casasimarro Spain 39°22N 2°3W 197 F2
Casatejada Spain 39°54N 5°40W 194 F5
Casavieja Spain 40°17N 4°46W 194 E6
Cascada de Basaseachic △
Mexico 28°9N 108°15W 318 B3
Cascade Seychelles 4°39S 55°29E 272 c
Cascade Idaho, U.S.A. 44°31N 116°2W 304 D5
Cascade Iowa, U.S.A. 42°18N 91°0W 310 D6
Cascade Mont., U.S.A. 47°16N 111°42W 304 C8
Cascade Heights U.S.A. 33°43N 84°26W 113 C2
Cascade Locks U.S.A. 45°40N 121°54W 306 E5
Cascade Pt. N.Z. 44°1S 168°20E 285 F2
Cascade Ra. U.S.A. 47°0N 121°30W 306 D5
Cascade Res. U.S.A. 44°32N 116°3W 304 D5
Cascades, Pte. des Réunion 21°9S 55°51E 272 f
Cascais Portugal 38°41N 9°25W 195 G1
Cascavel Ceará, Brazil 4°7S 38°14W 332 B4
Cascavel Paraná, Brazil 24°57S 53°28W 335 B5
Cáscina Italy 43°41N 10°33E 198 E7
Casco B. U.S.A. 43°45N 70°0W 309 D18
Case Noyale Mauritius 20°23S 57°22E 272 e
Case-Pilote Martinique 14°38N 61°9W 322 c
Caselle Torinese Italy 45°10N 7°39E 198 C4
Caserta Italy 41°4N 14°20E 201 A7
Casey Antarctica 66°0S 76°0E 151 C8
Casey Ill., U.S.A. 39°18N 87°59W 311 E9
Caseyr, Raas = Asir, Ras
Somali Rep. 11°55N 51°10E 267 B7
Cashel Ireland 52°30N 7°53W 166 D4
Casibare → Colombia 3°48N 72°18W 328 C3
Casiguran Phil. 16°22N 122°7E 232 C4
Casiguran Sound Phil. 16°6N 121°58E 232 C4
Casilda Argentina 33°10S 61°10W 334 C3
Casim = General Toshevo
Bulgaria 43°42N 28°6E 203 C12
Casimcea Romania 44°45N 28°23E 183 F13
Casino N.S.W., Australia 28°52S 153°3E 281 D5
Casino New Orleans, U.S.A. 131 b2
Casiquiare → Venezuela 2°1N 67°7W 328 C4
Casitas Peru 3°54S 80°39W 330 A1
Caslan → Canada 54°38N 112°31W 296 C6
Čáslav Czech Rep. 49°54N 15°22E 180 B8
Casma Peru 9°30S 78°20W 330 B2
Casmalia U.S.A. 34°50N 120°32W 307 L6
Cásola Valsénio Italy 44°12N 11°40E 199 D8
Cásoli Italy 42°7N 14°18E 199 F11
Caspe Spain 41°14N 0°1W 196 D4
Casper U.S.A. 42°51N 106°19W 304 E10
Caspian Depression Eurasia 47°0N 48°0E 191 G9
Caspian Sea Eurasia 43°0N 50°0E 187 F9
Cass City U.S.A. 43°36N 83°10W 312 D2
Cass Lake U.S.A. 47°23N 94°37W 308 B6
Cassà de la Selva Spain 41°53N 2°52E 196 D7
Cassadaga U.S.A. 42°20N 79°19W 312 D5
Cassai Angola 10°33S 21°59E 265 E4
Cassai → Angola 3°2S 16°57E 265 E4
Cassamba Angola 13°6S 20°18E 265 E4
Cassano allo Iónio Italy 39°47N 16°20E 201 C9
Cassel France 50°48N 2°30E 173 B9
Casselberry U.S.A. 28°41N 81°20W 317 G8
Casselman Canada 45°19N 75°5W 313 A9
Casselton U.S.A. 46°54N 97°13W 308 B5
Cassiar Mts. Canada 59°30N 130°30W 296 B2
Cassilândia Brazil 19°9S 51°45W 331 D7
Cassilis Australia 32°3S 149°58E 283 B4
Cassinga Angola 15°5S 16°4E 265 F3
Cassino Italy 41°30N 13°49E 200 A6
Cassis France 43°14N 5°32E 175 E9
Cassoalala Angola 9°30S 14°22E 265 D2
Cassoango Angola 13°42S 20°56E 265 E4
Cassongue Angola 11°53S 15°2E 265 D2
Cassopolis U.S.A. 41°55N 86°1W 311 C10
Cassunda Angola 10°57S 21°13E 265 E4
Cassville Mo., U.S.A. 36°41N 93°52W 308 G7
Cassville Wis., U.S.A. 42°43N 90°59W 310 B6
Castagneto Carducci Italy 43°9N 10°36E 198 E7
Castaic U.S.A. 34°30N 118°38W 307 L8
Castanhal Brazil 1°18S 47°55W 332 B2
Castara Trin. & Tob. 11°17N 60°42W 323 s
Castara B. Trin. & Tob. 11°17N 60°42W 323 s
Castéggio Italy 45°0N 9°7E 198 D6
Castejón de Monegros
Spain 41°37N 0°15W 196 D4
Castel Guadeloupe 16°15N 61°35W 322 e
Castèl di Leva Italy 41°46N 12°33E 136 C2
Castèl di Sangro Italy 41°47N 14°6E 199 G11
Castèl San Giovanni Italy 45°4N 9°26E 198 C6
Castèl San Pietro Terme
Italy 44°24N 11°35E 199 D8
Castèl Sant'Angelo Rome, Italy 136 b
Castelbuono Italy 37°56N 14°5E 201 E7
Casteldáccia Italy 43°28N 13°33E 199 E10
Castelfiorentino Italy 43°36N 10°58E 198 E7
Castelfranco Emília Italy 44°37N 11°3E 198 D8
Castelfranco Véneto Italy 45°40N 11°55E 199 C8
Casteljaloux France 44°19N 0°6E 174 D4
Castellabate Italy 40°17N 14°57E 201 B7
Castellammare, G. di Italy 38°8N 12°54E 200 D5
Castellammare del Golfo
Italy 38°1N 12°53E 200 D5
Castellammare di Stábia
Italy 40°42N 14°29E 201 B7
Castellamonte Italy 45°23N 7°42E 198 C4
Castellane France 43°50N 6°31E 175 E10
Castellaneta Italy 40°38N 16°56E 201 B9
Castelli Argentina 36°7S 57°47W 334 D4
Castelló de la Plana Spain 39°58N 0°3W 196 F4
Castellón de la Plana □
Spain 40°15N 0°5W 196 E4
Castellote Spain 40°48N 0°15W 196 E4
Castelmáuro Italy 41°50N 14°43E 199 G11
Castelnau-de-Médoc
France 45°2N 0°48W 174 C3
Castelnau-Magnoac
France 43°17N 0°31E 174 E4
Castelnaudary France 43°20N 1°58E 174 E5
Castelnovo ne' Monti
Italy 44°26N 10°24E 198 D7
Castelnuovo di Val di Cécina
Italy 43°12N 10°59E 198 E7
Castelo = Manuel Urbano
Brazil 8°53S 69°18W 330 B4
Castelo Brazil 20°33S 41°14W 333 F3
Castelo, Pta. do Azores 36°56N 25°1W 153 d4
Castelo Branco Azores 38°31N 28°44W 153 d1
Castelo Branco Portugal 39°50N 7°31W 194 F3
Castelo Branco □
Portugal 39°52N 7°45W 194 F3
Castelo de Paiva Portugal 41°2N 8°16W 194 D2
Castelo de Vide Portugal 39°25N 7°27W 195 F3
Castelo do Piauí Brazil 5°20S 41°33W 332 C3
Castelrosso = Megisti
Greece 36°8N 29°34E 205 E11
Castelsardo Italy 40°55N 8°43E 200 B1
Castelsarrasin France 44°2N 1°7E 174 D5
Castelvetrano Italy 37°41N 12°47E 200 E5
Castendo Angola 8°3S 14°10E 265 D2
Casterton Australia 37°30S 141°30E 282 D2
Castets France 43°52N 1°6W 174 E2
Castiglion Fiorentino
Italy 43°20N 11°55E 199 E8
Castiglione = Bou Ismaïl
Algeria 36°38N 2°42E 261 A5
Castiglione del Lago Italy 43°7N 12°3E 199 E9
Castiglione della Pescáia
Italy 42°46N 10°53E 198 F7
Castiglione delle Stiviere
Italy 45°23N 10°29E 198 C7
Castilblanco Spain 39°17N 5°5W 195 F5
Castile U.S.A. 42°38N 78°3W 312 D6
Castilla Peru 5°12S 80°38W 330 B1
Castilla, Playa de Spain 37°0N 6°33W 195 J4
Castilla-La Mancha □
Spain 39°30N 3°30W 195 F7
Castilla y Leon □ Spain 42°0N 5°0W 194 D6
Castillo de Locubín Spain 37°32N 3°56W 195 H7
Castillo de San Marcos ◻
U.S.A. 29°54N 81°19W 316 F8
Castillon-en-Couserans
France 42°56N 1°1E 174 F5
Castillonnès France 44°39N 0°37E 174 D4
Castillos Uruguay 34°12S 53°52W 335 C5
Castle Bruce Dominica 15°26N 61°16W 323 k
Castle Dale U.S.A. 39°13N 111°1W 304 G8
Castle Douglas U.K. 54°56N 3°56W 167 G5
Castle Harbour Bermuda 32°21N 64°40W 153 a
Castle Mt. Jamaica 18°8N 76°22W 320 a
Castle of Good Hope
Cape Town, S. Africa 118 c3
Castle Roads Bermuda 32°20N 64°40W 153 a
Castle Rock Colo.,
U.S.A. 39°22N 104°51W 304 G11
Castle Rock Wash.,
U.S.A. 46°17N 122°54W 306 D4
Castlebar Ireland 53°52N 9°18W 166 C2
Castlebay U.K. 56°57N 7°31W 167 E1
Castleblaney Ireland 54°7N 6°44W 166 B5
Castlecliff N.Z. 39°57S 175°5E 284 F4
Castleford U.K. 53°43N 1°21W 168 D6
Castlegar Canada 49°20N 117°40W 296 D5
Castleknock Ireland 53°22N 6°21W 120 A3
Castlemaine Vic.,
Australia 37°2S 144°12E 282 D6
Castlemaine Kerry, Ireland 52°10N 9°42W 166 D2
Castlemaine Harbour
Ireland 52°8N 9°50W 166 D2
Castlepollard Ireland 53°46N 7°18W 166 C4
Castlereagh → Australia 30°12S 147°32E 283 A7
Castlereagh B. Australia 12°10S 135°10E 280 A2
Castleton U.S.A. 43°37N 73°11W 313 C11
Castleton-on-Hudson
U.S.A. 42°31N 73°45W 313 D11
Castletown I. of Man 54°5N 4°38W 168 C3
Castletown Bearhaven
Ireland 51°39N 9°55W 166 E2
Castor Canada 52°15N 111°50W 296 C6
Castor → Canada 52°34N 78°58W 298 B4
Castorland U.S.A. 43°53N 75°31W 313 C9
Castres France 43°37N 2°13E 174 E6
Castricum Neths. 52°33N 4°40E 170 B6
Castries St. Lucia 14°2N 60°58W 323 m
Castril Spain 37°48N 2°46W 195 H8
Castro Brazil 24°45S 50°0W 335 A6
Castro Chile 42°30S 73°50W 336 B2
Castro Alves Brazil 12°46S 39°33W 333 D4
Castro del Río Spain 37°41N 4°29W 195 H6
Castro-Urdiales Spain 43°23N 3°11W 194 B7
Castro Valley U.S.A. 37°41N 122°5W 306 H4
Castro Verde Portugal 37°41N 8°4W 195 H2
Castrojeriz Spain 42°17N 4°9W 194 C6
Castropol Spain 43°32N 7°0W 194 B4
Castroreale Italy 38°6N 15°12E 201 D8
Castrovillari Italy 39°49N 16°12E 201 C9
Castroville U.S.A. 36°46N 121°45W 306 J5
Castrovirreyna Peru 13°20S 75°18W 330 C2
Castuera Spain 38°43N 5°37W 195 G5
Caswell Sound N.Z. 44°59S 167°8E 285 E2
Cat → Turkey 39°40N 41°3E 213 C9
Cat Ba, Dao Vietnam 20°50N 107°0E 236 B6
Cat Ba △ Vietnam 20°47N 107°3E 236 B6
Cat I. Bahamas 24°30N 75°30W 321 B4
Cat L. Canada 51°40N 91°50W 298 B1
Cat Lake Canada 51°40N 91°50W 298 B1
Cat Tien △ Vietnam 11°25N 107°17E 237 G6
Čata Slovak Rep. 47°58N 18°38E 181 D11
Catabola Angola 12°9S 17°16E 265 E3
Catacamas Honduras 14°54N 85°56W 320 D2
Catacaos Peru 5°20S 80°45W 330 B1
Cataguases Brazil 21°23S 42°39W 333 F3
Catagupan Phil. 8°1N 116°58E 233 G1
Cataingan Phil. 12°0N 124°0E 232 E4
Çatak Turkey 38°1N 43°8E 213 C10
Catalão Brazil 18°10S 47°57W 333 E2
Çatalca Turkey 41°8N 28°27E 203 E12
Catalina Nfld. & L., Canada 48°31N 53°4W 299 C9
Catalina Chile 25°13S 69°43W 334 B2
Catalina Ariz., U.S.A. 32°30N 110°50W 305 K8
Catalonia = Cataluña □
Spain 41°40N 1°15E 196 D6
Cataluña □ Spain 41°40N 1°15E 196 D6
Çatalzeytin Turkey 41°57N 34°12E 212 B6
Catamarca Argentina 28°30S 65°50W 334 B2
Catamarca □ Argentina 27°0S 65°50W 334 B2
Catanauan Phil. 13°36N 122°19E 232 E4
Catanduanes □ Phil. 13°50N 124°20E 232 E4
Catanduva Brazil 21°5S 48°58W 335 A6
Catánia Italy 37°30N 15°6E 201 E8
Catánia, G. di Italy 37°26N 15°19E 201 E8
Catanzaro Italy 38°54N 16°35E 201 D9
Cataouatche, L. U.S.A. 29°50N 90°14W 131 B1
Cataract N. Samar.,
Phil. 12°28N 124°35E 232 E5
Catatumbo → Venezuela 9°21N 71°45W 328 B3
Cataula U.S.A. 32°39N 84°52W 316 C5
Catbalogan Phil. 11°46N 124°53E 233 F5
Catchacoma Canada 44°44N 78°19W 312 B6
Cateco Cangola Angola 8°25S 15°51E 265 D3
Cateel Phil. 7°47N 126°24E 233 H6
Cateel Bay Phil. 7°54N 126°25E 233 H6
Catembe Mozam. 26°0S 32°33E 271 C5
Catende Brazil 8°40S 35°43W 332 C4
Catete Angola 9°6S 13°43E 265 D2
Cathair na Mart = Westport
Ireland 53°48N 9°31W 166 C2
Cathair Saidhbhín = Cahersiveen
Ireland 51°56N 10°14W 166 E1
Cathcart N.S.W.,
Australia 36°52S 149°24E 283 D8
Cathcart Eastern Cape,
S. Africa 32°18S 27°10E 270 D4
Cathedral City U.S.A. 33°47N 116°28W 307 M10
Cathedral Rock △
Australia 30°24S 152°15E 283 A10
Catherine, U.S.A. 42°54N 76°52W 312 D6
Cathlamet U.S.A. 46°12N 123°23W 306 D3
Cati Guinea-Biss. 11°55N 15°5W 262 C1
Catió Brazil 9°31S 43°1W 332 C3
Cativa Panama 9°21N 79°49W 320 c
Catlettsburg U.S.A. 38°25N 82°36W 309 F12
Catlin U.S.A. 40°4N 87°42W 311 D9
Catlins N.Z. 46°12S 169°17E 285 G4
Çatma Daği Turkey 38°25N 29°50E 205 C11
Çazma Croatia 45°45N 16°39E 199 C13
Cazombo Angola 11°54S 22°56E 265 E4
Cazorla Spain 37°55N 3°2W 195 H7
Cazorla, Sierra de Spain 38°5N 2°55W 195 G8
Cea → Spain 42°0N 5°36W 194 C5
Ceamurlia de Jos
Romania 44°43N 28°47E 183 F13
Ceanannus Mor Ireland 53°44N 6°53W 166 C5
Ceara = Fortaleza Brazil 3°45S 38°35W 332 B4
Ceará □ Brazil 5°0S 40°0W 332 C4
Ceará-Mirim Brazil 5°38S 35°25W 332 C4
Ceara Abyssal Plain Atl. Oc. 0°0 36°30W 152 F7
Ceara Rise Atl. Oc. 4°30N 43°30W 152 F7
Ceatharlach = Carlow
Ireland 52°50N 6°56W 166 D5
Cebaco, I. de Panama 7°33N 81°9W 320 E3
Cebeci Turkey 41°7N 28°52E 122 B1
Cebollar Argentina 29°10S 66°35W 334 B2
Cebollera, Sierra de Spain 42°0N 2°30W 196 D2
Cebreros Spain 40°27N 4°28W 194 E6
Cebu Phil. 10°18N 123°54E 233 F4
Cebu □ Phil. 10°20N 123°40E 233 F4
Cebu ✈ Phil. 10°18N 123°45E 233 F4
Čečava Bos.-H. 44°42N 17°44E 182 F7
Ceccano Italy 41°34N 13°20E 200 A6
Cecchignola Italy 41°48N 12°29E 136 C2
Čechi Ivory C. 6°15N 4°25W 262 D4
Cecil Plains Australia 27°30S 151°11E 281 D5
Cecilienhof, Schloss
Germany 52°35N 13°5E 115 B1
Cécina Italy 43°19N 10°33E 198 E7
Cécina → Italy 43°18N 10°29E 198 E7
Ceclavín Spain 39°50N 6°45W 194 F4
Cedar → U.S.A. 41°17N 91°21W 310 C5
Cedar City U.S.A. 37°41N 113°4W 305 H7
Cedar Creek Res. U.S.A. 32°11N 96°4W 314 E6
Cedar Falls Iowa, U.S.A. 42°32N 92°27W 310 B4
Cedar Falls Wash.,
U.S.A. 47°25N 121°45W 306 C5
Cedar Grove Georgia,
U.S.A. 33°40N 84°16W 113 C3
Cedar Grove Ind., U.S.A. 39°22N 84°56W 311 C12
Cedar Key U.S.A. 29°8N 83°2W 317 F6
Cedar L. Canada 53°10N 100°0W 297 C9
Cedar Lake U.S.A. 41°22N 87°26W 311 C9
Cedar Park U.S.A. 30°30N 97°49W 314 K6
Cedar Point U.S.A. 41°44N 83°21W 311 C13
Cedar Rapids U.S.A. 41°59N 91°40W 310 C5
Cedar Tree Pt.
Antigua & B. 17°42N 61°53W 322 c
Cedartown U.S.A. 34°1N 85°15W 316 A4
Cedarvale Canada 55°1N 128°22W 296 B3
Cedarvale Park Canada 43°42N 79°16W 141 A2
Cedarville S. Africa 30°23S 29°3E 271 D4
Cedarville Ohio, U.S.A. 39°44N 83°49W 311 E13
Cedeira Spain 43°39N 8°2W 194 B2
Cedral Mexico 23°50N 100°45W 318 C4
Cedrino → Italy 40°11N 9°24E 200 B2
Cedro Brazil 6°34S 39°3W 332 C4
Cedros Azores 38°38N 28°42W 153 d1
Cedros, I. Mexico 28°12N 115°15W 318 B1
Cedros B. Trin. & Tob. 10°16N 61°54W 323 t
Cedros Pt. Trin. & Tob. 10°7N 61°49W 323 t
Ceduna Australia 32°7S 133°46E 281 D1
Cedynia Poland 52°53N 14°12E 185 F1
Cée Spain 42°57N 9°10W 194 C1
Ceel Gaal Somali Rep. 10°58N 50°20E 267 B7
Ceel Waaq Kenya 2°49N 40°56E 266 B5
Ceelbuur = El Bur
Somali Rep. 4°40N 46°37E 267 D6
Ceeldheere Galguduud,
Somali Rep. 3°50N 47°8E 267 D6
Ceeldheere Galguduud,
Somali Rep. 5°22N 46°11E 267 D6
Ceerigaabo Somali Rep. 10°35N 47°20E 267 B6
Cefalù Italy 38°2N 14°1E 201 D7
Cega → Spain 41°33N 4°46W 194 D6
Ceglédi Hungary 47°11N 19°47E 182 C4
Céglie Messápico Italy 40°39N 17°31E 201 B10
Cehegín Spain 38°6N 1°48W 197 G3
Cehu-Silvaniei Romania 47°24N 23°9E 183 C8
Ceiba Puerto Rico 18°16N 65°39W 321 b
Ceica Romania 46°53N 22°10E 182 D7
Ceira → Portugal 40°13N 8°16W 194 E2
Çekerek Turkey 40°4N 35°29E 212 B6
Cekik Indonesia 8°12S 114°27E 231 J17
Cela Angola 11°25S 15°7E 265 E3
Čelákovice Czech Rep. 50°10N 14°43E 180 A7
Celano Italy 42°5N 13°33E 199 F10
Celanova Spain 42°9N 7°58W 194 C3
Celaque △ Honduras 14°30N 88°42W 320 D2
Celaya Mexico 20°31N 100°37W 318 C4
Celebes = Sulawesi
Indonesia 2°0S 120°0E 231 E6
Celebes Sea Indonesia 3°0N 123°0E 231 D6
Celendín Peru 6°52S 78°10W 330 B2
Celestial Mts. = Tian Shan
Asia 40°30N 76°0E 217 D9
Celica Ecuador 4°7S 79°59W 328 D2
Celina U.S.A. 40°33N 84°35W 311 D12
Celinac Bos.-H. 44°44N 17°12E 182 F7
Celje Slovenia 46°16N 15°18E 199 B12
Celldömölk Hungary 47°16N 17°10E 182 C2
Celle Germany 52°37N 10°4E 178 C6
Celorico da Beira Portugal 40°38N 7°24W 194 E3
Celtic Sea Atl. Oc. 50°9N 9°34W 165 F2
Çeltikçi Turkey 37°32N 30°28E 205 D12
Cempaka Putih Indonesia 6°10S 106°51E 122 A2
Cenderwasih, Teluk
Indonesia 3°0S 135°20E 231 E9
Cenepa → Peru 4°35S 78°10W 328 D2
Çengelköy Turkey 41°2N 29°3E 122 B1
Cengkareng Indonesia 6°9S 106°41E 122 A1
Cengong China 27°13N 108°44E 235 D7
Cenon France 44°50N 0°33W 174 D3
Centallo Italy 44°30N 7°35E 198 D4
Centelles Spain 41°48N 2°13E 196 D7
Centenario do Sul Brazil 22°48S 51°36W 333 F1
Centennial Olympic Park
U.S.A. 33°46N 84°23W 113 B2
Centennial Park
Australia 33°53S 151°14E 139 B2
Center N. Dak., U.S.A. 47°7N 101°18W 308 B3
Center Tex., U.S.A. 31°48N 94°11W 314 F7
Center Hill Fla., U.S.A. 28°38N 81°59W 317 G7
Center Hill Georgia,
U.S.A. 33°45N 84°29W 113 B2
Center Point U.S.A. 33°38N 86°41W 316 B5
Centerburg U.S.A. 40°18N 82°42W 312 F2
Centerville Calif., U.S.A. 36°44N 119°30W 307 J7
Centerville Iowa, U.S.A. 40°44N 92°52W 310 E4
Centerville Ohio, U.S.A. 39°38N 84°9W 311 F12
Centerville Tex., U.S.A. 31°16N 95°59W 314 F7
Central □ Kenya 0°30S 37°30E 266 C4
Central □ Zambia 14°25S 28°50E 269 E2
Central, Cordillera
Bolivia 18°30S 64°55W 331 D5
Central, Cordillera Colombia 5°0N 75°0W 328 C3
Central, Cordillera
Costa Rica 10°10N 84°5W 320 D3
Central, Cordillera
Dom. Rep. 19°15N 71°0W 321 C5
Central, Cordillera Peru 7°0S 77°30W 330 B2
Central, Cordillera Phil. 17°20N 120°57E 232 C3
Central, Cordillera
Puerto Rico 18°8N 66°35W 321 b
Central, Gare Montréal, Canada 130 C2
Central African Empire = Central
African Rep. ■ Africa 7°0N 20°0E 264 A4
Central African Rep. ■
Africa 7°0N 20°0E 264 A4
Central America America 12°0N 85°0W 292 H11
Central Australia ⊙
Australia 22°30S 128°30E 278 D4
Central Butte Canada 50°48N 106°31W 297 C7
Central City Colo.,
U.S.A. 39°48N 105°31W 304 G11
Central City Iowa, U.S.A. 42°12N 91°32W 310 B5
Central City Ky., U.S.A. 37°18N 87°7W 308 G10
Central City Nebr., U.S.A. 41°7N 98°0W 308 E4
Central Desert ⊙
Australia 19°56S 130°46E 278 C5
Central I. Kenya 3°30N 36°0E 266 B4
Central Island △ Kenya 2°33N 36°1E 268 B4
Central Japan Int. ✈ (CJI)
Japan 34°53N 136°45E 223 C8
Central Kalahari △
Botswana 22°36S 23°58E 270 B3
Central Makran Range
Pakistan 26°30N 64°15E 240 D2
Central Pacific Basin
Pac. Oc. 8°0N 175°0W 288 G10
Central Park New York, U.S.A. 132 a3
Central Park Zoo New York, U.S.A. 132 b2
Central Patricia Canada 51°30N 90°9W 298 B1
Central Point Canada 42°23N 122°55W 304 E2
Central Provinces = Madhya
Pradesh □ India 22°50N 78°0E 242 J8
Central Ra. Papua N. G. 5°0S 143°0E 286 C2
Central Ra. Trin. & Tob. 10°25N 61°15W 323 t
Central Range Wildlife Sanctuary
Trin. & Tob. 10°27N 61°14W 323 t
Central Russian Uplands
Europe 54°0N 36°0E 158 E13
Central Siberian Plateau
Russia 65°0N 105°0E 210 B12
Central Square U.S.A. 43°17N 76°9W 313 C8
Central Village Jamaica 17°59N 76°55W 320 a
Centralia Ont., Canada 43°17N 81°28W 312 C3
Centralia Ill., U.S.A. 38°32N 89°8W 310 F7
Centralia Mo., U.S.A. 39°13N 92°8W 310 F4
Centralia Wash., U.S.A. 46°43N 122°58W 306 D4
Centre □ Cameroon 4°45N 12°0E 263 E7
Centre de Flacq Mauritius 20°12S 57°43E 272 e
Centreville Mich.,
U.S.A. 41°55N 85°32W 311 C11
Centreville N.Y., U.S.A. 42°28N 78°14W 312 D6
Centreville Pa., U.S.A. 41°44N 79°45W 312 E5
Century U.S.A. 30°58N 87°16W 317 E2
Century City U.S.A. 34°3N 118°25W 132 b1
Cenxi China 22°57N 110°57E 229 F8
Čeotina → Bos.-H. 43°36N 18°50E 202 C2
Cephalonia = Kefalonia
Greece 38°15N 20°30E 207 C2
Čepin Croatia 45°32N 18°34E 182 E2
Ceprano Italy 41°33N 13°31E 200 A6
Ceptia Angola 12°56S 17°59E 265 E3
Ceptura Romania 45°1N 26°21E 183 E11
Cepu Indonesia 7°9S 111°35E 231 J24
Ceram = Seram Indonesia 3°10S 129°0E 231 E7
Ceram Sea = Seram Sea
Indonesia 2°30S 128°30E 231 E7
Cerbère France 42°26N 3°10E 174 F7
Cerbicales, Îs. France 41°33N 9°22E 175 G13
Cercal Portugal 37°48N 8°40W 195 H2
Cercemaggiore Italy 41°27N 14°43E 199 G11
Cerdanyola del Vallès
Spain 41°27N 2°8W 114 A1
Cère → France 44°55N 1°49E 174 D5
Cerea Italy 45°12N 11°13E 199 C8
Ceredigion □ U.K. 52°16N 4°15W 169 E3
Ceres Argentina 29°55S 61°55W 334 B3
Ceres Brazil 15°17S 49°35W 333 E1
Ceres S. Africa 33°21S 19°18E 270 D2
Ceres Calif., U.S.A. 37°35N 120°57W 306 H6
Céret France 42°30N 2°42E 174 F6
Cereté Colombia 8°53N 75°48W 328 B2
Cerf Seychelles 4°38S 55°40E 272 c
Cerfs, Îs. aux Mauritius 20°16S 57°47E 272 e
Cergy France 49°2N 2°4E 173 C9
Cerignola Italy 41°17N 15°53E 201 A8
Cerigo = Kythira Greece 36°8N 23°0E 204 E5
Cerillos Chile 33°29S 70°42W 137 B1
Cérilly France 46°37N 2°50E 173 F9
Cerisiers France 48°8N 3°30E 173 D10
Cerizay France 46°50N 0°40W 172 F6
Çerkeş Turkey 40°49N 32°52E 212 B5
Çerkezköy Turkey 41°17N 28°0E 203 E12
Cerknica Slovenia 45°48N 14°21E 199 C11
Cerkovica Serbia 43°35N 22°26E 202 C4
Cermerno Serbia 43°30N 20°52E 202 C4
Çermik Turkey 38°8N 39°26E 213 C8
Cerna Romania 44°4N 28°17E 183 C13
Cerna → Romania 44°38N 22°58E 183 F8
Cernăuţi = Chernivtsi
Ukraine 48°15N 25°52E 183 B10
Cernavodă Romania 44°22N 28°3E 183 F13
Cernay France 47°44N 7°10E 173 E14
Cernik Croatia 45°17N 17°22E 182 E2
Ceralvo, I. Mexico 24°15N 109°55W 318 C3
Cërrik Albania 41°2N 19°58E 202 E3
Cerritos Mexico 22°58N 100°16W 318 C4
Cerro Chato Uruguay 33°6S 55°8W 335 C4
Cerro Corá △ Paraguay 22°35S 56°2W 335 A4
Cerro de la Estrella △
Mexico 19°23N 99°5W 128 D2
Cerro de los Angeles
Spain 40°18N 3°41W 127 C1
Cerro de Pasco Peru 10°45S 76°10W 330 C2
Cerro Gordo U.S.A. 39°53N 88°44W 311 E8
Cerro Hoya △ Panama 7°17N 80°45W 320 E3
Cerro Navia Chile 33°25S 70°43W 137 B1
Cerro Saroche △
Venezuela 10°6N 69°38W 328 A4
Cerro Sombrero Chile 52°45S 69°15W 336 D2
Certaldo Italy 43°33N 11°2E 199 E8
Cervantes Phil. 17°0N 120°44E 232 C3
Cervaro → Italy 41°30N 15°52E 201 A8

Cervati, Monte Italy 40°17N 15°29E 201 B8
Cerventes Australia 30°31S 115°3E 279 F2
Cervera Spain 41°40N 1°16E 196 D6
Cervera de Pisuerga Spain 42°51N 4°30W 194 C6
Cervera del Río Alhama
  Spain 42°2N 1°58W 196 C3
Cervéteri Italy 42°0N 12°6E 199 F9
Cérvia Italy 44°15N 12°22E 199 D9
Cervignano del Friuli
  Italy 45°49N 13°20E 199 C10
Cervione France 42°20N 9°29E 175 F13
Cervo Spain 43°40N 7°24W 194 B3
Cesano Boscone Italy 45°26N 9°5E 129 B1
César → Italy 9°0N 73°3E 328 B3
Cesarò Italy 37°50N 14°38E 201 F7
Cesena Italy 44°8N 12°15E 199 D9
Cesenático Italy 44°12N 12°24E 199 D9
Cēsis Latvia 57°18N 25°15E 188 D3
Česká Lípa Czech Rep. 50°45N 14°30E 180 A7
Česká Rep. = Czech Rep. ■
  Europe 50°0N 15°0E 180 B8
Česká Třebová Czech Rep. 49°54N 16°27E 181 B9
České Budějovice
  Czech Rep. 48°55N 14°25E 180 C7
České Velenice Czech Rep. 48°45N 14°57E 180 D7
Českobudějovický □
  Czech Rep. 49°10N 14°30E 180 B7
Českomoravská Vrchovina
  Czech Rep. 49°30N 15°40E 180 B8
Český Brod Czech Rep. 50°4N 14°52E 180 A7
Český Krumlov
  Czech Rep. 48°43N 14°21E 180 C7
Český Těšín Czech Rep. 49°45N 18°39E 181 B13
Česma → Croatia 45°35N 16°29E 199 C13
Çeşme Turkey 38°20N 26°23E 205 D8
Cessnock Australia 32°50S 151°21E 283 B9
Cesson-Sévigné France 48°7N 1°36W 172 D5
Cestas France 44°44N 0°41W 174 D3
Cestos → Liberia 5°40N 9°10W 262 D3
Cestos Sehnkwehn △
  Liberia 5°40N 9°10W 262 D3
Cetate Romania 44°7N 23°2E 182 F8
Cetatea-Albă = Bilhorod-
  Dnistrovskyy Ukraine 46°11N 30°23E 189 J6
Cetin Grad Croatia 45°9N 15°45E 199 C12
Cetina → Croatia 43°26N 16°42E 199 E13
Cetinje Montenegro 42°23N 18°59E 202 D2
Çetm Turkey 36°52N 32°38E 250 B3
Cetraro Italy 39°31N 15°55E 201 E8
Ceuta N. Afr. 35°52N 5°18W 260 A3
Ceva Italy 44°23N 8°2E 198 D5
Ceve-i-Ra Fiji 21°46S 174°31E 277 E13
Cévennes France 44°10N 3°50E 174 D7
Cévennes △ France 44°15N 3°45E 174 D7
Ceyhan Turkey 37°4N 35°47E 250 A6
Ceyhan → Turkey 36°38N 35°40E 250 B6
Ceylanpınar Turkey 36°50N 40°2E 213 D9
Ceylon = Sri Lanka ■
  Asia 7°30N 80°50E 245 L5
Ceylon Plain Ind. Oc. 4°0S 82°0E 273 E7
Cèze → France 44°6N 4°43E 175 D8
Cha-am Thailand 12°48N 99°58E 236 F2
Cha Kwo Ling China 22°18N 114°13E 122 B2
Chá Pungana Angola 13°44S 18°39E 265 E3
Chabanais France 45°52N 0°43E 174 C4
Chabeuil France 44°54N 5°3E 175 D9
Chablais France 46°20N 6°36E 173 E13
Chablis France 47°47N 3°48E 173 E10
Chabounia Algeria 35°30N 2°38E 261 A5
Chacabuco Argentina 34°40S 60°27W 334 C3
Chachacare I.
  Trin. & Tob. 10°41N 61°45W 323 t
Chacao, Canal Chile 41°47S 73°42W 336 B2
Chacarita Argentina 34°35S 58°27W 117 B2
Chachani, Nevado Peru 16°11S 71°31W 330 D3
Chachapoyas Peru 6°15S 77°50W 330 B2
Chachasp Peru 15°30S 72°15W 330 D3
Chachoengsao Thailand 13°42N 101°5E 236 F3
Chachran Pakistan 28°55N 70°30E 242 E4
Chachro Pakistan 25°5N 70°15E 242 G4
Chaco □ U.S.A. 36°46N 108°39W 305 H9
Chaco □ Paraguay 26°0S 60°0W 334 B4
Chaco △ Argentina 27°0S 59°30W 334 B4
Chaco Culture △
  U.S.A. 36°3N 107°58W 305 H10
Chacon, C. U.S.A. 54°42N 132°0W 296 C2
Chad ■ Africa 15°0N 17°15E 259 F3
Chad, L. = Tchad, L.
  Chad 13°30N 14°30E 259 F2
Chadileuvú → Argentina 37°46S 66°0W 334 D2
Chadiza Zambia 14°45S 32°27E 269 E3
Chadron U.S.A. 42°50N 103°0W 311 D3
Chadwell Heath U.K. 51°34N 0°8E 125 A4
Chadyr-Lunga = Ciadâr-Lunga
  Moldova 46°3N 28°51E 183 D13
Chae Hom Thailand 18°43N 99°35E 236 C2
Chae Son △ Thailand 18°42N 99°20E 236 C2
Chaem → Thailand 18°11N 98°38E 236 C2
Chaeryŏng N. Korea 38°24N 125°36E 224 C2
Chafe Nigeria 11°59N 6°50E 263 C6
Chagai Hills = Chāh Gay Hills
  Afghan. 29°30N 64°0E 240 C2
Chagda Russia 58°45N 130°38E 215 D14
Chagdo Kangri China 34°15N 84°10E 217 F10
Chaghcharān Afghan. 34°31N 65°15E 240 B2
Chagne Ethiopia 10°57N 36°30E 266 B4
Chagny France 46°57N 4°45E 173 F11
Chagoda Russia 59°10N 35°15E 188 C8
Chagos Arch. ☑ Ind. Oc. 6°0S 72°0E 211 J9
Chagos-Laccadive Ridge
  Ind. Oc. 3°0N 73°0E 273 D6
Chagres → Panama 9°10N 79°40W 320 c
Chagres △ Panama 9°33N 79°37W 320 c
Chaguanas Trin. & Tob. 10°30N 61°26W 323 t
Chaguaramas Trin. & Tob. 10°41N 61°38W 323 t
Chāh Ākhvor Iran 32°41N 59°40E 247 C8
Chāh Bahar Iran 25°20N 60°40E 247 E9
Chāh-e Āb Afghan. 37°23N 69°48E 240 A3
Chāh-e Kavīr Iran 34°29N 56°52E 247 C8
Chāh Gay Hills Afghan. 29°30N 64°0E 240 C2
Chahār Borjak Iran 30°6N 45°59E 213 D11
Chahār Borjak Afghan. 30°17N 62°3E 240 C1
Chahār Mahāll va Bakhtīarī □
  Iran 32°0N 49°0E 247 C6
Chahtung Burma 26°41N 98°10E 241 B7
Chai Badan Thailand 15°12N 101°8E 236 E3
Chai Chee Singapore 1°19N 103°48E 138 d
Chai Wan China 22°16N 114°14E 122 B2
Chai Wan Kok China 22°22N 114°5E 122 A1
Chaibasa India 22°42N 85°49E 243 H11
Chaillé-les-Marais France 46°25N 1°2W 174 B2
Chaillot, Palais de Paris, France 134 b2
Chaillu, Massif du Gabon 2°32S 11°10E 266 C2
Chain Ridge Ind. Oc. 6°0N 54°0E 273 D4
Chainat Thailand 15°11N 100°8E 236 E2
Chaires U.S.A. 30°26N 84°7W 316 E5
Chaitén Chile 42°55S 72°43W 336 B2
Chaiya Thailand 9°23N 99°14E 237 H2
Chaiyaphum Thailand 15°48N 102°2E 236 E4
Chaj Doab Pakistan 32°15N 73°0E 242 C5
Chajari Argentina 30°42S 58°0W 334 C4
Chak Amru Pakistan 32°22N 75°11E 242 C6

Chaka Sudan 4°49N 31°14E 257 K6
Chakar → Pakistan 29°29N 68°2E 242 E3
Chakari Zimbabwe 18°5S 29°51E 271 A4
Chakaria Bangla. 21°45N 92°5E 241 G4
Chakarnada Chad 14°13N 20°51E 259 F4
Chakdaha India 22°28N 88°19E 124 C1
Chake Chake Tanzania 5°15S 39°45E 268 C4
Chakhānsūr Afghan. 31°10N 62°0E 240 C1
Chakonipau, L. Canada 56°18N 68°30W 299 A6
Chakradharpur India 22°45N 85°40E 243 H11
Chakrata India 30°42N 77°51E 242 D7
Chakwadam Burma 27°29N 98°31E 241 B7
Chakwal Pakistan 32°56N 72°53E 242 C5
Chala Peru 15°48S 74°20W 330 D3
Chalais France 45°16N 0°3E 174 C4
Chalakudi India 10°18N 76°20E 245 J3
Chalan Kanoa N. Marianas 15°9N 145°42E 302 e
Chalchihuites Mexico 23°29N 103°53W 318 C4
Chalcis = Halkida Greece 38°27N 23°42E 204 C5
Châlette-sur-Loing France 48°1N 2°44E 173 D9
Chaleur B. Canada 47°55N 65°30W 299 C6
Chalfant U.S.A. 37°32N 118°21W 306 H8
Chalhuanca Peru 14°15S 73°15W 330 C3
Chaliki Greece 39°36N 22°30E 204 B4
Chalindrey France 47°43N 5°26E 173 E12
Chaling China 26°58N 113°30E 229 D9
Chalisgaon India 20°30N 75°10E 244 D2
Chalk River Canada 46°1N 77°27W 298 C4
Chalkar, Ozero = Shalkar Köli
  Kazakhstan 50°35N 51°47E 190 E10
Chalky Inlet N.Z. 46°3S 166°31E 285 G1
Chalkyitsik U.S.A. 66°39N 143°43W 303 C12
Challakere India 14°19N 76°39E 245 G3
Challans France 46°50N 1°52W 172 F5
Challapata Bolivia 18°53S 66°50W 330 D4
Challenger Deep Pac. Oc. 11°30N 142°0E 288 F6
Challenger Fracture Zone
  Pac. Oc. 35°0S 105°0W 289 L17
Challis U.S.A. 44°30N 114°14W 304 D6
Chalmette U.S.A. 29°56N 89°57W 315 G10
Chalon-sur-Saône France 46°48N 4°50E 173 F11
Chalonnes-sur-Loire
  France 47°20N 0°45W 172 E6
Châlons-en-Champagne
  France 48°58N 4°20E 173 D11
Cháltén, Cerro = Fitz Roy, Cerro
  Argentina 49°17S 73°5W 336 C2
Châlus Haute-Vienne,
  France 45°39N 0°58E 174 C4
Chālūs Iran 36°38N 51°26E 247 B6
Cham Germany 49°13N 12°39E 179 F8
Cham, Cu Lao Vietnam 15°57N 108°30E 236 D7
Chama → U.S.A. 36°54N 106°35W 305 H10
Chamah, Gunong
  Malaysia 5°13N 101°35E 234 A2
Chamaicó Argentina 35°3S 64°58W 334 D3
Chaman Pakistan 30°58N 66°25E 240 C2
Chamartin Spain 40°27N 3°40W 127 B1
Chamba India 32°35N 76°10E 242 C7
Chamba Tanzania 11°37S 37°0E 269 E4
Chamberi Spain 40°26N 3°42W 127 B1
Chamberlain U.S.A. 43°49N 99°20W 308 D4
Chamberlain →
  Australia 15°30S 127°54E 278 C4
Chamberlain L. U.S.A. 46°14N 69°19W 309 B19
Chambers U.S.A. 35°11N 109°26W 305 J9
Chambersburg U.S.A. 39°56N 77°40W 309 F15
Chambéry France 45°34N 5°55E 175 C9
Chambeshi → Zambia 11°53S 29°48E 269 E3
Chambi, Jebel Tunisia 35°11N 8°39E 261 A6
Chamblee U.S.A. 33°53N 84°18W 316 B5
Chambly Canada 45°27N 73°17W 313 A11
Chambord Canada 48°25N 72°6W 299 C5
Chamboulive France 45°26N 1°42E 174 C5
Chambourcy France 48°54N 2°2E 134 A1
Chambri I. Papua N. G. 4°15S 143°10E 288 C5
Chamela Mexico 19°32N 105°5W 318 D3
Chamical Argentina 30°22S 66°27W 334 C2
Chamkar Luong
  Cambodia 11°0N 103°45E 237 G4
Chamois U.S.A. 38°41N 91°46W 310 F5
Chamoli India 30°24N 79°21E 243 D8
Chamonix-Mont Blanc
  France 45°55N 6°51E 175 C10
Chamouchouane =
Ashuapmushuan →
  Canada 48°37N 72°20W 298 C5
Champa India 22°2N 82°43E 243 H10
Champagne Canada 60°49N 136°30W 296 A1
Champagne France 48°40N 4°20E 173 D11
Champagnole France 46°45N 5°55E 173 F12
Champaign U.S.A. 40°7N 88°15W 311 D8
Champassak Laos 14°53N 105°52E 236 E5
Champaubert France 48°52N 3°45E 173 D10
Champawat India 29°20N 80°6E 243 E9
Champdeniers-St-Denis
  France 46°29N 0°25W 174 B3
Champdoré, L. Canada 55°55N 65°49W 299 A6
Champeix France 45°37N 3°8E 174 C7
Champigny-sur-Marne
  France 48°49N 2°30E 134 B4
Champion U.S.A. 41°19N 80°51W 312 E4
Champion B. Australia 28°30S 114°10E 279 E1
Champlain U.S.A. 44°40N 73°20W 313 B11
Champlain, Pont Canada 45°28N 73°31W 130 B2
Champlitte France 47°32N 5°31E 173 E12
Champotón Mexico 19°21N 90°43W 319 D6
Champs Elysées, Avenue des
  Paris, France 134 b2
Champs-sur-Marne
  France 48°50N 2°34E 134 A4
Champua India 22°5N 85°40E 243 H11
Chamrail India 22°38N 88°17E 124 B1
Chamusca Portugal 39°21N 8°29W 195 F2
Chan Chan Peru 8°5S 79°0W 330 B2
Chana Thailand 6°55N 100°44E 237 J3
Chanakyapuri India 28°35N 77°11E 120 B2
Chañaral Chile 26°23S 70°40W 334 B1
Chanasma India 23°44N 72°5E 242 H5
Chancay Peru 11°35S 77°25W 330 C2
Chancel, Î. Martinique 14°41N 60°53W 322 j

Chandler Okla., U.S.A. 35°42N 96°53W 314 D6
Chandless → Brazil 9°8S 69°53W 330 B4
Chandod India 21°59N 73°28E 242 J5
Chandpur Bangla. 23°8N 90°45E 241 F4
Chandra Greece 35°3N 26°8E 205 F8
Chandragiri India 13°35N 79°19E 245 H4
Chandragiri India 19°57N 79°12E 244 E4
Chandrapatla India 18°33N 80°42E 244 E5
Chânf Iran 26°38N 60°29E 247 E9
Chang, Ko Thailand 12°0N 102°23E 237 G4
Ch'ang Chiang = Chang Jiang →
  China 31°48N 121°10E 229 B13
Chang Jiang → China 31°48N 121°10E 229 B13
Chang-won S. Korea 35°16N 128°37E 224 E4
Changa India 33°53N 77°35E 243 C7
Changan = Xi'an China 34°15N 109°0E 226 C5
Changanacheri India 9°25N 76°31E 245 K3
Changanassery = Changanacheri
  India 9°25N 76°31E 245 K3
Changane → Mozam. 24°30S 33°30E 271 B5
Changbai China 41°25N 128°5E 224 B4
Changbai Shan China 42°20N 129°0E 224 A4
Changchiak'ou = Zhangjiakou
  China 40°48N 114°55E 226 D8
Changchih = Changzhi
  China 36°10N 113°6E 226 F7
Changchih Taiwan 22°34N 120°32E 225 E6
Ch'angchou = Changzhou
  China 31°47N 119°58E 229 B12
Changchow = Changzhou
  China 31°47N 119°58E 229 B12
Changchun China 43°57N 125°17E 227 C13
Changchunling China 45°18N 125°27E 227 B13
Changde China 29°4N 111°35E 229 C8
Changdo-ri N. Korea 38°30N 127°40E 224 C3
Changfeng China 32°28N 117°10E 229 A11
Changfeng Park China 31°14N 121°24E 138 B1
Changhai = Shanghai
  China 31°15N 121°26E 138 B2
Changhua Zhejiang,
  China 30°12N 119°12E 229 B12
Changhua Taiwan 24°2N 120°30E 225 B2
Changhua → Taiwan 24°2N 120°32E 225 B2
Changhüngni N. Korea 40°24N 128°19E 224 B4
Changi Singapore 1°23N 103°59E 138 A3
Changi, Singapore ✈ (SIN)
  Singapore 1°21N 103°59E 138 A3
Changji China 44°1N 87°19E 217 D11
Changjiang China 19°20N 108°55E 236 C7
Changjiang Shuiku
  China 22°29N 113°27E 219 G10
Changjin N. Korea 40°23N 127°15E 224 B3
Changjin-ho N. Korea 40°30N 127°15E 224 B3
Changle China 25°59N 119°27E 229 E12
Changli China 39°40N 119°13E 227 D10
Changling China 44°20N 123°58E 227 B12
Changlun Malaysia 6°25N 100°26E 237 J3
Changning Hunan,
  China 26°28N 112°22E 229 D9
Changning Shanghai,
  China 31°13N 121°24E 138 B1
Changning Sichuan,
  China 28°40N 104°56E 228 C5
Changning Yunnan, China 24°45N 99°30E 228 E2
Ch'angpin Taiwan 23°19N 121°27E 225 D6
Changqing China 40°14N 116°12E 226 D9
Changsha China 28°12N 113°0E 229 C9
Changshan China 28°55N 118°27E 229 C12
Changshan Qundao
  China 39°11N 122°32E 227 E12
Changshou China 31°38N 120°43E 229 B13
Changshu China 26°3N 106°25E 228 D6
Changtai China 24°35N 117°42E 229 E11
Changt'e = Chongde
  China 30°32N 120°26E 229 B13
Changting China 25°50N 116°22E 229 E11
Changuinola Panama 9°26N 82°31W 320 E3
Changwu China 35°10N 107°45E 226 G4
Changxing China 31°0N 119°50E 229 B12
Changyang China 30°30N 111°10E 229 B8
Changyi China 36°40N 119°30E 227 F10
Changyŏn N. Korea 38°15N 125°6E 224 C2
Changyuan Henan,
  China 35°15N 114°42E 226 G8
Changzhi Taiwan 23°25N 121°29E 225 C3
Changzhi China 36°10N 113°6E 226 F7
Changzhou China 31°47N 119°58E 229 B12
Chanhanga Angola 16°0S 14°8E 265 F2
Chania Greece 35°30N 24°4E 207 D6
Chania □ Greece 35°30N 24°4E 207 D5
Chania ✈ (CHQ) Greece 35°30N 24°6E 207 D5
Chanion, Kolpos Greece 35°33N 23°55E 207 D5
Chanlar = Xanlar
  Azerbaijan 40°37N 46°12E 191 K8
Channagiri India 14°1N 75°56E 245 G2
Channapatna India 12°40N 77°15E 245 H3
Channel Is. U.K. 49°19N 2°24W 169 H5
Channel Is. Calif.,
  U.S.A. 33°40N 119°15W 307 M7
Channel Islands △
  U.S.A. 34°0N 119°24W 307 L7
Channel-Port aux Basques
  Canada 47°30N 59°9W 299 C8
Channel Tunnel Europe 51°0N 1°30E 169 F9
Channing U.S.A. 35°41N 102°20W 314 A1
Chantada Spain 42°36N 7°46W 194 C3
Chanthaburi Thailand 12°38N 102°12E 236 F4
Chantian China 23°12N 113°16E 121 A2
Chantilly France 49°12N 2°29E 173 C9
Chantonnay France 46°40N 1°3W 172 F5
Chantrey Inlet Canada 67°48N 96°20W 294 D12
Chanumla India 8°19N 93°5E 245 K11
Chanute U.S.A. 37°41N 95°27W 308 G6
Chany, Ozero Russia 54°49N 77°29E 217 B9
Chanza → Spain 37°32N 7°30W 195 H3
Chao Hu China 31°30N 117°30E 229 B11
Chao Phraya →
  Thailand 13°40N 100°31E 236 F3
Chao Phraya Lowlands
  Thailand 15°30N 100°0E 236 E3
Chaocheng China 36°4N 115°37E 226 F8
Ch'aochou Taiwan 22°33N 120°32E 225 D2
Chaohu China 31°38N 117°50E 229 B11
Chaoyang Beijing, China 39°55N 116°26E 114 B2
Chaoyang Guangdong,
  China 23°17N 116°30E 229 F11
Chaoyang Liaoning,
  China 41°35N 120°22E 227 D11
Chaoyangmen China 39°54N 116°25E 114 B2
Chaozhou China 23°42N 116°32E 229 F11
Chapada Diamantina △
  Brazil 12°52S 41°30W 333 D3
Chapada dos Guimarães
  Brazil 15°26S 55°45W 331 D5
Chapada dos Guimarães △
  Brazil 15°18S 55°54W 331 D5
Chapada dos Veadeiros △
  Brazil 14°0S 47°30W 333 D2
Chapaevo Kazakhstan 50°25N 51°10E 190 E10
Chapaev Canada 49°47N 74°51W 298 C5
Chapala Mozam. 15°50S 37°35E 269 E4
Chapala, L. de Mexico 20°10N 103°20W 318 C4
Chaparé → Bolivia 15°58S 64°42W 331 D5

Chaparmukh India 26°12N 92°31E 241 B4
Chaparral Colombia 3°43N 75°28W 328 C2
Chapayevsk Russia 53°0N 49°40E 190 D9
Chapecó Brazil 27°14S 52°41W 335 B5
Chapel Hill U.S.A. 35°55N 79°4W 315 D15
Chapel-en-le-Frith U.K. 53°21N 1°54W 161 D6
Chapeltown Ireland 53°21N 6°21W 120 A1
Chapelton Jamaica 18°5N 77°16W 320 a
Chapin = Edinburg
  U.S.A. 26°18N 98°10W 314 H5
Chapin U.S.A. 39°46N 90°24W 310 E6
Chaplau Canada 47°50N 83°24W 298 C3
Chaplin Canada 50°28N 106°40W 297 C7
Chaplin L. Canada 50°22N 106°36W 297 C7
Chaplino Ukraine 48°8N 36°15E 189 H9
Chaplygin Russia 53°15N 40°0E 188 F11
Chappell U.S.A. 41°6N 102°28W 308 E2
Chappells U.S.A. 34°11N 81°52W 316 A1
Chapra = Chhapra India 25°48N 84°44E 243 G11
Chaptalu, Bosque de
  Mexico 19°25N 99°11W 128 B1
Chapultepec, Castillo de
  Mexico 19°25N 99°10W 128 B1
Chaqābel Iran 33°16N 47°30E 213 F12
Chār Mauritania 21°32N 12°45W 260 D2
Chār Russia 56°54N 118°20E 215 D12
Charadai Argentina 27°35S 59°55W 334 B4
Charagua Bolivia 19°45S 63°10W 331 D5
Charakas Greece 35°1N 25°7E 207 E6
Charal Colombia 6°17N 73°10W 328 B3
Charaña Bolivia 17°30S 69°25W 330 D4
Charantsavan Armenia 40°35N 44°41E 191 K7
Charanwala India 27°51N 72°10E 242 F5
Charapita Colombia 0°37S 74°21W 328 D3
Charata Argentina 27°13S 61°14W 334 B3
Charcas Mexico 23°8N 101°7W 318 C4
Charcot I. Antarctica 70°0S 70°0W 151 C17
Chard U.K. 50°52N 2°58W 169 G5
Chardon U.S.A. 41°35N 81°12W 312 E3
Charduar India 26°51N 92°46E 241 B4
Chardzhou = Türkmenabat
  Turkmenistan 39°6N 63°34E 247 B9
Charente □ France 45°50N 0°16E 174 C4
Charente → France 45°57N 1°5W 174 C2
Charente-Inférieure = Charente-
Maritime □ France 45°45N 0°45E 174 C3
Charente-Maritime □
  France 45°45N 0°45W 174 C3
Charenton-du-Cher
  France 46°44N 2°39E 173 F9
Charenton-le-Pont France 48°49N 2°25E 134 B3
Chari → Chad 12°58N 14°31E 259 F2
Chari-Baguirmi □ Chad 11°0N 17°0E 259 F3
Chārīkār Afghan. 35°0N 69°10E 240 B3
Charing U.K. 51°12N 0°49E 125 B4
Charing Cross London, U.K. 125 b4
Chariton U.S.A. 41°1N 93°19W 310 C3
Chariton → U.S.A. 39°19N 92°58W 310 E3
Charity Guyana 7°24N 58°36W 329 B6
Chärjew = Türkmenabat
  Turkmenistan 39°6N 63°34E 247 B9
Charkhari India 25°24N 79°45E 243 G8
Charkhi Dadri India 28°37N 76°17E 242 E7
Charleroi Belgium 50°24N 4°27E 170 D4
Charleroi U.S.A. 40°9N 79°57W 312 F5
Charleroi, Kanal de
  Belgium 50°55N 4°19E 116 B1
Charles, C. U.S.A. 37°7N 75°58W 309 G16
Charles, I. = Santa María, I.
  Ecuador 1°17S 90°26W 330 a
Charles, Peak Australia 32°52S 121°11E 279 F3
Charles Bridge = Karlův most
  Prague, Czech Rep. 135 b1
Charles de Gaulle, Paris ✈ (CDG)
  France 49°0N 2°32E 173 D9
Charles Gates Dawes House
  U.S.A. 42°2N 87°40W 119 A2
Charles I. Canada 62°39N 74°15W 295 E17
Charles L. Canada 59°50N 110°33W 297 B6
Charles Sound N.Z. 45°2S 167°4E 285 F2
Charles Square = Karlovo náměstí
  Prague, Czech Rep. 135 c1
Charles Town U.S.A. 39°17N 77°52W 309 F15
Charlesbourg Canada 46°51N 71°16W 309 C18
Charleston Ill., U.S.A. 39°30N 88°10W 311 E8
Charleston Miss., U.S.A. 34°1N 90°4W 315 D9
Charleston Mo., U.S.A. 36°55N 89°21W 308 G9
Charleston S.C., U.S.A. 32°46N 79°56W 316 C10
Charleston W. Va.,
  U.S.A. 38°21N 81°38W 309 F13
Charleston Peak
  U.S.A. 36°16N 115°42W 307 J11
Charleston of Aberlour
  Scotland 57°28N 3°14W 167 D5
Charleville = Rath Luirc
  Ireland 52°21N 8°40W 166 D3
Charleville Australia 26°24S 146°15E 281 D4
Charleville-Mézières
  France 49°44N 4°40E 173 C11
Charlevoix U.S.A. 45°19N 85°16W 309 C11
Charlie Gibbs Fracture Zone
  Atl. Oc. 52°45N 35°30W 152 A8
Charlieu France 46°10N 4°10E 173 F11
Charlotte Dominica 15°17N 61°24W 323 k
Charlotte Mich., U.S.A. 42°34N 84°50W 311 B12
Charlotte N.C., U.S.A. 35°13N 80°50W 315 D14
Charlotte Vt., U.S.A. 44°19N 73°16W 313 B11
Charlotte Amalie
  U.S. Virgin Is. 18°21N 64°56W 321 C7
Charlotte Harbor U.S.A. 26°57N 82°4W 317 J7
Charlotte L. Canada 52°12N 125°19W 296 C3
Charlottenberg Sweden 59°54N 12°17E 162 E6
Charlottenburg Germany 52°31N 13°14E 115 A2
Charlottenburg, Schloss
  Germany 52°31N 13°18E 115 A2
Charlottenlund Denmark 55°46N 12°35E 118 A3
Charlottesville U.S.A. 38°2N 78°30W 309 F14
Charlottetown Nfld. & L.,
  Canada 52°46N 56°7W 299 B8
Charlottetown P.E.I.,
  Canada 46°14N 63°8W 299 C7
Charlotteville Trin. & Tob. 11°16N 60°33W 323 s
Charlton Vic., Australia 36°16S 143°24E 282 D5
Charlton London, U.K. 125 B4
Charlton I. Canada 52°0N 79°20W 298 B4
Charmes France 48°22N 6°17E 173 D13
Charnes Canada 49°44N 4°0E 173 C11
Charneca Lisboa, Portugal 38°47N 9°9E 130 a
Charneca Setúbal, Portugal 38°41N 9°6E 130 a
Charny France 46°43N 71°15W 299 C15
Charnyany Belarus 51°28N 24°12E 185 G13

Charolles France 46°27N 4°16E 173 F11
Chârost France 47°0N 2°7E 173 F9
Charouine Algeria 29°0N 0°15W 261 C4
Charre Mozam. 17°13S 35°10E 269 F4
Charroux France 46°9N 0°25E 174 B4
Charsadda Pakistan 34°7N 71°45E 242 B4
Charshanga = Köytendag
  Turkmenistan 37°30N 66°1E 240 A2
Charters Towers
  Australia 20°5S 146°13E 280 C4
Chartres France 48°29N 1°30E 172 D8
Chartreuse △ France 45°22N 5°42E 175 C9
Charuma Trin. & Tob. 10°24N 61°9W 323 t
Charvein Fr. Guiana 5°27N 53°50W 329 B8
Charyshskoye Russia 48°13N 29°22E 183 B14
Chas Czech Rep. 50°9N 12°28E 180 A5
Chasbe Czech Rep. 41°0N 87°54W 311 D9
Chasong N. Korea 41°27N 126°38E 224 B3
Chassenon-sur-Bonnieure
  France 45°52N 0°29E 174 C4
Chechen, Ostrov Russia 43°59N 47°40E 191 H8
Ch'ech'eng Taiwan 22°5N 120°42E 225 D2
Chechnia = Chechenia □
  Russia 43°30N 45°29E 191 J7
Chechnya = Chechenia □
  Russia 43°30N 45°29E 191 J7
Chechyn Poland 50°46N 20°28E 185 H7
Checotah U.S.A. 35°28N 95°31W 314 D7
Chedabucto B. Canada 45°25N 61°8W 299 C7
Cheduba I. Burma 18°45N 93°40E 241 E4
Cheektowaga U.S.A. 42°54N 78°45W 312 D6
Cheepie Australia 26°33S 145°0E 281 D4
Cheeyou Trin. & Tob. 10°33N 61°8W 323 t
Chef-Boutonne France 46°7N 0°4W 174 B3
Chefchaouen Morocco 35°9N 5°15W 260 A3
Chefchaouen □ Morocco 35°9N 5°15W 260 A3
Cheffadine Niger 19°57N 12°11E 259 D2
Chefoo = Yantai China 37°34N 121°22E 227 F11
Chefornak U.S.A. 60°13N 164°12W 303 F6
Chegdomyn Russia 51°7N 133°1E 215 D14
Chegga Mauritania 25°27N 5°40W 260 C3
Chegutu Zimbabwe 18°10S 30°14E 269 F3
Chehalis U.S.A. 46°40N 122°58W 306 D4
Chehalis → U.S.A. 46°57N 123°50W 306 D4
Cheile Nerei-Beusnita △
  Romania 44°56N 21°52E 182 F6
Cheiron, Mt. France 43°49N 6°58E 175 E10
Cheju = Jeju S. Korea 33°31N 126°32E 224 a
Cheju-do = Jeju-do
  S. Korea 33°29N 126°34E 224 a
Chekalin Russia 54°10N 36°10E 188 E9
Chekhovo Russia 54°33N 20°43E 184 D7
Chekiang = Zhejiang □
  China 29°0N 120°0E 229 C13
Chel = Kuru, Bahr el →
  Sudan 8°10N 29°10E 257 J7
Chela, Sa. da Angola 16°20S 13°20E 265 F2
Chelan U.S.A. 47°51N 120°1W 304 B3
Chelan, L. U.S.A. 48°11N 120°30W 304 B3
Cheleken = Hazar
  Turkmenistan 39°34N 53°16E 187 D2
Cheleken Yarymadasy
  Turkmenistan 39°30N 53°15E 247 B2
Chelforó Argentina 39°0S 66°33W 336 A3
Chella Dahrania Algeria 33°2N 0°1E 261 B5
Chelles France 48°53N 2°35E 134 A4
Chelles, Canal de France 48°53N 2°35E 134 A4
Chells-le-Pin ✈ France 48°53N 2°36E 134 A4
Chełm Poland 51°8N 23°30E 185 G10
Chelmno Poland 53°20N 18°30E 185 B5
Chelmsford U.K. 51°44N 0°29E 169 F8
Chełmża Poland 53°10N 18°39E 185 B5
Chelsea Vic., Australia 38°5S 145°8E 283 E6
Chelsea London, U.K. 51°29N 0°10W 125 B2
Chelsea Mass., U.S.A. 42°23N 71°1W 116 A2
Chelsea Mich., U.S.A. 42°19N 84°1W 311 B12
Chelsea New York, U.S.A. 132 c1
Chelsea Vt., U.S.A. 43°59N 72°27W 313 C12
Cheltenham U.K. 51°54N 2°4W 169 F5
Chelva Spain 39°45N 1°0W 196 F4
Chelyabinsk Russia 55°10N 61°24E 216 A6
Chelyakobi = Kopeysk
  Russia 55°7N 61°37E 216 A6
Chelyuskin, C. = Chelyuskin, Mys
  Russia 77°30N 103°0E 215 B11
Chelyuskin, Mys Russia 77°30N 103°0E 215 B11
Chemainus Canada 48°55N 123°42W 306 B3
Chembar = Belinskiy
  Russia 53°0N 43°25E 190 D8
Chemillé France 47°14N 0°45W 172 E6
Chemin Grenier Mauritius 20°29S 57°28E 272 e
Chemnitz Germany 50°51N 12°54E 178 E8
Chemulpho = Incheon
  S. Korea 37°27N 126°40E 224 D3
Chemult U.S.A. 43°14N 121°47W 304 E3
Chen, Gora Russia 65°16N 141°50E 215 C15
Chenab → Pakistan 30°23N 71°2E 242 D4
Chenab Nagar Pakistan 31°45N 72°56E 242 D5
Chenachane Algeria 26°0N 4°15W 260 C4
Chenachane, O. →
  Algeria 25°20N 3°20W 260 C4
Chenango Forks U.S.A. 42°15N 75°51W 313 D9
Chencha Ethiopia 6°15N 37°32E 257 F4
Chenchiang = Zhenjiang
  China 32°11N 119°26E 229 A12
Chengbu China 26°18N 110°16E 229 D8
Chengcheng China 35°8N 109°56E 226 G5
Chengchou = Zhengzhou
  China 34°45N 113°34E 226 G7
Chengde China 40°59N 117°58E 227 D9
Chengdong Hu China 32°15N 116°10E 229 A11
Chengdu China 30°38N 104°2E 228 B5
Chengele India 28°41N 96°16E 241 A6
Chenggong China 24°55N 102°46E 228 E4
Chenggu China 33°10N 107°3E 228 B6
Chengjiang China 24°39N 103°0E 228 E4
Chengkou China 31°54N 108°30E 228 B7
Ch'engmai China 19°50N 109°58E 236 C7
Chengtu = Chengdu
  China 30°38N 104°2E 228 B5
Chengwu China 34°58N 115°50E 226 G8
Chengxi Hu China 32°15N 116°10E 229 A11
Chengyang China 34°23N 119°47E 227 G10
Chenkaladi Sri Lanka 7°47N 81°33E 245 L6

Chennai India 13°8N 80°19E 245 H5
Chennevières-sur-Marne France 48°47N 2°31E 134 B4
Chenoa U.S.A. 40°45N 88°43W 311 D8
Chenôve France 47°16N 5°1E 173 E12
Chenxi China 28°2N 110°12E 229 C8
Chenzhou China 25°47N 113°1E 229 E9
Cheò, Eilean a' = Skye U.K. 57°15N 6°10W 167 D2
Cheom Ksan Cambodia 14°13N 104°56E 236 E5
Cheonan S. Korea 36°48N 127°9E 224 D3
Cheongdam S. Korea 37°31N 127°2E 137 B2
Cheongdo S. Korea 35°38N 128°42E 224 E4
Cheongju S. Korea 36°39N 127°27E 224 D3
Cheongsando S. Korea 34°11N 126°53E 224 E3
Cheongsong S. Korea 36°25N 129°3E 224 D4
Cheonho S. Korea 37°32N 127°6E 137 B2
Cheonsumman S. Korea 36°33N 126°25E 224 D3
Cheops Egypt 29°58N 31°8E 117 B1
Cheorwon S. Korea 38°15N 127°10E 224 C3
Chepelare Bulgaria 41°44N 24°40E 203 E8
Chepén Peru 7°15S 79°23W 330 B2
Chépénéhé N. Cal. 20°47S 167°9E 288 d
Chepes Argentina 31°20S 66°35W 334 C2
Chepo Panama 9°10N 79°6W 320 E4
Chepstow U.K. 51°38N 2°41W 169 F5
Chequamegon B. U.S.A. 46°39N 90°51W 308 B8
Cher □ France 47°10N 2°30E 173 E9
Cher → France 47°21N 0°29E 172 E7
Chéradi Italy 40°27N 17°10E 201 B10
Cheran India 25°45N 90°44E 241 C3
Cherasco Italy 44°39N 7°51E 198 D4
Cheraw U.S.A. 34°42N 79°53W 315 D15
Cherbourg France 49°39N 1°40W 172 C5
Cherchell Algeria 36°35N 2°12E 261 A5
Cherdakly Russia 54°25N 48°50E 190 C9
Cherdyn Russia 60°24N 56°29E 186 B10
Cheremkhovo Russia 53°8N 103°1E 215 D11
Cherepanovo Russia 54°15N 83°30E 217 B10
Cherepkovo Russia 55°45N 37°21E 129 B2
Cherepovets Russia 59°5N 37°55E 188 C9
Chergui, Chott ech Algeria 34°21N 0°25E 261 B5
Chergui, Zahrez Algeria 35°11N 3°31E 261 B5
Cherial India 17°55N 78°59E 244 F4
Cheribon = Cirebon Indonesia 6°45S 108°32E 235 D3
Cherikov = Cherykaw Belarus 53°32N 31°20E 177 B16
Cheriyam I. India 10°9N 73°40E 245 J1
Cherkasy Ukraine 49°27N 32°4E 189 H7
Cherkasy □ Ukraine 48°55N 30°50E 189 H6
Cherkessk Russia 44°15N 42°5E 191 H6
Cherla India 18°5N 80°49E 244 E5
Cherlak Russia 54°15N 74°55E 217 B8
Chernaya Russia 70°30N 89°10E 215 B9
Chernelytsya Ukraine 48°49N 25°26E 183 B10
Cherni Bulgaria 42°35N 23°18E 202 D7
Chernigov = Chernihiv Ukraine 51°28N 31°20E 189 G6
Chernigovka Russia 44°19N 132°34E 220 B6
Chernihiv Ukraine 51°28N 31°20E 189 G6
Chernihiv □ Ukraine 51°10N 32°5E 189 G7
Chernivtsi Chernivtsi, Ukraine 48°15N 25°52E 183 B10
Chernivtsi Vinnyts'ka, Ukraine 48°32N 28°9E 183 B13
Chernivtsi □ Ukraine 48°5N 25°30E 183 B10
Chernobyl = Chornobyl Ukraine 51°20N 30°15E 177 C16
Chernogorsk Russia 53°49N 91°18E 217 B12
Chernomorskoye = Chornomorske Ukraine 45°31N 32°40E 189 K7
Chernorechye = Dzerzhinsk Russia 56°14N 43°30E 190 B6
Chernovtsy = Chernivtsi Ukraine 48°15N 25°52E 183 B10
Chernyakhovsk Russia 54°36N 21°48E 184 D8
Chernyanka Russia 50°56N 37°49E 189 G9
Chernyovo Russia 55°50N 37°17E 129 A1
Chernysheyskiy Russia 63°0N 112°30E 215 C12
Chernyye Zemli Russia 46°10N 46°0E 191 H8
Cherokee Iowa, U.S.A. 42°45N 95°33W 308 D6
Cherokee Okla., U.S.A. 36°45N 98°21W 314 C5
Cherokee Village U.S.A. 36°18N 91°31W 314 C9
Cherokees, Grand Lake O' The U.S.A. 36°28N 94°55W 314 C7
Cherquenco Chile 38°35S 72°0W 336 A2
Cherrapunji India 25°17N 91°47E 241 C3
Cherry Valley U.S.A. 42°48N 74°45W 313 D10
Cherryville U.S.A. 37°51N 91°16W 310 G5
Cherskiy Russia 68°45N 161°18E 215 C17
Cherskogo Khrebet Russia 65°0N 143°0E 215 C15
Chersonisos Akrotiri Greece 35°30N 24°10E 207 E5
Chertanovka → Russia 55°38N 37°48E 129 C3
Chertanovo Russia 55°38N 37°36E 129 C3
Cherthala = Shertallai India 9°42N 76°20E 245 K3
Chertkov = Chortkiv Ukraine 49°2N 25°46E 177 D13
Chertkovo Russia 49°25N 40°19E 189 H11
Cherven Belarus 53°45N 28°28E 177 B15
Cherven-Bryag Bulgaria 43°17N 24°7E 203 C8
Chervonoarmeyskoye = Volnansk Ukraine 48°2N 35°29E 189 H8
Chervonoarmiyske Ukraine 45°47N 28°44E 183 E13
Chervonohrad Ukraine 50°25N 24°10E 177 C13
Cherwell → U.K. 51°44N 1°14W 169 F6
Cherykaw Belarus 53°32N 31°20E 177 B16
Cheryomushki Russia 55°40N 37°35E 129 B3
Chesapeake U.S.A. 36°49N 76°16W 309 G15
Chesapeake B. U.S.A. 38°0N 76°10W 309 F14
Cheshire □ U.K. 53°14N 2°30W 168 D5
Cheshskaya Guba Russia 67°20N 47°0E 186 A8
Cheshunt U.K. 51°43N 0°1W 169 F7
Chesil Beach U.K. 50°37N 2°33W 169 G5
Chesley Canada 44°17N 81°5W 312 B3
Chesnokovka = Novoaltaysk Russia 53°30N 84°0E 217 B10
Cheste Spain 39°30N 0°41W 197 F4
Chester Ches., U.K. 53°12N 2°53W 168 D5
Chester Calif., U.S.A. 40°19N 121°14W 304 F3
Chester Ga., U.S.A. 32°24N 83°9W 316 C6
Chester Ill., U.S.A. 37°55N 89°49W 310 G7
Chester Mont., U.S.A. 48°31N 110°58W 304 B8
Chester Pa., U.S.A. 39°51N 75°22W 309 F16
Chester S.C., U.S.A. 34°43N 81°12W 315 D14
Chester Vt., U.S.A. 43°16N 72°36W 313 C12
Chester W. Va., U.S.A. 40°37N 80°34W 312 F4
Chester-le-Street U.K. 54°51N 1°34W 168 C6
Chesterfield Derby, U.K. 53°15N 1°25W 168 D6
Chesterfield Mo., U.S.A. 38°40N 90°35W 310 F6
Chesterfield, Îs. N. Cal. 19°52S 158°15E 277 D10
Chesterfield Inlet Canada 63°30N 90°45W 294 E13
Chesterton Ra. Australia 25°30S 147°27E 281 D4
Chesterton Range △ Australia 26°16S 147°22E 281 D4
Chestertown U.S.A. 43°40N 73°48W 313 C11
Chesterville Canada 45°6N 75°14W 313 A9
Chestnut Hill U.S.A. 42°19N 71°10W 116 B1
Chesuncook L. U.S.A. 46°0N 69°21W 309 C19
Chetamale India 10°43N 92°33E 245 J11
Chéticamp Canada 46°37N 60°59W 299 C7
Chetlat I. India 11°42N 72°42E 245 J1
Chetrosu Moldova 48°5N 27°54E 183 B12
Chetumal Mexico 18°30N 88°20W 319 D7
Chetumal, B. de Cent. Amer. 18°40N 88°10W 319 D7
Chetwynd Canada 55°45N 121°36W 296 B4
Cheung Sha Wan China 22°20N 114°8E 122 A1
Chevak U.S.A. 61°32N 165°35W 303 F6
Chevalier, Î. de Martinique 14°25N 60°50W 322 j
Chevanceaux France 45°18N 0°14W 174 C3
Cheverly U.S.A. 38°55N 76°54W 143 B4
Chevilly-Larue France 48°46N 2°21E 134 B3
Cheviot U.S.A. 39°9N 84°36W 311 E12
Cheviot, The U.K. 55°29N 2°9W 168 B5
Cheviot Hills Northumberland, U.K. 55°20N 2°30W 168 B5
Cheviot Hills Calif., U.S.A. 34°2N 118°24W 126 B2
Cheviot Ra. Australia 25°20S 143°45E 280 D3
Chevy Chase U.S.A. 38°59N 77°4W 143 B3
Chew Bahir Ethiopia 4°40N 36°50E 257 G4
Chewelah U.S.A. 48°17N 117°43W 304 B5
Chewore ⏢ Zimbabwe 16°0S 29°52E 269 F2
Cheyenne Okla., U.S.A. 35°37N 99°40W 314 D5
Cheyenne Wyo., U.S.A. 41°8N 104°49W 304 F11
Cheyenne → U.S.A. 44°41N 101°18W 308 C3
Cheyenne Wells U.S.A. 38°49N 102°21W 304 G12
Cheyne B. Australia 34°35S 118°50E 279 F2
Cheyur India 12°21N 80°0E 245 H5
Chhabra India 24°40N 76°54E 242 G7
Chhaktala India 22°6N 74°11E 242 H6
Chhapra India 25°48N 84°44E 243 G11
Chhata India 27°42N 77°30E 242 F7
Chhatak Bangla. 25°5N 91°37E 241 C3
Chhatarpur Jharkhand, India 24°23N 84°11E 243 G11
Chhatarpur Mad. P., India 24°55N 79°35E 243 G8
Chhati India 20°47N 81°40E 244 D5
Chhatrapati Shivaji, Mumbai ✈ (BOM) India 19°5N 72°51E 130 A2
Chhattisgarh □ India 22°0N 82°0E 243 J10
Chhaygaon India 26°3N 91°24E 241 B3
Chhep Cambodia 13°45N 105°24E 236 F5
Chhindwara Mad. P., India 23°3N 79°29E 243 H8
Chhindwara Mad. P., India 22°2N 78°59E 243 H8
Chhinhdipada India 21°6N 84°52E 244 D7
Chhlong Cambodia 12°15N 105°58E 237 F5
Chhota Tawa → India 22°14N 76°36E 242 H7
Chhoti Kali Sindh → India 24°2N 75°31E 242 G6
Chhuikhadan India 21°32N 80°59E 243 J9
Chhuk Cambodia 10°46N 104°28E 237 G5
Chi → Thailand 15°11N 104°43E 236 E5
Chia Keng Singapore 1°21N 103°52E 138 A3
Chiahsien Taiwan 23°5N 120°35E 225 C2
Chiai Taiwan 23°29N 120°25E 225 C2
Chiai □ Taiwan 23°30N 120°30E 225 C2
Chiaksan △ S. Korea 37°15N 128°0E 224 D4
Chiali Taiwan 23°9N 120°10E 225 C2
Chialiulantsun Taiwan 22°49N 121°11E 225 D3
Chiamboni Somali Rep. 1°39S 41°35E 267 E5
Chiamussu = Jiamusi China 46°40N 130°26E 219 B8
Chian Taiwan 23°59N 121°33E 225 C3
Chianapu Taiwan 22°47N 120°36E 225 D2
Chianciano Terme Italy 43°2N 11°49E 199 E8
Chiang Dao Thailand 19°22N 98°58E 236 C2
Chiang Kham Thailand 19°32N 100°18E 236 C3
Chiang Khan Thailand 17°52N 101°36E 236 D3
Chiang Khong Thailand 20°17N 100°24E 228 G3
Chiang Mai Thailand 18°47N 98°59E 236 C2
Chiang Rai Thailand 19°52N 99°50E 228 H2
Chiang Saen Thailand 20°16N 100°5E 228 G3
Chiangchun Taiwan 23°12N 120°5E 225 C2
Chiange Angola 15°35S 13°40E 265 F2
Chianti Italy 43°32N 11°25E 199 E8
Chiaohsi Taiwan 24°49N 121°46E 225 B3
Chiaotou Taiwan 22°45N 120°18E 225 D2
Chiapa → Mexico 16°42N 93°0W 319 D6
Chiapa de Corzo Mexico 16°42N 93°0W 319 D6
Chiapas □ Mexico 16°30N 92°30W 319 D6
Chiapas, Sa. Madre de Mexico 15°40N 93°0W 319 D6
Chiaramonte Gulfi Italy 37°2N 14°42E 201 E7
Chiaravalle Italy 43°36N 13°19E 199 E10
Chiaravalle Centrale Italy 38°41N 16°25E 201 D9
Chiaravalle Milanese Italy 45°24N 9°16E 128 B2
Chiari Italy 45°32N 9°56E 198 C6
Chiatung Taiwan 22°25N 120°32E 225 D2
Chiatura Georgia 42°15N 43°17E 191 J6
Chiautla de Tapia Mexico 18°18N 98°36W 319 D5
Chiávari Italy 44°19N 9°19E 198 D6
Chiavenna Italy 46°19N 9°24E 198 B6
Chiba Japan 35°30N 140°7E 223 B12
Chiba □ Japan 35°30N 140°20E 223 B12
Chibabava Mozam. 20°17S 33°35E 271 B5
Chibango Angola 13°38S 21°56E 265 E4
Chibemba Cunene, Angola 15°48S 14°8E 265 F2
Chibemba Huila, Angola 16°20S 15°20E 265 F3
Chibi Zimbabwe 20°18S 30°25E 271 B5
Chibia Angola 15°10S 13°42E 265 F2
Chibizovka = Zherdevka Russia 51°56N 41°29E 190 E5
Chibougamau Canada 49°56N 74°24W 298 C5
Chibougamau, L. Canada 49°50N 74°20W 298 C5
Chibuk Nigeria 10°52N 12°50E 263 C7
Chibuto Mozam. 24°40S 33°33E 271 B5
Chibyu = Ukhta Russia 63°34N 53°41E 186 B9
Chic-Chocs, Mts. Canada 48°55N 66°0W 299 C6
Chicacole = Srikakulam India 18°14N 83°58E 244 E6
Chicago U.S.A. 41°52N 87°38W 119 B3
Chicago, Univ. of U.S.A. 41°47N 87°35W 119 C3
Chicago Harbor Chicago, U.S.A. 119 d3
Chicago Heights U.S.A. 41°30N 87°38W 311 C9
Chicago Lawn U.S.A. 41°47N 87°40W 119 C2
Chicago-Midway ✈ (MDW) U.S.A. 41°47N 87°45W 119 C2
Chicago O'Hare Int. ✈ (ORD) U.S.A. 41°59N 87°54W 119 B1
Chicago Ridge U.S.A. 41°41N 87°46W 119 C2
Chicago River → Chicago, U.S.A. 119 b2
Chicago River, North Branch → U.S.A. 41°53N 87°42W 119 B2
Chicago Sanitary and Ship Canal U.S.A. 41°49N 87°45W 119 C2
Chicago State Univ. U.S.A. 41°43N 87°36W 119 C3
Chicago Zoo U.S.A. 41°50N 87°50W 119 B1
Chicapa → Dem. Rep. of the Congo 6°25S 20°48E 265 D4
Chicha Chad 16°57N 18°34E 259 E3
Chichagof I. U.S.A. 57°30N 135°30W 303 H14
Chichaoua Morocco 31°32N 8°44W 260 B3
Chichaoua □ Morocco 31°32N 8°45W 260 B3
Chichawatni Pakistan 30°32N 72°42E 242 D5
Chichén-Itzá Mexico 20°37N 88°35W 319 C7
Chicheng China 40°55N 115°55E 226 D8
Chichester U.K. 50°50N 0°47W 169 G7
Chichester Ra. Australia 22°12S 119°15E 278 D2
Chichi Hualien, Taiwan 23°44N 121°33E 225 C3
Chichi Nant'ou, Taiwan 23°49N 120°47E 225 C2
Chichibu Japan 35°59N 139°10E 223 A11
Chichibu-Tama △ Japan 35°52N 138°42E 223 B10
Ch'ich'ihaerh = Qiqihar China 47°26N 124°0E 219 B7
Chicholi India 22°1N 77°40E 242 H8
Chichou Taiwan 23°45N 120°33E 225 C2
Chickasaw ⏢ U.S.A. 34°26N 97°0W 314 D6
Chickasha U.S.A. 35°3N 97°58W 314 D6
Chicken U.S.A. 64°5N 141°56W 303 D12
Chiclana de la Frontera Spain 36°26N 6°9W 195 J4
Chiclayo Peru 6°42S 79°50W 330 B2
Chico U.S.A. 39°44N 121°50W 306 F5
Chico → Chubut, Argentina 44°0S 67°0W 336 B3
Chico → Santa Cruz, Argentina 50°0S 68°30W 336 D3
Chicoa Mozam. 15°36S 32°20E 269 F3
Chicomba Angola 14°10S 14°52E 265 E2
Chicomo Mozam. 24°31S 34°6E 271 B5
Chicomostoc Mexico 22°28N 102°46W 318 C4
Chiconi Mayotte 12°50S 45°7E 272 b
Chicontepec Mexico 20°58N 98°10W 319 C5
Chicopee U.S.A. 42°9N 72°37W 313 D12
Chicoutimi Canada 48°28N 71°5W 299 C5
Chicualacuala Mozam. 22°6S 31°42E 271 B5
Chicuma Angola 13°26S 14°50E 265 E2
Chidambaram India 11°20N 79°45E 245 J4
Chidenguele Mozam. 24°55S 34°11E 271 B5
Chidley, C. Canada 60°23N 64°26W 295 E19
Chiducuane Mozam. 24°35S 34°25E 271 B5
Chiede Angola 17°15S 16°22E 265 F3
Chiefland U.S.A. 29°29N 82°52W 317 F7
Chiefs Pt. Canada 44°41N 81°18W 312 B3
Chiehting Taiwan 22°54N 120°11E 225 D2
Chiem Hoa Vietnam 22°12N 105°17E 236 A5
Chiemsee Germany 47°53N 12°28E 179 H8
Chienchen Taiwan 22°35N 120°18E 225 D2
Chiengi Zambia 8°45S 29°10E 269 D2
Chiengmai = Chiang Mai Thailand 18°47N 98°59E 236 C2
Chiengo Angola 13°20S 21°55E 265 E4
Chienti → Italy 43°18N 13°45E 199 E10
Chienzui China 23°12N 113°22E 121 A3
Chieri Italy 45°1N 7°49E 198 C4
Chiers → France 49°39N 4°59E 173 C11
Chiesa in Valmalenco Italy 46°16N 9°51E 198 B6
Chiese → Italy 45°8N 10°25E 198 C7
Chieti Italy 42°21N 14°10E 199 F11
Chifeng China 42°18N 118°58E 227 C10
Chigasaki Japan 35°19N 139°24E 223 B11
Chigirin Ukraine 49°4N 32°38E 189 H7
Chignecto B. Canada 45°30N 64°40W 299 C7
Chignik U.S.A. 56°18N 158°24W 303 H8
Chigorodó Colombia 7°41N 76°42W 328 B2
Chiguana Bolivia 21°0S 67°58W 334 A2
Chigwell U.K. 51°37N 0°6E 169 F8
Chihli, G. of = Bo Hai China 39°0N 119°0E 227 E10
Ch'ihpen Taiwan 22°42N 121°2E 225 D3
Ch'ihshang Taiwan 23°7N 121°12E 225 C3
Chihsi = Jixi China 45°20N 130°50E 227 B16
Chihu Taiwan 23°54N 120°24E 225 C2
Chihuahua Mexico 28°38N 106°5W 318 B3
Chihuahua □ Mexico 28°30N 106°0W 318 B3
Chiili = Shieli Kazakhstan 44°20N 66°15E 217 D7
Chik Bollapur India 13°25N 77°45E 245 H3
Chik Sha China 22°17N 114°16E 122 B2
Chikalda India 21°24N 77°19E 244 D3
Chikhli Ahmadabad, India 20°45N 73°4E 244 D1
Chikhli Maharashtra, India 20°20N 76°18E 244 D3
Chikmagalur India 13°15N 75°45E 245 H2
Chiknayakanhalli India 13°26N 76°37E 245 H3
Chikodi India 16°26N 74°38E 245 F2
Chiku Taiwan 23°8N 120°7E 225 C2
Chikugo Japan 33°14N 130°28E 222 D2
Chikuma-Gawa → Japan 36°59N 138°35E 223 A10
Chikushino Japan 33°30N 130°30E 222 D2
Chikwawa Malawi 16°2S 34°50E 269 F3
Chila Angola 12°3S 14°29E 265 E2
Ch'ilaichu Shan Taiwan 24°5N 121°20E 225 B3
Chilanga Zambia 15°33S 28°16E 269 F2
Chilapa Mexico 17°36N 99°10W 319 D5
Chilas Pakistan 35°25N 74°5E 243 B6
Chilaw Sri Lanka 7°30N 79°50E 245 L4
Chilcotin → Canada 51°44N 122°23W 296 C4
Childers Australia 25°15S 152°17E 281 D5
Childersburg U.S.A. 33°16N 86°21W 316 B3
Children's Museum Boston, U.S.A. 116 c3
Children's Palace Beijing, China 114 b2
Childress U.S.A. 34°25N 100°13W 314 D4
Child's Hill U.K. 51°33N 0°12W 125 A2
Chile ■ S. Amer. 35°0S 72°0W 327 G3
Chile, Univ. de Chile 33°26S 70°39W 137 B2
Chile Basin Pac. Oc. 33°0S 80°0W 289 L20
Chile Chico Chile 46°33S 71°44W 336 C2
Chile Rise Pac. Oc. 38°0S 92°0W 289 L18
Chilecito Argentina 29°10S 67°30W 334 B2
Chilengue, Serra do Angola 13°18S 15°22E 265 E2
Chilesso Angola 11°35S 16°34E 265 E3
Chilete Peru 7°10S 78°50W 330 B2
Chilhowee U.S.A. 38°36N 93°51W 310 F3
Chilia, Braţul → Romania 45°14N 29°42E 183 E14
Chilibre Panama 9°9N 79°37W 320 c
Chilik = Shelek Kazakhstan 43°33N 78°17E 217 D9
Chililabombwe Zambia 12°18S 27°43E 269 E2
Chilim Pakistan 35°5N 75°5E 243 B6
Chilin = Jilin China 43°44N 126°30E 227 C14
Chiliomodi Greece 37°48N 22°51E 204 D4
Chilka L. India 19°40N 85°25E 244 E7
Chilko → Canada 52°0N 123°40W 296 C4
Chilko L. Canada 51°20N 124°10W 296 C4
Chilla Saroda India 28°35N 77°18E 120 B2
Chillagoe Australia 17°7S 144°33E 280 B3
Chillán Chile 36°40S 72°10W 334 D1
Chillicothe Ill., U.S.A. 40°55N 89°29W 310 D7
Chillicothe Mo., U.S.A. 39°48N 93°33W 310 E3
Chillicothe Ohio, U.S.A. 39°20N 82°59W 309 F12
Chilliwack Canada 49°10N 121°54W 296 D4
Chillum U.S.A. 38°56N 76°58W 143 B4
Chilly-Mazarin France 48°42N 2°17E 134 B2
Chilo India 27°25N 73°32E 242 F5
Chiloane, I. Mozam. 20°40S 34°55E 271 B5
Chiloé, I. de Chile 42°30S 73°50W 336 B2
Chiloé △ Chile 42°11S 73°59W 336 B2
Chilonda Angola 11°19S 16°12E 265 E3
Chilongo Angola 13°55S 16°35E 265 E3
Chilpancingo Mexico 17°33N 99°30W 319 D5
Chiltern Australia 36°10S 146°36E 283 D7
Chiltern Hills U.K. 51°40N 0°53W 169 F7
Chilton U.S.A. 44°2N 88°10W 308 C9
Chiluage Angola 9°30S 21°50E 265 D4
Chilubi Zambia 11°5S 29°58E 269 E2
Chilubula Zambia 10°14S 30°51E 269 E3
Chilumba Malawi 10°28S 34°12E 269 E3
Chilung Taiwan 25°3N 121°45E 225 A3
Chilwa, L. Malawi 15°15S 35°40E 269 F4
Chimalenga Angola 15°24S 16°58E 265 F3
Chimakudi India 25°47N 93°48E 241 C4
Chimaltitán Mexico 21°35N 103°50W 318 C4
Chimán Panama 8°45N 78°40W 320 E4
Chimanimani Zimbabwe 19°48S 32°52E 271 A5
Chimanimani △ Zimbabwe 19°48S 33°0E 271 A5
Chimay Belgium 50°3N 4°20E 170 D4
Chimayo U.S.A. 36°0N 105°56W 305 J11
Chimba Zambia 9°54S 31°28E 269 D3
Chimbay Uzbekistan 42°57N 59°47E 216 D5
Chimborazo Ecuador 1°29S 78°55W 328 D2
Chimborazo □ Ecuador 1°0S 78°40W 328 D2
Chimbote Peru 9°0S 78°35W 330 B2
Chimbu □ Papua N. G. 6°15S 144°50E 286 D3
Ch'imei Taiwan 23°12N 119°25E 225 C1
Ch'imei Yü Taiwan 23°13N 119°26E 225 C1
Chimichagua Colombia 9°15N 73°49W 328 B3
Chimkent = Shymkent Kazakhstan 42°18N 69°36E 217 D7
Chimoio Mozam. 19°4S 33°30E 269 F3
Chimpembe Zambia 9°31S 29°33E 269 D2
Chimur India 20°30N 79°23E 244 D4
Chin □ Burma 22°0N 93°0E 241 E4
Chin Hills Burma 22°30N 93°30E 241 D4
Chin Ling Shan = Qinling Shandi China 33°50N 108°10E 226 H5
China Mexico 25°42N 99°14W 319 B5
China ■ Asia 30°0N 110°0E 219 C6
China, Great Plain of Asia 35°0N 115°0E 210 E13
China Basin San Francisco, U.S.A. 136 c3
China Lake U.S.A. 35°44N 117°37W 307 K9
China Town Toronto, Canada 141 b1
Chinacota Colombia 7°37N 72°36W 328 B3
Chinan = Jinan China 36°38N 117°1E 226 F9
Chinandega Nic. 12°35N 87°12W 320 D2
Chinati Peak U.S.A. 29°57N 104°29W 314 G2
Chinatown Singapore 138 c2
Chinatown Boston, U.S.A. 116 c2
Chinatown Chicago, U.S.A. 119 f1
Chinatown Los Angeles, U.S.A. 127 a3
Chinatown New York, U.S.A. 132 e2
Chinatown San Francisco, U.S.A. 136 b2
Chincha Alta Peru 13°25S 76°7W 330 C2
Chinchaga → Canada 58°53N 118°20W 296 B5
Chincheros Peru 13°30S 73°44W 330 C3
Chinchilla Australia 26°45S 150°38E 281 D5
Chinchilla de Monte Aragón Spain 38°53N 1°40W 197 G3
Chincholi India 17°28N 77°26E 244 E3
Chinchorro, Banco Mexico 18°35N 87°22W 319 D7
Chinchou = Jinzhou China 41°5N 121°3E 227 D11
Chinchoua Gabon 0°1N 9°48E 264 B1
Chincoteague U.S.A. 37°56N 75°23W 309 G16
Chinde Mozam. 18°35S 36°30E 269 F4
Chindwin → Burma 21°26N 95°15E 241 E5
Chineni India 33°2N 75°15E 243 C6
Chinga Mozam. 15°13S 38°35E 269 F4
Chingaza △ Colombia 4°30N 73°40W 328 C3
Chingola Zambia 12°31S 27°53E 269 E2
Chingole Malawi 13°4S 34°17E 269 E3
Chingoni Mayotte 12°48S 45°8E 272 b
Chingpu Taiwan 23°28N 121°29E 225 C3
Ch'ingshui Changhua, Taiwan 24°16N 120°34E 225 B2
Chingshui Hualien, Taiwan 24°13N 121°41E 225 B3
Chingshui Ilan, Taiwan 24°39N 121°35E 225 B3
Ch'ingtao = Qingdao China 36°5N 120°20E 227 F11
Chinguar Angola 12°25S 16°45E 265 E3
Chinguetti Mauritania 20°25N 12°24W 260 D2
Chingune Mozam. 20°33S 34°58E 271 B5
Chingupota India 22°29N 88°14E 124 C1
Chinhanguanine Mozam. 25°21S 32°30E 271 C5
Chinhoyi Zimbabwe 17°20S 30°8E 269 F3
Chinhsien = Jinxian China 28°26N 116°17E 229 C11
Chini India 31°32N 78°15E 242 D8
Chiniot Pakistan 31°45N 73°0E 242 D5
Chínipas Mexico 27°23N 108°32W 318 B3
Chinji Pakistan 32°42N 72°22E 242 C5
Chinju = Jinju S. Korea 35°12N 128°2E 224 E4
Chinkai Afghan. 31°57N 67°26E 242 D2
Chinkapook Australia 35°11S 142°57E 282 C5
Chinkiang = Zhenjiang China 32°11N 119°26E 229 A12
Chinko → C.A.R. 4°50N 23°53E 264 B4
Chinle U.S.A. 36°9N 109°33W 305 H9
Ch'inlun Taiwan 22°32N 120°57E 225 D2
Chinmen Taiwan 24°26N 118°19E 225 a
Chinmen Tao Taiwan 24°26N 118°22E 225 a
Chinna Cr. → Pakistan 24°50N 67°0E 123 B2
Chinnamanur India 9°50N 77°24E 245 K3
Chinnampo = Namp'o N. Korea 38°52N 125°10E 224 C2
Chino Japan 35°59N 138°9E 223 B10
Chino Calif., U.S.A. 34°1N 117°41W 307 L9
Chino Valley U.S.A. 34°45N 112°27W 305 J7
Chinois, Quartier Montréal, Canada 130 b2
Chinon France 47°10N 0°15E 172 E7
Chinook U.S.A. 48°35N 109°14W 304 B9
Chinook Trough Pac. Oc. 44°0N 175°0W 288 C10
Chinoya Zambia 13°55S 23°16E 265 E4
Chinsali Zambia 10°30S 32°2E 269 E3
Chinshan Taiwan 25°13N 121°38E 225 A3
Chinsura = Chunchura India 22°53N 88°27E 243 H13
Chintalapudi India 17°4N 80°59E 244 F5
Chintamani India 13°26N 78°3E 245 H4
Chinwangtao = Qinhuangdao China 39°56N 119°30E 227 E10
Chióggia Italy 45°13N 12°17E 199 C9
Chíos = Hios Greece 38°27N 26°9E 205 C8
Chipata Zambia 13°38S 32°28E 269 E3
Chipei Tao Taiwan 23°45N 119°37E 225 C1
Chiperceni Moldova 47°31N 28°50E 183 C13
Chipindo Angola 13°49S 15°48E 265 E3
Chipinge Zimbabwe 20°13S 32°28E 269 G3
Chipinge △ Zimbabwe 20°14S 33°0E 269 G3
Chipiona Spain 36°44N 6°26W 195 J4
Chipley U.S.A. 30°47N 85°32W 316 E4
Chiplun India 17°31N 73°34E 244 F1
Chipman Canada 46°6N 65°53W 299 C6
Chipoka Malawi 13°57S 34°28E 269 E3
Chippenham U.K. 51°27N 2°6W 169 F5
Chippewa → U.S.A. 44°25N 92°5W 308 C7
Chippewa Falls U.S.A. 44°56N 91°24W 308 C8
Chipping Norton U.K. 51°56N 1°32W 169 F6
Chiprovtsi Bulgaria 43°24N 22°52E 202 C6
Chiputneticook Lakes N. Amer. 45°35N 67°35W 309 C20
Chiputo = Vila Vasco da Gama Mozam. 14°54S 32°14E 269 E3
Chiquelequele Angola 16°44S 19°25E 265 F3
Chiquián Peru 10°10S 77°0W 330 C2
Chiquibul △ Belize 16°49N 88°52W 320 C2
Chiquihuite, Cerro Mexico 19°32N 99°8W 128 A2
Chiquimula Guatemala 14°51N 89°37W 320 D2
Chiquinquira Colombia 5°37N 73°50W 328 B3
Chiquitos, Llanos de Bolivia 18°0S 61°30W 331 D5
Chir → Russia 48°30N 43°0E 191 F6
Chira → Peru 4°54S 81°8W 328 D1
Chirala India 15°50N 80°26E 245 G5
Chiramba Mozam. 16°55S 34°39E 269 F3
Chirawa India 28°14N 75°42E 242 E6
Chirayinkil India 8°41N 76°49E 245 K3
Chirchiq Uzbekistan 41°29N 69°35E 217 D7
Chiredzi Zimbabwe 21°0S 31°38E 271 B5
Chirfa Niger 20°55N 12°22E 259 D2
Chirgua → Venezuela 8°54N 67°58W 328 B4
Chiribiquete △ Colombia 0°31N 72°50W 328 C3
Chiricahua ⏢ U.S.A. 32°0N 109°20W 305 K9
Chiricahua Peak U.S.A. 31°51N 109°18W 305 L9
Chirikof I. U.S.A. 55°50N 155°40W 300 D8
Chiriquí, G. de Panama 8°0N 82°10W 320 E3
Chiriquí, L. de Panama 9°10N 82°0W 320 E3
Chirisa △ Zimbabwe 17°53S 28°15E 269 F2
Chirivira Falls Zimbabwe 21°10S 32°12E 269 G3
Chirmiri India 23°15N 82°20E 243 H10
Chirnogi Romania 44°7N 26°32E 183 F11
Chirongui Mayotte 12°55S 45°9E 272 b
Chirpan Bulgaria 42°10N 25°19E 203 D9
Chirripó Grande, Cerro Costa Rica 9°29N 83°29W 320 E3
Chirundu Zimbabwe 16°3S 28°50E 271 A4
Chisamba Zambia 14°55S 28°20E 269 E2
Chisapani Nepal 28°37N 81°16E 243 E9
Chisasa Zambia 12°6S 25°30E 265 E5
Chisasibi Canada 53°50N 79°0W 298 B4
Ch'ishan Taiwan 22°44N 120°31E 225 D2
Ch'ishan Hsi → Taiwan 22°51N 120°28E 225 C2
Chisholm Alta., Canada 54°55N 114°10W 296 C6
Chisholm Minn., U.S.A. 47°29N 92°53W 308 B7
Chishtian Mandi Pakistan 29°50N 72°55E 242 E5
Chishui China 28°30N 105°42E 228 C5
Chishui He → China 28°49N 105°50E 228 C5
Chisimaio = Kismaayo Somali Rep. 0°22S 42°32E 267 E5
Chisimba Falls Zambia 10°12S 30°56E 269 E3
Chişinău Moldova 47°2N 28°50E 183 C13
Chişinău ✈ (KIV) Moldova 47°3N 28°46E 183 C13
Chişineu Criş Romania 46°32N 21°37E 182 D6
Chislehurst U.K. 51°24N 0°6E 125 B4
Chisone → Italy 44°49N 7°25E 198 D4
Chisos Mts. U.S.A. 29°5N 103°15W 314 G3
Chissengue Angola 9°13S 20°34E 265 D4
Chissilo Angola 13°48S 16°31E 265 E3
Chistochina U.S.A. 62°34N 144°40W 303 E11
Chistopol Russia 55°25N 50°38E 190 C10
Chiswick U.K. 51°29N 0°16W 125 B2
Chiswick House U.K. 51°28N 0°15W 125 B2
Chita Colombia 6°11N 72°28W 328 B3
Chita Russia 52°0N 113°35E 215 D12
Chitado Angola 17°10S 14°8E 265 F2
Chitaldrug = Chitradurga India 14°14N 76°24E 245 G3
Chitan Taiwan 24°35N 121°29E 225 B3
Chitanda → Angola 16°1S 15°12E 265 F3
Chitapur India 17°10N 77°5E 244 F3
Chitembo Angola 13°30S 16°50E 265 E3
Chitina U.S.A. 61°31N 144°26W 303 F11
Chitipa Malawi 9°41S 33°19E 269 D3
Chitose Hokkaidō, Japan 42°49N 141°39E 220 C10
Chitose Kanagawa, Japan 35°33N 139°37E 140 B2
Chitradurga India 14°14N 76°24E 245 G3
Chitrakot India 19°10N 81°40E 244 E5
Chitral Pakistan 35°50N 71°56E 240 B3
Chitralada Palace Thailand 13°45N 100°31E 113 B2
Chitravati → India 14°45N 78°15E 245 G4
Chitré Panama 7°59N 80°27W 320 E3
Chittagong Bangla. 22°19N 91°48E 241 D3
Chittagong □ Bangla. 24°5N 91°0E 241 C3
Chittaurgarh India 24°52N 74°38E 242 G6
Chittoor India 13°15N 79°5E 245 H4
Chittur India 10°40N 76°45E 245 J3
Chitungwiza Zimbabwe 18°0S 31°6E 269 F3
Chiuju Taiwan 22°44N 120°29E 225 D2
Chiumbe → Dem. Rep. of the Congo 6°59S 21°12E 265 D4
Chiumbo Angola 12°29S 16°8E 265 E3
Chiume Angola 15°3S 21°14E 265 F4
Chiusi Italy 43°1N 11°57E 199 E8
Chiva Spain 39°27N 0°41W 197 F4
Chivacoa Venezuela 10°10N 68°54W 328 A4
Chivasso Italy 45°11N 7°53E 198 C4
Chivay Peru 15°40S 71°35W 330 D3
Chive Bolivia 12°23S 68°35W 330 C4
Chivhu Zimbabwe 19°2S 30°52E 269 F3
Chivilcoy Argentina 34°55S 60°0W 334 C4
Chiwanda Tanzania 11°23S 34°55E 269 E3
Chixi China 22°0N 112°58E 229 G9
Chiyoda Tokyo, Japan 140 b4
Chizarira Zimbabwe 17°36S 27°45E 269 F2
Chizarira △ Zimbabwe 17°44S 27°52E 269 F2
Chizela Zambia 13°8S 25°0E 265 E5
Chizu Japan 35°16N 134°14E 222 B6
Chkalov = Orenburg Russia 51°45N 55°6E 186 D10
Chkalova Russia 55°39N 37°56E 129 C5
Chkolovsk Russia 56°50N 43°10E 190 B6
Chloride U.S.A. 35°25N 114°12W 307 K12
Chlumec nad Cidlinou Czech Rep. 50°9N 15°29E 180 A8
Chmielnik Poland 50°37N 20°43E 185 H7
Cho Bo Vietnam 20°46N 105°10E 228 G5
Cho-do N. Korea 38°30N 124°40E 224 C2
Cho Phuoc Hai Vietnam 10°26N 107°18E 237 G6
Choa Chu Kang Singapore 1°22N 103°41E 138 A2
Choba Kenya 2°30N 38°5E 268 B4
Chobe △ Botswana 18°37S 24°23E 270 A4
Choboty Russia 55°39N 37°21E 129 C2
Choc B. St. Lucia 14°3N 60°59W 323 m
Choch'i Taiwan 23°20N 121°16E 225 C3
Chocianów Poland 51°27N 15°55E 185 G2
Chociwel Poland 53°29N 15°21E 184 E2
Chocó □ Colombia 6°0N 77°0W 328 B2
Chocolate Mts. U.S.A. 33°15N 115°15W 307 M11
Chocontá Colombia 5°9N 73°41W 328 B3
Choctawhatchee → U.S.A. 30°25N 86°8W 316 E3
Choctawhatchee B. U.S.A. 30°20N 86°20W 317 E3
Chodavaram Andhra Pradesh, India 17°50N 82°57E 244 F6
Chodavaram Andhra Pradesh, India 17°27N 81°46E 244 F5
Chodecz Poland 52°24N 19°2E 185 F6
Chodov Czech Rep. 50°15N 12°45E 180 A5
Chodov u Prahy Czech Rep. 50°1N 14°30E 135 B3
Chodzież Poland 52°58N 16°58E 185 F3
Choele Choel Argentina 39°11S 65°40W 336 A3
Chōfu Japan 35°38N 139°32E 140 B2
Choiseul St. Lucia 13°47N 61°3W 323 m
Choiseul Solomon Is. 7°0S 156°40E 287 L9
Choisy-le-Roi France 48°46N 2°24E 134 B3
Choix Mexico 26°43N 108°17W 318 B3
Chojna Poland 52°58N 14°25E 185 F1
Chojnice Poland 53°42N 17°32E 184 E4
Chojnów Poland 51°18N 15°58E 185 G2
Chok Chai Thailand 14°44N 102°10E 236 E4
Chōkai-San Japan 39°6N 140°3E 220 E10
Choke Canyon Res. U.S.A. 28°30N 98°20W 314 G5
Choke Mts. Ethiopia 11°18N 37°15E 257 E4
Chokurdakh Russia 70°38N 147°55E 215 B15
Chokwé Mozam. 24°32S 32°59E 271 B5
Cholame U.S.A. 35°44N 120°18W 306 K6
Cholan Taiwan 24°18N 120°49E 225 B2
Cholet France 47°4N 0°52W 172 E6
Cholguan Chile 37°10S 72°3W 334 D1
Choloma Honduras 15°37N 87°57W 320 C2
Cholpon-Ata Kyrgyzstan 42°40N 77°6E 217 D9
Cholupice Czech Rep. 49°59N 14°27E 135 C2
Choluteca Honduras 13°20N 87°14W 320 D2
Choluteca → Honduras 13°0N 87°20W 320 D2
Chom Bung Thailand 13°37N 99°36E 236 F2
Chom Thong Bangkok, Thailand 13°41N 100°29E 113 B1
Chom Thong Chiang Mai, Thailand 18°25N 98°41E 236 C2
Choma Zambia 16°48S 26°59E 269 F2
Chomolungma = Everest, Mt. Nepal 28°5N 86°58E 243 E12
Chomun India 27°15N 75°40E 242 F6
Chomutov Czech Rep. 50°28N 13°23E 180 A6
Chon Buri Thailand 13°21N 101°1E 236 F3
Chon Thanh Vietnam 11°24N 106°36E 237 G6
Chone Ecuador 0°40S 80°0W 328 D2
Chong Kai Cambodia 13°57N 103°35E 236 F4
Chong Mek Thailand 15°10N 105°27E 236 E5
Chong Pang Singapore 1°26N 103°49E 138 A2
Chong Phangan Thailand 9°39N 100°0E 237 b
Chong Samui Thailand 9°21N 99°50E 237 b
Chongde China 30°32N 120°26E 229 B13
Ch'ŏngjin N. Korea 41°47N 129°50E 224 B4
Chŏngju N. Korea 39°40N 125°5E 224 C2
Chongli China 40°58N 115°15E 226 D8
Chongming China 31°38N 121°23E 229 B13
Chongming Dao China 31°40N 121°30E 229 B13
Chongoroi Angola 13°37S 14°1E 265 E2
Chongoyape Peru 6°35S 79°25W 330 B2
Chŏngp'yŏng N. Korea 39°47N 127°23E 224 C3
Chongqing Chongqing, China 29°35N 106°25E 228 C6
Chongqing Sichuan, China 30°38N 103°40E 228 B4
Chongqing Shi □ China 30°0N 108°0E 228 C6
Chongren China 27°46N 116°3E 229 D11
Chonguene Mozam. 25°3S 33°49E 271 C5
Chongwe Zambia 15°21S 28°42E 269 F2
Chongwen Beijing, China 114 c2
Chongyi China 25°45N 114°29E 229 E10
Chongzuo China 22°23N 107°20E 228 F6
Chonos, Arch. de los Chile 45°0S 75°0W 336 C2
Chop Ukraine 48°26N 22°12E 182 B7
Chopda India 21°20N 75°15E 244 D2
Chopim → Brazil 25°35S 53°5W 335 B5
Chopin Museum Warsaw, Poland 142 b2
Chor Pakistan 25°31N 69°46E 242 G3
Chora Greece 37°3N 21°42E 204 D3
Chora Sfakion Greece 35°15N 24°9E 207 E5
Chorbat La India 34°42N 76°37E 243 B7
Chorley U.K. 53°39N 2°38W 168 D5
Chorna Ukraine 47°36N 29°20E 183 C14
Chornaya → Russia 55°41N 38°10E 129 B6
Chornobyl Ukraine 51°20N 30°15E 177 C16
Chornomorske Ukraine 45°31N 32°40E 189 K7
Chorolque, Cerro Bolivia 20°59S 66°5W 334 A2
Choroszcz Poland 53°10N 22°59E 185 E9
Chorregon Australia 22°40S 143°32E 280 C3
Chorrillos Peru 12°10S 77°1W 124 C2
Chortkiv Ukraine 49°2N 25°46E 177 D13
Chorzele Poland 53°15N 20°55E 185 E7
Chorzów Poland 50°18N 18°57E 185 H5
Chos-Malal Argentina 37°20S 70°15W 334 D1
Ch'osan N. Korea 40°50N 125°47E 224 B2
Chosheta Shan Taiwan 23°50N 121°6E 225 C3
Chōshi Japan 35°45N 140°51E 223 B12
Choshui Hsi → Taiwan 23°50N 120°15E 225 C2
Choszczno Poland 53°7N 15°25E 185 E2
Chota Peru 6°33S 78°39W 330 B2
Choteau U.S.A. 47°49N 112°11W 304 C7
Chotěboř Czech Rep. 49°43N 15°40E 180 B8
Chotila India 22°23N 71°15E 242 H4
Chotta Udepur India 22°19N 74°1E 242 H6
Choûm Mauritania 21°11N 13°3W 260 D2
Chounguі Mayotte 12°57S 45°8E 272 b
Chowchilla U.S.A. 37°7N 120°16W 306 H6
Chowpatty Beach Mumbai, India 130 b1
Choybalsan Mongolia 48°4N 114°30E 219 B6
Choyr Mongolia 46°24N 108°30E 215 E11
Chrisman U.S.A. 39°48N 87°41W 311 E9
Christ Church Cathedral Montréal, Canada 130 c2
Christburg = Dzierzgoń Poland 53°58N 19°20E 184 E6
Christchurch N.Z. 43°33S 172°47E 285 D7
Christchurch Dorset, U.K. 50°44N 1°47W 169 G6
Christian I. Canada 44°50N 80°12W 312 B4
Christian Quarter Jerusalem 123 b3
Christian Sd. U.S.A. 55°56N 134°40W 303 J14
Christiana Jamaica 18°10N 77°29W 320 a
Christiana North West, S. Africa 27°52S 25°8E 270 C4
Christiansborg Slot Copenhagen, Denmark 118 c2
Christiansfeld Denmark 55°21N 9°29E 163 J3
Christianshåb = Qasigiannguit Greenland 68°50N 51°18W 154 D5
Christianshavn Denmark 55°40N 12°35E 118 A3
Christiansted U.S. Virgin Is. 17°45N 64°42W 321 C7
Christie B. Canada 62°32N 111°10W 297 A6
Christina → Canada 56°40N 111°3W 297 B6
Christmas Cr. → Australia 18°29S 125°23E 278 C4
Christmas I. = Kiritimati Kiribati 1°58N 157°27W 289 G12
Christmas I. Ind. Oc. 10°30S 105°40E 273 F9
Christoffel Nat. Park △ Neth. Ant. 12°21N 69°8W 322 g
Christopher U.S.A. 37°59N 89°3W 310 G7
Christopher, L. Australia 24°49S 127°42E 279 D4
Christyakovo = Thorez Ukraine 48°4N 38°34E 189 H10
Chrudim Czech Rep. 49°58N 15°43E 180 B8
Chrysler Building New York, U.S.A. 132 c2
Chrzanów Malopolskie, Poland 50°10N 19°21E 185 H6
Chrzanów Warszawa, Poland 52°13N 20°53E 142 B1
Chtimba Malawi 10°35S 34°13E 269 E3
Chū = Shū Kazakhstan 43°36N 73°42E 217 D8
Chū = Shū → Kazakhstan 45°0N 67°44E 217 D7
Chu → Vietnam 19°53N 105°45E 236 C5
Chu Lai Vietnam 15°28N 108°45E 236 E7
Chuadanga Bangla. 23°38N 88°51E 241 D2
Chuak, Ko Thailand 9°28N 99°41E 237 b
Ch'uanchou = Quanzhou China 24°55N 118°34E 229 E12
Chüanchow = Quanzhou China 24°55N 118°34E 229 E12
Chuangwei Taiwan 24°45N 121°47E 225 B3
Chuankou China 34°20N 110°59E 226 G6
Chuathbaluk U.S.A. 61°40N 159°15W 303 F8
Chubarovka = Pology Ukraine 47°29N 36°15E 189 J9
Chubbuck U.S.A. 42°55N 112°28W 304 E7
Chūbu □ Japan 36°45N 137°30E 223 A9
Chubu-Sangaku △ Japan 36°30N 137°40E 223 A9
Chubut □ Argentina 43°30S 69°0W 336 B3
Chubut → Argentina 43°20S 65°5W 336 B3
Chuch'i Taiwan 23°31N 120°33E 225 C2

Chuchi L. *Canada* 55°12N 124°30W **296** B4
Chuchow = Zhuzhou *China* 27°49N 113°12E **229** D9
Chuda *India* 22°29N 71°41E **242** H4
Chudovo *Russia* 59°10N 31°41E **188** C6
Chudskoye, Ozero *Russia* 58°13N 27°30E **188** C4
Chuen Lung *China* 22°23N 114°6E **122** A1
Chugach Mts. *U.S.A.* 60°45N 147°0W **303** F11
Chuginadak I. *U.S.A.* 52°50N 169°45W **303** K5
Chūgoku □ *Japan* 35°0N 133°0E **222** C5
Chūgoku-Sanchi *Japan* 35°0N 133°0E **222** B5
Chuguyev = Chuhuyiv *Ukraine* 49°55N 36°45E **189** H9
Chugwater *U.S.A.* 41°46N 104°50W **304** F11
Chuhuyiv *Ukraine* 49°55N 36°45E **189** H9
Chuk Kok *China* 22°20N 114°15E **122** A2
Chuka *Kenya* 0°20S 37°39E **268** C4
Chukchi Plateau *Arctic* 78°0N 165°0W **150** B17
Chukchi Sea *Russia* 68°0N 175°0W **215** C19
Chukotskiy Mys *Russia* 64°14N 173°8W **300** C5
Chukotskiy Poluostrov *Russia* 66°0N 174°0W **300** B5
Chukotskoye Nagorye *Russia* 68°0N 175°0E **215** C18
Chula *U.S.A.* 31°33N 83°32W **316** D6
Chula Vista *U.S.A.* 32°38N 117°5W **307** N9
Chulalongkom Univ. *Thailand* 13°44N 100°31E **113** B2
Chulband → *India* 20°40N 79°54E **244** D4
Ch'ulin *Taiwan* 22°8N 120°42E **225** D2
Chulucanas *Peru* 5°8S 80°10W **330** B1
Chulumani *Bolivia* 16°24S 67°31W **330** D4
Chulym → *Russia* 57°43N 83°51E **214** D9
Chum Phae *Thailand* 16°40N 102°6E **236** D4
Chum Saeng *Thailand* 15°55N 100°15E **236** E3
Chuma *Bolivia* 15°24S 68°56W **330** D4
Chumar *India* 32°40N 78°35E **243** C8
Chumbicha *Argentina* 29°0S 66°10W **334** B2
Chumerna *Bulgaria* 42°45N 25°55E **203** D9
Chumikan *Russia* 54°40N 135°10E **215** D14
Chumphon *Thailand* 10°35N 99°14E **237** G2
Chumpi *Peru* 15°4S 73°46W **330** D3
Chumuare *Mozam.* 14°31S 31°50E **269** E3
Chuna → *Russia* 57°47N 94°37E **215** D10
Chun'an *Zhejiang, China* 29°35N 119°3E **229** C12
Chunan *Taiwan* 24°41N 120°52E **225** B2
Chuncheon *S. Korea* 37°58N 127°44E **224** D3
Chunchura *India* 22°53N 88°27E **243** H13
Chunga *Zambia* 15°0S 26°2E **269** F2
Chungcheongbuk-do □ *S. Korea* 36°45N 128°0E **224** D4
Chungcheonnam-do □ *S. Korea* 36°30N 127°0E **224** D3
Ch'ungch'ing = Chongqing *China* 29°35N 106°25E **228** C6
Chunggang-ŭp *N. Korea* 41°48N 126°48E **224** B3
Chungho *Taiwan* 25°0N 121°28E **225** A3
Chunghwa *N. Korea* 38°52N 125°47E **224** C2
Chungju *S. Korea* 36°58N 127°58E **224** D3
Chungking = Chongqing *China* 29°35N 106°25E **228** C6
Chungli *Taiwan* 24°57N 121°13E **225** B3
Chungpu *Taiwan* 23°26N 120°31E **225** C2
Chungt'iaoshan = Zhongtiao Shan *China* 35°0N 111°10E **226** G6
Chungtungwan *Taiwan* 24°31N 120°40E **225** B2
Chungyang Shanmo *Taiwan* 23°10N 121°0E **225** C3
Chunian *Pakistan* 30°57N 74°0E **242** D6
Chunya *Tanzania* 8°30S 33°27E **269** D3
Chunyang *China* 43°38N 129°23E **227** C15
Chuō *Tokyo, Japan* **140** b5
Chupara B. *Trin. & Tob.* 10°48N 61°22W **323** t
Chupara Pt. *Trin. & Tob.* 10°49N 61°22W **323** t
Chupei *Taiwan* 24°50N 121°0E **225** B3
Chuquibamba *Peru* 15°47S 72°44W **330** D3
Chuquibambilla *Peru* 14°7S 72°41W **330** C3
Chuquicamata *Chile* 22°15S 69°0W **334** A2
Chuquisaca □ *Bolivia* 20°30S 63°30W **331** E5
Chur *Switz.* 46°52N 9°32E **179** J5
Churachandpur *India* 24°20N 93°40E **241** C4
Church End *U.K.* 51°35N 0°11W **125** A2
Church of our Lady = Frauenkirche *Munich, Germany* **131** b2
Church Stretton *U.K.* 52°32N 2°48W **169** E5
Churchill *Vic., Australia* 38°19S 146°25E **283** E7
Churchill *Man., Canada* 58°47N 94°11W **297** B10
Churchill → *Man., Canada* 58°47N 94°12W **297** B10
Churchill → *Nfld. & L., Canada* 53°19N 60°10W **299** B7
Churchill, C. *Canada* 58°46N 93°12W **297** B10
Churchill Falls *Canada* 53°36N 64°19W **299** B7
Churchill L. *Canada* 55°55N 108°20W **297** B7
Churchill Pk. *Canada* 58°10N 125°10W **296** B3
Churchtown *Ireland* 53°18N 6°16W **120** B2
Churdan *U.S.A.* 42°9N 94°29W **310** D2
Churki *India* 23°50N 83°12E **243** H10
Churu *India* 28°20N 74°50E **242** E6
Churubusco *U.S.A.* 41°14N 85°19W **311** C11
Churún Merú = Angel Falls *Venezuela* 5°57N 62°30W **329** B5
Chushal *India* 33°40N 78°40E **243** C8
Chushan *Taiwan* 23°45N 120°40E **225** C2
Chuska Mts. *U.S.A.* 36°15N 108°50W **305** H9
Chusovoy *Russia* 58°22N 57°50E **186** C10
Chusovskoy Zavod = Chusovoy *Russia* 58°22N 57°50E **186** C10
Chuspipata *Bolivia* 16°18S 67°48W **330** D4
Chust = Khust *Ukraine* 48°10N 23°18E **183** B8
Chust *Uzbekistan* 41°0N 71°13E **217** D8
Chute-aux-Outardes *Canada* 49°7N 68°24W **299** C6
Chutung *Taiwan* 24°44N 121°5E **225** B3
Chuuk = Truk *Micronesia* 7°25N 151°46E **287** T17
Chuuk Lagoon *Micronesia* 7°24N 151°45E **287** T18
Chuvash Republic = Chuvashia □ *Russia* 55°30N 47°0E **190** C8
Chuvashia □ *Russia* 55°30N 47°0E **190** C8
Chuwārtah *Iraq* 35°43N 45°34E **213** E11
Chuwei *Taiwan* 25°6N 121°14E **225** A3
Chuxiong *China* 25°2N 101°28E **228** E3
Chüy *Kyrgyzstan* 42°55N 75°15E **217** D9
Chuy *Uruguay* 33°41S 53°27W **335** C5
Chüy □ *Kyrgyzstan* 42°25N 75°16E **217** D9
Chuzenji-Ko *Japan* 36°44N 139°27E **223** A11
Chuzhou *China* 32°19N 118°20E **229** A12
Chynadiyeve *Ukraine* 48°29N 22°50E **183** B7
Ci Xian *China* 36°20N 114°25E **226** F8
Ciacova *Romania* 45°35N 21°10E **182** E6
Ciadâr-Lunga *Moldova* 46°3N 28°51E **183** D13
Ciales *Puerto Rico* 18°20N 66°28W **321** b
Ciamis *Indonesia* 7°20S 108°21E **235** D3
Ciampino *Italy* 41°47N 12°36E **136** C2
Ciampino ✕ (CIA) *Italy* 41°47N 12°35E **136** C2
Cianjur *Indonesia* 6°49S 107°8E **234** D3
Cianorte *Brazil* 23°37S 52°37W **335** A5
Cibola *U.S.A.* 33°17N 114°42W **307** M12
Çiçekdağı *Turkey* 39°36N 34°24E **212** C6
Cicero *U.S.A.* 41°51N 87°44W **119** B2
Cicero Dantas *Brazil* 10°36S 38°23W **332** D4
Ciceron *St. Lucia* 13°59N 61°1W **323** m
Cicia *Fiji* 17°45S 179°18W **287** A3
Cidacos → *Spain* 42°21N 1°38W **196** C3
Cidade de Minas = Belo Horizonte *Brazil* 19°55S 43°56W **333** E3
Cide *Turkey* 41°53N 33°1E **212** B5
Cidra *Puerto Rico* 18°11N 66°10W **321** b
Ciechanów *Poland* 52°52N 20°38E **185** F7
Ciechanowiec *Poland* 52°40N 22°31E **185** F9
Ciechocinek *Poland* 52°53N 18°45E **185** F5
Ciego de Ávila *Cuba* 21°50N 78°50W **320** B4
Ciénaga *Colombia* 11°1N 74°15W **328** A3
Ciénaga de Oro *Colombia* 8°53N 75°37W **328** B2
Ciénagas del Catatumbo △ *Venezuela* 9°26N 72°8W **328** B3
Cienfuegos *Cuba* 22°10N 80°30W **320** B3
Cierp-Gaud *France* 42°55N 0°40E **174** F4
Cíes, Is. *Spain* 42°12N 8°55W **194** C2
Cieszanów *Poland* 50°14N 23°8E **185** H10
Cieszyn *Poland* 49°45N 18°35E **185** J5
Cieza *Spain* 38°17N 1°23W **197** G3
Çifteler *Turkey* 39°22N 31°2E **212** C4
Cifuentes *Spain* 40°47N 2°37W **196** E2
Cihanbeyli *Turkey* 38°40N 32°55E **212** C5
Cihuatlán *Mexico* 19°14N 104°35W **318** D4
Cijara, Embalse de *Spain* 39°18N 4°52W **195** F6
Cijara ⌂ *Spain* 39°18N 4°35W **195** F6
Cijulang *Indonesia* 7°42S 108°27E **231** G13
Cilacap *Indonesia* 7°43S 109°0E **235** D3
Cilandak *Indonesia* 6°17S 106°47E **122** B1
Cilao, Cirque de *Réunion* 21°7S 55°28E **272** f
Cilaos *Réunion* 21°8S 55°27E **272** f
Çıldır *Turkey* 41°7N 43°8E **213** B10
Çıldır Gölü *Turkey* 41°5N 43°15E **213** B10
Cilento e Vallo di Diano △ *Italy* 40°15N 15°20E **201** B8
Cili *China* 29°30N 111°8E **229** C8
Cilibia *Romania* 45°4N 27°4E **183** E12
Cilicia *Turkey* 36°30N 35°0E **250** B5
Cilincing *Indonesia* 6°6S 106°54E **122** A2
Ciliwung → *Indonesia* 6°6S 106°47E **122** B2
Cill Airne = Killarney *Ireland* 52°4N 9°30W **166** D2
Cill Chainnigh = Kilkenny *Ireland* 52°39N 7°15W **166** D4
Cill Dara = Kildare *Ireland* 53°9N 6°55W **166** C5
Cill Mhantáin = Wicklow *Ireland* 52°59N 6°3W **166** D5
Cilo Dağı *Turkey* 37°28N 43°55E **213** D10
Cima *U.S.A.* 35°14N 115°30W **307** K11
Cimarron *Kans., U.S.A.* 37°48N 100°21W **308** G3
Cimarron *N. Mex., U.S.A.* 36°31N 104°55W **305** H11
Cimarron → *U.S.A.* 36°10N 96°16W **314** C6
Čimice *Czech Rep.* 50°8N 14°25E **135** B2
Cimişlia *Moldova* 46°34N 28°44E **183** D13
Cimone, Mte. *Italy* 44°12N 10°42E **198** D7
Çinar *Turkey* 37°46N 40°19E **213** D9
Çınarcık *Turkey* 40°38N 29°5E **203** F13
Cinaruco-Capanaparo △ *Venezuela* 6°51N 67°32W **328** B4
Cinca → *Spain* 41°26N 0°21E **196** D5
Cincar *Bos.-H.* 43°55N 17°5E **182** G2
Cincinnati *Iowa, U.S.A.* 40°38N 92°56W **310** D4
Cincinnati *Ohio, U.S.A.* 39°9N 84°27W **311** E12
Cincinnati-Northern Kentucky Int. ✕ (CVG) *U.S.A.* 39°3N 84°40W **311** E12
Cincinnatus *U.S.A.* 42°33N 75°54W **313** D9
Çine *Turkey* 37°37N 28°2E **205** D10
Cinecittà *Italy* 41°51N 12°34E **136** B2
Ciney *Belgium* 50°18N 5°5E **170** D5
Cíngoli *Italy* 43°23N 13°10E **199** E10
Cinigiano *Italy* 42°53N 11°24E **199** F8
Cinisello Bálsamo *Italy* 45°33N 9°13E **129** A2
Cinkota *Hungary* 47°31N 19°14E **117** A3
Cinque I. *India* 11°16N 92°42E **245** J11
Cinto, Mte. *France* 42°24N 8°54E **175** F12
Cintra, G. de *W. Sahara* 23°0N 16°15W **260** D1
Cintruénigo *Spain* 42°5N 1°49W **196** C3
Ciocile *Romania* 44°49N 27°14E **183** F12
Ciolăneşti din Deal *Romania* 44°19N 25°5E **183** F10
Ciorani *Romania* 44°45N 26°25E **183** F11
Čiovo *Croatia* 43°30N 16°17E **199** E13
Cipero → *Trin. & Tob.* 10°16N 61°28W **323** t
Cipete *Indonesia* 6°15S 106°47E **122** B1
Cipó *Brazil* 11°6S 38°31W **332** D4
Cipolletti *Argentina* 38°56S 67°59W **336** A3
Circeo, Mte. *Italy* 41°14N 13°3E **200** A6
Çirçir *Turkey* 40°3N 36°47E **212** C7
Circle *Alaska, U.S.A.* 65°50N 144°4W **303** D11
Circle *Mont., U.S.A.* 47°25N 105°35W **304** C11
Circleville *U.S.A.* 39°36N 82°57W **309** F12
Circular Reef *Papua N. G.* 3°25S 147°47E **286** B4
Cirebon *Indonesia* 6°45S 108°32E **235** D3
Ciremay *Indonesia* 6°55S 108°27E **235** D3
Cirencester *U.K.* 51°43N 1°57W **169** F6
Cireşu *Romania* 44°47N 22°31E **182** F7
Cirey-sur-Vezouze *France* 48°35N 6°57E **173** D13
Ciriè *Italy* 45°14N 7°36E **198** C4
Cirium *Cyprus* 34°40N 32°53E **207** F8
Cirò *Italy* 39°23N 17°4E **201** C10
Cirò Marina *Italy* 39°22N 17°8E **201** C10
Ciron → *France* 44°36N 0°18W **174** D3
Cisco *U.S.A.* 32°23N 98°59W **314** E5
Cislău *Romania* 45°14N 26°20E **183** E11
Cisna *Poland* 49°12N 22°20E **185** J9
Cisnădie *Romania* 45°42N 24°9E **183** E9
Cisne *U.S.A.* 38°31N 88°26W **311** F8
Cisneros *Colombia* 6°33N 75°4W **328** B2
Cissna Park *U.S.A.* 40°34N 87°54W **311** D9
Cisterna di Latina *Italy* 41°35N 12°49E **200** A5
Cisternino *Italy* 40°44N 17°25E **201** B10
Cistierna *Spain* 42°48N 5°7W **194** C5
Citadel = Kastellet *Copenhagen, Denmark* **118** a3
Citadel *Budapest, Hungary* **117** c2
Citaré → *Brazil* 1°11N 54°41W **329** C7
Citeli-Ckaro = Tsiteli-Tsqaro *Georgia* 41°33N 46°0E **191** K8
Citlaltépetl = Orizaba, Pico de *Mexico* 18°58N 97°15W **319** D5
Citra *U.S.A.* 29°25N 82°7W **317** F7
Citron *Fr. Guiana* 4°44N 53°57W **329** C7
Citrus Heights *U.S.A.* 38°42N 121°17W **306** G5
Citrus Springs *U.S.A.* 29°2N 82°27W **317** F7
Citrusdal *S. Africa* 32°35S 19°0E **270** D2
Città degli Studi *Italy* 45°28N 9°12E **129** B2
Città del Vaticano = Vatican City ■ *Europe* 41°54N 12°27E **136** B1
Città della Pieve *Italy* 42°57N 12°1E **199** F9
Città di Castello *Italy* 43°27N 12°14E **199** E9
Città Sant' Angelo *Italy* 42°32N 14°5E **199** F11
Cittadella *Italy* 45°39N 11°47E **199** C8
Cittaducale *Italy* 42°23N 12°57E **199** F9
Cittanova *Italy* 38°21N 16°5E **201** D9
City, The *U.K.* 51°30N 0°6W **125** A3
City Hall = Rådhus *Oslo, Norway* **133** b1
City Hall = Stadshuset *Stockholm, Sweden* **139** b1
City of the Dead *Egypt* 30°0N 31°15E **117** A2
City Park *U.S.A.* 30°0N 90°5W **131** A2
City Terrace *U.S.A.* 34°3N 118°11W **126** B3
Ciuc, Munţii *Romania* 46°25N 26°5E **183** D11
Ciucaş, Vf. *Romania* 45°31N 25°56E **183** E10
Ciucea *Romania* 46°57N 22°49E **182** D7
Ciuciulea *Moldova* 47°40N 27°29E **183** C12
Ciuciuleni *Moldova* 47°2N 28°25E **183** C13
Ciudad Acuña *Mexico* 29°18N 100°55W **318** B4
Ciudad Altamirano *Mexico* 18°20N 100°40W **318** D4
Ciudad Anáhuac *Mexico* 27°14N 100°7W **318** B4
Ciudad Bolívar *Venezuela* 8°5N 63°36W **329** B5
Ciudad Bolivia *Venezuela* 8°21N 70°34W **328** B3
Ciudad Camargo *Mexico* 27°40N 105°10W **318** B3
Ciudad Cortés *Costa Rica* 8°55N 84°0W **320** E3
Ciudad de México *Mexico* 19°24N 99°9W **128** B2
Ciudad de Nutrias *Venezuela* 8°5N 69°18W **328** B4
Ciudad de Valles *Mexico* 22°0N 99°0W **319** C5
Ciudad del Carmen *Mexico* 18°38N 91°50W **319** D6
Ciudad del Este *Paraguay* 25°30S 54°50W **335** B5
Ciudad Delicias = Delicias *Mexico* 28°13N 105°28W **318** B3
Ciudad Deportiva *Mexico* 19°24N 99°5W **128** B2
Ciudad Fin de Semana *Spain* 40°26N 3°34W **127** B2
Ciudad Frontera *Mexico* 26°56N 101°27W **318** B4
Ciudad General Belgrano *Argentina* 34°43S 58°33W **117** C1
Ciudad Guayana *Venezuela* 8°0N 62°30W **329** B5
Ciudad Guerrero *Mexico* 28°33N 107°30W **318** B3
Ciudad Guzmán *Mexico* 19°41N 103°29W **318** D4
Ciudad Juárez *Mexico* 31°44N 106°29W **318** A3
Ciudad Lerdo *Mexico* 25°32N 103°32W **318** B4
Ciudad Lineál *Spain* 40°26N 3°38W **127** B2
Ciudad Madero *Mexico* 22°19N 97°50W **319** C5
Ciudad Mante *Mexico* 22°44N 98°59W **319** C5
Ciudad Obregón *Mexico* 27°29N 109°56W **318** B3
Ciudad Ojeda *Venezuela* 10°12N 71°19W **328** A3
Ciudad Piar *Venezuela* 7°27N 63°19W **329** B5
Ciudad Porfirio Díaz = Piedras Negras *Mexico* 28°42N 100°31W **318** B4
Ciudad Real *Spain* 38°59N 3°55W **195** G7
Ciudad Real □ *Spain* 38°50N 4°0W **195** G7
Ciudad Rodrigo *Spain* 40°35N 6°32W **194** E4
Ciudad Satélite *Mexico* 19°30N 99°13W **128** A1
Ciudad Trujillo = Santo Domingo *Dom. Rep.* 18°30N 69°59W **321** C6
Ciudad Universitaria *B. Aires, Argentina* 34°33S 58°27W **117** B2
Ciudad Universitaria *México, Mexico* 19°20N 99°11W **128** C1
Ciudad Victoria *Mexico* 23°44N 99°8W **319** C5
Ciudadela *Spain* 40°0N 3°50E **206** B4
Ciulniţa *Romania* 44°26N 27°22E **183** F12
Ciumeghiu *Romania* 46°44N 21°35E **182** D6
Ciuperceni *Romania* 44°54N 23°4E **182** F8
Ciutadella, Parc de la *Barcelona, Spain* **114** b3
Civa Burnu *Turkey* 41°21N 36°38E **212** B7
Civic Center *Los Angeles, U.S.A.* **127** b2
Cividale del Friuli *Italy* 46°6N 13°25E **199** B10
Civita Castellana *Italy* 42°18N 12°24E **199** F9
Civitanova Marche *Italy* 43°18N 13°44E **199** E10
Civitavécchia *Italy* 42°6N 11°48E **199** F8
Civray *France* 46°10N 0°17E **174** B4
Çivril *Turkey* 38°20N 29°43E **205** C11
Cixerri → *Italy* 39°17N 8°59E **200** C1
Cixi *China* 30°17N 121°9E **229** B13
Cizre *Turkey* 37°19N 42°10E **213** D10
Clackmannanshire □ *U.K.* 56°10N 3°43W **167** E5
Clacton-on-Sea *U.K.* 51°47N 1°11E **169** F9
Clain → *France* 46°47N 0°33E **172** F7
Claire, L. *Canada* 58°35N 112°5W **296** B6
Claireville Res. *Canada* 43°45N 79°39W **141** A1
Clairton *U.S.A.* 40°18N 79°53W **312** F5
Clairvaux-les-Lacs *France* 46°35N 5°45E **173** F12
Claise → *France* 46°56N 0°42E **174** B5
Clallam Bay *U.S.A.* 48°15N 124°16W **306** B2
Clam Gulch *U.S.A.* 60°15N 151°23W **303** F10
Clamart *France* 48°48N 2°15E **134** B2
Clamecy *France* 47°28N 3°30E **173** E10
Clanton *U.S.A.* 32°51N 86°38W **315** E11
Clanwilliam *S. Africa* 32°11S 18°52E **270** D2
Clapham *U.K.* 51°27N 0°8W **125** B3
Clapton *U.K.* 51°33N 0°3W **125** A3
Clara *Ireland* 53°21N 7°37W **166** C4
Claraville *U.S.A.* 35°24N 118°20W **307** K8
Clare *S. Austral., Australia* 33°50S 138°37E **282** B3
Clare *Mich., U.S.A.* 43°49N 84°46W **309** D11
Clare □ *Ireland* 52°45N 9°0W **166** D3
Clare → *Ireland* 53°20N 9°2W **166** C2
Clare I. *Ireland* 53°49N 10°0W **166** C1
Claremont *Jamaica* 18°19N 77°11W **320** a
Claremont *Western Cape, S. Africa* 34°8S 18°28E **118** A1
Claremont *Calif., U.S.A.* 34°6N 117°43W **307** L9
Claremont *N.H., U.S.A.* 43°23N 72°20W **313** C12
Claremont Pt. *Australia* 14°1S 143°41E **280** A3
Claremore *U.S.A.* 36°19N 95°36W **314** C7
Claremorris *Ireland* 53°45N 9°0W **166** C3
Clarence *U.S.A.* 39°45N 92°16W **310** E4
Clarence → *N.S.W., Australia* 29°25S 153°22E **281** D5
Clarence → *N.Z.* 42°10S 173°56E **285** C8
Clarence, I. *Chile* 54°0S 72°0W **336** D2
Clarence, Port *U.S.A.* 65°15N 166°40W **303** D6
Clarence B. *Ascension I.* 7°55S 14°25W **153** g
Clarence I. *Antarctica* 61°10S 54°0W **151** C18
Clarence Str. *Australia* 12°0S 131°0E **278** B5
Clarence Town *Bahamas* 23°6N 74°59W **321** B5
Clarendon *Pa., U.S.A.* 41°47N 79°6W **312** E5
Clarendon *Tex., U.S.A.* 34°56N 100°53W **314** D4
Clarenville *Canada* 48°10N 54°1W **299** C9
Claresholm *Canada* 50°2N 113°33W **296** D6
Clarie Coast *Antarctica* 68°0S 135°0E **151** C9
Clarinda *U.S.A.* 40°44N 95°2W **308** E6
Clarington *Canada* 43°55N 78°41W **312** C6
Clarion *Iowa, U.S.A.* 42°44N 93°44W **310** B3
Clarion *Pa., U.S.A.* 41°13N 79°23W **312** E5
Clarion → *U.S.A.* 41°7N 79°41W **312** E5
Clarion Fracture Zone *Pac. Oc.* 20°0N 120°0W **292** H7
Clark *Mo., U.S.A.* 39°17N 92°21W **310** E4
Clark *S. Dak., U.S.A.* 44°53N 97°44W **308** C5
Clark, Pt. *Canada* 44°4N 81°45W **312** B3
Clark Fork *U.S.A.* 48°9N 116°11W **304** B5
Clark Fork → *U.S.A.* 48°9N 116°15W **304** B5
Clarkdale *U.S.A.* 34°46N 112°3W **305** J7
Clarke City *Canada* 50°12N 66°38W **299** B6
Clarke I. *Australia* 40°32S 148°10E **281** G4
Clarke Ra. *Australia* 20°40S 148°30E **280** b
Clarks Fork Yellowstone → *U.S.A.* 45°32N 108°50W **304** D9
Clark's Harbour *Canada* 43°25N 65°38W **299** D6
Clarks Hill L. = J. Strom Thurmond L. *U.S.A.* 33°40N 82°12W **316** B7
Clarks Point *U.S.A.* 58°51N 158°33W **303** G8
Clarks Summit *U.S.A.* 41°30N 75°42W **313** E9
Clarks Town *Jamaica* 18°25N 77°33W **320** a
Clarksburg *U.S.A.* 39°17N 80°30W **309** F13
Clarksdale *U.S.A.* 34°12N 90°35W **315** D9
Clarkston *U.S.A.* 46°25N 117°3W **304** C5
Clarksville *Ark., U.S.A.* 35°28N 93°28W **314** D8
Clarksville *Ind., U.S.A.* 38°17N 85°45W **311** F11
Clarksville *Iowa, U.S.A.* 42°47N 92°40W **310** B4
Clarksville *Mo., U.S.A.* 39°22N 90°54W **310** E6
Clarksville *Tenn., U.S.A.* 36°32N 87°21W **315** C11
Clarksville *Tex., U.S.A.* 33°37N 95°3W **314** E7
Claro → *Brazil* 19°8S 50°40W **333** E1
Clatskanie *U.S.A.* 46°6N 123°12W **306** D3
Claude *U.S.A.* 35°7N 101°22W **314** D4
Claveria *Cagayan, Phil.* 18°37N 121°4E **232** B3
Claveria *Masbate, Phil.* 12°54N 123°15E **232** E4
Claveria *Mis. Or., Phil.* 8°38N 124°55E **233** G5
Clavering Ø *Greenland* 74°15N 21°0W **154** C8
Claxton *U.S.A.* 32°10N 81°55W **316** C8
Claxton B. *Trin. & Tob.* 10°21N 61°28W **323** t
Claxton Bay *Trin. & Tob.* 10°21N 61°28W **323** t
Clay *U.S.A.* 38°17N 121°10W **306** G5
Clay Center *U.S.A.* 39°23N 97°8W **308** F5
Clay City *Ind., U.S.A.* 39°17N 87°7W **311** E9
Clay City *Ky., U.S.A.* 37°52N 83°55W **311** G13
Clayhall *U.K.* 51°35N 0°3E **125** A4
Claypool *U.S.A.* 33°25N 110°51W **305** K8
Claysburg *U.S.A.* 40°17N 78°27W **312** F6
Claysville *U.S.A.* 40°7N 80°25W **312** F4
Clayton *Ont., Canada* 45°11N 76°19W **313** A8
Clayton *Ala., U.S.A.* 31°53N 85°27W **316** D4
Clayton *Ind., U.S.A.* 39°41N 86°31W **311** E10
Clayton *N. Mex., U.S.A.* 36°27N 103°11W **305** H12
Clayton *N.Y., U.S.A.* 44°14N 76°5W **313** B8
Clear, C. *Ireland* 51°25N 9°32W **166** E2
Clear, L. *Ont., Canada* 45°26N 77°12W **312** A7
Clear, L. *Fla., U.S.A.* 28°31N 81°24W **133** A2
Clear Hills *Canada* 56°40N 119°30W **296** B5
Clear I. *Ireland* 51°26N 9°30W **166** E2
Clear L. *U.S.A.* 39°2N 122°47W **306** F4
Clear Lake *Iowa, U.S.A.* 43°8N 93°23W **310** A3
Clear Lake *S. Dak., U.S.A.* 44°45N 96°41W **308** C5
Clear Lake Res. *U.S.A.* 41°56N 121°5W **304** F3
Clearfield *Pa., U.S.A.* 41°2N 78°27W **312** E6
Clearfield *Utah, U.S.A.* 41°7N 112°2W **304** F7
Clearlake *U.S.A.* 38°57N 122°38W **306** G4
Clearwater *B.C., Canada* 51°38N 120°2W **296** C4
Clearwater *Fla., U.S.A.* 27°59N 82°48W **317** H7
Clearwater → *Alta., Canada* 52°22N 114°57W **296** C6
Clearwater → *Alta., Canada* 56°44N 111°23W **297** B6
Clearwater L. *Canada* 53°34N 99°49W **297** C9
Clearwater Lake ⌂ *Canada* 54°0N 101°0W **297** C8
Clearwater Mts. *U.S.A.* 46°5N 115°20W **304** C6
Clearwater River ⌂ *Canada* 56°55N 109°10W **297** B7
Cleburne *U.S.A.* 32°21N 97°23W **314** E6
Clee Hills *U.K.* 52°26N 2°35W **169** E5
Cleethorpes *U.K.* 53°33N 0°3W **168** D7
Cleeve Cloud *U.K.* 51°56N 2°0W **169** F6
Clelles *France* 44°50N 5°38E **175** D9
Clemson *U.S.A.* 34°41N 82°50W **315** D13
Cleopatra Needle *Phil.* 10°7N 118°58E **233** F2
Clerke Reef *Australia* 17°22S 119°20E **278** C2
Clerkenwell *London, U.K.* **125** a4
Clermiston *U.K.* 55°57N 3°17W **121** B2
Clermont *Queens., Australia* 22°49S 147°39E **280** C4
Clermont *Oise, France* 49°23N 2°24E **173** C9
Clermont *Fla., U.S.A.* 28°33N 81°46W **317** G8
Clermont-en-Argonne *France* 49°5N 5°4E **173** C12
Clermont-Ferrand *France* 45°46N 3°4E **174** C7
Clermont-l'Hérault *France* 43°38N 3°26E **174** E7
Clerval *France* 47°25N 6°30E **173** E13
Clervaux *Lux.* 50°4N 6°2E **170** D6
Cles *Italy* 46°22N 11°2E **198** B8
Cleve *Australia* 33°43S 136°30E **282** B2
Clevedon *U.K.* 51°26N 2°52W **169** F5
Cleveland *Miss., U.S.A.* 33°45N 90°43W **315** E9
Cleveland *Ohio, U.S.A.* 41°29N 81°41W **312** E3
Cleveland *Okla., U.S.A.* 36°19N 96°28W **314** C6
Cleveland *Tenn., U.S.A.* 35°10N 84°53W **315** D12
Cleveland *Tex., U.S.A.* 30°21N 95°5W **314** F7
Cleveland, C. *Australia* 19°11S 147°1E **280** B4
Cleveland, Mt. *U.S.A.* 48°56N 113°51W **304** B7
Cleveland Heights *U.S.A.* 41°31N 81°33W **312** E3
Clevelândia *Brazil* 26°24S 52°23W **335** B5
Clevelândia do Norte *Brazil* 3°49N 51°52W **329** C7
Cleves *U.S.A.* 39°10N 84°45W **311** E12
Clew B. *Ireland* 53°50N 9°49W **166** C2
Clewiston *U.S.A.* 26°45N 80°56W **317** J9
Clichy *France* 48°54N 2°18E **134** A2
Clichy-sous-Bois *France* 48°54N 2°32E **134** A4
Clifden *Galway, Ireland* 53°29N 10°1W **166** C1
Clifden *N.Z.* 46°1S 167°42E **285** G2
Cliffdell *U.S.A.* 46°56N 121°5W **306** D5
Cliffside *Canada* 43°44N 79°14W **141** A3
Cliffside Park *U.S.A.* 40°49N 73°59W **132** B2
Cliffy Hd. *Australia* 35°1S 116°29E **279** G2
Clifton *Queens., Australia* 27°59S 151°53E **281** D5
Clifton *Sindh, Pakistan* 24°48N 67°1E **123** B2
Clifton *Western Cape, S. Africa* 33°56S 18°22E **118** A1
Clifton *Ariz., U.S.A.* 33°3N 109°18W **305** K9
Clifton *Colo., U.S.A.* 39°7N 108°25W **304** G9
Clifton *Ill., U.S.A.* 40°56N 87°56W **311** D9
Clifton *N.J., U.S.A.* 40°37N 74°4W **132** C1
Clifton *Tex., U.S.A.* 31°47N 97°35W **314** F6
Clifton Beach *Queens., Australia* 16°46S 145°39E **280** B4
Clifton Beach *Sindh, Pakistan* 24°48N 67°2E **123** B2
Clifton Pt. *Bahamas* 25°1N 77°34W **153** b
Cliftondale *U.S.A.* 42°26N 71°0W **116** A2
Climax *U.S.A.* 30°53N 84°26W **316** E5
Clinch → *U.S.A.* 35°53N 84°29W **315** D12
Clingmans Dome *U.S.A.* 35°34N 83°30W **315** D13
Clint *U.S.A.* 31°35N 106°14W **314** F1
Clinton *B.C., Canada* 51°6N 121°35W **296** C4
Clinton *Ont., Canada* 43°37N 81°32W **312** C3
Clinton *N.Z.* 46°12S 169°23E **285** G4
Clinton *Ark., U.S.A.* 35°36N 92°28W **314** D8
Clinton *Conn., U.S.A.* 41°17N 72°32W **313** E12
Clinton *Ill., U.S.A.* 40°9N 88°57W **310** D8
Clinton *Ind., U.S.A.* 39°40N 87°24W **311** E9
Clinton *Iowa, U.S.A.* 41°51N 90°12W **310** C6
Clinton *Mass., U.S.A.* 42°25N 71°41W **313** D13
Clinton *Mich., U.S.A.* 42°4N 83°58W **311** B13
Clinton *Miss., U.S.A.* 32°20N 90°20W **315** E9
Clinton *Mo., U.S.A.* 38°22N 93°46W **310** F3
Clinton *N.C., U.S.A.* 35°0N 78°22W **315** D15
Clinton *Okla., U.S.A.* 35°31N 98°58W **314** D5
Clinton *S.C., U.S.A.* 34°29N 81°53W **315** D14
Clinton *Tenn., U.S.A.* 36°6N 84°8W **315** C12
Clinton *Wash., U.S.A.* 47°59N 122°21W **306** C4
Clinton *Wis., U.S.A.* 42°34N 88°52W **311** B8
Clinton, C. *Australia* 22°30S 150°45E **280** C5
Clinton, L. *U.S.A.* 40°15N 88°45W **311** D8
Clinton Colden L. *Canada* 63°58N 107°27W **294** E10
Clintonville *U.S.A.* 44°37N 88°46W **308** C9
Clio *U.S.A.* 31°43N 85°37W **316** D4
Clipperton, I. *Pac. Oc.* 10°18N 109°13W **289** F17
Clipperton Fracture Zone *Pac. Oc.* 19°0N 122°0W **289** G16
Clisham *U.K.* 57°58N 6°49W **167** D2
Clisson *France* 47°5N 1°16W **172** E5
Clitheroe *U.K.* 53°53N 2°22W **168** D5
Clive *N.Z.* 39°36S 176°58E **284** F5
Clive *Iowa, U.S.A.* 41°36N 93°43W **310** C3
Cliza *Bolivia* 17°36S 65°56W **331** D4
Clo-oose *Canada* 48°39N 124°49W **306** B2
Cloates, Pt. *Australia* 22°43S 113°40E **278** D1
Clocolan *S. Africa* 28°55S 27°34E **271** C4
Clodomira *Argentina* 27°35S 64°14W **334** B3
Clogher Hd. *Ireland* 53°48N 6°14W **166** C5
Cloghran *Ireland* 53°27N 6°14W **120** A2
Clonakilty *Ireland* 51°37N 8°53W **166** E3
Clonakilty B. *Ireland* 51°35N 8°51W **166** E3
Cloncurry *Queens., Australia* 20°40S 140°28E **280** C3
Cloncurry *Kildare, Ireland* 53°25N 6°48W **166** C5
Cloncurry → *Australia* 18°37S 140°40E **280** B3
Clondalkin *Ireland* 53°19N 6°25W **166** C5
Clones *Ireland* 54°11N 7°15W **166** B4
Clonmel *Ireland* 52°21N 7°42W **166** D4
Clonskeagh *Ireland* 53°19N 6°14W **120** B2
Clontarf *N.S.W., Australia* 33°48S 151°16E **139** A2
Clontarf *Dublin, Ireland* 53°22N 6°11W **120** A2
Cloppenburg *Germany* 52°51N 8°1E **178** C4
Cloquet *U.S.A.* 46°43N 92°28W **308** B7
Clorinda *Argentina* 25°16S 57°45W **334** B4
Cloud Bay *Canada* 48°5N 89°26W **298** C2
Cloud Peak *U.S.A.* 44°23N 107°11W **304** D10
Cloudcroft *U.S.A.* 32°58N 105°45W **305** K11
Cloudy B. *N.Z.* 41°25S 174°10E **285** B9
Clovelly *Australia* 33°54S 151°15E **139** B2
Cloverdale *Calif., U.S.A.* 38°48N 123°1W **306** G4
Cloverdale *Ind., U.S.A.* 39°31N 86°48W **311** E10
Cloverport *U.S.A.* 37°50N 86°38W **311** G10
Clovis *Calif., U.S.A.* 36°49N 119°42W **306** J7
Clovis *N. Mex., U.S.A.* 34°24N 103°12W **305** J12
Cloyes-sur-le-Loir *France* 48°0N 1°14E **172** E8
Cloyne *Canada* 44°49N 77°11W **312** B7
Cluain Meala = Clonmel *Ireland* 52°21N 7°42W **166** D4
Club Terrace *Australia* 37°35S 148°58E **283** D8
Cluj □ *Romania* 46°45N 23°30E **183** D8
Cluj-Napoca *Romania* 46°47N 23°38E **183** D8
Clunes *Australia* 37°20S 143°45E **282** D5
Cluny *France* 46°26N 4°38E **173** F11
Cluses *France* 46°5N 6°35E **173** F13
Clusone *Italy* 45°53N 9°57E **198** C6
Clutha → *N.Z.* 46°20S 169°49E **285** G4
Clwyd → *U.K.* 53°19N 3°31W **168** D4
Clyattville *U.S.A.* 30°42N 83°19W **316** E6
Clyde *Alta., Canada* 54°9N 113°39W **296** C6
Clyde *N.Z.* 45°12S 169°20E **285** F4
Clyde *N.Y., U.S.A.* 43°5N 76°52W **312** C8
Clyde *Ohio, U.S.A.* 41°18N 82°59W **311** C14
Clyde → *U.K.* 55°55N 4°30W **167** F4
Clyde, Firth of *U.K.* 55°22N 5°1W **167** F3
Clyde Muirshiel △ *U.K.* 55°50N 4°40W **167** F4
Clyde River *Canada* 70°30N 68°30W **295** C18
Clydebank *U.K.* 55°54N 4°23W **167** F4
Clymer *N.Y., U.S.A.* 42°1N 79°37W **312** D5
Clymer *Pa., U.S.A.* 40°40N 79°1W **312** D5
Clyo *U.S.A.* 32°29N 81°16W **316** C8
Ćmielów *Poland* 50°53N 21°31E **185** H8
Côa → *Portugal* 41°5N 7°6W **194** D3
Coachella *U.S.A.* 33°41N 116°10W **307** M10
Coachella Canal *U.S.A.* 32°43N 114°57W **307** N12
Coahoma *U.S.A.* 32°18N 101°18W **314** E4
Coahuayana → *Mexico* 18°41N 103°45W **318** D4
Coahuila □ *Mexico* 27°20N 102°0W **318** B4
Coal → *Canada* 59°39N 126°57W **296** B3
Coal City *U.S.A.* 41°17N 88°17W **311** C8
Coal I. *N.Z.* 46°8S 166°40E **285** G1
Coalane *Mozam.* 17°48S 37°2E **269** F4
Coalcomán *Mexico* 18°47N 103°9W **318** D4
Coaldale *Canada* 49°45N 112°35W **296** D6
Coalgate *U.S.A.* 34°32N 96°13W **314** D6
Coalinga *U.S.A.* 36°9N 120°21W **306** J6
Coalisland *U.K.* 54°33N 6°42W **166** B5
Coalville *Leics., U.K.* 52°44N 1°23W **168** E6
Coalville *Utah, U.S.A.* 40°55N 111°24W **304** F8
Coamo *Puerto Rico* 18°5N 66°22W **321** b
Coaraci *Brazil* 14°38S 39°32W **333** D4
Coari *Brazil* 4°8S 63°7W **329** D5
Coari → *Brazil* 4°30S 63°33W **329** D5
Coari, L. *Brazil* 4°15S 63°22W **329** D5
Coast □ *Kenya* 2°40S 39°45E **268** C4
Coast Mts. *Canada* 55°0N 129°20W **296** C3
Coast Ranges *U.S.A.* 39°0N 123°0W **306** G4
Coatbridge *U.K.* 55°52N 4°6W **167** F4
Coatepec *Mexico* 19°27N 96°58W **319** D5
Coatepeque *Guatemala* 14°46N 91°55W **320** D1
Coatesville *U.S.A.* 39°59N 75°50W **309** F16
Coaticook *Canada* 45°10N 71°46W **313** A13
Coats I. *Canada* 62°30N 83°0W **295** E15
Coats Land *Antarctica* 77°0S 25°0W **151** D1
Coatzacoalcos *Mexico* 18°7N 94°25W **319** D6
Cobá *Mexico* 20°31N 87°45W **319** C7
Cobadin *Romania* 44°5N 28°13E **183** F13
Cobalt *Canada* 47°25N 79°42W **298** C4
Cobán *Guatemala* 15°30N 90°21W **320** C1
Çobanlar *Turkey* 38°41N 30°47E **205** C12
Cobar *Australia* 31°27S 145°48E **283** A6
Cobargo *Australia* 36°20S 149°55E **283** D8
Cobbannah *Australia* 37°37S 147°12E **283** D7
Cobberas, Mt. *Australia* 36°53S 148°12E **283** D8
Cobden *Australia* 38°20S 143°3E **282** E5
Cóbh *Ireland* 51°51N 8°17W **166** E3
Cobija *Bolivia* 11°0S 68°50W **330** C4
Cobleskill *U.S.A.* 42°41N 74°29W **313** D10
Coboconk *Canada* 44°39N 78°48W **312** B6
Cobourg *Canada* 43°58N 78°10W **312** C6
Cobourg Pen. *Australia* 11°20S 132°15E **278** B5
Cobram *Australia* 35°54S 145°40E **283** C6
Cobras, I. das *Brazil* 22°53S 43°9W **135** B2
Cóbué *Mozam.* 12°0S 34°58E **269** E3
Coburg *Vic., Australia* 37°44S 144°58E **128** A1
Coburg *Bayern, Germany* 50°15N 10°58E **179** E6
Coburg I. *Canada* 75°57N 79°26W **295** B16
Coca *Spain* 41°13N 4°32W **194** D6
Coca → *Ecuador* 0°29S 76°58W **328** D2
Cocachacra *Peru* 17°5S 71°45W **330** D3
Cocal *Brazil* 3°28S 41°34W **332** B3
Cocanada = Kakinada *India* 16°57N 82°11E **244** F6
Cocentaina *Spain* 38°45N 0°27W **197** G4
Cochabamba *Bolivia* 17°26S 66°10W **331** D4
Coche, I. *Venezuela* 10°47N 63°56W **329** A5
Cochem *Germany* 50°9N 7°9E **179** E3
Cochemane *Mozam.* 17°0S 32°54E **269** F3
Cochin *India* 9°58N 76°20E **245** K3
Cochin China = Nam-Phan *Vietnam* 10°30N 106°0E **237** G6
Cochran *U.S.A.* 32°23N 83°21W **316** C6
Cochrane *Alta., Canada* 51°11N 114°30W **296** C6
Cochrane *Ont., Canada* 49°0N 81°0W **298** C3
Cochrane *Chile* 47°15S 72°33W **336** C2
Cochrane → *Canada* 59°0N 103°40W **297** B8
Cochrane, L. *Chile* 47°10S 72°0W **336** C2
Cochranton *U.S.A.* 41°31N 80°3W **312** E4
Cockburn *Australia* 32°5S 141°0E **282** B4
Cockburn, Canal *Chile* 54°30S 72°0W **336** D2
Cockburn I. *Canada* 45°55N 83°22W **298** C3
Cockburn Ra. *Australia* 15°46S 128°0E **278** C4
Cockermouth *U.K.* 54°40N 3°22W **168** C4
Cocklebiddy *Australia* 32°0S 126°3E **279** F4
Cockpit *Jamaica* 18°16N 77°39W **320** a
Cockpit Country, The *Jamaica* 18°15N 77°45W **320** a
Côco → *Brazil* 9°27S 50°2W **332** C2
Coco → *Cent. Amer.* 15°0N 83°8W **320** D3
Coco, I. del *Pac. Oc.* 5°25N 87°55W **289** G19
Coco, Pta. *Colombia* 2°58N 77°43W **328** C2
Coco Channel *Asia* 13°45N 93°10E **245** H11
Cocoa *U.S.A.* 28°21N 80°44W **317** G9
Cocoa Beach *U.S.A.* 28°19N 80°37W **317** G9
Cocoa Point *Antigua & B.* 17°33N 61°46W **322** c
Cocobeach *Gabon* 0°59N 9°34E **264** B1
Cocoparra △ *Australia* 34°10S 146°12E **283** C7
Cocora *Romania* 44°45N 27°3E **183** F12
Cocos *Brazil* 14°10S 44°33W **333** D3
Cocos → *Brazil* 12°44S 44°48W **333** D3
Cocos B. *Trin. & Tob.* 10°25N 61°2W **323** t
Cocos Basin *Ind. Oc.* 1°0N 94°0E **273** D8
Cocos I. *Guam* 13°14N 144°39E **302** d
Cocos Is. *Ind. Oc.* 12°10S 96°55E **273** E8
Cocos Ridge *Pac. Oc.* 4°0N 88°0W **289** G19
Cocotá *Brazil* 22°48S 43°11W **135** A1
Cod, C. *U.S.A.* 42°5N 70°10W **309** D18
Codajás *Brazil* 3°55S 62°0W **329** D5
Codera, C. *Venezuela* 10°35N 66°4W **328** A4
Codfish I. *N.Z.* 46°47S 167°38E **285** G2
Codigoro *Italy* 44°49N 12°8E **199** D9
Codlea *Romania* 45°42N 25°27E **183** E10
Codó *Brazil* 4°30S 43°55W **332** B3
Codogno *Italy* 45°9N 9°42E **198** C6
Codpa *Chile* 18°50S 69°44W **330** D4
Codrington *Antigua & B.* 17°38N 61°50W **322** c
Codrington Lagoon *Antigua & B.* 17°39N 61°50W **322** c
Codróipo *Italy* 45°58N 13°0E **199** C10
Codru, Munţii *Romania* 46°30N 22°15E **182** D7
Cody *U.S.A.* 44°32N 109°3W **304** D9
Coe Hill *Canada* 44°52N 77°50W **312** B7
Coelemu *Chile* 36°30S 72°48W **334** D1
Coelho Neto *Brazil* 4°15S 43°0W **332** B3
Coen *Australia* 13°52S 143°12E **280** A3
Coeroeni *Suriname* 3°22N 57°21W **329** C6
Coeroeni → *Suriname* 3°21N 57°31W **329** C6
Coesfeld *Germany* 51°56N 7°10E **178** D3
Coetivy Is. *Seychelles* 7°8S 56°16E **273** E4
Cœuilly *France* 48°48N 2°32E **134** B4
Coeur d'Alene *U.S.A.* 47°41N 116°46W **304** C5
Coeur d'Alene L. *U.S.A.* 47°32N 116°49W **304** C5
Coevorden *Neths.* 52°40N 6°44E **170** B6
Cofete *Canary Is.* 28°6N 14°23W **153** e2
Coffeyville *U.S.A.* 37°2N 95°37W **308** G6
Coffin B. *Australia* 34°38S 135°28E **281** E2
Coffin Bay *Australia* 34°37S 135°29E **281** E2
Coffin Bay △ *Australia* 34°34S 135°19E **281** E2
Coffin Bay Peninsula *Australia* 34°32S 135°15E **281** E2
Coffs Harbour *Australia* 30°16S 153°5E **283** A10
Cofrentes *Spain* 39°13N 1°5W **197** F3
Cogalnic → *Moldova* 45°49N 29°40E **183** E14
Cogealac *Romania* 44°36N 28°36E **183** F13
Coghinas → *Italy* 40°55N 8°48E **200** B1
Coghinas, L. del *Italy* 40°46N 9°3E **200** B2
Cognac *France* 45°41N 0°20W **174** C3
Cogne *Italy* 45°37N 7°21E **198** C4
Cogolin *France* 43°15N 6°32E **175** E10
Cogolludo *Spain* 40°59N 3°10W **196** E1
Cohocton *U.S.A.* 42°30N 77°30W **312** D7
Cohocton → *U.S.A.* 42°9N 77°6W **312** D7
Cohoes *U.S.A.* 42°46N 73°42W **313** D11
Cohuna *Australia* 35°45S 144°15E **282** C6
Coiba, I. de *Panama* 7°30N 81°40W **320** E3
Coig → *Argentina* 51°0S 69°10W **336** D3
Coigeach, Rubha *U.K.* 58°6N 5°26W **167** C3
Coihaique *Chile* 45°30S 71°45W **336** C2
Coimbatore *India* 11°2N 76°59E **245** J3
Coimbra *Mato Grosso, Brazil* 19°55S 57°48W **331** D6
Coimbra *Portugal* 40°15N 8°27W **194** E2
Coimbra □ *Portugal* 40°12N 8°25W **194** E2
Coín *Spain* 36°40N 4°48W **195** J6
Coina *Portugal* 38°39N 9°5W **126** B2
Coipasa, L. de *Bolivia* 19°12S 68°7W **330** D4
Coipasa, Salar de *Bolivia* 19°26S 68°9W **330** D4
Coit Tower *San Francisco, U.S.A.* **136** a2
Cojata *Peru* 15°2S 69°25W **330** D4
Cojedes □ *Venezuela* 9°20N 68°20W **328** B4
Cojedes → *Venezuela* 8°34N 68°5W **328** B4
Cojimies *Ecuador* 0°20N 80°0W **328** C1
Cojocna *Romania* 46°45N 23°50E **183** D8
Cojutepequé *El Salv.* 13°41N 88°54W **320** D2
Čoka *Serbia* 45°57N 20°12E **182** E5
Coker *Nigeria* 6°28N 3°20E **124** B2
Cokeville *U.S.A.* 42°5N 110°57W **304** E8
Colaba *India* 18°53N 72°48E **130** B1
Colaba Pt. *India* 18°53N 72°48E **130** B1
Colac *Australia* 38°21S 143°35E **282** E5
Colachel = Kolachel *India* 8°10N 77°15E **245** K3
Colán *Peru* 5°0S 81°0W **330** B1
Colatina *Brazil* 19°32S 40°37W **333** E3
Colbeck, C. *Antarctica* 77°6S 157°48W **151** D13
Colbert *U.S.A.* 34°2N 83°13W **316** A6
Colborne *Canada* 44°0N 77°53W **312** C7
Colby *U.S.A.* 39°24N 101°3W **308** F3
Colca, Cañón del *Peru* 15°50S 72°20W **330** D3
Colchester *Essex, U.K.* 51°54N 0°55E **169** F8
Colchester *Conn., U.S.A.* 41°35N 72°20W **313** E12
Cold Bay *U.S.A.* 55°12N 162°42W **303** J7
Cold L. *Canada* 54°33N 110°5W **297** C7
Cold Lake *Canada* 54°27N 110°10W **297** C6
Coldstream *B.C., Canada* 50°13N 119°11W **296** C5
Coldstream *Borders, U.K.* 55°39N 2°15W **167** F6
Coldwater *Ont., Canada* 44°42N 79°40W **312** B5
Coldwater *Kans., U.S.A.* 37°16N 99°20W **308** G4
Coldwater *Mich., U.S.A.* 41°57N 85°0W **311** C11
Coldwater *Ohio, U.S.A.* 40°29N 84°38W **311** D12
Coldwater, L. *U.S.A.* 41°48N 84°59W **311** C12
Cole Camp *U.S.A.* 38°28N 93°12W **310** F3
Coleambally *Australia* 34°49S 145°52E **283** C6
Colebrook *U.S.A.* 44°54N 71°30W **313** B13
Colegiales *Argentina* 34°34S 58°27W **117** B2
Coleman *Alta., Canada* 49°40N 114°30W **296** D6
Coleman *Fla., U.S.A.* 28°48N 82°4W **317** G7
Coleman *Tex., U.S.A.* 31°50N 99°26W **314** F5
Coleman → *Australia* 15°6S 141°38E **280** B3
Colenso *S. Africa* 28°44S 29°50E **271** C4
Coleraine *Vic., Australia* 37°36S 141°40E **282** D4
Coleraine *L'derry., U.K.* 55°8N 6°41W **166** A5
Coleridge, L. *N.Z.* 43°17S 171°30E **285** D6
Coleroon → *India* 11°25N 79°50E **245** J4
Colesberg *S. Africa* 30°45S 25°5E **270** D4
Coleville *U.S.A.* 38°34N 119°30W **306** G7
Colfax *Calif., U.S.A.* 39°6N 120°57W **306** F6
Colfax *Ill., U.S.A.* 40°34N 88°37W **311** D8
Colfax *Ind., U.S.A.* 40°12N 86°40W **311** D10
Colfax *Iowa, U.S.A.* 41°41N 93°14W **310** C3
Colfax *La., U.S.A.* 31°31N 92°42W **314** F8
Colfax *Wash., U.S.A.* 46°53N 117°22W **304** C5
Colhué Huapi, L. *Argentina* 45°30S 69°0W **336** C3
Colibaşi *Moldova* 45°43N 28°11E **183** E13
Colibaşi *Romania* 44°56N 24°54E **183** F9
Colibris, Pte. des *Guadeloupe* 16°17N 61°5W **322** e
Cólico *Italy* 46°8N 9°22E **198** B6
Colider *Brazil* 10°45S 55°25W **331** C6
Coligny *Ain, France* 46°23N 5°21E **173** F12
Coligny *North West, S. Africa* 26°17S 26°15E **271** C4

Colihaut Dominica 15°29N 61°29W 323 k
Colima Mexico 19°14N 103°43W 318 D4
Colima □ Mexico 19°10N 104°0W 318 D4
Colima, Nevado de Mexico 19°33N 103°38W 318 D4
Colina Chile 33°13S 70°45W 334 C1
Colina do Norte Guinea-Biss. 12°28N 15°0W 262 C2
Colinas Goiás, Brazil 14°15S 48°2W 333 D2
Colinas Maranhão, Brazil 6°0S 44°10W 332 C3
Colindale U.K. 51°35N 0°15W 125 A2
Colindres Spain 43°24N 3°27W 194 B7
Colinton U.K. 55°55N 3°14W 121 B2
Coll U.K. 56°39N 6°34W 167 E2
Collahuasi Chile 21°5S 68°45W 334 A2
Collarada, Peña Spain 42°43N 0°29W 196 C4
Collarenebri Australia 29°33S 148°34E 281 D4
Colle di Val d'Elsa Italy 43°25N 11°7E 198 E8
Collécchio Italy 44°45N 10°13E 198 D7
Colleen Bawn Zimbabwe 21°0S 29°12E 269 G2
College U.S.A. 64°52N 147°49W 303 D11
College Park Ga., U.S.A. 33°39N 84°27W 113 C2
College Park Md., U.S.A. 38°59N 76°55W 143 B4
College Point U.S.A. 40°47N 73°50W 132 B2
College Station U.S.A. 30°37N 96°21W 314 F6
Collégien France 48°50N 2°41E 134 A4
Collesalvetti Italy 43°34N 10°27E 198 E7
Colli Euganei ⌓ Italy 45°18N 11°43E 199 C8
Collie N.S.W., Australia 31°41S 148°18E 283 A8
Collie W. Austral., Australia 33°22S 116°8E 279 F2
Collier B. Australia 16°10S 124°15E 278 C3
Collier Ra. Australia 24°45S 119°10E 279 D2
Collier Range △ Australia 24°39S 119°7E 279 D2
Collier Row U.K. 51°35N 0°9E 125 A4
Colliers Wood U.K. 51°24N 0°10W 125 B2
Collierville U.S.A. 35°3N 89°40W 315 D10
Collina, Passo di Italy 44°2N 10°56E 198 D7
Collingwood Ont., Canada 44°29N 80°13W 312 B4
Collingwood N.Z. 40°41S 172°40E 285 A7
Collins Ont., Canada 50°17N 89°27W 298 B2
Collins Ga., U.S.A. 32°11N 82°7W 316 C7
Collins Mo., U.S.A. 37°54N 93°37W 310 G3
Collins Bay Canada 44°14N 76°36W 313 B8
Collinson Pen. Canada 69°58N 101°24W 294 D11
Collinsville Queens., Australia 20°30S 147°56E 280 C4
Collinsville Ill., U.S.A. 38°40N 89°59W 310 F7
Collipulli Chile 37°55S 72°30W 334 D1
Collo Algeria 36°58N 6°37E 261 A6
Collooney Ireland 54°11N 8°29W 166 B3
Colma U.S.A. 37°40N 122°27W 136 B2
Colmar France 48°5N 7°20E 173 D14
Colmars France 44°11N 6°39E 175 D10
Colmenar Spain 36°54N 4°20W 195 J6
Colmenar de Oreja Spain 40°6N 3°25W 194 E7
Colmenar Viejo Spain 40°39N 3°47W 194 E7
Colney Hatch U.K. 51°36N 0°9W 125 A3
Colo ➜ Australia 33°25S 150°52E 283 B9
Cologne = Köln Germany 50°56N 6°57E 178 E2
Cologno Monzese Italy 45°31N 9°16E 129 A2
Colom, I. d'en Spain 39°58N 4°16E 206 B5
Coloma Calif., U.S.A. 38°48N 120°53W 306 G6
Coloma Mich., U.S.A. 42°11N 86°19W 311 B10
Colomb-Béchar = Béchar Algeria 31°38N 2°18W 261 B4
Colombes France 48°55N 2°15E 134 A2
Colombey-les-Belles France 48°32N 5°54E 173 D12
Colombey-les-Deux-Églises France 48°13N 4°50E 173 D11
Colômbia Brazil 20°10S 48°40W 333 F2
Colombia ■ S. Amer. 3°45N 73°0W 328 C3
Colombian Basin S. Amer. 14°0N 76°0W 321 D5
Colombier St.-Martin 18°5N 63°4W 322 a
Colombo Sri Lanka 6°56N 79°58E 245 L4
Colomiers France 43°36N 1°21E 174 E5
Colón B. Aires, Argentina 33°53S 61°7W 334 C3
Colón Entre Ríos, Argentina 32°12S 58°10W 334 C4
Colón Cuba 22°42N 80°54W 320 B3
Colón Panama 9°20N 79°54W 320 c
Colón, Arch. de Ecuador 0°0 91°0W 330 a
Colón, Monumente a Barcelona, Spain 114 c3
Colon, Plaza de Madrid, Spain 127 a3
Colón Ridge Pac. Oc. 2°0N 96°0W 289 G18
Colonarie St. Vincent 13°14N 61°8W 323 n
Colonia Micronesia 9°30N 138°10E 287 R16
Colonia 25 de Mayo Argentina 37°48S 67°41W 336 A3
Colònia de Sant Jordi Spain 39°19N 2°59E 206 B3
Colonia del Sacramento Uruguay 34°25S 57°50W 334 C4
Colonia Dora Argentina 28°34S 62°59W 334 B3
Colonia Güell Spain 41°21N 2°2E 114 A1
Colonial Beach U.S.A. 38°15N 76°58W 309 F15
Colonial Knob N.Z. 41°9S 174°48E 143 A1
Colonie U.S.A. 42°43N 73°50W 313 D11
Colonna, C. Italy 39°2N 17°12E 201 C10
Colonsay Sask., Canada 51°59N 105°52W 297 C7
Colonsay Argyll & Bute, U.K. 56°5N 6°12W 167 E2
Colorado □ U.S.A. 39°30N 105°30W 304 G11
Colorado ➜ Argentina 39°50S 62°8W 336 A4
Colorado ➜ N. Amer. 31°45N 114°40W 305 L6
Colorado ➜ Tex., U.S.A. 28°36N 95°59W 314 G7
Colorado City U.S.A. 32°24N 100°52W 314 E4
Colorado Plateau U.S.A. 37°0N 111°0W 305 H8
Colorado River Aqueduct U.S.A. 33°50N 117°23W 307 L12
Colorado Springs U.S.A. 38°50N 104°49W 304 G11
Colorno Italy 44°56N 10°23E 198 D7
Colosseo Rome, Italy 136 c3
Colosseum = Colosseo Rome, Italy 136 c3
Colotlán Mexico 22°6N 103°16W 318 C4
Colquechaca Bolivia 18°40S 66°1W 331 D4
Colquitt U.S.A. 31°10N 84°44W 316 D5
Colstrip U.S.A. 45°53N 106°38W 304 D10
Colton U.S.A. 44°33N 74°56W 313 B10
Columbia Ala., U.S.A. 31°18N 85°7W 316 D4
Columbia Ill., U.S.A. 38°27N 90°12W 310 F6
Columbia Ky., U.S.A. 37°6N 85°18W 309 G11
Columbia La., U.S.A. 32°6N 92°5W 314 E8
Columbia Miss., U.S.A. 31°15N 89°50W 315 F10
Columbia Mo., U.S.A. 38°57N 92°20W 310 F4
Columbia Pa., U.S.A. 40°2N 76°30W 313 F8
Columbia S.C., U.S.A. 34°0N 81°2W 316 A8
Columbia Tenn., U.S.A. 35°37N 87°2W 315 D11
Columbia ➜ N. Amer. 46°15N 124°5W 306 D2
Columbia, C. Canada 83°6N 69°57W 295 A18
Columbia, District of □ U.S.A. 38°55N 77°0W 309 F15
Columbia, Mt. Canada 52°8N 117°20W 296 C5
Columbia Basin U.S.A. 46°45N 119°5W 304 C4
Columbia City U.S.A. 41°10N 85°29W 311 C11
Columbia Falls U.S.A. 48°23N 114°11W 304 B6
Columbia Mts. Canada 52°0N 119°0W 296 C5
Columbia Plateau U.S.A. 44°0N 117°30W 304 E5
Columbiana U.S.A. 40°53N 80°42W 312 F4
Columbretes, Is. Spain 39°50N 0°50E 196 F5
Columbus Ga., U.S.A. 32°28N 84°59W 316 C5
Columbus Ind., U.S.A. 39°13N 85°55W 311 E11
Columbus Kans., U.S.A. 37°10N 94°50W 308 G6
Columbus Miss., U.S.A. 33°30N 88°25W 315 E10
Columbus Mont., U.S.A. 45°38N 109°15W 304 D9
Columbus N. Mex., U.S.A. 31°50N 107°38W 305 L10
Columbus Nebr., U.S.A. 41°26N 97°22W 308 E5
Columbus Ohio, U.S.A. 39°58N 83°0W 311 E13
Columbus Tex., U.S.A. 29°42N 96°33W 314 G6
Columbus Circle Washington, D.C., U.S.A. 143 b3
Columbus Circle New York, U.S.A. 132 b2
Columbus Grove U.S.A. 40°55N 84°4W 311 D12
Columbus Junction U.S.A. 41°17N 91°22W 310 C5
Columbus Monument = Colón, Monumente a Barcelona, Spain 114 c3
Columbus Park Jamaica 18°28N 77°25W 320 a
Columbus Park Boston, U.S.A. 116 b3
Colunga Spain 43°29N 5°16W 194 B5
Colusa U.S.A. 39°13N 122°1W 306 F4
Colville U.S.A. 48°33N 117°54W 304 B5
Colville ➜ U.S.A. 70°25N 150°30W 303 A10
Colville, C. N.Z. 36°29S 175°21E 284 C4
Colville Channel N.Z. 36°25S 175°27E 284 C4
Colville Ridge Pac. Oc. 30°0S 180°0E 277 G15
Colwood Canada 48°26N 123°29W 306 B3
Colwyn Bay U.K. 53°18N 3°44W 168 D4
Coma Ethiopia 8°29N 36°53E 257 F4
Comácchio Italy 44°42N 12°11E 199 D9
Comalcalco Mexico 18°16N 93°13W 319 D6
Comallo Argentina 41°0S 70°5W 336 B2
Comana Romania 44°10N 26°10E 183 F11
Comanche U.S.A. 31°54N 98°36W 314 F5
Comandante Arbues = Mirandópolis Brazil 21°9S 51°6W 335 A5
Comandante Ferraz Antarctica 62°30S 58°0W 151 C18
Comandante Luis Piedrabuena Argentina 49°59S 68°54W 336 C3
Comăneşti Romania 46°25N 26°26E 183 D11
Comarapa Bolivia 17°54S 64°29W 331 D5
Comarnic Romania 45°15N 25°38E 183 E10
Comayagua Honduras 14°25N 87°37W 320 D2
Combahee ➜ U.S.A. 32°31N 80°31W 315 E14
Combara Australia 31°10S 148°22E 283 A8
Combarbalá Chile 31°11S 71°2W 334 C1
Combault France 48°48N 2°37E 134 B4
Combe Martin U.K. 51°12N 4°3W 169 F3
Combeaufontaine France 47°38N 5°54E 173 E12
Comber Ont., Canada 42°14N 82°33W 312 D2
Comber Down, U.K. 54°33N 5°45W 166 B6
Combermere Canada 45°22N 77°37W 312 A7
Combermere Bay Burma 19°37N 93°34E 241 F4
Comblain-au-Pont Belgium 50°29N 5°35E 170 D5
Combourg France 48°25N 1°46W 172 D5
Comboyne Australia 31°34S 152°27E 283 A10
Combrailles France 46°8N 2°8E 173 F9
Combronde France 45°58N 3°5E 174 C7
Comer Ala., U.S.A. 32°2N 85°23W 316 C4
Comer Ga., U.S.A. 34°4N 83°8W 316 A6
Comeragh Mts. Ireland 52°18N 7°34W 166 D4
Comércio, Praça do Portugal 38°41N 9°9W 126 A2
Comerío Puerto Rico 18°12N 66°12W 321 b
Comet Australia 23°36S 148°38E 280 C4
Comilla Bangla. 23°28N 91°10E 241 D3
Comino Malta 36°1N 14°20E 206 E7
Comino, C. Italy 40°32N 9°49E 200 B2
Cómiso Italy 36°56N 14°36E 201 F7
Comitán de Domínguez Mexico 16°15N 92°8W 319 D6
Commentry France 46°20N 2°46E 173 F9
Commerce Calif., U.S.A. 34°0N 118°9W 126 B4
Commerce Ga., U.S.A. 34°12N 83°28W 315 D13
Commerce Tex., U.S.A. 33°15N 95°54W 314 E7
Commercy France 48°43N 5°34E 173 D12
Commissioner's Pt. Bermuda 32°19N 64°49W 153 a
Committee B. Canada 68°30N 86°30W 295 D14
Commodore, C. Canada 44°47N 80°54W 312 B4
Commonwealth B. Antarctica 67°0S 144°0E 151 C10
Commoron Cr. ➜ Australia 28°22S 150°8E 281 D5
Communism Pk. = imeni Ismail Samani, Pik Tajikistan 39°0N 72°2E 217 E8
Como Italy 45°47N 9°5E 198 C6
Como, Lago di Italy 46°0N 9°11E 198 B6
Comodoro Rivadavia Argentina 45°50S 67°40W 336 C3
Comoé ➜ Ivory C. 5°12N 3°44W 262 D4
Comoé △ Ivory C. 9°0N 3°35W 262 D4
Comorâşte Romania 45°10N 21°35E 182 E6
Comorin, C. = Kannyakumari India 8°3N 77°40E 245 K3
Comoros ■ Ind. Oc. 12°10S 44°15E 272 a
Comox Canada 49°42N 124°55W 296 D4
Company's Gardens Cape Town, S. Africa 118 c2
Compass Lake U.S.A. 30°36N 85°24W 316 E4
Compiègne France 49°24N 2°50E 173 C9
Comporta Portugal 38°22N 8°46W 195 G2
Compostela Nayarit, Mexico 21°14N 104°55W 318 C4
Compostela Phil. 7°40N 126°2E 233 H6
Comprida, I. Brazil 24°50S 47°42W 335 A6
Compton Qué., Canada 45°14N 71°49W 313 A13
Compton Calif., U.S.A. 33°53N 118°13W 307 M8
Comrat Moldova 46°18N 28°40E 183 D13
Comunidad Peru 13°59S 69°20W 330 C4
Con Cuong Vietnam 19°2N 104°54E 236 C5
Con Dao △ Vietnam 8°42N 106°35E 237 H6
Con Son Vietnam 8°41N 106°37E 237 H6
Cona Niyeu Argentina 41°58S 67°0W 336 B3
Conakry Guinea 9°29N 13°49W 262 D2
Conara Australia 41°50S 147°26E 281 G4
Conargo Australia 35°16S 145°10E 283 C6
Concarneau France 47°52N 3°56W 172 E3
Conceição Paraíba, Brazil 7°33S 38°31W 332 C4
Conceição Mozam. 18°47S 36°7E 269 F4
Conceição, I. da Brazil 22°52S 43°6W 135 B2
Conceição da Barra Brazil 18°35S 39°45W 333 E4
Conceição do Araguaia Brazil 8°0S 49°2W 332 C2
Conceição do Canindé Brazil 7°54S 41°34W 332 C3
Conceição do Maú Brazil 3°35N 59°53W 329 C6
Conceição do Paraíba = Capela Brazil 10°30S 37°0W 332 D4
Concepción Argentina 27°20S 65°35W 334 B2
Concepción Bolivia 16°15S 62°8W 331 D5
Concepción Chile 36°50S 73°0W 334 D1
Concepción Mexico 18°15N 90°5W 319 D6
Concepción Paraguay 23°22S 57°26W 334 A4
Concepción Peru 11°54S 75°19W 330 C2
Concepcion Tarlac, Phil. 15°27N 120°47E 232 D3
Concepción □ Chile 37°0S 72°30W 334 D1
Concepción ➜ Mexico 30°32N 113°2W 318 A2
Concepción, Est. de Chile 50°30S 74°55W 336 D2
Concepción, L. Bolivia 17°20S 61°20W 331 D5
Concepción, Pta. Mexico 26°53N 111°50W 318 B2
Concepción del Oro Mexico 24°38N 101°25W 318 C4
Concepción del Uruguay Argentina 32°35S 58°20W 334 C4
Conception, Pt. U.S.A. 34°27N 120°28W 307 L6
Conception B. Nfld. & L., Canada 47°45N 53°0W 299 C9
Conception B. Namibia 23°55S 14°22E 270 B1
Conception I. Bahamas 23°52N 75°9W 321 B4
Concession Zimbabwe 17°27S 30°56E 269 F3
Conchalí Chile 33°22S 70°39W 137 B2
Conchas Dam U.S.A. 35°22N 104°11W 305 J11
Conches-en-Ouche France 48°58N 0°56E 172 D7
Concho U.S.A. 34°28N 109°36W 305 J9
Concho ➜ U.S.A. 31°34N 99°43W 314 F5
Conchos ➜ Chihuahua, Mexico 29°35N 104°25W 318 B4
Conchos ➜ Chihuahua, Mexico 27°29N 106°45W 318 B3
Conchos ➜ Tamaulipas, Mexico 24°55N 97°38W 319 B5
Concord N.S.W., Australia 33°52S 151°6E 139 B1
Concord Ont., Canada 43°48N 79°29W 141 A2
Concord Grenada 12°17N 61°44W 323 q
Concord Calif., U.S.A. 37°59N 122°2W 306 H4
Concord Ga., U.S.A. 33°5N 84°27W 316 B5
Concord Mich., U.S.A. 42°11N 84°38W 311 B12
Concord Mo., U.S.A. 38°32N 90°23W 310 F6
Concord N.C., U.S.A. 35°25N 80°35W 315 D14
Concord N.H., U.S.A. 43°12N 71°32W 313 C13
Concorde, Place de la Paris, France 134 b3
Concordia Antarctica 75°6S 123°23E 151 D17
Concordia Argentina 31°20S 58°2W 334 C4
Concórdia Amazonas, Brazil 4°36S 66°36W 328 D4
Concórdia Sta. Catarina, Brazil 27°14S 52°1W 335 B5
Concordia Sinaloa, Mexico 23°17N 106°4W 318 C3
Concordia Kans., U.S.A. 39°34N 97°40W 308 F5
Concordia Mo., U.S.A. 38°59N 93°34W 310 F3
Concordia Univ. Montréal, Canada 130 c1
Concorezzo Italy 45°35N 9°19E 129 A2
Concrete U.S.A. 48°32N 121°45W 304 B3
Conda Angola 11°9S 14°20E 265 E2
Condah Australia 37°57S 141°44E 282 D4
Condamine Australia 26°56S 150°9E 281 D5
Condat France 45°21N 2°46E 174 C6
Condé Angola 10°50S 14°37E 265 E2
Conde Brazil 11°49S 37°37W 333 D4
Conde S. Dak., U.S.A. 45°9N 98°6W 308 C4
Condé-sur-Noireau France 48°51N 0°33W 172 D6
Condet Indonesia 6°17S 106°51E 122 A2
Condeúba Brazil 14°52S 42°0W 333 D3
Condobolin Australia 33°4S 147°6E 283 B7
Condom France 43°57N 0°22E 174 E4
Condon U.S.A. 45°14N 120°11W 304 D3
Conegliano Italy 45°53N 12°18E 199 C9
Conejera, I. = Conills, I. des Spain 39°11N 2°58E 206 B3
Conejos Mexico 26°14N 103°53W 318 B4
Conemaugh ➜ U.S.A. 40°28N 79°19W 312 F5
Conero ⌓ Italy 43°32N 13°35E 199 E10
Coney Island U.S.A. 40°34N 74°0W 132 C2
Conflict Group Papua N. G. 10°47S 151°45E 286 F6
Confolens France 46°2N 0°40E 174 B4
Confuso ➜ Paraguay 25°9S 57°34W 334 B4
Congaree ➜ U.S.A. 33°44N 80°38W 316 B9
Congaree △ U.S.A. 33°47N 80°47W 316 B9
Congaz Moldova 46°7N 28°36E 183 D13
Congerville U.S.A. 40°38N 89°11W 310 D7
Conghua China 23°36N 113°31E 229 F9
Congjiang China 25°43N 108°52E 228 E7
Congleton U.K. 53°10N 2°13W 168 D5
Congo Brazil 7°48S 36°40W 332 C4
Congo (Brazzaville) = Congo ■ Africa 1°0S 16°0E 264 C3
Congo (Kinshasa) = Congo, Dem. Rep. of the ■ Africa 3°0S 23°0E 265 C4
Congo ■ Africa 1°0S 16°0E 264 C3
Congo ➜ Africa 6°4S 12°24E 265 D2
Congo, Dem. Rep. of the ■ Africa 3°0S 23°0E 265 C4
Congo Basin Africa 0°10S 24°30E 254 G6
Congo Free State = Congo, Dem. Rep. of the ■ Africa 3°0S 23°0E 265 C4
Congonhas Brazil 20°30S 43°52W 333 F3
Congonhas São Paulo ✕ (CGH) Brazil 23°38S 46°39W 137 B2
Congress U.S.A. 34°9N 112°51W 305 J7
Conguillio △ Chile 38°40S 71°42W 336 A2
Conil de la Frontera Spain 36°17N 6°10W 195 J4
Conills, I. des Spain 39°11N 2°58E 206 B3
Conimbla △ Australia 33°45S 148°28E 283 B8
Coniston Canada 46°29N 80°51W 298 C3
Conjeeveram = Kanchipuram India 12°52N 79°45E 245 H4
Conklin Alta., Canada 55°38N 111°5W 297 B6
Conklin N.Y., U.S.A. 42°2N 75°49W 313 D9
Conkouati ⌓ Congo 3°50S 11°28E 264 C2
Conlendas, Pta. das Azores 38°38N 27°14W 153 d1
Conley ➜ U.S.A. 33°40N 84°17W 113 C3
Conn, L. Ireland 54°3N 9°15W 166 B2
Connacht □ Ireland 53°43N 9°12W 166 C2
Connaught Place Delhi, India 120 b2
Conneaut U.S.A. 41°57N 80°34W 312 E4
Conneautville U.S.A. 41°45N 80°22W 312 E4
Connecticut □ U.S.A. 41°30N 72°45W 313 E12
Connecticut ➜ U.S.A. 41°16N 72°20W 313 E12
Connell U.S.A. 46°40N 118°52W 304 C4
Connellsville U.S.A. 40°1N 79°35W 312 F5
Connemara Ireland 53°29N 9°45W 166 C2
Connemara △ Ireland 53°32N 9°52W 166 C2
Conner Phil. 17°48N 121°19E 232 C3
Connerré France 48°3N 0°30E 172 D7
Connersville U.S.A. 39°39N 85°8W 311 E11
Connors Ra. Australia 21°40S 149°10E 280 C4
Conoble Australia 32°55S 144°33E 283 B6
Conococha Peru 10°7S 77°18W 330 C2
Conoename ➜ Suriname 5°48N 55°55W 329 B6
Cononaco ➜ Ecuador 1°32S 75°35W 328 D2
Conques France 44°36N 2°23E 174 D6
Conquest Canada 51°32N 107°14W 297 C7
Conquista = Vitória da Conquista Brazil 14°51S 40°51W 333 D3
Conrad Iowa, U.S.A. 42°14N 92°52W 310 B4
Conrad Mont., U.S.A. 48°10N 111°57W 304 B8
Conrad Rise S. Ocean 53°0S 41°0E 151 B5
Conran, C. Australia 37°49S 148°44E 283 D8
Conroe U.S.A. 30°19N 95°27W 314 F7
Consecon Canada 44°0N 77°31W 312 C7
Conselheiro Lafaiete Brazil 20°40S 43°48W 333 F3
Conselheiro Pena Brazil 19°10S 41°30W 333 E3
Consell Spain 39°40N 2°49E 206 B3
Conselve Italy 45°14N 11°52E 199 C8
Conservatori, Palazzo dei Rome, Italy 136 c3
Consett U.K. 54°51N 1°50W 168 C6
Consolação Brazil 23°32S 46°38W 137 B2
Consort Canada 52°1N 110°46W 297 C6
Constance = Konstanz Germany 47°40N 9°10E 179 H5
Constance, L. = Bodensee Europe 47°35N 9°25E 179 H5
Constanţa Romania 44°14N 28°38E 183 F13
Constanţa □ Romania 44°15N 28°15E 183 F13
Constantia S. Africa 34°2S 18°26E 118 B1
Constantina Spain 37°51N 5°40W 195 H5
Constantine Algeria 36°25N 6°42E 261 A6
Constantine Mich., U.S.A. 41°50N 85°40W 311 C11
Constantine □ Algeria 36°30N 6°40E 261 A6
Constantine, Arch of = Costantino, Arco di Rome, Italy 136 c3
Constantine, C. U.S.A. 58°24N 158°54W 303 G8
Constantinople = İstanbul Turkey 41°0N 28°58E 122 C1
Constitución B. Aires, Argentina 34°38S 58°23W 117 B2
Constitución Chile 35°20S 72°30W 334 D1
Constitución Uruguay 31°0S 57°50W 334 C4
Constitución de 1857 △ Mexico 32°4N 115°55W 318 A1
Constitution U.S.A. 33°42N 84°20W 113 B2
Constitution Avenue Washington, D.C., U.S.A. 143 b2
Constitution Square = Syntagma Square Athens, Greece 112 b2
Consuegra Spain 39°28N 3°36W 195 F7
Consul Canada 49°20N 109°30W 297 D7
Contact U.S.A. 41°46N 114°45W 304 F6
Contagem Brazil 19°55S 44°6W 333 E3
Contai India 21°54N 87°46E 243 J12
Contamana Peru 7°19S 74°55W 330 B3
Contarina Italy 45°1N 12°13E 199 C9
Contas ➜ Brazil 14°17S 39°1W 333 D4
Contes France 43°49N 7°19E 175 E11
Continental U.S.A. 41°6N 84°16W 311 C12
Contoocook U.S.A. 43°13N 71°45W 313 C13
Contra Costa Mozam. 25°9S 33°30E 271 C5
Contres France 47°24N 1°26E 172 E8
Contrexéville France 48°10N 5°53E 173 D12
Controller B. U.S.A. 60°7N 144°15W 303 F11
Contumaza Peru 7°23S 78°57W 330 B2
Contwoyto L. Canada 65°42N 110°50W 294 D9
Convención Colombia 8°28N 73°21W 328 B3
Convention Center U.S.A. 34°3N 118°16W 126 B3
Conversano Italy 40°58N 17°7E 201 B10
Converse U.S.A. 40°35N 85°52W 311 D11
Convoy U.S.A. 40°55N 84°43W 311 D12
Conway = Conwy U.K. 53°17N 3°50W 168 D4
Conway = Conwy ➜ U.K. 53°17N 3°50W 168 D4
Conway Australia 20°24S 148°41E 280 b
Conway Ont., Canada 44°6N 76°54W 312 B8
Conway Ark., U.S.A. 35°5N 92°26W 314 D8
Conway Fla., U.S.A. 28°30N 81°19W 133 B2
Conway N.H., U.S.A. 43°59N 71°7W 313 C13
Conway S.C., U.S.A. 33°51N 79°3W 315 E15
Conway, C. Australia 20°34S 148°46E 280 b
Conway, L. S. Austral., Australia 28°17S 135°35E 281 D2
Conway, L. Fla., U.S.A. 28°28N 81°21W 133 B2
Conwy U.K. 53°17N 3°50W 168 D4
Conwy □ U.K. 53°10N 3°44W 168 D4
Conwy ➜ U.K. 53°17N 3°50W 168 D4
Conyers U.S.A. 33°40N 84°1W 316 B5
Coober Pedy Australia 29°1S 134°43E 281 D1
Cooch Behar = Koch Bihar India 26°22N 89°29E 241 B2
Coogee Australia 33°55S 151°16E 139 B2
Cooinda Australia 13°15S 130°5E 278 B5
Cook S. Austral., Australia 30°37S 130°25E 279 F5
Cook Minn., U.S.A. 47°51N 92°41W 308 B7
Cook, B. Chile 55°10S 70°0W 336 E3
Cook, C. Canada 50°8N 127°55W 296 C3
Cook, Mt. = Aoraki Mount Cook N.Z. 43°36S 170°9E 285 D5
Cook, Récif de N. Cal. 19°25S 163°50E 288 d
Cook B. Vanuatu 18°46S 169°15E 287 H7
Cook Inlet U.S.A. 60°0N 152°0W 303 G10
Cook Is. Pac. Oc. 17°0S 160°0W 289 J12
Cook Strait N.Z. 41°15S 174°29E 284 H3
Cooke Plains Australia 35°23S 139°34E 282 C3
Cookeville U.S.A. 36°10N 85°30W 315 C12
Cookhouse S. Africa 32°44S 25°47E 270 D4
Cooks Hammock U.S.A. 29°56N 83°17W 316 F6
Cooks Harbour Canada 51°36N 55°52W 299 B8
Cookshire Canada 45°25N 71°38W 313 A13
Cookstown Ont., Canada 44°11N 79°42W 312 B5
Cookstown Tyrone, U.K. 54°39N 6°45W 166 B5
Cooksville Canada 43°35N 79°38W 141 B1
Cooktown Australia 15°30S 145°16E 280 B4
Coolabah Australia 31°1S 146°43E 283 A7
Cooladdi Australia 26°37S 145°23E 281 D4
Coolah Australia 31°48S 149°41E 283 A8
Coolah Tops △ Australia 31°52S 150°0E 283 A9
Coolamon Australia 34°46S 147°8E 283 C7
Coolgardie Australia 30°55S 121°8E 279 F3
Coolidge Ariz., U.S.A. 32°59N 111°31W 305 K8
Coolidge Ga., U.S.A. 31°1N 83°52W 316 D6
Coolidge Dam U.S.A. 33°10N 110°32W 305 K8
Coolock Ireland 53°22N 6°12W 120 A2
Cooma Australia 36°12S 149°8E 283 D8
Coon Rapids Iowa, U.S.A. 41°53N 94°41W 310 C2
Coon Rapids Minn., U.S.A. 45°9N 93°19W 308 C7
Coonabarabran Australia 31°14S 149°18E 283 A8
Coonalpyn Australia 35°43S 139°52E 282 C3
Coonamble Australia 30°56S 148°27E 283 A8
Coonana Australia 31°0S 123°0E 279 F3
Coonana ☼ Australia 30°51S 122°53E 279 F3
Coondapoor India 13°42N 74°40E 245 H2
Cooninnie, L. Australia 26°4S 139°59E 281 D2
Coonoor India 11°21N 76°45E 245 J3
Cooper U.S.A. 33°23N 95°42W 314 E7
Cooper ➜ U.S.A. 32°50N 79°56W 316 C10
Cooper Cr. ➜ Australia 28°29S 137°46E 281 D2
Cooper Ridge Pac. Oc. 10°0N 150°30W 289 G12
Cooper's Hill Jamaica 18°4N 76°51W 320 a
Cooperstown N. Dak., U.S.A. 47°27N 98°8W 308 B4
Cooperstown N.Y., U.S.A. 42°42N 74°56W 313 D10
Coopersville U.S.A. 43°4N 85°57W 311 A11
Coopracambra △ Australia 37°20S 149°20E 283 D8
Coora ➜ Trin. & Tob. 10°10N 61°28W 323 t
Coorabie Australia 31°54S 132°18E 279 F5
Coorong, The Australia 35°50S 139°20E 282 C3
Coorong △ Australia 36°0S 139°29E 282 D3
Coorow Australia 29°53S 116°2E 279 E2
Cooroy Australia 26°22S 152°54E 281 D5
Coos Bay U.S.A. 43°22N 124°13W 304 E1
Coosa ➜ U.S.A. 32°30N 86°16W 315 E11
Cootamundra Australia 34°36S 148°1E 283 C8
Cootehill Ireland 54°4N 7°5W 166 B4
Copacabana Brazil 22°58S 43°11W 135 B1
Copahue Paso Argentina 37°49S 71°8W 334 D1
Copainalá Mexico 17°4N 93°18W 319 D6
Copake U.S.A. 42°7N 73°31W 313 D11
Copalnic Mănăştur Romania 47°30N 23°41E 183 C8
Copán Honduras 14°50N 89°9W 320 D2
Copatana Brazil 2°48S 67°4W 328 D4
Cope Colo., U.S.A. 39°40N 102°51W 304 G12
Cope S.C., U.S.A. 33°23N 81°0W 316 B8
Cope, C. Spain 37°26N 1°28W 197 H3
Copeland U.S.A. 25°57N 81°22W 317 K8
Copenhagen = København Denmark 55°40N 12°26E 118 A2
Copenhagen U.S.A. 43°54N 75°41W 313 C9
Copertino Italy 40°16N 18°3E 201 B11
Copiapó Chile 27°30S 70°20W 334 B1
Copiapó ➜ Chile 27°19S 70°56W 334 B1
Coplay U.S.A. 40°44N 75°29W 313 F9
Copley Australia 30°36S 138°26E 282 A3
Copo △ Argentina 25°53S 61°41W 334 B3
Copp L. Canada 60°14N 114°40W 296 A6
Copparo Italy 44°54N 11°49E 199 D8
Copper ➜ U.S.A. 60°18N 145°3W 303 F11
Copper Canyon = Barranca del Cobre ⌓ Mexico 27°18N 107°40W 318 B3
Copper Center U.S.A. 61°58N 145°18W 303 F11
Copper City = Invermere Canada 50°30N 116°2W 296 C5
Copper Harbor U.S.A. 47°28N 87°53W 308 B10
Copper Queen Zimbabwe 17°29S 29°18E 269 F2
Copperas Cove U.S.A. 31°8N 97°54W 314 F6
Copperbelt □ Zambia 13°15S 27°30E 269 E2
Coppermine = Kugluktuk Canada 67°50N 115°5W 294 D8
Coppermine ➜ Canada 67°49N 116°4W 294 D8
Copperopolis U.S.A. 37°58N 120°38W 306 H6
Copşa Mică Romania 46°7N 24°15E 183 D9
Coquet ➜ U.K. 55°20N 1°32W 168 B6
Coquilhatville = Mbandaka Dem. Rep. of the Congo 0°1N 18°18E 264 B3
Coquille U.S.A. 43°11N 124°11W 304 E1
Coquimbo Chile 30°0S 71°20W 334 C1
Coquimbo □ Chile 31°0S 71°0W 334 C1
Coquitlam Canada 49°17N 122°45W 296 D4
Corabia Romania 43°48N 24°30E 183 G9
Coração de Jesus Brazil 16°43S 44°22W 333 E3
Coracora Peru 15°5S 73°45W 330 D3
Coraki Australia 28°59S 153°17E 281 D5
Coral U.S.A. 40°29N 79°10W 312 F5
Coral Bay W. Austral., Australia 23°8S 113°46E 278 D1
Coral Bay Phil. 8°25N 117°20E 233 G1
Coral Gables U.S.A. 25°43N 80°16W 128 B2
Coral Harbour Bahamas 24°58N 77°28W 153 b
Coral Harbour Nunavut, Canada 64°8N 83°10W 295 E15
Coral Heights Bahamas 25°0N 77°27W 153 b
Coral Hills U.S.A. 38°51N 76°55W 143 B4
Coral Sea Pac. Oc. 15°0S 150°0E 286 F4
Coral Sea Basin Pac. Oc. 14°0S 152°0E 288 J7
Coral Sea Islands Terr. □ Australia 20°0S 155°0E 276 D9
Coral Springs U.S.A. 26°16N 80°16W 317 J9
Corales del Rosario △ Colombia 10°8N 75°46W 328 A2
Coralville U.S.A. 41°40N 91°35W 310 C5
Coralville L. U.S.A. 41°42N 91°33W 310 C5
Corangamite, L. Australia 38°5S 143°30E 282 E5
Corantijn ➜ Suriname 5°50N 57°8W 329 B6
Coraopolis U.S.A. 40°31N 80°10W 312 F4
Corato Italy 41°9N 16°25E 201 A9
Corbeil-Essonnes France 48°36N 2°26E 173 D9
Corbeiro, C. W. Sahara 21°50N 17°0W 260 D1
Corbett △ India 29°20N 79°0E 243 E8
Corbie France 49°54N 2°30E 173 C9
Corbières France 42°55N 2°35E 174 F6
Corbigny France 47°16N 3°40E 173 E10
Corbin U.S.A. 36°57N 84°6W 309 G11
Corbones ➜ Spain 37°36N 5°39W 195 H5
Corbu Romania 44°25N 28°39E 183 F13
Corby U.K. 52°30N 0°41W 169 E7
Corcaigh = Cork Ireland 51°54N 8°29W 166 E3
Corcoran U.S.A. 36°6N 119°33W 306 J7
Corcovado, Cristo Redentar Brazil 22°57S 43°12W 135 B1
Corcovado △ Costa Rica 8°33N 83°35W 320 E3
Cordele U.S.A. 31°58N 83°47W 316 D6
Cordell U.S.A. 35°17N 98°59W 314 D5
Cordenòns Italy 45°59N 12°42E 199 C9
Cordes-sur-Ciel France 44°5N 1°57E 174 D5
Cordillera Azul △ Peru 7°30S 76°30W 330 B2
Cordillera de los Picachos △ Colombia 2°39N 74°30W 328 C3
Cordisburgo Brazil 19°7S 44°21W 333 E3
Córdoba Argentina 31°20S 64°10W 334 C3
Córdoba Veracruz, Mexico 18°53N 96°56W 319 D5
Córdoba Spain 37°50N 4°50W 195 H6
Córdoba □ Argentina 31°22S 64°15W 334 C3
Córdoba □ Colombia 8°20N 75°40W 328 B2
Córdoba □ Spain 38°5N 5°0W 195 G6
Córdoba, Sierra de Argentina 31°10S 64°25W 334 C3
Cordon Phil. 16°42N 121°32E 232 C3
Cordova U.S.A. 60°33N 145°45W 303 F11
Corduff Ireland 53°23N 6°21W 120 A1
Corella Spain 42°7N 1°48W 196 C3
Corella ➜ Australia 19°34S 140°47E 280 B3
Coremas Brazil 7°1S 37°58W 332 C4
Corentyne ➜ Guyana 5°50N 57°8W 329 B6
Corfield Australia 21°40S 143°21E 280 C3
Corfu = Kerkyra Greece 39°38N 19°50E 206 B9
Corfu U.S.A. 42°57N 78°24W 312 D6
Corfu ✕ (CFU) Greece 39°35N 19°54E 204 B1
Corfu, Str. of = Kerkyras, Notio Steno Greece 39°34N 20°0E 206 B10
Corgo = O Corgo Spain 42°56N 7°25W 194 C3
Corguinho Brazil 19°53S 54°52W 331 D7
Cori Italy 41°39N 12°55E 200 A5
Coria Spain 39°58N 6°33W 194 F4
Coria del Río Spain 37°16N 6°3W 195 H4
Coricudgy Australia 32°51S 150°24E 283 B9
Corigliano Cálabro Italy 39°36N 16°31E 201 C9
Corimba, Barra de Angola 8°52S 13°9E 265 D2
Coringa Is. Australia 16°58S 149°58E 280 B4
Corinth = Korinthos Greece 37°56N 22°55E 204 D4
Corinth Grenada 12°2N 61°40W 323 q
Corinth Ky., U.S.A. 38°30N 84°34W 311 F12
Corinth Miss., U.S.A. 34°56N 88°31W 315 D10
Corinth N.Y., U.S.A. 43°15N 73°49W 313 C11
Corinth, G. of = Korinthiakos Kolpos Greece 38°16N 22°30E 204 C4
Corinth Canal Greece 37°58N 23°0E 204 D4
Corinto Brazil 18°20S 44°30W 333 E3
Corinto Nic. 12°30N 87°10W 320 D2
Coriole Somali Rep. 1°47N 44°32E 267 D5
Corisco Eq. Guin. 0°55N 9°18E 264 B1
Cork Ireland 51°54N 8°29W 166 E3
Cork □ Ireland 51°57N 8°40W 166 E3
Cork Harbour Ireland 51°47N 8°16W 166 E3
Corlay France 48°20N 3°5W 172 D3
Corleone Italy 37°49N 13°18E 200 E6
Corleto Perticara Italy 40°23N 16°2E 201 B9
Çorlu Turkey 41°11N 27°49E 203 E11
Cormack L. Canada 60°56N 121°37W 296 A4
Cormano Italy 45°32N 9°10E 129 A2
Cormòns Italy 45°58N 13°28E 199 C10
Cormorant Canada 54°14N 100°35W 297 C8
Cormorant L. Canada 54°15N 100°50W 297 C8
Corn Is. = Maíz, Is. del Nic. 12°15N 83°4W 320 D3
Cornalvo ⌓ Spain 39°1N 6°13W 195 F4
Cornaredo Italy 45°30N 9°1E 129 A1
Cornélio Procópio Brazil 23°7S 50°40W 335 A5
Cornell U.S.A. 41°0N 88°44W 311 D8
Corner Brook Canada 48°57N 57°58W 299 C8
Corner Inlet Australia 38°45S 146°20E 283 E7
Corner Seamounts Atl. Oc. 35°0N 52°0W 152 C6
Corneşti Moldova 47°21N 28°1E 183 C13
Corneto = Tarquínia Italy 42°15N 11°45E 199 F8
Corníglio Italy 44°29N 10°5E 198 D7
Corning Ark., U.S.A. 36°25N 90°35W 315 C9
Corning Calif., U.S.A. 39°56N 122°11W 304 G2
Corning Iowa, U.S.A. 40°59N 94°44W 310 D2
Corning N.Y., U.S.A. 42°9N 77°3W 312 D7
Corno Grande Italy 42°28N 13°34E 199 F10
Cornwall Ont., Canada 45°2N 74°44W 313 A10
Cornwall Pa., U.S.A. 40°17N 76°25W 313 F8
Cornwall □ Jamaica 18°15N 77°54W 320 a
Cornwall □ U.K. 50°26N 4°40W 169 G3
Cornwall I. Canada 77°37N 94°38W 295 B13
Cornwallis I. Canada 75°8N 95°0W 295 B13
Cornwell U.S.A. 27°23N 81°6W 317 H8
Corny Pt. Australia 34°55S 137°0E 282 C2
Coro Venezuela 11°25N 69°41W 328 A4
Coroaci Brazil 18°35S 42°17W 333 E3
Coroatá Brazil 4°8S 44°0W 332 B3
Corocoro Bolivia 17°15S 68°28W 330 D4
Corocoro, I. Venezuela 8°30N 60°10W 329 B5
Coroico Bolivia 16°0S 67°50W 330 D4
Coromandel Brazil 18°28S 47°13W 333 E2
Coromandel N.Z. 36°45S 175°31E 284 C4
Coromandel Coast India 12°30N 81°0E 245 H5
Coromandel Pen. N.Z. 37°0S 175°45E 284 D4
Coromandel Ra. N.Z. 37°0S 175°40E 284 D4
Coron Phil. 12°1N 120°12E 232 E3
Coron Bay Phil. 11°54N 120°8E 233 F3
Coron I. Phil. 11°55N 120°14E 233 F3
Corona Calif., U.S.A. 33°53N 117°34W 307 M9
Corona N. Mex., U.S.A. 34°15N 105°36W 305 J11
Coronado U.S.A. 32°41N 117°10W 307 N9
Coronado, B. de Costa Rica 9°0N 83°40W 320 E3
Coronados, G. de los Chile 41°40S 74°0W 336 B2
Coronados, Is. Los Mexico 32°26N 117°19W 307 N9
Coronation Canada 52°5N 111°27W 296 C6
Coronation Gulf Canada 68°25N 110°0W 294 D10
Coronation I. Antarctica 60°45S 46°0W 151 C18
Coronation Is. Australia 14°57S 124°55E 278 B3
Coronda Argentina 31°58S 60°56W 334 C3
Coronel Chile 37°0S 73°10W 334 D1
Coronel Bogado Paraguay 27°11S 56°18W 334 B4
Coronel Dorrego Argentina 38°40S 61°10W 334 D3
Coronel Fabriciano Brazil 19°31S 42°38W 333 E3
Coronel Murta Brazil 16°37S 42°11W 333 E3
Coronel Oviedo Paraguay 25°24S 56°30W 334 B4
Coronel Ponce Brazil 15°34S 55°1W 331 D6
Coronel Pringles Argentina 38°0S 61°30W 334 D3
Coronel Suárez Argentina 37°30S 61°52W 334 D3
Coronel Vidal Argentina 37°28S 57°45W 334 D4
Corongo Peru 8°30S 77°53W 330 B2
Coropuna, Nevado Peru 15°30S 72°41W 330 D3
Corossol St.-Martin 17°54N 62°51W 322 a
Çorovodë Albania 40°31N 20°14E 202 F4
Corowa Australia 35°58S 146°21E 283 C7
Corozal Colombia 9°19N 75°18W 328 B2
Corozal Puerto Rico 18°21N 66°19W 321 b
Corozal □ Belize 18°23N 88°23W 319 D7
Corozal Pt. Trin. & Tob. 10°45N 61°37W 323 t
Corps France 44°50N 5°56E 175 D9
Corpus Argentina 27°10S 55°30W 335 B4
Corpus Christi U.S.A. 27°47N 97°24W 314 H6
Corpus Christi, L. U.S.A. 28°2N 97°52W 314 G6
Corque Bolivia 18°20S 67°41W 330 D4
Corral Chile 39°52S 73°26W 336 A2
Corral de Almaguer Spain 39°45N 3°10W 194 F7
Corralejo Canary Is. 28°43N 13°53W 153 e2
Corraun Pen. Ireland 53°54N 9°54W 166 C2
Corréggio Italy 44°46N 10°47E 198 D7
Corregidor Phil. 14°23N 120°35E 232 D3
Corrente Brazil 10°27S 45°10W 332 D2
Corrente ➜ Brazil 13°8S 43°28W 333 D3
Correntes ➜ Brazil 17°38S 55°8W 331 D6
Correntes, C. das Mozam. 24°6S 35°34E 271 B6
Correntina Brazil 13°20S 44°39W 333 D3
Corrèze □ France 45°20N 1°45E 174 C5
Corrèze ➜ France 45°10N 1°28E 174 C5
Corrib, L. Ireland 53°27N 9°16W 166 C2
Corridónia Italy 43°15N 13°30E 199 E10
Corrientes Argentina 27°30S 58°45W 334 B4
Corrientes □ Argentina 28°0S 57°0W 334 B4
Corrientes ➜ Argentina 30°42S 59°38W 334 C4
Corrientes ➜ Peru 3°43S 74°35W 328 D3
Corrientes, C. Colombia 5°30N 77°34W 328 B2
Corrientes, C. Cuba 21°43N 84°30W 320 B3
Corrientes, C. Jalisco, Mexico 20°25N 105°42W 318 C3
Corrigan U.S.A. 31°0N 94°52W 314 F7
Corrigin Australia 32°20S 117°53E 279 F2
Corriverton Guyana 5°55N 57°20W 329 B6
Corry U.S.A. 41°55N 79°39W 312 E5
Corryong Australia 36°12S 147°53E 283 D7
Corse □ France 42°0N 9°0E 175 G13
Corse, C. France 43°1N 9°25E 175 E13
Corse ⌓ France 42°14N 9°10E 175 F13
Corse-du-Sud □ France 41°45N 9°0E 175 G13
Corsica = Corse □ France 42°0N 9°0E 175 G13
Corsicana U.S.A. 32°6N 96°28W 314 E6
Córsico Italy 45°25N 9°6E 129 B1
Corsini, Palazzo Rome, Italy 136 c1
Corstorphine U.K. 55°56N 3°17W 121 B2
Corte France 42°19N 9°11E 175 F13
Corte Pinto Portugal 37°42N 7°29W 195 H3
Cortegana Spain 37°52N 6°49W 195 H4
Cortes Phil. 9°17N 126°11E 233 G6
Cortés, Mar de = California, G. de Mexico 27°0N 111°0W 318 B2
Cortez U.S.A. 37°21N 108°35W 305 H9
Cortina d'Ampezzo Italy 46°32N 12°8E 199 B9
Cortland N.Y., U.S.A. 42°36N 76°11W 313 D8
Cortland Ohio, U.S.A. 41°20N 80°44W 312 E4
Cortona Italy 43°16N 11°59E 199 E8
Corubal ➜ Guinea-Biss. 11°57N 15°5W 262 C2
Coruche Portugal 38°57N 8°30W 195 G2
Çoruh ➜ Turkey 41°38N 41°38E 191 K5
Çorum Turkey 40°30N 34°57E 212 B6
Çorum □ Turkey 40°40N 35°0E 212 B6
Corumbá Brazil 19°0S 57°30W 331 D6
Corumbá ➜ Brazil 18°19S 48°55W 333 E2
Corumbá de Goiás Brazil 16°0S 48°50W 333 E2
Corumbaíba Brazil 18°9S 48°34W 333 E2
Corund Romania 46°30N 25°13E 183 D10
Corunna = A Coruña Spain 43°20N 8°25W 194 B2
Corunna U.S.A. 42°59N 84°7W 311 B12
Corvallis U.S.A. 44°34N 123°16W 304 D2
Corvette, L. de la Canada 53°25N 74°3W 298 B5
Corviale Italy 41°51N 12°25E 136 B1
Corvo Azores 39°42N 31°6W 153 d2
Coryal Trin. & Tob. 10°30N 61°11W 323 t
Corydon Ind., U.S.A. 38°13N 86°7W 311 F10
Corydon Iowa, U.S.A. 40°46N 93°19W 310 D3
Corydon Ky., U.S.A. 37°44N 87°43W 311 G9
Cosalá Mexico 24°23N 106°41W 318 C3
Cosamaloapan de Carpio Mexico 18°22N 95°48W 319 D5
Cosenza Italy 39°18N 16°15E 201 C9
Coşereni Romania 44°38N 26°35E 183 F11
Coshocton U.S.A. 40°16N 81°51W 312 F3
Coslada Spain 40°25N 3°35W 127 B2
Cosmo Newberry Australia 28°0S 122°54E 279 E3

Cosmo Newberry ◎
　Australia 27°59S 122°53E 279 E3
Cosmonaut Sea S. Ocean 66°30S 40°0E 151 C5
Cosne-Cours-sur-Loire
　France 47°24N 2°54E 173 E9
Coso Junction U.S.A. 36°3N 117°57W 307 J9
Coso Pk. U.S.A. 36°13N 117°44W 307 J9
Cospeito Spain 43°12N 7°34W 194 B3
Cosquín Argentina 31°15S 64°30W 334 C3
Cossato Italy 45°34N 8°10E 198 C5
Cossé-le-Vivien France 47°57N 0°54W 172 E6
Cossigny France 48°43N 2°40E 134 B4
Cosson → France 47°30N 1°15E 172 E8
Costa Blanca Spain 38°25N 0°10W 197 G4
Costa Brava Spain 41°30N 3°0E 196 D8
Costa Cálida Spain 37°30N 1°30W 197 H3
Costa Daurada Spain 41°12N 1°15E 196 D6
Costa del Sol Spain 36°30N 4°30W 195 J6
Costa del Pins Spain 39°38N 3°26E 206 B4
Costa Mesa U.S.A. 33°38N 117°55W 307 M9
Costa Rica ■ Cent. Amer. 10°0N 84°0W 320 E3
Costa Smeralda Italy 41°5N 9°35E 200 A2
Costantino, Arco di Rome, Italy k
Costermansville = Bukavu
　Dem. Rep. of the Congo 2°20S 28°52E 268 C2
Costeşti Romania 44°40N 24°53E 183 F9
Costigliole d'Asti Italy 44°47N 8°11E 198 D5
Cosumnes → U.S.A. 38°16N 121°26W 306 G5
Coswig Sachsen, Germany 51°7N 13°34E 178 D9
Coswig Sachsen-Anhalt,
　Germany 51°53N 12°27E 178 D8
Cotabato Phil. 7°14N 124°15E 233 H5
Cotabato □ Phil. 7°10N 125°0E 233 H5
Cotacajes → Bolivia 16°0S 67°1W 330 D4
Cotagaita Bolivia 20°45S 65°40W 330 E4
Cotahuasi Peru 15°12S 72°50W 330 D3
Cotao Portugal 38°45N 9°17E 196 b1
Côte d'Azur France 43°25N 7°10E 175 E11
Côte-d'Ivoire = Ivory Coast ■
　Africa 7°30N 5°0W 262 D4
Côte d'Or France 47°10N 4°50E 173 E11
Côte-d'Or □ France 47°30N 4°50E 173 E11
Côte-St-Luc Canada 45°28N 73°39W 130 B2
Coteau des Prairies
　U.S.A. 45°20N 97°50W 308 C6
Coteau du Missouri
　U.S.A. 47°0N 100°0W 308 B4
Cotegipe Brazil 12°2S 44°15W 333 D3
Cotentin France 49°15N 1°30W 172 C5
Côtes d'Armor □ France 48°25N 2°40W 172 D4
Côtes de Meuse France 49°15N 5°22E 173 C12
Côtes-du-Nord = Côtes d'Armor □
　France 48°25N 2°40W 172 D4
Cotiella Spain 42°31N 0°19E 196 C5
Cotillo Canary Is. 28°41N 14°1W 153 d2
Cotiujeni Moldova 47°51N 28°33E 183 C13
Cotoca Bolivia 17°49S 63°3W 331 D5
Cotonou Benin 6°20N 2°25E 263 D5
Cotopaxi Ecuador 0°40S 78°30W 328 D2
Cotopaxi □ Ecuador 0°5S 78°55W 328 D2
Cotopaxi ◭ Ecuador 0°39S 78°24W 328 D2
Cotronei Italy 39°9N 16°47E 201 C9
Cotswold Hills U.K. 51°42N 2°10W 169 F5
Cottage Grove U.S.A. 43°48N 123°3W 304 E2
Cottageville U.S.A. 32°56N 80°29W 316 C9
Cottam Canada 42°8N 82°45W 312 D2
Cottbus Germany 51°45N 14°20E 178 D10
Cotton Ground
　St. Kitts & Nevis 17°11N 62°36W 322 d
Cottondale U.S.A. 30°48N 85°23W 316 E4
Cottonwood Ala., U.S.A. 31°3N 85°18W 316 E4
Cottonwood Ariz., U.S.A. 34°45N 112°1W 305 J7
Cotulla U.S.A. 28°26N 99°14W 314 G5
Cotunduba, I. de Brazil 22°57S 43°8W 135 B2
Coubre, Pte. de la France 45°42N 1°15W 172 E4
Coubron France 48°54N 2°34E 134 A4
Couches France 46°53N 4°30E 173 F11
Couço Portugal 38°59N 8°17W 195 G2
Coudersport U.S.A. 41°46N 78°1W 312 E6
Couedic, C. du Australia 36°5S 136°40E 282 D2
Couëron France 47°13N 1°44W 172 E5
Couesnon → France 48°38N 1°32W 172 D5
Couhé France 46°17N 0°11E 174 B4
Coulanges-sur-Yonne
　France 47°31N 3°33E 173 E10
Coulee City U.S.A. 47°37N 119°17W 304 C4
Coulee Dam Nat. Recr. Area = Lake
　Roosevelt U.S.A. 48°5N 118°14W 304 B4
Coulibistri Dominica 15°27N 61°28W 323 k
Coulman I. Antarctica 73°35S 170°0E 151 D11
Coulommiers France 48°49N 3°3E 173 D10
Coulon → France 43°51N 5°6E 175 E9
Coulonge → Canada 45°52N 76°46W 298 C4
Coulonges-sur-l'Autize
　France 46°29N 0°36W 174 B3
Coulterville Calif.,
　U.S.A. 37°43N 120°12W 306 H6
Coulterville Ill., U.S.A. 38°11N 89°36W 310 F7
Council Alaska, U.S.A. 64°53N 163°41W 303 B7
Council Idaho, U.S.A. 44°44N 116°26W 304 D5
Council Bluffs U.S.A. 41°16N 95°52W 308 E6
Council Grove U.S.A. 38°40N 96°29W 308 F5
Countryside U.S.A. 41°47N 87°52W 119 C1
County Art Museum
　U.S.A. 34°4N 118°21W 126 B2
Coupeville U.S.A. 48°13N 122°41W 306 B4
Courantyne → S. Amer. 5°55N 57°5W 329 B6
Courbevoie France 48°53N 2°14E 134 A2
Courcelles Belgium 50°28N 4°22E 170 D4
Courchevel France 45°25N 6°36E 175 C10
Courçon France 46°15N 0°50W 174 B3
Courland = Tervel 11°13N 60°47W 323 s
Courmayeur Italy 45°48N 6°58E 198 C3
Couronne, C. France 43°19N 5°3E 175 E9
Cours-la-Ville France 46°7N 4°19E 173 F11
Coursan France 43°14N 3°4E 174 E7
Courseulles-sur-Mer
　France 49°20N 0°29W 172 C6
Courtenay B.C., Canada 49°45N 125°0W 296 D4
Courtenay Loiret, France 48°2N 3°3E 173 D10
Courtland Ont., Canada 42°51N 80°38W 312 D4
Courtland Calif., U.S.A. 38°20N 121°34W 306 G5
Courtrai = Kortrijk
　Belgium 50°50N 3°17E 170 D3
Courtright Canada 42°49N 82°28W 312 D2
Courtry France 48°55N 2°35E 134 A4
Coushatta U.S.A. 32°1N 93°21W 314 E8
Coutances France 49°3N 1°28W 172 C5
Coutras France 45°3N 0°8W 174 C3
Coutts Crossing
　Australia 29°49S 152°55E 281 D5
Couva Trin. & Tob. 10°25N 61°27W 323 t
Couvin Belgium 50°3N 4°29E 170 D4
Covarrubias Spain 42°4N 3°31W 194 C7
Covasna Romania 45°50N 26°10E 183 E11
Covasna □ Romania 45°50N 26°0E 183 E10
Cove I. Canada 45°17N 81°44W 312 A3
Coveñas Colombia 9°24N 75°44W 328 B2
Covent Garden London, U.K. 125 b4
Coventry U.K. 52°25N 1°28W 169 E6
Coverdale U.K. 31°38N 83°58W 168 C6
Covilhã Portugal 40°17N 7°31W 194 E3
Covington Ga., U.S.A. 33°36N 83°51W 316 B6

Covington Ind., U.S.A. 40°9N 87°24W 311 D9
Covington Ky., U.S.A. 39°5N 84°30W 311 E12
Covington Ohio, U.S.A. 40°7N 84°21W 311 D12
Covington Tenn., U.S.A. 35°34N 89°39W 315 D10
Covington Va., U.S.A. 37°47N 79°59W 309 G14
Cowal, L. Australia 33°40S 147°25E 283 B7
Cowan, Cerro Ecuador 0°12S 90°48W 330 a
Cowan Canada 54°0N 100°45W 297 C7
Cowan L. Canada 54°0N 107°15W 297 C7
Cowangie Australia 35°12S 141°26E 282 C4
Cowansville Canada 45°14N 72°46W 313 A12
Coward Springs
　Australia 29°24S 136°49E 281 D2
Cowcowing Lakes
　Australia 30°55S 117°20E 279 F2
Cowden U.S.A. 39°15N 88°52W 311 E8
Cowdenbeath U.K. 56°7N 3°21W 167 E5
Cowell Australia 33°39S 136°56E 282 B2
Cowes Australia 38°28S 145°14E 283 E6
Cowes I. of W., U.K. 50°45N 1°18W 169 G6
Cowgate Edinburgh, U.K. 121 b3
Cowichan L. Canada 48°53N 124°17W 306 B2
Cowley U.K. 51°31N 0°28W 125 A1
Cowlitz → U.S.A. 46°6N 122°55W 306 D4
Cowra Australia 33°49S 148°42E 283 B8
Coxilha Grande Brazil 28°18S 51°30W 335 B5
Coxim Brazil 18°30S 54°55W 331 D7
Coxim → Brazil 18°34S 54°46W 331 D7
Cox's Bazar Bangla. 21°26N 91°59E 241 E3
Coyah Guinea 9°42N 13°22W 262 D2
Coyoacán Mexico 19°21N 99°9W 128 B2
Coyote Wells U.S.A. 32°44N 115°58W 307 N11
Coyuca de Benitez Mexico 17°2N 100°4W 319 D4
Coyuca de Catalán
　Mexico 18°20N 100°39W 318 D4
Cozad U.S.A. 40°52N 99°59W 308 E4
Cozes France 45°34N 0°49W 174 C3
Cozumel Mexico 20°31N 86°55W 319 C7
Cozumel, Isla Mexico 20°30N 86°40W 319 C7
Crab Hill Barbados 13°19N 59°38W 323 r
Crabs Pen. Antigua & B. 17°7N 61°45W 322 b
Cracow = Kraków Poland 50°4N 19°57E 185 H6
Cracow Australia 25°17S 150°17E 281 D5
Craddock Channel N.Z. 36°10S 175°13E 284 C4
Cradle Mt.-Lake St. Clair △
　Australia 41°49S 147°56E 281 G4
Cradock S. Austral.,
　Australia 32°6S 138°31E 281 E2
Cradock Eastern Cape,
　S. Africa 32°8S 25°36E 270 D4
Crafers Australia 35°0S 138°42E 282 C3
Craig Alaska, U.S.A. 55°29N 133°9W 303 J14
Craig Colo., U.S.A. 40°31N 107°33W 304 F10
Craigavon U.K. 54°27N 6°23W 166 B6
Craighall Park S. Africa 26°7S 28°1E 123 A2
Craigieburn Australia 37°36S 144°56E 283 D6
Craiglockhart U.K. 55°55N 3°14W 121 B2
Craigmillar U.K. 55°56N 3°9W 121 B3
Craigmore Zimbabwe 20°28S 32°50E 269 G3
Craik Canada 51°3N 105°49W 297 C7
Crailsheim Germany 49°8N 10°5E 179 F6
Craiova Romania 44°21N 23°48E 183 F8
Cramond U.K. 55°58N 3°18W 121 B2
Cramond Bridge U.K. 55°57N 3°19W 121 B1
Cramond I. U.K. 55°59N 3°17W 121 B2
Cramsie Australia 23°20S 144°15E 281 C3
Cranberry L. U.S.A. 44°11N 74°50W 313 B10
Cranberry Portage
　Canada 54°35N 101°23W 297 C8
Cranbrook W. Austral.,
　Australia 34°18S 117°33E 279 F2
Cranbrook B.C., Canada 49°30N 115°46W 296 D5
Crandon U.S.A. 45°34N 88°54W 308 C9
Crane Oreg., U.S.A. 43°25N 118°35W 304 E4
Crane Tex., U.S.A. 31°24N 102°21W 314 F3
Crane, The Barbados 13°6N 59°27W 323 r
Cranford U.S.A. 51°29N 0°25W 125 B1
Cranganore India 10°13N 76°13E 245 J3
Cranston U.S.A. 41°47N 71°26W 313 E13
Craon France 47°50N 0°58W 172 E6
Craonne France 49°27N 3°46E 173 C10
Craponne-sur-Arzon
　France 45°19N 3°51E 174 C7
Crasna Romania 46°32N 27°51E 183 D12
Crasna → Romania 47°44N 22°35E 182 C7
Crasnei, Munţii Romania 47°0N 23°20E 183 C8
Crater, L. St. Vincent 13°17N 61°13W 323 h
Crater L. Oreg., U.S.A. 42°56N 122°6W 304 E2
Crater Lake △ U.S.A. 42°55N 122°10W 304 E2
Crater Mt. Papua N. G. 6°37S 145°7E 286 D3
Crater Pt. Papua N. G. 5°25S 152°9E 286 C7
Craters of the Moon △
　U.S.A. 43°25N 113°30W 304 E7
Crateús Brazil 5°10S 40°39W 332 C3
Crati → Italy 39°43N 16°31E 201 C9
Crato Portugal 7°10S 39°25W 332 C4
Crato Portugal 39°16N 7°39W 195 F3
Cravo Norte Colombia 6°18N 70°12W 328 B3
Cravo Norte → Colombia 6°18N 70°12W 328 B3
Crawford Western Cape,
　S. Africa 33°59S 18°30E 118 A2
Crawford Ala., U.S.A. 32°27N 85°11W 316 C4
Crawford Nebr., U.S.A. 42°41N 103°25W 308 D2
Crawfordsville Ind.,
　U.S.A. 40°2N 86°54W 311 D10
Crawfordsville Iowa,
　U.S.A. 41°12N 91°32W 310 C5
Crawfordville Fla., U.S.A. 30°11N 84°23W 316 E5
Crawfordville Ga., U.S.A. 33°33N 82°54W 316 B7
Crawley U.K. 51°7N 0°11W 169 F7
Crayford U.K. 51°27N 0°11E 125 B5
Crazy Mts. U.S.A. 46°1N 110°20W 304 C8
Crean L. Canada 54°5N 106°9W 297 C7
Crécy-en-Ponthieu France 50°15N 1°53E 173 B8
Crediton Ont., Canada 43°17N 81°33W 312 C3
Crediton Devon, U.K. 50°47N 3°40W 169 G4
Cree → Canada 58°57N 105°47W 297 B7
Cree → Dumf. & Gall.,
　U.K. 54°55N 4°25W 167 G4
Cree L. Canada 57°30N 106°30W 297 B7
Creekmouth U.K. 51°30N 0°6E 125 A4
Creekside U.S.A. 40°40N 79°11W 312 F5
Creel Mexico 27°45N 107°38W 318 B3
Creemore Canada 44°19N 80°6W 312 B4
Creighton Sask., Canada 54°45N 101°54W 297 C8
Creighton Nebr., U.S.A. 42°28N 97°54W 308 D5
Creil France 49°15N 2°34E 173 C9
Crema Italy 45°22N 9°41E 198 C6
Cremona Italy 45°7N 10°2E 198 C7
Crepaja Serbia 45°1N 20°38E 182 C5
Crepori → Brazil 5°42S 57°8W 331 D6
Crépy France 49°35N 3°32E 173 C10
Crépy-en-Valois France 49°14N 2°54E 173 C9
Cres Croatia 44°58N 14°25E 199 D11
Crescent, L. U.S.A. 28°30N 81°33W 133 A1
Crescent Beach U.S.A. 29°46N 81°31W 316 F8
Crescent City Calif.,
　U.S.A. 41°45N 124°12W 304 F1
Crescent City Fla., U.S.A. 29°26N 81°31W 316 F8
Crescent Hd. Australia 31°11S 152°59E 283 A10
Crescentino Italy 45°11N 8°6E 198 C5
Crescenzago Italy 45°30N 9°14E 129 A2

Crespo Argentina 32°2S 60°19W 334 C3
Cressely France 48°44N 2°6E 134 B1
Cresskill U.S.A. 40°56N 73°57W 132 A2
Cresson France 40°28N 78°36W 312 F6
Cressy Australia 38°2S 143°40E 282 E5
Crest France 44°44N 5°2E 175 D9
Cresta, Mt. Phil. 17°1N 122°6E 232 C4
Crestline Calif., U.S.A. 34°14N 117°18W 307 L9
Crestline Ohio, U.S.A. 40°47N 82°44W 312 F2
Creston B.C., Canada 49°10N 116°31W 296 D5
Creston Calif., U.S.A. 35°32N 120°33W 306 K6
Creston Iowa, U.S.A. 41°4N 94°22W 310 C2
Crestview Calif., U.S.A. 37°33N 118°58W 306 H8
Crestview Fla., U.S.A. 30°46N 86°34W 316 E3
Creswick Australia 37°25S 143°58E 282 D5
Crêt de la Neige France 46°16N 5°58E 173 F12
Crete = Kríti Greece 35°15N 25°0E 207 E6
Crete Ill., U.S.A. 41°27N 87°38W 311 C9
Crete, Sea of Greece 36°0N 25°0E 205 E7
Créteil France 48°47N 2°27E 134 B4
Cretin, C. Papua N. G. 6°40S 147°53E 286 D4
Creus, C. de Spain 42°20N 3°19E 196 C8
Creuse □ France 46°10N 2°0E 173 F9
Creuse → France 47°0N 0°34E 174 B4
Creutzwald France 49°12N 6°42E 173 C13
Creuzburg Germany 51°3N 10°14E 178 D6
Crèvecœur-le-Grand
　France 49°37N 2°5E 173 C9
Crevillent Spain 38°12N 0°48W 197 G4
Crewe U.K. 53°6N 2°26W 168 D5
Crewkerne U.K. 50°53N 2°48W 169 G5
Crianlarich U.K. 56°24N 4°37W 166 E4
Criciúma Brazil 28°40S 49°23W 335 B6
Cricklewood U.K. 51°33N 0°13W 125 A2
Cricova Moldova 47°8N 28°52E 183 C13
Cridersville U.S.A. 40°39N 84°9W 311 D12
Crieff U.K. 56°22N 3°50W 167 E5
Crikvenica Croatia 45°11N 14°40E 199 C11
Crimea □ Ukraine 45°30N 33°10E 189 K8
Crimean Pen. = Krymskyy
　Pivostriv Ukraine 45°0N 34°0E 189 K8
Crimmitschau Germany 50°48N 12°24E 178 E8
Cristal, Mts. de Gabon 0°30N 10°30E 264 B2
Cristalândia Brazil 10°36S 49°11W 332 D2
Cristino Castro Brazil 8°49S 44°13W 332 C3
Cristo Redentor, Corcovado
　Brazil 22°56S 43°12W 135 B1
Cristóbal Panama 9°19N 79°54W 322 C3
Cristóbal, Pta. Ecuador 0°54S 91°31W 330 a
Cristuru Secuiesc
　Romania 46°17N 25°2E 183 D10
Crişul Alb → Romania 46°42N 21°17E 182 D6
Crişul Negru → Romania 46°42N 21°17E 182 D6
Crişul Repede →
　Romania 46°55N 20°59E 182 D5
Crittenden U.S.A. 38°47N 84°36W 311 F12
Criuleni Moldova 47°13N 29°10E 183 C14
Crivitz Germany 53°34N 11°39E 178 B7
Crixás Brazil 14°27S 49°58W 333 D2
Crna → Macedonia 41°33N 21°59E 202 E5
Crna Gora = Montenegro ■
　Europe 42°40N 19°20E 202 D3
Crna Gora Macedonia 42°10N 21°30E 202 D5
Crna Reka = Crna →
　Macedonia 41°33N 21°59E 202 E5
Crna Trava Serbia 42°49N 22°19E 202 D6
Crni Drim → Macedonia 41°17N 20°40E 202 E4
Crni Timok → Serbia 43°53N 22°15E 202 C6
Crnoljeva Planina Kosovo 42°20N 21°0E 202 D5
Črnomelj Slovenia 45°33N 15°10E 199 C12
Croagh Patrick Ireland 53°46N 9°40W 166 C2
Croajingolong △
　Australia 37°45S 149°26E 283 D8
Croatia ■ Europe 45°20N 16°0E 199 C13
Crockenhill U.K. 51°22N 0°9E 125 B4
Crocker U.S.A. 37°57N 92°16W 310 G4
Crocker, Banjaran
　Malaysia 5°40N 116°30E 235 A5
Crocker, Cerro Ecuador 0°36S 90°21W 330 a
Crocker Range △
　Malaysia 5°33N 116°8E 235 A5
Crockett U.S.A. 31°19N 95°27W 314 F7
Crocodile = Umgwenya →
　Mozam. 25°14S 32°18E 271 C5
Crocodile → S. Africa 24°12S 26°53E 270 B4
Crocodile Is. Australia 12°3S 134°58E 280 A1
Crocq France 45°52N 2°21E 174 C6
Crocus B. Anguilla 18°13N 63°5W 322 a
Crodo Italy 46°13N 8°19E 198 B5
Crohy Hd. Ireland 54°55N 8°26W 166 B3
Croisette, C. France 43°14N 5°22E 175 E9
Croisic, Pte. du France 47°19N 2°31W 172 E4
Croissy-Beaubourg France 48°49N 2°39E 134 B4
Croissy-sur-Seine France 48°52N 2°8E 134 A1
Croix, L. la Canada 48°20N 92°15W 298 D6
Croker, C. N. Terr.,
　Australia 10°58S 132°35E 278 B5
Croker, C. Ont., Canada 44°58N 80°59W 312 B4
Croker I. Australia 11°12S 132°32E 278 B5
Croker Islands Seas ◎
　Australia 11°20S 132°30E 278 B5
Cromarty U.K. 57°40N 4°2W 167 D4
Cromer U.K. 52°56N 1°17E 168 E9
Crompton Pt. Dominica 15°35N 61°19W 323 k
Cromwell N.Z. 45°3S 169°14E 285 F4
Cromwell Conn., U.S.A. 41°36N 72°39W 313 E12
Cronat France 46°43N 3°40E 173 F10
Crook U.K. 54°43N 1°45W 168 C6
Crooked → B.C.,
　Canada 54°50N 122°54W 296 C4
Crooked → Oreg.,
　U.S.A. 44°32N 121°16W 304 D3
Crooked Creek U.S.A. 61°52N 158°7W 303 F8
Crooked I. Bahamas 22°50N 74°10W 321 B5
Crooked Island Passage
　Bahamas 22°55N 74°35W 321 B5
Crookston Minn., U.S.A. 47°47N 96°37W 308 B5
Crookston Nebr., U.S.A. 42°56N 100°45W 308 D3
Crookwell Australia 34°28S 149°24E 283 B8
Cropane-Micone → Italy 38°31N 16°18E 201 D9
Crosby Gauteng, S. Africa 26°11S 27°59E 123 B1
Crosby Mersey., U.K. 53°30N 3°3W 168 D4
Crosby N. Dak., U.S.A. 48°55N 103°18W 308 A2
Crosbyton U.S.A. 33°40N 101°14W 314 D4
Cross → Nigeria 4°42N 8°21E 263 D6
Cross City U.S.A. 29°38N 83°7W 317 F6
Cross Fell U.K. 54°43N 2°28W 168 C5
Cross I. India 18°56N 72°51E 130 B2
Cross L. Canada 54°45N 97°30W 297 C9
Cross Lake U.S.A. 54°37N 97°47W 297 C9
Cross River □ Nigeria 6°0N 8°0E 263 D6
Cross River □ Nigeria 6°0N 8°0E 263 D6
Cross Sound U.S.A. 58°0N 135°0W 303 E14
Cross Timbers U.S.A. 38°1N 93°14W 310 F2
Crossen = Krosno Odrzańskie
　Poland 52°3N 15°7E 185 F2
Crossett U.S.A. 33°8N 91°58W 314 E9
Crosshaven Ireland 51°47N 8°17W 166 F4
Crossley, Mt. N.Z. 42°50S 172°5E 285 E4
Crossmaglen U.K. 54°5N 6°36W 166 B5
Crossmolina Ireland 54°6N 9°20W 166 B2
Crossville Ill., U.S.A. 38°10N 88°4W 311 F8

Crossville Tenn., U.S.A. 35°57N 85°2W 315 D12
Croswell U.S.A. 43°16N 82°37W 312 C2
Croton-on-Hudson
　U.S.A. 41°12N 73°55W 313 E11
Crotone Italy 39°5N 17°8E 201 C10
Crouch End U.K. 51°34N 0°7W 125 A3
Crow → Canada 59°41N 124°20W 296 B4
Crow Agency U.S.A. 45°36N 107°28W 304 D10
Crow Hd. Ireland 51°35N 10°9W 166 F1
Crowdy Bay △
　Australia 31°45S 152°45E 283 A10
Crowell U.S.A. 33°59N 99°43W 314 E5
Crowl Cr. → Australia 32°0S 145°30E 283 B8
Crowley U.S.A. 30°13N 92°22W 314 F8
Crowley, L. U.S.A. 37°35N 118°42W 306 H8
Crown I. Papua N. G. 5°7S 146°58E 286 C4
Crown Mine = Crown 26°12S 27°57E 123 B1
Crown Point Ind., U.S.A. 41°25N 87°22W 311 C9
Crown Point N.Y.,
　U.S.A. 43°57N 73°26W 313 C11
Crown Point ✈ (TAB)
　Trin. & Tob. 11°9N 60°50W 323 s
Crown Pt. Trin. & Tob. 11°18N 60°51W 323 s
Crownpoint U.S.A. 35°41N 108°9W 305 J9
Crows Landing U.S.A. 37°23N 121°6W 306 H5
Crows Nest N.S.W.,
　Australia 33°49S 151°12E 139 A2
Crows Nest Queens.,
　Australia 27°16S 152°4E 281 D5
Crowsnest Pass Canada 49°40N 114°40W 296 D6
Croydon London, U.K. 51°22N 0°5W 125 B3
Croydon □ U.K. 51°22N 0°5W 169 F7
Croydon Park Australia 33°55S 151°7E 139 B1
Crozet, Is. Ind. Oc. 46°27S 52°0E 273 J4
Crozet Basin Ind. Oc. 39°0S 60°0E 273 H5
Crozon France 48°15N 4°30W 172 D2
Cruces, Punta Colombia 6°39N 77°32W 328 B2
Crumlin Ireland 53°19N 6°19W 122 D2
Crusheen Ireland 52°57N 8°53W 166 D3
Cruz, C. Cuba 19°50N 77°50W 320 C4
Cruz Alta Brazil 28°45S 53°40W 335 B5
Cruz Bay U.S. Virgin Is. 18°20N 64°48W 321 b
Cruz das Almas Brazil 12°0S 39°6W 333 D4
Cruz de Pau Portugal 38°37N 9°7W 126 B2
Cruz del Eje Argentina 30°45S 64°50W 334 C3
Cruzeiro Brazil 22°33S 45°0W 333 F3
Cruzeiro do Oeste Brazil 23°46S 53°4W 335 A5
Cruzeiro do Sul = Joaçaba
　Brazil 27°5S 51°31W 335 B5
Cruzeiro do Sul Brazil 7°35S 72°35W 330 B3
Cry L. Canada 58°45N 129°0W 296 B3
Crystal B. U.S.A. 28°50N 82°45W 317 G7
Crystal Bay U.S.A. 39°15N 120°0W 306 F7
Crystal Brook Australia 33°21S 138°12E 282 B3
Crystal City U.S.A. 38°13N 90°23W 310 F6
Crystal City Tex., U.S.A. 28°41N 99°50W 314 G5
Crystal Falls U.S.A. 46°5N 88°20W 308 B9
Crystal Lake Fla., U.S.A. 26°30N 85°42W 316 E4
Crystal Lake Ill., U.S.A. 42°14N 88°19W 311 B8
Crystal Palace U.K. 51°25N 0°4W 125 B3
Crystal River U.S.A. 28°54N 82°35W 317 G7
Crystal Springs U.S.A. 31°59N 90°21W 315 F9
Csenger Hungary 47°50N 22°41E 182 C7
Csepel Hungary 47°25N 19°4E 117 B2
Csepelsziget Hungary 47°25N 19°4E 117 B2
Csillaghegy Hungary 47°35N 19°2E 117 A2
Csillagtelep Hungary 47°24N 19°5E 117 B2
Csömör Hungary 47°33N 19°14E 117 A3
Csömöri-patak →
　Hungary 47°35N 19°2E 117 A3
Csongrád Hungary 46°43N 20°12E 182 D5
Csongrád □ Hungary 46°32N 20°15E 182 D5
Csorna Hungary 47°38N 17°18E 182 C2
Csurgo Hungary 46°16N 17°9E 182 D2
Cu Lao Hon Vietnam 10°54N 108°18E 237 G7
Cua Rao Vietnam 19°16N 104°27E 236 C5
Cuácua → Mozam. 17°54S 37°0W 269 F4
Cuále Angola 8°22S 16°10E 265 D3
Cuále → Angola 8°29S 15°1E 265 D3
Cuamato Angola 17°2S 15°7E 265 F3
Cuamba Mozam. 14°45S 36°22E 269 E4
Cuando → Angola 14°34S 19°1E 265 E3
Cuando → Angola 17°36S 18°39E 265 F3
Cuando Cubango □
　Angola 16°25S 20°0E 265 F4
Cuangar Angola 17°36S 18°39E 265 F3
Cuango = Kwango →
　Dem. Rep. of the Congo 3°14S 17°22E 264 C3
Cuango Lunda Norte, Angola 9°8S 18°3E 265 D3
Cuango Malange, Angola 9°21S 13°9E 265 D2
Cuango Uíge, Angola 6°15S 16°42E 265 D3
Cuanza → Angola 9°21S 13°9E 265 D2
Cuanza Norte □ Angola 8°50S 14°30E 265 D2
Cuanza Sul □ Angola 10°50S 14°50E 265 E2
Cuao → Venezuela 4°55N 67°40W 328 C4
Cuare → Trin. & Tob. 10°36N 61°6W 323 t
Cuarto → Argentina 33°25S 63°2W 334 C3
Cuatir → Angola 17°1S 18°9E 265 F3
Cuatro Vientos Spain 40°22N 3°47W 127 B1
Cuatrociénegas Mexico 26°59N 102°5W 318 B4
Cuauhtémoc Chihuahua,
　Mexico 28°25N 106°52W 318 B3
Cuauhtémoc México,
　Mexico 19°25N 99°9W 128 B2
Cuba Portugal 38°10N 7°54W 195 G3
Cuba Mo., U.S.A. 38°4N 91°24W 310 F5
Cuba N. Mex., U.S.A. 36°1N 107°4W 305 H10
Cuba N.Y., U.S.A. 42°13N 78°17W 312 D6
Cuba W. Indies 22°0N 79°0W 320 B6
Cubal Angola 13°0S 14°3E 265 E2
Cubal → Angola 15°9S 12°5E 265 E2
Cuban Museum U.S.A. 25°45N 80°13W 128 B2
Cubango → Africa 18°50S 22°25E 265 F4
Cubanja Angola 14°49S 21°20E 265 E4
Cubao Phil. 14°37N 121°3E 127 B2
Cubia → Angola 15°58S 21°42E 265 F4
Çubuk Turkey 40°14N 33°3E 212 B5
Cuc Phuong △ Vietnam 20°17N 105°38E 236 B5
Cuche Trin. & Tob. 10°22N 61°11W 323 t
Cuchi Angola 14°37S 16°58E 265 E3
Cuchi → Angola 15°13S 17°20E 265 E3
Cuchillo-Co Argentina 37°20S 64°37W 336 A4
Cuchivero → Venezuela 8°30N 65°57W 328 B4
Cuchumatanes, Sierra de los
　Guatemala 15°35N 91°25W 320 C1
Cuckfield U.K. 51°1N 0°8W 169 F7
Cucúi Brazil 1°12N 66°50W 328 C4
Cucurpé Mexico 30°20N 110°43W 318 A2
Cucurruí Colombia 2°5N 76°56W 328 C2
Cúcuta Colombia 7°54N 72°31W 328 B3
Cudahy Calif., U.S.A. 33°57N 118°11W 126 C2
Cudahy Wis., U.S.A. 42°57N 87°52W 311 B9
Cudalbi Romania 45°46N 27°41E 183 E12
Cudarebe = Kudarebe
　Aruba 12°37N 70°4W 322 f
Cuddalore India 11°46N 79°45E 245 G4
Cuddapah India 14°30N 78°47E 245 G4
Cudgewa Australia 36°10S 147°42E 283 D7

Cudjoehead Montserrat 16°47N 62°12W 323 p
Cue Australia 27°25S 117°54E 279 E2
Cuebe → Angola 15°46S 17°32E 265 F3
Cuéllar Spain 41°23N 4°21W 194 D6
Cuemba Angola 11°50S 17°42E 265 E3
Cuenca Ecuador 2°50S 79°9W 328 D2
Cuenca Spain 40°5N 2°10W 196 E2
Cuenca □ Spain 40°0N 2°0W 196 E3
Cuenca, Serranía de Spain 39°55N 1°50W 196 E2
Cuenca Alta del Manzanares △
　Spain 40°40N 3°55W 194 E7
Cuerda del Pozo, Embalse de la
　Spain 41°51N 2°44W 196 D2
Cuernavaca Mexico 18°55N 99°15W 319 D5
Cuero U.S.A. 29°6N 97°17W 314 G6
Cuers France 43°14N 6°5E 175 E10
Cueva de la Quebrada del Toro △
　Venezuela 10°36N 69°3W 328 A4
Cueva de los Guácharos △
　Colombia 1°35N 76°1W 328 C2
Cuevas, Cerro Bolivia 22°20S 65°12W 331 E4
Cuevas de Vera = Cuevas del
　Almanzora Spain 37°18N 1°58W 197 H3
Cuevas del Almanzora
　Spain 37°18N 1°58W 197 H3
Cuevo Bolivia 20°15S 63°30W 331 E5
Cugir Romania 45°48N 23°25E 183 E8
Cugnaux France 43°32N 1°20E 174 E5
Cuhai-Bakony →
　Hungary 47°35N 17°54E 182 C2
Cuiabá Brazil 15°30S 56°0W 331 D6
Cuiabá → Brazil 17°5S 56°36W 331 D6
Cuicuilco, Pirámide de
　Mexico 19°18N 99°11W 128 C1
Cuihangcun China 22°27N 113°32E 219 G10
Cuijk Neths. 51°44N 5°50E 170 C6
Cuilco Guatemala 15°24N 91°58W 320 C1
Cuillin Hills U.K. 57°13N 6°15W 167 D2
Cuillin Sd. U.K. 57°4N 6°20W 167 D2
Cuilo = Kwilu →
　Dem. Rep. of the Congo 3°22S 17°22E 265 C3
Cuilo Angola 8°21S 19°28E 265 D3
Cuilo-Futa Angola 8°12S 18°2E 265 D3
Cuima Angola 13°25S 15°45E 265 E2
Cuiseaux France 46°30N 5°22E 173 F12
Cuité Brazil 6°10S 14°41E 265 D2
Cuito → Angola 18°1S 20°48E 265 F4
Cuito Cuanavale Angola 15°10S 19°10E 265 F3
Cuitzeo, L. de Mexico 19°55N 101°5W 318 D4
Cuiuni → Brazil 0°45S 63°7W 329 D5
Cuivre → U.S.A. 44°13N 22°57E 182 F7
Cujmir Romania 44°13N 22°57E 182 F7
Cukai Malaysia 4°13N 103°25E 237 K4
Çukurca Turkey 37°14N 43°36E 213 D10
Cul-de-Sac St.-Maarten 18°2N 63°4W 322 a
Cul de Sac St.-Martin 18°7N 63°6W 322 a
Culasi Phil. 11°26N 122°3E 233 F4
Culbertson U.S.A. 48°9N 104°31W 304 B11
Culburra N.S.W.,
　Australia 34°56S 150°46E 283 C9
Culburra S. Austral.,
　Australia 35°50S 139°58E 282 C3
Culcairn Australia 35°41S 147°3E 283 C7
Culebra Puerto Rico 18°19N 65°18W 321 b
Culebra, Sierra de la
　Spain 41°55N 6°20W 194 D4
Culfa Azerbaijan 38°57N 45°38E 213 C11
Culgoa → Australia 29°56S 146°20E 281 D4
Culgoa Flood Plain △
　Australia 28°58S 147°5E 281 D4
Culiacán Mexico 24°50N 107°23W 318 C3
Culiacán → Mexico 24°30N 107°42W 318 C3
Culik Indonesia 8°21S 115°37E 231 J18
Culion Phil. 11°54N 119°58E 233 F3
Culion I. Phil. 11°50N 120°0E 233 F2
Culiseau → Brazil 12°14S 53°17W 331 C7
Cúllar Spain 37°35N 2°34W 195 H8
Cullarin Ra. Australia 34°30S 149°30E 283 B8
Cullen U.K. 57°42N 2°49W 167 D6
Cullen Bullen Australia 33°18S 150°2E 283 B9
Cullen Pt. Australia 11°57S 141°54E 281 A3
Cullera Spain 39°9N 0°17W 197 F4
Cullman U.S.A. 34°11N 86°51W 315 D11
Culloden U.K. 57°28N 4°4W 167 D4
Cullom U.S.A. 40°53N 88°16W 311 D8
Cullompton U.K. 50°51N 3°24W 169 G4
Culmore U.S.A. 38°51N 77°8W 143 B3
Culo → Angola 6°13S 15°3E 265 D3
Culoz France 45°47N 5°46E 175 C9
Culpeper U.S.A. 38°30N 78°0W 309 F14
Culuene → Brazil 12°56S 52°51W 331 C7
Culuã → Brazil 0°43S 47°50W 332 B2
Culuã → Brazil 4°27S 71°23W 330 B3
Culuene → Brazil 24°31S 55°42W 335 A4
Çürüksu Çayı = Büyük
　Menderes → Turkey 37°28N 27°11E 205 D9
Curup Indonesia 4°26S 102°13E 234 C2
Curupira, Serra S. Amer. 1°25N 64°30W 329 C5
Cururupu Brazil 1°50S 44°50W 332 B3
Cururupu Cuatiá Argentina 29°50S 58°5W 334 B4
Curvelo Brazil 18°45S 44°27W 333 E3
Cusago Italy 45°26N 9°1E 129 B1
Cusano Milanino Italy 45°33N 9°11E 129 A2
Cusco = Cuzco Peru 13°32S 72°0W 330 C3
Cushendall U.K. 55°5N 6°4W 166 A5
Cushing U.S.A. 35°59N 96°46W 314 D6
Cushing, Mt. Canada 57°35N 126°57W 296 B3
Cusihuiriáchic Mexico 28°14N 106°50W 318 B3
Cusna, Mte. Italy 44°17N 10°23E 198 D7
Cussabat = Al Qaşabāt
　Libya 32°39N 14°1E 258 B2
Cusset France 46°8N 3°28E 173 F10
Cussetta U.S.A. 32°18N 84°47W 316 C5
Cusso, Sa. do Angola 6°30S 14°58E 265 D2
Custer U.S.A. 43°46N 103°36W 308 D2
Custom House Dublin, Ireland 120 b3
Cut Bank U.S.A. 48°38N 112°20W 304 B7
Cutervo Peru 6°25S 78°55W 328 E3
Cuthbert U.S.A. 31°46N 84°48W 316 D5
Cutler U.S.A. 36°31N 119°17W 306 J7
Cutler Park U.S.A. 42°17N 71°12W 116 B1
Cutler Ridge U.S.A. 25°35N 80°20W 316 F8
Cutlerville U.S.A. 42°50N 85°40W 311 B11
Cutral-Có Argentina 38°58S 69°15W 336 A3
Cutro Italy 39°2N 16°59E 201 C9
Cuttaburra → Australia 29°43S 144°22E 281 D3
Cuttack India 20°25N 85°57E 244 D7
Cuva → Angola 11°42S 14°52E 265 E2
Cuvelai Angola 15°45S 15°50E 265 F3
Cuvier, C. Australia 23°14S 113°22E 279 D1
Cuvier I. N.Z. 36°27S 175°50E 284 C4
Çuvuşabaşı → Turkey 40°58N 28°51E 122 B1
Cuwei China 39°54N 116°15E 114 B1
Cuxhaven Germany 53°51N 8°41E 178 B4
Cuyabeno Ecuador 0°16S 75°53W 328 D2
Cuyahoga Falls U.S.A. 41°8N 81°29W 312 E3
Cuyahoga Valley △
　U.S.A. 41°15N 81°33W 312 E3
Cuyamaca Pk. U.S.A. 32°57N 116°35W 307 N10
Cuyo Phil. 10°51N 121°2E 233 F3
Cuyo East Pass Phil. 11°0N 121°0E 233 F3
Cuyo Group Phil. 10°54N 121°5E 233 F3
Cuyo West Pass Phil. 11°4N 120°50E 233 F3
Cuyuni → Guyana 6°23N 58°41W 329 B6

Cuzco Bolivia 20°0S 66°50W 330 E4
Cuzco Peru 13°32S 72°0W 330 C3
Cuzco □ Peru 13°31S 71°59W 330 C3
Čvrsnica Bos.-H. 43°36N 17°35E 182 G2
Cwmbran U.K. 51°39N 3°2W 169 F4
Cyangugu Rwanda 2°29S 28°54E 268 C2
Cybinka Poland 52°12N 14°46E 185 F1
Cyclades Greece 37°0N 24°30E 204 E6
Cyclades □ Greece 37°0N 25°0E 204 D6
Cygnet Australia 43°8S 147°1E 281 G4
Cynthiana U.S.A. 38°23N 84°18W 311 F12
Cypress Hills Canada 49°40N 109°30W 297 D7
Cypress Hills N.Y., U.S.A. 40°41N 73°53W 132 B2
Cypress Hills ⌂ Canada 49°40N 109°30W 297 D7
Cypress Park U.S.A. 34°6N 118°13W 126 B3
Cyprus ■ Asia 35°0N 33°0E 207 F9
Cyrenaica = Barqa Libya 27°0N 23°0E 258 B4
Cyrene Libya 32°53N 21°52E 258 B4
Czaplinek Poland 53°34N 16°14E 184 E3
Czar Canada 52°27N 110°50W 297 C6
Czarna → Łódzkie, Poland 51°18N 19°55E 185 G6
Czarna → Świętokrzyskie, Poland 50°28N 21°21E 185 H8
Czarna Białostocka Poland 53°18N 23°17E 185 E10
Czarna Woda Poland 53°51N 18°6E 184 E5
Czarne Poland 53°42N 16°58E 184 E3
Czarnków Poland 52°55N 16°38E 185 F3
Czaslau = Čáslav Czech Rep. 49°54N 15°22E 180 B8
Czech Rep. ■ Europe 50°0N 15°0E 180 B8
Czechowice-Dziedzice Poland 49°54N 18°59E 185 J5
Czempiń Poland 52°9N 16°43E 185 F3
Czeremcha Poland 52°31N 23°21E 185 F10
Czerniejewo Poland 52°26N 17°30E 185 F4
Czernowitz = Chernivtsi Ukraine 48°15N 25°52E 183 B10
Czerniaków Poland 52°11N 21°13E 142 B2
Czersk Poland 53°46N 17°58E 184 E4
Czerwieńsk Poland 52°1N 15°23E 185 F2
Czerwionka-Leszczyny Poland 50°7N 18°37E 185 H5
Częstochowa Poland 50°49N 19°7E 185 H6
Człopa Poland 53°6N 16°6E 185 E3
Człuchów Poland 53°41N 17°22E 184 E4
Czortów = Chortkiv Ukraine 49°2N 25°46E 177 D13
Czyste Poland 52°13N 20°57E 142 B1
Czyżew-Osada Poland 52°48N 22°19E 185 F9

D

D.C. War Memorial Washington, D.C., U.S.A. 143 b1
Da → Vietnam 21°15N 105°20E 228 G5
Da Hinggan Ling China 48°0N 121°0E 219 B7
Da Lat Vietnam 11°56N 108°25E 237 G7
Da Moóca → Brazil 23°35S 46°35W 137 B2
Da Nang Vietnam 16°4N 108°13E 236 D7
Da Qaidam China 37°50N 95°15E 218 C4
Da Yunhe → Hopei, China 39°10N 117°10E 227 E9
Da Yunhe → Jiangsu, China 34°25N 120°5E 227 G11
Da'an China 45°30N 124°7E 227 B13
Daan Viljoen ⌂ Namibia 22°2S 16°45E 270 B2
Daanbantayan Phil. 11°17N 124°2E 233 F5
Dab'a, Ras el Egypt 31°3N 28°31E 256 H6
Daba Shan China 32°0N 109°0E 228 B7
Dabai Nigeria 11°25N 5°15E 263 C6
Dabajuro Venezuela 11°2N 70°40W 328 A3
Dabakala Ivory C. 8°15N 4°20W 262 D4
Dabaro Somali Rep. 6°21N 48°43E 267 C6
Dabas Hungary 47°11N 19°19E 182 C4
Dabat Ethiopia 12°58N 37°41E 257 E4
Dabbagh, Jabal Si. Arabia 27°52N 35°45E 246 E2
Dabeiba Colombia 7°1N 76°16W 328 B2
Daber = Dobra Poland 53°34N 15°20E 184 E2
Dabhoi India 22°10N 73°20E 242 H5
Dąbie Poland 52°5N 18°50E 185 F5
Dabie Shan China 31°20N 115°20E 229 B10
Dabilda Cameroon 12°45N 14°35E 259 F2
Dabl, W. → Si. Arabia 29°5N 36°16E 251 J7
Dáblice Czech Rep. 50°8N 14°29E 135 B2
Dabnou Niger 14°10N 5°22E 263 C6
Dabo = Pasirkuning Indonesia 0°30S 104°33E 234 C2
Dabola Guinea 10°50N 11°5W 262 C2
Dabou Ivory C. 5°20N 4°23W 262 D4
Daboya Ghana 9°30N 1°20W 263 D4
Dabravolya Belarus 52°55N 23°59E 185 F10
Dąbrowa Poland 52°19N 20°52E 142 B1
Dąbrowa Białostocka Poland 53°40N 23°21E 184 E10
Dąbrowa Górnicza Poland 50°15N 19°10E 185 H6
Dąbrowa Tarnowska Poland 50°10N 20°59E 185 H7
Dabu China 24°22N 116°41E 229 E11
Dabugam India 19°27N 82°26E 244 E6
Dabung Malaysia 5°23N 102°1E 237 K4
Dabus → Ethiopia 10°48N 35°10E 257 E4
Dacato → Ethiopia 7°25N 42°40E 257 F5
Dacca = Dhaka Bangla. 23°43N 90°26E 241 D3
Dacca = Dhaka □ Bangla. 24°25N 90°25E 241 C3
Dachang China 31°17N 121°24E 138 B1
Dachang ✕ China 31°18N 121°25E 138 B1
Dachau Germany 48°15N 11°26E 131 A1
Dachau-Ost Germany 48°15N 11°27E 131 A1
Dachauer Moos Germany 48°13N 11°27E 131 A1
Dachigam ⌂ India 34°10N 75°0E 242 B6
Dachstein, Hoher Austria 47°28N 13°35E 180 D6
Dačice Czech Rep. 49°5N 15°26E 180 B8
Dacre Canada 45°22N 76°57W 312 A8
Dacula U.S.A. 33°59N 83°54W 316 B6
Dadanawa Guyana 2°50N 59°30W 329 C6
Dadar India 19°0N 72°49E 130 A1
Daday Turkey 41°28N 33°27E 212 B5
Dade City U.S.A. 28°22N 82°11W 317 G7
Dadès, Oued → Morocco 30°58N 6°44W 260 B3
Dadeville U.S.A. 32°50N 85°46W 316 C4
Dadhar Pakistan 29°28N 67°39E 242 E2
Dadiya Nigeria 9°35N 11°24E 263 D7
Ḑadnah U.A.E. 25°32N 56°22E 247 E8
Dadohae Maritime Nat. Park ⌂ S. Korea 34°0N 126°0E 224 E3
Dadra = Achalpur India 21°22N 77°32E 244 D3
Dadra & Nagar Haveli □ India 20°5N 73°0E 244 D1
Dadri = Charkhi Dadri India 28°37N 76°17E 242 E7
Dadu Pakistan 26°45N 67°45E 242 F2
Dadu He → China 29°31N 103°46E 228 C4
Daebang S. Korea 37°30N 126°55E 137 B1
Daebudo S. Korea 37°14N 126°35E 224 D3
Daecheongdo S. Korea 37°49N 124°42E 224 D2
Daechi S. Korea 37°30N 127°2E 137 B2
Daegu S. Korea 35°50N 128°37E 224 E4
Daejeon S. Korea 36°20N 127°28E 224 D3
Daejeon □ S. Korea 36°20N 127°25E 224 D3
Daejeong S. Korea 33°8N 126°17E 224 a
Daemodo S. Korea 34°11N 126°45E 224 E3
Daet Phil. 14°2N 122°55E 232 D4
Dafang China 27°9N 105°39E 228 D5
Dafdaf, J. Si. Arabia 28°16N 35°21E 251 K6
Dafnes Greece 35°13N 25°3E 207 E6
Dafni Athina, Greece 37°55N 23°44E 112 B2
Dafni Peloponnese, Greece 37°48N 22°1E 204 D4
Dafnoudi, Akra Greece 38°28N 20°32E 207 C2
Dağ Turkey 37°12N 30°31E 205 D12
Daga Post Sudan 9°13N 33°58E 266 C3
Dagali Norway 60°25N 8°28E 164 F3
Dagana Senegal 16°30N 15°35W 262 B1
Dagash Sudan 19°19N 33°25E 256 D3
Dagenham U.K. 51°32N 0°8E 125 A4
Dagestan □ Russia 42°30N 47°0E 191 J8
Dagestanskiye Ogni Russia 42°6N 48°12E 191 J9
Dagg Sd. N.Z. 45°23S 166°45E 285 F1
Daggett U.S.A. 34°52N 116°52W 307 L10
Daghestan Republic = Dagestan □ Russia 42°30N 47°0E 191 J8
Daghfeli Sudan 19°18N 32°40E 256 D3
Dagfling Germany 48°8N 11°39E 131 B2
Dağlıq Qarabağ = Nagorno-Karabakh □ Azerbaijan 39°55N 46°45E 213 C12
Dagö = Hiiumaa Estonia 58°50N 22°45E 188 C2
Dagu China 38°59N 117°40E 227 E9
Dagua Papua N. G. 3°27S 143°20E 286 B2
Daguan China 27°43N 103°56E 228 D4
Dagupan Phil. 16°3N 120°20E 232 C3
Daguragu Australia 17°33S 130°30E 278 C5
Daguragu ✪ Australia 17°24S 130°48E 278 C5
Dahab Egypt 28°31N 34°31E 251 K5
Dahab, Gezîret el Egypt 29°59N 31°13E 117 B2
Dahanu India 19°58N 72°44E 244 E1
Daheisha West Bank 31°42N 35°11E 123 B2
Dahivadi India 17°43N 74°33E 244 F2
Dahlak Kebir Eritrea 15°50N 40°10E 257 D5
Dahlak Marine ⌂ Eritrea 15°35N 40°1E 257 D5
Dahlem Germany 52°27N 13°16E 115 B2
Dahlenburg Germany 53°11N 10°44E 178 B6
Dahlonega U.S.A. 34°32N 83°59W 315 D13
Dahlwitz-Hoppegarten Germany 52°30N 13°41E 115 A5
Dahme Germany 51°52N 13°25E 178 D9
Dahod India 22°50N 74°15E 242 H6
Dahomey = Benin ■ Africa 10°0N 2°0E 263 D5
Dahong Shan China 31°25N 113°0E 229 B9
Dahongliutan China 35°45N 79°20E 243 B8
Dahongmen China 39°48N 116°21E 114 C2
Dahra Libya 29°30N 17°50E 258 C3
Dahra Senegal 15°22N 15°30W 262 B1
Dahra, Massif de Algeria 36°7N 1°21E 261 A5
Dahshûr Egypt 29°45N 31°14E 256 J7
Dahūk Iraq 36°50N 43°1E 213 D10
Dahūk □ Iraq 36°50N 42°50E 213 D10
Dahuofan Shuiku China 41°52N 124°12E 224 B2
Ḑahy, Nafūd ad Si. Arabia 22°0N 45°25E 248 B4
Dai Solomon Is. 7°54S 160°40E 287 L11
Dai Hao Vietnam 18°1N 106°25E 236 C6
Dai-Sen Japan 35°22N 133°32E 222 B5
Dai Shan China 30°25N 122°10E 229 B14
Dai Xian China 39°4N 112°58E 226 E7
Daicheng China 38°42N 116°38E 226 E9
Daigo Japan 36°46N 140°21E 223 A12
Daik-u Burma 17°47N 96°40E 241 G6
Daikondi = Day Kundī □ Afghan. 34°0N 66°0E 240 B2
Daimanji-San Japan 36°14N 133°20E 222 A5
Daimiel Spain 39°5N 3°35W 195 F7
Daingean Ireland 53°18N 7°17W 166 C4
Dainkog China 32°30N 97°58E 228 A1
Daintree Australia 16°20S 145°20E 280 B4
Daintree ⌂ Australia 16°8S 145°2E 280 B4
Daiō-Misaki Japan 34°15N 136°45E 223 C8
Dair, J. ed Sudan 12°27N 30°42E 257 E3
Dairen = Dalian China 38°50N 121°40E 227 E11
Dairût Egypt 27°34N 30°43E 256 B3
Daisen-Oki ⌂ Japan 35°23N 133°34E 222 B5
Daisetsu-Zan Japan 43°30N 142°57E 220 C11
Daisetsu-Zan ⌂ Japan 43°30N 142°55E 220 C11
Daitari India 21°10N 85°46E 244 D7
Daito Japan 35°19N 132°58E 222 B6
Dajarra Australia 21°42S 139°30E 280 C2
Dajiaoting China 39°51N 116°27E 114 B2
Dajiawa China 37°9N 119°0E 227 F10
Dajin Chuan → China 31°16N 101°59E 228 B3
Dak Dam Cambodia 12°20N 107°21E 236 F6
Dak Nhe Vietnam 15°28N 107°48E 236 E6
Dak Pek Vietnam 15°4N 107°44E 236 E6
Dak Song Vietnam 12°19N 107°35E 237 F6
Dak Sui Vietnam 14°55N 107°43E 236 E6
Dakar Senegal 14°34N 17°29W 262 C1
Dakar □ Senegal 14°45N 17°20W 262 C1
Dakhal, W. el → Egypt 28°48N 32°47E 251 K3
Dakhin Bangla. 22°30N 90°45E 241 D3
Dakhla W. Sahara 23°50N 15°53W 260 D1
Dakhla, El Wâhât el Egypt 25°30N 28°50E 256 B2
Dakhnoye Russia 59°49N 30°15E 137 C1
Dakingari Nigeria 11°37N 4°1E 263 C5
Dakoank India 7°2N 93°43E 245 L11
Dakor India 22°45N 73°11E 242 H5
Dakoro Niger 14°31N 6°46E 263 C6
Dakota City Iowa, U.S.A. 42°43N 94°12W 310 B2
Dakota City Nebr., U.S.A. 42°25N 96°25W 308 D5
Dakovica Kosovo 42°22N 20°26E 202 D4
Dakovo Croatia 45°19N 18°24E 182 E3
Daksum India 33°37N 75°22E 243 C6
Dal Norway 59°53N 8°40E 164 E5
Dala Lunda Sul, Angola 11°3S 20°17E 265 E4
Dala Uíge, Angola 8°5S 15°49E 265 D3
Dala Solomon Is. 8°30S 160°41E 287 M11
Dala-Cachibo Angola 10°30S 14°41E 265 E2
Dalaba Guinea 10°47N 12°12W 262 C2
Dalachi China 36°48N 105°0E 226 F3
Dalagan = San Antonio Phil. 14°57N 120°5E 232 D3
Dalaguete Phil. 9°46N 123°32E 233 G4
Dalai Nur China 43°20N 116°45E 226 C9
Dālakī Iran 29°26N 51°17E 247 D6
Dalälven → Sweden 60°12N 16°43E 162 D10
Dalaman Turkey 36°48N 28°47E 205 E10
Dalaman → Turkey 36°41N 28°43E 205 E10
Dalandzadgad Mongolia 43°27N 104°30E 226 C3
Dalanganem Is. Phil. 10°40N 120°17E 233 F3
Dalap-Uliga-Darrit = Majuro Marshall Is. 7°9N 171°12E 288 G9
Dalarna Sweden 61°0N 14°0E 162 D8
Dalarnas län □ Sweden 61°0N 14°15E 162 D8
Dalasýsla □ Iceland 65°15N 22°0W 155 B4
Dalat Malaysia 2°44N 111°56E 235 B4
Dālbandīn Pakistan 29°0N 64°23E 240 C2
Dalbeattie U.K. 54°56N 3°50W 167 G5
Dalbeg Australia 20°16S 147°18E 280 C4
Dalbosjön Sweden 58°40N 12°45E 163 F6
Dalby Queens., Australia 27°10S 151°17E 281 D5
Dalby Skåne, Sweden 55°40N 13°22E 163 J7
Dalby Söderskog ⌂ Sweden 55°41N 13°21E 163 J7
Dale Sogn og Fjordane, Norway 61°22N 5°23E 164 C2
Dale Ind., U.S.A. 38°10N 86°59W 311 F10
Dale City U.S.A. 38°38N 77°19W 309 F15
Dale Hollow L. U.S.A. 36°32N 85°27W 315 C12
Dalejsky potok → Czech Rep. 50°2N 14°24E 135 B2
Dalen Norway 59°26N 8°0E 164 E4
Dalet Burma 19°59N 93°51E 241 F4
Daletme Burma 21°36N 92°46E 241 E4
Daleville Ala., U.S.A. 31°19N 85°43W 316 D4
Daleville Ind., U.S.A. 40°7N 85°33W 311 D11
Dalga Egypt 27°39N 30°41E 256 B3
Dalgān Iran 27°31N 59°19E 247 E8
Dalgety Bay U.K. 56°2N 3°20W 121 A1
Dalhart U.S.A. 36°4N 102°31W 314 C3
Dalhousie N.B., Canada 48°5N 66°26W 299 C6
Dalhousie India 32°38N 75°58E 242 C6
Dali Shaanxi, China 34°48N 109°58E 226 G5
Dali Yunnan, China 25°40N 100°10E 228 E3
Dalian China 38°50N 121°40E 227 E11
Daliang Shan China 28°0N 102°45E 228 D4
Daling He → China 40°55N 121°40E 227 D11
Dāliyat el Karmel Israel 32°43N 35°2E 250 F6
Dalj Croatia 45°29N 18°59E 182 E3
Dalkeith Midloth., U.K. 55°54N 3°4W 121 B3
Dalkeith Fla., U.S.A. 30°0N 85°9W 316 E4
Dalkey Ireland 53°16N 6°6W 120 B3
Dalkey I. Ireland 53°17N 6°5W 120 B3
Dallas Ga., U.S.A. 33°55N 84°51W 316 B5
Dallas Oreg., U.S.A. 44°55N 123°19W 304 D2
Dallas Tex., U.S.A. 32°47N 96°48W 314 E6
Dallas Center U.S.A. 41°41N 93°58W 310 C3
Dallas City U.S.A. 40°38N 91°10W 310 D5
Dalle = Yirga Alem Ethiopia 6°48N 38°22E 257 F4
Dalles, The U.S.A. 45°36N 121°10W 304 D3
Dallgow Germany 52°32N 13°5E 115 A1
Dallol Ethiopia 14°14N 40°17E 257 E5
Dalmā U.A.E. 24°30N 52°20E 247 E7
Dalmacija Croatia 43°20N 17°0E 199 E13
Dalmas, L. Canada 53°30N 71°50W 299 B5
Dalmatia = Dalmacija Croatia 43°20N 17°0E 199 E13
Dalmau India 26°4N 81°2E 243 F9
Dalmellington U.K. 55°19N 4°23W 167 F4
Dalmeny N.S.W., Australia 36°10S 150°8E 283 D9
Dalmeny Edinburgh, U.K. 55°59N 3°22W 121 B1
Dalnegorsk Russia 44°32N 135°33E 220 B7
Dalnerechensk Russia 45°50N 133°40E 220 B6
Dalnevostochnyy □ Russia 67°0N 140°0E 215 C14
Dalny = Dalian China 38°50N 121°40E 227 E11
Daloa Ivory C. 7°0N 6°30W 262 D3
Dalou Shan China 28°15N 107°0E 228 C6
Dalry U.K. 55°42N 4°43W 167 F4
Dalrymple, L. Australia 20°40S 147°0E 280 C4
Dalrymple, Mt. Australia 21°1S 148°39E 280 b
Dals Långed Sweden 58°56N 12°18E 163 F6
Dalsætra Norway 61°28N 9°26E 164 C6
Dalsjöfors Sweden 57°46N 13°5E 163 G7
Dalsland Sweden 58°50N 12°15E 163 F6
Dalsmynni Iceland 64°48N 21°29W 155 C5
Dalston U.K. 51°32N 0°4W 125 A3
Daltenganj India 24°0N 84°4E 243 H11
Dalton Ga., U.S.A. 34°46N 84°58W 315 D12
Dalton Mass., U.S.A. 42°28N 73°11W 313 D11
Dalton Nebr., U.S.A. 41°25N 102°58W 308 E2
Dalton, Kap Greenland 69°25N 24°3W 154 D8
Dalton-in-Furness U.K. 54°10N 3°11W 168 C4
Dalupiri I. Cagayan, Phil. 19°5N 121°12E 232 B3
Dalupiri I. N. Samar, Phil. 12°25N 124°16E 232 E5
Dalvík Iceland 65°58N 18°32W 155 B8
Dálvvadis = Jokkmokk Sweden 66°35N 19°50E 160 C18
Dalwallinu Australia 30°17S 116°40E 279 F2
Daly → Australia 13°35S 130°19E 278 B5
Daly City U.S.A. 37°42N 122°27W 136 B2
Daly L. Canada 56°32N 105°39W 297 B7
Daly River Australia 13°46S 130°42E 278 B5
Daly River-Port Keats ✪ Australia 14°13S 129°36E 278 B4
Daly Waters Australia 16°15S 133°24E 280 B1
Dalyan Turkey 36°50N 28°39E 205 E10
Dam Amsterdam, Neths. 112 a2
Dam Doi Vietnam 8°50N 105°12E 237 H5
Dam Ha Vietnam 21°21N 107°36E 236 B6
Damachova Belarus 51°45N 23°36E 185 G10
Damaia Portugal 38°44N 9°12W 126 A1
Daman India 20°25N 72°57E 244 D1
Daman & Diu □ India 20°25N 72°58E 244 D1
Dāmaneh Iran 33°1N 50°29E 247 C6
Damanganga → India 20°25N 72°56E 244 D1
Damanhûr Egypt 31°0N 30°30E 256 H7
Damant L. Canada 61°45N 105°5W 297 A7
Damanzhuang China 38°5N 116°35E 226 E9
Damaq Iran 35°25N 48°49E 213 E13
Damar Indonesia 7°7S 128°40E 231 F7
Damara C.A.R. 4°58N 18°42E 264 B3
Damaraland Greece 37°58N 23°39E 112 B1
Damaraland Namibia 20°0S 15°0E 270 B2
Damascus = Dimashq Syria 33°30N 36°18E 250 E7
Damascus U.S.A. 31°18N 84°43W 316 D5
Damasi Greece 39°43N 22°11E 204 B4
Damaturu Nigeria 11°45N 11°55E 263 C7
Damāvand Iran 35°47N 52°0E 247 C7
Damāvand, Qolleh-ye Iran 35°56N 52°10E 247 C7
Damba Angola 6°44S 15°20E 265 D3
Damboa Nigeria 11°15N 12°55E 259 F2
Dâmboviţa □ Romania 45°0N 25°30E 183 F10
Dâmboviţa → Romania 44°12N 26°26E 183 F11
Dâmbovnic → Romania 44°28N 25°18E 183 F10
Dambrowica = Dubrovytsya Ukraine 51°31N 26°35E 177 C14
Dambulla Sri Lanka 7°51N 80°39E 245 L5
Dame Marie Haiti 18°36N 74°26W 321 C5
Dämeritzsee Germany 52°34N 13°43E 115 B5
Dāmghān Iran 36°10N 54°17E 247 B7
Dâmieneşti Romania 46°44N 26°59E 183 D11
Damietta = Dumyât Egypt 31°24N 31°48E 251 G2
Daming China 36°15N 115°6E 226 F8
Dāmir Qābū Syria 36°58N 41°51E 246 B4
Dammai I. Phil. 5°47N 120°25E 233 J3
Dammam = Ad Dammām Si. Arabia 26°20N 50°5E 247 E6
Dammarie-les-Lys France 48°31N 2°39E 173 D9
Dammartin-en-Goële France 49°3N 2°41E 173 C9
Damme Germany 52°32N 8°11E 178 C4
Damodar → India 23°17N 87°35E 243 H12
Damoh India 23°50N 79°28E 243 H8
Damous Algeria 36°31N 1°42E 261 A5
Dampier Australia 20°41S 116°42E 278 D2
Dampier, Selat Indonesia 0°40S 131°0E 231 E8
Dampier Arch. Australia 20°38S 116°32E 278 D2
Dampier Str. Papua N. G. 5°50S 148°0E 286 C5
Damqawt Yemen 16°34N 52°50E 249 C6
Damrak Amsterdam, Neths. 112 a2
Damrani Algeria 27°45N 2°56W 260 C4
Damrei, Chuor Phnum Cambodia 11°30N 103°0E 237 G4
Damroh India 28°26N 95°14E 241 A5
Damvillers France 49°20N 5°21E 173 C12
Damyang S. Korea 35°19N 126°59E 224 E3
Dan Gorayo Somali Rep. 8°43N 49°20E 267 C6
Dan-Gulbi Nigeria 11°40N 6°15E 263 C6
Dan Ryan Woods U.S.A. 41°44N 87°40W 119 C2
Dan-Sadau Nigeria 11°17N 6°29E 263 C6
Dana Indonesia 11°0S 122°52E 231 F6
Dana Jordan 30°41N 35°37E 251 H6
Dana, L. Canada 50°53N 77°20W 298 B4
Dana, Mt. U.S.A. 37°54N 119°12W 306 H7
Danakil Depression Ethiopia 13°0N 41°0E 267 B5
Danakil Desert Ethiopia 12°45N 41°0E 267 B5
Danan Ethiopia 6°31N 43°30E 267 C5
Danané Ivory C. 7°16N 8°9W 262 D3
Danao Phil. 10°31N 124°1E 233 F5
Danau Poso Indonesia 1°52S 120°35E 231 E6
Danba China 30°54N 101°48E 228 B3
Danbury U.S.A. 41°24N 73°28W 313 E11
Danby L. U.S.A. 34°13N 115°5W 305 J6
Dand Afghan. 31°28N 65°32E 242 D1
Dande → Angola 8°28S 13°21E 265 D2
Dande ⌂ Zimbabwe 15°56S 30°16E 269 F3
Dandeldhura Nepal 29°20N 80°35E 243 E9
Dandeli India 15°5N 74°30E 245 G2
Dandenong Australia 38°0S 145°15E 283 E6
Danderhall U.K. 55°55N 3°7W 121 B3
Danderyd Sweden 59°24N 18°1E 139 A2
Dandī Iran 36°32N 47°37E 213 D12
Dandîl Egypt 29°10N 31°2E 256 J7
Dandong China 40°10N 124°20E 224 B2
Danfeng China 33°45N 110°25E 226 H6
Danforth Canada 43°43N 79°16W 140 A2
Dangan Liedao China 22°2N 114°8E 229 F10
Dange Angola 7°56S 15°3E 265 D3
Dangé-St-Romain France 46°56N 0°36E 174 B4
Dângeni Romania 47°51N 26°58E 183 C11
Danger Is. = Pukapuka Cook Is. 10°53S 165°49W 289 J11
Danger Pt. S. Africa 34°40S 19°17E 270 D2
Danginpuri Indonesia 8°40S 115°13E 231 K18
Dangjin S. Korea 36°53N 126°37E 224 D3
Dangla Ethiopia 11°18N 36°56E 257 E4
Dangla Shan = Tanggula Shan China 32°40N 92°10E 218 C4
Dangora Nigeria 11°30N 8°7E 263 C6
Dangouadougou Burkina Faso 10°9N 4°56W 262 D4
Dangrek, Mts. = Dangrek, Phnom Thailand 14°20N 104°0E 236 E5
Dangrek, Phnom Thailand 14°20N 104°0E 236 E5
Dangriga Belize 17°0N 88°13W 320 C2
Dangshan China 34°27N 116°22E 226 G9
Dangtu China 31°32N 118°25E 229 B12
Dangyang China 30°52N 111°44E 229 B8
Daniel U.S.A. 42°52N 110°4W 304 E8
Daniel's Harbour Canada 50°13N 57°35W 299 B8
Danielskuil S. Africa 28°11S 23°33E 270 C3
Danielson U.S.A. 41°48N 71°53W 313 E13
Danielsville U.S.A. 34°8N 83°13W 316 A6
Danilov Russia 58°16N 40°13E 188 C11
Danilovgrad Montenegro 42°38N 19°4E 202 D3
Danilovka Russia 50°25N 44°12E 190 E7
Daning China 36°28N 110°45E 226 F6
Danish West Indies = Virgin Is. (U.S.) ☒ W. Indies 18°20N 65°0W 321 C7
Danissa Kenya 3°17N 40°59E 267 D5
Danja Nigeria 11°21N 7°30E 263 C6
Danje-la-Menha Angola 9°32S 14°39E 265 D2
Danjiangkou China 32°31N 111°30E 229 A8
Danjiangkou Shuiku China 32°37N 111°30E 229 A8
Ḑank Oman 23°33N 56°16E 247 F8
Dankalwa Nigeria 11°52N 12°12E 263 C7
Dankama Nigeria 13°20N 7°44E 263 C6
Dankhar Gompa India 32°10N 78°10E 242 C8
Dankov Russia 53°20N 39°5E 188 F10
Danleng China 30°1N 103°31E 228 B4
Danlí Honduras 14°4N 86°35W 320 D2
Danmark = Denmark ■ Europe 55°45N 10°0E 163 J3
Danmark Fjord Greenland 81°30N 22°0W 154 A8
Danmarkshavn Greenland 76°45N 18°50W 154 B9
Dannemora U.S.A. 44°43N 73°44W 313 B11
Dannenberg Germany 53°6N 11°5E 178 B7
Dannevirke N.Z. 40°12S 176°8E 284 G5
Dannhauser S. Africa 28°0S 30°3E 271 C5
Danot Ethiopia 7°33N 45°17E 267 C6
Dansalan = Marawi City Phil. 8°0N 124°21E 233 G5
Dansville U.S.A. 42°34N 77°42W 312 D7
Danta India 24°11N 72°46E 242 G5
Dantan India 21°57N 87°20E 243 J12
Dante = Xaafuun Somali Rep. 10°25N 51°16E 267 B7
Dantewara India 18°54N 81°21E 244 E5
Danube = Dunărea → Europe 45°20N 29°40E 183 E14
Danubyu Burma 17°15N 95°35E 241 G5
Danvers U.S.A. 42°34N 70°56W 313 D14
Danville Ga., U.S.A. 32°37N 83°15W 316 C6
Danville Ill., U.S.A. 40°8N 87°37W 311 D9
Danville Ind., U.S.A. 39°46N 86°32W 311 E10
Danville Ky., U.S.A. 37°39N 84°46W 311 G12
Danville Pa., U.S.A. 40°58N 76°37W 313 F8
Danville Va., U.S.A. 36°36N 79°23W 309 G14
Danville Vt., U.S.A. 44°25N 72°9W 313 B12
Danyang China 32°0N 119°31E 229 B12
Danzhai China 26°11N 107°48E 228 D6
Danzhou China 19°31N 109°33E 236 C7
Danzig = Gdańsk Poland 54°22N 18°40E 184 D5
Dao = Tobias Fornier Phil. 10°30N 121°57E 233 F3
Dao Phil. 11°24N 122°41E 233 F4
Dão → Portugal 40°20N 8°11W 194 E2
Dao Xian China 25°36N 111°31E 229 E8
Daocheng China 29°0N 100°10E 228 C3
Daora W. Sahara 27°25N 12°59W 260 C2
Daoud = Aïn Beïda Algeria 35°50N 7°29E 261 A6
Daoukro Ivory C. 7°10N 3°58W 262 D4
Dapa Phil. 9°46N 126°3E 233 G6
Dapaong Togo 10°55N 0°16E 263 C5
Dapchi Nigeria 12°32N 11°31E 263 C7
Dapiak, Mt. Phil. 8°15N 123°28E 233 G4
Dapitan Phil. 8°39N 123°25E 233 G4
Dapoli India 17°46N 73°11E 244 F1
Daqahlîya □ Egypt 30°55N 31°30E 251 H2
Daqing Shan China 40°40N 111°0E 226 D6
Daqq-e Sorkh, Kavīr Iran 33°45N 52°50E 247 C7
Daqu Shan China 30°25N 122°20E 229 B14
Dar Banda Africa 8°0N 23°0E 254 F6
Dar el Beida = Casablanca Morocco 33°36N 7°36W 260 B3
Dar es Salaam Tanzania 6°50S 39°12E 268 D4
Dar Mazār Iran 29°14N 57°20E 247 D8
Dar Rounga C.A.R. 0°45N 22°20E 264 A4
Dār Ta'izzah Syria 36°20N 36°52E 250 B7
Dar'ā Syria 32°36N 36°7E 250 F7
Dar'ā □ Syria 32°55N 36°10E 250 F7
Dara Dere = Zlatograd Bulgaria 41°22N 25°7E 203 E9
Dārāb Iran 28°50N 54°30E 247 D7
Daraban Pakistan 31°44N 70°20E 242 D4
Darabani Romania 48°10N 26°39E 183 B11
Darai Hills Papua N. G. 7°8S 143°33E 286 D2
Daraina Madag. 13°12S 49°40E 272 A2
Daraj Libya 30°10N 10°28E 258 B2
Darakeh Iran 35°49N 51°22E 141 A2
Daram Phil. 11°38N 124°48E 233 F5
Dārān Iran 32°59N 50°24E 247 C6
Đaravica Kosovo 42°32N 20°8E 202 D4
Daraw Egypt 24°22N 32°51E 256 C3
Dārayyā Syria 33°28N 36°15E 250 E7
Darazo Nigeria 11°1N 10°24E 263 C7
Darband Tehrān, Iran 35°49N 51°27E 141 A2
Darband Pakistan 34°20N 72°50E 242 B5
Darband, Kūh-e Iran 31°34N 57°8E 247 D8
Darbhanga India 26°15N 85°55E 243 F11
Darburruk Somali Rep. 9°44N 44°31E 267 C5
Darby, C. U.S.A. 64°19N 162°47W 303 D7
D'Arcy Canada 50°33N 122°29W 296 C4
Darda Croatia 45°40N 18°41E 182 E3
Dardanelle Ark., U.S.A. 35°13N 93°9W 314 D8
Dardanelle Calif., U.S.A. 38°20N 119°50W 306 G7
Dardanelles = Çanakkale Boğazı Turkey 40°17N 26°32E 203 F10
Dare → Ethiopia 7°20N 42°11E 257 F5
Darende Turkey 38°31N 37°30E 212 C7
Dārestān Iran 29°9N 58°42E 247 D8
Darfield N.Z. 43°29S 172°7E 285 D7
Darfo Italy 45°53N 10°11E 198 C7
Dârfûr Sudan 13°40N 24°0E 259 F4
Dargai Pakistan 34°25N 71°55E 242 B4
Dargaville N.Z. 35°57S 173°52E 284 B2
Dargol Niger 13°54N 1°22E 263 C5
Darhan Mongolia 49°37N 106°21E 218 B5
Darhan Muminggan Lianheqi China 41°40N 110°28E 226 D6
Dari Sudan 5°48N 30°26E 257 F3
Darıca Turkey 40°45N 29°23E 212 B3
Darien U.S.A. 31°23N 81°26W 316 D8
Darién, G. del Colombia 9°0N 77°0W 320 E4
Darién, Serranía del Colombia 8°30N 77°30W 320 E4
Darién ⌂ Panama 7°36N 77°57W 320 E4
Dariganga = Ovoot Mongolia 45°21N 113°45E 226 B7
Daringbadi India 19°54N 84°8E 244 E7
Darjeeling = Darjiling India 27°3N 88°18E 241 B2
Darjiling India 27°3N 88°18E 241 B2
Darkan Australia 33°20S 116°43E 279 F2
Darke Peak Australia 33°27S 136°12E 282 B2
Darkhana Pakistan 30°39N 72°11E 242 D5
Darkhazīneh Iran 31°54N 48°39E 247 D6
Darkot Pass Pakistan 36°45N 73°26E 243 A5
Darling → Australia 34°4S 141°54E 282 C4
Darling Downs Australia 27°30S 150°30E 281 D5
Darling Harbour Sydney, Australia 139 b1
Darling Point Australia 33°52S 151°15E 139 B2
Darling Ra. Australia 32°30S 116°20E 279 F2
Darlington Durham, U.K. 54°32N 1°33W 168 C6
Darlington Fla., U.S.A. 30°57N 86°3W 316 E3
Darlington S.C., U.S.A. 34°18N 79°52W 315 D15
Darlington Wis., U.S.A. 42°41N 90°7W 310 B6
Darlington □ U.K. 54°32N 1°33W 168 C6
Darlington, L. S. Africa 33°10S 25°9E 270 D4
Darlington Point Australia 34°37S 146°1E 283 C7
Darlot, L. Australia 27°48S 121°35E 279 E3
Darłowo Poland 54°25N 16°25E 184 D3
Dărmăneşti Bacău, Romania 46°21N 26°33E 183 D11
Dărmăneşti Suceava, Romania 47°44N 26°9E 183 C11
Darmstadt Germany 49°51N 8°39E 179 F4
Darnah Libya 32°45N 22°45E 258 B4
Darnall S. Africa 29°23S 31°18E 271 C5
Darndale Ireland 53°23N 6°12W 120 A2
Darney France 48°5N 6°2E 173 D13
Darnick Australia 32°48S 143°38E 282 B5
Darnley Australia 9°35S 143°46E 280 a
Darnley, C. Antarctica 68°0S 69°0E 151 C6
Darnley B. Canada 69°30N 123°30W 294 D7
Daroca Spain 41°9N 1°25W 196 D3
Daror Ethiopia 8°14N 44°42E 267 C5
Darou-Mousti Senegal 15°3N 16°3W 262 B1
Darr → Australia 23°39S 143°50E 280 C3
Darra Pezu Pakistan 32°19N 70°44E 242 C4
Darran Mts. N.Z. 44°37S 167°59E 285 E2
Darreh Shahr Iran 33°7N 47°22E 213 F12
Darrequeira Argentina 37°42S 63°10W 334 D3
Darrington U.S.A. 48°15N 121°36W 304 B3
Darrūs Iran 35°46N 51°27E 141 A2
Darsana Bangla. 23°35N 88°48E 241 D2
Darsi India 15°46N 79°44E 245 G4
Darsser Ort Germany 54°28N 12°32E 178 A8
Dart → U.K. 50°24N 3°39W 169 G4
Dart, C. Antarctica 73°6S 126°20W 151 D14
Dartford U.K. 51°26N 0°13E 125 B5
Dartmoor Vic., Australia 37°56S 141°19E 282 D4
Dartmoor Devon, U.K. 50°38N 3°57W 169 G4
Dartmoor ⌂ U.K. 50°37N 3°59W 169 G4
Dartmouth N.S., Canada 44°40N 63°30W 299 D7
Dartmouth Torbay, U.K. 50°21N 3°36W 169 G4
Dartmouth, Res. Australia 36°34S 147°32E 283 D7
Dartmouth Res. Australia 26°4S 145°18E 281 D4
Dartuch, C. = Artrutx, C. de Spain 39°55N 3°49E 206 B4
Daru Papua N. G. 9°3S 143°13E 286 E2
Daruvar Croatia 45°35N 17°14E 182 E2
Darvaza Turkmenistan 40°11N 58°24E 216 D5
Darvel, Teluk = Lahad Datu, Telok Malaysia 4°50N 118°20E 235 B5
Darvi Mongolia 46°27N 94°7E 217 C12
Darwen U.K. 53°42N 2°29W 168 D5
Darwendale Zimbabwe 17°41S 30°33E 271 A5
Darwha India 20°15N 77°45E 244 D3
Darwin N. Terr., Australia 12°25S 130°51E 278 B5
Darwin Calif., U.S.A. 36°15N 117°35W 307 J9
Darwin, Mt. Chile 54°47S 69°55W 336 D3
Darwin, Volcán Ecuador 0°10S 91°18W 330 a
Darya Ganj Delhi, India 120 a3
Darya Khan Pakistan 31°48N 71°6E 242 D4
Daryācheh-ye Bakhtegān Iran 29°40N 53°50E 247 D7
Daryapur India 20°55N 77°20E 244 D3
Daryoi Amu = Amudarya → Uzbekistan 43°58N 59°34E 216 D5
Dās U.A.E. 25°20N 53°30E 247 E7
Dashetai China 41°0N 109°5E 226 D5
Dashen, Ras Ethiopia 13°8N 38°26E 257 E4
Dasher U.S.A. 30°45N 83°13W 316 E6
Dashetai China 41°0N 109°5E 226 D5
Dashi China 23°1N 113°17E 121 B2
Dashkesan = Daşkäsän Azerbaijan 40°25N 46°0E 191 K7
Dashköpri Turkmenistan 36°16N 62°8E 247 B9
Dashoguz Turkmenistan 41°49N 59°58E 216 D5
Dasht → Pakistan 25°10N 61°40E 240 D1
Dasht-i-Tahlab Pakistan 28°40N 62°25E 240 C1
Daska Pakistan 32°20N 74°20E 242 C6
Daşkäsän Azerbaijan 40°25N 46°0E 191 K7
Dasmariñas Phil. 14°20N 120°56E 232 D3
Dassa Benin 7°46N 2°14E 263 D5
Dasuya India 31°49N 75°38E 242 D6
Datansha China 23°8N 113°12E 121 B2
Datça Turkey 36°46N 27°40E 205 E9
Datia India 25°39N 78°27E 243 G8
Datian China 25°40N 117°50E 229 E11
Datong Anhui, China 30°48N 117°44E 229 B11
Datong Shanxi, China 40°6N 113°18E 226 D7
Dattakhel Pakistan 32°54N 69°46E 242 C3
Dattapur = Dhamangaon India 20°48N 78°9E 244 D4
Datteln Germany 51°39N 7°21E 178 D3
Datu, Tanjung Indonesia 2°5N 109°39E 235 B3
Datu Piang Phil. 7°2N 124°30E 233 H5
Datuk, Tanjong = Datu, Tanjung Indonesia 2°5N 109°39E 235 B3
Datun China 40°0N 116°23E 114 B2
Daua = Dawa → Africa 4°11N 42°6E 257 G5
Daud Khel Pakistan 32°53N 71°34E 242 C4
Daudnagar India 25°2N 84°24E 243 G11
Daugava → Latvia 57°4N 24°3E 188 D3
Daugavpils Latvia 55°53N 26°32E 188 E4
Daulatabad India 19°57N 75°15E 244 E2
Daulatpur India 28°44N 77°6E 120 A1
Daule Ecuador 1°56S 79°56W 328 D2
Daule → Ecuador 2°10S 79°52W 328 D2
Daule-Peripa, Presa Ecuador 1°0S 79°35W 328 D2
Daulpur India 26°45N 77°59E 242 F7
Daun Germany 50°11N 6°49E 179 E2
Daund India 18°26N 74°40E 244 E2
Dauphin Man., Canada 51°9N 100°5W 297 C8
Dauphin Pa., U.S.A. 40°22N 76°56W 312 F8
Dauphin L. Canada 51°20N 99°45W 297 C9
Dauphiné France 45°15N 5°25E 175 C9
Daura Borno, Nigeria 11°31N 11°24E 263 C7
Daura Katsina, Nigeria 13°2N 8°21E 263 C6
Dausa India 26°52N 76°20E 242 F7
Däväçi Azerbaijan 41°15N 48°57E 191 K9
Davangere India 14°25N 75°55E 245 G2
Davao Phil. 7°0N 125°40E 233 H5
Davao □ Phil. 7°0N 125°55E 233 H5
Davao del Sur □ Phil. 6°30N 125°25E 233 H5
Davao G. Phil. 6°30N 125°48E 233 H5
Davao Oriental □ Phil. 7°10N 126°30E 233 H6
Dāvar Panāh = Sarāvān Iran 27°25N 62°15E 247 E9
Davenport Calif., U.S.A. 37°1N 122°12W 306 H4
Davenport Fla., U.S.A. 28°10N 81°36W 317 G8
Davenport Iowa, U.S.A. 41°32N 90°35W 310 C6
Davenport Wash., U.S.A. 47°39N 118°9W 304 C4
Davenport Ra. Australia 20°28S 134°0E 280 C1
Davenport Range ⌂ Australia 20°36S 134°22E 280 C1
Daventry U.K. 52°16N 1°10W 169 E6
David Panama 8°30N 82°30W 320 E3
David City U.S.A. 41°15N 97°8W 308 E5
David Glacier Antarctica 75°20S 162°0E 151 D21
David Gorodok = Davyd Haradok Belarus 52°4N 27°8E 177 B14
David's Citadel Jerusalem 123 b3
David's Tomb Jerusalem 123 b3
Davidson Canada 51°16N 105°59W 297 C7
Davidson, Mt. U.S.A. 37°44N 122°27W 136 B2
Davidson Mts. U.S.A. 68°41N 142°22W 303 B12
Davidson's Mains U.K. 55°58N 3°16W 121 B2
Davie U.S.A. 26°3N 80°14W 317 J9
Davis Antarctica 68°34S 77°55E 151 C6
Davis Calif., U.S.A. 38°33N 121°44W 306 G5
Davis Dam U.S.A. 35°12N 114°34W 307 K12
Davis Inlet Canada 55°50N 60°59W 299 A7
Davis Mts. U.S.A. 30°50N 103°55W 314 F3
Davis Sea Antarctica 66°0S 92°0E 151 C7
Davis Str. N. Amer. 65°0N 58°0W 295 D19
Davisboro U.S.A. 32°59N 82°36W 316 C7
Davison U.S.A. 43°2N 83°31W 311 A13
Davlos Cyprus 35°25N 33°54E 207 E9
Davo → Ivory C. 5°0N 6°10W 262 D3
Davos Switz. 46°48N 9°49E 179 J5
Dāvūdīyeh Iran 35°45N 51°25E 141 A2
Davutlar Turkey 37°43N 27°17E 205 D9
Davy L. Canada 58°53N 108°18W 297 B7
Davyd Haradok Belarus 52°4N 27°8E 177 B14
Davydkovo Russia 55°43N 37°29E 129 B2
Dawa → Africa 4°11N 42°6E 257 G5
Dawaki Bauchi, Nigeria 9°25N 9°33E 263 D6
Dawaki Kano, Nigeria 12°5N 8°23E 263 C6
Dawei = Tavoy Burma 14°2N 98°12E 236 E2
Dawes Ra. Australia 24°40S 150°40E 280 C5
Dawidy Poland 52°8N 20°58E 142 C1
Dawkah Oman 18°39N 54°2E 249 C6
Dawley = Telford U.K. 52°40N 2°27W 169 E5
Dawlish U.K. 50°35N 3°28W 169 G4
Dawna Ra. Burma 16°30N 98°30E 236 D2
Dawnyein Burma 15°54N 95°36E 241 G5
Dawqah Si. Arabia 19°36N 40°54E 248 C3
Dawros Hd. Ireland 54°50N 8°33W 166 B3
Dawson U.S.A. 31°46N 84°27W 316 D5
Dawson, I. Chile 53°50S 70°50W 336 D2
Dawson B. Canada 52°53N 100°49W 297 C8
Dawson City Canada 64°10N 139°30W 294 E4
Dawson Creek Canada 55°45N 120°15W 296 B4
Dawson Inlet Canada 61°50N 93°25W 297 A10
Dawson Ra. Australia 24°30S 149°48E 280 C4
Dawu Hubei, China 31°34N 114°7E 229 B9
Dawu Sichuan, China 30°55N 101°10E 228 B3
Dawwah Oman 20°33N 58°48E 249 B7
Dawwara, Ras id- Malta 35°52N 14°21E 206 F7
Dax France 43°44N 1°3W 174 E2
Daxian China 31°15N 107°23E 228 B6
Daxin China 22°50N 107°11E 228 F6
Daxindian China 37°30N 120°50E 227 F11
Daxing China 39°47N 116°24E 114 C2
Daxinggou China 43°25N 129°40E 227 C15
Daxue Shan Sichuan, China 30°30N 101°30E 228 B3
Daxue Shan Yunnan, China 23°42N 99°48E 228 F2
Day U.S.A. 30°12N 83°17W 316 E6
Day Kundī □ Afghan. 34°0N 66°0E 240 B2
Daya el Khadra Mauritania 25°14N 6°2W 260 C3
Dayang He → China 39°51N 123°38E 224 C1
Dayao China 25°43N 101°20E 228 E3
Daye China 30°6N 114°58E 229 B10
Dayet en Naharat Mali 17°39N 3°10W 262 B4
Dayi China 30°41N 103°29E 228 B4
Daylesford Australia 37°21S 144°9E 282 D6
Dayong China 29°11N 110°30E 229 C8
Dayr az Zawr Syria 35°20N 40°5E 213 E9
Dayr az Zawr □ Syria 34°50N 40°10E 213 E9
Days Bay N.Z. 41°17S 174°54E 143 B2
Daysland Canada 52°50N 112°20W 296 C6
Dayton Iowa, U.S.A. 42°16N 94°4W 310 B2
Dayton Nev., U.S.A. 39°14N 119°36W 306 F7
Dayton Ohio, U.S.A. 39°45N 84°12W 311 E12
Dayton Pa., U.S.A. 40°53N 79°15W 312 F5
Dayton Tenn., U.S.A. 35°30N 85°1W 315 D12
Dayton Wash., U.S.A. 46°19N 117°59W 304 C5
Dayton Wyo., U.S.A. 44°53N 107°16W 304 D10
Daytona Beach U.S.A. 29°13N 81°1W 317 F8
Dayu China 25°24N 114°22E 229 E10
Dayville U.S.A. 44°28N 119°32W 304 D4
Dazaifu Japan 33°32N 130°32E 222 D2
Dazhu China 30°41N 107°15E 228 B6
Dazkırı Turkey 37°57N 29°52E 205 D11
Dazu China 29°40N 105°42E 228 C5
De Aar S. Africa 30°39S 24°0E 270 D3
De Armanville U.S.A. 33°38N 85°54W 316 B4
De Bary U.S.A. 28°54N 81°18W 317 G8
De Biesbosch ⌂ Neths. 51°45N 4°48E 170 C4
De Forest U.S.A. 43°15N 89°20W 310 A7
De Funiak Springs U.S.A. 30°43N 86°7W 316 E3
De Grey → Australia 20°12S 119°13E 278 D2
De Haan Belgium 51°16N 3°2E 170 C3

De Hoge Veluwe △ Neths. 52°5N 5°46E 170 B5
De Hoop ⌓ S. Africa 34°30S 20°28E 270 D3
De Kalb Junction U.S.A. 44°30N 75°16W 313 B9
De Kennemerduinen △ Neths. 52°27N 4°33E 170 B4
De Land U.S.A. 29°2N 81°18W 317 F8
De Leon U.S.A. 32°7N 98°32W 314 E5
De Leon Springs U.S.A. 29°7N 81°21W 317 F8
De Long Mts. U.S.A. 68°10N 163°30W 303 B7
De Panne Belgium 51°6N 2°34E 170 C2
De Pere U.S.A. 44°27N 88°4W 308 C9
De Queen U.S.A. 34°2N 94°21W 314 D7
De Quincy U.S.A. 30°27N 93°26W 314 F8
De Ruyters U.S.A. 42°45N 75°53W 313 D9
De Smet U.S.A. 44°23N 97°33W 308 C5
De Soto U.S.A. 38°8N 90°34W 310 F6
De Soto City U.S.A. 27°27N 81°24W 317 H8
De Tour Village U.S.A. 46°0N 83°56W 309 B12
De Witt Ark., U.S.A. 34°18N 91°20W 314 D9
De Witt Iowa, U.S.A. 41°49N 90°33W 310 C6
De Witt Mich., U.S.A. 42°51N 84°34W 311 B12
Dead L. U.S.A. 30°10N 85°10W 316 E4
Dead Sea Asia 31°30N 35°30E 251 G6
Deadhorse U.S.A. 70°11N 148°27W 303 A10
Deadman B. U.S.A. 29°30N 83°30W 317 F6
Deadwood U.S.A. 44°23N 103°44W 308 C2
Deadwood L. Canada 59°10N 128°30W 296 B3
Deal U.K. 51°13N 1°25E 169 F9
Deal I. Australia 39°30S 147°20E 281 F4
Dealesville S. Africa 28°41S 25°44E 270 C4
De'an China 29°21N 115°46E 229 C10
Dean ➜ Canada 52°49N 126°58W 296 C3
Dean, Forest of U.K. 51°45N 2°33W 169 F5
Dean Chan. Canada 52°30N 127°15W 296 C3
Deán Funes Argentina 30°20S 64°20W 334 C3
Dearborn Mich., U.S.A. 42°19N 83°10W 311 B13
Dearborn Mo., U.S.A. 39°32N 94°46W 310 E2
Dease ➜ Canada 59°56N 128°32W 296 B3
Dease Inlet U.S.A. 71°2N 155°26W 303 A9
Dease L. Canada 58°40N 130°5W 296 B2
Dease Lake Canada 58°25N 130°6W 296 B2
Death Valley U.S.A. 36°15N 116°50W 307 J10
Death Valley △ U.S.A. 36°29N 117°6W 307 J9
Death Valley Junction U.S.A. 36°20N 116°25W 307 J10
Deauville France 49°23N 0°2E 172 C7
Deba Spain 43°18N 2°21W 196 B2
Deba Habe Nigeria 10°14N 11°20E 263 C7
Debagram India 23°51N 90°33E 243 H14
Debak Malaysia 1°34N 111°25E 235 B4
Debaltsevo Ukraine 48°22N 38°26E 189 H10
Debao China 23°21N 106°46E 228 F6
Debar Macedonia 41°31N 20°30E 202 E4
Debark Ethiopia 13°1N 37°48E 257 E4
Debden Canada 53°30N 106°50W 297 C7
Debdou Morocco 33°59N 3°0W 261 B4
Debe Trin. & Tob. 10°22N 61°27W 323 t
Dębica Poland 50°2N 21°27E 185 H8
Dęblin Poland 51°34N 21°50E 185 G8
Dębno Poland 52°44N 14°41E 185 F1
Débo, L. Mali 15°14N 4°15W 262 B4
DeBolt Canada 55°12N 118°1W 296 B5
Deborah East, L. Australia 30°45S 119°30E 279 F2
Deborah West, L. Australia 30°45S 119°5E 279 F2
Deboyne Is. Papua N. G. 10°43S 152°22E 286 F7
Debrc Serbia 44°38N 19°53E 202 B3
Debre Birhan Ethiopia 9°41N 39°31E 257 F4
Debre Markos Ethiopia 10°20N 37°40E 257 E4
Debre May Ethiopia 11°20N 37°25E 257 E4
Debre Sina Ethiopia 9°51N 39°50E 257 F4
Debre Tabor Ethiopia 11°50N 38°26E 257 E4
Debre Zebit Ethiopia 11°48N 38°30E 257 E4
Debre Zevit Ethiopia 8°50N 39°0E 257 F4
Debrecen Hungary 47°33N 21°42E 182 C6
Debrzno Poland 53°31N 17°14E 184 E4
Dečani Kosovo 42°30N 20°18E 202 D4
Decatur Ala., U.S.A. 34°36N 86°59W 315 D11
Decatur Ga., U.S.A. 33°46N 84°16W 113 B3
Decatur Ill., U.S.A. 39°51N 88°57W 310 E8
Decatur Ind., U.S.A. 40°50N 84°56W 311 D12
Decatur Mich., U.S.A. 42°7N 85°58W 311 B11
Decatur Tex., U.S.A. 33°14N 97°35W 314 E6
Decazeville France 44°34N 2°15E 174 D6
Deccan India 18°0N 79°0E 244 F4
Deception, Mt. Australia 30°42S 138°16E 282 A3
Deception B. Papua N. G. 7°45S 144°40E 286 D3
Deception Bay Australia 27°10S 153°5E 281 D5
Deception I. Antarctica 63°0S 60°15W 151 C17
Deception L. Canada 56°33N 104°13W 297 B8
Dechang China 27°25N 102°11E 228 D4
Dechhu India 26°46N 72°20E 242 F5
Děčín Czech Rep. 50°47N 14°12E 180 A7
Decize France 46°50N 3°28E 173 F10
Deckerville U.S.A. 43°32N 82°44W 312 C2
Decollatura Italy 39°3N 16°21E 201 C9
Decorah U.S.A. 43°18N 91°48W 308 D8
Deda Romania 46°56N 24°50E 183 D9
Dedaye Burma 16°24N 95°53E 241 G5
Dedéagach = Alexandroupoli Greece 40°50N 25°54E 203 F9
Dededo Guam 13°31N 144°50E 302 d
Deder Ethiopia 9°19N 41°27E 257 F5
Dedham U.S.A. 42°15N 71°10W 116 B1
Dedoplis Tskaro = Tsiteli-Tsqaro Georgia 41°33N 46°0E 191 K8
Dédougou Burkina Faso 12°30N 3°25W 262 C4
Dedovichi Russia 57°32N 29°56E 188 D5
Dedza Malawi 14°20S 34°20E 269 E3
Dee ➜ Aberds., U.K. 57°9N 2°5W 167 D6
Dee ➜ Dumf. & Gall., U.K. 54°51N 4°3W 167 G4
Dee ➜ Wales, U.K. 53°22N 3°17W 168 D4
Deep B. Canada 61°15N 116°35W 296 A5
Deep Bay = Chilumba Malawi 10°28S 34°12E 269 E3
Deep Bay = Shenzhen Wan China 22°27N 113°55E 219 G10
Deep Lead Australia 37°0S 142°43E 282 D5
Deepwater N.S.W., Australia 29°25S 151°51E 281 D5
Deepwater Mo., U.S.A. 38°16N 93°47W 310 F3
Deer ➜ Canada 58°23N 94°13W 297 B10
Deer I. U.S.A. 54°55N 162°18W 303 J7
Deer L. Canada 52°40N 94°20W 297 C10
Deer Lake Nfld. & L., Canada 49°11N 57°27W 299 C8
Deer Lake Ont., Canada 52°36N 94°20W 297 C10
Deer Lodge U.S.A. 46°24N 112°44W 304 C7
Deer Park Fla., U.S.A. 28°6N 80°54W 317 G9
Deer Park Ohio, U.S.A. 39°12N 84°23W 311 E12
Deer Park Wash., U.S.A. 47°57N 117°28W 304 C5
Deer River U.S.A. 47°20N 93°48W 308 B7
Deeragun Australia 19°16S 146°33E 280 B4
Deerdepoort S. Africa 24°37S 26°27E 270 B4
Deerfield Ill., U.S.A. 42°10N 87°51W 311 B9
Deerfield Mo., U.S.A. 37°50N 94°30W 310 G2
Deerfield Beach U.S.A. 26°19N 80°6W 317 J9
Deering U.S.A. 66°4N 162°42W 303 C7
Defensores del Chaco ⌓ Paraguay 20°13S 60°27W 331 E5
Defiance U.S.A. 41°17N 84°22W 311 C12
Dega Medo Ethiopia 7°59N 43°1E 267 C5
Degana India 26°50N 74°20E 242 F6
Dêgê China 31°44N 98°39E 228 B2
Degebe ➜ Portugal 38°13N 7°29W 195 G3
Degeberga Sweden 55°51N 14°5E 163 J8
Degeh Bur Ethiopia 8°11N 43°31E 267 C5
Dégelis Canada 47°30N 68°35W 299 C6
Degema Nigeria 4°50N 6°48E 263 E6
Degerfors Sweden 59°15N 14°27E 162 E8
Degerhamn Sweden 56°20N 16°24E 163 H10
Deggendorf Germany 48°50N 12°57E 179 G8
Degh ➜ Pakistan 31°3N 73°21E 242 D5
Değirmendere Turkey 40°42N 29°47E 203 F13
Değirmenlik = Kythréa Cyprus 35°15N 33°29E 207 E9
Degunino Russia 55°52N 37°33E 129 A3
Deh Bīd Iran 30°39N 53°11E 247 D7
Deh Dasht Iran 30°47N 50°33E 247 D6
Deh-e Shīr Iran 31°29N 53°45E 247 D7
Deh Nugaled = Nugaaleed, Dooxo Somali Rep. 8°35N 48°35E 267 C6
Dehaj Iran 30°42N 54°53E 247 D7
Dehak Iran 27°11N 62°37E 240 D1
Déhane Cameroon 3°30N 10°5E 264 B2
Dehdez Iran 31°43N 50°17E 247 D6
Dehej India 21°44N 72°40E 242 J5
Dehestān Iran 28°30N 55°35E 247 D7
Dehgolān Iran 35°17N 47°25E 213 E12
Dehibat Tunisia 32°0N 10°47E 258 B2
Dehiwala Sri Lanka 6°50N 79°51E 245 L4
Dehlorān Iran 32°41N 47°16E 213 F12
Dehnow-e Kūhestān Iran 27°58N 58°32E 247 E8
Dehra Dun India 30°20N 78°4E 242 D8
Dehri India 24°50N 84°15E 243 G11
Dehua China 25°26N 118°14E 229 E12
Dehui China 44°30N 125°40E 227 B13
Deim Zubeir Sudan 7°49N 26°16E 257 F2
Deinze Belgium 50°59N 3°32E 170 D3
Deir Dibwan West Bank 31°55N 35°16E 123 A2
Deir Ibzi'e West Bank 31°55N 35°7E 123 A1
Dej Romania 47°10N 23°52E 183 C8
Deje Sweden 59°35N 13°29E 162 E7
Dejiang China 28°18N 108°7E 228 C7
Dejvice Czech Rep. 50°6N 14°23E 135 B2
Deka ➜ Zimbabwe 18°4S 26°42E 270 A4
Dekabristov, Ostrov Russia 59°56N 30°15E 137 B1
DeKalb U.S.A. 41°56N 88°46W 311 C8
Dekemhare Eritrea 15°6N 39°0E 257 D4
Dekese Dem. Rep. of the Congo 3°24S 21°24E 264 C4
Dekoa C.A.R. 6°19N 19°4E 264 A3
Del Caño Rise Ind. Oc. 45°15S 44°15E 273 J3
Del Carmen Phil. 9°50N 126°0E 233 G6
Del Mar U.S.A. 32°58N 117°16W 307 N9
Del Norte U.S.A. 37°41N 106°21W 305 H10
Del Rey U.S.A. 33°59N 118°25W 126 C2
Del Rio U.S.A. 29°22N 100°54W 314 G4
Delai Sudan 17°21N 36°6E 256 D4
Delambre I. Australia 20°26S 117°5E 278 D2
Delami Sudan 11°38N 30°23E 257 E3
Delano Calif., U.S.A. 35°46N 119°15W 307 K7
Delano Peak U.S.A. 38°22N 112°22W 304 G7
Delārām Afghan. 32°9N 63°25E 240 B1
Delareyville S. Africa 26°41S 25°26E 270 C4
Delaronde L. Canada 54°3N 107°3W 297 C7
Delavan Ill., U.S.A. 40°22N 89°33W 310 D7
Delavan Wis., U.S.A. 42°38N 88°39W 311 B8
Delaware U.S.A. 40°18N 83°4W 311 D13
Delaware □ U.S.A. 39°0N 75°20W 309 F16
Delaware ➜ U.S.A. 39°15N 75°20W 313 G9
Delaware B. U.S.A. 39°0N 75°10W 309 F16
Delaware Water Gap ⌓ U.S.A. 41°10N 74°55W 313 E10
Delay ➜ Canada 56°56N 71°28W 299 A5
Delbrück Germany 51°46N 8°34E 178 D4
Delčevo Macedonia 41°58N 22°46E 202 E6
Delegate Australia 37°4S 148°56E 283 D8
Delémont Switz. 47°22N 7°20E 179 H3
Delevan U.S.A. 42°29N 78°29W 312 D6
Delft Neths. 52°1N 4°22E 170 B4
Delft I. Sri Lanka 9°30N 79°40E 245 K4
Delfzijl Neths. 53°20N 6°55E 170 A6
Delgada, Punta Chile 52°28S 69°32W 336 D3
Delgado, C. Mozam. 10°45S 40°40E 269 E5
Delgerhet Mongolia 45°50N 110°30E 226 B6
Delgo Sudan 20°6N 30°40E 256 C3
Delhi Ont., Canada 42°51N 80°30W 312 D4
Delhi India 28°39N 77°13E 120 B2
Delhi La., U.S.A. 32°28N 91°30W 314 E9
Delhi N.Y., U.S.A. 42°17N 74°55W 313 D10
Delhi Gate Delhi, India 120 b3
Delhi Indira Gandhi Int. ✕ (DEL) India 28°34N 77°5E 120 B1
Deli Jovan Serbia 44°13N 22°9E 202 B6
Delia Canada 51°38N 112°23W 296 C6
Delice Turkey 39°54N 34°2E 212 C6
Délices Dominica 15°17N 61°17W 323 k
Delicias Mexico 28°13N 105°28W 318 B3
Delījān Iran 33°59N 50°40E 247 C6
Delimara Point Malta 35°49N 14°34E 206 F8
Déline Canada 65°11N 123°25W 294 D7
Delisle Canada 51°55N 107°8W 297 C7
Delitzsch Germany 51°31N 12°20E 178 D8
Deliverance I. Australia 9°31S 141°34E 280 a
Dell City U.S.A. 31°56N 105°12W 314 F2
Dell Rapids U.S.A. 43°50N 96°43W 308 D5
Delle France 47°30N 7°2E 173 E14
Dellys Algeria 36°57N 3°57E 261 A5
Delmar Iowa, U.S.A. 42°0N 90°37W 310 C6
Delmar N.Y., U.S.A. 42°37N 73°47W 313 D11
Delmenhorst Germany 53°3N 8°37E 178 B4
Delmiro Gouveia Brazil 9°24S 38°6W 332 C4
Delnice Croatia 45°23N 14°50E 199 C11
Delonga, Ostrova Russia 76°40N 149°20E 215 B15
Deloraine Tas., Australia 41°30S 146°40E 281 G4
Deloraine Man., Canada 49°15N 100°29W 297 D8
Delphi Greece 38°28N 22°30E 204 C4
Delphi Ind., U.S.A. 40°36N 86°41W 311 D10
Delphos U.S.A. 40°51N 84°21W 311 D12
Delportshoop S. Africa 28°22S 24°20E 270 C3
Delray Beach U.S.A. 26°28N 80°4W 317 J9
Delsbo Sweden 61°48N 16°32E 162 C10
Delta Ala., U.S.A. 33°26N 85°42W 316 B4
Delta Colo., U.S.A. 38°44N 108°4W 304 G9
Delta Utah, U.S.A. 39°21N 112°35W 304 G7
Delta □ Nigeria 5°30N 6°0E 263 D6
Delta Amacuro □ Venezuela 8°30N 61°30W 329 B5
Delta del Ebre ⌓ Spain 40°43N 0°43E 196 E5
Delta del Po ⌓ Italy 44°50N 12°15E 199 D9
Delta du Saloum △ Senegal 13°42N 16°43W 262 C1
Delta Dunărea ⌓ Romania 45°15N 29°25E 183 E14
Delta Junction U.S.A. 64°2N 145°44W 303 D11
Deltona U.S.A. 28°54N 81°16W 317 G8
Delungra Australia 29°39S 150°51E 281 D5
Delvada India 20°46N 71°2E 242 J4
Delvinakí Greece 39°57N 20°32E 204 B2
Delvinë Albania 39°59N 20°6E 202 G4
Delyatyn Ukraine 48°32N 24°38E 183 B9
Demagiri India 22°55N 92°28E 241 D4
Demak Indonesia 6°53S 110°38E 235 D4
Demanda, Sierra de la Spain 42°15N 3°0W 196 C2
Demarcation Pt. U.S.A. 69°41N 141°18W 303 B12
Demarest U.S.A. 40°57N 73°57W 132 A2
Demavend = Damāvand, Qolleh-ye Iran 35°56N 52°10E 247 C7
Demba Dem. Rep. of the Congo 5°28S 22°15E 265 D4
Demba Chio Angola 9°41S 13°41E 265 D2
Dembecha Ethiopia 10°32N 37°30E 257 E4
Dembéni Comoros Is. 11°52S 43°23E 272 a
Dembéni Mayotte 12°50S 45°11E 272 b
Dembi Ethiopia 8°5N 36°25E 257 F4
Dembia C.A.R. 4°56N 23°53E 264 B4
Dembia Dem. Rep. of the Congo 3°33N 25°48E 268 B2
Dembica = Dębica Poland 50°2N 21°25E 185 H8
Dembidolo Ethiopia 8°34N 34°50E 257 F3
Demchok India 32°42N 79°29E 243 C8
Demer ➜ Belgium 50°57N 4°42E 170 D4
Demerara Abyssal Plain Atl. Oc. 10°0N 48°0W 152 F7
Demetrias Greece 39°22N 23°1E 204 B5
Demidov Russia 55°16N 31°30E 188 E6
Deming N. Mex., U.S.A. 32°16N 107°46W 305 K10
Deming Wash., U.S.A. 48°50N 122°13W 306 B4
Demini ➜ Brazil 0°46S 62°56W 329 D5
Demirci Turkey 39°2N 28°38E 205 B10
Demirköprü Barajı Turkey 38°42N 28°25E 205 C10
Demirköy Turkey 41°49N 27°45E 203 E11
Demirtas Turkey 36°25N 32°11E 250 B3
Demmin Germany 53°54N 13°2E 178 B9
Demnate Morocco 31°44N 6°59W 260 B3
Democracia Brazil 5°48S 61°26W 331 B5
Demonte Italy 44°19N 7°17E 198 D4
Demopolis U.S.A. 32°31N 87°50W 315 E11
Dempo Indonesia 4°2S 103°15E 234 C2
Demyansk Russia 57°40N 32°27E 188 D7
Den Bosch = 's-Hertogenbosch Neths. 51°42N 5°17E 170 C5
Den Burg Neths. 53°3N 4°47E 170 A4
Den Chai Thailand 17°59N 100°4E 236 D3
Den Haag = 's-Gravenhage Neths. 52°7N 4°17E 170 B4
Den Helder Neths. 52°57N 4°45E 170 B4
Den Ilp Neths. 52°27N 4°55E 112 A2
Den Lille Havfrue Copenhagen, Denmark 118 a3
Den Oever Neths. 52°56N 5°2E 170 B5
Denain France 50°20N 3°22E 173 B10
Denair U.S.A. 37°32N 120°48W 306 H6
Denali = McKinley, Mt. U.S.A. 63°4N 151°0W 303 E10
Denali △ U.S.A. 63°30N 152°0W 303 E10
Denau Uzbekistan 38°16N 67°54E 217 E7
Denbigh Ont., Canada 45°8N 77°15W 312 A7
Denbigh Denbs., U.K. 53°12N 3°25W 168 D4
Denbigh, C. U.S.A. 64°23N 161°32W 303 D7
Denbighshire □ U.K. 53°8N 3°22W 168 D4
Dendang Indonesia 3°7S 107°56E 235 C3
Dendé = Ndindi Gabon 3°46S 11°9E 264 C2
Dendermonde Belgium 51°2N 4°5E 170 C4
Deneba Ethiopia 9°47N 39°10E 257 F4
Deng Deng Cameroon 5°12N 13°31E 264 A2
Dengchuan China 25°59N 100°3E 228 E3
Denge Nigeria 12°52N 5°21E 263 C6
Dengfeng China 34°25N 113°2E 226 G7
Dengi Nigeria 9°25N 9°55E 263 D6
Dengkou China 40°18N 106°55E 226 D4
Dengzhou China 32°34N 112°4E 229 A9
Denham Australia 25°56S 113°31E 279 E1
Denham, Mt. Jamaica 18°13N 77°32W 320 a
Denham Ra. Australia 21°55S 147°46E 280 C4
Denham Sd. Australia 25°45S 113°15E 279 E1
Denholm Canada 52°39N 108°1W 297 C7
Denia Spain 38°49N 0°8E 197 G5
Denial B. Australia 32°14S 133°32E 281 E1
Deniliquin Australia 35°30S 144°58E 283 C6
Denimoo = Fort Resolution Canada 61°10N 113°40W 296 A6
Denis Gabon 0°19N 9°22E 264 B1
Denison Iowa, U.S.A. 42°1N 95°21W 308 D6
Denison Tex., U.S.A. 33°45N 96°33W 314 E6
Denison Plains Australia 18°35S 128°0E 278 C4
Denisovka Kazakhstan 52°27N 61°39E 216 B6
Denistone Heights Australia 33°48S 151°8E 139 A1
Deniyaya Sri Lanka 6°21N 80°33E 245 L5
Denizli Turkey 37°42N 29°2E 205 D11
Denizli □ Turkey 37°45N 29°5E 205 D11
Denman Australia 32°24S 150°42E 283 B9
Denman Glacier Antarctica 66°45S 99°25E 151 C7
Denmark W. Austral., Australia 34°59S 117°25E 279 F2
Denmark S.C., U.S.A. 33°19N 81°9W 316 B8
Denmark ■ Europe 55°45N 10°0E 163 J3
Denmark Str. Atl. Oc. 66°0N 30°0W 292 C17
Dennery St. Lucia 13°55N 60°54W 323 m
Dennison U.S.A. 40°24N 81°19W 312 F3
Denny U.K. 56°1N 3°55W 167 E5
Denpasar Indonesia 8°39S 115°13E 231 K18
Denpasar ✕ (DPS) Indonesia 8°44S 115°10E 231 K18
Denton Ga., U.S.A. 31°44N 82°42W 316 D7
Denton Mont., U.S.A. 47°19N 109°57W 304 C9
Denton Tex., U.S.A. 33°13N 97°8W 314 E6
Dentonia Park Canada 43°42N 79°17W 141 A3
D'Entrecasteaux, Ís. N. Cal. 18°0S 163°0E 277 D11
D'Entrecasteaux, Pt. Australia 34°50S 115°57E 279 F2
D'Entrecasteaux △ Australia 34°20S 115°33E 279 F2
D'Entrecasteaux Is. Papua N. G. 9°0S 151°0E 286 E6
Dentsville U.S.A. 34°4N 80°58W 316 A9
Denu Ghana 6°4N 1°8E 263 D5
Denver Colo., U.S.A. 39°42N 104°59W 304 G11
Denver Ind., U.S.A. 40°52N 86°5W 311 D10
Denver Iowa, U.S.A. 42°40N 92°20W 310 B4
Denver Pa., U.S.A. 40°14N 76°8W 313 F8
Denver City U.S.A. 32°58N 102°50W 314 E3
Denwood = Wainwright Canada 52°50N 110°50W 297 C6
Deoband India 29°42N 77°43E 242 E7
Deobhog India 19°53N 82°44E 244 E6
Deodrug India 16°26N 76°55E 245 F3
Deogarh Orissa, India 21°32N 84°45E 244 D7
Deogarh Raj., India 25°32N 73°54E 242 G5
Deoghar India 24°30N 86°42E 243 G12
Deogyusan △ S. Korea 35°45N 127°40E 224 E3
Deokjeokdo S. Korea 37°13N 126°7E 224 D3
Deolali India 19°58N 73°50E 244 E1
Deoli = Devli India 25°50N 75°20E 242 G6
Déols France 46°50N 1°43E 173 F8
Deora India 26°22N 70°55E 242 F4
Deorha = Jubbal India 31°5N 77°40E 242 D7
Deori India 23°24N 79°1E 243 H8
Deoria India 26°31N 83°48E 243 F10
Deosai Mts. Pakistan 35°40N 75°0E 243 B6
Deosri India 26°46N 90°29E 241 B3
Depalpur India 22°51N 75°33E 242 H6
DePaul Univ. U.S.A. 41°55N 87°39W 119 B3
Deping China 37°25N 116°58E 227 F9
Deposit U.S.A. 42°4N 75°25W 313 D9
Deptford U.K. 51°28N 0°1W 125 B3
Depuch I. Australia 20°37S 117°44E 278 D2
Deputati, Camera dei Rome, Italy 136 b2
Deputatskiy Russia 69°18N 139°54E 215 C14
Dêqên China 28°34N 98°51E 228 C2
Deqing China 23°8N 111°42E 229 F8
Dera, Lach ➜ Somali Rep. 0°15N 42°17E 267 D5
Dera Ghazi Khan Pakistan 30°5N 70°43E 242 D4
Dera Ismail Khan Pakistan 31°50N 70°50E 242 D4
Derabugti Pakistan 29°2N 69°9E 242 E3
Derawar Fort Pakistan 28°46N 71°20E 242 E4
Derbent Russia 42°5N 48°15E 191 J9
Derbent Turkey 38°11N 28°33E 205 C10
Derby W. Austral., Australia 17°18S 123°38E 278 C3
Derby Derby City, U.K. 52°56N 1°28W 168 E6
Derby Conn., U.S.A. 41°19N 73°5W 313 E11
Derby Kans., U.S.A. 37°33N 97°16W 308 G5
Derby N.Y., U.S.A. 42°41N 78°58W 312 D6
Derby City □ U.K. 52°56N 1°28W 168 E6
Derby Line U.S.A. 45°0N 72°6W 313 B12
Derbyshire □ U.K. 53°11N 1°38W 168 D6
Đerdap △ Serbia 44°40N 22°23E 202 B6
Derdepoort S. Africa 24°38S 26°24E 270 B4
Derecske Hungary 47°20N 21°33E 182 C6
Dereham U.K. 52°41N 0°57E 169 E8
Dereköy Turkey 41°55N 27°21E 203 E11
Dereli Turkey 40°44N 38°26E 213 B8
Derg ➜ U.K. 54°44N 7°26W 166 B4
Derg, L. Ireland 53°0N 8°20W 166 D3
Dergachi = Derhaci Ukraine 50°9N 36°11E 189 G9
Derhaci Ukraine 50°9N 36°11E 189 G9
Deridder U.S.A. 30°51N 93°17W 314 F8
Derik Turkey 37°21N 40°18E 213 D9
Derinkuyu Turkey 38°22N 34°45E 212 C6
Dermantsi Bulgaria 43°8N 24°17E 203 C8
Dermott U.S.A. 33°32N 91°26W 314 E9
Dernière Rivière St. Lucia 13°57N 60°55W 323 m
Dêrong China 28°44N 99°9E 228 C2
Derri Somali Rep. 4°20N 46°37E 267 D6
Derrinallum Australia 37°57S 143°15E 282 D5
Derry = Londonderry U.K. 55°0N 7°20W 166 B4
Derry = Londonderry □ U.K. 55°0N 7°20W 166 B4
Derry N.H., U.S.A. 42°53N 71°19W 313 D13
Derry Pa., U.S.A. 40°20N 79°18W 312 F5
Derryveagh Mts. Ireland 54°56N 8°11W 166 B3
Derudub Sudan 17°31N 36°7E 256 D4
Derval France 47°40N 1°41W 172 E5
Derveni Greece 38°8N 22°25E 204 C4
Derventa Bos.-H. 44°59N 17°55E 182 F2
Derwent ➜ Cumb., U.K. 54°39N 3°33W 168 C4
Derwent ➜ Derby, U.K. 52°57N 1°28W 168 E6
Derwent ➜ N. Yorks., U.K. 53°45N 0°58W 168 D7
Derwent Water U.K. 54°35N 3°9W 168 C4
Derzhavinsk Kazakhstan 51°6N 66°19E 217 B7
Des Moines Iowa, U.S.A. 41°35N 93°37W 310 C3
Des Moines N. Mex., U.S.A. 36°46N 103°50W 305 H12
Des Moines Wash., U.S.A. 47°24N 122°19W 306 C4
Des Moines ➜ U.S.A. 40°23N 91°25W 310 D5
Des Moines ✕ (DSM) U.S.A. 41°32N 93°40W 310 C3
Des Plaines U.S.A. 42°2N 87°54W 119 A1
Des Plaines ➜ U.S.A. 41°23N 88°15W 311 C8
Desa Romania 43°52N 23°2E 182 G8
Desaguadero Peru 16°34S 69°3W 330 D4
Desaguadero ➜ Argentina 34°30S 66°46W 334 C2
Desaguadero ➜ Bolivia 16°35S 69°5W 330 D4
Desantne Ukraine 45°34N 29°32E 183 E14
Désappointement, Is. du French Polynesia 14°10S 141°20W 289 f
Desar Malaysia 1°31N 104°17E 237 d
Descanso, Pta. Mexico 32°21N 117°3W 307 N9
Descartes France 46°59N 0°42E 174 B4
Deschaillons-sur-St-Laurent Canada 46°32N 72°7W 299 C5
Deschambault L. Canada 54°50N 103°50W 297 C8
Deschutes ➜ U.S.A. 45°38N 120°55W 304 D3
Descobrimento △ Brazil 16°53S 39°21W 333 E4
Dese Ethiopia 11°5N 39°40E 257 E4
Deseado, C. Chile 52°45S 74°42W 336 D2
Desenzano del Garda Italy 45°28N 10°32E 198 C7
Deseronto Canada 44°12N 77°3W 312 B7
Desert Center U.S.A. 33°43N 115°24W 307 M11
Desert Hot Springs U.S.A. 33°58N 116°30W 307 M10
Desert Wetlands Park U.S.A. 36°7N 115°2W 124 B2
Desertas, Ilhas Madeira 32°30N 16°30W 260 B1
Deset Norway 61°20N 11°26E 164 C8
Desfina Greece 38°25N 22°31E 204 C4
Deshaies Guadeloupe 16°18N 61°47W 322 e
Deshauteur Guadeloupe 16°15N 61°25W 322 e
Deshnok India 27°48N 73°21E 242 F5
Desierto Central de Baja California ⌓ Mexico 29°40N 114°50W 318 B2
Desjardins, Complexe Montréal, Canada 130 b2
Deskati Greece 39°55N 21°49E 202 G5
Desna ➜ Ukraine 50°33N 30°32E 177 C16
Desnătui ➜ Romania 43°53N 23°35E 183 G8
Desolación, I. Chile 53°0S 74°0W 336 D2
Despeñaperros, Paso Spain 38°24N 3°30W 195 G7
Despeñaperros ⌓ Spain 38°23N 3°32W 195 G7
Despotiko Greece 36°57N 24°58E 204 E6
Despotovac Serbia 44°6N 21°30E 202 B5
Dessau Germany 51°51N 12°14E 178 D8
Dessye = Dese Ethiopia 11°5N 39°40E 257 E4
Destin U.S.A. 30°24N 86°30W 317 E3
D'Estrees B. Australia 35°55S 137°45E 282 C2
Desuri India 25°18N 73°35E 242 G5
Desvres France 50°40N 1°48E 173 B8
Det Udom Thailand 14°54N 105°5E 236 E5
Deta Romania 45°24N 21°13E 182 E6
Dete Zimbabwe 18°38S 26°50E 270 A4
Detinja ➜ Serbia 43°51N 20°5E 202 C4
Detmold Germany 51°56N 8°52E 178 D4
Detour, Pt. U.S.A. 45°40N 86°40W 308 C10
Detroit U.S.A. 42°19N 83°12W 312 D1
Detroit Lakes U.S.A. 46°49N 95°51W 308 B6
Detroit Metropolitan Wayne County ✕ (DTW) U.S.A. 42°13N 83°21W 311 B13
Detskoye Selo = Pushkin Russia 59°45N 30°25E 188 C6
Dettifoss Iceland 65°48N 16°24W 155 B10
Detva Slovak Rep. 48°34N 19°25E 181 C12
Deua △ Australia 35°32S 149°46E 283 C8
Deurne Neths. 51°27N 5°49E 170 C5
Deutsch = Przemyśl Poland 49°50N 22°45E 185 J9
Deutsch Brod = Havlíčkův Brod Czech Rep. 49°36N 15°33E 180 B8
Deutsch-Eylau = Iława Poland 53°36N 19°34E 184 E6
Deutsch Krone = Wałcz Poland 53°17N 16°27E 185 E3
Deutsch-Luxemburgischer ⌓ Germany 49°58N 6°12E 179 F2
Deutsche Bucht Germany 54°15N 8°0E 178 A4
Deutsche Oper Germany 52°30N 13°19E 115 A2
Deutsches Museum Germany 48°7N 11°35E 131 B2
Deutschland = Germany ■ Europe 51°0N 10°0E 178 E6
Deutschlandsberg Austria 46°49N 15°14E 180 E8
Deux-Sèvres □ France 46°35N 0°20W 172 F6
Deva Romania 45°53N 22°55E 182 E7
Devakottai India 9°55N 78°45E 245 K4
Devaprayag India 30°13N 78°35E 243 D8
Devarkonda India 16°42N 78°56E 244 F4
Dévaványa Hungary 47°2N 20°59E 182 C5
Deveci Dağları Turkey 40°6N 36°15E 212 B7
Devecikonağı Turkey 39°55N 28°34E 203 G12
Devecser Hungary 47°6N 17°26E 182 C2
Develi Turkey 38°23N 35°29E 212 C6
Deventer Neths. 52°15N 6°10E 170 B6
Deveraux U.S.A. 33°13N 83°59W 316 B6
Deveron ➜ U.K. 57°41N 2°32W 167 D6
Devesel Romania 44°28N 22°41E 182 F7
Devgad I. India 14°48N 74°5E 245 G2
Devgadh Bariya India 22°40N 73°55E 242 H5
Devgarh India 16°23N 73°23E 245 F1
Devi ➜ India 19°59N 86°24E 244 E8
Devikot India 26°42N 71°12E 242 F4
Devil River Pk. N.Z. 40°56S 172°37E 285 A7
Devil's Bridge Antigua & B. 17°6N 61°41W 322 b
Devils Den U.S.A. 35°46N 119°58W 306 K7
Devils Hole = Death Valley △ U.S.A. 36°29N 117°6W 307 J9
Devils Island, I. = Diable, Île du Fr. Guiana 5°16N 52°34W 329 B7
Devils Lake U.S.A. 48°7N 98°52W 308 A4
Devils Paw Canada 58°47N 134°0W 296 B2
Devil's Peak S. Africa 33°57S 18°27E 118 A1
Devils Postpile ⌓ U.S.A. 37°37N 119°5W 306 H7
Devil's Pt. Sri Lanka 9°26N 80°6E 245 K5
Devils Tower U.S.A. 44°35N 104°42W 304 D11
Devils Tower △ U.S.A. 44°48N 104°55W 304 D11
Devil's Woodyard Mud Volcano Trin. & Tob. 10°16N 61°22W 323 t
Devin Bulgaria 41°44N 24°24E 203 E8
Devine U.S.A. 29°8N 98°54W 314 G5
Devipattinam India 9°29N 78°54E 245 K4
Devizes U.K. 51°22N 1°58W 169 F6
Devli India 25°50N 75°20E 242 G6
Devnya Bulgaria 43°13N 27°33E 203 C11
Devoll ➜ Albania 40°57N 20°15E 202 F4
Devon Canada 53°24N 113°44W 296 C6
Devon □ U.K. 50°50N 3°40W 169 G4
Devon I. Canada 75°10N 85°0W 295 B15
Devonport Australia 41°10S 146°22E 281 G4
Devrek Turkey 41°13N 31°57E 212 B4
Devrekâni Turkey 41°36N 33°50E 212 B5
Devrez ➜ Turkey 41°6N 34°25E 212 B6
Devrukh India 17°3N 73°37E 244 F1
Dewas India 22°59N 76°3E 242 H7
Dewetsdorp S. Africa 29°33S 26°39E 270 C4
Dewey Puerto Rico 18°18N 65°18W 321 b
Dexing China 28°46N 117°30E 229 C11
Dexter Maine, U.S.A. 45°1N 69°18W 309 C19
Dexter Mich., U.S.A. 42°20N 83°53W 311 B13
Dexter Mo., U.S.A. 36°48N 89°57W 308 G9
Dexter N. Mex., U.S.A. 33°12N 104°22W 305 K11
Dey-Dey, L. Australia 29°12S 131°4E 279 E5
Deyang China 31°3N 104°27E 228 B5
Deyhūk Iran 33°15N 57°30E 247 C8
Deyyer Iran 27°55N 51°55E 247 E6
Dez ➜ Iran 31°39N 48°52E 213 F13
Dezadeash L. Canada 60°28N 136°58W 296 A1
Dezfūl Iran 32°20N 48°30E 213 F13
Dezhneva, Mys Russia 66°5N 169°40W 215 C19
Dezhou China 37°26N 116°18E 226 F9
Dhadhar ➜ India 24°56N 85°24E 243 G11
Dhahabān Si. Arabia 21°58N 39°3E 248 B2
Dhahiriya = Az Ẓāhirīyah West Bank 31°25N 34°58E 251 G5
Dhahran = Aẓ Ẓahrān Si. Arabia 26°10N 50°7E 247 E6
Dhak Pakistan 32°25N 72°33E 242 C5
Dhaka Bangla. 23°43N 90°26E 241 D3
Dhaka □ Bangla. 24°25N 90°25E 241 C3
Dhakuria India 22°30N 88°22E 124 B2
Dhali Cyprus 35°1N 33°25E 207 E9
Dhamangaon India 20°48N 78°9E 244 D4
Dhamār Yemen 14°30N 44°20E 248 D4
Dhampur India 29°19N 78°33E 243 E8
Dhamra ➜ India 20°47N 86°58E 244 D8
Dhamtari India 20°42N 81°35E 244 D5
Dhanbad India 23°50N 86°30E 243 H12
Dhangarhi Nepal 28°55N 80°40E 243 E9
Dhankuta Nepal 26°55N 87°40E 243 F12
Dhanora India 20°20N 80°22E 244 D5
Dhanpuri India 23°13N 81°30E 244 C5
Dhanushkodi India 9°11N 79°24E 245 K4
Dhar India 22°35N 75°26E 242 H6
Dharampur Gujarat, India 20°32N 73°17E 244 D1
Dharampur Mad. P., India 22°13N 75°18E 242 H6
Dharamsala = Dharmsala India 32°16N 76°23E 242 C7
Dharan Nepal 26°49N 87°17E 243 F12
Dharangaon India 21°1N 75°16E 244 D2
Dharapuram India 10°45N 77°34E 245 J3
Dharavi India 19°1N 72°51E 130 A2
Dhariwal India 31°57N 75°19E 242 D6
Dharla ➜ Bangla. 25°46N 89°42E 243 G13
Dharmapuri India 12°10N 78°10E 245 H4
Dharmavaram India 14°29N 77°44E 245 G3
Dharmjaygarh India 22°28N 83°13E 243 H10
Dharmsala India 32°16N 76°23E 242 C7
Dharni India 21°33N 76°53E 242 J7
Dharug △ Australia 33°20S 151°2E 283 B9
Dharur India 18°3N 76°8E 244 E3
Dharwad India 15°30N 75°4E 245 G2
Dhasan ➜ India 25°48N 79°24E 243 G8
Dhaulagiri Nepal 28°39N 83°28E 243 E10
Dhebar, L. India 24°10N 74°0E 242 G6
Dheftera Cyprus 35°5N 33°16E 207 E9
Dhenkanal India 20°45N 85°35E 244 D7
Dherinia Cyprus 35°3N 33°57E 207 E9
Dheskáti = Deskati Greece 39°55N 21°49E 202 G5
Dhī Qār □ Iraq 31°0N 46°15E 246 D5
Dhiarrizos ➜ Cyprus 34°41N 32°34E 207 F8
Dhībān Jordan 31°30N 35°46E 251 G6
Dhilwan India 31°31N 75°21E 242 D6
Dhimarkhera India 23°28N 80°22E 243 H9
Dhodhekánisos = Dodecanese Greece 36°35N 27°0E 205 E8
Dholka India 22°44N 72°29E 242 H5
Dhomokós = Domokos Greece 39°10N 22°18E 204 B4
Dhond = Daund India 18°26N 74°40E 244 E2
Dhone India 15°25N 77°53E 245 G3
Dhoraji India 21°45N 70°37E 242 J4
Dhragonisi = Tragonhsi Greece 37°27N 25°29E 205 D7
Dhrangadhra India 22°59N 71°31E 242 H4
Dhrol India 22°33N 70°25E 242 H4
Dhubāb Yemen 12°56N 43°25E 248 D3
Dhuburi India 26°2N 89°59E 241 B2
Dhulasar Bangla. 21°52N 90°14E 241 E3
Dhule India 20°58N 74°50E 244 D2
Dhupdhara India 26°10N 91°4E 241 B3
Dhurbo Somali Rep. 11°37N 50°20E 267 B7
Dhuusamarreeb Somali Rep. 5°30N 46°15E 267 C6
Di-ib, W. ➜ Sudan 22°38N 36°6E 256 C4
Di Linh Vietnam 11°35N 108°4E 237 G7
Di Linh, Cao Nguyen Vietnam 11°30N 108°0E 237 G7
Dia Greece 35°28N 25°14E 207 E6
Diabakania Guinea 10°38N 10°58W 262 C2
Diable, Île du Fr. Guiana 5°16N 52°34W 329 B7
Diable, Pte. du Martinique 14°46N 60°53W 322 j
Diables, Morne aux Dominica 15°37N 61°27W 323 k
Diablo Pt. N. Marianas 15°0N 145°35E 302 e
Diablo Range U.S.A. 37°20N 121°25W 306 J5
Diablotins, Morne Dominica 15°30N 61°24W 323 k
Diadema Brazil 23°41S 46°37W 137 C2
Diafarabé Mali 14°9N 4°57W 262 C4
Diala Mali 14°10N 9°58W 262 C3
Dialakoro Mali 12°18N 7°54W 262 C3
Dialakoto Senegal 13°21N 13°19W 262 C2
Diallassagou Mali 13°47N 3°41W 262 C4
Diamant, Pte. du Martinique 14°27N 61°3W 322 j
Diamant, Rocher du Martinique 14°27N 61°2W 322 j
Diamante Argentina 32°5S 60°40W 334 C3
Diamante Italy 39°41N 15°49E 201 C8
Diamante ➜ Argentina 34°30S 66°46W 334 C2
Diamantina Brazil 18°17S 43°40W 333 E3
Diamantina ➜ Australia 26°45S 139°10E 281 D2
Diamantina △ Australia 23°33S 141°23E 280 C3
Diamantino Brazil 14°30S 56°30W 331 C6
Diamond Bar U.S.A. 34°1N 117°48W 307 L9
Diamond Harbour India 22°11N 88°14E 243 H13
Diamond Head U.S.A. 21°16N 157°49W 302 K14
Diamond I. Grenada 12°20N 61°35W 323 q
Diamond Is. Australia 17°25S 151°5E 280 B5
Diamond Mts. U.S.A. 39°40N 115°50W 304 G6
Diamond Springs U.S.A. 38°42N 120°49W 306 G6
Diamou Mali 14°5N 11°16W 262 C2
Dian Chi China 24°50N 102°43E 228 E4
Dianalund Denmark 55°32N 11°30E 163 J5
Dianbai China 21°33N 111°0E 229 G8
Diancheng China 21°30N 111°4E 229 G8
Dianjiang China 30°24N 107°20E 228 B6
Diano Marina Italy 43°54N 8°5E 198 E5
Dianópolis Brazil 11°38S 46°50W 333 D2
Dianra Ivory C. 8°45N 6°14W 262 D3
Diaoyu Tai = Senkaku-Shotō E. China Sea 25°45N 123°30E 221 M1
Diapaga Burkina Faso 12°5N 1°46E 263 C5
Diapangou Burkina Faso 12°5N 0°10E 263 C5
Diariguila Guinea 10°35N 10°2W 262 C2
Diavolo, Mt. India 12°40N 92°56E 245 H11
Dibā U.A.E. 25°45N 56°16E 247 E8
Dibagah Iraq 35°52N 43°48E 213 E10
Dibai India 28°13N 78°15E 242 E8
Dibaya Dem. Rep. of the Congo 6°30S 22°57E 265 D4
Dibaya-Lubue Dem. Rep. of the Congo 4°12S 19°54E 265 C3
Dibbeen △ Jordan 32°20N 35°45E 251 F6
Dibella Niger 17°32N 13°6E 259 E2
D'Iberville, Lac Canada 55°55N 73°15W 298 A5
Dibete Botswana 23°45S 26°32E 270 B4
Dibi Cameroon 7°8N 13°43E 264 A2
Dibru-Saikhowa △ India 27°40N 95°25E 241 B5
Dibrugarh India 27°29N 94°55E 241 B5
Diciosânmartin = Târnăveni Romania 46°19N 24°13E 183 D9
Dickens U.S.A. 33°37N 100°50W 314 E4
Dickeyville U.S.A. 42°38N 90°36W 310 B6
Dickinson U.S.A. 46°53N 102°47W 308 B2
Dickinson B. Antigua & B. 17°10N 61°51W 322 b
Dick's Pt. Bahamas 25°4N 77°18W 153 b
Dickson = Dikson Russia 73°40N 80°5E 214 B9
Dickson U.S.A. 36°5N 87°23W 315 C11
Dickson City U.S.A. 41°28N 75°36W 313 E9
Dicle Barajı Turkey 38°20N 40°11E 213 C9
Dicle Nehri ➜ Turkey 37°44N 41°10E 213 D9
Dicomano Italy 43°53N 11°31E 199 E8
Didesa, W. ➜ Ethiopia 10°2N 35°32E 257 E4
Didiéni Mali 13°53N 8°6W 262 C3
Didimbo Angola 17°30S 21°45E 265 F4
Didimoticho Greece 41°22N 26°29E 203 E10
Didsbury Canada 51°35N 114°10W 296 C6
Didwana India 27°23N 74°36E 242 F6
Die France 44°47N 5°22E 175 D9
Diébougou Burkina Faso 11°0N 3°15W 262 C4
Diecke Guinea 7°27N 8°54W 262 D3
Diedenhofen = Thionville France 49°20N 6°10E 173 C13
Diefenbaker, L. Canada 51°0N 106°55W 297 C7
Diegen Belgium 50°53N 4°26E 116 A2
Diego de Almagro Chile 26°22S 70°3W 334 B1
Diego Garcia Ind. Oc. 7°50S 72°50E 273 E6
Diego Martin Trin. & Tob. 10°43N 61°34W 323 t
Diego Ramirez, Islas Chile 56°30S 68°44W 336 E3
Diego Suarez = Antsiranana Madag. 12°25S 49°20E 272 A2
Diekirch Lux. 49°52N 6°10E 170 E6
Diéma Mali 14°32N 9°12W 262 C3
Diembéring Senegal 12°29N 16°47W 262 C1
Diemelsee ⌓ Germany 51°20N 8°40E 178 D4
Diemen Neths. 52°21N 4°58E 112 A2
Dien Ban Vietnam 15°53N 108°16E 236 E7
Dien Bien Vietnam 21°20N 103°0E 228 G4
Dien Khanh Vietnam 12°15N 109°6E 237 F7
Diepholz Germany 52°37N 8°22E 178 C4
Diepkloof S. Africa 26°14S 27°57E 123 B1
Dieppe France 49°54N 1°4E 172 C8
Dieppe Bay Town St. Kitts & Nevis 17°25N 62°48W 322 d
Dieprivier S. Africa 34°2S 18°27E 118 B1
Dierks U.S.A. 34°7N 94°1W 314 D7
Diest Belgium 50°58N 5°4E 170 D5
Dieterich U.S.A. 39°4N 88°23W 311 E8
Dietikon Switz. 47°24N 8°24E 179 H4
Dieulefit France 44°32N 5°4E 175 D9
Dieuze France 48°49N 6°43E 173 D13
Dievenow = Dziwnów Poland 54°2N 14°45E 184 D1
Dif Somali Rep. 0°59N 40°58E 267 D5
Diffa Niger 13°18N 12°36E 263 C7
Diffa □ Niger 14°0N 12°30E 263 C7
Differdange Lux. 49°31N 5°54E 170 E5
Difficult Run ➜ U.S.A. 38°55N 77°18W 143 B2
Diffun Phil. 16°36N 121°33E 232 C3
Dig India 27°28N 77°20E 242 F7
Digba Dem. Rep. of the Congo 4°25N 25°48E 268 B2
Digboi India 27°23N 95°38E 241 B5
Digby Canada 44°38N 65°50W 299 D6
Digges Is. Canada 62°40N 77°50W 295 E16
Diggi India 26°22N 75°26E 242 F6
Dighinala Bangla. 23°15N 92°5E 241 D4
Dighton U.S.A. 38°29N 100°28W 308 F3
Digity Mud Volcanoes Trin. & Tob. 10°12N 61°25W 323 t
Diglur India 18°34N 77°33E 244 E3
Digna Mali 14°48N 8°10W 262 C3
Digne-les-Bains France 44°5N 6°12E 175 D10

Digoin France 46°29N 4°1E 173 F11
Digor Turkey 40°22N 43°25E 213 B10
Digos Phil. 6°45N 125°20E 233 H5
Digranes Iceland 66°4N 14°44W 155 A12
Digras India 20°6N 77°45E 244 D3
Digul → Indonesia 7°7S 138°42E 231 F9
Digya △ Ghana 7°15N 0°5E 263 D5
Dihang = Brahmaputra → Asia 23°40N 90°35E 241 D3
Diinsoor Somali Rep. 2°24N 42°59E 267 D5
Dijlah, Nahr → Asia 31°0N 47°25E 246 D5
Dijon France 47°20N 5°3E 173 E12
Dikhil Djibouti 11°8N 42°20E 257 E5
Dikili Turkey 39°4N 26°53E 205 B8
Dikirnis Egypt 31°6N 31°35E 256 H7
Dikkil = Dikhil Djibouti 11°8N 42°20E 257 E5
Dikodougou Ivory C. 9°4N 5°45W 262 D3
Diksmuide Belgium 51°2N 2°52E 170 C2
Dikson Russia 73°40N 80°5E 214 B9
Dikti Oros Greece 35°8N 25°30E 207 E6
Dikwa Nigeria 12°4N 13°30E 263 C7
Dila Ethiopia 6°21N 38°22E 257 F4
Dilasag Phil. 16°25N 122°11E 232 C4
Dilbeek Belgium 50°51N 4°17E 116 A1
Dilek Yarimadisi △ Turkey 37°40N 27°10E 205 D9
Dili E. Timor 8°39S 125°34E 231 F7
Diligent Strait India 12°11N 92°57E 245 H11
Dilijan Armenia 40°46N 44°57E 191 K7
Dilinata Greece 38°13N 20°31E 207 C2
Dilizhan = Dilijan Armenia 40°46N 44°57E 191 K7
Dilj Croatia 45°29N 18°1E 182 E3
Dillenburg Germany 50°43N 8°17E 178 E4
Dilley U.S.A. 28°40N 99°10W 314 G5
Dilli = Delhi India 28°39N 77°13E 120 B2
Dilli Mali 15°1N 7°40W 262 C3
Dillia → Niger 14°9N 12°50E 259 F2
Dilling Sudan 12°3N 29°35E 257 E2
Dillingen Bayern, Germany 48°36N 10°30E 179 G6
Dillingen Saarland, Germany 49°22N 6°43E 179 F2
Dillingham U.S.A. 59°3N 158°28W 303 G8
Dillon Sask., Canada 55°56N 108°35W 297 B7
Dillon Mont., U.S.A. 45°13N 112°38W 304 D7
Dillon S.C., U.S.A. 34°25N 79°22W 315 D15
Dillon → Canada 55°56N 108°56W 297 B7
Dillsboro U.S.A. 39°1N 85°4W 311 E11
Dillsburg U.S.A. 40°7N 77°2W 312 F7
Dilolo Dem. Rep. of the Congo 10°28S 22°18E 265 E4
Dilos Greece 37°23N 25°15E 205 D7
Dilove Ukraine 47°56N 24°11E 183 C9
Dimapur India 25°54N 93°45E 241 C4
Dimas Mexico 23°43N 106°47W 318 C3
Dimasalang Phil. 12°12N 123°51E 232 E4
Dimashq Syria 33°30N 36°18E 250 E7
Dimashq □ Syria 33°30N 36°30E 250 E7
Dimbaza S. Africa 32°50S 27°14E 271 D4
Dimbelenge Dem. Rep. of the Congo 5°33S 23°7E 265 D4
Dimbokro Ivory C. 6°45N 4°46W 262 D4
Dimboola Australia 36°28S 142°7E 282 D5
Dîmbovița = Dâmbovița → Romania 44°12N 26°26E 183 F11
Dimbulah Australia 17°8S 145°4E 280 B4
Dimitrovgrad Bulgaria 42°5N 25°35E 203 D9
Dimitrovgrad Russia 54°14N 49°39E 190 C9
Dimitrovgrad Serbia 43°2N 22°48E 202 C6
Dimitrovo = Pernik Bulgaria 42°35N 23°2E 202 D7
Dimitsana Greece 37°36N 22°3E 204 D4
Dimmitt U.S.A. 34°33N 102°19W 314 D3
Dimo Sudan 5°19N 29°10E 257 F2
Dimona Israel 31°2N 35°1E 251 G6
Dimonika ⌓ Congo 4°13S 12°21E 264 C2
Dimovo Bulgaria 43°43N 22°50E 202 C6
Dinagat Phil. 10°10N 125°40E 233 F5
Dinagat □ Phil. 10°0N 125°35E 233 F5
Dinaig Phil. 7°11N 124°10E 233 H5
Dinajpur Bangla. 25°33N 88°43E 241 C2
Dinalupihan Phil. 14°52N 120°28E 232 D3
Dinan France 48°28N 2°2W 172 D4
Dīnān Āb Iran 32°4N 56°49E 247 C8
Dinant Belgium 50°16N 4°55E 170 D4
Dinapur India 25°38N 85°5E 243 G11
Dinar Turkey 38°5N 30°10E 205 C12
Dīnār, Kūh-e Iran 30°42N 51°46E 247 D6
Dinara Planina Croatia 44°0N 16°30E 199 D13
Dinard France 48°38N 2°6W 172 D4
Dinaric Alps = Dinara Planina Croatia 44°0N 16°30E 199 D13
Dinas Phil. 7°38N 123°20E 233 H4
Dindanko Mali 14°8N 9°30W 262 C3
Dinde Angola 14°17S 13°42E 265 E2
Dinder, Nahr ed → Sudan 14°6N 33°40E 257 E3
Dinder △ Sudan 12°30N 35°10E 257 E4
Dindi → India 16°24N 78°15E 245 F4
Dindigul India 10°25N 78°0E 245 J4
Dindori India 22°57N 81°5E 243 H9
Ding Xian = Dingzhou China 38°30N 114°59E 226 E8
Dinga Dem. Rep. of the Congo 5°17S 16°42E 265 D3
Dinga Pakistan 25°26N 67°10E 242 G2
Dingalan Phil. 15°18N 121°25E 232 D3
Dingalan Bay Phil. 15°18N 121°25E 232 D3
Ding'an China 19°42N 110°19E 236 C8
Dingbian China 37°35N 107°32E 226 F4
Dingelstädt Germany 51°18N 10°19E 178 D6
Dingle Kerry, Ireland 52°9N 10°17W 166 D1
Dingle Sweden 58°32N 11°35E 163 F5
Dingle B. Ireland 52°3N 10°20W 166 D1
Dingli Malta 35°52N 14°23E 206 F7
Dingmans Ferry U.S.A. 41°13N 74°55W 313 E10
Dingnan China 24°45N 115°0E 229 E10
Dingo Australia 23°38S 149°19E 280 C4
Dingolfing Germany 48°37N 12°30E 179 G8
Dingras Phil. 18°6N 120°42E 232 B3
Dingtao China 35°5N 115°35E 226 G8
Dinguiraye Guinea 11°18N 10°49W 262 C2
Dingwall U.K. 57°36N 4°26W 167 D4
Dingxi China 35°30N 104°33E 226 G3
Dingxiang China 38°30N 112°58E 226 E7
Dingyuan China 32°32N 117°41E 229 A11
Dingzhou China 38°30N 114°59E 226 E8
Dinh, Mui Vietnam 11°22N 109°1E 237 G7
Dinh Lap Vietnam 21°33N 107°6E 228 G6
Dinhata India 26°8N 89°27E 241 B2
Dinin → Ireland 52°43N 7°18W 166 D4
Dinira △ Venezuela 9°57N 70°6W 328 B3
Dinokwe Botswana 23°29S 26°37E 270 B4
Dinorwic Canada 49°41N 92°30W 297 D10
Dinosaur ⌓ Alta., Canada 50°47N 111°30W 296 C6
Dinosaur ⌓ Colo., U.S.A. 40°30N 108°45W 304 F9
Dinuba U.S.A. 36°32N 119°23W 306 J7
Diö Sweden 56°37N 14°15E 163 H8
Dioïla Mali 12°23N 6°50W 262 C3
Dioka Mali 14°57N 10°4W 262 C2
Diomede U.S.A. 65°47N 169°0W 303 D5
Diona Chad 17°51N 22°36E 259 E4
Diongoï Mali 14°38N 8°34W 262 C3
Dionisades Greece 35°20N 26°10E 207 E7
Dionysos, Theatro Athens, Greece 112 c2
Diósgyör Hungary 48°7N 20°43E 182 B5
Diosig Romania 47°18N 22°2E 182 C7
Diougani Mali 14°19N 2°44W 262 C4
Diouloulou Senegal 13°5N 16°38W 262 C1
Dioura Mali 14°59N 5°12W 262 C3
Diourbel Senegal 14°39N 16°12W 262 C1
Diourbel □ Senegal 14°45N 16°15W 262 C1
Dipaculao Phil. 15°51N 121°32E 232 D3
Dipalpur Pakistan 30°40N 73°39E 242 D5
Diphu India 25°50N 93°26E 241 C4
Dipkarpaz = Rizokarpaso Cyprus 35°36N 34°23E 207 E10
Diplo Pakistan 24°35N 69°35E 242 G3
Dipolog Phil. 8°36N 123°20E 233 G4
Dipperu △ Australia 21°56S 148°42E 280 C4
Dipton N.Z. 45°54S 168°22E 285 F3
Dir Pakistan 35°8N 71°59E 240 B3
Diré Mali 16°20N 3°25W 262 B4
Dire Dawa Ethiopia 9°35N 41°45E 257 F5
Dirfis Oros Greece 38°40N 23°54E 204 C5
Diriamba Nic. 11°51N 86°19W 320 D2
Dirico Angola 17°50S 20°42E 265 F4
Dirk Hartog I. Australia 25°50S 113°5E 279 E1
Dirkou Niger 19°1N 12°53E 259 E2
Dirnismaning Germany 48°13N 11°38E 131 A2
Dirranbandi Australia 28°33S 148°17E 281 D4
Dirs Si. Arabia 18°32N 42°5E 248 C3
Dirschau = Tczew Poland 54°8N 18°50E 184 D5
Disa India 24°18N 72°10E 242 G5
Disa Sudan 12°5N 34°15E 257 E3
Disappointment, C. U.S.A. 46°18N 124°5W 304 C1
Disappointment, L. Australia 23°20S 122°40E 278 D3
Disaster B. Australia 37°15S 149°58E 283 D8
Discovery B. Vic., Australia 38°10S 140°40E 282 E4
Discovery B. China 22°18N 114°1E 219 G11
Discovery Bay △ Australia 38°9S 141°16E 282 E4
Discovery Seamount Atl. Oc. 42°0S 0°10E 152 L12
Disentis Muster Switz. 46°42N 8°50E 179 J4
Dishna Egypt 26°9N 32°32E 256 B3
Disina Nigeria 11°35N 9°50E 263 C6
Disko = Qeqertarsuaq Greenland 69°45N 53°30W 154 D5
Disko Bugt Greenland 69°10N 52°0W 154 D5
Disna = Dzisna → Belarus 55°34N 28°12E 188 E5
Disney-M.G.M. Studios U.S.A. 28°21N 81°33W 133 B1
Disney Reef Tonga 19°17S 174°7W 287 P13
Disney Studios U.S.A. 34°9N 118°19W 126 B3
Dispur India 26°3N 91°52E 241 B3
Diss U.K. 52°23N 1°7E 169 E9
Disteghil Sar Pakistan 36°20N 75°12E 243 A6
District Heights U.S.A. 38°51N 76°53W 143 B4
District of Columbia □ U.S.A. 38°55N 77°0W 309 F15
Distrito Federal □ Brazil 15°45S 47°45W 333 E2
Distrito Federal □ Mexico 19°15N 99°10W 319 D5
Distrito Federal □ Venezuela 10°30N 66°55W 328 A4
Disûq Egypt 31°8N 30°35E 256 H7
Ditan Park Beijing, China 114 a2
Diu India 20°45N 70°58E 242 J4
Diuata Mts. Phil. 9°0N 125°50E 233 G5
Dīvāndarreh Iran 35°55N 47°2E 213 E12
Divarata Greece 38°20N 20°33E 207 C2
Divenié Congo 2°43S 12°1E 264 C2
Dives → France 49°18N 0°7W 172 C6
Dives-sur-Mer France 49°18N 0°8W 172 C6
Divi Pt. India 15°59N 81°9E 245 G5
Divichi = Däväçi Azerbaijan 41°15N 48°57E 191 K9
Divide U.S.A. 45°45N 112°45W 304 D7
Dividing Ra. Australia 27°45S 116°0E 279 E2
Divinópolis Brazil 20°10S 44°54W 333 F3
Divisões, Serra dos Brazil 17°0S 51°0W 333 E1
Divjake Albania 41°0N 19°32E 202 F3
Divnoye Russia 45°55N 43°21E 191 H6
Divo Ivory C. 5°48N 5°15W 262 D3
Divriği Turkey 39°22N 38°7E 213 C8
Dīwāl Kol Afghan. 34°23N 67°52E 242 B2
Dix → U.S.A. 37°49N 84°43W 311 G12
Dixie Mt. U.S.A. 39°55N 120°16W 306 F6
Dixie Union U.S.A. 31°20N 82°28W 316 D7
Dixon Calif., U.S.A. 38°27N 121°49W 306 G5
Dixon Ill., U.S.A. 41°50N 89°29W 310 C7
Dixon Mo., U.S.A. 37°59N 92°6W 310 G4
Dixon Entrance U.S.A. 54°30N 132°0W 303 J14
Dixville Canada 45°4N 71°46W 313 A13
Diyadin Turkey 39°33N 43°40E 213 C10
Diyālá □ Iraq 33°45N 44°50E 246 C5
Diyālá → Iraq 33°13N 44°30E 213 F11
Diyarb Nigm Egypt 30°45N 31°26E 251 H2
Diyarbakır Turkey 37°55N 40°18E 213 D9
Diyarbakır □ Turkey 38°0N 40°10E 213 D9
Diyodar India 24°8N 71°50E 242 G4
Dizangué Cameroon 3°46N 9°59E 264 B1
Dja ⌓ Cameroon 3°10N 12°58E 264 B2
Djadié → Gabon 0°46N 12°58E 264 B2
Djado Niger 21°4N 12°14E 259 D2
Djado, Plateau du Niger 21°29N 12°21E 259 D2
Djakarta = Jakarta Indonesia 6°9S 106°52E 122 A2
Djalma Dutra = Miguel Calmon Brazil 11°26S 40°36W 332 D3
Djalma Dutra = Poções Brazil 14°31S 40°21W 333 D3
Djamâa Algeria 33°32N 5°59E 261 B6
Djamba Angola 16°45S 13°58E 265 F2
Djambala Congo 2°32S 14°30E 264 C2
Djanet Algeria 24°35N 9°32E 261 D6
Djaul I. Papua N. G. 2°58S 150°57E 286 B6
Djawa = Jawa Indonesia 7°0S 110°0E 235 D4
Djebel Tazzeka △ Morocco 34°6N 4°11W 260 B4
Djebiniana Tunisia 35°1N 11°0E 258 A2
Djédaa Chad 13°31N 18°34E 259 F3
Djelfa Algeria 34°40N 3°15E 261 B5
Djelfa □ Algeria 34°20N 3°40E 261 B5
Djema C.A.R. 6°3N 25°15E 264 A5
Djember Chad 10°25N 17°50E 259 F3
Djembo Dem. Rep. of the Congo 9°54S 22°18E 265 D4
Djendel Algeria 36°15N 2°25E 261 A5
Djenné Mali 14°0N 4°30W 262 C4
Djenoun, Garet el Algeria 25°4N 5°31E 261 C6
Djerba Tunisia 33°48N 10°54E 258 B2
Djerba, Î. de Tunisia 33°50N 10°48E 258 B2
Djeréme → Cameroon 5°20N 13°24E 264 A2
Djerid, Chott Tunisia 33°42N 8°30E 258 B1
Djermaya Chad 12°24N 15°3E 259 F3
Djibo Burkina Faso 14°9N 1°35W 263 C4
Djibouti Djibouti 11°30N 43°5E 257 E5
Djibouti ■ Africa 12°0N 43°0E 257 E5
Djohong Cameroon 6°47N 14°20E 264 A2
Djolu Dem. Rep. of the Congo 0°35N 22°5E 264 B4
Djouab → Gabon 1°13N 13°12E 264 B2
Djougou Benin 9°40N 1°45E 263 D5
Djoum Cameroon 2°41N 12°35E 264 B2
Djouna Chad 10°27N 20°4E 259 F4
Djugu Dem. Rep. of the Congo 1°55N 30°35E 268 B3
Djukbinj △ Australia 12°11S 131°2E 278 B5
Djúpavík Iceland 65°57N 21°34W 155 B5
Djúpivogur Iceland 64°39N 14°17W 155 C12
Djupvasshytta Norway 62°2N 7°16E 164 B4
Djurås Sweden 60°34N 15°8E 162 D9
Djurdjura △ Algeria 35°20N 4°15E 261 A5
Djurö △ Sweden 58°52N 13°28E 163 F7
Djursholm Sweden 59°24N 18°5E 139 A2
Djursland Denmark 56°27N 10°45E 163 H4
Dmitriya Lapteva, Proliv Russia 73°0N 140°0E 215 B15
Dmitriyev Lgovskiy Russia 52°10N 35°0E 189 F8
Dmitriyevsk = Makiyivka Ukraine 48°0N 38°0E 189 H9
Dmitriyevskoye = Talas Kyrgyzstan 42°30N 72°13E 217 D8
Dmitrov Russia 56°25N 37°32E 188 D9
Dmitrovsk-Orlovskiy Russia 52°29N 35°10E 189 F8
Dnepr = Dnipro → Ukraine 46°30N 32°18E 189 J7
Dneprodzerzhinsk = Dniprodzerzhynsk Ukraine 48°32N 34°37E 189 H8
Dneprodzerzhinskoye Vdkhr. = Dniprodzerzhynske Vdskh. Ukraine 48°49N 34°8E 189 H8
Dnepropetrovsk = Dnipropetrovsk Ukraine 48°30N 35°0E 189 H8
Dneprorudnoye = Dniprorudne Ukraine 47°21N 34°58E 189 J8
Dnestr = Dnister → Europe 46°18N 30°17E 177 E16
Dnestrovski = Belgorod Russia 50°35N 36°35E 189 G9
Dnieper = Dnipro → Ukraine 46°30N 32°18E 189 J7
Dniester = Dnister → Europe 46°18N 30°17E 177 E16
Dnipro → Ukraine 46°30N 32°18E 189 J7
Dniprodzerzhynsk Ukraine 48°32N 34°37E 189 H8
Dniprodzerzhynske Vdskh. Ukraine 48°49N 34°8E 189 H8
Dnipropetrovsk Ukraine 48°30N 35°0E 189 H8
Dnipropetrovsk □ Ukraine 48°15N 34°50E 189 H8
Dniprorudne Ukraine 47°21N 34°58E 189 J8
Dnister → Europe 46°18N 30°17E 177 E16
Dnistrovskyy Lyman Ukraine 46°15N 30°17E 189 J6
Dno Russia 57°50N 29°58E 188 D5
Dnyapro = Dnipro → Ukraine 46°30N 32°18E 189 J7
Do Gonbadān = Gachsārān Iran 30°15N 50°45E 247 D6
Doabi Afghan. 36°1N 69°32E 240 A3
Doaktown Canada 46°33N 66°8W 299 C6
Doan Hung Vietnam 21°30N 105°10E 228 G5
Doany Madag. 14°21S 49°30E 272 A2
Doba Chad 8°40N 16°50E 259 G3
Dobandi Pakistan 31°13N 66°50E 242 D2
Dobbiaco Italy 46°44N 12°14E 199 B9
Dobbyn Australia 19°44S 140°2E 280 B3
Dobczyce Poland 49°52N 20°5E 185 J7
Dobele Latvia 56°37N 23°16E 184 B10
Dobele □ Latvia 56°35N 23°5E 184 B10
Döbeln Germany 51°6N 13°7E 178 D9
Doberai, Jazirah Indonesia 1°25S 133°0E 231 E8
Döberitz Germany 52°32N 13°3E 115 A1
Dobiegniew Poland 52°59N 15°45E 185 F2
Doblas Argentina 37°5S 64°0W 334 D3
Döbling Austria 48°14N 16°20E 142 A2
Dobo Dem. Rep. of the Congo 2°20N 22°11E 264 B4
Dobo Indonesia 5°45S 134°15E 231 F8
Doboj Bos.-H. 44°46N 18°4E 182 F3
Dobong S. Korea 37°39N 127°2E 137 B2
Dobongsan S. Korea 37°40N 127°0E 137 A2
Dobra Wielkopolskie, Poland 51°55N 18°37E 185 G5
Dobra Zachodnio-Pomorskie, Poland 53°34N 15°20E 184 E2
Dobra Dâmbovita, Romania 44°52N 25°40E 183 F10
Dobra Hunedoara, Romania 45°54N 22°36E 182 E7
Dobre Miasto Poland 53°58N 20°26E 184 E7
Dobreşti Romania 46°51N 22°18E 182 D7
Dobrich Bulgaria 43°37N 27°49E 203 C11
Dobrinishta Bulgaria 41°49N 23°34E 202 E7
Dobříš Czech Rep. 49°46N 14°10E 180 B7
Dobrodzień Poland 50°45N 18°25E 185 H5
Dobromyl Ukraine 49°34N 22°46E 185 J9
Dobron Ukraine 48°25N 22°23E 182 B7
Dobropole Ukraine 48°25N 37°2E 189 H9
Dobrovolsk Russia 54°46N 22°31E 184 D9
Dobruja Europe 44°30N 28°15E 183 F13
Dobrush Belarus 52°25N 31°22E 177 B16
Dobrzany Poland 53°22N 15°25E 184 E2
Dobrzyń nad Wisłą Poland 52°39N 19°22E 185 F6
Doc, Mui Vietnam 17°58N 106°30E 236 D6
Doc Can I. Phil. 5°55N 119°56E 233 J2
Doce → Brazil 19°37S 39°49W 333 E4
Docker River = Kaltukatjara Australia 24°52S 129°5E 279 D4
Docklands U.K. 51°30N 0°1W 125 A3
Docksta Sweden 63°3N 18°18E 162 A12
Doctor Arroyo Mexico 23°40N 100°11W 318 C4
Doctor Pedro P. Peña Paraguay 22°27S 62°21W 331 E5
Doctor Phillips U.S.A. 28°26N 81°29W 133 B2
Doctors Inlet U.S.A. 30°6N 81°47W 316 E8
Doda India 33°10N 75°34E 243 C6
Doda, L. Canada 49°25N 75°13W 298 C4
Doda Betta India 11°24N 76°44E 245 J3
Dodballapur India 13°18N 77°32E 245 H3
Dodder → Ireland 53°20N 6°13W 120 B1
Dodecanese Greece 36°35N 27°0E 205 E8
Dodekanisa = Dodecanese Greece 36°35N 27°0E 205 E8
Dodekanisa □ Greece 36°35N 27°0E 205 E8
Dodge City U.S.A. 37°45N 100°1W 308 G3
Dodge L. Canada 59°50N 105°36W 297 B7
Dodger Stadium U.S.A. 34°4N 118°14W 126 B3
Dodgeville U.S.A. 42°58N 90°8W 310 B6
Dodo Cameroon 7°30N 12°3E 263 D7
Dodo Sudan 5°10N 29°57E 257 F2
Dodola Ethiopia 6°59N 39°11E 257 F4
Dodoma Tanzania 6°8S 35°45E 268 D4
Dodoma □ Tanzania 6°0S 36°0E 268 D4
Dodoni Greece 39°40N 20°46E 204 B2
Dodori ⌓ Kenya 1°55S 41°7E 268 C5
Dodsland Canada 51°50N 108°45W 297 C7
Dodson U.S.A. 48°24N 108°15W 304 B9
Dodurga Turkey 39°49N 29°57E 205 B11
Doerun U.S.A. 31°19N 83°55W 316 D6
Doesburg Neths. 52°1N 6°9E 170 B6
Doetinchem Neths. 51°59N 6°18E 170 C6
Dog Creek Canada 51°35N 122°14W 296 C4
Dog I. U.S.A. 29°48N 84°36W 316 F5
Dog L. Man., Canada 51°2N 98°31W 297 C9
Dog L. Ont., Canada 48°48N 89°30W 298 C2
Doğankent Turkey 36°52N 35°18E 250 B6
Doğanşehir Turkey 38°5N 37°53E 212 C7
Dogliani Italy 44°32N 7°56E 198 D4
Dōgo Japan 36°15N 133°16E 222 A5
Dōgo-San Japan 35°2N 133°13E 222 B5
Dogondoutchi Niger 13°38N 4°2E 263 C5
Dogran Pakistan 31°48N 73°35E 242 D5
Dogs, Isle of U.K. 51°29N 0°1W 125 B3
Doğubayazıt Turkey 39°31N 44°5E 213 C11
Doguéraoua Niger 14°0N 5°31E 263 C6
Dogura Papua N. G. 10°6S 150°5E 286 F6
Doha = Ad Dawḩah Qatar 25°15N 51°35E 247 E6
Dohazari Bangla. 22°10N 92°5E 241 D4
Dohinog = Manukan Phil. 8°32N 123°12E 233 G4
Dohrighat India 26°16N 83°31E 243 F10
Doi Indonesia 2°14N 127°49E 231 D7
Doi Inthanon △ Thailand 18°33N 98°34E 236 C2
Doi Khuntan △ Thailand 18°33N 99°14E 236 C2
Doi Luang Thailand 18°30N 101°0E 236 C3
Doi Luang △ Thailand 19°22N 99°35E 236 C2
Doi Saket Thailand 18°52N 99°9E 236 C2
Doi Suthep △ Thailand 18°49N 98°53E 236 C2
Dois Irmãos, Sa. Brazil 9°0S 42°30W 332 C3
Dojransko Jezero Macedonia 41°13N 22°44E 202 E6
Doka Sudan 13°31N 35°46E 257 E4
Dokka Norway 60°49N 10°7E 164 D7
Dokka → Norway 60°49N 10°7E 164 D7
Dokkum Neths. 53°20N 5°59E 170 A5
Dokos Greece 37°20N 23°20E 204 D5
Dokri Pakistan 27°25N 68°7E 242 F3
Dokshukino = Nartkala Russia 43°33N 43°51E 191 J6
Dokuchayevsk Ukraine 47°44N 37°40E 189 J9
Dol-de-Bretagne France 48°34N 1°47W 172 D5
Dolac Kosovo 42°36N 20°36E 202 D4
Dolak, Pulau Indonesia 8°0S 138°30E 231 F9
Dolban = Liman Russia 45°45N 47°12E 191 H8
Dolbeau-Mistassini Canada 48°53N 72°14W 299 C5
Dole France 47°7N 5°31E 173 E12
Doleib, Wadi → Sudan 12°10N 33°15E 257 E3
Dolenji Logatec Slovenia 45°56N 14°15E 199 C11
Dolgellau U.K. 52°45N 3°53W 168 E4
Dolgelley = Dolgellau U.K. 52°45N 3°53W 168 E4
Dolgoe Ozero Russia 60°0N 30°15E 137 A1
Dolhasca Romania 47°26N 26°36E 183 C11
Doliana Greece 39°54N 20°32E 204 B2
Dolianova Italy 39°22N 9°10E 200 C2
Dolinsk Russia 47°21N 142°48E 215 E15
Dolinskaya = Dolynska Ukraine 48°6N 32°46E 189 H7
Dolj □ Romania 44°10N 23°30E 183 F8
Doll Museum Delhi, India 120 b3
Dollard Neths. 53°20N 7°10E 170 A7
Dollis Hill U.K. 51°33N 0°13W 125 A2
Dollymount Ireland 53°22N 6°11W 120 A2
Dolna Banya Bulgaria 42°18N 23°44E 202 D7
Dolni Czech Rep. 50°3N 14°33E 135 B3
Dolni Chabry Czech Rep. 50°8N 14°26E 135 B2
Dolni Chiflik Bulgaria 42°59N 27°43E 203 D11
Dolni Dŭbnik Bulgaria 43°24N 24°26E 203 C8
Dolni Počernice Czech Rep. 50°5N 14°34E 135 B3
Dolnośląskie □ Poland 51°10N 16°30E 185 G3
Dolný Kubín Slovak Rep. 49°12N 19°18E 181 B12
Dolo Ethiopia 4°11N 42°3E 257 G5
Dolo Italy 45°25N 12°5E 199 C9
Dolomites = Dolomiti Italy 46°23N 11°51E 199 B8
Dolomiti Italy 46°23N 11°51E 199 B8
Dolomiti Bellunesi △ Italy 46°10N 12°5E 199 B9
Dolores Argentina 36°20S 57°40W 334 D4
Dolores Phil. 12°2N 125°29E 232 E5
Dolores Uruguay 33°34S 58°15W 334 C4
Dolores Colo., U.S.A. 37°28N 108°30W 305 H9
Dolores → U.S.A. 38°49N 109°17W 304 G9
Dolovo Serbia 44°55N 20°52E 182 F5
Dolphin, C. Falk. Is. 51°10S 59°0W 153 f
Dolphin and Union Str. Canada 69°5N 114°45W 294 D9
Dolphin Head Jamaica 18°22N 78°10W 320 a
Dolphin I. Jamaica 17°48N 77°10W 320 a
Dolphins Barn Ireland 53°20N 6°17W 120 B2
Dolsk Poland 51°59N 17°3E 185 G4
Dolton U.S.A. 41°38N 87°36W 311 C9
Dolungmukh India 27°30N 94°18E 241 B5
Dolyna Ukraine 48°58N 24°1E 183 B9
Dolynska Ukraine 48°6N 32°46E 189 H7
Dolynske Ukraine 47°32N 29°55E 183 C14
Dolzhanskaya Russia 46°37N 37°48E 189 J9
Dom Joaquim Brazil 18°57S 43°16W 333 E3
Dom Pedrito Brazil 31°0S 54°40W 335 C5
Dom Pedro Brazil 4°59S 44°27W 332 B3
Dom Pedro II, Parque Brazil 23°33S 46°36W 137 B2
Doma = Gombe Nigeria 10°19N 11°2E 263 C7
Doma Nigeria 8°25N 8°18E 263 D6
Doma ⌓ Zimbabwe 16°28S 30°12E 269 F3
Domadare Somali Rep. 1°52N 41°15E 267 D5
Domain, The Sydney, Australia 139 b2
Domaniç Turkey 39°48N 29°36E 205 B11
Domar, E. → Chad 18°11N 18°4E 259 E3
Domariaganj → India 26°17N 83°44E 243 F10
Domasi Malawi 15°15S 35°22E 269 F4
Domažlice Czech Rep. 49°28N 12°58E 180 B5
Dombarovka = Dombarovskiy Russia 50°46N 59°32E 214 D6
Dombarovskiy Russia 50°46N 59°32E 214 D6
Dombås Norway 62°4N 9°8E 164 B6
Dombasle-sur-Meurthe France 48°38N 6°21E 173 D13
Dombe Grande Angola 12°57S 13°6E 265 E2
Dombes France 45°58N 5°0E 175 C9
Dombóvár Hungary 46°21N 18°9E 182 D3
Dombrád Hungary 48°13N 21°54E 182 B6
Dombrova = Dąbrowa Górnicza Poland 50°15N 19°10E 185 H6
Dombrowitsa = Dubrovytsya Ukraine 51°31N 26°35E 177 C14
Dome Argus Antarctica 80°50S 76°30E 151 E12
Dome C. Antarctica 75°12S 123°37E 151 D17
Dome Fuji Antarctica 77°20S 39°45E 151 D5
Dome of the Rock Jerusalem 123 b3
Domel I. = Letsôk-aw Kyun Burma 11°30N 98°25E 237 G2
Domérat France 46°21N 2°32E 173 F9
Domett N.Z. 42°53S 173°12E 285 C8
Domeyko Chile 29°0S 71°0W 334 B1
Domeyko, Cordillera Chile 24°30S 69°0W 334 A2
Domfront France 48°37N 0°40W 172 D6
Dominador Chile 24°21S 69°20W 334 A2
Dominica ■ W. Indies 15°20N 61°20W 321 C7
Dominica Passage W. Indies 15°10N 61°20W 321 C7
Dominican Rep. ■ W. Indies 19°0N 70°30W 321 C5
Dominion Centre Toronto, Canada 141 b2
Domiongo Dem. Rep. of the Congo 4°37S 21°15E 265 C4
Dömitz Germany 53°8N 11°15E 178 B7
Domme France 44°48N 1°12E 174 D5
Domneşti Romania 45°12N 24°50E 183 E9
Domo Ethiopia 7°50N 47°10E 267 C6
Domodóssola Italy 46°7N 8°17E 198 B5
Domogled-Valea Cernei △ Romania 44°52N 22°27E 182 F7
Domokos Greece 39°10N 22°18E 204 B4
Domoni Comoros Is. 12°15S 44°32E 272 a
Dompaire France 48°14N 6°14E 173 D13
Dompierre-sur-Besbre France 46°31N 3°41E 173 F10
Dompim Ghana 5°10N 2°5W 262 D4
Dompu Indonesia 8°32S 118°28E 235 D5
Domrémy-la-Pucelle France 48°26N 5°40E 173 D12
Domvena Greece 38°15N 22°59E 204 C4
Domville, Mt. Australia 28°1S 151°15E 281 D5
Domžale Slovenia 46°9N 14°35E 199 B11
Don → India 16°20N 76°15E 245 F3
Don → Russia 47°4N 39°18E 189 J10
Don → Aberds., U.K. 57°11N 2°5W 167 D6
Don → S. Yorks., U.K. 53°41N 0°52W 168 D7
Don, C. Australia 11°18S 131°46E 278 B5
Don Benito Spain 38°53N 5°51W 195 G5
Don Figuerero Mts. Jamaica 18°5N 77°36W 320 a
Don Mills Canada 43°44N 79°21W 141 A2
Don Muang Int. ✈ (BKK) Thailand 13°53N 100°36E 113 A2
Don Sak Thailand 9°18N 99°41E 237 b
Dona Ana = Nhamaabué Mozam. 17°25S 35°5E 269 F4
Doña Mencía Spain 37°33N 4°21W 195 H6
Donaghadee U.K. 54°39N 5°33W 166 B6
Donaghmede Ireland 53°23N 6°9W 120 A3
Donaghmore Ireland 52°52N 7°36W 166 D4
Donald Australia 36°23S 143°0E 282 D5
Donaldsonville U.S.A. 30°6N 90°59W 314 F9
Donalsonville U.S.A. 31°3N 84°53W 316 D5
Doñana △ Spain 36°59N 6°23W 195 J4
Donau = Dunărea → Europe 45°20N 29°40E 183 E14
Donau → Austria 48°10N 17°0E 181 C10
Donau Auen △ Austria 48°8N 16°44E 181 C9
Donau-Oder Kanal Austria 48°12N 16°32E 142 A3
Donaueschingen Germany 47°56N 8°29E 179 H4
Donaufeld Austria 48°15N 16°24E 142 A2
Donaupark Austria 48°14N 16°24E 142 A2
Donaustadt Austria 48°13N 16°29E 142 A2
Donauwörth Germany 48°43N 10°47E 179 G6
Doncaster U.K. 53°32N 1°6W 168 D6
Dondo Angola 9°45S 14°25E 265 D2
Dondo Dem. Rep. of the Congo 4°11N 21°39E 264 B4
Dondo Mozam. 19°33S 34°46E 269 F3
Dondo, Teluk Indonesia 0°50N 120°30E 231 D6
Dondra Head Sri Lanka 5°55N 80°40E 245 M5
Donduşeni Moldova 48°14N 27°36E 183 B12
Donegal Ireland 54°39N 8°5W 166 B3
Donegal □ Ireland 54°53N 8°0W 166 B4
Donegal B. Ireland 54°31N 8°49W 166 B3
Donets → Russia 47°33N 40°55E 191 G5
Donets Basin Ukraine 49°0N 38°0E 158 F13
Donetsk Ukraine 48°0N 37°45E 189 J9
Donetsk □ Ukraine 47°30N 37°50E 189 J9
Dong Ba Thin Vietnam 12°8N 109°13E 237 F7
Dong Dang Vietnam 21°54N 106°42E 228 G6
Dong Giam Vietnam 19°25N 105°31E 236 C5
Dong Ha Vietnam 16°55N 107°8E 236 D6
Dong Hene Laos 16°40N 105°18E 236 D5
Dong Hoi Vietnam 17°29N 106°36E 236 D6
Dong Jiang → China 23°6N 114°0E 229 F10
Dong Khe Vietnam 22°26N 106°27E 236 A6
Dong Ujimqin Qi China 45°32N 116°55E 226 B9
Dong Van Vietnam 23°16N 105°22E 236 A5
Dong Xoai Vietnam 11°32N 106°55E 237 G6
Donga Nigeria 7°45N 10°2E 263 D7
Donga → Nigeria 8°20N 9°58E 263 D7
Dong'an China 26°23N 111°12E 229 D8
Dongan Hills U.S.A. 40°35N 74°5W 132 C1
Dongara Australia 29°14S 114°57E 279 E1
Dongargarh India 21°10N 80°40E 244 D5
Dongbei China 45°0N 125°0E 220 A5
Dongcheng Beijing, China 114 b2
Dongchuan China 26°8N 103°1E 228 D4
Dongdaemung S. Korea 37°34N 127°2E 137 B2
Dongducheon S. Korea 37°54N 127°3E 224 D3
Donges France 47°18N 2°4W 172 E4
Dongfang China 18°50N 108°33E 236 C7
Dongfeng China 42°40N 125°34E 224 A2
Donggala Indonesia 0°30S 119°40E 231 E5
Donggan China 23°22N 105°9E 228 F5
Donggang China 39°52N 124°10E 224 C2
Donggou China 31°17N 121°33E 138 B2
Dongguan China 22°58N 113°44E 229 F9
Dongguang China 37°50N 116°30E 226 F9
Donghae S. Korea 37°29N 129°7E 224 D4
Donghai Dao China 21°0N 110°15E 229 G8
Dongjak S. Korea 37°30N 126°56E 137 B1
Dongjiao China 23°5N 113°12E 121 B2
Dongjingcheng China 44°5N 129°10E 227 B15
Dongkou China 27°6N 110°35E 229 D8
Donglan China 24°30N 107°21E 228 E6
Dongliu China 30°13N 116°55E 229 B11
Dongmen China 22°20N 107°48E 228 F6
Dongnae S. Korea 35°12N 129°5E 224 E4
Dongning China 44°2N 131°5E 227 B16
Dongnyi China 28°3N 100°15E 228 C3
Dongo Angola 14°36S 15°48E 265 E3
Dongobe Dem. Rep. of the Congo 4°35N 23°13E 264 B4
Dongola Sudan 19°9N 30°22E 256 D3
Dongou Congo 2°0N 18°5E 264 B3
Dongping China 35°55N 116°20E 226 G9
Dongri India 18°53N 72°57E 130 B2
Dongsha Dao S. China Sea 20°45N 116°43E 229 G11
Dongshan China 23°43N 117°30E 229 F11
Dongshanhu Park China 23°7N 113°17E 121 B2
Dongsheng China 39°50N 110°0E 226 E6
Dongsi Mosque Beijing, China 114 b2
Dongtai China 32°51N 120°21E 227 H11
Dongting Hu China 29°18N 112°45E 229 C9
Dongtou China 27°51N 121°10E 229 D13
Dongwe → Zambia 13°59S 23°53E 265 E4
Dongxiang China 28°11N 116°34E 229 C11
Dongxing China 21°34N 108°0E 228 G7
Dongyang China 29°13N 120°15E 229 C13
Dongzhi China 30°9N 117°0E 229 B11
Dongzhimen China 39°55N 116°24E 114 B2
Donington, C. Australia 34°45S 136°0E 282 C2
Doniphan U.S.A. 36°37N 90°50W 308 G8
Donja Stubica Croatia 45°59N 15°59E 199 C12
Donji Dušnik Serbia 43°12N 22°5E 202 C6
Donji Miholjac Croatia 45°45N 18°10E 182 E3
Donji Milanovac Serbia 44°28N 22°6E 202 B6
Donji Vakuf Bos.-H. 44°8N 17°24E 182 F2
Dønna Nordland, Norway 66°6N 12°30E 160 C15
Donna Tex., U.S.A. 26°9N 98°4W 314 H5
Donnacona Canada 46°41N 71°41W 299 C5
Donnelly's Crossing N.Z. 35°42S 173°38E 284 B2
Donnybrook W. Austral., Australia 33°34S 115°48E 279 F2
Donnybrook Dublin, Ireland 53°19N 6°14W 120 B2
Donnybrook KwaZulu Natal, S. Africa 29°59S 29°48E 271 C4
Donora U.S.A. 40°11N 79°52W 312 F5
Donostia = Donostia-San Sebastián Spain 43°17N 1°58W 196 B3
Donostia-San Sebastián Spain 43°17N 1°58W 196 B3
Donousa Greece 37°8N 25°48E 205 D7
Donovan U.S.A. 40°53N 87°37W 311 D9
Donque Angola 15°28S 14°6E 265 F2
Donskoy Russia 53°55N 38°15E 188 F10
Donsol Phil. 12°54N 123°36E 232 E4
Donwood Canada 44°19N 78°16W 312 B6
Donzère France 44°28N 4°43E 175 D8
Donzy France 47°20N 3°6E 173 E10
Dookie Australia 36°20S 145°41E 283 D6
Doomadgee Australia 17°56S 138°49E 280 B2
Doomadgee ◎ Australia 17°56S 138°49E 280 B2
Doon → U.K. 55°27N 4°39W 167 F4
Doon Doon ◎ Australia 16°18S 128°14E 278 C4
Doornfontein S. Africa 26°11S 28°3E 123 B2
Doornik = Tournai Belgium 50°35N 3°25E 170 D3
Dora, L. Australia 22°0S 123°0E 278 D3
Dora Báltea → Italy 45°11N 8°3E 198 C5
Dora Ripária → Italy 45°5N 7°44E 198 C4
Doran L. Canada 61°13N 108°6W 297 A7
Doraville U.S.A. 33°54N 84°17W 316 B5
Dorchester Dorset, U.K. 50°42N 2°27W 169 G5
Dorchester Mass., U.S.A. 42°17N 71°4W 116 B2
Dorchester, C. Canada 65°27N 77°27W 295 D16
Dorchester B. U.S.A. 42°18N 71°1W 116 B2
Dorchester Heights Nat. Historical Site ⌓ U.S.A. 42°20N 71°2W 116 B2
Dordabis Namibia 22°52S 17°38E 270 B2
Dordogne □ France 45°5N 0°40E 174 C4
Dordogne → France 45°2N 0°36W 174 C3
Dordrecht Neths. 51°48N 4°39E 170 C4
Dordrecht Eastern Cape, S. Africa 31°20S 27°3E 270 D4
Dore → France 45°50N 3°35E 174 C7
Dore, Mts. France 45°32N 2°50E 174 C6
Doré L. Canada 54°46N 107°17W 297 C7
Dorée → St. Lucia 13°46N 61°3W 323 m
Dores da Boa Esperança = Boa Esperança Brazil 3°21N 61°23W 329 C5
Dores do Indaiá Brazil 19°27S 45°36W 333 E2
Dorfen Germany 48°15N 12°8E 179 G8
Dorgali Italy 40°17N 9°35E 200 B2
Dori Burkina Faso 14°3N 0°2W 263 C4
Doring → S. Africa 31°54S 18°39E 270 D2
Doringbos S. Africa 31°59S 19°16E 270 D2
Dorking U.K. 51°14N 0°19W 169 F7
Dormaa-Ahenkro Ghana 7°15N 2°52W 262 D4
Dormans France 49°4N 3°38E 173 C10
Dormo, Ras Eritrea 13°14N 42°35E 257 E5
Dornach Germany 48°9N 11°41E 131 B3
Dornakal India 17°27N 80°10E 244 F5
Dornbirn Austria 47°25N 9°45E 180 D2
Dornes France 46°48N 3°18E 173 F10
Dorneşti Romania 47°52N 26°1E 183 C11
Dornie U.K. 57°17N 5°31W 167 D3
Dornoch Ont., Canada 44°18N 80°51W 312 B4
Dornoch Highl., U.K. 57°53N 4°2W 167 D4
Dornoch Firth U.K. 57°51N 4°4W 167 D4
Dornogovĭ □ Mongolia 44°0N 110°0E 226 C6
Doro Mali 16°9N 0°51W 263 B4
Doro, Kavo Greece 38°9N 24°38E 204 C6
Dorog Hungary 47°42N 18°45E 182 C3
Dorogobuzh Russia 54°50N 33°18E 188 E7
Dorohoi Romania 47°56N 26°23E 183 C11
Döröö Nuur Mongolia 48°0N 93°0E 217 C12
Dorpat = Tartu Estonia 58°20N 26°44E 188 C4
Dorr Iran 33°17N 50°38E 247 C6
Dorre I. Australia 25°13S 113°12E 279 E1
Dorrigo Australia 30°20S 152°44E 283 A10
Dorrigo △ Australia 30°22S 152°47E 283 A10
Dorris U.S.A. 41°58N 121°55W 304 F3
Dorset Ont., Canada 45°14N 78°54W 312 A6
Dorset Ohio, U.S.A. 41°40N 80°40W 312 E4
Dorset Vt., U.S.A. 43°15N 73°5W 313 C11
Dorset □ U.K. 50°45N 2°26W 169 G5
Dorsten Germany 51°40N 6°58E 178 D2
Dortmund Germany 51°30N 7°28E 178 D3
Dortmund-Ems-Kanal → Germany 51°50N 7°26E 178 D3
Dörtyol Turkey 36°50N 36°13E 250 B7
Doruk Turkey 36°53N 35°45E 250 B6
Dorum Germany 53°41N 8°34E 178 B4
Doruma Dem. Rep. of the Congo 4°42N 27°33E 268 B2
Dorūneh Iran 35°10N 57°18E 247 C8
Dorval Int., Montréal ✈ (YUL) Canada 45°28N 73°44W 130 B1
Dos Bahías, C. Argentina 44°58S 65°32W 336 B3
Dos d'Âne Réunion 20°58S 55°23E 272 f
Dos Hermanas Spain 37°16N 5°55W 195 H5
Dos Moninos → Brazil 23°40S 46°33W 137 C2
Dos Palos U.S.A. 36°59N 120°37W 306 J6
Döşemealtı Turkey 37°4N 30°36E 205 D12
Dosso Niger 13°0N 3°13E 263 C5
Dosso □ Niger 13°30N 3°30E 263 C5
Dosso ⌓ Niger 12°36N 2°36E 263 C5
Dostyq Kazakhstan 45°15N 82°29E 217 C10
Dot Lake U.S.A. 63°40N 144°4W 303 E11
Dothan U.S.A. 31°13N 85°24W 316 D4
Doty U.S.A. 46°38N 123°17W 306 D3
Douai France 50°21N 3°4E 173 B10
Douako Guinea 9°45N 10°8W 262 D2
Douala Cameroon 4°0N 9°45E 263 E6
Douala-Édéa ⌓ Cameroon 3°20N 9°41E 264 B1
Douamoungo, C. Mayotte 12°38S 45°8E 272 b
Douaouir Mali 20°45N 3°0W 260 D4
Douarnenez France 48°6N 4°21W 172 D2
Doubabougou Mali 14°13N 7°59W 262 C3
Double Cone N.Z. 45°4S 168°49E 285 F3
Double Island Pt. Australia 25°56S 153°11E 281 D5
Double Mountain Fork → U.S.A. 33°16N 100°0W 314 E4
Doubrava → Czech Rep. 50°2N 15°20E 180 A8
Doubs □ France 47°10N 6°20E 173 E13
Doubs → France 46°53N 5°1E 173 F12
Doubtful Sd. N.Z. 45°20S 166°49E 285 F1
Doubtless B. N.Z. 34°55S 173°26E 284 A2
Doudeville France 49°43N 0°47E 172 C7
Doué-la-Fontaine France 47°11N 0°16W 172 E6
Douentza Mali 14°58N 2°48W 262 C4
Douentza ⌓ Mali 15°40N 2°25W 262 B4
Dougga Tunisia 36°25N 9°13E 258 A1
Doughboy B. N.Z. 47°2S 167°40E 285 H2
Douglas Ont., Canada 45°31N 76°56W 312 A8
Douglas I. of Man 54°10N 4°28W 168 C3
Douglas Northern Cape, S. Africa 29°4S 23°46E 270 C3
Douglas Alaska, U.S.A. 58°17N 134°24W 303 G14
Douglas Ariz., U.S.A. 31°21N 109°33W 305 L9
Douglas Ga., U.S.A. 31°31N 82°51W 316 D7
Douglas Mich., U.S.A. 42°39N 86°14W 311 B10
Douglas Wyo., U.S.A. 42°45N 105°24W 304 E11
Douglas Apsley △ Australia 41°45S 148°11E 281 G4
Douglas B. Dominica 15°36N 61°29W 323 k
Douglas C. U.S.A. 58°51N 153°15W 303 G9
Douglas Chan. Canada 53°40N 129°20W 296 C3
Douglas Park U.S.A. 41°51N 87°42W 119 B2
Douglas Pt. Canada 44°19N 81°37W 312 B3
Douglasville U.S.A. 33°45N 84°45W 316 B5
Douirat Morocco 33°2N 4°11W 260 B4
Doukaton, Akra Greece 38°34N 20°33E 207 B2
Doukoula Cameroon 10°10N 15°0E 259 F2

Doulevant-le-Château France 48°23N 4°55E 173 D11
Doullens France 50°10N 2°20E 173 B9
Doumé Cameroon 4°15N 13°25E 264 B2
Doumen China 22°10N 113°18E 229 F9
Douna Mali 13°13N 6°0W 262 C3
Dounreay U.K. 58°35N 3°44W 167 C5
Dourada, Serra Brazil 13°10S 48°45W 333 D2
Dourados Brazil 22°9S 54°50W 335 A5
Dourados → Brazil 21°58S 54°18W 335 A5
Dourados, Serra dos Brazil 23°30S 53°30W 335 A5
Dourbali Chad 11°49N 15°52E 259 F3
Dourdan France 48°30N 2°1E 173 D9
Douro → Europe 41°8N 8°40W 194 D2
Douvaine France 46°19N 6°16E 173 F13
Douville Guadeloupe 16°15N 61°22W 322 e
Douvres-la-Délivrande France 49°17N 0°23W 172 C6
Douz Tunisia 33°25N 9°0E 258 B1
Douze → France 43°54N 0°30W 174 E3
Dove → U.K. 52°51N 1°36W 168 E6
Dove Creek U.S.A. 37°46N 108°54W 305 H9
Dover Tas., Australia 43°18S 147°2E 281 G4
Dover Kent, U.K. 51°7N 1°19E 169 F9
Dover Del., U.S.A. 39°10N 75°32W 309 F16
Dover Ky., U.S.A. 38°43N 83°52W 311 F13
Dover N.H., U.S.A. 43°12N 70°56W 313 C14
Dover N.J., U.S.A. 40°53N 74°34W 313 F10
Dover Ohio, U.S.A. 40°32N 81°29W 312 F3
Dover, Pt. Australia 32°32S 125°32E 279 F4
Dover, Str. of Europe 51°0N 1°30E 169 G9
Dover-Foxcroft U.S.A. 45°11N 69°13W 309 C19
Dover Heights Australia 33°52S 151°16E 139 B2
Dover Plains U.S.A. 41°43N 73°35W 313 E11
Dovey = Dyfi → U.K. 52°32N 4°3W 169 E3
Dovhe Ukraine 48°22N 23°17E 183 B8
Dovlen = Devin Bulgaria 41°44N 24°24E 203 E8
Dovre Norway 61°58N 9°15E 164 C6
Dovrefjell Norway 62°15N 9°33E 164 B6
Dovrefjell △ Norway 62°20N 9°25E 164 B6
Dovrefjell-Sunndalsfjella △ Norway 62°23N 9°11E 164 B6
Dow Rūd Iran 33°28N 49°4E 247 C6
Dowa Malawi 13°38S 33°58E 269 E3
Dowagiac U.S.A. 41°59N 86°6W 311 C10
Dowerin Australia 31°12S 117°2E 279 F2
Dowgha'i Iran 36°54N 58°32E 247 B8
Dowlat Yār Afghan. 34°30N 65°45E 240 B2
Dowlatābād Farāh, Afghan. 32°47N 62°40E 240 B1
Dowlatābād Fāryāb, Afghan. 36°26N 64°55E 240 A2
Dowlatābād Kermān, Iran 28°20N 56°40E 247 D8
Dowlatābād Khorāsān, Iran 35°16N 59°29E 247 C8
Dowlatābād Tehrān, Iran 35°38N 51°27E 141 B2
Dowling Park U.S.A. 30°15N 83°15W 316 E6
Down □ U.K. 54°23N 6°2W 166 B5
Down, L. U.S.A. 28°30N 81°31W 133 A1
Downers Grove U.S.A. 41°48N 88°1W 311 C8
Downey Calif., U.S.A. 33°56N 118°9W 126 C4
Downey Idaho, U.S.A. 42°26N 112°7W 304 E7
Downham Market U.K. 52°37N 0°23E 169 E8
Downieville U.S.A. 39°34N 120°50W 306 F6
Downing U.S.A. 40°29N 92°22W 310 D4
Downpatrick U.K. 54°20N 5°43W 166 B6
Downpatrick Hd. Ireland 54°20N 9°21W 166 B2
Downsview Canada 43°43N 79°30W 141 A1
Downsville U.S.A. 42°5N 75°0W 313 D10
Downton, Mt. Canada 52°42N 124°52W 296 C4
Dowsārī Iran 28°25N 57°59E 247 D8
Dowshī Afghan. 35°35N 68°43E 240 B3
Doxato Greece 41°9N 24°16E 203 E8
Doyle U.S.A. 40°2N 120°6W 306 E6
Doylestown U.S.A. 40°21N 75°10W 313 F9
Dozen Japan 36°5N 133°5E 222 A5
Dozois, Rés. Canada 47°30N 77°5W 298 C4
Dra Khel Pakistan 27°58N 66°45E 242 F2
Drâa, C. Morocco 28°47N 11°0W 260 C2
Drâa, Hamada du Algeria 28°0N 7°0W 260 C3
Drâa, Oued → Morocco 28°40N 11°10W 260 C2
Drac → France 45°12N 5°42E 175 C9
Drac, Coves del Spain 39°31N 3°19E 206 B4
Dračevo Macedonia 41°56N 21°31E 202 E5
Drachten Neths. 53°7N 6°5E 170 A6
Drăgănești Moldova 47°43N 28°15E 183 C13
Drăgănești-Olt Romania 44°9N 24°32E 183 F9
Drăgănești-Vlașca Romania 44°5N 25°33E 183 F10
Dragaš Kosovo 42°5N 20°41E 202 D4
Drăgășani Romania 44°39N 24°17E 183 F9
Dragichyn Belarus 52°15N 25°8E 177 B13
Dragocvet Serbia 43°58N 21°15E 202 C5
Dragon's Mouths Venezuela 11°0N 61°50W 323 t
Dragør Denmark 55°35N 12°38E 118 B3
Dragovishtitsa Bulgaria 42°22N 22°39E 202 D6
Draguignan France 43°32N 6°27E 175 E10
Drahove Ukraine 48°14N 23°33E 183 B8
Drain U.S.A. 43°40N 123°19W 304 E2
Drake U.S.A. 47°55N 100°23W 308 B3
Drake Passage S. Ocean 58°0S 68°0W 151 B17
Drakensberg S. Africa 31°0S 28°0E 271 D4
Drama Greece 41°9N 24°10E 203 E8
Drama □ Greece 41°20N 24°0E 203 E8
Dramburg = Drawsko Pomorskie Poland 53°35N 15°50E 184 E2
Drammen Norway 59°42N 10°12E 164 E7
Drancy France 48°55N 2°26E 134 A3
Dranesville U.S.A. 39°0N 77°20W 143 A1
Drangajökull Iceland 66°9N 22°15W 155 A4
Drangedal Norway 59°6N 9°3E 164 E6
Drangsnes Iceland 65°41N 21°27W 155 B5
Dranov, Ostrov Romania 44°55N 29°30E 183 F14
Drapetsona Greece 37°56N 23°37E 112 B1
Dras India 34°25N 75°48E 243 B6
Drastis, Akra Greece 39°48N 19°40E 206 B9
Drau = Drava → Croatia 45°33N 18°55E 182 E3
Drava → Croatia 45°33N 18°55E 182 E3
Dravograd Slovenia 46°36N 15°5E 199 B12
Drawa → Poland 52°52N 15°59E 185 F2
Drawieński △ Poland 53°6N 15°58E 185 E2
Drawno Poland 53°13N 15°46E 185 E2
Drawsko Pomorskie Poland 53°35N 15°50E 184 E2
Drayton Canada 43°46N 80°40W 312 C4
Drayton Plains U.S.A. 42°41N 83°23W 311 B13
Drayton Valley Canada 53°12N 114°58W 296 C6
Dreieich Germany 50°1N 8°41E 179 E4
Dreikikir Papua N. G. 3°35S 142°46E 286 B2
Dreilinden Germany 52°24N 13°10E 115 B2
Dren Kosovo 43°8N 20°46E 202 C4
Drenthe □ Neths. 52°52N 6°40E 170 B6
Drepano, Akra Greece 35°28N 24°14E 207 E5
Drepanum, C. Cyprus 34°54N 32°19E 207 E8
Dresden Ont., Canada 42°35N 82°11W 312 D2
Dresden Sachsen, Germany 51°3N 13°44E 178 D9
Dresden N.Y., U.S.A. 42°41N 76°57W 312 D8
Dreux France 48°44N 1°23E 172 D8
Drevsjø Norway 61°53N 12°1E 164 C9
Drewnica Poland 52°18N 21°6E 142 B2
Drexel U.S.A. 39°45N 84°18W 311 E12
Drezdenko Poland 52°50N 15°49E 185 F2
Driesen = Drezdenko Poland 52°50N 15°49E 185 F2
Driffield U.K. 54°0N 0°26W 168 C7
Driftwood U.S.A. 41°20N 78°8W 312 E6
Driggs U.S.A. 43°44N 111°6W 304 E8
Drigh Road Pakistan 24°52N 67°7E 123 A2
Drimnagh Ireland 53°19N 6°19W 120 B2
Drin → Albania 42°1N 19°38E 202 D3
Drin i Zi → Albania 41°37N 20°28E 202 E4
Drina → Bos.-H. 44°53N 19°21E 202 B3
Drincea → Romania 44°20N 22°55E 182 F7
Drinjača → Bos.-H. 44°15N 19°8E 182 F4
Driopida Greece 37°25N 24°26E 204 D6
Drissa = Vyerkhnyadzvinsk Belarus 55°45N 27°58E 188 E4
Driva → Norway 62°41N 9°31E 164 B6
Drivstoggo Norway 62°26N 9°47E 164 B6
Drniš Croatia 43°51N 16°10E 199 E13
Drøbak Norway 59°39N 10°39E 164 E7
Drobeta-Turnu Severin Romania 44°39N 22°41E 182 F7
Drobin Poland 52°42N 19°58E 185 F6
Drochia Moldova 48°2N 27°48E 183 B12
Drogenbos Belgium 50°47N 4°19E 116 B1
Drogheda Ireland 53°43N 6°22W 166 C5
Drogichyn = Dragichyn Belarus 52°15N 25°8E 177 B13
Drogobych = Drohobych Ukraine 49°20N 23°30E 185 J10
Drohiczyn Poland 52°24N 22°39E 185 F9
Drohobych Ukraine 49°20N 23°30E 185 J10
Droichead Atha = Drogheda Ireland 53°43N 6°22W 166 C5
Droichead na Bandan = Bandon Ireland 51°44N 8°44W 166 E3
Droichead Nua Ireland 53°11N 6°48W 166 C5
Droitwich U.K. 52°16N 2°8W 169 E5
Drôme □ France 44°38N 5°15E 175 D9
Drôme → France 44°46N 4°46E 175 D8
Dromedary, C. Australia 36°17S 150°10E 283 D9
Drömling ⌂ Germany 52°29N 11°5E 178 C7
Dromore U.K. 54°31N 7°28W 166 B4
Dromore West Ireland 54°15N 8°52W 166 B3
Dronero Italy 44°28N 7°22E 198 D4
Dronfield U.K. 53°19N 1°27W 168 D6
Dronne → France 45°2N 0°9W 174 C3
Dronning Ingrid Land Greenland 64°25N 52°5W 154 E5
Dronning Maud Land Antarctica 72°30S 12°0E 151 D3
Dronninglund Denmark 57°10N 10°19E 163 G4
Dronten Neths. 52°32N 5°43E 170 B5
Dropt → France 44°35N 0°6W 174 D3
Drosendorf Austria 48°52N 15°37E 180 C8
Drosh Pakistan 35°33N 71°48E 240 B3
Droué France 48°3N 1°6E 172 D8
Drouin Australia 38°10S 145°53E 283 E6
Druid Hills U.S.A. 33°47N 84°21W 113 B2
Drujba Uzbekistan 41°13N 61°18E 216 D6
Druk Yul = Bhutan ■ Asia 27°25N 90°30E 241 B3
Drum Tower Beijing, China 114 a3
Drumbo Canada 43°16N 80°35W 312 C4
Drumcliff Ireland 54°20N 8°29W 166 B3
Drumcondra Ireland 53°21N 6°16W 120 A2
Drumheller Canada 51°25N 112°40W 296 C6
Drummond U.S.A. 46°40N 113°9W 304 C7
Drummond I. U.S.A. 46°1N 83°39W 309 B12
Drummond Pt. Australia 34°9S 135°16E 281 E2
Drummond Ra. Australia 23°45S 147°10E 280 C4
Drummondville Canada 45°55N 72°25W 298 C5
Drummoyne Australia 33°51S 151°8E 139 B1
Drumright U.S.A. 35°59N 96°36W 314 D6
Druskeniki = Druskininkai Lithuania 54°3N 23°58E 188 E2
Druskininkai Lithuania 54°3N 23°58E 188 E2
Drut → Belarus 53°8N 30°5E 177 B16
Druya Belarus 55°45N 27°28E 188 E4
Druzhba Bulgaria 43°15N 28°1E 203 C12
Druzhina Russia 68°14N 145°18E 215 C15
Drvar Bos.-H. 44°21N 16°23E 199 D13
Drvenik Croatia 43°27N 16°3E 199 E13
Drwęca → Poland 53°0N 18°42E 185 E5
Dry Harbour Mts. Jamaica 18°19N 77°24W 320 a
Dry Tortugas U.S.A. 24°38N 82°55W 315 F13
Dryander △ Australia 20°13S 148°34E 280 b
Dryanovo Bulgaria 42°59N 25°28E 203 D9
Dryden Ont., Canada 49°47N 92°50W 297 D10
Dryden N.Y., U.S.A. 42°30N 76°18W 313 D8
Drygalski I. Antarctica 66°0S 92°0E 151 C7
Drygalski Ice Tongue Antarctica 75°24S 163°30E 151 D21
Drylaw U.K. 55°58N 3°15W 121 B2
Drysdale → Australia 13°59S 126°51E 278 B4
Drysdale I. Australia 11°41S 136°0E 280 A2
Drysdale River △ Australia 14°56S 127°2E 278 B4
Drzewica Poland 51°27N 20°29E 185 G7
Drzewiczka → Poland 51°36N 20°36E 185 G7
Dschang Cameroon 5°32N 10°3E 263 D7
Du Gué → Canada 57°21N 70°45W 298 A5
Du He China 32°48N 110°40E 229 A8
Du Quoin U.S.A. 38°1N 89°14W 310 G7
Du'an China 23°59N 108°3E 228 F7
Duanesburg U.S.A. 42°45N 74°11W 313 D10
Duaringa Australia 23°42S 149°42E 280 C4
Duarte, Pico Dom. Rep. 19°2N 70°59W 321 C5
Dubai = Dubayy U.A.E. 25°18N 55°20E 247 E7
Dubăsari Moldova 47°15N 29°10E 183 C14
Dubăsari Vdkhr. Moldova 47°30N 29°0E 183 C13
Dubawnt → Canada 64°33N 100°6W 297 A8
Dubawnt L. Canada 63°8N 101°28W 297 A8
Dubayy U.A.E. 25°18N 55°20E 247 E7
Dubbo Australia 32°11S 148°35E 283 B8
Dube → Liberia 5°16N 7°29W 262 D3
Dubeč Czech Rep. 50°3N 14°35E 135 B3
Dubele Dem. Rep. of the Congo 2°56N 29°35E 268 B2
Dübendorf Switz. 47°24N 8°37E 179 H4
Dubica Croatia 45°11N 16°48E 199 C13
Dublanc Dominica 15°31N 61°28W 323 k
Dublin Dublin, Ireland 53°21N 6°15W 120 A2
Dublin Ga., U.S.A. 32°32N 82°54W 316 C7
Dublin Ohio, U.S.A. 40°5N 83°7W 311 D13
Dublin Tex., U.S.A. 32°5N 98°21W 314 E5
Dublin □ Ireland 53°24N 6°20W 166 C5
Dublin ✕ (DUB) Ireland 53°26N 6°15W 120 A2
Dublin B. Ireland 53°19N 6°7W 120 B3
Dublin Castle Dublin, Ireland 120 c2
Dublin Harbour Ireland 53°21N 6°11W 120 A2
Dubna Russia 56°44N 37°10E 188 D9
Dubnica nad Váhom Slovak Rep. 48°58N 18°11E 181 C11
Dubno Ukraine 50°25N 25°45E 177 C13
Dubois Idaho, U.S.A. 44°10N 112°14W 304 D7
Dubois Ind., U.S.A. 38°27N 86°48W 311 F10
DuBois Pa., U.S.A. 41°7N 78°46W 312 E6
Dubossary = Dubăsari Moldova 47°15N 29°10E 183 C14
Dubossary Vdkhr. = Dubăsari Vdkhr. Moldova 47°30N 29°0E 183 C13
Dubove Ukraine 48°10N 23°53E 183 B8
Dubovka Russia 49°5N 44°50E 191 F7
Dubovskoye Russia 47°28N 42°46E 191 G6
Dubrajpur India 23°48N 87°25E 243 H12
Dubréka Guinea 9°46N 13°31W 262 D2
Dubrovitsa = Dubrovytsya Ukraine 51°31N 26°35E 177 C14
Dubrovnik Croatia 42°39N 18°6E 202 D2
Dubrovytsya Ukraine 51°31N 26°35E 177 C14
Dubulu Dem. Rep. of the Congo 4°18N 20°16E 264 B4
Dubuque U.S.A. 42°30N 90°41W 310 B6
Dubysa → Lithuania 55°5N 23°26E 184 C10
Duc de Gloucester, Îs. French Polynesia 20°38S 143°20W 289 f
Ducassous, Pte. Martinique 14°32N 60°50W 322 j
Duchang China 29°18N 116°12E 229 C11
Duchesne U.S.A. 40°10N 110°24W 304 F8
Duchess Australia 21°20S 139°50E 280 C2
Ducie I. Pac. Oc. 24°40S 124°48W 289 K15
Duck → U.S.A. 36°2N 87°52W 315 C11
Duck Cr. → Australia 22°37S 116°53E 278 D2
Duck Lake Canada 52°50N 106°16W 297 C7
Duck Mountain ⌂ Canada 51°45N 101°0W 297 C8
Duckwall, Mt. U.S.A. 37°58N 120°7W 306 H6
Ducos Martinique 14°33N 60°59W 322 j
Duda → Colombia 2°34N 74°3W 328 C3
Duddington U.K. 55°56N 3°8W 121 B3
Duderstadt Germany 51°31N 10°15E 178 D6
Dudhi India 24°15N 83°10E 243 G10
Dudhnai India 25°59N 90°47E 241 C3
Dudinka Russia 69°30N 86°13E 215 C9
Dudley W. Mids., U.K. 52°31N 2°5W 169 E5
Dudley Ga., U.S.A. 32°32N 83°5W 316 C6
Dudna → India 19°17N 76°54E 244 E3
Dudo Somali Rep. 9°20N 50°12E 267 C7
Dudo, W. → Somali Rep. 9°14N 50°40E 267 C7
Dudub Ethiopia 6°55N 46°43E 267 C6
Dudwa India 28°30N 80°41E 243 E9
Dudwa △ India 28°30N 80°40E 243 E9
Duékoué Ivory C. 6°40N 7°15W 262 D3
Duenas Phil. 11°4N 122°37E 233 F4
Dueñas Spain 41°52N 4°33W 194 D6
Duerë Brazil 11°20S 49°17W 333 D2
Duero = Douro → Europe 41°8N 8°40W 194 D2
Duff Is. Pac. Oc. 9°50S 167°10E 277 B12
Dufftown U.K. 57°27N 3°8W 167 D5
Dufourspitz Switz. 45°56N 7°52E 179 K3
Dugger U.S.A. 39°4N 87°18W 311 E9
Dugi Otok Croatia 44°0N 15°3E 199 D11
Dugiuma Somali Rep. 1°15N 42°34E 267 D5
Dugnano Italy 45°33N 9°11E 129 A2
Dugo Selo Croatia 45°51N 16°18E 199 C13
Duida-Marahuaca △ Venezuela 3°33N 65°33W 328 C4
Duisburg Germany 51°26N 6°45E 178 D2
Duitama Colombia 5°50N 73°2W 328 B3
Duivendrecht Neths. 52°20N 4°55E 112 B2
Duiwelskloof = Modjadjiskloof S. Africa 23°42S 30°10E 271 B5
Dujiangyan China 31°2N 103°38E 228 B4
Duk Fadiat Sudan 7°45N 31°25E 257 F3
Duk Faiwil Sudan 7°30N 31°29E 257 F3
Dukat Albania 40°16N 19°32E 202 F3
Dūkdamīn Iran 35°59N 57°43E 247 C8
Dukelský Průsmyk Slovak Rep. 49°25N 21°42E 181 B14
Dukhān Qatar 25°25N 50°50E 247 E6
Dukhovshchina Russia 55°15N 32°27E 188 E7
Duki Pakistan 30°14N 68°25E 240 C3
Dukla Poland 49°30N 21°35E 185 J8
Duku Bauchi, Nigeria 10°43N 10°43E 263 C7
Duku Sokoto, Nigeria 11°11N 4°55E 263 C5
Dula Dem. Rep. of the Congo 4°40N 20°21E 264 B4
Dūlāb Iran 35°39N 51°27E 141 B2
Dulag Phil. 10°57N 125°2E 233 F5
Dulawan = Datu Piang Phil. 7°2N 124°30E 233 H5
Dulce U.S.A. 36°56N 107°0W 305 H10
Dulce → Argentina 30°32S 62°33W 334 C3
Dulce, G. Costa Rica 8°40N 83°20W 320 E3
Dulcina Antigua & B. 17°35N 61°49W 322 c
Dulf Iraq 35°7N 45°51E 246 C5
Dŭlgopol Bulgaria 43°3N 27°22E 203 C11
Duliu China 39°2N 116°55E 226 E9
Dullabchara India 24°30N 92°26E 241 C4
Dulles Int. ✕ (IAD) U.S.A. 38°57N 77°27W 143 B1
Dullewala Pakistan 31°50N 71°25E 242 D4
Dullstroom S. Africa 25°27S 30°7E 271 C5
Dülmen Germany 51°49N 7°17E 178 D3
Dulovo Bulgaria 43°48N 27°9E 203 C11
Dulpetorpet Norway 60°34N 12°19E 164 D9
Dulq Maghār Syria 36°22N 38°39E 213 D8
Duluth Ga., U.S.A. 34°0N 84°9W 316 A5
Duluth Minn., U.S.A. 46°47N 92°6W 308 B7
Dulwich U.K. 51°27N 0°5W 125 B3
Dum Dum India 22°39N 88°26E 124 B2
Dum Dum Int. ✕ (CCU) India 22°38N 88°26E 124 B2
Dum Duma India 27°40N 95°40E 241 B5
Dūmā Syria 33°34N 36°24E 250 E7
Dumaguete Phil. 9°17N 123°15E 233 G4
Dumai Indonesia 1°35N 101°28E 234 B2
Dumalinao Phil. 7°49N 123°23E 233 H4
Dumanguilas Bay Phil. 7°34N 123°4E 233 H4
Dumanjug Phil. 10°4N 123°26E 233 F4
Dumaran Phil. 10°33N 119°50E 233 F2
Dumaran I. Phil. 10°33N 119°51E 233 F2
Dumarao Phil. 11°16N 122°41E 233 F4
Dumas Ark., U.S.A. 33°53N 91°29W 314 E9
Dumas Tex., U.S.A. 35°52N 101°58W 314 D4
Dumayr Syria 33°39N 36°42E 250 E7
Dumbarton U.K. 55°57N 4°33W 167 F4
Dumbéa N. Cal. 22°10S 166°27E 288 d
Ďumbier Slovak Rep. 48°56N 19°38E 181 C12
Dumbleyung Australia 33°17S 117°42E 279 F2
Dumbo Angola 14°6S 17°24E 265 E3
Dumbrăveni Romania 46°14N 24°34E 183 D9
Dumfries U.K. 55°4N 3°37W 167 F5
Dumfries & Galloway □ U.K. 55°9N 3°58W 167 F5
Dumingag Phil. 8°20N 123°20E 233 G4
Dumitrești Romania 45°33N 26°55E 183 E11
Dumka India 24°12N 87°15E 243 G12
Dumlupınar Turkey 38°53N 30°0E 205 C12
Dümmer Germany 52°31N 8°20E 178 C4
Dümmer ⌂ Germany 52°31N 8°21E 178 C4
Dumoine → Canada 46°13N 77°51W 298 C4
Dumoine, L. Canada 46°55N 77°55W 298 C4
Dumont U.S.A. 40°56N 73°59W 132 A2
Dumont d'Urville Antarctica 67°0S 110°0E 151 C10
Dumont d'Urville Sea S. Ocean 63°30S 138°0E 151 C9
Dumoulin Is. Papua N. G. 10°54S 150°46E 286 F6
Dumpu Papua N. G. 5°53S 145°44E 286 C3
Dumraon India 25°33N 84°8E 243 G11
Dumyât Egypt 31°24N 31°48E 251 G2
Dumyât, Far → Egypt 31°32N 31°51E 251 G2
Dumyât, Masabb Egypt 31°28N 31°51E 251 G2
Dún Dealgan = Dundalk Ireland 54°1N 6°24W 166 B5
Dún Garbhán = Dungarvan Ireland 52°5N 7°37W 166 D4
Dún Laoghaire Ireland 53°17N 6°8W 120 B3
Dun-le-Palestel France 46°18N 1°39E 173 F8
Dun-sur-Auron France 46°53N 2°33E 173 F9
Dun-sur-Meuse France 49°23N 5°11E 173 C12
Duna = Dunărea → Europe 45°20N 29°40E 183 E14
Duna-Drava △ Hungary 46°15N 18°50E 182 D3
Duna-völgyi-főcsatorna Hungary 46°40N 19°14E 182 D4
Dünaburg = Daugavpils Latvia 55°53N 26°32E 188 E4
Dunaföldvár Hungary 46°50N 18°57E 182 D3
Dunagiri India 30°31N 79°52E 243 D8
Dunaj = Dunărea → Europe 45°20N 29°40E 183 E14
Dunajec → Poland 50°15N 20°44E 185 H7
Dunajská Streda Slovak Rep. 48°0N 17°37E 181 C10
Dunakeszi Hungary 47°37N 19°8E 182 C4
Dunapataj Hungary 46°39N 19°4E 182 D4
Dunărea → Europe 45°20N 29°40E 183 E14
Dunaszekcső Hungary 46°6N 18°45E 182 D3
Dunaújváros Hungary 46°58N 18°57E 182 D3
Dunav = Dunărea → Europe 45°20N 29°40E 183 E14
Dunavățu de Jos Romania 44°59N 29°13E 183 F14
Dunavtsi Bulgaria 43°57N 22°53E 202 C6
Dunay Russia 42°52N 132°22E 220 C6
Dunayivtsi Ukraine 48°54N 26°50E 183 B11
Dunback N.Z. 45°23S 170°36E 285 F5
Dunbar U.K. 56°0N 2°31W 167 E6
Dunblane U.K. 56°11N 3°58W 167 E5
Duncan B.C., Canada 48°45N 123°40W 306 B3
Duncan Ariz., U.S.A. 32°43N 109°6W 305 K9
Duncan Okla., U.S.A. 34°30N 97°57W 314 D6
Duncan, L. Canada 53°29N 77°58W 298 B4
Duncan Dock Cape Town, S. Africa 118 a3
Duncan L. Canada 62°51N 113°58W 296 A6
Duncan Passage India 11°0N 92°0E 245 J11
Duncan Town Bahamas 22°15N 75°45W 320 B4
Duncannon U.S.A. 40°23N 77°2W 312 F7
Duncans Jamaica 18°27N 77°32W 320 a
Duncansby Head U.K. 58°38N 3°1W 167 C5
Duncansville U.S.A. 40°25N 78°26W 312 F6
Dund-Us Mongolia 48°1N 91°38E 217 C12
Dundaga Latvia 57°31N 22°21E 184 A9
Dundalk Ont., Canada 44°10N 80°24W 312 B4
Dundalk Louth, Ireland 54°1N 6°24W 166 B5
Dundalk Md., U.S.A. 39°15N 76°31W 309 F15
Dundalk Bay Ireland 53°55N 6°15W 166 C5
Dundas = Uummannaq Greenland 77°33N 68°52W 154 B4
Dundas Canada 43°17N 79°59W 312 C5
Dundas, L. Australia 32°35S 121°50E 279 F3
Dundas I. Canada 54°30N 130°50W 296 C2
Dundas Str. Australia 11°15S 131°35E 278 B5
Dundee KwaZulu Natal, S. Africa 28°11S 30°15E 271 C5
Dundee Dundee C., U.K. 56°28N 2°59W 167 E6
Dundee Mich., U.S.A. 41°57N 83°40W 311 C13
Dundee N.Y., U.S.A. 42°32N 76°59W 312 D8
Dundee City □ U.K. 56°30N 2°58W 167 E6
Dundgovĭ □ Mongolia 45°10N 106°0E 226 B4
Dundrum Dublin, Ireland 53°18N 6°14W 120 B2
Dundrum Down, U.K. 54°16N 5°52W 166 B6
Dundrum B. U.K. 54°13N 5°47W 166 B6
Dunearn Singapore 1°19N 103°49E 138 B2
Dunedin N.Z. 45°50S 170°33E 285 F5
Dunedin Fla., U.S.A. 28°1N 82°46W 317 G7
Dunedoo Australia 32°0S 149°25E 283 B8
Dunfanaghy Ireland 55°11N 7°58W 166 A4
Dunfermline U.K. 56°5N 3°27W 167 E5
Dungannon Ont., Canada 43°51N 81°36W 312 C3
Dungannon Tyrone, U.K. 54°31N 6°46W 166 B5
Dungarpur India 23°52N 73°45E 242 H5
Dungarvan Ireland 52°5N 7°37W 166 D4
Dungarvan Harbour Ireland 52°4N 7°35W 166 D4
Dungeness U.K. 50°54N 0°59E 169 G8
Dunglow Ireland 54°57N 8°21W 166 B3
Dungo, L. do Angola 17°15S 19°0E 265 F3
Dungog Australia 32°22S 151°46E 283 B9
Dungu Dem. Rep. of the Congo 3°40N 28°32E 268 B2
Dungun Malaysia 4°45N 103°25E 237 K4
Dungunâb Sudan 21°10N 37°9E 256 C4
Dungunâb, Khalîg Sudan 21°5N 37°12E 256 C4
Dunhua China 43°20N 128°14E 227 C15
Dunhuang China 40°8N 94°36E 218 B4
Dunk I. Australia 17°59S 146°29E 280 B4
Dunkassa Benin 10°21N 3°10E 263 C5
Dunkeld Queens., Australia 33°25S 149°29E 281 E4
Dunkeld Vic., Australia 37°40S 142°22E 282 D5
Dunkeld Perth & Kinr., U.K. 56°34N 3°35W 167 E5
Dunkerque France 51°2N 2°20E 173 A9
Dunkery Beacon U.K. 51°9N 3°36W 169 F4
Dunkirk = Dunkerque France 51°2N 2°20E 173 A9
Dunkirk U.S.A. 42°29N 79°20W 312 D5
Dunkuj Sudan 12°50N 32°49E 257 E3
Dunkwa Central, Ghana 6°0N 1°47W 262 D4
Dunkwa Central, Ghana 5°30N 1°0W 263 D4
Dúnleary = Dún Laoghaire Ireland 53°17N 6°8W 120 B3
Dunleer Ireland 53°50N 6°24W 166 C5
Dunmanus B. Ireland 51°31N 9°50W 166 E2
Dunmanway Ireland 51°43N 9°6W 166 E2
Dunmarra Australia 16°42S 133°25E 280 B1
Dunmore U.S.A. 41°25N 75°38W 313 E9
Dunmore East Ireland 52°9N 7°0W 166 D5
Dunmore Hd. Ireland 52°10N 10°35W 166 D1
Dunmore Town Bahamas 25°30N 76°39W 320 A4
Dunn U.S.A. 35°19N 78°37W 315 D15
Dunn Loring U.S.A. 38°54N 77°13W 143 B2
Dunnellon U.S.A. 29°3N 82°28W 317 F7
Dunnet Hd. U.K. 58°40N 3°21W 167 C5
Dunning Ill., U.S.A. 41°56N 87°48W 119 B2
Dunning Nebr., U.S.A. 41°50N 100°6W 308 E3
Dunn's River Falls Jamaica 18°25N 77°8W 320 a
Dunnville Canada 42°54N 79°36W 312 D5
Dunolly Australia 36°51S 143°44E 282 D5
Dunoon U.K. 55°57N 4°56W 167 F4
Dunqul Egypt 23°26N 31°37E 256 C3
Duns U.K. 55°47N 2°20W 167 F6
Dunseith U.S.A. 48°50N 100°3W 308 A3
Dunshaughlin Ireland 53°31N 6°33W 166 C5
Dunsmuir U.S.A. 41°13N 122°16W 304 F2
Dunstable U.K. 51°53N 0°32W 169 F7
Dunstan Mts. N.Z. 44°53S 169°35E 285 F4
Dunster Canada 53°8N 119°50W 296 C5
Duntroon N.Z. 44°51S 170°40E 285 F5
Dunvegan Gauteng, S. Africa 26°9S 28°8E 123 A2
Dunvegan Highl., U.K. 57°27N 6°35W 167 D2
Dunvegan L. Canada 60°8N 107°10W 297 A7
Duobiyi China 35°18N 102°7E 222 E9
Duolun China 42°12N 116°28E 226 C9
Duomo Italy 45°28N 9°11E 129 B2
Duomula China 34°8N 82°29E 217 F10
Duong Dong Vietnam 10°13N 103°58E 237 G4
Dupax Phil. 16°17N 121°5E 232 C3
Dupree U.S.A. 45°4N 101°35W 308 C3
Dupuyer U.S.A. 48°13N 112°30W 304 B7
Duqm Oman 19°39N 57°42E 249 C7
Duque de Caxias Brazil 22°46S 43°18W 135 A1
Duque de York, I. Chile 50°37S 75°25W 336 D1
Durack → Australia 15°33S 127°52E 278 C4
Durack Ra. Australia 16°50S 127°40E 278 C4
Durack River Australia 15°32S 127°39E 278 C4
Durağan Turkey 41°25N 35°3E 212 B6
Durak Turkey 39°42N 28°17E 205 B10
Ďurakovac Kosovo 42°43N 20°29E 202 D4
Durance → France 43°55N 4°45E 175 E8
Durand Ga., U.S.A. 32°55N 84°46W 316 C5
Durand Ill., U.S.A. 42°26N 89°20W 310 B7
Durand Mich., U.S.A. 42°55N 83°59W 311 B13
Durand Wis., U.S.A. 44°38N 91°58W 308 C8
Durandeau St. Lucia 13°56N 60°59W 323 m
Durango Mexico 24°3N 104°39W 318 C4
Durango Colo., U.S.A. 37°16N 107°53W 305 H10
Durango □ Mexico 24°50N 105°20W 318 C4
Durankulak Bulgaria 43°41N 28°32E 203 C12
Durant Iowa, U.S.A. 41°36N 90°54W 310 C6
Durant Miss., U.S.A. 33°4N 89°51W 315 E10
Durant Okla., U.S.A. 33°59N 96°25W 314 E6
Duratón → Spain 41°37N 4°7W 194 D6
Durazno Uruguay 33°25S 56°31W 334 C4
Durazzo = Durrës Albania 41°19N 19°28E 202 E3
Durban Aude, France 42°59N 2°49E 174 F6
Durban KwaZulu Natal, S. Africa 29°49S 31°1E 271 C5
Durbuy Belgium 50°21N 5°28E 170 D5
Dúrcal Spain 36°59N 3°34W 195 J7
Đurđevac Croatia 46°2N 17°3E 182 D2
Düren Germany 50°48N 6°29E 178 E2
Duren Sawit Indonesia 6°13S 106°54E 122 A2
Durg = Bhilainagar-Durg India 21°13N 81°26E 244 D5
Durgapur India 23°30N 87°20E 243 H12
Durham Ont., Canada 44°10N 80°49W 312 B4
Durham Darlington, U.K. 54°47N 1°34W 168 C6
Durham Calif., U.S.A. 39°39N 121°48W 306 F5
Durham N.C., U.S.A. 35°59N 78°54W 315 D15
Durham N.H., U.S.A. 43°8N 70°56W 313 C14
Durham □ U.K. 54°42N 1°45W 168 C6
Durlas = Thurles Ireland 52°41N 7°49W 166 D4
Durlești Moldova 47°1N 28°46E 183 C13
Ḑurmā Si. Arabia 24°37N 46°8E 246 E5
Durmitor Montenegro 43°10N 19°0E 202 C2
Durmitor △ Serbia 43°15N 19°5E 202 C3
Durness U.K. 58°34N 4°45W 167 C4
Durnford, Pta. W. Sahara 23°37N 16°0W 260 D1
Durrës Albania 41°19N 19°28E 202 E3
Durrow Ireland 52°51N 7°24W 166 D4
Dursey I. Ireland 51°36N 10°12W 166 E1
Dursley U.K. 51°40N 2°21W 169 F5
Dursunbey Turkey 39°35N 28°37E 205 B10
Durtal France 47°40N 0°18W 172 E6
Duru Dem. Rep. of the Congo 4°14N 28°50E 268 B2
Duru Gölü Turkey 41°20N 28°35E 203 E12
Durukhsi Ethiopia 8°31N 45°28E 267 C6
Durusu Turkey 41°17N 28°41E 203 E12
Durūz, Jabal ad Jordan 32°35N 36°40E 250 F7
D'Urville, Tanjung Indonesia 1°28S 137°54E 231 E9
D'Urville I. N.Z. 40°50S 173°55E 285 A8
Duryea U.S.A. 41°20N 75°45W 313 E9
Dusa Mareb = Dhuusamarreeb Somali Rep. 5°30N 46°15E 267 C6
Dûsh Egypt 24°35N 30°41E 256 C3
Dushak Turkmenistan 37°13N 60°1E 247 B9
Dushan China 25°48N 107°30E 228 E6
Dushanbe Tajikistan 38°33N 68°48E 217 E7
Dusheti Georgia 42°10N 44°42E 191 J7
Dushore U.S.A. 41°31N 76°24W 313 E8
Dusit Bangkok, Thailand 113 a2
Dusit Zoo Bangkok, Thailand 113 a2
Dusky Sd. N.Z. 45°47S 166°30E 285 F1
Dussejour, C. Australia 14°45S 128°13E 278 B4
Düsseldorf Germany 51°14N 6°47E 178 D2
Düsseldorf Rhein-Ruhr ✕ (DUS) Germany 51°17N 6°46E 178 D2
Dusti Tajikistan 37°20N 68°40E 217 E7
Duszniki-Zdrój Poland 50°24N 16°24E 185 H3
Dutch East Indies = Indonesia ■ Asia 5°0S 115°0E 235 C4
Dutch Guiana = Suriname ■ S. Amer. 4°0N 56°0W 329 C6
Dutch Harbor U.S.A. 53°53N 166°32W 303 K6
Dutlwe Botswana 23°58S 23°46E 270 B3
Dutsan Wai Nigeria 10°50N 8°10E 263 C6
Dutse Nigeria 11°46N 9°20E 263 C6
Dutton Canada 42°39N 81°30W 312 D3
Dutton → Australia 20°44S 143°10E 280 C3
Dutywa S. Africa 32°8S 28°18E 271 D4
Duved Sweden 63°23N 12°55E 162 A6
Düvertepe Turkey 39°14N 28°27E 205 B10
Dūvida = Roosevelt → Brazil 7°35S 60°20W 331 B5
Duwayhin, Khawr U.A.E. 24°20N 51°25E 247 E6
Duyfken Pt. Australia 12°33S 141°38E 280 A3
Duyun China 26°18N 107°29E 228 D6
Düzağac Turkey 38°48N 30°10E 205 C12
Düzce Turkey 40°50N 31°10E 212 B4
Düzce □ Turkey 40°50N 31°10E 212 B4
Duzdab = Zāhedān Iran 29°30N 60°50E 247 D9
Duzer Guadeloupe 16°20N 61°44W 322 e
Dve Mogili Bulgaria 43°35N 25°55E 203 C9
Dvigatelstroy = Kaspiysk Russia 42°52N 47°40E 191 J8
Dvina, Severnaya → Russia 64°32N 40°30E 186 B7
Dvinsk = Daugavpils Latvia 55°53N 26°32E 188 E4
Dvinskaya Guba Russia 65°0N 39°0E 186 B6
Dvor Croatia 45°4N 16°22E 199 C13
Dvůr Králové nad Labem Czech Rep. 50°27N 15°50E 180 A8
Dwarka India 22°18N 69°8E 242 H3
Dwellingup Australia 32°43S 116°4E 279 F2
Dwight Ont., Canada 45°20N 79°1W 312 A5
Dwight Ill., U.S.A. 41°5N 88°26W 311 C8
Dworp Belgium 50°44N 4°18E 116 B1
Dyakove Ukraine 48°1N 23°0E 182 B7
Dyakovo Russia 55°40N 37°39E 129 B3
Dyatkovo Russia 53°40N 34°27E 188 F8
Dyatlovo = Dzyatlava Belarus 53°28N 25°28E 177 B13
Dyce U.K. 57°13N 2°12W 167 D6
Dyer, C. Canada 66°37N 61°16W 295 D19
Dyer Bay Canada 45°10N 81°20W 312 A3
Dyer Plateau Antarctica 70°45S 65°30W 151 D17
Dyersburg U.S.A. 36°3N 89°23W 315 C10
Dyersville U.S.A. 42°29N 91°8W 310 B5
Dyfi → U.K. 52°32N 4°3W 169 E3
Dyhernfurth = Brzeg Dolny Poland 51°16N 16°41E 185 G3
Dyje → Czech Rep. 48°37N 16°56E 181 C9
Dyke Ackland B. Papua N. G. 9°0S 148°45E 286 E5
Dyker Beach Park U.S.A. 40°36N 74°1W 132 C1
Dymer Ukraine 50°47N 30°18E 177 C16
Dynów Poland 49°50N 22°11E 185 J9
Dyranut Norway 60°22N 7°31E 164 D4
Dyrhólaey Iceland 63°24N 19°8W 155 D7
Dyrnes Norway 63°25N 7°52E 164 A4
Dysart Queens., Australia 22°32S 148°23E 280 C4
Dysart Iowa, U.S.A. 42°10N 92°18W 310 B4
Dyushambe = Dushanbe Tajikistan 38°33N 68°48E 217 E7
Dyviziya Ukraine 45°55N 29°59E 183 E14
Dzamin Üüd = Borhoyn Tal Mongolia 43°50N 111°58E 226 C6
Dzaoudzi Mayotte 12°47S 45°16E 272 b
Dzaoudzi ✕ (DZA) Mayotte 12°48S 45°18E 272 b
Dzaudzhikau = Vladikavkaz Russia 43°0N 44°35E 191 J7
Dzavhan □ Mongolia 48°0N 96°0E 217 C13
Dzavhan Gol Mongolia 48°54N 93°23E 218 B4
Dzerzhinsk Russia 56°14N 43°30E 190 B6
Dzerzhinskiy Moskva, Russia 55°38N 37°51E 129 C5
Dzerzhinskiy Moskva, Russia 55°47N 37°37E 129 B3
Dzerzhinskiy Park Russia 55°50N 37°37E 129 B3
Dzhalal-Abad = Jalal-Abad Kyrgyzstan 40°56N 73°0E 217 D8
Dzhalal-Ogly = Stepanavan Armenia 41°1N 44°23E 191 K7
Dzhalinda Russia 53°26N 124°0E 215 D13
Dzhambeyty = Zhympity Kazakhstan 50°16N 52°35E 216 B4
Dzhambul = Taraz Kazakhstan 42°54N 71°22E 217 D8
Dzhankoy Ukraine 45°40N 34°20E 189 K8
Dzhanybek = Zhänibek Kazakhstan 49°25N 46°50E 190 F8
Dzhargalantu = Hovd □ Mongolia 48°2N 91°37E 217 C12
Dzharkent = Zharkent Kazakhstan 44°10N 80°0E 217 D10
Dzharylhach, Ostriv Ukraine 46°2N 32°55E 189 J7
Dzhezkazgan = Zhezqazghan Kazakhstan 47°44N 67°40E 217 C7
Dzhibkhalantu = Uliastay Mongolia 47°56N 97°28E 218 B4
Dzhizak = Jizzax Uzbekistan 40°6N 67°50E 217 D7
Dzhugdzur, Khrebet Russia 57°30N 138°0E 215 D14
Dzhulynk Ukraine 48°26N 29°45E 183 B14
Dzhumgoltau, Khrebet Kyrgyzstan 42°15N 74°30E 217 D8
Dzhungarskiye Vorota = Dzungarian Gate Asia 45°10N 82°0E 217 C10
Dzhuryn Ukraine 48°41N 28°18E 183 B13
Dzhvari = Jvari Georgia 42°42N 42°4E 191 J6
Działdowo Poland 53°15N 20°15E 185 E7
Działoszyce Poland 50°22N 20°20E 185 H7
Działoszyn Poland 51°6N 18°50E 185 G5
Dzibilchaltún Mexico 21°10N 89°35W 319 C7
Dzierzgoń Poland 53°58N 19°20E 184 E6
Dzierżoniów Poland 50°45N 16°39E 185 H3
Dzilam de Bravo Mexico 21°24N 88°53W 319 C7
Dzioua Algeria 33°14N 5°14E 261 B6
Dzisna Belarus 55°34N 28°12E 188 E5
Dzisna → Belarus 55°34N 28°12E 188 E5
Dziwnów Poland 54°2N 14°45E 184 D1
Dzūkija △ Lithuania 54°10N 24°30E 161 J21
Dzungarian Basin = Junggar Pendi China 44°30N 86°0E 217 D11
Dzungarian Gate Asia 45°10N 82°0E 217 C10
Dzur Mongolia 49°39N 95°46E 217 C13
Dzüünharaa Mongolia 48°52N 106°28E 218 B5
Dzüünmod Mongolia 47°45N 106°58E 218 B5
Dzyarzhynsk Belarus 53°40N 27°1E 177 B14
Dzyatlava Belarus 53°28N 25°28E 177 B13

E

E.C. Manning ⌂ Canada 49°5N 120°45W 296 D4
E.T. Joshua ✕ (SVD) St. Vincent 13°8N 61°13W 323 n
E.U.R. = Esposizione Universale di Roma Italy 41°49N 12°28E 136 C1
Eabamet L. Canada 51°30N 87°46W 298 B2
Eabametoong Canada 51°30N 88°0W 298 B2
Éadan Doire = Edenderry Ireland 53°21N 7°4W 166 C4
Eads U.S.A. 38°29N 102°47W 304 G12
Eagar U.S.A. 34°6N 109°17W 305 J9
Eagle Alaska, U.S.A. 64°47N 141°12W 303 D12
Eagle Colo., U.S.A. 39°39N 106°50W 304 G10
Eagle → Canada 53°36N 57°26W 299 B8
Eagle, Mt. U.S. Virgin Is. 17°46N 64°49W 321 b
Eagle Beach Aruba 12°32N 70°3W 322 f
Eagle Butte U.S.A. 45°0N 101°10W 308 C3
Eagle Cr. → U.S.A. 38°36N 85°4W 311 F11
Eagle Grove U.S.A. 42°40N 93°54W 310 B3
Eagle L. Ont., Canada 49°42N 93°13W 297 D10
Eagle L. Calif., U.S.A. 40°39N 120°45W 304 F3
Eagle L. Maine, U.S.A. 46°20N 69°22W 309 B19
Eagle Lake Ont., Canada 45°8N 78°29W 312 A6
Eagle Lake Maine, U.S.A. 47°3N 68°36W 309 B19
Eagle Lake Tex., U.S.A. 29°35N 96°20W 314 G6
Eagle Mountain U.S.A. 33°49N 115°27W 307 M11
Eagle Nest U.S.A. 36°33N 105°16W 305 H11
Eagle Pass U.S.A. 28°43N 100°30W 314 G4
Eagle Pk. U.S.A. 38°10N 119°25W 306 G7
Eagle Pt. Australia 16°11S 124°23E 278 C3
Eagle River Mich., U.S.A. 47°25N 88°18W 308 B9
Eagle River Wis., U.S.A. 45°55N 89°15W 308 C9
Eagle Rock U.S.A. 34°8N 118°12W 126 B3
Eaglehawk Australia 36°44S 144°15E 282 D6
Eagles Mere U.S.A. 41°25N 76°33W 313 E8
Eagleville U.S.A. 40°28N 93°59W 310 D3
Ealing □ U.K. 51°31N 0°20W 125 A2
Ear Falls Canada 50°38N 93°13W 297 C10
Earle U.S.A. 35°16N 90°28W 315 D9
Earlimart U.S.A. 35°53N 119°16W 307 K7
Earl's Court London, U.K. 125 c1
Earlsfield U.K. 51°26N 0°10W 125 B2
Earlville Ill., U.S.A. 41°35N 88°55W 311 C8
Earlville N.Y., U.S.A. 42°44N 75°32W 313 D9
Earlwood Australia 33°55S 151°8E 139 B1
Early Branch U.S.A. 32°45N 80°55W 316 C9
Earn → U.K. 56°21N 3°18W 167 E5
Earn, L. U.K. 56°23N 4°13W 167 E4
Earnslaw, Mt. N.Z. 44°32S 168°27E 285 E3
Earth U.S.A. 34°14N 102°24W 314 D3
Eas Vanuatu 16°20S 168°15E 287 F6
Easley U.S.A. 34°50N 82°36W 315 D13
East Anglia U.K. 52°30N 1°0E 168 E9
East Angus Canada 45°30N 71°40W 299 C5
East Antarctica Antarctica 80°0S 90°0E 151 D7
East Arlington Mass., U.S.A. 42°24N 71°8W 116 A2
East Arlington Va., U.S.A. 38°51N 77°4W 143 B3
East Aurora U.S.A. 42°46N 78°37W 312 D6
East Ayrshire □ U.K. 55°26N 4°11W 167 F4
East Bedfont U.K. 51°26N 0°28W 125 B1
East Beskids = Vychodné Beskydy Europe 49°20N 22°0E 181 B15
East Boston U.S.A. 42°22N 71°1W 116 A2
East Brady U.S.A. 40°59N 79°37W 312 F5
East Branch Clarion River L. U.S.A. 41°35N 78°35W 312 E6
East C. = Dezhneva, Mys Russia 66°5N 169°40W 215 C19
East C. N.Z. 37°42S 178°35E 284 D7
East C. Papua N. G. 10°13S 150°53E 286 F6
East Caroline Basin Pac. Oc. 4°0N 146°45E 288 G6
East Chicago U.S.A. 41°38N 87°27W 311 C9
East China Sea Asia 30°0N 126°0E 219 D7

East Coulee Canada 51°23N 112°27W 296 C6
East Dereham = Dereham
U.K. 52°41N 0°57E 169 E8
East Don → Canada 43°48N 79°25W 141 A2
East Don Parkland
Canada 43°47N 79°22W 141 A2
East Dublin U.S.A. 32°32N 82°52W 316 C7
East Dubuque U.S.A. 42°30N 90°39W 310 B6
East Dunbartonshire □
U.K. 55°57N 4°13W 167 F4
East Elmhurst U.S.A. 40°45N 73°52W 132 B2
East End Pt. Bahamas 25°3N 77°16W 153 b
East Falkland Falk. Is. 51°30S 58°30W 153 f
East Finchley U.K. 51°35N 0°10W 125 A2
East Flatbush U.S.A. 40°39N 73°55W 132 C2
East Fork White →
U.S.A. 38°33N 87°14W 311 F9
East Grand Forks U.S.A. 47°56N 97°1W 308 B5
East Grand Rapids
U.S.A. 42°58N 85°37W 311 B11
East Greenwich U.S.A. 41°40N 71°27W 313 E13
East Grinstead U.K. 51°7N 0°0 169 F8
East Ham U.K. 51°32N 0°3E 125 A4
East Hartford U.S.A. 41°46N 72°39W 313 E12
East Haydon Australia 18°0S 141°30E 280 B3
East Helena U.S.A. 46°35N 111°56W 304 C8
East Humber → Canada 43°47N 79°35W 141 A1
East Indies Asia 0°0 120°0E 210 J14
East Kilbride U.K. 55°47N 4°11W 167 F4
East Lamma Channel
China 22°14N 114°9E 122 B1
East Lansing U.S.A. 42°44N 84°29W 311 B12
East Las Vegas = Whitney
U.S.A. 36°4N 115°5W 124 B2
East Lexington U.S.A. 42°25N 71°12W 116 A1
East Livermore = Livermore Falls
U.S.A. 44°29N 70°11W 309 C18
East Liverpool U.S.A. 40°37N 80°35W 312 F4
East London S. Africa 33°0S 27°55E 271 D4
East Los Angeles U.S.A. 34°1N 118°10W 126 B3
East Lothian □ U.K. 55°58N 2°44W 167 F6
East Main = Eastmain
Canada 52°10N 78°30W 298 B4
East Mariana Basin
Pac. Oc. 12°0N 153°0E 288 F7
East Milwaukee = Shorewood
U.S.A. 43°5N 87°53W 311 A9
East Molesey U.K. 51°24N 0°21W 125 B1
East Moline U.S.A. 41°32N 90°26W 310 C6
East Naples U.S.A. 26°8N 81°46W 317 J8
East New Britain □
Papua N. G. 6°30S 152°30E 286 D7
East New York U.S.A. 40°40N 73°53W 132 B2
East Northport U.S.A. 40°53N 73°20W 313 F11
East Orange U.S.A. 40°46N 74°12W 313 F10
East Pacific Rise Pac. Oc. 15°0S 110°0W 289 J17
East Pakistan = Bangladesh ■
Asia 24°0N 90°0E 241 D3
East Palatka U.S.A. 29°39N 81°36W 316 F8
East Palestine U.S.A. 40°50N 80°33W 312 F4
East Peoria U.S.A. 40°40N 89°34W 310 D7
East Pine Canada 55°48N 120°12W 296 B4
East Pines U.S.A. 38°57N 76°54W 143 B4
East Point U.S.A. 33°41N 84°25W 113 B2
East Potomac Park
Washington, D.C., U.S.A. 143 c1
East Providence U.S.A. 41°49N 71°23W 313 E13
East Pt. Br. Virgin Is. 18°40N 64°18W 321 b
East Pt. N.S., Canada 46°27N 61°58W 299 C7
East Pt. U.S. Virgin Is. 17°45N 64°34W 321 b
East Renfrewshire □ U.K. 55°46N 4°21W 167 F4
East Retford = Retford
U.K. 53°19N 0°56W 168 D7
East Riding of Yorkshire □
U.K. 53°55N 0°30W 168 D7
East River → New York, U.S.A. 132 e3
East Rochester U.S.A. 43°7N 77°29W 312 C7
East Rutherford U.S.A. 40°50N 74°5W 132 A1
East St. Louis U.S.A. 38°37N 90°9W 310 F6
East Schelde = Oosterschelde →
Neths. 51°33N 4°0E 170 C4
East Sea = Japan, Sea of
Asia 40°0N 135°0E 220 E7
East Sepik □ Papua N. G. 4°0S 143°45E 286 C2
East Sheen U.K. 51°27N 0°16W 125 B2
East Siberian Sea Russia 73°0N 160°0E 215 B17
East Stroudsburg U.S.A. 41°1N 75°11W 313 E9
East Sussex □ U.K. 50°56N 0°19E 169 G8
East Talpiyot West Bank 31°45N 35°13E 123 B2
East Tasman Plateau
Pac. Oc. 43°30S 152°0E 288 M7
East Tawas U.S.A. 44°17N 83°29W 309 C12
East Timor ■ Asia 8°50S 126°0E 231 F7
East Toorale Australia 30°27S 145°28E 281 E4
East Troy U.S.A. 42°47N 88°24W 311 B8
East Village New York, U.S.A. 132 e2
East Walker → U.S.A. 38°52N 119°10W 306 G7
East Wickham U.K. 51°28N 0°5E 125 B4
East Windsor U.S.A. 40°17N 74°34W 313 F10
East York Canada 43°40N 79°22W 141 A2
East Youngstown = Campbell
U.S.A. 41°5N 80°37W 312 E4
Eastbourne N.Z. 41°19S 174°55E 143 B2
Eastbourne E. Sussex, U.K. 50°46N 0°18E 169 G8
Eastcote U.K. 51°34N 0°23W 125 A1
Eastend Canada 49°32N 108°50W 297 D7
Easter Fracture Zone
Pac. Oc. 25°0S 115°0W 289 K16
Easter Howgate U.K. 55°52N 3°12W 121 B2
Easter I. = Pascua, I. de
Chile 27°7S 109°23W 330 b
Eastern □ Ghana 6°30N 0°30W 263 D4
Eastern □ Kenya 0°0 38°30E 268 C4
Eastern □ S. Leone 8°15N 11°0W 262 D2
Eastern Cape □ S. Africa 32°0S 26°0E 270 D4
Eastern Cr. → Australia 20°40S 141°35E 280 C3
Eastern Desert = Es Sahrâ' Esh
Sharqîya Egypt 27°30N 32°30E 256 B3
Eastern Ghats India 14°0N 78°50E 245 H4
Eastern Group = Lau Group
Fiji 17°0S 178°30W 287 A3
Eastern Group Australia 33°30S 124°30E 279 F3
Eastern Guruma ☼
Australia 22°0S 117°30E 278 D2
Eastern Highlands □
Papua N. G. 6°30S 145°35E 286 D3
Eastern I. Midway Is. 28°12N 177°19W 302 c
Eastern Samar □ Phil. 11°40N 125°40E 233 F5
Eastern Transvaal =
Mpumalanga □ S. Africa 26°0S 30°0E 271 C5
Easterville Canada 53°8N 99°49W 297 C9
Easthampton U.S.A. 42°16N 72°40W 313 D12
Eastlake U.S.A. 41°40N 81°26W 312 E3
Eastland U.S.A. 32°24N 98°49W 314 E5
Eastleigh U.K. 50°58N 1°21W 169 G6
Eastmain Canada 52°10N 78°30W 298 B4
Eastmain → Canada 52°27N 78°26W 298 B4
Eastman Qué., Canada 45°18N 72°19W 313 A12
Eastman Ga., U.S.A. 32°12N 83°11W 316 C6
Eastman Wis., U.S.A. 43°10N 91°1W 310 A5
Easton Md., U.S.A. 38°47N 76°5W 309 F15
Easton Pa., U.S.A. 40°41N 75°13W 313 F9
Easton Wash., U.S.A. 47°14N 121°11W 306 C5
Eastover U.S.A. 33°52N 80°41W 316 B9
Eastpoint U.S.A. 29°44N 84°53W 316 F5
Eastpoint Park Canada 43°46N 79°10W 141 A4
Eastport U.S.A. 44°56N 67°0W 309 C20
Eastsound U.S.A. 48°42N 122°55W 306 B4
Eastwood Australia 33°47S 151°4E 139 A1
Eaton Colo., U.S.A. 40°32N 104°42W 304 F11
Eaton Ohio, U.S.A. 39°45N 84°38W 311 E12
Eaton Canyon Park
U.S.A. 34°10N 118°7W 126 A4
Eaton Centre Toronto, Canada 141 a2
Eaton Rapids U.S.A. 42°31N 84°39W 311 B12
Eatonia Canada 51°13N 109°25W 297 C7
Eatonton U.S.A. 33°20N 83°23W 316 B6
Eatontown U.S.A. 40°19N 74°4W 313 F10
Eatonville U.S.A. 46°52N 122°16W 306 D4
Eau Claire Fr. Guiana 3°30N 53°40W 329 C7
Eau Claire Wis., U.S.A. 44°49N 91°30W 308 C8
Eau Claire, L. à l' Canada 56°10N 74°25W 298 A5
Eauripik Rise Pac. Oc. 2°0N 142°0E 288 G6
Eauze France 43°53N 0°7E 174 E4
Eban Nigeria 9°40N 4°50E 263 D5
Ebanga Angola 12°45S 14°45E 265 E2
Ebangalakata
Dem. Rep. of the Congo 0°29S 21°29E 264 C4
Ebano Mexico 22°13N 98°24W 319 C5
Ebara Japan 35°35N 139°42E 140 B3
Ebbegebirge ⌂ Germany 51°10N 7°55E 178 D3
Ebbw Vale U.K. 51°46N 3°12W 169 F4
Ebebiyín Eq. Guin. 2°9N 11°20E 264 B2
Ebel Gabon 0°7N 11°5E 264 B2
Ebeltoft Denmark 56°12N 10°41E 163 H4
Ebeltoft Vig Denmark 56°10N 10°35E 163 H4
Ebensburg U.S.A. 40°29N 78°44W 312 F6
Ebensee Austria 47°48N 13°46E 180 D6
Eber Gölü Turkey 38°38N 31°11E 212 C4
Eberbach Germany 49°28N 8°59E 179 F4
Eberswalde-Finow
Germany 52°50N 13°49E 178 C9
Ebetsu Japan 43°7N 141°34E 220 C10
Ebey's Landing ⌂
U.S.A. 48°12N 122°41W 306 B4
Ebian China 29°11N 103°13E 228 C4
Ebingen Germany 48°13N 9°1E 179 G5
Ebino Japan 32°2N 130°48E 222 E2
Ebinur Hu China 44°55N 82°55E 217 D10
Ebisu Japan 35°38N 139°42E 140 B3
Ebla Syria 35°50N 36°48E 250 C7
Ebo Angola 11°40S 14°40E 265 E2
Ebola →
Dem. Rep. of the Congo 3°20N 20°57E 264 B4
Éboli Italy 40°39N 15°2E 201 B8
Ebolowa Cameroon 2°55N 11°10E 263 F7
Ebonda
Dem. Rep. of the Congo 2°12N 22°21E 264 B4
Ebonyi □ Nigeria 6°20N 8°0E 263 D6
Eboy Dem. Rep. of the Congo 2°50N 23°11E 264 B4
Ebrach Germany 49°51N 10°29E 179 F6
Ebre = Ebro → Spain 40°43N 0°54E 196 E5
Ébrié, Lagune Ivory C. 5°12N 4°26W 262 D4
Ebro → Spain 40°43N 0°54E 196 E5
Ebro, Embalse del Spain 43°0N 3°58W 194 C7
Ebstorf Germany 53°2N 10°24E 178 B6
Ebute-Ikorodu Nigeria 6°35N 3°29E 124 A2
Ebute-Metta Nigeria 6°28N 3°23E 124 B2
Ecatepec de Morelos
Mexico 19°36N 99°3W 319 D5
Ecbatana = Hamadān
Iran 34°52N 48°32E 213 E13
Ecclesville Trin. & Tob. 10°19N 61°8W 323 t
Eceabat Turkey 40°11N 26°21E 203 F10
Ech Chéliff Algeria 36°10N 1°20E 261 A5
Ech Chéliff □ Algeria 36°15N 1°30E 261 A5
Echeconnee → U.S.A. 32°39N 83°36W 316 C6
Echigo-Sammyaku
Japan 36°50N 139°50E 221 F9
Echinades Greece 38°25N 21°2E 207 C3
Echinos Greece 41°16N 25°1E 203 E9
Échirolles France 45°8N 5°44E 175 C9
Echizen-Misaki Japan 35°59N 135°57E 223 B7
Echmiadzin = Yejmiadzin
Armenia 40°12N 44°19E 191 K7
Echo U.S.A. 31°29N 85°28W 316 D4
Echo Bay N.W.T., Canada 66°5N 117°55W 294 D8
Echo Bay Ont., Canada 46°29N 84°4W 298 C3
Echo Park Los Angeles, U.S.A. 127 a1
Echoing → Canada 55°51N 92°5W 298 B1
Echterdingen, Stuttgart ✈ (STR)
Germany 48°42N 9°11E 179 G5
Echternach Lux. 49°49N 6°25E 170 E6
Echuca Australia 36°10S 144°45E 283 D6
Écija Spain 37°30N 5°10W 195 H5
Eckental Germany 49°35N 11°12E 179 F7
Eckernförde Germany 54°28N 9°50E 178 A5
Eclectic U.S.A. 32°38N 86°2W 316 C3
Eclipse I. Australia 35°5S 117°58E 279 G2
Eclipse Is. Australia 13°54S 126°19E 278 B4
Eclipse Sd. Canada 72°38N 79°0W 295 C16
Écommoy France 47°50N 0°17E 172 E7
Economy = Ambridge
U.S.A. 40°36N 80°14W 312 F4
Ecoporanga Brazil 18°23S 40°50W 333 E3
Écouché France 48°42N 0°10W 172 D6
Ecrins △ France 44°54N 6°18E 175 D10
Ecuador ■ S. Amer. 2°0S 78°0W 328 D2
Ecuador, Volcán Ecuador 1°1S 91°32W 330 a
Écueillé France 47°5N 1°21E 172 E8
Ed Sweden 58°55N 11°55E 163 F5
Ed Dabbura Sudan 17°40N 34°15E 256 D3
Ed Da'ein Sudan 11°26N 26°9E 257 E2
Ed Damazin Sudan 11°46N 34°21E 266 B3
Ed Dâmer Sudan 17°27N 34°0E 256 D3
Ed Dar el Beida = Casablanca
Morocco 33°36N 7°36W 260 B3
Ed Debba Sudan 18°0N 30°51E 256 D3
Ed Déffa Egypt 30°40N 26°30E 256 A2
Ed Deim Sudan 10°10N 28°20E 257 E2
Ed Dibeikir Sudan 10°23N 29°9E 266 B2
Ed Dueim Sudan 14°0N 32°10E 257 E3
Eda Japan 35°33N 139°33E 140 B2
Edam Sask., Canada 53°11N 108°46W 297 C7
Edam Neths. 52°31N 5°3E 170 B5
Edane Sweden 59°38N 12°49E 162 E6
Edapally India 11°19N 78°3E 245 J4
Eday U.K. 59°11N 2°47W 167 B6
Edchera W. Sahara 27°2N 13°4W 260 C2
Edd Eritrea 14°0N 41°38E 257 E5
Eddrachillis B. U.K. 58°17N 5°14W 167 C3
Eddystone U.K. 50°11N 4°16W 169 G3
Eddystone Pt. Australia 40°59S 148°20E 281 G4
Eddyville U.S.A. 41°9N 92°38W 310 C4
Ede Neths. 52°4N 5°40E 170 B5
Ede Nigeria 7°45N 4°29E 263 D5
Édéa Cameroon 3°51N 10°9E 263 E7
Edebäck Sweden 60°4N 13°32E 162 D7
Edehon L. Canada 60°25N 97°15W 297 A9
Edelény Hungary 48°18N 20°44E 182 B5
Eden = Bar Harbor
U.S.A. 44°23N 68°13W 309 C19
Eden N.S.W., Australia 37°3S 149°55E 283 D8
Eden N.C., U.S.A. 36°29N 79°53W 315 C15
Eden N.Y., U.S.A. 42°39N 78°55W 312 D6
Eden Tex., U.S.A. 31°13N 99°51W 314 F5
Eden → U.K. 54°57N 3°1W 168 C4
Edenburg S. Africa 29°43S 25°58E 270 C4
Edendale N.Z. 46°19S 168°48E 285 G3
Edendale Gauteng, S. Africa 26°8S 28°9E 123 A2
Edendale KwaZulu Natal,
S. Africa 29°39S 30°18E 271 C5
Edenderry Ireland 53°21N 7°4W 166 C4
Edenhope Australia 37°4S 141°19E 282 D4
Edenmore Ireland 53°22N 6°11W 120 A2
Edenton U.S.A. 36°4N 76°39W 315 C16
Edenville S. Africa 27°37S 27°34E 271 C4
Eder → Germany 51°12N 9°28E 178 D5
Eder-Stausee Germany 51°10N 8°57E 178 D4
Edessa Greece 40°48N 22°5E 202 F6
Edewecht Germany 53°8N 7°58E 178 B3
Edfu = Idfû Egypt 24°55N 32°49E 256 C3
Edgar U.S.A. 40°22N 97°58W 308 E5
Edgars Cr. → Australia 37°43S 144°58E 128 A1
Edgartown U.S.A. 41°23N 70°31W 313 E14
Edge Hill U.K. 52°8N 1°26W 169 E6
Edgecumbe N.Z. 37°59S 176°47E 284 D5
Edgefield U.S.A. 33°47N 81°56W 316 B8
Edgeley Ont., Canada 43°47N 79°31W 141 A1
Edgeley N. Dak., U.S.A. 46°22N 98°43W 308 B4
Edgemar U.S.A. 37°39N 122°29W 136 C2
Edgemont U.S.A. 43°18N 103°50W 308 D2
Edgeøya Svalbard 77°45N 22°30E 150 B9
Edgerton Ohio, U.S.A. 41°27N 84°45W 311 C12
Edgerton Wis., U.S.A. 42°50N 89°4W 310 B7
Edgewater Fla., U.S.A. 28°59N 80°54W 317 G9
Edgewater N.J., U.S.A. 40°49N 73°58W 132 B2
Edgewood Fla., U.S.A. 28°29N 81°22W 133 B2
Edgewood Ill., U.S.A. 38°55N 88°40W 311 F8
Édhessa = Edessa Greece 40°48N 22°5E 202 F6
Edievale N.Z. 45°49S 169°22E 285 F4
Edina Liberia 6°0N 10°10W 262 D2
Edina Mo., U.S.A. 40°10N 92°11W 310 D4
Edinboro U.S.A. 41°52N 80°8W 312 E4
Edinburg Ill., U.S.A. 39°39N 89°23W 310 E7
Edinburg Tex., U.S.A. 26°18N 98°10W 314 H5
Edinburgh Edinburgh, U.K. 55°57N 3°13W 121 B2
Edinburgh Ind., U.S.A. 39°21N 85°58W 311 E11
Edinburgh ✈ (EDI) U.K. 55°54N 3°22W 121 B1
Edinburgh, City of □ U.K. 55°57N 3°17W 167 F5
Edinburgh Castle Edinburgh, U.K. 121 b2
Edineţ Moldova 48°9N 27°18E 183 B12
Edirne Turkey 41°40N 26°34E 203 E10
Edirne □ Turkey 41°12N 26°30E 203 E10
Edison Ga., U.S.A. 31°34N 84°44W 316 D5
Edison Wash., U.S.A. 48°33N 122°27W 306 B4
Edison Park U.S.A. 42°1N 87°48W 119 A2
Edisto → U.S.A. 32°29N 80°21W 316 C9
Edisto Beach U.S.A. 32°29N 80°20W 316 C9
Edisto I. U.S.A. 32°35N 80°20W 316 C9
Edithburgh Australia 35°5S 137°43E 282 C2
Edjeleh Algeria 28°38N 9°50E 261 C6
Edmeston U.S.A. 42°42N 75°15W 313 D9
Edmond U.S.A. 35°39N 97°29W 314 D6
Edmonds U.S.A. 47°48N 122°22W 306 C4
Edmondston U.S.A. 38°56N 76°54W 143 B4
Edmondstown Ireland 53°17N 6°18W 120 B2
Edmonton Queens.,
Australia 17°2S 145°46E 280 B4
Edmonton Alta., Canada 53°30N 113°30W 296 C6
Edmund L. Canada 54°45N 93°17W 298 B1
Edmundston Canada 47°23N 68°20W 299 C6
Edna U.S.A. 28°59N 96°39W 314 G6
Edo □ Nigeria 6°30N 6°0E 263 D6
Edo → Japan 35°38N 139°52E 140 B4
Edogawa Japan 35°43N 139°52E 140 A4
Edolo Italy 46°10N 10°21E 198 B7
Edøya Norway 63°18N 8°10E 164 A5
Edremit Turkey 39°34N 27°0E 205 B9
Edremit Körfezi Turkey 39°30N 26°45E 205 B8
Edsberg Sweden 59°26N 17°57E 139 A1
Edsbro Sweden 59°54N 18°29E 162 E12
Edsbyn Sweden 61°23N 15°49E 162 C9
Edson Canada 53°35N 116°28W 296 C5
Eduardo Castex
Argentina 35°50S 64°18W 334 D3
Edward → Australia 35°5S 143°30E 282 C5
Edward, L. Africa 0°25S 29°40E 268 C2
Edward VII Land
Antarctica 80°0S 150°0W 151 E13
Edwardesabad = Bannu
Pakistan 33°0N 70°18E 240 B3
Edwards Calif., U.S.A. 34°50N 117°40W 307 L9
Edwards N.Y., U.S.A. 44°20N 75°15W 313 B9
Edwards → U.S.A. 41°9N 90°59W 310 C6
Edwards L. Australia 37°42S 144°59E 128 A1
Edwards Plateau U.S.A. 30°45N 101°20W 314 F4
Edwardsburg U.S.A. 41°48N 86°6W 311 C10
Edwardsville Ill., U.S.A. 38°49N 89°58W 310 F7
Edwardsville Pa., U.S.A. 41°15N 75°56W 313 E9
Edzná Mexico 19°39N 90°19W 319 D6
Edzo Canada 62°49N 116°4W 296 A5
Eek U.S.A. 60°14N 162°2W 303 F7
Eeklo Belgium 51°11N 3°33E 170 C3
Eel → Ind., U.S.A. 39°7N 86°57W 311 E10
Eel → Ind., U.S.A. 40°45N 86°22W 311 D10
Eesti = Estonia ■ Europe 58°30N 25°30E 188 C3
Efate, I. Vanuatu 17°40S 168°25E 287 G6
Eferding Austria 48°18N 14°1E 180 C7
Effigy Mounds ⌂ U.S.A. 43°5N 91°11W 310 A5
Effingham U.S.A. 39°7N 88°33W 311 E8
Eforie Romania 44°1N 28°37E 183 F13
Efoulen Cameroon 2°46N 10°43E 264 B2
Eftelot Norway 59°33N 9°49E 164 E6
Efxinoupoli Greece 39°12N 22°42E 204 B4
Efzonos Greece 37°55N 23°49E 112 B2
Ega → Spain 42°19N 1°55W 196 C3
Égadi, Ísole Italy 37°55N 12°16E 200 E5
Egaleo Greece 37°59N 23°40E 112 B2
Egaleo, Oros Greece 38°0N 23°36E 112 B1
Egan Range U.S.A. 39°35N 114°55W 304 G6
Eganville Canada 45°32N 77°5W 312 A7
Egedesminde = Aasiaat
Greenland 68°43N 52°56W 154 D5
Egegik U.S.A. 58°13N 157°22W 303 G8
Eger = Cheb Czech Rep. 50°9N 12°28E 180 A5
Eger Hungary 47°53N 20°27E 182 C5
Eger → Hungary 47°38N 20°50E 182 C5
Egersund Norway 58°26N 6°1E 164 F3
Egg I. St. Helena 15°58S 5°47W 153 h
Egg L. Canada 55°5N 105°30W 297 B7
Eggedal Norway 60°14N 9°22E 164 D6
Eggegebirge Südlicher Teutoburger
Wald ⌂ Germany 51°40N 8°59E 178 D4
Eggenburg Austria 48°38N 15°50E 180 C8
Eggenfelden Germany 48°23N 12°46E 179 G8
Egherta Somali Rep. 2°4N 43°11E 267 D5
Éghezée Belgium 50°35N 4°55E 170 D4
Egholo Solomon Is. 8°25S 157°25E 287 M9
Egilsstaðir Iceland 65°16N 14°25W 155 B12
Egina Greece 37°45N 23°26E 204 D5
Eginio Greece 40°28N 22°28E 202 F6
Egio Greece 38°15N 22°5E 204 C4
Egito Angola 12°4S 13°58E 265 E2
Égletons France 45°24N 2°3E 174 C6
Eglinton I. Canada 75°48N 118°30W 295 B8
Egmond Canada 49°45N 123°56W 296 D4
Egmont, C. N.Z. 39°16S 173°45E 284 F2
Egmont, Mt. = Taranaki, Mt.
N.Z. 39°17S 174°5E 284 F3
Egmont △ N.Z. 39°17S 174°4E 284 F3
Egra India 21°54N 87°32E 243 J12
Eğridir Turkey 37°52N 30°51E 212 D4
Eğridir Gölü Turkey 37°53N 30°50E 212 D4
Egtved Denmark 55°38N 9°18E 163 J3
Éguas → Brazil 13°26S 44°14W 333 D3
Egum Atoll Papua N. G. 9°25S 152°0E 286 E7
Éguzon-Chantôme France 46°27N 1°33E 173 F8
Egvekinot Russia 66°19N 179°50W 215 C19
Egyek Hungary 47°39N 20°52E 182 C5
Egypt ■ Africa 28°0N 31°0E 256 B3
Eha Amufu Nigeria 6°30N 7°46E 263 D6
Eheli Algeria 22°26N 4°30E 261 D5
Ehime □ Japan 33°30N 132°40E 222 D4
Ehingen Germany 48°16N 9°43E 179 G5
Ehrenberg U.S.A. 33°36N 114°31W 307 M12
Ehrhardt U.S.A. 33°6N 81°1W 316 B8
Ehrwald Austria 47°24N 10°56E 180 D3
Eiao French Polynesia 8°0S 140°40W 289 f
Eibar Spain 43°11N 2°28W 196 B2
Eibenschitz = Ivančice
Czech Rep. 49°6N 16°23E 181 B9
Eiche Germany 52°33N 13°35E 115 A4
Eiche Süd Germany 52°33N 13°35E 115 A4
Eichstätt Germany 48°54N 11°11E 179 G7
Eide Hordaland, Norway 60°31N 6°44E 164 D3
Eide Møre og Romsdal,
Norway 62°55N 7°27E 164 B4
Eider → Germany 54°19N 8°57E 178 A4
Eidsbugarden Norway 61°23N 8°16E 164 C5
Eidsbygda Norway 62°36N 7°30E 164 B4
Eidsdalen Norway 62°16N 7°10E 164 B4
Eidsvåg Norway 62°46N 8°2E 164 B5
Eidsvold Australia 25°25S 151°12E 281 D5
Eidsvoll Norway 60°19N 11°14E 164 D8
Eielson U.S.A. 64°40N 147°4W 303 D11
Eifel Germany 50°15N 6°50E 179 E2
Eiffel, Tour Paris, France 134 c2
Eiffel Flats Zimbabwe 18°20S 30°0E 269 F3
Eiger Switz. 46°34N 8°1E 198 B5
Eigg U.K. 56°54N 6°10W 167 E2
Eighty Mile Beach
Australia 19°30S 120°40E 278 C3
Eikefjord Norway 61°35N 5°27E 164 C2
Eikelandsosen Norway 60°15N 5°43E 164 D2
Eiken Norway 58°29N 7°14E 164 F4
Eikeren Norway 59°38N 9°58E 164 E6
Eikesdalen Norway 62°28N 8°12E 164 B5
Eil, L. U.K. 56°51N 5°16W 167 E3
Eil Malk Palau 7°10N 134°23E 288 c
Eildon Australia 37°14S 145°55E 283 D6
Eildon, L. Australia 37°10S 146°0E 283 D7
Eilean Sar = Western Isles □
U.K. 57°30N 7°10W 167 D1
Eilenburg Germany 51°27N 12°36E 178 D8
Ein Arik West Bank 31°54N 35°8E 123 A1
Ein el Luweiqa Sudan 14°5N 33°50E 257 E3
Ein Naquba Israel 31°47N 35°7E 123 B1
Ein Rafa Israel 31°47N 35°7E 123 B1
Eina Norway 60°38N 10°35E 164 D7
Einarsstaðir Iceland 65°44N 17°24W 155 B9
Einasleigh Australia 18°32S 144°5E 280 B3
Einasleigh → Australia 17°30S 142°17E 280 B3
Einbeck Germany 51°49N 9°53E 178 D5
Eindhoven Neths. 51°26N 5°28E 170 C5
Einsiedeln Switz. 47°7N 8°46E 179 H4
Eire = Ireland ■ Europe 53°50N 7°52W 166 C4
Eiríksjökull Iceland 64°46N 20°24W 155 C6
Eiríksstaðir Iceland 65°7N 15°25W 155 B11
Eirunepé Brazil 6°35S 69°53W 330 B4
Eiseb → Namibia 20°33S 20°59E 270 B2
Eisenach Germany 50°58N 10°19E 178 E6
Eisenberg Germany 50°58N 11°54E 178 E7
Eisenerz Austria 47°32N 14°54E 180 D7
Eisenhüttenstadt
Germany 52°9N 14°38E 178 C10
Eisenkappel Austria 46°29N 14°36E 180 E7
Eisenstadt Austria 47°51N 16°31E 181 D9
Eisenstein = Železná Ruda
Czech Rep. 49°8N 13°15E 180 B6
Eisfeld Germany 50°25N 10°54E 179 E6
Eisleben Germany 51°32N 11°32E 178 D7
Eislingen Germany 48°41N 9°42E 179 G5
Eivindvik Norway 60°59N 5°2E 164 D2
Eivissa Spain 38°54N 1°26E 206 D1
Eixe, Serra do Spain 42°24N 6°54W 194 C4
Eizariya West Bank 31°46N 35°16E 123 B2
Ejby Denmark 55°41N 12°24E 118 A2
Ejea de los Caballeros Spain 42°7N 1°9W 196 C3
Ejeda Madag. 24°20S 44°31E 272 C1
Ejigbo Nigeria 6°35N 3°16E 124 A1
Ejura Ghana 7°23N 1°15W 263 D4
Ejutla Mexico 16°34N 96°44W 319 D5
Ekalaka U.S.A. 45°53N 104°33W 304 D11
Ekalla Gabon 1°27S 14°0E 264 C2
Ekanga
Dem. Rep. of the Congo 2°23S 23°14E 264 C4
Ekaterinburg = Yekaterinburg
Russia 56°50N 60°30E 214 D7
Ekeberg Norway 59°53N 10°46E 133 A3
Ekenäs = Tammisaari
Finland 60°0N 23°26E 188 B2
Ekenässjön Sweden 57°28N 15°1E 163 G9
Ekerö Sweden 59°16N 17°45E 162 E11
Eket Nigeria 4°38N 7°56E 263 E6
Eketahuna N.Z. 40°38S 175°43E 284 G4
Ekibastuz Kazakhstan 51°50N 75°10E 217 B9
Ekiti □ Nigeria 7°25N 5°20E 263 D6
Eklutna U.S.A. 61°27N 149°22W 303 F10
Eknäs Sweden 59°18N 18°13E 139 B3
Ekoli Dem. Rep. of the Congo 0°23S 24°13E 264 C4
Ekoln Sweden 59°45N 17°37E 162 E11
Ekouamou Congo 0°8N 16°31E 264 B3
Ekoungounou Congo 1°10S 15°52E 264 C3
Ekshärad Sweden 60°10N 13°30E 162 D7
Eksjö Sweden 57°40N 14°58E 163 G8
Ekukola
Dem. Rep. of the Congo 0°31S 18°56E 264 C3
Ekuku
Dem. Rep. of the Congo 0°41S 21°42E 264 C4
Ekukula
Dem. Rep. of the Congo 0°15N 21°30E 264 B4
Ekuma → Namibia 18°40S 16°2E 270 A2
Ekuta Dem. Rep. of the Congo 3°0N 18°50E 264 B3
Ekwan → Canada 53°12N 82°15W 298 B3
Ekwan Pt. Canada 53°16N 82°7W 298 B3
Ekwok U.S.A. 59°22N 157°30W 303 G8
El Aaiún W. Sahara 27°9N 13°12W 260 C2
El Aargub Mauritania 23°37N 15°52W 260 D1
El Abanico Chile 37°20S 71°31W 334 D1
El 'Abbasiya El Qâhira,
Egypt 30°3N 31°16E 117 A2
El Abbasiya Sudan 12°10N 31°18E 257 E3
El Abiodh-Sidi-Cheikh
Algeria 32°53N 0°31E 261 B5
El Adde Somali Rep. 2°35N 46°9E 267 D6
El Adeb Larache Algeria 27°22N 8°52E 261 C6
El 'Agrûd Egypt 30°14N 34°24E 251 H5
El Agustino Peru 12°2S 77°0W 124 B2
El Agustino, Cerro Peru 12°3S 76°59W 124 B3
El Aïoun Morocco 34°33N 2°30W 260 B4
El Ait Sudan 12°22N 27°27E 257 E2
El 'Aiyat Egypt 29°36N 31°15E 256 J7
El Alamein Egypt 30°48N 28°58E 256 A2
El Alto Peru 4°15S 81°14W 330 A1
El Aouj Mauritania 22°53N 12°49W 260 D2
El 'Aqaba, W. → Egypt 30°7N 33°54E 251 H4
El 'Arag Egypt 28°40N 26°20E 256 B2
El Aricha Algeria 34°13N 1°10W 261 B4
El Arîḥā West Bank 31°52N 35°27E 251 G6
El 'Arîsh Egypt 31°8N 33°50E 251 G4
El 'Arîsh, W. → Egypt 31°8N 33°47E 251 G4
El Arrouch Algeria 36°37N 6°53E 261 A6
El Asnam = Ech Chéliff
Algeria 36°10N 1°20E 261 A5
El Astillero Spain 43°23N 3°49W 194 B7
El Avagi Somali Rep. 3°36N 46°57E 267 D6
El Badâri Egypt 27°4N 31°25E 256 B3
El Badrshein Egypt 29°51N 31°16E 251 J2
El Bagur Egypt 30°25N 31°2E 251 H2
El Bahrein Egypt 28°30N 26°25E 256 B2
El Ballâs Egypt 26°2N 32°43E 256 B3
El Balyana Egypt 26°10N 32°3E 256 B3
El Banco Colombia 9°0N 73°58W 328 B3
El Baqeir Sudan 18°40N 33°40E 256 D3
El Baragil Egypt 30°4N 31°9E 117 A1
El Barco de Ávila Spain 40°21N 5°31W 194 E5
El Barco de Valdeorras = O Barco
Spain 42°23N 6°58W 194 C4
El Basâlîn Egypt 29°58N 31°16E 117 B2
El Bauga Sudan 18°18N 33°52E 256 D3
El Baúl Venezuela 8°57N 68°17W 328 B4
El Bawiti Egypt 28°25N 28°45E 256 B2
El Bayadh Algeria 33°40N 1°1E 261 B5
El Bayadh □ Algeria 32°30N 1°10E 261 B5
El Bierzo Spain 42°45N 6°30W 194 C4
El Bira West Bank 31°54N 35°13E 123 A2
El Bluff Nic. 11°59N 83°40W 320 D3
El Bolsón Argentina 41°55S 71°30W 336 B2
El Bonillo Spain 38°57N 2°35W 197 G2
El Bosque Chile 33°32S 70°40W 137 C2
El Buheirat □ Sudan 7°0N 30°0E 257 F3
El Bur Somali Rep. 4°40N 46°37E 267 D6
El Burgo de Osma Spain 41°35N 3°4W 196 D1
El Caín Argentina 41°40S 68°19W 336 B3
El Cajon U.S.A. 32°48N 116°58W 307 N10
El Calafate Argentina 50°19S 72°15W 336 D2
El Callao Venezuela 7°18N 61°50W 329 B5
El Campello Spain 38°26N 0°24W 197 G4
El Campo U.S.A. 29°12N 96°16W 314 G6
El Capitan U.S.A. 37°44N 119°38W 306 H7
El Carbón Honduras 15°25N 85°32W 320 C2
El Carmen Bolivia 13°40S 63°55W 331 C5
El Carmen Santiago, Chile 33°22S 70°43W 137 B1
El Carmen Colombia 9°43N 75°8W 328 B2
El Centro U.S.A. 32°48N 115°34W 307 N11
El Cerro Bolivia 17°30S 61°40W 331 D5
El Cerro de Andévalo
Spain 37°45N 6°57W 195 H4
El Cocuy Colombia 6°25N 72°27W 328 B3
El Cocuy △ Colombia 6°33N 72°5W 328 B3
El Compadre Mexico 32°20N 116°14W 307 N10
El Corcovado Argentina 43°25S 71°35W 336 B2
El Coronil Spain 37°5N 5°38W 195 H5
El Cortijo Chile 33°22S 70°42W 137 B1
El Cristo, Vaso Regulador
Mexico 19°30N 99°5W 128 B1
El Cuy Argentina 39°55S 68°25W 336 A3
El Cuyo Mexico 21°31N 87°41W 319 C7
El Dab'a Egypt 31°0N 28°27E 256 H6
El Daheir Egypt 31°13N 34°10E 251 G5
El Dambahaddo
Somali Rep. 3°17N 46°40E 267 D6
El Deir Egypt 25°25N 32°20E 256 B3
El Dere = Ceeldheere
Somali Rep. 5°22N 46°11E 267 C6
El Dere Ethiopia 5°6N 43°5E 267 C5
El Descanso Mexico 32°12N 116°58W 307 N10
El Desemboque Mexico 30°33N 113°1W 318 A2
El Dilingat Egypt 30°50N 30°31E 256 H7
El Diviso Colombia 1°22N 78°14W 328 C2
El Djouf Africa 21°25N 6°40W 260 D3
El Djouf Mauritania 20°0N 9°0W 260 C3
El Dorado Sinaloa,
Mexico 24°17N 107°21W 318 C3
El Dorado Ark., U.S.A. 33°12N 92°40W 314 E8
El Dorado Kans., U.S.A. 37°49N 96°52W 308 G5
El Dorado Venezuela 6°55N 61°37W 329 B5
El Dorado Springs U.S.A. 37°52N 94°1W 310 G2
El Duqqi Egypt 30°1N 31°12E 117 A2
El Eglab Algeria 26°20N 4°30W 260 C4
El 'Ein Sudan 16°35N 29°22E 257 D2
El Ejido Spain 36°47N 2°49W 195 J8
El Encinar de los Reyes
Spain 40°30N 3°39W 127 A2
El Escorial Spain 40°35N 4°7W 194 E6
El Espinar Spain 41°43N 4°15W 194 D6
El Eulma Algeria 36°9N 5°42E 261 A6
El Faiyûm Egypt 29°19N 30°50E 256 J7
El Faourar Tunisia 33°22N 8°45E 258 B1
El Fâsher Sudan 13°33N 25°26E 257 E2
El Fashn Egypt 28°50N 30°54E 256 J7
El Ferrol = Ferrol Spain 43°29N 8°15W 194 B2
El Fifi Sudan 10°4N 25°0E 257 E2
El Fud Ethiopia 7°15N 42°52E 267 C5
El Fuerte Mexico 26°25N 108°39W 318 B3
El Ga'a Sudan 14°16N 29°59E 257 E2
El Gamâlîya Egypt 31°10N 31°52E 251 G2
El Garef Sudan 12°3N 34°19E 257 E3
El Gebir Sudan 13°40N 29°40E 257 E2
El Gedida Egypt 25°40N 28°30E 256 B2
El Geneina = Al Junaynah
Sudan 13°27N 22°45E 259 F4
El Geteina Sudan 14°50N 32°27E 257 E3
El Gezira Egypt 30°2N 31°13E 117 A2
El Gezira □ Sudan 15°0N 33°0E 257 E3
El Gharbîya □ Egypt 30°50N 31°0E 251 H2
El Ghurîya Egypt 30°2N 31°15E 117 A2
El Gir Sudan 19°50N 28°18E 256 D2
El Gîza Egypt 30°0N 31°12E 117 A2
El Gîza □ Egypt 29°46N 31°18E 251 J2
El Gogorrón △ Mexico 21°49N 100°57W 318 C4
El Goléa Algeria 30°30N 2°50E 261 B5
El Golfo de Santa Clara
Mexico 31°42N 114°30W 318 A2
El Gouna Egypt 27°5N 33°47E 256 B3
El Grau Spain 39°0N 0°7W 197 G4
El Hadjira Algeria 32°36N 5°30E 261 B6
El Hagiz Sudan 15°15N 35°50E 257 D4
El Hâi Egypt 29°39N 31°18E 256 J7
El Hajeb Morocco 33°43N 5°13W 260 B3
El Hamma Tunisia 33°54N 9°48E 258 B1
El Hammam Egypt 30°52N 29°25E 256 A2
El Hammâmi Mauritania 23°3N 11°30W 260 D2
El Hâmûl Egypt 31°18N 31°9E 251 G2
El Hamurre Somali Rep. 7°13N 48°54E 267 C6
El Hank Mauritania 24°30N 7°0W 260 D3
El Hasian W. Sahara 26°20N 14°0W 260 C2
El Hawata Sudan 13°25N 34°42E 257 E3
El Heiz Egypt 27°50N 28°40E 256 B2
El Hideib Sudan 13°0N 32°50E 257 E3
El Hilla Sudan 13°24N 27°2E 257 E2
El Homr Algeria 29°43N 1°45E 261 C5
El 'Idisât Egypt 25°30N 32°35E 256 B3
El Iskandarîya Egypt 31°13N 29°58E 256 H7
El Jadida Morocco 33°11N 8°17W 260 B3
El Jadida □ Morocco 32°45N 8°30W 260 B3
El Jardal Honduras 14°54N 88°50W 320 D2
El Jebelein Sudan 12°40N 32°55E 257 E3
El Jebha Morocco 35°11N 4°43W 260 A4
El Jem Tunisia 35°19N 10°41E 258 A2
El Kab Sudan 19°27N 32°46E 256 D3
El Kafr el Sharqi Egypt 31°16N 31°10E 256 H7
El Kala Algeria 36°53N 8°26E 261 A6
El Kamlin Sudan 15°3N 33°11E 257 D3
El Kantara Algeria 35°14N 5°45E 261 A6
El Kantara Tunisia 33°45N 10°58E 258 B2
El Karaba Sudan 18°32N 33°41E 256 D3
El Kef Tunisia 36°12N 8°47E 258 A1
El Kef □ Tunisia 36°0N 9°0E 261 A6
El Kelâa de Srahna
Morocco 32°4N 7°27W 260 B3
El Kelâa de Srahna □
Morocco 32°10N 7°45W 260 B3
El Kelaâ M'Gouna Morocco 31°14N 6°7W 260 B3
El Kere Ethiopia 5°50N 42°5E 257 F5
El Khadr West Bank 31°42N 35°10E 123 B1
El Khalîfa Egypt 30°0N 31°15E 117 A2
El Khandaq Sudan 18°30N 30°30E 256 D3
El Khânka Egypt 30°13N 31°21E 251 H2
El Khârga Egypt 25°30N 30°33E 256 B3
El Khartûm Sudan 15°31N 32°35E 257 D3
El Khartûm □ Sudan 16°0N 33°0E 257 D3
El Khartûm Bahrî Sudan 15°40N 32°31E 257 D3
El Khroub Algeria 36°10N 6°55E 261 A6
El Kôm el Ahmar Egypt 30°6N 31°10E 117 A2
El Kseur Algeria 36°46N 4°49E 261 A5
El Ksiba Morocco 32°45N 6°1W 260 B3
El Kuntilla Egypt 30°1N 34°45E 251 H5
El Laqâwa Sudan 11°25N 29°1E 257 E2
El Leh Ethiopia 3°46N 39°13E 257 G4
El Leiya Sudan 16°15N 35°28E 257 D4
El Leoncito △ Argentina 31°58S 69°10W 334 C2
El Limón Panama 9°15N 79°49W 320 c
El Lucero Mexico 30°37N 106°31W 318 A3
El Ma'âdi Egypt 29°57N 31°15E 117 B2
El Maestrazgo Spain 40°30N 0°25W 196 E4
El Mafâza Sudan 13°38N 34°30E 257 E3
El Maghra Egypt 30°15N 28°55E 256 A2
El Mahalla el Kubra Egypt 31°0N 31°0E 256 H7
El Mahârîq Egypt 25°35N 30°35E 256 B3
El Maîmûn Egypt 29°14N 31°12E 256 J7
El Maitén Argentina 42°3S 71°10W 336 B2
El Maiz Algeria 28°19N 0°9W 261 C4
El Maks el Bahari Egypt 24°30N 30°40E 256 C3
El Malpais ⌂ U.S.A. 34°53N 108°0W 305 J10
El Manshâh Egypt 26°26N 31°50E 256 B3
El Mansour Algeria 27°47N 0°14W 261 C4
El Mansûra Egypt 31°0N 31°19E 256 H7
El Manteco Venezuela 7°38N 62°45W 329 B5
El Manzala Egypt 31°10N 31°50E 256 H7
El Marâgha Egypt 26°35N 31°10E 256 B3
El Masid Sudan 15°15N 33°0E 257 D3
El Masnou Spain 41°28N 2°20E 196 D7
El Matarîya El Mansûra,
Egypt 31°15N 32°0E 256 H8
El Matarîya El Qâhira,
Egypt 30°7N 31°18E 117 A2
El Meda Ethiopia 5°39N 41°47E 257 F5
El Medano Canary Is. 28°3N 16°32W 153 e1
El Meghaier Algeria 33°55N 5°58E 261 B6
El Ménia = El Goléa
Algeria 30°30N 2°50E 261 B5
El Meraguen Algeria 28°0N 0°7W 261 C4
El Metemma Sudan 16°50N 33°10E 257 D3
El Miamo Venezuela 7°39N 61°46W 329 B5
El Milagro Argentina 30°59S 65°59W 334 C2
El Milia Algeria 36°51N 6°13E 261 A6
El Minûfîya □ Egypt 30°30N 31°0E 251 H2
El Minyâ Egypt 28°7N 30°33E 256 B3
El Mohandessin Egypt 30°2N 31°11E 117 A2
El Monte U.S.A. 34°4N 118°1W 126 B4
El Montseny Spain 41°55N 2°25E 196 D7
El Mreiti Mauritania 23°29N 7°51W 260 D3
El Mreyye Mauritania 18°0N 6°0W 262 B3
El Muqattam Egypt 30°1N 31°17E 117 A2
El Mûskî Egypt 30°3N 31°15E 117 A2
El Nido Phil. 11°10N 119°25E 233 F2
El Niybo Ethiopia 4°40N 39°55E 257 G4
El Obeid Sudan 13°8N 30°10E 257 E3
El Odaiya Sudan 12°8N 28°12E 257 E2
El Oro Mexico 19°51N 100°7W 319 D4
El Oro □ Ecuador 3°30S 79°50W 328 D2
El Oued Algeria 33°20N 6°58E 261 B6
El Oued □ Algeria 33°10N 7°15E 261 B6
El Palmar Bolivia 17°50S 63°9W 331 D5
El Palmar Venezuela 7°58N 61°53W 329 B5
El Palmar △ Argentina 32°10S 58°31W 334 C4
El Palmito, Presa
Mexico 25°40N 105°30W 318 B3
El Pardo Spain 40°30N 3°46W 127 A1
El Paso = Derby U.S.A. 37°33N 97°16W 308 G5
El Paso Ill., U.S.A. 40°44N 89°1W 310 D7
El Paso Tex., U.S.A. 31°45N 106°29W 314 F1
El Pedernoso Spain 39°29N 2°45W 197 F2
El Pedroso Spain 37°51N 5°45W 195 H5
El Pilar Venezuela 10°32N 63°9W 329 A5
El Pinacate y Gran Desierto de
Altar = Gran Desierto del
Pinacate ⌂ Mexico 31°51N 113°32W 318 A2
El Pobo de Dueñas Spain 40°46N 1°39W 196 E3
El Portal Calif., U.S.A. 37°41N 119°47W 306 H7
El Portal Fla., U.S.A. 25°51N 80°11W 128 A2
El Porvenir Mexico 31°15N 105°51W 318 A3
El Prat de Llobregat Spain 41°19N 2°5E 114 B1
El Progreso Galápagos Is.,
Ecuador 0°54S 89°33W 330 a
El Progreso Honduras 15°26N 87°51W 320 C2
El Pueblito Mexico 29°6N 105°7W 318 B3
El Pueblo Canary Is. 28°36N 17°47W 153 e1
El Pueblo de Los Angeles Historic
Park Los Angeles, U.S.A. 127 b2
El Puente del Arzobispo
Spain 39°48N 5°10W 194 F5
El Puerto de Santa María
Spain 36°36N 6°13W 195 J4
El Qâhira Egypt 30°2N 31°13E 117 A2
El Qâhira □ Egypt 30°2N 31°13E 251 H2
El Qanâyat Egypt 30°37N 31°27E 251 H2
El Qantara Egypt 30°51N 32°20E 251 H3
El Qasr Egypt 25°44N 28°42E 256 B2
El Qassâsîn Egypt 30°33N 31°55E 251 H2
El Qubâbât Egypt 29°28N 31°16E 256 J7
El Qubba Egypt 30°4N 31°16E 117 A2
El Quseima Egypt 30°40N 34°15E 251 H5
El Qusîya Egypt 27°29N 30°44E 256 B3
El Râshda Egypt 25°36N 28°57E 256 B2
El Reloj Mexico 19°19N 99°9W 128 C2
El Reno U.S.A. 35°32N 97°57W 301 H20
El Retiro Spain 40°25N 3°41W 127 B1
El Rey △ Argentina 24°40S 64°34W 334 A3
El Rîdisiya Egypt 24°56N 32°51E 256 C3
El Rio U.S.A. 34°14N 119°10W 307 L7
El Ronquillo Spain 37°44N 6°10W 195 H4
El Roque, Pta. Canary Is. 28°10N 15°25W 153 e1
El Rosarito Mexico 28°38N 114°4W 318 B2
El Rubio Spain 37°22N 5°0W 195 H5
El Saff Egypt 29°34N 31°16E 256 J7
El Salto Santiago, Chile 33°22S 70°38W 137 B2
El Salto Durango, Mexico 23°47N 105°22W 318 C3
El Salvador ■ Cent. Amer. 13°50N 89°0W 320 D2
El Sauce Nic. 13°0N 86°40W 320 D2
El Saucejo Spain 37°4N 5°6W 195 H5
El Sereno U.S.A. 34°4N 118°10W 126 B3
El Shallal Egypt 24°0N 32°53E 256 C3
El Simbillawein Egypt 30°48N 31°13E 256 H7
El Sombrero Venezuela 9°23N 67°3W 328 B4
El Sueco Mexico 29°54N 106°24W 318 B3
El Suweis Egypt 29°58N 32°31E 256 J8
El Suweis □ Egypt 29°30N 32°15E 251 J3
El Tabbin Egypt 29°47N 31°18E 256 J7
El Talibiya Egypt 29°59N 31°10E 117 B2
El Tamà △ S. Amer. 7°25N 72°25W 328 B3
El Tamarâni, W. → Egypt 30°7N 34°43E 251 H5
El Tarf Algeria 36°46N 8°19E 261 A6
El Tarf □ Algeria 36°45N 8°15E 261 A6
El Thamad Egypt 29°40N 34°28E 251 J5
El Tigre Venezuela 8°44N 64°15W 329 B5

El Tîh, Gebel Egypt 29°40N 33°50E 251 J4
El Tîna Egypt 31°3N 32°22E 256 H8
El Tocuyo Venezuela 9°47N 69°48W 328 B4
El Tofo Chile 29°22S 71°18W 334 B1
El Tránsito Chile 28°52S 70°17W 334 B1
El Tucuche Trin. & Tob. 10°43N 61°25W 323 t
El Tuparro △ Colombia 5°19N 68°28W 328 B4
El Tûr Egypt 28°14N 33°36E 251 K4
El Turbio Argentina 51°45S 72°5W 336 D2
El Uarre Somali Rep. 3°4N 45°20E 267 D6
El Uqsur Egypt 25°41N 32°38E 256 B3
El Valle ⌂ Spain 37°56N 1°6W 197 H3
El Vendrell Spain 41°10N 1°30E 196 D6
El Vergel Chihuahua, Mexico 26°28N 106°22W 318 B3
El Vergel Distrito Federal, Mexico 19°18N 99°5W 128 C2
El Vigía Venezuela 8°38N 71°39W 328 B3
El Viso del Alcor Spain 37°23N 5°43W 195 H5
El Wabeira Egypt 29°34N 33°6E 251 J4
El Wâhli Egypt 30°3N 31°16E 117 A2
El Wak Somali Rep. 2°44N 41°1E 267 D5
El Waqf Egypt 25°45N 32°15E 256 B3
El Weguet Ethiopia 5°28N 42°17E 257 F5
El Wuz Sudan 15°5N 30°7E 257 D3
El Yunque, Cerro Chile 33°39S 78°50W 330 c
El Yunque Puerto Rico 18°19N 65°48W 321 b
El Zamâlik Egypt 30°3N 31°12E 117 A2
El Zeitûn Egypt 30°6N 31°18E 117 A2
Elafonisos Greece 36°29N 22°56E 204 E4
Elamanchili India 17°33N 82°50E 244 F6
Élancourt France 48°47N 1°58E 173 D8
Elands Australia 31°37S 152°20E 283 A10
Elandsfontein Junc. = Germiston S. Africa 26°13S 28°10E 123 B2
Elasa Greece 35°18N 26°21E 205 F8
Elassona Greece 39°53N 22°12E 204 B4
Elat Israel 29°30N 34°56E 251 J5
Elati Oros Greece 38°43N 20°39E 207 B2
Elatia Greece 38°37N 22°46E 204 C4
Elâzığ Turkey 38°37N 39°14E 213 C8
Elâzığ □ Turkey 38°40N 39°15E 213 C8
Elba Italy 42°46N 10°17E 198 F7
Elba Ala., U.S.A. 31°25N 86°4W 316 D3
Elbasan Albania 41°9N 20°9E 202 E4
Elbe U.S.A. 46°45N 122°10W 306 D4
Elbe → Europe 53°50N 9°0E 178 B4
Elbe-Seitenkanal Germany 52°45N 10°32E 178 C6
Elberfeld U.S.A. 38°10N 87°27W 311 F9
Elbert, Mt. U.S.A. 39°7N 106°27W 304 G10
Elberton U.S.A. 34°7N 82°52W 316 A7
Elbeuf France 49°17N 1°2E 172 C8
Elbeyli Turkey 36°40N 37°27E 250 B8
Elbing = Elbląg Poland 54°10N 19°25E 184 D6
Elbistan Turkey 38°13N 37°15E 212 C7
Elbląg Poland 54°10N 19°25E 184 D6
Elbow Canada 51°7N 106°35W 297 C7
Elbrus Russia 43°21N 42°30E 191 J6
Elbufer-Drawehn ⌂ Germany 53°8N 10°58E 178 B6
Elburn U.S.A. 41°54N 88°28W 311 C8
Elburz Mts. = Alborz, Reshteh-ye Kûhhâ-ye Iran 36°0N 52°0E 247 C7
Elche Spain 38°15N 0°42W 197 G4
Elche de la Sierra Spain 38°27N 2°3W 197 G2
Elcho I. Australia 11°55S 135°45E 280 A2
Elda Spain 38°29N 0°47W 197 G4
Eldama Ravine Kenya 0°3N 35°43E 268 B4
Elde → Germany 53°7N 11°15E 178 B7
Eldey Iceland 63°45N 22°55W 155 D4
Eldon Iowa, U.S.A. 40°55N 92°13W 310 D4
Eldon Mo., U.S.A. 38°21N 92°35W 310 F4
Eldon Wash., U.S.A. 47°33N 123°3W 306 C3
Eldora U.S.A. 42°22N 93°5W 310 B3
Eldorado = Echo Bay Canada 66°5N 117°55W 294 D8
Eldorado Argentina 26°28S 54°43W 335 B5
Eldorado Ont., Canada 44°35N 77°31W 312 B7
Eldorado Ill., U.S.A. 37°49N 88°26W 311 G8
Eldorado Tex., U.S.A. 30°52N 100°36W 314 F4
Eldorendo U.S.A. 31°3N 84°39W 316 D5
Eldoret Kenya 0°30N 35°17E 268 B4
Eldred U.S.A. 41°58N 78°23W 312 E6
Eldridge U.S.A. 41°39N 90°35W 310 C6
Elea, C. Cyprus 35°19N 34°4E 207 E10
Eleanora, Pk. Australia 32°57S 121°9E 279 F3
Eleao U.S.A. 21°27N 157°52W 302 K14
Elefantes → Africa 24°10S 32°40E 271 B5
Elefantes, B. das Angola 13°13S 12°44E 265 E2
Elefantes, G. Chile 46°28S 73°49W 336 C2
Elefsina Greece 38°4N 23°26E 204 C5
Eleftherios Venizelos ✈ (ATH) Greece 37°56N 23°56E 112 A3
Elektrogorsk Russia 55°56N 38°50E 188 E10
Elektroperedacha = Elektrogorsk Russia 55°56N 38°50E 188 E10
Elektrostal Russia 55°41N 38°32E 188 E10
Elektrovoz = Stupino Russia 54°57N 38°2E 188 E10
Elele Nigeria 5°5N 6°50E 263 D6
Elemi Triangle Africa 5°0N 35°20E 257 G4
Elena Bulgaria 42°55N 25°53E 203 D9
Elephant Butte Res. U.S.A. 33°9N 107°11W 305 K10
Elephant I. Antarctica 61°0S 55°0W 151 C18
Elephant Pass Sri Lanka 9°35N 80°25E 245 K5
Elephanta Caves India 18°57N 72°57E 130 B2
Elephanta I. India 18°57N 72°56E 130 B2
Elesbão Veloso Brazil 6°13S 42°8W 332 C3
Eleshnitsa Bulgaria 41°52N 23°36E 202 E7
Eleşkirt Turkey 39°50N 42°50E 213 C10
Eleuthera Bahamas 25°0N 76°20W 320 B4
Eleutheroupoli Greece 40°52N 24°20E 203 F8
Elfin Cove U.S.A. 58°12N 136°22W 303 G13
Elgå Norway 62°10N 11°56E 164 B8
Elgin Ont., Canada 44°36N 76°13W 313 B8
Elgin Moray, U.K. 57°39N 3°19W 167 D5
Elgin Ill., U.S.A. 42°2N 88°17W 311 B8
Elgin N. Dak., U.S.A. 46°24N 101°51W 308 B3
Elgin Oreg., U.S.A. 45°34N 117°55W 304 D5
Elgin S.C., U.S.A. 34°10N 80°48W 316 A9
Elgin Tex., U.S.A. 30°21N 97°22W 314 F6
Elgoibar Spain 43°13N 2°24W 196 B2
Elgon, Mt. Africa 1°10N 34°30E 268 B3
Elgspiggen Norway 62°10N 11°21E 164 B8
Eliase Indonesia 8°21S 130°48E 231 F8
Elikonos Oros Greece 38°18N 22°45E 204 C4
Elim Namibia 17°48S 15°31E 270 A2
Elim Western Cape, S. Africa 34°35S 19°45E 270 D2
Elim Alaska, U.S.A. 64°37N 162°15W 303 D7
Elin Pelin Bulgaria 42°40N 23°36E 202 D7
Elingampangu Dem. Rep. of the Congo 2°0S 24°4E 264 C4
Elipa Dem. Rep. of the Congo 1°3S 24°20E 264 C4
Eliseu Martins Brazil 8°13S 43°42W 332 C3
Elista Russia 46°16N 44°14E 191 G7
Eliza, L. Australia 37°15S 139°50E 282 D3
Elizabeth S. Austral., Australia 34°42S 138°41E 282 C3
Elizabeth Ill., U.S.A. 42°19N 90°13W 310 B6
Elizabeth N.J., U.S.A. 40°39N 74°12W 313 F10
Elizabeth, B. Ecuador 0°36S 91°12W 330 a
Elizabeth City U.S.A. 36°18N 76°14W 315 C16
Elizabethton U.S.A. 36°21N 82°13W 315 C13
Elizabethtown Ky., U.S.A. 37°42N 85°52W 311 G11
Elizabethtown N.Y., U.S.A. 44°13N 73°36W 313 B11
Elizabethtown Pa., U.S.A. 40°9N 76°36W 313 F8
Elizabethville = Lubumbashi Dem. Rep. of the Congo 11°40S 27°28E 269 E2
Elizondo Spain 43°12N 1°30W 196 B3
Ełk Poland 53°50N 22°21E 184 E9
Elk → B.C., Canada 49°11N 115°14W 296 C5
Ełk → Poland 53°41N 22°28E 184 E9
Elk → Ala., U.S.A. 34°46N 87°16W 315 D11
Elk City U.S.A. 35°25N 99°25W 314 D5
Elk Creek U.S.A. 39°36N 122°32W 306 F4
Elk Grove U.S.A. 38°25N 121°22W 306 G5
Elk Island △ Canada 53°35N 112°59W 296 C6
Elk Lake Canada 47°40N 80°25W 298 C3
Elk Point Canada 53°54N 110°55W 297 C6
Elk River Idaho, U.S.A. 46°47N 116°11W 304 C5
Elk River Minn., U.S.A. 45°18N 93°35W 308 C7
Elkader U.S.A. 42°51N 91°24W 310 B5
Elkedra → Australia 21°8S 136°22E 280 C2
Elkhart Ind., U.S.A. 41°41N 85°58W 311 C11
Elkhart Kans., U.S.A. 37°0N 101°54W 308 G3
Elkhart → U.S.A. 41°41N 85°58W 311 C11
Elkhorn Man., Canada 49°59N 101°14W 297 D8
Elkhorn Wis., U.S.A. 42°40N 88°33W 311 B8
Elkhorn → U.S.A. 41°8N 96°19W 308 E5
Elkhovo Bulgaria 42°10N 26°35E 203 D10
Elkin U.S.A. 36°15N 80°51W 315 C14
Elkins U.S.A. 38°55N 79°51W 309 F14
Elkland U.S.A. 41°59N 77°19W 312 E7
Elko B.C., Canada 49°20N 115°10W 296 D5
Elko Nev., U.S.A. 40°50N 115°46W 304 F6
Elkton U.S.A. 43°49N 83°11W 312 C1
Ellas = Greece ■ Europe 40°0N 23°0E 204 B3
Ellaville Fla., U.S.A. 30°23N 83°10W 316 E6
Ellaville Ga., U.S.A. 32°14N 84°19W 316 C5
Ellboda Sweden 59°24N 18°15E 139 A3
Ellef Ringnes I. Canada 78°30N 102°2W 295 B11
Ellen, Mt. U.S.A. 44°9N 72°56W 313 B12
Ellenburg U.S.A. 44°54N 73°48W 313 B11
Ellendale U.S.A. 46°0N 98°32W 308 B4
Ellenor, L. U.S.A. 28°28N 81°25W 133 B2
Ellensburg U.S.A. 46°59N 120°34W 304 C3
Ellenville U.S.A. 41°43N 74°24W 313 E10
Ellerton Barbados 13°7N 59°33W 323 r
Ellery, Mt. Australia 37°28S 148°47E 283 D8
Ellesmere = Scottsdale Australia 41°9S 147°31E 281 G4
Ellesmere, L. N.Z. 43°47S 172°28E 285 H7
Ellesmere I. Canada 79°30N 80°0W 295 B16
Ellesmere Island = Quttinirpaaq △ Canada 82°13N 72°13W 295 A17
Ellesmere Port U.K. 53°17N 2°54W 168 D5
Ellettsville U.S.A. 39°14N 86°38W 311 E10
Ellice Is. = Tuvalu ■ Pac. Oc. 8°0S 178°0E 277 B14
Ellicottville U.S.A. 42°17N 78°40W 312 D6
Ellington U.S.A. 42°13N 79°6W 312 D5
Elliniko Olympic Complex Greece 37°50N 23°45E 112 B2
Elliot N. Terr., Australia 17°33S 133°32E 280 B1
Elliot Eastern Cape, S. Africa 31°22S 27°48E 271 D4
Elliot Lake Canada 46°25N 82°35W 298 C3
Elliotdale = Xhora S. Africa 31°55S 28°38E 271 D4
Elliott U.S.A. 34°6N 80°10W 316 A9
Elliott Key U.S.A. 25°27N 80°12W 317 K9
Ellipse, The Washington, D.C., U.S.A. 143 b1
Ellis U.S.A. 38°56N 99°34W 308 F4
Ellis I. U.S.A. 40°41N 74°2W 128 B1
Elliston Australia 33°39S 134°53E 281 E1
Ellisville U.S.A. 31°36N 89°12W 315 F10
Ellon U.K. 57°22N 2°4W 167 D6
Ellora India 20°1N 75°10E 244 D2
Ellore = Eluru India 16°48N 81°8E 244 F5
Elloree U.S.A. 33°32N 80°34W 316 B9
Ellsworth Kans., U.S.A. 38°44N 98°14W 308 F4
Ellsworth Maine, U.S.A. 44°33N 68°25W 309 C19
Ellsworth Land Antarctica 76°0S 89°0W 151 D16
Ellsworth Mts. Antarctica 78°30S 85°0W 151 D16
Ellwangen Germany 48°57N 10°8E 179 G6
Ellwood City U.S.A. 40°52N 80°17W 312 F4
Ellzey U.S.A. 29°19N 82°48W 317 F7
Elm Switz. 46°54N 9°10E 179 J5
Elm-Lappwald ⌂ Germany 52°15N 10°50E 178 C6
Elma Man., Canada 49°52N 95°55W 297 D9
Elma Wash., U.S.A. 47°0N 123°25W 306 D3
Elmadağ Turkey 39°55N 33°14E 212 C5
Elmalı Turkey 36°44N 29°56E 205 E11
Elmers End U.K. 51°23N 0°2W 125 B3
Elmhurst Ill., U.S.A. 41°53N 87°56W 311 C9
Elmhurst N.Y., U.S.A. 40°44N 73°53W 128 B2
Elmina Ghana 5°5N 1°21W 263 D4
Elmira Ont., Canada 43°36N 80°33W 312 C4
Elmira N.Y., U.S.A. 42°6N 76°48W 312 D8
Elmira Heights U.S.A. 42°8N 76°50W 312 D8
Elmodel U.S.A. 31°21N 84°29W 316 D5
Elmore Vic., Australia 36°30S 144°37E 282 D6
Elmore Ala., U.S.A. 32°32N 86°19W 316 C3
Elmore Ohio, U.S.A. 41°29N 83°18W 311 C13
Elmshorn Germany 53°43N 9°40E 178 B5
Elmstead U.K. 51°24N 0°2E 125 B4
Elmvale Canada 44°35N 79°52W 312 B5
Elmwood Ill., U.S.A. 40°47N 89°58W 310 D7
Elmwood La., U.S.A. 29°57N 90°11W 131 B1
Elmwood Park Ill., U.S.A. 41°55N 87°48W 119 B2
Elmwood Park N.J., U.S.A. 40°54N 74°7W 132 A1
Elne France 42°36N 2°58E 174 F6
Elnesvågen Norway 62°52N 7°10E 164 B4
Eloaua I. Papua N. G. 1°38S 149°40E 286 A5
Elobey, Is. de Eq. Guin. 1°0N 9°29E 264 B1
Elongo Dem. Rep. of the Congo 0°19S 21°39E 264 C4
Elora Canada 43°41N 80°26W 312 C4
Elorza Venezuela 7°3N 69°31W 328 B4
Elos Greece 36°46N 22°43E 204 E4
Elounda Greece 35°16N 25°42E 207 E6
Eloy U.S.A. 32°45N 111°33W 305 K8
Éloyes France 48°6N 6°36E 173 D13
Elphin Canada 44°55N 76°37W 313 B8
Elpitiya Sri Lanka 6°17N 80°10E 245 L5
Elrose Canada 51°12N 108°0W 297 C7
Elsberry U.S.A. 39°10N 90°47W 310 E6
Elsby △ Australia 14°55S 133°10E 278 B5
Elsdon N.Z. 41°8S 174°50E 143 A1
Elsdorf Germany 50°55N 6°34E 178 E2
Elsie Mich., U.S.A. 43°5N 84°23W 311 A12
Elsie Oreg., U.S.A. 45°52N 123°36W 306 E3
Elsiesrivier S. Africa 33°55S 18°35E 118 A2
Elsinore = Helsingør Denmark 56°2N 12°35E 163 H6
Elster → Germany 51°25N 11°57E 178 D7
Elsternwick Australia 37°52S 145°0E 128 B2
Elsterwerda Germany 51°27N 13°31E 178 D9
Eltanin Fracture Zone System S. Ocean 54°0S 130°0W 151 B14
Eltham N.Z. 39°26S 174°19E 284 F3
Eltham London, U.K. 51°27N 0°3E 125 B4
Elton Russia 49°5N 46°52E 191 F8
Elton, Ozero Russia 49°5N 46°42E 191 F8
Eltville Germany 50°2N 8°7E 179 E4
Eluru India 16°48N 81°8E 244 F5
Elvas Portugal 38°50N 7°10W 195 G3
Elven France 47°44N 2°36W 172 E4
Elverum Norway 60°53N 11°34E 164 D8
Elvire → Australia 17°51S 128°11E 278 C4
Elvire, Mt. Australia 29°22S 119°36E 279 E2
Elvo → Italy 45°23N 8°21E 198 C5
Elwell, L. = Tiber Res. U.S.A. 48°19N 111°6W 304 B8
Elwood Vic., Australia 37°53S 144°59E 128 B1
Elwood Ill., U.S.A. 41°24N 88°7W 311 C8
Elwood Ind., U.S.A. 40°17N 85°50W 311 D11
Elwood Nebr., U.S.A. 40°36N 99°52W 308 E4
Elx = Elche Spain 38°15N 0°42W 197 G4
Ely Cambs., U.K. 52°24N 0°16E 169 E8
Ely Minn., U.S.A. 47°55N 91°51W 308 B8
Ely Nev., U.S.A. 39°15N 114°54W 304 G6
Elyria U.S.A. 41°22N 82°7W 312 E2
Elyros Greece 35°15N 23°45E 204 F5
Élysée France 48°52N 2°19E 134 A2
Elysian Park Los Angeles, U.S.A. 127 a3
Elz → Germany 48°18N 7°44E 179 G3
Emådalen Sweden 61°20N 14°44E 162 C8
Émaé Vanuatu 17°4S 168°24E 287 G6
eMalahleni S. Africa 25°51S 29°14E 271 C4
Emāmrūd Iran 36°30N 55°0E 247 B7
Emāmzādeh Sāleh Iran 35°48N 51°26E 141 A2
Emån → Sweden 57°8N 16°30E 163 G10
Emao Vanuatu 17°29S 168°30E 287 G6
Emas △ Brazil 18°2S 52°50W 331 D7
Emateloa Dem. Rep. of the Congo 1°16N 18°42E 264 B3
Embajadores Madrid, Spain 127 c2
Embalenhle S. Africa 26°32S 29°4E 271 C4
Embarcación Argentina 23°10S 64°0W 334 A3
Embarcadero, The San Francisco, U.S.A. 136 b3
Embarras → U.S.A. 38°39N 87°37W 311 F9
Embetsu Japan 44°44N 141°47E 220 B10
Embi Kazakhstan 48°50N 58°8E 216 C5
Embi → Kazakhstan 46°55N 53°28E 187 E9
Embonas Greece 36°13N 27°51E 206 E11
Embro Canada 43°9N 80°54W 312 C4
Embrun France 44°34N 6°30E 175 D10
Embu Kenya 0°32S 37°38E 268 C4
Emden Germany 53°21N 7°12E 178 B3
Emecik Turkey 36°46N 27°49E 205 E9
Emek Refa'im Jerusalem 123 c2
Émerainville France 48°48N 2°37E 134 B4
Emerald Queens., Australia 23°32S 148°10E 280 C4
Emerald Vic., Australia 37°56S 145°29E 276 E8
Emerald Buddha = Phra Kaeo Bangkok, Thailand 113 b1
Emerald I. Canada 76°48N 114°10W 295 B9
Emerson Man., Canada 49°0N 97°10W 297 D9
Emerson Ga., U.S.A. 34°8N 84°45W 316 A5
Emeryville U.S.A. 37°49N 122°17W 136 A3
Emet Turkey 39°20N 29°15E 205 B11
Emeti Papua N. G. 7°53S 143°15E 286 D2
Emi Koussi Chad 19°45N 18°55E 259 E3
Emília-Romagna □ Italy 44°45N 11°0E 198 D8
Emilius, Mte. Italy 45°45N 7°20E 198 C4
Emin China 46°34N 83°36E 217 C10
Eminabad Pakistan 32°2N 74°8E 242 C6
Emine, Nos Bulgaria 42°40N 27°56E 203 D11
Eminence U.S.A. 38°22N 85°11W 311 F11
Eminönü Turkey 41°0N 28°57E 122 B1
Emirau I. Papua N. G. 1°40S 150°0E 286 A6
Emirdağ Turkey 39°2N 31°8E 212 C4
Emirgan Turkey 41°6N 29°2E 122 B2
Emissi, Tarso Chad 21°27N 18°36E 259 D3
Emlenton U.S.A. 41°11N 79°43W 312 E5
Emlichheim Germany 52°37N 6°51E 178 C2
Emmaboda Sweden 56°37N 15°32E 163 H9
Emmalane U.S.A. 32°46N 82°0W 316 C7
Emmarentia S. Africa 26°9S 28°0E 123 A2
Emmastad Neth. Ant. 12°8N 68°55W 322 g
Emmaus S. Africa 29°2S 25°15E 270 C4
Emmaus Pa., U.S.A. 40°32N 75°30W 313 F9
Emme → Switz. 47°14N 7°32E 179 H3
Emmeloord Neths. 52°44N 5°46E 170 B5
Emmen Neths. 52°48N 6°57E 170 B6
Emmen Switz. 47°5N 8°18E 179 H4
Emmendingen Germany 48°6N 7°51E 179 G3
Emmental Switz. 46°55N 7°40E 179 J3
Emmerich Germany 51°50N 6°14E 178 D2
Emmet Australia 24°45S 144°30E 280 C3
Emmetsburg U.S.A. 43°7N 94°41W 310 A2
Emmett Idaho, U.S.A. 43°52N 116°30W 304 E5
Emmett Mich., U.S.A. 42°59N 82°46W 312 D2
Emmiganuru = Yemmiganur India 15°44N 77°29E 245 G3
Emmonak U.S.A. 62°47N 164°31W 303 E6
Emo Canada 48°38N 93°50W 297 D10
Emőd Hungary 47°57N 20°47E 182 C5
Emona Bulgaria 42°43N 27°53E 203 D11
Empalme Mexico 27°58N 110°51W 318 B2
Empangeni S. Africa 28°50S 31°52E 271 C5
Empedrado Argentina 28°0S 58°46W 334 B4
Emperor Seamount Chain Pac. Oc. 40°0N 170°0E 288 D9
Emperor Trough Pac. Oc. 43°0N 175°30E 288 C9
Empingham Res. = Rutland Water U.K. 52°39N 0°38W 169 E7
Empire U.S.A. 32°21N 83°18W 316 C6
Empire State Building New York, U.S.A. 132 c2
Empoli Italy 43°43N 10°57E 198 E7
Emporia Kans., U.S.A. 38°25N 96°11W 308 F5
Emporia Va., U.S.A. 36°42N 77°32W 309 G15
Emporium U.S.A. 41°31N 78°14W 312 E6
Empress Canada 50°57N 110°0W 297 C7
Empty Quarter = Rub' al Khālī Si. Arabia 19°0N 48°0E 249 C5
Ems → Germany 53°20N 7°12E 178 B3
Emsdale Canada 45°32N 79°19W 312 A5
Emsdetten Germany 52°10N 7°32E 178 C3
Emu China 43°40N 128°6E 227 C15
Emu Park Australia 23°13S 150°50E 280 C5
eMuziwezinto S. Africa 30°15S 30°45E 271 D5
'En 'Avrona Israel 29°43N 35°0E 251 J6
'En Boqeq Israel 31°12N 35°21E 251 G6
En Gannim = Ramat Gan Israel 32°4N 34°48E 251 F5
'En Gedi Israel 31°28N 35°25E 251 G6
En Na'am Sudan 10°21N 27°58E 266 B2
En Nahrat Mali 22°55N 3°36W 260 D4
En Nahud Sudan 12°45N 28°25E 257 E2
En Nofalab Sudan 15°52N 32°32E 257 D3
En Nuqra Sudan 10°4N 28°10E 266 B2
Ena Japan 35°25N 137°25E 223 B9
Ena-San Japan 35°26N 137°36E 223 B9
Enambú Colombia 1°1N 70°17W 328 C3
Enana Namibia 17°30S 16°23E 270 A2
Enånger Sweden 61°30N 17°9E 162 C11
Enard B. U.K. 58°5N 5°20W 167 C3
Enare = Inarijärvi Finland 69°0N 28°0E 160 B23
Enarotali Indonesia 3°55S 136°21E 231 E9
Encampment U.S.A. 41°12N 106°47W 304 F10
Encantadas, Serra Brazil 30°40S 53°0W 335 C5
Encantado Brazil 22°53S 43°19W 135 B1
Encarnación Paraguay 27°15S 55°50W 335 B4
Encarnación de Díaz Mexico 21°31N 102°14W 318 C4
Enchi Ghana 5°53N 2°48W 262 D4
Encinitas U.S.A. 33°3N 117°17W 307 M9
Encino Calif., U.S.A. 34°9N 118°28W 126 B2
Encino N. Mex., U.S.A. 34°39N 105°28W 305 J11
Encino Res. U.S.A. 34°8N 118°30W 126 B1
Encontrados Venezuela 9°3N 72°14W 328 B3
Encounter B. Australia 35°45S 138°45E 282 C3
Encruzilhada Brazil 15°31S 40°54W 333 E3
Encs Hungary 48°20N 21°8E 182 B6
Endako Canada 54°6N 125°2W 296 C3
Endau Kenya 1°18S 38°31E 268 C4
Endau Rompin △ Malaysia 2°27N 103°45E 237 L4
Ende Indonesia 8°45S 121°40E 231 F6
Endeavour Str. Australia 10°45S 142°0E 286 F2
Endelave Denmark 55°46N 10°18E 163 J4
Enden Norway 61°47N 10°15E 164 C7
Enderbury I. Kiribati 3°8S 171°5W 277 A16
Enderby Canada 50°35N 119°10W 296 C5
Enderby Abyssal Plain S. Ocean 60°0S 40°0E 151 C5
Enderby I. Australia 20°35S 116°30E 278 D2
Enderby Land Antarctica 66°0S 53°0E 151 C5
Enderlin U.S.A. 46°38N 97°36W 308 B5
Enderrocat, C. Spain 39°28N 2°43E 206 B3
Endicott U.S.A. 42°6N 76°4W 313 D8
Endicott Mts. U.S.A. 68°0N 152°0W 303 C9
Endimari → Brazil 8°46S 66°7W 330 B3
Endwell U.S.A. 42°6N 76°2W 313 D8
Endyalgout I. Australia 11°40S 132°35E 278 B5
Ené → Peru 11°10S 74°18W 330 C3
Eneabba Australia 29°49S 115°16E 279 E2
Enebyberg Sweden 59°25N 17°59E 139 A1
Enewetak Atoll Marshall Is. 11°30N 162°15E 288 F8
Enez Turkey 40°45N 26°5E 203 F10
Enfer, Pte. d' Martinique 14°22N 60°54W 322 j
Enfield N.S.W., Australia 33°53S 151°6E 139 B1
Enfield N.S., Canada 44°56N 63°32W 299 D7
Enfield Conn., U.S.A. 41°58N 72°36W 313 E12
Enfield Ill., U.S.A. 38°6N 88°20W 311 F8
Enfield N.C., U.S.A. 36°11N 77°41W 315 C16
Enfield N.H., U.S.A. 43°39N 72°9W 313 C12
Enga □ Papua N. G. 5°30S 143°20E 286 C2
Engadin Switz. 46°45N 10°10E 179 J6
Engan Norway 63°8N 8°31E 164 A5
Engaño, C. Dom. Rep. 18°30N 68°20W 321 C6
Engaño, C. Phil. 18°35N 122°23E 232 B4
Engaru Japan 44°3N 143°31E 220 B11
Engcobo = Ngcobo S. Africa 31°37S 28°0E 271 D4
Engelberg Switz. 46°48N 8°26E 179 J4
Engels Russia 51°28N 46°6E 190 E8
Engemann L. Canada 58°0N 106°55W 297 B7
Engenho, I. do Brazil 22°50S 43°6W 135 B2
Engerdal Norway 61°45N 11°58E 164 C8
Engershatu Eritrea 16°7N 38°34E 257 D4
Enggano Indonesia 5°20S 102°40E 234 D2
Engineer Group Papua N. G. 10°35S 151°20E 286 F6
Engkilili Malaysia 1°3N 111°42E 235 B4
England U.S.A. 34°33N 91°58W 314 D9
England □ U.K. 53°0N 2°0W 169 E5
Englee Canada 50°45N 56°5W 299 B8
Englehart Canada 47°49N 79°52W 298 C4
Englewood Colo., U.S.A. 39°38N 104°59W 304 G11
Englewood Fla., U.S.A. 26°58N 82°21W 317 J7
Englewood Ill., U.S.A. 41°46N 87°38W 119 C3
Englewood N.J., U.S.A. 40°54N 73°58W 132 A2
Englewood Ohio, U.S.A. 39°53N 84°18W 311 E12
Englewood Cliffs U.S.A. 40°53N 73°59W 132 A2
English U.S.A. 38°20N 86°28W 311 F10
English → Ont., Canada 49°12N 91°5W 297 C10
English → Iowa, U.S.A. 41°29N 91°32W 310 C5
English B. Ascension I. 7°54S 14°23W 153 g
English Bazar = Ingraj Bazar India 24°58N 88°10E 243 G13
English Channel Europe 50°0N 2°0W 169 G6
English Company's Is., The Australia 11°50S 136°32E 280 A2
English Harbour Town Antigua & B. 17°1N 61°46W 322 b
English River Canada 49°14N 91°0W 298 C1
Engures ezers Latvia 57°16N 23°6E 184 A10
Enguri → Georgia 42°27N 41°38E 191 J5
Enid U.S.A. 36°24N 97°53W 314 C6
Enipeas → Greece 39°22N 22°17E 204 B4
Enkhuizen Neths. 52°42N 5°17E 170 B5
Enköping Sweden 59°37N 17°4E 162 E11
Enle China 24°0N 101°9E 228 F3
Enmore Australia 33°54S 151°10E 139 B2
Enna Italy 37°34N 14°16E 201 E7
Ennadai L. Canada 60°58N 101°20W 297 A8
Enné, O. → Chad 14°24N 18°45E 259 F3
Ennedi Chad 17°15N 22°0E 259 E4
Enneri Achelouma → Niger 21°55N 13°35E 261 D7
Enngonia Australia 29°21S 145°50E 281 D4
Ennigerloh Germany 51°50N 8°2E 178 D4
Ennis Clare, Ireland 52°51N 8°59W 166 D3
Ennis Mont., U.S.A. 45°21N 111°44W 304 D8
Ennis Tex., U.S.A. 32°20N 96°38W 314 E6
Enniscorthy Ireland 52°30N 6°34W 166 D5
Enniskillen U.K. 54°21N 7°39W 166 B4
Ennistimon Ireland 52°57N 9°17W 166 D2
Enns Austria 48°12N 14°28E 180 C7
Enns → Austria 48°14N 14°32E 180 C7
Eno Finland 62°47N 30°10E 160 E24
Enontekiö Finland 68°23N 23°37E 160 B20
Enosburg Falls U.S.A. 44°55N 72°48W 313 B12
Enping China 22°16N 112°21E 229 F9
Enrile Phil. 17°34N 121°42E 232 C3
Enriquillo, L. Dom. Rep. 18°20N 72°5W 321 C5
Enschede Neths. 52°13N 6°53E 170 B6
Ensenada Argentina 34°55S 57°55W 334 C4
Ensenada Chile 41°12S 72°33W 336 B2
Ensenada Baja Calif., Mexico 31°52N 116°37W 318 A1
Ensenada de los Muertos Mexico 23°59N 109°51W 318 C2
Enshi China 30°18N 109°29E 228 B7
Enshū-Nada Japan 34°27N 137°38E 223 C9
Ensiola, Pta. de n' Spain 39°7N 2°55E 206 B3
Ensisheim France 47°50N 7°20E 173 E14
Enskede Sweden 59°17N 18°4E 139 B2
Ensley U.S.A. 30°31N 87°16W 317 E2
Entebbe Uganda 0°4N 32°28E 268 B3
Enterprise N.W.T., Canada 60°47N 115°45W 296 A5
Enterprise Ala., U.S.A. 31°19N 85°51W 316 D4
Enterprise Nev., U.S.A. 36°13N 115°14W 124 B1
Enterprise Oreg., U.S.A. 45°25N 117°17W 304 D5
Entorno de Doñana ⌂ Spain 37°0N 6°26W 195 J4
Entrance, The Australia 33°21S 151°30E 283 B9
Entraygues-sur-Truyère France 44°38N 2°35E 174 D6
Entre-Deux Réunion 21°14S 55°28E 272 f
Entre Rios = Rio Brilhante Brazil 21°48S 54°33W 335 A5
Entre Rios = Três Rios Brazil 22°6S 43°15W 333 F3
Entre Ríos Bolivia 21°30S 64°25W 334 A3
Entre Rios Bahia, Brazil 11°56S 38°5W 333 D4
Entre Rios Pará, Brazil 5°24S 54°21W 331 B7
Entre Ríos □ Argentina 30°30S 58°30W 334 C4
Entrepeñas, Embalse de Spain 40°34N 2°42W 196 E2
Entrevias Spain 40°22N 3°40W 127 B1
Entroncamento Portugal 39°28N 8°28W 195 F2
Enugu Nigeria 6°30N 7°30E 263 D6
Enugu □ Nigeria 6°30N 7°45E 263 D6
Enugu Ezike Nigeria 7°0N 7°29E 263 D6
Enumclaw U.S.A. 47°12N 121°59W 306 C5
Envalira, Port d' Europe 42°33N 1°43E 196 C6
Envermeu France 49°53N 1°15E 172 C8
Envigado Colombia 6°10N 75°35W 328 B2
Enviken Sweden 60°49N 15°46E 162 D9
Envira Brazil 7°18S 70°13W 330 B3
Envira → Brazil 7°19S 70°15W 330 B3
Enying Hungary 46°56N 18°15E 182 D3
Enyonga Gabon 0°59S 9°22E 264 C1
Enza → Italy 44°54N 10°31E 198 D7
Enzan Japan 35°42N 138°44E 223 B10
Eochail = Youghal Ireland 51°56N 7°52W 166 E4
Eólie, Ís. Italy 38°30N 14°57E 201 D7
Eot I. Micronesia 7°23N 151°44E 287 T17
Epanomi Greece 40°25N 22°59E 202 F6
Epcot U.S.A. 28°21N 81°32W 133 B1
Epe Neths. 52°21N 5°59E 170 B5
Epe Nigeria 6°36N 3°59E 263 D5
Epéna Congo 1°22N 17°29E 264 B3
Épernay France 49°3N 3°56E 173 C10
Épernon France 48°35N 1°40E 173 D8
Ephesus Turkey 37°55N 27°22E 205 D9
Ephraim U.S.A. 39°22N 111°35W 304 G8
Ephrata Pa., U.S.A. 40°11N 76°11W 313 F8
Ephrata Wash., U.S.A. 47°19N 119°33W 304 C4
Epi Vanuatu 16°43S 168°15E 287 F6
Epidavros Limira Greece 36°46N 23°0E 204 E5
Épila Spain 41°36N 1°17W 196 D3
Épinac France 46°59N 4°31E 173 F11
Épinal France 48°10N 6°27E 173 D13
Epira Guyana 5°5N 57°20W 329 B6
Epiros □ Greece 39°30N 20°30E 204 B2
Episkopi Cyprus 34°40N 32°54E 207 F8
Episkopi Kriti, Greece 35°20N 24°20E 207 E5
Episkopi Bay Cyprus 34°35N 32°50E 207 F8
Epitalio Greece 37°37N 21°30E 204 D3
Eppalock, L. Australia 36°52S 144°34E 282 D6
Eppan = Appiano Italy 46°28N 11°15E 199 B8
Epping Australia 33°46S 151°5E 139 A1
Eppingen Germany 49°8N 8°53E 179 F4
Epsom U.K. 51°19N 0°16W 169 F7
Epukiro Namibia 21°40S 19°9E 270 B2
Equality U.S.A. 37°44N 88°20W 311 G8
Équateur □ Dem. Rep. of the Congo 2°0N 21°0E 264 B4
Equatorial Channel Maldives 0°0 73°10E 272 d
Equatorial Guinea ■ Africa 2°0N 8°0E 264 B1
Equeipa Venezuela 5°22N 62°43W 329 B5
Er Hai China 25°48N 100°11E 228 E3
Er Rachidia Morocco 31°58N 4°20W 260 B4
Er Rachidia □ Morocco 31°45N 4°30W 260 B4
Er Rahad Sudan 12°45N 30°32E 257 E3
Er Rif Morocco 35°1N 4°1W 261 A4
Er Rogel Sudan 18°10N 35°25E 256 D4
Er Roseires Sudan 11°55N 34°30E 257 E3
Er Rua'at Sudan 12°21N 32°17E 257 E3
Eraclea Italy 45°35N 12°40E 199 C9
Eran Phil. 9°4N 117°42E 233 G1
Erandol India 20°56N 75°20E 244 D2
Eranga Dem. Rep. of the Congo 1°52S 18°56E 264 C3
Erap Papua N. G. 6°37S 146°51E 286 D4
Erasmus = Bronkhorstspruit S. Africa 25°46S 28°45E 271 C4
Erave Papua N. G. 6°39S 144°0E 286 D2
Erave → Papua N. G. 6°54S 144°47E 286 D3
Erāwadī Myit = Irrawaddy → Burma 15°50N 95°6E 241 G5
Erāwadī Myitwanya = Irrawaddy, Mouths of the Burma 15°30N 95°0E 241 H5
Erawan △ Thailand 14°25N 98°58E 236 E2
Erba Italy 45°48N 9°15E 198 C6
Erba Sudan 19°5N 36°51E 256 D4
Erba, J. Sudan 20°48N 36°47E 256 C4
Erbaa Turkey 40°42N 36°36E 212 B7
Erbeng Shan China 42°50N 84°0E 217 D10
Erbeskopf Germany 49°44N 7°2E 179 F3
Erbil = Arbīl Iraq 36°15N 44°5E 213 D11
Erbu Ethiopia 6°44N 34°53E 257 E3
Ercan, Nicosia ✈ (ECN) Cyprus 35°10N 33°30E 207 E9
Erçek Turkey 38°39N 43°36E 246 B4
Erçiş Turkey 39°2N 43°21E 213 C10
Erciyaş Dağı Turkey 38°30N 35°30E 246 B2
Érd Hungary 47°22N 18°56E 182 C3
Erdao Jiang → China 42°37N 128°0E 224 A3
Erdek Turkey 40°23N 27°47E 203 F11
Erdély = Transilvania Romania 46°30N 24°0E 183 D9
Erdemli Turkey 36°36N 34°19E 250 B5
Erdene = Ulaan-Uul Mongolia 44°13N 111°10E 226 B6
Erdenet Mongolia 49°2N 104°5E 218 B5
Erdenetsogt Mongolia 42°55N 106°5E 226 C4
Erding Germany 48°18N 11°54E 179 G7
Erdre → France 47°13N 1°32W 172 E5
Erebato → Venezuela 5°54N 64°16W 329 B5
Erebus, Mt. Antarctica 77°35S 167°0E 151 D11
Erechim Brazil 27°35S 52°15W 335 B5
Ereğli Konya, Turkey 37°31N 34°4E 212 D6
Ereğli Zonguldak, Turkey 41°15N 31°24E 212 B4
Erei, Monti Italy 37°20N 14°20E 201 E7
Erenhot China 43°48N 112°2E 226 C7
Erenköy = Kokkina Cyprus 35°11N 32°36E 207 E8
Erenköy Turkey 40°58N 29°3E 122 C2
Eresfjord Norway 62°40N 8°8E 164 B5
Eresma → Spain 41°26N 4°45W 194 D6
Eresos Greece 39°11N 25°57E 205 B7
Ereymentaū Kazakhstan 51°37N 73°6E 217 B8
Erfelek Turkey 41°53N 34°55E 212 B6
Erfenisdam S. Africa 28°30S 26°50E 270 C4
Erfjord Norway 59°20N 6°14E 164 E3
Erfoud Morocco 31°30N 4°15W 260 B4
Erfstadt Germany 50°50N 6°50E 178 E2
Erft → Germany 51°11N 6°44E 178 D2
Erfurt Germany 50°58N 11°2E 178 E7
Ergani Turkey 38°17N 39°49E 213 C8
Ergel Mongolia 43°8N 109°5E 226 C5
Ergene → Turkey 41°1N 26°22E 203 E10
Ergeni Vozvyshennost Russia 47°0N 44°0E 191 G7
Ērgli Latvia 56°54N 25°38E 188 D3
Erhlin Taiwan 23°54N 120°22E 225 C2
Erhshui Taiwan 23°45N 120°37E 225 C2
Eria → Spain 42°3N 5°44W 194 C5
Eriba Sudan 16°40N 36°10E 257 D4
Eriboll, L. U.K. 58°30N 4°42W 167 C4
Érice Italy 38°2N 12°35E 200 D5
Eridu U.S.A. 30°18N 83°45W 316 E6
Erie Mich., U.S.A. 41°47N 83°31W 311 C13
Erie Pa., U.S.A. 42°8N 80°5W 312 D4
Erie, L. N. Amer. 42°15N 81°0W 312 D4
Erie Canal U.S.A. 43°5N 78°43W 312 C7
Erieau Canada 42°16N 81°57W 312 D3
Erigavo = Ceerigaabo Somali Rep. 10°35N 47°20E 267 B6
Erikoussa Greece 39°53N 19°34E 206 B9
Eriksdale Canada 50°52N 98°7W 297 C9
Erimanthos Greece 37°57N 21°50E 204 D3
Erimo-misaki Japan 41°50N 143°15E 220 D11
Erin Ont., Canada 43°45N 80°7W 312 C4
Erin Trin. & Tob. 10°5N 61°39W 323 t
Erin B. Trin. & Tob. 10°4N 61°43W 323 t
Erin Pt. Trin. & Tob. 10°3N 61°39W 323 t
Erinpura India 25°9N 73°3E 242 G5
Eriskay U.K. 57°4N 7°18W 167 D1
Erith U.K. 51°28N 0°11E 125 B5
Erithres Greece 38°13N 23°20E 204 C5
Eritrea ■ Africa 14°0N 38°30E 257 E4
Erivan = Yerevan Armenia 40°10N 44°31E 191 K7
Erjas → Portugal 39°40N 7°1W 194 F3
Erkech-Tam Pass Asia 39°46N 74°2E 217 E8
Erkelenz Germany 51°4N 6°19E 178 D2
Erkner Germany 52°25N 13°44E 178 C9
Erlaa Austria 48°9N 16°19E 142 B1
Erlangen Germany 49°36N 11°0E 179 F6
Erlanger U.S.A. 39°1N 84°36W 311 E12
Erldunda Australia 25°14S 133°12E 280 D1
Ermelo Neths. 52°18N 5°35E 170 B5
Ermelo Mpumalanga, S. Africa 26°31S 29°59E 271 C4
Ermenek Turkey 36°38N 33°0E 250 B4
Ermenek → Turkey 36°35N 33°23E 250 B4
Ermil Sudan 13°35N 27°40E 257 E2
Ermington Australia 33°48S 151°4E 139 A1
Ermioni Greece 37°23N 23°15E 204 D5
Ermita Phil. 14°35N 120°59E 127 B1
Ermones Greece 39°37N 19°46E 206 B9
Ermoupoli Greece 37°28N 24°57E 204 D6
Ernakulam India 9°59N 76°22E 245 K3
Erne → Ireland 54°30N 8°16W 166 B3
Erne, Lower L. U.K. 54°28N 7°47W 166 B4
Erne, Upper L. U.K. 54°14N 7°32W 166 B4
Ernée France 48°18N 0°56W 172 D6
Ernest Giles Ra. Australia 27°0S 123°45E 279 E3
Ernest N. Morial Convention Center New Orleans, U.S.A. 131 c3
Ernstberg Germany 50°13N 6°47E 179 E2
Erode India 11°24N 77°45E 245 J3
Eromanga Australia 26°40S 143°11E 281 D3
Erongo Namibia 21°39S 15°58E 270 B2
Erquy France 48°38N 2°29W 172 D4
Erramala Hills India 15°30N 78°15E 245 G4
Errentería Spain 43°19N 1°54W 196 B3
Errer → Ethiopia 7°32N 42°35E 257 F5
Erri-Nundra △ Australia 37°28S 148°5E 281 F4
Errigal Ireland 55°2N 8°6W 166 A3
Errinundra △ Australia 37°20S 148°47E 283 D8
Erris Hd. Ireland 54°19N 10°0W 166 B1
Erromango Vanuatu 18°45S 169°5E 287 H7
Ersekë Albania 40°22N 20°40E 202 F4
Ersekújvár = Nové Zámky Slovak Rep. 48°2N 18°8E 181 C11
Ershatou China 23°6N 113°18E 121 B2
Erskine U.S.A. 47°40N 96°0W 308 B6
Erskineville Australia 33°54S 151°12E 139 B2
Erstein France 48°25N 7°38E 173 D14
Ertai China 46°3N 90°5E 217 C12
Ertholmene Denmark 55°19N 15°11E 163 J9
Ertil Russia 51°55N 40°50E 190 E5
Ertis = Irtysh → Russia 61°4N 68°52E 214 C7
Ertis Kazakhstan 53°20N 75°27E 217 B9
Ertis → Kazakhstan 47°52N 84°16E 217 C10
Ertvågøy Norway 63°13N 8°26E 164 A5
Eruh Turkey 37°46N 42°13E 213 D10
Erunkan Nigeria 6°36N 3°23E 124 A2
Eruwa Nigeria 7°33N 3°26E 263 D5
Ervy-le-Châtel France 48°2N 3°55E 173 D10
Erwin U.S.A. 36°9N 82°25W 315 C13
Eryuan China 26°7N 99°57E 228 D2
Erzgebirge Germany 50°27N 12°55E 178 E8
Erzin Russia 50°15N 95°10E 217 B13
Erzin Turkey 36°57N 36°11E 250 B7
Erzincan Turkey 39°46N 39°30E 213 C8
Erzincan □ Turkey 39°45N 39°30E 213 C8
Erzsébet-Telep Hungary 47°27N 19°10E 117 B3
Erzurum Turkey 39°57N 41°15E 213 C9
Erzurum □ Turkey 39°55N 41°15E 213 C9
Es Caló Spain 38°40N 1°30E 206 D2
Es Canar Spain 39°2N 1°36E 206 C2
Es Mercadal Spain 39°59N 4°5E 206 B5
Es Migjorn Gran Spain 39°57N 4°3E 206 B5
Es Safiya Sudan 15°31N 30°7E 257 D3
Es Sahrâ al Beida Egypt 27°50N 28°45E 256 B2
Es Sahrâ' Esh Sharqîya Egypt 27°30N 32°30E 256 B3
Es Sînâ' Egypt 29°0N 34°0E 246 D2
Es Sûkî Sudan 13°20N 33°58E 257 E3
Es Vedrà Spain 38°52N 1°12E 206 D1
Esa'ala Papua N. G. 9°45S 150°49E 286 E6
Esambo Dem. Rep. of the Congo 3°48S 23°30E 264 C4
Esan-Misaki Japan 41°40N 141°10E 220 D10
Esashi Hokkaidō, Japan 44°56N 142°35E 220 B11
Esashi Hokkaidō, Japan 41°52N 140°7E 220 D10
Esbjerg Denmark 55°29N 8°29E 163 J2
Esbo = Espoo Finland 60°12N 24°40E 188 B3
Escada Brazil 8°22S 35°8W 332 C4
Escalante U.S.A. 37°47N 111°36W 305 H8
Escalante → U.S.A. 37°24N 110°57W 305 H8
Escalente Phil. 10°50N 123°33E 233 F4
Escalón Mexico 26°45N 104°20W 318 B4
Escambia → U.S.A. 30°32N 87°11W 317 E2
Escanaba U.S.A. 45°45N 87°4W 308 C10
Escarparda Pt. Phil. 18°31N 122°13E 232 B4
Escarpé, C. N. Cal. 20°41S 167°13E 288 d
Escaut = Schelde → Belgium 51°15N 4°16E 170 C4
Esch-sur-Alzette Lux. 49°32N 6°0E 170 E6
Eschede Germany 52°44N 10°14E 178 C6
Eschenried Germany 48°13N 11°24E 131 A1
Eschwege Germany 51°11N 10°2E 178 D6
Eschweiler Germany 50°49N 6°15E 178 E2
Escobal Panama 9°6N 80°1W 320 c
Escoma Bolivia 15°40S 69°8W 330 D4
Escondido U.S.A. 33°7N 117°5W 307 M9
Escravos → Nigeria 5°35N 5°10E 263 D6
Escuinapa de Hidalgo Mexico 22°50N 105°50W 318 C3
Escuintla Guatemala 14°20N 90°48W 320 D1
Eséka Cameroon 3°41N 10°44E 263 E7
Eşen → Turkey 36°27N 29°16E 205 E11
Esenguly Turkmenistan 37°37N 53°59E 216 E4
Esenler Turkey 41°1N 28°52E 122 B1
Esens Germany 53°38N 7°36E 178 B3
Esenyurt Turkey 41°3N 28°48E 203 E12
Esera → Spain 42°6N 0°15E 196 C5
Eşfahān Iran 32°39N 51°43E 247 C6
Eşfahān □ Iran 32°50N 51°50E 247 C6
Esfarāyen Iran 37°4N 57°30E 247 B8
Esfideh Iran 33°39N 59°46E 247 C8
Esgueva → Spain 41°40N 4°43W 194 D6
Esh Sham = Dimashq Syria 33°30N 36°18E 250 E7
Esh Shamâlîya □ Sudan 19°0N 29°0E 256 D2
Esha Ness U.K. 60°29N 1°38W 167 A7
Eshan China 24°11N 102°24E 228 E4
Esher U.K. 51°21N 0°20W 125 B1
Eshkāshem = Ishkashim Tajikistan 36°44N 71°37E 217 E8
Eshkol △ Israel 31°20N 34°30E 251 G5
Eshowe S. Africa 28°50S 31°30E 271 C5
Esiama Ghana 4°56N 2°25W 262 E4

INDEX Fayette 369

Esigodini Zimbabwe 20°18S 28°56E 271 B4
Esil = Ishim → Russia 57°45N 71°10E 214 D8
Esil Kazakhstan 51°57N 66°24E 217 B7
Esino → Italy 43°39N 13°22E 199 E10
Esira Madag. 24°20S 46°42E 272 C2
Esk → Dumf. & Gall., U.K. 54°58N 3°2W 167 G5
Esk → N. Yorks., U.K. 54°30N 0°37W 168 C7
Eskān Iran 26°48N 63°9E 240 D1
Eskbank U.K. 55°52N 3°4W 121 B3
Esker Siding Canada 53°53N 66°25W 299 B6
Eskifjörður Iceland 65°3N 13°55W 155 B13
Eskije = Xanthi Greece 41°10N 24°58E 203 E8
Eskilsäter Sweden 58°57N 13°10E 163 F7
Eskilstuna Sweden 59°22N 16°32E 162 E10
Eskimalatya Turkey 38°24N 38°22E 213 C8
Eskimo Point = Arviat Canada 61°6N 93°59W 297 A10
Eskişehir Turkey 39°50N 30°30E 205 B12
Eskişehir □ Turkey 39°40N 31°0E 205 B12
Esla → Spain 41°29N 6°3W 194 D4
Eslāmābād-e Gharb Iran 34°10N 46°30E 213 E12
Eslāmshahr Iran 35°40N 51°10E 247 C6
Eslöv Sweden 55°50N 13°20E 163 J7
Eşme Turkey 38°23N 28°58E 205 C10
Esmeralda, I. Chile 48°55S 75°25W 336 C1
Esmeraldas Ecuador 1°0N 79°40W 328 C2
Esmeraldas □ Ecuador 0°40N 79°30W 328 C2
Esmeraldas → Ecuador 0°58N 79°38W 328 C2
Esna = Isna Egypt 25°17N 32°30E 256 B3
Esnagi L. Canada 48°36N 84°33W 298 C3
Esom Hill U.S.A. 33°57N 85°23W 316 B4
Espa Norway 60°34N 11°16E 164 D8
Espada, Pta. Colombia 12°5N 71°7W 328 A3
Espalion France 44°32N 2°47E 174 D6
España = Spain ■ Europe 39°0N 4°0W 192 D3
Espanola Ont., Canada 46°15N 81°46W 298 C3
Espanola N. Mex., U.S.A. 35°59N 106°5W 305 J10
Española, I. Ecuador 1°23S 89°39W 330 a
Espanya, Plaça d' Barcelona, Spain 114 c1
Esparreguera Spain 41°33N 1°52E 196 D6
Esparza Costa Rica 9°59N 84°40W 320 E3
Espeland Norway 60°23N 5°28E 164 D2
Espelkamp Germany 52°24N 8°36E 178 C4
Espenberg, C. U.S.A. 66°33N 163°36W 303 C7
Esperança Amazonas, Brazil 4°24S 69°52W 328 D4
Esperança Paraíba, Brazil 7°1S 35°51W 332 C4
Esperance Australia 33°45S 121°55E 279 F3
Esperance, C. Solomon Is. 9°15S 159°43E 287 M10
Esperance B. Australia 33°48S 121°55E 279 F3
Esperantinópolis Brazil 4°53S 44°53W 332 B3
Esperanza Antarctica 65°0S 55°0W 151 C18
Esperanza Santa Cruz, Argentina 51°1S 70°49W 336 D2
Esperanza Santa Fe, Argentina 31°29S 61°3W 334 C3
Esperanza Mexico City, Mexico 128 c3
Esperanza Agusan del S., Phil. 8°43N 125°36E 233 G5
Esperanza Masbate, Phil. 11°45N 124°3E 233 F5
Esperanza Puerto Rico 18°6N 65°28W 321 b
Espéraza France 42°56N 2°14E 174 F6
Espevær Norway 59°35N 5°7E 164 E2
Espichel, C. Portugal 38°22N 9°16W 195 G1
Espiel Spain 38°11N 5°1W 195 G5
Espigão, Serra do Brazil 26°35S 50°30W 335 B5
Espinal Colombia 4°9N 74°53W 328 C3
Espinar Peru 14°51S 71°24W 330 C3
Espinazo, Sierra del = Espinhaço, Serra do Brazil 17°30S 43°30W 333 E3
Espinhaço, Serra do Brazil 17°30S 43°30W 333 E3
Espinho Portugal 41°1N 8°38W 194 D2
Espinilho, Serra do Brazil 28°30S 55°0W 335 B5
Espinosa de los Monteros Spain 43°5N 3°34W 194 B7
Espírito Santo □ Brazil 20°0S 40°45W 333 F3
Espírito Santo do Pinhal Brazil 22°10S 46°46W 335 A6
Espíritu Santo Vanuatu 15°15S 166°50E 287 E4
Espíritu Santo, B. del Mexico 19°20N 87°35W 319 D7
Espíritu Santo, I. Mexico 24°30N 110°22W 318 C2
Espita Mexico 21°1N 88°19W 319 C7
Espiye Turkey 40°56N 38°43E 213 B8
Esplanada Brazil 11°47S 37°57W 333 D4
Esplugas Spain 41°22N 2°5E 114 A1
Espoo Finland 60°12N 24°40E 188 B3
Esposizione Universale di Roma Italy 41°49N 12°28E 136 C1
Espuña, Sierra de Spain 37°51N 1°35W 197 H3
Espungabera Mozam. 20°29S 32°45E 271 B5
Esquel Argentina 42°55S 71°20W 336 B2
Esquimalt Canada 48°26N 123°25W 306 B3
Esquina Argentina 30°0S 59°30W 334 C4
Essandsjøen Norway 63°0N 12°0E 164 A8
Essaouira Morocco 31°32N 9°42W 260 B3
Essaouira □ Morocco 31°25N 9°30W 260 B3
Essebie Dem. Rep. of the Congo 2°58N 30°40E 268 B3
Essen Belgium 51°28N 4°28E 170 C4
Essen Nordrhein-Westfalen, Germany 51°28N 7°2E 178 D3
Essendon Australia 37°44S 144°55E 128 A1
Essendon ✕ (MEB) Australia 37°43S 144°54E 128 A1
Essendon, Mt. Australia 25°0S 120°29E 279 E3
Essequibo → Guyana 6°50N 58°30W 329 B6
Essex Ont., Canada 42°10N 82°49W 312 D2
Essex Calif., U.S.A. 34°44N 115°15W 307 L11
Essex N.Y., U.S.A. 44°19N 73°21W 313 B11
Essex □ U.K. 51°54N 0°27E 169 F8
Essex Junction U.S.A. 44°29N 73°7W 313 B11
Essingen Sweden 59°19N 17°59E 139 B1
Essling Austria 48°12N 16°30E 142 A3
Esslingen Germany 48°44N 9°18E 179 G5
Essonne □ France 48°30N 2°20E 173 D9
Est, Gare de l' Paris, France 134 a5
Estaca de Bares, C. de Spain 43°46N 7°42W 194 B3
Estación Camacho Mexico 24°25N 102°18W 318 C4
Estación Simón Mexico 24°42N 102°35W 318 C4
Estadilla Spain 42°4N 0°16E 196 C5
Estado, Parque do Brazil 23°38S 46°38W 137 B2
Estados, I. de Los Argentina 54°40S 64°30W 336 D4
Estagel France 42°47N 2°40E 174 F6
Eşţahbānāt Iran 29°8N 54°4E 247 D7
Estância Brazil 11°16S 37°26W 332 D4
Estancia N. Mex., U.S.A. 34°46N 106°4W 305 J10
Estancia Monte León Argentina 50°14S 68°55W 336 D3
Estārm Iran 28°21N 58°21E 247 D8
Estarreja Portugal 40°45N 8°35W 194 E2
Estats, Pic d' Spain 42°40N 1°24E 196 C6
Estcourt S. Africa 29°0S 29°53E 271 C4
Este Italy 45°14N 11°39E 199 C8
Este △ Dom. Rep. 18°14N 68°42W 321 C6
Estefânia Lisbon, Portugal 126 a2
Estelí Nic. 13°9N 86°22W 320 D2
Estella Spain 42°40N 2°2W 196 C2
Estelle U.S.A. 29°50N 90°6W 131 B2
Estellencs Spain 39°39N 2°29E 206 B3
Estena → Spain 39°23N 4°44W 195 F6
Estepa Spain 37°17N 4°52W 195 H6
Estepona Spain 36°24N 5°7W 195 J5
Esterhazy Canada 50°37N 102°5W 297 C8
Esterias, C. Gabon 0°40N 9°20E 264 B1
Esternay France 48°44N 3°33E 173 D10
Esterri d'Aneu Spain 42°38N 1°5E 196 C6
Estevan Canada 49°10N 102°59W 297 D8
Estevan Group Canada 53°3N 129°38W 296 C3
Estherville U.S.A. 43°24N 94°50W 308 D6
Estill U.S.A. 32°45N 81°15W 316 C8
Estissac France 48°16N 3°48E 173 D10
Eston Canada 51°8N 108°40W 297 C7
Estonia ■ Europe 58°30N 25°30E 188 C3
Estoril Portugal 38°42N 9°23W 195 G1
Estouk Mali 18°14N 1°2E 263 B5
Estrela, Basilica da Portugal 38°42N 9°9W 126 A2
Estrela, Serra da Portugal 40°10N 7°45W 194 E3
Estrella Spain 38°25N 3°35W 195 G7
Estremoz Portugal 38°51N 7°39W 195 G3
Estrondo, Serra do Brazil 7°20S 48°0W 332 C2
Esutoru = Uglegorsk Russia 49°5N 142°2E 215 E15
Esztergom Hungary 47°47N 18°44E 182 C3
Et Tîdra Mauritania 19°45N 16°20W 262 B1
Etah India 27°35N 78°40E 243 F8
Étain France 49°13N 5°38E 173 C12
Étampes France 48°26N 2°10E 173 D9
Étang-Salé-les-Bains Réunion 21°15S 55°20E 272 f
Etanga Namibia 17°55S 13°0E 270 A1
Étaples France 50°30N 1°39E 173 B8
Etawah India 26°48N 79°6E 243 F8
Etawney L. Canada 57°50N 96°50W 297 B9
Etchojoa Mexico 26°55N 109°38W 318 B3
Ete Nigeria 7°2N 7°28E 263 D6
Etéké Gabon 1°29S 11°35E 264 C2
eThekwini = Durban S. Africa 29°49S 31°1E 271 C5
Ethel U.S.A. 46°32N 122°46W 306 D4
Ethelbert Canada 51°32N 100°25W 297 C8
Ethiopia ■ Africa 8°0N 40°0E 267 C4
Ethiopian Highlands Ethiopia 10°0N 37°0E 254 E7
Etili Turkey 39°59N 26°54E 203 G10
Etive, L. U.K. 56°29N 5°10W 167 E3
Etna Italy 37°50N 14°55E 201 E7
Etna → Norway 60°49N 10°7E 164 C6
Etne Norway 59°40N 5°58E 164 E2
Etobicoke Canada 43°39N 79°34W 141 B1
Etobicoke Cr. → Canada 43°35N 79°32W 141 B1
Etoile Dem. Rep. of the Congo 11°33S 27°30E 269 E2
Etoliko Greece 38°26N 21°21E 204 C3
Etolin Strait U.S.A. 60°20N 165°15W 303 F6
Etoloakarnania □ Greece 38°45N 21°18E 204 C3
Etosha △ Namibia 19°0S 16°0E 270 A2
Etosha Pan Namibia 18°40S 16°30E 270 A2
Etoumbi Congo 0°1S 14°57E 264 C2
Etowah U.S.A. 35°20N 84°32W 315 D12
Étréchy France 48°30N 2°12E 173 D9
Etrek Turkmenistan 37°36N 54°46E 247 B7
Étrépagny France 49°18N 1°36E 173 C8
Étretat France 49°42N 0°12E 172 C7
Etropole Bulgaria 42°50N 24°0E 203 D8
Ettelbruck Lux. 49°51N 6°5E 170 E6
Etterbeek Belgium 50°50N 4°23E 116 B2
Ettlingen Germany 48°56N 8°25E 179 G4
Ettrick Water → U.K. 55°31N 2°55W 167 F6
Etuku Dem. Rep. of the Congo 3°42S 25°45E 264 C5
Etulia Moldova 45°32N 28°27E 183 E13
Etzná-Tixmucuy = Edzná Mexico 19°39N 90°19W 319 D6
Eu France 50°3N 1°26E 172 B8
Eua Tonga 21°22S 174°56W 287 Q13
Euboea = Evia Greece 38°30N 24°0E 204 C6
Eucaliptus = Tomás Barrón Bolivia 17°35S 67°31W 330 D4
Euchareena Australia 32°57S 149°6E 283 B8
Eucla Australia 31°41S 128°52E 279 F4
Euclid U.S.A. 41°34N 81°32W 312 E3
Euclides da Cunha Brazil 10°31S 39°1W 332 D4
Eucumbene, L. Australia 36°2S 148°40E 283 D8
Eudora U.S.A. 33°7N 91°16W 314 E9
Eudunda Australia 34°12S 139°7E 282 C3
Eufaula Ala., U.S.A. 31°54N 85°9W 316 D4
Eufaula Okla., U.S.A. 35°17N 95°35W 314 D7
Eufaula L. U.S.A. 35°18N 95°21W 314 D7
Eugene U.S.A. 44°5N 123°4W 304 D2
Eugowra Australia 33°22S 148°24E 283 B8
Eulo Australia 28°10S 145°3E 281 D4
Eulonia U.S.A. 31°32N 81°26W 316 D8
Eumungerie Australia 31°56S 148°36E 283 A8
Eung-am S. Korea 37°34N 126°55E 137 B1
Eungella △ Australia 20°57S 148°40E 280 b
Eunice La., U.S.A. 30°30N 92°25W 314 F8
Eunice N. Mex., U.S.A. 32°26N 103°10W 305 K12
Eunpyeong S. Korea 37°36N 126°56E 137 B1
Eupen Belgium 50°37N 6°3E 170 D6
Euphrates = Furāt, Nahr al → Asia 31°0N 47°25E 246 D5
Eure □ France 49°10N 1°0E 172 C8
Eure → France 49°18N 1°12E 172 C8
Eure-et-Loir □ France 48°22N 1°30E 172 D8
Eureka Nunavut, Canada 80°0N 85°56W 295 B14
Eureka Calif., U.S.A. 40°47N 124°9W 304 F1
Eureka Ill., U.S.A. 40°43N 89°16W 310 D7
Eureka Kans., U.S.A. 37°49N 96°17W 308 G5
Eureka Mo., U.S.A. 38°30N 90°38W 310 F6
Eureka Mont., U.S.A. 48°53N 115°3W 304 B6
Eureka Nev., U.S.A. 39°31N 115°58W 304 G6
Eureka S.C., U.S.A. 33°42N 81°46W 316 B8
Eureka S. Dak., U.S.A. 45°46N 99°38W 308 C4
Eureka, Mt. Australia 26°35S 121°35E 279 E3
Eureka Sd. Canada 79°0N 85°0W 295 B15
Eurelia Australia 32°33S 138°35E 282 B3
Eurinilla Cr. → Australia 30°53S 140°11E 282 A4
Euroa Australia 36°44S 145°35E 283 D6
Europa, Île Ind. Oc. 22°20S 40°22E 271 B7
Europa, Picos de Spain 43°10N 4°49W 194 B6
Europa, Pt. Gib. 36°3N 5°21W 195 J5
Europe 50°0N 20°0E 158 E10
Europoort Neths. 51°57N 4°10E 170 C4
Euskirchen Germany 50°39N 6°48E 178 E2
Eustis U.S.A. 28°51N 81°41W 317 G8
Euston N.S.W., Australia 34°30S 142°46E 282 C5
Euston London, U.K. 125 a3
Eutawville U.S.A. 33°24N 80°21W 316 B9
Eutin Germany 54°8N 10°36E 178 A6
Eutsuk L. Canada 53°20N 126°45W 296 C3
Eva Perón = La Pampa □ Argentina 36°50S 66°0W 334 D2
Eva Perón = La Plata Argentina 35°0S 57°55W 334 C4
Evale Angola 16°33S 15°44E 265 F3
Evanger Norway 60°39N 6°7E 164 D3
Evanlı Turkey 36°46N 34°26E 250 B5
Evans U.S.A. 40°23N 104°41W 304 F11
Evans, L. Canada 50°50N 77°0W 298 B4
Evans City U.S.A. 40°46N 80°4W 312 F4
Evans Head Australia 29°7S 153°27E 281 D5
Evansburg Canada 53°36N 114°59W 296 C5
Evansdale U.S.A. 42°30N 92°17W 310 B4
Evanston Ill., U.S.A. 42°3N 87°40W 119 A2
Evanston Wyo., U.S.A. 41°16N 110°58W 304 F8
Evansville Ill., U.S.A. 38°5N 89°56W 310 F7
Evansville Ind., U.S.A. 37°58N 87°35W 311 G9
Evansville Wis., U.S.A. 42°47N 89°18W 310 B7
Évaux-les-Bains France 46°12N 2°29E 173 F9
Evaz Iran 27°46N 53°59E 247 E7
Evciler Afyon, Turkey 38°4N 29°54E 205 C11
Evciler Çanakkale, Turkey 39°47N 26°44E 205 B8
Eveleth U.S.A. 47°28N 92°32W 308 B7
Even Sapir Israel 31°46N 35°8E 123 B1
Evensk Russia 62°12N 159°30E 215 C16
Evenstad Norway 61°25N 11°7E 164 C8
Everard, L. Australia 31°30S 135°0E 281 E2
Everard Ranges Australia 27°5S 132°28E 279 E5
Evere Belgium 50°52N 4°25E 116 A2
Everest, Mt. Nepal 28°5N 86°58E 243 E12
Everett Ga., U.S.A. 31°24N 81°38W 316 D8
Everett Mass., U.S.A. 42°24N 71°3W 116 A2
Everett Pa., U.S.A. 40°1N 78°23W 312 F6
Everett Wash., U.S.A. 47°59N 122°12W 306 C4
Everglades, The U.S.A. 25°50N 81°0W 317 K9
Everglades △ U.S.A. 25°30N 81°0W 317 K9
Everglades City U.S.A. 25°52N 81°23W 317 K8
Evergreen Ala., U.S.A. 31°26N 86°57W 315 F11
Evergreen Mont., U.S.A. 48°14N 114°17W 304 B6
Evergreen Park U.S.A. 41°43N 87°42W 119 C2
Everöd Sweden 55°53N 14°5E 163 J8
Everton Australia 36°25S 146°33E 283 D7
Evertsberg Sweden 61°8N 13°58E 162 C7
Evesham U.K. 52°6N 1°56W 169 E6
Evia Greece 38°30N 24°0E 204 C6
Evia □ Greece 38°40N 23°40E 204 C5
Évian-les-Bains France 46°24N 6°35E 173 F13
Evīn Iran 35°47N 51°23E 141 A2
Evinayong Eq. Guin. 1°26N 10°35E 264 B2
Evinos → Greece 38°27N 21°40E 204 C3
Évisa France 42°15N 8°48E 175 F12
Evje Norway 58°36N 7°51E 164 F4
Évora Portugal 38°33N 7°57W 195 G3
Évora □ Portugal 38°33N 7°50W 195 G3
Evowghlī Iran 38°43N 45°13E 213 C11
Évreux France 49°3N 1°8E 172 C8
Evritania □ Greece 39°5N 21°30E 204 B3
Évron France 48°10N 0°24W 172 D6
Evros □ Greece 41°10N 26°0E 203 E10
Evros → Greece 41°40N 26°34E 212 B2
Evrotas → Greece 36°50N 22°40E 204 E4
Évry France 48°38N 2°27E 173 D9
Évvoia = Evia Greece 38°30N 24°0E 204 C6
'Ewa Beach U.S.A. 21°19N 158°1W 302 K13
'Ewa District U.S.A. 21°25N 158°0W 302 K13
'Ewa Villages U.S.A. 21°20N 158°3W 302 K13
Ewarton Jamaica 18°11N 77°6W 320 a
Ewasse Papua N. G. 5°19S 151°1E 286 C6
Ewe, L. U.K. 57°49N 5°38W 167 D3
Ewing Mo., U.S.A. 40°6N 91°43W 310 E5
Ewing Nebr., U.S.A. 42°16N 98°21W 308 D4
Ewo Congo 0°48S 14°45E 264 C2
Ewu Nigeria 6°33N 3°19E 124 A1
Exaltación Bolivia 13°10S 65°20W 331 C4
Excelsior Springs U.S.A. 39°20N 94°13W 310 E2
Exchange Square Hong Kong, China 122 c1
Excideuil France 45°20N 1°4E 174 C5
Exe → U.K. 50°41N 3°29W 169 G4
Exeter Ont., Canada 43°21N 81°29W 312 C3
Exeter Devon, U.K. 50°43N 3°31W 169 G4
Exeter Calif., U.S.A. 36°18N 119°9W 306 J7
Exeter N.H., U.S.A. 42°59N 70°57W 313 D14
Exhibition Place Canada 43°38N 79°25W 141 B2
Exira U.S.A. 41°35N 94°52W 310 C2
Exmoor U.K. 51°12N 3°45W 169 F4
Exmoor △ U.K. 51°8N 3°42W 169 F4
Exmouth W. Austral., Australia 21°54S 114°10E 278 D1
Exmouth Devon, U.K. 50°37N 3°25W 169 G4
Exmouth G. Australia 22°15S 114°15E 278 D1
Exmouth Plateau Ind. Oc. 19°0S 114°0E 288 J3
Expedition △ Australia 25°41S 149°7E 281 D4
Expedition Ra. Australia 24°30S 149°12E 280 C4
Experiment = Highland Mills U.S.A. 33°17N 84°17W 316 B5
Exposições, Palácio das Brazil 22°53S 43°13W 135 B1
Extremadura □ Spain 39°30N 6°5W 195 F4
Extrême-Nord □ Cameroon 11°0N 14°30E 259 F2
Exuma Sound Bahamas 24°30N 76°20W 320 B4
Eyak U.S.A. 60°32N 145°36W 303 F11
Eyasi, L. Tanzania 3°30S 35°0E 268 C4
Eydehavn Norway 58°30N 8°53E 164 F5
Eydhafushi Maldives 5°7N 73°2E 272 d
Eye Pen. U.K. 58°13N 6°10W 167 C2
Eyemouth U.K. 55°52N 2°5W 167 F6
Eygues = Aigues → France 44°7N 4°43E 175 D8
Eygurande France 45°40N 2°26E 173 G9
Eyjafjallajökull Iceland 63°38N 19°36W 155 D7
Eyjafjarðarsýsla □ Iceland 65°30N 18°30W 155 B8
Eyjafjörður Iceland 66°15N 18°30W 155 A8
Eyl Somali Rep. 8°0N 49°50E 267 C6
Eymet France 44°40N 0°25E 174 D4
Eymoutiers France 45°40N 1°45E 174 C5
Eynesil Turkey 41°4N 39°9E 213 B8
Eyrarbakki Iceland 63°52N 21°9W 155 D5
Eyre (North), L. Australia 28°30S 137°20E 281 D2
Eyre (South), L. Australia 29°18S 137°25E 281 D2
Eyre, L. Australia 29°30S 137°26E 276 F6
Eyre Mts. N.Z. 45°25S 168°25E 285 F3
Eyre Pen. Australia 33°30S 136°17E 282 C1
Eysturoy Færoe Is. 62°13N 6°54W 160 E9
Eyüp Turkey 41°2N 28°55E 122 B1
Eyvān = Jūy Zar Iran 33°50N 46°18E 213 F12
Eyvānkī Iran 35°24N 51°56E 247 C6
Ez Zeidab Sudan 17°25N 33°55E 256 D3
Ezcaray Spain 42°19N 3°0W 196 C1
Ezeiza ✕ (EZE) Argentina 34°49S 58°32W 117 C1
Ežerėlis Lithuania 54°53N 23°37E 184 D10
Ezhou China 30°23N 114°50E 229 B10
Ezine Turkey 39°48N 26°20E 205 B8
Ezouza → Cyprus 34°44N 32°27E 207 F8

F

F.Y.R.O.M. = Macedonia ■ Europe 41°53N 21°40E 202 E5
Faaa Tahiti 17°34S 149°35W 289 e
Faaborg Denmark 55°6N 10°15E 163 J4
Faaone Tahiti 17°40S 149°21W 289 e
Fabala Guinea 9°44N 9°5W 262 D3
Fabens U.S.A. 31°30N 106°10W 314 F1
Fåberg Norway 61°10N 10°25E 164 C7
Fabero Spain 42°46N 6°37W 194 C4
Fabius U.S.A. 42°50N 75°59W 313 D9
Fabour, Mt. Singapore 1°16N 103°49E 138 B2
Fabriano Italy 43°20N 12°54E 199 E9
Făcăeni Romania 44°32N 27°53E 183 F12
Facatativá Colombia 4°49N 74°22W 328 C3
Faceville U.S.A. 30°45N 84°38W 316 E5
Fachi Niger 18°6N 11°34E 259 E2
Facundo Argentina 45°18S 69°58W 336 C3
Fada Chad 17°13N 21°34E 259 E4
Fada-n-Gourma Burkina Faso 12°10N 0°30E 263 C5
Fadd Hungary 46°28N 18°49E 182 D3
Faddeyevskiy, Ostrov Russia 76°0N 144°0E 215 B15
Faddor Sudan 8°7N 32°17E 257 F3
Fadghāmī Syria 35°53N 40°52E 213 E9
Fadiffolu Atoll Maldives 5°23N 73°29E 272 d
Fadlab Sudan 17°42N 34°2E 256 D3
Fadwel Sudan 8°11N 29°20E 266 C2
Fælledparken Denmark 55°42N 12°34E 118 A3
Faenza Italy 44°17N 11°53E 199 D8
Færingehavn = Kangerluarsoruseq Greenland 63°45N 51°27W 154 E5
Færoe Is. = Føroyar □ Atl. Oc. 62°0N 7°0W 160 F9
Fafa Mali 15°22N 0°48E 263 B5
Fafe Portugal 41°27N 8°11W 194 D2
Fafen → Ethiopia 5°59N 44°25E 267 C5
Fagam Nigeria 11°1N 10°1E 263 C7
Fagamalo Amer. Samoa 14°18S 170°48W 302 f
Făgăras Romania 45°48N 24°58E 183 E9
Făgăras, Munţii Romania 45°40N 24°40E 183 E9
Fagasa Amer. Samoa 14°17S 170°43W 302 f
Fagatogo Amer. Samoa 14°16S 170°41W 302 f
Fågelfors Sweden 57°12N 15°51E 163 G9
Fågelmara Sweden 56°16N 15°58E 163 H9
Fågelön Sweden 59°18N 17°55E 139 B1
Fagerheim Norway 60°26N 7°46E 164 D4
Fagerhult Sweden 57°8N 15°40E 163 G9
Fagernes Norway 60°59N 9°14E 164 D6
Fagersjö Sweden 59°14N 18°4E 139 B2
Fagersta Sweden 60°1N 15°46E 162 D9
Făget Romania 45°52N 22°10E 182 E7
Făget, Munţii Romania 47°40N 23°10E 183 C8
Faggo Nigeria 11°21N 9°57E 263 C6
Fagnano, L. Argentina 54°30S 68°0W 336 D3
Fagnières France 48°58N 4°20E 173 D11
Faguibine, L. Mali 16°45N 4°0W 262 B4
Fahlīān Iran 30°11N 51°28E 247 D6
Fahraj Kermān, Iran 29°0N 59°0E 247 D8
Fahraj Yazd, Iran 31°46N 54°36E 247 D7
Fai Tsi Long Vietnam 21°0N 107°30E 228 G6
Faial Azores 38°34N 28°42W 153 d1
Faial Madeira 32°47N 16°53W 153 c
Faial, Canal do Azores 38°33N 28°35W 153 d1
Faichan Kangri India 35°48N 76°34E 243 B7
Faichuk Micronesia 7°21N 151°38E 287 T17
Fair Haven N.Y., U.S.A. 43°18N 76°42W 313 C8
Fair Haven Vt., U.S.A. 43°36N 73°16W 309 D17
Fair Hd. U.K. 55°14N 6°9W 166 A5
Fair Isle U.K. 59°32N 1°38W 165 B6
Fair Oaks U.S.A. 38°39N 121°16W 306 G5
Fairbank U.S.A. 42°38N 92°3W 310 B4
Fairbanks Alaska, U.S.A. 64°51N 147°43W 303 D11
Fairbanks Fla., U.S.A. 29°44N 82°16W 316 F7
Fairborn U.S.A. 39°49N 84°2W 311 E12
Fairburn U.S.A. 33°34N 84°35W 316 B5
Fairbury Ill., U.S.A. 40°45N 88°31W 311 D8
Fairbury Nebr., U.S.A. 40°8N 97°11W 308 E5
Fairfax Ohio, U.S.A. 39°5N 83°37W 311 E13
Fairfax S.C., U.S.A. 32°59N 81°15W 316 C8
Fairfax Va., U.S.A. 38°50N 77°19W 143 B2
Fairfax Vt., U.S.A. 44°40N 73°1W 313 B11
Fairfax Station U.S.A. 38°48N 77°19W 143 C2
Fairfield N.S.W., Australia 33°53S 150°57E 283 B9
Fairfield Ala., U.S.A. 33°29N 86°55W 315 E11
Fairfield Calif., U.S.A. 38°15N 122°3W 306 G4
Fairfield Conn., U.S.A. 41°9N 73°16W 313 E11
Fairfield Idaho, U.S.A. 43°21N 114°44W 304 E6
Fairfield Ill., U.S.A. 38°23N 88°22W 311 F8
Fairfield Iowa, U.S.A. 40°56N 91°57W 310 D5
Fairfield Ohio, U.S.A. 39°20N 84°34W 311 E12
Fairfield Tex., U.S.A. 31°44N 96°10W 314 F6
Fairford Canada 51°37N 98°38W 297 C9
Fairhope U.S.A. 30°31N 87°54W 315 F11
Fairland S. Africa 26°8S 27°57E 123 A1
Fairlie N.Z. 44°5S 170°49E 285 E5
Fairmead U.S.A. 37°5N 120°10W 306 H6
Fairmilehead U.K. 55°54N 3°11W 121 B2
Fairmont Minn., U.S.A. 43°39N 94°28W 308 D6
Fairmont W. Va., U.S.A. 39°29N 80°9W 309 F13
Fairmount Calif., U.S.A. 34°45N 118°26W 307 L8
Fairmount N.Y., U.S.A. 43°5N 76°12W 313 C8
Fairmount Heights U.S.A. 38°54N 76°54W 143 B4
Fairplay U.S.A. 39°15N 106°2W 304 G10
Fairport Ont., Canada 43°49N 79°4W 141 A4
Fairport N.Y., U.S.A. 43°6N 77°27W 312 C7
Fairport Harbor U.S.A. 41°45N 81°17W 312 E3
Fairview Alta., Canada 56°5N 118°25W 296 B5
Fairview Mont., U.S.A. 47°51N 104°3W 304 C11
Fairview N.J., U.S.A. 40°48N 73°59W 132 B2
Fairview Okla., U.S.A. 36°16N 98°29W 314 C5
Fairview, L. U.S.A. 28°35N 81°24W 133 A2
Fairweather, Mt. U.S.A. 58°55N 137°32W 296 B1
Faisalabad Pakistan 31°30N 73°5E 242 D5
Faith U.S.A. 45°2N 102°2W 308 C2
Faizabad India 26°45N 82°10E 243 F10
Faizpur India 21°14N 75°49E 244 D2
Fajã Grande Azores 39°27N 31°16W 153 d2
Fajardo Puerto Rico 18°20N 65°39W 321 C6
Fajou, Îlet à Guadeloupe 16°21N 61°35W 322 e
Fajr, W. → Si. Arabia 29°10N 38°10E 246 D3
Fakaofo Pac. Oc. 9°23S 171°15W 277 B16
Fakarava French Polynesia 16°20S 145°37W 289 f
Fakenham U.K. 52°51N 0°51E 168 E8
Fåker Sweden 63°0N 14°34E 162 A8
Fakfak Indonesia 2°55S 132°18E 231 E8
Fakiya Bulgaria 42°10N 27°6E 203 D11
Fakobli Ivory C. 7°23N 7°23W 262 D3
Fakse Denmark 55°15N 12°8E 163 J6
Fakse Bugt Denmark 55°11N 12°15E 163 J6
Fakse Ladeplads Denmark 55°11N 12°9E 163 J6
Faku China 42°32N 123°21E 224 A1
Fala Beguets I. Micronesia 7°21N 151°41E 287 U17
Falaba S. Leone 9°54N 11°22W 262 D2
Falaise France 48°54N 0°12W 172 D6
Falaise, Mui Vietnam 19°6N 105°45E 236 C5
Falakro Oros Greece 41°15N 23°58E 202 E7
Falam Burma 23°0N 93°45E 241 D4
Falas I. Micronesia 7°31N 151°44E 287 T18
Falces Spain 42°24N 1°48W 196 C3
Fălciu Romania 46°17N 28°7E 183 D13
Falcó, C. des Spain 38°50N 1°23E 206 C7
Falcón □ Venezuela 11°0N 69°50W 328 A4
Falcon, C. Algeria 35°50N 0°50W 261 A4
Falcón, Presa Mexico 26°35N 99°10W 318 B5
Falcon Lake Canada 49°42N 95°15W 297 D9
Falcon Res. U.S.A. 26°34N 99°10W 314 H5
Falconara Marittima Italy 43°37N 13°24E 199 E10
Falcone, C. del Italy 40°58N 8°12E 200 B1
Falconer U.S.A. 42°7N 79°12W 312 D5
Faléa Mali 12°16N 11°17W 262 C2
Falefa Samoa 13°54S 171°31W 287 V20
Falelatai Samoa 13°55S 171°59W 287 V20
Falelima Samoa 13°32S 172°41W 287 V19
Falémé → Senegal 14°46N 12°14W 262 C2
Faleniu Amer. Samoa 14°19S 170°44W 302 f
Falenty Poland 52°8N 20°55E 142 C1
Falerum Sweden 58°8N 16°13E 163 F10
Faleshty = Făleşti Moldova 47°32N 27°44E 183 C12
Făleşti Moldova 47°32N 27°44E 183 C12
Falfurrias U.S.A. 27°14N 98°9W 314 H5
Falher Canada 55°44N 117°15W 296 B5
Faliraki Greece 36°22N 28°12E 206 E12
Faliro Greece 37°55N 23°39E 112 B1
Faliro, Ormos Greece 37°54N 23°40E 112 B2
Falkenberg Brandenburg, Germany 51°35N 13°14E 178 D9
Falkenberg Sweden 56°54N 12°30E 163 H6
Falkenburg = Niemodlin Poland 50°38N 17°38E 185 H4
Falkenburg Germany 52°34N 13°32E 115 A4
Falkenhagen Germany 52°34N 13°5E 115 A1
Falkensee Germany 52°34N 13°4E 115 A1
Falkirk U.K. 56°0N 3°47W 167 F5
Falkirk □ U.K. 55°58N 3°49W 167 F5
Falkland U.K. 56°16N 3°12W 167 E5
Falkland, East, I. Falk. Is. 51°40S 58°30W 336 D5
Falkland, West, I. Falk. Is. 51°40S 60°0W 336 D5
Falkland Is. □ Atl. Oc. 51°30S 59°0W 153 f
Falkland Plateau Atl. Oc. 51°0S 50°0W 152 M7
Falkland Ridge Atl. Oc. 49°20S 40°0W 152 L8
Falkland Sd. Falk. Is. 52°0S 60°0W 153 f
Falknov nad Ohří = Sokolov Czech Rep. 50°12N 12°40E 180 A5
Falkonera Greece 36°50N 23°52E 204 E5
Falköping Sweden 58°12N 13°33E 163 F7
Fall River U.S.A. 41°43N 71°10W 313 E13
Fallbrook U.S.A. 33°23N 117°15W 307 M9
Fallon U.S.A. 39°28N 118°47W 304 G4
Falls Church U.S.A. 38°53N 77°12W 143 B2
Falls City U.S.A. 40°3N 95°36W 308 E6
Falls Creek U.S.A. 41°9N 78°48W 312 E6
Falmouth Jamaica 18°30N 77°40W 320 a
Falmouth Corn., U.K. 50°9N 5°5W 169 G2
Falmouth Ky., U.S.A. 38°41N 84°20W 311 F12
Falmouth Mass., U.S.A. 41°33N 70°37W 313 E14
Falo I. Micronesia 7°28N 151°52E 287 T18
Falomo Nigeria 6°26N 3°26E 124 B2
Falsa, Pta. Mexico 27°51N 115°3W 318 B1
False B. S. Africa 34°15S 18°40E 270 D2
False Bay S. Africa 34°6S 18°33E 118 B2
False Divi Pt. India 15°43N 80°50E 245 G5
False Pass U.S.A. 54°51N 163°25W 303 J7
False Pt. India 20°18N 86°48E 244 D8
Falso, C. Honduras 15°12N 83°21W 320 C3
Falster Denmark 54°45N 11°55E 163 K5
Falsterbo Sweden 55°23N 12°50E 161 J15
Fălticeni Romania 47°21N 26°20E 183 C11
Falun Sweden 60°37N 15°37E 162 D9
Famagusta Cyprus 35°8N 33°55E 207 E9
Famagusta Bay Cyprus 35°15N 34°0E 207 E10
Famatina, Sierra de Argentina 27°30S 68°0W 334 B2
Famenin Iran 35°5N 48°58E 213 E13
Family L. Canada 51°54N 95°27W 297 C9
Famoso U.S.A. 35°37N 119°12W 307 K7
Fan Xian China 35°55N 115°38E 226 G8
Fana Mali 13°0N 6°56W 262 C3
Fanad Hd. Ireland 55°17N 7°38W 166 A4
Fanahammaren Norway 60°16N 5°20E 164 D2
Fanari Greece 39°24N 21°47E 204 B3
Fandriana Madag. 20°14S 47°21E 272 C2
Faneuil Hall Marketplace Boston, U.S.A. 116 b3
Fánes-Sénnes e Braies ⌓ Italy 46°38N 12°4E 199 B9
Fang Thailand 19°55N 99°13E 228 H2
Fang Xian China 32°3N 110°40E 229 A8
Fangak Sudan 9°4N 30°53E 257 F3
Fangataufa French Polynesia 22°15S 138°45W 289 f
Fangatufa French Polynesia 15°50S 140°52W 289 f
Fangchang China 31°5N 118°4E 229 B12
Fangcheng China 33°18N 112°59E 226 H7
Fangchenggang China 21°42N 108°21E 228 G7
Fangcun China 23°6N 113°13E 121 B2
Fangliao Taiwan 22°22N 120°38E 225 D2
Fangshan Shanxi, China 38°3N 111°25E 226 E6
Fangshan Taiwan 22°15N 120°39E 225 D2
Fangyuan Taiwan 23°56N 120°19E 225 C2
Fangzi China 36°33N 119°10E 227 F10
Fani i Madh → Albania 41°56N 20°16E 202 E4
Fanjakana Madag. 21°10S 46°53E 272 C2
Fanjiatun China 43°40N 125°15E 227 C13
Fanling China 22°30N 114°8E 219 F11
Fannich, L. U.K. 57°38N 4°59W 167 D4
Fannrem Norway 63°16N 9°50E 164 A6
Fannūj Iran 26°35N 59°38E 247 E8
Fanø Denmark 55°25N 8°25E 163 J2
Fano Italy 43°50N 13°1E 199 E10
Fanshi China 39°12N 113°20E 226 E7
Fantzuliao Hsi → Taiwan 22°42N 120°28E 225 D2
Fanuet I. Micronesia 7°32N 151°48E 287 T18
Fao = Al Fāw Iraq 30°0N 48°30E 247 D6
Faqirwali Pakistan 29°27N 73°0E 242 E5
Fâqûs Egypt 30°44N 31°47E 256 H7
Far East = Dalnevostochnyy □ Russia 67°0N 140°0E 215 C14
Far East Asia 40°0N 130°0E 210 E14
Fara in Sabina Italy 42°12N 12°43E 199 F9
Faradje Dem. Rep. of the Congo 3°50N 29°45E 268 B2
Farafangana Madag. 22°49S 47°50E 272 C2
Farafenni Gambia 13°34N 15°36W 262 C1
Farâfra, El Wâhât el Egypt 27°15N 28°20E 256 B2
Farāh Afghan. 32°20N 62°7E 240 B1
Farāh □ Afghan. 32°25N 62°10E 240 B1
Farāh → Afghan. 31°27N 61°28E 240 C1
Faraḩābād Iran 35°41N 51°30E 141 A2
Farahalana Madag. 14°26S 50°10E 272 A3
Faraid, Gebel Egypt 23°33N 35°19E 256 C4
Farako Ivory C. 10°45N 6°50W 262 D4
Farallon de Medinilla N. Marianas 16°1N 146°4E 302 a
Farallon de Pajaros N. Marianas 20°32N 144°54E 302 a
Farallones de Cali △ Colombia 3°13N 76°46W 328 C2
Faramana Burkina Faso 11°56N 4°45W 262 C4
Faranah Guinea 10°3N 10°45W 262 C2
Farap Turkmenistan 39°6N 63°36E 216 E6
Fararah Oman 17°55N 55°38E 249 C6
Farasān, Jazā'ir Si. Arabia 16°45N 41°55E 248 C3
Farasan Is. = Farasān, Jazā'ir Si. Arabia 16°45N 41°55E 248 C3
Faratsiho Madag. 19°24S 46°57E 272 B2
Farbaraki Somali Rep. 2°30N 45°30E 267 D6
Fardes → Spain 37°35N 3°0W 195 H7
Fareham U.K. 50°51N 1°11W 169 G6
Farewell U.S.A. 62°31N 153°54W 303 E9
Farewell, C. N.Z. 40°29S 172°43E 285 A7
Farewell C. = Nunap Isua Greenland 59°48N 43°55W 154 F6
Farewell Spit N.Z. 40°35S 173°0E 285 A8
Farforovskaya Russia 59°52N 30°27E 137 B2
Färgelanda Sweden 58°34N 12°0E 163 F5
Farghona Uzbekistan 40°23N 71°19E 217 D8
Farghona □ Uzbekistan 40°30N 71°15E 217 D8
Farghona Vodiysi Asia 40°46N 71°30E 217 D8
Fargo Ga., U.S.A. 30°41N 82°34W 316 E7
Fargo N. Dak., U.S.A. 46°53N 96°48W 308 B5
Fār'iah, W. al → West Bank 32°12N 35°27E 251 F6
Faribault U.S.A. 44°18N 93°16W 308 C7
Faridabad India 28°26N 77°19E 242 E6
Faridkot India 30°44N 74°45E 242 D6
Faridpur Bangla. 23°15N 89°55E 241 D2
Faridpur India 28°13N 79°33E 243 E8
Fārigh, W. al → Libya 30°20N 20°44E 259 B4
Färila Sweden 61°48N 15°50E 162 C9
Farim Guinea-Biss. 12°27N 15°9W 262 C1
Farīmān Iran 35°40N 59°49E 247 C8
Farinha → Brazil 6°51S 47°30W 332 C2
Fariones, Pta. Canary Is. 29°13N 13°28W 153 e2
Fâriskûr Egypt 31°20N 31°43E 256 H7
Färjestaden Sweden 56°39N 16°27E 163 H10
Farkadona Greece 39°36N 22°4E 204 B4
Farleigh Australia 21°4S 149°8E 280 b
Farley U.S.A. 42°27N 91°0W 310 B6
Farmakonisi Greece 37°17N 27°5E 205 D9
Farmer City U.S.A. 40°15N 88°39W 311 D8
Farmersburg U.S.A. 39°15N 87°23W 311 E9
Farmerville U.S.A. 32°47N 92°24W 314 E8
Farmingdale U.S.A. 40°12N 74°10W 313 F10
Farmington B.C., Canada 55°54N 120°30W 296 B4
Farmington Calif., U.S.A. 37°55N 120°59W 306 H6
Farmington Ga., U.S.A. 33°47N 83°26W 316 B6
Farmington Ill., U.S.A. 40°42N 90°0W 310 D7
Farmington Iowa, U.S.A. 40°38N 91°44W 310 D5
Farmington Maine, U.S.A. 44°40N 70°9W 309 C18
Farmington Mo., U.S.A. 37°47N 90°25W 310 G6
Farmington N.H., U.S.A. 43°24N 71°4W 313 C13
Farmington N. Mex., U.S.A. 36°44N 108°12W 305 H9
Farmington Utah, U.S.A. 40°59N 111°53W 304 F8
Farmington → U.S.A. 41°51N 72°38W 313 E12
Farmland U.S.A. 40°15N 85°5W 311 D11
Farmville U.S.A. 37°18N 78°24W 309 G14
Färnäs Sweden 61°0N 14°39E 162 D8
Farne Is. U.K. 55°38N 1°37W 168 B6
Färnebofjärden △ Sweden 60°10N 16°48E 162 D10
Farnham Canada 45°17N 72°59W 313 A12
Farnham, Mt. Canada 50°29N 116°30W 296 C5
Farningham U.K. 51°23N 0°12E 125 B5
Faro Brazil 2°10S 56°39W 329 D6
Faro Yukon, Canada 62°11N 133°22W 294 E5
Faro Portugal 37°2N 7°55W 195 H3
Fårö Gotland, Sweden 57°55N 19°5E 161 H18
Faro □ Portugal 37°12N 8°10W 195 H2
Faro ✕ (FAO) Portugal 37°2N 7°57W 195 H3
Faro ⌓ Cameroon 8°15N 12°37E 264 A2
Fårösund Sweden 57°52N 19°2E 163 G13
Farquhar, C. Australia 23°50S 113°36E 279 D1
Farquhar Is. Seychelles 11°0S 52°0E 273 F4
Farrars Cr. → Australia 25°35S 140°43E 280 D3
Farrāshband Iran 28°57N 52°5E 247 D7
Farrell U.S.A. 41°13N 80°30W 312 E4
Farrell Flat Australia 33°48S 138°48E 282 B3
Farrokhī Iran 33°50N 59°31E 247 C8
Farruch, C. = Ferrutx, C. de Spain 39°47N 3°21E 206 B4
Farrukhabad India 27°24N 79°34E 244 A4
Färs □ Iran 29°30N 55°0E 247 D7
Farsala Greece 39°17N 22°23E 204 B4
Fārsī Afghan. 33°47N 63°15E 240 B1
Fārsī Iran 27°58N 50°11E 247 E6
Farsø Denmark 56°46N 9°19E 163 H3
Farson U.S.A. 42°7N 109°26W 304 E9
Farsta Sweden 59°14N 18°5E 139 B2
Farsund Norway 58°5N 6°55E 164 F3
Fartak, Rās Si. Arabia 28°5N 34°34E 246 D2
Fartak, Ra's Yemen 15°38N 52°15E 249 D6
Fârţăneşti Romania 45°49N 27°59E 183 E12
Fartura, Serra da Brazil 26°21S 52°52W 335 B5
Faru Nigeria 12°48N 6°12E 263 C6
Farūj Iran 37°14N 58°14E 247 B8
Fårup Denmark 56°33N 9°51E 163 H3
Farvel, Kap = Nunap Isua Greenland 59°48N 43°55W 154 F6
Farwell U.S.A. 34°23N 103°2W 314 D3
Fāryāb □ Afghan. 36°0N 65°0E 240 B2
Fasā Iran 29°0N 53°39E 247 D7
Fasanerie-Nord Germany 48°11N 11°32E 131 A2
Fasangarten Germany 48°5N 11°36E 131 B2
Fasano Italy 40°50N 17°22E 201 B10
Fashoda Sudan 9°50N 32°2E 257 F3
Fasil Ghebbi Ethiopia 12°36N 37°28E 266 B4
Fáskrúðsfjörður Iceland 64°56N 14°1W 155 C12
Fassa Mali 13°26N 8°15W 262 C3
Fastiv Ukraine 50°7N 29°57E 177 C15
Fastnet Rock Ireland 51°22N 9°37W 166 E2
Fastov = Fastiv Ukraine 50°7N 29°57E 177 C15
Fatagar, Tanjung Indonesia 2°46S 131°57E 231 E8
Fataka Solomon Is. 11°55S 170°12E 277 C12
Fatatsu Ne Iwo Jima 24°45N 141°18E 288 b
Fatehabad Haryana, India 29°31N 75°27E 242 E6
Fatehabad Ut. P., India 27°1N 78°19E 242 F8
Fatehgarh India 27°25N 79°35E 243 F8
Fatehpur Bihar, India 24°38N 85°14E 243 G11
Fatehpur Raj., India 28°0N 74°40E 242 F6
Fatehpur Ut. P., India 25°56N 81°13E 243 G9
Fatehpur Ut. P., India 27°10N 81°13E 243 F9
Fatehpur Sikri India 27°6N 77°40E 242 F6
Fatesh Russia 52°8N 35°57E 189 F8
Fathai Sudan 8°5N 31°48E 257 F3
Fathom Five ⌓ Canada 45°17N 81°40W 312 A3
Fatick Senegal 14°19N 16°27W 262 C1
Fatick □ Senegal 14°15N 16°30W 262 C1
Fatih Turkey 41°0N 28°56E 122 B1
Fatima Qué., Canada 47°24N 61°53W 299 C7
Fátima Portugal 39°37N 8°39W 195 F2
Fatoya Guinea 11°37N 9°10W 262 C3
Fatsa Turkey 41°2N 37°31E 212 B7
Fatshan = Foshan China 23°6N 113°9E 121 B2
Faucille, Col de la France 46°22N 6°2E 173 F13
Faulkton U.S.A. 45°2N 99°8W 308 C4
Faulquemont France 49°3N 6°36E 173 C13
Faure I. Australia 25°52S 113°50E 279 E1
Făurei Romania 45°6N 27°19E 183 E12
Fauresmith S. Africa 29°44S 25°17E 270 C4
Fauro Solomon Is. 6°55S 156°7E 287 L9
Fauske Norway 67°17N 15°25E 160 C16
Fåvang Norway 61°27N 10°11E 164 C7
Favânia Brazil 3°7S 51°48W 329 D7
Favara Italy 37°19N 13°39E 200 E6
Faváritx, C. de Spain 40°0N 4°15E 206 B11
Faverges France 45°45N 6°17E 175 C10
Favignana Italy 37°56N 12°20E 200 E5
Favignana, I. Italy 37°56N 12°19E 200 E5
Favoriten Austria 48°9N 16°23E 142 B2
Fawcett, Pt. Australia 11°46S 130°2E 278 B5
Fawkner Australia 37°42S 144°56E 128 A1
Fawkner Park Australia 37°50S 144°58E 128 B1
Fawn → Canada 55°20N 87°35W 298 A2
Fawnskin U.S.A. 34°16N 116°56W 307 L10
Faxaflói Iceland 64°29N 23°0W 155 C3
Faxälven → Sweden 63°13N 17°13E 162 A10
Faya-Largeau Chad 17°58N 19°6E 259 E3
Fayaoué N. Cal. 20°38S 166°33E 288 d
Fayd Si. Arabia 27°1N 42°52E 246 E4
Fayence France 43°38N 6°42E 175 E10
Fayette Ala., U.S.A. 33°41N 87°50W 315 E11
Fayette Iowa, U.S.A. 42°51N 91°48W 310 B5

Fayette Mo., U.S.A. 39°9N 92°41W 310 E4
Fayette N.Y., U.S.A. 42°48N 76°48W 313 D8
Fayette Ohio, U.S.A. 41°40N 84°20W 311 C12
Fayetteville Ark., U.S.A. 36°4N 94°10W 314 C7
Fayetteville Ga., U.S.A. 33°27N 84°27W 316 B5
Fayetteville N.C., U.S.A. 35°3N 78°53W 315 D15
Fayetteville N.Y., U.S.A. 43°1N 76°0W 313 C9
Fayetteville Tenn., U.S.A. 35°9N 86°34W 315 D11
Fayied Egypt 30°18N 32°16E 256 H8
Faylakah Kuwait 29°27N 48°20E 247 D6
Fayón Spain 41°15N 0°20E 196 D5
Fazao-Malfakassa △ Togo 8°45N 0°50E 263 D5
Fazenda Libongo Angola 8°24S 13°24E 265 D2
Fazenda Nova Brazil 16°11S 50°48W 333 E1
Fazilka India 30°27N 74°2E 242 D6
Fazilpur Pakistan 29°18N 70°29E 242 E4
Fdérik Mauritania 22°40N 12°45W 260 D2
Feakle Ireland 52°56N 8°40W 166 D3
Feale ➜ Ireland 52°27N 9°37W 166 D2
Fear, C. U.S.A. 33°50N 77°58W 315 E16
Feather ➜ U.S.A. 38°47N 121°36W 304 G3
Feather Falls U.S.A. 39°36N 121°16W 306 F5
Featherston N.Z. 41°6S 175°20E 284 H4
Featherstone Zimbabwe 18°42S 30°55E 269 F3
Fécamp France 49°45N 0°22E 172 C7
Feda Norway 58°17N 6°50E 164 F3
Fedala = Mohammedia
Morocco 33°44N 7°21W 260 B3
Federación Argentina 31°0S 57°55W 334 C4
Federal Capital Terr. □
Nigeria 9°0N 7°10E 263 D6
Federal Way U.S.A. 47°18N 122°19W 306 C4
Fedeshküh Iran 28°49N 53°50E 247 D7
FedEx Stadium U.S.A. 38°54N 76°51W 143 B4
Fedje Norway 60°47N 4°43E 164 D1
Fedorovka Kazakhstan 53°37N 62°42E 216 B6
Fefan I. Pac. Oc. 7°21N 151°51E 287 T18
Fehérgyarmat Hungary 47°58N 22°30E 182 C7
Fehmarn Germany 54°27N 11°7E 178 A7
Fehmarn Bælt Europe 54°35N 11°20E 163 K5
Fehmarn Belt = Fehmarn Bælt
Europe 54°35N 11°20E 163 K5
Fei Xian China 35°18N 117°59E 227 G9
Feijó Brazil 8°9S 70°21W 330 B3
Feilding N.Z. 40°13S 175°35E 284 G4
Feira de Santana Brazil 12°15S 38°57W 333 D4
Feirān, W. ➜ Egypt 28°39N 33°12E 251 K4
Feirâni, G. Egypt 28°31N 34°19E 251 K5
Feiring Norway 60°30N 11°10E 164 D8
Feixi China 31°43N 117°59E 229 B11
Feixiang China 36°30N 114°45E 226 F8
Fejaj, Chott el Tunisia 33°52N 9°14E 258 B1
Fejér □ Hungary 47°9N 18°30E 182 C3
Fejø Denmark 54°55N 11°30E 163 K5
Feke Turkey 37°48N 35°56E 212 D6
Fekete ➜ Hungary 45°47N 18°15E 182 E3
Felanitx Spain 39°28N 3°9E 206 B4
Felda U.S.A. 26°34N 81°26W 317 J8
Feldbach Austria 46°57N 15°52E 180 E8
Feldberg Baden-W., Germany 47°52N 8°0E 179 H3
Feldberg Mecklenburg-Vorpommern,
Germany 53°20N 13°25E 178 B9
Feldkirch Austria 47°15N 9°37E 180 D2
Feldkirchen Austria 46°44N 14°6E 180 E7
Feldkirchen Oberbayern,
Germany 48°8N 11°43E 131 B3
Feldmoching Germany 48°14N 11°32E 131 A2
Félicité Seychelles 4°19S 55°52E 272 c
Felicity U.S.A. 38°51N 84°6W 311 F12
Felidhoo Maldives 3°29N 73°32E 272 d
Felidu Atoll Maldives 3°29N 73°29E 272 d
Felipe Carrillo Puerto
Mexico 19°38N 88°3W 319 D7
Felixburg Zimbabwe 19°29S 30°51E 271 A5
Felixlândia Brazil 18°47S 44°55W 333 E3
Felixstowe U.K. 51°58N 1°23E 169 F9
Felletin France 45°53N 2°11E 174 C6
Fellingsbro Sweden 59°26N 15°37E 162 E9
Fellsmere U.S.A. 27°46N 80°36W 317 H9
Felshtin = Gvardeyskoye
Ukraine 45°7N 34°1E 189 K8
Felsogalla = Tatabánya
Hungary 47°32N 18°25E 182 C3
Feltham U.K. 51°26N 0°24W 125 B1
Felton U.S.A. 37°3N 122°4W 306 H4
Feltre Italy 46°1N 11°54E 199 B8
Femer Bælt = Fehmarn Bælt
Europe 54°35N 11°20E 163 K5
Femø Denmark 54°58N 11°35E 163 K5
Femunden Norway 62°10N 11°53E 164 B8
Femundsmarka △
Norway 62°18N 12°6E 164 B9
Fen He ➜ China 35°36N 110°42E 226 G6
Fenchih Taiwan 23°30N 120°40E 225 C2
Fene Spain 43°27N 8°9W 194 B2
Fenelon Falls Canada 44°32N 78°45W 312 B6
Fener Turkey 41°1N 28°56E 122 B1
Fener Burnu Turkey 36°58N 27°18E 205 E9
Fenerbahçe Turkey 40°58N 29°2E 122 C2
Feneroa Ethiopia 13°5N 39°3E 257 E4
Feng Xian Jiangsu, China 34°43N 116°35E 226 G9
Feng Xian Shaanxi,
China 33°54N 106°40E 226 H4
Fengari Greece 40°25N 25°32E 203 F9
Fengcheng Jiangxi,
China 28°12N 115°48E 229 C10
Fengcheng Liaoning,
China 40°28N 124°5E 224 B2
Fengfeng China 36°28N 114°8E 226 F8
Fenggang China 27°57N 107°47E 228 D6
Fenghua China 29°40N 121°25E 229 C13
Fenghuang China 27°57N 109°29E 228 D7
Fengkai China 23°24N 111°30E 229 F8
Fengkang Taiwan 22°12N 120°41E 225 D2
Fengle China 31°29N 112°29E 229 B9
Fenglin Taiwan 23°45N 121°26E 225 C3
Fengning China 41°10N 116°33E 226 D9
Fengpin Taiwan 23°36N 121°31E 225 C3
Fengqing China 24°38N 99°55E 228 E2
Fengqiu China 35°2N 114°25E 226 G8
Fengrun China 39°48N 118°8E 227 E10
Fengshan Guangxi Zhuangzu,
China 24°39N 109°15E 228 E7
Fengshan Guangxi Zhuangzu,
China 24°31N 107°3E 228 E6
Fengshan Taiwan 22°38N 120°21E 225 D2
Fengshun China 23°46N 116°10E 229 F11
Fengtai Anhui, China 32°50N 116°40E 229 A11
Fengtai Beijing, China 39°49N 116°14E 114 C1
Fengtai Stadium China 39°51N 116°15E 114 B1
Fengxian China 30°55N 121°26E 229 B13
Fengxiang China 34°29N 107°25E 226 G4
Fengxin China 28°41N 115°18E 229 C10
Fengyang China 32°51N 117°29E 227 H9
Fengyi China 25°37N 100°20E 228 E3
Fengyüan Taiwan 24°15N 120°35E 225 B2
Fengzhen China 40°25N 113°2E 226 D7
Feni Is. Papua N. G. 4°0S 153°40E 286 C7
Fenino Russia 55°43N 37°56E 129 B5
Fennimore U.S.A. 42°59N 90°39W 310 B6
Fenny Bangla. 22°55N 91°32E 241 D3
Feno, C. de France 41°58N 8°33E 175 G12
Fenoarivo Fianarantsoa,
Madag. 21°43S 46°24E 272 C2
Fenoarivo Fianarantsoa,
Madag. 20°52S 46°53E 272 C2
Fenoarivo Afovoany
Madag. 18°26S 46°34E 272 B2
Fenoarivo Atsinanana
Madag. 17°22S 49°25E 272 B2
Fens, The U.K. 52°38N 0°2W 168 E7
Fensmark Denmark 55°17N 11°48E 163 J5
Fenton U.S.A. 42°48N 83°42W 311 B13
Fenxi China 36°40N 111°31E 226 F6
Fenyang China 37°18N 111°48E 226 F6
Fenyi China 27°45N 114°47E 229 D10
Fenyuan Taiwan 24°1N 120°37E 225 B2
Feodosiya Ukraine 45°2N 35°16E 189 K8
Fer, C. de Algeria 37°3N 7°10E 261 A6
Fera Solomon Is. 8°6S 159°37E 287 M10
Ferbane Ireland 53°16N 7°50W 166 C4
Ferdows Iran 33°58N 58°2E 247 C8
Fère-Champenoise
France 48°45N 3°59E 173 D10
Fère-en-Tardenois France 49°10N 3°30E 173 C10
Ferencváros Hungary 47°29N 19°5E 117 B2
Ferentino Italy 41°42N 13°15E 199 G10
Feres Greece 40°53N 26°10E 203 F10
Ferfer Somali Rep. 5°4N 45°9E 267 C6
Fergana = Farghona
Uzbekistan 40°23N 71°19E 217 D8
Fergana Range Asia 41°0N 73°50E 217 D8
Fergus Canada 43°43N 80°24W 312 C4
Fergus Falls U.S.A. 46°17N 96°4W 308 B5
Ferguson U.S.A. 38°44N 90°18W 310 F6
Fergusson I. Papua N. G. 9°30S 150°45E 286 E6
Fériana Tunisia 34°59N 8°33E 258 B1
Feričanci Croatia 45°32N 18°0E 182 E2
Ferihegy, Budapest ✕ (BUD)
Hungary 47°26N 19°14E 117 B3
Ferkane Algeria 34°37N 7°26E 261 B6
Ferkéssédougou Ivory C. 9°35N 5°6W 262 D3
Ferlach Austria 46°32N 14°18E 180 E7
Ferland Canada 50°19N 88°27W 298 B2
Ferlo, Vallée du Senegal 15°15N 14°15W 262 B2
Ferlo-Nord ⌓ Senegal 15°43N 14°0W 262 B2
Ferlo-Sud ⌓ Senegal 15°43N 14°0W 262 B2
Fermanagh □ U.K. 54°21N 7°40W 166 B4
Fermo Italy 43°9N 13°43E 199 E10
Fermont Canada 52°47N 67°5W 299 B6
Fermoselle Spain 41°19N 6°27W 194 D4
Fermoy Ireland 52°9N 8°16W 166 D3
Fern Creek U.S.A. 38°9N 85°36W 311 G11
Fern Gully Jamaica 18°22N 77°5W 320 a
Fernán Núñez Spain 37°40N 4°44W 195 H6
Fernández Argentina 27°55S 63°50W 334 B3
Fernandina, I. Ecuador 0°25S 91°30W 330 a
Fernandina Beach
U.S.A. 30°40N 81°27W 316 E8
Fernando de Noronha
Brazil 4°0S 33°10W 152 G8
Fernando Póo = Bioko
Eq. Guin. 3°30N 8°40E 263 E6
Fernandópolis Brazil 20°16S 50°14W 333 F1
Ferndale Ont., Canada 44°58N 81°17W 312 B3
Ferndale Gauteng, S. Africa 26°5S 28°0E 123 A2
Ferndale Wash., U.S.A. 48°51N 122°36W 306 B4
Fernie Canada 49°30N 115°5W 296 D5
Fernlees Australia 23°51S 148°7E 280 C4
Fernley U.S.A. 39°36N 119°15W 304 G4
Fernwood U.S.A. 43°16N 73°38W 313 C11
Feroke India 11°9N 75°46E 245 J2
Feroz Shah Kotla Cricket Stadium
Delhi, India 120 b3
Ferozepore = Firozpur
India 30°55N 74°40E 242 D6
Ferrandina Italy 40°29N 16°27E 201 B9
Ferrara Italy 44°50N 11°35E 199 D8
Ferrato, C. Italy 39°18N 9°38E 200 C2
Ferré, C. Martinique 14°27N 60°49W 322 j
Ferreira do Alentejo
Portugal 38°4N 8°6W 195 G2
Ferreira Gomes Brazil 0°48N 51°8W 332 A1
Ferreñafe Peru 6°42S 79°50W 330 B2
Ferrerías Spain 39°59N 4°1E 206 B5
Ferret, C. France 44°38N 1°15W 174 D2
Ferrette France 47°30N 7°20E 173 E14
Ferriday U.S.A. 31°38N 91°33W 314 F9
Ferriere Italy 44°40N 9°30E 198 D6
Ferrières France 48°5N 2°48E 173 D9
Ferro, Capo Italy 41°9N 9°31E 200 A2
Ferrol Spain 43°29N 8°15W 194 B2
Ferrol, Pen. de Peru 9°10S 78°35W 330 B2
Ferron U.S.A. 39°5N 111°8W 304 G8
Ferros Brazil 19°14S 43°2W 333 E3
Ferrutx, C. de Spain 39°47N 3°21E 206 B4
Ferry Pass U.S.A. 30°31N 87°13W 317 E2
Ferryland Canada 47°2N 52°53W 299 C9
Ferrysburg U.S.A. 43°5N 86°13W 311 A10
Ferryville = Menzel-Bourguiba
Tunisia 37°9N 9°49E 258 A1
Fertile U.S.A. 47°32N 96°17W 308 B5
Fertő-Hanság △ Hungary 47°25N 16°50E 182 C1
Fertőszentmiklós
Hungary 47°35N 16°53E 182 C1
Fès Morocco 34°0N 5°0W 260 B4
Fès □ Morocco 34°1N 5°0W 260 B4
Feshi Dem. Rep. of the Congo 6°8S 18°10E 265 D3
Fessenden U.S.A. 47°39N 99°38W 308 B4
Festenberg = Twardogóra
Poland 51°23N 17°28E 185 G4
Festøya Norway 62°22N 6°19E 164 B3
Festus U.S.A. 38°13N 90°24W 310 F6
Feté Bowé Senegal 14°56N 13°30W 262 C2
Fetești Romania 44°22N 27°51E 183 F12
Fethiye Turkey 36°36N 29°6E 205 E11
Fethiye Körfezi Turkey 36°40N 28°50E 205 E10
Fetlar U.K. 60°36N 0°52W 167 A8
Fetsund Norway 59°56N 11°10E 164 E8
Feuilles ➜ Canada 58°47N 70°4W 295 F17
Feurs France 45°45N 4°13E 175 C8
Fevik Norway 58°22N 8°39E 164 F5
Fevzipaşa Turkey 37°6N 36°37E 250 A7
Feyzābād Badakhshān,
Afghan. 37°7N 70°33E 240 A3
Feyzābād Fāryāb, Afghan. 36°17N 64°52E 240 A2
Fez = Fès Morocco 34°0N 5°0W 260 B4
Fezzan Libya 27°0N 13°0E 258 C2
Fia Congo 3°25S 14°49E 264 C2
Fiambalá Argentina 27°45S 67°37W 334 B2
Fianarantsoa Madag. 21°26S 47°5E 272 C2
Fianarantsoa □ Madag. 19°30S 47°0E 272 B2
Fianga Cameroon 9°55N 15°9E 259 G3
Fiche Ethiopia 9°50N 38°46E 257 F4
Fichtelgebirge Germany 50°2N 11°55E 179 E7
Fichtelgebirge ⌓ Germany 50°8N 12°0E 179 E8
Fichtenau Germany 52°27N 13°42E 115 B5
Ficksburg S. Africa 28°51S 27°53E 271 C4
Fidenza Italy 44°52N 10°3E 198 D7
Fiditi Nigeria 7°45N 3°53E 263 D5
Fidjeland Norway 58°57N 6°56E 164 F3
Field ➜ Australia 23°48S 138°0E 280 C2
Field I. Australia 12°5S 132°23E 278 B5
Field Museum of Natural History
Chicago, U.S.A. 119 e2
Fields Corner U.S.A. 42°18N 71°3W 116 B2
Fieni Romania 45°8N 25°25E 183 E10
Fier Albania 40°43N 19°33E 202 F3
Fiera Camp Italy 45°28N 9°8E 129 B1
Fierzë Albania 42°15N 20°1E 202 D4
Fife □ U.K. 56°16N 3°1W 167 E5
Fife ⌓ U.K. 56°15N 3°15W 167 E5
Fife Ness U.K. 56°17N 2°35W 167 E6
Fifth Cataract Sudan 18°22N 33°50E 256 D3
Fig Tree St. Kitts & Nevis 17°8N 62°35W 322 d
Figari France 41°29N 9°7E 175 G13
Figeac France 44°37N 2°2E 174 D6
Figeholm Sweden 57°22N 16°33E 163 G10
Figino Italy 45°29N 9°4E 129 B1
Figline Valdarno Italy 43°37N 11°28E 199 E8
Figtree Zimbabwe 20°22S 28°20E 269 G2
Figueira = Governador Valadares
Brazil 18°15S 41°57W 333 E3
Figueira Castelo Rodrigo
Portugal 40°57N 6°58W 194 E4
Figueira da Foz Portugal 40°7N 8°54W 194 E2
Figueiró dos Vinhos
Portugal 39°55N 8°16W 194 F2
Figueres Spain 42°18N 2°58E 196 C7
Figuig Morocco 32°5N 1°11W 261 B4
Figuig □ Morocco 32°50N 2°15W 261 B5
Fihaonana Madag. 18°36S 47°12E 272 B2
Fiherenana Madag. 18°29S 48°24E 272 B2
Fiherenana ➜ Madag. 23°19S 43°37E 272 C1
Fiji ■ Pac. Oc. 17°20S 179°0E 287 A2
Fijir Iraq 33°21N 44°21E 113 A2
Fik Ethiopia 8°10N 42°19E 257 F5
Fika Nigeria 11°15N 11°13E 263 C7
Filabres, Sierra de los
Spain 37°13N 2°20W 195 H8
Filabusi Zimbabwe 20°34S 29°20E 271 B4
Filadélfia Bolivia 11°20S 68°46W 330 C4
Filadélfia Brazil 7°21S 47°30W 332 C2
Filadelfia Athina, Greece 38°2N 23°43E 112 A2
Filadélfia Italy 38°47N 16°17E 201 D9
Filadelfia Paraguay 22°21S 60°2W 334 A3
Fil'akovo Slovak Rep. 48°17N 19°50E 181 C12
Filchner Ice Shelf
Antarctica 79°0S 40°0W 151 D1
Filefjell Norway 61°8N 8°10E 164 C5
Filey U.K. 54°12N 0°18W 168 C7
Filey B. U.K. 54°12N 0°15W 168 C7
Filfla Malta 35°47N 14°24E 206 F7
Fili-Mazilovo Russia 55°44N 37°29E 129 B2
Filiaşi Romania 44°32N 23°31E 183 F8
Filiates Greece 39°38N 20°16E 206 B10
Filiatra Greece 37°9N 21°35E 204 D3
Filicudi Italy 38°35N 14°33E 201 D7
Filim Oman 20°37N 58°12E 249 B7
Filingué Niger 14°21N 3°22E 263 C5
Filiouri = Lissos ➜
Greece 41°15N 25°40E 203 E9
Filipada Greece 39°12N 20°53E 204 B2
Filipstad Sweden 59°43N 14°9E 162 E8
Filisur Switz. 46°41N 9°40E 179 J5
Fillmore Calif., U.S.A. 34°24N 118°55W 307 L8
Fillmore Utah, U.S.A. 38°58N 112°20W 304 G7
Filothei Greece 38°2N 23°46E 112 A2
Filotio Greece 37°3N 25°30E 205 D7
Filottrano Italy 43°26N 13°21E 199 E10
Filtu Ethiopia 5°8N 40°35E 257 F5
Fimbul Ice Shelf S. Ocean 69°30S 1°0W 151 C2
Fimi ➜
Dem. Rep. of the Congo 3°1S 16°58E 264 C3
Fina ⌓ Mali 13°15N 8°46W 262 C3
Finale Emília Italy 44°50N 11°18E 199 D8
Finale Ligure Italy 44°10N 8°20E 198 D5
Finalmarina = Finale Ligure
Italy 44°10N 8°20E 198 D5
Fiñana Spain 37°10N 2°50W 195 H8
Financial District San Francisco, U.S.A. 136 b3
Finch Canada 45°11N 75°7W 313 A9
Finch Hatton Australia 20°25S 148°39E 280 b
Finchaa, L. Ethiopia 9°35N 37°20E 266 C4
Finchley U.K. 51°36N 0°11W 125 A2
Findhorn ➜ U.K. 57°38N 3°38W 167 D5
Findıklı Turkey 41°16N 41°9E 213 B9
Findlay U.S.A. 41°2N 83°39W 311 C13
Fine U.S.A. 44°14N 75°8W 313 B9
Fine Art, Museum of =
Kunsthistorischesmuseum
Vienna, Austria 142 b1
Fine Arts, Museum of
U.S.A. 42°20N 71°5W 116 A2
Finger L. Canada 53°33N 93°30W 298 B1
Finger Lakes U.S.A. 42°40N 76°30W 313 D8
Finglas Ireland 53°23N 6°19W 120 A2
Fingoè Mozam. 14°55S 31°50E 269 E3
Finike Turkey 36°21N 30°10E 205 E12
Finike Körfezi Turkey 36°17N 30°16E 205 E12
Finiq Albania 39°54N 20°3E 202 G4
Finistère □ France 48°20N 4°0W 172 D3
Finisterre = Fisterra Spain 42°54N 9°16W 194 C1
Finisterre, C. = Fisterra, C.
Spain 42°50N 9°19W 194 C1
Finisterre Ra. Papua N. G. 6°0S 146°30E 286 D4
Finke Australia 25°34S 134°35E 280 D1
Finke Gorge △ Australia 24°8S 132°49E 278 D5
Finland ■ Europe 63°0N 27°0E 160 E22
Finland, G. of Europe 60°0N 26°0E 188 C3
Finlay ➜ Canada 57°0N 125°10W 296 B3
Finley N.S.W., Australia 35°38S 145°35E 283 C6
Finley N. Dak., U.S.A. 47°31N 97°50W 308 B5
Finn ➜ Ireland 54°51N 7°28W 166 B4
Finnerödja Sweden 58°57N 14°24E 163 F8
Finnigan, Mt. Australia 15°49S 145°17E 280 B4
Finniss, C. Australia 33°8S 134°51E 281 E1
Finnmark Norway 69°37N 23°57E 160 B20
Finnsnes Norway 69°14N 18°0E 160 B18
Finsbury U.K. 51°31N 0°6W 125 A3
Finsbury Park U.K. 51°34N 0°6W 125 A3
Finschhafen Papua N. G. 6°33S 147°50E 286 D4
Finse Norway 60°36N 7°30E 164 D4
Finspång Sweden 58°43N 15°47E 163 F9
Finsteraarhorn Switz. 46°31N 8°10E 179 J4
Finsterwalde Germany 51°37N 13°42E 178 D9
Fiora ➜ Italy 42°20N 11°34E 199 F8
Fiordland △ N.Z. 45°46S 167°0E 285 F2
Fiorenzuola d'Arda Italy 44°56N 9°55E 198 D6
Fiorito Argentina 34°42S 58°26W 117 C2
Fiq Syria 32°46N 35°41E 250 F6
Firat = Furāt, Nahr al ➜
Asia 31°0N 47°25E 246 D5
Fire Island ⌓ U.S.A. 40°38N 73°8W 313 F11
Firebag ➜ Canada 57°45N 111°21W 297 B6
Firebaugh U.S.A. 36°52N 120°27W 306 J6
Firedrake L. Canada 61°25N 104°30W 297 A8
Firenze Italy 43°46N 11°15E 199 E8
Firenze Amerigo Vespucci ✕ (FLR)
Italy 43°49N 11°13E 199 E8
Firenze Pisa ✕ (PSA)
Italy 43°40N 10°22E 198 E7
Firenzuola Italy 44°7N 11°23E 199 D8
Firhouse Ireland 53°17N 6°20W 120 B2
Firk, Sha'ib ➜ Iraq 30°59N 44°34E 246 D5
Firkachi Niger 15°40N 14°20E 259 E2
Firmi France 44°33N 2°19E 174 D6
Firminy France 45°23N 4°18E 175 C8
Firozabad India 27°10N 78°25E 243 F8
Firozpur India 30°55N 74°40E 242 D6
Firozpur-Jhirka India 27°48N 76°57E 242 F7
Fīrūzābād Iran 28°52N 52°35E 247 D7
Fīrūzkūh Iran 35°50N 52°50E 247 C7
Firvale Canada 52°27N 126°13W 296 C3
Fischerhäuser Germany 48°14N 11°41E 131 A3
Fish ➜ Namibia 28°7S 17°10E 270 C2
Fish ➜ Northern Cape,
S. Africa 31°30S 20°16E 270 D3
Fish River Canyon
Namibia 27°40S 17°35E 270 C2
Fisheating Cr. ➜ U.S.A. 26°57N 81°7W 317 J8
Fisher B. Canada 51°35N 97°13W 297 C9
Fisher Island U.S.A. 25°45N 80°8W 128 B2
Fishermans Bend
Australia 37°49S 144°55E 128 A1
Fisherman's Wharf
San Francisco, U.S.A. 136 a1
Fishers I. U.S.A. 41°15N 72°0W 313 E13
Fisherville Canada 43°46N 79°28W 141 A2
Fishguard U.K. 52°0N 4°58W 169 E3
Fishing L. Canada 52°10N 95°24W 297 C9
Fishkill U.S.A. 41°32N 73°54W 313 E11
Fiskardo Greece 38°28N 20°35E 207 C2
Fiskenæsset = Qeqertarsuatsiaat
Greenland 63°5N 50°45W 154 E5
Fisksätra Sweden 59°17N 18°13E 139 B3
Fismes France 49°20N 3°40E 173 C10
Fisterra Spain 42°54N 9°16W 194 C1
Fisterra, C. Spain 42°50N 9°19W 194 C1
Fitchburg Mass., U.S.A. 42°35N 71°48W 313 D13
Fitchburg Wis., U.S.A. 42°58N 89°28W 310 B7
Fitjar Iceland 64°28N 21°18W 155 C5
Fitjar Hordaland, Norway 59°55N 5°17E 164 E2
Fitri, L. Chad 12°50N 17°28E 259 F3
Fitz Roy Argentina 47°0S 67°0W 336 F3
Fitz Roy, Cerro Argentina 49°17S 73°5W 336 F2
Fitzgerald Alta., Canada 59°51N 111°36W 296 B6
Fitzgerald Ga., U.S.A. 31°43N 83°15W 316 D6
Fitzgerald River △
Australia 33°53S 119°55E 279 F3
Fitzmaurice ➜ Australia 14°45S 130°5E 278 B5
Fitzroy ➜ Queens.,
Australia 23°32S 150°52E 280 C5
Fitzroy ➜ W. Austral.,
Australia 17°31S 123°35E 278 C3
Fitzroy Crossing Australia 18°9S 125°38E 278 C4
Fitzroy Gardens
Australia 37°48S 144°58E 128 A1
Fitzwilliam I. Canada 45°30N 81°45W 312 A3
Fiuggi Italy 41°48N 13°13E 199 G10
Fiume = Rijeka Croatia 45°20N 14°21E 199 C11
Fiumicino, Roma ✕ (FCO)
Italy 41°48N 12°15E 199 G9
Five Cowrie Cr. ➜ Nigeria 6°26N 3°24E 124 B2
Five Dock Australia 33°52S 151°8E 139 B1
Five Island Harbour
Antigua & B. 17°6N 61°54W 322 b
Five Points U.S.A. 36°26N 120°6W 306 J6
Fivizzano Italy 44°14N 10°8E 198 D7
Fizi Dem. Rep. of the Congo 4°17S 28°55E 268 C2
Fjæra Norway 59°52N 6°22E 164 E3
Fjærland Norway 61°24N 6°43E 164 C3
Fjærlandsfjorden Norway 61°17N 6°40E 164 C3
Fjällbacka Sweden 58°36N 11°17E 163 F5
Fjärdhundra Sweden 59°47N 16°56E 162 E10
Fjellerup Denmark 56°29N 10°34E 163 H4
Fjellstrand Norway 59°47N 10°36E 133 B2
Fjerritslev Denmark 57°5N 9°15E 163 G3
Fjugesta Sweden 59°11N 14°52E 162 E8
Fkih ben Salah Morocco 32°32N 6°45W 260 B3
Flå Norway 60°25N 9°28E 164 D6
Flacq Plain Mauritius 20°13S 57°43E 272 e
Flagler Beach U.S.A. 29°29N 81°8W 317 F8
Flagstaff U.S.A. 35°12N 111°39W 305 J8
Flagstaff B. St. Helena 15°54S 5°41W 153 h
Flagstaff L. U.S.A. 45°12N 70°18W 313 A14
Flaherty I. Canada 56°15N 79°15W 298 A4
Flåm Norway 60°50N 7°7E 164 D4
Flamands St.-Martin 17°55N 62°51W 322 a
Flambeau ➜ U.S.A. 45°18N 91°14W 308 C8
Flamborough Hd. U.K. 54°7N 0°5W 168 C7
Flamengo Brazil 22°56S 43°11W 135 B1
Flamengos Azores 38°33N 28°39W 153 d1
Fläming Germany 52°6N 12°23E 178 C8
Flaming Gorge ⌓
U.S.A. 41°10N 109°25W 304 F9
Flaming Gorge Res.
U.S.A. 41°10N 109°25W 304 F9
Flamingo Fla., U.S.A. 28°22N 81°22W 133 B2
Flamingo Fla., U.S.A. 25°8N 80°57W 317 K9
Flamingo, Teluk Indonesia 5°30S 138°0E 231 F9
Flaminio Italy 41°55N 12°28E 136 B1
Flanagan U.S.A. 40°53N 88°52W 311 D8
Flanagin Town
Trin. & Tob. 10°25N 61°19W 323 t
Flanders = Flandre Europe 50°50N 2°30E 173 B9
Flandre Europe 50°50N 2°30E 173 B9
Flandre-Occidentale = West-
Vlaanderen □ Belgium 51°0N 3°0E 170 D2
Flandre-Orientale = Oost-
Vlaanderen □ Belgium 51°5N 3°50E 170 C3
Flandreau U.S.A. 44°3N 96°36W 308 C5
Flanigan U.S.A. 40°10N 119°53W 306 E7
Flannan Is. U.K. 58°9N 7°52W 167 C1
Flåsjön Sweden 64°5N 15°40E 160 D16
Flaskebekk Norway 59°51N 10°39E 133 A2
Flat U.S.A. 62°28N 158°1W 303 E8
Flat ➜ N.W.T., Canada 61°33N 125°18W 296 A3
Flat ➜ Mich., U.S.A. 42°56N 85°20W 311 B11
Flat Pt. N.Z. 41°14S 175°57E 284 H4
Flat Rock U.S.A. 42°6N 83°17W 311 B13
Flatbush U.S.A. 40°39N 73°56W 132 C2
Flateby Norway 59°50N 11°10E 164 E8
Flaten Sweden 59°15N 18°9E 139 B2
Flatey Iceland 66°10N 17°52W 155 A9
Flateyri Iceland 66°3N 23°31W 155 A3
Flathead L. U.S.A. 47°51N 114°8W 304 C6
Flatiron Building New York, U.S.A. 132 d2
Flatlands U.S.A. 40°37N 73°56W 132 C2
Flatow = Złotów Poland 53°22N 17°2E 184 E4
Flatrock ➜ U.S.A. 39°12N 85°56W 311 F10
Flattery, C. Queens.,
Australia 14°58S 145°21E 280 A4
Flattery, C. Wash.,
U.S.A. 48°23N 124°29W 306 B2
Flatts Village Bermuda 32°18N 64°43W 153 a
Flatwoods U.S.A. 38°31N 82°43W 309 F12
Flecha Pt. Phil. 7°22N 123°24E 233 H4
Flechas Pt. Phil. 10°22N 119°34E 233 F2
Fleet Center Boston, U.S.A. 116 a2
Fleetwood Lancs., U.K. 53°55N 3°1W 168 D4
Fleetwood Pa., U.S.A. 40°27N 75°49W 313 F9
Flekke Norway 61°19N 5°20E 164 C2
Flekkefjord Norway 58°18N 6°39E 164 F3
Flemingsburg U.S.A. 38°25N 83°45W 311 F13
Flemington U.S.A. 41°7N 77°28W 312 E7
Flemington Racecourse
Australia 37°47S 144°54E 128 A1
Flemish Cap Atl. Oc. 47°0N 45°0W 152 B7
Flen Sweden 59°4N 16°35E 162 E10
Flensburg Germany 54°47N 9°27E 178 A5
Flers France 48°47N 0°33W 172 D6
Flesberg Norway 59°51N 9°22E 164 E6
Flesherton Canada 44°16N 80°33W 312 B4
Flesko, Tanjung
Indonesia 0°29N 124°30E 231 D6
Fletcher = Aurora
U.S.A. 39°43N 104°49W 304 G11
Fleurance France 43°52N 0°40E 174 E4
Fleurier Switz. 46°54N 6°35E 179 J2
Fleurieu Pen. Australia 35°40S 138°5E 282 C3
Flevoland □ Neths. 52°30N 5°30E 170 B5
Flin Flon Canada 54°46N 101°53W 297 C8
Flinders ➜ Australia 17°36S 140°36E 280 B3
Flinders B. Australia 34°19S 115°19E 279 F2
Flinders Chase △
Australia 35°50S 136°42E 282 C2
Flinders Group Australia 14°11S 144°15E 280 A3
Flinders I. S. Austral.,
Australia 33°44S 134°41E 281 E1
Flinders I. Tas., Australia 40°0S 148°0E 281 G4
Flinders Ranges
Australia 31°30S 138°30E 282 A3
Flinders Ranges △
Australia 31°30S 138°40E 282 A3
Flinders Reefs Australia 17°37S 148°31E 280 B4
Flint U.K. 53°15N 3°8W 168 D4
Flint Mich., U.S.A. 43°1N 83°41W 311 A13
Flint ➜ U.S.A. 30°57N 84°34W 316 E5
Flint I. Kiribati 11°26S 151°48W 289 f
Flint Pk. U.S.A. 34°9N 118°11W 126 B3
Flintshire □ U.K. 53°17N 3°17W 168 D4
Flipper Pt. Wake I. 19°18N 166°37E 302 b
Flisa Norway 60°37N 12°0E 164 D9
Flisa ➜ Norway 60°37N 12°0E 164 D9
Fliseryd Sweden 57°6N 16°15E 163 G10
Flix Spain 41°14N 0°32E 196 D5
Flixecourt France 50°1N 2°5E 173 B9
Floby Sweden 58°8N 13°20E 163 F7
Floda Sweden 57°49N 12°22E 163 G6
Flodden U.K. 55°37N 2°8W 168 B5
Flogny-la-Chapelle
France 47°57N 3°57E 173 E10
Floodplains △ Sri Lanka 8°10N 81°10E 245 K5
Floodwood U.S.A. 46°56N 92°55W 308 B7
Flora Apayao, Phil. 18°14N 121°5E 232 B3
Flora Ill., U.S.A. 38°40N 88°29W 310 F8
Flora Ind., U.S.A. 40°33N 86°31W 311 D10
Florac France 44°20N 3°37E 174 D7
Florahome U.S.A. 29°44N 81°54W 316 F8
Floral City U.S.A. 28°45N 82°17W 317 G7
Florala U.S.A. 31°0N 86°20W 315 F11
Florânia Brazil 6°8S 36°49W 332 C4
Floreana, I. = Santa María, I.
Ecuador 1°17S 90°26W 330 a
Florence = Firenze Italy 43°46N 11°15E 199 E8
Florence Ala., U.S.A. 34°48N 87°41W 315 D11
Florence Ariz., U.S.A. 33°2N 111°23W 305 K8
Florence Calif., U.S.A. 33°57N 118°13W 126 C3
Florence Colo., U.S.A. 38°23N 105°8W 304 G11
Florence Oreg., U.S.A. 43°58N 124°7W 304 D1
Florence S.C., U.S.A. 34°12N 79°46W 315 D15
Florence, L. Australia 28°53S 138°9E 281 D2
Florence Bay = Chitimba
Malawi 10°35S 34°13E 269 E3
Florence Bloom Bird Sanctuary ⌓
S. Africa 26°7S 28°0E 123 A2
Florencia Colombia 1°36N 75°36W 328 C2
Florennes Belgium 50°15N 4°35E 170 D4
Florensac France 43°23N 3°28E 174 E7
Florentia S. Africa 26°16S 28°8E 123 B2
Florenville Belgium 49°40N 5°19E 170 E5
Flores = Florânia Brazil 6°8S 36°49W 332 C4
Flores = Timon Brazil 5°8S 42°52W 332 C3
Flores B. Aires, Argentina 34°38S 58°27W 117 B2
Flores Azores 39°26N 31°13W 153 d2
Flores Brazil 7°51S 37°59W 332 C4
Flores Guatemala 16°59N 89°50W 320 C2
Flores Indonesia 8°35S 121°0E 231 F6
Flores, Mercado de
Mexico 19°19N 99°5W 128 C2
Flores I. Canada 49°20N 126°10W 296 D3
Flores Sea Indonesia 6°30S 120°0E 231 F6
Floresta B. Aires,
Argentina 34°37S 58°27W 117 B2
Floresta Brazil 8°40S 37°26W 332 C4
Florești Moldova 47°53N 28°17E 183 C13
Floresville U.S.A. 29°8N 98°10W 314 G5
Floriano Brazil 6°50S 43°0W 332 C3
Florianópolis Brazil 27°30S 48°30W 335 B6
Florida B. Aires, Argentina 34°31S 58°28W 117 B2
Florida Cuba 21°32N 78°14W 320 B4
Florida Puerto Rico 18°22N 66°34W 321 b
Florida Gauteng, S. Africa 26°10S 27°55E 123 B1
Florida Uruguay 34°7S 56°10W 335 C4
Florida □ U.S.A. 28°0N 82°0W 315 G14
Florida, Straits of U.S.A. 25°0N 80°0W 320 B4
Florida B. U.S.A. 25°0N 80°45W 320 B3
Florida City U.S.A. 25°27N 80°29W 317 K9
Florida Is. Solomon Is. 9°55S 160°15E 287 M11
Florida Keys U.S.A. 24°40N 81°0W 317 L8
Floridablanca Phil. 14°59N 120°31E 232 D3
Floridia Italy 37°5N 15°9E 201 E8
Floridsdorf Austria 48°15N 16°26E 142 A2
Florin U.S.A. 38°30N 121°24W 306 G5
Florina Greece 40°48N 21°26E 202 F5
Florina □ Greece 40°45N 21°20E 202 F5
Florissant U.S.A. 38°47N 90°19W 310 F6
Florø Norway 61°35N 5°1E 164 C2
Flotte, C. de N. Cal. 21°10S 167°25E 288 d
Flotten Station Canada 45°10N 76°41W 313 A8
Flowerpot I. Canada 45°18N 81°38W 312 A3
Floydada U.S.A. 33°59N 101°20W 314 E4
Fludir Iceland 64°7N 20°6W 155 C6
Flugumyri Iceland 65°34N 19°19W 155 B7
Fluk Indonesia 1°42S 127°44E 231 E7
Flúmen ➜ Spain 41°43N 0°9W 196 D4
Flumendosa ➜ Italy 39°26N 9°37E 200 C2
Fluminimaggiore Italy 39°26N 8°30E 200 C1
Flushing = Vlissingen
Neths. 51°26N 3°34E 170 C3
Flushing Mich., U.S.A. 43°4N 83°51W 311 A13
Flushing N.Y., U.S.A. 40°45N 73°49W 132 B3
Flushing Meadows Corona Park
U.S.A. 40°44N 73°50W 132 B3
Fluvià ➜ Spain 42°12N 3°7E 196 C8
Fly ➜ Papua N. G. 8°25S 143°0E 286 E2
Flying Fish, C.
Antarctica 72°6S 102°29W 151 D15
Flysta Sweden 59°22N 17°54E 139 A1
Fo Tan China 22°23N 114°11E 122 A2
Foa Tonga 19°45S 174°18W 287 P13
Foam Lake Canada 51°40N 103°32W 297 C8
Foča Bos.-H. 43°31N 18°47E 202 C2
Foça Turkey 38°39N 26°46E 205 C8
Fochabers U.K. 57°37N 3°6W 167 D5
Focșani Romania 45°41N 27°15E 183 E12
Fodé C.A.R. 5°29N 23°18E 264 A4
Fodécontéa Guinea 10°50N 14°22W 262 C2
Fogang China 23°52N 113°30E 229 F9
Foggaret el Arab Algeria 27°13N 2°49E 261 C5
Foggaret ez Zoua Algeria 27°20N 2°53E 261 C5
Fóggia Italy 41°27N 15°34E 201 A8
Foggy Bottom U.S.A. 38°54N 77°3W 143 B3
Foglia ➜ Italy 43°55N 12°54E 199 E9
Fogo Nfld. & L., Canada 49°43N 54°17W 299 C9
Fogo C. Verde Is. 15°5N 24°20W 153 j
Fogo I. Canada 49°40N 54°5W 299 C9
Fohnsdorf Austria 47°12N 14°40E 180 D7
Föhr Germany 54°43N 8°30E 178 A4
Föhrenhain Austria 48°19N 16°26E 142 A2
Foia Portugal 37°19N 8°37W 195 H2
Foix France 42°58N 1°38E 174 F5
Fojnica Bos.-H. 43°59N 17°51E 182 G2
Fokida □ Greece 38°30N 22°15E 204 C4
Fokino Russia 53°30N 34°22E 188 F8
Fokku Nigeria 11°36N 4°32E 263 C5
Fokstugu Norway 62°7N 9°17E 164 B6
Folda Nord-Trøndelag,
Norway 64°32N 10°30E 160 D14
Folda Nordland, Norway 67°38N 14°50E 160 C16
Földeák Hungary 46°19N 20°30E 182 D5
Folegandros Greece 36°40N 24°55E 204 E6
Foley Botswana 21°34S 27°21E 270 B4
Foley Ala., U.S.A. 30°24N 87°41W 315 F11
Foley Fla., U.S.A. 30°4N 83°32W 316 E6
Foleyet Canada 48°15N 82°25W 298 C3
Folgefonna Norway 60°3N 6°23E 164 D3
Folgefonna △ Norway 60°5N 6°15E 164 D3
Foligno Italy 42°57N 12°42E 199 F9
Folkestad Norway 62°7N 6°1E 164 B3
Folkestone U.K. 51°5N 1°12E 169 F9
Folkestone Underwater Park
Barbados 13°11N 59°38W 323 r
Folkston U.S.A. 30°50N 82°0W 316 E7
Folla ➜ Norway 62°7N 10°37E 164 B7
Follansbee U.S.A. 40°19N 80°35W 312 F4
Folldal Norway 62°8N 10°0E 164 B6
Folle Anse, Pte. de
Guadeloupe 15°56N 61°19W 322 e
Follebu Norway 61°13N 10°16E 164 C7
Follónica Italy 42°55N 10°45E 198 F7
Follónica, G. di Italy 42°54N 10°43E 198 F7
Folsom L. U.S.A. 38°42N 121°9W 306 G5
Foltești Romania 45°45N 28°3E 183 E13
Fomboni Comoros Is. 12°18S 43°46E 272 a
Fomm ir-Rih Bay Malta 35°54N 14°20E 206 F7
Fond-du-Lac Sask.,
Canada 59°19N 107°12W 297 B7
Fond du Lac Wis., U.S.A. 43°47N 88°27W 308 D9
Fond-du-Lac ➜ Canada 59°17N 106°0W 297 B7
Fond Rousseau Martinique 14°38N 61°6W 322 j
Fond St. Jacques St. Lucia 13°50N 61°1W 323 m
Fonda Iowa, U.S.A. 42°35N 94°51W 310 B2
Fonda N.Y., U.S.A. 42°57N 74°22W 313 D10
Fondi Italy 41°21N 13°25E 200 A6
Fonds-St-Denis Martinique 14°44N 61°8W 322 j
Fonfría Spain 41°37N 6°9W 194 D4
Fongafale Tuvalu 8°31S 179°13E 277 B14
Fongen Norway 63°11N 11°38E 164 A8
Fonni Italy 40°7N 9°15E 200 B2
Fonsagrada = A Fonsagrada
Spain 43°8N 7°4W 194 B3
Fonseca, G. de
Cent. Amer. 13°10N 87°40W 320 D2
Font-Romeu-Odeillo-Via
France 42°31N 2°3E 174 F5
Fontaine-Française
France 47°32N 5°21E 173 E12
Fontainebleau Seine-et-Marne,
France 48°24N 2°40E 173 D9
Fontainebleau Gauteng,
S. Africa 26°6S 27°57E 123 A1
Fontana U.S.A. 34°6N 117°26W 307 L9
Fontana, L. Argentina 44°55S 71°30W 336 B2
Fontas ➜ Canada 58°14N 121°48W 296 B4
Fonte Boa Brazil 2°33S 66°0W 328 D4
Fontem Cameroon 5°32N 9°52E 263 D6
Fontenay-aux-Roses
France 48°47N 2°17E 134 B2
Fontenay-le-Comte
France 46°28N 0°48W 174 B3
Fontenay-le-Fleury France 48°48N 2°2E 134 B1
Fontenay-sous-Bois
France 48°51N 2°28E 134 A3
Fontenelle Res. U.S.A. 42°1N 110°3W 304 E8
Fontur Iceland 66°23N 14°32W 155 A12
Fonuafo'ou Tonga 20°19S 175°25W 287 Q13
Fonuakula Cook Is. 19°2S 169°55W 289 g
Fonualei Tonga 18°1S 174°19W 287 P13
Fonyód Hungary 46°44N 17°33E 182 D2
Foochow = Fuzhou
China 26°5N 119°16E 229 D12
Foots Cray U.K. 51°24N 0°7E 125 B4
Footscray Australia 37°48S 144°56E 128 A1
Foping China 33°41N 108°0E 226 H5
Foraker, Mt. U.S.A. 62°58N 151°24W 303 E10
Forari Vanuatu 17°40S 168°31E 287 G6
Forbach France 49°10N 6°52E 173 C13
Forbes Australia 33°22S 148°5E 283 B8
Forbesganj India 26°17N 87°18E 243 F12
Forbidden City = Imperial Palace
Museum Beijing, China 114 b3
Forcados Nigeria 5°26N 5°26E 263 D6
Forcados ➜ Nigeria 5°25N 5°19E 263 D6
Forcalquier France 43°58N 5°47E 175 E9
Forchheim Germany 49°43N 11°2E 179 F7
Ford City Calif., U.S.A. 35°9N 119°27W 307 K7
Ford City Pa., U.S.A. 40°46N 79°32W 312 F5
Ford d'Or B. St. Lucia 13°56N 60°54W 323 m
Ford I. U.S.A. 21°22N 157°58W 302 K14
Førda ➜ Norway 62°57N 10°40E 164 B7
Førde Hordaland, Norway 59°36N 5°27E 164 E2
Førde Rogaland, Norway 59°26N 5°23E 164 E2
Førde Sogn og Fjordane,
Norway 61°27N 5°53E 164 C2
Førdefjorden Norway 61°29N 5°18E 164 C2
Fords Bridge Australia 29°41S 145°29E 281 D4
Ford's Theater Washington, D.C., U.S.A. 143 b2
Fordyce U.S.A. 33°49N 92°25W 314 E8
Forécariah Guinea 9°28N 13°10W 262 D2
Forel, Mt. Greenland 66°52N 36°55W 154 D7
Foremost Canada 49°26N 111°34W 296 D6
Foreshore Cape Town, S. Africa 118 a3
Forest Belgium 50°49N 4°20E 116 B1
Forest Ont., Canada 43°6N 82°0W 312 C3
Forest Miss., U.S.A. 32°22N 89°29W 315 E10
Forest Acres U.S.A. 34°1N 80°58W 316 A9
Forest City Iowa, U.S.A. 43°16N 93°39W 308 D7
Forest City N.C., U.S.A. 35°20N 81°52W 315 D14
Forest City Pa., U.S.A. 41°39N 75°28W 313 E9
Forest Gate U.K. 51°32N 0°1E 125 A4
Forest Grove U.S.A. 45°31N 123°7W 306 E3
Forest Heights U.S.A. 38°48N 77°0W 143 C3
Forest Hill Ont., Canada 43°41N 79°25W 141 A2
Forest Hill London, U.K. 51°26N 0°2W 125 B3
Forest Hills U.S.A. 40°42N 73°51W 132 B3
Forest Park Ga., U.S.A. 33°37N 84°22W 316 B5
Forest Park Ill., U.S.A. 41°51N 87°47W 119 B2
Forest Park N.Y., U.S.A. 40°42N 73°51W 132 B3
Forest Park Ohio, U.S.A. 39°17N 84°30W 311 E12
Forest View U.S.A. 41°48N 87°47W 119 C2
Forestburg Canada 52°35N 112°1W 296 C6
Foreste Casentinesi-Monte
Falterona-Campigna △
Italy 43°50N 11°48E 199 E8
Foresthill U.S.A. 39°1N 120°49W 306 F6
Forestier Pen. Australia 43°0S 148°0E 281 G4
Forestville Qué., Canada 48°48N 69°2W 299 C6
Forestville Calif., U.S.A. 38°28N 122°54W 306 G4
Forestville Md., U.S.A. 38°50N 76°52W 143 B4
Forestville N.Y., U.S.A. 42°28N 79°10W 312 D5
Forêt d'Orient ⌓ France 48°16N 4°25E 173 D11
Forêt du Day ⌓ Djibouti 11°56N 42°40E 267 B5
Forez, Mts. du France 45°40N 3°50E 174 C7
Forfar U.K. 56°39N 2°53W 167 E6
Forillon △ Canada 48°46N 64°12W 299 C7
Forks U.S.A. 47°57N 124°23W 306 C2
Forks, The = Merritt
Canada 50°10N 120°45W 296 C4
Forksville U.S.A. 41°29N 76°35W 313 E8
Forlì Italy 44°13N 12°3E 199 D9
Forman U.S.A. 46°7N 97°38W 308 B5
Formazza Italy 46°22N 8°26E 198 B5
Formby Pt. U.K. 53°33N 3°6W 168 D4
Formentera Spain 38°43N 1°27E 206 D1

Formentor, C. de Spain 39°58N 3°13E 206 B4
Formentor, Pen. de Spain 39°56N 3°11E 206 B4
Former Yugoslav Republic of Macedonia = Macedonia ■ Europe 41°53N 21°40E 202 E5
Fórmia Italy 41°15N 13°37E 200 A6
Formiga Brazil 20°27S 45°25W 333 F2
Formigine Italy 44°37N 10°51E 198 D7
Formosa = Taiwan ■ Asia 23°30N 121°0E 225 C3
Formosa Argentina 26°15S 58°10W 334 B4
Formosa Brazil 15°32S 47°20W 333 E2
Formosa ☐ Argentina 25°0S 60°0W 334 B4
Formosa, Serra Brazil 12°0S 55°0W 331 C7
Formosa B. = Ungwana B. Kenya 2°45S 40°20E 268 C5
Formosa do Rio Prêto Brazil 11°2S 45°3W 332 D2
Formosa Strait = Taiwan Strait Asia 24°40N 120°0E 229 E12
Formoso → Brazil 10°34S 49°56W 333 D2
Fornebu Norway 59°53N 10°36E 133 A2
Fornells Spain 40°3N 4°7E 206 A5
Fornos de Algodres Portugal 40°38N 7°32W 194 E3
Fornovo di Taro Italy 44°42N 10°6E 198 D7
Foro Romano Rome, Italy 136 c3
Føroyar ☐ Atl. Oc. 62°0N 7°0W 160 F9
Forres U.K. 57°37N 3°37W 167 D5
Forrest Vic., Australia 38°33S 143°47E 282 E5
Forrest W. Austral., Australia 30°51S 128°6E 279 F4
Forrest, Mt. Australia 24°48S 127°45E 279 D4
Forrest City U.S.A. 35°1N 90°47W 315 D9
Forreston U.S.A. 42°8N 89°35W 310 B7
Fors Sweden 60°14N 16°20E 162 D10
Forsand Norway 58°54N 6°5E 164 F3
Forsayth Australia 18°33S 143°34E 280 B3
Forshaga Sweden 59°33N 13°29E 162 E7
Förslöv Sweden 56°21N 12°48E 163 H6
Forsmo Sweden 63°16N 17°11E 162 A11
Forssa Finland 60°49N 23°38E 188 B2
Forst Germany 51°45N 14°37E 178 D10
Forstenried Germany 48°5N 11°29E 131 B1
Forstenrieder Park Germany 48°3N 11°27E 131 B1
Forster Australia 32°12S 152°31E 283 B10
Forsvik Sweden 58°35N 14°26E 163 F8
Forsyth Ga., U.S.A. 33°2N 83°56W 316 B6
Forsyth Mont., U.S.A. 46°16N 106°41W 304 C10
Forsyth I. N.Z. 40°58S 174°5E 285 A9
Fort Mumbai, India 130 c2
Fort Abbas Pakistan 29°12N 72°52E 242 E5
Fort Albany Canada 52°15N 81°35W 298 B3
Fort-Aleksandrovsky = Fort Shevchenko Kazakhstan 44°35N 50°23E 191 H10
Fort Archambault = Sarh Chad 9°5N 18°23E 259 G3
Fort Assiniboine Canada 54°20N 114°45W 296 C6
Fort Atkinson U.S.A. 42°56N 88°50W 311 B8
Fort Augustus U.K. 57°9N 4°42W 167 D4
Fort Bay Neth. Ant. 17°37N 63°15W 322 a
Fort Bayard = Zhanjiang China 21°15N 110°20E 229 G8
Fort Beaufort S. Africa 32°46S 26°40E 270 D4
Fort Benton U.S.A. 47°49N 110°40W 304 C8
Fort Bragg U.S.A. 39°26N 123°48W 304 G2
Fort Bridger U.S.A. 41°19N 110°23W 304 F8
Fort Canning Park Singapore 138 b2
Fort Caroline ⌂ U.S.A. 30°23N 81°30W 316 E8
Fort Charles Jamaica 17°55N 76°50W 320 a
Fort Charlotte St. Lucia 13°59N 61°0W 323 m
Fort Chipewyan Canada 58°42N 111°8W 297 B6
Fort Clatsop = Lewis and Clark ⌂ U.S.A. 46°8N 123°53W 306 D3
Fort Collins U.S.A. 40°35N 105°5W 304 F11
Fort-Coulonge Canada 45°50N 76°45W 298 C4
Fort Covington U.S.A. 44°59N 74°29W 313 B10
Fort Dauphin = Taolanaro Madag. 25°2S 47°0E 272 D2
Fort Davis Ala., U.S.A. 32°15N 85°43W 316 C4
Fort Davis Tex., U.S.A. 30°35N 103°54W 314 F3
Fort-de-France Martinique 14°36N 61°2W 322 j
Fort-de-France, B. de Martinique 14°34N 61°4W 322 j
Fort de Kock = Bukittinggi Indonesia 0°20S 100°20E 234 C2
Fort de Polignac = Illizi Algeria 26°31N 8°32E 261 C6
Fort de Possel = Possel C.A.R. 5°5N 19°10E 264 A3
Fort Defiance U.S.A. 35°45N 109°5W 305 J9
Fort Dodge U.S.A. 42°30N 94°11W 310 B2
Fort Drum U.S.A. 27°32N 80°48W 317 H9
Fort Dupont Park U.S.A. 38°52N 76°56W 143 B4
Fort Edward U.S.A. 43°16N 73°35W 313 C11
Fort Erie Canada 42°54N 78°56W 312 D6
Fort Fairfield U.S.A. 46°46N 67°50W 309 B20
Fort Flatters = Bordj Omar Driss Algeria 28°10N 6°40E 261 C6
Fort Foote Village U.S.A. 38°46N 77°1W 143 C3
Fort-Foureau = Kousseri Cameroon 12°0N 14°55E 259 F2
Fort Frances Canada 48°36N 93°24W 297 D10
Fort Franklin = Déline Canada 65°11N 123°25W 294 D7
Fort Frederica ⌂ U.S.A. 31°13N 81°23W 316 D8
Fort Gaines U.S.A. 31°36N 85°3W 316 D4
Fort Garland U.S.A. 37°26N 105°26W 305 H11
Fort George = Chisasibi Canada 53°50N 79°0W 298 B4
Fort George = Prince George Canada 53°55N 122°50W 296 C4
Fort George Grenada 12°3N 61°45W 323 q
Fort Good Hope Canada 66°14N 128°40W 294 D6
Fort Gouraud = Fdérik Mauritania 22°40N 12°45W 260 D2
Fort Hancock U.S.A. 31°18N 105°51W 314 F2
Fort Hertz = Putao Burma 27°28N 97°30E 241 B6
Fort Hill = Chitipa Malawi 9°41S 33°19E 269 D3
Fort Hope = Eabametoong Canada 51°30N 88°0W 298 B2
Fort Irwin U.S.A. 35°16N 116°41W 307 K10
Fort Jameson = Chipata Zambia 13°38S 32°28E 269 E3
Fort Jeudy, Pt. of Grenada 11°59N 61°42W 323 q
Fort Johnston = Mangochi Malawi 14°25S 35°16E 269 E4
Fort Kent U.S.A. 47°15N 68°36W 309 B19
Fort Klamath U.S.A. 42°42N 122°0W 304 D3
Fort Lamy = Ndjamena Chad 12°10N 15°0E 259 F3
Fort-Laperrine = Tamanrasset Algeria 22°50N 5°30E 261 D6
Fort Laramie U.S.A. 42°13N 104°31W 304 E11
Fort Lauderdale U.S.A. 26°7N 80°8W 317 J9
Fort Lee U.S.A. 40°50N 73°58W 132 A2
Fort Liard Canada 60°14N 123°30W 296 A4
Fort Liberté Haiti 19°42N 71°51W 321 C5
Fort Lupton U.S.A. 40°5N 104°49W 304 F11
Fort MacKay Canada 57°12N 111°41W 296 B6
Fort Macleod Canada 49°45N 113°30W 296 D6
Fort MacMahon = El Homr Algeria 29°43N 1°45E 261 C5
Fort McMurray Canada 56°44N 111°7W 296 B6
Fort McPherson Canada 67°30N 134°55W 294 D5
Fort Madison U.S.A. 40°38N 91°27W 310 D5
Fort Manning = Mchinji Malawi 13°47S 32°58E 269 E3
Fort Mason Center San Francisco, U.S.A. 136 a1
Fort Matanzas ⌂ U.S.A. 29°43N 81°14W 316 F8
Fort Meade U.S.A. 27°45N 81°48W 317 H8
Fort Mitchell U.S.A. 32°20N 85°1W 316 C4
Fort Morgan U.S.A. 40°15N 103°48W 304 F12
Fort Myers U.S.A. 26°39N 81°52W 317 J8
Fort Myers Beach U.S.A. 26°26N 81°52W 317 J8
Fort Myers Villas U.S.A. 26°33N 81°52W 317 J8
Fort Napoléon Guadeloupe 15°52N 61°35W 322 e
Fort Nelson Canada 58°50N 122°44W 296 B4
Fort Nelson → Canada 59°32N 124°0W 296 B4
Fort Norman = Tulita Canada 64°57N 125°30W 294 E6
Fort Ogden U.S.A. 27°5N 81°57W 317 H8
Fort Payne U.S.A. 34°26N 85°43W 315 D12
Fort Peck U.S.A. 48°1N 106°27W 304 B10
Fort Peck Dam U.S.A. 48°0N 106°26W 304 C10
Fort Peck L. U.S.A. 48°0N 106°26W 304 C10
Fort Pierce U.S.A. 27°27N 80°20W 317 H9
Fort Pierre U.S.A. 44°21N 100°22W 308 C3
Fort Pierre Bordes = Ti-n-Zaouatene Algeria 19°55N 2°55E 261 E5
Fort Plain U.S.A. 42°56N 74°37W 313 D10
Fort Portal Uganda 0°40N 30°20E 268 B3
Fort Providence Canada 61°3N 117°40W 296 A5
Fort Pulaski ⌂ U.S.A. 32°2N 80°56W 316 C9
Fort Qu'Appelle Canada 50°45N 103°50W 297 C8
Fort Recovery U.S.A. 40°25N 84°47W 311 D12
Fort Resolution Canada 61°10N 113°40W 296 A6
Fort Rixon Zimbabwe 20°2S 29°17E 269 G2
Fort Rosebery = Mansa Zambia 11°13S 28°55E 269 E2
Fort Ross U.S.A. 38°32N 123°13W 306 G3
Fort-Rousset = Owando Congo 0°29S 15°55E 264 C3
Fort Rupert = Waskaganish Canada 51°30N 78°40W 298 B4
Fort St. James Canada 54°30N 124°10W 296 C4
Fort St. John Canada 56°15N 120°50W 296 B4
Fort Sandeman = Zhob Pakistan 31°20N 69°31E 242 D3
Fort Saskatchewan Canada 53°40N 113°15W 296 C6
Fort Scott U.S.A. 37°50N 94°42W 308 G6
Fort Severn Canada 56°0N 87°40W 298 A2
Fort Shevchenko Kazakhstan 44°35N 50°23E 191 H10
Fort Simpson Canada 61°45N 121°15W 296 A4
Fort Smith Alta., Canada 60°0N 111°51W 296 B6
Fort Smith Ark., U.S.A. 35°23N 94°25W 314 D7
Fort Stockton U.S.A. 30°53N 102°53W 314 F3
Fort Sumner U.S.A. 34°28N 104°15W 305 J11
Fort Thomas U.S.A. 39°4N 84°26W 311 E12
Fort Thompson U.S.A. 44°3N 99°26W 308 C4
Fort Trinquet = Bîr Mogreïn Mauritania 25°10N 11°25W 260 C2
Fort Union ⌂ U.S.A. 35°54N 105°1W 305 J11
Fort Uritskogo = Fort Shevchenko Kazakhstan 44°35N 50°23E 191 H10
Fort Valley U.S.A. 32°33N 83°53W 316 C6
Fort Vermilion Canada 58°24N 116°0W 296 B5
Fort Walton Beach U.S.A. 30°25N 86°36W 317 E3
Fort Ware Canada 57°26N 125°41W 296 B3
Fort Wayne U.S.A. 41°4N 85°9W 311 C11
Fort White U.S.A. 29°55N 82°43W 316 F7
Fort William U.K. 56°49N 5°7W 167 E3
Fort Worth U.S.A. 32°43N 97°19W 314 E6
Fort Yates U.S.A. 46°5N 100°38W 308 B3
Fort Yukon U.S.A. 66°34N 145°16W 303 C11
Fortaleza = Pedra Azul Brazil 16°2S 41°17W 333 E3
Fortaleza Bolivia 12°6S 66°49W 330 C4
Fortaleza Brazil 3°45S 38°35W 332 B4
Forteau Canada 51°28N 56°58W 299 B8
Fortescue → Australia 21°0S 116°4E 278 D2
Fortescue River Roadhouse Australia 21°17S 116°8E 278 D2
Forth → U.K. 56°9N 3°50W 167 E5
Forth, Firth of U.K. 56°5N 2°55W 121 A3
Forth Rail Bridge U.K. 56°0N 3°23W 121 A1
Forth Road Bridge U.K. 56°0N 3°24W 121 A1
Forthassa Rharbia Algeria 32°52N 1°18W 261 B4
Fortín General Pando Paraguay 19°45S 59°47W 331 D6
Fortín Madrejón Paraguay 20°45S 59°52W 331 E6
Fortín Teniente Primero Ramiro Espinola Paraguay 21°27S 61°30W 331 E5
Fortín Uno Argentina 38°50S 65°18W 336 A3
Fortore → Italy 41°55N 15°17E 199 G12
Fortrose N.Z. 46°38S 168°45E 285 G3
Fortrose Highl., U.K. 57°35N 4°9W 167 D4
Fortuna Spain 38°11N 1°7W 197 G3
Fortuna Calif., U.S.A. 40°36N 124°9W 304 F1
Fortuna N. Dak., U.S.A. 48°55N 103°47W 308 A2
Fortuna Ledge = Marshall U.S.A. 61°53N 162°5W 303 F7
Fortune Canada 47°4N 55°50W 299 C8
Fortune B. Canada 47°30N 55°22W 299 C8
Forūr Iran 26°17N 54°32E 247 E7
Fos-sur-Mer France 43°26N 4°56E 175 E8
Fosen Norway 63°50N 10°20E 160 E14
Foshan China 23°6N 113°9E 121 B2
Fosnavåg Norway 62°22N 5°38E 164 B2
Foso Ghana 5°43N 1°15W 263 D4
Foss Iceland 63°51N 17°52W 155 D9
Fossano Italy 44°33N 7°43E 198 D4
Fossil U.S.A. 45°0N 120°9W 304 D3
Fossil Butte ⌂ U.S.A. 41°50N 110°27W 304 F8
Fossombrone Italy 43°41N 12°48E 199 E9
Fossvellir Iceland 65°27N 14°37W 155 B12
Foster Vic., Australia 38°40S 146°15E 283 E7
Foster Qué., Canada 45°17N 72°30W 313 A12
Foster Ky., U.S.A. 38°48N 84°13W 311 F12
Foster → Canada 55°47N 105°49W 297 B7
Foster Village U.S.A. 21°21N 157°55W 302 K14
Fosters Ra. Australia 21°35S 133°48E 280 C1
Fostoria U.S.A. 41°10N 83°25W 311 C13
Fót Hungary 47°35N 19°11E 117 A3
Fotadrevo Madag. 24°3S 45°1E 272 C2
Fouesnant France 47°53N 4°1W 172 E2
Fougamou Gabon 1°16S 10°30E 264 C2
Fougères France 48°21N 1°14W 172 D5
Foul Pt. Sri Lanka 8°35N 81°18E 245 K5
Foula U.K. 60°10N 2°5W 167 A6
Foulalaba Mali 10°40N 7°20W 262 C3
Foulness I. U.K. 51°36N 0°55E 169 F8
Foulpointe Madag. 17°41S 49°31E 272 B2
Foulwind, C. N.Z. 41°45S 171°28E 285 B6
Foum Assaka Morocco 29°8N 10°24W 260 C2
Foum Zguid Morocco 30°2N 6°59W 260 B3
Foumban Cameroon 5°45N 10°50E 263 D7
Foumbot Cameroon 5°31N 10°28E 263 D7
Foumbouni Comoros Is. 11°51S 43°29E 272 a
Foumirate Algeria 27°30N 3°12W 260 C4
Foundiougne Senegal 14°5N 16°32W 262 C1
Fountain Colo., U.S.A. 38°41N 104°42W 304 G11
Fountain Fla., U.S.A. 30°29N 85°25W 316 E4
Fountain Hills U.S.A. 33°37N 111°43W 305 K8
Fountain Springs U.S.A. 35°54N 118°51W 307 K8
Four Mountains, Is. of U.S.A. 53°0N 170°0W 303 K5
Four Roads Trin. & Tob. 10°41N 61°33W 323 t
Fourchambault France 47°2N 3°3E 173 E10
Fourchue, Île St.-Martin 17°58N 62°54W 322 a
Fouriesburg S. Africa 28°38S 28°14E 270 C4
Fourmies France 50°1N 4°2E 173 B11
Fourna Greece 39°3N 21°52E 204 B3
Fournaise, Piton de la Réunion 21°14S 55°43E 272 f
Fourni Greece 37°36N 26°32E 205 D8
Fourqueux France 48°53N 2°3E 134 A1
Fours France 46°50N 3°42E 173 F10
Fous, Pte. de Dominica 15°12N 61°20W 323 k
Fousinshin = Fuxin China 42°5N 121°48E 227 C11
Fouta Djallon Guinea 11°20N 12°10W 262 C2
Foux, Cap-à- Haiti 19°43N 73°27W 321 C5
Foveaux Str. N.Z. 46°42S 168°10E 285 G3
Fowey U.K. 50°20N 4°39W 169 G3
Fowler Calif., U.S.A. 36°38N 119°41W 306 J7
Fowler Colo., U.S.A. 38°8N 104°2W 304 G11
Fowler Ind., U.S.A. 40°37N 87°19W 311 D9
Fowler Mich., U.S.A. 43°0N 84°45W 311 B12
Fowler, Pt. Australia 32°2S 132°3E 279 F5
Fowlers B. Australia 31°59S 132°34E 279 F5
Fowlerville U.S.A. 42°40N 84°4W 311 B12
Fowman Iran 37°13N 49°19E 213 D13
Fox → Canada 56°3N 93°18W 297 B10
Fox Creek Canada 54°24N 116°48W 296 C5
Fox Is. U.S.A. 53°0N 168°0W 303 K6
Fox Lake Alta., Canada 58°28N 114°31W 296 B6
Fox Lake Ill., U.S.A. 42°24N 88°11W 311 B8
Fox Studios Australia 33°55S 151°13E 139 B2
Fox Valley Canada 50°30N 109°25W 297 C7
Foxboro Ont., Canada 44°14N 77°26W 312 B7
Foxboro Mass., U.S.A. 42°4N 71°16W 313 D13
Foxdale Australia 20°22S 148°35E 280 b
Foxe Basin Canada 66°0N 77°0W 295 D16
Foxe Chan. Canada 65°0N 80°0W 295 E16
Foxe Pen. Canada 65°0N 76°0W 295 E16
Foxen Sweden 59°25N 11°55E 162 E5
Foxford Ireland 53°59N 9°7W 166 C2
Foxrock Ireland 53°17N 6°11W 120 B2
Foxton N.Z. 40°29S 175°18E 284 G4
Foyle, Lough U.K. 55°7N 7°4W 166 A4
Foynes Ireland 52°37N 9°7W 166 D2
Foz Spain 43°33N 7°20W 194 B3
Foz do Copeá Brazil 3°52S 63°19W 329 D5
Foz do Cunene Angola 17°15S 11°48E 265 F2
Foz do Gregório Brazil 6°47S 70°44W 330 B3
Foz do Iguaçu Brazil 25°30S 54°30W 335 B5
Foz do Mamoriá Brazil 2°27S 66°32W 328 D4
Frackville U.S.A. 40°47N 76°14W 313 F8
Fraga Spain 41°32N 0°21E 196 D5
Fraile Muerto Uruguay 32°31S 54°32W 335 C5
Framingham U.S.A. 42°18N 71°24W 313 D13
Framnes Iceland 66°1N 20°26W 155 A6
Frampol Poland 50°41N 22°40E 185 H9
Franca Brazil 20°33S 47°30W 333 F2
Francavilla al Mare Italy 42°25N 14°17E 199 F11
Francavilla Fontana Italy 40°32N 17°35E 201 B10
France ■ Europe 47°0N 3°0E 171 C5
Frances Australia 36°41S 140°55E 282 D4
Frances → Canada 60°16N 129°10W 296 A3
Frances L. Canada 61°23N 129°30W 296 A3
Francesville U.S.A. 40°59N 86°53W 311 D10
Franceville Gabon 1°40S 13°32E 264 C2
Franche-Comté ☐ France 46°50N 5°55E 173 F12
Francis Case, L. U.S.A. 43°4N 98°34W 308 D4
Francisco Beltrão Brazil 26°5S 53°4W 335 B5
Francisco de Orellana Ecuador 0°28S 76°58W 328 D2
Francisco Ignacio Madero Coahuila, Mexico 25°48N 103°18W 318 B4
Francisco Ignacio Madero Durango, Mexico 24°26N 104°18W 318 C4
Francisco Ignacio Madero, Presa Mexico 28°10N 105°37W 318 B3
Francisco Sá Brazil 16°28S 43°30W 333 E3
Francistown Botswana 21°7S 27°33E 271 B4
Francofonte Italy 37°14N 14°53E 201 E7
François Canada 47°35N 56°45W 299 C8
François, B. du Martinique 14°38N 60°54W 322 j
François-Joseph, Chutes Dem. Rep. of the Congo 7°37S 17°17E 265 D3
François L. Canada 54°0N 125°30W 296 C3
Francois Peron △ Australia 25°42S 113°33E 279 E1
Franconia U.S.A. 38°47N 77°7W 143 C3
Francs Pk. U.S.A. 43°58N 109°20W 304 E9
Franeker Neths. 53°12N 5°33E 170 A5
Frank Hann △ Australia 32°52S 120°19E 279 F3
Frank Lloyd Wright Home U.S.A. 41°53N 87°47W 119 B2
Frankel Singapore 1°18N 103°55E 138 B3
Frankenberg Germany 51°3N 8°48E 178 D4
Frankenhöhe ⌂ Germany 49°20N 10°25E 179 F6
Frankenstein = Ząbkowice Śląskie Poland 50°35N 16°50E 185 H3
Frankenwald Germany 50°20N 11°30E 179 E7
Frankenwald ⌂ Germany 50°15N 11°30E 179 E7
Frankfield Jamaica 18°8N 77°22W 320 a
Frankford Ont., Canada 44°12N 77°36W 312 B7
Frankford Mo., U.S.A. 39°29N 91°19W 310 E5
Frankfort Free State, S. Africa 27°17S 28°30E 271 C4
Frankfort Ind., U.S.A. 40°17N 86°31W 311 D10
Frankfort Kans., U.S.A. 39°42N 96°25W 308 F5
Frankfort Ky., U.S.A. 38°12N 84°52W 311 F12
Frankfort N.Y., U.S.A. 43°2N 75°4W 313 C9
Frankfort Ohio, U.S.A. 39°24N 83°11W 311 E13
Frankfurt Brandenburg, Germany 52°20N 14°32E 178 C10
Frankfurt Hessen, Germany 50°7N 8°41E 179 E4
Frankfurt ✈ (FRA) Germany 50°1N 8°34E 179 E4
Fränkische Alb Germany 49°10N 11°23E 179 F7
Fränkische Rezat → Germany 49°11N 11°1E 179 F7
Fränkische Saale → Germany 50°3N 9°42E 179 E5
Fränkische Schweiz Germany 49°50N 11°16E 179 F7
Fränkische Schweiz-Veldensteiner Forst ⌂ Germany 49°45N 11°22E 179 F7
Frankland → Australia 35°0S 116°48E 279 G2
Franklin Ga., U.S.A. 33°17N 85°6W 316 B4
Franklin Ind., U.S.A. 39°29N 86°3W 311 E10
Franklin Ky., U.S.A. 36°43N 86°35W 308 G10
Franklin La., U.S.A. 29°48N 91°30W 314 G9
Franklin Mass., U.S.A. 42°5N 71°24W 313 D13
Franklin N.H., U.S.A. 43°27N 71°39W 313 C13
Franklin N.Y., U.S.A. 42°20N 75°9W 313 D9
Franklin Nebr., U.S.A. 40°6N 98°57W 308 E4
Franklin Ohio, U.S.A. 39°34N 84°18W 311 E12
Franklin Pa., U.S.A. 41°24N 79°50W 312 E5
Franklin Va., U.S.A. 36°41N 76°56W 309 G15
Franklin W. Va., U.S.A. 38°39N 79°20W 309 F14
Franklin, Pt. U.S.A. 70°55N 158°48W 303 A8
Franklin B. Canada 69°45N 126°0W 294 D6
Franklin D. Roosevelt L. U.S.A. 48°18N 118°9W 304 B4
Franklin-Gordon Wild Rivers △ Australia 42°19S 145°51E 281 G4
Franklin Harb. Australia 33°43S 136°55E 282 B2
Franklin I. Antarctica 76°10S 168°30E 151 D11
Franklin I. Ont., Canada 45°24N 80°20W 312 A4
Franklin L. U.S.A. 40°25N 115°22W 304 F6
Franklin Mts. N.W.T., Canada 65°0N 125°0W 294 D6
Franklin Mts. N.Z. 44°55S 167°45E 285 E2
Franklin Park Ill., U.S.A. 41°55N 87°52W 119 B1
Franklin Park Mass., U.S.A. 42°18N 71°5W 116 B2
Franklin Park Va., U.S.A. 38°55N 77°9W 143 B3
Franklin Res. U.S.A. 34°5N 118°24W 126 B2
Franklin Str. Canada 72°0N 96°0W 294 C12
Franklinton U.S.A. 30°51N 90°9W 315 F9
Franklinville U.S.A. 42°20N 78°27W 312 D6
Franklyn Mt. N.Z. 42°4S 172°42E 285 C7
Frankston Australia 38°8S 145°8E 283 E6
Frånö Sweden 62°55N 17°50E 162 B11
Fransfontein Namibia 20°12S 15°1E 270 B2
Fränsta Sweden 62°30N 16°11E 162 B10
Frantsa Iosifa, Zemlya Russia 82°0N 55°0E 214 A6
Franz Canada 48°25N 84°30W 298 C3
Franz Josef Land = Frantsa Iosifa, Zemlya Russia 82°0N 55°0E 214 A6
Franz Josef Strauss ✈ (MUC) Germany 48°21N 11°47E 131 A2
Franzburg Germany 54°11N 12°51E 178 A8
Frascati Italy 41°48N 12°41E 199 G9
Fraser U.S.A. 42°32N 82°57W 312 D2
Fraser → B.C., Canada 49°7N 123°11W 306 A3
Fraser → Nfld. & L., Canada 56°39N 62°10W 299 A7
Fraser, Mt. Australia 25°35S 118°20E 279 E2
Fraser I. Australia 25°15S 153°10E 281 D5
Fraser Lake Canada 54°0N 124°50W 296 C4
Fraserburg S. Africa 31°55S 21°30E 270 D3
Fraserburg Road = Leeu Gamka S. Africa 32°47S 21°59E 270 D3
Fraserburgh U.K. 57°42N 2°1W 167 D6
Fraserdale Canada 49°55N 81°37W 298 C3
Fraserpet = Kushalnagar India 12°14N 75°57E 245 H2
Frasertown N.Z. 38°58S 177°28E 284 E6
Fraserville = Rivière-du-Loup Canada 47°50N 69°30W 299 C6
Frashër Albania 40°23N 20°26E 202 F4
Frasne France 46°50N 6°10E 173 F13
Frătești Romania 43°58N 25°58E 183 G10
Frauenfeld Switz. 47°34N 8°54E 179 H4
Frauenkirche Munich, Germany 131 b2
Frauenstadt = Wadowice Poland 49°52N 19°30E 185 J6
Fraustadt = Wschowa Poland 51°48N 16°20E 185 G3
Fray Bentos Uruguay 33°10S 58°15W 334 C4
Fray Jorge ⌂ Chile 30°42S 71°40W 334 C1
Frazier Downs ❂ Australia 18°48S 121°42E 278 C3
Frechilla Spain 42°8N 4°50W 194 C6
Fredericia Denmark 55°34N 9°45E 163 J3
Frederick Md., U.S.A. 39°25N 77°25W 309 F15
Frederick Okla., U.S.A. 34°23N 99°1W 314 D5
Frederick S. Dak., U.S.A. 45°50N 98°31W 308 C4
Frederick E. Hyde Fjord Greenland 83°25N 29°0W 154 A8
Fredericksburg Pa., U.S.A. 40°27N 76°26W 313 F8
Fredericksburg Tex., U.S.A. 30°16N 98°52W 314 F5
Fredericksburg Va., U.S.A. 38°18N 77°28W 309 F15
Fredericktown Mo., U.S.A. 37°34N 90°18W 308 G8
Fredericktown Ohio, U.S.A. 40°29N 82°33W 312 F2
Frederico Westphalen Brazil 27°22S 53°24W 335 B5
Fredericton Canada 45°57N 66°40W 299 C6
Fredericton Junction Canada 45°41N 66°40W 299 C6
Frederiksberg Denmark 55°40N 12°33E 118 A3
Frederiksdal Denmark 55°46N 12°25E 118 A2
Frederikshåb = Paamiut Greenland 62°0N 49°43W 154 E6
Frederikshald = Halden Norway 59°9N 11°23E 164 E8
Frederikshamn = Hamina Finland 60°34N 27°12E 188 B4
Frederikshavn Denmark 57°28N 10°31E 163 G4
Frederikssund Denmark 55°50N 12°3E 163 J6
Frederiksted U.S. Virgin Is. 17°43N 64°53W 321 C7
Frederiksværk Denmark 55°58N 12°4E 163 J6
Fredersdorf Germany 52°31N 13°45E 115 A5
Fredonia Ariz., U.S.A. 36°57N 112°32W 305 H7
Fredonia Kans., U.S.A. 37°32N 95°49W 308 G6
Fredonia N.Y., U.S.A. 42°26N 79°20W 312 D5
Fredriksberg Sweden 60°8N 14°23E 162 D8
Fredrikstad Norway 59°13N 10°57E 164 E7
Fredriksvern = Stavern Norway 59°0N 10°1E 164 F7
Free State ☐ S. Africa 28°30S 27°0E 270 C4
Freeburg U.S.A. 38°19N 91°56W 310 F5
Freehold U.S.A. 40°16N 74°17W 313 F10
Freeland U.S.A. 41°1N 75°54W 313 E9
Freels, C. Nfld. & L., Canada 49°15N 53°30W 299 C9
Freels, C. Nfld. & L., Canada 46°37N 53°32W 299 C9
Freeman Calif., U.S.A. 35°35N 117°53W 307 K9
Freeman Mo., U.S.A. 38°37N 94°30W 310 F2
Freeman S. Dak., U.S.A. 43°21N 97°26W 308 D5
Freeport Bahamas 26°30N 78°47W 320 A4
Freeport Trin. & Tob. 10°27N 61°25W 323 t
Freeport Fla., U.S.A. 30°30N 86°8W 316 E3
Freeport Ill., U.S.A. 42°17N 89°36W 310 B7
Freeport N.Y., U.S.A. 40°39N 73°35W 313 F11
Freeport Ohio, U.S.A. 40°12N 81°15W 312 F3
Freeport Pa., U.S.A. 40°41N 79°41W 312 F5
Freeport Tex., U.S.A. 28°57N 95°21W 314 G7
Freetown Antigua & B. 17°3N 61°42W 322 b
Freetown S. Leone 8°30N 13°17W 262 D2
Freeville U.S.A. 42°30N 76°20W 313 D8
Frégate, L. de la Canada 53°15N 74°45W 298 B5
Fregate Island Nature Reserve St. Lucia 13°52N 60°53W 323 m
Fregenal de la Sierra Spain 38°10N 6°39W 195 G4
Fregene Italy 41°51N 12°12E 199 G9
Fregon Australia 26°45S 132°1E 279 E5
Freguesia Brazil 22°48S 43°10W 135 A1
Fréhel, C. France 48°40N 2°20W 172 D4
Freiberg Germany 50°55N 13°20E 178 E9
Freibourg = Fribourg Switz. 46°49N 7°9E 179 J3
Freiburg Baden-W., Germany 47°59N 7°51E 179 H3
Freiburg Niedersachsen, Germany 53°49N 9°16E 178 B5
Freiburg in Schlesien = Świebodzice Poland 50°51N 16°20E 185 H3
Freidrichshain, Volkspark Germany 52°31N 13°25E 115 A3
Freienwalde = Chociwel Poland 53°29N 15°21E 184 E2
Freiham Germany 48°8N 11°25E 131 B1
Freilassing Germany 47°50N 12°58E 179 H8
Freimann Germany 48°11N 11°36E 131 A2
Freire Chile 38°54S 72°38W 336 A2
Freirina Chile 28°30S 71°10W 334 B1
Freising Germany 48°24N 11°45E 179 G7
Freistadt Austria 48°30N 14°30E 180 C7
Freital Germany 51°1N 13°39E 178 D9
Freiwaldau = Jeseník Czech Rep. 50°14N 17°8E 181 A10
Fréjus France 43°25N 6°44E 175 E10
Fremantle Australia 32°7S 115°47E 279 F2
Fremont Calif., U.S.A. 37°32N 121°57W 306 H4
Fremont Ind., U.S.A. 41°44N 84°56W 311 C12
Fremont Iowa, U.S.A. 41°13N 92°26W 310 C4
Fremont Mich., U.S.A. 43°28N 85°57W 309 D11
Fremont Nebr., U.S.A. 41°26N 96°30W 308 E5
Fremont Ohio, U.S.A. 41°21N 83°7W 311 C13
Fremont → U.S.A. 38°24N 110°42W 304 G8
French Camp U.S.A. 37°53N 121°16W 306 H5
French Cays = Plana Cays Bahamas 22°38N 73°30W 321 B5
French Creek → U.S.A. 41°24N 79°50W 312 E5
French Frigate Shoals U.S.A. 23°45N 166°10W 302 G10
French Guiana ☐ S. Amer. 4°0N 53°0W 329 C7
French Guinea = Guinea ■ W. Afr. 10°20N 11°30W 262 C2
French I. Australia 38°20S 145°22E 283 E6
French Island △ Australia 38°20S 145°22E 283 E6
French Lick U.S.A. 38°33N 86°37W 311 F10
French Market New Orleans, U.S.A. 131 a3
French Pass N.Z. 40°55S 173°55E 285 A8
French Polynesia ☐ Pac. Oc. 20°0S 145°0W 289 f
French Quarter New Orleans, U.S.A. 131 a2
French Sudan = Mali ■ Africa 17°0N 3°0W 262 B4
French Territory of the Afars and Issas = Djibouti ■ Africa 12°0N 43°0E 257 E5
French Togoland = Togo ■ W. Afr. 8°30N 1°35E 263 D5
Frenchburg U.S.A. 37°57N 83°38W 311 G13
Frenchman Cr. → N. Amer. 48°31N 107°10W 304 B10
Frenchman Cr. → Nebr., U.S.A. 40°14N 100°50W 308 E3
Frenda Algeria 35°2N 1°1E 261 A5
Frenštát pod Radhoštěm Czech Rep. 49°33N 18°13E 181 B11
Fresco Ivory C. 5°3N 5°31W 262 D3
Fresco → Brazil 7°15S 51°30W 331 B7
Fresh Pond U.S.A. 42°22N 71°8W 116 A2
Freshfield, C. Antarctica 68°25S 151°10E 151 C10
Fresnay-sur-Sarthe France 48°17N 0°1E 172 D7
Fresnes France 48°45N 2°18E 134 B2
Fresnillo Mexico 23°10N 102°53W 318 C4
Fresno U.S.A. 36°44N 119°47W 306 J7
Fresno Alhándiga Spain 40°42N 5°37W 194 E5
Fresno Res. U.S.A. 48°36N 109°57W 304 B9
Fresvik Norway 61°4N 6°55E 164 C3
Freudenau Austria 48°11N 16°25E 142 A2
Freudenstadt Germany 48°27N 8°24E 179 G4
Freudenthal = Bruntál Czech Rep. 49°59N 17°27E 181 B10
Frévent France 50°15N 2°17E 173 B9
Frew → Australia 20°0S 135°38E 280 C2
Frewsburg U.S.A. 42°3N 79°10W 312 D5
Freycinet △ Australia 42°11S 148°19E 281 G4
Freycinet Pen. Australia 42°10S 148°25E 281 G4
Freyming-Merlebach France 49°8N 6°48E 173 C13
Freystadt = Kisielice Poland 53°36N 19°16E 184 E6
Freystadt = Kożuchów Poland 51°45N 15°31E 185 G2
Freyung Germany 48°48N 13°31E 179 G9
Fria Guinea 10°27N 13°38W 262 C2
Fria, C. Namibia 18°0S 12°0E 270 A1
Friant U.S.A. 36°59N 119°43W 306 J7
Friar's B. St. Kitts & Nevis 17°16N 62°40W 322 d
Friarstown Ireland 53°15N 6°21W 120 B1
Frías Argentina 28°40S 65°5W 334 B2
Fribourg Switz. 46°49N 7°9E 179 J3
Fribourg ☐ Switz. 46°40N 7°0E 179 J3
Frick Collection New York, U.S.A. 132 b3
Fridafors Sweden 56°25N 14°39E 163 H8
Friday Harbor U.S.A. 48°32N 123°1W 306 B3
Friedberg Bayern, Germany 48°21N 10°59E 179 G6
Friedberg Hessen, Germany 50°19N 8°45E 179 E4
Friedeberg = Mirsk Poland 50°58N 15°23E 185 H2
Friedeberg in Neumark = Strzelce Krajeńskie Poland 52°52N 15°33E 185 F2
Friedenau Germany 52°28N 13°22E 115 B3
Friedens U.S.A. 40°3N 78°59W 312 F6
Friedland = Mieroszów Poland 50°40N 16°11E 185 H3
Friedland = Pravdinsk Russia 56°29N 43°28E 190 B6
Friedland Germany 53°40N 13°33E 178 B9
Friedrichsfelde Germany 52°29N 13°33E 115 B4
Friedrichshafen Germany 47°39N 9°30E 179 H5
Friedrichshagen Germany 52°27N 13°37E 115 B4
Friedrichshain Germany 52°31N 13°25E 115 A3
Friedrichskoog Germany 54°1N 8°53E 178 A4
Friedrichslust Germany 52°33N 13°43E 115 A5
Friedrichstadt Germany 54°23N 9°6E 178 A5
Friendly Is. = Tonga ■ Pac. Oc. 19°50S 174°30W 287 P13
Friendship U.S.A. 42°12N 78°8W 312 D6
Friesach Austria 46°57N 14°24E 180 E7
Friesack Germany 52°44N 12°34E 178 C8
Friesland ☐ Neths. 53°5N 5°50E 170 A5
Friesoythe Germany 53°1N 7°51E 178 B3
Frigate Seychelles 4°35S 55°56E 272 c
Frigate Bay St. Kitts & Nevis 17°16N 62°41W 322 d
Frigate I. Grenada 12°25N 61°29W 323 q
Friggesund Sweden 61°54N 16°33E 162 C10
Friherrs Finland 60°16N 24°49E 121 B1
Frillesås Sweden 57°20N 12°12E 163 G6
Frilufts Museum Finland 60°12N 24°52E 121 B2
Frinnaryd Sweden 57°55N 14°50E 163 G8
Frio → U.S.A. 28°26N 98°11W 314 G5
Frio, C. Brazil 22°50S 41°50W 326 F6
Friol Spain 43°2N 7°47W 194 B3
Friona U.S.A. 34°38N 102°43W 314 D3
Frisches Haff = Zalew Wiślany Poland 54°20N 19°50E 184 D6
Fristad Sweden 57°50N 13°0E 163 G6
Fritch U.S.A. 35°38N 101°36W 314 D4
Fritsla Sweden 57°33N 12°47E 163 G6
Fritzlar Germany 51°7N 9°16E 178 D5
Friuli-Venézia Giulia ☐ Italy 46°0N 13°0E 199 B9
Frobisher B. Canada 62°30N 66°0W 295 E18
Frobisher Bay = Iqaluit Canada 63°44N 68°31W 295 E18
Frobisher L. Canada 56°20N 108°15W 297 B7
Frohavet Norway 64°0N 9°30E 160 E13
Frohnbruck = Veselí nad Lužnicí Czech Rep. 49°12N 14°43E 180 B7
Frohnleiten Austria 47°16N 15°19E 180 D8
Frolovo Russia 49°45N 43°40E 190 F6
Frombork Poland 54°21N 19°41E 184 D6
Frome U.K. 51°14N 2°19W 169 F5
Frome → U.K. 50°41N 2°6W 169 G5
Frome, L. Australia 30°45S 139°45E 282 A3
Frome Downs Australia 31°13S 139°45E 282 A3
Frómista Spain 42°16N 4°25W 194 C6
Front Range U.S.A. 40°25N 105°45W 301 G18
Front Royal U.S.A. 38°55N 78°12W 309 F14
Fronteira Portugal 39°3N 7°39W 195 F3
Fronteiras Brazil 7°5S 40°37W 332 C3
Frontenac ⌂ Canada 44°32N 76°30W 313 B8
Frontera Canary Is. 27°47N 17°59W 153 e1
Frontera Tabasco, Mexico 18°32N 92°38W 319 D6
Fronteras Mexico 30°56N 109°31W 318 A3
Frontignan France 43°27N 3°45E 174 E7
Frontón, I. Peru 12°7S 77°11W 124 B1
Frosinone Italy 41°38N 13°19E 200 A6
Frostburg U.S.A. 39°39N 78°56W 309 F14
Frostisen Norway 68°14N 17°10E 160 B17
Frostproof U.S.A. 27°45N 81°32W 317 H8
Frouard France 48°47N 6°8E 173 D13
Frövi Sweden 59°28N 15°24E 162 E9
Frøya Norway 63°43N 8°40E 160 E13
Fruithurst U.S.A. 33°44N 85°26W 316 B4
Fruitland Park U.S.A. 28°51N 81°54W 317 G8
Frumoasa Romania 46°28N 25°48E 183 D10
Frunze = Bishkek Kyrgyzstan 42°54N 74°46E 214 E8
Frunze Russia 55°47N 37°33E 129 B3
Frunzivka Ukraine 47°20N 29°45E 183 C14
Fruška Gora Serbia 45°7N 19°30E 182 E4
Fruška Gora △ Serbia 45°8N 19°40E 202 A3
Frutal Brazil 20°0S 49°0W 333 F2
Frutigen Switz. 46°35N 7°38E 179 J3
Frýdek-Místek Czech Rep. 49°40N 18°20E 181 B11
Frýdlant Czech Rep. 50°56N 15°9E 180 A8
Fryeburg U.S.A. 44°1N 70°59W 313 B14
Fryvaldov = Jeseník Czech Rep. 50°14N 17°8E 181 A10
Fthiotida ☐ Greece 38°50N 22°25E 204 C4
Fu Jiang → China 30°0N 106°16E 228 C6
Fu Xian = Wafangdian China 39°38N 121°58E 227 E11
Fu Xian China 36°0N 109°20E 226 G5
Fua Mulaku Maldives 0°17S 73°26E 272 d
Fu'an China 27°11N 119°36E 229 D12
Fubian China 31°17N 102°22E 228 B4
Fucécchio Italy 43°44N 10°48E 198 E7
Fucheng China 37°50N 116°10E 226 F9
Fuchou = Fuzhou China 26°5N 119°16E 229 D12
Fuchū Hiroshima, Japan 34°34N 133°14E 222 C5
Fuchū Tōkyō, Japan 35°40N 139°29E 140 A1
Fuchuan China 24°50N 111°5E 229 E8
Fuchun Jiang → China 30°5N 120°5E 229 B13
Fúcino, Piana del Italy 42°1N 13°31E 199 F10
Fuding China 27°20N 120°12E 229 D13
Fuencaliente Canary Is. 28°28N 17°50W 153 e1
Fuencaliente Spain 38°25N 4°18W 195 G6
Fuencaliente, Pta. Canary Is. 28°27N 17°51W 153 e1
Fuencarral Spain 40°29N 3°42W 127 B1
Fuengirola Spain 36°32N 4°41W 195 J6
Fuenlabrada Spain 40°17N 3°48W 127 C1
Fuensalida Spain 40°3N 4°12W 194 E6
Fuente-Álamo Spain 38°44N 1°24W 197 G3
Fuente Álamo de Murcia Spain 37°42N 1°6W 197 H3
Fuente de Cantos Spain 38°15N 6°18W 195 G4
Fuente del Maestre Spain 38°31N 6°28W 195 G4
Fuente el Fresno Spain 39°14N 3°46W 195 F7
Fuente Obejuna Spain 38°15N 5°25W 195 G5
Fuente Palmera Spain 37°42N 5°6W 195 H5
Fuentes de Andalucía Spain 37°28N 5°20W 195 H5
Fuentes de Ebro Spain 41°31N 0°38W 196 D4
Fuentes de León Spain 38°5N 6°32W 195 G4
Fuentes de Oñoro Spain 40°33N 6°52W 194 E4
Fuentesaúco Spain 41°15N 5°30W 194 D5
Fuerte → Mexico 25°54N 109°22W 318 B3
Fuerte Olimpo Paraguay 21°0S 57°51W 334 A4
Fuerteventura Canary Is. 28°30N 14°0W 153 e2
Fuerteventura ✈ (FUE) Canary Is. 28°24N 13°52W 153 e2
Fufeng China 34°22N 108°0E 226 G5
Fuga I. Phil. 18°52N 121°22E 232 B3
Fughmah Yemen 16°9N 49°26E 249 C5
Fugong China 27°5N 98°47E 228 D2
Fugou China 34°3N 114°25E 226 G8
Fugu China 39°2N 111°3E 226 E6
Fuhai China 47°2N 87°25E 217 C11
Fuḩaymī Iraq 34°16N 42°10E 213 E10
Fuhlsbüttel, Hamburg ✈ (HAM) Germany 53°35N 9°59E 178 B5
Fuhsien = Fu Xian China 36°0N 109°20E 226 G5
Fuhsing Changhua, Taiwan 24°3N 120°25E 225 B2
Fuhsing Kaohsiung, Taiwan 23°13N 120°48E 225 C2
Fuhsing Taoyüan, Taiwan 24°49N 121°21E 225 B3
Fuji Japan 35°9N 138°39E 223 B10
Fuji-Hakone-Izu △ Japan 35°15N 138°45E 223 B10
Fuji-San Japan 35°22N 138°44E 223 B10
Fuji-Yoshida Japan 35°30N 138°46E 223 B10
Fujian ☐ China 26°0N 118°0E 229 E12
Fujieda Japan 34°52N 138°16E 223 C10
Fujinomiya Japan 35°10N 138°40E 223 B10
Fujioka Japan 36°15N 139°3E 223 A11
Fujisawa Japan 35°22N 139°29E 223 B11
Fujiyama, Mt. = Fuji-San Japan 35°22N 138°44E 223 B10
Fukagawa Hokkaidō, Japan 43°43N 142°2E 220 C11
Fukagawa Tōkyō, Japan 35°39N 139°48E 140 B3
Fukang China 44°10N 87°59E 217 D11
Fukaya Japan 36°12N 139°12E 223 A11
Fukiage Japan 31°27N 130°17E 222 F2
Fukiage Imperial Garden Tokyo, Japan 140 a4
Fukien = Fujian ☐ China 26°0N 118°0E 229 E12
Fukuchiyama Japan 35°19N 135°9E 223 B7
Fukue-Shima Japan 32°40N 128°45E 221 H4
Fukuei Chiao Taiwan 25°17N 121°32E 225 A3
Fukui Japan 36°5N 136°10E 223 A8
Fukui ☐ Japan 36°0N 136°12E 223 B8
Fukuma Japan 33°46N 130°28E 222 D2
Fukuoka Japan 33°39N 130°21E 222 D2
Fukuoka ☐ Japan 33°30N 131°0E 222 D3
Fukuoka Int. ✈ (FUK) Japan 33°34N 130°28E 222 D2
Fukurei Japan 34°45N 137°55E 223 C9
Fukushima Fukushima, Japan 37°44N 140°28E 220 F10
Fukushima Ōsaka, Japan 34°41N 135°28E 133 A1
Fukushima ☐ Japan 37°30N 140°15E 220 F10
Fukuyama Japan 34°35N 133°20E 222 C5
Fulacunda Guinea-Biss. 11°44N 15°3W 262 C1
Fulaga Fiji 19°8S 178°33W 287 B3
Fulda Germany 50°32N 9°40E 178 E5
Fulda → Germany 51°25N 9°39E 178 D5
Fulford = North Miami Beach U.S.A. 25°55N 80°9W 128 A2
Fulford Harbour Canada 48°47N 123°27W 306 B3
Fulham U.K. 51°28N 0°12W 125 B2
Fuli Taiwan 23°11N 121°14E 225 C3

Fuliang China 29°23N 117°14E 229 C11
Fullarton Trin. & Tob. 10°5N 61°54W 323 t
Fullerton Calif., U.S.A. 33°53N 117°56W 307 M9
Fullerton Nebr., U.S.A. 41°22N 97°58W 308 E5
Fulongquan China 44°20N 124°42E 227 B13
Fülöpszállás Hungary 46°49N 19°15E 182 D4
Fulton Ill., U.S.A. 41°52N 90°11W 310 C6
Fulton Ind., U.S.A. 40°57N 86°16W 311 D10
Fulton N.Y., U.S.A. 43°19N 76°25W 313 C8
Fulton Mo., U.S.A. 38°52N 91°57W 310 F5
Fulufjället Sweden 61°32N 12°41E 162 C6
Fulun → Sweden 61°18N 13°4E 162 C7
Fumay France 49°58N 4°40E 173 C11
Fumel France 44°30N 0°58E 174 D4
Fumin China 25°10N 102°20E 228 E4
Funabashi Japan 35°45N 140°0E 223 B12
Funabori Japan 35°41N 139°52E 140 A4
Funafuti = Fongafale
Tuvalu 8°31S 179°13E 277 B14
Funafuti Pac. Oc. 8°31S 179°13E 277 B14
Funäsdalen Sweden 62°33N 12°32E 162 B6
Funchal Madeira 32°38N 16°54W 153 c
Funchal ✈ (FNC) Madeira 32°42N 16°45W 153 c
Fundación Colombia 10°31N 74°11W 328 A3
Fundão Brazil 19°55S 40°24W 333 E3
Fundão Portugal 40°8N 7°30W 194 E3
Fundão, I. do Brazil 22°51S 43°13W 135 B1
Fundong Cameroon 6°15N 10°16E 264 A2
Fundu Moldovei
Romania 47°32N 25°24E 183 C10
Fundulea Romania 44°28N 26°31E 183 F11
Fundy, B. of Canada 45°0N 66°0W 299 D6
Fundy △ Canada 45°35N 65°10W 299 D6
Fünfhaus Austria 48°11N 16°20E 142 A2
Fünfkirchen = Pécs
Hungary 46°5N 18°15E 182 D3
Funhalouro Mozam. 23°3S 34°25E 271 B5
Funing Hebei, China 39°53N 119°12E 227 E10
Funing Jiangsu, China 33°45N 119°50E 227 H10
Funing Yunnan, China 23°35N 105°45E 228 F5
Funiu Shan China 33°30N 112°20E 226 H7
Funsi Ghana 10°21N 1°54W 262 C4
Funtua Nigeria 11°30N 7°18E 263 C6
Fuping Hebei, China 38°48N 114°12E 226 E8
Fuping Shaanxi, China 34°42N 109°10E 226 G5
Fuqing China 25°41N 119°21E 229 E12
Fuquan China 26°40N 107°27E 228 D6
Furano Japan 43°21N 142°23E 220 C11
Furāt, Nahr al → Asia 31°0N 47°25E 246 D5
Fureso Denmark 55°47N 12°25E 118 A2
Fürg Iran 28°18N 55°13E 247 D7
Furkating India 26°28N 93°59E 241 B4
Furman U.S.A. 32°41N 81°11W 316 C8
Furmanov Russia 57°10N 41°9E 190 B5
Furnas Azores 37°46N 25°19W 153 d3
Furnás Spain 39°3N 1°32E 206 C2
Furnas, Represa de
Brazil 20°50S 45°30W 333 F2
Furneaux Group
Australia 40°10S 147°50E 281 G4
Furqlus Syria 34°36N 37°8E 250 D8
Fürstenau Germany 52°31N 7°40E 178 C3
Fürstenberg = Eisenhüttenstadt
Germany 52°9N 14°38E 178 C10
Fürstenberg Germany 53°10N 13°8E 178 B9
Fürstenfeld Austria 47°3N 16°3E 180 D9
Fürstenfeldbruck
Germany 48°11N 11°15E 179 G7
Fürstenwalde Germany 52°22N 14°3E 178 C10
Fürth Mittelfranken,
Germany 49°28N 10°59E 179 F6
Fürth Oberbayern, Germany 48°2N 11°35E 131 B2
Fürth im Wald Germany 49°18N 12°50E 179 F8
Furtwangen Germany 48°2N 8°12E 179 G4
Furudal Sweden 61°10N 15°11E 162 C9
Furukawa Gifu, Japan 36°14N 137°11E 223 A9
Furukawa Miyagi,
Japan 38°34N 140°58E 220 E10
Furulund Sweden 55°46N 13°6E 163 J7
Fury and Hecla Str.
Canada 69°56N 84°0W 295 D15
Fusagasugá Colombia 4°21N 74°22W 328 C3
Fuscaldo Italy 39°25N 16°2E 201 C9
Fushan Shandong, China 37°30N 121°15E 227 F11
Fushan Shanxi, China 35°58N 111°51E 226 G6
Fushë Arrëz Albania 42°4N 20°2E 202 D4
Fushë Krujë Albania 41°28N 19°43E 202 E3
Fushun Liaoning, China 41°50N 123°56E 224 B1
Fushun Sichuan, China 29°13N 104°52E 228 C5
Fusong China 42°20N 127°15E 224 A3
Füssen Germany 47°35N 10°43E 179 H6
Fusui China 22°40N 107°56E 228 F6
Futago-tamagawaen
Japan 35°36N 139°39E 140 B2
Futago-Yama Japan 33°35N 131°36E 222 D3
Futian China 22°32N 114°4E 219 F11
Futiga Amer. Samoa 14°21S 170°45W 302 f
Futog Serbia 45°15N 19°42E 182 E4
Futrono Chile 40°8S 72°24W 336 B2
Futtsu Japan 35°31N 139°49E 223 B11
Fuwa Egypt 31°12N 30°33E 256 H7
Fuxian Hu China 24°30N 102°58E 228 E4
Fuxin China 42°5N 121°48E 227 C11
Fuxinglu China 39°52N 116°16E 114 B1
Fuyang Anhui, China 33°0N 115°48E 226 H8
Fuyang Zhejiang, China 30°5N 119°57E 229 B12
Fuyang He → China 38°12N 117°0E 226 E9
Fuying Dao China 26°34N 120°9E 229 D13
Fuyong China 22°40N 113°49E 219 F10
Fuyu Heilongjiang, China 47°49N 124°27E 219 B7
Fuyu Jilin, China 45°12N 124°43E 227 B13
Fuyuan China 25°40N 104°16E 228 E5
Fuyun China 47°0N 89°28E 217 C11
Füzesgyarmat Hungary 47°6N 21°14E 182 C6
Fuzhou = Linchuan
China 27°57N 116°15E 229 D11
Fuzhou China 26°5N 119°16E 229 D12
Füzuli Azerbaijan 39°36N 47°8E 213 C12
Fyn Denmark 55°20N 10°30E 163 J4
Fyne, L. U.K. 55°59N 5°23W 167 F3
Fynshav Denmark 54°50N 9°59E 163 K3
Fyresdal Norway 59°11N 8°15E 164 E5
Fyresvatn Norway 59°6N 8°10E 164 E5
Fyzabad = Faizabad
India 26°45N 82°10E 243 F10
Fyzabad Trin. & Tob. 10°14N 61°33W 323 t

G

G. Ross Lord Park
Canada 43°47N 79°28W 141 A2
Ga Ghana 9°47N 2°30W 262 D4
Ga-eun S. Korea 36°38N 128°5E 224 D4
Gaa Fato Atoll Maldives 4°45N 73°26E 272 d
Gaanda Nigeria 10°10N 12°27E 263 C7
Gabas → France 43°46N 0°42W 174 E3
Gabba Australia 9°45S 142°38E 288 a
Gabela Angola 11°0S 14°24E 265 G2
Gaberones = Gaborone
Botswana 24°45S 25°57E 270 B4
Gabès Tunisia 33°53N 10°2E 258 B2
Gabès □ Tunisia 33°35N 9°30E 261 B6

Gabès, G. de Tunisia 34°0N 10°30E 258 B2
Gabgaba, W. → Egypt 22°10N 33°5E 256 C3
Gabia la Grande Spain 37°8N 3°40W 195 H7
Gablonz = Jablonec nad Nisou
Czech Rep. 50°43N 15°10E 180 A8
Gabon ■ Africa 0°10S 10°0E 264 C2
Gabon → Gabon 0°25N 9°20E 264 B1
Gaborone Botswana 24°45S 25°57E 270 B4
Gabras Sudan 10°16N 26°14E 257 F9
Gabriels U.S.A. 44°26N 74°12W 313 B10
Gäbrīk Iran 25°44N 58°28E 247 E8
Gabro Ethiopia 6°18N 43°16E 267 C5
Gabú = Nova Lamego
Guinea-Biss. 12°19N 14°11W 262 C2
Gacé France 48°49N 0°20E 172 D7
Gāch Sār Iran 36°7N 51°19E 247 B6
Gachsārān Iran 30°15N 50°45E 247 D6
Gacko Bos.-H. 43°10N 18°33E 202 C2
Gad Hinglaj India 16°14N 74°21E 245 F2
Gadag India 15°30N 75°45E 245 G2
Gadaisu Papua N. G. 10°22S 149°46E 286 F5
Gadamai Sudan 17°11N 36°10E 257 D4
Gadap Pakistan 25°5N 67°28E 242 G2
Gadarwara India 22°50N 78°50E 243 H8
Gaddebusch Germany 53°42N 11°7E 178 B7
Gadein Sudan 8°10N 28°5E 257 F7
Gador, Sierra de Spain 36°57N 2°45W 195 J8
Gadra Pakistan 25°40N 70°38E 242 G4
Gadsden Ala., U.S.A. 34°1N 86°1W 316 A3
Gadsden S.C., U.S.A. 33°51N 80°46W 316 B9
Gadwal India 16°10N 77°50E 245 F3
Gadyach = Hadyach
Ukraine 50°21N 34°0E 189 G8
Gadzi C.A.R. 4°47N 16°42E 264 B3
Gaebong S. Korea 37°29N 126°52E 137 C1
Gāeşti Romania 44°48N 25°19E 183 F10
Gaeta Italy 41°12N 13°35E 200 A6
Gaeta, G. di Italy 41°6N 13°30E 200 A6
Gaffney U.S.A. 35°5N 81°39W 315 D14
Gafsa Tunisia 34°24N 8°43E 258 B1
Gafsa □ Tunisia 34°30N 8°48E 261 B6
Gagarawa Nigeria 12°25N 9°32E 263 C6
Gagaria India 25°43N 70°46E 242 G4
Gagarin Russia 55°38N 35°0E 188 E8
Găgăuzia □ Moldova 46°10N 28°40E 183 D13
Gage Park U.S.A. 41°47N 87°42W 119 C2
Gaggenau Germany 48°48N 8°18E 179 G4
Gaghamni Sudan 11°41N 28°19E 257 E2
Gagil-Tomil, I. Pac. Oc. 9°31N 138°12E 287 R16
Gagino Russia 55°15N 45°1E 190 C7
Gagliano del Capo Italy 39°50N 18°22E 201 C11
Gagnef Sweden 60°36N 15°5E 162 D9
Gagnoa Ivory C. 6°56N 5°16W 262 D3
Gagnon Canada 51°50N 68°5W 299 B6
Gagnon, L. Canada 62°3N 110°27W 297 A5
Gagny France 48°53N 2°32E 134 A4
Gago Coutinho
São Tomé & Príncipe 0°1S 6°32E 265 a
Gagra Georgia 43°20N 40°10E 191 J5
Gahini Rwanda 1°50S 30°30E 268 C3
Gahmar India 25°27N 83°49E 243 G10
Gai Xian = Gaizhou
China 40°22N 122°20E 224 B1
Gaibanda Bangla. 25°20N 89°36E 241 C2
Gaïdouronísi Greece 34°53N 25°41E 207 F6
Gail → Austria 46°36N 13°53E 180 E5
Gail → Austria 32°46N 101°27W 314 E4
Gaillac France 43°54N 1°54E 174 E5
Gaillard Cut Panama 9°3N 79°40W 322 b
Gaillimh = Galway Ireland 53°17N 9°3W 166 C2
Gaillon France 49°10N 1°20E 172 C8
Gaimán Argentina 43°10S 65°25W 336 B3
Gaines U.S.A. 41°46N 77°35W 312 E7
Gainesville Fla., U.S.A. 29°40N 82°20W 317 F7
Gainesville Ga., U.S.A. 34°18N 83°50W 315 D13
Gainesville Mo., U.S.A. 36°36N 92°26W 308 G7
Gainesville Tex., U.S.A. 33°38N 97°8W 314 E6
Gainsborough U.K. 53°24N 0°46W 168 D7
Gairdner, L. Australia 31°30S 136°0E 282 A2
Gairloch U.K. 57°43N 5°41W 167 D3
Gairloch, L. U.K. 57°43N 5°45W 167 D3
Gaizhou China 40°22N 122°20E 224 B1
Gaj Croatia 45°28N 17°3E 182 E2
Gaj → Pakistan 26°26N 67°21E 242 F2
Gajendragarh India 15°44N 75°59E 245 G2
Gakona U.S.A. 62°18N 145°18W 303 E11
Gakuch Pakistan 36°7N 73°45E 243 A5
Gal Oya △ Sri Lanka 7°0N 81°0E 245 L5
Gal Oya Res. Sri Lanka 7°5N 81°30E 245 L5
Gal Tardo Somali Rep. 3°34N 45°58E 267 D6
Galachipa Bangla. 22°8N 90°26E 241 D3
Galāla, Gebel el Egypt 29°21N 32°22E 256 J8
Galāla el Bahariya, G. el
Egypt 29°22N 32°22E 251 J3
Galāla el Qiblīya, G. el
Egypt 28°42N 32°22E 251 K3
Galán, Cerro Argentina 25°55S 66°52W 334 B2
Galana → Kenya 3°9S 40°8E 268 C5
Galangue Angola 13°42S 16°9E 265 G3
Galangue, Serra Angola 14°18S 15°52E 265 G3
Galanta Slovak Rep. 48°11N 17°45E 181 C10
Galápagos Spain 40°36N 3°58W 194 E7
Galápagos = Colón, Arch. de
Ecuador 0°0 91°0W 330 a
Galápagos Fracture Zone
Pac. Oc. 3°0N 110°0W 289 G17
Galápagos Rise Pac. Oc. 15°0S 95°0W 289 J18
Galashiels U.K. 55°37N 2°49W 167 F6
Galatás Turkey 41°1N 28°58E 122 B1
Galata Tower Turkey 41°1N 28°59E 122 B1
Galatás Greece 37°30N 23°26E 204 D5
Galateia N.Z. 38°24S 176°45E 284 E5
Galateia Cyprus 35°25N 34°4E 207 E10
Galaţi Romania 45°27N 28°2E 183 E13
Galaţi □ Romania 45°45N 27°30E 183 E12
Galatia Turkey 39°30N 33°0E 212 C5
Galatina Italy 40°10N 18°10E 201 B11
Galátone Italy 40°9N 18°4E 201 B11
Galaţii Greece 38°1N 23°45E 122 A2
Galax U.S.A. 36°40N 80°56W 309 G13
Galaxídi Greece 38°22N 22°23E 204 C4
Galcaio = Gaalkacyo
Somali Rep. 6°30N 47°30E 267 D6
Gáldar Canary Is. 28°9N 15°30W 153 e1
Galdhøpiggen Norway 61°38N 8°18E 164 C5
Galeana Chihuahua,
Mexico 30°7N 107°38W 318 A3
Galeana Nuevo León,
Mexico 24°50N 100°4W 318 A3
Galeão, Int. de ✈ (GIG)
Brazil 22°49S 43°15W 135 A1
Galegu Sudan 12°49S 43°15W 257 E4
Galela Indonesia 1°50N 127°49E 231 D7
Galena Alaska, U.S.A. 64°44N 156°56W 303 D8
Galena Ill., U.S.A. 42°25N 90°26W 310 D6
Galena Mo., U.S.A. 36°48N 93°28W 310 G4
Galera Spain 37°45N 2°33W 197 H2
Galera, Pta. Chile 39°59S 73°43W 336 A2
Galera Pt. Trin. & Tob. 10°49N 60°54W 323 t
Galera, Pta. de Azores 37°42N 25°30W 153 d3
Galesburg Ill., U.S.A. 40°57N 90°22W 310 D6
Galesburg Mich., U.S.A. 42°17N 85°26W 311 B11

Galestan △ Iran 37°30N 56°0E 247 B8
Galeton U.S.A. 41°44N 77°39W 312 E7
Galets → Réunion 20°56S 55°17E 272 f
Galga → Hungary 6°39N 37°47E 257 F4
Galgasc Somali Rep. 0°11N 41°38E 267 D5
Galgeduud □ Somali Rep. 5°0N 47°0E 267 D6
Galheirão → Brazil 12°23S 45°5W 333 D2
Gali Georgia 42°37N 41°46E 191 J5
Galicea Mare Romania 44°4N 23°19E 183 F8
Galich Russia 58°22N 42°24E 190 A6
Galichina □ Spain 42°43N 7°45W 194 C3
Galicia □ Spain 42°43N 7°45W 194 C3
Galičica △ Macedonia 41°2N 20°55E 202 F4
Galien U.S.A. 41°48N 86°30W 311 C10
Galilee = Hagalil Israel 32°53N 35°18E 250 F6
Galilee, L. Australia 22°20S 145°50E 280 C4
Galilee, Sea of = Yam Kinneret
Israel 32°45N 35°35E 250 F6
Galim Cameroon 7°6N 12°25E 263 D7
Galina Pt. Jamaica 18°24N 76°58W 320 a
Galinoporni Cyprus 35°31N 34°18E 207 E10
Galion U.S.A. 40°44N 82°47W 312 F2
Galion, B. du Martinique 14°44N 60°56W 322 j
Galite, Îs. de la Tunisia 37°30N 8°59E 261 A6
Galiuro Mts. U.S.A. 32°30N 110°20W 305 K8
Galiwinku Australia 12°2S 135°34E 280 A2
Gallābāt Sudan 12°58N 36°11E 257 E4
Gallan Hd. U.K. 58°15N 7°2W 167 C1
Gallarate Italy 45°40N 8°48E 198 C5
Gallatin Mo., U.S.A. 39°55N 93°58W 310 E3
Gallatin Tenn., U.S.A. 36°24N 86°27W 315 C11
Galle Sri Lanka 6°5N 80°10E 245 L5
Gállego → Spain 41°39N 0°51W 196 D4
Gallegos → Argentina 51°35S 69°0W 336 D3
Gallery of Inuit Art = Dominion
Centre Toronto, Canada 141 b2
Galletti → Ethiopia 8°46N 41°10E 257 F5
Galley Hd. Ireland 51°32N 8°55W 166 E3
Galliate Italy 45°29N 8°42E 198 C5
Gallinas, Pta. Colombia 12°28N 71°40W 328 A3
Gallipoli = Gelibolu
Turkey 40°28N 26°43E 203 F10
Gallipoli Italy 40°3N 17°58E 201 B11
Gallipolis U.S.A. 38°49N 82°12W 309 F12
Gällivare Sweden 67°9N 20°40E 160 C19
Gällö Sweden 62°55N 15°13E 162 B8
Gallo, C. Italy 38°13N 13°19E 200 D6
Gallocanta, L. de Spain 40°58N 1°30W 196 D3
Galloo I. U.S.A. 43°55N 76°25W 313 C8
Galloway U.K. 55°1N 4°29W 167 G4
Galloway, Mull of U.K. 54°39N 4°52W 167 G4
Galloway □ U.K. 55°1N 4°29W 167 G4
Gallup U.S.A. 35°32N 108°45W 305 J9
Gallur Spain 41°52N 1°19W 196 D3
Galma Galla Kenya 1°1S 40°47E 267 C5
Galong Australia 34°37S 148°34E 283 C8
Galool Somali Rep. 3°38N 43°44E 267 C6
Galoya Sri Lanka 8°10N 80°55E 245 K5
Galt Calif., U.S.A. 38°15N 121°18W 306 G5
Galt Mo., U.S.A. 40°8N 93°23W 310 D3
Galten Denmark 56°9N 9°54E 163 H3
Galtür Austria 46°58N 10°11E 180 E3
Galty Mts. Ireland 52°22N 8°10W 166 D3
Galtymore Ireland 52°21N 8°11W 166 D3
Galugah Iran 36°43N 53°48E 247 B7
Galva U.S.A. 41°10N 90°3W 310 D6
Galvarino Chile 38°24S 72°47W 336 A2
Galve de Sorbe Spain 41°13N 3°10W 196 D1
Galveston Ind., U.S.A. 40°35N 86°11W 311 D10
Galveston Tex., U.S.A. 29°18N 94°48W 314 G7
Galveston B. U.S.A. 29°36N 94°50W 314 G7
Gálvez Argentina 32°0S 61°14W 334 C3
Galway Ireland 53°17N 9°3W 166 C2
Galway □ Ireland 53°22N 9°1W 166 C2
Galway B. Ireland 53°13N 9°10W 166 C2
Galvanovo Russia 55°48N 37°47E 129 B4
Gam → Vietnam 21°55N 105°12E 236 B5
Gamagōri Japan 34°50N 137°14E 223 B9
Gamari, L. Ethiopia 11°32N 41°40E 257 E5
Gamawa Nigeria 12°10N 10°31E 263 C7
Gamay Phil. 12°23S 125°18E 232 E5
Gamay Bay Phil. 12°21N 125°21E 232 E5
Gamba Angola 11°42S 17°14E 265 G3
Gambaga Ghana 10°30N 0°28W 262 C4
Gambat Pakistan 27°17N 68°26E 242 F3
Gambela Ethiopia 8°14N 34°38E 257 F4
Gambela □ Ethiopia 8°0N 34°0E 257 F3
Gambela Hizboch □ Ethiopia 8°0N 34°0E 257 F3
Gambell U.S.A. 63°47N 171°45W 303 E5
Gambhir → India 26°58N 77°27E 242 F6
Gambia ■ W. Afr. 13°25N 16°0W 262 C1
Gambia → W. Afr. 13°28N 16°34W 262 C1
Gambier U.S.A. 40°22N 82°23W 312 F2
Gambier, C. Australia 11°56S 130°57E 278 B5
Gambier, Îs.
French Polynesia 23°8S 134°58W 289 f
Gambier Is. Australia 35°3S 136°30E 282 C2
Gambier Village Bahamas 25°3N 77°33W 153 b
Gambir Indonesia 6°9S 106°48E 122 A1
Gambo Canada 48°47N 54°13W 299 C9
Gambo C.A.R. 4°39N 22°16E 264 B4
Gamboli Pakistan 29°53N 68°24E 242 E3
Gambomba → Congo 1°55S 15°52E 264 C3
Gamboula C.A.R. 4°8N 15°9E 264 B3
Gamka → S. Africa 33°18S 21°39E 270 D3
Gamkab → Namibia 28°4S 17°54E 270 C2
Gamla Stan Stockholm, Sweden 139 c2
Gamla Uppsala Sweden 59°54N 17°40E 162 E11
Gamlakarleby = Kokkola
Finland 63°50N 23°8E 160 E20
Gamleby Sweden 57°54N 16°24E 163 G10
Gamlebyen Norway 59°54N 10°46E 133 A3
Gammon → Canada 51°24N 95°44W 297 C9
Gammon Ranges △
Australia 30°38S 139°8E 281 E2
Gamo-Gofa Ethiopia 5°40N 36°40E 257 F4
Gamoda-Saki Japan 33°50N 134°45E 222 D6
Gamou Niger 14°20N 9°55E 259 F1
Gampaha Sri Lanka 7°4N 79°59E 245 L4
Gampo S. Korea 35°48N 129°31E 224 E4
Gamtoos → S. Africa 33°58S 25°1E 270 D3
Gan Gan Argentina 43°12N 0°27W 174 E3
Gan Gan Argentina 42°30N 68°21E 336 B3
Gan Goriama, Mts.
Cameroon 7°44N 12°45E 263 D7
Gan Jiang → China 29°15N 116°0E 229 C11
Ganado U.S.A. 35°43N 109°33W 305 J9
Gananita Sudan 18°22N 33°50E 256 D3
Gananoque Canada 44°20N 76°10W 313 B8
Ganāveh Iran 29°35N 50°35E 247 D6
Gäncä Azerbaijan 40°45N 46°20E 191 K8
Gancheng China 18°51N 108°37E 236 D5
Gand = Gent Belgium 51°2N 3°42E 173 C3
Ganda Angola 13°3S 14°35E 265 G2
Gandak → India 25°39N 85°13E 243 G11
Gandara Pakistan 28°32N 67°32E 242 F2
Gandava Pakistan 28°32N 67°32E 242 E2

Gander L. Canada 48°58N 54°35W 299 C9
Ganderkesee Germany 53°2N 8°32E 178 B4
Ganderowe Falls
Zimbabwe 17°20S 29°10E 269 F2
Gandesa Spain 41°3N 0°26E 196 D5
Gandhi Sagar India 24°40N 75°40E 242 G6
Gandhinagar India 23°15N 72°45E 242 H5
Gandi Nigeria 12°55N 5°49E 263 C6
Gandia Spain 38°58N 0°9W 197 G4
Gandino Italy 45°49N 9°54E 198 C6
Gando, Pta. Canary Is. 27°55N 15°22W 153 e1
Gando Nigeria 8°28N 11°35E 263 D7
Gandole Nigeria 8°28N 11°35E 263 D7
Gandu Brazil 13°45S 39°30W 333 D4
Ganedidalem = Gani
Indonesia 0°48S 128°14E 231 E7
Ganga → India 23°20N 90°30E 243 H14
Ganga Sagar India 21°38N 88°5E 243 J13
Gangafani Mali 14°20N 2°20W 262 C4
Gangakher India 18°57N 76°45E 244 E3
Gangan → India 28°38N 78°58E 243 E8
Ganganagar India 29°56N 73°56E 242 E5
Gangapur Maharashtra,
India 19°41N 75°1E 244 E2
Gangapur Raj., India 26°32N 76°49E 242 F7
Gangara Niger 14°35N 8°29E 259 F1
Gangaw Burma 22°5N 94°5E 241 D5
Gangaw Taungdan
Burma 24°55N 96°35E 241 C6
Gangawati India 15°30N 76°36E 245 G3
Gangdisê Shan China 31°20N 81°0E 243 D9
Gangdong S. Korea 37°30N 127°5E 137 B2
Ganges = Ganga →
India 23°20N 90°30E 243 H14
Ganges Canada 48°51N 123°31W 296 D4
Ganges France 43°56N 3°42E 174 E7
Ganges, Mouths of the
India 21°30N 90°0E 243 J13
Gangges S. Korea 36°10N 127°0E 224 D3
Gangneung S. Korea 37°45N 128°54E 224 D4
Gangoh India 29°46N 77°18E 242 E7
Gangotri India 30°50N 79°10E 243 D8
Gangotri △ India 30°50N 79°10E 243 D8
Gangseong S. Korea 37°32N 126°51E 137 B1
Gangseong S. Korea 38°24N 128°30E 224 D4
Gangtok India 27°20N 88°37E 241 B2
Gangtou China 23°12N 113°8E 121 A1
Gangu China 34°40N 105°15E 226 G3
Gangwa
Dem. Rep. of the Congo 3°30S 20°54E 264 C4
Gangwei China 23°4N 113°11E 121 B2
Gangwi China 32°32N 126°51E 137 B1
Gangyao China 44°12N 126°37E 227 B14
Gani Indonesia 0°48S 128°14E 231 E7
Ganj India 27°45N 78°57E 243 F8
Ganjam India 19°23N 85°4E 244 F7
Ganjiakou China 39°54N 116°16E 114 B1
Ganluc China 28°58N 102°59E 228 C4
Ganmain Australia 34°47S 147°1E 283 C7
Ganmuceheng China 47°2N 87°31E 217 C10
Ganna Sudan 7°30N 28°0E 266 C2
Gannat France 46°7N 3°11E 173 B10
Gannett Peak U.S.A. 43°11N 109°39W 304 E9
Ganquan China 36°20N 109°20E 226 F5
Gänserndorf Austria 48°20N 16°43E 181 C9
Ganshoren Belgium 50°52N 4°18E 116 A1
Ganshui China 28°40N 106°40E 228 C6
Gansu □ China 36°0N 104°0E 226 G3
Ganta Liberia 7°15N 8°59W 262 D3
Gantheaume, C.
Australia 36°4S 137°32E 282 D2
Gantheaume B.
Australia 27°40S 114°10E 279 E1
Gants Hill U.K. 51°34N 0°4E 125 A4
Gantsevichi = Hantsavichy
Belarus 52°49N 26°30E 177 B14
Ganye Nigeria 8°25N 12°4E 263 D7
Ganyem = Genyem
Indonesia 2°46S 140°12E 231 E10
Ganyu China 34°50N 119°8E 227 G10
Ganyushkino Kazakhstan 46°35N 49°20E 191 G9
Ganzhou China 25°51N 114°56E 229 E10
Gao Mali 16°15N 0°5W 263 B4
Gao Xian China 28°26N 104°32E 228 C5
Gao'an China 28°26N 115°17E 229 C10
Gaochun China 31°20N 118°49E 229 B12
Gaohe China 22°46N 112°57E 229 F9
Gaohebu China 30°40N 117°34E 229 B11
Gaokeng China 27°20N 113°25E 229 D9
Gaolan Dao China 21°55N 113°10E 229 G9
Gaoligong Shan China 24°45N 98°45E 228 E2
Gaomi China 36°20N 119°42E 227 F10
Gaoping China 35°45N 112°55E 226 G7
Gaoqiao China 31°21N 121°34E 138 A2
Gaotang China 36°50N 116°15E 226 F9
Gaouwiyak Australia 12°25S 135°43E 280 A2
Gar China 32°10N 79°58E 218 C2
Gara, L. Ireland 53°57N 8°26W 166 C3
Garāb Iran 33°27N 47°16E 213 F12
Garabogazköl Aylagy
Turkmenistan 41°0N 53°30E 187 F9
Garacad Somali Rep. 6°57N 49°24E 267 D6
Garachico Canary Is. 28°22N 16°46W 153 e1
Garachiné Panama 8°0N 78°12W 320 E4
Garafia Canary Is. 28°48N 17°57W 153 e1
Garagum Turkmenistan 39°30N 60°0E 247 B8
Garah Australia 29°5S 149°38E 281 D4
Garaina Papua N. G. 7°53S 147°9E 286 D4
Garamba △
Dem. Rep. of the Congo 4°10N 29°40E 268 B2
Garanhuns Brazil 8°50S 36°30W 332 D6
Garango Burkina Faso 11°48N 0°34W 263 C4
Garanhuns → China 29°15N 116°0E 229 C11
Garapan N. Marianas 15°12N 145°43E 302 e
Garautha India 25°34N 79°18E 243 G8
Garawa → Australia 16°43S 136°51E 280 B2
Garawe Liberia 4°35N 8°0W 262 E3
Garba Harre = Garbahaarrey
Somali Rep. 3°19N 42°13E 267 D5
Garba Tula Kenya 0°30S 38°32E 268 B4
Garbahaarrey
Somali Rep. 3°19N 42°13E 267 D5
Garberville U.S.A. 40°6N 123°48W 306 F2
Garbiyang India 30°8N 80°54E 243 D9
Garbsen Germany 52°24N 9°36E 178 C5
Gardo Somali Rep. 9°30N 49°6E 267 D6

Garz Germany 54°19N 13°20E 178 A9
Garzê China 31°38N 100°1E 228 B3
Garzón Colombia 2°10N 75°40W 328 C3
Gas City U.S.A. 40°29N 85°37W 311 D11
Gas-San Japan 38°32N 140°1E 220 E10
Gasa Bhutan 27°55N 89°40E 241 B2
Gasan Kuli = Esenguly
Turkmenistan 37°37N 53°59E 216 E4
Gascogne France 43°45N 0°20E 174 E4
Gascogne, G. de Europe 44°0N 2°0W 174 E2
Gasconade → U.S.A. 38°40N 91°33W 310 F5
Gascony = Gascogne
France 43°45N 0°20E 174 E4
Gascoyne → Australia 24°52S 113°37E 279 D1
Gascoyne Junction
Australia 25°2S 115°17E 279 E2
Gascueña Spain 40°18N 2°31W 196 E2
Gash, Wadi → Africa 16°48N 35°51E 257 D4
Gash Setit □ Eritrea 15°12N 36°58E 257 D4
Gåshaga Sweden 59°21N 18°13E 139 A3
Gashaka Nigeria 13°22N 12°47E 263 C7
Gashaka-Gumti △ Nigeria 7°23N 11°34E 263 D7
Gasherbrum Pakistan 35°40N 76°40E 243 B7
Gashua Nigeria 12°54N 11°0E 263 C7
Gasmata Papua N. G. 6°17S 150°20E 286 D6
Gasparilla I. U.S.A. 26°46N 82°16W 317 H7
Gasparillo Trin. & Tob. 10°18N 61°26W 323 t
Gasparito Neth. Ant. 12°8N 68°56W 322 g
Gaspé Canada 48°52N 64°30W 299 C7
Gaspé, C. de Canada 48°48N 64°7W 299 C7
Gaspé Pen. = Gaspésie, Pén. de la
Canada 48°45N 65°40W 299 C6
Gasper Grande Trin. & Tob. 10°40N 61°39W 323 t
Gaspésie, Pén. de la
Canada 48°45N 65°40W 299 C6
Gaspésie △ Canada 48°55N 66°10W 299 C6
Gassan Burkina Faso 12°49N 3°12W 262 C4
Gassen = Jasień Poland 51°46N 15°0E 185 G2
Gassol Nigeria 8°34N 10°25E 263 D7
Gasteiz = Vitoria-Gasteiz
Spain 42°50N 2°41W 196 C2
Gastonia U.S.A. 33°49N 81°5W 316 D8
Gastoúni Greece 35°16N 81°11W 315 D14
Gastouri Greece 37°51N 21°15E 204 D3
Gastre Argentina 39°34N 19°54E 206 B9
Gästrikland Sweden 42°20S 69°15W 336 B3
Gata, C. Cyprus 60°45N 16°40E 162 D10
Gata, C. de Spain 34°34N 33°2E 207 F9
Gata, Sierra de Spain 36°41N 2°13W 197 J2
Gataga → Canada 40°20N 6°45W 194 E4
Gataga → Canada 58°35N 126°59W 296 B3
Gătaia Romania 45°26N 21°30E 182 E6
Gatchina Russia 59°35N 30°9E 188 C6
Gatehouse of Fleet U.K. 54°53N 4°12W 167 G4
Gates U.S.A. 43°9N 77°42W 312 D7
Gates of the Arctic △
U.S.A. 67°45N 153°15W 303 C9
Gateshead I. Canada 70°36N 100°26W 294 C11
Gateshead U.K. 54°57N 1°35W 168 C6
Gateway △ U.S.A. 38°40N 108°58W 305 G9
Gateway of India India 18°55N 72°50E 130 B2
Gaths Zimbabwe 20°2S 30°32E 269 G3
Gâtinais France 48°5N 2°40E 173 D9
Gâtine, Hauteurs de
France 46°35N 0°45W 174 B3
Gatineau Canada 45°29N 75°39W 313 A9
Gatineau → Canada 45°27N 75°42W 298 C4
Gatineau △ Canada 45°40N 76°0W 298 C4
Gatow Germany 52°29N 13°11E 115 B1
Gattaran Phil. 18°4N 121°38E 232 B3
Gattinara Italy 45°37N 8°22E 198 C5
Gatton Australia 27°32S 152°17E 281 D5
Gatún, L. Panama 9°7N 79°56W 320 c
Gatún Dam Panama 9°16N 79°55W 320 c
Gatún Locks Panama 9°16N 79°55W 320 c
Gatwick, London ✈ (LGW)
U.K. 51°10N 0°11W 169 F7
Gatyana S. Africa 32°16S 28°31E 271 D4
Gau Fiji 18°2S 179°18E 287 D2
Gaua Vanuatu 14°15S 167°30E 287 D5
Gaucín Spain 36°31N 5°19W 195 J5
Gauer L. Canada 57°0N 97°50W 297 B9
Gauhati = Guwahati
India 26°10N 91°45E 241 B4
Gauja → Latvia 57°10N 24°16E 184 A11
Gaujas △ Latvia 57°10N 24°16E 161 H21
Gaula → Norway 63°21N 10°14E 164 A7
Gaupne Norway 61°25N 7°8E 164 C4
Gaurdak = Gowurdak
Turkmenistan 37°50N 66°4E 217 F7
Gauri Phanta India 28°41N 80°36E 243 E9
Gauribidanur India 13°37N 77°32E 245 H3
Gaustatoppen Norway 59°48N 8°40E 164 E5
Gauteng □ S. Africa 26°0S 28°0E 271 C4
Gāv Koshi Iran 28°38N 57°12E 247 D8
Gāvakān Iran 29°37N 53°10E 247 D7
Gavarnie France 41°1N 2°9W 114 B1
Gavāter Iran 25°10N 61°31E 247 E9
Gāvbandī Iran 27°12N 53°4E 247 E7
Gávdos Greece 34°50N 24°5E 207 F5
Gavião Portugal 39°28N 7°56W 195 F3
Gávios Brazil 22°58S 43°13W 135 B1
Gávea, Pedra da Brazil 22°59S 43°18W 135 B1
Gavi Italy 44°41N 8°49E 198 D5
Gavião Portugal 39°28N 7°56W 195 F3
Gaviota U.S.A. 34°29N 120°13W 307 L6
Gävle Sweden 60°40N 17°9E 162 D11
Gävleborgs län □
Sweden 61°30N 16°15E 162 C10
Gävlebukten Sweden 60°40N 17°27E 162 D11
Gavorrano Italy 42°55N 10°54E 198 F7
Gavray France 48°55N 1°20W 172 D5
Gavrilov Yam Russia 57°18N 39°49E 188 D10
Gawachab Namibia 27°4S 17°55E 270 C2
Gawai Burma 27°56N 97°30E 241 B6
Gawilgarh Hills India 21°15N 76°45E 244 D3
Gawler Australia 34°30S 138°42E 282 C2
Gawler Ranges Australia 32°30S 135°45E 282 C2
Gawu Nigeria 9°1N 6°52E 263 D6
Gaxun Nur China 42°22N 100°30E 226 A3
Gay Russia 51°27N 58°27E 186 D10
Gaya India 24°47N 85°4E 243 G11
Gaya Niger 11°52N 3°28E 263 C5
Gaya Nigeria 11°57N 9°0E 263 C6
Gayéri Burkina Faso 12°37N 0°30E 263 C5
Gaylord U.S.A. 45°2N 84°41W 311 B11
Gayndah Australia 25°35S 151°32E 281 D5
Gaysin = Haysyn
Ukraine 48°57N 29°25E 183 B14
Gayvoron = Hayvoron
Ukraine 48°22N 29°52E 183 B14
Gaza Gaza Strip 31°30N 34°28E 251 D3
Gaza □ Mozam. 23°10S 32°45E 271 B5
Gaza Strip ■ Asia 31°29N 34°25E 251 D3
Gazanjyk = Bereket
Turkmenistan 39°16N 55°32E 247 B8

Gazaoua Niger 13°32N 7°55E 263 C6
Gāzbor Iran 28°55N 58°51E 247 D8
Gazdagrét Hungary 47°29N 19°0E 117 B1
Gazelle Pen. Papua N. G. 4°40S 152°0E 286 C7
Gazi Dem. Rep. of the Congo 1°3N 24°30E 264 B4
Gaziantep Turkey 37°6N 37°23E 250 A8
Gaziantep □ Turkey 37°0N 37°0E 250 B8
Gazimağusa = Famagusta
  Cyprus 35°8N 33°55E 207 E19
Gaziosmanpaşa Turkey 41°5N 28°50E 122 B1
Gazipaşa Turkey 36°16N 32°18E 250 B3
Gazli Uzbekistan 40°8N 63°27E 216 D6
Gbadolite
  Dem. Rep. of the Congo 4°17N 21°1E 264 B4
Gbarnga Liberia 7°19N 9°13W 262 D3
Gboko Nigeria 7°17N 9°4E 263 D6
Gbongan Nigeria 7°28N 4°20E 263 D5
Gcoverega Botswana 19°8S 24°18E 270 A3
Gcuwa S. Africa 32°20S 28°11E 271 D4
Gdańsk Poland 54°22N 18°40E 184 D5
Gdańsk ✈ (GDN) Poland 54°22N 18°58E 184 D5
Gdańska, Zatoka Poland 54°30N 19°20E 184 D6
Gdingen = Gdynia
  Poland 54°35N 18°33E 184 D5
Gdov Russia 58°48N 27°55E 188 C4
Gdynia Poland 54°35N 18°33E 184 D5
Geba → Guinea-Biss. 11°46N 15°36W 262 C1
Gebe Indonesia 0°5N 129°25E 231 D7
Gebeciler Turkey 38°46N 30°46E 205 C12
Gebeit Mine Sudan 21°3N 36°29E 256 C4
Gebel Abyad Sudan 19°0N 28°0E 256 D2
Gebel el Ahmar Egypt 30°2N 31°21E 117 A3
Gebel el Muqattam Egypt 30°1N 31°17E 117 A2
Gebel el Tura Egypt 29°56N 31°16E 117 B2
Gebel Iweibid Egypt 30°8N 32°13E 256 H8
Gebiley Somali Rep. 9°42N 43°37E 267 C5
Gebze Turkey 40°47N 29°25E 203 F13
Gecha Ethiopia 7°30N 35°18E 257 F4
Gedaref Sudan 14°2N 35°28E 257 E4
Gedaref □ Sudan 14°0N 35°0E 257 E4
Gede, Tanjung Indonesia 6°46S 105°12E 234 D3
Gediz Turkey 39°1N 29°24E 205 B11
Gediz → Turkey 38°35N 26°48E 205 C8
Gedo Ethiopia 9°2N 37°25E 257 F4
Gedo □ Somali Rep. 2°15N 42°10E 267 D5
Gèdre France 42°47N 0°2E 174 F4
Gedser Denmark 54°35N 11°55E 163 K5
Gedung, Pulau Malaysia 5°17N 100°23E 237 c
Geegully Cr. →
  Australia 18°32S 123°41E 278 C3
Geel Belgium 51°10N 4°59E 170 C4
Geelong Australia 38°10S 144°22E 282 E6
Geelvink B. = Cenderawasih, Teluk
  Indonesia 3°0S 135°20E 231 E9
Geelvink Chan. Australia 28°30S 114°0E 279 E1
Geesthacht Germany 53°26N 10°22E 178 B6
Geidam Nigeria 12°57N 11°57E 263 C7
Geikie → Canada 57°45N 103°52W 297 B8
Geikie Gorge △ Australia 18°3S 125°41E 278 C4
Geilenkirchen Germany 50°57N 6°8E 178 E2
Geili Sudan 16°1N 32°37E 257 D3
Geilo Norway 60°32N 8°14E 164 D5
Geiselgasteig Germany 48°3N 11°33E 131 B2
Geisingen Germany 47°54N 8°38E 179 H4
Geislingen Germany 48°37N 9°50E 179 G5
Geistown U.S.A. 40°18N 78°52W 312 F6
Geita Tanzania 2°48S 32°12E 268 C3
Geitastrand Norway 63°20N 9°56E 164 A6
Geithus Norway 59°59N 9°56E 164 E6
Gejiu China 23°20N 103°10E 228 F4
Gel → Sudan 7°5N 29°10E 257 F2
Gel, Meydân-e Iran 29°4N 54°50E 247 D7
Gel River Sudan 7°5N 29°10E 257 F2
Gela Italy 37°4N 14°15E 201 F7
Gela, G. di Italy 37°0N 14°20E 201 F7
Geladi Ethiopia 6°59N 46°30E 267 C6
Gelahun Liberia 7°55N 10°28W 262 D2
Gelang Patah Malaysia 1°27N 103°35E 237 d
Gelderland □ Neths. 52°5N 6°10E 170 B6
Geldern Germany 51°31N 6°20E 178 D2
Geldrop Neths. 51°25N 5°32E 170 C5
Geleen Neths. 50°57N 5°49E 170 D5
Gelehun S. Leone 8°20N 10°40W 262 D2
Gelembe Turkey 39°10N 27°50E 205 B9
Gelemso Ethiopia 8°49N 40°31E 257 F5
Gelendost Turkey 38°7N 31°1E 212 C4
Gelendzhik Russia 44°33N 38°10E 189 K10
Gelib = Jilib Somali Rep. 0°29N 42°46E 267 D5
Gelibolu Turkey 40°28N 26°43E 203 F10
Gelibolu Yarımadası
  Turkey 40°20N 26°30E 203 F10
Gelidonya Burnu Turkey 36°12N 30°24E 212 D4
Gellinsoor Somali Rep. 6°28N 46°39E 267 C6
Gelnhausen Germany 50°11N 9°11E 179 E5
Gelnica Slovak Rep. 48°51N 20°55E 181 C13
Gelsenkirchen Germany 51°32N 7°6E 178 D3
Gelting Germany 54°45N 9°53E 178 A5
Gelugur Malaysia 5°22N 100°18E 237 c
Gemas Malaysia 2°37N 102°36E 237 L4
Gembloux Belgium 50°34N 4°43E 170 D4
Gembu Nigeria 6°42N 11°10E 263 D7
Gemena
  Dem. Rep. of the Congo 3°13N 19°48E 264 B3
Gemerek Turkey 39°15N 36°10E 212 C7
Gemla Sweden 56°48N 14°39E 163 H8
Gemlik Turkey 40°26N 29°9E 203 F13
Gemlik Körfezi Turkey 40°25N 28°52E 203 F12
Gemona del Friuli Italy 46°16N 13°9E 199 B10
Gemsa Egypt 27°39N 33°35E 256 B3
Gemsbok △ Botswana 25°5S 21°1E 270 C3
Gemünden Germany 50°3N 9°42E 179 F5
Genadi Greece 36°2N 27°56E 206 E11
Genale → Ethiopia 6°2N 39°1E 257 F4
Genç Turkey 38°44N 40°34E 213 C9
Gençay France 46°23N 0°23E 174 B4
Geneina, Gebel Egypt 29°2N 33°55E 256 B3
General Acha
  Argentina 37°20S 64°38W 334 D3
General Alvear B. Aires,
  Argentina 36°0S 60°0W 334 D4
General Alvear Mendoza,
  Argentina 35°0S 67°40W 334 D2
General Artigas
  Paraguay 26°52S 56°16W 334 B4
General Belgrano
  Argentina 36°35S 58°47W 334 D4
General Bernardo O'Higgins
  Antarctica 63°0S 58°3W 151 C18
General Cabrera
  Argentina 32°53S 63°52W 334 C3
General Carrera, L. Chile 46°35S 72°0W 336 C2
General Cepeda Mexico 25°21N 101°22W 318 B4
General Conesa Argentina 40°6S 64°25W 336 B4
General Eugenio A. Garay
  Paraguay 20°31S 62°8W 331 E5
General Germán Busch = Villa
  Abecia Bolivia 21°0S 68°18W 334 A2
General Guido Argentina 36°40S 57°50W 334 D4
General Juan Madariaga
  Argentina 37°0S 57°0W 334 D4
General La Madrid
  Argentina 37°17S 61°20W 334 D3
General Lorenzo Vintter
  Argentina 40°45S 64°26W 336 B4
General Luna Phil. 13°41N 122°10E 232 E4
General MacArthur
  Phil. 11°18N 125°28E 233 F5

General Martín Miguel de Güemes
  Argentina 24°50S 65°0W 334 A3
General Pico Argentina 35°45S 63°50W 334 D3
General Pinedo
  Argentina 27°15S 61°20W 334 B3
General Pinto Argentina 34°45S 61°50W 334 C3
General Sampaio Brazil 4°2S 39°29W 332 B4
General San Martin
  Argentina 34°35S 58°32W 117 B1
General Santos Phil. 6°5N 125°14E 233 H5
General Tinio Phil. 15°39N 121°10E 232 D3
General Toshevo Bulgaria 43°42N 28°6E 203 C12
General Treviño Mexico 26°14N 99°29W 319 B5
General Trias Mexico 28°21N 106°22W 318 B3
General Uriburu = Zárate
  Argentina 34°7S 59°0W 334 C4
General Viamonte
  Argentina 35°1S 61°3W 334 D3
General Villegas Argentina 35°5S 63°0W 334 D3
General Vintter, L.
  Argentina 43°55S 71°40W 336 B2
Generoso Ponce = Jaci-Paraná
  Brazil 9°15S 64°23W 331 B5
Genesee Idaho, U.S.A. 46°33N 116°56W 304 C5
Genesee Pa., U.S.A. 41°59N 77°54W 312 E7
Genesee → U.S.A. 43°16N 77°36W 312 C7
Geneseo Ill., U.S.A. 41°27N 90°9W 310 C6
Geneseo N.Y., U.S.A. 42°48N 77°49W 312 D7
Geneva = Genève Switz. 46°12N 6°9E 179 J2
Geneva Ala., U.S.A. 31°2N 85°52W 316 D4
Geneva Ga., U.S.A. 32°35N 84°33W 316 D5
Geneva Ill., U.S.A. 41°53N 88°18W 311 E8
Geneva Ind., U.S.A. 40°36N 84°58W 311 D12
Geneva N.Y., U.S.A. 42°52N 76°59W 312 D8
Geneva Nebr., U.S.A. 40°32N 97°36W 308 E5
Geneva Ohio, U.S.A. 41°48N 80°57W 312 E4
Geneva, L. = Léman, L.
  Europe 46°26N 6°30E 173 F13
Geneva, L., U.S.A. 42°38N 88°30W 311 E8
Genève Switz. 46°12N 6°9E 179 J2
Geng Afghan. 31°22N 61°28E 247 C9
Gengenbach Germany 48°24N 8°1E 179 G4
Gengma China 23°32N 99°20E 228 F2
Genichesk = Henichesk
  Ukraine 46°12N 34°50E 189 J8
Genil → Spain 37°42N 5°19W 195 H5
Génipa, B. de Martinique 14°33N 61°0W 322 j
Genisea Greece 41°1N 24°57E 203 E8
Genk Belgium 50°58N 5°32E 170 D5
Genkai-Nada Japan 34°0N 130°0E 222 D2
Genlis France 47°11N 5°12E 173 G12
Gennargentu, Mti. del Italy 40°1N 9°19E 200 B2
Gennes France 47°20N 0°17E 172 G7
Gennevilliers France 48°56N 2°17E 134 A2
Genoa = Génova Italy 44°25N 8°57E 198 D5
Genoa Vic., Australia 37°29S 149°35E 283 D8
Genoa Ill., U.S.A. 42°6N 88°42W 311 B8
Genoa N.Y., U.S.A. 42°40N 76°32W 312 D8
Genoa Nebr., U.S.A. 41°27N 97°44W 308 E5
Genoa Nev., U.S.A. 39°2N 119°50W 306 F7
Genoa → Argentina 44°55S 70°50W 336 B2
Genoa City U.S.A. 42°30N 88°20W 311 B8
Génova Italy 44°25N 8°57E 198 D5
Génova, G. di Italy 44°0N 9°0E 198 E5
Génova ✈ (GOA) Italy 44°25N 8°50E 198 D5
Genovesa, I. Ecuador 0°20N 89°58W 330 a
Genriyetty, Ostrov
  Russia 77°6N 156°30E 215 B16
Gent Belgium 51°2N 3°42E 170 C3
Genteng Bali, Indonesia 8°22S 114°9E 234 J17
Genteng Jawa Barat,
  Indonesia 7°22S 106°24E 231 G12
Genthin Germany 52°24N 12°9E 178 C8
Gentilly Val-de-Marne,
  France 48°48N 2°21E 134 B3
Gentilly La., U.S.A. 30°0N 90°2W 131 A2
Gentio do Ouro Brazil 11°25S 42°30W 332 D3
Gentofte Denmark 55°44N 12°32E 118 A3
Gentryville U.S.A. 38°6N 87°2W 311 F9
Genval Belgium 50°43N 4°29E 116 B2
Genyem Indonesia 2°46S 140°12E 231 E10
Genzano di Lucánia Italy 40°51N 16°2E 201 B9
Genzano di Roma Italy 41°42N 12°41E 199 G9
Geoagiu Romania 45°55N 23°12E 183 E8
Geochang S. Korea 35°41N 127°55E 224 E3
Geogeumdo S. Korea 34°27N 127°10E 224 E3
Geographe B. Australia 33°30S 115°15E 279 F2
Geographe Chan.
  Australia 24°30S 113°0E 279 D1
Geographical Society Ø
  Greenland 72°57N 23°15W 154 C8
Geoje S. Korea 34°51N 128°35E 224 E4
Geojedo S. Korea 34°51N 128°38E 224 E4
Geokchay = Göyçay
  Azerbaijan 40°42N 47°43E 191 K8
Georga, Zemlya Russia 80°30N 49°0E 214 A5
George S. Africa 33°58S 22°29E 270 D3
George → Canada 58°49N 66°10W 299 A6
George, L. N.S.W.,
  Australia 35°10S 149°25E 283 C8
George, L. S. Austral.,
  Australia 37°25S 140°0E 282 D4
George, L. W. Austral.,
  Australia 22°45S 123°40E 278 D3
George, L. Uganda 0°5N 30°10E 268 B3
George, L. Fla., U.S.A. 29°17N 81°36W 317 E6
George, L. N.Y., U.S.A. 43°37N 73°33W 313 C11
George Gill Ra. Australia 24°22S 131°45E 278 D5
George I. Hong Kong,
  China 22°13N 114°7E 122 B1
George I. St. Helena 15°58S 5°38W 153 b
George Pt. Australia 20°6S 148°36E 280 b
George River = Kangiqsualujjuaq
  Canada 58°30N 65°59W 295 F18
George Rogers Clark Nat.
  Memorial △ U.S.A. 38°41N 87°32W 311 F9
George Sound N.Z. 44°52S 167°25E 285 E2
George Town Tas.,
  Australia 41°6S 146°49E 281 A4
George Town Bahamas 23°33N 75°47W 320 B4
George Town Cayman Is. 19°20N 81°24W 320 C3
George Town Malaysia 5°25N 100°20E 237 c
George V Land Antarctica 69°0S 148°0E 151 C10
George VI Sound
  Antarctica 71°0S 68°0W 151 D17
George West U.S.A. 28°20N 98°7W 314 G5
Georges River Bridge
  Australia 34°0S 151°6E 139 C1
Georgetown = Janjanbureh
  Gambia 13°30N 14°47W 262 C2
Georgetown Ascension I. 7°56S 14°25W 153 g
Georgetown Queens.,
  Australia 18°17S 143°33E 280 B3
Georgetown Ont., Canada 43°40N 79°56W 312 D5
Georgetown P.E.I.,
  Canada 46°13N 62°24W 299 C7
Georgetown Guyana 6°50N 58°12W 329 B6
Georgetown St. Vincent 13°16N 61°7W 323 k
Georgetown Calif.,
  U.S.A. 38°54N 120°50W 306 G6
Georgetown Colo.,
  U.S.A. 39°42N 105°42W 304 G11
Georgetown Fla., U.S.A. 29°23N 81°38W 317 E6
Georgetown Ga., U.S.A. 31°53N 85°6W 316 D4
Georgetown Ill., U.S.A. 39°59N 87°38W 311 E10

Georgetown Ky., U.S.A. 38°13N 84°33W 311 F12
Georgetown N.Y., U.S.A. 42°46N 75°44W 313 D9
Georgetown Ohio,
  U.S.A. 38°52N 83°54W 311 F13
Georgetown S.C., U.S.A. 33°23N 79°17W 315 E15
Georgetown Tex., U.S.A. 30°38N 97°41W 314 F6
Georgia □ U.S.A. 32°50N 83°15W 316 C6
Georgia ■ Asia 42°0N 43°0E 191 J6
Georgia, Str. of N. Amer. 49°25N 124°0W 306 A3
Georgia Basin S. Ocean 55°0S 35°0W 151 B1
Georgia Dome U.S.A. 33°45N 84°23W 113 B2
Georgian B. Canada 45°15N 81°0W 312 A4
Georgian Bay Islands △
  Canada 44°53N 79°52W 312 B5
Georgievka Kazakhstan 49°19N 84°34E 217 C10
Georgina → Australia 23°30S 139°47E 280 C2
Georgina L. Canada 44°22N 79°17W 312 B5
Georgioupoli Greece 35°20N 24°15E 207 E5
Georgiu-Dezh = Liski
  Russia 51°3N 39°30E 189 G10
Georgiyevsk Russia 44°12N 43°28E 191 H6
Georgsmarienhütte
  Germany 52°13N 8°3E 178 C4
Gera Germany 50°53N 12°4E 178 E8
Geraardsbergen Belgium 50°45N 3°53E 170 D3
Geraki Greece 37°0N 22°42E 204 D4
Geraki, Akra Greece 36°42N 23°50E 207 D2
Geral, Serra Goiás, Brazil 14°0S 41°0W 333 D3
Geral, Serra Goiás, Brazil 11°15S 46°30W 332 D2
Geral, Serra Sta. Catarina,
  Brazil 26°25S 50°0W 335 B6
Geral de Goiás, Serra
  Brazil 12°0S 46°0W 333 D2
Geral do Paraná, Serra
  Brazil 15°0S 47°30W 333 E2
Gerald U.S.A. 38°24N 91°20W 310 F5
Geraldine N.Z. 44°5S 171°15E 285 E6
Geraldine Mont., U.S.A. 47°36N 110°16W 304 C8
Geraldton W. Austral.,
  Australia 28°48S 114°32E 279 E1
Geraldton Ont., Canada 49°44N 86°59W 298 C2
Geranium Australia 35°23S 140°11E 282 C4
Gérardmer France 48°3N 6°50E 173 D13
Gerasdorf bei Wien
  Austria 48°17N 16°28E 142 A2
Gerberau Germany 48°12N 11°27E 131 A1
Gerçüş Turkey 37°34N 41°23E 213 D9
Gerdine, Mt. U.S.A. 61°35N 152°27W 303 F9
Gerede Turkey 40°45N 32°10E 212 B5
Gerês, Sierra de Portugal 41°48N 8°0W 194 D3
Gereshk Afghan. 31°47N 64°35E 240 C2
Geretsried Germany 47°51N 11°28E 179 H7
Gérgal Spain 37°7N 2°31W 197 H2
Gerik Malaysia 5°50N 101°15E 237 K3
Gering U.S.A. 41°50N 103°40W 308 E2
Geriş Turkey 36°57N 31°43E 250 B2
Gerlach U.S.A. 40°39N 119°21W 304 F4
Gerlachovský štít
  Slovak Rep. 49°11N 20°7E 181 B13
Gerli Argentina 34°41S 58°22W 117 C2
Gerlogubi Ethiopia 6°53N 45°3E 267 C6
Ghent = Gent Belgium 51°2N 3°42E 170 C3
Gheorghe Gheorghiu = Oneşti
  Romania 46°17N 26°47E 183 D11
Gheorgheni Romania 46°43N 25°41E 183 D10
Gherla Romania 47°2N 23°57E 183 C8
Ghidigeni Romania 46°17N 27°33E 183 D11
Ghilarza Italy 40°7N 8°50E 200 B1
Ghimeş-Făget Romania 46°35N 26°5E 183 D11
Ghīnah, Wādī al →
  Si. Arabia 30°27N 38°14E 246 D3
Ghīrān, W. → Si. Arabia 30°52N 47°10E 248 B4
Ghirardelli Square San Francisco, U.S.A. 136 a1
Ghisonaccia France 42°1N 9°26E 175 F13
Ghisoni France 42°7N 9°12E 175 F13
Ghizar → Pakistan 36°15N 73°43E 243 A5
Ghizri Pakistan 24°47N 67°5E 123 B2
Ghizri Cr. → Pakistan 24°47N 67°5E 123 B2
Ghod → India 18°31N 74°35E 244 E2
Ghogha India 21°40N 72°20E 244 D1
Ghonda India 28°41N 77°16E 120 A2
Ghot Ogrein Egypt 31°10N 25°20E 256 A2
Ghotaru India 27°20N 70°1E 242 F4
Ghotki Pakistan 28°5N 69°21E 242 E3
Ghowr □ Afghan. 34°0N 64°20E 240 B2
Ghubbet el Bûs Egypt 29°39N 32°24E 256 H7
Ghughri India 22°39N 80°41E 243 H9
Ghugus India 19°58N 79°12E 244 E4

Ghadāmis Libya 30°11N 9°29E 258 B1
Ghadāmis □ Libya 30°25N 10°25E 258 B2
Ghaddūwah Libya 26°26N 14°19E 258 C2
Ghaghara → India 29°30N 74°53E 242 E6
Ghaghara → India 25°45N 84°40E 243 G11
Ghaghat → Bangla. 25°19N 89°38E 241 C2
Ghaghe Solomon Is. 7°24S 158°15E 287 C10
Ghagra India 23°17N 84°33E 243 H11
Ghagra → India 27°29N 81°9E 243 F9
Ghajn Tuffieha Bay
  Malta 35°56N 14°21E 206 F7
Ghajnsielem Malta 36°1N 14°17E 206 E7
Ghalla, Wadi el → Sudan 10°25N 27°32E 257 F2
Ghallamane Mauritania 23°15N 10°0W 260 D3
Ghallamane, Sebkhet
  Mauritania 23°41N 9°50W 260 D3
Ghamid az Zenad
  Si. Arabia 19°35N 41°24E 248 C3
Ghana ■ W. Afr. 8°0N 1°0W 263 D4
Ghansor India 22°39N 80°1E 243 H9
Ghanzi Botswana 21°50S 21°34E 270 C3
Gharapuri India 18°57N 72°57E 130 B2
Gharb el → Shahrak-e Qods
  Iran 35°47N 51°22E 141 A2
Gharb Malta 36°4N 14°13E 206 E6
Gharb Bahr el Ghazâl →
  Sudan 7°30N 27°30E 257 F2
Gharb Dârfûr □ Sudan 13°0N 23°0E 259 F4
Gharb el Istiwa'iya □ Sudan 5°0N 30°0E 257 G2
Gharb Kordofân □ Sudan 12°0N 28°0E 257 E2
Gharbîya, Es Sahrâ el
  Egypt 27°40N 26°30E 256 B2
Ghardaïa Algeria 32°20N 3°37E 261 B5
Ghardaïa □ Algeria 31°5N 3°10E 261 B5
Ghârib, G. Egypt 28°6N 32°54E 256 B3
Gharig Sudan 10°47N 27°33E 257 E2
Gharm Tajikistan 39°0N 70°20E 218 F8
Gharm, W. → Oman 19°57N 57°38E 249 C7
Gharyân Libya 32°10N 13°0E 258 B2
Gharyân □ Libya 30°35N 13°0E 258 B2
Ghat Libya 24°59N 10°11E 258 D2
Ghāt □ Libya 25°35N 10°15E 258 C2
Ghatal India 22°40N 87°46E 243 H12
Ghatampur India 26°8N 80°13E 243 F9
Ghatgaon India 21°24N 85°53E 244 D7
Ghatkopar India 19°4N 72°54E 130 A2
Ghatprabha → India 16°15N 75°20E 245 F2
Ghats, Eastern India 14°0N 78°50E 245 H4
Ghats, Western India 14°0N 75°0E 245 H2
Ghatsila India 22°36N 86°29E 243 H12
Ghaṭṭī Si. Arabia 31°16N 37°31E 246 D3
Ghawdex = Gozo Malta 36°3N 14°15E 206 E7
Ghayl Si. Arabia 21°40N 46°20E 248 B4
Ghazal, Bahr el → Chad 13°0N 15°47E 259 F3
Ghazâl, Bahr el → Sudan 9°31N 30°25E 257 F3
Ghazaouet Algeria 35°8N 1°50W 261 A4
Ghaziabad India 28°42N 77°26E 242 E7
Ghazipur Delhi, India 28°37N 77°19E 120 B2
Ghazipur Ut. P., India 25°38N 83°35E 243 G10
Ghaznī Afghan. 33°30N 68°28E 242 C3
Ghaznī □ Afghan. 32°10N 68°20E 240 B3
Ghedi Italy 45°24N 10°16E 198 C7
Ghelari Romania 45°40N 22°43E 183 E8

Giebnegáisi = Kebnekaise
  Sweden 67°53N 18°33E 160 C18
Gien France 47°40N 2°36E 173 E9
Giengen Germany 48°37N 10°14E 179 G6
Giesing Germany 48°6N 11°35E 131 B2
Giessen Germany 50°34N 8°41E 178 E4
Gīfān Iran 37°54N 57°28E 247 B8
Gifatin, Geziret Egypt 27°10N 33°50E 256 B3
Gifford U.S.A. 27°40N 80°25W 317 F6
Gifhorn Germany 52°30N 10°33E 178 C6
Gift Lake Canada 55°53N 115°49W 296 B5
Gifu Japan 35°30N 136°45E 223 B8
Gifu □ Japan 35°40N 137°0E 223 B9
Gigant Russia 46°28N 41°20E 191 G5
Giganta, Sa. de la Mexico 26°30N 111°30W 318 B2
Gigen Bulgaria 43°40N 24°28E 203 C8
Gīgha U.K. 55°42N 5°44E 167 F3
Gíglio Italy 42°20N 10°52E 198 F7
Gignac France 43°39N 3°32E 174 E7
Gigüela → Spain 39°8N 3°44W 195 F7
Gijang S. Korea 35°14N 129°12E 224 E4
Gijón Spain 43°32N 5°42W 194 B5
Gikongoro Rwanda 2°28S 29°54E 268 C2
Gil I. Canada 53°12N 129°15W 296 C3
Gila → U.S.A. 32°43N 114°33W 305 K6
Gila Bend U.S.A. 32°57N 112°43W 305 K7
Gila Bend Mts. U.S.A. 33°10N 113°0W 305 K7
Gila Cliff Dwellings △
  U.S.A. 33°12N 108°16W 305 K9
Gīlān □ Iran 37°0N 50°0E 247 B6
Gīlān-e Gharb Iran 34°8N 45°55E 213 E11
Gilău Romania 46°45N 23°23E 183 D8
Gilbert → Australia 16°35S 141°15E 280 B3
Gilbert Is. Kiribati 1°0N 172°0E 277 A14
Gilbert River Australia 18°9S 142°52E 280 B3
Gilbert Seamounts
  Pac. Oc. 52°50N 150°10W 150 D18
Gilbués Brazil 9°50S 46°21W 332 C2
Gilead U.S.A. 44°24N 70°59W 313 B14
Gilf el Kebîr, Hadabat el
  Egypt 23°50N 25°50E 256 C2
Gilford I. Canada 50°40N 126°30W 296 C3
Gilgandra Australia 31°43S 148°39E 283 A8
Gilgil Kenya 0°30S 36°20E 268 C4
Gilgit India 35°50N 74°15E 243 B6
Gilgit → Pakistan 35°44N 74°37E 243 B6
Gilgunnia Australia 32°26S 146°2E 283 B7
Gili Mozam. 16°39S 39°27E 269 F4
Giljeva Planina Europe 43°9N 20°0E 202 C3
Gill Pt. St. Helena 15°58S 5°38W 153 b
Gillam Canada 56°20N 94°40W 297 B10
Gilleleje Denmark 56°8N 12°19E 163 H6
Gillen, L. Australia 26°11S 124°38E 279 E3
Gilles, L. Australia 32°50S 136°45E 282 B2
Gillespie U.S.A. 39°8N 89°49W 310 F7
Gillespies Pt. N.Z. 43°24S 169°49E 285 E3
Gillette U.S.A. 44°18N 105°30W 304 D11
Gilliat Australia 20°40S 141°28E 280 C3
Gillingham U.K. 51°23N 0°33E 169 F8
Gilman Ill., U.S.A. 40°46N 88°0W 311 D9
Gilman City U.S.A. 40°8N 93°53W 310 D3
Gilmer U.S.A. 32°44N 94°57W 314 E7
Gilmerton U.K. 55°54N 3°7W 121 B3
Gilmore, L. Australia 32°29S 121°37E 279 F3
Gilmour Canada 44°48N 77°37W 312 B7
Gilo → Ethiopia 8°10N 33°15E 257 F3
Gilort → Romania 44°38N 23°32E 183 F8
Gilroy U.S.A. 37°1N 121°34W 306 H5
Giluwe, Mt. Papua N. G. 6°8S 143°52E 286 D2
Gimbi Ethiopia 9°3N 35°42E 257 F4
Gimcheon S. Korea 36°11N 128°4E 224 D4
Gimhae S. Korea 35°14N 128°53E 224 E4
Gimhwa S. Korea 38°17N 127°28E 224 C3
Gimie, Mt. St. Lucia 13°54N 61°0W 323 m
Gimje S. Korea 35°48N 126°45E 224 E3
Gimli Canada 50°40N 97°0W 297 C9
Gimmerstia Greece 38°11N 20°58E 204 C1
Gimnje → France 43°38N 0°52E 174 E4
Gimont France 43°38N 0°52E 174 E4
Gin Gin Australia 25°0S 151°58E 281 D5
Gin Gin Australia 25°0S 151°58E 281 D5
Ginâh Egypt 25°21N 30°30E 256 C5
Ginatilan Phil. 9°34N 123°19E 233 G6
Gineifa Egypt 30°12N 32°26E 256 H8
Gingee India 12°15N 79°25E 245 H4
Gingin Australia 31°22S 115°54E 279 F2
Gingindlovu S. Africa 29°2S 31°30E 271 C5
Gingoog Phil. 8°50N 125°7E 233 G6
Ginir Ethiopia 7°6N 40°40E 257 F5
Ginosa Italy 40°35N 16°45E 201 B9
Ginowan Japan 26°15N 127°45E 222 a
Ginza Tokyo, Japan 140 b5
Ginzo de Limia = Xinzo de Limia
  Spain 42°3N 7°47W 194 C3
Giofyros → Greece 35°20N 25°6E 207 E6
Giohar = Jawhar
  Somali Rep. 2°48N 45°30E 267 G4
Gióia, G. di Italy 38°30N 15°50E 201 D8
Gióia del Colle Italy 40°48N 16°55E 201 B9
Gióia Táuro Italy 38°26N 15°53E 201 D8
Gioiosa Iónica Italy 38°20N 16°19E 201 D9
Gioiosa Marea Italy 38°10N 14°54E 201 D7
Giona, Oros Greece 38°38N 22°14E 204 C4
Giovi, Passo dei Italy 44°33N 8°57E 198 D5
Giovinazzo Italy 41°11N 16°40E 201 A9
Gippsland Australia 37°45S 147°15E 283 C7
Gir → India 21°0N 71°0E 242 J4
Gir Hills India 21°0N 71°0E 242 J4
Gir National Park India 21°8N 70°50E 242 J4
Girab India 26°2N 70°38E 242 F4
Girâfi, W. → Egypt 29°58N 34°39E 251 F3
Giraltovce Slovak Rep. 49°7N 21°32E 181 B14
Girard Ga., U.S.A. 33°3N 81°43W 316 D8
Girard Ill., U.S.A. 39°27N 89°47W 310 F7
Girard Kans., U.S.A. 37°31N 94°51W 308 G6
Girard Ohio, U.S.A. 41°9N 80°42W 312 E4
Girard Pa., U.S.A. 42°0N 80°19W 312 D4
Girardot Colombia 4°18N 74°48W 328 C4
Giraud, Pte. Dominica 15°20N 61°15W 323 k
Girdle Ness U.K. 57°9N 2°3W 167 D6
Giresun Turkey 40°55N 38°30E 213 B8
Giresun □ Turkey 40°30N 38°0E 213 B8
Girga Egypt 26°17N 31°55E 256 B3
Girgaon Mumbai, India 130 b2
Girgir, C. Papua N. G. 3°50S 144°35E 286 B3
Giri →
  Dem. Rep. of the Congo 0°28N 17°58E 264 B3
Giridih India 24°10N 86°21E 243 G12
Girifalco Italy 38°49N 16°26E 201 D9
Girifu Kenya 1°59N 39°46E 267 D5
Girilambone Australia 31°16S 146°57E 283 B8
Girne = Kyrenia Cyprus 35°20N 33°20E 207 E18
Giro Nigeria 11°7N 4°42E 263 C6
Giro → France 47°45N 0°15E 172 G7
Giron = Kiruna Sweden 67°52N 20°15E 160 C19
Girona Spain 41°58N 2°46E 197 D7
Girona □ Spain 42°11N 2°30E 197 C7
Gironde □ France 44°45N 0°30W 174 D3
Gironde → France 45°32N 1°7W 174 C2

Gironella Spain 42°2N 1°53E 196 C6
Girraween △ Australia 28°46S 151°54E 281 D5
Girringun △ Australia 18°30S 145°50E 280 B4
Giru Australia 19°30S 147°5E 280 B4
Girvan U.K. 55°14N 4°51W 167 F4
Gisborne Vic., Australia 37°29S 144°36E 282 D6
Gisborne N.Z. 38°39S 178°5E 284 D6
Gisborne □ N.Z. 38°30S 178°0E 284 E6
Gisenyi Rwanda 1°41S 29°15E 268 C2
Gislaved Sweden 57°19N 13°32E 163 H7
Gisors France 49°15N 1°47E 173 C8
Gitarama Rwanda 2°4S 29°45E 268 C2
Gitega Burundi 3°26S 29°56E 268 C2
Githio Greece 36°46N 22°34E 204 E4
Gitschin = Jičín
  Czech Rep. 50°25N 15°28E 180 A8
Giuba = Juba →
  Somali Rep. 1°30N 42°35E 267 D5
Giugliano in Campania
  Italy 40°56N 14°12E 201 B7
Giulianova Italy 42°45N 13°57E 199 F10
Giura Greece 39°23N 24°10E 204 B6
Giurgeni Romania 44°45N 27°48E 183 F12
Giurgiu Romania 43°52N 25°57E 183 G10
Giurgiu □ Romania 44°20N 26°0E 183 F10
Giurgiulesti Moldova 45°29N 28°12E 183 E13
Giv'at Ram Israel 31°47N 35°12E 123 B2
Giv'at Ye'arim Israel 31°47N 35°5E 123 B1
Giv'at Ze'ev West Bank 31°52N 35°10E 123 B2
Give Denmark 55°51N 9°13E 163 J3
Givet France 50°8N 4°49E 173 B11
Giv'on West Bank 31°51N 35°10E 123 A1
Givors France 45°35N 4°45E 175 C8
Givry France 46°41N 4°46E 173 F11
Giyani S. Africa 23°19S 30°42E 271 A5
Giyon Ethiopia 8°33N 38°1E 257 F4
Giza = El Gîza Egypt 30°0N 31°12E 117 A2
Giza Pyramids Egypt 29°58N 31°9E 117 B1
Gizab Afghan. 33°22N 66°17E 242 C1
Gizhiga Russia 62°3N 160°30E 215 C17
Gizhiginskaya Guba
  Russia 61°0N 158°0E 215 C16
Gizo Solomon Is. 8°7S 156°50E 287 M9
Giżycko Poland 54°2N 21°48E 184 D8
Gizzeria Italy 38°59N 16°12E 201 D9
Gjälicë e Lumës, Mal.
  Albania 42°2N 20°25E 202 D4
Gjegjan Albania 41°58N 20°3E 202 D4
Gjendeshein Norway 61°30N 8°48E 164 D3
Gjermundshamn Norway 60°40N 5°55E 164 D2
Gjersjøen Norway 59°47N 10°47E 133 B3
Gjerstad Norway 58°54N 9°1E 164 F6
Gjevilvatnet Norway 62°43N 9°23E 164 A6
Gjirokastër Albania 40°7N 20°10E 202 E4
Gjoa Haven Canada 68°38N 95°53W 294 D12
Gjøra Norway 62°33N 9°4E 164 A6
Gjøvik Norway 60°47N 10°43E 164 D4
Gjuhës, Kep i Albania 40°28N 19°15E 202 F3
Glace Bay Canada 46°11N 59°58W 299 C8
Glacier △ B.C., Canada 51°15N 117°30W 296 C5
Glacier △ Mont., U.S.A. 48°42N 113°48W 304 B7
Glacier Bay U.S.A. 58°40N 136°0W 303 G14
Glacier Bay △ U.S.A. 58°45N 136°30W 296 B1
Glacier Peak U.S.A. 48°7N 121°7W 304 B3
Gladewater U.S.A. 32°33N 94°56W 314 E7
Gladsakse Denmark 55°45N 12°25E 118 A2
Gladstone Queens.,
  Australia 23°52S 151°16E 280 C5
Gladstone S. Austral.,
  Australia 33°15S 138°22E 282 B2
Gladstone Man., Canada 50°13N 98°57W 297 C9
Gladstone Ill., U.S.A. 40°52N 90°57W 310 D6
Gladstone Mich., U.S.A. 45°51N 87°1W 308 C10
Gladstone Mo., U.S.A. 39°13N 94°35W 310 F2
Gladwin U.S.A. 43°59N 84°29W 309 D11
Glafsfjorden Sweden 59°30N 12°37E 162 E6
Glagah Indonesia 8°13S 114°18E 231 J17
Głogów Małopolski
  Poland 50°10N 21°56E 185 H8
Glåma = Glomma →
  Norway 59°12N 10°57E 164 E2
Gláma Iceland 65°48N 23°0W 155 B4
Glamis U.S.A. 32°55N 115°4W 307 N11
Glamoč Bos.-H. 44°3N 16°51E 199 D13
Glamorgan, Vale of □
  U.K. 51°28N 3°25W 169 F4
Glåmos Norway 62°41N 11°12E 164 B8
Glamsbjerg Denmark 55°16N 10°6E 163 J4
Glanville Dominica 15°34N 61°28W 323 k
Glarus Switz. 47°3N 9°4E 179 H5
Glarus □ Switz. 47°0N 9°0E 179 H5
Glasco Kans., U.S.A. 39°22N 97°50W 308 F5
Glasco N.Y., U.S.A. 42°3N 73°57W 313 D11
Glasgow U.K. 55°51N 4°15W 167 F4
Glasgow Ky., U.S.A. 37°0N 85°55W 309 G11
Glasgow Mo., U.S.A. 39°14N 92°51W 310 E4
Glasgow Mont., U.S.A. 48°12N 106°38W 304 B10
Glasgow, City of □ U.K. 55°51N 4°15W 167 F4
Glasgow Int. ✈ (GLA)
  U.K. 55°51N 4°21W 167 F4
Glaslyn Canada 53°22N 108°21W 297 C7
Glasnevin Ireland 53°23N 6°15W 120 A2
Glassmanor U.S.A. 38°49N 77°0W 143 C4
Glasthule Ireland 53°17N 6°7W 120 B3
Glastonbury U.K. 51°9N 2°43W 169 F5
Glastonbury Somst., U.K. 51°9N 2°43W 169 F5
Glastonbury Conn.,
  U.S.A. 41°43N 72°37W 313 E11
Glatz = Kłodzko Poland 50°28N 16°38E 185 H3
Glauchau Germany 50°49N 12°10E 178 E8
Glava Sweden 59°36N 12°29E 162 E6
Glavice Croatia 43°43N 16°41E 199 E13
Glazov Russia 58°9N 52°40E 190 A11
Gleichen Canada 50°52N 113°3W 296 C6
Gleisdorf Austria 47°6N 15°44E 181 D9
Gleiwitz = Gliwice Poland 50°22N 18°41E 185 H5
Glen U.S.A. 44°7N 71°11W 313 B13
Glen Affric U.K. 57°17N 5°1W 167 D3
Glen Afton N.Z. 37°37S 175°4E 284 C5
Glen Canyon U.S.A. 37°30N 110°40W 305 H8
Glen Canyon △ U.S.A. 37°15N 111°0W 305 H8
Glen Canyon Dam
  U.S.A. 36°57N 111°29W 305 H8
Glen Coe U.K. 56°40N 5°0W 167 E3
Glen Cove U.S.A. 40°51N 73°38W 313 F11
Glen Garry U.K. 57°3N 5°7W 167 D3
Glen Innes Australia 29°44S 151°44E 281 D5
Glen Iris Australia 37°51S 145°3E 128 C2
Glen Lyon U.K. 56°37N 4°19W 167 E4
Glen Mar Park U.S.A. 39°11N 76°5W 143 B3
Glen Mor U.K. 57°9N 4°37W 167 D4
Glen Moriston U.K. 57°10N 4°58W 167 D4
Glen Robertson Canada 45°22N 74°30W 313 A10
Glen Rouge Park Canada 43°49N 79°10W 141 A4
Glen Spean U.K. 56°53N 4°40W 167 E4
Glen Ullin U.S.A. 46°49N 101°50W 308 B3
Glen Villa S. Africa 32°56S 27°51E 123 B1
Glenafooka U.K. 54°59N 6°11W 166 B5
Glénan, Îs. de France 47°43N 4°0W 172 E3
Glenarden U.S.A. 38°56N 76°52W 143 B4
Glenariff U.K. 55°2N 6°3W 166 A5
Glenariff △ Ireland 55°6N 6°0W 166 A5
Glenarm U.K. 54°57N 5°58W 166 B6
Glenavy N.Z. 44°54S 171°7E 285 F6
Glenbeigh Ireland 52°3N 9°58W 166 D2
Glenburn Australia 37°27S 145°26E 283 D6

Glencoe Ont., Canada 42°45N 81°43W 312 D3
Glencoe KwaZulu Natal, S. Africa 28°11S 30°11E 271 C5
Glencoe Ala., U.S.A. 33°57N 85°56W 316 B4
Glencoe Minn., U.S.A. 44°46N 94°9W 308 C6
Glencolumbkille Ireland 54°43N 8°42W 166 B3
Glencorse Res. U.K. 55°51N 3°15W 121 B2
Glencullen Ireland 53°14N 6°12W 120 B2
Glendale Ariz., U.S.A. 33°32N 112°11W 305 K7
Glendale Calif., U.S.A. 34°9N 118°15W 126 B3
Glendale Fla., U.S.A. 30°52N 86°7W 316 E3
Glendale Zimbabwe 17°22S 31°5E 269 F3
Glendive U.S.A. 47°7N 104°43W 304 C11
Glendo U.S.A. 42°30N 105°2W 304 E11
Glendoo Mt. Ireland 53°14N 6°16W 120 B2
Glenelg Australia 34°58S 138°31E 282 C3
Glenelg → Australia 38°4S 140°59E 282 E4
Glenfield U.S.A. 43°43N 75°24W 313 C9
Glengad Hd. Ireland 55°20N 7°10W 166 A4
Glengarriff Ireland 51°45N 9°34W 166 E2
Glengoffe Jamaica 18°10N 76°53W 320 a
Glenham N.Z. 46°26S 168°52E 285 G3
Glenhope N.Z. 41°40S 172°39E 285 B7
Glenhuntly Australia 37°52S 145°1E 128 B2
Glenmary, Mt. N.Z. 43°55S 169°55E 285 D4
Glenmont U.S.A. 40°31N 82°6W 312 F2
Glenmorgan Australia 27°14S 149°42E 281 D4
Glenn U.S.A. 39°31N 122°1W 306 F4
Glennallen U.S.A. 62°7N 145°33W 303 E11
Glennamaddy Ireland 53°37N 8°33W 166 C3
Glenns Ferry U.S.A. 42°57N 115°18W 304 E6
Glennville U.S.A. 31°56N 81°56W 316 D8
Glenora Canada 44°2N 77°3W 312 B7
Glenorchy Tas., Australia 42°49S 147°18E 281 G4
Glenorchy Vic., Australia 36°55S 142°41E 282 D5
Glenorchy N.Z. 44°51S 168°24E 285 E3
Glenore Australia 17°50S 141°12E 280 B3
Glenreagh Australia 30°2S 153°1E 281 E5
Glenrock U.S.A. 42°52N 105°52W 304 E11
Glenrothes U.K. 56°12N 3°10W 167 E5
Glenrowan Australia 36°29S 146°13E 283 D7
Glens Falls U.S.A. 43°19N 73°39W 313 C11
Glenside Wellington, N.Z. 41°12S 174°48E 143 B1
Glenside Pa., U.S.A. 40°6N 75°9W 313 F9
Glenthompson Australia 37°38S 142°38E 282 D5
Glenties Ireland 54°49N 8°16W 166 B3
Glenveagh △ Ireland 55°3N 8°1W 166 A3
Glenview U.S.A. 42°3N 87°48W 119 A2
Glenview Countryside U.S.A. 42°3N 87°49W 119 A2
Glenville U.S.A. 38°56N 80°50W 309 F13
Glenvista S. Africa 26°17S 28°3E 123 B2
Glenwood Nfld. & L., Canada 49°0N 54°58W 299 C9
Glenwood Ark., U.S.A. 34°20N 93°33W 314 D8
Glenwood Ga., U.S.A. 32°11N 82°40W 316 C7
Glenwood Hawai'i, U.S.A. 19°29N 155°9W 302 D6
Glenwood Iowa, U.S.A. 41°3N 95°45W 308 E6
Glenwood Minn., U.S.A. 45°39N 95°23W 308 C6
Glenwood Wash., U.S.A. 46°1N 121°17W 306 D5
Glenwood Springs U.S.A. 39°33N 107°19W 304 G10
Glettinganes Iceland 65°30N 13°37W 155 B13
Glidden U.S.A. 42°4N 94°44W 310 B2
Glifada Greece 37°52N 23°45E 112 B2
Glimåkra Sweden 56°19N 14°7E 163 H8
Glin Ireland 52°34N 9°17W 166 D2
Glina Croatia 45°20N 16°6E 199 C13
Glinojeck Poland 52°49N 20°21E 185 F7
Glittertind Norway 61°40N 8°32E 164 C5
Gliwice Poland 50°22N 18°41E 185 H5
Globe U.S.A. 33°24N 110°47W 305 K8
Glodeanu Siliştea Romania 44°50N 26°48E 183 F11
Glodeni Moldova 47°45N 27°31E 183 C12
Glödnitz Austria 46°53N 14°7E 180 E7
Głogau = Głogów Poland 51°37N 16°5E 185 G3
Gloggnitz Austria 47°41N 15°56E 180 D8
Głogów Poland 51°37N 16°5E 185 G3
Głogówek Poland 50°21N 17°53E 185 H4
Glomma → Norway 59°12N 10°57E 164 E7
Gloria Phil. 12°59N 121°30E 232 E3
Glorieuses, Îs. Ind. Oc. 11°30S 47°20E 272 A2
Glosa Greece 39°10N 23°45E 204 B5
Glossop U.K. 53°27N 1°56W 168 D6
Glostrup Denmark 55°39N 12°23E 118 B2
Gloucester N.S.W., Australia 32°0S 151°59E 283 B9
Gloucester Papua N. G. 5°31S 148°31E 286 C5
Gloucester Glouc., U.K. 51°53N 2°15W 169 F5
Gloucester Mass., U.S.A. 42°37N 70°40W 313 D14
Gloucester, C. Papua N. G. 5°26S 148°21E 286 C5
Gloucester I. Australia 20°0S 148°30E 280 b
Gloucester Island △ Australia 20°2S 148°30E 280 b
Gloucester Point U.S.A. 37°15N 76°30W 309 G15
Gloucestershire □ U.K. 51°46N 2°15W 169 F5
Glover I. Grenada 11°59N 61°47W 323 q
Gloversville U.S.A. 43°3N 74°21W 313 C10
Glovertown Canada 48°40N 54°3W 299 C9
Gloverville = Warrenville U.S.A. 33°33N 81°48W 316 B8
Głowno Poland 51°59N 19°42E 185 G6
Głubczyce Poland 50°13N 17°52E 185 H4
Glubokiy Russia 48°35N 40°25E 191 F5
Glubokoe Kazakhstan 50°8N 82°18E 217 B10
Glubokoye = Hlybokaye Belarus 55°10N 27°45E 188 E4
Głucholazy Poland 50°19N 17°24E 185 H4
Glücksburg Germany 54°50N 9°33E 178 A5
Glückstadt Germany 53°45N 9°25E 178 B5
Glukhov = Hlukhiv Ukraine 51°40N 33°58E 189 G7
Glusk Belarus 52°53N 28°41E 177 B15
Głuszyca Poland 50°41N 16°23E 185 H3
Glyngøre Denmark 56°46N 8°52E 163 H2
Gmünd Kärnten, Austria 46°54N 13°31E 180 E6
Gmünd Niederösterreich, Austria 48°45N 15°0E 180 C8
Gmunden Austria 47°55N 13°48E 180 D6
Gnali Gabon 2°34S 11°18E 264 C2
Gnarp Sweden 62°3N 17°16E 162 B11
Gnesen = Gniezno Poland 52°30N 17°35E 185 F4
Gnesta Sweden 59°3N 17°17E 162 E11
Gniew Poland 53°50N 18°50E 184 E5
Gniewkowo Poland 52°54N 18°25E 185 F5
Gniezno Poland 52°30N 17°35E 185 F4
Gnjilane Kosovo 42°28N 21°29E 202 D5
Gnoien Germany 53°58N 12°41E 178 B8
Gnosjö Sweden 57°22N 13°43E 163 G7
Gnowangerup Australia 33°58S 117°59E 279 F2
Go Cong Vietnam 10°22N 106°40E 237 G6
Gō-Gawa → Japan 35°2N 132°13E 222 B4
Gō-no-ura Japan 33°44N 129°40E 222 D1
Goa India 15°33N 73°59E 245 G1
Goa Phil. 13°42N 123°29E 232 E4
Goa □ India 15°33N 73°59E 245 G1
Goalen Hd. Australia 36°33S 150°4E 283 D9
Goalpara India 26°10N 90°40E 241 B3
Goaltor India 22°43N 87°10E 243 H12
Goalundo Ghat Bangla. 23°50N 89°47E 243 H13
Goaso Ghana 6°48N 2°30W 262 D4
Goat Fell U.K. 55°38N 5°11W 167 F3
Goat I. Antigua & B. 17°43N 61°51W 322 c
Goat Pt. Antigua & B. 17°44N 61°51W 322 c
Goba Ethiopia 7°1N 39°59E 257 F4
Goba Mozam. 26°15S 32°13E 271 C5
Gobabis Namibia 22°30S 19°0E 270 B2
Gobe Papua N. G. 9°4S 149°0E 286 E5
Göbel Turkey 40°0N 28°9E 203 F12
Gobernador Gregores Argentina 48°46S 70°15W 336 C2
Gobi Asia 44°0N 110°0E 226 C6
Gobichettipalayam India 11°31N 77°21E 245 J3
Gobles U.S.A. 42°22N 85°53W 311 B11
Gobō Japan 33°53N 135°10E 223 D7
Gobo Sudan 5°40N 31°10E 257 F3
Göçbeyli Turkey 39°13N 27°25E 205 B9
Goch Germany 51°41N 6°9E 178 D2
Gochang S. Korea 35°26N 126°42E 224 E3
Gochas Namibia 24°59S 18°55E 270 B2
God Dere Ethiopia 5°12N 44°1E 267 C5
Godalming U.K. 51°11N 0°36W 169 F7
Godavari → India 16°25N 82°18E 244 F6
Godavari Pt. India 17°0N 82°20E 244 F6
Godbout Canada 49°20N 67°38W 299 C6
Godda India 24°50N 87°13E 243 G12
Gode Ethiopia 5°53N 43°35E 267 C5
Godech Bulgaria 43°1N 23°4E 202 C7
Goderich Canada 43°45N 81°41W 312 C3
Goderville France 49°38N 0°22E 172 C7
Godfrey U.S.A. 38°58N 90°11W 310 F6
Godfrey Ra. Australia 24°0S 117°0E 279 D2
Goðafoss Iceland 65°41N 17°33W 155 B9
Godhavn = Qeqertarsuaq Greenland 69°15N 53°38W 154 D5
Goðdalir Iceland 65°20N 19°6W 155 B7
Godhra India 22°49N 73°40E 242 H5
Godinlabe Somali Rep. 5°54N 46°38E 267 C6
Gödöllő Hungary 47°38N 19°25E 182 C4
Godoy Cruz Argentina 32°56S 68°52W 334 C2
Gods → Canada 56°22N 92°51W 298 A1
Gods L. Canada 54°40N 94°15W 298 B1
Gods River Canada 54°50N 94°5W 297 C10
Godthåb = Nuuk Greenland 64°10N 51°35W 154 E5
Godwin Austen = K2 Pakistan 35°58N 76°32E 243 B7
Goeie Hoop, Kaap die = Good Hope, C. of S. Africa 34°24S 18°30E 270 D2
Goéland, L. au Canada 49°50N 76°48W 298 C4
Goélands, L. aux Canada 55°27N 64°17W 299 A7
Goeree Neths. 51°50N 4°0E 170 C3
Goes Neths. 51°30N 3°55E 170 C3
Gofca → Somali Rep. 1°10N 43°43E 267 D5
Goffstown U.S.A. 43°1N 71°36W 313 C13
Gogama Canada 47°35N 81°43W 298 C3
Gogar U.K. 55°56N 3°20W 121 B2
Gogebic, L. U.S.A. 46°30N 89°35W 308 B9
Goggetti Ethiopia 8°11N 38°35E 257 F4
Gogolin Poland 50°30N 18°0E 185 H5
Gogonou Benin 10°50N 2°50E 263 C5
Gogra = Ghaghara → India 25°45N 84°40E 243 G11
Gogrial Sudan 8°30N 28°8E 257 F2
Gogti Ethiopia 10°7N 42°51E 257 E5
Gohana India 29°8N 76°42E 242 E7
Goharganj India 23°1N 77°41E 242 H7
Goheung S. Korea 34°36N 127°17E 224 E3
Goi → India 22°4N 74°46E 242 H6
Goiana Brazil 7°33S 34°59W 332 C5
Goianésia Brazil 15°18S 49°7W 333 E2
Goiânia Brazil 16°43S 49°20W 333 E2
Goiás Brazil 15°55S 50°10W 333 E1
Goiás □ Brazil 12°10S 48°0W 332 D2
Goiatins Brazil 7°42S 47°10W 332 C2
Goiatuba Brazil 18°1S 49°23W 333 E2
Goidu Atoll Maldives 4°53N 72°54E 272 d
Goio-Erê Brazil 24°12S 53°1W 335 A5
Góis Portugal 40°10N 8°6W 194 E2
Gojam Ethiopia 10°55N 36°30E 257 E4
Gojeb, Wabi → Ethiopia 7°12N 36°40E 257 F4
Gojō Japan 34°21N 135°42E 223 C7
Gojra Pakistan 31°10N 72°40E 242 D5
Gokak India 16°11N 74°52E 245 F2
Gokarn India 14°33N 74°17E 245 G2
Gökçe = Sevana Lich Armenia 40°30N 45°20E 191 K7
Gökçeada Turkey 40°10N 25°50E 203 F9
Gökçedağ Turkey 39°33N 28°56E 205 B10
Gökçen Turkey 38°7N 27°53E 205 C9
Gökçeören Turkey 38°37N 28°35E 205 C10
Gökçeyazı Turkey 39°40N 27°40E 205 B9
Gökırmak → Turkey 41°25N 35°8E 212 B6
Gökova Turkey 37°1N 28°17E 205 D10
Gökova Körfezi Turkey 36°55N 27°50E 205 E9
Göksu → Turkey 36°19N 34°5E 250 B5
Göksun Turkey 38°2N 36°30E 212 C7
Gokteik Burma 22°26N 97°0E 241 D6
Göktepe Karaman, Turkey 36°37N 32°37E 250 B3
Göktepe Muğla, Turkey 37°25N 28°34E 205 D10
Göktürk Turkey 41°10N 28°53E 122 A1
Gokurt Pakistan 29°40N 67°26E 242 E2
Gokwe Zimbabwe 18°7S 28°58E 271 A4
Gol Norway 60°42N 8°55E 164 D5
Gol Gol Australia 34°12S 142°14E 282 C5
Gola India 28°3N 80°32E 243 E9
Golabari India 22°35N 88°20E 124 B2
Golakganj India 26°8N 89°52E 241 B2
Golan Heights = Hagolan Syria 33°0N 35°45E 250 F6
Golańcz Poland 52°57N 17°18E 185 F4
Golāshkerd Iran 27°59N 57°16E 247 E8
Golaya Pristen = Hola Prystan Ukraine 46°29N 32°32E 189 J7
Gölbaşı Adıyaman, Turkey 37°43N 37°25E 212 D7
Gölbaşı Ankara, Turkey 39°47N 32°49E 212 C5
Golchikha Russia 71°45N 83°30E 150 B12
Golconda India 17°24N 78°23E 244 F4
Golconda Nev., U.S.A. 40°58N 117°30W 304 F5
Gölcük Kocaeli, Turkey 40°42N 29°48E 203 F13
Gölcük Niğde, Turkey 38°14N 34°47E 212 C6
Gold U.S.A. 41°52N 77°50W 312 E7
Gold Beach U.S.A. 42°25N 124°25W 304 E1
Gold Coast = Ghana ■ W. Afr. 8°0N 1°0W 263 D4
Gold Coast Queens., Australia 28°0S 153°25E 276 F9
Gold Coast Chicago, U.S.A. 119 a2
Gold Coast W. Afr. 4°0N 1°40W 263 E4
Gold Creek U.S.A. 62°46N 149°41W 303 E10
Gold Hill U.S.A. 42°26N 123°3W 304 E2
Gold River Canada 49°46N 126°3W 296 D3
Goldap Poland 54°19N 22°18E 184 D9
Goldberg = Złotoryja Poland 51°8N 15°55E 185 G2
Goldberg Germany 53°35N 12°4E 178 B8
Golden B.C., Canada 51°20N 116°59W 296 C5
Golden Ill., U.S.A. 40°7N 91°1W 310 D5
Golden B. N.Z. 40°40S 172°50E 285 A7
Golden Buddha = Traimit Bangkok, Thailand 113 c2
Golden Gate U.S.A. 37°48N 122°29W 136 B2
Golden Gate ⌂ U.S.A. 37°49N 122°31W 136 A2
Golden Gate Bridge U.S.A. 37°49N 122°28W 136 B2
Golden Gate Highlands △ S. Africa 28°40S 28°40E 271 C4
Golden Gate Park U.S.A. 37°46N 122°28W 136 B2
Golden Grove Middlesex, Jamaica 18°19N 77°9W 320 a
Golden Grove Surrey, Jamaica 17°55N 76°16W 320 a
Golden Hinde Canada 49°40N 125°44W 296 D3
Golden Horn = Haliç Turkey 41°1N 28°57E 122 B1
Golden Lake Canada 45°34N 77°21W 312 A7
Golden Rock India 10°45N 78°48E 245 J4
Golden Spike ⌓ U.S.A. 41°37N 112°33W 304 F7
Golden Vale Ireland 52°33N 8°17W 166 D3
Goldendale U.S.A. 45°49N 120°50W 304 D3
Golders Green U.K. 51°34N 0°11W 125 A2
Goldfield U.S.A. 37°42N 117°14W 305 H5
Goldingen = Kuldīga Latvia 56°58N 21°59E 184 B8
Goldsand L. Canada 57°2N 101°8W 297 B8
Goldsboro U.S.A. 35°23N 77°59W 315 D16
Goldsmith U.S.A. 31°59N 102°37W 314 F3
Goldthwaite U.S.A. 31°27N 98°34W 314 F5
Golegã Portugal 39°24N 8°29W 195 F2
Goleniów Poland 53°35N 14°50E 184 E1
Golestān □ Iran 37°20N 55°25E 247 B7
Golestan Palace Iran 35°41N 51°25E 141 A2
Golestānak Iran 30°36N 54°14E 247 D7
Goleta U.S.A. 34°27N 119°50W 307 L7
Golfito Costa Rica 8°41N 83°5W 320 E3
Golfo Aranci Italy 40°59N 9°38E 200 B2
Golfo di Orosei e del Gennargentu △ Italy 40°5N 9°15E 200 B2
Gölgeli Dağları Turkey 37°10N 28°55E 205 D10
Gölhisar Turkey 37°8N 29°31E 205 D11
Goliad U.S.A. 28°40N 97°23W 314 G6
Golija Montenegro 43°5N 18°45E 202 C2
Golija Serbia 43°22N 20°15E 202 C4
Golina Poland 52°15N 18°4E 185 F5
Goljam Bratan = Morozov Bulgaria 42°30N 25°10E 203 D9
Gölköy Turkey 40°41N 37°37E 212 B7
Gollans Stream → N.Z. 41°22S 174°52E 143 B2
Gollel = Lavumisa Swaziland 27°20S 31°55E 271 C5
Göllersdorf Austria 48°29N 16°7E 180 C9
Gollnow = Goleniów Poland 53°35N 14°50E 184 E1
Gölmarmara Turkey 38°42N 27°55E 205 C9
Golo → France 42°31N 9°32E 175 F13
Gölova Turkey 36°48N 30°5E 205 E12
Golovin U.S.A. 64°33N 163°2W 303 D7
Golpāyegān Iran 33°27N 50°18E 247 C6
Gölpazarı Turkey 40°16N 30°18E 212 B4
Golra Pakistan 33°37N 72°56E 242 C5
Golspie U.K. 57°58N 3°59W 167 D5
Golub-Dobrzyń Poland 53°7N 19°2E 185 E6
Golubac Serbia 44°38N 21°38E 202 B5
Golungo Alto Angola 9°8S 14°46E 265 D2
Golyam Perelik Bulgaria 41°36N 24°33E 203 E8
Golyama Kamchiya → Bulgaria 43°10N 27°55E 203 C11
Golyevo Russia 55°48N 37°18E 129 B1
Golyshi = Vetluzhskiy Russia 58°23N 45°26E 190 A7
Goma Dem. Rep. of the Congo 1°37S 29°10E 268 C2
Gomal Pass Pakistan 31°56N 69°20E 242 D3
Gomati → India 25°32N 83°11E 243 G10
Gombari Dem. Rep. of the Congo 2°45N 29°3E 268 B2
Gombe Dem. Rep. of the Congo 0°45S 17°36E 264 C3
Gombe Nigeria 10°19N 11°2E 263 C7
Gömbe Turkey 36°33N 29°38E 205 E11
Gombe □ Nigeria 10°0N 11°0E 263 C7
Gombe → Tanzania 4°38S 31°40E 268 C3
Gombe Stream △ Tanzania 4°42S 29°37E 268 C2
Gombi Nigeria 10°12N 12°30E 263 C7
Gomel = Homyel Belarus 52°28N 31°0E 177 B16
Gomera Canary Is. 28°7N 17°14W 153 e1
Gómez Palacio Mexico 25°34N 103°30W 318 B4
Gomfi Greece 39°26N 21°36E 204 B3
Gomīshān Iran 37°4N 54°6E 247 B7
Gommern Germany 52°4N 11°50E 178 C7
Gomogomo Indonesia 6°39S 134°43E 231 F8
Gomoh India 23°52N 86°10E 243 H12
Gomotartsi Bulgaria 44°6N 22°57E 202 B6
Gompa = Ganta Liberia 7°15N 8°59W 262 D3
Gonābād Iran 34°15N 58°45E 247 C8
Gonaïves Haiti 19°20N 72°42W 321 C5
Gonarezhou △ Zimbabwe 21°32S 31°55E 269 G3
Gonâve, G. de la Haiti 19°29N 72°42W 321 C5
Gonâve, Île de la Haiti 18°51N 73°3W 321 C5
Gonbad-e Kāvūs Iran 37°20N 55°25E 247 B7
Gönc Hungary 48°28N 21°14E 182 B6
Gonda India 27°9N 81°58E 243 F9
Gondal India 21°58N 70°52E 242 J4
Gonder Ethiopia 12°39N 37°30E 257 E4
Gondia India 21°23N 80°10E 244 D5
Gondola Mozam. 19°10S 33°37E 269 F3
Gondomar Portugal 41°10N 8°35W 194 D2
Gondrecourt-le-Château France 48°31N 5°30E 173 D12
Gönen Israel 31°46N 35°13E 123 B2
Gönen Balıkesir, Turkey 40°6N 27°39E 203 F11
Gönen Isparta, Turkey 37°57N 30°31E 205 D12
Gönen → Turkey 40°6N 27°39E 203 F11
Gong Xian China 28°23N 104°47E 228 C5
Gong'an China 30°7N 112°12E 229 B9
Gongbei China 22°12N 113°32E 219 G10
Gongchangling China 41°7N 123°27E 224 B1
Gongcheng China 24°50N 110°49E 229 E8
Gongga Shan China 29°40N 101°55E 228 C3
Gongguan China 21°48N 109°36E 228 G7
Gonghe China 36°18N 100°32E 218 C5
Gongju S. Korea 36°27N 127°7E 224 D3
Gongliu China 43°28N 82°8E 217 D10
Gongming China 22°47N 113°53E 219 F10
Gongneung S. Korea 37°36N 127°5E 137 B2
Gongo Yembe Dem. Rep. of the Congo 1°58S 18°40E 264 C3
Gongola → Nigeria 9°30N 12°4E 263 D7
Gongolgon Australia 30°21S 146°54E 281 E4
Gongoué Gabon 0°31S 9°13E 264 C1
Gongshan China 27°43N 98°29E 228 D2
Gongtan China 28°55N 108°20E 228 C7
Gongzhuling China 43°30N 124°40E 227 C13
Goni Greece 39°52N 22°29E 204 B4
Goniadz Poland 53°30N 22°44E 184 E9
Goniri Nigeria 11°30N 12°15E 263 C7
Gonjo China 30°52N 98°17E 228 B2
Gonnesa Italy 39°16N 8°28E 200 C1
Gonnosfanádiga Italy 39°29N 8°39E 200 C1
Gonzaga Phil. 18°16N 122°0E 232 B4
Gonzales Calif., U.S.A. 36°30N 121°26W 306 J5
Gonzales Tex., U.S.A. 29°30N 97°27W 314 G6
González Mexico 22°48N 98°25W 319 C5
Goobang △ Australia 33°0S 148°32E 283 B8
Good Hope, C. of S. Africa 34°24S 18°30E 270 D2
Good Hope Lake Canada 59°16N 129°18W 296 B3
Good Hope Plantation Jamaica 18°25N 77°41W 320 a
Goodenough I. Papua N. G. 9°20S 150°15E 286 E6
Gooderham Canada 44°54N 78°21W 312 B6
Goodhouse S. Africa 28°57S 18°13E 270 C2
Gooding U.S.A. 42°56N 114°43W 304 E6
Goodland U.S.A. 39°21N 101°43W 308 F3
Goodlands Mauritius 20°2S 57°39E 272 e
Goodlow Canada 56°20N 120°8W 296 B4
Goodmayes U.K. 51°33N 0°6E 125 A4
Goodnews Bay U.S.A. 59°7N 161°35W 303 G7
Goodooga Australia 29°3S 147°28E 281 D4
Goodsprings U.S.A. 35°49N 115°27W 307 K11
Goodwater U.S.A. 33°4N 86°3W 316 B3
Goodwood S. Africa 33°55S 18°32E 118 A2
Goole U.K. 53°42N 0°53W 168 D7
Goolgowi Australia 33°58S 145°41E 283 B6
Goolwa Australia 35°30S 138°47E 282 C3
Goomalling Australia 31°15S 116°49E 279 F2
Goomeri Australia 26°12S 152°6E 281 D5
Goonda Mozam. 19°48S 33°57E 269 F3
Goondiwindi Australia 28°30S 150°21E 281 D5
Goongarrie, L. Australia 30°3S 121°9E 279 F3
Goongarrie △ Australia 30°7S 121°30E 279 F3
Goonyella Australia 21°47S 147°58E 280 C4
Goose → Canada 53°20N 60°35W 299 B7
Goose Creek U.S.A. 32°59N 80°2W 316 C9
Goose L. Calif., U.S.A. 41°56N 120°26W 304 F3
Goose L. Ill., U.S.A. 40°55N 89°27W 310 D7
Gooty India 15°7N 77°41E 245 G3
Gop India 22°5N 69°50E 242 H3
Gopalganj Bangla. 23°1N 89°50E 241 D2
Gopalganj India 26°28N 84°30E 243 F11
Gopalpur India 22°38N 88°26E 124 B2
Göppingen Germany 48°42N 9°39E 179 G5
Gor Spain 37°23N 2°58W 195 H8
Góra Dolnośląskie, Poland 51°40N 16°31E 185 G3
Góra Mazowieckie, Poland 52°39N 20°6E 185 F7
Góra Kalwaria Poland 51°59N 21°14E 185 G8
Gorakhpur India 26°47N 83°23E 243 F10
Goražde Bos.-H. 43°38N 18°58E 182 G3
Gorbatov Russia 56°12N 43°2E 190 B6
Gorbea, Peña Spain 43°1N 2°50W 196 B2
Górce Poland 52°15N 20°55E 142 B1
Gorczański △ Poland 49°30N 20°10E 185 J7
Gorda, Banco W. Indies 15°40N 80°27W 320 C3
Gorda, Pta. Canary Is. 28°45N 18°0W 153 e1
Gorda, Pta. Nic. 14°20N 83°10W 320 D3
Gordan B. Australia 11°35S 130°10E 278 B5
Gördes Turkey 38°54N 28°17E 205 C10
Gordon Ga., U.S.A. 32°54N 83°20W 316 C6
Gordon Nebr., U.S.A. 42°48N 102°12W 308 D2
Gordon Wis., U.S.A. 46°15N 91°48W 308 B8
Gordon → Australia 42°27S 145°30E 281 G4
Gordon, I. Chile 54°55S 69°30W 336 D3
Gordon Bay Canada 45°12N 79°47W 312 A5
Gordon L. Alta., Canada 56°30N 110°25W 297 B6
Gordon L. N.W.T., Canada 63°5N 113°11W 296 A6
Gordonvale Australia 17°5S 145°50E 280 B4
Goré Chad 7°59N 16°31E 259 G3
Gore Ethiopia 8°12N 35°32E 257 F4
Gore N.Z. 46°5S 168°58E 285 G3
Gore Bay Canada 45°57N 82°28W 298 C3
Gore Hill Australia 33°49S 151°10E 139 A2
Gorée, Île de Senegal 14°40N 17°23W 262 C1
Görele Turkey 41°2N 39°0E 213 B8
Gorelyy → Russia 60°1N 30°30E 137 A3
Goreme Turkey 38°35N 34°52E 212 C6
Gorenki Russia 55°47N 37°53E 129 B5
Gorey Ireland 52°41N 6°18W 166 D5
Gorg Iran 29°29N 59°43E 247 D8
Gorgān Iran 36°55N 54°30E 247 B7
Gorgie U.K. 55°56N 3°14W 121 B2
Gorgol □ Mauritania 15°45N 13°0W 262 B2
Gorgona Italy 43°26N 9°54E 198 E6
Gorgora Ethiopia 12°15N 37°17E 257 E4
Gorgoram Nigeria 12°40N 10°45E 263 C7
Gorham U.S.A. 44°23N 71°10W 313 B13
Gori Georgia 42°0N 44°7E 191 J7
Goribidnur = Gauribidanur India 13°37N 77°32E 245 H3
Goriganga → India 29°45N 80°23E 243 E9
Gorinchem Neths. 51°50N 4°59E 170 C4
Gorinhatã Brazil 19°15S 49°45W 333 E2
Goris Armenia 39°31N 46°22E 213 C12
Goritsy Russia 57°4N 36°43E 188 D9
Gorízia Italy 45°56N 13°37E 199 C10
Gorj □ Romania 45°5N 23°25E 183 E8
Gorki = Horki Belarus 54°17N 30°59E 188 E6
Gorkiy = Nizhniy Novgorod Russia 56°20N 44°0E 190 B7
Gorkovskoye Vdkhr. Russia 57°2N 43°4E 190 B6
Gorky Park Russia 55°43N 37°36E 129 B3
Gorleston U.K. 52°35N 1°44E 169 E9
Gorlice Poland 49°35N 21°11E 185 J8
Görlitz Germany 51°9N 14°58E 178 D10
Gorlovka = Horlivka Ukraine 48°19N 38°5E 189 H10
Gorman U.S.A. 34°47N 118°51W 307 L8
Gorna Djumayа = Blagoevgrad Bulgaria 42°2N 23°5E 202 D7
Gorna Dzhumayo = Blagoevgrad Bulgaria 42°2N 23°5E 202 D7
Gorna Oryakhovitsa Bulgaria 43°7N 25°40E 203 C9
Gornja Radgona Slovenia 46°40N 16°2E 199 B13
Gornja Tuzla Bos.-H. 44°35N 18°46E 182 F3
Gornji Grad Slovenia 46°20N 14°52E 199 B11
Gornji Milanovac Serbia 44°3N 20°29E 202 B4
Gornji Vakuf Bos.-H. 43°57N 17°34E 182 G2
Gorno Ablanovo Bulgaria 43°37N 25°43E 203 C9
Gorno-Altay □ Russia 51°0N 86°0E 217 B11
Gorno-Altaysk Russia 51°50N 86°5E 217 B11
Gorno-Badakhshan = Kŭhiston-Badakhshon □ Tajikistan 38°30N 73°0E 217 E8
Gornozavodsk Russia 46°33N 141°50E 215 E15
Gornyak Russia 50°59N 81°27E 217 B10
Gornyatski Russia 67°32N 64°3E 186 A11
Gornyatskiy Russia 48°18N 40°56E 191 F5
Gornyy Primorsk, Russia 44°57N 133°59E 220 B6
Gornyy Saratov, Russia 51°50N 48°30E 190 E9
Goro → C.A.R. 9°14N 21°16E 264 A4
Gorodenka = Horodenka Ukraine 48°41N 25°29E 183 B10
Gorodets Russia 56°38N 43°28E 190 B6
Gorodishche = Horodyshche Ukraine 49°17N 31°27E 189 H6
Gorodishche Russia 53°13N 45°40E 190 D7
Gorodnya = Horodnya Ukraine 51°55N 31°33E 189 G6
Gorodok = Haradok Belarus 55°30N 30°3E 188 E6
Gorodok = Horodok Ukraine 49°46N 23°32E 177 D12
Gorodok = Zakamensk Russia 50°23N 103°17E 215 D11
Gorodovikovsk Russia 46°8N 41°58E 191 G5
Goroka Papua N. G. 6°7S 145°25E 286 D3
Goroke Australia 36°43S 141°29E 282 D4
Gorokhov = Horokhiv Ukraine 50°30N 24°45E 177 C13
Gorokhovets Russia 56°13N 42°39E 190 B6
Gorom Gorom Burkina Faso 14°26N 0°14W 263 C4
Goromonzi Zimbabwe 17°52S 31°22E 269 F3
Gorong, Kepulauan Indonesia 3°59S 131°25E 231 E8
Gorongosa △ Mozam. 18°50S 34°29E 271 A5
Gorongose → Mozam. 20°30S 34°40E 271 B5
Gorongoza Mozam. 18°44S 34°2E 269 F3
Gorongoza, Sa. da Mozam. 18°27S 34°2E 269 F3
Gorontalo Indonesia 0°35N 123°5E 231 D6
Gorontalo □ Indonesia 0°50N 122°20E 231 D6
Goronyo Nigeria 13°29N 5°39E 263 C6
Górowo Iławeckie Poland 54°17N 20°30E 184 D7
Gorron France 48°25N 0°50W 172 D6
Gorror Micronesia 9°26N 138°4E 287 S16
Gorshechnoye Russia 51°31N 38°2E 189 G10
Gort Ireland 53°3N 8°49W 166 C3
Gortis Greece 35°4N 24°58E 207 E5
Gorumahisani India 22°20N 86°24E 244 C8
Góry Bystrzyckie Poland 50°16N 16°33E 185 H3
Goryachiy Klyuch Russia 44°38N 39°8E 191 H4
Goryeong S. Korea 35°44N 128°15E 224 E4
Gorzkowice Poland 51°13N 19°36E 185 G6
Górzno Poland 53°12N 19°38E 185 E6
Gorzów Śląski Poland 51°3N 18°22E 185 G5
Gorzów Wielkopolski Poland 52°43N 15°15E 185 F2
Gose Japan 34°27N 135°44E 223 C7
Gosen Germany 52°23N 13°43E 115 B5
Gosener kanal Germany 52°24N 13°42E 115 B5
Goseong S. Korea 34°58N 128°19E 224 E4
Gosford Australia 33°23S 151°18E 283 B9
Goshen Calif., U.S.A. 36°21N 119°25W 306 J7
Goshen Ind., U.S.A. 41°35N 85°50W 311 C11
Goshen N.Y., U.S.A. 41°24N 74°20W 313 E10
Goshogawara Japan 40°48N 140°27E 220 D10
Goskopi = Kopeysk Russia 55°7N 61°37E 216 A6
Goslar Germany 51°54N 10°25E 178 D6
Gospel Oak U.K. 51°32N 0°9W 125 A3
Gospič Croatia 44°35N 15°23E 199 D12
Gosport Hants., U.K. 50°48N 1°9W 169 G6
Gosport Ind., U.S.A. 39°21N 86°40W 311 E10
Gossa Norway 62°52N 6°50E 164 B3
Gossas Senegal 14°28N 16°0W 262 C1
Gosse → Australia 19°32S 134°37E 280 B1
Gossi Mali 15°48N 1°20W 263 B4
Gossinga Sudan 8°36N 25°59E 257 F2
Gostingen = Gostyń Poland 51°50N 17°3E 185 G4
Gostinopolye = Volkhov Russia 59°55N 32°15E 188 C7
Gostivar Macedonia 41°48N 20°57E 202 E4
Gostyń Poland 51°50N 17°3E 185 G4
Gostynin Poland 52°26N 19°29E 185 F6
Göta älv → Sweden 57°42N 11°54E 163 G5
Göta kanal Sweden 58°30N 15°58E 163 F9
Götaland Sweden 57°30N 14°30E 163 G8
Gotanda Japan 35°37N 139°43E 140 B3
Göteborg Sweden 57°43N 11°59E 163 G5
Gotemba Japan 35°18N 138°56E 223 B10
Götene Sweden 58°32N 13°30E 163 F7
Gotenhafen = Gdynia Poland 54°35N 18°33E 184 D5
Goteşti Moldova 46°9N 28°10E 183 D13
Goth Goli Mar Pakistan 24°53N 67°1E 123 A2
Goth Sher Shah Pakistan 24°53N 66°59E 123 A1
Gotha Thüringen, Germany 50°56N 10°42E 178 E6
Gotha Fla., U.S.A. 28°31N 81°33W 133 A1
Gothenburg = Göteborg Sweden 57°43N 11°59E 163 G5
Gothenburg U.S.A. 40°56N 100°10W 308 E3
Gothèye Niger 13°52N 1°34E 263 C5
Gotland Sweden 57°30N 18°33E 163 G12
Gotlands län □ Sweden 57°15N 18°30E 163 G12
Goto Meer Neth. Ant. 12°14N 68°22W 322 h
Gotō-Rettō Japan 32°55N 129°5E 221 H4
Gotse Delchev Bulgaria 41°36N 23°46E 202 E7
Gotska Sandön Sweden 58°24N 19°15E 161 G18
Gōtsu Japan 35°0N 132°14E 222 C4
Göttero, Monte Italy 44°22N 9°42E 198 D6
Gottesberg = Boguszów-Gorce Poland 50°45N 16°12E 185 H3
Göttingen Germany 51°31N 9°55E 178 D5
Gottschee = Kočevje Slovenia 45°39N 14°50E 199 C11
Gottwald = Zmiyev Ukraine 49°39N 36°27E 189 H9
Gottwaldov = Zlín Czech Rep. 49°14N 17°40E 181 B10
Goubangzi China 41°20N 121°52E 227 D11
Gouda Neths. 52°1N 4°42E 170 B4
Goudiri Senegal 14°15N 12°45W 262 C2
Goudoumaria Niger 13°40N 11°10E 259 F2
Goudouras, Akra Greece 34°59N 26°6E 207 F7
Gouéké Guinea 8°2N 8°43W 262 D3
Gough I. Atl. Oc. 40°10S 9°45W 152 L11
Gouin, Rés. Canada 48°35N 74°40W 298 C5
Gouitafla Ivory C. 7°30N 5°53W 262 D3
Goulburn Australia 34°44S 149°44E 283 C8
Goulburn Is. Australia 11°40S 133°20E 280 A1
Goulburn River △ Australia 32°19S 150°10E 283 B9
Goulds U.S.A. 25°33N 80°23W 317 K9
Goulia Ivory C. 10°1N 7°11W 262 C3
Goulimine Morocco 28°56N 10°0W 260 C3
Goulimine □ Morocco 29°8N 9°2W 260 C3
Goulmima Morocco 31°41N 4°57W 260 B4
Goumbou Mali 15°2N 7°25W 262 B3
Goumenissa Greece 40°56N 22°37E 202 F6
Gounatolo Solomon Is. 8°25S 160°52E 287 M11
Goundam Mali 16°27N 3°40W 262 B4
Goundi Chad 9°22N 17°21E 259 G3
Gounou-Gaya Chad 9°38N 15°31E 259 G3
Goura Greece 37°56N 22°20E 204 D4
Gouraya Algeria 36°31N 1°56E 261 A5
Gourbassi Mali 13°24N 11°38W 262 C2
Gourbeyre Guadeloupe 16°0N 61°40W 322 e
Gourde, Pt. Trin. & Tob. 10°40N 61°38W 323 t
Gourdon France 44°44N 1°23E 174 D5
Gouré Niger 14°0N 10°10E 259 F2
Gouri Chad 18°50N 16°49E 259 E3
Gourin France 48°8N 3°37W 172 D3
Gourits → S. Africa 34°21S 21°52E 270 D3
Gourma-Rharous Mali 16°55N 1°50W 263 B4
Gournay-en-Bray France 49°29N 1°44E 173 C8
Gournay-sur-Marne France 48°51N 2°34E 134 A4
Gournes Greece 35°19N 25°16E 207 E6
Gouro Chad 19°36N 19°36E 259 E3
Gourock U.K. 55°57N 4°49W 167 F4
Gourock Ra. Australia 36°0S 149°25E 283 D8
Goursi Burkina Faso 12°42N 2°37W 262 C4
Gouvea Brazil 18°27S 43°44W 333 E3
Gouverneur U.S.A. 44°20N 75°28W 313 B9
Gouvia Greece 39°39N 19°50E 206 B9
Gouyave Grenada 12°10N 61°44W 323 q
Gouzon France 46°12N 2°14E 173 F9
Gove, Barragem do Angola 13°26S 15°53E 265 E3
Gove Peninsula Australia 12°17S 136°49E 280 A2
Governador, I. do Brazil 22°48S 43°13W 135 A1
Governador Valadares Brazil 18°15S 41°57W 333 E3
Governor Generoso Phil. 6°39N 126°5E 233 H6
Governor's Harbour Bahamas 25°10N 76°14W 320 A4
Governors I. New York, U.S.A. 132 f1
Govĭaltay □ Mongolia 45°30N 96°0E 217 C13
Govindgarh India 24°23N 81°18E 243 G9
Gowan Ra. Australia 25°0S 145°0E 280 D4
Gowanda U.S.A. 42°28N 78°56W 312 D6
Gower U.K. 51°35N 4°10W 169 F3
Gowers Corner U.S.A. 28°20N 82°30W 317 G7
Gowna, L. Ireland 53°51N 7°34W 166 C4
Gowrie U.S.A. 42°17N 94°17W 310 B2
Gowurdak Turkmenistan 37°50N 66°4E 217 E7
Goya Argentina 29°10S 59°10W 334 B4
Goyang S. Korea 37°39N 126°50E 224 D3
Goyave Guadeloupe 16°8N 61°34W 322 e
Goyaves, Grande Rivière → Guadeloupe 16°18N 61°36W 322 e
Göyçay Azerbaijan 40°42N 47°43E 191 K8
Goyder Lagoon Australia 27°3S 138°58E 281 D2
Goyllarisquizga Peru 10°31S 76°24W 330 C2
Göynük Antalya, Turkey 36°41N 30°33E 205 E12
Göynük Bolu, Turkey 40°24N 30°48E 212 B4
Goz Beïda Chad 12°10N 21°20E 259 F4
Goz Regeb Sudan 16°3N 35°33E 257 D4
Gozdnica Poland 51°28N 15°4E 185 G2
Gözneköy Turkey 36°58N 34°33E 250 B5
Gozo Malta 36°3N 14°15E 206 E7
Graaff-Reinet S. Africa 32°13S 24°32E 270 D3
Graben Vienna, Austria 142 b2
Grabill U.S.A. 41°13N 84°57W 311 C12
Grabo Ivory C. 4°57N 7°30W 262 D3
Grabow Mecklenburg-Vorpommern, Germany 53°17N 11°34E 178 B7
Grabów Warszawa, Poland 52°8N 20°59E 142 C1
Grabów nad Prosną Poland 51°31N 18°7E 185 G5
Graça Lisbon, Portugal 126 b3
Gračac Croatia 44°18N 15°57E 199 D12
Gračanica Bos.-H. 44°43N 18°18E 182 F3
Graçay France 47°10N 1°50E 173 E8
Grace, Mt. N.Z. 41°20S 174°55E 143 B2
Grace Cathedral San Francisco, U.S.A. 136 b2
Gracefield N.Z. 41°14S 174°55E 143 B2
Graceville U.S.A. 30°58N 85°31W 316 E4
Gracewood U.S.A. 33°22N 82°2W 316 B7
Gràcia Spain 41°24N 2°10E 114 A2
Gracias a Dios, C. Honduras 15°0N 83°10W 320 D3
Graciosa Azores 39°4N 28°0W 153 d1
Graciosa, I. Canary Is. 29°15N 13°32W 153 e2
Grad Sofiya □ Bulgaria 42°35N 23°20E 202 D7
Gradac Montenegro 43°23N 19°9E 202 C3
Gradačac Bos.-H. 44°52N 18°26E 182 F3
Gradaús Brazil 7°43S 51°11W 332 C1
Gradaús, Serra dos Brazil 8°0S 50°45W 332 C1
Gradeška Planina Macedonia 41°30N 22°15E 202 E6
Gradets Bulgaria 42°46N 26°30E 203 D10
Gradište Slovenia 46°37N 15°50E 199 B12
Grădiştea de Munte Romania 45°37N 23°13E 183 E8
Grado Italy 45°40N 13°23E 199 C10
Grado Spain 43°23N 6°4W 194 B4
Grady U.S.A. 34°49N 103°19W 305 J12
Graeca, Lacul Romania 44°5N 26°10E 183 F11
Grafarnes Iceland 64°55N 23°16W 155 C3
Gräfelfing Germany 48°7N 11°25E 131 B1
Grafenau Germany 48°51N 13°22E 179 G9
Gräfenberg Germany 49°39N 11°14E 179 F7
Grafham Water U.K. 52°19N 0°18W 169 E7
Grafton N.S.W., Australia 29°38S 152°58E 281 D5
Grafton Ill., U.S.A. 38°58N 90°26W 310 F6
Grafton N. Dak., U.S.A. 48°25N 97°25W 308 A5
Grafton W. Va., U.S.A. 39°21N 80°2W 309 F13
Grafton Caledonia Wildlife Estate Trin. & Tob. 11°11N 60°47W 323 s
Grafton's Pt. Anguilla 18°20N 62°54W 322 a
Gragaotá Brazil 22°53S 43°8W 135 B2
Graham Ont., Canada 49°20N 90°30W 298 C1
Graham Ga., U.S.A. 31°50N 82°30W 316 D7
Graham Tex., U.S.A. 33°6N 98°35W 314 E5
Graham, Mt. U.S.A. 32°42N 109°52W 305 K9
Graham Bell, Ostrov = Greem-Bell, Ostrov Russia 81°0N 62°0E 214 A7
Graham I. B.C., Canada 53°40N 132°30W 296 C2
Graham I. Nunavut, Canada 77°25N 90°30W 295 B13
Graham Land Antarctica 65°0S 64°0W 151 C17
Grahamstown S. Africa 33°19S 26°31E 270 D4
Grahamsville U.S.A. 41°51N 74°33W 313 E10
Grahovo Montenegro 42°40N 18°40E 202 D2
Graïba Tunisia 34°30N 10°13E 258 B2
Graie, Alpi Europe 45°30N 7°10E 175 C11
Grain Coast W. Afr. 4°20N 10°0W 262 E3
Grajagan Indonesia 8°35S 114°13E 231 K17
Grajagan, Teluk Indonesia 8°40S 114°18E 231 K17
Grajaú Brazil 5°50S 46°4W 332 C2
Grajaú → Brazil 3°41S 44°48W 332 B3
Grajewo Poland 53°39N 22°30E 184 E9
Gramada Bulgaria 43°49N 22°39E 202 C6
Gramat France 44°48N 1°43E 174 D5
Grammichele Italy 37°13N 14°38E 201 E7
Grámmos, Óros Greece 40°18N 20°47E 202 F4
Grampian U.S.A. 40°58N 78°37W 312 F6
Grampian Highlands = Grampian Mts. U.K. 56°50N 4°0W 167 E5
Grampian Mts. U.K. 56°50N 4°0W 167 E5
Grampians, The Australia 37°15S 142°20E 282 D5
Grampians △ Australia 37°15S 142°28E 282 D5
Gramsh Albania 40°52N 20°12E 202 F4
Gran Norway 60°23N 10°31E 164 D7
Gran → Suriname 4°1N 55°30W 329 C6
Gran Altiplanicie Central Argentina 49°0S 69°30W 336 C3
Gran Canaria Canary Is. 27°55N 15°35W 153 e1
Gran Chaco S. Amer. 25°0S 61°0W 334 B3
Gran Couva Trin. & Tob. 10°24N 61°22W 323 t
Gran Desierto del Pinacate ⌓ Mexico 31°51N 113°32W 318 A2
Gran Laguna Salada Argentina 44°24S 67°23W 336 B3
Gran Pajonal Peru 10°45S 74°30W 330 C3
Gran Paradiso Italy 45°33N 7°17E 198 C4
Gran Sasso d'Itália Italy 42°27N 13°42E 199 F10
Gran Sasso e Monti Della Laga △ Italy 42°32N 13°22E 199 F10
Granada Nic. 11°58N 86°0W 320 D2
Granada Spain 37°10N 3°35W 195 H7
Granada Colo., U.S.A. 38°4N 102°19W 304 G12
Granada □ Spain 37°18N 3°0W 195 H7
Granadilla de Abona Canary Is. 28°7N 16°33W 153 e1
Granard Ireland 53°47N 7°30W 166 C4
Granbury U.S.A. 32°27N 97°47W 314 E6
Granby Qué., Canada 45°25N 72°45W 313 A12
Granby Colo., U.S.A. 40°5N 105°56W 304 F11
Grand → Ont., Canada 42°51N 79°34W 312 D5
Grand → Mich., U.S.A. 43°4N 86°15W 311 A10
Grand → Mo., U.S.A. 39°23N 93°7W 310 E3
Grand → S. Dak., U.S.A. 45°40N 100°45W 308 C3
Grand Abaque, Pte.du Guadeloupe 16°21N 61°0W 322 e
Grand Anse Grenada 12°1N 61°45W 323 q
Grand Anse B. Grenada 12°2N 61°45W 323 q
Grand B. Dominica 15°14N 61°18W 323 k
Grand Bahama I. Bahamas 26°40N 78°30W 320 A4
Grand Baie Mauritius 20°0S 57°35E 272 e
Grand Bank Canada 47°6N 55°48W 299 C8
Grand Banks Atl. Oc. 45°0N 52°0W 152 B6
Grand Bassam Ivory C. 5°10N 3°49W 262 D4
Grand Bassin Réunion 21°10S 55°32E 272 f

Grand Batanga Cameroon 2°50N 9°55E 264 B1
Grand Bazaar = Kapali Carsi Turkey 41°1N 28°58E 122 B1
Grand Bénare Réunion 21°6S 55°25E 272 f
Grand Bend Canada 43°18N 81°45W 312 C3
Grand Béréby Ivory C. 4°38N 6°55W 262 E3
Grand Blanc U.S.A. 42°56N 83°38W 311 B13
Grand Bois Mauritius 20°25S 57°32E 272 e
Grand-Bourg Guadeloupe 15°53N 61°19W 322 e
Grand Canal = Da Yunhe → China 39°10N 117°10E 227 E9
Grand Canyon U.S.A. 36°3N 112°9W 305 H7
Grand Canyon △ U.S.A. 36°15N 112°30W 305 H7
Grand Canyon-Parashant ⌓ U.S.A. 36°30N 113°45W 305 H7
Grand Case St.-Martin 18°6N 63°4W 322 a
Grand Cayman Cayman Is. 19°20N 81°20W 320 C3
Grand Central Station New York, U.S.A. 132 c2
Grand Cess Liberia 4°40N 8°12W 262 E3
Grand Coulee U.S.A. 47°57N 119°0W 304 C4
Grand Coulee Dam U.S.A. 47°57N 118°59W 304 C4
Grand Cul-de-Sac Marin Guadeloupe 16°20N 61°35W 322 e
Grand Erg de Bilma Niger 18°30N 14°0E 259 E2
Grand Étang △ Grenada 12°5N 61°42W 323 q
Grand Falls Canada 47°3N 67°44W 299 C6
Grand Falls-Windsor Canada 48°56N 55°40W 299 C8
Grand Fond St.-Martin 17°53N 62°48W 322 a
Grand Forks B.C., Canada 49°0N 118°30W 296 D5
Grand Forks N. Dak., U.S.A. 47°55N 97°3W 308 B5
Grand Galet Réunion 21°17S 55°38E 272 f
Grand Gaube Mauritius 20°0S 57°39E 272 e
Grand Gorge U.S.A. 42°21N 74°29W 313 D10
Grand Haven U.S.A. 43°4N 86°13W 311 A10
Grand I. Mich., U.S.A. 46°31N 86°40W 308 B10
Grand I. N.Y., U.S.A. 43°0N 78°58W 312 D6
Grand Îlet Guadeloupe 15°50N 61°35W 322 e
Grand Îlet Réunion 21°1S 55°29E 272 f
Grand Island U.S.A. 40°55N 98°21W 308 E4
Grand Isle La., U.S.A. 29°14N 90°0W 315 G9
Grand Isle Vt., U.S.A. 44°43N 73°18W 313 B11
Grand Junction Colo., U.S.A. 39°4N 108°33W 304 G9
Grand Junction Iowa, U.S.A. 42°2N 94°14W 310 B2
Grand L. N. B., Canada 45°57N 66°7W 299 C6
Grand L. Nfld. & L., Canada 49°0N 57°30W 299 C8
Grand L. Nfld. & L., Canada 53°40N 60°30W 299 B7
Grand L. La., U.S.A. 29°55N 92°47W 314 G8
Grand L. Ohio, U.S.A. 40°32N 84°25W 311 D12
Grand Lahou Ivory C. 5°10N 5°5W 262 D3
Grand Lake U.S.A. 40°15N 105°49W 304 F11
Grand Ledge U.S.A. 42°45N 84°45W 311 B12
Grand-Lieu, L. de France 47°6N 1°40W 172 E5
Grand Mal B. Grenada 12°4N 61°45W 323 q
Grand Manan I. Canada 44°45N 66°52W 299 D6
Grand Marais Mich., U.S.A. 46°40N 85°59W 309 B11
Grand Marais Minn., U.S.A. 47°45N 90°25W 298 C1
Grand Marigot B. Dominica 15°25N 61°16W 323 k
Grand-Mère Canada 46°36N 72°40W 298 C5
Grand Palace Bangkok, Thailand 113 b1
Grand Popo Benin 6°15N 1°57E 263 D5
Grand Portage U.S.A. 47°58N 89°41W 308 B9
Grand Prairie U.S.A. 32°44N 96°59W 314 E6
Grand Rapids = Wisconsin Rapids U.S.A. 44°23N 89°49W 308 C9
Grand Rapids Man., Canada 53°12N 99°19W 297 C9
Grand Rapids Mich., U.S.A. 42°58N 85°40W 311 B10
Grand Rapids Minn., U.S.A. 47°14N 93°31W 308 B7
Grand Rapids ✈ (GRR) U.S.A. 42°53N 85°31W 311 B11
Grand Récif Sud N. Cal. 22°47S 166°55E 288 d
Grand Ridge U.S.A. 30°43N 85°1W 316 E4
Grand River U.S.A. 40°49N 93°58W 310 D3
Grand River Bay Mauritius 20°9S 57°27E 272 e
Grand River South East → Mauritius 20°17S 57°46E 272 e
Grand' Rivière Martinique 14°52N 61°11W 322 j
Grand Roy Grenada 12°8N 61°45W 323 q
Grand St-Bernard, Col du Europe 45°50N 7°10E 179 K3
Grand Santi Fr. Guiana 4°20N 54°24W 329 C7
Grand Staircase-Escalante ⌓ U.S.A. 37°25N 111°33W 305 H8
Grand Teton U.S.A. 43°54N 110°50W 304 E8
Grand Teton △ U.S.A. 43°50N 110°50W 304 E8
Grand Union Canal U.K. 52°7N 0°53W 169 E7
Grandas de Salime Spain 43°13N 6°53W 194 B4
Grande → Jujuy, Argentina 24°20S 65°2W 334 A2
Grande → Mendoza, Argentina 36°52S 69°45W 334 D2
Grande → Bolivia 15°51S 64°39W 331 D5
Grande → Bahia, Brazil 11°30S 44°30W 332 D3
Grande → Minas Gerais, Brazil 20°6S 51°4W 333 F1
Grande → Venezuela 8°36N 61°39W 329 B5
Grande, B. Argentina 50°30S 68°20W 336 D3
Grande, I. Brazil 23°9S 44°14W 333 F3
Grande, Rio → N. Amer. 25°58N 97°9W 314 J6
Grande, Serra Piauí, Brazil 8°0S 45°10W 332 C2
Grande, Serra Tocantins, Brazil 11°15S 46°30W 332 D2
Grande Anse = Beauséjour Guadeloupe 16°18N 61°4W 322 e
Grande Anse Guadeloupe 16°19N 61°47W 322 e
Grande Anse Martinique 14°30N 61°5W 322 j
Grande Anse St. Lucia 14°1N 60°54W 323 m
Grande Anse Seychelles 4°18S 55°45E 272 c
Grande Baleine → Canada 55°16N 77°47W 298 A4
Grande Cache Canada 53°53N 119°8W 296 C5
Grande Casse, Pte. de la France 45°24N 6°49E 175 C10
Grande Comore Comoros Is. 11°35S 43°20E 272 a
Grande Cul de Sac B St. Lucia 13°59N 61°2W 323 m
Grande-Entrée Canada 47°30N 61°40W 299 C7
Grande Matelot Pt. Trin. & Tob. 10°49N 61°9W 323 t
Grande Place Brussels, Belgium 116 b2
Grande Prairie Canada 55°10N 118°50W 296 B5
Grande Pte. Guadeloupe 15°58N 61°37W 322 e
Grande-Rivière Qué., Canada 48°26N 64°30W 299 C7
Grande Riviere Trin. & Tob. 10°50N 61°3W 323 t
Grande Rivière, Pte. de la Guadeloupe 16°18N 61°36W 322 e
Grande Rivière Noire Mauritius 20°21S 57°21E 272 e
Grande Rivière Sud Est Mauritius 20°17S 57°46E 272 e
Grande Sertão Veredas △ Brazil 15°10S 45°40W 333 E2
Grande-Terre Guadeloupe 16°20N 61°25W 322 e
Grande Terre Mayotte 12°46S 45°7E 272 b
Grande-Vallée Canada 49°14N 65°8W 299 C6
Grande Vigie, Pte. de la Guadeloupe 16°32N 61°27W 322 e
Grandfalls U.S.A. 31°20N 102°51W 314 F3
Grândola Portugal 38°12N 8°35W 195 G2
Grandpré France 49°20N 4°50E 173 C11
Grands Causses ⌓ France 44°5N 2°58E 174 D6
Grands-Jardins ⌓ Canada 47°41N 70°51W 299 C5
Grandview Man., Canada 51°10N 100°42W 297 C8
Grandview Mo., U.S.A. 38°53N 94°32W 310 F2
Grandview Wash., U.S.A. 46°15N 119°54W 304 C4
Grandview Heights U.S.A. 39°58N 83°2W 311 E13
Grandvilliers France 49°40N 1°57E 173 C8
Graneros Chile 34°5S 70°45W 334 C1
Grange Hill Jamaica 18°18N 78°11W 320 a
Grangemouth U.K. 56°1N 3°42W 167 E5
Granger U.S.A. 41°35N 109°58W 304 F9
Grängesberg Sweden 60°6N 15°1E 162 D9
Grangeville U.S.A. 45°56N 116°7W 304 D5
Granisle Canada 54°53N 126°13W 296 C3
Granite City U.S.A. 38°42N 90°8W 310 F6
Granite Falls U.S.A. 44°49N 95°33W 308 C6
Granite L. Canada 48°8N 57°5W 299 C8
Granite Mt. U.S.A. 33°5N 116°28W 307 M10
Granite Pk. U.S.A. 45°10N 109°48W 304 D9
Graniteville S.C., U.S.A. 33°34N 81°49W 316 B8
Graniteville Vt., U.S.A. 44°8N 72°29W 313 B12
Granitola, C. Italy 37°34N 12°39E 200 E5
Granity N.Z. 41°39S 171°51E 285 B6
Granja Brazil 3°7S 40°50W 332 B3
Granja de Moreruela Spain 41°48N 5°44W 194 D5
Granja de Torrehermosa Spain 38°19N 5°35W 195 G5
Grankulla = Kauniainen Finland 60°13N 24°44E 121 B1
Gränna Sweden 58°1N 14°28E 163 F8
Granollers Spain 41°39N 2°18E 196 D7
Gransee Germany 53°1N 13°8E 178 B9
Grant Fla., U.S.A. 27°56N 80°32W 317 H9
Grant Nebr., U.S.A. 40°50N 101°43W 308 E3
Grant, Mt. U.S.A. 38°34N 118°48W 304 G4
Grant City U.S.A. 40°29N 94°25W 310 D2
Grant I. Australia 11°10S 132°52E 278 B5
Grant Park Chicago, U.S.A. 119 c2
Grant Range U.S.A. 38°30N 115°25W 304 G6
Grantham U.K. 52°55N 0°38W 168 E7
Grantley Adams Int. ✈ (BGI) Barbados 13°4N 59°29W 323 r
Granton U.K. 55°58N 3°14W 121 B2
Grantown-on-Spey U.K. 57°20N 3°36W 167 D5
Grants U.S.A. 35°9N 107°52W 305 J10
Grants Pass U.S.A. 42°26N 123°19W 304 E2
Grantsville U.S.A. 40°36N 112°28W 304 F7
Grantville U.S.A. 33°14N 84°50W 316 B5
Granville Manche, France 48°50N 1°35W 172 D5
Granville Trin. & Tob. 10°7N 61°48W 323 t
Granville Ill., U.S.A. 41°16N 89°14W 310 C7
Granville N. Dak., U.S.A. 48°16N 100°47W 308 A3
Granville N.Y., U.S.A. 43°24N 73°16W 313 C11
Granville Ohio, U.S.A. 40°4N 82°31W 312 F2
Granville L. Canada 56°18N 100°30W 297 B8
Granvin Norway 60°33N 6°45E 164 D3
Graskop S. Africa 24°56S 30°49E 271 B5
Gräsö Sweden 60°28N 18°35E 162 D12
Grass → Canada 56°3N 96°33W 297 B9
Grass Range U.S.A. 47°2N 108°48W 304 C9
Grass River △ Canada 54°40N 100°50W 297 C8
Grass Valley Calif., U.S.A. 39°13N 121°4W 306 F6
Grass Valley Oreg., U.S.A. 45°22N 120°47W 304 D3
Grassano Italy 40°38N 16°17E 201 B9
Grasse France 43°38N 6°56E 175 E10
Grassflat U.S.A. 41°0N 78°6W 312 E6
Grasslands △ Canada 49°11N 107°38W 297 D7
Grassy Australia 40°3S 144°5E 281 G3
Grassy Park S. Africa 34°3S 18°30E 118 B2
Gråsten Denmark 54°55N 9°35E 163 K3
Grästorp Sweden 58°20N 12°40E 163 F6
Gratis U.S.A. 39°38N 84°32W 311 E12
Gratkorn Austria 47°8N 15°21E 180 D8
Gratosóglio Italy 45°24N 9°1E 129 B2
Gratz U.S.A. 38°28N 84°57W 311 F12
Gratzwalde Germany 52°28N 13°42E 115 B5
Graubünden □ Switz. 46°45N 9°30E 179 J5
Graudenz = Grudziądz Poland 53°30N 18°47E 184 E5
Graulhet France 43°45N 1°59E 174 E5
Graus Spain 42°11N 0°20E 196 C5
Gravberget Norway 60°53N 12°14E 164 D9
Grave, Pte. de France 45°34N 1°4W 174 C2
Gravelbourg Canada 49°50N 106°35W 297 D7
Gravelines France 51°1N 2°10E 173 A9
's-Gravenhage Neths. 52°7N 4°17E 170 B4
Gravenhurst Canada 44°52N 79°20W 312 B5
Gravesend N.S.W., Australia 29°35S 150°20E 281 D5
Gravesend Kent, U.K. 51°26N 0°22E 169 F8
Gravesend N.Y., U.S.A. 40°36N 73°56W 132 C2
Gravina in Púglia Italy 40°49N 16°25E 201 B9
Gravois, Pointe-à- Haiti 18°15N 73°56W 321 C5
Gravone → France 41°58N 8°45E 175 G12
Gray Haute-Saône, France 47°22N 5°35E 173 E12
Gray Ga., U.S.A. 33°1N 83°32W 316 B6
Grayling Alaska, U.S.A. 62°57N 160°3W 303 E7
Grayling Mich., U.S.A. 44°40N 84°43W 309 C11
Grays U.K. 51°28N 0°21E 169 F8
Grays Harbor U.S.A. 46°59N 124°1W 304 C1
Grays L. U.S.A. 43°4N 111°26W 304 E8
Grays River U.S.A. 46°21N 123°37W 306 D3
Grayville U.S.A. 38°16N 88°0W 311 F9
Grayvoron Russia 50°29N 35°41E 189 G8
Graz Austria 47°4N 15°27E 180 D8
Grazhdanka Russia 59°59N 30°24E 137 B2
Grdelica Serbia 42°55N 22°3E 202 D6
Greåker Norway 59°16N 11°12E 164 E8
Greasy L. Canada 62°55N 122°12W 296 A4
Great Abaco I. = Abaco I. Bahamas 26°25N 77°10W 320 A4
Great Artesian Basin Australia 23°0S 144°0E 280 C3
Great Australian Bight Australia 33°30S 130°0E 279 F5
Great Bacolet Bay Grenada 12°4N 61°37W 323 q
Great Bahama Bank Bahamas 23°15N 78°0W 320 B4
Great Barrier I. N.Z. 36°11S 175°25E 284 C4
Great Barrier Reef Australia 18°0S 146°50E 280 B4
Great Barrier Reef ⌓ Australia 20°0S 150°0E 280 B4
Great Barrington U.S.A. 42°12N 73°22W 313 D11
Great Basalt Wall △ Australia 19°52S 145°43E 280 B4
Great Basin U.S.A. 40°0N 117°0W 304 G5
Great Basin △ U.S.A. 38°56N 114°15W 304 G6
Great Basses Sri Lanka 6°11N 81°29E 245 L5
Great Bear → Canada 65°0N 126°0W 294 E7
Great Bear L. Canada 65°30N 120°0W 294 D8
Great Belt = Store Bælt Denmark 55°20N 11°0E 163 J4
Great Bend Kans., U.S.A. 38°22N 98°46W 308 F4
Great Bend Pa., U.S.A. 41°58N 75°45W 313 E9
Great Blasket I. Ireland 52°6N 10°32W 166 D1
Great Britain Europe 54°0N 2°15W 158 E5
Great Camanoe Br. Virgin Is. 18°30N 64°35W 321 b
Great Channel Asia 6°0N 94°0E 245 L11
Great Coco I. = Koko Kyunzu Burma 14°7N 93°22E 245 G11
Great Codroy Canada 47°51N 59°16W 299 C8
Great Divide, The = Great Dividing Ra. Australia 23°0S 146°0E 280 C4
Great Divide Basin U.S.A. 42°0N 108°0W 304 E9
Great Dividing Ra. Australia 23°0S 146°0E 280 C4
Great Driffield = Driffield U.K. 54°0N 0°26W 168 C7
Great Exuma I. Bahamas 23°30N 75°50W 320 B4
Great Falls Guyana 5°35N 61°0W 329 B5
Great Falls Mont., U.S.A. 47°30N 111°17W 304 C8
Great Falls Va., U.S.A. 38°59N 77°17W 143 B2
Great Falls Park U.S.A. 38°59N 77°14W 143 B2
Great Fish = Groot-Vis → S. Africa 33°28S 27°5E 270 D4
Great Goat I. Jamaica 17°52N 77°3W 320 a
Great Guana Cay Bahamas 24°0N 76°20W 320 B4
Great Hall of the People Beijing, China 114 c3
Great Himalayan △ India 31°30N 77°30E 242 D7
Great Inagua I. Bahamas 21°0N 73°20W 321 B5
Great Indian Desert = Thar Desert India 28°0N 72°0E 242 F5
Great Karoo S. Africa 31°55S 21°0E 270 D3
Great Khingan Mts. = Da Hinggan Ling China 48°0N 121°0E 219 B7
Great Lake Australia 41°50S 146°40E 281 G4
Great Lakes N. Amer. 46°0N 84°0W 292 E11
Great Limpopo Transfrontier △ Africa 23°0S 31°45E 271 B5
Great Malvern U.K. 52°7N 2°18W 169 E5
Great Miami → U.S.A. 39°7N 84°49W 309 F11
Great Nicobar India 7°0N 93°50E 245 L11
Great Ormes Head U.K. 53°20N 3°52W 168 D4
Great Otway △ Australia 38°50S 143°50E 282 E5
Great Ouse → U.K. 52°48N 0°21E 168 E8
Great Palm I. Australia 18°45S 146°40E 280 B4
Great Pedro Bluff Jamaica 17°51N 77°44W 320 a
Great Pee Dee → U.S.A. 33°21N 79°10W 315 E15
Great Plains N. Amer. 47°0N 105°0W 292 E9
Great Ruaha → Tanzania 7°56S 37°52E 268 D4
Great Sacandaga L. U.S.A. 43°6N 74°16W 313 C10
Great Saint Bernard Pass = Grand St-Bernard, Col du Europe 45°50N 7°10E 179 K3
Great Salt Desert = Kavīr, Dasht-e Iran 34°30N 55°0E 247 C7
Great Salt Desert = Lūt, Dasht-e Iran 31°30N 58°0E 247 D8
Great Salt L. U.S.A. 41°15N 112°40W 304 F7
Great Salt Lake Desert U.S.A. 40°50N 113°30W 304 F7
Great Salt Plains L. U.S.A. 36°45N 98°8W 314 C5
Great Salt Pond St. Kitts & Nevis 17°14N 62°40W 322 d
Great Sand Dunes ⌓ U.S.A. 37°48N 105°45W 305 H11
Great Sand Sea Libya 29°0N 24°0E 258 C4
Great Sandy △ Australia 26°13S 153°2E 281 D5
Great Sandy Desert Australia 21°0S 124°0E 278 D3
Great Sangi = Sangihe, Pulau Indonesia 3°35N 125°30E 231 D7
Great Scarcies → S. Leone 9°0N 13°0W 262 D2
Great Sd. Bermuda 32°17N 64°51W 153 a
Great Sea Reef Fiji 16°15S 179°0E 287 A2
Great Sitkin I. U.S.A. 52°3N 176°6W 303 K3
Great Skellig Ireland 51°47N 10°33W 166 E1
Great Slave L. Canada 61°23N 115°38W 296 A5
Great Smoky Mts. △ U.S.A. 35°40N 83°40W 315 D13
Great Stour = Stour → U.K. 51°18N 1°22E 169 F9
Great Victoria Desert Australia 29°30S 126°30E 279 E4
Great Wall Antarctica 62°30S 58°0W 151 C18
Great Wall China 38°30N 109°30E 226 E5
Great Western Forum U.S.A. 33°57N 118°20W 126 C2
Great Whale River = Kuujjuarapik Canada 55°20N 77°35W 298 A4
Great Whernside U.K. 54°10N 1°58W 168 C6
Great Yarmouth U.K. 52°37N 1°44E 169 E9
Great Zab = Zāb al Kabīr → Iraq 36°1N 43°24E 213 D10
Great Zimbabwe Zimbabwe 20°16S 30°54E 269 G3
Greater Antilles W. Indies 17°40N 74°0W 321 C5
Greater London □ U.K. 51°31N 0°6W 169 F7
Greater Manchester □ U.K. 53°30N 2°15W 168 D5
Greater St. Lucia Wetlands ⌓ S. Africa 28°6S 32°27E 271 C5
Greater Sudbury = Sudbury Canada 46°30N 81°0W 298 C3
Greater Sunda Is. Indonesia 7°0S 112°0E 230 F4
Grebbestad Sweden 58°42N 11°15E 163 F5
Grebenka = Hrebenka Ukraine 50°9N 32°22E 189 G7
Greco Italy 45°30N 9°12E 129 A2
Greco, C. Cyprus 34°57N 34°5E 207 F10
Greco, Mte. Italy 41°48N 13°58E 199 G10
Gredos, Sierra de Spain 40°20N 5°0W 194 E6
Greece U.S.A. 43°13N 77°41W 312 C7
Greece ■ Europe 40°0N 23°0E 204 B3
Greeley Colo., U.S.A. 40°25N 104°42W 304 F11
Greeley Nebr., U.S.A. 41°33N 98°32W 308 E4
Greeleyville U.S.A. 33°40N 79°59W 316 B10
Greely Fd. Canada 80°30N 85°0W 295 A15
Greem-Bell, Ostrov Russia 81°0N 62°0E 214 A7
Green → Ky., U.S.A. 37°54N 87°30W 308 G10
Green → Utah, U.S.A. 38°11N 109°53W 304 G9
Green B. U.S.A. 45°0N 87°30W 308 C10
Green Bay U.S.A. 44°31N 88°0W 308 C9
Green C. Australia 37°13S 150°1E 283 D9
Green City U.S.A. 40°16N 92°57W 310 D4
Green Cove Springs U.S.A. 29°59N 81°42W 316 F8
Green I. = Lü Tao Taiwan 22°40N 121°30E 225 D3
Green I. Antigua & B. 17°2N 61°40W 322 b
Green I. Hong Kong, China 22°17N 114°6E 122 B1
Green I. Grenada 12°13N 61°35W 323 q
Green Is. Papua N. G. 4°35S 154°10E 286 C8
Green Island Jamaica 18°23N 78°17W 320 a
Green Island Bay Phil. 10°12N 119°22E 233 F2
Green Lake Canada 54°17N 107°47W 297 C7
Green Mts. U.S.A. 43°45N 72°45W 313 C12
Green Point S. Africa 33°54S 18°25E 118 A1
Green Pond U.S.A. 32°44N 80°37W 316 C9
Green River Papua N. G. 3°54S 141°11E 286 B1
Green River Utah, U.S.A. 38°59N 110°10W 304 G8
Green River Wyo., U.S.A. 41°32N 109°28W 304 F9
Green Valley U.S.A. 31°52N 110°56W 305 L8
Greenacres U.S.A. 26°38N 80°7W 317 J9
Greenbank U.S.A. 48°6N 122°34W 306 B4
Greenbelt U.S.A. 39°0N 76°53W 143 A4
Greenbelt Park U.S.A. 38°58N 76°53W 143 B4
Greenbush Mich., U.S.A. 44°35N 83°19W 312 B1
Greenbush Minn., U.S.A. 48°42N 96°11W 308 A5
Greencastle U.S.A. 39°38N 86°52W 311 E10
Greene Iowa, U.S.A. 42°54N 92°48W 310 B4
Greene N.Y., U.S.A. 42°20N 75°46W 313 D9
Greeneville U.S.A. 36°10N 82°50W 315 C13
Greenfield Calif., U.S.A. 36°19N 121°15W 306 J5
Greenfield Calif., U.S.A. 35°15N 119°0W 307 K8
Greenfield Ill., U.S.A. 39°21N 90°12W 310 E6
Greenfield Ind., U.S.A. 39°47N 85°46W 311 E11
Greenfield Iowa, U.S.A. 41°18N 94°28W 310 C2
Greenfield Mass., U.S.A. 42°35N 72°36W 313 D12
Greenfield Mo., U.S.A. 37°25N 93°51W 308 G7
Greenfield Ohio, U.S.A. 39°21N 83°23W 311 E13
Greenfield Park Canada 45°29N 73°28W 130 B3
Greenford U.K. 51°31N 0°21W 125 A1
Greenhill U.K. 51°34N 0°18W 125 A2
Greenhills Ireland 53°18N 6°20W 120 B1
Greenland ☑ N. Amer. 66°0N 45°0W 154 D6
Greenland Sea Arctic 73°0N 10°0W 154 B10
Greenmarket Square Cape Town, S. Africa 118 c2
Greenock U.K. 55°57N 4°46W 167 F4
Greenore Ireland 54°2N 6°8W 166 B5
Greenore Pt. Ireland 52°14N 6°19W 166 D5
Greenough Australia 28°58S 114°43E 279 E1
Greenough → Australia 28°51S 114°38E 279 E1
Greenough Pt. Canada 44°58N 81°26W 312 B3
Greenpoint New York, U.S.A. 132 e3
Greenport U.S.A. 41°6N 72°22W 313 E12
Greensboro Fla., U.S.A. 30°34N 84°45W 316 E5
Greensboro Ga., U.S.A. 33°35N 83°11W 316 B6
Greensboro N.C., U.S.A. 36°4N 79°48W 315 C15
Greensboro Vt., U.S.A. 44°36N 72°18W 313 B12
Greensburg Ind., U.S.A. 39°20N 85°29W 311 E11
Greensburg Kans., U.S.A. 37°36N 99°18W 308 G4
Greensburg Pa., U.S.A. 40°18N 79°33W 312 F5
Greenstone = Geraldton Canada 49°44N 87°10W 298 C2
Greenstone Pt. U.K. 57°55N 5°37W 167 D3
Greentown U.S.A. 40°29N 85°58W 311 D11
Greenup U.S.A. 39°15N 88°10W 311 E8
Greenvale Australia 18°59S 145°7E 280 B4
Greenville Liberia 5°1N 9°6W 262 D3
Greenville Ala., U.S.A. 31°50N 86°38W 315 F11
Greenville Calif., U.S.A. 40°8N 120°57W 306 E6
Greenville Fla., U.S.A. 30°28N 83°38W 316 E6
Greenville Ga., U.S.A. 33°2N 84°43W 316 B5
Greenville Ill., U.S.A. 38°53N 89°25W 310 F7
Greenville Ind., U.S.A. 38°22N 85°59W 311 F11
Greenville Maine, U.S.A. 45°28N 69°35W 309 C19
Greenville Mich., U.S.A. 43°11N 85°15W 311 A11
Greenville Miss., U.S.A. 33°24N 91°4W 315 E9
Greenville Mo., U.S.A. 37°8N 90°27W 308 G8
Greenville N.C., U.S.A. 35°37N 77°23W 315 D16
Greenville N.H., U.S.A. 42°46N 71°49W 313 D13
Greenville N.Y., U.S.A. 42°25N 74°1W 313 D10
Greenville Ohio, U.S.A. 40°6N 84°38W 311 D12
Greenville Pa., U.S.A. 41°24N 80°23W 312 E4
Greenville S.C., U.S.A. 34°51N 82°24W 315 D13
Greenville Tex., U.S.A. 33°8N 96°7W 314 E6
Greenwater Lake ⌓ Canada 52°32N 103°30W 297 C8
Greenwich Conn., U.S.A. 41°2N 73°38W 313 E11
Greenwich N.Y., U.S.A. 43°5N 73°30W 313 C11
Greenwich Ohio, U.S.A. 41°2N 82°31W 312 E2
Greenwich □ U.K. 51°29N 0°1E 125 B3
Greenwich Observatory U.K. 51°28N 0°0 125 B3
Greenwich Village New York, U.S.A. 132 d1
Greenwood B.C., Canada 49°10N 118°40W 296 D5
Greenwood Ark., U.S.A. 35°13N 94°16W 314 D7
Greenwood Fla., U.S.A. 30°52N 85°10W 316 E4
Greenwood Ind., U.S.A. 39°37N 86°7W 311 E10
Greenwood Mass., U.S.A. 42°29N 71°2W 116 A2
Greenwood Miss., U.S.A. 33°31N 90°11W 315 E9
Greenwood S.C., U.S.A. 34°12N 82°10W 315 D13
Greenwood, Mt. Australia 13°48S 130°4E 278 B5
Greenwood Great House Jamaica 18°29N 77°44W 320 a
Grefsen Norway 59°56N 10°47E 133 A3
Gregbe Ivory C. 6°48N 6°43W 262 D3
Gregório → Brazil 6°50S 70°46W 330 B3
Gregory U.S.A. 43°14N 99°26W 308 D4
Gregory → Australia 17°53S 139°17E 280 B2
Gregory, L. S. Austral., Australia 28°55S 139°0E 281 D2
Gregory, L. W. Austral., Australia 20°0S 127°40E 278 D4
Gregory, L. W. Austral., Australia 25°38S 119°58E 279 E2
Gregory △ Australia 15°38S 131°15E 278 C5
Gregory Downs Australia 18°35S 138°45E 280 B2
Gregory Ra. Queens., Australia 19°30S 143°40E 280 B3
Gregory Ra. W. Austral., Australia 21°20S 121°12E 278 D3
Greifenberg = Gryfice Poland 53°55N 15°13E 184 E2
Greifenhagen = Gryfino Poland 53°16N 14°29E 185 E1
Greiffenberg = Gryfów Śląski Poland 51°2N 15°24E 185 G2
Greiffenberg Germany 53°5N 13°57E 178 B9
Greifswald Germany 54°5N 13°23E 178 A9
Greifswalder Bodden Germany 54°12N 13°35E 178 A9
Grein Austria 48°14N 14°51E 180 C7
Greiz Germany 50°39N 12°10E 178 E8
Gremikha Russia 67°59N 39°47E 186 A6
Grenaa Denmark 56°25N 10°53E 163 H4
Grenada U.S.A. 33°47N 89°49W 315 E10
Grenada ■ W. Indies 12°10N 61°40W 323 q
Grenade France 43°47N 1°17E 174 E5
Grenadier I. U.S.A. 44°3N 76°22W 313 B8
Grenadines, The St. Vincent 12°40N 61°20W 323 n
Grenchen Switz. 47°12N 7°24E 179 H3
Grenen Denmark 57°44N 10°40E 163 G4
Grenfell N.S.W., Australia 33°52S 148°8E 283 B8
Grenfell Sask., Canada 50°30N 102°56W 297 C8
Grenivík Iceland 65°57N 18°11W 155 B8
Grenjaðarstaður Iceland 65°49N 17°21W 155 B9
Grenoble France 45°12N 5°42E 175 C9
Grenville Grenada 12°7N 61°37W 323 q
Grenville, C. Australia 12°0S 143°13E 286 F2
Grenville Chan. Canada 53°40N 129°46W 296 C3
Gréoux-les-Bains France 43°45N 5°52E 175 E9
Gresham U.S.A. 45°30N 122°25W 306 E4
Gresham Park U.S.A. 33°43N 84°20W 113 B2
Gresik Indonesia 7°13S 112°38E 235 D4
Gretna Dumf. & Gall., U.K. 55°0N 3°3W 167 F5
Gretna Fla., U.S.A. 30°37N 84°40W 316 E5
Gretna La., U.S.A. 29°54N 90°3W 131 B2
Gretna City Park U.S.A. 29°54N 90°3W 131 B2
Greve Strand Denmark 55°34N 12°18E 118 B1
Greven Germany 52°6N 7°37E 178 C3
Grevena Greece 40°4N 21°25E 202 F5
Grevena □ Greece 40°2N 21°25E 202 F5
Grevenbroich Germany 51°5N 6°35E 178 D2
Grevenmacher Lux. 49°41N 6°26E 170 E6
Grevesmühlen Germany 53°52N 11°12E 178 B7
Grey → Nfld. & L., Canada 47°34N 57°6W 299 C8
Grey → N.Z. 42°27S 171°12E 285 C6
Grey, C. Australia 13°0S 136°35E 280 A2
Grey Is. Canada 50°50N 55°35W 295 G20
Grey Ra. Australia 27°0S 143°30E 281 D3
Greybull U.S.A. 44°30N 108°3W 304 D9
Greyfriars Kirk Edinburgh, U.K. 121 c2
Greymouth N.Z. 42°29S 171°13E 285 C6
Greystones Ireland 53°9N 6°5W 166 C5
Greytown N.Z. 41°5S 175°29E 284 H4
Greytown KwaZulu Natal, S. Africa 29°1S 30°36E 271 C5
Gribanovskiy Russia 51°28N 41°50E 190 E5
Gribbell I. Canada 53°23N 129°0W 296 C3
Gribës, Mal i Albania 40°17N 19°45E 202 F3
Gribingui → C.A.R. 8°33N 19°5E 264 A3
Gribingui-Bamingui ⌓ C.A.R. 7°45N 19°17E 264 A3
Gridley U.S.A. 39°22N 121°42W 306 F5
Griebeg, Ras il- Malta 35°58N 14°23E 206 F7
Griebnitzsee Germany 52°23N 13°8E 115 B1
Griekwastad S. Africa 28°49S 23°15E 270 C3
Griesheim Germany 49°51N 8°33E 179 F4
Grieskirchen Austria 48°16N 13°48E 180 C6
Griffin U.S.A. 33°15N 84°16W 316 B5
Griffin, L. U.S.A. 28°52N 81°51W 317 G8
Griffith N.S.W., Australia 34°18S 146°2E 283 C7
Griffith Ont., Canada 45°15N 77°10W 312 A7
Griffith I. Canada 44°50N 80°55W 312 B4
Griffith Park U.S.A. 34°8N 118°17W 126 B3
Griggsville U.S.A. 39°43N 90°43W 310 E6
Grignols France 44°23N 0°2W 174 D3
Grigoriopol Moldova 47°9N 29°18E 183 C14
Grimari C.A.R. 5°43N 20°6E 264 A4
Grimaylov = Hrymayliv Ukraine 49°20N 26°5E 177 D14
Grimbergen Belgium 50°56N 4°22E 116 A2
Grimes U.S.A. 39°4N 121°54W 306 F5
Grimm = Kamenskiy Russia 50°48N 45°25E 190 E7
Grimma Germany 51°14N 12°43E 178 D8
Grimmen Germany 54°7N 13°3E 178 A9
Grimsay U.K. 57°29N 7°14W 167 D1
Grimsby Ont., Canada 43°12N 79°34W 312 C5
Grimsby N.E. Lincs., U.K. 53°34N 0°5W 168 D7
Grímsey Iceland 66°33N 17°58W 155 A9
Grimshaw Canada 56°10N 117°40W 296 B5
Grimslöv Sweden 56°44N 14°34E 163 H8
Grímsstaðir Iceland 65°39N 16°7W 155 B10
Grimstad Norway 58°20N 8°35E 164 F5
Grímsvötn Iceland 64°26N 17°22W 155 C9
Grindavík Iceland 63°50N 22°26W 155 D4
Grindelwald Switz. 46°38N 8°2E 179 J4
Grindsted Denmark 55°46N 8°55E 163 J2
Grindu Romania 44°44N 26°50E 183 F11
Grinnell U.S.A. 41°45N 92°43W 310 C4
Grinnell Pen. Canada 76°40N 95°0W 295 B13
Grintavec Slovenia 46°22N 14°32E 199 B11
Grinzing Austria 48°15N 16°20E 142 A2
Gris-Nez, C. France 50°52N 1°35E 173 B8
Grise Fiord Canada 76°25N 82°57W 295 B15
Grishino = Krasnoarmeisk Ukraine 48°18N 37°11E 189 H9
Grisolles France 43°49N 1°19E 174 E5
Grisons = Graubünden □ Switz. 46°45N 9°30E 179 J5
Grisslehamn Sweden 60°5N 18°49E 162 D12
Grmeč Planina Bos.-H. 44°43N 16°16E 199 D13
Groais I. Canada 50°55N 55°35W 299 B8
Gröbenried Germany 48°13N 11°25E 131 A1
Grobiņa Latvia 56°33N 21°10E 184 B8
Groblersdal S. Africa 25°15S 29°25E 271 C4
Grobming Austria 47°27N 13°54E 180 D6
Grochów Poland 52°15N 21°5E 142 B2
Grocka Serbia 44°40N 20°42E 202 B4
Gródek Poland 53°6N 23°40E 185 E10
Gródek Jagielloński = Horodok Ukraine 49°46N 23°32E 177 D12
Grodekovo = Pogranichnyy Russia 44°25N 131°24E 220 B5
Grodków Poland 50°43N 17°21E 185 H4
Grodno = Hrodna Belarus 53°42N 23°52E 184 E10
Grodzisk Poland 52°19N 21°4E 142 B2
Grodzisk Mazowiecki Poland 52°7N 20°37E 185 F7
Grodzisk Wielkopolski Poland 52°15N 16°22E 185 F3
Grodzyanka = Hrodzyanka Belarus 53°31N 28°42E 177 B15
Groenendaal Belgium 50°46N 4°26E 116 B2
Groesbeck U.S.A. 31°31N 96°32W 314 F6
Grogol Petamburin Indonesia 6°9S 106°46E 122 A1
Groix France 47°38N 3°29W 172 E3
Groix, Î. de France 47°38N 3°28W 172 E3
Grójec Poland 51°50N 20°58E 185 G7
Gronau Niedersachsen, Germany 52°5N 9°47E 178 C5
Gronau Nordrhein-Westfalen, Germany 52°12N 7°2E 178 C3
Grong Norway 64°25N 12°8E 160 D15
Grönhögen Sweden 56°16N 16°24E 163 H10
Groningen Neths. 53°15N 6°35E 170 A6
Groningen Suriname 5°48N 55°28W 329 B6
Groningen □ Neths. 53°16N 6°40E 170 A6
Grønnedal = Kangilinnguit Greenland 61°20N 47°57W 154 E6
Gronsdorf Germany 48°7N 11°42E 131 B3
Groom U.S.A. 35°12N 101°6W 314 D4
Groot → S. Africa 33°45S 24°36E 270 D3
Groot-Berg → S. Africa 32°47S 18°8E 270 D2
Groot-Brakrivier S. Africa 34°2S 22°18E 270 D3
Groot Karasberge Namibia 27°20S 18°40E 270 C2
Groot-Kei → S. Africa 32°41S 28°22E 271 D4
Groot-Vis → S. Africa 33°28S 27°5E 270 D4
Grootdrink S. Africa 28°33S 21°42E 270 C3
Groote Eylandt Australia 14°0S 136°40E 280 A2
Grootfontein Namibia 19°31S 18°6E 270 A2
Grootlaagte → Africa 20°55S 21°27E 270 B3
Grootvloer → S. Africa 30°0S 20°40E 270 D3
Grorud Norway 59°57N 10°52E 133 A4
Gros C. Canada 61°59N 113°32W 296 A6
Gros Cap Guadeloupe 16°24N 61°25W 322 e
Gros Islet St. Lucia 14°5N 60°58W 323 m
Gros-Morne Martinique 14°43N 61°2W 322 j
Gros Morne △ Canada 49°40N 57°50W 299 C8
Gros Piton St. Lucia 13°49N 61°5W 323 m
Grósio Italy 46°18N 10°16E 198 B7
Grosne → France 46°42N 4°56E 173 F11
Gross-Glienicke Germany 52°28N 13°6E 115 B1
Gross-Hadern Germany 48°6N 11°29E 131 B1
Gross-Lappen Germany 48°11N 11°35E 131 A2
Gross-Meseritsch = Velké Meziříčí Czech Rep. 49°21N 16°1E 180 B9
Gross-Strehlitz = Strzelce Opolskie Poland 50°31N 18°18E 185 H5
Gross Wartenberg = Syców Poland 51°19N 17°40E 185 G4
Grossa, Pta. Spain 39°6N 1°36E 206 C2
Grosse I. U.S.A. 42°8N 83°9W 311 B13
Grosse Krampe Germany 52°23N 13°40E 115 B5
Grosse Müggelsee Germany 52°26N 13°38E 115 B4
Grosse Point U.S.A. 42°23N 82°54W 312 D2
Grosse Point Lighthouse U.S.A. 42°2N 87°41W 119 A2
Grosse Pte. Guadeloupe 16°1N 61°17W 322 e
Grossenbrode Germany 54°21N 11°4E 178 A7
Grossenhain Germany 51°17N 13°32E 178 D9
Grossenzersdorf Austria 48°12N 16°33E 142 A3
Grossenzersdorfer Arm → Austria 48°12N 16°31E 142 A3
Grosser Arber Germany 49°6N 13°8E 179 F9
Grosser Biberhaufen Austria 48°12N 16°28E 142 A2
Grosser Plöner See Germany 54°10N 10°22E 178 A6
Grosser Wannsee Germany 52°25N 13°10E 115 B2
Grosseto Italy 42°46N 11°8E 199 F8
Grossfeld-Siedlung Austria 48°16N 16°26E 142 A2
Grossgerungs Austria 48°34N 14°57E 180 C7
Grossglockner Austria 47°5N 12°40E 180 D5
Grosshesselohe Germany 48°3N 11°32E 131 B2
Grossjedlersdorf Austria 48°16N 16°23E 142 A2
Grosswardein = Oradea Romania 47°2N 21°58E 182 C6
Grossziethen Germany 52°23N 13°26E 115 B3
Groswater B. Canada 54°20N 57°40W 299 B8
Grotli Norway 62°2N 7°42E 164 B4
Groton Conn., U.S.A. 41°21N 72°5W 313 E12
Groton N.Y., U.S.A. 42°36N 76°22W 313 D8
Groton S. Dak., U.S.A. 45°27N 98°6W 308 C4
Grottáglie Italy 40°32N 17°26E 201 B10
Grottaminarda Italy 41°4N 15°2E 201 A8
Grottammare Italy 42°59N 13°52E 199 F10
Grottkau = Grodków Poland 50°43N 17°21E 185 H4
Grouard Mission Canada 55°33N 116°9W 296 B5
Grouin, Pte. du France 48°43N 1°51W 172 D5
Ground Zero New York, U.S.A. 132 e1
Groundhog → Canada 48°45N 82°58W 298 C3
Grouw Neths. 53°5N 5°51E 170 A5
Grove, The U.S.A. 42°5N 87°52W 119 A1
Grove City Fla., U.S.A. 26°56N 82°19W 317 J7
Grove City Ohio, U.S.A. 39°53N 83°6W 311 E13
Grove City Pa., U.S.A. 41°10N 80°5W 312 E4
Grove Hall U.S.A. 42°18N 71°4W 116 B2
Grove Hill U.S.A. 31°42N 87°47W 315 F11
Grove Park Hounslow, U.K. 51°28N 0°15W 125 B2
Grove Park Lewisham, U.K. 51°25N 0°1E 125 B4
Grove Park Georgia, U.S.A. 33°46N 84°26W 113 B2
Groveland Calif., U.S.A. 37°50N 120°14W 306 H6
Groveland Fla., U.S.A. 28°34N 81°51W 317 G8
Grover = Tiltonsville U.S.A. 40°10N 80°41W 312 F4
Grover Beach U.S.A. 35°7N 120°37W 307 K6
Groves U.S.A. 29°57N 93°54W 314 G8
Groveton N.H., U.S.A. 44°36N 71°31W 313 B13
Groveton Va., U.S.A. 38°46N 77°6W 143 C3
Grovetown U.S.A. 33°27N 82°12W 316 B7
Grožnjan Croatia 45°22N 13°43E 199 C10
Groznyy Russia 43°20N 45°45E 191 J7
Grua Norway 60°16N 10°40E 164 D7
Grubišno Polje Croatia 45°44N 17°12E 182 E2
Grudovo Bulgaria 42°21N 27°10E 203 D11
Grudusk Poland 53°3N 20°38E 185 E7
Grudziądz Poland 53°30N 18°47E 184 E5
Gruinard B. U.K. 57°56N 5°35W 167 D3
Gruissan France 43°8N 3°7E 174 E7
Grumo Áppula Italy 41°1N 16°42E 201 A9
Grums Sweden 59°22N 13°5E 162 E7
Grünau Germany 52°25N 13°34E 115 B4
Grünberg Germany 50°35N 8°58E 178 E4
Grünberg in Schlesien = Zielona Góra Poland 51°57N 15°31E 185 G2
Grund Iceland 65°31N 18°9W 155 B8
Gründau Germany 50°10N 9°9E 179 E5
Grundy Center U.S.A. 42°22N 92°47W 310 B4
Grunewald Germany 52°28N 13°13E 115 B2
Grungedal Norway 59°44N 7°43E 164 E4
Grünstadt Germany 49°34N 8°9E 179 F4
Grünwald Germany 48°2N 11°31E 131 B2
Grünwalder Forst Germany 48°2N 11°33E 131 B2
Gruppo di Tessa ⌓ Italy 46°47N 11°0E 198 B8
Gruvberget Sweden 61°6N 16°10E 162 C10
Gruver U.S.A. 36°16N 101°24W 314 C4
Gruyères Switz. 46°35N 7°4E 179 J3
Gruža Serbia 43°54N 20°46E 202 C4
Gryazi Russia 52°30N 39°58E 189 F10
Gryazliv = Borovichi Russia 58°25N 33°55E 188 C7
Gryazovets Russia 58°50N 40°10E 188 C11
Grybów Poland 49°36N 20°55E 185 J7
Grycksbo Sweden 60°40N 15°29E 162 D9
Gryfice Poland 53°55N 15°13E 184 E2
Gryfino Poland 53°16N 14°29E 185 E1
Gryfów Śląski Poland 51°2N 15°24E 185 G2
Grymes Hill U.S.A. 40°36N 74°6W 132 C1
Grythyttan Sweden 59°41N 14°32E 162 E8
Grytviken S. Georgia 54°19S 36°33W 152 M8
Gstaad Switz. 46°28N 7°18E 179 J3
Gua India 22°18N 85°20E 243 H11
Gua Musang Malaysia 4°53N 101°58E 237 K3
Guabún, Pta. Chile 41°48S 74°2W 336 B2
Guacanayabo, G. de Cuba 20°40N 77°20W 320 B4
Guacara Venezuela 10°14N 67°53W 328 A4
Guachípas → Argentina 25°40S 65°30W 334 B2
Guadajoz → Spain 37°50N 4°51W 195 H6
Guadalajara Jalisco, Mexico 20°40N 103°20W 318 C4
Guadalajara Spain 40°37N 3°12W 196 E1
Guadalajara □ Spain 40°47N 2°30W 196 E2
Guadalcanal Solomon Is. 9°32S 160°12E 287 M11
Guadalcanal Spain 38°5N 5°52W 195 G5
Guadalén → Spain 38°5N 3°32W 195 G7
Guadales Argentina 34°30S 67°55W 334 C2
Guadalete → Spain 36°35N 6°13W 195 J4
Guadalimar → Spain 38°5N 3°28W 195 G7
Guadalmena → Spain 38°19N 2°56W 195 G8
Guadalmez → Spain 38°46N 5°4W 195 G5
Guadalope → Spain 41°15N 0°3W 196 D4
Guadalquivir → Spain 36°47N 6°22W 195 J4
Guadalupe = Guadeloupe ☑ W. Indies 16°20N 61°40W 322 e
Guadalupe Brazil 6°44S 43°47W 332 C3
Guadalupe Zacatecas, Mexico 22°45N 102°31W 318 C4
Guadalupe Manila, Phil. 14°34N 121°2E 127 B2
Guadalupe Spain 39°27N 5°17W 195 F5
Guadalupe Calif., U.S.A. 34°58N 120°34W 307 L6
Guadalupe → U.S.A. 28°27N 96°47W 314 G6
Guadalupe, Basilica de Mexico 19°29N 99°7W 128 B2
Guadalupe, Sierra de Spain 39°28N 5°30W 195 F5
Guadalupe Bravos Mexico 31°20N 106°10W 318 A3

376 Guadalupe I.
INDEX

Guadalupe I. Pac. Oc. 29°0N 118°50W 292 G8
Guadalupe Mts. △ U.S.A. 31°40N 104°30W 314 F2
Guadalupe Peak U.S.A. 31°50N 104°52W 314 F2
Guadalupe y Calvo Mexico 26°6N 106°58W 318 B3
Guadarrama, Sierra de Spain 41°0N 4°0W 194 E7
Guadeloupe ⊠ W. Indies 16°20N 61°40W 322 e
Guadeloupe △ Guadeloupe 16°10N 61°40W 322 e
Guadeloupe Passage W. Indies 16°50N 62°15W 322 e
Guadelupe Peru 7°15S 79°29W 330 B2
Guadiamar → Spain 36°55N 6°24W 195 J4
Guadiana → Portugal 37°14N 7°22W 195 H3
Guadiana Menor → Spain 37°56N 3°15W 195 H7
Guadiaro → Spain 36°17N 5°17W 195 J5
Guadiato → Spain 37°48N 5°5W 195 H5
Guadiela → Spain 40°22N 2°49W 196 E2
Guadix Spain 37°18N 3°11W 195 H7
Guafo, Boca del Chile 43°35S 74°0W 336 B2
Guafo, I. Chile 43°35S 74°50W 336 B2
Guaico Trin. & Tob. 10°35N 61°9W 323 t
Guainía □ Colombia 2°30N 69°0W 328 C4
Guainía → Colombia 2°1N 67°7W 328 C4
Guaíra Brazil 24°5S 54°10W 335 A5
Guaíra □ Paraguay 25°45S 56°30W 334 B4
Guaire = Gorey Ireland 52°41N 6°18W 166 D5
Guaitecas, Is. Chile 44°0S 74°30W 336 B2
Guajará-Mirim Brazil 10°50S 65°20W 331 C4
Guajira □ Colombia 11°30N 72°30W 328 A3
Guajira, Pen. de la Colombia 12°0N 72°0W 328 A3
Gualaceo Ecuador 2°54S 78°47W 328 D2
Gualán Guatemala 15°8N 89°22W 320 C2
Gualdo Tadino Italy 43°14N 12°47E 199 E9
Gualeguay Argentina 33°10S 59°14W 334 C4
Gualeguaychú Argentina 33°3S 59°31W 334 C4
Gualequay → Argentina 33°19S 59°39W 334 C4
Gualicho, Salina Argentina 40°25S 65°20W 336 B3
Gualjaina Argentina 42°45S 70°30W 336 B2
Guam ⊠ Pac. Oc. 13°27N 144°45E 302 d
Guamá → Brazil 1°29S 48°30W 332 B2
Guamblin, I. Chile 44°50S 75°0W 336 B2
Guaminí Argentina 37°1S 62°28W 334 D3
Guamote Ecuador 1°56S 78°43W 328 D2
Guampí, Sierra de Venezuela 6°0N 65°35W 329 B4
Guamúchil Mexico 25°28N 108°6W 318 B3
Guana I. Br. Virgin Is. 18°30N 64°30W 321 b
Guanabacoa Cuba 23°8N 82°18W 320 B3
Guanabara, B. de Brazil 22°52S 43°10W 135 B1
Guanabara, Jardim Brazil 22°48S 43°11W 135 A1
Guanabara, Palácio da Brazil 22°56S 43°11W 135 B1
Guanacaste, Cordillera de Costa Rica 10°40N 85°4W 320 D2
Guanacaste △ Costa Rica 10°57N 85°30W 320 D2
Guanaceví Mexico 25°56N 105°57W 318 B3
Guanahani = San Salvador I. Bahamas 24°0N 74°40W 321 B5
Guanaja Honduras 16°30N 85°55W 320 C2
Guanajay Cuba 22°56N 82°42W 320 B3
Guanajuato Mexico 21°1N 101°15W 318 C4
Guanajuato □ Mexico 21°0N 101°0W 318 C4
Guanambi Brazil 14°13S 42°47W 333 D3
Guanapo Trin. & Tob. 10°36N 61°15W 323 t
Guanare Venezuela 8°42N 69°12W 328 B4
Guanare → Venezuela 8°13N 67°46W 328 B4
Guandacol Argentina 29°30S 68°40W 334 B2
Guane Cuba 22°10N 84°7W 320 B3
Guang'an China 30°28N 106°35E 228 B6
Guang'anmen China 39°51N 116°18E 114 B1
Guangchang China 26°50N 116°21E 229 D11
Guangde China 30°54N 119°25E 229 B12
Guangdong □ China 23°0N 113°0E 229 F9
Guangfeng China 28°20N 118°15E 229 C12
Guanghan China 30°58N 104°17E 228 B5
Guangling China 39°47N 114°22E 226 E8
Guangnan China 24°5N 105°4E 228 E5
Guangning China 23°40N 112°22E 229 F9
Guangqumen China 39°52N 116°25E 114 B2
Guangrao China 37°5N 118°25E 227 F10
Guangshui China 31°37N 114°0E 229 B9
Guangshun China 26°8N 106°21E 228 D6
Guangwu China 37°48N 105°57E 226 F3
Guangxi Zhuangzu Zizhiqu □ China 24°0N 109°0E 228 F7
Guangyuan China 32°26N 105°51E 228 A5
Guangze China 27°30N 117°12E 229 D11
Guangzhou China 23°6N 113°13E 121 B2
Guanhães Brazil 18°47S 42°57W 333 E3
Guanica Puerto Rico 17°58N 66°55W 321 b
Guanipa → Venezuela 9°56N 62°26W 329 B5
Guanling China 25°56N 105°35E 228 E5
Guannan China 34°8N 119°21E 227 G10
Guanshuo China 23°4N 113°22E 121 B3
Guanta Venezuela 10°14N 64°36W 329 A5
Guantánamo Cuba 20°10N 75°14W 321 B4
Guantánamo B. Cuba 19°59N 75°10W 321 C4
Guantao China 36°42N 115°25E 226 F8
Guanyang China 25°30N 111°8E 229 E8
Guanyun China 34°20N 119°18E 227 G10
Guapay = Grande → Bolivia 15°51S 64°39W 331 D5
Guapí Colombia 2°36N 77°54W 328 C2
Guápiles Costa Rica 10°10N 83°46W 320 D3
Guapo → Trin. & Tob. 10°11N 61°40W 323 t
Guapo B. Trin. & Tob. 10°12N 61°41W 323 t
Guaporé = Rondônia Brazil 10°52S 61°57W 331 C5
Guaporé Brazil 28°51S 51°54W 335 B5
Guaporé → Brazil 11°55S 65°4W 331 C4
Guaqui Bolivia 16°41S 68°54W 330 D4
Guara, Sierra de Spain 42°19N 0°15W 196 C4
Guarabira Brazil 6°51S 35°29W 332 C4
Guaracara → Trin. & Tob. 10°18N 61°28W 323 t
Guarachirá → Colombia 5°27N 70°36W 328 B3
Guaranda Ecuador 1°36S 79°0W 328 D2
Guarani = Pacajus Brazil 4°10S 38°31W 332 B4
Guarapari Brazil 20°40S 40°30W 333 F3
Guarapuava Brazil 25°20S 51°30W 333 G1
Guaratinguetá Brazil 22°49S 45°9W 335 A6
Guaratuba Brazil 25°53S 48°38W 335 B6
Guarda Portugal 40°32N 7°20W 194 E3
Guarda □ Portugal 40°40N 7°20W 194 E3
Guardafui, C. = Asir, Ras Somali Rep. 11°55N 51°10E 267 B7
Guardamar del Segura Spain 38°5N 0°39W 197 G4
Guardavalle Italy 38°30N 16°30E 201 D9
Guárdia Sanframondi Italy 41°15N 14°36E 201 A7
Guardiagrele Italy 42°11N 14°13E 199 F11
Guardo Spain 42°47N 4°50W 194 C6
Guareña Spain 38°51N 6°6W 195 G4
Guareña → Spain 41°29N 5°23W 194 D5
Guari Papua N. G. 8°3S 146°52E 286 E4
Guárico □ Venezuela 8°40N 66°35W 328 B4
Guarrojo → Colombia 4°6N 70°42W 328 C3
Guarujá Brazil 24°2S 46°25W 335 A6
Guarulhos Brazil 23°29S 46°33W 335 A6
Guasave Mexico 25°34N 108°27W 318 B3
Guascama, Pta. Colombia 2°32N 78°24W 328 C2
Guasdualito Venezuela 7°15N 70°44W 328 B3
Guasipati Venezuela 7°28N 61°54W 329 B5
Guasopa Papua N. G. 9°12S 152°56E 286 E7
Guastalla Italy 44°55N 10°39E 198 D7
Guatemala Guatemala 14°40N 90°22W 320 D1
Guatemala ■ Cent. Amer. 15°40N 90°30W 320 C1
Guatemala Basin Pac. Oc. 11°0N 95°0W 289 F18
Guatemala Trench Pac. Oc. 14°0N 95°0W 292 H10
Guatire Venezuela 10°28N 66°32W 328 A4
Guatopo △ Venezuela 10°5N 66°30W 328 A4
Guatuaro Pt. Trin. & Tob. 10°19N 60°59W 323 t
Guavi → Papua N. G. 7°48S 143°16E 286 D2
Guaviare □ Colombia 2°0N 72°30W 328 C3
Guaviare → Colombia 4°3N 67°44W 328 C4
Guaxupé Brazil 21°10S 47°5W 335 A6
Guayabero → Colombia 2°36N 72°47W 328 C3
Guayaguayare Trin. & Tob. 10°8N 61°2W 323 t
Guayaguayare B. Trin. & Tob. 10°7N 61°2W 323 t
Guayama Puerto Rico 17°59N 66°7W 321 C6
Guayaneco, Arch. Chile 47°45S 75°10W 336 C1
Guayanilla Puerto Rico 18°1N 66°47W 321 b
Guayaquil Ecuador 2°15S 79°52W 328 D2
Guayaquil Baja Calif., Mexico 29°59N 115°4W 318 B1
Guayaquil, G. de Ecuador 3°10S 81°0W 328 D1
Guayaramerín Bolivia 10°48S 65°23W 331 C4
Guayas → Ecuador 2°36S 79°52W 328 D2
Guaymas Mexico 27°56N 110°54W 318 B2
Guaynabo Puerto Rico 18°22N 66°7W 321 b
Guba Dem. Rep. of the Congo 10°38S 26°27E 269 E2
Guba Ethiopia 11°17N 35°20E 257 E4
Gûbâl, Madîq Egypt 27°30N 34°0E 256 B3
Gubam Papua N. G. 8°39S 141°53E 286 E1
Guban Somali Rep. 10°30N 44°0E 267 B5
Gubat Phil. 12°55N 124°7E 232 E5
Gubbi India 13°19N 76°56E 245 H3
Gúbbio Italy 43°21N 12°35E 199 E9
Guben Germany 51°57N 14°42E 178 D10
Gubin Poland 51°57N 14°43E 185 G1
Gubio Nigeria 12°30N 12°42E 263 C7
Gubkin Russia 51°17N 37°32E 189 G9
Gubkinskiy Russia 64°27N 76°36E 214 C8
Guča Serbia 43°46N 20°15E 202 C4
Gucheng China 32°20N 111°30E 229 A8
Gudå Norway 63°27N 11°36E 164 A8
Gudalur India 11°30N 76°29E 245 J3
Gudauta Georgia 43°7N 40°32E 191 J5
Gudbrandsdalen Norway 61°33N 10°10E 164 C7
Guddu Barrage Pakistan 28°30N 69°50E 242 E3
Gudenå → Denmark 56°29N 10°13E 163 H4
Gudermes Russia 43°24N 46°5E 191 J8
Gudhjem Denmark 55°12N 14°58E 163 J8
Gudivada India 16°30N 81°3E 245 F5
Gudiyattam India 12°57N 78°55E 245 H4
Gudö Sweden 59°12N 18°12E 139 B3
Gudur India 14°12N 79°55E 245 G4
Gudvangen Norway 60°52N 6°49E 164 D3
Guebwiller France 47°55N 7°12E 173 E14
Guecho = Getxo Spain 43°21N 2°59W 196 B2
Guékédou Guinea 8°40N 10°5W 262 D2
Guelb er Rîchât Mauritania 21°7N 11°24W 260 D2
Guéle Mendouka Cameroon 4°23N 12°55E 263 E7
Guélengdeng Chad 10°55N 15°31E 259 F3
Güell, Parque de Spain 41°24N 2°10E 114 A2
Guelma Algeria 36°25N 7°29E 261 A6
Guelma □ Algeria 36°25N 7°25E 261 A6
Guelmine = Goulimine Morocco 28°56N 10°0W 260 C3
Guelph Canada 43°35N 80°20W 312 C4
Guelta Zemmur W. Sahara 25°8N 12°22W 260 C2
Guemar Algeria 33°30N 6°49E 261 B6
Guéméné-Penfao France 47°38N 1°50W 172 E5
Guéméné-sur-Scorff France 48°4N 3°13W 172 D3
Guéné Benin 11°44N 3°16E 263 C5
Güeppí Peru 0°7S 75°15W 328 D2
Guer France 47°54N 2°8W 172 E4
Güer Aike Argentina 51°39S 69°35W 336 D3
Guera Chad 11°55N 18°12E 259 F3
Guéra □ Chad 11°30N 18°30E 259 F3
Guérande France 47°20N 2°26W 172 E4
Guerara Algeria 32°51N 4°22E 261 B5
Guercif Morocco 34°14N 3°21W 261 B4
Guéréda Chad 14°31N 22°5E 259 F4
Guéret France 46°11N 1°51E 173 F8
Guérigny France 47°6N 3°10E 173 E10
Guerneville U.S.A. 38°30N 123°0W 306 G4
Guernica = Gernika-Lumo Spain 43°19N 2°40W 196 B2
Guernsey Chan. Is., U.K. 49°26N 2°35W 169 H5
Guernsey Wyo., U.S.A. 42°16N 104°45W 304 E11
Guerrara Algeria 28°5N 0°8W 261 C4
Guerrero Mexico City, Mexico 128 a1
Guerrero □ Mexico 17°40N 100°0W 319 D5
Guerzim Algeria 29°39N 1°40W 261 C4
Guessou-Sud Benin 10°3N 2°38E 263 C5
Gueugnon France 46°36N 4°4E 173 F11
Guéyo Ivory C. 5°25N 6°5W 262 D3
Gufuðalur Iceland 65°34N 22°25W 155 B4
Guggenheim Museum New York, U.S.A. 132 b3
Gughe Ethiopia 6°12N 37°30E 257 F4
Gūgher Iran 29°28N 56°27E 247 D8
Guglionesi Italy 41°55N 14°55E 199 G11
Guguan N. Marianas 17°18N 145°51E 302 a
Guhakolak, Tanjung Indonesia 6°50S 105°14E 231 G11
Guhrau = Góra Poland 51°40N 16°31E 185 G3
Gui Jiang → China 23°30N 111°15E 229 F8
Guia Canary Is. 28°8N 15°38W 153 e1
Guia de Isora Canary Is. 28°12N 16°46W 153 e1
Guia Lopes da Laguna Brazil 21°26S 56°7W 335 A4
Guiana Venezuela 5°9N 63°36W 329 B5
Guiana Highlands S. Amer. 5°10N 60°40W 326 C4
Guiana I. Antigua & B. 17°6N 61°44W 322 b
Guibéroua Ivory C. 6°14N 6°10W 262 D3
Guichen B. Australia 37°10S 139°45E 282 D3
Guichi China 30°39N 117°27E 229 B11
Guider Cameroon 9°56N 13°57E 263 D7
Guidiguir Niger 13°40N 9°50E 259 F1
Guidimaka □ Mauritania 15°20N 12°0W 262 B2
Guidimouni Niger 13°42N 9°31E 259 F1
Guiding China 26°34N 107°11E 228 D6
Guidong China 26°7N 113°57E 229 D9
Guidónia-Montecélio Italy 42°1N 12°45E 199 F9
Guiers, L. de Senegal 16°10N 15°50W 262 B1
Guigang China 23°8N 109°35E 228 F7
Guiglo Ivory C. 6°45N 7°30W 262 D3
Guihulñgan Phil. 10°7N 123°16E 233 F4
Guijá Mozam. 24°27S 33°0E 271 B5
Guijuelo Spain 40°33N 5°40W 194 E5
Guildford U.K. 51°14N 0°34W 169 F7
Guilford U.S.A. 41°17N 72°41W 313 E12
Guilin China 25°18N 110°15E 229 E8
Guillaume-Delisle, L. Canada 56°15N 76°17W 298 A4
Guillaumes France 44°5N 6°52E 175 D10
Guillestre France 44°39N 6°40E 175 D10
Guilvinec France 47°48N 4°17W 172 E2
Güimar Canary Is. 28°18N 16°24W 153 e1
Guimarães Brazil 2°9S 44°42W 332 B3
Guimarães Portugal 41°28N 8°24W 194 D2
Guimaras □ Phil. 10°35N 122°37E 233 F4
Guimba Phil. 15°40N 120°46E 232 D3
Guinardó Spain 41°24N 2°10E 114 A2
Guinayangan Phil. 13°54N 122°27E 232 E4
Guinda U.S.A. 38°50N 122°12W 306 G4
Guindulman Phil. 9°46N 124°29E 233 G5
Guinea Africa 8°0N 8°0E 254 F4
Guinea ■ W. Afr. 10°20N 11°30W 262 C2
Guinea, Gulf of Atl. Oc. 3°0N 2°30E 263 E5
Guinea Basin Atl. Oc. 0°0 5°0W 152 G11
Guinea-Bissau ■ Africa 12°0N 15°0W 262 C2
Güines Cuba 22°50N 82°0W 320 B3
Guingamp France 48°34N 3°10W 172 D3
Guinguinéo Senegal 14°20N 15°57W 262 C1
Guinobatan Phil. 13°11N 123°36E 232 E4
Guipavas France 48°26N 4°29W 172 D2
Guiping China 23°21N 110°2E 229 F8
Guipúzcoa □ Spain 43°12N 2°15W 196 B2
Guir Mali 18°52N 2°52W 262 B4
Guir, O. → Algeria 31°29N 2°17W 261 B4
Guiratinga Brazil 16°21S 53°45W 331 D7
Guirel Mauritania 15°30N 7°3W 262 B3
Güiria Venezuela 10°32N 62°18W 329 F8
Guiscard France 49°40N 3°1E 173 C10
Guise France 49°52N 3°35E 173 C10
Guita-Koulouba C.A.R. 5°58N 23°21E 264 A4
Guitiriz Spain 43°11N 7°50W 194 B3
Guitri Ivory C. 5°30N 5°14W 262 D3
Guiuan Phil. 11°5N 125°55E 233 F5
Guixi China 28°16N 117°15E 229 C11
Guiyang Guizhou, China 26°32N 106°40E 228 D6
Guiyang Hunan, China 25°46N 112°42E 229 E9
Guizhou □ China 27°0N 107°0E 228 D6
Gujan-Mestras France 44°38N 1°4W 174 D2
Gujar Khan Pakistan 33°16N 73°19E 242 C5
Gujarat □ India 23°20N 71°0E 242 H4
Gujiang China 27°11N 114°47E 229 D10
Gujranwala Pakistan 32°10N 74°12E 242 C6
Gujrat Pakistan 32°40N 74°2E 242 C6
Gukovo Russia 48°1N 39°58E 191 F5
Gulargambone Australia 31°20S 148°30E 283 A8
Gulbai Pakistan 24°52N 66°58E 123 A1
Gulbarga India 17°20N 76°50E 244 F3
Gulbene Latvia 57°8N 26°52E 188 D4
Gülchö Kyrgyzstan 40°19N 73°26E 217 D8
Guledagudda India 16°3N 75°48E 245 F2
Gülek Turkey 37°12N 34°48E 250 A5
Gulf □ Papua N. G. 8°0S 145°0E 286 D3
Gulf, The = Persian Gulf Asia 27°0N 50°0E 247 E6
Gulf Breeze U.S.A. 30°21N 87°9W 317 E2
Gulf Hammock U.S.A. 29°15N 82°43W 317 F7
Gulf Islands ⌂ U.S.A. 30°10N 87°10W 317 K2
Gulfport Fla., U.S.A. 27°44N 82°42W 317 H7
Gulfport Miss., U.S.A. 30°22N 89°6W 315 F10
Gulgong Australia 32°20S 149°49E 283 B8
Gulin China 28°1N 105°50E 228 C5
Gulistan Pakistan 30°30N 66°35E 242 D2
Guliston Uzbekistan 40°29N 68°46E 217 D7
Gulja = Yining China 43°58N 81°10E 217 D10
Gulkana U.S.A. 62°16N 145°23W 303 E11
Gull Lake Canada 50°10N 108°29W 297 C7
Gullbrå Norway 60°50N 6°17E 164 D3
Gullbrandstorp Sweden 56°42N 12°43E 163 H6
Gullbringusýsla □ Iceland 64°0N 22°0W 155 D4
Gullfoss Iceland 64°20N 20°8W 155 C6
Gullhaug Norway 59°30N 10°15E 164 E7
Gullivan B. U.S.A. 25°45N 81°40W 317 K8
Gullspång Sweden 58°59N 14°6E 163 F8
Gullstein Norway 63°13N 8°9E 164 A5
Güllük Turkey 37°14N 27°35E 205 D9
Güllük Dağı △ Turkey 37°0N 30°30E 205 E12
Güllük Korfezi Turkey 37°12N 27°30E 205 D9
Gulma Nigeria 12°40N 4°23E 263 C5
Gulmarg India 34°3N 74°25E 243 B6
Gülnar Turkey 36°19N 33°24E 250 B4
Gulnare Australia 33°27S 138°27E 282 B3
Gülpınar Turkey 39°32N 26°7E 205 B8
Gülşehir Turkey 38°44N 34°37E 212 C6
Gülshat Kazakhstan 46°38N 74°21E 217 C8
Gulsvik Norway 60°24N 9°38E 164 D6
Gulu Uganda 2°48N 32°17E 268 B3
Gŭlŭbovo Bulgaria 42°8N 25°55E 203 D9
Gulud, J. Sudan 11°41N 29°31E 257 E2
Gulwe Tanzania 6°30S 36°25E 268 D4
Gulyaypole = Hulyaypole Ukraine 47°45N 36°21E 189 J9
Gum Lake Australia 32°42S 143°9E 282 B5
Gumaca Phil. 13°55N 122°6E 232 E4
Gumal → Pakistan 31°40N 71°50E 242 D4
Gumbaz Pakistan 30°2N 69°0E 242 D3
Gumbinnen = Gusev Russia 54°35N 22°10E 184 D9
Gumdag Turkmenistan 39°9N 54°56E 216 E4
Gumel Nigeria 12°39N 9°22E 263 C6
Gumi S. Korea 36°10N 128°12E 224 D4
Gumiel de Hizán Spain 41°46N 3°41W 194 D7
Gumla India 23°3N 84°33E 243 H11
Gumlu Australia 19°53S 147°41E 280 B4
Gumma □ Japan 36°30N 138°20E 223 A10
Gummersbach Germany 51°1N 7°34E 178 D3
Gummi Nigeria 12°4N 5°9E 263 C6
Gümüldür Turkey 38°6N 27°0E 205 C9
Gumuljina = Komotini Greece 41°9N 25°26E 203 E9
Gümüşçay Turkey 40°16N 27°17E 203 F11
Gümüşhacıköy Turkey 40°50N 35°18E 212 B6
Gümüşhane Turkey 40°30N 39°30E 213 B8
Gümüşsu Turkey 38°14N 29°1E 205 C11
Gumzai Indonesia 5°28S 134°42E 231 F8
Gun Hill Tower Barbados 13°8N 59°33W 323 r
Gun Pt. Grenada 12°32N 61°37W 323 q
Guna Amara, Ethiopia 11°43N 38°14E 266 B4
Guna Oromiya, Ethiopia 8°18N 39°52E 257 F4
Guna India 24°40N 77°19E 242 G7
Gunbalanya Australia 12°20S 133°4E 278 B5
Gundabooka △ Australia 30°30S 145°20E 281 E4
Gundagai Australia 35°3S 148°6E 283 C8
Gundarehi India 20°57N 81°17E 244 D5
Gundelfingen Germany 48°34N 10°22E 179 G6
Gundih Indonesia 7°10S 110°56E 235 D4
Gundji Dem. Rep. of the Congo 2°5N 21°27E 264 B4
Gundlakamma → India 15°30N 80°15E 245 G5
Gundlupet India 11°48N 76°41E 245 J3
Gündoğmuş Turkey 36°48N 32°0E 250 B3
Gunebang Australia 33°1S 146°38E 283 B7
Güney Burdur, Turkey 37°29N 29°34E 205 D11
Güney Denizli, Turkey 38°9N 29°4E 205 C11
Güneydoğu Toroslar Turkey 38°20N 40°30E 213 C9
Gungal Australia 32°17S 150°32E 283 B9
Gungo Angola 10°58S 15°30E 265 E2
Güngören Turkey 41°1N 28°52E 122 B1
Gungu Dem. Rep. of the Congo 5°43S 19°20E 265 D3
Gunisao → Canada 53°56N 97°53W 297 C9
Gunisao L. Canada 53°33N 96°15W 297 C9
Gunjur Gambia 13°12N 16°44W 262 C1
Gunjyal Pakistan 32°20N 71°55E 242 C4
Günlüce Turkey 36°50N 28°20E 205 E10
Gunnarskog Sweden 59°49N 12°34E 162 E6
Gunnbjørn Fjeld Greenland 68°55N 29°47W 154 D8
Gunnebo Sweden 57°44N 16°32E 163 G10
Gunnedah Australia 30°59S 150°15E 283 A9
Gunnersbury U.K. 51°29N 0°17W 125 B2
Gunnewin Australia 25°59S 148°33E 281 D4
Gunningbar Cr. → Australia 31°14S 147°6E 283 A7
Gunnison Colo., U.S.A. 38°33N 106°56W 304 G10
Gunnison Utah, U.S.A. 39°9N 111°49W 304 G8
Gunnison → U.S.A. 39°4N 108°35W 304 G9
Gunsan S. Korea 35°59N 126°45E 224 E3
Guntakal India 15°11N 77°27E 245 G3
Gunter Canada 44°52N 77°32W 312 B7
Guntersville U.S.A. 34°21N 86°18W 315 D11
Guntong Malaysia 4°36N 101°3E 237 K3
Guntur India 16°23N 80°30E 245 F5
Gunung Gading Malaysia 2°2N 109°52E 235 B3
Gunung Leuser △ Indonesia 3°39N 97°32E 234 B1
Gunung Mulu △ Malaysia 4°6N 114°53E 235 B4
Gunung Palung △ Indonesia 1°9S 110°13E 235 C4
Gunungapi Indonesia 6°45S 126°30E 231 F7
Gunungsitoli Indonesia 1°15N 97°30E 234 B1
Gunupur India 19°5N 83°50E 244 E6
Günz → Germany 48°27N 10°16E 179 G6
Gunza Angola 10°50S 13°50E 265 E2
Günzburg Germany 48°26N 10°17E 179 G6
Gunzenhausen Germany 49°7N 10°44E 179 F6
Guo He → China 32°59N 117°10E 227 H9
Guomao China 39°54N 116°26E 114 B2
Guoyang China 33°32N 116°12E 226 H9
Gupis Pakistan 36°15N 73°20E 243 A5
Gura Humorului Romania 47°35N 25°53E 183 C10
Gura-Teghii Romania 45°30N 26°25E 183 E11
Gurabo Puerto Rico 18°16N 65°58W 321 b
Gurag Ethiopia 8°20N 38°20E 257 F4
Gurahonţ Romania 46°16N 22°21E 182 D7
Gurbantünggüt Shamo China 45°8N 87°20E 217 C11
Gurdaspur India 32°5N 75°31E 242 C6
Gurdon U.S.A. 33°55N 93°9W 314 E8
Güre Balıkesir, Turkey 39°36N 26°54E 205 B8
Güre Uşak, Turkey 38°39N 29°10E 205 C11
Gurgaon India 28°27N 77°1E 242 E7
Gürgentepe Turkey 40°51N 37°50E 212 B7
Gurghiu, Munţii Romania 46°41N 25°15E 183 D10
Gurgueia → Brazil 6°50S 43°24W 332 C3
Gurha India 25°12N 71°39E 242 G4
Guri, Embalse de Venezuela 7°50N 62°52W 329 B5
Gurimatu Papua N. G. 6°45S 144°45E 286 D3
Gurin Nigeria 9°5N 12°54E 263 D7
Gurinhatã Brazil 19°14S 49°48W 333 E2
Gurjaani Georgia 41°43N 45°52E 191 K7
Gurk → Austria 46°35N 14°31E 180 E7
Gurkfeld = Krško Slovenia 45°57N 15°30E 199 C12
Gurkha Nepal 28°5N 84°40E 243 E11
Gurla Mandhata = Naimona'nyi Feng Nepal 30°26N 81°18E 243 D9
Gurley Australia 29°45S 149°48E 281 D4
Gurnee U.S.A. 42°22N 87°55W 311 B9
Gurnet Point U.S.A. 42°1N 70°34W 313 D14
Guro Mozam. 17°26S 32°30E 269 F3
Gürpınar İstanbul, Turkey 40°59N 28°37E 203 F12
Gürpınar Van, Turkey 38°18N 43°25E 213 C10
Gürsu Turkey 40°13N 29°11E 203 F13
Gurué Mozam. 15°25S 36°58E 269 F4
Gurueragu Ethiopia 6°23N 45°31E 267 C6
Gurun Malaysia 5°49N 100°27E 237 K3
Gürün Turkey 38°43N 37°15E 212 C7
Gurupá Brazil 1°25S 51°35W 329 D7
Gurupá, I. Grande de Brazil 1°25S 51°45W 329 D7
Gurupi Brazil 11°43S 49°4W 333 D2
Gurupi → Brazil 1°13S 46°6W 332 B2
Gurupi, Serra do Brazil 5°0S 47°50W 332 C2
Guruwe Zimbabwe 16°40S 30°42E 271 A5
Gurvan Sayhan Uul Mongolia 43°50N 104°0E 218 B5
Guryev = Atyraū Kazakhstan 47°5N 52°0E 187 E9
Guryevsk Russia 54°47N 20°38E 184 D7
Gus-Khrustalnyy Russia 55°42N 40°44E 190 C5
Gusau Nigeria 12°12N 6°40E 263 C6
Gusev Russia 54°35N 22°10E 184 D9
Gushan China 39°50N 123°35E 224 C1
Gushgy = Serhetabat Turkmenistan 35°20N 62°18E 247 C9
Gushi China 32°11N 115°41E 229 A10
Gushiago Ghana 9°55N 0°15W 263 D4
Gushikami Japan 26°7N 127°44E 288 a
Gushikawa Japan 26°21N 127°52E 288 a
Gusinje Montenegro 42°35N 19°50E 202 D3
Gusinoozersk Russia 51°16N 106°27E 215 D11
Gúspini Italy 39°32N 8°37E 200 C1
Güssing Austria 47°3N 16°20E 181 D9
Gustav Holm, Kap Greenland 66°36N 34°15W 154 D7
Gustavia St.-Martin 17°53N 62°51W 322 a
Gustavo A. Madero Mexico 19°29N 99°8W 128 B2
Gustavsberg Sweden 59°19N 18°23E 162 E12
Gustavus U.S.A. 58°25N 135°44W 296 B1
Gustine U.S.A. 37°16N 121°0W 306 H6
Güstrow Germany 53°47N 12°10E 178 B8
Gusum Sweden 58°16N 16°30E 163 F10
Guta = Kolárovo Slovak Rep. 47°54N 18°0E 181 D10
Gütersloh Germany 51°54N 8°24E 178 D4
Gutha Australia 28°58S 115°55E 279 E2
Guthalungra Australia 19°52S 147°50E 280 B4
Guthrie Ont., Canada 44°28N 79°32W 312 B5
Guthrie Okla., U.S.A. 35°53N 97°25W 314 D6
Guthrie Tex., U.S.A. 33°37N 100°19W 314 E4
Guthrie Center U.S.A. 41°41N 94°30W 310 C2
Gutian China 26°32N 118°43E 229 D12
Gutiérrez Bolivia 19°25S 63°34W 331 D5
Guttenberg Iowa, U.S.A. 42°47N 91°6W 310 B5
Guttenberg New York, U.S.A. 132 a1
Guttentag = Dobrodzień Poland 50°45N 18°25E 185 H5
Guttstadt = Dobre Miasto Poland 53°58N 20°26E 184 E7
Gutu Zimbabwe 19°41S 31°9E 271 A5
Gutulia △ Norway 62°2N 12°11E 164 B9
Gutuyevskiy, Ostrov Russia 59°53N 30°15E 137 B1
Guwahati India 26°10N 91°45E 241 B3
Guy Fawkes River △ Australia 30°0S 152°20E 281 D5
Guy-Fayreau, Complexe Montréal, Canada 130 b2
Guyana ■ S. Amer. 5°0N 59°0W 329 C6
Guyancourt France 48°46N 2°4E 134 B1
Guyane française = French Guiana ⊠ S. Amer. 4°0N 53°0W 329 C7
Guyang China 41°0N 110°5E 226 D6
Guyenne France 44°30N 0°40E 174 D4
Guymon U.S.A. 36°41N 101°29W 314 C4
Guyotville = Aïn Benian Algeria 36°48N 2°55E 261 A5
Guyra Australia 30°15S 151°40E 281 E5
Guyton U.S.A. 32°20N 81°24W 316 C8
Guyuan Hebei, China 41°37N 115°40E 226 D8
Guyuan Ningxia Huizu, China 36°0N 106°20E 226 F4
Guzar Uzbekistan 38°36N 66°15E 217 E7
Güzelbağ Turkey 36°44N 31°53E 250 B2
Güzelbahçe Turkey 38°21N 26°54E 205 C8
Güzeloluk Turkey 36°47N 34°4E 250 B5
Güzelsu Turkey 36°53N 31°51E 250 B2
Güzelyurt = Morphou Cyprus 35°12N 32°59E 207 E8
Guzhang China 28°42N 109°58E 228 C7
Guzhen China 33°22N 117°18E 227 H9
Guzmán, L. de Mexico 31°20N 107°30W 318 A3
Gvardeysk Russia 54°39N 21°5E 184 D8
Gvardeyskoye Ukraine 45°7N 34°1E 189 K8
Gvarv Norway 59°23N 9°9E 164 E6
Gwa Burma 17°36N 94°34E 241 G5
Gwaai Zimbabwe 19°15S 27°45E 269 F2
Gwaai → Zimbabwe 17°59S 26°52E 269 F2
Gwabegar Australia 30°37S 148°59E 283 A8
Gwadabawa Nigeria 13°28N 5°15E 263 C6
Gwādar Pakistan 25°10N 62°18E 240 D1
Gwagwada Nigeria 10°15N 7°15E 263 C6
Gwaii Haanas △ Canada 52°21N 131°26W 296 C2
Gwalior India 26°12N 78°10E 242 F8
Gwanak S. Korea 37°29N 126°57E 137 C1
Gwanaksan S. Korea 37°27N 126°58E 137 C1
Gwanara Nigeria 8°55N 3°9E 263 D5
Gwanda Zimbabwe 20°55S 29°0E 269 G2
Gwandu Nigeria 12°30N 4°41E 263 C5
Gwane Dem. Rep. of the Congo 4°45N 25°48E 268 B2
Gwang-yang S. Korea 34°58N 127°35E 224 E3
Gwangju S. Korea 35°9N 126°54E 224 E3
Gwangju □ S. Korea 35°10N 126°45E 224 E3
Gwanju = Gwangju S. Korea 35°9N 126°54E 224 E3
Gwaram Nigeria 10°15N 10°25E 263 C7
Gwarzo Nigeria 12°20N 8°55E 263 C6
Gwasero Nigeria 9°29N 3°30E 263 D5
Gwda → Poland 53°3N 16°44E 185 E3
Gweebarra B. Ireland 54°51N 8°23W 166 B3
Gweedore Ireland 55°3N 8°13W 166 A3
Gweru Zimbabwe 19°28S 29°45E 269 F2
Gwi Nigeria 9°0N 7°10E 263 D6
Gwinn U.S.A. 46°19N 87°27W 308 B10
Gwio Kura Nigeria 12°40N 11°2E 263 C7
Gwoza Nigeria 11°5N 13°40E 263 C7
Gwydir → Australia 29°27S 149°48E 281 D4
Gwynedd □ U.K. 52°52N 4°10W 168 E3
Gyál Hungary 47°23N 19°13E 117 B3
Gyáli-patak → Hungary 47°23N 19°7E 117 B2
Gyandzha = Gäncä Azerbaijan 40°45N 46°20E 191 K8
Gyaring Hu China 34°50N 97°40E 218 C4
Gydanskiy Poluostrov Russia 70°0N 78°0E 214 C8
Gyeonggi-do □ S. Korea 36°37N 127°15E 224 D3
Gyeongju S. Korea 35°51N 129°14E 224 E4
Gyeongsan S. Korea 35°49N 128°44E 224 E4
Gyeongsangbuk-do □ S. Korea 36°20N 128°45E 224 D4
Gyeongsangnam-do □ S. Korea 35°15N 128°15E 224 E4
Gyeryongsan △ S. Korea 36°20N 127°15E 224 D3
Gyl Norway 62°57N 8°7E 164 B5
Gyldenløve Fjord Greenland 64°15N 40°30W 154 E6
Gympie Australia 26°11S 152°38E 281 D5
Gyobingauk Burma 18°13N 95°39E 241 F5
Gyōda Japan 36°10N 139°30E 223 A11
Gyodongdo S. Korea 37°47N 126°15E 224 D3
Gyomaendrőd Hungary 46°56N 20°50E 182 D5
Gyöngyös Hungary 47°48N 19°56E 182 C4
Győr Hungary 47°41N 17°40E 182 C2
Győr-Moson-Sopron □ Hungary 47°40N 17°20E 182 C2
Gypsum Pt. Canada 61°53N 114°35W 296 A6
Gypsumville Canada 51°45N 98°40W 297 C9
Gyueshevo Bulgaria 42°14N 22°28E 202 D6
Gyula Hungary 46°38N 21°17E 182 D6
Gyumri Armenia 40°47N 43°50E 191 K6
Gyzylarbat = Serdar Turkmenistan 39°4N 56°23E 247 B8
Gyzyletrek = Etrek Turkmenistan 37°36N 54°46E 247 B7
Gzhatsk = Gagarin Russia 55°38N 35°0E 188 E8
Gzira Malta 35°54N 14°29E 206 F7

H

H. Neely Henry L. U.S.A. 33°55N 86°2W 316 B3
Ha 'Arava → Israel 30°50N 35°20E 251 H6
Ha Coi Vietnam 21°26N 107°46E 228 G6
Ha Dong Vietnam 20°58N 105°46E 228 G5
Ha Giang Vietnam 22°50N 104°59E 228 F5
Ha Karmel △ Israel 32°45N 35°5E 250 F6
Ha Long, Vinh Vietnam 20°56N 107°3E 236 B6
Ha Tien Vietnam 10°23N 104°29E 237 G5
Ha Tinh Vietnam 18°20N 105°54E 236 C5
Ha Trung Vietnam 19°58N 105°50E 236 C5
Haaga Finland 60°13N 24°53E 121 B2
Haakon VII Topp Norway 71°0N 8°20W 154 C10
Haaksbergen Neths. 52°9N 6°45E 170 B6
Ha'ano Tonga 19°41S 174°18W 287 P13
Ha'apai Group Tonga 19°47S 174°27W 287 P13
Haapiti Moorea 17°34S 149°52W 289 e
Haapsalu Estonia 58°56N 23°30E 188 C2
Haar Germany 48°6N 11°43E 131 B3
Haarby Denmark 55°13N 10°7E 163 J4
Haarlem Neths. 52°23N 4°39E 170 B4
Haas-Lilienthal House San Francisco, U.S.A. 136 b1
Haast N.Z. 43°51S 169°1E 285 D4
Haast → N.Z. 43°50S 169°2E 285 D4
Haast Pass N.Z. 44°6S 169°21E 285 E4
Haasts Bluff Australia 23°22S 132°0E 278 D5
Haasts Bluff ☼ Australia 23°39S 130°34E 278 D5
Hab → Pakistan 24°53N 66°41E 242 G3
Hab Nadi Chauki Pakistan 25°0N 66°50E 242 G2
Habahe China 48°3N 86°23E 217 C11
Ḩabarūt Yemen 17°18N 52°44E 249 C6
Habaswein Kenya 1°2N 39°30E 268 B4
Ḩabawnah, W. → Si. Arabia 17°57N 44°58E 248 C4
Habay Alta., Canada 58°50N 118°44W 296 B5
Habay Manila, Phil. 14°27N 120°56E 127 C1
Ḩabbān Yemen 14°21N 47°5E 248 D4
Ḩabbānīyah Iraq 33°17N 43°29E 213 F10
Ḩabbānīyah, Hawr al Iraq 33°17N 43°29E 213 F10
Habelschwerdt = Bystrzyca Kłodzka Poland 50°19N 16°39E 185 H3
Habibas, Îles Algeria 35°44N 1°8W 197 K3
Habichtswald ⌂ Germany 51°15N 9°15E 178 D5
Habiganj Bangla. 24°24N 91°30E 241 C3
Habisa Sudan 15°38N 31°18E 266 A3
Habo Sweden 57°55N 14°6E 163 G8
Haboro Japan 44°22N 141°42E 220 B10
Ḩabshān U.A.E. 23°50N 53°37E 247 F7
Hachenburg Germany 50°40N 7°49E 178 E3
Hachi India 27°48N 94°2E 241 B5
Hachijō-Jima Japan 33°5N 139°45E 223 D11
Hachiman Japan 35°45N 136°57E 223 B8
Hachinohe Japan 40°30N 141°29E 220 D10
Hachiōji Japan 35°40N 139°20E 223 B11
Hacı Zeynalabdin Azerbaijan 40°37N 49°33E 213 B13
Hacıbektaş Turkey 38°56N 34°33E 212 C6
Hacılar Turkey 38°38N 35°26E 212 C6
Hack, Mt. Australia 30°45S 138°55E 282 A3
Hackås Sweden 62°56N 14°30E 162 B8
Hackbridge U.K. 51°23N 0°9W 125 B3
Hackensack U.S.A. 40°52N 74°4W 132 A1
Hackensack → U.S.A. 40°42N 74°7W 132 B1
Hackettstown U.S.A. 40°51N 74°50W 313 F10
Hackney □ U.K. 51°33N 0°3W 125 A3
Hackney Wick U.K. 51°32N 0°1W 125 A3
Haco Angola 10°15S 15°44E 265 E3
Hadali Pakistan 32°16N 72°11E 242 C5
Hadano Japan 35°22N 139°14E 223 B11
Hadarba, Ras Sudan 22°4N 36°51E 256 C4
Hadarom □ Israel 31°0N 35°0E 251 H6
Ḩaḑbaram Oman 17°27N 55°15E 249 C6
Ḩadd, Ra's al Oman 22°35N 59°50E 249 B7
Ḩaddā Si. Arabia 21°27N 39°34E 248 B2
Haddington U.K. 55°57N 2°47W 167 F6
Haddock U.S.A. 33°2N 83°26W 316 B6
Haddummati Atoll Maldives 2°0N 73°30E 272 d
Hadejia Nigeria 12°30N 10°5E 263 C7
Hadejia → Nigeria 12°50N 10°51E 263 C7
Hadera Israel 32°27N 34°55E 251 F5
Hadersleben = Haderslev Denmark 55°15N 9°30E 163 J3
Haderslev Denmark 55°15N 9°30E 163 J3
Hadgaon India 19°30N 77°40E 244 E3
Hadhramaut = Ḩaḑramawt Yemen 15°30N 49°30E 249 D5
Hadīboh Yemen 12°39N 54°2E 249 D6
Hadilik China 37°56N 86°6E 217 E11
Hadım Turkey 36°58N 32°26E 250 B3
Hadithah Si. Arabia 31°27N 37°9E 251 G8
Hadjadj, O. el → Algeria 28°18N 5°20E 261 C6
Hadjeb el Aïoun Tunisia 35°21N 9°32E 258 A1
Hadjer Kamaran Chad 12°41N 21°46E 259 F4
Hadjer-Lamis □ Chad 12°55N 16°0E 259 F3
Hadjer Mornou Chad 17°12N 23°8E 259 E4
Hadlaskar Norway 60°15N 7°9E 164 D4
Hadley B. Canada 72°31N 108°12W 294 C10
Hadong S. Korea 35°5N 127°44E 224 E3
Hadr, Warrâq el Egypt 30°5N 31°12E 117 A2
Ḩaḑramawt Yemen 15°30N 49°30E 249 D5
Ḩaḑramawt, W. → Yemen 15°10N 51°8E 249 D5
Ḩadrānīyah Iraq 35°38N 43°14E 246 C4
Hadrian's Wall U.K. 55°0N 2°30W 168 B5
Hadsten Denmark 56°19N 10°3E 163 H4
Hadsund Denmark 56°44N 10°8E 163 H4
Hadyach Ukraine 50°21N 34°0E 189 G8
Hae, Ko Thailand 7°44N 98°22E 237 a
Hægeland Norway 58°22N 7°45E 164 F4
Haeju N. Korea 38°3N 125°45E 224 C2
Haeju-man N. Korea 37°54N 125°45E 224 D2
Hä'ena U.S.A. 22°14N 159°34W 302 A2
Haenam S. Korea 34°34N 126°35E 224 E3
Haenertsburg S. Africa 24°0S 29°50E 271 B4
Haerhpin = Harbin China 45°48N 126°40E 227 B14
Hafar al Bāţin Si. Arabia 28°32N 45°52E 246 D5
Hafik Turkey 39°51N 37°23E 212 C7
Ḩafīrat al 'Aydā Si. Arabia 26°26N 39°12E 246 E3
Ḩafit Oman 23°59N 55°49E 247 F7
Hafizabad Pakistan 32°5N 73°40E 242 C5
Haflong India 25°10N 93°5E 241 C4
Hafnarfjörður Iceland 64°4N 21°57W 155 C5
Hafnir Iceland 63°56N 22°41W 155 D4
Hafslo Norway 61°19N 7°10E 164 C4
Haft Gel Iran 31°30N 49°32E 247 D6
Haga Sweden 59°21N 18°1E 139 A2
Hagalil Israel 32°53N 35°18E 250 F6
Hagari → India 15°40N 77°0E 245 G3
Hagby Sweden 56°34N 16°11E 163 H10
Hagemeister I. U.S.A. 58°39N 160°54W 303 G7
Hagen Germany 51°21N 7°27E 178 D3
Hagenbrunn Austria 48°19N 16°27E 142 A2
Hagenow Germany 53°26N 11°12E 178 B7
Hagere Hiywet Ethiopia 8°59N 37°51E 266 C4
Hagerman U.S.A. 33°7N 104°20W 305 K11
Hagerman Fossil Beds ⌂ U.S.A. 42°48N 114°57W 304 E6
Hägersten Sweden 59°18N 17°59E 139 B1
Hagerstown Ind., U.S.A. 39°55N 85°10W 311 E11
Hagerstown Md., U.S.A. 39°39N 77°43W 309 F15
Hagersville Canada 42°58N 80°3W 312 D4
Hagetmau France 43°39N 0°37W 174 E3
Hagfors Sweden 60°3N 13°45E 162 D7
Häggvik Sweden 59°26N 17°56E 139 A1
Hagi Iceland 65°28N 23°25W 155 B3
Hagi Japan 34°30N 131°22E 222 C3
Hagolan Syria 33°0N 35°45E 250 F6
Hagondange France 49°16N 6°11E 173 C13
Hágöngulón Iceland 64°35N 18°8W 155 C8
Hagonoy Bulacan, Phil. 14°50N 120°44E 232 D3
Hagonoy Manila, Phil. 14°31N 121°3E 127 B2
Hags Hd. Ireland 52°57N 9°28W 166 D2
Hague, C. de la France 49°44N 1°56W 172 C5
Hague, The = 's-Gravenhage Neths. 52°7N 4°17E 170 B4
Hague Park Canada 43°45N 79°14W 141 A3
Haguenau France 48°49N 7°47E 173 D14
Hagunía W. Sahara 27°26N 12°24W 260 C2
Hahira U.S.A. 30°59N 83°22W 316 E6
Hai Duong Vietnam 20°56N 106°19E 228 G6
Hai'an Guangdong, China 20°18N 110°11E 229 G8
Hai'an Jiangsu, China 32°37N 120°27E 229 A13
Haian Shanmo Taiwan 23°25N 121°25E 225 C3
Haicheng Fujian, China 24°23N 117°48E 229 E11
Haicheng Liaoning, China 40°50N 122°45E 224 B1
Haidar Khel Afghan. 33°58N 68°38E 242 C3
Haidarâbâd = Hyderabad India 17°22N 78°29E 244 F4
Haidargarh India 26°37N 81°22E 243 F9
Haidari Greece 38°2N 23°38E 112 A1
Haidarpur India 28°43N 77°8E 120 A1
Haidhausen Germany 48°7N 11°36E 131 B2
Haidian China 39°59N 116°16E 114 B1
Haifa = Hefa Israel 32°46N 35°0E 250 F6
Haifeng China 22°58N 115°10E 229 F10
Haiger Germany 50°43N 8°12E 178 E4
Haight-Ashbury U.S.A. 37°46N 122°26W 136 B2
Haikou China 20°1N 110°16E 236 B8
Haiku-Pauwela U.S.A. 20°56N 156°19W 302 C5
Ḩā'il □ Si. Arabia 26°40N 41°40E 246 E4
Hailakandi India 24°42N 92°34E 241 C4
Hailar China 49°10N 119°38E 219 B6
Hailey U.S.A. 43°31N 114°19W 304 E6
Haileybury Canada 47°30N 79°38W 298 C4
Hailin China 44°37N 129°30E 227 B15
Hailing Dao China 21°35N 111°47E 229 G8
Hailuoto Finland 65°3N 24°45E 160 D21
Haimen Guangdong, China 23°15N 116°38E 229 F11
Haimen Jiangsu, China 31°52N 121°10E 229 B13
Hainan □ China 19°0N 109°30E 236 C7
Hainan Dao China 19°0N 109°30E 236 C7
Hainan Str. = Qiongzhou Haixia China 20°10N 110°15E 236 B8

Hainault *U.K.* 51°36N 0°6E **125** A4
Hainaut □ *Belgium* 50°30N 4°0E **170** D4
Hainburg *Austria* 48°9N 16°56E **181** C9
Haines *Alaska, U.S.A.* 59°14N 135°26W **296** B1
Haines *Oreg., U.S.A.* 44°55N 117°56W **304** D5
Haines City *U.S.A.* 28°7N 81°38W **317** G8
Haines Junction *Canada* 60°45N 137°30W **296** A1
Hainfeld *Austria* 48°3N 15°48E **180** C8
Haining *China* 30°28N 120°40E **229** B13
Haiphong *Vietnam* 20°47N 106°41E **228** G6
Haitan Dao *China* 25°30N 119°45E **229** E12
Haiti ■ *W. Indies* 19°0N 72°30W **321** C5
Haiya *Sudan* 18°20N 36°21E **256** D4
Haiyan *Qinghai, China* 36°53N 100°59E **218** C5
Haiyan *Zhejiang, China* 30°28N 120°58E **229** B13
Haiyang *China* 36°47N 121°9E **227** F11
Haiyang Dao *China* 39°2N 123°10E **224** C1
Haiyuan *Guangxi Zhuangzu, China* 22°8N 107°35E **228** F6
Haiyuan *Ningxia Huizu, China* 36°35N 105°52E **226** F3
Haizhou *Guangdong, China* 23°5N 113°18E **121** B2
Haizhou *Jiangsu, China* 34°37N 119°7E **227** G10
Haizhou Wan *China* 34°50N 119°20E **227** G10
Haizhu Guangchang *China* 23°6N 113°14E **121** B2
Haj Ali Qoli, Kavīr *Iran* 35°55N 54°50E **247** C7
Hajar Bangar *Sudan* 10°40N 22°45E **259** F4
Hajdú-Bihar □ *Hungary* 47°30N 21°30E **182** C6
Hajdúböszörmény *Hungary* 47°40N 21°30E **182** C6
Hajdúdorog *Hungary* 47°48N 21°30E **182** C6
Hajdúhadház *Hungary* 47°40N 21°40E **182** C6
Hajdúnánás *Hungary* 47°50N 21°26E **182** C6
Hajdúsámson *Hungary* 47°37N 21°42E **182** C6
Hajdúszoboszló *Hungary* 47°27N 21°22E **182** C6
Haji Ibrahim *Iraq* 36°40N 44°30E **213** D11
Hajīābād *Iran* 33°37N 60°0E **247** C9
Hajiganj *Bangla.* 23°15N 90°50E **241** D3
Hajipur *India* 25°45N 85°13E **243** G11
Ḥajjah *Yemen* 15°42N 43°36E **248** D3
Ḥājjīābād *Iran* 28°19N 55°55E **247** D7
Ḥājjīābād-e Zarrīn *Iran* 33°9N 54°51E **247** C7
Hajnówka *Poland* 52°47N 23°35E **185** F10
Hajodo *S. Korea* 34°17N 126°3E **224** E3
Ḥajrah *Si. Arabia* 20°14N 41°3E **248** B3
Haka *Burma* 22°39N 93°37E **241** D4
Hakansson, Mts. *Dem. Rep. of the Congo* 8°40S 25°45E **265** D5
Hakataramea *N.Z.* 44°43S 170°30E **285** E5
Hakkâri *Turkey* 37°34N 43°44E **213** D10
Hakkâri □ *Turkey* 37°30N 44°0E **213** D10
Hakkâri Dağları *Turkey* 38°2N 42°58E **213** C10
Hakken-Zan *Japan* 34°10N 135°54E **223** C7
Hakodate *Japan* 41°45N 140°44E **220** D10
Hakos *Namibia* 23°13S 16°21E **270** B2
Hakota *Japan* 36°5N 140°30E **223** A12
Håksberg *Sweden* 60°11N 15°12E **162** D9
Hakskeenpan *S. Africa* 26°48S 20°13E **270** C3
Haku-San *Japan* 36°9N 136°46E **223** A8
Haku-San △ *Japan* 36°15N 136°45E **223** A8
Hakuba *Japan* 36°42N 137°51E **223** A9
Hakui *Japan* 36°53N 136°47E **221** F8
Hakun *Burma* 26°46N 95°42E **241** B5
Hakunila *Finland* 60°16N 25°6E **121** B3
Hakupu *Cook Is.* 19°6S 169°50W **289** g
Hala *Pakistan* 25°43N 68°20E **240** D3
Ḥalab *Syria* 36°10N 37°15E **250** B8
Ḥalab □ *Syria* 36°10N 37°10E **250** B8
Ḥalaban *Si. Arabia* 23°29N 44°23E **248** B4
Ḥalabjah *Iraq* 35°10N 45°58E **213** E11
Halaib *Sudan* 22°12N 36°30E **256** C4
Halaib Triangle *Africa* 22°30N 35°20E **256** C4
Halandri *Greece* 38°3N 23°48E **112** A2
Halangingie Pt. *Cook Is.* 19°2S 169°58W **289** g
Halasa *Sudan* 14°26N 30°39E **257** E3
Halásztelek *Hungary* 47°22N 19°0E **117** B1
Hālat 'Ammār *Si. Arabia* 29°10N 36°4E **246** D3
Hālawa, C. *U.S.A.* 21°10N 156°43W **302** B5
Hālawa Heights *U.S.A.* 21°23N 157°55W **302** K14
Halbā *Lebanon* 34°34N 36°6E **250** D7
Halberstadt *Germany* 51°54N 11°3E **178** D7
Halcombe *N.Z.* 40°8S 175°30E **284** G4
Halcon *Phil.* 13°0N 121°30E **231** B6
Halcon, Mt. *Phil.* 13°16N 121°0E **232** E3
Halde Fjäll = Haltiatunturi *Finland* 69°17N 21°18E **160** B19
Halden *Norway* 59°9N 11°23E **164** E8
Haldensleben *Germany* 52°17N 11°24E **178** C7
Haldia *Bangla.* 22°1N 88°3E **243** H13
Haldwani *India* 29°31N 79°30E **243** E8
Hale *U.S.A.* 39°36N 93°20W **310** E3
Hale → *Australia* 24°56S 135°53E **280** C2
Haleakalä △ *U.S.A.* 20°40N 156°15W **302** C5
Hale'iwa *U.S.A.* 21°36N 158°6W **302** J13
Halesowen *U.K.* 52°27N 2°3W **169** E5
Halesworth *U.K.* 52°20N 1°31E **169** E9
Haleyville *U.S.A.* 34°14N 87°37W **315** D11
Half Assini *Ghana* 5°1N 2°50W **262** D4
Half Dome *U.S.A.* 37°44N 119°32E **306** H7
Halfa al Jadidah *Sudan* 15°20N 35°35E **266** A4
Halfeti *Turkey* 37°15N 37°52E **212** D7
Halfmoon Bay *N.Z.* 46°50S 168°5E **285** G3
Halfway → *Canada* 56°12N 121°32W **296** B4
Halfway Tree *Jamaica* 18°0N 76°48W **320** a
Halia *India* 24°50N 82°19E **243** G10
Haliburton *Canada* 45°3N 78°30W **312** A6
Haliç *Turkey* 41°1N 28°57E **122** B1
Halifax *Queens., Australia* 18°32S 146°22E **280** B4
Halifax *N.S., Canada* 44°38N 63°35W **299** D7
Halifax *W. Yorks., U.K.* 53°43N 1°52W **168** D6
Halifax *Pa., U.S.A.* 40°25N 76°55W **312** F8
Halifax B. *Australia* 18°50S 147°0E **280** B4
Halifax Harbour *Grenada* 12°6N 61°45W **323** q
Halifax I. *Namibia* 26°38S 15°4E **270** C2
Halik Shan *China* 42°20N 81°22E **217** D10
Halīl → *Iran* 27°40N 58°30E **247** E8
Halim Perdana Kusuma Int. ✈ **(HLP)** *Indonesia* 6°16S 106°53E **122** B2
Halkett, C. *U.S.A.* 70°48N 152°11W **303** A9
Halki *Greece* 36°17N 27°35E **205** E9
Halkida *Greece* 38°27N 23°42E **204** C5
Halkidiki □ *Greece* 40°25N 23°20E **202** F7
Halkirk *U.K.* 58°30N 3°29W **167** C5
Hall Beach *Canada* 68°46N 81°12W **295** D15
Hall I. *U.S.A.* 60°40N 173°6W **303** F4
Hall in Tirol *Austria* 47°17N 11°30E **180** D4
Hall Pen. *Canada* 63°30N 66°0W **295** E18
Hall Pt. *Australia* 15°40S 124°23E **278** C3
Hallabro *Sweden* 56°22N 15°5E **163** H9
Halland *Sweden* 57°8N 12°47E **161** H15
Hallandale Beach *U.S.A.* 25°58N 80°9W **317** K9
Hallands län □ *Sweden* 57°0N 12°40E **163** H6
Hallands Väderö *Sweden* 56°27N 12°34E **163** H6
Hallandsås *Sweden* 56°22N 13°0E **163** H7
Hallāniyat, Ghubbat al *Oman* 17°40N 55°45E **249** C6
Hallāniyat, Jazā'ir al *Oman* 17°30N 55°58E **249** C6
Hallasan *S. Korea* 33°22N 126°32E **224** a
Hallasan △ *S. Korea* 33°20N 126°30E **224** a
Hällbybrunn *Sweden* 59°24N 16°25E **162** E10
Halle *Belgium* 50°44N 4°13E **116** B1
Halle *Nordrhein-Westfalen, Germany* 52°3N 8°22E **178** C4
Halle *Sachsen-Anhalt, Germany* 51°30N 11°56E **178** D7
Hällefors *Sweden* 59°47N 14°31E **162** E8
Hälleforsnäs *Sweden* 59°10N 16°30E **162** E10
Hallein *Austria* 47°40N 13°5E **180** D6
Hällekis *Sweden* 58°38N 13°27E **163** F7
Hallen *Sweden* 63°11N 14°4E **162** A8
Hallett *Australia* 33°25S 138°55E **282** B3
Hallettsville *U.S.A.* 29°27N 96°57W **314** G6
Halley *Antarctica* 75°35S 26°39W **151** D1
Hallia → *India* 16°55N 79°20E **244** F4
Hallim *S. Korea* 33°24N 126°15E **224** a
Hallingby *Norway* 60°7N 10°10E **164** D7
Hallingdal *Norway* 60°40N 9°8E **164** D6
Hallingdalselva → *Norway* 60°23N 9°35E **164** D6
Hallingskarvet *Norway* 60°36N 7°47E **164** D4
Hallingskarvet △ *Norway* 60°37N 7°45E **164** D4
Hallingskeid *Norway* 60°40N 7°17E **164** D4
Hallock *U.S.A.* 48°47N 96°57W **308** A5
Hallormsstaður *Iceland* 65°6N 14°45W **155** B12
Halls Creek *Australia* 18°16S 127°38E **278** C4
Halls Gap *Australia* 37°8S 142°34E **281** F3
Halls Lake *Canada* 45°7N 78°45W **312** A6
Hallsberg *Sweden* 59°5N 15°7E **162** E9
Hallstahammar *Sweden* 59°38N 16°15E **162** E10
Hallstatt *Austria* 47°33N 13°38E **180** D6
Hallstavik *Sweden* 60°5N 18°37E **162** D12
Hallstead *U.S.A.* 41°58N 75°45W **313** E9
Hallyeo △ *S. Korea* 34°45N 128°25E **224** E4
Halmahera *Indonesia* 0°40N 128°0E **231** D7
Halmeu *Romania* 47°57N 23°2E **182** C8
Halmstad *Sweden* 56°41N 12°52E **163** H6
Halq el Oued *Tunisia* 36°53N 10°18E **258** A2
Hals *Denmark* 57°0N 10°18E **163** H4
Halsa *Norway* 63°3N 8°14E **164** A5
Halsafjorden *Norway* 63°5N 8°10E **164** A5
Hälsingborg = Helsingborg *Sweden* 56°3N 12°42E **163** H6
Hälsingland *Sweden* 61°40N 16°5E **162** C10
Halstead *U.K.* 51°57N 0°40E **169** F8
Haltdalen *Norway* 62°56N 11°8E **164** B8
Haltern *Germany* 51°44N 7°11E **178** D3
Haltiala *Finland* 60°16N 24°57E **121** B2
Haltiatunturi *Finland* 69°17N 21°18E **160** B19
Haltiavuori *Finland* 60°16N 24°56E **121** B2
Halton □ *U.K.* 53°22N 2°45W **168** D5
Haltwhistle *U.K.* 54°58N 2°26W **168** C5
Ḥālūl *Qatar* 25°40N 52°40E **247** E7
Halvad *India* 23°1N 71°11E **242** H4
Ḥalvān *Iran* 33°57N 56°15E **247** C8
Halve Dag, Pt. *Neth. Ant.* 12°14N 69°7W **322** g
Ham *Chad* 10°1N 15°35E **259** F3
Ham *Somme, France* 49°45N 3°4E **173** C10
Ham *London, U.K.* 51°25N 0°18W **125** B2
Ham Tan *Vietnam* 10°40N 107°45E **237** G6
Ham Yen *Vietnam* 22°4N 105°3E **236** A5
Hamab *Namibia* 28°7S 19°16E **270** C2
Hamad *Sudan* 15°20N 33°32E **257** D3
Hamada *Japan* 34°56N 132°4E **222** C4
Hamadān *Iran* 34°52N 48°32E **213** E13
Hamadān □ *Iran* 35°0N 49°0E **247** C6
Hamadia *Algeria* 35°28N 1°57E **261** A5
Ḥamāh *Syria* 35°5N 36°40E **250** C7
Ḥamāh □ *Syria* 35°10N 37°0E **250** C8
Hamakita *Japan* 34°45N 137°47E **223** C9
Hamamatsu *Japan* 34°45N 137°45E **223** C9
Haman *S. Korea* 35°14N 128°28E **224** E4
Hamar *Norway* 60°48N 11°7E **164** D8
Hamâta, Gebel *Egypt* 24°17N 35°0E **246** E2
Hambantota *Sri Lanka* 6°10N 81°10E **245** L5
Hamber ⌓ *Canada* 52°20N 118°0W **296** C5
Hamburg *Hamburg, Germany* 53°33N 9°59E **178** B5
Hamburg *Ark., U.S.A.* 33°14N 91°48W **314** E9
Hamburg *N.Y., U.S.A.* 42°43N 78°50W **312** D6
Hamburg *Pa., U.S.A.* 40°33N 75°59W **313** F9
Hamburg □ *Germany* 53°30N 10°0E **178** B5
Hamburg Fuhlsbüttel ✈ **(HAM)** *Germany* 53°35N 9°59E **178** B5
Ḥamḍ, W. al → *Si. Arabia* 24°55N 36°20E **246** E3
Ḥamḍah *Si. Arabia* 19°2N 43°36E **248** C3
Ḥamdānah *Si. Arabia* 19°59N 40°34E **248** C3
Hamden *U.S.A.* 41°23N 72°54W **313** E12
Hamdibey *Turkey* 39°50N 27°15E **205** B9
Häme *Finland* 61°38N 25°10E **188** B2
Hämeenkylä *Finland* 60°16N 24°48E **121** B1
Hämeenlinna *Finland* 61°0N 24°28E **188** B3
Hamélé *Ghana* 10°56N 2°45W **262** C4
Hamelin Pool *Australia* 26°22S 114°20E **279** E1
Hameln *Germany* 52°6N 9°21E **178** C5
Hamerkaz □ *Israel* 32°15N 34°55E **251** F5
Hamero Hadad *Ethiopia* 7°27N 42°14E **267** C5
Hamersley Ra. *Australia* 22°0S 117°45E **278** D2
Hamgyŏng-sanmaek *N. Korea* 41°35N 129°15E **224** B4
Hamgyŏngbuk-do □ *N. Korea* 41°50N 129°25E **224** B4
Hamgyŏngnam-do □ *N. Korea* 40°0N 127°30E **224** C3
Hamhŭng *N. Korea* 39°54N 127°30E **224** C3
Hamhŭng-man *N. Korea* 39°48N 127°37E **224** C3
Hami *China* 42°55N 93°25E **218** B4
Hamili *Greece* 35°50N 26°15E **205** F8
Hamilton = Churchill → *Canada* 53°19N 60°10W **299** B7
Hamilton *Vic., Australia* 37°45S 142°2E **282** D5
Hamilton *Bermuda* 32°17N 64°47W **153** a
Hamilton *Ont., Canada* 43°15N 79°50W **312** C5
Hamilton *N.Z.* 37°47S 175°19E **284** D4
Hamilton *S. Lanarks., U.K.* 55°46N 4°2W **167** F4
Hamilton *Ala., U.S.A.* 34°9N 87°59W **315** D11
Hamilton *Alaska, U.S.A.* 62°54N 163°53W **303** E7
Hamilton *Ga., U.S.A.* 32°45N 84°53W **316** C5
Hamilton *Ill., U.S.A.* 40°24N 91°21W **310** D5
Hamilton *Ind., U.S.A.* 41°33N 84°56W **311** C12
Hamilton *Mo., U.S.A.* 39°45N 94°0W **310** E2
Hamilton *Mont., U.S.A.* 46°15N 114°10W **304** C6
Hamilton *N.Y., U.S.A.* 42°50N 75°33W **313** D9
Hamilton *Ohio, U.S.A.* 39°24N 84°34W **311** E12
Hamilton *Tex., U.S.A.* 31°42N 98°7W **314** F5
Hamilton → *Queens., Australia* 23°30S 139°47E **280** C2
Hamilton → *S. Austral., Australia* 26°40S 135°19E **281** D2
Hamilton City *U.S.A.* 39°45N 122°1W **306** F4
Hamilton I. *Australia* 20°21S 148°56E **280** b
Hamilton Inlet *Canada* 54°0N 57°30W **299** B8
Hamilton Mt. *U.S.A.* 43°25N 74°22W **313** C10
Hamina *Finland* 60°34N 27°12E **188** B4
Hamirpur *H.P., India* 31°41N 76°31E **242** D7
Hamirpur *Ut. P., India* 25°57N 80°9E **243** G9
Hamitabat *Turkey* 41°43N 27°12E **203** E11
Hamju *N. Korea* 39°51N 127°26E **224** C3
Hamlet *U.S.A.* 34°53N 79°42W **315** D15
Hamley Bridge *Australia* 34°17S 138°35E **282** C3
Hamlin = Hameln *Germany* 52°6N 9°21E **178** C5
Hamlin *N.Y., U.S.A.* 43°17N 77°55W **312** C7
Hamlin *Tex., U.S.A.* 32°53N 100°8W **314** E4
Hamm *Germany* 51°40N 7°50E **178** D3
Hammām al Alī *Iraq* 36°9N 43°15E **213** D10
Hammam Bouhadjar *Algeria* 35°23N 0°58W **261** A4
Hammamet *Tunisia* 36°24N 10°38E **258** A2
Hammamet, G. de *Tunisia* 36°10N 10°48E **258** A2
Ḥammār, Hawr al *Iraq* 30°50N 47°10E **246** D5
Hammarby *Sweden* 59°17N 18°5E **139** B2
Hammarstrand *Sweden* 63°7N 16°20E **162** A10
Hamme *Belgium* 50°55N 4°17E **116** A1
Hammelburg *Germany* 50°6N 9°53E **179** E5
Hammeren *Denmark* 55°18N 14°47E **163** J8
Hammerfest *Norway* 70°39N 23°41E **160** A20
Hammersmith *U.K.* 51°29N 0°14W **125** B2
Hammerstein = Czarne *Poland* 53°42N 16°58E **184** E3
Hammerum *Denmark* 56°8N 9°3E **163** H3
Hamminkeln *Germany* 51°43N 6°35E **178** D2
Hammond *Ind., U.S.A.* 41°38N 87°30W **311** C9
Hammond *La., U.S.A.* 30°30N 90°28W **315** F9
Hammond *N.Y., U.S.A.* 44°27N 75°42W **313** B9
Hammondsport *U.S.A.* 42°25N 77°13W **312** D7
Hammonton *U.S.A.* 39°39N 74°48W **309** F16
Hamneda *Sweden* 56°41N 13°51E **163** H7
Hamoyet, Jebel *Sudan* 17°33N 38°2E **256** D4
Hampden *N.Z.* 45°18S 170°50E **285** F5
Hampshire □ *U.K.* 51°7N 1°23W **169** F6
Hampshire Downs *U.K.* 51°15N 1°10W **169** F6
Hampstead *Qué., Canada* 45°28N 73°37W **130** B2
Hampstead *Dominica* 15°36N 61°23W **323** k
Hampstead *London, U.K.* 51°33N 0°10W **125** A2
Hampstead Garden Suburb *U.K.* 51°34N 0°11W **125** A2
Hampstead Heath *U.K.* 51°33N 0°10W **125** A2
Hampton *N.B., Canada* 45°32N 65°51W **299** C6
Hampton *Ont., Canada* 43°58N 78°45W **312** C6
Hampton *London, U.K.* 51°24N 0°21W **125** B1
Hampton *Ark., U.S.A.* 33°32N 92°28W **314** E8
Hampton *Ga., U.S.A.* 33°23N 84°17W **316** B5
Hampton *Iowa, U.S.A.* 42°45N 93°13W **310** B3
Hampton *N.H., U.S.A.* 42°57N 70°50W **313** D14
Hampton *S.C., U.S.A.* 32°52N 81°7W **316** C8
Hampton *Va., U.S.A.* 37°2N 76°21W **309** G15
Hampton Bays *U.S.A.* 40°53N 72°30W **313** F12
Hampton Court Palace *U.K.* 51°24N 0°20W **125** B1
Hampton Springs *U.S.A.* 30°5N 83°40W **316** E6
Hampton Tableland *Australia* 32°0S 127°0E **279** F4
Hampton Wick *U.K.* 51°24N 0°18W **125** B2
Hampyeong *S. Korea* 35°3N 126°31E **224** E3
Hampyeongman *S. Korea* 35°6N 126°23E **224** E3
Hamrā' *Baghdād, Iraq* 33°18N 44°18E **113** B1
Hamra *Gävleborg, Sweden* 61°39N 14°59E **162** C8
Hamra → *Chad* 12°52N 21°15E **259** F4
Ḥamrā, Al Ḥamādah al *Libya* 29°30N 12°57E **258** C2
Hamrat esh Sheykh *Sudan* 14°38N 27°55E **257** E2
Ḥamrīn, Jabal *Iraq* 34°30N 44°30E **213** E11
Hamrun *Malta* 35°53N 14°29E **206** F8
Hamtik *Phil.* 10°42N 121°59E **233** F3
Hamur *Turkey* 39°37N 43°3E **213** C10
Hamyang *S. Korea* 35°32N 127°42E **224** E3
Hamzalar *Turkey* 37°7N 32°33E **250** A3
Han i Hotit *Albania* 42°19N 19°27E **202** D3
Han Jiang → *China* 23°25N 116°40E **229** F11
Han Shui → *China* 30°34N 114°17E **229** B10
Hāna *U.S.A.* 20°45N 155°59W **302** C6
Hanahan *U.S.A.* 32°55N 80°0W **316** C10
Hanak *Si. Arabia* 25°32N 37°0E **246** E3
Hanak *Turkey* 41°14N 42°50E **213** B10
Hanala *Finland* 60°20N 25°4E **121** A3
Hanalei *U.S.A.* 22°12N 159°30W **302** A2
Hanamaki *Japan* 39°23N 141°7E **220** E10
Hanamaulu *U.S.A.* 21°59N 159°22W **302** B2
Hanang *Tanzania* 4°30S 35°25E **268** C4
Hanapēpē *U.S.A.* 21°55N 159°35W **302** B2
Hanare Iwa *Iwo Jima* 24°48N 141°21E **288** b
Hanau *Germany* 50°7N 8°56E **179** E4
Hanauma B. *U.S.A.* 21°15N 157°40W **302** K14
Hanbogd = Ihbulag *Mongolia* 43°11N 107°10E **226** C4
Hançalar *Turkey* 38°8N 29°24E **205** C11
Hânceşti *Moldova* 46°50N 28°36E **183** D13
Hancheng *China* 35°31N 110°25E **226** G6
Hanchuan *China* 30°40N 113°50E **229** B9
Hanchung = Hanzhong *China* 33°10N 107°1E **226** H4
Hancock *Mich., U.S.A.* 47°8N 88°35W **308** B9
Hancock *N.Y., U.S.A.* 41°57N 75°17W **313** E9
Hancock *Vt., U.S.A.* 43°55N 72°50W **313** C12
Handa *Japan* 34°53N 136°55E **223** C8
Handa I. *U.K.* 58°23N 5°11W **167** C3
Handan *China* 36°35N 114°28E **226** F8
Handeni *Tanzania* 5°25S 38°2E **268** D4
Handlová *Slovak Rep.* 48°45N 18°35E **181** C11
Handub *Sudan* 19°15N 37°16E **256** D4
Handwara *India* 34°21N 74°20E **243** B6
Haneda *Japan* 35°32N 139°44E **140** B3
Haneda, Tōkyō ✈ **(HND)** *Japan* 35°33N 139°46E **140** B3
Hanegev *Israel* 30°50N 35°0E **251** H6
Hanford *U.S.A.* 36°20N 119°39W **306** J7
Hanford Reach ⌓ *U.S.A.* 46°40N 119°30W **304** C4
Hang Chat *Thailand* 18°20N 99°21E **236** C2
Hang Dong *Thailand* 18°41N 98°55E **236** C2
Hang Hau *China* 22°19N 114°16E **122** B2
Hanga Roa *Chile* 27°8S 109°26W **330** b
Hangang → *S. Korea* 37°50N 126°30E **227** F14
Hangayn Nuruu *Mongolia* 47°30N 99°0E **218** B4
Hangchou = Hangzhou *China* 30°18N 120°11E **229** B13
Hanggin Houqi *China* 40°58N 107°4E **226** D4
Hanggin Qi *China* 39°52N 108°50E **226** E5
Hanging Gardens *Mumbai, India* **130** b1
Hangkow = Wuhan *China* 30°31N 114°18E **229** B10
Hangku = Hangu *China* 39°18N 117°53E **227** E9
Hangu *China* 39°18N 117°53E **227** E9
Hangzhou *China* 30°18N 120°11E **229** B13
Hangzhou Wan *China* 30°15N 120°45E **229** B13
Hanh *Mongolia* 51°32N 100°35E **218** A5
Hanhöhiy Uul *Mongolia* 49°30N 94°30E **217** C12
Hanhongor *Mongolia* 43°55N 104°28E **226** C3
Hani *Turkey* 38°24N 40°23E **213** C9
Hania = Chania *Greece* 35°30N 24°4E **207** E5
Ḥanīdh *Si. Arabia* 26°35N 48°38E **247** E6
Ḥanīsh *Yemen* 13°45N 42°46E **248** D3
Haniska *Slovak Rep.* 48°37N 21°15E **181** C14
Hanjiang *China* 25°26N 119°6E **229** E12
Hankinson *U.S.A.* 46°4N 96°54W **308** B5
Hankö *Finland* 59°50N 22°57E **188** C2
Hankou *China* 30°35N 114°30E **229** B10
Hanksville *U.S.A.* 38°22N 110°43W **304** G8
Hanle *India* 32°42N 79°4E **243** C8
Hanmer Springs *N.Z.* 42°32S 172°50E **285** C7
Hann → *Australia* 17°26S 126°17E **278** C4
Hann, Mt. *Australia* 15°45S 126°0E **278** C4
Hanna *Alta., Canada* 51°40N 111°54W **296** C6
Hanna *Wyo., U.S.A.* 41°52N 106°34W **304** F10
Hannah B. *Canada* 51°40N 80°0W **298** B4
Hannibal *Mo., U.S.A.* 39°42N 91°22W **310** E5
Hannibal *N.Y., U.S.A.* 43°19N 76°35W **313** C8
Hannik *Sudan* 18°12N 32°20E **256** D3
Hannover *Germany* 52°22N 9°46E **178** C5
Hanö *Sweden* 56°1N 14°50E **163** H8
Hanöbukten *Sweden* 55°35N 14°30E **163** J8
Hanoi *Vietnam* 21°5N 105°55E **228** G5
Hanover = Hannover *Germany* 52°22N 9°46E **178** C5
Hanover *Ont., Canada* 44°9N 81°2W **312** B3
Hanover *Northern Cape, S. Africa* 31°4S 24°29E **270** D3
Hanover *Ind., U.S.A.* 38°43N 85°28W **311** F11
Hanover *N.H., U.S.A.* 43°42N 72°17W **313** C12
Hanover *Ohio, U.S.A.* 40°4N 82°16W **312** F2
Hanover *Pa., U.S.A.* 39°48N 76°59W **309** F15
Hanover, I. *Chile* 51°0S 74°50W **336** D2
Hanpan, C. *Papua N. G.* 5°0S 154°35E **286** C8
Hans Lollik I. *U.S. Virgin Is.* 18°24N 64°53W **321** b
Hans Meyer Ra. *Papua N. G.* 4°20S 152°55E **286** C7
Hansdiha *India* 24°36N 87°5E **243** G12
Hanshou *China* 28°56N 111°50E **229** C8
Hansi *H.P., India* 32°27N 77°50E **242** C7
Hansi *Haryana, India* 29°10N 75°57E **242** E6
Hanson, L. *Australia* 31°0S 136°15E **282** A2
Hanstholm *Denmark* 57°7N 8°36E **163** G2
Hantan = Handan *China* 36°35N 114°28E **226** F8
Hantsavichy *Belarus* 52°49N 26°30E **177** B14
Hanumangarh *India* 29°35N 74°19E **242** E6
Hanwell *U.K.* 51°30N 0°20W **125** A1
Hanworth *U.K.* 51°26N 0°23W **125** B1
Hanyin *China* 32°54N 108°28E **228** A7
Hanyū *Japan* 36°10N 139°32E **223** A11
Hanyuan *China* 29°21N 102°40E **228** C4
Hanzhong *China* 33°10N 107°1E **226** H4
Hanzhuang *China* 34°33N 117°23E **227** G9
Hao *French Polynesia* 18°15S 140°54W **289** f
Haora *India* 22°34N 88°18E **124** B1
Haouach, O. → *Chad* 16°45N 19°35E **259** E4
Haoxue *China* 30°3N 112°24E **229** B9
Haparanda *Sweden* 65°52N 24°8E **160** D21
Hapdeok *S. Korea* 36°48N 126°46E **224** D3
Hapeville *U.S.A.* 33°39N 84°24W **113** C2
Happy *U.S.A.* 34°45N 101°52W **314** D4
Happy Camp *U.S.A.* 41°48N 123°23W **304** F2
Happy Valley *China* 22°16N 114°10E **122** B2
Happy Valley-Goose Bay *Canada* 53°15N 60°20W **299** B7
Hapsu *N. Korea* 41°13N 128°51E **224** B4
Hapur *India* 28°45N 77°45E **242** E7
Ḥaql *Si. Arabia* 29°10N 34°58E **251** J5
Haquira *Peru* 14°14S 72°12W **330** C3
Har *Indonesia* 5°16S 133°14E **231** F8
Har Adar *West Bank* 31°49N 35°8E **123** B1
Har-Ayrag *Mongolia* 45°47N 109°16E **226** B5
Har Gilo *West Bank* 31°43N 35°10E **123** B2
Har Homa *West Bank* 31°44N 35°12E **123** B2
Har Hu *China* 38°20N 97°38E **218** C4
Har Nof *Israel* 31°47N 35°11E **123** B2
Har Tsiyon *Jerusalem* **123** b3
Har Us Nuur *Mongolia* 48°0N 92°0E **217** C12
Har Yehuda *Israel* 31°35N 34°57E **251** G5
Ḥaraḍ *Si. Arabia* 24°22N 49°0E **249** A5
Ḥaraḍ *Yemen* 16°26N 43°5E **248** C3
Haradok *Belarus* 55°30N 30°3E **188** E6
Häradsbäck *Sweden* 56°32N 14°26E **163** H8
Harahan *U.S.A.* 29°56N 90°12W **131** B1
Haraiki *French Polynesia* 17°38S 143°27W **289** f
Haramosh *Pakistan* 35°50N 74°54E **243** B6
Haranomachi *Japan* 37°38N 140°58E **220** F10
Harare *Zimbabwe* 17°43S 31°2E **269** F3
Ḥarāsīs, Jiddat al *Oman* 19°30N 56°0E **249** C7
Harat *Eritrea* 16°5N 39°26E **257** D4
Haraz-Djombo *Chad* 14°20N 19°12E **259** F3
Harazé *Chad* 9°57N 20°48E **259** G4
Harbel *Liberia* 6°16N 10°20W **262** D2
Harbhanga *India* 20°38N 84°36E **244** D7
Harbin *China* 45°48N 126°40E **227** B14
Harbiye *Turkey* 36°10N 36°8E **250** B7
Harbo *Sweden* 60°7N 17°12E **162** D11
Harboøre *Denmark* 56°38N 8°10E **163** H2
Harbor Beach *U.S.A.* 43°51N 82°39W **312** C2
Harborcreek *U.S.A.* 42°9N 79°57W **312** D5
Harbour Breton *Canada* 47°29N 55°50W **299** C8
Harbour Deep *Canada* 50°25N 56°32W **299** B8
Harbour View *Jamaica* 17°59N 76°50W **320** a
Harburg *Germany* 53°27N 9°58E **178** B5
Harburger Berge ⌓ *Germany* 53°26N 9°51E **178** B5
Harda *India* 22°27N 77°5E **242** H7
Hardangerfjorden *Norway* 60°5N 6°0E **164** D3
Hardangerjøkulen *Norway* 60°30N 7°27E **164** D4
Hardangervidda *Norway* 60°7N 7°20E **164** D4
Hardangervidda △ *Norway* 60°10N 7°25E **164** D4
Hardap ⌓ *Namibia* 24°29S 17°45E **270** B2
Hardap Dam *Namibia* 24°32S 17°50E **270** B2
Hardeeville *U.S.A.* 32°17N 81°5W **316** C8
Harden *Australia* 34°32S 148°24E **283** C8
Hardenberg *Neths.* 52°34N 6°37E **170** B6
Harderwijk *Neths.* 52°21N 5°38E **170** B5
Hardey → *Australia* 22°45S 116°8E **278** D2
Hardin *Ill., U.S.A.* 39°10N 90°37W **310** E6
Hardin *Mont., U.S.A.* 45°44N 107°37W **304** D10
Harding *S. Africa* 30°35S 29°55E **271** D4
Harding, L. *U.S.A.* 32°40N 85°5W **316** C4
Harding Ra. *Australia* 16°17S 124°55E **278** C3
Hardinsburg *U.S.A.* 37°47N 86°28W **311** G10
Hardisty *Canada* 52°40N 111°18W **296** C6
Hardoi *India* 27°26N 80°6E **243** F9
Hardwar = Haridwar *India* 29°58N 78°9E **242** E8
Hardwick *Ga., U.S.A.* 33°4N 83°14W **316** B6
Hardwick *Vt., U.S.A.* 44°30N 72°22W **313** B12
Hardwicke B. *Australia* 34°55S 137°20E **282** C2
Hardwood Lake *Canada* 45°12N 77°26W **312** A7
Hardy, Pen. *Chile* 55°30S 68°20W **336** E3
Hardy, Pte. *St. Lucia* 14°6N 60°56W **323** m
Hare B. *Canada* 51°15N 55°45W **299** B8
Hareid *Norway* 62°22N 6°1E **164** B3
Haren *Brussels, Belgium* 50°53N 4°25E **116** A2
Haren *Niedersachsen, Germany* 52°47N 7°13E **178** C3
Harer *Ethiopia* 9°20N 42°8E **257** F5
Harerge *Ethiopia* 7°12N 42°0E **257** F5
Hareskovby *Denmark* 55°45N 12°23E **118** A2
Harestua *Norway* 60°11N 10°44E **164** D7
Hareto *Ethiopia* 9°23N 37°6E **257** F4
Harfleur *France* 49°30N 0°10E **172** C7
Hargeisa *Somali Rep.* 9°30N 44°2E **267** C5
Hargeisa □ *Somali Rep.* 10°2N 44°2E **267** B5
Harghita □ *Romania* 46°30N 25°30E **183** D10
Harghita, Munţii *Romania* 46°25N 25°35E **183** D10
Hargshamn *Sweden* 60°12N 18°30E **162** D12
Hari → *Indonesia* 1°16S 104°5E **234** C2
Haría *Canary Is.* 29°8N 13°32W **153** e2
Ḥarīb *Yemen* 14°56N 45°30E **248** D4
Haricha, Hamada el *Mali* 22°40N 3°15W **260** D4
Haridwar *India* 29°58N 78°9E **242** E8
Harihar *India* 14°32N 75°44E **245** G2
Harihari *N.Z.* 43°9S 170°33E **285** D5
Hārim *Syria* 36°14N 36°29E **250** B7
Harim, Jabal al *Oman* 25°58N 56°14E **247** E8
Harima-Nada *Japan* 34°30N 134°35E **222** C6
Haringey □ *U.K.* 51°34N 0°5W **125** A3
Haringhata → *Bangla.* 22°0N 89°58E **241** E2
Haripad *India* 9°14N 76°28E **245** K3
Harīr, W. al → *Syria* 32°44N 35°59E **250** F6
Harīrūd → *Asia* 37°24N 60°38E **240** A1
Härjedalen *Sweden* 62°22N 13°5E **162** B7
Harjusuo *Finland* 60°19N 25°0E **121** B3
Harlaching *Germany* 48°5N 11°33E **131** B2
Harlan *Iowa, U.S.A.* 41°39N 95°19W **308** E6
Harlan *Ky., U.S.A.* 36°51N 83°19W **309** G12
Hârlău *Romania* 47°23N 26°55E **183** C12
Harlaw Res. *U.K.* 55°52N 3°18W **121** B2
Harlech *U.K.* 52°52N 4°6W **168** E3
Harlem *Ga., U.S.A.* 33°25N 82°19W **316** B7
Harlem *Mont., U.S.A.* 48°32N 108°47W **304** B9
Harlem *New York, U.S.A.* **132** a3
Harlesden *U.K.* 51°32N 0°14W **125** A2
Hårlev *Denmark* 55°21N 12°14E **163** J6
Harleyville *U.S.A.* 33°13N 80°27W **316** B9
Harlingen *Neths.* 53°11N 5°25E **170** A5
Harlingen *Tex., U.S.A.* 26°12N 97°42W **314** H6
Harlington *U.K.* 51°29N 0°25W **125** B1
Harlow *U.K.* 51°46N 0°8E **169** F8
Harlowton *U.S.A.* 46°26N 109°50W **304** C9
Harmaja *Finland* 60°6N 24°58E **121** C2
Harmancık *Turkey* 39°41N 29°9E **205** B11
Harmånger *Sweden* 61°55N 17°20E **162** C11
Harmashatar hegy *Hungary* 47°33N 19°0E **117** A2
Harmil *Eritrea* 16°30N 40°10E **257** D5
Harnai *India* 17°48N 73°6E **244** F1
Harnai *Pakistan* 30°6N 67°56E **242** D2
Harney, L. *U.S.A.* 28°45N 81°3W **317** G8
Harney Basin *U.S.A.* 43°0N 119°30W **304** E4
Harney L. *U.S.A.* 43°14N 119°8W **304** E4
Harney Peak *U.S.A.* 43°52N 103°32W **308** D2
Härnön *Sweden* 62°36N 18°0E **162** B12
Härnösand *Sweden* 62°38N 17°55E **162** B11
Haro *Spain* 42°35N 2°55W **196** C2
Harold *U.S.A.* 30°40N 86°53W **317** E3
Harold Pond *Bahamas* 25°2N 77°22W **153** b
Harolds Cross *Ireland* 53°19N 6°16W **120** B2
Haroldswick *U.K.* 60°48N 0°50W **167** A8
Háros *Hungary* 47°23N 19°2E **117** B2
Harp L. *Canada* 55°5N 61°50W **299** A7
Harpanahalli *India* 14°47N 76°2E **245** G3
Harper = Costa Mesa *U.S.A.* 33°38N 117°55W **307** M9
Harper *Liberia* 4°25N 7°43W **262** E3
Harper, Mt. *U.S.A.* 64°14N 143°51W **303** D12
Harperrig Res. *U.K.* 55°50N 3°26W **121** B1
Harplinge *Sweden* 56°45N 12°45E **163** H6
Harrai *India* 22°37N 79°13E **243** H8
Harrand *Pakistan* 29°28N 70°3E **242** E4
Ḥarrat Khaybar *Si. Arabia* 25°30N 39°45E **256** B5
Ḥarrat Nawāṣīf *Si. Arabia* 21°20N 42°10E **256** C5
Harricana → *Canada* 50°56N 79°32W **298** B4
Harriman *U.S.A.* 35°56N 84°33W **315** D12
Harrington *Australia* 31°52S 152°42E **283** A10
Harrington Harbour *Canada* 50°31N 59°30W **299** B8
Harrington Sd. *Bermuda* 32°20N 64°44W **153** a
Harris *Montserrat* 16°44N 62°11W **323** p
Harris *W. Isles, U.K.* 57°50N 6°55W **167** D2
Harris, L. *S. Austral., Australia* 31°10S 135°10E **281** E2
Harris, L. *Fla., U.S.A.* 28°47N 81°49W **317** G8
Harris, Sd. of *U.K.* 57°44N 7°6W **167** D1
Harris Mts. *N.Z.* 44°49S 168°49E **285** E3
Harris Pt. *Canada* 43°6N 82°9W **312** C2
Harrisburg *Ill., U.S.A.* 37°44N 88°32W **311** G8
Harrisburg *Nebr., U.S.A.* 41°33N 103°44W **308** E2
Harrisburg *Pa., U.S.A.* 40°16N 76°53W **312** F8
Harrismith *S. Africa* 28°15S 29°8E **271** C4
Harrison *Ark., U.S.A.* 36°14N 93°7W **314** C8
Harrison *Maine, U.S.A.* 44°7N 70°39W **313** B14
Harrison *Nebr., U.S.A.* 42°41N 103°53W **308** D2
Harrison, C. *Canada* 54°55N 57°55W **299** B8
Harrison Bay *U.S.A.* 70°40N 151°0W **303** A10
Harrison L. *Canada* 49°33N 121°50W **296** D4
Harrisonburg *U.S.A.* 38°27N 78°52W **309** F14
Harrison's Cave *Barbados* 13°11N 59°34W **323** f
Harrisonville *U.S.A.* 38°39N 94°21W **310** F2
Harriston *Canada* 43°57N 80°53W **312** C4
Harrisville *Mich., U.S.A.* 44°39N 83°17W **312** B1
Harrisville *N.Y., U.S.A.* 44°9N 75°19W **313** B9
Harrisville *Pa., U.S.A.* 41°8N 80°0W **312** E5
Harrodsburg *Ind., U.S.A.* 39°1N 86°33W **311** E10
Harrodsburg *Ky., U.S.A.* 37°46N 84°51W **311** G11
Harrogate *U.K.* 54°0N 1°33W **168** C6
Harrow *Vic., Australia* 37°9S 141°35E **282** D4
Harrow *Ont., Canada* 42°2N 82°55W **312** D2
Harrow □ *U.K.* 51°35N 0°21W **125** A1
Harrow on the Hill *U.K.* 51°34N 0°20W **125** A1
Harrow School *U.K.* 51°34N 0°20W **125** A1
Harrow Weald *U.K.* 51°36N 0°20W **125** A1
Harrowsmith *Canada* 44°24N 76°40W **313** B8
Harry S. Truman Res. *U.S.A.* 38°16N 93°24W **310** F3
Harsefeld *Germany* 53°27N 9°30E **178** B5
Harsewinkel *Germany* 51°56N 8°14E **178** D4
Harsīn *Iran* 34°18N 47°33E **213** E12
Hârşova *Romania* 44°40N 27°59E **183** F12
Harstad *Norway* 68°48N 16°30E **160** B17
Harsud *India* 22°6N 76°44E **242** H7
Hart *U.S.A.* 43°42N 86°22W **308** D10
Hart, L. *Australia* 31°10S 136°25E **282** A2
Hartbees → *S. Africa* 28°45S 20°32E **270** C3
Hartberg *Austria* 47°17N 15°58E **180** D8
Hårteigen *Norway* 60°11N 7°3E **164** D4
Hartford *Ala., U.S.A.* 31°6N 85°42W **316** D4
Hartford *Conn., U.S.A.* 41°46N 72°41W **313** E12
Hartford *Ky., U.S.A.* 37°27N 86°55W **308** G10
Hartford *Mich., U.S.A.* 42°13N 86°10W **311** B10
Hartford *S. Dak., U.S.A.* 43°38N 96°57W **308** D5
Hartford *Vt., U.S.A.* 43°40N 72°20W **313** C12
Hartford *Wis., U.S.A.* 43°19N 88°22W **308** D9
Hartford City *U.S.A.* 40°27N 85°22W **311** D11
Hartingsburg = Bela Bela *S. Africa* 24°51S 28°19E **271** B4
Hartland *N.B., Canada* 46°20N 67°32W **299** C6
Hartland *Wis., U.S.A.* 43°6N 88°21W **311** A8
Hartland Pt. *U.K.* 51°1N 4°32W **169** F3
Hartlepool *U.K.* 54°42N 1°13W **168** C6
Hartlepool □ *U.K.* 54°42N 1°17W **168** C6
Hartley Bay *Canada* 53°25N 129°15W **296** C3
Hartmannberge *Namibia* 17°0S 13°0E **270** A1
Hartney *Canada* 49°30N 100°35W **297** D8
Hârtop *Moldova* 46°39N 28°40E **183** D13
Harts → *S. Africa* 28°24S 24°17E **270** C3
Harts Range *Australia* 23°6S 134°55E **280** C1
Hartselle *U.S.A.* 34°27N 86°56W **315** D11
Hartsfield-Atlanta Int. ✈ **(ATL)** *U.S.A.* 33°38N 84°26W **113** C2
Hartshorne *U.S.A.* 34°51N 95°34W **314** D7
Hartstown *U.S.A.* 41°33N 80°23W **312** E4
Hartsville *U.S.A.* 34°23N 80°4W **315** D14
Hartswater *S. Africa* 27°34S 24°43E **270** C3
Hartwell *U.S.A.* 34°21N 82°56W **315** D13
Harumi *Tokyo, Japan* **140** c5
Harunabad *Pakistan* 29°35N 73°8E **242** E5
Harur *India* 12°3N 78°29E **245** H4
Harūt → *Afghan.* 31°29N 61°24E **240** C1
Harvand *Iran* 28°25N 55°43E **247** D7
Harvard *U.S.A.* 42°25N 88°37W **311** B8
Harvard Univ. *U.S.A.* 42°22N 71°7W **116** A2
Harvey *W. Austral., Australia* 33°5S 115°54E **279** F2
Harvey *Ill., U.S.A.* 41°36N 87°50W **311** C9
Harvey *La., U.S.A.* 29°54N 90°4W **131** B2
Harvey *N. Dak., U.S.A.* 47°47N 99°56W **308** B4
Harwich *U.K.* 51°56N 1°17E **169** F9
Harwood Heights *U.S.A.* 41°57N 87°46W **119** B2
Haryana □ *India* 29°0N 76°10E **242** E7
Haryn → *Belarus* 52°7N 27°17E **177** B14
Harz *Germany* 51°38N 10°44E **178** D6
Harz △ *Germany* 51°40N 10°18E **178** D6
Harzgerode *Germany* 51°38N 11°8E **178** D7
Hasa *Si. Arabia* 25°50N 49°0E **247** E6
Ḥasā, W. al → *Jordan* 31°4N 35°29E **251** D4
Hasaheisa *Sudan* 14°44N 33°20E **257** E3
Ḥasanābād *Esfahan, Iran* 32°8N 52°44E **247** C7
Ḥasanābād *Tehrān, Iran* 35°44N 51°16E **141** A1
Hasankeyf *Turkey* 37°42N 41°24E **213** D9
Hasanparti *India* 18°4N 79°32E **244** E4
Hasawinah, Jabal al *Libya* 28°15N 14°0E **261** C7
Ḥasb, W. → *Iraq* 31°45N 44°17E **246** D5
Hasbrouck Heights *U.S.A.* 40°51N 74°6W **132** A1
Hasdo → *India* 21°44N 82°44E **243** J10
Haselhorst *Germany* 52°33N 13°14E **115** A2
Haselünne *Germany* 52°40N 7°29E **178** C3
Hashima *Japan* 35°20N 136°40E **223** B8
Hashimoto *Japan* 34°19N 135°37E **223** C7
Hashtjerd *Iran* 35°52N 50°40E **247** C6
Hashtpur = Tālesh *Iran* 37°58N 48°58E **213** D13
Hashtrud *Iran* 37°28N 47°4E **213** D12
Hasi Nueifed *W. Sahara* 24°54N 14°49W **260** D2
Hāsik *Oman* 17°22N 55°17E **249** C6
Haskell *U.S.A.* 33°10N 99°44W **314** E5
Haskovo = Khaskovo *Bulgaria* 41°56N 25°30E **203** E9
Hasköy *Edirne, Turkey* 41°38N 26°52E **203** E10
Hasköy *İstanbul, Turkey* 41°2N 28°57E **122** B1
Haslach *Germany* 48°16N 8°5E **179** G4
Hasle *Denmark* 55°11N 14°44E **163** J8
Hasle *Oslo, Norway* 59°46N 10°38E **133** B2
Haslemere *U.K.* 51°5N 0°43W **169** F7
Haslev *Denmark* 55°18N 11°57E **163** J5
Haslum *Norway* 59°55N 10°34E **133** A2
Hasparren *France* 43°24N 1°18W **174** E2
Hassa *Turkey* 36°48N 36°29E **250** B7
Hassan *India* 13°0N 76°5E **245** H3
Hassberge ⌓ *Germany* 50°8N 10°45E **179** E6
Hassela *Sweden* 62°7N 16°42E **162** B10
Hasselt *Belgium* 50°56N 5°21E **170** D5
Hassfurt *Germany* 50°2N 10°30E **179** E6
Hassi bel Guebbour *Algeria* 28°30N 6°41E **261** C6
Hassi bou Khelala *Algeria* 30°17N 0°18W **261** B4
Hassi Bourarchet *Algeria* 27°26N 9°19E **261** C6
Hassi Djafou *Algeria* 30°55N 3°35E **261** B5
Hassi el Hadjar *Algeria* 31°28N 4°45E **261** B5
Hassi Imoulaye *Algeria* 29°54N 9°10E **261** C6
Hassi Inifeg *Algeria* 28°15N 1°30W **261** C4
Hassi Inifel *Algeria* 29°50N 3°41E **261** C5
Hassi Mana *Algeria* 28°48N 2°37W **261** C4
Hassi Marroket *Algeria* 30°10N 3°0E **261** B5
Hassi Mengoub *Algeria* 29°49N 5°26W **260** C3
Hassi Messaoud *Algeria* 31°51N 6°1E **261** B6
Hassi Sougoued *Algeria* 26°50N 9°28E **261** C6
Hassi Tartrat *Algeria* 30°5N 6°28E **261** B6
Hassi Zerzour *Morocco* 30°51N 3°56W **260** B4
Hassi Zguilma *Algeria* 30°19N 6°10W **260** B4
Hässleholm *Sweden* 56°10N 13°46E **163** H7
Hassloch *Germany* 49°22N 8°16E **179** F4
Hästhagen *Sweden* 59°18N 18°9E **139** B2
Hästholmen *Sweden* 58°17N 14°38E **163** F8
Hastings *Vic., Australia* 38°18S 145°12E **283** E6
Hastings *Barbados* 13°4N 59°36W **323** r
Hastings *N.Z.* 39°39S 176°52E **284** F5
Hastings *E. Sussex, U.K.* 50°51N 0°35E **169** G8
Hastings *Fla., U.S.A.* 29°43N 81°31W **316** F8
Hastings *Mich., U.S.A.* 42°39N 85°17W **311** B11
Hastings *Minn., U.S.A.* 44°44N 92°51W **308** C7
Hastings *Nebr., U.S.A.* 40°35N 98°23W **308** E4
Hastings Ra. *Australia* 31°15S 152°14E **283** A10
Hästveda *Sweden* 56°17N 13°55E **163** H7
Hat *Ukraine* 48°19N 22°38E **182** B7
Hat Head △ *Australia* 31°3S 153°1E **283** A10
Hat Yai *Thailand* 7°1N 100°27E **237** J3
Hataitai *N.Z.* 41°18S 174°48E **143** B1
Hatanbulag = Ergel *Mongolia* 43°8N 109°5E **226** C5
Hatay *Turkey* 36°14N 36°10E **250** B7
Hatay □ *Turkey* 36°25N 36°15E **250** B7
Hatch *U.S.A.* 32°40N 107°9W **305** K10
Hatch End *U.K.* 51°36N 0°22W **125** A1
Hatchet L. *Canada* 58°36N 103°40W **297** B8
Haţeg *Romania* 45°36N 22°55E **182** E7
Hateruma-Shima *Japan* 24°3N 123°47E **221** M1
Hatfield *Australia* 33°54S 143°49E **282** B5
Hatgal *Mongolia* 50°26N 100°9E **218** A5
Hathras *India* 27°36N 78°6E **242** F8
Hatia *Bangla.* 22°30N 91°5E **241** D3
Hatia Is. *Bangla.* 22°30N 91°0E **241** D3
Hatiara *India* 22°36N 88°26E **124** B2
Ḥāṭibah, Ra's *Si. Arabia* 21°55N 38°57E **256** C4
Hatid *India* 17°17N 75°3E **244** F2
Hatillo *Puerto Rico* 18°29N 66°50W **321** b
Hato *Bonaire, Neth. Ant.* 12°11N 68°17W **322** h
Hato *Curaçao, Neth. Ant.* 12°11N 68°57W **322** g
Hato Caves *Neth. Ant.* 12°11N 68°57W **322** g
Hato Corozal *Colombia* 6°11N 71°45W **328** B3
Hato Mayor *Dom. Rep.* 18°46N 69°15W **321** C6
Hatsukaichi *Japan* 34°22N 132°22E **222** C4
Hatta *India* 24°7N 79°36E **243** G8
Hatta *U.A.E.* 24°45N 56°4E **247** E8
Hattah *Australia* 34°48S 142°17E **282** C5
Hattah Kulkyne △ *Australia* 34°16S 142°33E **282** C5
Hatteras, C. *U.S.A.* 35°14N 75°32W **315** D17
Hatteras Abyssal Plain *Atl. Oc.* 28°0N 72°0W **152** D4
Hattiesburg *U.S.A.* 31°20N 89°17W **315** F10
Hatutu *French Polynesia* 7°56S 140°38W **289** f
Hatvan *Hungary* 47°40N 19°45E **182** C4
Hau Duc *Vietnam* 15°20N 108°13E **236** E7
Haubstadt *U.S.A.* 38°12N 87°34W **311** F9
Haud *Ethiopia* 8°0N 45°0E **267** C6
Hauganes *Iceland* 65°56N 18°27W **155** B8
Haugastøl *Norway* 60°30N 7°50E **164** D4
Hauge *Norway* 58°20N 6°10E **164** F3
Haugesund *Norway* 59°23N 5°13E **164** E2
Hauhui *Solomon Is.* 9°10S 160°59E **287** M11
Hauhungaroa Ra. *N.Z.* 38°42S 175°40E **284** E4
Haukeligrend *Norway* 59°44N 7°33E **164** E4
Hauketo *Norway* 59°50N 10°48E **133** A3
Haukipudas *Finland* 65°12N 25°20E **160** D21
Haultain → *Canada* 55°51N 106°46W **297** B7
Haungpa *Burma* 25°29N 96°7E **241** C6
Hauraha *Solomon Is.* 10°46S 161°59E **287** N11
Hauraki G. *N.Z.* 36°35S 175°5E **284** C4
Hauroko L. *N.Z.* 45°59S 167°21E **285** F2
Hausruck *Austria* 48°6N 13°30E **180** C6
Haut Atlas *Morocco* 32°30N 5°0W **260** B4
Haut de la Montagne *Guadeloupe* 16°26N 61°28W **322** e
Haut-Jura ⌓ *France* 46°23N 6°23E **173** F9
Haut-Languedoc ⌓ *France* 43°30N 2°43E **174** E6
Haut-Niger ⌓ *Guinea* 10°20N 10°20W **262** C2
Haut-Rhin □ *France* 48°0N 7°15E **173** E14
Haut-Zaïre = Orientale □ *Dem. Rep. of the Congo* 2°20N 26°0E **268** B2

Haute-Corse □ France 42°30N 9°30E 175 F13
Haute-Garonne □ France 43°30N 1°30E 174 E5
Haute-Loire □ France 45°5N 3°50E 174 C7
Haute-Marne □ France 48°10N 5°20E 173 D12
Haute-Normandie □
France 49°20N 1°0E 172 C7
Haute-Saône □ France 47°45N 6°10E 173 E13
Haute-Savoie □ France 46°0N 6°20E 175 C10
Haute-Vienne □ France 45°50N 1°10E 174 C5
Hautes-Alpes □ France 44°40N 6°30E 175 D10
Hautes-Pyrénées □ France 43°0N 0°10E 174 F4
Hauteville-Lompnès
France 45°58N 5°36E 175 C9
Hautmont France 50°15N 3°55E 173 B10
Hauts-de-Seine □ France 48°52N 2°15E 173 D9
Hauts Plateaux Algeria 35°0N 1°0E 261 B5
Hau'ula U.S.A. 21°37N 157°55W 302 J14
Hauz Khas India 28°33N 77°11E 120 B2
Hauzenberg Germany 48°40N 13°37E 179 G9
Havana = La Habana
Cuba 23°8N 82°22W 320 B3
Havana Fla., U.S.A. 30°37N 84°25W 316 E5
Havana Ill., U.S.A. 40°18N 90°4W 310 D6
Havant U.K. 50°51N 0°58W 169 G7
Havârna Romania 48°4N 26°43E 183 B11
Havasor = Kız Turkey 38°26N 43°25E 246 B4
Havasu, L. U.S.A. 34°18N 114°28W 307 L12
Havdata Greece 38°12N 20°23E 207 D1
Havdhem Sweden 57°10N 18°20E 163 G12
Havel → Germany 52°50N 12°3E 178 A2
Havelian Pakistan 34°2N 73°10E 242 B5
Havelkanal Germany 52°36N 13°10E 115 A2
Havelock Ont., Canada 44°26N 77°53W 312 B7
Havelock N.Z. 41°17S 173°48E 286 D5
Havelock N.C., U.S.A. 34°53N 76°54W 315 D16
Havelock I. India 11°25N 93°0E 245 J11
Havelock North N.Z. 39°40S 176°53E 284 F5
Haverfordwest U.K. 51°48N 4°58W 169 F3
Haverhill Suffolk, U.K. 52°5N 0°28E 169 E8
Haverhill Fla., U.S.A. 26°42N 80°7W 317 J9
Haverhill Mass., U.S.A. 42°47N 71°5W 313 D13
Haveri India 14°53N 75°24E 245 G2
Havering □ U.K. 51°34N 0°13E 125 A5
Havering-atte-Bower U.K. 51°37N 0°11E 125 A5
Haverstraw U.S.A. 41°12N 73°58W 313 E11
Håverud Sweden 58°50N 12°28E 163 F6
Havirga Mongolia 45°41N 113°5E 226 B7
Havířov Czech Rep. 49°46N 18°20E 181 B11
Havlíčkův Brod
Czech Rep. 49°36N 15°33E 180 B8
Havneby Denmark 55°5N 8°34E 163 J2
Havran Turkey 39°33N 27°6E 205 B9
Havre U.S.A. 48°33N 109°41W 304 B9
Havre-Aubert Canada 47°12N 61°56W 297 B7
Havre-St.-Pierre Canada 50°18N 63°33W 299 B7
Havsa Turkey 41°31N 26°48E 203 E10
Havza Turkey 40°58N 35°38E 212 B6
Haw → U.S.A. 35°36N 79°3N 315 D15
Hawai'i U.S.A. 19°30N 155°30W 302 D6
Hawai'i I County U.S.A. 19°30N 156°30W 302 D6
Hawai'i Kai U.S.A. 21°16N 157°42W 302 K14
Hawai'i Volcanoes △
U.S.A. 19°25N 155°18W 302 D6
Hawaiian Is. Pac. Oc. 20°30N 156°0W 302 G12
Hawaiian Ridge Pac. Oc. 24°0N 165°0W 289 E11
Hawarden U.K. 43°0N 96°29W 308 D5
Hawashiyah, W. Egypt 28°31N 32°58E 251 K3
Hawea, L. N.Z. 44°28S 169°19E 285 E4
Hawea Flat N.Z. 44°40S 169°19E 285 E4
Hawera N.Z. 39°35S 174°19E 284 F3
Hawesville U.S.A. 37°54N 86°45W 311 G10
Hawi U.S.A. 20°14N 155°50W 302 D6
Hawick U.K. 55°26N 2°47W 167 F6
Hawk Junction Canada 48°5N 84°38W 298 C3
Hawk Point U.S.A. 38°58N 91°8W 310 F5
Hawkdun Ra. N.Z. 44°52S 170°5E 285 E5
Hawke B. N.Z. 39°25S 177°20E 284 F6
Hawker Australia 31°59S 138°22E 282 A3
Hawke's Bay Canada 50°36N 57°10W 299 B8
Hawke's Bay □ N.Z. 39°45S 176°35E 284 F5
Hawkesbury Canada 45°37N 74°37W 298 C5
Hawkesbury I. Canada 53°37N 129°3W 296 D5
Hawkesbury Pt. Australia 11°55S 134°5E 280 A1
Hawkinsville U.S.A. 32°17N 83°28W 316 C6
Hawks Nest Australia 32°41S 152°11E 283 B10
Hawley Minn., U.S.A. 46°53N 96°19W 308 B5
Hawley Pa., U.S.A. 41°28N 75°11W 313 E9
Haworth U.S.A. 40°57N 73°59W 132 A2
Hawrān, W. → Iraq 33°58N 42°34E 213 F10
Hawsh Mūssā Lebanon 33°45N 35°55E 248 B4
Hawthorne Fla., U.S.A. 29°36N 82°5W 317 F7
Hawthorne Nev., U.S.A. 38°32N 118°38W 304 G4
Hawthorne Racecourse
U.S.A. 41°49N 87°44W 119 C2
Hay Australia 34°30S 144°51E 283 C6
Hay → N. Terr., Australia 24°50S 138°0E 280 C2
Hay, C. Australia 14°5S 129°29E 278 B4
Hay, C. Canada 44°53N 80°58W 312 B4
Hay I. Canada 58°50N 118°50W 296 C6
Hay-on-Wye U.K. 52°5N 3°8W 169 E4
Hay Point Australia 21°18S 149°17E 280 C4
Hay River Canada 60°51N 115°44W 296 A5
Hay Springs U.S.A. 42°41N 102°41W 308 D2
Haya = Tehoru Indonesia 3°23S 129°30E 231 E7
Hayachine-San Japan 39°34N 141°29E 220 E10
Hayange France 49°20N 6°2E 173 C13
Hayastan = Armenia ■
Asia 40°20N 45°0E 191 K7
Hayato Japan 31°40N 130°42E 222 F2
Haydān, W. al → Jordan 31°29N 35°34E 251 G6
Haydarlı Turkey 38°16N 30°23E 205 C12
Hayden U.S.A. 40°30N 107°16W 304 F10
Hayes Jamaica 17°52N 77°14W 320 a
Hayes Kent, U.K. 51°22N 0°0 125 B4
Hayes Middlesex, U.K. 51°30N 0°25W 125 C2
Hayes S. Dak., U.S.A. 44°23N 101°1W 308 C3
Hayes → Canada 57°3N 92°12W 298 A1
Hayes, Mt. U.S.A. 63°37N 146°43W 303 E11
Hayes Creek Australia 13°43S 131°22E 278 B5
Hayes End U.S.A. 51°31N 0°25W 125 A1
Hayfield □ U.K. 51°35N 0°35W 125 A1
Hayford U.S.A. 41°45N 87°42W 119 C2
Hayle U.K. 50°11N 5°26W 169 G2
Hayling I. U.K. 50°48N 0°59W 169 G7
Haymā' Oman 19°56N 56°19E 249 C7
Hayman I. Australia 20°4S 148°53E 280 C4
Hayman Turkey 39°26N 32°31E 212 C5
Haynan Yemen 15°50N 48°18E 249 G5
Haynau = Chojnów
Poland 51°18N 15°58E 185 G2
Hayneville U.S.A. 32°23N 83°37W 316 C6
Hayrabolu Turkey 41°12N 27°5E 203 E10
Hays Alta., Canada 50°6N 111°48W 296 C6
Hays Kans., U.S.A. 38°53N 99°20W 308 F4
Haysville U.S.A. 38°28N 86°55W 115 C3
Hayvoron Ukraine 48°57N 29°25E 183 B14
Hayward Calif., U.S.A. 37°40N 122°4W 306 H4
Hayward Wis., U.S.A. 46°1N 91°29W 308 B8
Haywards N.Z. 41°9S 174°59E 143 A2
Haywards Heath U.K. 51°0N 0°5W 169 G7
Hazafon □ Israel 32°40N 35°20E 250 F6

Hazar Turkmenistan 39°34N 53°16E 187 G9
Hazarān, Kūh-e Iran 29°35N 57°20E 247 D8
Hazard U.S.A. 37°15N 83°12W 309 G12
Hazaribag India 23°58N 85°26E 243 H11
Hazaribag Road India 24°12N 85°57E 243 G11
Hazebrouck France 50°42N 2°31E 173 B9
Hazelton B.C., Canada 55°20N 127°42W 296 B3
Hazelton N. Dak., U.S.A. 46°29N 100°17W 308 B3
Hazen U.S.A. 47°18N 101°38W 308 B3
Hazen, L. Canada 81°47N 71°1W 154 A3
Hazlehurst Ga., U.S.A. 31°52N 82°36W 316 D7
Hazlehurst Miss., U.S.A. 31°52N 90°24W 315 F9
Hazlet U.S.A. 40°25N 74°12W 313 F10
Hazleton U.S.A. 38°29N 87°33W 311 F9
Hazleton Pa., U.S.A. 40°57N 75°59W 313 F9
Hazlett, L. Australia 21°30S 128°48E 278 D4
Hazro Turkey 38°15N 40°47E 246 B4
He Xian Anhui, China 31°45N 118°20E 229 B12
He Xian Guangxi Zhuangzu,
China 24°27N 111°30E 229 E8
Head of Bight Australia 31°30S 131°25E 279 F5
Headland U.S.A. 31°21N 85°21W 316 D4
Headlands Zimbabwe 18°15S 32°2E 269 F3
Healdsburg U.S.A. 38°37N 122°52W 306 G4
Healdton U.S.A. 34°14N 97°29W 314 D6
Healesville Australia 37°35S 145°30E 283 C6
Healy U.S.A. 63°52N 148°58W 303 E10
Heany Junction Zimbabwe 20°6S 28°54E 269 H2
Heard I. Ind. Oc. 53°6S 72°36E 273 K6
Hearne Canada 49°40N 83°41W 298 C3
Hearne U.S.A. 30°53N 96°36W 314 F6
Heart → Canada 49°40N 83°41W 298 C3
Heart → U.S.A. 46°46N 100°50W 308 B3
Heart's Content Canada 47°54N 53°27W 299 C9
Heath → Bolivia 12°31S 68°38W 330 C4
Heath, Pte. Canada 49°8N 61°40W 299 B7
Heath Mts. N.Z. 45°39S 167°9E 285 F2
Heathcote Australia 36°56S 144°45E 283 D6
Heather Canada 53°35N 116°28W 296 C5
Heathfield S. Africa 34°3S 18°27E 118 B1
Heathfield U.K. 51°28N 0°27W 125 B1
Heavener U.S.A. 34°53N 94°36W 314 D7
Hebbronville U.S.A. 27°18N 98°41W 314 H5
Hebe Haven China 22°21N 114°15E 122 A2
Hebei □ China 39°0N 116°0E 226 E9
Hebel Australia 28°58S 147°47E 283 A5
Heber U.S.A. 32°44N 115°32W 307 N11
Heber Springs U.S.A. 35°30N 92°2W 314 D8
Hebgen L. U.S.A. 44°52N 111°20W 304 D8
Hebi China 35°57N 114°7E 226 G8
Hebrides U.K. 57°30N 7°0W 158 D4
Hebrides, Sea of the U.K. 57°5N 7°0W 167 D2
Hebron = Al Khalīl
West Bank 31°32N 35°6E 251 G6
Hebron Nfld. & L., Canada 58°5N 62°30W 299 F5
Hebron N. Dak., U.S.A. 46°54N 102°3W 308 B2
Hebron Nebr., U.S.A. 40°10N 97°35W 308 E5
Heby Sweden 59°56N 16°53E 162 E10
Hecate Str. Canada 53°10N 130°30W 296 C2
Heceta I. U.S.A. 55°46N 133°40W 296 B2
Hechi China 24°40N 108°2E 228 E7
Hechingen Germany 48°21N 8°57E 179 G4
Hechuan China 30°2N 106°12E 228 B6
Hecla U.S.A. 45°53N 98°9W 308 C4
Hecla I. Canada 51°10N 96°43W 297 C9
Heddal Norway 59°36N 9°9E 163 F3
Hede Sweden 62°23N 13°30E 162 C6
Hédé Ille-et-Vilaine, France 48°18N 1°49W 172 D5
Hede Jämtland, Sweden 62°23N 13°30E 162 C6
Hedemora Sweden 60°18N 15°58E 162 D9
Hedensted Denmark 55°46N 9°42E 163 J3
Hedesunda Sweden 60°24N 17°0E 162 D10
Hedgehope N.Z. 46°12S 168°34E 285 G3
Hedmark □ Norway 61°17N 11°40E 164 C8
Hedo Japan 26°52N 128°15E 288 a
Hedo-misaki Japan 26°52N 128°15E 288 a
Hedong China 23°5N 113°14E 121 B2
Hedrick U.S.A. 41°11N 92°19W 310 C4
He'eia U.S.A. 21°25N 157°48W 302 K14
Heerde Neths. 52°24N 6°2E 170 B3
Heerenveen Neths. 52°57N 5°55E 170 B5
Heerhugowaard Neths. 52°40N 4°51E 170 B4
Heerlen Neths. 50°55N 5°58E 170 D5
Heerwegen = Polkowice
Poland 51°29N 16°3E 185 G3
Hefa Israel 32°46N 35°0E 250 F6
Hefa □ Israel 32°40N 35°0E 250 F6
Hefei China 31°52N 117°18E 229 B11
Hefeng China 29°55N 109°57E 229 C8
Heflin U.S.A. 33°39N 85°35W 316 B4
Hegalig Sudan 14°36N 34°54E 257 E5
Hegang China 47°20N 130°19E 219 B8
Heggenes Norway 61°9N 9°4E 164 C6
Hegra Norway 63°27N 11°8E 164 A8
Hei Ling Chau China 22°15N 114°2E 219 G11
Heiban Sudan 11°13N 30°31E 257 E3
Heichengzhen China 36°24N 106°3E 226 F4
Heidal Norway 61°45N 9°19E 164 C6
Heide Germany 54°11N 9°6E 178 A5
Heidelberg Baden-W.,
Germany 49°24N 8°42E 179 F4
Heidelberg Western Cape,
S. Africa 34°6S 20°59E 270 D3
Heidelberg Heights
Australia 37°45S 145°4E 128 A2
Heidelberg West Australia 37°45S 145°2E 128 A2
Heidelburg S. Africa 26°30S 28°21E 271 C4
Heidenheim Germany 52°29N 13°40E 115 B5
Heideveld S. Africa 33°58S 18°32E 118 A2
Heigun-Tō Japan 33°47N 132°14E 222 D4
Heihe China 50°10N 127°30E 219 A7
Heihe China 25°22N 101°44E 228 E3
Heijo = P'yŏngyang
N. Korea 39°0N 125°30E 224 C2
Heilbad Heiligenstadt
Germany 51°22N 10°8E 178 D6
Heilbron S. Africa 27°16S 27°59E 271 C4
Heilbronn Germany 49°9N 9°13E 179 F5
Heiligenblut Austria 47°2N 12°51E 180 D5
Heiligenhafen Germany 54°22N 10°59E 178 A6
Heiligensee Germany 52°36N 13°13E 115 A2
Heiligenstadt Austria 48°0N 126°0E 219 B7
Heilprin Land Greenland 80°30N 134°0W 154 A7
Heilongjiang □ China 48°0N 126°0E 219 B7
Heilunkiang = Heilongjiang □
China 48°0N 126°0E 219 B7
Heim Norway 63°26N 9°5E 164 A6
Heimaey Iceland 63°26N 20°17W 155 D6
Heimdal Norway 63°21N 10°17E 164 A7
Heineken Experience
Amsterdam, Neths. 112 c2
Heinola Finland 61°13N 26°2E 158 A8
Heinsberg Germany 51°3N 6°5E 170 C2
Heinze Kyun Burma 14°25N 97°45E 244 E1
Heirnkut Burma 25°14N 94°44E 241 C10
Heishan China 41°40N 122°5E 227 D12
Heishui Liaoning, China 42°8N 119°30E 227 C10

Heishui Sichuan, China 32°4N 103°2E 228 A4
Hejaz = Ḥijāz Si. Arabia 24°0N 40°0E 246 E3
Hejian China 38°25N 116°5E 226 E9
Hejiang China 28°43N 105°46E 228 C5
Hejin China 35°35N 110°42E 226 G6
Hejing China 42°18N 86°22E 217 D11
Hekimhan Turkey 38°50N 37°55E 212 C7
Hekinan Japan 34°52N 137°0E 223 C9
Hekla Iceland 63°56N 19°35W 155 D7
Hekou Guangdong, China 23°11N 112°45E 229 F9
Hekou Yunnan, China 22°30N 103°59E 228 F4
Hel Poland 54°37N 18°47E 185 A6
Helagsfjället Sweden 62°54N 12°25E 162 C5
Helan Shan China 38°30N 105°55E 226 E3
Heldenplatz Vienna, Austria 142 b1
Helden's Pt.
St. Kitts & Nevis 17°25N 62°51W 322 d
Helechosa de los Montes
Spain 39°22N 4°53W 195 F6
Helemano U.S.A. 21°35N 158°7W 302 J13
Helen Atoll Pac. Oc. 2°40N 132°0E 231 D8
Helena Ark., U.S.A. 34°32N 90°36W 315 D9
Helena Mont., U.S.A. 46°36N 112°2W 304 C7
Helendale U.S.A. 34°44N 117°19W 307 L9
Hélène de Champlain, Parc △
Canada 45°31N 73°32W 130 A2
Helenelund Sweden 59°24N 17°58E 139 A1
Helensburgh N.S.W.,
Australia 34°11S 151°1E 283 C9
Helensburgh Argyll & Bute,
U.K. 56°1N 4°43W 167 E4
Helensville N.Z. 36°41S 174°29E 284 E4
Helenvale Australia 15°43S 145°1E 280 B4
Helgasjön Sweden 56°55N 14°50E 163 H8
Helgeland Norway 66°7N 13°29E 160 C15
Helgoland Germany 54°10N 7°53E 178 A3
Helheim Gletscher
Greenland 66°24N 38°12W 154 D7
Heligoland = Helgoland
Germany 54°10N 7°53E 178 A3
Heligoland B. = Deutsche Bucht
Germany 54°15N 8°0E 178 A4
Heliopolis = Masr el Gedida
Egypt 30°5N 31°21E 117 A2
Hell Norway 63°26N 10°54E 164 A7
Hell-Bourg Réunion 21°3S 55°32E 272 f
Hell Hole Gorge △
Australia 25°31S 144°12E 280 D3
Hella Iceland 63°50N 20°24W 155 D6
Hellas = Greece ■ Europe 40°0N 23°0E 204 B3
Helleland Norway 58°33N 6°7E 164 F3
Hellertown U.S.A. 40°35N 75°21W 313 F9
Hellerup Denmark 55°44N 12°33E 118 A3
Hellespont = Çanakkale Boğazı
Turkey 40°17N 26°32E 203 F10
Hellesylt Norway 62°6N 6°51E 164 B3
Hellevoetsluis Neths. 51°50N 4°8E 170 C4
Hellin Spain 38°31N 1°40W 197 G3
Hellissandur Iceland 64°55N 23°54W 155 C3
Hells Canyon U.S.A. 45°30N 117°45W 304 D5
Hell's Gate Neth. Ant. 17°39N 63°14W 322 a
Hell's Gate △ Kenya 0°54S 36°19E 268 C4
Hellvik Norway 58°29N 5°52E 164 F2
Helmand □ Afghan. 31°20N 64°0E 242 D3
Helmand → Afghan. 31°12N 61°34E 240 C1
Helme → Germany 51°20N 11°21E 178 D7
Helmeringhausen
Namibia 25°54S 16°57E 270 C2
Helmond Neths. 51°29N 5°41E 170 C5
Helmsdale U.K. 58°7N 3°39W 167 C5
Helmsdale → U.K. 58°8N 3°43W 167 C5
Helmstedt Germany 52°12N 11°0E 178 C7
Helong China 42°40N 129°0E 224 A4
Helper U.S.A. 39°41N 110°51W 304 G8
Helsingborg Sweden 56°3N 12°42E 163 H6
Helsinge Denmark 56°2N 12°12E 163 H6
Helsingfors = Helsinki
Finland 60°10N 24°55E 121 B2
Helsingør Denmark 56°2N 12°35E 163 H6
Helsinki Finland 60°10N 24°55E 121 B2
Helsinki-Vantaa ✈ (HEL)
Finland 60°18N 24°58E 121 B2
Helska, Mierzeja Poland 54°45N 18°40E 185 A5
Helston U.K. 50°6N 5°17W 169 G2
Helvellyn U.K. 54°32N 3°1W 168 C4
Helwân Egypt 29°50N 31°20E 256 J7
Hemavati → India 12°30N 76°20E 245 H3
Hemel Hempstead U.K. 51°44N 0°28W 169 F7
Hemet U.S.A. 33°45N 116°58W 307 M10
Hemingford U.S.A. 42°19N 103°4W 308 D2
Hemis △ India 34°0N 77°35W 243 C8
Hemmingford Canada 45°3N 73°35W 313 A11
Hempstead N.Y., U.S.A. 40°42N 73°37W 313 F11
Hempstead Tex., U.S.A. 30°6N 96°5W 314 F6
Hemse Sweden 57°15N 18°22E 163 G12
Hemsedal Norway 60°51N 8°30E 164 D5
Hemsön Sweden 62°42N 18°5E 162 B12
Hen Norway 60°11N 10°14E 164 D7
Hen and Chicken B.
Australia 33°50S 151°7E 139 B1
Hen and Chickens Is.
N.Z. 35°58S 174°45E 284 B3
Henán Sweden 58°14N 11°40E 163 F5
Henan □ China 34°0N 114°0E 226 H8
Henares → Spain 40°24N 3°30W 194 B3
Henashi-Misaki Japan 40°37N 139°51E 220 D9
Hendaye France 43°23N 1°47W 174 E2
Hendek Turkey 40°48N 30°44E 212 B4
Henderson Argentina 36°18S 61°43W 334 D3
Henderson Ga., U.S.A. 32°21N 83°47W 316 C6
Henderson Ky., U.S.A. 37°50N 87°35W 311 G9
Henderson N.C., U.S.A. 36°20N 78°25W 315 C15
Henderson N.Y., U.S.A. 43°50N 76°10W 313 C8
Henderson Nev., U.S.A. 36°2N 114°58W 307 J12
Henderson Tenn., U.S.A. 35°26N 88°38W 315 D10
Henderson Tex., U.S.A. 32°9N 94°48W 314 E7
Henderson I. Pac. Oc. 24°22S 128°19W 289 K15
Hendersonville N.C.,
U.S.A. 35°19N 82°28W 315 D13
Hendersonville Tenn.,
U.S.A. 36°18N 86°37W 315 C11
Hendījān Iran 30°14N 49°43E 247 D6
Hendon U.K. 51°35N 0°14W 125 A2
Hendorābī Iran 26°40N 53°37E 247 E7
Heng Jiang → China 23°40N 109°17E 228 F7
Heng Xian China 22°40N 109°17E 228 F7
Hengām Iran 26°50N 54°40W 335 B5
Hengandofu Papua N. G. 6°15S 145°38E 286 B3
Hengcheng China 38°18N 106°28E 226 E4
Hěngch'un Taiwan 22°0N 120°44E 229 F13
Hengdaohezi China 44°52N 129°0E 219 B8
Hengduan Shan China 27°30N 99°0E 218 D4
Hengelo Neths. 52°3N 6°19E 170 B6
Hengfeng China 28°12N 117°48E 229 C11
Henggang China 22°39N 114°12E 121 C2
Hengmen China 22°33N 113°33E 121 B2
Hengqin Dao China 22°8N 113°34E 121 B1
Hengshan Shaanxi, China 37°58N 109°5E 226 F5
Hengshan Hunan, China 27°16N 112°45E 229 D9
Hengshui China 37°41N 115°40E 226 F8
Hengyang China 26°59N 112°22E 229 D9

Henichesk Ukraine 46°12N 34°50E 189 J8
Henima India 25°22N 93°36E 241 C4
Hénin-Beaumont France 50°25N 2°58E 173 B9
Hénin-Liétard = Hénin-Beaumont
France 50°25N 2°58E 173 B9
Henley-on-Thames U.K. 51°32N 0°54W 169 F7
Henlopen, C. U.S.A. 38°48N 75°6W 309 F16
Henna Japan 26°19N 127°53E 288 a
Hennenman S. Africa 27°59S 27°1E 270 C4
Hennepin U.S.A. 41°15N 89°21W 310 C7
Hennessey U.S.A. 36°6N 97°54W 314 C6
Hennigsdorf Germany 52°38N 13°12E 115 A2
Henrietta N.Y., U.S.A. 43°4N 77°37W 312 C7
Henrietta U.S.A. 33°49N 98°12W 314 E5
Henrietta, Ostrov = Genriyetty,
Ostrov Russia 77°6N 156°30E 215 B16
Henrietta Maria, C.
Canada 55°9N 82°20W 298 A3
Henry U.S.A. 41°7N 89°22W 310 C7
Henry Lawrence I. India 12°9N 93°5E 245 H11
Henryetta U.S.A. 35°27N 95°59W 314 D7
Henryków Poland 52°19N 20°58E 142 B1
Henryville Canada 45°8N 73°11W 313 A11
Hensall Canada 43°26N 81°30W 312 C3
Henson Cr. → U.S.A. 38°47N 76°58W 143 C4
Hentesbaai Namibia 22°8S 14°18E 270 B1
Hentiyn Nuruu
Mongolia 48°30N 108°30E 219 B5
Henttaa Finland 60°11N 24°45E 121 B3
Henty Australia 35°30S 147°3E 283 C7
Henzada Burma 17°38N 95°26E 241 G5
Hephaestia Greece 39°55N 25°14E 205 B7
Hephzibah U.S.A. 33°19N 82°6W 316 C7
Heping China 24°29N 115°0E 229 E10
Hepingli China 39°57N 116°23E 114 B2
Heppner U.S.A. 45°21N 119°33W 304 D4
Hepu China 21°40N 109°12E 228 G7
Hequ China 39°20N 111°15E 226 E6
Héraðsflói Iceland 65°42N 14°12W 155 B12
Héraðsvötn → Iceland 65°45N 19°25W 155 B7
Herald Cays Australia 16°58S 149°9E 280 B4
Herand Norway 60°20N 6°22E 164 D3
Herangi Ra. N.Z. 38°33S 174°44E 284 E3
Herāt Afghan. 34°20N 62°7E 240 B1
Herāt □ Afghan. 35°0N 62°0E 240 B1
Hérault → France 43°17N 3°26E 174 E7
Hérault □ France 43°34N 3°15E 174 E7
Herbault France 47°36N 1°8E 172 E8
Herbert Canada 50°30N 107°10W 297 C7
Herbert I. U.S.A. 52°45N 170°7W 303 K5
Herbertabad India 11°43N 92°37E 245 J11
Herberton Australia 17°20S 145°25E 280 B4
Herbertsdale S. Africa 34°1S 21°46E 270 D3
Herbertville N.Z. 40°30S 176°33E 284 G5
Herborn Germany 50°40N 8°18E 178 E4
Herby Poland 50°45N 18°50E 185 H5
Herceg-Novi Montenegro 42°30N 18°33E 202 D2
Hercegfalva = Mezőfalva
Hungary 46°55N 18°49E 182 D3
Herchmer Canada 57°22N 94°10W 297 B10
Herculaneum = Coxim
Brazil 18°30S 54°55W 331 D7
Heroubreið Iceland 65°11N 16°21W 155 B10
Hereford U.K. 52°4N 2°43W 169 E5
Hereford Tex., U.S.A. 34°49N 102°24W 314 D3
Herefordshire □ U.K. 52°8N 2°40W 169 E5
Herefoss Norway 58°32N 8°23E 164 F5
Héréhérétué
French Polynesia 19°45S 144°58W 289 f
Hereroa Sweden 61°44N 12°8E 164 C9
Hereke N.Z. 40°47N 29°38E 203 F13
Herekino N.Z. 35°18S 173°11E 284 B2
Herencia Spain 39°21N 3°21W 195 F7
Herentals Belgium 51°12N 4°51E 170 C4
Herford Germany 52°7N 8°39E 178 C4
Héricourt France 47°32N 6°45E 173 E13
Heriot N.Z. 45°40N 96°57W 308 F5
Heris Iran 38°14N 47°6E 213 C12
Herisau Switz. 47°22N 9°17E 179 H5
Hérisson France 46°32N 2°42E 173 F9
Herkimer U.S.A. 43°2N 74°59W 313 D10
Herlev Denmark 55°43N 12°27E 118 A2
Herlong U.S.A. 40°8N 120°8W 306 E6
Herm U.K. 49°30N 2°28W 169 H5
Hermakivka Ukraine 48°42N 26°11E 183 B11
Herman Eckstein Park
S. Africa 26°9S 28°1E 123 A2
Herman U.S.A. 45°48N 96°9W 308 C5
Hermannsbad = Ciechocinek
Poland 52°53N 18°45E 185 F5
Hermannsburg N. Terr.,
Australia 23°57S 132°45E 278 D5
Hermannsburg Niedersachsen,
Germany 52°50N 10°5E 178 C6
Hermannskogel Austria 48°16N 16°17E 142 A1
Hermannstadt = Sibiu
Romania 45°45N 24°9E 183 E8
Hermansverk Norway 61°11N 6°52E 164 C3
Hermanus S. Africa 34°27S 19°12E 270 D2
Herment France 45°45N 2°24E 174 C6
Hermidale Australia 31°30S 146°42E 283 A7
Hermiston U.S.A. 45°51N 119°17W 304 D4
Hermitage N.Z. 43°44N 170°5E 284 G3
Hermitage Mo., U.S.A. 37°56N 93°19W 310 G5
Hermitage and Winter Palace
Russia 59°56N 30°18E 137 B1
Hermon Ont., Canada 45°6N 77°37W 312 B7
Hermon U.S.A. 44°28N 75°14W 313 B9
Hermon, Mt. = Shaykh, J. ash
Lebanon 33°25N 35°50E 250 E6
Hermosilo Mexico 29°10N 111°0W 318 B2
Hermosa U.S.A. 43°21N 103°12W 308 D2
Hermoso de Magallanes △
Chile 54°0S 72°30W 335 D2
Hernani Spain 43°16N 1°58W 196 B3
Herndon U.S.A. 40°43N 76°51W 313 F8
Herne Germany 51°32N 7°14E 170 C3
Herne Bay U.K. 51°21N 1°8E 169 F9
Herne Hill U.K. 51°27N 0°6W 125 B3
Herning Denmark 56°8N 8°58E 163 H2
Herod U.S.A. 37°42N 84°20W 316 B6
Héroes de Churubusco
Mexico 19°21N 99°6W 120 B2

High Bridge U.S.A. 40°40N 74°54W 313 F10
High Desert U.S.A. 43°40N 120°20W 304 D5
High Island Res. China 22°22N 114°21E 219 G11
High Level Canada 58°31N 117°8W 296 B5
High Park Canada 43°38N 79°27W 141 B2
High Pk. St. Helena 15°29N 120°7E 232 D3
High Point U.S.A. 35°57N 80°0W 315 D15
High Prairie Canada 55°30N 116°30W 296 B5
High River Canada 50°30N 113°50W 296 C6
High Springs U.S.A. 29°50N 82°36W 316 F7
High Tatra = Tatry
Slovak Rep. 49°20N 20°0E 181 B13
High Veld Africa 27°0S 27°0E 254 J6
High Wycombe U.K. 51°37N 0°45W 169 F7
Highbank Canada 43°37S 171°45E 285 D6
Highbury U.K. 51°33N 0°6W 125 A3
Highgate Jamaica 18°16N 76°57W 320 a
Highgate London, U.K. 51°34N 0°9W 125 A3
Highland U.S.A. 38°44N 89°41W 310 F7
Highland Ind., U.S.A. 41°33N 87°28W 311 C9
Highland Wis., U.S.A. 43°4N 90°22W 310 A6
Highland □ U.K. 57°17N 4°21W 167 D4
Highland Cr. → Canada 27°58N 81°53W 317 H8
Highland Creek Canada 43°46N 79°9W 141 A3
Highland Home U.S.A. 31°57N 86°19W 316 D4
Highland Mills U.S.A. 33°17N 84°17W 316 B5
Highland Park Calif.,
U.S.A. 34°7N 118°13W 126 B3
Highland Park Ill.,
U.S.A. 42°11N 87°48W 311 B9
Highland View U.S.A. 29°50N 85°19W 316 F4
Highlands = Fort Thomas
U.S.A. 39°4N 84°26W 311 C12
Highlands, The
Antigua & B. 17°8N 61°47W 322 c
Highlands North S. Africa 26°8S 28°5E 123 A2
Highmore U.S.A. 44°31N 99°27W 308 C4
Highrock L. Canada 55°45N 100°30W 297 B8
Higüera, Pta. Puerto Rico 18°22N 67°16W 321 b
Higüey Dom. Rep. 18°37N 68°42W 321 C6
Hihya Egypt 30°40N 31°36E 256 H7
Hiiumaa = Somali Rep. 4°0N 45°0E 267 C5
Hiiumaa Estonia 58°50N 22°45E 188 C2
Hījar Spain 41°10N 0°27W 196 B4
Hijārah, Şaḥrā' al Iraq 30°25N 44°30E 246 D5
Hijāz Si. Arabia 24°0N 40°0E 246 E3
Hiji Japan 33°22N 131°32E 222 D2
Hijo = Tagum Phil. 7°33N 125°53E 233 H5
Hikari Japan 33°58N 131°58E 222 D2
Hiketa Japan 34°13N 134°24E 222 C7
Hikkaduwa Sri Lanka 6°8N 80°6E 245 L5
Hikmak, Ras el Egypt 31°15N 27°51E 256 A2
Hiko U.S.A. 37°32N 115°14W 306 H11
Hikone Japan 35°15N 136°10E 223 B8
Hikurangi Gisborne, N.Z. 37°55S 178°4E 284 E5
Hikurangi Northland,
N.Z. 35°36S 174°17E 284 B3
Hikutavake Cook Is. 18°56S 169°53W 289 g
Hilawe Burma 21°23N 93°48E 241 D4
Hilbert U.S.A. 44°8N 88°10W 310 B7
Hildburghausen Germany 50°25N 10°45E 178 E6
Hildesheim Germany 52°9N 9°56E 178 C5
Hillnarendal Iceland 63°44N 19°57W 155 D7
Hill → Australia 30°23S 115°3E 279 F2
Hill City Idaho, U.S.A. 43°18N 115°3W 304 E6
Hill City Kans., U.S.A. 39°22N 99°51W 308 F4
Hill City Minn., U.S.A. 46°59N 93°36W 308 B7
Hill City S. Dak., U.S.A. 43°56N 103°35W 308 D2
Hill Island L. Canada 60°30N 109°50W 297 A7
Hillaby, Mt. Barbados 13°12N 59°35W 323 r
Hillared Sweden 57°37N 13°10E 163 G7
Hillcrest Center U.S.A. 35°23N 118°57W 307 K8
Hillcrest Heights U.S.A. 38°49N 76°57W 143 C4
Hillegom Neths. 52°18N 4°35E 170 B4
Hillend U.K. 56°2N 3°22W 121 A1
Hillerød Denmark 55°56N 12°19E 163 J6
Hillerstorp Sweden 57°20N 13°52E 163 G7
Hilli Bangla. 25°17N 89°1E 241 C2
Hilliard U.S.A. 30°41N 81°55W 316 E8
Hillingdon □ U.K. 51°32N 0°27W 125 A1
Hillsboro = Deerfield Beach
U.S.A. 26°19N 80°6W 317 J9
Hillsboro Ga., U.S.A. 33°11N 83°38W 316 B6
Hillsboro Ill., U.S.A. 39°9N 89°29W 310 F7
Hillsboro Kans., U.S.A. 38°21N 97°12W 308 F5
Hillsboro Mo., U.S.A. 38°14N 90°34W 310 F8
Hillsboro N. Dak., U.S.A. 47°26N 97°3W 308 B5
Hillsboro Ohio, U.S.A. 39°12N 83°37W 311 E13
Hillsboro Oreg., U.S.A. 45°31N 122°59W 306 C4
Hillsboro Canal U.S.A. 26°30N 80°15W 317 J9
Hillsborough Grenada 12°28N 61°28W 323 q
Hillsborough N.H.,
U.S.A. 43°7N 71°54W 313 C14
Hillsborough Channel
Australia 20°56S 149°15E 280 b
Hillsborough Dam
Trin. & Tob. 11°13N 60°40W 323 s
Hillsborough Land = Belle Glade
U.S.A. 26°41N 80°40W 317 J9
Hillsdale Mich., U.S.A. 41°56N 84°38W 311 C12
Hillsdale N.Y., U.S.A. 42°11N 73°32W 313 D11
Hillsport Canada 49°27N 85°34W 298 C2
Hillston Australia 33°30S 145°31E 283 B8
Hilltonia U.S.A. 32°52N 81°36W 316 C7
Hillwood U.S.A. 38°52N 77°9W 143 A2
Hilmīya Egypt 30°6N 31°19E 117 A2
Hilo U.S.A. 19°44N 155°5W 302 D6
Hilo ✈ (ITO) U.S.A. 19°43N 155°2W 302 D6
Hilo Bay U.S.A. 19°45N 155°5W 302 D6
Hilton U.S.A. 43°17N 77°48W 312 C7
Hilton Head Island
U.S.A. 32°13N 80°45W 316 C9
Hilvan Turkey 37°34N 38°58E 213 D8
Hilversum Neths. 52°14N 5°10E 170 B5
Himachal Pradesh □
India 31°30N 77°0E 242 D7
Himalaya Asia 29°0N 84°0E 243 E11
Himalchuli Nepal 28°27N 84°38E 243 E11
Himamaylan Phil. 10°6N 122°52E 233 F4
Himarë Albania 40°8N 19°43E 202 F2
Himatnagar India 23°37N 72°57E 242 H5
Hime-jima Japan 33°43N 131°40E 222 D2
Himeji Japan 34°50N 134°40E 222 C6
Himi Japan 36°50N 136°55E 222 A7
Himmerland Denmark 56°45N 9°30E 163 H3
Ḥimṣ Syria 34°40N 36°45E 250 D5
Ḥimṣ □ Syria 34°30N 37°0E 250 D5
Hin Keng China 22°23N 114°11E 121 A2
Hinatuan Phil. 8°23N 126°20E 233 G6
Hinatuan Passage Phil. 9°45S 125°31E 233 G6
Hinche Haiti 19°9N 72°1W 321 C5
Hinckley I.
Australia 18°20S 146°15E 280 B4
Hinchinbrook Island △
Australia 18°14S 146°6E 280 B4
Hinckley Leics., U.K. 52°33N 1°22W 169 E6
Hinckley Minn., U.S.A. 46°1N 92°56W 308 B7
Hindaun India 26°44N 77°5E 242 F7
Hindenburg = Zabrze
Poland 50°18N 18°50E 185 H5
Hindmarsh, L. Australia 36°5S 141°55E 282 D4
Hindol India 20°40N 85°10E 244 D7
Hinds N.Z. 43°59S 171°36E 285 D6

Hindsholm *Denmark* 55°30N 10°40E **163** J4
Hindu Bagh *Pakistan* 30°56N 67°50E **242** D2
Hindu Kush *Asia* 36°0N 71°0E **240** B3
Hindupur *India* 13°49N 77°32E **245** H3
Hines Creek *Canada* 56°20N 118°40W **296** B5
Hinesville *U.S.A.* 31°51N 81°36W **316** D8
Hinganghat *India* 20°30N 78°52E **244** D4
Hingham *U.S.A.* 48°33N 110°25W **304** B8
Hinghwa = Xinghua *China* 32°58N 119°48E **227** H10
Hingir *India* 21°57N 83°41E **243** J10
Hingoli *India* 19°41N 77°15E **244** E3
Hinigaran *Phil.* 10°16N 122°50E **233** F4
Hinis *Turkey* 39°22N 41°43E **213** C9
Hinna = Imi *Ethiopia* 6°28N 42°10E **257** F5
Hinna *Nigeria* 10°25N 11°35E **263** C7
Hinnerup *Denmark* 56°16N 10°4E **163** H4
Hinnøya *Norway* 68°35N 15°50E **160** B16
Hino *Japan* 35°0N 136°15E **223** C8
Hinoba-an *Phil.* 9°35N 122°28E **233** G4
Hinojosa del Duque *Spain* 38°30N 5°9W **195** G5
Hinokage *Japan* 32°39N 131°24E **222** E3
Hinsdale *U.S.A.* 42°47N 72°29W **313** D12
Hinterrhein → *Switz.* 46°40N 9°25E **179** J5
Hinthada = Henzada *Burma* 17°38N 95°26E **241** G5
Hinton *Alta., Canada* 53°26N 117°34W **296** C5
Hinton *W. Va., U.S.A.* 37°40N 80°54W **309** G13
Hinubuan = Antipolo *Phil.* 14°35N 121°10E **232** D3
Hinunangan *Phil.* 10°25N 125°12E **233** F5
Hios *Greece* 38°27N 26°9E **205** C8
Hios □ *Greece* 38°27N 26°9E **205** C8
Hirado *Japan* 33°22N 129°33E **222** D1
Hirado-Shima *Japan* 33°20N 129°30E **222** D1
Hirakata *Japan* 34°48N 135°38E **223** C7
Hirakud Dam *India* 21°32N 83°45E **244** D6
Hiran → *India* 23°6N 79°21E **243** H8
Hirapur *India* 24°22N 79°13E **243** G8
Hirara *Japan* 24°48N 125°17E **221** M2
Hirata *Japan* 35°24N 132°49E **222** B4
Hiratsuka *Japan* 35°19N 139°21E **223** B11
Hirekerur *India* 14°28N 75°23E **245** G2
Hirfanlı Barajı *Turkey* 39°18N 33°31E **212** C5
Hirhafok *Algeria* 23°49N 5°45E **261** D6
Hiromi *Japan* 33°13N 132°36E **222** D4
Hiroo *Japan* 42°17N 143°19E **220** C11
Hirosaki *Japan* 40°34N 140°28E **220** D10
Hiroshima *Japan* 34°24N 132°30E **222** C4
Hiroshima □ *Japan* 34°50N 133°0E **222** C5
Hiroshima-Wan *Japan* 34°5N 132°20E **222** C4
Hirota *Japan* 34°45N 135°20E **133** A1
Hirschberg = Jelenia Góra *Poland* 50°50N 15°45E **185** H2
Hirschstetten *Austria* 48°14N 16°27E **142** A2
Hirson *France* 49°55N 4°4E **173** C11
Hirtshals *Denmark* 57°36N 9°57E **163** G3
Hisai *Japan* 34°40N 136°28E **223** C8
Hisar *India* 29°12N 75°45E **242** E6
Hisarcık *Turkey* 39°15N 29°14E **205** B11
Hisaria *Bulgaria* 42°30N 24°44E **203** D8
Hisb, Sha'ib = Ḩasb, W. → *Iraq* 31°45N 44°17E **246** D5
Ḩismá *Si. Arabia* 28°30N 36°0E **251** K7
Ḩişn al 'Abr *Yemen* 16°8N 47°14E **248** C4
Hispaniola *W. Indies* 19°0N 71°0W **321** C5
History Center *U.S.A.* 33°45N 84°22W **113** B2
Hīt *Iraq* 33°38N 42°49E **213** F10
Hita *Japan* 33°20N 130°58E **222** D2
Hitachi *Japan* 36°36N 140°39E **223** A12
Hitachi-Ōta *Japan* 36°30N 140°30E **223** A12
Hitchin *U.K.* 51°58N 0°16W **169** F7
Hithadhoo *Maldives* 0°36S 73°5E **272** d
Hither Green *U.K.* 51°26N 0°0 **125** B3
Hitiaa *Tahiti* 17°36S 149°18W **289** e
Hitoyoshi *Japan* 32°13N 130°45E **222** E2
Hitra *Norway* 63°30N 8°45E **164** A5
Hitzacker *Germany* 53°9N 11°2E **178** B7
Hiu *Vanuatu* 13°10S 166°35E **287** C4
Hiuchi-Nada *Japan* 34°5N 133°20E **222** C5
Hiva Oa *French Polynesia* 9°45S 139°0W **289** f
Hixon *Canada* 53°25N 122°35W **296** C4
Hiyoshi *Japan* 35°32N 139°38E **140** B2
Ḩiyyon, N. → *Israel* 30°25N 35°10E **251** H6
Hizma *West Bank* 31°50N 35°16E **123** B2
Hjalmar L. *Canada* 61°33N 109°25W **297** A7
Hjälmaren *Sweden* 59°18N 15°40E **162** E9
Hjältevad *Sweden* 57°38N 15°20E **163** G9
Hjaltyeri *Iceland* 65°55N 18°18W **155** B8
Hjartdal *Norway* 59°37N 8°41E **164** E5
Hjelmelandsvågen *Norway* 59°14N 6°10E **164** E3
Hjelset *Norway* 62°48N 7°30E **164** B4
Hjerkinn *Norway* 62°13N 9°33E **164** B6
Hjo *Sweden* 58°22N 14°17E **163** F8
Hjørring *Denmark* 57°29N 9°59E **163** G3
Hjörsey *Iceland* 64°32N 22°21W **155** C4
Hjort Trench *S. Ocean* 58°0S 157°30E **151** B10
Hjortekær *Denmark* 55°47N 12°32E **118** A3
Hjortespring *Denmark* 55°44N 12°25E **118** A2
Hjortkvarn *Sweden* 58°54N 15°26E **163** F9
Hjukse *Norway* 59°31N 9°19E **164** E6
Hkakabo Razi *Burma* 28°25N 97°23E **241** B6
Hkakabo Razi △ *Burma* 28°0N 97°55E **241** B6
Hkamti = Singkaling Hkamti *Burma* 26°0N 95°39E **241** C5
Hko-lam *Burma* 21°7N 98°5E **241** E7
Hko-ut *Burma* 20°58N 98°2E **241** E7
Hkyenhpa *Burma* 27°43N 97°25E **241** B6
Hlaingbwe *Burma* 17°8N 97°50E **241** G6
Hlinsko *Czech Rep.* 49°45N 15°54E **180** B8
Hlobane *S. Africa* 27°42S 31°0E **271** C5
Hlohovec *Slovak Rep.* 48°26N 17°49E **181** C10
Hluboč̌epy *Czech Rep.* 50°2N 14°23E **135** B2
Hlučín *Czech Rep.* 49°54N 18°11E **181** B11
Hluhluwe *S. Africa* 28°1S 32°15E **271** C5
Hluhluwe ⌓ *S. Africa* 22°10S 32°5E **271** B5
Hlukhiv *Ukraine* 51°40N 33°58E **189** G7
Hlwaze *Burma* 18°54N 96°37E **241** F6
Hlyboka *Ukraine* 48°5N 25°56E **183** B10
Hlybokaye *Belarus* 55°10N 27°45E **188** E4
Hnappadalssýsla □ *Iceland* 64°50N 22°30W **155** C4
Hnífsdalur *Iceland* 66°7N 23°8W **155** A3
Hnúšťa *Slovak Rep.* 48°35N 19°58E **181** C12
Ho *Ghana* 6°37N 0°27E **263** D5
Ho Chi Minh City = Thanh Pho Ho Chi Minh *Vietnam* 10°58N 106°40E **237** G6
Ho Chung *China* 22°21N 114°14E **122** A2
Ho Thuong *Vietnam* 19°32N 105°48E **236** C5
Hoa Binh *Vietnam* 20°50N 105°20E **228** G5
Hoa Da *Vietnam* 11°16N 108°40E **237** G7
Hoa Hiep *Vietnam* 11°34N 105°51E **237** G5
Hoai Nhon *Vietnam* 14°28N 109°1E **236** E7
Hoang Lien Son *Vietnam* 22°0N 104°0E **228** F4
Hoanib → *Namibia* 19°27S 12°46E **270** A2
Hoare B. *Canada* 65°17N 62°30W **295** D19
Hoarusib → *Namibia* 19°3S 12°36E **270** A2
Hobart *Tas., Australia* 42°50S 147°21E **281** G4
Hobart *Ind., U.S.A.* 41°32N 87°15W **311** C9
Hobart *Okla., U.S.A.* 35°1N 99°6W **314** D5
Hobbs *U.S.A.* 32°42N 103°8W **305** K12
Hobbs Coast *Antarctica* 74°50S 131°0W **151** D14
Hobe Sound *U.S.A.* 27°4N 80°8W **317** H9
Hobo *Colombia* 2°35N 75°30W **328** C2
Hoboken *Ga., U.S.A.* 31°11N 82°8W **316** D7
Hoboken *New York, U.S.A.* **132** d1
Hobro *Denmark* 56°39N 9°46E **163** H3
Hobsons B. *Australia* 37°51S 144°55E **128** B1
Hoburgen *Sweden* 56°55N 18°7E **163** H12
Hobyo *Somali Rep.* 5°25N 48°30E **267** C6
Hocalar *Turkey* 38°36N 30°0E **205** C11
Hochbrück *Germany* 48°14N 11°37E **131** A2
Hochelaga *Canada* 45°32N 73°33W **130** A2
Hochfeld *Namibia* 21°28S 17°58E **270** B2
Hochharz △ *Germany* 51°48N 10°38E **178** D6
Hochschwab *Austria* 47°35N 15°0E **180** D8
Höchstadt *Germany* 49°42N 10°47E **179** F6
Hochtaunus ⌓ *Germany* 50°20N 8°30E **179** E4
Hoch'uan = Hechuan *China* 30°2N 106°12E **228** B6
Hochwan = Hechuan *China* 30°2N 106°12E **228** B6
Hockenheim *Germany* 49°19N 8°32E **179** F4
Hockley = Levelland *U.S.A.* 33°35N 102°23W **314** E3
Hodaka-Dake *Japan* 36°17N 137°39E **223** A9
Hodeida = Al Ḩudaydah *Yemen* 14°50N 43°0E **248** D3
Hodgeville *Canada* 50°7N 106°58W **297** C7
Hodgkins *U.S.A.* 41°46N 87°53W **119** C1
Hodgson *Canada* 51°13N 97°36W **297** C9
Hodh El Gharbi □ *Mauritania* 16°30N 10°0W **262** B3
Hódmezővásárhely *Hungary* 46°28N 20°22E **182** D5
Hodna, Chott el *Algeria* 35°26N 4°43E **261** A6
Hodo-dan *N. Korea* 39°23N 127°32E **224** C3
Hodonín *Czech Rep.* 48°50N 17°10E **181** C10
Hœdic, Î. de *France* 47°20N 2°53W **172** E4
Hoegi *S. Korea* 37°35N 127°3E **137** B2
Hoeilaart *Belgium* 50°46N 4°28E **116** B2
Hoek van Holland *Neths.* 52°0N 4°7E **170** C4
Hoengseong *S. Korea* 37°29N 127°59E **224** D3
Hoeryong *N. Korea* 42°30N 129°45E **224** A4
Hoeyang *N. Korea* 38°43N 127°36E **224** C3
Hof *Bayern, Germany* 50°19N 11°55E **179** E7
Hof *Norður-Múlasýsla, Iceland* 65°39N 15°0W **155** B11
Hof *Suður-Múlasýsla, Iceland* 64°33N 14°40W **155** C12
Hof *Vestfold, Norway* 59°32N 10°5E **164** E7
Hofburg *Vienna, Austria* **142** b1
Hofei = Hefei *China* 31°52N 117°18E **229** B11
Hoffell *Iceland* 64°23N 15°20W **155** C11
Hoffman I. *U.S.A.* 40°34N 74°3W **132** C1
Hofgarten *Munich, Germany* **131** a3
Hofgeismar *Germany* 51°29N 9°23E **178** D5
Hofheim *Germany* 50°5N 8°26E **179** E4
Hofmeyr *S. Africa* 31°39S 25°50E **270** D4
Höfn *Iceland* 64°15N 15°13W **155** C11
Hofors *Sweden* 60°31N 16°15E **162** D10
Hofsjökull *Iceland* 64°49N 18°48W **155** C8
Hofsós *Iceland* 65°53N 19°26W **155** B7
Hōfu *Japan* 34°3N 131°34E **222** C3
Hog Harbour *Vanuatu* 15°8S 167°6E **287** E5
Hog I. = Paradise I. *Bahamas* 25°6N 77°19W **153** b
Hog I. *Grenada* 12°0N 61°44W **323** q
Hog Pt. *Antigua & B.* 17°41N 61°47W **322** c
Hogan Group *Australia* 39°13S 147°1E **281** F4
Höganäs *Sweden* 56°12N 12°33E **163** H6
Hogansville *U.S.A.* 33°10N 84°55W **316** B5
Hogarth, Mt. *Australia* 21°48S 136°58E **280** C2
Hoge Kempen △ *Belgium* 51°6N 5°35E **170** C5
Høgeloft *Norway* 61°3N 8°12E **164** C5
Hogenakai Falls *India* 12°6N 77°50E **245** H3
Hoggar = Ahaggar *Algeria* 23°0N 6°30E **261** D6
Högsäter *Sweden* 58°38N 12°5E **163** F6
Högsby *Sweden* 57°10N 16°1E **163** G10
Högsjö *Sweden* 59°4N 15°44E **162** E9
Hogsty Reef *Bahamas* 21°41N 73°48W **321** B5
Hoh → *U.S.A.* 47°45N 124°29W **306** C2
Hoh Xil Shan *China* 35°0N 89°0E **218** C3
Hohd ech Chargui □ *Mauritania* 19°0N 7°15W **260** E3
Hohe Acht *Germany* 50°22N 7°0E **179** E3
Hohe Tauern *Austria* 47°11N 12°40E **180** D5
Hohe Tauern △ *Austria* 47°5N 12°20E **180** D5
Hohenau *Austria* 48°36N 16°55E **181** C9
Hohenbrunn *Germany* 48°2N 11°42E **131** B3
Hohenelbe = Vrchlabí *Czech Rep.* 50°38N 15°37E **180** A8
Hohenems *Austria* 47°22N 9°42E **180** D2
Hohenloher Ebene *Germany* 49°14N 9°36E **179** F5
Hohenmauth = Vysoké Mýto *Czech Rep.* 49°58N 16°10E **181** B9
Hohensalza = Inowrocław *Poland* 52°50N 18°12E **185** F5
Hohensalzburg = Lunino *Russia* 53°38N 45°18E **190** D7
Hohenschönhausen *Germany* 52°33N 13°30E **115** A4
Hohenstadt = Zábřeh *Czech Rep.* 49°53N 16°52E **181** B9
Hohenstein = Olsztynek *Poland* 53°34N 20°19E **184** E7
Hohenwald *U.S.A.* 35°33N 87°33W **315** D11
Hohenwestedt *Germany* 54°5N 9°40E **178** A5
Hoher Rhön = Rhön *Germany* 50°24N 9°58E **178** E5
Hoher Vogelsberg ⌓ *Germany* 51°45N 9°35E **178** D5
Hohes Venn *Belgium* 50°30N 6°5E **170** D6
Hohes Venn-Eifel ⌓ *Europe* 50°30N 6°10E **178** E2
Hohhot *China* 40°52N 111°40E **226** D6
Hohoe *Ghana* 7°8N 0°32E **263** D5
Hoi An *Vietnam* 15°30N 108°19E **236** E7
Hoi Xuan *Vietnam* 20°25N 105°9E **228** G5
Hoihow = Haikou *China* 20°1N 110°16E **236** B8
Hoisington *U.S.A.* 38°31N 98°47W **308** F4
Hojai *India* 26°2N 92°54E **241** B4
Hojambaz *Turkmenistan* 38°7N 65°0E **216** E6
Højer *Denmark* 54°58N 8°42E **163** K2
Hōjō *Japan* 33°58N 132°46E **222** D4
Hok *Sweden* 57°31N 14°16E **163** G8
Hokang = Hegang *China* 47°20N 130°19E **219** B8
Hökensås *Sweden* 58°0N 14°5E **163** G8
Hökerum *Sweden* 57°51N 13°16E **163** G7
Hokianga Harbour *N.Z.* 35°31S 173°22E **284** B2
Hokitika *N.Z.* 42°42S 171°0E **285** C6
Hokkaidō □ *Japan* 43°30N 143°0E **220** C11
Hokksund *Norway* 59°48N 9°54E **164** E6
Hol-Hol *Djibouti* 11°20N 42°50E **257** E5
Hola *Kenya* 1°29S 40°2E **268** B4
Hola Pristan *Ukraine* 46°29N 32°32E **189** J7
Holakas *Greece* 35°57N 27°53E **206** F11
Holalkere *India* 14°2N 76°11E **245** G3
Hólar *Iceland* 65°44N 19°8W **155** B7
Holargos *Greece* 37°59N 23°48E **112** B2
Holbæk *Denmark* 55°43N 11°43E **163** J5
Holborn *London, U.K.* **125** a4
Holbrook *N.S.W., Australia* 35°42S 147°18E **283** C7
Holbrook *Ariz., U.S.A.* 34°54N 110°10W **305** J8
Holcomb *U.S.A.* 42°54N 77°25W **312** D7
Holden *Mo., U.S.A.* 38°43N 94°0W **310** F3
Holden *Utah, U.S.A.* 39°6N 112°16W **304** G7
Holden, L. *U.S.A.* 28°30N 81°23W **133** B2
Holdenville *U.S.A.* 35°5N 96°24W **314** D6
Holdich *Argentina* 45°57S 68°13W **336** C3
Holdrege *U.S.A.* 40°26N 99°23W **308** E4
Hole-Narsipur *India* 12°48N 76°16E **245** H3
Holešov *Czech Rep.* 49°20N 17°35E **181** B10
Holešovice *Czech Rep.* 50°6N 14°28E **135** B2
Holetown *Barbados* 13°11N 59°38W **323** r
Holgate *U.S.A.* 41°15N 84°8W **311** C12
Holguín *Cuba* 20°50N 76°20W **320** B4
Holíč *Slovak Rep.* 48°49N 17°10E **181** C10
Holice *Czech Rep.* 50°5N 16°0E **180** A8
Holiday *U.S.A.* 28°11N 82°44W **317** G7
Höljes *Sweden* 60°50N 12°35E **162** D6
Hollabrunn *Austria* 48°34N 16°5E **180** C9
Hollams Bird I. *Namibia* 24°40S 14°30E **270** B1
Holland = Netherlands ■ *Europe* 52°0N 5°30E **170** C5
Holland *Mich., U.S.A.* 42°47N 86°7W **311** B10
Holland *N.Y., U.S.A.* 42°38N 78°32W **312** D6
Holland B. *Jamaica* 17°57N 76°13W **320** a
Holland Centre *Canada* 44°23N 80°47W **312** B4
Holland Patent *U.S.A.* 43°14N 75°15W **313** C9
Holland Tunnel *New York, U.S.A.* **132** d1
Holland Village *Singapore* 1°18N 103°47E **138** B2
Hollandale *U.S.A.* 33°10N 90°51W **315** E9
Hollandia = Jayapura *Indonesia* 2°28S 140°38E **231** E10
Holley *U.S.A.* 43°14N 78°2W **312** C6
Hollfeld *Germany* 49°56N 11°18E **179** F7
Hollidaysburg *U.S.A.* 40°26N 78°24W **312** F6
Hollis *U.S.A.* 34°41N 99°55W **314** D5
Hollis Reservoir *Trin. & Tob.* 10°40N 61°10W **323** t
Hollister *Calif., U.S.A.* 36°51N 121°24W **306** J5
Hollister *Idaho, U.S.A.* 42°21N 114°35W **304** E6
Höllriegelskreuth *Germany* 48°2N 11°30E **131** B1
Höllviken = Höllviksnäs *Sweden* 55°26N 12°58E **163** J6
Höllviksnäs *Sweden* 55°26N 12°58E **163** J6
Holly *U.S.A.* 42°48N 83°38W **311** B13
Holly Hill *Fla., U.S.A.* 29°16N 81°3W **317** F8
Holly Hill *S.C., U.S.A.* 33°19N 80°25W **316** B9
Holly Springs *Ga., U.S.A.* 34°10N 84°30W **316** A5
Holly Springs *Miss., U.S.A.* 34°46N 89°27W **315** D10
Hollywood *Calif., U.S.A.* 34°5N 118°19W **126** B3
Hollywood *Fla., U.S.A.* 26°0N 80°8W **317** J9
Hollywood Bowl *U.S.A.* 34°7N 118°20W **126** B2
Holman *Canada* 70°44N 117°44W **294** C8
Hólmavík *Iceland* 65°42N 21°40W **155** B5
Holmen *Oppland, Norway* 60°40N 10°22E **164** D7
Holmen *Wis., U.S.A.* 43°58N 91°15W **308** D8
Holmenkollen *Norway* 59°57N 10°41E **133** A3
Holmes Beach *U.S.A.* 27°31N 82°43W **317** H7
Holmes Cr. → *U.S.A.* 30°30N 85°50W **316** E4
Holmes Reefs *Australia* 16°27S 148°0E **280** B4
Holmes Run Acres *U.S.A.* 38°51N 77°13W **143** B2
Holmestrand *Norway* 59°31N 10°14E **164** E7
Holmgård *Sweden* 59°14N 18°0E **139** B1
Holmlia *Norway* 59°49N 10°46E **133** B3
Holmsjö *Sweden* 56°25N 15°32E **163** H9
Holmsjön *Västernorrland, Sweden* 62°41N 16°33E **162** B10
Holmsjön *Västernorrland, Sweden* 62°26N 15°20E **162** B9
Holmslands Klit *Denmark* 56°0N 8°5E **163** J2
Holmsund *Sweden* 63°41N 20°20E **160** E19
Holocaust Memorial *Israel* 31°47N 35°11E **123** B2
Holocaust Memorial Park *Boston, U.S.A.* **116** b2
Holod *Romania* 46°49N 22°8E **182** D7
Holon *Israel* 32°0N 34°46E **251** G5
Holopaw *U.S.A.* 28°8N 81°5W **317** G8
Holovne *Ukraine* 51°20N 24°5E **185** G11
Høløydal *Norway* 62°12N 11°27E **164** B8
Holozubyntsi *Ukraine* 48°50N 26°55E **183** B11
Holroyd → *Australia* 14°10S 141°36E **280** A3
Holstebro *Denmark* 56°22N 8°37E **163** H2
Holsteinische Schweiz ⌓ *Germany* 54°8N 10°30E **178** A6
Holsteinsborg = Sisimiut *Greenland* 66°40N 53°30W **154** D5
Holsworthy *U.K.* 50°48N 4°22W **169** G3
Holt *Iceland* 63°33N 19°48W **155** D7
Holt *Fla., U.S.A.* 30°43N 86°45W **317** E3
Holt *Mich., U.S.A.* 42°39N 84°31W **311** B12
Holton *Nfld. & L., Canada* 54°31N 57°12W **299** B8
Holton *Kans., U.S.A.* 39°28N 95°44W **308** F6
Holts Summit *U.S.A.* 38°38N 92°7W **310** F4
Holtville *U.S.A.* 32°49N 115°23W **307** N11
Holualoa *U.S.A.* 19°37N 155°57W **302** D6
Holum *Norway* 58°6N 7°32E **164** F4
Holwerd *Neths.* 53°22N 5°54E **170** A5
Holy Cross *U.S.A.* 62°12N 159°46W **303** E8
Holy I. *Anglesey, U.K.* 53°17N 4°37W **168** D3
Holy I. *Northumberland, U.K.* 55°40N 1°47W **168** B6
Holyhead *U.K.* 53°18N 4°38W **168** D3
Holyoke *Colo., U.S.A.* 40°35N 102°18W **304** F12
Holyoke *Mass., U.S.A.* 42°12N 72°37W **313** D12
Holyrood *Canada* 47°27N 53°8W **299** C9
Holyrood House, Palace of *U.K.* 55°57N 3°10W **121** B3
Holysloot *Neths.* 52°25N 5°2E **112** A3
Holzkirchen *Germany* 47°52N 11°42E **179** H7
Holzminden *Germany* 51°50N 9°28E **178** D5
Homa Bay *Kenya* 0°36S 34°30E **268** C3
Homalin *Burma* 24°55N 95°0E **241** C5
Homand *Iran* 32°28N 59°37E **247** C8
Homathko → *Canada* 51°0N 124°56W **296** C4
Homberg *Germany* 51°2N 9°25E **178** D5
Hombori *Mali* 15°20N 1°38W **263** B4
Hombori Tondo *Mali* 15°16N 1°40W **263** B4
Homburg *Germany* 49°28N 7°18E **179** F3
Home B. *Canada* 68°40N 67°10W **295** D18
Home Hill *Australia* 19°43S 147°25E **280** B4
Home Reef *Tonga* 18°59S 174°47W **287** P13
Homedale *U.S.A.* 43°37N 116°56W **304** E5
Homei *Taiwan* 24°7N 120°29E **225** B2
Homeland *U.S.A.* 30°51N 82°1W **316** E7
Homer *Alaska, U.S.A.* 59°39N 151°33W **303** G10
Homer *Ill., U.S.A.* 40°4N 87°57W **311** D9
Homer *La., U.S.A.* 32°48N 93°4W **314** E8
Homer *Mich., U.S.A.* 42°9N 84°49W **311** B12
Homer *N.Y., U.S.A.* 42°38N 76°10W **313** D8
Homer City *U.S.A.* 40°32N 79°10W **312** F5
Homert ⌓ *Germany* 51°15N 8°0E **178** D4
Homerton *U.K.* 51°32N 0°2W **125** A3
Homerville *U.S.A.* 31°2N 82°45W **316** D7
Homestead *Queens., Australia* 20°20S 145°40E **280** C4
Homestead *Fla., U.S.A.* 25°28N 80°29W **317** K9
Homestead ⌓ *U.S.A.* 40°17N 96°50W **308** E5
Hometown *U.S.A.* 41°44N 87°42W **119** C2
Homewood *U.S.A.* 41°34N 87°40W **311** C9
Hommelvik *Norway* 63°25N 10°48E **164** A7
Hommersåk *Norway* 58°56N 5°50E **164** F2
Homnabad *India* 17°45N 77°11E **244** F3
Homoine *Mozam.* 23°55S 35°8E **271** B6
Homoljske Planina *Serbia* 44°10N 21°45E **202** B5
Homonhon I. *Phil.* 10°44N 125°43E **233** F5
Homorod *Romania* 46°5N 25°15E **183** D10
Homosassa Springs *U.S.A.* 28°48N 82°35W **317** G7
Homs = Al Khums *Libya* 32°40N 14°17E **258** B2
Homs = Ḩimş *Syria* 34°40N 36°45E **250** D7
Homyel *Belarus* 52°28N 31°0E **177** B16
Homyel □ *Belarus* 52°40N 30°10E **189** F6
Hon Chong *Vietnam* 10°25N 104°30E **237** G5
Hon Hai *Vietnam* 10°0N 109°0E **237** H7
Hon Me *Vietnam* 19°23N 105°56E **236** C5
Honan = Henan □ *China* 34°0N 114°0E **226** H8
Hōnanchō *Japan* 35°40N 139°39E **140** A2
Hōnaunau *U.S.A.* 19°26N 155°55W **302** D6
Honavar *India* 14°17N 74°27E **245** G2
Honaz *Turkey* 37°46N 29°18E **205** D11
Honbetsu *Japan* 43°7N 143°37E **220** C11
Honcho *Japan* 35°40N 139°41E **140** A3
Honcut *U.S.A.* 39°20N 121°32W **306** F5
Honda *Colombia* 5°12N 74°45W **328** B3
Honda, Bahía *Cuba* 22°54N 83°10W **320** B3
Honda Bay *Phil.* 9°53N 118°49E **233** G2
Hondarribia *Spain* 43°22N 1°47W **196** B3
Hondeklipbaai *S. Africa* 30°19S 17°17E **270** D2
Honden *Japan* 35°43N 139°50E **140** A4
Hondo *Japan* 32°27N 130°12E **222** E2
Hondo *Tex., U.S.A.* 29°21N 99°9W **314** G5
Hondo, Río → *Belize* 18°25N 88°21W **319** D7
Hondo, Rio → *Calif., U.S.A.* 34°2N 118°15W **126** B4
Honduras ■ *Cent. Amer.* 14°40N 86°30W **320** D2
Honduras, G. de *Caribbean* 16°50N 87°0W **320** C2
Hønefoss *Norway* 60°10N 10°18E **164** D7
Honesdale *U.S.A.* 41°34N 75°16W **313** E9
Honey Harbour *Canada* 44°52N 79°49W **312** B5
Honey L. *U.S.A.* 40°15N 120°19W **306** E6
Honfleur *France* 49°25N 0°13E **172** C7
Hong *Denmark* 55°31N 11°18E **163** J5
Hong Gai *Vietnam* 20°57N 107°5E **228** G6
Hong He → *China* 32°25N 115°35E **226** H8
Hong Hu *China* 29°54N 113°24E **229** C9
Hong Kong *China* 22°17N 114°11E **122** B1
Hong Kong □ *China* 22°11N 114°14E **219** G11
Hong Kong, Univ. of *China* 22°16N 114°8E **122** B1
Hong Kong I. *China* 22°16N 114°12E **122** B2
Hong Kong Int. ✈ (HKG) *China* 22°19N 113°57E **219** G10
Hong Kong Park *Hong Kong, China* **122** c1
Honga *Angola* 15°9S 15°12E **265** F3
Hong'an *China* 31°20N 114°40E **229** B10
Hongcheon *S. Korea* 37°44N 127°53E **224** D3
Hongdo *S. Korea* 34°41N 125°12E **224** E2
Honghai Wan *China* 22°40N 115°0E **229** F10
Honghe *China* 23°25N 102°25E **228** F4
Honghu *China* 29°50N 113°30E **229** C9
Hongje *S. Korea* 37°35N 126°56E **137** B1
Hongjiang *China* 27°7N 109°59E **228** D7
Hongjimun Tunnel *S. Korea* 37°37N 126°58E **137** B1
Hongkou *China* 31°16N 121°29E **138** B1
Hongliu He → *China* 38°0N 109°50E **226** F5
Hongor *Mongolia* 45°45N 112°50E **226** B7
Hongqiao *China* 31°11N 121°22E **138** B1
Hongsa *Laos* 19°43N 101°20E **236** C3
Hongseong *S. Korea* 36°37N 126°38E **224** D3
Hongshui He → *China* 23°48N 109°30E **228** F7
Hongtong *China* 36°16N 111°40E **226** F6
Honguedo, Détroit d' *Canada* 49°15N 64°0W **299** C7
Hongwon *N. Korea* 40°0N 127°56E **224** C4
Hongya *China* 29°57N 103°22E **228** C4
Hongyuan *China* 32°51N 102°40E **228** A4
Hongze Hu *China* 33°15N 118°35E **227** H10
Honiara *Solomon Is.* 9°27S 159°57E **287** M10
Honiton *U.K.* 50°47N 3°11W **169** G4
Honjō *Akita, Japan* 39°23N 140°3E **220** E10
Honjō *Gumma, Japan* 36°14N 139°11E **223** A11
Honjyo *Japan* 35°41N 139°48E **140** A3
Honkawane *Japan* 35°5N 138°5E **223** B10
Honkorâb, Ras *Egypt* 24°35N 35°10E **256** C4
Honnali *India* 14°15N 75°40E **245** G2
Honningsvåg *Norway* 70°59N 25°59E **160** A21
Hönö *Sweden* 57°41N 11°39E **163** G5
Honoka'a *U.S.A.* 20°5N 155°28W **302** C6
Honokai Hale *U.S.A.* 21°20N 158°6W **302** K13
Honolulu *U.S.A.* 21°19N 157°52W **302** K14
Honolulu District *U.S.A.* 21°19N 157°46W **302** K14
Honolulu Int. ✈ (HNL) *U.S.A.* 21°19N 157°55W **302** K14
Honomu *U.S.A.* 19°52N 155°7W **302** D6
Honoré Mercier, Pont *Canada* 45°24N 73°39W **130** B1
Honouliuli *U.S.A.* 21°22N 158°2W **302** K13
Hönow *Germany* 52°32N 13°38E **115** A4
Honshū *Japan* 36°0N 138°0E **223** A8
Hontoria del Pinar *Spain* 41°50N 3°10W **196** D1
Honu'apo B. *U.S.A.* 19°5N 155°33W **302** D6
Hood, I. = Española, I. *Ecuador* 1°23S 89°39W **330** a
Hood, Mt. *U.S.A.* 45°23N 121°42W **304** D3
Hood, Pt. *Australia* 34°23S 119°34E **279** F2
Hood Pt. *Papua N. G.* 10°4S 147°45E **286** F4
Hood River *U.S.A.* 45°43N 121°31W **304** D3
Hoodsport *U.S.A.* 47°24N 123°9W **306** C3
Hooge *Germany* 54°34N 8°33E **178** A4
Hoogeveen *Neths.* 52°44N 6°28E **170** B6
Hoogezand-Sappemeer *Neths.* 53°9N 6°45E **170** A6
Hooghly = Hugli → *India* 21°56N 88°4E **243** J13
Hooghly-Chinsura = Chunchura *India* 22°53N 88°27E **243** H13
Hook *U.K.* 51°22N 0°17W **125** B2
Hook Hd. *Ireland* 52°7N 6°56W **166** D5
Hook I. *Australia* 20°4S 149°0E **280** b
Hook of Holland = Hoek van Holland *Neths.* 52°0N 4°7E **170** C4
Hooker *U.S.A.* 36°52N 101°13W **314** C4
Hooker Creek = Lajamanu *Australia* 18°23S 130°38E **278** C5
Hooker Creek ◎ *Australia* 18°6S 130°23E **278** C5
Ho'olehua *U.S.A.* 21°10N 157°5W **302** B4
Hoonah *U.S.A.* 58°7N 135°27W **296** B1
Hoop *Neth. Ant.* 12°7N 68°17W **322** h
Hooper Bay *U.S.A.* 61°32N 166°6W **303** F6
Hoopeston *U.S.A.* 40°28N 87°40W **311** D9
Hoopstad *S. Africa* 27°50S 25°55E **270** C4
Höör *Sweden* 55°56N 13°33E **163** J7
Hoorn *Neths.* 52°38N 5°4E **170** B5
Hoover *U.S.A.* 33°24N 86°49W **315** E11
Hoover Dam *U.S.A.* 36°1N 114°44W **307** K12
Hooversville *U.S.A.* 40°9N 78°55W **312** F6
Hop Bottom *U.S.A.* 41°42N 75°46W **313** E9
Hopa *Turkey* 41°28N 41°30E **213** B9
Hope *B.C., Canada* 49°25N 121°25W **296** D4
Hope *Ariz., U.S.A.* 33°43N 113°42W **307** M13
Hope *Ark., U.S.A.* 33°40N 93°36W **314** E8
Hope *Ind., U.S.A.* 39°18N 85°46W **311** E11
Hope, L. *S. Austral., Australia* 28°24S 139°18E **281** D2
Hope, L. *W. Austral., Australia* 32°35S 120°15E **279** F3
Hope, Pt. *U.S.A.* 68°21N 166°47W **303** B6
Hope Bay *Jamaica* 18°12N 76°34W **320** a
Hope I. *Canada* 44°55N 80°11W **312** B4
Hope Town *Bahamas* 26°35N 76°57W **320** A4
Hope Vale *Australia* 15°16S 145°20E **280** B4
Hope Vale ◎ *Australia* 15°8S 145°15E **280** B4
Hopedale *Nfld. & L., Canada* 55°28N 60°13W **299** A7
Hopedale *Mass., U.S.A.* 42°8N 71°33W **313** D13
Hopefield *S. Africa* 33°3S 18°22E **270** D2
Hopei = Hebei □ *China* 39°0N 116°0E **226** E9
Hopelchén *Mexico* 19°46N 89°51W **319** D7
Hopetoun *Vic., Australia* 35°42S 142°22E **282** C5
Hopetoun *W. Austral., Australia* 33°57S 120°7E **279** F3
Hopetown *S. Africa* 29°34S 24°3E **270** C3
Hopewell *U.S.A.* 37°18N 77°17W **309** G15
Hopfgarten *Austria* 47°27N 12°10E **180** D5
Hopin *Burma* 24°58N 96°30E **241** C6
Hoping *Changhua, Taiwan* 24°10N 120°56E **225** B2
Hoping *T'aitung, Taiwan* 23°4N 121°20E **225** C3
Hopkins *U.S.A.* 40°33N 94°49W **310** D2
Hopkins, L. *Australia* 24°15S 128°35E **278** D4
Hopkinsville *U.S.A.* 36°52N 87°29W **308** G10
Hopland *U.S.A.* 38°58N 123°7W **306** G3
Hopong *Burma* 20°47N 97°11E **241** E6
Hopwood's Ferry = Echuca *Australia* 36°10S 144°45E **283** D6
Hoque *Angola* 14°40S 13°55E **265** E2
Hoquiam *U.S.A.* 46°59N 123°53W **306** D3
Hora Hoverla *Ukraine* 48°7N 24°47E **183** B9
Hora Sfakion = Chora Sfakion *Greece* 35°15N 24°9E **207** E5
Hōrai *Japan* 34°58N 137°32E **223** C9
Horana *Sri Lanka* 6°43N 80°4E **245** L5
Horasan *Turkey* 40°3N 42°11E **213** B10
Horažďovice *Czech Rep.* 49°19N 13°42E **180** B6
Horb *Germany* 48°26N 8°47E **179** G4
Hörby *Sweden* 55°51N 13°40E **163** J7
Horcajo de Santiago *Spain* 39°50N 3°1W **196** F1
Hordabø *Norway* 60°42N 4°54E **164** D1
Hordaland □ *Norway* 60°25N 6°15E **164** D3
Hordern Hills *Australia* 20°15S 130°0E **278** D5
Horezu *Romania* 45°6N 24°0E **183** E8
Horgen *Switz.* 47°15N 8°35E **179** H4
Horgoš *Serbia* 46°10N 20°0E **182** D4
Hořice *Czech Rep.* 50°21N 15°39E **180** A8
Horikiri *Japan* 35°44N 139°50E **140** A4
Horinchove *Ukraine* 48°16N 23°26E **183** B8
Horinger *China* 40°28N 111°48E **226** D6
Horizontina *Brazil* 27°37S 54°19W **335** B5
Horki *Belarus* 54°17N 30°59E **188** E6
Horlick Mts. *Antarctica* 84°0S 102°0W **151** E15
Horlivka *Ukraine* 48°19N 38°5E **189** H10
Hormak *Iran* 29°58N 60°51E **247** D9
Hormigueros *Puerto Rico* 18°8N 67°8W **321** b
Hormoz *Iran* 27°35N 55°0E **247** E7
Hormoz, Jaz.-ye *Iran* 27°8N 56°28E **247** E8
Hormozgān □ *Iran* 27°30N 56°0E **247** E8
Hormuz, Kūh-e *Iran* 27°27N 55°10E **247** E7
Hormuz, Str. of *The Gulf* 26°30N 56°30E **247** E8
Horn *Austria* 48°39N 15°40E **180** C8
Horn *Iceland* 66°28N 22°28W **155** A4
Horn *Sweden* 57°54N 15°51E **163** G9
Horn → *Canada* 61°30N 118°1W **296** A5
Horn, Cape = Hornos, C. de *Chile* 55°50S 67°30W **336** E3
Horn, Is. *Wall. & F. Is.* 14°16S 178°6W **277** C15
Horn Head *Ireland* 55°14N 8°0W **166** A3
Horn I. *Australia* 10°37S 142°17E **286** F2
Horn Plateau *Canada* 62°15N 119°15W **296** A5
Horn Pond *U.S.A.* 42°28N 71°9W **116** A1
Hornachuelos *Spain* 37°50N 5°14W **195** H5
Hornavan *Sweden* 66°15N 17°30E **160** C17
Hornbeck *U.S.A.* 31°20N 93°24W **314** F8
Hornbrook *U.S.A.* 41°55N 122°33W **304** F2
Hornburg *Germany* 52°2N 10°37E **178** C6
Hornby *N.Z.* 43°33S 172°33E **285** D7
Horncastle *U.K.* 53°13N 0°7W **168** D7
Hornchurch *U.K.* 51°33N 0°14E **125** A5
Horndal *Sweden* 60°18N 16°23E **162** D10
Hornell *U.S.A.* 42°20N 77°40W **312** D7
Hornell L. *Canada* 62°20N 119°25W **296** A5
Hornepayne *Canada* 49°14N 84°48W **298** C3
Horní Černošice *Czech Rep.* 50°2N 14°33E **135** B3
Horní Planá *Czech Rep.* 48°46N 14°2E **180** C7
Horní Počernice *Czech Rep.* 50°6N 14°36E **135** B3
Hornindal *Norway* 61°58N 6°30E **164** C3
Hornings Mills *Canada* 44°9N 80°12W **312** B4
Hornitos *U.S.A.* 37°30N 120°14W **306** H6
Hornopirén △ *Chile* 41°58S 72°17W **336** B2
Hornos, C. de *Chile* 55°50S 67°30W **336** E3
Hornos, Is. *Papua N. G.* 2°12S 147°45E **286** B4
Hornoy-le-Bourg *France* 49°50N 1°54E **173** C8
Hornsby *Australia* 33°42S 151°2E **283** B9
Hornsea *U.K.* 53°55N 0°11W **168** D7
Hornsey *U.K.* 51°35N 0°7W **125** A3
Hornsjø *Norway* 61°19N 10°38E **164** C7
Hornslandet *Sweden* 61°35N 17°37E **162** C11
Hörnum *Germany* 54°45N 8°17E **178** A4
Horobetsu = Noboribetsu *Japan* 42°24N 141°6E **220** C10
Horodenka *Ukraine* 48°41N 25°29E **183** B10
Horodnya *Ukraine* 51°55N 31°33E **189** G6
Horodok *Khmelnytskyy, Ukraine* 49°10N 26°34E **177** D14
Horodok *Lviv, Ukraine* 49°46N 23°32E **177** D12
Horodyshche *Ukraine* 49°17N 31°27E **189** H6
Horokhiv *Ukraine* 50°30N 24°45E **177** C13
Horoměřice *Czech Rep.* 50°8N 14°20E **135** B1
Horovice *Czech Rep.* 49°48N 13°53E **180** B6
Horqin Youyi Qianqi *China* 46°5N 122°3E **227** A12
Horqueta *Paraguay* 23°15S 56°55W **334** A4
Horred *Sweden* 57°22N 12°28E **163** G6
Horse Cr. → *U.S.A.* 41°57N 103°58W **304** F12
Horse I. *Canada* 53°20N 99°6W **297** C9
Horse Is. *Canada* 50°15N 55°50W **299** B8
Horsefly L. *Canada* 52°25N 121°0W **296** C4
Horseheads *U.S.A.* 42°10N 76°49W **312** D8
Horsens *Denmark* 55°52N 9°51E **163** J3
Horseshoe Bend ⌓ *U.S.A.* 32°59N 85°44W **316** C4
Horseshoe Lake *Canada* 45°17N 79°51W **312** A5
Horsham *Vic., Australia* 36°44S 142°13E **282** D5
Horsham *W. Susx., U.K.* 51°4N 0°20W **169** F7
Horšovský Týn *Czech Rep.* 49°31N 12°58E **180** B5
Horta *Azores* 38°32N 28°38W **153** d1
Hortaleza *Spain* 40°28N 3°38W **127** B2
Horten *Norway* 59°25N 10°32E **164** E7
Hortense *U.S.A.* 31°20N 81°57W **316** D8
Horti *India* 17°7N 75°47E **244** F2
Hortobágy → *Hungary* 47°30N 21°6E **182** C6
Hortobágyi △ *Hungary* 47°36N 21°10E **182** C6
Horton *Kans., U.S.A.* 39°40N 95°32W **308** F6
Horton *Mo., U.S.A.* 37°58N 94°22W **310** G2
Horton → *Canada* 69°56N 126°52W **294** D6
Hortus Botanicus *Amsterdam, Neths.* **112** b3
Horwood L. *Canada* 48°5N 82°20W **298** C3
Hosaina *Ethiopia* 7°30N 37°47E **257** F4
Hosapete = Hospet *India* 15°15N 76°20E **245** G3
Hosdrug = Kanhangad *India* 12°21N 74°58E **245** H2
Hosdurga *India* 13°49N 76°17E **245** H3
Hosenofu *Libya* 23°41N 21°4E **258** D4
Ḩoseynābād *Khuzestan, Iran* 32°45N 48°20E **247** C6
Ḩoseynābād *Kordestān, Iran* 35°33N 47°8E **213** E12
Hosford *U.S.A.* 30°23N 84°48W **316** E5
Hōsh 'Īsa *Egypt* 30°55N 30°17E **256** H7
Hoshangabad *India* 22°45N 77°45E **242** H7
Hoshiarpur *India* 31°30N 75°58E **242** D6
Hoskins *Papua N. G.* 5°29S 150°27E **286** C6
Hoskote *India* 13°4N 77°48E **245** H3
Hosoyama *Japan* 35°36N 139°31E **140** B2
Hospet *India* 15°15N 76°20E **245** G3
Hostafrancs *Spain* 41°21N 2°8E **114** A1
Hoste, I. *Chile* 55°0S 69°0W **336** E3
Hostens *France* 44°30N 0°40W **174** D3
Hostivař *Czech Rep.* 50°3N 14°31E **135** B3
Hosur *India* 12°43N 77°49E **245** H3
Hot *Thailand* 18°8N 98°29E **236** C2
Hot Creek Range *U.S.A.* 38°40N 116°20W **304** G5
Hot Springs = Truth or Consequences *U.S.A.* 33°8N 107°15W **305** K10
Hot Springs *Ark., U.S.A.* 34°31N 93°3W **314** D8
Hot Springs *S. Dak., U.S.A.* 43°26N 103°29W **308** D2
Hot Springs △ *U.S.A.* 34°31N 93°3W **314** D8
Hotagen *Sweden* 63°59N 14°12E **160** E16
Hotan *China* 37°25N 79°55E **217** E9
Hotan He → *China* 40°22N 80°56E **217** D10
Hotazel *S. Africa* 27°17S 22°58E **270** C3
Hotchkiss *U.S.A.* 38°48N 107°43W **304** G10
Hôtel des Invalides *Paris, France* **134** c2
Hotham, C. *Australia* 12°2S 131°18E **278** B5
Hoting *Sweden* 64°8N 16°15E **160** D17
Hotolisht *Albania* 41°10N 20°25E **202** E4
Hotspur Seamount *Atl. Oc.* 17°55S 35°55W **152** H8
Hotte, Massif de la *Haiti* 18°30N 73°45W **321** C5
Hottentotsbaai *Namibia* 26°8S 14°59E **270** C1
Hou Hai *China* 22°32N 113°56E **219** F10
Houailou *N. Cal.* 21°17S 165°38E **288** d
Houat, Î. de *France* 47°24N 2°58W **172** E4
Houbětín *Czech Rep.* 50°6N 14°33E **135** B3
Houdan *France* 48°48N 1°35E **173** D8
Houei Sai *Laos* 20°18N 100°26E **228** G3
Houeillès *France* 44°12N 0°2E **174** D4
Houffalize *Belgium* 50°8N 5°48E **170** D5
Houghton *Gauteng, S. Africa* 26°10S 28°3E **123** B2
Houghton *Mich., U.S.A.* 47°7N 88°34W **308** B9
Houghton *N.Y., U.S.A.* 42°25N 78°10W **312** D6
Houghton L. *U.S.A.* 44°21N 84°44W **309** C11
Houghton-le-Spring *U.K.* 54°51N 1°28W **168** C6
Houhora Heads *N.Z.* 34°49S 173°9E **284** A2
Houilles *France* 48°56N 2°11E **134** A2
Houli *Taiwan* 24°19N 120°44E **225** B2
Houlton *U.S.A.* 46°8N 67°51W **309** B20
Houlung *Taiwan* 24°37N 120°47E **225** B2
Houma *U.S.A.* 29°36N 90°43W **315** G9
Houmt Souk = Djerba *Tunisia* 33°48N 10°54E **258** B2
Houndé *Burkina Faso* 11°34N 3°31W **262** C4
Hounslow □ *U.K.* 51°28N 0°21W **125** B1
Houpi *Taiwan* 23°22N 120°21E **225** C2
Hourtin *France* 45°11N 1°4W **174** C2
Hourtin-Carcans, Étang d' *France* 45°10N 1°6W **174** C2
Housatonic → *U.S.A.* 41°10N 73°7W **313** E11
House of Nobility = Riddarhuset *Stockholm, Sweden* **139** c2
House of Parliament = Riksdagshuset *Stockholm, Sweden* **139** b2
Houses of Parliament *London, U.K.* **125** c3
Houston *B.C., Canada* 54°25N 126°39W **296** C3
Houston *Fla., U.S.A.* 30°15N 82°54W **316** E7
Houston *Mo., U.S.A.* 37°22N 91°58W **308** G8
Houston *Tex., U.S.A.* 29°45N 95°21W **314** G7
Hout = Mogwadi → *S. Africa* 23°4S 29°36E **271** B4
Hout Bay *S. Africa* 34°2S 18°23E **118** B1
Houtkraal *S. Africa* 30°23S 24°5E **270** D3
Houtman Abrolhos *Australia* 28°43S 113°48E **279** E1
Hov *Norway* 60°42N 10°20E **164** D7
Hovd □ *Mongolia* 48°2N 91°37E **217** C12
Hovda *Norway* 60°53N 9°11E **164** D6
Hovden *Aust-Agder, Norway* 59°33N 7°22E **164** E4
Hovden *Sogn og Fjordane, Norway* 61°41N 4°52E **164** C1
Hove *U.K.* 50°50N 0°10W **169** G7
Hove Å → *Denmark* 55°43N 12°7E **118** B2
Hovedøya *Norway* 59°53N 10°43E **133** A3
Hovedstaden □ *Denmark* 56°0N 10°0E **163** J6
Hovenweep ⌓ *U.S.A.* 37°20N 109°0W **305** H9
Hovet *Norway* 60°38N 8°8E **164** D5
Hoveyzeh *Iran* 31°27N 48°4E **247** D6
Hovgaard Ø *Greenland* 79°55N 18°50W **154** B9
Hovik *Norway* 59°54N 10°34E **133** A2
Hovin *Norway* 59°51N 9°0E **164** E6
Hovmantorp *Sweden* 56°47N 15°7E **163** H9
Hovorčovice *Czech Rep.* 50°10N 14°31E **135** A3
Hövsgöl *Mongolia* 43°37N 109°39E **226** C5
Hövsgöl Nuur *Mongolia* 51°0N 100°30E **218** A5
Hovsta *Sweden* 59°22N 15°15E **162** E9
Howakil *Eritrea* 15°10N 40°16E **257** D5
Howar, Wadi → *Sudan* 17°30N 27°8E **257** D2
Howard *Queens., Australia* 25°16S 152°32E **281** D5
Howard *Pa., U.S.A.* 41°1N 77°40W **312** F7
Howard *S. Dak., U.S.A.* 44°1N 97°32W **308** C5
Howard Beach *U.S.A.* 40°39N 73°50W **132** C2
Howe *U.S.A.* 43°48N 113°0W **304** E7
Howe, C. *Australia* 37°30S 150°0E **283** D9
Howe, West Cape *Australia* 35°8S 117°36E **279** G2
Howe I. *Canada* 44°16N 76°17W **313** B8
Howell *U.S.A.* 42°36N 83°56W **311** B13
Howick *Qué., Canada* 45°11N 73°51W **313** A11
Howick *N.Z.* 36°54S 174°56E **284** C3
Howick *KwaZulu Natal, S. Africa* 29°28S 30°14E **271** C5
Howick Group *Australia* 14°20S 145°30E **280** A4
Howitt, L. *Australia* 27°40S 138°40E **281** D2
Howland I. *Pac. Oc.* 0°48N 176°38W **288** G10
Howlong *Australia* 35°59S 146°38E **283** C7
Howrah = Haora *India* 22°34N 88°18E **124** B1
Howth *Ireland* 53°23N 6°6W **120** A3
Howth Hd. *Ireland* 53°22N 6°4W **120** A3
Höxter *Germany* 51°46N 9°22E **178** D5
Hoxtolgay *China* 46°35N 85°59E **217** C11
Hoxton *London, U.K.* **125** a5
Hoxud *China* 42°15N 86°51E **217** D11
Hoy *U.K.* 58°50N 3°15W **167** C5
Hoya *Niedersachsen, Germany* 52°49N 9°8E **178** C5
Hōya *Tōkyō, Japan* 35°44N 139°34E **140** A2
Høyanger *Norway* 61°13N 6°4E **164** C3
Hoyerswerda *Germany* 51°26N 14°14E **178** D10
Hoylake *U.K.* 53°24N 3°10W **168** D4
Hōyo-Kaikyō *Japan* 33°20N 131°58E **222** D3
Hoyos *Spain* 40°9N 6°45W **194** E4
Hpa-an = Pa-an *Burma* 16°51N 97°40E **241** G6
Hpawlum *Burma* 27°12N 98°12E **241** B7
Hpettintha *Burma* 24°14N 95°23E **241** C5
Hpizow *Burma* 26°57N 98°24E **241** B7
Hpunan Pass *Burma* 27°30N 96°55E **241** A6
Hradčany *Czech Rep.* 50°5N 14°24E **135** B2

Hradec Králové Czech Rep. 50°15N 15°50E 180 A8
Hrádek Czech Rep. 48°46N 16°16E 181 C9
Hrafnseyri Iceland 65°46N 23°28W 155 B3
Hranice Czech Rep. 49°34N 17°45E 181 B10
Hrazdan Armenia 40°30N 44°46E 191 K7
Hrebenka Ukraine 50°9N 32°22E 189 G7
Hrífunes Iceland 63°38N 18°30W 155 D8
Hrísey Iceland 66°0N 18°23W 155 B8
Hrisoupoli Greece 40°58N 24°42E 203 F8
Hristiana Greece 36°14N 25°13E 205 E7
Hrodna Belarus 53°42N 23°52E 184 E10
Hrodna □ Belarus 53°20N 24°45E 188 F3
Hrodzyanka Belarus 53°31N 28°42E 177 B15
Hron → Slovak Rep. 47°49N 18°45E 181 D11
Hrubieszów Poland 50°49N 23°51E 185 H10
Hrubý Jeseník Czech Rep. 50°5N 17°10E 181 A10
Hrvatska = Croatia ■ Europe 45°20N 16°0E 199 C13
Hrymayliv Ukraine 49°20N 26°5E 177 D14
Hrynyava Ukraine 47°59N 24°53E 183 C9
Hsa-paw Burma 19°1N 97°30E 241 F6
Hsenwi Burma 23°22N 97°55E 241 D6
Hsi-hkip Burma 20°25N 96°42E 241 E6
Hsiafu Taiwan 25°7N 121°17E 225 A3
Hsiamen = Xiamen China 24°25N 118°4E 229 E12
Hsian = Xi'an China 34°15N 109°0E 226 G5
Hsiangshan Taiwan 24°48N 120°54E 225 B2
Hsiaochinmen Tao Taiwan 24°26N 118°14E 225 a
Hsiaohungt'ou Hsü Taiwan 21°57N 121°36E 225 E3
Hsiaokang Taiwan 22°34N 120°20E 225 D2
Hsiatahsi Taiwan 22°28N 120°56E 225 D2
Hsiaying Taiwan 23°14N 120°15E 225 C2
Hsichih Taiwan 25°4N 121°39E 225 A3
Hsikang Taiwan 23°7N 120°12E 225 C2
Hsilo Taiwan 23°48N 120°27E 225 C2
Hsinche Taiwan 24°10N 120°50E 225 B2
Hsinch'eng Taiwan 24°8N 121°39E 225 B3
Hsinchu Taiwan 24°48N 120°58E 225 B2
Hsinchu □ Taiwan 24°45N 121°10E 225 B3
Hsinchuang Kaohsung, Taiwan 22°34N 120°29E 225 D2
Hsinchuang T'aipei, Taiwan 25°2N 121°27E 225 A3
Hsinfa Taiwan 23°1N 120°39E 225 C2
Hsinfeng Taiwan 24°54N 120°59E 225 B2
Hsinhailien = Lianyungang China 34°40N 119°11E 227 G10
Hsinhua Taiwan 23°2N 120°18E 225 C2
Hsini Taiwan 23°41N 120°51E 225 C2
Hsinking = Changchun China 43°57N 125°17E 227 C13
Hsinpi Taiwan 22°28N 120°33E 225 D2
Hsinshih Taiwan 23°4N 120°17E 225 C2
Hsintien Taiwan 24°57N 121°32E 225 B3
Hsinwu Taiwan 24°59N 121°6E 225 B3
Hsinying Taiwan 23°21N 120°17E 225 C2
Hsinyuan Taiwan 22°32N 120°27E 225 D2
Hsipaw Burma 22°37N 97°18E 241 D6
Hsiukuluan Hsi → Taiwan 23°28N 121°30E 225 C3
Hsiushui Taiwan 24°3N 120°30E 225 B2
Hsiyu Taiwan 23°36N 119°30E 225 C1
Hsopket Burma 23°11N 98°26E 228 F2
Hsüchou = Xuzhou China 34°18N 117°10E 227 G9
Hsüeh Shan China 24°24N 121°12E 225 B3
Hsüehchia Taiwan 23°14N 120°10E 225 C2
Hsühaitsun Taiwan 22°12N 120°52E 225 D2
Htapodia Greece 37°24N 25°34E 205 D7
Htawgaw Burma 25°57N 98°23E 241 C7
Hu Xian China 34°8N 108°42E 226 G5
Hua Hin Thailand 12°34N 99°58E 236 F2
Hua Lamphong Railway Station Bangkok, Thailand 113 c2
Hua Xian Henan, China 35°30N 114°30E 226 G8
Hua Xian Shaanxi, China 34°30N 109°48E 226 G5
Hua Yü Taiwan 23°24N 119°19E 225 C1
Hua'an China 25°1N 117°32E 229 E11
Huab → Namibia 20°52S 13°25E 270 A2
Huacaya Bolivia 20°45S 63°43W 331 E5
Huachacalla Bolivia 18°45S 68°17W 330 D4
Huacheng China 24°4N 115°37E 229 E10
Huachinera Mexico 30°9N 108°55W 318 A3
Huacho Peru 11°10S 77°35W 330 C2
Huachón Peru 10°35S 76°0W 330 C2
Huade China 41°55N 113°59E 226 D7
Huadian China 43°0N 126°40E 227 C14
Huadu China 23°22N 113°12E 229 F9
Huahine, Î. French Polynesia 16°46S 150°58W 289 f
Huai Hat △ Thailand 16°52N 104°17E 236 D5
Huai He → China 33°0N 118°30E 229 A12
Huai Nam Dang △ Thailand 19°30N 98°30E 236 C2
Huai Yot Thailand 7°45N 99°37E 237 J2
Huai'an Hebei, China 40°30N 114°20E 226 D8
Huai'an Jiangsu, China 33°30N 119°10E 227 H10
Huaibei China 34°0N 116°48E 226 G9
Huaibin China 32°32N 115°27E 229 A10
Huaicho = Puerto Acosta Bolivia 15°32S 69°15W 330 D4
Huaide = Gongzhuling China 43°30N 124°40E 227 C13
Huaidezhen China 43°48N 124°50E 227 C13
Huaihua China 27°32N 109°57E 228 D7
Huaiji China 23°55N 112°12E 229 F9
Huainan China 32°38N 116°58E 229 A11
Huaining China 30°24N 116°40E 229 B11
Huairen China 39°48N 113°20E 226 E7
Huairou China 40°20N 116°35E 226 D9
Huaiyang China 33°40N 114°52E 226 H8
Huaiyin China 33°30N 119°2E 227 H10
Huaiyuan Anhui, China 32°55N 117°10E 227 H9
Huaiyuan Guangxi Zhuangzu, China 24°31N 108°22E 228 E7
Huajuapán de León Mexico 17°48N 97°46W 319 D5
Hualālai U.S.A. 19°42N 155°52W 302 D6
Hualapai Peak U.S.A. 35°5N 113°54W 305 J7
Hualien Taiwan 23°59N 121°36E 225 C3
Hualien □ Taiwan 23°45N 121°25E 225 C3
Huallaga → Peru 5°15S 75°30W 330 B2
Huallanca Peru 8°50S 77°56W 330 B2
Huamachuco Peru 7°50S 78°5W 330 B2
Huambo Angola 12°42S 15°54E 265 E3
Huambo □ Angola 13°0S 16°0E 265 E3
Huan Jiang → China 34°28N 109°0E 226 G5
Huan Xian China 36°33N 107°7E 226 F4
Huancabamba Peru 5°10S 79°15W 330 B2
Huancane Peru 15°10S 69°44W 330 D4
Huancapi Peru 13°40S 74°0W 330 C3
Huancavelica Peru 12°50S 75°5W 330 C2
Huancavelica □ Peru 13°0S 75°0W 330 C3
Huancayo Peru 12°5S 75°12W 330 C2
Huanchaca Bolivia 20°15S 66°40W 330 E4
Huanchaca, Serranía de Bolivia 14°30S 60°39W 331 C5
Huang Hai = Yellow Sea China 35°0N 123°0E 227 G12
Huang He → China 37°55N 118°50E 227 F10
Huang Xian China 37°38N 120°30E 227 F11
Huangchuan China 32°15N 115°10E 229 A10
Huanggang China 30°29N 114°52E 229 B10
Huangguoshu China 26°0N 105°40E 228 E5
Huanghuagang Mausoleum China 23°9N 113°17E 121 B2
Huangling China 35°34N 109°15E 226 G5
Huanglong China 35°30N 109°59E 226 G5
Huanglongtan China 32°40N 110°33E 229 A8
Huangmei China 30°5N 115°56E 229 B10
Huangpi China 30°50N 114°22E 229 B10
Huangping China 26°52N 107°54E 228 D6
Huangpu China 31°14N 121°30E 138 B2
Huangpu Jiang → China 31°11N 121°29E 138 B1
Huangpu Park China 31°14N 121°29E 138 B1
Huangshan Anhui, China 30°8N 118°9E 229 B12
Huangshan Anhui, China 29°42N 118°25E 229 C12
Huangshi China 30°10N 115°3E 229 B10
Huangsongdian China 43°45N 127°25E 227 C14
Huangtugang China 39°49N 116°15E 114 C1
Huangyan China 28°38N 121°19E 229 C13
Huangyangsi China 26°33N 111°39E 229 D8
Huaning China 24°17N 102°56E 228 E4
Huanjiang China 24°50N 108°18E 228 E7
Huanren China 41°23N 125°20E 224 B2
Huanren Shuiku China 41°17N 125°34E 224 B2
Huanta Peru 12°55S 74°20W 330 C3
Huantai China 36°58N 117°56E 227 F9
Huánuco Peru 9°55S 76°15W 330 B2
Huánuco □ Peru 9°55S 76°14W 330 B2
Huanuni Bolivia 18°16S 66°51W 330 D4
Huanzo, Cordillera de Peru 14°35S 73°20W 330 C3
Huaping China 26°46N 101°25E 228 D3
Huara Chile 19°59S 69°47W 330 D4
Huaral Peru 11°32S 77°13W 330 C2
Huaraz Peru 9°30S 77°32W 330 B2
Huari Peru 9°14S 77°14W 330 B2
Huarmey Peru 10°5S 78°5W 330 C2
Huarochirí Peru 12°9S 76°15W 330 C2
Huarocondo Peru 13°26S 72°14W 330 C3
Huarong China 29°29N 112°30E 229 C9
Huascar Peru 11°59S 77°1W 124 A2
Huascarán, Nevado Peru 9°7S 77°37W 330 B2
Huasco Chile 28°30S 71°15W 334 B1
Huasco → Chile 28°27S 71°13W 334 B1
Huasna U.S.A. 35°6N 120°24W 307 K6
Huatabampo Mexico 26°50N 109°38W 318 B3
Huauchinango Mexico 20°12N 98°3W 319 C5
Huautla de Jiménez Mexico 18°8N 96°51W 319 D5
Huaxi China 26°25N 106°40E 228 D6
Huay Khwang Thailand 13°47N 100°33E 113 B2
Huayhuash, Cordillera Peru 10°30S 76°45W 330 B2
Huayin China 34°35N 110°5E 226 G6
Huayllay Peru 11°3S 76°21W 330 C2
Huayuan China 28°37N 109°29E 228 C7
Huayun China 30°14N 106°40E 228 B6
Huazhou China 21°33N 110°33E 229 G8
Hubballi = Hubli India 15°22N 75°15E 245 G2
Hubbard Iowa, U.S.A. 42°18N 93°18W 310 B3
Hubbard Ohio, U.S.A. 41°9N 80°34W 312 E4
Hubbard Tex., U.S.A. 31°51N 96°48W 314 F6
Hubbard, Mt. N. Amer. 60°19N 139°4W 303 F13
Hubbard Glacier Canada 60°18N 139°22W 294 E4
Hubbart Pt. Canada 59°21N 94°41W 297 B10
Hubei □ China 31°0N 112°0E 229 B9
Hubli India 15°22N 75°15E 245 G2
Huch'ang N. Korea 41°25N 127°2E 224 D3
Huchow = Huzhou China 30°51N 120°8E 229 B13
Hucknall U.K. 53°3N 1°13W 168 D6
Huddersfield U.K. 53°39N 1°47W 168 D6
Huddinge Sweden 59°14N 18°0E 139 B2
Hude Germany 53°7N 8°26E 178 B4
Hudi Sudan 17°43N 34°18E 256 D3
Hudiksvall Sweden 61°43N 17°10E 162 C11
Hudson Ont., Canada 50°6N 92°9W 298 B1
Hudson Fla., U.S.A. 28°22N 82°42W 317 G7
Hudson Mass., U.S.A. 42°23N 71°34W 313 D13
Hudson Mich., U.S.A. 41°51N 84°21W 311 C12
Hudson N.Y., U.S.A. 42°15N 73°46W 313 D11
Hudson Wis., U.S.A. 44°58N 92°45W 308 C7
Hudson Wyo., U.S.A. 42°54N 108°35W 304 E9
Hudson → U.S.A. 40°42N 74°2W 313 F10
Hudson, C. Antarctica 68°21S 153°45E 151 C20
Hudson, Vol. Chile 46°4S 72°55W 336 C2
Hudson Bay Nunavut, Canada 60°0N 86°0W 295 F14
Hudson Bay Sask., Canada 52°51N 102°23W 297 C8
Hudson Falls U.S.A. 43°18N 73°35W 313 C11
Hudson Mts. Antarctica 74°32S 99°20W 151 D16
Hudson Str. Canada 62°0N 70°0W 295 E18
Hudson's Hope Canada 56°0N 121°54W 296 B4
Hudsonville U.S.A. 42°52N 85°52W 311 B11
Hue Vietnam 16°30N 107°35E 236 D6
Huebra → Spain 41°2N 6°48W 194 D4
Huechuraba Chile 33°22S 70°39W 137 B1
Huedin Romania 46°52N 23°2E 182 D8
Huehuetenango Guatemala 15°20N 91°28W 320 C1
Huejúcar Mexico 22°21N 103°13W 318 C4
Huélamo Spain 40°17N 1°48W 196 E3
Huelgoat France 48°22N 3°46W 172 D3
Huelma Spain 37°39N 3°28W 195 H7
Huelva Spain 37°18N 6°57W 195 H4
Huelva □ Spain 37°40N 7°0W 195 H4
Huelva → Spain 37°27N 6°0W 195 H5
Hueneme = Port Hueneme U.S.A. 34°7N 119°12W 307 L7
Huentelauquén Chile 31°38S 71°33W 334 C1
Huércal-Overa Spain 37°23N 1°57W 197 H3
Huerquehue △ Chile 39°6S 71°42W 336 A2
Huerta, Sa. de la Argentina 31°10S 67°30W 334 C2
Huertas, C. de las Spain 38°21N 0°24W 197 G4
Huertas de San Beltran Spain 41°22N 2°9E 114 A1
Huerva → Spain 41°39N 0°52W 196 D4
Huesca Spain 42°8N 0°25W 196 C4
Huesca □ Spain 42°20N 0°1E 196 C5
Huéscar Spain 37°44N 2°35W 197 H2
Hueso Ballena, Pta. Chile 33°40S 78°46W 330 c
Huetamo Mexico 18°35N 100°53W 318 D4
Huete Spain 40°10N 2°43W 196 E2
Huevos I. Trin. & Tob. 10°42N 61°43W 323 t
Hug Point U.S.A. 45°52N 123°57W 124 A2
Hugh → Australia 25°1S 134°1E 280 D1
Hughenden Australia 20°52S 144°10E 280 C3
Hughes U.S.A. 66°3N 154°15W 303 C9
Hughesville U.S.A. 41°14N 76°44W 313 E8
Hugli → India 21°56N 88°4E 243 J13
Hugo Colo., U.S.A. 39°8N 103°28W 304 G12
Hugo Okla., U.S.A. 34°1N 95°31W 314 D7
Hugoton U.S.A. 37°11N 101°21W 308 G3
Huguang Opera Museum Beijing, China 114 c2
Huhehaote = Hohhot China 40°52N 111°40E 226 D6
Huhsi Taiwan 23°35N 119°39E 225 C1
Hui Xian = Huixian China 35°27N 113°12E 226 G7
Hui Xian China 33°50N 106°4E 226 H4
Hui'an China 25°1N 118°43E 229 E12
Hui'anbu China 37°28N 106°38E 226 F4
Huiarau Ra. N.Z. 38°45S 176°55E 284 E5
Huichang China 25°32N 115°45E 229 E10
Huichapan Mexico 20°23N 99°39W 319 C5
Huichon N. Korea 40°10N 126°16E 224 B3
Huidong Guangdong, China 22°58N 114°43E 229 F10
Huidong Sichuan, China 26°34N 102°35E 228 D4
Huifa He → China 43°0N 127°50E 227 C14
Huíla Angola 15°4S 13°32E 265 F2
Huíla □ Angola 14°0S 15°0E 265 E2
Huila □ Colombia 2°30N 75°45W 328 C2
Huila, Nevado del Colombia 3°0N 76°0W 328 C2
Huilai China 23°0N 116°18E 229 F11
Huili China 26°35N 102°17E 228 D4
Huimin China 37°27N 117°28E 227 F9
Huinan China 42°40N 126°2E 224 A3
Huinca Renancó Argentina 34°51S 64°22W 334 C3
Huining China 35°38N 105°0E 226 G3
Huinong China 39°5N 106°35E 226 E4
Huiroa N.Z. 39°15S 174°30E 284 F3
Huishui China 26°7N 106°38E 228 D6
Huisne → France 47°59N 0°11E 172 E7
Huiting China 34°5N 116°5E 226 G9
Huitong China 26°51N 109°45E 228 D7
Huixian China 35°27N 113°12E 226 G7
Huixtla Mexico 15°9N 92°28W 319 D6
Huize China 26°24N 103°15E 228 D4
Huizhou China 23°0N 114°23E 229 F10
Huizingen Belgium 50°45N 4°17E 116 B1
Hukawng Valley Burma 26°30N 96°30E 241 B6
Hukeri India 16°14N 74°36E 245 F2
Hukou Jiangxi, China 29°45N 116°21E 229 C11
Huk'ou Taiwan 24°54N 121°2E 225 B3
Hukuntsi Botswana 23°58S 21°45E 270 B3
Hula Papua N. G. 10°5S 147°43E 286 F4
Ḩulayfā' Si. Arabia 25°58N 40°45E 246 E4
Huld = Ulaanjirem Mongolia 45°5N 105°30E 226 B3
Hulin He → China 45°0N 122°10E 227 B12
Hull = Kingston upon Hull U.K. 53°45N 0°21W 168 D7
Hull Canada 45°26N 75°43W 313 A9
Hull → U.K. 53°44N 0°20W 168 D7
Hulst Neths. 51°17N 4°2E 170 C4
Hultschin = Hlučín Czech Rep. 49°54N 18°11E 181 B11
Hultsfred Sweden 57°30N 15°52E 163 G9
Hulun = Hailar China 49°10N 119°38E 219 B6
Hulun Nur China 49°0N 117°30E 219 B6
Hulyaypole Ukraine 47°45N 36°21E 189 J9
Huma, Tanjung Malaysia 5°29N 100°16E 237 c
Humacao Puerto Rico 18°9N 65°50W 321 b
Humahuaca Argentina 23°10S 65°25W 334 A2
Humaitá = Porto Walter Brazil 8°15S 72°40W 330 B3
Humaitá Brazil 7°35S 63°1W 331 B5
Humaitá Paraguay 27°2S 58°31W 334 B4
Humansdorp S. Africa 34°2S 24°46E 270 D3
Humansville U.S.A. 37°48N 93°35W 310 G3
Humara, J. Sudan 16°16N 30°59E 257 D3
Humayun's Tomb India 28°35N 77°15E 120 B2
Humbe Angola 16°40S 14°55E 265 F2
Humbe, Serra do Angola 12°10S 15°25E 265 E2
Humber → Ont., Canada 43°47N 79°38W 141 A1
Humber → England, U.K. 53°42N 0°27W 168 D7
Humber B. Canada 43°37N 79°27W 141 B2
Humber Bay Canada 43°38N 79°29W 141 B2
Humber Bay Park Canada 43°37N 79°28W 141 B2
Humber College Canada 43°35N 79°30W 141 B1
Humber Summit Canada 43°45N 79°32W 141 A1
Humber Valley Village Canada 43°40N 79°31W 141 A1
Humberlea Canada 43°43N 79°31W 141 A1
Humberwood Park Canada 43°44N 79°37W 141 A1
Humboldt Sask., Canada 52°15N 105°9W 297 C7
Humboldt Iowa, U.S.A. 42°44N 94°13W 310 B2
Humboldt Tenn., U.S.A. 35°50N 88°55W 315 D10
Humboldt → U.S.A. 39°59N 118°36W 304 G4
Humboldt Gletscher = Sermersuaq Greenland 79°30N 62°0W 154 B4
Humboldt Mts. N.Z. 44°30S 168°15E 285 E3
Humboldt Park U.S.A. 41°54N 87°42W 119 B2
Humbolt, Mt. N. Cal. 21°53S 166°25E 288 d
Hume U.S.A. 36°48N 118°54W 306 J8
Hume, L. Australia 36°0S 147°5E 283 D7
Humen China 22°50N 113°40E 219 F10
Humenné Slovak Rep. 48°55N 21°50E 181 C14
Humera Spain 40°25N 3°46W 127 B1
Humeston U.S.A. 40°52N 93°30W 310 D3
Hummelsta Sweden 59°34N 16°58E 162 E10
Hummelvika Norway 63°29N 8°19E 164 A5
Hummingbird Centre Toronto, Canada 141 c3
Hummock Hill = Whyalla Australia 33°2S 137°30E 282 B2
Humpata Angola 15°2S 13°24E 265 F2
Humphreys, Mt. U.S.A. 37°17N 118°40W 306 H8
Humphreys Peak U.S.A. 35°21N 111°41W 305 J8
Humpolec Czech Rep. 49°31N 15°20E 180 B8
Humptulips U.S.A. 47°14N 123°57W 306 C3
Humula Australia 35°30S 147°46E 283 C7
Hūn Libya 29°2N 16°0E 258 C3
Hun He → China 40°41N 122°8E 224 B1
Hun Jiang → China 40°50N 125°38E 227 D13
Húnaflói Iceland 65°50N 20°50W 155 B6
Hunan □ China 27°30N 112°0E 229 D9
Húnavatnssýsla □ Iceland 65°30N 20°25W 155 B6
Hunayḑī Iraq 33°18N 44°29E 113 B2
Hunchun China 42°52N 130°28E 227 C16
Hundested Denmark 55°58N 11°52E 163 J5
Hundewali Pakistan 31°55N 72°38E 242 D5
Hundige Denmark 55°35N 12°18E 118 B1
Hundige Strand Denmark 55°35N 12°20E 118 B1
Hundorp Norway 61°33N 9°59E 164 C7
Hundred Islands △ Phil. 16°10N 120°2E 232 C3
Hundred Mile House Canada 51°38N 121°18W 296 C4
Hundvåg Norway 59°0N 5°43E 164 E2
Hunedoara Romania 45°40N 22°50E 182 E7
Hunedoara □ Romania 45°50N 22°54E 182 E7
Hunei Taiwan 22°53N 120°14E 225 D2
Hünfeld Germany 50°39N 9°46E 178 E5
Hung Hom China 22°18N 114°11E 122 B2
Hung Yen Vietnam 20°39N 106°4E 228 G6
Hunga Ha'apai Tonga 20°41S 175°7W 287 Q13
Hungary ■ Europe 47°20N 19°20E 181 D12
Hungary, Plain of Europe 47°0N 20°0E 158 F10
Hungerford Australia 28°58S 144°24E 281 D3
Hŭngnam N. Korea 39°49N 127°45E 224 C3
Hungt'ou Hsü = Lan Yü Taiwan 22°4N 121°25E 225 D3
Hungund India 16°4N 76°3E 245 F3
Huni Valley Ghana 5°33N 1°56W 262 D4
Hunjiang China 41°54N 126°26E 224 B3
Hunneberg Sweden 58°18N 12°30E 163 F6
Hunnebostrand Sweden 58°27N 11°18E 163 F5
Hunsberge Namibia 27°45S 17°12E 270 C2
Hunsrück Germany 49°56N 7°27E 179 F3
Hunstanton U.K. 52°56N 0°29E 168 E8
Hunsur India 12°16N 76°16E 245 H3
Hunte → Germany 53°14N 8°28E 178 B4
Hunter N.Z. 44°36S 171°2E 285 E6
Hunter N.Y., U.S.A. 42°13N 74°13W 313 D10
Hunter → N.S.W., Australia 32°52S 151°46E 283 B9
Hunter → N.Z. 44°21S 169°27E 285 E4
Hunter, C. Solomon Is. 9°48S 159°50E 287 M10
Hunter Hills, The N.Z. 44°26S 170°46E 285 E5
Hunter I. Tas., Australia 40°30S 144°45E 281 G3
Hunter I. B.C., Canada 51°55N 128°0W 296 C3
Hunter Mts. N.Z. 45°43S 167°25E 285 F2
Hunter Ra. Australia 32°45S 150°15E 283 B9
Hunters Hill Australia 33°50S 151°9E 139 B1
Hunters Pt. U.S.A. 37°43N 122°21W 136 B2
Hunters Road Zimbabwe 19°9S 29°49E 269 F2
Hunters Valley U.S.A. 38°54N 77°17W 143 B2
Hunterville N.Z. 39°56S 175°35E 284 F4
Huntingburg U.S.A. 38°18N 86°57W 311 F10
Huntingdon Cambs., U.K. 52°20N 0°11W 169 E7
Huntingdon Pa., U.S.A. 40°30N 78°1W 312 F6
Huntington = Shelton U.S.A. 41°19N 73°5W 313 E11
Huntington Ind., U.S.A. 40°53N 85°30W 311 D11
Huntington N.Y., U.S.A. 40°52N 73°26W 313 F11
Huntington Oreg., U.S.A. 44°21N 117°16W 304 D5
Huntington Utah, U.S.A. 39°20N 110°58W 304 G8
Huntington Va., U.S.A. 38°47N 77°4W 143 C3
Huntington W. Va., U.S.A. 38°25N 82°27W 309 F12
Huntington Beach U.S.A. 33°40N 118°5W 307 M9
Huntington Park U.S.A. 33°58N 118°13W 126 C3
Huntley Jamaica 18°4N 77°35W 320 a
Huntley Ill., U.S.A. 42°10N 88°26W 311 B8
Huntly N.Z. 37°34S 175°11E 284 D4
Huntly Aberds., U.K. 57°27N 2°47W 167 D6
Huntsville Ont., Canada 45°20N 79°14W 312 A5
Huntsville Ala., U.S.A. 34°44N 86°35W 315 D11
Huntsville Mo., U.S.A. 39°26N 92°33W 310 E4
Huntsville Tex., U.S.A. 30°43N 95°33W 314 F7
Hunyani → Zimbabwe 15°57S 30°39E 269 F3
Hunyuan China 39°42N 113°42E 226 E7
Hunza → India 35°54N 74°20E 243 B6
Huo Xian = Huozhou China 36°36N 111°42E 226 F6
Huocheng China 44°0N 80°48E 217 D10
Huon G. Papua N. G. 7°0S 147°30E 286 D4
Huon Pen. Papua N. G. 6°20S 147°30E 286 D4
Huong Khe Vietnam 18°13N 105°41E 236 C5
Huonville Australia 43°0S 147°5E 281 G4
Huoqiu China 32°20N 116°12E 229 A11
Huoshan Anhui, China 32°28N 118°30E 229 A12
Huoshan Anhui, China 31°25N 116°20E 229 B11
Huoshao Dao = Lü Tao Taiwan 22°40N 121°30E 225 D3
Huozhou China 36°36N 111°42E 226 F6
Hupeh = Hubei □ China 31°0N 112°0E 229 B9
Ḩūr Iran 30°50N 57°7E 247 D8
Hurand Iran 38°51N 47°22E 247 B6
Ḩuraymila Si. Arabia 25°8N 46°8E 246 E5
Hurbanovo Slovak Rep. 47°51N 18°11E 181 D11
Hurd, C. Canada 45°13N 81°44W 312 A3
Hurdiyo Somali Rep. 10°33N 51°6E 267 B7
Hure Qi China 42°45N 121°45E 227 C11
Hurezani Romania 44°49N 23°40E 183 F8
Hurghada Egypt 27°15N 33°50E 256 B3
Hurīya Iraq 33°21N 44°19E 113 A1
Hurley N. Mex., U.S.A. 32°42N 108°8W 305 K9
Hurley Wis., U.S.A. 46°27N 90°11W 308 B8
Huron Calif., U.S.A. 36°12N 120°6W 306 J6
Huron Ohio, U.S.A. 41°24N 82°33W 312 E2
Huron S. Dak., U.S.A. 44°22N 98°13W 308 C4
Huron, L. U.S.A. 44°30N 82°40W 312 B2
Huron East Canada 43°37N 81°18W 312 C3
Hurricane U.S.A. 37°11N 113°17W 305 H7
Hurso Ethiopia 9°35N 41°33E 257 F5
Hurstville Australia 33°57S 151°6E 139 B1
Hurtsboro U.S.A. 32°15N 85°25W 316 C4
Hurungwe ⌂ Zimbabwe 16°7S 29°5E 269 F2
Hurunui → N.Z. 42°54S 173°18E 285 C8
Hurup Denmark 56°46N 8°25E 163 H2
Húsafell Iceland 64°42N 20°53W 155 C6
Husan West Bank 31°42N 35°8E 123 B1
Húsavík Iceland 66°3N 17°21W 155 A9
Husby Sweden 59°24N 17°56E 139 A1
Huşi Romania 46°41N 28°7E 183 D13
Huskisson Australia 35°2S 150°41E 283 C9
Huskvarna Sweden 57°47N 14°15E 163 G8
Huslia U.S.A. 65°41N 156°24W 303 D8
Husnes Norway 59°52N 5°45E 164 E2
Hustad Norway 62°57N 7°6E 164 B4
Hustadvika Norway 63°0N 7°6E 164 A3
Hustontown U.S.A. 40°3N 78°2W 312 F6
Hustopeče Czech Rep. 48°57N 16°43E 181 C9
Husum København, Denmark 55°42N 12°27E 118 A2
Husum Schleswig-Holstein, Germany 54°28N 9°4E 178 A5
Husum Sweden 63°21N 19°12E 162 A13
Huszt = Khust Ukraine 48°10N 23°18E 183 B8
Hutchinson Kans., U.S.A. 38°5N 97°56W 308 F5
Hutchinson Minn., U.S.A. 44°54N 94°22W 308 C6
Ḩūth Yemen 16°14N 43°58E 248 C3
Hutjena Papua N. G. 5°23S 154°42E 286 C8
Hutsonville U.S.A. 39°7N 87°40W 311 E9
Hutt → N.Z. 41°14S 174°54E 143 B2
Hutte Sauvage, L. de la Canada 56°15N 64°45W 299 A7
Hüttelldorf Austria 48°12N 16°15E 142 A1
Hüttenberg Austria 46°56N 14°33E 180 E7
Hüttenberger Berge ⌂ Germany 54°24N 9°40E 178 A5
Hutton, Mt. Australia 25°51S 148°20E 281 D4
Huvadu Atoll Maldives 0°30N 73°15E 272 d
Hüvösvölgy Hungary 47°32N 19°0E 117 A2
Huwei Taiwan 23°42N 120°26E 225 C2
Huwei Hsi → Taiwan 23°37N 120°22E 225 C2
Huwon Secret Garden S. Korea 37°34N 126°59E 137 B1
Huwun Ethiopia 4°23N 40°6E 257 G5
Huy Belgium 50°31N 5°15E 170 D5
Huzhou China 30°51N 120°8E 229 B13
Huzurabad India 18°12N 79°25E 244 E4
Huzurnagar India 16°54N 79°53E 244 F4
Hvalpsund Denmark 56°42N 9°11E 163 H3
Hvalstad Norway 59°51N 10°27E 133 A1
Hvalstrand Norway 59°50N 10°30E 133 A2
Hvammsfjörður Iceland 65°4N 22°5W 155 B4
Hvammstangi Iceland 65°24N 20°57W 155 B6
Hvammur Mýrasýsla, Iceland 64°50N 21°21W 155 C5
Hvammur Skagafjarðarsýsla, Iceland 65°53N 19°51W 155 B7
Hvannadalshnúkur Iceland 64°1N 16°41W 155 C10
Hvanneyri Iceland 64°34N 21°36W 155 C5
Hvar Croatia 43°11N 16°28E 199 E13
Hvarski Kanal Croatia 43°15N 16°35E 199 E13
Hveragerði Iceland 64°0N 21°12W 155 C5
Hvidovre Denmark 55°38N 12°27E 118 B2
Hvítá → Iceland 64°30N 21°58W 155 C5
Hvítárvatn Iceland 64°37N 19°50W 155 C7
Hvittingfoss Norway 59°29N 10°0E 164 F7
Hvizdets Ukraine 48°35N 25°17E 183 B10
Hvolsvöllur Iceland 63°45N 20°14W 155 D6
Hwacheon-Cheosuji S. Korea 38°5N 127°50E 224 C3
Hwagok S. Korea 37°32N 126°51E 137 B1
Hwainan = Huainan China 32°38N 116°58E 229 A11
Hwaiyin = Huaiyin China 33°30N 119°2E 227 H10
Hwang Ho = Huang He → China 37°55N 118°50E 227 F10
Hwange Zimbabwe 18°18S 26°30E 269 F2
Hwange △ Zimbabwe 19°0S 26°30E 270 A4
Hwanghaebuk-do □ N. Korea 38°30N 126°25E 224 C3
Hwanghaenam-do □ N. Korea 38°15N 125°30E 224 C2
Hwangju N. Korea 38°40N 125°46E 224 C2
Hwangshih = Huangshi China 30°10N 115°3E 229 B10
Hwaseong S. Korea 37°12N 126°48E 224 D3
Hwasun S. Korea 35°3N 126°59E 224 E3
Hwekum Burma 26°7N 95°22E 241 B5
Hyaing Burma 22°49N 94°44E 241 D5
Hyannis Mass., U.S.A. 41°39N 70°17W 309 E18
Hyannis Nebr., U.S.A. 42°0N 101°46W 308 E3
Hyargas Nuur Mongolia 49°0N 93°0E 217 C12
Hyattsville U.S.A. 38°57N 76°57W 143 B4
Hybo Sweden 61°49N 16°15E 162 C10
Hydaburg U.S.A. 55°15N 132°50W 296 B2
Hyde N.Z. 45°18S 170°16E 285 F5
Hyde Park N.S.W., Australia 33°52S 151°12E 139 B2
Hyde Park Guyana 6°30N 58°16W 329 B6
Hyde Park Gauteng, S. Africa 26°6S 28°2E 123 A2
Hyde Park London, U.K. 51°30N 0°10W 125 A2
Hyde Park Calif., U.S.A. 33°58N 118°19W 126 C3
Hyde Park Ill., U.S.A. 41°47N 87°35W 119 C3
Hyde Park Mass., U.S.A. 42°15N 71°7W 116 B2
Hyde Park N.Y., U.S.A. 41°47N 73°56W 313 E11
Hyden Australia 32°24S 118°53E 279 F2
Hyder U.S.A. 55°55N 130°5W 296 B2
Hyderabad India 17°22N 78°29E 244 F4
Hyderabad Pakistan 25°23N 68°24E 242 G3
Hydra Greece 37°20N 23°28E 204 D5
Hyen Norway 61°44N 5°56E 164 C2
Hyères France 43°8N 6°9E 175 E10
Hyères, Îs. d' France 43°0N 6°20E 175 F10
Hyesan N. Korea 41°20N 128°10E 224 B4
Hyland → Canada 59°52N 128°12W 296 B3
Hylestad Norway 59°6N 7°29E 164 E4
Hyllestad Norway 61°10N 5°17E 164 C2
Hyltebruk Sweden 56°59N 13°15E 163 H7
Hymia India 33°40N 78°2E 243 C8
Hyndman Peak U.S.A. 43°45N 114°8W 304 E6
Hynnekleiv Norway 58°36N 8°25E 164 F5
Hyōgo □ Japan 35°15N 134°50E 222 B6
Hyrra Banda C.A.R. 5°58N 22°1E 264 A4
Hyrum U.S.A. 41°38N 111°51W 304 F8
Hysham U.S.A. 46°18N 107°14W 304 C10
Hythe U.K. 51°4N 1°5E 169 F9
Hyūga Japan 32°25N 131°35E 222 E3
Hyvinge = Hyvinkää Finland 60°38N 24°50E 188 B3
Hyvinkää Finland 60°38N 24°50E 188 B3

I

I-n-Akhmed Mali 19°49N 0°56W 261 E4
I-n-Azaoua Illizi, Algeria 25°42N 6°54E 261 C6
I-n-Azaoua Tamanrasset, Algeria 20°46N 7°32E 261 D6
I-n-Échaï Mali 20°10N 2°5W 260 D4
I-n-Ezzane Algeria 23°29N 11°15E 261 D7
I-n-Gall Niger 16°51N 7°1E 263 B6
I-n-Kelemet Algeria 26°57N 5°47E 261 C6
I-n-Oudad Algeria 20°17N 4°38E 261 D5
I-n-Ouzzal Algeria 20°41N 2°34E 261 D5
I-n-Tadreft Niger 19°5N 6°38E 263 B6
Iabès, Erg Algeria 27°30N 2°2W 261 C4
Iablaniţa Romania 44°57N 22°19E 182 F7
Iaco → Brazil 9°3S 68°34W 330 B4
Iacobeni Romania 47°25N 25°20E 183 C10
Iaçu Brazil 12°45S 40°13W 333 D3
Iakora Madag. 23°6S 46°40E 272 C2
Ialibu Papua N. G. 6°17S 143°59E 286 D2
Ialissos Greece 36°24N 28°10E 206 E12
Ialomiţa □ Romania 44°30N 27°30E 183 F12
Ialomiţa → Romania 44°42N 27°51E 183 F12
Ialoveni Moldova 46°56N 28°47E 183 D13
Ialpug → Moldova 45°41N 28°35E 183 E13
Iamonia L. U.S.A. 30°38N 84°14W 316 E5
Ianca Romania 45°6N 27°29E 183 E12
Iara Romania 46°31N 23°35E 183 D8
Iarda Ethiopia 11°9N 35°53E 257 E4
Iargara Moldova 46°24N 28°23E 183 D13
Iaşi Romania 47°10N 27°40E 183 C12
Iaşi □ Romania 47°20N 27°0E 183 C12
Iasmos Greece 41°8N 25°11E 203 E9
Iauaretê Colombia 0°36N 69°12W 328 C4
Ib → India 21°34N 83°48E 243 J10
Iba Phil. 15°22N 120°0E 232 D2
Ibadan Nigeria 7°22N 3°58E 263 D5
Ibagué Colombia 4°20N 75°20W 328 C2
Ibaiti Brazil 23°50S 50°10W 333 F1
Ibajay Phil. 11°49N 122°10E 233 F4
Iballë Albania 42°12N 20°2E 202 D4
Ibăneşti Botoşani, Romania 48°4N 26°22E 183 B11
Ibăneşti Mureş, Romania 46°45N 24°57E 183 D9
Ibanshe Dem. Rep. of the Congo 4°58S 21°30E 265 C4
Ibar → Serbia 43°43N 20°45E 202 C4
Ibara Japan 34°36N 133°28E 222 C5
Ibaraki Japan 34°49N 135°34E 223 C7
Ibaraki □ Japan 36°10N 140°10E 223 A12
Ibarra Ecuador 0°21N 78°7W 328 C2
Ibb Yemen 14°2N 44°10E 248 D4
Ibba Sudan 4°49N 29°2E 257 G2
Ibba, Bahr el → Sudan 5°30N 28°55E 257 F2
Ibbenbüren Germany 52°16N 7°43E 178 C3
Ibeke Gembo Dem. Rep. of the Congo 1°24S 18°51E 264 C3
Ibembo Dem. Rep. of the Congo 2°35N 23°35E 264 B4
Ibenga → Congo 2°19N 18°9E 264 B3
Ibera, L. Argentina 28°30S 57°9W 334 B4
Iberia Peru 11°21S 69°35W 330 C4
Iberia Mo., U.S.A. 38°5N 92°18W 310 F4
Iberian Peninsula Europe 40°0N 5°0W 158 H5
Iberville Canada 45°19N 73°17W 313 A11
Iberville, Mt. d' Canada 58°50N 63°50W 295 F19
Ibese Nigeria 6°33N 3°28E 124 A2
Ibeto Nigeria 10°29N 5°8E 263 C6
Ibi Nigeria 8°15N 9°44E 263 D6
Ibi Spain 38°38N 0°34W 197 G4
Ibiá Brazil 19°30S 46°30W 333 E2
Ibiapaba, Sa. da Brazil 4°0S 41°30W 332 B3
Ibicaraí Brazil 14°51S 39°36W 333 D4
Ibicuí Brazil 14°51S 39°59W 333 D4
Ibicuí → Brazil 29°25S 56°47W 335 B4
Ibicuy Argentina 33°55S 59°10W 334 C4
Ibirapuera Brazil 23°36S 46°40W 137 B1
Ibirapuera, Parque do Brazil 23°35S 46°38W 137 B2
Ibitiara Brazil 12°39S 42°13W 333 D3
Ibiza = Eivissa Spain 38°54N 1°26E 206 D1
Ibiza ✕ (IBZ) Spain 38°53N 1°22E 197 G6
Iblei, Monti Italy 37°15N 14°45E 201 E7
Ibn Hāni', Ra's Syria 35°35N 35°43E 250 C6
Ibo Mozam. 12°22S 40°40E 269 E5
Ibonma Indonesia 3°29S 133°31E 231 E8
Ibotirama Brazil 12°13S 43°12W 333 D3
Iboundji Gabon 1°0S 11°51E 264 C2
Ibradı Turkey 37°4N 31°35E 250 A2
Ibrāhīm → Lebanon 34°4N 35°38E 250 D6
'Ibrī Oman 23°14N 56°30E 247 F8
İbriktepe Turkey 41°0N 26°30E 203 E10
Ibshawâi Egypt 29°21N 30°40E 256 J7
Ibu Indonesia 1°35N 127°33E 231 D7
Ibuki-Sanchi Japan 35°25N 136°18E 223 B8
Ibusuki Japan 31°12N 130°40E 222 F2
Ica Peru 14°0S 75°48W 330 C2
Ica □ Peru 14°20S 75°30W 330 C2
Içá → Brazil 2°55S 67°58W 330 A4
Icabarú Venezuela 4°20N 61°45W 329 C5
Icabarú → Venezuela 4°45N 62°15W 329 C5
Icacos Trin. & Tob. 10°3N 61°54W 323 t
Icacos Pt. Trin. & Tob. 10°3N 61°57W 323 t
Içana Brazil 0°21N 67°19W 328 C4
Içana → Brazil 0°26N 67°19W 328 C4
Icarai Brazil 22°54S 43°6W 135 B2
Icatu Brazil 2°46S 44°4W 332 B3
Icaturama = Santa Rosa de Viterbo Colombia 5°53N 72°59W 328 B3
İçel Turkey 36°51N 34°36E 250 B5
İçel □ Turkey 36°45N 34°0E 250 B5
Iceland ■ Europe 64°45N 19°0W 155 C8
Iceland Basin Atl. Oc. 61°0N 19°0W 150 C7
Icelandic Plateau Arctic 64°0N 10°0W 150 C7
İçerenköy Turkey 40°58N 29°6E 122 C2
İçeriçumra Turkey 37°34N 32°39E 212 D5
Ichalkaranji India 16°40N 74°33E 244 F2
Ich'ang = Yichang China 30°40N 111°20E 229 B8
Ichchapuram India 19°10N 84°40E 244 E7
Icheon S. Korea 37°17N 127°27E 224 D3
Ichgao Japan 35°32N 139°32E 140 B2
Ichhawar India 23°1N 77°1E 242 H7
Ichigaya Tokyo, Japan 140 a3
Ichihara Japan 35°28N 140°5E 223 B12
Ichikawa Japan 35°43N 139°54E 140 A4
Ichilo → Bolivia 15°57S 64°50W 331 D5
Ichinohe Japan 40°13N 141°17E 220 D10
Ichinomiya Gifu, Japan 35°18N 136°48E 223 B8
Ichinomiya Kumamoto, Japan 32°58N 131°5E 222 E3
Ichinoseki Japan 38°55N 141°8E 220 E10
Ichkeul △ Tunisia 37°5N 9°37E 258 A1
Ichnya Ukraine 50°52N 32°24E 189 G7
Icht Morocco 29°6N 8°54W 260 C3
Ichu Taiwan 23°20N 120°14E 225 C2
Ichun = Yichun China 47°44N 128°52E 219 B7
Ickenham U.K. 51°33N 0°26W 125 A1
Icó Brazil 6°24S 38°51W 332 C4
Icoca Angola 6°12S 16°20E 265 D3
Icod Canary Is. 28°22N 16°43W 153 e1
Iconi Comoros Is. 12°21S 43°51E 272 a
Icoraci Brazil 1°18S 48°28W 332 B2
Icy C. U.S.A. 70°20N 161°52W 303 A7
Ida Grove U.S.A. 42°21N 95°28W 308 D6
Idaan Somali Rep. 6°10N 48°55E 267 C6
Idabel U.S.A. 33°54N 94°50W 314 E7
Idaga Hamus Ethiopia 14°13N 39°48E 257 E4
Idah Nigeria 7°5N 6°40E 263 D6
Idaho □ U.S.A. 45°0N 115°0W 304 D6
Idaho City U.S.A. 43°50N 115°50W 304 E6
Idaho Falls U.S.A. 43°30N 112°2W 304 E7
Idalia △ Australia 24°49S 144°36E 280 C3
Idanha-a-Nova Portugal 39°50N 7°15W 194 F3
Idar-Oberstein Germany 49°43N 7°16E 179 F3
Iday Niger 14°54N 11°33E 259 F2
'Idd el Ghanam Sudan 11°30N 24°19E 259 F4
Iddo Nigeria 6°28N 3°22E 124 B2
Idelès Algeria 23°50N 5°53E 261 D6
Idensalmi = Iisalmi Finland 63°32N 27°10E 160 E22
Idfû Egypt 24°55N 32°49E 256 C3
Ídhra = Hydra Greece 37°20N 23°28E 204 D5
Idi Indonesia 5°2N 97°37E 234 A1
Idi, Oros = Psiloritis, Oros Greece 35°15N 24°45E 207 E5
Idi Amin Dada, L. = Edward, L. Africa 0°25S 29°40E 268 C2
Idi-Oro Nigeria 6°31N 3°21E 124 A2
İdil Turkey 37°20N 41°53E 213 D9
Idiofa Dem. Rep. of the Congo 4°55S 19°42E 265 C3
Idjil = Fdérik Mauritania 22°40N 12°45W 260 D2
Idkerberget Sweden 60°22N 15°15E 162 D9
Idku Egypt 31°18N 30°17E 256 H7
Idku, Bahra el Egypt 31°18N 30°18E 256 H7
Idlib Syria 35°55N 36°36E 250 C7
Idlib □ Syria 35°45N 36°45E 250 C7
Idre Sweden 61°52N 12°42E 162 C6
Idria U.S.A. 36°25N 120°41W 306 J6
Idrija Slovenia 46°0N 14°5E 199 C11
Idritsa Russia 56°17N 28°53E 188 D5
Idutywa = Dutywa S. Africa 32°8S 28°18E 271 D4
Ie Shima Japan 26°43N 127°48E 288 a
Ie Suido Japan 26°42N 127°51E 288 a
Ieper Belgium 50°51N 2°53E 170 D2
Ierapetra Greece 35°1N 25°44E 207 F6
Ierissos Greece 40°22N 23°52E 202 F7
Ierissos Kolpos Greece 40°27N 23°57E 202 F7
Iernut Romania 46°27N 24°15E 183 D9
Ieshima-Shotō Japan 34°40N 134°32E 222 C6
Iesi Italy 43°31N 13°14E 199 E10
Iésolo Italy 45°32N 12°38E 199 C9
Iet Ethiopia 4°33N 43°21E 267 D5
Ifac, Penyal d' Spain 38°38N 0°5E 197 G5
'Ifāl, W. al → Si. Arabia 28°7N 35°3E 251 K6
Ifanadiana Madag. 21°19S 47°39E 272 C2
Ife Nigeria 7°30N 4°31E 263 D5
Iférouâne Niger 19°5N 8°24E 259 E1
Ifetesene Algeria 25°30N 4°33E 261 C5
Iffley Australia 18°53S 141°12E 280 B3
Ifon Nigeria 6°58N 5°40E 263 D6
Iforas, Adrar des Africa 19°40N 1°40E 261 D5
Ifould, L. Australia 30°52S 132°6E 279 F5
Ifrane Morocco 33°33N 5°7W 260 B3
Ifrane □ Morocco 33°20N 5°15W 260 B3
Iga Phil. 16°40N 121°20E 232 C3
Iga Japan 34°45N 136°10E 223 C8
Igalo Montenegro 42°28N 18°30E 202 D2
Iganga Uganda 0°37N 33°28E 268 B3
Igantu Nigeria 6°28N 3°22E 124 B2
Iganmu Nigeria 6°28N 3°22E 124 B2
Igara-Paraná → Colombia 2°9S 71°47W 328 D3
Igarapava Brazil 20°3S 47°47W 333 F2
Igarapé-Açu Brazil 1°4S 47°33W 332 B2
Igarapé-Mirí Brazil 1°59S 48°58W 332 B2
Igarka Russia 67°30N 86°33E 214 C9
Igatpuri India 19°40N 73°35E 244 E1
Igbetti Nigeria 8°44N 4°8E 263 D5
Igbo-Ora Nigeria 7°29N 3°15E 263 D5
Igbobi Nigeria 6°31N 3°22E 124 A2
Igboho Nigeria 8°53N 3°50E 263 D5
Igbologun Nigeria 6°24N 3°19E 124 B1
Igbor Nigeria 7°27N 8°34E 263 D6

INDEX
Irosin 381

Iğdır Turkey 39°55N 44°2E 213 C11
Igelfors Sweden 58°52N 15°41E 163 F9
Iggesund Sweden 61°39N 17°10E 162 C11
Ighil Izane = Relizane Algeria 35°44N 0°31E 261 A5
Igiugig U.S.A. 59°20N 155°55W 303 G9
Iglau = Jihlava Czech Rep. 49°28N 15°35E 180 B8
Iglésias Italy 39°19N 8°32E 200 C1
Igli Algeria 30°25N 2°19W 261 B4
Igloolik = Iglulik Canada 69°20N 81°49W 295 D15
Igluligaarjuk = Chesterfield Inlet Canada 63°30N 90°45W 294 E13
Iglulik Canada 69°20N 81°49W 295 D15
'Igma, G. el Egypt 29°10N 34°0E 251 J5
'Igma, Gebel el Egypt 28°55N 34°0E 256 B3
Ignace Canada 49°30N 91°40W 298 C1
İğneada Turkey 41°52N 27°59E 203 E11
İğneada Burnu Turkey 41°53N 28°2E 203 E12
Igny France 48°44N 2°13E 134 B2
Igoumenitsa Greece 39°32N 20°18E 206 B10
Igrim Russia 63°12N 64°30E 214 C7
Iguaçu → Brazil 25°36S 54°36W 335 B5
Iguaçu, Cat. del Brazil 25°41S 54°26W 335 B5
Iguaçu △ Brazil 25°30S 54°0W 335 B5
Iguaçu Falls = Iguaçu, Cat. del Brazil 25°41S 54°26W 335 B5
Iguala Mexico 18°21N 99°32W 319 D5
Igualada Spain 41°37N 1°37E 196 D6
Iguape Brazil 24°43S 47°33W 333 F2
Iguaratinga = São Francisco do Maranhão Brazil 6°15S 42°52W 332 C3
Iguassu = Iguaçu → Brazil 25°36S 54°36W 335 B5
Iguatu Brazil 6°20S 39°18W 332 C4
Iguazú △ Argentina 25°42S 54°22W 335 B5
Iguéla Gabon 2°0S 9°16E 264 C1
Iguéla, Lagune Gabon 1°48S 9°16E 264 C2
Iguidi, Erg Africa 27°0N 6°0W 260 C3
Iguig Phil. 17°45N 121°44E 232 C3
Igumen = Cherven Belarus 53°45N 28°28E 177 B15
Iharana Madag. 13°25S 50°0E 272 A3
Ihavandiffulu Atoll Maldives 7°0N 72°50E 272 d
Ihbulag Mongolia 43°11N 107°10E 226 C4
Iheya-Shima Japan 27°4N 127°58E 221 L3
Ihiala Nigeria 5°51N 6°55E 263 D6
Ihirene → Algeria 20°28N 4°37E 261 D5
Ihosy Madag. 22°24S 46°8E 272 C2
Ihotry, Farihy Madag. 21°56S 43°41E 272 C1
Ihu Papua N. G. 7°55S 145°24E 286 D3
Ihugh Nigeria 7°2N 9°0E 263 D6
Ii Finland 65°19N 25°22E 160 D21
Ii-Shima Japan 26°43N 127°47E 221 L3
Iida Japan 35°35N 137°50E 223 B9
Iijoki → Finland 65°20N 25°20E 160 D21
Iisalmi Finland 63°32N 27°10E 160 E22
Iiyama Japan 36°51N 138°22E 221 F9
Iizuka Japan 33°38N 130°42E 222 D2
IJ, Het → Neths. 52°23N 4°54E 112 A2
IJ-meer Neths. 52°23N 4°54E 112 A3
Ijâfene Mauritania 20°40N 8°0W 260 D3
Ijebu-Igbo Nigeria 6°56N 4°1E 263 D5
Ijebu-Ode Nigeria 6°47N 3°58E 263 D5
Ijesa-Tedo Nigeria 6°29N 3°19E 124 B1
Ijevan Armenia 40°52N 45°8E 213 B11
Ijill, Sebkhet Mauritania 22°47N 12°53W 260 D2
IJmuiden Neths. 52°28N 4°35E 170 B4
Ijo älv = Iijoki → Finland 65°20N 25°20E 160 D21
Ijora Nigeria 6°27N 3°22E 124 B2
IJssel → Neths. 52°35N 5°50E 170 B5
IJsselmeer Neths. 52°45N 5°20E 170 B5
Ijuí Brazil 28°23S 53°55W 335 B5
Ijuí → Brazil 27°58S 55°20W 335 B4
Ijūin Japan 31°37N 130°24E 222 F2
Ikalamavony Madag. 21°9S 46°35E 272 C2
Ikale Nigeria 7°40N 5°37E 263 D6
Ikali Dem. Rep. of the Congo 2°2S 21°4E 264 C4
Ikamatua N.Z. 42°16S 171°41E 285 C6
Ikang Nigeria 4°49N 8°30E 263 E6
Ikanga Kenya 1°42S 38°4E 268 C4
Ikara Nigeria 11°12N 8°15E 263 C6
Ikare Nigeria 7°32N 5°40E 263 D6
Ikaria Greece 37°35N 26°10E 205 D8
Ikast Denmark 56°8N 9°10E 163 H3
Ikebe Japan 35°31N 139°34E 140 B2
Ikebukuro Japan 35°43N 139°42E 140 A3
Ikeda Japan 34°1N 133°48E 222 C5
Ikegami Japan 35°33N 139°42E 140 B3
Ikei-shima Japan 26°23N 127°59E 288 a
Ikeja Nigeria 6°35N 3°20E 124 A2
Ikela Dem. Rep. of the Congo 1°6S 23°6E 264 C4
Ikélemba Congo 1°12N 16°38E 264 B3
Ikélemba → Dem. Rep. of the Congo 0°7N 18°17E 264 B3
Ikengo Dem. Rep. of the Congo 0°8S 18°8E 264 C3
Ikere Nigeria 7°25N 5°19E 263 D6
Ikeuchi Japan 34°35N 135°32E 133 B2
Ikhtiman Bulgaria 42°27N 23°48E 202 D7
Iki Japan 33°45N 129°42E 222 D1
Iki-Kaikyō Japan 33°40N 129°45E 222 D1
Ikimba L. Tanzania 1°30S 31°20E 268 C3
Ikire Nigeria 7°23N 4°15E 263 D5
Ikitsuki-Shima Japan 33°23N 129°26E 222 D1
İkizdere Turkey 40°46N 40°32E 213 B9
Iko Congo 0°35S 16°0E 264 C3
Ikom Nigeria 6°0N 8°42E 263 D6
Ikomu Dem. Rep. of the Congo 1°54S 19°40E 264 C3
Ikongo Madag. 21°52S 47°27E 272 C2
Ikopa → Madag. 16°45S 46°40E 272 B2
Ikorongo △ Tanzania 1°50S 34°53E 268 C3
Ikot Ekpene Nigeria 5°12N 7°40E 263 D6
Ikoyi Nigeria 6°27N 3°26E 124 B2
Ikparjuk = Arctic Bay Canada 73°1N 85°7W 295 C14
Iksan S. Korea 35°59N 127°0E 224 E3
Ikuata Nigeria 6°24N 3°21E 124 B2
Ikungu Tanzania 1°33S 33°42E 268 C3
Ikuno Hyōgo, Japan 35°10N 134°48E 222 B6
Ikuno Ōsaka, Japan 34°40N 135°30E 133 A2
Ikuntji = Haasts Bluff Australia 23°22S 132°0E 278 D5
Ikurun Nigeria 7°54N 4°40E 263 D5
Ikuta Japan 35°36N 139°32E 140 B2
Il-Kullana Malta 35°50N 14°24E 206 F7
Il-Munxar Malta 35°51N 14°34E 206 F8
Ila Dem. Rep. of the Congo 2°53S 21°7E 264 C4
Ila Nigeria 8°0N 4°39E 263 D5
Ila Oslo, Norway 59°57N 10°35E 133 A2
Ilafer Algeria 21°40N 1°58E 261 D5
Ilagan Phil. 17°7N 121°53E 232 C3
Ilaka Madag. 19°33S 48°52E 272 B2
Īlām Iran 33°36N 46°36E 213 F12
Ilam Nepal 26°58N 87°58E 243 F12
Īlām □ Iran 33°0N 47°0E 246 C5
Ilan Taiwan 24°45N 121°44E 225 B3
Ilan □ Taiwan 24°30N 121°35E 225 B3
Ilanskiy Russia 56°14N 96°3E 215 D10
Ilaro Nigeria 6°53N 3°3E 263 D5
Ilatane Niger 16°30N 4°45E 263 B5
Ilave Peru 16°5S 69°40W 330 D4
Iława Poland 53°36N 19°34E 184 E6
Ilayangudi India 9°34N 78°37E 245 K4
Ile → Kazakhstan 45°53N 77°10E 217 C9
Île-à-la-Crosse Canada 55°27N 107°53W 297 B7
Île-à-la-Crosse, Lac Canada 55°40N 107°45W 297 B7
Île-de-France □ France 49°0N 2°20E 173 D9
Ileanda Romania 47°20N 23°38E 183 C8
Ilebo Dem. Rep. of the Congo 4°17S 20°55E 265 C4
Ilek Russia 51°32N 53°21E 216 B4
Ilek → Russia 51°30N 53°22E 186 B9
Iler, O. → Algeria 20°59N 3°14E 261 D5
Ilero Nigeria 8°0N 3°20E 263 D5
Ilesha Kwara, Nigeria 8°57N 3°28E 263 D5
Ilesha Oyo, Nigeria 7°37N 4°40E 263 D5
Ilet = Krasnogorskiy Russia 56°10N 48°28E 190 B9
Iletskaya = Sol Iletsk Russia 51°10N 55°0E 186 D10
Iletsky Gorodok = Ilek Russia 51°32N 53°21E 216 B4
Ilford Man., Canada 56°4N 95°35W 297 B9
Ilford London, U.K. 51°33N 0°4E 125 A4
Ilfracombe Queens., Australia 23°30S 144°30E 280 C3
Ilfracombe Devon, U.K. 51°12N 4°8W 169 F3
Ilgaz Turkey 40°55N 33°37E 212 B5
Ilgaz Dağları Turkey 41°10N 33°50E 212 B5
Ilgın Turkey 38°16N 31°55E 212 C4
Ilha, Pta. da Azores 38°25N 28°3W 153 d1
Ilha Grande Brazil 0°27S 65°2W 329 D4
Ilha Grande, B. da Brazil 23°9S 44°30W 333 F3
Ilha Grande, Represa Brazil 23°10S 53°5W 335 A5
Ilha Grande △ Brazil 23°10S 53°20W 335 A5
Ílhavo Portugal 40°33N 8°43W 194 E2
Ilhéus Brazil 14°49S 39°2W 333 D4
Ili = Ile → Kazakhstan 45°53N 77°10E 217 C9
Ilia Romania 45°57N 22°40E 182 E7
Ilía □ Greece 37°45N 21°35E 204 D3
Iliamna U.S.A. 59°45N 154°55W 303 G9
Iliamna L. U.S.A. 59°30N 155°0W 303 G9
Ilian, Mt. Phil. 10°26N 119°33E 233 F2
Ilias, Profitis Greece 36°17N 27°56E 206 E11
Iliç Turkey 39°27N 38°33E 213 C8
Ilıca Turkey 39°52N 27°46E 205 B9
Ilig, Ras Somali Rep. 7°47N 49°50E 267 C6
Iligan Phil. 8°12N 124°13E 233 G5
Iligan Bay Phil. 8°25N 124°5E 233 G5
Iligan Pt. Phil. 18°25N 122°25E 232 B4
Ilin I. Phil. 12°14N 121°5E 232 E3
'Ílio Pt. U.S.A. 21°13N 157°16W 302 B4
Ilion U.S.A. 43°1N 75°2W 313 D9
Ilioupoli Greece 37°54N 23°47E 112 B2
Ilirska-Bistrica Slovenia 45°34N 14°14E 199 C11
Iliwa = Rewa → Guyana 3°19N 58°42W 329 C6
Iliysk = Qapshaghay Kazakhstan 43°51N 77°14E 217 D9
Ilkal India 15°57N 76°8E 245 G3
Ilkenau = Olkusz Poland 50°18N 19°33E 185 H6
Ilkeston U.K. 52°58N 1°19W 168 E6
Ilkley U.K. 53°56N 1°48W 168 D6
Illampu = Ancohuma, Nevado Bolivia 16°0S 68°50W 330 D4
Illana B. Phil. 7°35N 123°45E 233 H4
Illapel Chile 32°0S 71°10W 334 C1
Ille-et-Vilaine □ France 48°10N 1°30W 172 D5
Ille-sur-Têt France 42°40N 2°38E 174 F6
Illéla Niger 14°32N 5°20E 263 C6
Iller → Germany 48°23N 9°58E 179 G5
Illertissen Germany 48°12N 10°7E 179 G6
Illescas Spain 40°8N 3°51W 194 E7
Illetas Spain 39°32N 2°35E 206 B3
Illichivsk Ukraine 46°20N 30°35E 189 J6
Illiers-Combray France 48°18N 1°15E 172 D8
Illimani, Nevado Bolivia 16°30S 67°50W 330 D4
Illinois □ U.S.A. 40°15N 89°30W 310 D7
Illinois → U.S.A. 38°58N 90°28W 310 F6
Illinois at Chicago, Univ. of U.S.A. 41°52N 87°38W 119 B3
Illinois Institute of Technology U.S.A. 41°50N 87°37W 119 B3
Illiopolis U.S.A. 39°51N 89°15W 310 E7
Illium = Troy Turkey 39°57N 26°12E 205 B8
Illizi Algeria 26°31N 8°32E 261 C6
Illizi □ Algeria 26°50N 8°10E 261 C6
Illkirch-Graffenstaden France 48°34N 7°42E 173 D14
Íllora Spain 37°17N 3°53W 195 H7
Illulissat Greenland 69°12N 51°10W 154 B5
Ilm → Germany 51°6N 11°40E 178 D7
Ilma, L. Australia 29°13S 127°46E 279 E4
Ilmajoki Finland 62°44N 22°34E 160 E20
Ilmen, Ozero Russia 58°15N 31°10E 188 C6
Ilmenau = Jordanów Poland 49°41N 19°49E 185 J6
Ilmenau = Limanowa Poland 49°42N 20°22E 185 J7
Ilmenau Germany 50°41N 10°54E 178 E6
Ilnytsya Ukraine 48°21N 23°5E 182 B8
Ilo Peru 17°40S 71°20W 330 D3
Ilobu Nigeria 7°45N 4°25E 263 D5
Ilocos Norte □ Phil. 18°10N 120°45E 232 B3
Ilocos Sur □ Phil. 17°20N 120°35E 232 C3
Iloilo Phil. 10°45N 122°33E 233 F4
Iloilo □ Phil. 11°0N 122°40E 233 F4
Ilomantsi Finland 62°38N 30°57E 160 E24
Ilora Nigeria 7°45N 3°50E 263 D5
Ilorin Nigeria 8°30N 4°35E 263 D5
Ilovatka Russia 50°30N 45°50E 190 E7
Ilovlya Russia 49°15N 44°2E 191 F7
Ilovlya → Russia 49°14N 44°0E 191 F7
Iłowa Poland 51°30N 15°10E 185 G2
Ilpendam Neths. 52°28N 4°57E 112 A2
Ilsos → Greece 37°55N 23°41E 112 B2
Ilubabor Ethiopia 7°25N 35°0E 257 F4
Ilva Mică Romania 47°17N 24°40E 183 C9
Ilwaco U.S.A. 46°19N 124°3W 306 D2
Ilwaki Indonesia 7°55S 126°30E 231 F7
Ilyichevsk = Illichivsk Ukraine 46°20N 30°35E 189 J6
Iłża Poland 51°10N 21°15E 185 G8
Iłżanka → Poland 51°14N 21°48E 185 G8
Imabari Japan 34°4N 133°0E 222 C5
Imagem e do Som, Museu da Rio de J., Brazil 135 b3
Imaichi Japan 36°43N 139°46E 223 A11
Imaloto → Madag. 23°27S 45°13E 272 C2
İmamoğlu Turkey 37°15N 35°38E 212 D6
Iman = Dalnerechensk Russia 45°50N 133°40E 220 B6
Imandra, Ozero Russia 67°30N 33°0E 160 C25
Imanombo Madag. 24°26S 45°49E 272 C2
Imari Japan 33°15N 129°52E 222 D1
Imasa Sudan 18°0N 36°12E 256 D4
Imathia □ Greece 40°30N 22°15E 202 F6
Imatra Finland 61°12N 28°48E 188 B5
Imazu Japan 35°24N 136°2E 223 B8
Imbâbah Egypt 30°3N 31°12E 117 A2
Imbabura □ Ecuador 0°30N 78°45W 328 C2
Imbaimadai Guyana 5°44N 60°17W 329 B5
Imbonga Dem. Rep. of the Congo 0°43S 19°44E 264 C3
Imdahane Morocco 32°8N 7°0W 260 B3
Iménas Mali 16°20N 0°40E 263 B5
imeni 26 Bakinskikh Komissarov = Neftçala Azerbaijan 39°19N 49°12E 213 C13
imeni 26 Bakinskikh Komissarov Turkmenistan 39°22N 54°10E 247 B7
imeni Dvadtsati Shesti Bakinskikh Komissarov = Neftçala Azerbaijan 39°19N 49°12E 213 C13
imeni Dzerzhinskogo = Naryan-Mar Russia 67°42N 53°12E 186 A9
imeni Ismail Samani, Pik Tajikistan 39°0N 72°2E 217 E8
imeni Mikoyana = Kara-Balta Kyrgyzstan 42°50N 73°49E 217 D8
imeni Petrovskogo G.I. = Horodyshche Ukraine 49°17N 31°27E 189 H6
imeni Sverdlova = Sverdlovsk Ukraine 48°5N 39°47E 189 H10
imeni Tovarishcha Khateyevicha = Synelnykove Ukraine 48°25N 35°30E 189 H8
imeni Tretyego Internatsionala = Novoshakhtinsk Russia 47°46N 39°58E 189 J10
Imeri, Serra Brazil 0°50N 65°25W 328 C4
Imerimandroso Madag. 17°26S 48°35E 272 B2
Imese Dem. Rep. of the Congo 2°6N 18°9E 264 B3
Imfolozi △ S. Africa 28°18S 31°50E 271 C5
Imi Ethiopia 6°28N 42°10E 257 F5
Imielin Poland 52°9N 21°0E 142 C2
Imirim Brazil 23°29S 46°39W 137 A2
Imishly = İmişli Azerbaijan 39°55N 48°4E 191 L9
İmişli Azerbaijan 39°55N 48°4E 191 L9
Imitek Morocco 29°43N 8°10W 260 C3
Imitos Greece 37°55N 23°45E 112 B2
Imitos, Oros Greece 37°53N 23°48E 112 B2
Imjado S. Korea 35°5N 126°5E 224 E3
Imjin-gang → N. Korea 37°47N 126°39E 224 D3
Imlay U.S.A. 40°40N 118°9W 304 F4
Imlay City U.S.A. 43°2N 83°5W 312 D1
Immaseri Sudan 15°40N 25°31E 257 D2
Immenstadt Germany 47°33N 10°13E 179 H6
Immingham U.K. 53°37N 0°13W 168 D7
Immokalee U.S.A. 26°25N 81°25W 317 J8
Imo □ Nigeria 5°30N 7°10E 263 D6
Imo → Nigeria 4°36N 7°35E 263 E6
Ímola Italy 44°20N 11°42E 199 D8
Imotski Croatia 43°27N 17°12E 199 E14
Impé Congo 2°45S 15°16E 264 C3
Imperatorskaya Gavan = Vanino Russia 48°50N 140°5E 215 E15
Imperatriz Amazonas, Brazil 5°18S 67°11W 330 B4
Imperatriz Maranhão, Brazil 5°30S 47°29W 332 C2
Impéria Italy 43°53N 8°3E 198 E5
Imperial Sask., Canada 51°21N 105°28W 297 C7
Imperial Peru 13°4S 76°21W 330 C2
Imperial Calif., U.S.A. 32°51N 115°34W 307 N11
Imperial Nebr., U.S.A. 40°31N 101°39W 308 E3
Imperial Beach U.S.A. 32°35N 117°6W 307 N9
Imperial Dam U.S.A. 32°55N 114°25W 307 N12
Imperial Palace = Paço Imperial Rio de J., Brazil 135 a2
Imperial Palace Museum Beijing, China 114 b3
Imperial Res. U.S.A. 32°53N 114°28W 307 N12
Imperial Valley U.S.A. 33°0N 115°30W 307 N11
Imperieuse Reef Australia 17°36S 118°50E 278 C2
Impfondo Congo 1°40N 18°0E 264 B3
Imphal India 24°48N 93°56E 241 C4
Imphy France 46°55N 3°16E 173 F10
Impulo Angola 13°51S 13°39E 265 E2
İmranlı Turkey 39°54N 38°7E 213 C8
İmroz = Gökçeada Turkey 40°10N 25°50E 203 F9
İmroz Turkey 40°10N 25°55E 203 F9
Imst Austria 47°15N 10°44E 180 D3
Imuris Mexico 30°47N 110°52W 318 A2
Imuruan B. Phil. 10°40N 119°10E 233 F2
Imus Phil. 14°26N 120°56E 232 D3
In Aleï Mali 17°42N 2°30W 262 B4
In Amenas Algeria 28°5N 9°33E 261 C6
In Amguel Algeria 23°41N 5°9E 261 D6
In Atei Algeria 20°33N 6°24E 261 D6
In Belbel Algeria 27°55N 1°12E 261 C5
In Delimane Mali 15°52N 1°31E 263 B5
In Ghar Algeria 27°10N 1°59E 261 C5
In Guezzam Algeria 19°37N 5°52E 261 E6
In Koufi Mali 19°11N 1°25E 263 B5
In Salah Algeria 27°10N 2°32E 261 C5
In Tallak Mali 16°19N 3°15E 263 B5
In Tebezas Mali 17°49N 1°53E 263 B5
Ina Japan 35°50N 137°55E 223 B9
Ina Ill., U.S.A. 38°9N 88°54W 311 F8
Ina-Bonchi Japan 35°45N 137°58E 223 B9
Inabanga Phil. 10°2N 124°4E 233 F5
Inaguan Phil. 9°33N 118°39E 233 G2
Inagi Japan 35°38N 139°31E 140 B2
Inajá Brazil 8°54S 37°49W 332 C4
Inambari → Peru 12°41S 69°44W 330 C4
Inangahua N.Z. 41°52S 171°59E 285 B6
Inanwatan Indonesia 2°8S 132°10E 231 E8
Iñapari Peru 11°0S 69°40W 330 C4
Inarajan Guam 13°16N 144°45E 302 d
Inari Finland 68°54N 27°1E 160 B22
Inarijärvi Finland 69°0N 28°0E 160 B23
Inawashiro-Ko Japan 37°29N 140°6E 220 F10
Inazawa Japan 35°15N 136°47E 223 B8
Inbin Burma 18°6N 95°16E 241 F5
Inca Spain 39°43N 2°54E 206 B3
Inca de Oro Chile 26°45S 69°54W 334 B2
Incahuasi Argentina 27°2S 68°18W 334 B2
Incahuasi Chile 29°12S 71°5W 334 B1
İnce Burun Turkey 42°7N 34°56E 212 A6
İncekum Burnu Turkey 36°13N 33°57E 250 B4
İncesu Turkey 38°38N 35°11E 212 C6
Inchcolm U.K. 56°2N 3°18W 121 A2
Incheon S. Korea 37°27N 126°40E 224 D3
Inchicore Ireland 53°20N 6°20W 120 A1
Inchiri □ Mauritania 20°0N 15°0W 260 E2
Inchkeith U.K. 56°2N 3°8W 121 A3
Inchmickery U.K. 56°0N 3°16W 121 A2
Incio = A Cruz do Incio Spain 42°39N 7°21W 194 C3
Incirano Italy 45°34N 9°9E 129 A1
İncirliova Turkey 37°50N 27°41E 205 D9
Incline Village U.S.A. 39°10N 119°58W 304 G4
Incomáti → Mozam. 25°46S 32°43E 271 C5
Incudine, Mte. France 41°50N 9°12E 175 G13
Inda Silase Ethiopia 14°10N 38°15E 257 E4
Indal Sweden 62°35N 17°5E 162 B11
Indalsälven → Sweden 62°36N 17°30E 162 B11
Indaw Burma 24°15N 96°5E 241 C6
Indawgyi, L. Burma 25°20N 96°20E 241 C6
Indbir Ethiopia 8°7N 37°52E 257 F4
Indefatigable, I. = Santa Cruz, I. Ecuador 0°38S 90°23W 330 a
Independence Calif., U.S.A. 36°48N 118°12W 306 J8
Independence Iowa, U.S.A. 42°28N 91°54W 310 B5
Independence Kans., U.S.A. 37°14N 95°42W 308 G6
Independence Ky., U.S.A. 38°57N 84°33W 311 F12
Independence Mo., U.S.A. 39°6N 94°25W 310 E2
Independence Avenue Washington, D.C., U.S.A. 143 c2
Independence Fjord Greenland 82°10N 29°0W 154 A8
Independence Mts. U.S.A. 41°20N 116°0W 304 F5
Independência Brazil 5°23S 40°19W 332 C3
Independencia Santiago, Chile 33°25S 70°39W 137 B2
Independencia Lima, Peru 11°59S 77°3W 124 A2
Independencia, I. Peru 14°16S 76°12W 330 C2
Independenţa Romania 45°25N 27°42E 183 E12
İnderbor Kazakhstan 48°33N 51°47E 216 C4
Index U.S.A. 47°50N 121°33W 306 C5
Indi India 17°10N 75°58E 244 F2
India ■ Asia 20°0N 78°0E 239 F11
India Gate Delhi, India 120 c2
Indialantic U.S.A. 28°6N 80°34W 317 G9
Indian → U.S.A. 27°59N 80°34W 317 G9
Indian Cabins Canada 59°52N 117°40W 296 B5
Indian Creek Village U.S.A. 25°52N 80°8W 128 A2
Indian Harbour Canada 54°27N 57°13W 299 B8
Indian Harbour Beach U.S.A. 28°10N 80°35W 317 G9
Indian Head Canada 50°30N 103°41W 297 C8
Indian L. U.S.A. 43°46N 74°16W 313 C10
Indian Lake U.S.A. 43°47N 74°16W 313 C10
Indian Ocean 5°0S 75°0E 273 E6
Indian Rocks Beach U.S.A. 27°52N 82°51W 317 H7
Indian Springs U.S.A. 36°35N 115°40W 307 J11
Indian Town Pt. Antigua & B. 17°6N 61°40W 322 b
Indian Walk Trin. & Tob. 10°16N 61°20W 323 t
Indiana U.S.A. 40°37N 79°9W 312 F5
Indiana □ U.S.A. 40°0N 86°0W 311 E11
Indiana Dunes △ U.S.A. 41°40N 87°0W 311 C9
Indianapolis U.S.A. 39°46N 86°9W 311 E10
Indianapolis Int. ✕ (IND) U.S.A. 39°43N 86°17W 311 E10
Indianola Iowa, U.S.A. 41°22N 93°34W 310 C3
Indianola Miss., U.S.A. 33°27N 90°39W 315 E9
Indianópolis Brazil 23°35S 46°38W 137 B2
Indiantown U.S.A. 27°1N 80°28W 317 H9
Indiapora Brazil 19°57S 50°17W 333 E1
Indiga Russia 67°38N 49°9E 186 A8
Indigirka → Russia 70°48N 148°54E 215 B15
Inđija Serbia 45°6N 20°7E 182 E5
Indio U.S.A. 33°43N 116°13W 307 M10
Indira Gandhi Canal India 28°0N 72°0E 242 F5
Indira Gandhi Int. ✕ (DEL) India 28°34N 77°5E 120 B1
Indira Pt. India 6°44N 93°49E 245 L11
Indira Sagar India 22°15N 76°40E 242 H7
Indispensable Str. Solomon Is. 9°0S 160°30E 287 M11
Indo-China Asia 15°0N 102°0E 210 G12
Indonesia ■ Asia 5°0S 115°0E 235 C4
Indore India 22°42N 75°53E 242 H6
Indramayu Indonesia 6°20S 108°19E 235 D3
Indrapura = Kerinci Indonesia 1°40S 101°15E 234 C2
Indravati → India 19°20N 80°20E 244 E5
Indre □ France 46°50N 1°39E 173 F8
Indre → France 47°16N 0°11E 172 E7
Indre Ålvik Norway 60°26N 6°26E 164 D3
Indre Arna Norway 60°26N 5°30E 164 D2
Indre-et-Loire □ France 47°20N 0°40E 172 E7
Indrio U.S.A. 27°31N 80°21W 317 H9
Indulkana Australia 26°58S 133°5E 281 D1
Indungo Angola 14°48S 16°17E 265 E3
Indura Belarus 53°26N 23°53E 184 E10
Indus → Pakistan 24°20N 67°47E 242 G2
Indus, Mouths of the Pakistan 24°0N 68°0E 242 H3
Industria S. Africa 26°11S 27°58E 123 B1
Industrial Canal U.S.A. 30°4N 90°4W 131 A2
Industry U.S.A. 40°20N 90°36W 310 D6
İnebolu Turkey 41°55N 33°40E 212 B5
İnecik Turkey 40°56N 27°16E 203 F11
İnegöl Turkey 40°5N 29°31E 203 F13
Inés, Mt. Argentina 48°30S 69°40W 336 C3
Ineu Romania 46°26N 21°51E 182 D6
Inezgane Morocco 30°25N 9°29W 260 B3
Infanta Phil. 14°45N 121°39E 232 D3
Infantes = Villanueva de los Infantes Spain 38°43N 3°1W 195 G7
Infiernillo, Presa del Mexico 18°35N 101°50W 318 D4
Infiesto Spain 43°21N 5°21W 194 B5
Inga, Barrage d' Dem. Rep. of the Congo 5°39S 13°39E 265 D2
Ingabu Burma 17°37N 95°20E 241 G5
Inganda Dem. Rep. of the Congo 0°5S 20°57E 264 C4
Ingapirca Ecuador 2°38S 78°56W 328 D2
Ingelstad Sweden 56°45N 14°56E 163 H8
Ingende Dem. Rep. of the Congo 0°12S 18°57E 264 C3
Ingeniero Jacobacci Argentina 41°20S 69°36W 336 B3
Ingenio Canary Is. 27°55N 15°26W 153 e1
Ingenio Santa Ana Argentina 27°25S 65°40W 334 B2
Ingersoll Canada 43°4N 80°55W 312 C4
Ingham Australia 18°43S 146°10E 280 B4
Ingierstrand Norway 59°49N 10°46E 133 B3
Ingleborough U.K. 54°10N 2°22W 168 C5
Inglefield Land Greenland 78°30N 70°0W 154 B4
Inglewood Queens., Australia 28°25S 151°2E 281 D5
Inglewood Vic., Australia 36°29S 143°53E 282 D5
Inglewood N.Z. 39°9S 174°14E 284 F3
Inglewood Calif., U.S.A. 33°58N 118°21W 126 C3
Inglis U.S.A. 29°2N 82°40W 317 F7
Ingliston U.K. 55°56N 3°23W 121 B1
Ingolf Fjord Greenland 80°35N 17°30W 154 A9
Ingólfshöfði Iceland 63°48N 16°39W 155 D10
Ingolstadt Germany 48°46N 11°26E 179 G7
Ingomar U.S.A. 46°35N 107°23W 304 C10
Ingonish Canada 46°42N 60°18W 299 C7
Ingore Guinea-Biss. 12°24N 15°48W 262 C1
Ingraj Bazar India 24°58N 88°10E 243 G13
Ingrid Christensen Coast Antarctica 69°30S 76°0E 151 C6
Ingul = Inhul → Ukraine 46°50N 32°0E 189 J7
Ingulec = Inhulec Ukraine 47°42N 33°14E 189 J7
Ingulets = Inhulets → Ukraine 46°46N 32°47E 189 J7
Inguri = Enguri → Georgia 42°27N 41°38E 191 J5
Ingushetia □ Russia 43°20N 44°50E 191 J7
Ingwavuma S. Africa 27°9S 31°59E 271 C5
Inhaca Mozam. 26°1S 32°57E 271 C5
Inhaca Pen. Mozam. 26°13S 32°55E 271 C5
Inhafenga Mozam. 20°36S 33°53E 271 B5
Inhambane Mozam. 23°54S 35°30E 271 B6
Inhambane □ Mozam. 22°30S 34°20E 271 B5
Inhambupe Brazil 11°47S 38°21W 333 D4
Inhaminga Mozam. 18°26S 35°0E 269 F4
Inharrime Mozam. 24°30S 35°0E 271 B6
Inharrime → Mozam. 24°30S 35°0E 271 B6
Inhaúma Brazil 22°51S 43°17W 135 B1
Inhisar Turkey 40°3N 30°23E 205 A12
Inhul → Ukraine 46°50N 32°0E 189 J7
Inhulec Ukraine 47°42N 33°14E 189 J7
Inhulets → Ukraine 46°46N 32°47E 189 J7
Inhuma Brazil 6°40S 41°42W 332 C3
Inhumas Brazil 16°22S 49°30W 333 E2
Iniesta Spain 39°27N 1°45W 197 F3
Ining = Yining China 43°58N 81°10E 217 D10
Inini □ Fr. Guiana 4°0N 53°0W 329 C7
Inírida → Colombia 3°55N 67°52W 328 C4
Inis = Ennis Ireland 52°51N 8°59W 166 D3
Inis Córthaidh = Enniscorthy Ireland 52°30N 6°34W 166 D5
Inishbofin Ireland 53°37N 10°13W 166 C1
Inisheer Ireland 53°3N 9°32W 166 C2
Inishfree B. Ireland 55°4N 8°23W 166 A3
Inishkea North Ireland 54°9N 10°11W 166 B1
Inishkea South Ireland 54°7N 10°12W 166 B1
Inishmaan Ireland 53°5N 9°35W 166 C2
Inishmore Ireland 53°8N 9°45W 166 C2
Inishmurray I. Ireland 54°26N 8°39W 166 B3
Inishowen Pen. Ireland 55°14N 7°15W 166 A4
Inishshark Ireland 53°37N 10°16W 166 C1
Inishturk Ireland 53°42N 10°7W 166 C1
Inishvickillane Ireland 52°3N 10°37W 166 D1
Injāna Iraq 34°29N 44°38E 213 E11
Injibara Ethiopia 10°59N 37°0E 257 E4
Injinoo © Australia 10°56S 142°15E 280 A3
Injune Australia 25°53S 148°32E 281 D4
Inkisi → Dem. Rep. of the Congo 4°46S 14°52E 265 D3
Inklin → N. Amer. 58°50N 133°10W 296 B2
Inland Kaikoura Ra. N.Z. 41°59S 173°41E 285 B8
Inland Sea = Setonaikai Japan 34°20N 133°30E 222 C5
Inle L. Burma 20°30N 96°58E 241 E6
Inlet U.S.A. 43°45N 74°48W 313 C10
Inn → Austria 48°35N 13°28E 180 C6
Innamincka Australia 27°44S 140°46E 281 D3
Innbygda Norway 61°19N 12°17E 164 C9
Inner Hebrides U.K. 57°0N 6°30W 167 E2
Inner Mongolia = Nei Monggol Zizhiqu □ China 42°0N 112°0E 226 D7
Inner Port Shelter China 22°22N 114°17E 122 A2
Inner Sound U.K. 57°30N 5°55W 167 D3
Innerkip Canada 43°13N 80°42W 312 C4
Innes △ Australia 35°52S 136°53E 282 C2
Innetalling I. Canada 56°0N 79°0W 298 A4
Innisfail Queens., Australia 17°33S 146°5E 280 B4
Innisfail Alta., Canada 52°2N 113°57W 296 C6
Innoko Nat. Wildlife Refuge △ U.S.A. 63°20N 158°25W 303 E8
In'noshima Japan 34°19N 133°10E 222 C5
Innsbruck Austria 47°16N 11°23E 180 D4
Innviertel Austria 48°15N 13°15E 180 C6
Innvik Norway 61°51N 6°37E 164 C3
Inny → Ireland 53°30N 7°50W 166 C4
Ino Japan 33°33N 133°26E 222 D5
Inocência Brazil 19°47S 51°48W 333 E1
Inongo Dem. Rep. of the Congo 1°55S 18°30E 264 C3
Inoni Congo 3°4S 15°39E 264 C3
İnönü Turkey 39°48N 30°9E 205 B12
Inoucdjouac = Inukjuak Canada 58°25N 78°15W 295 F16
Inousses Greece 38°33N 26°14E 205 C8
Inowrocław Poland 52°50N 18°12E 185 F5
Inquisivi Bolivia 16°50S 67°10W 330 D4
Inscription, C. Australia 25°29S 112°59E 279 E1
Insein Burma 16°50N 96°5E 241 G6
Insjön Sweden 60°41N 15°6E 162 D9
Ińsko Poland 53°25N 15°32E 184 E2
Insterberg = Chernyakhovsk Russia 54°36N 21°48E 184 D8
Însurăţei Romania 44°50N 27°40E 183 F12
Inta Russia 66°5N 60°8E 186 A11
Intendente Alvear Argentina 35°12S 63°32W 334 D3
İntepe Turkey 40°1N 26°20E 205 A8
Interlachen U.S.A. 29°37N 81°53W 317 F8
Interlagos Brazil 23°41S 46°42W 137 C1
Interlaken Switz. 46°41N 7°50E 179 J3
Interlaken N.Y., U.S.A. 42°37N 76°44W 313 D8
International Falls U.S.A. 48°36N 93°25W 308 A7
Interview I. India 12°55N 92°43E 245 H11
Intiyaco Argentina 28°43S 60°5W 334 B3
Întorsura Buzăului Romania 45°41N 26°2E 183 E11
Intramuros Phil. 14°35N 120°57E 127 B1
Intrepid Air and Space Museum New York, U.S.A. 132 b1
Intutu Peru 3°32S 74°48W 328 D3
Inubō-Zaki Japan 35°42N 140°52E 223 B12
Inukjuak Canada 58°25N 78°15W 295 F16
Inútil, B. Chile 53°30S 70°15W 336 D2
Inuvik Canada 68°16N 133°40W 294 D5
Inuyama Japan 35°23N 136°56E 223 B8
Invalides France 48°51N 2°18E 134 A2
Inveraray U.K. 56°14N 5°5W 167 E3
Inverbervie U.K. 56°51N 2°17W 167 E6
Invercargill N.Z. 46°24S 168°24E 285 G3
Inverclyde □ U.K. 55°55N 4°49W 167 F4
Inverell Australia 29°45S 151°8E 281 D5
Invergordon U.K. 57°41N 4°10W 167 D4
Inverkeithing U.K. 56°2N 3°24W 121 A1
Inverleigh Australia 38°6S 144°3E 282 E6
Inverloch Australia 38°38S 145°45E 281 F4
Invermere Canada 50°30N 116°2W 296 C5
Inverness N.S., Canada 46°15N 61°19W 299 C7
Inverness Highl., U.K. 57°29N 4°13W 167 D4
Inverness Ala., U.S.A. 32°1N 85°45W 316 C4
Inverness Fla., U.S.A. 28°50N 82°20W 317 G7
Inverurie U.K. 57°17N 2°23W 167 D6
Investigator Group Australia 34°45S 134°20E 281 E1
Investigator Ridge Ind. Oc. 11°30S 98°10E 273 F8
Investigator Str. Australia 35°30S 137°0E 282 C2
Inya Russia 50°28N 86°37E 217 B11
Inyanga Zimbabwe 18°12S 32°40E 269 F3
Inyangani Zimbabwe 18°5S 32°50E 269 F3
Inyantue Zimbabwe 18°33S 26°39E 270 A4
Inyo Mts. U.S.A. 36°40N 118°0W 306 J9
Inyokern U.S.A. 35°39N 117°49W 307 K9
Inyonga Tanzania 6°45S 32°5E 268 D3
Inywa Burma 23°56N 96°17E 241 D6
Inza Russia 53°55N 46°25E 190 D8
Inzersdorf Austria 48°8N 16°21E 142 B2
Inzhavino Russia 52°22N 42°30E 190 D6
Inzia → Dem. Rep. of the Congo 3°45S 17°57E 265 C3
Iō-Jima Japan 30°48N 130°18E 221 J5
Ioannina Greece 39°42N 20°47E 204 B2
Ioannina □ Greece 39°39N 20°57E 204 B2
Iokea Papua N. G. 8°25S 146°16E 286 E4
Iola U.S.A. 37°55N 95°24W 308 G6
Iolani Palace U.S.A. 21°18N 157°51W 302 K14
Ioma Papua N. G. 8°19S 147°52E 286 E4
Ion Corvin Romania 44°7N 27°50E 183 F12
Iona Angola 16°54S 12°34E 265 F2
Iona Argyll & Bute, U.K. 56°20N 6°25W 167 E2
Iona △ Angola 16°47S 12°20E 265 F2
Ione U.S.A. 38°21N 120°56W 306 G6
Iongo Angola 9°11S 17°45E 265 D3
Ionia U.S.A. 42°59N 85°4W 311 B11
Ionian Is. = Ionioi Nisoi Greece 38°40N 20°0E 204 C2
Ionian Sea Medit. S. 37°30N 17°30E 193 D7
Ionioi Nisoi Greece 38°40N 20°0E 204 C2
Ionioi Nisoi □ Greece 38°40N 20°0E 207 B2
Ios Greece 36°41N 25°20E 205 E7
Iowa □ U.S.A. 42°18N 93°30W 310 C3
Iowa → U.S.A. 41°10N 91°1W 310 C5
Iowa City U.S.A. 41°40N 91°32W 310 C5
Iowa Falls U.S.A. 42°31N 93°16W 310 B3
Iowa Park U.S.A. 33°57N 98°40W 314 E5
Ipala Tanzania 4°30S 32°52E 268 C3
Ipameri Brazil 17°44S 48°9W 333 E2
Ipanema Minas Gerais, Brazil 19°47S 41°44W 333 E3
Ipanema Rio de J., Brazil 22°59S 43°12W 135 B1
Iparía Peru 9°17S 74°29W 330 B3
Ipati Greece 38°52N 22°14E 204 C4
Ipatinga Brazil 19°32S 42°30W 333 E3
Ipatovo Russia 45°45N 42°50E 191 H6
Ipek = Peć Kosovo 42°40N 20°17E 202 D4
Ipel' → Europe 47°48N 18°53E 181 D11
Ipiales Colombia 0°50N 77°37W 328 C2
Ipiaú Brazil 14°8S 39°44W 333 D4
Ipil Phil. 7°47N 122°35E 233 H4
Ipin = Yibin China 28°45N 104°32E 228 C5
Ipirá Brazil 12°10S 39°44W 333 D4
Ipiranga Brazil 23°35S 46°36W 137 B2
Ipiranga → Brazil 23°37S 46°37W 137 B2
Ipixuna Brazil 7°0S 71°40W 330 B3
Ipixuna → Amazonas, Brazil 7°11S 71°51W 330 B3
Ipixuna → Amazonas, Brazil 5°45S 63°2W 331 B5
Ipoh Malaysia 4°35N 101°5E 237 K3
Iponri Nigeria 6°28N 3°22E 124 B2
Iporá Brazil 16°28S 51°7W 331 D7
Ipota Vanuatu 18°52S 169°20E 287 H7
Ippy C.A.R. 6°5N 21°7E 264 A4
Ipsala Turkey 40°55N 26°23E 203 F10
Ipsario, Oros Greece 40°40N 24°40E 203 F8
Ipsos Greece 39°43N 19°48E 206 B9
Ipswich Queens., Australia 27°35S 152°40E 281 D5
Ipswich Suffolk, U.K. 52°4N 1°10E 169 E9
Ipswich Mass., U.S.A. 42°41N 70°50W 313 D14
Ipswich S. Dak., U.S.A. 45°27N 99°2W 308 C4
Ipu Brazil 4°23S 40°44W 332 B3
Ipueiras Brazil 4°33S 40°43W 332 B3
Ipupiara Brazil 11°49S 42°37W 333 D3
Iqaluit Canada 63°44N 68°31W 295 E18
Iqaluktuutiaq = Cambridge Bay Canada 69°10N 105°0W 294 D11
Iquique Chile 20°19S 70°5W 330 E3
Iquitos Peru 3°45S 73°10W 328 D3
Ir Gannim = Bat Yam Israel 32°2N 34°44E 251 F5
Irabu-Jima Japan 24°50N 125°10E 221 M2
Iracoubo Fr. Guiana 5°30N 53°10W 329 B7
Īrafshān Iran 26°42N 61°56E 247 E9
Irahuan Phil. 9°48N 118°41E 233 G2
Iraklia Cyclades, Greece 36°50N 25°28E 205 E7
Iraklia Serres, Greece 41°10N 23°16E 202 E7
Iraklio Greece 35°20N 25°12E 207 E6
Iraklio □ Greece 35°10N 25°10E 207 E6
Iraklio ✕ (HER) Greece 35°20N 25°15E 207 E6
Iráklion = Iraklio Greece 35°20N 25°12E 207 E6
Irakliou, Kolpos Greece 35°23N 25°8E 207 E6
Irako-Zaki Japan 34°35N 137°1E 223 C9
Irala Paraguay 25°55S 54°35W 335 B5
Iran ■ Asia 33°0N 53°0E 247 C7
Iran, Pegunungan Malaysia 2°20N 114°50E 235 B4
Iran Ra. = Iran, Pegunungan Malaysia 2°20N 114°50E 235 B4
Iranamadu Tank Sri Lanka 9°23N 80°29E 245 K5
Īrānshahr Iran 27°15N 60°40E 247 E9
Irapa Venezuela 10°34N 62°35W 329 A5
Irapuato Mexico 20°41N 101°28W 318 C4
Iraq ■ Asia 33°0N 44°0E 213 F10
Irarrar, O. → Mali 20°0N 1°30E 261 E5
Irati Brazil 25°25S 50°38W 335 B5
Irbes saurums Latvia 57°45N 22°5E 184 A9
Irbid Jordan 32°35N 35°48E 251 F6
Irbid □ Jordan 32°30N 35°50E 250 F6
Irebu Dem. Rep. of the Congo 0°40S 17°46E 264 C3
Irecê Brazil 11°18S 41°52W 332 D3
Iregua → Spain 42°27N 2°24W 196 C7
Ireland ■ Europe 53°50N 7°52W 166 C4
Ireland I. Bermuda 32°19N 64°50W 153 a
Ireland Island Bermuda 32°19N 64°50W 153 a
Ireland's Eye Ireland 53°24N 6°4W 120 A3
Irele Nigeria 7°40N 5°40E 263 D6
Ireng → Brazil 3°33N 59°51W 329 C6
Irerrer, O. → Algeria 19°25N 5°47E 261 E6
Irgiz = Yrghyz Kazakhstan 48°37N 61°16E 216 C6
Irgiz = Yrghyz → Kazakhstan 48°6N 62°30E 216 C6
Irgiz, Bolshaya → Russia 52°10N 49°10E 190 D9
Irharhar, O. → Algeria 28°3N 6°15E 261 C6
Irherm Morocco 30°7N 8°18W 260 B3
Irhil M'Goun Morocco 31°30N 6°28W 260 B3
Iri = Iksan S. Korea 35°59N 127°0E 224 E3
Irian Barat = Papua □ Indonesia 4°0S 137°0E 231 E9
Irian Jaya = Papua □ Indonesia 4°0S 137°0E 231 E9
Irian Jaya Barat □ Indonesia 2°5S 132°50E 231 E8
Iriba Chad 15°7N 22°15E 259 E4
Irié Guinea 8°15N 9°10W 262 D3
Iriga Phil. 13°25N 123°25E 232 E4
Iriklinskoye Vdkhr. Russia 52°0N 59°0E 216 B5
Iringa Tanzania 7°48S 35°43E 268 D4
Iringa □ Tanzania 7°48S 35°43E 268 D4
Irinjalakuda India 10°21N 76°14E 245 J3
Iriomote △ Japan 24°29N 123°53E 221 M1
Iriomote-Jima Japan 24°19N 123°48E 221 M1
Iriona Honduras 15°57N 85°11W 320 C2
Iriri → Brazil 3°52S 52°37W 329 D7
Iriri Novo → Brazil 8°46S 53°22W 331 B7
Irish Republic ■ Europe 53°50N 7°52W 166 C4
Irish Sea Europe 53°38N 4°48W 168 D3
Irkeshtam Pass = Erkech-Tam Pass Asia 39°46N 74°2E 217 E8
Irkutsk Russia 52°18N 104°20E 215 D11
Irlığanlı Turkey 37°53N 29°15E 205 D11
Irma Canada 52°55N 111°14W 297 C6
Irō-Zaki Japan 34°36N 138°51E 223 C10
Iroise, Mer d' France 48°15N 4°45W 172 D2
Irois B. Trin. & Tob. 10°9N 61°45W 323 t
Iron Baron Australia 32°58S 137°11E 282 B2
Iron Gate = Portile de Fier Europe 44°44N 22°30E 182 F7
Iron Knob Australia 32°46S 137°8E 282 B2
Iron Mountain U.S.A. 45°49N 88°4W 308 C9
Iron Range △ Australia 12°34S 143°18E 280 A3
Iron River U.S.A. 46°6N 88°39W 308 B9
Irondequoit U.S.A. 43°13N 77°35W 312 C7
Ironton Mo., U.S.A. 37°36N 90°38W 308 G8
Ironton Ohio, U.S.A. 38°32N 82°41W 309 F12
Ironwood U.S.A. 46°27N 90°9W 308 B8
Ironwood Forest △ U.S.A. 32°32N 111°28W 305 K8
Iroquois Canada 44°51N 75°19W 313 B9
Iroquois → U.S.A. 41°5N 87°49W 311 C9
Iroquois Falls Canada 48°46N 80°41W 298 C3
Iroquois Point U.S.A. 21°19N 157°58W 302 K14
Irosin Phil. 12°42N 124°2E 232 E5

Irpin *Ukraine* 50°30N 30°15E **177** C16
Irqieqa, Ras I- *Malta* 35°56N 14°29E **206** F7
Irrara Cr. → *Australia* 29°35S 145°31E **281** D4
Irrawaddy ☐ *Burma* 17°0N 95°0E **241** G5
Irrawaddy → *Burma* 15°50N 95°6E **241** G5
Irrawaddy, Mouths of the *Burma* 15°30N 95°0E **241** H5
Irricana *Canada* 51°19N 113°37W **296** C6
Irrunytju *Australia* 26°3S 128°56E **279** E4
Irshava *Ukraine* 48°19N 23°3E **182** B8
Irsina *Italy* 40°45N 16°14E **201** B9
Irtysh → *Russia* 61°4N 68°52E **214** C7
Irumu *Dem. Rep. of the Congo* 1°32N 29°53E **268** B2
Irún *Spain* 43°20N 1°52W **196** B3
Irunea = Pamplona-Iruña *Spain* 42°48N 1°38W **196** C3
Irurzun *Spain* 42°55N 1°50W **196** C3
Irvine *Alta., Canada* 49°57N 110°16W **297** D6
Irvine *N. Ayrs., U.K.* 55°37N 4°41W **167** F4
Irvine *Calif., U.S.A.* 33°41N 117°46W **307** M9
Irvine *Ky., U.S.A.* 37°42N 83°58W **311** G13
Irvinestown *U.K.* 54°28N 7°39W **166** B4
Irving *U.S.A.* 32°48N 96°56W **314** E6
Irving Park *U.S.A.* 41°57N 87°42W **119** B2
Irvington *U.S.A.* 37°53N 86°17W **311** G10
Irvona *U.S.A.* 40°46N 78°33W **312** F6
Irwin → *Australia* 29°15S 114°54E **279** E1
Irwinton *U.S.A.* 32°49N 83°10W **316** C6
Irwinville *U.S.A.* 31°39N 83°23W **316** D6
Irymple *Australia* 34°14S 142°8E **282** C5
Is, Jebel *Sudan* 22°3N 35°28E **256** C4
Is-sur-Tille *France* 47°30N 5°8E **173** E12
Isa *Nigeria* 13°14N 6°24E **263** C6
Isa Khel *Pakistan* 32°41N 71°17E **242** C4
Isaac → *Australia* 22°55S 149°20E **280** C4
Isabel *Rio de J., Brazil* 22°55S 43°14W **135** B1
Isabel *S. Dak., U.S.A.* 45°24N 101°26W **308** C3
Isabel, I. *Mexico* 21°51N 105°55W **318** C3
Isabel Segunda *Puerto Rico* 18°9N 65°27W **321** b
Isabela *Basilan, Phil.* 6°40N 121°59E **233** H3
Isabela *Negros, Phil.* 10°12N 122°59E **233** F4
Isabela *Puerto Rico* 18°30N 67°2W **321** b
Isabela ☐ *Phil.* 17°0N 122°0E **232** C4
Isabela, Canal *Ecuador* 0°20S 90°55W **330** a
Isabela, I. *Ecuador* 0°30S 91°4W **330** a
Isabella, Cord. *Nic.* 13°30N 85°25W **320** D2
Isabella Ra. *Australia* 21°0S 121°4E **278** D3
Isaccea *Romania* 45°16N 28°28E **183** E13
Isachsen, C. *Canada* 79°20N 105°28W **295** B10
Ísafjarðardjúp *Iceland* 66°10N 23°0W **155** A3
Ísafjarðarsýsla ☐ *Iceland* 66°0N 23°0W **155** B3
Ísafjörður *Iceland* 66°5N 23°9W **155** A3
Isagarh *India* 24°48N 77°51E **242** G7
Isagatedo *Nigeria* 6°31N 3°19E **124** A1
Isahaya *Japan* 32°52N 130°2E **222** E2
Isaka *Dem. Rep. of the Congo* 2°33S 18°54E **264** C3
Isaka *Tanzania* 3°56S 32°59E **268** C3
Işalniţa *Romania* 44°24N 23°44E **183** F8
Isalo, Tangorombohitr' *Madag.* 22°45S 45°15E **272** C2
Isalo △ *Madag.* 22°23S 45°16E **272** C2
Isan → *India* 26°51N 80°7E **243** F9
Isana = Içana → *Brazil* 0°26N 67°19W **328** C4
Isandja *Dem. Rep. of the Congo* 2°59S 21°59E **264** C4
Isangano △ *Zambia* 11°8S 30°35E **269** E3
Isangi *Dem. Rep. of the Congo* 0°52N 24°10E **264** B4
Isanlu Makutu *Nigeria* 8°20N 5°50E **263** D6
Isar → *Bayern, Germany* 48°48N 12°57E **179** G8
Isar → *Oberbayern, Germany* 48°15N 11°41E **131** A3
Isarco → *Italy* 46°27N 11°18E **199** B8
Isaris *Greece* 37°22N 22°0E **204** D3
Isarog, Mt. *Phil.* 13°39N 123°23E **232** E4
Íscar *Spain* 41°22N 4°32W **194** D6
Iscayachi *Bolivia* 21°31S 65°3W **331** E4
İscehisar *Turkey* 38°51N 30°45E **205** C12
Íschia *Italy* 40°44N 13°57E **200** B6
Iscuandé *Colombia* 2°28N 77°59W **328** C2
Isdell → *Australia* 16°27S 124°51E **278** C3
Ise *Japan* 34°25N 136°45E **223** C8
Ise-Shima △ *Japan* 34°25N 136°48E **223** C8
Ise-Wan *Japan* 34°43N 136°43E **223** C8
Isefjord *Denmark* 55°53N 11°50E **163** J5
Isel → *Austria* 46°50N 12°47E **180** E5
Iseo *Italy* 45°39N 10°3E **198** C7
Iseo, L. d' *Italy* 45°43N 10°4E **198** C7
Iseramagazi *Tanzania* 4°37S 32°10E **268** C3
Isère ☐ *France* 45°15N 5°40E **175** C9
Isère → *France* 44°59N 4°51E **175** D8
Iserlohn *Germany* 51°22N 7°41E **178** D3
Isérnia *Italy* 41°36N 14°14E **201** A7
Isesaki *Japan* 36°19N 139°12E **223** A11
Iseyin *Nigeria* 8°0N 3°36E **263** D5
Isfahan = Eşfahān *Iran* 32°39N 51°43E **247** C6
Isfjorden *Norway* 62°35N 7°49E **164** B4
Ishbīlīya *Iraq* 33°21N 44°26E **113** A2
Ishëm *Albania* 41°33N 19°34E **202** E3
Ishenga Oshwe *Dem. Rep. of the Congo* 3°57S 22°33E **264** C4
Isherton *Guyana* 2°20N 59°25W **329** C6
Ishigaki *Japan* 24°26N 124°10E **221** M2
Ishigaki-Shima *Japan* 24°20N 124°10E **221** M2
Ishikari-Gawa → *Japan* 43°15N 141°23E **220** C10
Ishikari-Sammyaku *Japan* 43°30N 143°0E **220** C11
Ishikari-Wan *Japan* 43°25N 141°1E **220** C10
Ishikawa *Japan* 26°25N 127°49E **288** a
Ishikawa ☐ *Japan* 36°30N 136°30E **223** A8
Ishim *Russia* 56°10N 69°30E **214** D7
Ishim → *Russia* 57°45N 71°10E **214** D8
Ishimbay *Russia* 53°28N 56°2E **216** B5
Ishinomaki *Japan* 38°32N 141°20E **220** E10
Ishioka *Japan* 36°11N 140°16E **223** A12
Ishizuchi-Yama *Japan* 33°45N 133°6E **222** D5
Ishkashim *Tajikistan* 36°44N 71°37E **217** E8
Ishkoman *Pakistan* 36°30N 73°50E **243** A5
Ishøj Strand *Denmark* 55°36N 12°20E **118** B2
Ishpeming *U.S.A.* 46°29N 87°40W **308** B10
Ishurdi *Bangla.* 24°9N 89°3E **241** C2
Isiboro Sécure △ *Bolivia* 16°15S 65°50W **331** D4
Isigny-sur-Mer *France* 49°19N 1°6W **172** C5
Isıklar Dağı *Turkey* 40°45N 27°15E **203** F11
Işıklı *Turkey* 38°19N 29°51E **205** C11
Isil Kul *Russia* 54°55N 71°16E **217** B8
Ísili *Italy* 39°44N 9°6E **200** C2
Isiolo *Kenya* 0°24N 37°33E **268** B4
Isiro *Dem. Rep. of the Congo* 2°53N 27°40E **268** B2
Isisford *Australia* 24°15S 144°21E **280** C3
İskenderun *Turkey* 36°32N 36°10E **250** B7
İskenderun Körfezi *Turkey* 36°40N 35°50E **250** B6
İskilip *Turkey* 40°45N 34°29E **212** B6
Iskitim *Russia* 54°38N 83°18E **217** B10
Iskŭr → *Bulgaria* 43°45N 24°25E **203** C8
Iskŭr, Yazovir *Bulgaria* 42°23N 23°30E **202** D7
Iskushuban *Somali Rep.* 10°18N 50°12E **267** B7
Iskut → *Canada* 56°45N 131°49W **296** B2
Isla → *U.K.* 56°32N 3°20W **167** E5
Isla Coiba △ *Panama* 7°33N 81°36W **320** E4
Isla Cristina *Spain* 37°13N 7°17W **195** H3
Isla de Salamanca △ *Colombia* 10°59N 74°40W **328** A3
Isla Gorge △ *Australia* 25°10S 149°57E **280** D4
Isla Gorgona △ *Colombia* 2°59N 78°10W **328** C2
Isla Guamblin △ *Chile* 44°50S 75°4W **336** B1
Isla Isabel △ *Mexico* 21°54N 105°58W **318** C3
Isla Magdalena △ *Chile* 44°20S 73°13W **336** B2
Isla Tiburón y San Esteban ⌓ *Mexico* 29°0N 112°27W **318** B2
Isla Vista *U.S.A.* 34°25N 119°53W **307** L7
İslâhiye *Turkey* 37°0N 36°35E **250** B7
Islam Headworks *Pakistan* 29°49N 72°33E **242** E5
Islamabad *Pakistan* 33°40N 73°10E **242** C5
Islamgarh *Pakistan* 27°51N 70°48E **242** F4
Islamkot *Pakistan* 24°42N 70°13E **242** G4
Islamorada *U.S.A.* 24°56N 80°37W **317** L9
Islampur *Bihar, India* 25°9N 85°12E **243** G11
Islampur *Maharashtra, India* 17°2N 74°20E **244** F2
Islampur *W. Bengal, India* 26°16N 88°12E **243** F13
Island = Iceland ■ *Europe* 64°45N 19°0W **155** C8
Island Bay *N.Z.* 41°20S 174°46E **143** B1
Island Bay *Phil.* 9°6N 118°10E **233** G2
Island Harbour *Anguilla* 18°12N 63°0W **322** a
Island L. *Canada* 53°47N 94°25W **297** C10
Island Lagoon *Australia* 31°30S 136°40E **282** A2
Island Park *Canada* 43°37N 79°22W **141** B2
Island Pond *U.S.A.* 44°49N 71°53W **313** B13
Islands, B. of *Nfld. & L., Canada* 49°11N 58°15W **299** C8
Islands, B. of *N.Z.* 35°15S 174°6E **284** B3
Islay *U.K.* 55°46N 6°10W **167** F2
Isle → *France* 44°55N 0°15W **174** D3
Isle aux Morts *Canada* 47°35N 59°0W **299** C8
Isle of Hope *U.S.A.* 31°58N 81°5W **316** D8
Isle of Wight ☐ *U.K.* 50°41N 1°17W **169** G6
Isle Royale △ *U.S.A.* 48°0N 88°55W **308** B9
Isleton *U.S.A.* 38°10N 121°37W **306** G5
Islev *Denmark* 55°41N 12°27E **118** A2
Isleworth *U.K.* 51°28N 0°19W **125** B2
Islington *Canada* 43°38N 79°30W **141** B1
Islington ☐ *U.K.* 51°33N 0°5W **125** A3
Islote Pt. *Trin. & Tob.* 10°4N 61°47W **323** t
Ismail = Izmayil *Ukraine* 45°22N 28°46E **183** E13
Ismâ'ilîya *Egypt* 30°37N 32°18E **251** H3
Ismâ'ilîya ☐ *Egypt* 30°35N 32°16E **251** H3
Ismâ'ilîya, Tir'at el → *Egypt* 30°4N 31°16E **251** H2
Ismaning *Germany* 48°13N 11°40E **131** A3
Ismayloskiy Park *Russia* 55°46N 37°46E **129** B4
Isna *Egypt* 25°17N 32°30E **256** B3
Isoanala *Madag.* 23°50S 45°44E **272** C2
Ísola del Liri *Italy* 41°41N 13°34E **199** G10
Ísola della Scala *Italy* 45°16N 11°0E **198** C7
Ísola di Capo Rizzuto *Italy* 38°58N 17°6E **201** D10
Isolo *Nigeria* 6°31N 3°19E **124** A1
İsparta *Turkey* 37°47N 30°30E **205** D12
İsparta ☐ *Turkey* 38°0N 31°0E **212** D4
Isperikh *Bulgaria* 43°43N 26°50E **203** C10
Íspica *Italy* 36°47N 14°55E **201** F7
İspir *Turkey* 40°28N 40°59E **213** B9
Israel ■ *Asia* 32°0N 34°50E **251** G5
Isratu *Eritrea* 16°20N 39°53E **257** D4
Issakly *Russia* 54°8N 51°32E **190** C10
Issano *Guyana* 5°49N 59°26W **329** B6
Issaouane, Erg *Algeria* 26°58N 8°42E **258** C1
Issia *Ivory C.* 6°33N 6°33W **262** D3
Issoire *France* 45°32N 3°15E **174** C7
Issoudun *France* 46°57N 1°59E **173** F8
Issy-les-Moulineaux *France* 48°49N 2°15E **134** B2
Issyk-Kul = Balykchy *Kyrgyzstan* 42°26N 76°12E **217** D9
Issyk-Kul, Ozero = Ysyk-Köl *Kyrgyzstan* 42°25N 77°15E **217** D9
Ist *Croatia* 44°17N 14°47E **199** D11
Istaihah *U.A.E.* 23°19N 54°4E **249** B6
Istállós-kő *Hungary* 48°4N 20°26E **182** B5
İstanbul *Turkey* 41°0N 28°58E **122** C1
İstanbul ☐ *Turkey* 41°0N 29°0E **203** E12
İstanbul ✈ (IST) *Turkey* 40°59N 28°49E **203** F12
İstanbul Boğazı *Turkey* 41°5N 29°3E **122** B2
Istaravshan = Uroteppa *Tajikistan* 39°55N 69°1E **217** E7
Isteren *Norway* 61°58N 11°47E **164** B8
Istiea *Greece* 38°57N 23°9E **204** C5
Istinye *Turkey* 41°6N 29°3E **122** B2
Istmina *Colombia* 5°10N 76°39W **328** B2
Isto, Mt. *U.S.A.* 69°12N 143°48W **303** B12
Istok *Kosovo* 42°45N 20°24E **202** D4
Istokpoga, L. *U.S.A.* 27°23N 81°17W **317** H8
Istra *Croatia* 45°10N 14°0E **199** C10
Istres *France* 43°31N 4°59E **175** E8
Istria = Istra *Croatia* 45°10N 14°0E **199** C10
Isugod *Phil.* 9°19N 118°5E **233** G2
Isulan *Phil.* 6°30N 124°29E **233** H5
Itá *Paraguay* 25°29S 57°21W **334** B4
Itä Hakkila *Finland* 60°17N 25°7E **121** B3
Itabaiana *Paraíba, Brazil* 7°18S 35°19W **332** C4
Itabaiana *Sergipe, Brazil* 10°41S 37°37W **332** D4
Itabaianinha *Brazil* 11°16S 37°47W **332** D4
Itaberaba *Brazil* 12°32S 40°18W **333** D3
Itaberaí *Brazil* 16°2S 49°48W **333** E2
Itabira *Brazil* 19°37S 43°13W **333** E3
Itabirito *Brazil* 20°15S 43°48W **333** F3
Itaboca *Brazil* 4°50S 62°40W **329** D5
Itabuna *Brazil* 14°48S 39°16W **333** D4
Itacajá *Brazil* 8°19S 47°46W **332** C2
Itacaunas → *Brazil* 5°21S 49°8W **332** C2
Itaewon *S. Korea* 37°32N 126°58E **137** B1
Itaguari → *Brazil* 14°11S 44°40W **333** D3
Itaguatins *Brazil* 5°47S 47°29W **332** C2
Itaim → *Brazil* 7°2S 42°2W **332** C3
Itainópolis *Brazil* 7°24S 41°31W **332** C3
Itaipú, Represa de *Brazil* 25°30S 54°30W **335** B5
Itaituba *Brazil* 4°10S 55°50W **329** D6
Itajaí *Brazil* 27°50S 48°39W **335** B6
Itajany do Sul = Rio do Sul *Brazil* 27°13S 49°37W **335** B6
Itajubá *Brazil* 22°24S 45°30W **333** F2
Itajuípe *Brazil* 14°41S 39°22W **333** D4
Itaka *Tanzania* 8°50S 32°49E **269** D3
Itako *Japan* 35°56N 140°33E **223** B12
Itala ⌓ *S. Africa* 27°30S 31°7E **271** C5
Italy ■ *Europe* 42°0N 13°0E **192** C6
Itamaraju *Brazil* 17°4S 39°32W **333** E4
Itamarati *Brazil* 6°24S 68°15W **330** B4
Itamataré *Brazil* 2°16S 46°24W **332** B2
Itambacuri *Brazil* 18°1S 41°42W **333** E3
Itambé *Brazil* 15°15S 40°37W **333** E3
Itami *Japan* 34°46N 135°24E **133** A1
Itampolo *Madag.* 24°41S 43°57E **272** C1
Itanagar *India* 27°6N 93°37E **241** B4
Itandrano *Madag.* 21°47S 45°17E **272** C2
Itanhaém *Brazil* 24°11S 46°47W **333** F2
Itanhanga *Brazil* 22°59S 43°19W **135** B1
Itanhauã → *Brazil* 4°45S 63°48W **329** D5
Itanhém *Brazil* 17°9S 40°20W **333** E3
Itano *Japan* 34°7N 134°28E **222** C6
Itapaci *Brazil* 14°57S 49°34W **333** D2
Itapagé *Brazil* 3°41S 39°34W **332** B4
Itaparica = Petrolândia *Brazil* 9°5S 38°20W **332** C4
Itaparica, I. de *Brazil* 12°54S 38°42W **333** D4
Itaparica, Represa de *Brazil* 11°3S 42°47W **332** D3
Itapebi *Brazil* 15°56S 39°32W **333** E4
Itapecuru Mirim *Brazil* 3°24S 44°20W **332** B3
Itaperuna *Brazil* 21°10S 41°54W **333** F3
Itapetinga *Brazil* 15°15S 40°15W **333** E3
Itapetininga *Brazil* 23°36S 48°7W **335** A6
Itapeva *Brazil* 23°59S 48°59W **335** A6
Itapicuru → *Bahia, Brazil* 11°47S 37°32W **332** D4
Itapicuru → *Maranhão, Brazil* 2°52S 44°12W **332** B3
Itapipoca *Brazil* 3°30S 39°35W **332** B4
Itapira = Ubaitaba *Brazil* 14°18S 39°20W **333** D4
Itapiranga *Brazil* 2°45S 58°1W **329** D6
Itapiúna *Brazil* 4°33S 38°57W **332** B4
Itaporanga *Paraíba, Brazil* 7°18S 38°0W **332** C4
Itaporanga *São Paulo, Brazil* 23°42S 49°29W **333** F2
Itapuá ☐ *Paraguay* 26°40S 55°40W **335** B4
Itapuranga *Brazil* 15°40S 49°59W **333** E2
Itaquai → *Brazil* 4°20S 70°12W **330** A3
Itaquatiara *Brazil* 2°58S 58°30W **329** D6
Itaquí *Brazil* 29°8S 56°30W **334** B4
Itararé *Brazil* 24°6S 49°23W **335** A6
Itarsi *India* 22°36N 77°51E **242** H7
Itarumã *Brazil* 18°42S 51°25W **333** E1
Itatí *Argentina* 27°16S 58°15W **334** B4
Itatiaia △ *Brazil* 22°22S 44°38W **335** A7
Itatira *Brazil* 4°30S 39°37W **332** B4
Itatuba *Brazil* 5°46S 63°20W **331** B5
Itatupã *Brazil* 0°37S 51°12W **329** D7
Itaueira *Brazil* 7°36S 43°2W **332** C3
Itaueira → *Brazil* 6°41S 42°55W **332** C3
Itaúna *Brazil* 20°4S 44°34W **333** F3
Itbayat *Phil.* 20°47N 121°51E **232** A3
Itbayat I. *Phil.* 20°45N 121°50E **232** A3
Itchen → *U.K.* 50°55N 1°22W **169** G6
Itchouma *Niger* 20°14N 13°32E **261** D7
Ite *Peru* 17°55S 70°57W **330** D3
Itea *Greece* 38°25N 22°25E **204** C4
Itezhi Tezhi, L. *Zambia* 15°30S 25°30E **269** F2
Ithaca = Ithaki *Greece* 38°25N 20°40E **207** C2
Ithaca *U.S.A.* 42°27N 76°30W **313** D8
Ithaki *Greece* 38°25N 20°40E **207** C2
Ithakis, Stenon *Greece* 38°22N 20°39E **207** C2
Iti △ *Greece* 38°50N 22°15E **204** C4
Itimbiri → *Dem. Rep. of the Congo* 2°2N 22°44E **264** B4
Itinga *Brazil* 16°36S 41°47W **333** E3
Itiquira *Brazil* 17°12S 54°7W **331** D7
Itiquira → *Brazil* 17°18S 56°44W **331** D6
Itiruçu *Brazil* 13°31S 40°9W **333** D3
Itiúba *Brazil* 10°43S 39°51W **332** D4
Itiyuro → *Argentina* 22°40S 63°50W **334** A3
Itkilik → *U.S.A.* 70°9N 150°56W **303** A10
Itō *Japan* 34°58N 139°5E **223** C11
Itogon *Phil.* 16°22N 120°41E **232** C3
Itoigawa *Japan* 37°2N 137°51E **221** F8
Itoko *Dem. Rep. of the Congo* 1°0S 21°48E **264** C4
Itoman *Japan* 26°7N 127°40E **288** a
Iton → *France* 49°9N 1°12E **172** C8
Itonamas → *Bolivia* 12°28S 64°24W **331** C5
Itri *Italy* 41°17N 13°32E **200** A6
Itsa *Egypt* 29°15N 30°47E **256** J7
Itsamia *Comoros Is.* 12°21S 43°52E **272** a
Itsandra *Comoros Is.* 11°40S 43°15E **272** a
Itsuki *Japan* 32°24N 130°50E **222** E2
Íttiri *Italy* 40°36N 8°34E **200** B1
Ittoqqortoormiit *Greenland* 70°20N 23°0W **154** C8
Itu *Brazil* 23°17S 47°15W **335** A6
Itu *Nigeria* 5°10N 7°58E **263** D6
Itu Aba I. *S. China Sea* 10°23N 114°21E **230** B4
Ituaçu *Brazil* 13°50S 41°18W **333** D3
Ituango *Colombia* 7°4N 75°45W **328** B2
Ituí → *Brazil* 4°38S 70°19W **328** D3
Ituiutaba *Brazil* 19°0S 49°25W **333** E2
Itumbiara *Brazil* 18°20S 49°10W **333** E2
Ituna *Canada* 51°10N 103°24W **297** C8
Itunge Port *Tanzania* 9°40S 33°55E **269** D3
Ituni *Guyana* 5°28N 58°15W **329** B6
Itupiranga *Brazil* 5°9S 49°20W **332** C2
Iturama *Brazil* 19°44S 50°11W **333** E1
Iturbe *Argentina* 23°0S 65°25W **334** A2
Ituri → *Dem. Rep. of the Congo* 1°40N 27°1E **268** B2
Iturup, Ostrov *Russia* 45°0N 148°0E **215** E15
Ituverava *Brazil* 20°20S 47°47W **333** F2
Ituxi → *Brazil* 7°18S 64°51W **331** B5
Itzehoe *Germany* 53°55N 9°31E **178** B5
Iuka *U.S.A.* 38°37N 88°47W **311** F8
Iungsdalshytta *Norway* 60°49N 7°55E **164** D4
Ivahona *Madag.* 23°27S 46°10E **272** C2
Ivaí → *Brazil* 23°18S 53°42W **335** A5
Ivalo *Finland* 68°38N 27°35E **160** B22
Ivalojoki → *Finland* 68°40N 27°40E **160** B22
Ivanava *Belarus* 52°7N 25°29E **177** B13
Ivančice *Czech Rep.* 49°6N 16°23E **181** B9
Ivane-Puste *Ukraine* 48°39N 26°10E **183** B11
Ivăneşti *Romania* 46°39N 27°27E **183** D12
Ivangorod = Dęblin *Poland* 51°34N 21°50E **185** G8
Ivangorod *Russia* 59°27N 28°13E **188** C5
Ivanhoe *N.S.W., Australia* 32°56S 144°20E **282** B6
Ivanhoe *Vic., Australia* 37°45S 145°3E **128** A2
Ivanhoe *Ont., Canada* 44°23N 77°28W **312** B7
Ivanhoe *Calif., U.S.A.* 36°23N 119°13W **306** J7
Ivanhoe *Minn., U.S.A.* 44°28N 96°15W **308** C5
Ivanhorod *Ukraine* 48°48N 29°50E **183** B14
Ivanić Grad *Croatia* 45°41N 16°25E **199** C13
Ivanjica *Serbia* 43°35N 20°12E **202** C4
Ivanjska *Bos.-H.* 44°55N 17°4E **182** F2
Ivankoyskoye Vdkhr. *Russia* 56°37N 36°32E **188** D9
Ivano-Frankivsk *Ukraine* 48°40N 24°40E **183** B9
Ivano-Frankivsk ☐ *Ukraine* 48°45N 24°30E **183** B9
Ivanof Bay *U.S.A.* 55°54N 159°29W **303** J8
Ivanovo = Ivanava *Belarus* 52°7N 25°29E **177** B13
Ivanovo *Russia* 57°5N 41°0E **188** D11
Ivanovo ☐ *Russia* 57°10N 41°50E **190** B5
Ivanšćica *Croatia* 46°12N 16°13E **199** B13
Ivashchenkovo = Chapayevsk *Russia* 53°0N 49°40E **190** D9
Ivato *Madag.* 20°37S 47°10E **272** C2
Ivatsevichy *Belarus* 52°43N 25°21E **177** B13
Ivaylovgrad *Bulgaria* 41°32N 26°8E **203** E10
Ivdel *Russia* 60°42N 60°24E **186** B11
Ivgres = Komsomolsk *Russia* 57°2N 40°20E **188** D11
Ivindo → *Gabon* 0°9S 12°9E **264** C2
Ivinheima → *Brazil* 23°14S 53°42W **335** A5
Ivinhema *Brazil* 22°10S 53°37W **335** A5
Ivittuut *Greenland* 61°14N 48°12W **154** E6
Iviza = Eivissa *Spain* 38°54N 1°26E **206** D1
Ivohibe *Madag.* 22°31S 46°57E **272** C2
Ivolândia *Brazil* 16°34S 50°51W **333** E1
Ivory Coast *W. Afr.* 4°20N 5°0W **262** E4
Ivory Coast ■ *Africa* 7°30N 5°0W **262** D4
Ivösjön *Sweden* 56°8N 14°25E **163** H8
Ivrea *Italy* 45°28N 7°52E **198** C4
İvrindi *Turkey* 39°34N 27°30E **205** B9
Ivry-sur-Seine *France* 48°49N 2°22E **134** B3
Ivujivik *Canada* 62°24N 77°55W **295** E16
Ivvavik △ *Canada* 69°6N 139°30W **294** D4
Ivybridge *U.K.* 50°23N 3°56W **169** G4
Iwai-Jima *Japan* 33°47N 131°58E **222** D3
Iwaizumi *Japan* 39°50N 141°45E **220** E10
Iwaki *Japan* 37°3N 140°55E **221** F10
Iwakuni *Japan* 34°15N 132°8E **222** C4
Iwami *Japan* 35°32N 134°15E **222** B6
Iwamizawa *Japan* 43°12N 141°46E **220** C10
Iwanai *Japan* 42°58N 140°30E **220** C10
Iwase *Japan* 36°21N 140°6E **223** A12
Iwata *Japan* 34°42N 137°51E **223** C9
Iwate ☐ *Japan* 39°30N 141°30E **220** E10
Iwate-San *Japan* 39°51N 141°0E **220** E10
Iwo *Nigeria* 7°39N 4°9E **263** D5
Iwo Jima *Pac. Oc.* 24°47N 141°20E **288** b
Iwŏn *N. Korea* 40°19N 128°39E **224** B4
Iwonicz-Zdrój *Poland* 49°37N 21°47E **185** J8
Iwungu *Dem. Rep. of the Congo* 5°16S 19°17E **265** D3
Ixelles *Belgium* 50°50N 4°22E **116** B2
Ixiamas *Bolivia* 13°50S 68°5W **330** C4
Ixopo *S. Africa* 30°11S 30°5E **271** D5
Ixtepec *Mexico* 16°34N 95°6W **319** D5
Ixtlán del Río *Mexico* 21°2N 104°22W **318** C4
'Iyādh *Yemen* 14°59N 46°51E **248** D4
Iyal Bakhit *Sudan* 13°20N 28°39E **257** E2
Iyo *Japan* 33°45N 132°45E **222** D4
Iyo-Mishima *Japan* 33°58N 133°30E **222** D5
Iyo-Nada *Japan* 33°40N 132°20E **222** D4
Izabal, L. de *Guatemala* 15°30N 89°10W **320** C2
Izamal *Mexico* 20°56N 89°1W **319** C7
Izberbash *Russia* 42°35N 47°52E **191** J8
Izbica *Poland* 50°53N 23°10E **185** H10
Izbica Kujawska *Poland* 52°25N 18°40E **185** F5
Izbiceni *Romania* 43°45N 24°40E **183** G9
Izembek Nat. Wildlife Refuge ⌓ *U.S.A.* 55°15N 162°45W **303** J7
Izena-Shima *Japan* 26°56N 127°56E **221** L3
Izgrev *Bulgaria* 43°36N 26°58E **203** C10
Izhevsk *Russia* 56°51N 53°14E **186** C9
Izhma = Sosnogorsk *Russia* 63°37N 53°51E **186** B9
Izhma → *Russia* 65°19N 52°54E **186** A9
Izileg *Algeria* 20°20N 6°4E **261** D6
Izkī *Oman* 22°56N 57°46E **249** B7
Izmayil *Ukraine* 45°22N 28°46E **183** E13
Izmaylovo *Russia* 55°47N 37°47E **129** B4
İzmir *Turkey* 38°25N 27°8E **205** C9
İzmir ☐ *Turkey* 38°15N 27°40E **205** C9
İzmir Adnan Menderes ✈ (ADB) *Turkey* 38°23N 27°6E **205** C9
İzmir Körfezi *Turkey* 38°30N 26°50E **205** C8
İzmit = Kocaeli *Turkey* 40°45N 29°50E **203** F13
Iznájar *Spain* 37°15N 4°19W **195** H6
Iznalloz *Spain* 37°24N 3°30W **195** H7
İznik *Turkey* 40°23N 29°46E **212** B3
İznik Gölü *Turkey* 40°27N 29°30E **203** F13
Izobilno-Tishchenskoye = Izobil'nyy *Russia* 45°25N 41°44E **191** H5
Izobil'nyy *Russia* 45°25N 41°44E **191** H5
Izola *Slovenia* 45°32N 13°39E **199** C10
Izozog, Bañados de *Bolivia* 18°48S 62°10W **331** D5
Izra *Syria* 32°51N 36°15E **250** F7
Iztacalco *Mexico* 19°23N 99°5W **128** B2
Iztapalapa *Mexico* 19°21N 99°6W **128** B2
Iztochni Rodopi *Bulgaria* 41°45N 25°30E **203** E9
Izu-Hantō *Japan* 34°45N 139°0E **223** C11
Izu-Shotō *Japan* 34°30N 140°0E **221** G10
Izúcar de Matamoros *Mexico* 18°36N 98°28W **319** D5
Izuhara *Japan* 34°12N 129°17E **222** C1
Izumi *Kagoshima, Japan* 32°5N 130°22E **222** E2
Izumi *Ōsaka, Japan* 34°28N 135°24E **223** C7
Izumi-Sano *Japan* 34°23N 135°18E **223** C7
Izumo *Japan* 35°20N 132°46E **222** B4
Izyaslav *Ukraine* 50°5N 26°50E **177** C14
Izyum *Ukraine* 49°12N 37°19E **189** H9

J

J.F.K. Int. ✈ (JFK) *U.S.A.* 40°38N 73°47W **313** F11
J.F. Rodrigues *Brazil* 2°55S 50°20W **332** B1
J.P. Koch Fjord *Greenland* 82°45N 44°0W **154** A6
J. Strom Thurmond L. *U.S.A.* 33°40N 82°12W **316** B7
Ja-ela *Sri Lanka* 7°5N 79°53E **245** L4
Ja-eundo *S. Korea* 34°53N 126°2E **224** E3
Jaba *Ethiopia* 6°20N 35°7E **257** F4
Jaba *West Bank* 31°51N 35°16E **123** A2
Jabal al Awliya' *Sudan* 15°14N 32°29E **266** A3
Jabal at Ṭā'ir *Red Sea* 15°35N 41°52E **257** D5
Jabalón → *Spain* 38°53N 4°5W **195** G6
Jabalpur *India* 23°9N 79°58E **243** H8
Jabbūl *Syria* 36°4N 37°30E **246** B3
Jabiru *Australia* 12°40S 132°53E **278** B5
Jablah *Syria* 35°20N 36°0E **250** C7
Jablanac *Croatia* 44°42N 14°56E **199** D11
Jablanica *Bos.-H.* 43°40N 17°45E **182** G2
Jablonec nad Nisou *Czech Rep.* 50°43N 15°10E **180** A8
Jablonica *Slovak Rep.* 48°37N 17°26E **181** C10
Jabłonowo Pomorskie *Poland* 53°23N 19°10E **184** E6
Jablunkov *Czech Rep.* 49°35N 18°46E **181** B11
Jaboatão *Brazil* 8°7S 35°1W **332** C4
Jabonga *Phil.* 9°20N 125°32E **233** G5
Jaboticabal *Brazil* 21°15S 48°17W **335** A6
Jabukovac *Serbia* 44°22N 22°21E **202** B6
Jaburu *Brazil* 5°30S 64°0W **331** B5
Jaca *Spain* 42°35N 0°33W **196** C4
Jacaré *Brazil* 22°53S 43°14W **135** B1
Jacaré → *Brazil* 10°3S 42°13W **332** D3
Jacareí *Brazil* 23°20S 46°0W **335** A6
Jacarèzinho *Brazil* 23°5S 49°58W **335** A6
Jaci-Paraná *Brazil* 9°15S 64°23W **331** B5
Jaciara *Brazil* 15°59S 54°57W **331** D7
Jacinto *Brazil* 16°10S 40°17W **333** E3
Jack River △ *Australia* 14°58S 144°19E **280** A3
Jackman *U.S.A.* 45°37N 70°15W **309** C18
Jacksboro *U.S.A.* 33°13N 98°10W **314** E5
Jackson *Barbados* 13°7N 59°36W **323** r
Jackson *Ala., U.S.A.* 31°31N 87°53W **315** F11
Jackson *Calif., U.S.A.* 38°21N 120°46W **306** G6
Jackson *Ga., U.S.A.* 33°20N 83°57W **316** B6
Jackson *Ky., U.S.A.* 37°33N 83°23W **309** G12
Jackson *Mich., U.S.A.* 42°15N 84°24W **311** B12
Jackson *Minn., U.S.A.* 43°37N 95°1W **308** D6
Jackson *Miss., U.S.A.* 32°18N 90°12W **315** E9
Jackson *Mo., U.S.A.* 37°23N 89°40W **308** G9
Jackson *N.H., U.S.A.* 44°10N 71°11W **313** B13
Jackson *Ohio, U.S.A.* 39°3N 82°39W **309** F12
Jackson *S.C., U.S.A.* 33°20N 81°47W **316** B8
Jackson *Tenn., U.S.A.* 35°37N 88°49W **315** D10
Jackson *Wyo., U.S.A.* 43°29N 110°46W **304** E8
Jackson, C. *N.Z.* 40°59S 174°20E **285** A9
Jackson B. *N.Z.* 43°58S 168°42E **285** D3
Jackson Center *U.S.A.* 40°27N 84°4W **311** D12
Jackson Hd. *N.Z.* 43°58S 168°37E **285** D3
Jackson Heights *U.S.A.* 40°44N 73°53W **132** B2
Jackson L. *Fla., U.S.A.* 30°30N 84°17W **316** E5
Jackson L. *Ga., U.S.A.* 33°19N 83°50W **316** B6
Jackson L. *Wyo., U.S.A.* 43°52N 110°36W **304** E8
Jackson Park *U.S.A.* 41°46N 87°34W **119** C3
Jacksons *N.Z.* 42°46S 171°32E **285** C6
Jackson's Arm *Canada* 49°52N 56°47W **299** C8
Jacksonville *Ala., U.S.A.* 33°49N 85°46W **316** B4
Jacksonville *Ark., U.S.A.* 34°52N 92°7W **314** D8
Jacksonville *Calif., U.S.A.* 37°52N 120°24W **306** H6
Jacksonville *Fla., U.S.A.* 30°20N 81°39W **316** E8
Jacksonville *Ga., U.S.A.* 31°49N 82°59W **316** D7
Jacksonville *Ill., U.S.A.* 39°44N 90°14W **310** E6
Jacksonville *N.C., U.S.A.* 34°45N 77°26W **315** D16
Jacksonville *Tex., U.S.A.* 31°58N 95°17W **314** F7
Jacksonville Beach *U.S.A.* 30°17N 81°24W **316** E8
Jacksonville Int. ✈ (JAX) *U.S.A.* 30°30N 81°41W **316** E8
Jacmel *Haiti* 18°14N 72°32W **321** C5
Jaco, Pte. *Dominica* 15°39N 61°24W **323** k
Jacob Lake *U.S.A.* 36°43N 112°13W **305** H7
Jacobabad *Pakistan* 28°20N 68°29E **242** E3
Jacobina *Brazil* 11°11S 40°30W **332** D3
Jacobshagen = Dobrzany *Poland* 53°22N 15°25E **184** E2
Jacon Javits Convention Center *New York, U.S.A.* **132** c1
Jacotet, B. *Mauritius* 20°30S 57°26E **272** e
Jacqueline Kennedy Onassis Res. *New York, U.S.A.* **132** a3
Jacques-Cartier *Canada* 45°31N 73°27W **130** A3
Jacques-Cartier, Dét. de *Canada* 50°0N 63°30W **299** C7
Jacques-Cartier, Mt. *Canada* 48°57N 66°0W **299** C6
Jacques-Cartier, Pont *Canada* 45°31N 73°32W **130** A2
Jacques-Cartier ⌓ *Canada* 47°15N 71°33W **299** C5
Jacqueville *Ivory C.* 5°12N 4°25W **262** D4
Jacuí → *Brazil* 30°2S 51°15W **335** C5
Jacumba *U.S.A.* 32°37N 116°11W **307** N10
Jacundá → *Brazil* 1°57S 50°26W **332** B1
Jadavpur *India* 22°28N 88°22E **124** C2
Jadcherla *India* 16°46N 78°9E **244** F4
Jade *Germany* 53°20N 8°14E **178** B4
Jade Buddha Temple *China* 31°15N 121°25E **138** B1
Jade City *Canada* 59°15N 129°37W **296** B3
Jade Island *Beijing, China* **114** b2
Jade Mt. = Yü Shan *Taiwan* 23°25N 120°52E **225** C2
Jadebusen *Germany* 53°29N 8°12E **178** B4
Jadotville = Likasi *Dem. Rep. of the Congo* 10°55S 26°48E **269** E2
Jadovnik *Serbia* 43°20N 19°45E **202** C3
Jadraque *Spain* 40°55N 2°55W **196** E2
Jādū *Libya* 32°0N 12°0E **258** B2
Jægersborg *Denmark* 55°45N 12°31E **118** A3
Jægersborg Dyrehave *Denmark* 55°46N 12°33E **118** A3
Jaén *Peru* 5°25S 78°40W **330** B2
Jaén *Spain* 37°44N 3°43W **195** H7
Jaén ☐ *Spain* 37°50N 3°30W **195** H7
Jæren *Norway* 58°42N 5°47E **164** F2
Jærens Rev *Norway* 58°45N 5°45E **164** F2
Jafarabad *India* 20°52N 71°22E **242** J4
Jaffa = Tel Aviv-Yafo *Israel* 32°4N 34°48E **251** F5
Jaffa, C. *Australia* 36°58S 139°40E **282** D3
Jaffna *Sri Lanka* 9°45N 80°2E **245** K5
Jaffrey *U.S.A.* 42°49N 72°2W **313** D12
Jagadhri *India* 30°10N 77°20E **242** D7
Jagadishpur *Bihar, India* 25°30N 84°21E **243** G11
Jagadishpur *W. Bengal, India* 22°39N 88°17E **124** B1
Jagatpur *India* 28°44N 77°13E **120** A2
Jagdalpur *India* 19°3N 82°0E **244** E6
Jagersfontein *S. Africa* 29°44S 25°27E **270** C4
Jaghīn → *Iran* 27°17N 57°13E **247** E8
Jagna *Phil.* 9°39N 124°22E **233** G5
Jagodina *Serbia* 44°5N 21°15E **202** B5
Jagraon *India* 30°50N 75°25E **242** D6
Jagst → *Germany* 49°14N 9°10E **179** F5
Jagtial *India* 18°50N 79°0E **244** E4
Jaguaquara *Brazil* 13°32S 39°58W **333** D4
Jaguaré, Rib. do → *Brazil* 23°32S 46°45W **137** B1
Jaguariaíva *Brazil* 24°10S 49°50W **335** A6
Jaguaribe *Brazil* 5°53S 38°37W **332** C4
Jaguaribe → *Brazil* 4°25S 37°45W **332** B4
Jaguaruana *Brazil* 4°50S 37°47W **332** B4
Jagüey Grande *Cuba* 22°35N 81°7W **320** B3
Jagungal, Mt. *Australia* 36°8S 148°22E **283** D8
Jahanabad *India* 25°13N 84°59E **243** G11
Jahangirpur *India* 28°43N 77°12E **120** A2
Jahazpur *India* 25°37N 75°17E **242** G6
Jahrom *Iran* 28°30N 53°31E **247** D7
Jaicós *Brazil* 7°21S 41°8W **332** C3
Jaigarh *India* 17°17N 73°13E **244** F1
Jaijon *India* 31°21N 76°9E **242** D7
Jailolo *Indonesia* 1°5N 127°30E **231** D7
Jailolo, Selat *Indonesia* 0°5N 129°5E **231** D7
Jaintiapur *Bangla.* 25°8N 92°7E **241** C4
Jaipur *Assam, India* 27°16N 95°24E **241** B5
Jaipur *Raj., India* 27°0N 75°50E **242** F6
Jais *India* 26°15N 81°32E **243** F9
Jaisalmer *India* 26°55N 70°54E **242** F4
Jaisinghnagar *India* 23°38N 78°34E **243** H8
Jaitaran *India* 26°12N 73°56E **242** F5
Jaithari *India* 23°14N 78°37E **243** H8
Jājarm *Iran* 36°58N 56°27E **247** B8
Jajce *Bos.-H.* 44°19N 17°17E **182** F2
Jajpur *India* 20°53N 86°22E **244** D8
Jakam → *India* 23°54N 74°13E **242** H6
Jakar Dzong *Bhutan* 27°33N 90°43E **241** B3
Jakarta *Indonesia* 6°9S 106°52E **122** A2
Jakarta, Teluk *Indonesia* 6°5S 106°50E **122** A1
Jakarta Halim Perdana Kusuma Int. ✈ (HLP) *Indonesia* 6°16S 106°53E **122** B2
Jakhal *India* 29°48N 75°50E **242** E6
Jakharrah *Libya* 29°13N 21°34E **258** C4
Jakhau *India* 23°13N 68°43E **242** H3
Jakobshavn = Illulissat *Greenland* 69°12N 51°10W **154** D5
Jakobstad = Pietarsaari *Finland* 63°40N 22°43E **160** E20
Jakupica *Macedonia* 41°45N 21°22E **202** E5
Jal *U.S.A.* 32°7N 103°12W **305** K12
Jalaihai Pt. *Guam* 13°18N 144°46E **302** d
Jalājil *Si. Arabia* 25°40N 45°27E **246** E5
Jalal-Abad *Kyrgyzstan* 40°56N 73°0E **217** D8
Jalal-Abad ☐ *Kyrgyzstan* 41°30N 72°30E **217** D8
Jalālābād *Afghan.* 34°30N 70°29E **242** B4
Jalalabad *India* 27°41N 79°42E **243** F8
Jalalpur Jattan *Pakistan* 32°38N 74°11E **242** C6
Jalama *U.S.A.* 34°29N 120°29W **307** L6
Jalan Kayu *Singapore* 1°24N 103°52E **138** A3
Jalandhar = Jullundur *India* 31°20N 75°40E **242** D6
Jalapa *Guatemala* 14°39N 89°59W **320** D2
Jalapa Enríquez = Xalapa *Mexico* 19°32N 96°55W **319** D5
Jalasjärvi *Finland* 62°29N 22°47E **160** E20
Jalaun *India* 26°8N 79°25E **243** F8
Jalāzin *Afghan.* 37°2N 64°49E **240** A2
Jaldak *Afghan.* 31°58N 66°43E **240** C2
Jaldhaka → *Bangla.* 26°16N 89°16E **241** B2
Jales *Brazil* 20°10S 50°33W **333** F1
Jalesar *India* 27°29N 78°19E **242** F8
Jaleswar *Nepal* 26°38N 85°48E **243** F11
Jalgaon *India* 21°0N 75°42E **244** D2
Jalībah *Iraq* 30°35N 46°32E **246** D5
Jalingo *Nigeria* 8°55N 11°25E **263** D7
Jalisco ☐ *Mexico* 20°20N 103°40W **318** D4
Jalkot *Pakistan* 35°14N 73°24E **243** B5
Jalna *India* 19°48N 75°38E **244** E2
Jalón → *Spain* 41°47N 1°4W **196** D3
Jalor *India* 25°21N 72°37E **242** G5
Jalpa *Mexico* 21°38N 102°58W **318** C4
Jalpaiguri *India* 26°32N 88°46E **241** B2
Jalpan *Mexico* 21°14N 99°29W **319** C5
Jālq *Iran* 27°35N 62°46E **240** D1
Jālū *Libya* 29°2N 21°33E **258** C4
Jaluit I. *Marshall Is.* 6°0N 169°30E **288** G8
Jalūlā *Iraq* 34°16N 45°10E **213** E11
Jamaame *Somali Rep.* 0°4N 42°44E **267** D5
Jamaari *Nigeria* 11°44N 9°53E **263** C6
Jamaica ■ *W. Indies* 18°10N 77°30W **320** a
Jamaica B. *U.S.A.* 40°36N 73°50W **132** C3
Jamaica Channel *Jamaica* 17°0N 76°0W **321** C4
Jamaica Plain *U.S.A.* 42°18N 71°6W **116** B2
Jamakpuri *India* 28°37N 77°5E **120** B1
Jamalpur *Bangla.* 24°52N 89°56E **241** C2
Jamalpur *India* 25°18N 86°28E **243** G12
Jamalpurganj *India* 23°2N 87°59E **243** H13
Jamanota *Aruba* 12°29N 69°57W **322** f
Jamanxim → *Brazil* 4°43S 56°18W **331** A6
Jamari *Brazil* 8°45S 63°27W **331** B5
Jamari → *Brazil* 8°27S 63°30W **331** B5
Jamba *Angola* 14°40S 16°2E **265** E3
Jambewangi *Indonesia* 8°17S 114°7E **231** J17
Jambi *Indonesia* 1°38S 103°30E **234** C2
Jambi ☐ *Indonesia* 1°30S 102°30E **234** C2
Jambongan, Pulau *Malaysia* 6°45N 117°20E **235** A5
Jambusar *India* 22°3N 72°51E **242** H5
James *U.S.A.* 32°58N 83°29W **316** C6
James → *S. Dak., U.S.A.* 42°52N 97°18W **308** D5
James → *Va., U.S.A.* 36°56N 76°27W **309** G15
James, I. = San Salvador, I. *Ecuador* 0°16S 90°42W **330** a
James B. *Canada* 54°0N 80°0W **298** B3
James I. *Gambia* 13°19N 16°21W **262** C1
James Island *U.S.A.* 32°45N 79°55W **316** C10
James Ranges *Australia* 24°10S 132°30E **278** D5
James Ross I. *Antarctica* 63°58S 57°50W **151** C18
Jamesabad *Pakistan* 25°17N 69°15E **242** G3
Jameson Land *Greenland* 71°0N 23°30W **154** C8
Jamesport *U.S.A.* 39°58N 93°48W **310** E3
Jamestown = Wawa *Canada* 47°59N 84°47W **298** C3
Jamestown *S. Austral., Australia* 33°10S 138°32E **282** B3
Jamestown *St. Helena* 15°55S 5°43W **153** h
Jamestown *Eastern Cape, S. Africa* 31°6S 26°45E **270** D4
Jamestown *Ind., U.S.A.* 39°56N 86°38W **311** E10
Jamestown *Mo., U.S.A.* 38°48N 92°30W **310** F4
Jamestown *N. Dak., U.S.A.* 46°54N 98°42W **308** B4
Jamestown *N.Y., U.S.A.* 42°6N 79°14W **312** D5
Jamestown *Ohio, U.S.A.* 39°39N 83°33W **311** E13
Jamestown *Pa., U.S.A.* 41°29N 80°27W **312** E4
Jamestown *S.C., U.S.A.* 33°17N 79°42W **316** B10
Jamīlābād *Iran* 34°24N 48°28E **247** C6
Jamira → *India* 21°35N 88°28E **243** J13
Jämjö *Sweden* 56°12N 15°49E **163** H9
Jamkhandi *India* 16°30N 75°15E **244** F2
Jamkhed *India* 18°43N 75°19E **244** E2
Jammalamadugu *India* 14°51N 78°25E **245** G4
Jammerbugten *Denmark* 57°15N 9°20E **163** G3
Jammu *India* 32°43N 74°54E **242** C6
Jammu & Kashmir ☐ *India* 34°25N 77°0E **243** B7
Jamnagar *India* 22°30N 70°6E **242** H4
Jamner *India* 20°45N 75°52E **244** D2
Jamni → *India* 25°13N 78°35E **243** G8
Jampur *Pakistan* 29°39N 70°40E **242** E4
Jamrud *Pakistan* 33°59N 71°24E **242** C4
Jämsä *Finland* 61°53N 25°10E **188** B3
Jamshedpur *India* 22°44N 86°12E **243** H12
Jamshīdīyeh *Iran* 35°42N 51°22E **141** A2
Jamsil *S. Korea* 37°30N 127°4E **137** B2
Jamtara *India* 23°59N 86°49E **243** H12
Jämtland *Sweden* 63°31N 14°0E **160** E16
Jämtlands län ☐ *Sweden* 63°0N 14°40E **162** B7
Jamuna → *Bangla.* 23°51N 89°45E **241** D2
Jamunamukh *India* 26°6N 92°44E **241** B4
Jamurki *Bangla.* 24°9N 90°2E **241** C3
Jamwon *S. Korea* 37°30N 127°0E **137** B2
Jan L. *Canada* 54°56N 102°55W **297** C8
Jan Mayen *Arctic* 71°0N 9°0W **150** B7
Janakkala *Finland* 60°54N 24°36E **188** B3
Janakpur *India* 26°42N 85°55E **244** A7
Janaúba *Brazil* 15°48S 43°19W **333** E3
Janaucu, I. *Brazil* 0°30N 50°10W **332** A1
Jand *Pakistan* 33°30N 72°6E **242** C5
Jandaia *Brazil* 17°6S 50°7W **333** E1
Jandanku ⚙ *Australia* 16°20S 135°45E **280** B2
Jandaq *Iran* 34°3N 54°22E **247** C7
Jandía *Canary Is.* 28°6N 14°21W **153** e2
Jandía, Pta. de *Canary Is.* 28°3N 14°31W **153** e2
Jandía △ *Canary Is.* 28°4N 14°19W **153** e2
Jandiatuba → *Brazil* 3°28S 68°42W **328** D4
Jandola *Pakistan* 32°20N 70°9E **242** C4
Jandowae *Australia* 26°45S 151°7E **281** D5
Jándula → *Spain* 38°3N 4°6W **195** G6
Jane Pk. *N.Z.* 45°15S 168°20E **285** F3
Janesville *U.S.A.* 42°41N 89°1W **310** B7
Janga *Ghana* 10°5N 1°0W **263** C4
Jangamo *Mozam.* 24°6S 35°21E **271** B6
Janghai *India* 25°33N 82°19E **243** G10
Jangheung *S. Korea* 34°41N 126°52E **224** E3
Janghowon *S. Korea* 37°7N 127°37E **224** D3
Jangoon *India* 17°44N 79°5E **244** F4
Jangsu *S. Korea* 35°38N 127°31E **224** E3
Janhtang Ga *Burma* 26°32N 96°38E **241** B6
Jani Khel *Afghan.* 32°46N 68°24E **240** B3
Janikowo *Poland* 52°45N 18°7E **185** F5
Janinà = Ioannina ☐ *Greece* 39°39N 20°57E **204** B2
Janiuay *Phil.* 10°58N 122°30E **233** F4
Janja *Bos.-H.* 44°40N 19°14E **182** F4
Janjanbureh *Gambia* 13°30N 14°47W **262** C2
Janjevo *Kosovo* 42°35N 21°19E **202** D5
Janjgir *India* 22°1N 82°34E **243** J10
Janjina *Croatia* 42°58N 17°25E **199** F14
Janjina *Madag.* 20°30S 45°50E **272** C2
Jankau = Janikowo *Poland* 52°45N 18°7E **185** F5
Janki *Poland* 52°8N 20°52E **142** C1
Jannaale *Somali Rep.* 1°48N 44°42E **267** D5
Janos *Mexico* 30°54N 108°10W **318** A3
Jánoshalma *Hungary* 46°18N 19°21E **182** D4
Jánosháza *Hungary* 47°8N 17°12E **182** C2
Jánossomorja *Hungary* 47°47N 17°11E **182** C2
Janów *Poland* 50°44N 19°27E **185** H6
Janów Lubelski *Poland* 50°48N 22°23E **185** H9
Janów Podlaski *Poland* 52°11N 23°11E **185** F10
Janowiec Wielkopolski *Poland* 52°45N 17°30E **185** F4
Januária *Brazil* 15°25S 44°25W **333** E3
Janub △ *Sudan* 6°50N 28°45E **257** F2
Janub Dârfûr ☐ *Sudan* 11°0N 25°0E **257** E2

Janub Kordofân □ *Sudan* 12°0N 30°0E **257** E3
Janûb Sînî □ *Egypt* 29°30N 33°50E **251** J4
Janubio *Canary Is.* 28°56N 13°50W **153** e2
Janville *France* 48°10N 1°50E **173** D8
Janwada *India* 18°0N 77°29E **244** E3
Janzé *France* 47°55N 1°28W **172** E5
Jaora *India* 23°40N 75°10E **242** H6
Japan ■ *Asia* 36°0N 136°0E **221** G8
Japan, Sea of *Asia* 40°0N 135°0E **220** E7
Japan Center *San Francisco, U.S.A.* **136** c1
Japan Trench *Pac. Oc.* 32°0N 142°0E **288** D6
Japen = Yapen *Indonesia* 1°50S 136°0E **231** E9
Japiim *Brazil* 7°37S 72°54W **330** B3
Japla *India* 24°33N 84°1E **243** G11
Japurá *Brazil* 1°48S 66°34W **328** D4
Japurá → *Brazil* 3°8S 65°46W **328** D4
Jaquarão *Brazil* 32°34S 53°23W **335** C5
Jaqué *Panama* 7°27N 78°8W **320** E4
Jarābulus *Syria* 36°49N 38°1E **213** D8
Jaraguá *Goiás, Brazil* 15°45S 49°20W **333** E2
Jaraguá *São Paulo, Brazil* 23°27S 46°44W **137** A1
Jaraguá, Pico de *Brazil* 23°27S 46°46W **137** A1
Jaraguari *Brazil* 20°9S 54°35W **331** E7
Jaraicejo *Spain* 39°40N 5°49W **195** F5
Jaraíz de la Vera *Spain* 40°4N 5°45W **194** E5
Jarama → *Spain* 40°24N 3°32W **194** E7
Jaramānah *Syria* 33°29N 36°21E **250** E7
Jaramillo *Argentina* 47°10S 67°7W **336** C3
Jarandilla de la Vera *Spain* 40°8N 5°39W **194** E5
Jaranwala *Pakistan* 31°15N 73°26E **242** D5
Jarash *Jordan* 32°17N 35°54E **251** F6
Jarash □ *Jordan* 32°17N 35°54E **251** F6
Jarauçu → *Brazil* 1°48S 52°22W **329** D7
Järbo *Sweden* 60°43N 16°36E **162** D10
Jarboesville = Lexington Park *U.S.A.* 38°16N 76°27W **309** F15
Jardas al 'Abīd *Libya* 32°18N 20°59E **258** B4
Jardim *Brazil* 21°28S 56°2W **334** A4
Jardim Paulista *Brazil* 23°34S 46°41W **137** B1
Jardín → *Spain* 38°50N 2°10W **197** G2
Jardín América *Argentina* 27°3S 55°14W **335** B4
Jardin Botanique *Brussels, Belgium* **116** a3
Jardine River △ *Australia* 11°9S 142°21E **280** A3
Jardines de la Reina, Arch. de los *Cuba* 20°50N 78°50W **320** B4
Jargalang *China* 43°5N 122°55E **227** C12
Jargalant = Hovd □ *Mongolia* 48°2N 91°37E **217** C12
Jari → *Brazil* 1°9S 51°54W **329** D7
Jaria Janjail *Bangla.* 25°0N 90°40E **241** C3
Jarīr, W. al → *Si. Arabia* 25°38N 42°30E **246** E4
Järlåsa *Sweden* 59°53N 17°12E **162** E11
Jarlsberg og Larvik = Vestfold □ *Norway* 59°15N 10°0E **164** E7
Jarmen *Germany* 53°54N 13°20E **178** B9
Järna *Dalarna, Sweden* 60°33N 14°26E **162** D8
Järna *Stockholm, Sweden* 59°6N 17°34E **162** E11
Jarnac *France* 45°40N 0°11W **174** C3
Jarny *France* 49°9N 5°53E **173** C12
Jaro *Phil.* 11°11N 124°47E **233** F5
Jarocin *Poland* 51°59N 17°29E **185** G4
Jaroměř *Czech Rep.* 50°22N 15°52E **180** A8
Jarosław *Poland* 50°2N 22°42E **185** H9
Järpås *Sweden* 58°23N 12°57E **163** F6
Järpen *Sweden* 63°21N 13°26E **162** A7
Jarrahdale *Australia* 32°24S 116°5E **279** F2
Jarrahi → *Iran* 30°49N 48°48E **247** D6
Jarres, Plaine des *Laos* 19°27N 103°10E **236** C4
Jarso *Ethiopia* 5°15N 37°30E **257** F4
Jartai *China* 39°45N 105°48E **226** E3
Jaru *Brazil* 10°26S 62°27W **331** C5
Jaru → *Brazil* 10°5S 61°59W **331** C5
Jarud Qi *China* 44°28N 120°50E **227** B11
Järvatältet *Sweden* 59°25N 17°54E **139** A1
Järvenpää *Finland* 60°29N 25°5E **188** B3
Jarvis *Canada* 42°53N 80°6W **312** D4
Jarvis I. *Pac. Oc.* 0°15S 160°5W **289** H12
Jarvorník *Czech Rep.* 50°23N 17°2E **181** A10
Järvsö *Sweden* 61°43N 16°10E **162** C10
Jarwa *India* 27°38N 82°30E **243** F10
Jaša Tomić *Serbia* 45°26N 20°50E **182** E5
Jasaan *Phil.* 8°39N 124°45E **233** G5
Jasdan *India* 22°2N 71°12E **242** H4
Jashpurnagar *India* 22°54N 84°9E **243** H11
Jasidih *India* 24°31N 86°39E **243** G12
Jasień *Poland* 51°46N 15°0E **185** G2
Jāsimīyah *Iraq* 33°45N 44°41E **213** F11
Jasin *Malaysia* 2°20N 102°26E **237** L4
Jāsk *Iran* 25°38N 57°45E **247** E8
Jaskhar *India* 18°54N 72°58E **130** B2
Jasło *Poland* 49°45N 21°30E **185** J8
Jasmund *Germany* 54°32N 13°35E **178** A9
Jasmund △ *Germany* 54°31N 13°38E **178** A9
Jaso *India* 24°30N 80°29E **243** G9
Jason Is. *Falk. Is.* 51°0S 61°0W **153** f
Jasonville *U.S.A.* 39°10N 87°12W **311** E9
Jasper *Alta., Canada* 52°55N 118°5W **296** C5
Jasper *Ont., Canada* 44°52N 75°57W **313** B9
Jasper *Ala., U.S.A.* 33°50N 87°17W **315** E11
Jasper *Fla., U.S.A.* 30°31N 82°57W **316** E7
Jasper *Ind., U.S.A.* 38°24N 86°56W **311** F10
Jasper *Tex., U.S.A.* 30°56N 94°1W **314** F7
Jasper △ *Canada* 52°50N 118°8W **296** C5
Jasrasar *India* 27°43N 73°49E **242** F5
Jassān *Iraq* 32°58N 45°52E **213** G11
Jassey = Iaşi *Romania* 47°10N 27°40E **183** C12
Jastarnia *Poland* 54°42N 18°40E **184** D5
Jastrebarsko *Croatia* 45°41N 15°39E **199** C12
Jastrow = Jastrowie *Poland* 53°26N 16°49E **184** E3
Jastrowie *Poland* 53°26N 16°49E **184** E3
Jastrzębie Zdrój *Poland* 49°57N 18°35E **185** J5
Jász-Nagykun-Szolnok □ *Hungary* 47°15N 20°30E **182** C5
Jászapáti *Hungary* 47°32N 20°10E **182** C5
Jászárokszállás *Hungary* 47°39N 19°58E **182** C4
Jászberény *Hungary* 47°30N 19°55E **182** C4
Jászkisér *Hungary* 47°27N 20°20E **182** C5
Jászladány *Hungary* 47°23N 20°10E **182** C5
Jataí *Brazil* 17°58S 51°48W **333** E1
Jatapu → *Brazil* 2°13S 58°17W **329** D6
Jath *India* 17°3N 75°13E **244** F2
Jati *Pakistan* 24°20N 68°19E **242** G3
Jatibarang *Indonesia* 6°28S 108°18E **235** D3
Jatiluwih *Indonesia* 8°23S 115°8E **231** J18
Jatinegara *Indonesia* 6°13S 106°52E **122** B2
Játiva = Xátiva *Spain* 38°59N 0°32W **197** G4
Jatobá = Petrolândia *Brazil* 9°5S 38°20W **332** C4
Jättendal *Sweden* 61°58N 17°15E **162** C11
Jaú *Angola* 15°12S 13°31E **265** F2
Jaú *Brazil* 22°10S 48°30W **335** A6
Jaú → *Brazil* 1°54S 61°26W **329** D5
Jauaperi → *Brazil* 1°26S 61°35W **329** D5
Jauer = Jawor *Poland* 51°4N 16°11E **185** G3
Jauja *Peru* 11°45S 75°15W **330** C2
Jaunpur *India* 25°46N 82°44E **243** G10
Jauru → *Brazil* 16°22S 57°46W **331** D6
Java = Jawa *Indonesia* 7°0S 110°0E **235** D4
Java Sea *Indonesia* 4°35S 107°15E **235** C3
Java Trench *Ind. Oc.* 9°0S 105°0E **234** D2
Javadi Hills *India* 12°40N 78°40E **245** H4
Javādīyeh *Iran* 35°39N 51°22E **141** B2
Javalambre, Sa. de *Spain* 40°6N 1°0W **196** E4
Javānrud *Iran* 34°47N 46°31E **213** E12
Jávea *Spain* 38°48N 0°10E **197** G5
Javhlant = Uliastay *Mongolia* 47°56N 97°28E **218** B4
Javier, I. *Chile* 47°5S 74°25W **336** C2
Javla *India* 17°18N 75°9E **244** F2
Jawa *Indonesia* 7°0S 110°0E **235** D4
Jawa Barat □ *Indonesia* 7°0S 107°0E **231** G12
Jawa Tengah □ *Indonesia* 7°0S 110°0E **231** G14
Jawa Timur □ *Indonesia* 8°0S 113°0E **231** G15
Jawad *India* 24°36N 74°51E **242** G6
Jawf, W. al → *Yemen* 15°50N 45°30E **248** D4
Jawhar *India* 19°55N 73°14E **244** E1
Jawhar *Somali Rep.* 2°48N 45°30E **267** D6
Jawor *Poland* 51°4N 16°11E **185** G3
Jaworowa *Poland* 52°9N 20°56E **142** C1
Jaworzno *Poland* 50°13N 19°11E **185** H6
Jaworzyna Śląska *Poland* 50°55N 16°28E **185** H3
Jawoyn ☼ *Australia* 14°16S 132°28E **278** B5
Jay *U.S.A.* 30°57N 87°9W **317** E2
Jay Peak *U.S.A.* 44°55N 72°32W **313** B12
Jaya, Puncak *Indonesia* 3°57S 137°17E **231** E9
Jayanca *Peru* 6°24S 79°50W **330** B2
Jayanti *India* 26°45N 89°40E **241** B2
Jayapura *Indonesia* 2°28S 140°38E **231** E10
Jayawijaya, Pegunungan *Indonesia* 5°0S 139°0E **231** F9
Jaynagar *India* 26°43N 86°9E **243** F12
Jaypur = Jeypore *India* 18°50N 82°38E **244** E6
Jayrūd *Syria* 33°49N 36°44E **250** E7
Jayton *U.S.A.* 33°15N 100°34W **314** E4
Jāz Mūrīān, Hāmūn-e *Iran* 27°20N 58°55E **247** E8
Jazīreh-ye Shīf *Iran* 29°4N 50°54E **247** D6
Jazminal *Mexico* 24°52N 101°24W **318** C4
Jazz Museum *New Orleans, U.S.A.* **131** a3
Jazzīn *Lebanon* 33°31N 35°35E **250** E6
Jean *U.S.A.* 35°47N 115°20W **307** K11
Jean Lafitte Nat. Historical Park ⌂ *U.S.A.* 29°51N 90°9W **131** B1
Jean Marie River *Canada* 61°32N 120°38W **296** A4
Jean-Rabel *Haiti* 19°50N 73°5W **321** C5
Jeanerette *U.S.A.* 29°55N 91°40W **314** G9
Jeanette, Ostrov = Zhannetty, Ostrov *Russia* 76°43N 158°0E **215** B16
Jeanne-Mance, Parc *Montréal, Canada* **130** b1
Jeanneton, Morne *Guadeloupe* 16°14N 61°43W **322** e
Jeannette *U.S.A.* 40°20N 79°36W **312** F5
Jebāl Bārez, Kūh-e *Iran* 28°30N 58°20E **247** D8
Jebba *Nigeria* 9°9N 4°48E **263** D5
Jebel, Bahr el → *Sudan* 9°30N 30°25E **257** F3
Jebel Ali = Minā' Jabal 'Alī *U.A.E.* 25°2N 55°8E **247** E7
Jebel Dud *Sudan* 13°25N 33°9E **257** E3
Jebel Qerri *Sudan* 16°16N 32°50E **257** D3
Jeberos *Peru* 5°15S 76°10W **330** B2
Jecheon *S. Korea* 37°8N 128°12E **224** D4
Jedburgh *U.K.* 55°29N 2°33W **167** F6
Jedda = Jiddah *Si. Arabia* 21°29N 39°10E **248** B2
Jeddore L. *Canada* 48°3N 55°55W **299** C8
Jedlesee *Austria* 48°15N 16°23E **142** A2
Jedlicze *Poland* 49°43N 21°40E **185** J8
Jędrzejów *Poland* 50°35N 20°15E **185** H7
Jedwabne *Poland* 53°17N 22°18E **185** E9
Jeetzel → *Germany* 53°9N 11°3E **178** B7
Jefferson *Ga., U.S.A.* 34°7N 83°35W **316** A6
Jefferson *Iowa, U.S.A.* 42°1N 94°23W **310** B2
Jefferson *La., U.S.A.* 29°57N 90°9W **131** B2
Jefferson *Ohio, U.S.A.* 41°44N 80°46W **312** E4
Jefferson *Tex., U.S.A.* 32°46N 94°21W **314** E7
Jefferson *Wis., U.S.A.* 43°0N 88°48W **311** B8
Jefferson, Mt. *Nev., U.S.A.* 38°47N 116°56W **304** G5
Jefferson, Mt. *Oreg., U.S.A.* 44°41N 121°48W **304** D3
Jefferson City *Mo., U.S.A.* 38°34N 92°10W **310** F4
Jefferson City *Tenn., U.S.A.* 36°7N 83°30W **315** C13
Jefferson Memorial *Washington, D.C., U.S.A.* **143** c1
Jefferson Park *Calif., U.S.A.* 34°2N 118°19W **126** B3
Jefferson Park *Ill., U.S.A.* 41°58N 87°46W **119** B2
Jeffersontown *U.S.A.* 38°12N 85°35W **311** F11
Jeffersonville *Ga., U.S.A.* 32°41N 83°20W **316** C6
Jeffersonville *Ind., U.S.A.* 38°17N 85°44W **311** F11
Jeffersonville *Ohio, U.S.A.* 39°39N 83°34W **311** E13
Jeffrey City *U.S.A.* 42°30N 107°49W **304** E10
Jega *Nigeria* 12°15N 4°23E **263** C5
Jegi *S. Korea* 37°34N 127°1E **137** B2
Jejevo *Solomon Is.* 8°6S 159°8E **287** M10
Jeju *S. Korea* 33°31N 126°32E **224** a
Jeju-do *S. Korea* 33°29N 126°34E **224** a
Jeju-do □ *S. Korea* 33°25N 126°30E **224** a
Jēkabpils *Latvia* 56°29N 25°57E **188** D3
Jekyll I. *U.S.A.* 31°4N 81°25W **316** D8
Jelambar *Indonesia* 6°9S 106°47E **122** A1
Jelcz-Laskowice *Poland* 51°2N 17°19E **185** G4
Jelenia Góra *Poland* 50°50N 15°45E **185** H2
Jelgava *Latvia* 56°41N 23°49E **184** B10
Jelgava □ *Latvia* 56°35N 23°45E **184** B10
Jelica *Serbia* 43°50N 20°17E **202** C4
Jelli *Sudan* 5°25N 31°45E **257** F3
Jelonki *Poland* 52°14N 20°54E **142** B1
Jelšava *Slovak Rep.* 48°37N 20°15E **181** C13
Jema'a Mallam = Kafanchan *Nigeria* 9°40N 8°20E **263** D6
Jemaja *Indonesia* 3°5N 105°45E **237** L5
Jemaluang *Malaysia* 2°16N 103°52E **237** L4
Jember *Indonesia* 8°11S 113°41E **235** D4
Jena *Thüringen, Germany* 50°54N 11°35E **178** E7
Jena *La., U.S.A.* 31°41N 92°8W **314** F8
Jenai *Taiwan* 24°2N 121°8E **225** B3
Jenbach *Austria* 47°24N 11°47E **180** D4
Jendouba *Tunisia* 36°29N 8°47E **258** A1
Jendouba □ *Tunisia* 36°34N 8°52E **261** A6
Jenho *Taiwan* 23°54N 121°36E **225** C3
Jenīn *West Bank* 32°28N 35°18E **251** F6
Jenison *U.S.A.* 42°54N 85°47W **311** B11
Jenkins *U.S.A.* 37°10N 82°38W **309** G12
Jenner *U.S.A.* 38°27N 123°7W **306** G3
Jennings *Fla., U.S.A.* 30°36N 83°6W **316** E6
Jennings *La., U.S.A.* 30°13N 92°40W **314** F8
Jennings *Mo., U.S.A.* 38°43N 90°15W **310** F6
Jenny Pt. *Dominica* 15°28N 61°15W **323** k
Jensen Beach *U.S.A.* 27°15N 80°14W **317** H9
Jente *Taiwan* 22°58N 120°16E **225** D2
Jenwu *Taiwan* 22°42N 120°20E **225** D2
Jeollabuk-do □ *S. Korea* 35°45N 127°15E **224** E3
Jeollanam-do □ *S. Korea* 34°45N 127°0E **224** E3
Jeong-eup *S. Korea* 35°35N 126°50E **224** E3
Jeonju *S. Korea* 35°50N 127°4E **224** E3
Jepara *Indonesia* 7°40S 109°14E **235** D3
Jeparit *Australia* 36°8S 142°1E **282** D5
Jequié *Brazil* 13°51S 40°5W **333** D3
Jequitaí → *Brazil* 17°4S 44°50W **333** E3
Jequitinhonha *Brazil* 16°30S 41°0W **333** E3
Jequitinhonha → *Brazil* 15°51S 38°53W **333** E4
Jerada *Morocco* 34°17N 2°10W **261** B4
Jerantut *Malaysia* 3°56N 102°22E **237** L4
Jerejak, Pulau *Malaysia* 5°19N 100°19E **237** c
Jérémie *Haiti* 18°40N 74°10W **321** C5
Jeremoabo *Brazil* 10°4S 38°21W **332** D4
Jerez, Pta. *Mexico* 22°58N 97°40W **319** C5
Jerez de García Salinas *Mexico* 22°39N 103°0W **318** C4
Jerez de la Frontera *Spain* 36°41N 6°7W **195** J4
Jerez de los Caballeros *Spain* 38°20N 6°45W **195** G4
Jericho = El Arīḥā *West Bank* 31°52N 35°27E **251** G6
Jericho *Australia* 23°38S 146°6E **280** C4
Jerichow *Germany* 52°30N 12°1E **178** C8
Jerico Springs *U.S.A.* 37°37N 94°1W **310** G2
Jerid, Chott el = Djerid, Chott *Tunisia* 33°42N 8°30E **258** B1
Jerilderie *Australia* 35°20S 145°41E **283** C6
Jermyn *U.S.A.* 41°32N 75°33W **313** E9
Jerningham Junction *Trin. & Tob.* 10°33N 61°23W **323** t
Jerome *U.S.A.* 42°44N 114°31W **304** E6
Jerónimos, Mosteiro dos *Portugal* 38°41N 9°11W **126** A1
Jerramungup *Australia* 33°55S 118°55E **279** F2
Jersey *U.K.* 49°11N 2°7W **169** H5
Jersey City *U.S.A.* 40°42N 74°4W **132** B1
Jersey Shore *U.S.A.* 41°12N 77°15W **312** E7
Jerseyville *U.S.A.* 39°7N 90°20W **310** E6
Jerumenha *Brazil* 7°5S 43°30W **332** C3
Jerusalem *Israel/West Bank* 31°47N 35°10E **123** B2
Jervis B. *Australia* 35°8S 150°46E **283** C9
Jervis Bay △ *Australia* 35°9S 150°40E **283** C9
Jervis Inlet *Canada* 50°0N 123°57W **296** C4
Jerzu *Italy* 39°47N 9°31E **200** C2
Jesenice *Slovenia* 46°28N 14°3E **199** B11
Jeseník *Czech Rep.* 50°14N 17°8E **181** A10
Jesenké *Slovak Rep.* 48°20N 20°10E **181** C13
Jesi = Iesi *Italy* 43°31N 13°14E **199** E10
Jessamine, L. *U.S.A.* 28°28N 81°23W **133** B2
Jessel = Jasło *Poland* 49°45N 21°30E **185** J8
Jesselton = Kota Kinabalu *Malaysia* 6°0N 116°4E **235** A5
Jessheim *Norway* 60°9N 11°10E **164** D8
Jessnitz *Germany* 51°40N 12°18E **178** D8
Jessore *Bangla.* 23°10N 89°10E **241** D2
Jesup *Ga., U.S.A.* 31°36N 81°53W **316** D8
Jesup *Iowa, U.S.A.* 42°29N 92°4W **310** B4
Jesup, L. *U.S.A.* 28°43N 81°14W **317** G8
Jesús *Peru* 7°15S 78°25W **330** B2
Jésus, Î. *Canada* 45°36N 73°44W **130** A1
Jesús Carranza *Mexico* 17°26N 95°2W **319** D5
Jesús María *Argentina* 30°59S 64°5W **334** C3
Jesús Maria *Lima, Peru* 12°4S 77°3W **124** B2
Jetmore *U.S.A.* 38°4N 99°54W **308** F4
Jetpur *India* 21°45N 70°10E **242** J4
Jette *Belgium* 50°53N 4°20E **116** A1
Jeumont *France* 50°18N 4°6E **173** B11
Jeungdo *S. Korea* 34°56N 126°9E **224** E3
Jeungpyeong *S. Korea* 36°47N 127°34E **224** D3
Jevnaker *Norway* 60°15N 10°26E **164** D7
Jewell *U.S.A.* 42°20N 93°39W **310** B3
Jewett *U.S.A.* 40°22N 81°2W **312** F3
Jewett City *U.S.A.* 41°36N 71°59W **313** E13
Jewish Quarter *Jerusalem* **123** b3
Jey *Iran* 35°41N 51°20E **141** B2
Jeyḥūnābād *Iran* 34°58N 48°59E **247** C6
Jeypore *India* 18°50N 82°38E **244** E6
Jeziorak, Jezioro *Poland* 53°40N 19°35E **184** E6
Jeziorany *Poland* 53°58N 20°46E **184** E7
Jeziorka → *Poland* 52°8N 21°9E **185** F8
Jha Jha *India* 24°46N 86°22E **243** G12
Jhaarkand = Jharkhand □ *India* 24°0N 85°50E **243** H11
Jhabua *India* 22°46N 74°36E **242** H6
Jhajjar *India* 28°37N 76°42E **242** E7
Jhal *Pakistan* 28°17N 67°27E **242** E2
Jhal Jhao *Pakistan* 26°20N 65°35E **240** D2
Jhalakati *Bangla.* 22°39N 90°12E **241** D3
Jhalawar *India* 24°40N 76°10E **242** G7
Jhalida *India* 23°22N 85°58E **243** H11
Jhalrapatan *India* 24°33N 76°10E **242** G7
Jhang Maghiana *Pakistan* 31°15N 72°22E **242** D5
Jhansi *India* 25°30N 78°36E **243** G8
Jhargram *India* 22°27N 86°59E **243** H12
Jharia *India* 23°45N 86°26E **243** H12
Jharkhand □ *India* 24°0N 85°50E **243** H11
Jharsuguda *India* 21°56N 84°5E **244** D7
Jhelum *Pakistan* 33°0N 73°45E **242** C5
Jhelum → *Pakistan* 31°20N 72°10E **242** D5
Jhenaidah *Bangla.* 23°33N 89°10E **241** D2
Jhilmilli *India* 23°24N 82°51E **243** H10
Jhudo *Pakistan* 24°58N 69°18E **242** G3
Jhunjhunu *India* 28°10N 75°30E **242** E6
Ji-Paraná *Brazil* 10°50S 61°58W **331** C5
Ji Xian *Hebei, China* 37°35N 115°30E **226** F8
Ji Xian *Henan, China* 35°22N 114°5E **226** G8
Ji Xian *Shanxi, China* 36°7N 110°40E **226** F6
Jia Xian *Henan, China* 33°59N 113°12E **226** H7
Jia Xian *Shaanxi, China* 38°12N 110°28E **226** E6
Jiading *China* 31°22N 121°15E **229** B13
Jiahe *China* 25°38N 112°19E **229** E9
Jiaji = Qionghai *China* 19°15N 110°26E **236** C8
Jialing Jiang → *China* 29°30N 106°20E **228** C6
Jiamusi *China* 46°40N 130°26E **219** B8
Ji'an *Jiangxi, China* 27°6N 114°59E **229** D10
Ji'an *Jilin, China* 41°5N 126°10E **227** D14
Jianchang *China* 40°55N 120°35E **227** D11
Jianchangying *China* 40°10N 118°50E **227** D10
Jianchuan *China* 26°38N 99°55E **228** D2
Jiande *China* 29°23N 119°15E **229** C12
Jiang'an *China* 28°40N 105°3E **228** C5
Jiangbei *China* 29°40N 106°34E **228** C6
Jiangcheng *China* 22°36N 101°52E **228** F3
Jiangchuan *China* 24°8N 102°39E **228** E4
Jiangdi *China* 26°57N 103°37E **228** D4
Jiangdu *China* 32°27N 119°36E **229** A12
Jiange *China* 32°4N 105°32E **228** A5
Jianggao *China* 23°15N 113°13E **121** A2
Jianghua *China* 25°0N 111°47E **229** E8
Jiangjin *China* 29°14N 106°14E **228** C6
Jiangkou *China* 27°40N 108°49E **228** D7
Jiangle *China* 26°42N 117°23E **229** D11
Jiangling *China* 30°25N 112°12E **229** B9
Jiangmen *China* 22°32N 113°0E **229** F9
Jiangning *China* 31°55N 118°50E **229** B12
Jiangshan *China* 28°40N 118°37E **229** C12
Jiangsu □ *China* 33°0N 120°0E **227** H11
Jiangwan *China* 31°18N 121°28E **138** B1
Jiangxi □ *China* 27°30N 116°0E **229** D11
Jiangyan *China* 32°30N 120°7E **229** A13
Jiangyin *China* 31°54N 120°17E **229** B13
Jiangyong *China* 25°20N 111°22E **229** E8
Jiangyou *China* 31°44N 104°43E **228** B5
Jianhe *China* 26°37N 108°31E **228** D7
Jianli *China* 29°46N 112°56E **229** C9
Jianning *China* 26°50N 116°50E **229** D11
Jian'ou *China* 27°3N 118°17E **229** D12
Jianshi *China* 30°37N 109°38E **228** B7
Jianshui *China* 23°36N 102°43E **228** F4
Jianyang *Fujian, China* 27°20N 118°5E **229** D12
Jianyang *Sichuan, China* 30°24N 104°33E **228** B5
Jiao Xian = Jiaozhou *China* 36°18N 120°1E **227** F11
Jiaohe *Hebei, China* 38°2N 116°20E **226** E9
Jiaohe *Jilin, China* 43°40N 127°22E **227** C14
Jiaojiang *China* 28°40N 121°24E **229** C13
Jiaoling *China* 24°41N 116°12E **229** E11
Jiaozhou *China* 36°18N 120°1E **227** F11
Jiaozhou Wan *China* 36°5N 120°10E **227** F11
Jiaozuo *China* 35°16N 113°12E **226** G7
Jiashan *China* 30°55N 120°55E **229** B13
Jiawang *China* 34°28N 117°26E **227** G9
Jiaxiang *China* 35°25N 116°20E **226** G9
Jiaxing *China* 30°49N 120°45E **229** B13
Jiayi = Chiai *Taiwan* 23°29N 120°25E **225** C2
Jiayu *China* 29°55N 113°55E **229** C9
Jib *West Bank* 31°51N 35°11E **123** A2
Jibão, Serra do *Brazil* 14°48S 45°0W **333** D3
Jibiya *Nigeria* 13°5N 7°12E **263** C6
Jibou *Romania* 47°15N 23°17E **183** C8
Jibuti = Djibouti ■ *Africa* 12°0N 43°0E **257** E5
Jicarón, I. *Panama* 7°10N 81°50W **320** E3
Jičín *Czech Rep.* 50°25N 15°28E **180** A8
Jiddah *Si. Arabia* 21°29N 39°10E **248** B2
Jido *India* 29°2N 94°58E **241** A5
Jido *S. Korea* 35°4N 126°14E **224** E3
Jieshou *China* 33°18N 115°22E **226** H8
Jiexiu *China* 37°2N 111°55E **226** F6
Jieyang *China* 23°35N 116°21E **229** F11
Jigalong *Australia* 23°21S 120°47E **278** D3
Jigalong ☼ *Australia* 23°21S 120°46E **278** D3
Jigawa □ *Nigeria* 12°0N 9°45E **263** C6
Jigme Dorje △ *Bhutan* 28°0N 89°40E **241** B2
Jigme Singye Wangchuck *Bhutan* 27°20N 90°25E **241** B3
Jigni *India* 25°45N 79°25E **243** G8
Jihād *Iraq* 33°17N 44°19E **113** B1
Jihlava *Czech Rep.* 49°28N 15°35E **180** B8
Jihlava → *Czech Rep.* 48°55N 16°36E **181** C9
Jihlavský □ *Czech Rep.* 49°30N 15°30E **180** B8
Jihnan *Taiwan* 24°22N 120°39E **225** B2
Jihočeský □ *Czech Rep.* 49°8N 14°35E **180** B7
Jihomoravský □ *Czech Rep.* 49°5N 16°30E **181** B9
Jiigley *Somali Rep.* 5°25N 45°20E **267** C6
Jijel *Algeria* 36°52N 5°50E **261** A6
Jijel □ *Algeria* 36°45N 6°0E **261** A6
Jijiga *Ethiopia* 9°20N 42°50E **267** C5
Jikamshi *Nigeria* 12°12N 7°45E **263** C6
Jikau *Sudan* 8°28N 33°47E **257** F3
Jilib *Somali Rep.* 0°29N 42°46E **267** D5
Jilin *China* 43°44N 126°30E **227** C14
Jilin □ *China* 44°0N 127°0E **224** A3
Jiloca → *Spain* 41°21N 1°39W **196** D3
Jilong = Chilung *Taiwan* 25°3N 121°45E **225** A3
Jim Thompson's House *Bangkok, Thailand* **113** b3
Jim Thorpe *U.S.A.* 40°52N 75°44W **313** F9
Jima *Ethiopia* 7°40N 36°47E **257** F4
Jimbaran, Teluk *Indonesia* 8°46S 115°9E **231** K18
Jimbōchō *Tokyo, Japan* **140** a4
Jimbolia *Romania* 45°47N 20°43E **182** E5
Jimena de la Frontera *Spain* 36°27N 5°24W **195** J5
Jiménez *Chihuahua, Mexico* 27°8N 104°54W **318** B4
Jimenez *Phil.* 8°20N 123°50E **233** G4
Jimeta *Nigeria* 9°17N 12°28E **263** D7
Jimo *China* 36°23N 120°30E **227** F11
Jimsar *China* 43°59N 89°4E **217** D11
Jin Jiang → *China* 28°24N 115°48E **229** C10
Jin Xian = Jinzhou *Hebei, China* 38°2N 115°2E **226** E8
Jin Xian = Jinzhou *Liaoning, China* 38°55N 121°42E **227** E11
Jinan *China* 36°38N 117°1E **226** F9
Jinchang *China* 38°30N 102°10E **218** C5
Jincheng *China* 35°29N 112°50E **226** G7
Jinchuan *China* 31°30N 102°3E **228** B4
Jind *India* 29°19N 76°22E **242** E7
Jindabyne *Australia* 36°25S 148°35E **283** D8
Jinding *China* 22°22N 113°33E **219** G10
Jindo *S. Korea* 34°28N 126°15E **224** E3
Jindřichův Hradec *Czech Rep.* 49°10N 15°2E **180** B8
Jing He → *China* 34°27N 109°4E **226** G5
Jing Shan *China* 31°20N 111°35E **229** B8
Jing Xian *China* 30°38N 118°25E **229** B12
Jing'an *Jiangxi, China* 28°50N 115°17E **229** C10
Jingan *Shanghai, China* 31°14N 121°25E **138** B1
Jingbian *China* 37°20N 108°30E **226** F5
Jingchuan *China* 35°20N 107°20E **226** G4
Jingde *China* 30°15N 118°27E **229** B12
Jingdezhen *China* 29°20N 117°11E **229** C11
Jingdong *China* 24°23N 100°47E **228** E3
Jinggangshan *China* 26°58N 114°15E **229** D10
Jinggu *China* 23°35N 100°41E **228** F3
Jinghai *China* 38°55N 116°55E **226** E9
Jinghong *China* 22°0N 100°45E **228** G3
Jingjiang *China* 32°2N 120°16E **229** A13
Jingle *China* 38°20N 111°55E **226** E6
Jingmen *China* 31°0N 112°10E **229** B9
Jingning *China* 35°30N 105°43E **226** G3
Jingpo Hu *China* 43°55N 128°55E **227** C15
Jingshan *China* 31°1N 113°7E **229** B9
Jingtai *China* 37°10N 104°6E **226** F3
Jingu Outer Garden *Tokyo, Japan* **140** b2
Jingxi *China* 23°8N 106°27E **228** F6
Jingxing *China* 38°2N 114°8E **226** E8
Jingyang *China* 34°30N 108°50E **226** G5
Jingyu *China* 42°25N 126°45E **224** A3
Jingyuan *China* 36°30N 104°40E **226** F3
Jingzhou *China* 26°33N 109°40E **228** D7
Jingziguan *China* 33°15N 111°0E **226** H6
Jinhua *China* 29°8N 119°38E **229** C12
Jining *Nei Monggol Zizhiqu, China* 41°5N 113°0E **226** D7
Jining *Shandong, China* 35°22N 116°34E **226** G9
Jinja *Uganda* 0°25N 33°12E **268** B3
Jinjang *Malaysia* 3°13N 101°39E **237** L3
Jinji *China* 37°58N 106°8E **226** F4
Jinjiang *Fujian, China* 24°43N 118°33E **229** E12
Jinjiang *Yunnan, China* 26°14N 100°34E **228** D3
Jinjini *Ghana* 7°26N 2°42W **262** D4
Jinju *S. Korea* 35°12N 128°2E **224** E4
Jinkou *China* 30°20N 114°8E **229** B10
Jinkouhe *China* 29°18N 103°4E **228** C4
Jinmen Dao *China* 24°25N 118°25E **229** E12
Jinnah Barrage *Pakistan* 32°58N 71°33E **242** C4
Jinning *China* 24°38N 102°38E **228** E4
Jinočany *Czech Rep.* 50°2N 14°16E **135** B1
Jinonice *Czech Rep.* 50°3N 14°22E **135** B2
Jinotega *Nic.* 13°6N 85°59W **320** D2
Jinotepe *Nic.* 11°50N 86°10W **320** D2
Jinping *Guizhou, China* 26°41N 109°10E **228** D7
Jinping *Yunnan, China* 22°45N 103°18E **228** F4
Jinsha *China* 27°29N 106°12E **228** D6
Jinsha Jiang → *China* 28°50N 104°36E **228** C5
Jinshan *China* 30°54N 121°10E **229** B13
Jinshi *China* 29°40N 111°50E **229** C8
Jintan *China* 31°42N 119°36E **229** B12
Jintotolo Channel *Phil.* 11°48N 123°5E **233** F4
Jintur *India* 19°37N 76°42E **244** E3
Jinxi *Jiangxi, China* 27°56N 116°45E **229** D11
Jinxi *Liaoning, China* 40°52N 120°50E **227** D11
Jinxian *China* 28°26N 116°17E **229** C11
Jinxiang *China* 35°5N 116°22E **226** G9
Jinyang *China* 27°28N 103°5E **228** D4
Jinyun *China* 28°35N 120°5E **229** C13
Jinzhai *China* 31°40N 115°53E **229** B10
Jinzhong *China* 37°42N 112°46E **226** F7
Jinzhou *Hebei, China* 38°2N 115°2E **226** E8
Jinzhou *Liaoning, China* 38°55N 121°42E **227** E11
Jinzhou *Liaoning, China* 41°5N 121°3E **227** D11
Jiparaná → *Brazil* 8°3S 62°52W **331** B5
Jipijapa *Ecuador* 1°0S 80°40W **328** D1
Jiquilpan *Mexico* 19°59N 102°43W **318** D4
Jirisan *S. Korea* 35°20N 127°44E **224** E3
Jirisan △ *S. Korea* 35°15N 127°30E **224** E3
Jiroft *Iran* 28°45N 57°50E **247** D8
Jishan *China* 35°34N 110°58E **226** G6
Jishou *China* 28°21N 109°43E **228** C7
Jishui *China* 27°12N 115°8E **229** D10
Jisr ash Shughūr *Syria* 35°49N 36°18E **250** C7
Jitarning *Australia* 32°48S 117°57E **279** F2
Jitra *Malaysia* 6°16N 100°25E **237** J3
Jiu → *Romania* 43°47N 23°48E **183** G8
Jiudengkou *China* 39°56N 106°40E **226** E4
Jiujiang *Guangdong, China* 22°50N 113°0E **229** F9
Jiujiang *Jiangxi, China* 29°42N 115°58E **229** C10
Jiuling Shan *China* 28°40N 114°40E **229** C10
Jiulong = Kowloon *China* 22°19N 114°11E **122** B1
Jiulong *China* 28°57N 101°31E **228** C3
Jiuquan *China* 39°50N 98°20E **218** C4
Jiutai *China* 44°10N 125°50E **227** B13
Jiuxincheng *China* 39°17N 115°59E **226** E8
Jiuyuhang *China* 30°18N 119°56E **229** B12
Jiwa *U.A.E.* 23°0N 54°10E **249** B6
Jiwani *Pakistan* 25°1N 61°44E **240** D1
Jiwani, Ras *Pakistan* 25°1N 61°44E **240** D1
Jixi *Anhui, China* 30°5N 118°34E **229** B12
Jixi *Heilongjiang, China* 45°20N 130°50E **227** B16
Jiyang *China* 37°0N 117°12E **227** F9
Jiyuan *China* 35°7N 112°57E **226** G7
Jiyūgaoka *Japan* 35°35N 139°40E **140** B3
Jiz', W. → *Yemen* 16°12N 52°14E **249** C6
Jizā'ir *Iraq* 33°15N 44°23E **113** B2
Jīzān *Si. Arabia* 17°0N 42°20E **248** C3
Jize *China* 36°54N 114°56E **226** F8
Jizera → *Czech Rep.* 50°10N 14°43E **180** A7
Jizīra *Iraq* 33°15N 44°25E **113** B2
Jizl, Wādī al → *Si. Arabia* 25°39N 38°25E **246** E3
Jizō-Zaki *Japan* 35°34N 133°20E **222** B5
Jizzax *Uzbekistan* 40°6N 67°50E **217** D7
Jizzax □ *Uzbekistan* 40°20N 67°40E **217** D7
Joaçaba *Brazil* 27°5S 51°31W **335** B5
Joaíma *Brazil* 16°39S 41°2W **333** E3
Joal Fadiout *Senegal* 14°9N 16°50W **262** C1
João Amaro *Brazil* 12°46S 40°22W **333** D3
João Belo = Xai-Xai *Mozam.* 25°6S 33°31E **271** C5
João Câmara *Brazil* 5°32S 35°48W **332** C4
João Neiva *Brazil* 19°45S 40°24W **333** E3
João Pessoa = Eirunepé *Brazil* 6°35S 69°53W **330** B4
João Pessoa = Porto *Brazil* 3°54S 42°42W **332** B3
João Pessoa *Brazil* 7°10S 34°52W **332** C5
João Pinheiro *Brazil* 17°45S 46°10W **333** E2
Joaquín V. González *Argentina* 25°10S 64°0W **334** B3
Jobat *India* 22°25N 74°34E **242** H6
Jobourg, Nez de *France* 49°41N 1°57W **172** C5
Jódar *Spain* 37°50N 3°21W **195** H7
Jodhpur *India* 26°23N 73°8E **242** F5
Jodiya *India* 22°42N 70°18E **242** H4
Joensuu *Finland* 62°37N 29°49E **160** E23
Jōetsu *Japan* 37°12N 138°10E **221** F9
Jœuf *France* 49°12N 6°0E **173** C12
Jofane *Mozam.* 21°15S 34°18E **271** B5
Joffre, Morne = Moustique, Morne *Guadeloupe* 16°7N 61°44W **322** e
Jog Falls = Gersoppa Falls *India* 14°12N 74°46E **245** G2
Jogbani *India* 26°25N 87°15E **243** F12
Jõgeva *Estonia* 58°45N 26°24E **188** C4
Jogjakarta = Yogyakarta *Indonesia* 7°49S 110°22E **235** D4
Joglo *Indonesia* 6°13S 106°45E **122** B1
Jōhana *Japan* 36°30N 136°57E **223** A8
Johannesburg *Gauteng, S. Africa* 26°11S 28°2E **123** B2
Johannesburg *Calif., U.S.A.* 35°22N 117°38W **307** K9
Johannesburg, Univ. of *S. Africa* 26°11S 28°0E **123** B2
Johanneskirchen *Germany* 48°10N 11°38E **131** A2
Johannesstift *Germany* 52°34N 13°12E **115** A2
Johannisburg = Pisz *Poland* 53°38N 21°49E **184** E8
Johannisthal *Germany* 52°26N 13°30E **115** B4
Johansfors *Sweden* 56°42N 15°32E **163** H9
Johilla → *India* 23°37N 81°14E **243** H9
John Crow Mts. *Jamaica* 18°5N 76°25W **320** a
John Day *U.S.A.* 44°25N 118°57W **304** D4
John Day → *U.S.A.* 45°44N 120°39W **304** D3
John Day Fossil Beds ⌂ *U.S.A.* 44°33N 119°38W **304** D4
John D'or Prairie *Canada* 58°30N 115°8W **296** B5
John F. Kennedy Nat. Historic Site ⌂ *U.S.A.* 42°20N 71°7W **116** A2
John F. Kennedy Space Center *U.S.A.* 28°40N 80°42W **317** G9
John H. Kerr Res. *U.S.A.* 36°36N 78°18W **315** C15
John Hancock Center *Chicago, U.S.A.* **119** a2
John McLaren Park *U.S.A.* 37°43N 122°24W **136** B2
John o' Groats *U.K.* 58°38N 3°4W **167** C5
Johnnie *U.S.A.* 36°25N 116°5W **307** J10
Johns I. *U.S.A.* 32°47N 80°7W **316** C9
John's Ra. *Australia* 21°55S 133°23E **280** C1
Johnson *U.S.A.* 44°38N 72°41W **313** B12
Johnson City *Kans., U.S.A.* 37°34N 101°45W **308** G3
Johnson City *N.Y., U.S.A.* 42°7N 75°58W **313** D9
Johnson City *Tenn., U.S.A.* 36°19N 82°21W **315** C13
Johnson City *Tex., U.S.A.* 30°17N 98°25W **314** F5
Johnsonburg *U.S.A.* 41°29N 78°41W **312** E6
Johnsondale *U.S.A.* 35°58N 118°32W **307** K8
Johnsons Crossing *Canada* 60°29N 133°18W **296** A2
Johnsons Pt. *Antigua & B.* 17°2N 61°53W **322** b
Johnsonville *N.Z.* 41°13S 174°48E **143** B1
Johnston *U.S.A.* 33°50N 81°48W **316** B8
Johnston, L. *Australia* 32°25S 120°30E **279** F3
Johnston City *U.S.A.* 37°49N 88°56W **310** G8
Johnston Falls = Mambilima Falls *Zambia* 10°31S 28°45E **269** E2
Johnston I. *Pac. Oc.* 17°10N 169°8W **289** F11
Johnstone Str. *Canada* 50°28N 126°0W **296** C3
Johnstown *Kilkenny, Ireland* 52°45N 7°33W **166** D4
Johnstown *N.Y., U.S.A.* 43°0N 74°22W **313** C10
Johnstown *Ohio, U.S.A.* 40°9N 82°41W **312** F2
Johnstown *Pa., U.S.A.* 40°20N 78°55W **312** F6
Johor □ *Malaysia* 2°5N 103°20E **234** B2
Johor, Selat *Asia* 1°28N 103°47E **237** d
Johor Bahru *Malaysia* 1°28N 103°46E **237** d
Jõhvi *Estonia* 59°22N 27°27E **188** C4
Joigny *France* 47°58N 3°20E **173** E10
Joinville *Brazil* 26°15S 48°55W **335** B6
Joinville *Haute-Marne, France* 48°27N 5°10E **173** D12
Joinville I. *Antarctica* 65°0S 55°30W **151** C18
Joinville-le-Pont *France* 48°49N 2°27E **134** B3
Jojutla *Mexico* 18°37N 99°11W **319** D5
Jøkelbugten *Greenland* 78°25N 20°20W **154** B9
Jokkmokk *Sweden* 66°35N 19°50E **160** C18
Jökulsá á Bru → *Iceland* 65°40N 14°16W **155** B12
Jökulsá á Fjöllum → *Iceland* 66°10N 16°30W **155** A10
Jökulsárgljúfur △ *Iceland* 65°56N 16°31W **155** B10
Jolfā *Āzarbājān-e Sharqī, Iran* 38°57N 45°38E **213** C11
Jolfā *Eşfahan, Iran* 32°58N 51°37E **247** C6
Joli-Bois *Belgium* 50°42N 4°24E **116** B2
Joliet *U.S.A.* 41°32N 88°5W **311** C8
Joliette *Canada* 46°3N 73°24W **298** C5
Jollas *Finland* 60°10N 25°5E **121** B3
Jolo *Phil.* 6°0N 121°0E **233** H3
Jolo Group *Phil.* 6°0N 121°9E **233** J3
Jolon *U.S.A.* 35°58N 121°9W **306** K5
Jølstravatnet *Norway* 61°32N 6°23E **164** C3
Jomalig I. *Phil.* 14°42N 122°22E **232** D4
Jombang *Indonesia* 7°33S 112°14E **235** D4
Jomda *China* 31°28N 98°12E **228** B2
Jonava *Lithuania* 55°8N 24°12E **188** E3
Jondal *Norway* 60°16N 6°15E **164** D3
Jones *Phil.* 16°33N 121°42E **232** C3
Jones Sound *Canada* 76°0N 85°0W **295** B15
Jonesboro *Ark., U.S.A.* 35°50N 90°42W **315** D9
Jonesboro *Ga., U.S.A.* 33°31N 84°22W **316** B5
Jonesboro *La., U.S.A.* 32°15N 92°43W **314** E8
Jonesburg *U.S.A.* 38°51N 91°18W **310** F5
Jonesville *Ind., U.S.A.* 39°5N 85°54W **311** E11
Jonesville *Mich., U.S.A.* 41°59N 84°40W **311** C12
Jong → *S. Leone* 7°32N 12°23W **262** D2
Jonglei *Sudan* 6°25N 30°50E **257** F3
Jonglei □ *Sudan* 7°30N 32°30E **257** F3
Jonglei Canal *Sudan* 9°20N 31°39E **266** C3
Jongmyo Royal Shrine *S. Korea* 37°34N 126°59E **137** B1
Jongno *S. Korea* 37°35N 126°59E **137** B1
Joniškis *Lithuania* 56°13N 23°35E **184** B10
Jönköping *Sweden* 57°45N 14°8E **163** G8
Jönköpings län □ *Sweden* 57°30N 14°30E **163** G8
Jonquière *Canada* 48°27N 71°14W **299** C5
Jonsered *Sweden* 57°45N 12°10E **163** G6
Jonstrup *Denmark* 55°45N 12°20E **118** A2
Jonzac *France* 45°27N 0°28W **174** C3
Joplin *U.S.A.* 37°6N 94°31W **308** G6
Joppa *U.K.* 55°57N 3°6W **121** B3
Jora *India* 26°20N 77°49E **242** F6
Jordan *Guimaras, Phil.* 10°40N 122°35E **233** F4
Jordan *Mont., U.S.A.* 47°19N 106°55W **304** C10
Jordan *N.Y., U.S.A.* 43°4N 76°29W **313** C8
Jordan ■ *Asia* 31°0N 36°0E **251** H7
Jordan → *Asia* 31°48N 35°32E **251** G6
Jordan Valley *U.S.A.* 42°59N 117°3W **304** E5
Jordânia *Brazil* 15°55S 40°11W **333** E3
Jordanów *Poland* 49°41N 19°49E **185** J6
Jordet *Norway* 61°25N 12°8E **164** C9
Jorge, C. *Chile* 51°40S 75°35W **336** D1
Jorge Chavez, Int. ✈ **(LIM)** *Peru* 12°2S 77°8W **124** B2
Jorge Newbery ✈ **(AEP)** *Argentina* 34°34S 58°25W **117** B2
Jorgen Brønlund Fjord *Greenland* 82°30N 31°0W **154** A7
Jorhat *India* 26°45N 94°12E **241** B5
Jori → *Norway* 62°4N 9°5E **162** B3
Jorm *Afghan.* 36°50N 70°52E **240** A3
Jörn *Sweden* 65°4N 20°1E **160** D19
Jorong *Indonesia* 3°58S 114°56E **235** C4
Jørpeland *Norway* 59°3N 6°1E **164** E3
Jorquera → *Chile* 28°3S 69°58W **334** B2
Joru *S. Leone* 7°41N 11°3W **262** D2
Jos *Nigeria* 9°53N 8°51E **263** D6
Jos Plateau *Niger* 9°30N 9°0E **259** G1
Jos Plateau *Nigeria* 9°55N 9°0E **263** D6
Jošanička Banja *Serbia* 43°24N 20°47E **202** C4
Jose Abad Santos *Phil.* 5°55N 125°39E **233** J5
José Batlle y Ordóñez *Uruguay* 33°20S 55°10W **335** C4
José Bonifácio = Erechim *Brazil* 27°35S 52°15W **335** B5
José de San Martín *Argentina* 44°4S 70°26W **336** B2
Jose Panganiban *Phil.* 14°17N 122°41E **232** D4
Jósefa Piłsudskiego Park *Poland* 52°15N 21°2E **142** B1
Joseni *Romania* 46°42N 25°29E **183** D10
Joseph, L. *Canada* 45°10N 79°44W **312** A5
Joseph Banks Group *Australia* 34°36S 136°16E **282** C2
Joseph Bonaparte G. *Australia* 14°35S 128°50E **278** B4
Joseph L. *Canada* 52°45N 65°18W **299** B6
Joshinath *India* 30°34N 79°34E **243** D8
Joshinetsu-Kōgen △ *Japan* 36°42N 138°32E **223** A10
Joshua Tree *U.S.A.* 34°8N 116°19W **307** L10
Joshua Tree △ *U.S.A.* 33°55N 116°0W **307** M10
Josselin *France* 47°57N 2°33W **172** E4
Jost Van Dyke I. *Br. Virgin Is.* 18°29N 64°47W **321** b
Jostedal *Norway* 61°35N 7°15E **164** C4
Jostedalsbreen *Norway* 61°40N 6°59E **164** C3
Jōtō *Japan* 34°42N 135°33E **133** A2
Jotunheimen *Norway* 61°35N 8°25E **164** C5
Jotunheimen △ *Norway* 61°32N 8°25E **164** C5
Joubertberge *Namibia* 18°30S 14°0E **270** A1
Joué-lès-Tours *France* 47°21N 0°40E **172** E7
Jourdanton *U.S.A.* 28°55N 98°33W **314** G5
Joutseno *Finland* 61°7N 28°31E **188** B5
Jouy-en-Josas *France* 48°46N 2°10E **134** B2
Jovellanos *Cuba* 22°40N 81°10W **320** B3
Jovellar *Phil.* 13°4N 123°36E **232** E4
Jowai *India* 25°26N 92°12E **241** C4
Jowkār *Iran* 34°25N 48°40E **213** E13
Jowzjān □ *Afghan.* 36°10N 66°0E **240** A2
Joyeuse *France* 44°29N 4°16E **175** D8
Jōyō *Japan* 34°50N 135°47E **223** C7
Józefów *Lubelskie, Poland* 50°28N 23°2E **185** H10
Józefów *Mazowieckie, Poland* 52°10N 21°11E **185** F8
Ju Xian *China* 36°35N 118°20E **227** F10
Juan Aldama *Mexico* 24°19N 103°21W **318** C4
Juan Anchorena *Argentina* 34°30S 58°29W **117** A2
Juan Bautista Alberdi *Argentina* 34°26S 61°48W **334** C3
Juan de Bolas *Jamaica* 18°5N 77°9W **320** a
Juan de Fuca, Str of. *N. Amer.* 48°15N 124°0W **306** B3
Juán de Nova *Ind. Oc.* 17°3S 43°45E **271** A7
Juan Fernández, Arch. de *Pac. Oc.* 33°50S 80°0W **326** G2
Juan Fernández △ *Chile* 33°38S 78°52W **330** c
Juan González Romero *Mexico* 19°30N 99°3W **128** A2
Juan José Castelli *Argentina* 25°27S 60°57W **334** B3
Juan L. Lacaze *Uruguay* 34°26S 57°25W **334** C4
Juana Días *Puerto Rico* 18°3N 66°31W **321** b
Juanjuí *Peru* 7°10S 76°45W **330** B2
Juankoski *Finland* 63°3N 28°19E **160** E23
Juara *Brazil* 11°20S 57°25W **331** C6
Juárez *Mexico* 27°37N 100°44W **318** B4

384 Juárez, Sierra de INDEX

Juárez, Sierra de Mexico 32°0N 116°0W 318 A1
Juárez Int. ✈ (MEX) Mexico 19°25N 99°5W 128 B2
Juatinga, Pta. da Brazil 23°17S 44°30W 333 F3
Juàzeiro Brazil 9°30S 40°30W 332 C3
Juàzeiro do Norte Brazil 7°10S 39°18W 332 C4
Juazohn Liberia 5°22N 8°50W 262 D3
Jûbâ Sudan 4°50N 31°35E 257 G3
Juba → Somali Rep. 1°30N 42°35E 267 D5
Jubany Antarctica 62°30S 58°0W 151 C18
Jubayl Lebanon 34°5N 35°39E 250 D6
Jubbada Dhexe □ Somali Rep. 2°0N 41°30E 267 D5
Jubbada Hoose □ Somali Rep. 0°0 42°0E 267 E5
Jubbah Si. Arabia 28°2N 40°56E 246 D4
Jubbal India 31°5N 77°40E 242 D7
Jubbulpore = Jabalpur India 23°9N 79°58E 243 H8
Jübek Germany 54°33N 9°22E 178 A5
Jubga Russia 44°19N 38°48E 191 H4
Jubilee L. Australia 29°0S 126°50E 279 E4
Juby, C. Morocco 28°0N 12°59W 260 C2
Júcar = Xúquer → Spain 39°5N 0°10W 197 F4
Júcaro Cuba 21°37N 78°51W 320 B4
Juchitán de Zaragoza Mexico 16°26N 95°1W 319 D5
Judaberg Norway 59°10N 5°51E 164 E2
Judea = Har Yehuda Israel 31°35N 34°57E 251 G5
Judeira West Bank 31°52N 35°12E 123 A2
Judenburg Austria 47°12N 14°38E 180 D7
Judith → U.S.A. 47°44N 109°39W 304 C9
Judith, Pt. U.S.A. 41°22N 71°29W 313 E13
Judith Gap U.S.A. 46°41N 109°45W 304 C9
Juelsminde Denmark 55°43N 10°1E 163 J4
Jufari → Brazil 1°13S 62°0W 329 D5
Juhdum West Bank 31°42N 35°15E 123 B2
Juhu India 19°5N 73°0E 130 A2
Juifang Taiwan 25°7N 121°48E 225 A3
Juigalpa Nic. 12°6N 85°26W 320 D2
Juillac France 45°20N 1°19E 174 C5
Juist Germany 53°40N 6°59E 178 B2
Juisui Taiwan 23°30N 121°22E 225 C3
Juiz de Fora Brazil 21°43S 43°19W 333 F3
Jūjā Japan 35°45N 139°43E 140 A3
Jujuy □ Argentina 23°20S 65°40W 334 A2
Jukao = Rugao China 32°23N 120°31E 229 A13
Jukskeirivier → S. Africa 26°5S 28°6E 123 A2
Julesburg U.S.A. 40°59N 102°16W 304 F12
Juli Peru 16°10S 69°25W 330 D4
Julia Cr. → Australia 20°0S 141°11E 280 C3
Julia Creek Australia 20°39S 141°44E 280 C3
Juliaca Peru 15°25S 70°10W 330 D3
Julian U.S.A. 33°4N 116°38W 307 M10
Julian, L. Canada 54°25N 77°57W 298 B4
Julian Alps = Julijske Alpe Slovenia 46°15N 14°1E 199 B11
Juliana Top = Mandala, Puncak Indonesia 4°44S 140°20E 231 E10
Julianadorp Neth. Ant. 12°9N 68°57W 322 g
Julianatop Suriname 3°40N 56°30W 329 C6
Julianehåb = Qaqortoq Greenland 60°43N 46°0W 154 E6
Julianów Poland 52°10N 21°9E 142 B2
Jülich Germany 50°55N 6°22E 178 E2
Juliette, L. U.S.A. 33°2N 83°50W 316 B6
Julijske Alpe Slovenia 46°15N 14°1E 199 B11
Julimes Mexico 28°25N 105°27W 318 B3
Jullundur India 31°20N 75°40E 242 D6
Julu China 37°15N 115°2E 226 F8
Jumbo Zimbabwe 17°30S 30°58E 269 F3
Jumbo Pk. U.S.A. 36°12N 114°11W 307 J12
Jumentos Cays Bahamas 23°0N 75°40W 320 B4
Jumilla Spain 38°28N 1°19W 197 G3
Jumla Nepal 29°15N 82°13E 243 E10
Jumna = Yamuna → India 25°30N 81°53E 243 G9
Jumunjin S. Korea 37°55N 128°54E 224 D4
Junagadh India 21°30N 70°30E 242 J4
Juncos Puerto Rico 18°14N 65°55W 321 b
Junction Tex., U.S.A. 30°29N 99°46W 314 F5
Junction Utah, U.S.A. 38°14N 112°13W 305 G7
Junction B. Australia 11°52S 133°55E 280 A1
Junction City Ga., U.S.A. 32°36N 84°28W 316 C5
Junction City Kans., U.S.A. 39°2N 96°50W 308 F5
Junction City Oreg., U.S.A. 44°13N 123°12W 304 D2
Junction Pt. Australia 11°45S 133°50E 280 A1
Jundah Australia 24°46S 143°2E 280 C3
Jundiaí Brazil 24°30S 47°0W 335 A6
Juneau U.S.A. 58°18N 134°25W 296 B2
Junee Australia 34°53S 147°35E 283 C7
Jung S. Korea 37°33N 126°59E 137 B1
Jungbunzlau = Mladá Boleslav Czech Rep. 50°27N 14°53E 180 A7
Jungfernheide, Volkspark Germany 52°32N 13°18E 115 A2
Jungfernsee Germany 52°25N 13°6E 115 B1
Jungfrau Switz. 46°32N 7°58E 179 J3
Junggar Pendi China 44°30N 86°0E 217 D11
Junghwa S. Korea 37°35N 127°3E 137 B2
Jungnang S. Korea 37°36N 127°5E 137 B2
Jungnangcheon → S. Korea 37°32N 126°55E 137 B1
Jungsdalshytta = Iungsdalshytta Norway 60°49N 7°55E 164 D4
Jungshahi Pakistan 24°52N 67°44E 242 G2
Juniata → U.S.A. 40°24N 77°1W 312 F7
Junín Argentina 34°33S 60°57W 334 C3
Junín Peru 11°12S 76°0W 330 C2
Junín □ Peru 11°30S 75°0W 330 C3
Junín, L. de Peru 11°2S 76°6W 330 C2
Junín de los Andes Argentina 39°45S 71°0W 336 A2
Juniper Green U.K. 55°54N 3°16W 121 B2
Jūniyah Lebanon 33°59N 35°38E 250 E6
Junk B. China 22°17N 114°15E 122 B2
Junlian China 28°8N 104°29E 228 C5
Junnar India 19°12N 73°58E 244 E1
Juno Beach U.S.A. 26°52N 80°3W 317 J9
Juntas Chile 28°24S 69°58W 334 B2
Juntura U.S.A. 43°45N 118°5W 304 E4
Juparanã, L. Brazil 19°16S 40°8W 333 E3
Jupiter U.S.A. 26°57N 80°6W 317 J9
Juquiá Brazil 24°19S 47°38W 333 F2
Jur, Nahr el → Sudan 8°45N 29°15E 257 F2
Jura = Jura, Mts. du Europe 46°40N 6°5E 173 F13
Jura = Schwäbische Alb Germany 48°20N 9°30E 179 G5
Jura U.K. 56°0N 5°50W 167 F3
Jura □ France 46°47N 5°45E 173 F12
Jura □ Switz. 47°20N 7°20E 179 H3
Jūra → Lithuania 55°3N 22°9E 184 C9
Jura, Mts. du Europe 46°40N 6°5E 173 F13
Jura, Sd. of U.K. 55°57N 5°45W 167 F3
Juradó Colombia 7°7N 77°46W 328 B2
Jurbarkas Lithuania 55°4N 22°46E 184 C9
Jurien Bay Australia 30°18S 115°2E 279 F2
Jurilovca Romania 44°46N 28°52E 183 F13
Jūrmala Latvia 56°58N 23°34E 184 B10
Jurong Jiangsu, China 31°57N 119°9E 229 B12
Jurong Singapore 1°19N 103°42E 138 B2
Jurong, Selat Singapore 1°17N 103°42E 138 B2
Jurong Industrial Estate Singapore 1°19N 103°40E 138 B1
Juruá Brazil 3°27S 66°3W 328 D4
Juruá → Brazil 2°37S 65°44W 328 D4
Juruena Brazil 13°0S 58°10W 331 C6
Juruena → Brazil 7°20S 58°3W 331 B6
Jurujuba, Enseada de Brazil 22°54S 43°6W 135 B2
Juruti Brazil 2°9S 56°4W 329 D6
Jūsō Japan 34°42N 135°27E 133 A1
Jussey France 47°50N 5°55E 173 E12
Justice U.S.A. 41°44N 87°49W 119 C2
Justicia Madrid, Spain 127 a3
Justo Daract Argentina 33°52S 65°12W 334 C2
Jutaí Amazonas, Brazil 2°44S 66°57W 328 D4
Jutaí Amazonas, Brazil 5°11S 68°54W 330 B4
Jutaí → Brazil 2°43S 66°57W 328 D4
Jüterbog Germany 51°59N 13°5E 178 D9
Juticalpa Honduras 14°40N 86°12W 320 D2
Jutland = Jylland Denmark 56°25N 9°30E 163 H3
Juuka Finland 63°13N 29°17E 160 E23
Juventud, I. de la Cuba 21°40N 82°40W 320 B3
Juvigny-sous-Andaine France 48°32N 0°30W 172 D6
Juwangsan △ S. Korea 36°20N 129°15E 224 D4
Jūy Zar Iran 33°50N 46°18E 213 F12
Juye China 35°22N 116°5E 226 G9
Juzennecourt France 48°10N 4°58E 173 D11
Južni Brod = Brod Macedonia 41°32N 21°17E 202 E5
Jvari Georgia 42°42N 42°4E 191 J6
Jwalahari India 28°40N 77°6E 120 B1
Jyderup Denmark 55°40N 11°26E 163 J5
Jylland Denmark 56°25N 9°30E 163 H3
Jyväskylä Finland 62°14N 25°50E 188 A3

K

K2 Pakistan 35°58N 76°32E 243 B7
Ka → Nigeria 11°40N 4°10E 263 C5
Kaa-Iya △ Bolivia 18°35S 61°40W 331 D5
Ka'a'awa U.S.A. 21°33N 157°51W 302 J14
Kaakha = Kaka Turkmenistan 37°21N 59°36E 247 B8
Ka'ala U.S.A. 21°31N 158°9W 302 J13
Kaala-Gomén N. Cal. 20°40S 164°25E 288 d
Ka'alu'alu B. U.S.A. 18°58N 155°37W 302 E6
Kaap Plateau S. Africa 28°30S 24°0E 270 C3
Kaapkruis Namibia 21°55S 13°57E 270 B1
Kaapstad = Cape Town S. Africa 33°55S 18°22E 118 A1
Kaashidhoo Atoll Maldives 4°58N 73°28E 272 d
Kaashidhoo Channel Maldives 5°1N 73°28E 272 d
Kaataon, Mt. Phil. 8°10N 124°52E 233 G5
Kaba Guinea 10°9N 11°40W 262 C2
Kabacan Phil. 7°8N 124°49E 233 H5
Kabachishche = Zelenodolsk Russia 55°55N 48°30E 190 C9
Kabaena Indonesia 5°15S 122°0E 231 F6
Kabala S. Leone 9°38N 11°37W 262 D2
Kabale Uganda 1°15S 30°0E 268 C3
Kabalo Dem. Rep. of the Congo 6°0S 27°0E 265 D5
Kabambare Dem. Rep. of the Congo 4°41S 27°39E 268 C2
Kabango Dem. Rep. of the Congo 8°35S 28°30E 269 D2
Kabanjahe Indonesia 3°6N 98°30E 234 B1
Kabankalan Phil. 9°59N 122°49E 233 G4
Kabara Fiji 18°59S 178°56W 287 B3
Kabara Mali 16°40N 2°50W 262 B4
Kabardinka Russia 44°40N 37°57E 189 K10
Kabardino-Balkaria □ Russia 43°30N 43°30E 191 J6
Kabarega Falls = Murchison Falls Uganda 2°15N 31°30E 268 B3
Kabarnet Kenya 0°30N 35°45E 268 B4
Kabasalan Phil. 7°47N 122°44E 233 H4
Kabat Indonesia 8°16S 114°19E 231 J17
Kabaty Poland 52°8N 21°4E 142 C2
Kabba Nigeria 7°50N 6°3E 263 D6
Kabbani → India 12°13N 76°54E 245 H3
Kabi Niger 13°30N 12°35E 259 F2
Kabin Buri Thailand 13°57N 101°43E 236 F3
Kabinakagami L. Canada 48°54N 84°25W 298 C3
Kabinda Dem. Rep. of the Congo 6°10S 24°29E 265 D4
Kabkabīyah Sudan 13°50N 24°0E 259 F4
Kablungu, C. Papua N. G. 6°20S 150°1E 286 D6
Kabna Sudan 19°6N 32°40E 256 D3
Kabo C.A.R. 7°35N 18°38E 264 A3
Kabompo Zambia 13°36S 24°14E 265 E4
Kabompo → Zambia 14°11S 23°11E 265 E4
Kabondo Dem. Rep. of the Congo 8°58S 25°40E 265 D5
Kabongo Dem. Rep. of the Congo 7°22S 25°33E 265 D5
Kabot Guinea 10°48N 14°57W 262 C2
Kabou Togo 9°28N 0°55E 263 D5
Kaboudia, Rass Tunisia 35°13N 11°10E 258 A2
Kabr Sudan 10°54N 26°50E 257 E2
Kabrīt, G. el Egypt 29°42N 33°16E 251 J4
Kabrousse Senegal 12°25N 16°45W 262 C1
Kabubu Dem. Rep. of the Congo 9°42S 24°40E 265 D4
Kabūd Gonbad Iran 37°5N 59°45E 247 B8
Kabudar Ahang Iran 35°11N 48°43E 213 E13
Kabugao Phil. 18°2N 121°11E 232 B3
Kābul Afghan. 34°28N 69°11E 242 B3
Kābul □ Afghan. 34°30N 69°0E 240 B3
Kābul → Pakistan 33°55N 72°14E 242 C5
Kabuli Papua N. G. 2°7S 146°40E 286 B4
Kabunga Dem. Rep. of the Congo 1°38S 28°3E 268 C2
Kaburuang Indonesia 3°50N 126°30E 231 D7
Kabushiya Sudan 16°54N 33°41E 257 D3
Kabwanga Dem. Rep. of the Congo 7°2S 22°36E 265 D4
Kabwe Zambia 14°30S 28°29E 269 E2
Kabwum Papua N. G. 6°11S 147°15E 286 D4
Kačanik Kosovo 42°13N 21°12E 202 D5
Kačerginė Lithuania 54°56N 23°42E 184 D10
Kachar Kazakhstan 53°23N 62°55E 216 B6
Kachchh, Gulf of India 22°50N 69°15E 242 H3
Kachchh, Rann of India 24°0N 70°0E 242 H4
Kachchhidhana India 21°44N 78°46E 243 J8
Kachebera Zambia 13°50S 32°50E 269 E3
Kachia Nigeria 9°50N 7°55E 263 D6
Kachikau Botswana 18°8S 24°26E 270 A3
Kachin □ Burma 26°0N 97°30E 241 D6
Kachira, L. Uganda 0°40S 31°7E 268 C3
Kachiry Kazakhstan 53°10N 75°50E 217 B9
Kachisi Ethiopia 9°40N 37°50E 257 F4
Kachnara India 23°50N 75°6E 242 H6
Kachot Cambodia 11°30N 103°3E 237 G4
Kaçkar Turkey 40°45N 41°10E 212 B9
Kada Chad 19°20N 19°39E 259 E3
Kadaingti Burma 17°37N 97°32E 241 G6
Kadaiyanallur India 9°3N 77°22E 245 K3
Kadam, Mt. Uganda 1°45N 34°45E 268 B3
Kadan Czech Rep. 50°23N 13°16E 180 A6
Kadan Kyun Burma 12°30N 98°20E 236 F2
Kadanai → Afghan. 31°22N 65°45E 242 D1
Kadarkút Hungary 46°13N 17°39E 182 D2
Kadavu Fiji 19°0S 178°15E 287 B2
Kadavu Passage Fiji 18°45S 178°0E 287 B2
Kade Ghana 6°7N 0°56W 263 D4
Kadei → C.A.R. 3°31N 16°3E 264 B3
Kademlija = Triglav Slovenia 46°21N 13°50E 199 B10
Kadena Japan 26°22N 127°45E 288 a
Kadhimain = Al Kāẓimīyah Iraq 33°22N 44°18E 213 F11
Kadi India 23°18N 72°23E 242 H5
Kadiak I. = Kodiak I. U.S.A. 57°30N 152°45W 303 H9
Kadiana Mali 10°45N 6°30W 262 C3
Kadıköy Turkey 40°59N 29°1E 122 C2
Kadina Australia 33°55S 137°43E 282 B2
Kadınhanı Turkey 38°14N 32°13E 212 C5
Kadiolo Mali 10°35N 7°41W 262 C3
Kadipur India 26°10N 82°23E 243 F10
Kadirabad India 19°51N 75°54E 244 E2
Kadiri India 14°12N 78°13E 245 G4
Kadirli Turkey 37°23N 36°5E 212 D7
Kadiyevka = Stakhanov Ukraine 48°35N 38°40E 189 H10
Kadja, O. → Chad 12°2N 22°28E 259 F4
Kadmat I. India 11°14N 72°47E 245 J1
Kadodo Sudan 11°4N 29°31E 257 E2
Kadoka U.S.A. 43°50N 101°31W 308 D3
Kadom Russia 54°37N 42°30E 190 C6
Kadoma Ōsaka, Japan 34°44N 135°35E 133 A2
Kadoma Zimbabwe 18°20S 29°52E 269 F2
Kâdugli Sudan 11°0N 29°45E 257 E2
Kaduna Nigeria 10°30N 7°21E 263 C6
Kaduna □ Nigeria 11°0N 7°30E 263 C6
Kaduna → Nigeria 8°45N 5°48E 263 D6
Kadur India 13°34N 76°1E 245 H3
Kaduy Russia 59°12N 37°9E 188 C9
Kaédi Mauritania 16°9N 13°28W 262 B2
Kaélé Cameroon 10°7N 14°27E 259 F2
Ka'ena U.S.A. 21°34N 158°14W 302 J13
Ka'ena Pt. U.S.A. 21°35N 158°17W 302 J13
Kaeng Khoi Thailand 14°35N 101°0E 236 E3
Kaeng Krachan △ Thailand 12°57N 99°23E 236 F2
Kaeng Tana △ Thailand 15°25N 105°32E 236 E5
Kaeo N.Z. 35°6S 173°49E 284 B2
Kaesŏng N. Korea 37°58N 126°35E 224 D3
Kaesŏng □ N. Korea 38°0N 126°37E 224 D3
Kāf Si. Arabia 31°25N 37°29E 246 D3
Kafakumba Dem. Rep. of the Congo 9°38S 23°46E 265 D4
Kafan = Kapan Armenia 39°18N 46°27E 213 C12
Kafanchan Nigeria 9°40N 8°20E 263 D6
Kafareti Nigeria 10°25N 11°12E 263 C7
Kaffrine Senegal 14°8N 15°36W 262 C1
Kafia Kingi Sudan 9°20N 24°25E 264 A4
Kafin Nigeria 9°30N 7°4E 263 D6
Kafin Madaki Nigeria 10°41N 9°46E 263 C6
Kafinda Zambia 12°32S 30°20E 269 E3
Kafr 'Aqab West Bank 31°52N 35°13E 123 A2
Kafr el Battikh Egypt 31°25N 31°44E 256 H7
Kafr el Dauwâr Egypt 31°8N 30°8E 256 H7
Kafr el Sheikh Egypt 31°15N 30°50E 251 G1
Kafr el Sheikh □ Egypt 31°15N 30°55E 251 G1
Kafr el Zaiyât Egypt 30°49N 30°48E 256 H7
Kafue Zambia 15°46S 28°9E 269 F2
Kafue → Zambia 15°12S 25°38E 269 F2
Kafue Flats Zambia 15°40S 27°25E 269 F2
Kafulwe Zambia 9°0S 29°1E 269 D2
Kafumba Dem. Rep. of the Congo 5°23S 18°55E 265 D3
Kaga Afghan. 34°14N 70°10E 242 B4
Kaga Japan 36°16N 136°15E 223 A8
Kaga Bandoro C.A.R. 7°0N 19°10E 264 A3
Kagamil I. U.S.A. 53°0N 169°43W 303 K5
Kaganovich = Tovarkovskiy Russia 53°40N 38°14E 188 F10
Kagarko Nigeria 9°28N 7°36E 263 D6
Kagawa □ Japan 34°15N 134°0E 222 C6
Kagera □ Tanzania 2°0S 31°30E 268 C3
Kagera → Uganda 0°57S 31°47E 268 C3
Kâğıthane Turkey 41°4N 28°56E 122 B1
Kâğıthane → Turkey 41°9N 28°56E 122 B1
Kağızman Turkey 40°5N 43°10E 213 B10
Kagmar Sudan 14°24N 30°25E 257 E3
Kagopal Chad 8°16N 16°23E 259 G3
Kagoro Nigeria 9°36N 8°23E 263 D6
Kagoshima Japan 31°35N 130°33E 222 F2
Kagoshima □ Japan 31°30N 130°30E 222 F2
Kagoshima-Wan Japan 31°25N 130°40E 222 F2
Kagran Austria 48°14N 16°26E 142 A2
Kagua Papua N. G. 6°26S 143°48E 286 D2
Kagul = Cahul Moldova 45°50N 28°15E 183 E13
Kahak Iran 36°6N 49°46E 247 B6
Kāhala U.S.A. 21°16N 157°47W 302 K14
Kahalu'u U.S.A. 21°27N 157°50W 302 K14
Kahama Tanzania 4°8S 32°30E 268 C3
Kahan Pakistan 29°18N 68°54E 242 E3
Kahana U.S.A. 21°34N 157°53W 302 J14
Kahana B. U.S.A. 21°35N 157°50W 302 J14
Kahana Valley State Park ⌂ U.S.A. 21°32N 157°53W 302 J14
Kahang Malaysia 2°12N 103°32E 237 L4
Kahayan → Indonesia 3°40S 114°0E 235 C4
Kahe Tanzania 3°30S 37°25E 268 C4
Kahemba Dem. Rep. of the Congo 7°18S 18°55E 265 D3
Kaherekoau Mts. N.Z. 45°45S 167°15E 285 F2
Kahil, Djebel bou Algeria 34°26N 4°0E 261 B5
Kahnawake Canada 45°24N 73°40W 130 B1
Kahnūj Iran 27°55N 57°40E 247 E8
Kahoka U.S.A. 40°25N 91°44W 310 D5
Kaho'olawe U.S.A. 20°33N 156°37W 302 C5
Kahouanne Guadeloupe 16°15N 61°12W 322 e
Kahouanne, Îlet à Guadeloupe 16°22N 61°46W 322 e
Kahramanmaraş Turkey 37°37N 36°53E 212 D7
Kahramanmaraş □ Turkey 37°35N 36°33E 212 D7
Kâhta Turkey 37°46N 38°36E 213 D8
Kahuku U.S.A. 21°41N 157°57W 302 J14
Kahuku Pt. U.S.A. 21°43N 157°59W 302 J14
Kahul, Ozero Ukraine 45°24N 28°24E 183 E13
Kahului U.S.A. 20°54N 156°28W 302 C5
Kahului ✈ (OGG) U.S.A. 20°54N 156°26W 302 C5
Kahurangi △ N.Z. 41°10S 172°32E 285 B7
Kahurangi Pt. N.Z. 40°50S 172°10E 285 A7
Kahuta Pakistan 33°35N 73°24E 242 C5
Kahuzi-Biega △ Dem. Rep. of the Congo 1°50S 27°55E 268 C2
Kai, Kepulauan Indonesia 5°55S 132°45E 231 F8
Kai Besar Indonesia 5°35S 133°0E 231 F8
Kai Is. = Kai, Kepulauan Indonesia 5°55S 132°45E 231 F8
Kai Kecil Indonesia 5°45S 132°40E 231 F8
Kai Xian China 31°11N 108°21E 228 B7
Kaiama Nigeria 9°36N 4°1E 263 D5
Kaiapit Papua N. G. 6°18S 146°18E 286 D4
Kaiapoi N.Z. 43°24S 172°40E 285 D7
Kaidu He → China 41°46N 86°31E 218 B3
Kaieteur Falls Guyana 5°1N 59°10W 329 B6
Kaifeng China 34°48N 114°21E 226 G8
Kaihua China 29°12N 118°20E 229 C12
Kaijiang China 31°7N 107°55E 228 B6
Kaikohe N.Z. 35°25S 173°49E 284 B2
Kaikoura N.Z. 42°25S 173°43E 285 C8
Kaikoura Pen. N.Z. 42°25S 173°43E 285 C8
Kailahun S. Leone 8°18N 10°39W 262 D2
Kailash = Kangrinboqe Feng China 31°0N 81°25E 243 D9
Kailashahar India 24°19N 92°0E 241 C4
Kaileuna I. Papua N. G. 8°32S 150°57E 286 E6
Kaili China 26°33N 107°59E 228 D6
Kailu China 43°38N 121°18E 227 C11
Kailua U.S.A. 21°24N 157°44W 302 K14
Kailua B. U.S.A. 21°25N 157°40W 302 K14
Kailua Kona U.S.A. 19°39N 155°59W 302 D6
Kaim → Papua N. G. 6°55S 141°33E 286 D1
Kaimaktsalan Oros = Voras Oros Greece 40°57N 21°45E 202 F5
Kaimana Indonesia 3°39S 133°45E 231 E8
Kaimanawa Mts. N.Z. 39°15S 175°56E 284 F4
Kaimata N.Z. 42°34S 171°28E 285 C6
Kaimes U.K. 55°54N 3°10W 121 B2
Kaimganj India 27°33N 79°24E 243 F8
Kaimon-Dake Japan 31°11N 130°32E 222 F2
Kaimur Hills India 24°30N 82°0E 243 G10
Kainab → Namibia 28°32S 19°34E 270 C2
Kainan Japan 34°9N 135°12E 223 C7
Kainantu Papua N. G. 6°18S 145°52E 286 D3
Kainji Dam Nigeria 9°55N 4°35E 263 D5
Kainji Lake △ Nigeria 10°5N 4°6E 263 C5
Kainji Res. Nigeria 10°1N 4°40E 263 C5
Kainsk = Samara Russia 53°8N 50°6E 190 D10
Kainuu Finland 64°30N 29°7E 160 D23
Kaipara Harbour N.Z. 36°25S 174°14E 284 C3
Kaiping China 22°23N 112°42E 229 F9
Kaipokok B. Canada 54°54N 59°47W 299 B8
Kaira India 22°45N 72°50E 242 H5
Kairana India 29°24N 77°15E 242 E7
Kairiru I. Papua N. G. 3°21S 143°34E 286 B2
Kaironi Indonesia 0°47S 133°40E 231 E8
Kairouan Tunisia 35°45N 10°5E 258 A2
Kairouan □ Tunisia 35°30N 9°46E 261 A6
Kairuku Papua N. G. 8°51S 146°35E 286 E4
Kaiser Wilhelm Kanal = Nord-Ostsee-Kanal Germany 54°12N 9°32E 178 A5
Kaiser Wilhelm Kirche Berlin, Germany 115 b2
Kaiser-Wilhelmsland = Papua □ Indonesia 4°0S 137°0E 231 E9
Kaiserebersdorf Austria 48°9N 16°26E 142 B2
Kaiserslautern Germany 49°26N 7°45E 179 F3
Kaiserstuhl Germany 48°4N 7°40E 179 G3
Kaita Japan 34°22N 132°32E 222 C4
Kaitaia N.Z. 35°8S 173°17E 284 B2
Kaitangata N.Z. 46°17S 169°51E 285 G4
Kaithal India 29°48N 76°26E 242 E7
Kaitu → Pakistan 33°10N 70°30E 242 C4
Kaivoksela Finland 60°15N 24°53E 121 B2
Kaiwi Channel U.S.A. 21°15N 157°30W 302 K14
Kaiyang China 27°4N 106°59E 228 D6
Kaiyuan Liaoning, China 42°28N 124°1E 224 A2
Kaiyuan Yunnan, China 23°40N 103°12E 228 F4
Kaiyuh Mts. U.S.A. 64°30N 158°0W 303 D8
Kajaani Finland 64°17N 27°46E 160 D22
Kajabbi Australia 20°0S 140°1E 280 C3
Kajaki Afghan. 32°18N 65°5E 240 B2
Kajana = Kajaani Finland 64°17N 27°46E 160 D22
Kajang Malaysia 2°59N 101°48E 237 L3
Kajaran Armenia 39°10N 46°7E 213 C12
Kajiado Kenya 1°53S 36°48E 268 C4
Kajo Kaji Sudan 3°58N 31°40E 257 G3
Kajok Sudan 8°19N 28°0E 257 F2
Kajuru Nigeria 10°15N 7°34E 263 C6
Kaka Sudan 10°38N 32°10E 257 E3
Kaka Turkmenistan 37°21N 59°36E 247 B8
Kakabeka Falls Canada 48°24N 89°37W 298 C2
Kakadu △ Australia 12°0S 132°3E 278 B5
Kakamas S. Africa 28°45S 20°33E 270 C3
Kakamega Kenya 0°20N 34°46E 268 B3
Kakamigahara Japan 35°28N 136°48E 223 B8
Kakana India 9°7N 92°48E 245 K11
Kakanj Bos.-H. 44°4N 18°4E 182 F3
Kakanui Mts. N.Z. 45°10S 170°30E 285 F5
Kakata Liberia 6°35N 10°20W 262 D2
Kakdwip India 21°53N 88°11E 243 J13
Kake Japan 34°36N 132°19E 222 C4
Kake Alaska, U.S.A. 56°59N 133°57W 296 B2
Kakegawa Japan 34°45N 138°1E 223 C10
Kakeroma-Jima Japan 28°8N 129°14E 221 K4
Kākhak Iran 34°9N 58°38E 247 C8
Kakhib Russia 42°28N 46°34E 191 J8
Kakhonak U.S.A. 59°26N 154°51W 303 G9
Kakhovka Ukraine 46°45N 33°30E 189 J7
Kakhovske Vdskh. Ukraine 47°5N 34°0E 189 J7
Kakinada India 16°57N 82°11E 244 F6
Kakisa Canada 60°56N 117°25W 296 A5
Kakisa → Canada 61°3N 118°10W 296 A5
Kakisa L. Canada 60°56N 117°43W 296 A5
Kakisalmi = Priozersk Russia 61°2N 30°7E 188 B6
Kakogawa Japan 34°46N 134°51E 222 C6
Kaktovik U.S.A. 70°8N 143°38W 303 A12
Kakum △ Ghana 5°24N 1°20W 263 D4
Kakuma Kenya 3°43N 34°52E 268 B3
Kakwa → Canada 54°37N 118°28W 296 C5
Kāl Gūsheh Iran 30°59N 58°12E 247 D8
Kal Sefid Iran 34°52N 47°23E 213 E12
Kala Nigeria 12°2N 14°40E 263 C7
Kala Oya → Sri Lanka 8°20N 79°45E 245 K4
Kalaa-Kebira Tunisia 35°59N 10°32E 258 A2
Kalaallit Nunaat = Greenland ⊠ N. Amer. 66°0N 45°0W 154 D6
Kalabagh Pakistan 33°0N 71°28E 242 C4
Kalabahi Indonesia 8°13S 124°31E 231 F6
Kalabak = Radomir Bulgaria 42°37N 22°59E 202 D6
Kalabakan Malaysia 4°25N 117°29E 235 B5
Kalabana Mali 14°10N 8°35W 262 C3
Kalabo Zambia 14°58S 22°40E 265 E4
Kalach Russia 50°22N 41°0E 190 E5
Kalach na Donu Russia 48°43N 43°32E 191 F6
Kalachinsk Russia 55°3N 74°33E 217 A8
Kaladan → Burma 20°20N 93°5E 241 E4
Kaladar Canada 44°37N 77°5W 312 B7
Kalae U.S.A. 18°55N 155°41W 302 E6
Kalahari Africa 24°0S 21°30E 270 B3
Kalahari Gemsbok △ S. Africa 25°30S 20°30E 270 C3
Kalaheo U.S.A. 21°56N 159°32W 302 B2
Kalaikhum Tajikistan 38°28N 70°46E 217 E8
Kalajoki Finland 64°12N 24°10E 160 D21
Kalakamati Botswana 20°40S 27°25E 271 B4
Kalakan Russia 55°15N 116°45E 215 D12
Kalakol Kenya 3°33N 35°54E 266 D4
K'alak'unlun Shank'ou = Karakoram Pass Asia 35°33N 77°50E 243 B7
Kalam Pakistan 35°34N 72°30E 243 B5
Kalama Dem. Rep. of the Congo 2°52S 28°35E 268 C2
Kalama Wash., U.S.A. 46°1N 122°51W 306 E4
Kalamaki Greece 37°52N 23°43E 112 B2
Kalamaloué △ Cameroon 12°9N 14°58E 259 F2
Kalamansig Phil. 6°33N 124°3E 233 H5
Kalamaria Greece 40°33N 22°55E 202 F6
Kalamata Greece 37°3N 22°10E 204 D4
Kalamazoo U.S.A. 42°17N 85°35W 311 B11
Kalamazoo → U.S.A. 42°40N 86°10W 311 B10
Kalamb India 18°3N 74°48E 244 E2
Kalambaka Greece 39°42N 21°39E 204 B3
Kalambo Falls Tanzania 8°37S 31°35E 269 D3
Kalamitsi Greece 38°45N 20°36E 207 B2
Kalamnuri India 19°40N 77°20E 244 E3
Kalamos Attiki, Greece 38°17N 23°52E 204 C5
Kalamos Lefkada, Greece 38°37N 20°55E 207 B2
Kalangadoo Australia 37°34S 140°41E 282 D4
Kalankalan Guinea 10°7N 8°54W 262 C3
Kalannie Australia 30°22S 117°5E 279 F2
Kalāntarī Iran 32°10N 54°8E 247 C7
Kalao Indonesia 7°21S 121°0E 231 F6
Kalaoa U.S.A. 19°43N 155°58W 302 D6
Kalaotoa Indonesia 7°20S 121°50E 231 F6
Kalapana U.S.A. 19°21N 154°59W 302 D7
Kälarne Sweden 62°59N 16°5E 162 B10
Kalasin Thailand 16°26N 103°30E 236 D4
Kālat Iran 25°29N 59°22E 247 E8
Kalat Pakistan 29°8N 66°31E 240 C2
Kalāteh Iran 36°33N 55°41E 247 B7
Kalāteh-ye Ganj Iran 27°31N 57°55E 247 E8
Kalathos Greece 36°9N 28°8E 206 E12
Kalatungan Mt. Phil. 7°54N 124°50E 233 H5
Kalaupapa U.S.A. 21°12N 156°59W 302 B5
Kalaupapa ⌂ U.S.A. 21°10N 156°59W 302 B5
Kalaus → Russia 45°40N 44°7E 191 H7
Kalavrita Greece 38°3N 22°8E 204 C4
Kalaw Burma 20°38N 96°34E 241 E6
Kalawao County U.S.A. 21°11N 156°58W 302 B5
Kalbā U.A.E. 25°5N 56°22E 247 E8
Kalbadevi Mumbai, India 130 b2
Kalbān Oman 20°18N 58°38E 249 B7
Kalbarri Australia 27°40S 114°10E 279 E1
Kalbarri △ Australia 27°51S 114°30E 279 E1
Kalburgi = Gulbarga India 17°20N 76°50E 244 F3
Kalce Slovenia 45°54N 14°13E 176 F8
Kaldrananes Iceland 65°45N 21°25W 155 B5
Kale Antalya, Turkey 36°14N 30°0E 205 E12
Kale Denizli, Turkey 37°27N 28°49E 205 D10
Kalecik Turkey 40°4N 33°26E 212 B5
Kalegauk Kyun Burma 15°33N 97°35E 236 E1
Kalehe Dem. Rep. of the Congo 2°6S 28°50E 268 C2
Kalema Tanzania 1°12S 31°55E 268 C3
Kalemie Dem. Rep. of the Congo 5°55S 29°9E 268 D2
Kalemyo Burma 23°11N 94°4E 241 D5
Kalety Poland 50°35N 18°52E 185 H5
Kalewa Burma 23°10N 94°15E 241 D5
Kaleybar Iran 38°47N 47°2E 213 C12
Kálfafell Iceland 63°57N 17°41W 155 D9
Kalgan = Zhangjiakou China 40°48N 114°55E 226 D8
Kalghatgi India 15°11N 74°58E 245 G2
Kalgoorlie-Boulder Australia 30°40S 121°22E 279 F3
Kalhovd Norway 60°4N 8°21E 164 D5
Kali → India 27°6N 79°55E 243 F8
Kali Sindh → India 25°32N 76°17E 242 G6
Kaliakra, Nos Bulgaria 43°21N 28°30E 203 C12
Kalianda Indonesia 5°50S 105°45E 234 D3
Kalibo Phil. 11°43N 122°22E 233 F4
Kaliganj Bangla. 22°25N 89°8E 241 D2
Kalihi U.S.A. 21°20N 157°53W 302 K14
Kalihi Valley U.S.A. 21°20N 157°52W 302 K14
Kalima Dem. Rep. of the Congo 2°33S 26°32E 268 C2
Kalimantan Indonesia 0°0 114°0E 235 C4
Kalimantan Barat □ Indonesia 0°0 110°30E 235 C4
Kalimantan Selatan □ Indonesia 2°30S 115°30E 235 C4
Kalimantan Tengah □ Indonesia 2°0S 113°30E 235 C4
Kalimantan Timur □ Indonesia 1°30N 116°30E 235 B5
Kálimnos Greece 37°0N 27°0E 205 D8
Kalimpong India 27°4N 88°35E 241 B2
Kalinadi → India 14°50N 74°7E 245 G2
Kalinga □ Phil. 17°30N 121°20E 232 C3
Kalinikinsk Russia 51°29N 44°28E 216 B2
Kalinin = Tver Russia 56°55N 35°55E 188 D8
Kaliningrad Russia 54°42N 20°32E 184 D7
Kaliningrad ✈ (KGD) Russia 54°45N 20°33E 184 D7
Kalininsk = Petrozavodsk Russia 61°41N 34°20E 188 B8
Kalininsk Russia 51°30N 44°40E 190 E7
Kalinkavichy Belarus 52°12N 29°20E 177 B15
Kalinkovichi = Kalinkavichy Belarus 52°12N 29°20E 177 B15
Kalinovik Bos.-H. 43°31N 18°25E 202 C2
Kalipetrovo Bulgaria 44°5N 27°14E 203 B11
Kalipur India 22°40N 88°17E 124 A1
Kalirachi Greece 40°40N 24°35E 203 F8
Kaliro Uganda 0°56N 33°30E 268 B3
Kalispell U.S.A. 48°12N 114°19W 304 B6
Kalisz Poland 51°45N 18°8E 185 G5
Kalisz Pomorski Poland 53°17N 15°55E 185 E2
Kalithea Greece 37°56N 23°43E 112 B2
Kaliua Tanzania 5°5S 31°48E 268 D3
Kaliveli Tank India 12°5N 79°50E 245 H4
Kalivia Thorikou Greece 37°50N 23°55E 204 D5
Kalix = Kalixälven → Sweden 65°50N 23°11E 160 D20
Kalix Sweden 65°53N 23°12E 160 D20
Kalixälven → Sweden 65°50N 23°11E 160 D20
Kalka India 30°46N 76°57E 242 D7
Kalkaji India 28°32N 77°12E 120 B2
Kalkali Ghat India 24°36N 92°20E 241 C4
Kalkan Turkey 36°15N 29°23E 205 E11
Kalkarindji Australia 17°30S 130°47E 278 C5
Kalkaska U.S.A. 44°44N 85°11W 309 C11
Kalkfeld Namibia 20°57S 16°14E 270 B2
Kalkfontein Botswana 22°4S 20°57E 270 B3
Kalkım Turkey 39°48N 27°13E 205 B9
Kalkrand Namibia 24°1S 17°35E 270 B2
Kallakkurichchi India 11°44N 79°1E 245 J4
Kallam India 18°36N 76°2E 244 E3
Källandsö Sweden 58°40N 13°5E 163 F7
Kallavesi Finland 62°58N 27°30E 160 E22
Källby Sweden 58°30N 13°8E 163 F7
Kållered Sweden 57°32N 12°4E 163 G6
Kallidaikurichi India 8°38N 77°31E 245 K3
Kallies = Kalisz Pomorski Poland 53°17N 15°55E 185 E2
Kallimasia Greece 38°18N 26°6E 205 C8
Kallinge Sweden 56°15N 15°18E 163 H9
Kallmet Albania 41°51N 19°41E 202 E3
Kallsjön Sweden 63°38N 13°0E 160 E15
Kalmalo Nigeria 13°40N 5°20E 263 C6
Kalmanstunga Iceland 64°44N 20°48W 155 C6
Kalmar Sweden 56°40N 16°20E 163 H10
Kalmar län □ Sweden 57°25N 16°0E 163 G10
Kalmar sund Sweden 56°40N 16°25E 163 H10
Kalmunai Sri Lanka 7°25N 81°49E 245 L5
Kalmykia □ Russia 46°5N 46°1E 191 G8
Kalna India 23°13N 88°25E 243 H13
Kalnai India 22°46N 83°30E 243 H10
Kalni → Bangla. 24°21N 91°13E 241 C3
Kalo Papua N. G. 10°1S 147°48E 286 F4
Kalo Nero Greece 37°20N 21°38E 204 D3
Kalocsa Hungary 46°32N 19°0E 182 D4
Kalofer Bulgaria 42°37N 24°59E 203 D8
Kalohi Channel U.S.A. 21°0N 157°0W 302 C5
Kalokhorio Cyprus 34°51N 33°2E 207 F9
Kaloko Dem. Rep. of the Congo 6°47S 25°48E 265 D5
Kaloko-Honokōhau ⌂ U.S.A. 19°40N 156°1W 302 D5
Kalol Gujarat, India 22°37N 73°31E 242 H5
Kalol Gujarat, India 23°15N 72°33E 242 H5
Kalolimnos Greece 37°4N 27°5E 205 D9
Kalomo Zambia 17°0S 26°30E 269 F2
Kalona U.S.A. 41°29N 91°43W 310 C5
Kaloni Greece 39°14N 26°12E 205 B8
Kaloni, Kolpos Greece 39°10N 26°10E 205 B8
Kalookan = Caloocan Phil. 14°39N 120°58E 127 B1
Kalpeni I. India 10°5N 73°38E 245 J1
Kalpi India 26°8N 79°47E 243 F8
Kalpitiya Sri Lanka 8°14N 79°46E 245 K4
Kalputhi I. India 10°49N 72°10E 245 J1
Kalrayan Hills India 11°45N 78°40E 245 J4
Kalsubai India 19°35N 73°45E 244 E1
Kaltag U.S.A. 64°20N 158°43W 303 D8
Kaltern = Caldaro Italy 46°25N 11°14E 199 B8
Kaltukatjara Australia 24°52S 129°5E 279 D4
Kaltungo Nigeria 9°48N 11°19E 263 D7
Kalu Pakistan 25°5N 67°39E 242 G2
Kaluga Russia 54°35N 36°10E 188 E9
Kaluga □ Russia 54°15N 34°50E 188 E8
Kalulong, Bukit Malaysia 3°14N 114°39E 235 B4
Kalulushi Zambia 12°50S 28°3E 269 E2
Kalumburu Australia 13°55S 126°35E 278 B4
Kalumburu ✪ Australia 14°17S 126°38E 278 B4
Kalundborg Denmark 55°41N 11°5E 163 J5
Kalush Ukraine 49°3N 24°23E 177 D13
Kałuszyn Poland 52°13N 21°52E 185 F8
Kalutara Sri Lanka 6°35N 80°0E 245 L5
Kalvåg Norway 61°46N 4°51E 164 C1
Kalvarija Lithuania 54°24N 23°14E 184 D10
Kalvebod Fælled Denmark 55°35N 12°33E 118 B3
Kalveboderne Denmark 55°37N 12°31E 118 B3
Kalwakurti India 16°41N 78°30E 244 F4
Kalya Russia 60°15N 59°59E 186 B10
Kalyan Maharashtra, India 20°30N 74°3E 244 D2
Kalyan Maharashtra, India 19°15N 73°9E 244 E1
Kalyandurg India 14°33N 77°6E 245 G3
Kalyani India 17°52N 76°57E 244 F3
Kalyansingapuram India 19°30N 83°19E 244 E6
Kalyazin Russia 57°15N 37°55E 188 D9
Kam Albania 42°17N 20°18E 202 D4
Kam → Nigeria 8°15N 11°0E 263 D7
Kama Burma 19°1N 95°4E 241 E5
Kama Dem. Rep. of the Congo 3°30S 27°5E 268 C2
Kama → Russia 55°45N 52°0E 186 C9
Kama Iwa Iwo Jima 24°47N 141°17E 288 b
Kamachumu Tanzania 1°37S 31°37E 268 C3
Kamae Japan 32°48N 131°56E 222 E3
Kamaing Burma 25°26N 96°35E 241 C6
Kamaishi Japan 39°16N 141°53E 220 E10
Kamakou U.S.A. 21°7N 156°52W 302 B5
Kamakura Japan 35°19N 139°33E 223 B11
Kamalapurum India 14°35N 78°39E 245 G4
Kamalété Gabon 0°43S 11°49E 264 C2
Kamalia Pakistan 30°44N 72°42E 242 D5
Kaman India 27°39N 77°16E 242 F6
Kaman Turkey 39°22N 33°44E 212 C5
Kamana Dem. Rep. of the Congo 5°59S 24°58E 265 D4
Kamananui → U.S.A. 21°38N 158°4W 302 J13
Kamanjab Namibia 19°35S 14°51E 270 A2
Kamapanda Zambia 12°5S 24°0E 269 E1
Kamara Mali 14°38N 9°23W 262 C3
Kamarān Yemen 15°21N 42°35E 248 D3
Kamareddi India 18°19N 78°21E 244 E4
Kamarhati India 22°40N 88°23E 124 A2
Kamata Japan 35°33N 139°43E 140 B3
Kamativi Zimbabwe 18°20S 27°6E 270 A4
Kamba Dem. Rep. of the Congo 4°0S 22°22E 265 C4
Kamba Nigeria 11°50N 3°45E 263 C5
Kambalda West Australia 31°10S 121°37E 279 F3
Kambam India 9°45N 77°16E 245 K3
Kambar Pakistan 27°37N 68°1E 242 F3
Kambarka Russia 56°15N 54°11E 186 C9
Kambia S. Leone 9°3N 12°53W 262 D2
Kambolé Togo 8°43N 1°39E 263 D5
Kambolé Zambia 8°47S 30°48E 269 D3
Kambos Cyprus 35°2N 32°44E 207 E8
Kambove Dem. Rep. of the Congo 10°51S 26°33E 269 E2
Kambuie Dem. Rep. of the Congo 6°59S 22°19E 265 D4
Kambwata Zambia 14°3S 23°43E 265 E4
Kamchatka, Poluostrov Russia 57°0N 160°0E 215 D17
Kamchatka Pen. = Kamchatka, Poluostrov Russia 57°0N 160°0E 215 D17
Kamchiya → Bulgaria 43°4N 27°44E 203 C11
Kame Ruins Zimbabwe 20°7S 28°25E 269 G2
Kameari Japan 35°45N 139°50E 140 A4
Kameido Japan 35°42N 139°50E 140 A4
Kamen Russia 53°50N 81°30E 217 B10
Kamen-Rybolov Russia 44°46N 132°2E 220 B6
Kamende Dem. Rep. of the Congo 6°26S 24°35E 265 D4
Kamenica Serbia 43°27N 22°27E 202 C6
Kamenica Serbia 44°25N 19°45E 202 B3
Kamenice nad Lipou Czech Rep. 49°18N 15°2E 180 B8
Kamenjak, Rt Croatia 44°47N 13°55E 199 D10
Kamenka = Kaminka Ukraine 49°3N 32°6E 189 H7
Kamenka Kazakhstan 51°7N 50°19E 190 E10
Kamenka Arkhangelsk, Russia 65°58N 44°0E 186 A7
Kamenka Penza, Russia 53°10N 44°5E 190 D6
Kamenka Voronezh, Russia 50°47N 39°20E 189 G10
Kamenka Bugskaya = Kamyanka-Buzka Ukraine 50°8N 24°16E 177 C13
Kamenka Dneprovskaya = Kamyanka-Dniprovska Ukraine 47°29N 34°28E 189 J8
Kamenka-Shevchenkovskaya = Kamyanka-Buzka Ukraine 50°8N 24°16E 177 C13
Kamennomostskiy Russia 44°18N 40°13E 191 H5
Kameno Bulgaria 42°34N 27°18E 203 D11
Kamenolomini Russia 47°40N 40°14E 191 G5
Kamensk-Shakhtinskiy Russia 48°23N 40°20E 191 F5
Kamensk Uralskiy Russia 56°25N 62°2E 214 D7
Kamenskaya = Kamensk-Shakhtinskiy Russia 48°23N 40°20E 191 F5
Kamenskiy Russia 50°48N 45°25E 190 E7
Kamenskoye = Dniprodzerzhynsk Ukraine 48°32N 34°37E 189 H8
Kamenskoye Russia 62°45N 165°30E 215 C17
Kamenyak Bulgaria 43°24N 26°57E 203 C10
Kamenz Germany 51°15N 14°5E 178 D10
Kameoka Japan 35°0N 135°35E 223 C7
Kamet India 30°55N 79°35E 243 D8
Kameyama Japan 34°51N 136°27E 223 C8
Kami-Itabashi Japan 35°45N 139°40E 140 A3
Kami-Jima Japan 32°27N 130°20E 222 E2
Kami-Koshiki-Jima Japan 31°50N 129°52E 222 F1
Kamiagata Japan 34°40N 129°24E 222 C1

Kamiah U.S.A. 46°14N 116°2W 304 C5
Kamień Krajeński Poland 53°32N 17°32E 184 E4
Kamień Pomorski Poland 53°57N 14°43E 184 E1
Kamienna → Poland 51°6N 21°47E 185 G8
Kamienna Góra Poland 50°47N 16°2E 185 H3
Kamieńsk Poland 51°12N 19°29E 185 G6
Kamieskroon S. Africa 30°9S 17°56E 270 D2
Kamikitazawa Japan 35°39N 139°36E 140 B2
Kamilukuak L. Canada 62°22N 101°40W 297 A8
Kamin-Kashyrskyy Ukraine 51°39N 24°56E 177 C13
Kamina Dem. Rep. of the Congo 8°45S 25°0E 265 D5
Kaminak L. Canada 62°10N 95°0W 297 A10
Kaministiquia Canada 48°32N 89°35W 298 C1
Kaminka Ukraine 49°3N 32°6E 189 H7
Kaminoyama Japan 38°9N 140°17E 220 E10
Kamioka Japan 36°25N 137°15E 223 A9
Kamiros Greece 36°20N 27°56E 206 E11
Kamishak Bay U.S.A. 59°15N 153°45W 303 G9
Kamitsuruma Japan 35°30N 139°26E 140 B1
Kamitsushima Japan 34°50N 129°28E 222 C1
Kamituga Dem. Rep. of the Congo 3°2S 28°10E 268 C2
Kamla → India 25°35N 86°36E 243 G12
Kamloops Canada 50°40N 120°20W 296 C4
Kamnik Slovenia 46°14N 14°37E 199 B11
Kamo Armenia 40°21N 45°7E 191 K7
Kamo Japan 37°39N 139°3E 220 F9
Kamo N.Z. 35°42S 174°20E 284 B3
Kamoa Mts. Guyana 1°30N 59°0W 329 C6
Kamogawa Japan 35°5N 140°5E 223 B12
Kamojima Japan 34°4N 134°21E 222 C6
Kamoke Pakistan 32°4N 74°4E 242 C6
Kamo'oloa U.S.A. 21°34N 158°7W 302 J13
Kamoshida Japan 35°33N 139°31E 140 B2
Kamp → Austria 48°23N 15°42E 180 C8
Kampala Uganda 0°20N 32°30E 268 B3
Kampar Malaysia 4°18N 101°9E 237 K3
Kampar → Indonesia 0°30N 103°8E 234 B2
Kampen Neths. 52°33N 5°53E 170 B5
Kamphaeng Phet Thailand 16°28N 99°30E 236 D2
Kampinoski △ Poland 52°21N 20°40E 185 F7
Kampolombo, L. Zambia 11°37S 29°42E 269 E2
Kampong Chhnang Cambodia 12°20N 104°35E 237 F5
Kampong Landang Singapore 1°20N 103°55E 138 A3
Kampong Pengerang Malaysia 1°22N 104°7E 237 d
Kampong Punggai Malaysia 1°27N 104°18E 237 d
Kampong Saom Cambodia 10°38N 103°30E 237 G4
Kampong Saom, Chaak Cambodia 10°50N 103°32E 237 G4
Kampong Tanjong Langsat Malaysia 1°28N 104°1E 237 d
Kampong Tanjong Penjuru Singapore 1°18N 103°45E 138 B2
Kampong Telok Ramunia Malaysia 1°22N 104°15E 237 d
Kampot Cambodia 10°36N 104°10E 237 G5
Kampsville U.S.A. 39°18N 90°37W 310 E6
Kampti Burkina Faso 10°7N 3°25W 262 C4
Kampuchea = Cambodia ■ Asia 12°15N 105°0E 236 F5
Kampung Air Putih Malaysia 4°15N 103°10E 237 K4
Kampung Bali Indonesia 6°11S 106°48E 122 B1
Kampung Jerangau Malaysia 4°50N 103°10E 237 K4
Kampung Raja Malaysia 5°45N 102°35E 237 K4
Kampungbaru = Tolitoli Indonesia 1°5N 120°50E 231 D6
Kamrau, Teluk Indonesia 3°30S 133°36E 231 E8
Kamsack Canada 51°34N 101°54W 297 C8
Kamsar Guinea 10°40N 14°36W 262 C2
Kamskoye Ustye Russia 55°10N 49°20E 190 C9
Kamskoye Vdkhr. Russia 58°41N 56°7E 186 C10
Kamsuuma Somali Rep. 0°15N 42°46E 267 D5
Kamthi India 21°9N 79°19E 244 D4
Kamuchawie L. Canada 56°18N 101°59W 297 B8
Kamuela U.S.A. 20°1N 155°41W 302 C6
Kamui-Misaki Japan 43°20N 140°21E 220 C10
Kamyanets-Podilskyy Ukraine 48°45N 26°40E 183 B11
Kamyanka-Buzka Ukraine 50°8N 24°16E 177 C13
Kamyanka-Dniprovska Ukraine 47°29N 34°28E 189 J8
Kamyanyets Belarus 52°23N 23°49E 185 F10
Kamyanyuki Belarus 52°32N 23°49E 185 F10
Kāmyārān Iran 34°47N 46°56E 213 E12
Kamyshin Russia 50°10N 45°24E 190 E7
Kamyzyak Russia 46°4N 48°10E 191 G9
Kan = Gan Jiang → China 29°15N 116°0E 229 C11
Kan Burma 22°25N 94°5E 241 D5
Kan Sudan 9°1N 31°47E 257 F3
Kanaaupscow → Canada 54°2N 76°30W 298 B4
Kanab U.S.A. 37°3N 112°32W 305 H7
Kanab Cr. → U.S.A. 36°24N 112°38W 305 H7
Kanacea Lau Group, Fiji 17°15S 179°6W 287 A3
Kanacea Taveuni, Fiji 16°59S 179°56E 287 A2
Kanaga I. U.S.A. 51°45N 177°22W 303 L3
Kanagawa □ Japan 35°20N 139°20E 223 B11
Kanagi Japan 40°54N 140°27E 220 D10
Kanairiktok → Canada 55°2N 60°18W 299 A7
Kanakanak U.S.A. 59°0N 158°32W 303 G8
Kanakapura India 12°33N 77°28E 245 H3
Kanalia Greece 39°30N 22°53E 204 B4
Kanamori Japan 35°31N 139°27E 140 B1
Kananga Dem. Rep. of the Congo 5°55S 22°18E 265 D4
Kanangra-Boyd △ Australia 33°57S 150°15E 283 B9
Kanash Russia 55°30N 47°32E 190 C8
Kanaskat U.S.A. 47°19N 121°54W 306 C5
Kanastraíon, Ákra = Paliouri, Akra Greece 39°57N 23°45E 202 G7
Kanawha → U.S.A. 38°50N 82°9W 309 F12
Kanazawa Japan 36°30N 136°38E 223 A8
Kanbalu Burma 23°12N 95°31E 241 D5
Kanchanaburi Thailand 14°2N 99°31E 236 E2
Kanchenjunga Nepal 27°50N 88°10E 243 F13
Kanchipuram India 12°52N 79°45E 245 H4
Kanchow = Ganzhou China 25°51N 114°56E 229 E10
Kańczuga Poland 49°59N 22°25E 185 J9
Kanda Tokyo, Japan 140 a5
Kanda Kanda Dem. Rep. of the Congo 6°52S 23°48E 265 D4
Kandagach = Qandyaghash Kazakhstan 49°28N 57°25E 187 E10
Kandaghat India 30°59N 77°7E 242 D7
Kandahār Kandahār, Afghan. 31°32N 65°43E 240 C2
Kandahar India 18°52N 77°12E 244 E3
Kandahār □ Afghan. 31°0N 65°0E 240 C2
Kandala Dem. Rep. of the Congo 6°20S 19°40E 265 D3
Kandalaksha Russia 67°9N 32°30E 160 C25
Kandalakshskiy Zaliv Russia 66°0N 35°0E 186 A6
Kandangan Indonesia 2°50S 115°20E 235 C5
Kandanghaur Indonesia 6°21S 108°6E 231 G13
Kandanos Greece 35°19N 23°44E 207 E4
Kandava Latvia 57°2N 22°46E 184 A9
Kandavu = Kadavu Fiji 19°0S 178°15E 287 B2
Kandavu Passage = Kadavu Passage Fiji 18°45S 178°0E 287 B2
Kandep Papua N. G. 5°54S 143°32E 286 C2
Kandhkot Pakistan 28°16N 69°8E 242 E3
Kandhla India 29°18N 77°19E 242 E7
Kandi Benin 11°7N 2°55E 263 C5
Kandi India 23°58N 88°5E 243 H13
Kandiaro Pakistan 27°4N 68°13E 242 F3
Kandila Arkadia, Greece 37°46N 22°22E 204 D4
Kandila Etoloakarnania, Greece 38°42N 20°56E 207 B2
Kandilli Turkey 41°4N 29°3E 122 B2
Kandıra Turkey 41°4N 30°9E 212 B4
Kandla India 23°0N 70°10E 242 H4
Kandor, O. → Chad 17°13N 20°52E 259 E4
Kandos Australia 32°45S 149°58E 283 B8
Kandreho Madag. 17°29S 46°6E 272 B2
Kandrian Papua N. G. 6°14S 149°37E 286 D5
Kandy Sri Lanka 7°18N 80°43E 245 L5
Kane U.S.A. 41°40N 78°49W 312 E6
Kane Basin Greenland 79°1N 70°0W 154 B4
Kaneilio Pt. U.S.A. 21°27N 158°12W 302 K13
Kanel Senegal 15°30N 13°18W 262 B2
Kanem □ Chad 15°0N 16°0E 259 F3
Käne'ohe U.S.A. 21°25N 157°48W 302 K14
Käne'ohe B. U.S.A. 21°30N 157°50W 302 K14
Kaneohe Marine Corps Air Station U.S.A. 21°27N 157°46W 302 K14
Kanevskaya Russia 46°3N 38°57E 191 G4
Kanfanar Croatia 45°7N 13°50E 199 C10
Kang Botswana 23°41S 22°50E 270 B3
Kang Krung △ Thailand 9°30N 98°50E 237 H2
Kangaamiut Greenland 65°50N 53°20W 154 D5
Kangaba Mali 11°56N 8°25W 262 C3
Kangal Turkey 39°14N 37°23E 212 C7
Kangān Fārs, Iran 27°50N 52°3E 247 E7
Kangān Hormozgān, Iran 25°48N 57°28E 247 E8
Kangar Malaysia 6°27N 100°12E 237 J3
Kangaré Mali 11°36N 8°4W 262 C3
Kangaroo I. Australia 35°45S 137°0E 282 C2
Kangaroo Mts. Australia 23°29S 141°51E 280 C3
Kangasala Finland 61°28N 24°4E 188 B3
Kangāvar Iran 34°40N 48°0E 213 E12
Kangding China 30°2N 101°57E 228 B3
Kangdong N. Korea 39°9N 126°5E 224 C3
Kangean, Kepulauan Indonesia 6°55S 115°23E 235 D5
Kangean Is. = Kangean, Kepulauan Indonesia 6°55S 115°23E 235 D5
Kangen → Sudan 6°47N 33°9E 257 F3
Kangerdlugssuak Greenland 68°10N 32°20W 154 D7
Kangerluarsoruseq Greenland 63°45N 51°27W 154 E5
Kangerluarsoruset = Kangerluarsoruseq Greenland 63°45N 51°27W 154 E5
Kangerlussuaq Greenland 66°59N 50°40W 154 D5
Kangertittivaq = Scoresby Sund Greenland 70°28N 21°46W 154 C8
Kanggye N. Korea 41°0N 126°35E 224 B3
Kanghsi Taiwan 23°34N 120°8E 225 C2
Kangikajik Greenland 70°7N 22°0W 154 C8
Kangilinnguit Greenland 61°20N 47°57W 154 E6
Kangiqliniq = Rankin Inlet Canada 62°30N 93°0W 294 E13
Kangiqsualujjuaq Canada 58°30N 65°59W 295 F18
Kangiqsujuaq Canada 61°30N 72°0W 295 E17
Kangiqtugaapik = Clyde River Canada 70°30N 68°30W 295 C18
Kangirsuk Canada 60°0N 70°0W 295 F18
Kangkar Chemaran Malaysia 1°34N 104°12E 237 d
Kangkar Sungai Tiram Malaysia 1°35N 103°55E 237 d
Kangkar Teberau Malaysia 1°32N 103°51E 237 d
Kango Gabon 0°11N 10°5E 264 B2
Kangoku Iwa Iwo Jima 24°48N 141°17E 288 b
Kangoya Dem. Rep. of the Congo 9°55S 22°48E 265 D4
Kangping China 42°43N 123°18E 227 C12
Kangpokpi India 25°8N 93°58E 241 C4
Kangra India 32°6N 76°16E 242 C7
Kangrinboqe Feng China 31°0N 81°25E 243 D9
Kangshan Taiwan 22°48N 120°17E 225 D2
Kangto China 27°50N 92°35E 241 B4
Kangtzu Taiwan 22°8N 120°52E 225 D2
Kangwon-do □ N. Korea 38°47N 127°35E 224 C3
Kangyidaung Burma 16°56N 94°54E 241 G5
Kanha △ India 22°15N 80°40E 243 H9
Kanhan → India 21°4N 79°34E 244 D4
Kanhangad India 12°21N 74°58E 245 H2
Kanhar → India 24°28N 83°8E 243 G10
Kanheri India 19°13N 72°50E 244 E1
Kani Sagaing, Burma 23°52N 95°22E 241 D5
Kani Sagaing, Burma 22°26N 94°51E 241 D5
Kani Ivory C. 8°29N 6°36W 262 D3
Kani-Keli Mayotte 12°57S 45°6E 272 b
Kaniama Dem. Rep. of the Congo 7°30S 24°12E 265 D4
Kaniapiskau = Caniapiscau → Canada 56°40N 69°30W 299 A6
Kaniapiskau, L. = Caniapiscau, L. Canada 54°10N 69°55W 299 B6
Kaniere, L. N.Z. 42°50S 171°10E 285 C6
Kanif Micronesia 9°31N 138°5E 287 R16
Kanigiri India 15°24N 79°31E 245 G4
Kanin, Poluostrov Russia 68°0N 45°0E 186 A8
Kanin Nos, Mys Russia 68°39N 43°32E 186 A7
Kanin Pen. = Kanin, Poluostrov Russia 68°0N 45°0E 186 A8
Kaninë Albania 40°23N 19°30E 202 F3
Kaniva Australia 36°22S 141°18E 282 D4
Kanjiža Serbia 46°3N 20°4E 182 D5
Kanjut Sar Pakistan 36°7N 75°25E 243 A6
Kankaanpää Finland 61°44N 22°50E 188 B2
Kankakee U.S.A. 41°7N 87°52W 311 C9
Kankakee → U.S.A. 41°23N 88°15W 311 C8
Kankan Guinea 10°23N 9°15W 262 C3
Kankendy = Xankändi Azerbaijan 39°52N 46°49E 213 C12
Kanker India 20°10N 81°40E 244 D5
Kankesanturai Sri Lanka 9°49N 80°2E 245 K5
Kankossa Mauritania 15°54N 11°31W 262 B2
Kankroli India 25°4N 73°53E 242 G5
Kankurgachi India 22°34N 88°23E 124 B2
Kanlıca Turkey 41°5N 29°3E 122 B2
Kanmuri-Yama Japan 34°30N 132°4E 222 C4
Kannabe Japan 34°32N 133°23E 222 C5
Kannapolis U.S.A. 35°30N 80°37W 315 D14
Kannauj India 27°3N 79°56E 243 F8
Kanniyakumari India 8°5N 77°34E 245 K3
Kannur = Cannanore India 11°53N 75°27E 245 J2
Kannyakumari India 8°3N 77°40E 245 K3
Kano Nigeria 12°2N 8°30E 263 C6
Kano □ Nigeria 11°30N 8°30E 263 C6
Kanonerskiy, Ostrov Russia 59°53N 30°13E 137 B1
Kan'onji Japan 34°7N 133°39E 222 C5
Kanoroba Ivory C. 9°7N 6°8W 262 D3
Kanowha U.S.A. 42°57N 93°47W 310 B3
Kanowit Malaysia 2°14N 112°20E 235 B4
Kanoya Japan 31°25N 130°50E 222 F2
Kanpetlet Burma 21°10N 93°59E 241 E4
Kanpur India 26°28N 80°20E 243 F9
Kansai Int. ✈ (KIX) Japan 34°27N 135°12E 133 B2
Kansas U.S.A. 39°33N 87°56W 311 E9
Kansas □ U.S.A. 38°30N 99°0W 308 F4
Kansas → U.S.A. 39°7N 94°37W 308 F6
Kansas City Kans., U.S.A. 39°7N 94°38W 310 E2
Kansas City Mo., U.S.A. 39°6N 94°35W 310 E2
Kansas City Int. ✈ (MCI) U.S.A. 39°18N 94°43W 310 E2
Kansenia Dem. Rep. of the Congo 10°20S 26°0E 269 E2
Kansk Russia 56°20N 95°37E 215 D10
Kansu = Gansu □ China 36°0N 104°0E 226 G3
Kantaphor India 22°35N 76°34E 242 H7
Kantchari Burkina Faso 12°37N 1°37E 263 C5
Kantché Niger 13°31N 8°30E 259 F1
Kanté Togo 9°57N 1°3E 263 D5
Kantemirovka Russia 49°43N 39°55E 189 H10
Kanth = Kąty Wrocławskie Poland 51°2N 16°45E 185 G3
Kantharalak Thailand 14°39N 104°39E 236 E5
Kanthi = Contai India 21°54N 87°46E 243 J12
Kantishna U.S.A. 63°31N 150°57W 303 E10
Kantishna → U.S.A. 64°45N 149°58W 303 D10
Kantli → India 28°20N 75°30E 242 E6
Kantō □ Japan 36°15N 139°30E 223 A11
Kantō-Sanchi Japan 35°59N 138°50E 223 B10
Kantu-long Burma 19°57N 97°36E 241 F6
Kanturk Ireland 52°11N 8°54W 166 D3
Kanuma Japan 36°34N 139°42E 223 A11
Kanus Namibia 27°50S 18°39E 270 C2
Kanuti Nat. Wildlife Refuge ⌓ U.S.A. 66°25N 151°50W 303 C10
Kanye Botswana 24°55S 25°28E 270 B4
Kanzaki → Japan 34°41N 135°24E 133 A1
Kanzenze Dem. Rep. of the Congo 10°30S 25°12E 265 E5
Kanzi, Ras Tanzania 7°1S 39°33E 268 D4
Kanzoni, Chissioua Comoros Is. 12°23S 43°40E 272 a
Kao Tonga 19°40S 175°1W 287 P13
Kao Phara Thailand 8°3N 98°22E 237 a
Kaohsiung Taiwan 22°35N 120°16E 225 D2
Kaohsung □ Taiwan 23°0N 120°35E 225 D2
Kaoka Solomon Is. 9°42S 160°43E 287 M11
Kaokaona = Kirakira Solomon Is. 10°27S 161°56E 287 N11
Kaokoveld Namibia 19°15S 14°30E 270 A1
Kaolack Senegal 14°5N 16°8W 262 C1
Kaolack □ Senegal 14°0N 15°15W 262 C1
Kaolan = Lanzhou China 36°1N 103°52E 226 F2
Kaolo Solomon Is. 8°24S 159°38E 287 M10
Kaoma Zambia 14°47S 24°48E 265 E4
Kaoshan China 44°38N 124°50E 227 B13
Kaoshu Taiwan 22°49N 120°36E 225 D2
Kaouar Niger 19°5N 12°52E 259 E2
Kaoyao = Zhaoqing China 23°0N 112°20E 229 F9
Kapa'a U.S.A. 22°5N 159°19W 302 A2
Kapadvanj India 23°5N 73°0E 242 H5
Kapagere Papua N. G. 9°46S 147°42E 286 E4
Kapahulu U.S.A. 21°16N 157°49W 302 K14
Kapaklı Turkey 41°19N 27°59E 203 E11
Kapali Carsi Turkey 41°1N 28°58E 122 B1
Kapalua U.S.A. 20°59N 156°39W 302 C5
Kapan Armenia 39°18N 46°27E 213 C12
Kapanga Bandundu, Dem. Rep. of the Congo 5°4S 16°58E 265 D3
Kapanga Katanga, Dem. Rep. of the Congo 8°30S 22°40E 265 D4
Kapapa I. U.S.A. 21°29N 157°48W 302 K14
Kapatagan Phil. 7°52N 123°44E 233 H4
Kapchagai = Qapshaghay Kazakhstan 43°51N 77°14E 217 D9
Kapchagaiskoye Vdkhr. = Qapshaghay Bögeni Kazakhstan 43°45N 77°50E 217 D9
Kapedo Kenya 1°10N 36°6E 268 B4
Kapela = Velika Kapela Croatia 45°10N 15°5E 199 C12
Kapellerfeld Austria 48°18N 16°29E 142 A2
Kapelo, Akra Greece 36°9N 23°3E 204 E5
Kapema Dem. Rep. of the Congo 10°45S 28°22E 269 E2
Kapenguria Kenya 1°14N 35°7E 268 B4
Kapfenberg Austria 47°26N 15°18E 180 D8
Kapı Dağı Turkey 40°28N 27°50E 203 F11
Kapia Dem. Rep. of the Congo 4°17S 19°46E 265 C3
Kapiri Mposhi Zambia 13°59S 28°43E 269 E2
Kāpīsā □ Afghan. 35°0N 69°20E 240 B3
Kapiskau → Canada 52°47N 81°55W 298 B3
Kapit Malaysia 2°0N 112°55E 235 B4
Kapiti I. N.Z. 40°50S 174°56E 284 G3
Kapka, Massif du Chad 15°7N 21°45E 259 E4
Kaplan U.S.A. 30°0N 92°17W 314 F8
Kaplice Czech Rep. 48°42N 14°30E 180 C7
Kapoe Thailand 9°34N 98°32E 237 H2
Kapoeta Sudan 4°50N 33°35E 257 G3
Kapoho U.S.A. 19°30N 154°50W 302 D7
Kapolei U.S.A. 21°19N 158°5W 302 K13
Kápolnásnyék Hungary 47°16N 18°41E 182 C3
Kapombo Dem. Rep. of the Congo 10°40S 23°30E 265 E4
Kaponga N.Z. 39°29S 174°9E 284 F3
Kapos → Hungary 46°44N 18°30E 182 D3
Kaposvár Hungary 46°25N 17°47E 182 D2
Káposztásmegyer Hungary 47°35N 19°6E 117 A2
Kapotnya Russia 55°39N 37°48E 129 C4
Kapowsin U.S.A. 46°59N 122°13W 306 D4
Kapp Norway 60°43N 10°52E 164 D7
Käppala Sweden 59°21N 18°13E 139 A3
Kappeln Germany 54°40N 9°55E 178 A5
Kappelshamn Sweden 57°52N 18°47E 163 G12
Kapps Namibia 22°32S 17°18E 270 B2
Kaprije Croatia 43°42N 15°43E 199 E12
Kapsabet Kenya 0°12N 35°6E 268 B4
Kapsan N. Korea 41°4N 128°19E 224 B4
Kapsukas = Marijampolė Lithuania 54°33N 23°19E 184 D10
Kaptai Bangla. 22°21N 92°17E 241 D4
Kaptai L. Bangla. 22°40N 92°20E 241 D4
Kapuas Indonesia 3°10S 114°5E 235 C4
Kapuas → Indonesia 0°25S 109°20E 235 C3
Kapuas Hulu, Pegunungan Malaysia 1°30N 113°30E 235 B4
Kapuas Hulu Ra. = Kapuas Hulu, Pegunungan Malaysia 1°30N 113°30E 235 B4
Kapuk Indonesia 6°7S 106°44E 122 A1
Kapulo Dem. Rep. of the Congo 8°18S 29°15E 269 D2
Kapunda Australia 34°20S 138°56E 282 C3
Kapuni N.Z. 39°29S 174°8E 284 F3
Kapurthala India 31°23N 75°25E 242 D6
Kapuskasing Canada 49°25N 82°30W 298 C3
Kapuskasing → Canada 49°49N 82°0W 298 C3
Kapustin Yar Russia 48°37N 45°40E 191 F7
Kaputar, Mt. Australia 30°15S 150°10E 281 E5
Kaputir Kenya 2°5N 35°28E 268 B4
Kapuvár Hungary 47°36N 17°1E 182 C2
Käpylä Finland 60°13N 24°57E 121 B2
Kara Russia 69°10N 65°0E 214 C7
Karā, W. → Si. Arabia 20°45N 41°42E 256 C5
Kara Ada Turkey 36°58N 27°28E 205 E9
Kara-Balta Kyrgyzstan 42°50N 73°49E 217 D8
Kara Bogaz Gol, Zaliv = Garabogazköl Aylagy Turkmenistan 41°0N 53°30E 187 F9
Kara Burun Turkey 36°32N 27°58E 205 E9
Kara-Kala = Garrygala Turkmenistan 38°31N 56°29E 247 B8
Kara Kalpak Republic = Qoraqalpoghistan □ Uzbekistan 43°0N 58°0E 216 D5
Kara-Köl Kyrgyzstan 41°40N 72°43E 217 D8
Kara Kum = Garagum Turkmenistan 39°30N 60°0E 247 B8
Kara-Saki Japan 34°41N 129°30E 222 C1
Kara Sea Russia 75°0N 70°0E 214 B8
Karaadilli Turkey 38°18N 30°37E 205 C12
Karabiğa Turkey 40°23N 27°17E 203 F11
Karabük Turkey 41°12N 32°37E 212 B5
Karabük □ Turkey 41°10N 32°30E 212 B5
Karaburun Albania 40°25N 19°20E 202 F3
Karaburun Turkey 38°41N 26°28E 205 C8
Karabutak = Qarabutaq Kazakhstan 49°59N 60°14E 216 C6
Karacabey Turkey 40°12N 28°21E 203 F12
Karacakılavuz Turkey 41°8N 27°21E 203 E11
Karacaköy Turkey 41°24N 28°22E 203 E12
Karaçal Tepesi Turkey 36°21N 32°38E 250 B3
Karacasu Turkey 37°43N 28°35E 205 D10
Karachala = Qaraçala Azerbaijan 39°45N 48°53E 191 L9
Karachayevsk Russia 43°50N 41°55E 191 J5
Karachev Russia 53°10N 35°5E 189 F8
Karachey-Cherkessia □ Russia 43°40N 41°30E 191 J5
Karachi Pakistan 24°50N 67°0E 123 A2
Karachi Int. ✈ (KHI) Pakistan 24°53N 67°9E 123 A2
Karad India 17°15N 74°10E 244 F2
Karadirek Turkey 38°34N 30°11E 205 C12
Karaga Ghana 9°58N 0°28W 263 D4
Karaganda = Qaraghandy Kazakhstan 49°50N 73°10E 217 C8
Karagayly = Qaraghayly Kazakhstan 49°26N 76°0E 214 E8
Karaginskiy, Ostrov Russia 58°45N 164°0E 215 D17
Karagiye, Vpadina Kazakhstan 43°27N 51°45E 187 F9
Karagiye Depression = Karagiye, Vpadina Kazakhstan 43°27N 51°45E 187 F9
Karagola Road India 25°29N 87°23E 243 G12
Karagüney Dağları Turkey 40°30N 34°40E 212 B6
Karahallı Turkey 38°21N 29°33E 205 C11
Kárahnjúkar Iceland 64°57N 15°46W 155 C11
Karaikal India 10°59N 79°50E 245 J4
Karaikkudi India 10°5N 78°45E 245 J4
Karaisali Turkey 37°16N 35°2E 212 D6
Karaiskakis Greece 38°35N 21°4E 207 B3
Karaitivu I. Sri Lanka 9°45N 79°52E 245 K4
Karaj Iran 35°48N 51°0E 247 C6
Karajarri ☼ Australia 19°0S 122°30E 278 C3
Karak Malaysia 3°25N 102°2E 237 L4
Karakalpakstan = Qoraqalpoghistan □ Uzbekistan 43°0N 58°0E 216 D5
Karakaya Barajı Turkey 38°31N 38°23E 213 C8
Karakelong Indonesia 4°35N 126°50E 231 D7
Karakitang Indonesia 3°14N 125°28E 231 D7
Karaklis = Vanadzor Armenia 40°48N 44°30E 191 K7
Karakoçan Turkey 38°57N 40°2E 213 C9
Karakol Kyrgyzstan 42°30N 78°20E 217 D9
Karakoram Pass Asia 35°33N 77°50E 243 B7
Karakoram Ra. Pakistan 35°30N 77°0E 243 B7
Karakul = Qarakol Uzbekistan 39°32N 63°50E 216 E6
Karakul Tajikistan 39°2N 73°33E 217 E8
Karakul, Ozero Tajikistan 39°5N 73°25E 217 E8
Karakurt Turkey 40°10N 42°37E 213 B10
Karakuwisa Namibia 18°56S 19°40E 270 A2
Karal Chad 12°50N 14°46E 259 F2
Karalon Russia 57°5N 115°50E 215 D12
Karama Jordan 31°57N 35°35E 251 G6
Karaman Balıkesir, Turkey 39°39N 28°0E 205 B9
Karaman Konya, Turkey 37°14N 33°13E 212 D5
Karaman □ Turkey 37°5N 33°15E 250 A4
Karamanlı Turkey 37°23N 29°47E 205 D11
Karamay China 45°30N 84°58E 217 C10
Karambu Indonesia 3°53S 116°6E 235 C5
Karamea N.Z. 41°14S 172°6E 285 B7
Karamea → N.Z. 41°13S 172°26E 285 B7
Karamea Bight N.Z. 41°22S 171°40E 285 B6
Karamnasa → India 25°31N 83°52E 243 G10
Karamürsel Turkey 40°41N 29°36E 203 F13
Karān Si. Arabia 27°43N 49°49E 247 E6
Karand Iran 34°16N 46°15E 213 E12
Karangana Mali 12°15N 5°4W 262 C3
Karanganyar Indonesia 7°38S 109°37E 235 D3
Karangasem Indonesia 8°27S 115°37E 231 J18
Karanja Maharashtra, India 21°11N 78°24E 244 D4
Karanja Maharashtra, India 20°29N 77°31E 244 D3
Karanjia India 21°47N 85°58E 243 J11
Karankasso Burkina Faso 10°50N 3°53W 262 C4
Karaova Turkey 37°5N 27°40E 205 D9
Karapınar Turkey 37°41N 33°30E 212 D5
Karapiro N.Z. 37°53S 175°32E 284 D4
Karasburg Namibia 28°0S 18°44E 270 C2
Karasino Russia 66°50N 86°50E 214 C9
Karasjok Norway 69°27N 25°30E 160 B21
Karasu Turkey 41°4N 30°46E 212 B4
Karasu → Antalya, Turkey 36°18N 30°10E 205 E12
Karasu → Hatay, Turkey 36°20N 36°20E 250 B7
Karasubazar = Bilohirsk Ukraine 45°3N 34°35E 189 K8
Karasuk Russia 53°44N 78°2E 217 B9
Karasuyama Japan 36°39N 140°9E 223 A12
Karataş Adana, Turkey 36°36N 35°21E 250 B6
Karataş Manisa, Turkey 38°35N 28°16E 205 C10
Karataş Burnu Turkey 36°31N 35°24E 250 B6
Karatau, Khrebet = Qarataū Kazakhstan 43°30N 69°30E 217 D7
Karatax Shan China 35°57N 81°0E 217 E10
Karateki Shan China 40°40N 77°50E 217 D9
Karativu Sri Lanka 8°22N 79°47E 245 K4
Karatoprak Turkey 37°2N 27°15E 205 D9
Karatoya → India 24°7N 89°36E 241 C2
Karatsu Japan 33°26N 129°58E 222 D1
Karaul Russia 70°6N 82°15E 214 B9
Karauli India 26°30N 77°4E 242 F7
Karavastasë, L. e Albania 40°55N 19°30E 202 F3
Karavia Greece 36°49N 23°37E 204 E5
Karavostasi Cyprus 35°8N 32°50E 207 E8
Karawa Dem. Rep. of the Congo 3°18N 20°17E 264 B4
Karawang Indonesia 6°30S 107°15E 235 D3
Karawanken Europe 46°30N 14°40E 180 E7
Karayazı Turkey 39°41N 42°9E 213 C10
Karazhal = Qarazhal Kazakhstan 48°2N 70°49E 214 E8
Karbalā' Iraq 32°36N 44°3E 213 F11
Karbalā' □ Iraq 32°30N 43°50E 213 F10
Kårböle Sweden 61°59N 15°22E 162 C9
Karcag Hungary 47°19N 20°57E 182 C5
Karcha → Pakistan 34°45N 76°10E 243 B7
Karchana India 25°17N 81°56E 243 G9
Karczew Poland 52°5N 21°15E 185 F8
Kardakata Greece 38°17N 20°28E 207 C1
Kardam Bulgaria 43°45N 28°6E 203 C12
Kardamila Greece 38°35N 26°5E 205 C8
Kardamili Greece 36°53N 22°13E 204 E4
Kardeljovo = Ploče Croatia 43°4N 17°26E 199 E14
Karditsa Greece 39°23N 21°54E 204 B3
Karditsa □ Greece 39°15N 21°50E 204 B3
Kärdla Estonia 59°0N 22°45E 188 C2
Kareeberge S. Africa 30°59S 21°50E 270 D3
Kareha → India 25°44N 86°21E 243 G12
Kareima Sudan 18°30N 31°49E 256 D3
Karelia □ Russia 65°30N 32°30E 160 D25
Karelian Republic = Karelia □ Russia 65°30N 32°30E 160 D25
Karelo-Finnish S.S.R. = Karelia □ Russia 65°30N 32°30E 160 D25
Karema Papua N. G. 9°12S 147°18E 286 E4
Karen = Kayin □ Burma 18°0N 97°30E 241 G6
Karenni = Kayah □ Burma 19°15N 97°15E 241 F6
Karera India 25°32N 78°9E 242 G8
Kārevāndar Iran 27°53N 60°44E 247 E9
Kargasok Russia 59°3N 80°53E 214 D9
Kargat Russia 55°10N 80°15E 214 D9
Kargi Eastern, Kenya 2°31N 37°34E 268 B4
Kargı Turkey 41°11N 34°30E 212 B6
Kargil India 34°32N 76°12E 243 B7
Kargopol Russia 61°30N 38°58E 188 B10
Kargowa Poland 52°5N 15°51E 185 F2
Karguéri Niger 13°27N 10°30E 259 F2
Karhal India 27°1N 78°57E 243 F8
Karia Greece 38°45N 20°39E 207 B2
Karia ba Mohammed Morocco 34°22N 5°12W 260 B3
Karīān Iran 26°57N 57°14E 247 E8
Karianga Madag. 22°25S 47°22E 272 C2
Kariba Zimbabwe 16°28S 28°50E 269 F2
Kariba, L. Zimbabwe 16°40S 28°25E 269 F2
Kariba Dam Zimbabwe 16°30S 28°35E 269 F2
Kariba Gorge Zambia 16°30S 28°50E 269 F2
Karibib Namibia 22°0S 15°56E 270 B2
Karies Greece 40°14N 24°19E 203 F8
Karijini △ Australia 23°8S 118°15E 278 D2
Karikari, C. N.Z. 34°46S 173°24E 284 A2
Karimata, Kepulauan Indonesia 1°25S 109°0E 235 C3
Karimata, Selat Indonesia 2°0S 108°40E 235 C3
Karimata Is. = Karimata, Kepulauan Indonesia 1°25S 109°0E 235 C3
Karimganj India 24°52N 92°20E 241 C4
Karimnagar India 18°26N 79°10E 244 E4
Karimun Kecil, Pulau Indonesia 1°8N 103°22E 237 d
Karimunjawa, Kepulauan Indonesia 5°50S 110°30E 235 D4
Karin Bari, Somali Rep. 10°59N 49°13E 267 B6
Karin Woqooyi Galbeed, Somali Rep. 10°50N 45°52E 267 B6
Karistos Greece 38°1N 24°29E 204 C6
Karīt Iran 33°29N 56°55E 247 C8
Kariya Japan 34°58N 137°1E 223 C9
Kariyangwe Zimbabwe 18°0S 27°38E 271 A4
Karjala Finland 62°0N 30°25E 188 A5
Karjat India 18°33N 75°0E 244 E2
Karkal India 13°15N 74°56E 245 H2
Karkar Papua N. G. 4°32S 145°57E 286 C3
Karkar I. Papua N. G. 4°40S 146°0E 286 C4
Karkaralinsk = Qarqaraly Kazakhstan 49°26N 75°30E 217 C9
Karkh Iraq 33°20N 44°22E 113 A2
Karkheh → Iran 31°2N 47°29E 246 D5
Karkinitska Zatoka Ukraine 45°56N 33°0E 189 K7
Karkinitskiy Zaliv = Karkinitska Zatoka Ukraine 45°56N 33°0E 189 K7
Karkuk = Kirkūk Iraq 35°30N 44°21E 213 E11
Karkur Tohl Egypt 22°5N 25°5E 256 C2
Karl Liebknecht Russia 51°40N 35°35E 189 G8
Karl-Marx-Stadt = Chemnitz Germany 50°51N 12°54E 178 E8
Karla, L. = Volvi, L. Greece 40°40N 23°34E 202 F7
Karlantijpa North ☼ Australia 19°27S 133°33E 278 C5
Karlantijpa South ☼ Australia 20°31S 133°9E 278 D5
Karleby = Kokkola Finland 63°50N 23°8E 160 E20
Karlholmsbruk Sweden 60°31N 17°37E 162 D11
Karlin Czech Rep. 50°5N 14°26E 135 B2
Karlino Poland 54°3N 15°53E 184 D2
Karlıova Turkey 39°17N 41°0E 213 C9
Karlivka Ukraine 49°29N 35°8E 189 H8
Karlobag Croatia 44°32N 15°5E 199 D12
Karlovac Croatia 45°31N 15°36E 199 C12
Karlovarský □ Czech Rep. 50°10N 12°50E 180 A5
Karlovasi Greece 37°45N 26°42E 205 D8
Karlovka = Karlivka Ukraine 49°29N 35°8E 189 H8
Karlovo Bulgaria 42°38N 24°47E 203 D8
Karlovo náměstí Prague, Czech Rep. 135 c1
Karlovy Vary Czech Rep. 50°13N 12°51E 180 A5
Karlowitz = Sremski Karlovci Serbia 45°12N 19°56E 182 E4
Karlowitz = Velké Karlovice Czech Rep. 49°20N 18°17E 181 B11
Karlsbad = Karlovy Vary Czech Rep. 50°13N 12°51E 180 A5
Karlsborg Sweden 58°33N 14°33E 163 F8
Karlsburg = Alba-Iulia Romania 46°8N 23°39E 183 D8
Karlsena, Mys Russia 77°0N 67°42E 214 B7
Karlsfeld Germany 48°13N 11°28E 131 A1
Karlshamn Sweden 56°10N 14°51E 163 H8
Karlshorst Germany 52°29N 13°31E 115 B4
Karlshus Norway 59°21N 10°52E 164 E7
Karlskoga Sweden 59°28N 14°33E 162 E8
Karlskrona Sweden 56°10N 15°35E 163 H9
Karlsplatz Munich, Germany 131 b1
Karlsruhe Germany 49°0N 8°23E 179 F4
Karlstad = Karlovac Croatia 45°31N 15°36E 199 C12
Karlstad Sweden 59°23N 13°30E 162 E7
Karlstad Minn., U.S.A. 48°35N 96°31W 308 A5
Karlstadt Germany 49°57N 9°47E 179 F5
Karluk U.S.A. 57°34N 154°28W 303 H9
Karlův most Prague, Czech Rep. 135 b1
Karma Niger 13°38N 1°52E 263 C5
Karmala India 18°25N 75°12E 244 E2
Karmėlava Lithuania 54°58N 24°4E 184 D11
Karmi'el Israel 32°55N 35°18E 250 F6
Karmøy Norway 59°15N 5°15E 164 E2
Karnak Egypt 25°43N 32°39E 256 B3
Karnal India 29°42N 77°2E 242 E7
Karnali → Nepal 28°45N 81°16E 243 E9
Karnaphuli Res. = Kaptai L. Bangla. 22°40N 92°20E 241 D4
Karnaprayag India 30°16N 79°15E 243 D8
Karnataka □ India 13°15N 77°0E 245 H3
Karnes City U.S.A. 28°53N 97°54W 314 G6
Karnische Alpen Europe 46°36N 13°0E 180 E6
Karnobat Bulgaria 42°39N 26°59E 203 D10
Kärnten □ Austria 46°52N 13°30E 180 E6
Karntner Strasse Vienna, Austria 142 b2
Karo Mali 12°16N 3°18W 262 C4
Karoi Zimbabwe 16°48S 29°45E 269 F2
Karol Bagh India 28°39N 77°11E 120 B2
Karolinenhof Germany 52°23N 13°38E 115 B4
Karomatan Phil. 7°55N 123°44E 233 H4
Karon, Ao Thailand 7°51N 98°17E 237 a
Karonga Malawi 9°57S 33°55E 269 D3
Karoo △ S. Africa 32°18S 22°27E 270 D3
Karoonda Australia 35°1S 139°59E 282 C3
Karor Pakistan 31°15N 70°59E 242 D4
Karora Sudan 17°44N 38°15E 256 D4
Karori N.Z. 41°17S 174°44E 143 B1
Karounga Mali 15°20N 7°35W 262 B3
Karousades Greece 39°47N 19°45E 206 B9
Karow Germany 52°36N 13°29E 115 A3
Karpacz Poland 50°46N 15°46E 185 H2
Karpasia Cyprus 35°32N 34°15E 207 E10
Karpathos Greece 35°37N 27°10E 205 F9
Karpathos, Stenon Greece 36°0N 27°30E 205 F9
Karpatsky △ Ukraine 48°20N 24°35E 183 B9
Karpenisi Greece 38°55N 21°40E 204 C3
Karpilovka = Aktsyabrski Belarus 52°38N 28°53E 177 B15
Karpinsk Russia 59°45N 60°1E 186 C11
Karpogory Russia 64°0N 44°27E 186 B7
Karpuz Burnu = Apostolos Andreas, C. Cyprus 35°42N 34°35E 207 E10
Karpuzlu Turkey 37°33N 27°51E 205 D9
Karrādah Iraq 33°17N 44°23E 113 B2
Karratha Australia 20°44S 116°52E 278 D2
Kars Turkey 40°40N 43°5E 213 B10
Kars □ Turkey 40°40N 43°0E 213 B10
Karsakpay Kazakhstan 47°55N 66°40E 217 C7
Karsha Kazakhstan 49°45N 51°35E 190 F10
Karshi = Qarshi Uzbekistan 38°53N 65°48E 217 E7
Karsiyang India 26°56N 88°18E 241 B2
Karsog India 31°23N 77°12E 242 D7
Kärsön Sweden 59°19N 17°54E 139 B1
Karst = Kras Croatia 45°35N 14°0E 199 C10
Kartal Turkey 40°53N 29°11E 203 F13
Kartal Dağları Turkey 37°4N 36°55E 250 A7
Kartala Comoros Is. 11°45S 43°21E 272 a
Kartaly Russia 53°3N 60°40E 216 B6
Kartapur India 31°27N 75°32E 242 D6
Karthaus U.S.A. 41°8N 78°9W 312 E6
Kartuzy Poland 54°22N 18°10E 184 D5
Karuah Australia 32°37S 151°56E 283 B9
Karufa Indonesia 3°50S 133°20E 231 E8
Karuma ⌓ Uganda 2°5N 32°15E 268 B3
Karumba Australia 17°31S 140°50E 280 B3
Karumo Tanzania 2°25S 32°50E 268 C3
Karumwa Tanzania 3°12S 32°38E 268 C3
Kārūn → Iran 30°26N 48°10E 247 D6
Karungu Kenya 0°50S 34°10E 268 C3
Karup Denmark 56°19N 9°10E 163 H3
Karur India 10°59N 78°2E 245 J4
Karviná Czech Rep. 49°53N 18°31E 181 B11
Karwan → India 27°26N 78°4E 242 F8
Karwar India 14°55N 74°13E 245 G2
Karwendel ⌓ Austria 47°25N 11°30E 180 D4
Karwi India 25°12N 80°57E 243 G9
Karymskoye Russia 51°36N 114°21E 215 D12
Kas Sudan 12°30N 24°17E 259 F4
Kaş Turkey 36°11N 29°37E 205 E11
Kasaan U.S.A. 55°32N 132°24W 303 J14
Kasaba Turkey 36°18N 29°44E 205 E11
Kasabi Zambia 14°52S 23°45E 265 E4
Kasache Malawi 13°25S 34°20E 269 E3
Kasai Hyōgo, Japan 34°55N 134°52E 222 C6
Kasai Tōkyō, Japan 35°39N 139°52E 140 B4
Kasai → Dem. Rep. of the Congo 3°30S 16°10E 265 C3
Kasai-Occidental □ Dem. Rep. of the Congo 6°0S 22°0E 265 D4
Kasai-Oriental □ Dem. Rep. of the Congo 5°0S 24°30E 265 D4
Kasaji Dem. Rep. of the Congo 10°25S 23°27E 265 E4
Kasama Japan 36°23N 140°16E 223 A12
Kasama Zambia 10°16S 31°9E 269 E3
Kasan N. Korea 41°18N 126°55E 224 B3
Kasandra Greece 40°0N 23°30E 202 F7
Kasandra Kolpos Greece 40°5N 23°30E 202 F7
Kasandras, Akra Greece 39°57N 23°30E 202 G7
Kasane Namibia 17°34S 24°50E 270 A3
Kasanga Tanzania 8°30S 31°10E 269 D3
Kasangaie Dem. Rep. of the Congo 6°20S 22°42E 265 D4
Kasangulu Dem. Rep. of the Congo 4°33S 15°15E 265 C3
Kasanka △ Zambia 11°34S 30°15E 269 E3
Kasaoka Japan 34°30N 133°30E 222 C5
Kasar, Ras Sudan 18°2N 38°36E 256 D4
Kasaragod India 12°30N 74°58E 245 H2
Kasat Burma 15°56N 98°13E 241 G7
Kasba Bangla. 23°45N 91°2E 241 D3
Kasba L. Canada 60°20N 102°10W 297 A8
Kasba Tadla Morocco 32°36N 6°17W 260 B3
Kaschau = Košice Slovak Rep. 48°42N 21°15E 181 C14
Kaseda Japan 31°25N 130°19E 222 F2
Kāseh Garān Iran 34°5N 46°2E 246 C5
Kasempa Zambia 13°30S 25°44E 269 E2
Kasenga Dem. Rep. of the Congo 10°20S 28°45E 269 E2
Kasese Uganda 0°13N 30°3E 268 B3
Kasewa Zambia 14°28S 28°53E 269 E2
Kasganj India 27°48N 78°42E 243 F8
Kashabowie Canada 48°40N 90°26W 298 C1
Kashaf Iran 35°58N 61°7E 247 C9
Kāshān Iran 34°5N 51°30E 247 C6
Kashechewan Canada 52°18N 81°37W 298 B3
Kashgān → Iran 33°5N 47°31E 213 F12
Kashgar = Kashi China 39°30N 76°2E 217 E9
Kashi China 39°30N 76°2E 217 E9
Kashihara Japan 34°27N 135°46E 223 C7
Kashiji Plain Zambia 13°12S 22°20E 265 E4
Kashima Ibaraki, Japan 35°58N 140°38E 223 B12
Kashima Saga, Japan 33°7N 130°6E 222 D2
Kashima-Nada Japan 36°0N 140°45E 223 B12
Kashimbo Dem. Rep. of the Congo 11°12S 26°19E 269 E2
Kashin Russia 57°20N 37°36E 188 D9
Kashing = Jiaxing China 30°49N 120°45E 229 B13
Kashipur Orissa, India 19°16N 83°3E 244 E6
Kashipur Uttarakhand, India 29°15N 79°0E 243 E8
Kashira Russia 54°45N 38°10E 188 E10
Kashiwa Japan 35°52N 139°59E 223 B11
Kashiwabara = Severo-Kurilsk Russia 50°40N 156°8E 215 D16
Kashiwazaki Japan 37°22N 138°33E 221 F9
Kashk-e Kohneh Afghan. 34°55N 62°30E 240 B1
Kashksaray Iran 38°27N 45°34E 213 C11

Kashkū'īyeh *Iran* 30°31N 55°40E 247 D7
Kāshmar *Iran* 35°16N 58°26E 247 C8
Kashmir *Asia* 34°0N 76°0E 243 C7
Kashmor *Pakistan* 28°28N 69°32E 242 E3
Kashpirovka *Russia* 53°0N 48°30E 190 D9
Kashun Noerh = Gaxun Nur
 China 42°22N 100°30E 218 B3
Kasiari *India* 22°8N 87°14E 243 H12
Kasilof *U.S.A.* 60°23N 151°18W 303 F10
Kasimov *Russia* 54°55N 41°20E 190 C5
Kasinge
 Dem. Rep. of the Congo 6°15S 26°58E 268 C2
Kasipur *India* 22°37N 88°22E 124 B2
Kasiruta *Indonesia* 0°25S 127°12E 231 E7
Kaskaskia ↠ *U.S.A.* 37°58N 89°57W 310 G7
Kaskattama ↠ *Canada* 57°3N 90°4W 297 B8
Kaskinen *Finland* 62°22N 21°15E 160 E19
Kaskö = Kaskinen
 Finland 62°22N 21°15E 160 E19
Kaslo *Canada* 49°55N 116°55W 296 D5
Kasmere L. *Canada* 59°34N 101°10W 297 B8
Kasongan *Indonesia* 2°0S 113°23E 235 C4
Kasongo
 Dem. Rep. of the Congo 4°30S 26°33E 268 C2
Kasongo Lunda
 Dem. Rep. of the Congo 6°35S 16°49E 265 D3
Kasos *Greece* 35°20N 26°55E 205 F8
Kasos, Stenon *Greece* 35°30N 26°30E 205 F8
Kaspi *Georgia* 41°59N 44°26E 191 K7
Kaspichan *Bulgaria* 43°18N 27°11E 203 C11
Kaspiysk *Russia* 42°52N 47°40E 191 J8
Kaspiyskiy *Russia* 45°22N 47°23E 191 H8
Kassab *Syria* 35°55N 35°59E 250 C6
Kassab ed Doleib *Sudan* 13°30N 33°35E 257 E3
Kassaba *Egypt* 22°40N 29°55E 256 C2
Kassalâ *Sudan* 15°30N 36°0E 257 D4
Kassalâ □ *Sudan* 15°20N 36°26E 257 D4
Kassandrino *Greece* 40°1N 23°27E 202 F7
Kassel *Germany* 51°18N 9°26E 178 D5
Kasserine *Tunisia* 35°10N 8°50E 258 A1
Kasserine □ *Tunisia* 35°15N 9°0E 258 A1
Kassinger *Sudan* 18°46N 31°51E 256 D3
Kassiopi *Greece* 39°48N 19°53E 206 B9
Kasson *U.S.A.* 44°2N 92°45W 308 C7
Kastamonu *Turkey* 41°25N 33°43E 212 B5
Kastamonu □ *Turkey* 41°20N 34°0E 212 B5
Kastav *Croatia* 45°22N 14°20E 199 C11
Kasteli *Greece* 35°29N 23°38E 207 E4
Kastellet *Copenhagen, Denmark* 11a3d
Kastélli *Greece* 35°12N 25°20E 207 E6
Kastellórizon = Megísti
 Greece 36°8N 29°34E 205 E11
Kastelo, Ákra *Greece* 35°30N 27°15E 205 F9
Kasterlee *Belgium* 51°15N 4°59E 170 C4
Kastlösa *Sweden* 56°26N 16°25E 163 H10
Kastoria *Greece* 40°30N 21°19E 202 F5
Kastoria □ *Greece* 40°30N 21°15E 202 F5
Kastorias, L. *Greece* 40°30N 21°15E 202 F5
Kastório *Greece* 37°10N 22°17E 204 D4
Kastornoye *Russia* 51°55N 38°2E 189 G10
Kastos *Greece* 38°35N 20°55E 202 H3
Kastrosikia *Greece* 39°6N 20°38E 207 A2
Kastrup *Denmark* 55°38N 12°19E 118 B3
Kastrup, Kobenhavn ✈ (CPH)
 Denmark 55°37N 12°39E 118 B3
Kastsyukovichy *Belarus* 53°20N 32°4E 188 F7
Kasuga *Fukuoka, Japan* 33°32N 130°26E 222 D2
Kasuga *Hyōgo, Japan* 35°9N 135°9E 223 B8
Kasugai *Japan* 35°12N 136°59E 223 B8
Kasugai *Japan* 35°45N 139°49E 140 A3
Kasukabe *Japan* 35°58N 139°45E 223 B11
Kasumi *Japan* 35°38N 134°38E 222 B6
Kasumiga-Ura *Japan* 36°0N 140°25E 223 B12
Kasumigaseki *Tokyo, Japan* 1d b4
Kasumkent *Russia* 41°47N 48°15E 191 K9
Kasungu *Malawi* 13°0S 33°29E 269 E3
Kasungu △ *Malawi* 12°53S 33°9E 269 E3
Kasur *Pakistan* 31°5N 74°25E 242 D6
Kata, Ao *Thailand* 7°48N 98°18E 237 J2
Kata Archanes *Greece* 35°15N 25°10E 207 E6
Kata Tjuta *Australia* 25°20S 130°50E 279 E5
Kataba *Zambia* 16°5S 25°10E 269 F2
Katagum *Nigeria* 12°18N 10°21E 263 C7
Katahdin, Mt. *U.S.A.* 45°54N 68°56W 309 C19
Kataka = Cuttack *India* 20°25N 85°57E 244 D7
Katako Kombe
 Dem. Rep. of the Congo 3°25S 24°20E 264 C4
Katakolo *Greece* 37°38N 21°19E 204 D3
Katale *Tanzania* 4°52S 31°7E 268 C3
Katalla *U.S.A.* 60°12N 144°31W 303 F11
Katamatite *Australia* 36°6S 145°41E 283 D6
Katanda *Katanga,*
 Dem. Rep. of the Congo 7°52S 24°13E 265 D4
Katanda *Nord-Kivu,*
 Dem. Rep. of the Congo 0°55S 29°21E 268 C2
Katanga □
 Dem. Rep. of the Congo 8°0S 25°0E 268 D2
Katangi *India* 21°56N 79°50E 244 C4
Katanning *Australia* 33°40S 117°33E 279 F2
Katapakishi
 Dem. Rep. of the Congo 8°15S 22°49E 265 D4
Katastari *Greece* 37°50N 20°45E 207 D2
Katavi △ *Tanzania* 6°51S 31°3E 268 D3
Katavi Swamp *Tanzania* 6°51S 31°7E 268 D3
Katchall *India* 7°57N 93°22E 245 L11
Katchiungo *Angola* 12°35S 16°13E 265 E3
Katerini *Greece* 40°18N 22°37E 202 F6
Katghora *India* 22°30N 82°33E 243 H10
Katha *Burma* 24°10N 96°30E 241 C6
Kathapa ↠ *Burma* 22°20N 94°30E 241 D5
Katherine *Australia* 28°30N 33°57E 251 K4
Katherine *Australia* 14°27S 132°20E 278 B5
Katherine Gorge = Nitmiluk △
 Australia 14°6S 132°15E 278 B5
Kathi *India* 21°47N 74°3E 242 J6
Kathiawar *India* 22°20N 71°0E 242 H4
Kathikas *Cyprus* 34°55N 32°25E 207 F8
Kathleen *U.S.A.* 28°7N 82°2W 317 C2
Kathmandu *Nepal* 27°45N 85°20E 243 F11
Kathua *India* 32°23N 75°34E 242 C6
Kati *Mali* 12°41N 8°4W 262 C3
Katihar *India* 25°34N 87°36E 243 G12
Katikati *N.Z.* 37°32S 175°57E 284 D4
Katima Mulilo *Namibia* 17°28S 24°13E 270 A3
Katimbira *Malawi* 12°40S 34°0E 269 E3
Katingan = Mendawai ↠
 Indonesia 3°30S 113°0E 235 C4
Katiola *Ivory C.* 8°10N 5°10E 262 D3
Katipunan *Phil.* 8°31N 123°17E 233 G6
Katiti □ *Australia* 25°1S 131°11E 279 E5
Katla *Iceland* 63°36N 19°7W 155 D7
Katlabukh, Ozero
 Ukraine 45°28N 29°0E 183 E14
Katlanovo *Macedonia* 41°52N 21°40E 202 E5
Katmai △ *U.S.A.* 58°20N 155°0W 303 G9
Katmandu = Kathmandu
 Nepal 27°45N 85°20E 243 F11
Katni = Murwara *India* 23°46N 80°28E 243 H9
Katni *India* 23°51N 80°24E 243 H9
Kato Achaia *Greece* 38°8N 21°33E 204 C3
Kato Chorio *Greece* 35°3N 25°47E 207 E6
Kato Korakiana *Greece* 39°42N 19°47E 207 A3
Káto Pyrgos *Cyprus* 35°11N 32°41E 207 D8
Katochi *Greece* 38°26N 21°1E 204 C3
Katol *India* 21°17N 78°38E 244 D4

Katompe
 Dem. Rep. of the Congo 6°2S 26°23E 265 C5
Katong *Singapore* 1°18N 103°53E 138 B3
Katonga ↠ *Uganda* 0°34N 31°50E 268 B3
Katoomba *Australia* 33°41S 150°19E 283 B9
Katouna *Greece* 38°47N 21°7E 204 C3
Katowice *Poland* 50°17N 19°5E 185 H6
Katrancı Dağı *Turkey* 37°27N 30°25E 205 D12
Katrine, L. *U.K.* 56°15N 4°30W 167 E4
Katrineholm *Sweden* 59°9N 16°12E 162 E10
Katsepe *Madag.* 15°45S 46°15E 272 B2
Katsina *Nigeria* 13°0N 7°32E 263 C6
Katsina □ *Nigeria* 12°30N 7°30E 263 C6
Katsina Ala *Nigeria* 7°10N 9°20E 263 D6
Katsina Ala ↠ *Nigeria* 7°10N 9°20E 263 D6
Katsumoto *Japan* 33°51N 129°42E 222 C1
Katsushika *Japan* 35°44N 139°51E 140 A4
Katsuura *Japan* 36°35N 140°31E 223 B12
Katsuura *Fukui, Japan* 35°10N 140°0E 223 B12
Katsuyama *Japan* 36°3N 136°30E 223 A8
Katsuyama *Okayama,*
 Japan 35°5N 133°41E 222 B5
Kattaqūrghon *Uzbekistan* 39°55N 66°15E 217 F7
Kattavia *Greece* 35°57N 27°46E 206 F11
Kattegat *Denmark* 56°40N 11°0E 163 H5
Katthammarsvik
 Sweden 57°26N 18°51E 163 G12
Kattowitz = Katowice
 Poland 50°17N 19°5E 185 H6
Katul, J. *Sudan* 14°12N 29°25E 257 E2
Katumba
 Dem. Rep. of the Congo 7°40S 25°17E 265 D5
Katun ↠ *Russia* 52°25N 85°1E 217 B11
Katwa *India* 23°30N 88°5E 243 H13
Katwijk *Neths.* 52°12N 4°24E 170 B4
Katy Wrocławskie *Poland* 51°2N 16°45E 185 G3
Ka'ū Desert *U.S.A.* 19°21N 155°19W 302 D6
Kau Pai Chau *China* 22°12N 114°15E 122 B2
Kau Yi Chau *China* 22°17N 114°4E 122 B1
Kaua'i *U.S.A.* 22°3N 159°30W 302 A2
Kauai Channel *U.S.A.* 21°45N 158°50W 302 B3
Kauai Island Lihue Municipal ✈
 (LIH) *U.S.A.* 21°58N 159°20W 302 B2
Kaub *Germany* 50°5N 7°46E 179 E3
Kaudom △ *Namibia* 18°45S 20°51E 270 B3
Kauehi *French Polynesia* 15°49S 145°10W 289 f
Kaufbeuren *Germany* 47°53N 10°37E 179 H6
Kaufman *U.S.A.* 32°35N 96°19W 314 E6
Kauhajoki *Finland* 62°25N 22°10E 160 E20
Kauhava *Finland* 63°6N 23°5E 160 E20
Kaukauna *U.S.A.* 44°17N 88°17W 308 C9
Kaukauveld *Namibia* 20°0S 20°15E 270 B3
Kaukonahua ↠ *U.S.A.* 21°35S 158°7W 302 J13
Ka'ula I. *U.S.A.* 21°40N 160°30W 302 B1
Kaulakahi Channel
 U.S.A. 22°0N 159°55W 302 B2
Kaulsdorf *Germany* 52°29N 13°34E 115 B4
Kaunā Pt. *U.S.A.* 19°2N 155°53W 302 D6
Kaunakakai *U.S.A.* 21°6N 157°1W 302 B4
Kaunas *Lithuania* 54°54N 23°54E 184 D10
Kaunas ✈ (KUN)
 Lithuania 54°57N 24°3E 184 D11
Kaunchi = Yangiyul
 Uzbekistan 41°0N 69°3E 217 D7
Kaunia *Bangla.* 25°46N 89°26E 243 G13
Kauniainen *Finland* 60°13N 24°44E 121 B1
Kaunos *Turkey* 36°49N 28°39E 205 D6
Kaupangur *Iceland* 65°38N 18°2W 155 B8
Kaura Namoda *Nigeria* 12°37N 6°33E 263 C6
Kauru *Nigeria* 10°33N 8°12E 263 C6
Kautokeino *Norway* 69°0N 23°4E 160 B20
Kauwapur *India* 27°31N 82°18E 243 F10
Kavacha *Russia* 60°16N 169°51E 215 C17
Kavadarci *Macedonia* 41°26N 22°3E 202 E6
Kavajë *Albania* 41°11N 19°33E 202 E3
Kavak *Turkey* 41°4N 36°3E 212 B7
Kavak Dağı *Turkey* 37°10N 28°2E 205 D6
Kavaklı *Turkey* 41°39N 27°10E 203 E11
Kavaklıdere *Turkey* 37°27N 28°21E 205 D10
Kavala = Topolovgrad
 Bulgaria 42°5N 26°20E 203 D10
Kavala *Greece* 40°57N 24°28E 203 F8
Kavála □ *Greece* 41°5N 24°30E 203 F8
Kavala Kolpos *Greece* 40°50N 24°25E 203 F8
Kavalerovo *Russia* 44°15N 135°4E 220 B7
Kavali *India* 14°55N 80°1E 245 G5
Kavār *Iran* 29°11N 52°44E 247 D7
Kavaratti *India* 10°34N 72°37E 245 J11
Kavaratti I. *India* 10°33N 72°38E 245 J11
Kavarna *Bulgaria* 43°26N 28°22E 203 C12
Kavaya
 Dem. Rep. of the Congo 8°52S 22°19E 265 D4
Kavi *India* 22°12N 72°38E 242 H15
Kavieng *Papua N. G.* 2°36S 150°51E 286 B6
Kavimba *Botswana* 18°2S 24°38E 270 A3
Kavīr, Dasht-e *Iran* 34°30N 55°0E 247 C7
Kavīr △ *Iran* 34°40N 52°0E 247 C7
Kavirondo G. = Winam G.
 Kenya 0°20S 34°15E 268 C3
Kavkaz *Russia* 45°20N 36°40E 189 K9
Kävlinge *Sweden* 55°47N 13°9E 163 J7
Kavos *Greece* 39°23N 20°3E 206 C10
Kavousi *Greece* 35°7N 25°51E 207 E6
Kavungo *Angola* 11°31S 23°3E 265 E4
Kaw *Fr. Guiana* 4°30N 52°15W 329 C7
Kawa *Sudan* 13°42N 32°34E 257 E3
Kawachi-Nagano *Japan* 34°28N 135°31E 223 C7
Kawagama L. *Canada* 45°18N 78°45W 312 A6
Kawagoe *Japan* 35°55N 139°29E 223 B11
Kawaguchi *Japan* 35°52N 139°45E 223 B11
Kawaihae *U.S.A.* 20°3N 155°50W 302 D6
Kawaihoa Pt. *U.S.A.* 21°47N 160°12W 302 B1
Kawaikini *U.S.A.* 22°5N 159°29W 302 A2
Kawailoa *Australia* 21°36N 158°3W 302 J13
Kawailoa Beach *U.S.A.* 21°37N 158°5W 302 J13
Kawakawa *N.Z.* 35°23S 174°6E 284 B5
Kawambwa *Zambia* 9°48S 29°3E 268 D2
Kawana *Zambia* 13°5S 25°58E 265 E5
Kawanabe *Japan* 31°23N 130°24E 222 F2
Kawanoe *Japan* 34°1N 133°34E 222 C5
Kawardha *India* 22°0N 81°17E 243 J9
Kawasaki *Japan* 35°31N 139°43E 140 B3
Kawasi *Indonesia* 1°38S 127°28E 231 E7
Kawau I. *N.Z.* 36°25S 174°52E 284 D4
Kawawachikamach
 Canada 54°48N 66°50W 298 B6
Kawczyn *Poland* 51°56N 21°5E 142 B2
Kaweka Ra. *N.Z.* 39°17S 176°19E 284 F6
Kawela *U.S.A.* 21°42N 158°1W 302 J13
Kawerau *N.Z.* 38°7S 176°42E 284 F6
Kawhia *N.Z.* 38°4S 174°49E 284 F5
Kawhia Harbour *N.Z.* 38°5S 174°51E 284 F5
Kawio, Kepulauan
 Indonesia 4°30N 125°30E 231 D7
Kawlin *Burma* 16°33N 95°41E 241 D5
Kawnro *Burma* 22°37N 99°33E 241 C6
Kawthaung *Burma* 10°5N 98°36E 237 H2
Kawthoolei = Kayin □
 Burma 18°0N 97°30E 241 G6
Kawthule = Kayin □
 Burma 18°0N 97°30E 241 G6
Kawya *Burma* 24°5N 96°54E 241 C5
Kaxgar He ↠ *China* 39°45N 78°24E 217 C2
Kaxholmen *Sweden* 57°51N 14°19E 163 G8
Kaya *Burkina Faso* 13°4N 1°10W 263 C4

Kayah □ *Burma* 19°15N 97°15E 241 F6
Kayak I. *U.S.A.* 59°56N 144°23W 303 G11
Kayalıköy Baraji *Turkey* 41°50N 27°55E 203 E11
Kayan *Burma* 16°54N 96°34E 241 D6
Kayan ↠ *Indonesia* 2°55N 117°35E 235 B5
Kayan Mentarang △
 Indonesia 2°55N 115°0E 235 B5
Kayankulam *India* 9°10N 76°33E 245 K3
Kaycee *U.S.A.* 43°43N 106°38W 304 C10
Kayeli *Indonesia* 3°20S 127°10E 231 E7
Kayenda
 Dem. Rep. of the Congo 10°48S 23°6E 265 E4
Kayenta *U.S.A.* 36°44N 110°15W 305 H8
Kayes *Congo* 4°25S 11°41E 265 C2
Kayes *Mali* 14°25N 11°30W 262 C2
Kayes □ *Mali* 14°0N 11°0W 262 C2
Kayi *Turkey* 39°12N 30°46E 205 B12
Kayima *S. Leone* 8°54N 11°15N 262 D2
Kayin □ *Burma* 18°0N 97°30E 241 G6
Kaymakçı *Turkey* 38°28N 27°54E 205 C10
Kayoa *Indonesia* 0°1N 127°28E 231 D7
Kayomba *Zambia* 13°11S 24°2E 269 E1
Kayomba *Zambia* 13°3S 23°51E 265 E4
Kaysatskoye *Russia* 49°47N 46°49E 190 F8
Kayseri *Turkey* 38°45N 35°30E 212 C6
Kayseri □ *Turkey* 38°40N 36°0E 212 C7
Kaysville *U.S.A.* 41°2N 111°56W 304 F8
Kayts *Sri Lanka* 9°42N 79°51E 245 K4
Kayu Putih *Indonesia* 6°10S 106°53E 122 B2
Kayuagong *Indonesia* 3°24S 104°50E 234 C2
Kaz Dağ *Turkey* 39°42N 26°50E 205 B8
Kazachye *Russia* 70°52N 135°58E 215 B14
Kazak *Russia* 55°50N 49°10E 190 C9
Kazan *Russia* 55°50N 49°10E 190 C9
Kazan ↠ *Canada* 64°2N 95°29W 297 A9
Kazan-Rettō *Pac. Oc.* 25°0N 141°0E 288 E6
Kazanci *Turkey* 36°29N 32°51E 250 B3
Kazancı *Turkey* 36°49N 34°43E 250 B5
Kazanlŭk *Bulgaria* 42°38N 25°20E 203 D9
Kazanskaya *Russia* 49°50N 41°10E 190 F5
Kazatin = Kozyatyn
 Ukraine 49°45N 28°50E 177 D15
Kazaure *Nigeria* 12°42N 8°28E 263 C6
Kazbek *Russia* 42°42N 44°30E 191 J7
Kāzerūn *Iran* 29°38N 51°40E 247 D6
Kazi Magomed = Qazmämmäd
 Azerbaijan 40°3N 49°0E 191 K9
Kazimierz Dolny *Poland* 51°19N 21°57E 185 G8
Kazimierza Wielka
 Poland 50°15N 20°30E 185 H7
Kazincbarcika *Hungary* 48°17N 20°36E 182 D5
Kazipet *India* 17°58N 79°30E 244 F4
Kaziranga △ *India* 26°30N 93°30E 241 B4
Kaziza
 Dem. Rep. of the Congo 10°42S 23°52E 265 E4
Kazlŭ Rūda *Lithuania* 54°46N 23°30E 184 D10
Kazo *Japan* 36°7N 139°36E 223 A11
Kazteliovka *Kazakhstan* 48°47N 48°43E 190 F9
Kazu *Burma* 25°27N 97°46E 241 C6
Kazuma Pan △ *Zimbabwe* 18°20S 25°48E 269 F2
Kazumba
 Dem. Rep. of the Congo 6°25S 22°5E 265 D4
Kazungula *Zambia* 17°54S 25°25E 269 F2
Kazuno *Japan* 40°10N 140°45E 220 D10
Kazym ↠ *Russia* 63°54N 65°50E 214 C7
Kbely *Czech Rep.* 50°8N 14°32E 135 B3
Kcynia *Poland* 53°0N 17°30E 185 F4
Ke-hsi Mansam *Burma* 21°56N 97°50E 241 E6
Kē-Macina *Mali* 13°58N 5°22E 262 C3
Kea *Greece* 37°35N 24°22E 204 D6
Kea'au *U.S.A.* 19°37N 155°2W 302 D6
Keady *U.K.* 54°15N 6°42W 166 B5
Keahi Pt. *U.S.A.* 21°19N 157°59W 302 K14
Keahole Pt. *U.S.A.* 19°44N 156°4W 302 D5
Kealaikahiki Channel
 U.S.A. 20°35N 156°50W 302 C2
Kealakekua *U.S.A.* 19°31N 155°50W 302 D6
Kearney *Mo., U.S.A.* 39°22N 94°22W 310 E2
Kearney *Nebr., U.S.A.* 40°42N 99°5W 308 E4
Kearney ◎ *Australia* 20°10S 128°4E 278 C4
Kearny *U.S.A.* 33°3N 110°55W 305 K8
Kearsarge, Mt. *U.S.A.* 43°22N 71°50W 313 C13
Keban *Turkey* 38°50N 38°50E 213 C8
Keban Baraji *Turkey* 38°41N 38°33E 213 C8
Kebara *Congo* 2°27S 14°25E 264 C2
Kebayoran Baru
 Indonesia 6°14S 106°47E 122 B1
Kebayoran Lama
 Indonesia 6°13S 106°46E 122 B1
Kebbi □ *Nigeria* 11°35N 4°0E 263 C5
Kébémèr *Senegal* 15°23N 16°34W 262 B1
Kébi *Ivory C.* 9°18N 6°37W 262 D3
Kebi, Mayo ↠ *Cameroon* 9°18N 13°33E 264 A2
Kebili *Tunisia* 33°47N 9°0E 258 B1
Kebili □ *Tunisia* 33°30N 8°50E 261 B6
Kebnekaise *Sweden* 67°53N 18°33E 160 C18
Kebon Jeruk *Indonesia* 6°11S 106°46E 122 B1
Kebri Dehar *Ethiopia* 6°45N 44°17E 267 C5
Kebumen *Indonesia* 7°42S 109°40E 122 B3
Kecel *Hungary* 46°31N 19°16E 182 D4
Kechika ↠ *Canada* 59°41N 127°12W 296 B3
Keçiborlu *Turkey* 37°57N 30°18E 205 D12
Kecskemét *Hungary* 46°57N 19°42E 182 D4
Kedada *Ethiopia* 5°25N 35°58E 257 F4
Kedah □ *Malaysia* 5°50N 100°40E 237 D6
Kedainiai *Lithuania* 55°15N 24°2E 184 C11
Kedar Kanta *India* 31°0N 78°5E 243 D8
Kedarnath *India* 30°44N 79°4E 243 D8
Kedgwick *Canada* 47°40N 67°20W 299 C6
Kediet Ijill *Mauritania* 22°38N 12°30W 260 D2
Kediri *Indonesia* 7°51S 112°1E 235 D4
Kedja
 Dem. Rep. of the Congo 4°50N 19°16E 264 B3
Kedjebi *Ghana* 8°12N 0°25E 263 D5
Kédougou *Senegal* 12°35N 12°10W 262 C2
Kedoya *Indonesia* 6°10S 106°45E 122 B1
Kedros Oros *Greece* 35°11N 24°37E 207 E6
Kędzierzyn-Koźle *Poland* 50°20N 18°12E 185 H5
Ke'ehi Lagoon *U.S.A.* 21°20N 157°54W 302 K14
Keeler *U.S.A.* 36°29N 117°52W 306 J9
Keeley L. *Canada* 54°54N 108°8W 297 C7
Keeling Is. = Cocos Is.
 Ind. Oc. 12°10S 96°55E 273 F8
Keelung = Chilung
 Taiwan 25°3N 121°45E 225 A9
Keenapusan *Phil.* 6°50N 118°50E 233 H5
Keene *Canada* 44°15N 78°10W 312 B6
Keene *Calif., U.S.A.* 35°13N 118°33W 307 K8
Keene *N.H., U.S.A.* 42°56N 72°17W 313 D12
Keene *N.Y., U.S.A.* 44°16N 73°46W 313 B11
Keep River △ *Australia* 15°49S 129°8E 278 C4
Keeper Hill *Ireland* 52°45N 8°16W 166 D3
Keepit, L. *Australia* 30°50N 150°23W 283 A9
Keerweer, C. *Australia* 14°0S 141°32E 282 A3
Keeseville *U.S.A.* 44°29N 73°30E 313 B11
Keetmanshoop *Namibia* 26°35S 18°8E 270 D2
Keewatin *Canada* 49°46N 94°34W 297 D10
Keewatin ↠ *Canada* 56°29N 100°46W 297 B8
Kefa *Ethiopia* 6°55N 36°30E 267 C4
Kefalonia *Greece* 38°15N 20°30E 207 C2
Kefalonia *Greece* 38°20N 20°30E 207 C2
Kefalonia ✈ (EFL) *Greece* 38°7N 20°30E 207 C1
Kefalos *Greece* 36°44N 26°57E 205 E8
Kefamenanu *Indonesia* 9°28S 124°29E 231 F6
Kefar Sava *Israel* 32°11N 34°54E 251 F5
Keffi *Nigeria* 8°55N 7°43E 263 D6

Keffin Hausa *Nigeria* 12°13N 9°59E 263 C6
Keflavík *Iceland* 64°2N 22°35W 155 C4
Keflavík ✈ (KEF) *Iceland* 64°0N 22°45W 155 C4
Keftya *Ethiopia* 13°54N 37°7E 257 E4
Keg River *Canada* 57°54N 117°55W 296 B5
Kegalla *Sri Lanka* 7°15N 80°21E 245 L5
Keng Kok *Laos* 16°26N 105°12E 236 D5
Keng Tawng *Burma* 20°45N 98°18E 241 E7
Keng Tung *Burma* 21°0N 99°30E 228 G2
Kengani
 Dem. Rep. of the Congo 2°59S 17°36E 264 C3
Kenge *Dem. Rep. of the Congo* 4°50S 17°4E 265 C3
Kengeja *Tanzania* 5°26S 39°45E 268 D4
Kenhardt *S. Africa* 29°19S 21°12E 270 D3
Kenitra *Morocco* 34°15N 6°40W 260 B3
Kenli *China* 37°30N 118°20E 227 F10
Kenmare *Kerry, Ireland* 51°53N 9°36W 166 E2
Kenmare *N. Dak., U.S.A.* 48°41N 102°5W 308 A2
Kenmare River *Ireland* 51°48N 9°51W 166 E2
Kennebago Lake *U.S.A.* 45°3N 70°40W 313 A14
Kennebec *U.S.A.* 43°54N 99°52W 308 D4
Kennebec ↠ *U.S.A.* 43°45N 69°46W 309 D19
Kennebunk *U.S.A.* 43°23N 70°33W 313 C14
Kenhena, Is. *Tunisia* 34°42N 11°21E 261 B7
Kennedy *Zimbabwe* 18°52S 27°10E 270 A4
Kennedy, C. = Canaveral, C.
 U.S.A. 28°27N 80°32W 317 G9
Kennedy Channel *Arctic* 80°50N 66°0W 154 A4
Kennedy Entrance
 U.S.A. 59°1N 152°0W 303 G10
Kennedy Ra. *Australia* 24°45S 115°10E 279 D2
Kennedy Range △
 Australia 24°34S 115°2E 279 D2
Kennedy Space Center
 U.S.A. 28°40N 80°42W 317 G9
Kennet ↠ *U.K.* 51°27N 0°57W 169 F7
Kennett *U.S.A.* 36°14N 90°3W 308 G8
Kennewick *U.S.A.* 46°12N 119°7W 304 C4
Kénogami *Canada* 51°6N 84°28W 298 B3
Kenogami ↠ *Canada* 51°6N 84°28W 298 B3
Kenora *Canada* 49°47N 94°29W 297 D10
Kenosha *U.S.A.* 42°35N 87°49W 311 D9
Kensington *P.E.I.,*
 Canada 46°28N 63°34W 299 C7
Kensington *London, U.K.* 125 c4
Kensington *S. Africa* 26°11S 28°6E 123 B2
Kensington *London, U.K.* 125 c4
Kensington *Australia* 33°54S 151°13E 139 B2
Kensington *Canada* 51°30N 0°18W 125 c4
Kensington *S. Africa* 26°11S 28°6E 123 B2
Kent *Ohio, U.S.A.* 41°9N 81°22W 312 E3
Kent *Tex., U.S.A.* 31°4N 104°13W 314 F2
Kent *Wash., U.S.A.* 47°22N 122°14W 306 C4
Kent □ *U.K.* 51°12N 0°40E 169 F8
Kent Group *Australia* 39°30S 147°20E 281 F4
Kent Pen. *Canada* 68°30N 107°0W 294 C10
Kent Village *U.S.A.* 38°55N 76°53W 143 B8
Kentau *Kazakhstan* 43°32N 68°36E 217 D7
K'enting △ *Taiwan* 21°57N 120°48E 225 E2
Kentish Town *U.K.* 51°32N 0°9W 125 d5
Kentland *U.S.A.* 40°46N 87°27W 311 D9
Kenton *London, U.K.* 51°34N 0°17W 125 a2
Kenton *Ohio, U.S.A.* 40°39N 83°37W 311 D3
Kentucky □ *U.S.A.* 37°0N 84°0W 309 G4
Kentucky ↠ *U.S.A.* 38°41N 85°11W 311 F11
Kentucky L. *U.S.A.* 37°1N 88°16W 308 G9
Kentville *Canada* 45°6N 64°29W 299 C7
Kentwood *La., U.S.A.* 30°56N 90°31W 315 F9
Kentwood *Mich., U.S.A.* 42°52N 85°39W 311 B11
Kenwood *U.S.A.* 51°34N 0°9W 125 b5
Kenya ■ *Africa* 1°0N 38°0E 268 B4
Kenya, Mt. *Kenya* 0°10S 37°18E 268 C4
Kenyir, Tasik *Malaysia* 5°1N 102°54E 237 K4
Kenzou *Cameroon* 4°10N 15°2E 264 B3
Keo Neua, Deo *Vietnam* 18°23N 105°10E 236 C5
Keokuk *U.S.A.* 40°24N 91°24W 310 E8
Keoladeo △ *India* 27°0N 77°20E 242 F7
Keonjhargarh *India* 21°28N 85°35E 243 J11
Keosauqua *U.S.A.* 40°44N 91°58W 310 E8
Keota *U.S.A.* 41°22N 91°57W 310 E8
Kep *Cambodia* 10°29N 104°19E 237 G5
Kep *Vietnam* 21°24N 106°16E 236 B6
Kepa *Poland* 52°13N 21°3E 142 B2
Kepala Batas *Malaysia* 5°31N 100°26E 237 c
Kepez *Turkey* 36°50N 26°24E 203 F10
Kepi *Indonesia* 6°32S 139°19E 231 F9
Kepice *Poland* 54°16N 16°51E 184 D3
Kepler Mts. *N.Z.* 45°25S 167°20E 285 G4
Kepno *Poland* 51°18N 17°58E 185 G4
Keppel Harbour
 Singapore 1°15N 103°49E 138 B2
Keppel Pt., U.S.A. 10°10S 147°58E 185 G4
Kepuhi Pt., U.S.A. 21°29N 158°14W 302 K13
Kerala □ *India* 11°0N 76°15E 245 J3
Keram ↠ *Papua N. G.* 4°7S 144°5E 286 B7
Kerama-Rettō *Japan* 26°5N 127°15E 221 L3
Keramadion *Greece* 36°58N 27°50E 205 D8
Keran *Pakistan* 34°35N 73°59E 243 B5
Keran □ *Togo* 10°0N 1°0E 263 C5
Kerang *Australia* 35°40S 143°55E 283 C5
Keranyo *Ethiopia* 5°5N 36°35E 267 F4
Kerao ↠ *Sudan* 10°15N 34°5E 257 E3
Keratea *Greece* 37°48N 23°58E 204 D5
Keraudren, C. *Australia* 19°58S 119°45E 279 D2
Keravat *Papua N. G.* 4°21S 152°2E 286 C7
Keravi ↠ *Finland* 60°25N 25°5E 121 B2
Kerch *Ukraine* 45°20N 36°20E 189 K9
Kerchenskiy Proliv
 Black Sea 45°10N 36°30E 189 K9
Kerchoual *Mali* 17°12N 0°20E 263 B5
Kerema *Papua N. G.* 7°58S 145°50E 286 B7
Kerempe Burnu *Turkey* 42°2N 33°0E 212 B5
Keren *Eritrea* 15°45N 38°28E 257 D4
Kerewan *Gambia* 13°29N 16°10W 262 C1
Kerguelen *Ind. Oc.* 49°15S 69°10E 273 K6
Kerguelen Plateau *S. Ocean* 55°0S 75°0E 273 K6
Keri *Greece* 37°40N 20°49E 207 D2
Keri Kera *Sudan* 12°21N 32°42E 257 E3
Kericho *Kenya* 0°22S 35°15E 268 C4
Kerinci *Indonesia* 1°40S 101°15E 234 C1
Kerinci Seblat △ *Indonesia* 1°46S 101°15E 234 C1
Kerintji = Kerinci
 Indonesia 1°40S 101°15E 234 C1
Keriya He ↠ *China* 38°30N 82°10E 217 C10
Kerkenna, Is. = Kenhena, Is.
 Tunisia 34°42N 11°21E 261 B7
Kerki = Atamyrat
 Turkmenistan 37°50N 65°12E 217 F7
Kerki, L. *Canada* 41°12N 29°12W 312 B4
Kerkira *Greece* 39°38N 19°50E 206 B9
Kerkira ✈ (CFU) *Greece* 39°35N 19°54E 206 B2
Kerkrade *Neths.* 50°53N 6°4E 170 D6
Kerkyra *Greece* 39°38N 19°50E 206 B9
Kerkyra □ *Greece* 39°37N 19°50E 206 B9
Kerkyra ✈ (CFU) *Greece* 39°35N 19°54E 206 B2
Kerkyras, Notio Steno
 Greece 39°34N 20°0E 206 B10

Kerma *Sudan* 19°33N 30°32E 256 D3
Kermadec Is. *Pac. Oc.* 30°0S 178°15W 277 G15
Kermadec Trench
 Pac. Oc. 30°30S 176°0W 277 G15
Kermān *Iran* 30°15N 57°1E 247 D8
Kerman *Calif., U.S.A.* 36°43N 120°4W 306 J6
Kermān □ *Iran* 30°0N 57°0E 247 D8
Kermān, Bīābān-e *Iran* 28°45N 59°45E 247 D8
Kermānshāh *Iran* 34°23N 47°0E 213 C12
Kermānshāh □ *Iran* 34°0N 46°30E 246 C5
Kermen *Bulgaria* 42°30N 26°16E 203 D10
Kermine = Navoiy
 Uzbekistan 40°9N 65°22E 217 D7
Kermit *U.S.A.* 31°52N 103°6W 314 F3
Kernhof *Austria* 35°16N 119°18W 307 K7
Kernville *U.S.A.* 47°49N 15°32E 180 D4
Kernow = Cornwall □
 U.K. 50°26N 4°40W 169 G3
Keroh *Malaysia* 5°43N 101°1E 237 K3
Keros *Greece* 36°54N 25°40E 205 E7
Kérou *Benin* 10°50N 2°5E 263 C5
Kérouané *Guinea* 9°15N 9°0W 262 D3
Kerowagi *Papua N. G.* 5°51S 144°51E 286 C3
Kerpen *Germany* 50°51N 6°41E 178 E2
Kerrera *U.K.* 56°24N 5°33W 167 E3
Kerrobert *Canada* 51°56N 109°8W 297 C7
Kerrville *U.S.A.* 30°3N 99°8W 314 F5
Kerry □ *Ireland* 52°7N 9°35W 166 D2
Kerry Hd. *Ireland* 52°25N 9°56W 166 D2
Kersa *Ethiopia* 9°28N 41°48E 257 F5
Kertosono *Indonesia* 7°38S 112°9E 235 D4
Kerulen ↠ *Asia* 48°48N 117°0E 219 B6
Kervo = Kerava *Finland* 60°25N 25°5E 188 B3
Kerzaz *Algeria* 29°29N 1°37W 261 C4
Kesagami ↠ *Canada* 51°40N 79°45W 298 B4
Kesagami L. *Canada* 50°23N 80°15W 298 B3
Keşan *Turkey* 40°49N 26°38E 203 F10
Kesariani *Greece* 37°57N 23°46E 112 B2
Kesennuma *Japan* 38°54N 141°35E 220 E10
Keshāvar *Iran* 36°50N 46°22E 213 D12
Keshit *Iran* 29°43N 58°17E 247 D8
Kesigi = Kosgi *India* 15°51N 77°16E 245 G3
Keşiş Dağ *Turkey* 39°47N 39°46E 213 C8
Keskal *India* 20°5N 81°35E 244 D5
Keskin *Turkey* 39°40N 33°36E 212 C5
Kestenga *Russia* 65°50N 31°45E 160 D24
Keswick *U.K.* 54°36N 3°8W 168 C4
Keszthely *Hungary* 46°50N 17°15E 182 D2
Ket ↠ *Russia* 58°55N 81°32E 214 D9
Keta *Ghana* 5°49N 1°0E 263 D5
Keta Lagoon *Ghana* 5°55N 1°0E 263 D5
Ketapang *Bali, Indonesia* 8°9S 114°23E 231 J17
Ketapang *Kalimantan,*
 Indonesia 1°55S 110°0E 235 C4
Ketchenery *Russia* 47°18N 44°32E 191 G7
Ketchikan *U.S.A.* 55°21N 131°39W 296 B2
Ketchum *U.S.A.* 43°41N 114°22W 304 E6
Kete Krachi *Ghana* 7°46N 0°1W 263 D4
Ketef, Khalig Umm el
 Egypt 23°40N 35°35E 246 F2
Keti Bandar *Pakistan* 24°8N 67°27E 242 G2
Kétou *Benin* 7°25N 2°45E 263 D5
Ketri *India* 28°1N 75°50E 242 E6
Kętrzyn *Poland* 54°7N 21°22E 184 D8
Ketta *Congo* 1°28N 15°54E 264 B3
Kettering *Northants., U.K.* 52°24N 0°43W 169 E7
Kettering *Ohio, U.S.A.* 39°41N 84°10W 311 E12
Kettle ↠ *Canada* 56°40N 89°34W 297 B11
Kettle Falls *U.S.A.* 48°37N 118°3W 304 B4
Kettle Point *Canada* 43°13N 82°1W 312 C2
Kettle Pt. *Canada* 43°13N 82°1W 312 C2
Kettleman City *U.S.A.* 36°1N 119°58W 306 J7
Kęty *Poland* 49°51N 19°16E 185 J6
Keuka L. *U.S.A.* 42°30N 77°9W 312 D7
Keuruu *Finland* 62°16N 24°41E 188 A3
Kevelaer *Germany* 51°36N 6°15E 178 D2
Kew, Vic., *Australia* 37°48S 145°2E 128 a2
Kew *London, U.K.* 51°28N 0°17W 125 d5
Kew Gardens *Ont.,*
 Canada 43°39N 79°18W 141 A4
Kew Gardens *London,*
 U.K. 51°28N 0°17W 125 d5
Kewanee *U.S.A.* 41°14N 89°56W 310 C7
Kewanna *U.S.A.* 41°1N 86°25W 311 C10
Kewaunee *U.S.A.* 44°27N 87°31W 308 C10
Keweenaw B. *U.S.A.* 47°0N 88°15W 308 B9
Keweenaw Pen. *U.S.A.* 47°15N 88°15W 308 B9
Keweenaw Pt. *U.S.A.* 47°25N 87°43W 308 B10
Kexholm = Priozersk
 Russia 61°2N 30°7E 188 B6
Key, L. *Ireland* 54°0N 8°15W 166 C3
Key Biscayne *U.S.A.* 25°41N 80°9W 128 E2
Key Colony Beach
 U.S.A. 24°45N 80°57W 317 G9
Key Largo *U.S.A.* 25°5N 80°27W 317 G9
Key West *U.S.A.* 24°33N 81°48W 317 G9
Keyala *Sudan* 4°27N 32°52E 257 G3
Keynsham *U.K.* 51°24N 2°29W 169 F5
Keyser *U.S.A.* 39°26N 78°59W 309 F14
Keystone Heights *U.S.A.* 29°47N 82°2W 316 F7
Keytesville *U.S.A.* 39°26N 92°56W 310 F7
Kezhma *Russia* 58°59N 101°9E 215 D11
Kezi *Zimbabwe* 20°58S 28°32E 271 B4
Kežmarok *Slovak Rep.* 49°10N 20°28E 185 B7
Kgalagadi Transfrontier □
 Africa 25°10S 21°0E 270 C3
Kgalagadi *Russia* 28°51N 135°5E 215 E14
Khabarovsk *Russia* 48°30N 135°5E 215 E14
Khābūr ↠ *Syria* 35°17N 40°35E 213 C9
Khachmas = Xaçmaz
 Azerbaijan 41°31N 48°42E 191 K9
Khadari, W. el ↠ *Sudan* 10°29N 27°15E 257 E2
Khadro *Pakistan* 26°11N 68°50E 242 F3
Khadyzhensk *Russia* 44°26N 39°32E 191 H4
Khadzhilyangar = Dahongliutan
 China 35°45N 79°20E 243 B8
Khaga *India* 25°47N 81°7E 243 G9
Khagaria *India* 25°30N 86°32E 243 G12
Khaipur *India* 27°57N 74°46E 242 F5
Khair *India* 27°57N 77°46E 242 F7
Khairabad *India* 27°33N 80°47E 243 F9
Khairagarh *India* 21°27N 81°2E 243 J9
Khairpur *India* 27°32N 68°49E 242 F3
Khairpur Nathan Shah
 Pakistan 27°6N 67°44E 242 F2
Khairwara *India* 23°58N 73°38E 242 H5
Khaisor ↠ *Pakistan* 32°4N 69°51E 242 D3
Khāk Dow *Afghan.* 31°28N 62°16E 247 D9
Khakassia □ *Russia* 53°0N 90°0E 217 D10
Khakhea *Botswana* 24°48S 23°22E 270 B3
Khalafābād *Iran* 30°54N 49°24E 247 D6
Khalīlī *Yemen* 15°52N 52°10E 249 E5
Khalīlabad *India* 26°48N 83°5E 243 F10
Khaliabad *India* 26°48N 83°5E 243 F10
Khalkhāl *Iran* 37°37N 48°32E 213 D12
Khalkis = Halkida *Greece* 38°27N 23°42E 204 C5
Khalmer Yu *Russia* 67°58N 65°1E 214 C7
Khalmer-Sede = Tazovskiy
 Russia 67°30N 78°44E 214 C8
Khalturin *Russia* 58°40N 48°50E 186 B8

Kham Keut Laos 18°15N 104°43E 236 C5
Khamaria India 23°5N 80°48E 243 H9
Khambhaliya India 22°14N 69°41E 242 H3
Khambhat India 22°23N 72°33E 242 H5
Khambhat, G. of India 20°45N 72°30E 239 E10
Khamgaon India 20°42N 76°37E 244 D3
Khamir Iran 26°57N 55°36E 247 E7
Khamir Yemen 16°2N 44°0E 248 C4
Khamīs Mushayṭ Si. Arabia 18°18N 42°44E 248 C3
Khammam India 17°11N 80°6E 244 F5
Khamsa Egypt 30°27N 32°23E 251 H3
Khan → Namibia 22°37S 14°56E 270 B2
Khān Abū Shāmat Syria 33°39N 36°53E 250 E7
Khān al Baghdādī Iraq 33°51N 42°32E 213 G10
Khān al Ḥammād Iraq 32°19N 44°16E 213 G11
Khān Azād Iraq 33°7N 44°22E 246 C5
Khān Mujiddah Iraq 32°21N 43°48E 246 C4
Khān Shaykhūn Syria 35°26N 36°38E 212 E7
Khan Tengri, Pik Asia 42°12N 80°10E 217 D10
Khān Yūnis Gaza Strip 31°21N 34°18E 251 G5
Khānābād Afghan. 36°45N 69°5E 240 A3
Khanai Pakistan 30°30N 67°8E 242 D2
Khānaqīn Iraq 34°23N 45°25E 213 E11
Khanāşir Syria 35°45N 37°30E 250 C8
Khānbāghī Iran 36°10N 55°25E 247 B7
Khandallah N.Z. 41°15S 174°47E 143 B1
Khandwa India 21°49N 76°22E 244 D3
Khandyga Russia 62°42N 135°35E 215 C14
Khanewal Pakistan 30°20N 71°55E 242 D4
Khangah Dogran Pakistan 31°50N 73°37E 242 D5
Khanh Duong Vietnam 12°44N 108°44E 236 F7
Khaniá = Chania Greece 35°30N 24°4E 207 E5
Khaniadhana India 25°1N 78°8E 242 G8
Khanka, L. Asia 45°0N 132°24E 220 B6
Khankendy = Xankändi Azerbaijan 39°52N 46°49E 213 C12
Khanna India 30°42N 76°16E 242 D7
Khanozai Pakistan 30°37N 67°19E 242 D2
Khanpur Pakistan 28°42N 70°35E 242 E4
Khansā' Iraq 33°21N 44°28E 113 A2
Khanty-Mansiysk Russia 61°0N 69°0E 214 C7
Khanzira, Ras Somali Rep. 10°52N 45°48E 267 B6
Khao Laem △ Thailand 14°56N 98°31E 236 E2
Khao Laem Res. Thailand 14°50N 98°30E 236 E2
Khao Lak △ Malaysia 8°38N 98°18E 237 H2
Khao Luang △ Thailand 8°34N 99°42E 237 H2
Khao Phlu Thailand 9°29N 99°59E 237 b
Khao Pu-Khao Ya △ Thailand 7°26N 99°57E 237 J2
Khao Sam Roi Yot △ Thailand 12°13N 99°57E 237 F2
Khao Sok △ Thailand 8°55N 98°38E 237 H2
Khao Yai △ Thailand 14°21N 101°29E 236 E3
Khaoen Si Nakarin △ Thailand 14°47N 99°0E 236 E2
Khapalu Pakistan 35°10N 76°20E 243 B7
Khapcheranga Russia 49°42N 112°24E 215 E12
Khaptao △ Nepal 29°20N 81°10E 243 E9
Kharabali Russia 47°25N 47°15E 191 G8
Kharagauli Georgia 42°1N 43°12E 191 J6
Kharaghoda India 23°11N 71°46E 242 H4
Kharagpur India 22°20N 87°25E 243 H12
Kharan Kalat Pakistan 28°34N 65°21E 240 C2
Kharānaq Iran 32°20N 54°45E 247 C7
Kharavli India 18°54N 72°55E 130 B2
Kharda India 18°40N 75°34E 244 E2
Khardung La India 34°20N 77°43E 243 B7
Kharg = Khārk, Jazīreh-ye Iran 29°15N 50°28E 247 D6
Khârga, El Wâhât el Egypt 25°10N 30°35E 256 B3
Khargon India 21°45N 75°40E 244 D2
Khari → India 25°54N 74°31E 242 G6
Kharian Pakistan 32°49N 73°52E 242 C5
Khariar India 20°17N 82°46E 244 D6
Kharit, Wadi el → Egypt 24°26N 33°3E 256 C3
Khārk, Jazīreh-ye Iran 29°15N 50°28E 247 D6
Kharkiv Ukraine 49°58N 36°20E 189 H9
Kharkiv □ Ukraine 48°20N 36°20E 189 H9
Kharkov = Kharkiv Ukraine 49°58N 36°20E 189 H9
Kharmanli Bulgaria 41°55N 25°55E 203 E11
Kharovsk Russia 59°56N 40°13E 188 C11
Kharsawangarh India 22°48N 85°50E 243 H11
Kharta Turkey 40°55N 29°7E 212 B3
Khartoum = El Khartûm Sudan 15°31N 32°35E 257 D3
Khartum Canada 45°15N 77°5W 312 A7
Khasan Russia 42°25N 130°40E 220 C5
Khasavyurt Russia 43°16N 46°40E 191 J8
Khāsh Iran 28°15N 61°15E 240 C1
Khâsh, Dasht-e Afghan. 31°50N 62°30E 240 C1
Khashm el Girba Sudan 14°59N 35°58E 257 E4
Khashum Sudan 12°27N 28°12E 257 E2
Khashuri Georgia 42°3N 43°35E 191 J6
Khasi Hills India 25°30N 91°30E 241 C3
Khaskovo Bulgaria 41°56N 25°30E 203 E9
Khaskovo □ Bulgaria 42°0N 25°40E 203 E9
Khatanga Russia 72°0N 102°20E 215 B11
Khatanga → Russia 72°55N 106°0E 215 B11
Khatauli India 29°17N 77°43E 242 E7
Khatlon □ Tajikistan 37°50N 69°0E 217 E7
Khatra India 22°59N 86°51E 243 H12
Khātūnābād Iran 30°1N 55°25E 247 D7
Khatyrka Russia 62°3N 175°15E 215 C18
Khavda India 23°51N 69°43E 242 H3
Khawlaf, Ra's Yemen 12°40N 54°7E 249 D6
Khawr Fakkān U.A.E. 25°21N 56°22E 247 E8
Khay' Si. Arabia 18°45N 41°24E 248 C3
Khaybar, Ḥarrat Si. Arabia 25°45N 40°0E 246 E4
Khāzimiyah Iraq 34°46N 43°37E 246 C4
Khazzān Jabal al Awliyā Sudan 15°24N 32°20E 257 D3
Khe Bo Vietnam 19°8N 104°41E 236 C5
Khe Long Vietnam 21°29N 104°46E 236 B5
Khe Sanh Vietnam 16°37N 106°45E 236 D6
Khed Maharashtra, India 17°43N 73°27E 244 F1
Khed Maharashtra, India 18°51N 73°56E 244 E1
Khed Brahma India 24°7N 73°5E 242 G5
Khefren Egypt 29°58N 31°8E 117 B1
Khekra India 28°52N 77°20E 242 E7
Khem-Beldyr = Kyzyl Russia 51°50N 94°30E 217 B12
Khemarak Phouminville = Krong Kaoh Kong Cambodia 11°37N 102°59E 237 G4
Khemisset Morocco 33°50N 6°1W 260 B3
Khemisset □ Morocco 33°50N 6°1W 260 B3
Khemmarat Thailand 16°10N 105°15E 236 D5
Khenāmān Iran 30°27N 56°29E 247 D8
Khenchela Algeria 35°28N 7°11E 261 A6
Khenchela □ Algeria 35°0N 7°0E 261 B6
Khenifra Morocco 32°58N 5°46W 260 B3
Kherrata Algeria 36°27N 5°13E 261 A6
Khersān → Iran 31°33N 50°22E 247 D6
Kherson Ukraine 46°35N 32°35E 189 J7
Kherson □ Ukraine 46°15N 33°10E 189 J7
Kheta → Russia 71°54N 102°6E 215 B11
Khewari Pakistan 26°36N 68°52E 242 F3
Khibinogorsk = Kirovsk Russia 67°32N 33°41E 186 A5
Khichripur India 28°37N 77°18E 120 B2
Khidirpur India 22°32N 88°19E 124 B1
Khilchipur India 24°2N 76°34E 242 G7
Khilok Russia 51°30N 110°45E 215 D12
Khimki Russia 55°50N 37°20E 188 E9
Khimki-Khovrino Russia 55°51N 37°31E 129 A3
Khíos = Hios Greece 38°27N 26°9E 205 C8
Khirbet Batin Abu Lihyah West Bank 31°50N 35°6E 123 A1
Khirbet el-Misbah West Bank 31°53N 35°4E 123 A1
Khirbet Jub e-Rum West Bank 31°44N 35°16E 123 B2
Khirsadoh India 22°11N 78°47E 243 H8
Khiuma = Hiiumaa Estonia 58°50N 22°45E 188 C2
Khiva Uzbekistan 41°30N 60°18E 216 D6
Khlebarovo Bulgaria 43°37N 26°15E 203 C10
Khlong Khlung Thailand 16°12N 99°43E 236 D2
Khlong San Thailand 13°43N 100°29E 113 B2
Khlong Toey Thailand 13°43N 100°36E 113 B2
Khmelnik Ukraine 49°33N 27°58E 177 D14
Khmelnytskyy Ukraine 49°23N 27°0E 177 D14
Khmelnytskyy □ Ukraine 49°50N 26°40E 189 H4
Khmer Rep. = Cambodia ■ Asia 12°15N 105°0E 236 F5
Khoai, Hon Vietnam 8°26N 104°50E 237 H5
Khodoriv Ukraine 49°24N 24°19E 177 D13
Khodzent = Khŭjand Tajikistan 40°17N 69°37E 217 D7
Khojak Pass Afghan. 30°51N 66°34E 242 D2
Khojayli Uzbekistan 42°29N 59°31E 216 D5
Khok Kloi Thailand 8°17N 98°19E 237 a
Khok Pho Thailand 6°43N 101°6E 237 J3
Khok Samrong Thailand 15°3N 100°43E 236 E3
Khokhropār Pakistan 25°42N 70°12E 240 D3
Kholm Afghan. 36°45N 67°40E 240 A2
Kholm Russia 57°10N 31°15E 188 D6
Kholmsk Russia 47°40N 142°5E 215 E15
Khomārlu Iran 39°6N 47°3E 213 C12
Khomas Hochland Namibia 22°40S 16°0E 270 B2
Khombole Senegal 14°43N 16°42W 262 C1
Khomeyn Iran 33°40N 50°7E 247 C6
Khomeynī Shahr Iran 32°41N 51°31E 247 C6
Khomodino Botswana 22°46S 23°52E 270 B3
Khon Kaen Thailand 16°30N 102°47E 236 D4
Khong → Cambodia 13°32N 105°58E 236 F5
Khong Sedone Laos 15°34N 105°49E 236 E5
Khonuu Russia 66°30N 143°12E 215 C15
Khoper → Russia 49°30N 42°20E 190 F6
Khor el 'Atash Sudan 13°20N 34°15E 257 E3
Khorāsān □ Iran 34°0N 58°0E 247 C8
Khorāsān-e Razavī □ Iran 35°0N 59°0E 216 F5
Khorāsān-e Shemālī □ Iran 37°0N 57°0E 216 E5
Khorat = Nakhon Ratchasima Thailand 14°59N 102°12E 236 E4
Khorat, Cao Nguyen Thailand 15°30N 102°50E 236 E4
Khorazm = Xorazm □ Uzbekistan 43°0N 60°0E 216 D6
Khorb el Ethel Algeria 28°30N 6°17W 260 C3
Khorel India 22°41N 88°18E 124 A1
Khorixas Namibia 20°16S 14°59E 270 B1
Khorol Ukraine 49°48N 33°15E 189 H7
Khorosovo Russia 55°46N 37°27E 129 B2
Khorramābād Khorāsān, Iran 35°6N 57°57E 247 C8
Khorramābād Lorestān, Iran 33°30N 48°25E 247 C6
Khorramdarreh Iran 36°11N 49°11E 213 D13
Khorramshahr Iran 30°29N 48°15E 247 D6
Khorugh Tajikistan 37°30N 71°36E 240 A3
Khosravī Iran 30°48N 51°28E 247 D6
Khosrowābād Khuzestān, Iran 30°10N 48°25E 247 D6
Khosrowābād Kordestān, Iran 35°31N 47°38E 213 E12
Khost Pakistan 30°13N 67°35E 242 D2
Khosūyeh Iran 28°32N 54°26E 247 D7
Khotan = Hotan China 37°25N 79°55E 217 E9
Khotyn Ukraine 48°31N 26°27E 183 B11
Khouribga Morocco 32°58N 6°57W 260 B3
Khouribga □ Morocco 32°56N 6°36W 260 B3
Khowai Bangla. 24°5N 91°40E 241 C3
Khowst Afghan. 33°22N 69°58E 242 C3
Khowst □ Afghan. 33°20N 70°0E 240 B3
Khoyniki Belarus 51°54N 29°55E 177 C15
Khrami → Georgia 41°25N 45°0E 191 K7
Khrenovoye Russia 51°4N 40°16E 190 E5
Khromtaū Kazakhstan 50°17N 58°27E 216 B5
Khrysokhou B. Cyprus 35°6N 32°25E 207 E8
Khu Khan Thailand 14°42N 104°12E 236 E5
Khuan Wa Thailand 7°53N 98°17E 237 a
Khudrah, W. → Yemen 18°10N 50°20E 249 C5
Khudzhand = Khŭjand Tajikistan 40°17N 69°37E 217 D7
Khuff Si. Arabia 24°55N 44°53E 246 E5
Khūgīānī Afghan. 31°34N 66°32E 242 D2
Khuis Botswana 26°40S 21°49E 270 C3
Khuiyala India 27°9N 70°25E 242 F4
Khŭjand Tajikistan 40°17N 69°37E 217 D7
Khŭjayli = Khojayli Uzbekistan 42°29N 59°31E 216 D5
Khujner India 23°47N 76°36E 242 H7
Khulays Si. Arabia 22°9N 39°19E 248 B2
Khulna Bangla. 22°45N 89°34E 241 D2
Khulna □ Bangla. 22°25N 89°35E 241 D2
Khulo Georgia 41°33N 42°19E 191 K6
Khumago Botswana 20°26S 24°32E 270 B3
Khumrah Si. Arabia 21°22N 39°13E 248 B2
Khunjerab △ Pakistan 36°40N 75°30E 243 A6
Khunjerab Pass = Kinjirap Daban Asia 36°40N 75°25E 240 A4
Khūnsorkh Iran 27°9N 56°7E 247 E8
Khunti India 23°5N 85°17E 243 H11
Khūr Iran 32°55N 58°18E 247 C8
Khurai India 24°3N 78°23E 242 G8
Khuraydah Yemen 15°33N 48°18E 249 D5
Khurays Si. Arabia 25°6N 48°2E 247 E6
Khurda India 20°11N 85°37E 244 D7
Khureit Sudan 13°59N 26°3E 257 E2
Khurja India 28°15N 77°58E 242 E7
Khūrmāl Iraq 35°18N 46°2E 213 E12
Khurr, Wādī al Iraq 32°3N 43°52E 246 C4
Khūsf Iran 32°46N 58°53E 247 C8
Khushab Pakistan 32°20N 72°20E 242 C5
Khust Ukraine 48°10N 23°18E 183 B8
Khutse △ Botswana 23°31S 24°12E 270 B3
Khuwei Sudan 13°5N 29°14E 257 E2
Khuzdar Pakistan 27°52N 66°30E 242 F2
Khūzestān □ Iran 31°0N 49°0E 247 D6
Khvāf Iran 34°33N 60°8E 247 C9
Khvājeh Iran 38°9N 46°35E 246 B5
Khvājeh Moḥammad, Kūh-e Afghan. 36°22N 70°17E 240 A3
Khvalynsk Russia 52°30N 48°2E 190 D9
Khvānsār Iran 29°56N 54°8E 247 D7
Khvatovka Russia 52°24N 46°32E 190 D8
Khvor Iran 33°45N 55°0E 247 C7
Khvorgū Iran 27°34N 56°27E 247 E8
Khvormūj Iran 28°40N 51°30E 247 D6
Khvoy Iran 38°35N 45°0E 213 C11
Khvoynaya Russia 58°58N 34°28E 188 C8
Khyber Pass Afghan. 34°10N 71°8E 242 B4
Khyriv Ukraine 49°32N 22°50E 185 J9
Kia Fiji 16°16S 179°8E 287 A2
Kia Solomon Is. 7°32S 158°26E 287 L10
Kiabukwa Dem. Rep. of the Congo 8°40S 24°48E 265 D4
Kiadho → India 19°37N 77°40E 244 E3
Kiama N.S.W., Australia 34°40S 150°50E 283 C9
Kiama Dem. Rep. of the Congo 7°19S 17°49E 265 D3
Kiamari Pakistan 24°49N 66°58E 123 B1
Kiamba Phil. 6°2N 124°46E 233 H5
Kiambi Dem. Rep. of the Congo 7°15S 28°0E 268 D2
Kiambu Kenya 1°8S 36°50E 268 C4
Kiamusze = Jiamusi China 46°40N 130°26E 219 B8
Kian = Ji'an China 41°5N 126°10E 227 D14
Kiana U.S.A. 66°58N 160°26W 303 C7
Kiang West △ Gambia 13°25N 15°50W 262 C1
Kiangara Madag. 17°58S 47°2E 272 B2
Kiangsi = Jiangxi □ China 27°30N 116°0E 229 D11
Kiangsu = Jiangsu □ China 33°0N 120°0E 227 H11
Kiato Greece 38°1N 22°45E 204 C4
Kibæk Denmark 56°2N 8°51E 163 H2
Kibale △ Uganda 0°16N 30°18E 268 B3
Kibanga Port Uganda 0°10N 32°58E 268 B3
Kibangou Congo 3°26S 12°22E 264 C2
Kibara Tanzania 2°8S 33°30E 268 C3
Kibare, Mts. Dem. Rep. of the Congo 8°25S 27°10E 268 D2
Kibawe Phil. 7°34N 125°0E 233 H5
Kibenga Dem. Rep. of the Congo 7°56S 17°30E 265 D3
Kibira △ Burundi 3°6S 30°24E 268 C3
Kiboga Uganda 0°58N 31°45E 268 B3
Kibombo Dem. Rep. of the Congo 3°57S 25°53E 265 C5
Kibondo Tanzania 3°35S 30°45E 268 C3
Kibre Mengist Ethiopia 5°54N 38°59E 257 F4
Kıbrıs = Cyprus ■ Asia 35°0N 33°0E 207 F9
Kibumbu Burundi 3°32S 29°45E 268 C2
Kibungo Rwanda 2°10S 30°32E 268 C3
Kibuye Burundi 3°39S 29°59E 268 C2
Kibuye Rwanda 2°3S 29°21E 268 C2
Kibwesa Tanzania 6°30S 29°58E 268 D2
Kibwezi Kenya 2°27S 37°57E 268 C4
Kicasalih Turkey 41°23N 26°48E 203 E10
Kičevo Macedonia 41°34N 20°59E 202 E4
Kichha India 28°53N 79°30E 243 E8
Kichha → India 28°41N 79°18E 243 E8
Kichmengskiy Gorodok Russia 59°59N 45°48E 186 B8
Kicking Horse Pass Canada 51°28N 116°16W 296 C5
Kîd, W. → Egypt 28°9N 34°27E 251 K5
Kid I. Antigua & B. 17°42N 61°49W 322 c
Kidal Mali 18°26N 1°22E 263 B5
Kidal □ Mali 19°55N 1°5E 261 E5
Kidapawan Phil. 7°1N 125°3E 233 H5
Kidderminster U.K. 52°24N 2°15W 169 E5
Kidepo Valley △ Uganda 3°52N 33°50E 268 B3
Kidete Tanzania 6°25S 37°17E 268 D4
Kidira Senegal 14°28N 12°13W 262 C2
Kidnappers, C. N.Z. 39°38S 177°5E 284 F6
Kidsgrove U.K. 53°5N 2°14W 168 D5
Kidston Australia 18°52S 144°8E 280 B3
Kidugallo Tanzania 6°49S 38°15E 268 D4
Kidurong, Tanjong Malaysia 3°16N 113°3E 235 B4
Kiel Germany 54°19N 10°8E 178 A6
Kiel Canal = Nord-Ostsee-Kanal Germany 54°12N 9°32E 178 A5
Kiel-Kanal = Nord-Ostsee-Kanal Germany 54°12N 9°32E 178 A5
Kielce Poland 50°52N 20°42E 185 H7
Kielder Water U.K. 55°11N 2°31W 168 B5
Kieler Bucht Germany 54°35N 10°25E 178 A6
Kiembara Burkina Faso 13°15N 2°44W 262 C4
Kien Binh Vietnam 9°55N 105°19E 237 H5
Kien Tan Vietnam 10°7N 105°17E 237 G5
Kienge Dem. Rep. of the Congo 10°30S 27°30E 269 E2
Kierling Austria 48°18N 16°16E 142 A1
Kierlingbach → Austria 48°18N 16°19E 142 A1
Kiessé Niger 13°29N 4°1E 263 C5
Kieta Papua N. G. 6°12S 155°36E 286 D8
Kiev = Kyyiv Ukraine 50°30N 30°28E 177 C16
Kifaya Guinea 12°10N 13°4W 262 C2
Kiffa Mauritania 16°37N 11°24W 262 B2
Kifisos → Athina, Greece 37°58N 23°42E 112 B2
Kifisos → Voiotia, Greece 38°35N 23°20E 204 C5
Kifissia Greece 38°4N 23°49E 204 C5
Kifrī Iraq 34°45N 45°0E 213 E11
Kigali Rwanda 1°59S 30°4E 268 C3
Kigarama Tanzania 1°1S 31°50E 268 C3
Kigelle Sudan 8°40N 34°2E 257 F3
Kigezi △ Uganda 0°34S 29°55E 268 C2
Kiğı Turkey 39°18N 40°21E 213 C9
Kigoma □ Tanzania 5°0S 30°0E 268 D3
Kigoma-Ujiji Tanzania 4°55S 29°36E 268 C2
Kigomasha, Ras Tanzania 4°58S 38°58E 268 C4
Kigosi △ Tanzania 4°10S 31°45E 268 C3
Kığzı Turkey 38°18N 43°25E 246 B4
Kihei U.S.A. 20°47N 156°28W 302 C5
Kihikihi N.Z. 38°2S 175°22E 284 E4
Kihnu Estonia 58°9N 24°1E 188 C3
Kiholo B. U.S.A. 19°50N 155°55W 302 D6
Kii-Hantō Japan 34°0N 135°45E 223 D7
Kii-Nagashima Japan 34°12N 136°20E 223 C8
Kii-Sanchi Japan 34°20N 136°0E 223 C8
Kii-Suidō Japan 33°40N 134°45E 222 D6
Kiira Dam Uganda 0°25N 33°0E 268 B3
Kiire Japan 31°22N 130°33E 222 F2
Kijik U.S.A. 60°20N 154°20W 303 F9
Kikaiga-Shima Japan 28°19N 129°59E 221 K4
Kikiakhi = Rigolet Canada 54°10N 58°23W 299 B8
Kikinda Serbia 45°50N 20°30E 182 E5
Kikládhes = Cyclades Greece 37°0N 24°30E 204 E6
Kikoira Australia 33°39S 146°40E 283 B7
Kikombo Bandundu, Dem. Rep. of the Congo 5°37S 18°50E 265 D3
Kikombo Bandundu, Dem. Rep. of the Congo 5°49S 17°45E 265 D3
Kikongo Dem. Rep. of the Congo 4°16S 17°17E 265 C3
Kikori Papua N. G. 7°25S 144°15E 286 D3
Kikori → Papua N. G. 7°38S 144°20E 286 D3
Kikuchi Japan 32°59N 130°47E 222 E2
Kikuma Japan 35°30N 139°37E 143 C2
Kikwit Dem. Rep. of the Congo 5°0S 18°45E 265 D3
Kil Sweden 59°30N 13°20E 162 F7
Kilafors Sweden 61°14N 16°36E 162 C10
Kilakkarai India 9°12N 78°47E 245 K4
Kilar India 33°6N 76°25E 242 C7
Kilauea U.S.A. 22°13N 159°25W 302 A2
Kīlauea Caldera U.S.A. 19°25N 155°17W 302 D6
Kilbarrack Ireland 53°23N 6°9W 120 A3
Kilbeggan Ireland 53°22N 7°30W 166 C4
Kilbirnie N.Z. 41°19S 174°48E 143 B1
Kilbrannan Sd. U.K. 55°37N 5°26W 167 F3
Kilbuck Mts. U.S.A. 60°36N 159°53W 303 F8
Kilburn U.K. 51°32N 0°11W 125 A2
Kilchu N. Korea 40°57N 129°25E 224 B4
Kilcoy Australia 26°59S 152°30E 281 D5
Kildare Ireland 53°9N 6°55W 166 C5
Kildare □ Ireland 53°10N 6°50W 166 C5
Kildinstroy Russia 68°48N 33°6E 160 B25
Kileikli Sudan 11°25N 25°31E 257 E2
Kilembe Dem. Rep. of the Congo 5°42S 19°55E 265 D3
Kilen Norway 59°20N 8°49E 164 E5
Kilfinnane Ireland 52°21N 8°28W 166 D3
Kilgarvan Ireland 51°54N 9°27W 166 E2
Kilgore U.S.A. 32°23N 94°53W 314 E7
Kilgoris Kenya 1°0S 34°53E 268 C3
Kilibo Benin 8°32N 2°38E 263 D5
Kilifi Kenya 3°40S 39°48E 268 C4
Kilimanjaro Tanzania 3°7S 37°20E 268 C4
Kilimanjaro □ Tanzania 4°0S 38°0E 268 C4
Kilimanjaro △ Tanzania 3°2S 37°19E 268 C4
Kilimli Turkey 41°28N 31°50E 212 B4
Kilinailau Is. Papua N. G. 4°45S 155°20E 286 C8
Kilindini Kenya 4°4S 39°40E 268 C4
Kilis Turkey 36°42N 37°6E 250 B8
Kilis □ Turkey 36°50N 37°10E 212 D7
Kiliya Ukraine 45°28N 29°16E 183 E14
Kilkee Ireland 52°41N 9°39W 166 D2
Kilkeel U.K. 54°4N 6°0W 166 B5
Kilkenny Ireland 52°39N 7°15W 166 D4
Kilkenny □ Ireland 52°35N 7°15W 166 D4
Kilkieran B. Ireland 53°20N 9°41W 166 C2
Kilkís Greece 40°58N 22°57E 202 F6
Kilkís □ Greece 41°5N 22°50E 202 E6
Killakee Ireland 53°15N 6°19W 120 B2
Killala Ireland 54°13N 9°12W 166 B2
Killala B. Ireland 54°16N 9°8W 166 B2
Killaloe Ont., Canada 45°33N 77°25W 312 A7
Killaloe Clare, Ireland 52°48N 8°28W 166 D3
Killarney Queens., Australia 28°20S 152°18E 281 D5
Killarney Man., Canada 49°10N 99°40W 297 D9
Killarney Kerry, Ireland 52°4N 9°30W 166 D2
Killarney, L. Bahamas 25°3N 77°27W 153 b
Killarney △ Ireland 52°0N 9°33W 166 D2
Killary Harbour Ireland 53°38N 9°52W 166 C2
Killdeer U.S.A. 47°22N 102°45W 308 B2
Killeberg Sweden 56°29N 14°5E 163 H8
Killeen U.S.A. 31°7N 97°44W 314 F6
Killester Ireland 53°22N 6°11W 120 A2
Killin U.K. 56°28N 4°19W 167 E4
Killiney Ireland 53°15N 6°7W 120 B3
Killiney B. Ireland 53°16N 6°5W 120 B3
Killington Pk. U.S.A. 43°36N 72°49W 313 C12
Killini = Kyllini Greece 37°55N 21°8E 207 D3
Killini Greece 37°54N 22°25E 204 D4
Killorglin Ireland 52°6N 9°47W 166 D2
Killybegs Ireland 54°38N 8°26W 166 B3
Kilmacud Ireland 53°17N 6°13W 120 B2
Kilmainham Ireland 53°20N 6°17W 120 A2
Kilmainham Gaol Ireland 53°21N 6°19W 120 A2
Kilmarnock U.K. 55°37N 4°29W 167 F4
Kilmashogue Mt. Ireland 53°15N 6°15W 120 B2
Kilmez Russia 56°58N 50°55E 190 B10
Kilmez → Russia 56°58N 50°28E 190 B10
Kilmore Vic., Australia 37°25S 144°53E 283 D6
Kilmore Dublin, Ireland 53°23N 6°13W 120 A2
Kilmore Quay Ireland 52°10N 6°36W 166 D5
Kilnamanagh Ireland 53°18N 6°22W 120 B1
Kilo Finland 60°13N 24°47E 121 B1
Kilokri India 28°34N 77°15E 120 B2
Kilómetro 1082 = Joaquín V. González Argentina 25°10S 64°0W 334 B3
Kilondo Tanzania 9°45S 34°20E 269 D3
Kilosa Tanzania 6°48S 37°0E 268 D4
Kilrush Ireland 52°38N 9°29W 166 D2
Kiltan I. India 11°29N 73°0E 245 J1
Kiltiernan Ireland 53°15N 6°11W 120 B2
Kilwa Kisiwani Tanzania 8°58S 39°32E 269 D4
Kilwa Kivinje Tanzania 8°45S 39°25E 269 D4
Kilwa Masoko Tanzania 8°55S 39°30E 269 D4
Kilwinning U.K. 55°39N 4°43W 167 F4
Kim U.S.A. 37°15N 103°21W 305 H12
Kim → Cameroon 5°28N 11°7E 263 D7
Kimaam Indonesia 7°58S 138°53E 231 F9
Kimamba Tanzania 6°45S 37°10E 268 D4
Kimba Australia 33°8S 136°23E 282 B2
Kimball Nebr., U.S.A. 41°14N 103°40W 308 E2
Kimball S. Dak., U.S.A. 43°45N 98°57W 308 D4
Kimbanda Dem. Rep. of the Congo 4°16S 18°30E 265 C3
Kimbe Papua N. G. 5°33S 150°11E 286 C6
Kimbe B. Papua N. G. 5°15S 150°30E 286 C6
Kimberley W. Austral., Australia 16°20S 127°0E 278 C4
Kimberley B.C., Canada 49°40N 115°59W 296 D5
Kimberley Ont., Canada 44°23N 80°32W 312 B4
Kimberley Northern Cape, S. Africa 28°43S 24°46E 270 C3
Kimberly U.S.A. 42°32N 114°22W 304 E6
Kimbongo Dem. Rep. of the Congo 6°8S 18°1E 265 D3
Kimch'aek N. Korea 40°40N 129°10E 224 B4
Kimhae = Gimhae S. Korea 35°14N 128°53E 224 E4
Kimhwa N. Korea 38°25N 127°36E 224 C3
Kimi Greece 38°38N 24°6E 204 C6
Kimitsu Japan 35°19N 139°54E 223 B11
Kimjŏngsugŭp N. Korea 41°24N 127°45E 224 B3
Kimmage Ireland 53°18N 6°17W 120 B2
Kimmirut Canada 62°50N 69°50W 295 E18
Kimolos Greece 36°48N 24°37E 204 E6
Kimongo Congo 4°27S 12°53E 265 C2
Kimovsk Moskva, Russia 55°21N 37°28E 188 E9
Kimovsk Tula, Russia 54°0N 38°29E 188 E10
Kimpangu Dem. Rep. of the Congo 5°52S 15°3E 265 D3
Kimparana Mali 12°48N 5°0W 262 C4
Kimpese Congo 5°33S 14°26E 265 D2
Kimpese Dem. Rep. of the Congo 5°35S 14°26E 265 D2
Kimry Russia 56°55N 37°15E 188 D9
Kimstad Sweden 58°35N 15°58E 163 F9
Kimvula Dem. Rep. of the Congo 5°44S 15°58E 265 D3
Kin Burma 22°46N 94°42E 241 D5
Kin-u Burma 22°46N 95°37E 241 D5
Kin-wan Japan 26°23N 127°55E 288 a
Kinabalu, Gunung Malaysia 6°3N 116°14E 235 A5
Kinabalu △ Malaysia 6°0N 116°30E 235 A5
Kinango Kenya 4°8S 39°19E 268 C4
Kinard U.S.A. 30°16N 85°15W 316 E4
Kinaros Greece 36°59N 26°15E 205 E8
Kinaskan L. Canada 57°38N 130°8W 296 B2
Kinbasket L. Canada 52°0N 118°10W 296 C5
Kincaid U.S.A. 39°35N 89°25W 310 E7
Kincardine Canada 44°10N 81°40W 312 B3
Kinchafoonee Cr. → U.S.A. 31°38N 84°10W 316 D5
Kinchega △ Australia 32°27S 142°15E 282 B5
Kincolith Canada 55°0N 129°57W 296 C3
Kinda Kasai-Or., Dem. Rep. of the Congo 9°18S 25°4E 265 D5
Kinda Katanga, Dem. Rep. of the Congo 4°47S 21°48E 265 C4
Kindambi Dem. Rep. of the Congo 5°6S 18°14E 265 D3
Kindberg Austria 47°30N 15°27E 180 D8
Kinde U.S.A. 43°56N 83°0W 312 C2
Kindele Dem. Rep. of the Congo 8°39S 24°10E 265 D4
Kinder Scout U.K. 53°24N 1°52W 168 D6
Kinderhook U.S.A. 39°42N 91°10W 310 E5
Kindersley Canada 51°30N 109°10W 297 C7
Kindi Iraq 33°18N 44°22E 113 B2
Kindia Guinea 10°0N 12°52W 262 D2
Kindongo Dem. Rep. of the Congo 3°58S 17°30E 264 C3
Kindu Dem. Rep. of the Congo 2°55S 25°50E 264 C5
Kinel Russia 53°15N 50°40E 190 D10
Kineshma Russia 57°30N 42°5E 190 B6
Kinesi Tanzania 1°25S 33°50E 268 C3
King, L. Australia 33°10S 119°35E 279 F2
King, Mt. Australia 25°10S 147°30E 280 D4
King Christian I. Canada 77°48N 101°40W 295 B11
King City Calif., U.S.A. 36°13N 121°8W 306 J5
King City Mo., U.S.A. 40°3N 94°31W 310 D2
King Cove U.S.A. 55°3N 162°19W 303 J7
King Cr. → Australia 24°35S 139°30E 280 C2
King Edward → Australia 14°14S 126°35E 278 B4
King Edward Point S. Georgia 54°17S 36°30W 151 B1
King Frederick VI Land = Kong Frederik VI Kyst Greenland 63°0N 43°0W 154 E6
King George B. Falk. Is. 51°30S 60°30W 153 f
King George I. Antarctica 60°0S 60°0W 151 C18
King George Is. Canada 57°20N 80°30W 295 F15
King George Sd. Australia 35°5S 118°0E 279 G2
King George VI Falls Guyana 5°42N 61°5W 329 B5
King I. = Kadan Kyun Burma 12°30N 98°20E 236 F2
King I. Tas., Australia 39°50S 144°0E 281 F3
King I. B.C., Canada 52°10N 127°40W 296 C3
King Khalid Military City = Madinat al Malik Khālid al Askarīyah Si. Arabia 27°54N 45°31E 246 E5
King Leopold Ranges Australia 17°30S 125°45E 278 C4
King of Prussia U.S.A. 40°5N 75°23W 313 F9
King Salmon U.S.A. 58°42N 156°40W 303 G8
King Sd. Australia 16°50S 123°20E 278 C3
King Sejong Antarctica 62°30S 58°0W 151 C18
King William I. Canada 69°10N 97°25W 294 D12
King William's Town S. Africa 32°51S 27°22E 270 D4
Kingaok = Bathurst Inlet Canada 66°50N 108°1W 294 D10
Kingaroy Australia 26°32S 151°51E 281 D5
Kingdom City U.S.A. 38°56N 91°56W 310 F5
Kingfisher U.S.A. 35°52N 97°56W 314 D6
Kinghorn U.K. 56°5N 3°10W 121 A2
Kingirbān Iraq 34°40N 44°54E 246 C5
Kingisepp = Kuressaare Estonia 58°15N 22°30E 188 C2
Kingisepp Russia 59°25N 28°40E 188 C5
Kingking = Pantukan Phil. 7°9N 125°54E 233 H5
Kinglake △ Australia 37°30S 145°22E 283 D6
Kingman Ariz., U.S.A. 35°12N 114°4W 307 K12
Kingman Ind., U.S.A. 39°58N 87°18W 311 E9
Kingman Kans., U.S.A. 37°39N 98°7W 308 G4
Kingoonya Australia 30°55S 135°19E 281 E2
Kingri Pakistan 30°27N 69°49E 242 D3
Kings → U.S.A. 36°3N 119°50W 306 J7
Kings Canyon Australia 24°15S 131°34E 278 D5
Kings Canyon △ U.S.A. 36°50N 118°40W 306 J8
Kings County = Offaly □ Ireland 53°15N 7°30W 166 C4
Kings Cross Sydney, Australia 139 c3
King's Cross London, U.K. 125 a4
Kings Domain Australia 37°49S 144°58E 128 A1
Kings Forest = Kongelunden Denmark 55°34N 12°34E 118 B3
King's Lynn U.K. 52°45N 0°24E 168 E8
Kings Park N.Y., U.S.A. 40°53N 73°16W 313 F11
Kings Park Va., U.S.A. 38°48N 77°17W 143 C2
Kings Park West U.S.A. 38°48N 77°18W 143 C2
Kings Peak U.S.A. 40°46N 110°23W 304 F8
King's Trough Atl. Oc. 43°48N 22°0W 152 B9
Kingsbridge U.K. 50°17N 3°47W 169 G4
Kingsburg U.S.A. 36°31N 119°33W 306 J7
Kingsbury Vic., Australia 37°43S 145°2E 128 A2
Kingsbury London, U.K. 51°34N 0°15W 125 A2
Kingscote Australia 35°40S 137°38E 282 C2
Kingscourt Ireland 53°55N 6°48W 166 C5
Kingsford N.S.W., Australia 33°56S 151°14E 139 B2
Kingsford Mich., U.S.A. 45°48N 88°4W 308 C9
Kingsford Smith, Sydney ✈ (SYD) Australia 33°57S 151°11E 139 B2
Kingsland U.S.A. 30°48N 81°41W 316 E8
Kingsport U.S.A. 36°33N 82°33W 315 C13
Kingston Ont., Canada 44°14N 76°30W 313 B8
Kingston Jamaica 18°0N 76°50W 320 a
Kingston N.Z. 45°20S 168°43E 285 F3
Kingston N.H., U.S.A. 42°56N 71°3W 313 D13
Kingston N.Y., U.S.A. 41°56N 73°59W 313 E11
Kingston Pa., U.S.A. 41°16N 75°54W 313 E9
Kingston R.I., U.S.A. 41°29N 71°30W 313 E13
Kingston Pk. U.S.A. 35°44N 115°55W 307 K11
Kingston South East Australia 36°51S 139°55E 282 D3
Kingston upon Hull U.K. 53°45N 0°21W 168 D7
Kingston upon Hull □ U.K. 53°45N 0°21W 168 D7
Kingston-upon-Thames □ U.K. 51°24N 0°17W 125 B2
Kingston Vale U.K. 51°25N 0°25W 125 B2
Kingstown = Dún Laoghaire Ireland 53°17N 6°8W 120 B3
Kingstown N.S.W., Australia 30°29S 151°6E 283 A9
Kingstown St. Vincent 13°10N 61°10W 323 n
Kingstree U.S.A. 33°40N 79°50W 316 B10
Kingsville Ont., Canada 42°2N 82°45W 312 D2
Kingsville Tex., U.S.A. 27°31N 97°52W 314 H6
Kingsway Canada 43°38N 79°32W 141 B1
Kingtechen = Jingdezhen China 29°20N 117°11E 229 C11
Kingunda Dem. Rep. of the Congo 6°36S 16°58E 265 D3
Kingussie U.K. 57°6N 4°2W 167 D4
Kingwood U.S.A. 30°2N 95°16W 314 F7
Kinhwa = Jinhua China 29°8N 119°38E 229 C12
Kınık Antalya, Turkey 36°20N 29°20E 205 E11
Kınık İzmir, Turkey 39°6N 27°24E 205 B9
Kinistino Canada 52°57N 105°2W 297 C7
Kinjirap Daban Asia 36°40N 75°25E 240 A4
Kinkala Congo 4°18S 14°49E 265 C2
Kinki □ Japan 33°45N 136°0E 223 D8
Kinkony, Farihin' Madag. 16°8S 45°50E 272 B2
Kinleith N.Z. 38°20S 175°56E 284 E4
Kinlochleven U.K. 56°43N 5°0W 167 E4
Kinmount Canada 44°48N 78°45W 312 B6
Kinmundy U.S.A. 38°46N 88°51W 311 F8
Kinn Norway 61°34N 4°45E 164 D1
Kinna Sweden 57°32N 12°42E 163 G6
Kinnairds Hd. U.K. 57°43N 2°1W 167 D6
Kinnared Sweden 57°2N 13°7E 163 G7
Kinnarp Sweden 58°5N 13°32E 163 F7
Kinneviken Sweden 58°35N 13°15E 163 F7
Kinngait Canada 64°14N 76°32W 295 E16
Kino Nuevo Mexico 28°52N 112°3W 318 B2
Kinogitan Phil. 9°0N 124°48E 233 G5
Kinoje → Canada 52°8N 81°25W 298 B3
Kinomoto Japan 35°30N 136°13E 223 B8
Kinoni Uganda 0°41S 30°28E 268 C3
Kinoosao Canada 57°5N 102°1W 297 B8
Kinross U.K. 56°13N 3°25W 167 E5
Kinsale Cork, Ireland 51°42N 8°31W 166 E3
Kinsale Montserrat 16°42N 62°13W 323 p
Kinsale, Old Hd. of Ireland 51°37N 8°33W 166 E3
Kinsaley Ireland 53°24N 6°11W 120 A2
Kinsarvik Norway 60°22N 6°43E 164 D3
Kinsha = Chang Jiang → China 31°48N 121°10E 229 B13
Kinshasa Dem. Rep. of the Congo 4°20S 15°15E 265 C3
Kinsley U.S.A. 37°55N 99°25W 308 G4
Kinsman U.S.A. 41°26N 80°35W 312 E4
Kinston Ala., U.S.A. 31°13N 86°10W 316 D3
Kinston N.C., U.S.A. 35°16N 77°35W 315 D16
Kintamani Indonesia 8°14S 115°19E 231 J18
Kintampo Ghana 8°5N 1°41W 263 D4
Kintap Indonesia 3°51S 115°13E 235 C5
Kintore U.K. 57°14N 2°20W 167 D6
Kintore Ra. Australia 23°15S 128°47E 278 D4
Kintshua Dem. Rep. of the Congo 4°27S 19°38E 265 C3
Kintyre U.K. 55°30N 5°35W 167 F3
Kintyre, Mull of U.K. 55°17N 5°47W 167 F3
Kinu-Gawa → Japan 35°36N 139°57E 223 B11
Kinushseo → Canada 55°15N 83°45W 298 A3
Kinuso Canada 55°20N 115°25W 296 B5
Kinvarra Ireland 53°8N 8°56W 166 C3
Kinwat India 19°38N 78°12E 244 E4
Kinyangiri Tanzania 4°25S 34°37E 268 C3
Kinyeti Sudan 3°57N 32°54E 257 G3
Kinzia Dem. Rep. of the Congo 3°36S 18°26E 264 C3
Kinzig → Germany 48°36N 7°49E 179 G3
Kinzua U.S.A. 41°52N 78°58W 312 E6
Kioni Greece 38°27N 20°41E 207 C2
Kiosk Canada 46°6N 78°53W 298 C4
Kiowa Kans., U.S.A. 37°1N 98°29W 308 G4
Kiowa Okla., U.S.A. 34°43N 95°54W 314 D7
Kipahigan L. Canada 55°20N 101°55W 297 B8
Kipanga Tanzania 6°15S 35°20E 268 D4
Kipapa → U.S.A. 21°24N 158°1W 302 K13
Kiparissia Greece 37°15N 21°40E 204 D3
Kiparissiakos Kolpos Greece 37°25N 21°25E 204 D3
Kipawa, L. Canada 46°50N 79°0W 298 C4
Kipembawe Tanzania 7°38S 33°27E 268 D3
Kipengere Ra. Tanzania 9°12S 34°15E 269 D3
Kipili Tanzania 7°28S 30°32E 268 D3
Kipini Kenya 2°30S 40°32E 268 C5
Kipling Canada 50°6N 102°38W 297 C8
Kipling Heights Canada 43°43N 79°34W 141 A1
Kipnuk U.S.A. 59°56N 164°3W 303 G6
Kippure Ireland 53°11N 6°21W 166 C5
Kipseli Athens, Greece 112 a3
Kipushi Dem. Rep. of the Congo 11°48S 27°12E 269 E2
Kira Panagia Greece 39°17N 24°4E 204 B6
Kirakira Solomon Is. 10°27S 161°56E 287 N11
Kirandul India 18°33N 81°10E 244 E5
Kirane Mali 15°20N 10°20W 262 B2
Kiranomena Madag. 18°17S 46°2E 272 B2
Kiraz Turkey 38°14N 28°13E 205 C10
Kirazlı Turkey 40°2N 26°41E 203 F10
Kirchhain Germany 50°47N 8°56E 178 E4
Kirchheim Germany 48°39N 9°27E 179 G5
Kirchheimbolanden Germany 49°40N 8°0E 179 F3
Kirchschlag Austria 47°30N 16°19E 181 D9
Kirchstockbach Germany 48°1N 11°40E 131 B3
Kirchtrudering Germany 48°7N 11°40E 131 B3
Kirdâsa Egypt 30°2N 31°6E 251 H2
Kirdimi Chad 18°11N 18°31E 259 E3
Kireç Turkey 39°33N 28°22E 205 B10
Kirensk Russia 57°50N 107°55E 215 D11
Kirghiz Range Asia 42°40N 73°40E 217 D8
Kirghizia = Kyrgyzstan ■ Asia 42°0N 75°0E 217 D9
Kirgiz-Kulak = Chirchiq Uzbekistan 41°29N 69°35E 217 D7
Kirgiziya Steppe Eurasia 50°0N 55°0E 187 E10
Kiri Dem. Rep. of the Congo 1°29S 19°0E 264 C3
Kiri Buru India 22°0N 85°0E 244 D7
Kiribati ■ Pac. Oc. 3°0S 180°0E 277 A15
Kırıkhan Turkey 36°31N 36°21E 250 B7
Kirikiri Nigeria 6°26N 3°18E 124 B1
Kırıkkale Turkey 39°51N 33°32E 212 C5
Kirikopuni N.Z. 35°50S 174°1E 284 B3
Kirillov Russia 59°49N 38°24E 188 C10
Kirin = Jilin China 43°44N 126°30E 227 C14
Kirindi Oya → Sri Lanka 6°15N 81°20E 245 L5
Kirinyaga = Kenya, Mt. Kenya 0°10S 37°18E 268 C4
Kirirom △ Cambodia 11°18N 104°5E 237 G5
Kirishi Russia 59°28N 31°59E 188 C7
Kirishima Yaku △ Japan 31°24N 130°50E 221 J5
Kirishima-Yama Japan 31°58N 130°55E 222 F2
Kiritimati Kiribati 1°58N 157°27W 289 G12
Kiriwina I. Papua N. G. 8°40S 151°6E 286 E6
Kirka Turkey 39°17N 30°33E 205 B12
Kırkağaç Turkey 39°8N 27°40E 205 B9
Kirkby U.K. 53°30N 2°54W 168 D5
Kirkby-in-Ashfield U.K. 53°6N 1°14W 168 D6
Kirkby Lonsdale U.K. 54°12N 2°36W 168 C5
Kirkby Stephen U.K. 54°29N 2°21W 168 C5
Kirkcaldy U.K. 56°7N 3°9W 167 E5
Kirkcudbright U.K. 54°50N 4°2W 167 G4
Kirke Værløse Denmark 55°47N 12°19E 118 A1
Kirkehamn Norway 58°14N 6°31E 164 F3
Kirkenær Norway 60°27N 12°3E 164 D9
Kirkenes Norway 69°40N 30°5E 160 B24
Kirkfield Canada 44°34N 78°59W 312 B6
Kirkhill U.K. 55°50N 3°13W 121 B2
Kirkintilloch U.K. 55°56N 4°8W 167 F4
Kirkjubæjarklaustur Iceland 63°47N 18°4W 155 D8
Kirkkonummi Finland 60°8N 24°26E 188 B3
Kirkland Ill., U.S.A. 42°6N 88°51W 311 B8
Kirkland Wash., U.S.A. 47°40N 122°12W 306 C4
Kirkland Lake Canada 48°9N 80°2W 298 C3
Kırklareli Turkey 41°44N 27°15E 203 E11
Kırklareli □ Turkey 41°45N 27°15E 203 E11
Kirklin U.S.A. 40°12N 86°22W 311 D10
Kirkliston U.K. 55°57N 3°24W 121 B1
Kirkliston Ra. N.Z. 44°25S 170°34E 285 E5
Kirknewton U.K. 55°53N 3°25W 121 B1
Kirknitz = Cerknica Slovenia 45°48N 14°21E 199 C11
Kirksville U.S.A. 40°12N 92°35W 310 D4
Kirkūk Iraq 35°30N 44°21E 213 E11
Kirkwall U.K. 58°59N 2°58W 167 C6
Kirkwood Eastern Cape, S. Africa 33°22S 25°15E 270 D4
Kirkwood Mo., U.S.A. 38°35N 90°24W 310 F6
Kirlampudi India 17°12N 82°12E 244 F6
Kirmasti = Mustafakemalpaşa Turkey 40°2N 28°24E 203 F12
Kirn Germany 49°47N 7°26E 179 F3
Kirobasi Turkey 36°43N 33°52E 250 B4
Kirov Kaluga, Russia 54°3N 34°20E 188 E8
Kirov Kirov, Russia 58°35N 49°40E 186 C8

Kirov Palace of Culture Russia 59°55N 30°16E 137 B1
Kirovabad = Gäncä Azerbaijan 40°45N 46°20E 191 K8
Kirovakan = Vanadzor Armenia 40°48N 44°30E 191 K7
Kirovo = Kirovohrad Ukraine 48°35N 32°20E 189 H7
Kirovograd = Kirovohrad Ukraine 48°35N 32°20E 189 H7
Kirovohrad Ukraine 48°35N 32°20E 189 H7
Kirovohrad □ Ukraine 48°30N 31°30E 189 H6
Kirovsk Russia 67°32N 33°41E 186 A5
Kirovskiy = Balpyq Bī Kazakhstan 44°52N 78°12E 217 D9
Kirovskiy Astrakhan, Russia 45°51N 48°11E 191 H9
Kirovskiy Kamchatka, Russia 54°27N 155°42E 215 D16
Kirovskiy Primorsk, Russia 45°7N 133°30E 220 B6
Kirriemuir U.K. 56°41N 3°1W 167 E5
Kirsanov Russia 52°35N 42°40E 190 D6
Kırşehir Turkey 39°14N 34°5E 212 C6
Kirtachi Niger 12°52N 2°30E 263 C5
Kīrteh Afghan. 32°15N 63°0E 240 B1
Kirthar △ Pakistan 25°45N 67°30E 242 F2
Kirthar Range Pakistan 27°0N 67°0E 242 F2
Kirtland U.S.A. 36°44N 108°21W 305 H9
Kiruna Sweden 67°52N 20°15E 160 C19
Kirundu Dem. Rep. of the Congo 0°50S 25°35E 264 C5
Kirya Russia 55°8N 46°50E 190 C8
Kiryat Anavim Israel 31°49N 35°6E 123 B1
Kiryat Ha Yovel Israel 31°46N 35°10E 123 B1
Kiryū Japan 36°24N 139°20E 223 A11
Kisa Sweden 58°0N 15°39E 163 G9
Kisaga Tanzania 4°30S 34°23E 268 C3
Kisalföld Hungary 47°30N 17°0E 182 C2
Kisambo Dem. Rep. of the Congo 6°25S 18°14E 265 D3
Kisandji Dem. Rep. of the Congo 6°18S 19°16E 265 D3
Kisanga Dem. Rep. of the Congo 2°30N 26°35E 268 B2
Kisangani Dem. Rep. of the Congo 0°35N 25°15E 268 B2
Kisantu Dem. Rep. of the Congo 5°7S 15°5E 265 D3
Kisar Indonesia 8°5S 127°10E 231 F7
Kisaran Indonesia 3°0N 99°37E 234 B1
Kisarawe Tanzania 6°53S 39°0E 268 D4
Kisarazu Japan 35°23N 139°55E 223 B11
Kisbér Hungary 47°30N 18°2E 182 C3
Kiselevsk Russia 54°0N 86°39E 217 B11
Kish = Qeys Iran 26°32N 53°58E 249 A6
Kishanganga → Pakistan 34°18N 73°28E 243 B5
Kishanganj India 26°3N 88°14E 241 B2
Kishangarh Raj., India 26°34N 74°52E 242 F6
Kishangarh Raj., India 27°50N 70°30E 242 F4
Kishb, Ḥarrat al Si. Arabia 22°30N 40°15E 248 B3
Kishi Nigeria 9°1N 3°52E 263 D5
Kishinev = Chişinău Moldova 47°2N 28°50E 183 C13
Kishiwada Japan 34°28N 135°22E 223 C7
Kishkareny = Lazo Moldova 47°33N 28°2E 183 C13
Kishkenekól Kazakhstan 53°38N 72°20E 217 B8
Kishorganj Bangla. 24°26N 90°40E 241 C3
Kishtwar India 33°20N 75°48E 242 C6
Kishwaukee → U.S.A. 42°12N 89°8W 310 B7
Kisielice Poland 53°36N 19°16E 184 E6
Kisigo ⌂ Tanzania 6°27S 34°17E 268 D3
Kisii Kenya 0°40S 34°45E 268 C3
Kisiju Tanzania 7°23S 39°19E 268 D4
Kısıklı Turkey 41°1N 29°2E 122 B2
Kisir Turkey 41°0N 43°5E 213 B10
Kisizi Uganda 1°0S 29°58E 268 C2
Kiska I. U.S.A. 51°59N 177°30E 303 L2
Kiskomárom = Zalakomár Hungary 46°33N 17°10E 182 D2
Kiskőrei-víztároló Hungary 47°31N 20°36E 182 C5
Kiskőrös Hungary 46°37N 19°20E 182 D4
Kiskundorozsma Hungary 46°16N 20°5E 182 D5
Kiskunfélegyháza Hungary 46°42N 19°53E 182 D4
Kiskunhalas Hungary 46°28N 19°37E 182 D4
Kiskunmajsa Hungary 46°30N 19°48E 182 D4
Kiskunsági △ Hungary 46°39N 19°30E 182 D4
Kislovodsk Russia 43°50N 42°45E 191 J6
Kismaayo Somali Rep. 0°22S 42°32E 267 E5
Kismayu △ Somali Rep. 1°25N 41°30E 267 D5
Kiso-Gawa → Japan 35°20N 136°45E 223 B8
Kiso-Sammyaku Japan 35°45N 137°45E 223 B9
Kisofukushima Japan 35°52N 137°43E 223 B9
Kisoro Uganda 1°17S 29°48E 268 C2
Kispest Hungary 47°27N 19°8E 117 B2
Kissamos = Kasteli Greece 35°29N 23°38E 207 E4
Kissamos, Kolpos Greece 35°30N 23°38E 207 E4
Kissidougou Guinea 9°5N 10°5W 262 D2
Kissimmee U.S.A. 28°18N 81°24W 317 G8
Kissimmee → U.S.A. 27°9N 80°52W 317 H8
Kissimmee, L. U.S.A. 27°55N 81°17W 317 H8
Kississing L. Canada 55°10N 101°20W 297 B8
Kissónerga Cyprus 34°49N 32°24E 207 F8
Kissu, J. Sudan 21°37N 25°10E 256 C2
Kista Sweden 59°24N 17°57E 139 A1
Kistanje Croatia 43°58N 15°55E 199 E12
Kistna = Krishna → India 15°57N 80°59E 245 G5
Kisújszállás Hungary 47°12N 20°50E 182 C5
Kisuki Japan 35°17N 132°54E 222 B4
Kisumu Kenya 0°3S 34°45E 268 C3
Kisvárda Hungary 48°14N 22°4E 182 B7
Kiswani Tanzania 4°5S 37°57E 268 C4
Kiswere Tanzania 9°27S 39°30E 269 D4
Kit Carson U.S.A. 38°46N 102°48W 304 G12
Kita Ōsaka, Japan 34°41N 135°30E 133 A2
Kita Tōkyō, Japan 35°44N 139°44E 140 A3
Kita Mali 13°5N 9°25W 262 C3
Kita-Ura Japan 36°0N 140°34E 223 B12
Kitaa □ Greenland 70°0N 47°0W 154 C6
Kitaibaraki Japan 36°50N 140°45E 221 F10
Kitakami Japan 39°20N 141°10E 220 E10
Kitakami-Gawa → Japan 38°25N 141°19E 220 E10
Kitakami-Sammyaku Japan 39°30N 141°30E 220 E10
Kitakata Japan 37°39N 139°52E 220 F9
Kitakyūshū Japan 33°50N 130°50E 222 D2
Kitale Kenya 1°0N 35°0E 268 B4
Kitami Japan 43°48N 143°54E 220 C11
Kitami-Sammyaku Japan 44°22N 142°43E 220 B11
Kitangiri, L. Tanzania 4°5S 34°20E 268 C3
Kitano Hana Iwo Jima 24°49N 141°20E 288 b
Kitano-Kaikyō Japan 34°17N 134°58E 222 C6
Kitaotao Phil. 7°40N 125°1E 233 H5
Kitava I. Papua N. G. 8°40S 151°20E 286 E6
Kitaya Tanzania 10°38S 40°8E 269 E5
Kitazawa Japan 35°39N 139°40E 140 B3
Kitcharao Phil. 9°27N 125°36E 233 G5
Kitchener Canada 43°27N 80°29W 312 C4
Kitee Finland 62°5N 30°8E 188 A6
Kitega = Gitega Burundi 3°26S 29°56E 268 C2
Kitengo Dem. Rep. of the Congo 7°26S 24°8E 265 D4
Kitgum Uganda 3°17N 32°52E 268 B3
Kíthira = Kythira Greece 36°8N 23°0E 204 E5
Kíthnos Greece 37°26N 24°27E 204 D6
Kiti Cyprus 34°50N 33°34E 207 F9
Kiti, C. Cyprus 34°48N 33°36E 207 F9
Kitimat Canada 54°3N 128°38W 296 C3
Kitinen → Finland 67°14N 27°27E 160 C22
Kitiyab Sudan 17°13N 33°35E 257 D3
Kitombe Dem. Rep. of the Congo 5°22S 18°59E 265 D3
Kitridge Pt. Barbados 13°9N 59°25W 323 r
Kitros Greece 40°22N 22°34E 202 F6
Kitsman Ukraine 48°26N 25°46E 183 B10
Kitsuki Japan 33°25N 131°37E 222 D3
Kittakittaooloo, L. Australia 28°3S 138°14E 281 D2
Kittanning U.S.A. 40°49N 79°31W 312 F5
Kittatinny Mt. U.S.A. 41°19N 74°39W 313 F10
Kittery U.S.A. 43°5N 70°45W 313 C14
Kittilä Finland 67°40N 24°51E 160 C21
Kitui Kenya 1°17S 38°0E 268 C4
Kitwanga Canada 55°6N 128°4W 296 B3
Kitwe Zambia 12°54S 28°13E 269 E2
Kityang = Jieyang China 23°35N 116°21E 229 F11
Kitzbühel Austria 47°27N 12°24E 180 D5
Kitzbühler Alpen Austria 47°20N 12°20E 180 D5
Kitzingen Germany 49°44N 10°9E 179 F6
Kiu Tsiu China 22°22N 114°17E 122 A2
Kiukiang = Jiujiang China 29°42N 115°58E 229 C10
Kiunga Papua N. G. 6°7S 141°18E 286 D1
Kiunga Marine ⌂ Kenya 2°1S 41°14E 268 C5
Kivalina U.S.A. 67°44N 164°33W 303 C6
Kivarli India 24°33N 72°46E 242 G5
Kivertsi Ukraine 50°50N 25°28E 177 C13
Kividhes Cyprus 34°46N 32°51E 207 F8
Kivik Sweden 55°41N 14°13E 163 J8
Kivistö Finland 60°18N 24°50E 121 B2
Kivotos Greece 40°13N 21°26E 202 F5
Kivu, L. Dem. Rep. of the Congo 1°48S 29°0E 268 C2
Kiwai I. Papua N. G. 8°35S 143°30E 286 E2
Kiwirrkurra Australia 22°49S 127°45E 278 D4
Kiwirrkurra ✪ Australia 22°49S 127°45E 278 D4
Kiyev = Kyyiv Ukraine 50°30N 30°28E 177 C16
Kiyevskoye Vdkhr. = Kyyivske Vdskh. Ukraine 51°0N 30°25E 177 C16
Kıyıköy Turkey 41°38N 28°5E 203 E12
Kizel Russia 59°3N 57°40E 186 C10
Kiziba-Baluba ⌂ Congo 11°50S 28°0E 269 E2
Kiziguru Rwanda 1°46S 30°23E 268 C3
Kızıl Adalar Turkey 40°52N 29°5E 203 F13
Kızıl Dağ Turkey 36°19N 35°50E 250 B6
Kızıl Irmak → Turkey 41°44N 35°58E 212 B6
Kızıl Jilga China 35°26N 78°50E 243 B8
Kizil Yurt Russia 43°13N 46°54E 191 J8
Kızılcabölük Turkey 37°37N 29°1E 205 D11
Kızılcadağ Turkey 37°1N 29°58E 205 D11
Kızılcahamam Turkey 40°30N 32°30E 212 B5
Kızıldağ △ Turkey 38°5N 31°20E 246 B1
Kızılhisar Turkey 37°32N 29°17E 212 D3
Kızılırmak Turkey 40°21N 33°59E 212 B5
Kızılkaya Turkey 37°18N 30°27E 205 D12
Kızılören Turkey 38°15N 30°10E 205 C12
Kızıltepe Turkey 37°12N 40°35E 213 D9
Kızıltoprak Turkey 40°58N 29°3E 122 C2
Kizimkazi Tanzania 6°28S 39°30E 268 D4
Kizlyar Russia 43°51N 46°40E 191 J8
Kizuri Japan 34°38N 135°34E 133 B2
Kizyl-Arvat = Serdar Turkmenistan 39°4N 56°23E 247 B8
Kjellerup Denmark 56°17N 9°25E 163 H3
Kjellmyra Norway 60°39N 12°1E 164 D9
Kjelsås Norway 59°57N 10°47E 133 A3
Kjølen Norway 62°3N 8°45E 164 C5
Kjölur Iceland 64°50N 19°25W 155 C7
Kjósarsýsla □ Iceland 64°15N 21°30W 155 D3
Kladanj Bos.-H. 44°14N 18°42E 182 F3
Kladnica Serbia 43°23N 20°2E 202 C4
Kladno Czech Rep. 50°10N 14°7E 180 A7
Kladovo Serbia 44°36N 22°33E 202 B6
Kladow Germany 52°27N 13°9E 115 B1
Klæbu Norway 63°18N 10°29E 164 A7
Klaeng Thailand 12°47N 101°39E 236 F3
Klagan Malaysia 5°58N 117°27E 235 A5
Klagenfurt Austria 46°38N 14°20E 180 E7
Klaipėda Lithuania 55°43N 21°10E 184 C8
Klaipėda □ Lithuania 55°43N 21°7E 184 C8
Klaksvík Færoe Is. 62°14N 6°35W 160 E9
Klamath → U.S.A. 41°33N 124°5W 304 F1
Klamath Falls U.S.A. 42°13N 121°46W 304 E3
Klamath Mts. U.S.A. 41°50N 123°20W 304 F2
Klamono Indonesia 1°8S 131°30E 231 E8
Klampenborg Denmark 55°46N 12°35E 118 A3
Klang Malaysia 3°2N 101°26E 237 L3
Klangklang Burma 22°41N 93°26E 241 D4
Klanjec Croatia 46°3N 15°45E 199 B12
Klappan → Canada 58°0N 129°43W 296 B3
Klara = Trysilelva → Norway 61°2N 12°35E 164 C9
Klarälven → Sweden 59°23N 13°32E 162 E7
Klässbol Sweden 59°33N 12°45E 162 E6
Klaten Indonesia 7°43S 110°36E 235 D4
Klatovy Czech Rep. 49°23N 13°18E 180 B6
Klausenburg = Cluj-Napoca Romania 46°47N 23°38E 183 D8
Klawer S. Africa 31°44S 18°36E 270 D2
Klawock U.S.A. 55°33N 133°6W 303 J14
Klazienaveen Neths. 52°44N 7°0E 170 B6
Klé Mali 12°0N 6°28W 262 C3
Klečany Czech Rep. 50°10N 14°24E 135 A2
Klecko Poland 52°38N 17°25E 185 F4
Kleczew Poland 52°22N 18°9E 185 F5
Kledering Austria 48°8N 16°26E 142 B2
Kleena Kleene Canada 52°0N 124°59W 296 C4
Klein Bonaire Neth. Ant. 12°9N 68°18W 322 h
Klein Jukskei → S. Africa 26°6S 27°57E 123 A1
Klein-Karas Namibia 27°33S 18°7E 270 C2
Klein-Schlatten = Zlatna Romania 46°8N 23°11E 183 D8
Kleinbegin S. Africa 28°54S 21°40E 270 C3
Kleinmachnow Germany 52°24N 13°14E 115 B2
Kleinschönebeck Germany 52°29N 13°42E 115 B5
Klekovača Bos.-H. 44°25N 16°32E 199 D13
Klembivka Ukraine 48°23N 28°25E 183 B13
Klemetsrud Norway 59°50N 10°51E 133 A4
Klender Indonesia 6°12S 106°54E 122 B2
Klenoec Macedonia 41°32N 20°49E 202 E4
Klenovec Slovak Rep. 48°36N 19°54E 181 C12
Klerksdorp S. Africa 26°53S 26°38E 270 C4
Kleszczele Poland 52°35N 23°19E 185 F10
Kletnya Russia 53°23N 33°12E 188 F7
Kletsk = Klyetsk Belarus 53°5N 26°45E 177 B14
Kletskiy Russia 49°16N 43°11E 191 F6
Kleve Germany 51°47N 6°7E 178 D2
Kličany Czech Rep. 50°11N 14°25E 135 A2
Klickitat U.S.A. 45°49N 121°9W 304 D3
Klickitat → U.S.A. 45°42N 121°17W 306 E5
Klidhes Cyprus 35°42N 34°36E 207 E10
Klimovichi Belarus 53°36N 32°0E 188 F6
Klin Russia 56°20N 36°48E 188 D9
Klina Kosovo 42°37N 20°35E 202 D4
Klinaklini → Canada 51°21N 125°40W 296 C3
Klintehamn Sweden 57°24N 18°12E 163 G12
Klintsy Russia 52°50N 32°10E 189 F7
Klip → S. Africa 27°3S 29°3E 271 C4
Klipdale S. Africa 34°19S 19°57E 270 D2
Klippan Sweden 56°8N 13°10E 163 H7
Klipplaat S. Africa 33°1S 24°22E 270 D3
Kliprivierberg Nature Reserve S. Africa 26°16S 28°2E 123 B2
Klishkivtsi Ukraine 48°26N 26°16E 183 B11
Klisura Bulgaria 42°40N 24°28E 203 D8
Kljajićevo Serbia 45°45N 19°17E 182 E4
Ključ Bos.-H. 44°32N 16°48E 199 D13
Kłobuck Poland 50°55N 18°55E 185 H5
Klockestrand Sweden 62°53N 17°55E 162 B11
Kłodawa Poland 52°15N 18°55E 185 F5
Kłodzko Poland 50°28N 16°38E 185 H3
Kløfta Norway 60°4N 11°6E 164 D8
Klondike Canada 64°0N 139°26W 294 E4
Klondike Goldrush ⌂ U.S.A. 59°27N 135°19W 303 G14
Klong Wang Chao △ Thailand 16°20N 99°9E 236 D2
Klos Albania 41°28N 20°10E 202 E4
Klosterneuburg Austria 48°18N 16°19E 142 A1
Klosters Switz. 46°52N 9°52E 179 J5
Klötze Germany 52°37N 11°10E 178 C7
Klouto Togo 6°57N 0°44E 263 D5
Kluane △ Canada 60°45N 139°30W 296 A1
Kluane L. Canada 61°15N 138°40W 294 E4
Kluang Malaysia 2°3N 103°18E 237 L4
Kluczbork Poland 50°58N 18°12E 185 H5
Klukhori = Karachayevsk Russia 43°50N 41°55E 191 J5
Klukwan U.S.A. 59°24N 135°54W 296 B1
Klungkung Indonesia 8°32S 115°24E 231 K18
Klyetsk Belarus 53°5N 26°45E 177 B14
Klyuchevskaya, Gora Russia 55°50N 160°30E 215 D17
Klyuchi Russia 56°18N 160°51E 215 D17
Knaben Norway 58°40N 7°4E 164 F4
Knappavellir Iceland 63°54N 16°36W 155 D10
Knäred Sweden 56°31N 13°19E 163 H7
Knaresborough U.K. 54°1N 1°28W 168 C6
Knarvik Norway 60°32N 5°19E 164 D2
Knee L. Man., Canada 55°3N 94°45W 298 A1
Knee L. Sask., Canada 55°51N 107°0W 297 B7
Kneïss, Îs. Tunisia 34°22N 10°18E 258 B2
Knesset Jerusalem 123 b1
Knezha Bulgaria 43°30N 24°5E 203 C8
Knight I. U.S.A. 60°21N 147°45W 303 F11
Knight Inlet Canada 50°45N 125°40W 296 C3
Knighton U.K. 52°21N 3°3W 169 E4
Knights Ferry U.S.A. 37°50N 120°40W 306 H6
Knights Landing U.S.A. 38°48N 121°43W 306 G5
Knightsbridge London, U.K. 125 c2
Knightstown U.S.A. 39°48N 85°32W 311 E11
Knin Croatia 44°3N 16°17E 199 D13
Knislinge Sweden 56°12N 14°5E 163 H8
Knittelfeld Austria 47°13N 14°51E 180 D7
Knivsta Sweden 59°43N 17°48E 162 E11
Knjaževac Serbia 43°35N 22°18E 202 C6
Knob, C. Australia 34°32S 119°16E 279 F2
Knob Lake = Kawawachikamach Canada 54°48N 66°50W 299 B6
Knob Noster U.S.A. 38°46N 93°33W 310 F3
Knock Ireland 53°48N 8°55W 166 C3
Knockmealdown Mts. Ireland 52°14N 7°56W 166 D4
Knokke-Heist Belgium 51°21N 3°17E 170 C3
Knossos Greece 35°16N 25°10E 207 E6
Knowlton Canada 45°13N 72°31W 313 A12
Knox U.S.A. 41°18N 86°37W 311 C10
Knox Coast Antarctica 66°30S 108°0E 151 C8
Knoxville Ga., U.S.A. 32°47N 83°59W 316 C6
Knoxville Ill., U.S.A. 40°55N 90°17W 310 D6
Knoxville Iowa, U.S.A. 41°19N 93°6W 310 C4
Knoxville Pa., U.S.A. 41°57N 77°27W 312 E7
Knoxville Tenn., U.S.A. 35°58N 83°55W 315 D13
Knud Rasmussen Land Greenland 78°0N 60°0W 154 B4
Knysna S. Africa 34°2S 23°2E 270 D3
Knyszyn Poland 53°20N 22°56E 184 E9
Ko Kha Thailand 18°11N 99°24E 236 C2
Kō-Saki Japan 34°5N 129°13E 222 C1
Ko Tarutao △ Thailand 6°31N 99°26E 237 J2
Ko Yao Thailand 8°7N 98°35E 237 a
Koartac = Quaqtaq Canada 60°55N 69°40W 295 E18
Koba Aru, Indonesia 6°37S 134°37E 231 F8
Koba Bangka, Indonesia 2°26S 106°14E 234 C3
Kobánya Hungary 47°28N 19°9E 117 B2
Kobarid Slovenia 46°15N 13°30E 199 B10
Kobayashi Japan 31°56N 130°59E 222 F2
Kobbegem Belgium 50°55N 4°15E 116 A1
Kobdo = Hovd □ Mongolia 48°2N 91°37E 217 C12
Kōbe Japan 34°41N 135°13E 223 C7
Kobelyaky Ukraine 49°11N 34°9E 189 H8
København Denmark 55°40N 12°26E 118 A2
København ✕ (CPH) Denmark 55°37N 12°39E 118 B3
Kobenni Mauritania 15°58N 9°24W 262 B3
Kōbi-Sho Japan 25°56N 123°41E 221 M1
Koblenz Germany 50°21N 7°36E 179 E3
Kobo Dem. Rep. of the Congo 4°54S 17°9E 265 C3
Kobo Ethiopia 12°2N 39°56E 257 E4
Kobryn Belarus 52°15N 24°22E 177 B13
Kobuchizawa Japan 35°52N 138°19E 223 B10
Kobuk U.S.A. 66°55N 156°52W 303 C8
Kobuk → U.S.A. 66°54N 160°38W 303 C7
Kobuk Valley △ U.S.A. 67°0N 160°0W 303 C7
Kobuleti Georgia 41°55N 41°45E 191 K5
Kobyletska Polyana Ukraine 48°3N 24°4E 183 B9
Kobylin Poland 51°43N 17°12E 185 G4
Kobylisy Czech Rep. 50°7N 14°26E 135 B2
Kobyłka Poland 52°20N 21°10E 142 A3
Kobylkino Russia 54°8N 43°56E 190 C6
Koca → Turkey 40°8N 27°57E 203 F11
Kocabaş Turkey 37°49N 29°20E 205 D11
Kocaeli Turkey 40°45N 29°50E 203 F13
Kocaeli □ Turkey 40°45N 29°55E 203 F13
Kočane Serbia 43°12N 21°52E 202 C5
Kočani Macedonia 41°55N 22°25E 202 E6
Koçarlı Turkey 37°45N 27°43E 205 D9
Koceljevo Serbia 44°28N 19°50E 202 B3
Kočevje Slovenia 45°39N 14°50E 199 C11
Kocgiri = Zara Turkey 39°58N 37°43E 212 C7
Koch Bihar India 26°22N 89°29E 241 B2
Kochas India 25°15N 83°56E 243 G10
Kocher → Germany 49°13N 9°12E 179 F5
Kochi = Cochin India 9°58N 76°20E 245 K3
Kōchi Japan 33°30N 133°35E 222 D5
Kōchi □ Japan 33°40N 133°30E 222 D5
Kochiu = Gejiu China 23°20N 103°10E 228 F4
Kochkor Kyrgyzstan 42°13N 75°46E 217 D9
Kochubey Russia 44°23N 46°32E 191 H8
Kock Poland 51°38N 22°27E 185 G9
Kodaira Japan 35°43N 139°28E 140 A1
Kodala India 19°38N 84°57E 244 E7
Kodanaka Japan 35°34N 139°37E 140 B2
Kodarma India 24°28N 85°36E 243 G11
Koddiyar B. Sri Lanka 8°33N 81°15E 245 K5
Kode Sweden 57°57N 11°51E 163 G5
Kodenmacho Tokyo, Japan 140 a5
Kodi Dem. Rep. of the Congo 3°34S 22°12E 264 C4
Kodi Indonesia 9°33S 119°0E 278 A2
Kodiak U.S.A. 57°47N 152°24W 303 H9
Kodiak I. U.S.A. 57°30N 152°45W 303 H9
Kodikkarai = Point Calimere India 10°17N 79°49E 245 J4
Kodinar India 20°46N 70°46E 242 J4
Kodinsk Russia 58°40N 99°10E 215 D10
Kodlipet India 12°48N 75°53E 245 H2
Kodok Sudan 9°53N 32°7E 257 F3
Kodori → Georgia 42°47N 41°10E 191 J5
Kodoro Dem. Rep. of the Congo 1°16N 20°6E 264 B4
Kodungallur = Cranganore India 10°13N 76°13E 245 J3
Kodyma Ukraine 48°6N 29°7E 183 B14
Koedoesberge S. Africa 32°40S 20°11E 270 D3
Koekelberg Belgium 50°52N 4°20E 116 A1
Koes Namibia 26°0S 19°15E 270 C2
Kofarnihon Tajikistan 38°33N 69°1E 217 E7
Kofçaz Turkey 41°58N 27°12E 203 E11
Koffiefontein S. Africa 29°30S 25°0E 270 C4
Kofiau Indonesia 1°11S 129°50E 231 E7
Köflach Austria 47°4N 15°5E 180 D8
Koforidua Ghana 6°3N 0°17W 263 D4
Kōfu Japan 35°40N 138°30E 223 B10
Koga Japan 36°11N 139°43E 223 A11
Kogaluc → Canada 56°12N 61°44W 299 A7
Koganei Japan 35°42N 139°31E 140 A2
Kogarah Australia 33°57S 151°8E 139 B1
Køge Denmark 55°27N 12°11E 163 J6
Køge Bugt Denmark 55°34N 12°24E 163 J6
Kogi □ Nigeria 7°45N 6°45E 263 D6
Kogin Baba Nigeria 7°55N 11°35E 263 D7
Kogo Eq. Guin. 1°5N 9°42E 264 B1
Kogon Uzbekistan 39°43N 64°33E 216 E6
Koh-i-Khurd Afghan. 33°30N 65°59E 242 C1
Koh-i-Maran Pakistan 29°18N 66°50E 242 E2
Kohala Mts. U.S.A. 20°5N 155°45W 302 C6
Kohat Pakistan 33°40N 71°29E 242 C4
Kohima India 25°35N 94°10E 241 C5
Kohkīlūyeh va Būyer Aḥmadi □ Iran 31°30N 50°30E 247 D6
Kohler Ra. Antarctica 77°0S 110°0W 151 D15
Kohlfurt = Węgliniec Poland 51°18N 15°10E 185 G2
Kohlu Pakistan 29°54N 69°15E 242 E3
Kohtla-Järve Estonia 59°20N 27°20E 188 C4
Kohukohu N.Z. 35°22S 173°38E 284 B2
Kohylnyk → Ukraine 45°49N 29°40E 183 E14
Koi Sanjaq Iraq 36°5N 44°38E 213 D11
Koidu S. Leone 8°38N 10°59W 262 D2
Koihoa India 8°12N 93°29E 245 K11
Koilkuntla India 15°14N 78°19E 245 G4
Koillismaa Finland 65°44N 28°36E 160 D23
Koimbani Comoros Is. 11°37S 43°21E 272 a
Koin N. Korea 40°28N 126°18E 224 B3
Koinare Bulgaria 43°21N 24°8E 203 C8
Koindu S. Leone 8°26N 10°19W 262 D2
Koivisto = Primorsk Russia 60°22N 28°37E 188 B5
Koivupää Finland 60°18N 24°53E 121 B2
Koja Indonesia 6°8S 106°52E 122 A2
Koja Utara Indonesia 6°5S 106°53E 122 A2
Kojetín Czech Rep. 49°21N 17°20E 181 B10
Kojŏ N. Korea 38°58N 127°58E 224 C3
Kojonup Australia 33°48S 117°10E 279 F2
Kojūr Iran 36°23N 51°43E 247 B6
Kokand = Qŭqon Uzbekistan 40°31N 70°56E 217 D8
Kokas Indonesia 2°42S 132°26E 231 E8
Kokava Slovak Rep. 48°35N 19°50E 181 C12
Kokcha → Afghan. 37°9N 69°24E 240 A3
Kokchetav = Kökshetaū Kazakhstan 53°20N 69°25E 217 B7
Kōke'e State Park ⌂ U.S.A. 22°6N 159°40W 302 A2
Kokemäenjoki → Finland 61°32N 21°44E 188 B1
Kokerite Guyana 7°12N 59°35W 329 B6
Kokhav Ya'akov West Bank 31°53N 35°14E 123 A2
Kokhma Russia 56°57N 41°8E 190 B5
Koki Senegal 15°30N 15°59W 262 B1
Kokiu = Gejiu China 23°20N 103°10E 228 F4
Kokkilai Sri Lanka 9°0N 80°57E 245 K5
Kokkina Cyprus 35°11N 32°36E 207 E8
Kokkola Finland 63°50N 23°8E 160 E20
Koko Nigeria 11°28N 4°29E 263 C5
Koko Head U.S.A. 21°16N 157°43W 302 K14
Koko Kyunzu Burma 14°7N 93°22E 245 G11
Kokobunji Japan 35°42N 139°27E 140 A1
Kokobunji-Temple Japan 35°44N 139°55E 140 A4
Kokoda Papua N. G. 8°54S 147°47E 286 E4
Kokologo Burkina Faso 12°11N 1°53W 262 C4
Kokolopozo Ivory C. 5°8N 6°5W 262 D3
Kokomo U.S.A. 40°29N 86°8W 311 D10
Kokopo Papua N. G. 4°22S 152°19E 286 C7
Kokoro Niger 14°12N 0°55E 263 C5
Koksan N. Korea 38°46N 126°40E 224 C3
Kökshetaū Kazakhstan 53°20N 69°25E 217 B7
Koksoak → Canada 58°30N 68°10W 295 F18
Kokstad S. Africa 30°32S 29°29E 271 D4
Köktal Kazakhstan 44°8N 79°48E 217 D9
Kokubu Japan 31°44N 130°46E 222 F2
Kokyar China 37°23N 77°10E 217 E9
Kola Indonesia 5°35S 134°30E 231 F8
Kola Russia 68°45N 33°8E 160 B25
Kola Pen. = Kolskiy Poluostrov Russia 67°30N 38°0E 186 A6
Kolachel India 8°10N 77°15E 245 K3
Kolachi → Pakistan 27°8N 67°2E 242 F2
Kolahoi India 34°12N 75°22E 243 B6
Kolahun Liberia 8°15N 10°4W 262 D2
Kolaka Indonesia 4°3S 121°46E 231 E6
Kolar India 13°12N 78°15E 245 H4
Kolar Gold Fields India 12°58N 78°16E 245 H4
Kolarängen Sweden 59°16N 18°10E 139 B3
Kolaras India 25°14N 77°36E 242 G6
Kolari Finland 67°20N 23°48E 160 C20
Kolarovgrad = Shumen Bulgaria 43°18N 26°55E 203 C10
Kolárovo Slovak Rep. 47°54N 18°0E 181 D10
Kolašin Montenegro 42°50N 19°31E 202 D3
Kolayat India 27°50N 72°50E 242 F5
Kolbäck Sweden 59°34N 16°15E 162 E10
Kolbäcksån → Sweden 59°36N 16°16E 162 E10
Kolbeinsstaðir Iceland 64°59N 22°16W 155 C4
Kolberg = Kołobrzeg Poland 54°10N 15°35E 184 D2
Kolbermoor Germany 47°51N 12°4E 179 H8
Kolbio Kenya 1°8S 41°12E 267 E5
Kolbotn Norway 59°48N 10°48E 133 B3
Kolbu Norway 60°39N 10°45E 164 D7
Kolbuszowa Poland 50°15N 21°46E 185 H8
Kolchugino = Leninsk-Kuznetskiy Russia 54°44N 86°10E 217 B11
Kolchugino Russia 56°17N 39°22E 188 D10
Kolda Senegal 12°55N 14°57W 262 C2
Kolda □ Senegal 13°5N 14°50W 262 C2
Koldegi Sudan 12°3N 30°16E 257 E3
Kolding Denmark 55°30N 9°29E 163 J3
Kole Dem. Rep. of the Congo 3°16S 22°42E 264 C4
Koléa Algeria 36°38N 2°46E 261 A5
Kolepom = Dolak, Pulau Indonesia 8°0S 138°30E 231 F9
Kolguyev, Ostrov Russia 69°20N 48°30E 186 A8
Kolhapur India 16°43N 74°15E 244 F2
Kolia Ivory C. 9°46N 6°28W 262 D3
Koliganek U.S.A. 59°48N 157°25W 303 G8
Kolimbia Greece 36°15N 28°10E 206 E12
Kolín Czech Rep. 50°2N 15°9E 180 A8
Kolind Denmark 56°21N 10°34E 163 H4
Kolkas rags Latvia 57°46N 22°37E 184 A9
Kolkata India 22°34N 88°21E 124 B2
Kolkata Dum Dum Int. ✕ (CCU) India 22°38N 88°26E 124 B2
Kolkata Maidan India 22°33N 88°21E 124 B1
Kollam = Quilon India 8°50N 76°38E 245 K3
Kölleda Germany 51°11N 11°15E 178 D7
Kollegal India 12°9N 77°9E 245 H3
Kolleru L. India 16°40N 81°10E 244 F5
Kollum Neths. 53°17N 6°10E 170 A6
Kolmanskop Namibia 26°45S 15°14E 270 C2
Köln Germany 50°56N 6°57E 178 E2
Kolno Poland 53°25N 21°56E 184 E8
Koło Poland 52°14N 18°40E 185 F5
Koło Warszawa, Poland 52°14N 20°56E 142 B1
Koło Wielkopolskie, Poland 52°14N 18°40E 185 F5
Kołobrzeg Poland 54°10N 15°35E 184 D2
Kolochava Ukraine 48°26N 23°41E 183 B8
Kologi Sudan 10°51N 30°58E 257 E3
Kolokani Mali 13°35N 7°45W 262 C3
Kolokinthou Greece 38°0N 23°42E 112 B2
Koloko Burkina Faso 11°5N 5°19W 262 C3
Kololo Ethiopia 7°29N 41°58E 257 F5
Kolombangara Solomon Is. 8°0S 157°5E 287 M9
Kolomna Russia 55°8N 38°45E 188 E10
Kolomyagi Russia 60°0N 30°19E 137 A1
Kolomyya Ukraine 48°31N 25°2E 183 B10
Kolondiéba Mali 11°5N 6°54W 262 C3
Kolonodale Indonesia 2°0S 121°19E 231 E6
Kolonos Greece 37°59N 23°43E 112 B2
Kolonowskie Poland 50°39N 18°22E 185 H5
Kolosib India 24°15N 92°45E 241 C4
Kolpashevo Russia 58°20N 83°5E 214 D9
Kolpino Russia 59°44N 30°39E 188 C6
Kolpny Russia 52°17N 37°1E 189 F9
Kolsås Norway 59°55N 10°30E 133 A2
Kolskiy Poluostrov Russia 67°30N 38°0E 186 A6
Kolskiy Zaliv Russia 69°23N 34°0E 160 B26
Kolsva Sweden 59°36N 15°51E 162 E9
Kolubara → Serbia 44°35N 20°15E 202 B4
Kolumadulu Atoll Maldives 2°22N 73°7E 272 d
Koluszki Poland 51°45N 19°46E 185 G6
Kolwezi Dem. Rep. of the Congo 10°40S 25°25E 269 E2
Kolyma → Russia 69°30N 161°0E 215 C17
Kolymskoye Nagorye Russia 63°0N 157°0E 215 C16
Kôm Hamâda Egypt 30°46N 30°41E 256 H7
Kôm Ombo Egypt 24°25N 32°52E 256 C3
Komadugu Gana → Nigeria 13°5N 12°24E 263 C7
Komae Japan 35°37N 139°34E 140 B2
Komagane Japan 35°44N 137°58E 223 B9
Komagome Japan 35°43N 139°45E 140 A3
Komaki Japan 35°17N 136°55E 223 B8
Komandorskiye Is. = Komandorskiye Ostrova Russia 55°0N 167°0E 215 D17
Komandorskiye Ostrova Russia 55°0N 167°0E 215 D17
Komárno Slovak Rep. 47°49N 18°5E 181 D11
Komarnyky Ukraine 48°59N 23°3E 182 B8
Komárom Hungary 47°43N 18°7E 182 C3
Komárom-Esztergom □ Hungary 47°35N 18°20E 182 C3
Komáromújváros = Komárom Hungary 47°43N 18°7E 182 C3
Komatipoort S. Africa 25°25S 31°55E 271 C5
Komatou Yialou Cyprus 35°25N 34°8E 207 E10
Komatsu Japan 36°25N 136°30E 223 A8
Komatsushima Japan 34°0N 134°35E 222 D6
Komavangard = Sobinka Russia 56°0N 40°0E 188 E11
Komazawa Japan 35°37N 139°40E 140 B3
Komba Dem. Rep. of the Congo 2°52N 24°3E 264 B4
Kombissiri Burkina Faso 12°4N 1°20W 263 C4
Kombo Gabon 0°20S 12°22E 264 C2
Kombong India 28°7N 94°51E 241 A5
Kombori Burkina Faso 13°26N 3°56W 262 C4
Komboti Greece 39°6N 21°5E 204 B3
Kome Channel Uganda 0°10S 32°35E 268 C3
Komebail Lagoon Palau 7°25N 134°29E 288 c
Komen Slovenia 45°49N 13°45E 199 C10
Komenda Ghana 5°4N 1°28W 263 D4
Komi Cyprus 35°24N 34°0E 207 E10
Komi □ Russia 64°0N 55°0E 186 B10
Kominter = Novoshakhtinsk Russia 47°46N 39°58E 189 J10
Komintern = Marhanets Ukraine 47°40N 34°40E 189 J8
Komiža Croatia 43°3N 16°11E 199 E13
Komló Hungary 46°15N 18°16E 182 D3
Kommamur Canal India 16°0N 80°25E 245 G5
Kommunarsk = Alchevsk Ukraine 48°30N 38°45E 189 H10
Kommunizma, Pik = imeni Ismail Samani, Pik Tajikistan 39°0N 72°2E 217 E8
Komodo Indonesia 8°37S 119°20E 231 F5
Komono Congo 3°10S 13°20E 264 C2
Komoran, Pulau Indonesia 8°18S 138°45E 231 F9
Komoro Japan 36°19N 138°26E 223 A10
Komotau = Chomutov Czech Rep. 50°28N 13°23E 180 A6
Komotini Greece 41°9N 25°26E 203 E9
Komovi Montenegro 42°41N 19°39E 202 D3
Kompasberg S. Africa 31°45S 24°32E 270 D3
Kompong Cham Cambodia 12°0N 105°30E 237 G5
Kompong Chhnang = Kampong Chhnang Cambodia 12°20N 104°35E 237 F5
Kompong Chikreng Cambodia 13°5N 104°18E 236 F5
Kompong Kleang Cambodia 13°6N 104°8E 236 E5
Kompong Luong Cambodia 11°49N 104°48E 237 G5
Kompong Pranak Cambodia 13°35N 104°55E 236 F5
Kompong Som = Kampong Saom Cambodia 10°38N 103°30E 237 G4
Kompong Som, Chhung = Kampong Saom, Chaak Cambodia 10°50N 103°32E 237 G4
Kompong Speu Cambodia 11°26N 104°32E 237 G5
Kompong Sralau Cambodia 14°5N 105°46E 236 E5
Kompong Thom Cambodia 12°35N 104°51E 236 F5
Kompong Trabeck Cambodia 13°6N 105°14E 236 F5
Kompong Trabeck Cambodia 11°9N 105°28E 237 G5
Kompong Trach Cambodia 11°25N 105°48E 237 G5
Kompong Tralach Cambodia 11°54N 104°47E 237 G5
Komrat = Comrat Moldova 46°18N 28°40E 183 D13
Komsberg S. Africa 32°40S 20°45E 270 D3
Komsomolets = Qarabalyq Kazakhstan 53°45N 62°2E 216 B6
Komsomolets, Ostrov Russia 80°30N 95°0E 215 A10
Komsomolsk Russia 57°2N 40°20E 188 D11
Komsomolsk-na-Amur Russia 50°30N 137°0E 219 A8
Komsomolskiy Russia 54°27N 45°33E 190 C7
Komsomolskoe Kazakhstan 50°25N 60°5E 216 B6
Komsomolsky = Chirchiq Uzbekistan 41°29N 69°35E 217 D7
Kömür Burnu Turkey 38°39N 26°12E 205 C8
Kon Tum Vietnam 14°24N 108°0E 236 E7
Kon Tum, Plateau du Vietnam 14°30N 108°30E 236 E7
Kona W. Bengal, India 22°37N 88°18E 124 B1
Kona Mali 14°57N 3°53W 262 C4
Kona Nigeria 8°57N 11°21E 263 D7
Kona ✕ (KOA) U.S.A. 19°44N 156°3W 302 D5
Konāhuanui U.S.A. 21°21N 157°47W 302 K14
Konakovo Russia 56°40N 36°51E 188 D9
Konala Finland 60°14N 24°52E 121 B2
Konar □ Afghan. 34°30N 71°3E 240 B3
Konarak India 19°54N 86°7E 244 E8
Konārak Iran 25°21N 60°23E 249 A8
Konārī Iran 28°13N 51°36E 247 D6
Konch India 26°0N 79°10E 243 G8
Kondagaon India 19°35N 81°35E 244 E5
Konde Tanzania 4°57S 39°45E 268 C4
Kondias Greece 39°49N 25°10E 205 B7
Kondinin Australia 32°34S 118°8E 279 F2
Kondli India 28°36N 77°19E 120 B2
Kondo Dem. Rep. of the Congo 5°35S 13°0E 265 D2
Kondoa Tanzania 4°55S 35°50E 268 C4
Kondopoga Russia 62°12N 34°17E 188 A8
Kondratyevo Russia 57°22N 98°15E 215 D10
Kondrovo Russia 54°48N 35°56E 188 E8
Konduga Nigeria 11°35N 13°26E 263 C7
Kondukur India 15°12N 79°57E 245 G4
Kondūz Afghan. 36°50N 68°50E 240 A3
Kondūz □ Afghan. 36°50N 68°50E 240 A3
Koné Cameroon 8°50N 13°17E 259 G2
Koné N. Cal. 21°4S 164°52E 288 d
Koneürgench Turkmenistan 42°19N 59°10E 216 D5
Konevo Russia 62°8N 39°20E 188 A10
Kong = Khong → Cambodia 13°32N 105°58E 236 F5
Kong Ivory C. 8°54N 4°36W 262 D4
Kong, Koh Cambodia 11°20N 103°0E 237 G4
Kong Christian IX Land Greenland 68°0N 36°0W 154 D7
Kong Christian X Land Greenland 74°0N 29°0W 154 C8
Kong Frederik IX Land Greenland 67°0N 52°0W 154 D5
Kong Frederik VI Kyst Greenland 63°0N 43°0W 154 E6
Kong Frederik VIII Land Greenland 78°30N 26°0W 154 B8
Kong Karls Land Svalbard 79°0N 28°0E 154 B13
Kong Oscar Fjord Greenland 72°20N 24°0W 154 C8
Kongauru I. Palau 7°3N 134°16E 288 c
Kongbo C.A.R. 4°44N 21°23E 264 B4
Kongeå → Denmark 55°23N 8°39E 163 J2
Kongelunden Denmark 55°34N 12°34E 118 B3
Kongens Lyngby Denmark 55°46N 12°30E 118 A3
Kongerslev Denmark 56°54N 10°6E 163 H4
Kongkemul Indonesia 1°52N 112°11E 235 B4
Konglu Burma 27°13N 97°57E 241 B6
Kongmoon = Jiangmen China 22°32N 113°0E 229 F9
Kongo Finland 60°20N 24°47E 121 A1
Kongola Namibia 17°45S 23°20E 270 A3
Kongolo Kasai-Or., Dem. Rep. of the Congo 5°26S 24°49E 265 D4
Kongolo Katanga, Dem. Rep. of the Congo 5°22S 27°0E 268 D2
Kongor Sudan 7°1N 31°27E 257 F3
Kongossambougou ⌂ Mali 14°0N 8°30W 262 C3
Kongoulou Cameroon 2°59N 11°7E 264 B2
Kongoussi Burkina Faso 13°19N 1°32W 263 C4
Kongsberg Norway 59°39N 9°39E 164 E6
Kongsvinger Norway 60°12N 12°2E 164 D9
Kongur Shan China 38°34N 75°18E 217 E9
Kongwa Tanzania 6°11S 36°26E 268 D4
Koni Dem. Rep. of the Congo 10°40S 27°11E 269 E2
Koni, Mts. Dem. Rep. of the Congo 10°36S 27°10E 269 E2
Koniakari Mali 14°35N 10°50W 262 C2
Koniecpol Poland 50°46N 19°40E 185 H6
Königgrätz = Hradec Králové Czech Rep. 50°15N 15°50E 180 A8
Königs Wusterhausen Germany 52°19N 13°38E 178 C9
Königsberg = Chojna Poland 52°58N 14°25E 185 F1
Königsberg = Kaliningrad Russia 54°42N 20°32E 184 D7
Königsbrunn Germany 48°16N 10°54E 179 G6
Königshütte = Chorzów Poland 50°18N 18°57E 185 H5
Königslutter Germany 52°15N 10°49E 178 C6
Konin Poland 52°12N 18°15E 185 F5
Königinhof an der Elbe = Dvůr Králové nad Labem Czech Rep. 50°27N 15°50E 180 A8
Koninklijk Paleis Amsterdam, Neths. 112 a2
Konispol Albania 39°42N 20°10E 206 B10
Konitsa Greece 40°5N 20°48E 204 A2
Konjic Bos.-H. 43°42N 17°58E 182 G2
Konkiep Namibia 26°49S 17°15E 270 C2
Konkō Japan 34°33N 133°36E 222 C4
Konkouré → Guinea 9°50N 13°42W 262 D2
Konnagar India 22°42N 88°21E 124 A2
Könnern Germany 51°41N 11°47E 178 D7
Konnur India 16°14N 74°49E 245 F2
Kono S. Leone 8°30N 11°5W 262 D2
Konogogo Papua N. G. 3°29S 152°10E 286 B7
Konohana Japan 34°40N 135°26E 133 A1
Konongo Ghana 6°40N 1°15W 263 D4
Konos Papua N. G. 3°10S 151°44E 286 B6
Konosha Russia 61°0N 40°5E 188 B11
Kōnosu Japan 36°3N 139°31E 223 A11
Konotop Ukraine 51°12N 33°7E 189 G7
Konqi He → China 41°0N 86°0E 217 D11
Konradshof = Skawina Poland 49°59N 19°50E 185 J6
Konradshöhe Germany 52°35N 13°13E 115 A2
Konrei Palau 7°43N 134°36E 288 c
Konsankoro Guinea 9°2N 9°0W 262 D3
Końskie Poland 51°15N 20°23E 185 G7
Konsmo Norway 58°16N 7°23E 164 F4
Konstadt = Wołczyn Poland 51°1N 18°3E 185 G5

Konstancin-Jeziorna Poland 52°5N 21°7E 185 F8
Konstantinograd = Krasnohrad Ukraine 49°27N 35°27E 189 H8
Konstantinovka = Kostyantynivka Ukraine 48°32N 37°39E 189 H9
Konstantinovsk Russia 47°33N 41°10E 191 G5
Konstantynów Łódzki Poland 51°45N 19°20E 185 G6
Konstanz Germany 47°40N 9°10E 179 H5
Kont Iran 26°55N 61°50E 247 E9
Konta India 17°48N 81°23E 244 F5
Kontagora Nigeria 10°23N 5°27E 263 C6
Kontcha Cameroon 7°59N 12°15E 263 D7
Kontiolahti Finland 62°46N 29°50E 160 E23
Kontokali Greece 39°38N 19°51E 206 B9
Konya Turkey 37°52N 32°35E 212 D5
Konya □ Turkey 37°46N 32°35E 250 A3
Konya Ovasi Turkey 38°30N 33°5E 212 C5
Konyin Burma 22°58N 94°42E 241 D5
Konz Germany 49°42N 6°34E 179 F2
Konza Kenya 1°45S 37°7E 268 C4
Koo-wee-rup Australia 38°13S 145°28E 283 E6
Koocanusa, L. Canada 49°20N 115°15W 304 B6
Kookynie Australia 29°17S 121°22E 279 F3
Ko'olauloa District U.S.A. 21°35N 157°55W 302 J14
Ko'olauloa District U.S.A. 21°35N 157°50W 302 K14
Kö'Ölina U.S.A. 21°19N 158°7W 302 K13
Koolyanobbing Australia 30°48S 119°36E 279 F2
Koondrook Australia 35°33S 144°8E 282 C6
Koonibba Australia 31°54S 133°25E 281 E1
Koorawatha Australia 34°2S 148°33E 283 C8
Koorda Australia 30°48S 117°35E 279 F2
Kooskia U.S.A. 46°9N 115°59W 304 C6
Kootenay → U.S.A. 49°19N 117°39W 296 D5
Kootenay L. Canada 51°0N 116°0W 296 C5
Kootenay L. Canada 49°45N 116°50W 304 B5
Kootingal Australia 31°3S 151°4E 283 A9
Kootjieskolk S. Africa 31°15S 20°21E 270 D3
Kopanina Czech Rep. 50°3N 14°17E 180 A5
Kopaonik Serbia 43°10N 20°50E 202 C4
Kopaonik △ Serbia 43°20N 20°50E 202 C4
Kopargaon India 19°51N 74°28E 244 E2
Koparkhairna India 19°6N 72°59E 130 A2
Kópasker Iceland 66°18N 16°27W 155 A10
Kópavogur Iceland 64°6N 21°55W 155 C5
Kopayhorod Ukraine 48°52N 27°47E 183 B12
Koper Slovenia 45°31N 13°44E 199 C10
Kopervik Norway 59°17N 5°17E 164 E2
Kopet Dagh Asia 38°0N 58°0E 247 B8
Kopeysk Russia 55°7N 61°37E 216 A6
Kopi Australia 33°24S 135°40E 281 E2
Köping Sweden 59°31N 16°3E 162 E10
Köpingsvik Sweden 56°53N 16°43E 163 H10
Kopište Croatia 42°48N 16°42E 199 F13
Koplik Albania 42°15N 19°25E 202 D3
Köpmanholmen Sweden 63°10N 18°35E 162 A12
Koppa India 13°33N 75°21E 245 H2
Koppal India 15°23N 76°6E 245 G3
Koppang Norway 61°34N 11°3E 164 C8
Kopparberg Sweden 59°52N 15°0E 162 E9
Koppeh Dägh = Kopet Dagh Asia 38°0N 58°0E 247 B8
Kopperå Norway 63°24N 11°50E 164 A8
Koppies S. Africa 27°20S 27°30E 271 C4
Koppom Sweden 59°43N 12°10E 162 E6
Koprivlen Bulgaria 41°31N 23°53E 202 E7
Koprivnica Croatia 46°12N 16°45E 199 B13
Kopřivnice Czech Rep. 49°36N 18°9E 181 B11
Koprivshtitsa Bulgaria 42°40N 24°19E 203 D8
Köprü → Turkey 36°48N 31°11E 250 B2
Köprübaşı Turkey 38°43N 28°23E 205 C10
Köprülü Turkey 36°43N 32°10E 250 B3
Köprülü △ Turkey 37°20N 31°5E 250 B3
Kopychyntsi Ukraine 49°7N 25°58E 177 D13
Kor Aban Somali Rep. 3°58N 42°44E 267 D5
Kora △ Kenya 0°14S 38°44E 268 C4
Koraa Shiir Somali Rep. 3°16N 46°16E 267 D6
Korab Macedonia 41°44N 20°40E 202 E4
Korahe Ethiopia 6°39N 44°5E 267 C5
Koral India 21°50N 73°12E 242 J5
Korangal India 17°6N 77°36E 244 E3
Korangi Pakistan 24°47N 67°8E 123 B2
Koraput India 18°50N 82°40E 244 E6
Korarou, L. Mali 15°15N 3°15W 262 B4
Korba India 22°20N 82°45E 243 H10
Korbach Germany 51°16N 8°52E 178 D4
Korbu, G. Malaysia 4°41N 101°18E 237 K3
Korçë Albania 40°37N 20°50E 202 F4
Korčula Croatia 42°56N 16°57E 199 F13
Korčulanski Kanal Croatia 43°3N 16°40E 199 E13
Kord Küy Iran 36°48N 54°7E 247 B7
Kord Sheykh Iran 28°31N 52°53E 247 D7
Kordestan = Kurdistan Asia 37°20N 43°30E 213 D10
Kordestän □ Iran 36°0N 47°0E 246 C5
Kordié Burkina Faso 12°36N 2°22W 262 C4
Koré Mayroua Niger 13°18N 3°55E 263 C5
Korea, North ■ Asia 40°0N 127°0E 227 E14
Korea, South ■ Asia 36°0N 128°0E 227 G15
Korea Bay Korea 39°0N 124°0E 224 C2
Korea Strait Asia 34°0N 129°30E 227 H15
Koregaon India 17°40N 74°10E 244 F2
Korem India 12°30N 39°32E 257 E4
Koremasa Japan 35°39N 139°29E 140 B1
Korenevo Kursk, Russia 51°27N 35°14E 189 H9
Korenevo Moskva, Russia 55°40N 38°10E 129 B6
Korenica = Titova Korenica Croatia 44°45N 15°41E 199 D12
Korenovsk Russia 45°30N 39°22E 191 H4
Korfantów Poland 50°29N 17°36E 185 H4
Korgan Turkey 40°44N 37°13E 212 B7
Korgus Sudan 19°16N 33°29E 256 D3
Korhogo Ivory C. 9°29N 5°28W 262 D3
Koribundu S. Leone 7°41N 11°46W 262 D2
Koridalos Greece 37°59N 23°39E 112 B1
Korienzé Mali 15°22N 3°50W 262 B4
Korinthia □ Greece 37°50N 22°35E 204 C4
Korinthiakos Kolpos Greece 38°16N 22°30E 204 C4
Korinthos Greece 37°56N 22°55E 204 C4
Korioumé Mali 16°35N 3°0W 262 B4
Korissia Greece 37°31N 24°19E 207 D2
Korithi Greece 37°55N 20°42E 207 D2
Kōriyama Japan 37°24N 140°23E 220 F10
Korkino Russia 54°54N 61°23E 216 B6
Korkuteli Turkey 37°4N 30°13E 205 D12
Korla China 41°45N 86°4E 217 D11
Kormakiti, C. Cyprus 35°23N 32°56E 207 E18
Körmend Hungary 47°5N 16°35E 182 C1
Kormor Iraq 35°8N 44°50E 213 E11
Kornat Croatia 43°50N 15°20E 199 E12
Kornat △ Croatia 43°48N 15°12E 199 E12
Korneshty = Corneşti Moldova 47°21N 28°1E 183 C13
Korneuburg Austria 48°20N 16°20E 181 C9
Kórnik Poland 52°9N 17°1E 185 F4
Kornsjø Norway 58°57N 11°39E 164 F8
Koro Fiji 17°19S 179°23E 287 A2

Koro Ivory C. 8°32N 7°30W 262 D3
Koro Mali 14°1N 2°58W 262 C4
Koro Sea Fiji 17°30S 179°45W 287 A3
Koro Toro Chad 16°5N 18°30E 253 F9
Koroba Papua N. G. 5°44S 142°47E 286 C2
Korobovo = Gubkin Russia 51°17N 37°32E 189 G9
Korocha Russia 50°55N 37°30E 189 G9
Köroğlu Dağları Turkey 40°38N 33°0E 212 B5
Korogwe Tanzania 5°5S 38°25E 268 C4
Koroit Australia 38°18S 142°24E 282 E5
Korokoro N.Z. 41°13S 174°52E 143 B2
Korokoro Stream → N.Z. 41°14S 174°52E 143 B2
Korona U.S.A. 29°25N 81°12W 317 F8
Koronadal Phil. 6°12N 125°1E 233 H5
Korong Vale Australia 36°22S 143°45E 282 C5
Koroni Greece 36°48N 21°57E 204 E3
Koronia, L. Greece 40°47N 23°10E 202 F7
Koronos Greece 37°12N 25°35E 206 D7
Koronowo Poland 53°19N 17°55E 185 E4
Koropelē C.A.R. 4°44N 17°11E 264 B3
Koropets Ukraine 48°56N 25°10E 183 B10
Koror Palau 7°20N 134°28E 288 c
Körös → Hungary 46°43N 20°12E 182 D5
Köröstarcsa Hungary 46°53N 21°3E 182 D6
Korosten Ukraine 50°54N 28°36E 177 C15
Korostyshev Ukraine 50°19N 29°4E 177 C15
Korotoyak Russia 51°1N 39°2E 189 G10
Korovou Fiji 17°47S 178°32E 287 A2
Koroyanitu △ Fiji 17°40S 177°35E 287 A1
Korraraika, Helodranon' i Madag. 17°45S 43°57E 272 B1
Korror I. Palau 7°20N 134°29E 288 c
Korsakov Russia 46°36N 142°42E 215 E15
Korsberga Sweden 57°19N 15°7E 163 G9
Korshiv Ukraine 48°39N 25°1E 183 B10
Korshunovo Russia 58°37N 110°10E 215 D12
Korsør Denmark 55°20N 11°9E 163 J5
Korsun Shevchenkovskiy Ukraine 49°26N 31°16E 189 H6
Korsze Poland 54°11N 21°9E 184 D8
Korti Sudan 18°6N 31°33E 256 D3
Kortrijk Belgium 50°50N 3°17E 170 D3
Korucu Turkey 39°28N 27°22E 205 B9
Korumburra Australia 38°26S 145°50E 283 E6
Korup △ Cameroon 5°15N 9°2E 264 A1
Korwai India 24°7N 78°5E 242 G8
Koryakskoye Nagorye Russia 61°0N 171°0E 215 C18
Koryukivka Ukraine 51°46N 32°16E 189 G7
Kos Greece 36°50N 27°15E 205 E9
Kosa Ethiopia 7°50N 36°50E 257 F4
Kosai Japan 34°42N 137°32E 223 C9
Kosan N. Korea 38°52N 127°25E 224 C3
Kosaya Gora Russia 54°10N 37°30E 188 C9
Kościan Poland 52°5N 16°40E 185 F3
Kościerzyna Poland 54°8N 17°59E 184 D4
Kosciusko U.S.A. 33°4N 89°35W 315 E10
Kosciuszko, Mt. Australia 36°27S 148°16E 283 C8
Kosciuszko △ Australia 36°30S 148°20E 283 C8
Kösely → Hungary 47°25N 21°15E 182 C6
Kosgi Andhra Pradesh, India 16°58N 77°43E 244 F3
Kosgi Andhra Pradesh, India 15°51N 77°16E 245 G3
Kosha Sudan 20°50N 30°30E 256 C3
Koshava Bulgaria 44°4N 23°2E 202 B7
Koshigaya Japan 35°54N 139°48E 223 B11
K'oshih = Kashi China 39°30N 76°2E 222 F2
Koshiki-Rettō Japan 31°45N 129°49E 222 L1
Koshim = Kazakhstan 42°20N 50°30E 190 F10
Koshkonong, L. U.S.A. 42°52N 88°58W 311 E8
Koshoku Japan 36°38N 138°6E 223 A10
Koshu-Kavak = Krumovgrad Bulgaria 41°29N 25°38E 203 E9
Kosi India 27°48N 77°29E 242 F7
Kosi → India 28°41N 78°57E 243 E8
Košice Slovak Rep. 48°42N 21°15E 181 C14
Košický □ Slovak Rep. 48°45N 21°10E 181 C14
Kosino Russia 55°43N 37°50E 129 B5
Kosiv Ukraine 48°19N 25°6E 183 B10
Kosjerić Serbia 44°0N 19°55E 202 B3
Kösk Turkey 37°50N 28°3E 205 D10
Koskinou Greece 36°23N 28°13E 206 E12
Koslan Russia 63°34N 49°14E 186 B8
Köslin = Koszalin Poland 54°11N 16°8E 184 D3
Kosmach Ukraine 48°20N 24°50E 183 B9
Kosŏng N. Korea 38°40N 128°22E 224 C4
Kosovo □ Europe 42°30N 21°0E 202 C2
Kosovo Polje Kosovo 42°40N 21°5E 202 C2
Kosovska Kamenica Kosovo 42°35N 21°35E 202 D3
Kosovska Mitrovica Kosovo 42°54N 20°52E 202 D2
Kossou, L. de Ivory C. 6°59N 5°31W 262 D3
Kosta Sweden 56°50N 15°24E 163 H9
Kostajnica Croatia 45°17N 16°30E 199 C13
Kostanjevica Slovenia 45°51N 15°27E 199 C12
Kostenets Bulgaria 42°15N 23°52E 202 D7
Kostenets = Pernik Bulgaria 42°35N 23°2E 202 D7
Koster S. Africa 25°52S 26°54E 270 C4
Kösti Sudan 13°8N 32°43E 257 E3
Kostinbrod Bulgaria 42°49N 23°13E 202 D7
Kostolac Serbia 44°37N 21°15E 202 B5
Kostopil Ukraine 50°51N 26°22E 177 C14
Kostroma Russia 57°50N 40°58E 188 C11
Kostromskoye Vdkhr. Russia 57°52N 40°49E 188 D11
Kostryzhivka Ukraine 48°39N 25°43E 183 B10
Kostrzyn Lubuskie, Poland 52°35N 14°39E 185 F1
Kostrzyn Wielkopolskie, Poland 52°24N 17°14E 185 F4
Kostyantynivka Ukraine 48°32N 37°39E 189 H9
Kostyukovichi = Kastsyukovichy Belarus 53°20N 32°4E 188 F7
Kosugi Japan 35°34N 139°39E 140 B2
Koszalin Poland 54°11N 16°8E 184 D3
Kőszeg Hungary 47°23N 16°33E 182 C1

Kotcho L. Canada 59°7N 121°12W 296 F4
Kotdwara India 29°45N 78°32E 243 E8
Kotel Bulgaria 42°52N 26°26E 203 D10
Kotelnich Russia 58°22N 48°24E 190 A9
Kotelnikovo Russia 47°38N 43°8E 191 G6
Kotelny, Ostrov Russia 75°10N 139°0E 215 B14
Kothagudem India 17°30N 80°40E 244 F5
Kothapet India 19°21N 79°29E 244 E4
Kothari → India 25°20N 75°4E 242 G6
Kothi Chhattisgarh, India 23°21N 82°3E 243 H10
Kothi Mad. P., India 24°45N 80°40E 243 G9
Kotiro Pakistan 26°17N 67°13E 242 F2
Kotka Finland 60°28N 26°58E 188 B4
Kotlas Russia 61°17N 46°43E 186 B8
Kotlenska Planina Bulgaria 42°56N 26°30E 203 D10
Kotli Pakistan 33°30N 73°55E 242 C5
Kotlik U.S.A. 63°2N 163°33W 303 E7
Kotma India 23°12N 81°58E 243 H9
Kotohira Japan 34°11N 133°49E 222 C5
Koton-Karifi Nigeria 8°0N 6°48E 263 D6
Kotonkoro Nigeria 11°3N 5°58E 263 C6
Kotor Montenegro 42°25N 18°47E 202 D2
Kotor Varoš Bos.-H. 44°38N 17°22E 182 F2
Kotoriba Croatia 46°23N 16°48E 199 B13
Kotovo Russia 50°22N 44°45E 190 E7
Kotovsk Russia 52°36N 41°32E 190 D5
Kotovsk Ukraine 47°45N 29°35E 177 E15
Kotputli India 27°43N 76°12E 242 F7
Kotri → India 26°30N 65°30E 247 C9
Kotri India 25°22N 68°22E 242 G3
Kotturu India 14°45N 76°10E 245 G3
Kotuy → Russia 71°54N 102°6E 215 B11
Kotzebue U.S.A. 66°53N 162°39W 303 C7
Kotzebue Sound U.S.A. 66°20N 163°0W 303 C7
Kotzenau = Chocianów Poland 51°27N 15°55E 185 G2
Kouango C.A.R. 5°0N 20°10E 264 B4
Kouchibouguac △ Canada 46°50N 65°0W 299 C6
Koudougou Burkina Faso 12°10N 2°20W 262 C4
Koufey Niger 13°57N 7°56E 259 F1
Koufonisi Iraklio, Greece 34°56N 26°8E 207 F7
Koufonisi Notio Aigaio, Greece 36°57N 25°35E 205 E7
Kougaberge S. Africa 33°48S 23°50E 270 D3
K'ouhu Taiwan 23°35N 120°11E 225 C2
Kouibli Ivory C. 7°15N 7°14W 262 D3
Kouilou → Congo 4°10S 12°5E 265 C2
Koukdjuak → Canada 66°43N 73°0W 295 D17
Kouki C.A.R. 7°22N 17°3E 264 A3
Koukoulé, Mt. Comoros Is. 12°18S 43°41E 272 a
Koukourou → C.A.R. 7°19N 20°2E 264 A4
Koula Greece 41°23N 24°44E 203 E8
Koula Moutou Gabon 1°15S 12°25E 264 C2
Koulen = Kulen Cambodia 13°50N 104°40E 236 F5
Koulikoro Mali 12°40N 7°50W 262 C3
Koulikoro □ Mali 14°0N 7°45W 262 C3
Kouloura Greece 39°42N 19°54E 206 B9
Koumac N. Cal. 20°33S 164°17E 288 d
Koumala Australia 21°38S 149°15E 280 C4
Koumameveng Gabon 0°11N 11°51E 264 B2
Koumankou Mali 11°58N 6°6W 262 C3
Koumbia Burkina Faso 11°10N 3°50W 262 C4
Koumbia Guinea 11°48N 13°29W 262 C2
Koumboum Guinea 10°25N 13°0W 262 C2
Koumpenntoum Senegal 13°59N 14°34W 262 C2
Koumra Chad 8°50N 17°35E 259 G3
Koun-Fao Ivory C. 7°30N 3°15W 262 D4
Koundara Guinea 12°29N 13°18W 262 C2
Koundé C.A.R. 6°1N 14°38E 264 A2
Koundian Guinea 13°10N 10°35W 262 C2
Koungheul Senegal 14°0N 14°50W 262 C2
Koungou Mayotte 12°43S 45°12E 272 b
Koungoulou Congo 3°31S 13°20E 264 C2
Kountze U.S.A. 30°22N 94°19W 314 F7
Koupéla Burkina Faso 12°11N 0°21W 263 C4
Kouponia Greece 37°57N 23°47E 112 B2
Kourémalé Mali 11°59N 8°42W 262 C3
Kouri-shima Japan 26°42N 128°1E 288 a
Kouris → Cyprus 34°38N 32°54E 207 F8
Kourou, P. de Chad 20°28N 15°52E 258 D3
Kourou Fr. Guiana 5°9N 52°39W 329 B7
Kourouba Mali 13°22N 10°57W 262 C2
Koûroudjel Mauritania 16°12N 11°30W 262 B2
Kouroukoto Mali 12°35N 10°5W 262 C2
Kourouma Burkina Faso 11°35N 4°50W 262 C4
Kourouninkoto Mali 13°52N 9°35W 262 C3
Koussanar Senegal 13°52N 14°5W 262 C2
Koussané Senegal 14°53N 11°14W 262 C2
Kousséri Cameroon 12°0N 14°55E 259 F2
Koutiala Mali 12°25N 5°23W 262 C3
Kouto Ivory C. 9°53N 6°25W 262 D3
Kouts U.S.A. 41°19N 87°2W 311 C9
Kouvé Togo 6°25N 1°25E 263 D5
Kouvola Finland 60°52N 26°43E 188 B4
Kouyi Congo 2°29S 12°25E 264 C2
Kouyou → Congo 0°44S 16°38E 264 C3
Kovačica Serbia 45°5N 20°38E 182 E5
Kovdor Russia 67°34N 30°24E 160 C24
Kovel Ukraine 51°11N 24°38E 177 C13
Kovilpatti India 9°10N 77°50E 245 K3
Kovin Serbia 44°44N 20°59E 182 F5
Kovno = Kaunas Lithuania 54°54N 23°54E 184 D10
Kovrov Russia 56°25N 41°38E 186 C7
Kovur Andhra Pradesh, India 17°3N 81°39E 244 F5
Kovur Andhra Pradesh, India 14°30N 80°1E 245 G5
Kowal Poland 52°32N 19°7E 185 F6
Kowalewo Pomorskie Poland 53°10N 18°52E 185 E5
Kowanyama Australia 15°29S 141°44E 280 B3
Kowanyama ◇ Australia 15°29S 141°44E 280 B3
Kowlīni Afghan. 32°29N 65°58E 240 C4
Kowloon China 122 A2
Kowloon Peak Hong Kong, China 122 A2
Kowloon Park Hong Kong, China 122 A2
Kowloon Res. China 22°21N 114°9E 122 A1
Kowloon Tong China 22°20N 114°10E 122 A1
Kowŏn N. Korea 39°26N 127°14E 224 C3
Koyampattur = Coimbatore India 11°2N 76°59E 245 J3
Köyceğiz Turkey 36°57N 28°40E 205 E10
Köyceğiz Gölü Turkey 36°53N 28°40E 205 E10
Köytendag Turkmenistan 37°30N 66°12E 240 A2
Koyuk U.S.A. 64°56N 161°9W 303 D7

Koyukuk U.S.A. 64°53N 157°42W 303 D8
Koyukuk → U.S.A. 64°55N 157°32W 303 D8
Koyukuk Nat. Wildlife Refuge △ U.S.A. 66°35N 156°30W 303 D8
Koyulhisar Turkey 40°20N 37°52E 212 B7
Koyunyeri Turkey 40°50N 26°26E 203 F10
Kozak Turkey 39°15N 27°6E 205 B9
Kozakli Turkey 39°11N 34°49E 212 C6
Kozan Turkey 37°26N 35°50E 212 D6
Kozani Greece 40°19N 21°47E 202 F5
Kozani □ Greece 40°18N 21°45E 202 F5
Kozara △ Bos.-H. 45°0N 17°0E 182 F2
Kozara Bos.-H. 45°0N 17°0E 182 F2
Kozarac Bos.-H. 44°58N 16°48E 199 D13
Kozelets Ukraine 50°55N 31°17E 189 G6
Kozelsk Russia 54°2N 35°48E 188 E8
Kozhikode = Calicut India 11°15N 75°43E 245 J2
Kozhukhovo Russia 55°43N 37°53E 129 B5
Kozhva Russia 65°10N 57°0E 186 A10
Koziegłowy Poland 50°37N 19°8E 185 H6
Kozienice Poland 51°35N 21°34E 185 G8
Kozje Slovenia 46°5N 15°35E 199 B12
Kozloduy Bulgaria 43°45N 23°42E 202 C7
Kozlov = Michurinsk Russia 52°58N 40°27E 190 D5
Kozlovets Bulgaria 43°30N 25°20E 203 D9
Kozlovka Russia 55°52N 48°14E 190 C9
Kozova Ukraine 49°25N 25°9E 177 D13
Kozu Turkey 41°26N 31°45E 212 B4
Kozluk Turkey 38°11N 41°31E 213 C9
Kozmin Poland 51°48N 17°27E 185 G4
Kozmodemyansk Russia 56°20N 46°36E 190 B8
Kōzu-Shima Japan 34°13N 139°10E 223 C11
Kōzuchów Poland 51°45N 15°31E 185 G2
Kozyatyn Ukraine 49°45N 28°50E 177 D15
Kozyrevsk Russia 56°3N 159°51E 215 D16
Kpabia Ghana 9°10N 0°20W 263 D4
Kpalimé Togo 6°57N 0°44E 263 D5
Kpandae Ghana 8°30N 0°2W 263 D4
Kpessi Togo 8°4N 1°16E 263 D5
Kra, Isthmus of = Kra, Kho Khot Thailand 10°15N 99°30E 237 G2
Kra, Kho Khot Thailand 10°15N 99°30E 237 G2
Kra Buri Thailand 10°22N 98°46E 237 G2
Kraai → S. Africa 30°40S 26°45E 270 D4
Kraainem Belgium 50°52N 4°28E 116 A2
Krabi Thailand 8°4N 98°55E 237 H2
Kracheh Cambodia 12°32N 106°10E 236 F6
Kratke Ra. Papua N. G. 6°45S 146°0E 286 D4
Kratovo Macedonia 42°6N 22°10E 202 D6
Krau Indonesia 3°19S 140°5E 231 E10
Kraulshavn = Nuussuaq Greenland 74°8N 57°3W 154 C5
Kravanh, Chuor Phnum Cambodia 12°0N 103°32E 237 G4
Krč Czech Rep. 50°2N 14°26E 135 B2
Krefeld Germany 51°20N 6°33E 178 D2
Kremaston, L. Greece 38°52N 21°30E 204 C3
Kremen Croatia 44°28N 15°53E 199 D12
Kremenchuk Ukraine 49°5N 33°25E 189 H7
Kremenchuksk Vdskh. Ukraine 49°20N 32°30E 189 H7
Kremenets Ukraine 50°8N 25°43E 177 C13
Kremenki Ukraine 49°1N 38°10E 189 H10
Kremennaya Ukraine 49°1N 38°10E 189 H10
Kremges = Svitlovodsk Ukraine 49°2N 33°13E 189 H7
Kremlin Moscow, Russia 129 C2
Kremmen Germany 52°45N 13°1E 178 C9
Kremmling U.S.A. 40°4N 106°24W 304 F10
Kremnica Slovak Rep. 48°45N 18°50E 181 C11
Krems Austria 48°3N 15°36E 180 C8
Kremsmünster Austria 48°3N 14°8E 180 C7
Krenau = Chrzanów Poland 50°10N 19°21E 185 H6
Krestena Greece 37°35N 21°37E 204 D3
Krestovskiye, Ostrov Russia 59°57N 30°14E 137 B1
Krestsy Russia 58°15N 32°30E 188 C7
Kretinga Lithuania 55°53N 21°15E 184 D9
Krettamia Algeria 28°47N 3°27W 260 C4
Krettsy Russia 58°15N 32°30E 188 C7
Kreuzberg Bayern, Germany 50°22N 9°58E 179 E5
Kreuzberg Berlin, Germany 129 B3
Kreuzburg = Kluczbork Poland 50°58N 18°12E 185 H5
Kreuztal Germany 50°57N 8°0E 178 E4
Kria Vrisi Greece 40°41N 22°18E 202 F6
Kribi Cameroon 2°57N 9°56E 263 E6
Krichem Bulgaria 42°8N 24°28E 203 D8
Krichev = Krychaw Belarus 53°40N 31°41E 177 B16
Kril'on, Mys Russia 45°53N 142°5E 220 B11
Krim Slovenia 45°53N 14°30E 199 C11
Krim-Krim Chad 9°10N 15°24E 259 G3
Krindachyovka = Krasnyy Luch Ukraine 48°13N 39°0E 189 H10
Krios, Akra Greece 35°13N 23°34E 207 E14
Krishna → India 15°57N 80°59E 245 G5
Krishnagiri India 12°32N 78°16E 245 H4
Krishnanagar India 23°24N 88°33E 243 H13
Krishnaraja Sagar India 12°20N 76°32E 245 H3
Kristdala Sweden 57°24N 16°13E 163 G10
Kristians = Oppland □ Norway 61°15N 9°40E 164 C6
Kristiansand Norway 58°8N 8°1E 164 F6
Kristianstad Sweden 56°2N 14°9E 163 H8
Kristiansund Norway 63°7N 7°45E 164 A4
Kristiinankaupunki Finland 62°16N 21°21E 160 E19
Kristinehamn Sweden 59°18N 14°7E 162 E8
Kristinestad = Kristiinankaupunki Finland 62°16N 21°21E 160 E19
Kriti Greece 35°15N 25°0E 207 E6
Kritsa Greece 35°10N 25°41E 207 E6
Kritzendorf Austria 48°19N 16°18E 142 A1
Kriva → Macedonia 42°5N 21°47E 202 D5
Kriva Palanka Macedonia 42°11N 22°19E 202 D6
Krivaja → Bos.-H. 44°27N 18°9E 182 F3
Krivelj Serbia 44°6N 22°5E 202 B5
Křivoklát △ Czech Rep. 50°1N 13°51E 180 A6
Krivoy Rog = Kryvyy Rih Ukraine 47°51N 33°20E 189 J7
Križevci Croatia 46°3N 16°32E 199 B13
Krk Croatia 45°8N 14°40E 199 C11
Krka → Slovenia 45°50N 15°30E 199 C12
Krka △ Croatia 43°55N 15°55E 199 E12
Krkonoše Czech Rep. 50°50N 15°35E 180 A8
Krokeai Greece 36°53N 22°32E 204 E4
Kroken Sweden 65°24N 14°16E 163 C8
Krokodil = Umgwenya → Mozam. 25°14S 32°18E 271 C5
Krokom Sweden 63°20N 14°30E 162 A8
Krókfjorður Iceland 65°45N 22°50W 155 B3
Krokowa Poland 54°47N 18°9E 185 D5
Kroksfjarðarnes Iceland 65°28N 21°40W 155 B3
Kroměříž Czech Rep. 49°18N 17°21E 181 B10
Krompachy Slovak Rep. 48°54N 20°52E 181 C13
Kromy Russia 52°48N 35°48E 189 F8
Kronach Germany 50°14N 11°19E 179 E7
Kronau = Kranjska Gora Slovenia 46°29N 13°48E 199 B10
Krong Kaoh Kong Cambodia 11°37N 102°59E 237 G4
Kronobergs län □ Sweden 56°45N 14°30E 163 H8
Kronprins Christian Land Greenland 80°30N 22°0W 154 A8
Kronprins Frederik Land Greenland 81°0N 45°0W 154 A6
Kronprins Olav Kyst Antarctica 69°0S 42°0E 151 C5
Kronprinsesse Märtha Kyst Antarctica 73°30S 10°0W 151 D2
Kronshtadt = Braşov Romania 45°38N 25°35E 183 E10
Kronstadt Russia 59°57N 29°51E 188 C5
Kroonstad S. Africa 27°43S 27°19E 270 C4
Kröpelin Germany 54°4N 11°47E 178 A7
Kropotkin Russia 45°28N 40°28E 191 H5
Kropp Germany 54°24N 9°31E 178 A5
Krosna Lithuania 54°32N 23°33E 184 D10
Krośniewice Poland 52°15N 19°11E 185 F6
Krosno Poland 49°42N 21°46E 185 J8
Krosno Odrzańskie Poland 52°3N 15°7E 185 F2
Krotoszyn Poland 51°42N 17°23E 185 G4
Krotovka Russia 53°18N 51°10E 190 D10
Krousonas Greece 35°13N 24°59E 207 E6
Krrabë Albania 41°13N 20°0E 202 E4
Krško Slovenia 45°57N 15°30E 199 C12
Krstača Serbia 42°57N 20°8E 202 D4
Kruger △ S. Africa 24°50S 26°10E 271 B4
Krugersdorp S. Africa 26°5S 27°46E 271 C4
Kruisfontein S. Africa 33°59S 24°43E 270 D3
Krujë Albania 41°32N 19°46E 202 E3
Krulevshchina = Krulyewshchyna Belarus 55°5N 27°45E 188 E4
Krulyewshchyna Belarus 55°5N 27°45E 188 E4
Krumbach Germany 48°13N 10°22E 179 G6
Krumë Albania 42°14N 20°28E 202 D4
Krummau = Český Krumlov Czech Rep. 48°43N 14°21E 180 C7
Krumme Lanke Germany 52°27N 13°14E 115 A5
Krummensee Germany 52°35N 13°41E 115 A5
Krummhübel = Karpacz Poland 50°46N 15°46E 185 H2
Krumovgrad Bulgaria 41°29N 25°38E 203 E9
Krung Thep = Bangkok Thailand 13°45N 100°35E 113 B2
Krupanj Serbia 44°25N 19°22E 202 B3
Krupina Slovak Rep. 48°22N 19°5E 181 C12
Krupinica → Slovak Rep. 48°4N 18°55E 181 C11
Krupki Belarus 54°19N 29°8E 177 A15
Krusboda Sweden 59°13N 18°14E 139 B3
Krusenstern, C. U.S.A. 67°8N 163°45W 303 C7
Kruševac Serbia 43°35N 21°28E 202 C5
Kruševo Macedonia 41°23N 21°19E 202 E5
Krushevo = Svitlovodsk Ukraine 49°2N 33°13E 189 H7
Krushelnyksya Ukraine 49°2N 23°29E 185 J10
Kruszwica Poland 52°40N 18°20E 185 F5
Krychaw Belarus 53°40N 31°41E 177 B16
Krylatskoye Russia 55°44N 37°23E 129 B4
Krymsk Russia 44°50N 38°0E 189 K10
Krymskiy Poluostrov = Krymskyy Pivostriv Ukraine 45°0N 34°0E 189 K8
Krymskyy Pivostriv Ukraine 45°0N 34°0E 189 K8
Krynica Ukraine 49°25N 20°57E 185 J7
Krynica Morska Poland 54°23N 19°25E 184 D6
Krynki Poland 53°17N 23°43E 185 E10
Krynychne Ukraine 48°32N 28°40E 183 B13
Kryvyy Rih Ukraine 47°51N 33°20E 189 J7
Kryzhopil Ukraine 48°23N 28°53E 183 B13
Krzemieniec = Kremenets Ukraine 50°8N 25°43E 177 C13
Krzepice Poland 50°58N 18°45E 185 H5
Krzeszów Poland 50°24N 22°21E 185 H9
Krzna → Poland 52°0N 23°2E 185 F10
Krzywiń Poland 51°58N 16°50E 185 G3
Krzyż Wielkopolski Poland 52°52N 16°0E 185 F3
Ksabi Morocco 32°51N 4°13W 260 B4
Ksar Chellala Algeria 35°13N 2°19E 261 A5
Ksar el Boukhari Algeria 35°51N 2°52E 261 A5
Ksar el Kebir Morocco 35°0N 6°0W 260 B3
Ksar es Souk = Er Rachidia Morocco 31°58N 4°20W 260 B4
Ksar Rhilane Tunisia 33°0N 9°39E 258 B1
Ksiąz Wielkopolski Poland 52°4N 17°14E 185 F4
Ksour, Mts. des Algeria 32°45N 0°30W 260 B4
Kstovo Russia 56°12N 44°13E 187 C8
Ku, W. el → Sudan 13°37N 25°15E 257 E2
Ku-Ring-Gai Chase △ Australia 33°39S 151°14E 283 B9
Ku Tree Res. U.S.A. 21°30N 157°59W 302 J14
Kuah Malaysia 6°19N 99°51E 237 J2
Kuala Indonesia 2°55N 105°47E 234 B3
Kuala Belait Malaysia 4°35N 114°11E 235 B4
Kuala Berang Malaysia 5°5N 103°1E 237 K4
Kuala Dungun = Dungun Malaysia 4°45N 103°25E 237 K4
Kuala Kangsar Malaysia 4°46N 100°56E 237 K3
Kuala Kelawang Malaysia 2°56N 102°5E 237 L4
Kuala Kerai Malaysia 5°30N 102°12E 237 K4
Kuala Kerian Malaysia 5°14N 100°37E 237 c
Kuala Kubu Bharu Malaysia 3°34N 101°39E 237 L3
Kuala Lipis Malaysia 4°10N 102°3E 237 K4
Kuala Lumpur Malaysia 3°9N 101°41E 237 L3
Kuala Nerang Malaysia 6°16N 100°37E 237 J3
Kuala Pilah Malaysia 2°45N 102°15E 237 L4
Kuala Rompin Malaysia 2°49N 103°29E 237 L4
Kuala Selangor Malaysia 3°20N 101°15E 237 L3
Kuala Sepetang Malaysia 4°49N 100°28E 237 K3
Kuala Terengganu Malaysia 5°20N 103°8E 237 K4
Kualajelai Indonesia 2°58S 110°46E 235 C4
Kualakapuas Indonesia 2°55S 114°20E 235 C4
Kualakurun Indonesia 1°1S 113°50E 235 C4
Kualapembuang Indonesia 3°14S 112°38E 235 C4
Kualapu'u U.S.A. 21°9N 157°2W 302 B2
Kualasimpang Indonesia 4°17N 98°3E 235 A1
Kualoa Pt. U.S.A. 21°31N 157°50W 302 J14
Kuamut Malaysia 5°13N 117°30E 235 A5
Kuan Shan Taiwan 23°4N 121°11E 225 b
Kuanao Taiwan 24°31N 121°55E 225 a
Kuancheng China 40°37N 118°30E 222 D10
Kuandang Indonesia 0°56N 123°1E 231 D6
Kuandian China 40°45N 124°45E 224 A2
Kuangchou = Guangzhou China 23°6N 113°13E 121 B2
Kuanhsi Taiwan 24°48N 121°10E 225 b
Kuanmiao Taiwan 22°58N 120°19E 225 C2
Kuantan Malaysia 3°49N 103°20E 237 L4
Kuanyin Ilan, Taiwan 24°34N 121°44E 225 a
Kuanyin Taoyüan, Taiwan 25°2N 121°4E 225 A3
Kuapä Pond U.S.A. 21°17N 157°43W 302 K14

La Guardia, New York ✈ (LGA)
  U.S.A.   40°46N 73°52W **132** B2
La Gudiña = A Gudiña
  Spain   42°4N 7°8W **194** C3
La Güera Mauritania   20°51N 17°0W **260** D1
La Guerche-de-Bretagne
  France   47°57N 1°16W **172** E5
La Guerche-sur-l'Aubois
  France   46°58N 2°56E **173** F9
La Habana Cuba   23°8N 82°22W **320** B3
La Harpe U.S.A.   40°35N 90°58W **310** D6
La Haute Vallée de Chevreuse △
  France   48°35N 1°58E **173** D8
La Haye-du-Puits France   49°17N 1°33W **172** C5
La Horqueta Venezuela   7°55N 60°20W **329** B5
La Horra Spain   41°44N 3°53W **194** D7
La Hulpe Belgium   50°43N 4°30E **116** B2
La Independencia Mexico   16°15N 92°1W **319** D6
La Isabela Dom. Rep.   19°58N 71°2W **321** C5
La Jonquera Spain   42°25N 2°53E **196** C7
La Joya Peru   16°43S 71°52W **330** D3
La Junta U.S.A.   37°59N 103°33W **304** H12
La Laguna Canary Is.   28°28N 16°18W **153** e1
La Lézarde ➤ Martinique   14°35N 61°1W **322** j
La Libertad = Puerto Libertad
  Mexico   29°55N 112°43W **318** B2
La Libertad Guatemala   16°47N 90°7W **320** C1
La Libertad □ Peru   8°0S 78°30W **330** B2
La Ligua Chile   32°30S 71°16W **334** C1
La Línea de la Concepción
  Spain   36°15N 5°23W **195** d3
La Llacuna Spain   41°24N 2°12E **114** A2
La Loche Canada   56°29N 109°26W **297** B7
La Loma Mexico   19°31N 99°11W **128** A1
La Londe-les-Maures
  France   43°8N 6°14E **175** E10
La Lora Spain   42°45N 4°0W **194** C7
La Loupe France   48°29N 1°0E **172** D8
La Louvière Belgium   50°27N 4°10E **170** D4
La Lucila Argentina   34°30S 58°29W **117** C2
La Lune Trin. & Tob.   10°3N 61°22W **323** t
La Machine France   46°54N 3°27E **173** F10
La Maddalena Italy   41°13N 9°24E **200** A2
La Maladrerie France   48°54N 2°1E **134** A1
La Malbaie Canada   47°40N 70°10W **299** C5
La Malinche △ Mexico   19°15N 98°3W **319** D5
La Mancha Spain   39°10N 2°54W **197** F2
La Manche ➤ Martinique   14°33N 61°0W **322** j
La Mariña Spain   43°30N 7°40W **194** B3
La Martre, L. Canada   63°15N 117°55W **296** A5
La Merced Peru   11°3S 75°19W **330** C2
La Mesa Baja Calif.,
  Mexico   32°30N 116°57W **307** N10
La Mesa Calif., U.S.A.   32°46N 117°1W **307** N9
La Mesilla U.S.A.   32°16N 106°48W **305** K10
La Milla, Cerro Peru   12°2S 77°5W **124** B2
La Misión Mexico   32°6N 116°53W **318** A1
La Moille U.S.A.   41°32N 89°17W **310** C7
La Moine ➤ U.S.A.   39°59N 90°31W **310** E6
La Monachina Italy   41°53N 12°21E **136** B1
La Montagne Réunion   20°53S 55°26E **272** f
La Monte U.S.A.   38°46N 93°26W **310** F3
La Moraleja Spain   40°30N 3°38W **127** A2
La Mothe-Achard France   46°37N 1°40W **172** F5
La Motte-Chalançon
  France   44°30N 5°21E **175** D9
La Motte-du-Caire France   44°20N 6°3E **175** D10
La Motte-Servolex France   45°35N 5°53E **175** C9
La Moure U.S.A.   46°21N 98°18W **308** B4
La Moustique ➤
  Guadeloupe   16°10N 61°34W **322** e
La Muela Spain   41°36N 1°7W **196** D3
La Mure France   44°55N 5°48E **175** D9
La Negra Chile   23°46S 70°18W **334** A1
La Nopalera Mexico   19°18N 99°5W **128** C2
La Oliva Canary Is.   28°36N 13°57W **153** e2
La Oroya Peru   11°32S 75°54W **330** C2
La Orotava Canary Is.   28°22N 16°31W **153** e1
La Oroya Peru   11°32S 75°54W **330** C2
La Pacaudière France   46°11N 3°52E **173** F10
La Pagerie Martinique   14°32N 61°3W **322** j
La Palma Canary Is.   28°40N 17°50W **153** e1
La Palma Panama   8°15N 78°0W **320** E4
La Palma del Condado
  Spain   37°21N 6°38W **195** H4
La Paloma Chile   30°35S 71°0W **334** C1
La Pampa □ Argentina   36°50S 66°0W **334** D2
La Paragua Venezuela   6°50N 63°20W **329** B5
La Pastora Trin. & Tob.   10°42N 61°19W **323** t
La Paternal Argentina   34°35S 58°26W **117** B2
La Paya △ Colombia   0°0 75°5W **328** C2
La Paz Entre Ríos,
  Argentina   30°50S 59°45W **334** C4
La Paz San Luis, Argentina   33°30S 67°20W **334** C2
La Paz Bolivia   16°20S 68°10W **330** D4
La Paz Honduras   14°20N 87°47W **320** D2
La Paz Baja Calif. S.,
  Mexico   24°10N 110°18W **318** C2
La Paz Abra, Phil.   17°40N 120°41E **232** C3
La Paz Tarlac, Phil.   15°26N 120°45E **232** D3
La Paz □ Bolivia   15°30S 68°0W **330** D4
La Paz Centro Nic.   12°20N 86°41W **320** D2
La Pedrera Colombia   1°18S 69°43W **328** D4
La Pérade Canada   46°35N 72°12W **299** C5
La Perla Chihuahua,
  Mexico   28°18N 104°32W **318** B4
La Perla Lima, Peru   12°4S 77°7W **124** B2
La Perouse Australia   33°59S 151°14E **139** B2
La Perouse, Bahía Chile   27°55S 109°18W **330** b
La Perouse Str. Asia   23°46N 97°47W **319** C5
La Pesca Mexico   20°21N 102°0W **318** C4
La Piedad Mexico   40°40N 121°30W **304** E3
La Pine U.S.A.   41°51N 12°23E **136** B1
La Pisana Italy   15°20N 61°15W **323** k
La Plaine Dominica   21°13S 55°33E **272** f
La Plaine des Cafres
  Réunion   21°7S 55°38E **272** f
La Plaine des Palmistes
  Réunion   21°2S 55°38E **272** f
La Plata Argentina   35°0S 57°55W **334** C4
La Plata Colombia   2°23N 75°53W **328** C2
La Plata Mo., U.S.A.   40°2N 92°29W **310** D3
La Plata, L. Argentina   44°55S 71°50W **336** B2
La Pobla de Lillet Spain   42°16N 1°59E **196** C6
La Pobla de Segur Spain   42°15N 0°58E **196** C5
La Pocatière Canada   47°22N 70°2W **299** C5
La Pola de Gordón Spain   42°51N 5°41W **194** C5
La Porte U.S.A.   42°25N 9°21E **175** F13
La Porte U.S.A.   29°40N 95°1W **314** C2
La Porte City U.S.A.   42°19N 92°12W **310** D2
La Possession Réunion   20°55S 55°21E **272** f
La Prairie Canada   45°25N 73°29W **130** C8
La Presanella Italy   46°13N 10°40E **198** B7
La Puebla = Sa Pobla Spain   39°46N 3°1E **206** B4
La Puebla de Cazalla
  Spain   37°14N 5°19W **195** H5
La Puebla de los Infantes
  Spain   37°47N 5°24W **195** H5
La Puebla de Montalbán
  Spain   39°52N 4°22W **194** F6
La Puebla del Río Spain   37°16N 6°3W **195** H4
La Puerta de Segura
  Spain   38°22N 2°45W **195** G8
La Punta Peru   12°4S 77°10W **124** B2
La Puntigala Spain   41°27N 2°13E **114** A2
La Purísima Mexico   26°10N 112°4W **318** B2

La Push U.S.A.   47°55N 124°38W **306** C2
La Queue-en-Brie France   48°47N 2°34E **134** B4
La Quiaca Argentina   22°5S 65°35W **334** A2
La Reina Chile   33°26S 70°33W **187** B2
La Réole France   44°35N 0°1W **174** D3
La Republica, Plaza de
  Mexico City, Mexico   **128** b1
La Restinga Canary Is.   27°38N 17°59W **153** e1
La Ribera Spain   41°21N 2°4E **114** A1
La Rioja Argentina   29°20S 67°0W **334** B2
La Rioja □ Argentina   29°30S 67°0W **334** B2
La Rioja □ Spain   42°20N 2°20W **196** C2
La Rivière des Pluies
  Réunion   20°54S 55°31E **272** f
La Robla Spain   42°50N 5°41W **194** C5
La Roche N. Cal.   21°26S 168°2E **288** d
La Roche-Bernard France   47°31N 2°19W **172** E4
La Roche-Canillac France   45°12N 1°57E **174** C5
La Roche-en-Ardenne
  Belgium   50°11N 5°35E **170** D5
La Roche-sur-Foron
  France   46°4N 6°19E **173** F13
La Roche-sur-Yon France   46°40N 1°25W **172** F5
La Rochefoucauld France   45°44N 0°24E **174** C4
La Rochelle France   46°10N 1°9W **174** B2
La Roda Spain   39°13N 2°15W **197** F2
La Roda de Andalucía
  Spain   37°12N 4°46W **195** H6
La Romaine Canada   50°13N 60°40W **299** B7
La Romana Dom. Rep.   18°27N 68°57W **321** C6
La Ronge Canada   55°5N 105°20W **297** B7
La Rue U.S.A.   40°35N 83°23W **311** D13
La Rumorosa Mexico   32°34N 116°6W **307** N10
La Sabina = Sa Savina
  Spain   38°44N 1°25E **206** D1
La Sagra Spain   37°57N 2°35W **197** H2
La Sagrera Spain   41°25N 2°11E **114** A2
La Salada Argentina   34°43S 58°28W **117** C2
La Saline Réunion   21°4S 55°16E **272** f
La Salle U.S.A.   41°20N 89°6W **310** C7
La Sanabria Spain   42°0N 6°30W **194** C4
La Santa Canary Is.   29°5N 13°40W **153** e2
La Sarre Canada   48°45N 79°15W **298** C4
La Scala Italy   45°28N 9°11E **129** B2
La Scie Canada   49°57N 55°36W **299** C8
La Selva Spain   42°0N 2°45E **196** C7
La Selva Beach U.S.A.   36°56N 121°51W **306** J5
La Selva del Camp Spain   41°13N 1°8E **196** D6
La Serena Chile   29°55S 71°10W **334** B1
La Serena Spain   38°55N 5°40W **195** G5
La Seu d'Urgell Spain   42°22N 1°23E **196** C6
La Seyne-sur-Mer France   43°7N 5°52E **175** E9
La Sila Italy   39°15N 16°35E **209** C9
La Solana Spain   38°59N 3°14W **195** G7
La Soufrière St. Vincent   13°20N 61°11W **323** n
La Souterraine France   46°15N 1°30E **173** F8
La Spézia Italy   44°7N 9°50E **198** D6
La Storta Italy   41°59N 12°26E **136** A1
La Suze-sur-Sarthe France   47°53N 0°2E **172** E7
La Tagua Colombia   0°3N 74°40W **328** C3
La Taxonera Spain   41°25N 2°10E **114** A2
La Teste-de-Buch France   44°37N 1°8W **174** D2
La Tortuga Venezuela   11°0N 65°22W **326** D6
La Tour-du-Pin France   45°33N 5°27E **175** C9
La Tranche-sur-Mer
  France   46°20N 1°27W **172** F5
La Tremblade France   45°46N 1°8W **174** C2
La Trinidad Phil.   16°28N 120°35E **232** C3
La Trinité Martinique   14°45N 60°58W **322** j
La Tuque Canada   47°30N 72°50W **298** C5
La Unión Chile   40°10S 73°0W **336** B2
La Unión Colombia   1°35N 77°5W **328** C2
La Unión El Salv.   13°20N 87°50W **320** D2
La Unión Guerrero,
  Mexico   17°58N 101°49W **318** D4
La Unión Peru   9°43S 76°40W **330** B2
La Unión Phil.   37°38N 0°53W **197** H4
La Unión □ Phil.   16°30N 120°25E **232** C3
La Urbana Venezuela   7°8N 66°56W **328** B5
La Vache B. Trin. & Tob.   10°45N 61°29W **323** t
La Vache Pt. Trin. & Tob.   10°47N 61°28W **323** t
La Vall d'Uixó Spain   39°49N 0°15W **196** F4
La Vecilla Spain   42°51N 5°27W **194** C5
La Vega Dom. Rep.   19°20N 70°30W **321** C5
La Vega Peru   10°41S 77°44W **330** C2
La Vela de Coro
  Venezuela   11°27N 69°34W **328** A4
La Veleta Spain   37°1N 3°22W **195** H7
La Venta Mexico   18°5N 94°3W **319** D6
La Venturosa Colombia   6°8N 68°48W **328** B4
La Vergne U.S.A.   36°1N 86°35W **315** C11
La Veronica Trin. & Tob.   10°42N 61°21W **323** t
La Victoria Peru   12°3S 77°2W **124** B2
La Victoria Venezuela   10°14N 67°20W **328** A4
La Villa Joiosa = Villajoyosa
  Spain   38°30N 0°12W **197** G4
La Voulte-sur-Rhône
  France   44°48N 4°46E **175** D8
Laa an der Thaya Austria   48°43N 16°23E **181** C9
Laaber, Grosse ➤
  Germany   48°57N 12°8E **181** D7
Laage Germany   53°55N 12°21E **178** B8
Laajalahti Finland   60°11N 24°48E **121** B1
Laajasalo Finland   60°10N 25°1E **121** B3
Laaksolahti Finland   60°14N 24°45E **121** B1
Laas Dawaco Somali Rep.   10°28N 49°0E **267** B6
Laascaanood = Las Anod
  Somali Rep.   8°26N 47°19E **267** C4
Laasqoray Somali Rep.   11°10N 48°20E **267** B6
Laatzen Germany   52°19N 9°48E **178** C5
Lā'au Pt. U.S.A.   21°6N 157°19W **302** B4
Laba ➤ Russia   45°11N 39°42E **191** H4
Labagou National Forest Park
  China   40°1N 116°22E **114** A2
Laban Burma   25°52N 96°40E **241** C6
Labasa Fiji   16°30S 179°27E **287** F7
Labason Phil.   8°4N 122°31E **233** G4
Labastide-Murat France   44°39N 1°33E **174** D5
Labastide-Rouairoux
  France   43°28N 2°39E **174** E6
Labbézanga Mali   15°2N 0°48E **263** B5
Labdah = Leptis Magna
  Libya   32°40N 14°12E **258** B2
Labe = Elbe ➤ Europe   53°50N 9°0E **178** B4
Labé Guinea   11°24N 12°16W **262** C2
Laberge, L. Canada   61°11N 135°12W **296** A1
Labes = Lobez Poland   53°38N 15°39E **184** B2
Labian, Tanjong Malaysia   6°45N 118°19E **235** A5
Labiau = Polessk Russia   54°50N 21°5E **184** A8
Labig Pt. = Iligan Pt.
  Phil.   18°25N 122°25E **232** B4
Labin Croatia   45°5N 14°8E **199** C11
Labinsk Russia   44°40N 40°48E **191** H5
Labis Malaysia   2°22N 103°2E **234** B2
Labiszyn Poland   52°57N 17°54E **185** F4
Lablába, W. el ➤ Egypt   30°1N 31°19E **117** A2
Labo Phil.   14°9N 122°51E **232** D4
Laboe Germany   54°25N 10°13E **178** A6
Laborec ➤ Slovak Rep.   48°37N 21°58E **181** C14
Laborie St. Lucia   13°45N 61°0W **323** m
Labouheyre France   44°13N 0°55W **174** D3
Laboulaye Argentina   34°10S 63°30W **334** C3
Labrador Canada   53°20N 61°0W **299** B7
Labrador City Canada   52°57N 66°55W **299** B6
Labrador Sea Atl. Oc.   57°0N 54°0W **295** F21
Lábrea Brazil   7°15S 64°51W **331** B5

Labruguière France   43°31N 2°16E **174** E6
Labuan
  Somali Rep.   1°16S 41°49E **267** C5
Laghmān □ Afghan.   34°20N 70°0E **240** B3
Laghouat Algeria   33°50N 2°59E **261** B5
Laghouat □ Algeria   33°35N 2°40E **261** B5
Lagnieu France   45°55N 5°20E **175** C9
Lagny-sur-Marne France   48°52N 2°44E **173** D9
Lago ➤ Niassa □ Mozam.   13°30S 36°0E **269** E4
Lago Italy   39°10N 16°9E **201** C9
Lago Agrio Ecuador   0°5N 76°52W **328** C2
Lago de Sanabria y Entorno △
  Spain   42°9N 6°45W **194** C4
Lago Posadas Argentina   47°30S 71°50W **336** C2
Lago Puela □ Argentina   42°0S 71°30W **336** B2
Lago Ranco Chile   40°19S 72°30W **336** B2
Lagoa Azores   37°45N 25°20W **153** d3
Lagoa Rio de J., Brazil   22°58S 43°11W **135** B1
Lagôa Portugal   37°8N 8°27W **195** H2
Lagoa do Peixe △ Brazil   31°12S 50°55W **335** D5
Lagoa Vermelha Brazil   28°13S 51°32W **335** B5
Lagôaça Portugal   41°11N 6°44W **194** D4
Lagodekhi Georgia   41°50N 46°22E **191** K8
Lagong = Laguna Beach
  U.S.A.   33°33N 117°47W **307** M9
Lagonegro Italy   40°8N 15°45E **201** B8
Lagonoy G. Phil.   13°35N 123°50E **232** E4
Lagos Angola   11°1N 25°6E **203** E9
Lagos Greece   6°25N 3°27E **124** B2
Lagos Nigeria   6°25N 3°27E **124** B2
Lagos Portugal   37°5N 8°41W **195** H2
Lagos □ Nigeria   6°28N 3°25E **124** B2
Lagos de Moreno
  Mexico   21°21N 101°55W **318** C4
Lagos Harbour Nigeria   6°26N 3°23E **124** B2
Lagos-Ikeja ✈ (LOS)
  Nigeria   6°34N 3°19E **124** A1
Lagos Island Nigeria   6°26N 3°23E **124** B2
Lagos Lagoon Nigeria   6°30N 3°28E **124** B2
Lagrange U.S.A.   18°45S 121°43E **278** C3
Lagrange U.S.A.   41°39N 85°25W **311** C11
Lagrange B. Australia   18°38S 121°42E **278** C3
Laguardia Spain   42°33N 2°35W **196** C2
Laguépie France   44°8N 1°57E **174** D5
Lagún Neth. Ant.   12°19N 69°10W **322** g
Laguna = Padilla Bolivia   19°19S 64°20W **331** D5
Laguna Brazil   28°30S 48°50W **335** B6
Laguna N. Mex., U.S.A.   35°2N 107°25W **305** J10
Laguna U.S.A.   38°42N 121°25E **232** D2
Laguna, Sa. de la
  Mexico   23°35N 109°55W **318** C3
Laguna Beach U.S.A.   33°33N 117°47W **307** M9
Laguna Blanca △
  Argentina   39°0S 70°5W **336** A2
Laguna de B. Phil.   14°29N 121°6E **127** C2
Laguna de Duera Spain   41°29N 4°44W **194** D6
Laguna de Lachuá △
  Guatemala   15°55N 90°40W **320** C1
Laguna de Tacarigua △
  Venezuela   10°59N 64°7W **328** A4
Laguna del Laja △ Chile   37°27S 71°20W **334** D1
Laguna del Tigre △
  Guatemala   17°0N 90°45W **320** C1
Laguna Limpia Argentina   26°32S 59°45W **334** B4
Laguna San Rafael △
  Chile   46°54S 73°31W **336** C2
Lagunas Chile   21°0S 69°45W **334** A2
Lagunas Peru   5°10S 75°35W **330** B2
Lagunas de Chacahua △
  Mexico   16°0N 97°43W **319** D5
Lagunas de Montebello △
  Mexico   16°4N 91°42W **319** D6
Lagunas de Ruidera △
  Spain   38°57N 2°52W **197** G2
Lagunillas Bolivia   19°38S 63°43W **331** D5
Lahad Datu Malaysia   5°0N 118°20E **235** A5
Lahad Datu, Telok
  Malaysia   4°50N 118°20E **235** B5
Lahaina U.S.A.   20°53N 156°41W **302** C5
Lahan Sai Thailand   14°25N 102°52E **236** E4
Lahanam Laos   16°16N 105°16E **236** D5
Lahar India   26°12N 78°57E **243** F8
Laharpur India   27°43N 80°56E **243** F9
Lahat Indonesia   3°45S 103°30E **234** C2
Lahe Burma   26°20N 95°26E **241** B5
Lahewa Indonesia   1°22N 97°12E **234** B1
Lahij Yemen   13°4N 44°53E **248** E3
Lāhijān Iran   37°10N 50°6E **247** B6
Lahilahi Pt. U.S.A.   21°28N 158°13W **302** K13
Lähn = Wleń Poland   50°59N 77°37E **179** E3
Lahn ➤ Germany   50°19N 7°37E **179** E3
Laholm Sweden   56°30N 13°2E **163** H7
Laholmsbukten Sweden   56°30N 12°45E **163** H6
Lahontan Res. U.S.A.   31°32N 74°22E **242** D6
Lahore Pakistan   31°32N 74°22E **242** D6
Lahr Germany   48°20N 7°52E **179** G3
Lahri Pakistan   29°11N 68°13E **242** E3
Lähröd Iran   38°30N 47°52E **213** C12
Lahti = Lahtis Finland   60°58N 25°40E **188** B3
Lahtis Finland   60°58N 25°40E **188** B3
Lahugala Kitulana △
  Sri Lanka   6°50N 81°40E **245** L5
Laï Chad   9°25N 16°18E **259** G3
Lai Chau Vietnam   22°5N 103°3E **228** F4
Lai'è U.S.A.   21°39N 157°56W **302** J14
Laifeng China   29°27N 109°20E **228** D7
L'Aigle France   48°46N 0°38E **172** D7
Laignes France   47°50N 4°20E **173** E11
L'Aiguillon-sur-Mer
  France   46°20N 1°18W **174** B2
Laila = Layla Si. Arabia   22°10N 46°40E **248** B4
Laim Germany   48°7N 11°30E **131** B2
Lainate Italy   45°34N 9°1E **129** A1
Laingsburg S. Africa   33°9S 20°52E **270** D3
Lainioälven ➤ Sweden   67°35N 22°40E **160** C20
Lainz Austria   48°10N 16°16E **142** B1
Lafontaine, Parc Canada   45°32N 73°34W **130** A2
Laful India   7°10N 93°52E **245** L11
Lagan ➤ Papua N. G.   5°4S 142°52E **286** C2
Lagan = Kaspiyskiy
  Russia   45°22N 47°23E **191** H8
Lagan Sweden   56°56N 13°58E **163** H7
Lagan ➤ Antrim, U.K.   54°36N 5°55W **166** B6
Lagan ➤ Sweden   56°56N 13°58E **163** H7
Lagana, Kolpos Greece   37°45N 20°53E **207** D2
Laganas Greece   37°44N 20°50E **207** D2
Lagangilang Phil.   17°37N 120°44E **232** C3
Lagarfljót ➤ Iceland   65°40N 14°18W **155** D6
Lagarto Brazil   10°54S 37°41W **332** D4
Lagawe Phil.   16°49N 121°6E **232** C4
Lagdo, L. de Cameroon   8°40N 14°43E **264** A2
Lage Germany   51°58N 8°48E **178** C4
Lage-Mierde Neths.   51°24N 5°9E **170** C3
Lagen ➤ Oppland, Norway   61°8N 10°25E **163** D6
Lågen ➤ Vestfold, Norway   59°3N 10°3E **163** D6
Lägerdorf Germany   53°53N 9°34E **178** B5
Lages Brazil   27°48N 27°6W **153** d3
Lages do N., Brazil
  Brazil   5°41S 36°14W **332** C4
Laggan = Lake Louise
  Canada   51°30N 116°10W **296** C5

Lajes do Pico Azores   38°23N 28°16W **153** d1
Lajinha Brazil   20°9S 41°37W **333** F3
Lajkovac Serbia   44°27N 20°14E **202** B4
Lajosmizse Hungary   47°3N 19°32E **182** C4
Lak Sao Laos   18°11N 104°59E **236** C5
Lakamané Mali   14°35N 9°44W **262** C3
Lakatoro Vanuatu   16°5S 167°25E **287** F5
Lake U.S.A.   44°33N 110°24W **304** D8
Lake Alfred U.S.A.   28°6N 81°44W **317** G3
Lake Alpine U.S.A.   38°29N 120°0W **306** G7
Lake Andes U.S.A.   43°9N 98°32W **308** D4
Lake Arthur U.S.A.   30°5N 92°41W **314** F8
Lake Bindegolly △
  Australia   28°0S 144°12E **281** A3
Lake Boga Australia   35°26S 143°38E **282** C5
Lake Buena Vista U.S.A.   28°23N 81°32W **133** B1
Lake Butler U.S.A.   30°1N 82°21W **316** E7
Lake Cain Hills U.S.A.   28°29N 81°28W **133** B1
Lake Cargelligo
  Australia   33°15S 146°22E **283** B7
Lake Charles U.S.A.   30°14N 93°13W **314** F8
Lake City Colo., U.S.A.   38°2N 107°19W **304** G10
Lake City Fla., U.S.A.   30°11N 82°38W **316** E7
Lake City Iowa, U.S.A.   42°16N 94°44W **310** D2
Lake City Mich., U.S.A.   44°20N 85°13W **309** C11
Lake City Minn., U.S.A.   44°27N 92°16W **308** C7
Lake City Pa., U.S.A.   42°1N 80°21W **312** D4
Lake City S.C., U.S.A.   33°52N 79°45W **316** D10
Lake Clark △ U.S.A.   61°0N 154°0W **303** F9
Lake Coeur d'Alene Shores
  U.S.A.   26°39N 80°5W **317** J9
Lake Coleridge U.S.A.   43°17S 171°30E **285** D6
Lake Cowichan Canada   48°49N 124°3W **296** D4
Lake District △ U.K.   54°30N 3°21W **168** C4
Lake Eildon △ Australia   10°15S 145°56E **283** D6
Lake Elsinore U.S.A.   33°38N 117°20W **307** M9
Lake Eyre △ Australia   28°40S 137°31E **281** D2
Lake Fairfax Park
  U.S.A.   38°57N 77°19W **143** B2
Lake Geneva U.S.A.   42°36N 88°26W **311** B8
Lake George U.S.A.   43°26N 73°43W **313** C11
Lake Grace Australia   33°7S 118°28E **279** F2
Lake Gregory ◎
  Australia   20°12S 127°27E **278** D4
Lake Harbour = Kimmirut
  Canada   62°50N 69°50W **295** E18
Lake Havasu City
  U.S.A.   34°27N 114°22W **307** L12
Lake Helen U.S.A.   28°59N 81°14W **317** G3
Lake Hughes U.S.A.   34°41N 118°26W **307** L8
Lake Isabella U.S.A.   35°38N 118°28W **307** K8
Lake Jackson U.S.A.   29°3N 95°27W **314** G7
Lake King Australia   33°5S 119°45E **279** F2
Lake Kopiago Papua N. G.   5°23S 142°31E **286** C2
Lake Kutubu Papua N. G.   6°20S 143°18E **286** C2
Lake Lenore Canada   52°24N 104°59W **297** C8
Lake Louise Canada   51°30N 116°10W **296** C5
Lake Mackay ◎
  Australia   21°48S 129°46E **278** D4
Lake Mburo △ Uganda   0°33S 30°56E **268** C3
Lake Mead △ U.S.A.   36°30N 114°22W **307** K12
Lake Meredith △
  U.S.A.   35°50N 101°50W **314** D4
Lake Mills Iowa, U.S.A.   43°25N 93°32W **308** D7
Lake Mills Wis., U.S.A.   43°5N 88°55W **311** A8
Lake Murray Papua N. G.   6°48S 141°29E **286** D1
Lake Nakuru △ Kenya   0°23S 36°8E **268** C4
Lake Naujan △ Phil.   13°0N 121°22E **232** E3
Lake Odessa U.S.A.   42°47N 85°8W **311** B11
Lake Orion U.S.A.   42°47N 83°14W **311** B13
Lake Park U.S.A.   26°48N 80°3W **317** J9
Lake Park U.S.A.   30°41N 83°11W **316** E6
Lake Placid Fla., U.S.A.   27°18N 81°22W **317** H3
Lake Placid N.Y., U.S.A.   44°17N 73°59W **313** B11
Lake Pleasant U.S.A.   43°28N 74°25W **313** C10
Lake Point Tower Chicago, U.S.A. **119** b3
Lake Providence U.S.A.   32°48N 91°10W **314** E9
Lake Pukaki N.Z.   44°11S 170°8E **285** E5
Lake Roosevelt △ U.S.A.   48°5N 118°14W **306** B4
Lake St. Peter Canada   45°18N 78°2W **312** A6
Lake Shore Drive Chicago, U.S.A. **119** a2
Lake Shore Park Chicago, U.S.A. **119** a1
Lake Superior △ Canada   47°45N 84°45W **298** C3
Lake Tekapo N.Z.   44°0S 170°30E **285** E5
Lake Torrens △
  Australia   30°55S 137°40E **281** E2
Lake View U.S.A.   38°47N 80°52W **310** D3
Lake Villa U.S.A.   42°25N 88°4W **311** A8
Lake Village U.S.A.   33°20N 91°17W **314** E9
Lake Wales U.S.A.   27°54N 81°35W **317** H3
Lake Worth U.S.A.   26°37N 80°3W **317** J9
Lake Zurich U.S.A.   42°12N 88°5W **311** A8
Lakeba Fiji   18°13S 178°47W **287** D2
Lakeba Passage Fiji   18°15S 178°45W **287** D2
Lakefield Canada   44°25N 78°16W **312** B6
Lakefield △ Australia   15°24S 144°6E **280** B4
Lakehurst U.S.A.   40°1N 74°19W **313** F10
Lakeland Australia   15°49S 144°57E **280** B4
Lakeland Fla., U.S.A.   28°3N 81°57W **317** G8
Lakeland Ga., U.S.A.   31°2N 83°4W **316** E6
Lakemba = Lakeba Fiji   18°13S 178°47W **287** D2
Lakemba Australia   33°55S 151°5E **139** B1
Lakepa Cook Is.   18°59S 169°48W **289** g
Lakeport Calif., U.S.A.   39°3N 122°55W **306** F4
Lakeport Mich., U.S.A.   43°7N 82°30W **312** B2
Lakes Entrance Australia   37°50S 148°0E **283** D8
Lakeside Gauteng, S. Africa   26°5S 28°8E **123** A2
Lakeside Calif., U.S.A.   32°52N 116°55W **307** N10
Lakeside Ariz., U.S.A.   34°9N 109°58W **305** J9
Lakeside Center Chicago, U.S.A. **119** f3
Lakeview Ill., U.S.A.   41°56N 87°38W **119** B3
Lakeview Ca., U.S.A.   30°0N 90°6W **131** A2
Lakeview Oreg., U.S.A.   42°11N 120°21W **304** E4
Lakeville U.S.A.   44°39N 93°14W **308** C7
Lakewood Colo., U.S.A.   39°42N 105°4W **304** G11
Lakewood N.J., U.S.A.   40°6N 74°13W **313** F10
Lakewood N.Y., U.S.A.   42°6N 79°19W **312** D5
Lakewood Ohio, U.S.A.   41°29N 81°48W **312** E3
Lakewood Wash.,
  U.S.A.   47°11N 122°32W **306** C4
Lakewood Park Fla.,
  U.S.A.   27°33N 80°24W **317** H9
Lakewood Park Georgia,
  U.S.A.   33°43N 84°24W **113** B2
Lakha India   27°57N 80°46E **243** F9
Lakhimpur Assam, India   24°48N 93°0E **241** C4
Lakhimpur Ut. P., India   27°57N 80°46E **243** F9
Lakhisarai India   25°11N 86°5E **243** G11
Lakhnadon India   22°36N 79°36E **243** H8
Lakhnau = Lucknow
  India   26°50N 81°0E **243** F9
Lakhonpheng Laos   15°54N 105°34E **236** E5
Lakhpat India   23°48N 68°47E **242** H3
Lakhtinskiy Razliv, Oz.
  Russia   59°59N 30°9E **137** B1
Läki Azerbaijan   40°34N 47°22E **191** K8

Laki Iceland   64°4N 18°14W **155** C8
Lakin U.S.A.   37°57N 101°15W **308** G3
Lakitusaki ➤ Canada   54°21N 82°25W **298** B3
Lakka Greece   39°17N 20°9E **206** C10
Lakki Greece   35°24N 23°57E **207** E4
Lakki Pakistan   32°36N 70°55E **242** C4
Lakonia □ Greece   36°55N 22°30E **204** E4
Lakonikos Kolpos Greece   36°40N 22°40E **204** E4
Lakor Indonesia   8°15S 128°17E **231** F7
Lakota Ivory C.   5°50N 5°30W **262** D3
Lakota N. Dak., U.S.A.   48°2N 98°21W **308** A4
Laksar India   29°46N 78°3E **242** E8
Laksefjorden Norway   70°45N 26°50E **160** A22
Lakselv Norway   70°2N 25°0E **160** A21
Laksettipet India   18°52N 79°13E **244** E4
Lakshadweep □ India   10°0N 72°30E **245** J1
Lakshadweep Is. India   10°0N 72°30E **245** J1
Laksham Bangla.   23°14N 91°8E **241** D3
Lakshmanpur India   22°58N 83°3E **243** H10
Lakshmeshwar India   15°9N 75°28E **245** G2
Lakshmikantapur India   22°5N 88°20E **243** H13
Laksi Thailand   13°53N 100°35E **113** A2
Lakuramau Papua N. G.   2°54S 151°15E **286** B6
Lal-lo Phil.   18°12N 121°40E **232** B3
Lala Dem. Rep. of the Congo   4°10S 20°30E **265** C4
Lala Musa Pakistan   32°40N 73°57E **242** C5
Lalaghat India   24°30N 92°40E **241** C4
Lalago Tanzania   3°28S 33°58E **268** C3
Lalapanzi Zimbabwe   19°20S 30°15E **269** F3
Lalapaşa Turkey   41°49N 26°44E **203** E10
Lalara France   0°19N 11°32E **264** B2
Lalbenque France   44°19N 1°34E **174** D5
Lalbert Australia   35°38S 143°20E **282** C5
L'Albufera Spain   39°20N 0°27W **197** F4
L'Alcora Spain   40°5N 0°14W **196** E4
L'Alfàs del Pi Spain   38°35N 0°9W **197** G4
Lalganj India   25°52N 85°13E **243** G13
Lalgola India   24°25N 88°15E **243** G13
Lālī Iran   32°21N 49°6E **247** C6
Lalibela Ethiopia   12°3N 39°0E **257** E4
Lalin Heilongjiang, China   45°12N 127°0E **227** B14
Lalín Spain   42°40N 8°5W **194** C2
Lalin He ➤ China   45°32N 125°40E **227** B13
Lalinde France   44°50N 0°44E **174** D4
Lalitapur Nepal   27°40N 85°20E **243** F11
Lalitpur India   24°42N 78°28E **243** G8
Lalkua India   29°5N 79°31E **243** E8
Lalm Norway   61°50N 9°17E **164** C6
Lalsot India   26°34N 76°20E **242** F7
Lam Pao Res. Thailand   16°50N 103°15E **236** D4
Lam Tin China   22°18N 114°14E **122** B2
Lama Kara Togo   9°30N 1°15E **263** D5
Lamae Thailand   9°51N 99°9E **237** H2
Lamag Malaysia   5°29N 117°49E **235** A5
Lamaing Burma   15°25N 97°53E **236** E1
Lamaipum Burma   25°40N 97°57E **241** C6
Lamap Vanuatu   16°26S 167°43E **287** F5
Lamar Colo., U.S.A.   38°5N 102°37W **304** G12
Lamar Mo., U.S.A.   37°30N 94°16W **308** G6
Lamarque Argentina   39°24S 65°42W **336** A3
Lamas Peru   6°28S 76°31W **330** B2
Lamastre France   44°59N 4°35E **175** D8
Lamayuru India   34°25N 76°56E **243** B7
Lambach Austria   48°6N 13°51E **180** C6
Lamballe France   48°29N 2°31E **172** D4
Lambaréné Gabon   0°41S 10°12E **264** C2
Lambasa = Labasa Fiji   16°30S 179°27E **287** A2
Lambay I. Ireland   53°29N 6°1W **166** C5
Lambayeque □ Peru   6°45S 80°0W **330** B2
Lamberg Norway   59°52N 10°48E **133** A3
Lambert, C. Papua N. G.   4°21S 151°31E **286** C6
Lambert-St. Louis Int. ✈ (STL)
  U.S.A.   38°45N 90°22W **310** F6
Lambert's Bay S. Africa   32°5S 18°17E **270** D2
Lambertville U.S.A.   41°46N 83°35W **311** C13
Lambesc France   43°39N 5°16E **175** E9
Lambèse = Tazoult Algeria   35°29N 6°11E **261** A6
Lambeth U.S.A.   42°54N 81°18W **312** D3
Lambeth □ U.K.   51°28N 0°6W **125** A3
Lambi Solomon Is.   9°22S 159°39E **287** M10
Lambia Greece   37°52N 21°53E **204** D3
Lambir Hills △ Malaysia   4°12N 114°1E **235** B4
Lambomakondro Madag.   22°41S 44°44E **272** C1
Lambon Papua N. G.   4°45S 152°48E **286** C7
Lambrate Italy   45°28N 9°16E **129** B2
Lambro ➤ Italy   45°8N 9°32E **198** C6
Lambro, Parco Italy   45°29N 9°14E **129** A2
Lambton Mills Canada   43°39N 79°30W **141** B1
Lambu Papua N. G.   3°18S 151°43E **286** B6
Lamé Chad   9°19N 14°32E **259** G2
Lame Nigeria   10°30N 9°20E **263** C6
Lame Deer U.S.A.   45°37N 106°40W **304** D10
Lamego Portugal   41°5N 7°52W **194** D3
Lamèque Canada   47°45N 64°38W **299** C7
Lameroo Australia   35°19S 140°33E **281** F3
Lamesa U.S.A.   32°44N 101°58W **314** D4
Lamia Greece   38°55N 22°26E **204** D4
Lamigan Pt. Phil.   6°48N 126°21E **233** H6
Lamine ➤ U.S.A.   38°59N 92°51W **310** F3
Lamington △ Australia   28°13S 153°12E **281** D5
Lamitan Phil.   6°39N 122°8E **233** H4
Lamlam, Mt. Guam   13°22N 144°41E **302** d
Lamma I. China   22°12N 114°7E **122** B1
Lammermuir Hills U.K.   55°50N 2°40W **167** F6
Lammhult Sweden   57°2N 14°34E **163** G8
Lamoille ➤ U.S.A.   44°38N 73°13W **313** B11
Lamon B. Phil.   14°30N 122°20E **232** D4
Lamont Canada   53°46N 112°50W **296** C6
Lamont Calif., U.S.A.   35°15N 118°55W **307** K8
Lamont Fla., U.S.A.   30°23N 83°49W **316** E6
Lamont Iowa, U.S.A.   42°36N 91°39W **310** D5
Lamont Wyo., U.S.A.   42°13N 107°29W **304** E10
Lamotte-Beuvron France   47°36N 2°1E **173** E9
Lampa Peru   15°22S 70°22W **330** D3
Lampang Thailand   18°16N 99°32E **236** C2
Lampasas U.S.A.   31°4N 98°11W **314** F5
Lampazos de Naranjo
  Mexico   27°1N 100°31W **318** B4
Lampedusa Medit. S.   35°36N 12°40E **261** A7
Lampeter U.K.   49°35N 7°24W **169** E3
Lampione Medit. S.   35°33N 12°20E **258** A2
Lampman Canada   49°25N 102°50W **297** D8
Lamprechtshausen
  Austria   48°0N 12°58E **180** D5
Lampung □ Indonesia   5°30S 104°30E **234** D2
Lamta India   22°8N 80°7E **243** H9
Lamu Burma   19°14N 94°10E **241** F5
Lamu Coast, Kenya   2°16S 40°55E **268** C5
Lamud Peru   6°10S 77°57W **330** B2
Lamy U.S.A.   35°29N 105°53W **305** J11
Lan Xian China   38°15N 111°35E **226** E6
Lan Yü Taiwan   22°4N 121°25E **229** G13
Lāna'i I. U.S.A.   20°50N 156°55W **302** C5
Lāna'i City U.S.A.   20°50N 156°55W **302** C5
Lāna'ihale U.S.A.   20°49N 156°53W **302** C5

Lanak La China 34°27N 79°32E 243 B8
Lanak'o Shank'ou = Lanak La China 34°27N 79°32E 243 B8
Lanao, L. Phil. 7°52N 124°15E 233 H5
Lanao del Norte □ Phil. 8°0N 124°10E 233 H5
Lanao del Sur □ Phil. 7°40N 124°15E 233 H5
Lanark Ont., Canada 45°1N 76°22W 313 A8
Lanark S. Lanarks., U.K. 55°40N 3°47W 167 F5
Lanark Ill., U.S.A. 42°6N 89°50W 310 B7
Lanbi Kyun Burma 10°50N 98°20E 237 G2
Lancang China 22°36N 99°58E 228 F2
Lancang Jiang → China 21°40N 101°10E 228 G3
Lancashire □ U.K. 53°50N 2°48W 168 D5
Lancaster Ont., Canada 45°10N 74°30W 313 A10
Lancaster Lancs., U.K. 54°3N 2°48W 168 C5
Lancaster Calif., U.S.A. 34°42N 118°8W 307 L8
Lancaster Ky., U.S.A. 37°37N 84°35W 309 G11
Lancaster Mo., U.S.A. 40°31N 92°32W 310 D4
Lancaster N.H., U.S.A. 44°29N 71°34W 313 B13
Lancaster Ohio, U.S.A. 39°43N 82°36W 309 F12
Lancaster Pa., U.S.A. 40°2N 76°19W 313 F8
Lancaster S.C., U.S.A. 34°43N 80°46W 315 D14
Lancaster Wis., U.S.A. 42°51N 90°43W 310 B6
Lancaster, Récif = Neilson, Récif Pac. Oc. 27°1S 146°2W 289 f
Lancaster Sd. Canada 74°13N 84°0W 295 C15
Lancelin Australia 31°0S 115°18E 279 F2
Lanchow = Lanzhou China 36°1N 103°52E 226 F2
Lanchyn Ukraine 48°33N 24°45E 183 B9
Lanciano Italy 42°14N 14°23E 199 F11
Lanco Chile 39°24S 72°46W 336 A2
Lancones Peru 4°30S 80°30W 330 A1
Lancun China 36°25N 120°10E 227 F11
Łańcut Poland 50°10N 22°13E 185 H9
Land Between the Lakes ⌂ U.S.A. 36°25N 88°0W 315 C11
Landau Bayern, Germany 48°40N 12°41E 179 G8
Landau Rhld-Pfz., Germany 49°12N 8°6E 179 F4
Landay Afghan. 30°31N 63°47E 240 C1
Landeck Austria 47°9N 10°34E 180 D3
Lander U.S.A. 42°50N 108°44W 304 E9
Lander → Australia 22°0S 132°0E 278 D5
Landerneau France 48°28N 4°17W 172 D2
Landeryd Sweden 57°7N 13°15E 163 G7
Landes France 44°0N 1°0W 174 D2
Landes □ France 43°57N 0°48W 174 E3
Landes de Gascogne ⌂ France 44°23N 0°50W 174 D3
Landeshut = Kamienna Góra Poland 50°47N 16°2E 185 H3
Landete Spain 39°56N 1°25W 196 F3
Landfall I. India 13°40N 93°2E 245 H11
Landi Kotal Pakistan 34°7N 71°6E 242 B4
Landianchang China 39°56N 116°17E 114 B1
Landisburg U.S.A. 40°21N 77°19W 312 F7
Landivisiau France 48°31N 4°6W 172 D2
Landmannalaugar Iceland 63°59N 19°4W 155 D7
Landover Hills U.S.A. 38°56N 76°54W 143 B4
Landquart Switz. 46°58N 9°32E 179 J5
Landrecies France 50°7N 3°40E 173 B10
Land's End U.K. 50°4N 5°44W 169 G2
Landsberg = Górowo Iławeckie Poland 54°17N 20°30E 184 D7
Landsberg Germany 48°2N 10°53E 179 G6
Landsberg an der Warthe = Gorzów Wielkopolski Poland 52°43N 15°15E 185 F2
Landsberg in Oberschlesien = Gorzów Śląski Poland 51°3N 18°22E 185 G5
Landsborough Cr. → Australia 22°28S 144°35E 280 C3
Landsbro Sweden 57°24N 14°56E 163 G8
Landshut Germany 48°34N 12°8E 179 G8
Landskrona Sweden 55°53N 12°50E 163 J6
Landsmeer Neths. 52°26N 4°55E 112 A2
Landstrasse Austria 48°12N 16°23E 142 A2
Landstuhl Germany 49°24N 7°33E 179 F3
Landvetter Sweden 57°41N 12°17E 163 G6
Landwehr kanal Germany 52°29N 13°24E 115 B3
Lane U.S.A. 33°32N 79°53W 316 B10
Lane Cove Australia 33°48S 151°9E 134 B1
Lane Cove Nat. Park △ Australia 33°47S 151°8E 139 A1
Lanesboro U.S.A. 41°57N 75°34W 313 E9
Lanester France 47°46N 3°22W 172 E3
Lanett U.S.A. 32°52N 85°12W 316 C4
Lang Shan China 41°0N 106°30E 226 D4
Lang Son Vietnam 21°52N 106°42E 228 G6
Lang Suan Thailand 9°57N 99°4E 237 H2
Langå Midtjylland, Denmark 56°23N 9°54E 163 H3
Langa Western Cape, S. Africa 33°57S 18°31E 118 A2
La'nga Co China 30°45N 81°15E 243 D9
Langa-Langa Dem. Rep. of the Congo 3°50S 15°59E 264 C3
Langadas Greece 40°46N 23°6E 202 F7
Langadia Greece 37°43N 22°1E 204 D4
Långan → Sweden 63°19N 14°44E 162 A8
Langanes Iceland 66°20N 14°53W 155 A12
Langano, L. Ethiopia 7°36N 38°43E 257 F4
Langar Afghan. 37°2N 73°47E 240 A4
Langar Iran 35°23N 60°25E 247 C9
Langara I. Canada 54°14N 133°1W 296 C2
Langarūd Iran 37°11N 50°8E 247 B6
Långås Sweden 56°58N 12°26E 163 H6
Langatabbetje Suriname 4°59N 54°28W 329 C7
Langdai China 26°6N 105°21E 228 D5
Langdon U.S.A. 48°45N 98°22W 308 A4
Långe Jan = Ölands södra udde Sweden 56°12N 16°23E 163 H10
Langeac France 45°7N 3°29E 174 C7
Langeais France 47°20N 0°24E 172 E7
Langeb Baraka → Sudan 17°28N 36°50E 256 D4
Langeberg S. Africa 33°55S 21°0E 270 D3
Langeberge S. Africa 28°15S 22°33E 270 C3
Langeland Denmark 54°56N 10°48E 163 K4
Langelands Bælt Denmark 54°50N 10°55E 163 K4
Langen Hessen, Germany 49°59N 8°40E 179 F4
Langen Niedersachsen, Germany 53°36N 8°36E 178 B4
Langenbielau = Bielawa Poland 50°43N 16°37E 185 H3
Langenburg Canada 50°51N 101°43W 297 C8
Langeneß Germany 54°38N 8°36E 178 A4
Langenlois Austria 48°29N 15°40E 180 C8
Langenzersdorf Austria 48°18N 16°21E 142 A2
Langeoog Germany 53°45N 7°32E 178 B3
Langer See Germany 52°24N 13°37E 115 B4
Langeskov Denmark 55°22N 10°35E 163 J4
Langesund Norway 59°0N 9°45E 164 F6
Langevåg Norway 62°26N 6°13E 164 B3
Långhem Sweden 57°36N 13°14E 163 G7
Langhirano Italy 44°37N 10°16E 198 D7
Langholm U.K. 55°9N 3°0W 167 F5
Langisjór Iceland 64°11N 18°15W 155 C8
Langjökull Iceland 64°39N 20°12W 155 C6
Langkawi, Pulau Malaysia 6°25N 99°45E 237 J2
Langklip S. Africa 28°12S 20°20E 270 C3
Langkon Malaysia 6°30N 116°40E 235 A5
Langley B.C., Canada 49°7N 122°39W 306 A4
Langley Va., U.S.A. 38°57N 77°11W 143 B2
Langley Park U.S.A. 38°59N 76°58W 143 B4
Langnau Switz. 46°56N 7°47E 179 J3
Langogne France 44°43N 3°50E 174 D7
Langon France 44°33N 0°16W 174 D3
Langøya Norway 68°45N 14°50E 160 B16
Langreo Spain 43°18N 5°40W 194 B5
Langres France 47°52N 5°20E 173 E12
Langres, Plateau de France 47°45N 5°3E 173 E12
Langsa Indonesia 4°30N 97°57E 234 B1
Långsele Sweden 63°12N 17°4E 162 A11
Långshyttan Sweden 60°27N 16°2E 162 D10
Langtang △ Nepal 28°10N 85°30E 243 E11
Langtao Burma 27°15N 97°34E 241 B6
Langting India 25°31N 93°7E 241 C4
Langtry U.S.A. 29°49N 101°34W 314 G4
Langu Thailand 6°53N 99°47E 237 J2
Langue de Barbarie △ Senegal 14°54N 16°30W 262 C1
Languedoc France 43°58N 3°55E 174 E7
Languedoc-Roussillon □ France 43°25N 3°0E 174 E6
Langwald Germany 48°10N 11°25E 131 A1
Langwang China 22°38N 113°27E 219 F9
Langxi China 31°10N 119°12E 229 B12
Langxiangzhen China 39°43N 116°8E 226 E9
Langzhong China 31°38N 105°58E 228 B5
Lanham U.S.A. 38°59N 76°51W 143 B4
Lanigan Canada 51°51N 105°2W 297 C7
Lanikai U.S.A. 21°23N 157°42W 302 K14
Lanín △ Argentina 40°0S 71°58W 336 A2
Lanjigarh India 19°43N 83°23E 244 E6
Lankao China 34°48N 114°50E 226 G8
Länkäran Azerbaijan 38°48N 48°52E 213 C13
Lankwitz Germany 52°25N 13°21E 115 B3
Lanmeur France 48°39N 3°43W 172 D3
Lannemezan France 43°8N 0°23E 174 E4
Lannilis France 48°35N 4°32W 172 D2
Lannion France 48°46N 3°29W 172 D3
L'Annonciation Canada 46°25N 74°55W 298 C5
L'Annunziatella Italy 41°49N 12°33E 136 C2
Lanouaille France 45°24N 1°9E 174 C5
Lanping China 26°28N 99°15E 228 D2
Lansdale U.S.A. 40°14N 75°17W 313 F9
Lansdowne N.S.W., Australia 31°48S 152°30E 283 A10
Lansdowne Ont., Canada 44°24N 76°1W 313 B8
Lansdowne India 29°50N 78°41E 243 E8
Lansdowne Western Cape, S. Africa 33°59S 18°30E 118 A2
Lansdowne House = Neskantaga Canada 52°14N 87°53W 298 B2
L'Anse U.S.A. 46°45N 88°27W 308 B9
L'Anse à l'Âne Martinique 14°32N 61°4W 322 j
L'Anse au Loup Canada 51°32N 56°50W 299 B8
L'Anse Aux Epines Grenada 11°59N 61°45W 323 q
L'Anse aux Meadows Canada 51°36N 55°32W 299 B8
L'Anse la Raye St. Lucia 13°55N 61°3W 323 m
L'Anse Mitan Martinique 14°32N 61°3W 322 j
Lansford U.S.A. 40°50N 75°53W 313 F9
Lanshan China 25°24N 112°10E 229 E9
Lansing Ont., Canada 43°45N 79°24W 141 A2
Lansing Mich., U.S.A. 42°44N 84°33W 311 B12
Lanslebourg-Mont-Cenis France 45°17N 6°52E 175 C10
Lanta Yai, Ko Thailand 7°35N 99°3E 237 J2
Lantana U.S.A. 26°35N 80°3W 317 J9
Lantau I. China 22°15N 113°56E 219 G10
Lantewa Nigeria 12°16N 11°44E 263 C7
Lantian China 34°11N 109°20E 226 G5
Lanus Argentina 34°42S 58°23W 117 C2
Lanusei Italy 39°52N 9°34E 200 C2
Lanuza Phil. 9°14N 126°4E 233 G6
Lanxi China 29°13N 119°28E 229 C12
Lanyang Hsi → Taiwan 24°43N 121°49E 225 B3
Lanyü Taiwan 22°2N 121°33E 225 D3
Lanzarote Canary Is. 29°0N 13°40W 153 e2
Lanzarote ✈ (ACE) Canary Is. 28°57N 13°40W 153 e2
Lanzhou China 36°1N 103°52E 226 F2
Lanzo Torinese Italy 45°16N 7°28E 198 C4
Lao → Italy 39°47N 15°48E 201 C8
Lao Bao Laos 16°35N 106°30E 236 D6
Lao Cai Vietnam 22°30N 103°57E 228 F4
Laoag Phil. 18°7N 120°34E 232 B3
Laoang Phil. 12°32N 125°8E 232 E5
Laoha He → China 43°25N 120°35E 227 C11
Laohekou China 32°22N 111°38E 229 A8
Laois □ Ireland 52°57N 7°36W 166 D4
Laon France 49°33N 3°35E 173 C10
Laona U.S.A. 45°34N 88°40W 308 C9
Laonung Hsi → Taiwan 22°47N 120°27E 225 D2
Laos ■ Asia 17°45N 105°0E 236 D5
Lapa Paraná, Brazil 25°46S 49°44W 335 B6
Lapa Rio de J., Brazil 22°54S 43°10W 135 B1
Lapac I. Phil. 5°32N 120°47E 233 J3
Lapai Nigeria 9°5N 6°32E 263 D6
Lapalisse France 46°15N 3°38E 173 F10
Lapara I. Phil. 5°57N 120°0E 233 J2
Lapeer U.S.A. 43°3N 83°19W 311 A13
Lapeyrade France 44°4N 0°3W 174 D3
Lapithos Cyprus 35°21N 33°11E 207 E9
Lapland = Lappland Europe 68°7N 24°0E 160 B21
LaPorte Ind., U.S.A. 41°36N 86°43W 311 C10
Laporte Pa., U.S.A. 41°25N 76°30W 313 E8
Lapovo Serbia 44°10N 21°7E 202 B5
Lappeenranta Finland 61°3N 28°12E 188 B5
Lappland Europe 68°7N 24°0E 160 B21
Lappo = Lapua Finland 62°58N 23°0E 160 E20
Laprida Argentina 37°34S 60°45W 334 D3
Lâpseki Turkey 40°20N 26°41E 203 F10
Laptev Sea Russia 76°0N 125°0E 215 B13
Lapu-Lapu Phil. 10°20N 123°55E 233 F4
Lapua Finland 62°58N 23°0E 160 E20
Lăpuş → Romania 47°25N 23°40E 183 C8
Lăpuş, Munţii Romania 47°20N 23°50E 183 C8
Lăpuşna Moldova 46°53N 28°25E 183 D13
Łapy Poland 52°59N 22°52E 185 F9
Laqiya Arba'in Sudan 20°1N 28°1E 256 C2
Laqiya Umran Sudan 19°55N 28°18E 256 C2
L'Àquila Italy 42°22N 13°22E 199 F10
Lār Iran 27°40N 54°14E 247 E7
Lara Australia 38°2S 144°26E 282 E6
Lara □ Venezuela 10°10N 69°50W 328 A4
Larabanga Ghana 9°16N 1°56W 262 D4
Larache Morocco 35°10N 6°5W 260 A3
Larache □ Morocco 35°10N 5°50W 260 A3
Laragaran = Plaridel Phil. 8°37N 123°43E 233 G4
Laragne-Montéglin France 44°18N 5°49E 175 D9
Lārak Iran 26°51N 56°21E 249 A7
Laramie U.S.A. 41°19N 105°35W 304 F11
Laramie Mts. U.S.A. 42°0N 105°30W 304 F11
Laranjal do Jari Brazil 0°51S 52°32W 329 D7
Laranjeiras Brazil 22°55S 43°10W 135 B1
Laranjeiras do Sul Brazil 25°23S 52°23W 335 B5
Larantuka Indonesia 8°21S 122°55E 231 F6
Larat Indonesia 7°0S 132°0E 231 F8
L'Arbresle France 45°50N 4°36E 175 C8
Lärbro Sweden 57°47N 18°50E 163 G12
Lårdal Norway 59°25N 8°10E 164 E5
Larde Mozam. 16°28S 39°43E 269 F4
Larder Lake Canada 48°5N 79°40W 298 C4
Lardos Greece 36°6N 28°1E 206 E12
Lardos, Akra = Lindos, Akra Greece 36°4N 28°10E 206 E12
Lardos, Ormos Greece 36°4N 28°2E 206 E12
Lare Kenya 0°20N 37°56E 268 C4
Laredo Spain 43°26N 3°28W 194 B7
Laredo Tex., U.S.A. 27°30N 99°30W 314 H5
Laredo Sd. Canada 52°30N 128°53W 296 C3
Larena Phil. 9°15N 123°35E 233 G4
Lares Puerto Rico 18°18N 66°53W 321 b
Large I. Grenada 12°24N 61°30W 323 q
Largentière France 44°34N 4°18E 175 D8
L'Argentière-la-Bessée France 44°47N 6°33E 175 D10
Largo U.S.A. 27°54N 82°47W 317 H7
Largo, Key U.S.A. 25°15N 80°15W 317 K9
Largs U.K. 55°47N 4°52W 167 F4
Lari Italy 43°34N 10°35E 198 E7
Lariang Indonesia 1°26S 119°17E 231 E5
Larimore U.S.A. 47°54N 97°38W 308 B5
Larino Italy 41°48N 14°54E 199 G11
Larisa Greece 39°36N 22°27E 204 B4
Larisis Station Athens, Greece 112 a1
Larissa = Larisa Greece 39°36N 22°27E 204 B4
Larissas □ Greece 39°39N 22°24E 204 B4
Larkana Pakistan 27°32N 68°18E 242 F3
Larkins = South Miami U.S.A. 25°42N 80°17W 128 B1
Larnaca Cyprus 34°55N 33°38E 207 F9
Larnaca ✈ (LCA) Cyprus 34°50N 33°34E 207 F9
Larnaca Bay Cyprus 34°53N 33°45E 207 F9
Larnare, Pte. Martinique 14°47N 61°13W 322 j
Larne U.K. 54°51N 5°51W 166 B6
Larned U.S.A. 38°11N 99°6W 308 F4
Laroquebrou France 44°58N 2°12E 174 D6
Larose U.S.A. 29°34N 90°23W 315 G9
Larose, Pte. Martinique 14°39N 60°53W 322 j
Larrimah Australia 15°35S 133°12E 278 C5
Larsen Bay U.S.A. 57°32N 153°59W 303 H9
Larsen Ice Shelf Antarctica 67°0S 62°0W 151 C17
Laruns France 43°0N 0°26W 174 F3
Larvik Norway 59°4N 10°2E 164 E7
Larzac, Causse du France 43°50N 3°17E 174 E7
Las Palmas 52°13N 21°6E 142 B2
Las Alpujarras Spain 36°55N 3°20W 197 J1
Las Animas U.S.A. 38°4N 103°13W 304 G12
Las Anod Somali Rep. 8°26N 47°19E 267 C6
Las Arenas Spain 43°17N 4°50W 194 B6
Las Batuecas ⌂ Spain 40°32N 6°5W 194 E4
Las Bonitas Venezuela 7°52N 65°40W 328 B4
Las Brenãs Argentina 27°5S 61°7W 334 B3
Las Cabezas de San Juan Spain 36°57N 5°58W 195 J5
Las Cañadas del Teide ⌂ Canary Is. 28°15N 16°37W 153 e1
Las Chimeneas Mexico 32°8N 116°5W 307 N10
Las Coloradas Argentina 39°34S 70°36W 336 A2
Las Corts Spain 41°23N 2°9E 114 A1
Las Cruces U.S.A. 32°19N 106°47W 305 K10
Las Flores Argentina 36°10S 59°7W 334 D4
Las Gabias = Gabia la Grande Spain 37°8N 3°40W 195 H7
Las Heras Mendoza, Argentina 32°51S 68°49W 334 C2
Las Heras Santa Cruz, Argentina 46°33S 68°57W 336 C3
Las Hermosas △ Colombia 3°48N 75°51W 328 C2
Las Horquetas Argentina 48°14S 71°11W 336 C2
Las Kabacki Poland 52°7N 21°2E 142 C2
Las Khoreh = Laasqoray Somali Rep. 11°10N 48°20E 267 B6
Las Lajas Argentina 38°30S 70°25W 336 A2
Las Lomas Peru 4°40S 80°10W 330 A1
Las Lomitas Argentina 24°43S 60°35W 334 A3
Las Marismas Spain 37°5N 6°20W 195 H4
Las Mercedes Venezuela 9°7N 66°24W 328 B4
Las Minas Spain 38°20N 1°41W 197 G3
Las Navas de la Concepción Spain 37°56N 5°30W 195 H5
Las Navas del Marqués Spain 40°36N 4°20W 194 E6
Las Nieves Phil. 8°46N 125°34E 233 G5
Las Orquideas △ Colombia 6°36N 76°16W 328 B2
Las Palmas Argentina 27°8S 58°45W 334 B4
Las Palmas Canary Is. 28°7N 15°26W 153 e1
Las Palmas → Mexico 32°31N 116°58W 307 N10
Las Palmas ✈ (LPA) Canary Is. 27°55N 15°25W 153 e1
Las Pedroñas Spain 39°26N 2°40W 197 F2
Las Piedras Puerto Rico 18°11N 65°52W 321 b
Las Piedras Uruguay 34°44S 56°14W 335 C4
Las Pinas Phil. 14°29N 120°58E 127 C1
Las Pipinas Argentina 35°30S 57°19W 334 D4
Las Plumas Argentina 43°40S 67°15W 336 B3
Las Rejas Chile 33°27S 70°42W 137 B1
Las Rosas Argentina 32°30S 61°35W 334 C3
Las Rozas Spain 40°29N 3°52W 194 E7
Las Tablas Panama 7°49N 80°14W 320 E3
Las Toscas Argentina 28°21S 59°18W 334 B4
Las Truchas Mexico 17°57N 102°13W 318 D4
Las Tunas Cuba 20°58N 76°59W 320 B4
Las Varillas Argentina 31°50S 62°50W 334 C3
Las Vegas N. Mex., U.S.A. 35°36N 105°13W 305 J11
Las Vegas Nev., U.S.A. 36°10N 115°8W 124 A2
Las Vegas McCarran Int. ✈ (LAS) U.S.A. 36°5N 115°9W 124 B2
Lasa = Lhasa China 29°25N 90°58E 218 D4
LaSalle Canada 45°26N 73°38W 130 B2
LaSalle Street Chicago, U.S.A. 119 a1
LaSalle Street Station Chicago, U.S.A. 119 d1
Lasanga I. Papua N. G. 7°25S 147°15E 286 D4
Lasarte-Oria Spain 43°16N 2°1W 196 B2
Lascano Uruguay 33°35S 54°12W 335 C5
Lascelles Australia 35°34S 142°34E 282 C5
Lasek Bielański Poland 52°17N 20°57E 142 B1
Lasek Na Kole Poland 52°15N 20°56E 142 B1
Lash-e Joveyn Afghan. 31°45N 61°30E 240 D1
Lashburn Canada 53°10N 109°40W 297 C7
Lashio Burma 22°56N 97°45E 241 D6
Lashkar India 26°10N 78°10E 242 F8
Lashkar Gāh Afghan. 31°35N 64°21E 240 D2
Lasin Poland 53°30N 19°2E 184 E6
Lasithi Greece 35°11N 25°31E 207 E6
Lasithi □ Greece 35°5N 25°50E 207 E6
Lāsjerd Iran 35°24N 53°4E 247 C7
Lask Poland 51°34N 19°8E 185 G6
Łaskarzew Poland 51°48N 21°36E 185 G8
Laško Slovenia 46°10N 15°16E 199 B12
Lassance Brazil 17°54S 44°34W 333 E3
Lassay-les-Châteaux France 48°27N 0°30W 172 D6
Lassen Pk. U.S.A. 40°29N 121°30W 304 F3
Lassen Volcanic △ U.S.A. 40°30N 121°20W 304 F3
Lassongo Angola 12°5S 22°46E 265 E4
Last Mountain L. Canada 51°5N 105°14W 297 C7
Lastchance Cr. → U.S.A. 40°2N 121°15W 306 E5
Lastoursville Gabon 0°55S 12°38E 264 C2
Lastovo Croatia 42°46N 16°55E 199 F13
Lastovski Kanal Croatia 42°50N 17°0E 199 F14
Lat Yao Thailand 15°45N 99°48E 236 E2
Lata Mt. Amer. Samoa 14°14S 169°27W 302 f
Latacunga Ecuador 0°50S 78°35W 328 D2
Latakia = Al Lādhiqīyah Syria 35°30N 35°45E 250 C6
Latchford Canada 47°20N 79°50W 298 C4
Late Tonga 18°48S 174°39W 287 P13
Latehar India 23°45N 84°30E 243 H11
Laterza Italy 40°37N 16°48E 201 B9
Latham Australia 29°44S 116°20E 279 E2
Lathen Germany 52°52N 7°19E 178 C3
Lathi India 27°43N 71°23E 242 F4
Lathi Vanuatu 14°57S 167°8E 287 D5
Lathrop U.S.A. 39°33N 94°20W 310 E2
Lathrop Wells U.S.A. 36°39N 116°24W 307 J10
Latiano Italy 40°33N 17°43E 201 B10
Latin, Quartier Montréal, Canada 130 b2
Latina Italy 41°28N 12°52E 200 A5
Latina Madrid, Spain 40°24N 3°44W 127 B1
Latisana Italy 45°47N 13°0E 199 C10
Latium = Lazio □ Italy 42°10N 12°30E 199 F9
Laton U.S.A. 36°26N 119°41W 306 J7
Latorytsya → Slovak Rep. 48°28N 21°50E 181 C14
Latouche Treville, C. Australia 18°27S 121°49E 278 C3
Latouma Niger 22°10N 14°50E 259 D2
Látrar Iceland 66°24N 23°2W 155 A3
Latrobe Tas., Australia 41°14S 146°30E 281 G4
Latrobe Pa., U.S.A. 40°19N 79°23W 312 F5
Latrónico Italy 40°5N 16°1E 201 B9
Latur India 18°25N 76°40E 244 E3
Latvia ■ Europe 56°50N 24°0E 188 D2
Lau Nigeria 9°11N 11°19E 263 D7
Lau Basin Pac. Oc. 20°0S 177°0W 277 E15
Lau Fau Shan China 22°28N 113°59E 219 G10
Lau Group Fiji 17°0S 178°30W 287 A3
Lau Ridge Pac. Oc. 21°0S 178°0W 277 E15
Lauban = Lubań Poland 51°5N 15°15E 185 G2
Lauca → Bolivia 19°9S 68°10W 330 D4
Lauchhammer Germany 51°29N 13°47E 178 D9
Lauda-Königshofen Germany 49°33N 9°42E 179 F5
Laudal Norway 58°15N 7°30E 164 F4
Laudat Dominica 15°20N 61°21W 323 k
Lauenburg = Lębork Poland 54°33N 17°46E 184 D4
Lauenburg Germany 53°22N 10°32E 178 B6
Lauenburgische Seen ⌂ Germany 53°38N 10°45E 178 B6
Lauf Germany 49°30N 11°16E 179 F7
Laufás Iceland 65°53N 18°4W 155 B8
Laugar Iceland 65°15N 21°48W 155 B5
Laugarbakki Iceland 65°20N 20°55W 155 B6
Laugarvatn Iceland 64°13N 20°44W 155 C6
Lauge Koch Kyst Greenland 75°45N 57°45W 295 B20
Laughlin U.S.A. 35°10N 114°34W 305 J6
Laujar de Andarax Spain 37°0N 2°54W 197 H2
Laukaa Finland 62°24N 25°56E 160 E21
Laulau, Bahia N. Marianas 15°8N 145°45E 302 e
Launceston Tas., Australia 41°24S 147°8E 281 G4
Launceston Corn., U.K. 50°38N 4°22W 169 G3
Laune → Ireland 52°7N 9°47W 166 D2
Launglon Bok Burma 13°50N 97°54E 236 F1
Laupheim Germany 48°14N 9°52E 179 G5
Laura Queens., Australia 15°32S 144°32E 280 B3
Laura S. Austral., Australia 33°10S 138°18E 282 B3
Laureana di Borrello Italy 38°30N 16°5E 201 D9
Laurel Fla., U.S.A. 27°8N 82°27W 317 H7
Laurel Ind., U.S.A. 39°30N 85°11W 311 E11
Laurel Miss., U.S.A. 31°41N 89°8W 315 F10
Laurel Mont., U.S.A. 45°40N 108°46W 304 D9
Laurel Bay U.S.A. 32°27N 80°47W 316 C9
Laurel Hill U.S.A. 40°14N 79°6W 312 F5
Laurencekirk U.K. 56°50N 2°28W 167 E6
Laurens Iowa, U.S.A. 42°51N 94°52W 310 B2
Laurens S.C., U.S.A. 34°30N 82°1W 315 D13
Laurentian Plateau Canada 52°0N 70°0W 299 B6
Lauria Italy 40°2N 15°50E 201 B8
Laurie L. Canada 56°35N 101°57W 297 B8
Laurinburg U.S.A. 34°47N 79°28W 315 D15
Laurium U.S.A. 47°14N 88°27W 308 B9
Lausanne Switz. 46°32N 6°38E 179 J2
Laut Indonesia 4°45N 108°0E 235 B3
Laut, Pulau Indonesia 3°40S 116°10E 235 C5
Laut Kecil, Kepulauan Indonesia 4°45S 115°40E 235 C5
Lautaro Chile 38°31S 72°27W 336 A2
Lauterbach Germany 50°37N 9°24E 178 E5
Lauterecken Germany 49°38N 7°35E 179 F3
Lautoka Fiji 17°37S 177°27E 287 A1
L'Autre Bord Guadeloupe 16°20N 61°20W 322 e
Lauttasaari Finland 60°9N 24°53E 121 C2
Lauzès France 44°34N 1°35E 174 D5
Lava → Russia 54°37N 21°14E 184 D8
Lava Beds ⌂ U.S.A. 41°40N 121°30W 304 F3
Lavagh More Ireland 54°46N 8°6W 166 B3
Lavagna Italy 44°18N 9°20E 198 D6
Laval France 48°4N 0°48W 172 D6
Laval-des-Rapides Canada 45°33N 73°42W 130 A1
Lavalle Argentina 28°15S 65°15W 334 B2
Lāvān Iran 26°48N 53°22E 247 E7
Lavanggu Solomon Is. 11°36S 160°16E 287 N11
Lavant Canada 45°3N 76°42W 313 A8
Lāvar Meydān Iran 30°20N 54°30E 247 D7
Lavara Greece 41°19N 26°22E 203 E10
Lavardac France 44°12N 0°20E 174 D4
Lavaur France 43°40N 1°49E 174 E5
Lavelanet France 42°57N 1°51E 174 F5
Lavello Italy 41°3N 15°48E 201 A8
L'Averdy, C. Papua N. G. 5°33S 155°4E 286 C8
Lavers Hill Australia 38°40S 143°25E 282 E5
Laverton Australia 28°44S 122°29E 279 E3
Lavik Norway 61°6N 5°25E 164 C2
Lavis Italy 46°8N 11°7E 198 B8
Lavīzān Iran 35°47N 51°30E 141 A2
Lavos Portugal 40°6N 8°49W 194 E2
Lavoutte, Anse St. Lucia 14°5N 60°55W 323 m
Lavradio Portugal 38°40N 9°2W 126 A2
Lavras Brazil 21°20S 45°0W 333 F3
Lavre Portugal 38°46N 8°22W 195 G2
Lavrio Greece 37°40N 24°4E 204 D6
Lavris Greece 35°25N 24°40E 207 E5
Lavumisa Swaziland 27°20S 31°55E 271 C5
Lavushi Manda △ Zambia 12°46S 31°0E 269 E3
Lawa Phil. 6°21N 125°41E 233 H5
Lawa-an Phil. 11°51N 125°5E 233 F5
Lawaki Fiji 17°40S 178°35E 287 A2
Lawas Malaysia 4°55N 115°25E 235 B5
Lawdar Yemen 13°53N 45°52E 248 D4
Lawele Indonesia 5°13S 122°57E 231 F6
Lawksawk Burma 21°15N 96°52E 241 E6
Lawn Hill = Boodjamulla △ Australia 18°15S 138°6E 280 B2
Lawndale U.S.A. 41°50N 87°42W 119 B2
Lawne L. U.S.A. 28°33N 81°26W 133 A2
Lawqah Si. Arabia 29°49N 42°45E 246 D4
Lawra Ghana 10°39N 2°51W 262 C4
Lawrence N.Z. 45°55S 169°41E 285 F4
Lawrence Ind., U.S.A. 39°50N 86°2W 311 E10
Lawrence Kans., U.S.A. 38°58N 95°14W 308 F6
Lawrence Mass., U.S.A. 42°43N 71°10W 313 D13
Lawrence Heights Canada 43°43N 79°25W 141 A2
Lawrenceburg Ind., U.S.A. 39°6N 84°52W 311 E12
Lawrenceburg Ky., U.S.A. 38°2N 84°54W 311 F12
Lawrenceburg Tenn., U.S.A. 35°14N 87°20W 315 D11
Lawrenceville Ga., U.S.A. 33°57N 83°59W 316 B6
Lawrenceville Ill., U.S.A. 38°44N 87°41W 311 F9
Lawrenceville Pa., U.S.A. 41°59N 77°8W 312 E7
Laws U.S.A. 37°24N 118°20W 306 H8
Lawson U.S.A. 39°26N 94°12W 310 E2
Lawtey U.S.A. 30°3N 82°5W 316 E7
Lawton Mich., U.S.A. 42°10N 85°50W 311 B11
Lawton Okla., U.S.A. 34°37N 98°25W 314 D5
Lawu Indonesia 7°40S 111°13E 235 D4
Lawz, J. al Si. Arabia 28°39N 35°18E 251 K6
Laxå Sweden 58°59N 14°37E 163 F8
Laxamýri Iceland 65°58N 17°24W 155 B9
Laxford, L. U.K. 58°24N 5°6W 167 C3
Laxou France 48°41N 6°8E 173 D13
Lay → France 46°18N 1°17W 174 B2
Layari Pakistan 24°52N 67°0E 123 A2
Layari → Pakistan 24°53N 66°58E 123 A1
Layla Si. Arabia 22°10N 46°40E 248 B4
Laylān Iraq 35°18N 44°31E 246 C5
Layon → France 47°20N 0°45W 172 E6
Layou St. Vincent 13°12N 61°17W 323 n
Layou → Dominica 15°23N 61°21W 323 k
Laysan I. U.S.A. 25°50N 171°50W 302 F9
Layton Fla., U.S.A. 24°50N 80°47W 317 L9
Layton Utah, U.S.A. 41°4N 111°58W 304 F8
Laytonville U.S.A. 39°41N 123°29W 304 G2
Laza Burma 26°30N 97°38E 241 B6
Lazarata Greece 38°47N 20°40E 207 B2
Lazarev Russia 52°13N 141°30E 215 D15
Lazarev Sea S. Ocean 67°30S 3°0W 151 C2
Lazarevac Serbia 44°23N 20°17E 202 B4
Lazarevskoye Russia 43°55N 39°21E 191 J4
Lazarivo Madag. 23°54S 44°59E 272 C1
Lázaro Cárdenas Mexico 17°55N 102°11W 318 D4
Lazdijai Lithuania 54°14N 23°31E 184 D10
Lazhuglung China 34°52N 81°24E 217 F10
Lazi Phil. 9°8N 123°38E 233 G4
Lazienki Palace Warsaw, Poland 142 c3
Łazienkowski Park Poland 52°13N 21°1E 142 B2
Lazio □ Italy 42°10N 12°30E 199 F9
Lazo Moldova 47°33N 28°2E 183 C13
Lazo Russia 43°25S 133°55E 220 C6
Lbishchensk = Chapaev Kazakhstan 50°25N 51°10E 190 E10
Le Beausset France 43°12N 5°48E 175 E9
Le Bélier Réunion 21°2S 55°28E 272 f
Le Bic Canada 48°20N 68°41W 299 C6
Le Blanc France 46°37N 1°3E 174 B5
Le Blanc-Mesnil France 48°56N 2°27E 134 A3
Le Bleymard France 44°30N 3°42E 174 D7
Le Bourget France 48°56N 2°25E 134 A3
Le Bourgneuf-la-Fôret France 48°10N 0°59W 172 D6
Le Bugue France 44°55N 0°56E 174 D4
Le Carbet Martinique 14°42N 61°11W 322 j
Le Cateau Cambrésis France 50°7N 3°32E 173 B10
Le Caylar France 43°51N 3°19E 174 E7
Le Chambon-Feugerolles France 45°24N 4°19E 175 C8
Le Chameau Guadeloupe 15°51N 61°35W 322 e
Le Châtelet France 46°38N 2°16E 173 F9
Le Chenoi Belgium 50°41N 4°18E 116 B2
Le Chesnay France 48°49N 2°8E 134 B1
Le Chesne France 49°30N 4°45E 173 C11
Le Cheylard France 44°55N 4°25E 175 D8
Le Christ de Saclay France 48°43N 1°59E 134 B2
Le Claire U.S.A. 41°36N 90°21W 310 C6
Le Conquet France 48°21N 4°46W 172 D2
Le Creusot France 46°48N 4°24E 173 F11
Le Croisic France 47°18N 2°30W 172 E4
Le Diamant Martinique 14°28N 61°2W 322 j
Le Donjon France 46°22N 3°48E 173 F10
Le Dorat France 46°14N 1°5E 174 B5
Le François Martinique 14°38N 60°57W 322 j
Le Gosier Guadeloupe 16°14N 61°29W 322 e
Le Grand Brûlé Réunion 21°14S 55°47E 272 f
Le Grand-Lucé France 47°52N 0°28E 172 E7
Le Grand-Pressigny France 46°55N 0°48E 172 F7
Le Grand-Quevilly France 49°24N 1°3E 172 C8
Le Gris Gris Mauritius 20°31S 57°32E 272 e
Le Gros Morne Réunion 21°5S 55°28E 272 f
Le Havre France 49°30N 0°5E 172 C7
Le Kremlin-Bicêtre France 48°48N 2°21E 134 B3
Le Lamentin Martinique 14°35N 61°2W 322 j
Le Lavandou France 43°8N 6°22E 175 E10
Le Lion-d'Angers France 47°37N 0°43W 172 E6
Le Lorrain Martinique 14°48N 61°3W 322 j
Le Louroux-Béconnais France 47°30N 0°55W 172 E6
Le Luc France 43°23N 6°21E 175 E10
Le Lude France 47°39N 0°9E 172 E7
Le Maire, Estr. de Argentina 54°50S 65°0W 336 D4
Le Mans France 48°0N 0°10E 172 E7
Le Marigot Martinique 14°50N 61°4W 322 j
Le Marin Martinique 14°27N 60°55W 322 j
Le Mars U.S.A. 42°47N 96°10W 308 D5
Le Mayet-de-Montagne France 46°4N 3°40E 173 F10
Le Mêle-sur-Sarthe France 48°31N 0°22E 172 D7
Le Mesnil-le-Roi France 48°56N 2°7E 134 A1
Le Monastier-sur-Gazeille France 44°57N 3°59E 174 D7
Le Monêtier-les-Bains France 44°58N 6°30E 175 D10
Le Mont-Dore France 45°35N 2°49E 174 C6
Le Mont-St-Michel France 48°40N 1°30W 172 D5
Le Morne Brabant Mauritius 20°27S 57°19E 272 e
Le Morne Rouge Martinique 14°47N 61°8W 322 j
Le Morne-Vert Martinique 14°42N 61°8W 322 j
Le Moule Guadeloupe 16°20N 61°22W 322 e
Le Moyne, L. Canada 56°45N 68°47W 299 A6
Le Muy France 43°28N 6°34E 175 E10
Le Palais France 47°20N 3°10W 172 E3
Le Pecq France 48°53N 2°6E 134 A1
Le Perreux France 48°50N 2°29E 134 A3
Le Perthus France 42°30N 2°53E 174 F6
Le Pin France 48°54N 2°37E 134 A4
Le Plessis-Robinson France 48°47N 2°15E 134 B2
Le Plessis-Trévise France 48°48N 2°34E 134 B4
Le Port Réunion 20°56S 55°18E 272 f
Le Port-Marly France 48°52N 2°6E 134 A1
Le Pré-St-Gervais France 48°53N 2°23E 134 A3
Le Prêcheur Martinique 14°50N 61°12W 322 j
Le Puy-en-Velay France 45°3N 3°52E 174 C7
Le Raincy France 48°53N 2°31E 134 A4
Le Raysville U.S.A. 41°50N 76°10W 313 E8
Le Robert Martinique 14°40N 60°56W 322 j
Le Roy Ill., U.S.A. 40°21N 88°46W 311 D8
Le Roy N.Y., U.S.A. 42°58N 77°59W 312 D7
Le St-Esprit Martinique 14°34N 60°56W 322 j
Le Souffleur Guadeloupe 16°19N 61°2W 322 e
Le Sueur U.S.A. 44°28N 93°55W 308 C7
Le Tampon Réunion 21°16S 55°32E 272 f
Le Teil France 44°33N 4°40E 175 D8
Le Teilleul France 48°32N 0°53W 172 D6
Le Theil France 48°16N 0°42E 172 D7
Le Thillot France 47°53N 6°46E 173 E13
Le Thuy Vietnam 17°14N 106°49E 236 D6
Le Touquet-Paris-Plage France 50°30N 1°36E 173 B8
Le Tréport France 50°3N 1°20E 172 B8
Le Trou à Diable Guadeloupe 15°57N 61°14W 322 e
Le Val-d'Ajol France 47°55N 6°30E 173 E13
Le Val Nature Park Mauritius 20°22S 57°37E 272 e
Le Vauclin Martinique 14°33N 60°52W 322 j
Le Verdon-sur-Mer France 45°33N 1°4W 174 C2
Le Vésinet France 48°54N 2°8E 134 A1
Le Vigan France 43°59N 3°36E 174 E7
Lea → U.K. 51°31N 0°1E 169 F8
Lea Bridge U.K. 51°33N 0°2W 125 A3
Lea Lea Papua N. G. 9°17S 146°59E 286 E4
Leach Cambodia 12°21N 103°46E 237 F4
Lead U.S.A. 44°21N 103°46W 308 C2
Leader Canada 50°50N 109°30W 297 C7
Leadville U.S.A. 39°15N 106°18W 304 G10
Leaf → U.S.A. 30°59N 88°44W 315 F10
Leaf Rapids Canada 56°30N 99°59W 297 B9
Leaghur, L. Australia 33°35S 143°3E 282 B5
Leaksville = Eden U.S.A. 36°29N 79°53W 315 C15
Lealui Zambia 15°10S 23°2E 265 F4
Leamington Ont., Canada 42°3N 82°36W 312 D2
Leamington N.Z. 37°55S 175°30E 284 D4
Leamington Utah, U.S.A. 39°32N 112°17W 304 G7
Leamington Spa = Royal Leamington Spa U.K. 52°18N 1°31W 169 E6
Le'an China 27°22N 115°48E 229 D10
Leandro Norte Alem Argentina 27°34S 55°15W 335 B4
Leane, L. Ireland 52°2N 9°32W 166 D2
Learmonth Australia 22°13S 114°10E 278 D1
Leary U.S.A. 31°29N 84°31W 316 D5
Leaside Canada 43°42N 79°22W 141 A2
Leask Canada 53°5N 106°45W 297 C7
Leatherhead U.K. 51°18N 0°20W 169 F7
Leavenworth Ind., U.S.A. 38°12N 86°21W 311 F10
Leavenworth Kans., U.S.A. 39°19N 94°55W 308 F6
Leavenworth Wash., U.S.A. 47°36N 120°40W 304 C3
Leawood U.S.A. 38°58N 94°37W 310 F2
Łeba Poland 54°45N 17°32E 184 D4
Łeba → Poland 54°46N 17°33E 184 D4
Lebach Germany 49°25N 6°54E 179 F2
Lebak Phil. 6°32N 124°5E 233 H5
Lebam U.S.A. 46°34N 123°33W 306 D3
Lebane Serbia 42°56N 21°44E 202 D5
Lebango Congo 0°39N 14°21E 264 B2
Lebango → Congo 0°2N 14°52E 264 B2
Lebanon Fla., U.S.A. 29°10N 82°37W 317 F7
Lebanon Ill., U.S.A. 38°38N 89°49W 310 F7
Lebanon Ind., U.S.A. 40°3N 86°28W 311 D10
Lebanon Kans., U.S.A. 39°49N 98°33W 308 F4
Lebanon Ky., U.S.A. 37°34N 85°15W 309 G11
Lebanon Mo., U.S.A. 37°41N 92°40W 310 G4
Lebanon N.H., U.S.A. 43°39N 72°15W 313 C12
Lebanon Ohio, U.S.A. 39°26N 84°13W 311 E12
Lebanon Oreg., U.S.A. 44°32N 122°55W 304 D2
Lebanon Pa., U.S.A. 40°20N 76°26W 313 F8
Lebanon Tenn., U.S.A. 36°12N 86°18W 315 C11
Lebanon ■ Asia 34°0N 36°0E 250 E7
Lebanon Junction U.S.A. 37°50N 85°44W 311 G11
Lebap □ Turkmenistan 40°0N 63°0E 216 D6
Lebec U.S.A. 34°51N 118°52W 307 L8
Lebedyan Russia 53°0N 39°10E 189 F10
Lebedyn Ukraine 50°35N 34°30E 189 G8
Lebel-sur-Quévillon Canada 49°3N 76°59W 298 C4
Leblon Brazil 22°59S 43°14W 135 B1
Lebo Dem. Rep. of the Congo 4°30N 23°58E 264 B4
Lebomboberge S. Africa 24°30S 32°0E 271 B5
Lębork Poland 54°33N 17°46E 184 D4
Lebowakgomo S. Africa 24°12S 29°30E 271 B4
Lebrija Spain 36°53N 6°5W 195 J4
Lebsko, Jezioro Poland 54°40N 17°25E 184 D4
Lebu Chile 37°40S 73°47W 334 D1
Leca da Palmeira Portugal 41°12N 8°42W 194 D2
Lecce Italy 40°23N 18°11E 201 B11
Lecco Italy 45°51N 9°23E 198 C6
Lecco, L. di Italy 45°55N 9°19E 198 C6
Lécera Spain 41°13N 0°43W 196 D4
Lech Austria 47°13N 10°9E 180 D3
Lech → Germany 48°43N 10°56E 179 G6
Lechang China 25°10N 113°20E 229 E9
Lechena Greece 37°57N 21°16E 204 D3
Lechtaler Alpen Austria 47°15N 10°30E 180 D3
Lecontes Mills U.S.A. 41°5N 78°17W 312 E6
Lectoure France 43°56N 0°38E 174 E4
Łęczna Poland 51°18N 22°53E 185 G9
Łęczyca Poland 52°5N 19°15E 185 F6
Ledang, Gunung Malaysia 2°22N 102°37E 234 B2
Ledesma Spain 41°6N 5°59W 194 D5
Lediba Dem. Rep. of the Congo 3°1S 16°34E 264 C3
Lédo, Cabo Angola 9°43S 13°12E 265 D2
Ledong China 18°41N 109°5E 236 C7
Leduc Canada 53°15N 113°30W 296 C6
Lee London, U.K. 51°27N 0°0 125 B3
Lee Fla., U.S.A. 30°25N 83°18W 316 E6
Lee Mass., U.S.A. 42°19N 73°15W 313 D11
Lee → Ireland 51°53N 8°56W 166 E3
Lee Vining U.S.A. 37°58N 119°7W 306 H7
Leech L. U.S.A. 47°10N 94°24W 308 B6
Leechburg U.S.A. 40°37N 79°36W 312 F5
Leeds W. Yorks., U.K. 53°48N 1°33W 168 D6
Leeds Ala., U.S.A. 33°33N 86°33W 315 E11
Leek Neths. 53°10N 6°24E 170 A6
Leek Staffs., U.K. 53°7N 2°1W 168 D5
Leeman Australia 29°57S 114°58E 279 E1
Leeper U.S.A. 41°22N 79°18W 312 E5
Leer Germany 53°13N 7°26E 178 B3
Lee's Summit U.S.A. 38°55N 94°23W 310 F2
Leesburg Fla., U.S.A. 28°49N 81°53W 317 G8
Leesburg Ga., U.S.A. 31°44N 84°10W 316 D5
Leesburg Ohio, U.S.A. 39°21N 83°33W 311 E13
Leeston N.Z. 43°45S 172°19E 285 D7
Leesville U.S.A. 31°8N 93°16W 314 F8
Leeton Australia 34°33S 146°23E 283 C7
Leetonia U.S.A. 40°53N 80°45W 312 F4
Leeu Gamka S. Africa 32°47S 21°59E 270 D3
Leeuwarden Neths. 53°15N 5°48E 170 A5
Leeuwin, C. Australia 34°20S 115°9E 279 F2
Leeuwin Naturaliste △ Australia 34°6S 115°3E 279 F2
Leeward Is. Atl. Oc. 16°30N 63°30W 321 C7
Léfini Congo 2°55S 15°39E 264 C3
Léfini → Congo 2°56S 16°9E 264 C3
Léfini ⌂ Congo 2°55S 15°20E 264 C3
Lefka Cyprus 35°6N 32°51E 207 E8
Lefkada Greece 38°40N 20°43E 207 B2
Lefkimi Greece 39°25N 20°3E 206 C10
Lefkimis, Akra Greece 39°29N 20°4E 206 C10
Lefkoniko Cyprus 35°18N 33°44E 207 E9
Lefroy Canada 44°16N 79°34W 312 B5
Lefroy, L. Australia 31°21S 121°40E 279 F3

INDEX Linapacan I. 393

Leg → *Poland* 50°42N 21°50E **185** H8
Leganés *Spain* 40°19N 3°45W **127** C1
Legazpi *Phil.* 13°10N 123°45E **232** E4
Legazpi *Madrid, Spain* 40°23N 3°41W **127** B1
Lège-Cap-Ferret *France* 44°48N 1°9W **174** D2
Lege Hida *Ethiopia* 7°56N 41°4E **257** F5
Legendre I. *Australia* 20°22S 116°55E **278** D2
Leghorn = Livorno *Italy* 43°33N 10°19E **198** E7
Legionowo *Poland* 52°25N 20°50E **185** F7
Legnago *Italy* 45°11N 11°18E **199** C8
Legnano *Italy* 45°36N 8°54E **198** C5
Legnica *Poland* 51°12N 16°10E **185** G3
Legrad *Croatia* 46°17N 16°51E **199** B13
Leh *India* 34°9N 77°35E **243** B7
Lehigh Acres *U.S.A.* 26°36N 81°39W **317** J8
Lehighton *U.S.A.* 40°50N 75°43W **313** F9
Lehliu *Romania* 44°29N 26°50E **183** F11
Leho *Sudan* 7°7N 33°52E **257** F3
Lehrte *Germany* 52°22N 9°58E **178** C5
Lehtisaari *Finland* 60°10N 24°51E **121** B2
Lehua I. *U.S.A.* 22°1N 160°6W **302** A1
Lehututu *Botswana* 23°54S 21°55E **270** B3
Lei Shui → *China* 26°55N 112°35E **229** D9
Lei Yue Mun *China* 22°17N 114°14E **122** B2
Leiah *Pakistan* 30°58N 70°58E **242** D4
Leião *Portugal* 38°43N 9°17W **126** A1
Leibnitz *Austria* 46°47N 15°34E **180** E8
Leibo *China* 28°11N 103°34E **228** C4
Leicester *U.K.* 52°38N 1°8W **169** E6
Leicester City ☐ *U.K.* 52°38N 1°8W **169** E6
Leicester Square *London, U.K.* **125** b3
Leicestershire ☐ *U.K.* 52°41N 1°17W **169** E6
Leichhardt *Australia* 33°53S 151°9E **139** B1
Leichhardt → *Australia* 17°35S 139°48E **280** B2
Leichhardt Ra. *Australia* 20°46S 147°40E **280** C4
Leiden *Neths.* 52°9N 4°30E **170** B4
Leie → *Belgium* 51°2N 3°45E **170** C3
Leifers = Làives *Italy* 46°26N 11°20E **199** B8
Leigh → *Australia* 38°18S 144°30E **282** E6
Leigh Creek *Australia* 30°38S 138°26E **282** A3
Leikang *Norway* 62°15N 5°47E **164** B2
Leikanger *Sogn og Fjordane, Norway* 62°8N 5°18E **164** B2
Leikanger *Sogn og Fjordane, Norway* 61°10N 6°51E **164** C3
Leiktho *Burma* 19°13N 96°35E **241** F6
Leimen *Germany* 49°21N 8°41E **179** F4
Leimus *Nic.* 14°40N 84°3W **320** D3
Leine → *Germany* 52°43N 9°36E **178** C5
Leinefelde *Germany* 51°23N 10°19E **178** D6
Leinster *Australia* 27°51S 120°36E **279** E3
Leinster ☐ *Ireland* 53°3N 7°8W **166** C4
Leinster, Mt. *Ireland* 52°37N 6°46W **166** D5
Leipalingis *Lithuania* 54°5N 23°51E **184** D10
Leipe = Lipno *Poland* 52°49N 19°15E **185** F6
Leipzig *Germany* 51°18N 12°22E **178** D8
Leira *Norway* 60°58N 9°17E **164** D6
Leiria *Portugal* 39°46N 8°53W **194** F2
Leiria ☐ *Portugal* 39°46N 8°53W **194** F2
Leirvassbu *Norway* 61°33N 8°13E **164** C5
Leirvik *Norway* 59°47N 5°28E **164** E2
Leishan *China* 26°15N 108°20E **228** D7
Leisler, Mt. *Australia* 23°23S 129°20E **278** D4
Leisure City *U.S.A.* 25°30N 80°26W **317** K9
Leith *U.K.* 55°59N 3°11W **121** B3
Leith Hill *U.K.* 51°11N 0°22W **169** F7
Leitha → *Europe* 47°50N 17°15E **181** D10
Leitir Ceanainn = Letterkenny *Ireland* 54°57N 7°45W **166** B4
Leitrim *Ireland* 54°0N 8°5W **166** B3
Leitrim ☐ *Ireland* 54°8N 8°0W **166** B4
Leitza *Spain* 43°5N 1°55W **196** B3
Leiyang *China* 26°27N 112°45E **229** D9
Leizhou *China* 20°52N 110°8E **229** G8
Leizhou Bandao *China* 21°0N 110°0E **228** G7
Leizhou Wan *China* 20°50N 110°20E **229** G8
Lek → *Neths.* 51°54N 4°35E **170** C4
Leka *Norway* 65°5N 11°35E **160** D14
Lekani *Greece* 41°10N 24°35E **203** E8
Lekbibaj *Albania* 42°17N 19°56E **202** D3
Lekeitio *Spain* 43°20N 2°32W **196** B2
Lékéti, Mt. *Congo* 2°34S 14°17E **264** C2
Lekki *Nigeria* 6°26N 3°28E **124** B2
Lekki Lagoon *Nigeria* 6°30N 4°7E **263** D5
Léko *Mali* 13°37N 9°2W **262** C3
Lékoli-Pandaka ⌂ *Congo* 0°41N 14°50E **264** B2
Lékoni *Gabon* 1°35S 14°14E **264** C2
Lékoni → *Gabon* 1°11S 13°16E **264** C2
Lekoui *Burkina Faso* 12°37N 3°40W **262** C4
Leksand *Sweden* 60°44N 15°1E **162** D9
Leksura = Lentekhi *Georgia* 42°47N 42°45E **191** J6
Leland *Mich., U.S.A.* 45°1N 85°45W **309** C11
Leland *Miss., U.S.A.* 33°24N 90°54W **315** E9
Lelång *Sweden* 59°10N 12°5E **162** E6
Lelepa *Vanuatu* 17°35S 168°11E **287** G6
Leleque *Argentina* 42°28S 71°0W **336** B2
Leli *Solomon Is.* 8°42S 161°4E **287** M11
Lélouma *Guinea* 11°11N 12°56W **262** C2
Lelu *Burma* 19°4N 95°30E **241** F5
Lelydorp *Suriname* 5°42N 55°14W **329** B6
Lelystad *Neths.* 52°30N 5°25E **170** B5
Lem *Denmark* 56°1N 8°24E **163** H2
Lema *Nigeria* 12°58N 4°13E **263** C5
Lema Shilindi *Ethiopia* 4°50N 42°6E **257** G5
Léman, L. *Europe* 46°26N 6°30E **173** F13
Lemankoa *Papua N. G.* 5°3S 154°34E **286** C8
Lembar *Indonesia* 8°45S 116°4E **231** K19
Lemberg = Lviv *Ukraine* 49°50N 24°0E **177** D13
Lembuak *Indonesia* 8°36S 116°11E **231** K19
Leme *Brazil* 22°58S 43°10W **135** B1
Lemera *Dem. Rep. of the Congo* 3°0S 28°55E **268** C2
Lemery *Phil.* 13°51N 120°56E **232** E3
Lemfu *Dem. Rep. of the Congo* 5°18S 15°13E **265** D3
Lemhi Ra. *U.S.A.* 44°0N 113°0W **304** D7
Lemmer *Neths.* 52°51N 5°43E **170** B5
Lemmon *U.S.A.* 45°57N 102°10W **308** C2
Lemon Grove *U.S.A.* 32°44N 117°1W **307** N9
Lemoore *U.S.A.* 36°18N 119°46W **306** J7
Lemotol B. *Micronesia* 7°21N 151°35E **287** T17
Lemoyne *Canada* 45°29N 73°29W **130** B3
Lempdes *France* 45°22N 3°17E **174** C7
Lemsid *W. Sahara* 26°33N 13°51W **260** C2
Lemvig *Denmark* 56°33N 8°20E **163** H2
Lemyethna *Burma* 17°36N 95°9E **241** G5
Lena *U.S.A.* 42°23N 89°49W **310** B7
Lena → *Russia* 72°52N 126°40E **215** B13
Lenadoon Pt. *Ireland* 54°18N 9°3W **166** B2
Lenakel *Vanuatu* 19°38S 169°16E **287** J7
Lenart *Slovenia* 46°36N 15°48E **199** B12
Lenartovce *Slovak Rep.* 48°18N 20°19E **181** C13
Lencloître *France* 46°50N 0°20E **172** F7
Lençóis *Brazil* 12°35S 41°24W **333** D3
Lençóis Maranhenses △ *Brazil* 2°30S 43°0W **332** B3
Lendava *Slovenia* 46°35N 16°25E **199** B13
Lendinara *Italy* 45°5N 11°36E **199** C8
Lenger *Kazakhstan* 42°12N 69°54E **217** E7
Lengerich *Germany* 52°11N 7°52E **178** C3
Lenggong *Malaysia* 5°6N 100°58E **237** K3
Lenggries *Germany* 47°41N 11°35E **179** H7
Léngoué *Congo* 1°15N 15°38E **264** B3
Lengshuijiang *China* 27°40N 111°26E **229** D8
Lengshuitan *China* 26°27N 111°35E **229** D8
Lengua de Vaca, Pta. *Chile* 30°14S 71°38W **334** C1
Lengwe △ *Malawi* 16°14S 34°45E **269** F3
Lengwethen = Lunino *Russia* 53°38N 45°18E **190** D7
Lengyeltóti *Hungary* 46°40N 17°40E **182** D2
Lengyeltótihács = Lengyeltóti *Hungary* 46°40N 17°40E **182** D2
Lenhovda *Sweden* 57°0N 15°16E **163** G9
Lenin *Russia* 55°43N 37°34E **129** B3
Lenin Mausoleum *Moscow, Russia* **129** b2
Lenina, Kanal → *Russia* 43°44N 45°17E **191** J7
Leninabad = Khŭjand *Tajikistan* 40°17N 69°37E **217** D7
Leninakan = Gyumri *Armenia* 40°47N 43°50E **191** K6
Leningrad = Sankt-Peterburg *Russia* 59°55N 30°20E **137** B1
Leningrad ☐ *Russia* 59°40N 32°0E **188** C7
Lenino = Leninsk-Kuznetskiy *Russia* 54°44N 86°10E **217** B11
Lenino *Moskva, Russia* 55°38N 37°39E **129** C3
Lenino *Ukraine* 45°17N 35°46E **189** K8
Leninogorsk *Kazakhstan* 50°20N 83°30E **217** B10
Leninogorsk *Russia* 54°36N 52°30E **216** B4
Leninsk = Petrodvorets *Russia* 59°52N 29°54E **188** C5
Leninsk *Russia* 48°40N 45°15E **191** F7
Leninsk-Kuznetskiy *Russia* 54°44N 86°10E **217** B11
Leninsk-Turkmensky = Türkmenabat *Turkmenistan* 39°6N 63°34E **247** B9
Leninskiye Gory *Russia* 55°41N 37°32E **129** B3
Leninskoye *Russia* 58°23N 47°3E **190** A8
Lenk *Switz.* 46°27N 7°28E **179** J3
Lenkoran = Länkäran *Azerbaijan* 38°48N 48°52E **213** C13
Lenmalu *Indonesia* 1°45S 130°15E **231** E8
Lenne → *Germany* 51°25N 7°29E **178** D3
Lennestadt *Germany* 51°8N 8°2E **178** D4
Lennox *Calif., U.S.A.* 33°56N 118°20W **126** C2
Lennox *S. Dak., U.S.A.* 43°21N 96°53W **308** D5
Lennox, I. *Chile* 55°18S 66°50W **336** E3
Lennoxville *Canada* 45°22N 71°51W **313** A13
Leno *Italy* 45°22N 10°13E **198** C7
Lenoir *U.S.A.* 35°55N 81°32W **315** D14
Lenoir City *U.S.A.* 35°48N 84°16W **315** D12
Lenore L. *Canada* 52°30N 104°59W **297** C8
Lenox *Ga., U.S.A.* 31°16N 83°28W **316** D6
Lenox *Iowa, U.S.A.* 40°53N 94°34W **310** D2
Lenox *Mass., U.S.A.* 42°22N 73°17W **313** D11
Lens *France* 50°26N 2°50E **173** B9
Lensahn *Germany* 54°13N 10°53E **178** A6
Lensk *Russia* 60°48N 114°55E **215** C12
Lensvik *Norway* 63°31N 9°48E **164** A6
Lentas *Greece* 34°56N 24°56E **207** F5
Lentekhi *Georgia* 42°47N 42°45E **191** J6
Lenti *Hungary* 46°37N 16°33E **182** D1
Lentini *Italy* 37°17N 15°0E **201** E8
Lentschütz = Łęczyca *Poland* 52°5N 19°15E **185** F6
Lenwood *U.S.A.* 34°53N 117°7W **307** L9
Lenya *Burma* 11°33N 98°57E **237** G2
Lenzen *Germany* 53°5N 11°29E **178** B7
Léo *Burkina Faso* 11°3N 2°2W **262** C4
Leoben *Austria* 47°22N 15°5E **180** D8
Leobschütz = Głubczyce *Poland* 50°13N 17°52E **185** H4
Leodhas = Lewis *U.K.* 58°9N 6°40W **167** C2
Leola *U.S.A.* 45°43N 98°56W **308** C4
Leominster *Hereford, U.K.* 52°14N 2°43W **169** E5
Leominster *Mass., U.S.A.* 42°32N 71°46W **313** D13
León = Cotopaxi ☐ *Ecuador* 0°5S 78°55W **328** D2
León *Landes, France* 43°53N 1°18W **174** E2
León *Guanajuato, Mexico* 21°6N 101°41W **318** C4
León *Nic.* 12°20N 86°51W **320** D2
León *Spain* 42°38N 5°34W **194** C5
Leon *Iowa, U.S.A.* 40°44N 93°45W **310** D3
León ☐ *Spain* 42°40N 5°55W **194** C5
Leon → *U.S.A.* 31°14N 97°28W **314** F6
León, Montes de *Spain* 42°30N 6°18W **194** C4
Leonardo da Vinci, Roma ✈ (FCO) *Italy* 41°48N 12°15E **199** G9
Leonardtown *U.S.A.* 38°17N 76°38W **309** F15
Leonardville *Namibia* 23°29S 18°49E **270** B2
Leonberg *Germany* 48°48N 9°1E **179** G5
Leonding *Austria* 48°16N 14°15E **180** C7
Leone *Amer. Samoa* 14°23S 170°48W **302** f
Leonessa *Italy* 42°34N 12°58E **199** F9
Leonforte *Italy* 37°38N 14°23E **201** E7
Leongatha *Australia* 38°30S 145°58E **283** E6
Leonia *Fla., U.S.A.* 30°55N 86°1W **316** E3
Leonia *N.J., U.S.A.* 40°51N 73°59W **132** A2
Leonidio *Greece* 37°9N 22°52E **204** D4
Leonora *Australia* 28°49S 121°19E **279** E3
Leopardstown *Ireland* 53°16N 6°11W **120** B2
Leopold II, L. = Mai-Ndombe, L. *Dem. Rep. of the Congo* 2°0S 18°20E **264** C3
Leopoldau *Austria* 48°15N 16°26E **142** A2
Leopoldina = Aruanã *Brazil* 14°54S 51°10W **333** D1
Leopoldina = Parnamirim *Brazil* 8°5S 39°34W **332** C4
Leopoldina *Brazil* 21°28S 42°40W **333** F3
Leopoldo Bulhões *Brazil* 16°37S 48°46W **333** E2
Leopoldsburg *Belgium* 51°7N 5°13E **170** C5
Leopoldsdorf *Austria* 48°7N 16°23E **142** B2
Leopoldstadt *Austria* 48°13N 16°22E **142** A2
Leopoldville = Kinshasa *Dem. Rep. of the Congo* 4°20S 15°15E **265** C3
Leoti *U.S.A.* 38°29N 101°21W **308** F3
Leova *Moldova* 46°28N 28°15E **183** D13
Leoville *Canada* 53°39N 107°33W **297** C7
Lepe *Spain* 37°15N 7°12W **195** H3
Lepel = Lyepyel *Belarus* 54°50N 28°40E **188** E5
Lepenou *Greece* 38°42N 21°17E **204** C3
Leping *China* 28°47N 117°7E **229** C11
Lépo, L. do *Angola* 17°0S 19°0E **265** F3
Lepontine, Alpi *Italy* 46°22N 8°27E **198** B5
Leportovo *Russia* 55°46N 37°43E **129** B4
Leposavić *Kosovo* 43°6N 20°48E **202** C4
Leppävaara *Finland* 60°13N 24°49E **121** B1
Leppävirta *Finland* 62°29N 27°46E **160** E22
Lepsény *Hungary* 47°0N 18°15E **182** D3
Leptis Magna *Libya* 32°40N 14°12E **258** B2
Lequeitio = Lekeitio *Spain* 43°20N 2°32W **196** B2
Lercara Friddi *Italy* 37°45N 13°36E **200** E6
Léré *C.A.R.* 6°46N 17°25E **264** A3
Léré *Chad* 9°39N 14°13E **259** G8
Léré *Mali* 15°45N 4°55W **262** B4
Lere *Bauchi, Nigeria* 9°43N 9°18E **263** D6
Lere *Kaduna, Nigeria* 10°23N 8°35E **263** C6
Leribe *Lesotho* 28°51S 28°3E **271** C4
Lérici *Italy* 44°4N 9°55E **198** D6
Lérida = Lleida *Spain* 41°37N 0°39E **196** D5
Lérins, Îs. de *France* 43°31N 7°3E **175** E11
Lerma *Spain* 42°0N 3°47W **194** C7
Leros *Greece* 37°10N 26°50E **205** D8
Lérouville *France* 48°44N 5°30E **173** D12
Lerum *Sweden* 57°46N 12°16E **163** G6
Lerwick *U.K.* 60°9N 1°9W **167** A7
Leş *Romania* 46°58N 21°50E **182** D6
Les Abrets *France* 45°32N 5°35E **175** C9
Les Abymes *Guadeloupe* 16°17N 61°32W **322** e
Les Andelys *France* 49°15N 1°25E **172** C8
Les Anses-d'Arlets *Martinique* 14°28N 61°6W **322** j
Les Avirons *Réunion* 21°14S 55°20E **272** f
Les Borges Blanques *Spain* 41°31N 0°52E **196** D5
Les Cayes *Haiti* 18°15N 73°46W **321** C5
Les Coteaux *Canada* 45°15N 74°13W **313** A10
Les Escoumins *Canada* 48°21N 69°24W **299** C6
Les Essarts *France* 46°47N 1°12W **172** F5
Les Grands Fonds *Guadeloupe* 16°16N 61°26W **322** e
Les Herbiers *France* 46°52N 1°1W **172** F5
Les Lilas *France* 48°52N 2°25E **134** A3
Les Loges-en-Josas *France* 48°45N 2°8E **134** B1
Les Mangles *Guadeloupe* 16°23N 61°27W **322** e
Les Minquiers, Plateau des *Chan. Is.* 48°58N 2°8W **172** D4
Les Moroubas *C.A.R.* 6°11N 20°13E **264** A4
Les Pavillons-sous-Bois *France* 48°54N 2°30E **134** A4
Les Pieux *France* 49°30N 1°48W **172** C5
Les Ponts-de-Cé *France* 47°25N 0°30W **172** E6
Les Riceys *France* 47°59N 4°22E **173** E11
Les Sables-d'Olonne *France* 46°30N 1°45W **174** B2
Les Tantes *Grenada* 12°19N 61°33W **323** q
Les Trois-Bassins *Réunion* 21°5S 55°18E **272** f
Les Trois-Îlets *Martinique* 14°32N 61°2W **322** j
Les Vans *France* 44°25N 4°7E **175** D8
Lesbos *Greece* 39°10N 26°20E **205** B8
L'Escala *Spain* 42°7N 3°8E **196** C8
L'Escalier *Mauritius* 20°28S 57°36E **272** e
Leschnitz = Leśnica *Poland* 50°26N 18°11E **185** H5
Leshan *China* 29°33N 103°41E **228** C4
Leshukonskoye *Russia* 64°54N 45°46E **186** B8
Leshwe ⌂ *Dem. Rep. of the Congo* 12°45S 29°30E **269** E2
Lésigny *France* 48°44N 2°37E **134** B4
Lésina *Italy* 41°52N 15°21E **199** G12
Lésina, L. di *Italy* 41°53N 15°26E **199** G12
Lesjaskog *Norway* 62°14N 8°22E **164** B5
Lesjaverk *Norway* 62°12N 8°34E **164** B5
Lesjöfors *Sweden* 59°58N 14°11E **162** E8
Leskhimstroy = Syeverodonetsk *Ukraine* 48°58N 38°35E **189** H10
Lesko *Poland* 49°30N 22°23E **185** J9
Leskov I. *Antarctica* 56°0S 28°0W **151** B1
Leskovac *Serbia* 43°0N 21°58E **202** C5
Leskovik *Albania* 40°10N 20°34E **202** F4
Leslau = Włocławek *Poland* 52°40N 19°3E **185** F6
Leslie *Ga., U.S.A.* 31°57N 84°5W **316** D5
Leslie *Mich., U.S.A.* 42°27N 84°26W **311** B12
Leśna *Poland* 51°1N 15°15E **185** G2
Lesneven *France* 48°35N 4°20W **172** D2
Leśnica *Poland* 50°26N 18°11E **185** H5
Lešnica *Serbia* 44°39N 19°20E **202** B3
Lesnoi = Umba *Russia* 66°42N 34°11E **186** A5
Lesnoye *Russia* 58°15N 35°18E **188** C8
Lesnozavodskaya *Russia* 59°51N 30°29E **137** B2
Lesopilnoye *Russia* 46°44N 134°20E **220** A7
Lesotho ■ *Africa* 29°40S 28°0E **271** C4
Lesozavodsk *Russia* 45°30N 133°29E **220** B6
Lesparre-Médoc *France* 45°18N 0°57W **174** C3
L'Espluga de Francolí *Spain* 41°24N 1°7E **196** D6
Lessay *France* 49°14N 1°30W **172** C5
Lesse → *Belgium* 50°15N 4°54E **170** D4
Lesse et Lomme ⌂ *Belgium* 50°8N 5°9E **170** D5
Lessebo *Sweden* 56°45N 15°16E **163** H9
Lesser Antilles *W. Indies* 15°0N 61°0W **321** D7
Lesser Slave L. *Canada* 55°30N 115°25W **296** B5
Lesser Sunda Is. *Indonesia* 8°0S 120°0E **235** D5
Lessines *Belgium* 50°42N 3°50E **170** D3
Lester B. Pearson Int., Toronto ✈ (YYZ) *Canada* 43°46N 79°35W **141** A1
L'Esterre *Grenada* 12°28N 61°29W **323** q
Lestershire = Johnson City *U.S.A.* 42°7N 75°58W **313** D9
Lestock *Canada* 51°19N 103°59W **297** C8
Lesueur I. *Australia* 13°50S 127°17E **278** B4
Lesueur △ *Australia* 30°11S 115°10E **279** F2
Lésvos = Lesbos *Greece* 39°10N 26°20E **205** B8
Leszno *Poland* 51°50N 16°30E **185** G3
Letaba *S. Africa* 23°59S 31°50E **271** B5
Letälven → *Sweden* 59°5N 14°20E **162** E8
L'Étang-la-Ville *France* 48°52N 2°4E **134** A1
L'Étang-Salé *Réunion* 21°15S 55°23E **272** f
Létavértes *Hungary* 47°23N 21°55E **182** C6
Letchworth *U.K.* 51°59N 0°13W **169** F7
Letea, Ostrov *Romania* 45°18N 29°20E **183** E14
Lethbridge *Canada* 49°45N 112°45W **296** D6
Lethem *Guyana* 3°20N 59°50W **329** C6
Leti, Kepulauan *Indonesia* 8°10S 128°0E **231** F7
Leti Is. = Leti, Kepulauan *Indonesia* 8°10S 128°0E **231** F7
Letiahau → *Botswana* 21°16S 24°0E **270** B3
Leticia *Colombia* 4°9S 70°0W **328** D4
Leting *China* 39°23N 118°55E **227** E10
Letjiesbos *S. Africa* 32°34S 22°16E **270** D3
Letlhakane *Botswana* 21°27S 25°30E **270** B4
Letlhakeng *Botswana* 24°0S 24°59E **270** B3
Letná *Prague, Czech Rep.* **135** a2
Letňany *Czech Rep.* 50°8N 14°30E **135** B3
Letopolis = Ausîm *Egypt* 30°7N 31°8E **117** A1
Letpadan *Burma* 17°45N 95°45E **241** G5
Letpan *Burma* 19°28N 94°10E **241** F5
Letsôk-aw Kyun *Burma* 11°30N 98°25E **237** G2
Letterkenny *Ireland* 54°57N 7°45W **166** B4
Leu *Romania* 44°10N 24°0E **183** F9
Léua *Angola* 11°34S 20°32E **265** E4
Leucadia *U.S.A.* 33°4N 117°18W **307** M9
Leucate *France* 42°56N 3°3E **174** F7
Leucate, Étang de *France* 42°50N 3°0E **174** F7
Leuchars *U.K.* 56°24N 2°53W **167** E6
Leuk *Switz.* 46°19N 7°37E **179** J3
Leuşeni *Moldova* 46°49N 28°12E **183** D13
Leuser, G. *Indonesia* 3°46N 97°12E **234** B1
Leusoalii *Amer. Samoa* 14°14S 169°25W **302** f
Leutkirch *Germany* 47°49N 10°1E **179** H6
Leutschau = Levoča *Slovak Rep.* 49°2N 20°35E **181** B13
Leuven *Belgium* 50°52N 4°42E **170** D4
Leuze-en-Hainaut *Belgium* 50°36N 3°37E **170** D3
Lev Tolstoy *Russia* 53°13N 39°29E **188** F10
Levallois-Perret *France* 48°53N 2°16E **134** A2
Levan *Albania* 40°40N 19°28E **202** F3
Levanger *Norway* 63°45N 11°19E **160** E14
Levant, Î. du *France* 43°3N 6°28E **175** E10
Lévanto *Italy* 44°10N 9°38E **198** D6
Lévanzo *Italy* 38°0N 12°20E **200** D5
Leveld *Norway* 60°44N 8°33E **164** D5
Levelland *U.S.A.* 33°35N 102°23W **314** E3
Levelock *U.S.A.* 59°7N 156°51W **303** G8
Leven *U.K.* 56°12N 3°0W **167** E6
Leven, L. *U.K.* 56°12N 3°22W **167** E5
Leven, Toraka *Madag.* 12°30S 47°45E **272** A2
Levent *Turkey* 41°5N 29°0E **122** B2
Leveque C. *Australia* 16°20S 123°0E **278** C3
Levera △ *Grenada* 12°13N 61°38W **323** q
Leverano *Italy* 40°17N 18°0E **201** B10
Leverger = Santo Antônio do Leverger *Brazil* 15°52S 56°5W **331** D6
Leverkusen *Germany* 51°1N 7°1E **178** D3
Levice *Slovak Rep.* 48°13N 18°35E **181** C11
Lévico Terme *Italy* 46°0N 11°18E **199** C8
Levie *France* 41°40N 9°7E **175** G13
Levier *France* 46°58N 6°8E **173** F13
Levin *N.Z.* 40°37S 175°18E **284** G4
Lévis *Canada* 46°48N 71°9W **299** C5
Levis, L. *Canada* 62°37N 117°58W **296** A5
Levitha *Greece* 37°0N 26°28E **205** D8
Levittown *N.Y., U.S.A.* 40°44N 73°31W **313** F11
Levittown *Pa., U.S.A.* 40°9N 74°51W **313** F10
Levka *Bulgaria* 41°52N 26°15E **203** E10
Levka Oros *Greece* 35°18N 24°3E **207** E5
Levkada ☐ *Greece* 38°45N 20°40E **207** B2
Levkás = Lefkada *Greece* 38°40N 20°43E **207** B2
Levkôsia = Nicosia *Cyprus* 35°10N 33°25E **207** E9
Levoča *Slovak Rep.* 49°2N 20°35E **181** B13
Levroux *France* 46°59N 1°38E **173** F8
Levski *Bulgaria* 43°21N 25°10E **203** C9
Levskigrad = Karlovo *Bulgaria* 42°38N 24°47E **203** D8
Levuka *Fiji* 17°34S 179°0E **287** A2
Lewe *Burma* 19°38N 96°7E **241** F6
Lewes *E. Sussex, U.K.* 50°52N 0°1E **169** G8
Lewes *Del., U.S.A.* 38°46N 75°9W **309** F16
Lewin Brzeski *Poland* 50°45N 17°37E **185** H4
Lewis *U.K.* 58°9N 6°40W **167** C2
Lewis → *U.S.A.* 45°51N 122°48W **306** E4
Lewis, Butt of *U.K.* 58°31N 6°16W **167** C2
Lewis and Clark ⌂ *U.S.A.* 46°8N 123°53W **306** D3
Lewis Pass *N.Z.* 42°31S 172°11E **285** C7
Lewis Ra. *Australia* 20°3S 128°50E **278** D4
Lewis Range *U.S.A.* 48°5N 113°5W **304** B7
Lewis Run *U.S.A.* 41°52N 78°40W **312** E6
Lewisburg *Ohio, U.S.A.* 39°51N 84°33W **311** E12
Lewisburg *Pa., U.S.A.* 40°58N 76°54W **312** F8
Lewisburg *Tenn., U.S.A.* 35°27N 86°48W **315** D11
Lewisburg *W. Va., U.S.A.* 37°48N 80°27W **309** G13
Lewisdale *U.S.A.* 38°58N 76°59W **143** B4
Lewisham ☐ *U.K.* 51°27N 0°1W **125** B3
Lewisport *U.S.A.* 37°56N 86°54W **311** G10
Lewisporte *Canada* 49°15N 55°3W **299** C8
Lewiston *Idaho, U.S.A.* 46°25N 117°1W **304** C5
Lewiston *Maine, U.S.A.* 44°6N 70°13W **309** C18
Lewiston *N.Y., U.S.A.* 43°11N 79°3W **312** C5
Lewistown *Ill., U.S.A.* 40°24N 90°9W **310** D6
Lewistown *Mo., U.S.A.* 40°5N 91°49W **310** D5
Lewistown *Mont., U.S.A.* 47°4N 109°26W **304** C9
Lewistown *Pa., U.S.A.* 40°36N 77°34W **312** F7
Lexington *Ga., U.S.A.* 33°52N 83°7W **316** B6
Lexington *Ill., U.S.A.* 40°39N 88°47W **311** D8
Lexington *Ky., U.S.A.* 38°3N 84°30W **311** F12
Lexington *Mass., U.S.A.* 42°25N 71°12W **116** A1
Lexington *Mich., U.S.A.* 43°16N 82°32W **312** C2
Lexington *Mo., U.S.A.* 39°11N 93°52W **310** E3
Lexington *N.C., U.S.A.* 35°49N 80°15W **315** D14
Lexington *N.Y., U.S.A.* 42°15N 74°22W **313** D10
Lexington *Nebr., U.S.A.* 40°47N 99°45W **308** E4
Lexington *Ohio, U.S.A.* 40°41N 82°35W **312** F2
Lexington *S.C., U.S.A.* 33°59N 81°11W **316** B8
Lexington *Tenn., U.S.A.* 35°39N 88°24W **315** D10
Lexington *Va., U.S.A.* 37°47N 79°27W **309** G14
Lexington Park *U.S.A.* 38°16N 76°27W **309** F15
Leyburn *U.K.* 54°19N 1°48W **168** C6
Leye *China* 24°48N 106°29E **228** E6
Leyeh *Taiwan* 23°28N 120°42E **225** C2
Leyland *U.K.* 53°42N 2°43W **168** D5
Leyre → *France* 44°39N 1°1W **174** D2
Leyte *Phil.* 10°30N 125°0E **233** F5
Leyte ☐ *Phil.* 11°0N 125°0E **233** F5
Leyte Gulf *Phil.* 10°50N 125°25E **233** F5
Leyton *U.K.* 51°33N 0°1W **125** A3
Leytonstone *U.K.* 51°34N 0°0 **125** A4
Leżajsk *Poland* 50°16N 22°25E **185** H9
Lezay *France* 46°15N 0°1W **174** B3
Lezhë *Albania* 41°47N 19°39E **202** E3
Lezhi *China* 30°19N 104°58E **228** B5
Lézignan-Corbières *France* 43°13N 2°43E **174** E6
Lezoux *France* 45°49N 3°21E **174** C7
Lgov *Russia* 51°42N 35°16E **189** G8
Lhasa *China* 29°25N 90°58E **218** D4
L'Haÿ-les-Roses *France* 48°46N 2°20E **134** B3
Lhazê *China* 29°5N 87°38E **218** D3
L'Hermite, I. *Chile* 55°50S 68°0W **336** E3
Lhokkruet *Indonesia* 4°55N 95°24E **234** B1
Lhokseumawe *Indonesia* 5°10N 97°10E **234** A1
L'Hospitalet de Llobregat *Spain* 41°21N 2°6E **114** A1
Lhotka *Czech Rep.* 50°1N 14°26E **135** B2
Lhuntsi Dzong *Bhutan* 27°39N 91°10E **241** B3
Lhut, W. → *Somali Rep.* 10°17N 50°9E **267** B7
Li *Thailand* 17°48N 98°57E **236** D2
Li Jiang → *China* 24°40N 110°40E **229** E8
Li Shui → *China* 29°24N 112°1E **229** C9
Li Xian *Gansu, China* 34°10N 105°5E **226** G3
Li Xian *Hebei, China* 38°30N 115°35E **226** E8
Li Xian *Hunan, China* 29°36N 111°42E **229** C8
Lia-Moya *C.A.R.* 6°54N 16°17E **264** A3
Liadi *Greece* 36°50N 26°11E **205** E8
Liamuiga, Mt. *St. Kitts & Nevis* 17°22N 62°48W **322** d
Lian *Phil.* 14°3N 120°39E **232** D3
Liancheng *China* 25°42N 116°40E **229** E11
Liancourt Rocks = Tokdo *Asia* 37°15N 131°52E **221** F5
Liang Tao *Taiwan* 26°23N 128°28E **225** b
Lianga *Phil.* 8°38N 126°6E **233** G6
Liangcheng *Nei Monggol Zizhiqu, China* 40°28N 112°25E **226** D7
Liangcheng *Shandong, China* 35°32N 119°37E **227** G10
Liangdang *China* 33°56N 106°18E **226** H4
Lianghe *China* 24°50N 98°20E **228** E2
Lianghekou *China* 29°11N 108°44E **228** C7
Liangping *China* 30°38N 107°47E **228** B6
Liangpran *Indonesia* 1°4N 114°23E **234** B4
Liangshui He → *China* 39°48N 116°23E **114** C2
Lianhua *China* 27°3N 113°54E **229** D9
Lianhua Chi *China* 39°52N 116°16E **114** B1
Lianhua He → *China* 39°52N 116°13E **114** B1
Lianjiang *Fujian, China* 26°12N 119°27E **229** D12
Lianjiang *Guangdong, China* 21°40N 110°20E **229** G8
Lianping *China* 24°26N 114°30E **229** E10
Lianshan *China* 24°38N 112°8E **229** E9
Lianshanguan *China* 40°53N 123°43E **224** B1
Lianshui *China* 33°42N 119°20E **227** H10
Lianyuan *China* 27°40N 111°38E **229** D8
Lianyungang *China* 34°40N 119°11E **227** G10
Lianzhou *China* 24°51N 112°22E **229** E9
Liao He → *China* 41°0N 121°50E **227** D11
Liaocheng *China* 36°28N 115°58E **226** F8
Liaodong Bandao *China* 40°0N 122°30E **227** E12
Liaodong Wan *China* 40°20N 121°10E **227** D11
Liaoning ☐ *China* 41°40N 122°30E **227** D12
Liaotung, G. of = Liaodong Wan *China* 40°20N 121°10E **227** D11
Liaoyang *China* 41°15N 122°58E **224** B1
Liaoyuan *China* 42°58N 125°2E **227** C13
Liaozhong *China* 41°23N 122°50E **224** B1
Liapades *Greece* 39°42N 19°40E **206** B9
Liard → *Canada* 61°51N 121°18W **296** A4
Liard River *Canada* 59°25N 126°5W **296** B3
Liari *Pakistan* 25°37N 66°30E **242** G2
Líbano *Colombia* 4°55N 75°4W **328** C2
Libau = Liepāja *Latvia* 56°30N 21°0E **184** B8
Libby *U.S.A.* 48°23N 115°33W **304** B6
Libčice nad Vltavou *Czech Rep.* 50°11N 14°22E **135** A2
Libeň *Czech Rep.* 50°6N 14°27E **135** B2
Libenge *Dem. Rep. of the Congo* 3°40N 18°55E **264** B3
Liberal *U.S.A.* 37°3N 100°55W **308** G3
Liberdade *Acre, Brazil* 10°5S 70°20W **330** C3
Liberdade *São Paulo, Brazil* 23°33S 46°37W **137** B2
Liberdade → *Brazil* 9°40S 52°17W **331** B7
Liberdade, Avenida da *Lisbon, Portugal* **126** b1
Liberec *Czech Rep.* 50°47N 15°7E **180** A8
Liberecký ☐ *Czech Rep.* 50°45N 15°0E **180** A8
Liberia *Costa Rica* 10°40N 85°30W **320** D2
Liberia ■ *W. Afr.* 6°30N 9°30W **262** D3
Libertad *Antique, Phil.* 11°46N 121°55E **233** F3
Libertad *Venezuela* 8°20N 69°37W **328** B4
Libertador ☐ *Chile* 34°15S 70°45W **334** C1
Liberton *U.K.* 55°54N 3°9W **121** B3
Liberty *Ind., U.S.A.* 39°38N 84°56W **311** E12
Liberty *Mo., U.S.A.* 39°15N 94°25W **310** E2
Liberty *N.Y., U.S.A.* 41°48N 74°45W **313** E10
Liberty *Pa., U.S.A.* 41°34N 77°6W **312** E7
Liberty *Tex., U.S.A.* 30°3N 94°48W **314** F7
Liberty Center *U.S.A.* 41°27N 84°1W **311** C12
Liberty I. *U.S.A.* 40°41N 74°2W **132** B1
Liberty-Newark Int. ✈ (EWR) *U.S.A.* 40°42N 74°10W **313** F10
Liberty Osaka Museum *Japan* 34°38N 135°29E **133** B1
Liberty State Park ⌂ *U.S.A.* 40°42N 74°2W **132** B1
Libertyville *U.S.A.* 42°18N 87°57W **311** B9
Libeznice *Czech Rep.* 50°11N 14°29E **135** A2
Libiąż *Poland* 50°7N 19°21E **185** H6
Libibi *Angola* 14°42S 17°44E **265** E3
Lîbîya, Sahrâ' *Africa* 25°0N 25°0E **258** C4
Libjo *Phil.* 10°12N 125°32E **233** F5
Libmanan *Phil.* 13°42N 123°4E **232** E4
Libo *China* 25°22N 107°53E **228** E6
Libobo, Tanjung *Indonesia* 0°54S 128°28E **231** E7
Libode *S. Africa* 31°33S 29°2E **271** D4
Libohovë *Albania* 40°3N 20°10E **202** F4
Liboi *Kenya* 0°24N 40°57E **267** D5
Libona *Phil.* 8°20N 124°44E **233** G5
Libonda *Zambia* 14°28S 23°12E **265** E4
Libong, Ko *Thailand* 7°15N 99°23E **237** J2
Libourne *France* 44°55N 0°14W **174** D3
Libramont *Belgium* 49°55N 5°23E **170** E5
Library of Congress *Washington, D.C., U.S.A.* **143** b3
Librazhd *Albania* 41°12N 20°22E **202** E4
Libreville *Gabon* 0°25N 9°26E **264** B1
Libuš *Czech Rep.* 50°0N 14°27E **135** B2
Libya ■ *N. Afr.* 27°0N 17°0E **258** C3
Libyan Desert = Lîbîya, Sahrâ' *Africa* 25°0N 25°0E **258** C4
Libyan Plateau = Ed Déffa *Egypt* 30°40N 26°30E **256** A2
Licantén *Chile* 35°55S 72°0W **334** D1
Licata *Italy* 37°6N 13°56E **200** E6
Lice *Turkey* 38°27N 40°39E **213** C9
Licheng *China* 36°28N 113°20E **226** F7
Lichfield *U.K.* 52°41N 1°49W **169** E6
Lichia *Taiwan* 22°47N 121°3E **225** D3
Lichiao *China* 23°3N 113°18E **121** B2
Lichinga *Mozam.* 13°13S 35°11E **269** E4
Lichtenberg *Berlin, Germany* 52°31N 13°30E **115** A4
Lichtenburg *North West, S. Africa* 26°8S 26°8E **270** C4
Lichtenfels *Germany* 50°8N 11°4E **179** E7
Lichterfelde *Germany* 52°25N 13°19E **115** B2
Lichuan *Hubei, China* 30°18N 108°57E **228** B7
Lichuan *Jiangxi, China* 27°18N 116°55E **229** D11
Licking → *U.S.A.* 39°6N 84°30W **311** F12
Licosa, Punta *Italy* 40°15N 14°54E **201** B7
Licungo → *Mozam.* 17°40S 37°15E **269** F4
Lida *Belarus* 53°53N 25°15E **177** B13
Liden *Sweden* 62°42N 16°48E **162** B10
Lidhult *Sweden* 56°50N 13°27E **163** H7
Lidingö *Sweden* 59°21N 18°8E **139** A2
Lidköping *Sweden* 58°31N 13°7E **163** F7
Lido *Italy* 45°25N 12°22E **199** C9
Lido *Niger* 12°54N 3°44E **263** C5
Lido di Roma = Ostia, Lido di *Italy* 41°43N 12°17E **199** G9
Lidoriki *Greece* 38°32N 22°12E **204** C4
Lidzbark *Poland* 53°15N 19°49E **185** E6
Lidzbark Warmiński *Poland* 54°7N 20°34E **184** D7
Liebenthal = Lubomierz *Poland* 51°1N 15°31E **185** G2
Liebenwalde *Germany* 52°52N 13°24E **178** C9
Lieberose *Germany* 51°59N 14°17E **178** D10
Liebig, Mt. *Australia* 23°18S 131°22E **278** D5
Liebling *Romania* 45°36N 21°20E **182** E6
Liechtenstein ■ *Europe* 47°8N 9°35E **179** H5
Liège *Belgium* 50°38N 5°35E **170** D5
Liège ☐ *Belgium* 50°32N 5°35E **170** D5
Liegnitz = Legnica *Poland* 51°12N 16°10E **185** G3
Lieksa *Finland* 63°18N 30°2E **160** E24
Lienart *Dem. Rep. of the Congo* 3°3N 25°31E **268** B2
Lienyünchiangshih = Lianyungang *China* 34°40N 119°11E **227** G10
Lienz *Austria* 46°50N 12°46E **180** E5
Liepāja *Latvia* 56°30N 21°0E **184** B8
Liepāja ☐ *Latvia* 56°30N 21°0E **184** B8
Liepājas ezers *Latvia* 56°27N 21°3E **184** B8
Lier *Belgium* 51°7N 4°34E **170** C4
Lierais *France* 47°13N 4°16E **173** E11
Lieshi Lingyuan *China* 23°7N 113°16E **121** B2
Liesing *Austria* 48°8N 16°17E **142** B1
Liesing → *Austria* 48°8N 16°22E **142** B2
Lieşti *Romania* 45°38N 27°34E **183** E12
Lietuva = Lithuania ■ *Europe* 55°30N 24°0E **188** E2
Liévin *France* 50°24N 2°47E **173** B9
Lièvre → *Canada* 45°31N 75°26W **298** C4
Liezen *Austria* 47°34N 14°15E **180** D7
Liffey → *Ireland* 53°21N 6°13W **166** C5
Lifford *Ireland* 54°51N 7°29W **166** B4
Liffré *France* 48°12N 1°30W **172** D5
Lifjell *Norway* 59°27N 8°45E **164** E5
Lifou, Î. *N. Cal.* 20°53S 167°13E **288** d
Lifudzin *Russia* 44°21N 134°58E **220** B7
Lifuka *Tonga* 19°48S 174°21W **287** P13
Ligao *Phil.* 13°14N 123°32E **232** E4
Ligasa *Dem. Rep. of the Congo* 0°44N 23°49E **264** B4
Lighthouse Point *U.S.A.* 26°15N 80°7W **317** J9
Lighthouse Pt. *U.S.A.* 29°54N 84°21W **316** F5
Lightning Ridge *Australia* 29°22S 148°0E **281** D4
Lignano Sabbiadoro *Italy* 45°42N 13°9E **199** C10
Ligny-en-Barrois *France* 48°36N 5°20E **173** D12
Ligonha → *Mozam.* 16°54S 39°9E **269** F4
Ligonier *Ind., U.S.A.* 41°28N 85°35W **311** C11
Ligonier *Pa., U.S.A.* 40°15N 79°14W **312** F5
Ligourio *Greece* 37°37N 23°4E **204** D5
Ligovo *Russia* 59°49N 30°10E **137** C1
Ligueil *France* 47°2N 0°49E **172** E7
Liguria ☐ *Italy* 44°30N 8°50E **198** D5
Ligurian Sea *Medit. S.* 43°20N 9°0E **198** E5
Lihir Group *Papua N. G.* 3°0S 152°35E **286** B7
Lihir I. *Papua N. G.* 3°5S 152°35E **286** B7
Lihou Reefs and Cays *Australia* 17°25S 151°40E **280** B5
Lihu'e *U.S.A.* 21°59N 159°23W **302** B2
Lihué Calel △ *Argentina* 38°0S 65°10W **334** D2
Lijiang *China* 26°55N 100°20E **228** D3
Lijordet *Norway* 59°56N 10°36E **133** A2
Likala *Dem. Rep. of the Congo* 0°9N 19°12E **264** B3
Likang *Taiwan* 22°47N 120°29E **225** D2
Likasi *Dem. Rep. of the Congo* 10°55S 26°48E **269** E2
Likati *Dem. Rep. of the Congo* 3°20N 24°0E **264** B4
Likati → *Dem. Rep. of the Congo* 2°53N 24°3E **264** B4
Likenäs *Sweden* 60°37N 13°3E **162** D7
Likete *Dem. Rep. of the Congo* 0°48S 21°31E **264** C4
Likhaya = Likhovskoy *Russia* 48°10N 40°10E **189** H11
Likhoborka → *Russia* 55°50N 37°37E **129** A3
Likhoslavl *Russia* 57°12N 35°30E **188** D8
Likhovskoy *Russia* 48°10N 40°10E **189** H11
Likhvin = Chekalin *Russia* 54°10N 36°10E **188** E9
Likimi *Dem. Rep. of the Congo* 2°44N 20°47E **264** B4
Likita *Dem. Rep. of the Congo* 4°15N 23°36E **264** B4
Liknes *Norway* 58°19N 6°59E **164** F3
Likokou *Gabon* 0°12S 12°48E **264** C2
Likoma I. *Malawi* 12°3S 34°45E **269** E3
Likouala → *Congo* 0°2N 14°53E **264** C3
Likouala aux Herbes → *Congo* 0°52S 17°8E **264** C3
Liku *Cook Is.* 19°2S 168°47W **289** g
Likumburu *Tanzania* 9°43S 35°8E **269** D4
Lilanga *Dem. Rep. of the Congo* 0°34S 23°56E **264** C4
L'Île-Bouchard *France* 47°7N 0°26E **172** E7
L'Île-Rousse *France* 42°38N 8°57E **175** F12
Lilenga *Dem. Rep. of the Congo* 1°4N 22°6E **264** B4
Liling *China* 27°42N 113°29E **229** D9
Lilla Edet *Sweden* 58°9N 12°8E **163** F6
Lilla Värtan *Sweden* 59°20N 18°11E **139** A3
Lille *France* 50°38N 3°3E **173** B10
Lille Bælt *Denmark* 55°20N 9°45E **163** J3
Lille Værløse *Denmark* 55°47N 12°22E **118** A2
Lillebonne *France* 49°30N 0°32E **172** C7
Lillehammer *Norway* 61°8N 10°30E **164** C7
Lillesand *Norway* 58°15N 8°23E **164** F5
Lillestrøm *Norway* 59°58N 11°5E **164** E8
Lillhärdal *Sweden* 61°51N 14°5E **162** C8
Lillian Pt. *Australia* 27°40S 126°6E **279** E4
Lillo *Spain* 39°45N 3°20W **194** F7
Lillooet *Canada* 50°44N 121°57W **296** C4
Lillooet → *Canada* 49°15N 121°57W **296** D4
Lilongwe *Malawi* 14°0S 33°48E **269** E3
Liloy *Phil.* 8°4N 122°39E **233** G4
Liluah *India* 22°37N 88°19E **124** B1
Lim → *Europe* 43°45N 19°15E **202** C3
Lim Chu Kang *Singapore* 1°26N 103°43E **138** A2
Lima *Brazil* 4°36S 63°40W **329** D5
Lima *Indonesia* 3°39S 127°58E **231** E7
Lima *Peru* 12°3S 77°2W **124** B2
Lima *Ill., U.S.A.* 40°11N 91°23W **310** D5
Lima *Mont., U.S.A.* 44°38N 112°36W **304** D7
Lima *N.Y., U.S.A.* 42°54N 77°36W **312** D7
Lima *Ohio, U.S.A.* 40°44N 84°6W **311** D12
Lima ☐ *Peru* 12°3S 77°3W **330** C2
Lima → *Portugal* 41°41N 8°50W **194** D2
Lima Jorge Chavez, Int. ✈ (LIM) *Peru* 12°2S 77°8W **124** B2
Liman = Krasnyy Liman *Ukraine* 48°58N 37°50E **189** H9
Liman *Indonesia* 7°48S 111°45E **231** G14
Liman *Russia* 45°45N 47°12E **191** H8
Limanowa *Poland* 49°42N 20°22E **185** J7
Limassol *Cyprus* 34°42N 33°1E **207** F9
Limavady *U.K.* 55°3N 6°56W **166** A5
Limay → *Argentina* 39°0S 68°0W **336** A3
Limay Mahuida *Argentina* 37°10S 66°45W **334** D2
Limbach-Oberfrohna *Germany* 50°52N 12°43E **178** E8
Limbang *Brunei* 4°42N 115°6E **235** B5
Limbara, Mte. *Italy* 40°51N 9°10E **200** B2
Limbaži *Latvia* 57°31N 24°42E **188** D3
Limbdi *India* 22°34N 71°51E **242** H4
Limbe *Cameroon* 4°1N 9°10E **263** E6
Limbiate *Italy* 45°35N 9°7E **129** A1
Limbueta *Angola* 12°30S 18°42E **265** E3
Limbuhan = Pio V. Corpuz *Phil.* 11°55N 124°2E **233** F5
Limburg *Germany* 50°22N 8°4E **179** E4
Limburg ☐ *Belgium* 51°2N 5°25E **170** C5
Limburg ☐ *Neths.* 51°20N 5°55E **170** C5
Lime Village *U.S.A.* 61°21N 155°28W **303** F9
Limedsforsen *Sweden* 60°52N 13°25E **162** D7
Limehouse *U.K.* 51°30N 0°1W **125** A3
Limeil-Brévannes *France* 48°44N 2°29E **134** B3
Limeira = Joaçaba *Brazil* 27°5S 51°31W **335** B5
Limeira *Brazil* 22°35S 47°28W **335** A6
Limenaria *Greece* 40°38N 24°32E **203** F8
Limenas Chersonisou *Greece* 35°18N 25°21E **207** E6
Limerick *Limerick, Ireland* 52°40N 8°37W **166** D3
Limerick *Maine, U.S.A.* 43°41N 70°48W **313** C14
Limerick ☐ *Ireland* 52°30N 8°50W **166** D3
Limestone *U.S.A.* 42°2N 78°38W **312** D6
Limestone → *Canada* 56°31N 94°7W **297** B10
Limestone Hill = Lackawanna *U.S.A.* 42°50N 78°50W **312** D6
Limfjorden *Denmark* 56°55N 9°0E **163** H3
Limia = Lima → *Portugal* 41°41N 8°50W **194** D2
Limingen *Norway* 64°48N 13°35E **160** D15
Liminka *Sweden* 57°34N 13°20E **163** G7
Limmen ✪ *Australia* 15°15S 135°30E **280** B2
Limmen Bight *Australia* 14°40S 135°35E **280** A2
Limmen Bight → *Australia* 15°7S 135°44E **280** B2
Limni *Greece* 38°43N 23°18E **204** C5
Limnos *Greece* 39°50N 25°5E **205** B7
Limoeiro *Brazil* 7°52S 35°27W **332** C4
Limoeiro do Norte *Brazil* 5°5S 38°0W **332** B4
Limoges *Ont., Canada* 45°20N 75°16W **313** A9
Limoges *Haute-Vienne, France* 45°50N 1°15E **174** C5
Limón *Costa Rica* 10°0N 83°2W **320** E3
Limon *Colo., U.S.A.* 39°16N 103°41W **304** G12
Limone Piemonte *Italy* 44°12N 7°34E **198** D4
Limonlu *Turkey* 36°34N 34°15E **250** B5
Limousin ☐ *France* 45°30N 1°30E **174** C5
Limousin, Plateaux du *France* 45°45N 1°15E **174** C5
Limoux *France* 43°4N 2°12E **174** E6
Limpopo ☐ *S. Africa* 24°5S 29°0E **271** B4
Limpopo → *Africa* 25°5S 33°30E **271** C5
Limuru *Kenya* 1°2S 36°35E **268** C4
Lin Xian *China* 37°57N 110°58E **226** F6
Lin'an *China* 30°15N 119°42E **229** B12
Linao Pt. *Phil.* 6°46N 123°58E **233** H4
Linapacan *Phil.* 11°30N 119°52E **233** F2
Linapacan I. *Phil.* 11°27N 119°49E **233** F2

Linapacan Str. *Phil.* 11°37N 119°56E **233** F2
Linares *Chile* 35°50S 71°40W **334** D1
Linares *Colombia* 1°23N 77°31W **328** C2
Linares *Nuevo León, Mexico* 24°52N 99°34W **319** C5
Linares *Spain* 38°10N 3°40W **195** G7
Linaria *Greece* 38°52N 24°31E **204** C6
Linaro, Capo *Italy* 42°2N 11°50E **199** F8
Línas Mte. *Italy* 39°25N 8°38E **200** C1
Linate, Milano ✈ (LIN) *Italy* 45°27N 9°16E **129** B2
Linbropark *S. Africa* 26°5S 28°7E **123** A2
Lincang *China* 23°58N 100°1E **228** F3
Lincheng *China* 37°25N 114°30E **226** F8
Linchuan *China* 27°57N 116°15E **229** D11
Lincoln = Beamsville *Canada* 43°12N 79°28W **312** C5
Lincoln *Argentina* 34°55S 61°30W **334** C3
Lincoln *N.Z.* 43°38S 172°30E **285** D7
Lincoln *Lincs., U.K.* 53°14N 0°32W **168** D7
Lincoln *Calif., U.S.A.* 38°54N 121°17W **306** G5
Lincoln *Ill., U.S.A.* 40°9N 89°22W **310** D7
Lincoln *Kans., U.S.A.* 39°3N 98°9W **308** F4
Lincoln *Maine, U.S.A.* 45°22N 68°30W **309** C19
Lincoln *N.H., U.S.A.* 44°3N 71°40W **313** B13
Lincoln *N. Mex., U.S.A.* 33°30N 105°23W **305** K11
Lincoln *Nebr., U.S.A.* 40°49N 96°41W **308** E5
Lincoln Boyhood ⌂ *U.S.A.* 38°7N 86°59W **311** F10
Lincoln Center for Performing Arts *New York, U.S.A.* **132** b2
Lincoln City *U.S.A.* 44°57N 124°1W **304** D1
Lincoln Hav = Lincoln Sea *Arctic* 84°0N 55°0W **154** A5
Lincoln Heights *U.S.A.* 34°4N 118°12W **126** B3
Lincoln Memorial *U.S.A.* 38°52N 77°4W **143** B3
Lincoln Park *Calif., U.S.A.* 37°47N 122°30W **136** B1
Lincoln Park *Ga., U.S.A.* 32°52N 84°20W **316** C5
Lincoln Park *Ill., U.S.A.* 41°57N 87°38W **119** B3
Lincoln Park *Mich., U.S.A.* 42°15N 83°11W **311** B13
Lincoln Park *N.J., U.S.A.* 40°55N 74°18W **132** B1
Lincoln Park Zoo *U.S.A.* 41°55N 87°38W **119** B3
Lincoln Sea *Arctic* 84°0N 55°0W **154** A5
Lincoln Tunnel *New York, U.S.A.* **132** c1
Lincolnshire ☐ *U.K.* 53°14N 0°32W **168** D7
Lincolnshire Wolds *U.K.* 53°26N 0°13W **168** D7
Lincolnton *Ga., U.S.A.* 33°48N 82°29W **316** B7
Lincolnton *N.C., U.S.A.* 35°29N 81°16W **315** D14
Lincolnwood *U.S.A.* 42°1N 87°43W **119** A2
Lind *U.S.A.* 46°58N 118°37W **304** C4
Linda *U.S.A.* 39°8N 121°34W **306** F5
Linda-a-Pastora *Portugal* 38°42N 9°15W **126** A1
Lindale *U.S.A.* 34°11N 85°11W **316** A4
Lindås *Norway* 60°44N 5°9E **164** D2
Lindau *Germany* 47°33N 9°42E **179** H5
Lindeman I. *Australia* 20°27S 149°3E **280** b
Lindeman Islands △ *Australia* 20°28S 149°5E **280** b
Linden = Gladstone *U.S.A.* 39°13N 94°35W **310** E2
Linden *Guyana* 6°0N 58°10W **329** B6
Linden *Wellington, N.Z.* 41°10S 174°50E **143** A1
Linden *Gauteng, S. Africa* 26°8S 28°0E **123** A2
Linden *Ala., U.S.A.* 32°18N 87°48W **315** E11
Linden *Calif., U.S.A.* 38°1N 121°5W **306** G5
Linden *Ind., U.S.A.* 40°11N 86°54W **311** D10
Linden *Mich., U.S.A.* 42°49N 83°47W **311** B13
Linden *Tex., U.S.A.* 33°1N 94°22W **314** E7
Lindenberg *Germany* 52°36N 13°31E **115** A4
Lindenhurst *U.S.A.* 40°41N 73°23W **313** F11
Lindenow Fjord *Greenland* 60°30N 43°25W **154** E6
Lindesberg *Sweden* 59°36N 15°15E **162** E9
Lindesnes *Norway* 57°58N 7°3E **164** G4
Lindi *Tanzania* 9°58S 39°38E **269** D4
Lindi ☐ *Tanzania* 9°40S 38°30E **269** D4
Lindi ➔ *Dem. Rep. of the Congo* 0°33N 25°5E **268** B2
Lindley *U.S.A.* 42°1N 77°8W **312** D7
Lindö *Sweden* 58°37N 16°15E **163** F10
Lindome *Sweden* 57°35N 12°5E **163** G6
Lindos *Greece* 36°6N 28°4E **206** E12
Lindos, Akra *Greece* 36°4N 28°10E **206** E12
Lindoso *Portugal* 41°52N 8°11W **194** D2
Lindow *Germany* 52°58N 12°59E **178** C8
Lindøya *Norway* 59°53N 10°42E **133** A3
Lindsay *Ont., Canada* 44°22N 78°43W **312** B6
Lindsay *Calif., U.S.A.* 36°12N 119°5W **306** J7
Lindsay *Okla., U.S.A.* 34°50N 97°38W **314** D6
Lindsborg *U.S.A.* 38°35N 97°40W **308** F5
Lindsdal *Sweden* 56°44N 16°18E **163** H10
Line Islands *Pac. Oc.* 7°0N 160°0W **289** H12
Linesville *U.S.A.* 41°39N 80°26W **312** E4
Lineville *Ala., U.S.A.* 33°19N 85°45W **316** B4
Lineville *Iowa, U.S.A.* 40°35N 93°32W **310** D3
Linfen *China* 36°3N 111°30E **226** F6
Ling Xian *Hunan, China* 26°29N 113°48E **229** D9
Ling Xian *Shandong, China* 37°22N 116°30E **226** F9
Lingal *India* 16°17N 78°31E **245** F4
Linganamakki Res. *India* 14°6N 74°52E **245** G2
Lingao *China* 19°56N 109°42E **236** C7
Lingayen *Phil.* 16°1N 120°14E **232** C3
Lingayen G. *Phil.* 16°10N 120°15E **232** C3
Lingbi *China* 33°33N 117°33E **227** H9
Lingbo *Sweden* 61°3N 16°41E **162** C10
Lingchuan *Guangxi Zhuangzu, China* 25°26N 110°21E **229** E8
Lingchuan *Shanxi, China* 35°45N 113°12E **226** G7
Lingding Yang *China* 22°25N 113°44E **219** G10
Lingen *Germany* 52°31N 7°19E **178** C3
Lingga *Indonesia* 0°12S 104°37E **234** C2
Lingga, Kepulauan *Indonesia* 0°10S 104°30E **234** C2
Lingga Arch. = Lingga, Kepulauan *Indonesia* 0°10S 104°30E **234** C2
Linghem *Sweden* 58°26N 15°47E **163** F9
Lingig *Phil.* 8°2N 126°24E **233** G6
Lingle *U.S.A.* 42°8N 104°21W **304** E11
Lingomo *Dem. Rep. of the Congo* 0°38N 22°3E **264** B4
Lingqiu *China* 39°28N 114°22E **226** E8
Lingshan *China* 22°25N 109°18E **228** F7
Lingshi *China* 36°48N 111°48E **226** F6
Lingshou *China* 38°20N 114°20E **226** E8
Lingshui *China* 18°27N 110°0E **236** C8
Lingsugur *India* 16°10N 76°31E **245** F3
Lingtai *China* 35°0N 107°40E **226** G4
Linguère *Senegal* 15°25N 15°5W **262** B1
Lingui *China* 25°12N 110°2E **229** E8
Lingunda *Dem. Rep. of the Congo* 0°49N 21°8E **264** C3
Lingwu *China* 38°6N 106°20E **226** E4
Lingyuan *China* 41°10N 119°15E **227** D10
Lingyun *China* 25°2N 106°35E **228** E6
Linhai *China* 28°50N 121°8E **229** C13
Linhares *Brazil* 19°25S 40°4W **333** E3
Linhe *China* 40°48N 107°20E **226** D4
Liniers *Argentina* 34°39S 58°30W **117** B1
Linjiang *China* 41°50N 127°0E **224** B3
Linkebeek *Belgium* 50°46N 4°20E **116** B2
Linköping *Sweden* 58°28N 15°36E **163** F9
Linkou *China* 45°15N 130°18E **227** B16
Linksfield *S. Africa* 26°9S 28°6E **123** A2
Linli *China* 29°27N 111°30E **229** C8
Linlithgow = West Lothian ☐ *U.K.* 55°54N 3°36W **167** F5
Linmeyer *S. Africa* 26°15S 28°4E **123** B2
Linn *U.S.A.* 38°29N 91°51W **310** F5
Linna *Finland* 60°20N 24°50E **121** A2
Linnei *Taiwan* 23°45N 120°36E **225** C2
Linneus *U.S.A.* 39°53N 93°11W **310** E3
Linnhe, L. *U.K.* 56°36N 5°25W **167** E3
Linosa *Medit. S.* 35°51N 12°50E **258** A2
Linpien *Taiwan* 22°26N 120°30E **225** D2
Linqi *China* 35°45N 113°52E **226** G7
Linqing *China* 36°50N 115°42E **226** F8
Linqu *China* 36°25N 118°30E **227** F10
Linru *China* 34°11N 112°52E **226** G7
Lins *Brazil* 21°40S 49°44W **335** A6
Linshui *China* 30°21N 106°57E **228** B6
Linsia = Linxia *China* 35°36N 103°10E **218** C5
Linstead *Jamaica* 18°8N 77°2W **320** a
Linta ➔ *Madag.* 25°2S 44°5E **272** D1
Linth ➔ *Switz.* 47°7N 9°7E **179** H5
Linthal *Switz.* 46°54N 9°0E **179** J5
Linton *Ind., U.S.A.* 39°2N 87°10W **311** F9
Linton *N. Dak., U.S.A.* 46°16N 100°14W **308** B3
Lintong *China* 34°20N 109°10E **226** G5
Lintuvaara *Finland* 60°14N 24°49E **121** B1
Linwood *Canada* 43°35N 80°43W **312** C4
Linwu *China* 25°19N 112°31E **229** E9
Linxi *China* 43°36N 118°2E **227** C10
Linxia *China* 35°36N 103°10E **218** C5
Linxiang *China* 29°28N 113°23E **229** C9
Linyanti ➔ *Africa* 17°50S 25°5E **270** A4
Linyi *China* 35°5N 118°21E **227** G10
Linyuan *Taiwan* 22°30N 120°23E **225** D2
Linz *Austria* 48°18N 14°18E **180** C7
Linz *Rhld-Pfz., Germany* 50°34N 7°17E **178** E3
Linzhenzhen *China* 36°30N 109°59E **226** F5
Linzi *China* 36°50N 118°20E **227** F10
Lioko *Équateur, Dem. Rep. of the Congo* 0°2N 22°4E **264** B4
Lioko *Orientale, Dem. Rep. of the Congo* 1°25N 23°7E **264** B4
Liomseter *Norway* 61°15N 9°35E **164** C6
Lion, G. du *France* 43°10N 4°0E **174** E7
Lion Rock Country Park ⌂ *China* 22°21N 114°11E **122** A2
Lionárisso *Cyprus* 35°28N 34°8E **207** E10
Lionel Town *Jamaica* 17°50N 77°15W **320** a
Lioni *Italy* 40°52N 15°11E **201** B8
Lions, G. of = Lion, G. du *France* 43°10N 4°0E **174** E7
Lion's Den *Zimbabwe* 17°15S 30°5E **269** F3
Lion's Head *Ont., Canada* 44°58N 81°15W **312** B3
Lion's Head *Western Cape, S. Africa* 33°56S 18°23E **118** A1
Liouesso *Congo* 1°2N 15°43E **264** B3
Lioumi *Greece* 38°0N 23°40E **112** B2
Liozno = Lyozna *Belarus* 55°0N 30°50E **188** E6
Lipa *Phil.* 13°57N 121°10E **232** E3
Lipali *Mozam.* 15°50S 35°50E **269** F4
Lipany *Slovak Rep.* 49°9N 20°58E **181** B13
Lípari *Italy* 38°26N 14°58E **201** D7
Lípari, I. *Italy* 38°29N 14°56E **201** D7
Lípari, Is. = Eólie, Ís. *Italy* 38°30N 14°57E **201** D7
Lipcani *Moldova* 48°14N 26°48E **183** B11
Liperi *Finland* 62°31N 29°24E **160** E23
Lipetsk *Russia* 52°37N 39°35E **189** F10
Lipetsk ☐ *Russia* 52°50N 38°50E **190** D4
Lipiany *Poland* 53°2N 14°58E **185** E1
Liping *China* 26°15N 109°7E **228** D7
Lipisi *Greece* 37°19N 26°50E **205** D8
Lipkany = Lipcani *Moldova* 48°14N 26°48E **183** B11
Lipljan *Kosovo* 42°31N 21°7E **202** D5
Lipník nad Bečvou *Czech Rep.* 49°32N 17°36E **181** B10
Lipno *Poland* 52°49N 19°15E **185** F6
Lipova *Romania* 46°8N 21°42E **182** D6
Lipovets *Ukraine* 49°12N 29°1E **177** D15
Lippe ➔ *Germany* 51°39N 6°36E **178** D2
Lippehne = Lipiany *Poland* 53°2N 14°58E **185** E1
Lippstadt *Germany* 51°41N 8°22E **178** D4
Lipscomb *U.S.A.* 36°14N 100°16W **314** C4
Lipsk *Poland* 53°44N 23°24E **184** E10
Lipsko *Poland* 51°9N 21°40E **185** G8
Liptovský Hrádok *Slovak Rep.* 49°2N 19°44E **181** B12
Liptovský Milkuláš *Slovak Rep.* 49°6N 19°35E **181** B12
Liptrap, C. *Australia* 38°50S 145°55E **283** E6
Lipu *China* 24°30N 110°22E **229** E8
Lira *Uganda* 2°17N 32°57E **268** B3
Liranga *Congo* 0°43S 17°32E **264** C3
Liri ➔ *Italy* 41°25N 13°52E **200** A6
Liria = Lliria *Spain* 39°37N 0°35W **197** F4
Līsakovsk *Kazakhstan* 52°33N 62°37E **216** B6
Lisala *Dem. Rep. of the Congo* 2°12N 21°38E **264** B4
Lisboa *Portugal* 38°42N 9°8W **126** A2
Lisboa ☐ *Portugal* 39°0N 9°12W **195** F1
Lisboa ✈ (LIS) *Portugal* 38°46N 9°8W **126** A2
Lisbon = Lisboa *Portugal* 38°42N 9°8W **126** A2
Lisbon *N. Dak., U.S.A.* 46°27N 97°41W **308** B5
Lisbon *N.H., U.S.A.* 44°13N 71°55W **313** B13
Lisbon *N.Y., U.S.A.* 44°43N 75°19W **313** B9
Lisbon *Ohio, U.S.A.* 40°46N 80°46W **312** F4
Lisbon Falls *U.S.A.* 44°0N 70°4W **309** D18
Lisburn *U.K.* 54°31N 6°3W **166** B5
Lisburn, C. *Vanuatu* 15°39S 166°46E **287** E4
Lisburne, C. *U.S.A.* 68°53N 166°13W **303** B6
Liscannor B. *Ireland* 52°55N 9°24W **166** D2
Liscia ➔ *Italy* 41°11N 9°9E **200** A2
Lisdoonvarna *Ireland* 53°2N 9°18W **166** C2
Lishan *Taiwan* 24°16N 121°14E **225** B3
Lishe Jiang ➔ *China* 24°15N 101°35E **228** E3
Lishi *China* 37°31N 111°8E **226** F6
Lishu *China* 43°20N 124°18E **227** C13
Lishui *Guangdong, China* 23°12N 113°9E **121** A1
Lishui *Jiangsu, China* 31°38N 119°2E **229** B12
Lishui *Zhejiang, China* 28°28N 119°54E **229** C12
Lisianski I. *U.S.A.* 26°2N 174°0W **302** F9
Lisichansk = Lysychansk *Ukraine* 48°55N 38°30E **189** H10
Lisieux *France* 49°10N 0°12E **172** C7
Liski *Russia* 51°3N 39°30E **189** G10
L'Isle-Jourdain *Gers, France* 43°36N 1°5E **174** E5
L'Isle-Jourdain *Vienne, France* 46°13N 0°31E **174** B4
L'Isle-sur-la-Sorgue *France* 43°54N 5°2E **175** E9
Lisle-sur-Tarn *France* 43°52N 1°49E **174** E5
Lismore *N.S.W., Australia* 28°44S 153°21E **281** D5
Lismore *Waterford, Ireland* 52°8N 7°55W **166** D4
Lissa = Leszno *Poland* 51°50N 16°30E **185** G3
Lissos ➔ *Greece* 41°15N 25°40E **203** E9
Lista *Norway* 58°7N 6°39E **164** F3
Lister, Mt. *Antarctica* 78°0S 162°0E **151** D11
Lister og Mandals = Vest-Agder ☐ *Norway* 58°30N 7°15E **164** F4
Liston *Australia* 28°39S 152°6E **281** D5
Listowel *Ont., Canada* 43°44N 80°58W **312** C4
Listowel *Kerry, Ireland* 52°27N 9°29W **166** D2
Lit *Sweden* 63°19N 14°51E **162** A8
Lit-et-Mixe *France* 44°2N 1°15W **174** D2
Litang *Guangxi Zhuangzu, China* 23°12N 109°8E **228** F7
Litang *Sichuan, China* 30°1N 100°17E **228** B3
Litang *Malaysia* 5°27N 118°31E **235** A5
Litang Qu ➔ *China* 28°4N 101°32E **228** C3
Litani ➔ *Lebanon* 33°20N 35°15E **250** E6
Litchfield *Vic., Australia* 36°18S 142°52E **282** D5
Litchfield *Calif., U.S.A.* 40°24N 120°23W **306** E6
Litchfield *Conn., U.S.A.* 41°45N 73°11W **313** E11
Litchfield *Ill., U.S.A.* 39°11N 89°39W **310** E7
Litchfield *Minn., U.S.A.* 45°8N 94°32W **308** C6
Litchfield △ *Australia* 13°14S 131°1E **278** B5
Liteni *Romania* 47°32N 26°32E **183** C11
Lithakia *Greece* 37°43N 20°50E **207** D2
Lithgow *Australia* 33°25S 150°8E **283** B9
Lithino, Akra *Greece* 34°55N 24°44E **207** F5
Lithuania ■ *Europe* 55°30N 24°0E **188** E2
Litija *Slovenia* 46°3N 14°50E **199** B11
Lititz *U.S.A.* 40°9N 76°18W **313** F8
Litochoro *Greece* 40°8N 22°34E **202** F6
Litoko *Dem. Rep. of the Congo* 1°13S 24°47E **264** C4
Litoměřice *Czech Rep.* 50°33N 14°10E **180** A7
Litomyšl *Czech Rep.* 49°52N 16°20E **181** B9
Litschau *Austria* 48°58N 15°4E **180** C8
Little Abaco *Bahamas* 26°50N 77°30W **320** A4
Little Andaman I. *India* 10°45N 92°30E **245** J11
Little Aral Sea = Northern Aral Sea *Kazakhstan* 46°20N 60°30E **216** C6
Little B. *N.S.W., Australia* 33°58S 151°15E **139** B2
Little B. *Montserrat* 16°43N 62°11W **323** p
Little Barrier I. *N.Z.* 36°12S 175°8E **284** C4
Little Basses *Sri Lanka* 6°24N 81°43E **245** L5
Little Belt Mts. *U.S.A.* 46°40N 110°45W **304** C8
Little Bighorn Battlefield ⌂ *U.S.A.* 45°34N 107°25W **304** D10
Little Blue ➔ *U.S.A.* 39°42N 96°41W **308** F5
Little Buffalo ➔ *Canada* 61°0N 113°46W **296** A6
Little Calumet ➔ *U.S.A.* 41°39N 87°34W **119** D3
Little Cayman *Cayman Is.* 19°41N 80°3W **320** C3
Little Churchill ➔ *Canada* 57°30N 95°22W **297** B9
Little Coco I. *Burma* 14°0N 93°13E **245** H11
Little Colorado ➔ *U.S.A.* 36°12N 111°48W **305** H8
Little Current *Canada* 45°55N 82°0W **298** C3
Little Current ➔ *Canada* 50°57N 84°36W **298** B3
Little Desert △ *Australia* 37°25S 141°30E **282** D4
Little Diomede I. *U.S.A.* 65°45N 168°56W **303** D5
Little Falls *Minn., U.S.A.* 45°59N 94°22W **308** C6
Little Falls *N.Y., U.S.A.* 43°3N 74°51W **313** C10
Little Ferry *U.S.A.* 40°50N 74°2W **132** A1
Little Fork ➔ *U.S.A.* 48°31N 93°35W **308** A7
Little Grand Rapids *Canada* 52°0N 95°29W **297** C9
Little Humboldt ➔ *U.S.A.* 41°1N 117°43W **304** F5
Little Inagua I. *Bahamas* 21°40N 73°50W **321** B5
Little Italy *New York, U.S.A.* **132** e2
Little Karoo *S. Africa* 33°45S 21°0E **270** D3
Little Khingan Mts. = Xiao Hinggan Ling *China* 49°0N 127°0E **219** B7
Little Lake *U.S.A.* 35°56N 117°55W **307** K9
Little Lake Conway *U.S.A.* 28°29N 81°21W **133** B2
Little Laut Is. = Laut Kecil, Kepulauan *Indonesia* 4°45S 115°40E **235** C5
Little London *Jamaica* 18°15N 78°13W **320** a
Little Mecatina = Petit-Mécatina ➔ *Canada* 50°40N 59°30W **299** B8
Little Mermaid = Den Lille Havfrue *Copenhagen, Denmark* **118** a3
Little Minch *U.K.* 57°35N 6°45W **167** D2
Little Missouri ➔ *U.S.A.* 47°36N 102°25W **308** B2
Little Nicobar *India* 7°20N 93°40E **245** L11
Little Ouse ➔ *U.K.* 52°22N 1°12E **169** E9
Little Rann *India* 23°25N 71°25E **242** H4
Little Red ➔ *U.S.A.* 35°11N 91°27W **314** D9
Little Red School House Nature Center *U.S.A.* 41°42N 87°51W **119** C1
Little River *N.Z.* 43°45S 172°49E **285** D7
Little Rock *U.S.A.* 34°45N 92°17W **314** D8
Little Rouge ➔ *Canada* 43°45N 79°11W **141** A4
Little Ruaha ➔ *Tanzania* 7°57S 37°53E **268** D4
Little Sable Pt. *U.S.A.* 43°38N 86°33W **308** D10
Little Scarcies ➔ *S. Leone* 8°50N 13°10W **262** D2
Little Sioux ➔ *U.S.A.* 41°48N 96°4W **308** E5
Little Sitkin I. *U.S.A.* 51°57N 178°31E **303** L2
Little Smoky ➔ *Canada* 54°44N 117°11W **296** C5
Little Snake ➔ *U.S.A.* 40°27N 108°26W **304** F9
Little Sound *Bermuda* 32°15N 64°50W **153** a
Little Tokyo *Los Angeles, U.S.A.* **127** c2
Little Valley *U.S.A.* 42°15N 78°48W **312** D6
Little Wabash ➔ *U.S.A.* 37°55N 88°5W **311** G8
Little White ➔ *U.S.A.* 43°40N 100°40W **308** D3
Little York *U.S.A.* 41°1N 90°45W **310** C6
Little Zab = Zāb aş Şaghīr ➔ *Iraq* 35°17N 43°29E **213** E10
Littlefield *U.S.A.* 33°55N 102°20W **314** E3
Littlehampton *U.K.* 50°49N 0°32W **169** G7
Littleton *U.S.A.* 44°18N 71°46W **313** B13
Littoral ☐ *Cameroon* 4°0N 10°0E **263** E7
Littoria = Latina *Italy* 41°28N 12°52E **200** A5
Litunga *Angola* 13°19S 16°48E **265** E3
Litvinov *Czech Rep.* 50°36N 13°37E **180** A6
Liu He ➔ *Jilin, China* 42°46N 126°13E **224** A3
Liu He ➔ *Liaoning, China* 40°55N 121°35E **227** D11
Liu Jiang ➔ *China* 23°55N 109°30E **228** F7
Liuba *China* 33°38N 106°55E **226** H4
Liucheng *China* 24°38N 109°14E **228** E7
Liuchia *Taiwan* 23°13N 120°21E **225** C2
Liuch'iu *Taiwan* 22°21N 120°23E **225** D2
Liuch'iu Yü *Taiwan* 22°21N 120°22E **225** D2
Liugou *China* 40°57N 118°15E **227** D10
Liuhang *China* 31°21N 121°21E **138** A1
Liuhe *China* 42°17N 125°43E **224** A2
Liuheng Dao *China* 29°40N 122°5E **229** C14
Liujiang *China* 24°26N 109°11E **228** E7
Liukang Tenggaja = Sabalana, Kepulauan *Indonesia* 6°45S 118°50E **231** F5
Liuli *Tanzania* 11°3S 34°38E **269** E3
Liupanshui *China* 26°38N 104°48E **228** D5
Liurong Temple *China* 23°8N 113°15E **121** B2
Liuwa Plain *Zambia* 14°20S 22°30E **265** E4
Liuwa Plain △ *Zambia* 14°45S 22°35E **265** E4
Liuyang *China* 28°10N 113°37E **229** C9
Liuying *Taiwan* 23°17N 120°18E **225** C2
Liuzhou *China* 24°22N 109°22E **228** E7
Liuzhuang *China* 33°12N 120°18E **227** H11
Livada *Romania* 47°52N 23°5E **182** C8
Livadero *Greece* 40°2N 21°57E **202** F5
Livadhia *Cyprus* 34°57N 33°38E **207** F9
Livadhje *Albania* 39°47N 20°7E **206** B10
Livadi *Greece* 40°8N 22°9E **204** A4
Livadia *Greece* 38°27N 22°54E **204** C4
Livarot *France* 48°58N 0°9E **172** D7
Live Oak *Calif., U.S.A.* 39°17N 121°40W **306** F5
Live Oak *Fla., U.S.A.* 30°18N 82°59W **316** E7
Live Oak Manor *U.S.A.* 29°57N 90°14W **131** B1
Lively *Canada* 46°26N 81°9W **309** B13
Livengood *U.S.A.* 65°32N 148°33W **303** D10
Liveras *Cyprus* 35°23N 32°57E **207** E8
Livermore *U.S.A.* 37°41N 121°47W **306** H5
Livermore, Mt. *U.S.A.* 30°38N 104°11W **314** F2
Livermore Falls *U.S.A.* 44°29N 70°11W **309** C18
Liverpool *N.S.W., Australia* 33°54S 150°58E **283** B9
Liverpool *N.S., Canada* 44°5N 64°41W **299** D7
Liverpool *Mersey., U.K.* 53°25N 3°0W **168** D4
Liverpool *N.Y., U.S.A.* 43°6N 76°13W **313** C8
Liverpool Bay *U.K.* 53°30N 3°20W **168** D4
Liverpool Plains *Australia* 31°15S 150°15E **283** A9
Liverpool Ra. *Australia* 31°50S 150°30E **283** A9
Liverpool Street *London, U.K.* **125** a5
Livigno *Italy* 46°35N 10°10E **198** B7
Livingston *Guatemala* 15°50N 88°50W **320** C2
Livingston *W. Loth., U.K.* 55°54N 3°30W **167** F5
Livingston *Ala., U.S.A.* 32°35N 88°11W **315** E10
Livingston *Calif., U.S.A.* 37°23N 120°43W **306** H6
Livingston *Mont., U.S.A.* 45°40N 110°34W **304** D8
Livingston *S.C., U.S.A.* 33°38N 81°7W **315** E14
Livingston *Tenn., U.S.A.* 36°23N 85°19W **315** C12
Livingston *Tex., U.S.A.* 30°43N 94°56W **314** F7
Livingston *Wis., U.S.A.* 42°54N 90°26W **310** B6
Livingston, L. *U.S.A.* 30°50N 95°10W **314** F7
Livingston Manor *U.S.A.* 41°54N 74°50W **313** E10
Livingstone *Zambia* 17°46S 25°52E **269** F2
Livingstone △ *Australia* 35°22S 147°22E **283** C7
Livingstone Mts. *N.Z.* 45°15S 168°9E **285** F3
Livingstone Mts. *Tanzania* 9°40S 34°20E **269** D3
Livingstonia *Malawi* 10°38S 34°5E **269** E3
Livno *Bos.-H.* 43°50N 17°1E **182** G2
Livny *Russia* 52°30N 37°30E **189** F9
Livonia *Mich., U.S.A.* 42°23N 83°23W **311** B13
Livonia *N.Y., U.S.A.* 42°49N 77°40W **312** D7
Livorno *Italy* 43°33N 10°19E **198** E7
Livradois-Forez ⌂ *France* 44°0N 3°0E **174** E7
Livramento = Nossa Senhora do Livramento *Brazil* 15°48S 56°22W **331** D6
Livramento *Brazil* 30°55S 55°30W **335** C4
Livramento do Brumado *Brazil* 13°39S 41°50W **333** D3
Livron-sur-Drôme *France* 44°46N 4°51E **175** D8
Livry-Gargan *France* 48°55N 2°31E **134** A4
Livyntsi *Ukraine* 48°25N 26°37E **183** B11
Liwale *Tanzania* 9°48S 37°58E **269** D4
Liwan *China* 23°3N 113°13E **121** B2
Liwiec ➔ *Poland* 52°36N 21°34E **185** F8
Liwonde *Malaysia* 15°4S 35°13E **269** F4
Liwonde △ *Malawi* 14°48S 35°20E **269** E4
Lixi *China* 26°23N 101°59E **228** D3
Lixian *China* 31°23N 103°13E **228** B4
Lixouri *Greece* 38°12N 20°26E **207** C2
Liyang *China* 31°26N 119°28E **229** B12
Lizard ➔ *Trin. & Tob.* 10°9N 61°1W **323** t
Lizard I. *Australia* 14°42S 145°30E **280** A4
Lizard Pt. *U.K.* 49°57N 5°13W **169** H2
Lizarda *Brazil* 9°36S 46°41W **332** C2
Lizarra = Estella *Spain* 42°40N 2°2W **196** C2
Lizella *U.S.A.* 32°48N 83°49W **316** C6
Lizzano *Italy* 40°23N 17°27E **201** B10
Ljan *Norway* 59°50N 10°46E **133** A3
Ljig *Serbia* 44°13N 20°18E **202** B4
Ljøra ➔ *Norway* 61°24N 12°35E **164** C9
Ljørdalen *Norway* 61°23N 12°41E **164** C9
Ljosland *Norway* 58°47N 7°22E **164** F4
Ljubija *Bos.-H.* 44°55N 16°35E **199** D13
Ljubinje *Bos.-H.* 42°58N 18°5E **202** D2
Ljubišnja *Europe* 43°18N 19°6E **202** C3
Ljubljana *Slovenia* 46°4N 14°33E **199** B11
Ljubljana ✈ (LJU) *Slovenia* 46°14N 14°33E **199** B11
Ljubno *Slovenia* 46°25N 14°46E **199** B11
Ljubovija *Serbia* 44°11N 19°22E **202** B3
Ljugarn *Sweden* 57°20N 18°43E **163** G12
Ljung *Sweden* 57°59N 13°3E **163** G7
Ljungan ➔ *Sweden* 62°18N 17°23E **162** B11
Ljungaverk *Sweden* 62°30N 16°5E **162** B10
Ljungby *Sweden* 56°49N 13°55E **163** H7
Ljungbyholm *Sweden* 56°39N 16°5E **163** H10
Ljungdalen *Sweden* 62°51N 12°47E **162** B6
Ljungsbro *Sweden* 58°31N 15°30E **163** F9
Ljungskile *Sweden* 58°14N 11°55E **163** F5
Ljusdal *Sweden* 61°46N 16°3E **162** C10
Ljusfallshammar *Sweden* 58°48N 15°30E **163** F9
Ljusnan ➔ *Sweden* 61°12N 17°8E **162** C11
Ljusne *Sweden* 61°13N 17°7E **162** C11
Ljutomer *Slovenia* 46°31N 16°11E **199** B13
Llagostera *Spain* 41°50N 2°54E **196** D7
Llamellín *Peru* 9°0S 76°54W **330** B2
Llancanelo, Salina *Argentina* 35°40S 69°8W **334** D2
Llandeilo *U.K.* 51°53N 3°59W **169** F4
Llandovery *U.K.* 51°59N 3°48W **169** F4
Llandrindod Wells *U.K.* 52°14N 3°22W **169** E4
Llandudno *U.K.* 53°19N 3°50W **168** D4
Llanelli *U.K.* 51°41N 4°10W **169** F3
Llanes *Spain* 43°25N 4°50W **194** B6
Llanganates △ *Ecuador* 0°51S 72°20W **328** D3
Llangollen *U.K.* 52°58N 3°11W **168** E4
Llanidloes *U.K.* 52°27N 3°31W **169** E4
Llano *U.S.A.* 30°45N 98°41W **314** F5
Llano ➔ *U.S.A.* 30°39N 98°26W **314** F5
Llano de Can Gineu *Spain* 41°27N 2°10E **114** A2
Llano Estacado *U.S.A.* 33°30N 103°0W **314** E3
Llanos *S. Amer.* 5°0N 71°35W **326** C3
Llanos de Challe △ *Chile* 28°8S 71°1W **334** B1
Llanquihue, L. *Chile* 41°10S 72°50W **336** B1
Llanwrtyd Wells *U.K.* 52°7N 3°38W **169** E4
Llata *Peru* 9°25S 76°47W **330** B2
Llebeig, C. des *Spain* 39°33N 2°18E **206** B3
Lleida *Spain* 41°37N 0°39E **196** D5
Lleida ☐ *Spain* 42°6N 1°0E **196** C6
Llentrisca, C. *Spain* 38°52N 1°15E **206** D1
Llera de Canales *Mexico* 23°19N 99°1W **319** C5
Llerena *Spain* 38°17N 6°0W **195** G5
Llevant, Sa. de *Spain* 39°35N 3°17E **206** B4
Lleyn Peninsula *U.K.* 52°51N 4°36W **168** E3
Llica *Bolivia* 19°52S 68°16W **330** D4
Llico *Chile* 34°46S 72°5W **334** C1
Lliria *Spain* 39°37N 0°35W **197** F4
Llívia *Spain* 42°28N 1°59E **174** F5
Llobregat ➔ *Spain* 41°19N 2°5E **196** D7
Llodio *Spain* 43°9N 2°58W **196** B2
Llorente *Phil.* 11°25N 125°33E **233** F5
Lloret de Mar *Spain* 41°41N 2°53E **196** D7
Lloseta *Spain* 39°43N 2°52E **206** B3
Lloyd B. *Australia* 12°45S 143°27E **280** A3
Lloyd L. *Canada* 57°22N 108°57W **297** B7
Lloydminster *Canada* 53°17N 110°0W **297** C7
Llubí *Spain* 39°42N 3°0E **206** B4
Llucena del Cid *Spain* 40°9N 0°17W **196** E4
Llucmajor *Spain* 39°29N 2°53E **206** B3
Lluidas Vale *Jamaica* 18°6N 77°5W **320** a
Llullaillaco, Volcán *S. Amer.* 24°43S 68°30W **334** A2
Llullaillaco △ *Chile* 24°50S 68°51W **334** A2
Lo ➔ *Vietnam* 21°18N 105°25E **236** B5
Lo Aranguiz *Chile* 33°23S 70°40W **137** B2
Lo Boza *Chile* 33°23S 70°43W **137** B1
Lo Chau *China* 22°11N 114°15E **122** B2
Lo Chau Pak Mai *China* 22°11N 114°14E **122** B2
Lo Espejo *Chile* 33°31S 70°42W **137** C1
Lo Hermida *Chile* 33°28S 70°33W **137** B2
Lo Prado *Chile* 33°26S 70°42W **137** B1
Lo So Shing *China* 22°12N 114°7E **122** B1
Lo Wai *China* 22°22N 114°8E **122** A1
Loa *U.S.A.* 38°24N 111°39W **304** G8
Loa ➔ *Chile* 21°26S 70°41W **334** A1
Loagan Bunut △ *Malaysia* 3°32N 114°40E **235** B4
Loaita I. *S. China Sea* 10°41N 114°25E **230** B4
Loange ➔ *Dem. Rep. of the Congo* 4°17S 20°2E **265** C4
Loango *Congo* 4°38S 11°50E **265** C2
Loanhead *U.K.* 55°53N 3°9W **121** B3
Loano *Italy* 44°8N 8°15E **198** D5
Loay *Phil.* 9°36N 124°1E **233** G5
Lobamba *Swaziland* 26°28S 31°12E **271** C5
Lobatse *Botswana* 25°12S 25°40E **270** C4
Lobau *Wien, Austria* 48°10N 16°31E **142** A3
Löbau *Sachsen, Germany* 51°5N 14°40E **178** D10
Lobaye ➔ *C.A.R.* 3°41N 18°35E **264** B3
Loben = Lubliniec *Poland* 50°43N 18°45E **185** H5
Lobenstein *Germany* 50°25N 11°39E **178** E7
Lobería *Argentina* 38°10S 58°40W **334** D4
Löberöd *Sweden* 55°47N 13°31E **163** J7
Łobez *Poland* 53°38N 15°39E **184** E2
Lobito *Angola* 12°18S 13°35E **265** E2
Lobo *Phil.* 13°39N 121°13E **232** E3
Lobo ➔ *Ivory C.* 6°2N 6°45W **262** D3
Lobos *Argentina* 35°10S 59°0W **334** D4
Lobos, I. *Mexico* 27°20N 110°36W **318** B2
Lobos, I. de *Canary Is.* 28°45N 13°50W **153** e2
Lobos, Pt. *U.S.A.* 37°46N 122°30W **136** B1
Lobos de Afuera, Islas *Peru* 6°57S 80°42W **330** B1
Lobos de Tierra, I. *Peru* 6°27S 80°52W **330** B1
Łobżenica *Poland* 53°18N 17°15E **185** E4
Loc Binh *Vietnam* 21°46N 106°54E **236** B6
Loc Ninh *Vietnam* 11°50N 106°34E **237** G6
Locarno *Switz.* 46°10N 8°47E **179** J4
Loch Baghasdail = Lochboisdale *U.K.* 57°9N 7°20W **167** D1
Loch Garman = Wexford *Ireland* 52°20N 6°28W **166** D5
Loch Lomond and the Trossachs △ *U.K.* 56°10N 4°40W **167** E4
Loch Nam Madadh = Lochmaddy *U.K.* 57°36N 7°10W **167** D1
Lochaber *U.K.* 56°59N 5°1W **167** E3
Locham *Germany* 48°7N 11°26E **131** B1
Locharbriggs *U.K.* 55°7N 3°35W **167** F5
Lochboisdale *U.K.* 57°9N 7°20W **167** D1
Loche, L. La *Canada* 56°30N 109°30W **297** B7
Lochem *Neths.* 52°9N 6°26E **170** B6
Loches *France* 47°7N 1°0E **172** E7
Lochgilphead *U.K.* 56°2N 5°26W **167** E3
Lochino *Russia* 55°41N 37°17E **129** B1
Lochinvar △ *Zambia* 15°55S 27°15E **269** F2
Lochinver *U.K.* 58°9N 5°14W **167** C3
Lochkov *Czech Rep.* 50°0N 14°21E **135** B2
Lochloosa L. *U.S.A.* 29°30N 82°7W **317** F7
Lochmaddy *U.K.* 57°36N 7°10W **167** D1
Lochnagar *Queens., Australia* 23°33S 145°38E **280** C4
Lochnagar *Aberds., U.K.* 56°57N 3°15W **167** E5
Łochów *Poland* 52°33N 21°42E **185** F8
Lochy, L. *U.K.* 57°0N 4°53W **167** E4
Lock *Australia* 33°34S 135°46E **281** E2
Lock Haven *U.S.A.* 41°8N 77°28W **312** E7
Lockeford *U.S.A.* 38°10N 121°9W **306** G5
Lockeport *Canada* 43°47N 65°4W **299** D6
Lockerbie *U.K.* 55°7N 3°21W **167** F5
Lockhart *N.S.W., Australia* 35°14S 146°40E **283** C7
Lockhart *Tex., U.S.A.* 29°53N 97°40W **314** G6
Lockhart, L. *Australia* 33°15S 119°3E **279** F2
Lockhart River *Australia* 12°58S 143°30E **280** A3
Lockhart River ✪ *Australia* 12°47S 143°20E **280** A3
Lockhausen *Germany* 48°10N 11°24E **131** A1
Lockney *U.S.A.* 34°7N 101°27W **314** D4
Lockport *Ill., U.S.A.* 41°35N 88°3W **311** C8
Lockport *N.Y., U.S.A.* 43°10N 78°42W **312** C6
Locminé *France* 47°54N 2°51W **172** E4
Locri *Italy* 38°14N 16°16E **201** D9
Locronan *France* 48°7N 4°15W **172** D2
Locust Cr. ➔ *U.S.A.* 39°40N 93°17W **310** E3
Locust Grove *U.S.A.* 33°21N 84°7W **316** B5
Lod *Israel* 31°57N 34°54E **251** G5
Lodalskåpa *Norway* 61°47N 7°13E **164** C4
Lodeinoye Pole *Russia* 60°44N 33°33E **188** B7
Lodève *France* 43°44N 3°19E **174** E7
Lodge Bay *Canada* 52°14N 55°51W **299** B8
Lodge Grass *U.S.A.* 45°19N 107°22W **304** D10
Lodhran *Pakistan* 29°32N 71°30E **242** E4
Lodi *Italy* 45°19N 9°30E **198** C6
Lodi *Calif., U.S.A.* 38°8N 121°16W **306** G5
Lodi *N.J., U.S.A.* 40°52N 74°5W **132** A1
Lodi *Ohio, U.S.A.* 41°2N 82°1W **312** E3
Lodi Estate *India* 28°36N 77°15E **120** B2
Lodja *Dem. Rep. of the Congo* 3°30S 23°23E **264** C4
Lodosa *Spain* 42°25N 2°4W **196** C2
Lödöse *Sweden* 58°2N 12°9E **163** F6
Lodwar *Kenya* 3°7N 35°36E **268** B4
Łódź *Poland* 51°45N 19°27E **185** G6
Łódzkie ☐ *Poland* 51°30N 19°30E **185** G6
Loei *Thailand* 17°29N 101°35E **236** D3
Loengo *Dem. Rep. of the Congo* 4°48S 26°30E **265** C5
Loeriesfontein *S. Africa* 31°0S 19°26E **270** D2
Lofa ➔ *Liberia* 6°35N 11°8W **263** D2
Lofa Mano △ *Liberia* 7°55N 10°25W **262** D2
Lofer *Austria* 47°35N 12°41E **180** D5
Lofoten *Norway* 68°30N 13°59E **160** B16
Lofsdalen *Sweden* 62°10N 13°20E **162** B7
Lofsen ➔ *Sweden* 62°7N 13°57E **162** B7
Loftahammar *Sweden* 57°54N 16°41E **163** G10
Loga *Niger* 13°40N 3°15E **263** C5
Logan *Iowa, U.S.A.* 41°39N 95°47W **308** E6
Logan *Ohio, U.S.A.* 39°32N 82°25W **309** F12
Logan *Utah, U.S.A.* 41°44N 111°50W **304** F8
Logan *W. Va., U.S.A.* 37°51N 81°59W **309** G13
Logan, Mt. *Canada* 60°34N 140°23W **294** E3
Logan Int., Boston ✈ (BOS) *U.S.A.* 42°22N 71°1W **116** A2
Logan Martin L. *U.S.A.* 33°26N 86°20W **316** B3
Logan Square *U.S.A.* 41°55N 87°42W **119** B2
Logandale *U.S.A.* 36°36N 114°29W **307** J12
Logansport *Ind., U.S.A.* 40°45N 86°22W **311** D10
Logansport *La., U.S.A.* 31°58N 94°0W **314** F8
Logirim *Sudan* 4°43N 33°14E **257** G3
Lognes-Émerainville ✈ (XLG) *France* 48°49N 2°37E **134** B4
Logo *Sudan* 5°20N 30°18E **257** F3
Logone ➔ *Chad* 12°6N 15°2E **259** F3
Logone Gana *Chad* 11°36N 15°4E **259** F3
Logone Occidental ☐ *Chad* 8°30N 16°0E **259** G3
Logone Occidental ➔ *Chad* 8°50N 16°0E **259** G3
Logone Oriental ☐ *Chad* 8°30N 16°30E **259** G3
Logone Orientale ➔ *Chad* 9°7N 16°26E **259** G3
Logroño *Spain* 42°28N 2°27W **196** C2
Logrosán *Spain* 39°20N 5°32W **195** F5
Løgstør *Denmark* 56°58N 9°14E **163** H3
Logtak L. *India* 24°33N 93°50E **241** C4
Løgumkloster *Denmark* 55°4N 8°57E **163** J2
Loh *Vanuatu* 13°21S 166°38E **287** C4
Lohals *Denmark* 55°8N 10°55E **163** J4
Lohardaga *India* 23°27N 84°45E **243** H11
Loharia *India* 23°45N 74°14E **242** H6
Loharu *India* 28°27N 75°49E **242** E6
Lohja *Finland* 60°12N 24°5E **188** B3
Löhme *Germany* 52°37N 13°40E **115** A5
Löhne *Germany* 52°11N 8°40E **178** C4
Loho = Luohe *China* 33°32N 114°2E **226** H8
Lohr *Germany* 49°59N 9°35E **179** F5
Lohri Wah ➔ *Pakistan* 27°27N 67°37E **242** F2
Loi-kaw *Burma* 19°40N 97°17E **241** F6
Loi-lem *Burma* 20°52N 97°28E **241** E6
Loimaa *Finland* 60°50N 23°5E **188** B2
Loir ➔ *France* 47°33N 0°32W **172** E6
Loir-et-Cher ☐ *France* 47°40N 1°20E **172** E8
Loire ☐ *France* 45°40N 4°5E **175** C8
Loire ➔ *France* 47°16N 2°10W **172** E4
Loire Anjou Touraine ⌂ *France* 47°14N 0°5W **172** E6
Loire-Atlantique ☐ *France* 47°25N 1°40W **172** E5
Loire Inférieure = Loire-Atlantique ☐ *France* 47°25N 1°40W **172** E5
Loiret ☐ *France* 47°55N 2°30E **173** E9
Loitz *Germany* 53°58N 13°8E **178** B9
Loja *Ecuador* 3°59S 79°16W **330** A2
Loja *Spain* 37°10N 4°10W **195** H6
Loja ☐ *Ecuador* 4°0S 79°13W **328** D2
Loje ➔ *Angola* 7°49S 13°6E **265** D2
Loji = Kawasi *Indonesia* 1°38S 127°28E **231** E7
Lojo = Lohja *Finland* 60°12N 24°5E **188** B3
Løjt Kirkeby *Denmark* 55°7N 9°26E **163** J3
Lojung *China* 24°27N 109°36E **228** E7
Loka *Dem. Rep. of the Congo* 0°22N 18°2E **264** B3
Loka *Sudan* 4°13N 31°0E **257** G3
Lokako *Dem. Rep. of the Congo* 0°57S 18°55E **264** C4
Lokandu *Dem. Rep. of the Congo* 2°30S 25°45E **264** C5
Lokaw *Dem. Rep. of the Congo* 2°40S 20°12E **264** C4
Løken *Norway* 59°48N 11°29E **164** E8
Lokeren *Belgium* 51°6N 3°59E **170** C3
Lokgwabe *Botswana* 24°10S 21°50E **270** B3
Lokhvitsa *Ukraine* 50°25N 33°18E **189** G7
Lokichar *Kenya* 2°23N 35°39E **268** B4
Lokichokio *Kenya* 4°19N 34°13E **268** B3
Lokitaung *Kenya* 4°12N 35°48E **268** B4
Lokkan tekojärvi *Finland* 67°55N 27°35E **160** C22
Løkken *Denmark* 57°22N 9°41E **163** G3
Løkken *Sør-Trøndelag, Norway* 63°9N 9°41E **164** A6
Loknya *Russia* 56°49N 30°4E **188** D6
Loko *C.A.R.* 3°38N 18°2E **264** B3
Loko *Nigeria* 8°1N 7°53E **263** D6
Lokoja *Nigeria* 7°47N 6°45E **263** D6
Lokolama *Dem. Rep. of the Congo* 2°35S 19°50E **264** C3
Lokolenge *Dem. Rep. of the Congo* 1°12N 22°38E **264** B4
Lokolo ➔ *Dem. Rep. of the Congo* 1°43S 18°23E **264** C3
Lokot *Russia* 52°34N 34°36E **189** F8
Loktak L. = Logtak L. *India* 24°33N 93°50E **241** C4
Lokuru *Solomon Is.* 8°20S 157°0E **287** M9
Lol *Sudan* 6°26N 29°37E **257** F2
Lol ➔ *Sudan* 9°13N 26°30E **257** F2
Lola *Angola* 14°19S 13°37E **265** E2
Lola *Guinea* 7°52N 8°29W **262** D3
Lola, Mt. *U.S.A.* 39°26N 120°22W **306** F6
Lolgorien *Kenya* 1°14S 34°48E **268** C3
Lolibai, Gebel *Sudan* 3°50N 33°0E **257** G3
Lolimi *Sudan* 4°35N 34°0E **257** G3
Loliondo *Tanzania* 2°2S 35°39E **268** C4
Lolland *Denmark* 54°45N 11°30E **163** K5
Lollar *Germany* 50°37N 8°43E **178** E4
Lolo *U.S.A.* 46°45N 114°5W **304** C6
Lolo ➔ *Eq. Guin.* 1°36N 9°37E **264** B1
Lolo ➔ *Gabon* 0°18S 12°18E **264** C2
Lolobau I. *Papua N. G.* 4°55S 151°10E **286** C6
Lolodorf *Cameroon* 3°16N 10°49E **263** E7
Lolokhet *Pakistan* 24°54N 67°2E **123** A2
Loloma *Zambia* 13°24S 24°21E **265** E4
Loltong *Vanuatu* 15°32S 168°10E **287** E6
Lom *Bulgaria* 43°48N 23°12E **202** C7
Lom *Oppland, Norway* 61°50N 8°34E **164** C5
Lom ➔ *Bulgaria* 43°45N 23°15E **202** C7
Lom ➔ *Cameroon* 5°20N 13°24E **264** A2
Lom Kao *Thailand* 16°53N 101°14E **236** D3
Lom Sak *Thailand* 16°47N 101°15E **236** D3
Loma *U.S.A.* 47°56N 110°30W **304** C8
Loma Linda *U.S.A.* 34°3N 117°16W **307** L9
Loma Mansa *S. Leone* 9°13N 11°7W **262** D2
Loma Mts. *S. Leone* 9°10N 11°7W **262** D2
Lomako ➔ *Dem. Rep. of the Congo* 0°50N 20°50E **264** B4
Lomaloma *Fiji* 17°17S 178°59W **287** A3
Lomami ➔ *Dem. Rep. of the Congo* 0°46N 24°16E **264** B4
Lomas Chapultepec *Mexico* 19°25N 99°12W **128** B1
Lomas de San Angel Inn *Mexico* 19°20N 99°13W **128** B1
Lomas de Zamora *Argentina* 34°45S 58°24W **334** C4
Lombadina *Australia* 16°31S 122°54E **278** C3
Lombard *U.S.A.* 41°53N 88°1W **311** C8
Lombárdia ☐ *Italy* 45°40N 9°30E **198** C6
Lombardy = Lombárdia ☐ *Italy* 45°40N 9°30E **198** C6
Lombardy East *S. Africa* 26°6S 28°7E **123** A2
Lombe *Angola* 9°27S 16°13E **265** D3
Lombez *France* 43°29N 0°55E **174** E4
Lomblen *Indonesia* 8°30S 123°32E **231** F6
Lombok *Indonesia* 8°45S 116°30E **235** D5
Lombok, Selat *Indonesia* 8°30S 115°50E **231** K18
Lomé *Togo* 6°9N 1°20E **263** D5
Lomela *Dem. Rep. of the Congo* 2°19S 23°15E **264** C4
Lomela ➔ *Dem. Rep. of the Congo* 0°15S 20°40E **264** C4
Lomianki *Poland* 52°21N 20°54E **142** A1
Lomié *Cameroon* 3°13N 13°38E **264** B2
Lomma *Sweden* 55°43N 13°6E **163** J7
Lommel *Belgium* 51°14N 5°19E **170** C5
Lomond *Canada* 50°24N 112°36W **296** C6
Lomond, L. *U.K.* 56°8N 4°38W **167** E4
Lomonosov Ridge *Arctic* 88°0N 140°0E **150** A
Lomphat *Cambodia* 13°30N 106°59E **236** F6
Lompobatang *Indonesia* 5°24S 119°56E **231** F5
Lompoc *U.S.A.* 34°38N 120°28W **307** L6
Lomseggje *Norway* 61°49N 8°21E **164** C5
Lomus Reforma *Mexico* 19°24N 99°14W **128** B1
Łomża *Poland* 53°10N 22°2E **185** E9
Lon, Ko *Thailand* 7°47N 98°23E **237** a
Lonavale *India* 18°46N 73°29E **244** E1
Loncoche *Chile* 39°20S 72°50W **336** A2
Loncopué *Argentina* 38°4S 70°37W **336** A2
Londa *India* 15°30N 74°30E **245** G2
Londiani *Kenya* 0°10S 35°33E **268** C4
Londinières *France* 49°50N 1°25E **172** C8
London *Ont., Canada* 42°59N 81°15W **312** D3
London *London, U.K.* 51°30N 0°3W **125** B3
London *Ky., U.S.A.* 37°8N 84°5W **309** G11
London *Ohio, U.S.A.* 39°53N 83°27W **311** E13
London, Greater ☐ *U.K.* 51°36N 0°5W **169** F7
London Avenue Canal *U.S.A.* 30°3N 90°6W **131** A2
London Bridge *Grenada* 12°15N 61°35W **323** q
London Bridge *London, U.K.* **125** b5
London City ✈ (LCY) *U.K.* 51°30N 0°3E **125** A4
London Gatwick ✈ (LGW) *U.K.* 51°10N 0°11W **169** F7

London Heathrow ✈ (LHR) U.K. 51°28N 0°27W **125** B1
London Mills U.S.A. 40°43N 90°11W **310** D6
London Stansted ✈ (STN) U.K. 51°54N 0°14E **169** F8
London Zoo U.K. 51°31N 0°9W **125** A3
Londonderry U.K. 55°0N 7°20W **166** B4
Londonderry □ U.K. 55°0N 7°20W **166** B4
Londonderry, C. Australia 13°45S 126°55E **278** B4
Londonderry, I. Chile 55°0S 71°0W **336** E2
Londrina Brazil 23°18S 51°10W **335** A5
Londuimbale Angola 12°15S 15°19E **265** E3
Lone Pine U.S.A. 36°36N 118°4W **306** J8
Lonely Mine Zimbabwe 19°30S 28°49E **271** A4
Long, Î. Martinique 14°36N 60°51W **322** j
Long Akah Malaysia 3°19N 114°47E **235** B4
Long B. N.S.W., Australia 33°59S 151°15E **139** B2
Long B. Cornwall, Jamaica 18°20N 78°20W **320** a
Long B. S.C., U.S.A. 33°35N 78°45W **315** E15
Long Beach Calif., U.S.A. 33°46N 118°11W **307** M8
Long Beach N.Y., U.S.A. 40°35N 73°39W **313** F11
Long Beach Wash., U.S.A. 46°21N 124°3W **306** D2
Long Branch Ont., Canada 43°35N 79°31W **141** B1
Long Branch N.J., U.S.A. 40°18N 74°0W **313** F11
Long Brook ➝ U.S.A. 38°49N 77°15W **143** C2
Long Cay Bahamas 25°6N 77°22W **153** b
Long Creek U.S.A. 44°43N 119°6W **304** D4
Long Ditton U.K. 51°22N 0°19W **125** B2
Long Eaton U.K. 52°53N 1°15W **168** E6
Long I. Antigua & B. 17°8N 61°45W **322** b
Long I. Queens., Australia 20°22S 148°51E **280** b
Long I. Bahamas 23°20N 75°10W **321** B4
Long I. Nunavut, Canada 54°50N 79°20W **298** B4
Long I. Cork, Ireland 51°30N 9°34W **166** E2
Long I. Papua N. G. 5°20S 147°5E **286** C4
Long I. N.Y., U.S.A. 40°45N 73°30W **313** F11
Long Island City U.S.A. 40°45N 73°56W **132** B2
Long Island Sd. U.S.A. 41°10N 73°0W **313** E12
Long L. Ont., Canada 49°30N 86°50W **298** C2
Long L. N.Y., U.S.A. 44°0N 74°23W **313** C10
Long Lake U.S.A. 43°58N 74°25W **313** C10
Long Mountain Mauritius 20°8S 57°33E **272** e
Long Point Canada 42°34N 80°25W **312** D4
Long Point B. Canada 42°40N 80°10W **312** D4
Long Prairie U.S.A. 45°59N 94°52W **308** C6
Long Prairie ➝ U.S.A. 46°20N 94°36W **308** B6
Long Pt. Bahamas 25°1N 77°20W **153** b
Long Pt. Ont., Canada 42°35N 80°2W **312** D4
Long Pt. Ont., Canada 43°56N 76°53W **313** C8
Long Pt. Otago, N.Z. 46°34S 169°36E **285** G4
Long Range Mts. Canada 49°30N 57°30W **299** C8
Long Reef Australia 14°1S 125°48E **278** B4
Long Sault Canada 45°2N 74°53W **313** A10
Long Str. = Longa, Proliv Russia 70°0N 175°0E **215** C18
Long Street Cape Town, S. Africa **118** c2
Long Thanh Vietnam 10°47N 106°57E **237** G6
Long Xian China 34°55N 106°55E **226** G4
Long Xuyen Vietnam 10°19N 105°28E **237** G5
Longa Angola 14°42S 18°32E **265** E3
Longa Greece 36°53N 21°55E **204** E3
Longa ➝ Angola 10°14S 13°29E **265** E2
Longa, Proliv Russia 70°0N 175°0E **215** C18
Longa Mavinga ⌂ Angola 16°20S 20°15E **265** F4
Long'an China 23°10N 107°40E **228** F6
Longana Vanuatu 15°18S 168°0E **287** E5
Longarone Italy 46°16N 12°18E **199** B9
Longbenton U.K. 55°1N 1°31W **168** B6
Longboat Key U.S.A. 27°23N 82°39W **317** H7
Longburn N.Z. 40°23S 175°35E **284** G4
Longchamp, Hippodrome de France 48°51N 2°13E **134** A2
Longchang China 29°18N 105°15E **228** C5
Longchi China 29°25N 103°24E **228** C4
Longchuan Guangdong, China 24°5N 115°17E **229** E10
Longchuan Yunnan, China 24°23N 97°58E **228** E1
Longde China 35°30N 106°20E **226** G4
Longdenville Trin. & Tob. 10°31N 61°23W **323** t
Longeau France 47°47N 5°20E **173** E12
Longford Tas., Australia 41°32S 147°3E **281** G4
Longford Longf., Ireland 53°43N 7°49W **166** C4
Longford □ Ireland 53°42N 7°45W **166** C4
Longgan Shan China 24°12N 120°36E **224** A3
Longhai China 24°25N 117°46E **229** E11
Longhua Guangdong, China 22°39N 114°0E **219** F11
Longhua Hebei, China 41°18N 117°45E **227** D9
Longhua Pagoda China 31°10N 121°26E **138** B1
Longhua Park China 31°10N 121°26E **138** B1
Longhui China 27°7N 111°2E **229** D8
Longido Tanzania 2°43S 36°42E **268** C4
Longiram Indonesia 0°5S 115°45E **235** C5
Longjohn Slough U.S.A. 41°42N 87°52W **119** C1
Longkou Jiangxi, China 26°8N 115°10E **229** D10
Longkou Shandong, China 37°40N 120°18E **227** F11
Longlac Canada 49°45N 86°25W **298** C2
Longli China 26°25N 106°58E **228** D6
Longlin China 24°47N 105°20E **228** E5
Longling China 24°37N 98°39E **228** E2
Longmeadow U.S.A. 42°3N 72°34W **313** D12
Longmen China 23°40N 114°18E **229** F10
Longming China 22°59N 107°7E **228** F6
Longmont U.S.A. 40°10N 105°6W **304** F11
Longnan China 24°55N 114°47E **229** E10
Longnawan Indonesia 1°51N 114°55E **235** B4
Longobucco Italy 39°27N 16°37E **201** C9
Longoni, B. de Mayotte 12°41S 45°8E **272** b
Longonot △ Kenya 0°55S 36°28E **266** E4
Longos Greece 39°16N 20°7E **206** C10
Longquan China 28°7N 119°10E **229** C12
Longreach Australia 23°28S 144°14E **280** C3
Longshan China 29°29N 109°25E **228** C7
Longsheng China 25°48N 110°0E **229** E8
Longtan He ➝ China 39°51N 116°24E **114** B2
Longué-Jumelles France 47°22N 0°8W **172** E6
Longue-Pointe Canada 45°35N 73°31W **130** A2
Longueau France 49°52N 2°21E **173** C9
Longueuil Canada 45°31N 73°29W **130** A3
Longuy Cameroon 3°5N 9°58E **264** B1
Longuyon France 49°27N 5°35E **173** C12
Longvic France 47°17N 5°4E **173** E12
Longview Tex., U.S.A. 32°30N 94°44W **314** E7
Longview Wash., U.S.A. 46°8N 122°57W **306** D4
Longwood St. Helena 15°57S 5°41W **153** h
Longwood Fla., U.S.A. 28°42N 81°21W **317** G8
Longwy France 49°30N 5°46E **173** C12
Longxi China 34°53N 104°40E **226** G3
Longxue Dao China 22°41N 113°38E **219** F10
Longyan China 25°10N 117°0E **229** E11
Longyearbyen Svalbard 78°13N 15°40E **150** B8
Longyou China 29°1N 119°8E **229** C12
Longzhou China 22°22N 106°50E **228** F6
Loni India 28°45N 77°17E **120** A2
Lonigo Italy 45°23N 11°23E **199** C8
Löningen Germany 52°44N 7°46E **178** C3
Lonja ➝ Croatia 45°22N 16°40E **199** C13
Lonkala Dem. Rep. of the Congo 4°37S 23°14E **265** C4
Lonkin Burma 25°39N 96°22E **241** C6
Lonoke U.S.A. 34°47N 91°54W **314** D9
Lonquimay Chile 38°26S 71°14W **336** A2
Lons-le-Saunier France 46°40N 5°31E **173** F12
Lönsboda Sweden 56°24N 14°20E **163** H8
Lønset Norway 62°46N 7°24E **164** B4
Lonton Burma 25°6N 96°17E **241** C6
Looe U.K. 50°22N 4°28W **169** G3
Loogootee U.S.A. 38°41N 86°55W **311** F10
Lookout, C. Canada 55°18N 83°56W **298** A3
Lookout, C. N.C., U.S.A. 34°35N 76°32W **315** D16
Loolmalasin Tanzania 3°0S 35°53E **268** C4
Loon ➝ Alta., Canada 57°8N 115°3W **296** B5
Loon ➝ Man., Canada 55°53N 101°59W **297** B8
Loon Lake Canada 54°2N 109°10W **297** C7
Loongana Australia 30°52S 127°5E **279** F4
Loop, The Chicago, U.S.A. **119** c1
Loop Hd. Ireland 52°34N 9°56W **166** D2
Lop China 37°3N 80°11E **217** E10
Lop Buri Thailand 14°48N 100°37E **236** E3
Lop Nor = Lop Nur China 40°20N 90°10E **217** D12
Lop Nur China 40°20N 90°10E **217** D12
Lopare Bos.-H. 44°39N 18°46E **182** F3
Lopatin Russia 43°50N 47°35E **191** J8
Lopatina, Gora Russia 50°47N 143°10E **215** D15
Lopatino = Volzhsk Russia 55°57N 48°23E **190** C9
Lopatka, Mys Russia 50°52N 156°40E **215** D16
Lopaye Sudan 6°37N 33°40E **257** F3
Lopé-Okanda ⌂ Gabon 0°45S 11°34E **264** C2
Lopevi Vanuatu 16°30S 168°21E **287** F6
Lopez Phil. 13°53N 122°15E **232** E4
Lopez Pa., U.S.A. 41°27N 76°20W **313** E8
Lopez, C. Gabon 0°47S 8°40E **264** C1
López de Filippis = Mariscal Estigarribia Paraguay 22°3S 60°40W **334** A3
Lopinot Trin. & Tob. 10°41N 61°19W **323** t
Lopori ➝ Dem. Rep. of the Congo 1°14N 19°49E **264** B3
Lopphavet Norway 70°27N 21°15E **160** A19
Lora Norway 62°8N 8°45E **164** B5
Lora ➝ Afghan. 31°35N 66°32E **240** C2
Lora ➝ Oppland, Norway 62°8N 8°42E **164** B5
Lora, Hāmūn-i- Pakistan 29°38N 64°58E **240** C2
Lora Cr. ➝ Australia 28°10S 135°22E **281** D2
Lora del Río Spain 37°39N 5°33W **195** H5
Lorain U.S.A. 41°28N 82°11W **312** E2
Loraine U.S.A. 40°9N 91°13W **310** D5
Loralai Pakistan 30°20N 68°41E **242** D3
Lorca Spain 37°41N 1°42W **197** H3
Lord Howe I. Pac. Oc. 31°33S 159°6E **277** G10
Lord Howe Rise Pac. Oc. 30°0S 162°30E **277** H12
Lord Howe Seamount Chain Pac. Oc. 28°0S 159°0E **277** F10
Lord's Cricket Ground U.K. 51°31N 0°10W **125** A2
Lordsburg U.S.A. 32°21N 108°43W **305** K9
Lorengau Papua N. G. 2°1S 147°15E **286** B4
Lorestān □ Iran 33°30N 48°40E **247** C6
Loreto Bolivia 15°13S 64°40W **331** D5
Loreto Brazil 7°5S 45°10W **332** C2
Loreto Marche, Italy 43°26N 13°36E **199** E10
Loreto Piemonte, Italy 45°29N 9°12E **129** B2
Loreto Baja Calif. S., Mexico 26°0N 111°21W **318** B2
Loreto Surigao N., Phil. 10°21N 125°34E **233** F5
Loreto □ Peru 5°0S 75°0W **328** E3
Lorgues France 43°28N 6°22E **175** E10
Lorhosso Burkina Faso 10°17N 3°38W **262** C4
Lorian Swamp Kenya 0°40N 39°35E **267** D4
Lorica Colombia 9°14N 75°49W **328** B2
Lorient Morbihan, France 47°45N 3°23W **172** E3
Lorient St.-Martin 17°54N 62°49W **322** a
Lorimor U.S.A. 41°8N 94°3W **310** C2
Lőrinci Hungary 47°44N 19°41E **182** C4
Lormi India 22°17N 81°41E **243** H9
Lorn U.K. 56°26N 5°10W **167** E3
Lorn, Firth of U.K. 56°20N 5°40W **167** E3
Lorne Australia 38°33S 143°59E **282** E5
Lorono Sudan 4°38N 32°38E **257** G3
Lorovouno Cyprus 35°8N 32°36E **207** E8
Lörrach Germany 47°36N 7°40E **179** H3
Lorrain ➝ Martinique 14°50N 61°3W **322** j
Lorraine = Baker U.S.A. 46°22N 104°17W **304** C11
Lorraine □ France 48°53N 6°0E **173** D13
Lorraine ⌂ France 48°55N 5°50E **173** D12
Los Sweden 61°45N 15°10E **162** C9
Los, Îles de Guinea 9°30N 13°50W **262** D2
Los Alamos Calif., U.S.A. 34°44N 120°17W **307** L6
Los Alamos N. Mex., U.S.A. 35°53N 106°19W **305** J10
Los Alcornocales ⌂ Spain 36°21N 5°32W **195** J5
Los Alerces △ Argentina 42°55S 71°55W **336** B2
Los Altos U.S.A. 37°23N 122°7W **306** H4
Los Andes Chile 32°50S 70°40W **334** C1
Los Angeles Chile 37°28S 72°23W **334** D1
Los Angeles Calif., U.S.A. 34°4N 118°15W **126** B3
Los Angeles, Bahia de Mexico 28°56N 113°34W **318** B2
Los Angeles Aqueduct U.S.A. 35°22N 118°5W **307** K9
Los Angeles Int. ✈ (LAX) U.S.A. 33°57N 118°25W **126** C2
Los Antiguos Argentina 46°35S 71°40W **336** C2
Los Banos U.S.A. 37°4N 120°51W **306** H6
Los Barrios Spain 36°11N 5°30W **195** J5
Los Blancos Argentina 23°40S 62°30W **334** A3
Los Cardones △ Argentina 25°8S 65°55W **334** B2
Los Cerrillos ✈ (ULC) Chile 33°29S 70°42W **137** B1
Los Chiles Costa Rica 11°2N 84°43W **320** D3
Los Corrales de Buelna Spain 43°16N 4°4W **194** B6
Los Cristianos Canary Is. 28°3N 16°42W **153** e1
Los Gallardos Spain 37°10N 1°57W **197** H3
Los Gallos Pt. Trin. & Tob. 10°5N 61°55W **323** t
Los Gatos U.S.A. 37°14N 121°59W **306** H5
Los Glaciares △ Argentina 50°0S 73°55W **336** C2
Los Haïtises △ Dom. Rep. 19°4N 69°36W **321** C6
Los Hermanos Is. Venezuela 11°45N 64°25W **321** D7
Los Huemules △ Chile 46°10S 73°23W **336** C2
Los Islotes Canary Is. 29°4N 13°44W **153** e2
Los Katios △ Colombia 7°50N 77°10W **328** B2
Los Lagos Chile 39°51S 72°50W **336** A2
Los Llanos de Aridane Canary Is. 28°38N 17°54W **153** e1
Los Loros Chile 27°50S 70°6W **334** B1
Los Lunas U.S.A. 34°48N 106°44W **305** J10
Los Menucos Argentina 40°50S 68°10W **336** B3
Los Mochis Mexico 25°45N 108°57W **318** B3
Los Monegros Spain 41°29N 0°13W **196** D4
Los Monos Argentina 46°1S 69°36W **336** C3
Los Muermos Chile 41°24S 73°29W **336** B2
Los Nevados △ Colombia 4°41N 75°21W **328** C2
Los Nietos Spain 37°39N 0°47W **197** H4
Los Nietos Calif., U.S.A. 33°57N 118°4W **126** C4
Los Olivos Lima, Peru 11°59S 77°5W **124** A2
Los Olivos Calif., U.S.A. 34°40N 120°7W **307** L6
Los Palacios Cuba 22°35N 83°15W **320** B3
Los Palacios y Villafranca Spain 37°10N 5°55W **195** H5
Los Queñes Chile 35°1S 70°48W **334** D1
Los Remedios △ Mexico 19°28N 99°17W **128** B1
Los Reyes Mexico 19°21N 99°6W **128** B2
Los Reyes de Salgado Mexico 19°35N 102°29W **318** D4
Los Ríos □ Ecuador 1°30S 79°25W **328** D2
Los Roques Is. Venezuela 11°50N 66°45W **321** D6
Los Santos de Maimona Spain 38°27N 6°22W **195** G4
Los Teques Venezuela 10°21N 67°2W **328** A4
Los Testigos, Is. Venezuela 11°23N 63°6W **329** A5
Los Vilos Chile 32°10S 71°30W **334** C1
Los Yébenes Spain 39°36N 3°55W **195** F7
Loshan = Leshan China 29°33N 103°41E **228** C4
Losice Poland 52°13N 22°43E **185** F9
Lošinj Croatia 44°30N 14°30E **199** D11
Loskop Dam S. Africa 25°23S 29°20E **271** C4
Løsning Denmark 55°48N 9°42E **163** J3
Losombo Dem. Rep. of the Congo 1°2N 19°4E **264** B3
Lossiemouth U.K. 57°42N 3°17W **167** D5
Lossnen △ Sweden 62°26N 12°45E **162** B6
Lostwithiel U.K. 50°24N 4°41W **169** G3
Losuia Papua N. G. 8°30S 151°4E **286** E6
Lot Belgium 50°46N 4°16E **116** B1
Lot □ France 44°39N 1°40E **174** D5
Lot ➝ France 44°18N 0°20E **174** D4
Lot-et-Garonne □ France 44°22N 0°30E **174** D4
Lota Chile 37°5S 73°10W **334** D1
Lotagipi Swamp Sudan 4°36N 34°55E **257** G3
Løten Norway 60°51N 11°21E **164** D8
Lotfābād Iran 37°32N 59°20E **247** B8
Lothair S. Africa 26°22S 30°27E **271** C5
Loto Dem. Rep. of the Congo 2°48S 22°3E **264** C4
Lotoi ➝ Dem. Rep. of the Congo 1°35S 18°30E **264** C3
Lotorp Sweden 58°44N 15°50E **163** F9
Lötschbergtunnel Switz. 46°26N 7°43E **179** J3
Lotta ➝ Europe 68°42N 31°6E **160** B24
Löttorp Sweden 57°10N 17°0E **163** G11
Lotung Taiwan 24°41N 121°46E **225** B3
Lotus River S. Africa 34°4S 18°31E **118** B2
Lotus Temple India 28°33N 77°15E **120** B2
Lötzen = Giżycko Poland 54°2N 21°48E **184** D8
Lou I. Papua N. G. 2°25S 147°22E **286** B4
Loubière Dominica 15°16N 61°23W **323** k
Loubomo Congo 4°9S 12°47E **264** C2
Loudéac France 48°11N 2°47W **172** D4
Loudi China 27°42N 111°59E **229** D8
Loudima Congo 4°6S 13°5E **264** C2
Loudonville U.S.A. 40°38N 82°14W **312** F2
Loudun France 47°3N 0°5E **172** E7
Loue ➝ France 47°1N 5°28E **173** E12
Louga Senegal 15°45N 16°5W **262** B1
Louga □ Senegal 15°20N 15°35W **262** B1
Loughborough U.K. 52°47N 1°11W **168** E6
Lougheed I. Canada 77°26N 105°6W **295** B10
Loughlinstown Ireland 53°15N 6°7W **120** B3
Loughman U.S.A. 28°14N 81°34W **317** G8
Loughrea Ireland 53°12N 8°33W **166** C3
Loughros More B. Ireland 54°48N 8°32W **166** B3
Louhans France 46°38N 5°12E **173** F12
Louis Armstrong New Orleans Int. ✈ (MSY) U.S.A. 30°0N 90°15W **131** A1
Louis Armstrong Park New Orleans, U.S.A. **131** a2
Louis-Gentil = Youssoufia Morocco 32°16N 8°31W **260** B3
Louis Trichardt S. Africa 23°1S 29°43E **271** B4
Louis XIV, Pte. Canada 54°37N 79°45W **298** B4
Louisa U.S.A. 38°7N 82°36W **309** F12
Louisbourg Canada 45°55N 60°0W **299** C8
Louisburg U.S.A. 38°37N 94°41W **310** F2
Louisburgh Ireland 53°46N 9°49W **166** C2
Louise, L. U.S.A. 28°28N 81°32W **133** B1
Louise I. Canada 52°55N 131°50W **296** C2
Louiseville Canada 46°20N 72°56W **298** C5
Louisiade Arch. Papua N. G. 11°10S 153°0E **286** F7
Louisiana U.S.A. 39°27N 91°3W **310** E6
Louisiana □ U.S.A. 30°50N 92°0W **314** F9
Louisiana Superdome New Orleans, U.S.A. **131** b1
Louisville Ala., U.S.A. 31°47N 85°33W **316** D4
Louisville Ga., U.S.A. 33°0N 82°25W **316** B7
Louisville Ill., U.S.A. 38°46N 88°30W **311** F8
Louisville Ky., U.S.A. 38°15N 85°46W **311** F11
Louisville Miss., U.S.A. 33°7N 89°3W **315** E10
Louisville Ohio, U.S.A. 40°50N 81°16W **312** F3
Louisville Ridge Pac. Oc. 31°0S 172°30W **288** L10
Loukoléla Congo 1°4S 17°10E **264** C3
Loukouo Congo 3°38S 14°39E **264** C2
Loulay France 46°3N 0°30W **174** B3
Loulé Portugal 37°9N 8°0W **195** H3
Louloui Mali 10°54N 5°36W **262** C3
Loum Cameroon 4°42N 9°44E **264** B1
Louny Czech Rep. 50°20N 13°48E **180** A6
Loup City U.S.A. 41°17N 98°58W **308** E4
Loups Marins, Lacs des Canada 56°30N 73°45W **298** A5
Lourdes France 43°6N 0°3W **174** E3
Lourdes-du-Blanc-Sablon Canada 51°24N 57°12W **299** B8
Lourenço Brazil 2°30N 51°40W **329** C7
Lourenço Marques = Maputo Mozam. 25°58S 32°32E **271** C5
Loures Portugal 38°49N 9°10W **126** A1
Lourinhã Portugal 39°14N 9°17W **195** F1
Louros Greece 39°30N 20°47E **207** A2
Louroujina Cyprus 35°0N 33°28E **207** F9
Lousã Portugal 40°7N 8°14W **194** E2
Louta Burkina Faso 13°30N 3°10W **262** C4
Louth N.S.W., Australia 30°30S 145°8E **283** A6
Louth Louth, Ireland 53°58N 6°32W **166** C5
Louth Lincs., U.K. 53°22N 0°1W **168** D7
Louth □ Ireland 53°56N 6°34W **166** C5
Louth B. Australia 34°33S 135°56E **282** C1
Loutra Edipsou Greece 38°54N 23°2E **204** C5
Loutra Kyllinis Greece 37°52N 21°7E **207** D3
Loutraki Greece 37°58N 22°57E **204** D4
Loutropoli Thermis Greece 39°11N 26°29E **205** B8
Louvain = Leuven Belgium 50°52N 4°42E **170** D4
Louvale U.S.A. 32°10N 84°50W **316** C5
Louveciennes France 48°51N 2°8E **134** A1
Louviers France 49°12N 1°10E **172** C8
Louvre, Musée du Paris, France **134** b4
Louvre, Palais du Paris, France **134** b4
Louwsburg S. Africa 27°37S 31°7E **271** C5
Lovat ➝ Russia 58°14N 31°28E **188** C6
Lovćen Montenegro 42°23N 18°51E **202** D2
Lovćen △ Montenegro 42°20N 18°50E **202** D2
Lovech Bulgaria 43°8N 24°42E **203** C8
Lovech □ Bulgaria 43°15N 24°45E **203** C8
Loveland Colo., U.S.A. 40°24N 105°5W **304** F11
Loveland Ohio, U.S.A. 39°16N 84°16W **311** E12
Lovell U.S.A. 44°50N 108°24W **304** D9
Lovelock U.S.A. 40°11N 118°28W **304** F4
Lòvere Italy 45°49N 10°4E **198** C7
Lovers Leap Jamaica 17°52N 77°39W **320** a
Loves Park U.S.A. 42°19N 89°3W **310** B7
Lövestad Sweden 55°40N 13°54E **163** J7
Loviisa Finland 60°28N 26°12E **188** B4
Lovilia U.S.A. 41°8N 92°55W **310** C4
Loving U.S.A. 32°17N 104°6W **305** K11
Lovington Ill., U.S.A. 39°43N 88°38W **311** E8
Lovington N. Mex., U.S.A. 32°57N 103°21W **305** K12
Lovisa = Loviisa Finland 60°28N 26°12E **188** B4
Lovosice Czech Rep. 50°30N 14°2E **180** A7
Lovran Croatia 45°18N 14°15E **199** C11
Lovrin Romania 45°58N 20°48E **182** E5
Lövstabruk Sweden 60°25N 17°53E **162** D11
Lövstabukten Sweden 60°35N 17°45E **162** D11
Lóvua Lunda Norte, Angola 7°19S 20°12E **265** D4
Lóvua Moxico, Angola 11°33S 23°33E **265** E4
Lóvua ➝ Dem. Rep. of the Congo 6°6S 20°37E **265** D4
Low, L. Canada 52°29N 76°17W **298** B4
Low B. Antigua & B. 17°39N 61°54W **322** b
Low Pt. Australia 32°25S 127°25E **279** F4
Low Tatra = Nízké Tatry Slovak Rep. 48°55N 19°30E **181** C12
Lowa Dem. Rep. of the Congo 1°25S 25°47E **268** C2
Lowa ➝ Dem. Rep. of the Congo 1°24S 25°51E **268** C2
Lowden U.S.A. 41°52N 90°56W **310** C6
Lowell Ind., U.S.A. 41°18N 87°25W **311** C9
Lowell Mass., U.S.A. 42°38N 71°19W **313** D13
Lowell Mich., U.S.A. 42°56N 85°20W **311** B11
Lowellville U.S.A. 41°2N 80°32W **312** E4
Löwen = Lewin Brzeski Poland 50°45N 17°37E **185** H4
Löwen ➝ Namibia 26°51S 18°17E **270** C2
Löwenberg = Lwówek Śląski Poland 51°7N 15°38E **185** G2
Löwenstadt = Brzeziny Poland 51°49N 19°42E **185** G6
Lower Alkali L. U.S.A. 41°16N 120°2W **304** F3
Lower Arrow L. Canada 49°40N 118°5W **296** D5
Lower Austria = Niederösterreich □ Austria 48°25N 15°40E **180** C8
Lower B. U.S.A. 40°32N 74°5W **132** C1
Lower California = Baja California Mexico 31°10N 115°12W **318** A1
Lower East Side New York, U.S.A. **132** e2
Lower Glenelg △ Australia 38°4S 141°41E **282** E4
Lower Hutt N.Z. 41°10S 174°55E **143** B2
Lower Kalskag U.S.A. 61°31N 160°22W **303** F7
Lower Lake U.S.A. 38°55N 122°37W **306** G4
Lower Manhattan New York, U.S.A. **132** e1
Lower Manitou L. Canada 49°15N 93°0W **297** D10
Lower Manzanilla Trin. & Tob. 10°31N 61°3W **323** t
Lower New York B. = Lower B. U.S.A. 40°32N 74°5W **132** C1
Lower Paia U.S.A. 20°55N 156°23W **302** C5
Lower Post Canada 59°58N 128°30W **296** B3
Lower Red L. U.S.A. 47°58N 95°0W **308** B6
Lower Saxony = Niedersachsen □ Germany 52°50N 9°0E **178** C4
Lower Shing Mun Res. China 22°22N 114°9E **122** A1
Lower Tunguska = Tunguska, Nizhnyaya ➝ Russia 65°48N 88°4E **215** C9
Lower Zambezi △ Zambia 15°25S 29°40E **269** F2
Lowestoft U.K. 52°29N 1°45E **169** E9
Lowgar □ Afghan. 34°0N 69°0E **240** B3
Łowicz Poland 52°6N 19°55E **185** F6
Lowly, Pt. Australia 33°0S 137°46E **282** B2
Lowry Bay N.Z. 41°15S 174°55E **143** B2
Lowry City U.S.A. 38°8N 93°44W **310** F3
Lowther I. Canada 74°33N 97°30W **295** C12
Lowville U.S.A. 43°47N 75°29W **313** C9
Loxton S. Austral., Australia 34°28S 140°31E **282** C4
Loxton Northern Cape, S. Africa 31°30S 22°22E **270** D3
Loyalton U.S.A. 39°41N 120°14W **306** F6
Loyalty Is. = Loyauté, Îs. N. Cal. 20°50S 166°30E **288** d
Loyang = Luoyang China 34°40N 112°26E **226** G7
Loyauté, Îs. N. Cal. 20°50S 166°30E **288** d
Loyev = Loyew Belarus 51°56N 30°46E **177** C16
Loyew Belarus 51°56N 30°46E **177** C16
Loyola Univ. U.S.A. 42°0N 87°39W **119** B3
Loyoro Uganda 3°22N 34°14E **268** B3
Lož Slovenia 45°43N 14°30E **199** C11
Lozère □ France 44°35N 3°30E **174** D7
Loznica Serbia 44°32N 19°12E **202** B3
Lozova Ukraine 49°0N 36°20E **189** H9
Ltalaltuma ✪ Australia 23°57S 132°25E **278** D5
Lu India 26°58N 95°14E **241** B5
Lü Shan China 29°30N 115°55E **229** C11
Lü Tao Taiwan 22°40N 121°30E **225** D3
Lu Verne U.S.A. 42°55N 94°5W **310** B2
Lu Wo China 22°33N 114°6E **219** F11
Lu Xun, Tomb of China 31°17N 121°29E **138** B1
Lu Xun Museum Beijing, China **114** b1
Lu Xun Park China 31°17N 121°28E **138** B1
Lua ➝ Dem. Rep. of the Congo 2°46N 18°26E **264** B3
Lua Makiki U.S.A. 20°33N 156°37W **302** C5
Luachimo Angola 7°23S 20°48E **265** D4
Luacono Angola 11°15S 21°37E **265** E4
Luajan ➝ India 24°44N 85°1E **243** G11
Lualaba ➝ Dem. Rep. of the Congo 0°26N 25°20E **264** B5
Luale Dem. Rep. of the Congo 1°9N 23°5E **264** B4
Lualualei Naval Reserve U.S.A. 21°27N 158°6W **302** K13
Luambe △ Zambia 12°30S 32°15E **269** E3
Luampa Zambia 15°4S 24°20E **265** F4
Lu'an China 31°45N 116°29E **229** B11
Luan Chau Vietnam 21°38N 103°24E **228** G4
Luan He ➝ China 39°20N 119°5E **227** E10
Luan Xian China 39°40N 118°40E **227** E10
Luancheng Guangxi Zhuangzu, China 22°48N 108°55E **228** F7
Luancheng Hebei, China 37°53N 114°40E **226** F8
Luanco Spain 43°37N 5°48W **194** B5
Luanda Angola 8°50S 13°15E **265** D2
Luando ➝ Angola 10°21S 16°27E **265** E3
Luando ⌂ Angola 11°0S 17°32E **265** E3
Luang, Thale Thailand 7°30N 100°15E **237** J3
Luang Prabang Laos 19°52N 102°10E **228** H4
Luanginga ➝ Zambia 15°11S 22°55E **265** F4
Luangwa Zambia 15°35S 30°16E **269** F3
Luangwa ➝ Zambia 14°25S 30°25E **269** E3
Luangwa Valley Zambia 13°30S 31°30E **269** E3
Luangwe = Loange ➝ Dem. Rep. of the Congo 4°17S 20°2E **265** C4
Luania-Bubi Dem. Rep. of the Congo 7°28S 24°49E **265** D4
Luanne China 40°55N 117°40E **227** D9
Luanping China 40°53N 117°23E **227** D9
Luanshya Zambia 13°3S 28°28E **269** E2
Luapula □ Zambia 11°0S 29°0E **269** E2
Luapula ➝ Africa 9°26S 28°33E **269** D2
Luarca Spain 43°32N 6°32W **194** B4
Luashi Dem. Rep. of the Congo 10°50S 23°36E **265** E4
Luatamba Angola 12°6S 20°19E **265** E4
Luatira Angola 12°52S 17°14E **265** E3
Luau Angola 10°40S 22°10E **265** E4
Luba Phil. 17°19N 120°42E **232** C3
Lubaczów Poland 50°10N 23°8E **185** H10
Lubalo Angola 9°10S 19°15E **265** D3
Lubamiti Dem. Rep. of the Congo 2°28S 17°47E **264** C3
Lubań Poland 51°5N 15°15E **185** G2
Lubana, Ozero = Lubānas Ezers Latvia 56°45N 27°0E **188** D4
Lubānas Ezers Latvia 56°45N 27°0E **188** D4
Lubang Phil. 13°52N 120°7E **232** E3
Lubang Is. Phil. 13°50N 120°12E **232** E3
Lubango Angola 14°55S 13°30E **265** E2
Lubao Dem. Rep. of the Congo 5°17S 25°42E **265** D5
Lübars Germany 52°37N 13°21E **115** A3
Lubartów Poland 51°28N 22°42E **185** G9
Lubawa Poland 53°30N 19°48E **184** E6
Lübbecke Germany 52°18N 8°37E **178** C4
Lübben Germany 51°56N 13°54E **178** D9
Lübbenau Germany 51°52N 13°57E **178** D9
Lubbock U.S.A. 33°35N 101°51W **314** E4
Lübeck Germany 53°52N 10°40E **178** B6
Lübecker Bucht Germany 54°3N 10°54E **178** A6
Lubefu Dem. Rep. of the Congo 4°47S 24°27E **265** C4
Lubefu ➝ Dem. Rep. of the Congo 4°10S 23°0E **265** C4
Lubelskie □ Poland 51°20N 22°30E **185** G9
Lüben = Lubin Poland 51°24N 16°11E **185** G3
Lubero = Luofu Dem. Rep. of the Congo 0°10S 29°15E **268** C2
Luberon ⌂ France 43°52N 5°25E **175** E9
Lubersac France 45°26N 1°23E **174** C5
Lubicon L. Canada 56°23N 115°56W **296** B5
Lubień Kujawski Poland 52°23N 19°9E **185** F6
Lubilash ➝ Dem. Rep. of the Congo 6°2S 23°45E **265** D4
Lubin Poland 51°24N 16°11E **185** G3
Lublin Poland 51°12N 22°38E **185** G9
Lubliniec Poland 50°43N 18°45E **185** H5
Lubnān = Lebanon ■ Asia 34°0N 36°0E **250** E7
Lubnān, Jabal Lebanon 33°45N 35°40E **250** E6
Lubniewice Poland 52°31N 15°15E **185** F2
Lubny Ukraine 50°3N 32°58E **189** G7
Lubomierz Poland 51°1N 15°31E **185** G2
Luboń Poland 52°21N 16°51E **185** F3
Lubondaie Dem. Rep. of the Congo 8°1S 26°32E **265** D4
Lubongola Dem. Rep. of the Congo 2°35S 27°50E **268** C2
L'ubotín Slovak Rep. 49°17N 20°53E **181** B13
Lubraniec Poland 52°33N 18°50E **185** F5
Lubsko Poland 51°45N 14°57E **185** G1
Lübtheen Germany 53°18N 11°5E **178** B7
Lubuagan Phil. 17°21N 121°10E **232** C3
Lubudi Dem. Rep. of the Congo 6°51S 21°18E **265** D4
Lubudi ➝ Kasai-Occ., Dem. Rep. of the Congo 4°19S 20°25E **265** C4
Lubudi ➝ Katanga, Dem. Rep. of the Congo 9°0S 25°35E **265** D5
Lubuklinggau Indonesia 3°15S 102°55E **234** C2
Lubuksikaping Indonesia 0°10N 100°15E **234** B2
Lubumbashi Dem. Rep. of the Congo 11°40S 27°28E **269** E2
Lubunda Dem. Rep. of the Congo 5°12S 26°41E **265** D5
Lubungu Zambia 14°35S 26°24E **269** E2
Lubuskie □ Poland 52°10N 15°20E **185** F2
Lubutu Dem. Rep. of the Congo 0°45S 26°30E **268** C2
Luc An Chau Vietnam 22°6N 104°43E **236** A5
Luc-en-Diois France 44°36N 5°28E **175** D9
Lucala Angola 9°7S 15°58E **265** D3
Lucala ➝ Angola 9°38S 14°14E **265** D2
Lucan Canada 43°11N 81°24W **312** C3
Lucania, Mt. Canada 61°1N 140°27W **294** E3
Lucapa Angola 8°25S 20°45E **265** D4
Lucas U.S.A. 41°2N 93°29W **310** C3
Lucas Channel = Main Channel Canada 45°21N 81°45W **312** A3
Lucban Phil. 14°6N 121°33E **232** D3
Lucca Italy 43°50N 10°29E **198** E7
Lucé France 48°26N 1°27E **172** D8
Luce Bay U.K. 54°45N 4°48W **167** G4
Lucea Jamaica 18°27N 78°10W **320** a
Lucedale U.S.A. 30°56N 88°35W **315** F10
Lucena Phil. 13°56N 121°37E **232** E3
Lucena Spain 37°27N 4°31W **195** H6
Lučenec Slovak Rep. 48°18N 19°42E **181** C12
Lucera Italy 41°30N 15°20E **201** A8
Lucerne = Lake Worth U.S.A. 26°37N 80°3W **317** J9
Lucerne = Luzern Switz. 47°3N 8°18E **179** H4
Lucerne U.S.A. 39°6N 122°48W **306** F4
Lucerne Valley U.S.A. 34°27N 116°57W **307** L10
Lucero Mexico 30°49N 106°30W **318** A3
Luchena ➝ Spain 37°44N 1°50W **197** H3
Lucheng China 36°20N 113°11E **226** F7
Lucheringo ➝ Mozam. 11°43S 36°17E **269** E4
Luchow = Luzhou China 28°52N 105°20E **228** C5
Lüchow Germany 52°58N 11°8E **178** C7
Luchu Taiwan 22°52N 120°15E **225** D2
Luchuan China 22°21N 110°12E **229** F8
Lucia U.S.A. 36°2N 121°33W **306** J5
Luciara Brazil 10°45S 50°34W **333** D1
Lucie ➝ Suriname 3°35N 57°38W **329** C6
Lucinda Australia 18°32S 146°20E **280** B4
Lucindale Australia 36°58S 140°26E **282** D4
Lucira Angola 14°0S 12°35E **265** E2
Luciras, B. das Angola 13°52S 12°31E **265** E2
Luckau Germany 51°50N 13°42E **178** D9
Luckenwalde Germany 52°5N 13°10E **178** C9
Luckey U.S.A. 41°27N 83°29W **311** C13
Luckhoff S. Africa 29°44S 24°43E **270** C3
Lucknow Ont., Canada 43°57N 81°31W **312** C3
Lucknow India 26°50N 81°0E **243** F9
Luçon France 46°28N 1°10W **174** B2
Lucusse Angola 12°32S 20°48E **265** E4
Lucy, L. U.S.A. 28°34N 81°29W **133** A2
Lüda = Dalian China 38°50N 121°40E **227** E11
Luda Kamchiya ➝ Bulgaria 43°3N 27°29E **203** C11
Ludbreg Croatia 46°15N 16°38E **199** B13
Lüdenscheid Germany 51°13N 7°37E **178** D3
Lüderitz Namibia 26°41S 15°8E **270** C2
Lüderitzbaai Namibia 26°36S 15°8E **270** C2
Ludhiana India 30°57N 75°56E **242** D6
Ludian China 27°10N 103°33E **228** D4
Luding Qiao China 29°53N 102°12E **228** C4
Lüdinghausen Germany 51°46N 7°27E **178** D3
Ludington U.S.A. 43°57N 86°27W **308** D10
Ludlow U.K. 52°22N 2°42W **169** E5
Ludlow Calif., U.S.A. 34°43N 116°10W **307** L10
Ludlow Pa., U.S.A. 41°43N 78°56W **312** E6
Ludlow Vt., U.S.A. 43°24N 72°42W **313** C12
Ludowici U.S.A. 31°43N 81°45W **316** D8
Luduş Romania 46°29N 24°5E **183** D9
Ludvika Sweden 60°8N 15°14E **162** D9
Ludwigsburg Germany 48°53N 9°11E **179** G5
Ludwigsfeld Germany 48°12N 11°27E **131** A1
Ludwigsfelde Germany 52°17N 13°17E **178** C9
Ludwigshafen Germany 49°29N 8°26E **179** F4
Ludwigslust Germany 53°19N 11°30E **178** B7
Ludza Latvia 56°32N 27°43E **188** D4
Lue Australia 32°38S 149°50E **283** B8
Luebo Dem. Rep. of the Congo 5°21S 21°23E **265** D4
Lueki Dem. Rep. of the Congo 3°20S 25°48E **264** C5
Luena Angola 12°13S 19°51E **265** E3
Luena Dem. Rep. of the Congo 9°28S 25°43E **269** D2
Luena Zambia 10°40S 30°25E **269** E3
Luena ➝ Angola 12°30S 22°34E **265** E4
Luena ➝ Zambia 14°46S 23°30E **265** E4
Luena Flats Zambia 14°47S 23°17E **265** E4
Luengué ⌂ Angola 16°55S 19°55E **265** F3
Luenha = Ruenya ➝ Africa 16°24S 33°48E **269** F3
Luepa Venezuela 5°43N 61°31W **329** B5
Lueta ➝ Dem. Rep. of the Congo 7°4S 21°40E **265** D4
Luete ➝ Zambia 15°46S 23°10E **265** F4
Lüeyang China 33°22N 106°10E **226** H4
Lufeng Guangdong, China 22°57N 115°38E **229** F10
Lufeng Yunnan, China 25°0N 102°5E **228** E4
Lufico Angola 6°24S 13°23E **265** D2
Lufira ➝ Dem. Rep. of the Congo 9°30S 27°0E **269** D2
Lufkin U.S.A. 31°21N 94°44W **314** F7
Lufupa Dem. Rep. of the Congo 10°37S 24°56E **265** E4
Luga Russia 58°40N 29°55E **188** C5
Luga ➝ Russia 59°40N 28°18E **188** C5
Lugano Switz. 46°1N 8°57E **179** J4
Lugano, L. di Switz. 46°0N 9°0E **198** C6
Lugansk = Luhansk Ukraine 48°38N 39°15E **189** H10
Luganville Vanuatu 15°27S 167°10E **287** E5
Lugard's Falls Kenya 3°6S 38°41E **268** C4
Lugela Mozam. 16°25S 36°43E **269** F4
Lugenda ➝ Mozam. 11°25S 38°33E **269** E4
Lugh Ganana = Luuq Somali Rep. 3°48N 42°34E **267** D5
Lugnaquillia Ireland 52°58N 6°28W **166** D5
Lugo Italy 44°25N 11°54E **199** D8
Lugo Spain 43°2N 7°35W **194** B3
Lugo □ Spain 43°0N 7°30W **194** C3
Lugoj Romania 45°42N 21°57E **182** E6
Lugovoy = Qulan Kazakhstan 42°55N 72°43E **214** E8
Lugus I. Phil. 5°41N 120°50E **233** J3
Luhansk Ukraine 48°38N 39°15E **189** H10
Luhansk □ Ukraine 49°10N 38°40E **189** H10
Luhe China 32°19N 118°50E **229** A12
Luhe ➝ Germany 53°23N 10°13E **178** B6
Luhit ➝ India 27°48N 95°28E **241** B5
Luhu China 23°9N 113°16E **121** B2
Luhuo China 31°21N 100°48E **228** B3
Lui ➝ Angola 8°21S 17°33E **265** D3
Lui ➝ Zambia 16°18S 23°17E **265** F4
Luia Angola 8°10S 21°32E **265** D4
Luia ➝ Angola 8°32S 21°47E **265** D4
Luiana Angola 17°25S 22°59E **265** F4
Luiana ➝ Angola 17°24S 23°3E **265** F4
Luiana ⌂ Angola 16°55S 22°15E **265** F4
Luichow = Liuzhou China 24°22N 109°22E **228** E7
Luichow Pen. = Leizhou Bandao China 21°0N 110°0E **228** G7
Luikuei Taiwan 23°0N 120°38E **225** D2
Luilaka ➝ Dem. Rep. of the Congo 0°52S 20°12E **264** C4
Luimneach = Limerick Ireland 52°40N 8°37W **166** D3
Luing U.K. 56°14N 5°39W **167** E3
Luino Italy 45°59N 8°44E **198** C5
Luio ➝ Angola 13°15S 21°37E **265** E4
Luís Correia Brazil 3°0S 41°35W **332** B3
Luís Gonçalves Brazil 5°37S 50°25W **332** C1
Luitpold Coast Antarctica 78°30S 32°0W **151** D1
Luiza Dem. Rep. of the Congo 7°40S 22°30E **265** D4
Luizi Dem. Rep. of the Congo 6°0S 27°25E **268** D2
Luján Argentina 34°45S 59°5W **334** C4
Lujiang China 31°20N 117°15E **229** B11
Lukala Dem. Rep. of the Congo 5°31S 14°32E **265** D2
Lukang Taiwan 24°1N 120°22E **225** B2
Lukanga Bandundu, Dem. Rep. of the Congo 1°41S 18°9E **264** C3
Lukanga Équateur, Dem. Rep. of the Congo 1°0S 18°8E **264** C3
Lukanga Swamp Zambia 14°30S 27°40E **269** E2
Lukavac Bos.-H. 44°33N 18°32E **182** F3
Lukenie ➝ Dem. Rep. of the Congo 3°0S 18°50E **264** C3
Lŭki Bulgaria 41°50N 24°43E **203** E8
Lukk Libya 32°1N 24°46E **258** B4
Lukolela Équateur, Dem. Rep. of the Congo 1°10S 17°12E **264** C3
Lukolela Kasai-Or., Dem. Rep. of the Congo 5°23S 24°32E **265** D4
Lukosi Zimbabwe 18°30S 26°30E **269** F2
Lukovë Albania 39°59N 19°54E **202** G3
Lukovit Bulgaria 43°13N 24°11E **203** C8
Łuków Poland 51°55N 22°23E **185** G9
Lukoyanov Russia 55°2N 44°29E **190** C7
Luksefjell Norway 59°23N 9°34E **164** E6
Luku Taiwan 23°44N 120°45E **225** C2
Lukulu Zambia 14°23S 23°15E **265** E4
Lukuni Dem. Rep. of the Congo 5°50S 17°16E **265** D3
Lukusuzi △ Zambia 12°43S 32°36E **269** E3
Lula Dem. Rep. of the Congo 5°22S 16°2E **265** D3
Luleå Sweden 65°35N 22°10E **160** D20
Luleälven ➝ Sweden 65°35N 22°10E **160** D20
Lüleburgaz Turkey 41°23N 27°22E **203** E11
Luliang China 25°0N 103°40E **228** E4
Lulima Dem. Rep. of the Congo 4°12S 25°36E **268** C2
Luling U.S.A. 29°41N 97°39W **314** G6
Lulong China 39°53N 118°51E **227** E10
Lulonga ➝ Dem. Rep. of the Congo 1°0N 18°10E **264** B3
Lulu U.S.A. 30°7N 82°29W **316** E7
Lulu ➝ Dem. Rep. of the Congo 1°18N 23°42E **264** B4
Lulua ➝ Dem. Rep. of the Congo 4°30S 20°30E **265** C4
Luluaburg = Kananga Dem. Rep. of the Congo 5°55S 22°18E **265** D4
Luma Amer. Samoa 14°16S 169°33W **302** f
Lumai Angola 13°13S 21°25E **265** E4
Lumajang Indonesia 8°8S 113°13E **235** D4
Lumaku, Gunong Malaysia 4°52N 115°38E **235** B5
Lumār Iran 33°33N 46°49E **213** F12
Lumbala ➝ Angola 12°39S 22°35E **265** E4
Lumbala Kaquengue Angola 12°39S 22°34E **265** E4
Lumbala N'guimbo Angola 14°18S 21°18E **265** E4
Lumbe ➝ Zambia 16°44S 23°41E **265** F4
Lumber City U.S.A. 31°56N 82°41W **316** D7
Lumberton U.S.A. 34°37N 79°0W **315** D15
Lumding India 25°46N 93°10E **241** C4
Lumi Papua N. G. 3°30S 142°2E **286** B2
Lumiar Portugal 38°46N 9°10W **126** A2
Lumpkin U.S.A. 32°3N 84°48W **316** C5
Lumsden Sask., Canada 50°39N 104°52W **297** C8
Lumsden N.Z. 45°44S 168°27E **285** F3
Lumut Malaysia 4°13N 100°37E **237** K3
Lumut, Tanjung Indonesia 3°50S 105°58E **234** C3
Luna India 23°43N 69°16E **242** H3

Luna Apayao, Phil. 18°18N 121°21E 232 B3
Lunan China 24°40N 103°18E 228 E4
Lunavada India 23°8N 73°37E 242 H5
Lunca Romania 47°22N 25°1E 183 C10
Lunca Corbului Romania 44°42N 24°45E 183 F9
Lund Sweden 55°44N 13°12E 163 J7
Lunda Norte □ Angola 8°0S 20°0E 265 D4
Lunda Sul □ Angola 10°0S 20°0E 265 E4
Lundamo Norway 63°9N 10°19E 164 A7
Lundazi Zambia 12°20S 33°7E 269 E3
Lundenburg = Břeclav Czech Rep. 48°46N 16°53E 181 C9
Lunderskov Denmark 55°29N 9°19E 163 J3
Lundi → Zimbabwe 21°43S 32°34E 269 G3
Lundtofte Denmark 55°47N 12°32E 118 A3
Lundu Malaysia 1°40N 109°50E 235 B3
Lundy U.K. 51°10N 4°41W 169 F3
Lune → U.K. 54°0N 2°51W 168 C5
Lüneburg Germany 53°15N 10°24E 178 B6
Lüneburg Heath = Lüneburger Heide Germany 53°10N 10°12E 178 B6
Lüneburger Heide Germany 53°10N 10°12E 178 B6
Lunel France 43°39N 4°9E 175 E8
Lünen Germany 51°37N 7°32E 178 D3
Lunenburg Canada 44°22N 64°18W 299 D7
Lunéville France 48°36N 6°30E 173 D13
Lung Mei China 22°23N 114°15E 122 A2
Lunga Dem. Rep. of the Congo 5°46S 12°14E 265 C4
Lunga → Zambia 14°34S 26°25E 269 E2
Lunga Lunga Kenya 4°33S 39°7E 268 C4
Lungchin Taiwan 24°12N 120°31E 225 B2
Lunge Angola 12°13S 16°7E 265 E3
Lungga Solomon Is. 9°25S 160°3E 287 M11
Lungi S. Leone 8°40N 13°17W 262 D2
Lunglei India 22°55N 92°45E 241 D4
Lungngo Burma 21°57N 93°36E 241 E4
Lung'tan Taiwan 24°52N 121°12E 225 B3
Lungwebungu → Zambia 14°19S 23°14E 265 E4
Luni India 26°0N 73°6E 242 G5
Luni → India 24°41N 71°14E 242 G4
Luninets = Luninyets Belarus 52°15N 26°50E 177 B14
Luning U.S.A. 38°30N 118°11W 304 G4
Lunino Russia 53°38N 45°18E 190 D7
Luninyets Belarus 52°15N 26°50E 177 B14
Lunkaransar India 28°29N 73°44E 242 E5
Lunner Norway 60°19N 10°35E 164 D7
Lunpei Taiwan 24°45N 120°21E 225 C2
Lunsar S. Leone 8°41N 12°32W 262 D2
Lunsemfwa → Zambia 14°54S 30°12E 269 E3
Lunsemfwa Falls Zambia 14°30S 29°6E 269 E2
Luntai China 41°46N 84°14E 217 D10
Luo He → China 34°35N 110°20E 226 G6
Luocheng China 24°48N 108°53E 228 E7
Luochuan China 35°45N 109°26E 226 G5
Luoci China 25°19N 102°18E 228 E4
Luodian China 25°24N 106°43E 228 E6
Luoding China 22°45N 111°40E 229 F8
Luofu Dem. Rep. of the Congo 0°10S 29°15E 268 C2
Luohe China 33°32N 114°2E 226 H8
Luojiang Guangdong, China 23°5N 113°17E 121 B2
Luojiang Sichuan, China 31°18N 104°33E 228 B5
Luonan China 34°5N 110°10E 226 G6
Luoning China 34°35N 111°40E 226 G6
Luoshan China 32°13N 114°30E 229 A10
Luotian China 30°46N 115°22E 229 B10
Luoxiao Shan China 26°30N 114°1E 229 D10
Luoyang China 34°40N 112°26E 226 G7
Luoyuan China 26°28N 119°30E 229 D12
Luozi Dem. Rep. of the Congo 4°54S 14°0E 265 C2
Luozigou China 43°42N 130°18E 227 C16
Lupeni Romania 45°21N 23°13E 183 E8
Lupilichi Mozam. 11°47S 35°13E 269 E4
Lupire Angola 14°36S 19°29E 265 E3
Łupków Poland 49°15N 22°4E 185 J9
Lupoing China 24°53N 104°21E 228 E5
Lupon Phil. 6°54N 126°0E 233 H6
Luputa Dem. Rep. of the Congo 7°7S 23°43E 265 D4
Luqa Malta 35°52N 14°29E 206 F7
Luquan China 25°35N 102°25E 228 E4
Luque Paraguay 25°19S 57°25W 334 B4
Luquembo Angola 10°44S 17°43E 265 E3
Luquillo Puerto Rico 18°23N 65°43W 321 b
Luquillo, Sierra de Puerto Rico 18°20N 65°47W 321 b
Lúras Italy 40°56N 9°10E 200 B2
Luray U.S.A. 38°40N 78°28W 309 F14
Lure France 47°40N 6°30E 173 E13
Luremo Angola 8°30S 17°50E 265 D3
Lurgan U.K. 54°28N 6°19W 166 B5
Luribay Bolivia 17°6S 67°39W 330 D4
Lurín Peru 12°17S 76°52W 330 C2
Lúrio Mozam. 13°32S 40°30E 269 E5
Lusaka Zambia 15°28S 28°16E 269 F2
Lusaka □ Zambia 15°30S 29°0E 269 F2
Lusambo Dem. Rep. of the Congo 4°58S 23°28E 265 C4
Lusancay Is. and Reefs Papua N. G. 8°30S 150°30E 286 E6
Lusangaye Dem. Rep. of the Congo 4°54S 26°0E 265 C5
Luseland Canada 52°5N 109°24W 297 C7
Lusenga Plain △ Zambia 9°22S 29°14E 269 D2
Lusengo Dem. Rep. of the Congo 1°47N 19°31E 264 B3
Lushan Henan, China 33°45N 112°55E 226 H7
Lushan Sichuan, China 30°12N 102°52E 228 B4
Lushi China 34°3N 111°3E 226 G6
Lushnjë Albania 40°55N 19°41E 202 F3
Lushoto Tanzania 4°47S 38°20E 268 C4
Lushui China 25°58N 98°44E 228 E2
Lushuihe China 42°31N 127°47E 224 A3
Lüshun China 38°45N 121°15E 227 E11
Lusignan France 46°26N 0°8E 174 B4
Lusigny-sur-Barse France 48°16N 4°15E 173 D11
Lusiye Zambia 15°30S 23°57E 265 F4
Lusk U.S.A. 42°46N 104°27W 304 E11
Lussac-les-Châteaux France 46°24N 0°43E 174 B4
Lustenau Austria 47°26N 9°39E 180 D2
Lustheim Germany 48°14N 11°34E 131 A2
Lustrafjorden Norway 61°23N 7°25E 164 C4
Lūt, Dasht-e Iran 31°30N 58°0E 247 D8
Luta = Dalian China 38°50N 121°40E 227 E11
Lutao Taiwan 22°40N 121°29E 225 D3
Lutembo Angola 13°26S 21°16E 265 E4
Lutherstadt Wittenberg Germany 51°53N 12°39E 178 D8
Luthersville U.S.A. 33°13N 84°45W 316 B5
Luti Solomon Is. 7°14S 157°0E 287 L9
Luton U.K. 51°53N 0°24W 169 F7
Luton □ U.K. 51°53N 0°24W 169 F7
Lutong Malaysia 4°28N 114°0E 235 B4
Lutsel K'e Canada 62°24N 110°44W 297 A6
Lutshima → Dem. Rep. of the Congo 5°22S 18°59E 265 D3
Lutsk Ukraine 50°50N 25°15E 177 C13
Luttenberg = Ljutomer Slovenia 46°31N 16°11E 199 B13
Lutto = Lotta → Europe 68°42N 31°6E 160 B24
Lutuai Angola 12°41S 20°7E 265 E4
Lutz U.S.A. 28°9N 82°28W 317 G7
Lützow Holmbukta Antarctica 69°10S 37°30E 151 C4
Lutzputs S. Africa 28°3S 20°40E 270 C3
Luuk Phil. 5°58N 121°18E 233 J3
Luuq Somali Rep. 3°48N 42°34E 267 D8
Luverne Ala., U.S.A. 31°43N 86°16W 316 D3
Luverne Minn., U.S.A. 43°39N 96°13W 308 D5
Luvo Angola 5°51S 14°5E 265 D2
Luvua Dem. Rep. of the Congo 8°48S 25°17E 265 D5
Luvua → Dem. Rep. of the Congo 6°50S 27°30E 268 D2
Luvuvhu → S. Africa 22°25S 31°18E 271 B5
Luwan China 31°12N 121°27E 138 B1
Luwegu → Tanzania 8°31S 37°23E 269 D4
Luwero Uganda 0°50N 32°28E 268 B3
Luwuk Indonesia 0°56S 122°47E 231 E6
Luxembourg Lux. 49°37N 6°9E 170 E6
Luxembourg □ Belgium 49°58N 5°30E 170 E5
Luxembourg ■ Europe 49°45N 6°0E 170 E5
Luxembourg ✈ (LUX) Lux. 49°37N 6°10E 170 E6
Luxembourg, Palais du Paris, France 134 c4
Luxemburg U.S.A. 42°36N 91°5W 310 B5
Luxeuil-les-Bains France 47°49N 6°24E 173 E13
Luxi Hunan, China 28°20N 110°7E 229 C8
Luxi Yunnan, China 24°40N 103°55E 228 E4
Luxi Yunnan, China 24°27N 98°36E 228 E2
Luxor = El Uqsur Egypt 25°41N 32°38E 256 B3
Luy-de-Béarn → France 43°39N 0°48W 174 E3
Luy-de-France → France 43°39N 0°48W 174 E3
Luyeh Hualien, Taiwan 23°35N 121°32E 225 C3
Luyeh T'aitung, Taiwan 22°55N 121°8E 225 D3
Luyi China 33°50N 115°35E 226 H8
Luz Azores 39°1N 28°0W 153 d1
Luz-St-Sauveur France 42°53N 0°0 174 F4
Luza Russia 60°39N 47°10E 186 B8
Luzern Switz. 47°3N 8°18E 179 H4
Luzern □ Switz. 47°2N 7°55E 179 H3
Luzhai China 24°29N 109°42E 228 E7
Luzhany Ukraine 48°22N 25°47E 183 B10
Luzhi China 26°21N 105°16E 228 D5
Luzhniki Sports Centre Russia 55°43N 37°31E 129 B3
Luzhou China 28°52N 105°20E 228 C5
Luziânia Brazil 16°20S 48°0W 333 E2
Luzilândia Brazil 3°28S 42°22W 332 B3
Lužnice → Czech Rep. 49°14N 14°23E 180 B7
Luzon Phil. 16°0N 121°0E 232 C3
Luzon Strait Asia 21°0N 120°40E 229 G13
Luzy France 46°47N 3°58E 173 F10
Luzzi Italy 39°27N 16°17E 201 C9
Lviv Ukraine 49°50N 24°0E 177 D13
Lviv □ Ukraine 49°30N 23°45E 189 H2
Lvov = Lviv Ukraine 49°50N 24°0E 177 D13
Lwówek Poland 52°28N 16°10E 185 F3
Lwówek Śląski Poland 51°7N 15°38E 185 G2
Lyakhavichy Belarus 53°2N 26°32E 177 B14
Lyakhovskiye, Ostrova Russia 73°40N 141°0E 215 B15
Lyaki = Läki Azerbaijan 40°34N 47°22E 191 K8
Lyal I. Canada 44°57N 81°24W 312 B3
Lyall Mt. N.Z. 45°16S 167°32E 285 F2
Lyallpur = Faisalabad Pakistan 31°30N 73°5E 242 D5
Lyaskovets Bulgaria 43°6N 25°44E 203 C9
Lyasnaya Belarus 52°9N 23°31E 185 F10
Lybster U.K. 58°18N 3°15W 167 C5
Lycabettus Athens, Greece 112 b3
Lycaonia Turkey 38°0N 33°0E 212 D5
Lychen Germany 53°12N 13°18E 178 B9
Lychkova Russia 57°55N 32°24E 188 D7
Lycia Turkey 36°30N 29°30E 205 E11
Lyck = Ełk Poland 53°50N 22°21E 184 E9
Lyckebyån → Sweden 56°12N 15°39E 163 H9
Lycksele Sweden 64°38N 18°40E 160 D18
Lycosura Greece 37°20N 22°3E 204 D4
Lydda = Lod Israel 31°57N 34°54E 251 G5
Lyddan I. Antarctica 74°0S 21°0W 151 D2
Lydenburg S. Africa 25°10S 30°29E 271 C5
Lydia Turkey 38°48N 28°19E 205 C10
Lydynia → Poland 52°43N 20°26E 185 F7
Lyell N.Z. 41°48S 172°4E 285 B7
Lyell I. Canada 52°40N 131°35W 296 C2
Lyepyel Belarus 54°50N 28°40E 188 E5
Lyford Cay Bahamas 25°2N 77°33W 153 b
Lygnern Sweden 57°30N 12°15E 163 G6
Lykavittos Hill = Lycabettus Athens, Greece 112 b3
Lykens U.S.A. 40°34N 76°42W 313 F8
Lyman Ukraine 45°41N 29°45E 183 E14
Lyman Wyo., U.S.A. 41°20N 110°18W 304 F8
Lymanske Ukraine 46°40N 29°58E 183 D14
Lyme B. U.K. 50°42N 2°53W 169 G4
Lyme Regis U.K. 50°43N 2°57W 169 G5
Lymington U.K. 50°45N 1°32W 169 G6
Lyna → Poland 54°37N 21°14E 184 D8
Lynchburg Ohio, U.S.A. 39°15N 83°48W 311 E13
Lynchburg S.C., U.S.A. 34°3N 80°4W 316 A9
Lynchburg Va., U.S.A. 37°25N 79°9W 309 G14
Lynd → Australia 16°28S 143°18E 280 B3
Lynd Ra. Australia 25°30S 149°20E 281 D4
Lynden Ont., Canada 43°14N 80°9W 312 C4
Lynden Wash., U.S.A. 48°57N 122°27W 306 B4
Lyndhurst S. Austral., Australia 30°15S 138°18E 281 E2
Lyndhurst N.J., U.S.A. 40°49N 74°7W 132 B1
Lyndon → Australia 23°29S 114°6E 279 D1
Lyndonville N.Y., U.S.A. 43°20N 78°23W 312 C6
Lyndonville Vt., U.S.A. 44°31N 72°1W 313 B12
Lyngdal Buskerud, Norway 59°54N 9°32E 164 E6
Lyngdal Vest-Agder, Norway 58°8N 7°7E 164 F4
Lyngen Norway 69°45N 20°30E 160 B19
Lyngør Norway 58°38N 9°8E 164 F6
Lynher Reef Australia 15°27S 121°55E 278 C3
Lynn Ind., U.S.A. 40°3N 84°56W 311 D12
Lynn Mass., U.S.A. 42°28N 70°57W 313 D14
Lynn Canal U.S.A. 58°50N 135°15W 303 G14
Lynn Haven U.S.A. 30°15N 85°39W 316 E4
Lynn Lake Canada 56°51N 101°3W 297 B8
Lynn Woods Res. U.S.A. 42°29N 71°0W 116 A2
Lynne U.S.A. 29°12N 81°55W 317 F8
Lynnville U.S.A. 38°12N 87°18W 311 F9
Lynnwood U.S.A. 47°49N 122°18W 306 C4
Lynton U.K. 51°13N 3°50W 169 F4
Lyntupy Belarus 55°4N 26°23E 188 E4
Lynx L. Canada 62°25N 106°15W 297 A7
Lyon France 45°46N 4°50E 175 C8
Lyon, Gare de Paris, France 134 c5
Lyon St-Exupery ✈ (LYS) France 45°44N 5°2E 175 C9
Lyonnais France 45°45N 4°15E 175 C8
Lyons = Lyon France 45°46N 4°50E 175 C8
Lyons Ga., U.S.A. 32°12N 82°19W 316 C7
Lyons Ill., U.S.A. 41°48N 87°49W 119 C2
Lyons Kans., U.S.A. 38°21N 98°12W 308 F4
Lyons N.Y., U.S.A. 43°5N 77°0W 312 C8
Lyons → Australia 25°2S 115°9E 279 E2
Lyons Falls U.S.A. 43°37N 75°22W 313 C9
Lyozna Belarus 55°0N 30°50E 188 E6
Lyra Reef Papua N. G. 1°50S 153°35E 286 A7
Lys = Leie → Belgium 51°2N 3°45E 170 C3
Lysá nad Labem Czech Rep. 50°11N 14°51E 180 A7
Lysaker Norway 59°54N 10°38E 133 A2
Lysakerselva → Norway 59°54N 10°38E 133 A2
Lyseboth Norway 59°3N 6°37E 164 E3
Lysefjorden Norway 59°0N 6°23E 164 E3
Lysekil Sweden 58°17N 11°26E 163 F5
Lysi Cyprus 35°6N 33°41E 207 E9
Lyskovo Russia 56°0N 45°3E 190 B7
Lysolaje Czech Rep. 50°8N 14°22E 135 B2
Lystrup Denmark 56°14N 10°14E 163 H4
Lysva Russia 58°7N 57°49E 186 C10
Lysvik Sweden 60°1N 13°9E 162 D7
Lysychansk Ukraine 48°55N 38°30E 189 H10
Lytham St. Anne's U.K. 53°45N 3°0W 168 D4
Lyttelton N.Z. 43°35S 172°44E 285 D7
Lytton Canada 50°13N 121°31W 296 C4
Lyuban Russia 59°16N 31°18E 188 C6
Lyubertsy Russia 55°40N 37°51E 129 B5
Lyubim Russia 58°20N 40°39E 188 C11
Lyubimets Bulgaria 41°50N 26°5E 203 E10
Lyublino Russia 55°41N 37°44E 129 B4
Lyuboml Ukraine 51°11N 24°4E 185 G11
Lyubotyn Ukraine 50°0N 36°0E 189 H8
Lyubytino Russia 58°50N 33°16E 188 C7
Lyudinovo Russia 53°52N 34°28E 188 F8

M

M.R. Stefanik, Bratislava ✈ (BTS) Slovak Rep. 48°11N 17°9E 181 C10
Ma → Vietnam 19°47N 105°56E 228 H5
Ma, O. el → Algeria 27°45N 7°52W 260 C3
Ma Nam Wat China 22°21N 114°16E 122 A2
Ma On Shan Country Park ⌂ China 22°22N 114°14E 122 A2
Ma'adaba Jordan 30°43N 35°47E 251 H6
Maafushi Maldives 3°59N 73°27E 272 d
Ma'ale Adumim West Bank 31°49N 35°17E 123 B2
Ma'ale Ha Khamisha Israel 31°49N 35°7E 123 B1
Ma'ale Mikhmas West Bank 31°52N 35°18E 123 A2
Maamba Zambia 17°17S 26°28E 270 A4
Ma'ān Jordan 30°12N 35°44E 251 H6
Ma'ān □ Jordan 30°0N 36°0E 251 J7
Maana'oba Solomon Is. 8°17S 160°50E 287 M11
Maanselkä Finland 63°52N 28°32E 160 E23
Ma'anshan China 31°44N 118°29E 229 B12
Maantiekylä Finland 60°20N 25°0E 121 A3
Maarianhamina = Mariehamn Finland 60°5N 19°55E 161 F18
Maarifa Iraq 33°15N 44°21E 113 B2
Maarmorilik Greenland 71°3N 51°0W 154 C5
Ma'arrat an Nu'mān Syria 35°43N 36°43E 250 C7
Maas → Neths. 51°45N 4°32E 170 C4
Maaseik Belgium 51°6N 5°45E 170 C5
Maasim Phil. 5°52N 125°0E 233 J5
Maasin Phil. 10°8N 124°50E 233 F5
Maastricht Neths. 50°50N 5°40E 170 D5
Maasupa Solomon Is. 9°16S 161°17E 287 M11
Maave Mozam. 21°4S 34°47E 271 B5
Mababe Depression Botswana 18°50S 24°15E 270 A3
Mabaia Angola 7°12S 14°2E 265 D2
Mabalane Mozam. 23°37S 32°31E 271 B5
Mabanga Dem. Rep. of the Congo 1°30N 19°6E 264 B3
Ma'bar Yemen 14°48N 44°17E 248 D4
Mabaruma Guyana 8°10N 59°50W 329 B6
Mabato Pt. Phil. 14°29N 121°3E 127 C2
Mabein Burma 23°29N 96°37E 241 D6
Mabel, L. U.S.A. 28°25N 81°32W 133 B1
Mabel L. Canada 50°35N 118°43W 296 C5
Mabenga Dem. Rep. of the Congo 3°39S 18°40E 264 C3
Mabenge Dem. Rep. of the Congo 4°15N 24°12E 264 B4
Maberly Canada 44°50N 76°32W 313 B8
Mabesi, L. S. Leone 7°10N 11°42W 262 D2
Mabian China 28°47N 103°37E 228 C4
Mabil Ethiopia 10°26N 36°52E 257 E4
Mabinay Phil. 9°48N 122°54E 233 G4
Mabirou Congo 1°3S 15°42E 264 C3
Mablethorpe U.K. 53°20N 0°15E 168 D8
Mableton U.S.A. 33°49N 84°35W 316 B5
Mably France 46°5N 4°4E 173 F11
Maboma Dem. Rep. of the Congo 2°30N 28°10E 268 B2
Mabonto S. Leone 8°53N 11°50W 262 D2
Maboukou Congo 3°39S 12°31E 264 C2
Mabouya I. Grenada 12°29N 61°30W 323 q
Mabroûk Mali 19°29N 1°15W 261 E4
Mabrous Niger 21°14N 13°35E 259 D2
Mabuasehube ⌂ Botswana 25°5S 21°10E 270 C3
Mabudis Phil. 20°55N 121°55E 232 A3
Mabuiag Australia 9°57S 142°11E 280 a
Mac Bac Vietnam 9°46N 106°7E 237 H6
Macachín Argentina 37°10S 63°43W 334 D3
Macaco, Morro do Brazil 22°56S 43°6W 135 B2
Macaé Brazil 22°20S 41°43W 333 F3
Macael Spain 37°20N 2°18W 197 H2
Macaíba Brazil 5°51S 35°21W 332 C4
Macajuba Brazil 12°9S 40°22W 333 D3
McAlester U.S.A. 34°56N 95°46W 314 D7
McAllen U.S.A. 26°12N 98°14W 314 H5
McAlpin U.S.A. 30°8N 82°57W 316 E7
MacAlpine L. Canada 66°32N 102°45W 294 D11
Macamic Canada 48°45N 79°0W 298 C4
Macao = Macau China 22°12N 113°33E 219 G10
Macão Portugal 39°35N 7°59W 195 F3
Macapá Brazil 0°5N 51°4W 329 C7
Macaque, Morne Dominica 15°20N 61°20W 323 k
Macará Ecuador 4°23S 79°57W 328 D2
Macarani Brazil 15°33S 40°24W 333 E3
Macarena, Serranía de la Colombia 2°45N 73°55W 328 C3
Macareo, Caño → Venezuela 9°47N 61°36W 329 B5
Macarthur Australia 38°5S 142°0E 282 E5
McArthur → Australia 15°54S 136°40E 280 B2
McArthur, Port Australia 16°4S 136°23E 280 B2
Macas Ecuador 2°19S 78°7W 328 D2
Macate Peru 8°48S 78°7W 330 B2
Macau Brazil 5°15S 36°40W 332 C4
Macau China 22°12N 113°33E 219 G10
Macaúbas Brazil 13°2S 42°42W 333 D3
Macauley I. Pac. Oc. 30°12S 178°28W 277 G15
Macaya → Colombia 0°59N 72°20W 328 C3
McBride Canada 53°20N 120°19W 296 C4
McCall U.S.A. 44°55N 116°6W 304 D5
McCamey U.S.A. 31°8N 102°14W 314 F3
McCammon U.S.A. 42°39N 112°12W 304 E7
McCarran Int., Las Vegas ✈ (LAS) U.S.A. 36°5N 115°9W 124 B2
McCarthy U.S.A. 61°26N 142°56W 303 F12
McCauley I. Canada 53°40N 130°15W 296 C3
McCleary U.S.A. 47°3N 123°16W 306 C3
Macclenny U.S.A. 30°17N 82°7W 316 E7
Macclesfield U.K. 53°15N 2°8W 168 D5
M'Clintock Chan. Canada 72°0N 102°0W 294 C11
McClintock Ra. Australia 18°44S 127°38E 278 C4
McCloud U.S.A. 41°15N 122°8W 304 F2
McCluer I. Australia 11°5S 133°0E 278 B5
McClure U.S.A. 40°42N 77°19W 312 F7
McClure, L. U.S.A. 37°35N 120°16W 306 H6
M'Clure Str. Canada 75°0N 119°0W 295 C8
McClusky U.S.A. 47°29N 100°27W 308 B3
McComb U.S.A. 31°15N 90°27W 315 F9
McCook Ill., U.S.A. 41°47N 87°49W 119 C2
McCook Nebr., U.S.A. 40°12N 100°38W 308 E3
McCormick U.S.A. 33°55N 82°17W 316 B7
McCreary Canada 50°47N 99°29W 297 C9
McCullough Mt. U.S.A. 35°35N 115°13W 307 K11
McCusker → Canada 55°32N 108°39W 297 B7
McDavid U.S.A. 30°52N 87°19W 317 E2
McDermitt U.S.A. 41°59N 117°43W 304 F5
McDonald U.S.A. 40°22N 80°14W 312 F4
Macdonald, L. Australia 23°30S 129°0E 278 D4
Macdonald, Mt. Vanuatu 17°36S 168°23E 287 G6
McDonald Is. Ind. Oc. 53°0S 73°0E 273 K6
MacDonnell Ranges Australia 23°40S 133°0E 278 D5
McDonough U.S.A. 33°27N 84°9W 316 B5
McDougalls Well Australia 31°8S 141°15E 282 A4
MacDowell L. Canada 52°15N 92°45W 298 B1
Macduff U.K. 57°40N 2°31W 167 D6
Maceda Spain 42°16N 7°39W 194 C3
Macedonia U.S.A. 41°19N 81°31W 312 E3
Macedonia ■ Europe 41°53N 21°40E 202 E5
Maceió Brazil 9°40S 35°41W 332 C4
Maceira Portugal 39°41N 8°55W 194 F2
Macenta Guinea 8°35N 9°32W 262 D3
Macerata Italy 43°18N 13°27E 199 E10
McFarland U.S.A. 35°41N 119°14W 307 K7
McFarlane → Canada 59°12N 107°58W 297 B7
Macfarlane, L. Australia 32°0S 136°40E 282 B2
McGehee U.S.A. 33°38N 91°24W 314 E9
McGill U.S.A. 39°23N 114°47W 304 G6
McGill Univ. Montréal, Canada 130 b1
Macgillycuddy's Reeks Ireland 51°58N 9°45W 166 E2
McGrath U.S.A. 62°58N 155°36W 303 E9
McGraw U.S.A. 42°36N 76°8W 313 D8
McGregor U.S.A. 43°1N 91°11W 310 A5
McGregor Ra. Australia 27°0S 142°45E 281 D3
McGuire, Mt. Australia 20°18S 148°23E 280 b
Mach Pakistan 29°50N 67°20E 242 E2
Māch Kowr Iran 25°48N 61°28E 247 E9
Machacalis Brazil 17°5S 40°45W 333 E3
Machado = Jiparaná → Brazil 8°3S 62°52W 331 B5
Machagai Argentina 26°56S 60°2W 334 B3
Machakos Kenya 1°30S 37°15E 268 C4
Machala Ecuador 3°20S 79°57W 328 D2
Machalilla △ Ecuador 1°24S 80°42W 328 D1
Machanga Mozam. 20°59S 35°0E 271 B6
Machattie, L. Australia 24°50S 139°48E 280 C2
Machault France 49°21N 4°29E 173 C11
Machava Mozam. 25°54S 32°28E 271 C5
Machece Mozam. 19°15S 35°32E 269 F4
Machecoul France 47°0N 1°49W 172 F5
Macheke Zimbabwe 18°5S 31°51E 271 A5
Machelen Belgium 50°55N 4°26E 116 A2
Macheng China 31°12N 115°2E 229 B10
McHenry U.S.A. 42°21N 88°16W 311 B8
Macherado Greece 37°46N 20°49E 207 D2
Macherla India 16°29N 79°26E 244 F4
Machero Spain 39°21N 4°20W 195 F6
Machgaon India 20°5N 86°17E 244 D8
Machhu → India 23°6N 70°46E 242 H4
Machiara △ Pakistan 34°40N 73°30E 242 B5
Machias Maine, U.S.A. 44°43N 67°28W 309 C20
Machias N.Y., U.S.A. 42°25N 78°29W 312 D6
Machichi → Canada 57°3N 92°6W 297 B10
Machico Madeira 32°43N 16°44W 153 c
Machida Japan 35°32N 139°26E 140 B1
Machilipatnam India 16°12N 81°8E 245 F5
Machiques Venezuela 10°4N 72°34W 328 A3
Machu Pichu Peru 13°8S 72°30W 330 C3
Machynlleth U.K. 52°35N 3°50W 169 E4
Macia Mozam. 25°2S 33°8E 271 C5
Macias Nguema Biyoga = Bioko Eq. Guin. 3°30N 8°40E 263 E6
Maciejowice Poland 51°36N 21°26E 185 G8
McIlwraith Ra. Australia 13°50S 143°20E 280 A3
Măcin Romania 45°16N 28°8E 183 E13
Macina Mali 14°50N 5°0W 262 C4
McInnes L. Canada 52°13N 93°45W 297 C10
McIntosh U.S.A. 45°55N 101°21W 308 C3
McIntosh L. Canada 55°45N 105°0W 297 B8
Macintosh Ra. Australia 27°39S 125°32E 279 E4
Macintyre → Australia 28°37S 150°47E 281 D5
Maciolki Poland 52°19N 21°9E 142 B2
Macizo Galaico Spain 42°30N 7°30W 194 C3
Macka Turkey 40°49N 39°36E 213 B8
Mackay Queens., Australia 21°8S 149°11E 280 K7
Mackay Idaho, U.S.A. 43°55N 113°37W 304 E7
MacKay → Canada 57°10N 111°38W 296 B6
Mackay, L. Australia 22°30S 129°0E 278 D4
McKay Ra. Australia 23°0S 122°30E 278 D3
McKean Kiribati 3°36S 174°8W 277 A16
McKeesport U.S.A. 40°20N 79°51W 312 F5
McKellar Canada 45°30N 79°55W 312 A5
McKenna U.S.A. 46°56N 122°33W 306 D4
Mackenzie Canada 55°20N 123°5W 296 B4
McKenzie U.S.A. 36°8N 88°31W 315 C10
Mackenzie → Queens., Australia 23°38S 149°46E 280 C4
Mackenzie → N.W.T., Canada 69°10N 134°20W 294 D5
McKenzie → U.S.A. 44°7N 123°6W 304 D2
Mackenzie Bay Canada 69°0N 137°30W 292 C6
Mackenzie City = Linden Guyana 6°0N 58°10W 329 B6
Mackenzie King I. Canada 77°45N 111°0W 295 B9
Mackenzie Mts. Canada 64°0N 130°0W 294 E6
Mackenzie Plains N.Z. 44°10S 170°25E 285 E5
McKerrow, L. N.Z. 44°25S 168°5E 285 E3
McKerrow, Mt. N.Z. 41°19S 174°58E 143 B2
Mackheim = Maków Mazowiecki Poland 52°52N 21°6E 185 F8
Mackinac, Straits of U.S.A. 45°50N 84°40W 301 F23
Mackinaw U.S.A. 40°32N 89°21W 310 D7
Mackinaw → U.S.A. 40°33N 89°44W 310 D7
Mackinaw City U.S.A. 45°47N 84°44W 309 C11
McKinlay Australia 21°16S 141°18E 280 C3
McKinlay → Australia 20°50S 141°28E 280 C3
McKinley, Mt. U.S.A. 63°4N 151°0W 303 E10
McKinley Park Alaska, U.S.A. 63°44N 148°55W 303 E10
McKinley Park Ill., U.S.A. 41°49N 87°40W 119 C2
McKinley Sea Arctic 82°0N 0°0 154 A11
McKinney U.S.A. 33°12N 96°37W 314 E6
Mackinnon Road Kenya 3°40S 39°1E 268 C4
McKittrick Calif., U.S.A. 35°18N 119°37W 307 K7
McKittrick Mo., U.S.A. 38°44N 91°27W 310 F5
Macklin Canada 52°20N 109°56W 297 C7
Macksville Australia 30°40S 152°56E 283 A10
McLaren Vale Australia 35°13S 138°31E 282 C3
McLaughlin U.S.A. 45°49N 100°49W 308 C3
Maclean Australia 29°26S 153°16E 281 D5
McLean Ill., U.S.A. 40°19N 89°10W 310 D7
McLean Tex., U.S.A. 35°14N 100°36W 314 D4
McLean Va., U.S.A. 38°56N 77°10W 143 B2
McLeansboro U.S.A. 38°6N 88°32W 311 F8
Maclear S. Africa 31°2S 28°23E 271 D4
Maclear, C. Malawi 13°58S 34°49E 269 E3
Macleay → Australia 30°56S 153°0E 283 A10
McLennan Canada 55°42N 116°50W 296 B5
MacLeod = Fort Macleod Canada 49°45N 113°30W 296 D6
McLeod → Canada 54°9N 115°44W 296 C5
MacLeod, L. Australia 24°9S 113°47E 279 D1
MacLeod B. Canada 62°53N 110°0W 297 A7
MacLeod Lake Canada 54°58N 123°0W 296 C4
McLoughlin, Mt. U.S.A. 42°27N 122°19W 304 E2
MacMahon = Aïn Touta Algeria 35°26N 5°54E 261 A6
McMechen U.S.A. 39°57N 80°44W 312 G4
McMinnville Oreg., U.S.A. 45°13N 123°12W 304 D2
McMinnville Tenn., U.S.A. 35°41N 85°46W 315 D12
McMurdo Antarctica 77°0S 140°0E 151 D11
McMurdo Sd. Antarctica 77°0S 170°0E 151 D11
McMurray = Fort McMurray Canada 56°44N 111°7W 296 B6
McMurray U.S.A. 48°19N 122°14W 306 B4
Maco Phil. 7°20N 125°50E 233 H5
Maçobere Mozam. 21°13S 32°47E 269 G3
Macocolo Angola 6°47S 16°8E 265 D3
Macodoene Mozam. 23°32S 35°5E 271 B6
Macolo Angola 7°5S 16°42E 265 D3
Macomb U.S.A. 40°27N 90°40W 310 D6
Macomer Italy 40°16N 8°47E 200 B1
Mâcon Saône-et-Loire, France 46°19N 4°50E 173 F11
Macon Ga., U.S.A. 32°51N 83°38W 316 C6
Macon Ill., U.S.A. 39°43N 89°0W 310 E8
Macon Miss., U.S.A. 33°7N 88°34W 315 E10
Macon Mo., U.S.A. 39°44N 92°28W 310 E4
Macondo Angola 12°37S 23°46E 265 E4
Macopocho → Chile 33°24S 70°40W 137 B1
Macossa Mozam. 17°55S 33°56E 269 F3
Macou → Dominica 15°25N 61°27W 323 k
Macou, Pte. Guadeloupe 16°21N 61°31W 322 e
Macouba Martinique 14°52N 61°9W 322 j
Macoun L. Canada 56°32N 103°40W 297 B8
Macoupin Cr. → U.S.A. 39°11N 90°38W 310 E6
Macovane Mozam. 21°30S 35°2E 271 B6
MacPherson = Kapuskasing Canada 49°25N 82°30W 298 C3
McPherson U.S.A. 38°22N 97°40W 308 F5
McPherson Pk. U.S.A. 34°53N 119°53W 307 L7
McPherson Ra. Australia 28°15S 153°15E 281 D5
Macquarie → Australia 30°7S 147°24E 283 A7
Macquarie Harbour Australia 42°15S 145°23E 281 G4
Macquarie Is. Pac. Oc. 54°36S 158°55E 288 N7
Macquarie Ridge S. Ocean 57°0S 159°0E 151 B10
Macqueripe B. Trin. & Tob. 10°44N 61°37W 323 t
McRae U.S.A. 32°4N 82°54W 316 C7
MacRitchie Res. Singapore 1°20N 103°49E 138 A2
MacRobertson Land Antarctica 71°0S 64°0E 151 D6
Macroom Ireland 51°54N 8°57W 166 E3
MacTier Canada 45°8N 79°47W 312 A5
Macubela Mozam. 16°53S 37°49E 269 F4
Macugnaga Italy 45°58N 7°58E 198 C4
Macuira △ Colombia 12°9N 71°21W 328 A3
Macuiza Mozam. 18°7S 34°29E 269 F3
Macuje Colombia 0°24N 73°10W 328 C3
Macul Chile 33°30S 70°35W 137 C2
Macumba → Australia 27°52S 137°12E 281 D2
Macuro Venezuela 10°42N 61°55W 329 F9
Macusani Peru 14°4S 70°29W 330 C3
Macuse Mozam. 17°45S 37°10E 269 F4
Macuspana Mexico 17°46N 92°36W 319 D6
Macusse Angola 17°48S 20°23E 265 F4
Mada → Nigeria 7°59N 7°55E 263 D6
Ma'dabā □ Jordan 31°43N 35°47E 251 G6
Madadeni S. Africa 27°43S 30°3E 271 C5
Madadi Chad 18°28N 20°45E 259 E4
Madagali Nigeria 10°56N 13°33E 263 C7
Madagascar ■ Africa 20°0S 47°0E 272 B2
Madagoi → Somali Rep. 0°49N 42°58E 267 D5
Madā'in Sālih Si. Arabia 26°46N 37°57E 246 E3
Madakasira India 13°56N 77°16E 245 H3
Madalena Azores 38°32N 28°32W 153 d1
Madama Niger 22°0N 13°40E 259 D2
Madame, I. Canada 45°30N 60°58W 299 C7
Madame Tussaud's London, U.K. 125 a3
Madan Bulgaria 41°30N 24°57E 203 E8
Madanapalle India 13°33N 78°28E 245 H4
Madang Papua N. G. 5°12S 145°49E 286 C3
Madang □ Papua N. G. 5°0S 145°30E 286 C3
Madaoua Niger 14°5N 6°27E 263 C6
Madara Nigeria 11°45N 10°35E 263 C7
Madaripur Bangla. 23°19N 90°15E 241 D3
Madau I. Papua N. G. 8°58S 152°28E 286 E7
Madauk Burma 17°56N 96°52E 241 G6
Madawaska Canada 45°30N 78°0W 312 A7
Madawaska → Canada 45°27N 76°21W 312 A8
Madaxmaroodi Somali Rep. 2°39N 44°36E 267 D5
Madaya Burma 22°12N 96°10E 241 D6
Madbar Sudan 6°17N 30°45E 257 F3
Maddalena Italy 41°16N 9°23E 200 A2
Maddaloni Italy 41°2N 14°23E 201 A7
Maddela Phil. 16°21N 121°41E 232 C3
Maddur India 12°36N 77°4E 245 H3
Madeira Atl. Oc. 32°50N 17°0W 153 c
Madeira Ohio, U.S.A. 39°11N 84°21W 311 E12
Madeira → Brazil 3°22S 58°45W 329 D6
Madeleine, Îs. de la Canada 47°30N 61°40W 299 C7
Maden Turkey 38°23N 39°40E 213 C8
Madera Chihuahua, Mexico 29°12N 108°7W 318 B3
Madera Calif., U.S.A. 36°57N 120°3W 306 J6
Madera Pa., U.S.A. 40°49N 78°26W 312 F6
Madgaon India 15°12N 73°58E 245 G1
Madha India 18°0N 75°30E 244 F2
Madhavpur India 21°15N 69°58E 242 J3
Madhepura India 26°11N 86°23E 243 F12
Madhira India 16°55N 80°22E 244 F5
Madhubani India 26°21N 86°7E 243 F12
Madhugiri India 13°40N 77°12E 245 H3
Madhumati → Bangla. 22°53N 89°52E 241 D2
Madhupur Bangla. 24°37N 90°2E 241 C3
Madhupur India 24°16N 86°39E 243 G12
Madhya Pradesh □ India 22°50N 78°0E 242 J8
Madhyamgram India 22°41N 88°26E 124 A2
Madidi → Bolivia 12°32S 66°52W 330 C4
Madikeri India 12°30N 75°45E 245 H2
Madikwe ⌂ S. Africa 27°38S 32°15E 271 C5
Madill U.S.A. 34°6N 96°46W 314 D6
Madimba Angola 6°36S 14°23E 265 D2
Madimba Dem. Rep. of the Congo 4°58S 15°5E 265 C3
Madīn México, Mexico 19°32N 99°16W 128 A1
Ma'dīn Syria 35°45N 39°36E 213 E8
Madin, L. Mexico 19°31N 99°16W 128 A1
Madina Mali 13°25N 8°50W 262 C3
Madīnah Al Manṣūr Iraq 33°18N 44°20E 113 B2
Madinani Ivory C. 9°37N 6°57W 262 D3
Madīnat al Malik Khālid al Askarīyah Si. Arabia 27°54N 45°31E 246 E5
Madīnat ash Sha'b Yemen 12°50N 45°0E 248 D4
Madīnat ath Thawrah Syria 35°50N 38°32E 213 E8
Mâdinet Nasr Egypt 30°4N 31°18E 117 A2
Madingo Congo 4°5S 11°24E 264 C2
Madingou Congo 4°10S 13°33E 264 C2
Madīq Gûbâl Egypt 27°47N 33°55E 251 L4
Madīq Tirân Egypt 27°55N 34°30E 251 L5
Madirovalo Madag. 16°26S 46°32E 272 B2
Madison Calif., U.S.A. 38°41N 121°59W 306 G5
Madison Fla., U.S.A. 30°28N 83°25W 316 E6
Madison Ga., U.S.A. 33°36N 83°28W 316 B6
Madison Ind., U.S.A. 38°44N 85°23W 311 F11
Madison Mo., U.S.A. 39°28N 92°13W 310 E4
Madison Nebr., U.S.A. 41°50N 97°27W 308 E5
Madison Ohio, U.S.A. 41°46N 81°3W 312 E3
Madison S. Dak., U.S.A. 44°0N 97°7W 308 D5
Madison Wis., U.S.A. 43°4N 89°24W 310 A7
Madison → U.S.A. 45°56N 111°31W 304 D8
Madison Avenue New York, U.S.A. 132 c2
Madison Heights U.S.A. 37°25N 79°8W 309 G14
Madison Square New York, U.S.A. 132 d2
Madison Square Garden New York, U.S.A. 132 c2
Madisonville Ky., U.S.A. 37°20N 87°30W 308 G10
Madisonville Tex., U.S.A. 30°57N 95°55W 314 F7
Madista Botswana 21°15S 25°6E 270 B4
Madiun Indonesia 7°38S 111°32E 235 D4
Madjingo Gabon 1°20N 14°4E 264 B2
Mado Gashi Kenya 0°44N 39°10E 268 B4
Madoc Canada 44°30N 77°28W 312 B7
Madon → France 48°36N 6°6E 173 D13
Madona Latvia 56°53N 26°5E 188 D4
Madonie Italy 37°50N 13°50E 200 E6
Madonna di Campiglio Italy 46°14N 10°49E 198 B7
Madra Dağı Turkey 39°23N 27°12E 205 B9
Madrakah, Ra's al Oman 19°0N 57°50E 249 C7
Madras = Chennai India 13°8N 80°19E 245 H5
Madras = Tamil Nadu □ India 11°0N 77°0E 245 J3
Madras U.S.A. 44°38N 121°8W 304 D3
Madre, L. U.S.A. 25°15N 97°30W 314 J6
Madre, Sierra Phil. 17°0N 122°0E 232 C4
Madre de Dios □ Peru 12°0S 70°15W 330 C3
Madre de Dios → Bolivia 10°59S 66°8W 330 C4
Madre de Dios, I. Chile 50°20S 75°10W 336 D1
Madre del Sur, Sierra Mexico 17°30N 100°0W 319 D5
Madre Occidental, Sierra Mexico 27°0N 107°0W 318 B3
Madre Oriental, Sierra Mexico 25°0N 100°0W 318 C5
Madri India 24°16N 73°32E 242 G5
Madrid Spain 40°24N 3°42W 127 B1
Madrid Ala., U.S.A. 31°2N 85°24W 316 D4
Madrid Iowa, U.S.A. 41°53N 93°49W 310 C3
Madrid N.Y., U.S.A. 44°45N 75°8W 313 B9
Madrid □ Spain 40°30N 3°45W 194 E7
Madrid Barajas ✈ (MAD) Spain 40°26N 3°34W 127 B2
Madridejos Spain 39°28N 3°33W 195 F7
Madrigal de las Altas Torres Spain 41°5N 5°0W 194 D6
Madrona Spain 41°27N 2°1E 114 A1
Madrona, Sierra Spain 38°27N 4°16W 195 G6
Madroñera Spain 39°26N 5°42W 195 F5
Madrusah Libya 24°48N 14°32E 258 D2
Madu Sudan 14°37N 26°4E 257 E2
Madula Dem. Rep. of the Congo 0°27N 25°22E 264 B5
Maduo Dem. Rep. of the Congo 1°24S 20°44E 264 C4
Madura W. Austral., Australia 31°55S 127°0E 279 F4
Madura Indonesia 7°30S 114°0E 231 G15
Madura, Selat Indonesia 7°30S 113°20E 235 D4
Madura Oya △ Sri Lanka 7°20N 81°10E 245 L5
Madurai India 9°55N 78°10E 245 K4
Madurantakam India 12°30N 79°50E 245 H4
Madzhalis Russia 42°9N 47°47E 191 J8
Mae Chan Thailand 20°9N 99°52E 236 B2
Mae Hong Son Thailand 19°16N 97°56E 236 C2
Mae Khlong → Thailand 13°24N 100°0E 236 F3
Mae Phrik Thailand 17°27N 99°7E 236 D2
Mae Ping △ Thailand 17°37N 98°51E 236 D2
Mae Ramat Thailand 16°58N 98°31E 236 D2
Mae Rim Thailand 18°54N 98°57E 236 C2
Mae Sai Thailand 20°20N 99°55E 228 G2
Mae Sot Thailand 16°43N 98°34E 236 D2
Mae Suai Thailand 19°39N 99°33E 228 H2
Mae Tha Thailand 18°28N 99°8E 236 C2
Mae Wong △ Thailand 15°54N 99°12E 236 E2
Mae Yom △ Thailand 18°43N 100°15E 236 C3
Maebaru Japan 33°33N 130°12E 222 D2
Maebashi Japan 36°24N 139°4E 223 A11
Maella Spain 41°8N 0°7E 196 D5
Maelpaeg L. Canada 48°20N 56°30W 299 C8
Maesawa Japan 35°44N 139°31E 140 A2
Maesteg U.K. 51°36N 3°40W 169 F4
Maestra, Sierra Cuba 20°15N 77°0W 320 B4
Maestre de Campo I. Phil. 12°56N 121°42E 232 E3
Maetambe, Mt. Solomon Is. 7°3S 157°1E 287 L9
Maevatanana Madag. 16°56S 46°49E 272 B2
Maéwo Vanuatu 15°10S 168°10E 287 E6
Mafadi S. Africa 29°12S 29°21E 271 C4
Mafate, Cirque de Réunion 21°3S 55°25E 272 f
Mafeking = Mafikeng S. Africa 25°50S 25°38E 270 C4
Mafeking Canada 52°40N 101°10W 297 C8
Maféré Ivory C. 5°30N 3°2W 262 D4
Mafeteng Lesotho 29°51S 27°15E 270 C4
Maffra Australia 37°53S 146°58E 283 D7
Mafia I. Tanzania 7°45S 39°50E 268 D4
Mafikeng S. Africa 25°50S 25°38E 270 C4
Mafra Brazil 26°10S 49°55W 335 B6
Mafra Portugal 38°55N 9°20W 195 G1
Mafungabusi Plateau Zimbabwe 18°30S 29°8E 269 F2
Magadan Russia 59°38N 150°50E 215 D16
Magadi India 12°58N 77°14E 245 H3
Magadi Rift Valley, Kenya 1°54S 36°19E 268 C4
Magadi, L. Kenya 1°54S 36°19E 268 C4
Magaliesburg S. Africa 26°0S 27°32E 271 C4
Magallanes = Punta Arenas Chile 53°10S 71°0W 336 D2
Magallanes Phil. 12°50N 123°50E 232 E4
Magallanes □ Chile 52°0S 72°0W 336 D2
Magallanes, Estrecho de Chile 52°30S 75°0W 336 D2
Magaluf Spain 39°29N 2°32E 206 B3
Magangué Colombia 9°14N 74°45W 328 B3
Maganoy Phil. 6°51N 124°31E 233 H5
Magaria Niger 13°4N 9°5E 259 F1
Magarida Papua N. G. 10°18S 149°20E 286 F5
Magburaka S. Leone 8°47N 12°0W 262 D2
Magdagachi Russia 53°27N 125°48E 215 D13
Magdalen Is. = Madeleine, Îs. de la Canada 47°30N 61°40W 299 C7

INDEX
Manasquan 397

Magdalena Argentina 35°5S 57°30W 334 D4
Magdalena Bolivia 13°13S 63°57W 331 C5
Magdalena Lima, Peru 12°5S 77°5W 124 B2
Magdalena N. Mex., U.S.A. 34°7N 107°15W 305 J10
Magdalena □ Colombia 10°0N 74°0W 328 B3
Magdalena ➝ Colombia 11°6N 74°51W 328 A3
Magdalena ➝ Mexico 30°40N 112°25W 318 A2
Magdalena, B. Mexico 24°35N 112°0W 318 C2
Magdalena, I. Chile 44°40S 73°0W 336 B2
Magdalena, I. Mexico 24°40N 112°15W 318 C2
Magdalena, Llano de Mexico 25°0N 111°25W 318 C2
Magdalena Contreras Mexico 19°20N 99°13W 128 C1
Magdalena de Kino Mexico 30°38N 110°57W 318 A2
Magdeburg Germany 52°7N 11°38E 178 C7
Magdelaine Cays Australia 16°33S 150°18E 280 B5
Magdub Sudan 13°42N 25°5E 257 E2
Magee U.S.A. 31°52N 89°44W 315 F10
Magelang Indonesia 7°29S 110°13E 235 D4
Magellan's Str. = Magallanes, Estrecho de Chile 52°30S 75°0W 336 D2
Magenta Italy 45°28N 8°53E 198 C5
Magenta, L. Australia 33°30S 119°2E 279 F2
Magerøya Norway 71°3N 25°40E 160 A21
Maggea Australia 34°28S 140°2E 282 C4
Maggia ➝ Switz. 46°18N 8°36E 179 J4
Maggiorasca, Mte. Italy 44°33N 9°29E 198 D6
Maggiore, Lago Italy 45°57N 8°39E 198 B5
Maggotty Jamaica 18°9N 77°46W 320 a
Maghâgha Egypt 28°38N 30°50E 256 B3
Maghama Mauritania 15°32N 12°57W 262 B2
Magherafelt U.K. 54°45N 6°37W 166 B5
Maghnia Algeria 34°50N 1°43W 261 B4
Maghreb Baghdād, Iraq 33°23N 44°22E 113 A2
Maghreb N. Afr. 32°0N 4°0W 254 C3
Maginu Japan 35°34N 139°34E 140 B2
Magione Italy 43°8N 12°12E 199 E9
Magistralnyy Russia 56°16N 107°36E 215 D11
Maglaj Bos.-H. 44°33N 18°7E 182 F3
Magliana Italy 41°50N 12°26E 136 B1
Magliano in Toscana Italy 42°36N 11°17E 199 F8
Máglie Italy 40°7N 18°18E 201 B11
Magnac-Laval France 46°13N 1°11E 174 B5
Magnetic Pole (North) Canada 82°42N 114°24W 150 A2
Magnetic Pole (South) Antarctica 64°8S 138°8E 151 C9
Magnisia □ Greece 39°15N 23°0E 204 B5
Magnitogorsk Russia 53°27N 59°4E 186 D10
Magnolia Ark., U.S.A. 33°16N 93°14W 314 E8
Magnolia Miss., U.S.A. 31°9N 90°28W 315 F9
Magnor Norway 59°56N 12°15E 164 E9
Magny-en-Vexin France 49°9N 1°47E 173 C8
Magny-les-Hameaux France 48°44N 2°3E 134 B1
Mago Fiji 17°26S 179°8W 287 A3
Mago △ Ethiopia 5°40N 36°18E 257 F4
Magog Canada 45°18N 72°9W 313 A12
Magoro Uganda 1°45N 34°12E 268 B3
Magoša = Famagusta Cyprus 35°8N 33°55E 207 E9
Magoye Zambia 16°1S 27°30E 269 F2
Magpie, L. Canada 51°0N 64°41W 299 B7
Magrath Canada 49°25N 112°50W 296 D6
Magre ➝ Spain 39°11N 0°25W 197 F4
Magrur Sudan 14°1N 30°27E 257 E3
Magrur, Wadi ➝ Sudan 16°5N 26°30E 257 D2
Magsingal Phil. 17°41N 120°25E 232 C3
Magta Lahjar Mauritania 17°28N 13°17W 262 B2
Magu Tanzania 2°30S 33°30E 268 C3
Maguan China 23°0N 104°21E 228 F5
Maguarinho, C. Brazil 0°15S 48°30W 332 B2
Magude Mozam. 25°2S 32°40E 271 C5
Maguindanao □ Phil. 7°5N 124°40E 233 H5
Magurski △ Poland 49°30N 21°30E 185 J8
Magusa = Famagusta Cyprus 35°8N 33°55E 207 E9
Maguse L. Canada 61°37N 95°10W 297 A9
Maguse Pt. Canada 61°20N 93°50W 297 A10
Magvana India 23°13N 69°22E 242 H3
Magwe Burma 20°10N 95°0E 241 E5
Magwe Sudan 4°8N 32°17E 257 G3
Magwe □ Burma 20°0N 95°0E 241 F5
Magyarorszag = Hungary ■ Europe 47°20N 19°20E 181 D12
Maha Oya Sri Lanka 7°31N 81°22E 245 L5
Maha Sarakham Thailand 16°12N 103°16E 236 D4
Mahābād Iran 36°50N 45°45E 213 D11
Mahabaleshwar India 17°58N 73°43E 244 F1
Mahabharat Lekh Nepal 28°30N 82°0E 243 E10
Mahabo Madag. 20°23S 44°40E 272 C1
Mahad India 18°6N 73°29E 244 E1
Mahaddayweyne Somali Rep. 2°58N 45°32E 267 D6
Mahadeo Hills India 22°20N 78°30E 243 H8
Mahadeopur India 18°48N 80°0E 244 E5
Mahaffey U.S.A. 40°53N 78°44W 312 F6
Mahagi Dem. Rep. of the Congo 2°20N 31°0E 268 B3
Mahaicony Guyana 6°36N 57°48W 329 B6
Mahajamba ➝ Madag. 15°33S 47°8E 272 B2
Mahajamba, Helodranon' i Madag. 15°24S 47°5E 272 B2
Mahajan India 28°48N 73°56E 242 E5
Mahajanga Madag. 15°40S 46°25E 272 B2
Mahajanga □ Madag. 17°0S 47°0E 272 B2
Mahajilo ➝ Madag. 19°42S 45°22E 272 B2
Mahakam ➝ Indonesia 0°35S 117°17E 235 C5
Mahalapye Botswana 23°1S 26°51E 270 B4
Mahalaxmi Mumbai, India 130 a1
Mahalchhar Bangla. 22°55N 92°2E 241 D4
Mahale Mts. Tanzania 6°20S 30°0E 268 D3
Mahale Mts. △ Tanzania 6°10S 29°50E 268 D2
Maḩallāt Iran 33°55N 50°30E 247 C6
Māhān Iran 30°5N 57°18E 247 D8
Mahan ➝ India 23°30N 82°50E 243 H10
Mahanadi ➝ India 20°20N 86°25E 244 D8
Mahananda ➝ India 25°12N 87°52E 243 G12
Mahanoro Madag. 19°54S 48°48E 272 B2
Mahanoy City U.S.A. 40°49N 76°9W 313 F8
Mahaplag Phil. 10°35N 124°57E 233 F5
Maharashtra □ India 20°30N 75°30E 244 D2
Maharès Tunisia 34°32N 10°29E 258 B2
Maharivo Madag. 20°26S 44°10E 272 C1
Mahasamund India 21°6N 82°6E 244 D6
Mahasham, W. ➝ Egypt 30°15N 34°10E 251 H5
Mahasoa Madag. 23°23S 45°41E 272 C2
Mahasolo Madag. 19°7S 46°22E 272 B2
Mahattat ash Shīdīyah Jordan 29°55N 35°55E 251 J6
Mahattat 'Unayzah Jordan 30°30N 35°47E 251 H6
Mahaut Dominica 15°21N 61°24W 323 k
Mahaut Guadeloupe 16°11N 61°46W 322 e
Mahavavy ➝ Madag. 15°57S 45°54E 272 B2
Mahaweli Ganga ➝ Sri Lanka 8°27N 81°13E 245 K5
Mahaxay Laos 17°22N 105°12E 236 D5
Mahbubabad India 17°42N 80°2E 244 F5
Mahbubnagar India 16°45N 77°59E 244 F3
Mahd adh Dhahab Si. Arabia 23°30N 40°52E 248 B3
Mahda U.A.E. 25°20N 56°15E 247 E8
Maḩḑah Oman 24°24N 55°59E 247 E7
Mahdia Guyana 5°13N 59°8W 329 B6
Mahdia Tunisia 35°28N 11°0E 258 A2
Mahdia □ Tunisia 35°20N 10°35E 261 A7
Mahe Jammu & Kashmir, India 33°10N 78°32E 243 C8
Mahé Pondicherry, India 11°42N 75°34E 245 J2
Mahé Seychelles 5°0S 55°30E 272 c
Mahé ✕ (SEZ) Seychelles 4°40S 55°31E 272 c
Mahébourg Mauritius 20°24S 57°42E 272 e
Mahendra Giri India 8°20N 77°30E 245 K3
Mahendraganj India 25°20N 89°45E 241 C2
Mahendragarh India 28°17N 76°14E 242 E7
Mahendranagar Nepal 28°55N 80°20E 243 E9
Mahenge Tanzania 8°45S 36°41E 269 D4
Maheno N.Z. 45°10S 170°50E 285 F5
Mahesana India 23°39N 72°26E 242 H5
Maheshtala India 22°29N 88°15E 124 C1
Maheshwar India 22°11N 75°35E 242 H6
Mahgawan India 26°29N 78°37E 243 F8
Mahi ➝ India 22°15N 72°55E 242 H5
Mahia Pen. N.Z. 39°9S 177°55E 284 F6
Mahibadhoo Maldives 3°47N 72°58E 272 d
Mahighe Solomon Is. 8°30S 159°58E 287 M10
Mahilyow Belarus 53°55N 30°18E 177 B16
Mahilyow □ Belarus 54°10N 30°50E 188 E6
Mahim Maharashtra, India 19°2N 72°50E 130 A2
Mahim Maharashtra, India 19°39N 72°44E 244 E1
Mahim B. India 19°2N 72°49E 130 A1
Mahina Tahiti 17°30S 149°27W 289 e
Mahirija Morocco 34°0N 3°16W 261 B4
Mahlaing Burma 21°6N 95°39E 241 E5
Mahlsdorf Germany 52°30N 13°37E 115 A4
Mahmiya Sudan 17°12N 33°43E 257 D3
Mahmoodabad Pakistan 24°51N 67°4E 123 A2
Mahmud Kot Pakistan 30°16N 71°0E 242 D4
Mahmudia Romania 45°5N 29°5E 183 E14
Mahmudiye Turkey 39°48N 30°15E 205 B12
Mahmutbey Turkey 41°3N 28°49E 203 E12
Mahmutlar Turkey 36°29N 32°5E 250 B3
Māhneshān Iran 36°44N 47°39E 213 D12
Mahnomen U.S.A. 47°19N 95°58W 308 B6
Maho Sri Lanka 7°49N 80°16E 245 L5
Mahoba India 25°15N 79°55E 243 G8
Mahomet U.S.A. 40°12N 88°24W 311 D8
Mahón = Maó Spain 39°53N 4°16E 206 B5
Mahon, Menorca ✕ (MAH) Spain 39°50N 4°16E 196 F9
Mahone Bay Canada 44°27N 64°23W 299 D7
Mahongo ⌓ Namibia 18°0S 23°15E 270 B3
Mahopac U.S.A. 41°22N 73°45W 313 E11
Mahoua Chad 11°49N 18°26E 259 F3
Mahrauli India 28°31N 77°10E 120 B2
Mährisch-Budwitz = Moravské Budějovice Czech Rep. 49°4N 15°49E 180 B8
Mährisch-Schönberg = Šumperk Czech Rep. 49°59N 16°59E 181 B9
Mährisch-Trubau = Moravská Třebová Czech Rep. 49°45N 16°40E 181 B9
Mahul India 19°0N 72°53E 130 A2
Mahuta Nigeria 11°32N 4°58E 263 C5
Mahuva India 21°5N 71°48E 242 J4
Mahya Daği Turkey 41°47N 27°36E 203 E11
Mai-Ndombe, L. Dem. Rep. of the Congo 2°0S 18°20E 264 C3
Mai Thon, Ko Thailand 7°40N 98°28E 237 a
Maia Amer. Samoa 14°13S 169°25W 302 g
Maia Azores 36°56N 25°1W 153 d4
Maia Portugal 41°14N 8°37W 194 D2
Maials Spain 41°22N 0°30E 196 D5
Maibong India 25°18N 93°10E 241 C4
Maicao Colombia 11°23N 72°13W 328 A3
Maîche France 47°16N 6°48E 173 E13
Maici ➝ Brazil 6°30S 61°43W 331 B5
Maicuru ➝ Brazil 2°14S 54°17W 329 D7
Máida Italy 38°51N 16°22E 201 D9
Maida Vale London, U.K. 125 a1
Maidan Khula Afghan. 33°36N 69°50E 242 C3
Maidenhead U.K. 51°31N 0°42W 169 F7
Maidstone Vic., Australia 37°47S 144°52E 128 A1
Maidstone Sask., Canada 53°5N 109°20W 297 C7
Maidstone Kent, U.K. 51°16N 0°32E 169 F8
Maiduguri Nigeria 12°0N 13°20E 263 C7
Maiella △ Italy 42°5N 14°5E 199 F11
Măieruş Romania 45°53N 25°31E 183 E10
Maigatari Nigeria 12°46N 9°27E 263 C6
Maigh Nuad = Maynooth Ireland 53°23N 6°34W 166 C5
Maignelay Montigny France 49°32N 2°30E 173 C9
Maigo Phil. 8°10N 123°57E 233 G4
Maigualida, Sierra Venezuela 5°30N 65°10W 329 B4
Maigudo Ethiopia 7°30N 37°8E 257 F4
Maihar India 24°16N 80°45E 243 G9
Maihara Japan 35°19N 136°17E 223 B8
Maikala Ra. India 22°0N 81°0E 244 D5
Maiko △ Dem. Rep. of the Congo 0°30S 27°50E 268 C2
Mailani India 28°17N 80°21E 243 E9
Mā'ili U.S.A. 21°25N 158°11W 302 K13
Mā'ili Pt. U.S.A. 21°24N 158°11W 302 K13
Maillezais France 46°22N 0°45W 174 B3
Mailsi Pakistan 29°48N 72°15E 242 E5
Maimbung Phil. 5°56N 121°2E 233 J3
Main ➝ Bayern, Germany 50°0N 8°18E 179 F4
Main ➝ Antrim, U.K. 54°48N 6°18W 166 B5
Main Channel Canada 45°21N 81°45W 312 A3
Main Range △ Australia 28°11S 152°27E 281 D5
Main Ridge Trin. & Tob. 11°16N 60°40W 323 s
Mainburg Germany 48°38N 11°47E 179 G7
Maindargi India 17°28N 76°18E 244 F3
Maine France 48°20N 0°15W 172 D6
Maine □ U.S.A. 45°20N 69°0W 309 C19
Maine ➝ Ireland 52°9N 9°45W 166 D2
Maine, G. of U.S.A. 43°0N 68°30W 309 D19
Maine-et-Loire □ France 47°31N 0°30W 172 E6
Maïne-Soroa Niger 13°13N 12°2E 263 C7
Maingkaing Burma 24°48N 95°16E 241 C5
Maingkwan Burma 26°15N 96°37E 241 B6
Mainistir an Corann = Midleton Ireland 51°55N 8°10W 166 E3
Mainit Phil. 9°32N 125°32E 233 G5
Mainit, L. Phil. 9°31N 125°30E 233 G5
Mainland Orkney, U.K. 58°59N 3°8W 167 C5
Mainland Shet., U.K. 60°15N 1°22W 167 A7
Mainpuri India 27°18N 79°4E 243 F8
Maintal Germany 50°7N 8°52E 179 E4
Maintenon France 48°35N 1°35E 173 D8
Maintirano Madag. 18°3S 44°1E 272 B1
Mainz Germany 50°1N 8°14E 179 E4
Maio C. Verde Is. 15°10N 23°10W 153 j
Maipú Argentina 36°52S 57°50W 334 D4
Maipú Santiago, Chile 33°30S 70°45W 137 C1
Maiquetía Venezuela 10°36N 66°57W 328 A4
Máira ➝ Italy 44°49N 7°38E 198 D4
Mairabari India 26°30N 92°22E 241 B4
Mairipotaba Brazil 17°18S 49°28W 333 E2
Maisi Cuba 20°17N 74°9W 321 B5
Maisí, Pta. de Cuba 20°10N 74°10W 321 B5
Maiskhal I. Bangla. 21°36N 91°56E 241 E3
Maison Coloniale Guadeloupe 16°18N 61°16W 322 e
Maisonneuve, Parc Canada 45°32N 73°33W 130 A2
Maisons-Alfort France 48°48N 2°26E 134 B3
Maisons-Laffitte France 48°57N 2°8E 134 A1
Maissoneuve Canada 45°32N 73°33W 130 A2
Maitland N.S.W., Australia 32°33S 151°36E 283 B9
Maitland S. Austral., Australia 34°23S 137°40E 282 C2
Maitland Western Cape, S. Africa 33°53S 18°29E 118 A1
Maitland ➝ Canada 43°45N 81°43W 312 C3
Maitland, Banjaran Malaysia 4°55N 116°37E 235 B5
Maitri Antarctica 70°0S 3°0W 151 D3
Maitum Phil. 6°2N 124°30E 233 H5
Maiyema Nigeria 12°5N 4°25E 263 C5
Maiyuan China 25°34N 117°28E 229 E11
Maiz, Is. del Nic. 12°15N 83°4W 320 D3
Maizuru Japan 35°25N 135°22E 223 B7
Majagual Colombia 8°33N 74°38W 328 B3
Majalengka Indonesia 6°50S 108°13E 235 D3
Majanji Uganda 0°16N 34°0E 268 B3
Majari ➝ Brazil 3°29N 60°58W 329 C5
Majdūl Libya 25°51N 15°57E 258 C3
Majene Indonesia 3°38S 118°57E 231 E5
Majes ➝ Peru 16°40S 72°44W 330 D3
Majete ⌓ Malawi 15°54S 34°34E 269 F3
Majevica Bos.-H. 44°45N 18°50E 182 F3
Maji Ethiopia 6°12N 35°30E 257 F4
Majiang China 26°28N 107°32E 228 D6
Majorca = Mallorca Spain 39°30N 3°0E 206 B4
Majors Creek Australia 35°33S 149°45E 283 C8
Majuriã Brazil 7°30S 64°55W 331 B5
Majuro Marshall Is. 7°9N 171°12E 288 G9
Maka Senegal 13°40N 14°10W 262 C2
Mākaha Hawai'i, U.S.A. 21°29N 158°13W 302 K13
Makaha Zimbabwe 17°20S 32°39E 271 A5
Makahu'ena Pt. U.S.A. 21°41N 157°56W 302 J14
Makak Cameroon 3°36N 11°0E 263 E7
Makaka Congo 3°45S 13°39E 264 C2
Makakilo City U.S.A. 21°22N 158°5W 302 K13
Makakou Gabon 0°11S 12°12E 264 C2
Makalamabedi Botswana 20°19S 23°51E 270 B3
Makale Indonesia 3°6S 119°51E 231 E5
Makalu-Barun △ Nepal 27°45N 87°10E 243 F12
Makamba Burundi 4°8S 29°49E 268 C2
Makapu'u Pt. U.S.A. 21°19N 157°39W 302 K14
Makarewa Junction N.Z. 46°20S 168°21E 285 G3
Makari Cameroon 12°35N 10°27E 259 F2
Makarikari = Makgadikgadi Salt Pans Botswana 20°40S 25°45E 270 B4
Makarov Basin Arctic 87°0N 150°0W 150 A4
Makarovo Russia 57°40N 107°45E 215 D11
Makarska Croatia 43°20N 17°2E 199 E14
Makaryev Russia 57°52N 43°50E 190 B6
Makasar = Ujung Pandang Indonesia 5°10S 119°20E 231 F5
Makasar Indonesia 6°17S 106°52E 122 A2
Makasar, Selat Indonesia 1°0S 118°20E 235 C5
Makasar, Str. of = Makasar, Selat Indonesia 1°0S 118°20E 235 C5
Makat = Maqat Kazakhstan 47°39N 53°19E 187 E9
Makati Phil. 14°33N 121°7E 127 B2
Makaw Dem. Rep. of the Congo 3°29S 18°20E 264 C3
Makawao U.S.A. 20°52N 156°17W 302 C5
Makaya Dem. Rep. of the Congo 3°21S 18°1E 264 C3
Makedonija = Macedonia ■ Europe 41°53N 21°40E 202 E5
Makefu Cook Is. 18°59S 169°55W 289 g
Makemo French Polynesia 16°35S 143°40W 289 f
Makeni S. Leone 8°55N 12°5W 262 D2
Makeyevka = Makiyivka Ukraine 48°0N 38°0E 189 H9
Makgadikgadi △ Botswana 20°27S 24°47E 270 B3
Makgadikgadi Salt Pans Botswana 20°40S 25°45E 270 B4
Makhachkala Russia 43°0N 47°30E 191 J8
Makhado = Louis Trichardt S. Africa 23°1S 29°43E 271 B4
Makham, Ao Thailand 7°51N 98°25E 237 a
Makharadze = Ozurgeti Georgia 41°55N 42°0E 191 K5
Makhfar al Buşayyah Iraq 30°0N 46°10E 246 D5
Makhmūr Iraq 35°46N 43°35E 213 E10
Makhu India 31°6N 74°59E 242 D6
Makhyah, W. ➝ Yemen 17°40N 49°1E 249 C5
Makian Indonesia 0°20N 127°20E 231 D7
Makina Solomon Is. 9°50S 160°50E 287 M11
Makindu Kenya 2°18S 37°50E 268 C4
Mäkiniitty Finland 60°20N 24°58E 121 A2
Makinka = Makinsk Kazakhstan 52°37N 70°26E 217 B8
Makinsk Kazakhstan 52°37N 70°26E 217 B8
Makira = San Cristóbal Solomon Is. 10°30S 161°0E 287 N11
Makiv Ukraine 48°48N 26°43E 183 B11
Makiyivka Ukraine 48°0N 38°0E 189 H9
Makkah Si. Arabia 21°30N 39°54E 248 B2
Makkah □ Si. Arabia 21°30N 42°30E 248 B3
Makkovik Canada 55°10N 59°10W 299 A8
Makó Hungary 46°14N 20°33E 182 D5
Mako Senegal 12°52N 12°20W 262 C2
Makogai Fiji 17°28S 179°0E 287 A2
Makok Gabon 0°1S 9°35E 264 C1
Makokou Gabon 0°40N 12°50E 264 B2
Makongo Dem. Rep. of the Congo 3°25N 26°17E 268 B2
Makoro Dem. Rep. of the Congo 3°10N 29°59E 268 B2
Makoua Congo 0°5S 15°50E 264 C3
Maków Mazowiecki Poland 52°52N 21°6E 185 F8
Maków Podhalański Poland 49°43N 19°45E 185 J6
Makra Greece 36°15N 25°54E 205 E7
Makrai India 22°2N 77°0E 242 H7
Makran Asia 26°13N 61°30E 240 D1
Makran Coast Range Pakistan 25°40N 64°0E 240 D2
Makrana India 27°2N 74°46E 242 F6
Makrany Belarus 51°48N 24°17E 185 G11
Makri Greece 40°52N 25°40E 203 F9
Makri India 19°46N 81°55E 244 E5
Makrigialos Greece 35°2N 25°59E 207 E6
Makthar Tunisia 35°48N 9°12E 258 A1
Mākū Iran 39°15N 44°31E 213 C11
Mākua U.S.A. 21°32N 158°13W 302 J13
Makua Military Reservation U.S.A. 21°32N 158°14W 302 J13
Makum India 27°30N 95°23E 241 B6
Makumbi Dem. Rep. of the Congo 5°50S 20°43E 265 D4
Makunda Botswana 22°30S 20°7E 270 B3
Makung Taiwan 23°34N 119°34E 225 C1
Makungo Somali Rep. 0°49N 42°35E 267 D5
Makunudu Atoll Maldives 6°20N 72°35E 272 d
Makunza Dem. Rep. of the Congo 8°52S 24°19E 265 D4
Makurazaki Japan 31°15N 130°20E 222 F2
Makurdi Nigeria 7°43N 8°35E 263 D6
Makushin Volcano U.S.A. 53°53N 166°55W 303 K6
Mākūyeh Iran 28°7N 53°9E 247 D7
Makwassie S. Africa 27°17S 26°0E 270 C4
Makwiro Zimbabwe 17°58S 30°25E 271 A5
Mal India 26°51N 88°45E 241 B2
Mâl Mauritania 16°58N 13°23W 262 B2
Mal B. Ireland 52°50N 9°30W 166 D2
Mala = Mallow Ireland 52°8N 8°39W 166 D3
Mala Peru 12°40S 76°38W 330 C2
Mala ✪ Australia 21°39S 130°45E 278 D5
Mala, Pta. Panama 7°28N 80°2W 320 E3
Mala Belozërka Ukraine 47°12N 34°56E 189 J8
Malá Fatra △ Slovak Rep. 49°10N 19°0E 181 B12
Mala Kapela Croatia 44°45N 15°30E 199 D12
Mala Panew ➝ Poland 50°43N 17°54E 185 H4
Malá Strana Czech Rep. 50°4N 14°24E 135 B2
Mala Vyska Ukraine 48°39N 31°36E 189 H6
Malabang Phil. 7°36N 124°3E 233 H5
Malabar N.S.W., Australia 33°58S 151°14E 139 B2
Malabar Fla., U.S.A. 28°0N 80°34W 317 H9
Malabar Coast India 11°0N 75°0E 245 J2
Malabar Hill India 18°57N 72°48E 130 B1
Malabar Pt. India 18°56N 72°48E 130 B1
Malabo = Rey Malabo Eq. Guin. 3°45N 8°50E 263 E6
Malabon Phil. 14°39N 120°56E 127 B1
Malabrigo = Puerto Chicama Peru 7°45S 79°20W 330 B2
Malabrigo Pt. Phil. 13°36N 121°15E 232 E3
Malabu Nigeria 9°32N 12°48E 263 D7
Malabuñgan Phil. 9°3N 117°38E 233 G1
Malacañang Palace Phil. 14°35N 120°59E 127 B1
Malacca, Straits of Indonesia 3°0N 101°0E 237 L3
Malacky Slovak Rep. 48°27N 17°0E 181 C10
Malad City U.S.A. 42°12N 112°15W 304 E7
Maladeta Spain 42°39N 0°39E 196 C5
Maladzyechna Belarus 54°20N 26°50E 177 A14
Málaga Colombia 6°42N 72°44W 328 B3
Málaga Spain 36°43N 4°23W 195 J6
Málaga □ Spain 36°38N 4°58W 195 J6
Malagarasi Tanzania 5°5S 30°50E 268 D3
Malagarasi ➝ Tanzania 5°12S 29°47E 268 D2
Malagasy Rep. = Madagascar ■ Africa 20°0S 47°0E 272 B2
Malagón Spain 39°11N 3°52W 195 F7
Malagón ➝ Spain 37°35N 7°29W 195 H3
Malah Syria 32°33N 36°54E 251 F7
Malahide Ireland 53°26N 6°9W 120 A3
Malaimbandy Madag. 20°20S 45°36E 272 C2
Malaita Solomon Is. 9°0S 161°0E 287 M11
Malakâl Sudan 9°33N 31°40E 257 F3
Malakal Harb. Palau 7°19N 134°27E 288 c
Malakanagiri India 18°21N 81°54E 244 E5
Malakand Pakistan 34°40N 71°55E 242 B4
Malakhovka Russia 55°39N 38°0E 129 C6
Malakoff France 48°49N 2°18E 134 B2
Malakula Vanuatu 16°15S 167°30E 287 F5
Malakwal Pakistan 32°34N 73°13E 242 C5
Malalag Phil. 6°36N 125°24E 233 H5
Malalaua Papua N. G. 8°4S 146°10E 286 E4
Malam Chad 11°27N 20°59E 259 F4
Malamala Indonesia 3°21S 120°55E 231 E6
Malanda Australia 17°22S 145°35E 280 B4
Malang Indonesia 7°59S 112°45E 235 D4
Malanga Mozam. 13°28S 36°7E 269 E4
Malangas Phil. 7°37N 123°1E 233 H4
Malange □ Angola 9°30S 16°0E 265 D3
Malangen Norway 69°24N 18°37E 160 B18
Malanje Angola 9°36S 16°17E 265 D3
Malapatan Phil. 5°59N 125°18E 233 J5
Mälaren Sweden 59°30N 17°10E 162 E11
Malargüe Argentina 35°32S 69°30W 334 D2
Mälarhöjaen Sweden 59°18N 17°58E 139 B1
Malartic Canada 48°9N 78°9W 298 C4
Malaryta Belarus 51°50N 24°3E 185 G11
Malaspina Glacier U.S.A. 59°50N 140°30W 303 G12
Malate Phil. 14°34N 120°59E 127 B1
Malatya Turkey 38°25N 38°20E 213 C8
Malatya □ Turkey 38°15N 38°0E 212 C7
Malawali Malaysia 7°3N 117°18E 235 A5
Malawi ■ Africa 11°55S 34°0E 269 E3
Malawi, L. Africa 12°30S 34°30E 269 E3
Malay Phil. 11°54N 121°55E 233 F3
Malay Pen. Asia 7°25N 100°0E 237 J3
Malay Quarter Cape Town, S. Africa 118 c2
Malaya Belozërka = Mala Belozërka Ukraine 47°12N 34°56E 189 J8
Malaya Neva Russia 59°56N 30°16E 137 B1
Malaya Okhta Russia 59°55N 30°25E 137 B2
Malaya Vishera Russia 58°55N 32°25E 188 C7
Malaya Viska = Mala Vyska Ukraine 48°39N 31°36E 189 H6
Malaybalay Phil. 8°5N 125°7E 233 G5
Malāyer Iran 34°19N 48°51E 213 E13
Malaysia ■ Asia 5°0N 110°0E 237 K4
Malazgirt Turkey 39°10N 42°33E 213 C10
Malbaza Niger 13°59N 5°38E 263 C6
Malbon Australia 21°5S 140°17E 280 C3
Malbooma Australia 30°41S 134°11E 281 E1
Malbork Poland 54°3N 19°1E 184 D6
Malca Dube Ethiopia 6°47N 42°4E 267 C5
Malcésine Italy 45°46N 10°48E 198 C7
Malchin Germany 53°44N 12°44E 178 B8
Malchow Berlin, Germany 52°34N 13°29E 115 A3
Malchow Mecklenburg-Vorpommern, Germany 53°28N 12°25E 178 B8
Malcolm Australia 28°51S 121°25E 279 E3
Malcolm, Pt. Australia 33°48S 123°45E 279 F3
Malczyce Poland 51°14N 16°29E 185 G3
Maldah India 25°2N 88°9E 243 G13
Maldegem Belgium 51°14N 3°26E 170 C3
Malden London, U.K. 51°23N 0°15W 125 B2
Malden Mass., U.S.A. 42°26N 71°3W 116 A2
Malden Mo., U.S.A. 36°34N 89°57W 308 G9
Malden I. Kiribati 4°3S 155°1W 289 H12
Maldives ■ Ind. Oc. 5°0N 73°0E 272 d
Maldon Vic., Australia 37°0S 144°6E 282 D6
Maldon Essex, U.K. 51°44N 0°42E 169 F8
Maldonado Uruguay 34°59S 55°0W 335 C5
Maldonado, Pta. Mexico 16°20N 98°33W 319 D5
Malè Italy 46°21N 10°55E 198 B7
Malé Maldives 4°10N 73°28E 272 d
Malé ✕ (MLE) Maldives 4°11N 73°28E 272 d
Malé Atoll Maldives 4°45N 73°15E 272 d
Malé Karpaty Slovak Rep. 48°30N 17°20E 181 C10
Maleas, Akra Greece 36°28N 23°7E 204 E5
Malebo, Pool Africa 4°17S 15°20E 265 C3
Malegaon India 20°30N 74°38E 244 D2
Malei Mozam. 17°12S 36°58E 269 F4
Maleizen Belgium 50°45N 4°31E 116 B3
Malek Sudan 6°4N 31°36E 257 F3
Malek Kandī Iran 37°9N 46°6E 213 D12
Malela Bas-Congo, Dem. Rep. of the Congo 5°59S 12°37E 265 D2
Malela Maniema, Dem. Rep. of the Congo 4°22S 26°8E 265 C5
Malema Mozam. 14°57S 37°20E 269 E4
Maleme Greece 35°31N 23°49E 207 E4
Malendok I. Papua N. G. 3°28S 153°16E 286 B7
Målerås Sweden 56°54N 15°34E 163 H9
Malerkotla India 30°32N 75°58E 242 D6
Males Greece 35°6N 25°35E 207 E6
Malesherbes France 48°15N 2°24E 173 D9
Maleshevska Planina Europe 41°38N 23°7E 202 E7
Malešice Czech Rep. 50°5N 14°30E 135 B3
Malesina Greece 38°37N 23°14E 204 C5
Malestroit France 47°49N 2°25W 172 E4
Malfa Italy 38°35N 14°50E 201 D7
Malgobek Russia 43°30N 44°34E 191 J7
Malgomaj Sweden 64°40N 16°30E 160 D17
Malgrat de Mar Spain 41°39N 2°46E 196 D7
Malha Sudan 15°8N 25°10E 257 D2
Malhada Brazil 14°21S 43°47W 333 D3
Malhargarh India 24°17N 74°59E 242 G6
Malheur ➝ U.S.A. 44°4N 116°59W 304 D5
Malheur L. U.S.A. 43°20N 118°48W 304 E4
Mali Guinea 12°10N 12°20W 262 C2
Mali ■ Africa 17°0N 3°0W 262 B4
Mali ➝ Burma 25°42N 97°30E 241 C6
Mali Kanal Serbia 45°36N 19°24E 182 E4
Mali Kyun Burma 13°0N 98°20E 236 F2
Malia Greece 35°17N 25°32E 207 E6
Malia, Kolpos Greece 35°19N 25°27E 207 E6
Maliao Taiwan 23°48N 120°13E 225 C2
Malibu U.S.A. 34°2N 118°41W 307 L8
Maligaya = Gloria Phil. 12°59N 121°30E 232 E3
Maliku Indonesia 0°39S 123°16E 231 E6
Malili Indonesia 2°42S 121°6E 231 E6
Målilla Sweden 57°23N 15°48E 163 G9
Malimba, Mts. Dem. Rep. of the Congo 7°30S 29°30E 268 D2
Malin Hd. Ireland 55°23N 7°23W 166 A4
Malin Pen. Ireland 55°20N 7°17W 166 A4
Malindang, Mt. Phil. 8°13N 123°38E 233 G4
Malindi Kenya 3°12S 40°5E 268 C5
Malindi Marine ⌓ Kenya 3°15S 40°7E 268 C5
Malines = Mechelen Belgium 51°2N 4°29E 170 C4
Malino Indonesia 1°0N 121°0E 231 D6
Malinyi Tanzania 8°56S 36°0E 269 D4
Malipo China 23°7N 104°42E 228 F5
Maliq Albania 40°45N 20°48E 202 F4
Malir ➝ Pakistan 24°49N 67°4E 123 B2
Malita Phil. 6°19N 125°39E 233 H5
Maliwun Burma 10°17N 98°40E 237 G2
Maliya India 23°5N 70°46E 242 H4
Maljenik Serbia 43°54N 21°43E 202 C5
Malka Mari △ Kenya 4°11N 40°46E 268 B5
Malkapur India 20°53N 76°12E 244 D3
Malkara Turkey 40°53N 26°53E 203 F10
Malkhangiri = Malakanagiri India 18°21N 81°54E 244 E5
Małkinia Górna Poland 52°42N 22°5E 185 F9
Malko Tŭrnovo Bulgaria 41°59N 27°31E 203 E11
Mall, The Washington, D.C., U.S.A. 143 b2
Mallacoota Australia 37°40S 149°40E 283 D8
Mallacoota Inlet Australia 37°34S 149°40E 283 D8
Mallaig U.K. 57°0N 5°50W 167 D3
Mallala Australia 34°26S 138°30E 282 C3
Mallaoua Niger 13°2N 9°36E 263 C6
Mallard U.S.A. 42°56N 94°41W 310 B2
Mallawan India 27°4N 80°12E 243 F9
Mallawi Egypt 27°44N 30°44E 256 B3
Mallee Cliffs △ Australia 34°16S 142°32E 282 C5
Mallembe Gabon 3°34S 10°53E 264 C2
Mallemort France 43°43N 5°11E 175 E9
Malleny Mills U.K. 55°52N 3°20W 121 B2
Mallès Venosta Italy 46°41N 10°32E 198 B7
Mallicolo = Malakula Vanuatu 16°15S 167°30E 287 F5
Mallorca Spain 39°30N 3°0E 206 B4
Mallorytown Canada 44°29N 75°53W 313 B9
Mallow Ireland 52°8N 8°39W 166 D3
Malmbäck Sweden 57°34N 14°28E 163 G8
Malmberget Sweden 67°11N 20°40E 160 C19
Malmédy Belgium 50°25N 6°2E 170 D6
Malmesbury S. Africa 33°28S 18°41E 270 D2
Malmi Finland 60°15N 24°59E 121 B2
Malmivaara = Malmberget Sweden 67°11N 20°40E 160 C19
Malmköping Sweden 59°8N 16°44E 162 E10
Malmö Sweden 55°36N 12°59E 163 J7
Malmok Aruba 12°36N 70°4W 322 f
Malmøya Norway 59°52N 10°45E 133 A3
Malmslätt Sweden 58°27N 15°33E 163 F9
Malmyzh Russia 56°31N 50°41E 190 B10
Malnaş Romania 46°2N 25°49E 183 D10
Malo Vanuatu 15°40S 167°11E 287 E5
Malo Konare Bulgaria 42°12N 24°24E 203 D8
Maloarkhangelsk Russia 52°28N 36°30E 189 F9
Maloca Brazil 0°43N 55°57W 329 C6
Malolo Fiji 17°45S 177°11E 287 A1
Malolos Phil. 14°50N 120°49E 232 D3
Malolotja ⌓ Swaziland 26°4S 31°6E 271 C5
Malombe L. Malawi 14°40S 35°15E 269 E4
Małomice Poland 51°34N 15°29E 185 G2
Malomir Bulgaria 42°16N 26°30E 203 D10
Malone Fla., U.S.A. 30°57N 85°10W 316 E4
Malone N.Y., U.S.A. 44°51N 74°18W 313 B10
Malong China 25°24N 103°34E 228 E4
Malonga Dem. Rep. of the Congo 10°24S 23°10E 265 E4
Małopolskie □ Poland 49°50N 20°20E 185 J7
Malorad Bulgaria 43°28N 23°41E 202 C7
Måløy Norway 61°57N 5°6E 164 C2
Maloyaroslovets Russia 55°2N 36°20E 188 E9
Malpartida de Cáceres Spain 39°26N 6°30W 195 F4
Malpaso Canary Is. 27°43N 18°3W 153 e1
Malpaso, Presa = Netzahualcóyotl, Presa Mexico 17°8N 93°35W 319 D6
Malpelo, I. de Colombia 4°3N 81°35W 289 G19
Malpica de Bergantiños Spain 43°19N 8°50W 194 B2
Malprabha ➝ India 16°20N 76°5E 245 F3
Malpur India 23°21N 73°27E 242 H5
Malpura India 26°17N 75°23E 242 F6
Mals = Mállès Venosta Italy 46°41N 10°32E 198 B7
Malsiras India 17°52N 74°55E 244 F2
Malta Brazil 6°54S 37°31W 332 C4
Malta Idaho, U.S.A. 42°18N 113°22W 304 E7
Malta Mont., U.S.A. 48°21N 107°52W 304 B10
Malta ■ Europe 35°55N 14°26E 206 F7
Malta ✕ (MLA) Malta 35°52N 14°29E 206 F7
Maltahöhe Namibia 24°55S 17°0E 270 B2
Maltepe Turkey 40°55N 29°8E 203 F13
Malton Ont., Canada 43°42N 79°38W 141 A1
Malton N. Yorks., U.K. 54°8N 0°49W 168 C7
Malu'a Solomon Is. 8°20S 160°38E 287 M11
Maluku = Manolo Fortich Phil. 8°28N 124°50E 233 G5
Maluku Indonesia 1°0S 127°0E 231 E7
Maluku □ Indonesia 3°0S 128°0E 231 E7
Maluku Sea = Molucca Sea Indonesia 0°0 125°0E 231 E6
Malumfashi Nigeria 11°48N 7°39E 263 C6
Malundo Angola 14°51S 22°0E 265 E4
Malung Sweden 60°42N 13°44E 162 D7
Malungon Phil. 6°16N 125°14E 233 H5
Malungsfors Sweden 60°44N 13°33E 162 D7
Malur India 13°0N 77°55E 245 H3
Maluso Phil. 6°33N 121°53E 233 H3
Maluwe Ghana 8°40N 2°17W 262 D4
Malvalli India 12°28N 77°8E 245 H3
Malvan India 16°2N 73°30E 245 F1
Malvern Vic., Australia 37°50S 145°2E 128 B2
Malvern Ont., Canada 43°48N 79°13W 141 A3
Malvern Gauteng, S. Africa 26°11S 28°5E 123 B2
Malvern Ark., U.S.A. 34°22N 92°49W 314 D8
Malvern Hills U.K. 52°0N 2°19W 169 E5
Malvik Norway 63°25N 10°40E 164 A7
Malvinas, Is. = Falkland Is. ∅ Atl. Oc. 51°30S 59°0W 153 f
Malwal Sudan 9°19N 31°35E 257 F3
Malý Dunaj ➝ Slovak Rep. 47°45N 18°9E 181 D11
Malya Tanzania 3°5S 33°38E 268 C3
Malye Derbety Russia 47°57N 44°42E 191 G7
Malyn Ukraine 50°46N 29°3E 177 C15
Malyy Lyakhovskiy, Ostrov Russia 74°7N 140°36E 215 B15
Malyy Taymyr, Ostrov Russia 78°6N 107°15E 215 B11
Mama Russia 58°18N 112°54E 215 D12
Mamadysh Russia 55°44N 51°23E 190 C10
Mamaku N.Z. 38°5S 176°8E 284 E5
Māmala B. U.S.A. 21°15N 157°55W 302 K14
Mamanguape Brazil 6°50S 35°4W 332 C4
Mamanuca Group Fiji 17°35S 177°5E 287 A1
Mamarr Mitlā Egypt 30°2N 32°54E 251 H3
Mamasa Indonesia 2°55S 119°20E 231 E5
Mambajao Phil. 9°15N 124°43E 233 G5
Mambasa Dem. Rep. of the Congo 1°22N 29°3E 268 B2
Mamberamo ➝ Indonesia 2°0S 137°50E 231 E9
Mambéré ➝ C.A.R. 3°31N 16°3E 264 B3
Mambili ➝ Congo 0°6N 16°5E 264 B3
Mambilima Falls Zambia 10°31S 28°45E 269 E2
Mambirima Dem. Rep. of the Congo 11°25S 27°33E 269 E2
Mambo Tanzania 4°52S 38°22E 268 C4
Mambrui Kenya 3°5S 40°5E 268 C5
Mamburao Phil. 13°13N 120°39E 232 E3
Mamedkala Russia 42°10N 48°7E 213 A13
Mameigwess L. Canada 52°35N 87°50W 298 B2
Mamers France 48°21N 0°22E 172 D7
Mamfé Cameroon 5°50N 9°15E 263 D6
Māmī, Ra's Yemen 12°32N 54°30E 249 D6
Mamili △ Namibia 18°2S 24°1E 270 A3
Mamiña Chile 20°5S 69°14W 330 E4
Mamlyutka Kazakhstan 54°56N 68°32E 217 B7
Mammoth U.S.A. 32°43N 110°39W 305 K8
Mammoth Cave △ U.S.A. 37°8N 86°13W 308 G10
Mamonovo Kaliningrad, Russia 54°28N 19°55E 184 D6
Mamonovo Moskva, Russia 55°41N 37°18E 129 B2
Mamoré ➝ Bolivia 10°23S 65°53W 331 C4
Mamou Guinea 10°15N 12°0W 262 C2
Mamoudzou Mayotte 12°48S 45°14E 272 b
Mampang Prapatan Indonesia 6°15S 106°49E 122 B1
Mampikony Madag. 16°6S 47°38E 272 B2
Mampoko Dem. Rep. of the Congo 0°51N 18°42E 264 B3
Mampong Ghana 7°6N 1°26W 263 D4
Mampukuji Japan 35°36N 139°31E 140 B2
Mamry, Jezioro Poland 54°5N 21°50E 184 D8
Mamuil Malal, Paso S. Amer. 39°35S 71°28W 336 A2
Mamuju Indonesia 2°41S 118°50E 231 E5
Ma'mūl Oman 18°8N 55°16E 249 C6
Mamuno Botswana 22°16S 20°1E 270 B3
Mamuras Albania 41°34N 19°41E 202 E3
Man Ivory C. 7°30N 7°40W 262 D3
Man ➝ India 17°31N 75°32E 244 F2
Man, I. of India 8°28N 93°36E 245 K11
Man, I. of U.K. 54°15N 4°30W 168 C3
Man-Bazar India 23°4N 86°39E 243 H12
Man Bndrukh India 19°2N 72°55E 130 A2
Mān Kat Burma 22°5N 98°1E 241 D7
Man Khurd India 19°3N 72°55E 130 A2
Man Na Burma 23°27N 97°19E 241 D6
Man-of-War B. Trin. & Tob. 11°19N 60°34W 323 s
Man Tun Burma 23°52N 98°38E 241 D7
Mana Fr. Guiana 5°45N 53°55W 329 B7
Manā Hawai'i, U.S.A. 22°2N 159°47W 302 A2
Mana ➝ Fr. Guiana 5°45N 53°55W 329 B7
Mana Pools △ Zimbabwe 15°56S 29°25E 269 F2
Manaar, G. of = Mannar, G. of Asia 8°30N 79°0E 245 K4
Manabí □ Ecuador 0°40S 80°5W 328 D1
Manacacías ➝ Colombia 4°23N 72°4W 328 C3
Manacapuru Brazil 3°16S 60°37W 329 D5
Manacapuru ➝ Brazil 3°18S 60°37W 329 D5
Manacor Spain 39°34N 3°13E 206 B4
Manadas Azores 38°38N 28°6W 153 d1
Manado Indonesia 1°29N 124°51E 231 D6
Managua Nic. 12°6N 86°20W 320 D2
Managua, L. de Nic. 12°20N 86°30W 320 D2
Manaia N.Z. 39°33S 174°8E 284 F3
Manakara Madag. 22°8S 48°1E 272 C2
Manakau N.Z. 42°15S 173°42E 285 C8
Manākhah Yemen 15°5N 43°44E 248 D3
Manakhat Israel 31°45N 35°11E 123 B2
Manali India 32°16N 77°10E 242 C7
Manam I. Papua N. G. 4°5S 145°0E 286 C3
Manama = Al Manāmah Bahrain 26°10N 50°30E 247 E6
Manambao ➝ Madag. 17°35S 44°0E 272 B1
Manambato Madag. 13°43S 49°7E 272 A2
Manambolo ➝ Madag. 19°18S 44°22E 272 B1
Manambolosy Madag. 16°2S 49°40E 272 B2
Mánamo, Caño ➝ Venezuela 9°55N 62°16W 329 B5
Mānana I. U.S.A. 21°20N 157°40W 302 K14
Mananara Madag. 16°10S 49°46E 272 B2
Mananara ➝ Madag. 23°21S 47°42E 272 C2
Mananara ⌓ Madag. 16°14S 49°45E 272 B2
Manangatang Australia 35°5S 142°54E 282 C5
Manànjary Madag. 21°13S 48°20E 272 C2
Manankoro Mali 10°28N 7°25W 262 C3
Manantali, L. de Mali 13°12N 10°28W 262 C2
Manantavadi India 11°49N 76°1E 245 J3
Manantenina Madag. 24°17S 47°19E 272 C2
Manaos = Manaus Brazil 3°0S 60°0W 329 D6
Manapala Phil. 10°58N 123°5E 233 F4
Manapire ➝ Venezuela 7°42N 66°7W 328 B4
Manapouri N.Z. 45°34S 167°39E 285 F2
Manapouri, L. N.Z. 45°32S 167°32E 285 F2
Manapparai India 10°36N 78°25E 245 J4
Manaqil Sudan 14°15N 32°59E 257 E3
Manar ➝ India 18°50N 77°20E 244 E3
Manār, Jabal Yemen 14°2N 44°17E 248 D3
Manaravolo Madag. 23°59S 45°39E 272 C2
Manas Xinjiang Uygur, China 44°17N 85°56E 217 D11
Manas Somali Rep. 2°57N 43°28E 267 D5
Manas ➝ India 26°12N 90°40E 241 B3
Manas △ India 26°40N 91°0E 241 B3
Manas He ➝ China 45°38N 85°12E 218 B3
Manas Hu China 45°45N 85°55E 217 C11
Manaslu Nepal 28°33N 84°33E 243 E11
Manasquan U.S.A. 40°8N 74°3W 313 F10

Manassa U.S.A. 37°11N 105°56W 305 H11
Manatí Puerto Rico 18°26N 66°29W 321 b
Manati B. St. Helena 16°0S 5°46W 153 h
Manau Papua N. G. 8°4S 148°0E 286 E4
Manaung Burma 18°45N 93°40E 241 F4
Manaus Brazil 3°0S 60°0W 329 D6
Manavgat Turkey 36°47N 31°26E 250 B2
Manavgat → Turkey 36°43N 31°27E 250 B2
Manawan = Rizal Phil. 17°51N 121°21E 232 C3
Manawan L. Canada 55°24N 103°14W 297 B8
Manawatu → N.Z. 40°28S 175°12E 284 G4
Manawatu-Wanganui □ N.Z. 39°50S 175°30E 284 F4
Manay Phil. 7°17N 126°33E 233 H6
Manbij Syria 36°31N 37°57E 212 D7
Mancha Real Spain 37°48N 3°39W 195 H7
Manche □ France 49°10N 1°20W 172 C5
Manchegorsk Russia 67°54N 32°58E 214 C4
Manchester Gt. Man., U.K. 53°29N 2°12W 168 D5
Manchester Calif., U.S.A. 38°58N 123°41W 306 G3
Manchester Conn., U.S.A. 41°47N 72°31W 313 E12
Manchester Ga., U.S.A. 32°51N 84°37W 316 C5
Manchester Iowa, U.S.A. 42°29N 91°27W 310 B5
Manchester Ky., U.S.A. 37°9N 83°46W 309 G12
Manchester Mich., U.S.A. 42°9N 84°2W 311 B12
Manchester N.H., U.S.A. 42°59N 71°28W 313 D13
Manchester N.Y., U.S.A. 42°56N 77°16W 312 D7
Manchester Ohio, U.S.A. 38°41N 83°36W 311 F13
Manchester Pa., U.S.A. 40°4N 76°43W 313 F8
Manchester Tenn., U.S.A. 35°29N 86°5W 315 D11
Manchester Vt., U.S.A. 43°10N 73°5W 313 C11
Manchester Int. ✈ (MAN) U.K. 53°21N 2°17W 168 D5
Manchester L. Canada 61°28N 107°29W 297 A7
Manchhar L. Pakistan 26°25N 67°39E 242 F2
Manchineel Bay Grenada 12°26N 61°29W 323 q
Manchou Taiwan 22°1N 120°50E 225 D2
Manchuria = Dongbei China 45°0N 125°0E 220 A5
Manchurian Plain China 47°0N 124°0E 210 D14
Manciano Italy 42°35N 11°31E 199 F8
Mancifa Ethiopia 6°53N 41°50E 257 F5
Máncora Peru 4°9S 81°1W 330 A1
Mand → India 21°42N 83°15E 243 J10
Mand → Iran 28°20N 52°30E 247 D7
Manda Ludewe, Tanzania 10°30S 34°40E 269 E3
Manda Mbeya, Tanzania 7°58S 32°29E 268 D3
Manda Mbeya, Tanzania 8°30S 32°49E 269 D3
Manda △ Chad 9°45N 17°52E 259 G3
Mandabé Madag. 21°0S 44°55E 272 C1
Mandaguari Brazil 23°32S 51°42W 335 A5
Mandah = Töhöm Mongolia 44°27N 108°2E 226 B5
Mandal Norway 58°2N 7°25E 164 F4
Mandala, Puncak Indonesia 4°44S 140°20E 231 E10
Mandalay Burma 22°0N 96°4E 241 E6
Mandalay □ Burma 22°0N 96°5E 241 E5
Mandale = Mandalay Burma 22°0N 96°4E 241 E6
Mandalgarh India 25°12N 75°6E 242 G6
Mandalgovĭ Mongolia 45°45N 106°10E 226 B4
Mandalī Iraq 33°43N 45°28E 213 F11
Mandalselva → Norway 58°2N 7°28E 164 F4
Mandaluyong Phil. 14°35N 121°1E 127 B2
Mandan U.S.A. 46°50N 100°54W 308 B3
Mandaoli India 28°37N 77°17E 120 B2
Mandaon Phil. 12°13N 123°17E 232 E4
Mandaqui → Brazil 23°30S 46°40W 137 A2
Mandar, Teluk Indonesia 3°35S 119°15E 231 E5
Mandara Mts. Nigeria 10°40N 13°40E 259 F2
Mandas Italy 39°40N 9°8E 200 C2
Mandasor = Mandsaur India 24°3N 75°8E 242 G6
Mandaue Phil. 10°20N 123°56E 233 F4
Mandelieu-la-Napoule France 43°34N 6°57E 175 E10
Mandera Kenya 3°55N 41°53E 268 B5
Mandeville Jamaica 18°2N 77°31W 320 a
Mandi India 31°39N 76°58E 242 D7
Mandi Burewala Pakistan 30°9N 72°41E 242 D5
Mandi Dabwali India 29°58N 74°42E 242 E6
Mandiana Guinea 10°37N 8°39W 262 C3
Mandigos = Manica Mozam. 18°58S 32°59E 271 A5
Mandimba Mozam. 14°20S 35°40E 269 E4
Mandioli Indonesia 0°40S 127°20E 231 E7
Mandioré, L. S. Amer. 18°8S 57°33W 331 D6
Mandla India 22°39N 80°30E 243 H9
Mandø Denmark 55°18N 8°33E 163 J2
Mandoli India 28°41N 77°18E 120 A2
Mandorah Australia 12°32S 130°42E 278 B5
Mandoto Madag. 19°34S 46°17E 272 B2
Mandoudi Greece 38°48N 23°29E 204 C5
Mandoul Chad 9°40N 15°30E 259 G3
Mandra Greece 38°4N 23°30E 204 C5
Mandra Pakistan 33°23N 73°12E 242 C5
Mandraki Greece 36°36N 27°11E 205 E9
Mandrare → Madag. 25°10S 46°30E 272 D2
Mandritsara Madag. 15°50S 48°49E 272 B2
Mandronarivo Madag. 21°7S 45°38E 272 C2
Mandsaur India 24°3N 75°8E 242 G6
Mandurah Australia 32°36S 115°48E 279 F2
Mandúria Italy 40°24N 17°38E 201 B10
Mandvi Gujarat, India 22°51N 69°22E 242 H3
Mandvi Maharashtra, India 18°56N 72°50E 130 B2
Mandya India 12°30N 77°0E 245 H3
Mandzai Pakistan 30°55N 67°6E 242 D2
Mané Burkina Faso 12°59N 1°21W 263 C4
Maneh Iran 37°39N 57°7E 247 B8
Manenberg S. Africa 33°58S 18°33E 118 A2
Manengouba, Mts. Cameroon 5°0N 9°50E 263 E6
Maner → India 18°30N 79°40E 244 E4
Manera Madag. 22°55S 44°20E 272 C1
Manérbio Italy 45°21N 10°8E 198 C7
Maneroo Cr. → Australia 23°21S 143°53E 280 C3
Manfalût Egypt 27°20N 30°52E 256 B3
Manfred Australia 33°19S 143°45E 282 B5
Manfredónia Italy 41°38N 15°55E 199 G12
Manfredónia, G. di Italy 41°35N 16°5E 199 G13
Mang Kung Uk China 22°18N 114°16E 122 B2
Mang-won S. Korea 37°33N 126°55E 137 B1
Manga Brazil 14°46S 43°56W 333 D3
Manga Burkina Faso 11°40N 1°4W 263 C4
Manga Congo 0°13S 16°5E 264 C3
Manga Niger 15°0N 14°0E 259 F2
Mangabeiras, Chapada das Brazil 10°0S 46°30W 332 D2
Mangai Dem. Rep. of the Congo 4°2S 19°33E 265 C3
Mangaia Cook Is. 21°55S 157°55W 289 K12
Mangakino N.Z. 38°22S 175°47E 284 E4
Mangal Phil. 6°25N 121°58E 233 H3
Mangalagiri India 16°26N 80°36E 245 F5
Mangaldai India 26°26N 92°2E 241 B4
Mangaldan Phil. 16°4N 120°24E 232 C3
Mangalia Romania 43°50N 28°35E 183 G13
Mangalmé Chad 12°26N 19°37E 259 F3
Mangalore India 12°55N 74°47E 245 H2
Mangaluru = Mangalore India 12°55N 74°47E 245 H2
Mangalvedha India 17°31N 75°28E 244 F2
Mangan India 27°31N 88°32E 241 B2
Mangaon India 18°15N 73°20E 244 E1
Mangawan India 24°41N 81°33E 243 G9
Mangaweka N.Z. 39°48S 175°47E 284 F4
Mangaweka, Mt. N.Z. 39°49S 176°5E 284 F5
Mange Dem. Rep. of the Congo 0°54N 20°30E 264 B4
Manger Norway 60°38N 5°3E 164 D2
Manggar Indonesia 2°50S 108°10E 235 C3
Manggawitu Indonesia 4°8S 133°32E 231 E8
Mangghystaū Kazakhstan 43°40N 51°13E 216 D4
Mangghystaū □ Kazakhstan 45°0N 53°0E 216 D4
Mangghystaū Tübegi Kazakhstan 44°30N 52°30E 216 D4
Manggis Indonesia 8°29S 115°31E 231 J18
Mangin Taungdan Burma 24°15N 95°45E 241 C5
Mangindrano Madag. 14°17S 48°58E 272 A2
Mangkalihat, Tanjung Indonesia 1°2N 118°59E 235 B5
Mangkururrpa ◎ Australia 20°35S 129°43E 278 D4
Mangla Pakistan 33°7N 73°39E 242 C5
Mangla Dam Pakistan 33°9N 73°44E 243 C5
Manglares, C. Colombia 1°36N 79°2W 328 C2
Manglaur India 29°44N 77°49E 242 E7
Manglisi Georgia 41°41N 44°22E 191 K7
Mangnai China 37°52N 91°43E 218 C4
Mangnai Zhen China 38°24N 90°14E 217 E12
Mango Togo 10°20N 0°30E 263 C5
Mango Tonga 20°17S 174°29W 287 U13
Mangoche Malawi 14°25S 35°16E 269 E4
Mangoky → Madag. 21°29S 43°41E 272 C1
Mangole Indonesia 1°50S 125°55E 231 E6
Mangolpuri India 28°41N 77°6E 120 A1
Mangombe Dem. Rep. of the Congo 1°20S 26°48E 268 C2
Mangonui N.Z. 35°1S 173°32E 284 B2
Mangoro → Madag. 20°0S 48°45E 272 C2
Mangrol Mad. P., India 21°7N 70°7E 242 J4
Mangrol Raj., India 25°20N 76°31E 242 G6
Mangrul Pir India 20°19N 77°21E 244 D3
Manguaba = Pilar Brazil 9°36S 35°56W 332 C4
Mangualde Portugal 40°38N 7°48W 194 E3
Mangueigne Chad 10°30N 21°15E 259 F4
Mangueira, L. da Brazil 33°0S 52°50W 335 C5
Manguéni, Hamada Niger 22°35N 12°40E 258 D2
Manguinhos ✈ Brazil 22°52S 43°14W 135 B1
Mangum U.S.A. 34°53N 99°30W 314 D5
Mangungu Dem. Rep. of the Congo 5°16S 19°36E 265 D3
Mangurri Australia 28°58S 134°22E 281 A1
Mangyshlak, Poluostrov = Mangghystaū Tübegi Kazakhstan 44°30N 52°30E 216 D4
Manhattan Kans., U.S.A. 39°11N 96°35W 308 F5
Manhattan New York, U.S.A. 132 d2
Manhattan Beach U.S.A. 40°34N 73°56W 132 C2
Manhattan Bridge New York, U.S.A. 132 f2
Manhattan U.S.A. 41°26N 87°59W 311 C9
Manhiça Mozam. 25°23S 32°49E 271 C5
Manhuaçu Brazil 20°15S 42°2W 333 F3
Manhumirim Brazil 20°22S 41°57W 333 F3
Mani Colombia 4°49N 72°17W 328 C3
Mania → Madag. 19°42S 45°22E 272 B2
Maniago Italy 46°10N 12°43E 199 B9
Manica Mozam. 18°58S 32°59E 271 A5
Manica □ Mozam. 19°10S 33°45E 271 A5
Manicaland □ Zimbabwe 19°0S 32°30E 269 F3
Manicoré Brazil 5°48S 61°16W 331 B5
Manicoré → Brazil 5°51S 61°19W 331 B5
Manicouagan → Canada 49°30N 68°30W 299 C6
Manicouagan, Rés. Canada 51°5N 68°40W 299 B6
Maniema □ Dem. Rep. of the Congo 3°0S 26°0E 268 C2
Manīfah Si. Arabia 27°44N 49°0E 247 E6
Manifold, C. Australia 22°41S 150°50E 280 C5
Maniganggo China 31°56N 99°10E 228 B2
Manigotagan Canada 51°6N 96°18W 297 C9
Manigotagan → Canada 51°7N 96°20W 297 C9
Manihari India 25°21N 87°38E 243 G12
Manihi French Polynesia 14°24S 145°56W 289 f
Manihiki Cook Is. 10°24S 161°1W 289 J11
Manihiki Plateau Pac. Oc. 11°0S 164°0W 289 J11
Maniitsoq Greenland 65°26N 52°55W 154 D5
Manika, Plateau de la Dem. Rep. of the Congo 10°0S 25°5E 269 E2
Manikchhari Bangla. 22°51N 91°50E 241 D3
Manikganj Bangla. 23°52N 90°0E 241 D3
Manikpur India 25°4N 81°7E 243 G9
Manila Phil. 14°35N 120°58E 127 B1
Manila U.S.A. 40°59N 109°43W 304 F9
Manila B. Phil. 14°40N 120°35E 232 D3
Manila Ninoy Aquino Int. ✈ (MNL) Phil. 14°31N 121°0E 127 B2
Manildra Australia 33°11S 148°41E 283 B8
Manilla Australia 30°45S 150°43E 283 A9
Manimpé Mali 14°11N 5°28W 262 C3
Maningrida Australia 12°3S 134°13E 280 A1
Maninian Ivory C. 10°3N 7°52W 262 C3
Manipur □ India 25°0N 94°0E 241 C5
Manipur → Burma 23°45N 94°20E 241 D5
Manisa Turkey 38°38N 27°30E 205 C9
Manisa □ Turkey 38°40N 28°0E 205 C9
Manistee U.S.A. 44°15N 86°19W 308 C10
Manistee → U.S.A. 44°15N 86°21W 308 C10
Manistique U.S.A. 45°57N 86°15W 308 C10
Manito U.S.A. 40°26N 89°47W 310 D7
Manitoba □ Canada 53°30N 97°0W 297 B9
Manitoba, L. Canada 51°0N 98°45W 297 C9
Manitou Canada 49°15N 98°32W 297 D9
Manitou, L. Canada 50°55N 65°17W 299 B6
Manitou Beach U.S.A. 41°58N 84°19W 311 C12
Manitou Is. U.S.A. 45°8N 86°0W 308 C10
Manitou L. Canada 52°43N 109°43W 297 C7
Manitou Springs U.S.A. 38°52N 104°55W 304 G11
Manitoulin I. Canada 45°40N 82°30W 298 C3
Manitouwadge Canada 49°8N 85°48W 298 C2
Manitowoc U.S.A. 44°5N 87°40W 308 C10
Manitsauá-Missu → Brazil 10°58S 53°20W 331 C7
Maniyachi India 8°51N 77°55E 245 K3
Manizales Colombia 5°5N 75°32W 328 B2
Manja Madag. 21°26S 44°20E 272 C1
Manjacaze Mozam. 24°45S 34°0E 271 B5
Manjakandriana Madag. 18°55S 47°47E 272 B2
Manjeri India 11°7N 76°11E 245 J3
Manjhand Pakistan 25°50N 68°10E 242 G3
Manjiang China 41°56N 127°35E 224 B3
Manjimup Australia 34°15S 116°6E 279 F2
Manjlegaon India 19°9N 76°14E 244 E3
Manjo Cameroon 4°50N 9°49E 264 B1
Manjra → India 18°49N 77°52E 244 E3
Mankato Kans., U.S.A. 39°47N 98°13W 308 F4
Mankato Minn., U.S.A. 44°10N 94°0W 308 C6
Mankayan Phil. 16°52N 120°47E 232 C3
Mankayane Swaziland 26°40S 31°4E 271 C5
Mankera Pakistan 31°23N 71°26E 242 D4
Mankim Cameroon 5°6N 12°3E 263 D7
Mankkaa Finland 60°11N 24°47E 121 B1
Mankono Ivory C. 8°1N 6°10W 262 D3
Mankota Canada 49°25N 107°5W 297 D7
Mankulam Sri Lanka 9°8N 80°26E 245 K5
Manlay = Üydzin Mongolia 44°9N 107°0E 226 B4
Manley Hot Springs U.S.A. 65°0N 150°38W 303 D10
Manlleu Spain 42°2N 2°17E 196 C7
Manly Australia 33°47S 151°17E 139 A2
Manmad India 20°18N 74°28E 244 D2
Mann, L. U.S.A. 28°32N 81°35W 133 A2
Mann Ranges Australia 26°6S 130°5E 279 E5
Manna Indonesia 4°25S 102°55E 234 C2
Mannahill Australia 32°25S 140°0E 282 B4
Mannar Sri Lanka 9°1N 79°54E 245 K4
Mannar, G. of Asia 8°30N 79°0E 245 K4
Mannar I. Sri Lanka 9°5N 79°45E 245 K4
Mannargudi India 10°45N 79°51E 245 J4
Mannheim Germany 49°29N 8°29E 179 F4
Manning Alta., Canada 56°53N 117°39W 296 B5
Manning Oreg., U.S.A. 45°45N 123°13W 306 E3
Manning S.C., U.S.A. 33°42N 80°13W 316 B9
Manning → Australia 31°52S 152°43E 283 A10
Manning Str. Solomon Is. 7°30S 158°0E 287 L10
Mann's Chinese Theatre U.S.A. 34°6N 118°20W 126 B2
Mannswörth Austria 48°8N 16°30E 142 B3
Mannu → Italy 39°16N 9°0E 200 C2
Mannu, C. Italy 40°3N 8°21E 200 B1
Mannum Australia 34°50S 139°20E 282 C3
Mano S. Leone 8°3N 12°2W 262 D2
Mano → Liberia 6°56N 11°30W 262 D2
Mano River Liberia 7°20N 11°6W 262 D2
Manoa Bolivia 9°40S 65°27W 331 B4
Manoharpur India 22°23N 85°12E 243 H11
Manokotak U.S.A. 58°58N 159°3W 303 G8
Manokwari Indonesia 0°54S 134°0E 231 E8
Manolada Greece 38°4N 21°21E 204 C3
Manolo Fortich Phil. 8°28N 124°50E 233 G5
Manombo Madag. 22°57S 43°28E 272 C1
Manono Dem. Rep. of the Congo 7°15S 27°25E 268 D2
Manono Samoa 13°50S 172°5W 287 V19
Manoppello Italy 42°15N 14°3E 199 F11
Manor Park Wellington, N.Z. 41°10S 174°59E 143 A2
Manor Park London, U.K. 51°32N 0°1E 125 A4
Manora Pakistan 24°47N 66°58E 123 B1
Manora Pt. Pakistan 24°47N 66°58E 123 B1
Manorhamilton Ireland 54°18N 8°9W 166 B3
Manosque France 43°49N 5°47E 175 E9
Manotick Canada 45°13N 75°41W 313 A9
Manouane → Canada 49°30N 71°10W 299 C5
Manouane, L. Canada 50°45N 70°45W 299 B5
Manovo-Gounda Saint Floris △ C.A.R. 9°30N 21°25E 264 A4
Manp'o N. Korea 41°6N 126°24E 224 B3
Manpojin = Manp'o N. Korea 41°6N 126°24E 224 B3
Manpur Chhattisgarh, India 23°17N 83°35E 243 H10
Manpur Chhattisgarh, India 20°22N 80°43E 244 D5
Manpur Mad. P., India 22°26N 75°37E 242 H6
Manquehue, Cerro Chile 33°21S 70°35W 137 B2
Manra Kiribati 4°27S 171°15W 277 A16
Manresa Spain 41°48N 1°50E 196 D6
Mansa Gujarat, India 23°27N 72°45E 242 H5
Mansa Punjab, India 30°0N 75°27E 242 E6
Mansa Zambia 11°13S 28°55E 269 E2
Mansa Konko Gambia 13°28N 15°33W 262 C1
Mansalay Phil. 12°31N 121°26E 232 E3
Månsåsen Sweden 63°5N 14°18E 162 A8
Mansehra Pakistan 34°20N 73°15E 242 B5
Mansel I. Canada 62°0N 80°0W 295 E15
Mansfield Vic., Australia 37°4S 146°6E 283 D7
Mansfield Notts., U.K. 53°9N 1°11W 168 D6
Mansfield Ga., U.S.A. 33°31N 83°44W 316 B6
Mansfield La., U.S.A. 32°2N 93°43W 314 E8
Mansfield Mass., U.S.A. 42°2N 71°13W 313 D13
Mansfield Ohio, U.S.A. 40°45N 82°31W 312 F2
Mansfield Pa., U.S.A. 41°48N 77°5W 312 E7
Mansfield Tex., U.S.A. 32°33N 97°8W 314 E6
Mansfield, Mt. U.S.A. 44°33N 72°49W 313 B12
Mansi Burma 24°48N 95°52E 241 C5
Mansidão Brazil 10°43S 44°2W 332 D3
Mansilla de las Mulas Spain 42°30N 5°25W 194 C5
Mansle France 45°52N 0°12E 174 C4
Manso → Brazil 13°50S 47°0W 333 D2
Mansôa Guinea-Biss. 12°0N 15°20W 262 C1
Manson U.S.A. 42°32N 94°32W 310 B2
Manson Creek Canada 55°37N 124°32W 296 B4
Mansoura Algeria 36°1N 4°31E 261 A5
Manta Ecuador 1°0S 80°40W 328 D1
Manta, B. de Ecuador 0°54S 80°44W 328 D1
Mantadia △ Madag. 18°54S 48°21E 272 B2
Mantalingajan, Mt. Phil. 8°55N 117°45E 233 G1
Mantantale Dem. Rep. of the Congo 2°10S 20°11E 264 C4
Mantare Tanzania 2°42S 33°13E 268 C3
Mantaro → Peru 12°16S 73°57W 330 C3
Manteca U.S.A. 37°48N 121°13W 306 H5
Mantecal Venezuela 7°34N 69°17W 328 B4
Mantena Brazil 18°47S 40°59W 333 E3
Manteno U.S.A. 41°15N 87°50W 311 C9
Manteo U.S.A. 35°55N 75°40W 315 D17
Mantes-la-Jolie France 48°58N 1°41E 173 D8
Mantha India 19°40N 76°23E 244 E3
Manthani India 18°40N 79°35E 244 E4
Manti U.S.A. 39°16N 111°38W 304 G8
Mantiqueira, Serra da Brazil 22°0S 44°0W 333 F3
Manton U.S.A. 44°25N 85°24W 309 C11
Mantorp Sweden 58°21N 15°20E 163 F9
Mántova Italy 45°9N 10°48E 198 C7
Mänttä Finland 62°3N 24°40E 188 A3
Mantua = Mántova Italy 45°9N 10°48E 198 C7
Mantung Australia 34°35S 140°3E 282 C4
Manturovo Russia 58°23N 44°45E 190 A7
Manú Peru 12°10S 70°51W 330 C3
Manú → Peru 12°16S 70°55W 330 C3
Manu'a Is. Amer. Samoa 14°13S 169°35W 287 W21
Manuel Alves → Brazil 11°19S 48°28W 333 D2
Manuel Alves Grande → Brazil 7°27S 47°35W 332 C2
Manuel Urbano Brazil 8°53S 69°18W 330 B4
Manui Indonesia 3°35S 123°5E 231 E6
Manukan Phil. 8°32N 123°5E 233 G4
Manukau N.Z. 37°0S 174°52E 284 D3
Manukau Harbour N.Z. 37°3S 174°45E 284 D3
Manunui N.Z. 38°54S 175°21E 284 E4
Manuoha N.Z. 38°42S 177°7E 284 E6
Manuripi → Bolivia 11°6S 67°36W 330 C4
Manus □ Papua N. G. 2°0S 147°0E 286 B4
Manus I. Papua N. G. 2°0S 147°0E 286 B4
Manvi India 15°57N 76°59E 245 G3
Manwath India 19°19N 76°32E 244 E3
Many U.S.A. 31°34N 93°29W 314 F8
Manyallaluk ◎ Australia 14°16S 132°49E 278 B5
Manyani Kenya 3°5S 38°30E 268 C4
Manyara, L. Tanzania 3°40S 35°50E 268 C4
Manyara △ Tanzania 3°35S 35°50E 268 C4
Manyas Turkey 40°2N 27°59E 203 F11
Manyas Gölü = Kus Gölü Turkey 40°10N 27°55E 203 F11
Manyava Ukraine 48°39N 24°21E 183 B9
Manych → Russia 47°13N 40°40E 191 G5
Manych-Gudilo, Ozero Russia 46°24N 42°38E 191 G6
Manyonga → Tanzania 4°10S 34°15E 268 C3
Manyoni Tanzania 5°45S 34°55E 268 D3
Manzai Pakistan 32°12N 70°15E 242 C4
Manzala, Bahra el Egypt 31°10N 31°56E 256 H7
Manzanar ⌂ U.S.A. 36°44N 118°9W 306 J7
Manzanares Spain 39°2N 3°22W 195 F7
Manzanares, Canal de Spain 40°19N 3°38W 127 C2
Manzaneda Spain 42°12N 7°15W 194 C3
Manzanilla Pt. Trin. & Tob. 10°31N 61°1W 323 t
Manzanillo Cuba 20°20N 77°31W 320 B4
Manzanillo Colima, Mexico 19°3N 104°20W 318 D4
Manzanillo, Pta. Panama 9°30N 79°40W 320 E4
Manzano Mts. U.S.A. 34°40N 106°20W 305 J10
Manzarīyeh Iran 34°53N 50°50E 247 C6
Manzhouli China 49°35N 117°25E 219 B6
Manzini Swaziland 26°30S 31°25E 271 C5
Manzur Vadisi △ Turkey 39°10N 39°30E 246 B3
Mao Chad 14°4N 15°19E 259 F3
Maó Spain 39°53N 4°16E 206 B5
Mao Mausoleum Beijing, China 114 c3
Maoka = Kholmsk Russia 47°40N 142°5E 215 E15
Maoke, Pegunungan Indonesia 3°40S 137°30E 231 E9
Maolin China 43°58N 123°30E 227 C12
Maoming China 21°50N 110°54E 229 G8
Maopi T'ou China 21°56N 120°43E 225 E2
Maouri, Dallol → Niger 12°5N 3°30E 263 C5
Maoxian China 31°41N 103°49E 228 B4
Maoxing China 45°28N 124°40E 227 B13
Map Micronesia 9°35N 138°10E 287 R16
Mapalma Dem. Rep. of the Congo 2°3N 24°30E 264 B4
Mapam Yumco China 30°45N 81°28E 243 D9
Mapastepec Mexico 15°26N 92°54W 319 D6
Mapfongui Gabon 1°15S 12°59E 264 C2
Maphrao, Ko Thailand 7°56N 98°26E 233 b
Mapia, Kepulauan Indonesia 0°50N 134°20E 231 D8
Mapimí Mexico 25°49N 103°51W 318 B4
Mapimí, Bolsón de Mexico 27°0N 104°15W 318 B4
Maping China 31°34N 113°32E 229 B9
Mapinga Tanzania 6°40S 39°12E 268 D4
Mapinhane Mozam. 22°20S 35°0E 271 B6
Mapire Venezuela 7°45N 64°42W 329 B5
Maple → U.S.A. 42°59N 84°57W 311 B12
Maple Creek Canada 49°55N 109°29W 297 D7
Maple Valley U.S.A. 47°25N 122°3W 306 C4
Mapleton U.S.A. 44°2N 123°52W 304 D2
Mapo S. Korea 37°32N 126°56E 137 B1
Mapoon ◎ Australia 11°44S 142°8E 280 A3
Mapourika, L. N.Z. 43°16S 170°12E 285 D5
Maprik Papua N. G. 3°44S 143°3E 286 B2
Mapuca India 15°36N 73°46E 245 G1
Mapuera → Brazil 1°5S 57°2W 329 D6
Mapulanguene Mozam. 24°29S 32°6E 271 B5
Mapungubwe △ S. Africa 22°12S 29°22E 271 B4
Maputo Mozam. 25°58S 32°32E 271 C5
Maputo □ Mozam. 26°0S 32°25E 271 C5
Maputo, B. de Mozam. 25°50S 32°45E 271 C5
Maputo ⌂ Mozam. 26°23S 32°48E 271 C5
Maqanshy Kazakhstan 46°47N 82°1E 217 C10
Maqat Kazakhstan 47°39N 53°19E 187 E9
Maqên China 34°24N 100°6E 218 C5
Maqiaohe China 44°40N 130°30E 227 B16
Maqnā Si. Arabia 28°25N 34°50E 251 K5
Maqran, W. → Si. Arabia 20°55N 47°12E 248 B4
Maqteïr Mauritania 21°50N 11°40W 260 D2
Maquan He = Brahmaputra → Asia 23°40N 90°35E 241 D3
Maqueda Spain 40°4N 4°22W 194 E6
Maqueda Channel Phil. 13°42N 124°12E 232 E5
Maquela do Zombo Angola 6°0S 15°15E 265 D3
Maquinchao Argentina 41°15S 68°50W 336 B3
Maquoketa U.S.A. 42°4N 90°40W 310 B6
Mar Canada 44°49N 81°12W 312 B3
Mar, Serra do Brazil 25°30S 49°0W 335 B6
Mar Chiquita, L. Argentina 30°40S 62°50W 334 C3
Mar del Plata Argentina 38°0S 57°30W 334 D4
Mar Menor Spain 37°40N 0°45W 197 H4
Mar Vista U.S.A. 34°0N 118°25W 126 B2
Mara Guyana 6°0N 57°36W 329 B6
Mara India 28°11N 94°14E 241 A5
Mara Tanzania 1°30S 34°32E 268 C3
Mara □ Tanzania 1°45S 34°20E 268 C3
Maraã Brazil 1°52S 65°25W 328 D4
Maraa Tahiti 17°46S 149°34W 289 e
Marabá Brazil 5°20S 49°5W 332 C2
Maraboon, L. Australia 23°41S 148°0E 280 C4
Maracá, I. de Brazil 2°10N 50°30W 329 C7
Maracaibo Venezuela 10°40N 71°37W 328 A3
Maracaibo, L. de Venezuela 9°40N 71°30W 328 B3
Maracaju Brazil 21°38S 55°9W 335 A4
Maracajú, Serra de Brazil 20°57S 55°1W 331 E6
Maracanã Pará, Brazil 0°46S 47°27W 332 B2
Maracanã Rio de J., Brazil 22°54S 43°13W 135 B1
Maracanaú Brazil 3°52S 38°38W 332 B4
Maracás Brazil 13°26S 40°18W 333 D3
Maracas Trin. & Tob. 10°41N 61°24W 323 t
Maracas → Trin. & Tob. 10°34N 61°25W 323 t
Maracas B. Trin. & Tob. 10°45N 61°26W 323 t
Maracas Bay Village Trin. & Tob. 10°46N 61°28W 323 t
Maracas Falls Trin. & Tob. 10°44N 61°24W 323 t
Maracay Venezuela 10°15N 67°28W 328 A4
Maracena Spain 37°12N 3°38W 195 H7
Marādah Libya 29°15N 19°15E 258 C3
Maradi Niger 13°29N 7°20E 263 C6
Maradi □ Niger 14°15N 7°15E 263 C6
Marāgheh Iran 37°30N 46°12E 213 D12
Maragogipe Brazil 12°46S 38°55W 333 D4
Marāh Si. Arabia 25°0N 45°35E 246 E5
Marahoue △ Ivory C. 8°0N 7°8W 262 D3
Marais du Cotentin et du Bessin ⌂ France 49°10N 1°30W 172 C5
Marais Poitevin, Val de Sèvre et Vendée ⌂ France 46°18N 0°35W 174 B3
Maraisburg = Hofmeyr S. Africa 31°39S 25°50E 270 D4
Marajó, B. de Brazil 1°0S 48°30W 332 B2
Marajo, I. de Brazil 1°0S 49°30W 332 B2
Marākand Iran 38°51N 45°16E 246 B5
Marakele △ S. Africa 32°14S 25°27E 271 D4
Maralal Kenya 1°0N 36°38E 268 B4
Maralinga Australia 30°13S 131°32E 279 F5
Maralinga Tjarutja ◎ Australia 29°30S 131°0E 279 E5
Maram India 25°25N 94°6E 241 C5
Marama Australia 35°10S 140°10E 282 C4
Maramag Phil. 7°46N 125°0E 233 G5
Maramaraereğlisi Turkey 40°57N 27°57E 203 F11
Maramasike Solomon Is. 9°30S 161°25E 287 M11
Marambio Antarctica 64°0S 56°0W 151 C18
Maramureș □ Romania 47°45N 24°0E 183 C9
Maran Malaysia 3°35N 102°45E 237 L4
Marana U.S.A. 32°27N 111°13W 305 K8
Maranboy Australia 14°40S 132°39E 278 B5
Maranchón Spain 41°6N 2°15W 196 D2
Marand Iran 38°30N 45°45E 213 C11
Marandochori Greece 38°38N 20°39E 207 B2
Marang Malaysia 5°12N 103°13E 237 K4
Maranguape Brazil 3°55S 38°50W 332 B4
Maranhão = São Luís Brazil 2°39S 44°15W 332 B3
Maranhão □ Brazil 5°0S 46°0W 332 C2
Marano, L. di Italy 45°44N 13°10E 199 C10
Maranoa → Australia 27°50S 148°37E 281 D4
Marañón → Peru 4°30S 73°35W 330 A3
Marão Mozam. 24°18S 34°2E 271 B5
Maraoli India 19°2N 72°53E 130 A2
Marapi → Brazil 0°37N 55°58W 329 C6
Marari Brazil 5°43S 67°47W 330 B4
Maraş = Kahramanmaraş Turkey 37°37N 36°53E 212 D7
Mărășești Romania 45°52N 27°14E 183 E12
Maratea Italy 39°59N 15°43E 201 C8
Marateca Portugal 38°34N 8°40W 195 G2
Marathasa Cyprus 34°59N 32°51E 207 F8
Marathia, Akra Greece 37°39N 20°50E 207 D2
Marathokambos Greece 37°43N 26°42E 205 D8
Marathon Queens., Australia 20°51S 143°32E 280 C3
Marathon Ont., Canada 48°44N 86°23W 298 C2
Marathon Fla., U.S.A. 24°43N 81°5W 317 L8
Marathon N.Y., U.S.A. 42°27N 76°2W 313 D8
Marathon Tex., U.S.A. 30°12N 103°15W 314 F3
Marathonas Greece 38°11N 23°58E 204 C5
Marathóvouno Cyprus 35°13N 33°37E 207 E9
Maratua Indonesia 2°10N 118°35E 235 B5
Maraú Brazil 14°6S 39°0W 333 D4
Marau Solomon Is. 10°31S 161°31E 287 N11
Maraval Trin. & Tob. 10°42N 61°31W 323 t
Maraval → Trin. & Tob. 10°39N 61°32W 323 t
Maravari Solomon Is. 7°50S 156°42E 287 L9
Maravatío Mexico 19°54N 100°27W 318 D4
Marawi City Phil. 8°0N 124°21E 233 G5
Marāwih U.A.E. 24°18N 53°18E 247 E7
Marazliyivka Ukraine 46°8N 30°3E 183 D15
Marbella Spain 36°30N 4°57W 195 J6
Marble Bar Australia 21°9S 119°44E 278 D2
Marble Falls U.S.A. 30°35N 98°16W 314 F5
Marblehead Mass., U.S.A. 42°29N 70°51W 313 D14
Marblehead Ohio, U.S.A. 41°32N 82°44W 312 E2
Mårbu Norway 60°11N 8°9E 164 D5
Marburg = Maribor Slovenia 46°36N 15°40E 199 B12
Marburg Germany 50°47N 8°46E 178 E4
Marca, Pta. do Angola 16°31S 11°43E 265 F2
Marcal → Hungary 47°41N 17°40E 182 C2
Marcali Hungary 46°35N 17°25E 182 D2
Marcapata Peru 13°31S 70°52W 330 C3
Marcaria Italy 45°7N 10°32E 198 C7
Mărcăuți Moldova 48°20N 27°14E 183 B12
Marcelin Poland 52°19N 20°59E 142 B1
Marceline U.S.A. 39°43N 92°57W 310 E4
March U.K. 52°33N 0°5E 169 E8
Marchal Dem. Rep. of the Congo 5°16S 14°58E 265 D2
Marchand = Rommani Morocco 33°31N 6°40W 260 B3
Marche France 46°5N 1°20E 174 B5
Marche □ Italy 43°30N 13°15E 199 E10
Marché Bonsecours Montréal, Canada 130 b3
Marche-en-Famenne Belgium 50°14N 5°19E 170 D5
Marchena Spain 37°18N 5°23W 195 H5
Marchena, Canal de Ecuador 0°19N 90°12W 330 a
Marchena, I. Ecuador 0°19N 90°29W 330 a
Marches = Marche □ Italy 43°30N 13°15E 199 E10
Marchesale ⌂ Italy 38°32N 16°13E 201 D9
Marciana Marina Italy 42°48N 10°12E 198 F7
Marcianise Italy 41°2N 14°17E 201 A7
Marcigny France 46°17N 4°2E 173 F11
Marcillat-en-Combraille France 46°12N 2°38E 173 F9
Marck France 50°57N 1°57E 173 B8
Marckolsheim France 48°10N 7°30E 173 D14
Marco Island U.S.A. 25°58N 81°44W 317 K8
Marco Rondon Brazil 12°0S 60°56W 331 C5
Marcona Peru 15°10S 75°0W 330 D3
Marcos Juárez Argentina 32°42S 62°5W 334 C3
Mărculești Moldova 47°52N 28°14E 183 C13
Marcus Baker, Mt. U.S.A. 61°26N 147°45W 303 F11
Marcus I. = Minami-Tori-Shima Pac. Oc. 24°20N 153°58E 288 E7
Marcy, Mt. U.S.A. 44°7N 73°56W 313 B11
Mardan Pakistan 34°20N 72°0E 242 B5
Mardarivka Ukraine 47°32N 29°44E 183 C14
Mardie Australia 21°12S 115°59E 278 D2
Mardin Turkey 37°20N 40°43E 213 D9
Mårdsjö Sweden 63°18N 15°35E 162 A9
Maré, Î. N. Cal. 21°30S 168°0E 277 E12
Marécchia → Italy 44°4N 12°34E 199 D9
Marechal Deodoro Brazil 9°43S 35°54W 332 C4
Marechal Floriano = Piranhas Brazil 9°27S 37°46W 332 C4
Maree, L. U.K. 57°40N 5°26W 167 D3
Mareeba Australia 16°59S 145°28E 280 B4
Mareeg Somali Rep. 3°46N 47°18E 267 D6
Mareetsane S. Africa 26°9S 25°25E 270 C4
Mareil-Marly France 48°52N 2°4E 134 A1
Maremma Italy 42°30N 11°30E 199 F8
Maremma ⌂ Italy 42°35N 11°8E 198 F8
Maréna Kayes, Mali 14°36N 10°45W 262 C2
Maréna Koulikouro, Mali 13°55N 7°20W 262 C3
Marengo Ind., U.S.A. 38°22N 86°21W 311 F10
Marengo Iowa, U.S.A. 41°48N 92°4W 310 C4
Marennes France 45°49N 1°7W 174 C2
Marerano Madag. 21°23S 44°52E 272 C1
Maréttimo Italy 37°58N 12°4E 200 E5
Mareuil France 45°26N 0°29E 174 C4
Marfa U.S.A. 30°19N 104°1W 314 F2
Marganets = Marhanets Ukraine 47°40N 34°40E 189 J8
Margao = Madgaon India 15°12N 73°58E 245 G1
Margaret → Australia 18°9S 125°41E 278 C4
Margaret Bay Canada 51°20N 127°35W 296 C3
Margaret L. Canada 58°56N 115°25W 296 B5
Margaret River Australia 33°57S 115°4E 279 F2
Margareten Austria 48°11N 16°20E 142 A2
Margarita, I. de Venezuela 11°0N 64°0W 329 A5
Margariti Greece 39°22N 20°26E 204 B2
Margaritovo Russia 43°25N 134°45E 220 C7
Margate KwaZulu Natal, S. Africa 30°50S 30°20E 271 D5
Margate Kent, U.K. 51°23N 1°23E 169 F9
Margate Fla., U.S.A. 26°15N 80°12W 317 J9
Margeride, Mts. de la France 44°43N 3°38E 174 D7
Marggrabowa = Olecko Poland 54°2N 22°31E 184 D9
Margherita India 27°16N 95°40E 241 B5
Margherita di Savòia Italy 41°22N 16°9E 201 A9
Margherita Pk. Uganda 0°22N 29°51E 268 B3
Marghilon Uzbekistan 40°27N 71°42E 217 D8
Marghita Romania 47°22N 22°22E 182 C7
Margonin Poland 52°58N 17°5E 185 F4
Margosatubig Phil. 7°34N 123°10E 233 H4
Margow, Dasht-e Afghan. 30°40N 62°30E 240 C1
Marguerite Canada 52°30N 122°25W 296 C4
Marhanets Ukraine 47°40N 34°40E 189 J8
Marhoum Algeria 34°27N 0°11W 261 B4
Mari Papua N. G. 9°11S 141°42E 286 E1
Māri' Syria 36°29N 37°10E 250 B8
Mari El □ Russia 56°30N 48°0E 190 B8
Mari Indus Pakistan 32°57N 71°34E 242 C4
Mari Republic = Mari El □ Russia 56°30N 48°0E 190 B8
Maria Austria 48°11N 16°21E 142 A2
Maria, Îs. French Polynesia 21°48S 154°41W 289 f
María, Sa. de Spain 37°39N 2°14W 197 H2
Maria Aurora Phil. 15°48N 121°28E 232 D3
María de la Salut Spain 39°40N 3°5E 206 B4
María Elena Chile 22°18S 69°40W 334 A2
María Grande Argentina 31°45S 59°55W 334 C4
Maria I. N. Terr., Australia 14°52S 135°45E 280 A2
Maria I. Tas., Australia 42°35S 148°0E 281 G4
Maria Is. St. Lucia 13°44N 60°56W 323 m
Maria Island △ Australia 42°38S 148°5E 281 G4
Maria Pereira = Mombaça Brazil 5°43S 39°45W 332 C4
Maria Theresiopel = Subotica Serbia 46°6N 19°39E 182 D4
Maria van Diemen, C. N.Z. 34°29S 172°40E 284 A1
Mariager Denmark 56°40N 9°59E 163 H3
Mariager Fjord Denmark 56°42N 10°19E 163 H4
Mariahilferstrasse Vienna, Austria 142 b1
Mariakani Kenya 3°50S 39°27E 268 C4
Mariala △ Australia 25°57S 145°2E 281 D4
Marian Australia 21°9S 148°57E 280 b
Marian L. Canada 63°0N 116°15W 296 A5
Mariana Islands N. Marianas 15°15N 145°48E 302 a
Mariana Trench Pac. Oc. 13°0N 145°0E 302 a
Mariani India 26°39N 94°19E 241 B5
Marianica, Cord. = Morena, Sierra Spain 38°20N 4°0W 195 G7
Marianna Ark., U.S.A. 34°46N 90°46W 315 D9
Marianna Fla., U.S.A. 30°46N 85°14W 316 E4
Mariannelund Sweden 57°37N 15°35E 163 G9
Mariánské Lázně Czech Rep. 49°58N 12°41E 180 B5
Marias → U.S.A. 47°56N 110°30W 304 C8
Marías, Islas Mexico 21°25N 106°28W 318 C3
Mariato, Punta Panama 7°12N 80°52W 320 E3
Mariazell Austria 47°47N 15°19E 180 D8
Ma'rib Yemen 15°25N 45°21E 248 D4
Maribo Denmark 54°48N 11°30E 163 K5
Maribor Slovenia 46°36N 15°40E 199 B12
Maricaban I. Phil. 13°39N 120°53E 232 E3
Maricao Puerto Rico 18°11N 66°59W 321 b
Marico → Africa 23°35S 26°57E 270 B4
Maricopa Ariz., U.S.A. 33°4N 112°3W 305 K7
Maricopa Calif., U.S.A. 35°4N 119°24W 307 K7
Maridalen Norway 59°59N 10°45E 133 A3
Maridalsvatnet Norway 59°59N 10°46E 133 A3
Marīdī Sudan 4°55N 29°25E 257 G2
Marīdī, Wadi → Sudan 6°15N 29°21E 257 F2
Marié → Brazil 0°27S 66°26W 328 D4
Marie Byrd Land Antarctica 79°30S 125°0W 151 D14
Marie-Galante Guadeloupe 15°56N 61°16W 322 e
Marie-Galante, Canal de Guadeloupe 16°0N 61°25W 322 e
Mariecourt = Kangiqsujuaq Canada 61°30N 72°0W 295 E17
Mariefred Sweden 59°15N 17°12E 162 E11
Mariehamn Finland 60°5N 19°55E 161 F18
Marieholm Sweden 55°53N 13°10E 163 J7
Mariembourg Belgium 50°6N 4°31E 170 D4
Marienbad = Mariánské Lázně Czech Rep. 49°58N 12°41E 180 B5
Marienberg Germany 50°39N 13°9E 178 E9
Marienburg = Malbork Poland 54°3N 19°1E 184 D6
Mariendorf Germany 52°26N 13°23E 115 B3
Marienfelde Germany 52°24N 13°23E 115 B3
Marienplatz Munich, Germany 131 b2
Mariental Namibia 24°36S 18°0E 270 B2
Marienville U.S.A. 41°28N 79°8W 312 E5
Mariestad Sweden 58°43N 13°50E 163 F7
Marietta Ga., U.S.A. 33°57N 84°33W 316 B5
Marietta Ohio, U.S.A. 39°25N 81°27W 309 F13
Marieville Canada 45°26N 73°10W 313 A11
Mariga → Nigeria 9°40N 5°55E 263 C6
Marignane France 43°25N 5°13E 175 E9
Marigot Dominica 15°33N 61°18W 323 k
Marigot Guadeloupe 16°5N 61°14W 322 e
Marigot St.-Martin 18°4N 63°5W 322 a
Marigot Bay St. Lucia 13°58N 61°1W 323 m
Marihatag Phil. 8°48N 126°18E 233 G6
Mariinsk Russia 56°10N 87°20E 214 D9
Mariinsk Water = Volgo-Baltiyskiy Kanal Russia 60°0N 38°0E 188 B9
Mariinskiy Posad Russia 56°10N 47°45E 190 B8
Marijampolė Lithuania 54°33N 23°19E 184 D10
Marijampolės □ Lithuania 54°34N 23°21E 184 D10
Marikina Phil. 14°37N 121°5E 127 B2
Marikina → Phil. 14°33N 121°5E 127 B2
Marília Brazil 22°13S 50°0W 335 A6
Marimba Angola 8°28S 17°8E 265 D3
Marin Spain 42°23N 8°42W 194 C2
Marin, Cul-de-Sac du Martinique 14°27N 60°53W 322 j
Marin City U.S.A. 37°52N 122°30W 136 A1
Marin Pen. U.S.A. 37°50N 122°30W 136 B1
Marina U.S.A. 36°41N 121°48W 306 J5
Marina del Rey U.S.A. 33°58N 118°27W 126 C2
Marinduque Phil. 13°25N 122°0E 231 B6
Marinduque □ Phil. 13°18N 122°0E 232 E4
Marine City U.S.A. 42°43N 82°30W 312 D2
Marine Drive Mumbai, India 130 b1
Marineland U.S.A. 29°40N 81°13W 316 F8
Marineo Italy 37°57N 13°25E 200 E6
Marinette U.S.A. 45°6N 87°38W 308 C10
Maringá Brazil 23°26S 52°2W 335 A5
Maringa → Dem. Rep. of the Congo 1°14N 19°48E 264 B3
Marinha Grande Portugal 39°45N 8°56W 194 F2
Marinho dos Abrolhos △ Brazil 17°50S 39°0W 333 E4
Marino Dublin, Ireland 53°22N 6°14W 120 A2
Marino Italy 41°46N 12°39E 199 G9
Marion Ala., U.S.A. 32°38N 87°19W 315 E11
Marion Ill., U.S.A. 37°44N 88°56W 310 G8
Marion Ind., U.S.A. 40°32N 85°40W 311 D11
Marion Iowa, U.S.A. 42°2N 91°36W 310 B5
Marion Kans., U.S.A. 38°21N 97°1W 308 F5
Marion N.C., U.S.A. 35°41N 82°1W 315 D13
Marion Ohio, U.S.A. 40°35N 83°8W 311 D13
Marion S.C., U.S.A. 34°11N 79°24W 315 D15
Marion Va., U.S.A. 36°50N 81°31W 309 G13
Marion, L. U.S.A. 33°28N 80°10W 316 B9
Marion Bay Australia 35°12S 136°59E 282 C2

Marion I. *Ind. Oc.* 47°0S 38°0E **273** J2
Maripa *Venezuela* 7°26N 65°9W **329** B4
Maripasoula *Fr. Guiana* 3°40N 54°4W **329** C7
Mariposa *U.S.A.* 37°29N 119°58W **306** H7
Mariscal Estigarribia *Paraguay* 22°3S 60°40W **334** A3
Marisco, Ponta do *Brazil* 23°1S 43°18W **135** C1
Maritime Alps = Maritimes, Alpes *Europe* 44°10N 7°10E **175** D11
Maritimes, Alpes *Europe* 44°10N 7°10E **175** D11
Maritsa = Evros → *Greece* 41°40N 26°34E **212** B2
Maritsa *Greece* 36°22N 28°8E **206** E12
Mariupol *Ukraine* 47°5N 37°31E **189** J9
Marīvān *Iran* 35°30N 46°25E **213** E12
Mariveles *Phil.* 14°26N 120°29E **232** D3
Marj 'Uyūn *Lebanon* 33°21N 35°34E **250** E6
Marjan = Wazikhwah *Afghan.* 32°11N 68°21E **240** B3
Mark Twain L. *U.S.A.* 39°28N 91°55W **310** E5
Marka *Si. Arabia* 18°14N 41°19E **256** D5
Marka *Somali Rep.* 1°48N 44°50E **267** D5
Markam *China* 29°42N 98°38E **228** C2
Markapur *India* 15°44N 79°19E **245** G4
Markaryd *Sweden* 56°28N 13°35E **163** H7
Markat *Albania* 39°44N 20°12E **206** B10
Markazī □ *Iran* 35°0N 49°30E **216** F3
Markdale *Canada* 44°19N 80°39W **312** B4
Marked Tree *U.S.A.* 35°32N 90°25W **315** D9
Markelsdorfer Huk *Germany* 54°33N 11°4E **178** A7
Market Drayton *U.K.* 52°54N 2°29W **168** E5
Market Harborough *U.K.* 52°29N 0°55W **169** E7
Market Rasen *U.K.* 53°24N 0°20W **168** D7
Markham *Canada* 43°52N 79°16W **141** A2
Markham → *Papua N. G.* 6°41S 147°2E **286** D4
Markham, Mt. *Antarctica* 83°0S 164°0E **151** E11
Marki *Poland* 52°19N 21°6E **142** B2
Märkisch Friedland = Mirosławiec *Poland* 53°20N 16°5E **184** E3
Märkische Schweiz ⌂ *Germany* 52°34N 14°2E **178** C10
Markit *China* 38°54N 77°40E **217** E9
Markkleeberg *Germany* 51°16N 12°23E **178** D8
Markland Wood *Canada* 43°38N 79°34W **141** B1
Markleeville *U.S.A.* 38°42N 119°47W **306** G7
Markopoulo *Greece* 37°53N 23°57E **204** D5
Markounda *C.A.R.* 7°39N 16°55E **264** A3
Markovac *Serbia* 44°14N 21°7E **202** B5
Markovo *Russia* 64°40N 170°24E **215** C17
Markoye *Burkina Faso* 14°39N 0°2E **263** C5
Marks *Russia* 51°45N 46°50E **190** E8
Marksshtadt = Marks *Russia* 51°45N 46°50E **190** E8
Marksville *U.S.A.* 31°8N 92°4W **314** F8
Markt Schwaben *Germany* 48°11N 11°52E **179** G7
Marktoberdorf *Germany* 47°45N 10°37E **179** H6
Marktredwitz *Germany* 50°1N 12°6E **179** E8
Marl *Germany* 51°39N 7°4E **178** D3
Marla *Australia* 27°19S 133°33E **281** D1
Marlbank *Canada* 44°26N 77°6W **312** B7
Marlboro *U.S.A.* 41°36N 73°59W **313** E11
Marlborough *Queens., Australia* 22°46S 149°52E **280** C4
Marlborough *Wilts., U.K.* 51°25N 1°43W **169** F6
Marlborough *Mass., U.S.A.* 42°21N 71°33W **313** D13
Marlborough □ *N.Z.* 41°40S 173°50E **285** B8
Marlborough Downs *U.K.* 51°27N 1°53W **169** F6
Marle *France* 49°43N 3°47E **173** C10
Marlin *U.S.A.* 31°18N 96°54W **314** F6
Marlow *Mecklenburg-Vorpommern, Germany* 54°9N 12°33E **178** A8
Marlow *Bucks., U.K.* 51°34N 0°46W **169** F7
Marlow *Okla., U.S.A.* 34°39N 97°58W **314** D6
Marly, Forêt de *France* 48°52N 2°2E **134** A1
Marly-le-Roi *France* 48°52N 2°5E **134** A1
Marmagao *India* 15°25N 73°56E **245** G1
Marmande *France* 44°30N 0°10E **174** D4
Marmara *Turkey* 40°35N 27°34E **203** F11
Marmara, Sea of = Marmara Denizi *Turkey* 40°45N 28°15E **203** F12
Marmara Denizi *Turkey* 40°45N 28°15E **203** F12
Marmara Gölü *Turkey* 38°37N 28°2E **205** C10
Marmaris *Turkey* 36°50N 28°14E **205** E10
Marmaris Limanı *Turkey* 36°50N 28°19E **205** E10
Marmelos → *Brazil* 6°6S 61°46W **331** B5
Marmion, Mt. *Australia* 29°16S 119°50E **279** E2
Marmion L. *Canada* 48°55N 91°20W **298** C1
Marmolada, Mte. *Italy* 46°26N 11°51E **199** B8
Marmolejo *Spain* 38°3N 4°13W **195** G6
Marmora *Canada* 44°28N 77°41W **312** B7
Mármora, La *Italy* 39°59N 9°20E **200** C2
Marmugao = Marmagao *India* 15°25N 73°56E **245** G1
Marnay *France* 47°16N 5°48E **173** E12
Marne *Germany* 53°56N 9°2E **178** B5
Marne □ *France* 48°50N 4°10E **173** D11
Marne → *France* 48°47N 2°29E **173** D9
Marne-la-Vallée *France* 48°50N 2°37E **134** A4
Marneuli *Georgia* 41°30N 44°48E **191** K7
Marnia = Maghnia *Algeria* 34°50N 1°43W **261** B4
Marnoo *Australia* 36°40S 142°52E **282** D5
Maro *Chad* 8°30N 19°0E **259** G3
Maro Reef *U.S.A.* 25°25N 170°35W **302** F9
Maro Rosa *Brazil* 13°58S 49°9W **333** D2
Maroa *Ill., U.S.A.* 40°2N 88°57W **310** D8
Maroa *Venezuela* 2°43N 67°33W **328** C4
Maroala *Madag.* 15°23S 47°59E **272** B2
Maroantsetra *Madag.* 15°26S 49°44E **272** B2
Maroelaboom *Namibia* 19°15S 18°53E **270** A2
Marofandilia *Madag.* 20°7S 44°34E **272** C1
Marojejy ⌂ *Madag.* 14°26S 49°21E **272** A2
Marokau *French Polynesia* 18°2S 142°17W **289** f
Marolambo *Madag.* 20°2S 48°7E **272** C2
Marolles-en-Brie *France* 48°44N 2°33E **134** B4
Maromandia *Madag.* 14°13S 48°5E **272** A2
Maromokotro *Madag.* 14°0S 49°0E **272** A2
Marondera *Zimbabwe* 18°5S 31°42E **269** F3
Maroni → *Fr. Guiana* 5°30N 54°0W **329** B7
Maronia *Greece* 40°53N 25°30E **203** F9
Maronne → *France* 45°5N 1°56E **174** C5
Maroochydore *Australia* 26°29S 153°5E **281** D5
Maroon Town *Jamaica* 18°22N 77°48W **320** a
Maroona *Australia* 37°27S 142°54E **282** D5
Maros → *Hungary* 46°15N 20°13E **182** D5
Marosakoa *Madag.* 15°26S 46°38E **272** B2
Maroseranana *Madag.* 18°32S 48°51E **272** B2
Maróstica *Italy* 45°44N 11°40E **199** C8
Marotandrano *Madag.* 16°10S 48°50E **272** B2
Marotaolano *Madag.* 12°47S 49°15E **272** A2
Marotiri, Îs. = Bass, Îs. de *French Polynesia* 27°55S 143°26W **289** f
Maroua *Cameroon* 10°40N 14°20E **259** F2
Maroubra *Australia* 33°56S 151°16E **139** B2
Marovato *Madag.* 15°48S 48°5E **272** B2
Marovoay *Madag.* 16°6S 46°39E **272** B2
Marowijne □ *Suriname* 4°0N 55°0W **329** C7
Marowijne → *Suriname* 5°45N 53°58W **329** B7
Marqaköl *Kazakhstan* 48°45N 85°45E **217** C11
Marquard *S. Africa* 28°40S 27°28E **270** C4
Marquesas Fracture Zone *Pac. Oc.* 9°0S 125°0W **289** H15
Marquesas Is. = Marquises, Îs. *French Polynesia* 9°30S 140°0W **289** f
Marquesas Keys *U.S.A.* 24°35N 82°10W **317** L7
Marquette *U.S.A.* 46°33N 87°24W **308** B10
Marquette Park *U.S.A.* 41°46N 87°42W **119** C2
Marquis *St. Lucia* 14°2N 60°54W **323** m
Marquis, C. *St. Lucia* 14°3N 60°54W **323** m
Marquis I. *Grenada* 12°5N 61°37W **323** q
Marquise *France* 50°50N 1°40E **173** B8
Marquises, Îs. *French Polynesia* 9°30S 140°0W **289** f
Marra, Gebel *Sudan* 7°20N 27°35E **257** F2
Marra, Pta. da *Angola* 16°31S 11°43E **265** F2
Marra Cr. → *Australia* 30°8S 147°15E **283** A7
Marra-Marra △ *Australia* 33°30S 151°4E **283** B9
Marracuene *Mozam.* 25°45S 32°35E **271** C5
Marradi *Italy* 44°4N 11°37E **199** D8
Marrakech *Morocco* 31°9N 8°0W **260** B3
Marrakech □ *Morocco* 31°30N 7°30W **260** B3
Marratxí *Spain* 39°39N 2°48E **206** B3
Marrawah *Australia* 40°55S 144°42E **281** G3
Marrecas, Serra das *Brazil* 9°0S 41°0W **332** C3
Marree *Australia* 29°39S 138°1E **281** D2
Marrero *U.S.A.* 29°53N 90°6W **131** B2
Marrickville *Australia* 33°54S 151°9E **139** B1
Marrimane *Mozam.* 22°58S 33°34E **271** B5
Marromeu *Mozam.* 18°15S 36°25E **271** A6
Marromeu ⌂ *Mozam.* 19°0S 36°0E **271** A6
Marroquí, Punta *Spain* 36°0N 5°37W **195** K5
Marrowie Cr. → *Australia* 33°23S 145°40E **283** B6
Marruás = Porto *Brazil* 3°54S 42°42W **332** B3
Marrubane *Mozam.* 18°0S 37°0E **269** F4
Marrúbiu *Italy* 39°40N 8°35E **200** C1
Marrupa *Mozam.* 13°8S 37°30E **269** E4
Mars B. *Ascension I.* 7°59S 14°24W **153** g
Mars Hill *U.S.A.* 46°31N 67°52W **309** B20
Marsá al Burayqah *Libya* 30°24N 19°37E **258** B3
Marsá 'Alam *Egypt* 25°5N 34°54E **256** B3
Marsá Matrûh *Egypt* 31°19N 27°9E **256** A2
Marsá Sha'b *Sudan* 22°52N 35°47E **256** C4
Marsabit *Kenya* 2°18N 38°0E **268** B4
Marsabit △ *Kenya* 2°23N 37°56E **268** B4
Marsala *Italy* 37°48N 12°26E **200** E5
Marsalforn *Malta* 36°4N 14°16E **206** E7
Marşani *Romania* 44°1N 24°1E **183** F9
Marsaskala *Malta* 35°52N 14°34E **206** F8
Marsaxlokk *Malta* 35°51N 14°33E **206** F8
Marsaxlokk Bay *Malta* 35°49N 14°33E **206** F8
Marsberg *Germany* 51°28N 8°52E **178** D4
Marsciano *Italy* 42°54N 12°20E **199** F9
Marsden *Australia* 33°47S 147°32E **283** B7
Marseillan *France* 43°23N 3°31E **174** E7
Marseille *France* 43°18N 5°23E **175** E9
Marseille-Marignane ✈ (MRS) *France* 43°26N 5°14E **175** E9
Marseilles = Marseille *France* 43°18N 5°23E **175** E9
Marseilles *U.S.A.* 41°20N 88°43W **311** C8
Marsfield *Australia* 33°46S 151°7E **139** A1
Marsh I. *U.S.A.* 29°34N 91°53W **314** G9
Marsha, L. *U.S.A.* 28°29N 81°29W **133** B2
Marshall *Liberia* 6°8N 10°22W **262** D2
Marshall *Alaska, U.S.A.* 61°53N 162°5W **303** F7
Marshall *Ark., U.S.A.* 35°55N 92°38W **314** D8
Marshall *Ill., U.S.A.* 39°23N 87°42W **311** E9
Marshall *Mich., U.S.A.* 42°16N 84°58W **311** B12
Marshall *Minn., U.S.A.* 44°27N 95°47W **308** C6
Marshall *Mo., U.S.A.* 39°7N 93°12W **310** E3
Marshall *Tex., U.S.A.* 32°33N 94°23W **314** E7
Marshall → *Australia* 22°59S 136°59E **280** C2
Marshall, C. *Ecuador* 0°1S 91°12W **330** a
Marshall Bennett Is. *Papua N. G.* 8°50S 151°55E **286** E6
Marshall Field's *Chicago, U.S.A.* **119** c2
Marshall Is. ■ *Pac. Oc.* 9°0N 171°0E **288** G9
Marshalltown *U.S.A.* 42°3N 92°55W **310** B4
Marshallville = Lewisporte *Canada* 49°15N 55°3W **299** C8
Marshallville *U.S.A.* 32°27N 83°56W **316** C6
Marshbrook *Zimbabwe* 18°33S 31°9E **271** A5
Marshfield = Coos Bay *U.S.A.* 43°22N 124°13W **304** E1
Marshfield *Mo., U.S.A.* 37°15N 92°54W **308** G7
Marshfield *Vt., U.S.A.* 44°20N 72°20W **313** B12
Marshfield *Wis., U.S.A.* 44°40N 90°10W **308** C8
Marshūn *Iran* 36°19N 49°23E **247** B6
Mársico Nuovo *Italy* 40°25N 15°44E **201** B8
Marsouins, R. des → *Réunion* 21°1S 55°44E **272** f
Märsta *Sweden* 59°37N 17°52E **162** E11
Marstal *Denmark* 54°51N 10°30E **163** K4
Marstrand *Sweden* 57°53N 11°35E **163** G5
Mart *U.S.A.* 31°33N 96°50W **314** F6
Marta → *Italy* 42°14N 11°42E **199** F8
Martaban *Burma* 16°30N 97°35E **241** G6
Martaban, G. of *Burma* 16°5N 96°30E **241** G6
Martano *Italy* 40°12N 18°18E **201** B11
Martapura *Kalimantan, Indonesia* 3°22S 114°47E **235** C4
Martapura *Sumatera, Indonesia* 4°19S 104°22E **234** C2
Marte *Nigeria* 12°23N 13°46E **263** C7
Marte, Campo de *Brazil* 23°30S 46°38W **137** B2
Marte R. Gómez, Presa *Mexico* 26°10N 99°0W **319** B5
Martel *France* 44°57N 1°37E **174** D5
Martelange *Belgium* 49°49N 5°43E **170** E5
Martellago *Italy* 45°33N 12°9E **199** C9
Martés, Sierra *Spain* 39°20N 1°0W **197** F4
Martesana, Navíglio della *Italy* 45°31N 9°17E **129** A2
Martfű *Hungary* 47°1N 20°17E **182** C5
Marthaguy Cr. → *Australia* 30°16S 147°35E **283** A7
Marthapal *India* 19°24N 81°37E **244** E5
Martha's Vineyard *U.S.A.* 41°25N 70°38W **313** E14
Martigné-Ferchaud *France* 47°50N 1°20W **172** E5
Martigny *Switz.* 46°6N 7°3E **179** J3
Martigues *France* 43°24N 5°4E **175** E9
Martil *Morocco* 35°36N 5°15W **260** A3
Martin *Slovak Rep.* 49°6N 18°58E **181** B11
Martin *S. Dak., U.S.A.* 43°11N 101°44W **308** D3
Martin *Tenn., U.S.A.* 36°21N 88°51W **315** C10
Martín → *Spain* 41°18N 0°19W **196** D4
Martin L. *U.S.A.* 32°41N 85°55W **316** C4
Martin Luther King Nat. Historic Site ⌂ *U.S.A.* 33°45N 84°22W **113** B2
Martin Pt. *U.S.A.* 70°8N 143°16W **303** A12
Martin Vaz *Atl. Oc.* 20°30S 28°51W **152** J9
Martina Franca *Italy* 40°42N 17°20E **201** B10
Martinborough *N.Z.* 41°14S 175°29E **284** H4
Martinez *B. Aires, Argentina* 34°29S 58°31W **117** A1
Martinez *Calif., U.S.A.* 38°1N 122°8W **306** G4
Martinez *Ga., U.S.A.* 33°31N 82°5W **315** E13
Martinho Campos *Brazil* 19°20S 45°13W **333** E2
Martinique ☒ *W. Indies* 14°40N 61°0W **322** j
Martinique Channel *St. Vincent* 12°34N 61°25W **323** n
Martinique Passage *W. Indies* 15°15N 61°0W **321** C7
Martinkylä *Finland* 60°17N 24°51E **121** B2
Martino *Greece* 38°35N 23°12E **204** C5
Martinópolis *Brazil* 22°11S 51°12W **335** A5
Martins Ferry *U.S.A.* 40°6N 80°44W **312** F4
Martinsberg *Austria* 48°22N 15°9E **180** C8
Martinsburg *Pa., U.S.A.* 40°19N 78°20W **312** F6
Martinsburg *W. Va., U.S.A.* 39°27N 77°58W **309** F15
Martinsicuro *Italy* 42°54N 13°54E **199** F10
Martinsried *Germany* 48°6N 11°27E **131** B1
Martinsville *Ill., U.S.A.* 39°20N 87°53W **311** E9
Martinsville *Ind., U.S.A.* 39°26N 86°25W **310** E10
Martinsville *Va., U.S.A.* 36°41N 79°52W **309** G14
Marton *N.Z.* 40°4S 175°23E **284** G4
Martorell *Spain* 41°28N 1°56E **196** D6
Martos *Spain* 37°44N 3°58W **195** H7
Martu ✪ *Australia* 22°30S 122°30E **278** D3
Martūbah *Libya* 32°35N 22°46E **258** B4
Martuni *Armenia* 40°8N 45°20E **191** K7
Maru *Nigeria* 12°22N 6°22E **263** C6
Marudi *Malaysia* 4°11N 114°19E **235** B4
Maruf *Afghan.* 31°30N 67°6E **240** C2
Marugame *Japan* 34°15N 133°40E **222** C5
Marui = Pagwi *Papua N. G.* 4°4S 143°2E **286** C2
Maruia → *N.Z.* 41°47S 172°13E **285** B7
Marūim *Brazil* 10°45S 37°5W **332** D4
Maruko *Japan* 35°33N 139°40E **140** B3
Marulan *Australia* 34°43S 150°3E **283** C9
Marum, Mt. *Vanuatu* 16°15S 168°7E **287** F6
Marunga *Angola* 17°28S 20°2E **265** F4
Marungu, Mts. *Dem. Rep. of the Congo* 7°30S 30°0E **268** D3
Marunouchi *Tokyo, Japan* **140** b4
Maruoka *Japan* 36°9N 136°16E **223** A8
Marusino *Russia* 55°41N 37°58E **129** B5
Maruwa ✪ *Australia* 22°30S 127°30E **278** D4
Marv Dasht *Iran* 29°50N 52°40E **247** D7
Marvão = Castelo do Piaui *Brazil* 5°20S 41°33W **332** C3
Marvast *Iran* 30°30N 54°15E **247** D7
Marvejols *France* 44°33N 3°19E **174** D7
Marvel Loch *Australia* 31°28S 119°29E **279** F2
Marwar *India* 25°43N 73°45E **242** G5
Mary *Turkmenistan* 37°40N 61°50E **247** B9
Mary Esther *U.S.A.* 30°25N 86°40W **317** E3
Maryborough = Port Laoise *Ireland* 53°2N 7°18W **166** C4
Maryborough *Queens., Australia* 25°31S 152°37E **281** D5
Maryborough *Vic., Australia* 37°3S 143°44E **282** D5
Maryfield *Canada* 49°50N 101°35W **297** D8
Maryino = Pristen *Russia* 51°15N 36°44E **189** G9
Maryino *Russia* 55°40N 37°45E **129** B4
Maryland *Singapore* 1°19N 103°47E **138** B2
Maryland □ *U.S.A.* 39°0N 76°30W **309** F15
Maryland Junction *Zimbabwe* 17°45S 30°31E **269** F3
Marylebone *London, U.K.* **125** a2
Marymont *Poland* 52°16N 20°58E **142** B1
Maryport *U.K.* 54°44N 3°28W **168** C4
Mary's Harbour *Canada* 52°18N 55°51W **299** B8
Marysin Wawerski *Poland* 52°14N 21°9E **142** B2
Marystown *Canada* 47°10N 55°10W **299** C8
Marysville *Calif., U.S.A.* 39°9N 121°35W **306** F5
Marysville *Kans., U.S.A.* 39°51N 96°39W **308** F5
Marysville *Mich., U.S.A.* 42°54N 82°29W **312** D2
Marysville *Ohio, U.S.A.* 40°14N 83°22W **311** D13
Marysville *Wash., U.S.A.* 48°3N 122°11W **306** B4
Maryville *Mo., U.S.A.* 40°21N 94°52W **310** D2
Maryville *Tenn., U.S.A.* 35°46N 83°58W **315** D13
Marzahn *Germany* 52°32N 13°34E **115** A4
Marzo, Punta *Colombia* 6°50N 77°42W **328** B2
Marzūq *Libya* 25°53N 13°57E **258** C2
Marzūq □ *Libya* 25°0N 16°0E **258** D3
Marzūq, Idehān *Libya* 24°50N 13°51E **258** D2
Masada = Mesada *Israel* 31°20N 35°19E **251** G6
Mas'ada *Syria* 33°13N 35°45E **250** E6
Masahunga *Tanzania* 2°6S 33°18E **268** C3
Masai *Malaysia* 1°29N 103°55E **237** d
Masai Mara △ *Kenya* 1°25S 35°5E **268** C4
Masai Steppe *Tanzania* 4°30S 36°30E **268** C4
Masaka *Uganda* 0°21S 31°45E **268** C3
Māsāl *Iran* 37°23N 49°8E **213** D12
Masalembo, Kepulauan *Indonesia* 5°35S 114°30E **235** D4
Masalima, Kepulauan *Indonesia* 5°4S 117°5E **235** D5
Masallı *Azerbaijan* 39°3N 48°40E **213** C13
Masalog Pt. *N. Marianas* 15°1N 145°40E **302** e
Masamba *Indonesia* 2°30S 120°15E **231** E6
Masan *S. Korea* 35°11N 128°32E **224** E4
Masandam, Ra's *Oman* 26°30N 56°30E **247** E8
Masasi *Tanzania* 10°45S 38°52E **269** E4
Masaya *Nic.* 12°0N 86°7W **320** D2
Masba *Nigeria* 11°35N 13°1E **263** C7
Masbate *Phil.* 12°21N 123°36E **232** E4
Masbate □ *Phil.* 12°20N 123°30E **232** E4
Masbate Pass *Phil.* 12°30N 123°35E **232** E4
Máscali *Italy* 37°45N 15°12E **201** E8
Mascara *Algeria* 35°26N 0°6E **261** A5
Mascara □ *Algeria* 35°25N 0°10E **261** A5
Mascarene Is. *Ind. Oc.* 22°0S 55°0E **273** G4
Mascot *Australia* 33°55S 151°12E **139** B2
Mascota *Mexico* 20°32N 104°49W **318** C4
Mascoutah *U.S.A.* 38°29N 89°48W **310** F7
Masefau B. *Amer. Samoa* 14°15S 170°37W **302** f
Masein *Burma* 23°22N 94°21E **241** D5
Masela *Indonesia* 8°9S 129°51E **231** F7
Maseru *Lesotho* 29°18S 27°30E **270** C4
Masfjorden *Norway* 60°48N 5°18E **164** D2
Mashaba *Zimbabwe* 20°2S 30°29E **269** G3
Mashābih *Si. Arabia* 25°35N 36°30E **246** E3
Mashan *China* 23°40N 108°11E **228** F7
Mashar *Sudan* 9°16N 26°51E **257** F2
Mashatu ⌂ *Botswana* 22°45S 29°5E **271** B4
Mashegu *Nigeria* 10°0N 5°35E **263** D6
Masherbrum *Pakistan* 35°38N 76°18E **243** B7
Mashhad *Iran* 36°20N 59°35E **247** B8
Mashi *Nigeria* 13°0N 7°54E **263** C6
Mashiki *Japan* 32°51N 130°53E **222** E2
Mashīz *Iran* 29°56N 56°37E **247** D8
Mashkal → *Pakistan* 26°2N 65°19E **240** D2
Māshkel, Hāmūn-i- *Pakistan* 28°20N 62°56E **240** C1
Mashki Chāh *Pakistan* 29°5N 62°30E **240** C1
Mashonaland Central □ *Zimbabwe* 17°30S 31°0E **271** A5
Mashonaland East □ *Zimbabwe* 18°0S 32°0E **271** A5
Mashonaland West □ *Zimbabwe* 17°30S 29°30E **271** A4
Mashrakh *India* 26°7N 84°48E **243** F11
Mashtaga = Maştağa *Azerbaijan* 40°35N 50°1E **191** K10
Masi Manimba *Dem. Rep. of the Congo* 4°40S 17°54E **265** C3
Masibi *Angola* 11°6S 22°11E **265** E4
Masig *Australia* 9°45S 143°24E **280** a
Masindi *Uganda* 1°40N 31°43E **268** B3
Masindi Port *Uganda* 1°43N 32°2E **268** B3
Masinga Res. *Kenya* 0°58S 37°38E **268** C4
Masinloc *Phil.* 15°32N 119°57E **232** D2
Maşirah, Jazīrat *Oman* 21°0N 58°50E **249** B7
Maşirah, Khalīj *Oman* 20°10N 58°10E **249** B7
Maşirah, Tur'at *Oman* 20°30N 58°40E **249** B7
Masisea *Peru* 8°35S 74°22W **330** B3
Masisi *Dem. Rep. of the Congo* 1°23S 28°49E **268** C2
Masjed Soleyman *Iran* 31°55N 49°18E **247** D6
Mask, L. *Ireland* 53°36N 9°22W **166** C2
Maskelyne Is. *Vanuatu* 16°32S 167°49E **287** F5
Maski *India* 15°56N 76°46E **245** G3
Maskin *Oman* 23°44N 56°52E **247** F8
Maslen Nos *Bulgaria* 42°18N 27°48E **203** D11
Maslinica *Croatia* 43°24N 16°13E **199** E13
Masmo *Sweden* 59°15N 17°53E **139** B1
Maşna'ah *Yemen* 14°27N 48°17E **249** D5
Masnou = El Masnou *Spain* 41°28N 2°20E **196** D7
Masoala, Tanjon' i *Madag.* 15°59S 50°13E **272** B3
Masoala △ *Madag.* 15°30S 50°12E **272** B3
Masoarivo *Madag.* 19°3S 44°19E **272** B1
Masohi = Amahai *Indonesia* 3°20S 128°55E **231** E7
Masomeloka *Madag.* 20°17S 48°37E **272** C2
Mason *Mich., U.S.A.* 42°35N 84°27W **311** B12
Mason *Nev., U.S.A.* 38°56N 119°8W **306** G7
Mason *Ohio, U.S.A.* 39°22N 84°19W **311** E12
Mason *Tex., U.S.A.* 30°45N 99°14W **314** F5
Mason B. *N.Z.* 46°55S 167°45E **285** G2
Mason City *Ill., U.S.A.* 40°12N 89°42W **310** D7
Mason City *Iowa, U.S.A.* 43°9N 93°12W **310** A3
Mason Hall *Trin. & Tob.* 11°13N 60°43W **323** s
Maspalomas *Canary Is.* 27°46N 15°35W **153** e1
Maspalomas, Pta. *Canary Is.* 27°43N 15°36W **153** e1
Maspeth *U.S.A.* 40°43N 73°55W **132** B2
Masqat *Oman* 23°37N 58°36E **249** B7
Masr el Gedîda *Egypt* 30°5N 31°21E **117** A2
Masr el Qadîma *Egypt* 30°0N 31°14E **117** A2
Massa *Congo* 3°45S 15°29E **264** C3
Massa *Italy* 44°1N 10°9E **198** D7
Massa, O. → *Morocco* 30°2N 9°40W **260** B3
Massa Marittima *Italy* 43°3N 10°52E **198** E7
Massachusetts □ *U.S.A.* 42°30N 72°0W **313** D13
Massachusetts Avenue *Washington, D.C., U.S.A.* **143** a2
Massachusetts B. *U.S.A.* 42°25N 70°50W **313** D14
Massachusetts Inst. of Tech. *U.S.A.* 42°21N 71°5W **116** A2
Massacre *Dominica* 15°20N 61°25W **323** k
Massafra *Italy* 40°35N 17°7E **201** B10
Massaguet *Chad* 12°28N 15°26E **259** F3
Massakory *Chad* 13°0N 15°49E **259** F3
Massamá *Portugal* 38°45N 9°16W **126** A1
Massamba *Mozam.* 15°58S 33°31E **269** F3
Massanella *Spain* 39°48N 2°51E **206** B3
Massangano *Angola* 9°40S 14°13E **265** D2
Massangena *Mozam.* 21°34S 33°0E **271** B5
Massango *Angola* 8°1S 16°10E **265** D3
Massapê *Brazil* 3°31S 40°19W **332** B3
Massat *France* 42°53N 1°21E **174** F5
Massawa = Mitsiwa *Eritrea* 15°35N 39°25E **257** D4
Massena *U.S.A.* 44°56N 74°54W **313** B10
Massenya *Chad* 11°21N 16°9E **259** F3
Masset *Canada* 54°2N 132°10W **296** C2
Masseube *France* 43°25N 0°34E **174** E4
Massey → *Canada* 43°42N 79°19W **141** A3
Massey Hall *Toronto, Canada* **141** a3
Massiac *France* 45°15N 3°11E **174** C7
Massif Central *France* 44°55N 3°0E **174** D7
Massif des Bauges ⌂ *France* 45°40N 6°10E **173** G13
Massigui *Mali* 11°48N 6°50W **262** C3
Massillon *U.S.A.* 40°48N 81°32W **312** F3
Massima *Gabon* 1°27S 11°33E **264** C2
Massine, O. → *Algeria* 36°13N 2°12E **261** A5
Massinga *Mozam.* 23°15S 35°22E **271** B6
Massingir *Mozam.* 23°51S 32°4E **271** B5
Masson-Angers *Canada* 45°32N 75°25W **313** A9
Masson I. *Antarctica* 66°10S 93°20E **151** C7
Massouka *Gabon* 1°37S 9°56E **264** C1
Massow = Maszewo *Poland* 53°29N 15°3E **184** E2
Massy *France* 48°43N 2°16E **134** B2
Mastābah *Si. Arabia* 20°49N 39°26E **248** B2
Maştağa *Azerbaijan* 40°35N 50°1E **191** K10
Mastanli = Momchilgrad *Bulgaria* 41°33N 25°23E **203** E9
Masterton *N.Z.* 40°56S 175°39E **284** G4
Mastic *U.S.A.* 40°47N 72°54W **313** F12
Mastuj *Pakistan* 36°20N 72°36E **243** A5
Mastung *Pakistan* 29°50N 66°56E **240** C2
Mastūrah *Si. Arabia* 23°7N 38°52E **248** B2
Masty *Belarus* 53°27N 24°38E **177** B13
Masuda *Japan* 34°40N 131°51E **222** C3
Masuika *Dem. Rep. of the Congo* 7°37S 22°32E **265** D4
Masuku = Franceville *Gabon* 1°40S 13°32E **264** C2
Masurian Lakes = Mazurski, Pojezierze *Poland* 53°50N 21°0E **184** E7
Masvingo *Zimbabwe* 20°8S 30°49E **269** G3
Masvingo □ *Zimbabwe* 21°0S 31°30E **269** G3
Maswa ⌂ *Tanzania* 2°58S 34°19E **268** C3
Maşyāf *Syria* 35°4N 36°20E **250** C7
Maszewo *Poland* 53°29N 15°3E **184** E2
Mat → *Albania* 41°40N 19°35E **202** E3
Mât → *Réunion* 20°57S 55°42E **272** f
Mata *Israel* 31°43N 35°4E **123** B1
Mata-au = Clutha → *N.Z.* 46°20S 169°49E **285** G4
Mata de São João *Brazil* 12°31S 38°17W **333** D4
Mata-Utu *Wall. & F. Is.* 13°17S 176°8W **277** C15
Matabele Plain *Zambia* 16°20S 23°10E **265** F4
Matabeleland North □ *Zimbabwe* 19°0S 28°0E **269** F2
Matabeleland South □ *Zimbabwe* 21°0S 29°0E **269** G2
Matachel → *Spain* 38°50N 6°17W **195** G4
Matachewan *Canada* 47°56N 80°39W **298** C3
Matacuni → *Venezuela* 3°2N 65°16W **329** C4
Matadi *Dem. Rep. of the Congo* 5°52S 13°31E **265** D2
Matafao, Mt. *Amer. Samoa* 14°17S 170°42W **302** f
Matagalpa *Nic.* 13°0N 85°58W **320** D2
Matagami *Canada* 49°45N 77°34W **298** C4
Matagami, L. *Canada* 49°50N 77°40W **298** C4
Matagorda B. *U.S.A.* 28°40N 96°12W **314** G6
Matagorda I. *U.S.A.* 28°15N 96°30W **314** G6
Mataguinao *Phil.* 12°5N 124°55E **232** E5
Matahiva *French Polynesia* 17°32S 149°20W **289** f
Mataiea *Tahiti* 17°46S 149°25W **289** e
Matak *Indonesia* 3°18N 106°16E **234** B3
Matakana *N.S.W., Australia* 32°59S 145°54E **283** B6
Matakana *N.Z.* 36°21S 174°43E **284** C3
Matala *Angola* 14°46S 15°4E **265** E3
Matala *Kriti, Greece* 34°59N 24°45E **207** F5
Matalaque *Peru* 16°26S 70°49W **330** D3
Matale *Sri Lanka* 7°30N 80°37E **245** L5
Matam *Senegal* 15°34N 13°17W **262** B2
Matam □ *Senegal* 15°37N 13°19W **262** B2
Matamata *N.Z.* 37°48S 175°47E **284** D4
Matameye *Niger* 13°26N 8°28E **259** F1
Matamoros *Campeche, Mexico* 18°50N 90°50W **319** D6
Matamoros *Coahuila, Mexico* 25°32N 103°15W **318** B4
Matamoros *Tamaulipas, Mexico* 25°53N 97°30W **319** B5
Ma'ṭan as Sarra *Libya* 21°45N 22°0E **259** D4
Ma'ṭan Bishārah *Libya* 23°0N 22°32E **258** D4
Matandu → *Tanzania* 8°45S 34°19E **269** D3
Matane *Canada* 48°50N 67°33W **299** C6
Matang *China* 23°30N 104°7E **228** F5
Matankari *Niger* 13°46N 4°1E **263** C5
Matanomadh *India* 23°33N 68°57E **242** H3
Matanzas *Cuba* 23°0N 81°40W **320** B3
Matapa *Botswana* 23°11S 24°39E **270** B3
Matapan, C. = Tenaro, Akra *Greece* 36°22N 22°27E **204** E4
Matapédia *Canada* 48°0N 66°59W **299** C6
Matapo △ *Zimbabwe* 20°30S 29°40E **269** G2
Matara *Sri Lanka* 5°58N 80°30E **245** M5
Mataram *Indonesia* 8°35S 116°7E **231** K19
Matarani *Peru* 17°0S 72°10W **330** D3
Mataranka *Australia* 14°55S 133°4E **278** B5
Matarma, Râs *Egypt* 30°27N 32°44E **251** H3
Mataró *Spain* 41°32N 2°29E **196** D7
Matarraña → *Spain* 41°14N 0°22E **196** D5
Mataruška Banja *Serbia* 43°40N 20°40E **202** C4
Mataso *Vanuatu* 17°14S 168°26E **287** G6
Matata *N.Z.* 37°54S 176°48E **284** D5
Matatiele *S. Africa* 30°20S 28°49E **271** D4
Matatila Dam *India* 25°0N 78°22E **244** B4
Matatula, C. *Amer. Samoa* 14°15S 170°33W **302** f
Mataura *N.Z.* 46°11S 168°51E **285** G3
Mataura → *N.Z.* 46°34S 168°44E **285** G3
Matavai, B. de *Tahiti* 17°30S 149°23W **289** e
Matavera *Cook Is.* 21°13S 159°44W **289** h
Mataveri *Chile* 27°9S 109°27W **330** b
Mategua *Bolivia* 13°1S 62°48W **331** C5
Matehuala *Mexico* 23°39N 100°39W **318** C4
Mateke *Dem. Rep. of the Congo* 4°52S 24°25E **264** C3
Mateke Hills *Zimbabwe* 21°48S 31°0E **269** G3
Matelot *Trin. & Tob.* 10°50N 61°7W **323** t
Matera *Italy* 40°40N 16°36E **201** B9
Matese, Monti del *Italy* 41°27N 14°22E **201** A7
Matese ⌂ *Italy* 41°24N 14°23E **201** A7
Mátészalka *Hungary* 47°58N 22°20E **182** C7
Matetsi *Zimbabwe* 18°12S 26°0E **269** F2
Mateur *Tunisia* 37°0N 9°40E **258** A1
Matfors *Sweden* 62°21N 17°2E **162** B11
Matha *France* 45°52N 0°20W **174** C3
Matheniko ⌂ *Uganda* 2°49N 34°27E **268** B3
Mathis *U.S.A.* 28°6N 97°50W **314** G6
Mathoura *Australia* 35°50S 144°55E **283** C6
Mathraki *Greece* 39°48N 19°31E **206** B9
Mathura *India* 27°30N 77°40E **242** F7
Mati *Phil.* 6°55N 126°15E **233** H6
Matiakoali *Burkina Faso* 12°28N 1°2E **263** C5
Matiali *India* 26°56N 88°49E **243** F13
Matías Romero *Mexico* 16°53N 95°2W **319** D5
Matibane *Mozam.* 14°49S 40°45E **269** E5
Matinha *Portugal* 38°45N 9°5W **126** A2
Matinhos *Brazil* 25°49S 48°32W **333** G2
Matiri Ra. *N.Z.* 41°38S 172°20E **285** B7
Matjiesfontein *S. Africa* 33°14S 20°35E **270** D3
Matla → *India* 21°40N 88°40E **243** J13
Matlamanyane *Botswana* 19°33S 25°57E **270** A4
Matli *Pakistan* 25°2N 68°39E **242** G3
Matlock *U.K.* 53°9N 1°33W **168** D6
Matmata *Tunisia* 33°37N 9°59E **258** B1
Matna *Sudan* 13°49N 35°10E **257** E4
Matnog *Phil.* 12°35N 124°5E **232** E5
Mato *Dem. Rep. of the Congo* 8°1S 24°24E **265** D4
Mato → *Venezuela* 7°9N 65°7W **329** B4
Mato, Serrania de *Venezuela* 6°25N 65°25W **328** B4
Mato Grosso □ *Brazil* 14°0S 55°0W **331** C7
Mato Grosso, Planalto do *Brazil* 15°0S 55°0W **331** D7
Mato Grosso do Sul □ *Brazil* 18°0S 55°0W **331** D7
Matobo = Matapo △ *Zimbabwe* 20°30S 29°40E **269** G2
Matochkin Shar, Proliv *Russia* 73°23N 55°12E **214** B6
Matola *Mozam.* 25°57S 32°27E **271** C5
Matong *Papua N. G.* 5°36S 151°50E **286** C6
Matopo Hills *Zimbabwe* 20°36S 28°20E **269** G2
Matopos *Zimbabwe* 20°20S 28°29E **269** G2
Matosinhos *Portugal* 41°11N 8°42W **194** D2
Matou *Taiwan* 23°11N 120°15E **225** C2
Matouba *Guadeloupe* 16°2N 61°41W **322** e
Matour *France* 46°19N 4°29E **173** F11
Matramam *Indonesia* 6°12S 106°51E **122** B2
Matroosberg *S. Africa* 33°23S 19°40E **270** D2
Maţruḩ *Oman* 23°37N 58°30E **249** B7
Matsena *Nigeria* 13°5N 10°5E **263** C7
Matsesta *Russia* 43°34N 39°51E **191** J4
Matsu Tao *Taiwan* 26°8N 119°56E **225** b
Matsubara = Takahagi *Japan* 36°43N 140°45E **221** F10
Matsubara *Japan* 34°34N 135°33E **133** B2
Matsudo *Japan* 35°47N 139°54E **223** B11
Matsue *Japan* 35°25N 133°10E **222** B5
Matsum, Ko *Thailand* 9°22N 99°59E **237** b
Matsumae *Japan* 41°26N 140°7E **220** D10
Matsumoto *Japan* 36°15N 138°0E **223** A10
Matsusaka *Japan* 34°34N 136°32E **223** C8
Matsushima *Japan* 32°30N 130°25E **222** E2
Matsuura *Japan* 33°20N 129°49E **222** D1
Matsuyama *Japan* 33°45N 132°45E **222** D4
Matsuzaki *Japan* 34°43N 138°50E **223** C10
Mattagami → *Canada* 50°43N 81°29W **298** B3
Mattancheri *India* 9°50N 76°15E **245** K3
Mattapan *U.S.A.* 42°16N 71°6W **116** B2
Mattawa *Canada* 46°20N 78°45W **298** C4
Matterhorn *Switz.* 45°58N 7°39E **179** K3
Mattersburg *Austria* 47°44N 16°24E **181** D9
Matteson *U.S.A.* 41°30N 87°42W **311** C9
Matthew, Î. *N. Cal.* 22°29S 171°15E **277** E13
Matthew Town *Bahamas* 20°57N 73°40W **321** B5
Matthews *U.S.A.* 40°23N 85°30W **311** D11
Matthews Ridge *Guyana* 7°37N 60°10W **329** B5
Mattias Church *Budapest, Hungary* **117** b1
Mattice *Canada* 49°40N 83°20W **298** C3
Mattili *India* 18°33N 82°12E **244** E6
Mattituck *U.S.A.* 40°59N 72°32W **313** F12
Mattō *Japan* 36°31N 136°34E **223** A8
Mattoon *U.S.A.* 39°29N 88°23W **311** E8
Matuba *Mozam.* 24°28S 32°49E **271** B5
Matucana *Peru* 11°55S 76°25W **330** C2
Matugama *Sri Lanka* 6°31N 80°7E **245** L5
Matuka *Papua N. G.* 4°54S 145°47E **286** C3
Matuku *Fiji* 19°10S 179°44E **287** B2
Matūn = Khowst *Afghan.* 33°22N 69°58E **242** C3
Matura *Trin. & Tob.* 10°40N 61°4W **323** t
Matura B. *Trin. & Tob.* 10°39N 61°1W **323** t
Maturín *Venezuela* 9°45N 63°11W **329** B5
Matusadona △ *Zimbabwe* 16°58S 28°42E **269** F2
Matutum, Mt. *Phil.* 6°22N 125°5E **233** H5
Matveyev Kurgan *Russia* 47°35N 38°57E **189** J10
Matxitxako, C. *Spain* 43°28N 2°47W **196** B2
Mátyásföld *Hungary* 47°30N 19°12E **117** A3
Mau *Mad. P., India* 26°17N 78°41E **243** F8
Mau *Ut. P., India* 25°56N 83°33E **243** G10
Mau *Ut. P., India* 25°17N 81°23E **243** G9
Mau Escarpment *Kenya* 0°40S 36°0E **268** C4
Mau Ranipur *India* 25°16N 79°8E **243** G8
Mau Tso Ngam *China* 22°22N 114°13E **122** A2
Maua *Eastern, Kenya* 0°14N 37°56E **268** C4
Maua *Mozam.* 13°53S 37°10E **269** E4
Mauban *Phil.* 14°12N 121°44E **232** D3
Maubeuge *France* 50°17N 3°57E **173** B10
Maubin *Burma* 16°44N 95°39E **241** G5
Maubourguet *France* 43°29N 0°1E **174** E4
Maud, Pt. *Australia* 23°6S 113°45E **278** D1
Maud Rise *S. Ocean* 66°0S 3°0E **151** C3
Maude *Australia* 34°29S 144°18E **282** C6
Maudin Sun *Burma* 16°0N 94°30E **241** G5
Mauer *Austria* 48°9N 16°16E **142** B1
Maués *Brazil* 3°20S 57°45W **329** D6
Maués-Acu → *Brazil* 3°22S 57°44W **329** D6
Maug Is. *N. Marianas* 20°1N 145°13E **302** a
Mauganj *India* 24°50N 81°55E **243** G9
Maughold Hd. *I. of Man* 54°18N 4°18W **168** C3
Mauguio *France* 43°37N 4°1E **174** E7
Maui *U.S.A.* 20°48N 156°20W **302** C5
Maulamyaing = Moulmein *Burma* 16°30N 97°40E **241** G6
Maule □ *Chile* 36°5S 72°30W **334** D1
Mauléon-Licharre *France* 43°14N 0°54W **174** E3
Maullín *Chile* 41°38S 73°37W **336** B2
Maulvibazar *Bangla.* 24°29N 91°42E **241** C3
Maumee *U.S.A.* 41°34N 83°39W **311** C13
Maumee → *U.S.A.* 41°42N 83°28W **311** C13
Maumere *Indonesia* 8°38S 122°13E **231** F6
Maumusson, Pertuis de *France* 45°48N 1°14W **174** C2
Maun *Botswana* 20°0S 23°26E **270** B3
Mauna Kea *U.S.A.* 19°50N 155°28W **302** D6
Mauna Loa *U.S.A.* 19°30N 155°35W **302** D6
Mauna Loa Forest Reserve *U.S.A.* 19°35N 155°33W **302** D6
Maunabo *Puerto Rico* 18°1N 65°54W **321** b
Maunaloa *U.S.A.* 21°8N 157°13W **302** B4
Maunalua B. *U.S.A.* 21°15N 157°45W **302** K14
Maunath Bhanjan = Mau *India* 25°56N 83°33E **243** G10
Maunawili *U.S.A.* 21°23N 157°46W **302** K14
Maunga Orito *Chile* 27°10S 109°25W **330** b
Maunga Puakatiki *Chile* 27°6S 109°15W **330** b
Maunga Terevaka *Chile* 27°5S 109°23W **330** b
Maungaroa *Cook Is.* 21°13S 159°48W **289** h
Maungatongaiti *Cook Is.* 21°14S 159°48W **289** h
Maungaturoto *N.Z.* 36°6S 174°23E **284** C3
Maungdow *Burma* 20°50N 92°21E **241** E4
Maungmagan Kyunzu *Burma* 14°0N 97°48E **236** E1
Maungu *Kenya* 3°33S 38°45E **268** C4
Maupihaa *French Polynesia* 16°50S 153°55W **289** f
Maupin *U.S.A.* 45°11N 121°5W **304** D3
Maupiti *French Polynesia* 16°27S 152°15W **289** f
Maure-de-Bretagne *France* 47°59N 1°58W **172** E5
Maurepas, L. *U.S.A.* 30°15N 90°30W **315** F9
Maures *France* 43°15N 6°15E **175** E10
Mauriac *France* 45°13N 2°19E **174** C6
Maurice, L. *Australia* 29°30S 131°0E **279** E5
Mauriceville *N.Z.* 40°45S 175°42E **284** G4
Mauricie △ *Canada* 46°45N 73°0W **298** C5
Maurienne *France* 45°13N 6°30E **175** C10
Mauripur *Pakistan* 24°52N 66°55E **123** A1
Mauritania ■ *Africa* 20°50N 10°0W **260** D3
Mauritius ■ *Ind. Oc.* 20°0S 57°0E **272** e
Mauritius ✈ (MRU) *Mauritius* 20°25S 57°40E **272** e
Mauron *France* 48°9N 2°18W **172** D4
Maurs *France* 44°43N 2°12E **174** D6
Mauston *U.S.A.* 43°48N 90°5W **308** D8
Mauterndorf *Austria* 47°9N 13°40E **180** D6
Mauthen *Austria* 46°40N 13°0E **180** E6
Mauvezin *France* 43°44N 0°53E **174** E4
Mauzé-sur-le-Mignon *France* 46°12N 0°41W **174** B3
Mavaca → *Venezuela* 2°31N 65°11W **329** C4
Mavinga *Angola* 15°50S 20°21E **265** F4
Mavli *India* 24°45N 73°55E **242** G5
Mavrata *Greece* 38°4N 20°44E **207** C2
Mavrovë *Albania* 40°26N 19°32E **202** F3
Mavrovo △ *Macedonia* 41°36N 20°45E **202** E4
Mavuradonha Mts. *Zimbabwe* 16°30S 31°30E **269** F3
Mawa *Dem. Rep. of the Congo* 2°45N 26°40E **268** B2
Mawai *India* 22°30N 81°4E **243** H9
Mawana *India* 29°6N 77°58E **242** E7
Mawand *Pakistan* 29°33N 68°38E **242** E3
Mawat *Iraq* 35°54N 45°24E **213** E11
Mawjib, W. al → *Jordan* 31°28N 35°36E **251** G6
Mawk Mai *Burma* 20°14N 97°37E **241** E6
Mawlaik *Burma* 23°40N 94°26E **241** D5
Mawlamyine = Moulmein *Burma* 16°30N 97°40E **241** G6
Mawlawkho *Burma* 17°50N 97°38E **241** G6
Mawqaq *Si. Arabia* 27°25N 41°8E **246** E4
Mawshij *Yemen* 13°43N 43°17E **248** D3
Mawson Base *Antarctica* 67°30S 62°53E **151** C6
Mawson Coast *Antarctica* 68°30S 63°0E **151** C6
Mawson Pk. *Heard I.* 53°6S 73°31E **273** K6
Mawsynram *India* 25°15N 91°30E **241** C3
Max *U.S.A.* 47°49N 101°18W **308** B3
Maxambamba = Nova Iguaçu *Brazil* 22°45S 43°28W **333** F3
Maxcanú *Mexico* 20°35N 90°0W **319** C6
Maxesibeni *S. Africa* 30°49S 29°23E **271** D4
Maxeys *U.S.A.* 33°45N 83°11W **316** B6
Maxhamish L. *Canada* 59°50N 123°17W **296** B4
Maxhof *Germany* 48°4N 11°29E **131** B1
Maxixe *Mozam.* 23°54S 35°17E **271** B6
Maxville *Canada* 45°17N 74°51W **313** A10
Maxwell *N.Z.* 39°51S 174°49E **284** F3
Maxwell *Calif., U.S.A.* 39°17N 122°11W **306** F4
Maxwelton *Australia* 20°43S 142°41E **280** C3
May, C. *U.S.A.* 38°56N 74°58W **309** F16
May Jirgui *Niger* 13°44N 8°8E **259** F1
May Pen *Jamaica* 17°58N 77°15W **320** a
May River *Papua N. G.* 4°19S 141°58E **286** C1
Maya *Indonesia* 1°10S 109°35E **235** C3
Maya → *Russia* 60°28N 134°28E **215** D14
Maya Mts. *Belize* 16°30N 89°0W **320** C2
Mayabandar *India* 12°56N 92°56E **245** H11
Mayaguana *Bahamas* 22°30N 72°44W **321** B5
Mayagüez *Puerto Rico* 18°12N 67°9W **321** C6
Mayahi *Niger* 13°58N 7°40E **263** C6
Mayaky *Ukraine* 47°26N 29°33E **183** C14
Mayals = Maials *Spain* 41°22N 0°30E **196** D5
Mayama *Congo* 3°51S 14°54E **264** C2
Mayāmey *Iran* 36°24N 55°42E **247** B7
Mayang *China* 27°53N 109°49E **228** D7
Mayanup *Australia* 33°57S 116°27E **279** F2
Mayapán *Mexico* 20°29N 89°11W **319** C7
Mayarí *Cuba* 20°40N 75°41W **321** B4
Mayaro *Trin. & Tob.* 10°12N 61°1W **323** t
Mayaro □ *Trin. & Tob.* 10°10N 61°5W **323** t
Mayaro B. *Trin. & Tob.* 10°14N 60°59W **323** t
Mayavaram = Mayiladuthurai *India* 11°3N 79°42E **245** J4
Maybell *U.S.A.* 40°31N 108°5W **304** F9
Maybole *U.K.* 55°21N 4°42W **167** F4
Maychew *Ethiopia* 12°50N 39°31E **257** E4
Maydān *Iraq* 34°55N 45°37E **213** E11
Maydan *Ukraine* 48°36N 23°29E **183** B8

Maydī Yemen 16°19N 42°48E 248 C3
Mayen Germany 50°19N 7°13E 179 E3
Mayenne France 48°20N 0°38W 172 D6
Mayenne □ France 48°10N 0°40W 172 D6
Mayenne ➜ France 47°30N 0°32W 172 E6
Mayer U.S.A. 34°24N 112°14W 305 J7
Mayerthorpe Canada 53°57N 115°8W 296 C5
Mayesville U.S.A. 34°0N 80°12W 316 A9
Mayfair Gauteng, S. Africa 26°11S 28°0E 123 B2
Mayfair London, U.K. 125 b3
Mayfield Ky., U.S.A. 36°44N 88°38W 308 G9
Mayfield N.Y., U.S.A. 43°6N 74°16W 313 C10
Mayhill U.S.A. 32°53N 105°29W 305 K11
Mayiladuthurai India 11°3N 79°42E 245 J4
Maykop Russia 44°35N 40°10E 191 H5
Mayma Russia 52°3N 85°55E 217 B11
Maymyo Burma 22°2N 96°28E 236 A1
Maynard Mass., U.S.A. 42°26N 71°27W 313 D13
Maynard Wash., U.S.A. 47°59N 122°55W 306 C4
Maynard Hills Australia 28°28S 119°49E 279 E2
Mayne ➜ Australia 23°40S 141°55E 280 C3
Maynooth Ont., Canada 45°13N 77°56W 312 A7
Maynooth Kildare, Ireland 53°23N 6°34W 166 C5
Mayo Yukon, Canada 63°38N 135°57W 294 E4
Mayo Trin. & Tob. 10°21N 61°23W 323 t
Mayo Fla., U.S.A. 30°3N 83°10W 316 E6
Mayo □ Ireland 53°53N 9°3W 166 C2
Mayo ➜ Argentina 45°45S 69°45W 336 C3
Mayo ➜ Peru 6°38S 76°15W 330 B2
Mayo Bay Phil. 6°56N 126°22E 233 H6
Mayo Daga Nigeria 6°59N 11°25E 263 D7
Mayo Faran Nigeria 8°57N 12°4E 263 D7
Mayo-Kébbi Est □ Chad 10°20N 15°30E 259 F3
Mayo-Kébbi Ouest □
Chad 9°40N 17°50E 259 G3
Mayoko Congo 2°18S 12°49E 264 C2
Mayoko
Dem. Rep. of the Congo 1°6S 23°50E 264 C4
Mayon Volcano Phil. 13°15N 123°41E 232 E4
Mayor Buratovich
Argentina 39°15S 62°37W 336 A4
Mayor I. N.Z. 37°16S 176°17E 284 D5
Mayor Pablo Lagerenza
Paraguay 19°55S 60°47W 331 D5
Mayorga Spain 42°10N 5°16W 194 C5
Mayotte ☑ Ind. Oc. 12°50S 45°10E 272 b
Mayoyao Phil. 16°59N 121°14E 232 C3
Mayqayyng Kazakhstan 51°27N 75°47E 217 B9
Mayraira Pt. Phil. 18°39N 120°51E 232 B3
Mayreau St. Vincent 12°39N 61°23W 323 n
Maysān □ Iraq 31°55N 47°15E 246 D5
Mayskiy Russia 43°47N 44°2E 191 J7
Maysville Ky., U.S.A. 38°39N 83°46W 311 F13
Maysville Mo., U.S.A. 39°53N 94°22W 310 E2
Mayu Indonesia 1°30N 126°30E 231 D7
Mayumba Gabon 3°25S 10°39E 264 C2
Mayuram = Mayiladuthurai
India 11°3N 79°42E 245 J4
Mayville N. Dak., U.S.A. 47°30N 97°20W 308 B5
Mayville N.Y., U.S.A. 42°15N 79°30W 312 D5
Maywood Calif., U.S.A. 33°59N 118°12W 126 C3
Maywood Ill., U.S.A. 41°52N 87°51W 119 B1
Maywood N.J., U.S.A. 40°53N 74°3W 132 A1
Maywood Park Race Track
U.S.A. 41°54N 87°50W 119 B1
Mazabuka Zambia 15°52S 27°44E 269 F2
Mazagán = El Jadida
Morocco 33°11N 8°17W 260 B3
Mazagão Brazil 0°7S 51°16W 329 D7
Mazagaon Mumbai, India 130 a2
Mazamet France 43°30N 2°20E 174 E6
Mazán Peru 3°30S 73°0W 328 D3
Māzandarān □ Iran 36°30N 52°0E 247 B7
Mazapil Mexico 24°39N 101°34W 318 C4
Mazar China 36°32N 77°1E 217 E9
Mazar, O. ➜ Algeria 31°50N 1°36E 261 B5
Mazār-e Sharīf Afghan. 36°41N 67°0E 240 A2
Mazara del Vallo Italy 37°39N 12°35E 200 E5
Mazarredo Argentina 47°10S 66°50W 336 C3
Mazarrón Spain 37°38N 1°19W 197 H3
Mazarrón, G. de Spain 37°27N 1°19W 197 H3
Mazaruni ➜ Guyana 6°25N 58°35W 329 B6
Mazatán Mexico 29°0N 110°8W 318 B2
Mazatenango Guatemala 14°35N 91°30W 320 D1
Mazatlán Mexico 23°13N 106°25W 318 C3
Mažeikiai Lithuania 56°20N 22°20E 184 B9
Mazhafa, J. Si. Arabia 28°52N 35°5E 251 K6
Māzhān Iran 32°30N 59°0E 247 C8
Mazdağı Turkey 37°28N 40°29E 213 D9
Mazīnān Iran 36°19N 56°56E 247 B8
Mazo Cruz Peru 16°45S 69°44W 330 D4
Mazoe Mozam. 16°42S 33°7E 269 F3
Mazoe ➜ Mozam. 16°20S 33°30E 269 F3
Mazomanie U.S.A. 43°11N 89°48W 310 A7
Mazon U.S.A. 41°14N 88°25W 311 C8
Mazowe Zimbabwe 17°28S 30°58E 269 F3
Mazowieckie □ Poland 52°40N 21°0E 185 F8
Mazrûb Sudan 14°0N 29°20E 257 E2
Mazu Dao China 26°10N 119°55E 229 D12
Mazurski, Pojezierze
Poland 53°50N 21°0E 184 E7
Mazyr Belarus 51°59N 29°15E 177 B15
Mba Fiji 17°33S 177°41E 287 A1
Mbaba Senegal 14°59N 16°44W 262 C1
Mbabane Swaziland 26°18S 31°6E 271 C5
Mbaéré ➜ C.A.R. 3°47N 17°31E 264 B3
Mbagne Mauritania 16°6N 14°47W 262 B2
M'bahiakro Ivory C. 7°33N 4°19W 262 D4
Mbaïki C.A.R. 3°53N 18°1E 264 B3
Mbakana, Mt. de Cameroon 7°57N 15°6E 264 A3
Mbala Zambia 8°46S 31°24E 269 D3
Mbalabala Zimbabwe 20°27S 29°3E 271 B4
Mbalam Cameroon 2°13N 13°49E 264 B2
Mbale Uganda 1°8N 34°12E 268 B3
Mbali ➜ C.A.R. 4°27N 18°20E 264 B3
Mbalmayo Cameroon 3°33N 11°33E 263 E7
Mbam ➜ Cameroon 4°24N 11°17E 263 E7
Mbamba Bay Tanzania 11°13S 34°49E 269 E3
Mbandaka
Dem. Rep. of the Congo 0°1N 18°18E 264 B3
Mbandjok Cameroon 4°27N 11°54E 264 B2
Mbanga Cameroon 4°30N 9°33E 263 E6
M'Banio, Lagune Gabon 3°35S 11°0E 264 C2
Mbanza Congo Angola 6°18S 14°16E 265 D2
Mbanza Ngungu
Dem. Rep. of the Congo 5°12S 14°53E 265 D2
Mbarangandu Tanzania 10°11S 36°48E 269 D4
Mbarara Uganda 0°35S 30°40E 268 C3
Mbari ➜ C.A.R. 4°34N 22°43E 264 B4
Mbatto Ivory C. 6°28N 4°22W 262 D4
Mbava Solomon Is. 7°47S 156°33E 287 L9
Mbé Congo 3°14S 15°50E 264 C3
Mbe Eq. Guin. 1°47N 9°56E 264 B1
Mbengga = Beqa Fiji 18°23S 178°8E 287 B2
Mbengué Gabon 2°2S 11°7E 264 C2
Mbengui Gabon 2°3S 10°4E 264 C2
Mbéni Comoros Is. 11°30S 43°22E 272 a
Mbenkuru ➜ Tanzania 9°25S 39°50E 269 D4
Mbéré ➜ Cameroon 7°45N 15°36E 264 A3
Mberengwa Zimbabwe 20°29S 29°57E 269 G2
Mberengwa, Mt.
Zimbabwe 20°37S 29°55E 269 G2
Mberubu Nigeria 6°10N 7°38E 263 D6
Mbesuma Zambia 10°0S 32°2E 269 E3
Mbeya Tanzania 8°54S 33°29E 269 D3
Mbeya □ Tanzania 8°15S 33°30E 268 D3
Mbhashe ➜ S. Africa 32°15S 28°54E 271 D4
Mbigou Gabon 1°53S 11°56E 264 C2
M'bili Sudan 7°35N 28°15E 257 F2
Mbinga Tanzania 10°50S 35°0E 269 E4
Mbini = Río Muni □
Eq. Guin. 1°30N 10°0E 264 B2
Mbini Eq. Guin. 1°35N 9°37E 264 B1
Mbizi Zimbabwe 21°23S 31°1E 269 G3
Mboi Dem. Rep. of the Congo 6°57S 21°54E 265 D4
Mboki C.A.R. 5°19N 25°58E 257 F2
Mbokonimbeti
Solomon Is. 8°57S 160°7E 287 M11
Mboli Dem. Rep. of the Congo 4°8N 23°9E 264 B4
Mbomo Congo 0°25N 14°42E 264 B2
M'bonge Cameroon 4°33N 9°5E 263 E6
Mboro Senegal 15°9N 16°54W 262 B1
Mboua Cameroon 4°25N 14°16E 264 A2
Mbouda Cameroon 5°38N 10°15E 264 A2
M'boukou, L. de Cameroon 6°23N 12°50E 263 D7
Mboune Senegal 14°42N 13°34W 262 C2
Mbouoma Congo 0°52S 15°4E 264 C3
Mbour Senegal 14°22N 16°54W 262 C1
Mbout Mauritania 16°1N 12°38W 262 B2
Mbrés C.A.R. 6°40N 19°48E 264 A3
M'Bridge ➜ Angola 7°12S 12°51E 265 D2
Mbuji-Mayi
Dem. Rep. of the Congo 6°9S 23°40E 265 D4
Mbulu Tanzania 3°45S 35°30E 268 C4
Mbuma
Dem. Rep. of the Congo 3°32N 24°50E 264 B4
Mbuma Solomon Is. 8°59S 160°46E 287 M11
Mburucuyá Argentina 28°1S 58°14W 334 B4
Mburucuyá △ Argentina 28°1S 58°12W 334 B4
M'bwat Cameroon 6°29N 10°45E 264 A2
Mcherrah Algeria 27°0N 4°30W 260 C4
Mchinja Tanzania 9°44S 39°45E 269 D4
Mchinji Malawi 13°47S 32°58E 269 E3
Mdantsane S. Africa 32°56S 27°46E 271 D4
Mdennah Mauritania 24°37N 6°0W 260 D3
Me'a She' Arim Jerusalem 123 a2
Mead, L. U.S.A. 36°0N 114°44W 307 J12
Meade = Atqasuk ➜
U.S.A. 70°52N 155°55W 303 A9
Meade U.S.A. 37°17N 100°20W 308 G3
Meade River = Atqasuk
U.S.A. 70°28N 157°24W 303 A8
Meadow Lake Canada 54°10N 108°26W 297 C7
Meadow Lake ⌂ Canada 54°27N 109°0W 297 C7
Meadow Valley Wash ➜
U.S.A. 36°40N 114°34W 307 J12
Meadowbank Park
Australia 33°49S 151°6E 139 A1
Meadville Mo., U.S.A. 39°47N 93°18W 310 E3
Meadville Pa., U.S.A. 41°39N 80°9W 312 E4
Meaford Canada 44°36N 80°35W 312 B4
Mealhada Portugal 40°22N 8°27W 194 E2
Mealy Mts. Canada 53°10N 58°0W 299 B8
Meander River Canada 59°2N 117°42W 296 B5
Meares, C. U.S.A. 45°37N 124°0W 304 D1
Mearim ➜ Brazil 3°4S 44°35W 332 B3
Meath □ Ireland 53°40N 6°57W 166 C5
Meath Park Canada 53°27N 105°22W 297 C7
Meaulne France 46°36N 2°36E 173 F9
Meaux France 48°58N 2°50E 173 D9
Mebechi-Gawa ➜
Japan 40°31N 141°31E 220 D10
Mebonden Norway 63°13N 11°2E 164 A8
Mebulu, Tanjung
Indonesia 8°50S 115°5E 231 K18
Mecanhelas Mozam. 15°12S 35°54E 269 F4
Mecaya ➜ Colombia 0°29N 75°11W 328 C2
Mecca = Makkah
Si. Arabia 21°30N 39°54E 248 B2
Mecca U.S.A. 33°34N 116°5W 307 M10
Mechanicsburg Ohio,
U.S.A. 40°4N 83°33W 311 D13
Mechanicsburg Pa.,
U.S.A. 40°13N 77°1W 312 F8
Mechanicsville U.S.A. 41°54N 91°16W 310 C5
Mechanicville U.S.A. 42°54N 73°41W 313 D11
Mechara Ethiopia 8°36N 40°20E 257 F5
Mechelen Belgium 51°2N 4°29E 170 C4
Mecheria Algeria 33°35N 0°18W 261 B4
Mechernich Germany 50°35N 6°39E 178 E2
Mechetinskaya Russia 46°45N 40°32E 191 G5
Mechol Micronesia 9°37N 138°9E 287 R16
Mecholupy Czech Rep. 50°3N 14°32E 135 B3
Mechra Bel Ksiri Morocco 34°34N 5°57W 260 B3
Mechra Benâbbou
Morocco 32°39N 7°48W 260 B3
Měčice Czech Rep. 50°11N 14°31E 135 A3
Mecidiye Turkey 40°38N 26°32E 203 F10
Mecidiyeköy Turkey 41°4N 29°0E 122 B2
Mecitözü Turkey 40°32N 35°17E 212 B6
Mecklenburg Germany 53°33N 11°40E 176 B7
Mecklenburg-Vorpommern □
Germany 53°45N 12°15E 178 B8
Mecklenburger Bucht
Germany 54°20N 11°40E 178 A7
Meconta Mozam. 14°59S 39°50E 269 E4
Mecsek Hungary 46°10N 18°18E 182 D3
Mecubúri Mozam. 14°39S 38°54E 269 E4
Mecubúri ➜ Mozam. 14°10S 40°30E 269 E5
Mecúfi Mozam. 13°20S 40°32E 269 E5
Meda Portugal 40°57N 7°18W 194 E3
Medak India 18°1N 78°15E 244 E4
Medan Indonesia 3°40N 98°38E 234 B1
Médanos Argentina 38°50S 62°42W 336 A4
Médanos de Coro △
Venezuela 11°35N 69°44W 328 A4
Medanosa, Pta. Argentina 48°8S 66°0W 336 C3
Medart U.S.A. 30°5N 84°23W 316 E5
Medaryville U.S.A. 41°5N 86°55W 311 C10
Medawachchiya Sri Lanka 8°30N 80°30E 245 K5
Medchal India 17°37N 78°29E 244 F4
Mede Italy 45°6N 8°44E 198 C5
Médéa Algeria 36°12N 2°50E 261 A5
Médéa □ Algeria 35°0N 3°0E 261 B5
Mededa Bos.-H. 43°44N 19°15E 182 G4
Medégué Gabon 0°37N 10°8E 264 B2
Medeiros Neto Brazil 17°20S 40°14W 333 E3
Medellín Colombia 6°15N 75°35W 328 B2
Medelpad Sweden 62°33N 16°30E 162 B10
Medemblik Neths. 52°46N 5°8E 170 B5
Médenine Tunisia 33°21N 10°30E 258 B2
Médenine □ Tunisia 32°20N 10°0E 261 B7
Mederdra Mauritania 17°0N 15°38W 262 B1
Medford Mass., U.S.A. 42°25N 71°7W 116 A2
Medford Oreg., U.S.A. 42°19N 122°52W 304 E2
Medford Wis., U.S.A. 45°9N 90°20W 308 C8
Medgidia Romania 44°15N 28°19E 183 F13
Medi Sudan 5°4N 30°42E 257 F3
Media Agua Argentina 31°58S 68°25W 334 C2
Media Luna Argentina 34°45S 66°44W 334 C2
Medianeira Brazil 25°17S 54°5W 335 B5
Mediapolis U.S.A. 41°0N 91°10W 310 D5
Mediaş Romania 46°9N 24°22E 183 D9
Medicilândia Brazil 3°33S 53°8W 329 D7
Medicina Italy 44°28N 11°38E 199 D8
Medicine Bow U.S.A. 41°54N 106°12W 304 F10
Medicine Bow Mts.
U.S.A. 40°40N 106°0W 304 F10
Medicine Bow Pk.
U.S.A. 41°21N 106°19W 304 F10
Medicine Hat Canada 50°0N 110°45W 297 D6
Medicine Lake U.S.A. 48°30N 104°30W 304 B11
Medicine Lodge U.S.A. 37°17N 98°35W 308 G4
Medina = Al Madīnah
Si. Arabia 24°35N 39°52E 246 E3
Medina Brazil 16°15S 41°29W 333 E3
Medina Colombia 4°30N 73°21W 328 C3
Medina Mis. Or., Phil. 8°55N 125°0E 233 G5
Medina N. Dak., U.S.A. 46°54N 99°18W 308 B4
Medina N.Y., U.S.A. 43°13N 78°23W 312 C6
Medina Ohio, U.S.A. 41°8N 81°52W 312 E3
Medina ➜ U.S.A. 29°16N 98°29W 314 G5
Medina de Pomar Spain 42°56N 3°29W 194 C7
Medina de Rioseco Spain 41°53N 5°3W 194 D5
Medina del Campo Spain 41°18N 4°55W 194 D6
Médina Gounas Senegal 13°8N 13°45W 262 C2
Medina L. U.S.A. 29°32N 98°56W 314 G5
Medina Sidonia Spain 36°28N 5°57W 195 J5
Medinaceli Spain 41°12N 2°30W 196 D2
Medinipur India 22°25N 87°21E 243 H12
Mediodia Spain 40°22N 3°39W 127 B2
Mediterranean Sea Europe 35°0N 15°0E 193 D7
Medjerda, O. ➜ Tunisia 37°7N 10°13E 258 A2
Mednogorsk Russia 51°24N 57°37E 216 B5
Medny = Mednogorsk
Russia 51°24N 57°37E 216 B5
Médoc France 45°10N 0°50W 174 C3
Medora U.S.A. 38°49N 86°10W 311 F10
Médouneu Gabon 0°57N 10°47E 264 B2
Medulin Croatia 44°49N 13°55E 199 D10
Medveđa Serbia 42°50N 21°32E 202 D5
Medvedevo Russia 56°37N 47°47E 190 B8
Medveditsa ➜ Tver,
Russia 57°5N 37°30E 188 D9
Medveditsa ➜ Volgograd,
Russia 49°35N 42°41E 190 F6
Medvedok Russia 57°20N 50°1E 190 B10
Medvezhi, Ostrava
Russia 71°0N 161°0E 215 B17
Medvezhiy Ozyora
Russia 55°52N 37°59E 129 A5
Medvezhye = Krasnogvardeyskoye
Russia 45°52N 41°33E 191 H5
Medvezhyegorsk Russia 63°0N 34°25E 186 B5
Medway □ U.K. 51°25N 0°32E 169 F8
Medway ➜ U.K. 51°27N 0°46E 169 F8
Medzev Slovak Rep. 48°43N 20°55E 181 C13
Medzilaborce Slovak Rep. 49°17N 21°52E 181 B14
Medžitlija Macedonia 40°56N 21°26E 202 F5
Meekatharra Australia 26°32S 118°29E 279 E2
Meeker U.S.A. 40°2N 107°55W 304 F10
Meeniyan Australia 38°35S 146°3E 283 E7
Meersburg Germany 47°41N 9°16E 179 H5
Meerut India 29°1N 77°42E 242 E7
Meeteetse U.S.A. 44°9N 108°52W 304 D9
Mega Ethiopia 3°57N 38°19E 257 G4
Mega Indonesia 4°0S 101°2E 234 C2
Megalo Ethiopia 6°51N 40°47E 267 C5
Megalo Horio Greece 36°27N 27°24E 205 E9
Megalonisos Greece 38°0N 24°15E 204 D6
Megalopoli Greece 37°25N 22°7E 204 D4
Meganisi Greece 38°38N 20°46E 207 B2
Megara Greece 37°58N 23°22E 204 D5
Megasini India 21°38N 86°21E 243 J12
Megdovas = Tavropos ➜
Greece 39°10N 21°45E 204 B3
Megève France 45°51N 6°37E 175 C10
Meghalaya □ India 25°50N 91°0E 241 C3
Meghezez Ethiopia 9°18N 39°26E 257 F4
Meghna ➜ Bangla. 22°50N 90°50E 241 D3
Megion Russia 61°3N 76°6E 214 C8
Mégiscane, L. Canada 48°35N 75°55W 298 C4
Megiste Greece 36°8N 29°35E 205 E11
Megisti Greece 36°8N 29°34E 205 E11
Megra Russia 60°11N 37°14E 188 B9
Meguro Japan 35°37N 139°42E 140 B3
Meguro ➜ Japan 35°37N 139°45E 140 B3
Mehadia Romania 44°56N 22°23E 182 F7
Mehaïguene, O. ➜
Algeria 32°15N 2°59E 261 B5
Meharry, Mt. Australia 22°59S 118°35E 278 D2
Mehedeby Sweden 60°27N 17°25E 162 D11
Mehedinți □ Romania 44°40N 22°45E 182 F7
Meheisa Sudan 19°38N 32°57E 256 D3
Mehekar India 20°9N 76°34E 244 D3
Méhétia French Polynesia 17°52S 148°3W 289 f
Mehlville U.S.A. 38°31N 90°19W 308 F8
Mehndawal India 26°58N 83°5E 243 F10
Mehpalpur India 28°32N 77°7E 120 B1
Mehr Jān Iran 33°50N 55°6E 247 C7
Mehrābād Iran 36°53N 47°55E 213 D12
Mehrābād ✕ (THR) Iran 35°41N 51°18E 141 A1
Mehrābān Iran 38°4N 47°7E 213 C12
Mehram Nagar India 28°34N 77°8E 120 B1
Mehrān Iran 33°7N 46°10E 213 F12
Mehrān ➜ Iran 26°45N 55°26E 247 E7
Mehrgarh Pakistan 29°30N 67°30E 242 E2
Mehrīz Iran 31°35N 54°28E 247 D7
Mehrow Germany 52°34N 13°37E 115 A4
Mehun-sur-Yèvre France 47°10N 2°13E 173 E9
Mei Jiang ➜ China 24°25N 116°35E 229 E11
Mei Lanfang, Pantheon of
Beijing, China 114 a2
Mei Xian China 34°18N 107°55E 226 G4
Meia Ponte ➜ Brazil 18°32S 49°36W 333 E2
Meicheng China 29°29N 119°16E 229 C12
Meichengzhen China 28°9N 111°40E 229 C8
Meichuan China 30°8N 115°31E 229 B10
Meidling Austria 48°10N 16°20E 142 A2
Meidougou Cameroon 6°25N 14°13E 264 A2
Méier Brazil 22°52S 43°15W 135 B1
Meiganga Cameroon 6°30N 14°25E 264 A2
Meighen I. Canada 80°0N 99°30W 295 B12
Meigs U.S.A. 31°4N 84°6W 316 D5
Meigu China 28°16N 103°20E 228 C4
Meihekou China 42°32N 125°40E 224 A2
Meiji Shrine Tokyo, Japan 140 b1
Meiktila Burma 20°53N 95°54E 241 E5
Meinerzhagen Germany 51°6N 7°38E 178 D3
Meiningen Germany 50°34N 10°25E 178 E6
Meinung Taiwan 22°54N 120°32E 225 D2
Meio ➜ Brazil 13°36S 44°7W 333 D3
Meira, Serra de Spain 43°15N 7°15W 194 B3
Meiringen Switz. 46°43N 8°12E 179 J4
Meise Belgium 50°56N 4°20E 116 A1
Meishan Sichuan, China 30°3N 103°23E 228 B4
Meishan Taiwan 23°35N 120°33E 225 C2
Meissen Germany 51°9N 13°29E 178 D9
Meissner Germany 51°13N 9°51E 178 D5
Meissner-Kaufunger Wald ⌂
Germany 51°16N 9°45E 178 D5
Meitan China 27°45N 107°29E 228 D6
Meizhou China 24°16N 116°6E 229 E11
Meja India 25°9N 82°7E 243 G10
Mejillones Chile 23°10S 70°30W 334 A1
Mejiro Japan 35°43N 139°43E 140 A3
Mékambo Gabon 1°2N 13°50E 264 B2
Mekdela Ethiopia 11°24N 39°10E 257 E4
Mekele Ethiopia 13°33N 39°30E 257 E4
Mekerghene, Sebkra
Algeria 26°21N 1°30E 261 C5
Mékhé Senegal 15°7N 16°38W 262 B1
Mekhomiya = Razlog
Bulgaria 41°53N 23°28E 202 E7
Mekhtar Pakistan 30°30N 69°15E 240 C3
Meknès Morocco 33°57N 5°33W 260 B3
Meknès □ Morocco 33°3N 5°35W 260 B3
Meko Nigeria 7°27N 2°52E 263 D5
Mekong ➜ Asia 9°30N 106°15E 237 H6
Mekongga Indonesia 3°39S 121°15E 231 E6
Mekoryuk U.S.A. 60°23N 166°11W 303 F6
Mekrou ➜ Benin 12°25N 2°50E 263 C5
Mekvari = Kür ➜
Azerbaijan 39°29N 49°15E 213 C13
Mel Italy 46°4N 12°5E 199 B9
Melagiri Hills India 12°20N 77°30E 245 H3
Melah, Oued el ➜ Algeria 32°20N 2°28E 261 B5
Melaka Malaysia 2°15N 102°15E 237 L4
Melaka □ Malaysia 2°15N 102°15E 234 B2
Melalap Malaysia 5°10N 116°5E 235 A5
Melambes Greece 35°8N 24°40E 207 E5
Melanesia Pac. Oc. 4°0S 155°0E 277 A10
Melanesian Basin Pac. Oc. 0°5N 160°35E 288 G8
Melapalaiyam India 8°39N 77°44E 245 K3
Melawi ➜ Indonesia 0°5N 111°29E 235 B4
Melaya Indonesia 8°17S 114°30E 231 J17
Melbourne Vic.,
Australia 37°48S 144°58E 128 A1
Melbourne Fla., U.S.A. 28°5N 80°37W 317 G9
Melbourne Iowa, U.S.A. 41°57N 93°6W 310 C3
Melbourne ✕ (MEL)
Australia 37°40S 144°50E 128 A1
Melcher-Dallas U.S.A. 41°14N 93°15W 310 C3
Melchor Múzquiz
Mexico 27°53N 101°31W 318 B4
Melchor Ocampo
Mexico 24°51N 101°39W 318 C4
Meldal Norway 63°3N 9°44E 164 A6
Méldola Italy 44°7N 12°5E 199 D9
Meldorf Germany 54°5N 9°5E 178 A5
Mélé C.A.R. 9°46N 21°33E 264 A4
Mele B. Vanuatu 17°44S 168°14E 287 G6
Meleden Somali Rep. 10°25N 49°51E 267 B6
Melegnano Italy 45°21N 9°19E 198 C6
Meleizem Mauritania 22°19N 11°24W 260 D2
Melekeok Palau 7°27N 134°38E 288 c
Melekess = Dimitrovgrad
Russia 54°14N 49°39E 190 C9
Melenci Serbia 45°32N 20°20E 182 E5
Melenki Russia 55°20N 41°37E 190 C5
Meleuz Russia 52°58N 55°55E 216 B5
Mélèzes ➜ Canada 57°40N 69°29W 298 A5
Melfi Chad 11°0N 17°59E 259 F3
Melfi Italy 41°0N 15°39E 201 B8
Melfort Sask., Canada 52°50N 104°37W 297 C8
Melfort Zimbabwe 18°0S 31°25E 269 F3
Melgaço Portugal 42°7N 8°15W 194 C2
Melgar de Fernamental
Spain 42°27N 4°17W 194 C6
Melgraseyri Iceland 66°1N 22°27W 155 A4
Melhus Norway 63°17N 10°18E 164 A7
Melide Spain 42°55N 8°1W 194 C2
Meligales Greece 37°15N 21°59E 204 D3
Melilla N. Afr. 35°21N 2°57W 261 A4
Melilli Italy 37°11N 15°7E 201 E8
Melipilla Chile 33°42S 71°15W 334 C1
Melissa Canada 45°24N 79°14W 312 A5
Melissa, Akra Greece 35°6N 24°33E 207 D6
Melissa Oros Greece 37°32N 26°4E 205 D8
Melissani Cave Greece 38°15N 20°38E 207 C2
Melita Canada 49°15N 101°0W 297 D8
Mélito di Porto Salvo
Italy 37°55N 15°47E 201 E8
Melitopol Ukraine 46°50N 35°22E 189 J8
Melk Austria 48°13N 15°20E 180 C8
Melkki Finland 60°8N 24°53E 121 C2
Mellan Fryken Sweden 59°45N 13°10E 162 E7
Mellansel Sweden 63°26N 18°19E 160 E18
Mellbystrand Sweden 56°30N 12°56E 163 H6
Melle Deux-Sèvres, France 46°14N 0°10W 174 B3
Melle Niedersachsen,
Germany 52°12N 8°20E 178 C4
Mellègue, O. ➜ Tunisia 36°36N 9°14E 258 A1
Mellen U.S.A. 46°20N 90°40W 308 B8
Mellerud Sweden 58°41N 12°28E 163 F6
Mellette U.S.A. 45°9N 98°30W 308 C4
Mellid = Melide Spain 42°55N 8°1W 194 C2
Mellieħa Malta 35°57N 14°22E 206 F1
Mellieħa Bay Malta 35°59N 14°22E 206 F1
Mellit Sudan 14°7N 25°34E 257 E2
Mellizo Sur, Cerro Chile 48°33S 73°10W 336 C2
Mellrichstadt Germany 50°25N 10°17E 178 E6
Mellunkylä Finland 60°14N 25°5E 121 B3
Mellunmäki Finland 60°14N 25°6E 121 B3
Melnik Bulgaria 41°30N 23°25E 202 E7
Mělník Czech Rep. 50°22N 14°23E 180 A7
Melnytsya Podilska
Ukraine 48°37N 26°10E 183 B11
Melo Uruguay 32°20S 54°10W 335 C5
Melolo Indonesia 9°53S 120°40E 231 F6
Melouprey Cambodia 13°48N 105°16E 236 F5
Melrhir, Chott Algeria 34°13N 6°30E 261 B6
Melrose N.S.W.,
Australia 32°42S 146°57E 283 B7
Melrose Borders, U.K. 55°36N 2°43W 167 F6
Melrose Mass., U.S.A. 42°27N 71°2W 116 A2
Melrose Minn., U.S.A. 45°40N 94°49W 308 C6
Melrose N. Mex.,
U.S.A. 34°26N 103°38W 305 J12
Melrose N.Y., U.S.A. 40°49N 73°55W 132 B2
Melrose Park U.S.A. 41°53N 87°50W 119 B1
Melsbroek Belgium 50°55N 4°29E 116 A2
Melsisi Vanuatu 15°46S 168°10E 287 E6
Melstone U.S.A. 46°36N 107°52W 304 C10
Melsungen Germany 51°7N 9°32E 178 D5
Melton Australia 37°41S 144°35E 282 D6
Melton Mowbray U.K. 52°47N 0°54W 168 E7
Melun France 48°32N 2°39E 173 D9
Melur India 10°2N 78°23E 245 J4
Melut Sudan 10°30N 32°13E 257 E3
Melville Sask., Canada 50°55N 102°50W 297 C8
Melville Gauteng, S. Africa 26°11S 28°1E 123 B2
Melville, C. Queens.,
Australia 14°11S 144°30E 280 A3
Melville, C. Phil. 7°49N 117°0E 233 H1
Melville, L. Canada 53°30N 60°0W 299 B8
Melville B. N. Terr.,
Australia 12°0S 136°45E 280 A2
Melville B. Greenland 75°30N 63°0W 154 B4
Melville I. N. Terr.,
Australia 11°30S 131°0E 278 B5
Melville I. Canada 75°30N 112°0W 295 B9
Melville Pen. Canada 68°0N 84°0W 295 D15
Melvin, Lough Ireland 54°26N 8°10W 166 B3
Mélykút Hungary 46°11N 19°25E 182 D4
Memaliaj Albania 40°25N 19°56E 202 F3
Memba Mozam. 14°11S 40°30E 269 E5
Memboro Indonesia 9°30S 119°30E 278 A2
Membrilla Spain 38°59N 3°21W 195 G7
Memel = Klaipėda
Lithuania 55°43N 21°10E 184 C8
Memel S. Africa 27°38S 29°36E 271 C4
Memmingen Germany 47°58N 10°10E 179 H6
Mempawah Indonesia 0°30N 109°5E 235 B3
Memphis Egypt 29°52N 31°12E 256 J7
Memphis Mich., U.S.A. 42°54N 82°46W 312 D2
Memphis Mo., U.S.A. 40°28N 92°10W 310 D4
Memphis Tenn., U.S.A. 35°8N 90°2W 315 D9
Memphis Tex., U.S.A. 34°44N 100°33W 314 D4
Memphrémagog, L.
N. Amer. 45°8N 72°17W 313 B12
Mena Ukraine 51°31N 32°13E 189 G7
Mena Ark., U.S.A. 34°35N 94°15W 314 D7
Mena ➜ Ethiopia 5°40N 40°50E 257 F5
Menai Strait U.K. 53°11N 4°13W 168 D3
Ménaka Mali 15°59N 2°18E 263 B5
Menam = Chao Phraya ➜
Thailand 13°40N 100°31E 236 F3
Menarandra ➜ Madag. 25°17S 44°30E 272 D1
Menard U.S.A. 30°55N 99°47W 314 F5
Menard Fracture Zone
Pac. Oc. 43°0S 97°0W 289 M18
Menate Indonesia 0°12S 113°3E 235 C4
Menawashei Sudan 12°41N 24°59E 257 E1
Mendaña Fracture Zone
Pac. Oc. 16°0S 91°0W 289 J18
Mendawai ➜ Indonesia 3°30S 113°0E 235 C4
Mende France 44°31N 3°30E 174 D7
Mendebo Mts. Ethiopia 7°0N 39°22E 257 F4
Mendeleyev Ridge Arctic 80°0N 178°0W 150 B17
Menden Germany 51°26N 7°47E 178 D3
Mendenhall, C. U.S.A. 59°45N 166°10W 303 G6
Menderes Turkey 38°14N 27°8E 205 C9
Mendhar India 33°35N 74°10E 243 C6
Mendi Ethiopia 9°47N 35°4E 257 F4
Mendi Papua N. G. 6°11S 143°39E 286 D2
Mendip Hills U.K. 51°17N 2°40W 169 F5
Mendocino U.S.A. 39°19N 123°48W 304 G2
Mendocino, C. U.S.A. 40°26N 124°25W 304 F1
Mendocino Fracture Zone
Pac. Oc. 40°0N 142°0W 289 D13
Mendol Indonesia 0°36N 103°13E 234 B2
Mendon U.S.A. 42°0N 85°27W 311 B11
Mendooran Australia 31°50S 149°6E 283 A8
Mendota Calif., U.S.A. 36°45N 120°23W 306 J6
Mendota Ill., U.S.A. 41°33N 89°7W 310 C7
Mendoyo Indonesia 8°23S 114°42E 231 J17
Mendoza Argentina 32°50S 68°52W 334 C2
Mendoza □ Argentina 33°0S 69°0W 334 C2
Mene Grande Venezuela 9°49N 70°56W 328 B3
Menemen Turkey 38°34N 27°3E 205 C9
Menen Belgium 50°47N 3°7E 170 D3
Menéndez, L. Argentina 42°40S 71°51W 336 B2
Menfi Italy 37°36N 12°58E 200 E5
Mengdingjie China 23°31N 98°58E 228 F2
Mengeš Slovenia 46°10N 14°35E 199 B11
Menggala Indonesia 4°30S 105°15E 234 C3
Menghai China 21°49N 100°55E 228 G3
Mengibar Spain 37°58N 3°48W 195 H7
Mengjin China 34°55N 112°45E 226 G7
Mengla China 21°20N 101°25E 228 G3
Menglian China 22°21N 99°27E 228 F2
Mengong Cameroon 2°56N 11°25E 264 B2
Mengshan China 24°14N 110°55E 229 E8
Mengyin China 35°40N 117°58E 227 G9
Mengzhe China 22°2N 100°15E 228 F3
Mengzi China 23°20N 103°22E 228 F4
Menihek Canada 54°28N 56°36W 299 B6
Menihek L. Canada 54°0N 67°0W 299 B6
Menin = Menen Belgium 50°47N 3°7E 170 D3
Menindee Australia 32°20S 142°25E 282 B5
Menindee L. Australia 32°20S 142°25E 282 B5
Meningie Australia 35°50S 139°18E 282 C3
Menjangan, Pulau
Indonesia 8°7S 114°31E 231 J17
Menkrour Algeria 26°27N 8°9E 261 C6
Menlo Park U.S.A. 37°27N 122°12W 306 H4
Menngen ⊘ Australia 15°21S 131°16E 278 C5
Menominee U.S.A. 45°6N 87°37W 308 C10
Menominee ➜ U.S.A. 45°6N 87°35W 308 C10
Menomonee Falls U.S.A. 43°10N 88°7W 311 A8
Menomonie U.S.A. 44°53N 91°55W 308 C8
Menongue Angola 14°48S 17°52E 265 E3
Menorca Spain 40°0N 4°0E 206 B5
Menorca ✕ (MAH) Spain 39°50N 4°16E 196 F9
Mentakab Malaysia 3°29N 102°21E 237 L4
Mentasta Lake U.S.A. 62°55N 143°45W 303 E12
Mentawai, Kepulauan
Indonesia 2°0S 99°0E 234 C1
Menteng Indonesia 6°11S 106°49E 122 B1
Menton France 43°50N 7°29E 175 E11
Mentone U.S.A. 41°10N 86°2W 311 C10
Mentor U.S.A. 41°40N 81°21W 312 E3
Menyamya Papua N. G. 7°10S 145°59E 286 D3
Menzel-Bourguiba Tunisia 37°9N 9°49E 258 A1
Menzel-Chaker Tunisia 35°0N 10°26E 258 B2
Menzel-Temime Tunisia 36°46N 11°0E 258 A2
Menzelinsk Russia 55°47N 53°11E 186 C9
Menzies Australia 29°40S 121°2E 279 E3
Meob B. Namibia 24°25S 14°34E 270 B1
Me'ona Israel 33°1N 35°15E 250 E6
Meoqui Mexico 28°17N 105°29W 318 B3
Mepaco Mozam. 15°57S 30°48E 269 F3
Meppel Neths. 52°42N 6°12E 170 B6
Meppen Germany 52°42N 7°17E 178 C3
Mequinenza Spain 41°22N 0°17E 196 D5
Mequinenza, Embalse de
Spain 41°25N 0°15E 196 D5
Mequon U.S.A. 43°14N 87°59W 311 A9
Mer France 47°42N 1°30E 172 E8
Merai Papua N. G. 4°52S 152°19E 286 C7
Merak Indonesia 6°10N 106°26E 231 F12
Meråker Norway 63°25N 11°46E 164 A8
Meramangye, L.
Australia 28°25S 132°13E 279 E5
Meramec ➜ U.S.A. 38°24N 90°21W 310 F6
Meran = Merano Italy 46°40N 11°9E 199 B8
Merano Italy 46°40N 11°9E 199 B8
Mérantaise ➜ France 48°42N 2°8E 134 B1
Merapi Indonesia 7°32S 110°26E 235 D4
Merate Italy 45°42N 9°25E 198 C6
Merauke Indonesia 8°29S 140°24E 231 F10
Merbabu Indonesia 7°30S 110°40E 235 D4
Merbein Australia 34°10S 142°2E 282 C5
Merbuk, Gunung
Indonesia 8°13S 114°39E 231 J17
Merca = Marka
Somali Rep. 1°48N 44°50E 267 D5
Mercamadrid Spain 40°21N 3°39W 127 B2
Mercantour △ France 44°16N 6°43E 175 D10
Mercato Saraceno Italy 43°57N 12°12E 199 E9
Merced U.S.A. 37°18N 120°29W 306 H6
Merced ➜ U.S.A. 37°21N 120°59W 306 H6
Merced, L. U.S.A. 37°43N 122°29W 136 B2
Merced Pk. U.S.A. 37°36N 119°24W 306 H7
Mercedes B. Aires,
Argentina 34°40S 59°30W 334 C4
Mercedes Corrientes,
Argentina 29°10S 58°5W 334 B4
Mercedes San Luis,
Argentina 33°40S 65°21W 334 C2
Mercedes Camarines N.,
Phil. 14°7N 123°1E 232 D4
Mercedes Uruguay 33°12S 58°0W 334 C4
Merceditas Chile 28°20S 70°35W 334 B1
Mercer N.Z. 37°16S 175°5E 284 D4
Mercer Mo., U.S.A. 40°31N 93°32W 310 D3
Mercer Pa., U.S.A. 41°14N 80°15W 312 E4
Mercer Island U.S.A. 47°34N 122°13W 306 C4
Merchandise Mart Chicago, U.S.A. 119 b1
Mercier Bolivia 10°42S 68°5W 330 C4
Mercury U.S.A. 36°40N 115°59W 307 J11
Mercury B. N.Z. 36°48S 175°45E 284 C4
Mercury Is. N.Z. 36°37S 175°52E 284 C4
Mercy, C. Canada 65°0N 63°30W 295 E19
Merdrignac France 48°11N 2°27W 172 D4
Mere U.K. 51°6N 2°16W 169 F5
Mere Lava Vanuatu 14°25S 168°3E 287 D6
Meredale S. Africa 26°16S 27°58E 123 B1
Meredith Australia 37°49S 144°5E 282 D6
Meredith, C. Falk. Is. 52°15S 60°40W 153 f
Meredith, L. U.S.A. 35°43N 101°33W 314 D4
Meredosia U.S.A. 39°50N 90°34W 310 E6
Merefa Ukraine 49°48N 36°3E 189 H9
Merei Romania 45°7N 26°43E 183 E11
Merga = Nukheila Sudan 19°1N 26°21E 256 D2
Mergui Burma 12°26N 98°34E 236 F2
Mergui Arch. = Myeik Kyunzu
Burma 11°30N 97°30E 237 G1
Meribah Australia 34°43S 140°51E 282 C4
Méribel-les-Allues France 45°25N 6°34E 175 C10
Meriç Turkey 41°11N 26°25E 203 E10
Meriç ➜ Turkey 40°52N 26°12E 203 F10
Mérida Yucatán, Mexico 20°58N 89°37W 319 C7
Merida Phil. 10°55N 124°32E 233 F5
Mérida Spain 38°55N 6°25W 195 G4
Mérida Venezuela 8°24N 71°8W 328 B3
Mérida □ Venezuela 8°30N 71°10W 328 B3
Mérida, Cord. de Venezuela 9°0N 71°0W 328 B3
Meriden W. Mids., U.K. 52°26N 1°38W 169 E6
Meriden Conn., U.S.A. 41°32N 72°48W 313 E12
Meridian Calif., U.S.A. 39°9N 121°55W 306 F5
Meridian Ga., U.S.A. 31°27N 81°23W 316 D8
Meridian Idaho, U.S.A. 43°37N 116°24W 304 E5
Meridian Miss., U.S.A. 32°22N 88°42W 315 E10
Mérignac France 44°51N 0°39W 174 D3
Merimbula Australia 36°53S 149°54E 283 D8
Merin Gubai Somali Rep. 1°26N 44°20E 267 D5
Merinda Australia 20°2S 148°11E 280 C4
Mering Germany 48°16N 10°59E 179 G6
Meringa Nigeria 10°44N 12°9E 263 C7
Meringur Australia 34°20S 141°19E 282 C4
Merir Pac. Oc. 4°10N 132°30E 231 D8
Merirumã Brazil 1°15N 54°50W 329 C7
Merizo Guam 13°16N 144°40E 302 d
Merkel U.S.A. 32°28N 100°1W 314 E4
Merlimau, Pulau
Singapore 1°17N 103°42E 138 B2
Mermaid Reef Australia 17°6S 119°36E 278 C2
Mero Dominica 15°25N 61°26W 323 k
Meroe India 7°33N 93°33E 245 L11
Merowe Sudan 18°29N 31°46E 256 D3
Merowe Dam Sudan 18°47N 32°3E 256 D3
Merredin Australia 31°28S 118°18E 279 F2
Merri Cr. ➜ Australia 37°47S 144°59E 128 A1
Merrick U.K. 55°8N 4°28W 167 F4
Merrickville Canada 44°55N 75°50W 313 B9
Merrill Oreg., U.S.A. 42°1N 121°36W 304 E3
Merrill Wis., U.S.A. 45°11N 89°41W 308 C9
Merrillville U.S.A. 41°29N 87°20W 311 C9
Merrimack ➜ U.S.A. 42°49N 70°49W 313 D14
Merriman U.S.A. 42°55N 101°42W 308 D3
Merrion Ireland 53°19N 6°12W 120 B2
Merrionette Park U.S.A. 41°41N 87°40W 119 C2
Merritt Canada 50°10N 120°45W 296 C4
Merritt Island U.S.A. 28°21N 80°42W 317 G9
Merriwa Australia 32°6S 150°22E 283 B9
Merriwagga Australia 33°47S 145°43E 283 B6
Merry I. Canada 55°29N 77°31W 298 A4
Merrygoen Australia 31°51S 149°12E 283 A8
Merryville U.S.A. 30°45N 93°33W 314 F8
Mersa Fatma Eritrea 14°57N 40°17E 257 E5
Mersch Lux. 49°44N 6°7E 170 E6
Merse ➜ Italy 43°5N 11°22E 199 E8
Mersea I. U.K. 51°47N 0°58E 169 F8
Merseburg Germany 51°22N 11°59E 178 D7
Mersey ➜ U.K. 53°25N 3°1W 168 D4
Merseyside □ U.K. 53°31N 3°2W 168 D4
Mersin = İçel Turkey 36°51N 34°36E 250 B5
Mersing Malaysia 2°25N 103°50E 237 L4
Merta India 26°39N 74°4E 242 F6
Merta Road India 26°43N 73°55E 242 F5
Merthyr Tydfil U.K. 51°45N 3°22W 169 F4
Merthyr Tydfil □ U.K. 51°46N 3°21W 169 F4
Merti Kenya 1°4N 38°40E 268 B4
Mértola Portugal 37°40N 7°40W 195 H3
Merton □ U.K. 51°25N 0°11W 125 B2
Mertzon U.S.A. 31°16N 100°49W 314 F4
Méru Oise, France 49°13N 2°8E 173 C9
Meru Eastern, Kenya 0°3N 37°40E 268 B4
Meru Tanzania 3°15S 36°46E 268 C4
Meru △ Kenya 0°5N 38°10E 268 B4
Meru Betiri △ Indonesia 8°27S 113°51E 235 D4
Merv = Mary
Turkmenistan 37°40N 61°50E 247 B9
Merville France 50°38N 2°38E 173 B9
Méry-sur-Seine France 48°31N 3°54E 173 D10
Merzifon Turkey 40°53N 35°32E 212 B6
Merzig Germany 49°26N 6°38E 179 F2
Merzouga, Erg Tin Algeria 24°0N 11°4E 261 D7
Mesa U.S.A. 33°25N 111°50W 305 K8
Mesa Verde △ U.S.A. 37°11N 108°29W 305 H9
Mesach Mellet Libya 24°30N 11°30E 258 D2
Mesada Israel 31°20N 35°19E 251 G6
Mesagne Italy 40°34N 17°48E 201 B10
Mesanagros Greece 36°1N 27°49E 206 E11
Mesaoría Cyprus 35°12N 33°14E 207 E9
Meschede Germany 51°20N 8°18E 178 D4
Mescit Turkey 40°21N 41°11E 213 B9
Mesemvriya = Nesebŭr
Bulgaria 42°41N 27°46E 203 D11
Mesfinto Ethiopia 13°20N 37°22E 257 E4
Mesgarābād Iran 35°27N 51°30E 141 B3
Mesgouez, L. Canada 51°20N 75°0W 298 B5
Meshcherskiy Russia 55°40N 37°23E 129 B2
Meshchovsk Russia 54°22N 35°17E 188 E8
Meshed = Mashhad Iran 36°20N 59°35E 247 B8
Meshgīn Shahr Iran 38°30N 47°45E 213 C12
Meshkede-Ser = Bābol Sar
Iran 36°45N 52°45E 247 B7
Meshoppen U.S.A. 41°36N 76°3W 313 E8
Meshra er Req Sudan 8°25N 29°18E 257 F2
Mesilinka ➜ Canada 56°6N 124°30W 296 B4
Meslay-du-Maine France 47°58N 0°33W 172 E6
Mesocco Switz. 46°23N 9°12E 179 J5
Mesologi Greece 38°21N 21°28E 204 C3
Mesongi Greece 39°29N 19°56E 207 B3
Mesopotamia = Al Jazirah
Iraq 33°30N 44°0E 213 E10
Mesopotamia U.S.A. 41°27N 80°57W 312 E4
Mesopotamo Greece 39°14N 20°32E 204 B2
Mesoraca Italy 39°5N 16°48E 201 C9
Mésou Volimais = Volimes
Greece 37°52N 20°39E 207 D2
Mesquite U.S.A. 36°48N 114°4W 305 H6
Messaad Algeria 34°8N 3°30E 261 B5
Messac France 47°49N 1°50W 172 E5
Messalo ➜ Mozam. 12°25S 39°15E 269 E4
Messaména Cameroon 3°48N 12°49E 264 B2
Messara, Kolpos Greece 35°6N 24°47E 207 E5
Messe Austria 48°13N 16°24E 142 A2
Messier, Canal Chile 48°20S 74°33W 336 C2
Messina = Musina
S. Africa 22°20S 30°5E 271 B5
Messina Italy 38°11N 15°34E 201 D8
Messina, Str. di Italy 38°15N 15°35E 201 D8
Messini Greece 37°4N 22°1E 204 D4
Messinia □ Greece 37°10N 22°0E 204 D3
Messiniakos Kolpos
Greece 36°45N 22°5E 204 E4
Messkirch Germany 47°59N 9°7E 179 H5
Messlingen Sweden 62°40N 12°50E 162 B6
Mesta = Nestos ➜
Europe 40°54N 24°49E 203 E8
Mesta, Akra Greece 38°16N 25°53E 205 C7

Mestanza *Spain* 38°35N 4°4W **195** G6
Mestersvig *Greenland* 72°10N 23°40W **154** C8
Mestre *Italy* 45°29N 12°15E **199** C9
Mestre, Espigão *Brazil* 12°30S 46°10W **333** D2
Mesudiye *Turkey* 40°28N 37°46E **242** B7
Meta □ 38°19N 92°10W **310** F4
Meta ➔ *S. Amer.* 6°12N 67°28W **328** B4
Meta □ *Colombia* 3°30N 73°0W **328** C3
Meta ➔ *S. Amer.* 6°12N 67°28W **328** B4
Meta Incognita Pen.
Canada 62°45N 68°30W **295** E18
Metabetchouan *Canada* 48°26N 71°52W **299** C5
Metairie *U.S.A.* 29°59N 90°9W **131** A2
Metaline Falls *U.S.A.* 48°52N 117°22W **304** B5
Metallifere, Colline *Italy* 43°10N 11°0E **198** E8
Metamora *U.S.A.* 40°47N 89°22W **310** D7
Metán *Argentina* 25°30S 65°0W **334** B3
Metangula *Mozam.* 12°40S 34°50E **269** E3
Metánopoli *Italy* 45°24N 9°15E **129** B2
Metauro ➔ *Italy* 43°50N 13°3E **199** E10
Metcalf *U.S.A.* 30°43N 83°59W **316** E6
Metcalfe *Canada* 45°14N 75°28W **299** C4
Metema *Ethiopia* 12°58N 36°12E **257** E4
Metengobalame *Mozam.* 14°49S 34°30E **269** E3
Methana *Greece* 37°35N 23°23E **204** D5
Methoni *Greece* 36°49N 21°42E **204** E3
Methven *N.Z.* 43°38S 171°40E **285** D6
Metil *Mozam.* 16°24S 39°0E **269** F4
Metković *Croatia* 43°6N 17°39E **199** E14
Metlakatla *U.S.A.* 55°8N 131°35W **303** J15
Metlaoui *Tunisia* 34°24N 8°24E **258** B1
Metlika *Slovenia* 45°40N 15°20E **199** C12
Metlili Chaamba *Algeria* 32°16N 3°38E **261** B5
Metro *Indonesia* 5°5S 105°20E **234** D3
Metro-Dade Cultural Centre
U.S.A. 25°46N 80°12W **128** B2
Metro Toronto Zoo
Canada 43°48N 79°10W **141** A3
Metropolis *U.S.A.* 37°9N 88°44W **308** G9
Metropolitan Museum of Art
New York, U.S.A. **132** b3
Metropolitana □ *Chile* 33°30S 70°50W **334** C1
Metsovo *Greece* 39°48N 21°12E **204** B3
Metter *U.S.A.* 32°24N 82°3W **316** C7
Mettuppalaiyam *India* 11°18N 76°59E **245** J3
Mettur *India* 11°48N 77°47E **245** J3
Metu *Ethiopia* 8°18N 35°35E **257** F4
Metz *France* 49°8N 6°10E **173** C13
Metzingen *Germany* 48°31N 9°17E **179** G5
Meudon *France* 48°48N 2°14E **134** B2
Meulaboh *Indonesia* 4°11N 96°3E **234** B1
Meung-sur-Loire *France* 47°50N 1°40E **173** E8
Meureudu *Indonesia* 5°19N 96°10E **234** A1
Meurthe ➔ *France* 48°47N 6°9E **173** D13
Meurthe-et-Moselle □
France 48°52N 6°0E **173** D13
Meuse □ *France* 49°8N 5°25E **173** C12
Meuse ➔ *Europe* 50°45N 5°41E **170** D5
Meuselwitz *Germany* 51°2N 12°17E **179** E8
Meutapok, Mt. *Malaysia* 5°40N 117°0E **235** A5
Mevaseret Tsiyon *Israel* 31°48N 35°9E **123** B1
Mevo Beitar *Israel* 31°43N 35°6E **123** B1
Mexia *U.S.A.* 31°41N 96°29W **314** F6
Mexiana, I. *Brazil* 0°0 49°30W **332** B2
Mexicali *Mexico* 32°40N 115°30W **307** N11
Mexican Plateau *Mexico* 25°0N 104°0W **292** D7
Mexican Water *U.S.A.* 36°57N 109°32W **305** H9
México *Distrito Federal.*
Mexico 19°24N 99°9W **128** B2
Mexico *Maine, U.S.A.* 44°34N 70°33W **313** B14
Mexico *Mo., U.S.A.* 39°10N 91°53W **310** E5
Mexico *N.Y., U.S.A.* 43°28N 76°14W **313** C8
México □ *Mexico* 19°20N 99°30W **319** D5
Mexico ■ *Cent. Amer.* 25°0N 105°0W **318** C4
México, Ciudad de *Cent. Amer.* 19°24N 99°9W **128** B2
Mexico, G. of *Cent. Amer.* 25°0N 90°0W **319** C7
Mexico B. *U.S.A.* 43°35N 76°20W **313** C8
Mexico Beach *U.S.A.* 29°57N 85°25W **316** F4
Mexico City Int. ✈ (MEX)
Mexico 19°25N 99°5W **128** B2
Meydân-e Naftûn *Iran* 31°56N 49°18E **247** D6
Meydani, Ra's-e *Iran* 25°24N 59°6E **247** E8
Meyenburg *Germany* 53°18N 12°14E **178** B8
Meyers Chuck *U.S.A.* 55°45N 132°15W **296** B2
Meyersdal *S. Africa* 26°17S 28°5E **123** B2
Meymac *France* 45°32N 2°10E **174** C6
Meymaneh *Afghan.* 35°53N 64°38E **240** B2
Meyo *Cameroon* 2°50N 11°1E **264** B2
Meyrueis *France* 44°12N 3°27E **174** D7
Meyssac *France* 45°3N 1°40E **174** C5
Meyzieu *France* 45°46N 4°59E **175** C8
Mezdra *Bulgaria* 43°12N 23°42E **202** C7
Mèze *France* 43°25N 3°36E **174** E7
Mezen *Russia* 65°50N 44°20E **186** A7
Mezen ➔ *Russia* 65°44N 44°22E **186** A7
Mézenc, Mt. *France* 44°54N 4°11E **175** D8
Mezeş, Munţii *Romania* 47°5N 23°5E **183** B8
Mezha ➔ *Russia* 55°44N 31°33E **188** E6
Mezhdurechensk *Russia* 53°41N 88°3E **217** B11
Mezhdurechenskiy
Russia 59°36N 65°56E **214** D7
Mezhdurechye = Shali
Russia 43°9N 45°55E **191** J7
Mézidon-Canon *France* 49°5N 0°1W **172** C6
Mézières-en-Brenne
France 46°49N 1°13E **174** B5
Mézilhac *France* 44°49N 4°21E **175** D8
Mézin *France* 44°4N 0°16E **174** D4
Mezőtiti *Turkey* 36°45N 34°29E **250** B5
Mezőberény *Hungary* 46°49N 21°3E **182** D6
Mezőfalva *Hungary* 46°55N 18°49E **182** D3
Mezőhegyes *Hungary* 46°19N 20°49E **182** D5
Mezőkövácsháza
Hungary 46°25N 20°57E **182** D5
Mezőkövesd *Hungary* 47°49N 20°35E **182** C5
Mézos *France* 44°5N 1°10W **174** D2
Mezőtúr *Hungary* 47°1N 20°41E **182** C5
Mezquital *Mexico* 23°29N 104°23W **318** C4
Mezzate *Italy* 45°26N 9°17E **129** B2
Mezzolombardo *Italy* 46°13N 11°5E **198** B8
Mfolozi ➔ *S. Africa* 28°25S 32°26E **271** C5
Mgarr *Malta* 35°55N 14°22E **206** F7
Mgarr *Gozo, Malta* 36°2N 14°18E **206** E7
Mgeta *Tanzania* 8°22S 36°56E **269** D4
Mglin *Russia* 53°2N 32°50E **188** F6
Mhamid *Morocco* 29°49N 5°43W **260** C3
Mhlaba Hills *Zimbabwe* 18°30S 30°30E **269** F3
Mhow *India* 22°33N 75°50E **242** H6
Mi-Shima *Japan* 34°46N 131°9E **222** D2
Miadong *S. Korea* 10°37N 122°14E **137** B2
Miagao *Phil.* 10°39N 122°14E **233** F4
Miahuatlán *Mexico* 16°20N 96°36W **319** D5
Miajadas *Spain* 39°9N 5°54W **195** F5
Miami *Fla., U.S.A.* 25°46N 80°11W **128** B2
Miami *Okla., U.S.A.* 36°53N 94°53W **314** C7
Miami *Tex., U.S.A.* 35°42N 100°38W **314** D4
Miami Beach *U.S.A.* 25°47N 80°7W **128** B2
Miami Canal *U.S.A.* 25°45N 80°12W **128** A2
Miami Int. ✈ (MIA)
U.S.A. 25°47N 80°11W **128** B2
Miami Shores *U.S.A.* 25°51N 80°11W **128** B2
Miami Springs *U.S.A.* 25°49N 80°17W **128** B1

Miamisburg *U.S.A.* 39°38N 84°17W **311** E12
Mian Xian *China* 33°10N 106°32E **226** H4
Mianchi *China* 34°48N 111°48E **226** G6
Miandarreh *Iran* 35°37N 53°39E **247** C7
Miandowāb *Iran* 37°0N 46°5E **213** D12
Miāneh *Iran* 37°30N 47°40E **213** D12
Mianning *China* 28°32N 102°9E **228** C4
Mianwali *Pakistan* 32°38N 71°28E **242** C4
Mianyang *China* 31°22N 104°47E **228** B5
Mianzhu *China* 31°22N 104°7E **228** B5
Miaoli □ *Taiwan* 24°37N 120°49E **225** B2
Miaoli □ *Taiwan* 24°30N 120°49E **225** B2
Miarinarivo *Antananarivo,*
Madag. 18°57S 46°55E **272** B2
Miarinarivo *Toamasina,*
Madag. 16°38S 48°15E **272** B2
Miarivaratra *Madag.* 20°13S 47°31E **272** C2
Miass *Russia* 54°59N 60°6E **186** D11
Miasteczko Krajeńskie
Poland 53°7N 17°1E **185** E4
Miastko *Poland* 54°0N 16°58E **184** E3
Miasto *Poland* 52°15N 21°0E **142** B2
Mica *S. Africa* 24°10S 30°48E **271** B5
Micanopy *U.S.A.* 29°30N 82°17W **317** F7
Micásasa *Romania* 46°7N 24°7E **183** D9
Micco *U.S.A.* 27°53N 80°30W **317** H9
Miccosukee *U.S.A.* 30°36N 84°3W **316** E5
Miccosukee, L. *U.S.A.* 30°33N 83°53W **316** E6
Michael, Mt. *Papua N. G.* 6°27S 145°22E **286** D3
Michalovce *Slovak Rep.* 48°47N 21°58E **181** C14
Michalowice *Poland* 52°10N 20°52E **142** B1
Michigan □ *U.S.A.* 44°0N 85°0W **309** C11
Michigan, L. *U.S.A.* 44°0N 87°0W **311** B9
Michigan Avenue *Chicago, U.S.A.* **141** B2
Michigan Center *U.S.A.* 42°14N 84°20W **311** B12
Michigan City *U.S.A.* 41°43N 86°54W **311** C10
Michika *Nigeria* 10°36N 13°23E **263** C7
Michipicoten I. *Canada* 47°40N 85°40W **298** C2
Michle *Czech Rep.* 50°3N 14°28E **135** B2
Michoacán □ *Mexico* 19°10N 101°50W **318** D4
Michurin *Bulgaria* 42°9N 27°51E **203** D11
Michurinsk *Russia* 52°58N 40°27E **190** D5
Miconje *Angola* 4°26S 12°48E **265** C2
Micoud *St. Lucia* 13°49N 60°54W **323** a
Micronesia *Pac. Oc.* 11°0N 160°0E **288** G7
Micronesia, Federated States of ■
Pac. Oc. 9°0N 150°0E **288** G7
Mid-Atlantic Ridge *Atl. Oc.* 0°0 20°0W **152** J11
Mid-City *Calif., U.S.A.* 34°4N 118°20W **126** B2
Mid-City *La., U.S.A.* 29°58N 90°6W **131** B2
Mid-Indian Ocean Basin
Ind. Oc. 10°0S 80°0E **273** F7
Mid-Indian Ridge *Ind. Oc.* 30°0S 75°0E **273** H6
Mid-Pacific Seamounts
Pac. Oc. 18°0N 177°0W **288** F10
Midai *Indonesia* 3°0N 107°47E **235** B3
Midale *Canada* 49°25N 103°20W **297** D8
Middelburg *Neths.* 51°30N 3°36E **170** C3
Middelburg *Eastern Cape,*
S. Africa 31°30S 25°0E **270** E4
Middelburg *Mpumalanga,*
S. Africa 25°49S 29°28E **271** C4
Middelfart *Denmark* 55°30N 9°43E **163** J3
Middelpos *S. Africa* 31°55S 20°17E **270** E3
Middelwit *S. Africa* 24°51S 27°3E **270** B4
Middle ➔ *U.S.A.* 41°26N 93°30W **310** C3
Middle Alkali L. *U.S.A.* 41°27N 120°5W **304** F3
Middle America Trench =
Guatemala Trench
Pac. Oc. 14°0N 95°0W **292** H10
Middle Andaman I.
India 12°30N 92°50E **245** H11
Middle Bass I. *U.S.A.* 41°41N 82°48W **312** E2
Middle East *Asia* 35°0N 40°0E **210** E5
Middle Fork Feather ➔
U.S.A. 38°33N 121°30W **306** F5
Middle Ground
Midway Is. 28°14N 177°24W **302** c
Middle Harbour
Australia 33°47S 151°14E **139** A2
Middle Hd. *Australia* 33°49S 151°16E **139** A2
Middle I. *Australia* 34°6S 123°11E **279** F3
Middle Island
St. Kitts & Nevis 17°20N 62°48W **322** d
Middle Loup ➔ *U.S.A.* 41°17N 98°24W **308** E5
Middle Park *Australia* 37°50S 144°57E **128** B1
Middle Raccoon ➔
U.S.A. 41°35N 93°30W **310** C3
Middle Village *U.S.A.* 40°43N 73°52W **132** B2
Middleboro *U.S.A.* 41°54N 70°55W **313** E14
Middleburg *Fla., U.S.A.* 30°4N 81°52W **316** E8
Middleburg *Pa., U.S.A.* 40°47N 77°3W **312** F7
Middleburgh *U.S.A.* 42°36N 74°20W **313** D10
Middlebury *Ind., U.S.A.* 41°41N 85°42W **311** C11
Middlebury *Vt., U.S.A.* 44°1N 73°10W **313** B11
Middlefield *U.S.A.* 41°27N 81°4W **312** E3
Middlemarch *N.Z.* 45°30S 170°9E **285** F5
Middlemount *Australia* 22°50S 148°40E **280** C4
Middleport *N.Y., U.S.A.* 43°13N 78°29W **312** C6
Middleport *Ohio, U.S.A.* 39°0N 82°3W **309** F12
Middlesboro *U.S.A.* 36°36N 83°43W **309** G12
Middlesbrough *U.K.* 54°35N 1°13W **168** C6
Middlesbrough □ *U.K.* 54°28N 1°13W **168** C6
Middlesex *Belize* 17°2N 88°31W **320** C2
Middlesex *N.J., U.S.A.* 40°36N 74°30W **313** F10
Middlesex *N.Y., U.S.A.* 42°42N 77°16W **312** D7
Middlesex □ *Jamaica* 18°10N 77°5W **320** a
Middlesex Fells Reservation
U.S.A. 42°27N 71°6W **116** A2
Middleton *Queens.,*
Australia 22°22S 141°32E **280** C3
Middleton *N.S., Canada* 44°57N 65°4W **299** D6
Middleton *Wis., U.S.A.* 43°6N 89°30W **310** A7
Middleton *Calif.,*
U.S.A. 38°45N 122°37W **306** G4
Middleton I. *U.S.A.* 59°26N 146°20W **303** G11
Middletown *Armagh, U.K.* 54°17N 6°51W **166** B8
Middletown *Calif.,*
U.S.A. 38°45N 122°37W **306** G4
Middletown *Conn.,*
U.S.A. 41°34N 72°39W **313** E12
Middletown *Ky., U.S.A.* 38°14N 85°32W **311** F11
Middletown *N.Y.,*
U.S.A. 41°27N 74°25W **313** E10
Middletown *Ohio,*
U.S.A. 39°31N 84°24W **311** E12
Middleville *U.S.A.* 42°43N 85°28W **311** B11
Midelt *Morocco* 32°46N 4°44W **260** B4
Midge Point *Australia* 20°39S 148°43E **280** b
Midhirst *N.Z.* 39°17S 174°18E **284** F3
Midian = Madyan *Si. Arabia* 28°0N 35°0E **246** E3
Midhurst *Ont., Canada* 44°26N 79°43W **312** B5
Midhurst *W. Susx., U.K.* 50°59N 0°44W **169** G7
Midi, Canal du ➔ *France* 43°45N 1°21E **174** E5
Midi, Gare du *Brussels, Belgium* **116** c1
Midi d'Ossau, Pic du
France 42°50N 0°26W **174** F3
Midi-Pyrénées □ *France* 43°55N 1°45E **174** E5
Midland *W. Austral.,*
Australia 31°54S 116°1E **279** F2
Midland *Ont., Canada* 44°45N 79°50W **312** B5
Midland *Calif., U.S.A.* 33°52N 114°48W **307** M12
Midland *Mich., U.S.A.* 43°37N 84°14W **309** D11
Midland *Pa., U.S.A.* 40°39N 80°27W **312** F4

Midland *Tex., U.S.A.* 32°0N 102°3W **314** F3
Midland Beach *U.S.A.* 40°34N 74°6W **132** C1
Midlands □ *Zimbabwe* 19°40S 29°0E **269** F2
Midleton *Ireland* 51°55N 8°10W **166** E3
Midlothian *U.S.A.* 32°30N 97°0W **314** F5
Midlothian □ *U.K.* 55°51N 3°5W **167** F5
Midnapore = Medinipur
India 22°25N 87°21E **243** H12
Midongy, Tangorombohitr' i
Madag. 23°35S 47°0E **272** C2
Midongy Atsimo *Madag.* 23°35S 47°1E **272** C2
Midou ➔ *France* 43°54N 0°30W **174** E3
Midouze ➔ *France* 43°48N 0°51W **174** E3
Midsayap *Phil.* 7°12N 124°32E **233** H5
Midsund *Norway* 62°41N 6°40E **164** B3
Midtgulen *Norway* 61°44N 5°11E **164** C2
Midtjylland □ *Denmark* 56°30N 9°0E **163** H2
Midu *China* 25°18N 100°30E **228** E3
Midville *U.S.A.* 32°49N 82°14W **316** C7
Midway *Ala., U.S.A.* 32°5N 85°31W **316** C4
Midway *Fla., U.S.A.* 30°30N 84°27W **316** E5
Midway Is. *Pac. Oc.* 28°13N 177°22W **302** c
Midway Wells *U.S.A.* 32°41N 115°7W **307** N11
Midwest *U.S.A.* 42°0N 90°0W **301** G22
Midwest *Wyo., U.S.A.* 43°25N 106°16W **304** G10
Midwest City *U.S.A.* 35°27N 97°24W **314** D6
Midwood *U.S.A.* 40°37N 73°57W **132** C2
Midyat *Turkey* 37°25N 41°23E **213** D9
Midzŏr *Bulgaria* 43°24N 22°40E **202** C6
Mie □ *Japan* 32°58N 131°35E **222** E3
Mie □ *Japan* 34°30N 136°10E **223** C8
Miechów *Poland* 50°21N 20°5E **185** H7
Miedwie, Jezioro *Poland* 53°17N 14°54E **185** E1
Międzyzecz *Poland* 52°10N 21°11E **142** B2
Międzybórz *Poland* 51°25N 17°36E **185** G4
Międzychód *Poland* 52°35N 15°53E **184** F2
Międzylesie *Dolnośląskie,*
Poland 50°8N 16°40E **185** H3
Międzylesie *Warszawa,*
Poland 52°12N 21°10E **142** B3
Międzyrzec Podlaski
Poland 51°58N 22°45E **185** G9
Międzyrzecz *Poland* 52°26N 15°35E **185** F2
Międzyzdroje *Poland* 53°56N 14°26E **184** E1
Miejska Górka *Poland* 51°39N 16°58E **185** G3
Miélan *France* 43°27N 0°19E **174** E4
Mielau = Mława *Poland* 53°9N 20°25E **185** E7
Mielec *Poland* 50°15N 21°25E **185** H8
Mienga *Angola* 17°12S 19°48E **265** F3
Miercurea-Ciuc
Romania 46°21N 25°48E **183** D10
Miercurea Sibiului
Romania 45°53N 23°48E **183** E8
Mieres *Spain* 43°18N 5°48W **194** B3
Mieresz *Stříbro *Czech Rep.* 50°40N 16°11E **185** H3
Mieso *Ethiopia* 9°15N 40°43E **257** F5
Miesjaunt *Finland* 60°8N 24°47E **121** C1
Mieszkowice *Poland* 52°47N 14°30E **185** F1
Mifflintown *U.S.A.* 40°34N 77°24W **312** F7
Migennes *France* 47°58N 3°31E **173** E10
Migliarino *Italy* 44°46N 11°56E **199** D8
Migliarino-San Rossore-
Massaciuccoli ○ *Italy* 43°44N 10°20E **198** E7
Migori *Kenya* 1°4S 34°28E **268** C3
Miguel Alemán, Presa
Mexico 18°15N 96°32W **319** D5
Miguel Alves *Brazil* 4°11S 42°55W **332** B3
Miguel Calmon *Brazil* 11°26S 40°36W **332** D3
Miguel Hidalgo *Mexico* 19°25N 99°12W **128** B1
Miguelturra *Spain* 38°58N 3°53W **195** F4
Mihăileni *Romania* 47°58N 26°9E **183** C11
Mihăilești *Romania* 44°20N 25°54E **183** F10
Mihailovca *Moldova* 46°33N 28°56E **183** D13
Mihalgazi *Turkey* 40°2N 30°34E **205** A12
Mihaliçcik *Turkey* 39°53N 31°30E **212** C4
Mihara *Japan* 34°24N 133°5E **222** C5
Mihara-Yama *Japan* 34°43N 139°23E **223** C11
Mihăeşu de Cîmpie
Romania 46°41N 24°9E **183** D9
Mijas *Spain* 36°36N 4°40W **195** J6
Mikese *Tanzania* 6°48S 37°55E **268** D4
Mikha-Tskhakaya = Senaki
Georgia 42°15N 42°7E **191** J6
Mikhailovka = Mykhaylivka
Ukraine 47°12N 35°15E **189** J8
Mikhaylov *Russia* 54°14N 39°0E **188** E10
Mikhaylovgrad = Montana
Bulgaria 43°27N 23°16E **202** C7
Mikhaylovka = Kimovsk
Russia 54°0N 38°29E **188** E10
Mikhaylovka *Russia* 50°3N 43°5E **190** E6
Mikhelysona *Russia* 55°42N 37°52E **129** B5
Mikhnevo *Russia* 55°4N 37°59E **188** E9
Miki *Hyōgo, Japan* 34°48N 134°59E **222** C6
Miki *Kagawa, Japan* 34°21N 134°7E **222** C6
Mikines *Greece* 37°43N 22°46E **204** D4
Mikir Hills *India* 26°10N 93°30E **241** B4
Mikkeli *Finland* 61°43N 27°15E **165** E9
Mikkwa ➔ *Canada* 58°25N 114°46W **296** B6
Mikniya *Sudan* 17°0N 33°45E **257** D3
Mikolajki *Poland* 53°49N 21°37E **184** E8
Mikonos = Mykonos
Greece 37°30N 25°25E **205** D7
Mikopke
Dem. Rep. of the Congo 4°58S 20°43E **265** C4
Mikoyan-Shakhar =
Karachayevsk *Russia* 43°50N 41°55E **191** J5
Mikri Prespa, L. *Greece* 40°47N 21°3E **204** C3
Mikri Derio *Greece* 41°19N 26°6E **203** E10
Mikstat *Poland* 51°32N 17°59E **185** G4
Mikulov *Czech Rep.* 48°48N 16°39E **181** D9
Mikumi *Tanzania* 7°26S 37°0E **268** D4
Mikumi △ *Tanzania* 7°35S 37°15E **268** D4
Mikun *Russia* 62°20N 50°0E **186** B9
Mikuni-Tōge *Japan* 36°50N 138°50E **223** A10
Mikura-Jima *Japan* 33°52N 139°36E **223** D11
Mila *Algeria* 36°27N 6°16E **261** A6
Mila □ *Algeria* 36°20N 6°16E **261** A6
Milaca *U.S.A.* 45°45N 93°39W **308** C7
Miladummadulu Atoll
Maldives 5°50N 73°30E **272** d
Milagro *Ecuador* 2°11S 79°36W **328** D2
Milagros *U.S.A.* 12°13N 123°30E **232** E4
Milan = Milano *Italy* 45°28N 9°10E **198** C6
Milan *Ga., U.S.A.* 32°1N 83°4W **316** D6
Milan *Mich., U.S.A.* 42°5N 83°41W **311** B13
Milan *Mo., U.S.A.* 40°12N 93°7W **310** D3
Milan *Tenn., U.S.A.* 35°55N 88°46W **315** D10
Milange *Mozam.* 16°3S 35°45E **269** F4
Milano *Italy* 45°28N 9°10E **198** C6
Milano Due *Italy* 45°29N 9°16E **129** B2
Milano Linate ✈ (LIN)
Italy 45°27N 9°16E **129** B2
Milano San Felice *Italy* 45°28N 9°22E **129** B2
Milâs *Turkey* 37°20N 27°50E **205** D9
Milatos *Greece* 35°18N 25°34E **207** D6

Milazzo *Italy* 38°13N 15°15E **201** D8
Milbank *U.S.A.* 45°13N 96°38W **308** C5
Milbanke Sd. *Canada* 52°19N 128°33W **296** C3
Milbertshofen *Germany* 48°10N 11°34E **131** A2
Mildenhall *U.S.A.* 52°21N 0°32E **169** E8
Mildmay *Canada* 44°3N 81°7W **312** B3
Mildura *Australia* 34°13S 142°9E **282** C5
Mile *China* 24°28N 103°20E **228** E4
Mile and a Quarter
Barbados 13°16N 59°37W **323** r
Miles *Australia* 26°40S 150°9E **281** D5
Miles City *U.S.A.* 46°25N 105°51W **304** C11
Milești *Moldova* 47°13N 28°3E **183** C13
Mina Pirquitas *Argentina* 22°40S 66°30W **334** A2
Minà Su'ud *Si. Arabia* 28°45N 48°28E **247** D6
Minà al Aḥmadī *Kuwait* 29°5N 48°10E **247** D6
Minago ➔ *Canada* 54°33N 98°59W **297** C9
Minakami *Japan* 36°49N 138°59E **223** A10
Minaki *Canada* 49°59N 94°40W **297** D10
Minakuchi *Japan* 34°58N 136°10E **223** C8
Minamata *Japan* 32°10N 130°30E **222** E2
Minami *Japan* 34°40N 135°33E **133** A2
Minami-Arapusa △
Japan 35°30N 138°9E **223** B10
Minami-Tori-Shima
Pac. Oc. 24°20N 153°58E **288** E7
Minamitsunashima
Japan 35°32N 139°37E **140** B2
Minami *Japan* 34°40N 135°33E **133** A2
Minas *Uruguay* 34°20S 55°10W **335** C4
Minas, Sierra de las
Guatemala 15°9N 89°31W **320** C2
Minas Basin *Canada* 45°20N 64°12W **299** C7
Minas de Riotinto *Spain* 37°42N 6°35W **195** H4
Minas Gerais □ *Brazil* 18°50S 46°0W **333** E2
Minas Novas *Brazil* 17°15S 42°36W **333** E3
Minatitlán *Mexico* 17°59N 94°31W **319** D6
Minato *Ōsaka, Japan* 34°39N 135°25E **133** B1
Minato *Tokyo, Japan* **140** c3
Minbu *Burma* 20°10N 94°52E **241** E5
Minbya *Burma* 20°22N 93°16E **241** E4
Minchinabad *Pakistan* 30°10N 73°34E **242** D5
Mincio ➔ *Italy* 45°4N 10°59E **198** C7
Minčol *Slovak Rep.* 49°15N 20°58E **181** B13
Mindanao *Phil.* 8°0N 125°0E **233** H5
Mindanao Sea = Bohol Sea
Phil. 9°0N 124°0E **233** G5
Mindanao Trench *Pac. Oc.* 12°0N 126°6E **232** E5
Mindel ➔ *Germany* 48°31N 10°23E **179** G6
Mindelheim *Germany* 48°2N 10°28E **179** G6
Mindelo *C. Verde Is.* 16°24N 25°0W **153** f
Minden *Canada* 44°55N 78°43W **312** B6
Minden *Nordrhein-Westfalen,*
Germany 52°17N 8°55E **178** C4
Minden *La., U.S.A.* 32°37N 93°17W **314** E8
Minden *Nev., U.S.A.* 38°57N 119°46W **306** G7
Mindiptana *Indonesia* 5°55S 140°22E **231** F10
Mindona L. *Australia* 33°6S 142°6E **282** B5
Mindoro *Phil.* 13°0N 121°0E **232** E3
Mindoro Occidental □
Phil. 13°0N 120°30E **232** E3
Mindoro Oriental □ *Phil.* 13°0N 121°30E **232** E3
Mindoro Str. *Phil.* 12°30N 120°30E **232** E3
Mine *Japan* 34°12N 131°7E **222** C2
Minehead *U.K.* 51°12N 3°29W **169** F4
Mineiros *Brazil* 17°34S 52°34W **331** H7
Miner ➔ *Canada* 56°6N 81°26W **312** A3
Miner L. *U.S.A.* 41°51N 87°49W **119** B2
Miner Meadow *U.S.A.* 41°5N 87°49W **119** B2
Mineola *Tex., U.S.A.* 32°40N 95°29W **314** E7
Mineola *N.Y., U.S.A.* 40°44N 73°38W **313** F11
Mineral *Tex., U.S.A.* 28°34N 97°54W **314** G6
Mineral Bath *Jamaica* 17°58N 76°22W **320** a
Mineral King *U.S.A.* 36°27N 118°36W **306** J8
Mineral Point *U.S.A.* 42°52N 90°11W **310** B6
Mineral Wells *U.S.A.* 32°48N 98°7W **314** E5
Mineralnyye Vody *Russia* 44°15N 43°8E **191** H6
Miners Bay *Canada* 44°49N 78°46W **312** B6
Minersville *U.S.A.* 40°41N 76°16W **313** F8
Minerva *Ohio, U.S.A.* 40°44N 81°6W **312** F3
Minervino Murge *Italy* 41°5N 16°5E **201** A9
Minetto *U.S.A.* 43°24N 76°28W **313** C8
Minfeng *China* 37°4N 82°46E **217** E10
Ming-Kush *Kyrgyzstan* 41°40N 74°28E **217** D8
Mingäçevir *Azerbaijan* 40°45N 47°0E **191** K8
Mingala *C.A.R.* 5°6N 21°49E **264** A4
Mingan *Canada* 50°20N 64°0W **299** B7
Mingary *Australia* 32°8S 140°45E **282** B4
Mingechaurskoye Vdkhr. =
Mingäçevir Su Anbarı
Azerbaijan 40°57N 46°50E **191** K8
Mingela *Australia* 19°52S 146°38E **280** B4
Mingenew *Australia* 29°12S 115°21E **279** E2
Mingera Cr. ➔
Australia 20°38S 137°45E **280** C2
Minggang *China* 32°24N 114°3E **226** H7
Mingguang *China* 32°46N 117°59E **227** H11
Mingin *Burma* 22°50N 94°30E **241** D5
Mingir *Moldova* 46°40N 28°20E **183** D13
Mingo Junction *U.S.A.* 40°19N 80°37W **312** F4
Mingora *Pakistan* 34°48N 72°22E **243** B5
Mingorría *Spain* 40°45N 4°40W **194** E6
Mingshan *China* 30°5N 103°10E **228** B4
Mingteke Daban = Mintaka Pass
Pakistan 37°0N 74°58E **243** A6
Mingxi *China* 26°18N 117°12E **229** D11
Mingyuegue *China* 43°2N 128°50E **227** C15
Minhe *China* 36°15N 102°55E **226** F2
Minhla *Magwe, Burma* 19°58N 95°4E **241** F5
Minhla *Pegu, Burma* 17°59N 95°43E **241** G5
Minho = Miño ➔ *Spain* 41°52N 8°40W **194** D2
Minhou *China* 26°0N 119°15E **229** E12
Minicoy I. *India* 8°17N 73°28E **245** L1
Minidoka *U.S.A.* 42°45N 113°29W **304** E7
Minier ➔ *U.S.A.* 42°45N 113°50W **304** E7
Minigwal, L. *Australia* 29°31S 123°14E **279** E3
Minilya *Australia* 23°55S 114°0E **279** D1
Minilya Roadhouse
Australia 23°55S 114°0E **279** D1
Mininera *Australia* 37°37S 142°58E **282** D5
Minipi L. *Canada* 52°25N 60°45W **299** B7
Minj *Papua N. G.* 5°54S 144°37E **286** C3
Mink L. *Canada* 61°54N 117°40W **296** A5
Minkamba *Congo* 0°38S 16°34E **264** E3
Minkébé *Gabon* 1°45N 12°45E **264** D2
Minna *Nigeria* 9°37N 6°30E **263** C6
Minna-shima *Japan* 26°39N 127°58E **223** L3
Minneapolis *Kans., U.S.A.* 39°8N 97°42W **308** F5
Minneapolis *Minn.,*
U.S.A. 44°57N 93°16W **308** C7
Minnedosa *Canada* 50°14N 99°50W **297** D9
Minnesota □ *U.S.A.* 46°0N 94°15W **308** B7
Minnesota ➔ *U.S.A.* 44°54N 93°9W **308** C7
Minnesund *Norway* 60°23N 11°14E **164** D4
Minnewaukan *U.S.A.* 48°4N 99°15W **308** A4

Minnipa *Australia* 32°51S 135°9E **281** E2
Minnitaki L. *Canada* 49°57N 92°10W **298** C1
Mino *Japan* 35°32N 136°55E **223** B8
Miño *Japan* 43°21N 8°12W **194** B2
Miño ➔ *Spain* 41°52N 8°40W **194** D2
Mino-Kamo *Japan* 35°23N 137°2E **223** B9
Mino-Mikawa-Kōgen
Japan 35°10N 137°23E **223** B9
Minoa *Greece* 35°6N 25°45E **205** F7
Minobu *Japan* 35°22N 138°26E **223** B10
Minobu-Sanchi *Japan* 35°14N 138°20E **223** B10
Minonk *U.S.A.* 40°54N 89°2W **310** D7
Minooka *U.S.A.* 41°27N 88°16W **311** C8
Minorca = Menorca *Spain* 40°0N 4°0E **206** B5
Minore *Australia* 32°14S 148°27E **283** B8
Minot *U.S.A.* 48°14N 101°18W **308** A3
Minqin *China* 38°38N 103°20E **226** E2
Minqing *China* 26°15N 118°50E **229** D12
Minshât el Bekkarî *Egypt* 30°0N 31°8E **117** A1
Minsk *Belarus* 53°52N 27°30E **188** F14
Minsk □ *Belarus* 53°15N 27°30E **188** F14
Mińsk Mazowiecki
Poland 52°10N 21°33E **185** F8
Minster *Australia* 27°15S 133°7E **281** D1
Mintabie *Australia* 27°15S 133°7E **281** D1
Mintaka Pass *Pakistan* 37°0N 74°58E **243** A6
Minthami *Burma* 23°55N 94°16E **241** D5
Minto N. S. *Canada* 46°5N 66°5W **299** C6
Minto, Alaska, U.S.A.* 64°53N 149°10W **303** D10
Minto, L. *Canada* 57°13N 75°0W **298** A5
Minton *Canada* 49°10N 104°35W **297** D8
Mintoum *Gabon* 0°27N 12°16E **264** B2
Minturn *U.S.A.* 39°35N 106°26W **304** G10
Minturno *Italy* 41°15N 13°45E **200** A6
Minudasht *Iran* 37°17N 56°7E **247** B8
Minûf *Egypt* 30°26N 30°52E **256** H7
Minusinsk *Russia* 53°43N 91°20E **217** B12
Minutang *India* 28°15N 96°30E **241** A6
Minvoul *Gabon* 2°9N 12°8E **264** B2
Minwakh *Yemen* 16°48N 48°2E **246** D5
Minya el Qamh *Egypt* 30°31N 31°21E **256** H7
Minya Konka = Gongga Shan
China 29°40N 101°55E **228** C3
Minyip *Australia* 36°29S 142°36E **282** D5
Minzhong *China* 22°37N 113°30E **219** F10
Mionica *Bos.-H.* 44°51N 18°29E **182** F3
Mionica *Serbia* 44°14N 20°6E **202** B4
Miquan *China* 43°58N 87°42E **217** D11
Miquelon *Qué., Canada* 49°25N 76°27W **298** C4
Miquelon St-P. & M.* 47°8N 56°22W **299** C8
Mir *Niger* 14°5N 11°59E **259** F2
Mīr Kūh *Iran* 26°22N 58°55E **247** E8
Mīr Shahdād *Iran* 26°15N 58°29E **247** E8
Mira *Italy* 45°26N 12°8E **199** C9
Mira *Portugal* 40°26N 8°44W **194** E2
Mira ➔ *Colombia* 1°36N 79°1W **328** C2
Mira ➔ *Portugal* 37°43N 8°47W **195** H2
Mira por vos Cay
Bahamas 22°9N 74°30W **321** B5
Mīrābād *Afghan.* 30°25N 61°50E **247** D9
Mirabella Eclano *Italy* 41°2N 14°59E **201** A7
Mirabello, Kolpos *Greece* 35°10N 25°50E **207** D6
Miracema do Norte *Brazil* 9°33S 48°24W **332** D2
Mirador *Brazil* 6°22S 44°22W **332** D3
Mirador-Río Azul △
Guatemala 17°45N 89°50W **320** C1
Miraflores = Rovira
Colombia 4°15N 75°20W **328** C2
Miraflores *Colombia* 1°25N 72°13W **328** C3
Miraflores *Lima, Peru* 12°7S 77°2W **124** E2
Miraflores, L. *Panama* 9°1N 79°36W **320** c
Miraflores Locks *Panama* 9°0N 79°36W **320** c
Miraj *India* 16°50N 74°45E **244** F2
Miram Shah *Pakistan* 33°0N 70°2E **242** C4
Miramar *Argentina* 38°15S 57°50W **334** D4
Miramar *Mozam.* 23°50S 35°35E **269** G4
Miramar *N.Z.* 41°18S 174°49E **143** B1
Miramas *France* 43°33N 4°59E **175** E8
Mirambeau *France* 45°23N 0°35W **174** C3
Miramichi *Canada* 47°2N 65°28W **299** C7
Miramichi B. *Canada* 47°15N 65°0W **299** C7
Miramont-de-Guyenne
France 44°37N 0°21E **174** D4
Miranda *Brazil* 20°10S 56°15W **331** H6
Miranda □ *Venezuela* 10°15N 66°25W **328** A5
Miranda ➔ *Brazil* 19°25S 57°20W **331** H6
Miranda de Corvo *Portugal* 40°6N 8°20W **194** E2
Miranda de Ebro *Spain* 42°41N 2°57W **196** C2
Miranda do Corvo *Portugal* 40°6N 8°20W **194** E2
Miranda do Douro
Portugal 41°30N 6°16W **194** D4
Mirande *France* 43°31N 0°25E **174** E4
Mirandela *Portugal* 41°32N 7°10W **194** D3
Mirándola *Italy* 44°53N 11°4E **198** D8
Mirandópolis *Brazil* 21°9S 51°6W **333** F1
Mirango *Malawi* 13°32S 34°58E **269** E3
Mirani *Australia* 21°9S 148°53E **280** b
Mirano *Italy* 45°30N 12°7E **199** C9
Miras *Albania* 40°28N 20°53E **204** C2
Mirassol *Brazil* 20°46S 49°28W **333** F1
Mirbāt *Oman* 17°0N 54°45E **249** D5
Mirboo North *Australia* 38°24S 146°10E **283** F7
Mirear *Egypt* 23°15N 35°41E **256** D4
Mirebeau *France* 46°49N 0°10E **172** F7
Mirebeau-sur-Bèze
France 47°25N 5°20E **173** E12
Mirecourt *France* 48°20N 6°10E **173** D13
Mires *Greece* 35°4N 24°56E **207** D5
Mirgorod = Myrhorod
Ukraine 49°58N 33°37E **189** H7
Miri *Malaysia* 4°23N 113°59E **234** B4
Miriala *India* 16°52N 79°35E **244** F4
Miriam Vale *Australia* 24°20S 151°33E **280** C5
Miribel *France* 45°50N 4°57E **173** G11
Mirigama *Sri Lanka* 7°15N 80°8E **245** L5
Mirim, L. *S. Amer.* 32°45S 52°50W **335** C5
Mirimire *Venezuela* 11°10N 68°43W **328** A4
Miringoni *Comoros Is.* 12°17S 43°38E **272** a
Miriti *Brazil* 6°15S 59°0W **331** B6
Miriuwung Gajerrong ○
Australia 15°0S 128°45E **278** C4
Mirnyy *Antarctica* 66°50S 93°30E **151** C14
Mirnyy *Russia* 62°33N 113°53E **215** C12
Miroč *Serbia* 44°32N 22°16E **202** B6
Mirokhan *Pakistan* 27°46N 68°6E **242** F3
Mirond L. *Canada* 55°6N 102°47W **297** B8
Mirosławiec *Poland* 53°20N 16°5E **184** E3
Mirpur *Pakistan* 33°32N 73°56E **243** C5
Mirpur Batoro *Pakistan* 24°44N 68°58E **242** G3
Mirpur Bibiwari *Pakistan* 28°33N 67°44E **242** F2
Mirpur Khas *Pakistan* 25°30N 69°0E **242** G3
Mirpur Sakro *Pakistan* 24°33N 67°41E **242** G2
Mirria *Niger* 13°43N 9°1E **259** F1
Mirrool *Australia* 34°19S 147°10E **283** B7
Mirs Bay = Tai Pang Wan
China 22°33N 114°24E **219** F11
Mirsale *Somali Rep.* 5°56N 48°29E **257** F5
Mirsk *Poland* 50°58N 15°23E **185** H2
Mirtağ *Turkey* 38°23N 41°56E **213** C10
Mirtoa Sea *Greece* 37°0N 23°20E **204** D5
Mirtou, Kolpos *Greece* 38°30N 20°27E **204** C2
Miryang *S. Korea* 35°31N 128°44E **224** E4
Mirzaani *Georgia* 41°24N 46°5E **191** K8
Mirzachul = Guliston
Uzbekistan 40°29N 68°46E **217** D7

Mirzapur *India* 25°10N 82°34E **243** G10
Mirzapur-cum-Vindhyachal = Mirzapur *India* 25°10N 82°34E **243** G10
Mirzoyan = Taraz *Kazakhstan* 42°54N 71°22E **217** D8
Misaki *Japan* 34°18N 135°9E **223** C7
Misamis = Ozamiz *Phil.* 8°15N 123°50E **233** G4
Misamis Occidental □ *Phil.* 8°20N 123°42E **233** G4
Misamis Oriental □ *Phil.* 8°45N 125°0E **233** G5
Misantla *Mexico* 19°56N 96°50W **319** D5
Misawa *Japan* 40°41N 141°24E **220** D10
Miscou I. *Canada* 47°57N 64°31W **299** C7
Misdroy = Międzyzdroje *Poland* 53°56N 14°26E **184** E1
Misericordia = Itaporanga *Brazil* 7°18S 38°0W **332** C4
Misericordia, Sa. da *Brazil* 22°51S 43°17W **135** B1
Misha *India* 7°59N 93°20E **245** L10
Mish'āb, Ra's al *Si. Arabia* 28°15N 48°43E **247** D6
Mishagua ➜ *Peru* 11°12S 72°58W **330** C3
Mishamo *Tanzania* 5°41S 30°41E **268** D3
Mishan *China* 45°37N 131°48E **220** B5
Mishawaka *U.S.A.* 41°40N 86°11W **311** C10
Mishbih, Gebel *Egypt* 22°38N 34°44E **256** C3
Mishima *Japan* 35°10N 138°52E **223** B10
Mishmi Hills *India* 29°0N 96°0E **241** A6
Mishō *Japan* 32°57N 132°35E **222** E4
Misima I. *Papua N. G.* 10°40S 152°45E **286** F7
Misión *Mexico* 32°6N 116°53W **307** N10
Misión Fagnano *Argentina* 54°32S 67°17W **336** D3
Misiones □ *Argentina* 27°0S 55°0W **335** B5
Misiones □ *Paraguay* 27°0S 56°0W **334** B4
Miskah *Si. Arabia* 24°49N 42°56E **246** E4
Miski, E. ➜ *Chad* 20°0N 17°55E **259** E3
Miskitos, Cayos *Nic.* 14°26N 82°50W **320** D3
Miskolc *Hungary* 48°7N 20°50E **182** B5
Misoke *Dem. Rep. of the Congo* 0°42S 28°2E **268** C2
Misool *Indonesia* 1°52S 130°10E **231** E8
Mişr = Egypt ■ *Africa* 28°0N 31°0E **256** B3
Mişrātah *Libya* 32°24N 15°3E **258** B3
Mişrātah □ *Libya* 33°30N 15°0E **258** C3
Missanabie *Canada* 48°20N 84°6W **298** C3
Missão Catrimani *Brazil* 2°48N 62°18W **329** C5
Missão Velha *Brazil* 7°15S 39°10W **332** C4
Missinaibi ➜ *Canada* 50°43N 81°29W **298** B3
Missinaibi L. *Canada* 48°23N 83°40W **298** C3
Mission *B.C., Canada* 49°10N 122°15W **296** D4
Mission *Calif., U.S.A.* 37°44N 122°25W **136** B2
Mission *S. Dak., U.S.A.* 43°18N 100°39W **308** D3
Mission *Tex., U.S.A.* 26°13N 98°20W **314** H5
Mission Beach *Australia* 17°53S 146°6E **280** B4
Mission Viejo *U.S.A.* 33°36N 117°40W **307** M9
Missirah *Senegal* 13°40N 16°30W **262** C1
Missisa L. *Canada* 52°20N 85°7W **298** B2
Missisicabi ➜ *Canada* 51°14N 79°31W **298** B4
Mississagi ➜ *Canada* 46°15N 83°9W **298** C3
Mississauga *Canada* 43°32N 79°35W **141** B1
Mississinewa L. *U.S.A.* 40°42N 85°52W **311** D10
Mississippi □ *U.S.A.* 33°0N 90°0W **315** E10
Mississippi ➜ *U.S.A.* 29°9N 89°15W **310** E5
Mississippi L. *Canada* 45°5N 76°10W **313** A8
Mississippi River Delta *U.S.A.* 29°10N 89°15W **315** G10
Mississippi Sd. *U.S.A.* 30°20N 89°0W **315** F10
Missoula *U.S.A.* 46°52N 114°1W **304** C6
Missour *Morocco* 33°3N 4°0W **260** B4
Missouri □ *U.S.A.* 38°25N 92°30W **310** E3
Missouri ➜ *U.S.A.* 38°49N 90°7W **310** F6
Missouri City *U.S.A.* 29°37N 95°32W **314** G7
Missouri Valley *U.S.A.* 41°34N 95°53W **308** E6
Mist *U.S.A.* 45°59N 123°15W **306** E3
Mistassibi ➜ *Canada* 48°53N 72°13W **299** B5
Mistassini *Canada* 48°53N 72°12W **299** C5
Mistassini ➜ *Canada* 48°42N 72°20W **299** C5
Mistassini, L. *Canada* 51°0N 73°30W **298** B5
Mistastin L. *Canada* 55°57N 63°20W **299** A7
Mistelbach *Austria* 48°34N 16°34E **181** C9
Misterbianco *Italy* 37°31N 15°1E **201** E8
Misteriosa Bank *W. Indies* 18°50N 83°50W **320** C3
Misti, Volcán *Peru* 16°18S 71°24W **330** D3
Mistinibi, L. *Canada* 55°56N 64°17W **299** A7
Mistissini *Canada* 48°53N 72°12W **299** C5
Mistretta *Italy* 37°56N 14°22E **201** E7
Misty Fjords Nat. Monument ⌂ *U.S.A.* 55°40N 130°40W **303** J15
Misty L. *Canada* 58°53N 101°40W **297** B8
Misugi *Japan* 34°31N 136°16E **223** C8
Misumi *Japan* 32°37N 130°27E **222** E2
Misurata = Mişrātah *Libya* 32°24N 15°3E **258** B3
Mît Ghamr *Egypt* 30°42N 31°12E **256** H7
Mitaka *Japan* 35°41N 139°34E **140** A2
Mitande *Mozam.* 14°6S 35°58E **269** E4
Mitatib *Sudan* 15°59N 36°12E **257** D4
Mitau = Jelgava *Latvia* 56°41N 23°49E **184** B10
Mitava = Jelgava *Latvia* 56°41N 23°49E **184** B10
Mitcham *U.K.* 51°23N 0°10W **125** B2
Mitcham Common *U.K.* 51°23N 0°8W **125** B3
Mitchell *Queens., Australia* 26°29S 147°58E **281** D4
Mitchell *Ont., Canada* 43°28N 81°12W **312** C3
Mitchell *Ga., U.S.A.* 33°13N 82°42W **316** B7
Mitchell *Ind., U.S.A.* 38°44N 86°28W **311** F10
Mitchell *Nebr., U.S.A.* 41°57N 103°49W **308** E2
Mitchell *Oreg., U.S.A.* 44°34N 120°9W **304** D3
Mitchell *S. Dak., U.S.A.* 43°43N 98°2W **308** D4
Mitchell ➜ *Australia* 15°12S 141°35E **280** B3
Mitchell, Mt. *U.S.A.* 35°46N 82°16W **315** D13
Mitchell-Alice Rivers △ *Australia* 15°28S 142°5E **280** B3
Mitchell Museum of the American Indian *U.S.A.* 42°4N 87°43W **119** A2
Mitchell Ra. *Australia* 12°49S 135°36E **280** A2
Mitchell River △ *Australia* 37°37S 147°22E **283** D7
Mitchell's Plain *S. Africa* 34°4S 18°35E **118** B2
Mitchelstown *Ireland* 52°15N 8°16W **166** D3
Mitha Tiwana *Pakistan* 32°13N 72°6E **242** C5
Mithi *Pakistan* 24°44N 69°48E **242** G3
Mithimna *Greece* 39°20N 26°12E **205** B8
Mithrao *Pakistan* 27°28N 69°40E **242** F3
Mitiamo *Australia* 36°12S 144°15E **282** D6
Mitikas *Etoloakarnania, Greece* 38°40N 20°56E **207** B2
Mitikas *Preveza, Greece* 39°0N 20°42E **207** B2
Mitilini *Greece* 39°6N 26°35E **205** B8
Mitilinii *Greece* 37°42N 26°56E **205** D8
Mitino *Russia* 55°51N 37°20E **129** A2
Mitla Pass = Mamarr Mitlā *Egypt* 30°2N 32°54E **251** H3
Mito *Japan* 36°20N 140°30E **223** A12
Mitra, Mt. *Eq. Guin.* 1°23N 9°19E **264** B1
Mitre, Mt. *N.Z.* 40°50S 175°30E **284** G4
Mitrofanovka *Russia* 49°58N 39°42E **189** H10
Mitrovica = Kosovska Mitrovica *Kosovo* 42°54N 20°52E **202** D4
Mitrowitz = Sremska Mitrovica *Serbia* 44°59N 19°38E **182** F4
Mitsamiouli *Comoros Is.* 11°20S 43°16E **272** a
Mitsang *Gabon* 0°42N 12°33E **264** B2
Mitsinjo *Madag.* 16°1S 45°52E **272** B2
Mitsiwa *Eritrea* 15°35N 39°25E **257** D4
Mitsiwa Channel *Eritrea* 15°30N 40°0E **257** D5
Mitsoudjé *Comoros Is.* 11°48S 43°16E **272** a
Mitsukaidō *Japan* 36°1N 139°59E **223** A11
Mitsushima *Japan* 34°15N 129°20E **222** C1
Mittagong *Australia* 34°28S 150°29E **283** C9
Mitte *Germany* 52°32N 13°24E **115** A3
Mittel Isarkanal ➜ *Germany* 48°12N 11°40E **131** A3
Mittel Schreiberhau = Szklarska Poreba *Poland* 50°50N 15°33E **185** H2
Mittelberg *Austria* 47°20N 10°10E **180** D3
Mittelfranken □ *Germany* 49°25N 10°40E **179** F6
Mittellandkanal ➜ *Germany* 52°20N 8°28E **178** C4
Mittelwalde = Międzylesie *Poland* 50°8N 16°40E **185** H3
Mittenwalde *Germany* 52°15N 13°31E **178** C9
Mittersill *Austria* 47°16N 12°29E **180** D5
Mitterteich *Germany* 49°57N 12°14E **179** F8
Mittimatalik = Pond Inlet *Canada* 72°40N 77°0W **295** C16
Mittweida *Germany* 50°59N 12°59E **178** E8
Mitú *Colombia* 1°15N 70°13W **328** C3
Mituas *Colombia* 3°52N 68°49W **328** C4
Mitumba *Tanzania* 7°8S 31°2E **268** D3
Mitumba, Mts. *Dem. Rep. of the Congo* 7°0S 27°30E **268** D2
Mitwaba *Dem. Rep. of the Congo* 8°2S 27°17E **269** D2
Mityana *Uganda* 0°23N 32°2E **268** B3
Mitzic *Gabon* 0°45N 11°40E **264** B2
Miura *Japan* 35°12N 139°40E **223** B11
Mixcoac *Mexico* 19°23N 99°11W **128** B1
Mixteco ➜ *Mexico* 18°11N 98°30W **319** D5
Miyagi □ *Japan* 38°15N 140°45E **220** E10
Miyāh, W. el ➜ *Egypt* 25°0N 33°23E **256** C3
Miyāh, W. el ➜ *Syria* 34°44N 39°57E **246** C3
Miyake-Jima *Japan* 34°5N 139°30E **223** C11
Miyako *Japan* 39°40N 141°59E **220** E10
Miyako-Jima *Japan* 24°45N 125°20E **221** M2
Miyako-Rettō *Japan* 24°24N 125°0E **221** M2
Miyakojima *Japan* 34°42N 135°31E **133** A2
Miyakonojō *Japan* 31°40N 131°5E **222** F3
Miyān Rahan *Iran* 34°34N 47°26E **213** E12
Miyani *India* 21°50N 69°26E **242** J3
Miyanojō *Japan* 31°54N 130°27E **222** F2
Miyanoura-Dake *Japan* 30°20N 130°31E **221** J5
Miyata *Japan* 33°49N 130°42E **222** D2
Miyazaki *Japan* 31°56N 131°30E **222** F3
Miyazaki □ *Japan* 32°30N 131°30E **222** E3
Miyazu *Japan* 35°35N 135°10E **223** B7
Miyet, Bahr el = Dead Sea *Asia* 31°30N 35°30E **251** G6
Miyi *China* 26°47N 102°9E **228** D4
Miyoshi *Japan* 34°48N 132°51E **222** C4
Miyun *China* 40°28N 116°50E **226** D9
Miyun Shuiku *China* 40°30N 117°0E **227** D9
Mizan Teferi *Ethiopia* 6°57N 35°3E **257** F4
Mizdah *Libya* 31°30N 13°0E **258** B2
Mizdah □ *Libya* 31°26N 12°59E **258** B2
Mizen Hd. *Cork, Ireland* 51°27N 9°50W **166** E2
Mizen Hd. *Wicklow, Ireland* 52°51N 6°4W **166** D5
Mizhhirya *Ukraine* 48°32N 23°30E **183** B8
Mizhi *China* 37°47N 110°12E **226** F6
Mizil *Romania* 44°59N 26°29E **183** F11
Mizo Hills = Mizoram □ *India* 23°30N 92°40E **241** D4
Mizonokuchi *Japan* 35°35N 139°34E **140** B2
Mizoram □ *India* 23°30N 92°40E **241** D4
Mizpe Ramon *Israel* 30°34N 34°49E **251** H5
Mizue *Japan* 35°41N 139°54E **140** A4
Mizuho *Antarctica* 70°30S 41°0E **151** D5
Mizuho *Japan* 35°6N 135°17E **223** B7
Mizunami *Japan* 35°22N 137°15E **223** B9
Mizusawa *Japan* 39°8N 141°8E **220** E10
Mjällby *Sweden* 56°3N 14°40E **163** H8
Mjöbäck *Sweden* 57°28N 12°53E **163** G6
Mjölby *Sweden* 58°20N 15°10E **163** F9
Mjølfjell *Norway* 60°41N 6°55E **164** D3
Mjømna *Norway* 60°55N 4°55E **164** D1
Mjörn *Sweden* 57°55N 12°25E **163** G6
Mjøsa *Norway* 60°40N 11°0E **164** D8
Mkata *Tanzania* 5°45S 38°20E **268** D4
Mkhaya ⌂ *Swaziland* 26°34S 31°45E **271** C5
Mkhuze ⌂ *S. Africa* 29°27S 29°30E **271** C4
Mkokotoni *Tanzania* 5°55S 39°15E **268** D4
Mkomazi *Tanzania* 4°40S 38°7E **268** C4
Mkomazi ➜ *S. Africa* 30°12S 30°50E **271** D5
Mkomazi ⌂ *Tanzania* 4°4S 30°2E **268** C3
Mkulwe *Tanzania* 8°37S 32°20E **269** D3
Mkumbi, Ras *Tanzania* 7°38S 39°55E **268** D4
Mkushi *Zambia* 14°25S 29°15E **269** E2
Mkushi River *Zambia* 13°32S 29°45E **269** E2
Mkuze *S. Africa* 27°10S 32°0E **271** C5
Mladá Boleslav *Czech Rep.* 50°27N 14°53E **180** A7
Mladenovac *Serbia* 44°28N 20°44E **202** B4
Mlala Hills *Tanzania* 6°50S 31°40E **268** D3
Mlange = Mulanje, Mt. *Malawi* 16°2S 35°33E **269** F4
Mlava ➜ *Serbia* 44°45N 21°13E **202** B5
Mława *Poland* 53°9N 20°25E **185** E7
Mlawula ⌂ *Swaziland* 26°12S 32°2E **271** C5
Mlinište *Bos.-H.* 44°15N 16°50E **199** D13
Mljet *Croatia* 42°43N 17°30E **199** F14
Mljet △ *Croatia* 42°45N 17°25E **199** F14
Mljetski Kanal *Croatia* 42°48N 17°35E **199** F14
Młocinski Park *Poland* 52°19N 20°57E **142** B1
Młociny *Poland* 52°18N 20°55E **142** B1
Młynary *Poland* 54°12N 19°46E **184** D6
Mmabatho *S. Africa* 25°49S 25°30E **270** C4
Mme *Cameroon* 6°18N 10°14E **263** D7
Mnevniki *Russia* 55°45N 37°28E **129** B2
Mnichovo Hradiště *Czech Rep.* 50°32N 14°59E **180** A7
Mo *Hordaland, Norway* 60°49N 5°48E **164** D2
Mo *Møre og Romsdal, Norway* 63°0N 8°59E **164** A5
Mo *Telemark, Norway* 59°28N 7°50E **164** E4
Mo i Rana *Norway* 66°20N 14°7E **160** C16
Moa *Queens., Australia* 10°11S 142°16E **280** a
Moa *Cuba* 20°40N 74°56W **321** B4
Moa *Indonesia* 8°0S 128°0E **231** F7
Moa ➜ *S. Leone* 6°59N 11°36W **262** D2
Moab *U.S.A.* 38°35N 109°33W **304** G9
Moabi *Gabon* 2°24S 10°59E **264** C2
Moaco ➜ *Brazil* 7°41S 68°18W **330** B4
Moala *Fiji* 18°36S 179°53E **287** B2
Moama *Australia* 36°7S 144°46E **281** F3
Moamba *Mozam.* 25°36S 32°15E **271** C5
Moapa *U.S.A.* 36°40N 114°37W **307** J12
Moate *Ireland* 53°24N 7°44W **166** C4
Moba *Dem. Rep. of the Congo* 7°0S 29°48E **268** D2
Moba *Lagos, Nigeria* 6°26N 3°28E **124** B2
Mobara *Japan* 35°25N 140°18E **223** B12
Mobārakābād *Iran* 28°24N 53°20E **247** D7
Mobaye *C.A.R.* 4°25N 21°5E **264** B4
Mobayi *Dem. Rep. of the Congo* 4°15N 21°8E **264** B4
Mobeka *Dem. Rep. of the Congo* 1°52N 19°49E **264** B3
Mobenzélé *Congo* 0°56N 17°50E **264** B3
Moberly *U.S.A.* 39°25N 92°26W **310** E4
Moberly Lake *Canada* 55°50N 121°44W **296** B4
Mobile *U.S.A.* 30°41N 88°3W **315** F10
Mobile B. *U.S.A.* 30°30N 88°0W **315** F11
Mobridge *U.S.A.* 45°32N 100°26W **308** C3
Mobutu Sese Seko, L. = Albert, L. *Africa* 1°30N 31°0E **268** B3
Moc Chau *Vietnam* 20°50N 104°38E **236** B5
Moc Hoa *Vietnam* 10°46N 105°56E **237** G5
Moca *Puerto Rico* 18°24N 67°10W **321** b
Mocabe Kasari *Dem. Rep. of the Congo* 9°58S 26°12E **269** D2
Mocajuba *Brazil* 2°35S 49°30W **332** B2
Moçambique = Mozambique ■ *Africa* 19°0S 35°0E **269** F4
Moçambique *Mozam.* 15°3S 40°42E **269** F5
Moçâmedes = Namibe *Angola* 15°7S 12°11E **265** F2
Mocanaqua *U.S.A.* 41°9N 76°8W **313** E8
Mocapra ➜ *Venezuela* 7°56N 66°46W **328** B4
Mocco, Morro de *Angola* 12°28S 15°11E **265** E3
Moce *Fiji* 18°40S 178°29W **287** B3
Mocha = Al Mukhā *Yemen* 13°18N 43°15E **248** D3
Mocha, I. *Chile* 38°22S 73°56W **336** A2
Mochos *Greece* 35°16N 25°27E **207** E6
Mochudi *Botswana* 24°27S 26°7E **270** B4
Mocimboa da Praia *Mozam.* 11°25S 40°20E **269** E5
Mociu *Romania* 46°46N 24°3E **183** D9
Möckeln *Sweden* 56°40N 14°15E **163** H8
Mockfjärd *Sweden* 60°30N 14°57E **162** D8
Moclips *U.S.A.* 47°14N 124°13W **306** C2
Mocoa *Colombia* 1°7N 76°35W **328** C2
Mococa *Brazil* 21°28S 47°0W **335** A6
Mocorito *Mexico* 25°29N 107°55W **318** B3
Moctezuma *Mexico* 29°48N 109°42W **318** B3
Moctezuma ➜ *Mexico* 21°59N 98°34W **319** C5
Mocuba *Mozam.* 16°54S 36°57E **269** F4
Moczydło *Poland* 52°8N 21°2E **142** C2
Moda *Burma* 24°22N 96°29E **241** C6
Modane *France* 45°12N 6°40E **175** C10
Modasa *India* 23°30N 73°21E **242** H5
Modder ➜ *S. Africa* 29°2S 24°37E **270** C3
Modderfontein = Niekerkshoop *S. Africa* 29°19S 22°51E **270** C3
Modderfontein *S. Africa* 26°5S 28°10E **123** A2
Modderrivier *S. Africa* 29°2S 24°38E **270** C3
Módena *Italy* 44°40N 10°55E **198** D7
Modena *Utah, U.S.A.* 37°48N 113°56W **305** H7
Modernamuseet *Stockholm, Sweden* **139** b3
Modesto *U.S.A.* 37°39N 121°0W **306** H6
Möðrudalur *Iceland* 65°22N 15°53W **155** B11
Möðruvellir *Iceland* 65°46N 18°15W **155** B8
Módica *Italy* 36°52N 14°46E **201** F7
Modimolle *S. Africa* 24°42S 28°22E **271** B4
Modjadjiskloof *S. Africa* 23°42S 30°10E **271** B5
Modjamboli *Dem. Rep. of the Congo* 2°28N 22°6E **264** B4
Mödling *Austria* 48°5N 16°17E **181** C9
Modo *Sudan* 5°31N 30°33E **257** F3
Modoc *U.S.A.* 33°44N 82°13W **316** B7
Modra *Slovak Rep.* 48°19N 17°20E **181** C10
Modřany *Czech Rep.* 50°0N 14°24E **135** B2
Modriča *Bos.-H.* 44°57N 18°17E **182** F3
Moe *Australia* 38°12S 146°19E **283** E7
Moebase *Mozam.* 17°3S 38°41E **269** F4
Moëlan-sur-Mer *France* 47°49N 3°38W **172** E3
Moelv *Norway* 60°56N 10°43E **164** D7
Moen I. = Weno *Pac. Oc.* 7°27N 151°52E **287** T18
Moengo *Suriname* 5°45N 54°20W **329** B7
Moerewa *N.Z.* 35°8S 174°1E **284** B3
Moffat *U.K.* 55°21N 3°27W **167** F5
Moga *India* 30°48N 75°8E **242** D6
Mogadishu = Muqdisho *Somali Rep.* 2°2N 45°25E **267** D6
Mogador = Essaouira *Morocco* 31°32N 9°42W **260** B3
Mogadouro *Portugal* 41°22N 6°47W **194** D4
Mogalakwena ➜ *S. Africa* 22°38S 28°40E **271** B4
Mogami-Gawa ➜ *Japan* 38°45N 140°0E **220** E10
Mogán *Canary Is.* 27°53N 15°43W **153** e1
Mogandjo *Dem. Rep. of the Congo* 1°23N 24°15E **264** B4
Mogaung *Burma* 25°20N 97°0E **241** C6
Mogen *Norway* 60°2N 7°52E **164** D4
Mogente = Moixent *Spain* 38°52N 0°45W **197** G4
Mogho *Ethiopia* 4°54N 40°16E **257** G5
Mogi das Cruzes *Brazil* 23°31S 46°11W **335** A6
Mogi-Guaçu ➜ *Brazil* 20°53S 48°10W **335** A6
Mogielnica *Poland* 51°42N 20°41E **185** G7
Mogige *Ethiopia* 5°24N 36°14E **257** F4
Mogilev = Mahilyow *Belarus* 53°55N 30°18E **177** B16
Mogilev-Podolskiy = Mohyliv-Podilskyy *Ukraine* 48°26N 27°48E **183** B12
Mogilno *Poland* 52°39N 17°55E **185** F4
Mogincual *Mozam.* 15°35S 40°25E **269** F5
Mogliano Véneto *Italy* 45°33N 12°14E **199** C9
Mogocha *Russia* 53°40N 119°50E **215** D12
Mogoditshane *Botswana* 24°37S 25°51E **270** B4
Mogok *Burma* 23°0N 96°40E **241** D6
Mogollon Rim *U.S.A.* 34°10N 110°50W **305** J8
Mógoro *Italy* 39°41N 8°47E **200** C1
Mograt *Sudan* 19°28N 33°16E **256** D3
Mogroum *Chad* 11°6N 15°25E **259** F3
Moguer *Spain* 37°15N 6°52W **195** H4
Mogumber *Australia* 31°2S 116°3E **279** F2
Mogwadi ➜ *S. Africa* 23°4S 29°36E **271** B4
Mogyoród *Hungary* 47°35N 19°14E **117** A3
Mohács *Hungary* 45°58N 18°41E **182** E3
Mohaka ➜ *N.Z.* 39°7S 177°12E **284** F6
Mohala *India* 20°35N 80°44E **244** D5
Mohales Hoek *Lesotho* 30°7S 27°26E **270** D4
Mohali *Congo* 0°15N 15°29E **264** B3
Mohall *U.S.A.* 48°46N 101°31W **308** A3
Moḩammadābād *Iran* 37°52N 59°5E **247** B8
Mohammadia *Algeria* 35°33N 0°3E **261** A5
Mohammedia *Morocco* 33°44N 7°21W **260** B3
Mohammerah = Khorrāmshahr *Iran* 30°29N 48°15E **247** D6
Mohana *India* 19°27N 84°16E **244** E7
Mohana ➜ *India* 24°43N 85°0E **243** G11
Mohanganj *Bangla.* 24°54N 90°59E **241** C3
Mohanlalganj *India* 26°41N 80°58E **243** F9
Mohave, L. *U.S.A.* 35°12N 114°34W **307** K12
Mohawk ➜ *U.S.A.* 42°47N 73°41W **313** D11
Moheda *Sweden* 57°1N 14°35E **163** G8
Mohéli *Comoros Is.* 12°20S 43°40E **272** a
Mohéli ✈ (NWA) *Comoros Is.* 12°19S 43°47E **272** a
Mohenjodaro *Pakistan* 27°19N 68°7E **242** F3
Moher, Cliffs of *Ireland* 52°58N 9°27W **166** D2
Mohican, C. *U.S.A.* 60°12N 167°25W **303** F6
Mohicanville Res. *U.S.A.* 40°45N 82°9W **312** F2
Möhne ➜ *Germany* 51°29N 7°57E **178** D3
Mohns Ridge *Arctic* 72°30N 5°0W **150** B7
Mohnyin *Burma* 24°47N 96°22E **241** C6
Mohoro *Tanzania* 8°6S 39°8E **268** D4
Mohrin = Moryń *Poland* 52°51N 14°22E **185** F1
Mohsenābād *Iran* 36°40N 59°35E **247** B8
Mohyliv-Podilskyy *Ukraine* 48°26N 27°48E **183** B12
Moi *Norway* 58°27N 6°32E **164** F3
Moia *Sudan* 5°3N 28°2E **257** F2
Moidart, L. *U.K.* 56°47N 5°52W **167** E3
Moinabad *India* 17°44N 77°16E **244** F3
Moinești *Romania* 46°28N 26°31E **183** D11
Moinho Velho, Cor. ➜ *Brazil* 23°35S 46°35W **137** B2
Moira ➜ *Canada* 44°21N 77°24W **312** B7
Moirang *India* 24°30N 93°46E **241** C4
Moirans *France* 45°20N 5°33E **175** C9
Moirans-en-Montagne *France* 46°26N 5°43E **173** F12
Moisaküla *Estonia* 58°3N 25°12E **188** C3
Moisie *Canada* 50°12N 66°1W **299** B6
Moisie ➜ *Canada* 50°14N 66°5W **299** B6
Moissac *France* 44°7N 1°5E **174** D5
Moïssala *Chad* 8°21N 17°46E **259** G3
Moita *Portugal* 38°38N 8°58W **195** G2
Moixent *Spain* 38°52N 0°45W **197** G4
Möja *Sweden* 59°26N 18°55E **162** E12
Mojácar *Spain* 37°6N 1°55W **197** H3
Mojados *Spain* 41°26N 4°40W **194** D6
Mojave *U.S.A.* 35°3N 118°10W **307** K8
Mojave ⌂ *U.S.A.* 35°7N 115°32W **307** K11
Mojave Desert *U.S.A.* 35°0N 116°30W **307** L10
Moji-Guaçu *Brazil* 22°22S 46°57W **333** F2
Mojiang *China* 23°37N 101°35E **228** F3
Mojjo ➜ *Ethiopia* 7°55N 42°0E **257** F5
Mojkovac *Montenegro* 42°58N 19°35E **202** D3
Mojo *Bolivia* 21°48S 65°33W **334** A2
Mojo *Ethiopia* 8°35N 39°5E **257** F4
Mojokerto *Indonesia* 7°28S 112°26E **235** D4
Mojos, Llanos de *Bolivia* 15°10S 65°0W **331** D5
Moju *Brazil* 1°53S 48°46W **332** B2
Moju ➜ *Brazil* 1°40S 48°25W **332** B2
Mok *S. Korea* 37°32N 126°52E **137** B1
Moka *Mauritius* 20°13S 57°29E **272** e
Mokai *N.Z.* 38°32S 175°56E **284** E4
Mokala △ *S. Africa* 29°10S 24°10E **270** C3
Mokambo *Dem. Rep. of the Congo* 12°25S 28°20E **269** E2
Mokameh *India* 25°24N 85°55E **243** G11
Mokane *U.S.A.* 38°41N 91°53W **310** F5
Mōkapu Peninsula *U.S.A.* 21°25N 157°45W **302** K14
Mokau *N.Z.* 38°42S 174°39E **284** E3
Mokau ➜ *N.Z.* 38°35S 174°35E **284** E3
Mokelumne ➜ *U.S.A.* 38°13N 121°28W **306** G5
Mokelumne Hill *U.S.A.* 38°18N 120°43W **306** G6
Mokhotlong *Lesotho* 29°22S 29°2E **271** C4
Mokihinui ➜ *N.Z.* 41°33S 171°58E **285** B6
Möklinta *Sweden* 60°4N 16°33E **162** D10
Moknine *Tunisia* 35°35N 10°58E **258** A2
Mokoan, L. *Australia* 36°27S 146°5E **283** D7
Mokokchung *India* 26°15N 94°30E **241** B5
Mökölea Rock *U.S.A.* 21°27N 157°44W **302** K14
Mokolo *Cameroon* 10°49N 13°54E **259** F2
Mokolo *Dem. Rep. of the Congo* 1°55N 18°6E **264** B3
Mokolo ➜ *S. Africa* 23°14S 27°43E **271** B4
Mokombe *Dem. Rep. of the Congo* 0°14S 23°48E **264** C4
Mokopane *S. Africa* 24°10S 28°55E **271** B4
Mokotów *Poland* 52°12N 21°0E **142** B2
Mokpalin *Burma* 17°26N 96°53E **241** G6
Mokpo *S. Korea* 34°50N 126°25E **224** E3
Mokra Gora *Europe* 42°50N 20°30E **202** D4
Mokronog *Slovenia* 45°57N 15°9E **199** C12
Moksha ➜ *Russia* 54°45N 41°53E **190** C6
Mokshan *Russia* 53°25N 44°35E **190** D7
Mokuauia I. *U.S.A.* 21°40N 157°56W **302** J14
Mokulē'ia *U.S.A.* 21°35N 158°9W **302** J13
Mokulua Is. *U.S.A.* 21°24N 157°42W **302** K14
Mokumanu *U.S.A.* 21°28N 157°43W **302** K14
Mokwa *Nigeria* 9°19N 5°0E **263** D6
Mol *Belgium* 51°11N 5°5E **170** C5
Mola di Bari *Italy* 41°4N 17°5E **201** A10
Molai *Greece* 36°49N 22°56E **204** E4
Molakalmuru *India* 14°55N 76°50E **245** G3
Molale *Ethiopia* 10°10N 39°41E **257** E4
Molaly *Kazakhstan* 45°27N 78°18E **217** C9
Molanda *Dem. Rep. of the Congo* 2°28N 20°48E **264** B4
Molara *Italy* 40°52N 9°43E **200** B2
Molat *Croatia* 44°15N 14°50E **199** D11
Molave *Phil.* 8°5N 123°30E **233** G4
Molchanovo *Russia* 57°40N 83°50E **214** D9
Mold *U.K.* 53°9N 3°8W **168** D4
Moldava nad Bodvou *Slovak Rep.* 48°38N 21°0E **181** C14
Moldavia = Moldova ■ *Europe* 47°0N 28°0E **183** C13
Moldavia *Romania* 46°30N 27°0E **183** D12
Molde *Norway* 62°45N 7°9E **164** B4
Moldova ■ *Europe* 47°0N 28°0E **183** C13
Moldova Nouă *Romania* 44°45N 21°41E **182** F6
Moldoveanu, Vf. *Romania* 45°36N 24°45E **183** E9
Moldovița *Romania* 47°41N 25°32E **183** C10
Mole ➜ *U.K.* 51°24N 0°21W **169** F7
Mole △ *Ghana* 9°43N 1°44W **263** D4
Molegbwe *Dem. Rep. of the Congo* 4°12N 20°53E **264** B4
Molenbeek-St-Jean *Belgium* 50°51N 4°19E **116** A1
Molepolole *Botswana* 24°28S 25°28E **270** B4
Molesworth *N.Z.* 42°5S 173°16E **285** C8
Molfetta *Italy* 41°12N 16°36E **201** A9
Möli'i Pond *U.S.A.* 21°31N 157°51W **302** J14
Molina de Aragón *Spain* 40°46N 1°52W **196** E3
Molina de Segura *Spain* 38°3N 1°12W **197** G3
Moline *U.S.A.* 41°30N 90°31W **310** C6
Molinella *Italy* 44°37N 11°40E **199** D8
Molino *U.S.A.* 30°43N 87°20W **317** E2
Molino de Rosas *Mexico* 19°21N 99°14W **128** B1
Molinos *Argentina* 25°28S 66°15W **334** B2
Moliro *Dem. Rep. of the Congo* 8°12S 30°30E **268** D3
Moliterno *Italy* 40°14N 15°52E **201** B8
Molkom *Sweden* 59°37N 13°44E **162** E7
Mölle *Sweden* 56°17N 12°31E **163** H6
Molledo *Spain* 43°8N 4°6W **194** B6
Mollem *Belgium* 50°56N 4°13E **116** A1
Mollendo *Peru* 17°0S 72°0W **330** D3
Mollerin, L. *Australia* 30°30S 117°35E **279** F2
Mollerussa *Spain* 41°37N 0°54E **196** D5
Mollina *Spain* 37°8N 4°38W **195** H6
Mollins de Rey *Spain* 41°24N 2°1E **114** A1
Mölln *Germany* 53°39N 10°32E **178** B6
Mölltorp *Sweden* 58°30N 14°26E **163** F8
Mölnlycke *Sweden* 57°40N 12°8E **163** G6
Molo *Burma* 23°22N 96°53E **241** D6
Molo *Rift Valley, Kenya* 0°15S 35°44E **268** C4
Molochansk *Ukraine* 47°15N 35°35E **189** J8
Molochnoye, Ozero *Ukraine* 46°30N 35°20E **189** J8
Molodechno = Maladzyechna *Belarus* 54°20N 26°50E **177** A14
Molodezhnaya *Antarctica* 67°40S 45°51E **151** C9
Molodove *Ukraine* 46°13N 29°39E **183** D14
Moloka'i *U.S.A.* 21°8N 157°0W **302** B4
Molokai Fracture Zone *Pac. Oc.* 28°0N 125°0W **289** E15
Molokini I. *U.S.A.* 20°38N 156°30W **302** C5
Molong *Australia* 33°5S 148°54E **283** B8
Molopo ➜ *Africa* 28°30S 20°12E **270** C3
Molos *Greece* 38°47N 22°37E **204** C4
Molotov = Perm *Russia* 58°0N 56°10E **186** C10
Molotov, Mys = Arkticheskiy, Mys *Russia* 81°10N 95°0E **215** A10
Molotovsk = Nolinsk *Russia* 57°28N 49°57E **190** B9
Molotovsk = Severodvinsk *Russia* 64°27N 39°58E **186** B6
Molotovskoye = Krasnogvardeyskoye *Russia* 45°52N 41°33E **191** H5
Moloundou *Cameroon* 2°8N 15°15E **264** B3
Molowaie *Dem. Rep. of the Congo* 5°47S 23°18E **265** D4
Molsheim *France* 48°33N 7°29E **173** D14
Molson L. *Canada* 54°22N 96°40W **297** C9
Molteno *S. Africa* 31°22S 26°22E **270** D4
Molu *Indonesia* 6°45S 131°40E **231** F8
Molucca Sea *Indonesia* 0°0 125°0E **231** E6
Moluccas = Maluku *Indonesia* 1°0S 127°0E **231** E7
Molundo *Phil.* 7°57N 124°23E **233** H5
Moma *Dem. Rep. of the Congo* 1°35S 23°52E **264** C4
Moma *Mozam.* 16°47S 39°4E **269** F4
Momba *Australia* 30°58S 143°30E **282** A5
Mombaça *Brazil* 5°43S 39°45W **332** C4
Mombango *Dem. Rep. of the Congo* 1°45N 24°26E **264** B4
Mombasa *Kenya* 4°3S 39°40E **268** C4
Mombetsu *Japan* 44°21N 143°22E **220** B11
Mombil *Burma* 27°46N 98°6E **241** B7
Momboyo ➜ *Dem. Rep. of the Congo* 0°16S 19°0E **264** C3
Mombuey *Spain* 42°3N 6°20W **194** C4
Momchilgrad *Bulgaria* 41°33N 25°23E **203** E9
Momence *U.S.A.* 41°10N 87°40W **311** C9
Momi *Dem. Rep. of the Congo* 1°42S 27°0E **268** C2
Momote *Papua N. G.* 2°4S 147°27E **286** B4
Mompog Pass *Phil.* 13°34N 122°13E **232** E4
Mompós *Colombia* 9°14N 74°26W **328** B3
Møn *Denmark* 54°57N 12°20E **163** K6
Møn *Hordaland, Norway* 60°37N 6°31E **164** D3
Mon □ *Burma* 16°0N 97°30E **241** G6
Mona, Canal de la = Mona Passage *W. Indies* 18°30N 67°45W **321** C6
Mona, Isla *Puerto Rico* 18°5N 67°54W **321** C6
Mona, Pta. *Costa Rica* 9°37N 82°36W **320** E3
Mona Passage *W. Indies* 18°30N 67°45W **321** C6
Mona Quimbundo *Angola* 9°55S 19°58E **265** D3
Monaca *U.S.A.* 40°41N 80°17W **312** F4
Monaco ■ *Europe* 43°46N 7°23E **175** E11
Monadhliath Mts. *U.K.* 57°10N 4°4W **167** D4
Monadnock, Mt. *U.S.A.* 42°52N 72°7W **313** D12
Monagas □ *Venezuela* 9°20N 63°0W **329** B5
Monaghan *Ireland* 54°15N 6°57W **166** B5
Monaghan □ *Ireland* 54°11N 6°56W **166** B5
Monahans *U.S.A.* 31°36N 102°54W **314** F3
Monapo *Mozam.* 14°56S 40°19E **269** E5
Monar, L. *U.K.* 57°26N 5°8W **167** D3
Monaragala *Sri Lanka* 6°52N 81°22E **245** L5
Monarch Mt. *Canada* 51°55N 125°57W **296** C3
Monashee Mts. *Canada* 51°0N 118°43W **296** C5
Monasterevin *Ireland* 53°8N 7°4W **166** C4
Monastir = Bitola *Macedonia* 41°1N 21°20E **202** E5
Monastir *Tunisia* 35°50N 10°49E **258** A2
Monastir □ *Tunisia* 35°37N 10°45E **261** A7
Moncada *Phil.* 15°44N 120°34E **232** D3
Moncalieri *Italy* 45°0N 7°41E **198** D4
Moncalvo *Italy* 45°3N 8°16E **198** C5
Moncão *Portugal* 42°4N 8°27W **194** C2
Moncarapacho *Portugal* 37°5N 7°46W **195** H3
Moncayo, Sierra del *Spain* 41°48N 1°50W **196** D3
Moncha-Guba = Monchegorsk *Russia* 67°54N 32°58E **160** C25
Monchegorsk *Russia* 67°54N 32°58E **160** C25
Mönchengladbach *Germany* 51°11N 6°27E **178** D2
Monchique *Portugal* 37°19N 8°38W **195** H2
Moncks Corner *U.S.A.* 33°12N 80°1W **316** B9
Monclova *Mexico* 26°54N 101°25W **318** B4
Moncontour *France* 48°22N 2°38W **172** D4
Moncton *Canada* 46°7N 64°51W **299** C7
Mondariz *Spain* 42°14N 8°27W **194** C2
Mondego ➜ *Portugal* 40°9N 8°52W **194** E2
Mondego, C. *Portugal* 40°11N 8°54W **194** E2
Mondeodo *Indonesia* 3°34S 122°9E **231** E6
Mondeor *S. Africa* 26°16S 28°0E **123** B2
Mondeville *France* 49°10N 0°18W **172** C6
Mondimbi *Dem. Rep. of the Congo* 1°48N 22°46E **264** B4
Mondjuku *Dem. Rep. of the Congo* 1°41S 21°12E **264** C4
Mondlo *S. Africa* 27°59S 30°43E **271** C5
Mondo *Chad* 13°47N 15°32E **259** F3
Mondolfo *Italy* 43°45N 13°6E **199** E10
Mondoñedo *Spain* 43°25N 7°23W **194** B3
Mondovì *Italy* 44°23N 7°49E **198** D4
Mondragó *Spain* 39°21N 3°12E **206** B4
Mondragon = Arrasate *Spain* 43°4N 2°30W **196** B2
Mondragon *Phil.* 12°31N 124°45E **232** E5
Mondragone *Italy* 41°7N 13°53E **200** A6
Mondrain I. *Australia* 34°9S 122°14E **279** F3
Moneague *Jamaica* 18°16N 77°7W **320** a
Moneda, Palacio de la *Chile* 33°26S 70°39W **137** B2
Monemvasia *Greece* 36°41N 23°3E **204** E5
Moneró *Brazil* 22°48S 43°11W **135** A1
Moneron, Ostrov *Russia* 46°15N 141°16E **220** A10
Monessen *U.S.A.* 40°9N 79°54W **312** F5
Monesterio *Spain* 38°6N 6°15W **195** G4
Monestier-de-Clermont *France* 44°55N 5°38E **175** D9
Monett *U.S.A.* 36°55N 93°55W **308** G7
Moneymore *U.K.* 54°41N 6°40W **166** B5
Monfalcone *Italy* 45°49N 13°32E **199** C10
Monflanquin *France* 44°32N 0°47E **174** D4
Monforte *Portugal* 39°6N 7°25W **195** F3
Monforte de Lemos *Spain* 42°31N 7°33W **194** C3
Mong Cai *Vietnam* 21°27N 107°54E **236** B6
Mong Hsu *Burma* 21°54N 98°30E **228** G2
Mong Hta *Burma* 19°50N 98°35E **241** F7
Mong Ket *Burma* 23°8N 98°22E **241** D7
Mong Kok *China* 22°19N 114°10E **122** B2
Mong Kung *Burma* 21°35N 97°35E **241** E6
Mong Kyawt *Burma* 19°56N 98°45E **241** F7
Mong Long *Burma* 22°47N 96°37E **241** D6
Mong Mit *Burma* 23°7N 96°41E **241** D6
Mong Nai *Burma* 20°32N 97°46E **241** E6
Mong Pan *Burma* 20°19N 98°22E **241** E7
Mong Ping *Burma* 21°22N 99°2E **228** G2
Mong Pu *Burma* 20°55N 98°44E **241** E7
Mong Ton *Burma* 20°17N 98°45E **241** E7
Mong Tung *Burma* 22°2N 97°41E **241** D6
Mong Yai *Burma* 22°21N 98°3E **241** D7
Mong Yu *Burma* 23°30N 97°47E **241** D6
Monga *Dem. Rep. of the Congo* 4°12N 22°49E **264** B4
Mongala ➜ *Dem. Rep. of the Congo* 1°53N 19°46E **264** B3
Mongalla *Sudan* 5°8N 31°42E **257** F3
Mongandia *Congo* 0°45N 17°11E **264** B3
Mongers, L. *Australia* 29°25S 117°5E **279** E2
Mongga *Solomon Is.* 7°52S 157°0E **287** L9
Monghyr = Munger *India* 25°23N 86°30E **243** G12
Mongibello = Etna *Italy* 37°50N 14°55E **201** E7
Mongla *Bangla.* 22°8N 89°35E **241** D2
Mongmong *Guam* 13°28N 144°45E **302** d
Mongngaw *Burma* 22°47N 96°59E **241** D6
Mongo *Chad* 12°14N 18°43E **259** F3
Mongó *Eq. Guin.* 1°52N 10°10E **264** B2
Mongo ➜ *S. Leone* 9°35N 12°10W **262** D2
Mongolia ■ *Asia* 47°0N 103°0E **218** B5
Mongolia, Plateau of *Asia* 45°0N 105°0E **210** D12
Mongomo *Eq. Guin.* 1°38N 11°19E **264** B2
Mongonu *Nigeria* 12°40N 13°32E **263** C7
Mongororo *Chad* 12°3N 22°26E **259** F4
Mongstad *Norway* 60°49N 5°2E **164** D2
Mongu *Zambia* 15°16S 23°12E **265** F4
Môngua *Angola* 16°43S 15°20E **265** F3
Moniac *U.S.A.* 30°31N 82°14W **316** E7
Monifieth *U.K.* 56°30N 2°48W **167** E6
Monistrol-sur-Loire *France* 45°17N 4°11E **175** C8
Monkayo *Phil.* 7°50N 126°5E **233** H6
Monkey Bay *Malawi* 14°7S 35°1E **269** E4
Monkey Mia *Australia* 25°48S 113°43E **279** E1
Monkey River *Belize* 16°22N 88°29W **320** C2
Monkey Town *Trin. & Tob.* 10°12N 61°25W **323** t
Mońki *Poland* 53°23N 22°48E **184** E9
Monkland *Canada* 45°11N 74°52W **313** A10
Monkoto *Dem. Rep. of the Congo* 1°38S 20°35E **264** C4
Monkstown *Ireland* 53°18N 6°10W **120** B3
Monkton *Canada* 43°35N 81°5W **312** C3
Monmouth *Monmouths., U.K.* 51°48N 2°42W **169** F5
Monmouth *Ill., U.S.A.* 40°55N 90°39W **310** D6
Monmouth *Oreg., U.S.A.* 44°51N 123°14W **304** D2
Monmouthshire □ *U.K.* 51°48N 2°54W **169** F5
Monnickendam *Neths.* 52°28N 5°2E **112** A3
Mono *Solomon Is.* 7°20S 155°35E **287** L8
Mono ➜ *Togo* 6°17N 1°51E **263** D5
Mono, Pta. *Nic.* 12°0N 83°30W **320** D3
Mono L. *U.S.A.* 38°1N 119°1W **306** H7
Monolith *U.S.A.* 35°7N 118°22W **307** K8
Monolithos *Greece* 36°7N 27°45E **206** E11
Monon *U.S.A.* 40°52N 86°53W **311** D10
Monona *Iowa, U.S.A.* 43°3N 91°23W **310** A5
Monona *Wis., U.S.A.* 43°4N 89°20W **310** A7
Monongahela *U.S.A.* 40°12N 79°56W **312** F5
Monópoli *Italy* 40°57N 17°18E **201** B10
Monor *Hungary* 47°21N 19°27E **182** C4
Monos I. *Trin. & Tob.* 10°42N 61°44W **323** t
Monóvar *Spain* 38°28N 0°53W **197** G4
Monowai *N.Z.* 45°53S 167°31E **285** F2
Monowai, L. *N.Z.* 45°53S 167°25E **285** F2
Monqoumba *C.A.R.* 3°33N 18°40E **264** B3
Monreal del Campo *Spain* 40°47N 1°20W **196** E3
Monreale *Italy* 38°5N 13°17E **200** D6
Monroe *Ga., U.S.A.* 33°47N 83°43W **316** B6
Monroe *Iowa, U.S.A.* 41°31N 93°6W **310** C3
Monroe *La., U.S.A.* 32°30N 92°7W **314** E8
Monroe *Mich., U.S.A.* 41°55N 83°24W **311** C13
Monroe *N.C., U.S.A.* 34°59N 80°33W **315** D14
Monroe *N.Y., U.S.A.* 41°20N 74°11W **313** E10
Monroe *Ohio, U.S.A.* 39°27N 84°22W **311** E12
Monroe *Utah, U.S.A.* 38°38N 112°7W **304** G7
Monroe *Wash., U.S.A.* 47°51N 121°58W **306** C5
Monroe *Wis., U.S.A.* 42°36N 89°38W **310** B7
Monroe, L. *U.S.A.* 28°50N 81°19W **317** G8
Monroe City *Ind., U.S.A.* 38°37N 87°20W **311** F9
Monroe City *Mo., U.S.A.* 39°39N 91°44W **310** E5
Monroe L. *U.S.A.* 39°1N 86°31W **311** E10
Monroeton *U.S.A.* 41°43N 76°29W **313** E8
Monroeville *Ala., U.S.A.* 31°31N 87°20W **315** F11
Monroeville *Ind., U.S.A.* 40°59N 84°52W **311** D12
Monroeville *Pa., U.S.A.* 40°26N 79°45W **312** F5
Monrovia *Liberia* 6°18N 10°47W **262** D2
Monrovia *Calif., U.S.A.* 34°9N 118°1W **126** B4
Mons *Belgium* 50°27N 3°58E **170** D3
Møns Klint *Denmark* 54°57N 12°33E **163** K6
Monsanto *Portugal* 38°44N 9°12W **126** A1
Monsanto, Parque Florestal de *Portugal* 38°43N 9°11W **126** A1
Monsaraz *Portugal* 38°28N 7°22W **195** G3
Monse *Indonesia* 4°7S 123°15E **231** E6
Monsefú *Peru* 6°52S 79°52W **330** B2
Monségur *France* 44°38N 0°4E **174** D4
Monsélice *Italy* 45°14N 11°45E **199** C8
Mönsterås *Sweden* 57°3N 16°26E **163** G10
Mont Cenis, Col du *France* 45°15N 6°55E **175** C10
Mont-de-Marsan *France* 43°54N 0°31W **174** E3
Mont-Dore *N. Cal.* 22°16S 166°34E **288** d
Mont Fouari ⌂ *Congo* 2°52S 11°32E **264** C2
Mont-Joli *Canada* 48°37N 68°10W **299** C6
Mont-Laurier *Canada* 46°35N 75°30W **298** C4
Mont-Louis *Canada* 49°15N 65°44W **299** C6
Mont Peko △ *Ivory C.* 9°5N 7°15W **262** D3
Mont-roig del Camp *Spain* 41°5N 0°58E **196** D5
Mont-Royal *Canada* 45°30N 73°38W **130** A2
Mont-Royal, Parc *Canada* 45°30N 73°36W **130** A2
Mont-St-Michel, Le *France* 48°40N 1°30W **172** D5
Mont Sangbé △ *Ivory C.* 8°0N 7°10W **262** D3
Mont-Tremblant ⌂ *Canada* 46°30N 74°30W **298** C5
Montabaur *Germany* 50°25N 7°50E **178** E3
Montagnac = Remchi *Algeria* 35°2N 1°26W **261** A4
Montagnac *France* 43°29N 3°28E **174** E7
Montagnana *Italy* 45°14N 11°28E **199** C8
Montagne Blanche *Mauritius* 20°16S 57°39E **272** e
Montagne d'Ambre △ *Madag.* 12°37S 49°8E **272** A2
Montagne de Reims ⌂ *France* 49°8N 4°0E **173** C11
Montagu *S. Africa* 33°45S 20°8E **270** D3
Montagu I. *Antarctica* 58°25S 26°20W **151** B1
Montague *Canada* 46°10N 62°39W **299** C7
Montague, I. *Mexico* 31°45N 114°48W **318** A2
Montague I. *N.S.W., Australia* 36°16S 150°13E **283** D9
Montague I. *Alaska, U.S.A.* 60°0N 147°30W **303** G11
Montague Ra. *Australia* 27°15S 119°30E **279** E2
Montague Sd. *Australia* 14°28S 125°20E **278** B4
Montaigu *France* 46°59N 1°18W **172** F5
Montalbán *Spain* 40°50N 0°45W **196** E4
Montalbano Iónico *Italy* 40°17N 16°34E **201** B9
Montalbo *Spain* 39°53N 2°42W **196** F2
Montalcino *Italy* 43°3N 11°29E **199** E8
Montalegre *Angola* 8°45S 17°4E **265** D3
Montalegre *Portugal* 41°49N 7°47W **194** D3
Montalto *Italy* 38°10N 15°55E **201** D8
Montalto di Castro *Italy* 42°21N 11°37E **199** F8
Montalto Uffugo *Italy* 39°24N 16°9E **201** C9
Montalvo *U.S.A.* 34°15N 119°12W **307** L7
Montamarta *Spain* 41°39N 5°49W **194** D5
Montana *Bulgaria* 43°27N 23°16E **202** C7
Montaña *Peru* 6°0S 73°0W **330** B3
Montana □ *Bulgaria* 43°30N 23°20E **202** C7
Montana □ *U.S.A.* 47°0N 110°0W **304** C9
Montaña Clara, I. *Canary Is.* 29°17N 13°33W **153** e2
Montana de Montjuich *Spain* 41°21N 2°9E **114** A1

Montañas de Malaga ⌂ Spain 36°48N 4°32W **195** J6
Montánchez Spain 39°15N 6°8W **195** F4
Montanhas do Tumucumaque Brazil 2°5N 53°0W **329** C7
Montañita Colombia 1°22N 75°28W **328** C2
Montargil Portugal 39°5N 8°10W **195** F2
Montargis France 47°59N 2°43E **173** E9
Montauban France 44°2N 1°21E **174** D5
Montauk U.S.A. 41°3N 71°57W **313** E13
Montauk Pt. U.S.A. 41°4N 71°51W **313** E13
Montbard France 47°38N 4°20E **173** E11
Montbarrey France 47°1N 5°39E **173** E12
Montbéliard France 47°31N 6°48E **173** E13
Montblanc Spain 41°23N 1°4E **196** D6
Montbrison France 45°36N 4°3E **175** C8
Montcada i Reixac Spain 41°29N 2°12W **114** A2
Montcalm, Pic de France 42°40N 1°25E **174** F5
Montceau-les-Mines France 46°40N 4°23E **173** F11
Montcenis France 46°47N 4°23E **175** B8
Montclair U.S.A. 40°49N 74°12W **313** F10
Montcornet France 49°40N 4°1E **173** C11
Montcuq France 44°21N 1°13E **174** D5
Montdidier France 49°38N 2°35E **173** C9
Monte Albán Mexico 17°2N 96°46W **319** D5
Monte Alegre Brazil 2°0S 54°0W **329** D7
Monte Alegre de Goiás Brazil 13°14S 47°10W **333** D2
Monte Alegre de Minas Brazil 18°52S 48°52W **333** E2
Monte Alegre do Piauí Brazil 9°46S 45°18W **332** C2
Monte Azul Brazil 15°9S 42°53W **333** E3
Monte-Carlo Monaco 43°44N 7°25E **175** E11
Monte Carmelo Brazil 18°43S 47°29W **333** E2
Monte Caseros Argentina 30°10S 57°50W **334** C4
Monte Chingolo Argentina 34°43S 58°22W **117** C2
Monte Comán Argentina 34°40S 67°53W **334** C2
Monte Cristi Dom. Rep. 19°52N 71°39W **321** C5
Monte Cucco ⌂ Italy 43°22N 12°43E **199** E9
Monte Dinero Argentina 52°18S 68°33W **336** D3
Monte Dourado Brazil 0°52S 52°31W **329** D7
Monte Lindo → Paraguay 23°56S 57°12W **334** A4
Monte Palatino Rome, Italy **136** c3
Monte Pascoal △ Brazil 16°51S 39°21W **333** E4
Monte Patria Chile 30°42S 70°58W **334** C1
Monte Quemado Argentina 25°53S 62°41W **334** B3
Monte Redondo Portugal 39°53N 8°50W **194** F2
Monte Rio U.S.A. 38°28N 123°0W **306** G4
Monte San Giovanni Campano Italy 41°38N 13°31E **200** A6
Monte San Giuliano = Érice Italy 38°2N 12°35E **200** D5
Monte San Savino Italy 43°20N 11°43E **199** E8
Monte Sant' Ángelo Italy 41°42N 15°59E **199** G12
Monte Santu, C. di Italy 40°5N 9°44E **200** B2
Monte Sibillini △ Italy 42°55N 13°15E **199** F10
Monte Subasio ⌂ Italy 43°5N 12°40E **199** E9
Monte Vista U.S.A. 37°35N 106°9W **305** H10
Monteagudo Argentina 27°14S 54°8W **335** B5
Monteagudo Bolivia 19°49S 63°59W **331** D5
Montealegre del Castillo Spain 38°48N 1°17W **197** G3
Montebello Qué., Canada 45°40N 74°55W **298** C5
Montebello Guadeloupe 16°10N 61°36W **322** e
Montebello Calif., U.S.A. 34°1N 118°8W **126** B4
Montebello Iónico Italy 37°59N 15°45E **201** E8
Montebello Is. Australia 20°30S 115°45E **278** D2
Montebelluna Italy 45°47N 12°3E **199** C9
Montebourg France 49°30N 1°20W **172** C5
Montecarlo Argentina 26°34S 54°47W **335** B5
Montecastrilli Italy 42°39N 12°29E **199** F9
Montecatini Terme Italy 43°53N 10°46E **198** E7
Montecito U.S.A. 34°26N 119°40W **307** L7
Montecristi Ecuador 1°0S 80°40W **328** D1
Montecristo Italy 42°20N 10°19E **198** F7
Montefalco Italy 42°54N 12°39E **199** F9
Montefiascone Italy 42°32N 12°2E **199** F9
Montefrío Spain 37°20N 4°0W **195** H7
Montegiórgio Italy 43°6N 13°33E **199** E10
Montego B. Jamaica 18°28N 77°56W **320** a
Montego Bay Jamaica 18°28N 77°55W **320** a
Montehermoso Spain 40°5N 6°21W **194** E4
Monteiro Brazil 7°48S 37°2W **332** C4
Montejicar Spain 37°33N 3°30W **195** H7
Montelbaanstoren Amsterdam, Neths. **112** b3
Monteleone di Calabria = Vibo Valéntia Italy 38°40N 16°6E **201** D9
Montelíbano Colombia 8°5N 75°29W **328** B2
Montélimar France 44°33N 4°45E **175** D8
Montella Italy 40°51N 15°1E **201** B8
Montellano Spain 36°59N 5°29W **195** J5
Montello U.S.A. 43°48N 89°20W **308** D9
Montemayor, Meseta de Argentina 44°20S 66°10W **336** B3
Montemor Portugal 38°49N 9°12W **126** A1
Montemor-o-Novo Portugal 38°40N 8°12W **195** G2
Montemor-o-Velho Portugal 40°11N 8°40W **194** E2
Montemorelos Mexico 25°12N 99°49W **319** B5
Montendre France 45°16N 0°26W **174** C3
Montenegro Brazil 29°39S 51°29W **335** B5
Montenegro ■ Europe 42°40N 19°20E **202** D3
Montenero di Bisáccia Italy 41°57N 14°47E **199** G11
Montepuez Mozam. 13°8S 38°59E **269** E4
Montepuez → Mozam. 12°32S 40°27E **269** E5
Montepulciano Italy 43°5N 11°47E **199** E8
Montereale Italy 42°31N 13°15E **199** F10
Montereau-Faut-Yonne France 48°22N 2°57E **173** D9
Monterey Calif., U.S.A. 36°37N 121°55W **306** J5
Monterey Ind., U.S.A. 41°11N 86°30W **311** C10
Monterey B. U.S.A. 36°45N 122°0W **306** J5
Monterey Hills U.S.A. 34°6N 118°10W **126** B3
Monterey Park U.S.A. 34°3N 118°7W **126** B4
Montería Colombia 8°46N 75°53W **328** B2
Montero Bolivia 17°20S 63°15W **331** D5
Monteros Argentina 27°11S 65°30W **334** B2
Monterotondo Italy 42°3N 12°37E **199** F9
Monterrey Mexico 25°40N 100°19W **318** B4
Montes Altos Brazil 5°50S 47°4W **332** C2
Montes Azules ⌂ Mexico 16°21N 91°3W **319** D6
Montes Claros Brazil 16°30S 43°50W **333** E3
Montesano U.S.A. 46°59N 123°36W **306** D3
Montesano sulla Marcellana Italy 40°16N 15°42E **201** B8
Montesárchio Italy 41°4N 14°38E **201** A7
Montescaglioso Italy 40°33N 16°40E **201** B9
Montesilvano Italy 42°29N 14°8E **199** F11
Montesinho ⌂ Portugal 41°54N 6°52W **194** D4
Montespaccato Italy 41°54N 12°23E **136** B1
Montesson France 48°54N 2°8E **134** A1
Montevarchi Italy 43°31N 11°34E **199** E8
Monteverde Nuovo Italy 41°52N 12°26E **136** B1
Montevideo Uruguay 34°50S 56°11W **335** C4
Montevideo Minn., U.S.A. 44°57N 95°43W **308** C6
Montezuma Ga., U.S.A. 32°18N 84°2W **316** C5
Montezuma Ind., U.S.A. 39°48N 87°22W **311** E9
Montezuma Iowa, U.S.A. 41°35N 92°32W **310** C4
Montezuma Castle ⌂ U.S.A. 34°39N 111°45W **305** J8
Montfaucon France 47°6N 1°7W **172** E5
Montfaucon-d'Argonne France 49°16N 5°8E **173** C12
Montfaucon-en-Velay France 45°11N 4°20E **175** C8
Montfermeil France 48°54N 2°33E **134** A4
Montfort-le-Gesnois France 48°3N 0°25E **172** D7
Montfort-sur-Meu France 48°9N 1°58W **172** D5
Montfragüe ⌂ Spain 39°48N 5°52W **194** F5
Montgenèvre France 44°56N 6°43E **175** D10
Montgomery = Sahiwal Pakistan 30°45N 73°8E **242** D5
Montgomery Powys, U.K. 52°34N 3°8W **169** E4
Montgomery Ala., U.S.A. 32°23N 86°19W **316** C3
Montgomery Ill., U.S.A. 41°44N 88°21W **311** C8
Montgomery Pa., U.S.A. 41°10N 76°53W **312** E8
Montgomery W. Va., U.S.A. 38°11N 81°19W **309** F13
Montgomery City U.S.A. 38°59N 91°30W **310** F5
Montguyon France 45°12N 0°12W **174** C3
Monthermé France 49°52N 4°42E **173** C11
Monthey Switz. 46°15N 6°56E **179** J2
Monthois France 49°19N 4°43E **173** C11
Monti Italy 40°49N 9°19E **200** B2
Monti Lucrétili ⌂ Italy 42°5N 12°50E **199** F9
Monti Picentini ⌂ Italy 40°45N 15°2E **201** B8
Monti Simbruini ⌂ Italy 41°55N 13°13E **199** G10
Monticelli d'Ongina Italy 45°5N 9°56E **198** C6
Monticello Ark., U.S.A. 33°38N 91°47W **314** E9
Monticello Fla., U.S.A. 30°33N 83°52W **316** E6
Monticello Ga., U.S.A. 33°18N 83°40W **316** B6
Monticello Ill., U.S.A. 40°1N 88°34W **311** D8
Monticello Ind., U.S.A. 40°45N 86°46W **311** D10
Monticello Iowa, U.S.A. 42°15N 91°12W **310** B5
Monticello Ky., U.S.A. 36°50N 84°51W **309** G11
Monticello Minn., U.S.A. 45°18N 93°48W **308** C7
Monticello Miss., U.S.A. 31°33N 90°7W **315** F9
Monticello Mo., U.S.A. 40°7N 91°43W **310** D5
Monticello N.Y., U.S.A. 41°39N 74°42W **313** E10
Monticello Utah, U.S.A. 37°52N 109°21W **305** H9
Montichiari Italy 45°25N 10°23E **198** C7
Montier-en-Der France 48°30N 4°45E **173** D11
Montignac France 45°4N 1°10E **174** C5
Montigny-le-Bretonneux France 48°46N 2°1E **134** B1
Montigny-les-Metz France 49°7N 6°10E **173** C13
Montigny-sur-Aube France 47°57N 4°45E **173** E11
Montijo Portugal 38°41N 8°54W **195** G2
Montijo Spain 38°52N 6°39W **195** G4
Montilla Spain 37°36N 4°40W **195** H6
Montivilliers France 49°33N 0°12E **172** C7
Montjay-la-Tour France 48°54N 2°40E **134** A4
Montjuïc Spain 41°22N 2°10E **114** A2
Montjuïc, Parc de Barcelona, Spain **114** c1
Montluçon France 46°22N 2°36E **173** F9
Montmagny Canada 46°58N 70°34W **299** C5
Montmarault France 46°19N 2°57E **173** F9
Montmartre Canada 50°14N 103°27W **297** C8
Montmédy France 49°30N 5°20E **173** C12
Montmélian France 45°30N 6°4E **175** C10
Montmirail France 48°51N 3°30E **173** D10
Montmoreau-St-Cybard France 45°23N 0°8E **174** C4
Montmorillon France 46°26N 0°50E **174** B4
Montmort-Lucy France 48°55N 3°49E **173** D10
Monto Australia 24°52S 151°6E **280** C5
Montoire-sur-le-Loir France 47°45N 0°52E **172** E7
Montongbuwoh Indonesia 8°33S 116°4E **231** K19
Montório al Vomano Italy 42°35N 13°38E **199** F10
Montoro Spain 38°1N 4°27W **195** G6
Montour Falls U.S.A. 42°21N 76°51W **312** D8
Montoursville U.S.A. 41°15N 76°55W **312** E8
Montparnasse, Gare France 48°50N 2°19E **134** A2
Montpelier Idaho, U.S.A. 42°19N 111°18W **304** E8
Montpelier Ind., U.S.A. 40°33N 85°17W **311** D11
Montpelier Ohio, U.S.A. 41°35N 84°37W **311** C12
Montpelier Vt., U.S.A. 44°16N 72°35W **313** B12
Montpellier France 43°37N 3°52E **174** E7
Montpezat-de-Quercy France 44°15N 1°30E **174** D5
Montpon-Ménestérol France 45°0N 0°11E **174** D4
Montréal Qué., Canada 45°30N 73°33W **130** A2
Montréal Aude, France 43°13N 2°8E **174** E6
Montréal Gers, France 43°56N 0°11E **174** E4
Montreal → Canada 47°14N 84°39W **298** C3
Montréal, Î. de Canada 45°30N 73°40W **130** A2
Montréal, Univ. de Canada 45°29N 73°37W **130** B2
Montréal Est Canada 45°37N 73°31W **130** A2
Montreal L. Canada 54°20N 105°45W **297** C7
Montreal Lake Canada 54°3N 105°46W **297** C7
Montréal-Nord Canada 45°36N 73°36W **130** A2
Montréal-Ouest Canada 45°27N 73°39W **130** B1
Montréal Trudeau Int. ✕ (YUL) Canada 45°28N 73°44W **130** B1
Montredon-Labessonnié France 43°45N 2°18E **174** E6
Montrésor France 47°10N 1°10E **172** E8
Montret France 46°40N 5°7E **173** F12
Montreuil Pas-de-Calais, France 50°27N 1°45E **173** B8
Montreuil Seine-St-Denis, France 48°51N 2°27E **134** A3
Montreuil-Bellay France 47°8N 0°9W **172** E6
Montreux Switz. 46°26N 6°55E **179** J2
Montrevel-en-Bresse France 46°21N 5°8E **173** F12
Montrichard France 47°20N 1°10E **172** E8
Montrose Angus, U.K. 56°44N 2°27W **167** E6
Montrose Colo., U.S.A. 38°29N 107°53W **304** G10
Montrose Pa., U.S.A. 41°50N 75°53W **313** E9
Montrose, L. U.S.A. 38°18N 93°50W **310** F3
Montrouge France 48°48N 2°18E **134** B2
Monts, Pte. des Canada 49°20N 67°12W **299** C6
Montsalvy France 44°41N 2°30E **174** D6
Montsant, Serra de Spain 41°17N 1°0E **196** D6
Montsauche-les-Settons France 47°13N 4°2E **173** E11
Montsec, Serra del Spain 42°0N 0°45E **196** C5
Montseny ⌂ Spain 41°43N 2°22E **196** D7
Montserrat B. Aires, Argentina 34°37S 58°24W **117** B2
Montserrat Spain 41°36N 1°49E **196** D6
Montserrat ☑ W. Indies 16°40N 62°10W **323** p
Montserrat Hills Trin. & Tob. 10°23N 61°21W **323** t
Montuenga Spain 41°3N 4°38W **194** D6
Montuiri Spain 39°34N 2°59E **206** B3
Montvert-les-Bas Réunion 21°19S 55°32E **272** f
Monveda Dem. Rep. of the Congo 2°52N 21°30E **264** B4
Monyo Burma 17°59N 95°30E **241** G5
Monywa Burma 22°7N 95°11E **241** D5
Monza Italy 45°35N 9°16E **129** A2
Monze Zambia 16°17S 27°29E **269** F2
Monze, C. Pakistan 24°47N 66°37E **242** G2
Monzón Spain 41°52N 0°10E **196** D5
Monzoro Italy 45°27N 9°2E **129** B1
Moóca Brazil 23°33S 46°35W **137** B2
Moodyville = North Vancouver Canada 49°19N 123°4W **306** A3
Mooers U.S.A. 44°58N 73°35W **313** B11
Mooi → S. Africa 28°45S 30°34E **271** C5
Mooi River S. Africa 29°13S 29°50E **271** C4
Mo'oka Japan 36°26N 140°1E **223** A12
Mookgophong = Mookgopong S. Africa 24°31S 28°44E **271** B4
Mookgopong S. Africa 24°31S 28°44E **271** B4
Moomba Australia 28°6S 140°12E **281** A3
Moonachie U.S.A. 40°50N 74°2W **132** B1
Moonah → Australia 22°3S 138°33E **280** C2
Moonda, L. Australia 25°52S 140°25E **280** D3
Moonee Ponds Australia 37°45S 144°53E **128** A1
Moonee Valley Racecourse Australia 37°45S 144°55E **128** A1
Moonie Australia 27°46S 150°20E **281** D5
Moonie → Australia 29°19S 148°43E **281** D4
Moonta Australia 34°6S 137°32E **282** C2
Moora Australia 30°37S 115°58E **279** F2
Moorcroft U.S.A. 44°16N 104°57W **304** D11
Moore → Australia 31°22S 115°30E **279** F2
Moore, L. Australia 29°50S 117°35E **279** E2
Moore Falls Canada 44°48N 78°48W **312** B6
Moore Haven U.S.A. 26°50N 81°6W **317** J8
Moore Park Australia 24°43S 152°17E **280** C5
Moore Res. U.S.A. 44°20N 71°53W **313** B13
Moore River △ Australia 31°7S 115°39E **279** F2
Moorea French Polynesia 17°30S 149°50W **289** e
Moorefield U.S.A. 39°4N 78°58W **309** F14
Mooresville U.S.A. 39°37N 86°22W **311** E10
Moorfoot Hills U.K. 55°44N 3°8W **167** F5
Moorhead U.S.A. 46°53N 96°45W **308** B5
Moorland U.S.A. 42°26N 94°18W **310** B2
Moormerland Germany 53°20N 7°20E **178** B3
Moornanyah L. Australia 33°15S 143°42E **282** B5
Mooroopna Australia 36°25S 145°22E **283** D6
Moorpark U.S.A. 34°17N 118°53W **307** L8
Moorreesburg S. Africa 33°6S 18°38E **270** D2
Moorrinya △ Australia 21°42S 144°58E **280** C3
Moosach Germany 48°10N 11°30E **131** A2
Moosburg Germany 48°27N 11°56E **179** G7
Moose → Ont., Canada 51°20N 80°25W **298** B3
Moose → N.Y., U.S.A. 43°38N 75°24W **313** C9
Moose Creek Canada 45°15N 74°58W **313** A10
Moose Factory Canada 51°16N 80°32W **298** B3
Moose Jaw Canada 50°24N 105°30W **297** C7
Moose Jaw → Canada 50°34N 105°18W **297** C7
Moose Lake Man., Canada 53°46N 100°8W **297** C8
Moose Lake Minn., U.S.A. 46°27N 92°46W **308** B7
Moose Mountain ⌂ Canada 49°48N 102°25W **297** D8
Moose Pass U.S.A. 60°29N 149°22W **303** F10
Moosehead L. U.S.A. 45°38N 69°40W **309** C19
Mooselookmeguntic L. U.S.A. 44°55N 70°49W **313** B14
Moosilauke, Mt. U.S.A. 44°3N 71°40W **313** B13
Moosomin Canada 50°9N 101°40W **297** C8
Moosonee Canada 51°17N 80°39W **298** B3
Moosup U.S.A. 41°43N 71°53W **313** E13
Mootwingee △ Australia 31°10S 142°30E **282** A5
Mopane S. Africa 22°37S 29°52E **271** B4
Mopeia Velha Mozam. 17°30S 35°40E **269** F4
Mopipi Botswana 21°6S 24°55E **270** B3
Mopoi C.A.R. 5°6N 26°54E **268** A2
Mopti Mali 14°30N 4°0W **262** C4
Mopti □ Mali 14°40N 4°0W **262** C4
Moqatta Sudan 14°38N 35°50E **257** E4
Moqor Afghan. 32°50N 67°42E **242** C2
Moquegua Peru 17°15S 70°46W **330** D3
Moquegua □ Peru 16°50S 70°55W **330** D3
Mór Hungary 47°25N 18°12E **182** C3
Mora Cameroon 11°2N 14°7E **259** F2
Mora Maharashtra, India 18°54N 72°55E **130** B2
Móra Portugal 38°55N 8°10W **195** G2
Mora Spain 39°41N 3°46W **195** F7
Mora Sweden 61°2N 14°38E **162** C8
Mora Minn., U.S.A. 45°53N 93°18W **308** C7
Mora N. Mex., U.S.A. 35°58N 105°20W **305** J11
Mora de Rubielos Spain 40°15N 0°45W **196** E4
Móra d'Ebre Spain 41°6N 0°38E **196** D5
Móra la Nova Spain 41°7N 0°39E **196** D5
Moraća → Montenegro 42°20N 19°9E **202** D3
Morada Nova Brazil 5°7S 38°23W **332** C4
Morada Nova de Minas Brazil 18°37S 45°22W **333** E2
Moradabad India 28°50N 78°50E **243** E8
Morafenobe Madag. 17°50S 44°53E **272** B1
Morąg Poland 53°55N 19°56E **184** E6
Moral de Calatrava Spain 38°51N 3°33W **195** G7
Moraleda, Canal Chile 44°30S 73°30W **336** B2
Moraleja Spain 40°6N 6°43W **194** E4
Morales Bolívar, Colombia 8°17N 73°52W **328** B3
Morales Cauca, Colombia 2°45N 76°38W **328** C2
Moramanga Madag. 18°56S 48°12E **272** B2
Moran Kans., U.S.A. 37°55N 95°10W **308** G6
Moran Wyo., U.S.A. 43°50N 110°31W **304** E8
Moranbah Australia 22°1S 148°6E **280** C4
Morané French Polynesia 23°10S 137°7W **289** f
Morang = Biratnagar Nepal 26°27N 87°17E **243** F12
Moranhat India 27°10N 94°50E **241** B5
Morano Cálabro Italy 39°50N 16°8E **201** C9
Morant Bay Jamaica 17°53N 76°25W **320** a
Morant Cays Jamaica 17°22N 76°0W **320** C4
Morant Pt. Jamaica 17°55N 76°12W **320** a
Morar India 26°14N 78°14E **242** F8
Morar, L. U.K. 56°57N 5°40W **167** E3
Moratalaz Spain 40°24N 3°39W **127** B2
Moratalla Spain 38°14N 1°49W **197** G3
Moratuwa Sri Lanka 6°45N 79°55E **245** L4
Morava → Slovak Rep. 48°10N 16°59E **181** C9
Moravia Iowa, U.S.A. 40°53N 92°49W **310** D4
Moravia N.Y., U.S.A. 42°43N 76°25W **313** D8
Moravian Hts. = Českomoravská Vrchovina Czech Rep. 49°30N 15°40E **180** B8
Moravica → Serbia 43°52N 20°8E **202** C4
Moravița Romania 45°17N 21°14E **182** E6
Moravská Třebová Czech Rep. 49°45N 16°40E **181** B9
Moravské Budějovice Czech Rep. 49°4N 15°49E **180** B8
Morawa Australia 29°13S 116°0E **279** E2
Morawhanna Guyana 8°30N 59°40W **329** B6
Moray □ U.K. 57°31N 3°18W **167** D5
Moray Firth U.K. 57°40N 3°52W **167** D5
Morbach Germany 49°48N 7°6E **179** F3
Morbegno Italy 46°8N 9°34E **198** B6
Morbi India 22°50N 70°42E **242** H4
Morbihan □ France 47°55N 2°50W **172** E4
Mörby Sweden 59°23N 18°3E **139** A2
Mörbylånga Sweden 56°32N 16°22E **163** H10
Morcenx France 44°3N 0°55W **174** D3
Morcone Italy 41°20N 14°40E **201** A7
Mordelles France 48°5N 1°52W **172** D5
Morden Man., Canada 49°15N 98°10W **297** D9
Morden London, U.K. 51°24N 0°13W **125** B2
Mordoğan Turkey 38°30N 26°37E **205** C8
Mordovian Republic = Mordvinia □ Russia 54°20N 44°30E **190** C7
Mordovo Russia 52°6N 40°50E **190** D5
Mordvinia □ Russia 54°20N 44°30E **190** C7
Mordy Poland 52°13N 22°31E **185** F9
Møre og Romsdal □ Norway 62°30N 8°0E **164** B4
Moreau → U.S.A. 45°18N 100°43W **308** C3
Morebeng S. Africa 23°30S 29°55E **271** B4
Morecambe U.K. 54°5N 2°52W **168** C5
Morecambe B. U.K. 54°7N 3°0W **168** C5
Moree Australia 29°28S 149°54E **281** D4
Morée → France 48°57N 2°25E **134** A3
Morehead Papua N. G. 8°41S 141°41E **286** E1
Morehead Ky., U.S.A. 38°11N 83°26W **311** F13
Morehead City U.S.A. 34°43N 76°43W **315** D16
Morel → India 26°13N 76°36E **242** F7
Moreland U.S.A. 33°17N 84°46W **316** B5
Morelia Mexico 19°42N 101°7W **318** D4
Morella Queens., Australia 23°0S 143°52E **280** C3
Morella Spain 40°35N 0°5W **196** E4
Morelos Mexico 26°42N 107°40W **318** B3
Morelos □ Mexico 18°45N 99°0W **319** D5
Moremi ⌂ Botswana 19°18S 23°10E **270** A3
Morena India 26°30N 78°4E **242** F8
Morena, Sierra Spain 38°20N 4°0W **195** G7
Morenci U.S.A. 41°43N 84°13W **311** C12
Moreni Romania 44°59N 25°36E **183** F10
Moreno Bolivia 11°9S 66°15W **330** C4
Moreno Valley U.S.A. 33°56N 117°14W **307** M10
Moreru → Brazil 10°10S 59°15W **331** C6
Moresby I. Canada 52°30N 131°40W **296** C2
Morestel France 45°40N 5°28E **175** C9
Moreton I. Australia 27°10S 153°25E **281** D5
Moreton Island △ Australia 27°2S 153°24E **281** D5
Moreuil France 49°46N 2°30E **173** C9
Morez France 46°31N 6°2E **173** F13
Morgan S. Austral., Australia 34°2S 139°35E **282** C3
Morgan Ga., U.S.A. 31°32N 84°36W **316** D5
Morgan Utah, U.S.A. 41°2N 111°41W **304** F8
Morgan City U.S.A. 29°42N 91°12W **314** G9
Morgan Hill U.S.A. 37°8N 121°39W **306** H5
Morgan Park U.S.A. 41°41N 87°38W **119** C3
Morganfield U.S.A. 37°41N 87°55W **308** G10
Morganton U.S.A. 35°45N 81°41W **315** D14
Morgantown Ind., U.S.A. 39°22N 86°16W **311** E10
Morgantown W. Va., U.S.A. 39°38N 79°57W **309** F14
Morgenzon S. Africa 26°45S 29°36E **271** C4
Morges Switz. 46°31N 6°29E **179** J2
Morghak Iran 29°7N 57°54E **247** D8
Morgongåva Sweden 59°57N 16°58E **162** E10
Morhange France 48°55N 6°38E **173** D13
Morhar → India 25°29N 85°11E **243** G11
Mori China 43°49N 90°11E **217** D12
Mori Italy 45°51N 10°59E **198** C7
Mori Japan 42°6N 140°35E **220** C10
Moriah Trin. & Tob. 11°15N 60°43W **323** s
Moriarty U.S.A. 34°59N 106°3W **305** J10
Moribaya Guinea 9°53N 9°32W **262** D3
Morice L. Canada 53°50N 127°40W **296** C3
Morichal Largo → Venezuela 9°27N 62°25W **329** B5
Morichal Viejo Colombia 2°13N 70°2W **328** C3
Moriguchi Japan 34°43N 135°34E **133** A2
Moriki Nigeria 12°52N 6°30E **263** C6
Morinville Canada 53°49N 113°41W **296** C6
Morioka Japan 39°45N 141°8E **220** E10
Moris Mexico 28°10N 108°32W **318** B3
Morisset Australia 33°6S 151°30E **283** B9
Morivione Italy 45°26N 9°12E **129** B2
Moriyama Japan 35°4N 135°59E **223** B7
Morlaàs France 43°21N 0°18W **174** E3
Morlaix France 48°36N 3°52W **172** D3
Mörlunda Sweden 57°19N 15°52E **163** G9
Mormanno Italy 39°53N 15°59E **201** C8
Mormant France 48°37N 2°52E **173** D9
Morne-à-l'Eau Guadeloupe 16°20N 61°27W **322** e
Morne des Esses Martinique 14°44N 61°1W **322** j
Morne Diablotins Dominica 15°30N 61°24W **323** k
Morne Fendue Grenada 12°12N 61°38W **323** q
Morne Raquette Dominica 15°27N 61°27W **323** k
Morne Trois Pitons △ Dominica 15°22N 61°20W **323** k
Morningside Gauteng, S. Africa 26°4S 28°3E **123** A2
Morningside Edinburgh, U.K. 55°56N 3°12W **121** B2
Morningside Md., U.S.A. 38°49N 76°53W **143** C4
Morningside Park Ont., Canada 43°47N 79°12W **141** A3
Morningside Park Fla., U.S.A. 28°26N 81°24W **133** B2
Mornington Australia 38°15S 145°5E **283** E6
Mornington, I. Chile 49°50S 75°30W **336** C1
Mornington I. Australia 16°30S 139°30E **280** B2
Mornington Peninsula △ Australia 38°28S 144°53E **283** E6
Mornos → Greece 38°25N 21°50E **204** C3
Moro Pakistan 26°40N 68°0E **242** F2
Moro Sudan 10°50N 30°9E **257** E3
Moro → Pakistan 29°42N 67°22E **242** E2
Moro G. Phil. 6°30N 123°0E **233** H4
Morobe Papua N. G. 7°49S 147°38E **286** D4
Morobe □ Papua N. G. 7°0S 147°0E **286** D4
Morocco U.S.A. 40°57N 87°27W **311** D9
Morocco ■ N. Afr. 32°0N 5°50W **260** B3
Morococha Peru 11°40S 76°5W **330** C2
Morogoro Tanzania 6°50S 37°40E **268** D4
Morogoro □ Tanzania 8°0S 37°0E **268** D4
Moroleón Mexico 20°8N 101°12W **318** C4
Morombe Madag. 21°45S 43°22E **272** C1
Moron = Morong Phil. 14°41N 120°16E **232** D3
Morón Argentina 34°39S 58°37W **334** C4
Morón Cuba 22°8N 78°39W **320** B4
Mörön Mongolia 49°38N 100°9E **218** B4
Morón de Almazán Spain 41°29N 2°27W **196** D2
Morón de la Frontera Spain 37°6N 5°28W **195** H5
Morona → Peru 4°40S 77°10W **328** D2
Morona-Santiago □ Ecuador 2°30S 78°0W **328** D2
Morondava Madag. 20°17S 44°17E **272** C1
Morondo Ivory C. 8°57N 6°47W **262** D3
Morong Phil. 14°41N 120°16E **232** D3
Morongo Valley U.S.A. 34°3N 116°37W **307** L10
Moroni Comoros Is. 11°40S 43°16E **272** a
Moroni Utah, U.S.A. 39°32N 111°35W **304** G8
Moroni Iconi ✕ (YVA) Comoros Is. 11°32S 43°15E **272** a
Moronou Ivory C. 6°16N 4°59W **262** D4
Morotai Indonesia 2°10N 128°30E **231** D7
Moroto Uganda 2°28N 34°42E **268** B3
Moroto, Mt. Uganda 2°30N 34°43E **268** B3
Morozov Bulgaria 42°30N 25°10E **203** D9
Morozovsk Russia 48°25N 41°50E **191** F5
Morpeth Ont., Canada 42°23N 81°50W **312** D3
Morpeth Northumberland, U.K. 55°10N 1°41W **168** B6
Morphou Cyprus 35°12N 32°59E **207** E8
Morphou Bay Cyprus 35°15N 32°50E **207** E8
Morrelganj Bangla. 22°28N 89°51E **241** D2
Morrilton U.S.A. 35°9N 92°44W **314** D8
Morrinhos Ceará, Brazil 3°14S 40°7W **332** B3
Morrinhos Minas Gerais, Brazil 17°45S 49°10W **333** E2
Morrinsville N.Z. 37°40S 175°32E **284** D4
Morris Man., Canada 49°25N 97°22W **297** D9
Morris Ill., U.S.A. 41°22N 88°26W **311** C8
Morris Minn., U.S.A. 45°35N 95°55W **308** C6
Morris N.Y., U.S.A. 42°33N 75°15W **313** D9
Morris Pa., U.S.A. 41°35N 77°17W **312** E7
Morris, Mt. Australia 26°9S 131°4E **279** E5
Morris Jesup, Kap Greenland 83°40N 34°0W **154** A7
Morrisburg Canada 44°55N 75°7W **313** B9
Morrison U.S.A. 41°49N 89°58W **310** C7
Morrisonville U.S.A. 39°25N 89°27W **310** E7
Morristown Ariz., U.S.A. 33°51N 112°37W **305** K7
Morristown Ind., U.S.A. 39°40N 85°42W **311** E11
Morristown N.J., U.S.A. 40°48N 74°29W **313** F10
Morristown N.Y., U.S.A. 44°35N 75°39W **313** B9
Morristown Tenn., U.S.A. 36°13N 83°18W **315** C13
Morrisville N.Y., U.S.A. 42°53N 75°35W **313** D9
Morrisville Pa., U.S.A. 40°13N 74°47W **313** F10
Morrisville Vt., U.S.A. 44°34N 72°36W **313** B12
Morro, Pta. Chile 27°6S 71°0W **334** B1
Morro Bay U.S.A. 35°22N 120°51W **306** K6
Morro Chico Chile 52°2S 71°26W **336** D2
Morro del Jable Canary Is. 28°3N 14°23W **153** e2
Morro do Chapéu Brazil 11°33S 41°9W **333** D3
Morro Grande = Barão de Cocais Brazil 19°56S 43°28W **333** E3
Morro Jable, Pta. de Canary Is. 28°2N 14°20W **153** e2
Morro Solar, Cerro Peru 12°11S 77°1W **124** C2
Morrocoy ⌂ Venezuela 10°48N 68°13W **328** A4
Morros Brazil 2°52S 44°3W **332** B3
Morrosquillo, G. de Colombia 9°35N 75°40W **320** E4
Morrow U.S.A. 39°21N 84°8W **311** E12
Mörrum Sweden 56°12N 14°45E **163** H8
Morrumbene Mozam. 23°31S 35°16E **271** B6
Mörrumsån → Sweden 56°10N 14°45E **163** H8
Mors Denmark 56°50N 8°45E **163** H2
Morshansk Russia 53°28N 41°50E **190** D5
Morsi India 21°21N 78°0E **244** D4
Mörsil Sweden 63°19N 13°40E **162** A7
Mortagne → France 48°33N 6°27E **173** D13
Mortagne-au-Perche France 48°31N 0°33E **172** D7
Mortagne-sur-Gironde France 45°28N 0°47W **174** C3
Mortagne-sur-Sèvre France 47°0N 0°59W **172** F6
Mortain France 48°40N 0°57W **172** D6
Mortara Italy 45°15N 8°44E **198** C5
Morteau France 47°3N 6°35E **173** E13
Morteros Argentina 30°50S 62°0W **334** C3
Mortes, R. das → Brazil 11°45S 50°44W **333** D1
Mortlach Canada 50°27N 106°4W **297** C7
Mortlake N.S.W., Australia 33°50S 151°6E **139** B1
Mortlake Vic., Australia 38°5S 142°50E **282** E5
Mortlake London, U.K. 51°27N 0°15W **125** B2
Morton Ill., U.S.A. 40°37N 89°28W **310** D7
Morton Tex., U.S.A. 33°44N 102°46W **314** E3
Morton Wash., U.S.A. 46°34N 122°17W **306** D4
Morton △ Australia 35°0S 150°12E **283** C9
Morton Grove U.S.A. 42°2N 87°46W **119** A2
Moruga Trin. & Tob. 10°4N 61°16W **323** t
Moruga → Trin. & Tob. 10°5N 61°16W **323** t
Morumbi Brazil 23°35S 46°42W **137** B1
Morundah Australia 34°57S 146°19E **283** C7
Morung Sudan 10°32N 31°3E **266** B3
Moruya Australia 35°58S 150°3E **283** C9
Morvan France 47°5N 4°3E **173** E11
Morvan ⌂ France 47°12N 4°3E **173** E11
Morvant Trin. & Tob. 10°40N 61°29W **323** t
Morven Queens., Australia 26°22S 147°5E **281** D4
Morven N.Z. 44°50S 171°6E **285** E6
Morven Ga., U.S.A. 30°57N 83°30W **316** E6
Morvern U.K. 56°38N 5°44W **167** E3
Morwell Australia 38°10S 146°22E **283** E7
Morwell △ Australia 38°14S 146°23E **283** E7
Moryń Poland 52°51N 14°22E **185** F1
Morzhovets, Ostrov Russia 66°44N 42°35E **186** A7
Morzine France 46°11N 6°42E **173** F13
Mosakahiken = Moose Lake Canada 53°46N 100°8W **297** C8
Mosalsk Russia 54°30N 34°55E **188** E8
Mosbach Germany 49°21N 9°9E **179** F5
Mosby Norway 58°12N 7°55E **164** F4
Moscavide Portugal 38°47N 9°6W **126** A2
Mošćenice Croatia 45°17N 14°16E **199** C11
Moschato Greece 37°55N 23°40E **112** B2
Mosciano Sant' Ángelo Italy 42°42N 13°52E **199** F10
Moscone Convention Center San Francisco, U.S.A. **136** c2
Moscos Is. Burma 14°0N 97°30E **236** F1
Moscow = Moskva Russia 55°45N 37°37E **129** B3
Moscow Idaho, U.S.A. 46°44N 117°0W **304** C5
Moscow Mich., U.S.A. 42°3N 84°30W **311** B12
Moscow Pa., U.S.A. 41°20N 75°31W **313** E9
Moscow Mills U.S.A. 38°57N 90°55W **310** F6
Mosel → Europe 50°22N 7°36E **173** B14
Moselle = Mosel → Europe 50°22N 7°36E **173** B14
Moselle □ France 48°59N 6°33E **173** D13
Moses Lake U.S.A. 47°8N 119°17W **304** C4
Mosgiel N.Z. 45°53S 170°21E **285** F5
Moshaweng → S. Africa 26°35S 22°50E **270** C3
Moshchnyy, Ostrov Russia 60°1N 27°50E **188** B4
Moshi Tanzania 3°22S 37°18E **268** C4
Moshi → Nigeria 9°18N 4°38E **263** D5
Moshupa Botswana 24°46S 25°29E **270** B4
Mosina Poland 52°15N 16°50E **185** F3
Mosite Dem. Rep. of the Congo 0°53N 23°40E **264** B4
Mosjøen Norway 65°51N 13°12E **160** D15
Moskenesøya Norway 67°58N 13°0E **160** C15
Moskenstraumen Norway 67°47N 12°45E **160** C15
Moskog Norway 61°26N 6°0E **164** C2
Moskva Russia 55°45N 37°37E **129** B3
Moskva □ Russia 56°20N 37°20E **188** D9
Moskva → Russia 55°5N 38°51E **188** E10
Moskvitsy Russia 55°42N 37°25E **129** B2
Moslavačka Gora Croatia 45°40N 16°37E **199** C13
Mosman Australia 33°49S 151°15E **139** B2
Moso Vanuatu 17°30S 168°15E **287** G6
Mosomane Botswana 24°2S 26°19E **270** B4
Mosonmagyaróvár Hungary 47°52N 17°18E **182** C2
Mošorin Serbia 45°19N 20°4E **182** E5
Mospino Ukraine 47°52N 38°0E **189** J9
Mosqueiro Brazil 1°10S 48°20W **332** B2
Mosquera Colombia 2°35N 78°24W **328** C2
Mosquero U.S.A. 35°47N 103°58W **305** J12
Mosqueruela Spain 40°21N 0°27W **196** E4
Mosquitia Honduras 15°20N 84°10W **320** C3
Mosquito Coast = Mosquitia Honduras 15°20N 84°10W **320** C3
Mosquito Creek L. U.S.A. 41°18N 80°46W **312** E4
Mosquito L. Canada 62°35N 103°20W **297** A8
Mosquitos, G. de los Panama 9°15N 81°10W **320** E3
Moss Norway 59°27N 10°40E **164** E7
Moss Vale Australia 34°32S 150°25E **283** C9
Mossaka Congo 1°15S 16°45E **264** C3
Mossâmedes Brazil 16°7S 50°11W **333** E1
Mossbank Canada 49°56N 105°56W **297** D7
Mossburn N.Z. 45°41S 168°15E **285** F3
Mosselbaai S. Africa 34°11S 22°8E **270** D3
Mossendjo Congo 2°55S 12°42E **264** C2
Mossfellsbær Iceland 64°11N 21°45W **155** C5
Mossgiel Australia 33°15S 144°5E **282** B6
Mössingen Germany 48°24N 9°4E **179** G5
Mossman Australia 16°21S 145°15E **280** B4
Mossoró Brazil 5°10S 37°15W **332** C4
Mossuril Mozam. 14°58S 40°42E **269** E5
Mossy Head U.S.A. 30°45N 86°19W **317** E3
Mossy Point Australia 35°50S 150°11E **283** C9
Most Czech Rep. 50°31N 13°38E **180** A6
Mosta Malta 35°55N 14°26E **206** F7
Mostaganem Algeria 35°54N 0°5E **261** A5
Mostaganem □ Algeria 35°40N 0°15E **261** A5
Mostar Bos.-H. 43°22N 17°50E **182** G2
Mostardas Brazil 31°2S 50°51W **335** C5
Mostefa, Rass Tunisia 36°55N 11°3E **258** A2
Mosteiros Azores 37°53N 25°49W **153** d3
Mosterhamn Norway 59°42N 5°21E **164** E2
Mostiska = Mostyska Ukraine 49°48N 23°4E **185** J10
Móstoles Spain 40°19N 3°53W **194** E7
Mosty = Masty Belarus 53°27N 24°38E **177** B13
Mostyska Ukraine 49°48N 23°4E **185** J10
Mosul = Al Mawşil Iraq 36°15N 43°5E **213** D10
Møsvatnet Norway 59°52N 8°5E **164** E5
Mota Ethiopia 11°5N 37°52E **257** E4
Mota Vanuatu 13°49S 167°42E **287** C5
Mota del Cuervo Spain 39°30N 2°52W **197** F2
Mota del Marqués Spain 41°38N 5°11W **194** D5
Mota Lava Vanuatu 13°40S 167°40E **287** C5
Motaba Congo 2°6N 18°2E **264** B3
Motagua → Guatemala 15°44N 88°14W **320** C2
Motala Sweden 58°32N 15°1E **163** F9
Motaze Mozam. 24°48S 32°52E **271** B5
Moţca Romania 47°15N 26°37E **183** C11
Motegi Japan 36°32N 140°11E **223** A12
Moth India 25°43N 78°57E **243** G8
Motherwell U.K. 55°47N 3°58W **167** F5
Moti Bagh India 28°33N 77°10E **120** B2
Motihari India 26°30N 84°55E **243** F11
Motilla del Palancar Spain 39°34N 1°55W **197** F3
Motiti I. N.Z. 37°38S 176°25E **284** D5
Motnik Slovenia 46°14N 14°54E **199** B11
Motobu Japan 26°39N 127°53E **288** a
Motocurunya Venezuela 4°24N 64°5W **329** C5
Motol Czech Rep. 50°3N 14°21E **125** B2
Motovun Croatia 45°20N 13°50E **199** C10
Motozintla de Mendoza Mexico 15°22N 92°14W **319** D6
Motril Spain 36°31N 3°37W **195** J7
Motru Romania 44°48N 22°59E **182** F7
Motru → Romania 44°32N 23°31E **183** F8
Motsa Israel 31°47N 35°9E **123** B2
Motsa Ilit Israel 31°48N 35°9E **123** B1
Motspur Park U.K. 51°23N 0°14W **125** B2
Mott U.S.A. 46°23N 102°20W **308** B2
Mottingham U.K. 51°26N 0°1E **125** B4
Möttling = Metlika Slovenia 45°40N 15°20E **199** C12
Móttola Italy 40°38N 17°2E **201** B10
Motu → N.Z. 37°52S 177°36E **284** D6
Motu Nui Chile 27°12S 109°28W **330** b
Motu Tapu Cook Is. 21°14S 159°43W **289** h
Motuba Dem. Rep. of the Congo 2°20N 18°34E **264** B3
Motueka N.Z. 41°7S 173°1E **285** B8
Motueka → N.Z. 41°5S 173°1E **285** B8
Motul Mexico 21°6N 89°17W **319** C7
Motupena Pt. Papua N. G. 6°30S 155°10E **286** D8
Mou N. Cal. 21°5S 167°52E **288** d
Mouanda Gabon 1°28S 13°7E **264** C2
Mouchalagane → Canada 50°56N 68°41W **299** B6
Mouchoir Bank W. Indies 20°57N 70°47W **321** B5
Mouding China 25°20N 101°28E **228** E3
Moudjeria Mauritania 17°50N 12°28W **262** B2
Moudon Switz. 46°40N 6°49E **179** J2
Moudros Greece 39°50N 25°18E **205** B7
Mougoundou Congo 2°40S 12°41E **264** C2
Mouhoun = Black Volta → Africa 8°41N 1°33W **262** D4
Mouila Gabon 1°50S 11°0E **264** C2
Mouka C.A.R. 7°16N 21°52E **264** A4
Moukalaba ⌂ Gabon 2°50S 10°35E **264** C2
Moukambo Gabon 3°5S 11°38E **264** C2
Moul Niger 15°5N 13°11E **259** F2
Moulamein Australia 35°3S 144°1E **282** C6
Moule à Chique, C. St. Lucia 13°43N 60°57W **323** m
Moulhoulé Djibouti 11°58N 42°58E **267** B5
Mouliana Greece 35°10N 25°59E **207** E6
Moulin Rouge Paris, France **134** a3
Moulins France 46°35N 3°19E **173** F10
Moulmein Burma 16°30N 97°40E **241** G6
Moulmeingyun Burma 16°23N 95°16E **241** G5
Moulouya, O. → Morocco 35°5N 2°25W **261** A4
Moulton U.S.A. 40°41N 92°41W **310** D4
Moultrie U.S.A. 31°11N 83°47W **316** D6
Moultrie, L. U.S.A. 33°20N 80°5W **316** B9
Mounana Gabon 1°18S 13°13E **264** C2
Mound City Mo., U.S.A. 40°7N 95°14W **308** E6
Mound City S. Dak., U.S.A. 45°44N 100°4W **308** C3
Moundou Chad 8°40N 16°10E **259** G3
Moundsville U.S.A. 39°55N 80°44W **312** G4
Mounembé Congo 3°20S 12°32E **264** C2
Moung Cambodia 12°46N 103°27E **236** F4
Moungoudi Congo 2°45S 11°46E **264** C2
Mount Airy U.S.A. 36°31N 80°37W **315** C14
Mount Albert Canada 44°8N 79°19W **312** B5
Mount Apo △ Phil. 7°0N 125°10E **233** H5
Mount Aspiring △ N.Z. 44°19S 168°47E **285** E3
Mount Ayliff = Maxesibeni S. Africa 30°49S 29°23E **271** D4
Mount Ayr U.S.A. 40°43N 94°14W **310** D2
Mount Barker S. Austral., Australia 35°5S 138°52E **282** C3
Mount Barker W. Austral., Australia 34°38S 117°40E **279** F2
Mount Barnett Roadhouse Australia 16°39S 125°57E **278** C4
Mount Beauty Australia 36°47S 147°10E **283** D7
Mount Bellew Bridge Ireland 53°28N 8°31W **166** C3
Mount Brydges Canada 42°54N 81°29W **312** D3
Mount Buffalo △ Australia 36°43S 146°46E **283** D7
Mount Burr Australia 37°34S 140°26E **281** F3
Mount Carmel = Ha Karmel △ Israel 32°45N 35°5E **250** F6
Mount Carmel Ill., U.S.A. 38°25N 87°46W **311** F9

INDEX
Naples Park 405

Mürz → Austria 47°30N 15°25E 180 D8
Mürzzuschlag Austria 47°36N 15°41E 180 D8
Mus India 9°14N 92°47E 245 K11
Muş Turkey 38°45N 41°30E 213 C9
Muş ☐ Turkey 38°45N 41°30E 213 C9
Musa Dem. Rep. of the Congo 2°40N 19°18E 264 B3
Musa → Papua N. G. 9°3S 148°55E 286 E5
Mûsa, Gebel Egypt 28°33N 33°59E 251 K4
Musa Khel Pakistan 30°59N 69°52E 242 D3
Mūsa Qal'eh Afghan. 32°20N 64°50E 240 B2
Musabeyli Turkey 36°53N 36°55E 250 B7
Musadi
Dem. Rep. of the Congo 2°31S 22°50E 264 C4
Musafirkhana India 26°22N 81°48E 243 F9
Musā'id Iraq 31°40N 47°16E 213 H12
Musala Bulgaria 42°13N 23°37E 202 D7
Musala Indonesia 1°41N 98°28E 234 B1
Musan N. Korea 42°12N 129°12E 224 A4
Musandam, Ra's Oman 26°20N 56°20E 249 A7
Musangu
Dem. Rep. of the Congo 10°28S 23°55E 265 E4
Musasa Tanzania 3°25S 31°30E 268 C3
Musashino Japan 35°42N 139°33E 140 A2
Musay'īd Qatar 25°0N 51°33E 247 E6
Musaymīr Yemen 13°27N 44°37E 248 D4
Muscat = Masqat Oman 23°37N 58°36E 249 B7
Muscat & Oman = Oman ■
Asia 23°0N 58°0E 249 B7
Muscatatuck → U.S.A. 38°46N 86°10W 311 F10
Muscatine U.S.A. 41°25N 91°3W 310 C5
Muschu I. Papua N. G. 3°25S 143°35E 286 B2
Muscle Shoals U.S.A. 34°45N 87°40W 315 D11
Muscoda U.S.A. 43°11N 90°27W 310 A6
Musengezi = Unsengedsi →
Zimbabwe 15°43S 31°14E 269 F3
Museu Nacional Brazil 22°59S 43°13W 135 B1
Museumquartier Vienna, Austria 142 c1
Musgrave Harbour
Canada 49°27N 53°58W 299 C9
Musgrave Ranges
Australia 26°0S 132°0E 279 E5
Mushie
Dem. Rep. of the Congo 2°56S 16°55E 264 C3
Mushima Zambia 14°10S 24°56E 265 E4
Mushin Nigeria 6°31N 3°21E 124 A2
Musi → India 16°41N 79°40E 244 F4
Musi → Indonesia 2°20S 104°56E 234 C2
Musiektheater Amsterdam, Neths. 112 b3
Musina S. Africa 22°20S 30°5E 271 B5
Musiri India 10°56N 78°27E 245 J4
Muskeg → Canada 60°20N 123°20W 296 A4
Muskego U.S.A. 42°55N 88°8W 311 B8
Muskegon U.S.A. 43°14N 86°16W 311 A10
Muskegon → U.S.A. 43°14N 86°21W 308 D10
Muskegon Heights
U.S.A. 43°12N 86°16W 311 A10
Muskogee U.S.A. 35°45N 95°22W 314 D7
Muskoka, L. Canada 45°0N 79°25W 312 B5
Muskoka Falls Canada 44°59N 79°17W 312 B5
Muskwa → Canada 58°47N 122°48W 296 B4
Muslim Quarter Jerusalem 123 a3
Muslimīyah Syria 36°19N 37°12E 246 B3
Musmar Sudan 18°13N 35°40E 256 D4
Musocco Italy 45°29N 9°28E 129 B1
Musofu Zambia 13°30S 29°0E 269 E2
Musoma Tanzania 1°30S 33°48E 268 C3
Musquaro, L. Canada 50°38N 61°5W 299 B7
Musquodoboit Harbour
Canada 44°50N 63°9W 299 D7
Mussau I. Papua N. G. 1°30S 149°40E 286 A5
Musselburgh U.K. 55°57N 3°2W 167 F5
Musselshell → U.S.A. 47°21N 107°57W 304 C10
Mussende Angola 10°32S 16°5E 265 E3
Musserra Angola 7°37S 13°2E 265 D2
Mussidan France 45°2N 0°22E 174 C4
Mussolinea di Sardegna = Arborèa
Italy 39°46N 8°35E 200 C1
Mussolo Angola 9°59S 17°19E 265 D3
Mussomeli Italy 37°35N 13°45E 200 E6
Mussoorie India 30°27N 78°6E 242 D8
Mussuco Angola 17°2S 19°3E 265 F3
Mustafakemalpaşa
Turkey 40°2N 28°24E 203 F12
Mustahil Ethiopia 5°16N 44°45E 267 C5
Mustang Nepal 29°10N 83°55E 243 E10
Mustansiriya Iraq 33°22N 44°24E 113 A2
Musters, L. Argentina 45°20S 69°25W 336 C3
Mustique I. St. Vincent 12°52N 61°11W 323 n
Musturud Egypt 30°8N 31°17E 117 A2
Musudan N. Korea 40°50N 129°43E 224 B4
Muswell Hill U.K. 51°35N 0°8W 125 A3
Muswellbrook Australia 32°16S 150°56E 283 B9
Muszyna Poland 49°22N 20°55E 185 J7
Mût Egypt 25°28N 28°58E 256 B2
Mut Turkey 36°40N 33°28E 250 B4
Mutalau Cook Is. 18°56S 169°50W 289 g
Mutanabi Iraq 33°19N 44°21E 113 B2
Mutanda
Dem. Rep. of the Congo 5°17S 16°34E 265 D3
Mutanda Mozam. 21°0S 33°34E 271 B5
Mutanda Zambia 12°24S 26°13E 269 E2
Mutankiang = Mudanjiang
China 44°38N 129°30E 227 B15
Mutanshe Taiwan 22°9N 120°48E 225 D2
Mutare Zimbabwe 18°58S 32°38E 269 F3
Mutawintji △ Australia 31°10S 142°30E 281 E3
Mutha Kenya 1°48S 38°26E 268 C4
Muthana Iraq 33°19N 44°27E 113 B2
Muting Indonesia 7°23S 140°20E 231 F10
Mutki = Mirtağ Turkey 38°23N 41°56E 246 B4
Mutoko Zimbabwe 17°24S 32°13E 271 A5
Mutomo Kenya 1°51S 38°12E 268 C4
Mutoray Russia 60°56N 101°0E 215 C11
Mutoto
Dem. Rep. of the Congo 5°42S 22°42E 265 D4
Mutoxo Angola 12°17S 21°40E 265 E4
Mutsamudu Comoros Is. 12°10S 44°25E 272 a
Mutshatsha
Dem. Rep. of the Congo 10°35S 24°20E 265 E4
Mutsu Japan 41°5N 140°55E 220 D10
Mutsu-Wan Japan 41°5N 140°55E 220 D10
Muttaburra Australia 22°38S 144°29E 280 C3
Muttalip Turkey 39°50N 30°32E 205 B12
Mutton I. Ireland 52°49N 9°32W 166 D2
Muttra = Mathura India 27°30N 77°40E 242 F7
Muttukuru India 14°16N 80°6E 245 G5
Mutuáli Mozam. 14°55S 37°0E 269 E4
Mutum Biyu Nigeria 8°40N 10°50E 263 D7
Mutumba Burundi 3°25S 29°21E 268 C2
Mutunópolis Brazil 13°40S 49°15W 333 D2
Mutur Sri Lanka 8°27N 81°16E 245 K5
Muweilih Egypt 30°42N 34°19E 251 H5
Muxaluando Angola 8°8S 14°18E 265 D2
Muxía Spain 43°3N 9°10W 194 B1
Muxima Angola 9°33S 13°58E 265 D2
Muy Muy Nic. 12°39N 85°36W 320 D2
Muyinga Burundi 3°14S 30°33E 268 C3
Muynak Uzbekistan 43°44N 59°10E 216 D5
Muyunkum, Peski = Moyynqum
Kazakhstan 44°12N 71°0E 217 D8
Muz Tag China 36°25N 87°25E 217 E11
Muzaffarabad Pakistan 34°25N 73°30E 243 B5
Muzaffargarh Pakistan 30°5N 71°14E 242 D4
Muzaffarnagar India 29°26N 77°40E 242 E7
Muzaffarpur India 26°7N 85°23E 243 F11
Muzafirpur Pakistan 30°58N 69°9E 242 D3
Muzeze Angola 15°3S 17°43E 265 F3
Muzhi Russia 65°25N 64°40E 186 A11
Muzillac France 47°35N 2°30W 172 E4
Muzon, C. U.S.A. 54°40N 132°42W 303 J14
Muztagh-Ata China 38°17N 75°7E 217 E9
Muztor = Toktogul
Kyrgyzstan 41°50N 72°50E 217 D8
Muzūra Egypt 28°53N 30°48E 256 J7
Mvadhi-Ousyé Gabon 1°13N 13°12E 264 B2
Mvam Gabon 0°13S 9°39E 264 C1
Mvangan Cameroon 2°17N 11°43E 264 B2
Mvôlô Sudan 6°2N 29°53E 257 F2
Mvuma Zimbabwe 19°16S 30°30E 269 F3
Mvurwi Zimbabwe 17°0S 30°57E 269 F3
Mwabvi ⌂ Malawi 16°42S 35°0E 269 F3
Mwadi-Kalumbu
Dem. Rep. of the Congo 7°53S 18°43E 265 D3
Mwadui Tanzania 3°26S 33°32E 268 C3
Mwali = Mohéli
Comoros Is. 12°20S 43°40E 272 a
Mwambo Tanzania 10°30S 40°22E 269 E5
Mwandi Zambia 17°30S 24°51E 269 F1
Mwanza Katanga,
Dem. Rep. of the Congo 7°55S 26°43E 265 D5
Mwanza Tanzania 2°30S 32°58E 268 C3
Mwanza Zambia 16°58S 24°28E 265 F4
Mwanza ☐ Tanzania 2°0S 33°0E 268 C3
Mwaya Tanzania 9°32S 33°55E 269 D3
Mweelrea Ireland 53°39N 9°49W 166 C2
Mweka
Dem. Rep. of the Congo 4°50S 21°34E 265 C4
Mwendjila
Dem. Rep. of the Congo 7°12S 18°51E 265 D3
Mwene-Ditu
Dem. Rep. of the Congo 6°35S 22°27E 265 D4
Mwenezi Zimbabwe 21°15S 30°48E 269 G3
Mwenezi → Mozam. 22°40S 31°50E 269 G3
Mwenga
Dem. Rep. of the Congo 3°1S 28°28E 268 C2
Mweru, L. Zambia 9°0S 28°40E 269 D2
Mweru Wantipa △
Zambia 8°39S 29°25E 269 D2
Mwetshi
Dem. Rep. of the Congo 4°50S 22°38E 265 C4
Mweza Range Zimbabwe 21°0S 30°0E 269 G3
Mwilambwe
Dem. Rep. of the Congo 8°7S 25°5E 265 D5
Mwimbi Tanzania 8°38S 31°39E 269 D3
Mwingi Kenya 0°56S 38°4E 268 C4
Mwinilunga Zambia 11°43S 24°25E 265 E4
My Tho Vietnam 10°29N 106°23E 237 G6
Mya, O. → Algeria 30°46N 4°54E 261 B5
Myajlar India 26°15N 70°20E 242 F4
Myakinino Russia 55°48N 37°22E 129 B2
Myakka → U.S.A. 26°56N 82°11W 317 J7
Myall Lakes △
Australia 32°25S 152°30E 283 B10
Myanaung Burma 18°18N 95°22E 241 F5
Myanmar = Burma ■
Asia 21°0N 96°30E 241 E6
Myaung Burma 21°50N 95°25E 241 E5
Myaungmya Burma 16°30N 94°40E 241 G5
Mycenæ = Mikines
Greece 37°43N 22°46E 204 D4
Myebon Burma 20°3N 93°22E 241 E4
Myedna Belarus 51°52N 23°42E 185 G10
Myeik Kyunzu Burma 11°30N 97°30E 237 G1
Myerstown U.S.A. 40°22N 76°19W 313 F8
Myingyan Burma 21°30N 95°20E 241 E5
Myitkyina Burma 25°24N 97°26E 241 C6
Myitson Burma 23°16N 96°34E 241 D6
Myittha Burma 21°25N 96°8E 241 E6
Myittha → Burma 23°12N 94°17E 241 D5
Myjava Slovak Rep. 48°41N 17°37E 181 C10
Mykerinos Egypt 29°58N 31°8E 117 B1
Mykhaylivka Ukraine 47°12N 35°15E 189 J8
Mykines Faroe Is. 62°7N 7°35W 160 E9
Myking Norway 60°41N 5°19E 164 D2
Mykolayiv Ukraine 46°58N 32°0E 189 J6
Mykolayiv ☐ Ukraine 47°20N 31°50E 189 J6
Mykonos Greece 37°30N 25°25E 205 D7
Mylius Erichsen Land
Greenland 81°30N 27°0W 154 A8
Myllypuro Finland 60°13N 25°3E 121 B3
Mymensingh Bangla. 24°45N 90°24E 241 C3
Mynydd Du U.K. 51°52N 3°50W 169 F4
Myo-gyi Burma 21°27N 96°22E 241 E6
Myohaung Burma 20°35N 93°11E 241 E4
Myohla Burma 19°16N 95°25E 241 F5
Myotha Burma 21°41N 95°43E 241 E5
Myothit Kachin, Burma 24°24N 97°24E 241 C6
Myothit Magwe, Burma 20°12N 95°27E 241 E5
Myrasýsla ☐ Iceland 64°45N 21°30W 155 C5
Mýrdalsjökull Iceland 63°40N 19°6W 155 D7
Myrhorod Ukraine 49°58N 33°37E 189 H7
Mýri Iceland 65°23N 17°23W 155 B9
Myrtle Beach U.S.A. 33°42N 78°53W 315 E15
Myrtle Creek U.S.A. 43°1N 123°17W 304 E2
Myrtle Grove U.S.A. 30°23N 87°17W 317 E2
Myrtle Point U.S.A. 43°4N 124°8W 304 E1
Myrtleford Australia 36°34S 146°44E 283 D7
Myrtou Cyprus 35°18N 33°4E 207 E9
Mysen Norway 59°33N 11°20E 164 E8
Mysia Turkey 39°50N 27°0E 203 G11
Myślenice Poland 49°51N 19°57E 185 J6
Myślibórz Poland 52°55N 14°50E 185 F1
Mysłowice Poland 50°15N 19°12E 185 H6
Myslowitz = Mysłowice
Poland 50°15N 19°12E 185 H6
Mysore = Karnataka ☐
India 13°15N 77°0E 245 H3
Mysore India 12°17N 76°41E 245 H3
Mystic Conn., U.S.A. 41°21N 71°58W 313 E13
Mystic Iowa, U.S.A. 40°47N 92°57W 310 D4
Mystic → U.S.A. 42°22N 71°3W 116 A2
Mysuru = Mysore India 12°17N 76°41E 245 H3
Myszków Poland 50°45N 19°22E 185 H6
Myszyniec Poland 53°23N 21°21E 184 E8
Mytishchi Russia 55°50N 37°50E 188 E9
Mývatn Iceland 65°36N 17°0W 155 B10
M'zab, Oued → Algeria 32°15N 5°0E 261 B6
Mže → Czech Rep. 49°46N 13°24E 180 B6
Mzimba Malawi 11°55S 33°39E 269 E3
Mzimkulu → S. Africa 30°44S 30°28E 271 D5
Mzimvubu → S. Africa 31°38S 29°33E 271 D4
Mzuzu Malawi 11°30S 33°55E 269 E3

N

Na Clocha Liatha = Greystones
Ireland 53°9N 6°5W 166 C5
Na Hearadh = Harris
U.K. 57°50N 6°55W 167 D2
Na-lang Burma 22°42N 97°33E 241 D6
Na Noi Thailand 18°19N 100°43E 236 C3
Na Phao Laos 17°35N 105°44E 236 D5
Na Sam Vietnam 22°3N 106°37E 228 F6
Na San Vietnam 21°12N 104°2E 236 B5
Na Thon Thailand 9°32N 99°56E 237 b
Naab → Germany 49°1N 12°2E 179 F8
Nā'ālehu U.S.A. 19°4N 155°35W 302 D6
Na'am Sudan 9°42N 28°27E 257 F2
Na'am → Sudan 6°48N 29°57E 257 F2
Naama Algeria 33°16N 0°19E 261 B5
Naama ☐ Algeria 33°15N 0°45E 261 B5
Naantali Finland 60°29N 22°2E 188 B1
Naas Ireland 53°12N 6°40W 166 C5
Nababeep S. Africa 29°36S 17°46E 270 C2
Nabadwip = Navadwip
India 23°34N 88°20E 243 H13
Nabari Japan 34°37N 136°5E 223 C8
Nabawa Australia 28°30S 114°48E 279 E1
Nabberu, L. Australia 25°50S 120°30E 279 E3
Nabburg Germany 49°27N 12°11E 179 F8
Naberezhnyye Chelny
Russia 55°42N 52°19E 190 C11
Nabesna U.S.A. 62°22N 143°0W 303 E12
Nabeul Tunisia 36°30N 10°44E 258 A2
Nabeul ☐ Tunisia 36°30N 10°40E 261 A7
Nabha India 30°26N 76°14E 242 D7
Nabī Sālih Egypt 28°37N 33°59E 251 K4
Nabīd Iran 29°40N 57°38E 247 D8
Nabire Indonesia 3°15S 135°26E 231 E9
Nabisar Pakistan 25°8N 69°40E 242 G3
Nabisipi → Canada 50°14N 62°13W 299 B7
Nabiswera Uganda 1°27N 32°15E 268 B3
Nāblus = Nābulus
West Bank 32°14N 35°15E 251 F6
Naboomspruit S. Africa 24°32S 28°40E 271 B4
Nabou Burkina Faso 11°25N 2°50W 262 C4
Nabouwalu Fiji 17°0S 178°45E 287 A2
Nabq Egypt 28°6N 34°25E 251 K5
Nabua Phil. 13°24N 123°22E 232 E4
Nābulus West Bank 32°14N 35°15E 251 F6
Nabunturan Phil. 7°35N 125°58E 233 H5
Nacala Mozam. 14°32S 40°34E 269 E5
Nacaome Honduras 13°31N 87°30W 320 D2
Nacaroa Mozam. 14°22S 39°56E 269 E4
Naches U.S.A. 46°44N 120°42W 304 C3
Naches → U.S.A. 46°38N 120°31W 306 D6
Nachicapau, L. Canada 56°40N 68°5W 299 A6
Nachikatsuura Japan 33°33N 135°58E 223 D7
Nachingwea Tanzania 10°23S 38°49E 269 E4
Nachna India 27°34N 71°41E 242 F4
Náchod Czech Rep. 50°25N 16°8E 180 A9
Nachuge India 10°47N 92°21E 245 J11
Nacimiento, L. U.S.A. 35°46N 120°53W 306 K6
Nacka Sweden 59°19N 18°10E 139 B3
Nackara Australia 32°48S 139°12E 282 B3
Naco Mexico 31°19N 109°56W 318 A3
Nacogdoches U.S.A. 31°36N 94°39W 314 F7
Nácori Chico Mexico 29°40N 108°57W 318 B3
Nacozari de García
Mexico 30°25N 109°38W 318 A3
Nacula Fiji 16°54S 177°27E 287 A1
Nådendal = Naantali
Finland 60°29N 22°2E 188 B1
Nadezhdinsky = Serov
Russia 59°29N 60°35E 186 C11
Nadi Fiji 17°42S 177°20E 287 A1
Nadi Sudan 18°40N 33°41E 256 D3
Nadiad India 22°41N 72°56E 242 H5
Nădlac Romania 46°10N 20°50E 182 D5
Nador Morocco 35°14N 2°58W 261 A4
Nadur Malta 35°54N 14°22E 206 F7
Nadur Gozo, Malta 36°2N 14°18E 206 E7
Nadūshan Iran 32°2N 53°35E 247 C7
Nadvirna Ukraine 48°37N 24°30E 183 B9
Nadvoitsy Russia 63°52N 34°14E 186 B5
Nadvornaya = Nadvirna
Ukraine 48°37N 24°30E 183 B9
Nadym Russia 65°35N 72°42E 214 C8
Nadym → Russia 66°12N 72°0E 214 C8
Naenae N.Z. 41°12S 174°57E 143 B2
Nærbø Norway 58°40N 5°39E 164 F2
Nærsnes Norway 59°45N 10°27E 133 B1
Næstved Denmark 55°13N 11°44E 163 J5
Nafada Nigeria 11°8N 11°20E 263 C7
Nafpaktos Greece 38°24N 21°50E 204 C3
Nafplio Greece 37°33N 22°50E 204 D4
Naft-e Safīd Iran 31°40N 49°17E 247 D6
Naftan Pt. N. Marianas 15°5N 145°45E 302 e
Naftshahr Iran 34°0N 45°30E 213 E11
Nafud Desert = An Nafūd
Si. Arabia 28°15N 41°0E 246 D4
Nafūsah, Jabal Libya 32°12N 12°30E 258 B2
Nag Hammâdi Egypt 26°2N 32°18E 256 B3
Naga Japan 26°34N 127°43E 288 a
Naga Camarines S., Phil. 13°38N 123°15E 232 E4
Naga Cebu, Phil. 10°13N 123°45E 233 F4
Naga Zamboanga del S.,
Phil. 7°46N 122°45E 233 H4
Naga, Kreb en Africa 24°12N 6°0W 260 D3
Naga Hills = Nagaland ☐
India 26°0N 94°30E 241 C5
Naga-Shima Kagoshima,
Japan 32°10N 130°9E 222 E2
Naga-Shima Yamaguchi,
Japan 33°49N 132°5E 222 D4
Nagagami Canada 50°23N 84°20W 298 B3
Nagahama Ehime, Japan 33°36N 132°29E 222 D4
Nagahama Shiga, Japan 35°23N 136°16E 223 B8
Nagai Japan 38°6N 140°2E 220 E10
Nagai I. U.S.A. 55°5N 160°0W 303 J8
Nagaland ☐ India 26°0N 94°30E 241 C5
Nagambie Australia 36°47S 145°10E 283 D6
Nagano Japan 36°40N 138°10E 223 A10
Nagano ☐ Japan 36°15N 138°0E 223 A10
Nagaoka Japan 37°27N 138°51E 221 F9
Nagaon = Nowgong
India 26°20N 92°50E 241 B4
Nagappattinam India 10°46N 79°51E 245 J4
Nagar → Bangla. 24°27N 89°12E 241 C2
Nagar Karnul India 16°29N 78°20E 245 F4
Nagar Parkar Pakistan 24°28N 70°46E 242 G4
Nagara-Gawa → Japan 35°40N 136°43E 223 B8
Nagaram India 18°21N 80°26E 244 E5
Nagarhole △ India 12°0N 76°10E 245 J3
Nagari Hills India 13°3N 79°45E 245 H4
Nagarjuna Sagar India 16°30N 79°13E 245 F4
Nagasaki Japan 32°47N 129°50E 222 E1
Nagasaki ☐ Japan 32°50N 129°40E 222 E1
Nagato Japan 34°19N 131°5E 222 C3
Nagatsuta Japan 35°32N 139°31E 140 B2
Nagaur India 27°15N 73°45E 242 F5
Nagbhir India 20°34N 79°55E 244 D4
Nagda India 23°27N 75°25E 242 H6
Nagercoil India 8°12N 77°26E 245 K3
Nagina India 29°30N 78°30E 243 E8
Nagīneh Iran 34°20N 57°15E 247 C8
Naginimara India 26°49N 94°50E 241 B5
Nagir Pakistan 36°12N 74°42E 243 A6
Naglarby Sweden 60°25N 15°34E 162 D9
Nagles Mts. Ireland 52°8N 8°30W 166 D3
Nago-wan Japan 26°34N 127°52E 288 a
Nagod India 24°34N 80°36E 243 G9
Nagold Germany 48°32N 8°43E 179 G4
Nagold → Germany 48°52N 8°42E 179 G4
Nagoorin Australia 24°17S 151°15E 280 C5
Nagorno-Karabakh ☐
Azerbaijan 39°55N 46°45E 213 C12
Nagornyy Russia 55°58N 124°57E 215 D13
Nagoya Japan 35°10N 136°50E 223 B8
Nagoya ✈ (NGO) Japan 35°14N 136°57E 223 B8
Nagpartian = Burgos
Phil. 18°31N 120°39E 232 B3
Nagpur India 21°8N 79°10E 244 D4
Nags Head
St. Kitts & Nevis 17°13N 62°38W 322 d
Nagua Dom. Rep. 19°23N 69°50W 321 C6
Naguabo Puerto Rico 18°13N 65°44W 321 b
Nagurunguru ☼
Australia 16°45S 129°45E 278 C4
Nagyatád Hungary 46°14N 17°22E 182 D2
Nagyecsed Hungary 47°53N 22°24E 182 C7
Nagykálló Hungary 47°53N 21°51E 182 C6
Nagykanizsa Hungary 46°28N 17°0E 182 D2
Nagykáta Hungary 47°25N 19°45E 182 C4
Nagykőrös Hungary 47°5N 19°48E 182 C4
Nagyszombat = Trnava
Slovak Rep. 48°23N 17°35E 181 C10
Nagytétény Hungary 47°23N 18°59E 117 B1
Nagyvárad = Oradea
Romania 47°2N 21°58E 182 C6
Naha Japan 26°13N 127°42E 288 a
Nahalin West Bank 31°41N 35°7E 123 B1
Nahan India 30°33N 77°18E 242 D7
Nahanni △ Canada 61°36N 125°41W 296 A4
Nahanni Butte Canada 61°2N 123°31W 296 A4
Nahargarh Mad. P., India 24°10N 75°14E 242 G6
Nahargarh Raj., India 24°55N 76°50E 242 G7
Nahariyya Israel 33°1N 35°5E 250 F6
Nahāvand Iran 34°10N 48°22E 213 E13
Nahe → Germany 49°58N 7°54E 179 F3
Nahirne Ukraine 45°26N 28°27E 183 E13
Nahîya, W. → Egypt 28°55N 31°0E 256 B3
Nahuel Huapi, L.
Argentina 41°0S 71°32W 336 B2
Nahuel Huapi △
Argentina 41°3S 71°59W 336 B2
Nahuelbuta △ Chile 37°44S 72°57W 334 D1
Nahunta U.S.A. 31°12N 81°59W 316 D8
Nai Yong Thailand 8°14N 98°22E 237 a
Naic Phil. 14°19N 120°46E 232 D3
Naicá Mexico 27°53N 105°31W 318 B3
Naicam Canada 52°30N 104°30W 297 C8
Naifaru Maldives 5°26N 73°20E 272 d
Naikoon ⌂ Canada 53°55N 131°55W 296 C2
Naikul India 21°20N 84°58E 244 D7
Naila Germany 50°19N 11°42E 179 E7
Naimisharanya India 27°21N 80°30E 243 F9
Naimona'nyi Feng Nepal 30°26N 81°18E 243 D9
Nain Nfld. & L., Canada 56°34N 61°40W 299 A7
Nā'īn Iran 32°54N 53°0E 247 C7
Nain Jamaica 17°57N 77°38W 320 a
Naini Tal India 29°30N 79°30E 243 E8
Nainpur India 22°30N 80°10E 243 H9
Naintré France 46°46N 0°29E 172 F7
Nainwa India 25°46N 75°51E 242 G6
Naipu Romania 44°12N 25°47E 183 F10
Nairai Fiji 17°49S 179°15E 287 A2
Nairn U.K. 57°35N 3°53W 167 D5
Nairobi Kenya 1°17S 36°48E 268 C4
Nairobi △ Kenya 1°22S 36°50E 268 C4
Naissaar Estonia 59°34N 24°29E 188 C3
Naita, Mt. Ethiopia 5°30N 35°18E 257 F4
Naitaba Fiji 17°0S 179°16W 287 A3
Naivasha Kenya 0°40S 36°30E 268 C4
Naivasha, L. Kenya 0°48S 36°20E 268 C4
Najac France 44°14N 1°58E 174 D5
Najaf = An Najaf Iraq 32°3N 44°15E 213 G11
Najafābād Iran 32°40N 51°15E 247 C6
Najafgarh Drain → India 28°39N 77°4E 120 B1
Najd Si. Arabia 26°30N 42°0E 248 A3
Nájera Spain 42°26N 2°48W 196 C2
Najerilla → Spain 42°32N 2°48W 196 C2
Najibabad India 29°40N 78°20E 242 E8
Najin N. Korea 42°12N 130°15E 224 A5
Najmah Si. Arabia 26°42N 50°6E 247 E6
Najrān Si. Arabia 17°34N 44°18E 248 C4
Najrān ☐ Si. Arabia 18°30N 45°50E 248 C4
Naju S. Korea 35°3N 126°43E 224 E3
Naka-Gawa → Japan 36°20N 140°36E 223 A12
Nakadōri-Shima Japan 32°57N 129°4E 221 H4
Nakagusuku-wan Japan 26°14N 127°53E 288 a
Nakahara Japan 35°33N 139°37E 140 B2
Nakał = Nakło nad Notecią
Poland 53°9N 17°38E 185 E4
Nakalagba
Dem. Rep. of the Congo 2°50N 27°58E 268 B2
Nakalele Pt. U.S.A. 21°2N 156°35W 302 B5
Nakama Japan 33°56N 130°43E 222 D2
Nakambé = White Volta →
Ghana 9°10N 1°15W 263 D4
Nakaminato Japan 36°21N 140°36E 223 A12
Nakamura Japan 32°59N 132°56E 222 E4
Nakanai Mts. Papua N. G. 5°40S 151°0E 286 C6
Nakano Nagano, Japan 36°45N 138°22E 223 A10
Nakano Tōkyō, Japan 35°42N 139°39E 140 A2
Nakano-Shima Japan 29°51N 129°52E 221 K4
Nakanojō Japan 36°35N 138°51E 223 A10
Nakashibetsu Japan 43°33N 144°59E 220 C12
Nakatsu Japan 33°34N 131°15E 222 D3
Nakatsugawa Japan 35°29N 137°30E 223 B9
Nakfa Eritrea 16°40N 38°32E 257 D4
Nakfa ⌂ Eritrea 17°28N 38°55E 257 D4
Nakha Yai, Ko Thailand 8°3N 98°28E 237 a
Nakhichevan = Naxçıvan
Azerbaijan 39°12N 45°15E 213 C11
Nakhichevan Rep. = Naxçıvan ☐
Azerbaijan 39°25N 45°26E 213 C11
Nakhl Egypt 29°55N 33°43E 251 J4
Nakhl-e Taqī Iran 27°28N 52°36E 247 E7
Nakhodka Russia 42°53N 132°54E 220 C6
Nakhon Nayok Thailand 14°12N 101°13E 236 E3
Nakhon Pathom Thailand 13°49N 100°3E 236 F3
Nakhon Phanom
Thailand 17°23N 104°43E 236 D5
Nakhon Ratchasima
Thailand 14°59N 102°12E 236 E4
Nakhon Sawan Thailand 15°35N 100°10E 236 E3
Nakhon Si Thammarat
Thailand 8°29N 100°0E 237 H3
Nakhon Thai Thailand 17°5N 100°44E 236 D3
Nakhtarana India 23°20N 69°15E 242 H3
Nakijin Japan 26°40N 127°58E 288 a
Nakina Canada 50°10N 86°40W 298 B2
Nakło nad Notecią Poland 53°9N 17°38E 185 E4
Naknek U.S.A. 58°44N 157°1W 303 G8
Nako Burkina Faso 10°40N 3°4W 262 C4
Nakodar India 31°8N 75°31E 242 D6
Nakskov Denmark 54°50N 11°8E 163 K5
Naktong → S. Korea 35°7N 128°57E 227 G15
Nakuru Kenya 0°15S 36°4E 268 C4
Nakuru, L. Kenya 0°23S 36°5E 268 C4
Nakusp Canada 50°20N 117°45W 296 C5
Nal Pakistan 27°40N 66°12E 242 F2
Nal → Pakistan 25°20N 65°30E 242 G1
Nalázi Mozam. 24°3S 33°20E 271 B5
Nalchik Russia 43°30N 43°33E 191 J6
Nałęczów Poland 51°17N 22°9E 185 G9
Nalerigu Ghana 10°35N 0°25W 263 C4
Nalgonda India 17°6N 79°15E 244 F4
Nalhati India 24°17N 87°52E 243 G12
Naliya India 23°16N 68°50E 242 H3
Nallamalai Hills India 15°30N 78°50E 245 G4
Nallıhan Turkey 40°11N 31°20E 212 B4
Nalolo Zambia 15°33S 23°7E 265 F4
Nalón → Spain 43°32N 6°4W 194 B4
Nalong Burma 24°44N 97°28E 241 C6
Nalubaale Dam Uganda 0°30N 33°5E 268 B3
Nālūt Libya 31°54N 11°0E 258 B2
Nālūt ☐ Libya 31°52N 10°58E 258 B2
Nam Can Vietnam 8°46N 104°59E 237 H5
Nam-ch'on N. Korea 38°15N 126°26E 224 C3
Nam Co China 30°30N 90°45E 218 C4
Nam Dinh Vietnam 20°25N 106°5E 228 G6
Nam Du, Hon Vietnam 9°41N 104°21E 237 H5
Nam Nao △ Thailand 16°44N 101°32E 236 D3
Nam Ngum Res. Laos 18°35N 102°34E 236 C4
Nam-Phan Vietnam 10°30N 106°0E 237 G6
Nam Phong Thailand 16°42N 102°52E 236 D4
Nam Tha Laos 20°58N 101°30E 228 G3
Nam Tok Thailand 14°21N 99°4E 236 E2
Namachire Angola 11°26S 22°43E 265 E4
Namacunde Angola 17°18S 15°50E 265 F3
Namacurra Mozam. 17°30S 36°50E 271 A6
Namadgi △ Australia 35°42S 149°0E 283 C8
Namai B. Palau 7°31N 134°38E 288 c
Namak, Daryācheh-ye
Iran 34°30N 52°0E 247 C7
Namak, Kavir-e Iran 34°30N 57°30E 247 C8
Namakkal India 11°13N 78°13E 245 J4
Namakzār, Daryācheh-ye
Iran 34°0N 60°30E 240 B1
Namaland Namibia 26°0S 17°0E 270 B2
Namanga Kenya 2°33S 36°47E 268 C4
Namangan Uzbekistan 41°0N 71°40E 217 D8
Namangan ☐ Uzbekistan 41°0N 71°15E 217 D8
Namapa Mozam. 13°43S 39°50E 269 E4
Namaqua △ S. Africa 30°0S 17°20E 270 D2
Namaqualand S. Africa 30°0S 17°25E 270 D2
Namasagali Uganda 1°2N 33°0E 268 B3
Namatanai Papua N. G. 3°40S 152°29E 286 B7
Namber Indonesia 1°2S 134°49E 231 E8
Nambour Australia 26°32S 152°58E 281 D5
Nambouwalu = Nabouwalu
Fiji 17°0S 178°45E 287 A2
Nambuangongo Angola 8°1S 14°12E 265 D2
Nambucca Heads
Australia 30°37S 153°0E 283 A10
Nambung △ Australia 30°30S 115°5E 279 F2
Namcha Barwa China 29°40N 95°10E 218 D4
Namche Bazar Nepal 27°51N 86°47E 243 F12
Namchonjŏm = Nam-ch'on
N. Korea 38°15N 126°26E 224 C3
Namdapha △ India 27°30N 96°50E 241 B6
Namecunda Mozam. 14°54S 37°37E 269 E4
Nameh Indonesia 2°34N 116°21E 235 B5
Namen = Namur Belgium 50°27N 4°52E 170 D4
Namenalala Fiji 17°8S 179°9E 287 A2
Nameponda Mozam. 15°50S 39°50E 269 F4
Nameri △ India 26°55N 92°55E 241 B4
Namerikawa Japan 36°46N 137°20E 223 A9
Náměšť nad Oslavou
Czech Rep. 49°12N 16°10E 181 B9
Námestovo Slovak Rep. 49°24N 19°25E 181 B12
Nametil Mozam. 15°40S 39°21E 269 F4
Namew L. Canada 54°14N 101°56W 297 C8
Namgia India 31°48N 78°40E 243 D8
Namhkam Burma 23°50N 97°41E 228 E1
Namho Burma 22°4N 99°1E 241 D7
Namhsan Burma 22°48N 97°2E 241 D6
Namialo Mozam. 14°55S 39°59E 269 E4
Namib Desert Namibia 22°30S 15°0E 270 B2
Namib-Naukluft ⌂
Namibia 24°40S 15°16E 270 B2
Namibe Angola 15°7S 12°11E 265 F2
Namibe ☐ Angola 16°35S 12°30E 265 F2
Namibe ⌂ Angola 16°35S 12°15E 265 F2
Namibia ■ Africa 22°0S 18°9E 270 B2
Namibia Abyssal Plain
Atl. Oc. 30°0S 5°30E 152 J12
Namibwoestyn = Namib Desert
Namibia 22°30S 15°0E 270 B2
Namīn Iran 38°25N 48°30E 213 C13
Namjeju S. Korea 33°14N 126°33E 224 a
Namlan Burma 22°15N 97°24E 241 D6
Namlea Indonesia 3°18S 127°5E 231 E7
Namoi → Australia 30°12S 149°30E 283 A8
Namous, O. en → Algeria 31°0N 0°15W 261 B4
Nampa U.S.A. 43°34N 116°34W 304 E5
Nampala Mali 15°20N 5°30W 262 B3
Namp'o N. Korea 38°52N 125°10E 224 C2
Namp'o ☐ N. Korea 38°52N 125°25E 224 C2
Nampō-Shotō Japan 32°0N 140°0E 221 J10
Nampula Mozam. 15°6S 39°15E 269 F4
Namrole Indonesia 3°46S 126°46E 231 E7
Namsan Park S. Korea 37°32N 126°59E 137 B1
Namsang Burma 20°53N 97°43E 241 E6
Namse Shankou China 30°0N 82°25E 243 E10
Namsen → Norway 64°28N 11°37E 160 D14
Namslau = Namysłów
Poland 51°6N 17°42E 185 G4
Namsos Norway 64°29N 11°30E 160 D14
Namtok Chat Trakan △
Thailand 17°17N 100°40E 236 D3
Namtok Mae Surin △
Thailand 18°55N 98°2E 236 C2
Namtsy Russia 62°43N 129°37E 215 C13
Namtu Burma 23°5N 97°28E 241 D6
Namtumbo Tanzania 10°30S 36°4E 269 E4
Namu Canada 51°52N 127°50W 296 C3
Namuka-i-Lau Fiji 18°53S 178°37W 287 B3
Namukulu Cook Is. 18°57S 169°54W 289 g
Namumea Tuvalu 5°41S 176°9E 277 B14
Namur Belgium 50°27N 4°52E 170 D4
Namur ☐ Belgium 50°17N 5°0E 170 D4
Namuruputh Kenya 4°34N 35°57E 268 B4
Namutoni Namibia 18°49S 16°55E 270 A2
Namwala Zambia 15°44S 26°30E 269 F2
Namwon Jeju-do, S. Korea 33°16N 126°43E 224 a
Namwon Jeollabuk-do,
S. Korea 35°23N 127°23E 224 E3
Namyang N. Korea 42°57N 129°52E 224 A4
Namyangju S. Korea 37°38N 127°12E 224 D3
Namyeong S. Korea 37°32N 126°57E 137 B1
Namysłów Poland 51°6N 17°42E 185 G4
Nan Thailand 18°48N 100°46E 236 C3
Nan → Thailand 15°42N 100°9E 236 E3
Nan-ch'ang = Nanchang
China 28°42N 115°55E 229 C10
Nan Ling China 25°0N 112°30E 229 E8
Nan Xian China 29°20N 112°22E 229 C9
Nana C.A.R. 5°0N 15°50E 264 A3
Nana Romania 44°17N 26°34E 183 F11
Nana-Barya ⌂ C.A.R. 7°40N 17°29E 264 A3
Nana Kru Liberia 4°55N 8°45W 262 E3
Nanaimo Canada 49°10N 124°0W 296 D4
Nānākuli U.S.A. 21°24N 158°9W 302 K13
Nanam N. Korea 41°44N 129°40E 224 B4
Nanan China 24°59N 118°21E 229 E12
Nanango Australia 26°40S 152°0E 281 D5
Nan'ao Guangdong, China 23°28N 117°5E 229 F11
Nanao Japan 37°0N 137°0E 221 F8
Nanao Taiwan 24°28N 121°48E 225 B3
Nanbiancun China 23°4N 113°10E 121 B1
Nanbu China 31°18N 106°3E 228 B6
Nanchang China 28°42N 115°55E 229 C10
Nanchang He → China 39°58N 116°14E 114 B1
Nancheng China 27°33N 116°35E 229 D11
Nanching = Nanjing
China 32°2N 118°47E 229 A12
Nanchong China 30°43N 106°2E 228 B6
Nanchuan China 29°9N 107°6E 228 C6
Nanchung = Nanchong
China 30°43N 106°2E 228 B6
Nancowry India 7°59N 93°32E 245 L11
Nancy France 48°42N 6°12E 173 D13
Nanda Devi India 30°23N 79°59E 243 D8
Nanda Devi △ India 30°30N 79°50E 243 D8
Nanda Kot India 30°17N 80°5E 243 D9
Nandan Guangxi Zhuangzu,
China 24°58N 107°29E 228 E6
Nandan Japan 34°10N 134°42E 222 C6
Nandang China 23°6N 113°12E 121 B2
Nanded India 19°10N 77°20E 244 E3
Nandewar Ra. Australia 30°15S 150°35E 281 E5
Nandgaon India 20°19N 74°39E 244 D2
Nandi = Nadi Fiji 17°42S 177°20E 287 A1
Nandi Zimbabwe 20°58S 31°44E 269 G3
Nandigama India 16°47N 80°18E 244 F5
Nandigram India 22°1N 87°58E 243 H12
Nandikotkur India 15°52N 78°18E 245 G4
Nandura India 20°52N 76°25E 244 D3
Nandurbar India 21°20N 74°15E 244 D2
Nandyal India 15°30N 78°30E 245 G4
Nanfeng Guangdong,
China 23°45N 111°47E 229 F8
Nanfeng Jiangxi, China 27°12N 116°28E 229 D11
Nang Rong Thailand 14°38N 102°48E 236 E4
Nanga-Eboko Cameroon 4°41N 12°22E 263 E7
Nanga Parbat Pakistan 35°10N 74°35E 243 B6
Nangade Mozam. 11°5S 39°36E 269 E4
Nangal Dewat India 28°33N 77°7E 120 B1
Nangapinoh Indonesia 0°20S 111°44E 235 C4
Nangar △ Australia 33°23S 148°7E 283 B8
Nangarhār ☐ Afghan. 34°20N 70°0E 240 B3
Nangatayap Indonesia 1°32S 110°34E 235 C4
Nangbéto, L. de Togo 7°26N 1°25E 262 D5
Nangeya Mts. Uganda 3°30N 33°30E 268 B3
Nangis France 48°33N 3°1E 173 D10
Nangnim-sanmaek
N. Korea 40°13N 126°51E 224 B3
Nangong China 37°23N 115°22E 226 F8
Nangtud, Mt. Phil. 11°17N 122°11E 233 F4
Nanguneri India 8°29N 77°40E 245 K3
Nangwarry Australia 37°33S 140°48E 282 D4
Nanhua Yunnan, China 25°13N 101°21E 228 E3
Nanhua Taiwan 23°2N 120°28E 225 C2
Nanhuang China 36°58N 121°48E 227 F11
Nanhui China 31°5N 121°44E 229 B13
Nanhunan Shan Taiwan 24°21N 121°26E 225 B3
Nanisivik Canada 73°2N 84°33W 295 C15
Naniwa Japan 34°39N 135°29E 133 B1
Nanjangud India 12°6N 76°43E 245 H3
Nanjeko Zambia 15°31S 23°30E 269 F1
Nanji Shan China 27°27N 121°4E 229 D13
Nanjian China 25°2N 100°25E 228 E3
Nanjiang China 32°28N 106°51E 228 A6
Nanjing Fujian, China 24°25N 117°20E 229 E11
Nanjing Jiangsu, China 32°2N 118°47E 229 A12
Nanjirinji Tanzania 9°41S 39°5E 269 D4
Nankana Sahib Pakistan 31°27N 73°38E 242 D5
Nankang Jiangxi, China 25°40N 114°45E 229 E10
Nankang Taiwan 25°3N 121°35E 225 A3
Nanking = Nanjing
China 32°2N 118°47E 229 A12
Nankoku Japan 33°39N 133°44E 222 D5
Nanlang China 22°30N 113°32E 219 G10
Nanliao Taiwan 24°50N 120°55E 225 B2
Nanling China 30°55N 118°20E 229 B12
Nannial India 19°4N 79°38E 244 E4
Nanning China 22°48N 108°20E 228 F7
Nannup Australia 33°59S 115°48E 279 F2
Nanole India 19°0N 72°55E 130 A2
Nanortalik Greenland 60°10N 45°17W 154 E6
Nanpan Jiang → China 25°10N 106°5E 228 E6
Nanpara India 27°52N 81°33E 243 F9
Nanpi China 38°2N 116°45E 226 E9
Nanping Fujian, China 26°38N 118°10E 229 D12
Nanping Henan, China 29°55N 112°3E 229 C9
Nanpu Bridge China 31°12N 121°30E 138 B2
Nanri Dao China 25°15N 119°25E 229 E12
Nanripe Mozam. 13°52S 38°52E 269 E4
Nansei-Shotō = Ryūkyū-rettō
Japan 26°0N 126°0E 221 M3
Nansen Basin Arctic 84°0N 50°0E 150 A10
Nansen Land Greenland 83°0N 43°0W 154 A6
Nansen Sd. Canada 81°0N 91°0W 295 A13
Nansha China 22°45N 113°34E 219 F10
Nanshan I. S. China Sea 10°45N 115°49E 230 B5
Nanshi China 31°12N 121°29E 138 B1
Nansio Tanzania 2°3S 33°4E 268 C3
Nant France 44°1N 3°18E 174 D7
Nantawarrinna ☼
Australia 30°49S 138°58E 281 B2
Nanterre France 48°53N 2°12E 134 A2
Nantes France 47°12N 1°33W 172 E5
Nantiat France 46°1N 1°11E 174 B5
Nanticoke U.S.A. 41°12N 76°0W 313 E8
Nanton Canada 50°21N 113°46W 296 C6
Nanton Pt. Antigua & B. 17°0N 61°45W 322 b
Nantong China 32°1N 120°52E 229 A13
Nantou China 22°32N 113°55E 219 F10
Nant'ou Taiwan 23°55N 120°41E 225 C2
Nant'ou ☐ Taiwan 23°50N 121°0E 225 C3
Nantua France 46°10N 5°35E 173 F12
Nantucket U.S.A. 41°17N 70°6W 309 E18
Nantucket I. U.S.A. 41°16N 70°5W 309 E18
Nantulo Mozam. 12°32S 38°45E 269 E4
Nantung = Nantong
China 32°1N 120°52E 229 A13
Nantwich U.K. 53°4N 2°31W 168 D5
Nanty Glo U.S.A. 40°28N 78°50W 312 F6
Nantzu Taiwan 22°44N 120°19E 225 D2
Nanuku Passage Fiji 16°45S 179°15W 287 A3
Nanumanga Pac. Oc. 6°18S 176°20E 277 B14
Nanuque Brazil 17°50S 40°21W 333 E3
Nanusa, Kepulauan
Indonesia 4°45N 127°1E 231 D7
Nanutarra Roadhouse
Australia 22°32S 115°30E 278 D2
Nanwan Taiwan 21°57N 120°46E 225 E2
Nanxi China 28°54N 104°59E 228 C5
Nanxiong China 25°6N 114°15E 229 E10
Nanyang China 33°11N 112°30E 226 H7
Nanyi Hu China 31°5N 119°0E 229 B12
Nanyuki Kenya 0°2N 37°4E 268 B4
Nanzhang China 31°45N 111°50E 229 B8
Nao, C. de la Spain 38°44N 0°14E 197 G5
Naococane, L. Canada 52°50N 70°45W 299 B5
Naogaon Bangla. 24°52N 88°52E 241 C2
Naoné Vanuatu 15°0S 168°8E 287 E6
Naoussa Cyclades, Greece 37°7N 25°14E 205 D7
Naoussa Imathia, Greece 40°42N 22°9E 202 F6
Naozhou Dao China 20°55N 110°20E 229 G8
Napa U.S.A. 38°18N 122°17W 306 G4
Napa → U.S.A. 38°10N 122°19W 306 G4
Napaimiut U.S.A. 61°33N 158°42W 303 F8
Napakiak U.S.A. 60°42N 161°57W 303 F7
Napali Coast U.S.A. 22°11N 159°39W 302 A2
Napanee Canada 44°15N 77°0W 312 B8
Napanoch U.S.A. 41°44N 74°22W 313 E10
Napaskiak U.S.A. 60°43N 161°55W 303 F7
Nape Laos 18°18N 105°6E 236 C5
Nape Pass = Keo Neua, Deo
Vietnam 18°23N 105°10E 236 C5
Naperville U.S.A. 41°46N 88°9W 311 C8
Napier N.Z. 39°30S 176°56E 284 F5
Napier Broome B.
Australia 14°2S 126°37E 278 B4
Napier Mole Pakistan 24°49N 66°58E 123 B1
Napier Pen. Australia 12°4S 135°43E 280 A2
Napierville Canada 45°11N 73°25W 313 A11
Napili-Honokowai
U.S.A. 20°58N 156°39W 302 C5
Naples = Nápoli Italy 40°50N 14°15E 201 B7
Naples U.S.A. 26°8N 81°48W 317 J8
Naples Park U.S.A. 26°17N 81°46W 317 J8

Napo China 23°22N 105°50E 228 F5
Napo □ Ecuador 0°30S 77°0W 328 D2
Napo ➜ Peru 3°20S 72°40W 328 D3
Napoleon N. Dak., U.S.A. 46°30N 99°46W 308 B4
Napoleon Ohio, U.S.A. 41°23N 84°8W 311 C12
Napoleon's Tomb St. Helena 15°56S 5°42W 153 h
Nápoli Italy 40°50N 14°15E 201 B7
Nápoli, G. di Italy 40°43N 14°10E 201 B7
Nápoli Capodichino ✈ (NAP) Italy 40°53N 14°16E 201 B7
Napopo Dem. Rep. of the Congo 4°15N 28°0E 268 B2
Nappanee U.S.A. 41°27N 86°0W 311 C11
Napperby Australia 33°9S 138°7E 282 B3
Naqâda Egypt 25°53N 32°42E 256 B3
Naqadeh Iran 36°57N 45°23E 213 D11
Naqb, Ra's an Jordan 29°48N 35°44E 251 J6
Naqqāsh Iran 35°40N 49°6E 247 C6
Nara Japan 34°40N 135°49E 223 C7
Nara Mali 15°10N 7°20W 262 B3
Nara □ Japan 34°30N 136°0E 223 C8
Nara Canal Pakistan 24°30N 69°20E 242 G3
Nara Visa U.S.A. 35°37N 103°6W 305 J12
Naracoorte Australia 36°58S 140°45E 282 D4
Naradhan Australia 33°34S 146°17E 283 B7
Naraina India 28°36N 77°8E 120 B1
Naraini India 25°11N 80°29E 243 G9
Naranjos Mexico 21°21N 97°41W 319 C5
Narasannapeta India 18°25N 84°3E 244 E7
Narasapur India 16°26N 81°40E 245 F5
Narasaropet India 16°14N 80°4E 245 F5
Narathiwat Thailand 6°30N 101°48E 237 J3
Narayanapatnam India 18°53N 83°10E 244 E6
Narayangadh = Bharatpur Nepal 27°34N 84°10E 243 F11
Narayanganj Bangla. 23°40N 90°33E 241 D3
Narayanpet India 16°45N 77°30E 244 F3
Narbada = Narmada ➜ India 21°38N 72°36E 242 J5
Narberth U.K. 51°47N 4°44W 169 F3
Narbonne France 43°11N 3°0E 174 E7
Narborough, I. = Fernandina, I. Ecuador 0°25S 91°30W 330 a
Narbuvoll Norway 62°21N 11°27E 164 B8
Narcea ➜ Spain 43°33N 6°44W 194 B4
Narcondam I. India 13°20N 94°16E 245 H12
Nardīn Iran 37°3N 55°59E 247 B7
Nardò Italy 40°11N 18°2E 201 B11
Narembeen Australia 32°7S 118°24E 279 F2
Narendranagar India 30°10N 78°18E 242 D8
Nares Abyssal Plain Atl. Oc. 22°0N 67°0W 152 D5
Nares Str. Arctic 80°0N 70°0W 154 B3
Naretha Australia 31°0S 124°45E 279 F3
Narew ➜ Poland 52°26N 20°41E 185 F7
Nari ➜ Pakistan 28°0N 67°40E 242 F2
Nariman Point Mumbai, India 130 c1
Nariman Pt. India 18°55N 72°49E 130 B1
Narin Afghan. 36°5N 69°0E 240 A3
Narindra, Helodranon' i Madag. 14°55S 47°30E 272 A2
Narino □ Colombia 1°30N 78°0W 328 C2
Narita Japan 35°47N 140°19E 223 B12
Narita, Tōkyō ✈ (NRT) Japan 35°45N 140°25E 223 B12
Nariva □ Trin. & Tob. 10°22N 61°10W 323 t
Nariva ➜ Trin. & Tob. 10°24N 61°14W 323 t
Nariva Swamp Trin. & Tob. 10°26N 61°4W 323 t
Närke Sweden 59°10N 15°0E 162 E8
Narmada ➜ India 21°38N 72°36E 242 J5
Narmada Canal India 22°20N 73°45E 244 C1
Nārmak Iran 35°42N 51°28E 141 A2
Narman Turkey 40°26N 41°57E 213 B9
Narnaul India 28°5N 76°11E 242 E7
Narni Italy 42°30N 12°30E 199 F9
Naro Ghana 10°22N 2°27W 262 C4
Naro Fominsk Russia 55°23N 36°43E 188 E9
Narodnaya Russia 65°5N 59°58E 186 A10
Narok Kenya 1°55S 35°52E 268 C4
Narón Spain 43°32N 8°9W 194 B2
Narooma Australia 36°14S 150°4E 283 D9
Narowal Pakistan 32°6N 74°52E 242 C6
Narra Phil. 9°18N 118°28E 233 G2
Narrabri Australia 30°19S 149°46E 281 E4
Narran ➜ Australia 28°37S 148°12E 281 D4
Narrandera Australia 34°42S 146°31E 283 C7
Narrogin Australia 32°58S 117°14E 279 F2
Narromine Australia 32°12S 148°12E 283 B8
Narrow Hills ⌂ Canada 54°0N 104°37W 297 C8
Narrows, The St. Kitts & Nevis 17°12N 62°40W 322 d
Narsampet India 17°57N 79°58E 244 F4
Narsaq Greenland 60°57N 46°4W 154 E6
Narsimhapur India 22°54N 79°14E 243 H8
Narsinghgarh India 23°45N 76°40E 242 H7
Narsinghpur India 20°28N 85°5E 244 D7
Narsipatnam India 17°40N 82°37E 244 F6
Nartes, L. e Albania 40°32N 19°25E 202 F3
Nartkala Russia 43°33N 43°51E 191 J6
Naruo Japan 34°43N 135°22E 133 A1
Naruto Kantō, Japan 34°11N 134°37E 222 C6
Narutō Shikoku, Japan 35°36N 140°25E 223 B12
Naruto-Kaikyō Japan 34°14N 134°39E 222 C6
Narva Estonia 59°23N 28°12E 188 C5
Narva ➜ Russia 59°27N 28°2E 188 C4
Narva Bay = Narva Laht Estonia 59°35N 27°35E 161 G22
Narva Laht Estonia 59°35N 27°35E 161 G22
Narvacan Phil. 17°25N 120°28E 232 C3
Narvik Norway 68°28N 17°26E 160 B17
Narvskoye Vdkhr. Russia 59°18N 28°14E 188 C5
Narwana India 29°39N 76°6E 242 E7
Narwiański △ Poland 52°5N 22°53E 185 F9
Narwinbi ✪ Australia 16°7S 136°17E 280 B2
Naryan-Mar Russia 67°42N 53°12E 186 A9
Narym Russia 59°0N 81°30E 214 D9
Naryn Kyrgyzstan 41°26N 75°58E 217 D9
Naryn □ Kyrgyzstan 41°26N 75°58E 217 D9
Naryn ➜ Uzbekistan 40°52N 71°36E 217 D8
Naryn Qum Kazakhstan 47°30N 49°0E 191 G9
Nasa Norway 66°29N 15°23E 160 C16
Nasau Fiji 17°19S 179°27E 287 A2
Năsăud Romania 47°19N 24°29E 183 C9
Nasawa Vanuatu 15°12S 168°9E 287 E6
Naşb, W. ➜ Egypt 28°29N 34°31E 251 K5
Näsby Sweden 59°25N 18°5E 139 A2
Näsbypark Sweden 59°25N 18°5E 139 A2
Nasca = Nazca Peru 14°50S 74°57W 330 C3
Naseby N.Z. 45°1S 170°10E 285 F5
Naselle U.S.A. 46°22N 123°49W 306 D3
Naser, Buheirat en Egypt 23°0N 32°30E 256 C3
Nashik = Nasik India 19°58N 73°50E 244 E1
Nashua Iowa, U.S.A. 42°57N 92°32W 310 B4
Nashua Mont., U.S.A. 48°8N 106°22W 304 B10
Nashua N.H., U.S.A. 42°45N 71°28W 313 D13
Nashville Ark., U.S.A. 33°57N 93°51W 314 E8
Nashville Ga., U.S.A. 31°12N 83°15W 316 D6
Nashville Ill., U.S.A. 38°21N 89°23W 310 F7
Nashville Ind., U.S.A. 39°12N 86°15W 311 E10
Nashville Mich., U.S.A. 42°36N 85°5W 311 B11
Nashville Tenn., U.S.A. 36°10N 86°47W 315 C11
Našice Croatia 45°32N 18°4E 182 E3
Nasielsk Poland 52°35N 20°50E 185 F7
Nasik India 19°58N 73°50E 244 E1
Nasipit Phil. 8°57N 125°19E 233 G5
Nasir Sudan 8°36N 33°4E 257 F3
Nasirabad = Mymensingh Bangla. 24°45N 90°24E 241 C3
Nasirabad India 26°15N 74°45E 242 F6
Nasirabad Pakistan 28°23N 68°24E 242 E3
Nasiri = Ahvāz Iran 31°20N 48°40E 247 D6
Nasiriyah = An Nāşirīyah Iraq 31°0N 46°15E 246 D5
Naskaupi ➜ Canada 53°47N 60°51W 299 B7
Naso Italy 38°7N 14°47E 201 D7
Naso Pt. Phil. 10°25N 121°57E 233 F3
Naşrābād Iran 34°8N 51°26E 247 C6
Naşriān-e Pā'īn Iran 32°52N 46°52E 246 C5
Nass ➜ Canada 55°0N 129°40W 296 C3
Nassarawa Nigeria 8°32N 7°41E 263 D6
Nassarawa □ Nigeria 8°30N 8°20E 263 D6
Nassau Bahamas 25°5N 77°20W 153 b
Nassau N.Y., U.S.A. 42°31N 73°37W 313 D11
Nassau, B. Chile 55°20S 68°0W 336 E3
Nassau Int. ✈ (NAS) Bahamas 25°3N 77°28W 153 b
Nasser, L. = Naser, Buheirat en Egypt 23°0N 32°30E 256 C3
Nasser City = Kôm Ombo Egypt 24°25N 32°52E 256 C3
Nassian Ivory C. 8°28N 3°28W 262 D4
Nässjö Sweden 57°39N 14°42E 163 G8
Nastapoka ➜ Canada 56°55N 76°33W 298 A4
Nastapoka, Is. Canada 56°55N 76°50W 298 A4
Nasugbu Phil. 14°5N 120°38E 232 D3
Näsum Sweden 56°10N 14°29E 163 H8
Näsviken Sweden 61°46N 16°52E 162 C10
Nata Botswana 20°12S 26°12E 270 B4
Nata ➜ Botswana 20°14S 26°10E 270 B4
Natagaima Colombia 3°37N 75°6W 328 C2
Natal Brazil 5°47S 35°13W 332 C4
Natal Indonesia 0°35N 99°7E 234 B1
Natal Drakensberg ⌂ S. Africa 29°27S 29°30E 271 C4
Natalinci Serbia 44°15N 20°49E 182 F5
Naţanz Iran 33°30N 51°55E 247 C6
Natashquan Canada 50°14N 61°46W 299 B7
Natashquan ➜ Canada 50°7N 61°50W 299 B7
Natchez U.S.A. 31°34N 91°24W 314 F9
Natchitoches U.S.A. 31°46N 93°5W 314 F8
Natewa B. Fiji 16°35S 179°40E 287 A2
Nathalia Australia 36°1S 145°13E 283 D6
Nathan Philips Square Toronto, Canada 141 b2
Nathan Road Hong Kong, China 122 a2
Nathdwara India 24°55N 73°50E 242 G5
Nathu La China 27°24N 88°49E 241 B2
Nati, Pta. Spain 40°3N 3°50E 206 A4
Natimuk Australia 36°42S 142°0E 282 D5
Nation ➜ Canada 55°30N 123°32W 296 B4
National Arboretum U.S.A. 38°54N 76°59W 143 B3
National Art Gallery Beijing, China 114 b2
National Capital District □ Papua N. G. 9°25S 147°10E 286 E4
National City U.S.A. 32°40N 117°5W 307 N9
National Grand Theatre Beijing, China 114 c2
National Place Washington, D.C., U.S.A. 143 b2
National Zoological Park U.S.A. 38°55N 77°4W 143 B3
Nationals Park U.S.A. 38°53N 77°1W 143 B3
Natitingou Benin 10°20N 1°26E 263 C5
Natividad, I. Mexico 27°52N 115°11W 318 B1
Natividade Brazil 11°43S 47°47W 333 D2
Nativity, Basilica of West Bank 31°42N 33°12E 123 B2
Natkyizin Burma 14°57N 97°59E 236 E1
Natmauk Burma 20°20N 95°24E 241 E5
Natogyi Burma 21°25N 95°39E 241 E5
Natolin Poland 52°8N 21°4E 142 C2
Natonin Phil. 17°6N 121°18E 232 C3
Natron, L. Tanzania 2°20S 36°0E 268 C4
Natrona Heights U.S.A. 40°37N 79°44W 312 F5
Natrûn, W. el ➜ Egypt 30°25N 30°13E 256 H7
Nattai △ Australia 34°12S 150°22E 283 C9
Nättraby Sweden 56°13N 15°31E 163 H9
Natukanaoka Pan Namibia 18°40S 15°45E 270 A2
Natuna Besar, Kepulauan Indonesia 4°0N 108°15E 234 B3
Natuna Is. = Natuna Besar, Kepulauan Indonesia 4°0N 108°15E 234 B3
Natuna Selatan, Kepulauan Indonesia 2°45N 109°0E 235 B3
Natural Bridge U.S.A. 44°5N 75°30W 313 B9
Natural Bridges ⌂ U.S.A. 37°36N 110°0W 305 H9
Naturaliste, C. Tas., Australia 40°50S 148°15E 281 G4
Naturaliste, C. W. Austral., Australia 33°32S 115°0E 279 F2
Naturaliste Plateau Ind. Oc. 34°0S 112°0E 276 G1
Nau Qala Afghan. 34°5N 68°5E 242 B3
Naucalpan de Juárez Mexico 19°28N 99°14W 128 B1
Naucelle France 44°13N 2°20E 174 D6
Nauders Austria 46°54N 10°30E 180 E3
Nauen Germany 52°36N 12°52E 178 C8
Naugard = Nowogard Poland 53°41N 15°10E 184 E2
Naugatuck U.S.A. 41°30N 73°3W 313 E11
Naujaat = Repulse Bay Canada 66°30N 86°30W 295 D14
Naujan Phil. 13°20N 121°18E 232 E3
Naujoji Akmenė Lithuania 56°19N 22°54E 184 B9
Naulila Angola 17°13S 14°39E 265 F2
Naumburg Germany 51°9N 11°47E 178 D7
Naumburg am Queis = Nowogrodziec Poland 51°12N 15°24E 185 G2
Naupada Andhra Pradesh, India 18°34N 84°18E 244 E7
Naupada Maharashtra, India 19°3N 72°50E 130 A2
Nā'ūr Jordan 31°53N 35°50E 251 G6
Nauru ■ Pac. Oc. 1°0S 166°0E 288 H8
Naushahra = Nowshera Pakistan 34°0N 72°0E 240 B4
Naushahro Pakistan 26°50N 68°7E 242 F3
Naushon I. U.S.A. 41°29N 70°45W 313 E14
Nausori Fiji 18°2S 178°32E 287 B2
Naustdal Norway 61°31N 5°43E 164 C2
Nauta Peru 4°31S 73°35W 328 D3
Nautanwa India 27°20N 83°25E 243 F10
Naute ⌂ Namibia 26°55S 17°57E 270 C2
Nautla Mexico 20°13N 96°47W 319 C5
Nauvoo U.S.A. 40°33N 91°23W 310 D5
Nava Coahuila, Mexico 28°25N 100°45W 318 B4
Nava Spain 43°21N 5°31W 194 B5
Nava del Rey Spain 41°22N 5°6W 194 D5
Navadwip India 23°34N 88°20E 243 H13
Navahermosa Spain 39°41N 4°28W 195 F6
Navahrudak Belarus 53°40N 25°50E 177 B13
Navai Fiji 17°36S 177°57E 287 A1
Navajo Res. U.S.A. 36°48N 107°36W 305 H10
Naval Phil. 11°34N 124°23E 233 F5
Navalcarnero Spain 40°17N 4°5W 194 E6
Navalgund India 15°34N 75°22E 245 G2
Navalmoral de la Mata Spain 39°52N 5°33W 194 F5
Navalvillar de Pela Spain 39°9N 5°24W 195 F5
Navan = An Uaimh Ireland 53°39N 6°41W 166 C5
Navanagar = Jamnagar India 22°30N 70°6E 242 H4
Navapolatsk Belarus 55°32N 28°37E 188 E5
Navarin, Mys Russia 62°15N 179°5E 215 C18
Navarino, I. Chile 55°0S 67°40W 336 E3
Navarra □ Spain 42°40N 1°40W 196 C3
Navarre Fla., U.S.A. 30°24N 86°52W 317 E3
Navarre Ohio, U.S.A. 40°43N 81°31W 312 F3
Navarro ➜ U.S.A. 39°11N 123°45W 306 F3
Navas de San Juan Spain 38°30N 3°19W 195 G7
Navasota U.S.A. 30°23N 96°5W 314 F6
Navassa I. W. Indies 18°30N 75°0W 321 C5
Nävekvarn Sweden 58°38N 16°49E 163 F10
Naver ➜ U.K. 58°32N 4°14W 167 C4
Navet Trin. & Tob. 10°21N 61°10W 323 t
Navet ➜ Trin. & Tob. 10°24N 61°5W 323 t
Navet Res. Trin. & Tob. 10°24N 61°15W 323 t
Navi Mumbai India 19°5N 73°0E 130 A2
Navia Spain 43°35N 6°42W 194 B4
Navia ➜ Spain 43°15N 6°50W 194 B4
Navia de Suarna = A Pobre Spain 42°58N 7°3W 194 C3
Navibandar India 21°26N 69°48E 242 J3
Navidad Chile 33°57S 71°50W 334 C1
Navidad Bank W. Indies 20°0N 68°58W 321 B6
Navíglio di Pavia Italy 45°24N 9°9E 129 B1
Navíglio Grande Italy 45°25N 9°5E 129 B1
Naviraí Brazil 23°8S 54°13W 335 A5
Naviti Fiji 17°7S 177°15E 287 A1
Navlakhi India 22°58N 70°28E 242 H4
Navlya Russia 52°53N 34°30E 189 F8
Năvodari Romania 44°19N 28°36E 183 F13
Navoiy Uzbekistan 40°9N 65°22E 217 D7
Navojoa Mexico 27°6N 109°26W 318 B3
Navolato Mexico 24°47N 107°42W 318 C3
Navona, Piazza Rome, Italy 136 b2
Navotas Phil. 14°39N 120°56E 127 B1
Navrongo Ghana 10°51N 1°3W 263 C4
Navsari India 20°57N 72°59E 244 D1
Navua Fiji 18°12S 178°11E 287 B2
Navy Pier Chicago, U.S.A. 119 b3
Nawa Kot Pakistan 28°21N 71°24E 242 E4
Nawab Khan Pakistan 30°17N 69°12E 242 D3
Nawabganj Bangla. 24°35N 88°14E 241 C2
Nawabganj Ut. P., India 26°56N 81°14E 243 F9
Nawabganj Ut. P., India 28°32N 79°40E 243 E8
Nawabshah Pakistan 26°15N 68°25E 242 F3
Nawada India 24°50N 85°33E 243 G11
Nāwah Afghan. 32°19N 67°53E 240 B2
Nawakot Nepal 27°55N 85°10E 243 F11
Nawalgarh India 27°50N 75°15E 242 F6
Nawanshahr India 32°33N 74°48E 243 C6
Nawapara India 20°46N 82°33E 244 D6
Nawar, Dasht-i- Afghan. 33°52N 68°0E 242 C3
Nawāsīf, Ḩarrat Si. Arabia 21°20N 42°10E 248 B3
Nawi Sudan 18°32N 30°50E 256 D3
Nawng Hpa Burma 22°30N 98°30E 241 D7
Nawoiy = Navoiy Uzbekistan 40°9N 65°22E 217 D7
Nawş, Ra's Oman 17°15N 55°16E 249 C6
Naxçıvan Azerbaijan 39°12N 45°15E 213 C11
Naxçıvan □ Azerbaijan 39°25N 45°26E 213 C11
Naxos Greece 37°8N 25°25E 205 D7
Naxxar Malta 35°55N 14°27E 206 F7
Nay France 43°10N 0°18W 174 E3
Nay, Mui = Varella, Mui Vietnam 12°54N 109°26E 236 F7
Nāy Band Būshehr, Iran 27°20N 52°40E 247 E7
Nāy Band Khorāsān, Iran 32°20N 57°34E 247 C8
Naya ➜ Colombia 3°13N 77°22W 328 C2
Nayagarh India 20°8N 85°6E 244 D7
Nayakhan Russia 61°56N 159°0E 215 C16
Nayarit □ Mexico 22°0N 105°0W 318 C4
Nayé Senegal 14°28N 12°12W 262 C2
Nayong China 26°50N 105°20E 228 D5
Nayoro Japan 44°21N 142°28E 220 B11
Naypyidaw Burma 19°44N 96°12E 236 C1
Nayudupeta India 13°54N 79°54E 245 H4
Nayyāl, W. ➜ Si. Arabia 28°35N 39°4E 246 D3
Nazal Hikmat Beg Iraq 33°23N 44°25E 113 A2
Nazar Kahrizi Iran 37°20N 46°45E 213 D12
Nazaré Bahia, Brazil 13°2S 39°0W 333 D4
Nazaré Pará, Brazil 6°25S 52°29W 331 B7
Nazaré Tocantins, Brazil 6°23S 47°40W 332 C2
Nazaré Portugal 39°36N 9°4W 195 F1
Nazareth = Nazerat Israel 32°42N 35°17E 250 F6
Nazareth U.S.A. 40°44N 75°19W 313 F9
Nazarovo Russia 57°2N 90°40E 215 D10
Nazas Mexico 25°14N 104°8W 318 B4
Nazas ➜ Mexico 25°12N 104°12W 318 B4
Nazca Peru 14°50S 74°57W 330 C3
Nazca Ridge Pac. Oc. 20°0S 80°0W 289 K19
Naze Japan 28°22N 129°27E 221 K4
Naze, The U.K. 51°53N 1°18E 169 F9
Nazerat Israel 32°42N 35°17E 250 F6
Nāzīk Iran 39°1N 45°4E 213 C11
Nazilli Turkey 37°55N 28°15E 205 D10
Nazimabad Pakistan 24°54N 67°1E 123 A2
Nazinon = Red Volta ➜ Africa 10°34N 0°30W 263 C4
Nazir Hat Bangla. 22°35N 91°49E 241 D3
Nazko Canada 53°1N 123°37W 296 C4
Nazko ➜ Canada 53°7N 123°34W 296 C4
Nazlet el Simmân Egypt 29°59N 31°9E 117 B1
Nāzlu Iran 37°41N 45°0E 213 D11
Nazret Ethiopia 8°32N 39°22E 257 F4
Ncama Eq. Guin. 1°55N 10°56E 264 B2
Nchanga Zambia 12°30S 27°49E 269 E2
Ncheu Malawi 14°50S 34°47E 269 E3
Ncue Eq. Guin. 2°1N 10°28E 264 B2
Ndala Tanzania 4°45S 33°15E 268 C3
Ndalatando Angola 9°12S 14°48E 265 D2
Ndali Benin 9°50N 2°46E 263 D5
Ndareda Tanzania 4°12S 35°30E 268 C4
Ndélé C.A.R. 8°25N 20°36E 264 A4
Ndendé Gabon 2°22S 11°23E 264 C2
Ndiael ⌂ Senegal 16°15N 16°0W 262 B1
Ndikinimeki Cameroon 4°46N 10°50E 263 E7
Ndim Cameroon 5°10N 10°41E 264 A2
Ndindi Gabon 3°46S 11°9E 264 C2
N'Dioum Senegal 16°31N 14°39W 262 B2
Ndjamena Chad 12°10N 15°0E 259 F3
Ndjolé Gabon 0°10S 10°45E 264 C2
Ndogo, Lagune Gabon 2°35S 10°0E 264 C2
Ndok Cameroon 7°57N 14°42E 264 A2
Ndoki-Nouabalé ⌂ Congo 2°32N 16°32E 264 B3
Ndola Zambia 13°0S 28°34E 269 E2
Ndomo ⌂ S. Africa 26°52S 32°15E 271 C5
Ndoto Mts. Kenya 2°0N 37°0E 268 B4
Ndoua, C. N. Cal. 22°24S 166°56E 288 d
Ndouba Congo 0°9S 14°4E 264 C2
Ndoukou C.A.R. 4°33N 20°39E 264 B4
Nduguti Tanzania 4°18S 34°41E 268 C3
Nea ➜ Norway 63°15N 11°0E 164 A8
Nea Alexandria Greece 37°52N 23°46E 112 B2
Nea Alikarnassos Greece 35°18N 25°13E 205 F7
Nea Anchialos Greece 39°16N 22°49E 204 B4
Nea Epidavros Greece 37°40N 23°7E 204 D5
Nea Ionia Athina, Greece 38°3N 23°45E 112 A2
Nea Ionia Magnisia, Greece 39°21N 22°56E 204 B4
Nea Kalikratia Greece 40°21N 23°3E 202 F7
Nea Liosia Greece 38°3N 23°43E 112 A2
Nea Makri Greece 38°5N 23°59E 204 C5
Nea Moudania Greece 40°15N 23°17E 202 F7
Nea Peramos Attiki, Greece 38°0N 23°26E 204 C5
Nea Peramos Kavala, Greece 40°50N 24°18E 203 F8
Nea Samsounda Greece 39°5N 20°45E 207 A2
Nea Smirni Greece 37°54N 23°43E 112 B2
Nea Visa Greece 41°34N 26°33E 203 E10
Nea Zichni Greece 41°2N 23°49E 202 E7
Neagari Japan 36°26N 136°25E 223 A8
Neagh, Lough U.K. 54°37N 6°25W 166 B5
Neah Bay U.S.A. 48°22N 124°37W 306 B2
Neale, L. Australia 24°15S 130°0E 278 D5
Neales ➜ Australia 28°8S 136°47E 281 D2
Neamati India 26°50N 94°20E 241 B5
Neamţ □ Romania 47°0N 26°20E 183 C11
Neapoli Athens, Greece 112 a3
Neapoli Kozani, Greece 40°20N 21°24E 202 F5
Neapoli Kriti, Greece 35°15N 25°37E 207 E6
Neapoli Lakonia, Greece 36°27N 23°8E 204 E5
Near Is. U.S.A. 52°30N 174°0E 303 K1
Near North Chicago, U.S.A. 119 b1
Neath U.K. 51°39N 3°48W 169 F4
Neath Port Talbot □ U.K. 51°42N 3°45W 169 F4
Nebbi Uganda 2°28N 31°6E 268 B3
Nebbou Burkina Faso 11°9N 1°51W 263 C4
Nebelat el Hagana Sudan 13°13N 29°2E 257 E2
Nebine Cr. ➜ Australia 29°27S 146°56E 281 D4
Nebitdag = Balkanabat Turkmenistan 39°30N 54°22E 247 B7
Nebka Algeria 27°28N 3°12W 260 C4
Neblina, Pico da Brazil 0°48N 66°0W 328 C4
Nebo Australia 21°42S 148°42E 280 C4
Nebolchy Russia 59°8N 33°18E 188 C7
Nebraska □ U.S.A. 41°30N 99°30W 308 E4
Nebraska City U.S.A. 40°41N 95°52W 308 E6
Nébrodi, Monti Italy 37°54N 14°35E 201 E7
Nebušice Czech Rep. 50°6N 14°19E 135 B1
Necedah U.S.A. 44°2N 90°4W 308 C8
Nechako ➜ Canada 53°55N 122°42W 296 C4
Neches ➜ U.S.A. 29°58N 93°51W 314 G8
Nechisar △ Ethiopia 5°58N 37°55E 257 F4
Neckar ➜ Germany 49°27N 8°29E 179 F4
Neckartal-Odenwald ⌂ Germany 49°30N 9°5E 179 F5
Necker I. U.S.A. 23°35N 164°42W 302 G11
Necochea Argentina 38°30S 58°50W 334 D4
Nectar Brook Australia 32°43S 137°57E 282 B2
Neda Spain 43°30N 8°9W 194 B2
Neda ➜ Greece 37°25N 21°45E 204 D3
Nedalshytta Norway 62°59N 12°3E 164 B9
Nedelino Bulgaria 41°27N 25°3E 203 E9
Nedelišće Croatia 46°23N 16°22E 199 B13
Nederhorst Neths. 52°16N 5°3E 112 B3
Nederland = Netherlands ■ Europe 52°0N 5°30E 170 C5
Nedlitz Germany 52°25N 13°3E 115 B1
Nedoboyivtsi Ukraine 48°26N 26°21E 183 B11
Nedreberg Norway 60°59N 11°41E 164 D8
Nedroma Algeria 35°1N 1°45W 261 A4
Nedstrand Norway 59°21N 5°49E 164 E2
Nee Soon Singapore 1°24N 103°49E 138 A2
Needham U.S.A. 42°17N 71°14W 116 B1
Needham Heights U.S.A. 42°17N 71°14W 116 B1
Needles B.C., Canada 49°53N 118°7W 296 D5
Needles Calif., U.S.A. 34°51N 114°37W 307 L12
Needles, The U.K. 50°39N 1°35W 169 G6
Needles Pt. N.Z. 36°3S 175°25E 284 C4
Neembucú □ Paraguay 27°0S 58°0W 334 B4
Neemuch = Nimach India 24°30N 74°56E 242 G6
Neenah U.S.A. 44°11N 88°28W 308 C9
Neepawa Canada 50°15N 99°30W 297 C9
Neeses U.S.A. 33°33N 81°7W 316 B8
Nefta Tunisia 33°53N 7°50E 258 B1
Neftçala Azerbaijan 39°19N 49°12E 213 C13
Neftechala = Neftçala Azerbaijan 39°19N 49°12E 213 C13
Neftegorsk Krasnodar, Russia 44°25N 39°45E 191 H4
Neftegorsk Sakhalin, Russia 53°1N 142°58E 215 D15
Neftekumsk Russia 44°46N 44°50E 191 H7
Nefteyugansk Russia 61°5N 72°42E 214 C8
Nefyn U.K. 52°56N 4°31W 168 E3
Négala Mali 12°52N 8°30W 262 C3
Negapatam = Nagappattinam India 10°46N 79°51E 245 J4
Negara Indonesia 8°22S 114°37E 231 J17
Negaunee U.S.A. 46°30N 87°36W 308 B10
Negele Oromiya, Ethiopia 5°20N 39°36E 257 F4
Negele Oromiya, Ethiopia 7°21N 38°42E 266 C4
Negeri Sembilan □ Malaysia 2°45N 102°10E 234 B2
Negev Desert = Hanegev Israel 30°50N 35°0E 251 H6
Negoiul, Vf. Romania 45°38N 24°35E 183 E9
Negombo Sri Lanka 7°12N 79°50E 245 L4
Negotin Serbia 44°16N 22°37E 202 B6
Negotino Macedonia 41°29N 22°7E 202 E6
Negra, Peña Spain 42°11N 6°30W 194 C4
Negra, Pta. Mauritania 22°54N 16°18W 260 D1
Negra, Pta. Peru 6°6S 81°10W 330 B1
Negra Pt. Phil. 18°40N 120°50E 232 B3
Negra Pt. Trin. & Tob. 10°4N 61°23W 323 t
Negrais, C. = Maudin Sun Burma 16°0N 94°30E 241 G5
Nègres, Pte. des Martinique 14°35N 61°5W 322 j
Negreşti Romania 46°50N 27°30E 183 D12
Negreşti-Oaş Romania 47°52N 23°26E 183 C8
Negril Jamaica 18°22N 78°20W 320 a
Négrine Algeria 34°30N 7°30E 261 B6
Negro ➜ Argentina 41°2S 62°47W 336 B4
Negro ➜ Bolivia 14°11S 63°7W 331 C5
Negro ➜ Brazil 3°0S 60°0W 329 D6
Negro ➜ Uruguay 33°24S 58°22W 334 C4
Negro, C. = Tarf, Ras Morocco 35°40N 5°11W 260 A3
Negros Phil. 9°30N 122°40E 233 G4
Negros Occidental □ Phil. 10°0N 122°55E 233 F4
Negros Oriental □ Phil. 9°45N 123°0E 233 G4
Negru Vodă Romania 43°47N 28°21E 183 G13
Neguac Canada 47°15N 65°5W 299 C6
Nehalem ➜ U.S.A. 45°40N 123°56W 306 E3
Nehāvand Iran 35°56N 49°31E 247 C6
Nehbandān Iran 31°35N 60°5E 247 D9
Nehoiu Romania 45°24N 26°20E 183 E11
Nei Monggol Zizhiqu □ China 42°0N 112°0E 226 D7
Neiafu Tonga 18°39S 173°59W 287 P14
Neidenburg = Nidzica Poland 53°25N 20°28E 185 E7
Neiges, Piton des Réunion 21°5S 55°29E 272 f
Neijiang China 29°35N 104°55E 228 C5
Neikiang = Neijiang China 29°35N 104°55E 228 C5
Neilingding Dao China 22°25N 113°48E 219 G10
Neill I. India 11°50N 93°3E 245 J11
Neillsville U.S.A. 44°34N 90°36W 308 C8
Neilson, Récif Pac. Oc. 27°1S 146°2W 289 f
Neilton U.S.A. 47°25N 123°53W 304 C2
Neipu Taiwan 22°37N 120°33E 225 D2
Neiqiu China 37°15N 114°30E 226 F8
Neisse = Nysa ➜ Europe 52°4N 14°46E 178 C10
Neiva Colombia 2°56N 75°18W 328 C2
Neiwan Taiwan 24°42N 121°10E 225 B3
Neixiang China 33°10N 111°52E 226 H6
Nejanilini L. Canada 59°33N 97°48W 297 B9
Nejd = Najd Si. Arabia 26°30N 42°0E 248 A3
Nejo Ethiopia 9°30N 35°28E 257 F4
Nekā Iran 36°39N 53°19E 247 B7
Nekemte Ethiopia 9°4N 36°30E 257 F4
Nêkheb Egypt 25°10N 32°48E 256 B3
Nekrasovka Russia 55°41N 37°55E 129 B5
Neksø Denmark 55°4N 15°8E 163 J9
Nelamangala India 13°6N 77°24E 245 H3
Nelas Portugal 40°32N 7°52W 194 E3
Nelaug Norway 58°39N 8°40E 164 F5
Nelia Australia 20°39S 142°12E 280 C3
Nelidovo Russia 56°13N 32°49E 188 D7
Neligh U.S.A. 42°8N 98°2W 308 D4
Nelkan Russia 57°40N 136°4E 215 D14
Nellikuppam India 11°46N 79°43E 245 J4
Nellis Air Force Base ✈ (LSV) U.S.A. 36°14N 115°2W 124 A2
Nellore India 14°27N 79°59E 245 G4
Nelson B.C., Canada 49°30N 117°20W 296 D5
Nelson N.Z. 41°18S 173°16E 285 B8
Nelson Lancs., U.K. 53°50N 2°13W 168 D5
Nelson Ariz., U.S.A. 35°31N 113°19W 305 J7
Nelson Nev., U.S.A. 35°42N 114°49W 307 K12
Nelson □ N.Z. 41°20S 173°20E 285 B8
Nelson ➜ Canada 54°33N 98°2W 297 C9
Nelson, C. Vic., Australia 38°26S 141°32E 282 E4
Nelson, C. Papua N. G. 9°0S 149°20E 286 E5
Nelson, Estrecho Chile 51°30S 75°0W 336 D2
Nelson Bay Australia 32°43S 152°9E 283 B10
Nelson Forks Canada 59°30N 124°0W 296 B4
Nelson House Canada 55°47N 98°51W 297 B9
Nelson L. Canada 55°48N 100°7W 297 B8
Nelson Lakes △ N.Z. 41°55S 172°44E 285 B7
Nelson's Dockyard Antigua & B. 17°1N 61°46W 322 b
Nelspoort S. Africa 32°7S 23°0E 270 D3
Nelspruit S. Africa 25°29S 30°59E 271 C5
Néma Mauritania 16°40N 7°15W 262 B3
Neman = Nemunas ➜ Lithuania 55°25N 21°10E 184 C8
Neman Russia 55°2N 22°2E 184 C9
N'ematābād Iran 35°38N 51°21E 141 B2
Nembe Nigeria 4°32N 6°24E 263 E6
Nembrala Indonesia 10°53S 122°50E 278 B3
Nemchinovka Russia 55°42N 37°19E 129 B1
Nemea Greece 37°49N 22°40E 204 D4
Nemecký Brod = Havlíčkův Brod Czech Rep. 49°36N 15°33E 180 B8
Nemeiben L. Canada 55°20N 105°20W 297 B7
Nemërçkë, Mal Albania 40°15N 20°15E 202 F4
Nemira, Vf. Romania 46°17N 26°19E 183 D11
Nemiscau Canada 51°18N 76°54W 298 B4
Nemiscau, L. Canada 51°25N 76°40W 298 B4
Nemours = Ghazaouet Algeria 35°8N 1°50W 261 A4
Nemours France 48°16N 2°40E 173 D9
Nemrut Daği △ Turkey 38°0N 38°55E 213 C8
Nemšová Slovak Rep. 48°58N 18°7E 181 C11
Nemunas ➜ Lithuania 55°25N 21°10E 184 C8
Nemuro Japan 43°20N 145°35E 220 C12
Nemuro-Kaikyō Japan 43°30N 145°30E 220 C12
Nemyriv Ukraine 50°7N 23°27E 185 H10
Nen Jiang ➜ China 45°28N 124°30E 227 B13
Nenagh Ireland 52°52N 8°11W 166 D3
Nenana U.S.A. 64°34N 149°5W 303 D10
Nenasi Malaysia 3°9N 103°23E 237 L4
Nendo Pac. Oc. 10°45S 165°54E 277 C12
Nene ➜ U.K. 52°49N 0°11E 169 E8
Nengkao Shan Taiwan 23°58N 121°16E 225 C3
Nengonengo French Polynesia 18°47S 141°48W 289 f
Nenita Greece 38°14N 26°6E 205 C8
Nenjiang China 49°10N 125°10E 219 B7
Neno Malawi 15°25S 34°40E 269 F3
Neo Chori Greece 38°25N 21°17E 204 C3
Neochori Greece 39°4N 21°0E 204 B2
Neodesha U.S.A. 37°25N 95°41W 308 G6
Neoga U.S.A. 39°19N 88°27W 311 E8
Neon Petritsi Greece 41°16N 23°15E 202 E7
Neópolis Brazil 10°18S 36°35W 332 D4
Neora Valley △ India 27°0N 88°45E 241 B2
Neosho U.S.A. 36°52N 94°22W 308 G6
Neosho ➜ U.S.A. 36°48N 95°18W 314 C7
Nepal ■ Asia 28°0N 84°30E 243 F11
Nepalganj Nepal 28°5N 81°40E 243 E9
Nepalganj Road India 28°1N 81°41E 243 E9
Nepean B. Australia 35°42S 137°37E 282 C2
Nephi U.S.A. 39°43N 111°50W 304 G8
Nephin Ireland 54°1N 9°22W 166 B2
Nephin Beg Range Ireland 54°0N 9°40W 166 C2
Nepi Italy 42°14N 12°21E 199 F9
Nepomuk Czech Rep. 49°29N 13°35E 180 B6
Neppel = Moses Lake U.S.A. 47°8N 119°17W 304 C4
Neptune U.S.A. 40°13N 74°2W 313 F10
Neptune Is. Australia 35°17S 136°10E 282 C2
Neqāb Iran 36°42N 57°25E 247 B8
Nera ➜ Italy 42°26N 12°24E 199 F9
Nera ➜ Romania 44°48N 21°25E 182 F6
Nérac France 44°8N 0°21E 174 D4
Nerang Australia 27°58S 153°20E 281 D5
Nerastro, Sarīr Libya 24°20N 20°37E 258 D4
Neratovice Czech Rep. 50°16N 14°31E 180 A7
Nerchinsk Russia 52°0N 116°39E 215 D12
Nereju Romania 45°43N 26°43E 183 E11
Nerekhta Russia 57°26N 40°38E 188 D11
Neresnytsya Ukraine 48°7N 23°46E 183 B8
Néret, L. Canada 54°45N 70°44W 299 B5
Neretvanski Kanal Croatia 43°7N 17°10E 199 E14
Nerima Japan 35°44N 139°40E 140 A3
Neringa Lithuania 55°20N 21°5E 184 C8
Neris ➜ Lithuania 55°8N 24°16E 188 E3
Nerja Spain 36°43N 3°55W 195 J7
Nerl ➜ Russia 56°11N 40°34E 188 D11
Nerpio Spain 38°11N 2°16W 197 G2
Nerva Spain 37°42N 6°30W 195 H4
Nervi Italy 44°23N 9°2E 198 D6
Neryungri Russia 57°38N 124°28E 215 D13
Nes Iceland 65°53N 17°24W 155 B9
Nes Buskerud, Norway 60°34N 9°59E 164 D6
Nesbyen Norway 60°34N 9°8E 164 D6
Nescopeck U.S.A. 41°3N 76°12W 313 E8
Nesebŭr Bulgaria 42°41N 27°46E 203 D11
Neset Norway 61°53N 10°7E 164 C7
Nesflaten Norway 59°38N 6°48E 164 E3
Nesjahverfi Iceland 64°20N 15°15W 155 C11
Neskantaga Canada 52°14N 87°53W 298 B2
Neskaupstaður Iceland 65°9N 13°42W 155 B13
Nesland Norway 59°31N 7°59E 164 E4
Neslandsvatn Norway 58°57N 9°10E 164 F6
Nesodden Norway 59°48N 10°41E 133 B3
Nesoddtangen Norway 59°48N 10°40E 133 A3
Nesøya Norway 59°52N 10°31E 133 A2
Ness, L. U.K. 57°15N 4°32W 167 D4
Ness City U.S.A. 38°27N 99°54W 308 F4
Nesterov Russia 54°38N 22°41E 184 D9
Nesterov Ukraine 50°4N 23°58E 177 C12
Nestorio Greece 40°24N 21°5E 202 F5
Nestos ➜ Europe 40°54N 24°49E 203 E8
Nesttun Norway 60°19N 5°20E 164 D2
Nesvady Slovak Rep. 47°56N 18°7E 181 D11
Nesvizh = Nyasvizh Belarus 53°14N 26°38E 177 B14
Netanya Israel 32°20N 34°51E 251 F5
Netarhat India 23°29N 84°16E 243 H11
Nete ➜ Belgium 51°7N 4°14E 170 C4
Netherdale Australia 21°10S 148°33E 280 b
Netherlands ■ Europe 52°0N 5°30E 170 C5
Netherlands Antilles ⊘ W. Indies 12°15N 69°0W 328 A4
Netherlands East Indies = Indonesia ■ Asia 5°0S 115°0E 235 C4
Netherlands Guiana = Suriname ■ S. Amer. 4°0N 56°0W 329 C6
Neto ➜ Italy 39°12N 17°9E 201 C10
Netrakona Bangla. 24°53N 90°47E 241 C3
Netrang India 21°39N 73°21E 242 J5
Nettancourt France 48°51N 4°57E 173 D11
Nettetal Germany 51°19N 6°12E 178 D2
Nettilling L. Canada 66°30N 71°0W 295 D17
Nettuno Italy 41°27N 12°39E 200 A5
Netzahualcóyotl, Presa Mexico 17°8N 93°35W 319 D6
Neu Aubing Germany 48°8N 11°25E 131 B1
Neu-Bentschen = Zbąszynek Poland 52°16N 15°51E 185 F2
Neu Buch Germany 52°37N 13°31E 115 A4
Neu Buchhorst Germany 52°24N 13°44E 115 B5
Neu Fahrland Germany 52°26N 13°3E 115 B1
Neu-Isenburg Germany 50°3N 8°42E 179 E4
Neu-Langenburg = Tukuyu Tanzania 9°17S 33°35E 269 D3
Neu Lindenberg Germany 52°36N 13°33E 115 A4
Neu-Mecklenberg = New Ireland Papua N. G. 3°20S 151°50E 286 B6
Neu Pommern = New Britain Papua N. G. 5°50S 150°20E 286 C6
Neu-Sandec = Nowy Sącz Poland 49°40N 20°41E 185 J7
Neu Sandez = Nowy Sącz Poland 49°40N 20°41E 185 J7
Neu-Ulm Germany 48°22N 10°0E 179 G6
Neubiberg Germany 48°4N 11°40E 131 B3
Neubrandenburg Germany 53°33N 13°15E 178 B9
Neubukow Germany 54°2N 11°39E 178 A7
Neuburg Germany 48°44N 11°11E 179 G7
Neuchâtel Switz. 47°0N 6°55E 179 J2
Neuchâtel □ Switz. 47°0N 6°55E 179 J2
Neuchâtel, Lac de Switz. 46°53N 6°50E 179 J2
Neudau Austria 47°11N 16°6E 180 D9
Neuenberg an der Elbe = Nymburk Czech Rep. 50°10N 15°1E 180 A8
Neuenhagen Germany 52°32N 13°38E 115 A4
Neuenhaus Germany 52°30N 6°58E 178 C2
Neuessling Austria 48°15N 16°32E 142 A3
Neuf-Brisach France 48°1N 7°30E 173 D14
Neufahrn Bayern, Germany 48°41N 12°11E 179 G8
Neufahrn Bayern, Germany 48°18N 11°40E 179 G7
Neufchâteau Belgium 49°50N 5°25E 170 E5
Neufchâteau Vosges, France 48°21N 5°40E 173 D12
Neufchâtel-en-Bray France 49°44N 1°26E 172 C8
Neufchâtel-sur-Aisne France 49°26N 4°1E 173 C11
Neuhaus = Jindřichův Hradec Czech Rep. 49°10N 15°2E 180 B8
Neuhaus Germany 53°17N 10°56E 178 B6
Neuhäusel = Nové Zámky Slovak Rep. 48°2N 18°8E 181 C11
Neuhausen Germany 48°9N 11°32E 131 B2
Neuherberg Germany 48°13N 11°35E 131 A2
Neuhönow Germany 52°34N 13°44E 115 A5
Neuillé-Pont-Pierre France 47°33N 0°33E 172 E7
Neuilly-Plaisance France 48°51N 2°30E 134 A4
Neuilly-St-Front France 49°10N 3°15E 173 C10
Neuilly-sur-Marne France 48°51N 2°31E 134 A4
Neuilly-sur-Seine France 48°53N 2°15E 134 A2
Neukagran Austria 48°14N 16°27E 142 A2
Neukalen Germany 53°49N 12°46E 178 B8
Neukettenhof Austria 48°7N 16°28E 142 B2
Neukölln Germany 52°28N 13°25E 115 B3
Neumarkt = Nowy Targ Poland 49°29N 20°2E 185 J7
Neumarkt = Środa Śląska Poland 51°10N 16°36E 185 G3
Neumarkt Germany 49°26N 11°27E 179 F7
Neumarktl = Tržič Slovenia 46°22N 14°18E 199 B11
Neumayer Antarctica 71°0S 68°30W 151 D17
Neumittelwalde = Międzybórz Poland 51°25N 17°34E 185 G4
Neumünster Germany 54°4N 9°58E 178 A5
Neung-sur-Beuvron France 47°30N 1°50E 173 E8
Neunkirchen Austria 47°43N 16°4E 180 D9
Neunkirchen Saarland, Germany 49°20N 7°9E 179 F3
Neuperlach Germany 48°6N 11°37E 131 B2
Neuquén Argentina 38°55S 68°0W 336 A3
Neuquén □ Argentina 38°0S 69°50W 334 D2
Neuquén ➜ Argentina 38°59S 68°0W 336 A3
Neuried Germany 48°5N 11°27E 131 B1
Neuruppin Germany 52°55N 12°48E 178 C8
Neusalz an der Oder = Nowa Sól Poland 51°48N 15°44E 185 G2
Neusäss Germany 48°24N 10°50E 179 G6
Neusatz = Novi Sad Serbia 45°18N 19°52E 182 E4
Neuse ➜ U.S.A. 35°6N 76°29W 315 D16
Neusiedl Austria 47°57N 16°50E 181 D9
Neusiedler See Austria 47°50N 16°47E 181 D9
Neusiedler See-Seewinkel △ Austria 47°50N 16°45E 181 D9
Neusohl = Banská Bystrica Slovak Rep. 48°46N 19°14E 181 C12
Neuss Germany 51°11N 6°42E 178 D2
Neussargues-Moissac France 45°9N 3°0E 174 C7
Neustadt = Lwówek Poland 52°28N 16°10E 185 F3
Neustadt = Prudnik Poland 50°20N 17°38E 185 H4
Neustadt = Wejherowo Poland 54°35N 18°12E 184 D5
Neustadt Bayern, Germany 49°44N 12°10E 179 F8
Neustadt Bayern, Germany 48°48N 11°46E 179 G7
Neustadt Bayern, Germany 49°34N 10°37E 179 F6
Neustadt Bayern, Germany 50°19N 11°7E 179 E7
Neustadt Brandenburg, Germany 52°50N 12°27E 178 C8
Neustadt Hessen, Germany 50°51N 9°9E 178 E5
Neustadt Niedersachsen, Germany 52°30N 9°30E 178 C5
Neustadt Rhld-Pfz., Germany 49°21N 8°10E 179 F4
Neustadt Sachsen, Germany 51°2N 14°12E 178 D10
Neustadt Schleswig-Holstein, Germany 54°6N 10°49E 178 A6
Neustadt Thüringen, Germany 50°45N 11°43E 178 E7
Neustädtel = Nowe Miasteczko Poland 51°42N 15°42E 185 G2

Neustädtl = Novo Mesto *Slovenia* 45°47N 15°12E **199** C12
Neustettin = Szczecinek *Poland* 53°43N 16°41E **184** E3
Neustift am Walde *Austria* 48°14N 16°17E **142** A1
Neustrelitz *Germany* 53°21N 13°4E **178** B9
Neusüssenbrunn *Austria* 48°16N 16°29E **142** A2
Neutitschein = Nový Jičín *Czech Rep.* 49°30N 18°2E **181** B11
Neuvic *France* 45°23N 2°16E **174** C6
Neuville-sur-Saône *France* 45°52N 4°51E **175** C8
Neuvy-le-Roi *France* 47°36N 0°36E **172** E7
Neuvy-St-Sépulchre *France* 46°35N 1°48E **173** F8
Neuvy-sur-Barangeon *France* 47°20N 2°15E **173** E9
Neuwaldegg *Austria* 48°14N 16°17E **142** A1
Neuwedell = Drawno *Poland* 53°13N 15°46E **185** E2
Neuwerk *Germany* 53°55N 8°30E **178** B4
Neuwied *Germany* 50°26N 7°29E **178** E3
Neva → *Russia* 59°56N 30°20E **188** C6
Nevada *Iowa, U.S.A.* 42°1N 93°27W **310** B3
Nevada *Mo., U.S.A.* 37°51N 94°22W **310** G2
Nevada □ *U.S.A.* 39°0N 117°0W **304** G5
Nevada City *U.S.A.* 39°16N 121°1W **306** F6
Nevado, Cerro *Argentina* 35°30S 68°32W **334** D2
Nevado de Colima = Volcán de Colima △ *Mexico* 19°30N 103°40W **318** D4
Nevado de Tres Cruces △ *Chile* 27°13S 69°5W **334** B2
Nevado del Huila △ *Colombia* 3°5N 75°58W **328** C2
Nevasa *India* 19°34N 75°0E **244** E2
Neve, Sa. da *Angola* 13°43S 13°10E **265** E2
Neve Ya'akov *West Bank* 31°50N 35°14E **123** A2
Nevel *Russia* 56°0N 29°55E **188** D5
Nevelsk *Russia* 46°40N 141°51E **215** E15
Nevers *France* 47°0N 3°9E **173** F10
Nevertire *Australia* 31°50S 147°44E **283** A7
Neves *Brazil* 22°51S 43°5W **135** B2
Nevesinje *Bos.-H.* 43°14N 18°6E **202** C2
Neville *Canada* 49°58N 107°39W **297** D7
Nevinnomyssk *Russia* 44°40N 42°0E **191** H6
Nevis *St. Kitts & Nevis* 17°0N 62°30W **322** d
Nevis Pk. *St. Kitts & Nevis* 17°9N 62°34W **322** d
Nevlunghavn *Norway* 58°58N 9°53E **164** F6
Nevoso, Mte. = Snežnik *Slovenia* 45°36N 14°35E **199** C11
Nevrokop = Gotse Delchev *Bulgaria* 41°36N 23°46E **202** E7
Nevşehir *Turkey* 38°33N 34°40E **212** C6
Nevşehir □ *Turkey* 38°50N 34°40E **212** C6
Nevskoye *Russia* 54°32N 22°39E **184** D9
Nevyansk *Russia* 57°30N 60°13E **186** C11
New → *Guyana* 3°20N 57°37W **329** C6
New → *W. Va., U.S.A.* 38°10N 81°12W **309** F13
New Aiyansh *Canada* 55°12N 129°4W **296** B3
New Albany *Ind., U.S.A.* 38°18N 85°49W **311** F11
New Albany *Miss., U.S.A.* 34°29N 89°0W **315** D10
New Albany *Pa., U.S.A.* 41°36N 76°27W **313** E8
New Amsterdam *Guyana* 6°15N 57°36W **329** B6
New Athens *U.S.A.* 38°19N 89°53W **310** F7
New Baghdād *Iraq* 33°18N 44°28E **113** B2
New Baltimore *U.S.A.* 42°41N 82°44W **312** D2
New Barakpur *India* 22°40N 88°26E **124** A2
New Barbadoes = Hackensack *U.S.A.* 40°52N 74°4W **132** A1
New Bedford *U.S.A.* 41°38N 70°56W **313** E14
New Berlin = North Canton *U.S.A.* 40°53N 81°24W **312** F3
New Berlin *Ill., U.S.A.* 39°44N 89°55W **310** E7
New Berlin *N.Y., U.S.A.* 42°37N 75°20W **313** D9
New Berlin *Pa., U.S.A.* 40°50N 76°57W **312** F8
New Berlin *Wis., U.S.A.* 42°59N 88°6W **311** B8
New Bern *U.S.A.* 35°7N 77°3W **315** D16
New Bethlehem *U.S.A.* 41°0N 79°20W **312** F5
New Bight *Bahamas* 24°19N 75°24W **321** B4
New Bloomfield *U.S.A.* 40°25N 77°11W **312** F7
New Boston *U.S.A.* 33°28N 94°25W **314** E7
New Braunfels *U.S.A.* 29°42N 98°8W **314** G5
New Brighton *N.Z.* 43°29S 172°43E **285** D7
New Brighton *N.Y., U.S.A.* 40°38N 74°5W **132** C1
New Brighton *Pa., U.S.A.* 40°42N 80°19W **312** F4
New Britain *Papua N. G.* 5°50S 150°20E **286** C6
New Britain *Conn., U.S.A.* 41°40N 72°47W **313** E12
New Britain Trench *Pac. Oc.* 6°0S 153°0E **276** J3
New Brockton *U.S.A.* 31°23N 85°56W **316** D4
New Brookland = West Columbia *U.S.A.* 33°59N 81°4W **316** B8
New Brunswick *U.S.A.* 40°30N 74°27W **313** F10
New Brunswick □ *Canada* 46°50N 66°30W **299** C6
New Buffalo *U.S.A.* 41°47N 86°45W **311** C10
New Bussa *Nigeria* 9°53N 4°31E **263** F5
New Caledonia ☑ *Pac. Oc.* 21°0S 165°0E **288** d
New Caledonia Trough *Pac. Oc.* 30°0S 165°0E **288** L8
New Canada *S. Africa* 26°12S 27°56E **123** B1
New Canada Dam *S. Africa* 26°12S 27°56E **123** B1
New Carlisle *Ind., U.S.A.* 41°45N 86°32W **311** C10
New Carlisle *Ohio, U.S.A.* 39°56N 84°2W **311** E12
New Carrollton *U.S.A.* 38°58N 76°53W **143** B4
New Castile = Castilla-La Mancha □ *Spain* 39°30N 3°30W **195** F7
New Castle *Ind., U.S.A.* 39°55N 85°22W **311** E11
New Castle *Ky., U.S.A.* 38°26N 85°10W **311** F11
New Castle *Pa., U.S.A.* 41°0N 80°21W **312** F4
New City *U.S.A.* 41°9N 73°59W **313** E11
New Concord *U.S.A.* 39°59N 81°54W **312** G3
New Cross *U.K.* 51°28N 0°1W **125** B3
New Cumberland *U.S.A.* 40°30N 80°36W **312** F4
New Cuyama *U.S.A.* 34°57N 119°38W **307** L7
New Delhi *India* 28°36N 77°11E **120** B2
New Denver *Canada* 50°0N 117°25W **296** D5
New Don Pedro Res. *U.S.A.* 37°43N 120°24W **306** H6
New Dorp *U.S.A.* 40°34N 74°7W **132** C1
New Dorp Beach *U.S.A.* 40°33N 74°6W **132** C1
New Ellenton *U.S.A.* 33°28N 81°41W **316** B8
New England *U.S.A.* 43°0N 71°0W **301** G25
New England *N. Dak., U.S.A.* 46°32N 102°52W **308** B2
New England △ *Australia* 30°25S 152°30E **283** A10
New England Aquarium *Boston, U.S.A.* **116** b3
New England Ra. *Australia* 30°20S 151°45E **281** E5
New England Seamounts *Atl. Oc.* 38°0N 63°0W **152** C5
New Forest △ *U.K.* 50°53N 1°34W **169** G6
New Franklin *U.S.A.* 39°1N 92°44W **310** E4
New Galloway *U.K.* 55°5N 4°9W **167** F4
New Georgia Is. *Solomon Is.* 8°15S 157°30E **287** M9
New Georgia Sound *Solomon Is.* 8°0S 158°20E **287** L9
New Glarus *U.S.A.* 42°49N 89°38W **310** B7
New Glasgow *Canada* 45°35N 62°36W **299** C7
New Grant *Trin. & Tob.* 10°17N 61°19W **323** t
New Guinea *Oceania* 4°0S 136°0E **276** B7
New Halfa = Halfa al Jadidah *Sudan* 15°20N 35°35E **266** A4
New Hamburg *Canada* 43°23N 80°42W **312** C4
New Hampshire □ *U.S.A.* 44°0N 71°30W **313** C13
New Hampton *U.S.A.* 43°3N 92°19W **310** A4
New Hanover *Papua N. G.* 2°30S 150°10E **286** B6
New Hanover *KwaZulu Natal, S. Africa* 29°22S 30°31E **271** C5
New Harmony *U.S.A.* 38°8N 87°56W **311** F9
New Hartford *U.S.A.* 43°4N 75°18W **313** C9
New Haven *Conn., U.S.A.* 41°18N 72°55W **313** E12
New Haven *Ill., U.S.A.* 37°55N 88°8W **311** G8
New Haven *Ind., U.S.A.* 41°4N 85°1W **311** C11
New Haven *Mich., U.S.A.* 42°44N 82°48W **312** D2
New Haven *Mo., U.S.A.* 38°37N 91°13W **310** F5
New Haven *N.Y., U.S.A.* 43°28N 76°18W **313** C8
New Hazelton *Canada* 55°20N 127°30W **296** B3
New Hebrides = Vanuatu ■ *Pac. Oc.* 15°0S 168°0E **287** E6
New Holland *U.S.A.* 40°6N 76°5W **313** F8
New Iberia *U.S.A.* 30°1N 91°49W **314** F9
New Ireland *Papua N. G.* 3°20S 151°50E **286** B6
New Ireland □ *Papua N. G.* 3°0S 151°30E **286** B6
New Jersey □ *U.S.A.* 40°0N 74°30W **309** F16
New Kensington *U.S.A.* 40°34N 79°46W **312** F5
New Lexington *U.S.A.* 39°43N 82°13W **309** F12
New Liskeard *Canada* 47°31N 79°41W **298** C4
New London *Conn., U.S.A.* 41°22N 72°6W **313** E12
New London *Iowa, U.S.A.* 40°55N 91°24W **310** D5
New London *Mo., U.S.A.* 39°35N 91°24W **310** E5
New London *Ohio, U.S.A.* 41°5N 82°24W **312** E2
New London *Wis., U.S.A.* 44°23N 88°45W **308** C9
New Madrid *U.S.A.* 36°36N 89°32W **308** G9
New Malden *U.K.* 51°24N 0°15W **125** B2
New Martinsville *U.S.A.* 39°39N 80°52W **309** F13
New Meadows *U.S.A.* 44°58N 116°18W **304** D5
New Melones L. *U.S.A.* 37°57N 120°31W **306** H6
New Mexico □ *U.S.A.* 34°30N 106°0W **305** J11
New Miami *U.S.A.* 39°26N 84°32W **311** E12
New Milford *Conn., U.S.A.* 41°35N 73°25W **313** E11
New Milford *N.Y., U.S.A.* 40°56N 74°0W **132** A1
New Milford *Pa., U.S.A.* 41°52N 75°44W **313** E9
New Moore I. *Ind. Oc.* 21°37N 89°10E **243** J13
New Mumbai = Navi Mumbai *India* 19°5N 73°0E **130** A2
New Norcia *Australia* 30°57S 116°13E **279** F2
New Norfolk *Australia* 42°46S 147°2E **281** G4
New Orleans *U.S.A.* 29°57N 90°4W **131** B2
New Orleans Int. ✕ (MSY) *U.S.A.* 30°0N 90°15W **131** A1
New Palestine *U.S.A.* 39°45N 85°52W **311** E11
New Panamao *Phil.* 5°59N 121°13E **233** J3
New Paris *U.S.A.* 39°51N 84°48W **311** E12
New Pekin *U.S.A.* 38°30N 86°0W **311** F10
New Philadelphia *U.S.A.* 40°30N 81°27W **312** F3
New Plymouth *N.Z.* 39°4S 174°5E **284** F3
New Plymouth *Idaho, U.S.A.* 43°58N 116°49W **304** E5
New Pomerania = New Britain *Papua N. G.* 5°50S 150°20E **286** C6
New Port Richey *U.S.A.* 28°16N 82°43W **317** G7
New Providence *Bahamas* 25°25N 78°35W **153** b
New Quay *U.K.* 52°13N 4°21W **169** E3
New Radnor *U.K.* 52°15N 3°9W **169** E4
New Richmond *Qué., Canada* 48°15N 65°45W **299** C6
New Richmond *Ohio, U.S.A.* 38°57N 84°17W **311** F12
New Richmond *Wis., U.S.A.* 45°7N 92°32W **308** C7
New River Gorge ⌂ *U.S.A.* 37°53N 81°5W **309** G13
New Roads *U.S.A.* 30°42N 91°26W **314** F9
New Rochelle *U.S.A.* 40°55N 73°46W **313** F11
New Rockford *U.S.A.* 47°41N 99°8W **308** B4
New Romney *U.K.* 50°59N 0°57E **169** G8
New Ross *Ireland* 52°23N 6°57W **166** D5
New Salem *U.S.A.* 46°51N 101°25W **308** B3
New Scone = Scone *U.K.* 56°25N 3°24W **167** E5
New Sharon *U.S.A.* 41°28N 92°39W **310** C4
New Siberian I. = Novaya Sibir, Ostrov *Russia* 75°10N 150°0E **215** B16
New Siberian Is. = Novosibirskiye Ostrova *Russia* 75°0N 142°0E **215** B15
New Smyrna Beach *U.S.A.* 29°1N 80°56W **317** F9
New South Wales □ *Australia* 33°0S 146°0E **283** B7
New Stuyahok *U.S.A.* 59°29N 157°20W **303** G8
New Tecumseth = Alliston *Canada* 44°9N 79°52W **312** B5
New Territories *China* 22°23N 114°10E **122** A1
New Toronto *Canada* 43°35N 79°30W **141** B1
New Town = Nowe Miasto *Warsaw, Poland* **142** a2
New Town *Edinburgh, U.K.* **121** a2
New Town *N. Dak., U.S.A.* 47°59N 102°30W **308** B2
New Tredegar *U.K.* 51°44N 3°16W **169** F4
New Ulm *U.S.A.* 44°19N 94°28W **308** C6
New Utrecht *U.S.A.* 40°36N 73°59W **132** C2
New Vienna *U.S.A.* 39°19N 83°42W **311** E13
New Washington *Phil.* 11°39N 122°26E **233** F4
New Waterford *Canada* 46°13N 60°4W **299** C7
New Westminster *Canada* 49°13N 122°55W **306** A4
New York *U.S.A.* 40°43N 74°0W **132** B3
New York □ *U.S.A.* 43°0N 75°0W **313** D9
New York Avenue *Washington, D.C., U.S.A.* **143** a2
New York J.F. Kennedy Int. ✕ (JFK) *U.S.A.* 40°38N 73°47W **313** F11
New York La Guardia ✕ (LGA) *U.S.A.* 40°46N 73°52W **132** B2
New York University *New York, U.S.A.* **132** d2
New Zealand ■ *Oceania* 40°0S 176°0E **284** G5
Newaj → *India* 24°24N 76°49E **242** G7
Newala *Tanzania* 10°58S 39°18E **269** E4
Newark *Del., U.S.A.* 39°41N 75°46W **309** F16
Newark *N.J., U.S.A.* 40°44N 74°10W **313** F10
Newark *N.Y., U.S.A.* 43°3N 77°6W **312** C7
Newark *Ohio, U.S.A.* 40°3N 82°24W **312** F2
Newark B. *U.S.A.* 40°40N 74°8W **132** B1
Newark Liberty Int. ✕ (EWR) *U.S.A.* 40°42N 74°10W **313** F10
Newark-on-Trent *U.K.* 53°5N 0°48W **168** D7
Newark Valley *U.S.A.* 42°14N 76°11W **313** D8
Newbattle *U.K.* 55°53N 3°4W **121** B3
Newberg *U.S.A.* 45°18N 122°58W **304** D2
Newberry *Fla., U.S.A.* 29°39N 82°37W **317** F7
Newberry *Mich., U.S.A.* 46°21N 85°30W **309** B11
Newberry *S.C., U.S.A.* 34°17N 81°37W **315** D14
Newberry Springs *U.S.A.* 34°50N 116°41W **307** L10
Newboro L. *Canada* 44°38N 76°20W **313** B8
Newbridge = Droichead Nua *Ireland* 53°11N 6°48W **166** C5
Newburg *U.S.A.* 37°55N 91°54W **310** G5
Newburgh *Ont., Canada* 44°19N 76°52W **312** B8
Newburgh *Ind., U.S.A.* 37°57N 87°24W **311** G9
Newburgh *N.Y., U.S.A.* 41°30N 74°1W **313** E10
Newbury *W. Berkshire, U.K.* 51°24N 1°20W **169** F6
Newbury *N.H., U.S.A.* 43°19N 72°3W **313** B12
Newbury *Vt., U.S.A.* 44°5N 72°4W **313** B12
Newbury Park *U.K.* 51°34N 0°5E **125** A4
Newburyport *U.S.A.* 42°49N 70°53W **313** D14
Newcastle *N.S.W., Australia* 33°0S 151°46E **283** B9
Newcastle *N.B., Canada* 47°1N 65°38W **299** C6
Newcastle *Ont., Canada* 43°55N 78°35W **298** D4
Newcastle *St. Kitts & Nevis* 17°14N 62°42W **322** d
Newcastle *KwaZulu Natal, S. Africa* 27°45S 29°58E **271** C4
Newcastle *Down, U.K.* 54°13N 5°54W **166** B6
Newcastle *Calif., U.S.A.* 38°53N 121°8W **306** G5
Newcastle *Wyo., U.S.A.* 43°50N 104°11W **304** E11
Newcastle Emlyn *U.K.* 52°2N 4°28W **169** E3
Newcastle Ra. *Australia* 15°45S 130°15E **278** C5
Newcastle-under-Lyme *U.K.* 53°1N 2°14W **168** D5
Newcastle-upon-Tyne *U.K.* 54°58N 1°36W **168** C6
Newcastle Waters *Australia* 17°30S 133°28E **280** B1
Newcastle West *Ireland* 52°27N 9°3W **166** D2
Newcomb *U.S.A.* 43°58N 74°10W **313** C10
Newcomerstown *U.S.A.* 40°16N 81°36W **312** F3
Newcraighall *U.K.* 55°56N 3°5W **121** B3
Newdegate *Australia* 33°6S 119°0E **279** F2
Newell *Queens., Australia* 16°20S 145°16E **280** B4
Newell *Iowa, U.S.A.* 42°36N 95°0W **310** B1
Newell *S. Dak., U.S.A.* 44°43N 103°25W **308** C2
Newenham, C. *U.S.A.* 58°39N 162°11W **303** G7
Newfane *U.S.A.* 43°17N 78°43W **312** C6
Newfield *U.S.A.* 42°18N 76°33W **313** D8
Newfound L. *U.S.A.* 43°40N 71°47W **313** C13
Newfoundland *Canada* 49°0N 55°0W **299** C8
Newfoundland *Pa., U.S.A.* 41°18N 75°19W **313** E9
Newfoundland & Labrador □ *Canada* 53°0N 58°0W **299** B8
Newhalen *U.S.A.* 59°43N 154°54W **303** G9
Newham □ *U.K.* 51°31N 0°3E **125** A4
Newhaven *E. Sussex, U.K.* 50°47N 0°3E **169** G8
Newhaven *Edinburgh, U.K.* 55°59N 3°11W **121** B2
Newington *Edinburgh, U.K.* 55°56N 3°10W **121** B2
Newington *London, U.K.* **125** c5
Newington *Ga., U.S.A.* 32°35N 81°30W **316** C8
Newkirk *U.S.A.* 36°53N 97°3W **314** C6
Newlands *Wellington, N.Z.* 41°13S 174°49E **143** B1
Newlands *Gauteng, S. Africa* 26°10S 27°57E **123** B1
Newlyn *U.K.* 50°6N 5°34W **169** G2
Newman *W. Austral., Australia* 23°18S 119°45E **278** D2
Newman *Calif., U.S.A.* 37°19N 121°1W **306** H5
Newman *Ill., U.S.A.* 39°48N 87°59W **311** E9
Newmarket *Ont., Canada* 44°3N 79°28W **312** B5
Newmarket *Cork, Ireland* 52°13N 9°0W **166** D2
Newmarket *Jamaica* 18°9N 77°55W **320** a
Newmarket *Suffolk, U.K.* 52°15N 0°25E **169** E8
Newmarket *N.H., U.S.A.* 43°5N 70°56W **313** C14
Newnan *U.S.A.* 33°23N 84°48W **316** B5
Newport = Nieuwpoort *Neth. Ant.* 12°3N 68°49W **322** g
Newport *Vic., Australia* 37°50S 144°51E **128** B1
Newport *Mayo, Ireland* 53°53N 9°33W **166** C2
Newport *I. of W., U.K.* 50°42N 1°17W **169** G6
Newport *Newport, U.K.* 51°35N 3°0W **169** F5
Newport *Ark., U.S.A.* 35°37N 91°16W **314** D9
Newport *Fla., U.S.A.* 30°11N 84°10W **316** E5
Newport *Ind., U.S.A.* 39°53N 87°25W **311** E9
Newport *Ky., U.S.A.* 39°5N 84°29W **311** E12
Newport *N.H., U.S.A.* 43°22N 72°10W **313** C12
Newport *N.Y., U.S.A.* 43°11N 75°1W **313** C9
Newport *Oreg., U.S.A.* 44°39N 124°3W **304** D1
Newport *Pa., U.S.A.* 40°29N 77°8W **312** F7
Newport *R.I., U.S.A.* 41°29N 71°19W **313** E13
Newport *Tenn., U.S.A.* 35°58N 83°11W **315** D13
Newport *Vt., U.S.A.* 44°56N 72°13W **313** B12
Newport *Wash., U.S.A.* 48°11N 117°3W **304** B5
Newport □ *U.K.* 51°33N 3°1W **169** F4
Newport Beach *U.S.A.* 33°37N 117°56W **307** M9
Newport News *U.S.A.* 36°58N 76°25W **309** G15
Newport Pagnell *U.K.* 52°5N 0°43W **169** E7
Newquay *U.K.* 50°25N 5°6W **169** G2
Newry *U.K.* 54°11N 6°21W **166** B5
Newry Islands △ *Australia* 20°51S 148°56E **280** b
Newtok *U.S.A.* 60°56N 164°38W **303** F6
Newton *Ga., U.S.A.* 31°19N 84°20W **316** D5
Newton *Ill., U.S.A.* 38°59N 88°10W **311** F8
Newton *Iowa, U.S.A.* 41°42N 93°3W **310** C3
Newton *Kans., U.S.A.* 38°3N 97°21W **308** F5
Newton *Mass., U.S.A.* 42°21N 71°12W **116** B1
Newton *Miss., U.S.A.* 32°19N 89°10W **315** E10
Newton *N.C., U.S.A.* 35°40N 81°13W **315** D14
Newton *N.J., U.S.A.* 41°3N 74°45W **313** E10
Newton *Tex., U.S.A.* 30°51N 93°46W **314** F8
Newton Abbot *U.K.* 50°32N 3°37W **169** G4
Newton Aycliffe *U.K.* 54°37N 1°34W **168** C6
Newton Falls *N.Y., U.S.A.* 44°12N 74°59W **313** B10
Newton Falls *Ohio, U.S.A.* 41°11N 80°59W **312** E4
Newton L. *U.S.A.* 38°55N 88°15W **311** F8
Newton Stewart *U.K.* 54°57N 4°30W **167** G4
Newton Terrace *Barbados* 13°4N 59°32W **323** r
Newtonbrook *Canada* 43°47N 79°24W **141** A2
Newtongrange *U.K.* 55°53N 3°3W **121** B3
Newtonmore *U.K.* 57°4N 4°8W **167** D4
Newtontoppen *Svalbard* 79°0N 17°30E **154** B12
Newtonville *U.S.A.* 42°20N 71°11W **116** A1
Newtown *N.S.W., Australia* 33°54S 151°11E **139** B2
Newtown *Powys, U.K.* 52°31N 3°19W **169** E4
Newtown *Ind., U.S.A.* 40°13N 87°9W **311** D9
Newtown *Mo., U.S.A.* 40°22N 93°20W **310** D3
Newtownabbey *U.K.* 54°40N 5°56W **166** B6
Newtownards *U.K.* 54°36N 5°42W **166** B6
Newtownbarry = Bunclody *Ireland* 52°39N 6°40W **166** D5
Newtownstewart *U.K.* 54°43N 7°23W **166** B4
Newville *U.S.A.* 40°10N 77°24W **312** F7
Nexon *France* 45°41N 1°11E **174** C5
Neya *Russia* 58°21N 43°49E **190** A6
Neyrīz *Iran* 29°15N 54°19E **247** D7
Neyshābūr *Iran* 36°10N 58°50E **247** B8
Neyveli *India* 11°32N 79°29E **245** J4
Neyyattinkara *India* 8°26N 77°5E **245** K3
Nezametny = Aldan *Russia* 58°40N 125°30E **215** D13
Nezhin = Nizhyn *Ukraine* 51°5N 31°55E **189** G6
Nezperce *U.S.A.* 46°14N 116°14W **304** C5
Nezvysko *Ukraine* 48°46N 25°15E **183** B10
Ngaanyatjarra ⊙ *Australia* 22°40S 127°0E **278** D4
Ngabang *Indonesia* 0°23N 109°55E **235** B3
Ngabe *Congo* 3°12S 16°12E **264** C3
Ngabordamlu, Tanjung *Indonesia* 6°56S 134°11E **231** F8
N'Gage *Angola* 7°46S 15°15E **265** D3
Ngaio *N.Z.* 41°15S 174°46E **143** B1
Ngaiphaipi *Burma* 22°14N 93°15E **241** D4
Ngala *Nigeria* 12°20N 14°11E **263** C7
Ngaliwurru Nungali ⊙ *Australia* 15°42S 130°4E **278** C5
Ngalurrtju ⊙ *Australia* 22°44S 132°5E **278** D5
Ngama *Chad* 11°45N 17°6E **259** F3
Ngambé *Centre, Cameroon* 5°48N 11°29E **263** D7
Ngambé *Littoral, Cameroon* 4°21N 10°40E **263** E7
Ngami Depression *Botswana* 20°30S 22°46E **270** B3
Ngamo *Zimbabwe* 19°3S 27°32E **269** F2
Nganbéto, L. de *Togo* 7°26N 1°25E **263** D5
Ngangala *Sudan* 4°42N 31°55E **257** G3
Nganglong Kangri *China* 33°0N 81°0E **243** C9
Nganjuk *Indonesia* 7°32S 111°55E **235** D4
Ngao *Thailand* 18°46N 99°59E **236** C2
Ngaoundéré *Cameroon* 7°15N 13°35E **264** A2
Ngapali *Burma* 18°26N 94°19E **241** F5
Ngapara *N.Z.* 44°57S 170°46E **285** E5
Ngape *Burma* 20°2N 94°28E **241** E5
Ngara *Tanzania* 2°29S 30°40E **268** C3
Ngardmau *Palau* 7°37N 134°34E **288** c
Ngardmau B. *Palau* 7°38N 134°34E **288** c
Ngardololok *Palau* 7°0N 134°14E **288** c
Ngaregur *Palau* 7°45N 134°37E **288** c
Ngarluma ⊙ *Australia* 21°30S 118°30E **278** D2
Ngaruawahia *N.Z.* 37°42S 175°11E **284** D4
Ngaruroro → *N.Z.* 39°34S 176°55E **284** F5
Ngatangiia *Cook Is.* 21°14S 159°43W **289** h
Ngatapa *N.Z.* 38°32S 177°45E **284** E6
Ngathainggyaung *Burma* 17°24N 95°5E **241** G5
Ngau Chi Wan *China* 22°20N 114°12E **122** A2
Ngau Tau Kok *China* 22°19N 114°12E **122** B2
Ngauranga *N.Z.* 41°15S 174°49E **143** B1
Ngauruhoe, Mt. *N.Z.* 39°13S 175°45E **284** F4
Ngawi *Indonesia* 7°24S 111°26E **235** D4
Ngcobo *S. Africa* 31°37S 28°0E **271** D4
Ngele *Dem. Rep. of the Congo* 0°30S 20°22E **264** C4
Ngelebok *Cameroon* 4°16N 14°3E **264** B2
Ngeregong *Palau* 7°6N 134°21E **288** c
Ngergoi *Palau* 7°5N 134°15E **288** c
Ngeru *Uganda* 0°27N 33°10E **268** B3
Ngesebus I. *Palau* 7°3N 134°15E **288** c
Nggatokae *Solomon Is.* 8°45S 158°15E **287** M10
Nggela Pile *Solomon Is.* 9°2S 160°20E **287** M11
Nggela Sule *Solomon Is.* 9°2S 160°12E **287** M11
Nghia Lo *Vietnam* 21°33N 104°28E **228** G5
Ngidinga *Dem. Rep. of the Congo* 5°37S 15°17E **265** D3
Ngo *Congo* 2°29S 15°45E **264** C3
Ngoap *Cameroon* 4°9N 12°51E **264** B2
Ngobasangel *Palau* 7°16N 134°19E **288** c
Ngoboli *Sudan* 4°57N 32°37E **257** G3
N'Gola *Angola* 14°10S 14°30E **265** E2
Ngoma *Malawi* 13°8S 33°45E **269** E3
Ngomahura *Zimbabwe* 20°26S 30°43E **269** G3
Ngomba *Tanzania* 8°20S 32°53E **269** D3
Ngomeni, Ras *Kenya* 2°59S 40°14E **268** C5
Ngong *Kenya* 1°22S 36°39E **268** C4
Ngong Shuen Chau *China* 22°19N 114°8E **122** B1
Ngongotaha *N.Z.* 38°5S 176°12E **284** E5
Ngonye Falls *Zambia* 16°40S 23°25E **265** F4
Ngop *Sudan* 6°17N 30°9E **257** F3
Ngoring Hu *China* 34°55N 97°5E **218** C4
Ngorkou *Mali* 15°40N 3°41W **262** B4
Ngorongoro *Tanzania* 3°11S 35°32E **268** C4
Ngorongoro ⌂ *Tanzania* 2°40S 35°30E **268** C4
Ngoto *C.A.R.* 3°59N 17°19E **264** B3
Ngouo, Dj. *C.A.R.* 7°55N 24°38E **264** A4
Ngoura *Chad* 12°44N 16°21E **259** F3
Ngouri *Chad* 13°38N 15°22E **259** F3
Ngourti *Niger* 15°19N 13°12E **259** E2
Ngoussou *Gabon* 3°0S 11°7E **264** C2
Ngozi *Burundi* 2°54S 29°50E **268** C2
Ngua Kok Wan *China* 22°21N 114°5E **122** A1
Ngudu *Tanzania* 2°58S 33°25E **268** C3
Nguigmi *Niger* 14°20N 13°20E **259** F2
Nguila *Cameroon* 4°41N 11°43E **263** E7
Nguiu *Australia* 11°46S 130°38E **278** B5
Ngukurr *Australia* 14°44S 134°44E **280** A1
Nguna *Vanuatu* 17°26S 168°22E **287** G6
Ngundu *Zimbabwe* 18°11S 31°15E **269** F3
Ngunga *Tanzania* 3°37S 33°37E **268** C3
Nguru *Nigeria* 12°56N 10°29E **263** C7
Nguru Mts. *Tanzania* 6°0S 37°30E **268** D4
Ngusi *Malawi* 14°0S 34°50E **269** E3
Nguyen Binh *Vietnam* 22°39N 105°56E **228** F5
Ngwedaung *Burma* 19°31N 97°12E **241** F6
Nha Trang *Vietnam* 12°16N 109°10E **237** F7
Nhacoongo *Mozam.* 24°18S 35°14E **271** B6
Nhamaabué *Mozam.* 17°25S 35°5E **269** F4
Nhambiquara *Brazil* 12°50S 59°49W **331** C6
Nhamundá *Brazil* 2°14S 56°43W **329** D6
Nhamundá → *Brazil* 2°12S 56°41W **329** D6
Nhangulaze, L. *Mozam.* 24°0S 34°30E **271** B5
Nharêa *Angola* 11°38S 16°58E **265** E3
Nharnuwangga, Wajarri and Ngarlawangga ⊙ *Australia* 24°50S 118°0E **279** D2
Nhava Sheva *India* 18°58N 72°55E **130** B2
Nhecolândia *Brazil* 19°17S 56°58W **331** D6
Nhill *Australia* 36°18S 141°40E **282** D4
Nho Quan *Vietnam* 20°18N 105°45E **228** G5
Nhulunbuy *Australia* 12°10S 137°20E **280** A2
Nhundo *Angola* 14°25S 21°23E **265** E4
Nia-nia *Dem. Rep. of the Congo* 1°30N 27°40E **268** B2
Niafounké *Mali* 16°0N 4°5W **262** B4
Niagara Falls *Ont., Canada* 43°7N 79°5W **312** C5
Niagara Falls *N.Y., U.S.A.* 43°5N 79°4W **312** C6
Niagara-on-the-Lake *Canada* 43°15N 79°4W **312** C5
Niah *Malaysia* 3°58N 113°46E **235** B4
Nialaha'u Pt. *Solomon Is.* 9°47S 161°34E **287** M11
Niamey *Niger* 13°27N 2°6E **263** C5
Niamtougou *Togo* 9°46N 1°6E **263** D5
Niandan-Koro *Guinea* 11°5N 9°15W **262** C3
Nianforando *Guinea* 9°37N 10°36W **262** D2
Niangara *Dem. Rep. of the Congo* 3°42N 27°50E **268** B2
Niangay, L. *Mali* 15°50N 3°0W **262** B4
Niangbo *Ivory C.* 8°49N 5°10W **262** D3
Niangoloko *Burkina Faso* 10°15N 4°55W **262** C4
Niangua → *U.S.A.* 38°58N 92°48W **310** G4
Niantic *U.S.A.* 41°20N 72°11W **313** E12
Niari *Congo* 4°9S 14°9E **264** C2
Niaro *Sudan* 10°38N 31°31E **257** E3
Nias *Indonesia* 1°0N 97°30E **234** B1
Niassa □ *Mozam.* 13°30S 36°0E **269** E4
Niassa ⌂ *Mozam.* 12°4S 36°57E **269** E4
Niāvarān *Iran* 35°47N 51°29E **141** A2
Nibāk *Si. Arabia* 24°25N 50°50E **247** E7
Nibe *Denmark* 56°59N 9°38E **163** H3
Nibra *India* 22°36N 88°15E **124** B1
Nicaragua ■ *Cent. Amer.* 11°40N 85°30W **320** D2
Nicaragua, L. de *Nic.* 12°0N 85°30W **320** D2
Nicastro *Italy* 38°59N 16°19E **201** D9
Nice *France* 43°42N 7°14E **175** E11
Nice-Côte-d'Azur ✕ (NCE) *France* 43°41N 7°12E **175** E11
Niceville *U.S.A.* 30°31N 86°30W **317** E3
Nichicun, L. *Canada* 53°5N 71°0W **299** B5
Nichinan *Japan* 31°38N 131°23E **222** F3
Nicholás, Canal *W. Indies* 23°30N 80°5W **320** B3
Nicholasville *U.S.A.* 37°53N 84°34W **311** G12
Nichols *U.S.A.* 42°1N 76°22W **313** D8
Nicholson *W. Austral., Australia* 18°2S 128°54E **278** C4
Nicholson *Pa., U.S.A.* 41°37N 75°47W **313** E9
Nicholson → *Australia* 17°31S 139°36E **280** B2
Nicholson L. *Canada* 62°40N 102°40W **297** A8
Nicholson Ra. *Australia* 27°15S 116°45E **279** E2
Nicholville *U.S.A.* 44°41N 74°39W **313** B10
Nickerie → *Suriname* 5°58N 57°0W **329** B6
Nico Pérez = José Batlle y Ordóñez *Uruguay* 33°20S 55°10W **335** C4
Nicobar Is. *Ind. Oc.* 8°0N 93°30E **245** L11
Nicola *Canada* 50°12N 120°40W **296** C4
Nicolls Town *Bahamas* 25°8N 78°0W **320** A4
Nicosia *Cyprus* 35°10N 33°25E **207** E9
Nicosia *Italy* 37°45N 14°24E **201** E7
Nicótera *Italy* 38°33N 15°56E **201** D8
Nicoya *Costa Rica* 10°9N 85°27W **320** D2
Nicoya, G. de *Costa Rica* 10°0N 85°0W **320** E3
Nicoya, Pen. de *Costa Rica* 9°45N 85°40W **320** E2
Nictheroy = Niterói *Brazil* 22°53S 43°7W **135** B2
Nida *Lithuania* 55°20N 21°4E **184** C8
Nidāl *Iraq* 33°19N 44°25E **113** B2
Nidaros = Trondheim *Norway* 63°36N 10°25E **164** A7
Nidd → *U.K.* 53°59N 1°23W **168** D6
Nidda *Germany* 50°23N 9°1E **179** E5
Nidda → *Germany* 50°17N 8°48E **179** E4
Niddrie *Vic., Australia* 37°44S 144°51E **128** A1
Niddrie *Edinburgh, U.K.* 55°56N 3°7W **121** B3
Nidri *Greece* 38°43N 20°42E **207** B2
Nidwalden □ *Switz.* 46°50N 8°25E **179** J4
Nidzica *Poland* 53°25N 20°28E **185** E7
Niebüll *Germany* 54°46N 8°48E **178** A4
Nied → *Germany* 49°23N 6°40E **179** F2
Nieder Neuendorf *Germany* 52°36N 13°12E **115** A2
Niederaula *Germany* 50°47N 9°36E **178** E5
Niederbayern □ *Germany* 48°40N 12°50E **179** G8
Niederbronn-les-Bains *France* 48°57N 7°39E **173** D14
Niedere Tauern *Austria* 47°20N 14°0E **180** D7
Niederlausitz *Germany* 51°42N 13°59E **178** D9
Niederösterreich □ *Austria* 48°25N 15°40E **180** C8
Niedersachsen □ *Germany* 52°50N 9°0E **178** C4
Niedersächsisches Wattenmeer △ *Germany* 53°45N 7°30E **178** B3
Niederschöneweide *Germany* 52°27N 13°30E **115** B3
Niederschönhausen *Germany* 52°35N 13°25E **115** A3
Niefang *Eq. Guin.* 1°50N 10°14E **264** B2
Niekerkshoop *S. Africa* 29°19S 22°51E **270** C3
Niel *Belgium* 51°7N 4°20E **170** C4
Niellé *Ivory C.* 10°5N 5°38W **262** C3
Niellim *Chad* 9°42N 17°49E **259** G3
Niem *C.A.R.* 6°12N 15°14E **264** A3
Niemba *Dem. Rep. of the Congo* 5°58S 28°24E **268** D2
Niemen = Nemunas → *Lithuania* 55°25N 21°10E **184** C8
Niemeyer *Brazil* 22°59S 43°16W **135** B1
Niemodlin *Poland* 50°38N 17°38E **185** H4
Niemur *Australia* 35°17S 144°9E **282** C6
Nienburg *Germany* 52°39N 9°13E **178** C5
Niepołomice *Poland* 50°3N 20°13E **185** H7
Niers → *Germany* 51°43N 5°57E **178** D1
Niesky *Germany* 51°17N 14°49E **178** D10
Nieszawa *Poland* 52°52N 18°50E **185** F5
Nieu Bethesda *S. Africa* 31°51S 24°34E **270** D3
Nieuw Amsterdam *Suriname* 5°53N 55°5W **329** B6
Nieuw Nickerie *Suriname* 6°0N 56°59W **329** B6
Nieuwe Kerk *Amsterdam, Neths.* **112** a2
Nieuwendam *Neths.* 52°23N 4°57E **112** A2
Nieuwoudtville *S. Africa* 31°23S 19°7E **270** D2
Nieuwpoort *Belgium* 51°8N 2°45E **170** C2
Nieuwpoort *Neth. Ant.* 12°3N 68°49W **322** g
Nieves, Pico de las *Canary Is.* 27°57N 15°35W **153** e1
Nièvre □ *France* 47°10N 3°40E **173** E10
Nif *Micronesia* 9°28N 138°4E **287** S16
Niğde *Turkey* 37°58N 34°40E **212** D6
Niğde □ *Turkey* 38°0N 34°30E **212** D6
Nigel *S. Africa* 26°27S 28°25E **271** C4
Niger ■ *W. Afr.* 17°30N 10°0E **259** E2
Niger → *W. Afr.* 5°33N 6°33E **263** E6
Niger Delta *Africa* 5°0N 6°0E **263** E6
Nigeria ■ *W. Afr.* 8°30N 8°0E **263** D6
Nighasin *India* 28°14N 80°52E **243** E9
Nightcaps *N.Z.* 45°57S 168°2E **285** F3
Nightmute *U.S.A.* 60°29N 164°44W **303** F6
Nigrita *Greece* 40°56N 23°29E **202** F7
Nihoa *U.S.A.* 23°6N 161°58W **302** G11
Nihon = Japan ■ *Asia* 36°0N 136°0E **221** G8
Nihonbashi *Tokyo, Japan* **140** b5
Nii-Jima *Japan* 34°20N 139°15E **223** C11
Niigata *Japan* 37°58N 139°0E **220** F9
Niigata □ *Japan* 37°15N 138°45E **221** F9
Niihama *Japan* 33°55N 133°16E **222** D5
Ni'ihau *U.S.A.* 21°54N 160°9W **302** B1
Niimi *Japan* 34°59N 133°28E **222** C5
Niipperi *Finland* 60°18N 24°45E **121** B1
Niislel Khureheh = Ulaanbaatar *Mongolia* 47°55N 106°53E **218** B5
Niitsu *Japan* 37°48N 139°7E **220** F9
Nij Laluk *India* 27°7N 93°56E **241** B4
Nijar *Spain* 36°53N 2°15W **197** J2
Nijil *Jordan* 30°32N 35°33E **251** H6
Nijkerk *Neths.* 52°13N 5°30E **170** B5
Nijmegen *Neths.* 51°50N 5°52E **170** C5
Nijverdal *Neths.* 52°22N 6°28E **170** B6
Nīk Pey *Iran* 36°50N 48°10E **213** D13
Nikao *Cook Is.* 21°12S 159°48W **289** h
Nikaweratiya *Sri Lanka* 7°45N 80°7E **245** L5
Nike *Nigeria* 6°26N 7°29E **263** D6
Nikea *Greece* 37°57N 23°38E **112** B1
Nikel *Russia* 69°24N 30°13E **160** B24
Nikiboko *Neth. Ant.* 12°9N 68°16W **322** h
Nikiniki *Indonesia* 9°49S 124°30E **278** A3
Nikisiani *Greece* 40°57N 24°9E **203** F8
Nikiski *U.S.A.* 61°41N 151°18W **303** F10
Nikiti *Greece* 40°13N 23°43E **202** F7
Nikitinskiye promysly = Kirovskiy *Russia* 45°51N 48°11E **191** H9
Nikki *Benin* 9°58N 3°12E **263** D5
Nikkō *Japan* 36°45N 139°35E **223** A11
Nikkō △ *Japan* 36°56N 139°37E **221** F9
Nikolai *U.S.A.* 62°58N 154°10W **303** F9
Nikolainkaupunki = Vaasa *Finland* 63°6N 21°38E **160** E19
Nikolaistad = Vaasa *Finland* 63°6N 21°38E **160** E19
Nikolassee *Germany* 52°25N 13°12E **115** B2
Nikolayev = Mykolayiv *Ukraine* 46°58N 32°0E **189** J7
Nikolayevsk *Russia* 50°0N 45°35E **190** E7
Nikolayevsk-na-Amur *Russia* 53°8N 140°44E **215** D15
Nikolsburg = Mikulov *Czech Rep.* 48°48N 16°39E **181** C9
Nikolsk *Russia* 53°49N 46°4E **190** D8
Nikolsk-Ussuriysky = Ussuriysk *Russia* 43°48N 131°59E **220** C5
Nikolskaya Pestravka = Nikolsk *Russia* 53°49N 46°4E **190** D8
Nikolski *U.S.A.* 52°56N 168°52W **303** K5
Nikolskiy *Russia* 55°49N 37°29E **129** B2
Nikolskoye = Ussuriysk *Russia* 43°48N 131°59E **220** C5
Nikolskoye *Russia* 55°12N 166°0E **215** D17
Nikolsky Khutor = Sursk *Russia* 53°3N 45°40E **190** D7
Nikolyskoye *Russia* 55°46N 37°53E **129** B5
Nikopol *Bulgaria* 43°43N 24°54E **203** C8
Nikopol *Ukraine* 47°35N 34°25E **189** J8
Nikopolis *Greece* 39°5N 20°43E **207** A2
Niksar *Turkey* 40°31N 37°2E **212** B7
Nīkshahr *Iran* 26°15N 60°10E **247** E9
Nikšić *Montenegro* 42°50N 18°57E **202** D2
Nikulino *Russia* 55°40N 37°25E **129** B2
Nikumaroro *Kiribati* 4°40S 174°32W **277** A16
Nikunau *Kiribati* 1°22S 176°28E **277** A14
Nîl, Nahr en → *Africa* 30°10N 31°6E **256** H7
Nîl el Abyad → *Sudan* 15°38N 32°31E **257** D3
Nîl el Azraq → *Sudan* 15°38N 32°31E **257** D3
Nila *Indonesia* 6°44S 129°31E **231** F7
Nilakkottai *India* 10°10N 77°52E **245** J3
Niland *U.S.A.* 33°14N 115°31W **307** M11
Nilanga *India* 18°6N 76°46E **244** E3
Nile = Nîl, Nahr en → *Africa* 30°10N 31°6E **256** H7
Nile Delta *Egypt* 31°40N 31°0E **256** H7
Niles *Ill., U.S.A.* 42°1N 87°48W **119** A2
Niles *Mich., U.S.A.* 41°50N 86°15W **311** C10
Niles *Ohio, U.S.A.* 41°11N 80°46W **312** E4
Niles Center = Skokie *U.S.A.* 42°2N 87°43W **119** A2
Nileshwar *India* 12°15N 75°6E **245** H2
Nilgiri Hills *India* 11°30N 76°30E **245** J3
Nilo Peçanha *Brazil* 13°37S 39°6W **333** D4
Nilsebu *Norway* 59°11N 6°39E **164** E3
Nilüfer → *Turkey* 40°18N 28°27E **203** F12
Nim Ka Thana *India* 27°44N 75°48E **242** F6
Nimach *India* 24°30N 74°56E **242** G6
Nimba, Mts. *Africa* 7°37N 8°25W **262** D3
Nimbahera *India* 24°37N 74°45E **242** G6
Nîmes *France* 43°50N 4°23E **175** E8
Nimfaíon, Ákra = Pines, Akra *Greece* 40°5N 24°20E **203** F8
Nimmitabel *Australia* 36°29S 149°15E **283** D8
Nīmrūz □ *Afghan.* 30°0N 62°0E **240** C1
Nimta *India* 22°40N 88°24E **124** A2
Nimule *Sudan* 3°32N 32°3E **257** G3
Nimule △ *Sudan* 3°38N 32°2E **257** G3
Nin *Croatia* 44°16N 15°12E **199** D12
Nīnawá *Iraq* 36°25N 43°10E **213** D10
Nīnawá □ *Iraq* 36°15N 43°0E **246** B4
Ninda *Angola* 14°47S 21°24E **265** E4
Nindigully *Australia* 28°21S 148°50E **281** D4
Nine Degree Channel *India* 9°0N 73°0E **245** K1
Ninepin Group *China* 22°16N 114°21E **219** G11
Ninety Mile Beach *N.Z.* 34°48S 173°0E **284** A2
Ninety Mile Beach, The *Australia* 38°15S 147°24E **283** E7
Ninety Six *U.S.A.* 34°11N 82°1W **316** A7
Ninetyeast Ridge *Ind. Oc.* 1°0S 90°0E **273** E7
Nineveh = Nīnawá *Iraq* 36°25N 43°10E **213** D10
Ning Xian *China* 35°30N 107°58E **226** G4
Ningaloo Marine ⌂ *Australia* 22°23S 113°32E **278** D1
Ning'an *China* 44°22N 129°20E **227** B15
Ningbo *China* 29°51N 121°28E **229** C13
Ningcheng *China* 41°32N 119°53E **227** D10
Ningde *China* 26°38N 119°23E **229** D12
Ningdu *China* 26°25N 115°59E **229** D10
Ningerum *Papua N. G.* 5°41S 141°8E **286** C1
Ningguo *China* 30°35N 119°0E **229** B12
Ninghai *China* 29°15N 121°27E **229** C13
Ninghua *China* 26°14N 116°45E **229** D11
Ningi *Nigeria* 10°55N 9°30E **263** C6
Ningjin *China* 37°35N 114°57E **226** F8
Ningjing Shan *China* 30°0N 98°20E **228** C2
Ninglang *China* 27°20N 100°52E **228** D3
Ningling *China* 34°25N 115°22E **226** G8
Ningming *China* 22°8N 107°4E **228** F6
Ningnan *China* 27°5N 102°36E **228** D4
Ningpo = Ningbo *China* 29°51N 121°28E **229** C13
Ningqiang *China* 32°47N 106°15E **226** H4
Ningshan *China* 33°21N 108°21E **226** H5
Ningsia Hui A.R. = Ningxia Huizu Zizhiqu □ *China* 38°0N 106°0E **226** F4
Ningwu *China* 39°0N 112°18E **226** E7
Ningxia Huizu Zizhiqu □ *China* 38°0N 106°0E **226** F4
Ningxiang *China* 28°15N 112°30E **229** C9
Ningyang *China* 35°47N 116°45E **226** G9
Ningyuan *China* 25°37N 111°57E **229** E8
Ninh Binh *Vietnam* 20°15N 105°55E **228** G5
Ninh Giang *Vietnam* 20°44N 106°24E **236** B6
Ninh Hoa *Vietnam* 12°30N 109°7E **236** F7
Ninh Ma *Vietnam* 12°48N 109°21E **236** F7
Nini-Suhien △ *Ghana* 5°20N 2°34W **262** D4
Ninigo Group *Papua N. G.* 1°22S 144°17E **286** A3
Ninove *Belgium* 50°51N 4°2E **170** D4
Ninoy Aquino Int. ✕ (MNL) *Phil.* 14°31N 121°0E **127** B2
Nioaque *Brazil* 21°5S 55°50W **335** A4
Niobrara *U.S.A.* 42°45N 98°2W **308** D4
Niobrara → *U.S.A.* 42°46N 98°3W **308** D4
Niokolo-Koba △ *Senegal* 13°3N 13°2W **262** C2
Niono *Mali* 14°15N 6°0W **262** C3
Nionsamoridougou *Guinea* 8°45N 8°50W **262** D3
Nioro du Rip *Senegal* 13°40N 15°50W **262** C1
Nioro du Sahel *Mali* 15°15N 9°30W **262** B3
Niort *France* 46°19N 0°29W **174** B3
Nioumachoua *Comoros Is.* 12°21S 43°42E **272** a
Nipa *Papua N. G.* 6°9S 143°29E **286** D2
Nipani *India* 16°20N 74°25E **245** F2
Nipawin *Canada* 53°20N 104°0W **297** C8
Nipfjället *Sweden* 61°59N 12°50E **162** C6
Nipigon *Canada* 49°0N 88°17W **298** C2
Nipigon, L. *Canada* 49°50N 88°30W **298** C2
Nipishish L. *Canada* 54°12N 60°45W **299** B7
Nipissing, L. *Canada* 46°20N 80°0W **298** C4
Nipomo *U.S.A.* 35°3N 120°29W **307** K6
Nippa *Japan* 35°32N 139°36E **140** B2
Nippon = Japan ■ *Asia* 36°0N 136°0E **221** G8
Nippori *Japan* 35°43N 139°45E **140** A3
Nipton *U.S.A.* 35°28N 115°16W **307** K11
Niquelândia *Brazil* 14°33S 48°23W **333** D2
Nīr *Iran* 38°2N 47°59E **213** C12
Nira → *India* 17°58N 75°8E **244** F2
Nirasaki *Japan* 35°42N 138°27E **223** B10
Nirmal *India* 19°3N 78°20E **244** E4
Nirmali *India* 26°20N 86°35E **243** F12
Niš *Serbia* 43°19N 21°58E **202** C5
Nisa = Nysa → *Europe* 52°4N 14°46E **178** C10
Nisa *Portugal* 39°30N 7°41W **195** F3

Nişāb Si. Arabia 29°11N 44°43E 246 D5
Nişāb Yemen 14°25N 46°29E 248 D4
Nišava → Serbia 43°20N 21°46E 202 C5
Niscemi Italy 37°9N 14°23E 201 E7
Nishi Japan 34°40N 135°28E 133 A1
Nishi-Sonogi-Hantō Japan 32°55N 129°45E 222 E1
Nishi-Tosa Japan 33°13N 132°46E 222 D4
Nishinari Japan 34°37N 135°28E 133 B1
Nishinomiya Japan 34°45N 135°20E 133 A1
Nishino'omote Japan 30°43N 130°59E 221 J5
Nishio Japan 34°52N 137°3E 223 C9
Nishiwaki Japan 34°59N 134°58E 222 C6
Nishiyodogawa Japan 34°41N 135°24E 133 A1
Nisibin = Nusaybin Turkey 37°3N 41°10E 213 D9
Niška Banja Serbia 43°18N 22°1E 202 C6
Niskibi → Canada 56°29N 88°9W 298 A2
Nisko Poland 50°35N 22°7E 185 H9
Nisporeni Moldova 47°4N 28°10E 183 C13
Nisqually → U.S.A. 47°7N 122°42W 306 C4
Nissaki Greece 39°43N 19°52E 206 B9
Nissan → Sweden 56°40N 12°51E 163 H6
Nissedal Norway 59°10N 8°30E 164 E5
Nisser Norway 59°7N 8°28E 164 E5
Nissiros Greece 36°35N 27°12E 205 E9
Nissum Bredning Denmark 56°40N 8°20E 163 H2
Nissum Fjord Denmark 56°20N 8°11E 163 H2
Nistru = Dnister → Europe 46°18N 30°17E 177 E16
Nisutlin → Canada 60°14N 132°34W 296 A2
Nitchequon Canada 53°10N 70°58W 299 B5
Niterói Brazil 22°53S 43°7W 135 B2
Nith → Ont., Canada 43°12N 80°23W 312 C4
Nith → Dumf. & Gall., U.K. 55°14N 3°33W 167 F5
Nitmiluk △ Australia 14°6S 132°15E 278 B5
Nitra Slovak Rep. 48°19N 18°4E 181 C11
Nitra → Slovak Rep. 47°46N 18°10E 181 D11
Nitriansky ☐ Slovak Rep. 48°10N 18°30E 181 C11
Nittenau Germany 49°12N 12°16E 179 F8
Niu Valley U.S.A. 21°19N 157°44W 302 K14
Niua Group Tonga 15°57S 173°45W 277 D16
Niuafo'ou Tonga 15°30S 175°58W 277 D15
Niuatoputapu Tonga 15°57S 173°45W 277 D16
Niue Pac. Oc. 19°2S 169°54W 289 g
Niulakita Pac. Oc. 10°45S 179°30E 277 C14
Niulan Jiang → China 27°30N 103°5E 228 D4
Niulanstun Taiwan 25°1N 121°2E 225 A3
Niur Indonesia 0°26S 103°30E 234 C2
Niut Indonesia 0°55N 110°6E 235 B4
Niutao Pac. Oc. 6°7S 177°18E 277 B14
Niutou Shan China 29°5N 121°59E 229 C13
Niuzhuang China 40°58N 122°28E 224 B11
Nivala Finland 63°56N 24°57E 160 E21
Nivelles Belgium 50°35N 4°20E 170 D4
Nivernais France 47°15N 3°30E 173 E10
Niverville Canada 49°36N 97°3W 297 D9
Niwas India 23°3N 80°26E 243 H9
Nixa U.S.A. 37°3N 93°18W 308 G7
Nixon U.S.A. 29°16N 97°46W 314 G6
Nizam Sagar India 18°10N 77°58E 244 E3
Nizamabad India 18°45N 78°7E 244 E4
Nizamghat India 28°20N 95°45E 241 A5
Nizhne Kolymsk Russia 68°34N 160°55E 215 C17
Nizhnegorskiy = Nyzhnohirskyy Ukraine 45°27N 34°38E 189 K8
Nizhnekamsk Russia 55°38N 51°49E 190 C10
Nizhneudinsk Russia 54°54N 99°3E 215 D10
Nizhnevartovsk Russia 60°56N 76°38E 214 C8
Nizhniy Bestyakh Russia 61°57N 129°54E 215 C13
Nizhniy Chir Russia 48°22N 43°5E 191 F6
Nizhniy Lomov Russia 53°34N 43°38E 190 D6
Nizhniy Novgorod Russia 56°20N 44°0E 190 B7
Nizhniy Novgorod ☐ Russia 56°30N 44°20E 190 B7
Nizhniy Tagil Russia 57°55N 59°57E 186 C10
Nizhniye Kresty = Cherskiy Russia 68°45N 161°18E 215 C17
Nizhyn Ukraine 51°5N 31°55E 189 G6
Nizina Mazowiecka Poland 52°30N 21°0E 185 F8
Nizip Turkey 37°5N 37°50E 212 D7
Nízké Tatry Slovak Rep. 48°55N 19°30E 181 C12
Nízké Tatry △ Slovak Rep. 48°55N 19°37E 181 C12
Nízký Jeseník Czech Rep. 49°50N 17°30E 181 B10
Nizwá Oman 22°56N 57°32E 249 B7
Nizza Monferrato Italy 44°46N 8°21E 198 D5
Njakwa Malawi 11°1S 33°56E 269 E3
Njanji Zambia 14°25S 31°46E 269 E3
Njarðvík Iceland 63°59N 22°32W 155 D4
Njazidja = Grande Comore Comoros Is. 11°35S 43°20E 272 a
Njegoš Montenegro 42°53N 18°45E 202 D2
Njinjo Tanzania 8°48S 38°54E 269 D4
Njoko → Zambia 17°8S 24°4E 265 F4
Njombe Tanzania 9°20S 34°50E 269 D3
Njombe → Tanzania 6°56S 35°6E 268 D4
Njurundabommen Sweden 62°15N 17°25E 162 B11
Nkambe Cameroon 6°35N 10°40E 263 D7
Nkana Zambia 12°50S 28°8E 269 E2
Nkandla S. Africa 28°37S 31°5E 271 C5
Nkawkaw Ghana 6°36N 0°49W 263 D4
Nkayi Congo 4°9S 13°17E 264 C2
Nkayi Zimbabwe 19°41S 29°20E 269 F2
Nkhotakota Malawi 12°56S 34°15E 269 E3
Nkhotakota ⌓ Malawi 12°50S 34°0E 269 E3
Nkolabona Gabon 1°14N 11°43E 264 B2
Nkomi, Lagune Gabon 1°35S 9°17E 264 C1
Nkondwe Tanzania 5°51S 30°51E 268 D3
Nkone Dem. Rep. of the Congo 1°25S 22°20E 264 C4
Nkongsamba Cameroon 4°55N 9°55E 263 E6
Nkoteng Cameroon 4°31N 12°2E 264 B2
Nkunga Dem. Rep. of the Congo 4°41S 18°34E 265 C3
Nkurenkuru Namibia 17°42S 18°32E 270 A2
Nkwanta Ghana 6°10N 2°10W 262 D4
Nmai → Burma 25°30N 97°25E 228 F2
Noakhali Bangla. 22°48N 91°10E 241 D3
Noatak U.S.A. 67°34N 162°58W 303 C7
Noatak ⌓ U.S.A. 68°10N 160°0W 303 B8
Nob Hill San Francisco, U.S.A. 136 b1
Nobel Canada 45°25N 80°6W 312 A4
Nobeoka Japan 32°36N 131°41E 222 E3
Noble U.S.A. 38°42N 88°14W 311 F8
Noblejas Spain 39°58N 3°26W 194 F7
Noblesville U.S.A. 40°3N 86°1W 311 D11
Noboribetsu Japan 42°24N 141°6E 220 C10
Nocatee U.S.A. 27°10N 81°53W 317 H8
Noccundra Australia 27°50S 142°36E 281 D3
Noce → Italy 46°9N 11°4E 198 B8
Nocera Inferiore Italy 40°44N 14°38E 201 B7
Nocera Umbra Italy 43°5N 12°47E 199 E9
Noci Italy 40°48N 17°7E 201 B10
Nockeby Sweden 59°19N 17°56E 139 B1
Nocona U.S.A. 33°47N 97°44W 314 E6
Nocrich Romania 45°55N 24°26E 183 E9
Noda Japan 35°56N 139°52E 223 B11
Nodeland Norway 58°8N 7°51E 164 F4
Noel Kempff Mercado △ Bolivia 14°9S 60°49W 331 C5
Noel Park U.K. 51°35N 0°5W 125 A3
Nogal Valley = Nugaaleed, Dooxo Somali Rep. 8°35N 48°35E 267 C6
Nogales Sonora, Mexico 31°19N 110°56W 318 A2
Nogales Ariz., U.S.A. 31°21N 110°56W 305 L8
Nogaro France 43°45N 0°2W 174 E3
Nogat → Poland 54°17N 19°17E 184 D6
Nōgata Japan 33°48N 130°44E 222 D2
Nogatino Russia 55°41N 37°41E 129 B4
Nogaysk = Prymorskoye Ukraine 46°48N 36°20E 189 J9
Nogent France 48°1N 5°20E 173 D12
Nogent-le-Rotrou France 48°20N 0°50E 172 D7
Nogent-sur-Marne France 48°50N 2°28E 134 A3
Nogent-sur-Seine France 48°30N 3°30E 173 D10
Noggara Ethiopia 13°54N 36°35E 257 E4
Noggerup Australia 33°32S 116°5E 279 F2
Noginsk Moskva, Russia 55°50N 38°25E 188 E10
Noginsk Tunguska, Russia 64°30N 90°50E 215 C10
Nogliki Russia 51°50N 143°10E 215 D15
Nogoa → Australia 23°40S 147°55E 280 C4
Nogoyá Argentina 32°24S 59°48W 334 C4
Nógrád ☐ Hungary 48°0N 19°30E 182 C4
Noguera Pallaresa → Spain 41°55N 0°55E 196 D5
Noguera Ribagorçana → Spain 41°40N 0°43E 196 D5
Nohar India 29°11N 74°49E 242 E6
Nohfelden Germany 49°35N 7°7E 179 F3
Nohili Pt. U.S.A. 22°4N 159°47W 302 A2
Nohta India 23°40N 79°34E 243 H8
Nohwa S. Korea 34°10N 126°34E 224 E3
Nohwado S. Korea 34°12N 126°35E 224 E3
Noia Spain 42°48N 8°53W 194 C2
Noichi Japan 33°33N 133°42E 222 D5
Noida India 28°36N 77°19E 120 B2
Noing Phil. 5°40N 125°28E 233 J5
Noipuos Papua N. G. 2°25S 150°7E 286 B6
Noire, Montagne France 43°28N 2°18E 174 E6
Noires, Mts. France 48°11N 3°40W 172 D3
Noirétable France 45°48N 3°46E 174 C7
Noirmoutier, Î. de France 46°58N 2°10W 172 F4
Noirmoutier-en-l'Île France 47°0N 2°14W 172 F4
Noiseau France 48°46N 2°32E 134 B4
Noisiel France 48°51N 2°37E 134 A4
Noisy-le-Grand France 48°50N 2°33E 134 A4
Noisy-le-Roi France 48°50N 2°3E 134 A1
Noisy-le-Sec France 48°53N 2°27E 134 A3
Nojane Botswana 23°15S 20°14E 270 B3
Nojima-Zaki Japan 34°54N 139°53E 223 C11
Nok Kundi Pakistan 28°50N 62°45E 240 C1
Nok Ta Phao, Ko Thailand 9°23N 99°40E 237 b
Nokaneng Botswana 19°40S 22°17E 270 A3
Nokia Finland 61°30N 23°30E 188 B2
Nokkala Finland 60°8N 24°45E 121 C1
Nokkeushi = Kitami Japan 43°48N 143°54E 220 C11
Nokomis Sask., Canada 51°35N 105°0W 297 C8
Nokomis Fla., U.S.A. 27°7N 82°27W 317 H7
Nokomis Ill., U.S.A. 39°18N 89°18W 310 E7
Nokomis L. Canada 57°0N 103°0W 297 B8
Nokou Chad 14°35N 14°47E 259 F2
Nokuku Vanuatu 14°54S 166°35E 287 D4
Nola C.A.R. 3°35N 16°4E 264 B3
Nola Italy 40°55N 14°33E 201 B7
Nolay France 46°58N 4°35E 173 F11
Noli, C. di Italy 44°12N 8°25E 198 D5
Nolinsk Russia 57°28N 49°57E 190 B9
Noma U.S.A. 30°59N 85°37W 316 E4
Noma Omuramba → Namibia 18°52S 20°53E 270 A3
Noma-Saki Japan 31°25N 130°7E 222 F2
Nomad Papua N. G. 6°19S 142°13E 286 D2
Nombre de Dios Panama 9°34N 79°28W 320 E4
Nome U.S.A. 64°30N 165°25W 303 D6
Nomentano Italy 41°55N 12°30E 136 B2
Nomo-Zaki Japan 32°35N 129°44E 222 E1
Nomoneas Micronesia 7°24N 151°53E 287 T18
Nomuka Tonga 20°17S 174°48W 287 Q13
Nomuka Group Tonga 20°20S 174°48W 287 Q13
Nonacho L. Canada 61°42N 109°40W 297 A7
Nonakashinden Japan 35°44N 139°30E 140 A2
Nonancourt France 48°47N 1°11E 172 D8
Nonda Australia 20°40S 142°28E 280 C3
Nondalton U.S.A. 60°0N 154°51W 303 F9
None Italy 44°56N 7°32E 198 D4
Nong Chang Thailand 15°23N 99°51E 236 E2
Nong Het Laos 19°29N 103°59E 236 C4
Nong Khai Thailand 17°50N 102°46E 236 D4
Nong'an China 44°25N 125°5E 227 B13
Nongjrong India 25°29N 92°6E 241 C4
Nongminyundong Jiangxisuo China 23°7N 113°15E 121 B2
Nongoma S. Africa 27°58S 31°35E 271 C5
Nongsa Indonesia 1°11N 104°8E 237 d
Nongstoin India 25°31N 91°16E 241 C3
Nonhyeon S. Korea 37°30N 127°1E 137 B2
Nono Ethiopia 8°32N 37°26E 266 C4
Nonoava Mexico 27°28N 106°44W 318 B3
Nonoc I. Phil. 9°51N 125°37E 233 G5
Nonsan S. Korea 36°12N 127°5E 224 D3
Nonsuch B. Antigua & B. 17°3N 61°42W 322 b
Nonthaburi Thailand 13°50N 100°29E 113 A1
Nontron France 45°31N 0°40E 174 C4
Nonza France 42°47N 9°21E 175 F13
Noon Gun Cape Town, S. Africa 118 b1
Noonamah Australia 12°40S 131°4E 278 B5
Noondie, L. Australia 28°30S 119°30E 279 E2
Noonkanbah ☼ Australia 18°30S 124°50E 278 C3
Noord Aruba 12°34N 70°1W 322 f
Noord Brabant ☐ Neths. 51°40N 5°0E 170 C5
Noord Holland ☐ Neths. 52°30N 4°45E 170 B4
Noord Saliña Neth. Ant. 12°11N 68°16W 322 h
Noordbeveland Neths. 51°35N 3°50E 170 C3
Noorderkerk Amsterdam, Neths. 112 a1
Noordgesig S. Africa 26°13S 27°56E 123 B1
Noordkaap Aruba 12°34N 70°1W 322 f
Noordoostpolder Neths. 52°45N 5°45E 170 B5
Noordpunt Bonaire, Neth. Ant. 12°18N 68°23W 322 h
Noordpunt Curaçao, Neth. Ant. 12°24N 69°10W 322 g
Noordwijk Neths. 52°14N 4°26E 170 B4
Noordzeekanaal Neths. 52°28N 4°37E 112 A1
Noorvik U.S.A. 66°50N 161°3W 303 C7
Noosa Heads Australia 26°25S 153°6E 281 D5
Nootka I. Canada 49°32N 126°42W 296 D3
Nopiming ⌓ Canada 50°30N 95°37W 297 C9
Nóqui Angola 5°55S 13°30E 265 D2
Nor-Bayzzet = Kamo Armenia 40°21N 45°7E 191 K7
Nora Eritrea 16°6N 40°4E 257 D5
Nora Sweden 59°32N 15°2E 162 E9
Nora Springs U.S.A. 43°9N 93°0W 310 A4
Norala Phil. 6°32N 124°40E 233 H5
Noralee Canada 53°59N 126°26W 296 C3
Noranda = Rouyn-Noranda Canada 48°20N 79°0W 298 C4
Norberg Sweden 60°4N 15°56E 162 D9
Norborne U.S.A. 39°18N 93°40W 310 E3
Nòrcia Italy 42°48N 13°5E 199 F10
Norco U.S.A. 33°56N 117°33W 307 M9
Norcross U.S.A. 33°56N 84°13W 316 B5
Nord ☐ Cameroon 8°30N 14°0E 263 D7
Nord ☐ France 50°15N 3°30E 173 B10
Nord, Gare du Paris, France 134 a4
Nord, Pt. Comoros Is. 11°22S 43°19E 272 a
Nord-Kivu ☐ Dem. Rep. of the Congo 1°0S 29°0E 268 C2
Nord-og-Østgrønland △ Greenland 75°0N 35°0W 154 C7
Nord-Ostsee-Kanal Germany 54°12N 9°32E 178 A5
Nord-Ouest ☐ Cameroon 6°20N 10°30E 263 D7
Nord-Pas-de-Calais ☐ France 50°30N 2°50E 173 B9
Nordagutu Norway 59°25N 9°20E 164 E6
Nordaustlandet Svalbard 79°14N 23°0E 150 B9
Nordberg Norway 61°54N 8°10E 164 C5
Nordborg Denmark 55°5N 9°50E 163 J3
Nordby Denmark 55°27N 8°24E 163 J2
Norddeich Germany 53°36N 7°9E 178 B3
Nordegg Canada 52°29N 116°5W 296 C5
Norden Germany 53°35N 7°12E 178 B3
Nordenham Germany 53°30N 8°30E 178 B4
Nordenskjöld Sea = Laptev Sea Russia 76°0N 125°0E 215 B13
Norderhov Norway 60°7N 10°17E 164 D7
Norderney Germany 53°42N 7°9E 178 B3
Norderstedt Germany 53°42N 10°1E 178 B6
Nordeste Azores 37°50N 25°10W 153 d3
Nordfjord Norway 61°55N 5°30E 164 C2
Nordfjordeid Norway 61°54N 6°0E 164 C2
Nordfriesische Inseln Germany 54°40N 8°20E 178 A4
Nordgrønland = Avannaarsua ☐ Greenland 80°0N 55°0W 154 B5
Nordhausen Germany 51°30N 10°47E 178 D6
Nordhorn Germany 52°26N 7°4E 178 C3
Norðoyar Færoe Is. 62°17N 6°35W 160 E9
Norðtunga Iceland 64°44N 21°24W 155 C5
Norður-múlasýsla ☐ Iceland 65°30N 15°0W 155 B11
Norðurbotn Iceland 65°36N 23°46W 155 B3
Nördinge-Nol Sweden 57°56N 12°5E 163 G6
Nordingrå Sweden 62°56N 18°17E 162 B12
Nordjylland ☐ Denmark 57°0N 9°30E 163 G3
Nordkapp Finnmark, Norway 71°10N 25°50E 160 A21
Nordkapp Svalbard 80°31N 20°0E 150 A9
Nordkinnhalvøya Norway 70°55N 27°40E 160 A22
Nördlicher Teutoburger Wald-Wiehengebirge ⌓ Germany 52°18N 8°10E 178 C4
Nördlingen Germany 48°48N 10°30E 179 G6
Nordmarka Norway 59°58N 10°41E 133 A3
Nordmøre Norway 63°6N 8°15E 164 B4
Nordostrundingen Greenland 81°22N 11°40W 154 A9
Nordøyane Norway 62°40N 6°0E 164 B3
Nordrand-Siedlung Austria 48°16N 16°26E 142 A2
Nordre Bergenhus = Sogn og Fjordane ☐ Norway 61°40N 6°45E 164 C3
Nørdre Osa Norway 61°18N 11°45E 164 C8
Nordre Strømfjord Greenland 67°10N 53°35W 154 D5
Nordrhein-Westfalen ☐ Germany 51°45N 7°30E 178 D3
Nordsinni Norway 60°50N 9°57E 164 D6
Nordstedalsseter Norway 61°40N 7°48E 164 C4
Nordstrand Schleswig-Holstein, Germany 54°30N 8°52E 178 A4
Nordstrand Oslo, Norway 59°52N 10°48E 133 A3
Nordvik Russia 74°2N 111°32E 215 B12
Nore → Ireland 52°25N 6°58W 166 D4
Norefjell Norway 60°16N 9°29E 164 D6
Noreland Canada 44°43N 78°48W 312 B6
Noresund Norway 60°11N 9°37E 164 D6
Norfolk = Simcoe Canada 42°50N 80°23W 312 D4
Norfolk N.Y., U.S.A. 44°48N 74°59W 313 B10
Norfolk Nebr., U.S.A. 42°2N 97°25W 308 D5
Norfolk Va., U.S.A. 36°50N 76°17W 309 G15
Norfolk ☐ U.K. 52°39N 0°54E 169 E8
Norfolk Basin Pac. Oc. 32°0S 170°0E 277 G13
Norfolk Broads ⌓ U.K. 52°45N 1°30E 169 E9
Norfolk I. Pac. Oc. 28°58S 168°3E 277 F12
Norfolk Ridge Pac. Oc. 29°0S 168°0E 288 K8
Norfork L. U.S.A. 36°15N 92°14W 314 C8
Norge = Norway ■ Europe 63°0N 11°0E 160 E14
Norheimsund Norway 60°23N 6°8E 164 D3
Norilsk Russia 69°20N 88°6E 215 C9
Norma, Mt. Australia 20°55S 140°42E 280 C3
Normal U.S.A. 40°31N 88°59W 310 D8
Norman U.S.A. 35°13N 97°26W 314 D6
Norman → Australia 19°18S 141°51E 280 B3
Norman Manley Int. ✕ (KIN) Jamaica 17°56N 76°47W 320 a
Norman Park U.S.A. 31°16N 83°41W 316 D6
Norman Wells Canada 65°17N 126°51W 294 D6
Normanby N.Z. 39°32S 174°18E 284 F3
Normanby → Australia 14°23S 144°10E 280 A3
Normanby I. Papua N. G. 10°55S 151°5E 286 F6
Normandale N.Z. 41°12S 174°53E 143 B2
Normandie France 48°45N 0°10E 171 B4
Normandie-Maine ⌓ France 48°30N 0°20W 172 D6
Normandin Canada 48°49N 72°31W 298 C5
Normandy = Normandie France 48°45N 0°10E 171 B4
Normanhurst, Mt. Australia 25°4S 122°30E 279 E3
Normanton Australia 17°40S 141°10E 280 B3
Normanville Australia 35°27S 138°18E 282 C3
Normétal Canada 49°0N 79°22W 298 C4
Norquay Canada 51°53N 102°5W 297 C8
Norquinco Argentina 41°51S 70°55W 336 B2
Norra Dellen Sweden 61°53N 16°43E 162 C10
Norra Kvill △ Sweden 57°46N 15°35E 163 G9
Norra Ulvön Sweden 63°3N 18°40E 162 A12
Norrahammar Sweden 57°43N 14°7E 163 G8
Norrbottens län ☐ Sweden 66°50N 20°0E 160 C19
Nørre Åby Denmark 55°27N 9°52E 163 J3
Nørre Alslev Denmark 54°54N 11°52E 163 K5
Nørrebro Copenhagen, Denmark 118 a1
Nørresundby Denmark 57°5N 9°52E 163 G3
Norrhult-Klavreström Sweden 57°7N 15°10E 163 G9
Norridge U.S.A. 41°57N 87°49W 119 B2
Norris City U.S.A. 37°59N 88°20W 311 G8
Norris Point Canada 49°31N 57°53W 299 C8
Norristown Ga., U.S.A. 32°30N 82°30W 316 C7
Norristown Pa., U.S.A. 40°7N 75°21W 313 F9
Norrköping Sweden 58°37N 16°11E 163 F10
Norrland Sweden 62°15N 15°45E 160 E16
Norrmalm Stockholm, Sweden 139 a1
Norrsundet Sweden 60°56N 17°8E 162 D11
Norrtälje Sweden 59°46N 18°42E 162 E12
Norseman Australia 32°8S 121°43E 279 F3
Norsewood N.Z. 40°3S 176°13E 284 G5
Norsjø Norway 59°18N 9°20E 164 E6
Norsk Russia 52°30N 130°5E 215 D14
Norsup Vanuatu 16°3S 167°24E 287 F5
Norte, C. Chile 27°3S 109°24W 330 b
Norte, Canal do → Brazil 0°40N 50°20W 329 C7
Norte, Pta. Argentina 42°5S 63°46W 336 B4
Norte, Pta. Chile 33°36S 78°54W 330 c
Norte, Pta. del Canary Is. 27°51N 17°57W 153 e1
Norte, Serra do Azores 37°1N 25°4W 153 d4
Norte, Serra do Brazil 11°20S 59°0W 331 C6
Norte de Santander ☐ Colombia 8°0N 73°0W 328 B3
Norte Grande Azores 38°40N 28°4W 153 d1
Nortelândia Brazil 14°25S 56°48W 331 C6
North U.S.A. 33°37N 81°6W 316 B8
North, C. Canada 47°2N 60°20W 299 C7
North Adams U.S.A. 42°42N 73°7W 313 D11
North America 40°0N 100°0W 292 F10
North Andaman I. India 13°15N 92°55E 245 H11
North Arlington U.S.A. 40°47N 74°7W 132 B1
North Arm Canada 62°0N 114°30W 296 A5
North Atlantic Ocean Atl. Oc. 30°0N 50°0W 152 C7
North Augusta U.S.A. 33°30N 81°59W 316 B8
North Australian Basin Ind. Oc. 14°30S 116°30E 278 B2
North Ayrshire ☐ U.K. 55°45N 4°44W 167 F4
North Baltimore U.S.A. 41°11N 83°41W 311 C13
North Bass I. U.S.A. 41°40N 82°56W 312 E2
North Battleford Canada 52°50N 108°17W 297 C7
North Bay Canada 46°20N 79°30W 298 C4
North Bay Village U.S.A. 25°50N 80°9W 128 A2
North Beach San Francisco, U.S.A. 136 a2
North Belcher Is. Canada 56°50N 79°50W 298 A4
North Bend Oreg., U.S.A. 43°24N 124°14W 304 E1
North Bend Pa., U.S.A. 41°20N 77°42W 312 E7
North Bend Wash., U.S.A. 47°30N 121°47W 306 C5
North Bennington U.S.A. 42°56N 73°15W 313 D11
North Bergen U.S.A. 40°48N 74°0W 132 B1
North Berwick E. Loth., U.K. 56°4N 2°42W 167 E6
North Berwick Maine, U.S.A. 43°18N 70°44W 313 C14
North Borneo = Sabah ☐ Malaysia 6°0N 117°0E 235 A5
North Breakers Midway Is. 28°13N 177°24W 302 c
North Brother I. India 10°59N 92°40E 245 J11
North Bruce Canada 44°22N 81°26W 312 B3
North Bull I. Ireland 53°22N 6°9W 120 A3
North C. N.B., Canada 47°5N 64°0W 299 C7
North C. N.Z. 34°23S 173°4E 284 A2
North C. Papua N. G. 2°32S 150°50E 286 B6
North Canadian → U.S.A. 35°22N 95°37W 314 D7
North Canton U.S.A. 40°53N 81°24W 312 F3
North Cape = Nordkapp Norway 71°10N 25°50E 160 A21
North Caribou L. Canada 52°50N 90°40W 298 B1
North Carolina ☐ U.S.A. 35°30N 80°0W 315 D15
North Cascades △ U.S.A. 48°45N 121°10W 304 B3
North Cay Bahamas 25°6N 77°26W 153 b
North Channel Ont., Canada 46°0N 83°0W 298 C3
North Channel U.K. 55°13N 5°52W 167 F3
North Charleston U.S.A. 32°53N 79°58W 316 C10
North Cheam U.K. 51°22N 0°11W 125 B2
North Chicago U.S.A. 42°19N 87°51W 311 B9
North College Hill U.S.A. 39°13N 84°33W 311 E12
North Collins U.S.A. 42°35N 78°56W 312 D6
North Comino Channel Malta 36°1N 14°20E 206 E7
North Cray U.K. 51°25N 0°8E 125 B4
North Creek U.S.A. 43°42N 73°59W 313 C11
North Dakota ☐ U.S.A. 47°30N 100°15W 308 B3
North Decatur U.S.A. 33°48N 84°17W 113 B3
North Downs U.K. 51°19N 0°21E 169 F8
North Druid Hills U.S.A. 33°49N 84°17W 113 B3
North East U.S.A. 42°13N 79°50W 312 D5
North East B. Ascension I. 7°55S 14°21W 153 g
North East Frontier Agency = Arunachal Pradesh ☐ India 28°0N 95°0E 241 B5
North East Lincolnshire ☐ U.K. 53°34N 0°2W 168 D7
North Eastern ☐ Kenya 1°30N 40°0E 268 B5
North End Boston, U.S.A. 116 a3
North Esk → Angus, U.K. 56°46N 2°24W 167 E6
North Esk → Midloth., U.K. 55°54N 3°4W 121 B2
North European Plain Europe 55°0N 25°0E 158 E10
North Fabius → U.S.A. 39°54N 91°30W 310 E5
North Foreland U.K. 51°22N 1°28E 169 F9
North Fork U.S.A. 37°14N 119°21W 306 H7
North Fork, Salt → U.S.A. 39°26N 91°53W 310 E5
North Fork American → U.S.A. 38°57N 120°59W 306 G5
North Fork Edisto → U.S.A. 33°16N 80°54W 316 B9
North Fork Feather → U.S.A. 38°33N 121°30W 306 F5
North Fork Grand → U.S.A. 45°47N 102°16W 308 C2
North Fork Red → U.S.A. 34°24N 99°14W 314 D5
North Fort Myers U.S.A. 26°41N 81°53W 317 J8
North Frisian Is. = Nordfriesische Inseln Germany 54°40N 8°20E 178 A4
North Gower Canada 45°8N 75°43W 313 A9
North Greenfield = West Allis U.S.A. 43°1N 88°0W 311 B8
North Gyle U.K. 55°57N 3°19W 121 B2
North Hackensack U.S.A. 40°54N 74°2W 132 A1
North Harbor Phil. 14°37N 120°57E 127 B1
North Hd. N.S.W., Australia 33°49S 151°18E 139 A2
North Hd. W. Austral., Australia 30°14S 114°59E 279 F1
North Henik L. Canada 61°45N 97°40W 297 A9
North Highlands U.S.A. 38°40N 121°23W 306 G5
North Hollywood U.S.A. 34°9N 118°22W 126 B2
North Horr Kenya 3°20N 37°8E 268 B4
North I. India 10°8N 72°20E 245 J1
North I. Rift Valley, Kenya 4°5N 36°5E 268 B4
North I. N.Z. 38°0S 175°0E 284 E4
North I. Seychelles 4°25S 55°13E 272 c
North Judson U.S.A. 41°13N 86°46W 311 C10
North Kingsville U.S.A. 41°54N 80°42W 312 E4
North Kitui ⌓ Kenya 0°15S 38°29E 268 C4
North Knife → Canada 58°53N 94°45W 297 B10
North Koel → India 24°45N 83°50E 243 G10
North Korea ■ Asia 40°0N 127°0E 227 E14
North L. Australia 32°30S 143°5E 282 B5
North Lakhimpur India 27°14N 94°7E 241 B5
North Lanarkshire ☐ U.K. 55°52N 3°56W 167 F5
North Las Vegas U.S.A. 36°11N 115°7W 124 A1
North Las Vegas ✕ (VGT) U.S.A. 36°12N 115°11W 124 A1
North Lexington U.S.A. 42°27N 71°14W 116 A1
North Liberty U.S.A. 41°32N 86°26W 311 C10
North Lincolnshire ☐ U.K. 53°36N 0°30W 168 D7
North Little Rock U.S.A. 34°45N 92°16W 314 D8
North Loup → U.S.A. 41°17N 98°24W 308 E4
North Luangwa △ Zambia 11°49S 32°9E 269 E3
North Magnetic Pole Canada 82°42N 114°24W 150 A2
North Malé Atoll Maldives 4°25N 73°55E 272 d
North Malosmadulu Atoll Maldives 5°37N 72°55E 272 d
North Manchester U.S.A. 41°0N 85°46W 311 D11
North Mankato U.S.A. 44°10N 94°2W 308 C6
North Miami U.S.A. 25°53N 80°11W 128 A2
North Miami Beach U.S.A. 25°55N 80°9W 128 A2
North Minch U.K. 58°5N 5°55W 167 C3
North Moose L. Canada 54°4N 100°12W 297 C8
North Myrtle Beach U.S.A. 33°48N 78°42W 315 E15
North Nahanni → Canada 62°15N 123°20W 296 A4
North Naples U.S.A. 26°12N 81°48W 317 J8
North Nazimabad Pakistan 24°55N 67°3E 123 A2
North New River Canal U.S.A. 26°30N 80°30W 317 J9
North Nilandu Atoll Maldives 3°14N 72°56E 272 d
North Olmsted U.S.A. 41°25N 81°56W 312 E3
North Ossetia ☐ Russia 43°30N 44°30E 191 J7
North Pagai, I. = Pagai Utara, Pulau Indonesia 2°35S 100°0E 234 C2
North Palisade U.S.A. 37°6N 118°31W 306 H8
North Platte U.S.A. 41°8N 100°46W 308 E3
North Platte → U.S.A. 41°7N 100°42W 308 E3
North Point Park Boston, U.S.A. 116 a1
North Pole Arctic 90°0N 0°0 150 A
North Pole Alaska, U.S.A. 64°45N 147°21W 303 D11
North Portal Canada 49°0N 102°33W 297 D8
North Powder U.S.A. 45°2N 117°55W 304 D5
North Pt. Ascension I. 7°53S 14°23W 153 g
North Pt. Barbados 13°20N 59°37W 323 r
North Pt. Hong Kong, China 22°17N 114°12E 122 B2
North Pt. Mich., U.S.A. 45°2N 83°16W 312 A1
North Pt. Vanuatu 14°56S 168°6E 287 D6
North Queensferry U.K. 56°1N 3°24W 121 A1
North Quincy U.S.A. 42°16N 71°1W 116 B2
North Reef I. India 13°5N 92°43E 245 H11
North Res. U.S.A. 42°27N 71°6W 116 A2
North Rhine Westphalia = Nordrhein-Westfalen ☐ Germany 51°45N 7°30E 178 D3
North River Canada 53°49N 57°6W 299 B8
North Riverside U.S.A. 41°50N 87°48W 119 B2
North Ronaldsay U.K. 59°22N 2°26W 167 B6
North Salem U.S.A. 39°52N 86°39W 311 E10
North Saskatchewan → Canada 53°15N 105°5W 297 C7
North Saugus U.S.A. 42°29N 71°0W 116 A2
North Sea Europe 56°0N 4°0E 158 D6
North Seal → Canada 58°50N 98°7W 297 B9
North Sentinel I. India 11°33N 92°15E 245 J11
North Shields Australia 34°38S 135°52E 282 C1
North Shore U.S.A. 21°39N 158°30W 302 J13
North Shore Channel → U.S.A. 41°58N 87°42W 119 B2
North Slope U.S.A. 69°15N 152°0W 300 B9
North Solomons ☐ Papua N. G. 4°0S 155°0E 286 B8
North Somerset ☐ U.K. 51°24N 2°45W 169 F5
North Springfield U.S.A. 38°48N 77°11W 143 C2
North Station Boston, U.S.A. 116 a2
North Sydney N.S.W., Australia 33°50S 151°13E 139 B2
North Sydney N.S., Canada 46°12N 60°15W 299 C7
North Syracuse U.S.A. 43°8N 76°7W 313 C8
North Taranaki Bight N.Z. 38°50S 174°15E 284 E3
North Thompson → Canada 50°40N 120°20W 296 C4
North Tonawanda U.S.A. 43°2N 78°53W 312 C6
North Troy U.S.A. 45°0N 72°24W 313 B12
North Twin I. Canada 53°20N 80°0W 298 B4
North Tyne → U.K. 55°0N 2°8W 168 B5
North Ubian I. Phil. 6°9N 120°25E 233 H3
North Uist U.K. 57°40N 7°15W 167 D1
North Union = Shaker Heights U.S.A. 41°28N 81°32W 312 E3
North Union St. Vincent 13°13N 61°8W 323 n
North Vancouver Canada 49°19N 123°4W 306 A3
North Vernon U.S.A. 39°0N 85°38W 311 F11
North Wabasca L. Canada 56°0N 113°55W 296 B6
North Walsham U.K. 52°50N 1°22E 168 E9
North Webster U.S.A. 41°25N 85°48W 311 C11
North West = Severo-Zapadnyy ☐ Russia 65°0N 40°0E 214 C4
North-West ☐ S. Africa 27°0S 25°0E 270 C4
North West Bluff Montserrat 16°49N 62°12W 323 p
North West C. Australia 21°45S 114°9E 278 D1
North West Frontier ☐ Pakistan 34°0N 72°0E 242 C4
North West Highlands U.K. 57°33N 4°58W 167 D4
North West Pt. Jamaica 18°27N 78°13W 320 a
North West River Canada 53°30N 60°10W 299 B7
North Western ☐ Zambia 13°30S 25°30E 269 E2
North-Western Provinces and Oudh = Uttar Pradesh ☐ India 27°0N 80°0E 243 F9
North Wildwood U.S.A. 39°0N 74°48W 309 F16
North Woolwich U.K. 51°30N 0°3E 125 A4
North Yakima = Yakima U.S.A. 46°36N 120°31W 304 C3
North York Canada 43°45N 79°27W 141 A2
North York Moors U.K. 54°23N 0°53W 168 C7
North York Moors △ U.K. 54°27N 0°51W 168 C7
North Yorkshire ☐ U.K. 54°15N 1°25W 168 C6
Northallerton U.K. 54°20N 1°26W 168 C6
Northam W. Austral., Australia 31°35S 116°42E 279 F2
Northam Limpopo, S. Africa 24°56S 27°18E 270 B4
Northampton W. Austral., Australia 28°27S 114°33E 279 E1
Northampton Northants., U.K. 52°15N 0°53W 169 E7
Northampton Mass., U.S.A. 42°19N 72°38W 313 D12
Northampton Pa., U.S.A. 40°41N 75°30W 313 F9
Northamptonshire ☐ U.K. 52°16N 0°55W 169 E7
Northbridge N.S.W., Australia 33°49S 151°15E 139 A2
Northbridge Mass., U.S.A. 42°9N 71°39W 313 D13
Northbridge Park Australia 33°49S 151°15E 139 A2
Northbrook Canada 44°44N 77°9W 312 B7
Northcliff S. Africa 26°8S 27°58E 123 A1
Northcliffe Australia 34°39S 116°7E 279 F2
Northcote Australia 37°46S 145°0E 128 A2
Northeast C. U.S.A. 63°18N 168°42W 303 E5
Northeast Pacific Basin Pac. Oc. 32°0N 145°0W 289 D13
Northeast Providence Chan. W. Indies 26°0N 76°0W 320 A4
Northeastern Univ. U.S.A. 42°20N 71°4W 116 A2
Northeim Germany 51°42N 10°0E 178 D6
Northern = Limpopo ☐ S. Africa 24°5S 29°0E 271 B4
Northern ☐ Ghana 9°30N 1°0W 263 D4
Northern ☐ Malawi 11°0S 34°0E 269 E3
Northern ☐ Papua N. G. 9°0S 148°30E 286 E5
Northern ☐ S. Leone 9°15N 11°30W 262 D2
Northern ☐ Zambia 10°30S 31°0E 269 E3
Northern Aral Sea Kazakhstan 46°20N 60°30E 216 C6
Northern Areas ☐ Pakistan 36°30N 73°0E 243 A5
Northern Cape ☐ S. Africa 30°0S 20°0E 270 C3
Northern Circars India 17°30N 82°30E 244 F6
Northern Indian L. Canada 57°20N 97°20W 297 B9
Northern Ireland ☐ U.K. 54°45N 7°0W 166 B5
Northern Lau Group Fiji 17°30S 178°59W 287 A3
Northern Light L. Canada 48°15N 90°39W 298 C1
Northern Marianas ⊠ Pac. Oc. 17°0N 145°0E 302 a
Northern Province ☐ S. Africa 24°0S 29°0E 271 B4
Northern Range Trin. & Tob. 10°46N 61°15W 323 t
Northern Rhodesia = Zambia ■ Africa 15°0S 28°0E 269 F2
Northern Samar ☐ Phil. 12°30N 124°40E 232 E5
Northern Sporades Greece 39°15N 23°30E 204 B5
Northern Territory ☐ Australia 20°0S 133°0E 278 D5
Northern Virginia Regional Park ⌓ U.S.A. 38°55N 77°6W 143 B3
Northfield Minn., U.S.A. 44°27N 93°9W 308 C7
Northfield Vt., U.S.A. 44°9N 72°40W 313 B12
Northgate Canada 49°0N 102°16W 297 D8
Northlake U.S.A. 41°54N 87°53W 119 B1
Northland ☐ N.Z. 35°30S 173°30E 284 B2
Northmount Canada 43°46N 79°23W 141 A2
Northolt U.K. 51°32N 0°22W 125 A1
Northome U.S.A. 47°52N 94°17W 308 B6
Northport Ala., U.S.A. 33°14N 87°35W 315 E11
Northport Wash., U.S.A. 48°55N 117°48W 304 B5
Northumberland ☐ U.K. 55°12N 2°0W 168 B6
Northumberland, C. Australia 38°5S 140°40E 282 E4
Northumberland Heath U.K. 51°28N 0°10E 125 B5
Northumberland Is. Australia 21°30S 149°50E 280 C4
Northumberland Str. Canada 46°20N 64°0W 299 C7
Northville Ont., Canada 43°10N 81°56W 312 C3
Northville N.Y., U.S.A. 43°13N 74°11W 313 C10
Northway U.S.A. 62°58N 141°56W 303 E12
Northwest Atlantic Mid-Ocean Canyon Atl. Oc. 54°0N 48°0W 152 A7
Northwest Pacific Basin Pac. Oc. 32°0N 165°0E 288 D8
Northwest Providence Channel W. Indies 26°0N 78°0W 320 A4
Northwest Pt. Bahamas 25°4N 77°31W 153 b
Northwest Territories ☐ Canada 63°0N 118°0W 294 E8
Northwestern Hawaiian Is. Marine Nat. Monument = Papahānaumokuākea Marine Nat. Monument U.S.A. 25°25N 170°35W 302 F9
Northwestern Station U.S.A. 41°52N 87°38W 119 B3
Northwestern Univ. U.S.A. 42°3N 87°40W 119 A2
Northwich U.K. 53°15N 2°31W 168 D5
Northwood London, U.K. 51°36N 0°25W 125 A1
Northwood Iowa, U.S.A. 43°27N 93°13W 308 D7
Northwood N. Dak., U.S.A. 47°44N 97°34W 308 B5
Northwood Park Canada 43°45N 79°30W 141 A1
Norton Kans., U.S.A. 39°50N 99°53W 308 F4
Norton Zimbabwe 17°52S 30°40E 269 F3
Norton B. U.S.A. 64°45N 161°15W 303 D7
Norton Sd. U.S.A. 63°50N 164°0W 303 E7
Norton Shores U.S.A. 43°10N 86°16W 311 A10
Nortorf Germany 54°10N 9°50E 178 A5
Norwalk Calif., U.S.A. 33°54N 118°4W 307 M8
Norwalk Conn., U.S.A. 41°7N 73°22W 313 E11
Norwalk Iowa, U.S.A. 41°29N 93°41W 310 C3
Norwalk Ohio, U.S.A. 41°15N 82°37W 312 E2
Norway Maine, U.S.A. 44°13N 70°32W 309 C18
Norway Mich., U.S.A. 45°47N 87°55W 308 C10
Norway ■ Europe 63°0N 11°0E 160 E14
Norway House Canada 53°59N 97°50W 297 C9
Norwegian B. Canada 77°30N 90°0W 295 B14
Norwegian Basin Atl. Oc. 68°0N 2°0W 150 C7
Norwegian Sea Atl. Oc. 66°0N 1°0E 158 B6
Norwich Ont., Canada 42°59N 80°36W 312 D4
Norwich Norfolk, U.K. 52°38N 1°18E 169 E9
Norwich Conn., U.S.A. 41°31N 72°5W 313 E12
Norwich N.Y., U.S.A. 42°32N 75°32W 313 D9
Norwood Ont., Canada 44°23N 77°59W 312 B7
Norwood Gauteng, S. Africa 26°9S 28°4E 123 A2
Norwood N.Y., U.S.A. 44°45N 75°0W 313 B10
Norwood Ohio, U.S.A. 39°9N 84°27W 311 E12
Norwood Park U.S.A. 41°59N 87°48W 119 B2
Noryangjin S. Korea 37°30N 126°56E 137 B1
Nosappu-Misaki Japan 45°26N 141°39E 220 C12
Noshaq Pakistan 36°24N 71°49E 240 A3
Noshiro Japan 40°12N 140°0E 220 D10
Nosivka Ukraine 50°50N 31°37E 189 G6
Nosovka = Nosivka Ukraine 50°50N 31°37E 189 G6
Noşratābād Iran 29°55N 60°0E 247 D8
Noss Hd. U.K. 58°28N 3°3W 167 C5
Nossa Senhora da Glória Brazil 10°14S 37°25W 332 D4
Nossa Senhora das Dores Brazil 10°29S 37°13W 332 D4
Nossa Senhora de Candelária Rio de J., Brazil 135 a2
Nossa Senhora do Livramento Brazil 15°48S 56°22W 331 D6
Nossa Senhora do Ó Brazil 23°30S 46°41W 137 B1
Nossa Senhora do Socorro Brazil 10°52S 37°7W 332 D4
Nossebro Sweden 58°12N 12°43E 163 F6
Nossegem Belgium 50°53N 4°30E 116 A3
Nossob → S. Africa 26°55S 20°45E 270 C3
Nossombougou Mali 13°5N 7°55W 262 C3
Nosy Barren Madag. 18°25S 43°40E 272 B1
Nosy Bé Madag. 13°25S 48°15E 272 A2
Nosy Boraha Madag. 16°50S 49°55E 272 B2
Nosy Lava Madag. 14°33S 47°36E 272 A2
Nosy Mitsio Madag. 12°54S 48°36E 272 A2

Nosy Varika *Madag.* 20°35S 48°32E **272** C2
Notasulga *U.S.A.* 32°34N 85°41W **316** C4
Noteć → *Poland* 52°44N 15°26E **185** F2
Notikewin → *Canada* 57°2N 117°38W **296** B5
Notio Aigaio □ 36°52N 25°34E **205** E7
Notios Evvoikos Kolpos
  Greece 38°20N 24°0E **204** C5
Notion Aigaio = Notio
  Aigaio □ 36°52N 25°34E **205** E7
Noto *Italy* 36°53N 15°4E **201** F8
Noto, G. di *Italy* 36°50N 15°12E **201** F8
Notodden *Norway* 59°35N 9°17E **164** E6
Notre-Dame *Paris, France* **134** c4
Notre-Dame, Basilique
  Montréal, Canada **130** c3
Notre-Dame, Bois *France* 48°45N 3°24E **134** B4
Notre Dame B. *Canada* 49°45N 55°30W **299** C8
Notre-Dame-de-Grace
  Canada 45°28N 73°38W **130** B2
Notre-Dame-de-Koartac = Quaqtaq
  Canada 60°55N 69°40W **295** E18
Notre-Dame-des-Bois
  Canada 45°24N 71°4W **313** A13
Notre-Dame-d'Ivugivic = Ivujivik
  Canada 62°24N 77°55W **295** E16
Notre-Dame-du-Nord
  Canada 47°36N 79°30W **298** C4
Notsé *Togo* 7°0N 1°17E **263** D5
Nottawasaga B. *Canada* 44°35N 80°15W **312** B4
Nottaway = Senneterre
  Canada 48°25N 77°15W **298** C4
Nottaway → *Canada* 51°22N 78°55W **298** B4
Notting Hill *London, U.K.* **125** b1
Nottingham *U.K.* 52°58N 1°10W **168** E6
Nottingham, City of □
  U.K. 52°58N 1°10W **168** E6
Nottingham I. *Canada* 63°20N 77°55W **295** E16
Nottinghamshire □ *U.K.* 53°10N 1°3W **168** E6
Nottoway → *U.S.A.* 36°33N 76°55W **309** G15
Notwane → *Botswana* 23°35S 26°58E **270** D4
Nouâdhibou *Mauritania* 20°54N 17°0W **260** D1
Nouâdhibou, Dakhlet
  Mauritania 20°55N 16°52W **260** D1
Nouâdhibou, Râs
  Mauritania 20°50N 17°0W **260** D1
Nouakchott *Mauritania* 18°9N 15°58W **262** B1
Nouâmghâr *Mauritania* 19°20N 16°20W **262** B1
Nouméa *N. Cal.* 22°17S 166°30E **288** d
Nouna *Burkina Faso* 12°42N 3°41W **262** C4
Noupoort *S. Africa* 31°10S 24°57E **270** D3
Nouveau Comptoir = Wemindji
  Canada 53°0N 78°49W **298** B4
Nouvelle Amsterdam, Î.
  Ind. Oc. 38°30S 77°30E **273** H6
Nouvelle-Calédonie = New
  Caledonia ☑ *Pac. Oc.* 21°0S 165°0E **288** d
Nouvelle France *Mauritius* 20°22S 57°33E **272** a
Nouzonville *France* 49°48N 4°44E **173** C11
Nová Baňa *Slovak Rep.* 48°28N 18°39E **181** C11
Nová Bystřice *Czech Rep.* 49°2N 15°8E **180** B8
Nova Cruz *Brazil* 6°28S 35°25W **332** C4
Nova Era *Brazil* 19°45S 43°3W **333** E3
Nova Esperança *Brazil* 23°8S 52°24W **335** A5
Nova Fontesvila = Vila Machado
  Mozam. 19°15S 34°14E **269** F3
Nova-Freixo = Cuamba
  Mozam. 14°45S 36°22E **269** E4
Nova Friburgo *Brazil* 22°16S 42°30W **333** F3
Nova Gaia = Cambundi-Catembo
  Angola 10°10S 17°35E **265** E3
Nova Gorica *Slovenia* 45°57N 13°39E **199** C10
Nova Gradiška *Croatia* 45°17N 17°28E **182** E2
Nova Granada *Brazil* 20°30S 49°20W **333** F2
Nova Iguaçu *Brazil* 22°45S 43°28W **333** F3
Nova Iorque *Brazil* 7°0S 44°5W **332** C3
Nova Kakhovka *Ukraine* 46°42N 33°27E **189** J7
Nova Lamego
  Guinea-Biss. 12°19N 14°11W **262** C2
Nova Lisboa = Huambo
  Angola 12°42S 15°54E **265** E3
Nova Lusitânia *Mozam.* 19°50S 34°34E **269** F3
Nova Mambone *Mozam.* 21°0S 35°3E **271** B6
Nova Milanese *Italy* 45°35N 9°12E **224** C6
Nova Odesa *Ukraine* 47°19N 31°47E **189** J6
Nova Olinda do Norte
  Brazil 3°45S 59°3W **329** D6
Nová Paka *Czech Rep.* 50°29N 15°30E **180** A8
Nova Pavova *Serbia* 44°56N 20°14E **182** F5
Nova Ponte *Brazil* 19°8S 47°41W **333** E2
Nova Russas *Brazil* 4°42S 40°34W **332** B3
Nova Scotia □ *Canada* 45°10N 63°0W **299** C7
Nova Siri *Italy* 40°10N 16°35E **201** B9
Nova Sofala *Mozam.* 20°7S 34°42E **271** B6
Nova Ushytsya *Ukraine* 48°50N 27°17E **183** B12
Nova Varoš *Serbia* 43°29N 19°48E **202** C3
Nova Venécia *Brazil* 18°45S 40°24W **333** E3
Nova Vida *Brazil* 10°11S 62°47W **331** C5
Nova Zagora *Bulgaria* 42°32N 26°1E **203** D10
Novaci *Macedonia* 41°5N 21°29E **202** E5
Novaci *Romania* 45°10N 23°42E **183** E8
Novafeltria *Italy* 43°53N 12°17E **199** E9
Novannenskiy = Novoannenskiy
  Russia 50°32N 42°39E **190** E6
Novar *Canada* 45°27N 79°15W **312** A5
Novara *Italy* 45°28N 8°38E **198** C5
Novate Milanese *Italy* 45°30N 9°8E **129** A1
Novato *U.S.A.* 38°6N 122°35W **306** G4
Novaya Aleksandriya = Puławy
  Poland 51°23N 21°59E **185** G8
Novaya Bukhara = Kogon
  Uzbekistan 39°43N 64°33E **216** E6
Novaya Derevnya *Russia* 60°59N 30°16W **137** A1
Novaya Kakhovka = Nova
  Kakhovka *Ukraine* 46°42N 33°27E **189** J7
Novaya Kazanka = Zhangaqala
  Kazakhstan 48°58N 49°36E **191** F9
Novaya Ladoga *Russia* 60°7N 32°16E **188** B7
Novaya Lyalya *Russia* 59°4N 60°45E **186** C11
Novaya Pismyanka = Leninogorsk
  Kazakhstan 50°20N 83°30E **217** B10
Novaya Sibir, Ostrov
  Russia 75°10N 150°0E **215** B16
Novaya Zemlya *Russia* 75°0N 56°0E **214** B6
Nové Město Praha,
  Czech Rep. 50°4N 14°25E **135** B2
Nové Město *Slovak Rep.* 48°45N 17°50E **181** C10
Nové Město na Moravě
  Czech Rep. 49°34N 16°5E **180** B8
Nové Město nad Metují
  Czech Rep. 50°20N 16°10E **181** A4
Nové Zámky *Slovak Rep.* 48°2N 18°8E **181** C11
Noveldia *Spain* 38°24N 0°45W **197** G4
Novellara *Italy* 44°51N 10°44E **198** D7
Novelty *U.S.A.* 40°1N 92°13W **310** D4
Noventa Vicentina *Italy* 45°17N 11°32E **199** C8
Novgorod □ *Russia* 58°30N 32°0E **188** C6
Novgorod □ *Russia* 58°50N 32°0E **188** C6
Novgorod-Seversky = Novhorod-
  Siverskyy *Ukraine* 52°2N 33°10E **189** G7
Novgradets = Suvorovo
  Bulgaria 43°20N 27°35E **203** C11
Novhorod-Siverskyy
  Ukraine 52°2N 33°10E **189** G7
Novi Iskar *Bulgaria* 42°48N 23°21E **202** D7
Novi Kneževac *Serbia* 46°4N 20°8E **182** D5

Novi Lígure *Italy* 44°46N 8°47E **198** D5
Novi Pazar *Bulgaria* 43°25N 27°15E **203** C11
Novi Pazar *Serbia* 43°12N 20°28E **202** C4
Novi Sad *Serbia* 45°18N 19°52E **182** E4
Novi Slankamen *Serbia* 45°8N 20°15E **182** E5
Novi Travnik *Bos.-H.* 44°10N 17°40E **182** F2
Novi Vinodolski *Croatia* 45°10N 14°48E **199** C11
Novigrad *Istra, Croatia* 45°19N 13°33E **199** C10
Novigrad *Zadar, Croatia* 44°10N 15°32E **199** D12
Novigradsko More
  Croatia 44°12N 15°33E **199** D12
Novinger *U.S.A.* 40°14N 92°43W **310** D4
Novo Acôrdo *Brazil* 10°10S 46°48W **332** D2
Novo Airão *Brazil* 2°40S 60°59W **329** D5
Novo Aripuanã *Brazil* 5°8S 60°22W **329** E5
Novo Cruzeiro *Brazil* 17°20S 41°53W **333** E3
Novo Hamburgo *Brazil* 29°37S 51°7W **335** B5
Novo Horizonte *Brazil* 21°25S 49°10W **333** E2
Novo Ivanivka *Ukraine* 45°55N 29°5E **183** E14
Novo-Mariinsk = Anadyr
  Russia 64°35N 177°20E **215** C19
Novo Mesto *Slovenia* 45°47N 15°12E **199** C12
Novo Miloševo *Serbia* 45°43N 20°20E **182** E5
Novo Nikolaevsk = Novosibirsk
  Russia 55°0N 83°5E **217** B10
Novo Paraíso *Brazil* 1°17N 60°28W **329** C5
Novo-Starobinsk = Salihorsk
  Belarus 52°51N 27°27E **177** B14
Novo Urgench = Urganch
  Uzbekistan 41°40N 60°41E **216** D6
Novoaleksandrovsk = Zarasai
  Lithuania 55°40N 26°20E **188** E4
Novoaleksandrovsk
  Russia 45°29N 41°17E **191** H5
Novoaleksandrovskaya =
  Novoaleksandrovsk
  Russia 45°29N 41°17E **191** H5
Novoaleksandrovskoye
  Russia 59°50N 30°31E **137** B2
Novoaltaysk *Russia* 53°30N 84°0E **217** B10
Novoannenskiy *Russia* 50°32N 42°39E **190** E6
Novoazovsk *Ukraine* 47°15N 38°4E **189** J11
Novocheboksarsk *Russia* 56°5N 47°27E **190** B8
Novocherkassk *Russia* 47°27N 40°15E **191** G5
Novodevichye *Russia* 53°37N 48°50E **190** D9
Novodvinsk *Russia* 64°25N 40°42E **188** B9
Novogireyevo *Russia* 55°45N 37°46E **129** B4
Novogrudok = Navahrudak
  Belarus 53°40N 25°50E **177** B13
Novohrad-Volynskyy
  Ukraine 50°34N 27°35E **177** C14
Novoivanovskaya *Russia* 55°42N 37°21E **129** B3
Novokachalinsk *Russia* 45°5N 132°0E **220** B5
Novokazalinsk = Zhangaqazaly
  Kazakhstan 45°48N 62°6E **216** C6
Novokhopersk *Russia* 51°5N 41°39E **190** E5
Novokiyevskiy = Krasnino
  Russia 42°44N 130°48E **220** C5
Novokuybyshevsk *Russia* 53°7N 49°58E **190** D9
Novokuznetsk *Russia* 53°45N 87°10E **217** B11
Novolazarevskaya
  Antarctica 71°0S 12°0E **151** D3
Novolyalinsky = Novaya Lyalya
  Russia 59°4N 60°45E **186** C11
Novomirgorod *Ukraine* 48°45N 31°33E **189** H6
Novomoskovsk *Russia* 54°5N 38°15E **188** D10
Novomoskovsk *Ukraine* 48°33N 35°17E **189** H8
Novonikolayevka = Novosibirsk
  Ukraine 47°15N 38°4E **189** J10
Novonikolysko *Russia* 55°50N 37°14E **129** A1
Novopolotsk = Navapolatsk
  Belarus 55°32N 28°37E **188** E5
Novorossiysk *Russia* 44°43N 37°46E **189** K9
Novorybnoye *Russia* 72°50N 105°50E **215** B11
Novorzhev *Russia* 57°3N 29°25E **188** D5
Novosaratovka *Russia* 59°50N 30°32E **137** B3
Novosej *Albania* 41°56N 20°35E **202** E4
Novoselytsya *Ukraine* 48°14N 26°15E **183** B11
Novoshakhtinsk *Russia* 47°46N 39°58E **189** J10
Novosibirsk *Russia* 55°0N 83°5E **217** B10
Novosibirskiye Ostrova
  Russia 75°0N 142°0E **215** B15
Novosibirskoye Vdkhr.
  Russia 54°35N 82°35E **217** B10
Novosil *Russia* 52°59N 37°2E **188** D9
Novosokolniki *Russia* 56°20N 30°2E **188** D6
Novotitarovskaya *Russia* 45°17N 39°2E **191** H4
Novotroitsk *Russia* 51°10N 58°15E **186** D10
Novotroitskoye = Tőle Bı
  Kazakhstan 43°42N 73°46E **217** D8
Novoukrayinka *Ukraine* 48°25N 31°30E **189** H6
Novouljanovsk *Russia* 54°8N 48°24E **190** C9
Novouzensk *Russia* 50°32N 48°17E **190** D9
Novovolynsk *Ukraine* 50°45N 24°4E **185** H11
Novovoronezhskiy
  Russia 51°19N 39°13E **189** G10
Novoyavorivske *Ukraine* 49°53N 23°33E **185** J10
Novozybkov *Russia* 52°30N 32°0E **189** F6
Novska *Croatia* 45°19N 17°0E **199** C13
Nový Bor *Czech Rep.* 50°46N 14°35E **180** A7
Novy Bug = Novyy Buh
  Ukraine 47°34N 32°29E **189** J7
Nový Bydžov *Czech Rep.* 50°14N 15°29E **180** A8
Nový Dvor *Belarus* 52°50N 24°21E **185** F11
Nowy Dwór Mazowiecki
  Poland 52°26N 20°44E **185** F7
Nový Jičín *Czech Rep.* 49°30N 18°0E **181** B11
Novy Margelan = Farghona
  Uzbekistan 40°23N 71°19E **217** D8
Novyy Afon *Georgia* 43°7N 40°50E **191** J5
Novyy Bor *Russia* 66°43N 52°19E **186** B9
Novyy Buh *Ukraine* 47°34N 32°29E **189** J7
Novyy Oskol *Russia* 50°44N 37°55E **189** G9
Novyy Port *Russia* 67°40N 72°30E **214** C8
Novyy Urengoy *Russia* 65°48N 76°52E **214** C8
Novyy Yarkyno *Russia* 50°26N 21°41E **185** H8
Nowa Nowa *Australia* 37°44S 148°3E **283** D8
Nowa Ruda *Poland* 50°35N 16°30E **185** H3
Nowa Sarzyna *Poland* 50°21N 22°21E **185** H9
Nowa Sól *Poland* 51°48N 15°44E **185** G2
Nowata *U.S.A.* 36°42N 95°38W **310** G7
Nowbarān *Iran* 35°8N 49°42E **247** C6
Nowe *Poland* 53°41N 18°44E **185** E5
Nowe-Babice *Poland* 52°14N 20°51E **142** B1
Nowe Miasto *Poland* 51°38N 20°34E **185** G7
Nowe Miasto *Mazowieckie,
  Poland* 53°27N 19°33E **184** E6
Nowe Miasto *Warsaw, Poland* **142** a2
Nowe Miasto Lubawskie
  Poland 53°27N 19°33E **184** E6
Nowe Skalmierzyce
  Poland 51°43N 18°0E **185** G4
Nowe Warpno *Poland* 53°42N 14°18E **184** E1
Nowendoc *Australia* 31°32S 151°44E **283** A4
Nowendoc → *Australia* 31°33S 151°54E **283** A9
Nowghāb *Iran* 33°53N 59°4E **247** C8
Nowgong *Assam, India* 26°20N 92°50E **248** F8
Nowgong *Mad. P., India* 25°4N 79°27E **243** G8
Nowitna Nat. Wildlife Refuge △
  U.S.A. 64°40N 154°16W **303** D9
Nowogard *Poland* 53°41N 15°10E **184** E2
Nowogród *Poland* 53°14N 21°53E **185** E8
Nowogród Bobrzanski
  Poland 51°48N 15°15E **185** G2
Nowogrodziec *Poland* 51°12N 15°24E **185** G2
Noworadomsk = Radomsko
  Poland 51°5N 19°28E **185** G6

Nowra *Australia* 34°53S 150°35E **283** C9
Nowrangapur *India* 19°14N 82°33E **244** E6
Nowshāk = Noshaq
  Pakistan 36°24N 71°49E **240** A3
Nowshera *Pakistan* 34°0N 72°0E **240** B4
Nowy Dwór Gdański
  Poland 54°13N 19°7E **184** D6
Nowy Sącz *Poland* 49°40N 20°41E **185** J7
Nowy Staw *Poland* 54°13N 19°2E **184** D6
Nowy Targ *Poland* 49°29N 20°2E **185** J7
Nowy Tomyśl *Poland* 52°19N 16°10E **185** F3
Nowy Wiśnicz *Poland* 49°55N 20°28E **185** J7
Noxen *U.S.A.* 41°25N 76°4W **313** E8
Noyabr'sk *Russia* 64°34N 76°21E **214** C8
Noyant *France* 47°30N 0°6E **172** E7
Noyers *France* 47°40N 4°0E **173** E10
Noyon *France* 49°34N 2°59E **173** C9
Noyon *Mongolia* 43°2N 102°4E **226** C2
Nozay *France* 47°34N 1°38W **172** E5
Nqutu *S. Africa* 28°13S 30°32E **271** C5
Nsa *Congo* 2°22S 15°19E **264** C3
Nsa, O. en → *Algeria* 32°28N 5°24E **261** B6
Nsanje *Malawi* 16°55S 35°12E **269** F4
Nsawam *Ghana* 5°50N 0°24W **263** D4
Nseluka *Zambia* 9°58S 31°16E **269** D3
Nsok *Eq. Guin.* 1°10N 11°19E **264** D2
Nsomba *Zambia* 10°45S 29°51E **269** E2
Nsontin
  Dem. Rep. of the Congo 3°7S 17°56E **264** C3
Nsopzup *Burma* 25°51N 97°30E **241** C6
Nsukka *Nigeria* 6°51N 7°29E **263** D6
Ntaria ♥ *Australia* 24°0S 132°41E **278** D5
Ntem → *Cameroon* 2°21N 9°49E **264** D1
Ntingui, Mt. *Comoros Is.* 12°12S 44°22E **264** a1
Ntoum *Gabon* 0°53S 14°44E **264** C2
N'Tsama *Congo* 0°53S 14°44E **264** C2
Ntsaoueni *Comoros Is.* 11°27S 43°15E **272** a
Ntsoudjini *Comoros Is.* 11°39S 43°15E **272** a
Ntui *Cameroon* 4°27N 11°38E **263** E7
Ntungamo *Uganda* 0°56S 30°17E **268** C3
Nu Jiang → *China* 29°58N 97°25E **228** E2
Nu Shan *China* 26°0N 99°20E **228** E2
Nuakata I. *Papua N. G.* 10°17S 151°12E **286** F4
Nuba Mts. = Nubah, Jibalan
  Sudan 12°0N 31°0E **257** E3
Nubah, Jibalan *Sudan* 12°0N 31°0E **257** E3
Nubia *Africa* 21°0N 32°0E **254** D7
Nubian Desert = Nûbiya, Es Sahrâ
  Sudan 21°30N 33°30E **256** C3
Nûbiya, Es Sahrâ en
  Sudan 21°30N 33°30E **256** C3
Nubl *Syria* 36°22N 36°59E **250** B7
Nubledo *Spain* 43°31N 5°52W **194** B5
Nuboai *Indonesia* 2°10S 136°30E **231** E9
Nubra → *India* 34°35N 77°35E **243** B7
Nucet *Romania* 46°28N 22°35E **182** D7
Nueces → *U.S.A.* 27°51N 97°30W **314** H6
Nueltin L. *Canada* 60°30N 99°30W **297** A9
Nuestra Señora del Rosario de
  Caá-Catí *Argentina* 27°45S 57°36W **334** B4
Nueva, I. *Chile* 55°13S 66°30W **336** E3
Nueva Antioquia *Colombia* 6°5N 69°26W **328** B4
Nueva Atzacoalco *Mexico* 19°29N 99°4W **128** B2
Nueva Carteya *Spain* 37°35N 4°28W **195** H6
Nueva Ciudad Guerrero
  Mexico 26°34N 99°12W **319** B5
Nueva Ecija □ *Phil.* 15°30N 121°0E **232** D3
Nueva Esparta □ *Venezuela* 11°0N 64°0W **329** A5
Nueva Gerona *Cuba* 21°53N 82°49W **320** B3
Nueva Imperial *Chile* 38°45S 72°58W **336** A2
Nueva Loja = Lago Agrio
  Ecuador 0°5N 76°52W **328** C2
Nueva Palmira *Uruguay* 33°52S 58°20W **334** C4
Nueva Pompeya
  Argentina 24°40S 58°25W **117** C2
Nueva Rosita *Mexico* 27°57N 101°13W **318** B4
Nueva San Salvador
  El Salv. 13°40N 89°18W **320** D2
Nueva Tabarca *Spain* 38°17N 0°30W **197** G4
Nueva Tenochtitlán
  Mexico 16°20N 91°5W **128** B2
Nueva Vizcaya □ *Phil.* 16°20N 121°0E **232** C3
Nuéve de Julio *Argentina* 35°30S 61°0W **334** D3
Nuevitas *Cuba* 21°30N 77°20W **320** B4
Nuevo, G. *Argentina* 43°0S 64°30W **336** B4
Nuevo Casas Grandes
  Mexico 30°25N 107°55W **318** A3
Nuevo Laredo *Mexico* 27°30N 99°31W **319** B5
Nuevo León □ *Mexico* 25°20N 100°0W **318** C5
Nuevo Mundo, Cerro
  Bolivia 21°55S 66°53W **330** E4
Nuevo Rocafuerte
  Ecuador 0°55S 75°27W **328** D2
Nugaal □ *Somali Rep.* 8°10N 49°0E **267** C4
Nugaal → *Somali Rep.* 8°0N 49°47E **267** C6
Nugaaleed, Dooxo
  Somali Rep. 8°35N 48°35E **267** C6
Nugget Pt. *N.Z.* 46°27S 169°50E **285** G4
Nugrus, Gebel *Egypt* 24°47N 34°35E **256** C3
Nuguria Is. *Papua N. G.* 3°20S 154°45E **286** B8
Nuhaka *N.Z.* 39°3S 177°45E **284** C6
Nuijala *Finland* 61°20N 24°46E **164** B8
Nuits-St-Georges *France* 47°10N 4°56E **173** E11
Nukey Bluff *Australia* 32°26S 135°29E **281** E2
Nukha = Şaki *Azerbaijan* 41°10N 47°5E **191** K8
Nukhayb *Iraq* 32°4N 42°3E **243** F10
Nukiki *Solomon Is.* 6°46S 156°35E **287** L8
Nuku *Papua N. G.* 3°41S 142°28E **286** B2
Nuku Hiva *French Polynesia* 8°54S 140°6W **289** f
Nuku'alofa *Tonga* 21°10S 175°12W **287** O13
Nukuhu *Papua N. G.* 5°34S 149°22E **286** C5
Nukulaelae *Tuvalu* 9°23S 179°52E **277** B14
Nukunonu *Pac. Oc.* 9°12S 171°54W **277** B16
Nukus *Uzbekistan* 42°27N 59°41E **216** D5
Nulato *U.S.A.* 64°43N 158°6W **303** D8
Nules *Spain* 39°51N 0°9W **196** F4
Nullagine *Australia* 21°53S 120°7E **278** D3
Nullagine → *Australia* 21°20S 120°20E **278** D3
Nullarbor *Australia* 31°28S 130°55E **279** F5
Nullarbor △ *Australia* 31°45S 130°54E **279** F5
Nullarbor Plain *Australia* 31°10S 129°0E **279** F4
Numalla, L. *Australia* 28°43S 144°20E **281** D3
Numan *Nigeria* 9°29N 12°3E **263** C7
Numanuma *Papua N. G.* 9°41S 150°55E **286** E6
Numata *Japan* 36°45N 139°4E **223** A11
Numatinna → *Sudan* 7°38N 27°2E **257** F2
Numazu *Japan* 35°7N 138°51E **223** B10
Numbulwar *Australia* 14°15S 135°45E **280** A2
Numedal *Norway* 60°42N 9°0E **164** D6
Numfoor *Indonesia* 1°0S 134°50E **231** E8
Numurkah *Australia* 36°5S 145°26E **283** C6
Nunaksaluk I. *Canada* 55°49N 60°20W **299** A7
Nunap Isua *Greenland* 59°48N 43°55W **117** C5
Nunavik *Canada* 71°50N 54°50W **154** C5
Nunavut □ *Canada* 66°0N 85°0W **295** D15
Nunda *U.S.A.* 42°35N 77°56W **312** D7
Nuneaton *U.K.* 52°32N 1°27W **169** E6
Nuñez *Argentina* 34°32S 58°27W **117** B2
Nungarin *Australia* 31°12S 118°6E **279** F2

Nungo *Mozam.* 13°23S 37°43E **269** E4
Nungwe *Tanzania* 2°48S 32°2E **268** C3
Nunhead *U.K.* 51°27N 0°3W **125** B3
Nunivak I. *U.S.A.* 60°10N 166°30W **303** F6
Ñuñoa *Chile* 33°27S 70°35W **137** B2
Núoro *Italy* 40°20N 9°20E **200** B2
Nupe *Iceland* 65°56N 23°36W **155** B3
Nuqay, Jabal *Libya* 23°11N 19°30E **258** D3
Nuqūb *Yemen* 14°59N 45°48E **248** E4
Nuqui *Colombia* 5°42N 77°17W **328** B2
Nūr *Iran* 36°33N 52°1E **247** B7
Nur Daǧ *Turkey* 36°54N 35°39E **250** B6
Nur Dağları *Turkey* 36°50N 36°23E **250** B6
Nura → *Kazakhstan* 50°30N 69°59E **217** B7
Nûrâbâd *Hormozgan, Iran* 27°47N 57°12E **247** E8
Nûrâbâd *Lorestan, Iran* 34°4N 47°58E **213** E12
Nurabad *Uzbekistan* 39°36N 66°17E **217** E7
Nure → *Italy* 45°3N 9°49E **198** C6
Nuremberg = Nürnberg
  Germany 49°27N 11°3E **179** F7
Nuri *Sonora, Mexico* 28°5N 109°22W **318** B3
Nuri *Sudan* 18°29N 31°59E **256** D3
Nuriootpa *Australia* 34°27S 139°0E **282** C3
Nūristān □ *Afghan.* 35°20N 71°0E **217** E8
Nurlat *Russia* 54°29N 50°45E **190** C9
Nurmes *Finland* 63°33N 29°10E **160** E23
Nürnberg *Germany* 49°27N 11°3E **179** F7
Nurpur *Pakistan* 31°53N 71°54E **242** D4
Nurra, Li *Italy* 40°45N 8°15E **200** B1
Nurran, L. = Terewah, L.
  Australia 29°52S 147°35E **281** D4
Nurrari Lakes *Australia* 29°1S 130°5E **279** E5
Nurri *Italy* 39°43N 9°14E **200** C2
Nürtingen *Germany* 48°37N 9°19E **179** G5
Nurzec → *Poland* 52°37N 22°25E **185** F9
Nus *Italy* 45°45N 7°28E **198** C4
Nusa Barung *Indonesia* 8°30S 113°30E **235** D4
Nusa Dua *Indonesia* 8°48S 115°14E **231** K18
Nusa Kambangan
  Indonesia 7°40S 108°10E **235** D3
Nusa Tenggara Barat □
  Indonesia 8°50S 117°30E **235** D5
Nusa Tenggara Timur □
  Indonesia 9°30S 122°0E **231** F6
Nusaybin *Turkey* 37°3N 41°10E **213** D9
Nuşayrīyah, J. an *Syria* 35°20N 36°13E **250** C7
Nushki *Pakistan* 29°35N 66°0E **242** E2
Nusle *Czech Rep.* 50°3N 14°26E **135** B3
Nussdorf *Austria* 48°15N 16°21E **142** A2
Nuuk *Greenland* 64°10N 51°35W **154** E5
Nuupere, Pte. *Moorea* 17°36S 149°47W **289** e
Nuussuaq *Greenland* 74°8N 57°3W **154** B5
Nu'uuli *Amer. Samoa* 14°19S 170°42W **302** f
Nuwakot *Nepal* 28°10N 83°55E **243** E10
Nuwara Eliya *Sri Lanka* 6°58N 80°48E **245** L5
Nuwayb'ī, W. an →
  Si. Arabia 29°18N 34°57E **251** A5
Nuweiba' *Egypt* 28°59N 34°39E **251** A5
Nuwerus *S. Africa* 31°8S 18°24E **270** D2
Nuweveldberge *S. Africa* 32°10S 21°45E **270** D3
Nuyts, Pt. *Australia* 35°4S 116°38E **279** G2
Nuyts Arch. *Australia* 32°35S 133°20E **281** E1
N'Vinda *Angola* 13°8S 19°2E **265** E3
Nxai Pan △ *Botswana* 19°50S 24°46E **270** A3
Nxaunxau *Botswana* 18°57S 21°4E **270** A3
Nyaake *Liberia* 4°52N 7°37W **262** E3
Nyabessan *Cameroon* 2°28N 10°24E **264** B2
Nyabing *Australia* 33°33S 118°9E **279** F2
Nyack *U.S.A.* 41°5N 73°55W **313** E11
Nyagan *Russia* 62°30N 65°38E **214** C7
Nyah West *Australia* 35°16S 143°21E **282** C5
Nyahanga *Tanzania* 2°20S 33°37E **268** C3
Nyahua *Tanzania* 5°25S 33°23E **268** D3
Nyahururu *Kenya* 0°2N 36°27E **268** B4
Nyaingêntanglha Shan
  China 30°0N 90°0E **218** D3
Nyakanazi *Tanzania* 3°2S 31°10E **268** C3
Nyakrom *Ghana* 5°40N 0°50W **263** D4
Nyâlâ *Sudan* 12°2N 24°58E **257** F1
Nyamandhlovu *Zimbabwe* 19°55S 28°16E **269** H2
Nyambiti *Tanzania* 2°48S 33°27E **268** C3
Nyamira *Kenya* 0°36S 34°52E **268** C4
Nyamwaga *Tanzania* 1°27S 34°33E **268** C3
Nyandekwa *Tanzania* 3°57S 32°32E **268** C3
Nyanding → *Sudan* 8°40N 32°41E **257** F3
Nyandoma *Russia* 61°40N 40°12E **188** B11
Nyanga *Congo* 2°52S 11°57E **264** C2
Nyanga *Western Cape,
  S. Africa* 33°59S 18°35E **118** A2
Nyanga → *Gabon* 2°58S 10°15E **264** C2
Nyanga △ *Zimbabwe* 18°17S 32°46E **269** F3
Nyanga *Namibia* 18°0S 20°40E **270** A3
Nyanguge *Tanzania* 2°30S 33°12E **268** C3
Nyankpala *Ghana* 9°21N 0°58W **263** D4
Nyanza *Rwanda* 2°20S 29°42E **268** C2
Nyanza □ *Kenya* 0°10S 34°15E **268** C3
Nyanza-Lac *Burundi* 4°21S 29°36E **268** C2
Nyapongeta *Sudan* 5°5N 33°45E **257** G3
Nyasa, L. = Malawi, L.
  Africa 12°0S 34°30E **269** E3
Nyasaland = Malawi ■
  Africa 11°55S 34°0E **269** E3
Nyasvizh *Belarus* 53°14N 26°38E **177** B14
Nyaunglebin *Burma* 17°52N 96°42E **241** J6
Nyazepetrovsk *Russia* 56°3N 59°36E **186** C10
Nyazura *Zimbabwe* 18°40S 32°16E **269** F3
Nyazwidzi → *Zimbabwe* 20°0S 31°17E **269** G3
Nybergsund *Norway* 61°15N 12°19E **164** C9
Nyborg *Denmark* 55°18N 10°47E **163** J4
Nybro *Sweden* 56°44N 15°55E **163** H9
Nyda *Russia* 66°40N 72°58E **214** C8
Nyeboe Land *Greenland* 82°0N 57°0W **154** A5
Nyengo Swamp *Zambia* 14°51S 22°7E **265** E4
Nyeri *Kenya* 0°23S 36°56E **268** C4
Nyerol *Sudan* 8°41N 32°1E **257** F3
Nyhammar *Sweden* 60°17N 14°58E **164** D8
Nyika △ *Zambia* 10°30S 33°50E **269** E3
Nyimba *Zambia* 14°33S 30°50E **269** E3
Nyinahin *Ghana* 6°43N 2°3W **262** D4
Nyíradony *Hungary* 47°41N 21°55E **182** C6
Nyírbátor *Hungary* 47°49N 22°9E **182** C7
Nyíregyháza *Hungary* 47°58N 21°47E **182** C6
Nyiru, Mt. *Kenya* 2°8N 36°50E **268** B4
Nykarleby = Uusikaarlepyy
  Finland 63°32N 22°31E **160** E20
Nykirke *Norway* 60°54N 10°19E **164** D5
Nykøbing *Nordjylland,
  Denmark* 56°48N 8°51E **163** H2
Nykøbing *Sjælland,
  Denmark* 54°56N 11°52E **168** K5
Nykøbing *Sjælland,
  Denmark* 55°55N 11°40E **163** J5
Nyköping *Sweden* 58°45N 17°1E **163** F11
Nykroppa *Sweden* 59°37N 14°18E **162** E8
Nykvarn *Sweden* 59°11N 17°25E **162** E11
Nyland *Sweden* 62°57N 17°45E **162** A11
Nylstroom = Modimolle
  S. Africa 24°42S 28°22E **271** B4
Nymagee *Australia* 32°7S 146°20E **283** B7
Nymboida *Australia* 29°59S 152°48E **283** A5
Nymboida → *Australia* 29°40N 14°0E **180** D6
Nymburk *Czech Rep.* 50°10N 15°1E **180** A8
Nymphenburg, Schloss
  Germany 48°9N 11°30E **131** B2

Nynäshamn *Sweden* 58°54N 17°57E **163** F11
Nyngan *Australia* 31°30S 147°8E **283** A7
Nyoma Rap *India* 33°10N 78°40E **243** C8
Nyoman = Nemunas →
  Lithuania 55°25N 21°10E **184** C8
Nyon *Switz.* 46°23N 6°14E **179** J2
Nyong → *Cameroon* 3°17N 9°54E **263** E6
Nyons *France* 44°22N 5°10E **175** D9
Nýrsko *Czech Rep.* 49°18N 13°9E **180** B6
Nysa *Poland* 50°30N 17°22E **185** H4
Nysa → *Europe* 52°4N 14°46E **178** C10
Nysa Kłodzka → *Poland* 50°49N 17°40E **185** H4
Nysetre *Norway* 62°10N 9°1E **163** B3
Nysäter *Sweden* 59°17N 12°47E **162** E6
Nyslott = Savonlinna
  Finland 61°52N 28°53E **188** B5
Nyssa *U.S.A.* 43°53N 117°0W **304** E5
Nystad = Uusikaupunki
  Finland 60°47N 21°25E **188** B1
Nysted *Denmark* 54°40N 11°44E **163** K5
Nyunzu
  Dem. Rep. of the Congo 5°57S 27°58E **268** D2
Nyurba *Russia* 63°17N 118°28E **215** C12
Nyíregyháza *Hungary* 47°58N 21°47E **182** C6
Nyzhankovychi *Ukraine* 49°40N 22°49E **185** J9
Nyzhnohirskyy *Ukraine* 45°27N 34°38E **189** K8
Nyzhny Vorota *Ukraine* 48°46N 23°6E **182** B8
Nzébéla *Guinea* 8°9N 9°7W **262** D3
Nzérékoré *Guinea* 7°49N 8°48W **262** D3
Nzeto *Angola* 7°10S 12°52E **265** D2
Nzilo, Chutes de
  Dem. Rep. of the Congo 10°18S 25°27E **265** E5
Nzilo, L.
  Dem. Rep. of the Congo 10°35S 25°39E **265** E5
N'zo → *Ivory C.* 6°15N 7°3W **262** D3
N'zo → *Ivory C.* 6°15N 7°15W **262** D3
Nzubuka *Tanzania* 4°45S 32°50E **268** C3
Nzwani = Anjouan
  Comoros Is. 12°15S 44°20E **272** a

O

O Barco *Spain* 42°23N 6°58W **194** C4
O Carballiño *Spain* 42°26N 8°5W **194** C2
O Corgo *Spain* 42°56N 7°25W **194** C3
O Le Pupū Pu'e △
  Samoa 13°59S 171°43W **287** V20
O Pino *Spain* 42°56N 8°20W **194** C2
O Porriño *Spain* 42°10N 8°37W **194** C2
Ō-Shima *Hokkaidō, Japan* 41°30N 139°22E **220** D9
Ō-Shima *Nagasaki, Japan* 32°29N 129°33E **222** D1
Ō-Shima *Shizuoka,
  Japan* 34°44N 139°24E **223** C11
Oa, Mull of *U.K.* 55°35N 6°20W **167** F2
Oacoma *U.S.A.* 43°48N 99°24W **308** D4
Oahe, L. *U.S.A.* 44°27N 100°24W **308** C3
Oahe Dam *U.S.A.* 44°27N 100°24W **308** C3
O'ahu *U.S.A.* 21°28N 157°58W **302** K14
Oak Creek *U.S.A.* 42°52N 87°55W **311** B9
Oak Grove *U.S.A.* 33°50N 84°18W **113** A3
Oak Harbor *U.S.A.* 48°18N 122°39W **306** B4
Oak Hill *Fla., U.S.A.* 28°52N 80°51W **317** G9
Oak Hill *W. Va., U.S.A.* 37°59N 81°9W **309** G13
Oak Island *U.S.A.* 33°55S 78°10W **315** E15
Oak Lawn *U.S.A.* 41°42N 87°45W **119** E2
Oak Park *La., U.S.A.* 32°22N 82°19W **316** D7
Oak Park *Ill., U.S.A.* 41°52N 87°47W **119** B2
Oak Ridge *U.S.A.* 36°1N 84°16W **315** C12
Oak Street Beach *Chicago, U.S.A.* **119** a2
Oak View *Calif., U.S.A.* 34°24N 119°18W **307** L7
Oak View *Md., U.S.A.* 39°1N 76°58W **143** A4
Oakan-Dake *Japan* 43°27N 144°10E **220** C12
Oakbank *Australia* 33°4S 140°33E **282** B4
Oakdale *Calif., U.S.A.* 37°46N 120°51W **306** H6
Oakdale *Georgia, U.S.A.* 33°51N 84°30W **113** A2
Oakdale *La., U.S.A.* 30°49N 92°40W **314** F8
Oakes *U.S.A.* 46°8N 98°6W **308** B4
Oakesdale *U.S.A.* 47°8N 117°15W **304** C5
Oakey *Australia* 27°25S 151°43E **281** D5
Oakfield *Ga., U.S.A.* 31°45N 83°58W **316** D6
Oakfield *N.Y., U.S.A.* 43°4N 78°16W **312** C6
Oakford *U.S.A.* 40°6N 89°58W **310** D7
Oakham *U.K.* 52°40N 0°43W **169** E7
Oakhurst *U.S.A.* 37°19N 119°40N **306** H7
Oakland *Calif., U.S.A.* 37°48N 122°16W **136** B3
Oakland *Ill., U.S.A.* 39°39N 88°2W **311** E8
Oakland *Md., U.S.A.* 39°25N 79°14W **309** F14
Oakland *Nebr., U.S.A.* 41°50N 96°28W **308** E6
Oakland City *U.S.A.* 38°20N 87°21W **311** F9
Oakland Park *U.S.A.* 26°10N 80°7W **317** J4
Oaklands *Australia* 35°34S 146°10E **283** C7
Oaklawn *U.S.A.* 37°40N 97°20W **310** G6
Oakleigh *Australia* 37°54S 145°5E **128** B2
Oakley *Idaho, U.S.A.* 42°15N 113°53W **304** E7
Oakley *Kans., U.S.A.* 39°8N 100°51W **308** F3
Oakover → *Australia* 21°0S 120°40E **278** D3
Oakridge *U.S.A.* 43°45N 122°28W **304** E2
Oaks, The *Australia* 34°3S 150°34E **283** C9
Oakton *U.S.A.* 38°52N 77°18W **143** B2
Oaktown *U.S.A.* 38°52N 87°27W **311** F9
Oakville *Ont., Canada* 43°27N 79°41W **312** D5
Oakville *Wash., U.S.A.* 46°51N 123°14W **306** D3
Oakwood *U.S.A.* 41°6N 84°23W **311** E12
Oakwood Beach *U.S.A.* 40°33N 74°7W **132** C1
Oamaru *N.Z.* 45°5S 170°59E **285** F5
Ōamishirasato *Japan* 35°31N 140°18E **223** B12
Oancea *Romania* 45°21N 27°42E **183** E12
Oasi *U.S.A.* 35°1N 133°45E **222** B5
Oasi *U.S.A.* 56°14N 3°40W **167** E5
Oaklockonee → *U.S.A.* 30°58N 84°0W **316** E5
Ocha → *Russia* 49°4N 84°7W **298** C3
Ocala *U.S.A.* 29°11N 82°8W **317** F7
Ocamo → *Venezuela* 2°48N 65°14W **329** C4
Ocampo *Chihuahua,
  Mexico* 28°11N 108°23W **318** B3
Ocampo *Tamaulipas,
  Mexico* 22°50N 99°20W **319** C5
Ocaña *Colombia* 8°15N 73°20W **328** B3
Ocaña *Spain* 39°55N 3°30W **194** F7
Occidental, Cordillera
  Colombia 5°0N 76°0W **328** C2
Occidental, Cordillera *Peru* 14°0S 74°0W **330** C3
Occidental, Grand Erg
  Algeria 30°20N 1°0E **261** B5
Ocean City *Md., U.S.A.* 38°20N 75°5W **309** F16
Ocean City *N.J., U.S.A.* 39°17N 74°35W **309** F16
Ocean City *Wash., U.S.A.* 47°4N 124°10W **306** C2
Ocean Falls *Canada* 52°18N 127°48W **296** C3
Ocean I. = Banaba
  Kiribati 0°45S 169°50E **288** H8
Ocean Park *Hong Kong,
  China* 22°13N 114°10E **122** B2
Ocean Park *Wash.,
  U.S.A.* 46°30N 124°3W **306** D2
Oceano *U.S.A.* 35°6N 120°37W **307** K6
Oceanport *U.S.A.* 40°19N 74°3W **313** F10
Oceanside *U.S.A.* 33°12N 117°23W **307** M9
Ochagavía *Spain* 42°55N 1°5W **196** C3
Ochakiv *Ukraine* 46°37N 31°33E **189** J6
Ochakovo *Russia* 55°41N 37°26E **129** B3
Ochamchira *Georgia* 42°46N 41°32E **191** J5
Ochi, Oros *Greece* 38°5N 24°25E **204** C6
Ochiai *Japan* 35°1N 133°45E **222** B5
Ochil Hills *U.K.* 56°14N 3°40W **167** E5
Ochlockonee → *U.S.A.* 30°58N 84°3W **316** E5
Ochlockonee → *U.S.A.* 29°59N 84°26W **316** F5
Ocho Rios *Jamaica* 18°24N 77°6W **320** a
Ochopee *U.S.A.* 25°54N 81°18W **317** K8
Ochota *Poland* 52°13N 20°58E **142** B1
Ochsenfurt *Germany* 49°40N 10°4E **179** F6
Ochsenhausen *Germany* 48°4N 9°57E **179** G5
Ocilla *U.S.A.* 31°36N 83°15W **316** D6
Ockelbo *Sweden* 60°54N 16°45E **162** D10
Ocmulgee → *U.S.A.* 31°58N 82°33W **316** D6
Ocmulgee △ *U.S.A.* 32°49N 83°37W **316** D6
Ocna Mureș *Romania* 46°23N 23°55E **183** D8
Ocnele Mari *Romania* 45°8N 24°18E **183** E8
Ocoee *U.S.A.* 28°34N 81°32W **133** A1
Ocós *Guatemala* 14°31S 92°11W **320** D1
Ocoña *Peru* 16°26S 73°8W **330** D3
Ocoña → *Peru* 16°28S 73°9W **330** D3
Oconee, L. *U.S.A.* 33°28N 83°15W **316** B6
O'Connell Street *Dublin, Ireland* **120** D2
Oconomowoc *U.S.A.* 43°7N 88°30W **311** A8
Oconto *U.S.A.* 44°53N 87°52W **308** D10
Oconto Falls *U.S.A.* 44°52N 88°9W **308** D9
Ocosingo *Mexico* 16°53N 92°9W **319** D6
Ocotal *Nic.* 13°41N 86°31W **320** D2
Ocotlán *Jalisco, Mexico* 20°21N 102°46W **318** C4
Ocotlán *Oaxaca, Mexico* 16°48N 96°40W **319** D5
Ocreza → *Portugal* 39°32N 7°50W **195** F3
Ócsa *Hungary* 47°17N 19°15E **182** C4
Octeville *France* 49°38N 1°40W **172** C5
Ocumare del Tuy
  Venezuela 10°7N 66°46W **328** A4

Ocurí Bolivia 18°45S 65°50W 331 D4
Oda Ghana 5°50N 0°51W 263 D4
Oda Shimane, Japan 35°11N 132°30E 222 B4
Oda, J. Sudan 20°21N 36°39E 256 C4
Ódáðahraun Iceland 65°5N 17°0W 155 B9
Ödaejin N. Korea 41°34N 129°40E 224 B4
Odaesan △ S. Korea 37°40N 128°30E 224 D4
Ödåkra Sweden 56°7N 12°45E 163 H6
Ōdana Japan 35°33N 139°35E 140 B2
Ōdate Japan 40°16N 140°34E 220 D10
Ōdawara Japan 35°20N 139°6E 223 B11
Odda Norway 60°3N 6°35E 164 D3
Odder = Xuddur Somali Rep. 4°11N 43°52E 267 D5
Odder Denmark 55°58N 10°10E 163 J4
Odei → Canada 56°6N 96°54W 297 B9
Odell U.S.A. 41°0N 88°31W 311 C8
Odemira Portugal 37°35N 8°40W 195 H2
Ödemiş Turkey 38°15N 28°0E 205 C9
Öden-Stockach Germany 48°5N 11°41E 131 B3
Ödenburg = Sopron Hungary 47°45N 16°32E 182 C1
Odendaalsrus S. Africa 27°48S 26°45E 270 C4
Odensbacken Sweden 59°10N 15°32E 162 E9
Odense Denmark 55°22N 10°23E 163 J4
Odenwald = Neckartal-Odenwald △ Germany 49°30N 9°5E 179 F5
Odenwald Germany 49°35N 9°0E 179 F5
Oder → Europe 53°33N 14°38E 178 B10
Oder-Havel Kanal Germany 52°52N 14°2E 178 C10
Oderzo Italy 45°47N 12°29E 199 C9
Odesa Ukraine 46°30N 30°45E 189 J6
Odesa □ Ukraine 47°20N 29°55E 189 J5
Ödeshög Sweden 58°14N 14°39E 163 F8
Odessa = Odesa Ukraine 46°30N 30°45E 189 J6
Odessa Ont., Canada 44°17N 76°43W 313 B8
Odessa Mo., U.S.A. 39°0N 93°57W 310 F3
Odessa Tex., U.S.A. 31°52N 102°23W 314 F3
Odessa Wash., U.S.A. 47°20N 118°41W 304 C4
Odiakwe Botswana 20°12S 25°17E 270 B4
Odiel → Spain 37°10N 6°55W 195 H4
Odienné Ivory C. 9°30N 7°34W 262 D3
Odilampi Finland 60°18N 24°45E 121 B1
Odimba Gabon 2°2S 9°33E 264 C2
Odintsovo Russia 55°40N 37°16E 129 B1
Odiongan Phil. 12°24N 121°59E 232 E3
Odivelas Portugal 38°47N 9°10W 126 A1
Odobești Romania 45°43N 27°4E 183 E12
Odolanów Poland 51°34N 17°40E 185 G4
Odolany Poland 52°13N 20°55E 142 B1
O'Donnell U.S.A. 32°58N 101°50W 314 E4
O'Donnell Pt. Canada 45°5N 80°5W 312 A4
Odorheiu Secuiesc Romania 46°21N 25°21E 183 D10
Odoyevo Russia 53°56N 36°42E 188 F9
Odra = Oder → Europe 53°33N 14°38E 178 B10
Odra → Spain * 42°14N 4°17W 194 C6
Odum U.S.A. 31°40N 82°2W 316 D7
Odžaci Serbia 45°30N 19°17E 182 E4
Odžak Bos.-H. 45°3N 18°18E 182 E3
Odzala Congo 0°37N 14°37E 264 B2
Odzala △ Congo 0°55N 14°55E 264 B2
Odzi Zimbabwe 19°0S 32°20E 271 A5
Odzi → Zimbabwe 19°45S 32°23E 271 A5
Oebisfelde Germany 52°27N 10°57E 178 C6
Oedong S. Korea 35°42N 129°14E 224 E5
Oeiras Brazil 7°0S 42°8W 332 C3
Oeiras Portugal 38°41N 9°18W 126 A1
Oeiras do Para Brazil 1°58S 49°51W 329 D8
Oelrichs U.S.A. 43°11N 103°14W 308 D2
Oels in Schlesien = Oleśnica Poland 51°13N 17°22E 185 G4
Oelsnitz Germany 50°24N 12°10E 179 E8
Oelwein U.S.A. 42°41N 91°55W 310 B5
Oenarodo S. Korea 34°26N 127°30E 224 E3
Oeno I. Pac. Oc. 24°0S 131°0W 289 K14
Oenpelli = Gunbalanya Australia 12°20S 133°4E 278 B5
Oetz Austria 47°13N 10°53E 180 D3
Of Turkey 40°59N 40°23E 213 B9
O'Fallon U.S.A. 38°49N 90°42W 310 F6
Ofanto → Italy 41°22N 16°13E 201 A9
Offa Nigeria 8°13N 4°42E 263 D5
Offaly □ Ireland 53°15N 7°30W 166 C4
Offenbach Germany 50°6N 8°44E 179 E4
Offenburg Germany 48°28N 7°56E 179 G3
Officer Cr. → Australia 27°46S 132°30E 279 E5
Offida Italy 42°56N 13°41E 199 F10
Offoué → Gabon 0°4S 11°44E 264 C2
Ofidousa Greece 36°33N 26°8E 205 E8
Ofin Nigeria 6°32N 3°30E 124 A3
Ofolanga Tonga 19°38S 174°27W 287 P13
Ofotfjorden Norway 68°27N 17°0E 160 B17
Ofte Norway 59°30N 8°12E 164 E5
Ofu Amer. Samoa 14°11S 169°41W 302 g
Ōfunato Japan 39°4N 141°43E 220 E10
Oga Japan 39°55N 139°50E 220 E9
Oga-Hantō Japan 39°58N 139°47E 220 E9
Ogaden Ethiopia 7°30N 45°30E 267 C6
Ōgaki Japan 35°21N 136°37E 223 B8
Ogallala U.S.A. 41°8N 101°43W 308 E3
Ogan → Indonesia 3°1S 104°44E 234 C2
Ogasawara Gunto Pac. Oc. 27°0N 142°0E 211 F16
Ogawa Japan 35°44N 139°28E 140 A1
Ogbomosho Nigeria 8°1N 4°11E 263 D5
Ogden Iowa, U.S.A. 42°2N 94°2W 310 B2
Ogden Utah, U.S.A. 41°13N 111°58W 304 F8
Ogden Park U.S.A. 41°46N 87°39W 119 C2
Ogden Slip Chicago, U.S.A. 119 b3
Ogdensburg U.S.A. 44°42N 75°30W 313 B9
Ogea Driki Fiji 19°12S 178°27W 287 B3
Ogea Levu Fiji 19°8S 178°24W 287 B3
Ogeechee → U.S.A. 31°50N 81°3W 316 D8
Ogikubo Japan 35°42N 139°37E 140 A2
Ogilby U.S.A. 32°49N 114°50W 307 N12
Oglat Beraber Algeria 30°15N 3°34W 260 B4
Oglat el Khnâchich Mali 21°51N 3°58W 260 D4
Oglesby U.S.A. 41°18N 89°4W 310 C7
Oglethorpe U.S.A. 32°18N 84°4W 316 C5
Óglio → Italy 45°2N 10°39E 198 C7
Óglio Nord △ Italy 45°22N 9°54E 198 C6
Óglio Sud △ Italy 45°7N 10°24E 198 C7
Ogmore Australia 22°37S 149°35E 280 C4
Ognon → France 47°16N 5°28E 173 E12
Ogogoro Nigeria 6°25N 3°24E 124 B2
Ogoja Nigeria 6°38N 8°39E 263 D6
Ogoki Canada 51°38N 85°58W 298 B2
Ogoki → Canada 51°38N 85°57W 298 B2
Ogoki L. Canada 50°50N 87°10W 298 B2
Ogoki Res. Canada 50°45N 88°15W 298 B2
Ogooué → Gabon 1°0S 9°0E 264 C1
Ogōri Japan 34°6N 131°24E 222 C3
Ogosta → Bulgaria 43°48N 23°55E 202 C7
Ogou → Togo 7°50N 1°19E 263 D5
Ogoueïleten Nmâdi Mauritania 19°46N 11°1W 260 E2
Ogowe = Ogooué → Gabon 1°0S 9°0E 264 C1
Ogoyo Nigeria 6°25N 3°29E 124 B2
Ogr = Sharafa Sudan 11°59N 27°7E 257 E2
Ograżden Macedonia 41°30N 22°50E 202 E6
Ogre Latvia 56°49N 24°36E 188 D3
Ogrein Sudan 17°55N 34°50E 256 D3
Ogudu Nigeria 6°34N 3°24E 124 A2
Ogulin Croatia 45°16N 15°16E 199 C12
Ogun □ Nigeria 7°0N 3°0E 263 D5
Oguni Japan 33°11N 131°8E 222 D3
Ögur Iceland 66°2N 22°44W 155 A4
Ogurchinskiy, Ostrov Turkmenistan 38°55N 53°2E 247 B7
Oguta Nigeria 5°44N 6°44E 263 D6
Oğuzeli Turkey 36°57N 37°30E 250 B8
Ogwashi-Uku Nigeria 6°15N 6°30E 263 D6
Ogwe Nigeria 5°0N 7°14E 263 E6
Ohai N.Z. 45°55S 168°0E 285 F3
Ohakune N.Z. 39°24S 175°24E 284 F4
Ohanet Algeria 28°44N 8°46E 261 C6
Ōhara Japan 35°15N 140°23E 223 B12
O'Hare Int., Chicago ✈ (ORD) U.S.A. 41°59N 87°54W 119 B1
Ohariu Stream → N.Z. 41°12S 174°47E 143 B1
Ohata Japan 41°24N 141°10E 220 D10
Ohatchee U.S.A. 33°47N 86°0W 316 B4
Ohau, L. N.Z. 44°15S 169°53E 285 E4
Ohaupo N.Z. 37°56S 175°20E 284 D4
O'Higgins, C. Chile 27°5S 109°15W 330 b
O'Higgins, Parque Chile 33°27S 70°40W 137 B2
O'Higgins, Pta. Chile 33°41S 79°0W 330 c
Ohio □ U.S.A. 40°15N 82°45W 312 F2
Ohio → U.S.A. 36°59N 89°8W 311 G8
Ohio City U.S.A. 40°46N 84°37W 311 D12
Ohiwa Harbour N.Z. 37°59S 177°10E 284 D6
Ohlau = Oława Poland 50°57N 17°20E 185 H4
Ohře → Czech Rep. 50°30N 14°10E 180 A7
Ohre → Sachsen-Anhalt, Germany 52°18N 11°46E 178 C7
Ohrid Macedonia 41°8N 20°52E 202 E4
Ohridsko Jezero Macedonia 41°8N 20°52E 202 E4
Ohrigstad S. Africa 24°39S 30°36E 271 B5
Öhringen Germany 49°12N 9°31E 179 F5
Ohura N.Z. 38°51S 174°59E 284 E3
Oi Qu China 28°37N 98°16E 228 C2
Oiapoque Brazil 3°50N 51°50W 329 C7
Oiapoque → S. Amer. 4°8N 51°40W 329 C7
Oikou China 38°35N 117°42E 227 E9
Oil City U.S.A. 41°26N 79°42W 312 E5
Oil Springs Canada 42°47N 82°7W 312 D2
Oildale U.S.A. 35°25N 119°1W 307 K7
Ōimachi Japan 35°35N 139°43E 140 B3
Oinousa = Inousses Greece 38°33N 26°14E 205 C8
Oise □ France 49°28N 2°30E 173 C9
Oise → France 49°0N 2°4E 173 C9
Oiseaux du Djoudj △ Senegal 16°24N 16°14W 262 B1
Oistins Barbados 13°4N 59°33W 323 r
Ōita Japan 33°14N 131°36E 222 D3
Ōita □ Japan 33°15N 131°30E 222 D3
Ojai U.S.A. 34°27N 119°15W 307 L7
Ojcowski △ Poland 50°15N 19°50E 185 H6
Ojhar India 20°6N 73°56E 244 D1
Ojinaga Mexico 29°34N 104°25W 318 B4
Ojiya Japan 37°18N 138°48E 221 F9
Ojo Caliente Mexico 21°53N 102°15W 318 C4
Ojo de Liebre, L. Mexico 27°45N 114°15W 318 B2
Ojos del Salado, Cerro Argentina 27°0S 68°40W 334 B2
Ojota Nigeria 6°35N 3°23E 124 A2
Oka Nigeria 7°9N 3°38E 263 D5
Oka → Russia 56°20N 43°59E 190 B7
Okaba Indonesia 8°6S 139°42E 231 F9
Okahandja Namibia 22°0S 16°59E 270 B2
Okahukura N.Z. 38°48S 175°14E 284 E4
Okaihau N.Z. 35°19S 173°47E 284 B2
Okalataka Congo 0°18S 14°54E 264 C2
Okanagan L. Canada 50°0N 119°30W 296 D5
Okandja Gabon 0°35S 13°45E 264 C2
Okano → Gabon 0°5S 10°57E 264 C2
Okanogan U.S.A. 48°22N 119°35W 304 B4
Okanogan → U.S.A. 48°6N 119°44W 304 B4
Okanogan Range N. Amer. 49°0N 119°55W 296 D5
Okány Hungary 46°52N 21°21E 182 D6
Okapa Papua N. G. 6°38S 145°39E 286 D3
Okapi △ Dem. Rep. of the Congo 2°30N 27°20E 268 B2
Okaputa Namibia 20°5S 17°0E 270 B2
Okara Pakistan 30°50N 73°31E 242 D5
Okarito N.Z. 43°15S 170°9E 285 D5
Okato N.Z. 39°12S 173°53E 284 F2
Okau Micronesia 9°32N 138°6E 287 R16
Okaukuejo Namibia 19°10S 16°0E 270 A2
Okavango Delta Botswana 18°45S 22°45E 270 A3
Okavango Swamp = Okavango Delta Botswana 18°45S 22°45E 270 A3
Ōkawa Japan 33°9N 130°21E 222 D2
Okawville U.S.A. 38°26N 89°33W 310 F7
Okaya Japan 36°5N 138°10E 223 A10
Okayama Japan 34°40N 133°54E 222 C5
Okayama □ Japan 35°0N 133°50E 222 C5
Okazaki Japan 34°57N 137°10E 223 C9
Oke-Iho Nigeria 8°1N 3°18E 263 D5
Oke-Ira Nigeria 6°29N 3°22E 124 B2
Okęcie Poland 52°11N 20°56E 142 B1
Okęcie, Warszawa ✈ (WAW) Poland 52°9N 20°59E 142 B1
Okeechobee U.S.A. 27°15N 80°50W 317 H9
Okeechobee, L. U.S.A. 27°0N 80°50W 317 J9
Okefenokee △ U.S.A. 30°45N 82°18W 316 E7
Okefenokee Swamp U.S.A. 30°40N 82°20W 316 E7
Okehampton U.K. 50°44N 4°0W 169 G4
Okemos U.S.A. 42°43N 84°26W 311 B12
Okene Nigeria 7°32N 6°11E 263 D6
Okeogbe Nigeria 6°24N 3°23E 124 B2
Oker → Germany 52°32N 10°22E 178 C6
Okha Gujarat, India 22°27N 69°4E 242 H3
Okha Russia 53°40N 143°0E 215 D15
Okhla India 28°33N 77°16E 120 B2
Okhotsk Russia 59°20N 143°10E 215 D15
Okhotsk, Sea of Asia 55°0N 145°0E 215 D15
Okhotskiy Perevoz Russia 61°52N 135°35E 215 C14
Okhta → Russia 59°56N 30°25E 137 B2
Okhtyrka Ukraine 50°25N 35°0E 189 G8
Oki-no-Shima Japan 32°44N 132°33E 222 E4
Oki-Shotō Japan 36°5N 133°15E 222 A5
Okiep S. Africa 29°39S 17°53E 270 C2
Okigwi Nigeria 5°52N 7°20E 263 D6
Okija Nigeria 5°54N 6°55E 263 D6
Okinawa Japan 26°19N 127°46E 288 a
Okinawa □ Japan 26°40N 128°0E 288 a
Okinawa-Guntō Japan 26°40N 128°0E 221 L4
Okinawa-Jima Japan 26°32N 128°0E 221 L4
Okino-erabu-Shima Japan 27°21N 128°33E 221 L4
Okitipupa Nigeria 6°31N 4°50E 263 D5
Okkervil → Russia 59°56N 30°30E 137 B2
Oklahoma □ U.S.A. 35°20N 97°30W 314 D6
Oklahoma City U.S.A. 35°30N 97°30W 314 D6
Oklawaha → U.S.A. 29°28N 81°41W 317 F8
Okmulgee U.S.A. 35°37N 95°58W 314 D7
Oknitsa = Ocnița Moldova 48°25N 27°30E 183 B12
Oko, W. → Sudan 21°15N 35°56E 256 C4
Okolo Uganda 2°37N 31°8E 268 B3
Okolona Ky., U.S.A. 38°8N 85°41W 311 F11
Okolona Miss., U.S.A. 34°0N 88°45W 315 E10
Okombahe Namibia 21°23S 15°22E 270 B2
Okonek Poland 53°32N 16°51E 184 E3
Okotoks Canada 50°43N 113°58W 296 C6
Okoyo Congo 1°28S 15°0E 264 C3
Okrika Nigeria 4°40N 7°10E 263 E6
Okrzeszyn Poland 52°8N 21°8E 142 C2
Oksapmin Papua N. G. 5°17S 142°15E 286 C2
Øksendalsøra Norway 62°42N 8°27E 164 B5
Oksibil Indonesia 4°59S 140°35E 231 E10
Øksna Norway 60°58N 11°27E 164 D8
Oksovskiy Russia 62°33N 39°57E 186 B6
Oksval Norway 59°51N 10°40E 133 A3
Oktwin Burma 18°49N 96°26E 241 F6
Oktyabr'sk = Qandyaghash Kazakhstan 49°28N 57°25E 187 E10
Oktyabrsk Russia 53°11N 48°40E 190 D9
Oktyabrskiy = Aktsyabrski Belarus 52°38N 28°53E 177 B15
Oktyabrskiy Bashkortostan, Russia 54°28N 53°28E 186 D9
Oktyabrskiy Kamchatka, Russia 52°39N 156°14E 215 D16
Oktyabrskiy Moskva, Russia 55°41N 37°35E 129 B3
Oktyabrskiy Rostov, Russia 47°30N 40°4E 191 G5
Oktyabrskoy Revolyutsii, Ostrov Russia 79°30N 97°0E 215 B10
Oktyabrskoye = Zhovtneve Ukraine 46°54N 32°3E 189 J7
Okubo Tokyo, Japan 140 a2
Ōkuchi Japan 32°4N 130°37E 222 E2
Okulovka Russia 58°25N 33°19E 188 C7
Ōkura Japan 35°35N 139°27E 140 B1
Okuru N.Z. 43°55S 168°55E 285 D3
Okushiri-Tō Japan 42°15N 139°30E 220 C9
Okuta Nigeria 9°14N 3°12E 263 D5
Okwa → Botswana 22°30S 23°0E 270 B3
Ola Russia 59°35N 151°17E 215 D16
Ola Ark., U.S.A. 35°2N 93°13W 314 D8
Ólafsfjörður Iceland 66°4N 18°39W 155 A8
Ólafsvík Iceland 64°53N 23°43W 155 C3
Olaine Latvia 56°48N 23°59E 184 B10
Olancha U.S.A. 36°17N 118°1W 307 J8
Olancha Pk. U.S.A. 36°16N 118°7W 307 J8
Olanchito Honduras 15°30N 86°30W 320 C2
Öland Sweden 56°45N 16°38E 163 H10
Ölands norra udde Sweden 57°22N 17°5E 163 G11
Ölands södra udde Sweden 56°12N 16°23E 163 H10
Olanta U.S.A. 33°56N 79°56W 316 B10
Olar U.S.A. 33°11N 81°11W 316 B8
Olargues France 43°34N 2°53E 174 E6
Olari Finland 60°10N 24°44E 121 B1
Olaria Brazil 22°50S 43°16W 135 B1
Olary Australia 32°18S 140°19E 282 B4
Olascoaga Argentina 35°15S 60°39W 334 D3
Olathe U.S.A. 38°53N 94°49W 308 F6
Olavarría Argentina 36°55S 60°20W 334 D3
Oława Poland 50°57N 17°20E 185 H4
Olbernhau Germany 50°40N 13°19E 178 E9
Ólbia Italy 40°55N 9°31E 200 B2
Ólbia, G. di Italy 40°55N 9°39E 200 B2
Olching Germany 48°12N 11°21E 179 G7
Olcott U.S.A. 43°20N 78°42W 312 C6
Old Admiralty Russia 59°55N 30°20E 137 B1
Old Bahama Chan. = Bahama, Canal Viejo de W. Indies 22°10N 77°30W 320 B4
Old Baldy Pk. = San Antonio, Mt. U.S.A. 34°17N 117°38W 307 L9
Old Bar Australia 31°58S 152°35E 283 A10
Old Bridge U.S.A. 40°25N 74°22W 313 F10
Old Castile = Castilla y Leon □ Spain 42°0N 5°0W 194 D6
Old City Shanghai, China 31°13N 121°29E 138 B1
Old City Delhi, India 120 a3
Old City Jerusalem 123 b3
Old Crow Canada 67°30N 139°55W 294 D4
Old Dale U.S.A. 34°8N 115°47W 307 L11
Old Forge N.Y., U.S.A. 43°43N 74°58W 313 C10
Old Forge Pa., U.S.A. 41°22N 75°45W 313 E9
Old Fort = Purana Qila Delhi, India 120 c3
Old Fort B. Bahamas 25°3N 77°32W 153 b
Old Fort Pt. Montserrat 16°40N 62°11W 323 p
Old Fort York Canada 43°39N 79°24W 141 B2
Old Harbor Alaska, U.S.A. 57°12N 153°18W 303 H9
Old Harbor Mass., U.S.A. 42°19N 71°1W 116 B2
Old Harbour Jamaica 17°56N 77°7W 320 a
Old Harbour Bay Jamaica 17°54N 77°6W 320 a
Old Ironside Boston, U.S.A. 116 a3
Old Mapoon ✪ Australia 11°5S 142°22E 280 A3
Old Perlican Canada 48°5N 53°1W 299 C9
Old Road Bluff Antigua & B. 16°59N 61°50W 322 b
Old Road Town St. Kitts & Nevis 17°17N 62°47W 322 d
Old Roundhouse Toronto, Canada 141 c2
Old Shinyanga Tanzania 3°33S 33°27E 268 C3
Old Speck Mt. U.S.A. 44°34N 70°57W 313 B14
Old Town = Stare Miasto Warsaw, Poland 142 a2
Old Town Edinburgh, U.K. 121 a2
Old Town Fla., U.S.A. 29°36N 82°59W 317 F7
Old Town Ill., U.S.A. 41°54N 87°37W 119 B3
Old Town Maine, U.S.A. 44°56N 68°39W 309 C19
Old Town Hall = Altes Rathaus Munich, Germany 131 b3
Old Town Square Warsaw, Poland 142 a2
Old Washington U.S.A. 40°2N 81°27W 312 F3
Old Wives L. Canada 50°5N 106°0W 297 C7
Oldbawn Ireland 53°17N 6°21W 120 B1
Oldbury U.K. 51°38N 2°33W 169 F5
Oldcastle Ireland 53°46N 7°10W 166 C4
Oldeani Tanzania 3°22S 35°35E 268 C4
Olden Norway 61°49N 6°49E 164 C3
Oldenburg Niedersachsen, Germany 53°9N 8°13E 178 B4
Oldenburg Schleswig-Holstein, Germany 54°17N 10°52E 178 A6
Oldenzaal Neths. 52°19N 6°53E 170 B6
Oldham U.K. 53°33N 2°7W 168 D5
Oldman → Canada 49°57N 111°42W 296 D6
Oldmeldrum U.K. 57°20N 2°19W 167 D6
Olds Canada 51°50N 114°10W 296 C6
Oldsmar U.S.A. 28°2N 82°39W 317 G7
Olduvai Gorge Tanzania 2°57S 35°23E 268 C4
Oldziyt Mongolia 44°40N 109°1E 226 B5
Ole Rømer Land Greenland 74°10N 24°30W 154 C8
Olean U.S.A. 42°5N 78°26W 312 D6
Olecko Poland 54°2N 22°31E 184 D9
Oléggio Italy 45°36N 8°38E 198 C5
Oleiros Portugal 39°56N 7°56W 194 F3
Oleiros Spain 43°20N 8°19W 194 B2
Olekma → Russia 60°22N 120°42E 215 C13
Olekminsk Russia 60°25N 120°30E 215 C13
Oleksandriya Kirovohrad, Ukraine 48°42N 33°3E 189 H7
Oleksandriya Rivne, Ukraine 50°37N 26°19E 177 C14
Oleksandrovka Ukraine 48°55N 32°20E 189 H7
Olema U.S.A. 38°3N 122°47W 306 G4
Ølen Norway 59°36N 5°48E 164 E2
Olenegorsk Russia 68°9N 33°18E 160 B25
Olenek Russia 68°28N 112°18E 215 C12
Olenek → Russia 73°0N 120°10E 215 B13
Olenino Russia 56°15N 33°30E 188 D7
Olenya = Olenegorsk Russia 68°9N 33°18E 160 B25
Oléron, Î. d' France 45°55N 1°15W 174 C2
Olesk Ukraine 51°6N 24°11E 185 G11
Oleśnica Poland 51°13N 17°22E 185 G4
Olesno Poland 50°51N 18°26E 185 H5
Olevsk Ukraine 51°12N 27°39E 177 C14
Olga, L. Canada 49°47N 77°15W 298 C4
Olgas, The = Kata Tjuta Australia 25°20S 130°50E 279 E5
Olgino Russia 60°0N 30°10E 137 A1
Ölgiy Mongolia 48°56N 89°57E 217 C11
Ølgod Denmark 55°49N 8°36E 163 J2
Olhão Portugal 37°3N 7°48W 195 H3
Olhopil Ukraine 48°12N 29°30E 183 B14
Olhovatka Russia 54°30N 22°18E 184 D9
Olib Croatia 44°23N 14°44E 199 D11
Oliena Italy 40°16N 9°24E 200 B2
Oliete Spain 41°1N 0°41W 196 D4
Olifants = Elefantes → Africa 24°10S 32°40E 271 B5
Olifants → Namibia 25°30S 19°30E 270 B2
Olifantshoek S. Africa 27°57S 22°42E 270 C3
Ólimbos Greece 35°44N 27°11E 205 F9
Ólimbos, Óros = Olymbos Oros Greece 40°6N 22°23E 202 F6
Olímpia Brazil 20°44S 48°54W 335 A6
Olimpico, Estadio Mexico 19°20N 99°11W 128 C1
Olimpos-Beydaglari △ Turkey 36°36N 30°30E 205 E12
Olin U.S.A. 42°0N 91°9W 310 B5
Olinda Brazil 8°1S 34°51W 332 C5
Olite Spain 42°29N 1°40W 196 C3
Oliva Argentina 32°0S 63°38W 334 C3
Oliva Spain 38°58N 0°9W 197 G4
Oliva, Punta del Spain 43°37N 5°28W 194 B5
Oliva de la Frontera Spain 38°17N 6°54W 195 G4
Olivais Portugal 38°45N 9°7W 126 A2
Olivar de los Padres Mexico 19°21N 99°14W 128 B1
Olivar del Conde Mexico 19°22N 99°12W 128 B1
Olivares, Cerro los Argentina 30°18S 69°55W 334 C2
Olivares de Júcar Spain 39°46N 2°20W 196 F2
Olive Branch U.S.A. 34°57N 89°49W 315 D10
Olive Hill U.S.A. 38°18N 83°13W 311 F13
Olive Park Chicago, U.S.A. 119 b3
Olivehurst U.S.A. 39°6N 121°34W 306 F5
Oliveira Brazil 20°39S 44°50W 333 F3
Oliveira de Azeméis Portugal 40°49N 8°29W 194 E2
Oliveira do Douro Portugal 41°5N 8°2W 194 D2
Oliveira dos Brejinhos Brazil 12°19S 42°54W 333 D3
Olivenza Spain 38°41N 7°9W 195 G3
Oliver Canada 49°13N 119°37W 296 D5
Oliver L. Canada 56°56N 103°22W 297 B8
Olives, Mt. of West Bank 31°46N 35°15E 123 B2
Olivet Loiret, France 47°51N 1°55E 173 E8
Olivet Mich., U.S.A. 42°27N 84°56W 311 B12
Olivia, L. U.S.A. 28°31N 81°31W 133 A1
Olivine Ra. N.Z. 44°15S 168°30E 285 E3
Olivos Argentina 34°30S 58°28W 117 B2
Olkhovka Russia 49°48N 44°32E 190 F7
Olkusz Poland 50°18N 19°33E 185 H6
Ollachea Peru 13°49S 70°29W 330 C3
Ollagüe Chile 21°15S 68°10W 334 A2
Ollombo Congo 1°18S 15°53E 264 C3
Olloua Congo 0°54S 14°34E 264 C2
Olmaliq Uzbekistan 40°50N 69°35E 217 D7
Olmedo Spain 41°20N 4°43W 194 D6
Olmeto France 41°43N 8°55E 175 G12
Olmos Peru 5°59S 79°46W 330 B2
Olmütz = Olomouc Czech Rep. 49°38N 17°12E 181 B10
Olney Ill., U.S.A. 38°44N 88°5W 311 F8
Olney Tex., U.S.A. 33°22N 98°45W 314 E5
Olofström Sweden 56°17N 14°32E 163 H8
Oloitokitok Kenya 2°56S 37°30E 268 C4
Ololi Congo 0°15S 14°36E 264 C2
Oloma Cameroon 3°29N 11°19E 263 E7
Olomane → Canada 50°14N 60°37W 299 B7
Olomouc Czech Rep. 49°38N 17°12E 181 B10
Olomoucký □ Czech Rep. 49°45N 17°5E 181 B10
Olona → Italy 45°29N 9°6E 129 B1
Olonets Russia 61°0N 32°54E 188 B7
Olongapo Phil. 14°50N 120°18E 232 D3
Olonne-sur-Mer France 46°32N 1°47W 174 B2
Oloron, Gave d' → France 43°33N 1°5W 174 E2
Oloron-Ste-Marie France 43°11N 0°38W 174 E3
Olosega Amer. Samoa 14°10S 169°37W 302 g
Olosenga = Swains I. Amer. Samoa 11°11S 171°4W 289 J11
Olot Spain 42°11N 2°30E 196 C7
Olovo Bos.-H. 44°8N 18°35E 182 F3
Olovyannaya Russia 50°58N 115°35E 215 D12
Oloy → Russia 66°29N 159°29E 215 C16
Olsberg Germany 51°21N 8°31E 178 D4
Olshammar Sweden 58°45N 14°48E 163 F8
Olshanka Ukraine 48°16N 30°58E 189 H6
Olshany Ukraine 50°3N 35°53E 189 G8
Olsztyn Poland 53°48N 20°29E 184 E7
Olsztynek Poland 53°34N 20°19E 184 E7
Olt □ Romania 44°20N 24°30E 183 F9
Olt → Romania 43°43N 24°51E 183 G9
Oltedal Norway 58°49N 6°2E 164 F3
Olten Switz. 47°21N 7°53E 179 H3
Oltenița Romania 44°7N 26°42E 183 F11
Olton U.S.A. 34°11N 102°8W 314 D3
Oltu Turkey 40°35N 41°58E 213 B9
Oluan Pi Taiwan 21°53N 120°51E 225 E2
Oluanpi Taiwan 21°54N 120°51E 225 E2
Olula del Rio Spain 37°21N 2°18W 197 H2
Olur Turkey 40°49N 42°8E 213 B10
Olustee U.S.A. 30°12N 82°26W 316 E7
Olutanga Phil. 7°26N 122°54E 233 H4
Olutanga I. Phil. 7°22N 122°52E 233 H4
Olvega Spain 41°47N 2°0W 196 D2
Olvera Spain 36°55N 5°18W 195 J5
Olymbos Cyprus 35°21N 33°45E 207 E9
Olymbos Oros Greece 40°6N 22°23E 202 F6
Olympia Greece 37°39N 21°39E 204 D3
Olympia London, U.K. 125 c1
Olympia Wash., U.S.A. 47°3N 122°53W 306 D4
Olympia, L. U.S.A. 28°34N 81°31W 133 A1
Olympic △ U.S.A. 47°45N 123°43W 306 C3
Olympic Dam Australia 30°30S 136°55E 282 A2
Olympic Green China 39°59N 116°23E 114 B2
Olympic Mts. U.S.A. 47°55N 123°45W 306 C3
Olympic Stadium = Turner Field U.S.A. 33°44N 84°23W 113 B2
Olympic Stadium Beijing, China 39°59N 116°23E 114 B2
Olympic Stadium Helsinki, Finland 60°11N 24°55E 121 B2
Olympique, Stade Canada 45°33N 73°33W 130 A2
Olympus Cyprus 34°56N 32°52E 207 F8
Olympus, Mt. = Olymbos Oros Greece 40°6N 22°23E 202 F6
Olympus, Mt. = Uludağ Turkey 40°4N 29°13E 203 F13
Olympus, Mt. U.S.A. 47°48N 123°43W 306 C3
Olyphant U.S.A. 41°27N 75°36W 313 E9
Olyutorskiy, Mys Russia 59°55N 170°27E 215 D18
Om → Russia 54°59N 73°22E 217 B8
Om Hajer Eritrea 14°20N 36°41E 257 E4
Om Koi Thailand 17°48N 98°22E 236 D2
Ōma Japan 41°45N 141°5E 220 D10
Ōmachi Japan 36°30N 137°50E 223 A9
Omae-Zaki Japan 34°36N 138°14E 223 C10
Ōmagari Japan 39°27N 140°29E 220 E10
Omagh U.K. 54°36N 7°19W 166 B4
Omagh □ U.K. 54°35N 7°15W 166 B4
Omaha U.S.A. 41°17N 95°58W 308 E6
Omak U.S.A. 48°25N 119°31W 304 B4
Omalos Greece 35°19N 23°55E 207 E4
Omalur India 11°44N 78°4E 245 J4
Oman ■ Asia 23°0N 58°0E 249 B7
Oman, G. of Asia 24°30N 58°30E 247 E8
Omapere N.Z. 35°37S 173°25E 284 B2
Omar Combon Somali Rep. 3°10N 45°47E 267 D6
Omaruru Namibia 21°26S 16°0E 270 B2
Omaruru → Namibia 22°7S 14°15E 270 B1
Omate Peru 16°45S 71°0W 330 D3
Ombai, Selat Indonesia 8°30S 124°50E 231 F6
Omboué Gabon 1°35S 9°15E 264 C1
Ombrone → Italy 42°42N 11°5E 198 F8
Omchi Chad 21°22N 17°53E 259 D3
Omdurmân Sudan 15°40N 32°28E 257 D3
Ōme Japan 35°47N 139°15E 223 B11
Omega U.S.A. 31°21N 83°36W 316 D6
Omegna Italy 45°53N 8°24E 198 C5
Omemee Canada 44°18N 78°33W 312 B6
Omeo Australia 37°6S 147°36E 283 D7
Omeonga Dem. Rep. of the Congo 3°40S 24°22E 264 C4
Ometepe, I. de Nic. 11°32N 85°35W 320 D2
Ometepec Mexico 16°41N 98°25W 319 D5
Ōmi-Shima Ehime, Japan 34°15N 133°0E 222 C5
Ōmi-Shima Yamaguchi, Japan 34°25N 131°9E 222 C3
Omihachiman Japan 35°7N 136°3E 223 B8
Omin Micronesia 9°36N 138°9E 287 R16
Ominato Japan 41°17N 141°10E 220 D10
Omineca → Canada 56°3N 124°16W 296 B4
Omineca Mts. Canada 56°30N 125°30W 296 B3
Omiš Croatia 43°28N 16°40E 199 E13
Omišalj Croatia 45°13N 14°32E 199 C11
Omitara Namibia 22°16S 18°2E 270 B2
Ōmiya = Saitama Japan 35°54N 139°38E 223 B11
Ommaney, C. U.S.A. 56°10N 134°40W 303 H14
Omme Å → Denmark 55°56N 8°32E 163 J2
Ommen Neths. 52°31N 6°26E 170 B6
Ömnögovĭ □ Mongolia 43°15N 104°0E 226 C3
Omo → Ethiopia 6°25N 36°10E 257 F4
Omo △ Ethiopia 5°54N 35°55E 257 F4
Omo Valley Ethiopia 5°7N 36°7E 257 F4
Omodeo, L. Italy 40°8N 8°56E 200 B1
Omodhos Cyprus 34°51N 32°48E 207 F8
Omoï Congo 2°56S 13°13E 264 C2
Omoko Nigeria 5°19N 6°40E 263 D6
Omolon → Russia 68°42N 158°36E 215 C16
Omona Solomon Is. 7°30S 158°43E 287 L10
Omonia Square Athens, Greece 112 b1
Omono-Gawa → Japan 39°46N 140°3E 220 E10
Ōmori Japan 35°34N 139°43E 140 B3
Ompha Canada 45°0N 76°50W 313 B8
Omsk Russia 55°0N 73°12E 217 B8
Omsukchan Russia 62°32N 155°48E 215 C16
Ōmu Japan 44°34N 142°58E 220 B11
Omul, Vf. Romania 45°27N 25°29E 183 E10
Omulew → Poland 53°5N 21°33E 185 E8
Ōmura Japan 32°56N 129°57E 222 E1
Ōmura-Wan Japan 32°57N 129°52E 222 E1
Omuramba Omatako → Namibia 17°45S 20°25E 270 A2
Omuramba Ovambo → Namibia 18°45S 16°59E 270 A2
Omurtag Bulgaria 43°8N 26°26E 203 C10
Ōmuta Japan 33°5N 130°26E 222 D2
On-na-thi Burma 22°17N 96°41E 241 D6
On-Take Japan 31°35N 130°39E 222 F2
Oña Spain 42°43N 3°25W 194 C7
Ona Fla., U.S.A. 27°29N 81°55W 317 H8
Ona Dikonde Dem. Rep. of the Congo 3°51S 24°11E 264 C4
Onaga U.S.A. 39°29N 96°10W 308 F5
Onalaska U.S.A. 43°53N 91°14W 308 D8
Onancock U.S.A. 37°43N 75°45W 309 G16
Onang Indonesia 3°2S 118°49E 231 E5
Onangue, L. Gabon 0°57S 10°4E 264 C1
Onaping L. Canada 47°3N 81°30W 298 C3
Onarga U.S.A. 40°43N 88°1W 311 D8
Oñati Spain 43°3N 2°25W 196 B2
Onavas Mexico 28°31N 109°35W 318 B3
Onawa U.S.A. 42°2N 96°6W 308 D5
Oncócua Angola 16°30S 13°25E 265 F2
Onda Spain 39°55N 0°17W 196 F4
Ondangwa Namibia 17°57S 16°4E 270 A2
Ondarroa Spain 43°19N 2°25W 196 B2
Ondas → Brazil 12°8S 44°55W 333 D3
Ondava → Slovak Rep. 48°27N 21°48E 181 C14
Ondjiva Angola 16°48S 15°50E 265 F3
Ondo Japan 34°11N 132°32E 222 C4
Ondo Nigeria 7°4N 4°47E 263 D5
Ondo □ Nigeria 6°45N 5°0E 263 D6
Öndörshil Mongolia 45°13N 108°5E 226 B5
Öndverðarnes Iceland 64°52N 24°0W 155 C2
One and a Half Degree Channel Maldives 1°30N 73°20E 272 d
One Arm Point Australia 16°26S 123°3E 278 C3
One Arm Point ✪ Australia 16°31S 122°53E 278 C3
One Tree Australia 34°11S 144°43E 281 E3
Oneata Fiji 18°26S 178°25W 287 B3
Oneco U.S.A. 27°25N 82°31W 317 H7
Onega Russia 64°0N 38°10E 186 B6
Onega → Russia 63°58N 38°2E 186 B6
Onega, G. of = Onezhskaya Guba Russia 64°24N 36°38E 186 B6
Onega, L. = Onezhskoye Ozero Russia 61°44N 35°22E 188 B8
Onehunga N.Z. 36°55S 174°48E 284 C3
Oneida Ill., U.S.A. 41°4N 90°13W 310 C6
Oneida N.Y., U.S.A. 43°6N 75°39W 313 C9
Oneida L. U.S.A. 43°12N 75°54W 313 C9
O'Neill U.S.A. 42°27N 98°39W 308 D4
Onekotan, Ostrov Russia 49°25N 154°45E 215 E16
Onema Dem. Rep. of the Congo 4°35S 24°30E 265 C4
Oneonta U.S.A. 42°27N 75°4W 313 D9
Onerahi N.Z. 35°45S 174°22E 284 B3
Oneroa Cook Is. 21°15S 159°43W 289 h
Onești Romania 46°17N 26°47E 183 D11
Onezhskaya Guba Russia 64°24N 36°38E 186 B6
Onezhskoye Ozero Russia 61°44N 35°22E 188 B8
Ongarue N.Z. 38°42S 175°19E 284 E4
Ongea Levu = Ogea Levu Fiji 19°8S 178°24W 287 B3
Ongers → S. Africa 31°4S 23°13E 270 D3
Ongerup Australia 33°58S 118°28E 279 F2
Ongjin N. Korea 37°56N 125°21E 224 D2
Ongkharak Thailand 14°8N 101°1E 236 E3
Ongniud Qi China 43°0N 118°38E 227 C10
Ongoka Dem. Rep. of the Congo 1°20S 26°0E 268 C2
Ongole India 15°33N 80°2E 245 G5
Ongon = Havirga Mongolia 45°41N 113°5E 226 B7
Ongouendjo Gabon 1°23S 9°5E 264 C1
Ongoujou Comoros Is. 12°18S 44°30E 272 a
Ongtüstik Qazaqstan □ Kazakhstan 43°0N 68°0E 217 D7
Oni Georgia 42°33N 43°26E 191 J6
Onida U.S.A. 44°42N 100°4W 308 C3
Onilahy → Madag. 23°34S 43°45E 272 C1
Onima Neth. Ant. 12°15N 68°19W 322 h
Onisigun Nigeria 6°35N 3°24E 124 A2
Onitsha Nigeria 6°6N 6°42E 263 D6
Onna Japan 26°29N 127°51E 288 a
Ono Fiji 18°55S 178°29E 287 B2
Ono Fukui, Japan 35°59N 136°29E 223 B8
Ono Hyōgo, Japan 34°51N 134°56E 222 C6
Onoda Japan 33°59N 131°11E 222 C3
Onohara Japan 34°5N 133°40E 222 C5
Onoke, L. N.Z. 41°22S 175°8E 284 H4
Onomichi Japan 34°25N 133°12E 222 C5
Onotoa Kiribati 1°52S 175°34E 277 A14
Ons, I. de Spain 42°23N 8°55W 194 C2
Onsala Sweden 57°26N 12°0E 163 G6
Onslow Australia 21°40S 115°12E 278 D2
Onslow B. U.S.A. 34°20N 77°15W 315 D16
Ontake-San Japan 35°53N 137°29E 223 B9
Ontar Vanuatu 14°17S 167°27E 287 D5
Ontario Calif., U.S.A. 34°4N 117°39W 307 L9
Ontario Oreg., U.S.A. 44°2N 116°58W 304 D5
Ontario □ Canada 48°0N 83°0W 298 B2
Ontario, L. N. Amer. 43°20N 78°0W 312 C7
Ontario Science Centre Canada 43°43N 79°20W 141 A2
Ontinyent Spain 38°50N 0°35W 197 G4
Ontonagon U.S.A. 46°52N 89°19W 308 B9
Ontong Java Plateau Pac. Oc. 1°0N 157°0E 277 A10
Ontur Spain 38°38N 1°29W 197 G3
Onverwacht Suriname 5°35N 55°11W 329 B6
Onyx U.S.A. 35°41N 118°14W 307 K8
Oodnadatta Australia 27°33S 135°30E 281 D2
Oodweyne Somali Rep. 9°25N 45°4E 267 C6
'Ō'ōkala U.S.A. 20°1N 155°17W 302 C6
Ōokayama Japan 35°36N 139°40E 140 B3
Ooku = Ōma Japan 41°45N 141°5E 220 D10
Ooldea Australia 30°27S 131°50E 279 F5
Oombulgurri Australia 15°15S 127°45E 278 C4
Oombulgurri ✪ Australia 15°10S 127°50E 278 C4
Oorindi Australia 20°40S 141°1E 280 C3
Oost-Vlaanderen □ Belgium 51°5N 3°50E 170 C3
Oostende Belgium 51°15N 2°54E 170 C2
Oosterhout Neths. 51°39N 4°47E 170 C4
Oosterschelde → Neths. 51°33N 4°0E 170 C4
Oosterwolde Neths. 53°0N 6°17E 170 B6
Oostpunt Neth. Ant. 12°2N 68°44W 322 g
Oostzaan Tuindorp Neths. 52°25N 4°54E 112 A2
Ootacamund = Udagamandalam India 11°30N 76°44E 245 J3
Ootha Australia 33°6S 147°29E 283 B7
Ootsa L. Canada 53°50N 126°2W 296 C3
Ooty = Udagamandalam India 11°30N 76°44E 245 J3
Op Luang △ Thailand 18°12N 98°32E 236 C2
Opa-Locka U.S.A. 25°54N 80°15W 128 A1
Opa-Locka ✈ (OPF) U.S.A. 25°54N 80°16W 128 A1
Opacz Poland 52°10N 20°53E 142 B1
Opaka Bulgaria 43°28N 26°10E 203 C10
Opala Dem. Rep. of the Congo 0°40S 24°20E 264 C4
Opalenica Poland 52°18N 16°24E 185 F3
Opan Bulgaria 42°13N 25°41E 203 D9
Opanake Sri Lanka 6°35N 80°40E 245 L5
Opapa N.Z. 39°47S 176°42E 284 F5
Opasatika Canada 49°30N 82°50W 298 C3
Opasquia △ Canada 53°33N 93°5W 298 B1
Opatija Croatia 45°21N 14°17E 199 C11
Opatów Poland 50°50N 21°27E 185 H8
Opava Czech Rep. 49°57N 17°58E 181 B10
Opelika U.S.A. 32°39N 85°23W 316 C4
Opelousas U.S.A. 30°32N 92°5W 314 F8
Opémisca, L. Canada 49°56N 74°52W 298 C5
Opheim U.S.A. 48°51N 106°24W 304 B10
Ophir U.S.A. 63°10N 156°31W 303 E8
Ophirton S. Africa 26°13S 28°1E 123 B2
Ophthalmia Ra. Australia 23°15S 119°30E 278 D2
Opi Nigeria 6°36N 7°28E 263 D6
Opihikao U.S.A. 19°26N 154°53W 302 D7
Opinaca → Canada 52°15N 78°2W 298 B4
Opinaca, Rés. Canada 52°39N 76°20W 298 B4
Opinnagau → Canada 54°12N 82°25W 298 B3
Opiscotéo, L. Canada 53°10N 68°10W 299 B6
Opobo Nigeria 4°35N 7°34E 263 E6
Opochka Russia 56°42N 28°45E 188 D5
Opoczno Poland 51°22N 20°18E 185 G7
Opol Phil. 8°31N 124°34E 233 G5
Opole Poland 50°42N 17°58E 185 H4
Opole Lubelskie Poland 51°9N 21°58E 185 G8
Opolskie □ Poland 50°30N 18°0E 185 H5
Opon = Lapu-Lapu Phil. 10°20N 123°55E 233 F4
Opononi L. Namibia 18°8S 15°45E 270 A2
Opornyy Kazakhstan 46°11N 54°25E 216 C4
Oporto = Porto Portugal 41°8N 8°40W 194 D2
Opotiki N.Z. 38°1S 177°19E 284 E6
Opp U.S.A. 31°17N 86°16W 316 D3
Oppdal Norway 62°35N 9°41E 164 B6
Oppegård Norway 59°45N 10°49E 133 B3
Oppeln = Opole Poland 50°42N 17°58E 185 H4
Oppem Belgium 50°56N 4°18E 116 A1
Óppido Mamertina Italy 38°16N 15°59E 201 D8
Oppland □ Norway 61°15N 9°40E 164 C6
Opportunity U.S.A. 47°39N 117°15W 304 C5
Oppsal Norway 59°53N 10°50E 133 A4
Oprișor Romania 44°17N 23°5E 182 F8
Oprtalj Croatia 45°23N 13°50E 199 C10
Opua N.Z. 35°19S 174°9E 284 B3
Opunake N.Z. 39°26S 173°52E 284 F2
Opuwo Namibia 18°3S 13°45E 270 A1
Opuzen Croatia 43°1N 17°34E 199 E14
Oquawka U.S.A. 40°56N 90°57W 310 D6
Or → Kazakhstan 51°11N 58°32E 216 B5
Ora Cyprus 34°51N 33°12E 207 F9
Ora Israel 31°45N 35°9E 123 B1
Oracabessa Jamaica 18°24N 76°57W 320 a
Oracle U.S.A. 32°37N 110°46W 305 K8
Oracuzar Peru 4°42S 78°28W 328 D2
Oradea Romania 47°2N 21°58E 182 C6
Oradell U.S.A. 40°57N 74°2W 132 A1
Oradell Res. U.S.A. 40°57N 74°1W 132 A1
Öræfajökull Iceland 64°2N 16°39W 155 C10
Orahovac Kosovo 42°24N 20°40E 202 D4
Orahovica Croatia 45°35N 17°52E 182 E2
Orai India 25°58N 79°30E 243 G8
Oraison France 43°55N 5°55E 175 E9
Oral = Zhayyq → Kazakhstan 47°0N 51°48E 187 E9
Oral Kazakhstan 51°20N 51°20E 190 E10
Oran Algeria 35°45N 0°39W 261 A4
Oran □ Algeria 35°0N 0°45W 261 B4
Orange N.S.W., Australia 33°15S 149°7E 283 B8

Orange Vaucluse, France 44°8N 4°47E 175 D8
Orange Calif., U.S.A. 33°47N 117°51W 307 M9
Orange Mass., U.S.A. 42°35N 72°19W 313 D12
Orange Tex., U.S.A. 30°6N 93°44W 314 F8
Orange Va., U.S.A. 38°15N 78°7W 309 F14
Orange → S. Africa 28°41S 16°28E 270 C2
Orange, C. Brazil 4°20N 51°30W 329 C7
Orange Bowl Stadium U.S.A. 25°46N 80°14W 128 B2
Orange City U.S.A. 28°57N 81°18W 317 G8
Orange Cove U.S.A. 36°38N 119°19W 306 J7
Orange Free State = Free State □ S. Africa 28°30S 27°0E 270 C4
Orange Grove U.S.A. 27°58N 97°56W 314 H6
Orange Hill Barbados 13°12N 59°36W 323 r
Orange Hill Jamaica 18°16N 77°59W 320 a
Orange Hill St. Vincent 13°19N 61°7W 323 n
Orange L. U.S.A. 29°25N 82°13W 317 F7
Orange Park U.S.A. 30°10N 81°42W 316 E8
Orange River Colony = Free State □ S. Africa 28°30S 27°0E 270 C4
Orange Walk Belize 18°6N 88°33W 319 D7
Orangeburg U.S.A. 33°30N 80°52W 316 B9
Orangeville Ont., Canada 43°55N 80°5W 312 C4
Orangeville Ill., U.S.A. 42°28N 89°39W 310 B7
Orangi Pakistan 24°54N 67°0E 123 A2
Orango Guinea-Biss. 11°5N 16°0W 262 C1
Orani Phil. 14°49N 120°32E 232 D3
Oranienburg Germany 52°45N 13°14E 178 C9
Oranje = Orange → S. Africa 28°41S 16°28E 270 C2
Oranjemund Namibia 28°38S 16°29E 270 C2
Oranjerivier S. Africa 29°40S 24°12E 270 C3
Oranjestad Aruba 12°32N 70°2W 322 f
Oranjestad Neth. Ant. 17°28N 62°59W 322 a
Orap Vanuatu 15°58S 167°20E 287 E5
Oras Phil. 12°9N 125°28E 232 E5
Orašje Bos.-H. 45°1N 18°42E 182 E3
Orăştie Romania 45°50N 23°10E 183 E8
Orava → Slovak Rep. 49°9N 19°8E 181 B12
Orava, Vodna nádrž Slovak Rep. 49°25N 19°35E 181 B12
Oravița Romania 45°2N 21°43E 182 E6
Orawia N.Z. 46°1S 167°50E 285 G2
Orb → France 43°15N 3°18E 174 E7
Orba → Italy 44°53N 8°37E 198 D5
Ørbæk Denmark 55°17N 10°39E 163 J4
Orbe Switz. 46°43N 6°32E 179 J2
Orbec France 49°1N 0°23E 172 C7
Orbetello Italy 42°27N 11°13E 199 F8
Órbigo → Spain 42°5N 5°42W 194 C5
Orbisonia U.S.A. 40°15N 77°54W 312 F7
Orbost Australia 37°40S 148°29E 283 D8
Örbyhus Sweden 60°15N 17°43E 162 D11
Orcadas Antarctica 60°44S 44°37W 151 C18
Orcas I. U.S.A. 48°42N 122°56W 306 B4
Orce Spain 37°44N 2°28W 197 H2
Orce → Spain 37°44N 2°28W 197 H2
Orchard City U.S.A. 38°50N 107°58W 304 G10
Orchard Homes U.S.A. 46°55N 114°4W 304 C6
Orchard Road Singapore 138 a1
Orchid I. = Lan Yü Taiwan 22°4N 121°25E 225 D3
Orchies France 50°28N 3°14E 173 B10
Orchila, I. Venezuela 11°48N 66°10W 321 D6
Orchilla, Pta. Canary Is. 27°42N 18°10W 153 e1
Órcia → Italy 42°58N 11°21E 199 F8
Orco → Italy 45°10N 7°52E 198 C4
Orcopampa Peru 15°20S 72°23W 330 D3
Orcutt U.S.A. 34°52N 120°27W 307 L6
Ord U.S.A. 41°36N 98°56W 308 E4
Ord → Australia 15°33S 128°15E 278 C4
Ord, Mt. Australia 17°20S 125°34E 278 C4
Ord Mts. U.S.A. 34°39N 116°45W 307 L10
Ordenes = Ordes Spain 43°5N 8°29W 194 B2
Orderville U.S.A. 37°17N 112°38W 305 H7
Ordes Spain 43°5N 8°29W 194 B2
Ordesa y Monte Perido △ Spain 42°40N 0°10W 196 C4
Ording = St-Peter-Ording Germany 54°20N 8°36E 178 A4
Ordos = Mu Us Shamo China 39°0N 109°0E 226 E5
Ordrup Denmark 55°45N 12°34E 118 A3
Ordu Turkey 40°55N 37°53E 212 B7
Ordu □ Turkey 41°0N 37°50E 212 B7
Ordubad Azerbaijan 38°54N 46°1E 213 C12
Orduña Álava, Spain 42°58N 2°58W 196 C2
Orduña Granada, Spain 37°20N 3°30W 195 H7
Ordway U.S.A. 38°13N 103°46W 304 G12
Ordzhonikidze = Denisovka Kazakhstan 52°27N 61°39E 216 B6
Ordzhonikidze = Vladikavkaz Russia 43°0N 44°35E 191 J7
Ordzhonikidze = Yenakiyeve Ukraine 48°15N 38°15E 189 H10
Ordzhonikidze Ukraine 47°39N 34°3E 189 J8
Ore Dem. Rep. of the Congo 3°17N 29°30E 268 B2
Ore Mts. = Erzgebirge Germany 50°27N 12°55E 178 E8
Orealla Guyana 5°15N 57°23W 329 B6
Orebić Croatia 43°0N 17°11E 199 F14
Örebro Sweden 59°20N 15°18E 162 E9
Örebro län □ Sweden 59°27N 15°0E 162 E8
Orecchiella ⌓ Italy 44°16N 10°22E 198 D7
Orech Czech Rep. 50°1N 14°17E 135 B1
Oregon Ill., U.S.A. 42°1N 89°20W 310 B7
Oregon Ohio, U.S.A. 41°38N 83°25W 311 C13
Oregon Wis., U.S.A. 42°56N 89°23W 310 B7
Oregon □ U.S.A. 44°0N 121°0W 304 E3
Oregon City U.S.A. 45°21N 122°36W 306 E4
Oregon Dunes ⌓ U.S.A. 43°40N 124°10W 304 E1
Öregrund Sweden 60°21N 18°30E 162 D12
Öregrundsgrepen Sweden 60°25N 18°15E 162 D12
Oregun Nigeria 6°35N 3°22E 124 A2
Orekhov = Orikhiv Ukraine 47°30N 35°48E 189 J8
Orekhovo-Zuyevo Russia 55°50N 38°55E 188 E10
Orel Russia 52°57N 36°3E 189 F9
Orel □ Russia 52°30N 36°40E 189 F9
Orel → Ukraine 48°40N 34°39E 189 H8
Orellana □ Ecuador 0°45S 76°25W 328 D2
Orellana, Canal de Spain 39°2N 6°0W 195 F5
Orellana, Embalse de Spain 39°5N 5°10W 195 F5
Orellana la Vieja Spain 39°1N 5°32W 195 F5
Orem U.S.A. 40°19N 111°42W 304 F8
Ören Turkey 37°3N 27°57E 205 D9
Orenburg Russia 51°45N 55°6E 186 D10
Örencik Turkey 39°16N 29°33E 205 B11
Orense = Ourense Spain 42°19N 7°55W 194 C3
Orepuki N.Z. 46°19S 167°46E 285 G2
Orestes Pereyra Mexico 26°30N 105°39W 318 B3
Orestiada Greece 41°30N 26°33E 203 E10
Øresund Europe 55°45N 12°40E 163 J6
Oretana, Cordillera = Toledo, Montes de Spain 39°33N 4°20W 195 F6
Oreti → N.Z. 46°28S 168°14E 285 G3
Orfanos Kolpos Greece 40°33N 24°0E 203 F7
Orford Ness U.K. 52°5N 1°35E 169 E9
Organ Pipe Cactus ⌓ U.S.A. 32°0N 112°52W 305 K7
Organos, Pta. de los Canary Is. 28°12N 17°17W 153 e1
Organyà Spain 42°13N 1°20E 196 C6
Orgaz Spain 39°39N 3°53W 195 F7
Ørgenvika Norway 60°17N 9°42E 164 D6
Orgeyev = Orhei Moldova 47°24N 28°50E 183 C13
Orgūn Afghan. 32°55N 69°12E 240 B3
Orhaneli Turkey 39°54N 28°59E 203 G12
Orhaneli → Turkey 39°50N 28°55E 203 G12
Orhangazi Turkey 40°29N 29°18E 203 F13
Orhei Moldova 47°24N 28°50E 183 C13
Orhon Gol → Mongolia 50°21N 106°0E 218 A5
Ória Italy 40°30N 17°38E 201 B10
Orida Niger 21°20N 12°15E 261 D7
Orient Heights U.S.A. 42°23N 70°59W 116 A3
Oriental, Cordillera Bolivia 17°0S 66°0W 331 D4
Oriental, Cordillera Colombia 6°0N 73°0W 328 B3
Oriental, Grand Erg Algeria 30°0N 6°30E 261 C6
Orientale □ Dem. Rep. of the Congo 2°20N 26°0E 268 B2
Oriente Argentina 38°44S 60°37W 334 D3
Orihuela Spain 38°7N 0°55W 197 G4
Orihuela del Tremedal Spain 40°33N 1°39W 196 E3
Orikhiv Ukraine 47°30N 35°48E 189 J8
Orikum Albania 40°20N 19°26E 202 F3
Orillia Canada 44°40N 79°24W 312 B5
Orinduik Guyana 4°40N 60°3W 329 C5
Orinoco → Venezuela 9°15N 61°30W 329 B5
Orinoco, Delta del Venezuela 9°0N 61°30W 329 B5
Orion Canada 49°27N 110°49W 297 D6
Orion Ala., U.S.A. 31°58N 86°0W 316 D4
Orion Ill., U.S.A. 41°21N 90°23W 310 C6
Oriskany U.S.A. 43°10N 75°20W 313 C9
Orissa □ India 20°0N 84°0E 244 E7
Orissaare Estonia 58°34N 23°5E 188 C2
Oristano Italy 39°54N 8°36E 200 C1
Oristano, G. di Italy 39°50N 8°29E 200 C1
Orituco → Venezuela 8°45N 67°27W 328 B4
Oriximina Brazil 1°45S 55°52W 329 D6
Orizaba Mexico 18°51N 97°6W 319 D5
Orizaba, Pico de Mexico 18°58N 97°15W 319 D5
Orizare Bulgaria 42°44N 27°39E 203 D11
Orizona Brazil 17°3S 48°18W 333 E2
Orje Norway 59°29N 11°39E 164 E8
Orjen Bos.-H. 42°35N 18°34E 202 D2
Orjiva Spain 36°53N 3°24W 195 J7
Orkanger Norway 63°18N 9°52E 164 A6
Örkelljunga Sweden 56°17N 13°17E 163 H7
Örken Sweden 57°6N 15°1E 163 G9
Örkény Hungary 47°9N 19°26E 182 C4
Orkhaniye = Botevgrad Bulgaria 42°55N 23°47E 202 D7
Orkla → Norway 63°18N 9°51E 164 A6
Orkney S. Africa 26°58S 26°40E 270 C4
Orkney □ U.K. 59°2N 3°13W 167 B5
Orkney Is. U.K. 59°0N 3°0W 167 B6
Orland Calif., U.S.A. 39°45N 122°12W 306 F4
Orland Ind., U.S.A. 41°47N 85°12W 311 C11
Orland Park U.S.A. 41°38N 87°52W 311 C8
Orlando U.S.A. 28°32N 81°22W 133 A2
Orlando, C. d' Italy 38°10N 14°43E 201 D7
Orlando Dam S. Africa 26°15S 27°55E 123 B1
Orlando East S. Africa 26°14S 27°55E 123 B1
Orlando Executive ✕ (ORL) U.S.A. 28°32N 81°20W 133 A2
Orlando Int. ✕ (MCO) U.S.A. 28°26N 81°19W 133 B3
Orléanais France 48°0N 2°0E 173 E9
Orléans Loiret, France 47°54N 1°52E 173 E8
Orleans Ind., U.S.A. 38°40N 86°27W 311 F10
Orleans Vt., U.S.A. 44°49N 72°12W 313 B12
Orléans, Î. d' Canada 46°54N 70°58W 299 C5
Orléansville = Ech Chéliff Algeria 36°10N 1°20E 261 A5
Orlice → Czech Rep. 50°13N 15°50E 180 A8
Orlivka Ukraine 45°19N 28°27E 183 E13
Orlov = Khalturin Russia 58°40N 48°50E 186 C8
Orlov Slovak Rep. 49°17N 20°51E 181 B13
Orlov Gay Russia 50°56N 48°19E 190 E9
Orlová Czech Rep. 49°51N 18°26E 181 B11
Orlovat Serbia 45°14N 20°33E 182 E5
Orlovista U.S.A. 28°32N 81°27W 133 A2
Orlovo Russia 55°38N 37°22E 129 C2
Orly France 48°45N 2°23E 134 B3
Orly, Paris ✕ (ORY) France 48°44N 2°23E 134 B3
Ormara Pakistan 25°16N 64°33E 240 D2
Ormea Italy 44°9N 7°54E 198 D4
Ormesson-sur-Marne France 48°47N 2°32E 134 B4
Ormilia Greece 40°16N 23°39E 202 F7
Ormoc Phil. 11°0N 124°37E 233 F5
Ormond Vic., Australia 37°54S 145°1E 128 B2
Ormond N.Z. 38°33S 177°56E 284 E6
Ormond Beach U.S.A. 29°17N 81°3W 317 F8
Ormond-by-the-Sea U.S.A. 29°21N 81°4W 317 F8
Ormondville N.Z. 40°5S 176°19E 284 G5
Ormøya Norway 59°52N 10°45E 133 A3
Ormož Slovenia 46°25N 16°10E 199 B13
Ormskirk U.K. 53°35N 2°54W 168 D5
Ormstown Canada 45°8N 74°0W 313 A11
Ormtjernkampen △ Norway 61°12N 9°48E 164 C6
Ornans France 47°7N 6°10E 173 E13
Orne □ France 48°40N 0°5E 172 D7
Orne → France 49°18N 0°15W 172 C6
Orneta Poland 54°8N 20°9E 184 D7
Ornö Sweden 59°4N 18°24E 162 E12
Örnsköldsvik Sweden 63°17N 18°40E 162 A12
Oro N. Korea 40°1N 127°27E 224 D3
Oro → Mexico 25°35N 105°2W 318 B3
Oro Grande U.S.A. 34°36N 117°20W 307 L9
Oro Valley U.S.A. 32°26N 110°58W 305 K8
Orobie, Alpi Italy 46°7N 10°0E 198 B6
Orobie Bergamasche ⌓ Italy 46°0N 9°45E 198 C6
Orobie Valtellinesi ⌓ Italy 46°5N 9°45E 198 B6
Orocué Colombia 4°48N 71°20W 328 C3
Orodara Burkina Faso 11°0N 4°55W 262 C4
Orodo Nigeria 5°34N 7°4E 263 D6
Orofino U.S.A. 46°29N 116°15W 304 C5
Orohena, Mt. Tahiti 17°37S 149°28W 289 e
Orol Dengizi = Aral Sea Asia 44°30N 60°0E 216 C5
Oromiya □ Ethiopia 7°0N 40°0E 257 F5
Oromocto Canada 45°54N 66°29W 299 C6
Oron Nigeria 4°48N 8°14E 263 E6
Orona Kiribati 4°31S 172°11W 277 A16
Orongo Chile 27°11S 109°27W 330 b
Orono Canada 43°59N 78°37W 312 C6
Orono Maine, U.S.A. 44°53N 68°40W 309 C19
Oronsay U.K. 56°1N 6°15W 167 E2
Oropesa Spain 39°57N 5°10W 194 F5
Oropuche → Trin. & Tob. 10°36N 61°6W 323 t
Oropuche Lagoon Trin. & Tob. 10°14N 61°31W 323 t
Oroqen Zizhiqi China 50°34N 123°43E 219 A7
Oroquieta Phil. 8°32N 123°44E 233 G4
Orós Brazil 6°15S 38°55W 332 C4
Orosei Italy 40°23N 9°42E 200 B2
Orosei, G. di Italy 40°15N 9°44E 200 B2
Orosháza Hungary 46°32N 20°42E 182 D5
Oroszlány Hungary 47°29N 18°19E 182 C3
Orote Pen. Guam 13°26N 144°38E 302 d
Orotukan Russia 62°16N 151°42E 215 C16
Oroville Calif., U.S.A. 39°31N 121°33W 306 F5
Oroville Wash., U.S.A. 48°56N 119°26W 304 B4
Oroville, L. U.S.A. 39°33N 121°29W 306 F5
Orpington U.K. 51°22N 0°6E 125 B4
Orrefors Sweden 56°50N 15°45E 163 H9
Orrick U.S.A. 39°13N 94°7W 310 E2
Orroroo Australia 32°43S 138°38E 282 B3
Orrville U.S.A. 40°50N 81°46W 312 F3
Orrviken Sweden 63°6N 14°26E 162 A8
Orsa Sweden 61°7N 14°37E 162 C8
Orsara di Púglia Italy 41°17N 15°16E 201 A8
Orsasjön Sweden 61°7N 14°37E 162 C8
Orsay, Musée d' Paris, France 134 b3
Orsha Belarus 54°30N 30°25E 188 E6
Örsjö Sweden 56°42N 15°45E 163 H9
Orsk Russia 51°12N 58°34E 216 B5
Orşova Romania 44°41N 22°25E 182 F7
Ørsta Norway 62°13N 6°8E 164 B3
Ørsted Denmark 56°30N 10°20E 163 H4
Örsundsbro Sweden 59°44N 17°18E 162 E11
Országos Levétár Budapest, Hungary 117 b1
Orta Turkey 40°38N 33°6E 212 B5
Orta, L. d' Italy 45°49N 8°24E 198 C5
Orta Nova Italy 41°19N 15°42E 201 A8
Ortaca Turkey 36°49N 28°45E 205 E10
Ortakent Turkey 37°5N 27°21E 205 D9
Ortaklar Turkey 37°53N 27°30E 205 D9
Ortaköy Çorum, Turkey 40°16N 35°15E 212 B6
Ortaköy İstanbul, Turkey 41°3N 29°1E 122 B2
Ortaköy Niğde, Turkey 38°44N 34°3E 212 C6
Orte Italy 42°27N 12°23E 199 F9
Ortegal, C. Spain 43°43N 7°52W 194 B3
Orteguaza → Colombia 0°43N 75°16W 328 C2
Ortelsburg = Szczytno Poland 53°33N 21°0E 184 E7
Orthez France 43°29N 0°48W 174 E3
Ortica Italy 45°28N 9°16E 129 B2
Ortigueira Spain 43°40N 7°50W 194 B3
Orting U.S.A. 47°6N 122°12W 306 C4
Ortisei Italy 46°34N 11°40E 199 B8
Ortles Italy 46°31N 10°33E 198 B7
Ortnevik Norway 61°6N 6°7E 164 C3
Ortoire → Trin. & Tob. 10°20N 61°0W 323 t
Ortón → Bolivia 10°50S 67°0W 330 C4
Ortona Italy 42°21N 14°24E 199 F11
Ortonville U.S.A. 45°19N 96°27W 308 C5
Oruba Nigeria 6°34N 3°24E 124 A2
Orukuizu Palau 7°10N 134°15E 288 c
Orūmīyeh Iran 37°40N 45°0E 213 D11
Orūmīyeh, Daryācheh-ye Iran 37°50N 45°30E 213 D11
Orune Italy 40°24N 9°22E 200 B2
Oruro Bolivia 18°0S 67°9W 330 D4
Oruro □ Bolivia 18°40S 67°30W 330 D4
Orust Sweden 58°10N 11°40E 163 F5
Oruzgān □ Afghan. 33°0N 66°0E 240 B2
Orvault France 47°17N 1°38W 172 E5
Orvieto Italy 42°43N 12°7E 199 F9
Orwell N.Y., U.S.A. 43°35N 75°50W 313 C9
Orwell Ohio, U.S.A. 41°32N 80°52W 312 E4
Orwell → U.K. 51°59N 1°18E 169 F9
Orwigsburg U.S.A. 40°38N 76°6W 313 F8
Oryakhovo Bulgaria 43°40N 23°57E 202 C7
Orynyn Ukraine 48°46N 26°24E 183 B11
Oryol = Orel Russia 52°57N 36°3E 189 F9
Orzinuovi Italy 45°24N 9°55E 198 C6
Orzyc → Poland 52°46N 21°14E 185 F8
Orzysz Poland 53°50N 21°58E 184 E8
Os Norway 62°30N 11°14E 164 B8
Osa Russia 57°17N 55°26E 186 C10
Osa → Poland 53°33N 18°46E 184 E5
Osa, Pen. de Costa Rica 8°0N 84°0W 320 E3
Osage Iowa, U.S.A. 43°17N 92°49W 308 D7
Osage → U.S.A. 38°36N 91°57W 310 F5
Osage City U.S.A. 38°38N 95°50W 308 F6
Ōsaka Japan 34°42N 135°30E 133 B2
Ōsaka □ Japan 34°30N 135°30E 223 C7
Osaka Castle Japan 34°41N 135°32E 133 A2
Ōsaka Harbour Japan 34°38N 135°25E 133 B1
Ōsaka Itami Int. ✕ (ITM) Japan 34°46N 135°26E 133 A1
Ōsaka Kansai Int. ✕ (KIX) Japan 34°27N 135°12E 133 B2
Ōsaka-Wan Japan 34°30N 135°18E 223 C7
Osakarovka Kazakhstan 50°33N 72°34E 217 B8
Ōsaki Kagoshima, Japan 31°25N 131°2E 222 F3
Ōsaki Tōkyō, Japan 35°36N 139°42E 140 B3
Osan S. Korea 37°11N 127°4E 224 D3
Osasco Brazil 23°31S 46°46W 137 B1
Osawatomie U.S.A. 38°31N 94°57W 308 F6
Osborn Plateau Ind. Oc. 14°45S 87°0E 273 F7
Osborne U.S.A. 39°26N 98°42W 308 F4
Osby Sweden 56°23N 13°59E 163 H7
Osceola Ark., U.S.A. 35°42N 89°58W 315 D10
Osceola Iowa, U.S.A. 41°2N 93°46W 310 C3
Osceola Mo., U.S.A. 38°3N 93°42W 310 F3
Oschatz Germany 51°17N 13°6E 178 D9
Oschersleben Germany 52°2N 11°13E 178 C7
Óschiri Italy 40°43N 9°6E 200 B2
Oscoda U.S.A. 44°26N 83°20W 312 B1
Osdorf Germany 52°24N 13°20E 115 B3
Osdorp Neths. 52°22N 4°47E 112 A1
Osečina Serbia 44°23N 19°34E 202 B3
Ösel = Saaremaa Estonia 58°30N 22°30E 188 C2
Osenjøen Norway 61°13N 11°50E 164 C8
Osery Russia 54°52N 38°28E 188 E10
Osgood U.S.A. 39°8N 85°18W 311 E11
Osgoode Canada 45°8N 75°36W 313 A9
Osgoode Hall Toronto, Canada 141 b2
Osh Kyrgyzstan 40°37N 72°49E 217 D8
Osh □ Kyrgyzstan 40°0N 73°0E 217 E8
Oshawa Canada 43°50N 78°50W 312 C6
Oshigambo Namibia 17°45S 16°5E 270 A2
Oshivelo Namibia 18°37S 17°10E 270 A2
Oshkosh Nebr., U.S.A. 41°24N 102°21W 308 E2
Oshkosh Wis., U.S.A. 44°1N 88°33W 308 C9
Oshmyany = Ashmyany Belarus 54°26N 25°52E 177 A13
Oshnovīyeh Iran 37°2N 45°6E 213 D11
Oshodi Nigeria 6°33N 3°21E 124 A2
Oshogbo Nigeria 7°48N 4°37E 263 D5
Oshtorīnān Iran 34°1N 48°38E 213 E13
Oshwe Dem. Rep. of the Congo 3°25S 19°28E 264 C3
Osi Nigeria 8°8N 5°14E 263 D6
Osieczna Poland 51°55N 16°40E 185 G3
Osijek Croatia 45°34N 18°41E 182 E3
Ósilo Italy 40°45N 8°40E 200 B1
Ósimo Italy 43°28N 13°29E 199 E10
Osintorf Belarus 54°40N 30°39E 188 E6
Osipenko = Berdyansk Ukraine 46°45N 36°50E 189 J9
Osipovichi = Asipovichy Belarus 53°19N 28°33E 177 B15
Osiyan India 26°43N 72°55E 242 F5
Osizweni S. Africa 27°49S 30°7E 271 C5
Oskaloosa U.S.A. 41°18N 92°39W 310 C4
Oskarshamn Sweden 57°15N 16°27E 163 G10
Oskarström Sweden 56°48N 12°58E 163 H6
Oskélanéo Canada 48°5N 75°15W 298 C4
Öskemen Kazakhstan 50°0N 82°36E 217 C10
Oskol → Ukraine 49°6N 37°25E 189 H9
Osku Iran 37°54N 46°8E 213 D12
Oslo Norway 59°54N 10°43E 133 A3
Oslo □ Norway 59°54N 10°43E 164 D7
Oslo ✕ (OSL) Norway 60°11N 11°6E 133 A4
Oslob Phil. 9°31N 123°26E 233 G4
Oslofjorden Norway 59°20N 10°35E 164 E7
Osmanabad India 18°5N 76°10E 244 E3
Osmancık Turkey 40°58N 34°47E 212 B6
Osmaniye Turkey 37°5N 36°10E 212 D7
Osmanlı Turkey 41°35N 26°51E 203 E10
Osmannagar India 18°32N 79°20E 244 E4
Ösmo Sweden 58°58N 17°55E 162 F11
Osnabrück Germany 52°17N 8°3E 178 C4
Ośno Lubuskie Poland 52°28N 14°51E 185 F1
Osoblaha Czech Rep. 50°17N 17°44E 181 A10
Osogovska Planina Macedonia 42°10N 22°30E 202 D6
Osone Japan 35°31N 139°37E 140 B2
Osor Italy 44°42N 14°24E 199 D11
Osório Brazil 29°53S 50°17W 335 B5
Osório da Fonseca Brazil 3°52S 58°14W 329 D6
Osorno Chile 40°25S 73°0W 336 B2
Osorno Spain 42°24N 4°22W 194 C6
Osorno □ Chile 40°34S 73°9W 336 B2
Osorno, Vol. Chile 41°0S 72°30W 336 B2
Osorun Nigeria 6°33N 3°29E 124 B3
Osoyoos Canada 49°0N 119°30W 296 D5
Osøyro Norway 60°9N 5°30E 164 D2
Óspakseyri Iceland 65°27N 21°26W 155 B5
Ospiate Italy 45°32N 9°6E 129 A1
Ospika → Canada 56°20N 124°0W 296 B4
Osprey U.S.A. 27°12N 82°29W 317 H7
Osprey Reef Australia 13°52S 146°36E 280 A4
Oss Neths. 51°46N 5°32E 170 C5
Ossa, Mt. Australia 41°52S 146°3E 281 G4
Ossa, Oros Greece 39°47N 22°42E 204 B4
Ossa de Montiel Spain 38°58N 2°45W 197 G2
Ossabaw I. U.S.A. 31°50N 81°5W 316 D8
Ossabaw Sd. U.S.A. 31°50N 81°6W 316 D8
Osse → Lot-et-Garonne, France 44°7N 0°17E 174 D4
Osse → Nigeria 6°10N 5°20E 263 D6
Ossersee = Zarasai Lithuania 55°40N 26°20E 188 E4
Ossi Italy 40°40N 8°35E 200 B1
Ossining U.S.A. 41°10N 73°55W 313 E11
Ossipee U.S.A. 43°41N 71°7W 313 C13
Ossokmanuan L. Canada 53°25N 65°0W 299 B7
Ossora Russia 59°20N 163°13E 215 D17
Ostankino Russia 55°49N 37°37E 129 B3
Ostashkov Russia 57°4N 33°2E 188 D7
Östavall Sweden 62°26N 15°29E 162 B9
Østby Norway 61°15N 12°33E 164 C9
Oste → Germany 53°49N 9°2E 178 B5
Ostenburg = Pułtusk Poland 52°43N 21°6E 185 F8
Ostend = Oostende Belgium 51°15N 2°54E 170 C2
Ostend N.Z. 36°48S 175°2E 284 C4
Oster Ukraine 50°57N 30°53E 177 C16
Österbotten = Pohjanmaa Finland 62°58N 22°50E 160 E20
Østerbro Copenhagen, Denmark 118 a1
Osterburg Sachsen-Anhalt, Germany 52°47N 11°45E 178 C7
Osterburg Pa., U.S.A. 40°16N 78°31W 312 F6
Österburken Germany 49°25N 9°26E 179 F5
Österbybruk Sweden 60°13N 17°55E 162 D11
Österbymo Sweden 57°49N 15°15E 163 G9
Österdalälven Sweden 61°30N 13°45E 162 C7
Østerdalen Norway 61°40N 10°50E 162 C4
Österfärnebo Sweden 60°19N 16°48E 162 D10
Österforse Sweden 63°9N 17°3E 162 A11
Östergötlands län □ Sweden 58°35N 15°45E 163 F9
Osterholz-Scharmbeck Germany 53°13N 8°47E 178 B4
Østerild Denmark 57°2N 8°51E 163 G2
Osterley U.K. 51°28N 0°21W 125 B1
Osterley Park U.K. 51°29N 0°21W 125 B1
Östermalm Stockholm, Sweden 139 a3
Östermyra = Seinäjoki Finland 62°40N 22°51E 160 E20
Osterode Germany 51°43N 10°15E 178 D6
Osterode in Ostpreussen = Ostróda Poland 53°42N 19°58E 184 E6
Österreich = Austria ■ Europe 47°0N 14°0E 180 E7
Österreich ober der Ems = Oberösterreich □ Austria 48°10N 14°0E 180 C7
Österskär Sweden 59°26N 18°16E 139 A3
Östersund Sweden 63°10N 14°38E 162 A8
Östervåla Sweden 60°11N 17°11E 162 D11
Østfold □ Norway 59°25N 11°25E 164 E8
Ostfriesische Inseln Germany 53°42N 7°0E 178 B3
Ostfriesland Germany 53°20N 7°30E 178 B3
Østgrønland = Tunu □ Greenland 75°0N 30°0W 154 C7
Östhammar Sweden 60°16N 18°22E 162 D12
Óstia, Lido di Italy 41°43N 12°17E 199 G9
Óstia Malpasso Italy 41°47N 12°26E 136 C1
Ostiense Italy 41°51N 12°29E 136 B1
Ostíglia Italy 45°4N 11°8E 199 C8
Östmark Sweden 60°17N 12°45E 162 D6
Østmarkkapellet Norway 59°52N 10°51E 133 A4
Ostøya Norway 59°52N 10°34E 133 A2
Östra Husby Sweden 58°35N 16°33E 163 F10
Ostrava Czech Rep. 49°51N 18°18E 181 B11
Ostravský □ Czech Rep. 49°55N 17°58E 181 B10
Østre Aker Norway 59°54N 10°49E 133 A3
Ostróda Poland 53°42N 19°58E 184 E6
Ostrogozhsk Russia 50°55N 39°7E 189 G10
Ostroh Ukraine 50°20N 26°30E 177 C14
Ostrołęka Poland 53°4N 21°32E 185 E8
Ostrov Bulgaria 43°40N 24°9E 203 C8
Ostrov Czech Rep. 50°18N 12°57E 180 A5
Ostrov Romania 44°6N 27°24E 183 F12
Ostrov Russia 57°25N 28°20E 188 D5
Ostrów Lubelski Poland 51°29N 22°51E 185 G9
Ostrów Mazowiecka Poland 52°50N 21°51E 185 F8
Ostrów Wielkopolski Poland 51°36N 17°44E 185 G4
Ostrowiec-Świętokrzyski Poland 50°55N 21°22E 185 H8
Ostrowo = Ostrów Wielkopolski Poland 51°36N 17°44E 185 G4
Ostrožac Bos.-H. 43°43N 17°49E 182 G2
Ostrzeszów Poland 51°25N 17°52E 185 G4
Ostseebad Kühlungsborn Germany 54°8N 11°44E 178 A7
Osttirol □ Austria 46°50N 12°30E 180 E5
Ostuni Italy 40°44N 17°35E 201 B10
Ostyako-Vogulsk = Khanty-Mansiysk Russia 61°0N 69°0E 214 C7
Osum → Albania 40°40N 20°10E 202 F4
Osŭm → Bulgaria 43°40N 24°50E 203 C8
Ōsumi-Hantō Japan 31°20N 130°55E 222 F2
Ōsumi-Kaikyō Japan 30°55N 131°0E 221 J5
Ōsumi-Shotō Japan 30°30N 130°0E 221 J5
Osun □ Nigeria 7°30N 4°30E 263 D5
Osuna Spain 37°14N 5°8W 195 H5
Oswegatchie → U.S.A. 44°42N 75°30W 313 B9
Oswego U.S.A. 43°27N 76°31W 313 C8
Oswego → U.S.A. 43°27N 76°30W 313 C8
Oswestry U.K. 52°52N 3°3W 168 E4
Oświęcim Poland 50°2N 19°11E 185 H6
Ōta Fukui, Japan 35°57N 136°3E 223 B8
Ōta Gumma, Japan 36°18N 139°22E 223 A11
Ōta Tōkyō, Japan 35°34N 139°41E 140 B3
Ōta-Gawa → Japan 34°21N 132°18E 222 C4
Otaci Moldova 48°27N 27°47E 183 B12
Otago □ N.Z. 45°15S 170°0E 285 E4
Otago Harbour N.Z. 45°47S 170°42E 285 F5
Otago Pen. N.Z. 45°48S 170°39E 285 F5
Otaheite B. Trin. & Tob. 10°15N 61°30W 323 t
Otahuhu N.Z. 36°56S 174°51E 284 C3
Ōtake Japan 34°12N 132°13E 222 C4
Otaki Japan 35°17N 140°15E 223 B12
Otaki N.Z. 40°45S 175°10E 284 G4
Otane N.Z. 39°54S 176°39E 284 F5
Otaniemi Finland 60°11N 24°49E 121 B1
Otari Open Air Museum N.Z. 41°16S 174°46E 143 B1
Otaru Japan 43°10N 141°0E 220 C10
Otaru-Wan = Ishikari-Wan Japan 43°25N 141°1E 220 C10
Otautau N.Z. 46°9S 168°1E 285 G3
Otava → Czech Rep. 49°26N 14°12E 180 B7
Otavalo Ecuador 0°13N 78°20W 328 C2
Otavi Namibia 19°40S 17°24E 270 A2
Otchinjau Angola 16°30S 13°56E 265 F2
Otego U.S.A. 42°23N 75°10W 313 D9
Oteiza = Marihatag Phil. 8°48N 126°18E 233 G6
Otelec Romania 45°36N 20°50E 182 E5
Otelnuk, L. Canada 56°9N 68°12W 299 A6
Oteļu Roşu Romania 45°32N 22°22E 182 E7
Otero de Rey = Outeiro de Rei Spain 43°6N 7°36W 194 B3
Othello U.S.A. 46°50N 119°10W 304 C4
Othoni Greece 39°52N 19°22E 206 B9
Othris, Oros Greece 39°2N 22°37E 204 B4
Oti → Africa 7°48N 0°8E 263 D5
Oti ⌓ Togo 10°40N 0°35E 263 C5
Otira N.Z. 42°49S 171°35E 285 C6
Otira Gorge N.Z. 42°53S 171°33E 285 C6
Otish, Mts. Canada 52°22N 70°30W 299 B5
Otjiwarongo Namibia 20°30S 16°33E 270 B2
Otmuchów Poland 50°28N 17°10E 185 H4
Oto Tolu Group Tonga 20°21S 174°32W 287 D13
Otočac Croatia 44°53N 15°12E 199 D12
Otoineppu Japan 44°44N 142°16E 220 B11
Otok Croatia 43°42N 16°44E 199 E13
Otomavi = Korsakov Russia 46°36N 142°42E 215 E15
Oton Phil. 10°42N 122°29E 233 F4
Otopeni, Bucureşti ✕ (OTP) Romania 44°30N 26°11E 183 F11
Otorohanga N.Z. 38°12S 175°14E 284 E4
Otoskwin → Canada 52°13N 88°6W 298 B2
Ōtoyo Japan 33°43N 133°45E 222 D5
Otpor = Zabaykalsk Russia 49°40N 117°25E 215 E12
Otra → Norway 58°9N 8°1E 164 F5
Otradnyy Russia 53°22N 51°21E 190 D10
Otranto Italy 40°9N 18°28E 201 B11
Otranto, C. d' Italy 40°7N 18°30E 201 B11
Otranto, Str. of Italy 40°15N 18°40E 201 B11
Otrobanda Neth. Ant. 12°7N 68°57W 322 g
Otrokovice Czech Rep. 49°12N 17°32E 181 B10
Otse S. Africa 25°2S 25°45E 270 C4
Otsego U.S.A. 42°27N 85°42W 311 B11
Otsego L. U.S.A. 42°45N 74°53W 313 D10
Ōtsu Japan 35°0N 135°50E 223 C7
Otsuka Japan 35°43N 139°44E 140 A3
Ōtsuki Japan 35°36N 138°57E 223 B10
Otta Norway 61°46N 9°32E 164 C6
Otta → Norway 61°46N 9°31E 164 C6
Ottakring Austria 48°12N 16°18E 142 A1
Ottapalam India 10°46N 76°23E 245 J3
Ottávia Italy 41°57N 12°24E 136 B1
Ottawa = Outaouais → Canada 45°27N 74°8W 298 C5
Ottawa Ont., Canada 45°26N 75°42W 313 A9
Ottawa Ill., U.S.A. 41°21N 88°51W 311 C8
Ottawa Kans., U.S.A. 38°37N 95°16W 308 F6
Ottawa Ohio, U.S.A. 41°1N 84°3W 311 C12
Ottawa Is. Canada 59°35N 80°10W 295 F15
Ottélé Cameroon 3°38N 11°19E 263 E7
Ottensheim Austria 48°21N 14°12E 180 C7
Otter Cr. → U.S.A. 44°13N 73°17W 313 B11
Otter Creek U.S.A. 29°19N 82°46W 317 F7
Otter Lake Canada 45°17N 79°56W 312 A5
Otterbein U.S.A. 40°29N 87°6W 311 D9
Otterndorf Germany 53°48N 8°53E 178 B4
Otterøya Norway 62°45N 6°50E 164 B3
Otterup Denmark 55°30N 10°22E 163 J4
Otterville Ont., Canada 42°55N 80°36W 312 D4
Otterville Mo., U.S.A. 38°42N 93°0W 310 F4
Ottery S. Africa 34°1S 18°32E 118 B2
Ottery St. Mary U.K. 50°44N 3°17W 169 G4
Ottilien Reef Papua N. G. 4°33S 148°49E 286 C5
Ottmachau = Otmuchów Poland 50°28N 17°10E 185 H4
Otto Beit Bridge Zimbabwe 15°59S 28°56E 269 F2
Ottobrunn Germany 48°3N 11°40E 131 B3
Ottosdal S. Africa 26°46S 25°59E 270 C4
Ottoville U.S.A. 40°57N 84°22W 311 D12
Ottumwa U.S.A. 41°1N 92°25W 310 D4
Otu Nigeria 8°14N 3°22E 263 D5
Otukpa Nigeria 7°9N 7°41E 263 D6
Otuquis △ Bolivia 19°45S 58°44W 331 D6
Oturkpo Nigeria 7°16N 8°8E 263 D6
Otvazhnoye = Zhigulevsk Russia 53°28N 49°30E 190 D9
Otvazhny = Zhigulevsk Russia 53°28N 49°30E 190 D9
Otway, B. Chile 53°30S 74°0W 336 D2
Otway, C. Australia 38°52S 143°30E 282 E5
Otway, Seno de Chile 53°0S 71°30W 336 D2
Otway △ Australia 38°47S 143°34E 282 E5
Otwock Poland 52°5N 21°20E 185 F8
Otyniya Ukraine 48°44N 24°51E 183 B9
Ötztaler Ache → Austria 47°14N 10°50E 180 D3
Ötztaler Alpen Austria 46°56N 11°0E 180 E3
Ou → Laos 20°4N 102°13E 236 B4
Ou Neua Laos 22°18N 101°48E 228 F3
Ou-Sammyaku Japan 39°20N 140°35E 220 E10
Ouachita → U.S.A. 31°38N 91°49W 314 F9
Ouachita, L. U.S.A. 34°34N 93°12W 314 D8
Ouachita Mts. U.S.A. 34°30N 94°30W 314 D7
Ouadâne Mauritania 20°50N 11°40W 260 D2
Ouadda C.A.R. 8°15N 22°20E 264 A4
Ouaddaï □ Chad 13°0N 21°0E 259 F4
Ouagadougou Burkina Faso 12°25N 1°30W 263 C4
Ouahigouya Burkina Faso 13°31N 2°25W 262 C4
Ouahran = Oran Algeria 35°45N 0°39W 261 A4
Oualâta Mauritania 17°20N 6°55W 262 B3
Ouallah Comoros Is. 12°19S 43°39E 272 a
Ouallam Niger 14°23N 2°10E 263 C5
Ouallene Algeria 24°41N 1°11E 261 D5
Ouanary Fr. Guiana 4°13N 51°40W 329 C7
Ouanda Djallé C.A.R. 8°55N 22°53E 264 A4
Ouandago C.A.R. 7°13N 18°50E 264 A3
Ouandja C.A.R. 8°28N 23°17E 264 A4
Ouandjia, Bahr → C.A.R. 9°35N 21°43E 264 A4
Ouandjia-Vakaga ⌓ C.A.R. 9°2N 22°18E 264 A4
Ouangani Mayotte 12°50S 45°8E 272 b
Ouango C.A.R. 4°19N 22°30E 264 B4
Ouani Comoros Is. 12°9S 44°18E 272 a
Ouantonou C.A.R. 7°19N 15°18E 264 A3
Ouarâne Mauritania 21°0N 10°30W 260 D2
Ouargaye Burkina Faso 11°40N 0°5E 263 C5
Ouargla Algeria 31°59N 5°16E 261 B6
Ouargla □ Algeria 30°30N 6°10E 261 B6
Ouarkoye Burkina Faso 12°5N 3°40W 262 C4
Ouarkziz, Jebel Algeria 28°50N 8°0W 260 C3
Ouarra → C.A.R. 5°5N 24°26E 264 A4
Ouarzazate Morocco 30°55N 6°50W 260 B3
Ouarzazate □ Morocco 30°45N 6°30W 260 B3
Ouassouas Mali 16°10N 1°23E 263 B5
Ouatagouna Mali 15°11N 0°43E 263 B5
Ouatere C.A.R. 5°30N 19°8E 264 A3
Oubangi → Dem. Rep. of the Congo 0°30S 17°50E 264 C3
Oubarakai, O. → Algeria 27°20N 9°0E 261 C6
Ouche → France 47°6N 5°16E 173 E12
Oud Zuid Amsterdam, Neths. 112 c1
Ouddorp Neths. 51°50N 3°57E 170 C3
Oude Kerk Amsterdam, Neths. 112 a2
Oude Rijn → Neths. 52°12N 4°24E 170 B4
Oudeïka Mali 17°30N 1°40W 263 B4
Oudenaarde Belgium 50°50N 3°37E 170 D3
Ouderkerk Neths. 52°18N 4°55E 112 B2
Oudon → France 47°41N 0°53W 172 E6
Oudtshoorn S. Africa 33°35S 22°14E 270 D3
Oued Zem Morocco 32°52N 6°34W 260 B3
Ouégoa N. Cal. 20°20S 164°26E 288 d
Oueita Chad 17°47N 20°39E 259 E4
Ouella Niger 14°48N 3°38E 263 C5
Ouellé Ivory C. 7°26N 4°1W 262 D4
Ouémé → Benin 6°30N 2°30E 263 D5
Ouenza Algeria 35°57N 8°4E 261 A6
Ouessa Burkina Faso 11°4N 2°47W 262 C4
Ouessant, Î. d' France 48°28N 5°6W 172 D1
Ouesso Congo 1°37N 16°5E 264 B3
Ouest □ Cameroon 5°30N 10°30E 263 D7
Ouest, Pte. de l' Canada 49°52N 64°40W 299 C7
Ouezzane Morocco 34°51N 5°35W 260 B3
Ougarou Burkina Faso 12°10N 0°58E 263 C5
Oughter, L. Ireland 54°1N 7°28W 166 B4
Oughterard Ireland 53°26N 9°18W 166 C2
Ouham → C.A.R. 6°35N 15°12E 264 A3
Ouhan → Chad 9°18N 18°14E 259 G3
Ouidah Benin 6°25N 2°0E 263 D5
Ouidi Niger 14°10N 13°0E 259 F2
Ouissongo Angola 7°40S 15°41E 265 E3
Ouistreham France 49°17N 0°18W 172 C6
Oujda Morocco 34°41N 1°55W 261 B4
Oujda □ Morocco 33°18N 2°24W 260 B4
Oujeft Mauritania 20°2N 13°0W 260 D2
Oulad-Teïma Morocco 30°24N 9°12W 260 B3
Oulainen Finland 64°17N 24°47E 160 D21
Ould Yenjé Mauritania 15°38N 12°16W 262 B2
Ouled Djellal Algeria 34°28N 5°2E 261 B6
Ouled Naïl, Mts. des Algeria 34°30N 3°30E 261 B5
Ouli Cameroon 5°12N 14°33E 264 A2
Oullins France 45°43N 4°49E 175 C8
Oulmès Morocco 33°17N 6°0W 260 B3
Oulou, Bahr → C.A.R. 9°48N 21°32E 264 A4
Oulu Finland 65°1N 25°29E 160 D21
Oulujärvi Finland 64°25N 27°15E 160 D22
Oulujoki → Finland 65°1N 25°30E 160 D21
Oulunkylä Finland 60°13N 24°58E 121 B2
Oulx Italy 45°2N 6°50E 198 C3
Oum Chalouba Chad 15°48N 20°46E 259 E4
Oum-el-Bouaghi Algeria 35°55N 7°6E 261 A6
Oum-el-Bouaghi □ Algeria 35°50N 7°5E 261 A6
Oum el Ksi Algeria 29°4N 6°59W 260 C3
Oum-er-Rbia, O. → Morocco 33°19N 8°21W 260 B3
Oum Hadjer Chad 13°18N 19°41E 259 F3
Oum Hadjer, O. → Chad 16°38N 20°14E 259 E4
Oumé Ivory C. 6°21N 5°27W 262 D3
Oumm ed Droûs Guebli, Sebkhet Mauritania 24°3N 11°45W 260 D2
Oumm ed Droûs Telli, Sebkhet Mauritania 24°20N 11°30W 260 D2
Ounane, Dj. Algeria 25°4N 7°19E 261 C6
Ounasjoki → Finland 66°31N 25°40E 160 C21
Ounguati Namibia 22°0S 15°46E 270 B2
Ounianga Kébir Chad 19°4N 20°29E 259 E4
Ounianga Sérir Chad 18°54N 20°51E 259 E4
Ounissoui Niger 17°34N 12°13E 259 E2
Our → Lux. 49°55N 6°5E 170 E6
Oura, Akra Greece 38°10N 26°2E 205 C8
Oura-wan Japan 26°32N 128°4E 288 a
Ouranoupoli Greece 40°20N 23°59E 202 F7
Ourârene Niger 19°30N 7°10E 263 B6
Ourari, Tarso Chad 21°27N 17°27E 259 D3
Ouray U.S.A. 38°1N 107°40W 305 G10
Ourcq → France 49°1N 3°1E 173 C10
Ourcq, Canal de l' France 48°54N 2°28E 134 A3
Ourém Brazil 1°33S 47°6W 332 B2
Ourense Spain 42°19N 7°55W 194 C3
Ourense □ Spain 42°15N 7°51W 194 C3
Ouricuri Brazil 7°53S 40°5W 332 C3
Ourinhos Brazil 23°0S 49°54W 335 A6
Ourique Portugal 37°38N 8°16W 195 H2
Ouro Fino Brazil 22°16S 46°25W 335 A6
Ouro-Ndia Mali 15°8N 4°35W 262 B4
Ouro Prêto Brazil 20°20S 43°30W 333 F3
Ouro Prêto do Oeste Brazil 10°40S 62°18W 331 C5
Ouro Sogui Senegal 15°36N 13°19W 262 B2
Oursi Burkina Faso 14°41N 0°27W 263 C4
Ourthe → Belgium 50°29N 5°35E 170 D5
Ouse → E. Sussex, U.K. 50°47N 0°4E 169 G8
Ouse → N. Yorks., U.K. 53°44N 0°55W 168 D7
Oust France 42°52N 1°13E 174 F5
Oust → France 47°35N 2°6W 172 E4
Outamba-Kilimi △ S. Leone 9°50N 12°40W 262 D2
Outaouais → Canada 45°27N 74°8W 298 C5
Outardes → Canada 49°24N 69°30W 299 C6
Outat Oulad el Haj Morocco 33°22N 3°42W 261 B4
Outeiro de Rei Spain 43°6N 7°36W 194 B3
Outer Hebrides U.K. 57°30N 7°40W 167 D1
Outer Mission U.S.A. 37°43N 122°26W 136 B2
Outes = A Serra de Outes Spain 42°52N 8°55W 194 C2
Outjo Namibia 20°5S 16°7E 270 B2
Outlook Canada 51°30N 107°0W 297 C7
Outokumpu Finland 62°43N 29°1E 160 E23
Outreau France 50°40N 1°36E 173 B8
Outremont Canada 45°31N 73°36W 130 A2
Ouvéa, Î. N. Cal. 20°35S 166°35E 288 d
Ouvèze → France 43°59N 4°51E 175 E8
Ouyen Australia 35°1S 142°22E 282 C5
Ouzinkie U.S.A. 57°56N 152°30W 303 H9
Ouzouer-le-Marché France 47°54N 1°32E 173 E8
Ovacık Turkey 36°11N 33°40E 250 B4
Ovada Italy 44°38N 8°38E 198 D5
Ovahe Chile 27°5S 109°19W 330 b
Ovalau Fiji 17°40S 178°48E 287 A2
Ovalle Chile 30°33S 71°18W 334 C1
Ovamboland Namibia 18°30S 16°0E 270 A2
Ovan Gabon 0°19N 12°10E 264 B2
Ovanåker Sweden 61°22N 15°53E 162 C9
Ovar Portugal 40°51N 8°40W 194 E2
Ovau Solomon Is. 6°40S 156°8E 287 L9
Overath Germany 50°56N 7°17E 178 E3
Overflakkee Neths. 51°44N 4°10E 170 C4
Overijse Belgium 50°47N 4°32E 116 B3

Overijssel □ *Neths.* 52°25N 6°35E **170** B6
Overland *U.S.A.* 38°42N 90°21W **310** F6
Overland Park *U.S.A.* 38°58N 94°40W **308** F6
Overlander Roadhouse
Australia 26°19S 114°28E **279** E1
Overton *U.S.A.* 36°33N 114°27W **307** J12
Övertorneå *Sweden* 66°23N 23°38E **160** C20
Överum *Sweden* 58°0N 16°20E **163** F10
Ovid *Mich., U.S.A.* 43°1N 84°22W **311** A12
Ovid *N.Y., U.S.A.* 42°41N 76°49W **313** D8
Ovidiopol *Ukraine* 46°15N 30°30E **189** J6
Ovidiu *Romania* 44°16N 28°34E **183** F13
Oviedo *Spain* 43°25N 5°50W **194** B5
Oviedo *Fla., U.S.A.* 28°40N 81°13W **317** G8
Oviksfjällen *Sweden* 63°0N 13°49E **162** A7
Ovišrags *Latvia* 57°33N 21°44E **184** A8
Ovoot *Mongolia* 45°21N 113°45E **226** B7
Övör Hangay □ *Mongolia* 45°0N 102°30E **226** B2
Ovoro *Nigeria* 5°26N 7°16E **263** D6
Øvre Årdal *Norway* 61°19N 7°48E **164** C4
Övre Fryken *Sweden* 60°0N 13°7E **162** E7
Øvre Rendal *Norway* 61°54N 11°4E **164** C8
Øvre Rindal *Norway* 63°6N 9°10E **164** A6
Øvre Sirdal *Norway* 58°48N 6°43E **164** F3
Ovruch *Ukraine* 51°25N 28°45E **177** C15
Owaka *N.Z.* 46°27S 169°40E **285** G4
Owambo = **Ovamboland**
Namibia 18°30S 16°0E **270** A2
Owando *Congo* 0°29S 15°55E **264** C3
Owasco L. *U.S.A.* 42°50N 76°31W **313** D8
Owase *Japan* 34°7N 136°12E **223** C8
Owatonna *U.S.A.* 44°5N 93°14W **308** C7
Owbeh *Afghan.* 34°28N 63°10E **240** B1
Owego *U.S.A.* 42°6N 76°16W **313** D8
Owen *Australia* 34°15S 138°32E **282** C3
Owen, Mt. *N.Z.* 41°35S 172°33E **285** B7
Owen Falls Dam = **Nalubaale Dam**
Uganda 0°30N 33°5E **268** B3
Owen Sound *Canada* 44°35N 80°55W **312** B4
Owen Stanley Ra.
Papua N. G. 8°30S 147°0E **286** E4
Owendo *Gabon* 0°17N 9°30E **264** B1
Oweniny ➔ *Ireland* 54°8N 9°34W **166** B2
Owens ➔ *U.S.A.* 36°32N 117°59W **306** J9
Owens L. *U.S.A.* 36°26N 117°57W **307** J9
Owensboro *U.S.A.* 37°46N 87°7W **311** G9
Owensville *Ind., U.S.A.* 38°16N 87°41W **311** F9
Owensville *Mo., U.S.A.* 38°21N 91°30W **310** F5
Owenteik *Guyana* 4°27N 59°35W **329** C6
Owenton *U.S.A.* 38°32N 84°50W **311** F12
Owerri *Nigeria* 5°29N 7°0E **263** D6
Owhango *N.Z.* 39°0S 175°23E **284** F4
Owhiro Bay *N.Z.* 41°21S 174°45E **143** C1
Owingsville *U.S.A.* 38°9N 83°46W **311** F13
Owl ➔ *Canada* 57°51N 92°44W **297** B10
Owo *Nigeria* 7°10N 5°39E **263** D6
Oworonsoki *Nigeria* 6°32N 3°24E **124** A2
Owosso *U.S.A.* 43°0N 84°10W **311** B12
Owyhee *U.S.A.* 41°57N 116°6W **304** F5
Owyhee ➔ *U.S.A.* 43°49N 117°2W **304** E5
Owyhee, L. *U.S.A.* 43°38N 117°14W **304** E5
Ox Mts. = **Slieve Gamph**
Ireland 54°6N 9°0W **166** B3
Oxapampa *Peru* 10°33S 75°26W **330** C2
Öxarfjörður *Iceland* 66°15N 16°45W **155** A10
Oxbow *Canada* 49°14N 102°10W **297** D8
Oxelösund *Sweden* 58°43N 17°5E **163** F11
Oxford *N.Z.* 43°18S 172°11E **285** D7
Oxford *Oxon., U.K.* 51°46N 1°15W **169** F6
Oxford *Ala., U.S.A.* 33°36N 85°51W **316** B4
Oxford *Iowa, U.S.A.* 41°43N 91°47W **310** C5
Oxford *Mass., U.S.A.* 42°7N 71°52W **313** D13
Oxford *Mich., U.S.A.* 42°49N 83°16W **311** B13
Oxford *Miss., U.S.A.* 34°22N 89°31W **315** D10
Oxford *N.C., U.S.A.* 36°19N 78°35W **315** C15
Oxford *N.Y., U.S.A.* 42°27N 75°36W **313** D9
Oxford *Ohio, U.S.A.* 39°31N 84°45W **311** E12
Oxford L. *Canada* 54°51N 95°37W **297** C9
Oxford Street *London, U.K.* **125** b3
Oxfordshire □ *U.K.* 51°48N 1°16W **169** F6
Oxgangs *U.K.* 55°54N 3°13W **121** B2
Oxia *Greece* 38°16N 21°5E **207** C3
Oxie *Sweden* 55°33N 13°6E **163** J7
Oxilithos *Greece* 38°35N 24°7E **204** C6
Oxley *Australia* 34°11S 144°6E **282** C6
Oxley Wild Rivers △
Australia 30°57S 152°12E **283** A10
Oxnard *U.S.A.* 34°12N 119°11W **307** L7
Oxon Hill *U.S.A.* 38°48N 76°59W **143** C4
Oxsjövålen *Sweden* 62°34N 13°57E **162** B7
Oxus = **Amudarya** ➔
Uzbekistan 43°58N 59°34E **216** D5
Oya *Malaysia* 2°55N 111°55E **235** B4
Oyabe *Japan* 36°47N 136°56E **223** A8
Oyama *Japan* 36°18N 139°48E **223** A11
Oyambre ⌂ *Spain* 43°22N 4°21W **194** B6
Oyapock ➔ *Fr. Guiana* 4°8N 51°40W **329** C7
Øye *Norway* 58°16N 6°49E **164** F3
Oyem *Gabon* 1°34N 11°31E **264** B2
Oyen *Canada* 51°22N 110°28W **297** C6
Øyer *Norway* 61°16N 10°25E **164** C7
Øyeren *Norway* 59°50N 11°15E **164** E8
Oykel ➔ *U.K.* 57°56N 4°26W **167** D4
Oymyakon *Russia* 63°25N 142°44E **215** C15
Oyo *Congo* 0°0 15°51E **264** C3
Oyo *Nigeria* 7°46N 3°56E **263** D5
Oyo *Sudan* 21°58N 36°10E **256** C4
Oyo □ *Nigeria* 8°15N 3°30E **263** D5
Oyodo *Japan* 34°42N 135°29E **133** A1
Oyón *Peru* 10°37S 76°47W **330** C2
Oyonnax *France* 46°16N 5°40E **173** F12
Oyrot = **Gorno-Altay** □
Russia 51°0N 86°0E **217** B11
Oyrot-Tura = **Gorno-Altaysk**
Russia 51°50N 86°5E **217** B11
Øyslebø *Norway* 58°9N 7°34E **164** F4
Oyster Bay *U.S.A.* 40°52N 73°32W **313** F11
Oyster Harbour = **Ladysmith**
Canada 49°0N 123°49W **306** B3
Oyster Rock *India* 18°54N 72°49E **130** B1
Oyster Rocks *Pakistan* 24°48N 66°59E **123** B2
Øystese *Norway* 60°22N 6°9E **164** D3
Ōyūbari *Japan* 43°1N 142°5E **220** C11
Oyyl ➔ *Kazakhstan* 49°4N 54°40E **216** C4
Özalp *Turkey* 38°39N 43°59E **213** C10
Ozamiz *Phil.* 8°15N 123°50E **233** G4
Ozar = **Ojhar** *India* 20°6N 73°56E **244** D1
Ozark *Ala., U.S.A.* 31°28N 85°39W **316** D4
Ozark *Ark., U.S.A.* 35°29N 93°50W **314** D8
Ozark *Mo., U.S.A.* 37°1N 93°12W **308** G7
Ozark Plateau *U.S.A.* 37°20N 91°40W **308** G8
Ozarks, L. of the *U.S.A.* 38°12N 92°38W **310** F4
Ożarów *Poland* 50°53N 21°40E **185** H8
Ózd *Hungary* 48°14N 20°15E **182** B5
Ozernovskiy *Russia* 51°30N 156°31E **215** D16
Ozernoye *Russia* 51°46N 51°28E **190** E10
Ozero Svityaz *Ukraine* 51°30N 23°50E **185** G10
Ozersk *Russia* 54°25N 22°0E **184** D8
Ozette, L. *U.S.A.* 48°6N 124°38W **306** B2
Ozieri *Italy* 40°35N 9°0E **200** B2
Ozimek *Poland* 50°41N 18°11E **185** H5
Ozinki *Russia* 51°12N 49°44E **190** E9
Ozoir-la-Ferrière *France* 48°46N 2°40E **134** B4
Ozona *U.S.A.* 30°43N 101°12W **314** F4
Ozone Park *U.S.A.* 40°40N 73°50W **132** B2
Ozorków *Poland* 51°57N 19°16E **185** G6
Ozren *Bos.-H.* 43°55N 18°29E **182** G3
Özu *Ehime, Japan* 33°30N 132°33E **222** D4
Özu *Kumamoto, Japan* 32°52N 130°52E **222** E2
Ozuluama *Mexico* 21°40N 97°51W **319** C5
Ozun *Romania* 45°47N 25°50E **183** E10
Ozurgeti *Georgia* 41°55N 42°0E **191** K5

P

Pa *Burkina Faso* 11°33N 3°19W **262** C4
Pa-an *Burma* 16°51N 97°40E **241** G6
Pa Mong Dam *Thailand* 18°0N 102°22E **236** D4
Pa Sak ➔ *Thailand* 15°30N 101°0E **236** E3
Paama *Vanuatu* 16°28S 168°14E **287** F6
Paamiut *Greenland* 62°0N 49°43W **154** E6
Paar ➔ *Germany* 48°46N 11°36E **179** G7
Paarl *S. Africa* 33°45S 18°56E **270** D2
Pa'auilo *U.S.A.* 20°2N 155°22W **302** C6
Pab Hills *Pakistan* 26°30N 66°45E **242** F2
Pabbay *U.K.* 57°46N 7°14W **167** D1
Pabianice *Poland* 51°40N 19°20E **185** G6
Pabna *Bangla.* 24°1N 89°18E **241** C2
Pabo *Uganda* 3°1N 32°10E **268** B3
Pacaás Novos, Serra dos
Brazil 10°45S 64°15W **331** C5
Pacaás Novos △ *Brazil* 11°0S 63°0W **331** C5
Pacaipampa *Peru* 5°35S 79°39W **330** B2
Pacajá ➔ *Brazil* 1°56S 50°50W **332** B1
Pacajus *Brazil* 4°10S 38°31W **332** B4
Pacaraima, Sa. *S. Amer.* 4°0N 62°30W **329** C5
Pacarán *Peru* 12°50S 76°3W **330** C2
Pacaraos *Peru* 11°12S 76°42W **330** C2
Pacasmayo *Peru* 7°20S 79°35W **330** B2
Pace *U.S.A.* 30°36N 87°10W **317** E2
Paceco *Italy* 37°59N 12°33E **200** E5
Pachacamac *Peru* 12°14S 77°53W **330** C2
Pachang Hsi ➔ *Taiwan* 23°20N 120°7E **225** C2
Pachao Yü *Taiwan* 23°22N 119°29E **225** C1
Pachia *Greece* 36°17N 25°50E **205** E7
Pachino *Italy* 36°43N 15°5E **201** F8
Pachitea ➔ *Peru* 8°46S 74°33W **330** B3
Pachiza *Peru* 7°16S 76°46W **330** B2
Pachmarhi *India* 22°28N 78°26E **243** H8
Pachnai *India* 26°57N 92°19E **241** B4
Pachnes *Greece* 35°16N 24°4E **207** E5
Pacho *Colombia* 5°8N 74°10W **328** B3
Pachora *India* 20°38N 75°29E **244** D2
Pachpadra *India* 25°58N 72°10E **242** G5
Pachuca *Mexico* 20°7N 98°44W **319** C5
Pacific *U.S.A.* 38°29N 90°45W **310** F6
Pacific Antarctic Ridge
Pac. Oc. 43°0S 115°0W **151** B13
Pacific City = **Huntington Beach**
U.S.A. 33°40N 118°5W **307** M9
Pacific Grove *U.S.A.* 36°38N 121°56W **306** J5
Pacific Heights *U.S.A.* 37°47N 122°26W **136** B2
Pacific Manor *U.S.A.* 37°38N 122°27W **136** C2
Pacific Ocean 10°0N 140°0W **289** G14
Pacific Palisades *Calif., U.S.A.* 34°2N 118°32W **126** B1
Pacific Palisades *Hawai'i, U.S.A.* 21°25N 157°58W **302** K14
Pacific Rim △ *Canada* 48°40N 124°45W **306** B2
Pacifica *U.S.A.* 37°37N 122°27W **136** C2
Pacitan *Indonesia* 8°12S 111°7E **235** D4
Packsaddle *Australia* 30°36S 141°58E **282** A4
Packwood *U.S.A.* 46°36N 121°40W **306** D5
Paco *Phil.* 14°35N 120°59E **127** B1
Paço de Arcos *Portugal* 38°41N 9°17W **126** A1
Paço Imperial *Rio de J., Brazil* **135** a2
Pacov *Czech Rep.* 49°27N 15°0E **180** B8
Pacoval *Brazil* 2°40S 54°11W **329** D7
Pacuí ➔ *Brazil* 16°46S 45°1W **333** E2
Pacy-sur-Eure *France* 49°1N 1°23E **172** C8
Padaido, Kepulauan
Indonesia 1°15S 136°30E **231** E9
Padali = **Amursk**
Russia 50°14N 136°54E **215** D14
Padampur *India* 20°59N 83°4E **244** D6
Padang *Riau, Indonesia* 1°30N 102°30E **237** M4
Padang *Sumatera Barat, Indonesia* 1°0S 100°20E **234** C2
Padang Endau *Malaysia* 2°40N 103°38E **237** L4
Padangpanjang *Indonesia* 0°40S 100°20E **234** C2
Padangsidempuan
Indonesia 1°30N 99°15E **234** B1
Padangtikar *Indonesia* 0°44S 109°15E **235** C3
Padatchaung *Burma* 19°46N 94°48E **241** F5
Padauari ➔ *Brazil* 0°15S 64°5W **329** D5
Padaung *Burma* 18°43N 95°9E **241** F5
Padborg *Denmark* 54°49N 9°21E **163** K3
Padcaya *Bolivia* 21°52S 64°48W **331** E5
Paddington *N.S.W., Australia* 33°53S 151°14E **139** B2
Paddington *London, U.K.* **125** b2
Paddle Prairie *Canada* 57°57N 117°29W **296** B5
Paderborn *Germany* 51°42N 8°45E **178** D4
Paderno *Italy* 45°33N 9°9E **129** A1
Paderoo *India* 18°5N 82°40E **244** E6
Padeș, Vf. *Romania* 45°40N 22°22E **182** E7
Padilla *Bolivia* 19°19S 64°20W **331** D5
Padina *Romania* 44°50N 27°8E **183** F12
Padma *India* 24°12N 85°22E **243** G11
Padma ➔ *Bangla.* 23°22N 90°32E **241** D3
Pádova *Italy* 45°25N 11°53E **199** C8
Padra *India* 22°15N 73°7E **242** H5
Padrão, Pta. *Angola* 6°5S 12°20E **265** D2
Padrauna *India* 26°54N 83°59E **243** F10
Padre Burgos *Phil.* 10°1N 125°0E **233** F5
Padre I. *U.S.A.* 27°10N 97°25W **314** H6
Padre Island ⌂ *U.S.A.* 27°0N 97°25W **314** H6
Padrón *Spain* 42°41N 8°39W **194** C2
Padstow *U.K.* 50°33N 4°58W **169** G3
Padthaway *Australia* 36°36S 140°31E **282** D4
Padua = **Pádova** *Italy* 45°25N 11°53E **199** C8
Paducah *Ky., U.S.A.* 37°5N 88°37W **308** G9
Paducah *Tex., U.S.A.* 34°1N 100°18W **314** D4
Padukka *Sri Lanka* 6°50N 80°5E **245** L5
Padul *Spain* 37°1N 3°38W **195** H7
Padwa *India* 18°27N 82°47E **244** E6
Paea *Tahiti* 17°41S 149°35W **289** e
Paekakariki *N.Z.* 40°59S 174°58E **284** G3
Paektu-san *N. Korea* 41°59N 128°4E **224** B4
Paengaroa *N.Z.* 37°49S 176°29E **284** D5
Paeroa *N.Z.* 37°23S 175°41E **284** D4
Paesana *Italy* 44°41N 7°16E **198** D4
Paete *Phil.* 14°23N 121°29E **232** D3
Pafúri *Mozam.* 22°28S 31°17E **271** B5
Pag *Croatia* 44°25N 15°3E **199** D12
Paga *Gabon* 0°45S 10°21E **264** C2
Paga *Ghana* 11°1N 1°8W **263** C4
Pagadian *Phil.* 7°55N 123°30E **233** H4
Pagai Selatan, Pulau
Indonesia 3°0S 100°15E **234** C2
Pagai Utara, Pulau
Indonesia 2°35S 100°0E **234** C2
Pagalu = **Annobón** *Atl. Oc.* 1°25S 5°36E **255** G4
Pagalungan *Phil.* 7°4N 124°41E **233** H5
Pagan *Burma* 21°10N 94°52E **241** E5
Pagan *N. Marianas* 18°7N 145°46E **302** a
Pagara *India* 24°22N 80°1E **243** G9
Pagastikos Kolpos *Greece* 39°15N 23°0E **204** B5
Pagatan *Indonesia* 3°33S 115°59E **235** C5
Page *U.S.A.* 36°57N 111°27W **305** H8
Pagėgiai *Lithuania* 55°9N 21°54E **184** C8
Pagei *Papua N. G.* 3°2S 141°10E **286** B1
Paget, Mt. *S. Georgia* 54°26S 36°31W **326** H6
Paget I. *India* 13°26N 92°50E **245** H11
Pagewood *Australia* 33°56S 151°14E **139** B2
Pago B. *Guam* 13°25N 144°47E **302** d
Pago Pago *Amer. Samoa* 14°16S 170°43W **302** f
Pago Pago Harbor
Amer. Samoa 14°17S 170°40W **302** f
Pagosa Springs *U.S.A.* 37°16N 107°1W **305** H10
Pagote *India* 18°53N 72°59E **130** B2
Pagua B. *Dominica* 15°32N 61°17W **323** k
Pagudpud *Phil.* 18°34N 120°47E **232** B3
Pagwa River *Canada* 50°2N 85°14W **298** B2
Pagwi *Papua N. G.* 4°4S 143°2E **286** C2
Pāhala *U.S.A.* 19°12N 155°29W **302** D6
Pahang □ *Malaysia* 3°30N 102°45E **234** B2
Pahang ➔ *Malaysia* 3°30N 103°9E **237** L4
Paharpur *Bangla.* 24°51N 88°44E **241** C2
Pahia Pt. *N.Z.* 46°20S 167°41E **285** G2
Pahiatua *N.Z.* 40°27S 175°50E **284** G4
Pāhoa *U.S.A.* 19°30N 154°57W **302** D7
Pahokee *U.S.A.* 26°50N 80°40W **317** J9
Pahrump *U.S.A.* 36°12N 115°59W **307** J11
Pahute Mesa *U.S.A.* 37°20N 116°45W **306** H10
Pai *Thailand* 19°19N 98°27E **236** C2
Pai, I. do *Brazil* 22°59S 43°5W **135** B2
Paia *U.S.A.* 20°54N 156°22W **302** C5
Paichuan Liehtao *Taiwan* 25°58N 119°57E **225** b
Paicines *U.S.A.* 36°44N 121°17W **306** J5
Paide *Estonia* 58°53N 25°33E **188** C3
Paignton *U.K.* 50°26N 3°35W **169** G4
Paihia *N.Z.* 35°17S 174°6E **284** B3
Paiho *Taiwan* 23°21N 120°25E **225** C2
Paiján *Peru* 7°42S 79°20W **330** B2
Päijänne *Finland* 61°30N 25°30E **188** B3
Pailani *India* 25°45N 80°26E **243** G9
Pailin *Cambodia* 12°46N 102°36E **236** F4
Pailolo Channel *U.S.A.* 21°0N 156°40W **302** B5
Paimpol *France* 48°48N 3°4W **172** D3
Painan *Indonesia* 1°21S 100°34E **234** C2
Paine Grande, Cerro *Chile* 50°59S 73°4W **336** D2
Painesville *U.S.A.* 41°43N 81°15W **312** E3
Paint Hills = **Wemindji**
Canada 53°0N 78°49W **298** B4
Paint L. *Canada* 55°28N 97°57W **297** B9
Painted Desert *U.S.A.* 36°0N 111°0W **305** H8
Paintsville *U.S.A.* 37°49N 82°48W **309** G12
País Vasco □ *Spain* 42°50N 2°45W **196** C2
Paisha *Taiwan* 23°40N 119°35E **225** C1
Paisley *Ont., Canada* 44°18N 81°16W **312** B3
Paisley *Renf., U.K.* 55°50N 4°25W **167** F4
Paisley *Oreg., U.S.A.* 42°42N 120°32W **304** E3
Païta *N. Cal.* 22°8S 166°22E **288** d
Paita *Peru* 5°11S 81°9W **330** B1
Paithan *India* 19°29N 75°23E **244** E2
Paiva ➔ *Portugal* 41°4N 8°16W **194** D2
Paizhou *China* 30°12N 113°55E **229** B9
Paja, Cerro *Ecuador* 1°17S 90°26W **330** a
Pájara *Canary Is.* 28°21N 14°6W **153** e2
Pajares *Spain* 43°1N 5°46W **194** B5
Pajares, Puerto de *Spain* 42°58N 5°46W **194** C5
Pajarito *Colombia* 5°17N 72°43W **328** B3
Pajęczno *Poland* 51°10N 19°0E **185** G5
Paju *S. Korea* 37°45N 126°46E **224** D3
Pak Kok *China* 22°14N 114°7E **122** B1
Pak Kong *China* 22°22N 114°12E **122** A2
Pak Lay *Laos* 18°15N 101°27E **236** C3
Pak Phanang *Thailand* 8°21N 100°12E **237** H3
Pak Sane *Laos* 18°22N 103°39E **236** C4
Pak Song *Laos* 15°11N 106°14E **236** E6
Pak Suong *Laos* 19°58N 102°15E **228** H4
Pak Tam Chung *China* 22°24N 114°19E **219** G11
Pakala *India* 13°29N 79°8E **245** H4
Pakaraima Mts. *Guyana* 6°0N 60°0W **329** B6
Pakaur *India* 24°38N 87°51E **243** G12
Pakch'ŏn *N. Korea* 39°44N 125°35E **224** C2
Pakenham *Vic., Australia* 38°6S 145°30E **283** E6
Pakenham *Ont., Canada* 45°18N 76°18W **313** A8
Pakhoi = **Beihai** *China* 21°28N 109°6E **228** G7
Pakhuis *S. Africa* 32°9S 19°5E **270** D2
Pakila *Finland* 60°15N 24°55E **121** B2
Pakistan ■ *Asia* 30°0N 70°0E **242** E4
Pakkading *Laos* 18°19N 103°59E **236** C4
Paklay = **Sayaboury**
Laos 19°15N 101°45E **236** C3
Paklenica △ *Croatia* 44°20N 15°39E **199** D12
Pakokku *Burma* 21°20N 95°0E **241** E5
Pakość *Poland* 52°48N 18°6E **185** F5
Pakowki L. *Canada* 49°20N 111°0W **297** D6
Pakpattan *Pakistan* 30°25N 73°27E **242** D5
Pakrac *Croatia* 45°27N 17°12E **182** E2
Pakruojis *Lithuania* 55°58N 23°52E **184** C10
Paks *Hungary* 46°38N 18°55E **182** D3
Paktīā □ *Afghan.* 33°30N 69°15E **240** B3
Paktīkā □ *Afghan.* 32°30N 69°0E **240** B3
Pakwach *Uganda* 2°28N 31°27E **268** B3
Pakxe *Laos* 15°5N 105°52E **236** E5
Pal Lahara *India* 21°27N 85°11E **243** J11
Pala *Chad* 9°25N 15°5E **259** G3
Pala *Dem. Rep. of the Congo* 6°45S 29°30E **268** D2
Pala *Calif., U.S.A.* 33°22N 117°5W **307** M9
Palabek *Uganda* 3°22N 32°33E **268** B3
Palacio Real *Madrid, Spain* **127** b1
Palacios *U.S.A.* 28°42N 96°13W **314** G6
Palafrugell *Spain* 41°55N 3°10E **196** D8
Palagiano *Italy* 40°35N 17°2E **201** B10
Palagonia *Italy* 37°19N 14°45E **201** E7
Palagruža *Croatia* 42°24N 16°15E **199** F13
Palais Royal *Brussels, Belgium* **116** b3
Palaiseau *France* 48°42N 2°14E **134** B2
Palakkad = **Palghat**
India 10°46N 76°42E **245** J3
Palakol *India* 16°31N 81°46E **245** F5
Palalankwe *India* 10°52N 92°29E **245** J11
Palam *India* 19°0N 77°0E **244** E3
Palamas *Greece* 39°26N 22°4E **204** B4
Palamós *Spain* 41°50N 3°10E **196** D8
Palampur *India* 32°10N 76°30E **242** C7
Palamut *Turkey* 38°59N 27°41E **205** C9
Palana *Tas., Australia* 39°45S 147°55E **281** F4
Palana *Russia* 59°10N 159°59E **215** D16
Palanan *Phil.* 17°8N 122°29E **232** C4
Palanan Bay *Phil.* 17°9N 122°27E **232** C4
Palanan Pt. *Phil.* 17°17N 122°30E **232** C4
Palandri *Pakistan* 33°42N 73°40E **243** C5
Palanga *Lithuania* 55°58N 21°3E **184** C8
Palanganene
Dem. Rep. of the Congo 6°32S 18°52E **265** D3
Palangkaraya *Indonesia* 2°16S 113°56E **235** C4
Palani *India* 10°30N 77°30E **245** J3
Palani Hills *India* 10°14N 77°33E **245** J3
Palanpur *India* 24°10N 72°25E **242** G5
Palaoa Pt. *U.S.A.* 20°44N 156°58W **302** C5
Palapag *Phil.* 12°33N 125°7E **232** E5
Palapye *Botswana* 22°30S 27°7E **270** B4
Palar ➔ *India* 12°27N 80°13E **245** H5
Palas *Pakistan* 35°4N 73°14E **243** B5
Palas de Rei *Spain* 42°52N 7°52W **194** C3
Palasponga *India* 21°47N 85°34E **243** J11
Palatine *U.S.A.* 42°7N 88°3W **311** B8
Palatka *Russia* 60°6N 150°54E **215** C16
Palatka *Fla., U.S.A.* 29°39N 81°38W **316** F8
Palau *Italy* 41°11N 9°23E **200** A2
Palau ■ *Palau* 7°30N 134°30E **288** c
Palauig *Phil.* 15°26N 119°54E **232** D2
Palauk *Burma* 13°10N 98°40E **236** F2
Palawan *Phil.* 9°30N 118°30E **233** G2
Palawan □ *Phil.* 10°0N 119°0E **233** G2
Palawan Passage *Phil.* 10°0N 118°0E **233** G2
Palayan *Phil.* 15°36N 121°8E **232** D3
Palayankottai *India* 8°45N 77°45E **245** K3
Palazzo, Pte. *France* 42°28N 8°30E **175** F12
Palazzo San Gervásio
Italy 40°56N 15°59E **201** B8
Palazzolo *Italy* 45°34N 9°9E **129** A1
Palazzolo Acrēide *Italy* 37°4N 14°54E **201** E7
Palca *Chile* 19°7S 69°9W **330** D4
Paldiski *Estonia* 59°23N 24°9E **188** C3
Pale *Bos.-H.* 43°50N 18°38E **182** G3
Palekastro *Greece* 35°12N 26°15E **207** E7
Palel *India* 24°27N 94°2E **241** C5
Paleleh *Indonesia* 1°10N 121°50E **231** D6
Palembang *Indonesia* 3°0S 104°50E **234** C2
Palena ➔ *Chile* 43°50S 73°50W **336** B2
Palena, L. *Chile* 43°55S 71°40W **336** B2
Palencia *Spain* 42°1N 4°34W **194** C6
Palencia □ *Spain* 42°31N 4°33W **194** C6
Paleng *Taiwan* 24°41N 121°23E **225** B3
Palenque *Mexico* 17°29N 92°1W **319** D6
Paleo Faliro *Greece* 37°53N 23°42E **112** B2
Paleochora *Greece* 35°16N 23°39E **207** E4
Paleokastritsa *Greece* 39°40N 19°41E **206** B9
Paleometokho *Cyprus* 35°7N 33°11E **207** E9
Paleopoli *Greece* 37°49N 24°50E **204** D6
Palermo *B. Aires, Argentina* 34°35S 58°24W **117** B2
Palermo *Colombia* 2°54N 75°26W **328** C2
Palermo *Italy* 38°7N 13°22E **200** D6
Palermo *Calif., U.S.A.* 39°26N 121°33W **304** G3
Palermo ✕ (**PMO**) *Italy* 38°11N 13°5E **200** D6
Pales *Greece* 38°47N 20°53E **207** B2
Palestina = **Jordânia**
Brazil 15°55S 40°11W **333** E3
Palestine *Asia* 32°0N 35°0E **251** G6
Palestine *Ill., U.S.A.* 39°0N 87°37W **311** F9
Palestine *Tex., U.S.A.* 31°46N 95°38W **314** F7
Palestrina *Italy* 41°50N 12°53E **199** G9
Paletwa *Burma* 21°10N 92°50E **241** E4
Palghat *India* 10°46N 76°42E **245** J3
Palgrave, Mt. *Australia* 23°22S 115°58E **278** D2
Palhais *Portugal* 38°37N 9°2W **126** B2
Pali *India* 25°50N 73°20E **242** G5
Pali *Taiwan* 25°8N 121°23E **225** A3
Palika-Aike △ *Chile* 52°6S 69°44W **336** D3
Palikea *U.S.A.* 21°26N 158°6W **302** K13
Palikir *Micronesia* 6°55N 158°9E **288** G7
Palimbang *Phil.* 6°12N 124°12E **233** H5
Palin, Mt. *Malaysia* 6°10N 117°10E **235** A5
Palinuro *Italy* 40°2N 15°17E **201** B8
Palinuro, C. *Italy* 40°2N 15°16E **201** B8
Paliouri, Akra *Greece* 39°57N 23°45E **202** G7
Palisades Park *U.S.A.* 40°50N 74°1W **132** A1
Palisades Res. *U.S.A.* 43°20N 111°12W **304** E8
Palisadoes, The *Jamaica* 17°57N 76°48W **320** a
Paliseul *Belgium* 49°54N 5°8E **170** E5
Palitana *India* 21°32N 71°49E **242** J4
Palizada *Mexico* 18°15N 92°5W **319** D6
Palk Bay *Asia* 9°30N 79°15E **245** K4
Palk Strait *Asia* 10°0N 79°45E **245** K4
Palkānah *Iraq* 35°49N 44°26E **246** C5
Palkonda *India* 18°36N 83°48E **244** E6
Palkonda Ra. *India* 13°50N 79°20E **245** H4
Palkot *India* 22°53N 84°39E **243** H11
Palla Road = **Dinokwe**
Botswana 23°29S 26°37E **270** B4
Pallanza = **Verbánia** *Italy* 45°56N 8°33E **198** C5
Pallarenda *Australia* 19°12S 146°46E **280** B4
Pallasovka *Russia* 50°4N 47°0E **190** E8
Pallëri ➔ *India* 16°45N 80°2E **245** F5
Pallës, Bishti i *Albania* 41°24N 19°24E **202** E3
Pallinup ➔ *Australia* 34°27S 118°50E **279** F2
Pallisa *Uganda* 1°12N 33°43E **268** B3
Palliser, C. *N.Z.* 41°37S 175°14E **284** H4
Palliser, Îs.
French Polynesia 15°30S 146°30W **289** f
Palliser B. *N.Z.* 41°26S 175°5E **284** H4
Pallu *India* 28°59N 74°14E **242** E6
Palm Bay *U.S.A.* 28°2N 80°35W **317** G9
Palm Beach *Aruba* 12°34N 70°2W **322** b
Palm Beach *Fla., U.S.A.* 26°43N 80°2W **317** J9
Palm Coast *U.S.A.* 29°35N 81°12W **317** F8
Palm Desert *U.S.A.* 33°43N 116°22W **307** M10
Palm-Grove △ *Australia* 24°57S 149°21E **280** C4
Palm Harbor *U.S.A.* 28°5N 82°46W **317** G7
Palm Is. *Australia* 18°40S 146°35E **280** B4
Palm Springs *U.S.A.* 33°50N 116°33W **307** M10
Palm Valley *U.S.A.* 30°11N 81°23W **316** E8
Palma = **Paraná** *Brazil* 12°30S 47°48W **333** D2
Palma *Mozam.* 10°46S 40°29E **269** E5
Palma ➔ *Brazil* 12°33S 47°52W **333** D2
Palma, B. de *Spain* 39°30N 2°39E **206** B3
Palma de Mallorca *Spain* 39°35N 2°39E **206** B3
Palma de Mallorca ✕ (**PMI**)
Spain 39°34N 2°43E **197** F7
Palma del Río *Spain* 37°43N 5°17W **195** H5
Palma di Montechiaro
Italy 37°11N 13°46E **200** E6
Palma Nova = **Palmanova**
Spain 39°32N 2°34E **206** B3
Palma Soriano *Cuba* 20°15N 76°0W **320** B4
Palmaner *India* 13°12N 78°45E **245** H4
Palmanova *Spain* 39°32N 2°34E **206** B3
Palmares *Brazil* 8°41S 35°28W **332** C4
Palmarito *Venezuela* 7°37N 70°10W **328** B3
Palmarola *Italy* 40°56N 12°51E **200** B5
Palmas *Paraná, Brazil* 26°29S 52°0W **335** B5
Palmas *Tocantins, Brazil* 10°13S 48°16W **332** D2
Palmas, C. *Liberia* 4°27N 7°46W **262** E3
Palmas, G. di *Italy* 39°0N 8°30E **200** D1
Palmas de Monte Alto
Brazil 14°16S 43°10W **333** D3
Palmdale *Calif., U.S.A.* 34°35N 118°7W **307** L8
Palmdale *Fla., U.S.A.* 26°57N 81°19W **317** J8
Palmeira *Brazil* 25°25S 50°0W **333** G2
Palmeira das Missões
Brazil 27°55S 53°17W **335** B5
Palmeira dos Índios
Brazil 9°25S 36°37W **332** C4
Palmeirais *Brazil* 6°0S 43°0W **332** C3
Palmeiras *Brazil* 12°31S 41°34W **333** D3
Palmeiras ➔ *Brazil* 12°22S 47°8W **333** D2
Palmeirinhas, Pta. das
Angola 9°2S 12°57E **265** D2
Palmela *Portugal* 38°32N 8°57W **195** G2
Palmelo *Brazil* 17°20S 48°27W **333** E2
Palmer *Antarctica* 64°35S 65°0W **151** C17
Palmer *Alaska, U.S.A.* 61°36N 149°7W **303** F10
Palmer ➔ *Australia* 16°0S 142°26E **280** B3
Palmer Arch. *Antarctica* 64°15S 65°0W **151** C17
Palmer Lake *U.S.A.* 39°7N 104°55W **304** G11
Palmer Land *Antarctica* 73°0S 63°0W **151** D18
Palmer Park *U.S.A.* 38°55N 76°52W **143** B4
Palmerston = **Darwin**
Australia 12°25S 130°51E **278** B5
Palmerston *N. Terr., Australia* 12°31S 130°59E **278** B5
Palmerston *Ont., Canada* 43°50N 80°51W **312** C4
Palmerston *Dublin, Ireland* 53°20N 6°22W **120** A1
Palmerston *N.Z.* 45°29S 170°43E **285** F5
Palmerston North *N.Z.* 40°21S 175°39E **284** G4
Palmerton *U.S.A.* 40°48N 75°37W **313** F9
Palmetto *Fla., U.S.A.* 27°31N 82°34W **317** H7
Palmetto *Ga., U.S.A.* 33°31N 84°40W **316** B5
Palmetto Pt. *Antigua & B.* 17°37N 61°51W **322** c
Palmetto Pt.
St. Kitts & Nevis 17°18N 62°46W **322** d
Palmi *Italy* 38°21N 15°51E **201** D8
Palmira *Argentina* 32°59S 68°34W **334** C2
Palmira *Colombia* 3°32N 76°16W **328** C2
Palms *U.S.A.* 34°1N 118°24W **126** B2
Palmyra = **Tudmur** *Syria* 34°36N 38°15E **213** E8
Palmyra *Ill., U.S.A.* 39°26N 90°0W **310** E7
Palmyra *Mo., U.S.A.* 39°48N 91°32W **310** E5
Palmyra *N.J., U.S.A.* 40°0N 75°1W **313** F9
Palmyra *N.Y., U.S.A.* 43°5N 77°18W **312** C7
Palmyra *Pa., U.S.A.* 40°18N 76°36W **313** F8
Palmyra *Wis., U.S.A.* 42°52N 88°36W **311** B8
Palmyra Is. *Pac. Oc.* 5°52N 162°5W **289** G11
Palmyras = **Santos Dumont**
Brazil 22°55S 43°10W **333** F3
Palmyras Pt. *India* 20°46N 87°1E **244** D8
Palo *Phil.* 11°10N 124°59E **233** F5
Palo Alto *U.S.A.* 37°27N 122°10W **306** H4
Palo Seco *Trin. & Tob.* 10°4N 61°36W **323** B1
Palo Verde *U.S.A.* 33°26N 114°44W **307** M12
Palo Verde △ *Costa Rica* 10°21N 85°21W **320** D2
Paloheinä *Finland* 60°15N 24°56E **121** B2
Paloich *Sudan* 10°28N 32°32E **257** E3
Palomar Mt. *U.S.A.* 33°22N 116°50W **307** M10
Palomeras *Spain* 40°22N 3°39W **127** B2
Palompon *Phil.* 11°3N 124°23E **233** F5
Palopo *Indonesia* 3°0S 120°16E **231** E6
Palos, C. de *Spain* 37°38N 0°40W **197** H4
Palos de la Frontera *Spain* 37°14N 6°53W **195** H4
Palos Heights *U.S.A.* 41°39N 87°47W **119** D2
Palos Hills *U.S.A.* 41°42N 87°49W **119** C2
Palos Hills Forest *U.S.A.* 41°40N 87°52W **119** C1
Palos Park *U.S.A.* 41°40N 87°50W **119** C1
Palos Verdes, Pt.
U.S.A. 33°46N 118°25W **307** M8
Palos Verdes Estates
U.S.A. 33°48N 118°23W **307** M8
Palpa *Peru* 14°30S 75°15W **330** C2
Palpara *India* 22°38N 88°22E **124** B2
Pålsboda *Sweden* 59°3N 15°22E **162** E9
Palu *Indonesia* 1°0S 119°52E **231** E5
Palu *Turkey* 38°45N 40°0E **213** C9
Paluan *Phil.* 13°26N 120°29E **232** E3
Paluke *Liberia* 5°2N 8°5W **262** D3
Paluma Ra. *Australia* 19°9S 146°22E **280** B4
Paluzza *Italy* 46°32N 13°1E **199** B10
Palwal *India* 28°8N 77°19E **242** E7
Pama *Burkina Faso* 11°19N 0°44E **263** C5
Pama ➔ *C.A.R.* 4°23N 18°43E **264** B3
Pama △ *Burkina Faso* 11°27N 0°40E **263** C5
Pamandzi *Mayotte* 12°47S 45°16E **272** b
Pamanukan *Indonesia* 6°16S 107°49E **235** D3
Pamban I. *India* 9°15N 79°20E **245** K4
Pamekasan *Indonesia* 7°10S 113°28E **235** D4
Pamenang *Indonesia* 8°24S 116°6E **231** J19
Pamiers *France* 43°7N 1°39E **174** E5
Pamir *Tajikistan* 37°40N 73°0E **217** E8
Pamirsky Post = **Murghob**
Tajikistan 38°10N 74°2E **217** E8
Pamlico ➔ *U.S.A.* 35°20N 76°28W **315** D16
Pamlico Sd. *U.S.A.* 35°20N 76°0W **315** D17
Pampa *U.S.A.* 35°32N 100°58W **314** D4
Pampa de Agma
Argentina 43°45S 69°40W **336** B3
Pampa de las Salinas
Argentina 32°1S 66°58W **334** C2
Pampa Grande *Bolivia* 18°5S 64°6W **331** D5
Pampa Hermosa *Peru* 7°7S 75°4W **330** B2
Pampanga □ *Phil.* 15°4N 120°40E **232** D3
Pampanua *Indonesia* 4°16S 120°8E **231** E6
Pampas *Argentina* 35°0S 63°0W **334** D3
Pampas *Peru* 12°20S 74°50W **330** C3
Pampas ➔ *Peru* 13°24S 73°12W **330** C3
Pamphylia *Turkey* 37°0N 31°20E **250** B2
Pamplemousses *Mauritius* 20°6S 57°34E **272** e
Pamplona *Colombia* 7°23N 72°39W **328** B3
Pamplona *Phil.* 18°31N 121°20E **232** B3
Pamplona-Iruña *Spain* 42°48N 1°38W **196** C3
Pampoenpoort *S. Africa* 31°3S 22°40E **270** D3
Pamuk ➔ *Turkey* 37°2N 34°49E **250** A5
Pamukçu *Turkey* 39°30N 27°54E **205** B9
Pamukkale *Turkey* 37°55N 29°8E **205** D11
Pan de Azúcar *Chile* 24°5S 68°10W **334** A2
Pan de Azúcar △ *Chile* 26°0S 70°40W **334** B1
Pan Xian *China* 25°46N 104°38E **228** E5
Pana *U.S.A.* 39°23N 89°5W **310** E7
Panabo *Phil.* 7°19N 125°42E **233** H5
Panaca *U.S.A.* 37°47N 114°23W **305** H6
Panacea *U.S.A.* 30°2N 84°23W **316** E5
Panagyurishte *Bulgaria* 42°30N 24°15E **203** D8
Panaitan *Indonesia* 6°36S 105°12E **234** D3
Panaji *India* 15°25N 73°50E **245** G1
Panamá *Panama* 9°0N 79°25W **320** c
Panama *Sri Lanka* 6°45N 81°48E **245** L5
Panama ■ *Cent. Amer.* 8°48N 79°55W **320** E4
Panamá, G. de *Panama* 8°4N 79°20W **320** E4
Panama, Isthmus of
Cent. Amer. 9°0N 79°0W **320** E4
Panama Basin *Pac. Oc.* 5°0N 83°30W **289** G19
Panama Canal *Panama* 9°10N 79°37W **320** c
Panama City *U.S.A.* 30°10N 85°40W **316** E4
Panama City Beach
U.S.A. 30°11N 85°48W **316** E4
Panamint Range *U.S.A.* 36°20N 117°20W **307** J9
Panamint Springs
U.S.A. 36°20N 117°28W **307** J9
Panão *Peru* 9°55S 75°55W **330** B2
Panaon I. *Phil.* 10°3N 125°13E **233** F5
Panare *Thailand* 6°51N 101°30E **237** J3
Panarea *Italy* 38°38N 15°4E **201** D8
Panaro ➔ *Italy* 44°55N 11°25E **199** D8
Panarukan *Indonesia* 7°42S 113°56E **235** D4
Panay *Phil.* 11°10N 122°30E **233** F4
Panay, G. *Phil.* 11°0N 122°30E **233** F4
Panayarvi △ *Russia* 66°16N 30°10E **160** C24
Pančevo *Serbia* 44°52N 20°41E **182** F5
Panch'iao *Taiwan* 25°1N 121°27E **225** A3
Panchur *India* 22°32N 88°16E **124** B1
Panciu *Romania* 45°54N 27°8E **183** E12
Pancol *Phil.* 10°52N 119°25E **233** F2
Pancorbo, Desfiladero
Spain 42°32N 3°5W **194** C7
Pâncota *Romania* 46°20N 21°45E **182** D6
Panda *Mozam.* 24°2S 34°45E **271** B5
Pandacan *Phil.* 14°35N 121°0E **127** B2
Pandan *Malaysia* 1°32N 103°46E **237** d
Pandan *Antique, Phil.* 11°45N 122°10E **233** F4
Pandan *Catanduanes, Phil.* 14°3N 124°10E **232** D5
Pandan, Selat *Singapore* 1°15N 103°44E **237** d
Pandan Bay *Phil.* 11°43N 122°0E **233** F4
Pandan Res. *Singapore* 1°18N 103°44E **138** B2
Pandan Tampoi = **Tampoi**
Malaysia 1°30N 103°39E **237** d
Pandegelang *Indonesia* 6°25S 106°5E **234** D3
Pandhana *India* 21°42N 76°13E **242** J7
Pandharkawada *India* 20°1N 78°32E **244** D4
Pandharpur *India* 17°41N 75°20E **244** F2
Pandhurna *India* 21°36N 78°35E **244** D4
Pando *Uruguay* 34°44S 56°0W **335** C4
Pando □ *Bolivia* 11°20S 67°40W **330** C4
Pando, L. = **Hope, L.**
Australia 28°24S 139°18E **281** D2
Pandokrator *Greece* 39°45N 19°50E **206** B9
Pandora *Costa Rica* 9°43N 83°3W **320** E3
Pandrup *Denmark* 57°14N 9°40E **163** G3
Pandu
Dem. Rep. of the Congo 4°59N 19°16E **264** B3
Panepistimio *Athens, Greece* **112** b2
Paneväggio-Pale di San Martino ⌂
Italy 46°11N 11°46E **199** B8
Panevėžys *Lithuania* 55°42N 24°25E **188** E3
Panfilov = **Zharkent**
Kazakhstan 44°10N 80°0E **217** D10
Panfilovo *Russia* 50°25N 42°46E **190** E6
Pang Sida △ *Thailand* 14°5N 102°17E **236** E4
Panga
Dem. Rep. of the Congo 1°52N 26°18E **268** B2
Pangaion Óros *Greece* 40°50N 24°0E **203** F8
Pangala *Congo* 3°16S 14°34E **264** C2
Pangalanes, Canal des = **Ampangalana, Lakandranon'**
Madag. 22°48S 47°50E **272** C2
Pangani *Tanzania* 5°25S 38°58E **268** D4
Pangani ➔ *Tanzania* 5°26S 38°58E **268** D4
Pangantocan *Phil.* 7°50N 124°49E **233** H5
Pangar Djerémé ⌂
Cameroon 5°50N 13°10E **263** D7
Pangasinan □ *Phil.* 15°55N 120°20E **232** D3
Pangfou = **Bengbu**
China 32°58N 117°20E **227** H9
Pangil
Dem. Rep. of the Congo 3°10S 26°35E **268** C2
Pangkah, Tanjung
Indonesia 6°51S 112°33E **235** D4
Pangkai *Burma* 22°40N 98°40E **241** D7
Pangkajene *Indonesia* 4°46S 119°34E **231** E5
Pangkalanbrandan
Indonesia 4°1N 98°20E **234** B1
Pangkalanbuun
Indonesia 2°41S 111°37E **235** C4
Pangkalansusu *Indonesia* 4°2N 98°13E **234** B1
Pangkalpinang *Indonesia* 2°0S 106°0E **234** C3
Pangkoh *Indonesia* 3°5S 114°8E **235** C4
Pangkor, P. *Malaysia* 4°13N 100°34E **237** K3
Panglao *Phil.* 9°35N 123°45E **233** G4
Panglao I. *Phil.* 9°35N 123°48E **233** G4
Pangniqtuuq = **Pangnirtung**
Canada 66°8N 65°43W **295** D18
Pangnirtung *Canada* 66°8N 65°43W **295** D18
Pango Alucuem *Angola* 8°43S 14°33E **265** D2
Pangody *Russia* 65°52N 74°27E **214** C8
Pangong Tso = **Bangong Co**
China 33°45N 78°43E **243** C8
Pangrango *Indonesia* 6°46S 107°1E **234** D3
Pangrati *Greece* 37°56N 23°45E **112** B2
Pangsau Pass *Burma* 27°15N 96°10E **241** B6
Pangsua, Sungei ➔
Singapore 1°25N 103°45E **138** A2
Pangtara *Burma* 20°57N 96°40E **241** E6
Panguipulli *Chile* 39°38S 72°20W **336** A2
Panguitch *U.S.A.* 37°50N 112°26W **305** H7
Panguna *Papua N. G.* 6°21S 155°25E **286** D8
Pangutaran *Phil.* 6°18N 120°35E **233** H3
Pangutaran Group *Phil.* 6°18N 120°34E **233** H3
Panhala *India* 16°49N 74°7E **244** F2
Panhandle *U.S.A.* 35°21N 101°23W **314** D4
Pani Mines *India* 22°29N 73°50E **242** H5
Pania-Mutombo
Dem. Rep. of the Congo 5°11S 23°51E **265** D4
Pāni'au *U.S.A.* 21°56N 160°5W **302** B1
Panié, Mt. *N. Cal.* 20°36S 164°46E **288** d
Panihati *India* 22°41N 88°22E **124** A2
Panikota I. *India* 20°46N 71°21E **242** J4
Panipat *India* 29°25N 77°2E **242** E7
Panitan *Phil.* 11°28N 122°46E **233** F4
Panj = **Pyandzh** ➔ *Asia* 37°6N 68°20E **240** A2
Panjab *Afghan.* 34°23N 67°1E **240** B2
Panjakent = **Pendzhikent**
Tajikistan 39°29N 67°37E **217** E7
Panjal Range = **Pir Panjal Range**
India 32°30N 76°50E **242** C7
Panjang, Bukit *Singapore* 1°22N 103°45E **138** A2
Panjang, Hon *Vietnam* 9°20N 103°28E **237** H4
Panjgur *Pakistan* 27°0N 64°5E **240** D2
Panjhra ➔ *India* 21°13N 74°57E **244** D2
Panjim = **Panaji** *India* 15°25N 73°50E **245** G1
Panjin *China* 41°3N 122°2E **227** D12
Panjnad ➔ *Pakistan* 28°57N 70°30E **242** E4
Panjnad Barrage *Pakistan* 29°22N 71°15E **242** E4
Panjsher □ *Afghan.* 35°50N 69°45E **240** B3
Panjwai *Afghan.* 31°26N 65°27E **242** D1
Panke ➔ *Germany* 52°31N 13°24E **115** A3
Pankow *Germany* 52°34N 13°23E **115** A3
Pankshin *Nigeria* 9°16N 9°25E **263** D6
Panmunjŏm *N. Korea* 37°59N 126°38E **224** D3
Panna *India* 24°40N 80°15E **243** G9
Panna △ *India* 24°40N 80°0E **243** G8
Panna Hills *India* 24°40N 81°15E **243** G9
Pannawonica *Australia* 21°39S 116°19E **278** D2
Pannga, Tanjung
Indonesia 8°54S 116°2E **231** K19
Panngi *Vanuatu* 15°58S 168°12E **287** E6
Pano Akil *Pakistan* 27°51N 69°7E **242** F3
Pano Lefkara *Cyprus* 34°53N 33°20E **207** F9
Pano Panayia *Cyprus* 34°55N 32°38E **207** F8
Panora *U.S.A.* 41°42N 94°22W **310** C2
Panorama *Brazil* 21°21S 51°51W **335** A5
Panormos *Greece* 35°25N 24°41E **207** E5
Panruti *India* 11°46N 79°35E **245** J4
Pansemal *India* 21°39N 74°42E **242** J6
Panshan = **Panjin** *China* 41°3N 122°2E **227** D12
Panshi *China* 42°58N 126°5E **227** C14
Pantanal Matogrossense △
Brazil 17°35S 57°27W **331** D6
Pantanaw *Burma* 16°59N 95°28E **241** G5
Pantanos de Centla ⌂
Mexico 18°25N 92°25W **319** D6
Pantar *Indonesia* 8°28S 124°10E **231** F6
Pante Macassar *E. Timor* 9°30S 123°58E **231** F6
Pantelleria *Italy* 36°50N 11°57E **200** F4
Panthéon *Paris, France* **134** c4
Pantheon *Rome, Italy* **136** b2
Panthersville *U.S.A.* 33°43N 84°16W **113** B3
Pantin *France* 48°53N 2°24E **134** A3
Pantin Sakan *Burma* 18°38N 97°33E **241** F6
Pantitlán *Mexico* 19°24N 99°4W **128** B2
Pantoja *Peru* 0°58S 75°10W **328** D2
Pantón *Spain* 42°31N 7°37W **196** C3
Pantukan *Phil.* 7°9N 125°54E **233** H5
Panu *Dem. Rep. of the Congo* 3°50S 19°10E **264** C3
Pánuco *Mexico* 22°3N 98°10W **319** C5
Panukulan *Phil.* 14°56N 121°49E **232** D3
Panvel *India* 18°59N 73°4E **244** E1
Panyam *Nigeria* 9°27N 9°8E **263** D6
Panyu = **Guangzhou**
China 23°6N 113°13E **121** B2
Panyu *Guangdong, China* 23°1N 113°21E **121** B2
Panyu *Guangdong, China* 22°51N 113°20E **229** F9
Panzhihua *China* 26°33N 101°44E **228** D3
Panzi *Dem. Rep. of the Congo* 7°17S 18°1E **265** D3
Pao ➔ *Anzoátegui, Venezuela* 8°6N 64°17W **329** B5
Pao ➔ *Apure, Venezuela* 8°33N 68°1W **328** B4
Paochi = **Baoji** *China* 34°20N 107°5E **226** G4
Paoki = **Baoji** *China* 34°20N 107°5E **226** G4
Páola *Italy* 39°21N 16°2E **201** C9
Paola *Malta* 35°52N 14°30E **206** F8
Paola *Kans., U.S.A.* 38°35N 94°53W **308** F6
Paoli *U.S.A.* 38°33N 86°28W **311** F10

Paonia U.S.A. 38°52N 107°36W 304 G10
Paopao Moorea 17°30S 149°49W 289 e
Paoting = Baoding China 38°50N 115°28E 226 E8
Paot'ou = Baotou China 40°32N 110°2E 226 D6
Paoua C.A.R. 7°9N 16°20E 264 A3
Pápa Hungary 47°22N 17°30E 182 C2
Pāpā Hawai'i, U.S.A. 19°13N 155°52W 302 D6
Papa Stour U.K. 60°20N 1°42W 167 A7
Papa Westray U.K. 59°20N 2°55W 167 B6
Pāpa'aloa U.S.A. 19°59N 155°13W 302 D6
Papagayo → Mexico 16°46N 99°43W 319 D5
Papagayo, G. de Costa Rica 10°30N 85°50W 320 D2
Papagni → India 15°35N 77°45E 245 G3
Papahānaumokuākea Marine Nat. Monument U.S.A. 25°25N 170°35W 302 F9
Papaïchton Fr. Guiana 3°48N 54°10W 329 C7
Pāpa'ikou U.S.A. 19°47N 155°6W 302 D6
Papakura N.Z. 37°4S 174°59E 284 D3
Papantla Mexico 20°27N 97°19W 319 C5
Papar Malaysia 5°45N 116°0E 235 A5
Papara Tahiti 17°43S 149°31W 289 e
Paparangi N.Z. 41°12S 174°48E 143 B1
Paparoa N.Z. 36°6S 174°16E 284 C3
Paparoa △ N.Z. 42°7S 171°26E 285 C6
Paparoa Ra. N.Z. 42°5S 171°35E 285 C6
Papas, Akra Greece 38°13N 21°20E 204 C3
Papatoetoe N.Z. 36°59S 174°51E 284 C3
Papatura Solomon Is. 7°32S 158°47E 287 L10
Papeete Tahiti 17°32S 149°34W 289 e
Papenburg Germany 53°5N 7°23E 178 B3
Papenoo Tahiti 17°30S 149°25W 289 e
Papenoo → Tahiti 17°30S 149°25W 289 e
Papetoai Moorea 17°29S 149°52W 289 e
Paphlagonia Turkey 41°30N 33°0E 212 B5
Paphos Cyprus 34°46N 32°25E 207 F8
Paphos ✕ (PFO) Cyprus 34°43N 32°30E 207 F8
Papien Chiang = Da → Vietnam 21°15N 105°20E 228 G5
Papikio Oros Greece 41°15N 25°13E 203 E9
Papiol Spain 41°25N 2°0E 114 A1
Paposo Chile 25°0S 70°30W 334 B1
Papoutsa Cyprus 34°54N 33°4E 207 F9
Papua □ Indonesia 4°0S 137°0E 231 E9
Papua, G. of Papua N. G. 9°0S 144°50E 286 E3
Papua New Guinea ■ Oceania 8°0S 145°0E 286 E3
Papudo Chile 32°29S 71°27W 334 C1
Papuk Croatia 45°30N 17°30E 182 E2
Papun Burma 18°2N 97°30E 241 F6
Papunya Australia 23°15S 131°54E 278 D5
Pará = Belém Brazil 1°20S 48°30W 332 B2
Pará □ Brazil 3°20S 52°0W 331 A7
Paraburdoo Australia 23°14S 117°32E 278 D2
Paracale Phil. 14°17N 122°48E 232 D4
Paracas, Pen. de Peru 13°53S 76°20W 330 C2
Paracatu Brazil 17°10S 46°50W 333 E2
Paracatu → Brazil 16°30S 45°4W 333 E2
Paracel Is. S. China Sea 15°50N 112°0E 230 A4
Parachilna Australia 31°10S 138°21E 282 A3
Parachinar Pakistan 33°55N 70°5E 242 C4
Paraćin Serbia 43°54N 21°27E 202 C5
Paracuru Brazil 3°24S 39°4W 332 B4
Parada, Punta Peru 15°22S 75°11W 330 D2
Paradas Spain 37°18N 5°29W 195 H5
Paradela Spain 42°44N 7°37W 194 C3
Paradera Aruba 12°32N 70°0W 322 f
Paradip India 20°15N 86°35E 244 D8
Paradise Calif., U.S.A. 39°46N 121°37W 306 F5
Paradise Nev., U.S.A. 36°5N 115°8W 124 B2
Paradise → Canada 53°27N 57°19W 299 B8
Paradise Hill Canada 53°32N 109°28W 297 C7
Paradise I. Bahamas 25°6N 77°19W 153 b
Paradise River Canada 53°27N 57°17W 299 B8
Paradise Valley U.S.A. 41°30N 117°32W 304 F5
Paradisi Greece 36°18N 28°7E 206 E12
Parado Indonesia 8°42S 118°30E 235 D5
Paragould U.S.A. 36°3N 90°29W 315 C9
Paragua = Palawan Phil. 9°30N 118°30E 233 G2
Paraguá → Bolivia 13°34S 61°53W 331 C5
Paragua → Venezuela 6°55N 62°55W 329 B5
Paraguaçu = Paraguaçu Paulista Brazil 22°22S 50°35W 335 A5
Paraguaçu → Brazil 12°45S 38°54W 333 D4
Paraguaçu Paulista Brazil 22°22S 50°35W 335 A5
Paraguaipoa Venezuela 11°21N 71°57W 328 A3
Paraguaná, Pen. de Venezuela 12°0N 70°0W 328 A4
Paraguarí Paraguay 25°36S 57°0W 334 B4
Paraguarí □ Paraguay 26°0S 57°10W 334 B4
Paraguay ■ S. Amer. 23°0S 57°0W 334 A4
Paraguay → Paraguay 27°18S 58°38W 334 B4
Paraíba = João Pessoa Brazil 7°10S 34°52W 332 C5
Paraíba □ Brazil 7°0S 36°0W 332 C4
Paraíba do Sul → Brazil 21°37S 41°3W 333 F3
Parainen Finland 60°18N 22°18E 188 B2
Paraiso Brazil 19°3S 52°59W 331 D7
Paraíso Tabasco, Mexico 18°24N 93°14W 319 D6
Paraiso Panama 9°3N 79°38W 320 c
Parak Iran 27°38N 52°25E 247 E7
Parakhino Paddubye Russia 58°26N 33°10E 188 C7
Parakou Benin 9°25N 2°40E 263 D5
Parakylia Australia 30°24S 136°25E 282 A2
Paralimni Cyprus 35°2N 33°58E 207 E9
Paralio Astros Greece 37°25N 22°45E 204 D4
Paralkote India 19°47N 80°41E 244 E5
Param I. Micronesia 7°22N 151°47E 287 T18
Parama I. Papua N. G. 9°0S 143°25E 286 E2
Paramaribo Suriname 5°50N 55°10W 329 B6
Parambu Brazil 6°13S 40°43W 332 C3
Paramillo, Cerro Colombia 7°4N 75°55W 328 B2
Paramillo △ Colombia 7°37N 76°13W 328 B2
Paramirim Brazil 13°26S 42°15W 333 D3
Paramirim → Brazil 11°34S 43°18W 333 D3
Paramithia Greece 39°30N 20°35E 204 B2
Paramonga Peru 10°40S 77°50W 330 C2
Paramount Studios U.S.A. 34°5N 118°19W 126 B3
Paramus U.S.A. 40°56N 74°2W 132 A1
Paramushir, Ostrov Russia 50°24N 156°0E 215 D16
Paran → Israel 30°20N 35°10E 251 H6
Paraná Argentina 31°45S 60°30W 334 C3
Paraná Brazil 12°30S 47°48W 333 D2
Paraná □ Brazil 24°30S 51°0W 335 A5
Paraná → Argentina 33°43S 59°15W 334 C4
Paraná → Brazil 12°30S 48°14W 333 D2
Paranaguá Brazil 25°30S 48°30W 335 B6
Paranaíba Brazil 19°40S 51°11W 331 D7
Paranaíba → Brazil 20°6S 51°4W 333 F1
Paranapanema → Brazil 22°40S 53°9W 335 A5
Paranapiacaba, Serra do Brazil 24°31S 48°35W 335 A6
Paranaque Phil. 14°30N 120°59E 127 B1
Paranas Phil. 11°42N 125°2E 233 F5
Paranavaí Brazil 23°4S 52°56W 335 A5
Parang Maguindanao, Phil. 7°23N 124°16E 233 H5
Parang Sulu, Phil. 5°55N 120°54E 233 J3
Parangippettai India 11°30N 79°38E 245 J4
Parângul Mare, Vf. Romania 45°20N 23°37E 183 E8
Paranthan Sri Lanka 9°26N 80°24E 245 K5
Paraoa French Polynesia 19°9S 140°43W 289 f
Paraparaumu N.Z. 40°57S 175°3E 284 G4
Parapetí → Bolivia 18°58S 62°21W 331 D5
Paraspori, Akra Greece 35°55N 27°15E 205 F9
Paratinga Brazil 12°40S 43°10W 333 D3
Paratoo Australia 32°42S 139°20E 282 B3
Paraúna Brazil 16°55S 50°26W 333 E1
Paray-le-Monial France 46°27N 4°7E 173 F11
Paray-Vieille-Poste France 48°42N 2°20E 134 B3
Parbati → Mad. P., India 25°50N 76°30E 242 G7
Parbati → Raj., India 26°54N 77°53E 242 F7
Parbatipur Bangla. 25°39N 88°55E 241 C2
Parbhani India 19°8N 76°52E 244 E3
Parchim Germany 53°26N 11°52E 178 B7
Parchwitz = Prochowice Poland 51°17N 16°20E 185 G3
Parco = Sinclair U.S.A. 41°47N 107°7W 304 F10
Parczew Poland 51°40N 22°52E 185 G9
Pardes Hanna-Karkur Israel 32°28N 34°57E 251 F5
Pardilla Spain 41°33N 3°43W 194 D7
Pardisān Nature Park Iran 35°44N 51°22E 141 A2
Pardo → Bahia, Brazil 15°40S 39°0W 333 E4
Pardo → Mato Grosso, Brazil 21°46S 52°9W 335 A5
Pardo → Minas Gerais, Brazil 15°48S 44°48W 333 E3
Pardo → São Paulo, Brazil 20°10S 48°38W 333 F2
Pardoo Roadhouse Australia 20°6S 119°3E 278 D2
Pardubice Czech Rep. 50°3N 15°45E 180 A8
Pardubický □ Czech Rep. 49°50N 16°0E 180 B8
Pardubitz = Pardubice Czech Rep. 50°3N 15°45E 180 A8
Pare Indonesia 7°43S 112°12E 235 D4
Pare Mts. Tanzania 4°0S 37°45E 268 C4
Parecis, Serra dos Brazil 13°0S 60°0W 331 C6
Paredes de Nava Spain 42°9N 4°42W 194 C6
Parel India 18°59N 72°49E 130 B1
Parelhas Brazil 6°41S 36°39W 332 C4
Paren Russia 62°30N 163°15E 215 C17
Parenda India 18°16N 75°28E 244 E2
Parengarenga Harbour N.Z. 34°31S 173°0E 284 A2
Parent Canada 47°55N 74°35W 298 C5
Parent, L. Canada 48°31N 77°1W 298 C4
Parentis-en-Born France 44°21N 1°4W 174 D2
Parepare Indonesia 4°0S 119°40E 231 E5
Parfino Russia 57°59N 31°34E 188 D6
Parga Greece 39°15N 20°29E 204 B2
Pargas = Parainen Finland 60°18N 22°18E 188 B2
Pargi India 17°11N 77°53E 244 E3
Pargo, Pta. do Madeira 32°49N 17°17W 153 c
Parguera Puerto Rico 17°59N 67°3W 321 b
Parham Canada 44°39N 76°43W 313 B8
Pari Brazil 23°32S 46°36W 137 B2
Paria → U.S.A. 36°52N 111°36W 305 H8
Paria, G. de Venezuela 10°20N 62°0W 323 t
Paria, Pen. de Venezuela 10°50N 62°30W 329 A5
Pariaguán Venezuela 8°51N 64°34W 329 B5
Pariaman Indonesia 0°47S 100°11E 234 C2
Paricatuba Brazil 4°26S 61°53W 329 D5
Paricutín, Cerro Mexico 19°28N 102°15W 318 D4
Parigi Java, Indonesia 7°42S 108°29E 235 D3
Parigi Sulawesi, Indonesia 0°50S 120°5E 231 E6
Parika Guyana 6°50N 58°20W 329 B6
Parikkia Greece 37°6N 25°11E 205 D7
Parikkala Finland 61°33N 29°31E 188 B5
Parima, Serra Brazil 2°30N 64°0W 329 C5
Parinari Peru 4°35S 74°25W 330 A3
Pariñas, Pta. Peru 4°30S 82°0W 330 A1
Parincea Romania 46°27N 27°9E 183 D12
Paringa Australia 34°10S 140°46E 282 C4
Parintins Brazil 2°40S 56°50W 329 D6
Parioli Italy 41°55N 12°29E 136 B1
Pariparit Kyun Burma 14°52N 93°41E 245 G11
Paris Ont., Canada 43°12N 80°25W 312 C4
Paris Paris, France 48°53N 2°20E 134 A3
Paris Idaho, U.S.A. 42°14N 111°24W 304 E8
Paris Ill., U.S.A. 39°36N 87°42W 311 E9
Paris Ky., U.S.A. 38°13N 84°15W 311 F12
Paris Mo., U.S.A. 39°29N 92°0W 310 E5
Paris Tenn., U.S.A. 36°18N 88°19W 315 C10
Paris Tex., U.S.A. 33°40N 95°33W 314 E7
Paris, Ville de □ France 48°50N 2°20E 173 D9
Paris Charles de Gaulle ✕ (CDG) France 49°0N 2°32E 173 D9
Paris Orly ✕ (ORY) France 48°44N 2°23E 134 B3
Parish U.S.A. 43°25N 76°8W 313 C8
Parishville U.S.A. 44°38N 74°49W 313 B10
Pariti Indonesia 10°1S 123°45E 278 B3
Parjé India 18°54N 72°57E 130 B2
Park U.S.A. 48°45N 122°18W 306 B4
Park City U.S.A. 37°48N 97°20W 308 G5
Pārk-e Āzādegān Iran 35°37N 51°28E 141 B2
Pārk-e Mellat Iran 35°47N 51°24E 141 A2
Park Falls U.S.A. 45°56N 90°27W 308 C8
Park Forest U.S.A. 41°29N 87°40W 311 C9
Park Head Canada 44°36N 81°9W 312 B3
Park Hills U.S.A. 37°51N 90°51W 310 G6
Park Range U.S.A. 40°41N 106°41W 304 F10
Park Rapids U.S.A. 46°55N 95°4W 308 B6
Park Ridge U.S.A. 42°2N 87°51W 119 A1
Park River U.S.A. 48°24N 97°45W 308 A5
Park Royal U.K. 51°31N 0°16W 125 A2
Park Rynie S. Africa 30°25S 30°45E 271 D5
Parka Bandar Iran 25°55N 59°35E 247 E8
Parkal India 18°12N 79°43E 244 E4
Parkán = Štúrovo Slovak Rep. 47°48N 18°41E 181 D11
Parkano Finland 62°1N 23°0E 188 A2
Parkchester U.S.A. 40°49N 73°50W 132 B2
Parkdale Canada 43°38N 79°25W 141 B2
Parkent Uzbekistan 41°18N 69°40E 217 D7
Parker Ariz., U.S.A. 34°9N 114°17W 307 L12
Parker Pa., U.S.A. 41°5N 79°41W 312 E5
Parker Center Los Angeles, U.S.A. 127 b2
Parker Dam U.S.A. 34°18N 114°8W 307 L12
Parkersburg Iowa, U.S.A. 42°35N 92°47W 310 B4
Parkersburg W. Va., U.S.A. 39°16N 81°34W 309 F13
Parkes Australia 33°9S 148°11E 283 B8
Parkfield U.S.A. 35°54N 120°26W 306 K6
Parkhill Canada 43°15N 81°38W 312 C3
Parkhurst S. Africa 26°8S 28°1E 123 A2
Parkland U.S.A. 47°9N 122°26W 306 C4
Parklawn U.S.A. 38°50N 77°7W 143 B3
Parkmore S. Africa 26°5S 28°2E 123 A2
Parkside U.S.A. 37°44N 122°29W 136 B2
Parkston U.S.A. 43°24N 97°59W 308 D5
Parksville Canada 49°20N 124°21W 296 D4
Parktown S. Africa 26°10S 28°2E 123 B2
Parkview S. Africa 26°9S 28°1E 123 A2
Parkville U.S.A. 39°22N 76°32W 144 A2
Parkway U.S.A. 38°32N 121°26W 306 G5
Parkwood Gauteng, S. Africa 26°9S 28°2E 123 A2
Parkwood Western Cape, S. Africa 34°2S 18°30E 118 B1
Parla Spain 40°14N 3°46W 194 E7
Parlakimidi India 18°45N 84°5E 244 E7
Parlatuvier Trin. & Tob. 11°18N 60°39W 323 s
Parli India 18°50N 76°35E 244 E3
Parliament Budapest, Hungary 117 b2
Pârliţa Moldova 47°19N 27°52E 183 C12
Parma Italy 44°48N 10°20E 198 D7
Parma Idaho, U.S.A. 43°47N 116°57W 304 E5
Parma Ohio, U.S.A. 41°24N 81°43W 312 E3
Parma → Italy 44°56N 10°26E 198 D7
Parnaguá Brazil 10°10S 44°38W 332 D3
Parnaíba Brazil 2°54S 41°47W 332 B3
Parnaíba → Brazil 3°0S 41°50W 332 B3
Parnamirim Pernambuco, Brazil 8°5S 39°34W 332 C4
Parnamirim Rio Grande do N., Brazil 5°55S 35°15W 332 C4
Parnarama Brazil 5°31S 43°6W 332 C3
Parnassos Greece 38°35N 22°30E 204 C4
Parnassus N.Z. 42°42S 173°23E 285 C8
Parndana Australia 35°48S 137°12E 282 C2
Parner India 19°0N 74°26E 244 E2
Parnitha Greece 38°14N 23°45E 204 C5
Parnitha △ Greece 38°12N 23°44E 204 C5
Parnonas Oros Greece 37°15N 22°45E 204 D4
Pärnu Estonia 58°28N 24°33E 188 C3
Paro Dzong Bhutan 27°32N 89°53E 241 B2
Parola India 20°47N 75°7E 244 D2
Paroo → Australia 31°28S 143°32E 282 A5
Paros Greece 37°5N 25°12E 205 D7
Parow S. Africa 33°53S 18°37E 118 A2
Parowan U.S.A. 37°51N 112°50W 305 H7
Parpaillon France 44°30N 6°40E 175 D10
Parque Chacabuco Argentina 34°39S 58°26W 117 B2
Parque Patricios Argentina 34°39S 58°23W 117 B2
Parral Chile 36°10S 71°52W 334 D1
Parramatta Australia 33°48S 151°1E 283 B9
Parramatta → Australia 33°49S 151°3E 139 A1
Parras Mexico 25°25N 102°11W 318 B4
Parrett → U.K. 51°12N 3°1W 169 F4
Parris I. U.S.A. 32°20N 80°41W 316 C9
Parrish U.S.A. 27°35N 82°26W 317 H7
Parrsboro Canada 45°30N 64°25W 299 C7
Parry Channel Canada 74°15N 94°0W 295 C13
Parry I. Canada 45°18N 80°10W 312 A4
Parry Is. Canada 77°0N 110°0W 295 B10
Parry Sound Canada 45°20N 80°0W 312 A5
Parsābād Iran 39°39N 48°16E 213 C13
Parsaloi Kenya 1°16N 36°51E 268 B4
Parsberg Germany 49°10N 11°43E 179 F7
Parsęta → Poland 54°11N 15°34E 184 D2
Parsnip → Canada 55°10N 123°2W 296 B4
Parsons U.S.A. 37°20N 95°16W 308 G6
Parsons Ra. Australia 13°30S 135°15E 280 A2
Partabpur India 20°0N 80°42E 244 E5
Partanna Italy 37°43N 12°53E 200 E5
Partenio △ Italy 40°56N 14°38E 201 B7
Parthenay France 46°38N 0°16W 172 F6
Parthenon Athens, Greece 112 c2
Partinico Italy 38°3N 13°7E 200 D6
Partizansk Russia 43°8N 133°9E 220 C6
Partizánske Slovak Rep. 48°38N 18°23E 181 C11
Partridge I. Canada 55°59N 87°37W 298 A2
Partry Mts. Ireland 53°40N 9°28W 166 C2
Paru → Brazil 19°40N 76°14E 244 E3
Paru → Brazil 1°33S 52°38W 329 D7
Parú → Venezuela 4°20N 66°27W 328 C4
Paru de Oeste → Brazil 1°30N 56°0W 329 C6
Parucito → Venezuela 5°18N 65°59W 328 B4
Parur India 10°13N 76°14E 245 J3
Paruro Peru 13°45S 71°50W 330 C3
Parvān □ Afghan. 35°0N 69°0E 240 B3
Parvatipuram India 18°50N 83°25E 244 E6
Parvatsar India 26°52N 74°49E 242 F6
Påryd Sweden 56°34N 15°55E 163 H9
Parys S. Africa 26°54S 27°27E 271 C4
Pas, Pta. des Spain 38°46N 1°26E 206 D1
Pas, The Canada 53°45N 101°15W 297 C8
Pas-de-Calais □ France 50°30N 2°10E 173 B9
Paşabahçe Turkey 41°6N 29°5E 122 B2
Pasada Spain 43°23N 5°40W 194 B5
Pasadena Nfld. & L., Canada 49°1N 57°36W 299 C8
Pasadena Calif., U.S.A. 34°9N 118°8W 126 B4
Pasadena Tex., U.S.A. 29°43N 95°13W 314 G7
Pasaje Ecuador 3°23S 79°50W 328 D2
Pasaje → Argentina 25°39S 63°56W 334 B3
Paşalimanı Turkey 40°29N 27°36E 203 F11
Pasar Indonesia 8°27S 114°54E 231 J17
Pasar Minggu Indonesia 6°16S 106°49E 122 B1
Pasay Phil. 14°32N 120°59E 127 B1
Pascagoula U.S.A. 30°21N 88°33W 315 F10
Pascagoula → U.S.A. 30°23N 88°37W 315 F10
Paşcani Romania 47°14N 26°45E 183 C11
Pasco U.S.A. 46°14N 119°6W 304 C4
Pasco □ Peru 10°40S 75°0W 330 C2
Pasco I. Australia 20°57S 115°20E 278 D2
Pascoag U.S.A. 41°57N 71°42W 313 E13
Pascoe Vale Australia 37°43S 144°55E 128 A1
Pascua, I. de Chile 27°7S 109°23W 330 b
Paseo de la Reforma Mexico City, Mexico 128 b2
Pasewalk Germany 53°30N 13°58E 178 B9
Pasfield L. Canada 58°24N 105°20W 297 B7
Pasha → Russia 60°29N 32°55E 188 B7
Pashmakli = Smolyan Bulgaria 41°36N 24°38E 203 E8
Pasig Phil. 14°33N 121°4E 127 B2
Pasig → Phil. 14°31N 121°6E 127 B2
Pasighat India 28°4N 95°21E 241 A5
Pasila Finland 60°12N 24°56E 121 B2
Pasing Germany 48°8N 11°28E 131 B1
Pasinler Turkey 39°59N 41°41E 213 C9
Pasir Mas Malaysia 6°2N 102°8E 237 J4
Pasir Panjang Singapore 1°18N 103°46E 138 B2
Pasir Putih Malaysia 5°50N 102°24E 237 K4
Pasir Ris Singapore 1°22N 103°56E 138 A3
Pasirian Indonesia 8°13S 113°8E 235 D4
Pasirkuning Indonesia 0°30S 104°33E 234 C2
Påskallavik Sweden 57°10N 16°26E 163 G10
Paskūh Iran 27°34N 61°39E 247 E9
Pasłęk Poland 54°3N 19°41E 184 D6
Pasłęka → Poland 54°26N 19°46E 184 D6
Pasley, C. Australia 33°52S 123°35E 279 F3
Pašman Croatia 43°58N 15°20E 199 E12
Pasmore → Australia 31°5S 139°49E 282 A3
Pasni Pakistan 25°15N 63°27E 240 D1
Paso Bravo △ Paraguay 22°32S 57°5W 334 A4
Paso Cantinela Mexico 32°33N 115°47W 307 N11
Paso de Indios Argentina 43°55S 69°0W 336 B3
Paso de los Indios Argentina 38°32S 69°25W 336 A3
Paso de los Libres Argentina 29°44S 57°10W 334 B4
Paso de los Toros Uruguay 32°45S 56°30W 334 C4
Paso Flores Argentina 40°35S 70°38W 336 B2
Paso Robles U.S.A. 35°38N 120°41W 306 K6
Pasorapa Bolivia 18°16S 64°37W 331 D5
Paspébiac Canada 48°3N 65°17W 299 C6
Pasrur Pakistan 32°16N 74°43E 242 C6
Passage East Ireland 52°14N 7°0W 166 D5
Passage West Ireland 51°52N 8°21W 166 E3
Passaic U.S.A. 40°51N 74°7W 132 A1
Passaic → U.S.A. 40°42N 74°10W 132 B1
Passam Papua N. G. 3°41S 143°38E 286 B2
Passau Germany 48°34N 13°28E 179 G9
Passenheim = Pasym Poland 53°48N 20°49E 184 E7
Passero, C. Italy 36°41N 15°10E 201 F8
Passi Phil. 11°6N 122°38E 233 F4
Passirana Italy 45°32N 9°2E 129 A1
Passo Fundo Brazil 28°10S 52°20W 335 B5
Passos Brazil 20°45S 46°37W 333 F2
Passow Germany 53°8N 14°6E 178 B10
Passy France 45°55N 6°41E 175 C10
Pastavy Belarus 55°4N 26°50E 188 E4
Pastaza □ Ecuador 2°0S 77°0W 328 D2
Pastaza → Peru 4°50S 76°52W 328 D2
Pasto Colombia 1°13N 77°17W 328 C2
Pastol B. U.S.A. 63°7N 163°15W 303 E7
Pastos Bons Brazil 6°36S 44°5W 332 C3
Pastrana Spain 40°27N 2°53W 196 E2
Pasuquin Phil. 18°20N 120°37E 232 B3
Pasuruan Indonesia 7°40S 112°44E 235 D4
Pasym Poland 53°48N 20°49E 184 E7
Pásztó Hungary 47°52N 19°43E 182 C4
Pata Phil. 5°51N 121°10E 233 J3
Pata I. Phil. 5°49N 121°10E 233 J3
Patagonia Argentina 45°0S 69°0W 336 C3
Patagonia Ariz., U.S.A. 31°33N 110°45W 305 L8
Patambar Iran 29°45N 60°17E 247 D9
Patan = Lalitapur Nepal 27°40N 85°20E 243 F11
Patan = Somnath India 20°53N 70°22E 242 J4
Patan Gujarat, India 23°54N 72°14E 242 H5
Patan Maharashtra, India 17°22N 73°57E 244 F1
Patani Indonesia 0°20N 128°50E 231 D7
Pătârlagele Romania 45°19N 26°21E 183 E11
Pataudi India 28°18N 76°48E 242 E7
Patchewollock Australia 35°22S 142°12E 282 C5
Patchogue U.S.A. 40°46N 73°1W 313 F11
Pate Coast, Kenya 2°10S 41°0E 268 C5
Pate Taiwan 24°56N 121°17E 225 B3
Patea N.Z. 39°45S 174°30E 284 F3
Pategi Nigeria 8°50N 5°45E 263 D6
Patel Nagar India 28°39N 77°10E 120 B1
Patensie S. Africa 33°46S 24°49E 270 D3
Paterna Spain 39°30N 0°26W 197 F4
Paternion Austria 46°43N 13°38E 180 E6
Paternò Italy 37°34N 14°54E 201 E7
Pateros Manila, Phil. 14°32N 121°3E 127 B2
Pateros Wash., U.S.A. 48°3N 119°54W 304 B4
Paterson N.S.W., Australia 32°35S 151°36E 283 B9
Paterson N.J., U.S.A. 40°54N 74°9W 313 F10
Paterson Inlet N.Z. 46°56S 168°12E 285 G3
Paterson Ra. Australia 21°45S 122°10E 278 D3
Pathankot India 32°18N 75°45E 242 C6
Pathardi India 19°10N 75°11E 244 E2
Patharghata Bangla. 22°2N 89°58E 241 D2
Pathein = Bassein Burma 16°45N 94°30E 241 G5
Pathfinder Res. U.S.A. 42°28N 106°51W 304 E10
Pathiu Thailand 10°42N 99°19E 237 G2
Pathri India 19°15N 76°27E 244 E3
Pathum Thani Thailand 14°1N 100°32E 236 E3
Pathumwan Thailand 13°44N 100°31E 138 B2
Pati Indonesia 6°45S 111°1E 235 D4
Pati Pt. Guam 13°35N 144°57E 302 d
Patía Colombia 2°4N 77°4W 328 C2
Patía → Colombia 2°13N 78°40W 328 C2
Patiala Punjab, India 30°23N 76°26E 242 D7
Patiala Ut. P., India 27°43N 79°1E 243 F8
Patine Kouka Senegal 12°45N 13°45W 262 C2
Patipukur India 22°36N 88°24E 124 B2
Patisia Greece 38°2N 23°45E 112 A2
Patitiri Greece 39°8N 23°50E 204 B5
Patkai Bum India 27°0N 95°30E 241 B5
Patmos Greece 37°21N 26°36E 205 D8
Patna India 25°35N 85°12E 243 G11
Patnagarh India 20°43N 83°9E 244 D6
Patnanongan I. Phil. 14°48N 122°11E 232 D4
Patnongon Phil. 10°55N 122°0E 233 F4
Patnos Turkey 39°13N 42°51E 213 C10
Pato Branco Brazil 26°13S 52°40W 335 B5
Patoka L. U.S.A. 38°20N 86°40W 311 F10
Patong, Ao Thailand 7°54N 98°17E 237 a
Patonga Uganda 2°45N 33°15E 268 B3
Patos Albania 40°42N 19°38E 202 F3
Patos Brazil 6°55S 37°16W 332 C4
Patos, L. dos Brazil 31°20S 51°0W 335 C5
Patos, Río de los → Argentina 31°18S 69°25W 334 C2
Patos de Minas Brazil 18°35S 46°32W 333 E2
Patquía Argentina 30°2S 66°55W 334 C2
Patra Greece 38°14N 21°47E 204 C3
Patraikos Kolpos Greece 38°17N 21°30E 204 C3
Patras = Patra Greece 38°14N 21°47E 204 C3
Patreksfjörður Iceland 65°35N 24°0W 155 B2
Patriarsheye = Donskoy Russia 53°55N 38°15E 188 F10
Patricio Lynch, I. Chile 48°35S 75°30W 336 C1
Patriot Hills Antarctica 82°20S 81°25W 151 E16
Patrocínio Brazil 18°57S 47°0W 333 E2
Pattada Italy 40°35N 9°6E 200 B2
Pattani Thailand 6°48N 101°15E 237 J3
Pattaya Thailand 12°52N 100°55E 236 F3
Patten U.S.A. 46°0N 68°38W 309 B19
Patterson Calif., U.S.A. 37°28N 121°8W 306 H5
Patterson Ga., U.S.A. 31°23N 82°8W 316 D7
Patterson La., U.S.A. 29°42N 91°18W 314 G9
Patterson, Mt. U.S.A. 38°29N 119°20W 306 G7
Patteson, Passage Vanuatu 15°26S 168°12E 287 E6
Patti Punjab, India 31°17N 74°54E 242 D6
Patti Ut. P., India 25°55N 82°12E 243 G10
Patti Italy 38°8N 14°58E 201 D7
Pattoki Pakistan 31°5N 73°52E 242 D5
Patton = Monroeville U.S.A. 40°26N 79°45W 312 F5
Patton U.S.A. 40°38N 78°39W 312 F6
Pattonsburg U.S.A. 40°3N 94°8W 310 D2
Pattukkattai India 10°25N 79°20E 245 J4
Patu Brazil 6°6S 37°38W 332 C4
Patuakhali Bangla. 22°20N 90°25E 241 D3
Patuanak Canada 55°55N 107°43W 297 B7
Patuca → Honduras 15°50N 84°18W 320 C3
Patuca, Punta Honduras 15°49N 84°14W 320 C3
Patuca △ Honduras 14°30N 85°30W 320 D2
Pătulele Romania 44°21N 22°47E 182 F7
Patur India 20°27N 76°56E 244 D3
Patvinsuo △ Finland 63°7N 30°45E 160 E24
Pátzcuaro Mexico 19°31N 101°38W 318 D4
Pau France 43°19N 0°25W 174 E3
Pau, Gave de → France 43°33N 1°12W 174 E2
Pau d' Arco Brazil 7°30S 49°22W 332 C2
Pau dos Ferros Brazil 6°7S 38°10W 332 C4
Pauanui N.Z. 37°1S 175°52E 284 D4
Paucartambo Peru 13°19S 71°35W 330 C3
Paudash Canada 44°59N 77°58W 312 B7
Pauillac France 45°11N 0°46W 174 C3
Pauini Brazil 7°40S 66°58W 330 B4
Pauini → Brazil 1°42S 62°50W 329 D5
Pauk Burma 21°27N 94°30E 241 E5
Paukkaung Burma 18°54N 95°33E 241 F5
Paukphyu Burma 20°11N 93°54E 241 E4
Paul I. Canada 56°30N 61°20W 299 A7
Paul Isnard Fr. Guiana 4°47N 54°1W 329 C7
Paul Revere Park Boston, U.S.A. 116 a2
Paul Smiths U.S.A. 44°26N 74°15W 313 B10
Paulatuk Canada 69°25N 124°0W 294 D7
Paulding U.S.A. 41°8N 84°35W 311 C12
Paulding Bay S. Ocean 66°0S 118°0E 151 C8
Paulhan France 43°33N 3°28E 174 E7
Paulis = Isiro Dem. Rep. of the Congo 2°53N 27°40E 268 B2
Paulista = Paulistana Brazil 8°9S 41°9W 332 C3
Paulista Brazil 7°57S 34°53W 332 C5
Paulistana Brazil 8°9S 41°9W 332 C3
Paulo Afonso Brazil 9°21S 38°15W 332 C4
Paulo de Faria Brazil 20°2S 49°24W 333 F2
Paulo E. Virginia, Gruta Brazil 22°56S 43°16W 135 B1
Paulpietersburg S. Africa 27°23S 30°50E 271 C5
Pauls Valley U.S.A. 34°44N 97°13W 314 D6
Paulshof Germany 52°34N 13°42E 115 A5
Pauma Valley U.S.A. 33°16N 116°58W 307 M10
Paung Burma 16°37N 94°28E 241 G5
Paungde Burma 18°29N 95°30E 241 F5
Pauni India 20°48N 79°40E 244 D4
Pauri India 30°9N 78°47E 243 D8
Pausa Peru 15°16S 73°22W 330 D3
Pauto → Colombia 5°9N 70°55W 328 B3
Pavagada India 14°6N 77°16E 245 G3
Pāveh Iran 35°3N 46°22E 213 E12
Pavelets Russia 53°49N 39°14E 188 F10
Pavia Italy 45°7N 9°8E 198 C6
Pavilion U.S.A. 42°52N 78°1W 312 D6
Pavilly France 49°34N 0°57E 172 C7
Pāvilosta Latvia 56°53N 21°14E 184 B8
Pavlikeni Bulgaria 43°14N 25°20E 203 C9
Pavlodar Kazakhstan 52°33N 77°0E 217 B9
Pavlograd = Pavlohrad Ukraine 48°30N 35°52E 189 H8
Pavlohrad Ukraine 48°30N 35°52E 189 H8
Pavlovo Russia 55°58N 43°5E 190 C6
Pavlovsk Russia 50°26N 40°5E 190 E5
Pavlovskaya Russia 46°17N 39°47E 191 G4
Pavlovskiy-Posad Russia 55°47N 38°42E 188 E10
Pavo U.S.A. 30°58N 83°45W 316 E6
Pavshino Russia 55°49N 37°20E 129 B1
Pavullo nel Frignano Italy 44°20N 10°50E 198 D7
Pavuvu Solomon Is. 9°4S 159°8E 287 M10
Paw Paw Ill., U.S.A. 41°41N 88°59W 310 C8
Paw Paw Mich., U.S.A. 42°13N 85°53W 311 B11
Pawahku Burma 26°11N 98°40E 241 B7
Pawai, Pulau Singapore 1°11N 103°44E 237 d
Pawan → Indonesia 1°55S 110°0E 235 C4
Pawayan India 28°4N 80°6E 243 E9
Pawhuska U.S.A. 36°40N 96°20W 314 C6
Pawling U.S.A. 41°34N 73°36W 313 E11
Pawnee Ill., U.S.A. 39°36N 89°35W 310 E7
Pawnee Okla., U.S.A. 36°20N 96°48W 314 C6
Pawnee City U.S.A. 40°7N 96°9W 308 E5
Pawtucket U.S.A. 41°53N 71°23W 313 E13
Paxi Greece 39°14N 20°12E 206 C10
Paximadia Greece 35°0N 24°35E 207 F5
Paxson U.S.A. 63°2N 145°30W 303 E11
Paxton U.S.A. 40°27N 88°6W 311 D8
Paya Lebar Singapore 1°21N 103°52E 138 A3
Payagyi Burma 17°29N 96°32E 241 G6
Payakumbuh Indonesia 0°20S 100°35E 234 C2
Payapa = General Tinio Phil. 15°39N 121°10E 232 D3
Payas = Yakacık Turkey 36°46N 36°11E 250 B7
Payerne Switz. 46°49N 6°56E 179 J2
Payette U.S.A. 44°5N 116°56W 304 D5
Paymogo Spain 37°44N 7°21W 195 H3
Payne U.S.A. 41°5N 84°44W 311 C12
Payne Bay = Kangirsuk Canada 60°0N 70°0W 295 F18
Payne L. Canada 59°30N 74°30W 295 F17
Payne Pt. Ascension I. 7°57S 14°25W 153 g
Paynes Find Australia 29°15S 117°42E 279 E2
Paynesville Liberia 6°20N 10°45W 262 D2
Paynesville Minn., U.S.A. 45°23N 94°43W 308 C6
Payo Obispo = Chetumal Mexico 18°30N 88°20W 319 D7
Pays de la Loire □ France 47°45N 0°25W 172 E6
Paysandú Uruguay 32°19S 58°8W 334 C4
Payson Ariz., U.S.A. 34°14N 111°20W 305 J8
Payson Utah, U.S.A. 40°3N 111°44W 304 F8
Paz → Guatemala 13°44N 90°10W 320 D1
Paz, B. de la Mexico 24°9N 110°25W 318 C2
Pāzanān Iran 30°35N 49°59E 247 D6
Pazar Turkey 41°10N 40°50E 213 B9
Pazarcık Turkey 37°30N 37°17E 212 D7
Pazardzhik Bulgaria 42°12N 24°20E 203 D8
Pazarköy Turkey 39°51N 27°24E 205 B9
Pazarlar Turkey 39°0N 29°7E 205 C11
Pazaryeri Turkey 40°0N 29°56E 205 B11
Pazaryolu Turkey 40°21N 40°47E 213 B9
Pazin Croatia 45°14N 13°56E 199 C10
Pazña Bolivia 18°36S 66°55W 330 D4
Pčinja → Macedonia 41°50N 21°45E 202 E5
Pe Ell U.S.A. 46°34N 123°18W 306 D3
Pea → U.S.A. 31°1N 85°51W 316 D4
Peabody U.S.A. 42°31N 70°56W 313 D14
Peace → Alta., Canada 59°0N 111°25W 296 B6
Peace → Fla., U.S.A. 26°56N 82°6W 317 J7
Peace Point Canada 59°7N 112°27W 296 B6
Peace River Canada 56°15N 117°18W 296 B5
Peach Springs U.S.A. 35°32N 113°25W 305 J7
Peachland Canada 49°47N 119°45W 296 D5
Peachtree City U.S.A. 33°25N 84°35W 316 B5
Peacock Pt. Wake I. 19°16N 166°37E 302 b
Peak, The = Kinder Scout U.K. 53°24N 1°52W 168 D6
Peak, The Ascension I. 7°57S 14°20W 153 g
Peak Charles △ Australia 32°42S 121°10E 279 F3
Peak District △ U.K. 53°24N 1°46W 168 D6
Peak Hill Australia 32°47S 148°11E 283 B8
Peak Ra. Australia 22°50S 148°20E 280 C4
Peake Australia 35°25S 139°55E 282 C3
Peake Cr. → Australia 28°2S 136°7E 281 D2
Peakhurst Australia 33°57S 151°3E 139 B1
Peal de Becerro Spain 37°55N 3°7W 195 H7
Peale, Mt. U.S.A. 38°26N 109°14W 304 G9
Peale I. Wake I. 19°18N 166°37E 302 b
Peania Greece 37°56N 23°52E 112 B3
Pearblossom U.S.A. 34°30N 117°55W 307 L9
Pearl → U.S.A. 30°11N 89°32W 315 F10
Pearl and Hermes Reef U.S.A. 27°55N 175°45W 302 F8
Pearl Banks Sri Lanka 8°45N 79°45E 245 K4
Pearl City U.S.A. 21°24N 157°59W 302 K14
Pearl Harbor U.S.A. 21°21N 157°57W 302 K14
Pearl Harbor Nat. Wildlife Refuge △ U.S.A. 21°23N 157°59W 302 K14
Pearl River = Zhu Jiang → China 22°45N 113°37E 229 F9
Pearl River U.S.A. 41°4N 74°2W 313 E10
Pearls Grenada 12°9N 61°37W 323 q
Pearls Rock Grenada 12°9N 61°36W 323 q
Pearsall U.S.A. 28°54N 99°6W 314 G5
Pearson U.S.A. 31°18N 82°51W 316 D7
Pearson Int. Toronto ✕ (YYZ) Canada 43°46N 79°35W 141 A1
Peary Land Greenland 82°40N 33°0W 154 A7
Pease → U.S.A. 34°12N 99°2W 314 D5
Peawanuck Canada 55°15N 85°12W 298 A2
Pebane Mozam. 17°10S 38°8E 269 F4
Pebas Peru 3°10S 71°46W 328 D3
Pebble, I. Falk. Is. 51°20S 59°40W 153 f
Pebble Beach U.S.A. 36°34N 121°57W 306 J5
Peć Kosovo 42°40N 20°17E 202 D4
Peçanha Brazil 18°33S 42°34W 333 E3
Pecatonica U.S.A. 42°19N 89°22W 310 B7
Pecatonica → U.S.A. 42°26N 89°12W 310 B7
Péccioli Italy 43°33N 10°43E 198 E7
Pechea Romania 45°36N 27°49E 183 E12
Pechenga Russia 69°29N 31°4E 160 B24
Pechenizhyn Ukraine 48°30N 24°48E 183 B9
Pechiguera, Pta. Canary Is. 28°51N 13°53W 153 e2
Pechnezhskoye Vdkhr. Ukraine 50°5N 36°54E 189 G9
Pechora Russia 65°10N 57°11E 186 A10
Pechora → Russia 68°13N 54°15E 186 A9
Pechorskaya Guba Russia 68°40N 54°0E 186 A9
Pechory Russia 57°48N 27°40E 188 D4
Pecica Romania 46°10N 21°3E 182 D6
Pecka Serbia 44°18N 19°33E 202 B3
Peckham U.K. 51°28N 0°3W 125 B3
Pécora, C. Italy 39°27N 8°23E 200 C1
Pecos N. Mex., U.S.A. 35°35N 105°41W 305 J11
Pecos Tex., U.S.A. 31°26N 103°30W 314 F3
Pecos → U.S.A. 29°42N 101°22W 314 G4
Pécs Hungary 46°5N 18°15E 182 D3
Pedasí Panama 7°32N 80°2W 320 E3
Pedda Bellala India 19°4N 78°49E 244 E4
Peddapalli India 18°40N 79°24E 244 E4
Peddapuram India 17°6N 82°8E 244 F6
Pedder, L. Australia 42°55S 146°10E 281 G4
Peddie S. Africa 33°14S 27°7E 271 D4
Pedernales Dom. Rep. 18°2N 71°44W 321 C5
Pedernales Ecuador 0°5N 80°3W 328 C1
Pederstrup Denmark 55°44N 12°20E 118 A2
Pedieos → Cyprus 35°10N 33°54E 207 E9
Pedirka Desert Australia 26°47S 134°11E 281 A1
Pedra Azul Brazil 16°2S 41°17W 333 E3
Pedra Branca Brazil 0°51N 51°58W 329 C7
Pedra Grande, Recifes de Brazil 17°45S 38°58W 333 E4
Pedra Lume C. Verde Is. 16°40N 22°52W 153 j
Pedralbes Spain 41°23N 2°7E 114 A1
Pedras Negras Brazil 12°51S 62°54W 331 C5
Pedras Tinhosas, I. São Tomé & Príncipe 1°22N 7°17E 265 a
Pedregal de San Angel, Jardines del Mexico 19°19N 99°12W 128 C1
Pedreguer Spain 38°48N 0°3E 197 G5
Pedreiras Brazil 4°32S 44°40W 332 B3
Pedro Afonso Brazil 9°0S 48°10W 332 C2
Pedro Bank W. Indies 17°5N 78°20W 320 C4
Pedro Bay U.S.A. 59°47N 154°7W 303 G9
Pedro Cays Jamaica 17°5N 77°48W 320 C4
Pedro Chico Colombia 1°4N 70°25W 328 C3
Pedro de Valdivia Chile 22°55S 69°38W 334 A2
Pedro Dorado Colombia 1°0N 70°14W 328 C3
Pedro Juan Caballero Paraguay 22°30S 55°40W 335 A4
Pedro Miguel Locks Panama 9°1N 79°36W 320 c
Pedro Muñoz Spain 39°25N 2°56W 195 F8
Pedro Pt. = North West Pt. Jamaica 18°27N 78°13W 320 a
Pedrógão Grande Portugal 39°55N 8°9W 194 F2
Pee Dee = Great Pee Dee → U.S.A. 33°21N 79°10W 315 E15
Peebinga Australia 34°52S 140°57E 282 C4
Peebles Borders, U.K. 55°40N 3°11W 167 F5
Peebles Ohio, U.S.A. 38°57N 83°24W 311 F13
Peekskill U.S.A. 41°17N 73°55W 313 E11
Peel I. of Man 54°13N 4°40W 168 C3
Peel → N.S.W., Australia 30°50S 150°29E 283 A9
Peel → Canada 67°0N 135°0W 294 D5
Peel Sd. Canada 73°0N 96°0W 294 C12
Peene → Germany 54°9N 13°46E 178 A9
Peera Peera Poolanna L. Australia 26°30S 138°0E 281 D2
Peerless Lake Canada 56°37N 114°40W 296 B6
Peers Canada 53°40N 116°0W 296 C5
Peery L. Australia 30°45S 143°35E 282 A5
Pegasus Bay N.Z. 43°20S 173°10E 285 D8
Peggau Austria 47°12N 15°21E 180 D8
Pegnitz Germany 49°44N 11°31E 179 F7
Pegnitz → Germany 49°30N 10°59E 179 F6
Pego Spain 38°51N 0°8W 197 G4
Pegu Burma 17°20N 96°29E 241 G6
Pegu □ Burma 17°30N 96°30E 241 G6
Pegu Yoma Burma 19°0N 96°0E 241 F6
Peguera Spain 39°32N 2°26E 206 B3
Pehčevo Macedonia 41°41N 22°55E 202 E6
Pehlivanköy Turkey 41°20N 26°55E 203 E10
Pehuajó Argentina 35°45S 62°0W 334 D3
Pei Xian = Pizhou China 34°44N 116°55E 226 G9
Peian = Bei'an China 48°10N 126°20E 219 B7
Peihai = Beihai China 21°28N 109°6E 228 G7
Peikang Taiwan 23°34N 120°18E 225 C2
Peikang Hsi → Taiwan 24°2N 120°50E 225 B2
Peikant'ang Taiwan 26°13N 120°0E 225 b
Peimen Taiwan 23°16N 120°7E 225 C2
Peinan Taiwan 22°47N 121°7E 225 D3
Peinan Hsi → Taiwan 22°46N 121°10E 225 D3
Peinanhsu Shan Taiwan 23°3N 120°52E 225 C2
Peine Chile 23°45S 68°8W 334 A2
Peine Niedersachsen, Germany 52°19N 10°14E 178 C6
Pei'ping = Beijing China 39°53N 116°21E 114 B1
Peipu Taiwan 24°2N 121°36E 225 B3
Peipus, L. = Chudskoye, Ozero Russia 58°13N 27°30E 188 C4
Peissenberg Germany 47°48N 11°4E 179 H7
Peitawu Shan Taiwan 22°38N 120°46E 225 D2
Peitou Chinhua, Taiwan 23°52N 120°32E 225 C2
Peitou T'aipei, Taiwan 25°11N 121°27E 225 A3
Peitun Taiwan 24°10N 120°41E 225 B2
Peitz Germany 51°51N 14°24E 178 D10
Peixe Brazil 12°0S 48°40W 333 D2
Peixe → Brazil 21°31S 51°58W 333 F1
Peixoto de Azeredo → Brazil 10°6S 55°31W 331 C6
Pek → Serbia 44°45N 21°29E 202 B5
Pekalongan Indonesia 6°53S 109°40E 235 D3
Pekan Malaysia 3°30N 103°25E 237 L4
Pekan Nenas Malaysia 1°31N 103°31E 237 d
Pekanbaru Indonesia 0°30N 101°15E 234 B2
Pekhorka → Russia 55°37N 38°2E 129 C6
Pekhra-Pokrovskoye Russia 55°50N 37°56E 129 A5
Pekhra-Yakovlevskaya Russia 55°47N 37°57E 129 B5
Pekin U.S.A. 40°35N 89°40W 310 D7
Peking = Beijing China 39°53N 116°21E 114 B1
Pekutatan Indonesia 8°25S 114°49E 231 J17
Pela Greece 40°46N 22°23E 202 F6
Péla Guinea 7°37N 9°7W 262 D3
Pelabuhan Klang Malaysia 3°0N 101°23E 237 L3
Pelabuhan Ratu, Teluk Indonesia 7°5S 106°30E 234 D3
Pelabuhanratu Indonesia 7°0S 106°32E 234 D3
Pelagos = Kira Panagia Greece 39°17N 24°4E 204 B6
Pelaihari Indonesia 3°55S 114°45E 235 C4
Pelat, Mt. France 44°16N 6°42E 175 D10
Pelczyce Poland 53°3N 15°16E 185 E2
Peleaga, Vf. Romania 45°22N 22°55E 182 E7
Pelechuco Bolivia 14°48S 69°4W 330 C4
Pelée, Mt. Martinique 14°48N 61°10W 322 j
Pelee, Pt. Canada 41°54N 82°31W 298 D3

Pelee I. *Canada* 41°47N 82°40W **312** E2
Pelejo *Peru* 6°10S 75°49W **330** B2
Pelekech *Kenya* 3°52N 35°8E **268** B4
Peleliu I. *Palau* 7°1N 134°15E **288** c
Peleng *Indonesia* 1°20S 123°30E **231** E6
Pelenge *Dem. Rep. of the Congo* 2°44S 22°39E **264** C4
Pelentong *Malaysia* 1°32N 103°49E **237** d
Pélézi *Ivory C.* 7°17N 6°54W **262** D3
Pelham *U.S.A.* 31°8N 84°9W **316** D5
Pelhřimov *Czech Rep.* 49°24N 15°12E **180** B8
Pelican *U.S.A.* 57°58N 136°14W **296** B1
Pelican L. *Canada* 52°28N 100°20W **297** C8
Pelican Narrows *Canada* 55°10N 102°56W **297** B8
Pelion *U.S.A.* 33°46N 81°15W **316** B8
Pelister △ *Macedonia* 41°0N 21°10E **202** F5
Pelješac *Croatia* 42°55N 17°25E **199** F14
Pelkosenniemi *Finland* 67°6N 27°28E **160** C22
Pell City *U.S.A.* 33°35N 86°17W **316** B3
Pella *Northern Cape, S. Africa* 29°1S 19°6E **270** C2
Pella *Iowa, U.S.A.* 41°25N 92°55W **310** C4
Pella □ *Greece* 40°52N 22°0E **202** F6
Pello *Finland* 66°47N 23°59E **160** C20
Pellworm *Germany* 54°31N 8°39E **178** A4
Pelly ➜ *Canada* 62°47N 137°19W **296** A1
Pelly Bay *Canada* 68°38N 89°50W **295** D14
Peloponnese □ *Greece* 37°10N 22°0E **204** D4
Peloponnisos Station *Athens, Greece* **112** a1
Peloritani, Monti *Italy* 38°3N 15°20E **201** D8
Pelorus ➜ *N.Z.* 41°16S 173°45E **285** B8
Pelorus Sd. *N.Z.* 40°59S 173°59E **285** A8
Pelotas *Brazil* 31°42S 52°23W **335** C5
Pelotas ➜ *Brazil* 27°28S 51°55W **335** B5
Pelovo *Bulgaria* 43°26N 24°17E **203** C8
Pelplin *Poland* 53°55N 18°42E **184** E5
Pelvoux, Massif du *France* 44°52N 6°20E **175** D10
Pemalang *Indonesia* 6°53S 109°23E **235** D3
Pemanggil, Pulau *Malaysia* 2°37N 104°21E **237** L5
Pematangsiantar *Indonesia* 2°57N 99°5E **234** B1
Pemba *Mozam.* 12°58S 40°30E **269** E5
Pemba *Zambia* 16°30S 27°28E **269** F2
Pemba Channel *Tanzania* 5°0S 39°37E **268** D4
Pemba I. *Tanzania* 5°0S 39°45E **268** D4
Pemberton *W. Austral., Australia* 34°30S 116°0E **279** F2
Pemberton *B.C., Canada* 50°25N 122°50W **296** C4
Pembina ➜ *Canada* 54°45N 114°17W **296** C6
Pembroke *Ont., Canada* 45°50N 77°7W **298** C4
Pembroke *Trin. & Tob.* 11°13N 60°37W **323** s
Pembroke *Pembs., U.K.* 51°41N 4°55W **169** F3
Pembroke *Ga., U.S.A.* 32°8N 81°37W **316** C8
Pembroke Pines *U.S.A.* 26°0N 80°13W **317** J9
Pembrokeshire □ *U.K.* 51°52N 4°56W **169** F3
Pembrokeshire Coast △ *U.K.* 51°50N 5°2W **169** F2
Pembuang ➜ *Indonesia* 3°24S 112°32E **235** C4
Pen *India* 18°45N 73°5E **244** E1
Pen-y-Ghent *U.K.* 54°10N 2°14W **168** C5
Peña, Sierra de la *Spain* 42°32N 0°45W **196** C4
Peña de Francia, Sierra de la *Spain* 40°32N 6°10W **194** E4
Penafiel *Portugal* 41°12N 8°17W **194** D2
Peñafiel *Spain* 41°35N 4°7W **194** D6
Peñaflor *Spain* 37°43N 5°21W **195** H5
Penal *Trin. & Tob.* 10°9N 61°29W **323** t
Peñalara *Spain* 40°51N 3°57W **194** E7
Peñalolén *Chile* 33°28S 70°32W **137** B2
Penalva *Brazil* 3°18S 45°10W **332** B2
Penamacôr *Portugal* 40°10N 7°10W **194** E3
Penang = Pinang *Malaysia* 5°25N 100°15E **237** c
Penápolis *Brazil* 21°30S 50°0W **335** A6
Peñaranda de Bracamonte *Spain* 40°53N 5°13W **194** E5
Peñarroya *Spain* 40°25N 0°40W **196** E4
Peñarroya-Pueblonuevo *Spain* 38°19N 5°16W **195** G5
Penarth *U.K.* 51°26N 3°11W **169** F4
Peñas, C. de *Spain* 43°42N 5°52W **194** B5
Peñas, G. de *Chile* 47°0S 75°0W **336** C2
Peñas, Pta. *Venezuela* 11°17N 62°0W **329** A5
Peñas de San Pedro *Spain* 38°44N 2°0W **197** G3
Peñas del Chache *Canary Is.* 29°6N 13°33W **153** e2
Peñausende *Spain* 41°17N 5°52W **194** D5
Pencarrow Hd. *N.Z.* 41°22S 174°51E **143** C2
Pench ➜ *India* 21°17N 79°10E **244** D4
Pench △ *India* 21°45N 79°20E **243** J8
Pench'i = Benxi *China* 41°20N 123°48E **224** B1
Pend Oreille ➜ *U.S.A.* 49°4N 117°37W **304** B5
Pend Oreille, L. *U.S.A.* 48°10N 116°21W **304** B5
Pendalofos *Greece* 40°14N 21°12E **202** F5
Pendé ➜ *C.A.R.* 7°55N 16°36E **264** A3
Pendembu *Eastern, S. Leone* 8°10N 10°42W **262** D2
Pendembu *Northern, S. Leone* 9°7N 11°14W **262** D2
Pendências *Brazil* 5°15S 36°43W **332** C4
Pender B. *Australia* 16°45S 122°42E **278** C3
Pendik *Turkey* 40°53N 29°13E **203** F13
Pendjari ➜ *Benin* 10°55N 0°50E **263** C5
Pendjari △ *Benin* 11°15N 1°32E **263** C5
Pendleton *Ind., U.S.A.* 40°0N 85°45W **311** E11
Pendleton *Oreg., U.S.A.* 45°40N 118°47W **304** D4
Pendra *India* 22°46N 81°57E **243** H9
Pendzhikent *Tajikistan* 39°29N 67°37E **217** E7
Peneda-Gerês △ *Portugal* 41°57N 8°15W **194** D2
Penedo *Brazil* 10°15S 36°36W **332** D4
Penelokan *Indonesia* 8°17S 115°22E **231** J18
Penetanguishene *Canada* 44°50N 79°55W **312** B5
Penfield *U.S.A.* 41°13N 78°35W **312** E6
Peng Chau *China* 22°17N 114°2E **219** G11
Peng Siang ➜ *Singapore* 1°24N 103°43E **138** A2
Pengalengan *Indonesia* 7°9S 107°30E **235** D3
Penganga ➜ *India* 19°53N 79°9E **244** E4
Penge *Kasai-Or., Dem. Rep. of the Congo* 5°30S 24°33E **265** D4
Penge *Sud-Kivu, Dem. Rep. of the Congo* 4°27S 28°25E **268** C2
Penge *London, U.K.* 51°24N 0°3W **125** B3
P'enghu □ *Taiwan* 23°30N 119°30E **225** C1
P'enghu Ch'üntou *Taiwan* 23°34N 119°30E **225** C1
P'enghu Tao *Taiwan* 23°34N 119°37E **225** C1
Penglai *China* 37°48N 120°42E **227** F11
Pengshan *China* 30°14N 103°58E **228** B4
Pengshui *China* 29°17N 108°12E **228** C7
Penguin *Australia* 41°8S 146°6E **281** G4
Pengxi *China* 30°44N 105°45E **228** B5
Pengze *China* 29°52N 116°32E **229** C11
Penha *Brazil* 22°49S 43°17W **141** C2
Penhalonga *Zimbabwe* 18°52S 32°40E **269** F3
Peniche *Portugal* 39°19N 9°22W **195** F1
Penicuik *U.K.* 55°50N 3°13W **121** B2
Penida, Nusa *Indonesia* 8°45S 115°30E **231** K18
Peninnes, Alpes = Pennine, Alpi *Alps* 46°4N 7°30E **179** J3
Peninsular Malaysia □ *Malaysia* 4°0N 102°0E **237** L4
Peñíscola *Spain* 40°22N 0°24E **196** E5
Penitente, Serra do *Brazil* 8°45S 46°20W **332** C2
Penjaringan *Indonesia* 6°7S 106°48E **122** A1
Pěnjwīn *Iraq* 35°37N 45°56E **213** E11
Penki = Benxi *China* 41°20N 123°48E **224** B1
Penkridge *U.K.* 52°44N 2°6W **168** E5
Penmarch *France* 47°49N 4°21W **172** E2
Penmarch, Pte. de *France* 47°48N 4°22W **172** E2
Penn = Penn Hills *U.S.A.* 40°28N 79°52W **312** F5
Penn Hills *U.S.A.* 40°28N 79°52W **312** F5
Penn Station *New York, U.S.A.* **132** c2
Penn Yan *U.S.A.* 42°40N 77°3W **312** D7
Penna, Punta della *Italy* 42°10N 14°43E **199** F11
Pennant *Canada* 50°32N 108°14W **297** C7
Penne *Italy* 42°27N 13°55E **199** F10
Penner ➜ *India* 14°35N 80°10E **245** G5
Penneshaw *Australia* 35°44S 137°56E **282** C2
Pennine, Alpi *Alps* 46°4N 7°30E **179** J3
Pennines *U.K.* 54°45N 2°27W **168** C5
Pennington *U.S.A.* 39°15N 121°47W **306** F5
Pennington ➜ *Nigeria* 4°45N 5°35E **263** E6
Pennino, Mte. *Italy* 43°6N 12°53E **199** E9
Pennsburg *U.S.A.* 40°23N 75°29W **313** F9
Pennsylvania □ *U.S.A.* 40°45N 77°30W **309** E15
Pennsylvania Avenue *Washington, D.C., U.S.A.* **143** b2
Pennville *U.S.A.* 40°30N 85°9W **311** D11
Penny *Canada* 53°51N 121°20W **296** C4
Peno *Russia* 57°2N 32°49E **188** D7
Penobscot ➜ *U.S.A.* 44°30N 68°48W **309** C19
Penobscot B. *U.S.A.* 44°35N 68°50W **309** C19
Penola *Australia* 37°25S 140°48E **282** D4
Penong *Australia* 31°56S 133°1E **279** F5
Penonomé *Panama* 8°31N 80°21W **320** E3
Penot, Mt. *Vanuatu* 16°20S 167°31E **287** F5
Penrhyn *Cook Is.* 9°0S 158°0W **289** H12
Penrith *N.S.W., Australia* 33°43S 150°38E **283** B9
Penrith *Cumb., U.K.* 54°40N 2°45W **168** C5
Penryn *U.K.* 50°9N 5°7W **169** G2
Pensacola *U.S.A.* 30°25N 87°13W **317** E2
Pensacola B. *U.S.A.* 30°25N 87°5W **317** E2
Pensacola Mts. *Antarctica* 84°0S 40°0W **151** E1
Pense *Canada* 50°25N 104°59W **297** C8
Penshurst *Australia* 37°49S 142°20E **282** D5
Pensiangan *Malaysia* 4°33N 116°19E **235** B5
Pentagon *U.S.A.* 38°53N 77°3W **143** B3
Pentecost = Pentecôte *Vanuatu* 15°42S 168°10E **287** E6
Pentecostes *Brazil* 3°48S 39°17W **332** B4
Pentecôte *Vanuatu* 15°42S 168°10E **287** E6
Penticton *Canada* 49°30N 119°38W **296** D5
Pentland *Australia* 20°32S 145°25E **280** C4
Pentland Firth *U.K.* 58°43N 3°10W **167** C5
Pentland Hills *U.K.* 55°48N 3°25W **167** F5
Pentland Hills ⌓ *U.K.* 55°50N 3°20W **167** F5
Penukonda *India* 14°5N 77°38E **245** G3
Penyagino *Russia* 55°50N 37°20E **129** A2
Penza *Russia* 53°15N 45°5E **190** D7
Penza □ *Russia* 52°50N 44°50E **190** D7
Penzance *U.K.* 50°7N 5°33W **169** G2
Penzberg *Germany* 47°45N 11°22E **179** H7
Penzhino *Russia* 63°30N 167°55E **215** C17
Penzhinskaya Guba *Russia* 61°30N 163°0E **215** C17
Penzhou *China* 31°4N 103°32E **228** B4
Penzing *Austria* 48°11N 16°18E **142** A1
Penzlin *Germany* 53°30N 13°5E **178** B9
People's Park *China* 31°13N 121°28E **138** B1
People's Square *China* 31°13N 121°28E **138** B1
Peoria *Ariz., U.S.A.* 33°43N 112°14W **305** K7
Peoria *Ill., U.S.A.* 40°42N 89°36W **310** D7
Peoria Heights *U.S.A.* 40°45N 89°35W **310** D7
Peotone *U.S.A.* 41°20N 87°48W **311** C9
Pepacton Res. *U.S.A.* 42°5N 74°58W **313** D10
Pepani ➜ *S. Africa* 25°49S 22°47E **270** C3
Pepeekeo *U.S.A.* 19°51N 155°6W **302** D6
Pepel *S. Leone* 8°40N 13°5W **262** D2
Peqin *Albania* 41°3N 19°44E **202** E3
Pera Hd. *Australia* 12°55S 141°37E **280** A3
Perabumulih *Indonesia* 3°27S 104°15E **234** C2
Perachora *Greece* 38°2N 22°56E **204** C4
Perachori *Greece* 38°21N 20°43E **207** C2
Perak □ *Malaysia* 5°0N 101°0E **234** A2
Perak ➜ *Malaysia* 4°0N 100°50E **237** K3
Perales del Alfambra *Spain* 40°38N 1°0W **196** E4
Perales del Puerto *Spain* 40°10N 6°40W **194** E4
Perales del Rio *Spain* 40°18N 3°38W **127** C2
Perama *Kerkyra, Greece* 39°34N 19°54E **206** B9
Perama *Kriti, Greece* 35°20N 24°40E **207** E5
Perancak *Indonesia* 8°24S 114°37E **231** J17
Peräpohjola *Finland* 66°16N 26°10E **160** C22
Perast *Montenegro* 42°31N 18°47E **202** D2
Peratia *Greece* 38°49N 20°45E **207** B2
Peravillo *Mexico City, Mexico* **128** a3
Percé *Canada* 48°31N 64°13W **299** C7
Perche *France* 48°31N 1°1E **172** D8
Perche, Collines du *France* 48°30N 0°40E **171** B4
Perche ⌓ *France* 48°24N 0°46E **172** D7
Perchtoldsdorf *Austria* 48°7N 16°17E **142** B1
Percival Lakes *Australia* 21°25S 125°0E **278** D4
Percy *Manche, France* 48°55N 1°11W **172** D5
Percy *Ill., U.S.A.* 38°5N 89°41W **310** F7
Percy Is. *Australia* 21°39S 150°16E **280** C5
Perdido ➜ *Argentina* 42°55S 67°0W **336** B3
Perdido, Mte. *Spain* 42°40N 0°5E **196** C5
Perdizes *Brazil* 23°32S 46°39W **137** B2
Perdu, Mt. = Perdido, Mte. *Spain* 42°40N 0°5E **196** C5
Perechyn *Ukraine* 48°44N 22°28E **182** B7
Peredelkino *Russia* 55°38N 37°20E **129** C2
Perehinske *Ukraine* 48°49N 24°11E **183** B9
Pereira *Colombia* 4°49N 75°43W **328** C2
Perelazovskiy *Russia* 49°8N 42°35E **191** F6
Peremul Par *India* 11°10N 72°4E **245** J1
Peremyshl = Przemyśl *Poland* 49°50N 22°45E **185** J9
Perené ➜ *Peru* 11°9S 74°14W **330** C3
Perenjori *Australia* 29°26S 116°16E **279** E2
Peresecina *Moldova* 47°16N 28°46E **183** C13
Pereslavl-Zalesskiy *Russia* 56°45N 38°50E **188** D10
Peretu *Romania* 44°3N 25°5E **183** F10
Pereyaslav-Khmelnytskyy *Ukraine* 50°3N 31°28E **189** G6
Pereyma *Ukraine* 48°4N 29°30E **183** B14
Pérez, I. *Mexico* 22°24N 89°42W **319** C7
Perg *Austria* 48°15N 14°38E **180** C7
Pergamino *Argentina* 33°52S 60°30W **334** C3
Pergamon Museum *Berlin, Germany* **115** a4
Pergau ➜ *Malaysia* 5°23N 102°2E **237** K3
Perge *Turkey* 37°3N 30°56E **250** A1
Pergine Valsugana *Italy* 46°4N 11°14E **199** B8
Pérgola *Italy* 43°34N 12°50E **199** E9
Perham *U.S.A.* 46°36N 95°34W **308** B6
Perhentian, Kepulauan *Malaysia* 5°54N 102°42E **237** K4
Peri ➜ *Turkey* 38°53N 39°52E **213** C8
Periam *Romania* 46°2N 20°52E **182** D5
Péribonka ➜ *Canada* 48°45N 72°5W **299** C5
Péribonka, L. *Canada* 50°1N 71°10W **299** B5
Perico *Argentina* 24°20S 65°5W **334** A2
Pericos *Mexico* 25°3N 107°42W **318** B3
Périers *France* 49°11N 1°25W **172** C5
Périgord *France* 45°0N 0°40E **174** D4
Périgord-Limousin ⌓ *France* 45°40N 0°50E **174** C4
Périgueux *France* 45°10N 0°42E **174** C4
Perijá, Sierra de *Colombia* 9°30N 73°3W **328** B3
Perijá △ *Venezuela* 9°30N 72°55W **328** B3
Perisher Valley *Australia* 36°27S 148°25E **283** D8
Peristera *Greece* 39°15N 23°58E **204** B5
Peristeri *Greece* 38°1N 23°42E **112** A2
Peristerona ➜ *Cyprus* 35°8N 33°5E **207** E9
Perito Moreno *Argentina* 46°36S 70°56W **336** C2
Perito Moreno △ *Argentina* 47°49S 72°17W **336** C2
Peritoró *Brazil* 4°20S 44°18W **332** B3
Perivale *U.K.* 51°31N 0°18W **125** A2
Perivol = Dragovishtitsa *Bulgaria* 42°22N 22°39E **202** D6
Periyakulam *India* 10°5N 77°30E **245** J3
Periyar ➜ *India* 10°15N 76°10E **245** J3
Periyar, L. *India* 9°25N 77°10E **245** K3
Periyar △ *India* 9°25N 77°10E **245** K3
Perk *Belgium* 50°56N 4°30E **116** A2
Perkasie *U.S.A.* 40°22N 75°18W **313** F9
Perković *Croatia* 43°41N 16°10E **199** E13
Perlach *Germany* 48°5N 11°37E **131** B2
Perlacher Forst *Germany* 48°4N 11°34E **131** B2
Perlas, Arch. de las *Panama* 8°41N 79°7W **320** E4
Perlas, Punta de *Nic.* 12°30N 83°30W **320** D3
Perleberg *Germany* 53°5N 11°52E **178** B7
Perlez *Serbia* 45°11N 20°22E **182** E5
Perlis □ *Malaysia* 6°30N 100°15E **234** A2
Perm *Russia* 58°0N 56°10E **186** C10
Përmet *Albania* 40°15N 20°21E **202** F4
Permskoye = Komsomolsk-na-Amur *Russia* 50°30N 137°0E **219** A8
Pernambuco = Recife *Brazil* 8°0S 35°0W **332** C5
Pernambuco □ *Brazil* 8°0S 37°0W **332** C4
Pernambuco Abyssal Plain *Atl. Oc.* 5°0S 24°0W **152** G9
Pernatty Lagoon *Australia* 31°30S 137°12E **282** A2
Pernik *Bulgaria* 42°35N 23°2E **202** D7
Pernov = Pärnu *Estonia* 58°28N 24°33E **188** C3
Pero *Italy* 45°30N 9°5E **129** A1
Peron Is. *Australia* 13°9S 130°4E **278** B5
Peron Pen. *Australia* 26°0S 113°10E **279** E1
Péronne *France* 49°55N 2°57E **173** C9
Peropok, Bukit *Singapore* 1°19N 103°42E **138** B2
Perosa Argentina *Italy* 44°58N 7°10E **198** D4
Perovo *Russia* 55°44N 37°45E **129** B4
Perovsk = Qyzylorda *Kazakhstan* 44°48N 65°28E **217** D7
Perow *Canada* 54°35N 126°10W **296** C3
Perparim = Pogradec *Albania* 40°54N 20°37E **202** F4
Perpignan *France* 42°42N 2°53E **174** F6
Perrégaux = Mohammadia *Algeria* 35°33N 0°3E **261** A5
Perrine *U.S.A.* 25°36N 80°21W **317** K9
Perris *U.S.A.* 33°47N 117°14W **307** M9
Perros-Guirec *France* 48°49N 3°28W **172** D3
Perry *Fla., U.S.A.* 30°7N 83°35W **316** E6
Perry *Ga., U.S.A.* 32°28N 83°44W **316** C6
Perry *Iowa, U.S.A.* 41°51N 94°6W **310** C2
Perry *Mich., U.S.A.* 42°50N 84°13W **311** B12
Perry *Mo., U.S.A.* 39°26N 91°40W **310** E5
Perry *N.Y., U.S.A.* 42°42N 78°0W **312** D7
Perry *Okla., U.S.A.* 36°17N 97°14W **314** C6
Perrysburg *U.S.A.* 41°34N 83°38W **311** C13
Perryton *U.S.A.* 36°24N 100°48W **314** C4
Perryville *Alaska, U.S.A.* 55°55N 159°9W **303** J8
Perryville *Mo., U.S.A.* 37°43N 89°52W **310** G7
Persan *France* 49°9N 2°16E **173** C9
Persberg *Sweden* 59°47N 14°15E **162** E8
Perşembe *Turkey* 41°5N 37°46E **212** B7
Persepolis *Iran* 29°55N 52°50E **247** D7
Perseverancia *Bolivia* 14°44S 62°48W **331** C5
Pershing Square *Los Angeles, U.S.A.* **127** c1
Pershotravensk *Ukraine* 50°13N 27°40E **177** C14
Pershotravneyoe = Pershotravensk *Ukraine* 50°13N 27°40E **177** C14
Persia = Iran ■ *Asia* 33°0N 53°0E **247** C7
Persian Gulf *Asia* 27°0N 50°0E **247** E6
Perstorp *Sweden* 56°10N 13°25E **163** H7
Pertek *Turkey* 38°51N 39°19E **213** C8
Perth *W. Austral., Australia* 31°57S 115°52E **279** F2
Perth *Ont., Canada* 44°55N 76°15W **313** B8
Perth *Perth & Kinr., U.K.* 56°24N 3°26W **167** E5
Perth & Kinross □ *U.K.* 56°45N 3°55W **167** E5
Perth Amboy *U.S.A.* 40°30N 74°15W **313** F10
Perth-Andover *Canada* 46°44N 67°42W **299** C6
Pertuis *France* 43°42N 5°30E **175** E9
Pertusato, C. *France* 41°21N 9°11E **175** G13
Pertusella *Italy* 45°35N 9°3E **129** A1
Peru *Ill., U.S.A.* 41°20N 89°8W **310** C7
Peru *Ind., U.S.A.* 40°45N 86°4W **311** D10
Peru *N.Y., U.S.A.* 44°35N 73°32W **313** B11
Peru ■ *S. Amer.* 4°0S 75°0W **328** D3
Peru Basin *Pac. Oc.* 20°0S 95°0W **289** J18
Peru-Chile Trench *Pac. Oc.* 20°0S 72°0W **326** E3
Perúgia *Italy* 43°7N 12°23E **199** E9
Perušić *Croatia* 44°40N 15°22E **199** D12
Peruvian Vale *St. Vincent* 13°13N 61°12W **323** n
Pervomaysk *Russia* 54°56N 43°58E **190** C6
Pervomaysk *Ukraine* 48°10N 30°46E **189** H6
Pervomayskiy *Kazakhstan* 50°16N 82°0E **217** B10
Pervouralsk *Russia* 56°59N 59°59E **186** C10
Pervouralsky = Pervouralsk *Russia* 56°59N 59°59E **186** C10
Pesada *Greece* 38°7N 20°35E **207** C2
Pesagot *West Bank* 31°54N 35°13E **123** A2
Pesanggrahag, Kali ➜ *Indonesia* 6°10S 106°44E **122** B1
Pésaro *Italy* 43°54N 12°55E **199** E9
Pescadores = P'enghu Ch'üntou *Taiwan* 23°34N 119°30E **225** C1
Pescara *Italy* 42°28N 14°13E **199** F11
Pescara ➜ *Italy* 42°28N 14°13E **199** F11
Peschanokopskoye *Russia* 46°14N 41°4E **191** G5
Peschanoye = Yashkul *Russia* 46°11N 45°21E **191** G7
Peschiera Borromeo *Italy* 45°26N 9°19E **129** B2
Péscia *Italy* 43°54N 10°41E **198** E7
Pescina *Italy* 42°2N 13°39E **199** F10
Pesek, Pulau *Singapore* 1°17N 103°41E **138** B2
Peshawar *Pakistan* 34°2N 71°37E **242** B4
Peshkopi *Albania* 41°41N 20°25E **202** E4
Peshtera *Bulgaria* 42°2N 24°18E **203** D8
Peshtigo *U.S.A.* 45°3N 87°45W **308** C10
Peski *Russia* 51°14N 42°29E **190** E6
Peski *Turkmenistan* 38°11N 62°59E **216** E6
Pêso da Régua *Portugal* 41°10N 7°47W **194** D3
Pesochnya = Kirov *Russia* 54°3N 34°20E **188** E8
Pesqueira *Brazil* 8°20S 36°42W **332** C4
Pessac *France* 44°48N 0°37W **174** D3
Pest *Hungary* 47°29N 19°4E **117** B2
Pest □ *Hungary* 47°29N 19°5E **182** C4
Pesterzsébet *Hungary* 47°26N 19°6E **117** B2
Pesthidegkút *Hungary* 47°33N 18°57E **117** A1
Pestimre *Hungary* 47°24N 19°11E **117** B3
Pestlőrinc *Hungary* 47°25N 19°11E **117** B3
Pestovo = Zavolzhye *Russia* 56°37N 43°26E **190** B6
Pestovo *Russia* 58°33N 35°42E **188** C8
Pestravka *Russia* 52°28N 49°57E **190** D9
Pestújhely *Hungary* 47°32N 19°7E **117** A2
Petah Tiqwa *Israel* 32°6N 34°53E **251** F5
Petalas *Greece* 38°25N 21°5E **207** C3
Petalidi *Greece* 36°57N 21°55E **204** E3
Petaling Jaya *Malaysia* 3°4N 101°42E **237** L3
Petaloudes *Greece* 36°18N 28°5E **206** E12
Petaluma *U.S.A.* 38°14N 122°39W **306** G4
Pétange *Lux.* 49°33N 5°55E **170** E5
Petaro *Pakistan* 25°31N 68°18E **242** G3
Petas *Helsinki, Finland* 60°15N 24°50E **121** B2
Petas *Greece* 39°10N 21°2E **204** B3
Petatlán *Mexico* 17°31N 101°16W **318** D4
Petauke *Zambia* 14°14S 31°20E **269** E3
Petawawa *Canada* 45°54N 77°17W **298** C4
Petén Itzá, L. *Guatemala* 16°58N 89°50W **320** C2
Peter I. *Br. Virgin Is.* 18°22N 64°35W **321** b
Peter I. Øy *Antarctica* 69°0S 91°0W **151** C16
Peter Pond L. *Canada* 55°55N 108°44W **297** B7
Peterbell *Canada* 48°36N 83°21W **298** C3
Peterborough *S. Austral., Australia* 32°58S 138°51E **282** B3
Peterborough *Ont., Canada* 44°20N 78°20W **312** B6
Peterborough *Peterborough, U.K.* 52°35N 0°15W **169** E7
Peterborough *N.H., U.S.A.* 42°53N 71°57W **313** D13
Peterborough □ *U.K.* 52°35N 0°15W **169** E7
Peterculter *U.K.* 57°6N 2°16W **167** D6
Peterhead *U.K.* 57°31N 1°48W **167** D7
Peterhof = Petrodvorets *Russia* 59°52N 29°54E **188** C5
Peterlee *U.K.* 54°47N 1°20W **168** C6
Petermann ☼ *Australia* 24°58S 130°0E **279** E4
Petermann Bjerg *Greenland* 73°7N 28°25W **154** C8
Petermann Gletscher *Greenland* 80°30N 60°0W **154** A4
Petermann Ranges *Australia* 26°0S 130°30E **279** E5
Peter's Mine *Guyana* 6°14N 59°20W **329** B6
Petersburg = Peterborough *Australia* 32°58S 138°51E **282** B3
Petersburg *Alaska, U.S.A.* 56°48N 132°58W **303** H14
Petersburg *Ill., U.S.A.* 40°1N 89°51W **310** D7
Petersburg *Ind., U.S.A.* 38°30N 87°17W **311** F9
Petersburg *Mich., U.S.A.* 41°54N 83°43W **311** C13
Petersburg *Pa., U.S.A.* 40°34N 78°3W **312** F6
Petersburg *Va., U.S.A.* 37°14N 77°24W **309** G15
Petersburg *W. Va., U.S.A.* 39°1N 79°5W **309** F14
Petersfield *U.K.* 51°1N 0°56W **169** F7
Petershagen *Germany* 52°23N 8°58E **178** C4
Petilia Policastro *Italy* 39°7N 16°48E **201** C9
Petit Batanga *Cameroon* 3°15N 9°54E **264** B1
Petit-Bourg *Guadeloupe* 16°11N 61°37W **322** b
Petit-Canal *Guadeloupe* 16°25N 61°31W **322** b
Petit Cul-de-Sac Marin *Guadeloupe* 16°12N 61°33W **322** b
Petit Dominique *Grenada* 12°30N 61°24W **323** q
Petit Goâve *Haiti* 18°27N 72°51W **321** C5
Petit Lac Manicouagan *Canada* 51°25N 67°40W **299** B6
Petit Loango ⌓ *Gabon* 2°20S 9°40E **264** C1
Petit-Mécatina ➜ *Canada* 50°40N 59°30W **299** B8
Petit-Mécatina, Î. du *Canada* 50°30N 59°25W **299** B8
Petit Piton *St. Lucia* 13°51N 61°5W **323** m
Petit Raffray *Mauritius* 20°0S 57°36E **272** b
Petit-Saguenay *Canada* 48°15N 70°4W **299** C5
Petit Saint Bernard, Col du *Italy* 45°40N 6°52E **175** C10
Petit Soufrière B. *Dominica* 15°23N 61°15W **323** k
Petitcodiac *Canada* 45°57N 65°11W **299** C6
Petite Anse *Martinique* 14°28N 61°4W **322** j
Petite-Île *Réunion* 21°20S 55°35E **272** f
Petite Martinique *Grenada* 12°31N 61°23W **323** q
Petite Rivière *Mauritius* 20°11S 57°26E **272** b
Petite Savane *Dominica* 15°15N 61°17W **323** k
Petite Terre = Pamandzi *Mayotte* 12°47S 45°16E **272** b
Petite Terre, Îles de la *Guadeloupe* 16°13N 61°9W **322** b
Petites-Anses *Guadeloupe* 15°51N 61°38W **322** b
Petitjean = Sidi Kacem *Morocco* 34°12N 5°42W **260** B3
Petitot ➜ *Canada* 60°14N 123°29W **296** A4
Petitsikapau L. *Canada* 54°37N 66°25W **299** B6
Petlad *India* 22°30N 72°45E **242** H5
Peto *Mexico* 20°8N 88°55W **319** C7
Petone *N.Z.* 41°13S 174°53E **143** B2
Petorca *Chile* 32°15S 70°56W **334** C1
Petoskey *U.S.A.* 45°22N 84°57W **309** C11
Petra *Jordan* 30°20N 35°22E **251** H6
Petra *Spain* 39°37N 3°6E **206** B4
Petra, Ostrova *Russia* 76°15N 118°30E **215** B12
Petra Velikogo, Zaliv *Russia* 42°40N 132°0E **220** C6
Petre, Pt. *Canada* 43°50N 77°9W **312** C7
Petrel = Petrer *Spain* 38°30N 0°46W **197** G4
Petrella, Monte *Italy* 41°18N 13°40E **200** A6
Petrer *Spain* 38°30N 0°46W **197** G4
Petreto-Bicchisano *France* 41°47N 8°58E **175** G12
Petrich *Bulgaria* 41°24N 23°13E **202** E7
Petrified Forest △ *U.S.A.* 35°0N 109°30W **305** J9
Petrijanec *Croatia* 46°23N 16°17E **199** B13
Petrikov = Pyetrikaw *Belarus* 52°11N 28°29E **177** B15
Petrila *Romania* 45°29N 23°29E **183** E8
Petrinja *Croatia* 45°28N 16°18E **199** C13
Petrodvorets *Russia* 59°52N 29°54E **188** C5
Petrograd = Sankt-Peterburg *Russia* 59°55N 30°20E **137** B1
Petrogradskaya Storona *Russia* 59°56N 30°20E **137** B2
Petrolândia *Brazil* 9°5S 38°20W **332** C4
Petrolia *Canada* 42°54N 82°9W **312** D2
Petrolina *Brazil* 9°24S 40°30W **332** C3
Petromaryevka = Pervomaysk *Ukraine* 48°10N 30°46E **189** H6
Petropavl *Kazakhstan* 54°53N 69°13E **217** B7
Petropavlovsk = Petropavl *Kazakhstan* 54°53N 69°13E **217** B7
Petropavlovsk-Kamchatskiy *Russia* 53°3N 158°43E **215** D16
Petropavlovskiy = Akhtubinsk *Russia* 48°13N 46°7E **191** F8
Petropavlovskiy = Severouralsk *Russia* 60°9N 59°57E **186** B10
Petrópolis *Brazil* 22°33S 43°9W **333** F3
Petroşani *Romania* 45°28N 23°20E **183** E8
Petroupoli *Greece* 38°3N 23°40E **112** A2
Petrova Gora *Croatia* 45°15N 15°45E **199** C12
Petrovac *Montenegro* 42°13N 18°57E **202** D2
Petrovac *Serbia* 44°22N 21°26E **202** B5
Petrovaradin *Serbia* 45°16N 19°55E **182** E4
Petrovgrad = Zrenjanin *Serbia* 45°22N 20°23E **182** E5
Petrovice *Czech Rep.* 50°2N 14°33E **135** B3
Petrovsk *Russia* 52°22N 45°19E **190** D7
Petrovsk-Port = Makhachkala *Russia* 43°0N 47°30E **191** J8
Petrovsk-Zabaykalskiy *Russia* 51°20N 108°55E **215** D11
Petrovskaya *Russia* 45°25N 37°58E **189** K9
Petrovskiy Park *Russia* 55°47N 37°34E **129** B3
Petrovsko-Razumovskoye *Russia* 55°49N 37°34E **129** B3
Petrovskoye = Svetlograd *Russia* 45°25N 42°58E **191** H6
Petrovsky Zavod = Petrovsk-Zabaykalskiy *Russia* 51°20N 108°55E **215** D11
Petrozavodsk *Russia* 61°41N 34°20E **188** B8
Petrus Steyn *S. Africa* 27°38S 28°8E **271** C4
Petrusburg *S. Africa* 29°4S 25°26E **270** C4
Petsamo = Pechenga *Russia* 69°29N 31°4E **160** B24
Pettycur *U.K.* 56°4N 3°10W **121** A2
Petukhovo *Russia* 55°6N 67°58E **217** A7
Petuna = Fuyu *China* 45°12N 124°43E **227** B13
Petzeck *Austria* 46°57N 12°48E **180** E5
Peumo *Chile* 34°21S 71°12W **334** C1
Peureulak *Indonesia* 4°48N 97°45E **234** B1
Peusangan ➜ *Indonesia* 5°16N 96°51E **234** A1
Peutie *Belgium* 50°56N 4°27E **116** A2
Pevek *Russia* 69°41N 171°19E **215** C18
Pevely *U.S.A.* 38°17N 90°24W **310** F6
Peveragno *Italy* 44°20N 7°37E **198** D4
Peyrehorade *France* 43°34N 1°7W **174** E2
Peyruis *France* 44°1N 5°56E **175** D9
Pézenas *France* 43°28N 3°24E **174** E7
Pezinok *Slovak Rep.* 48°17N 17°17E **181** C10
Pfaffenhofen *Germany* 48°31N 11°31E **179** G7
Pfälzerwald ⌓ *Germany* 49°18N 9°55E **179** F5
Pfarrkirchen *Germany* 48°25N 12°56E **179** G8
Pfaueninsel *Germany* 52°26N 13°7E **115** B1
Pfeffenhausen *Germany* 48°39N 11°58E **179** G7
Pforzheim *Germany* 48°52N 8°41E **179** G4
Pfullendorf *Germany* 47°55N 9°15E **179** H5
Pfungstadt *Germany* 49°48N 8°35E **179** F4
Pha Taem △ *Thailand* 15°32N 105°30E **236** E5
Phaestos *Greece* 35°2N 24°50E **207** E5
Phagwara *India* 31°10N 75°40E **242** D6
Phala *Botswana* 23°45S 26°50E **270** B4
Phalaborwa *S. Africa* 23°57S 31°7E **271** B5
Phalera = Phulera *India* 26°52N 75°16E **242** F6
Phalodi *India* 27°12N 72°24E **242** F5
Phalsbourg *France* 48°46N 7°15E **173** D14
Phaltan *India* 17°59N 74°26E **244** F2
Phaluai, Ko *Thailand* 9°32N 99°41E **237** b
Phan *Thailand* 19°28N 99°43E **236** C2
Phan Rang *Vietnam* 11°34N 109°0E **237** G7
Phan Ri = Hoa Da *Vietnam* 11°16N 108°40E **237** G7
Phan Si Pan *Vietnam* 22°18N 103°46E **236** A4
Phan Thiet *Vietnam* 11°1N 108°9E **237** G7
Phanae *Greece* 38°8N 25°57E **205** C7
Phanat Nikhom *Thailand* 13°27N 101°11E **236** F3
Phangan, Ko *Thailand* 9°45N 100°0E **237** H3
Phangnga *Thailand* 8°28N 98°30E **237** H2
Phangnga, Ao *Thailand* 8°16N 98°33E **237** a
Phanom Sarakham *Thailand* 13°45N 101°21E **236** F3
Phaphund *India* 26°36N 79°28E **243** F8
Pharenda *India* 27°5N 83°17E **243** F10
Pharr *U.S.A.* 26°12N 98°11W **314** H5
Phatthalung *Thailand* 7°39N 100°6E **237** J3
Phaya Thai *Thailand* 13°45N 100°37E **113** B2
Phayao *Thailand* 19°11N 99°55E **236** C2
Phelps *U.S.A.* 42°58N 77°3W **312** D7
Phelps L. *Canada* 59°15N 103°15W **297** B8
Phenix City *U.S.A.* 32°28N 85°0W **315** E12
Phet Buri *Thailand* 13°1N 99°55E **236** F2
Phetchabun *Thailand* 16°25N 101°8E **236** D3
Phetchabun, Thiu Khao *Thailand* 16°0N 101°20E **236** E3
Phetchaburi = Phet Buri *Thailand* 13°1N 99°55E **236** F2
Phi Phi, Ko *Thailand* 7°45N 98°46E **237** J2
Phiafay *Laos* 14°48N 106°0E **236** E6
Phibun Mangsahan *Thailand* 15°14N 105°14E **236** E5
Phichai *Thailand* 17°22N 100°10E **236** D3
Phichit *Thailand* 16°26N 100°22E **236** D3
Phihai *Pakistan* 24°50N 67°8E **123** A2
Philadelphia *Miss., U.S.A.* 32°46N 89°7W **315** E10
Philadelphia *N.Y., U.S.A.* 44°9N 75°43W **313** B9
Philadelphia *Pa., U.S.A.* 39°57N 75°9W **313** G9
Philip *U.S.A.* 44°2N 101°40W **308** C3
Philip Smith Mts. *U.S.A.* 68°0N 148°0W **303** C10
Philipi *Greece* 41°1N 24°16E **203** E8
Philippeville = Skikda *Algeria* 36°50N 6°58E **261** A6
Philippeville *Belgium* 50°12N 4°33E **170** D4
Philippi *U.S.A.* 39°9N 80°3W **309** F13
Philippi L. *Australia* 24°20S 138°55E **280** C2
Philippine Basin *Pac. Oc.* 17°0N 132°0E **288** F5
Philippine Sea *Pac. Oc.* 18°0N 125°0E **288** F4
Philippine Trench = Mindanao Trench *Pac. Oc.* 12°0N 126°6E **232** E5
Philippines ■ *Asia* 12°0N 123°0E **232** E4
Philippolis *S. Africa* 30°15S 25°16E **270** D4
Philippopolis = Plovdiv *Bulgaria* 42°8N 24°44E **203** D8
Philipsburg *Qué., Canada* 45°2N 73°5W **313** A11
Philipsburg *St.-Maarten* 18°3N 63°5W **322** a
Philipsburg *Mont., U.S.A.* 46°20N 113°18W **304** C7
Philipsburg *Pa., U.S.A.* 40°54N 78°13W **312** F6
Philipstown = Daingean *Ireland* 53°18N 7°17W **166** C4
Philipstown *S. Africa* 30°28S 24°30E **270** D3
Phillip B. *Australia* 33°58S 151°14E **139** B2
Phillip I. *Australia* 38°30S 145°12E **283** E6
Phillips *U.S.A.* 45°42N 90°24W **308** C8
Phillipsburg *Ga., U.S.A.* 31°25N 83°30W **316** D6
Phillipsburg *Kans., U.S.A.* 39°45N 99°19W **308** F4
Phillipsburg *N.J., U.S.A.* 40°42N 75°12W **313** F9
Philmont *U.S.A.* 42°15N 73°39W **313** D11
Philomath *Ga., U.S.A.* 33°44N 82°59W **316** B7
Philomath *Oreg., U.S.A.* 44°32N 123°22W **304** D2
Phimai *Thailand* 15°13N 102°30E **236** E4
Phitsanulok *Thailand* 16°50N 100°12E **236** D3
Phnom Kulen △ *Cambodia* 13°38N 104°15E **236** F5
Phnom Penh *Cambodia* 11°33N 104°55E **237** G5
Phnum Penh = Phnom Penh *Cambodia* 11°33N 104°55E **237** G5
Phoenicia *U.S.A.* 42°5N 74°14W **313** D10
Phoenix *Mauritius* 20°17S 57°30E **272** b
Phoenix *Ariz., U.S.A.* 33°26N 112°4W **305** K7
Phoenix *N.Y., U.S.A.* 43°14N 76°18W **313** C8
Phoenix Is. *Kiribati* 3°30S 172°0W **277** A16
Phoenix Park *Ireland* 53°21N 6°20W **120** A2
Phoenixville *U.S.A.* 40°8N 75°31W **313** F9
Phon *Thailand* 15°49N 102°36E **236** E4
Phon Tiou *Laos* 17°53N 104°37E **236** D5
Phong ➜ *Thailand* 16°23N 102°56E **236** D4
Phong Saly *Laos* 21°42N 102°9E **228** G4
Phong Tho *Vietnam* 22°32N 103°21E **236** A4
Phonhong *Laos* 18°30N 102°25E **236** C4
Phonum *Thailand* 8°49N 98°48E **237** H2
Phosphate Hill *Australia* 21°53S 139°58E **280** C2
Photharam *Thailand* 13°41N 99°51E **236** F2
Phra Kaeo *Bangkok, Thailand* **113** b1
Phra Khanong *Thailand* 13°40N 100°36E **113** B2
Phra Nakhon *Thailand* 13°45N 100°30E **113** B2
Phra Nakhon Si Ayutthaya *Thailand* 14°25N 100°30E **236** E3
Phra Pradaeng *Thailand* 13°39N 100°33E **113** C2
Phra Thong, Ko *Thailand* 9°5N 98°17E **237** H2
Phrae *Thailand* 18°7N 100°9E **236** C3
Phranakhon *Thailand* 13°44N 100°29E **113** B1
Phrom Phiram *Thailand* 17°2N 100°12E **236** D3
Phrygia *Turkey* 38°40N 30°0E **212** C4
Phu Bia *Laos* 19°10N 103°0E **236** C4
Phu Chong-Na Yoi △ *Thailand* 14°25N 105°30E **236** E5
Phu Dien *Vietnam* 18°58N 105°31E **236** C5
Phu Hin Rang Ka △ *Thailand* 17°0N 100°59E **236** D3
Phu Kradung △ *Thailand* 17°2N 101°44E **236** D3
Phu Loi *Laos* 20°14N 103°14E **236** B4
Phu Luang △ *Thailand* 17°15N 101°29E **236** D3
Phu Ly *Vietnam* 20°35N 105°50E **228** G5
Phu Phan △ *Thailand* 17°0N 103°56E **236** D4
Phu Quoc, Dao *Vietnam* 10°20N 104°0E **237** G4
Phu Tho *Vietnam* 21°24N 105°13E **228** G5
Phu Wiang △ *Thailand* 16°39N 102°23E **236** D4
Phuc Yen *Vietnam* 21°16N 105°45E **228** G5
Phuket *Thailand* 7°53N 98°24E **237** a
Phuket, Ko *Thailand* 8°0N 98°22E **237** a
Phul *India* 30°19N 75°14E **242** D6
Phulad *India* 25°38N 73°49E **242** G5
Phulbani *India* 20°28N 84°14E **244** D7
Phulbari *India* 25°55N 90°2E **241** C3
Phulchari *Bangla.* 25°11N 89°37E **241** C2
Phulera *India* 26°52N 75°16E **242** F6
Phulpur *India* 25°31N 82°49E **243** G10
Phun Phin *Thailand* 9°7N 99°12E **237** H2
Phuntsholing *Bhutan* 26°51N 89°23E **243** F13
Phuthaditjhaba *S. Africa* 28°29S 28°48E **271** C4
Pia ☼ *Australia* 27°7S 116°23E **279** E2
Piaçabuçu *Brazil* 10°24S 36°25W **332** D4
Piacenza *Italy* 45°1N 9°40E **198** C6
Piai, Tanjung *Malaysia* 1°17N 103°30E **237** d
Piako ➜ *N.Z.* 37°12S 175°30E **284** D4
Pian Cr. ➜ *Australia* 30°2S 148°12E **281** E4
Pian-Upe ⌓ *Uganda* 1°44N 34°20E **268** B3
Piana *France* 42°15N 8°34E **175** F12
Pianella *Italy* 42°24N 14°2E **199** F11
Piangil *Australia* 35°5S 143°20E **282** C5
Pianosa *Puglia, Italy* 42°12N 15°44E **199** F12
Pianosa *Toscana, Italy* 42°35N 10°5E **198** F7
Piapot *Canada* 49°59N 109°8W **297** D7
Piarco *Trin. & Tob.* 10°35N 61°20W **323** t
Piarco Int. ✈ (POS) *Trin. & Tob.* 10°36N 61°20W **323** t
Pias *Portugal* 38°1N 7°29W **195** G3
Piaseczno *Poland* 52°5N 21°2E **185** F8
Piaski *Poland* 51°8N 22°52E **185** G9
Piastów *Poland* 52°12N 20°48E **185** F7
Piatã *Brazil* 13°9S 41°48W **333** D3
Piatra *Romania* 43°51N 25°9E **183** G10
Piatra Craiului △ *Romania* 45°30N 25°12E **183** E10
Piatra Neamţ *Romania* 46°56N 26°21E **183** D11
Piatra Olt *Romania* 44°22N 24°16E **183** F9
Piauí □ *Brazil* 7°0S 43°0W **332** C3
Piauí ➜ *Brazil* 6°38S 42°42W **332** C3
Piave ➜ *Italy* 45°32N 12°44E **199** C9
Piazza Ármerina *Italy* 37°21N 14°20E **201** E7
Pibor ➜ *Sudan* 7°35N 33°0E **257** F3
Pibor Post *Sudan* 6°47N 33°3E **257** F3
Pica *Chile* 20°35S 69°25W **330** E4
Picardie □ *France* 49°50N 3°0E **173** C10
Picardie, Plaine de *France* 50°0N 2°0E **173** C9
Picardy = Picardie □ *France* 49°50N 3°0E **173** C10
Picasso, Museu *Barcelona, Spain* **114** c2
Picayune *U.S.A.* 30°32N 89°41W **315** F10
Piccadilly *London, U.K.* **125** b3
Picerno *Italy* 40°38N 15°38E **201** B8
Pichhor *India* 25°58N 78°20E **243** G8
Pichilemu *Chile* 34°22S 72°0W **334** C1
Pichincha, □ *Ecuador* 0°10S 78°40W **328** D2
Pichor *India* 25°11N 78°11E **242** G8
Pickerel L. *Canada* 48°40N 91°25W **298** C1
Pickering *U.K.* 54°15N 0°46W **168** C7
Pickering, Vale of *U.K.* 54°14N 0°45W **168** C7
Pickle Lake *Canada* 51°30N 90°12W **298** B1
Pickwick L. *U.S.A.* 35°4N 88°15W **315** D10
Pico *Azores* 38°28N 28°20W **153** d1
Pico, Ponta do *Azores* 38°28N 28°25W **153** d1
Pico Bonito △ *Honduras* 15°34N 86°48W **320** C2
Pico da Neblina △ *Brazil* 0°19N 66°28W **328** C4
Pico Rivera *U.S.A.* 33°59N 118°5W **126** C4
Pico Truncado *Argentina* 46°40S 68°0W **336** C3
Picos = Colinas *Brazil* 6°0S 44°10W **332** C3
Picos *Brazil* 7°5S 41°28W **332** C3
Picos de Europa △ *Spain* 43°13N 4°59W **194** B6
Picota *Peru* 6°54S 76°24W **330** B2
Picton *N.S.W., Australia* 34°12S 150°34E **283** C9
Picton *Ont., Canada* 44°1N 77°9W **312** B7
Picton *N.Z.* 41°18S 174°3E **285** B9
Picton, I. *Chile* 55°2S 66°57W **336** E3
Pictou *Canada* 45°41N 62°42W **299** C7
Picture Butte *Canada* 49°55N 112°45W **296** D6
Pictured Rocks △ *U.S.A.* 46°30N 86°30W **308** B10
Picuí *Brazil* 6°31S 36°21W **332** C4
Picún Leufú *Argentina* 39°30S 69°5W **336** A3
Pidbuzh *Ukraine* 49°19N 23°14E **185** J10
Pidurutalagala *Sri Lanka* 7°10N 80°50E **245** L5
Piechowice *Poland* 50°51N 15°36E **185** H2
Piedade *Rio de J., Brazil* 22°52S 43°18W **135** B1
Piedade *Lisboa, Portugal* 38°49N 9°16W **126** A1
Piedade, Cova da *Portugal* 38°40N 9°8W **126** A2
Piedecuesta *Colombia* 6°59N 73°3W **328** B3
Piedimonte Matese *Italy* 41°22N 14°22E **201** A7
Piedmont = Piemonte □ *Italy* 45°0N 8°0E **198** D5
Piedmont *Ala., U.S.A.* 33°55N 85°37W **316** B4
Piedmont *S.C., U.S.A.* 34°42N 82°28W **292** F11
Piedmont Park *U.S.A.* 33°47N 84°22W **113** B2
Piedra ➜ *Spain* 41°18N 1°47W **196** D3
Piedra del Águila *Argentina* 40°2S 70°4W **336** B2
Piedra del Águila, Embalse *Argentina* 40°15S 70°4W **336** B2
Piedra Lais *Venezuela* 3°10N 65°50W **328** C4
Piedrabuena *Spain* 39°0N 4°10W **195** G6
Piedrahita *Spain* 40°28N 5°23W **194** E5
Piedralaves *Spain* 40°19N 4°42W **194** E6
Piedras, R. de las ➜ *Peru* 12°30S 69°15W **330** C4
Piedras Blancas *Spain* 43°33N 5°58W **194** B5
Piedras Negras *Mexico* 28°42N 100°31W **318** B4
Piedras Pt. *Phil.* 10°11N 118°48E **233** F2
Piekar = Piekary Śląskie *Poland* 50°24N 18°57E **185** H5
Piekary Śląskie *Poland* 50°24N 18°57E **185** H5
Pieksämäki *Finland* 62°18N 27°10E **188** A4
Pielinen *Finland* 63°15N 29°40E **160** E23
Piemonte □ *Italy* 45°0N 8°0E **198** D5
Pienaarsrivier *S. Africa* 25°15S 28°18E **271** C4
Pieniężno *Poland* 54°14N 20°8E **184** D7
Pieninský △ *Europe* 49°25N 20°28E **181** B13
Pieńsk *Poland* 51°16N 15°2E **185** G2
Piercefield *U.S.A.* 44°13N 74°35W **313** B10
Pierceland *Canada* 54°20N 109°46W **297** C7
Pieria □ *Greece* 40°13N 22°25E **202** F6
Pierpont *U.S.A.* 41°45N 80°34W **312** E4
Pierre *U.S.A.* 44°22N 100°21W **308** C3

Pierre-Buffière France 45°41N 1°22E 174 C5
Pierre-de-Bresse France 46°54N 5°13E 173 F12
Pierre Elliott Trudeau ✈ (YUL) Canada 45°28N 73°44W 130 B1
Pierrefonds Canada 45°29N 73°51W 313 A11
Pierrefontaine-les-Varans France 47°14N 6°32E 173 E13
Pierrefort France 44°55N 2°50E 174 D6
Pierrelatte France 44°23N 4°43E 175 D8
Pierson U.S.A. 29°14N 81°28W 317 F8
Piešťany Slovak Rep. 48°38N 17°55E 181 C10
Piesting → Austria 48°6N 16°40E 181 C9
Pieszyce Poland 50°43N 16°33E 185 H3
Piet Retief S. Africa 27°1S 30°50E 271 C5
Pietarsaari Finland 63°40N 22°43E 160 E20
Pieter Both Mauritius 20°11S 57°32E 272 e
Pietermaritzburg S. Africa 29°35S 30°25E 271 C5
Pietersburg = Polokwane S. Africa 23°54S 29°25E 271 B4
Pietragalla Italy 40°45N 15°53E 201 B8
Pietralata Italy 41°55N 12°33E 136 B2
Pietrasanta Italy 43°57N 10°14E 198 E7
Pietroşiţa Romania 45°11N 25°26E 183 E10
Pietrosul, Vf. Maramureş, Romania 47°35N 24°43E 183 C9
Pietrosul, Vf. Suceava, Romania 47°12N 25°18E 183 C10
Pieve di Cadore Italy 46°26N 12°22E 199 B9
Pieve di Teco Italy 44°3N 7°56E 198 D4
Pievepélago Italy 44°12N 10°37E 198 D7
Pigaditsa Greece 39°59N 21°23E 202 G5
Pigeon Guadeloupe 16°9N 61°46W 322 e
Pigeon I. India 14°2N 74°20E 245 G2
Pigeon I. St. Lucia 14°6N 60°58W 323 m
Pigeon L. Canada 44°27N 78°30W 312 B6
Piges Greece 39°17N 21°25E 204 B3
Piggott U.S.A. 36°23N 90°11W 315 C9
Pigna Italy 43°56N 7°40E 198 E4
Pigüe Argentina 37°36S 62°25W 334 D3
Piha N.Z. 36°57S 174°28E 284 C3
Pihani India 27°36N 80°15E 243 F9
Pihlajamäki Finland 60°14N 24°58E 121 B2
Pihlajasaari Finland 60°8N 24°55E 121 C2
Pihlajavesi Finland 61°45N 28°45E 188 B5
Pijijiapan Mexico 15°42N 93°14W 319 D6
Pikalevo Russia 59°37N 34°9E 188 C8
Pikangikum Canada 51°49N 94°0W 297 C10
Pikes Peak U.S.A. 38°50N 105°3W 304 G11
Piketberg S. Africa 32°55S 18°40E 270 D2
Pikeville U.S.A. 37°29N 82°31W 309 G12
Pikit Phil. 7°4N 124°41E 233 H5
Pikou China 39°18N 122°22E 227 E12
Pikounda Congo 0°30N 16°44E 264 B3
Pikwitonei Canada 55°35N 97°9W 297 B9
Piła Poland 53°10N 16°48E 185 E3
Pila Spain 38°16N 1°11W 197 G3
Pilanesberg △ S. Africa 25°15S 27°4E 270 C4
Pilani India 28°22N 75°33E 242 E6
Pilar Brazil 9°36S 35°56W 332 C4
Pilar Paraguay 26°50S 58°20W 334 B4
Pilar Capiz, Phil. 11°29N 123°0E 233 F4
Pilar Sorsogon, Phil. 12°56N 123°40E 232 E4
Pilar de la Horadada Spain 37°52N 0°47W 197 H4
Pilares Brazil 22°52S 43°18W 135 B1
Pilas Group Phil. 6°45N 121°35E 233 H3
Pilat ⌓ France 45°20N 4°30E 175 C8
Pilawa Poland 51°57N 21°32E 185 G8
Pilaya → Bolivia 20°55S 64°4W 331 E5
Pilbara Australia 21°15S 118°16E 278 D2
Pilcomaya → Paraguay 25°21S 57°42W 334 B4
Pilea Greece 40°32N 22°59E 202 F6
Pilgrim's Rest S. Africa 24°55S 30°44E 271 B5
Pilgrimstad Sweden 62°57N 15°2E 162 B9
Pili Greece 36°50N 27°15E 205 E9
Pili Phil. 13°33N 123°19E 232 E4
Pilibhit India 28°40N 79°50E 243 E8
Pilica → Poland 51°52N 21°17E 185 G8
Pilio, Oros Greece 39°27N 23°3E 204 B5
Pilipinas = Philippines ■ Asia 12°0N 123°0E 232 E4
Pilis Hungary 47°17N 19°35E 182 C4
Pilisvörösvár Hungary 47°38N 18°56E 182 C3
Pilkhawa India 28°43N 77°42E 242 E7
Pillar B. Ascension I. 7°59S 14°21W 153 g
Pillaro Ecuador 1°10S 78°32W 328 D2
Pillau = Baltiysk Russia 54°41N 19°58E 184 D6
Pilliga Australia 30°21S 148°54E 281 E4
Pilos Greece 36°55N 21°42E 204 E3
Pilot Grove U.S.A. 38°53N 92°55W 310 F4
Pilot Mound Canada 49°15N 98°54W 297 D9
Pilot Point Alaska, U.S.A. 57°34N 157°35W 303 H8
Pilot Point Tex., U.S.A. 33°24N 96°58W 314 E6
Pilot Rock U.S.A. 45°29N 118°50W 304 D4
Pilot Station U.S.A. 61°56N 162°53W 303 F7
Pilote → Martinique 14°28N 60°55W 322 j
Pilsen = Pilzno Poland 49°58N 21°16E 185 J8
Pilsen = Plzeň Czech Rep. 49°45N 13°22E 180 B6
Pilštanj Slovenia 46°8N 15°39E 199 B12
Piltene Latvia 57°13N 21°40E 184 A8
Pilton U.K. 55°58N 3°13W 121 B2
Pilzno Poland 49°58N 21°16E 185 J8
Pima U.S.A. 32°54N 109°50W 305 K9
Pimba Australia 31°18S 136°46E 282 A2
Pimenta Bueno Brazil 11°35S 61°10W 331 C5
Pimenteiras Brazil 13°40S 60°58W 331 C5
Pimentel Peru 6°45S 79°55W 330 B2
Pimlico London, U.K. 125 c3
Pimmit Hills U.S.A. 38°54N 77°12W 143 B2
Pimpri Chinchwad India 18°37N 73°47E 244 E1
Pimu Dem. Rep. of the Congo 1°42N 20°58E 264 B4
Pin Valley △ India 31°50N 77°50E 242 D7
Pina de Ebro Spain 41°29N 0°33W 196 D4
Pinamalayan Phil. 13°2N 121°29E 232 E3
Pinang Malaysia 5°25N 100°15E 237 c
Pinang □ Malaysia 5°20N 100°20E 234 A2
Pinar, C. des Spain 39°53N 3°12E 206 B4
Pinar del Río Cuba 22°26N 83°40W 320 B3
Pınarbaşı Çanakkale, Turkey 39°53N 26°15E 205 B8
Pınarbaşı Kayseri, Turkey 38°43N 36°23E 212 C7
Pınarhisar Turkey 41°37N 27°30E 203 E11
Pinatubo, Mt. Phil. 15°8N 120°21E 232 D3
Pinawa Canada 50°9N 95°50W 297 C9
Pincehely Hungary 46°41N 18°27E 182 D3
Pinchang China 31°36N 107°3E 228 B6
Pincher Creek Canada 49°30N 113°57W 296 D6
Pinchi L. Canada 54°38N 124°30W 296 C4
Pinckard U.S.A. 31°19N 85°33W 316 D4
Pinckneyville U.S.A. 38°5N 89°23W 310 F7
Pińczów Poland 50°32N 20°32E 185 H7
Pind Dadan Khan Pakistan 32°36N 73°7E 217 F8
Pindar Australia 28°30S 115°47E 279 E2
Pindaré → Brazil 3°17S 44°47W 332 B3
Pindaré-Mirim Brazil 3°37S 45°21W 332 B2
Pindera Downs ☼ Australia 29°24S 142°37E 281 A3
Pindi Gheb Pakistan 33°14N 72°21E 242 C5
Pindiga Nigeria 9°58N 10°53E 263 D7
Pindobal Brazil 3°16S 48°25W 332 B2
Pindos △ Greece 39°52N 21°11E 204 B3
Pindos Oros Greece 40°0N 21°0E 204 B3
Pindus Mts. = Pindos Oros Greece 40°0N 21°0E 204 B3
Pine → B.C., Canada 56°8N 120°43W 296 B4
Pine → Sask., Canada 58°50N 105°38W 297 B7
Pine Bluff U.S.A. 34°13N 92°1W 314 D8
Pine Bluffs U.S.A. 41°11N 104°4W 304 F11
Pine Castle U.S.A. 28°28N 81°22W 133 B2
Pine City U.S.A. 45°50N 92°59W 308 C7
Pine Cr. → U.S.A. 41°10N 77°16W 312 E7
Pine Creek Australia 13°50S 131°50E 278 B5
Pine Falls Canada 50°34N 96°11W 297 C9
Pine Flat L. U.S.A. 36°50N 119°20W 306 J7
Pine Grove Ont., Canada 43°47N 79°34W 141 A1
Pine Grove Pa., U.S.A. 40°33N 76°23W 313 F8
Pine Hill Australia 23°38S 146°57E 280 C4
Pine Hills U.S.A. 28°33N 81°27W 133 A2
Pine I. U.S.A. 26°36N 82°7W 317 J7
Pine Level U.S.A. 32°4N 86°4W 316 C3
Pine Mountain U.S.A. 32°49N 84°51W 316 C5
Pine Pass Canada 55°25N 122°42W 296 B4
Pine Point Canada 60°50N 114°28W 296 A6
Pine Ridge N.S.W., Australia 31°30S 150°28E 283 A9
Pine Ridge S. Dak., U.S.A. 43°2N 102°33W 308 D2
Pine River Man., Canada 51°45N 100°30W 297 C8
Pine River Minn., U.S.A. 46°43N 94°24W 308 B6
Pine Valley U.S.A. 32°50N 116°32W 307 N10
Pinecrest U.S.A. 38°12N 120°1W 306 G6
Pineda de Mar Spain 41°37N 2°42E 196 D7
Pinedale Calif., U.S.A. 36°50N 119°48W 306 J7
Pinedale Wyo., U.S.A. 42°52N 109°52W 304 E9
Pinega → Russia 64°30N 44°19E 186 B8
Pinehouse L. Canada 55°32N 106°35W 297 B7
Pineimuta → Canada 52°8N 88°33W 298 B1
Pinellas Park U.S.A. 27°50N 82°41W 317 H7
Pinerolo Italy 44°53N 7°21E 198 D4
Pines, Akra Greece 40°5N 24°20E 203 F8
Pineto Italy 42°36N 14°4E 199 F11
Pinetop-Lakeside U.S.A. 34°9N 109°58W 305 J9
Pinetown S. Africa 29°48S 30°54E 271 C5
Pinetta U.S.A. 30°36N 83°21W 316 E6
Pineview U.S.A. 32°7N 83°30W 316 C6
Pineville La., U.S.A. 31°19N 92°26W 314 F8
Pineville S.C., U.S.A. 33°26N 80°1W 316 B9
Pinewood U.S.A. 33°44N 80°27W 316 B9
Pinewood Park U.S.A. 25°52N 80°13W 128 A2
Piney France 48°22N 4°21E 173 D11
Piney Run → U.S.A. 38°58N 77°14W 143 B2
Ping → Thailand 15°42N 100°9E 236 E3
Pingaring Australia 32°40S 118°32E 279 F2
Pingba China 26°23N 106°12E 228 D6
Pingbian China 23°0N 103°45E 228 F4
Pingchuan China 27°35N 101°55E 228 D3
Pingding China 37°47N 113°38E 226 F7
Pingdingshan China 33°43N 113°27E 226 H7
Pingdong Taiwan 22°39N 120°30E 229 F13
Pingdu China 36°42N 119°59E 227 F10
Pingelly Australia 32°32S 117°5E 279 F2
Pingguo China 23°19N 107°36E 228 F6
Pinghe China 24°17N 117°21E 229 E11
Pinghu China 30°40N 121°2E 229 B13
Pingjiang China 28°45N 113°36E 229 C9
Pingle China 24°40N 110°40E 229 E8
Pingli China 32°27N 109°22E 228 A7
Pingliang China 35°35N 106°31E 226 G4
Pinglin Taiwan 24°56N 121°42E 225 B3
Pinglu China 39°31N 112°30E 226 E7
Pingluo China 38°52N 106°30E 226 E4
Pingnan Fujian, China 26°55N 119°0E 229 D12
Pingnan Guangxi Zhuangzu, China 23°33N 110°22E 229 F8
Pingo Gabon 1°19S 10°55E 264 C2
Pingquan China 41°1N 118°37E 227 D10
Pingrup Australia 33°32S 118°29E 279 F2
Pingshan China 28°39N 104°3E 228 C5
Pingtan China 25°31N 119°47E 229 E12
Pingtang China 25°49N 107°17E 228 E6
P'ingtung Taiwan 22°38N 120°30E 225 D2
P'ingtung □ Taiwan 22°30N 120°40E 225 D2
Pingwu China 32°25N 104°30E 226 H3
Pingxiang Guangxi Zhuangzu, China 22°6N 106°46E 228 F6
Pingxiang Jiangxi, China 27°43N 113°48E 229 D9
Pingyao China 37°12N 112°10E 226 F7
Pingyi China 35°30N 117°35E 227 G9
Pingyin China 36°20N 116°25E 226 F9
Pingyuan Guangdong, China 24°37N 115°57E 229 E10
Pingyuan Shandong, China 37°10N 116°22E 226 F9
Pingyuanjie China 23°45N 103°48E 228 F4
Pingzhou China 23°1N 113°11E 121 B2
Pinhal Novo Portugal 38°38N 8°55W 195 G2
Pinheiro = Icoraci Brazil 1°18S 48°28W 332 B2
Pinheiro Brazil 2°31S 45°5W 332 B2
Pinheiro Machado Brazil 31°34S 53°23W 335 C5
Pinheiros → Brazil 23°37S 46°44W 137 B1
Pinhel Portugal 40°50N 7°1W 194 E3
Pinhuá → Brazil 6°21S 65°0W 331 B5
Pini Indonesia 0°10N 98°40E 234 B1
Pinios → Ilia, Greece 37°48N 21°20E 204 D3
Pinios → Trikala, Greece 39°55N 22°41E 204 B4
Pinjarra Australia 32°37S 115°52E 279 F2
Pinjrapur Pakistan 24°53N 67°4E 123 A2
Pink Beach Neth. Ant. 12°5N 68°17W 322 h
Pink Mountain Canada 57°3N 122°52W 296 B4
Pinkafeld Austria 47°22N 16°9E 181 D9
Pinlaung Burma 20°8N 96°47E 241 E6
Pinlebu Burma 24°5N 95°22E 241 C5
Pinnacles ⌓ U.S.A. 36°25N 121°12W 306 J5
Pinnaroo Australia 35°17S 140°53E 282 C4
Pinneberg Germany 53°40N 9°48E 178 B5
Pinner U.K. 51°35N 0°22W 125 A1
Pinner Green U.K. 51°35N 0°23W 125 A1
Pino Hachado, Paso S. Amer. 38°39S 70°54W 336 A2
Pinon Hills U.S.A. 34°26N 117°39W 307 L9
Pinos Mexico 22°18N 101°34W 318 C4
Pinos, Mt. U.S.A. 34°49N 119°8W 307 L7
Pinos Pt. U.S.A. 36°38N 121°57W 305 H3
Pinos Puente Spain 37°15N 3°45W 195 H7
Pinrang Indonesia 3°46S 119°41E 231 E5
Pins, Î. des N. Cal. 22°37S 167°30E 288 d
Pins, Pte. aux Canada 42°15N 81°51W 312 D3
Pinsk Belarus 52°10N 26°1E 177 B14
Pinta, Canal de Ecuador 0°27N 90°38W 330 a
Pinta, I. Ecuador 0°35N 90°44W 330 a
Pintados Chile 20°35S 69°40W 330 E4
Pintuyan Phil. 9°57N 125°15E 233 G5
Pinukpuk Phil. 17°35N 121°22E 232 C3
Pinyang China 27°42N 120°31E 229 D13
Pinyug Russia 60°5N 48°0E 186 B8
Pio Duran Phil. 13°2N 123°25E 232 E4
Pio V. Corpuz Phil. 11°55N 124°2E 233 F5
Pio XII Brazil 3°53S 45°17W 332 B2
Pioche U.S.A. 37°56N 114°27W 305 H6
Pioltello Italy 45°30N 9°19E 129 A2
Piombino Italy 42°55N 10°32E 198 F7
Piombino, Canale di Italy 42°53N 10°30E 198 F7
Pioner, Ostrov Russia 79°50N 92°0E 215 B10
Pionerskiy Russia 54°56N 20°14E 184 D7
Pionki Poland 51°29N 21°28E 185 G8
Piopiotaki = Milford Sd. N.Z. 44°41S 167°47E 285 E2
Piorini → Brazil 3°23S 63°30W 329 D5
Piorini, L. Brazil 3°15S 62°35W 329 D5
Piotrków Trybunalski Poland 51°23N 19°43E 185 G6
Piove di Sacco Italy 45°18N 12°2E 199 C9
Pip Iran 26°45N 60°10E 247 E9
Pipar India 26°25N 73°31E 242 F5
Pipar Road India 26°27N 73°27E 242 F5
Piparia Mad. P., India 22°45N 78°23E 242 H8
Piparia Mad. P., India 21°49N 77°37E 242 J7
Piparo Trin. & Tob. 10°20N 61°20W 323 t
Pipas Angola 14°57S 12°11E 265 E2
Piperi Greece 39°20N 24°19E 204 B6
Piperno = Priverno Italy 41°28N 13°11E 200 A6
Pipestone U.S.A. 44°0N 96°19W 308 D5
Pipestone → Canada 52°53N 89°23W 298 B2
Pipestone Cr. → Canada 49°38N 100°15W 297 D8
Pipinui Pt. N.Z. 41°10S 174°44E 143 A1
Pipiriki N.Z. 39°28S 175°5E 284 F4
Piplan Pakistan 32°17N 71°21E 242 C4
Piploda India 23°37N 74°56E 242 H6
Pipmuacan, Rés. Canada 49°45N 70°30W 299 C5
Pippingarra Australia 20°27S 118°42E 278 D2
Pipriac France 47°59N 1°58W 172 E5
Piqua U.S.A. 40°9N 84°15W 311 D12
Piquet Carneiro Brazil 5°48S 39°25W 332 C4
Piquiri → Brazil 24°3S 54°14W 335 A5
Pir Panjal Range India 32°30N 76°50E 242 C7
Pīr Sohrāb Iran 25°44N 60°54E 247 E9
Pira Benin 8°28N 1°48E 263 D5
Piracanjuba Brazil 17°18S 49°1W 333 E2
Piracicaba Brazil 22°45S 47°40W 335 A6
Piracuruca Brazil 3°50S 41°50W 332 B3
Pirae Tahiti 17°31S 149°32W 289 e
Piræus = Pireas Greece 37°57N 23°42E 112 B1
Piraiévs = Pireas Greece 37°57N 23°42E 112 B1
Pirajuçara → Brazil 23°33S 46°42W 137 B1
Pirajui Brazil 21°59S 49°29W 335 A6
Piram I. India 21°36N 72°21E 242 J5
Piran Slovenia 45°31N 13°33E 199 C10
Pirané Argentina 25°42S 59°6W 334 B4
Piranhas Brazil 9°27S 37°46W 332 C4
Pirano = Piran Slovenia 45°31N 13°33E 199 C10
Pīrānshahr Iran 36°41N 45°8E 213 D11
Pirapemas Brazil 3°43S 44°14W 332 B3
Pirapora Brazil 17°20S 44°56W 333 E3
Pirara Guyana 3°37N 59°40W 329 C6
Pirawa India 24°10N 76°2E 242 G7
Piray → Bolivia 16°32S 63°45W 331 D5
Pirdop Bulgaria 42°40N 24°10E 203 D8
Pireas Greece 37°57N 23°42E 112 B1
Pires do Rio Brazil 17°18S 48°17W 333 E2
Pirganj Bangla. 25°51N 88°24E 241 C2
Pirgi Greece 38°13N 25°59E 205 C7
Pirgos Ilia, Greece 37°40N 21°27E 204 D3
Pirgos Kriti, Greece 35°0N 25°9E 207 E6
Pirgovo Bulgaria 43°44N 25°43E 203 C9
Piribebuy Paraguay 25°26S 57°2W 334 B4
Pirimapun Indonesia 6°20S 138°24E 231 F9
Pirin △ Bulgaria 41°48N 23°22E 202 E7
Pirin Planina Bulgaria 41°40N 23°30E 202 E7
Pirinççi Turkey 41°10N 28°52E 122 B1
Pirineos = Pyrénées Europe 42°45N 0°18E 174 F4
Piripiri Brazil 4°15S 41°46W 332 B3
Piritu Venezuela 9°23N 69°12W 328 B4
Pirituba Brazil 23°29S 46°44W 137 A1
Pirkkola Finland 60°14N 24°55E 121 B2
Pirlangimpi Australia 11°24S 130°26E 278 B5
Pirmasens Germany 49°12N 7°36E 179 F3
Pirna Germany 50°57N 13°56E 178 E9
Pirojpur Bangla. 22°35N 90°1E 241 D3
Pirot Serbia 43°9N 22°33E 202 C6
Piru Indonesia 3°4S 128°12E 231 E7
Piru Calif., U.S.A. 34°25N 118°48W 307 L8
Piryatin = Pyryatyn Ukraine 50°15N 32°25E 189 G7
Pisa Italy 43°43N 10°23E 198 E7
Pisa → Poland 53°14N 21°52E 185 E8
Pisa, Firenze ✈ (PSA) Italy 43°40N 10°22E 198 E7
Pisa Ra. N.Z. 44°52S 169°12E 285 E4
Pisac Peru 13°25S 71°50W 330 C3
Pisagne Italy 45°45N 10°10E 198 C7
Pisagua Chile 19°40S 70°15W 330 D3
Pisarovina Croatia 45°35N 15°50E 199 C12
Pisau, Tanjong Malaysia 6°4N 117°59E 235 A5
Pisba △ Colombia 10°39N 74°30W 328 A3
Pisco Peru 13°50S 76°12W 330 C2
Piscu Romania 45°30N 27°43E 183 E12
Písek Czech Rep. 49°19N 14°10E 180 B7
Pisgat O'mer West Bank 31°49N 35°14E 123 B2
Pisgat Ze'ev West Bank 31°49N 35°14E 123 B2
Pishan China 37°30N 78°33E 217 E9
Pishcha Ukraine 51°35N 23°50E 185 G10
Pishchanka Ukraine 48°12N 28°54E 183 B13
Pīshīn Iran 26°6N 61°47E 247 E9
Pishin Pakistan 30°35N 67°0E 242 D2
Pishin Lora → Pakistan 29°9N 64°5E 242 E1
Pishpek = Bishkek Kyrgyzstan 42°54N 74°46E 214 E8
Pisidia Turkey 37°30N 31°40E 212 D4
Pising Indonesia 5°8S 121°53E 231 F6
Pisiou, Pte. Guadeloupe 15°59N 61°13W 322 e
Pismo Beach U.S.A. 35°9N 120°38W 307 K6
Písnice Czech Rep. 49°59N 14°28E 135 C2
Piso, L. Liberia 6°50N 11°15W 262 D2
Pissila Burkina Faso 13°7N 0°50W 263 C4
Pissis, Cerro Argentina 27°45S 68°48W 334 B2
Pissos France 44°19N 0°49W 174 D3
Pissouri Cyprus 34°40N 32°42E 207 F8
Pisticci Italy 40°23N 16°33E 201 B9
Pistóia Italy 43°55N 10°54E 198 E7
Pistol B. Canada 62°25N 92°37W 297 A10
Pisuerga → Spain 41°33N 4°52W 194 D6
Pisz Poland 53°38N 21°49E 184 E8
Pit → U.S.A. 40°47N 122°6W 304 F2
Pita Guinea 11°5N 12°15W 262 C2
Pitalito Colombia 1°51N 76°2W 328 C2
Pitampura India 28°41N 77°7E 120 A1
Pitanga Brazil 24°46S 51°44W 333 F1
Pitangui Brazil 19°40S 44°54W 333 E3
Pitarpunga L. Australia 34°24S 143°30E 282 C5
Pitcairn I. Pac. Oc. 25°5S 130°5W 289 K14
Pitch Pt. Trin. & Tob. 10°15N 61°37W 323 t
Piteå Sweden 65°20N 21°25E 160 D19
Piteälven → Sweden 65°20N 21°25E 160 D19
Piterka Russia 50°41N 47°29E 190 E8
Piteşti Romania 44°52N 24°54E 183 F9
Pithapuram India 17°10N 82°15E 244 F6
Pithara Australia 30°20S 116°35E 279 F2
Pithio Greece 41°24N 26°40E 203 E10
Pithiviers France 48°10N 2°13E 173 D9
Pithora India 21°16N 82°31E 244 D6
Pithoragarh India 29°35N 80°13E 243 E9
Pithoro Pakistan 25°31N 69°23E 242 G3
Piti Guam 13°28N 144°41E 302 d
Pitigliano Italy 42°38N 11°40E 199 F8
Pitkäjärvi Finland 60°15N 24°45E 121 B1
Pitkyaranta Russia 61°34N 31°37E 188 B6
Pitlochry U.K. 56°42N 3°44W 167 E5
Pitnak = Drujba Uzbekistan 41°13N 61°18E 216 D6
Pitoa Cameroon 9°23N 13°32E 264 A2
Pitogo Phil. 13°47N 122°5E 232 E4
Piton, Pte. du Guadeloupe 16°30N 61°26W 322 e
Piton de la Petite Rivière Noire Mauritius 20°24S 57°23E 272 e
Pitons, Anses des St. Lucia 13°49N 61°4W 323 m
Pitou Taiwan 23°53N 120°27E 225 C2
Pitou Chiao Taiwan 25°8N 121°55E 225 A3
Pitrufquén Chile 38°59S 72°39W 336 A2
Pitschen = Byczyna Poland 51°7N 18°12E 185 G5
Pitsilia Cyprus 34°55N 33°0E 207 F9
Pitt, Pta. Ecuador 0°43S 89°14W 330 a
Pitt I. B.C., Canada 53°30N 129°50W 296 C3
Pitt I. N.Z. 44°15S 176°15W 285 a
Pitti I. India 10°50N 72°38E 245 J1
Pittsburg Calif., U.S.A. 38°2N 121°53W 306 G5
Pittsburg Kans., U.S.A. 37°25N 94°42W 308 G6
Pittsburg Tex., U.S.A. 33°0N 94°59W 314 E7
Pittsburgh U.S.A. 40°26N 79°58W 312 F5
Pittsfield Ill., U.S.A. 39°36N 90°49W 310 E6
Pittsfield Maine, U.S.A. 44°47N 69°23W 309 C19
Pittsfield Mass., U.S.A. 42°27N 73°15W 313 D11
Pittsfield N.H., U.S.A. 43°18N 71°20W 313 C13
Pittston U.S.A. 41°19N 75°47W 313 E9
Pittsview U.S.A. 32°11N 85°10W 316 C4
Pittsworth Australia 27°41S 151°37E 281 D5
Pituri → Australia 22°35S 138°30E 280 C2
Pium Brazil 10°27S 49°11W 332 D2
Piumafua Mt. Amer. Samoa 14°11S 169°37W 302 f
Piumhi Brazil 20°28S 45°58W 333 F2
Piura Peru 5°15S 80°38W 330 B1
Piura □ Peru 5°10S 80°0W 330 B2
Piva → Montenegro 43°20N 18°50E 202 C2
Pivijay Colombia 10°28N 74°37W 328 A3
Piwniczna Poland 49°27N 20°42E 185 J7
Pixley U.S.A. 35°58N 119°18W 306 K7
Pizarra Spain 36°36N 4°42W 195 J6
Pizarro Colombia 4°58N 77°22W 328 C2
Pizhou China 34°44N 116°55E 226 G9
Pizzo Italy 38°44N 16°10E 201 D9
Placentia Canada 47°20N 54°0W 299 C9
Placentia B. Canada 47°0N 54°40W 299 C9
Placer Masbate, Phil. 11°52N 123°55E 233 F4
Placer Surigao N., Phil. 9°36N 125°38E 233 G5
Placerville U.S.A. 38°44N 120°48W 306 G6
Placetas Cuba 22°15N 79°44W 320 B4
Plácido de Castro Brazil 10°20S 67°11W 330 C4
Plačkovica Macedonia 41°45N 22°30E 202 E6
Plaine Magnien Mauritius 20°25S 57°39E 272 e
Plaines des Papayes Mauritius 20°3S 57°34E 272 e
Plainfield Ill., U.S.A. 41°37N 88°12W 311 C8
Plainfield Ind., U.S.A. 39°42N 86°24W 311 E10
Plainfield N.J., U.S.A. 40°37N 74°25W 313 F10
Plainfield Ohio, U.S.A. 40°13N 81°43W 312 F3
Plainfield Vt., U.S.A. 44°17N 72°26W 313 B12
Plains Ga., U.S.A. 32°2N 84°24W 316 C5
Plains Mont., U.S.A. 47°28N 114°53W 304 C6
Plains Tex., U.S.A. 33°11N 102°50W 314 E3
Plainview Nebr., U.S.A. 42°21N 97°47W 308 D5
Plainview Tex., U.S.A. 34°11N 101°43W 314 D4
Plainwell U.S.A. 42°27N 85°38W 311 B11
Plaisance France 43°36N 0°3E 174 E4
Plaistow U.S.A. 42°50N 71°6W 313 D13
Plaka Greece 40°0N 25°24E 205 B7
Plaka, Akra Greece 35°11N 26°19E 207 E7
Plakenska Planina Macedonia 41°14N 21°2E 202 E5
Planá Czech Rep. 49°50N 12°44E 180 B5
Plana Cays Bahamas 22°38N 73°30W 321 B5
Planada U.S.A. 37°16N 120°19W 306 H6
Planchón Peru 12°14S 69°11W 330 C4
Plancoët France 48°32N 2°13W 172 D4
Plandište Serbia 45°16N 21°10E 182 E6
Planegg Germany 48°6N 11°25E 131 B1
Planeta Rica Colombia 8°25N 75°36W 328 B2
Plano U.S.A. 33°1N 96°42W 314 E6
Plant City U.S.A. 28°1N 82°7W 317 G7
Plantation U.S.A. 26°7N 80°14W 317 J9
Plaquemine U.S.A. 30°17N 91°14W 314 F9
Plaridel Phil. 8°37N 123°43E 233 G4
Plasencia Spain 40°3N 6°8W 194 E4
Plaški Croatia 45°4N 15°22E 199 C12
Plassen Norway 61°9N 12°30E 164 C9
Plast Russia 54°22N 60°50E 216 B6
Plaster City U.S.A. 32°47N 115°51W 307 N11
Plaster Rock Canada 46°53N 67°22W 299 C6
Plastun Russia 44°45N 136°19E 220 B8
Plasy Czech Rep. 49°56N 13°24E 180 B6
Plata, Río de la → S. Amer. 34°45S 57°30W 334 C4
Plátani → Italy 37°23N 13°16E 200 E6
Platanos Greece 35°28N 23°33E 207 E4
Plataria Greece 39°27N 20°16E 206 C10
Plateau □ Nigeria 8°0N 9°0E 263 D6
Plateau d'Ipassa ⌓ Gabon 0°26N 12°40E 264 B2
Plathe = Płoty Poland 53°48N 15°18E 184 E2
Platinum U.S.A. 59°1N 161°49W 303 G7
Plato Colombia 9°47N 74°47W 328 B3
Platte U.S.A. 43°23N 98°51W 308 D4
Platte → Mo., U.S.A. 39°16N 94°50W 310 E2
Platte → Nebr., U.S.A. 41°4N 95°53W 308 E6
Platte City U.S.A. 39°22N 94°47W 310 E2
Platteville U.S.A. 42°44N 90°29W 310 B6
Plattling Germany 48°46N 12°53E 179 G8
Plattsburg U.S.A. 39°34N 94°27W 310 E2
Plattsburgh U.S.A. 44°42N 73°28W 313 B11
Plattsmouth U.S.A. 41°1N 95°53W 308 E6
Plau Germany 53°27N 12°15E 178 B8
Plauen Germany 50°30N 12°8E 178 E8
Plauer See Germany 53°28N 12°17E 178 B8
Plav Montenegro 42°38N 19°57E 202 D3
Plavinas Latvia 56°35N 25°46E 188 D3
Plavnica Montenegro 42°20N 19°13E 202 D3
Plavno Croatia 44°9N 16°10E 199 D13
Plavsk Russia 53°40N 37°18E 188 F9
Playa Blanca Sur Canary Is. 28°51N 13°50W 153 e2
Playa de las Americas Canary Is. 28°5N 16°43W 153 e1
Playa de Mogán Canary Is. 27°48N 15°47W 153 e1
Playa del Carmen Mexico 20°37N 87°4W 319 C7
Playa del Inglés Canary Is. 27°45N 15°33W 153 e1
Playa Esmerelda Canary Is. 28°8N 14°16W 153 e2
Playas Ecuador 2°38S 80°23W 328 D1
Playgreen L. Canada 54°0N 98°15W 297 C9
Plaza Mayor Madrid, Spain 127 b2
Pleasant Bay Canada 46°51N 60°48W 299 C7
Pleasant Hill Calif., U.S.A. 37°57N 122°4W 306 H4
Pleasant Hill Ill., U.S.A. 39°27N 90°52W 310 E6
Pleasant Hill Mo., U.S.A. 38°47N 94°16W 310 F2
Pleasant Mount U.S.A. 41°44N 75°26W 313 E9
Pleasant Point N.Z. 44°16S 171°9E 285 E6
Pleasant Prairie U.S.A. 42°33N 87°56W 311 B9
Pleasanton Calif., U.S.A. 37°39N 121°52W 306 H5
Pleasanton Tex., U.S.A. 28°58N 98°29W 314 G5
Pleasantville Iowa, U.S.A. 41°23N 93°18W 310 C3
Pleasantville N.J., U.S.A. 39°24N 74°32W 309 F16
Pleasantville Pa., U.S.A. 41°35N 79°34W 312 E5
Pleasure Island U.S.A. 28°21N 81°31W 133 B1
Pleasure Ridge Park U.S.A. 38°9N 85°50W 311 F11
Pléaux France 45°8N 2°13E 174 C6
Plei Ku Vietnam 13°57N 108°0E 236 F7
Plélan-le-Grand France 48°0N 2°7W 172 D4
Pléneuf-Val-André France 48°35N 2°32W 172 D4
Pleniţa Romania 44°14N 23°10E 183 F8
Plenty → Australia 23°25S 136°31E 280 C2
Plenty, B. of N.Z. 37°45S 177°0E 284 D6
Plentywood U.S.A. 48°47N 104°34W 304 B11
Plérin France 48°32N 2°46W 172 D4
Plesetsk Russia 62°43N 40°20E 186 B7
Pleskau = Pskov Russia 57°50N 28°25E 188 D5
Plessisville Canada 46°14N 71°47W 299 C5
Plestin-les-Grèves France 48°40N 3°39W 172 D3
Pleszew Poland 51°53N 17°47E 185 G4
Pleternica Croatia 45°17N 17°48E 182 E2
Plétipi, L. Canada 51°44N 70°6W 299 B5
Pleven Bulgaria 43°26N 24°37E 203 C8
Plevlja Montenegro 43°21N 19°21E 202 C3
Plevna Canada 44°58N 76°59W 312 B8
Plitvička Jezera △ Croatia 44°54N 15°35E 199 D12
Plješevica Croatia 44°45N 15°45E 199 D12
Ploaghe Italy 40°40N 8°45E 200 B1
Ploče Croatia 43°4N 17°26E 199 E14
Plock Poland 52°32N 19°40E 185 F6
Plöckenpass Italy 46°37N 12°57E 199 B9
Plöckenstein Germany 48°46N 13°51E 179 G9
Ploemeur France 47°44N 3°26W 172 E3
Ploërmel France 47°55N 2°26W 172 E4
Plöhnen = Płońsk Poland 52°37N 20°21E 185 F7
Ploieşti Romania 44°57N 26°5E 183 F11
Plomari Greece 38°59N 26°22E 205 C8
Plombières-les-Bains France 47°58N 6°27E 173 E13
Plomin Croatia 45°8N 14°10E 199 C11
Plön Germany 54°9N 10°24E 178 A6
Plonge, Lac la Canada 55°8N 107°20W 297 B7
Płońsk Poland 52°37N 20°21E 185 F7
Plopeni Romania 45°4N 25°59E 183 E10
Plopişului, Munţii Romania 47°5N 22°30E 182 C7
Plotsk = Plock Poland 52°32N 19°40E 185 F6
Płoty Poland 53°48N 15°18E 184 E2
Plouaret France 48°37N 3°28W 172 D3
Plouay France 47°55N 3°21W 172 E3
Ploučnice → Czech Rep. 50°46N 14°13E 180 A7
Ploudalmézeau France 48°34N 4°41W 172 D2
Plouescat France 48°39N 4°10W 172 D2
Plougasnou France 48°42N 3°49W 172 D3
Plougastel-Daoulas France 48°22N 4°17W 172 D2
Plouguerneau France 48°36N 4°30W 172 D2
Plouha France 48°41N 2°57W 172 D4
Plouhinec France 48°0N 4°29W 172 E2
Plovdiv Bulgaria 42°8N 24°44E 203 D8
Plovdiv □ Bulgaria 42°15N 24°30E 203 D8
Plover Cove Res. China 22°28N 114°15E 219 G11
Pluies, R. des → Réunion 20°52S 55°31E 272 f
Plum U.S.A. 40°29N 79°47W 312 F5
Plum I. U.S.A. 41°11N 72°12W 313 E12
Plumas U.S.A. 39°45N 120°4W 306 F6
Plummer U.S.A. 47°20N 116°53W 304 C5
Plumridge Lakes Australia 29°26S 125°16E 279 E4
Plumstead Western Cape, S. Africa 34°1S 18°28E 118 B1
Plumstead London, U.K. 51°29N 0°5E 125 B4
Plumtree Zimbabwe 20°27S 27°55E 269 G2
Plungė Lithuania 55°53N 21°59E 184 C8
Pluvigner France 47°46N 3°1W 172 E3
Plužine Montenegro 43°8N 18°51E 202 C2
Plymouth Montserrat 16°41N 62°12W 323 p
Plymouth Trin. & Tob. 11°14N 60°48W 323 s
Plymouth Plymouth, U.K. 50°22N 4°10W 169 G3
Plymouth Calif., U.S.A. 38°29N 120°51W 306 G6
Plymouth Ill., U.S.A. 40°18N 90°58W 310 D6
Plymouth Ind., U.S.A. 41°21N 86°19W 311 C10
Plymouth Mass., U.S.A. 41°57N 70°40W 313 E14
Plymouth N.C., U.S.A. 35°52N 76°43W 315 D16
Plymouth N.H., U.S.A. 43°46N 71°41W 313 C13
Plymouth Pa., U.S.A. 41°14N 75°57W 313 E9
Plymouth Wis., U.S.A. 43°45N 87°59W 308 D10
Plympton-Wyoming = Wyoming Canada 42°57N 82°7W 312 D2
Plynlimon = Pumlumon Fawr U.K. 52°28N 3°46W 169 E4
Plyusa Russia 58°28N 29°27E 188 C5
Plyusa → Russia 59°4N 28°6E 188 C5
Plyushchevo Russia 55°44N 37°45E 129 B4
Plzeň Czech Rep. 49°45N 13°22E 180 B6
Plzeňský □ Czech Rep. 49°35N 13°0E 180 B6
Pmere Nyente ☼ Australia 24°15S 136°10E 280 C2
Pniewy Poland 52°31N 16°16E 185 F3
Pnika Athens, Greece 112 c1
Pô Burkina Faso 11°14N 1°5W 263 C4
Po → Italy 44°57N 12°4E 199 D9
Po, Foci del Italy 44°55N 12°30E 199 D9
Pô △ Burkina Faso 11°25N 1°5W 263 C4
Po Hai = Bo Hai China 39°0N 119°0E 227 E10
Po Toi China 22°10N 114°16E 122 B2
Po Toi O China 22°16N 114°17E 122 B2
Poasco Italy 45°24N 9°16E 129 B2
Pobé Benin 7°0N 2°56E 263 D5
Pobé Burkina Faso 13°53N 1°42W 263 C4
Pobeda Russia 65°12N 146°12E 215 C15
Pobedy, Pik Kyrgyzstan 42°0N 79°58E 217 D9
Pobiedziska Poland 52°29N 17°11E 185 F4
Pobladura del Valle Spain 42°6N 5°44W 194 C5
Pobra de Trives Spain 42°20N 7°10W 194 C3
Pocahontas Ark., U.S.A. 36°16N 90°58W 315 C9
Pocahontas Ill., U.S.A. 38°50N 89°33W 310 F7
Pocahontas Iowa, U.S.A. 42°44N 94°40W 310 B2
Pocatello U.S.A. 42°52N 112°27W 304 E7
Počátky Czech Rep. 49°15N 15°14E 180 B8
Pocheon S. Korea 37°53N 127°13E 224 D3
Pochep Russia 52°58N 33°29E 189 F7
Pochinki Russia 54°41N 44°59E 190 C7
Pochinok Russia 54°28N 32°29E 188 E7
Pöchlarn Austria 48°12N 15°12E 180 C8
Poci Venezuela 5°57N 61°29W 329 B5
Pocinhos Brazil 7°4S 36°3W 332 C4
Pocking Germany 48°23N 13°19E 179 G9
Pocklington Reef Papua N. G. 10°51S 155°44E 286 F8
Poções Brazil 14°31S 40°21W 333 D3
Pocomoke City U.S.A. 38°5N 75°34W 309 F16
Poconé Brazil 16°15S 56°37W 331 D6
Poços de Caldas Brazil 21°50S 46°33W 335 A6
Podbaba Czech Rep. 50°7N 14°22E 135 B2
Podbořany Czech Rep. 50°14N 13°25E 180 A6
Poddębice Poland 51°54N 18°58E 185 G5
Poděbrady Czech Rep. 50°9N 15°8E 180 A8
Podensac France 44°40N 0°22W 174 D3
Podenzano Italy 44°57N 9°41E 198 D6
Podgorač Croatia 45°27N 18°13E 182 E3
Podgorica Montenegro 42°30N 19°19E 202 D3
Podgorie Albania 40°49N 20°48E 202 F4
Podile India 15°37N 79°37E 245 G4
Podilska Vysochyna Ukraine 49°0N 28°0E 183 B13
Podkarpackie □ Poland 50°0N 22°10E 185 H9
Podkova Bulgaria 41°24N 25°24E 203 E9
Podlapača Croatia 44°37N 15°47E 199 D12
Podlaskie □ Poland 53°10N 23°0E 185 E10
Podocarpus △ Ecuador 4°13S 79°29W 328 D2
Podoleni Romania 46°46N 26°39E 183 D11
Podoli Czech Rep. 50°2N 14°25E 135 B2
Podolínec Slovak Rep. 49°16N 20°31E 181 B13
Podolsk Russia 55°25N 37°30E 188 E9
Podor Senegal 16°40N 15°2W 262 B1
Podporozhye Russia 60°55N 34°2E 188 B8
Podu Iloaiei Romania 47°13N 27°16E 183 C12
Podu Turcului Romania 46°11N 27°25E 183 D12
Podujevo Kosovo 42°54N 21°10E 202 D5
Poduskino Russia 55°43N 37°15E 129 B1
Podyji △ Czech Rep. 48°51N 15°57E 180 C8
Poechos Peru 4°41S 80°34W 328 D1
Poel Germany 54°0N 11°25E 178 B6
Pofadder S. Africa 29°10S 19°22E 270 C2
Poggiardo Italy 40°3N 18°23E 201 B11
Poggibonsi Italy 43°28N 11°9E 198 E8
Póggio Mirteto Italy 42°16N 12°41E 199 F9
Pogoanele Romania 44°55N 27°0E 183 F12
Pogorzela Poland 51°50N 17°12E 185 G4
Pogoso Dem. Rep. of the Congo 6°46S 17°12E 265 D3
Pogradec Albania 40°54N 20°37E 202 F4
Pogranichnyy Russia 44°25N 131°24E 220 B5
Poh Indonesia 0°46S 122°51E 231 E6
Pohang S. Korea 36°1N 129°23E 224 D4
Pohick Creek → U.S.A. 38°48N 77°15W 143 C2
Pohjanmaa Finland 62°58N 22°50E 160 E20
Pohjois-Pirkkala = Nokia Finland 61°30N 23°30E 188 B2
Pohnpei Micronesia 6°55N 158°10E 288 G7
Pohorelá Slovak Rep. 48°50N 20°2E 181 C13
Pohořelice Czech Rep. 48°59N 16°31E 181 C9
Pohorje Slovenia 46°30N 15°20E 199 B12
Pohri India 25°32N 77°22E 242 G6
Pöhue B. U.S.A. 19°0N 155°48W 302 E6
Poi Solomon Is. 10°9S 161°42E 287 N11
Poiana Mare Romania 43°57N 23°5E 182 G8
Poiana Ruscăi, Munţii Romania 45°45N 22°25E 182 E7
Poiana Stampei Romania 47°19N 25°8E 183 C10
Poie Dem. Rep. of the Congo 2°50S 23°14E 264 C4
Poike, Península Chile 27°6S 109°15W 330 b
Poindimié N. Cal. 20°56S 165°20E 288 d
Poinsett, C. Antarctica 65°42S 113°18E 151 C8
Point Arena U.S.A. 38°55N 123°41W 306 G3
Point Baker U.S.A. 56°21N 133°37W 296 B2
Point Calimere India 10°17N 79°49E 245 J4
Point Fortin Trin. & Tob. 10°10N 61°42W 323 t
Point Hope U.S.A. 68°21N 166°47W 303 B6
Point L. Canada 65°15N 113°4W 294 D9
Point Lay U.S.A. 69°46N 163°3W 303 B7
Point Lisas Trin. & Tob. 10°24N 61°29W 323 t
Point Pedro Sri Lanka 9°50N 80°15E 245 K5
Point Pelee △ Canada 41°57N 82°31W 312 E2
Point Pleasant N.J., U.S.A. 40°5N 74°4W 313 F10
Point Pleasant W. Va., U.S.A. 38°51N 82°8W 309 F12
Point Reyes ⌓ U.S.A. 38°10N 122°55W 306 G2
Point Salines Int. ✈ (GND) Grenada 12°0N 61°46W 323 q
Pointe-à-Pierre Trin. & Tob. 10°19N 61°28W 323 t
Pointe-à-Pitre Guadeloupe 16°10N 61°32W 322 e
Pointe-au-Pic = La Malbaie Canada 47°40N 70°10W 299 C5
Pointe-Aux-Trembles Canada 45°38N 73°30W 130 A2
Pointe-Claire Canada 45°26N 73°50W 313 A11
Pointe-Gatineau Canada 45°27N 75°41W 313 A9
Pointe Michel Dominica 15°15N 61°23W 323 k
Pointe-Noire Congo 4°48S 11°53E 265 C2
Pointe-Noire Guadeloupe 16°14N 61°47W 322 e
Poio Spain 42°28N 8°41W 194 C2
Poipet Cambodia 13°39N 102°33E 236 F4
Poirino Italy 44°56N 7°48E 198 D4
Poisonbush Ra. Australia 22°30S 121°30E 278 D3
Poissonnier Pt. Australia 19°57S 119°10E 278 C2
Poissy France 48°55N 2°2E 134 A1
Poitiers France 46°35N 0°20E 172 F7
Poitou France 46°40N 0°10W 174 B3
Poitou-Charentes □ France 46°10N 0°15E 174 B4
Poix-de-Picardie France 49°47N 1°58E 173 C8
Poix-Terron France 49°38N 4°38E 173 C11
Pojoaque U.S.A. 35°54N 106°1W 305 J10
Pok Fu Lam China 22°16N 114°7E 122 B1
Pōka'ī B. U.S.A. 21°27N 158°12W 302 K13
Pokaran India 27°0N 71°50E 242 F4
Pokataroo Australia 29°30S 148°36E 281 D4
Pokcheong S. Korea 37°28N 127°8E 137 C2
Pokhara Nepal 28°14N 83°58E 243 E10
Pokhvistnevo Russia 53°36N 52°0E 190 D11
Pokigron Suriname 4°30N 55°22W 329 C6
Poko Dem. Rep. of the Congo 3°7N 26°52E 268 B2
Poko Sudan 5°41N 31°55E 257 F3
Pokrov Russia 55°55N 39°7E 188 E10
Pokrovka = Kyzyl-Suu Kyrgyzstan 42°20N 78°0E 217 D9
Pokrovsk = Engels Russia 51°28N 46°6E 190 E8
Pokrovsk Russia 61°29N 129°0E 215 C13
Pokrovsko-Sresnevo Russia 55°48N 37°27E 129 B2
Pokrovskoy = Priazovskoye Ukraine 46°44N 35°40E 189 J8
Pokrovskoye Russia 47°25N 38°54E 189 J10
Pol-e Dokhtar Iran 33°9N 47°42E 213 F12
Pol-e Khomrī Afghan. 35°56N 68°42E 240 B3
Pol-e Zahāb Iran 34°27N 45°51E 213 E11
Pola = Istra Croatia 45°10N 14°0E 199 C10
Pola = Pula Croatia 44°54N 13°57E 199 D10
Pola Russia 57°55N 32°0E 188 D7
Pola de Allande Spain 43°16N 6°37W 194 B4
Pola de Lena Spain 43°10N 5°49W 194 B5
Pola de Siero Spain 43°24N 5°39W 194 B5
Pola de Somiedo Spain 43°5N 6°15W 194 B4
Pola I. Amer. Samoa 14°14S 170°40W 302 f
Polacca U.S.A. 35°50N 110°23W 305 J8
Polan Iran 25°30N 61°10E 247 E9
Pol'ana Slovak Rep. 48°38N 19°29E 181 C12
Poland U.S.A. 43°13N 75°3W 313 C9
Poland ■ Europe 52°0N 20°0E 185 G3
Polanica-Zdrój Poland 50°24N 16°32E 185 H3
Połaniec Poland 50°26N 21°17E 185 H8
Polanów Poland 54°7N 16°41E 184 D3
Polar Bear ⌓ Canada 55°0N 83°45W 298 A2
Polatlı Turkey 39°36N 32°9E 212 C5
Polatsk Belarus 55°30N 28°50E 188 E5
Polavaram India 17°15N 81°38E 244 F5
Polcura Chile 37°17S 71°43W 334 D1
Połczyn-Zdrój Poland 53°47N 16°5E 184 E3
Poldasht Iran 39°20N 45°4E 213 C11
Poleski △ Poland 51°29N 23°5E 185 G10
Polessk Russia 54°50N 21°8E 184 D8
Polesye = Pripet Marshes Europe 52°10N 28°10E 177 B15
Polevskoy Russia 56°26N 60°11E 186 C11
Polgar Hungary 47°54N 21°6E 182 C6
Poli Cameroon 8°34N 13°15E 263 C7
Policastro, G. di Italy 40°0N 15°35E 201 C8
Police Poland 53°33N 14°33E 184 E1
Police, Pte. Seychelles 4°51S 55°32E 272 c
Polichnitos Greece 39°6N 26°10E 205 B8
Polička Czech Rep. 49°43N 16°15E 181 B9
Policoro Italy 40°13N 16°41E 201 B9
Poliegos Greece 36°45N 24°38E 204 E6
Poligiros Greece 40°23N 23°25E 202 F7

Polignano a Mare Italy 41°0N 17°13E 201 A9
Poligny France 46°50N 5°42E 173 F12
Polillo Phil. 14°43N 121°56E 232 D3
Polillo Is. Phil. 14°56N 122°0E 232 D4
Polillo Strait Phil. 14°44N 121°51E 232 D3
Polis Cyprus 35°2N 32°26E 207 E8
Polístena Italy 38°24N 16°4E 201 D9
Pölitz = Police Poland 53°33N 14°33E 184 E1
Polk U.S.A. 41°22N 79°56W 312 E5
Polkowice Poland 51°29N 16°3E 185 G3
Polkwitz = Polkowice Poland 51°29N 16°3E 185 G3
Polla Italy 40°31N 15°29E 201 B8
Pollachi India 10°35N 77°0E 245 J3
Pollença Spain 39°54N 3°1E 206 B4
Pollença, B. de Spain 39°53N 3°8E 206 B4
Pollfoss Norway 61°58N 7°54E 164 C4
Póllica Italy 40°11N 15°3E 201 B8
Pollino, Mte. Italy 39°55N 16°11E 201 C9
Pollino △ Italy 40°0N 16°12E 201 C9
Polna Russia 58°31N 28°5E 188 C5
Polnovat Russia 63°50N 65°54E 214 C7
Polo Ill., U.S.A. 41°59N 89°35W 310 C7
Polo Mo., U.S.A. 39°33N 94°3W 310 E2
Pology Ukraine 47°29N 36°15E 189 J9
Polokwane S. Africa 23°54S 29°25E 271 B4
Polokwane → S. Africa 22°25S 30°5E 271 B5
Polonnaruwa Sri Lanka 7°56N 81°0E 245 L5
Polonne Ukraine 50°6N 27°30E 177 C14
Polonnoye = Polonne Ukraine 50°6N 27°30E 177 C14
Polski Trŭmbesh Bulgaria 43°20N 25°38E 203 C9
Polsko Kosovo Bulgaria 43°23N 25°38E 203 C9
Polson U.S.A. 47°41N 114°9W 304 C6
Poltár Slovak Rep. 48°26N 19°48E 181 C12
Poltava Ukraine 49°35N 34°35E 189 H8
Poltava □ Ukraine 50°15N 33°15E 189 G7
Polton U.K. 55°52N 3°7W 121 B3
Poltoratsk = Ashgabat Turkmenistan 38°0N 57°50E 247 B8
Põltsamaa Estonia 58°39N 25°58E 188 C3
Polunochnoye Russia 60°52N 60°25E 214 C7
Polur India 12°32N 79°11E 245 H4
Põlva Estonia 58°3N 27°3E 188 C4
Polvoranca, Parque de Spain 40°19N 3°48W 127 C1
Polyana Ukraine 48°38N 22°58E 182 B7
Polyarny Russia 69°8N 33°20E 160 B25
Polyarnyye Zori Russia 67°22N 32°30E 160 C25
Polynesia Pac. Oc. 10°0S 162°0W 289 F11
Polynesian Cultural Center U.S.A. 21°38N 157°55W 302 J14
Polynésie française = French Polynesia ⊠ Pac. Oc. 20°0S 145°0W 289 f
Polyustrovo Russia 59°57N 30°25E 137 B2
Pomabamba = Azurduy Bolivia 19°59S 64°29W 331 D5
Pomabamba Peru 8°50S 77°28W 330 B2
Pomarance Italy 43°18N 10°52E 198 E7
Pombal Brazil 6°45S 37°50W 332 C4
Pombal Portugal 39°55N 8°40W 194 F2
Pombia Greece 35°0N 24°51E 207 F5
Pombos, B. dos Angola 11°40S 13°47E 265 E2
Pomene Mozam. 22°53S 35°33E 271 B6
Pomeroy Ohio, U.S.A. 39°2N 82°2W 309 F12
Pomeroy Wash., U.S.A. 46°28N 117°36W 304 C5
Pomézia Italy 41°40N 12°30E 200 A5
Pomichna Ukraine 48°13N 31°36E 189 H6
Pomio Papua N. G. 5°32S 151°33E 286 C6
Pomme de Terre L. U.S.A. 37°54N 93°19W 310 G3
Pomme Rose Grenada 12°3N 61°39W 323 q
Pomona Queens., Australia 26°22S 152°52E 281 D5
Pomona Calif., U.S.A. 34°4N 117°45W 307 L9
Pomona Park U.S.A. 29°30N 81°36W 317 F8
Pomorie Bulgaria 42°32N 27°41E 203 D11
Pomorskie □ Poland 54°30N 18°0E 184 D5
Pomorskie, Pojezierze Poland 53°40N 16°37E 184 E3
Pomos Cyprus 35°9N 32°33E 207 E8
Pomos, C. Cyprus 35°10N 32°33E 207 E8
Pompano Beach U.S.A. 26°14N 80°7W 317 J9
Pompei Italy 40°45N 14°30E 201 B7
Pompey France 48°46N 6°6E 173 D13
Pompeys Pillar U.S.A. 45°59N 107°57W 304 D10
Pompeys Pillar ⌂ U.S.A. 46°0N 108°0W 304 D10
Pompidou, Centre Paris, France 134 b4
Pomprap Thailand 13°44N 100°30E 113 B2
Pompton Lakes U.S.A. 41°0N 74°17W 313 F10
Ponape = Pohnpei Micronesia 6°55N 158°10E 288 G7
Ponask L. Canada 54°0N 92°41W 298 B1
Ponca U.S.A. 42°34N 96°43W 308 D5
Ponca City U.S.A. 36°42N 97°5W 314 C6
Ponce Puerto Rico 18°1N 66°37W 321 C6
Ponce de Leon U.S.A. 30°44N 85°56W 316 E4
Ponce de Leon B. U.S.A. 25°15N 81°10W 317 K8
Ponchatoula U.S.A. 30°26N 90°26W 315 F9
Poncheville, L. Canada 50°10N 76°55W 298 B4
Pond U.S.A. 35°43N 119°20W 307 K7
Pond Inlet Canada 72°40N 77°0W 295 C16
Pondicherry = Puducherry India 11°59N 79°50E 245 J4
Pondo Papua N. G. 4°33S 151°38E 286 C6
Pondok Gede Indonesia 6°20S 106°55E 122 A2
Pondok Indah Indonesia 6°16S 106°46E 122 B1
Ponds, I. of Canada 53°27N 55°52W 299 B8
Ponérihouen N. Cal. 21°5S 165°24E 288 d
Ponferrada Spain 42°32N 6°35W 194 C4
Pongo, Wadi → Sudan 8°42N 27°40E 257 F2
Poniatowa Poland 51°11N 22°3E 185 G9
Poniec Poland 51°48N 16°50E 185 G3
Ponikva Slovenia 46°16N 15°26E 199 B12
Ponizovkino = Krasnyy Profintern Russia 57°45N 40°27E 188 D11
Ponnaiyar → India 11°50N 79°45E 245 J4
Ponnani India 10°45N 75°59E 245 J2
Ponneri India 13°20N 80°15E 245 H5
Ponnuru India 16°5N 80°34E 245 F5
Ponoka Canada 52°42N 113°40W 296 C6
Ponorogo Indonesia 7°52S 111°27E 235 D4
Ponot Phil. 8°25N 123°0E 233 G4
Ponoy Russia 67°0N 41°13E 186 A7
Ponoy → Russia 66°59N 41°17E 186 A7
Pons = Ponts Spain 41°55N 1°12E 196 D6
Pons France 45°35N 0°34W 174 C3
Ponsul → Portugal 39°40N 7°31W 194 F3
Pont-à-Mousson France 48°54N 6°1E 173 D13
Pont-Audemer France 49°21N 0°30E 172 C7
Pont-Aven France 47°51N 3°47W 172 E3
Pont Canavese Italy 45°25N 7°36E 198 C4
Pont Casse Dominica 15°22N 61°21W 323 k
Pont-d'Ain France 46°3N 5°21E 173 F12
Pont-de-Roide France 47°23N 6°45E 173 E13
Pont-de-Salars France 44°18N 2°44E 174 D6
Pont-de-Vaux France 46°26N 4°56E 173 F11
Pont-de-Veyle France 46°17N 4°53E 173 F11
Pont-du-Château France 45°47N 3°15E 173 G10
Pont-l'Abbé France 47°52N 4°15W 172 E2
Pont-l'Évêque France 49°18N 0°11E 172 C7
Pont-St-Esprit France 44°16N 4°40E 175 D8
Pont-St-Martin Italy 45°36N 7°48E 198 C4
Pont-Ste-Maxence France 49°18N 2°36E 173 C9
Pont-sur-Yonne France 48°18N 3°10E 173 D10
Pont-Viau Canada 45°35N 73°41W 130 A1
Ponta de Pedras Brazil 1°23S 48°52W 332 B2
Ponta Delgada Flores, Azores 39°31N 31°13W 153 d2
Ponta Delgada São Miguel, Azores 37°44N 25°40W 153 d3
Ponta Delgada ✈ (PDL) Azores 37°44N 25°41W 153 d3
Ponta do Sol Madeira 32°42N 17°7W 153 c
Ponta Grossa Brazil 25°7S 50°10W 335 B5
Ponta Porã Brazil 22°20S 55°35W 335 A4
Pontacq France 43°11N 0°8W 174 E3
Pontailler-sur-Saône France 47°13N 5°25E 173 E12
Pontal → Brazil 9°8S 40°12W 332 C3
Pontalina Brazil 17°31S 49°27W 333 E2
Pontarlier France 46°54N 6°20E 173 F13
Pontassieve Italy 43°46N 11°26E 199 E8
Pontault-Combault France 48°47N 2°36E 134 B4
Pontaumur France 45°52N 2°40E 174 C6
Pontcharra France 45°26N 6°1E 175 C10
Pontchartrain, L. U.S.A. 30°5N 90°5W 315 F9
Pontchâteau France 47°25N 2°5W 172 E4
Ponte Alta, Serra do Brazil 19°42S 47°40W 333 E2
Ponte Alta do Norte Brazil 10°45S 47°34W 332 D2
Ponte Branca Brazil 16°27S 52°40W 331 D7
Ponte da Barca Portugal 41°48N 8°25W 194 D2
Ponte de Sor Portugal 39°17N 8°1W 195 F2
Ponte dell'Ólio Italy 44°52N 9°39E 198 D6
Ponte di Legno Italy 46°16N 10°31E 198 B7
Ponte do Lima Portugal 41°46N 8°35W 194 D2
Ponte do Pungué Mozam. 19°30S 34°33E 269 F3
Ponte-Leccia France 42°28N 9°13E 175 F13
Ponte nelle Alpi Italy 46°11N 12°16E 199 B9
Ponte Nova Brazil 20°25S 42°54W 333 F3
Ponte Vedra Beach U.S.A. 30°15N 81°23W 316 E8
Ponteareas Spain 42°10N 8°28W 194 C2
Pontebba Italy 46°30N 13°18E 199 B10
Ponteceso Spain 43°15N 8°54W 194 B2
Pontecorvo Italy 41°27N 13°40E 200 A6
Pontedeume Spain 43°24N 8°10W 194 B2
Ponteix Canada 49°46N 107°29W 297 D7
Pontes e Lacerda Brazil 15°12S 59°22W 331 D6
Pontevedra Capiz, Phil. 11°29N 122°50E 233 F4
Pontevedra Neg. Occ., Phil. 10°22N 122°52E 233 F4
Pontevedra Spain 42°26N 8°40W 194 C2
Pontevedra □ Spain 42°25N 8°39W 194 C2
Pontevedra, R. de → Spain 42°22N 8°45W 194 C2
Pontevico Italy 45°16N 10°5E 198 C7
Pontiac Ill., U.S.A. 40°53N 88°38W 311 D8
Pontiac Mich., U.S.A. 42°38N 83°18W 311 B13
Pontian Kechil Malaysia 1°29N 103°23E 237 d
Pontianak Indonesia 0°3S 109°15E 235 C3
Pontine Is. = Ponziane, Ísole Italy 40°55N 12°57E 200 B5
Pontine Mts. = Kuzey Anadolu Dağları Turkey 41°0N 36°45E 212 B7
Pontinha Portugal 38°45N 9°11W 126 A1
Pontínia Italy 41°25N 13°2E 200 A6
Pontivy France 48°5N 2°58W 172 D4
Pontoise France 49°3N 2°5E 173 C9
Ponton → Canada 58°27N 116°11W 296 B5
Pontorson France 48°34N 1°30W 172 D5
Pontrémoli Italy 44°22N 9°53E 198 D6
Pontrieux France 48°42N 3°10W 172 D3
Ponts Spain 41°55N 1°12E 196 D6
Pontypool Ont., Canada 44°6N 78°38W 312 B6
Pontypool Torf., U.K. 51°42N 3°2W 169 F4
Ponza Italy 40°54N 12°58E 200 B5
Ponziane, Ísole Italy 40°55N 12°57E 200 B5
Poochera Australia 32°43S 134°51E 281 E1
Poole Trin. & Tob. 10°17N 61°14W 323 t
Poole Poole, U.K. 50°43N 1°59W 169 G6
Poole □ U.K. 50°43N 1°59W 169 G6
Poole → Trin. & Tob. 10°15N 61°5W 323 t
Pooler U.S.A. 32°7N 81°15W 316 C8
Poona = Pune India 18°29N 73°57E 244 E1
Poonamallee India 13°3N 80°10E 245 H5
Pooncarie Australia 33°22S 142°31E 282 B5
Poopelloe L. Australia 31°40S 144°0E 282 A6
Poopó Bolivia 18°23S 66°59W 330 D4
Poopó, L. de Bolivia 18°30S 67°35W 330 D4
Poor Knights Is. N.Z. 35°29S 174°43E 284 B3
Poorman U.S.A. 64°5N 155°33W 303 D9
Popa Gabon 1°35S 12°32E 264 C2
Popa, Mt. Burma 20°55N 95°15E 241 E5
Popayán Colombia 2°27N 76°36W 328 C2
Poperinge Belgium 50°51N 2°42E 170 D2
Popiltah L. Australia 33°10S 141°42E 282 B4
Popina Bulgaria 44°7N 26°57E 203 B10
Popio L. Australia 33°10S 141°52E 282 B4
Poplar London, U.K. 51°30N 0°0 125 A3
Poplar Mont., U.S.A. 48°7N 105°12W 304 B11
Poplar → Canada 53°0N 97°19W 297 C9
Poplar Bluff U.S.A. 36°46N 90°24W 308 G8
Poplar Head = Dothan U.S.A. 31°13N 85°24W 316 D4
Poplarville U.S.A. 30°51N 89°32W 315 F10
Popocatépetl, Volcán Mexico 19°2N 98°38W 319 D5
Popokabaka Dem. Rep. of the Congo 5°41S 16°40E 265 D3
Pópoli Italy 42°10N 13°50E 199 F10
Popolo Dem. Rep. of the Congo 2°22N 21°8E 264 B4
Popolo, Porta del Rome, Italy 136 a2
Popomanaseu, Mt. Solomon Is. 9°40S 160°1E 287 M11
Popondetta Papua N. G. 8°48S 148°17E 286 E5
Popovača Croatia 45°30N 16°41E 199 C13
Popovo Bulgaria 43°21N 26°18E 203 C10
Poppberg Germany 49°26N 11°37E 179 F7
Poppi Italy 43°43N 11°46E 199 E8
Poppintree Ireland 53°23N 6°17W 120 A2
Poprad Slovak Rep. 49°3N 20°18E 181 B13
Poprad → Slovak Rep. 49°38N 20°42E 181 B13
Poradaha Bangla. 23°51N 89°1E 241 D2
Porali → Pakistan 25°58N 66°26E 242 G2
Porangaba Brazil 8°48S 70°36W 330 B3
Porangahau N.Z. 40°17S 176°37E 284 G5
Porangatu Brazil 13°26S 49°10W 333 D2
Porbandar India 21°44N 69°43E 242 J3
Porce → Colombia 7°28N 74°53W 328 B3
Porcher I. Canada 53°50N 130°30W 296 C2
Porco Bolivia 19°50S 65°59W 331 D4
Porcos → Brazil 12°42S 45°7W 333 D2
Porcuna Spain 37°52N 4°11W 195 H6
Porcupine → Sask., Canada 59°11N 104°46W 297 B8
Porcupine → Alaska, U.S.A. 66°34N 145°19W 303 C11
Porcupine Abyssal Plain Atl. Oc. 48°0N 8°0W 152 B10
Porcupine Gorge △ Australia 20°22S 144°26E 280 C3
Pordenone Italy 45°57N 12°39E 199 C9
Pordim Bulgaria 43°23N 24°51E 203 C8
Pore Colombia 5°43N 72°0W 328 B3
Poreč Croatia 45°14N 13°36E 199 C10
Porecatu Brazil 22°43S 51°24W 333 F1
Porechye = Demidov Russia 55°16N 31°30E 188 E6
Poretskoye Russia 55°9N 46°21E 190 C8
Porgera Papua N. G. 5°28S 143°12E 286 C2
Pori Finland 61°29N 21°48E 188 B1
Pori Greece 35°58N 23°13E 204 F5
Porirua N.Z. 41°8S 174°52E 143 A2
Porirua East N.Z. 41°8S 174°52E 143 A2
Porkhov Russia 57°45N 29°38E 188 D5
Porlamar Venezuela 10°57N 63°51W 329 A5
Porlezza Italy 46°2N 9°7E 198 B6
Porma → Spain 42°49N 5°28W 194 C5
Pormpuraaw Australia 14°59S 141°26E 280 A3
Pormpuraaw ☼ Australia 14°55S 141°47E 280 A3
Pornic France 47°7N 2°5W 172 E4
Poronaysk Russia 49°13N 143°0E 215 E15
Poros Attiki, Greece 37°30N 23°30E 204 D5
Poros Kefalonia, Greece 38°9N 20°47E 207 C2
Poros Lefkada, Greece 38°38N 20°43E 207 B2
Poroshiri-Dake Japan 42°41N 142°52E 220 C11
Poroszló Hungary 47°39N 20°40E 182 C5
Poroto Mts. Tanzania 9°0S 33°30E 269 D3
Porpoise B. Antarctica 66°0S 127°0E 151 C9
Porpoise Pt. Ascension I. 7°54S 14°21W 153 g
Porquerolles, Î. de France 43°0N 6°13E 175 F10
Porrentruy Switz. 47°25N 7°6E 179 H3
Porreres Spain 39°31N 3°2E 206 B4
Porsangerfjorden Norway 70°40N 25°40E 160 A21
Porsgrunn Norway 59°10N 9°40E 164 E6
Port Adelaide Australia 34°50S 138°30E 282 C3
Port Alberni Canada 49°14N 124°50W 296 D4
Port Albert Australia 38°42S 146°42E 283 E7
Port Alexander U.S.A. 56°15N 134°38W 303 H14
Port Alfred S. Africa 33°36S 26°55E 270 D4
Port Alice Canada 50°20N 127°25W 296 C3
Port Allegany U.S.A. 41°48N 78°17W 312 E6
Port Allen U.S.A. 30°27N 91°12W 314 F9
Port Alma Queens., Australia 23°38S 150°53E 280 C5
Port Alma Ont., Canada 42°10N 82°14W 312 D2
Port Angeles U.S.A. 48°7N 123°27W 306 B3
Port Antonio Jamaica 18°10N 76°26W 320 a
Port Aransas U.S.A. 27°50N 97°4W 314 H6
Port Arthur Tas., Australia 43°7S 147°50E 281 G4
Port Arthur Tex., U.S.A. 29°54N 93°56W 314 G8
Port au Choix Canada 50°43N 57°22W 299 B8
Port au Port B. Canada 48°40N 58°50W 299 C8
Port-au-Prince Haiti 18°40N 72°20W 321 C5
Port Augusta Australia 32°30S 137°50E 282 B2
Port Austin U.S.A. 44°3N 83°1W 312 B2
Port Authority Bus Terminal New York, U.S.A. 132 c2
Port-aux-Français Kerguelen 49°21S 70°13E 273 J6
Port Bell Uganda 0°18N 32°35E 268 B3
Port Bergé Vaovao Madag. 15°33S 47°40E 272 B2
Port Blair India 11°40N 92°45E 245 J11
Port Blandford Canada 48°20N 54°10W 299 C9
Port Botany Australia 33°58S 151°13E 139 B2
Port-Bouët Ivory C. 5°16N 3°57W 262 D4
Port Bradshaw Australia 12°30S 137°20E 280 A2
Port Broughton Australia 33°37S 137°56E 282 B2
Port Bruce Canada 42°39N 81°0W 312 D4
Port Burwell Canada 42°40N 80°48W 312 D4
Port Byron U.S.A. 41°36N 90°20W 310 C6
Port Campbell Vic., Australia 38°37S 143°1E 282 E5
Port Campbell India 11°56N 92°37E 245 J11
Port Campbell △ Australia 38°8S 143°6E 282 E5
Port Canning India 22°23N 88°40E 243 H13
Port Carling Canada 45°7N 79°35W 312 A5
Port-Cartier Canada 50°2N 66°50W 299 B6
Port Chalmers N.Z. 45°49S 170°30E 285 F5
Port Charles N.Z. 36°33S 175°30E 284 C4
Port Charlotte U.S.A. 26°59N 82°6W 317 J7
Port Chester U.S.A. 41°0N 73°40W 313 F11
Port Clements Canada 53°40N 132°10W 296 C2
Port Clinton U.S.A. 41°31N 82°56W 311 C14
Port Colborne Canada 42°50N 79°10W 312 D5
Port Coquitlam Canada 49°15N 122°45W 306 A4
Port Cornwallis India 13°17N 93°5E 245 H11
Port Credit Canada 43°33N 79°35W 312 C5
Port-Cros △ France 43°0N 6°24E 175 F10
Port Curtis Australia 23°57S 151°20E 280 C5
Port d'Alcúdia Spain 39°50N 3°7E 206 B4
Port Dalhousie Canada 43°13N 79°16W 312 C5
Port d'Andratx Spain 39°32N 2°23E 206 B3
Port Darwin N. Terr., Australia 12°24S 130°45E 278 B5
Port Darwin Falk. Is. 51°50S 59°0W 153 f
Port Davey Australia 43°16S 145°55E 281 G4
Port-de-Bouc France 43°24N 4°59E 175 E8
Port-de-Paix Haiti 19°50N 72°50W 321 C5
Port de Pollença Spain 39°54N 3°4E 206 B4
Port de Sóller Spain 39°48N 2°42E 206 B3
Port Dickson Malaysia 2°30N 101°49E 237 L3
Port Douglas Australia 16°30S 145°30E 280 B4
Port Dover Canada 42°47N 80°12W 312 D4
Port Edward Canada 54°12N 130°10W 296 C2
Port Elgin Canada 44°25N 81°25W 312 B3
Port Elizabeth S. Africa 33°58S 25°40E 270 D4
Port Ellen U.K. 55°38N 6°11W 167 F2
Port Elliot Australia 35°32S 138°41E 282 C3
Port-en-Bessin-Huppain France 49°21N 0°45W 172 C6
Port Erin I. of Man 54°5N 4°45W 168 C3
Port Essington Australia 11°15S 132°10E 278 B5
Port Etienne = Nouâdhibou Mauritania 20°54N 17°0W 260 D1
Port Ewen U.S.A. 41°54N 73°59W 313 E11
Port Fairy Australia 38°22S 142°12E 282 E5
Port Fitzroy N.Z. 36°8S 175°20E 284 C4
Port Florence = Kisumu Kenya 0°3S 34°45E 268 C3
Port Fouâd = Bûr Fuad Egypt 31°15N 32°20E 256 H8
Port Francqui = Ilebo Dem. Rep. of the Congo 4°17S 20°55E 265 C4
Port Gamble U.S.A. 47°51N 122°34W 306 C4
Port-Gentil Gabon 0°40S 8°50E 264 C1
Port Germein Australia 33°1S 138°1E 281 E2
Port Ghalib Egypt 25°20N 34°50E 246 E2
Port Gibson U.S.A. 31°58N 90°59W 314 F9
Port Glasgow U.K. 55°56N 4°41W 167 F4
Port-Gueydon = Azeffoun Algeria 36°51N 4°26E 261 A5
Port Harcourt Nigeria 4°40N 7°10E 263 E6
Port Hardy Canada 50°41N 127°30W 296 C3
Port Harrison = Inukjuak Canada 58°25N 78°15W 295 F16
Port Hawkesbury Canada 45°36N 61°22W 299 C7
Port Hedland Australia 20°25S 118°35E 278 D2
Port Heiden U.S.A. 56°55N 158°41W 303 H8
Port Henry U.S.A. 44°3N 73°28W 313 B11
Port Herald = Nsanje Malawi 16°55S 35°12E 269 F4
Port Hood Canada 46°0N 61°32W 299 C7
Port Hope Ont., Canada 43°56N 78°20W 312 C6
Port Hope Mich., U.S.A. 43°57N 82°43W 312 C2
Port Hope Simpson Canada 52°33N 56°18W 299 B8
Port Hueneme U.S.A. 34°7N 119°12W 307 L7
Port Huron U.S.A. 42°58N 82°26W 312 D2
Port Iliç Azerbaijan 38°53N 48°47E 213 C13
Port Jefferson U.S.A. 40°57N 73°3W 313 F11
Port Jervis U.S.A. 41°22N 74°41W 313 E10
Port-Joinville France 46°45N 2°23W 172 F4
Port Katon Russia 46°52N 38°46E 189 J10
Port Kelang = Pelabuhan Klang Malaysia 3°0N 101°23E 237 L3
Port Kembla Australia 34°52S 150°49E 283 C9
Port Kenny Australia 33°10S 134°41E 281 E1
Port-la-Nouvelle France 43°1N 3°3E 174 E7
Port Lairge = Waterford Ireland 52°15N 7°8W 166 D4
Port Laoise Ireland 53°2N 7°18W 166 C4
Port Lavaca U.S.A. 28°37N 96°38W 314 G6
Port Leyden U.S.A. 43°35N 75°21W 313 C9
Port Lincoln Australia 34°42S 135°52E 282 C1
Port Lions U.S.A. 57°52N 152°53W 303 H9
Port Loko S. Leone 8°48N 12°46W 262 D2
Port Louis Morbihan, France 47°42N 3°22W 172 E3
Port-Louis Guadeloupe 16°28N 61°32W 322 e
Port Louis Mauritius 20°10S 57°30E 272 e
Port Lyautey = Kenitra Morocco 34°15N 6°40W 260 B3
Port MacDonnell Australia 38°5S 140°48E 282 E4
Port McNeill Canada 50°35N 127°6W 296 C3
Port Macquarie Australia 31°25S 152°25E 283 A10
Port Maria Jamaica 18°22N 76°54W 320 a
Port Mathurin Rodrigues 19°41S 63°25E 273 F5
Port Matilda U.S.A. 40°48N 78°3W 312 F6
Port Mayaca U.S.A. 26°59N 80°36W 317 J9
Port McNicoll Canada 44°44N 79°48W 312 B5
Port Mearnóg = Portmarnock Ireland 53°26N 6°8W 120 A3
Port Melbourne Australia 37°50S 144°54E 128 B1
Port Mellon Canada 49°32N 123°31W 296 D4
Port-Menier Canada 49°51N 64°15W 299 C7
Port Moller U.S.A. 55°59N 160°34W 303 J7
Port Moody Canada 49°17N 122°51W 306 A4
Port Morant Jamaica 17°54N 76°19W 320 a
Port Moresby Papua N. G. 9°24S 147°8E 286 E4
Port Mourant Guyana 6°15N 57°20W 329 B6
Port Musgrave Australia 11°55S 141°50E 280 A3
Port Narevin Vanuatu 18°45S 169°10E 287 H7
Port-Navalo France 47°34N 2°54W 172 E4
Port Neches U.S.A. 30°0N 93°59W 314 G8
Port Nicholson N.Z. 41°20S 174°52E 143 B2
Port Nolloth S. Africa 29°17S 16°52E 270 C2
Port Nouveau-Québec = Kangiqsualujjuaq Canada 58°30N 65°59W 295 F18
Port of Climax Canada 49°10N 108°20W 297 D7
Port of Coronach Canada 49°7N 105°31W 297 D7
Port of Spain Trin. & Tob. 10°40N 61°31W 323 t
Port Olry Vanuatu 15°1S 167°4E 287 E5
Port Orange U.S.A. 29°9N 80°59W 317 F9
Port Orchard U.S.A. 47°32N 122°38W 306 C4
Port Orford U.S.A. 42°45N 124°30W 304 E1
Port Pegasus N.Z. 47°12S 167°41E 285 H2
Port Perry Canada 44°6N 78°56W 312 B6
Port Phillip B. Australia 38°10S 144°50E 283 E6
Port Pirie Australia 33°10S 138°1E 282 B3
Port Renfrew Canada 48°30N 124°20W 306 B2
Port Richmond U.S.A. 40°38N 74°7W 132 C1
Port Roper Australia 14°45S 135°25E 280 A2
Port Rowan Canada 42°40N 80°30W 312 D4
Port Royal Jamaica 17°56N 76°51W 320 a
Port Royal Sd. U.S.A. 32°15N 80°40W 316 C9
Port Safaga = Bûr Safâga Egypt 26°43N 33°57E 246 E2
Port Said = Bûr Sa'îd Egypt 31°16N 32°18E 256 H8
Port St. Joe U.S.A. 29°49N 85°18W 316 F4
Port St. John U.S.A. 28°29N 80°47W 317 G9
Port St. Johns = Umzimvubu S. Africa 31°38S 29°33E 271 D4
Port-St-Louis-du-Rhône France 43°23N 4°49E 175 E8
Port St. Lucie U.S.A. 27°18N 80°21W 317 H9
Port-Ste-Marie France 44°15N 0°25E 174 D4
Port Salerno U.S.A. 27°9N 80°12W 317 H9
Port Sanilac U.S.A. 43°26N 82°33W 312 C2
Port Severn Canada 44°48N 79°43W 312 B5
Port Shelter China 22°20N 114°17E 122 A2
Port Shepstone S. Africa 30°44S 30°28E 271 D5
Port Simpson Canada 54°30N 130°20W 296 C2
Port Stanley = Stanley Falk. Is. 51°40S 59°51W 153 f
Port Stanley Canada 42°40N 81°10W 312 D3
Port Sudan = Bûr Sûdân Sudan 19°32N 37°9E 256 D4
Port Sulphur U.S.A. 29°29N 89°42W 315 G10
Port-sur-Saône France 47°42N 6°2E 173 E13
Port Swettenham = Pelabuhan Klang Malaysia 3°0N 101°23E 237 L3
Port Talbot U.K. 51°35N 3°47W 169 F4
Port Taufiq = Bûr Taufiq Egypt 29°54N 32°32E 256 J8
Port Townsend U.S.A. 48°7N 122°45W 306 B4
Port Union Canada 43°47N 79°7W 141 A4
Port-Vato Vanuatu 16°20S 168°1E 287 F6
Port-Vendres France 42°32N 3°8E 174 F7
Port Victoria Australia 34°30S 137°29E 282 C2
Port Vila Vanuatu 17°45S 168°18E 287 G6
Port Vladimir Russia 69°25N 33°6E 160 B25
Port Wakefield Australia 34°12S 138°10E 282 C3
Port Washington U.S.A. 43°23N 87°53W 308 D10
Port Weld = Kuala Sepetang Malaysia 4°49N 100°28E 237 K3
Port Wentworth U.S.A. 32°9N 81°10W 316 C8
Porta Orientalis Romania 45°6N 22°18E 177 F12
Portachuelo Bolivia 17°10S 63°20W 331 D5
Portacloy Ireland 54°20N 9°46W 166 B2
Portadown U.K. 54°25N 6°27W 166 B5
Portaferry U.K. 54°23N 5°33W 166 B6
Portage Ind., U.S.A. 41°34N 87°11W 311 C10
Portage Mich., U.S.A. 42°12N 85°35W 311 B11
Portage Pa., U.S.A. 40°23N 78°41W 312 F6
Portage Wis., U.S.A. 43°33N 89°28W 308 D9
Portage → U.S.A. 41°31N 83°5W 311 C14
Portage la Prairie Canada 49°58N 98°18W 297 D9
Portage Park U.S.A. 41°56N 87°45W 119 B2
Portageville U.S.A. 36°26N 89°42W 308 G9
Portal U.S.A. 32°33N 81°56W 316 C8
Portal de la Pau, Plaza Barcelona, Spain 114 c2
Portalegre Portugal 39°19N 7°25W 195 F3
Portalegre □ Portugal 39°20N 7°40W 195 F3
Portales U.S.A. 34°11N 103°20W 305 J12
Portarlington Ireland 53°9N 7°14W 166 C4
Portbou Spain 42°25N 3°9E 196 C8
Porteira Brazil 1°5S 57°4W 329 D6
Porteirinha Brazil 15°44S 43°2W 333 E3
Portel Brazil 1°57S 50°49W 332 B1
Portel Portugal 38°19N 7°41W 195 G3
Portela, Lisboa ✈ (LIS) Portugal 38°46N 9°8W 126 A2
Porter U.S.A. 41°36N 87°4W 311 C9
Porter, L. U.S.A. 28°30N 81°19W 133 A3
Porter L. N.W.T., Canada 61°41N 108°5W 297 A7
Porter L. Sask., Canada 56°20N 107°20W 297 B7
Porterville Western Cape, S. Africa 33°0S 19°0E 270 D2
Porterville Calif., U.S.A. 36°4N 119°1W 306 J8
Portes-lès-Valence France 44°52N 4°54E 175 D8
Porthcawl U.K. 51°29N 3°42W 169 F4
Porthill U.S.A. 48°59N 116°30W 304 B5
Porthmadog U.K. 52°55N 4°8W 168 E3
Portile de Fier Europe 44°44N 22°30E 182 F7
Portimão Portugal 37°8N 8°32W 195 H2
Portishead U.K. 51°29N 2°46W 169 F5
Portiţei, Gura Romania 44°41N 29°0E 183 F14
Portknockie U.K. 57°42N 2°51W 167 D6
Portland N.S.W., Australia 33°20S 150°0E 283 B9
Portland Vic., Australia 38°20S 141°35E 282 E4
Portland Ont., Canada 44°42N 76°12W 313 B8
Portland Conn., U.S.A. 41°34N 72°38W 313 E12
Portland Fla., U.S.A. 30°31N 86°12W 316 E3
Portland Ind., U.S.A. 40°26N 84°59W 311 D12
Portland Maine, U.S.A. 43°39N 70°16W 309 D18
Portland Mich., U.S.A. 42°52N 84°54W 311 B12
Portland Oreg., U.S.A. 45°32N 122°37W 306 E4
Portland Pa., U.S.A. 40°55N 75°6W 313 F9
Portland Tex., U.S.A. 27°53N 97°20W 314 H6
Portland, I. of U.K. 50°33N 2°26W 169 G5
Portland, Récif French Polynesia 23°42S 134°30W 289 f
Portland B. Australia 38°15S 141°45E 282 E4
Portland Bight Jamaica 17°52N 77°5W 320 a
Portland Bill U.K. 50°31N 2°28W 169 G5
Portland Canal U.S.A. 55°56N 130°0W 296 B2
Portland I. N.Z. 39°20S 177°51E 284 F6
Portland Int. ✈ (PDX) U.S.A. 45°35N 122°36W 306 E4
Portland Pt. Ascension I. 7°59S 14°25W 153 g
Portland Pt. Jamaica 17°42N 77°11W 320 a
Portmadoc = Porthmadog U.K. 52°55N 4°8W 168 E3
Portmarnock Ireland 53°26N 6°8W 120 A3
Portmore Jamaica 17°53N 76°53W 320 a
Porto Brazil 3°54S 42°42W 332 B3
Porto Corse-du-Sud, France 42°16N 8°42E 175 F12
Porto Portugal 41°8N 8°40W 194 D2
Porto □ Portugal 41°8N 8°20W 194 D2
Porto, G. de France 42°17N 8°34E 175 F12
Porto Acre Brazil 9°34S 67°31W 330 B4
Pôrto Alegre = Luzilândia Brazil 3°28S 42°22W 332 B3
Pôrto Alegre Pará, Brazil 4°22S 52°44W 329 D7
Pôrto Alegre Rio Grande do S., Brazil 30°5S 51°10W 335 C5
Porto Alegre São Tomé & Príncipe 0°2N 6°32E 265 a
Porto Amboim = Gunza Angola 10°50S 13°50E 265 E2
Porto Amélia = Pemba Mozam. 12°58S 40°30E 269 E5
Porto Azzurro Italy 42°46N 10°24E 198 F7
Porto Brandão Portugal 38°40N 9°12W 126 A1
Pôrto Cajueiro Brazil 11°3S 55°53W 331 C6
Porto Colom Spain 39°26N 3°15E 206 B4
Porto Cristo Spain 39°33N 3°20E 206 B4
Pôrto da Fôlha Brazil 9°55S 37°17W 332 C4
Porto de Moz Brazil 1°41S 52°13W 329 D7
Porto de Pedras Brazil 9°10S 35°17W 332 C4
Pôrto des Meinacos Brazil 12°33S 53°7W 331 C7
Pôrto dos Gaúchos Brazil 11°32S 57°16W 331 C6
Porto Empédocle Italy 37°17N 13°32E 200 E6
Porto Esperança Brazil 19°37S 57°29W 331 D6
Porto Espirdão Brazil 15°51S 58°28W 331 D6
Porto Formoso Azores 37°49N 25°25W 153 d3
Porto Franco Brazil 6°20S 47°24W 332 C2
Porto Grande Brazil 0°42N 51°24W 329 C7
Porto Inglês C. Verde Is. 15°21N 23°10W 153 j
Porto Jofre Brazil 17°20S 56°48W 331 D6
Porto Lengone = Porto Azzurro Italy 42°46N 10°24E 198 F7
Porto Maurizio = Impéria Italy 43°53N 8°3E 198 E5
Porto Mendes Brazil 24°30S 54°15W 335 A5
Porto Moniz Madeira 32°52N 17°11W 153 c
Porto Murtinho Brazil 21°45S 57°55W 331 E6
Porto Nacional Brazil 10°40S 48°30W 332 D2
Porto-Novo Benin 6°23N 2°42E 263 D5
Pôrto Novo Rio de J., Brazil 22°50S 43°7W 135 A2
Porto Novo Cr. → Nigeria 6°25N 3°22E 124 B2
Porto Primavera, Represa Brazil 22°10S 52°45W 335 A5
Porto San Giórgio Italy 43°11N 13°48E 199 E10
Porto Sant' Elpídio Italy 43°15N 13°43E 199 E10
Porto Santana Brazil 0°3S 51°11W 329 D7
Porto Santo, I. de Madeira 33°45N 16°25W 260 B1
Porto Santo Stéfano Italy 42°26N 11°7E 198 F8
Porto São José Brazil 22°43S 53°10W 335 A5
Porto Seguro = Guadalupe Brazil 6°44S 43°47W 332 C3
Porto Seguro Brazil 16°26S 39°5W 333 E4
Porto Tolle Italy 44°56N 12°22E 199 D9
Porto Tórres Italy 40°50N 8°24E 200 B1
Porto União Brazil 26°10S 51°10W 335 B5
Porto-Vecchio France 41°35N 9°16E 175 G13
Pôrto Velho Brazil 8°46S 63°54W 331 B5
Porto Walter Brazil 8°15S 72°40W 330 B3
Portobello U.K. 55°57N 3°7W 121 B3
Portobelo Panama 9°35N 79°42W 320 E4
Portoferráio Italy 42°48N 10°20E 198 F7
Portogruaro Italy 45°47N 12°50E 199 C9
Portola U.S.A. 39°49N 120°28W 306 F6
Portomaggiore Italy 44°42N 11°48E 199 D8
Portopetro Spain 39°22N 3°13E 206 B4
Portør Norway 58°48N 9°28E 164 F6
Portoscuso Italy 39°12N 8°24E 200 C1
Portovénere Italy 44°3N 9°51E 198 D6
Portoviejo Ecuador 1°7S 80°28W 328 D1
Portpatrick U.K. 54°51N 5°7W 167 G3
Portree U.K. 57°25N 6°12W 167 D2
Portrero U.S.A. 37°46N 122°25W 136 B3
Portrush U.K. 55°12N 6°40W 166 A5
Portsmouth Dominica 15°34N 61°27W 323 k
Portsmouth Portsmouth, U.K. 50°48N 1°6W 169 G6
Portsmouth N.H., U.S.A. 43°5N 70°45W 313 C14
Portsmouth Ohio, U.S.A. 38°44N 82°57W 309 F12
Portsmouth R.I., U.S.A. 41°36N 71°15W 313 E13
Portsmouth Va., U.S.A. 36°58N 76°23W 309 G15
Portsmouth □ U.K. 50°48N 1°6W 169 G6
Portsoy U.K. 57°41N 2°41W 167 D6
Portstewart U.K. 55°11N 6°43W 166 A5
Porttipahdan tekojärvi Finland 68°5N 26°40E 160 B22
Portugal ■ Europe 40°0N 8°0W 194 F3
Portugalete Spain 43°19N 3°4W 196 B1
Portuguesa □ Venezuela 9°10N 69°15W 328 B4
Portuguese East Africa = Mozambique ■ Africa 19°0S 35°0E 269 F4
Portuguese Guinea = Guinea-Bissau ■ Africa 12°0N 15°0W 262 C2
Portuguese Timor = East Timor ■ Asia 8°50S 126°0E 231 F7
Portuguese West Africa = Angola ■ Africa 12°0S 18°0E 265 E3
Portumna Ireland 53°6N 8°14W 166 C3
Portville U.S.A. 42°3N 78°20W 312 D6
Poruma Australia 10°2S 143°4E 280 a
Porus Jamaica 18°2N 77°25W 320 a
Porvenir Bolivia 11°10S 68°50W 330 C4
Porvenir Chile 53°10S 70°16W 336 D2
Porvoo Finland 60°24N 25°40E 188 B3
Porzuna Spain 39°9N 4°9W 195 F6
Pos Chiquito Aruba 12°27N 69°57W 322 f
Posada Italy 40°38N 9°43E 200 B2
Posada → Italy 40°39N 9°45E 200 B2
Posadas Argentina 27°30S 55°50W 335 B4
Posadas Spain 37°47N 5°11W 195 H5
Poschiavo Switz. 46°19N 10°4E 179 J6
Posen = Poznań Poland 52°25N 16°55E 185 F3
Posets Spain 42°39N 0°25E 196 C5
Poseyville U.S.A. 38°10N 87°47W 311 F9
Poshan = Boshan China 36°28N 117°49E 227 F9
Posht-e Badam Iran 33°2N 55°23E 247 C7
Posidium Greece 35°30N 27°10E 205 F9
Poso Indonesia 1°20S 120°55E 231 E6
Posoegroenoe Suriname 4°23N 55°43W 329 C6
Posof Turkey 41°30N 42°43E 213 B10
Pospelikha Russia 51°57N 81°46E 217 B10
Posse Brazil 14°4S 46°18W 333 D2
Possedimenti Italiani dell'Egeo = Dodecanese Greece 36°35N 27°0E 205 E8
Possel C.A.R. 5°5N 19°10E 264 A3
Possession I. Antarctica 72°4S 172°0E 151 D11
Pössneck Germany 50°42N 11°35E 178 E7
Possum Kingdom L. U.S.A. 32°52N 98°26W 314 E5
Post U.S.A. 33°12N 101°23W 314 E4
Post Falls U.S.A. 47°43N 116°57W 304 C5
Postavy = Pastavy Belarus 55°4N 26°50E 188 E4
Poste, R. du Mauritius 20°29S 57°36E 272 e
Poste de Flacq Mauritius 20°9S 57°43E 272 e
Poste de Flacq → Mauritius 20°9S 57°44E 272 e
Poste-de-la-Baleine = Kuujjuarapik Canada 55°20N 77°35W 298 A4
Postmasburg S. Africa 28°18S 23°5E 270 C3
Postojna Slovenia 45°46N 14°12E 199 C11
Poston U.S.A. 34°0N 114°24W 307 M12
Postumia = Postojna Slovenia 45°46N 14°12E 199 C11
Postville Nfld. & L., Canada 54°54N 59°47W 299 B8
Postville Iowa, U.S.A. 43°5N 91°34W 310 A5
Posyet Russia 42°39N 130°48E 220 C5
Potamos Antikythira, Greece 35°52N 23°15E 204 F5
Potamos Kythira, Greece 36°15N 22°58E 204 E4
Potchefstroom S. Africa 26°41S 27°7E 270 C4
Potcoava Romania 44°30N 24°39E 183 F9
Poté Brazil 17°49S 41°49W 333 E3
Poteau U.S.A. 35°3N 94°37W 314 D7
Poteet U.S.A. 29°2N 98°35W 314 G5
Potenza Italy 40°38N 15°48E 201 B8
Potenza → Italy 43°25N 13°40E 199 E10
Potenza Picena Italy 43°22N 13°37E 199 E10
Poteriteri, L. N.Z. 46°5S 167°10E 285 G2
Potgietersrus = Mokopane S. Africa 24°10S 28°55E 271 B4
Poti Georgia 42°10N 41°38E 191 J5
Potiraguá Brazil 15°36S 39°53W 333 E4
Potiskum Nigeria 11°39N 11°2E 263 C7
Potlogi Romania 44°34N 25°34E 183 F10
Potomac U.S.A. 38°59N 77°13W 143 A2
Potomac → U.S.A. 38°0N 76°23W 309 F14
Potomac Park Washington, D.C., U.S.A. 143 c1
Potosí Bolivia 19°38S 65°50W 331 D4
Potosi Mo., U.S.A. 37°56N 90°47W 310 G6
Potosí □ Bolivia 20°31S 67°0W 330 E4
Potosi Mt. U.S.A. 35°57N 115°29W 307 K11
Pototan Phil. 10°54N 122°38E 233 F4
Potrerillos Chile 26°30S 69°30W 334 B2
Potrero Pt. U.S.A. 37°45N 122°22W 136 B2
Potsdam Brandenburg, Germany 52°23N 13°3E 115 B1
Potsdam N.Y., U.S.A. 44°40N 74°59W 313 B10
Potsdamer Platz Berlin, Germany 115 b3
Pottangi India 18°34N 82°58E 244 E6
Pottenstein Germany 49°46N 11°24E 179 F7
Potters Village Antigua & B. 17°5N 61°49W 322 b
Pottersville U.S.A. 43°43N 73°50W 313 C11
Pottery Hill = Abu Ballas Egypt 24°26N 27°36E 256 C2
Pottstown U.S.A. 40°15N 75°39W 313 F9
Pottsville U.S.A. 40°41N 76°12W 313 F8
Pottuvil Sri Lanka 6°55N 81°50E 245 L5
Potzham Germany 48°1N 11°36E 131 B2
Pötzleinsdorf Austria 48°14N 16°17E 142 A1
P'otzu Taiwan 23°28N 120°15E 225 C2
Pouancé France 47°44N 1°10W 172 E5
Pouce Coupé Canada 55°40N 120°10W 296 B4
Pouébo N. Cal. 20°24S 164°36E 288 d
Poughkeepsie U.S.A. 41°42N 73°56W 313 E11
Pouilly-sur-Loire France 47°17N 2°57E 173 E9
Poulan U.S.A. 31°31N 83°47W 316 D6
Poulaphouca Res. Ireland 53°8N 6°30W 166 C5
Poulata Greece 38°14N 20°36E 207 C2
Poulsbo U.S.A. 47°44N 122°38W 306 C4
Poultney U.S.A. 43°31N 73°14W 313 C11
Poulton-le-Fylde U.K. 53°51N 2°58W 168 D5
Poum N. Cal. 20°14S 164°2E 288 d
Pounga-Nganda Gabon 2°58S 10°51E 264 C2
Pouso Alegre Mato Grosso, Brazil 11°46S 57°16W 331 C6
Pouso Alegre Minas Gerais, Brazil 22°14S 45°57W 335 A6
Pouso Alto = Piracanjuba Brazil 17°18S 49°1W 333 E2
Pout Senegal 14°45N 17°0W 262 C1
Pouthisat Cambodia 12°34N 103°50E 236 F4
Pouytenga Burkina Faso 12°15N 0°25W 263 C4
Pouzauges France 46°47N 0°50W 172 F6
Pova de Santa Iria Portugal 38°51N 9°4W 195 G1
Považská Bystrica Slovak Rep. 49°8N 18°27E 181 B11
Povenets Russia 62°50N 34°50E 186 B5
Poverty B. N.Z. 38°43S 178°2E 284 E7
Povlen Serbia 44°9N 19°44E 202 B3
Póvoa de Lanhosa Portugal 41°33N 8°15W 194 D2
Póvoa de Santo Adriao Portugal 38°47N 9°9W 126 A2
Póvoa de Varzim Portugal 41°25N 8°46W 194 D2
Povoação Azores 37°45N 25°15W 153 d3
Povorino Russia 51°12N 42°5E 190 E6
Povorotnyy, Mys Russia 42°40N 133°2E 220 C6
Povungnituk = Puvirnituq Canada 60°2N 77°10W 295 E16
Powassan Canada 46°5N 79°25W 298 C4
Poway U.S.A. 32°58N 117°2W 307 N9
Powązki Poland 52°15N 20°58E 142 B1
Powder → U.S.A. 46°45N 105°26W 304 C11
Powder River U.S.A. 43°2N 106°59W 304 E10
Powder Springs U.S.A. 33°52N 84°41W 316 B5
Powell U.S.A. 44°45N 108°46W 304 D9
Powell, L. U.S.A. 36°57N 111°29W 305 H8
Powell River Canada 49°50N 124°35W 296 D4
Powelton U.S.A. 33°26N 82°52W 316 B7
Power House = Drayton Valley Canada 53°12N 114°58W 296 C6
Powers U.S.A. 45°41N 87°32W 308 C10
Powiśle Poland 52°14N 21°1E 142 B2
Pownal U.S.A. 42°45N 73°14W 313 D11

Powsin *Poland* 52°8N 21°6E **142** C2
Powsinek *Poland* 52°9N 21°6E **142** C2
Powys □ *U.K.* 52°20N 3°20W **169** E4
Poxoréo *Brazil* 15°50S 54°23W **331** B9
Poya *N. Cal.* 21°19S 165°7E **288** d
Poyan Res. *Singapore* 1°22N 103°40E **138** A2
Poyang Hu *China* 29°5N 116°20E **229** C11
Poyarkovo *Russia* 49°36N 128°41E **215** E13
Poysdorf *Austria* 48°40N 16°37E **181** C9
Poza de la Sal *Spain* 42°35N 3°31W **194** C7
Poza Rica *Mexico* 20°33N 97°27W **319** C5
Požarevac *Serbia* 44°35N 21°18E **202** B5
Pozazal, Puerto *Spain* 42°56N 4°10W **194** C6
Požega *Croatia* 45°20N 17°41E **182** E2
Požega *Serbia* 43°53N 20°2E **202** C4
Poznań *Poland* 52°25N 16°55E **185** F3
Poznań ✕ (POZ) *Poland* 52°26N 16°45E **185** F3
Pozo *U.S.A.* 35°20N 120°24W **307** K6
Pozo Alcón *Spain* 37°42N 2°56W **195** H8
Pozo Almonte *Chile* 20°10S 69°50W **334** A2
Pozo Colorado *Paraguay* 23°30S 58°45W **334** A4
Pozoblanco *Spain* 38°23N 4°51W **195** G6
Pozorrubio *Phil.* 16°7N 120°33E **232** C3
Pozuelo de Alarcón *Spain* 40°24N 3°53W **127** B1
Pozuzo *Peru* 10°5S 75°35W **330** C2
Pozzallo *Italy* 36°43N 14°51E **201** F7
Pozzuoli *Italy* 40°49N 14°7E **201** D6
Pra ➤ *Ghana* 5°1N 1°37W **263** D4
Prabuty *Poland* 53°47N 19°15E **184** E6
Prača *Bos.-H.* 43°47N 18°43E **182** G3
Prachatice *Czech Rep.* 49°1N 14°0E **180** B6
Prachin Buri *Thailand* 14°0N 101°25E **236** F3
Prachuap Khiri Khan
    Thailand 11°49N 99°48E **237** G2
Pradelles *France* 44°46N 3°52E **174** D7
Pradera *Colombia* 3°25N 76°15W **328** C2
Prades *France* 42°38N 2°23E **174** F6
Prado *Brazil* 17°20S 39°13W **333** E4
Prado, Museo del *Madrid, Spain* **127** b3
Prado Churubusco
    Mexico 19°20N 99°8W **128** B2
Prado del Rey *Spain* 36°48N 5°33W **195** J5
Præstø *Denmark* 55°8N 12°2E **163** J6
Praga *Poland* 52°15N 21°2E **142** B2
Pragersko *Slovenia* 46°27N 15°42E **199** B12
Prague = Praha *Czech Rep.* 50°4N 14°25E **135** B2
Praha *Czech Rep.* 50°4N 14°25E **135** B2
Praha ✕ (PRG) *Czech Rep.* 50°6N 14°16E **135** B1
Prahecq *France* 46°19N 0°26W **174** B3
Prahita ➤ *India* 19°0N 79°55E **244** E4
Prahova □ *Romania* 45°10N 26°0E **183** E10
Prahova ➤ *Romania* 44°50N 25°50E **183** F10
Prahovo *Serbia* 44°18N 22°39E **202** B6
Praia *Azores* 39°3N 27°58W **153** d1
Praia *C. Verde Is.* 15°2N 23°34W **153** j
Praia a Mare *Italy* 39°50N 15°45E **201** C8
Praia da Vitória *Azores* 38°44N 27°4W **153** d1
Praia do Norte *Azores* 38°36N 28°46W **153** d1
Praia Grande *Brazil* 24°0S 46°24W **333** F2
Praid *Romania* 46°32N 25°10E **183** D10
Prainha *Amazonas, Brazil* 7°10S 60°30W **331** B5
Prainha *Pará, Brazil* 1°45S 53°30W **329** D7
Prainha Nova *Brazil* 7°10S 60°30W **331** B5
Praires, R. des ➤
    Canada 45°38N 73°36W **130** a2
Prairie *Australia* 20°50S 144°35E **280** C3
Prairie City *U.S.A.* 44°28N 118°43W **304** D4
Prairie Dog Town Fork Red ➤
    U.S.A. 34°34N 99°58W **314** D5
Prairie du Chien *U.S.A.* 43°3N 91°9W **310** A5
Prairie du Rocher *U.S.A.* 38°5N 90°6W **310** F2
Prairie Village *U.S.A.* 38°58N 94°38W **310** F2
Prairies, L. of the
    Canada 51°16N 101°32W **297** C8
Pramanda *Greece* 39°32N 21°8E **204** B3
Prampram *Ghana* 5°43N 0°8E **263** D5
Pran Buri *Thailand* 12°23N 99°55E **236** F2
Prándjarökull *Iceland* 64°40N 14°55W **155** C12
Prang *Ghana* 8°1N 0°56W **263** D4
Prapat *Indonesia* 2°41N 98°58E **234** B1
Praslin *St. Lucia* 13°52N 60°54W **323** m
Praslin *Seychelles* 4°18S 55°45E **272** c
Prasonisi, Ákra *Greece* 35°42N 27°46E **206** F11
Prassberg = Mozirje
    Slovenia 46°22N 14°58E **199** B11
Prästmon *Sweden* 63°5N 17°45E **162** A11
Praszka *Poland* 51°5N 18°31E **185** G5
Prata *Brazil* 19°25S 48°54W **333** E2
Pratabpur *India* 23°28N 83°15E **243** H10
Pratapgarh *Raj., India* 24°2N 74°40E **242** G6
Pratapgarh *U. P., India* 25°56N 81°59E **243** G9
Pratas Is. = Dongsha Dao
    S. China Sea 20°45N 116°43E **229** G11
Prater *Austria* 48°12N 16°25E **142** A2
Prato *Italy* 43°53N 11°6E **198** E8
Prátola Peligna *Italy* 42°6N 13°52E **199** F10
Prats-de-Mollo-la-Preste
    France 42°25N 2°27E **174** F6
Pratt *U.S.A.* 37°39N 98°44W **308** G4
Prattville *U.S.A.* 32°28N 86°29W **315** E11
Praust = Pruszcz Gdański
    Poland 54°17N 18°40E **184** D5
Pravara ➤ *India* 19°35N 74°45E **244** E2
Pravdinsk *Kaliningrad,
    Russia* 54°27N 21°1E **184** D8
Pravdinsk *Nizhniy Novgorod,
    Russia* 56°29N 43°28E **190** B6
Pravets *Bulgaria* 42°53N 23°55E **202** D7
Pravia *Spain* 43°30N 6°12W **194** B4
Praya *Indonesia* 8°39S 116°17E **235** D5
Prayag = Allahabad
    India 25°25N 81°58E **243** G9
Pré-en-Pail *France* 48°28N 0°12W **172** D6
Preau *Trin. & Tob.* 10°12N 61°19W **323** t
Preble *U.S.A.* 42°44N 76°8W **313** D8
Prêcheur *Martinique* 14°48N 61°13W **322** j
Precipice △ *Australia* 25°18S 150°5E **281** D5
Precordillera *Argentina* 30°0S 69°1W **334** C2
Precotto *Italy* 45°30N 9°13E **129** A2
Predáppio *Italy* 44°6N 11°59E **199** D8
Predazzo *Italy* 46°19N 11°36E **199** B8
Predeal *Romania* 45°30N 25°34E **183** E10
Predejane *Serbia* 42°51N 22°9E **202** D6
Preeceville *Canada* 51°57N 102°40W **297** C8
Preetz *Germany* 54°14N 10°18E **178** A6
Pregrada *Croatia* 46°11N 15°45E **199** B12
Preili *Latvia* 56°18N 26°43E **188** D4
Preko *Croatia* 44°7N 15°10E **199** D11
Prelog *Croatia* 46°18N 16°32E **199** B13
Premer *Australia* 31°29S 149°56E **283** A8
Prémery *France* 47°10N 3°19E **172** E6
Premià de Mar *Spain* 41°29N 2°22E **196** D7
Premont *U.S.A.* 27°22N 98°7W **314** H5
Premuda *Croatia* 44°20N 14°36E **199** D11
Prenestino Labicano
    Italy 41°53N 12°33E **136** B2
Prentice *U.S.A.* 45°33N 90°17W **308** C8
Prenzlau *Germany* 53°19N 13°51E **178** B9
Prenzlauerberg *Germany* 52°32N 13°24E **115** A3
Preobrazheniye *Russia* 42°54N 133°54E **220** C6
Preparis I. = Pariparit Kyun
    Burma 14°52N 93°41E **245** G11
Preparis North Channel
    Ind. Oc. 15°27N 94°5E **245** G11

Preparis South Channel
    Ind. Oc. 14°33N 93°30E **245** G11
Přerov *Czech Rep.* 49°28N 17°27E **181** B10
Prescott *Ont., Canada* 44°45N 75°30W **313** B9
Prescott *Ariz., U.S.A.* 34°33N 112°28W **305** J7
Prescott *Ark., U.S.A.* 33°48N 93°23W **314** E8
Prescott Valley *U.S.A.* 34°40N 112°18W **305** J7
Preservation Inlet *N.Z.* 46°8S 166°35E **285** G1
Preševo *Serbia* 42°19N 21°39E **202** D5
Presho *U.S.A.* 43°54N 100°3W **308** D3
Presicce *Italy* 39°54N 18°16E **201** C11
Presidencia de la Plaza
    Argentina 27°0S 59°50W **334** B4
Presidencia Roque Saenz Peña
    Argentina 26°45S 60°30W **334** B3
Président-Thiers, Récif
    French Polynesia 24°30S 146°0W **289** f
Presidente Dutra *Brazil* 5°15S 44°30W **332** C3
Presidente Epitácio *Brazil* 21°56S 52°6W **333** F1
Presidente Figueiredo
    Brazil 1°57S 60°2W **329** D5
Presidente Hayes □
    Paraguay 24°0S 59°0W **334** A4
Presidente Juán Perón = Chaco □
    Argentina 26°30S 61°0W **334** B3
Presidente Médici *Brazil* 11°17S 61°55W **331** C5
Presidente Prudente
    Brazil 22°5S 51°25W **335** A5
Presidente Vargas = Nova Era
    Brazil 19°45S 43°3W **333** E3
Presidio *Mexico* 29°29N 104°23W **318** B4
Presidio *Tex., U.S.A.* 29°34N 104°22W **314** G2
Preslav *Bulgaria* 43°10N 26°52E **203** C10
Preslavska Planina
    Bulgaria 43°10N 26°45E **203** C10
Prešov *Slovak Rep.* 49°0N 21°15E **181** B14
Prešovský □ *Slovak Rep.* 49°8N 21°15E **181** B13
Prespa *Bulgaria* 41°44N 24°55E **203** E8
Prespa, L. = Prespansko Jezero
    Macedonia 40°55N 21°0E **202** F5
Prespa △ *Greece* 40°55N 21°4E **202** F5
Prespansko Jezero
    Macedonia 40°55N 21°0E **202** F5
Presque I. *U.S.A.* 42°10N 80°6W **312** D4
Presque Isle *U.S.A.* 46°41N 68°1W **309** B19
Pressburg = Bratislava
    Slovak Rep. 48°10N 17°7E **181** C10
Prestatyn *U.K.* 53°20N 3°24W **168** D4
Prestea *Ghana* 5°22N 2°7W **262** D4
Presteigne *U.K.* 52°17N 3°0W **169** E5
Přeštice *Czech Rep.* 49°34N 13°20E **180** B6
Presto *Bolivia* 18°55S 64°56W **331** D5
Preston *Vic., Australia* 37°44S 145°0E **128** A1
Preston *Ont., Canada* 43°23N 80°21W **312** C4
Preston *Lancs., U.K.* 53°46N 2°42W **168** E5
Preston *Ga., U.S.A.* 32°4N 84°32W **316** C5
Preston *Idaho, U.S.A.* 42°6N 111°53W **304** E8
Preston *Iowa, U.S.A.* 42°3N 90°24W **310** B6
Preston *Minn., U.S.A.* 43°40N 92°5W **310** C4
Preston *Mo., U.S.A.* 37°56N 93°13W **310** G3
Preston, C. *Australia* 20°51S 116°12E **278** D2
Prestonsburg *U.S.A.* 37°40N 82°47W **309** G12
Prestrand *Norway* 59°6N 9°4E **162** E3
Prestwick *U.K.* 55°29N 4°37W **167** F4
Prêto ➤ *Amazonas, Brazil* 0°8S 64°6W **329** D5
Prêto ➤ *Bahia, Brazil* 11°21S 43°52W **332** D3
Prêto do Igapó-Açu ➤
    Brazil 4°26S 59°48W **329** D6
Pretoria *S. Africa* 25°44S 28°12E **271** C4
Pretos Forros, Sa. dos
    Brazil 22°54S 43°17W **135** B1
Preuilly-sur-Claise *France* 46°51N 0°56E **172** F7
Preussisch-Eylau = Bagrationovsk
    Russia 54°23N 20°39E **184** D7
Preussisch Friedland = Debrzno
    Poland 53°33N 17°14E **184** E4
Preussisch Holland = Pasłęk
    Poland 54°3N 19°41E **184** D6
Preussisch-Stargard = Starogard
    Gdański *Poland* 53°59N 18°30E **184** E5
Preveza *Greece* 38°57N 20°45E **207** B2
Preveza □ *Greece* 39°10N 20°40E **204** B2
Preveza-Lefkada ✕ (PVK)
    Greece 38°57N 20°45E **207** B2
Préville *Canada* 45°28N 73°29W **130** B3
Prey Veng *Cambodia* 11°35N 105°29E **237** G5
Přeštětice *Czech Rep.* 50°9N 14°34E **135** B3
Priazovskoye *Ukraine* 46°44N 35°40E **189** J8
Pribalkhash = Balqash
    Kazakhstan 46°50N 74°50E **214** E8
Pribilof Is. *U.S.A.* 57°0N 170°0W **303** H5
Příbor *Serbia* 43°35N 19°32E **202** C3
Příbram *Czech Rep.* 49°41N 14°2E **180** B7
Price *U.S.A.* 39°36N 110°49W **304** G8
Price, C. *India* 13°34N 93°3E **245** H11
Price I. *Canada* 52°23N 128°41W **296** C3
Prichard *U.S.A.* 30°44N 88°5W **315** F10
Prickly Pear Cays
    Anguilla 18°16N 63°11W **322** a
Prickly Pt. *Grenada* 11°59N 61°45W **323** q
Priego *Spain* 40°26N 2°21W **196** E2
Priego de Córdoba *Spain* 37°27N 4°12W **195** H6
Priekule *Latvia* 56°26N 21°35E **184** B8
Priekule *Lithuania* 55°33N 21°19E **184** C8
Prien *Germany* 47°51N 12°20E **179** H8
Prienai *Lithuania* 54°38N 23°57E **184** D10
Prieska *S. Africa* 29°40S 22°42E **270** C3
Priest L. *U.S.A.* 48°35N 116°52W **304** B5
Priest River *U.S.A.* 48°11N 116°55W **304** B5
Priest Valley *U.S.A.* 36°10N 120°39W **306** J6
Prieto Diaz *Phil.* 13°2N 124°12E **232** E5
Prievidza *Slovak Rep.* 48°46N 18°36E **181** C11
Prignitz *Germany* 53°6N 11°45E **178** B7
Prijedor *Bos.-H.* 44°58N 16°41E **199** D13
Prijepolje *Serbia* 43°27N 19°40E **202** C3
Prikaspiyskaya Nizmennost =
    Caspian Depression
    Eurasia 47°0N 48°0E **191** G9
Prikro *Ivory C.* 7°40N 3°59W **262** D4
Prikubanskaya Nizmennost
    Russia 45°0N 38°55E **191** H4
Prilep *Macedonia* 41°21N 21°32E **202** F5
Priluki = Pryluky
    Ukraine 50°30N 32°24E **189** G7
Prima Porta *Italy* 42°0N 12°30E **136** B1
Primavalle *Italy* 41°54N 12°23E **136** B1
Prime Seal I. *Australia* 40°3S 147°43E **281** G4
Primeira Cruz *Brazil* 2°30S 43°26W **332** B3
Primkenau = Przemków
    Poland 51°31N 15°48E **185** G3
Primo Tapia *Mexico* 32°16N 116°54W **307** N10
Primorsk *Kaliningrad,
    Russia* 54°44N 20°0E **184** D6
Primorsk *St. Petersburg,
    Russia* 60°20N 28°37E **188** B5
Primorskiy Kray □ *Russia* 45°0N 135°0E **220** B7
Primorsko *Bulgaria* 42°15N 27°44E **203** D11
Primorsko-Akhtarsk
    Russia 46°2N 38°10E **189** J10
Primorskoye *Ukraine* 46°48N 36°20E **189** J9
Primrose *S. Africa* 26°11S 28°9E **123** B2
Primrose L. *Canada* 54°55N 109°45W **297** C7
Prince Albert *Canada* 53°15N 105°50W **297** C7
Prince Albert *Western Cape,
    S. Africa* 33°12S 22°2E **270** D3

Prince Albert △ *Canada* 54°0N 106°25W **297** C7
Prince Albert Mts.
    Antarctica 76°0S 161°30E **151** D11
Prince Albert Pen.
    Canada 72°30N 116°0W **294** C8
Prince Albert Sd. *Canada* 70°25N 115°0W **294** C9
Prince Alfred, C. *Canada* 74°20N 124°40W **150** B1
Prince Charles I.
    Canada 67°47N 76°12W **295** D16
Prince Charles Mts.
    Antarctica 72°0S 67°0E **151** D6
Prince Edward Fracture Zone
    Ind. Oc. 46°0S 35°0E **151** A4
Prince Edward I. □
    Canada 46°20N 63°20W **299** C7
Prince Edward Is. *Ind. Oc.* 46°35S 38°0E **273** J2
Prince George *Canada* 53°55N 122°50W **296** C4
Prince of Wales, C.
    U.S.A. 65°36N 168°5W **303** D5
Prince of Wales I. *Queens.,
    Australia* 10°40S 142°10E **286** F2
Prince of Wales I. *Nunavut,
    Canada* 73°0N 99°0W **294** C12
Prince of Wales I. *Alaska,
    Canada* 55°47N 132°50W **303** J14
Prince of Wales Icefield
    Canada 78°15N 79°0W **295** B16
Prince of Wales Str.
    Canada 73°0N 117°0W **294** C8
Prince Patrick I. *Canada* 77°0N 120°0W **295** B8
Prince Regent Inlet
    Canada 73°0N 90°0W **295** C14
Prince Rupert *Canada* 54°20N 130°20W **296** C2
Prince Rupert B. *Dominica* 15°34N 61°29W **323** k
Prince Rupert Bluff Pt.
    Dominica 15°35N 61°29W **323** k
Prince William Sd.
    U.S.A. 60°40N 147°0W **303** F11
Princes Street *Edinburgh, U.K.* **121** b2
Princes Town *Trin. & Tob.* 10°16N 61°23W **323** t
Princesa Isabel *Brazil* 7°44S 38°0W **332** C4
Princess Charlotte B.
    Australia 14°25S 144°0E **286** A3
Princess Elizabeth Trough
    S. Ocean 64°10S 83°0E **151** C7
Princess May Ranges
    Australia 15°30S 125°30E **278** C4
Princess Royal I. *Canada* 53°0N 128°40W **296** C3
Princeton *B.C., Canada* 49°27N 120°30W **296** D4
Princeton *Calif., U.S.A.* 39°24N 122°1W **306** F4
Princeton *Ill., U.S.A.* 41°23N 89°28W **310** C7
Princeton *Ind., U.S.A.* 38°21N 87°34W **311** F9
Princeton *Ky., U.S.A.* 37°7N 87°53W **308** G10
Princeton *Mo., U.S.A.* 40°24N 93°35W **310** D3
Princeton *N.J., U.S.A.* 40°21N 74°39W **313** F10
Princeton *W. Va., U.S.A.* 37°22N 81°6W **309** G13
Princeville *Hawai'i,
    U.S.A.* 22°13N 159°29W **302** A2
Princeville *Ill., U.S.A.* 40°56N 89°46W **310** D7
Príncipe *São Tomé & Príncipe* 1°37N 7°25E **265** a
Príncipe da Beira *Brazil* 12°20S 64°30W **331** C5
Prineville *U.S.A.* 44°18N 120°51W **304** D3
Pringles Bay *Dominica* 15°21N 61°25W **323** k
Prins Christian Sund
    Greenland 60°4N 43°10W **4** D5
Prins Harald Kyst
    Antarctica 70°0S 35°1E **151** D4
Prins Karls Forland
    Svalbard 78°30N 11°0E **154** B12
Prinsesse Astrid Kyst
    Antarctica 70°45S 12°30E **151** D3
Prinsesse Ragnhild Kyst
    Antarctica 70°15S 27°30E **151** D4
Printer's Row *Chicago, U.S.A.* **119** d2
Prinzapolca *Nic.* 13°20N 83°35W **320** D3
Prior, C. *Spain* 43°34N 8°17W **194** B2
Priozersk *Russia* 61°2N 30°7E **188** B6
Pripet = Prypyat ➤
    Europe 51°20N 30°15E **177** C16
Pripet Marshes = Prypyat
    Marshes *Europe* 52°10N 28°10E **177** B15
Pripyat Marshes = Pripet Marshes
    Europe 52°10N 28°10E **177** B15
Pripyats = Prypyat ➤
    Europe 51°20N 30°15E **177** C16
Prishib = Leninsk *Russia* 48°40N 45°15E **191** F7
Prislop, Pasul *Romania* 47°37N 24°48E **183** C9
Pristen *Russia* 51°15N 36°44E **189** G9
Priština *Kosovo* 42°40N 21°13E **202** D5
Pritzwalk *Germany* 53°9N 12°10E **178** B8
Privas *France* 44°45N 4°37E **175** D8
Priverno *Italy* 41°28N 13°11E **200** A6
Privolzhsk *Russia* 57°23N 41°16E **190** B5
Privolzhskaya Vozvyshennost
    Russia 51°0N 46°0E **190** E7
Privolzhskiy *Russia* 51°25N 46°3E **190** E8
Privolzhskiy □ *Russia* 56°0N 50°0E **190** B10
Privolzhsk *Russia* 52°52N 48°33E **190** D9
Priyutnoye *Russia* 46°12N 43°40E **191** G6
Prizren *Kosovo* 42°13N 20°45E **202** D4
Prizzi *Italy* 37°43N 13°26E **200** E6
Prnjavor *Bos.-H.* 44°52N 17°43E **182** F2
Probolinggo *Indonesia* 7°46S 113°13E **235** D4
Prochowice *Poland* 51°17N 16°20E **185** G3
Proctor *U.S.A.* 43°40N 73°2W **313** C11
Proddatur *India* 14°45N 78°30E **245** G4
Prodhromos *Cyprus* 34°57N 32°50E **207** F8
Proença-a-Nova *Portugal* 39°45N 7°54W **194** F3
Profília *Greece* 36°5N 27°51E **206** E11
Profondeville *Belgium* 50°23N 4°52E **170** D4
Progreso *Coahuila,
    Mexico* 27°28N 100°59W **318** B4
Progreso *Yucatán, Mexico* 21°20N 89°40W **319** C7
Progress *Antarctica* 66°22S 76°22E **151** C12
Progress *Russia* 49°45S 129°37E **215** E13
Prokhladnyy *Russia* 43°50N 44°2E **191** J7
Prokletije *Albania* 42°30N 19°45E **202** D3
Prokopyevsk *Russia* 54°0N 86°45E **217** B11
Prokuplje *Serbia* 43°16N 21°36E **202** C5
Proletarskaya = Proletarsk
    Russia 46°42N 41°50E **191** G5
Prome *Burma* 18°49N 95°13E **241** F5
Promise City *U.S.A.* 40°45N 93°9W **310** D3
Promzino = Surskoye
    Russia 54°20N 46°56E **190** C8
Prophet ➤ *Canada* 58°48N 122°40W **296** B4
Prophet River *Canada* 58°6N 122°43W **296** B4
Prophetstown *U.S.A.* 41°40N 89°56W **310** C7
Propriá *Brazil* 10°13S 36°51W **332** D4
Propriano *France* 41°41N 8°52E **175** G12
Prosek *Czech Rep.* 50°7N 14°30E **135** B3
Proserpine *Australia* 20°21S 148°36E **280** b
Proskurov = Khmelnytskyy
    Ukraine 49°23N 27°0E **177** D14
Prosna ➤ *Poland* 52°6N 17°44E **185** F4
Prospect *N.Y., U.S.A.* 43°18N 75°9W **313** C9
Prospect *Oreg., U.S.A.* 42°45N 122°29W **304** E2
Prospect Hill Park
    U.S.A. 42°23N 71°13W **116** A1
Prosperidad *Phil.* 8°34N 125°52E **233** G5
Prosperity *S. Africa* 30°51N 105°54W **318** b
Prosperous B. *St. Helena* 15°58S 5°39W **153** h
Prosser *U.S.A.* 46°12N 119°46W **304** C4
Prostějov = Prostĕjov
    Czech Rep. 49°30N 17°9E **181** B10

Prostĕjov *Czech Rep.* 49°30N 17°9E **181** B10
Prostki *Poland* 53°42N 22°25E **184** E9
Proston *Australia* 26°8S 151°32E **281** D5
Proszowice *Poland* 50°13N 20°16E **185** H7
Proti *Greece* 37°5N 21°32E **204** D3
Provadiya *Bulgaria* 43°12N 27°30E **203** C11
Provence *France* 43°40N 5°46E **175** E9
Provence-Alpes-Côte d'Azur □
    France 44°0N 6°15E **175** D10
Providence *Seychelles* 9°14S 51°2E **273** E4
Providence *Ky., U.S.A.* 37°24N 87°46W **308** G10
Providence *R.I., U.S.A.* 41°49N 71°24W **313** E13
Providence, C. *N.Z.* 45°51S 166°29E **285** F1
Providence Bay *Canada* 45°41N 82°15W **298** C3
Providence Mts.
    U.S.A. 35°10N 115°15W **307** K11
Providencia *Chile* 33°25S 70°36W **132** C2
Providencia, I. de
    Colombia 13°25N 81°26W **320** D3
Provideniya *Russia* 64°23N 173°18W **215** C19
Provincetown *U.S.A.* 42°3N 70°11W **309** D18
Provins *France* 48°33N 3°15E **173** D10
Provo *U.S.A.* 40°14N 111°39W **304** F8
Provost *Canada* 52°25N 110°20W **297** C6
Prozor *Bos.-H.* 43°50N 17°34E **182** G2
Prrenjas *Albania* 41°4N 20°32E **202** E4
Prudential Building *Chicago, U.S.A.* **119** c2
Prudentópolis *Brazil* 25°12S 50°57W **333** G1
Prudhoe Bay *U.S.A.* 70°18N 148°22W **303** A10
Prudhoe I. *Australia* 21°19S 149°41E **280** C4
Prud'homme *Canada* 52°20N 105°54W **297** C7
Prudnik *Poland* 50°20N 17°38E **185** H4
Průhonice *Czech Rep.* 50°0N 14°33E **135** C3
Prüm *Germany* 50°12N 6°25E **179** E2
Prundu *Romania* 44°16N 26°14E **183** F11
Pruszcz Gdański *Poland* 54°17N 18°40E **184** D5
Pruszków *Poland* 52°9N 20°49E **185** F7
Prut ➤ *Romania* 45°28N 28°10E **183** E13
Pruzhany *Belarus* 52°33N 24°28E **177** B13
Prvić *Croatia* 44°55N 14°47E **199** D11
Prydz B. *Antarctica* 69°0S 74°0E **151** C6
Pryluky *Ukraine* 50°30N 32°24E **189** G7
Pryor *U.S.A.* 36°19N 95°19W **314** C7
Prypyat ➤ *Europe* 51°20N 30°15E **177** C16
Prząsnysz *Poland* 53°2N 20°54E **185** E7
Przedbórz *Poland* 51°6N 19°53E **185** G6
Przedecz *Poland* 52°20N 18°53E **185** F5
Przemków *Poland* 51°31N 15°48E **185** G2
Przemyśl *Poland* 49°50N 22°45E **185** H9
Przeworsk *Poland* 50°6N 22°32E **185** H9
Przewóz *Poland* 51°28N 14°57E **185** G1
Przhevalsk = Karakol
    Kyrgyzstan 42°30N 78°20E **217** D9
Przysucha *Poland* 51°22N 20°38E **185** G7
Psachna *Greece* 38°34N 23°35E **204** C5
Psara *Greece* 38°37N 25°38E **205** C5
Psathoura *Greece* 39°30N 24°12E **204** B6
Pselpalos *Greece* 38°56N 27°8E **205** E9
Psël ➤ *Ukraine* 49°5N 33°20E **189** H7
Pserimos *Greece* 36°56N 27°8E **205** E9
Psíchiko *Greece* 38°1N 23°46E **112** A2
Psiloritis, Oros *Greece* 35°15N 24°45E **207** E5
Psíra *Greece* 35°12N 25°52E **207** E6
Pskov *Russia* 57°50N 28°25E **188** D5
Pskov □ *Russia* 57°30N 29°0E **188** D5
Pskovskoye, Ozero *Russia* 58°0N 27°58E **188** D5
Psunj *Croatia* 45°25N 17°19E **182** E2
Pteleos *Greece* 39°3N 22°57E **204** B4
Ptich = Ptsich ➤ *Belarus* 52°9N 28°52E **177** B15
Ptichia = Vidos *Greece* 39°38N 19°55E **208** B6
Ptolemaida *Greece* 40°30N 21°43E **202** F5
Ptsich ➤ *Belarus* 52°9N 28°52E **177** B15
Ptuj *Slovenia* 46°28N 15°50E **199** B12
Ptujska Gora *Slovenia* 46°23N 15°47E **199** B12
Pu Xian *China* 36°24N 111°6E **226** F6
Pua *Thailand* 19°11N 100°55E **236** C3
Pua'ena Pt. *U.S.A.* 21°36N 158°6W **302** J13
Puán *Argentina* 37°30S 62°45W **334** D3
Pu'an *Guizhou, China* 25°46N 104°57E **228** E5
Pu'apu'a *Samoa* 13°34S 172°9W **287** V19
Pubei *China* 22°16N 109°31E **228** F7
Pucacuro ➤ *Peru* 3°20S 74°58W **328** D3
Pucallpa *Peru* 8°25S 74°30W **330** B3
Pucará *Bolivia* 18°43S 64°11N **331** D5
Pucará *Cajamarca, Peru* 6°0S 79°7W **330** B2
Pucará *Puno, Peru* 15°5S 70°24W **330** D4
Pucheng *China* 27°59N 118°31E **229** D12
Pucheni *Romania* 45°12N 25°17E **183** E10
Puchheim *Germany* 48°9N 11°21E **179** G7
Puch'on = Bucheon
    S. Korea 37°30N 126°45E **224** D3
Púchov *Slovak Rep.* 49°8N 18°20E **181** B11
Pucio Pt. *Phil.* 11°46N 121°51E **233** F3
Pucioasa *Romania* 45°5N 25°28E **183** E10
Pučišča *Croatia* 43°22N 16°43E **199** E13
Puck *Poland* 54°45N 18°23E **184** D5
Pucka, Zatoka *Poland* 54°30N 18°40E **184** D5
Puçol *Spain* 39°37N 0°18W **197** F4
Pudasjärvi *Finland* 65°23N 26°53E **160** D22
Puding *China* 26°18N 105°44E **228** D5
Pudong New Area
    China 31°13N 121°30E **138** B2
Pudozh *Russia* 61°48N 36°32E **188** B9
Pudu = Suizhou *China* 31°42N 113°50E **229** C9
Puducherry *India* 11°59N 79°50E **245** G4
Pudukkottai *India* 10°28N 78°47E **245** J4
Pue *Cook Is.* 21°12S 159°45W **289** h
Puebla *Mexico* 19°3N 98°12W **319** D5
Puebla □ *Mexico* 18°50N 98°0W **319** D5
Puebla de Alcocer *Spain* 38°59N 5°14W **195** G5
Puebla de Don Fadrique
    Spain 37°58N 2°25W **195** H8
Puebla de Don Rodrigo
    Spain 39°5N 4°37W **195** F6
Puebla de Guzmán *Spain* 37°37N 7°15W **195** H3
Puebla de la Calzada
    Spain 38°54N 6°37W **195** G4
Puebla de Sanabria *Spain* 42°4N 6°38W **194** C4
Puebla de Trives = Pobra de Trives
    Spain 42°20N 7°10W **194** C3
Pueblo *U.S.A.* 38°16N 104°37W **304** H11
Pueblo Libre *Peru* 12°5S 77°4W **124** D2
Pueblo Nuevo *Barcelona,
    Spain* 41°23N 2°11E **114** A2
Pueblo Nuevo *Madrid,
    Spain* 40°25N 3°37W **127** B2
Puelches *Argentina* 38°5S 66°0W **334** D2
Puelén *Argentina* 37°32S 67°38W **334** D2
Puente Alto *Chile* 33°32S 70°35W **132** C2
Puente-Genil *Spain* 37°22N 4°47W **195** H6
Puente la Reina *Spain* 42°40N 1°49W **194** C8
Puente San Miguel *Spain* 43°23N 4°10W **194** B6
Puentearas = Ponteareas
    Spain 42°10N 8°28W **194** C2
Puerco ➤ *U.S.A.* 34°22N 107°50W **305** J10
Puerta del Sol, Plaza *Madrid, Spain* **127** b2
Púglia □ *Italy* 41°0N 16°30E **201** B9
Pugŏdong *N. Korea* 42°5N 130°0E **224** A5
Pugu *Tanzania* 6°55S 39°4E **266** C4
Puhár *India* 11°15N 79°49E **245** G4
Puhi *N.Z.* 38°30S 177°50E **284** C6

Puhuangyu *China* 39°50N 116°22E **114** B2
Pui *Romania* 45°30N 23°4E **182** E8
Puica *Peru* 15°0S 72°33W **330** D3
Puieşti *Romania* 46°25N 27°33E **183** D12
Puig Major *Spain* 39°48N 2°47E **206** B9
Puigcerdà *Spain* 42°24N 1°50E **196** C6
Puigmal *Spain* 42°23N 2°7E **196** C7
Puijiang *China* 42°23N 2°32E **206** B3
Puisaye, Collines de la
    France 47°37N 3°20E **173** E10
Puiseaux *France* 48°11N 2°30E **173** D9
Puistola *Finland* 60°16N 25°2E **121** A4
Pujehun *S. Leone* 7°23N 11°45W **262** D2
Pujiang *China* 29°29N 119°54E **229** C12
Pujili *Ecuador* 0°57S 78°41W **328** D2
Pujols *France* 44°48N 0°2E **174** D3
Pujon-ho *N. Korea* 40°35N 127°35E **224** B3
Puka *French Polynesia* 14°49S 138°48W **289** f
Puka Ruha
    French Polynesia 18°20S 137°2W **289** f
Pukaki, L. *N.Z.* 44°4S 170°1E **285** E5
Pukalani *U.S.A.* 20°51N 156°20W **302** C5
Pukapuka *Cook Is.* 10°53S 165°49W **289** J11
Pukaskwa △ *Canada* 48°20N 86°0W **298** C2
Pukatawagan *Canada* 55°45N 101°20W **297** B8
Pukchin *N. Korea* 40°12N 125°45E **224** B2
Pukch'ŏng *N. Korea* 40°14N 128°10E **224** B4
Pukë *Albania* 42°2N 19°53E **202** D3
Pukearuhe *N.Z.* 38°55S 174°31E **284** C5
Pukekohe *N.Z.* 37°12S 174°55E **284** B5
Puketerakai Ra. *N.Z.* 42°58S 172°13E **285** C7
Puketoi Ra. *N.Z.* 40°30S 176°5E **284** G5
Pukeuri *N.Z.* 45°4S 171°2E **285** F6
Pukhrayan *India* 26°14N 79°51E **243** F8
Pukinmäki *Finland* 60°15N 24°57E **121** B2
Pukou *China* 32°7N 118°38E **229** A12
Puksubaek-san
    N. Korea 40°42N 127°45E **224** B3
Pula *Croatia* 44°54N 13°57E **199** D10
Pula *Italy* 39°1N 9°0E **200** C1
Pulacayo *Bolivia* 20°25S 66°41W **330** E4
Pulai *Malaysia* 1°20N 103°31E **237** d
Pulandian *China* 39°25N 121°58E **227** E11
Pulaski *N.Y., U.S.A.* 43°34N 76°8W **313** C8
Pulaski *Tenn., U.S.A.* 35°12N 87°2W **315** D11
Pulaski *Va., U.S.A.* 37°3N 80°47W **309** G13
Pulau = Indonesia □ *Asia* 5°50S 138°15E **234** E9
Pulau Miangas *Indonesia* 5°35N 126°34E **233** J6
Pulawy *Poland* 51°23N 21°59E **185** G8
Pulga *U.S.A.* 39°48N 121°29W **306** F5
Pulgaon *India* 20°44N 78°21E **244** D4
Puli *Taiwan* 23°58N 120°57E **225** C2
Pulicat *India* 13°25N 80°19E **245** H5
Pulicat L. *India* 13°40N 80°15E **245** H5
Pulivendla *India* 14°25N 78°14E **245** G4
Puliyangudi *India* 9°11N 77°24E **245** K3
Pulkovo Int. ✕ (LED)
    Russia 59°48N 30°18E **137** C1
Pullach *Germany* 48°3N 11°31E **131** B1
Pullman *U.S.A.* 46°44N 117°10W **304** C5
Pullman Historic District
    U.S.A. 41°41N 87°36W **119** C3
Pulo Gadung *Indonesia* 6°11S 106°54E **122** B2
Pulog, Mt. *Phil.* 16°40N 120°50E **232** C3
Pultusk *Poland* 52°43N 21°6E **185** F8
Pülümür *Turkey* 39°30N 39°51E **213** C8
Pumlumon Fawr *U.K.* 52°28N 3°46W **169** E4
Puna *Bolivia* 19°45S 65°28W **331** D5
Puná, I. *Ecuador* 2°55S 80°5W **328** D1
Punaauia *Tahiti* 17°37S 149°34W **289** e
Pünak *Iran* 35°46N 51°20E **141** A2
Punakha Dzong *Bhutan* 27°42N 89°52E **241** B2
Punalur *India* 9°0N 76°56E **245** K3
Punalu'u *U.S.A.* 21°35N 157°53W **302** J14
Punasar *India* 27°6N 73°6E **242** F5
Punata *Bolivia* 17°32S 65°50W **331** D4
Punch *India* 33°48N 74°4E **242** C6
Punch ➤ *Pakistan* 33°12N 73°40E **242** C5
Punchbowl *Australia* 33°55S 151°3E **139** B1
Punda Maria *S. Africa* 22°40S 31°5E **271** B5
Pünde *India* 18°53N 72°57E **130** B2
Pune *India* 18°29N 73°57E **244** F1
Punggol *Singapore* 1°23N 103°54E **138** A3
Punggol, Sungei ➤
    Singapore 1°24N 103°54E **138** A3
Punggol Pt. *Singapore* 1°24N 103°54E **138** A3
Pungo Andongo *Angola* 9°44S 15°35E **265** D3
P'ungsan *N. Korea* 40°50N 128°9E **224** B4
Pungsan *S. Korea* 40°48N 128°9E **269** F3
Pungue, Ponte de *Mozam.* 19°0S 34°0E **269** F3
Puning *China* 23°20N 116°12E **229** F11
Punjab □ *India* 31°0N 76°0E **242** D7
Punjab □ *Pakistan* 32°0N 72°30E **242** E6
Punjabi Bagh *India* 28°40N 77°6E **120** A1
Puno *Peru* 15°55S 70°3W **330** D3
Puno □ *Peru* 15°0S 70°0W **330** D4
Punpun ➤ *India* 25°31N 85°18E **243** G11
Punta, Cerro de
    Puerto Rico 18°10N 66°37W **321** b
Punta Alta *Argentina* 38°53S 62°4W **334** D3
Punta Arenas *Chile* 53°10S 71°0W **336** D2
Punta Cardón *Venezuela* 11°38N 70°14W **328** A4
Punta Colés *Peru* 17°43S 71°23W **330** D3
Punta de Bombón *Peru* 17°10S 71°48W **330** D3
Punta del Díaz *Chile* 28°0S 70°45W **334** B1
Punta del Hidalgo
    Canary Is. 28°33N 16°19W **153** e1
Punta Delgada *Argentina* 42°43S 63°38W **334** B4
Punta Gorda *Belize* 16°10N 88°45W **320** D2
Punta Gorda *Fla., U.S.A.* 26°56N 82°3W **317** J7
Punta Prieta *Mexico* 28°58N 114°17W **318** B2
Punta Prima *Spain* 39°48N 4°16E **206** B5
Punta Umbría *Spain* 37°10N 6°56W **195** H4
Puntarenas *Costa Rica* 10°0N 84°50W **320** E3
Puntland *Somali Rep.* 8°0N 49°0E **267** C6
Punto Fijo *Venezuela* 11°50N 70°13W **328** A4
Punxsutawney *U.S.A.* 40°57N 78°59W **312** F6
Punyu = Guangzhou
    China 23°6N 113°13E **121** B2
Puotila *Finland* 60°13N 25°6E **121** B3
Pupuan *Indonesia* 8°19S 115°0E **231** J18
Püpükea *U.S.A.* 21°40N 158°3W **302** J13
Puqi *China* 29°40N 113°50E **229** C9
Puquio *Peru* 14°45S 74°10W **330** C3
Pur ➤ *Russia* 67°31N 77°55E **214** C8
Puracé, Vol. *Colombia* 2°21N 76°23W **328** C2
Puracé △ *Colombia* 2°10N 76°21W **328** C2
Puračić *Bos.-H.* 44°33N 18°29E **182** F3
Puralia = Puruliya *India* 23°17N 86°24E **243** H12
Purana Qila *Delhi, India* **120** c3
Puranpur *India* 28°31N 80°9E **243** E9
Purari ➤ *Papua N. G.* 7°49S 145°0E **288** D2
Purbeck, Isle of *U.K.* 50°39N 1°59W **169** G5
Purcell *U.S.A.* 35°1N 97°22W **314** D6
Purcell Mts. *Canada* 49°55N 116°15W **296** D5
Purdy *Canada* 45°19N 77°4W **312** A7
Puri *India* 19°50N 85°58E **244** F7
Purificación *Colombia* 3°51N 74°55W **328** C2
Purmerend *Neths.* 52°32N 4°58E **170** B4
Purna ➤ *India* 19°7N 77°2E **244** E3
Purnia *India* 25°45N 87°31E **243** G12
Pursat = Pouthisat
    Cambodia 12°34N 103°50E **236** F4

Purukcahu Indonesia 0°35S 114°35E 235 C4
Puruliya India 23°17N 86°24E 243 H12
Purus → Brazil 3°42S 61°28W 329 D5
Purutu I. Papua N. G. 8°24S 143°27E 286 E2
Puruvesi Finland 61°50N 29°30E 188 B5
Purvis U.S.A. 31°9N 89°25W 315 F10
Pŭrvomay Bulgaria 42°8N 25°17E 203 D9
Purwa India 26°28N 80°47E 243 F9
Purwakarta Indonesia 6°35S 107°29E 235 D3
Purwo, Tanjung Indonesia 8°44S 114°21E 231 K18
Purwodadi Indonesia 7°7S 110°55E 235 D4
Purwokerto Indonesia 7°25S 109°14E 235 D3
Purworejo Indonesia 7°43S 110°2E 235 D4
Puryŏng N. Korea 42°5N 129°43E 224 A4
Pus → India 19°55N 77°55E 244 E3
Pusa India 25°59N 85°41E 243 G11
Pusad India 19°56N 77°36E 244 E3
Pusan = Busan S. Korea 35°5N 129°0E 224 E4
Pushkin Russia 59°45N 30°25E 188 C6
Pushkino Moskva, Russia 56°2N 37°49E 188 D9
Pushkino Saratov, Russia 51°16N 47°0E 190 E8
Püspökladány Hungary 47°19N 21°6E 182 C6
Pustoshka Russia 56°20N 29°30E 188 D5
Puszczykowo Poland 52°18N 16°49E 185 F3
Put-in-Bay U.S.A. 41°39N 82°49W 312 E2
Putahow L. Canada 59°54N 100°40W 297 B8
Putai Taiwan 23°23N 120°9E 225 C2
Putao Burma 27°28N 97°30E 241 B6
Putaruru N.Z. 38°2S 175°50E 284 E4
Putatan Malaysia 5°53N 116°3E 235 A5
Putbus Germany 54°22N 13°28E 178 A9
Puteaux France 48°52N 2°14E 134 A2
Putian China 25°23N 119°0E 229 E12
Putignano Italy 40°51N 17°7E 201 B10
Putilkovo Russia 55°51N 37°22E 129 A2
Putina Peru 14°55S 69°55W 330 C4
Puting, Tanjung Indonesia 3°31S 111°46E 235 C4
Putlitz Germany 53°15N 12°2E 178 B8
Putna Romania 47°50N 25°33E 183 C10
Putna → Romania 45°42N 27°26E 183 E12
Putnam U.S.A. 41°55N 71°55W 313 E13
Putney London, U.K. 51°27N 0°13W 125 B2
Putney Ga., U.S.A. 31°29N 84°8W 316 D5
Putnok Hungary 48°18N 20°26E 182 B5
Putorana, Gory Russia 69°0N 95°0E 215 C10
Putorino N.Z. 39°4S 176°58E 284 F5
Putrajaya Malaysia 2°55N 101°40E 237 L3
Putre Chile 18°12S 69°35W 330 D4
Puttalam Sri Lanka 8°1N 79°55E 245 K5
Puttalam Lagoon Sri Lanka 8°15N 79°45E 245 K4
Puttegga Norway 62°13N 7°42E 164 B4
Puttgarden Germany 54°30N 11°10E 178 A7
Püttlingen Germany 49°17N 6°53E 179 F2
Puttur Andhra Pradesh, India 13°27N 79°33E 245 H4
Puttur Karnataka, India 12°46N 75°12E 245 H2
Putty Australia 32°57S 150°42E 283 B9
Putumayo → S. Amer. 3°7S 67°58W 328 D4
Putuo Shanghai, China 31°15N 121°24E 138 B1
Putuo Zhejiang, China 29°56N 122°20E 229 C14
Putussibau Indonesia 0°50N 112°56E 235 B4
Pututahi N.Z. 38°39S 177°53E 284 E6
Putxet Spain 41°24N 2°8E 114 A1
Putyla Ukraine 48°0N 25°5E 183 B10
Pu'uanahulu U.S.A. 19°49N 155°51W 302 D6
Pu'uhonua o Hōnaunau ⌂ U.S.A. 19°25N 155°54W 302 D6
Pu'uka'aumakua U.S.A. 21°30N 157°54W 302 J14
Pu'ukeahiakahoe U.S.A. 21°23N 157°49W 302 K14
Pu'ukoholā Heiau ⌂ U.S.A. 20°1N 155°49W 302 C6
Pu'ula'ula U.S.A. 20°42N 156°15W 302 C5
Pu'u'oke'oke'o U.S.A. 19°13N 155°44W 302 D6
Pu'uwai U.S.A. 21°54N 160°12W 302 B1
Puvirnituq Canada 60°2N 77°10W 295 E16
Puxi China 31°12N 121°30E 138 B1
Puy-de-Dôme France 45°46N 2°57E 174 C6
Puy-de-Dôme □ France 45°40N 3°5E 174 C7
Puy-l'Évêque France 44°31N 1°9E 174 D5
Puyallup U.S.A. 47°12N 122°18W 306 C4
Puyang China 35°40N 115°1E 226 G8
Puyehue Chile 40°40S 72°37W 336 B2
Puyehue △ Chile 40°27S 72°6W 336 B2
Puylaurens France 43°35N 2°0E 174 E6
Puyo Ecuador 1°28S 77°59W 328 D2
Puysegur Pt. N.Z. 46°9S 166°37E 285 G1
Pūzeh Rīg Iran 27°20N 58°40E 247 E8
Puzhaykove Ukraine 48°7N 29°50E 183 B14
Pwani □ Tanzania 7°0S 39°0E 268 D4
Pweto Dem. Rep. of the Congo 8°25S 28°51E 269 D2
Pwinbyu Burma 20°23N 94°40E 241 E5
Pwllheli U.K. 52°53N 4°25W 168 E3
Pyana → Russia 55°43N 46°1E 190 C8
Pyandzh = Dusti Tajikistan 37°20N 68°40E 217 E7
Pyandzh → Asia 37°6N 68°20E 240 A2
Pyaozero, Ozero Russia 66°5N 30°58E 160 C24
Pyapon Burma 16°20N 95°40E 241 G5
Pyasina → Russia 73°30N 87°0E 215 B9
Pyatigorsk Russia 44°2N 43°6E 191 H6
Pyatykhatky Ukraine 48°28N 33°38E 189 H7
Pyawbwe Burma 20°35N 96°4E 241 E6
Pyaye Burma 19°12N 95°10E 241 F5
Pydhuni Mumbai, India 130 b2
Pydna Greece 40°20N 22°34E 202 F6
Pyè = Prome Burma 18°49N 95°13E 241 F5
Pyeonghae S. Korea 36°43N 129°26E 224 D4
Pyeongtaek S. Korea 37°1N 127°4E 224 D3
Pyetrikaw Belarus 52°11N 28°29E 177 B15
Pyhäjoki Finland 64°28N 24°14E 160 D21
Pyinbauk Burma 19°10N 95°12E 241 F5
Pyingaing Burma 23°9N 94°50E 241 D5
Pyinkayaing Burma 15°58N 94°24E 241 H5
Pyinmana Burma 19°45N 96°12E 241 F6
Pyinyaung Burma 20°49N 96°25E 241 E6
Pyla Cyprus 35°1N 33°41E 250 C4
Pyla, C. Cyprus 34°56N 33°51E 207 F9
Pymatuning Res. U.S.A. 41°30N 80°28W 312 E4
Pyŏktong N. Korea 40°50N 125°50E 224 B2
P'yŏnganbuk-do □ N. Korea 40°0N 125°15E 224 C2
P'yŏngannam-do □ N. Korea 39°30N 126°24E 224 C3
Pyŏnggang N. Korea 38°24N 127°17E 224 C3
P'yŏngsong N. Korea 39°14N 125°52E 224 C2
P'yŏngyang N. Korea 39°0N 125°30E 224 C2
P'yŏngyang □ N. Korea 39°4N 125°50E 224 C2
Pyote U.S.A. 31°32N 103°8W 314 F3
Pyramid L. U.S.A. 40°1N 119°35W 304 F4
Pyramid Pk. U.S.A. 36°25N 116°37W 307 J10
Pyramid Pt. Ascension I. 7°55S 14°24W 153 g
Pyramids Egypt 29°58N 31°9E 117 B1
Pyrénées Europe 42°45N 0°18E 174 F4
Pyrénées △ France 42°52N 0°10W 174 F3
Pyrénées-Atlantiques □ France 43°10N 0°50W 174 E3
Pyrénées-Orientales □ France 42°35N 2°26E 174 F6
Pyry Poland 52°8N 21°0E 142 C1
Pyryatyn Ukraine 50°15N 32°25E 189 G7
Pyrzyce Poland 53°10N 14°55E 185 E1
Pyskowice Poland 50°24N 18°38E 185 H5
Pytalovo Russia 57°5N 27°55E 188 D4
Pyttegga = Puttegga Norway 62°13N 7°42E 164 B4
Pyu Burma 18°30N 96°28E 241 F6
Pyzdry Poland 52°11N 17°42E 185 F4

Q

Qaanaaq Greenland 77°30N 69°10W 154 B4
Qabanbay Kazakhstan 45°50N 80°37E 217 C10
Qabirri → Azerbaijan 41°3N 46°17E 191 K8
Qabr Hūd Yemen 16°9N 49°34E 249 C5
Qachasnek S. Africa 30°6S 28°42E 271 D4
Qādisiyah, Buhayrat al Iraq 34°20N 42°12E 213 E10
Qādub Yemen 12°37N 53°57E 249 D6
Qa'el Jafr Jordan 30°20N 36°25E 251 H7
Qa'emābād Iran 31°44N 60°2E 247 D9
Qā'emshahr Iran 36°30N 52°53E 247 B7
Qagan Nur China 43°30N 114°55E 226 C8
Qahar Youyi Zhongqi China 41°12N 112°40E 226 D7
Qahremānshahr = Kermānshāh Iran 34°23N 47°0E 213 E12
Qaidam Pendi China 37°0N 95°0E 218 C4
Qaiyara Iraq 35°48N 43°17E 213 E10
Qajarīyeh Iran 31°1N 48°22E 247 D6
Qala Malta 36°2N 14°19E 206 E7
Qala, Ras il Malta 36°2N 14°20E 206 E7
Qala-i-Jadid = Spīn Būldak Afghan. 31°1N 66°25E 242 D2
Qala Point = Qala, Ras il Malta 36°2N 14°20E 206 E7
Qala Viala Pakistan 30°49N 67°17E 242 D2
Qala Yangi Afghan. 34°20N 66°30E 242 B2
Qalācheh Afghan. 35°30N 67°43E 240 B2
Qalaikhum = Kalaikhum Tajikistan 38°28N 70°46E 217 E8
Qalandiya West Bank 31°52N 35°12E 123 A2
Qalansīyah Yemen 12°41N 53°29E 249 D6
Qal'at al Akhḍar Si. Arabia 28°4N 37°9E 251 K8
Qal'at Bīshah Si. Arabia 20°0N 42°36E 248 C3
Qal'at Dīzah Iraq 36°11N 45°7E 213 D11
Qalāt-i-Ghilzai Afghan. 32°15N 66°58E 240 B2
Qal'at Ṣāliḥ Iraq 31°31N 47°16E 246 D5
Qal'at Sukkar Iraq 31°51N 46°5E 213 G12
Qal'eh Morghī Iran 35°38N 51°22E 141 B2
Qal'eh-ye Bost Afghan. 31°30N 64°21E 240 C2
Qal'eh-ye Now Afghan. 35°0N 63°5E 240 B1
Qal'eh-ye Panjeh Afghan. 37°0N 72°35E 240 A4
Qal'eh-ye Sarkari Afghan. 35°54N 67°17E 240 B2
Qal'eh-ye Valī Afghan. 35°46N 63°45E 240 B1
Qalyūb Egypt 30°12N 31°11E 251 H2
Qalyûbiya □ Egypt 30°18N 31°18E 251 H2
Qamani'tuaq = Baker Lake Canada 64°20N 96°3W 294 E12
Qamar, Ghubbat al Yemen 16°20N 52°30E 249 C6
Qamar, Jabal al Oman 16°48N 53°15E 249 C6
Qamdo China 31°15N 97°6E 228 B1
Qamea Fiji 16°45S 179°45W 287 A3
Qamīnis Libya 31°40N 20°1E 258 B4
Qammieh Point Malta 35°58N 14°19E 206 F7
Qamruddin Karez Pakistan 31°45N 68°20E 242 D3
Qanâ el Ismâ'ilîya Egypt 30°7N 31°17E 117 A2
Qandahār = Kandahār Afghan. 31°32N 65°43E 240 C2
Qandahār = Kandahār □ Afghan. 31°0N 65°0E 240 C2
Qandala Somali Rep. 11°30N 49°58E 267 B6
Qandyaghash Kazakhstan 49°28N 57°25E 187 E10
Qapān Iran 37°40N 55°47E 247 B7
Qapqal China 43°48N 81°5E 217 D10
Qapshaghay Kazakhstan 43°51N 77°14E 217 D9
Qapshaghay Bögeni Kazakhstan 43°45N 77°50E 217 D9
Qaqortoq Greenland 60°43N 46°0W 154 E6
Qâra Egypt 29°38N 26°30E 256 B2
Qarā', Jabal al Oman 17°15N 54°15E 249 C6
Qara Dāgh Iraq 35°18N 45°18E 213 E11
Qara Qash → China 35°0N 78°30E 243 B8
Qarabalyq Kazakhstan 53°45N 62°2E 216 B6
Qarabutaq Kazakhstan 49°59N 60°14E 216 C6
Qaraçala Azerbaijan 39°45N 48°53E 191 L9
Qaraghandy Kazakhstan 49°50N 73°10E 217 C8
Qaraghayly Kazakhstan 49°26N 76°0E 214 E8
Qārah Si. Arabia 29°55N 40°3E 246 D4
Qarah Āghāj Iran 37°8N 46°58E 213 D12
Qarakol Uzbekistan 39°32N 63°50E 216 E6
Qaraoba Kazakhstan 47°6N 56°15E 216 C5
Qaraqīya Oyysy Kazakhstan 43°27N 51°45E 216 D4
Qarasū Iraq 36°16N 43°22E 213 D10
Qarataū Ongtüstik Qazaqstan, Kazakhstan 43°30N 69°30E 217 D7
Qarataū Zhambyl, Kazakhstan 43°10N 70°28E 217 D8
Qarāvol Afghan. 37°14N 68°46E 240 A3
Qarazhal Kazakhstan 48°2N 70°49E 214 E8
Qardho Somali Rep. 9°30N 49°6E 267 C6
Qardud Sudan 10°20N 29°56E 257 E2
Qareh → Iran 39°25N 47°22E 213 C12
Qareh Tekān Iran 36°38N 49°29E 247 B6
Qarnein U.A.E. 24°56N 52°52E 247 E7
Qarqan He → China 39°30N 88°30E 217 E11
Qarqaraly Kazakhstan 49°26N 75°30E 217 C9
Qarqin Afghan. 37°24N 66°4E 240 A2
Qarrasa Sudan 14°38N 32°5E 257 E3
Qarshi Uzbekistan 38°53N 65°48E 217 E7
Qartabā Lebanon 34°4N 35°50E 250 D6
Qārūh Kuwait 28°49N 48°46E 247 D6
Qaryat al Gharab Iraq 31°27N 44°48E 246 D5
Qaryat al 'Ulyā Si. Arabia 27°33N 47°42E 246 E5
Qarynzharyq Oyysy Kazakhstan 42°55N 54°25E 216 D4
Qaşbah, Râs al Si. Arabia 28°2N 34°38E 251 K5
Qāsemābād Iran 35°46N 51°30E 141 A3
Qashqadaryo □ Uzbekistan 38°35N 66°0E 217 E7
Qasigiannguit Greenland 68°50N 51°18W 154 D5
Qasr 'Amra Jordan 31°48N 36°35E 246 D3
Qaşr Bū Hadi Libya 31°1N 16°45E 258 B3
Qaşr-e Fīrūzeh Iran 35°29N 51°31E 141 B3
Qaşr-e Qand Iran 26°15N 60°45E 247 E9
Qaşr-e Shīrīn Iran 34°31N 45°35E 213 E11
Qasr Farâfra Egypt 27°0N 28°1E 256 B2
Qaşr Larocu Libya 26°32N 13°19E 258 C2
Qasuittuq = Resolute Canada 74°42N 94°54W 295 C13
Qa'ṭabah Yemen 13°51N 44°42E 248 D4
Qaṭanā Syria 33°26N 36°4E 250 E7
Qaṭanan, Ra's Yemen 12°21N 53°33E 249 D6
Qatane West Bank 31°50N 35°6E 123 B1
Qatar ■ Asia 25°30N 51°15E 247 E6
Qatlīsh Iran 37°50N 57°19E 247 B8
Qattâra Egypt 30°12N 27°3E 256 A2
Qattâra, Munkhafed el Egypt 29°30N 27°30E 256 B2
Qattâra Depression = Qattâra, Munkhafed el Egypt 29°30N 27°30E 256 B2
Qawām al Ḥamzah = Al Ḥamzah Iraq 31°43N 44°58E 246 D5
Qawra Point Malta 35°58N 14°26E 206 F7
Qāyen Iran 33°40N 59°10E 247 C8
Qaynar Kazakhstan 49°12N 77°22E 217 C9
Qazaly Kazakhstan 45°45N 62°6E 216 C6
Qazaqstan = Kazakhstan ■ Asia 50°0N 70°0E 217 C8
Qazaqtyng Usaqshogylyghy Kazakhstan 50°0N 72°0E 217 C8
Qazax Azerbaijan 41°5N 45°21E 191 K7
Qazmämmäd Azerbaijan 40°3N 49°0E 191 K9
Qazvīn Iran 36°15N 50°0E 247 B6
Qazvīn □ Iran 36°20N 50°0E 247 B6
Qazyghurt Kazakhstan 41°45N 69°23E 217 D7
Qeisari = Caesarea Israel 32°30N 34°53E 251 F5
Qeissan Sudan 11°4N 34°40E 257 E3
Qena Egypt 26°10N 32°43E 256 B3
Qena, W. → Egypt 26°12N 32°44E 256 B3
Qeqertarsuaq Greenland 69°45N 53°30W 154 D5
Qeqertarsuaq Greenland 69°15N 53°38W 154 D5
Qeqertarsuatsiaat Greenland 63°5N 50°45W 154 E5
Qeshlāq Iran 34°55N 46°28E 213 E12
Qeshm Iran 26°55N 56°10E 247 E8
Qeydār Iran 36°6N 48°35E 213 D13
Qeys Iran 26°32N 53°58E 249 A6
Qezel Owzen → Iran 36°45N 49°22E 247 B6
Qezi'ot Israel 30°52N 34°26E 251 H5
Qi Xian China 34°40N 114°48E 226 G8
Qian Gorlos China 45°5N 124°42E 227 B13
Qian Hai China 22°32N 113°54E 219 F10
Qian Xian China 34°31N 108°15E 226 G5
Qiancheng China 27°12N 109°50E 228 D7
Qianjiang Guangxi Zhuangzu, China 23°38N 108°58E 228 F7
Qianjiang Hubei, China 30°24N 112°55E 229 B9
Qianjiang Sichuan, China 29°33N 108°47E 228 C7
Qianmen China 39°51N 116°21E 114 B2
Qianshan Anhui, China 30°37N 116°35E 229 B11
Qianshan Guangdong, China 22°15N 113°31E 219 G10
Qianwei China 29°13N 103°56E 228 C4
Qianxi China 27°3N 106°3E 228 D6
Qianyang Hunan, China 27°18N 110°10E 229 D8
Qianyang Shaanxi, China 34°40N 107°8E 226 G4
Qianyang Zhejiang, China 30°11N 119°25E 229 B12
Qi'ao China 22°25N 113°39E 219 G10
Qi'ao Dao China 22°25N 113°38E 219 G10
Qiaojia China 26°56N 102°58E 228 D4
Qichun China 30°18N 115°25E 229 B10
Qidong Hunan, China 26°49N 112°7E 229 D9
Qidong Jiangsu, China 31°48N 121°38E 229 B13
Qiemo China 38°8N 85°32E 217 E11
Qijiang China 28°57N 106°35E 228 C6
Qijiaojing China 43°28N 91°36E 217 D12
Qikiqtarjuaq Canada 67°33N 63°0W 295 D19
Qila Saifullāh Pakistan 30°45N 68°17E 242 D3
Qilian Shan China 38°30N 96°0E 218 C4
Qimen China 29°50N 117°42E 229 C11
Qin He → China 35°1N 113°22E 226 G7
Qin Jiang → Guangxi Zhuangzu, China 21°53N 108°35E 228 F7
Qin Jiang → Jiangxi, China 26°15N 115°55E 229 D10
Qin Ling = Qinling Shandi China 33°50N 108°10E 226 H5
Qināb, W. → Yemen 17°55N 49°59E 249 C5
Qin'an China 34°48N 105°40E 226 G3
Qing Xian China 38°35N 116°45E 226 E9
Qingcheng China 37°15N 117°40E 227 F9
Qingdao China 36°5N 120°20E 227 F11
Qingfeng China 35°52N 115°8E 226 G8
Qinghai □ China 36°0N 98°0E 218 C4
Qinghai Hu China 36°40N 100°10E 218 C5
Qinghe China 46°37N 90°25E 217 C12
Qinghecheng China 41°28N 124°15E 224 B2
Qinghemen China 41°48N 121°25E 227 D11
Qinghuayuan China 39°59N 116°19E 114 B1
Qingjian China 37°8N 110°8E 226 F6
Qingjiang = Huaiyin China 33°30N 119°2E 227 H10
Qingliu China 26°11N 116°48E 229 D11
Qinglong China 25°49N 105°12E 228 E5
Qingningsi China 31°16N 121°33E 138 B2
Qingping China 26°39N 107°47E 228 D6
Qingpu China 31°10N 121°6E 229 B13
Qingshui China 34°48N 106°8E 226 G4
Qingshuihe China 39°55N 111°35E 226 E6
Qingtian China 28°12N 120°15E 229 C13
Qingtongxia Shuiku China 37°50N 105°58E 226 F3
Qingxi China 27°8N 108°43E 228 D7
Qingxu China 37°34N 112°22E 226 F7
Qingyang Anhui, China 30°38N 117°50E 229 B11
Qingyang Gansu, China 36°2N 107°55E 226 F4
Qingyi Jiang → China 29°32N 103°44E 228 C4
Qingyuan Guangdong, China 23°40N 112°59E 229 F9
Qingyuan Liaoning, China 42°10N 124°55E 224 A2
Qingyuan Zhejiang, China 27°36N 119°3E 229 D12
Qingyun China 37°45N 117°20E 227 F9
Qingzhen China 26°31N 106°25E 228 D6
Qinhuangdao China 39°56N 119°30E 227 E10
Qinling Shandi China 33°50N 108°10E 226 H5
Qinshui China 35°40N 112°8E 226 G7
Qinyang = Jiyuan China 35°7N 112°57E 226 G7
Qinyuan China 36°29N 112°20E 226 F7
Qinzhou China 21°58N 108°38E 228 G7
Qionghai China 19°15N 110°26E 236 C8
Qionglai China 30°25N 103°31E 228 B4
Qionglai Shan China 31°0N 102°30E 228 B4
Qiongzhou Haixia China 20°10N 110°15E 236 B8
Qiqihar China 47°26N 124°0E 219 B7
Qira China 37°0N 80°48E 217 E10
Qiraîya, W. → Egypt 30°27N 34°0E 251 H5
Qiryat Ata Israel 32°47N 35°6E 250 F6
Qiryat Gat Israel 31°32N 34°46E 251 G5
Qiryat Mal'akhi Israel 31°44N 34°44E 251 G5
Qiryat Shemona Israel 33°13N 35°35E 250 E6
Qiryat Yam Israel 32°51N 35°4E 250 F6
Qirzah, W. → Libya 30°56N 14°31E 258 B2
Qishan China 34°25N 107°38E 226 G4
Qishn Yemen 15°26N 51°40E 249 D5
Qitai China 44°2N 89°35E 217 D11
Qitaihe China 45°48N 130°51E 220 B5
Qitbit, W. → Oman 19°15N 54°23E 249 C6
Qiubei China 24°2N 104°12E 228 E5
Qixia China 37°17N 120°52E 227 F11
Qiyang China 26°35N 111°50E 229 D8
Qızılağac Körfäzi Azerbaijan 39°9N 49°0E 213 C13
Qobda Kazakhstan 50°55N 54°31E 216 B4
Qojūr Iran 36°12N 47°55E 246 B5
Qolhak Iran 35°45N 51°26E 141 A2
Qom Iran 34°40N 51°0E 247 C6
Qom □ Iran 34°40N 51°0E 247 C6
Qomolangma Feng = Everest, Mt. Nepal 28°5N 86°58E 243 E12
Qomsheh Iran 32°0N 51°55E 247 D6
Qondūz = Kondūz Afghan. 36°50N 68°50E 240 A3
Qondūz → Afghan. 37°0N 68°16E 240 A3
Qong Muztag China 35°42N 82°22E 217 E10
Qoqek = Tacheng China 46°40N 82°58E 217 C10
Qoqon = Qŭqon Uzbekistan 40°31N 70°56E 217 D8
Qoraqalpoghiston □ Uzbekistan 43°0N 58°0E 216 D5
Qormi Malta 35°53N 14°28E 206 F7
Qorveh Iran 35°10N 47°48E 213 E12
Qosshaghyl Kazakhstan 46°40N 54°0E 187 E9
Qostanay Kazakhstan 53°10N 63°35E 216 B6
Qotanqaraghay Kazakhstan 49°10N 85°36E 217 C11
Qoṭūr Iran 38°28N 44°25E 213 C11
Qoz Salsilgo C.A.R. 10°45N 22°54E 264 A4
Qrejten Point Malta 35°57N 14°27E 206 F7
Qu Jiang → China 30°1N 106°24E 228 B6
Qu Xian China 30°48N 106°58E 228 B6
Quabbin Res. U.S.A. 42°20N 72°20W 313 D12
Quadraro Italy 41°51N 12°33E 136 B2
Quaid-i-Azam Pakistan 24°50N 66°59E 123 A1
Quairading Australia 32°0S 117°21E 279 F2
Quakenbrück Germany 52°41N 7°57E 178 C3
Quakertown U.S.A. 40°26N 75°21W 313 F9
Qualicum Beach Canada 49°22N 124°26W 296 D4
Quambatook Australia 35°49S 143°34E 282 C5
Quambone Australia 30°57S 147°53E 283 A7
Quamby Australia 20°22S 140°17E 280 C3
Quan Long = Ca Mau Vietnam 9°7N 105°8E 237 H5
Quanah U.S.A. 34°18N 99°44W 314 D5
Quandialla Australia 34°1S 147°47E 283 C7
Quang Ngai Vietnam 15°13N 108°58E 236 E7
Quang Tri Vietnam 16°45N 107°13E 236 D6
Quang Yen Vietnam 20°56N 106°52E 228 G6
Quannan China 24°45N 114°33E 229 E10
Quantock Hills U.K. 51°8N 3°10W 169 F4
Quanzhou Fujian, China 24°55N 118°34E 229 E12
Quanzhou Guangxi Zhuangzu, China 25°57N 111°5E 229 E8
Qu'Appelle → Canada 50°33N 103°53W 297 C8
Quaqtaq Canada 60°55N 69°40W 295 E18
Quaraí Brazil 30°15S 56°20W 334 C4
Quarré-les-Tombes France 47°21N 4°0E 173 E11
Quarteira Portugal 37°4N 8°6W 195 H2
Quarter, The Anguilla 18°13N 63°3W 322 a
Quartier D'Orléans St.-Martin 18°5N 63°2W 322 a
Quartier Militaire Mauritius 20°14S 57°35E 272 e
Quartiere Zingone Italy 45°25N 9°3E 129 B1
Quartu Sant'Élena Italy 39°15N 9°10E 200 C2
Quartzsite U.S.A. 33°40N 114°13W 307 M12
Quatre, I. à St. Vincent 12°59N 61°15W 323 n
Quatre Bornes Mauritius 20°15S 57°28E 272 e
Quatsino Sd. Canada 50°25N 127°58W 296 C3
Quba Azerbaijan 41°21N 48°32E 191 K9
Qubeiba West Bank 31°50N 35°8E 123 B1
Qūchān Iran 37°10N 58°27E 247 B8
Quds Iraq 33°23N 44°24E 113 A2
Queanbeyan Australia 35°17S 149°14E 283 C8
Québec Canada 46°52N 71°13W 299 C5
Québec □ Canada 48°0N 74°0W 299 C6
Quebo Guinea-Biss. 11°20N 14°56W 262 C2
Quebrada del Condorito △ Argentina 31°49S 64°40W 334 C3
Quebradillas Puerto Rico 18°29N 66°56W 321 b
Quedlinburg Germany 51°47N 11°8E 178 D7
Queen Alexandra Ra. Antarctica 85°0S 170°0E 151 E11
Queen Charlotte B. Falk. Is. 51°50S 60°40W 153 f
Queen Charlotte City Canada 53°15N 132°2W 296 C2
Queen Charlotte Is. Canada 53°20N 132°10W 296 C2
Queen Charlotte Sd. B.C., Canada 51°0N 128°0W 296 C3
Queen Charlotte Sd. N.Z. 41°10S 174°15E 285 B9
Queen Charlotte Strait Canada 50°45N 127°10W 296 C3
Queen City U.S.A. 40°25N 92°34W 310 D4
Queen Elizabeth △ Uganda 0°0 30°0E 268 C3
Queen Elizabeth ⌂ U.K. 56°7N 4°30W 167 E4
Queen Elizabeth Is. Canada 76°0N 95°0W 295 B13
Queen Elizabeth Nat. Park = Ruwenzori △ Uganda 0°20N 30°0E 268 B2
Queen Mary Land Antarctica 70°0S 95°0E 151 D7
Queen Mary Res. U.K. 51°24N 0°27W 125 B1
Queen Maud G. Canada 68°15N 102°30W 294 D11
Queen Maud Land = Dronning Maud Land Antarctica 72°30S 12°0E 151 D3
Queen Maud Mts. Antarctica 86°0S 160°0W 151 E13
Queen Street Edinburgh, U.K. 121 a1
Queen Victoria Market Australia 37°47S 144°57W 128 A1
Queens Channel Australia 15°0S 129°30E 278 C4
Queens-Midtown Tunnel New York, U.S.A. 132 d2
Queen's Quay Terminal Toronto, Canada 141 c2
Queensboro Bridge New York, U.S.A. 132 c3
Queensbury U.K. 51°35N 0°16W 125 A2
Queenscliff Australia 38°16S 144°39E 282 E6
Queenscliffe Australia 33°47S 151°17E 139 A2
Queensferry U.K. 55°59N 3°23W 121 B1
Queensland U.S.A. 31°46N 83°14W 316 D6
Queensland □ Australia 22°0S 142°0E 280 C3
Queensland Plateau Pac. Oc. 17°0S 150°0E 276 D8
Queenstown = Cóbh Ireland 51°51N 8°17W 166 E3
Queenstown Tas., Australia 42°4S 145°35E 281 G4
Queenstown N.Z. 45°1S 168°40E 285 F3
Queenstown Singapore 1°18N 103°48E 138 B2
Queenstown Eastern Cape, S. Africa 31°52S 26°52E 270 D4
Queets U.S.A. 47°32N 124°19W 306 C2
Queguay Grande → Uruguay 32°9S 58°9W 334 C4
Queimada, Pta. da Azores 38°23N 28°14W 153 d1
Queimadas Brazil 11°0S 39°38W 332 D4
Queiros, C. Vanuatu 14°55S 167°1E 287 D5
Quela Angola 9°10S 16°56E 265 D3
Quelimane Mozam. 17°53S 36°58E 269 F4
Quellerina S. Africa 26°9S 27°56E 123 A1
Quellón Chile 43°7S 73°37W 336 B2
Quelo Angola 6°29S 12°56E 265 D2
Quelpart = Jeju-do S. Korea 33°29N 126°34E 224 a
Queluz Portugal 38°45N 9°14W 126 A1
Quemado N. Mex., U.S.A. 34°20N 108°30W 305 J9
Quemado Tex., U.S.A. 28°56N 100°37W 314 G4
Quemoy = Chinmen Taiwan 24°26N 118°19E 225 a
Quemú-Quemú Argentina 36°3S 63°36W 334 D3
Quepem India 15°13N 74°3E 245 G2
Quequén Argentina 38°30S 58°30W 334 D4
Querco Peru 13°50S 74°52W 330 C3
Querétaro Mexico 20°36N 100°23W 318 C4
Querétaro □ Mexico 21°0N 99°55W 318 C5
Querfurt Germany 51°23N 11°35E 178 D7
Quérigut France 42°42N 2°6E 174 F6
Querqueville France 49°40N 1°42W 172 C5
Quesada Spain 37°51N 3°4W 195 H7
Queshan China 32°55N 114°2E 226 H8
Quesnel Canada 53°0N 122°30W 296 C4
Quesnel → Canada 52°58N 122°29W 296 C4
Quesnel L. Canada 52°30N 121°20W 296 C4
Questa U.S.A. 36°42N 105°36W 305 H11
Questembert France 47°40N 2°28W 172 E4
Quetena Bolivia 22°10S 67°25W 330 E4
Quetico ⌂ Canada 48°30N 91°45W 298 C1
Quetrequile Argentina 41°33S 69°22W 336 B3
Quetta Pakistan 30°15N 66°55E 242 D2
Queulat △ Chile 44°29S 72°24W 336 B2
Quevedo Ecuador 1°2S 79°29W 328 D2
Queyras ⌂ France 44°45N 6°50E 175 D10
Quezaltenango Guatemala 14°50N 91°30W 320 D1
Quezon Phil. 9°15N 117°59E 233 G1
Quezon □ Phil. 14°40N 121°30E 232 D3
Quezon △ Phil. 14°0N 121°55E 232 D3
Quezon City Phil. 14°37N 121°2E 127 B2
Qufār Si. Arabia 27°26N 41°37E 246 E4
Qui Nhon Vietnam 13°40N 109°13E 236 F7
Quibala Angola 10°46S 14°59E 265 E2
Quibaxe Angola 8°24S 14°27E 265 D2
Quibdó Colombia 5°42N 76°40W 328 B2
Quiberon France 47°29N 3°9W 172 E3
Quiberon, Presqu'île de France 47°30N 3°8W 172 E3
Quiçama △ Angola 9°41S 13°35E 265 D2
Quickborn Germany 53°42N 9°52E 178 B5
Quiet L. Canada 61°5N 133°5W 296 A2
Quiindy Paraguay 25°58S 57°14W 334 B4
Quilá Mexico 24°23N 107°13W 318 C3
Quilán, C. Chile 43°15S 74°30W 336 B2
Quilcene U.S.A. 47°49N 122°53W 306 C4
Quilenda Angola 10°39S 14°23E 265 E2
Quilengues Angola 14°12S 14°12E 265 E2
Quilicura Chile 33°22S 70°43W 137 B1
Quilimarí Chile 32°5S 71°30W 334 C1
Quilino Argentina 30°14S 64°29W 334 C3
Quill, The Neth. Ant. 17°28N 62°57W 322 a
Quillabamba Peru 12°50S 72°50W 330 C3
Quillacollo Bolivia 17°26S 66°17W 330 D4
Quillagua Chile 21°40S 69°40W 334 A2
Quillan France 42°53N 2°10E 174 F6
Quillota Chile 32°54S 71°16W 334 C1
Quilmes Argentina 34°43S 58°15W 334 C4
Quilon India 8°50N 76°38E 245 K3
Quilpie Australia 26°35S 144°11E 281 D3
Quilpué Chile 33°5S 71°33W 334 C1
Quilua Mozam. 16°17S 39°54E 269 F4
Quimbele Angola 6°17S 16°41E 265 D3
Quimbo Angola 14°4S 16°11E 265 E3
Quimbonge Angola 8°36S 18°30E 265 D3
Quime Bolivia 17°2S 67°15W 330 D4
Quimilí Argentina 27°40S 62°30W 334 B3
Quimper France 48°0N 4°9W 172 E2
Quimperlé France 47°53N 3°33W 172 E3
Quinam B. Trin. & Tob. 10°4N 61°30W 323 t
Quinault → U.S.A. 47°21N 124°18W 306 C2
Quince Mil Peru 13°15S 70°40W 330 C3
Quincy Calif., U.S.A. 39°56N 120°57W 306 F6
Quincy Fla., U.S.A. 30°35N 84°34W 316 E5
Quincy Ill., U.S.A. 39°56N 91°23W 310 E5
Quincy Mass., U.S.A. 42°14N 71°0W 116 B2
Quincy Mich., U.S.A. 41°57N 84°53W 311 C12
Quincy Wash., U.S.A. 47°14N 119°51W 304 C4
Quincy B. U.S.A. 42°16N 70°59W 116 B3
Quines Argentina 32°13S 65°48W 334 C2
Quinga Mozam. 15°49S 40°15E 269 F5
Quingey France 47°7N 5°52E 173 E12
Quingombe Angola 6°38S 13°1E 265 D2
Quinhagak U.S.A. 59°45N 161°54W 303 G7
Quinhámel Guinea-Biss. 11°53N 15°51W 262 C1
Quiniluban Group Phil. 11°27N 120°48E 233 F3
Quinta Normal Chile 33°26S 70°42W 137 B1
Quintana de la Serena Spain 38°45N 5°40W 195 G5
Quintana Roo □ Mexico 19°40N 88°30W 319 D7
Quintanar de la Orden Spain 39°36N 3°5W 195 F7
Quintanar de la Sierra Spain 41°57N 2°55W 196 D2
Quintanar del Rey Spain 39°21N 1°56W 197 F3
Quintero Chile 32°45S 71°30W 334 C1
Quintin France 48°26N 2°56W 172 D4
Quinto Spain 41°25N 0°32W 196 D4
Quinto de Stampi Italy 45°24N 9°10E 129 B2
Quinto Romano Italy 45°28N 9°7E 129 B1
Quinzáu Angola 6°51S 12°44E 265 D2
Quípar → Spain 38°15N 1°40W 197 G3
Quipeio Angola 12°27S 15°30E 265 E3
Quirihue Chile 36°15S 72°35W 334 D1
Quirima Angola 10°47S 18°6E 265 E3
Quirimbas △ Mozam. 12°30S 40°15E 269 E5
Quirimbo Angola 10°36S 14°12E 265 E2
Quirinale Italy 41°53N 12°29E 136 B1
Quirinale, Palazzo dei Rome, Italy 136 b3
Quirindi Australia 31°28S 150°40E 283 A9
Quirinópolis Brazil 18°32S 50°30W 333 E1
Quiroga Spain 42°28N 7°18W 194 C3
Quiruvilca Peru 8°1S 78°19W 330 B2
Quissac France 43°55N 4°0E 175 E8
Quissanga Mozam. 12°24S 40°28E 269 E5
Quissico Mozam. 24°42S 34°44E 271 B5
Quitapa Angola 10°20S 18°19E 265 E3
Quitilipi Argentina 26°50S 60°13W 334 B3
Quitman U.S.A. 30°47N 83°34W 316 E6
Quito Ecuador 0°15S 78°35W 328 D2
Quitralco △ Chile 45°43S 73°25W 336 C2
Quixadá Brazil 4°55S 39°0W 332 B4
Quixaxe Mozam. 15°17S 40°4E 269 F5
Quixeramobim Brazil 5°12S 39°17W 332 C4
Quixico Angola 7°59S 14°25E 265 D2
Quixinge Angola 9°52S 14°23E 265 D2
Quizenga Angola 9°21S 15°28E 265 D3
Qujing China 25°32N 103°41E 228 E4
Qulan Kazakhstan 42°55N 72°43E 214 E8
Qul'ân, Jazâ'ir Egypt 24°22N 35°31E 246 E2
Qulsary Kazakhstan 46°59N 54°1E 187 E9
Qumbu S. Africa 31°10S 28°48E 271 D4
Qunayyin, Sabkhat al Libya 30°10N 21°0E 258 B4
Qŭnghirot Uzbekistan 43°2N 58°50E 216 D5
Qu'nyido China 31°15N 98°6E 228 B2
Quoin I. Australia 14°54S 129°32E 278 B4
Quoin Pt. S. Africa 34°46S 19°37E 270 D2
Quorn Australia 32°25S 138°5E 282 B3
Qŭqon Uzbekistan 40°31N 70°56E 217 D8
Qurein Sudan 13°30N 34°50E 257 E3
Qŭrghonteppa Tajikistan 37°50N 68°47E 217 E7
Qurnat as Sawdā' Lebanon 34°18N 36°6E 250 D7
Quryq Kazakhstan 43°12N 51°39E 216 D4
Qûs Egypt 25°55N 32°50E 256 B3
Qusar Azerbaijan 41°25N 48°26E 191 K9
Quşaybā' Si. Arabia 26°53N 43°35E 246 E4
Qusaybah Iraq 34°24N 40°59E 213 E9
Quşay'ir Yemen 14°55N 50°20E 249 D5
Quseir Egypt 26°7N 34°16E 246 E2
Qūshchī Iran 37°59N 45°3E 213 D11
Qusmuryn Kazakhstan 52°27N 64°36E 216 B6
Qusmuryn Köli Kazakhstan 52°41N 64°48E 216 B6
Quthing Lesotho 30°25S 27°36E 271 D4
Qūţīābād Iran 35°47N 48°30E 213 E13
Quttinirpaaq △ Canada 82°13N 72°13W 295 A17
Quwayq → Syria 36°20N 37°10E 250 B8
Quweisna Egypt 30°34N 31°9E 251 H2
Quwo China 35°38N 111°25E 226 G6
Quyang China 38°35N 114°40E 226 E8
Quynh Nhai Vietnam 21°49N 103°33E 236 B4
Quyon Canada 45°31N 76°14W 313 A8
Quzhou China 28°57N 118°54E 229 C12
Quzi China 36°20N 107°20E 226 F4
Qvareli Georgia 41°57N 45°47E 191 K7
Qytet Stalin = Kuçovë Albania 40°47N 19°57E 202 F3
Qyzylorda Kazakhstan 44°48N 65°28E 217 D7
Qyzylorda □ Kazakhstan 45°0N 65°0E 216 D6
Qyzylzhar Kazakhstan 48°17N 69°38E 217 C7

R

R.F.K. Memorial Stadium U.S.A. 38°52N 76°58W 143 B4
Ra, Ko Thailand 9°13N 98°16E 237 H2
Raab Austria 48°21N 13°39E 180 C6
Raahe Finland 64°40N 24°28E 160 D21
Raalte Neths. 52°23N 6°16E 170 B6
Ra'ananna Israel 32°10N 34°52E 251 F5
Raasay U.K. 57°25N 6°4W 167 D2
Raasay, Sd. of U.K. 57°30N 6°8W 167 D2
Raasdorf Austria 48°14N 16°33E 142 A3
Rab Croatia 44°45N 14°45E 199 D11
Raba Indonesia 8°36S 118°55E 235 D5
Rába → Hungary 47°38N 17°38E 182 C2
Raba → Poland 50°8N 20°30E 185 H7
Rabaçal → Portugal 41°30N 7°12W 194 D3
Rabah Nigeria 13°5N 5°30E 263 C6
Rabai Kenya 3°50S 39°31E 268 C4
Rabak Sudan 13°9N 32°44E 257 E3
Rabaraba Papua N. G. 9°58S 149°49E 286 E5
Rabastens France 43°50N 1°43E 174 E5
Rabastens-de-Bigorre France 43°23N 0°9E 174 E4
Rabat = Victoria Malta 36°3N 14°14E 206 E6
Rabat Malta 35°53N 14°24E 206 F7
Rabat Morocco 34°2N 6°48W 260 B3
Rabat □ Morocco 34°10N 6°45W 260 B3
Rabaul Papua N. G. 4°24S 152°18E 286 C7
Rabbit Flat Australia 20°11S 130°1E 278 D5
Rabbit Lake Mine Canada 58°4N 104°5W 297 B8
Rabi Fiji 16°30S 179°59W 287 A3
Rābigh Si. Arabia 22°50N 39°5E 248 B2
Rabka Poland 49°37N 19°59E 185 J6
Râbniţa Moldova 47°45N 29°0E 183 C14
Rābor Iran 29°17N 56°55E 247 D8
Rabwah = Chenab Nagar Pakistan 31°45N 72°55E 242 D5
Rabyānah Libya 24°15N 22°0E 258 D4
Rača Serbia 44°14N 21°0E 202 B4
Răcăciuni Romania 46°20N 26°59E 183 D11
Răcăşdia Romania 44°59N 21°36E 182 F6
Racconigi Italy 44°46N 7°46E 198 D4
Raccoon → U.S.A. 41°35N 93°37W 310 C3
Raccoon Cr. → U.S.A. 39°47N 87°23W 311 E9
Race, C. Canada 46°40N 53°5W 299 C9
Race Course Jamaica 17°51N 77°20W 320 a
Race Pond U.S.A. 31°1N 82°8W 316 D7
Rach Gia Vietnam 10°5N 105°5E 237 G5
Rachid Mauritania 18°45N 11°35W 262 B2
Raciąż Poland 52°46N 20°10E 185 F7
Racibórz Poland 50°7N 18°18E 185 H5
Racichy Belarus 53°44N 23°42E 184 E10
Racine U.S.A. 42°44N 87°47W 311 B9
Račisdorf = Rača Serbia 44°14N 21°0E 202 B4
Rackerby U.S.A. 39°26N 121°22W 306 F5
Radama, Nosy Madag. 14°0S 47°47E 272 A2
Radama, Saikanosy Madag. 14°16S 47°53E 272 A2
Radan Serbia 42°59N 21°29E 202 D5
Rădăuţi Romania 47°50N 25°59E 183 C10
Rădăuţi-Prut Romania 48°14N 26°48E 183 B11
Radbuza → Czech Rep. 49°45N 13°22E 180 B6
Radcliff U.S.A. 37°51N 85°57W 311 G11
Radcliffe College U.S.A. 42°22N 71°7W 116 A2
Radeberg Germany 51°7N 13°55E 178 D9
Radebeul Germany 51°6N 13°39E 178 D9
Radeče Slovenia 46°5N 15°14E 199 B12
Radekhiv Ukraine 50°25N 24°32E 177 C13
Radekhov = Radekhiv Ukraine 50°25N 24°32E 177 C13
Radenthein Austria 46°48N 13°43E 180 E6
Radew → Poland 54°2N 15°52E 184 D2
Radford U.S.A. 37°8N 80°34W 309 G13
Radhanpur India 23°50N 71°38E 242 H4
Rådhus Oslo, Norway 133 b1
Radhwa, Jabal Si. Arabia 24°34N 38°18E 246 E3
Radika → Macedonia 41°38N 20°37E 202 E4
Radisson Qué., Canada 53°47N 77°37W 298 B4
Radisson Sask., Canada 52°30N 107°20W 297 C7
Radium Hot Springs Canada 50°35N 116°2W 296 C5
Radlice Czech Rep. 50°3N 14°23E 135 B2
Radlje ob Dravi Slovenia 46°38N 15°13E 199 B12
Radmannsdorf = Radovljica Slovenia 46°22N 14°12E 199 B11
Radnevo Bulgaria 42°17N 25°58E 203 D9
Radnice Czech Rep. 49°51N 13°35E 180 B6
Radnor Forest U.K. 52°17N 3°10W 169 E4
Radolfzell Germany 47°39N 8°59E 179 H4
Radom Poland 51°23N 21°12E 185 G8
Radom △ Sudan 9°20N 23°50E 264 A4
Radomir Bulgaria 42°37N 22°56E 202 D6
Radomka → Poland 51°43N 21°28E 185 G8
Radomsko Poland 51°5N 19°28E 185 G6
Radomyshl Ukraine 50°30N 29°12E 177 C15
Radomyśl Wielki Poland 50°14N 21°15E 185 H8
Radość Poland 52°11N 21°11E 142 B3
Radoszyce Poland 51°4N 20°15E 185 G7
Radotín Czech Rep. 49°59N 14°21E 135 C2
Radoviš Macedonia 41°38N 22°28E 202 E6
Radovljica Slovenia 46°22N 14°12E 199 B11
Radstadt Austria 47°24N 13°28E 180 D6
Radstock, C. Australia 33°12S 134°20E 281 E1
Răducăneni Romania 46°58N 27°54E 183 D12
Raduša Macedonia 42°7N 21°15E 202 D5
Raduzhnyy Russia 62°5N 77°28E 214 C8
Radvanichy Belarus 52°1N 24°0E 185 F11
Radviliškis Lithuania 55°49N 23°33E 184 C10
Radville Canada 49°30N 104°15W 297 D8
Radwá, J. Si. Arabia 24°34N 38°18E 256 C4
Radymno Poland 49°59N 22°52E 185 J9
Radzanów Poland 52°56N 20°8E 185 F7
Radziejów Poland 52°40N 18°30E 185 F5
Radzyń Chełmiński Poland 53°23N 18°55E 184 E5
Radzyń Podlaski Poland 51°47N 22°37E 185 G9
Rae Canada 62°50N 116°3W 296 A5
Rae Bareli India 26°18N 81°20E 243 F9
Rae Isthmus Canada 66°40N 87°30W 295 D14
Raeren Belgium 50°41N 6°7E 170 D6

Raeside, L. Australia 29°20S 122°0E 279 E3
Raetihi N.Z. 39°25S 175°17E 284 F4
Rafaela Argentina 31°10S 61°30W 334 C3
Rafah Gaza Strip 31°18N 34°14E 251 G5
Rafai C.A.R. 4°59N 23°58E 264 B4
Rafat West Bank 31°52N 35°11E 123 A2
Raffadali Italy 37°24N 13°32E 200 E6
Raffili Sudan 6°50N 28°0E 257 F2
Raffles Hotel Singapore 138 b3
Raffles Park Singapore 1°19N 103°48E 138 B2
Rafḩā Si. Arabia 29°35N 43°35E 246 D4
Rafina Greece 38°2N 24°0E 204 C6
Rafsanjān Iran 30°30N 56°5E 247 D8
Raft Pt. Australia 16°4S 124°26E 278 C3
Râgâ Sudan 8°28N 25°41E 257 F2
Raga → Sudan 8°41N 25°52E 257 F2
Ragachow Belarus 53°8N 30°5E 177 B16
Ragag Sudan 10°59N 24°40E 257 E1
Ragang, Mt. Phil. 7°43N 124°32E 233 H5
Ragay Phil. 13°49N 122°47E 232 E4
Ragay G. Phil. 13°30N 122°45E 232 E4
Ragged, Mt. Australia 33°27S 123°25E 279 F3
Rāgh Afghan. 37°32N 70°27E 240 A3
Raghunathpalli India 22°14N 84°48E 243 H11
Raghunathpur India 23°33N 86°40E 243 H12
Raglan N.Z. 37°55S 174°55E 284 D3
Raglan Harbour N.Z. 37°47S 174°50E 284 D3
Ragland U.S.A. 33°45N 86°9W 316 B3
Ragnit = Neman Russia 55°2N 22°2E 184 C9
Raguda, Ghubbet Somali Rep. 10°43N 46°22E 267 B6
Ragusa = Dubrovnik Croatia 42°39N 18°6E 202 D2
Ragusa Italy 36°55N 14°44E 201 F7
Raha Indonesia 4°55S 123°0E 231 E6
Rahad, Nahr ed → Sudan 14°28N 33°31E 257 E3
Rahad al Bardī Sudan 11°20N 23°40E 259 F4
Rahaeng = Tak Thailand 16°52N 99°8E 236 D2
Rahat, Şarrat Si. Arabia 23°0N 40°5E 256 C5
Rahatgarh India 23°47N 78°22E 243 H8
Rahden Germany 52°26N 8°36E 178 C4
Raheb, Ras ir- Malta 35°54N 14°20E 206 F7
Raheita Eritrea 12°46N 43°4E 257 E5
Raheng = Tak Thailand 16°52N 99°8E 236 D2
Raheny Ireland 53°22N 6°10W 120 A3
Rahimyar Khan Pakistan 28°30N 70°25E 242 E4
Rāhjerd Iran 34°22N 50°22E 247 C6
Rahnsdorf Germany 52°25N 13°41E 115 B5
Rahole ⌓ Kenya 0°5N 38°57E 268 B4
Råholt Norway 60°16N 11°11E 164 D8
Rahon India 31°3N 76°7E 242 D7
Rahotu N.Z. 39°20S 173°49E 284 F2
Rahuri India 19°23N 74°39E 244 E2
Raiatéa, Î. French Polynesia 16°50S 151°25W 289 f
Raichur India 16°10N 77°20E 245 F3
Raiford U.S.A. 30°4N 82°14W 316 E7
Raiganj India 25°37N 88°10E 243 G13
Raigarh India 21°56N 83°25E 244 D6
Raighar India 19°51N 82°6E 244 E6
Raijua Indonesia 10°37S 121°36E 231 F6
Raikot India 30°41N 75°42E 242 D6
Railton Australia 41°25S 146°28E 281 G4
Rainbow Bridge ⌓ U.S.A. 37°5N 110°58W 305 H8
Rainbow City U.S.A. 33°57N 86°5W 316 B3
Rainbow Lake Canada 58°30N 119°23W 296 B5
Rainier U.S.A. 46°53N 122°41W 306 D4
Rainier, Mt. U.S.A. 46°52N 121°46W 306 D5
Rainy L. Canada 48°42N 93°10W 297 D10
Rainy River Canada 48°43N 94°29W 297 D10
Raippaluoto Finland 63°13N 21°14E 160 E19
Raipur India 21°17N 81°45E 244 D5
Rairakhol India 21°4N 84°21E 244 D7
Ra'is Si. Arabia 23°33N 38°43E 256 C4
Raisen India 23°20N 77°48E 242 H8
Raisio Finland 60°28N 22°11E 188 B2
Raivavae French Polynesia 23°52S 147°40W 289 f
Raj Ghat Delhi, India 120 b3
Raj Nandgaon India 21°5N 81°5E 244 D5
Raj Nilgiri India 21°28N 86°46E 243 J12
Raja, Ujung Indonesia 3°40N 96°25E 234 B1
Raja Ampat, Kepulauan Indonesia 0°30S 130°0E 231 E8
Rajah Sikatuna △ Phil. 9°40N 124°20E 233 G5
Rajahmundry India 17°1N 81°48E 244 F5
Rajaji △ India 30°10N 78°20E 242 D8
Rajakylä Finland 60°15N 25°5E 121 B3
Rajampet India 14°11N 79°10E 245 G4
Rajang → Malaysia 2°30N 112°0E 235 B4
Rajanpur Pakistan 29°6N 70°19E 242 E4
Rajapalaiyam India 9°25N 77°35E 245 K3
Rajapur India 16°40N 73°31E 244 F1
Rajasthan □ India 26°45N 73°30E 242 F5
Rajasthan Canal = Indira Gandhi Canal India 28°0N 72°0E 242 F5
Rajauri India 33°25N 74°21E 243 C6
Rajbari Bangla. 23°47N 89°41E 241 D2
Rajendranagar India 17°18N 78°27E 244 F4
Rajgarh Mad. P., India 24°2N 76°45E 242 G7
Rajgarh Raj., India 27°14N 76°38E 242 F7
Rajgarh Raj., India 28°40N 75°25E 242 E6
Rajghat Dam India 24°45N 78°20E 244 B4
Rajgir India 25°2N 85°25E 243 G11
Rajgród Poland 53°42N 22°42E 184 E9
Rajim India 20°58N 81°53E 244 D5
Rajkot India 22°15N 70°56E 242 H4
Rajmahal Hills India 24°30N 87°30E 243 G12
Rajpath Delhi, India 120 c2
Rajpipla India 21°50N 73°30E 244 D1
Rajpur India 22°18N 74°21E 242 H6
Rajpura Delhi, India 28°41N 77°12E 120 A2
Rajpura Punjab, India 30°25N 76°32E 242 D7
Rajputana = Rajasthan □ India 26°45N 73°30E 242 F5
Rajsamand = Kankroli India 25°4N 73°53E 242 G5
Rajshahi Bangla. 24°22N 88°39E 241 C2
Rajshahi □ Bangla. 25°0N 89°0E 241 C2
Rājū Syria 36°40N 36°40E 250 B7
Rajula India 21°3N 71°26E 242 J4
Rajur India 20°7N 78°55E 244 D4
Rajura India 19°47N 79°22E 244 E4
Rakaia N.Z. 43°45S 172°1E 285 D7
Rakaia → N.Z. 43°36S 172°15E 285 D7
Rakan, Ra's Qatar 26°10N 51°20E 247 E6
Rakaposhi Pakistan 36°10N 74°25E 243 A6
Rakata, Pulau Indonesia 6°10S 105°20E 234 D3
Rakbah, Sahl Si. Arabia 22°15N 41°0E 256 C5
Rakhiv Ukraine 48°3N 24°12E 183 B9
Rakhni Pakistan 30°4N 69°56E 242 D3
Rakhni → Pakistan 29°31N 69°36E 242 E3
Rakhny-Lisovi Ukraine 48°47N 28°29E 183 B13
Rakhyūt Oman 16°44N 53°20E 249 C6
Rakiraki Fiji 17°22S 178°11E 287 A2
Rakitnoye Russia 45°36N 134°17E 220 B7
Rakitovo Bulgaria 41°59N 24°5E 203 E8
Rakiura = Stewart I. N.Z. 46°58S 167°54E 285 G2
Rakkestad Norway 59°25N 11°21E 164 E8
Rakoniewice Poland 52°10N 16°16E 185 F3
Rakops Botswana 21°1S 24°28E 270 B3
Rákos-patak → Hungary 47°29N 19°12E 117 B3
Rákoshegy Hungary 47°27N 19°14E 117 B3
Rákoskeresztúr Hungary 47°29N 19°15E 117 B3
Rákoskert Hungary 47°27N 19°18E 117 B3
Rákosliget Hungary 47°29N 19°16E 117 B3
Rákospalota Hungary 47°34N 19°7E 117 A2
Rákosszentmihály Hungary 47°31N 19°8E 117 A2
Rakovica Croatia 44°59N 15°38E 199 D12
Rakovník Czech Rep. 50°6N 13°42E 180 A6
Rakovski Bulgaria 42°21N 24°57E 203 D8
Raków Poland 52°11N 20°56E 142 B1
Rakshan → Pakistan 27°10N 63°25E 240 D1
Rakvere Estonia 59°20N 26°25E 188 C4
Raleigh Fla., U.S.A. 29°25N 82°32W 317 F7
Raleigh N.C., U.S.A. 35°47N 78°39W 315 D15
Ralik Chain Pac. Oc. 8°0N 168°0E 288 G8
Ralja Serbia 44°33N 20°34E 202 B4
Ralls U.S.A. 33°41N 101°24W 314 E4
Ralston U.S.A. 41°30N 76°57W 312 E8
Ram West Bank 31°51N 35°14E 123 A2
Ram → Canada 62°1N 123°41W 296 A4
Rām Allāh West Bank 31°55N 35°10E 123 A2
Rama Nic. 12°9N 84°15W 320 D3
Ramacca Italy 37°23N 14°42E 201 E7
Ramachandrapuram India 16°50N 82°4E 244 F6
Ramadān Iraq 33°19N 44°20E 113 B2
Ramagiri Udayagiri India 19°5N 84°18E 244 E7
Ramagundam India 18°55N 79°15E 244 E4
Ramakona India 21°43N 78°50E 243 J8
Ramakrishna Puram India 28°32N 77°10E 120 B1
Ramales de la Victoria Spain 43°15N 3°28W 194 B7
Ramalho, Serra do Brazil 13°45S 44°0W 333 D3
Rāmallāh = Rām Allāh West Bank 31°55N 35°10E 123 A2
Raman Thailand 6°29N 101°18E 237 J3
Ramanathapuram India 9°25N 78°55E 245 K4
Ramanathpur India 22°41N 88°14E 124 A1
Ramanujganj India 23°48N 83°42E 243 H10
Ramas C. India 15°5N 73°55E 245 G1
Ramat Allon West Bank 31°49N 35°12E 123 B2
Ramat Eshkol West Bank 31°48N 35°13E 123 B2
Ramat Gan Israel 32°4N 34°48E 251 F5
Ramat Razi'el Israel 31°46N 35°4E 123 B1
Ramat Shafet West Bank 31°48N 35°12E 123 B2
Ramatlhabama S. Africa 25°37S 25°33E 270 C4
Ramban India 33°14N 75°12E 243 C6
Rambervillers France 48°20N 6°38E 173 D13
Rambi = Rabi Fiji 16°30S 179°59W 287 A3
Rambipuji Indonesia 8°12S 113°37E 235 D4
Rambla, La Barcelona, Spain 114 b2
Rambler Channel China 22°21N 114°6E 122 A1
Rambouillet France 48°39N 1°50E 173 D8
Rambrai India 25°40N 91°19E 241 C3
Rambutyo I. Papua N. G. 2°18S 147°49E 286 B4
Ramdurg India 15°58N 75°22E 245 G2
Rame Hd. Australia 37°47S 149°30E 283 D8
Ramechhap Nepal 27°25N 86°10E 243 F12
Ramenki Russia 55°41N 37°28E 129 B2
Ramenskoye Russia 55°32N 38°15E 188 E10
Ramer U.S.A. 32°3N 86°13W 316 C3
Ramersdorf Germany 48°6N 11°35E 131 B2
Rameses Station Egypt 30°3N 31°15E 117 A2
Rameswaram India 9°17N 79°18E 245 K4
Ramganga → India 27°5N 79°58E 243 F8
Ramgarh Bangla. 22°59N 91°44E 241 D3
Ramgarh Jharkhand, India 23°40N 85°35E 243 H11
Ramgarh Raj., India 27°16N 75°14E 242 F6
Ramgarh Raj., India 27°30N 70°36E 242 F4
Rāmhormoz Iran 31°15N 49°35E 247 D6
Ramīān Iran 37°3N 55°16E 247 B7
Ramingining Australia 12°19S 135°3E 280 A2
Ramla Israel 31°55N 34°52E 251 G5
Ramlat Zalṭan Libya 28°30N 19°30E 258 C3
Ramlu Eritrea 13°32N 41°40E 257 E5
Ramm = Rum Jordan 29°39N 35°26E 251 J6
Râmna → Romania 45°36N 27°3E 183 E12
Ramnad = Ramanathapuram India 9°25N 78°55E 245 K4
Ramnagar Jammu & Kashmir, India 32°47N 75°18E 243 C6
Ramnagar Uttarakhand, India 29°24N 79°7E 243 E8
Ramnäs Sweden 59°46N 16°12E 162 E10
Râmnicu Sărat Romania 45°26N 27°3E 183 E12
Râmnicu Vâlcea Romania 45°9N 24°21E 183 E9
Ramnous Greece 38°12N 24°3E 204 C6
Ramon Isabela, Phil. 16°50N 121°31E 232 C3
Ramon Russia 51°55N 39°21E 189 G10
Ramona U.S.A. 33°2N 116°52W 307 M10
Ramonville-St-Agne France 43°33N 1°28E 174 E5
Ramore Canada 48°30N 80°25W 298 C3
Ramos Brazil 22°50S 43°14W 135 B1
Ramos → Nigeria 5°8N 5°22E 263 D6
Ramos Mejía Argentina 34°39S 58°33W 117 B1
Ramot West Bank 31°48N 35°13E 123 B2
Ramotswa Botswana 24°50S 25°52E 270 B4
Rampanalgas Trin. & Tob. 10°44N 60°59W 323 t
Rampart U.S.A. 65°30N 150°10W 303 D10
Rampur H.P., India 31°26N 77°43E 242 D7
Rampur Mad. P., India 23°25N 73°53E 242 H5
Rampur Orissa, India 21°48N 83°58E 244 D6
Rampur Ut. P., India 28°44N 77°18E 120 A2
Rampur Ut. P., India 28°50N 79°5E 243 E8
Rampur Hat India 24°10N 87°50E 243 G12
Rampura India 24°30N 75°27E 242 G6
Ramrama Tola India 21°52N 79°55E 243 J8
Ramree I. Burma 19°0N 93°40E 241 F5
Rāmsar Iran 36°53N 50°41E 247 B6
Ramsey I. of Man 54°20N 4°22W 168 C3
Ramsey Ill., U.S.A. 39°8N 89°7W 310 E7
Ramsey N.J., U.S.A. 41°4N 74°9W 313 E10
Ramsey L. Canada 47°13N 82°15W 298 C3
Ramsgate N.S.W., Australia 33°58S 151°8E 139 B1
Ramsgate Kent, U.K. 51°20N 1°25E 169 F9
Ramshai India 26°44N 88°51E 241 B2
Ramsjö Sweden 62°11N 15°37E 162 B9
Ramstein Germany 49°27N 7°32E 179 F3
Ramtek India 21°20N 79°15E 244 D4
Ramu Kenya 3°55N 41°10E 268 B5
Ramu → Papua N. G. 4°0S 144°41E 286 C3
Ramvik Sweden 62°49N 17°51E 162 B11
Ramville, Î. = Chancel, Î. Martinique 14°41N 60°53W 322 j
Rana Pratap Sagar Dam India 24°58N 75°38E 242 G6
Ranaghat India 23°15N 88°35E 243 H13
Ranahu Pakistan 25°55N 69°45E 242 G3
Ranau Malaysia 6°2N 116°40E 235 A5
Rancagua Chile 34°10S 70°50W 334 C1
Rance → France 48°34N 1°59W 172 D5
Rancharia Brazil 22°15S 50°55W 333 F1
Rancheria → Canada 60°13N 129°7W 296 A3
Ranchester U.S.A. 44°54N 107°10W 304 D10
Ranchi India 23°19N 85°27E 243 H11
Rancho Cordova U.S.A. 38°36N 121°18W 306 G5
Rancho Cucamonga U.S.A. 34°10N 117°30W 307 L9
Rancho Park U.S.A. 34°3N 118°26W 126 B2
Ranco, L. Chile 40°15S 72°25W 336 B2
Rand Australia 35°33S 146°32E 283 C7
Rand ✕ (QRA) S. Africa 26°14S 28°8E 123 B2
Randaberg Norway 59°1N 5°36E 164 E2
Randabygda Norway 61°51N 6°20E 164 C3
Randalls I. U.S.A. 40°47N 73°55W 132 B2
Randalstown U.K. 54°45N 6°19W 166 B5
Randan France 46°2N 3°21E 173 F10
Randazzo Italy 37°53N 14°57E 201 E7
Randburg S. Africa 26°5S 27°57E 123 A1
Rander India 21°14N 72°47E 244 D1
Randers Denmark 56°29N 10°1E 163 H4
Randers Fjord Denmark 56°37N 10°20E 163 H4
Randfontein S. Africa 26°8S 27°45E 271 C4
Randhart S. Africa 26°16S 28°7E 123 B2
Randle U.S.A. 46°32N 121°57W 306 D5
Randolph Mass., U.S.A. 42°10N 71°2W 313 D13
Randolph N.Y., U.S.A. 42°10N 78°59W 312 D6
Randolph Utah, U.S.A. 41°40N 111°11W 304 F8
Randolph Vt., U.S.A. 43°55N 72°40W 313 C12
Randpark Ridge S. Africa 26°6S 27°58E 123 A1
Randsburg U.S.A. 35°22N 117°39W 307 K9
Randsfjorden Norway 60°25N 10°24E 164 D7
Randsverk Norway 61°44N 9°3E 164 C6
Randwick Australia 33°54S 151°14E 139 B2
Råneälven → Sweden 65°50N 22°20E 160 D20
Ranelagh Ireland 53°20N 6°15W 120 A2
Ranenburg = Chaplygin Russia 53°15N 40°0E 188 F11
Ranfurly N.Z. 45°7S 170°6E 285 F5
Rangae Thailand 6°19N 101°44E 237 J3
Rangamati Bangla. 22°38N 92°12E 241 D4
Rangapara India 26°49N 92°39E 241 B4
Rangárvallasýsla □ Iceland 63°55N 20°0W 155 D7
Rangataua N.Z. 39°26S 175°28E 284 F4
Rangaunu B. N.Z. 34°51S 173°15E 284 A2
Range, The Zimbabwe 19°2S 31°2E 269 F3
Rangeley U.S.A. 44°58N 70°39W 313 B14
Rangeley L. U.S.A. 44°55N 70°43W 313 B14
Rangely U.S.A. 40°5N 108°48W 304 F9
Ranger U.S.A. 32°28N 98°41W 314 E5
Rangia India 26°28N 91°38E 241 B3
Rangiora N.Z. 43°19S 172°36E 285 D7
Rangiroa French Polynesia 15°10S 147°35W 289 f
Rangitaiki N.Z. 38°52S 176°24E 284 E5
Rangitaiki → N.Z. 37°54S 176°49E 284 D5
Rangitata → N.Z. 43°45S 171°15E 285 D6
Rangitikei → N.Z. 40°17S 175°15E 284 G4
Rangitoto ke te tonga = D'Urville I. N.Z. 40°50S 173°55E 285 A8
Rangitoto Ra. N.Z. 38°25S 175°35E 284 E4
Rangkasbitung Indonesia 6°21S 106°15E 234 D3
Rangoon Burma 16°45N 96°20E 241 G6
Rangoon □ Burma 17°0N 96°10E 241 G6
Rangpur Bangla. 25°42N 89°22E 241 C2
Rangpuri India 28°32N 77°8E 120 B1
Rangsang Indonesia 1°20N 103°30E 237 M4
Rangsit Thailand 13°59N 100°37E 236 F3
Rangwe Kenya 0°36S 34°35E 266 E3
Ranibennur India 14°35N 75°30E 245 G2
Raniganj India 27°3N 82°13E 243 F9
Ranikhet India 29°39N 79°25E 243 E8
Ranippettai India 12°56N 79°23E 245 H4
Raniwara India 24°50N 72°10E 242 G5
Rāniyah Iraq 36°15N 44°53E 213 D11
Ranka India 23°59N 83°47E 243 H10
Ranken → Australia 20°31S 137°36E 280 C2
Rankin Ill., U.S.A. 40°28N 87°54W 311 D9
Rankin Tex., U.S.A. 31°13N 101°56W 314 F4
Rankin Inlet Canada 62°30N 93°0W 294 E13
Rankins Springs Australia 33°49S 146°14E 283 B7
Rankovicevo = Kraljevo Serbia 43°44N 20°41E 202 C4
Rankweil Austria 47°17N 9°39E 180 D2
Rannersdorf Austria 48°7N 16°27E 142 B2
Rannoch, L. U.K. 56°41N 4°20W 167 E4
Rannoch Moor U.K. 56°38N 4°48W 167 E4
Rano Kau Chile 27°11S 109°26W 330 b
Rano Raraku, Volcán Chile 27°7S 109°17W 330 b
Ranobe Madag. 17°10S 44°8E 272 B1
Ranobe, Helodranon' i Madag. 23°3S 43°33E 272 C1
Ranohira Madag. 22°29S 45°24E 272 C2
Ranomafana Toamasina, Madag. 18°57S 48°50E 272 B2
Ranomafana Toliara, Madag. 24°34S 47°0E 272 C2
Ranomafana △ Madag. 21°16S 47°25E 272 C2
Ranomena Madag. 23°25S 47°17E 272 C2
Ranon Vanuatu 16°8S 168°7E 287 F6
Ranong Thailand 9°56N 98°40E 237 H2
Ranongga Solomon Is. 8°5S 156°35E 287 M9
Ranotsara Nord Madag. 22°48S 46°36E 272 C2
Ranpur India 20°5N 85°20E 244 D7
Rānsa Iran 33°39N 48°18E 247 C6
Ransbèche Belgium 50°56N 4°27E 116 B2
Ransdorp Neths. 52°24N 5°0E 112 A2
Ransiki Indonesia 1°30S 134°10E 231 E8
Ransom U.S.A. 41°9N 88°39W 311 C8
Rantabe Madag. 15°42S 49°39E 272 B2
Rantau Indonesia 2°56S 115°9E 235 C5
Rantauprapat Indonesia 2°15N 99°50E 234 B1
Rantemario Indonesia 3°15S 119°57E 231 E5
Ranthambore △ India 26°10N 76°30E 242 F7
Rantoul U.S.A. 40°19N 88°9W 311 D8
Ranum Denmark 56°54N 9°14E 163 H3
Ranvad India 18°53N 72°55E 130 B2
Ranyah, W. → Si. Arabia 21°18N 43°20E 248 B3
Raohe China 46°47N 134°0E 220 A7
Raon l'Étape France 48°24N 6°50E 173 D13
Raoping China 23°42N 117°1E 229 F11
Raoui, Erg er Algeria 29°0N 2°0W 261 C4
Raoul I. Pac. Oc. 29°16S 177°54W 277 F15
Raoyang China 38°15N 115°45E 226 E8
Rap, Ko Thailand 9°19N 99°58E 237 b
Rapa French Polynesia 27°35S 144°20W 289 f
Rapa Nui = Pascua, I. de Chile 27°7S 109°23W 330 b
Rapallo Italy 44°21N 9°14E 198 D6
Rapar India 23°34N 70°38E 242 H4
Rāpch Iran 25°40N 59°15E 247 E8
Rapel, Lago Chile 34°20S 71°14W 334 C1
Raper, C. Canada 69°44N 67°6W 295 D18
Rapid City U.S.A. 44°5N 103°14W 308 C2
Rapid River U.S.A. 45°55N 86°58W 308 C10
Rapla Estonia 59°1N 24°52E 188 C3
Raposo Portugal 38°40N 9°11W 126 A1
Rapti → India 26°18N 83°41E 243 F10
Rapu Rapu I. Phil. 13°12N 124°9E 232 E5
Raqaba ez Zarqa → Sudan 9°14N 29°44E 257 F2
Rāqūbah Libya 28°58N 19°2E 258 C3
Raquette → U.S.A. 45°0N 74°42W 313 B10
Raquette Lake U.S.A. 43°49N 74°40W 313 C10
Rara △ Nepal 29°30N 82°10E 243 E10
Raraka French Polynesia 16°10S 144°54W 289 f
Raroia French Polynesia 16°1S 142°27W 289 f
Rarotonga Cook Is. 21°30S 160°0W 289 h
Ras Abu Soma Egypt 26°51N 33°58E 256 B3
Ra's al 'Ayn Syria 36°45N 40°12E 213 D9
Ras al Hadd Oman 22°30N 59°50E 249 B7
Ra's al Khaymah U.A.E. 25°50N 55°59E 247 E7
Ra's aṭ Tib Tunisia 37°1N 11°2E 258 A2
Ras el Ma Algeria 34°26N 0°50W 261 B4
Râs el Mâ Mali 16°35N 4°30W 262 B4
Râs el Oued Algeria 35°57N 5°2E 261 A6
Râs Ghârib Egypt 28°6N 33°18E 256 B3
Rās Kōh Pakistan 28°43N 64°55E 240 C2
Ra's Lānūf Libya 30°46N 18°11E 258 B3
Râs Muhammad △ Egypt 27°45N 34°16E 256 B3
Ra's Shamrah Syria 35°35N 35°45E 250 C6
Râs Sudr Egypt 29°40N 32°42E 256 B3
Rasa, Pta. Argentina 36°20S 56°41W 334 D4
Rasa, Punta Argentina 40°50S 62°15W 336 B4
Rasca, Pta. de la Canary Is. 27°59N 16°41W 153 e1
Răşcani Moldova 47°58N 27°33E 183 C12
Rasdhoo Maldives 4°17N 72°58E 272 d
Rasdu Atoll Maldives 4°18N 72°58E 272 d
Raseiniai Lithuania 55°25N 23°5E 184 C10
Rashad Sudan 11°55N 31°0E 257 E3
Rashîd Egypt 31°21N 30°22E 256 H7
Rashîd, Masabb Egypt 31°22N 30°17E 256 H7
Rashin = Najin N. Korea 42°12N 130°15E 224 A5
Rashmi India 25°4N 74°22E 242 G6
Rasht Iran 37°20N 49°40E 213 D13
Rashtrapati Bhawan Delhi, India 120 c1
Rasi Salai Thailand 15°20N 104°9E 236 E5
Rasipuram India 11°30N 78°15E 245 J4
Raška Serbia 43°19N 20°39E 202 C4
Râsnov Romania 45°35N 25°27E 183 E10
Rason L. Australia 28°45S 124°25E 279 E3
Raşova Romania 44°15N 27°55E 183 F12
Rasovo Bulgaria 43°42N 23°17E 202 C7
Rasra India 25°50N 83°50E 243 G10
Rasskazovka Russia 55°38N 37°20E 129 C2
Rasskazovo Russia 52°35N 41°50E 190 D5
Rast Romania 43°53N 23°16E 183 G8
Rastaala Finland 60°15N 24°47E 121 B1
Rastatt Germany 48°50N 8°11E 179 G4
Rastede Germany 53°15N 8°12E 178 B4
Rastenburg = Kętrzyn Poland 54°7N 21°22E 184 D8
Rastila Finland 60°12N 25°7E 121 B3
Răstolița Romania 46°59N 24°58E 183 D9
Rastyapino = Dzerzhinsk Russia 56°14N 43°30E 190 B6
Rasul Pakistan 32°42N 73°34E 242 C5
Raszków Poland 51°43N 17°40E 185 G4
Raszyn Poland 52°9N 20°54E 142 C1
Rat → Canada 49°35N 97°10W 297 D9
Rat Buri Thailand 13°30N 99°54E 236 F2
Rat I. St. Lucia 14°2N 60°58W 323 m
Rat I. Alaska, U.S.A. 51°48N 178°15E 303 L2
Rat Islands U.S.A. 52°0N 178°0E 303 L2
Rat L. Canada 56°10N 99°40W 297 B9
Ratak Chain Pac. Oc. 1°0N 170°0E 288 G8
Rätan Sweden 62°29N 14°33E 162 B8
Ratangarh India 28°5N 74°35E 242 E6
Raţāwī Iraq 30°38N 47°13E 246 D5
Ratcatchers L. Australia 32°30S 143°12E 282 B5
Rath India 25°36N 79°37E 243 G8
Rath Luirc Ireland 52°21N 8°40W 166 D3
Rathangan Ireland 53°13N 7°1W 166 C4
Rathbun L. U.S.A. 40°54N 93°5W 310 D4
Rathdrum Ireland 52°56N 6°14W 166 D5
Rathedaung Burma 20°29N 92°45E 241 E4
Rathenow Germany 52°37N 12°19E 178 C8
Rathfarnham Ireland 53°18N 6°16W 120 B2
Rathkeale Ireland 52°32N 8°56W 166 D3
Rathlin I. U.K. 55°18N 6°14W 166 A5
Rathmelton Ireland 55°2N 7°38W 166 A4
Ratho U.K. 55°55N 3°23W 121 B1
Ratho Station U.K. 55°56N 3°23W 121 B1
Ratibor = Racibórz Poland 50°7N 18°18E 185 H5
Rätikon Austria 47°0N 9°55E 180 D2
Ratingen Germany 51°18N 6°52E 178 D2
Ratlam India 23°20N 75°0E 242 H6
Ratmanova Ostrov Russia 65°46N 169°6W 300 B6
Ratnagiri India 16°57N 73°18E 244 F1
Ratnapura Sri Lanka 6°40N 80°20E 245 L5
Rato Portugal 38°43N 9°8W 126 A2
Ratodero Pakistan 27°48N 68°18E 242 F3
Raton U.S.A. 36°54N 104°24W 305 H11
Ratschach = Radeče Slovenia 46°5N 15°14E 199 B12
Rattaphum Thailand 7°8N 100°16E 237 J3
Ratten Austria 47°28N 15°44E 180 D8
Rattray Hd. U.K. 57°38N 1°50W 167 D7
Rättvik Sweden 60°52N 15°7E 162 D9
Ratz, Mt. Canada 57°23N 132°12W 296 B2
Ratzebuhr = Okonek Poland 53°32N 16°51E 184 E3
Ratzeburg Germany 53°40N 10°46E 178 B6
Raub Malaysia 3°47N 101°52E 237 L3
Rauch Argentina 36°45S 59°5W 334 D4
Raudales Mexico 17°27N 93°39W 319 D6
Raudeberg Norway 61°59N 5°7E 164 C2
Raufarhöfn Iceland 66°27N 15°57W 155 A11
Raufoss Norway 60°44N 10°37E 164 D7
Rauhellern Norway 60°15N 7°50E 164 D4
Raukumara Ra. N.Z. 38°5S 177°55E 284 E6
Raul Soares Brazil 20°5S 42°22W 333 F3
Rauma Finland 61°10N 21°30E 188 B1
Rauma → Norway 62°34N 7°43E 164 B4
Raumo = Rauma Finland 61°10N 21°30E 188 B1
Raung, Gunung Indonesia 8°8S 114°3E 231 J17
Raurkela India 22°14N 84°50E 243 H11
Rausu-Dake Japan 44°4N 145°7E 220 B12
Răut → Moldova 47°15N 29°9E 183 C14
Rava-Ruska Ukraine 50°15N 23°42E 185 H10
Rava Russkaya = Rava-Ruska Ukraine 50°15N 23°42E 185 H10
Ravahere French Polynesia 18°14S 142°9W 289 f
Ravalli U.S.A. 47°17N 114°11W 304 C6
Ravānsar Iran 34°43N 46°40E 213 E12
Ravanusa Italy 37°16N 13°58E 200 E6
Rāvar Iran 31°20N 56°51E 247 D8
Ravelston U.K. 55°57N 3°14W 121 B2
Ravena U.S.A. 42°28N 73°49W 313 D11
Ravenel U.S.A. 32°46N 80°15W 316 C9
Ravenna Italy 44°25N 12°12E 199 D9
Ravenna Ky., U.S.A. 37°41N 83°57W 311 G13
Ravenna Nebr., U.S.A. 41°1N 98°55W 308 E4
Ravenna Ohio, U.S.A. 41°9N 81°15W 312 E3
Ravensburg Germany 47°46N 9°36E 179 H5
Ravenshoe Australia 17°37S 145°29E 280 B4
Ravensthorpe Australia 33°35S 120°2E 279 F3
Ravenswood Queens., Australia 20°6S 146°54E 280 C4
Ravenswood W. Va., U.S.A. 38°57N 81°46W 309 F13
Ravensworth Australia 32°26S 151°4E 283 B9
Ravenwood U.S.A. 40°22N 94°41W 310 D2
Raver India 21°15N 76°2E 244 D3
Ravi → Pakistan 30°35N 71°49E 242 D4
Ravine Chaude Guadeloupe 16°14N 61°40W 322 e
Ravna Gora Croatia 45°24N 14°50E 199 C11
Ravna Reka Serbia 44°1N 21°35E 202 B5
Ravne na Koroškem Slovenia 46°36N 14°59E 199 B11
Rawa Mazowiecka Poland 51°46N 20°12E 185 G7
Rawaki Kiribati 3°43S 170°43W 277 A16
Rawalpindi Pakistan 33°38N 73°8E 242 C5
Rawamangun Indonesia 6°11S 106°52E 122 B2
Rawang Malaysia 3°20N 101°35E 237 L3
Rawene N.Z. 35°25S 173°32E 284 B2
Rawicz Poland 51°36N 16°52E 185 G3
Rawitsch = Rawicz Poland 51°36N 16°52E 185 G3
Rawka → Poland 52°9N 20°8E 185 F7
Rawlinna Australia 30°58S 125°28E 279 F4
Rawlins U.S.A. 41°47N 107°14W 304 F10
Rawlinson Ra. Australia 24°40S 128°30E 279 D4
Rawson Argentina 43°15S 65°5W 336 B3
Raxaul India 26°59N 84°51E 243 F11
Ray U.S.A. 48°21N 103°10W 308 A2
Ray, C. Canada 47°33N 59°15W 299 C8
Ray City U.S.A. 31°5N 83°11W 316 D6
Ray Mts. U.S.A. 66°0N 152°0W 303 D10
Raya Ring, Ko Thailand 8°18N 98°29E 237 a
Rayachoti India 14°4N 78°50E 245 G4
Rayadurg India 14°40N 76°50E 245 G3
Rayagada India 19°15N 83°20E 244 E6
Raychikhinsk Russia 49°46N 129°25E 215 E13
Rāyen Iran 29°34N 57°26E 247 D8
Rayle U.S.A. 33°48N 82°54W 316 B7
Rayleigh U.K. 51°36N 0°37E 169 F8
Raymond Alta., Canada 49°30N 112°35W 296 D6
Raymond Calif., U.S.A. 37°13N 119°54W 306 H7
Raymond Ill., U.S.A. 39°19N 89°34W 310 E7
Raymond N.H., U.S.A. 43°2N 71°11W 313 C13
Raymond Wash., U.S.A. 46°41N 123°44W 306 D3
Raymond Terrace Australia 32°45S 151°44E 283 B9
Raymondville U.S.A. 26°29N 97°47W 314 H6
Raymore Canada 51°25N 104°31W 297 C8
Rayners Lane U.K. 51°34N 0°23W 125 A1
Raynes Park U.K. 51°24N 0°12W 125 B2
Rayón Mexico 29°43N 110°35W 318 B2
Rayong Thailand 12°40N 101°20E 236 F3
Raypur India 22°28N 88°22E 124 C2
Raystown L. U.S.A. 40°25N 78°5W 312 F6
Raytown U.S.A. 39°1N 94°28W 310 E2
Rayville U.S.A. 32°29N 91°46W 314 E9
Raz, Pte. du France 48°2N 4°47W 172 D2
Razan Iran 35°23N 49°2E 213 E13
Ražana Serbia 44°6N 19°55E 202 B3
Ražanj Serbia 43°40N 21°31E 202 C5
Razāzah, Buḩayrat ar Iraq 32°40N 43°35E 213 F10
Razazah, L. = Razāzah, Buḩayrat ar Iraq 32°40N 43°35E 213 F10
Razdelna Bulgaria 43°13N 27°41E 203 C11
Razdel'naya = Rozdilna Ukraine 46°50N 30°2E 183 D15
Razdolnoye Russia 43°30N 131°52E 220 C5
Razdolnoye Ukraine 45°46N 33°29E 189 K7
Razdory Russia 55°44N 37°17E 129 B1
Razeh Iran 32°47N 48°9E 247 C6
Razgrad Bulgaria 43°33N 26°34E 203 C10
Razim, Lacul Romania 44°50N 29°0E 183 F14
Razlog Bulgaria 41°53N 23°28E 202 E7
Razmak Pakistan 32°45N 69°50E 242 C3
Re, Cu Lao Vietnam 15°22N 109°8E 236 E7
Ré, Î. de France 46°12N 1°30W 174 B2
Reach Falls Jamaica 18°2N 76°18W 320 a
Reading Reading, U.K. 51°27N 0°58W 169 F7
Reading Mich., U.S.A. 41°50N 84°45W 311 C12
Reading Ohio, U.S.A. 39°13N 84°26W 311 E12
Reading Pa., U.S.A. 40°20N 75°56W 313 F9
Reading □ U.K. 51°27N 0°58W 169 F7
Real, Cordillera Bolivia 17°0S 67°10W 330 D4
Real Felipe, Fuerte Peru 12°4S 77°9W 124 B2
Realejo Alto Canary Is. 28°22N 16°34W 153 e1
Realicó Argentina 35°0S 64°15W 334 D3
Réalmont France 43°48N 2°10E 174 E6
Ream Cambodia 10°34N 103°39E 237 G4
Ream △ Cambodia 10°30N 103°45E 237 G4
Reams, L. U.S.A. 28°26N 81°34W 133 B1
Réao French Polynesia 18°31S 136°23W 289 f
Reay Forest U.K. 58°22N 4°55W 167 C4
Rebais France 48°50N 3°10E 173 D10
Rebecca, L. Australia 30°0S 122°15E 279 F3
Rebi Indonesia 6°23S 134°7E 231 F8
Rebiana Libya 24°12N 22°10E 258 D4
Rebiana, Sahrâ' Libya 24°30N 21°0E 258 D3
Reboly Russia 63°49N 30°47E 160 E24
Rebun-Tō Japan 45°23N 141°2E 220 B10
Recanati Italy 43°24N 13°32E 199 E10
Recaş Romania 45°46N 21°30E 182 E6
Recco Italy 44°22N 9°9E 198 D6
Recherche, Arch. of the Australia 34°15S 122°50E 279 F3
Rechna Doab Pakistan 31°35N 73°30E 242 D5
Rechytsa Belarus 52°21N 30°24E 177 B16
Recife Brazil 8°0S 35°0W 332 C5
Recife Seychelles 4°36S 55°42E 272 c
Recklinghausen Germany 51°37N 7°12E 170 C7
Reclining Buddha = Wat Pho Bangkok, Thailand 113 b1
Recoleta B. Aires, Argentina 34°36S 58°24W 117 B2
Recoleta Santiago, Chile 33°25S 70°40W 137 B2
Reconquista Argentina 29°10S 59°45W 334 B4
Recreio Brazil 8°0S 58°25W 331 B6
Recreo Argentina 29°25S 65°10W 334 B2
Recuay Peru 9°43S 77°28W 330 B2
Recz Poland 53°16N 15°31E 185 E2
Red → U.S.A. 31°1N 91°45W 314 F9
Red Bank U.S.A. 40°21N 74°5W 313 F10
Red Bay Canada 51°44N 56°25W 299 B8
Red Bluff U.S.A. 40°11N 122°15W 304 F2
Red Bluff Res. U.S.A. 31°54N 103°55W 305 L12
Red Bud U.S.A. 38°13N 89°59W 310 F7
Red Cliffs Australia 34°19S 142°11E 282 C5
Red Cloud U.S.A. 40°5N 98°32W 308 E4
Red Creek U.S.A. 43°14N 76°45W 313 C8
Red Deer Canada 52°20N 113°50W 296 C6
Red Deer → Alta., Canada 50°58N 110°0W 297 C7
Red Deer → Man., Canada 52°53N 101°1W 297 C8
Red Deer L. Canada 52°55N 101°20W 297 C8
Red Devil U.S.A. 61°46N 157°19W 303 F8
Red Fort = Lal Qila Delhi, India 120 a3
Red Hook U.S.A. 41°55N 73°53W 313 E11
Red Indian L. Canada 48°35N 57°0W 299 C8
Red L. Canada 51°3N 93°49W 297 C10
Red Lake Canada 51°3N 93°49W 297 C10
Red Lake Falls U.S.A. 47°53N 96°16W 308 B5
Red Lake Road Canada 49°59N 93°25W 297 C10
Red Lodge U.S.A. 45°11N 109°15W 304 D9
Red Mountain U.S.A. 35°37N 117°38W 307 K9
Red Oak U.S.A. 41°1N 95°14W 308 E6
Red River of the North → N. Amer. 49°0N 97°15W 308 A5
Red Rock Canada 48°55N 88°15W 298 C2
Red Rock, L. U.S.A. 41°22N 92°59W 310 C3
Red Rocks Pt. Australia 32°13S 127°32E 279 F4
Red Sea Asia 25°0N 36°0E 238 E3
Red Slate Mt. U.S.A. 37°31N 118°52W 306 H8
Red Square Moscow, Russia 129 b2
Red Sucker L. Canada 54°9N 93°40W 298 B1
Red Tower Pass = Turnu Roşu, P. Romania 45°33N 24°17E 183 E9
Red Volta → Africa 10°34N 0°30W 263 C4
Red Wing U.S.A. 44°34N 92°31W 308 C7
Reda Poland 54°40N 18°19E 184 D5
Redang Malaysia 5°49N 103°2E 237 K4
Redange Lux. 49°46N 5°52E 170 E5
Redbridge □ U.K. 51°35N 0°7E 125 A4
Redcar U.K. 54°37N 1°4W 168 C6
Redcar & Cleveland □ U.K. 54°29N 1°0W 168 C7
Redcliff Canada 50°10N 110°50W 304 A8
Redcliffe Australia 27°12S 153°6E 281 D5
Redcliffe, Mt. Australia 28°30S 121°30E 279 E3
Reddersburg S. Africa 29°41S 26°10E 270 C4
Reddick Fla., U.S.A. 29°22N 82°12W 317 F7
Reddick Ill., U.S.A. 41°6N 88°15W 311 C8
Redding Calif., U.S.A. 40°35N 122°24W 304 F2
Redding Iowa, U.S.A. 40°36N 94°23W 310 D2
Redditch U.K. 52°18N 1°55W 169 E6
Redenção Brazil 4°13S 38°43W 332 B4
Redfern Australia 33°54S 151°12E 139 B2
Redfield U.S.A. 44°53N 98°31W 308 C4
Redford U.S.A. 44°38N 73°48W 313 B11
Redhead Trin. & Tob. 10°44N 60°58W 323 t
Redkey U.S.A. 40°21N 85°9W 311 D11
Redkino Russia 56°39N 36°16E 188 D9
Redlands U.S.A. 34°4N 117°11W 307 M9
Redmond Oreg., U.S.A. 44°17N 121°11W 304 D3
Redmond Wash., U.S.A. 47°40N 122°7W 306 C4
Redon France 47°40N 2°6W 172 E4
Redonda Antigua & B. 16°58N 62°19W 321 C7
Redonda, Pta. Chile 27°10S 109°22W 330 b
Redondela Spain 42°15N 8°38W 194 C2
Redondo Portugal 38°39N 7°37W 195 G3
Redondo Beach U.S.A. 33°50N 118°23W 307 M8
Redoubt Volcano U.S.A. 60°29N 152°45W 303 F9
Redpath Sugar Museum Toronto, Canada 141 c3
Redruth U.K. 50°14N 5°14W 169 G2
Redvers Canada 49°35N 101°40W 297 D8
Redwater Canada 53°55N 113°6W 296 C6
Redwood Wellington, N.Z. 41°11S 174°49E 143 B1
Redwood N.Y., U.S.A. 44°18N 75°48W 313 B9
Redwood △ U.S.A. 41°40N 124°5W 304 F1
Redwood City U.S.A. 37°30N 122°15W 306 H4
Redwood Falls U.S.A. 44°32N 95°7W 308 C6
Ree, L. Ireland 53°35N 8°0W 166 C3
Reed City U.S.A. 43°53N 85°31W 309 D11
Reed L. Canada 54°38N 100°30W 297 C8
Reedley U.S.A. 36°36N 119°27W 306 J7
Reedsburg U.S.A. 43°32N 90°0W 308 D8
Reedsport U.S.A. 43°42N 124°6W 304 E1
Reedsville U.S.A. 40°39N 77°35W 312 F7
Reedy Creek Australia 36°58S 140°2E 282 D4
Reef Is. Pac. Oc. 10°15S 166°10E 277 C12
Reefton N.Z. 42°6S 171°51E 285 C6
Rees Germany 51°46N 6°24E 178 D2
Reese → U.S.A. 40°48N 117°4W 304 F5
Reetz = Recz Poland 53°16N 15°31E 185 E2
Refahiye Turkey 39°54N 38°47E 213 C8
Reflecting Pool Washington, D.C., U.S.A. 143 b1
Refshaleøen Denmark 55°41N 12°36E 118 A3
Reftele Sweden 57°11N 13°35E 163 G7
Refugio U.S.A. 28°18N 97°17W 314 G6
Rega → Poland 54°10N 15°18E 184 D2
Regalbuto Italy 37°39N 14°38E 201 E7
Regana, C. de Spain 39°25N 2°43E 206 B3
Regen Germany 48°58N 13°8E 179 G9
Regen → Germany 49°1N 12°6E 179 F8
Regeneração Brazil 6°15S 42°41W 332 C3
Regensburg Germany 49°1N 12°6E 179 F8
Regenstauf Germany 49°7N 12°8E 179 F8
Regents Park Gauteng, S. Africa 26°14S 28°3E 123 B2
Regent's Park London, U.K. 125 a2
Regenwalde = Resko Poland 53°47N 15°25E 184 E2
Reggâne = Zaouiet Reggâne Algeria 26°32N 0°3E 261 C5
Reggello Italy 43°41N 11°32E 199 E8
Réggio di Calábria Italy 38°6N 15°39E 201 D8
Réggio nell'Emília Italy 44°43N 10°36E 198 D7
Reghin Romania 46°46N 24°42E 183 D9
Regina Sask., Canada 50°27N 104°35W 297 C8
Régina Fr. Guiana 4°19N 52°8W 329 C7
Regina Beach Canada 50°47N 105°0W 297 C8
Register U.S.A. 32°22N 81°53W 316 C8
Registro Brazil 24°29S 47°49W 335 A6
Rego Park U.S.A. 40°43N 73°51W 132 B2
Reguengos de Monsaraz Portugal 38°25N 7°32W 195 G3
Rehar → India 23°55N 82°40E 243 H10
Rehli India 23°38N 79°5E 243 H8
Rehoboth Namibia 23°15S 17°4E 270 B2
Rehovot Israel 31°54N 34°48E 251 G5
Reïbell = Ksar Chellala Algeria 35°13N 2°19E 261 A5
Reichenau = Rychnov nad Kněžnou Czech Rep. 50°10N 16°17E 181 A9
Reichenbach = Dzierżoniów Poland 50°45N 16°39E 185 H3
Reichenbach Germany 50°37N 12°17E 178 E8
Reichenberg = Liberec Czech Rep. 50°47N 15°7E 180 A8
Reichshof = Rzeszów Poland 50°5N 21°58E 185 H8
Reichstag Berlin, Germany 115 a3
Reid Australia 30°49S 128°26E 279 F4
Reidsville Ga., U.S.A. 32°6N 82°7W 316 C7
Reidsville N.C., U.S.A. 36°21N 79°40W 315 C15
Reifnig = Ribnica Slovenia 45°45N 14°45E 199 C11
Reigate U.K. 51°14N 0°12W 169 F7
Reillo Spain 39°54N 1°53W 196 F3
Reims France 49°15N 4°1E 173 C11
Reina Adelaida, Arch. Chile 52°20S 74°0W 336 D2
Reina Beatrix Int. ✕ (AUA) Aruba 12°30N 70°1W 322 f
Reina Sofía, Centro de Arte Madrid, Spain 127 c3
Reina Sofia, Tenerife ✕ (TFS) Canary Is. 28°3N 16°33W 153 e1
Reinbeck U.S.A. 42°19N 92°36W 310 B4
Reinbek Germany 53°30N 10°16E 178 B6
Reindeer → Canada 55°36N 103°11W 297 B8
Reindeer I. Canada 52°30N 98°0W 297 C9
Reindeer L. Canada 57°15N 102°15W 297 B8
Reinga, C. N.Z. 34°25S 172°43E 284 A1
Reinheimen △ Norway 62°10N 8°5E 164 B5
Reinickendorf Germany 52°34N 13°22E 115 A3
Reinosa Spain 43°2N 4°15W 194 B6
Reinsvoll Norway 60°40N 10°38E 164 D7
Reitan Norway 62°49N 11°22E 164 B8
Reitz S. Africa 27°48S 28°29E 271 C4
Reivilo S. Africa 27°36S 24°8E 270 C3
Rejaf Sudan 4°45N 31°35E 257 G3
Rejmyre Sweden 58°50N 15°55E 163 F9
Rejowiec Fabryczny Poland 51°5N 23°17E 185 G10
Reka → Slovenia 45°40N 14°0E 199 C11
Rekohu = Chatham I. N.Z. 43°50S 176°20W 285 a
Rekola Finland 60°19N 25°4E 121 B3
Rekovac Serbia 43°51N 21°3E 202 C5
Reliance Canada 63°0N 109°20W 297 A7
Relizane Algeria 35°44N 0°31E 261 A5
Relizane □ Algeria 35°45N 0°55E 261 A5
Remad, Oued → Algeria 33°28N 1°20W 261 B4
Rémalard France 48°26N 0°47E 172 D7
Remanso Brazil 9°41S 42°4W 332 C3
Remarkable, Mt. Australia 32°48S 138°10E 282 B3
Remarkables, The N.Z. 45°10S 168°50E 285 F3
Rembang Indonesia 6°42S 111°21E 235 D4

Rembau *Malaysia* 2°35N 102°6E **234** B2
Rembert *U.S.A.* 34°6N 80°32W **316** A9
Rembertów *Poland* 52°15N 21°9E **142** B2
Rembrandthuis *Amsterdam, Neths.* **112** b3
Rembrandtpark *Neths.* 52°22N 4°51E **112** A2
Rembrandtplein *Amsterdam, Neths.* **112** b2
Remchi *Algeria* 35°2N 1°26W **261** A4
Remedios *Colombia* 7°2N 74°41W **328** B3
Remedios *Panama* 8°15N 81°50W **320** E3
Remedios de Escalada *Argentina* 34°43S 58°24W **117** C2
Remeshk *Iran* 26°55N 58°50E **247** E8
Remetea *Romania* 46°45N 25°29E **183** D10
Remich *Lux.* 49°32N 6°22E **170** E6
Remington *U.S.A.* 40°46N 87°9W **311** D9
Rémire *Fr. Guiana* 4°53N 52°17W **329** C7
Remiremont *France* 48°2N 6°36E **173** D13
Remo *Ethiopia* 6°48N 41°20E **257** F5
Rémola, Estany del *Spain* 41°16N 2°4E **114** B1
Remontnoye *Russia* 46°34N 43°37E **191** G6
Remoulins *France* 43°55N 4°35E **175** E8
Rempart → *Mauritius* 20°19S 57°22E **272** e
Remparts → *Réunion* 21°22S 55°37E **272** f
Remscheid *Germany* 51°11N 7°12E **170** C7
Ren Xian *China* 37°8N 114°40E **226** F8
Rena *Norway* 61°8N 11°20E **164** C8
Rena → *Norway* 61°8N 11°23E **164** C8
Renascença *Brazil* 3°50S 66°21W **328** D4
Renca *Chile* 33°24S 70°42W **137** B1
Rend Lake *U.S.A.* 38°2N 88°58W **310** F8
Rendang *Indonesia* 8°26S 115°25E **231** J18
Rende *Italy* 39°20N 16°11E **201** C9
Rendezvous *Barbados* 13°4N 59°35W **323** r
Rendina *Greece* 39°4N 21°58E **204** B3
Rendova *Solomon Is.* 8°33S 157°17E **287** M9
Rendsburg *Germany* 54°17N 9°39E **178** A5
Renfrew *Canada* 45°30N 76°40W **313** A8
Renfrewshire □ *U.K.* 55°49N 4°38W **167** F4
Renfroe *U.S.A.* 32°14N 84°43W **316** C5
Rengat *Indonesia* 0°30S 102°45E **234** C2
Rengo *Chile* 34°24S 70°50W **334** C1
Renhua *China* 25°5N 113°40E **229** E9
Renhuai *China* 27°48N 106°24E **228** D6
Reni = Taranagar *India* 28°43N 74°50E **242** E6
Reni *Ukraine* 45°28N 28°15E **183** E13
Renigunta *India* 13°38N 79°30E **245** H4
Renk *Sudan* 11°50N 32°50E **257** E3
Renland *Greenland* 71°10N 26°30W **154** C8
Renmark *Australia* 34°11S 140°43E **282** C4
Rennebu *Norway* 62°52N 9°49E **164** B6
Rennell *Solomon Is.* 11°40S 160°10E **287** N11
Rennell Sd. *Canada* 53°23N 132°35W **296** C2
Rennemoulin *France* 48°50N 2°2E **134** A1
Renner Springs *Australia* 18°20S 133°47E **280** B1
Rennes *France* 48°7N 1°41W **172** D5
Rennick Glacier *Antarctica* 70°30S 161°45E **151** D21
Rennie L. *Canada* 61°32N 105°35W **297** A7
Reno *U.S.A.* 39°31N 119°48W **306** F7
Reno → *Italy* 44°38N 12°16E **199** D9
Renovo *U.S.A.* 41°20N 77°45W **312** E7
Renqiu *China* 38°43N 116°5E **226** E9
Rens *Denmark* 54°54N 9°5E **163** K3
Renshou *China* 30°3N 104°9E **228** E5
Rensselaer *Ind., U.S.A.* 40°57N 87°9W **311** D9
Rensselaer *N.Y., U.S.A.* 42°38N 73°45W **313** D11
Renton *U.S.A.* 47°28N 122°12W **306** C4
Renukoot *India* 24°12N 83°2E **243** G10
Renwick *N.Z.* 41°30S 173°51E **285** B8
Renwick Gallery *Washington, D.C., U.S.A.* **143** a1
Réo *Burkina Faso* 12°28N 2°35W **262** C4
Reocín = Puente San Miguel *Spain* 43°21N 4°5W **194** B6
Reotipur *India* 25°33N 83°45E **243** G10
Repalle *India* 16°2N 80°45E **245** F5
Répcelak *Hungary* 47°24N 17°1E **182** C2
Řeporyje *Czech Rep.* 50°1N 14°18E **135** B1
Reppen = Rzepin *Poland* 52°20N 14°49E **185** F1
Republic *Mo., U.S.A.* 37°7N 93°29W **308** G7
Republic *Wash., U.S.A.* 48°39N 118°44W **304** B4
Republican → *U.S.A.* 39°4N 96°48W **308** F5
Republiek *Suriname* 5°30N 55°13W **329** B6
République, Place de la *Paris, France* **134** b5
Repulse B. *Australia* 20°35S 148°46E **280** b
Repulse Bay *Nunavut, Canada* 66°30N 86°30W **295** D14
Repulse Bay *Hong Kong, China* 22°13N 114°10E **122** B2
Repy *Czech Rep.* 50°4N 14°17E **135** B1
Requena *Peru* 5°5S 73°52W **330** B3
Requena *Spain* 39°30N 1°4W **197** F3
Requin Bay *Grenada* 12°2N 61°39W **323** q
Réquista *France* 44°1N 2°32E **174** D6
Reşadiye *Muğla, Turkey* 36°45N 27°39E **205** E9
Reşadiye *Tokat, Turkey* 40°23N 37°20E **212** B7
Reşadiye Yarımadası *Turkey* 36°40N 27°45E **205** E9
Resavica *Serbia* 44°4N 21°31E **202** B5
Resen *Macedonia* 41°5N 21°0E **202** E5
Reserve *U.S.A.* 33°43N 108°45W **305** K9
Resht = Rasht *Iran* 37°20N 49°40E **213** D13
Residenz *Germany* 48°8N 11°34E **131** B2
Residenzmuseum *Munich, Germany* **131** b3
Resistencia *Argentina* 27°30S 59°0W **334** B4
Reşiţa *Romania* 45°18N 21°53E **182** E6
Resko *Poland* 53°47N 15°25E **184** E2
Reso = Raisio *Finland* 60°28N 22°11E **188** B2
Resolute *Canada* 74°42N 94°54W **295** C13
Resolution I. *Nunavut, Canada* 61°30N 65°0W **295** E19
Resolution I. *N.Z.* 45°40S 166°40E **285** F1
Resplendes *Brazil* 6°17S 45°13W **332** C2
Resplendor *Brazil* 19°20S 41°15W **333** E3
Ressano Garcia *Mozam.* 25°25S 32°0E **271** C5
Restinga de Jurubatiba △ *Brazil* 22°5S 41°20W **333** F3
Reston *Man., Canada* 49°33N 101°6W **297** D8
Reston *Va., U.S.A.* 38°57N 77°20W **143** B2
Resulayn = Ceylanpınar *Turkey* 36°50N 40°2E **213** D9
Reszel *Poland* 54°4N 21°10E **184** D8
Retalhuleu *Guatemala* 14°33N 91°46W **320** D1
Retenue, L. de *Dem. Rep. of the Congo* 11°0S 27°0E **269** E2
Retezat, Munţii *Romania* 45°25N 23°0E **182** E8
Retezat △ *Romania* 45°23N 22°56E **182** E7
Retford *U.K.* 53°19N 0°56W **168** D7
Rethel *France* 49°30N 4°20E **173** C11
Rethem *Germany* 52°47N 9°22E **178** C5
Rethimno *Greece* 35°18N 24°30E **207** E5
Rethimno □ *Greece* 35°23N 24°28E **207** E5
Reti *Pakistan* 28°5N 69°48E **242** E3
Retiche, Alpi *Switz.* 46°30N 10°0E **179** J6
Retiers *France* 47°55N 1°23W **172** E5
Retiro *B. Aires, Argentina* 34°35S 58°23W **117** B2
Retiro *Madrid, Spain* 40°24N 3°40W **127** B1
Retiro, Puerto *Argentina* 34°36S 58°21W **117** B2
Retortillo *Spain* 40°48N 6°21W **194** E4
Retournac *France* 45°12N 4°2E **175** C8
Retreat *S. Africa* 34°4S 18°28E **118** B1
Rétság *Hungary* 47°58N 19°10E **182** C4
Réunion ☑ *Ind. Oc.* 21°0S 56°0E **272** f
Reus *Spain* 41°10N 1°5E **196** D6
Reuterstadt Stavenhagen *Germany* 53°42N 12°54E **178** B8
Reutlingen *Germany* 48°29N 9°12E **179** G5
Reutov *Russia* 55°45N 37°50E **129** B5
Reutte *Austria* 47°29N 10°42E **180** D3
Reval = Tallinn *Estonia* 59°22N 24°48E **188** C3
Revda *Russia* 56°48N 59°57E **186** C10
Réveillon → *France* 48°42N 2°30E **134** B4
Revel = Tallinn *Estonia* 59°22N 24°48E **188** C3
Revel *France* 43°28N 2°1E **174** E6
Revelganj *India* 25°50N 84°40E **243** G11
Revelstoke *Canada* 51°0N 118°10W **296** C5
Reventazón *Peru* 6°10S 80°58W **330** B1
Revere *U.S.A.* 42°25N 71°0W **116** A2
Revere House *Boston, U.S.A.* **116** b3
Revigny-sur-Ornain *France* 48°49N 4°59E **173** D11
Revillagigedo, Is. de *Pac. Oc.* 18°40N 112°0W **318** D2
Revin *France* 49°55N 4°39E **173** C11
Revúca *Slovak Rep.* 48°41N 20°7E **181** C13
Revuè → *Mozam.* 19°50S 34°0E **269** F3
Rewa *India* 24°33N 81°25E **243** G9
Rewa → *Guyana* 3°19N 58°42W **329** C6
Rewari *India* 28°15N 76°40E **242** E7
Rexburg *U.S.A.* 43°49N 111°47W **304** E8
Rexdale *Canada* 43°43N 79°35W **141** A1
Rey *Iran* 35°35N 51°25E **247** C6
Rey, I. del *Panama* 8°20N 78°30W **320** E4
Rey, L. del *Mexico* 27°1N 103°26W **318** B4
Rey, Mayo → *Cameroon* 8°47N 14°1E **264** B2
Rey, Rio-del- → *Cameroon* 4°31N 8°45E **264** B1
Rey Bouba *Cameroon* 8°40N 14°15E **264** A2
Rey Malabo *Eq. Guin.* 3°45N 8°50E **263** E6
Reyðarfjörður *Iceland* 65°2N 14°13W **155** B12
Reyes *Bolivia* 14°19S 67°23W **330** C4
Reyes, Pt. *U.S.A.* 38°0N 123°0W **306** H3
Reyhanlı *Turkey* 36°16N 36°35E **250** B7
Reykhólar *Iceland* 65°27N 22°12W **155** B4
Reykholt *Árnessýsla, Iceland* 64°40N 21°18W **155** C5
Reykholt *Borgarfjarðarsýsla, Iceland* 64°10N 20°25W **155** C6
Reykjahlíð *Iceland* 65°40N 16°55W **155** B10
Reykjanes *Iceland* 63°48N 22°40W **155** D4
Reykjanes Ridge *Atl. Oc.* 59°0N 31°0W **152** A8
Reykjavík *Iceland* 64°10N 21°57W **155** C5
Reykjavík Keflavík ✕ **(KEF)** *Iceland* 64°0N 22°45W **155** C4
Reynolds *Ga., U.S.A.* 32°33N 84°6W **316** C5
Reynolds *Ill., U.S.A.* 41°20N 90°40W **310** C6
Reynolds Ra. *Australia* 22°30S 133°0E **278** D5
Reynoldsville *Ga., U.S.A.* 30°51N 84°47W **316** E5
Reynoldsville *Pa., U.S.A.* 41°6N 78°53W **312** E6
Reynosa *Mexico* 26°7N 98°18W **319** B5
Reynosa Tamaulipas *Mexico* 19°30N 99°10W **128** A1
Reza'iyeh = Orūmīyeh *Iran* 37°40N 45°0E **213** D11
Reza'iyeh, L. = Orūmīyeh, Daryācheh-ye *Iran* 37°50N 45°30E **213** D11
Rēzekne *Latvia* 56°30N 27°17E **188** D4
Rezhitsa = Rēzekne *Latvia* 56°30N 27°17E **188** D4
Rezina *Moldova* 47°45N 28°58E **183** C13
Rezovo *Bulgaria* 42°0N 28°0E **203** D12
Rezvān *Iran* 27°34N 56°6E **247** E8
Rezvānshahr *Iran* 37°32N 49°7E **213** D13
Rgotina *Serbia* 44°1N 22°17E **202** B6
Rharbi, Zahrez *Algeria* 34°50N 2°55E **261** B5
Rharis, O. → *Algeria* 26°0N 5°4E **261** C6
Rhayader *U.K.* 52°18N 3°29W **169** E4
Rheda-Wiedenbrück *Germany* 51°50N 8°20E **178** D4
Rhede *Germany* 51°50N 6°42E **178** D2
Rhein → *Europe* 51°52N 6°2E **170** C6
Rhein-Main-Donau-Kanal *Germany* 49°1N 11°27E **179** F7
Rhein-Ruhr, Düsseldorf ✕ **(DUS)** *Germany* 51°17N 6°46E **178** D2
Rhein-Taunus ⌂ *Germany* 50°10N 8°10E **179** E4
Rhein-Westerwald ⌂ *Germany* 50°32N 7°20E **178** E3
Rheinbach *Germany* 50°38N 6°57E **178** E2
Rheine *Germany* 52°17N 7°26E **178** C3
Rheinfelden *Germany* 47°33N 7°47E **179** H3
Rheinhessen-Pfalz □ *Germany* 49°20N 8°0E **179** F3
Rheinland-Pfalz □ *Germany* 50°0N 7°0E **179** E2
Rheinsberg *Germany* 53°6N 12°54E **178** B8
Rheris, Oued → *Morocco* 30°50N 4°34W **260** B4
Rhin = Rhein → *Europe* 51°52N 6°2E **170** C6
Rhine = Rhein → *Europe* 51°52N 6°2E **170** C6
Rhine *U.S.A.* 31°59N 83°12W **316** D6
Rhinebeck *U.S.A.* 41°56N 73°55W **313** E11
Rhineland-Palatinate = Rheinland-Pfalz □ *Germany* 50°0N 7°0E **179** E2
Rhinelander *U.S.A.* 45°38N 89°25W **308** C9
Rhinns Pt. *U.K.* 55°40N 6°29W **167** F2
Rhino Camp *Uganda* 3°0N 31°22E **268** B3
Rhir, Cap *Morocco* 30°38N 9°54W **260** B3
Rho *Italy* 45°31N 9°2E **198** C6
Rhode Island □ *U.S.A.* 41°40N 71°30W **313** E13
Rhodes *N.S.W., Australia* 33°49S 151°5E **138** B2
Rhodes *Greece* 36°15N 28°10E **206** E12
Rhodes ✕ **(RHO)** *Greece* 36°23N 28°12E **205** E10
Rhodesia = Zimbabwe ■ *Africa* 19°0S 30°0E **269** F3
Rhodon *France* 48°42N 2°3E **134** B1
Rhodon → *France* 48°42N 2°4E **134** B1
Rhodope Mts. = Rhodopi Planina *Bulgaria* 41°40N 24°20E **203** E8
Rhodopi Planina *Bulgaria* 41°40N 24°20E **203** E8
Rhön *Germany* 50°24N 9°58E **178** E5
Rhondda *U.K.* 51°39N 3°31W **169** F4
Rhondda Cynon Taff □ *U.K.* 51°42N 3°27W **169** F4
Rhône □ *France* 45°54N 4°35E **175** C8
Rhône → *France* 43°28N 4°42E **175** E8
Rhône-Alpes □ *France* 45°40N 6°0E **175** C9
Rhum *U.K.* 57°0N 6°20W **167** E2
Rhyl *U.K.* 53°20N 3°29W **168** D4
Ri-Aba *Eq. Guin.* 3°28N 8°40E **263** E6
Ria Formosa ⌂ *Portugal* 37°1N 7°48W **195** H3
Riachão *Brazil* 7°20S 46°37W **332** C2
Riacho de Santana *Brazil* 13°37S 42°57W **333** D3
Rialma *Brazil* 15°18S 49°34W **333** E2
Rialto Towers *Australia* 37°49S 144°57W **128** A1
Riang *India* 27°31N 92°56E **241** B4
Riangnom *Sudan* 9°55N 30°1E **257** F3
Riaño *Spain* 42°59N 4°59W **194** C6
Rians *France* 43°37N 5°44E **175** E9
Riansáres → *Spain* 39°32N 3°18W **195** F7
Riasi *India* 33°10N 74°50E **242** C6
Riau □ *Indonesia* 0°0 102°35E **234** B2
Riau, Kepulauan *Indonesia* 0°30N 104°20E **234** B2
Riau Arch. = Riau, Kepulauan *Indonesia* 0°30N 104°20E **234** B2
Riaza *Spain* 41°18N 3°30W **194** D7
Riaza → *Spain* 41°42N 3°55W **194** D7
Riba de Saelices *Spain* 40°55N 2°17W **196** E2
Riba-roja de Túria *Spain* 39°33N 0°34W **197** F4
Ribadavia *Spain* 42°17N 8°8W **194** C2
Ribadeo *Spain* 43°35N 7°5W **194** B3
Ribadesella *Spain* 43°30N 5°7W **194** B5
Ribado *Nigeria* 9°16N 12°47E **263** D7
Ribao *Cameroon* 6°32N 11°30E **263** D7
Ribas = Ribes de Freser *Spain* 42°19N 2°15E **196** C7
Ribas do Rio Pardo *Brazil* 20°27S 53°46W **331** E7
Ribauè *Mozam.* 14°57S 38°17E **269** E4
Ribble → *U.K.* 53°52N 2°25W **168** D5
Ribe *Denmark* 55°19N 8°44E **163** J2
Ribeauvillé *France* 48°10N 7°20E **173** D14
Ribécourt-Dreslincourt *France* 49°30N 2°55E **173** C9
Ribeira = Santa Uxía de Ribeira *Spain* 42°36N 8°58W **194** C2
Ribeira *Brazil* 22°49S 43°10W **135** A1
Ribeira Brava *Madeira* 32°41N 17°4W **153** c
Ribeira do Pombal *Brazil* 10°50S 38°32W **332** D4
Ribeira Grande *Azores* 37°49N 25°31W **153** d3
Ribeira Grande *C. Verde Is.* 17°0N 25°4W **153** j
Ribeirão *Brazil* 8°31S 35°23W **332** C4
Ribeirão Prêto *Brazil* 21°10S 47°50W **335** A6
Ribeiro Gonçalves *Brazil* 7°32S 45°14W **332** C2
Ribemont *France* 49°47N 3°27E **173** C10
Ribera *Italy* 37°30N 13°16E **200** E6
Ribérac *France* 45°15N 0°20E **174** C4
Riberalta *Bolivia* 11°0S 66°0W **331** C4
Ribes de Freser *Spain* 42°19N 2°15E **196** C7
Ribnica *Slovenia* 45°45N 14°45E **199** C11
Ribnitz-Damgarten *Germany* 54°15N 12°27E **178** A8
Ričany *Czech Rep.* 50°0N 14°40E **180** B7
Ricarda, Estany de la *Spain* 41°17N 2°6E **114** B1
Riccarton *N.Z.* 43°32S 172°37E **285** D7
Riccia *Italy* 41°30N 14°50E **201** A7
Riccione *Italy* 43°59N 12°39E **199** E9
Rice *U.S.A.* 34°5N 114°51W **307** L12
Rice L. *Canada* 44°12N 78°10W **312** B6
Rice Lake *U.S.A.* 45°30N 91°44W **308** C8
Riceboro *U.S.A.* 31°44N 81°26W **316** D8
Rich *Morocco* 32°16N 4°30W **260** B4
Rich, C. *Canada* 44°43N 80°38W **312** B4
Richard Toll *Senegal* 16°25N 15°42W **262** B1
Richards Bay *S. Africa* 28°48S 32°6E **271** C5
Richardson → *Canada* 58°25N 111°14W **297** B6
Richardson Lakes *U.S.A.* 44°46N 70°58W **309** C18
Richardson Mts. *N.Z.* 44°49S 168°34E **285** E3
Richardson Springs *U.S.A.* 39°51N 121°46W **306** F5
Riche, C. *Australia* 34°36S 118°47E **279** F2
Richelieu *France* 47°1N 0°20E **172** E7
Richey *U.S.A.* 47°39N 105°4W **304** C11
Richfield *U.S.A.* 38°46N 112°5W **304** G7
Richfield Springs *U.S.A.* 42°51N 74°59W **313** D10
Richford *U.S.A.* 45°0N 72°40W **313** B12
Richibucto *Canada* 46°42N 64°54W **299** C7
Richland *Ga., U.S.A.* 32°5N 84°40W **316** C5
Richland *Iowa, U.S.A.* 41°13N 92°0W **310** C5
Richland *Mo., U.S.A.* 37°51N 92°26W **310** G4
Richland *Wash., U.S.A.* 46°17N 119°18W **304** C4
Richland Center *U.S.A.* 43°21N 90°23W **308** D8
Richlands *U.S.A.* 37°6N 81°48W **309** G13
Richmond *N.S.W., Australia* 33°35S 150°42E **283** B9
Richmond *Queens., Australia* 20°43S 143°8E **280** C3
Richmond *Vic., Australia* 37°48S 145°0E **128** A2
Richmond *Nelson-Marlborough, N.Z.* 41°20S 173°12E **285** B8
Richmond *N. Yorks., U.K.* 54°25N 1°43W **168** C6
Richmond *Calif., U.S.A.* 37°46N 122°27W **136** B2
Richmond *Calif., U.S.A.* 37°56N 122°21W **306** H4
Richmond *Ind., U.S.A.* 39°50N 84°53W **311** E12
Richmond *Ky., U.S.A.* 37°45N 84°18W **311** G12
Richmond *Mich., U.S.A.* 42°49N 82°45W **312** D2
Richmond *Mo., U.S.A.* 39°17N 93°58W **310** E3
Richmond *Tex., U.S.A.* 29°35N 95°46W **314** G7
Richmond *Utah, U.S.A.* 41°56N 111°48W **304** F8
Richmond *Va., U.S.A.* 37°33N 77°27W **309** G15
Richmond *Vt., U.S.A.* 44°24N 72°59W **313** B12
Richmond, Mt. *N.Z.* 41°32S 173°22E **285** B8
Richmond Hill *Ont., Canada* 43°52N 79°27W **312** C5
Richmond Hill *Ga., U.S.A.* 31°56N 81°18W **316** D8
Richmond Hill *N.Y., U.S.A.* 40°41N 73°51W **132** B2
Richmond Park *U.K.* 51°26N 0°16W **125** B2
Richmond Peak *St. Vincent* 13°17N 61°13W **323** n
Richmond Ra. *N.S.W., Australia* 29°0S 152°45E **281** D5
Richmond Ra. *N.Z.* 41°32S 173°22E **285** B8
Richmond-upon-Thames □ *U.K.* 51°27N 0°17W **125** B2
Richmondville *U.S.A.* 42°38N 74°33W **313** D10
Richtersveld △ *S. Africa* 28°15S 17°10E **270** C2
Richville *U.S.A.* 44°25N 75°23W **313** B9
Richwood *Ohio, U.S.A.* 40°26N 83°18W **311** D13
Richwood *W. Va., U.S.A.* 38°14N 80°32W **309** F13
Ricla *Spain* 41°31N 1°24W **196** D3
Ricoge *Angola* 14°37S 21°25E **265** E4
Ridā' *Yemen* 14°25N 44°50E **248** D4
Riddarholmen *Stockholm, Sweden* **139** c1
Riddarhuset *Stockholm, Sweden* **139** c2
Ridder = Leninogorsk *Kazakhstan* 50°20N 83°30E **217** B10
Riddlesburg *U.S.A.* 40°9N 78°15W **312** F6
Ridge, The *India* 28°37N 77°12E **120** B2
Ridge Farm *U.S.A.* 39°54N 87°39W **311** E9
Ridge Spring *U.S.A.* 33°51N 81°40W **316** B8
Ridgecrest *U.S.A.* 35°38N 117°40W **307** K9
Ridgefield *Conn., U.S.A.* 41°17N 73°30W **313** E11
Ridgefield *N.J., U.S.A.* 40°49N 74°0W **132** B1
Ridgefield *Wash., U.S.A.* 45°49N 122°45W **306** E4
Ridgefield Park *U.S.A.* 40°52N 74°1W **132** A1
Ridgeland *Miss., U.S.A.* 32°26N 90°8W **315** E9
Ridgeland *S.C., U.S.A.* 32°29N 80°59W **316** C9
Ridgetown *Canada* 42°26N 81°52W **312** D3
Ridgeville *Ind., U.S.A.* 40°18N 85°2W **311** D11
Ridgeville *S.C., U.S.A.* 33°6N 80°19W **316** B9
Ridgewood *N.J., U.S.A.* 40°59N 74°7W **313** F10
Ridgewood *N.Y., U.S.A.* 40°42N 73°53W **132** B2
Ridgway *Ill., U.S.A.* 37°48N 88°16W **311** G8
Ridgway *Pa., U.S.A.* 41°25N 78°44W **312** E6
Riding Mountain △ *Canada* 50°50N 100°0W **297** C9
Ridley, Mt. *Australia* 33°12S 122°7E **279** F3
Riebeek-Oos *S. Africa* 33°10S 26°10E **270** D4
Ried *Austria* 48°14N 13°30E **180** C6
Riedlingen *Germany* 48°9N 9°28E **179** G5
Riedstadt *Germany* 49°45N 8°30E **179** F4
Riem *Germany* 48°8N 11°41E **131** B3
Rienza → *Italy* 46°49N 11°47E **199** B8
Riesa *Germany* 51°17N 13°17E **178** D9
Riesco, I. *Chile* 52°55S 72°40W **336** D2
Riesenburg = Prabuty *Poland* 53°47N 19°15E **184** E6
Riesenrad *Austria* 48°14N 16°23E **142** A2
Riesi *Italy* 37°17N 14°5E **201** E7
Riet → *S. Africa* 29°0S 23°54E **270** C3
Rietavas *Lithuania* 55°44N 21°56E **184** C8
Rietbron *S. Africa* 32°54S 23°10E **270** D3
Rietfontein *Namibia* 21°58S 20°58E **270** B3
Rieti *Italy* 42°24N 12°51E **199** F9
Rieupeyroux *France* 44°19N 2°12E **174** D6
Riez *France* 43°49N 6°6E **175** E10
Rif = Er Rif *Morocco* 35°1N 4°1W **261** A4
Rif *Iceland* 64°56N 23°49W **155** C3
Riffe L. *U.S.A.* 46°32N 122°26W **306** D4
Rifle *U.S.A.* 39°32N 107°47W **304** G10
Rifstangi *Iceland* 66°32N 16°12W **155** A10
Rift Valley *Africa* 7°0N 30°0E **254** G7
Rift Valley □ *Kenya* 0°20N 36°0E **268** B4
Rig Rig *Chad* 14°13N 14°25E **259** F2
Riga *India* 28°26N 95°2E **241** A5
Riga *Latvia* 56°53N 24°8E **184** B11
Riga ✕ **(RIX)** *Latvia* 56°54N 23°58E **184** B10
Riga, G. of *Latvia* 57°40N 23°45E **184** A10
Rigacikun *Nigeria* 10°40N 7°28E **263** C6
Rīgān *Iran* 28°37N 58°58E **247** D8
Rigas Jūras Līcis = Riga, G. of *Latvia* 57°40N 23°45E **184** A10
Rigaud *Canada* 45°29N 74°18W **313** A10
Rigby *U.S.A.* 43°40N 111°55W **304** E8
Rīgestān *Afghan.* 30°15N 65°0E **240** C2
Riggins *U.S.A.* 45°25N 116°19W **304** D5
Rignac *France* 44°25N 2°16E **174** D6
Rigolet *Canada* 54°10N 58°23W **299** B8
Rigu *Ghana* 9°59N 0°48W **263** D4
Rihand Dam *India* 24°9N 83°2E **243** G10
Riihimäki *Finland* 60°45N 24°48E **188** B3
Riiser-Larsen-halvøya *Antarctica* 68°0S 35°0E **151** C4
Riiser-Larsen Ice Shelf *S. Ocean* 74°0S 19°0W **151** D2
Riiser-Larsen Sea *S. Ocean* 67°30S 22°0E **151** C4
Rijau *Nigeria* 11°8N 5°17E **263** C6
Rijeka *Croatia* 45°20N 14°21E **199** C11
Rijeka Crnojevića *Montenegro* 42°24N 19°1E **202** D3
Rijksmuseum *Amsterdam, Neths.* **112** c1
Rijssen *Neths.* 52°19N 6°31E **170** B6
Rika → *Ukraine* 48°11N 23°16E **183** B8
Rikā', W. ar → *Si. Arabia* 22°25N 44°50E **248** B4
Rike *Ethiopia* 10°50N 39°53E **257** E4
Rikers I. *U.S.A.* 40°47N 73°53W **132** B2
Riksdagshuset *Stockholm, Sweden* **139** b2
Rikuchū-Kaigan △ *Japan* 39°20N 142°0E **220** E11
Rikuzentakada *Japan* 39°0N 141°40E **220** E10
Rila *Bulgaria* 42°7N 23°7E **202** D7
Rila Planina *Bulgaria* 42°10N 23°20E **202** D7
Riley *U.S.A.* 43°32N 119°28W **304** E4
Rima → *Nigeria* 13°4N 5°10E **263** C6
Rimac *Peru* 12°2S 77°2W **124** B2
Rimah, Wadi ar → *Si. Arabia* 26°5N 41°30E **246** E4
Rimatara *French Polynesia* 22°38S 152°51W **289** f
Rimau, Pulau *Malaysia* 5°15N 100°16E **237** c
Rimavská Sobota *Slovak Rep.* 48°22N 20°2E **181** C13
Rimbey *Canada* 52°35N 114°15W **296** C6
Rimbo *Sweden* 59°44N 18°21E **162** E12
Rimé, O. → *Chad* 14°2N 18°3E **259** F3
Rimersburg *U.S.A.* 41°3N 79°30W **312** E5
Rimforsa *Sweden* 58°6N 15°43E **163** F9
Rimi *Nigeria* 12°58N 7°43E **263** C6
Rimini *Italy* 44°3N 12°33E **199** D9
Rimouski *Canada* 48°27N 68°30W **299** C6
Rimrock *U.S.A.* 46°40N 121°7W **306** D5
Rinca *Indonesia* 8°45S 119°35E **231** F5
Rincon *Neth. Ant.* 12°14N 68°20W **322** h
Rincon *Puerto Rico* 18°20N 67°15W **321** b
Rincon *Ga., U.S.A.* 32°18N 81°14W **316** C8
Rincón de la Victoria *Spain* 36°43N 4°18W **195** J6
Rincón de Romos *Mexico* 22°14N 102°18W **318** C4
Rincon Falls *Trin. & Tob.* 10°46N 61°24W **323** t
Rinconada *Argentina* 22°26S 66°10W **334** A2
Rind → *India* 25°53N 80°33E **243** G9
Rindal *Norway* 63°3N 9°13E **164** A6
Ringarum *Sweden* 58°21N 16°26E **163** F10
Ringas *India* 27°21N 75°34E **242** F6
Ringdove *Vanuatu* 16°40S 168°10E **287** F6
Ringe *Denmark* 55°13N 10°28E **163** J4
Ringebu *Norway* 61°32N 10°7E **164** C7
Ringgi *Solomon Is.* 8°5S 157°10E **287** M9
Ringgold Is. *Fiji* 16°15S 179°25W **287** A3
Ringim *Nigeria* 12°13N 9°10E **263** C6
Ringkøbing *Denmark* 56°5N 8°15E **163** H2
Ringkøbing Fjord *Denmark* 56°0N 8°15E **163** H2
Ringoma *Angola* 12°25S 17°32E **265** E3
Ringsaker *Norway* 60°54N 10°45E **164** D7
Ringsend *Ireland* 53°20N 6°12W **120** A2
Ringsjön *Sweden* 55°55N 13°30E **163** J7
Ringsted *Denmark* 55°25N 11°46E **163** J5
Ringvassøya *Norway* 69°56N 19°15E **160** B18
Ringwood *U.S.A.* 41°7N 74°15W **313** E10
Rinia *Greece* 37°23N 25°13E **205** D7
Rinjani *Indonesia* 8°24S 116°28E **235** D5
Rinkeby *Sweden* 59°23N 17°55E **139** A1
Rinteln *Germany* 52°10N 9°8E **178** C5
Río, Punta del *Spain* 36°49N 2°24W **197** J2
Rio Bonito = Caiapônia *Brazil* 16°57S 51°49W **331** D7
Rio Branco = Arcoverde *Brazil* 8°25S 37°4W **332** C4
Rio Branco = Paratinga *Brazil* 12°40S 43°10W **333** D3
Rio Branco = Roraima □ *Brazil* 2°0N 61°30W **329** C5
Rio Branco *Brazil* 9°58S 67°49W **330** B4
Río Branco *Uruguay* 32°40S 53°40W **335** C5
Río Bravo *Mexico* 25°59N 98°6W **319** B5
Rio Bravo ⌂ *N. Amer.* 29°2N 102°45W **318** B4
Rio Bravo del Norte → *Mexico* 25°57N 97°9W **319** B5
Rio Brilhante *Brazil* 21°48S 54°33W **335** A5
Río Bueno *Chile* 40°19S 72°58W **336** B2
Rio Bueno *Jamaica* 18°28N 77°28W **320** a
Río Caribe *Venezuela* 10°42N 63°7W **329** A5
Río Chico *Venezuela* 10°19N 65°59W **328** A4
Rio Claro *Brazil* 22°19S 47°35W **335** A6
Rio Claro *Trin. & Tob.* 10°20N 61°25W **323** t
Rio Cobre → *Jamaica* 17°59N 76°52W **320** a
Río Colorado *Argentina* 39°0S 64°0W **336** A4
Rio Comprido *Brazil* 22°55S 43°13W **135** B1
Río Cuarto *Argentina* 33°10S 64°25W **334** C3
Rio das Pedras *Mozam.* 23°8S 35°28E **271** B6
Rio de Contas *Brazil* 13°36S 41°48W **333** D3
Rio de Janeiro *Brazil* 22°54S 43°12W **135** B1
Rio de Janeiro □ *Brazil* 22°50S 43°0W **333** F3
Rio de Janeiro Galeão ✕ **(GIG)** *Brazil* 22°49S 43°15W **135** A1
Rio de Mouro *Portugal* 38°46N 9°15W **126** A1
Río de Oro, B. de *W. Sahara* 23°45N 15°50W **260** D1
Rio do Prado *Brazil* 16°35S 40°34W **333** E3
Rio do Sul *Brazil* 27°13S 49°37W **335** B6
Río Dulce △ *Guatemala* 15°43N 88°50W **320** C2
Río Gallegos *Argentina* 51°35S 69°15W **336** D3
Río Grande *Argentina* 53°50S 67°45W **336** D3
Río Grande *Bolivia* 20°51S 67°17W **330** E4
Rio Grande *Brazil* 32°0S 52°20W **335** C5
Río Grande *Zacatecas, Mexico* 23°50N 103°2W **318** C4
Río Grande *Puerto Rico* 18°23N 65°50W **321** b
Rio Grande → *N. Amer.* 25°58N 97°9W **314** J6
Rio Grande City *U.S.A.* 26°23N 98°49W **314** H5
Río Grande de Santiago → *Mexico* 21°36N 105°26W **318** C3
Rio Grande do Norte □ *Brazil* 5°40S 36°0W **332** C4
Rio Grande do Sul □ *Brazil* 30°0S 53°0W **335** C5
Rio Grande Rise *Atl. Oc.* 31°0S 35°0W **152** K8
Río Hato *Panama* 8°22N 80°10W **320** E3
Río Lagartos *Mexico* 21°36N 88°10W **319** C7
Rio Largo *Brazil* 9°28S 35°50W **332** C4
Rio Maior *Portugal* 39°19N 8°57W **195** F2
Rio Marina *Italy* 42°49N 10°25E **198** F7
Río Mayo *Argentina* 45°40S 70°15W **336** C2
Río Mulatos *Bolivia* 19°40S 66°50W **330** D4
Río Muni □ *Eq. Guin.* 1°30N 10°0E **264** B2
Rio Negro *Brazil* 26°0S 49°55W **335** B6
Rio Negro *Chile* 40°47S 73°14W **336** B2
Rio Negro, Pantanal do *Brazil* 19°0S 56°0W **331** D6
Rio Novo = Ipiaú *Brazil* 14°8S 39°44W **333** D4
Rio Pardo = Ribas do Rio Pardo *Brazil* 20°27S 53°46W **331** E7
Rio Pardo *Brazil* 30°0S 52°30W **335** C5
Río Pico *Argentina* 44°0S 70°22W **336** B2
Rio Pilcomayo △ *Argentina* 25°5S 58°5W **334** B4
Río Platano □ *Honduras* 15°45N 85°0W **320** C2
Rio Prêto = Santa Rita de Cássia *Brazil* 11°0S 44°32W **332** D3
Rio Preto da Eva *Brazil* 2°46S 59°41W **329** D6
Río Rancho *U.S.A.* 35°14N 106°41W **305** J10
Rio Real *Brazil* 11°28S 37°56W **333** D4
Río Seco = Villa de María *Argentina* 29°55S 63°43W **334** B3
Río Segundo *Argentina* 31°40S 63°59W **334** C3
Río Simpson △ *Chile* 45°27S 73°30W **336** C2
Río Tercero *Argentina* 32°15S 64°8W **334** C3
Rio Tinto *Brazil* 6°48S 35°5W **332** C4
Rio Tinto *Portugal* 41°11N 8°34W **194** D2
Río Turbio *Argentina* 51°32S 72°18W **336** D2
Rio Verde *Brazil* 17°50S 51°0W **333** E1
Río Verde *San Luis Potosí, Mexico* 21°56N 99°59W **319** C5
Rio Verde de Mato Grosso *Brazil* 18°56S 54°52W **331** D7
Rio Viejo △ *Venezuela* 7°15N 71°20W **328** B3
Rio Vista *U.S.A.* 38°10N 121°42W **306** G5
Riobamba *Ecuador* 1°50S 78°45W **328** D2
Riohacha *Colombia* 11°33N 72°55W **328** A3
Rioja *Peru* 6°11S 77°5W **330** B2
Riom *France* 45°54N 3°7E **174** C7
Riom-ès-Montagnes *France* 45°17N 2°39E **174** C6
Rion-des-Landes *France* 43°55N 0°56W **174** E3
Rionegro *Antioquia, Colombia* 6°9N 75°22W **328** B2
Rionegro *Santander, Colombia* 7°15N 73°9W **328** B3
Rionero in Vúlture *Italy* 40°55N 15°40E **201** B8
Rioni → *Georgia* 42°14N 41°44E **191** J5
Riós *Spain* 41°58N 7°16W **194** D3
Riosinho → *Brazil* 7°7S 51°39W **331** B7
Riosucio *Caldas, Colombia* 5°30N 75°40W **328** B2
Riosucio *Choco, Colombia* 7°27N 77°7W **328** B2
Riou L. *Canada* 59°7N 106°25W **297** B7
Rioz *France* 47°26N 6°5E **173** E13
Riozinho → *Brazil* 2°55S 67°7W **328** D4
Ripatransone *Italy* 42°59N 13°46E **199** F10
Ripley *Ont., Canada* 44°4N 81°35W **312** B3
Ripley *Calif., U.S.A.* 33°32N 114°39W **307** M12
Ripley *N.Y., U.S.A.* 42°16N 79°43W **312** D5
Ripley *Ohio, U.S.A.* 38°45N 83°51W **311** F13
Ripley *Tenn., U.S.A.* 35°45N 89°32W **315** D10
Ripley *W. Va., U.S.A.* 38°49N 81°43W **309** F13
Ripoll *Spain* 42°15N 2°13E **196** C7
Ripollet *Spain* 41°26N 2°10E **114** A1
Ripon *N. Yorks., U.K.* 54°9N 1°31W **168** C6
Ripon *Calif., U.S.A.* 37°44N 121°7W **306** H5
Ripon *Wis., U.S.A.* 43°51N 88°50W **308** D9
Riposto *Italy* 37°44N 15°12E **201** E8
Rippin = Rypin *Poland* 53°3N 19°25E **185** E6
Ris *Norway* 59°56N 10°41E **133** A3
Risan *Montenegro* 42°32N 18°42E **202** D2
Risaralda □ *Colombia* 5°0N 76°10W **328** C2
Risby *Denmark* 55°41N 12°19E **118** A1
Riscle *France* 43°39N 0°5W **174** E3
Rishā', W. ar → *Si. Arabia* 25°33N 44°5E **246** E5
Rishiri-Rebun-Sarobetsu △ *Japan* 45°26N 141°30E **220** B10
Rishiri-Tō *Japan* 45°11N 141°15E **220** B10
Rishon le Ẕiyyon *Israel* 31°58N 34°48E **251** G5
Rishra *India* 22°42N 88°20E **124** A2
Rising Sun *U.S.A.* 38°57N 84°51W **311** F12
Risle → *France* 49°26N 0°23E **172** C7
Risnjak △ *Croatia* 45°25N 14°36E **199** C11
Rison *U.S.A.* 33°58N 92°11W **314** E8
Risør *Norway* 58°43N 9°13E **164** F6
Rissani *Morocco* 31°18N 4°12W **260** B4
Rita Blanca Cr. → *U.S.A.* 35°40N 102°29W **314** D3
Ritchie *U.S.A.* 38°52N 76°51W **143** B4
Ritchie's Arch. *India* 12°14N 93°10E **245** H11
Rithala *India* 28°43N 77°6E **120** A1
Riti *Nigeria* 7°57N 9°41E **263** D6
Ritidian Pt. *Guam* 13°39N 144°51E **302** d
Ritter, Mt. *U.S.A.* 37°41N 119°12W **306** H7
Rittman *U.S.A.* 40°58N 81°47W **312** F3
Ritzville *U.S.A.* 47°8N 118°23W **304** C4
Riu *India* 28°19N 95°3E **241** A5
Riva del Garda *Italy* 45°53N 10°50E **198** C7
Riva Lígure *Italy* 43°50N 7°50E **198** E4
Rivadavia *B. Aires, Argentina* 35°29S 62°59W **334** D3
Rivadavia *Mendoza, Argentina* 33°13S 68°30W **334** C2
Rivadavia *Salta, Argentina* 24°5S 62°54W **334** A3
Rivadavia *Chile* 29°57S 70°35W **334** B1
Rivarolo Canavese *Italy* 45°19N 7°42E **198** C4
Rivas *Nic.* 11°30N 85°50W **320** D2
Rivash *Iran* 35°28N 58°26E **247** C8
Rive-de-Gier *France* 45°32N 4°37E **175** C8
Rive Sud, Canal de la *Canada* 45°24N 73°31W **130** B2
River Cess *Liberia* 5°30N 9°32W **262** D3
River Edge *U.S.A.* 40°56N 74°1W **132** A1
River Estate & Waterwheel *Trin. & Tob.* 10°41N 61°33W **323** t
River Forest *U.S.A.* 41°53N 87°49W **119** B2
River Grove *U.S.A.* 41°55N 87°50W **119** B1
River Jordan *Canada* 48°26N 124°3W **306** B2
River North *Chicago, U.S.A.* **119** b1
River Ridge *U.S.A.* 29°57N 90°13W **131** B1
Rivera *Argentina* 37°12S 63°14W **334** D3
Rivera *Uruguay* 31°0S 55°50W **335** C4
Riverbank *U.S.A.* 37°44N 120°56W **306** H6
Riverdale *Calif., U.S.A.* 36°26N 119°52W **306** J7
Riverdale *Ga., U.S.A.* 33°34N 84°25W **316** B5
Riverdale *Md., U.S.A.* 38°57N 76°54W **143** B4
Riverdale *N.Y., U.S.A.* 40°59N 74°17W **132** B2
Riverdale Park *Canada* 43°40N 79°21W **141** A2
Riverhead *U.S.A.* 40°55N 72°40W **313** F12
Riverhurst *Canada* 50°55N 106°50W **297** C7
Riverlea *S. Africa* 26°12S 27°58E **123** B1
Rivers *Canada* 50°2N 100°14W **297** C8
Rivers □ *Nigeria* 4°30N 7°10E **263** E6
Rivers Inlet *Canada* 51°42N 127°15W **296** C3
Riversdale *Ont., Canada* 44°5N 81°20W **312** B3
Riversdale *N.Z.* 45°54S 168°44E **285** F3
Riversdale *Western Cape, S. Africa* 34°7S 21°15E **270** D3
Riverside *Calif., U.S.A.* 33°59N 117°22W **307** M9
Riverside *Ill., U.S.A.* 41°49N 87°49W **119** C2
Riverton *S. Austral., Australia* 34°10S 138°46E **282** C3
Riverton *Man., Canada* 51°1N 97°0W **297** C9
Riverton *N.Z.* 46°21S 168°0E **285** G3
Riverton *Ill., U.S.A.* 39°51N 89°33W **310** E7
Riverton *Wyo., U.S.A.* 43°2N 108°23W **304** E9
Riverview *Fla., U.S.A.* 27°52N 82°20W **317** H7
Riverview *Fla., U.S.A.* 30°32N 87°12W **317** E2
Riverwood *Australia* 33°57S 151°3E **139** B1
Rives *France* 45°21N 5°31E **175** C9
Rivesaltes *France* 42°47N 2°50E **174** F6
Riviera *U.S.A.* 35°4N 114°35W **307** K12
Riviera Beach *U.S.A.* 26°47N 80°3W **317** J9
Riviera di Levante *Italy* 44°15N 9°30E **198** D6
Riviera di Ponente *Italy* 44°10N 8°20E **198** D5
Rivière à Goyave, Pte. de la *Guadeloupe* 16°8N 61°33W **322** e
Rivière-au-Renard *Canada* 48°59N 64°23W **299** C7
Rivière des Anguilles *Mauritius* 20°29S 57°33E **272** e
Rivière-des-Praires *Canada* 45°38N 73°34W **130** A2
Rivière-du-Loup *Canada* 47°50N 69°30W **299** C6
Rivière du Rempart *Mauritius* 20°6S 57°41E **272** e
Rivière-Pentecôte *Canada* 49°57N 67°1W **299** C6
Rivière-Pilote *Martinique* 14°26N 60°53W **322** j
Rivière St-Paul *Canada* 51°28N 57°45W **299** B8
Rivière-Salée *Martinique* 14°31N 61°0W **322** j
Rivne *Odesa, Ukraine* 46°1N 29°10E **183** D14
Rivne *Rivne, Ukraine* 50°40N 26°10E **177** C14
Rivne □ *Ukraine* 51°15N 26°30E **189** G4
Rivoli *Italy* 45°3N 7°31E **198** C4
Rivoli B. *Australia* 37°32S 140°3E **282** D4
Riwaka *N.Z.* 41°5S 172°59E **285** B7
Rixensart *Belgium* 50°43N 4°32E **116** B3
Rixheim *France* 47°40N 7°24E **173** E14
Riyad *Iraq* 33°18N 44°27E **113** B2
Riyadh = Ar Riyāḍ *Si. Arabia* 24°41N 46°42E **246** E5
Riyadh al Khabrā' *Si. Arabia* 26°2N 43°33E **246** E4
Riza *Greece* 40°31N 23°15E **202** F7
Rizal *Cagayan, Phil.* 17°51N 121°21E **232** C3
Rizal *Nueva Ecija, Phil.* 15°43N 121°6E **232** D3
Rizal *Zamboanga del N., Phil.* 8°35N 123°26E **233** G4
Rizal Park *Phil.* 14°35N 120°58E **127** B1
Rizal Stadium *Phil.* 14°34N 120°59E **127** B1
Rize *Turkey* 41°0N 40°30E **213** B9
Rize □ *Turkey* 41°0N 40°30E **213** B9
Rizhao *China* 35°25N 119°30E **227** G10
Rizokarpaso *Cyprus* 35°36N 34°23E **207** E10
Rizzuto, C. *Italy* 38°53N 17°5E **201** D10
Rjukan *Norway* 59°54N 8°33E **164** E5
Rjuven *Norway* 59°9N 7°8E **164** E4
Rkîz, L. *Mauritania* 16°50N 15°23W **262** B1
Ro *Greece* 36°9N 29°33E **205** E11
Roa *Dem. Rep. of the Congo* 3°49N 24°56E **264** B4
Roa *Oppland, Norway* 60°17N 10°37E **164** D7
Røa *Oslo, Norway* 59°57N 10°39E **133** A2
Roa *Spain* 41°41N 3°56W **194** D7
Roachdale *U.S.A.* 39°51N 86°48W **311** E10
Road Town *Br. Virgin Is.* 18°27N 64°37W **321** C7
Roan Plateau *U.S.A.* 39°20N 109°20W **304** G9
Roanne *France* 46°3N 4°4E **173** F11
Roanoke *Ala., U.S.A.* 33°9N 85°22W **316** B4
Roanoke *Ind., U.S.A.* 40°58N 85°22W **311** D11
Roanoke *Va., U.S.A.* 37°16N 79°56W **309** G14
Roanoke → *U.S.A.* 35°57N 76°42W **315** D16
Roanoke I. *U.S.A.* 35°53N 75°39W **315** D17
Roanoke Rapids *U.S.A.* 36°28N 77°40W **315** C16
Roatán *Honduras* 16°18N 86°35W **320** C2
Rob Roy *Solomon Is.* 7°23S 157°36E **287** L9
Robāt *Iran* 34°16N 46°47E **213** E12
Robāt Sang *Iran* 35°35N 59°10E **247** C8
Robātkarīm *Iran* 35°25N 50°59E **247** C6
Robbins *U.S.A.* 41°38N 87°42W **119** D2
Robbins I. *Australia* 40°42S 145°0E **281** G4
Róbbio *Italy* 45°17N 8°35E **198** C5
Robe *Australia* 37°11S 139°45E **282** D3
Robe → *Australia* 21°42S 116°15E **278** D2
Röbel *Germany* 53°22N 12°35E **178** B8
Robert, Havre du *Martinique* 14°40N 60°55W **322** j
Robert Bourassa, Rés. *Canada* 53°40N 76°55W **298** B4
Robert Lee *U.S.A.* 31°54N 100°29W **314** F4
Roberta *U.S.A.* 32°43N 84°1W **316** C5
Roberts *U.S.A.* 40°37N 88°11W **311** D8
Roberts, Mt. *Trin. & Tob.* 10°47N 61°10W **323** t
Roberts, Mt. *Alaska, U.S.A.* 60°2N 166°16W **303** F6
Robertsdale *U.S.A.* 40°11N 78°6W **312** F6
Robertsganj *India* 24°44N 83°4E **243** G10
Robertsham *S. Africa* 26°15S 28°1E **123** B2
Robertson *S. Africa* 33°46S 19°50E **270** D2
Robertson I. *Antarctica* 65°15S 59°30W **151** C18
Robertson Ra. *Australia* 23°15S 121°0E **278** D3
Robertsport *Liberia* 6°45N 11°26W **262** D2
Robertstown *Australia* 33°58S 139°5E **282** B3
Roberval *Canada* 48°32N 72°15W **299** C5
Robeson Chan. *N. Amer.* 82°0N 61°30W **154** A4
Robesonia *U.S.A.* 40°21N 76°8W **313** F8
Robi *Ethiopia* 7°52N 39°38E **257** F4
Robinson *U.S.A.* 39°0N 87°44W **311** F9
Robinson → *Australia* 16°3S 137°16E **280** B2
Robinson Crusoe I. *Pac. Oc.* 33°38S 78°52W **330** c
Robinson Ra. *Australia* 25°40S 119°0E **279** E2
Robinvale *Australia* 34°40S 142°45E **282** C5
Robledo *Spain* 38°46N 2°26W **197** G2
Roblin *Canada* 51°14N 101°21W **297** C8
Roboré *Bolivia* 18°10S 59°45W **331** D6
Robson, Mt. *Canada* 53°10N 119°10W **296** C5
Robstown *U.S.A.* 27°47N 97°40W **314** H6
Roca, C. da *Portugal* 38°40N 9°31W **195** G1
Roca Partida, I. *Mexico* 19°1N 112°2W **318** D2
Rocamadour *France* 44°48N 1°37E **174** D5
Rocca San Casciano *Italy* 44°3N 11°50E **199** D8
Roccadáspide *Italy* 40°27N 15°10E **201** B8
Roccastrada *Italy* 43°0N 11°10E **199** F8
Roccella Iónica *Italy* 38°19N 16°24E **201** D9
Rocciamelone, Monte = Roche Melon *Italy* 45°12N 7°5E **175** C11
Rocha *Uruguay* 34°30S 54°25W **335** C5
Rochdale *U.K.* 53°38N 2°9W **168** D5
Roche Melon *Italy* 45°12N 7°5E **175** C11
Rochechouart *France* 45°50N 0°49E **174** C4
Rochedo *Brazil* 19°57S 54°52W **331** D7
Rochefort *Belgium* 50°9N 5°12E **170** D5
Rochefort *Charente-Maritime, France* 45°56N 0°57W **174** C3
Rochefort-en-Terre *France* 47°42N 2°22W **172** E4
Rochelle *Ga., U.S.A.* 31°57N 83°27W **316** D6
Rochelle *Ill., U.S.A.* 41°56N 89°4W **310** C7
Rocher Park *U.S.A.* 40°54N 74°4W **132** A1
Rocher River *Canada* 61°23N 112°44W **296** A6
Roches, R. des → *Réunion* 21°0S 55°42E **272** f
Roche's Bluff *Montserrat* 16°42N 62°9W **323** p

Roches Noires *Mauritius* 20°6S 57°42E **272** e
Rocheservière *France* 46°57N 1°30W **172** F5
Rochester *Vic., Australia* 36°22S 144°41E **282** D6
Rochester *Medway, U.K.* 51°23N 0°31E **169** F8
Rochester *Ind., U.S.A.* 41°4N 86°13W **311** C10
Rochester *Minn., U.S.A.* 44°1N 92°28W **308** C7
Rochester *N.H., U.S.A.* 43°18N 70°59W **313** C14
Rochester *N.Y., U.S.A.* 43°10N 77°37W **312** C7
Rochester Hills *U.S.A.* 42°41N 83°8W **311** B13
Rociu *Romania* 44°43N 25°2E **183** F10
Rock ➔ *Yukon, Canada* 60°7N 127°7W **296** A3
Rock ➔ *Ill., U.S.A.* 41°29N 90°37W **310** C6
Rock, The *Australia* 35°15S 147°2E **283** C7
Rock Cr. ➔ *U.S.A.* 38°54N 77°3W **143** B3
Rock Creek *U.S.A.* 41°40N 80°52W **312** E4
Rock Creek Park *U.S.A.* 38°56N 77°2W **143** B3
Rock Falls *U.S.A.* 41°47N 89°41W **310** C7
Rock Flat *Australia* 36°21S 149°13E **283** D8
Rock Hall *Barbados* 13°11N 59°36W **323** r
Rock Hill *U.S.A.* 34°56N 81°1W **315** D14
Rock Island *U.S.A.* 41°30N 90°34W **310** C6
Rock Port *U.S.A.* 40°25N 95°31W **308** E6
Rock Pt. *N.Z.* 41°8S 174°47E **143** A1
Rock Rapids *U.S.A.* 43°26N 96°10W **308** D5
Rock Sound *Bahamas* 24°54N 76°12W **320** B4
Rock Springs *Mont., U.S.A.* 46°49N 106°15W **304** C10
Rock Springs *Wyo., U.S.A.* 41°35N 109°14W **304** F9
Rock Valley *U.S.A.* 43°12N 96°18W **308** D5
Rockall *Atl. Oc.* 57°37N 13°42W **158** D3
Rockall Trough *Atl. Oc.* 57°0N 12°0W **152** A10
Rockaway Beach *U.S.A.* 40°34N 73°49W **132** C3
Rockaway Pt. *U.S.A.* 40°33N 73°54W **132** C2
Rockdale *N.S.W., Australia* 33°57S 151°8E **139** B1
Rockdale *Tex., U.S.A.* 30°39N 97°0W **314** F6
Rockdale *Wash., U.S.A.* 47°22N 121°28W **306** C5
Rockeby = Mungkan Kandju △ *Australia* 13°35S 142°52E **280** A3
Rockefeller Center *New York, U.S.A.* **132** c2
Rockefeller Plateau *Antarctica* 76°0S 130°0W **151** E14
Rockford *Ala., U.S.A.* 32°53N 86°13W **316** C3
Rockford *Ill., U.S.A.* 42°16N 89°6W **310** B7
Rockford *Iowa, U.S.A.* 43°3N 92°57W **310** A4
Rockford *Mich., U.S.A.* 43°7N 85°34W **311** A11
Rockford *Ohio, U.S.A.* 40°41N 84°39W **311** D12
Rockglen *Canada* 49°11N 105°57W **297** D7
Rockhampton *Australia* 23°22S 150°32E **280** C5
Rockingham *W. Austral., Australia* 32°15S 115°38E **279** F2
Rockingham *N.C., U.S.A.* 34°57N 79°46W **315** D15
Rockingham *Vt., U.S.A.* 43°11N 72°29W **313** C12
Rockingham B. *Australia* 18°5S 146°10E **280** B4
Rocklake *U.S.A.* 48°47N 99°15W **308** A4
Rockland *Ont., Canada* 45°33N 75°17W **313** A9
Rockland *Idaho, U.S.A.* 42°34N 112°53W **304** E7
Rockland *Maine, U.S.A.* 44°6N 69°7W **309** C19
Rockland *Mich., U.S.A.* 46°44N 89°11W **308** B9
Rocklands Bird Sanctuary *Jamaica* 18°24N 77°55W **320** a
Rocklands Reservoir *Australia* 37°15S 142°5E **282** D5
Rockledge *U.S.A.* 28°20N 80°43W **317** G9
Rocklin *U.S.A.* 38°48N 121°14W **306** G5
Rockly B. *Trin. & Tob.* 11°9N 60°46W **323** s
Rockmart *U.S.A.* 34°0N 85°3W **315** D12
Rockport *Ind., U.S.A.* 37°53N 87°3W **311** G9
Rockport *Mass., U.S.A.* 42°39N 70°37W **313** D14
Rockport *Tex., U.S.A.* 28°2N 97°3W **314** G6
Rocksprings *U.S.A.* 30°1N 100°13W **314** F4
Rockstone *Guyana* 5°59N 58°33W **329** B6
Rockville *Conn., U.S.A.* 41°52N 72°28W **313** E12
Rockville *Ind., U.S.A.* 39°46N 87°14W **311** E9
Rockville *Md., U.S.A.* 39°5N 77°9W **309** F15
Rockwall *U.S.A.* 32°56N 96°28W **314** E6
Rockwell City *U.S.A.* 42°24N 94°38W **310** B2
Rockwood *Ont., Canada* 43°37N 80°8W **312** C4
Rockwood *Maine, U.S.A.* 45°41N 69°45W **309** C19
Rockwood *Tenn., U.S.A.* 35°52N 84°41W **315** D12
Rocky Ford *U.S.A.* 38°3N 103°43W **304** G12
Rocky Fork L. *U.S.A.* 39°11N 83°26W **311** E13
Rocky Gully *Australia* 34°30S 116°57E **279** F2
Rocky Harbour *Canada* 49°36N 57°55W **299** C8
Rocky Island L. *Canada* 46°55N 83°0W **298** C3
Rocky Lane *Canada* 58°31N 116°22W **296** B5
Rocky Mount *U.S.A.* 35°57N 77°48W **315** D16
Rocky Mountain △ *U.S.A.* 40°25N 105°45W **304** F11
Rocky Mountain House *Canada* 52°22N 114°55W **296** C6
Rocky Mts. *N. Amer.* 49°0N 115°0W **304** B6
Rocky Point *Namibia* 19°3S 12°30E **270** A2
Rocky Run ➔ *U.S.A.* 38°58N 77°14W **143** B2
Rocroi *France* 49°55N 4°30E **173** C11
Rod *Pakistan* 28°10N 63°5E **240** C1
Roda = Stadtroda *Germany* 50°52N 11°44E **178** E7
Roda *Greece* 39°48N 19°46E **206** B9
Roda, Gezîret el *Egypt* 30°1N 31°13E **117** A2
Roda I. = Roda, Gezîret el *Egypt* 30°1N 31°13E **117** A2
Rodaon *Austria* 48°8N 16°16E **142** B1
Rødberg *Norway* 60°17N 8°56E **164** D5
Rødby *Denmark* 54°41N 11°23E **163** K5
Rødbyhavn *Denmark* 54°39N 11°22E **163** K5
Roddickton *Canada* 50°51N 56°8W **299** B8
Rødding *Denmark* 55°23N 9°3E **163** J3
Rödeby *Sweden* 56°15N 15°37E **163** H9
Rødekro *Denmark* 55°4N 9°20E **163** J3
Rodenkirchen *Germany* 53°23N 8°26E **178** B4
Rodez *France* 44°21N 2°33E **174** D6
Ródhos = Rhodes *Greece* 36°15N 28°10E **206** E12
Rodi Gargánico *Italy* 41°55N 15°53E **199** G12
Rodia *Greece* 35°22N 25°1E **207** E6
Rodīna *Kazakhstan* 50°16N 66°53E **217** B7
Rodna *Romania* 47°25N 24°50E **183** C9
Rodna ☼ *Australia* 23°45S 132°4E **278** D5
Rodnei, Munţii *Romania* 47°35N 24°35E **183** C9
Rodney *Canada* 42°34N 81°41W **312** D3
Rodney, C. *N.Z.* 36°17S 174°50E **284** C3
Rodney B. *St. Lucia* 14°5N 60°58W **323** m
Rodniki *Russia* 57°7N 41°47E **190** B5
Rodolivos *Greece* 40°55N 24°0E **204** F7
Rodonit, Kepi i *Albania* 41°35N 19°27E **202** E3
Rodopi □ *Greece* 41°5N 25°30E **203** E9
Rodopos *Greece* 35°34N 23°45E **207** E4
Rødovre *Denmark* 55°40N 12°26E **118** A2
Rodrigo de Freitas, L. *Brazil* 22°58S 43°12W **135** B1
Rodrigues *Ind. Oc.* 19°45S 63°20E **273** F5
Roe ➔ *U.K.* 55°6N 6°59W **166** A5
Roebling *U.S.A.* 40°7N 74°47W **313** F10
Roebourne *Australia* 20°44S 117°9E **278** D2
Roebuck B. *Australia* 18°5S 122°20E **278** C3
Roebuck Roadhouse *Australia* 17°59S 122°36E **278** C3
Roehampton *U.K.* 51°27N 0°15W **125** B2
Roermond *Neths.* 51°12N 6°0E **170** C6
Roes Welcome Sd. *Canada* 65°0N 87°0W **295** E14
Roeselare *Belgium* 50°57N 3°7E **170** D3
Rogachev = Ragachow *Belarus* 53°8N 30°5E **177** B16
Rogačica *Serbia* 44°4N 19°40E **202** B3
Rogagua, L. *Bolivia* 13°43S 66°50W **330** C4
Rogaland □ *Norway* 59°12N 6°20E **164** E3
Rogaška Slatina *Slovenia* 46°15N 15°42E **199** B12
Rogatec *Slovenia* 46°15N 15°46E **199** B12
Rogatica *Bos.-H.* 43°47N 19°0E **182** G4
Rogatyn *Ukraine* 49°24N 24°36E **177** D13
Rogers *U.S.A.* 36°20N 94°7W **314** C7
Rogers Centre *Toronto, Canada* **141** c1
Rogers City *U.S.A.* 45°25N 83°49W **309** C12
Rogers Park *U.S.A.* 42°0N 87°40W **119** A3
Rogersville *Canada* 46°44N 65°26W **299** C6
Roggan ➔ *Canada* 54°24N 79°25W **298** B4
Roggan L. *Canada* 54°8N 77°50W **298** B4
Roggeveen Basin *Pac. Oc.* 31°30S 95°30W **289** L18
Roggeveldberge *S. Africa* 32°10S 20°10E **270** D3
Roggiano Gravina *Italy* 39°37N 16°9E **201** C9
Rogliano *Haute-Corse, France* 42°57N 9°30E **175** F13
Rogliano *Italy* 39°10N 16°19E **201** C9
Rogoaguado, L. *Bolivia* 13°0S 65°30W **331** C4
Rogojampi *Indonesia* 8°19S 114°17E **231** J17
Rogoźno *Poland* 52°45N 16°59E **185** F3
Rogue ➔ *U.S.A.* 42°26N 124°26W **304** E1
Roha *India* 18°26N 73°7E **244** E1
Rohan *France* 48°4N 2°45W **172** D4
Rohnert Park *U.S.A.* 38°16N 122°40W **306** G4
Rohri *Pakistan* 27°45N 68°51E **242** F3
Rohri Canal *Pakistan* 26°15N 68°27E **242** F3
Rohtak *India* 28°55N 76°43E **242** E7
Rohtsich-Sauerbrunn = Rogaška Slatina *Slovenia* 46°15N 15°42E **199** B12
Roi Et *Thailand* 16°4N 103°40E **236** D4
Roi-Georges, Îs. du *French Polynesia* 14°32S 145°8W **289** f
Roihuvuori *Finland* 60°11N 25°2E **121** B3
Roissy-en-Brie *France* 48°48N 2°39E **134** B4
Roja *Latvia* 57°29N 22°43E **184** A9
Rojas *Argentina* 34°10S 60°45W **334** C3
Rojiște *Romania* 44°4N 23°56E **183** F8
Rojo, C. *Mexico* 21°33N 97°20W **319** C5
Rokan ➔ *Indonesia* 2°0N 100°50E **234** B2
Rokel ➔ *S. Leone* 8°30N 12°48W **262** D2
Rokin *Amsterdam, Neths.* **112** b2
Rokiškis *Lithuania* 55°55N 25°35E **188** E3
Rokitno *Russia* 50°57N 35°56E **189** G8
Rokycany *Czech Rep.* 49°43N 13°35E **180** B6
Rokytka ➔ *Czech Rep.* 50°6N 14°27E **135** B3
Rolândia *Brazil* 23°18S 51°23W **335** A5
Røldal *Norway* 59°47N 6°50E **164** E3
Rolfe *U.S.A.* 42°49N 94°31W **310** B2
Rolla *Mo., U.S.A.* 37°57N 91°46W **310** G5
Rolla *N. Dak., U.S.A.* 48°52N 99°37W **308** A4
Rolleston *Queens., Australia* 24°28S 148°35E **280** C4
Rolleston *N.Z.* 43°35S 172°24E **285** D7
Rolling Fork ➔ *U.S.A.* 37°55N 85°50W **311** G11
Rollingstone *Australia* 19°2S 146°24E **280** B4
Rom *Vest-Agder, Norway* 58°8N 7°56E **164** F4
Rom *Sudan* 9°54N 32°16E **257** F3
Roma *Queens., Australia* 26°32S 148°49E **281** D4
Roma *Italy* 41°54N 12°28E **136** B1
Roma *Sweden* 57°32N 18°26E **163** G12
Roma Fiumicino ✈ **(FCO)** *Italy* 41°48N 12°15E **199** G9
Roma-Los Saenz *U.S.A.* 26°24N 99°1W **314** H5
Roma Urbe ✕ *Italy* 41°57N 12°30E **136** B2
Római-Fürdő *Hungary* 47°34N 19°4E **117** A2
Romain, C. *U.S.A.* 33°0N 79°22W **315** E15
Romaine ➔ *Canada* 50°18N 63°47W **299** B7
Romainville *France* 48°52N 2°26E **134** A3
Roman *Bulgaria* 43°8N 23°57E **202** C7
Roman *Romania* 46°57N 26°55E **183** D11
Roman Forum = Foro Romano *Rome, Italy* **136** c3
Roman-Kosh, Gora *Ukraine* 44°37N 34°15E **189** K8
Romanche ➔ *France* 45°5N 5°43E **175** C9
Romang *Indonesia* 7°30S 127°20E **231** F7
Români *Egypt* 30°59N 32°38E **251** H3
Romania ■ *Europe* 46°0N 25°0E **183** D10
Romanija *Bos.-H.* 43°50N 18°45E **182** G3
Romano, C. *U.S.A.* 25°51N 81°41W **317** K8
Romano, Cayo *Cuba* 22°0N 77°30W **320** B4
Romano Banco *Italy* 45°25N 9°6E **129** B1
Romanov-Borisoglebsk = Tutayev *Russia* 57°53N 39°32E **188** D10
Romanovka = Basarabeasca *Moldova* 46°21N 28°58E **183** D13
Romanovna-Murmane = Murmansk *Russia* 68°57N 33°10E **160** B25
Romanovsk = Kropotkin *Russia* 45°28N 40°28E **191** H5
Romanovskiy Khutor = Kropotkin *Russia* 45°28N 40°28E **191** H5
Romans-sur-Isère *France* 45°3N 5°3E **175** C9
Romanshorn *Switz.* 47°33N 9°22E **179** H5
Romanzof C. *U.S.A.* 61°49N 166°6W **303** F6
Romashkovo *Russia* 55°43N 37°19E **129** B1
Rombari *Sudan* 4°33N 31°2E **257** G3
Romblon *Phil.* 12°33N 122°17E **232** E4
Romblon □ *Phil.* 12°30N 122°15E **232** E4
Romblon Pass *Phil.* 12°27N 122°12E **232** E4
Rome = Roma *Italy* 41°54N 12°28E **136** B1
Rome *Ga., U.S.A.* 34°15N 85°10W **315** D12
Rome *N.Y., U.S.A.* 43°13N 75°27W **313** C9
Rome *Pa., U.S.A.* 41°51N 76°21W **313** E8
Romema *Israel* 31°48N 35°12E **123** B2
Romeoville *U.S.A.* 41°39N 88°3W **311** C8
Rometta *Italy* 38°10N 15°25E **201** D8
Romford *U.K.* 51°34N 0°11E **125** A5
Romilly-sur-Seine *France* 48°31N 3°44E **173** D10
Romiton *Uzbekistan* 39°56N 64°23E **216** E6
Rommani *Morocco* 33°31N 6°40W **260** B3
Romney *U.S.A.* 39°21N 78°45W **309** F14
Romney Marsh *U.K.* 51°2N 0°54E **169** F8
Romny *Ukraine* 50°48N 33°28E **189** G7
Rømø *Denmark* 55°10N 8°30E **163** J2
Romodan *Ukraine* 49°55N 33°15E **189** G7
Romodanovo *Russia* 54°26N 45°23E **190** C7
Romont *Switz.* 46°42N 6°54E **179** J2
Romorantin-Lanthenay *France* 47°21N 1°45E **173** E8
Rompin ➔ *Malaysia* 2°49N 103°29E **234** B2
Romsdalen *Norway* 62°25N 7°52E **164** B4
Romsdalsfjorden *Norway* 62°25N 7°20E **164** B4
Romsey *U.K.* 51°0N 1°29W **169** G6
Ron *India* 15°40N 75°44E **245** G2
Ron *Vietnam* 17°53N 106°27E **236** D6
Rona *U.K.* 57°34N 5°59W **167** D3
Ronald Reagan Nat. Washington ✕ **(DCA)** *U.S.A.* 38°51N 77°2W **143** B3
Ronan *U.S.A.* 47°32N 114°6W **304** C6
Roncador, Cayos *Colombia* 13°32N 80°4W **320** D3
Roncador, Serra do *Brazil* 12°30S 52°30W **333** D1
Ronciglione *Italy* 42°17N 12°12E **199** F9
Ronco ➔ *Italy* 44°24N 12°12E **199** D9
Ronda *Spain* 36°46N 5°12W **195** J5
Ronda, Serranía de *Spain* 36°44N 5°3W **195** J5
Rondane *Norway* 61°57N 9°50E **164** C6
Rondane △ *Norway* 61°55N 9°44E **164** C6
Ronde, Pt. *Dominica* 15°33N 61°29W **323** k
Ronde I. *Grenada* 12°29N 61°36W **323** q
Rondebosch *S. Africa* 33°58S 18°28E **118** A1
Rondón *Colombia* 6°17N 71°6W **328** B3
Rondônia *Brazil* 10°52S 61°57W **331** C5
Rondônia □ *Brazil* 11°0S 63°0W **331** C5
Rondonópolis *Brazil* 16°28S 54°38W **331** D7
Rondslottet *Norway* 61°55N 9°45E **164** C6
Rondu *Pakistan* 35°32N 75°10E **243** B6
Rong, Koh *Cambodia* 10°45N 103°15E **237** G4
Rong Jiang ➔ *China* 24°35N 109°20E **228** E7
Rong Xian *Guangxi Zhuangzu, China* 22°50N 110°31E **229** F8
Rong Xian *Sichuan, China* 29°23N 104°22E **228** C5
Rong'an *China* 25°14N 109°22E **228** E7
Rongchang *China* 29°20N 105°32E **228** C5
Ronge, L. la *Canada* 55°6N 105°17W **297** B7
Rongjiang *China* 25°57N 108°28E **228** E7
Rongotea *N.Z.* 40°19S 175°25E **284** G4
Rongshui *China* 25°5N 109°12E **228** E7
Rønne *Denmark* 55°6N 14°43E **163** J8
Ronne Ice Shelf *Antarctica* 77°30S 60°0W **151** D18
Ronneby *Sweden* 56°12N 15°17E **163** H9
Ronnebyån ➔ *Sweden* 56°11N 15°18E **163** H9
Rönneshytta *Sweden* 58°56N 15°2E **163** F9
Ronsard, C. *Australia* 24°46S 113°10E **279** D1
Ronse *Belgium* 50°45N 3°35E **170** D3
Ronuro ➔ *Brazil* 11°56S 53°33W **331** C7
Roodepoort *S. Africa* 26°11S 27°54E **271** C4
Roodhouse *U.S.A.* 39°29N 90°24W **310** E6
Roof Butte *U.S.A.* 36°28N 109°5W **305** H9
Rooiboklaagte ➔ *Namibia* 20°50S 21°0E **270** B3
Rooniu, Mt. *Tahiti* 17°49S 149°12W **289** e
Roopville *U.S.A.* 33°27N 85°8W **316** B4
Roorkee *India* 29°52N 77°59E **242** E7
Roosendaal *Neths.* 51°32N 4°29E **170** C4
Roosevelt *U.S.A.* 40°18N 109°59W **304** F9
Roosevelt ➔ *Brazil* 7°35S 60°20W **330** B5
Roosevelt, Mt. *Canada* 58°26N 125°20W **296** B3
Roosevelt I. *Antarctica* 79°30S 162°0W **151** D12
Roosevelt Island *New York, U.S.A.* **132** c3
Ropczyce *Poland* 50°4N 21°38E **185** H8
Roper ➔ *Australia* 14°43S 135°27E **280** A2
Roper Bar *Australia* 14°44S 134°44E **280** A1
Roper River = St. Vidgeon's ☼ *Australia* 14°47S 134°53E **280** A1
Roppongi *Tokyo, Japan* **140** c3
Roque Pérez *Argentina* 35°25S 59°24W **334** D4
Roquefort *France* 44°2N 0°20W **174** D3
Roquemaure *France* 44°3N 4°48E **175** D8
Roquetas de Mar *Spain* 36°46N 2°36W **197** J2
Roquetes *Spain* 40°50N 0°30E **196** E5
Roquevaire *France* 43°20N 5°36E **175** E9
Roraima □ *Brazil* 2°0N 61°30W **329** C5
Roraima, Mt. *Venezuela* 5°10N 60°40W **329** B5
Røros *Norway* 62°35N 11°23E **164** B8
Rorschach *Switz.* 47°28N 9°28E **179** H5
Ros Comáin = Roscommon *Ireland* 53°38N 8°11W **166** C3
Rosa *Zambia* 9°33S 31°15E **269** D3
Rosa, C. *Algeria* 37°0N 8°16E **261** A6
Rosa, C. *Galápagos Is., Ecuador* 1°4S 91°10W **330** a
Rosa, Monte *Europe* 45°57N 7°53E **198** C4
Rosais, Pta. dos *Azores* 38°45N 28°19W **153** d1
Rosal de la Frontera *Spain* 37°59N 7°13W **195** H3
Rosales *Phil.* 15°54N 120°38E **232** D3
Rosalia *U.S.A.* 47°14N 117°22W **304** C5
Rosalie *Dominica* 15°22N 61°16W **323** k
Rosalie ➔ *Dominica* 15°22N 61°15W **323** k
Rosalind Bank *W. Indies* 16°30N 80°30W **320** C3
Rosamond *U.S.A.* 34°52N 118°10W **307** L8
Rosans *France* 44°24N 5°29E **175** D9
Rosario *Argentina* 33°0S 60°40W **334** C3
Rosário *Maranhão, Brazil* 3°0S 44°15W **332** B3
Rosario *Baja Calif., Mexico* 30°0N 115°50W **318** B1
Rosario *Sinaloa, Mexico* 22°58N 105°53W **318** C3
Rosario *Paraguay* 24°30S 57°35W **334** A4
Rosario *Phil.* 8°24N 125°59E **233** G5
Rosario, Villa del *Venezuela* 10°19N 72°19W **328** A3
Rosario de la Frontera *Argentina* 25°50S 65°0W **334** B3
Rosario de Lerma *Argentina* 24°59S 65°35W **334** A2
Rosario del Tala *Argentina* 32°20S 59°10W **334** C4
Rosário do Sul *Brazil* 30°15S 54°55W **335** C5
Rosário Oeste *Brazil* 14°50S 56°25W **331** C6
Rosarito *Mexico* 32°20N 117°2W **307** N9
Rosarno *Italy* 38°29N 15°58E **201** D8
Rosas = Roses *Spain* 42°19N 3°10E **196** C8
Roscoe *Mo., U.S.A.* 37°58N 93°48W **310** G3
Roscoe *N.Y., U.S.A.* 41°56N 74°55W **313** E10
Roscoff *France* 48°44N 3°58W **172** D3
Roscommon *Ireland* 53°38N 8°11W **166** C3
Roscommon □ *Ireland* 53°49N 8°23W **166** C3
Roscrea *Ireland* 52°57N 7°49W **166** D4
Rose ➔ *Australia* 14°16S 135°45E **280** A2
Rose, L. *Bahamas* 21°0N 73°30W **321** B5
Rose, L. *Fla., U.S.A.* 28°32N 81°30W **133** A1
Rose Belle *Mauritius* 20°24S 57°36E **272** e
Rose Blanche *Canada* 47°38N 58°45W **299** C8
Rose Bowl *U.S.A.* 34°9N 118°10W **126** B4
Rose Hall Great House *Jamaica* 18°31N 77°49W **320** a
Rose Hill = Port Mourant *Guyana* 6°15N 57°20W **329** B6
Rose Hill *Mauritius* 20°14S 57°27E **272** e
Rose Hill *Va., U.S.A.* 38°47N 77°6W **143** C3
Rose Pt. *Canada* 54°11N 131°39W **296** C2
Rose Rock *Grenada* 12°24N 61°28W **323** q
Rose Valley *Canada* 52°19N 103°49W **297** C8
Roseau *Dominica* 15°17N 61°24W **323** k
Roseau *Minn., U.S.A.* 48°51N 95°46W **308** A6
Rosebank *Gauteng, S. Africa* 26°8S 28°2E **123** A2
Rosebank *N.Y., U.S.A.* 40°36N 74°4W **132** C1
Rosebery *N.S.W., Australia* 33°55S 151°12E **139** B2
Rosebery *Tas., Australia* 41°46S 145°33E **281** G4
Rosebud *Vic., Australia* 38°21S 144°54E **282** E6
Rosebud *S. Dak., U.S.A.* 43°14N 100°51W **308** D3
Rosebud *Tex., U.S.A.* 31°4N 96°59W **314** F6
Roseburg *U.S.A.* 43°13N 123°20W **304** E2
Rosedal La Candelaria *Mexico* 19°20N 99°10W **128** B2
Rosedale *U.S.A.* 33°51N 91°2W **315** E9
Rosehearty *U.K.* 57°42N 2°7W **167** D6
Roseires Res. *Sudan* 11°51N 34°23E **266** B3
Roseland *Calif., U.S.A.* 38°25N 122°43W **306** G4
Roseland *Ill., U.S.A.* 41°42N 87°37W **119** C3
Rosemary *Canada* 50°46N 112°5W **296** C6
Rosemead *U.S.A.* 34°4N 118°4W **126** B4
Rosemont *Qué., Canada* 45°34N 73°33W **130** A2
Rosemont *Ill., U.S.A.* 41°59N 87°53W **119** B1
Rosenberg = Olesno *Poland* 50°51N 18°26E **185** H5
Rosenberg = Susz *Poland* 53°44N 19°20E **184** E6
Rosenberg *U.S.A.* 29°34N 95°49W **314** G7
Rosenborg Slot *Copenhagen, Denmark* **118** b2
Rosendaël *France* 51°3N 2°24E **173** A9
Rosendal *Norway* 59°59N 6°0E **164** E3
Rosendale *U.S.A.* 40°4N 94°51W **310** D2
Rosenheim *Germany* 47°51N 12°7E **179** H8
Rosenthal *Germany* 52°35N 13°22E **115** A3
Roses *Spain* 42°19N 3°10E **196** C8
Roses, G. de *Spain* 42°10N 3°15E **196** C8
Roseto degli Abruzzi *Italy* 42°41N 14°1E **199** F11
Rosetown *Canada* 51°35N 107°59W **297** C7
Rosetta = Rashîd *Egypt* 31°21N 30°22E **256** H7
Rosettenville *S. Africa* 26°15S 28°3E **123** B2
Roseville *Calif., U.S.A.* 38°45N 121°17W **306** G5
Roseville *Ill., U.S.A.* 40°44N 90°40W **310** D6
Roseville *Mich., U.S.A.* 42°30N 82°56W **312** D2
Roseville *Pa., U.S.A.* 41°51N 76°57W **313** E8
Rosewell *U.K.* 55°51N 3°8W **121** B3
Rosewood *Australia* 27°38S 152°36E **281** D5
Rosherville Dam *S. Africa* 26°13S 28°6E **123** B2
Roshkhvār *Iran* 34°58N 59°37E **247** C8
Rosières-en-Santerre *France* 49°49N 2°42E **173** C9
Rosignano Maríttimo *Italy* 43°24N 10°28E **198** E7
Rosignol *Guyana* 6°15N 57°30W **329** B6
Roşiori de Vede *Romania* 44°9N 25°0E **183** F10
Rositsa *Bulgaria* 43°57N 27°57E **203** C11
Rositsa ➔ *Bulgaria* 43°10N 25°30E **203** C9
Rösjön *Sweden* 59°26N 18°0E **139** A2
Roskilde *Denmark* 55°38N 12°3E **163** J6
Roskovec *Albania* 40°44N 19°43E **202** F3
Roslags-Näsby *Sweden* 59°25N 18°2E **139** A2
Roslavl *Russia* 53°57N 32°55E **188** F7
Roslin *U.K.* 55°51N 3°11W **121** B3
Roslindale *U.S.A.* 42°17N 71°7W **116** B2
Rosmaninhal *Portugal* 39°44N 7°5W **194** F3
Rosmead *S. Africa* 31°29S 25°8E **270** D4
Røsnæs *Denmark* 55°44N 10°55E **163** J4
Rosny-sous-Bois *France* 48°52N 2°30E **134** A4
Rosolini *Italy* 36°49N 14°57E **201** F7
Rosporden *France* 47°57N 3°50W **172** E3
Ross *Tas., Australia* 42°2S 147°30E **281** G4
Ross *N.Z.* 42°53S 170°49E **285** C5
Ross Béthio *Mauritania* 16°15N 16°8W **262** B1
Ross Dependency *Antarctica* 76°0S 170°0W **151** D12
Ross I. *Antarctica* 77°30S 168°0E **151** D11
Ross Ice Shelf *Antarctica* 80°0S 180°0E **151** E12
Ross L. *U.S.A.* 48°44N 121°4W **304** B3
Ross Mhic Thriúin = New Ross *Ireland* 52°23N 6°57W **166** D5
Ross-on-Wye *U.K.* 51°54N 2°34W **169** F5
Ross River *N. Terr., Australia* 23°44S 134°30E **280** C1
Ross River *Yukon, Canada* 62°30N 131°30W **296** A2
Ross Sea *Antarctica* 74°0S 178°0E **151** D11
Rossall Pt. *U.K.* 53°55N 3°3W **168** D4
Rossan Pt. *Ireland* 54°42N 8°47W **166** B3
Rossano *Italy* 39°36N 16°39E **201** C9
Rossburn *Canada* 50°40N 100°49W **297** C8
Rosseau *Canada* 45°16N 79°39W **312** A5
Rosseau, L. *Canada* 45°10N 79°35W **312** A5
Rössel = Reszel *Poland* 54°4N 21°10E **184** D8
Rossel I. *Papua N. G.* 11°21S 154°9E **286** F8
Rosses, The *Ireland* 55°2N 8°20W **166** A3
Rossford *U.S.A.* 41°36N 83°34W **311** C13
Rossignol, L. *Canada* 52°43N 73°40W **298** B5
Rossignol L. *Canada* 44°12N 65°10W **299** D6
Rossiya = Russia ■ *Eurasia* 62°0N 105°0E **215** C11
Rosskreppfjorden *Norway* 59°4N 7°10E **164** E4
Rossland *Canada* 49°6N 117°50W **296** D5
Rosslare *Ireland* 52°17N 6°24W **166** D5
Rosslare Harbour *Ireland* 52°15N 6°20W **166** D5
Rosslau *Germany* 51°52N 12°15E **178** D8
Rosslyn *U.S.A.* 38°53N 77°4W **143** B3
Rossmore *Canada* 44°8N 77°23W **312** B7
Rosso *Mauritania* 16°40N 15°45W **262** B1
Rosso, C. *France* 42°13N 8°32E **175** F12
Rossosh *Russia* 50°15N 39°28E **189** G10
Røssvatnet *Norway* 65°45N 14°5E **160** D16
Rossville *Ill., U.S.A.* 40°23N 87°40W **311** D9
Rossville *Ind., U.S.A.* 40°25N 86°36W **311** D10
Røst *Norway* 67°32N 12°0E **160** C15
Rostāq *Afghan.* 37°7N 69°49E **240** A3
Rosthern *Canada* 52°40N 106°20W **297** C7
Rostock *Germany* 54°5N 12°8E **178** A8
Rostov *Don, Russia* 47°15N 39°45E **189** J10
Rostov *Yaroslavl, Russia* 57°14N 39°25E **188** D10
Rostov □ *Russia* 48°50N 41°10E **191** F5
Rostrenen *France* 48°14N 3°21W **172** D3
Roswell *Ga., U.S.A.* 34°2N 84°22W **316** A5
Roswell *N. Mex., U.S.A.* 33°24N 104°32W **305** K11
Rosyth *U.K.* 56°2N 3°25W **121** A1
Rot-Front = Dobropole *Ukraine* 48°25N 37°2E **189** H9
Rota *N. Marianas* 14°9N 145°12E **302** a
Rota *Spain* 36°37N 6°20W **195** J4
Rotan *U.S.A.* 32°51N 100°28W **314** E4
Rotenburg *Hessen, Germany* 50°59N 9°44E **178** E5
Rotenburg *Niedersachsen, Germany* 53°6N 9°25E **178** B5
Roth *Germany* 49°15N 11°5E **179** F7
Rothaargebirge *Germany* 51°2N 8°13E **178** D4
Rothaargebirge △ *Germany* 51°0N 8°15E **178** E4
Rothenburg ob der Tauber *Germany* 49°23N 10°11E **179** F6
Rother ➔ *U.K.* 50°59N 0°45E **169** G8
Rothera *Antarctica* 67°34S 68°8W **151** C17
Rotherham *U.K.* 53°26N 1°20W **168** D6
Rotherhithe *U.K.* 51°29N 0°2W **125** B3
Rothes *U.K.* 57°32N 3°13W **167** D5
Rothesay *N.B., Canada* 45°23N 66°0W **299** C6
Rothesay *Argyll & Bute, U.K.* 55°50N 5°3W **167** F3
Rothneusiedl *Austria* 48°8N 16°23E **142** B2
Rothschwaige *Germany* 48°14N 11°27E **131** A1
Roti *Indonesia* 10°50S 123°0E **231** F6
Rotja, Pta. *Spain* 38°38N 1°35E **206** D2
Rotnes *Norway* 60°3N 10°51E **164** D7
Roto *Australia* 33°0S 145°30E **283** B6
Rotoaira, L. *N.Z.* 39°3S 175°45E **284** F4
Rotoehu, L. *N.Z.* 38°1S 176°32E **284** E5
Rotoiti, L. *Bay of Plenty, N.Z.* 38°2S 176°26E **284** E5
Rotoiti, L. *W. Coast, N.Z.* 41°51S 172°49E **285** B7
Rotoma, L. *N.Z.* 38°2S 176°35E **284** E5
Rotondo, Mte. *France* 42°14N 9°8E **175** F13
Rotoroa, L. *N.Z.* 41°55S 172°39E **285** B7
Rotorua *N.Z.* 38°9S 176°16E **284** E5
Rotorua, L. *N.Z.* 38°5S 176°18E **284** E5
Rott ➔ *Germany* 48°27N 13°25E **179** G9
Rottenburg *Germany* 48°28N 8°55E **179** G4
Rottenmann *Austria* 47°31N 14°22E **180** D7
Rotterdam *Neths.* 51°55N 4°30E **170** C4
Rotterdam *N.Y., U.S.A.* 42°48N 74°1W **313** D10
Rottne *Sweden* 57°1N 14°54E **163** G8
Rottnest I. *Australia* 32°0S 115°27E **279** F2
Rottumeroog *Neths.* 53°33N 6°34E **170** A6
Rottweil *Germany* 48°9N 8°37E **179** G4
Rotuma *Fiji* 12°25S 177°5E **277** C14
Roubaix *France* 50°40N 3°10E **173** B10
Roudnice nad Labem *Czech Rep.* 50°25N 14°15E **180** A7
Rouen *France* 49°27N 1°4E **172** C8
Rouergue *France* 44°15N 2°0E **174** D5
Rouge Hill *Canada* 43°48N 79°6W **141** A4
Rough Ridge *N.Z.* 45°10S 169°55E **285** F4
Rouillac *France* 45°47N 0°4W **174** C3
Rouissat *Algeria* 31°55N 5°20E **261** B6
Rouleau *Canada* 50°10N 104°56W **297** C8
Roulers = Roeselare *Belgium* 50°57N 3°7E **170** D3
Roulpmaulpma ☼ *Australia* 23°52S 133°0E **278** D5
Round Hill *Jamaica* 17°50N 77°23W **320** a
Round Hill *St. Kitts & Nevis* 17°11N 62°36W **322** d
Round I. *China* 22°13N 114°11E **122** B2
Round Mountain *U.S.A.* 38°43N 117°4W **304** G5
Round Mt. *Australia* 30°26S 152°16E **283** A10
Round Rock *U.S.A.* 30°31N 97°41W **314** F6
Roundhouse Park *Toronto, Canada* **141** c2
Roundup *U.S.A.* 46°27N 108°33W **304** C9
Roura *Fr. Guiana* 4°44N 52°20W **329** C7
Rousay *U.K.* 59°10N 3°2W **167** B5
Rouses Point *U.S.A.* 44°59N 73°22W **313** B11
Rouseville *U.S.A.* 41°28N 79°42W **312** E5
Rousse = Ruse *Bulgaria* 43°48N 25°59E **203** C9
Roussenski Lom △ *Bulgaria* 43°40N 26°10E **203** C10
Roussillac Swamp *Trin. & Tob.* 10°14N 61°35W **323** t
Roussillon *Isère, France* 45°24N 4°49E **175** C8
Roussillon *Pyrénées-Or., France* 42°30N 2°35E **174** F6
Rouxville *S. Africa* 30°25S 26°50E **270** D4
Rouyn-Noranda *Canada* 48°20N 79°0W **298** C4
Rovaniemi *Finland* 66°29N 25°41E **160** C21
Rovato *Italy* 45°34N 10°0E **198** C7
Rovenki *Ukraine* 48°5N 39°21E **189** H10
Rovereto *Italy* 45°53N 11°3E **198** C8
Roverud *Norway* 60°15N 12°3E **164** D9
Rovigno = Rovinj *Croatia* 45°5N 13°40E **199** C10
Rovigo *Italy* 45°4N 11°47E **199** C8
Rovinj *Croatia* 45°5N 13°40E **199** C10
Rovira *Colombia* 4°15N 75°20W **328** C3
Rovno = Rivne *Ukraine* 50°40N 26°10E **177** C14
Rovnoye *Russia* 50°52N 46°3E **190** E8
Rovuma = Ruvuma ➔ *Tanzania* 10°29S 40°28E **269** E5
Row'ān *Iran* 35°8N 48°51E **247** C6
Rowena *Australia* 29°48S 148°55E **281** D4
Rowley I. *Canada* 69°6N 77°52W **295** D16
Rowley Shoals *Australia* 17°30S 119°0E **278** C2
Roxa *Guinea-Biss.* 11°15N 15°45W **262** C1
Roxas *Capiz, Phil.* 11°36N 122°49E **233** F4
Roxas *Isabela, Phil.* 17°8N 121°36E **232** C3
Roxas *Mind. Or., Phil.* 12°35N 121°31E **232** E3
Roxas *Palawan, Phil.* 10°20N 119°21E **233** F2
Roxboro *U.S.A.* 36°24N 78°59W **315** C15
Roxborough *Trin. & Tob.* 11°15N 60°35W **323** s
Roxburgh *N.Z.* 45°33S 169°19E **285** F4
Roxbury *Mass., U.S.A.* 42°19N 71°5W **116** B2
Roxbury *N.Y., U.S.A.* 42°17N 74°33W **313** D10
Roxbury *Pa., U.S.A.* 40°6N 77°39W **312** F7
Roxby Downs *Australia* 30°43S 136°46E **281** E2
Roxen *Sweden* 58°30N 15°40E **163** F9
Roxeth *U.K.* 51°33N 0°20W **125** A1
Roy *Mont., U.S.A.* 47°20N 108°58W **304** C9
Roy *N. Mex., U.S.A.* 35°57N 104°12W **305** J11
Roy *Utah, U.S.A.* 41°10N 112°2W **304** F7
Roy Thomson Hall *Toronto, Canada* **141** b2
Royal △ *Australia* 34°5S 151°5E **283** C9
Royal Bardia △ *Nepal* 28°20N 81°20E **243** E9
Royal Botanic Gardens *Sydney, Australia* **139** b2
Royal Botanic Gardens *Edinburgh, U.K.* 55°58N 3°12W **121** B2
Royal Canal *Ireland* 53°30N 7°13W **166** C4
Royal Center *U.S.A.* 40°52N 86°30W **311** D10
Royal Chitawan △ *Nepal* 26°30N 84°30E **243** F11
Royal Geographical Society Is. *Canada* 68°56N 100°15W **294** D11
Royal Leamington Spa *U.K.* 52°18N 1°31W **169** E6
Royal Manas △ *Bhutan* 26°45N 90°50E **241** B3
Royal Natal △ *S. Africa* 28°43S 28°51E **271** C4
Royal Oak *U.S.A.* 42°30N 83°9W **311** B13
Royal Observatory *U.K.* 55°55N 3°12W **121** B2
Royal Palace = Koninklijk Paleis *Amsterdam, Neths.* **112** a2
Royal Palace = Kungliga Slottet *Stockholm, Sweden* **139** b2
Royal Palace = Palacio Real *Madrid, Spain* **127** b1
Royal Palace = Palais Royal *Brussels, Belgium* **116** b3
Royal Palace = Slottet *Oslo, Norway* **133** a1
Royal Palm Beach *U.S.A.* 26°42N 80°14W **317** J9
Royal Park *Australia* 37°46S 144°57E **128** A1
Royal Tunbridge Wells *U.K.* 51°7N 0°16E **169** F8
Royal Turf Club *Bangkok, Thailand* **113** b2
Royale, Isle *U.S.A.* 48°0N 88°54W **308** B9
Royalla *Australia* 35°30S 149°9E **283** C8
Royan *France* 45°37N 1°2W **174** C2
Roye *France* 49°42N 2°48E **173** C9
Röylä *Finland* 60°18N 24°42E **121** B1
Royston *U.K.* 52°3N 0°0 **169** E7
Rožaj *Montenegro* 42°50N 20°11E **202** D4
Różan *Poland* 52°52N 21°25E **185** F8
Rozas, Portilleros de las *Spain* 40°29N 3°49W **127** B1
Rozay-en-Brie *France* 48°41N 2°58E **173** D9
Rozdilna *Ukraine* 46°50N 30°2E **183** D15
Rozhnyativ *Ukraine* 48°56N 24°9E **183** B9
Rozhyshche *Ukraine* 50°54N 25°15E **177** C13
Rožmitál pod Třemšínem *Czech Rep.* 49°36N 13°53E **180** B6
Rožňava *Slovak Rep.* 48°37N 20°35E **181** C13
Rozogi *Poland* 53°28N 21°19E **184** E8
Rozoy-sur-Serre *France* 49°40N 4°8E **173** C11
Roztoczański △ *Poland* 50°37N 23°5E **185** H10
Roztoky *Czech Rep.* 50°9N 14°23E **135** B2
Rozzano *Italy* 45°22N 9°10E **129** B1
Rrëshen *Albania* 41°47N 19°49E **202** E3
Rrogozhine *Albania* 41°4N 19°50E **202** E3
Rtanj *Serbia* 43°45N 21°50E **202** C5
Rtem, O. er ➔ *Algeria* 33°29N 5°38E **261** B6
Rtishchevo *Russia* 52°18N 43°46E **190** D6
Rúa = A Rúa *Spain* 42°24N 7°6W **194** C3
Ruacaná *Namibia* 17°27S 14°21E **265** F2
Ruaha △ *Tanzania* 7°41S 34°30E **268** D3
Ruahine Ra. *N.Z.* 39°55S 176°2E **284** F5
Ruamahanga ➔ *N.Z.* 41°24S 175°8E **284** H4
Ruapehu *N.Z.* 39°17S 175°35E **284** F4
Ruapuke I. *N.Z.* 46°46S 168°31E **285** G3
Ruâq, W. ➔ *Egypt* 30°0N 33°49E **251** J4
Ruatoria *N.Z.* 37°55S 178°20E **284** D7
Ruavatu *Solomon Is.* 9°26S 160°26E **287** M11
Ruawai *N.Z.* 36°8S 173°59E **284** C2
Rub' al Khālī *Si. Arabia* 19°0N 48°0E **249** C5
Rubeho Mts. *Tanzania* 6°50S 36°25E **268** D4
Rubezhnoe = Rubizhne *Ukraine* 49°6N 38°25E **189** H10
Rubh a' Mhail *U.K.* 55°56N 6°8W **167** F2
Rubha Hunish *U.K.* 57°42N 6°20W **167** D2
Rubha Robhanais = Lewis, Butt of *U.K.* 58°31N 6°16W **167** C2
Rubí *Spain* 41°29N 2°2E **196** D7
Rubi ➔ *Dem. Rep. of the Congo* 2°48N 23°54E **264** B4
Rubí ➔ *Barcelona, Spain* 41°26N 2°0E **114** A1
Rubiataba *Brazil* 15°8S 49°48W **333** E2
Rubicon ➔ *U.S.A.* 38°53N 121°4W **306** G5
Rubicone ➔ *Italy* 44°8N 12°28E **199** D9
Rubik *Albania* 41°46N 19°47E **202** E3
Rubinéia *Brazil* 20°13S 51°2W **333** F1
Rubino *Ivory C.* 6°4N 4°18W **262** D4
Rubio *Venezuela* 7°43N 72°22W **328** B3
Rubizhne *Ukraine* 49°6N 38°25E **189** H10
Rublovo *Russia* 55°47N 37°21E **129** B2
Rubondo △ *Tanzania* 2°18S 31°58E **268** C3
Rubtsovsk *Russia* 51°30N 81°10E **217** B10
Ruby *U.S.A.* 64°45N 155°30W **303** D9
Ruby Beach = Jacksonville Beach *U.S.A.* 30°17N 81°24W **316** E8
Ruby L. *U.S.A.* 40°10N 115°28W **304** F6
Ruby Mts. *U.S.A.* 40°30N 115°20W **304** F6
Rubyvale *Australia* 23°25S 147°42E **280** C4
Rucheng *China* 25°33N 113°38E **229** E9
Ruciane-Nida *Poland* 53°40N 21°32E **184** E8
Rūd Sar *Iran* 37°8N 50°18E **247** B6
Ruda *Sweden* 57°6N 16°7E **163** G10
Ruda Śląska *Poland* 50°16N 18°50E **185** H5
Rudall *Australia* 33°43S 136°17E **282** B2
Rudall ➔ *Australia* 22°34S 122°13E **278** D3
Rudall River △ *Australia* 22°38S 122°30E **278** D3
Rūdbār *Afghan.* 30°9N 62°36E **240** C1
Rūdbār *Iran* 36°48N 49°23E **247** B6
Rüdersdorf *Germany* 52°27N 13°47E **178** C9
Rudewa *Tanzania* 10°7S 34°40E **269** E3
Rudkøbing *Denmark* 54°56N 10°41E **163** K4
Rudky *Ukraine* 49°38N 23°29E **185** J10
Rudna *Poland* 51°30N 16°17E **185** G3
Rudnevka ➔ *Russia* 55°43N 37°56E **129** B3
Rudnik *Bulgaria* 42°36N 27°30E **203** D11
Rudnik *Poland* 50°26N 22°15E **185** H9
Rudnik *Serbia* 44°7N 20°35E **202** B4
Rudnya *Russia* 54°55N 31°7E **188** E6
Rudnytsa *Ukraine* 48°16N 28°54E **183** B13
Rudnyy *Kazakhstan* 52°57N 63°7E **216** B6
Rudo *Bos.-H.* 43°41N 19°23E **182** G4
Rudolfa, Ostrov *Russia* 81°45N 58°30E **214** A6
Rudolfsheim *Austria* 48°12N 16°20E **142** A2
Rudolfshöhe *Germany* 52°37N 13°34E **115** A5
Rudolstadt *Germany* 50°44N 11°19E **178** E7
Rudong *China* 32°20N 121°12E **229** A13
Rudow *Germany* 52°24N 13°29E **115** B3
Rudozem *Bulgaria* 41°29N 24°51E **203** E8
Rudyard *U.S.A.* 46°14N 84°36W **309** B11
Rue *France* 50°15N 1°40E **173** B8
Rueil-Malmaison *France* 48°52N 2°11E **134** A2
Ruenya ➔ *Africa* 16°24S 33°48E **269** F3
Rufa'a *Sudan* 14°44N 33°22E **257** E3
Rufflin *U.S.A.* 33°0N 80°49W **316** B9
Ruffling Pt. *Br. Virgin Is.* 18°44N 64°27W **321** b
Rufiji ➔ *Tanzania* 7°50S 39°15E **268** D4
Rufino *Argentina* 34°20S 62°50W **334** C3
Rufisque *Senegal* 14°40N 17°15W **262** C1
Rufunsa *Zambia* 15°4S 29°34E **269** F2
Rugao *China* 32°23N 120°31E **229** A13
Rugby *Warks., U.K.* 52°23N 1°16W **169** E6
Rugby *N. Dak., U.S.A.* 48°22N 100°0W **308** A4
Rügen *Germany* 54°22N 13°24E **178** A9
Rügen ⌓ *Germany* 54°25N 13°25E **178** A9
Rugles *France* 48°50N 0°40E **172** D7
Ruhea *Bangla.* 26°10N 88°25E **241** B2
Ruhengeri *Rwanda* 1°30S 29°36E **268** C2
Ruhla *Germany* 50°54N 10°23E **178** E6
Ruhland *Germany* 51°27N 13°51E **178** D9
Ruhnu *Estonia* 57°48N 23°15E **184** A10
Ruhr ➔ *Germany* 51°27N 6°43E **178** D2
Ruhuhu ➔ *Tanzania* 10°31S 34°34E **269** E3
Rui Barbosa *Brazil* 12°18S 40°27W **333** D3
Rui'an *China* 27°47N 120°40E **229** D13
Ruichang *China* 29°40N 115°39E **229** C10
Ruidoso *U.S.A.* 33°20N 105°41W **305** K11
Ruijin *China* 25°48N 116°0E **229** E10
Ruili *China* 24°1N 97°43E **228** E1
Ruisbroek *Belgium* 50°47N 4°18E **116** B1
Ruislip *U.K.* 51°34N 0°24W **125** A1
Ruivo, Pico *Madeira* 32°45N 16°56W **153** c
Ruj *Bulgaria* 42°52N 22°34E **202** D6
Rujen *Macedonia* 42°9N 22°30E **202** D6
Rujm Tal'at al Jamā'ah *Jordan* 30°24N 35°30E **251** H6
Ruk *Pakistan* 27°50N 68°42E **242** F3
Rukan-sho *Japan* 26°6N 127°32E **288** a
Rukhla *Pakistan* 32°27N 71°57E **242** C4
Rukwa □ *Tanzania* 7°0S 31°30E **268** D3
Rukwa, L. *Tanzania* 8°0S 32°20E **268** D3
Rulenge *Burundi* 2°43S 30°37E **268** C3
Rulhieres, C. *Australia* 13°56S 127°22E **278** B4
Rum = Rhum *U.K.* 57°0N 6°20W **167** E2
Rum *Jordan* 29°39N 35°26E **251** J6
Rum Cay *Bahamas* 23°40N 74°58W **321** B5
Rum Jungle *Australia* 13°0S 130°59E **278** B5
Ruma *Serbia* 45°0N 19°50E **182** E4
Ruma △ *Kenya* 0°39S 34°18E **268** C3
Rumāḩ *Si. Arabia* 25°29N 47°10E **246** E5
Rumania = Romania ■ *Europe* 46°0N 25°0E **183** D10
Rumaylah *Iraq* 30°47N 47°37E **246** D5
Rumaylah, 'Urūq ar *Si. Arabia* 22°0N 48°30E **249** B5
Rumbêk *Sudan* 6°54N 29°37E **257** F2
Rumburk *Czech Rep.* 50°57N 14°32E **180** A7
Rumelihisarı *Turkey* 41°4N 29°2E **122** B2
Rumford *U.S.A.* 44°33N 70°33W **313** B14
Rumia *Poland* 54°37N 18°25E **184** D5
Rumilly *France* 45°53N 5°56E **175** C9
Rummelsburg = Miastko *Poland* 54°0N 16°58E **184** E3
Rumoi *Japan* 43°56N 141°39E **220** C10
Rumonge *Burundi* 3°59S 29°26E **268** C2
Rumphi *Malaysia* 11°1S 33°52E **269** E3
Rumson *U.S.A.* 40°23N 74°0W **313** F11
Rumung *Micronesia* 9°37N 138°9E **287** R16
Rumuruti *Kenya* 0°17N 36°32E **268** B4
Rumyantsevo *Russia* 55°38N 37°25E **129** C2
Runan *China* 33°0N 114°30E **226** H8
Runanga *N.Z.* 42°25S 171°15E **285** C6
Runaway, C. *N.Z.* 37°32S 177°59E **284** D6
Runaway B. *Antigua & B.* 17°9N 61°51W **322** b
Runaway Bay *Jamaica* 18°27N 77°20W **320** a
Runcorn *U.K.* 53°21N 2°44W **168** D5
Rundu *Namibia* 17°52S 19°43E **270** A2
Rungis *France* 48°44N 2°20E **134** B3
Rungwa *Tanzania* 6°55S 33°32E **268** D3
Rungwa ➔ *Tanzania* 7°36S 31°50E **268** D3
Rungwa ⌓ *Tanzania* 6°53S 34°2E **268** D3
Rungwe *Tanzania* 9°11S 33°32E **269** D3
Runka *Nigeria* 12°28N 7°20E **263** C6
Runn *Sweden* 60°30N 15°40E **162** D9
Runton Ra. *Australia* 23°31S 123°6E **278** D3
Runu *Micronesia* 9°35N 138°8E **287** R16
Ruo Shui ➔ *China* 41°0N 100°16E **218** B5
Ruokolahti *Finland* 61°17N 28°50E **188** B5
Ruoqiang *China* 38°55N 88°10E **217** E11
Rupa *India* 27°15N 92°21E **241** B4
Rupar *India* 31°2N 76°38E **242** D7
Rupat *Indonesia* 1°45N 101°40E **234** B2
Rupea *Romania* 46°2N 25°13E **183** D10
Rupen ➔ *India* 23°28N 71°31E **242** H4

Rupert *U.S.A.* 42°37N 113°41W **304** E7
Rupert → *Canada* 51°29N 78°45W **298** B4
Rupert B. *Canada* 51°35N 79°00W **298** B4
Rupert House = Waskaganish
   Canada 51°30N 78°40W **298** B4
Rupsa *India* 21°37N 87°1E **243** J12
Rupununi → *Guyana* 4°0N 58°30W **324** C7
Rur → *Germany* 51°11N 5°59E **178** D1
Rurópolis *Brazil* 4°3S 54°59W **329** D7
Rurrenabaque *Bolivia* 14°30S 67°32W **330** C4
Rururtu *French Polynesia* 22°26S 151°20W **289** f
Rus → *Spain* 39°30N 3°24W **197** F2
Rusăfa *Iraq* 33°21N 44°23E **113** A2
Rusambo *Zimbabwe* 16°30S 32°4E **269** F3
Rusape *Zimbabwe* 18°35S 32°8E **269** F3
Ruschuk = Ruse *Bulgaria* 43°48N 25°59E **203** C9
Ruse *Bulgaria* 43°48N 25°59E **203** C9
Ruse □ *Bulgaria* 43°35N 26°20E **203** C10
Ruşeţu *Romania* 44°57N 27°14E **183** F12
Rush *Ireland* 53°31N 6°6W **166** C5
Rush Green *U.K.* 51°33N 0°10E **125** A5
Rushan *China* 36°56N 121°30E **227** F11
Rushden *U.K.* 52°18N 0°35W **169** E7
Rushikulya → *India* 19°23N 85°5E **244** E7
Rushmore, Mt. *U.S.A.* 43°53N 103°28W **308** D2
Rushville *Ill., U.S.A.* 40°7N 90°34W **310** D6
Rushville *Ind., U.S.A.* 39°37N 85°27W **311** E11
Rushville *Nebr., U.S.A.* 42°43N 102°28W **308** D2
Rushworth *Australia* 36°32S 145°1E **283** D6
Ruskin *U.S.A.* 27°43N 82°26W **317** H7
Russa *India* 22°29N 88°21E **124** C2
Russas *Brazil* 4°55S 37°50W **332** B4
Russell *Man., Canada* 50°50N 101°20W **297** C8
Russell *N.Z.* 35°16S 174°10E **284** B3
Russell *Fla., U.S.A.* 30°3N 81°45N **316** A5
Russell *Kans., U.S.A.* 38°54N 98°52W **308** F4
Russell *N.Y., U.S.A.* 44°27N 75°9W **313** B9
Russell *Pa., U.S.A.* 41°56N 79°8W **312** E5
Russell Cave △ *U.S.A.* 34°59N 85°49W **315** D12
Russell Is. *Solomon Is.* 9°4S 159°12E **287** M10
Russell L. *Man., Canada* 56°15N 101°30W **297** B8
Russell L. *N.W.T., Canada* 63°5N 115°44W **296** A5
Russellkonda *India* 19°57N 84°42E **244** E7
Russells Point *U.S.A.* 40°28N 83°54W **311** D13
Russellville *Ala., U.S.A.* 34°30N 87°44W **315** D11
Russellville *Ark., U.S.A.* 35°17N 93°8W **314** D8
Russellville *Ky., U.S.A.* 36°51N 86°53W **308** G10
Rüsselsheim *Germany* 49°59N 8°23E **179** F4
Russi *Italy* 44°22N 12°2E **199** D9
Russia ■ *Eurasia* 62°0N 105°0E **215** C11
Russian → *U.S.A.* 38°27N 123°8W **306** G3
Russian Hill *San Francisco, U.S.A.* **136** a1
Russian Mission *U.S.A.* 61°47N 161°19W **303** F7
Russiaville *U.S.A.* 40°25N 86°16W **311** D10
Rust *Austria* 47°49N 16°42E **181** D9
Rustam Shahr *Pakistan* 26°58N 66°6E **242** F2
Rustavi *Georgia* 41°30N 45°0E **191** K7
Rustenburg *S. Africa* 25°41S 27°14E **270** C4
Ruston *U.S.A.* 32°32N 92°38W **314** E8
Rutana *Burundi* 3°55S 30°0E **268** C3
Rute *Spain* 37°19N 4°23W **195** H6
Ruteng *Indonesia* 8°35S 120°30E **231** F6
Rutenga *Zimbabwe* 21°15S 30°44E **269** C5
Ruth *U.S.A.* 43°42N 82°45W **312** C2
Rutherford *Calif., U.S.A.* 38°26N 122°24W **306** G4
Rutherford *N.J., U.S.A.* 40°49N 74°6W **137** A10
Rutherglen *Australia* 36°5S 146°29E **283** D7
Rutland *U.K.* 52°38N 0°40W **169** E7
Rutland □ *U.K.* 52°38N 0°40W **169** E7
Rutland I. *India* 11°25N 92°10E **245** J11
Rutland Water *U.K.* 52°39N 0°38W **169** E7
Rutledal *Norway* 61°4N 5°10E **164** C2
Rutledge → *Canada* 33°38N 83°37W **316** B6
Rutledge → *Canada* 61°4N 112°0W **297** A6
Rutledge L. *Canada* 61°33N 110°47W **297** A6
Rutog *China* 33°27N 79°42E **217** F9
Rutqa → *Syria* 34°30N 41°3E **113** B4
Rutshuru
   Dem. Rep. of the Congo 1°13S 29°25E **268** C2
Ruvo di Púglia *Italy* 41°7N 16°29E **201** A9
Ruvu *Tanzania* 6°49S 38°43E **268** D4
Ruvu → *Tanzania* 6°23S 38°52E **268** D4
Ruvuba △ *Burundi* 3°3S 29°33E **268** C2
Ruvuma □ *Tanzania* 10°20S 36°0E **269** E4
Ruvuma → *Tanzania* 10°29S 40°28E **269** E5
Ruwais *U.A.E.* 24°5N 52°50E **247** E7
Ruwenzori *Africa* 0°30N 29°55E **268** B2
Ruwenzori △ *Uganda* 0°20N 30°0E **268** B2
Ruya → *Zimbabwe* 16°27S 32°5E **271** A5
Ruyigi *Burundi* 3°29S 30°15E **268** C3
Ruyuan *China* 24°46N 113°16E **229** E9
Rūzaevka *Kazakhstan* 52°49N 66°56E **217** D7
Ruzayevka *Russia* 54°4N 45°0E **190** C7
Ružhevo Konare
   Bulgaria 42°23N 24°46E **203** D8
Ružomberok *Slovak Rep.* 49°3N 19°17E **181** B12
Ruzyně, Praha ✈ (PRG)
   Czech Rep. 50°6N 14°16E **135** B1
Rwanda ■ *Africa* 2°0S 30°0E **268** C3
Ryakhovo *Bulgaria* 43°58N 26°18E **203** C10
Ryan, L. *U.K.* 55°0N 5°2W **167** G3
Ryazan *Russia* 54°40N 39°40E **188** E10
Ryazan *Russia* 54°5N 39°30E **190** C4
Ryazhsk *Russia* 53°45N 40°3E **188** F11
Rybachiy *Russia* 55°10N 20°50E **184** C7
Rybachiy Poluostrov
   Russia 69°43N 32°0E **160** B25
Rybachye = Balykchy
   Kyrgyzstan 42°26N 76°12E **217** D9
Rybatskaya *Russia* 59°59N 30°29E **137** B2
Rybinsk *Russia* 58°5N 38°50E **188** C10
Rybinskoye Vdkhr.
   Russia 58°30N 38°25E **188** C10
Rybnik *Poland* 50°6N 18°32E **185** H6
Rybnitsa = Râbnița
   Moldova 47°45N 29°0E **183** C14
Rybnoye *Russia* 54°45N 39°30E **188** E10
Rychnov nad Kněžnou
   Czech Rep. 50°10N 16°17E **181** A9
Rychwal *Poland* 52°4N 18°10E **185** F5
Rycroft *Canada* 55°45N 118°40W **296** B5
Ryd *Sweden* 56°27N 14°42E **163** H8
Rydaholm *Sweden* 56°59N 14°18E **163** H8
Rydboholm *Sweden* 59°26N 18°12E **139** A3
Ryde *N.S.W., Australia* 33°48S 151°6E **139** A1
Ryde *I. of W., U.K.* 50°43N 1°9W **169** G6
Ryderwood *U.S.A.* 46°20N 123°3W **306** D2
Rydzyna *Poland* 51°47N 16°39E **185** G3
Rye *U.K.* 50°57N 0°45E **168** G5
Rye → *U.K.* 54°11N 0°44W **168** C7
Rye Bay *U.K.* 50°52N 0°49E **169** G8
Rye Patch Res. *U.S.A.* 40°28N 118°19W **304** C9
Ryegate *U.S.A.* 46°18N 109°15W **304** C9
Ryerson University *Toronto, Canada* **141** a3
Ryfylke *Norway* 59°25N 6°25E **164** E3
Rykene *Norway* 58°24N 8°37E **164** F5
Ryki *Poland* 51°38N 21°56E **185** G8
Rykovo = Yenakiyeve
   Ukraine 48°15N 38°15E **189** H10
Ryley *Canada* 53°17N 112°26W **296** C6
Rylsk *Russia* 51°36N 34°43E **189** G8
Rylstone *Australia* 32°46S 149°58E **283** B8
Rymanów *Poland* 49°35N 21°51E **185** J8
Ryn *Poland* 53°57N 21°34E **184** E8
Ryn Peski = Naryn Qum
   Kazakhstan 47°30N 49°0E **191** G9

S

Sa *Thailand* 18°34N 100°45E **236** C3
Sa Cabaneta *Spain* 39°37N 2°45E **206** B3
Sa Canal *Spain* 38°51N 1°23E **206** D1
Sa Conillera *Spain* 38°59N 1°13E **206** D1
Sa Dec *Vietnam* 10°20N 105°46E **237** G5
Sa Dragonera *Spain* 39°35N 2°19E **206** B3
Sa Kaeo *Thailand* 13°49N 102°4E **236** F4
Sa-koi *Burma* 19°54N 97°3E **241** F6
Sa Mesquida *Spain* 39°55N 4°16E **206** B5
Sa Pa *Vietnam* 22°20N 103°47E **236** A4
Sa Pobla *Spain* 39°46N 3°1E **206** B4
Sa Savina *Spain* 38°44N 1°25E **206** D1
Sa'a *Solomon Is.* 9°43S 161°35E **287** M11
Saʿādah *Iraq* 33°19N 44°25E **113** B2
Sádaba *Spain* 42°19N 1°12W **196** C2
Sadabad *India* 27°27N 78°3E **242** F8
Sa'ad Yemen 16°15N 43°37E **248** D3
Sadang *S. Korea* 37°29N 126°58E **137** C1
Sadani *Tanzania* 5°58S 38°35E **268** D4
Sadani → *Tanzania* 6°3S 38°47E **268** D4
Sadao *Thailand* 6°38N 100°26E **237** J3
Sadar Bazar *Delhi, India* **120** a1
Sadaseopet *India* 17°38N 77°59E **244** F3
Sadd el Aali *Egypt* 23°54N 32°54E **256** C3
Saddle → *U.S.A.* 40°51N 74°5W **132** A1
Saddle Brook *U.S.A.* 40°53N 74°5W **132** A1
Saddle Hill *St. Kitts & Nevis* 17°7N 62°33W **322** d
Saddle Mt. *U.S.A.* 45°58N 123°41W **306** E3
Saddle Pk. *India* 13°9N 93°1E **245** H11
Saddle Pt. *St. Helena* 15°57S 5°38W **153** h
Sade *Nigeria* 11°22N 10°45E **263** C7
Şadh *Oman* 17°3N 55°4E **249** C6
Sadhoowa *Trin. & Tob.* 10°8N 61°27W **323** l
Sadimi
   Dem. Rep. of the Congo 9°25S 23°32E **265** D4
Sadiola *Mali* 13°50N 11°40W **262** C2
Sadiya *India* 27°50N 95°40E **241** B5
Sa'diyah, Hawr as *Iraq* 32°15N 46°20E **213** F12
Sadlers *St. Kitts & Nevis* 17°24N 62°47W **322** d
Sado *Japan* 38°0N 138°25E **222** E9
Sado → *Portugal* 38°29N 8°55W **195** G2
Sadon *Russia* 42°52N 43°58E **191** J6
Sadovoye *Russia* 47°47N 44°31E **191** G7
Sadowara *Japan* 32°2N 131°26E **222** G5
Sadr *Pakistan* 24°51N 67°2E **123** A2
Sadr City *Iraq* 33°23N 44°30E **124** B2
Sadra *India* 23°21N 72°43E **242** H5
Sadri *India* 25°11N 73°26E **242** G5
Sadrinsk *Russia* 56°26N 63°40W **217** C6 ... Sadybo *Poland* 52°11N 21°3E **142** B2
Sæbøvik *Norway* 59°47N 5°46E **164** E2
Sæby *Denmark* 57°21N 10°30E **163** G4
Saegertown *U.S.A.* 41°43N 80°9W **312** E4
Saelices *Spain* 39°55N 2°49W **196** F2
Sætre *Norway* 59°41N 10°33E **164** E7
Sævareid *Norway* 60°11N 5°46E **164** D2
Safaalan *Turkey* 41°26N 28°6E **203** E12
Safaga *Egypt* 26°42N 34°0E **256** B3
Şafājah *Si. Arabia* 26°25N 39°0E **246** E3
Safárikovo = Tornaľa
   Slovak Rep. 48°25N 20°20E **181** C13
Safata B. *Samoa* 14°0S 171°50W **287** W20
Safdar Jang's Tomb *India* 28°35N 77°12E **120** B2
Säffle *Sweden* 59°8N 12°55E **162** G6
Safford *U.S.A.* 32°50N 109°43W **305** K9
Saffron Walden *U.K.* 52°1N 0°16E **169** E8
Safi *Morocco* 32°18N 9°20W **260** B3
Safi □ *Morocco* 32°10N 8°50W **260** B3
Safia *Papua N. G.* 9°35S 148°38E **286** C5
Safia, Hamada *Mali* 23°10N 4°15W **260** D4
Şafiābād *Iran* 36°45N 57°58E **247** B8
Safid Dasht *Iran* 33°27N 48°11E **247** C6
Safid Kūh *Afghan.* 34°45N 63°0E **240** B3
Safid Rūd → *Iran* 37°23N 50°11E **247** B6
Safipur *India* 26°44N 80°21E **243** F9
Şāfītā *Syria* 34°48N 36°7E **250** D7
Safonovo *Russia* 55°4N 33°16E **188** D8
Safranbolu *Turkey* 41°15N 32°41E **212** B5
Saft el Laban *Egypt* 30°1N 31°10E **117** A2
Saft Rashin *Egypt* 28°58N 30°53E **256** J7
Safune *Samoa* 13°25S 172°21W **287** V19
Safwan *Iraq* 30°7N 47°43E **246** D5
Sag Sag *Papua N. G.* 5°32S 148°23E **286** C5
Saga *Kōchi, Japan* 33°5N 133°3E **222** D5
Saga *Saga, Japan* 33°15N 130°16E **222** D2
Saga □ *Japan* 33°15N 130°20E **222** D2
Sagae *Japan* 38°22N 140°17E **222** E10
Sagaing *Burma* 21°52N 95°59E **241** E5
Sagaing □ *Burma* 23°55N 95°56E **241** D5
Sagala *Mali* 14°9N 6°38W **262** C3
Sagami-Nada *Japan* 34°58N 139°30E **223** C11
Sagami-Wan *Japan* 35°15N 139°25E **223** B11
Sagamihara *Japan* 35°33N 139°25E **223** B11
Sagamore *U.S.A.* 40°46N 79°14W **312** F5
Sagan = Żagań *Poland* 51°39N 15°22E **185** G2
Saganaga L. *Canada* 48°14N 90°52W **308** A8
Saganashkee Slough
   U.S.A. 41°41N 87°53W **119** C1
Saganoseki *Japan* 33°15N 131°53E **222** D4
Sagar *Karnataka, India* 14°36N 76°48E **244** F3
Sagar *Karnataka, India* 14°14N 75°6E **245** G2
Sagar *Mad. P., India* 23°50N 78°44E **243** H8
Sagara *Japan* 34°41N 138°12E **223** C10
Sagara, L. *Tanzania* 5°20S 31°0E **268** D3
Sagarejo *Georgia* 41°44N 45°19E **191** K7
Sagarmatha = Everest, Mt.
   Nepal 28°5N 86°58E **243** F12
Sagarmatha △ *Nepal* 27°55N 86°45E **243** F12
Sagavanirktok →
   U.S.A. 70°19N 147°53W **303** A11
Sagay *Phil.* 10°57N 123°25E **233** F4
Şabyā *Si. Arabia* 17°9N 42°37E **248** D3
Sabzevār *Iran* 36°15N 57°40E **247** B8
Sabzi Mandi *India* 28°40N 77°12E **120** A2
Sabzvārān = Jiroft *Iran* 28°45N 57°50E **247** D8
Sac City *U.S.A.* 42°25N 95°0W **310** D3
Sacaoja *Angola* 12°58S 22°28E **265** D4
Sacatepeo *Angola* 13°16S 21°20E **265** D4
Sacavém *Portugal* 38°47N 9°5W **195** G1
Sacedón *Spain* 40°29N 2°41W **196** E2
Săcele *Romania* 45°37N 25°41E **183** E10
Sacheon *S. Korea* 35°0N 128°6E **224** E4
Sachigo → *Canada* 55°6N 88°58W **298** A2
Sachigo, L. *Canada* 53°50N 92°12W **298** B1
Sachimbo *Angola* 9°14S 20°16E **265** D4
Sachin *India* 21°5N 72°53E **244** D1
Sachkhere *Georgia* 42°25N 43°28E **191** J6
Sachsen □ *Germany* 50°55N 13°10E **178** E9
Sachsen-Anhalt □
   Germany 52°0N 12°0E **178** D7
Sächsische Schweiz △
   Germany 50°55N 14°10E **178** E10
Sacile *Italy* 45°57N 12°30E **199** C9
Sackets Harbor *U.S.A.* 43°57N 76°7W **313** C8
Sackville *Canada* 45°54N 64°22W **299** C7
Saclay *France* 48°43N 2°10E **134** B2
Saclay, Étang de *France* 48°44N 2°9E **134** B1
Saco *Maine, U.S.A.* 43°30N 70°27W **313** C14
Saco *Mont., U.S.A.* 48°28N 107°21W **304** B10
Sacomã *Brazil* 23°36S 46°35W **137** B2
Sacramento
   Brazil 0°37S 51°12W **329** D7
Sacramento *Brazil* 19°53S 47°27W **333** E2
Sacramento *Calif.,*
   U.S.A. 38°35N 121°29W **306** G5
Sacramento → *U.S.A.* 38°3N 121°56W **306** G5
Sacramento Mts.
   U.S.A. 32°30N 105°30W **305** K11
Sacramento Valley
   U.S.A. 39°30N 122°0W **306** G5
Sacratif, C. *Spain* 36°42N 3°28W **195** J7
Sacré Cœur *Paris, France* **134** a4
Sacrow *Germany* 52°25N 13°6E **115** B1
Sacrower See *Germany* 52°26N 13°6E **115** B1
Săcueni *Romania* 47°20N 22°5E **182** C7
Sada *Mayotte* 12°51S 45°6E **272** b
Sada *Spain* 43°22N 8°15W **194** B2
Sada-Misaki *Japan* 33°20N 132°5E **222** D4
Sada-Misaki-Hantō
   Japan 33°22N 132°1E **222** D4
Sádaba *Spain* 42°19N 1°12W **196** C2
Sadabad *India* 27°27N 78°3E **242** F8

St-Julien-de-Vouvantes France 47°38N 1°13W 172 E5
St-Julien-en-Genevois France 46°9N 6°5E 173 F13
St-Junien France 45°53N 0°55E 174 C4
St-Just-en-Chaussée France 49°30N 2°25E 173 C9
St-Just-en-Chevalet France 45°55N 3°50E 174 C7
St. Kilda Vic., Australia 37°51S 144°58E 128 B1
St. Kilda N.Z. 45°53S 170°31E 285 F5
St. Kilda W. Isles, U.K. 57°49N 8°34W 165 C2
St. Kitts W. Indies 17°20N 62°40W 322 d
St. Kitts & Nevis ■ W. Indies 17°20N 62°40W 322 d
St-Lambert Qué., Canada 45°30N 73°29W 130 A3
St-Lambert Yvelines, France 48°43N 2°1E 134 B1
St. Laurent Canada 50°25N 97°58W 297 C9
St-Laurent Canada 45°30N 73°43W 130 A1
St-Laurent-de-la-Salanque France 42°46N 2°59E 174 F6
St-Laurent du Maroni Fr. Guiana 5°29N 54°3W 329 B7
St-Laurent-du-Pont France 45°23N 5°45E 175 C9
St-Laurent-en-Grandvaux France 46°35N 5°58E 173 F12
St-Laurent-Médoc France 45°8N 0°49W 174 C3
St. Lawrence Queens., Australia 22°16S 149°31E 280 C4
St. Lawrence Nfld. & L., Canada 46°54N 55°23W 299 C8
St. Lawrence → Canada 49°30N 66°0W 299 C6
St. Lawrence, Gulf of Canada 48°25N 62°0W 299 C7
St. Lawrence I. U.S.A. 63°30N 170°30W 303 E5
St. Lawrence Islands △ Canada 44°27N 75°52W 313 B9
St. Lawrence Market Toronto, Canada 141 b3
St-Lazare, Gare Paris, France 134 a3
St. Léonard Canada 47°12N 67°58W 299 C6
St-Léonard Canada 45°35N 73°34W 130 A2
St-Léonard-de-Noblat France 45°49N 1°29E 174 C5
St-Leu Réunion 21°9S 55°18E 272 f
St. Lewis → Canada 52°26N 56°11W 299 B8
St-Lô France 49°7N 1°5W 172 C5
St-Louis Montréal, Canada 130 b2
St-Louis Haut-Rhin, France 47°30N 7°34E 173 E14
St-Louis Guadeloupe 15°56N 61°19W 322 e
St-Louis Réunion 21°16S 55°25E 272 f
St. Louis Senegal 16°8N 16°27W 262 B1
St. Louis Mo., U.S.A. 38°37N 90°11W 310 F6
St. Louis ☐ Senegal 16°20N 15°0W 262 B2
St. Louis → U.S.A. 46°44N 92°9W 308 B7
St. Louis Lambert Int. ✕ (STL) U.S.A. 38°45N 90°22W 310 F6
St-Loup-sur-Semouse France 47°53N 6°16E 173 E13
St-Luc Canada 45°22N 73°18W 313 A11
St. Lucia ■ W. Indies 14°0N 60°57W 323 m
St. Lucia, L. S. Africa 28°5S 32°30E 271 C5
St. Lucia Channel W. Indies 14°15N 61°0W 321 D7
St. Lucie U.S.A. 27°29N 80°20W 317 H9
St. Lucie Canal U.S.A. 27°10N 80°18W 317 H9
St. Maarten ☒ W. Indies 18°0N 63°5W 322 a
St. Magelungen Sweden 59°13N 18°4E 139 B2
St. Magnus B. U.K. 60°25N 1°35W 167 A7
St-Maixent-l'École France 46°24N 0°12W 174 B3
St-Malo France 48°39N 2°1W 172 D4
St-Malo, G. de France 48°50N 2°30W 172 D4
St-Mandé France 48°50N 2°24E 134 A3
St-Mandrier-sur-Mer France 43°4N 5°57E 175 E9
St-Marc Haiti 19°10N 72°41W 321 C5
St-Marcellin France 45°9N 5°20E 175 C9
St-Marcouf, Îs. France 49°30N 1°10W 172 C5
St. Margaret's Ireland 53°25N 6°18W 120 A2
St. Maries U.S.A. 47°19N 116°35W 304 C5
St. Mark B. Grenada 12°11N 61°42W 323 q
St. Marks U.S.A. 30°9N 84°12W 316 E5
St-Martin ☒ W. Indies 18°0N 63°0W 322 a
St-Martin, Bois France 48°48N 2°35E 134 B4
St-Martin, C. Martinique 14°52N 61°14W 322 j
St. Martin, L. Canada 51°40N 98°30W 297 C9
St-Martin-de-Crau France 43°38N 4°48E 175 E8
St-Martin-de-Ré France 46°12N 1°21W 174 B2
St-Martin-d'Hères France 45°9N 5°45E 175 C9
St-Martin-Vésubie France 44°4N 7°15E 175 D11
St. Martin's I. Bangla. 20°36N 92°20E 241 E4
St-Martory France 43°9N 0°56E 174 E4
St. Mary U.S.A. 37°53N 89°57W 310 G7
St. Mary, Mt. Papua N. G. 8°8S 147°2E 286 E4
St. Mary Cray U.K. 51°23N 0°7E 125 B4
St. Mary Is. India 13°20N 74°35E 245 H2
St. Mary Pk. Australia 31°32S 138°34E 282 A3
St. Marys Tas., Australia 41°35S 148°11E 281 G4
St. Marys Ont., Canada 43°20N 81°10W 312 C3
St. Mary's Trin. & Tob. 10°14N 61°33W 323 t
St. Mary's Corn., U.K. 49°55N 6°18W 169 H1
St. Mary's Orkney, U.K. 58°54N 2°54W 167 C6
St. Marys Alaska, U.S.A. 62°4N 163°10W 303 E7
St. Marys Ga., U.S.A. 30°44N 81°33W 316 E8
St. Marys Ohio, U.S.A. 40°33N 84°24W 311 D12
St. Marys Pa., U.S.A. 41°26N 78°34W 312 E6
St. Marys → U.S.A. 30°43N 81°27W 316 E8
St. Mary's, C. Canada 46°50N 54°12W 299 C9
St. Mary's B. Canada 46°50N 53°50W 299 C9
St. Mary's Bay Canada 44°25N 66°10W 299 D6
St. Mary's Cathedral San Francisco, U.S.A. 136 c1
St-Mathieu, Pte. France 48°20N 4°45W 172 D2
St. Matthew I. U.S.A. 60°24N 172°42W 303 F4
St. Matthews Ky., U.S.A. 38°15N 85°39W 311 F11
St. Matthews S.C., U.S.A. 33°40N 80°46W 316 B9
St. Matthews, I. = Zadetkyi Kyun Burma 10°0N 98°25E 237 G2
St. Matthias Group Papua N. G. 1°30S 150°0E 286 A6
St-Maur-des-Fossés France 48°48N 2°29E 134 B3
St-Maurice France 48°49N 2°24E 134 B3
St-Maurice → Canada 46°21N 72°31W 298 C5
St. Mawes U.K. 50°10N 5°2W 169 G2
St-Maximin-la-Ste-Baume France 43°27N 5°52E 175 E9
St-Médard-en-Jalles France 44°53N 0°43W 174 D3
St-Méen-le-Grand France 48°11N 2°12W 172 D4
St. Meinrad U.S.A. 38°10N 86°49W 311 F10
St. Michael U.S.A. 63°29N 162°2W 303 E7
St. Michael's Cathedral Toronto, Canada 141 a3
St-Michel Canada 45°34N 73°37W 130 A2
St-Mihiel France 48°54N 5°32E 173 D12
St-Nazaire France 47°17N 2°12W 172 E4
St. Neots U.K. 52°14N 0°15W 169 E7
St-Nicolas-de-Port France 48°38N 6°18E 173 D13
St. Niklaas Belgium 51°10N 4°8E 170 C4
St. Nikolaus-Kirken Czech Rep. 50°5N 14°23E 135 B2
St-Omer France 50°45N 2°15E 173 B9
St-Ouen France 48°56N 2°20E 134 A3
St-Palais-sur-Mer France 45°38N 1°5W 174 C2
St-Pamphile Canada 46°58N 69°48W 299 C6
St-Pardoux-la-Rivière France 45°29N 0°45E 174 C4
St. Paris U.S.A. 40°8N 83°58W 311 D13
St-Pascal Canada 47°32N 69°48W 299 C6
St. Patrick ☐ Trin. & Tob. 10°10N 61°35W 323 t
St. Patricks Barbados 13°6N 59°30W 323 r
St. Patrick's Cathedral Dublin, Ireland 120 c1
St. Patrick's Cathedral New York, U.S.A. 132 c2
St. Patrick's Church Toronto, Canada 141 a1
St. Paul Canada 54°0N 111°17W 296 C6
St-Paul Alpes-de-Haute-Provence, France 44°31N 6°45E 175 D10
St-Paul Réunion 20°59S 55°17E 272 f
St. Paul Alaska, U.S.A. 57°7N 170°17W 303 H5
St. Paul Ind., U.S.A. 39°26N 85°38W 311 E11
St. Paul Minn., U.S.A. 44°56N 93°5W 308 C7
St. Paul Nebr., U.S.A. 41°13N 98°27W 308 E4
St-Paul → Canada 51°27N 57°42W 299 B8
St. Paul → Liberia 6°25N 10°48W 262 D2
St. Paul, I. Ind. Oc. 38°55S 77°34E 273 H6
St-Paul-de-Fenouillet France 42°48N 2°30E 174 F6
St. Paul I. N.S., Canada 47°12N 60°9W 299 C7
St. Paul I. Alaska, U.S.A. 57°10N 170°15W 303 H5
St-Paul-lès-Dax France 43°44N 1°3W 174 E2
St. Paul Subterranean River △ Phil. 10°10N 118°55E 233 F2
St. Paul's Bay Malta 35°57N 14°24E 206 F7
St. Paul's Cathedral London, U.K. 125 b4
St. Paul's Cray U.K. 51°23N 0°6E 125 B4
St-Péray France 44°57N 4°50E 175 D8
St. Pete Beach U.S.A. 27°43N 82°44W 317 H7
St. Peter U.S.A. 44°20N 93°57W 308 C7
St. Peter & St. Paul San Francisco, U.S.A. 136 a2
St-Peter-Ording Germany 54°20N 8°36E 178 A4
St. Peter Port U.K. 49°26N 2°33W 169 H5
St. Peters N.S.W., Australia 33°55S 151°11E 139 B2
St. Peters N.S., Canada 45°40N 60°53W 299 C7
St. Peters P.E.I., Canada 46°25N 62°35W 299 C7
St. Peters Montserrat 16°43N 62°13W 323 p
St. Peters Mo., U.S.A. 38°48N 90°37W 310 F6
St. Peter's Square = San Pietro, Piazza Rome, Italy 136 b1
St. Petersburg = Sankt-Peterburg Russia 59°55N 30°20E 137 B1
St. Petersburg U.S.A. 27°46N 82°40W 317 H7
St. Petersburg Pulkovo Int. ✕ (LED) Russia 59°48N 30°18E 137 C1
St-Philbert-de-Grand-Lieu France 47°2N 1°39W 172 E5
St-Philippe Réunion 21°21S 55°44E 272 f
St-Pie Canada 45°30N 72°54W 313 A12
St-Pierre Qué., Canada 45°27N 73°38W 130 B2
St-Pierre Martinique 14°45N 61°10W 322 j
St. Pierre Mauritius 20°13S 57°31E 272 e
St-Pierre Réunion 21°19S 55°28E 272 f
St-Pierre St-P. & M. 46°46N 56°12W 299 C8
St. Pierre Seychelles 9°20S 46°0E 273 E3
St-Pierre, L. Canada 46°12N 72°52W 298 C5
St-Pierre, Rade de Martinique 14°44N 61°11W 322 j
St-Pierre-de-la-Pointe-aux-Esquimaux = Havre-St.-Pierre Canada 50°18N 63°33W 299 B7
St-Pierre-d'Oléron France 45°57N 1°19W 174 C2
St-Pierre-en-Port France 49°48N 0°30E 172 C7
St-Pierre-et-Miquelon ☒ N. Amer. 46°55N 56°10W 299 C8
St-Pierre-le-Moûtier France 46°47N 3°7E 173 F10
St-Pierre-sur-Dives France 49°2N 0°1W 172 C6
St. Pieters Leew Belgium 50°47N 4°16E 116 B1
St-Pol-de-Léon France 48°41N 4°0W 172 D3
St-Pol-sur-Mer France 51°1N 2°20E 173 A9
St-Pol-sur-Ternoise France 50°23N 2°20E 173 B9
St-Pons France 43°30N 2°45E 174 E6
St-Pourçain-sur-Sioule France 46°18N 3°18E 173 F10
St-Priest France 45°42N 4°57E 175 C8
St-Quay-Portrieux France 48°39N 2°51W 172 D4
St-Quentin N.B., Canada 47°30N 67°23W 299 C6
St-Quentin Aisne, France 49°50N 3°16E 173 C10
St-Quentin, Étang de France 48°47N 2°0E 134 B1
St-Rambert-d'Albon France 45°17N 4°49E 175 C8
St-Raphaël France 43°25N 6°46E 175 E10
St. Regis U.S.A. 47°18N 115°6W 304 C6
St. Regis Falls U.S.A. 44°40N 74°32W 313 B10
St-Renan France 48°26N 4°37W 172 D2
St. Robert U.S.A. 37°50N 92°11W 310 G4
St-Saëns France 49°41N 1°16E 172 C8
St-Savin France 46°34N 0°53E 174 B4
St-Savinien France 45°53N 0°42W 174 C3
St. Sebastien, Tanjon' i Madag. 12°26S 48°44E 272 A2
St-Seine-l'Abbaye France 47°26N 4°47E 173 E11
St-Sernin-sur-Rance France 43°54N 2°35E 174 E6
St-Sever France 43°45N 0°35W 174 E3
St-Siméon Canada 47°51N 69°54W 299 C6
St. Simons I. U.S.A. 31°12N 81°15W 316 D8
St. Simons Island U.S.A. 31°9N 81°22W 315 F14
St. Stephen N.B., Canada 45°16N 67°17W 299 C6
St. Stephen S.C., U.S.A. 33°24N 79°55W 316 B10
St. Stephen's Basilica Budapest, Hungary 117 b2
St. Stephens Cathedral = Stephansdom Vienna, Austria 142 b2
St. Stephen's Green Dublin, Ireland 120 c3
St-Stevens-Woluwe Belgium 50°52N 4°26E 116 A2
St-Sulpice France 43°46N 1°41E 174 E5
St-Sulpice-Laurière France 46°3N 1°29E 174 B5
St-Sulpice-les-Feuilles France 46°19N 1°21E 174 B5
St-Syprien = St-Cyprien France 42°37N 3°2E 174 F7
St. Teresa U.S.A. 29°55N 84°27W 316 F5
St-Thégonnec France 48°31N 3°57W 172 D3
St. Thomas = Charlotte Amalie U.S. Virgin Is. 18°21N 64°56W 321 C7
St. Thomas Canada 42°45N 81°10W 312 D3
St. Thomas Bay Malta 35°51N 14°34E 206 F8
St. Thomas I. U.S. Virgin Is. 18°20N 64°55W 321 C7
St-Tite Canada 46°45N 72°34W 298 C5
St-Tropez France 43°17N 6°38E 175 E10
St-Troud = St. Truiden Belgium 50°48N 5°10E 170 D5
St. Truiden Belgium 50°48N 5°10E 170 D5
St-Vaast-la-Hougue France 49°35N 1°17W 172 C5
St-Valery-en-Caux France 49°52N 0°43E 172 C7
St-Valéry-sur-Somme France 50°11N 1°38E 173 B8
St-Vallier France 46°38N 4°22E 173 F11
St-Vallier-de-Thiey France 43°42N 6°51E 175 E10
St-Varent France 46°53N 0°13W 172 F6
St-Vaury France 46°12N 1°46E 174 B5
St. Vidgeon's ◎ Australia 14°47S 134°53E 280 A1
St. Vincent = São Vicente C. Verde Is. 17°0N 25°0W 153 j
St. Vincent Italy 45°45N 7°39E 198 C4
St. Vincent W. Indies 13°10N 61°10W 323 n
St. Vincent, G. Australia 35°0S 138°0E 282 C3
St. Vincent & the Grenadines ■ W. Indies 13°0N 61°10W 323 n
St-Vincent-de-Paul Canada 45°36N 73°39W 130 A2
St-Vincent-de-Tyrosse France 43°39N 1°19W 174 E2
St. Vincent I. U.S.A. 29°42N 85°3W 317 F4
St. Vincent Passage W. Indies 13°30N 61°0W 321 D7
St-Vith Belgium 50°17N 6°9E 170 D6
St-Vivien-de-Médoc France 45°25N 1°2W 174 C2
St. Walburg Canada 53°39N 109°12W 297 C7
St. Xavier Univ. U.S.A. 41°42N 87°42W 119 C2
St-Yrieix-la-Perche France 45°31N 1°12E 174 C5
Saintala India 20°26N 83°20E 244 D6
Ste-Adresse France 49°31N 0°5E 172 C7
Ste-Agathe-des-Monts Canada 46°3N 74°17W 298 C5
Ste-Anne Guadeloupe 16°13N 61°24W 322 e
Ste-Anne Martinique 14°25N 60°54W 322 j
Ste-Anne Réunion 21°4S 55°45E 272 f
Ste-Anne Seychelles 4°36S 55°31E 272 c
Ste-Anne, L. Canada 50°0N 67°42W 299 B6
Ste-Anne-des-Monts Canada 49°8N 66°30W 299 C6
Ste-Catherine Canada 45°24N 73°34W 130 B2
Ste-Croix Switz. 46°49N 6°34E 179 J2
Ste-Enimie France 44°22N 3°26E 174 D7
Ste-Foy-la-Grande France 44°50N 0°13E 174 D4
Ste. Genevieve U.S.A. 37°59N 90°2W 310 G6
Ste-Hélène, Î. Canada 45°31N 73°32W 130 A2
Ste-Hermine France 46°32N 1°4W 174 B2
Ste-Livrade-sur-Lot France 44°24N 0°36E 174 D4
Ste-Luce Martinique 14°28N 60°55W 322 j
Ste. Madeleine Trin. & Tob. 10°16N 61°26W 323 t
Ste-Marguerite Guadeloupe 16°23N 61°24W 322 e
Ste-Marguerite → Canada 50°9N 66°36W 299 B6
Ste-Marie Canada 46°26N 71°0W 299 C5
Ste. Marie Gabon 3°48S 11°1E 264 C2
Ste-Marie Guadeloupe 16°6N 61°33W 322 e
Ste-Marie Martinique 14°48N 61°1W 322 j
Ste-Marie Réunion 20°53S 55°33E 272 f
Ste-Marie, Ile = Nosy Boraha Madag. 16°50S 49°55E 272 B2
Ste-Marie-aux-Mines France 48°15N 7°12E 173 D14
Ste-Marthe Guadeloupe 16°15N 61°15W 322 e
Ste-Maure-de-Touraine France 47°7N 0°37E 172 E7
Ste-Maxime France 43°19N 6°39E 175 E10
Ste-Menehould France 49°5N 4°54E 173 C11
Ste-Mère-Église France 49°24N 1°19W 172 C5
Ste-Rose Guadeloupe 16°20N 61°45W 322 e
Ste-Rose Réunion 21°8S 55°45E 272 f
Ste. Rose du Lac Canada 51°4N 99°30W 297 C9
Ste-Savine France 48°18N 4°3E 173 D11
Ste-Sigolène France 45°15N 4°14E 175 C8
Ste-Suzanne Réunion 20°54S 55°36E 272 f
Saintes France 45°45N 0°37W 174 C3
Saintes, Canal des Guadeloupe 15°55N 61°40W 322 e
Saintes, Îs. des Guadeloupe 15°50N 61°35W 322 e
Stes-Maries-de-la-Mer France 43°26N 4°26E 175 E8
Saintfield U.K. 54°28N 5°49W 166 B6
Saintonge France 45°40N 0°50W 174 C3
Saipan N. Marianas 15°12N 145°45E 302 e
Saipan Channel N. Marianas 15°5N 145°41E 302 e
Sairang India 23°50N 92°45E 241 D4
Sairecábur, Cerro Bolivia 22°43S 67°54W 334 A2
Saitama Japan 35°54N 139°38E 223 B11
Saitama ☐ Japan 36°25N 139°30E 223 A11
Saiteli = Kadınhanı Turkey 38°14N 32°13E 212 C5
Saiţi Moldova 46°30N 29°24E 183 D14
Saito Japan 32°3N 131°24E 222 E3
Saiwai Japan 35°32N 139°41E 140 B3
Saiyid Pakistan 33°7N 73°2E 242 C5
Saja-Besaya ⌂ Spain 43°10N 4°9W 194 B6
Sajama Bolivia 18°7S 69°0W 330 D4
Sajama, Nevado Bolivia 18°6S 68°54W 330 D4
Sajan Serbia 45°50N 20°20E 182 E5
Sajó → Hungary 47°56N 21°7E 182 C6
Sajókazinc = Kazincbarcika Hungary 48°17N 20°36E 182 B5
Sajószentpéter Hungary 48°12N 20°44E 182 B5
Sajum India 33°20N 79°0E 243 C8
Sak → S. Africa 30°52S 20°25E 270 D3
Saka Kenya 0°9S 39°20E 268 B4
Saka Kalat Pakistan 27°3N 65°3E 240 D2
Sakaba Nigeria 11°4N 5°35E 263 C6
Sakai Japan 34°34N 135°27E 133 B1
Sakai Harbour Japan 34°36N 135°26E 133 B1
Sakaide Japan 34°19N 133°50E 222 C5
Sakaiminato Japan 35°38N 133°11E 222 B5
Sakākah Si. Arabia 30°0N 40°8E 246 D4
Sakakawea, L. U.S.A. 47°30N 101°25W 308 B3
Sakami → Canada 53°40N 76°40W 298 B4
Sakami, L. Canada 53°15N 77°0W 298 B4
Sâkâne, 'Erg i-n Mali 20°30N 1°30W 260 D4
Sakania Dem. Rep. of the Congo 12°43S 28°30E 269 E2
Sakar I. Papua N. G. 5°25S 148°6E 286 C5
Sakaraha Madag. 22°55S 44°32E 272 C1
Sakartvelo = Georgia ■ Asia 42°0N 43°0E 191 J6
Sakarya Turkey 40°48N 30°25E 212 B4
Sakarya ☐ Turkey 40°45N 30°25E 212 B4
Sakarya → Turkey 41°7N 30°39E 212 B4
Sakashima-Guntō Japan 24°46N 124°0E 221 M2
Sakassou Ivory C. 7°29N 5°19W 262 D3
Sakata Japan 38°55N 139°50E 220 E9
Sakawa Japan 33°28N 133°11E 222 D5
Sakchu N. Korea 40°23N 125°2E 224 B2
Sakeny → Madag. 20°0S 45°25E 272 C2
Sakété Benin 6°40N 2°45E 263 D5
Sakha ☐ Russia 66°0N 130°0E 215 C14
Sakhalin Russia 51°0N 143°0E 215 D15
Sakhalinskiy Zaliv Russia 54°0N 141°0E 215 D15
Sakhi Gopal India 19°58N 85°50E 244 E7
Şaki Azerbaijan 41°10N 47°5E 191 K8
Šakiai Lithuania 54°59N 23°2E 184 D10
Sakiz-Adasi = Hios Greece 38°27N 26°9E 205 C8
Sakmara → Russia 51°46N 55°1E 216 B5
Sakoli India 21°5N 79°59E 244 D4
Sakon Nakhon Thailand 17°10N 104°9E 236 D5
Sakra, Pulau Singapore 1°15N 103°41E 138 B2
Sakrand Pakistan 26°10N 68°15E 242 F3
Sakri Maharashtra, India 26°13N 86°5E 243 F12
Sakri Maharashtra, India 21°2N 74°20E 244 D2
Sakrivier S. Africa 30°54S 20°28E 270 D3
Sakskøbing Denmark 54°49N 11°39E 163 K5
Sakti India 22°2N 82°58E 243 H10
Saku Japan 36°17N 138°31E 223 A10
Sakuma Japan 35°3N 137°49E 223 B9
Sakura Japan 35°43N 140°14E 223 B12
Sakurai Japan 34°30N 135°51E 223 C7
Saky Ukraine 45°9N 33°34E 189 K7
Sal → Russia 47°31N 40°45E 191 G5
Sal Rei C. Verde Is. 16°11N 22°53W 153 j
Sala Eritrea 16°53N 37°56E 257 D4
Šal'a Slovak Rep. 48°10N 17°50E 181 C10
Sala Sweden 59°58N 16°35E 162 E10
Sala → Eritrea 16°53N 37°56E 257 D4
Sala, O. → Chad 17°0N 20°53E 259 E4
Sala Consilina Italy 40°23N 15°36E 201 B8
Sala-y-Gómez Pac. Oc. 26°28S 105°28W 289 K17
Sala y Gómez Ridge Pac. Oc. 25°0S 98°0W 289 K18
Salaberry-de-Valleyfield Canada 45°15N 74°8W 313 A10
Salacgrīva Latvia 57°45N 24°21E 184 A11
Salada, L. Mexico 32°20N 115°40W 305 K6
Saladas Argentina 28°15S 58°40W 334 B4
Saladillo Argentina 35°40S 59°55W 334 D4
Salado → B. Aires, Argentina 35°44S 57°22W 334 D4
Salado → La Pampa, Argentina 37°30S 67°0W 336 A3
Salado → Río Negro, Argentina 41°34S 65°3W 336 B3
Salado → Santa Fe, Argentina 31°40S 60°41W 334 C3
Salado → Tamaulipas, Mexico 26°52N 99°19W 314 H5
Salaga Ghana 8°31N 0°31W 263 D4
Şalāh Syria 32°40N 36°45E 250 F7
Şalāḩ ad Dīn ☐ Iraq 34°35N 43°35E 246 C4
Sălaj ☐ Romania 47°15N 23°0E 182 C8
Salakos Greece 36°17N 27°57E 206 E11
Salal Chad 14°48N 17°12E 259 F3
Salala Liberia 6°42N 10°7W 262 D2
Salala Sudan 21°17N 36°16E 256 C4
Salālah Oman 16°56N 53°59E 249 C6
Salam Iraq 33°20N 44°20E 113 A2
Salamanca Chile 31°46S 70°59W 334 C1
Salamanca Madrid, Spain 40°25N 3°41W 127 B1
Salamanca Salamanca, Spain 40°58N 5°39W 194 E5
Salamanca N.Y., U.S.A. 42°10N 78°43W 312 D6
Salamanca ☐ Spain 40°57N 5°40W 194 E5
Salamat ☐ Chad 11°0N 20°30E 259 F4
Salamat, Bahr → Chad 9°20N 18°0E 259 G3
Salāmatābād Iran 35°39N 47°50E 246 C5
Salamina Colombia 5°25N 75°29W 328 B2
Salamina Greece 37°56N 23°30E 204 D5
Salamis Cyprus 35°11N 33°54E 207 E9
Salamonie L. U.S.A. 40°46N 85°37W 311 D11
Salar de Atacama Chile 23°30S 68°25W 334 A2
Salar de Uyuni Bolivia 20°30S 67°45W 330 E4
Sălard Romania 47°12N 22°3E 182 C7
Salas Spain 43°25N 6°15W 194 B4
Salas de los Infantes Spain 42°2N 3°17W 194 C7
Salatiga Indonesia 7°19S 110°30E 235 D4
Salavat Russia 53°21N 55°55E 186 D10
Salaverry Peru 8°15S 79°0W 330 B2
Salawati Indonesia 1°7S 130°52E 231 E8
Salay Phil. 8°52N 124°47E 233 G5
Salaya India 22°19N 69°35E 242 H3
Salayar Indonesia 6°7S 120°30E 231 F6
Salazar → Spain 42°40N 1°20W 196 C3
Salazie Réunion 21°2S 55°32E 272 f
Salazie, Cirque de Réunion 21°3S 55°30E 272 f
Salbris France 47°25N 2°3E 173 E9
S'Albufera Spain 39°47N 3°7E 206 B4
S'albufera d'es Grau Spain 39°56N 4°16E 206 B5
Salcantay, Nevado Peru 13°19S 72°33W 330 C3
Salcedo Phil. 11°9N 125°40E 233 F5
Salcia Romania 43°56N 24°55E 183 G9
Sălciua Romania 46°24N 23°26E 183 D8
Salcombe U.K. 50°14N 3°47W 169 G4
Saldaña Spain 42°32N 4°48W 194 C6
Saldanha S. Africa 33°0S 17°58E 270 D2
Saldanha B. S. Africa 33°6S 18°0E 270 D2
Saldus Latvia 56°38N 22°30E 184 B9
Saldus ☐ Latvia 56°35N 22°30E 184 B9
Sale Vic., Australia 38°6S 147°6E 283 E7
Sale Burma 20°50N 94°45E 241 E5
Sale Italy 44°59N 8°48E 198 D5
Salé Morocco 34°3N 6°48W 260 B3
Sale Gt. Man., U.K. 53°26N 2°19W 168 D5
Sale City U.S.A. 31°16N 84°1W 316 D5
Salée, Rivière Guadeloupe 16°17N 61°33W 322 e
Salegard = Salekhard Russia 66°30N 66°35E 214 C7
Salekhard Russia 66°30N 66°35E 214 C7
Salelologa Samoa 13°41S 172°11W 287 V19
Salem India 11°40N 78°11E 245 J4
Salem Montserrat 16°45N 62°13W 323 p
Salem Fla., U.S.A. 29°53N 83°25W 316 F6
Salem Ill., U.S.A. 38°38N 88°57W 310 F8
Salem Ind., U.S.A. 38°36N 86°6W 311 F10
Salem Mass., U.S.A. 42°31N 70°53W 313 D14
Salem Mo., U.S.A. 37°39N 91°32W 308 G8
Salem N.H., U.S.A. 42°45N 71°12W 313 D13
Salem N.J., U.S.A. 39°34N 75°28W 309 F16
Salem N.Y., U.S.A. 43°10N 73°20W 313 C11
Salem Ohio, U.S.A. 40°54N 80°52W 312 F4
Salem Oreg., U.S.A. 44°56N 123°2W 304 D2
Salem S. Dak., U.S.A. 43°44N 97°23W 308 D5
Salem Va., U.S.A. 37°18N 80°3W 309 G13
Salemi Italy 37°49N 12°48E 200 E5
Sälen Sweden 61°15N 13°22E 162 C7
Salernes France 43°34N 6°15E 175 E10
Salerno Italy 40°41N 14°47E 201 B7
Salerno, G. di Italy 40°32N 14°42E 201 B7
Sales Brazil 4°2S 63°40W 329 D5
Salford U.K. 53°30N 2°18W 168 D5
Salgir → Ukraine 45°38N 35°1E 189 K8
Salgótarján Hungary 48°5N 19°47E 182 B4
Salgueiro Brazil 8°4S 39°6W 332 C4
Salher India 20°40N 73°55E 244 D1
Salhus Norway 60°30N 5°15E 164 D2
Salibabu Indonesia 3°51N 126°40E 231 D7
Salibea = Salybia Trin. & Tob. 10°43N 61°2W 323 t
Salibia Dominica 15°30N 61°16W 323 k
Salida U.S.A. 38°32N 106°0W 301 H18
Salies-de-Béarn France 43°28N 0°56W 174 E3
Şalif Yemen 15°18N 42°41E 248 D3
Salihli Turkey 38°28N 28°8E 212 C3
Salihorsk Belarus 52°51N 27°27E 177 B14
Salin Burma 20°35N 94°40E 241 E5
Salina Italy 38°34N 14°50E 201 D7
Salina Kans., U.S.A. 38°50N 97°37W 308 F5
Salina Utah, U.S.A. 38°58N 111°51W 304 G8
Salina Cruz Mexico 16°10N 95°12W 319 D5
Salina di Margherita di Savoia ⌂ Italy 41°23N 16°4E 201 A9
Salinas = Salinópolis Brazil 0°40S 47°20W 332 B2
Salinas Brazil 16°10S 42°10W 333 E3
Salinas Ecuador 2°10S 80°58W 328 D1
Salinas Calif., U.S.A. 36°40N 121°39W 306 J5
Salinas → Guatemala 16°28N 90°31W 319 D6
Salinas → Calif., U.S.A. 36°45N 121°48W 306 J5
Salinas, B. das Angola 14°11S 12°21E 265 E2
Salinas, B. de Nic. 11°4N 85°45W 320 D2
Salinas, Pampa de las Argentina 31°58S 66°42W 334 C2
Salinas Ambargasta Argentina 29°0S 65°0W 334 B3
Salinas de Hidalgo Mexico 22°38N 101°43W 318 C4
Salinas Grandes Argentina 30°0S 65°0W 334 C3
Salinas Pueblo Missions ⌂ U.S.A. 34°6N 106°4W 305 J10
Salinas Valley U.S.A. 36°15N 121°15W 306 J5
Saline U.S.A. 42°10N 83°47W 311 B13
Saline → Ark., U.S.A. 33°10N 92°8W 314 E8
Saline → Kans., U.S.A. 38°52N 97°30W 308 F5
Saline B. Trin. & Tob. 10°42N 61°2W 323 t
Saline di Trapani e Paceco ⌂ Italy 37°59N 12°28E 200 E5
Saline I. Grenada 12°26N 61°28W 323 q
Salines, C. de ses Spain 39°16N 3°4E 206 B4
Salines, Étang des Martinique 14°24N 60°52W 322 j
Salines, Pt. Grenada 12°0N 61°48W 323 q
Salines, Pte. de Martinique 14°23N 60°53W 322 j
Salinópolis Brazil 0°40S 47°20W 332 B2
Salins-les-Bains France 46°58N 5°52E 173 F12
Salir Portugal 37°14N 8°2W 195 H2
Salisbury = Harare Zimbabwe 17°43S 31°2E 269 F3
Salisbury S. Austral., Australia 34°46S 138°38E 282 C3
Salisbury Dominica 15°26N 61°27W 323 k
Salisbury Wilts., U.K. 51°4N 1°47W 169 F6
Salisbury Md., U.S.A. 38°22N 75°36W 309 F16
Salisbury Mo., U.S.A. 39°25N 92°48W 310 E4
Salisbury N.C., U.S.A. 35°40N 80°29W 315 D14
Salisbury I. Canada 63°30N 77°0W 295 E16
Salisbury Plain U.K. 51°14N 1°55W 169 F6
Săliște Romania 45°45N 23°56E 183 E8
Salitre → Brazil 9°29S 40°39W 332 C3
Salka Nigeria 10°20N 4°58E 263 C5
Salkehatchie → U.S.A. 32°37N 80°53W 316 C9
Şalkhad Syria 32°29N 36°43E 251 F7
Salkove Ukraine 48°15N 29°59E 183 B14
Salla Finland 66°50N 28°49E 160 C23
Sallanches France 45°55N 6°38E 175 C10
Sallent Spain 41°49N 1°54E 196 D6
Salles France 44°33N 0°52W 174 D3
Salles-Curan France 44°11N 2°48E 174 D6
Salling Denmark 56°40N 8°55E 163 H2
Salliq = Coral Harbour Canada 64°8N 83°10W 295 E15
Sallisaw U.S.A. 35°28N 94°47W 314 D7
Sallom Sudan 19°17N 37°6E 256 D4
Salluit Canada 62°14N 75°38W 295 E16
Sallynoggin Ireland 53°17N 6°8W 120 B3
Salmān Pak Iraq 33°6N 44°34E 213 G11
Salmannsdorf Austria 48°14N 16°14E 142 A1
Salmās Iran 38°11N 44°47E 213 C11
Salmedina Spain 40°18N 3°35W 127 C2
Salmerón Spain 40°33N 2°29W 196 E2
Salmo Canada 49°10N 117°20W 296 D5
Salmon U.S.A. 45°11N 113°54W 304 D7
Salmon → B.C., Canada 54°3N 122°40W 296 C4
Salmon → Idaho, U.S.A. 45°51N 116°47W 304 D5
Salmon Arm Canada 50°40N 119°15W 296 C5
Salmon Gums Australia 32°59S 121°38E 279 F3
Salmon Pt. Canada 43°52N 77°15W 312 C7
Salmon River Mts. U.S.A. 44°50N 115°30W 304 D6
Salmon River Res. U.S.A. 43°32N 75°55W 313 C9
Salo C.A.R. 3°10N 16°8E 264 B3
Salo Finland 60°22N 23°10E 188 B2
Salò Italy 45°36N 10°31E 198 C7
Salobreña Spain 36°44N 3°35W 195 J7
Salome U.S.A. 33°47N 113°37W 307 M13
Salomea Poland 52°11N 20°55E 142 B1
Salomon, C. Martinique 14°30N 61°6W 322 j
Salon India 26°2N 81°27E 243 F9
Salon-de-Provence France 43°39N 5°6E 175 E9
Salonga → Dem. Rep. of the Congo 0°10S 19°50E 264 C4
Salonga-Nord △ Dem. Rep. of the Congo 1°55S 21°45E 264 C4
Salonga-Sud △ Dem. Rep. of the Congo 2°25S 21°0E 264 C4
Salonica = Thessaloniki Greece 40°38N 22°58E 202 F6
Salonta Romania 46°49N 21°42E 182 D6
Salop = Shropshire ☐ U.K. 52°36N 2°45W 169 E5
Salor → Spain 39°39N 7°3W 195 F3
Salou Spain 41°4N 1°8E 196 D6
Salou, C. de Spain 41°3N 1°10E 196 D6
Saloum → Senegal 13°50N 16°45W 262 C1
Salpausselkä Finland 61°3N 26°15E 188 B4
Salsacate Argentina 31°20S 65°5W 334 C2
Salses France 42°50N 2°55E 174 F6
Salsette I. India 19°2N 72°53E 130 A2
Salsk Russia 46°28N 41°30E 191 G5
Salso → Italy 37°6N 13°57E 200 E6
Salsomaggiore Terme Italy 44°49N 9°59E 198 D6
Salt Spain 41°59N 2°47E 196 D7
Salt → Alta., Canada 60°0N 112°25W 296 B6
Salt → Ariz., U.S.A. 33°23N 112°19W 305 K7
Salt → Mo., U.S.A. 39°28N 91°4W 310 E5
Salt Cay Bahamas 25°6N 77°18W 153 b
Salt Flats = Witte Pan Neth. Ant. 12°3N 68°17W 322 h
Salt Fork Red → U.S.A. 34°27N 99°21W 314 D5
Salt L. N.S.W., Australia 30°6S 142°8E 281 E3
Salt L. Hawai'i, U.S.A. 21°21N 157°55W 302 K14
Salt Lake City = Bidhan Nagar India 22°35N 88°25E 124 B2
Salt Lake City U.S.A. 40°45N 111°53W 304 F8
Salt Range Pakistan 32°30N 72°25E 242 C5
Salt River S. Africa 34°6S 18°28E 118 A1
Salt Springs U.S.A. 29°21N 81°44W 317 F8
Salt Water L. India 22°33N 88°26E 124 B2
Salta Argentina 24°57S 65°25W 334 A2
Salta ☐ Argentina 24°48S 65°30W 334 A2
Saltara Italy 43°45N 12°50E 199 E9
Saltash U.K. 50°24N 4°14W 169 G3
Saltburn by the Sea U.K. 54°35N 0°58W 168 C7
Saltcoats U.K. 55°38N 4°47W 167 F4
Saltee Is. Ireland 52°7N 6°37W 166 D5
Salters U.S.A. 33°36N 79°51W 316 B10
Saltfjellet Norway 66°40N 15°15E 160 C16
Saltfjorden Norway 67°15N 14°10E 160 C16
Saltholm Denmark 55°38N 12°43E 163 J6
Salthólmavík Iceland 65°24N 21°57W 155 B5
Saltillo Mexico 25°25N 101°0W 318 B4
Salto Argentina 34°20S 60°15W 334 C3
Salto Uruguay 31°27S 57°50W 334 C4
Salto da Divisa Brazil 16°0S 39°57W 333 E4
Salto del Guaíra Paraguay 24°3S 54°17W 335 A5
Salton City U.S.A. 33°18N 115°57W 307 M11
Salton Sea U.S.A. 33°15N 115°45W 307 M11
Saltpond Ghana 5°15N 1°3W 263 D4
Saltrød Norway 58°30N 8°49E 164 F5
Saltsburg U.S.A. 40°29N 79°27W 312 F5
Saltsjö-Duvnäs Sweden 59°18N 18°12E 139 B3
Saltsjöbaden Sweden 59°15N 18°20E 162 E12
Saltykovka Russia 55°45N 37°54E 129 B5
Saluda U.S.A. 34°0N 81°46W 316 A8
Saluda → U.S.A. 34°1N 81°4W 315 D14
Salug Phil. 8°7N 122°47E 233 G4
Salûm Egypt 31°31N 25°7E 256 A2
Salûm, Khâlig el Egypt 31°35N 25°24E 256 A2
Salur India 18°27N 83°18E 244 E6
Salut, Is. du Fr. Guiana 5°15N 52°35W 329 B7
Saluzzo Italy 44°39N 7°29E 198 D4
Salvación, B. Chile 50°50S 75°10W 336 D1
Salvador Brazil 13°0S 38°30W 333 D4
Salvador Sask., Canada 52°10N 109°32W 297 C7
Salvador, El ■ Cent. Amer. 13°50N 89°0W 320 D2
Salvador, L. U.S.A. 29°43N 90°15W 315 G9
Salvaterra Brazil 0°46S 48°31W 332 B2
Salvaterra de Magos Portugal 39°1N 8°47W 195 F2
Salvisa U.S.A. 37°54N 84°51W 311 G12
Sálvora, I. de Spain 42°30N 8°58W 194 C2
Salween → Burma 16°31N 97°37E 241 G6
Salyan Azerbaijan 39°33N 48°59E 213 C13
Salybia Trin. & Tob. 10°43N 61°2W 323 t
Salza → Austria 47°40N 14°43E 180 D7
Salzach → Austria 48°12N 12°56E 180 C5
Salzburg Austria 47°48N 13°2E 180 D6
Salzburg ☐ Austria 47°15N 13°0E 180 D6
Salzburgen = Château-Salins France 48°50N 6°30E 173 D13
Salzgitter Germany 52°9N 10°19E 178 C6
Salzkotten Germany 51°40N 8°37E 178 D4
Salzwedel Germany 52°52N 11°10E 178 C7
Sam Gabon 0°58N 11°16E 264 B2
Sam India 26°50N 70°31E 242 F4
Sam Neua Laos 20°29N 104°5E 228 G5
Sam Ngao Thailand 17°18N 99°0E 236 D2
Sam Rayburn Res. U.S.A. 31°4N 94°5W 314 F7
Sam Son Vietnam 19°44N 105°54E 236 C5
Sam Teu Laos 19°59N 104°38E 236 C5
Sama de Langreo = Langreo Spain 43°18N 5°40W 194 B5
Samacimbo Angola 13°33S 16°59E 265 E3
Şamad Oman 22°48N 58°9E 249 B7
Samagaltay Russia 50°36N 95°3E 217 B13
Samā'il Oman 23°40N 57°50E 249 B7
Samaipata Bolivia 18°9S 63°52W 331 D5
Samal Phil. 7°5N 125°42E 233 H5
Samal I. Phil. 7°3N 125°44E 233 H5
Samales Group Phil. 6°0N 122°0E 233 J3
Samalkot India 17°3N 82°13E 244 F6
Samâlût Egypt 28°20N 30°42E 256 B3
Samana India 30°10N 76°13E 242 D7
Samana Cay Bahamas 23°3N 73°45W 321 B5
Samandağ Turkey 36°5N 35°59E 250 B6
Samandıra Turkey 40°59N 29°13E 203 F13
Samanga Tanzania 8°20S 39°13E 269 D4
Samangān ☐ Afghan. 36°15N 68°3E 240 A3
Samangwa Dem. Rep. of the Congo 4°23S 24°10E 265 C4
Samani Japan 42°7N 142°56E 220 C11
Samanli Dağları Turkey 40°32N 29°10E 203 F13
Samannûd Egypt 30°57N 31°14E 251 H2
Samar Phil. 12°0N 125°0E 233 E5
Samar ☐ Phil. 11°50N 125°0E 233 F5
Samar Sea Phil. 12°0N 124°15E 232 E5
Samara Russia 53°8N 50°6E 190 D10
Samara → Russia 53°10N 50°4E 190 D10
Samara → Ukraine 48°28N 35°7E 189 H8
Samarai Papua N. G. 10°39S 150°41E 286 F6
Samaria = Shōmrōn West Bank 32°15N 35°13E 251 F6
Samaria West Bank 32°17N 35°12E 251 F6
Samaria △ Greece 35°17N 23°58E 207 E4
Samariapo Venezuela 5°15N 67°48W 328 B4
Samarinda Indonesia 0°30S 117°9E 235 C5
Samarkand = Samarqand Uzbekistan 39°40N 66°55E 217 E7
Samarkandsky = Temirtau Kazakhstan 50°5N 72°56E 217 B8
Samarqand Uzbekistan 39°40N 66°55E 217 E7
Samarqand ☐ Uzbekistan 39°35N 66°25E 217 E7
Sāmarrā' Iraq 34°12N 43°52E 213 E10
Samastipur India 25°50N 85°50E 243 G11
Samatya Turkey 40°59N 28°55E 122 C1
Samaúma Brazil 7°50S 60°2W 331 B5
Şamaxi Azerbaijan 40°38N 48°37E 191 K9
Samba Équateur, Dem. Rep. of the Congo 0°13N 21°25E 264 B4
Samba Maniema, Dem. Rep. of the Congo 4°38S 26°22E 265 C5
Samba Jammu & Kashmir, India 32°32N 75°10E 243 C6
Samba Caju Angola 8°46S 15°24E 265 D3
Sambaíba Brazil 7°8S 45°21W 332 C2
Sambalpur India 21°28N 84°4E 244 D7
Sambar, Tanjung Indonesia 2°59S 110°19E 235 C4
Sambas Indonesia 1°20N 109°20E 235 B3
Sambava Madag. 14°16S 50°10E 272 A3
Sambawizi Zimbabwe 18°24S 26°13E 269 F2
Sambhajinagar = Aurangabad India 19°50N 75°23E 244 E2
Sambhal India 28°35N 78°37E 243 E8
Sambhar India 26°52N 75°6E 242 F6
Sambhar L. India 26°55N 75°12E 242 F6
Sambiase Italy 38°58N 16°17E 201 D9
Sambir Ukraine 49°30N 23°10E 185 J10
Sambo Angola 13°3S 16°8E 265 E3
Sambor Cambodia 12°46N 106°0E 236 F6
Samborombón, B. Argentina 36°5S 57°20W 334 D4
Sambuca di Sicilia Italy 37°39N 13°7E 200 E6
Samburu ⌂ Kenya 0°37N 37°31E 268 B4
Samcheok S. Korea 37°30N 129°10E 224 D4
Same Tanzania 4°2S 37°38E 268 C4
Samer France 50°38N 1°44E 173 B8
Samfya Zambia 11°22S 29°31E 269 E2
Samḩān, Jabal Oman 17°12N 54°55E 249 C6
Sami Greece 38°15N 20°39E 207 C2
Samka Burma 20°9N 96°57E 241 E6
Şämkir Azerbaijan 40°50N 46°0E 191 K8
Şamlı Turkey 39°48N 27°51E 205 B9
Sammanturai Sri Lanka 7°36N 81°39E 245 L5
Samnah Si. Arabia 25°10N 37°15E 246 E3
Samnū Libya 27°15N 14°55E 258 C2
Samo Alto Chile 30°22S 71°0W 334 C1
Samoa ■ Pac. Oc. 14°0S 172°0W 287 V20
Samoan Is. Pac. Oc. 14°0S 171°0W 287 V20
Samobor Croatia 45°47N 15°44E 199 C12
Samoëns France 46°5N 6°45E 173 F13
Samokov Bulgaria 42°18N 23°35E 202 D7
Šamorín Slovak Rep. 48°2N 17°19E 181 C10
Samorogouan Burkina Faso 11°21N 4°57W 262 C4
Samos Greece 37°45N 26°50E 205 D8
Samoš Serbia 45°13N 20°46E 182 E5
Samos Spain 42°44N 7°20W 194 C3
Samos ☐ Greece 37°45N 26°50E 205 D8
Samoset U.S.A. 27°28N 82°33W 317 H7
Samosir Indonesia 2°55N 98°50E 234 B1
Samothráki = Mathraki Greece 39°48N 19°31E 206 B9
Samothraki Greece 40°28N 25°28E 203 F9
Samoylovka Russia 51°12N 43°43E 190 E6
Sampa Angola 10°38S 18°56E 265 E3
Sampa Ghana 8°0N 2°36W 262 D4
Sampacho Argentina 33°20S 64°50W 334 C3
Sampalan Indonesia 8°41S 115°34E 231 K18
Sampaloc Phil. 14°36N 120°59E 127 B1
Sampang Indonesia 7°11S 113°13E 235 D4
Samper de Calanda Spain 41°11N 0°28W 196 D4

Sampéyre *Italy* 44°34N 7°11E **198** D4
Samphan Thawong *Thailand* 13°44N 100°31E **113** B2
Sampit *Indonesia* 2°34S 113°0E **235** C4
Sampit → *Indonesia* 2°44S 112°54E **235** C4
Sampit, Teluk *Indonesia* 3°5S 113°3E **235** C4
Sampun *Papua N. G.* 5°21S 152°8E **286** C7
Samrong *Cambodia* 14°15N 103°30E **236** E4
Samrong *Thailand* 15°10N 100°40E **236** E3
Samseon *S. Korea* 37°34N 127°0E **137** B2
Samsø *Denmark* 55°50N 10°35E **163** J4
Samsø Bælt *Denmark* 55°45N 10°45E **163** J4
Samson *U.S.A.* 31°7N 86°3W **316** D3
Samsun *Turkey* 41°15N 36°22E **212** B7
Samsun □ *Turkey* 41°10N 36°10E **212** B7
Samtah *Si. Arabia* 16°36N 42°56E **248** C3
Samtredia *Georgia* 42°7N 42°24E **191** J6
Samuel Smith Park *Canada* 43°35N 79°30W **141** B1
Samui, Ko *Thailand* 9°30N 100°0E **237** b
Samur → *Russia* 41°53N 48°32E **191** K9
Samurskiy Khrebet *Russia* 41°55N 47°11E **191** K8
Samusole *Dem. Rep. of the Congo* 10°2S 24°0E **265** E4
Samut Prakan *Thailand* 13°40N 100°36E **113** B2
Samut Songkhram *Thailand* 13°24N 100°1E **236** F3
Samwari *Pakistan* 28°30N 66°46E **242** E2
San *Mali* 13°15N 4°57W **262** C4
San → *Cambodia* 13°32N 105°57E **236** F5
San → *Poland* 50°45N 21°51E **185** H8
San Adrián *Spain* 42°20N 1°56W **196** C3
San Adrián, C. de *Spain* 43°21N 8°50W **194** B2
San Agustín *Colombia* 1°53N 76°16W **328** C2
San Agustin *Romblon, Phil.* 12°34N 122°6E **232** E4
San Agustin, C. *Phil.* 6°20N 126°13E **233** H6
San Agustín de Valle Fértil *Argentina* 30°35S 67°30W **334** C2
San Ambrosio *Pac. Oc.* 26°28S 79°53W **326** F3
San Andreas *U.S.A.* 38°12N 120°41W **306** G6
San Andres *Catanduanes, Phil.* 13°36N 124°6E **232** E5
San Andres *Romblon, Phil.* 13°19N 122°41E **232** E4
San Andres *Romblon, Phil.* 12°31N 122°2E **232** E4
San Andrés *Barcelona, Spain* 41°26N 2°11E **114** A2
San Andrés, I. de *Caribbean* 12°42N 81°46W **320** D3
San Andrês del Rabanedo *Spain* 42°37N 5°36W **194** C5
San Andres Mts. *U.S.A.* 33°0N 106°30W **305** K10
San Andrés Tuxtla *Mexico* 18°27N 95°13W **319** D5
San Angel *Mexico* 19°20N 99°11W **128** B1
San Angelo *U.S.A.* 31°28N 100°26W **314** F4
San Anselmo *U.S.A.* 37°59N 122°34W **306** H4
San Antonio *Belize* 16°15N 89°2W **320** C2
San Antonio *Chile* 33°40S 71°40W **334** C1
San Antonio *Phil.* 14°57N 120°5E **232** D3
San Antonio *N. Mex., U.S.A.* 33°55N 106°52W **305** K10
San Antonio *Tex., U.S.A.* 29°25N 98°29W **314** G5
San Antonio *Venezuela* 3°30N 66°44W **328** C4
San Antonio → *U.S.A.* 28°30N 96°54W **314** G6
San Antonio, C. *Argentina* 36°15S 56°40W **334** D4
San Antonio, C. de *Cuba* 21°50N 84°57W **320** B3
San Antonio, C. de *Spain* 38°48N 0°12E **197** G5
San Antonio, Mt. *U.S.A.* 34°17N 117°38W **307** L9
San Antonio Bay *Phil.* 8°38N 117°35E **233** G1
San Antonio de los Baños *Cuba* 22°54N 82°31W **320** B3
San Antonio de los Cobres *Argentina* 24°10S 66°17W **334** A2
San Antonio Oeste *Argentina* 40°40S 65°0W **336** B4
San Arcángelo *Italy* 40°14N 16°14E **201** B9
San Ardo *U.S.A.* 36°1N 120°54W **306** J6
San Augustin *Canary Is.* 27°47N 15°32W **153** e1
San Augustine *U.S.A.* 31°32N 94°7W **314** F7
San Bartolomé *Canary Is.* 28°59N 13°37W **153** e2
San Bartolomé de Tirajana *Canary Is.* 27°54N 15°34W **153** e1
San Bartolomeo in Galdo *Italy* 41°24N 15°1E **201** A8
San Basilio *Italy* 41°56N 12°35E **126** B2
San Benedetto del Tronto *Italy* 42°57N 13°53E **199** F10
San Benedetto Po *Italy* 45°2N 10°55E **198** C7
San Benedicto, I. *Mexico* 19°18N 110°49W **318** D2
San Benito *U.S.A.* 26°8N 97°38W **314** H6
San Benito → *U.S.A.* 36°53N 121°34W **306** J5
San Benito Mt. *U.S.A.* 36°22N 120°37W **306** J6
San Bernardino *U.S.A.* 34°7N 117°19W **307** L9
San Bernardino Mts. *U.S.A.* 34°10N 116°45W **307** L10
San Bernardino Str. *Phil.* 13°0N 125°0E **232** E5
San Bernardo *Chile* 33°40S 70°50W **334** C1
San Bernardo, I. de *Colombia* 9°45N 75°50W **328** B2
San-Beyse = Choybalsan *Mongolia* 48°4N 114°30E **219** B6
San Blas *Mexico* 26°5N 108°46W **318** B3
San Blas, Arch. de *Panama* 9°50N 78°31W **320** E4
San Blas, C. *U.S.A.* 29°40N 85°21W **316** F4
San Bonifacio *Italy* 45°24N 11°16E **199** C8
San Borja *Bolivia* 14°50S 66°52W **330** C4
San Borja *Lima, Peru* 12°6S 76°59W **124** B3
San Bóvio *Italy* 45°27N 9°18E **129** B2
San Bruno, Pt. *U.S.A.* 37°39N 122°22W **136** C2
San Bruno Mountain State Park ⌂ *U.S.A.* 37°41N 122°26W **136** B2
San Buenaventura = Ventura *U.S.A.* 34°17N 119°18W **307** L7
San Buenaventura *Bolivia* 14°28S 67°35W **330** C4
San Buenaventura *Coahuila, Mexico* 27°5N 101°32W **318** B4
San Carlos = Butuku-Luba *Eq. Guin.* 3°29N 8°33E **263** E6
San Carlos = Sant Carles *Spain* 39°3N 1°34E **206** C2
San Carlos *Argentina* 33°50S 69°0W **334** C2
San Carlos *Bolivia* 17°24S 63°45W **331** D5
San Carlos *Chile* 36°10S 72°0W **334** D1
San Carlos *Baja Calif. S., Mexico* 24°47N 112°7W **318** C2
San Carlos *Coahuila, Mexico* 29°1N 100°51W **318** B4
San Carlos *Nic.* 11°12N 84°50W **320** D3
San Carlos *Neg. Occ., Phil.* 10°29N 123°25E **233** F4
San Carlos *Pangasinan, Phil.* 15°55N 120°20E **232** D3
San Carlos *Uruguay* 34°46S 54°58W **335** C5
San Carlos *Ariz., U.S.A.* 33°21N 110°27W **305** K8
San Carlos *Amazonas, Venezuela* 1°55N 67°4W **328** C4
San Carlos *Cojedes, Venezuela* 9°40N 68°36W **328** B4
San Carlos de Bariloche *Argentina* 41°10S 71°25W **336** B2
San Carlos de Bolívar *Argentina* 36°15S 61°6W **334** D3
San Carlos de la Ràpita = Sant Carles de la Ràpita *Spain* 40°37N 0°35E **196** E5
San Carlos de Río Negro *Venezuela* 1°55N 67°4W **328** C4
San Carlos del Zulia *Venezuela* 9°1N 71°55W **328** B3
San Carlos L. *U.S.A.* 33°11N 110°32W **305** K8
San Carlos Park *U.S.A.* 26°28N 81°49W **317** J8
San Cataldo *Italy* 37°29N 13°59E **200** E6
San Celoni = Sant Celoni *Spain* 41°42N 2°30E **196** D7
San Clemente *Chile* 35°30S 71°29W **334** D1
San Clemente *Spain* 39°24N 2°25W **197** F2
San Clemente *Calif., U.S.A.* 33°26N 117°37W **307** M9
San Clemente I. *U.S.A.* 32°53N 118°29W **307** N8
San Cristóbal = Es Migjorn Gran *Spain* 39°57N 4°3E **206** B5
San Cristóbal *B. Aires, Argentina* 34°38S 58°23W **117** B2
San Cristóbal *Santa Fe, Argentina* 30°20S 61°10W **334** C3
San Cristóbal *Colombia* 2°18S 73°2W **328** D3
San Cristóbal *Dom. Rep.* 18°25N 70°6W **321** C5
San Cristóbal *Solomon Is.* 10°30S 161°0E **287** N11
San Cristóbal *Madrid, Spain* 40°25N 3°35W **127** B2
San Cristóbal *Venezuela* 7°46N 72°14W **328** B3
San Cristóbal, Cerro *Chile* 33°25S 70°38W **137** B2
San Cristóbal, I. *Ecuador* 0°50S 89°26W **330** a
San Cristóbal, Virgen del *Chile* 33°25S 70°38W **137** B2
San Cristóbal de las Casas *Mexico* 16°45N 92°38W **319** D6
San Cristoforo *Italy* 45°26N 9°9E **129** B1
San Damiano d'Asti *Italy* 44°50N 8°4E **198** D5
San Daniele del Friuli *Italy* 46°9N 13°1E **199** B10
San Diego *Calif., U.S.A.* 32°42N 117°9W **307** N9
San Diego *Tex., U.S.A.* 27°46N 98°14W **314** H5
San Diego, C. *Argentina* 54°40S 65°10W **336** D3
San Diego de la Unión *Mexico* 21°28N 100°52W **318** C4
San Diego Int. ✈ (SAN) *U.S.A.* 32°44N 117°11W **307** N9
San Dimitri, Ras *Malta* 36°4N 14°11E **206** E6
San Dimitri Point = San Dimitri, Ras *Malta* 36°4N 14°11E **206** E6
San Donà di Piave *Italy* 45°38N 12°34E **199** C9
San Donato Milanese *Italy* 45°24N 9°16E **129** B2
Sân el Hagar *Egypt* 30°58N 31°52E **251** H2
San Estanislao *Paraguay* 24°39S 56°26W **334** A4
San Esteban △ *Venezuela* 10°24N 67°58W **328** A4
San Esteban de Gormaz *Spain* 41°34N 3°13W **196** D1
San Eugenio = Artigas *Uruguay* 30°20S 56°30W **334** C4
San Felice Circeo *Italy* 41°14N 13°5E **200** A6
San Felice sul Panaro *Italy* 44°50N 11°8E **199** D8
San Felipe *Chile* 32°43S 70°42W **334** C1
San Felipe *Colombia* 1°55N 67°6W **328** C4
San Felipe *Baja Calif., Mexico* 31°1N 114°52W **318** A2
San Felipe *Phil.* 15°4N 120°4E **232** D3
San Felipe *Venezuela* 10°20N 68°44W **328** A4
San Felipe → *U.S.A.* 33°10N 115°49W **307** M11
San Félix *Chile* 28°56S 70°28W **334** B1
San Félix *Pac. Oc.* 26°23S 80°0W **326** F2
San Fernando = Sant Ferran *Spain* 38°42N 1°28E **206** D1
San Fernando *Chile* 34°30S 71°0W **334** C1
San Fernando *Tamaulipas, Mexico* 24°51N 98°10W **319** C5
San Fernando *Cebu, Phil.* 10°10N 123°42E **233** F4
San Fernando *La Union, Phil.* 16°40N 120°23E **232** C3
San Fernando *Pampanga, Phil.* 15°5N 120°37E **232** D3
San Fernando *Romblon, Phil.* 12°18N 122°36E **232** E4
San Fernando *Cádiz, Spain* 36°28N 6°17W **195** J4
San Fernando *Trin. & Tob.* 10°16N 61°28W **323** t
San Fernando *Calif., U.S.A.* 34°17N 118°26W **307** L8
San Fernando de Apure *Venezuela* 7°54N 67°15W **328** B4
San Fernando de Atabapo *Venezuela* 4°3N 67°42W **328** C4
San Fernando di Púglia *Italy* 41°18N 16°5E **201** A9
San Francique = Erin *Trin. & Tob.* 10°5N 61°39W **323** t
San Francisco *Córdoba, Argentina* 31°30S 62°5W **334** C3
San Francisco *Bolivia* 15°16S 65°31W **331** D4
San Francisco *Peru* 12°36S 73°49W **330** C3
San Francisco *Agusan del S., Phil.* 8°30N 125°56E **233** G5
San Francisco *Cebu, Phil.* 10°39N 124°23E **233** F5
San Francisco *Quezon, Phil.* 13°21N 122°31E **232** E4
San Francisco *S. Leyte, Phil.* 10°4N 125°9E **233** F5
San Francisco *Calif., U.S.A.* 37°46N 122°23W **136** B2
San Francisco → *U.S.A.* 32°59N 109°22W **305** K9
San Francisco, C. de *Colombia* 6°18N 77°29W **328** B2
San Francisco, Paso de *S. Amer.* 27°0S 68°0W **334** B2
San Francisco B. *U.S.A.* 37°39N 122°14W **136** B3
San Francisco Culhuacán *Mexico* 19°19N 99°8W **128** C2
San Francisco de Macorís *Dom. Rep.* 19°19N 70°15W **321** C5
San Francisco del Monte de Oro *Argentina* 32°36S 66°8W **334** C2
San Francisco del Oro *Mexico* 26°52N 105°51W **318** B3
San Francisco Int. ✈ (SFO) *U.S.A.* 37°37N 122°22W **306** H4
San Francisco Javier = Sant Francesc de Formentera *Spain* 38°42N 1°26E **206** D1
San Fratello *Italy* 38°1N 14°36E **201** D7
San Fruttuoso *Italy* 45°34N 9°14E **129** A2
San Gabriel *Chile* 33°47S 70°15W **334** C1
San Gabriel *Ecuador* 0°36N 77°49W **328** C2
San Gabriel *Calif., U.S.A.* 34°5N 118°5W **126** B4
San Gabriel → *U.S.A.* 33°58N 118°5W **126** C4
San Gabriel Chilac *Mexico* 18°19N 97°21W **319** D5
San Gabriel Mts. *U.S.A.* 34°17N 117°38W **307** L9
San Gavino Monreale *Italy* 39°33N 8°47E **200** C1
San German *Puerto Rico* 18°4N 67°4W **321** b
San Gil *Colombia* 6°33N 73°8W **328** B3
San Giljan = St. Julian's *Malta* 35°55N 14°29E **206** F7
San Gimignano *Italy* 43°28N 11°2E **198** E8
San Giórgio di Nogaro *Italy* 45°50N 13°13E **199** C10
San Giórgio Iónico *Italy* 40°27N 17°23E **201** B10
San Giovanni Bianco *Italy* 45°52N 9°39E **198** C6
San Giovanni in Fiore *Italy* 39°15N 16°42E **201** C9
San Giovanni in Persiceto *Italy* 44°38N 11°11E **199** D8
San Giovanni Rotondo *Italy* 41°42N 15°44E **199** G12
San Giovanni Valdarno *Italy* 43°34N 11°32E **199** E8
San Giuliano Milanese *Italy* 45°24N 9°17E **129** B2
San Giuliano Terme *Italy* 43°46N 10°26E **198** E7
San Gorgonio Mt. *U.S.A.* 34°6N 116°50W **307** L10
San Gottardo, P. del *Switz.* 46°33N 8°33E **179** J4
San Gregorio *Uruguay* 32°37S 55°40W **335** C4
San Gregorio *Calif., U.S.A.* 37°20N 122°23W **306** H4
San Guillermo △ *Argentina* 27°50S 69°45W **334** B2
San Guiseppe Jato *Italy* 37°57N 13°11E **200** E6
San Ignacio *Belize* 17°10N 89°5W **320** C2
San Ignacio *Beni, Bolivia* 14°53S 65°36W **331** C4
San Ignacio *Santa Cruz, Bolivia* 16°20S 60°55W **331** D5
San Ignacio *Baja Calif. S., Mexico* 27°27N 112°51W **318** B2
San Ignacio *Paraguay* 26°52S 57°3W **334** B4
San Ignacio *Peru* 5°8S 78°59W **330** B2
San Ignacio, L. *Mexico* 26°54N 113°13W **318** B2
San Ildefonso, C. *Phil.* 16°0N 122°1E **232** C4
San Isidro *Argentina* 34°29S 58°31W **334** C4
San Isidro *Lima, Peru* 12°5S 77°2W **124** B2
San Isidro *Phil.* 6°50N 126°5E **233** H6
San Isidro de Potot = Burgos *Phil.* 16°4N 119°52E **232** C2
San Jacinto *Colombia* 9°50N 75°8W **328** B2
San Jacinto *Phil.* 12°34N 123°44E **232** E4
San Jacinto *Calif., U.S.A.* 33°47N 116°57W **307** M10
San Jaime = Sant Jaume *Spain* 39°54N 4°4E **206** B5
San Javier *Misiones, Argentina* 27°55S 55°5W **335** B4
San Javier *Santa Fe, Argentina* 30°40S 59°55W **334** C4
San Javier *Beni, Bolivia* 14°34S 64°42W **331** C5
San Javier *Santa Cruz, Bolivia* 16°18S 62°30W **331** D5
San Javier *Chile* 35°40S 71°45W **334** D1
San Javier *Spain* 37°49N 0°50W **197** H4
San Jerónimo Lidice *Mexico* 19°19N 99°14W **128** C1
San Jerónimo Taviche *Mexico* 16°44N 96°35W **319** D5
San Joaquín *Bolivia* 13°4S 64°49W **331** C5
San Joaquín *Santiago, Chile* 33°29S 70°35W **137** B2
San Joaquin *Phil.* 10°35N 122°8E **233** F4
San Joaquin *Calif., U.S.A.* 36°36N 120°11W **306** J6
San Joaquín → *Bolivia* 13°8S 63°41W **331** C5
San Joaquin → *Calif., U.S.A.* 38°4N 121°51W **306** G5
San Joaquín, Cerro *Ecuador* 0°53S 89°30W **330** a
San Joaquin Valley *U.S.A.* 37°20N 121°0W **306** J6
San Jon *U.S.A.* 35°6N 103°20W **305** J12
San Jordi = Sant Jordi *Spain* 39°33N 2°46E **206** B3
San Jorge *Argentina* 31°54S 61°50W **334** C3
San Jorge *Solomon Is.* 8°28S 159°38E **287** M10
San Jorge, B. *Mexico* 31°20N 113°20W **318** A2
San Jorge, G. *Argentina* 46°0S 66°0W **336** C3
San José = San Josep *Spain* 38°55N 1°18E **206** D1
San José *Argentina* 32°12S 58°15W **334** C4
San José *Costa Rica* 9°55N 84°2W **320** E3
San José *Guatemala* 14°0N 90°50W **320** D1
San Jose *N. Marianas* 14°58N 145°37E **302** e
San Jose *Mind. Occ., Phil.* 12°27N 121°4E **232** E3
San Jose *Nueva Ecija, Phil.* 15°45N 120°55E **232** D3
San Jose *Calif., U.S.A.* 37°20N 121°53W **306** H5
San Jose *Ill., U.S.A.* 40°18N 89°36W **310** D7
San Jose → *U.S.A.* 34°25N 106°45W **305** J10
San José, Golfo *Argentina* 42°20S 64°18W **336** B4
San José, I. *Mexico* 25°0N 110°38W **318** C2
San Jose de Buenavista *Phil.* 10°45N 121°56E **233** F3
San José de Chiquitos *Bolivia* 17°53S 60°50W **331** D5
San José de Feliciano *Argentina* 30°26S 58°46W **334** C4
San José de Guanipa *Venezuela* 8°53N 64°9W **329** B5
San José de Jáchal *Argentina* 30°15S 68°46W **334** C2
San José de Mayo *Uruguay* 34°27S 56°40W **334** C4
San José de Ocuné *Colombia* 4°15N 70°20W **328** C3
San José de Uchapiamonas *Bolivia* 14°13S 68°5W **330** C4
San José del Cabo *Mexico* 23°3N 109°41W **318** C3
San José del Guaviare *Colombia* 2°35N 72°38W **328** C3
San Jose del Monte *Phil.* 14°49N 121°3E **232** D3
San José do Anauá *Brazil* 0°58N 61°22W **329** C5
San José Río Hondo *Mexico* 19°26N 99°14W **128** B1
San Josep *Spain* 38°55N 1°18E **206** D1
San Juan *Argentina* 31°30S 68°30W **334** C2
San Juan *Antioquia, Colombia* 8°46N 76°32W **328** B2
San Juan *Neth. Ant.* 12°15N 69°6W **322** g
San Juan *Ica, Peru* 15°22S 75°7W **330** D2
San Juan *Batangas, Phil.* 13°50N 121°24E **232** E3
San Juan *S. Leyte, Phil.* 10°16N 125°10E **233** F5
San Juan *Puerto Rico* 18°28N 66°7W **321** C6
San Juan *Trin. & Tob.* 10°39N 61°29W **323** t
San Juan □ *Argentina* 31°9S 69°0W **334** C2
San Juan → *Argentina* 32°20S 67°25W **334** C2
San Juan → *Bolivia* 21°2S 65°19W **331** E4
San Juan → *Colombia* 4°3N 77°27W **328** C2
San Juan → *Nic.* 10°56N 83°42W **320** D3
San Juan → *Manila, Phil.* 14°35N 121°0E **127** B2
San Juan → *Utah, U.S.A.* 37°16N 110°26W **305** H8
San Juan → *Venezuela* 10°14N 62°38W **329** A5
San Juan, C. *Argentina* 54°44S 63°44W **336** D4
San Juan, C. *Eq. Guin.* 1°5N 9°20E **264** B1
San Juan Bautista = Sant Joan de Labritja *Spain* 39°5N 1°31E **206** C2
San Juan Bautista = Villahermosa *Mexico* 17°59N 92°55W **319** D6
San Juan Bautista *Chile* 33°37S 78°50W **330** c
San Juan Bautista *Paraguay* 26°37S 57°6W **334** B4
San Juan Bautista *Calif., U.S.A.* 36°51N 121°32W **306** J5
San Juan Capistrano *U.S.A.* 33°30N 117°40W **307** M9
San Juan Cr. → *U.S.A.* 35°40N 120°22W **306** J5
San Juan de Aragón *Mexico* 19°28N 99°4W **128** B2
San Juan de Aragón, Parque *Mexico* 19°27N 99°4W **128** B2
San Juan de Guadelupe *Mexico* 24°38N 102°44W **318** C4
San Juan de Guía, Cabo de *Colombia* 11°21N 73°59W **328** A3
San Juan de la Costa *Mexico* 24°20N 110°41W **318** C2
San Juan de los Lagos *Mexico* 21°15N 102°18W **318** C4
San Juan de los Morros *Venezuela* 9°55N 67°21W **328** B4
San Juan de Lurigancho *Peru* 11°59S 77°0W **124** A2
San Juan de Manapiare *Venezuela* 5°15N 66°5W **328** B4
San Juan de Villa Hermosa = Villahermosa *Mexico* 17°59N 92°55W **319** D6
San Juan del César *Colombia* 10°46N 73°1W **328** A3
San Juan del Monte *Phil.* 14°36N 121°1E **127** B2
San Juan del Norte *Nic.* 10°58N 83°40W **320** D3
San Juan del Norte, B. de *Nic.* 11°0N 83°40W **320** D3
San Juan del Río *Mexico* 20°23N 100°0W **319** C5
San Juan del Sur *Nic.* 11°20N 85°51W **320** D2
San Juan I. *U.S.A.* 48°32N 123°5W **306** B3
San Juan Island ⌂ *U.S.A.* 48°35N 123°8W **306** B4
San Juan Ixtacala *Mexico* 19°31N 99°10W **128** A1
San Juan Mts. *U.S.A.* 37°30N 107°0W **305** H10
San Julian *Phil.* 11°45N 125°27E **233** F5
San Just, Sierra de *Spain* 40°45N 0°49W **196** E4
San Just Desvern *Spain* 41°22N 2°4E **114** A1
San Justo *B. Aires, Argentina* 34°40S 58°33W **117** C1
San Justo *Santa Fe, Argentina* 30°47S 60°30W **334** C3
San Kamphaeng *Thailand* 18°45N 99°8E **236** C2
San Lázaro, C. *Mexico* 24°50N 112°18W **318** C2
San Leandro *U.S.A.* 37°42N 122°9W **306** H4
San Leonardo de Yagüe *Spain* 41°51N 3°5W **196** D1
San Lorenzo = Sant Llorenç des Cardassar *Spain* 39°37N 3°17E **206** B4
San Lorenzo *Argentina* 32°45S 60°45W **334** C3
San Lorenzo *Beni, Bolivia* 15°22S 65°48W **331** D4
San Lorenzo *Tarija, Bolivia* 21°26S 64°47W **331** E5
San Lorenzo *Ecuador* 1°15N 78°50W **328** C2
San Lorenzo *Paraguay* 25°20S 57°32W **334** B4
San Lorenzo → *Mexico* 24°15N 107°24W **318** C3
San Lorenzo, I. *Baja Calif., Mexico* 28°38N 112°51W **318** B2
San Lorenzo, I. *Peru* 12°7S 77°15W **330** C2
San Lorenzo, Mte. *Argentina* 47°40S 72°20W **336** C2
San Lorenzo de la Parrilla *Spain* 39°51N 2°22W **196** F2
San Lorenzo de Morunys = Sant Llorenç de Morunys *Spain* 42°8N 1°35E **196** C6
San Lorenzo Tezonco *Mexico* 19°19N 99°3W **128** C2
San Lucas = Cabo San Lucas *Mexico* 22°53N 109°54W **318** C3
San Lucas *Bolivia* 20°5S 65°7W **331** E4
San Lucas *Baja Calif. S., Mexico* 27°10N 112°14W **318** B2
San Lucas *Calif., U.S.A.* 36°8N 121°1W **306** J5
San Lucas, C. *Mexico* 22°52N 109°53W **318** C3
San Lúcido *Italy* 39°18N 16°3E **201** C9
San Luis = Entre Ríos *Bolivia* 21°30S 64°25W **334** A3
San Luis = Sevilla *Colombia* 4°16N 75°57W **328** C2
San Luis *Argentina* 33°20S 66°20W **334** C2
San Luis *Pinar del Río, Cuba* 22°17N 83°46W **320** B3
San Luis *Guatemala* 16°14N 89°27W **320** C2
San Luis *Lima, Peru* 12°4S 77°0W **124** B2
San Luis *Ariz., U.S.A.* 32°29N 114°47W **305** K6
San Luis *Colo., U.S.A.* 37°12N 105°25W **305** H11
San Luis □ *Argentina* 34°0S 66°0W **334** C2
San Luis, I. *Mexico* 29°58N 114°26W **318** B2
San Luis, L. de *Bolivia* 13°45S 64°0W **331** C5
San Luis, Sierra de *Argentina* 32°30S 66°10W **334** C2
San Luis de la Paz *Mexico* 21°18N 100°31W **318** C4
San Luis Obispo *U.S.A.* 35°17N 120°40W **307** K6
San Luis Potosí *Mexico* 22°9N 100°59W **318** C4
San Luis Potosí □ *Mexico* 23°0N 101°0W **318** C4
San Luis Res. *U.S.A.* 37°4N 121°5W **306** H5
San Luis Río Colorado *Mexico* 32°29N 114°58W **318** A2
San Manuel *Phil.* 16°4N 120°40E **232** C3
San Manuel *Ariz., U.S.A.* 32°36N 110°38W **305** K8
San Marco, C. *Italy* 39°51N 8°26E **200** C1
San Marco Argentano *Italy* 39°33N 16°7E **201** C9
San Marco in Lámis *Italy* 41°43N 15°38E **199** G12
San Marcos *Colombia* 8°39N 75°8W **328** B2
San Marcos *Guatemala* 14°59N 91°52W **320** D1
San Marcos *Calif., U.S.A.* 33°9N 117°10W **307** M9
San Marcos *Tex., U.S.A.* 29°53N 97°56W **314** G6
San Marcos, I. *Mexico* 27°13N 112°6W **318** B2
San Mariano *Phil.* 17°0N 122°2E **232** C4
San Marino *San Marino* 43°55N 12°30E **199** E9
San Marino *Calif., U.S.A.* 34°7N 118°5W **126** B4
San Marino ■ *Europe* 43°56N 12°25E **199** E9
San Martín = Tarapoto *Peru* 6°30S 76°20W **330** B2
San Martín *Antarctica* 68°11S 67°0W **151** C17
San Martín *Argentina* 33°5S 68°28W **334** C2
San Martín *Colombia* 3°42N 73°42W **328** C3
San Martín *Barcelona, Spain* 41°24N 2°11E **114** A2
San Martín □ *Peru* 7°0S 76°50W **330** B2
San Martín → *Bolivia* 13°8S 63°43W **331** C5
San Martín, L. *Argentina* 48°50S 72°50W **336** C2
San Martín de la Vega *Spain* 40°13N 3°34W **194** E7
San Martín de los Andes *Argentina* 40°10S 71°20W **336** B2
San Martín de Porras *Peru* 12°1S 77°5W **124** B2
San Martín de Valdeiglesias *Spain* 40°21N 4°24W **194** E6
San Mateo = Sant Mateu *Baleares, Spain* 39°3N 1°23E **206** C1
San Mateo = Sant Mateu *Valencia, Spain* 40°28N 0°10E **196** E5
San Mateo *Isabela, Phil.* 16°54N 121°33E **232** C3
San Mateo *Calif., U.S.A.* 37°34N 122°19W **306** H4
San Mateo Tlaltenango *Mexico* 19°20N 99°16W **128** B1
San Matías *Bolivia* 16°25S 58°20W **331** D6
San Matías, G. *Argentina* 41°30S 64°0W **336** B4
San Miguel = Linapacan *Phil.* 11°30N 119°52E **233** F2
San Miguel = Sant Miquel *Spain* 39°3N 1°26E **206** C1
San Miguel = Sarrat *Phil.* 18°9N 120°39E **232** B3
San Miguel *Bolivia* 16°42S 61°1W **331** C5
San Miguel *Santiago, Chile* 33°29S 70°39W **137** B2
San Miguel *El Salv.* 13°30N 88°12W **320** D2
San Miguel *Panama* 8°27N 78°55W **320** E4
San Miguel *Lima, Peru* 12°5S 77°6W **124** B2
San Miguel *Bulacan, Phil.* 15°9N 120°59E **232** D3
San Miguel *Palawan, Phil.* 11°30N 119°51E **233** F2
San Miguel *Surigao S., Phil.* 9°3N 125°59E **233** G5
San Miguel *Calif., U.S.A.* 35°45N 120°42W **306** K6
San Miguel → *Bolivia* 13°52S 63°56W **331** C5
San Miguel → *Ecuador* 0°25N 76°30W **328** C2
San Miguel, Golfo de *Panama* 8°22N 78°17W **328** B2
San Miguel de Huachi *Bolivia* 15°40S 67°15W **330** D4
San Miguel de Tucumán *Argentina* 26°50S 65°20W **334** B2
San Miguel del Monte *Argentina* 35°23S 58°50W **334** D4
San Miguel I. *U.S.A.* 34°2N 120°23W **307** L6
San Miguel Is. *Phil.* 7°45N 118°28E **233** H2
San Miniato *Italy* 43°41N 10°51E **198** E7
San Narciso *Phil.* 13°34N 122°34E **232** E4
San Nicolas = Sint Nicolaas *Neth. Ant.* 12°17N 69°8W **322** g
San Nicolás *B. Aires, Argentina* 34°36S 58°22W **117** B2
San Nicolás *Canary Is.* 27°58N 15°47W **153** e1
San Nicolas *Phil.* 18°10N 120°36E **232** B3
San Nicolás de los Arroyos *Argentina* 33°25S 60°10W **334** C3
San Nicolas I. *U.S.A.* 33°15N 119°30W **307** M7
San Onofre *Colombia* 9°44N 75°32W **328** B2
San Onofre *Calif., U.S.A.* 33°22N 117°34W **307** M9
San Onófrio *Italy* 41°57N 12°25E **136** B1
San Pablo *Bolivia* 21°43S 66°38W **334** A2
San Pablo *Isabela, Phil.* 17°27N 121°48E **232** C3
San Pablo *Laguna, Phil.* 14°11N 121°31E **232** D3
San Pablo *Calif., U.S.A.* 37°58N 122°21W **306** H4
San Pablo de Manta = Manta *Ecuador* 1°0S 80°40W **328** D1
San Páolo di Civitate *Italy* 41°44N 15°15E **199** G12
San Pascual *Phil.* 13°8N 122°59E **232** E4
San Pedro *B. Aires, Argentina* 33°40S 59°40W **334** C4
San Pedro *Misiones, Argentina* 26°30S 54°10W **335** B5
San Pedro *Chile* 33°54S 71°28W **334** C1
San Pedro *Colombia* 4°56N 71°53W **328** C3
San Pedro *Ivory C.* 4°50N 6°33W **262** E3
San Pedro *Baja Calif. S., Mexico* 23°55N 110°17W **318** C2
San Pedro *Peru* 14°49S 74°5W **330** C3
San Pedro □ *Paraguay* 24°0S 57°0W **334** A4
San Pedro → *Chihuahua, Mexico* 28°20N 106°10W **318** B3
San Pedro → *Nayarit, Mexico* 21°45N 105°30W **318** C3
San Pedro → *Ariz., U.S.A.* 32°59N 110°47W **305** K8
San Pedro, Pta. *Chile* 25°30S 70°38W **334** B1
San Pedro, Sierra de *Spain* 39°18N 6°40W **195** F4
San Pedro Channel *U.S.A.* 33°30N 118°25W **307** M8
San Pedro de Arimena *Colombia* 4°37N 71°42W **328** C3
San Pedro de Atacama *Chile* 22°55S 68°15W **334** A2
San Pedro de Jujuy *Argentina* 24°12S 64°55W **334** A3
San Pedro de las Colonias *Mexico* 25°45N 102°59W **318** B4
San Pedro de Lloc *Peru* 7°15S 79°28W **330** B2
San Pedro de Macorís *Dom. Rep.* 18°30N 69°18W **321** C6
San Pedro del Norte *Nic.* 13°4N 84°33W **320** D3
San Pedro del Paraná *Paraguay* 26°43S 56°13W **334** B4
San Pedro del Pinatar *Spain* 37°50N 0°50W **197** H4
San Pedro Mártir *Spain* 41°23N 2°6E **114** A1
San Pedro Mártir, Sierra *Mexico* 31°0N 115°30W **318** A1
San Pedro Mártir △ *Mexico* 31°0N 115°21W **318** A1
San Pedro Ocampo = Melchor Ocampo *Mexico* 24°51N 101°39W **318** C4
San Pedro Pochutla *Mexico* 15°44N 96°28W **319** D5
San Pedro Sula *Honduras* 15°30N 88°0W **320** C2
San Pedro Tututepec *Mexico* 16°9N 97°38W **319** D5
San Pedro Zacatenco *Mexico* 19°30N 99°6W **128** A2
San Pietro *Italy* 39°8N 8°17E **200** C1
San Pietro, Piazza *Rome, Italy* **136** b1
San Pietro Vernótico *Italy* 40°29N 18°0E **201** B11
San Po Kong *China* 22°20N 114°11E **122** A2
San Rafael *Argentina* 34°40S 68°21W **334** C2
San Rafael *Bolivia* 16°45S 60°34W **331** D5
San Rafael *Trin. & Tob.* 10°34N 61°16W **323** t
San Rafael *Calif., U.S.A.* 37°58N 122°32W **306** H4
San Rafael *N. Mex., U.S.A.* 35°7N 107°53W **305** J10
San Rafael *Venezuela* 10°58N 71°46W **328** A3
San Rafael Chamapa *Mexico* 19°27N 99°15W **128** B1
San Rafael Hills *U.S.A.* 34°10N 118°12W **126** A3
San Rafael Mt. *U.S.A.* 34°41N 119°52W **307** L7
San Rafael Mts. *U.S.A.* 34°40N 119°50W **307** L7
San Ramón *Bolivia* 13°17S 64°43W **331** C5
San Ramón de la Nueva Orán *Argentina* 23°10S 64°20W **334** A3
San Remo *Italy* 43°49N 7°46E **198** E4
San Román, C. *Venezuela* 12°12N 70°0W **328** A4
San Roque *Argentina* 28°25S 58°45W **334** B4
San Roque *Manila, Phil.* 14°34N 121°5E **127** B2
San Roque *N. Samar, Phil.* 12°37N 124°52E **232** E5
San Roque *Spain* 36°17N 5°21W **195** J5
San Rosendo *Chile* 37°16S 72°43W **334** D1
San Saba *U.S.A.* 31°12N 98°43W **314** F5
San Salvador *El Salv.* 13°40N 89°10W **320** D2
San Salvador, Canal de *Ecuador* 0°25S 90°30W **330** a
San Salvador, I. *Ecuador* 0°16S 90°42W **330** a
San Salvador de Jujuy *Argentina* 24°10S 64°48W **334** A3
San Salvador I. *Bahamas* 24°0N 74°40W **321** B5
San Salvo *Italy* 42°3N 14°44E **199** F11
San Sebastián = Donostia-San Sebastián *Spain* 43°17N 1°58W **196** B3
San Sebastián *Argentina* 53°10S 68°30W **336** D3
San Sebastián *Puerto Rico* 18°20N 66°59W **321** b
San Sebastián de la Gomera *Canary Is.* 28°5N 17°7W **153** e1
San Serra = Son Serra *Spain* 39°43N 3°13E **206** B4
San Serverino Marche *Italy* 43°13N 13°10E **199** E10
San Severo *Italy* 41°41N 15°23E **199** G12
San Simeon *U.S.A.* 35°39N 121°11W **306** K5
San Simon *U.S.A.* 32°16N 109°14W **305** K9
San Siro *Italy* 45°28N 9°7E **129** B1
San Souci *Australia* 33°59S 151°8E **139** B1
San Stéfano di Cadore *Italy* 46°34N 12°33E **199** B9
San Stino di Livenza *Italy* 45°44N 12°41E **199** C9
San Telmo = Sant Elm *Spain* 39°35N 2°21E **206** B3
San Telmo *B. Aires, Argentina* 34°37S 58°23W **117** B2
San Telmo *Baja Calif., Mexico* 30°58N 116°6W **318** A1
San Teodoro *Phil.* 13°26N 121°1E **232** E3
San Tiburcio *Mexico* 24°8N 101°32W **318** C4
San Valentin, Mte. *Chile* 46°30S 73°30W **336** C2
San Vicenç dels Horts *Spain* 41°23N 2°0E **114** A1
San Vicente de Alcántara *Spain* 39°22N 7°8W **195** F3
San Vicente de Cañete *Peru* 13°8S 76°30W **330** C2
San Vicente de la Barquera *Spain* 43°23N 4°29W **194** B6
San Vicente del Caguán *Colombia* 2°7N 74°46W **328** C3
San Vincenzo *Italy* 43°6N 10°32E **198** E7
San Vito *Costa Rica* 8°50N 82°58W **320** E3
San Vito *Italy* 39°26N 9°32E **200** C2
San Vito, C. *Italy* 38°11N 12°41E **200** D5
San Vito al Tagliamento *Italy* 45°54N 12°52E **199** C9
San Vito Chietino *Italy* 42°18N 14°27E **199** F11
San Vito dei Normanni *Italy* 40°39N 17°42E **201** B10
San Yanaro *Colombia* 2°47N 69°42W **328** C4
Saña *Peru* 6°54S 79°36W **330** B2
Sana' *Yemen* 15°27N 44°12E **248** D4
Sana → *Bos.-H.* 45°3N 16°23E **199** C13
Sanaag □ *Somali Rep.* 10°30N 48°0E **267** B6
Sanaba *Burkina Faso* 12°25N 3°47W **262** C4
Sanae IV *Antarctica* 70°20S 9°0W **151** D2
Şanāfīr *Si. Arabia* 27°56N 34°42E **251** L5
Sanaga → *Cameroon* 3°35N 9°38E **263** E6
Sanak I. *U.S.A.* 54°25N 162°40W **303** J7
Sanaloa, Presa *Mexico* 24°50N 107°20W **318** C3
Sanām *Si. Arabia* 23°40N 44°45E **248** B4
Sanana *Indonesia* 2°4S 125°58E **231** E7
Sanand *India* 22°59N 72°25E **242** H5
Sanandaj *Iran* 35°18N 47°1E **213** E12
Sanandita *Bolivia* 21°40S 63°45W **334** A3
Sanaroa I. *Papua N. G.* 9°37S 151°0E **286** E6
Sanary-sur-Mer *France* 43°7N 5°49E **175** E9
Sanāw *Yemen* 17°50N 51°5E **249** C5
Sanawad *India* 22°11N 76°5E **242** H7
Sanbancho *Tokyo, Japan* **140** a3
Sanbe-San *Japan* 35°6N 132°38E **222** B4
Sancellas = Sencelles *Spain* 39°39N 2°54E **206** B3
Sancergues *France* 47°10N 2°54E **173** E9
Sancerre *France* 47°20N 2°50E **173** E9
Sancerrois, Collines du *France* 47°20N 2°40E **173** E9
Sancha He → *China* 26°48N 106°7E **228** D6
Sanchahe *China* 44°50N 126°2E **227** B14
Sánchez *Dom. Rep.* 19°15N 69°36W **321** C6
Sanchez-Mira *Phil.* 18°34N 121°14E **232** B3
Sanchih *Taiwan* 25°15N 121°30E **225** A3
Sanchor *India* 24°45N 71°55E **242** G4
Sanch'ung *Taiwan* 25°4N 121°30E **225** A3
Sanco Pt. *Phil.* 8°15N 126°27E **233** G6
Sancoins *France* 46°47N 2°55E **173** F9
Sancti Spíritus *Cuba* 21°52N 79°33W **320** B4
Sancy, Puy de *France* 45°32N 2°50E **174** C6
Sand = Polokwane → *S. Africa* 22°25S 30°5E **271** B5
Sand *Norway* 59°29N 6°16E **164** E3
Sand Bank B. *St. Kitts & Nevis* 17°15N 62°38W **322** d
Sand Cr. → *U.S.A.* 39°3N 85°51W **311** E11
Sand Hills *Guyana* 6°27N 58°19W **329** B6
Sand Hills *Nebr., U.S.A.* 42°10N 101°30W **308** D3
Sand I. *Midway Is.* 28°12N 177°23W **302** c
Sand I. *Hawai'i, U.S.A.* 21°19N 157°53W **302** K14
Sand Islet *Midway Is.* 28°16N 177°22W **302** c
Sand Lakes ⌂ *Canada* 57°51N 98°32W **297** B9
Sand Point *U.S.A.* 55°20N 160°30W **303** J7
Sand Springs *U.S.A.* 36°9N 96°7W **314** C6
Sanda *Japan* 34°53N 135°14E **223** C7
Sandakan *Malaysia* 5°53N 118°4E **235** A5
Sandalwood *Australia* 34°55S 140°9E **282** C4
Sandan = Sambor *Cambodia* 12°46N 106°0E **236** F6
Sandane *Norway* 61°46N 6°13E **164** C3
Sandanski *Bulgaria* 41°35N 23°16E **202** E7
Sandaré *Mali* 14°40N 10°15W **262** C2
Sandared *Sweden* 57°43N 12°47E **163** G6
Sandarne *Sweden* 61°16N 17°9E **162** C11
Sanday *U.K.* 59°16N 2°31W **167** B6
Sande *Møre og Romsdal, Norway* 62°15N 5°27E **164** B2
Sande *Sogn og Fjordane, Norway* 61°20N 5°47E **164** C2
Sande *Vestfold, Norway* 59°36N 10°12E **162** E4
Sandefjord *Norway* 59°10N 10°15E **164** F7
Sandeid *Norway* 59°33N 5°52E **164** E2
Sanders *Ariz., U.S.A.* 35°13N 109°20W **305** J9
Sanders *Ky., U.S.A.* 38°40N 84°56W **311** F12
Sanderson *Fla., U.S.A.* 30°15N 82°16W **316** E7
Sanderson *Tex., U.S.A.* 30°9N 102°24W **314** F3
Sandersville *U.S.A.* 32°59N 82°48W **316** C7
Sandfire Roadhouse *Australia* 19°45S 121°15E **278** C3
Sandfloegga *Norway* 59°58N 7°10E **164** E4
Sandfly L. *Canada* 55°43N 106°6W **297** B7
Sandfontein *Namibia* 23°48S 19°1E **270** B2
Sandhammaren *Sweden* 55°23N 14°14E **163** J8
Sandheads, The *India* 21°10N 88°20E **241** E2
Sandgerði *Iceland* 64°3N 22°42W **155** C4
Sandia *Peru* 14°10S 69°30W **330** C4
Sandıklı *Turkey* 38°28N 30°17E **205** C12
Sandila *India* 27°5N 80°31E **243** F9
Sandilands *Bahamas* 25°3N 77°19W **153** b
Sanding *Indonesia* 3°28S 100°40E **234** C2
Sandnes *Aust-Agder, Norway* 58°53N 7°45E **164** F4
Sandnes *Rogaland, Norway* 58°50N 5°45E **164** F2
Sandnessjøen *Norway* 66°2N 12°38E **160** C15
Sandoa *Dem. Rep. of the Congo* 9°41S 23°0E **265** D4
Sandomierz *Poland* 50°40N 21°43E **185** H8
Sândominic *Romania* 46°35N 25°47E **183** D10
Sandona *Colombia* 1°17N 77°28W **328** C2
Sandongo *Angola* 15°30S 21°28E **265** F4
Sandoval *U.S.A.* 38°37N 89°7W **310** F7
Sandover → *Australia* 21°43S 136°32E **280** C2
Sandoway = Thandwe *Burma* 18°20N 94°30E **241** F5

Sandown *S. Africa* 26°5S 28°4E **123** A2
Sandown Park Races *U.K.* 51°22N 0°21W **125** B1
Sandoy *Færoe Is.* 61°52N 6°46W **160** F9
Sandpoint *U.S.A.* 48°17N 116°33W **304** B5
Sandray *U.K.* 56°53N 7°31W **167** E1
Sandringham *U.K.* 52°51N 0°31E **168** E8
Sandstone *Australia* 27°59S 119°16E **279** E2
Sandton *S. Africa* 26°5S 28°4E **123** A2
Sandu *China* 26°0N 107°52E **228** E6
Sandumba *Angola* 13°45S 17°34E **265** E3
Sandur *India* 15°6N 76°33E **245** F3
Sandusky *Mich., U.S.A.* 43°25N 82°50W **312** C2
Sandusky *Ohio, U.S.A.* 41°27N 82°42W **312** E2
Sandusky → *U.S.A.* 41°27N 83°0W **311** C14
Sandveld *Namibia* 21°25S 20°0E **270** B3
Sandvig *Denmark* 55°18N 14°47E **163** J8
Sandvika *Norway* 59°54N 10°31E **133** A2
Sandviken *Sweden* 60°38N 16°46E **162** D10
Sandwich *U.S.A.* 41°39N 88°37W **311** C8
Sandwich, C. *Australia* 18°14S 146°18E **280** B4
Sandwich B. *Nfld. & L., Canada* 53°40N 57°15W **299** B8
Sandwich B. *Namibia* 23°25S 14°20E **270** B1
Sandwip I. *Bangla.* 22°30N 91°25E **241** D3
Sandy *Oreg., U.S.A.* 45°24N 122°16W **306** E4
Sandy *Pa., U.S.A.* 41°6N 78°46W **312** E6
Sandy *Utah, U.S.A.* 40°32N 111°50W **304** F8
Sandy B. *St. Helena* 16°0S 5°43W **153** h
Sandy Bay *Canada* 55°31N 102°19W **297** B8
Sandy Bight *Australia* 33°50S 123°20E **279** F3
Sandy C. *Queens., Australia* 24°42S 153°15E **280** C5
Sandy C. *Tas., Australia* 41°25S 144°45E **281** G3
Sandy Cay *Bahamas* 23°13N 75°18W **321** B4
Sandy Cr. → *N.S.W., Australia* 31°54S 145°18E **281** B4
Sandy Cr. → *Wyo., U.S.A.* 41°51N 109°47W **304** F9
Sandy Creek *U.S.A.* 43°38N 76°5W **313** C8
Sandy Ground Village *Anguilla* 18°12N 63°6W **322** a
Sandy Hill Bay *Anguilla* 18°13N 63°1W **322** a
Sandy I. *Anguilla* 18°13N 63°7W **322** a
Sandy I. *Grenada* 12°29N 61°29W **323** q
Sandy I. *Grenada* 12°13N 61°35W **323** q
Sandy L. *Canada* 53°2N 93°0W **298** B1
Sandy Lake *Canada* 53°0N 93°15W **298** B1
Sandy Point *India* 10°32N 92°22E **245** J11
Sandy Point Town *St. Kitts & Nevis* 17°22N 62°51W **322** d
Sandy Springs *U.S.A.* 33°56N 84°23W **316** B5
Sandy Valley *U.S.A.* 35°49N 115°38W **307** K11
Sandyford *Ireland* 53°17N 6°13W **120** B2
Sandymount *Ireland* 53°20N 6°13W **120** B2
Sånfjällets △ *Sweden* 62°17N 13°35E **162** B7
Sanford *Fla., U.S.A.* 28°48N 81°16W **317** G8
Sanford *Maine, U.S.A.* 43°27N 70°47W **313** C14
Sanford *N.C., U.S.A.* 35°29N 79°10W **315** D15
Sanford → *Australia* 27°22S 115°53E **279** E2
Sanford, Mt. *U.S.A.* 62°13N 144°8W **303** E11
Sang-i-Masha *Afghan.* 33°8N 67°27E **242** C2
Sanga *Angola* 11°9S 15°21E **265** E3
Sanga *Mozam.* 12°22S 35°21E **269** E4
Sanga → *Congo* 1°5S 17°0E **264** C3
Sangaie *Dem. Rep. of the Congo* 6°48S 22°46E **265** D4
Sangamner *India* 19°37N 74°15E **244** E2
Sangamon → *U.S.A.* 40°1N 90°26W **310** D6
Sangān *Iran* 34°23N 60°15E **247** C9
Sanganeb Atoll △ *Sudan* 19°33N 37°11E **256** D4
Sangar *Afghan.* 32°56N 65°30E **242** C1
Sangar *Russia* 64°2N 127°31E **215** C13
Sangar Sarai *Afghan.* 34°27N 70°35E **242** B4
Sangareddi *India* 17°38N 78°7E **244** F4
Sangaredi *Guinea* 11°7N 13°52W **262** C2
Sangarh → *Pakistan* 30°43N 70°44E **242** D4
Sangasangadalam *Indonesia* 0°36S 117°13E **235** C5
Sangasso *Mali* 12°5N 5°35W **262** C3
Sangatte *France* 50°56N 1°44E **173** B8
Sangāw *Iraq* 35°17N 45°10E **213** E11
Sangay *Ecuador* 2°0S 78°20W **328** D2
Sangay △ *Ecuador* 2°15S 78°26W **328** D2
Sangbé *Cameroon* 6°3N 12°28E **264** A2
Sangchris L. *U.S.A.* 39°39N 89°29W **310** E7
Sangdong *S. Korea* 37°7N 128°49E **224** D4
Sange *Dem. Rep. of the Congo* 6°58S 28°21E **268** D2
Sangeang *Indonesia* 8°12S 119°6E **235** D5
Sangenjaya *Japan* 35°37N 139°39E **140** B2
Sângeorz-Băi *Romania* 47°22N 24°41E **183** C9
Sanger *U.S.A.* 36°42N 119°33W **306** J7
Sângera *Moldova* 46°55N 28°58E **183** D13
Sangerhausen *Germany* 51°28N 11°18E **178** D7
Sanggan He → *China* 38°12N 117°15E **226** E9
Sanggau *Indonesia* 0°5N 110°30E **235** B4
Sanggye *S. Korea* 37°38N 127°3E **137** B2
Sanghar *Pakistan* 26°2N 68°57E **242** F3
Sangihe, Kepulauan *Indonesia* 3°0N 125°30E **231** D7
Sangihe, Pulau *Indonesia* 3°35N 125°30E **231** D7
Sangju *S. Korea* 36°25N 128°10E **224** D4
Sangkapura *Indonesia* 5°52S 112°40E **235** D4
Sangkhla Buri *Thailand* 14°57N 98°28E **236** E2
Sangkulirang *Indonesia* 0°59N 117°58E **230** D5
Sangla *Pakistan* 31°43N 73°23E **242** D5
Sangley Pt. *Phil.* 14°29N 120°54E **127** C1
Sangli *India* 16°55N 74°33E **244** F2
Sangmélima *Cameroon* 2°57N 12°1E **263** E7
Sango *Angola* 9°51S 15°44E **265** D2
Sango *Zimbabwe* 18°44S 31°44E **269** F3
Sangod *India* 24°55N 76°17E **242** G7
Sangole *India* 17°26N 75°12E **244** F2
Sangorodok = Ust-Vorkuta *Russia* 67°24N 64°0E **186** A11
Sangpang Bum *Burma* 26°30N 95°50E **241** B5
Sangre de Cristo Mts. *U.S.A.* 37°30N 105°20W **305** H11
Sangre Grande *Trin. & Tob.* 10°35N 61°8W **323** t
Sangro → *Italy* 42°14N 14°32E **199** F11
Sangrur *India* 30°14N 75°50E **242** D6
Sangudo *Canada* 53°50N 114°54W **296** C6
Sangue → *Brazil* 11°1S 58°39W **331** C6
Sangüesa *Spain* 42°37N 1°17W **196** C3
Sanguinaires, Îs. *France* 41°51N 8°36E **175** G12
Sangzhi *China* 29°25N 110°12E **229** C8
Sanhala *Ivory C.* 10°3N 6°51W **262** C3
Sanhsia *Taiwan* 24°56N 121°22E **225** B3
Sanhsien *Hualien, Taiwan* 23°8N 121°25E **225** C3
Sanhsien *T'aitung, Taiwan* 23°24N 121°19E **225** C3
Sanhsing *Taiwan* 24°40N 121°36E **225** B3
Sani *Taiwan* 24°24N 120°46E **225** B2
Sanibel *U.S.A.* 26°27N 82°1W **317** J7
Sanibel I. *U.S.A.* 26°26N 82°6W **317** J7
Sanikluaq *Canada* 56°32N 79°14W **298** A4
Sanin-Kaigan △ *Japan* 35°39N 134°37E **222** B6
Sanirajak = Hall Beach *Canada* 68°46N 81°12W **295** D15
Sanjawi *Pakistan* 30°17N 68°21E **242** D3
Sanje *Uganda* 0°49S 31°30E **268** C3
Sanjiang *China* 25°48N 109°37E **228** E7
Sanjo *Japan* 37°37N 138°57E **220** F9
Sankarankovil *India* 9°10N 77°35E **245** K3
Sankeshwar *India* 16°23N 74°32E **245** F2
Sankh → *India* 22°15N 84°48E **243** H11
Sankosh → *India* 26°24N 89°47E **241** B2
Sankrail *India* 22°33N 88°13E **124** B1
Sankt Andrä *Austria* 46°46N 14°50E **180** F7
Sankt Anton *Austria* 47°8N 10°16E **179** H6
Sankt Augustin *Germany* 50°45N 7°10E **178** E3
Sankt Blasien *Germany* 47°47N 8°7E **179** H4
Sankt Gallen *Switz.* 47°26N 9°22E **179** H5
Sankt Gallen □ *Switz.* 47°25N 9°22E **179** H5
Sankt Goar *Germany* 50°12N 7°43E **179** E3
Sankt Ingbert *Germany* 49°16N 7°6E **179** F3
Sankt Johann im Pongau *Austria* 47°22N 13°12E **180** D6
Sankt Johann in Tirol *Austria* 47°30N 12°25E **180** D5
Sankt Marein = Smarje *Slovenia* 46°15N 15°34E **199** B12
Sankt Michel = Mikkeli *Finland* 61°43N 27°15E **188** B4
Sankt Moritz *Switz.* 46°30N 9°51E **179** J5
Sankt-Peterburg *Russia* 59°55N 30°20E **137** B1
Sankt Pölten *Austria* 48°12N 15°38E **180** C8
Sankt Ulrich = Ortisei *Italy* 46°34N 11°40E **199** B8
Sankt Valentin *Austria* 48°11N 14°33E **180** C7
Sankt Veit *Austria* 48°11N 16°16E **142** A1
Sankt Veit an der Glan *Austria* 46°47N 14°22E **180** E7
Sankt Wendel *Germany* 49°27N 7°9E **179** F3
Sankt Wolfgang *Austria* 47°43N 13°27E **180** D6
Sankuru → *Dem. Rep. of the Congo* 4°17S 20°25E **265** C4
Sanlihe *China* 39°53N 116°18E **114** B1
Sanlintang *China* 31°9N 121°29E **138** C1
Sanliurfa *Turkey* 37°12N 38°50E **213** D8
Sanliurfa □ *Turkey* 37°0N 39°0E **213** D8
Sanlúcar de Barrameda *Spain* 36°46N 6°21W **195** J4
Sanluri *Italy* 39°34N 8°54E **200** C1
Sânmartin *Romania* 46°19N 25°58E **183** D10
Sanmen *China* 29°5N 121°35E **229** C13
Sanmenxia *China* 34°47N 111°12E **226** G6
Sanming *China* 26°15N 117°40E **229** D11
Sannan *Japan* 35°2N 135°1E **223** B7
Sannat *Malta* 36°1N 14°15E **206** E6
Sannicandro Gargánico *Italy* 41°50N 15°34E **199** G12
Sânnicolau Mare *Romania* 46°5N 20°39E **182** D5
Sannieshof *S. Africa* 26°30S 25°47E **270** C4
Sannīn, J. *Lebanon* 33°57N 35°52E **250** E6
Sanniquellie *Liberia* 7°19N 8°38W **262** D3
Sannûr *Egypt* 28°58N 31°3E **251** K2
Sannûr, W. → *Egypt* 28°59N 31°3E **251** K2
Sano *Japan* 36°19N 139°35E **223** A11
Sanok *Poland* 49°35N 22°10E **185** J9
Sanquhar *U.K.* 55°22N 3°54W **167** F5
Sanquianga △ *Colombia* 2°33N 78°14W **328** C2
Sans *Spain* 41°22N 2°7E **114** A1
Sans Souci *St. Vincent* 13°13N 61°7W **323** n
Sans Souci *Trin. & Tob.* 10°50N 61°0W **323** t
Sansanding *Mali* 13°48N 6°0W **262** C3
Sansané *Niger* 13°50N 1°36E **263** C5
Sansepolcro *Italy* 43°34N 12°8E **199** E9
Sansha *China* 26°58N 120°12E **229** D13
Sanshui *China* 23°10N 112°56E **229** F9
Sanski Most *Bos.-H.* 44°46N 16°40E **199** D13
Sanssouci *Germany* 52°23N 13°2E **115** B1
Sansui *China* 26°58N 108°39E **228** D7
Sant Agusti *Barcelona, Spain* **114** c2
Sant Ambrogio, Basilica di *Italy* 45°27N 9°10E **129** B2
Sant Antoni de Portmany *Spain* 38°59N 1°19E **206** D1
Sant Boi de Llobregat *Spain* 41°20N 2°2E **114** A1
Sant Carles *Spain* 39°3N 1°34E **206** C2
Sant Carles de la Ràpita *Spain* 40°37N 0°35E **196** E5
Sant Celoni *Spain* 41°42N 2°30E **196** D7
Sant Cugat *Spain* 41°28N 2°5E **114** A1
Sant Elm *Spain* 39°35N 2°21E **206** B3
Sant Feliu de Guíxols *Spain* 41°45N 3°1E **196** D8
Sant Feliu de Llobregat *Spain* 41°22N 2°2E **114** A1
Sant Ferran *Spain* 38°42N 1°28E **206** D1
Sant Francesc de Formentera *Spain* 38°42N 1°26E **206** D1
Sant Jaume *Spain* 39°54N 4°4E **206** B5
Sant Joan *Spain* 39°36N 3°4E **206** B4
Sant Joan d'Alacant *Spain* 38°24N 0°26W **197** G4
Sant Joan de Labritja *Spain* 39°5N 1°31E **206** C2
Sant Joan Despi *Spain* 41°22N 2°2E **114** A1
Sant Jordi *Ibiza, Spain* 38°53N 1°24E **206** D1
Sant Jordi *Mallorca, Spain* 39°33N 2°46E **206** B3
Sant Jordi, G. de *Spain* 40°53N 1°2E **196** E6
Sant Llorenç de Morunys *Spain* 42°8N 1°35E **196** C6
Sant Llorenç del Munt y l'Obac ⌂ *Spain* 41°39N 1°55W **196** D3
Sant Llorenç des Cardassar *Spain* 39°37N 3°17E **206** B4
Sant Maria del Mar *Barcelona, Spain* **114** b3
Sant Mateu *Baleares, Spain* 39°3N 1°23E **206** C1
Sant Mateu *Valencia, Spain* 40°28N 0°10E **196** E5
Sant Miquel *Spain* 39°3N 1°26E **206** C1
Sant Pau del Camp *Barcelona, Spain* **114** c2
Sant Salvador *Spain* 39°27N 3°11E **206** B4
Sant Vicent del Raspeig *Spain* 38°24N 0°31W **197** G4
Santa *Peru* 8°59S 78°40W **330** B2
Sant' Ágata Militello *Italy* 38°2N 14°8E **201** D7
Santa Agnés *Spain* 39°3N 1°21E **206** C1
Santa Ana *Beni, Bolivia* 13°50S 65°40W **331** C4
Santa Ana *La Paz, Bolivia* 15°31S 67°30W **330** D4
Santa Ana *Santa Cruz, Bolivia* 18°43S 58°44W **331** D6
Santa Ana *Santa Cruz, Bolivia* 16°37S 60°43W **331** D5
Santa Ana *Ecuador* 1°16S 80°20W **328** D1
Santa Ana *El Salv.* 14°0N 89°31W **320** D2
Santa Ana *Guam* 13°32N 145°46E **302** d
Santa Ana *Sonora, Mexico* 30°33N 111°7W **318** A2
Santa Ana *Cagayan, Phil.* 18°28N 122°20E **232** B4
Santa Ana *Manila, Phil.* 14°34N 121°0E **127** B2
Santa Ana *Solomon Is.* 10°50S 162°30E **287** N12
Santa Ana *Calif., U.S.A.* 33°46N 117°52W **307** M9
Santa Ana → *Venezuela* 9°30N 71°57W **328** B3
Sant' Ángelo Lodigiano *Italy* 45°14N 9°25E **198** C6
Santa Anita Park *U.S.A.* 34°8N 118°5W **126** B4
Sant' Antíoco *Italy* 39°4N 8°27E **200** C1
Santa Bárbara *Santa Maria, Azores* 36°59N 25°4W **153** d4
Santa Bárbara *Terceira, Azores* 38°41N 27°20W **153** d1
Santa Bárbara *Chile* 37°40S 72°1W **334** D1
Santa Bárbara *Colombia* 5°53N 75°35W **328** B2
Santa Bárbara *Honduras* 14°53N 88°14W **320** D2
Santa Bárbara *Chihuahua, Mexico* 26°48N 105°49W **318** B3
Santa Barbara *Neth. Ant.* 12°5N 68°51W **322** g
Santa Barbara *Phil.* 10°50N 122°32E **233** F4
Santa Barbara *Spain* 40°42N 0°29E **196** E5
Santa Barbara *Calif., U.S.A.* 34°25N 119°42W **307** L7
Santa Bárbara *Amazonas, Venezuela* 3°57N 67°6W **328** C4
Santa Bárbara *Barinas, Venezuela* 7°47N 71°10W **328** B3
Santa Bárbara, Mt. *Spain* 37°23N 2°50W **197** H2
Santa Bárbara, Serra de *Azores* 38°44N 27°19W **153** d1
Santa Barbara Channel *U.S.A.* 34°15N 120°0W **307** L7
Santa Barbara I. *U.S.A.* 33°29N 119°2W **307** M7
Santa Catalina *Colombia* 10°36N 75°17W **328** A2
Santa Catalina *Neg. Or., Phil.* 9°20N 122°52E **233** G4
Santa Catalina *Solomon Is.* 10°53S 162°29E **287** N12
Santa Catalina, Gulf of *U.S.A.* 33°10N 117°50W **307** N9
Santa Catalina, I. *Mexico* 25°40N 110°47W **318** B2
Santa Catalina I. *U.S.A.* 33°23N 118°25W **307** M8
Santa Catarina □ *Brazil* 27°25S 48°30W **335** B6
Santa Catarina, I. de *Brazil* 27°30S 48°40W **335** B6
Santa Caterina di Pittinuri *Italy* 40°6N 8°27E **200** B1
Santa Caterina Villarmosa *Italy* 37°35N 14°2E **201** E7
Santa Cecília *Brazil* 26°56S 50°18W **335** B5
Santa Clara *Cuba* 22°20N 80°0W **320** B4
Santa Clara *Calif., U.S.A.* 37°21N 121°57W **306** H5
Santa Clara *N.Y., U.S.A.* 44°38N 74°27W **313** B10
Santa Clara *Utah, U.S.A.* 37°8N 113°39W **305** H7
Santa Clara, I. *Chile* 33°42S 79°0W **330** c
Santa Clara de Olimar *Uruguay* 32°50S 54°54W **335** C5
Santa Clara Valley *U.S.A.* 36°50N 121°30W **306** J5
Santa Clarita *U.S.A.* 34°24N 118°33W **307** L8
Santa Clotilde *Peru* 2°33S 73°45W **328** D3
Santa Coloma de Farners *Spain* 41°50N 2°39E **196** D7
Santa Coloma de Gramenet *Spain* 41°27N 2°13E **114** A2
Santa Comba *Spain* 43°2N 8°49W **194** B2
Santa Croce Camerina *Italy* 36°50N 14°31E **201** F7
Santa Croce di Magliano *Italy* 41°42N 14°59E **199** G11
Santa Cruz *Aruba* 12°30N 69°59W **322** f
Santa Cruz *Bolivia* 17°43S 63°10W **331** D5
Santa Cruz *Brazil* 6°13S 36°1W **332** C4
Santa Cruz *Chile* 34°38S 71°27W **334** C1
Santa Cruz *Costa Rica* 10°15N 85°35W **320** D2
Santa Cruz *Maharashtra, India* 19°4N 72°51E **130** A1
Santa Cruz *Jamaica* 18°3N 77°43W **320** a
Santa Cruz *Madeira* 32°42N 16°46W **153** c
Santa Cruz *Neth. Ant.* 12°18N 69°7W **322** g
Santa Cruz *Peru* 5°40S 75°56W **330** B2
Santa Cruz *Davao del S., Phil.* 6°50N 125°25E **233** H5
Santa Cruz *Laguna, Phil.* 14°20N 121°24E **232** D3
Santa Cruz *Manila, Phil.* 14°36N 120°58E **127** B1
Santa Cruz *Marinduque, Phil.* 13°28N 122°2E **232** E4
Santa Cruz *Mind. Occ., Phil.* 13°4N 120°43E **232** E3
Santa Cruz *Zambales, Phil.* 15°46N 119°55E **232** D2
Santa Cruz *Calif., U.S.A.* 36°58N 122°1W **306** J4
Santa Cruz *Venezuela* 8°3N 64°27W **329** B5
Santa Cruz □ *Argentina* 49°0S 70°0W **336** C3
Santa Cruz □ *Bolivia* 17°43S 63°10W **331** D5
Santa Cruz → *Argentina* 50°10S 68°20W **336** D3
Santa Cruz, B. *Neth. Ant.* 12°18N 69°10W **322** g
Santa Cruz, I. *Ecuador* 0°38S 90°23W **330** a
Santa Cruz, I. de *Brazil* 22°51S 43°7W **135** B2
Santa Cruz Cabrália *Brazil* 16°17S 39°2W **333** E4
Santa Cruz da Graciosa *Azores* 39°5N 28°1W **153** d1
Santa Cruz das Flores *Azores* 39°27N 31°7W **153** d2
Santa Cruz de Bravo = Felipe Carrillo Puerto *Mexico* 19°38N 88°3W **319** D7
Santa Cruz de la Palma *Canary Is.* 28°41N 17°46W **153** e1
Santa Cruz de la Palma ✕ (SPC) *Canary Is.* 28°40N 17°45W **153** e1
Santa Cruz de Mudela *Spain* 38°39N 3°28W **195** G7
Santa Cruz de Olorde *Spain* 41°25N 2°3E **114** A1
Santa Cruz de Tenerife *Canary Is.* 28°28N 16°15W **153** e1
Santa Cruz del Norte *Cuba* 23°9N 81°55W **320** B3
Santa Cruz del Retamar *Spain* 40°8N 4°14W **194** E6
Santa Cruz del Sur *Cuba* 20°44N 78°0W **320** B4
Santa Cruz do Rio Pardo *Brazil* 22°54S 49°37W **335** A6
Santa Cruz do Sul *Brazil* 29°42S 52°25W **335** B5
Santa Cruz I. *U.S.A.* 34°1N 119°43W **307** M7
Santa Cruz Is. *Solomon Is.* 10°30S 166°0E **277** C12
Santa Cruz la Vieja △ *Bolivia* 17°55S 60°50W **331** D5
Santa Cruz Mts. *Jamaica* 17°58N 77°43W **320** a
Santa Domingo, Cay *Bahamas* 21°25N 75°15W **320** B4
Santa Efigênia *Brazil* 23°32S 46°38W **137** B2
Sant' Egídio alla Vibrata *Italy* 42°49N 13°42E **199** F10
Santa Elena *Argentina* 30°58S 59°47W **334** C4
Santa Elena *Ecuador* 2°16S 80°52W **328** D1
Santa Elena *Camarines N., Phil.* 14°12N 122°24E **232** D4
Santa Elena *Manila, Phil.* 14°38N 121°5E **127** B2
Santa Elena, C. *Costa Rica* 10°54N 85°56W **320** D2
Santa Elena del Gomero *Chile* 33°28S 70°45W **137** B1
Sant' Eufêmia, G. di *Italy* 38°51N 16°4E **201** D9
Santa Eulalia *Spain* 41°25N 2°10E **114** A2
Santa Eulària des Riu *Spain* 38°59N 1°32E **206** D2
Santa Fé *Argentina* 31°35S 60°41W **334** C3
Santa Fe *Nueva Viscaya, Phil.* 16°10N 120°57E **232** C3
Santa Fe *Romblon, Phil.* 12°10N 122°0E **232** E4
Santa Fé *Spain* 37°11N 3°43W **195** H7
Santa Fe *N. Mex., U.S.A.* 35°41N 105°57W **305** J11
Santa Fé □ *Argentina* 31°50S 60°55W **334** C3
Santa Fé, Canal de *Ecuador* 0°48S 89°55W **330** a
Santa Fé, I. *Ecuador* 0°49S 90°5W **330** a
Santa Fé do Sul *Brazil* 20°13S 50°56W **333** F1
Santa Fe Springs *U.S.A.* 33°56N 118°3W **126** C4
Santa Filomena *Brazil* 9°6S 45°50W **332** C2
Santa Fiora *Italy* 42°50N 11°35E **199** F8
Santa Gertrudis *Spain* 39°0N 1°26E **206** C1
Santa Giustina *Italy* 46°10N 12°5E **199** B9
Santa Helena *Brazil* 2°14S 45°18W **332** B2
Santa Helena de Goiás *Brazil* 17°53S 50°35W **333** E1
Santa Inês *Bahia, Brazil* 13°17S 39°48W **333** D4
Santa Inês *Maranhão, Brazil* 3°39S 45°20W **332** B2
Santa Inés *Extremadura, Spain* 38°32N 5°37W **195** G5
Santa Inés, I. *Chile* 54°0S 73°0W **336** D2
Santa Iria da Azóia *Portugal* 38°49N 9°5W **126** A2
Santa Isabel = Rey Malabo *Eq. Guin.* 3°45N 8°50E **263** E6
Santa Isabel *Argentina* 36°10S 66°54W **334** D2
Santa Isabel *Puerto Rico* 17°58N 66°24W **321** b
Santa Isabel *Solomon Is.* 8°0S 159°0E **287** M10
Santa Isabel do Araguaia *Brazil* 6°7S 48°19W **332** C2
Santa Isabel do Morro *Brazil* 11°34S 50°40W **333** D1
Santa Isabel do Rio Negro *Brazil* 0°24S 65°2W **329** D4
Santa Julia *Chile* 33°30S 70°35W **137** C2
Santa Lucía *Corrientes, Argentina* 28°58S 59°5W **334** B4
Santa Lucía *San Juan, Argentina* 31°30S 68°30W **334** C2
Santa Lucía *Canary Is.* 27°55N 15°32W **153** e1
Santa Lucia *Phil.* 17°7N 120°27E **232** C3
Santa Lucía *Spain* 37°35N 0°58W **197** H4
Santa Lucía *Uruguay* 34°27S 56°24W **334** C4
Santa Lucia Range *U.S.A.* 36°0N 121°20W **306** K5
Santa Luzia = Luziânia *Brazil* 16°20S 48°0W **333** E2
Santa Luzia *Brazil* 19°47S 43°52W **333** E3
Santa Luzia *C. Verde Is.* 16°50N 24°35W **153** j
Santa Margalida *Spain* 39°42N 3°6E **206** B4
Santa Margarita *Argentina* 38°28S 61°35W **334** D3
Santa Margarita *Calif., U.S.A.* 35°23N 120°37W **306** K6
Santa Margarita → *U.S.A.* 33°13N 117°23W **307** M9
Santa Margarita, I. *Mexico* 24°27N 111°50W **318** C2
Santa Margherita *Italy* 38°58N 8°58E **200** D1
Santa Margherita Ligure *Italy* 44°20N 9°11E **198** D6
Santa María *Argentina* 26°40S 66°0W **334** B2
Santa Maria *Azores* 36°58N 25°6W **153** d4
Santa Maria *Brazil* 29°40S 53°48W **335** B5
Santa Maria *C. Verde Is.* 16°31N 22°53W **153** j
Santa María *Mexico City, Mexico* **128** a1
Santa Maria *Ilocos S., Phil.* 17°22N 120°29E **232** C3
Santa Maria *Isabela, Phil.* 17°28N 121°45E **232** C3
Santa Maria *Calif., U.S.A.* 34°57N 120°26W **307** L6
Santa María → *Mexico* 31°0N 107°14W **318** A3
Santa María, B. de *Mexico* 25°4N 108°6W **318** B3
Santa Maria, C. de *Portugal* 36°58N 7°53W **195** J3
Santa María, I. *Ecuador* 1°17S 90°26W **330** a
Santa Maria Cápua Vétere *Italy* 41°5N 14°15E **201** A7
Santa Maria da Feira *Portugal* 40°55N 8°35W **194** E2
Santa Maria da Vitória *Brazil* 13°24S 44°12W **333** D3
Santa María de Ipire *Venezuela* 8°49N 65°19W **329** B4
Santa María del Camí *Spain* 39°38N 2°47E **206** B3
Santa Maria di Léuca, C. *Italy* 39°47N 18°22E **201** C11
Santa Maria do Boiaçu *Brazil* 0°25S 61°48W **329** D5
Santa Maria do Suaçuí *Brazil* 18°12S 42°25W **333** E3
Santa Maria dos Marmelos *Brazil* 6°7S 61°51W **331** B5
Santa María la Real de Nieva *Spain* 41°4N 4°24W **194** D6
Santa Marinella *Italy* 42°2N 11°52E **199** F8
Santa Marta *Colombia* 11°15N 74°13W **328** A3
Santa Marta, Sierra Nevada de *Colombia* 10°55N 73°50W **328** A3
Santa Marta de Tormes *Spain* 40°57N 5°38W **194** E5
Santa Marta Grande, C. *Brazil* 28°43S 48°50W **335** B6
Santa Marta Ortigueira, Ría de *Spain* 43°44N 7°45W **194** B3
Santa Martabaai = Sint Marthabaai *Neth. Ant.* 12°17N 69°8W **322** g
Santa Maura = Lefkada *Greece* 38°40N 20°43E **207** B2
Santa Monica *U.S.A.* 34°1N 118°29W **126** B2
Santa Monica Mts. *U.S.A.* 34°6N 118°29W **126** B2
Santa Monica Mts. ⌂ *U.S.A.* 34°4N 118°44W **307** L8
Santa Olalla *Spain* 40°2N 4°25W **194** E6
Santa Olalla del Cala *Spain* 37°54N 6°14W **195** H4
Santa Paula *U.S.A.* 34°21N 119°4W **307** L7
Santa Pola *Spain* 38°13N 0°35W **197** G4
Santa Ponça *Spain* 39°30N 2°28E **206** B3
Santa Quitéria *Brazil* 4°20S 40°10W **332** B3
Santa Rita = Itumbiara *Brazil* 18°20S 49°10W **333** E2
Santa Rita *Amazonas, Brazil* 3°29S 69°19W **328** D4
Santa Rita *Paraíba, Brazil* 7°8S 34°58W **332** C5
Santa Rita *Colombia* 4°53N 68°24W **328** C4
Santa Rita *Guam* 13°23N 144°40E **302** d
Santa Rita *Samar, Phil.* 11°27N 124°56E **233** F5
Santa Rita *Zulia, Venezuela* 10°32N 71°32W **328** A3
Santa Rita de Cássia *Brazil* 11°0S 44°32W **332** D3
Santa Rita do Araguaia = Guiratinga *Brazil* 16°21S 53°45W **331** D7
Santa Rita do Araguaia *Brazil* 17°20S 53°12W **331** D7
Santa Rosa = Bella Unión *Uruguay* 30°15S 57°40W **334** C4
Santa Rosa *La Pampa, Argentina* 36°40S 64°17W **334** D3
Santa Rosa *San Luis, Argentina* 32°21S 65°10W **334** C2
Santa Rosa *Beni, Bolivia* 14°10S 66°53W **330** C4
Santa Rosa *Pando, Bolivia* 10°36S 67°20W **330** C4
Santa Rosa *Santa Cruz, Bolivia* 17°7S 63°35W **331** D5
Santa Rosa *Brazil* 27°52S 54°29W **335** B5
Santa Rosa *Colombia* 3°32N 69°48W **328** C4
Santa Rosa *El Oro, Ecuador* 3°27S 79°58W **328** D2
Santa Rosa *Galápagos Is., Ecuador* 0°40S 90°25W **330** a
Santa Rosa *Neth. Ant.* 12°7N 68°53W **322** g
Santa Rosa *Puno, Peru* 14°30S 70°50W **330** C3
Santa Rosa *San Martín, Peru* 6°41S 76°37W **330** B2
Santa Rosa *Phil.* 15°25N 120°57E **232** D3
Santa Rosa *Calif., U.S.A.* 38°26N 122°43W **306** G4
Santa Rosa *N. Mex., U.S.A.* 34°57N 104°41W **305** J11
Santa Rosa *Amazonas, Venezuela* 1°29N 66°55W **328** C4
Santa Rosa, Mt. *Guam* 13°32N 144°55E **302** d
Santa Rosa and San Jacinto Mts. ⌂ *U.S.A.* 33°28N 116°20W **307** M10
Santa Rosa Beach *U.S.A.* 30°22N 86°14W **316** E3
Santa Rosa de Amanadona *Venezuela* 1°29N 66°55W **328** C4
Santa Rosa de Cabal *Colombia* 4°52N 75°38W **328** C2
Santa Rosa de Copán *Honduras* 14°47N 88°46W **320** D2
Santa Rosa de la Roca *Bolivia* 16°3S 61°34W **331** D5
Santa Rosa de Locobe *Chile* 33°25S 70°33W **137** B2
Santa Rosa de Osos *Colombia* 6°39N 75°28W **328** B2
Santa Rosa de Río Primero *Argentina* 31°8S 63°20W **334** C3
Santa Rosa de Viterbo *Colombia* 5°53N 72°59W **328** B3
Santa Rosa del Palmar *Bolivia* 16°54S 62°24W **331** D5
Santa Rosa I. *Calif., U.S.A.* 33°58N 120°6W **307** M6
Santa Rosa I. *Fla., U.S.A.* 30°20N 86°50W **317** E3
Santa Rosa Range *U.S.A.* 41°45N 117°40W **304** F5
Santa Rosalía *Mexico* 27°19N 112°17W **318** B2
Santa Sylvina *Argentina* 27°50S 61°10W **334** B3
Santa Tecla = Nueva San Salvador *El Salv.* 13°40N 89°18W **320** D2
Santa Teresa *Argentina* 33°25S 60°47W **334** C3
Santa Teresa *N. Terr., Australia* 24°8S 134°22E **280** C1
Santa Teresa *Brazil* 19°55S 40°36W **333** E3
Santa Teresa *Tamaulipas, Mexico* 25°17N 97°51W **319** B5
Santa Teresa *Venezuela* 4°43N 61°4W **329** C5
Santa Teresa △ *Uruguay* 33°57S 53°31W **335** C5
Santa Teresa de la Ovalle *Chile* 33°22S 70°44W **137** B1
Santa Teresa di Riva *Italy* 37°57N 15°22E **201** E8
Santa Teresa Gallura *Italy* 41°14N 9°11E **200** A2
Santa Teresinha *Brazil* 10°28S 50°31W **332** D1
Santa Teresita *Argentina* 36°32S 56°41W **334** D4
Santa Uxía de Ribeira *Spain* 42°36N 8°58W **194** C2
Santa Vitória *Brazil* 18°50S 50°8W **333** E1
Santa Vitória do Palmar *Brazil* 33°32S 53°25W **335** C5
Santa Ynez → *U.S.A.* 34°41N 120°36W **307** L6
Santa Ynez Mts. *U.S.A.* 34°30N 120°0W **307** L6
Santa Ysabel *U.S.A.* 33°7N 116°40W **307** M10
Santadi *Italy* 39°5N 8°43E **200** C1
Santaella *Spain* 37°34N 4°51W **195** H6
Santahamina *Finland* 60°8N 25°2E **121** C3
Santahar *Bangla.* 24°48N 88°59E **241** C2
Santai *China* 31°5N 104°58E **228** B5
Santaluz *Brazil* 11°15S 39°22W **332** D4
Santana = Uruaçu *Brazil* 14°30S 49°10W **333** D2
Santana *Bahia, Brazil* 13°2S 44°5W **333** D3
Santana *São Paulo, Brazil* 23°29S 46°36W **137** A2
Santana *Madeira* 32°48N 16°52W **153** c
Santana *Romania* 46°20N 21°30E **182** D6
Santana, Coxilha de *Brazil* 30°50S 55°35W **335** C4
Santana do Ipanema *Brazil* 9°22S 37°14W **332** C4
Santana do Livramento *Brazil* 30°55S 55°30W **335** C4
Santana do Paranaíba = Paranaíba *Brazil* 19°40S 51°11W **331** D7
Santander *Colombia* 3°1N 76°28W **328** C2
Santander *Phil.* 9°25N 123°20E **233** G4
Santander *Spain* 43°27N 3°51W **194** B7
Santander □ *Colombia* 7°0N 73°15W **328** B3
Santander Jiménez *Mexico* 24°13N 98°28W **319** C5
Sant'Angelo, Castel *Rome, Italy* **136** b1
Santanilla, Is. *Honduras* 17°22N 83°57W **320** C3
Santanyí *Spain* 39°20N 3°5E **206** B4
Santaquin *U.S.A.* 39°59N 111°47W **304** G8
Santarcángelo di Romagna *Italy* 44°4N 12°26E **199** D9
Santarém *Brazil* 2°25S 54°42W **329** D7
Santarém *Portugal* 39°12N 8°42W **195** F2
Santarém □ *Portugal* 39°10N 8°40W **195** F2
Santaren Channel *W. Indies* 24°0N 79°30W **320** B4
Santee *U.S.A.* 32°50N 116°58W **307** N10
Santee → *U.S.A.* 33°7N 79°17W **315** E15
Santeny *France* 48°43N 2°34E **134** B4
Santéramo in Colle *Italy* 40°49N 16°45E **201** B9
Santerno → *Italy* 44°34N 11°58E **199** D8
Santhià *Italy* 45°22N 8°10E **198** C5
Santi *Taiwan* 22°43N 120°39E **225** D2
Santi-Quaranta = Sarandë *Albania* 39°52N 19°55E **206** B9
Santiago = Río Grande de Santiago → *Mexico* 21°36N 105°26W **318** C3
Santiago = São Tiago *C. Verde Is.* 15°0N 23°40W **153** j
Santiago *Brazil* 29°11S 54°52W **335** B5
Santiago *Canary Is.* 28°2N 17°12W **153** e1
Santiago *Chile* 33°26S 70°40W **137** B2
Santiago *Panama* 8°0N 81°0W **320** E3
Santiago *Peru* 14°11S 75°43W **330** C2
Santiago *Ilocos S., Phil.* 17°18N 120°27E **232** C3
Santiago *Isabela, Phil.* 16°41N 121°33E **232** C3
Santiago → *Peru* 4°27S 77°38W **328** D2
Santiago, C. *Chile* 50°46S 75°27W **336** D1
Santiago, I. = San Salvador, I. *Ecuador* 0°16S 90°42W **330** a
Santiago, Punta de *Eq. Guin.* 3°12N 8°40E **263** E6
Santiago, Sierra de *Bolivia* 18°25S 59°25W **331** D6
Santiago Benítez ✕ (SCL) *Chile* 33°33S 70°42W **137** B1
Santiago de Chiquitos *Bolivia* 18°19S 59°34W **331** D6
Santiago de Chuco *Peru* 8°9S 78°11W **330** B2
Santiago de Compostela *Spain* 42°52N 8°37W **194** C2
Santiago de Cuba *Cuba* 20°0N 75°49W **320** C4
Santiago de los Caballeros *Dom. Rep.* 19°30N 70°40W **321** C5
Santiago de Surco *Peru* 12°9S 77°0W **124** B2
Santiago del Estero *Argentina* 27°50S 64°15W **334** B3
Santiago del Estero □ *Argentina* 27°40S 63°15W **334** B3
Santiago del Teide *Canary Is.* 28°17N 16°48W **153** e1
Santiago do Boqueirão = Santiago *Brazil* 29°11S 54°52W **335** B5
Santiago do Cacém *Portugal* 38°1N 8°42W **195** G2
Santiago Ixcuintla *Mexico* 21°49N 105°13W **318** C3
Santiago Jamiltepec *Mexico* 16°17N 97°49W **319** D5
Santiago Papasquiaro *Mexico* 25°3N 105°25W **318** C3
Santiago Pinotepa Nacional *Mexico* 16°19N 98°1W **319** D5
Santiaguillo, L. de *Mexico* 24°48N 104°48W **318** C4
Santialing *Taiwan* 25°5N 121°51E **225** A3
Santiao Chiao *Taiwan* 25°1N 122°0E **225** A3
Santiaolun *Taiwan* 23°39N 120°9E **225** C2
Santiguila *Mali* 12°42N 7°25W **262** C3
Santillana del Mar *Spain* 43°24N 4°6W **194** B6
Santisteban del Puerto *Spain* 38°17N 3°15W **195** G7
Santo → *Peru* 8°56S 78°37W **330** B2
Santo Amaro *Bahia, Brazil* 12°30S 38°43W **333** D4
Santo Amaro *São Paulo, Brazil* 23°39S 46°42W **137** B1
Santo Amaro *Lisboa, Portugal* 38°42N 9°11W **126** A1
Santo Anastácio *Brazil* 21°58S 51°39W **335** A5
Santo André *Brazil* 23°39S 46°29W **335** A6
Santo André *Lisboa, Portugal* 38°38N 9°3W **126** B2
Santo Ângelo *Brazil* 28°15S 54°15W **335** B5
Santo Antão *C. Verde Is.* 16°52N 25°10W **153** j
Santo Antão do Tojal *Portugal* 38°49N 9°9W **126** A2
Santo Antônio *São Tomé & Principe* 1°37N 7°27E **265** a
Santo Antônio *Brazil* 2°24S 60°58W **329** D5
Santo Antônio, Qta. de *Portugal* 38°39N 9°15W **126** B1
Santo Antônio da Cachoeira = Itaguatins *Brazil* 5°47S 47°29W **332** C2
Santo Antônio de Jesus *Brazil* 12°58S 39°16W **333** D4
Santo Antônio do Abaixo = Santo Antônio do Leverger *Brazil* 15°52S 56°5W **331** D6
Santo Antônio do Içá *Brazil* 3°5S 67°57W **328** D4
Santo Antônio do Leverger *Brazil* 15°52S 56°5W **331** D6
Santo Corazón *Bolivia* 18°0S 58°45W **331** D6
Santo Domingo *Dom. Rep.* 18°30N 69°59W **321** C6
Santo Domingo *Baja Calif., Mexico* 30°43N 116°2W **318** A1
Santo Domingo *Baja Calif. S., Mexico* 25°29N 111°55W **318** B2
Santo Domingo *Nic.* 12°14N 84°59W **320** D3
Santo Domingo de la Calzada *Spain* 42°26N 2°57W **196** C2
Santo Domingo de los Colorados *Ecuador* 0°15S 79°9W **328** D2
Santo Domingo Pueblo *U.S.A.* 35°31N 106°22W **305** J10
Santo Stéfano di Camastro *Italy* 38°1N 14°22E **201** D7
Santo Tirso *Portugal* 41°21N 8°28W **194** D2
Santo Tomás *Galápagos Is., Ecuador* 0°51S 91°2W **330** a
Santo Tomás *Baja Calif., Mexico* 31°33N 116°24W **318** A1
Santo Tomás *Peru* 14°26S 72°8W **330** C3
Santo Tomas, Univ. of *Phil.* 14°36N 120°59E **127** B1
Santo Tomás, Volcán *Ecuador* 0°48S 91°7W **330** a
Santo Tomé *Argentina* 28°40S 56°5W **335** B4
Santo Tomé de Guayana = Ciudad Guayana *Venezuela* 8°0N 62°30W **329** B5
Santomera *Spain* 38°4N 1°3W **197** G3
Santoña *Spain* 43°29N 3°27W **194** B7
Santorini *Greece* 36°23N 25°27E **205** E7
Santos *Brazil* 24°0S 46°20W **335** A6
Santos, Sierra de los *Spain* 38°7N 5°12W **195** G5
Santos Dumont *Brazil* 22°55S 43°10W **333** F3
Santos Dumont ✕ (SDU) *Brazil* 22°54S 43°9W **135** B2
Santoshpur *India* 22°31N 88°16E **124** B1
Santragachi *India* 22°35N 88°17E **124** B1
Santry *Ireland* 53°24N 6°15W **120** A2
Santuario de Aves Laguna Colorada △ *Bolivia* 22°10S 67°45W **334** A2
Sanur *Indonesia* 8°41S 115°15E **231** K18
Sanwan *Taiwan* 24°39N 120°57E **225** B2
Sanwer *India* 22°59N 75°50E **242** H6
Sanxenxo *Spain* 42°24N 8°49W **194** C2
Sanxia Shuiku *China* 30°10N 108°0E **219** C5
Sanxiang *China* 22°21N 113°25E **219** G9
Sanya *China* 18°14N 109°29E **236** C7
San'yō *Japan* 34°2N 131°5E **222** C3
Sanyuan *China* 34°35N 108°58E **226** G5
Sanyuanli *China* 23°8N 113°14E **121** B2
Sanyuki-Sammyaku *Japan* 34°5N 134°0E **222** C6
Sanza Pombo *Angola* 7°18S 15°56E **265** D3
São Bartolomeu de Messines *Portugal* 37°15N 8°17W **195** H2
São Benedito = Beneditinos *Brazil* 5°27S 42°22W **332** C3
São Benedito *Brazil* 4°3S 40°53W **332** B3
São Benedito → *Brazil* 9°11S 57°2W **331** B6
São Bento *Brazil* 2°42S 44°50W **332** B3
São Bento do Norte *Brazil* 5°4S 36°2W **332** C4
São Bernardo do Campo *Brazil* 23°45S 46°34W **333** F2
São Borja *Brazil* 28°39S 56°0W **335** B4
São Brás de Alportel *Portugal* 37°8N 7°37W **195** H3
São Braz, C. de *Angola* 9°58S 13°19E **265** D2
São Caetano do Sul *Brazil* 23°37S 46°34W **137** B2
São Caitano *Brazil* 8°21S 36°6W **332** C4
São Carlos *Brazil* 22°0S 47°50W **335** A6
São Conrado *Brazil* 23°5S 43°17W **135** B1
São Cristóvão *Rio de J., Brazil* 22°53S 43°13W **135** B1
São Cristóvão *Sergipe, Brazil* 11°1S 37°15W **332** D4
São Domingo do Capim *Brazil* 1°41S 47°47W **332** B2
São Domingos *Brazil* 13°25S 46°19W **333** D2
São Domingos *Guinea-Biss.* 12°19N 16°13W **262** C1
São Domingos da Boa Vista = São Domingo do Capim *Brazil* 1°41S 47°47W **332** B2
São Domingos do Maranhão *Brazil* 5°42S 44°22W **332** C3
São Felipe = Içana *Brazil* 0°21N 67°19W **328** C4
São Felippe = Eirunepé *Brazil* 6°35S 69°53W **330** B4
São Félix *Brazil* 11°36S 50°39W **333** D1
São Félix do Xingu *Brazil* 6°38S 51°59W **331** B7
São Filipe *C. Verde Is.* 15°2N 24°30W **153** j
São Francisco = Itapagé *Brazil* 3°41S 39°34W **332** B4
São Francisco *Brazil* 16°0S 44°50W **333** E3
São Francisco → *Brazil* 10°30S 36°24W **332** D4

São Francisco do Maranhão Brazil 6°15S 42°52W 332 C3
São Francisco do Sul Brazil 26°15S 48°36W 335 B6
São Francisco Penitência Rio de J., Brazil 135 b1
São Gabriel Brazil 30°20S 54°20W 335 C5
São Gabriel da Cachoeira Brazil 0°8S 67°5W 328 D4
São Gabriel da Palha Brazil 18°47S 40°39W 333 E3
São Gonçalo = Araripina Brazil 7°33S 40°34W 332 C3
São Gonçalo Brazil 22°48S 43°5W 333 F3
São Gotardo Brazil 19°19S 46°3W 333 E2
Sao Hill Tanzania 8°20S 35°12E 269 D4
São João Guinea-Biss. 11°32N 15°25W 262 C1
São João da Baliza Brazil 0°52N 59°52W 329 C6
São João da Barra Brazil 21°38S 41°3W 333 F3
São João da Boa Vista Brazil 22°0S 46°52W 335 A6
São João da Madeira Portugal 40°54N 8°30W 194 E2
São João da Pesqueira Portugal 41°8N 7°24W 194 D3
São João da Ponte Brazil 15°56S 44°1W 333 E3
São João de Meriti Brazil 22°48S 43°21W 333 F3
São João de Montenegro = Montenegro Brazil 29°39S 51°29W 335 B5
São João del Rei Brazil 21°8S 44°15W 333 F3
São João do Araguaia Brazil 5°23S 48°46W 332 C2
São João do Paraíso Brazil 15°19S 42°1W 333 E3
São João do Piauí Brazil 8°21S 42°15W 332 C3
São João do Sul Angola 15°46S 12°0E 265 F2
São João dos Patos Brazil 6°30S 43°42W 332 C3
São Joaquim Amazonas, Brazil 0°1S 67°16W 328 D4
São Joaquim Sta. Catarina, Brazil 28°18S 49°56W 335 B6
São Joaquim △ Brazil 28°12S 49°37W 335 B6
São Joaquim da Barra Brazil 20°35S 47°53W 333 F2
São Jorge Azores 38°38N 28°3W 153 d1
São Jorge, Canal de Azores 38°30N 28°0W 153 d1
São Jorge, Castelo de Portugal 38°42N 9°8W 126 A2
São Jorge, Pta. de Azores 38°42N 27°3W 153 d1
São Jorge, Pta. de Madeira 32°50N 16°53W 153 c
São José Brazil 27°38S 48°39W 335 B5
São José, B. de Brazil 2°38S 44°4W 332 B3
São José da Lagoa = Nova Era Brazil 19°45S 43°3W 333 E3
São José da Laje Brazil 9°1S 36°3W 332 C4
São José de Mipibu Brazil 6°5S 35°15W 332 C4
São José de Ribamar Brazil 2°33S 44°3W 332 B3
São José de Tocantins = Niquelândia Brazil 14°33S 48°23W 333 D2
São José do Norte Brazil 32°1S 52°3W 335 C5
São José do Peixe Brazil 7°24S 42°34W 332 C3
São José do Rio Preto Brazil 20°50S 49°20W 335 A6
São José dos Campos Brazil 23°7S 45°52W 335 A6
São José dos Cocais = Nossa Senhora do Livramento Brazil 15°48S 56°22W 331 D6
São José dos Matões = Parnarama Brazil 5°31S 43°6W 332 C3
São Julião do Tojal Portugal 38°49N 9°8W 126 A2
São Leopoldo Brazil 29°50S 51°10W 335 B5
São Lourenço Brazil 22°7S 45°3W 333 F2
São Lourenço → Brazil 17°53S 57°27W 331 D6
São Lourenço, Pantanal do Brazil 17°30S 56°20W 331 D6
São Lourenço, Pta. de Madeira 32°44N 16°39W 153 c
São Lourenço do Sul Brazil 31°22S 51°58W 335 C5
São Luís Brazil 2°39S 44°15W 332 B3
São Luís do Curu Brazil 3°40S 39°14W 332 B4
São Luís do Tapajós Brazil 4°25S 56°12W 329 D6
São Luís Gonzaga = Ipixuna Brazil 7°0S 71°40W 330 B3
São Luís Gonzaga Brazil 28°25S 55°0W 335 B5
São Marcos → Brazil 18°15S 47°37W 333 E2
São Marcos, B. de Brazil 2°0S 44°0W 332 B3
São Martinho da Cortiça Portugal 40°18N 8°8W 194 E2
São Mateus Azores 38°26N 28°27W 153 d1
São Mateus Brazil 18°44S 39°50W 333 E4
São Mateus → Brazil 18°35S 39°44W 333 E4
São Mateus do Sul Brazil 25°52S 50°23W 335 B5
São Miguel Azores 37°47N 25°30W 153 d3
São Miguel do Araguaia Brazil 13°19S 50°13W 333 D1
São Miguel do Guamá Brazil 1°37S 47°29W 332 B2
São Miguel do Oeste Brazil 26°45S 53°34W 335 B5
São Miguel dos Campos Brazil 9°47S 36°5W 332 C4
São Nicolau C. Verde Is. 16°20N 24°20W 153 j
São Nicolau → Angola 14°16S 12°22E 265 E2
São Nicolau → Brazil 5°45S 42°2W 332 C3
São Paulo Brazil 23°32S 46°38W 137 B2
São Paulo □ Brazil 22°0S 49°0W 335 A6
São Paulo, I. Atl. Oc. 0°56N 29°22W 152 F9
São Paulo Congonhas ✕ (CGH) Brazil 23°38S 46°39W 137 B2
São Paulo de Olivença Brazil 3°27S 68°48W 328 D4
São Pedro Atl. Oc. 0°56N 29°22W 152 F9
São Pedro do Sul Portugal 40°46N 8°4W 194 E2
São Rafael Brazil 5°47S 36°55W 332 C4
São Raimundo das Mangabeiras Brazil 7°1S 45°29W 332 C2
São Raimundo Nonato Brazil 9°1S 42°42W 332 C3
São Romão Brazil 16°22S 45°4W 333 E2
São Roque Madeira 32°46N 16°48W 153 c
São Roque, C. de Brazil 5°30S 35°16W 332 C4
São Roque do Pico Azores 38°31N 28°19W 153 d1
São Salvador do Congo = Mbanza Congo Angola 6°18S 14°16E 265 D2
São Sebastião Azores 38°39N 27°6W 153 d1
São Sebastião, I. de Brazil 23°50S 45°18W 335 A6
São Sebastião do Paraíso Brazil 20°54S 46°59W 335 A6
São Simão Brazil 18°56S 50°30W 333 E1
São Teotónio Portugal 37°30N 8°42W 195 H2
São Tiago C. Verde Is. 15°0N 23°40W 153 j
São Tomé Brazil 5°58S 36°4W 332 C4
São Tomé São Tomé & Príncipe 0°10N 6°39E 265 a
São Tomé, C. de Brazil 22°0S 40°59W 333 F3
São Tomé, Pico de São Tomé & Príncipe 0°16N 6°33E 265 a
São Tomé & Príncipe ■ Africa 0°12N 6°39E 265 a
São Vicente = Araguatins Brazil 5°38S 48°7W 332 C2
São Vicente Brazil 23°57S 46°23W 335 A6
São Vicente C. Verde Is. 17°0N 25°0W 153 j
São Vicente Madeira 32°48N 17°3W 153 c
São Vicente, C. de Portugal 37°0N 9°0W 195 H1
Saona, I. Dom. Rep. 18°10N 68°40W 321 C6
Saône → France 45°44N 4°50E 173 G11
Saône-et-Loire □ France 46°30N 4°50E 173 F11
Saonek Indonesia 0°22S 130°55E 231 E8
Saoura, O. → Algeria 29°0N 0°55W 261 C4
Sapa India 22°30N 88°15E 124 B1
Sapam, Ao Thailand 8°0N 98°26E 237 a
Sapanca Turkey 40°41N 30°16E 212 B4
Sapão → Brazil 11°1S 45°32W 332 D2
Saparua Indonesia 3°33S 128°40E 231 E7
Sapateiro, Cor. do → Brazil 23°35S 46°41W 137 B1
Sapé Brazil 7°6S 35°13W 332 C4
Sape Indonesia 8°34S 118°59E 235 D5
Sapele Nigeria 5°50N 5°40E 263 D6
Sapelo I. U.S.A. 31°25N 81°12W 316 D8
Sapelo Sound U.S.A. 31°30N 81°10W 316 D8
Sapes Greece 41°2N 25°43E 203 E9
Şaphane Turkey 39°1N 29°13E 205 B11
Sapi ⌂ Zimbabwe 15°48S 29°42E 269 F2
Sapienza Greece 36°45N 21°43E 204 E3
Sapindji Dem. Rep. of the Congo 9°39S 23°12E 265 D4
Sapo △ Liberia 5°15N 8°30W 262 D3
Sapone Burkina Faso 12°3N 1°35W 263 C4
Saposoa Peru 6°55S 76°45W 330 B2
Sapotskina Belarus 53°49N 23°40E 184 E10
Sapouy Burkina Faso 11°34N 1°44W 263 C4
Sapozhok Russia 53°59N 40°41E 190 D5
Sapphire Australia 23°28S 147°43E 280 C4
Sappho U.S.A. 48°4N 124°16W 306 B2
Sapporo Japan 43°0N 141°21E 220 C10
Sapri Italy 40°4N 15°38E 201 B8
Sapu Angola 12°28S 19°26E 265 E3
Sapudi Indonesia 7°6S 114°20E 235 D4
Sapulpa U.S.A. 35°59N 96°5W 314 D6
Saqqez Iran 36°15N 46°20E 213 D12
Sar Dasht Āzarbāyjān-e Gharbī, Iran 36°9N 45°28E 213 D11
Sar Dasht Khuzestān, Iran 32°32N 48°52E 247 C6
Sar-e Pol Afghan. 36°10N 66°0E 240 A2
Sar-e Pol □ Afghan. 36°20N 65°50E 240 A2
Sar Gachīneh = Yāsūj Iran 30°31N 51°31E 247 D6
Sar Passage Palau 7°12N 134°22E 288 c
Sar Planina Macedonia 42°0N 21°0E 202 E4
Sara Burkina Faso 11°40N 3°53W 262 C4
Sara Niger 20°46N 12°35E 259 D2
Sara Phil. 11°16N 123°1E 233 F4
Šara △ Serbia 42°12N 21°0E 202 D5
Sara Buri = Saraburi Thailand 14°30N 100°55E 236 E3
Sarāb Iran 37°55N 47°40E 213 D12
Sarābādī Iraq 33°1N 44°48E 246 C5
Sarabit el Khâdim Egypt 29°3N 33°25E 251 J4
Sarābleh Iran 33°44N 46°34E 213 F12
Saraburi Thailand 14°30N 100°55E 236 E3
Saradiya India 21°34N 70°2E 242 J4
Saraféré Mali 15°50N 3°40W 262 B4
Saragossa = Zaragoza Spain 41°39N 0°53W 196 D4
Saraguro Ecuador 3°35S 79°16W 328 D2
Sarahs Turkmenistan 36°32N 61°13E 247 B9
Sarai Naurang Pakistan 32°50N 70°47E 242 C4
Saraikela India 22°42N 85°56E 243 H11
Saraipali India 21°20N 82°59E 244 D6
Saraiu Romania 44°43N 28°10E 183 F13
Sarajevo Bos.-H. 43°52N 18°26E 182 G3
Sarakhs = Sarahs Turkmenistan 36°32N 61°13E 247 B9
Sarakhs Iran 36°32N 61°9E 216 E6
Saramacca → Suriname 5°50N 55°55W 329 B6
Saramati Burma 25°44N 95°2E 241 C5
Saran, Gunung Indonesia 0°30S 111°25E 235 C4
Saranac U.S.A. 42°56N 85°13W 311 B11
Saranac Lake U.S.A. 44°20N 74°10W 313 B10
Saranac Lakes U.S.A. 44°20N 74°28W 313 B10
Saranda Tanzania 5°45S 34°59E 268 D3
Sarandë Albania 39°52N 19°55E 206 B9
Sarandí Argentina 34°40S 58°20W 117 C2
Sarandí del Yí Uruguay 33°18S 55°38W 335 C4
Sarandí Grande Uruguay 33°44S 56°20W 334 C4
Sarangani □ Phil. 5°45N 125°20E 233 J5
Sarangani B. Phil. 6°0N 125°13E 233 J5
Sarangani Is. Phil. 5°25N 125°25E 233 J5
Sarangarh India 21°30N 83°5E 244 D6
Saranovo = Septemvri Bulgaria 42°13N 24°6E 203 D8
Saransk Russia 54°10N 45°10E 190 C7
Sarapul Russia 56°28N 53°48E 186 C9
Sarāqib Syria 35°52N 36°47E 250 C7
Sarar Plain = Bannaanka Saraar Somali Rep. 9°25N 46°17E 267 C6
Sarasota U.S.A. 27°20N 82°32W 317 H7
Saraswati → India 22°46N 88°15E 124 A1
Sarata Ukraine 46°1N 29°40E 183 D14
Sarata → Ukraine 45°51N 29°41E 183 E14
Saratoga Calif., U.S.A. 37°16N 122°2W 306 H4
Saratoga Wyo., U.S.A. 41°27N 106°49W 304 F10
Saratoga ⌂ U.S.A. 43°0N 73°38W 313 D11
Saratoga L. U.S.A. 43°1N 73°44W 313 C11
Saratoga Springs U.S.A. 43°5N 73°47W 313 C11
Saratok Malaysia 1°55N 111°17E 235 B4
Saratov Russia 51°30N 46°2E 190 E7
Saratov □ Russia 51°50N 46°20E 190 E8
Sarāvān Iran 27°25N 62°15E 247 E9
Saravane Laos 15°43N 106°25E 236 E6
Sarawak □ Malaysia 2°0N 113°0E 235 B4
Saray Tekirdağ, Turkey 41°26N 27°55E 203 E11
Saray Van, Turkey 38°38N 44°9E 213 C11
Saraya Senegal 12°50N 11°45W 262 C2
Sarayçık Turkey 39°1N 29°49E 205 B11
Sarayköy Turkey 37°55N 28°54E 205 D10
Saraylar Turkey 40°39N 27°40E 203 F11
Sarayönü Turkey 38°16N 32°24E 212 C5
Sarbāz Iran 26°38N 61°19E 247 E9
Sarbīsheh Iran 32°30N 59°40E 247 C8
Sárbogárd Hungary 46°50N 18°40E 182 D3
Sarca → Italy 45°52N 10°52E 198 C7
Sarcelles France 49°1N 2°23E 173 D9
Sarda → India 27°21N 81°23E 243 F9
Sardalas Libya 25°50N 10°34E 258 C2
Sardar Sarovar Dam India 21°50N 73°50E 244 D1
Sardarshahr India 28°30N 74°29E 242 E6
Sardegna □ Italy 40°0N 9°0E 200 B1
Sardhana India 29°9N 77°39E 242 E7
Sardina, Pta. Canary Is. 28°9N 15°44W 153 e1
Sardinata Colombia 8°5N 72°48W 328 B3
Sardinia = Sardegna □ Italy 40°0N 9°0E 200 B1
Sardinia U.S.A. 39°0N 83°49W 311 F13
Sardis Turkey 38°28N 27°58E 205 C10
Sardis Ga., U.S.A. 32°58N 81°46W 316 C8
Sardūīyeh = Dar Mazār Iran 29°14N 57°20E 247 D8
Sarecky potok → Czech Rep. 50°7N 14°23E 135 B2
Saren Indonesia 8°26S 115°34E 231 J18
S'Arenal Spain 39°30N 2°45E 206 B3
Sarentino Italy 46°38N 11°21E 199 B8
Saréyamou Mali 16°7N 3°10W 262 B4
Sargasso Sea Atl. Oc. 27°0N 72°0W 292 G13
Sargent U.S.A. 33°26N 84°52W 316 B5
Sargodha Pakistan 32°10N 72°40E 242 C5
Sarh Chad 9°5N 18°23E 259 G3
Sarhala Ivory C. 8°22N 6°8W 262 D3
Sarhro, Jebel Morocco 31°6N 5°0W 260 B4
Sārī Iran 36°30N 53°4E 247 B7
Sari d'Orcino France 42°3N 8°49E 175 F12
Saria Greece 35°54N 27°17E 205 F9
Saria India 21°38N 83°22E 243 J10
Sariab Pakistan 30°6N 66°59E 242 D2
Sarıbeyler Turkey 39°24N 27°35E 205 B9
Saricumbe Angola 12°12S 19°46E 265 E3
Sarigan N. Marianas 16°43N 145°47E 302 a
Sarıgöl Turkey 38°14N 28°41E 212 C3
Sarıkamış Turkey 40°22N 42°35E 213 B10
Sarikei Malaysia 2°8N 111°30E 235 B4
Sarıköy Turkey 40°12N 27°37E 203 F11
Sarila India 25°46N 79°41E 243 G8
Sarimbun Singapore 1°24N 103°40E 138 A2
Sarimbun Res. Singapore 1°25N 103°41E 138 A2
Sarina Australia 21°22S 149°13E 280 C4
Sariñena Spain 41°47N 0°10W 196 D4
Sarinleey Somali Rep. 2°22N 42°17E 267 D5
Sarıoğlan Turkey 39°5N 35°59E 212 C6
Sariri Papua N. G. 9°11S 148°35E 286 E5
Sarita U.S.A. 27°13N 97°47W 314 H6
Sarıveliler Turkey 36°41N 32°37E 250 B3
Sariwŏn N. Korea 38°31N 125°46E 224 C2
Sariyar Barajı Turkey 40°2N 31°33E 212 B4
Sarıyer Turkey 41°10N 29°3E 122 A2
Sarız Turkey 38°28N 36°30E 212 C7
Sarju → India 27°21N 81°23E 243 F9
Sark U.K. 49°25N 2°22W 169 H5
Sarkad Hungary 46°47N 21°23E 182 D6
Sarkari Tala India 27°39N 70°52E 242 F4
Şarkışla Turkey 39°21N 36°25E 212 C7
Şarköy Turkey 40°36N 27°6E 203 F11
Sarlat-la-Canéda France 44°54N 1°13E 174 D5
Sărmăşag Romania 47°21N 22°50E 182 C7
Sărmaşu Romania 46°45N 24°13E 183 D9
Sarmi Indonesia 1°49S 138°44E 231 E9
Sarmiento Argentina 45°35S 69°5W 336 C3
Sarmizegetusa Romania 45°31N 22°47E 182 E7
Särna Sweden 61°41N 13°8E 162 C7
Sarnano Italy 43°2N 13°18E 199 E10
Sarnen Switz. 46°53N 8°13E 179 J4
Sarnia Canada 42°58N 82°23W 312 D2
Sarno Italy 40°49N 14°37E 201 B7
Sarnthein = Sarentino Italy 46°38N 11°21E 199 B8
Särö Sweden 57°31N 11°57E 163 G5
Sarolangun Indonesia 2°19S 102°42E 234 C2
Saronikos Kolpos Greece 37°45N 23°45E 204 D5
Saronno Italy 45°38N 9°2E 198 C6
Saros Körfezi Turkey 40°30N 26°15E 203 F10
Sárospatak Hungary 48°18N 21°33E 182 B6
Sarowbī Afghan. 34°36N 69°44E 240 B3
Sarpsborg Norway 59°16N 11°7E 164 E8
Sarqan Kazakhstan 45°24N 79°55E 217 C9
Sarracín Spain 42°15N 3°45W 196 C7
Sarralbe France 49°0N 7°1E 173 D14
Sarrat Phil. 18°9N 120°39E 232 B3
Sarre = Saar → Europe 49°41N 6°32E 170 E6
Sarre Italy 45°40N 7°15E 198 C4
Sarre-Union France 48°57N 7°4E 173 D14
Sarrebourg France 48°43N 7°3E 173 D14
Sarreguemines France 49°5N 7°4E 173 C14
Sarriá Barcelona, Spain 41°22N 2°8E 114 A1
Sarria Galicia, Spain 42°49N 7°29W 194 C3
Sarrión Spain 40°9N 0°49W 196 E4
Sarro Mali 13°40N 5°15W 262 C3
Sarsing Iraq 37°2N 43°20E 213 D10
Sarstedt Germany 52°14N 9°52E 178 C5
Sarsuna India 22°28N 88°17E 124 C1
Sartène France 41°38N 8°58E 175 G12
Sarthe □ France 47°58N 0°10E 172 D7
Sarthe → France 47°33N 0°31W 172 E6
Sartilly France 48°45N 1°28W 172 D5
Sartrouville France 48°56N 2°10E 134 A2
Saruhanlı Turkey 38°44N 27°36E 205 C9
Sărulești Romania 44°25N 26°39E 183 F11
Saruna → Pakistan 26°31N 67°7E 242 F2
Sarupeta India 26°30N 91°5E 241 B3
Sārur Azerbaijan 39°22N 45°5E 213 C11
Saruwaged Ra. Papua N. G. 6°13S 146°35E 286 D4
Sárvár Hungary 47°15N 16°56E 182 C1
Sarvar India 26°4N 75°0E 242 F6
Sarvestān Iran 29°20N 53°10E 247 D7
Särvfjället Sweden 62°42N 13°30E 162 B7
Sárvíz → Hungary 46°24N 18°41E 182 D3
Sary-Tash Kyrgyzstan 39°44N 73°15E 217 E8
Sarych, Mys Ukraine 44°25N 33°45E 189 K7
Sarycsik-Atyraū Qumy Kazakhstan 45°30N 76°0E 217 C9
Sarykamyshskoye, Ozero = Saryqamysh Köli Turkmenistan 41°56N 57°25E 216 D5
Sarykemer Kazakhstan 43°0N 71°30E 217 D8
Sarykenggir → Kazakhstan 48°22N 67°59E 217 C7
Sarykol' Kazakhstan 53°20N 65°12E 216 B7
Sarykolskiy Khrebet Tajikistan 38°30N 74°30E 217 E8
Saryözek Kazakhstan 44°22N 77°59E 217 D9
Saryqamysh Köli Turkmenistan 41°56N 57°25E 216 D5
Saryshaghan Kazakhstan 46°12N 73°38E 217 C8
Sarysū → Kazakhstan 45°12N 66°36E 217 C7
Sarzana Italy 44°7N 9°58E 198 D6
Sarzeau France 47°31N 2°48W 172 E4
Sasabeneh Ethiopia 7°59N 44°43E 267 C5
Sasad Hungary 47°28N 19°0E 117 B2
Sasamungga Solomon Is. 7°0S 156°50E 287 L9
Sasan Gir India 21°10N 70°36E 242 J4
Sasaram India 24°57N 84°5E 243 G11
Sasari, Mt. Solomon Is. 8°10S 159°30E 287 M10
Sasayama Japan 35°4N 135°13E 223 B7
Sasebo Japan 33°10N 129°43E 222 D1
Saser Kangri India 34°50N 77°50E 243 B7
Sashalom Hungary 47°30N 19°10E 117 A3
Saska Poland 52°14N 21°3E 132 B2
Saskatchewan □ Canada 54°40N 106°0W 297 C7
Saskatchewan → Canada 53°37N 100°40W 297 C8
Saskatoon Canada 52°10N 106°38W 297 C7
Saskylakh Russia 71°55N 114°1E 215 B12
Sasolburg S. Africa 26°46S 27°49E 271 C4
Sason Turkey 38°19N 41°24E 213 C9
Sasovo Russia 54°25N 41°55E 190 C5
Sassandra Ivory C. 4°55N 6°8W 262 E3
Sassandra → Ivory C. 4°58N 6°5W 262 E3
Sássari Italy 40°43N 8°34E 200 B1
Sassie Australia 10°2S 142°51E 280 a
Sassnitz Germany 54°29N 13°39E 178 A9
Sasso Marconi Italy 44°24N 11°15E 199 D8
Sassocorvaro Italy 43°47N 12°30E 199 E9
Sassoferrato Italy 43°26N 12°51E 199 E9
Sasstown Liberia 4°45N 8°27W 262 E3
Sassuolo Italy 44°33N 10°47E 198 D7
Sástago Spain 41°19N 0°21W 196 D4
Sasvad India 18°20N 74°2E 244 E2
Sasyk, Ozero Ukraine 45°45N 29°20E 183 E14
Sasyqköl Kazakhstan 46°35N 81°0E 217 C10
Sata-Misaki Japan 31°0N 130°40E 222 F2
Satadougou Mali 12°25N 11°25W 262 C2
Satakunda = Satakunta Finland 61°45N 23°0E 188 B2
Satakunta Finland 61°45N 23°0E 188 B2
Satalice Czech Rep. 50°7N 14°34E 135 B3
Satama-Soukoura Ivory C. 7°55N 4°27W 262 D4
Satara India 17°44N 73°58E 244 F1
Satara S. Africa 24°29S 31°47E 271 B5
Sätbaev Kazakhstan 48°10N 67°31E 217 C7
Satbarwa India 23°55N 84°16E 243 H11
Satellite Beach U.S.A. 28°10N 80°36W 317 G9
Såtenäs Sweden 58°27N 12°41E 163 F6
Säter Sweden 60°21N 15°45E 162 D9
Satevó Mexico 27°57N 106°7W 318 B3
Satgachi India 22°37N 88°25E 124 B2
Satilla → U.S.A. 30°59N 81°29W 316 E8
Satipo Peru 11°15S 74°25W 330 C3
Satka Russia 55°3N 59°1E 186 C10
Satkania Bangla. 22°4N 92°3E 241 D4
Satkhira Bangla. 22°43N 89°8E 241 D2
Satmala Hills Andhra Pradesh, India 19°45N 78°45E 244 E4
Satmala Hills Maharashtra, India 20°15N 74°40E 244 D2
Satna India 24°35N 80°50E 243 G9
Šator Bos.-H. 44°11N 16°37E 199 D13
Sátoraljaújhely Hungary 48°25N 21°41E 182 B6
Satpukur India 22°37N 88°24E 124 B2
Satpura △ India 22°40N 78°15E 242 H8
Satpura Ra. India 21°25N 76°10E 244 D3
Sätra Sweden 59°17N 17°54E 139 B1
Satrup Germany 54°41N 9°36E 178 A5
Satsuma-Hantō Japan 31°25N 130°25E 222 F2
Satsuna-Shotō Japan 30°0N 130°0E 221 K5
Sattahip Thailand 12°41N 100°54E 236 F3
Sattenapalle India 16°25N 80°6E 245 F5
Sattru Phet Bangkok, Thailand 113 b2
Satu Mare Romania 47°46N 22°55E 182 C7
Satu Mare □ Romania 47°45N 23°0E 182 C8
Satui Indonesia 3°50S 115°27E 235 C5
Satun Thailand 6°43N 100°2E 237 J3
Satupa'itea Samoa 13°45S 172°18W 287 V19
Saturnina → Brazil 12°15S 58°10W 331 C6
Sauce = Juan L. Lacaze Uruguay 34°26S 57°25W 334 C4
Sauce Argentina 30°5S 58°46W 334 C4
Sauceda Mexico 25°46N 101°19W 318 B4
Saucillo Mexico 28°1N 105°17W 318 B3
Sauda Norway 59°40N 6°20E 164 E3
Saudasjøen Norway 59°38N 6°17E 164 E3
Saudé Bahia, Brazil 10°56S 40°24W 332 D3
Saúde São Paulo, Brazil 23°36S 46°37W 137 B2
Sauðárkrókur Iceland 65°45N 19°40W 155 D4
Saudi Arabia ■ Asia 26°0N 44°0E 246 B3
Sauerland Germany 51°12N 7°59E 176 C4
Saugatuck U.S.A. 42°40N 86°12W 311 B10
Saugeen → Canada 44°30N 81°22W 312 B3
Saugerties U.S.A. 42°5N 73°57W 313 D11
Saugues France 44°58N 3°32E 174 D7
Saugus Calif., U.S.A. 34°25N 118°32W 307 L8
Saugus Mass., U.S.A. 42°28N 71°0W 116 A2
Saugus → U.S.A. 42°27N 70°58W 116 A2
Saujbulagh = Mahābād Iran 36°50N 45°45E 213 D11
Saujon France 45°41N 0°55W 174 C3
Sauk Centre U.S.A. 45°44N 94°57W 308 C6
Sauk City U.S.A. 43°17N 89°43W 310 A7
Sauk Rapids U.S.A. 45°35N 94°10W 308 C6
Saül Fr. Guiana 3°37N 53°12W 329 C7
Sauland Norway 59°37N 8°56E 164 E5
Saulgau Germany 48°1N 9°29E 179 G5
Saulieu France 47°17N 4°14E 173 E11
Sault France 44°6N 5°24E 175 D9
Sault-au-Récollet Canada 45°35N 73°39W 130 A2
Sault Ste. Marie Ont., Canada 46°30N 84°20W 298 C3
Sault Ste. Marie Mich., U.S.A. 46°30N 84°21W 309 B11
Saūmalkol Kazakhstan 53°17N 68°6E 217 B7
Saumlaki Indonesia 7°55S 131°20E 231 F8
Saumur France 47°15N 0°5W 172 E6
Saundatti India 15°47N 75°7E 245 G2
Saunders, C. N.Z. 45°53S 170°45E 285 F5
Saunders I. Antarctica 57°48S 26°28W 151 B1
Saunders Pt. Australia 27°52S 125°38E 279 E4
Saunemin U.S.A. 40°54N 88°24W 311 D8
Saupite Angola 13°54S 17°43E 265 E3
Saurbær Borgarfjarðarsýsla, Iceland 64°24N 21°35W 155 C5
Saurbær Eyjafjarðarsýsla, Iceland 65°27N 18°13W 155 B8
Sauri Nigeria 11°42N 6°44E 263 C6
Saurimo Angola 9°40S 20°12E 265 D4
Sausalito U.S.A. 37°51N 122°29W 136 A2
Sautatá Colombia 7°50N 77°4W 328 B2
Sauteurs Grenada 12°14N 61°38W 323 q
Sauveterre-de-Béarn France 43°24N 0°57W 174 E3
Sauzé-Vaussais France 46°8N 0°8E 174 B4
Savá Honduras 15°32N 86°15W 320 C2
Sava Italy 40°24N 17°33E 201 B10
Sava → Serbia 44°50N 20°26E 182 F5
Savage U.S.A. 47°27N 104°21W 304 C11
Savage I. = Niue Pac. Oc. 19°2S 169°54W 289 g
Savage River Australia 41°31S 145°14E 281 G4
Savai'i Samoa 13°28S 172°24W 287 V19
Savalou Benin 7°57N 1°58E 263 D5
Savane Mozam. 19°37S 35°8E 269 F4
Savaneta Aruba 12°27N 69°56W 322 f
Savanna U.S.A. 42°5N 90°8W 310 B6
Savanna-la-Mar Jamaica 18°10N 78°10W 320 a
Savannah Ga., U.S.A. 32°5N 81°6W 316 C8
Savannah Mo., U.S.A. 39°56N 94°50W 310 E2
Savannah Tenn., U.S.A. 35°14N 88°15W 315 D10
Savannah → U.S.A. 32°2N 80°53W 316 C9
Savannah Beach = Tybee Island U.S.A. 32°1N 80°51W 316 C9
Savannakhet Laos 16°30N 104°49E 236 D5
Savanne, Piton Mauritius 20°26S 57°29E 272 e
Savannes B. St. Lucia 13°45N 60°56W 323 m
Savant L. Canada 50°16N 90°44W 298 B1
Savant Lake Canada 50°14N 90°40W 298 B1
Savantvadi India 15°55N 73°54E 245 G1
Savanur India 14°59N 75°21E 245 G2
Savarkundla = Kundla India 21°21N 71°25E 242 J4
Săvârșin Romania 46°1N 22°14E 182 D7
Savaştepe Turkey 39°22N 27°42E 205 B9
Savda India 21°9N 75°56E 244 D2
Savé Benin 8°2N 2°29E 263 D5
Save → Haute-Garonne, France 43°47N 1°17E 174 E5
Save → Mozam. 21°16S 34°0E 271 B5
Sāveh Iran 35°2N 50°20E 247 C6
Savelugu Ghana 9°38N 0°54W 263 D4
Savenay France 47°20N 1°55W 172 E5
Săveni Romania 47°57N 26°52E 183 C11
Saverdun France 43°14N 1°34E 174 E5
Saverne France 48°43N 7°20E 173 D14
Savigliano Italy 44°39N 7°40E 198 D4
Savigny-sur-Braye France 47°53N 0°49E 172 E7
Sávio → Italy 44°19N 12°20E 199 D9
Šavnik Montenegro 42°59N 19°10E 202 D3
Savo Finland 62°45N 27°30E 188 A5
Savo Solomon Is. 9°8S 159°48E 287 M10
Savoie □ France 45°26N 6°25E 175 C10
Savolax = Savo Finland 62°45N 27°30E 160 E22
Savona Italy 44°17N 8°30E 198 D5
Savona N.Y., U.S.A. 42°17N 77°13W 312 D7
Savonet Neth. Ant. 12°21N 69°7W 322 g
Savonlinna Finland 61°52N 28°53E 188 B5
Savoonga U.S.A. 63°42N 170°29W 303 E5
Savoy = Savoie □ France 45°26N 6°25E 175 C10
Şavşat Turkey 41°15N 42°20E 213 B10
Sävsjö Sweden 57°20N 14°40E 163 G8
Savur Turkey 37°34N 40°53E 246 B4
Savusavu Fiji 16°34S 179°15E 287 A2
Savusavu B. Fiji 16°45S 179°15E 287 A2
Sawa Besar Indonesia 6°8S 106°49E 122 A1
Sawahlunto Indonesia 0°40S 100°52E 234 C2
Sawai Indonesia 3°0S 129°5E 231 E7
Sawai Madhopur India 26°0N 76°25E 242 G7
Sawaleke Fiji 17°59S 179°18E 287 A2
Sawang Daen Din Thailand 17°28N 103°28E 236 D4
Sawankhalok Thailand 17°19N 99°50E 236 D2
Sawara Japan 35°55N 140°30E 223 B12
Sawatch Range U.S.A. 39°0N 106°30W 304 G10
Sawdā', Jabal as Libya 28°51N 15°12E 258 C3
Sawel Mt. U.K. 54°50N 7°2W 166 B4
Sawfajjin, W. → Libya 31°41N 14°44E 258 B2
Sawi Thailand 10°14N 99°5E 237 G2
Sawla Ghana 9°17N 2°25W 262 D4
Sawmills Zimbabwe 19°30S 28°2E 269 F2
Şawqirah Oman 18°7N 56°32E 249 C7
Şawqirah, Ghubbat Oman 18°35N 57°0E 249 C7
Sawtell Australia 30°19S 153°6E 283 A10
Sawtelle U.S.A. 34°2N 118°27W 126 B2
Sawtooth ⌂ U.S.A. 44°0N 114°50W 304 D6
Sawtooth Range U.S.A. 44°3N 114°58W 304 D6
Sawu Indonesia 10°35S 121°50E 231 F6
Sawu Sea Indonesia 9°30S 121°50E 231 F6
Saxby → Australia 18°25S 140°53E 280 B3
Saxmundham U.K. 52°13N 1°30E 169 E9
Saxony = Sachsen □ Germany 50°55N 13°10E 178 E9
Saxony, Lower = Niedersachsen □ Germany 52°50N 9°0E 178 C4
Saxton U.S.A. 40°13N 78°15W 312 F6
Say Mali 13°50N 4°57W 262 C4
Say Niger 13°8N 2°22E 263 C5
Saya Nigeria 9°30N 3°18E 263 D5
Sayabec Canada 48°35N 67°41W 299 C6
Sayaboury Laos 19°15N 101°45E 236 C3
Sayán Peru 11°8S 77°12W 330 C2
Sayan, Vostochnyy Russia 54°0N 96°0E 215 D10
Sayan, Zapadnyy Russia 52°30N 94°0E 217 B12
Sayanogorsk Russia 53°5N 91°23E 215 D10
Saydā Lebanon 33°35N 35°25E 250 E6
Sayghān Afghan. 35°10N 67°55E 240 B2
Sayhandulaan = Oldziyt Mongolia 44°40N 109°1E 226 B5
Sayhūt Yemen 15°12N 51°10E 249 D5
Saykhin Kazakhstan 48°50N 46°47E 191 F8
Saylac Somali Rep. 11°21N 43°30E 267 B5
Saylorville L. U.S.A. 41°48N 93°46W 310 C3
Saynshand = Buyant-Uhaa Mongolia 44°55N 110°11E 219 B6
Sayō Japan 34°59N 134°22E 222 C6
Sayre Okla., U.S.A. 35°18N 99°38W 314 D5
Sayre Pa., U.S.A. 41°59N 76°32W 313 E8
Sayreville U.S.A. 40°28N 74°22W 313 F10
Sayula Mexico 19°52N 103°36W 318 D4
Sayward Canada 50°21N 125°55W 296 C3
Saywūn Yemen 15°56N 48°47E 249 D5
Saza Japan 33°14N 129°39E 222 D1
Sazanit Albania 40°30N 19°20E 202 F3
Sázava → Czech Rep. 49°53N 14°24E 180 B7
Sazin Pakistan 35°35N 73°30E 243 B5
Sazlika → Bulgaria 41°59N 25°50E 203 E9
Sbeïtla Tunisia 35°12N 9°7E 258 A1
Scaër France 48°2N 3°42W 172 D3
Scafell Pike U.K. 54°27N 3°14W 168 C4
Scald Law U.K. 55°50N 3°17W 121 B2
Scalea Italy 39°49N 15°47E 201 C8
Scalloway U.K. 60°9N 1°17W 167 A7
Scalpay U.K. 57°18N 6°0W 167 D3
Scammon Bay U.S.A. 61°51N 165°35W 303 F6
Scandia Canada 50°20N 112°2W 296 C6
Scandiano Italy 44°36N 10°43E 198 D7
Scandicci Italy 43°45N 11°11E 199 E8
Scandinavia Europe 64°0N 12°0E 160 E15
Scansano Italy 42°41N 11°20E 199 F8
Scapa Flow U.K. 58°53N 3°3W 167 C5
Scappoose U.S.A. 45°45N 122°53W 306 E4
Scarámia, Capo Italy 36°47N 14°29E 201 F7
Scarba U.K. 56°11N 5°43W 167 E3
Scarborough Ont., Canada 43°44N 79°14W 141 A3
Scarborough Trin. & Tob. 11°11N 60°42W 323 s
Scarborough N. Yorks., U.K. 54°17N 0°24W 168 C7
Scarborough Bluffs Canada 43°42N 79°14W 141 A3
Scarborough Shoal S. China Sea 15°0N 117°50E 232 D1
Scargill N.Z. 42°56S 172°58E 285 C7
Scariff I. Ireland 51°44N 10°15W 166 E1
Scarp U.K. 58°1N 7°8W 167 C1
Scarpanto = Karpathos Greece 35°37N 27°10E 205 F9
Scarpe-Escaut ⌂ France 50°26N 3°23E 173 B10
Scarsdale Australia 37°41S 143°39E 282 D5
Sceaux France 48°46N 2°17E 134 B2
Scebeli = Shabeelle → Somali Rep. 2°0N 44°0E 267 D5
Šćedro Croatia 43°6N 16°43E 199 E13
Scenery, Mt. Neth. Ant. 17°38N 63°14W 322 a
Schaal See Germany 53°36N 10°55E 178 B6
Schaalsee ⌂ Germany 53°40N 10°59E 178 B6
Schaerbeek Belgium 50°52N 4°22E 116 A2
Schaffhausen Switz. 47°42N 8°39E 179 H4
Schagen Neths. 52°49N 4°48E 170 B4
Schaghticoke U.S.A. 42°54N 73°35W 313 D11
Schärding Austria 48°27N 13°27E 180 C6
Scharfenberg Germany 52°35N 13°15E 115 A2
Scharfenwiese = Ostrołęka Poland 53°4N 21°32E 185 E8
Scharhörn Germany 53°57N 8°24E 178 B4
Schässburg = Sighişoara Romania 46°12N 24°50E 183 D9
Scheessel Germany 53°10N 9°29E 178 B5
Schefferville Canada 54°48N 66°50W 299 B6
Scheibbs Austria 48°1N 15°9E 180 C8
Scheidt = Schelde → Belgium 51°15N 4°16E 170 C4
Schelde → Belgium 51°15N 4°16E 170 C4
Schell City U.S.A. 38°1N 94°7W 310 F2
Schell Creek Ra. U.S.A. 39°25N 114°40W 304 G6
Schellsburg U.S.A. 40°3N 78°39W 312 F6
Schemnitz = Banská Štiavnica Slovak Rep. 48°25N 18°55E 181 C11
Schenectady U.S.A. 42°49N 73°57W 313 D11
Schenevus U.S.A. 42°33N 74°50W 313 D10
Scherfede Germany 51°32N 9°2E 178 D5
Schesslitz Germany 49°58N 11°2E 179 F7
Schiedam Neths. 51°55N 4°25E 170 C4
Schierstein = Sieradz Poland 51°37N 18°41E 185 G5
Schiermonnikoog Neths. 53°30N 6°15E 170 A6
Schiller Park U.S.A. 41°56N 87°52W 119 B1
Schiller Woods U.S.A. 41°57N 87°51W 119 B1
Schiltigheim France 48°35N 7°45E 173 D14
Schinousa Greece 36°53N 25°31E 205 E7
Schio Italy 45°43N 11°21E 199 C8
Schiphol, Amsterdam ✕ (AMS) Neths. 52°18N 4°45E 112 B1
Schippenbeil = Sępopol Poland 54°16N 21°2E 184 D8
Schivelbein = Świdwin Poland 53°47N 15°49E 184 E2
Schlachtensee Germany 52°26N 13°13E 115 B2
Schladming Austria 47°23N 13°41E 180 D6
Schlanders = Silandro Italy 46°38N 10°46E 198 B7
Schlawa = Sława Poland 51°52N 16°2E 185 G3
Schlei → Germany 54°40N 10°0E 178 A5
Schleiden Germany 50°31N 6°28E 178 E2
Schleinitz Ra. Papua N. G. 3°0S 151°30E 286 B6
Schleiz Germany 50°35N 11°49E 178 E7
Schlesiersee = Sława Poland 51°52N 16°2E 185 G3
Schleswig Germany 54°31N 9°34E 178 A5
Schleswig-Holstein □ Germany 54°30N 9°30E 178 A5
Schlettstadt = Sélestat France 48°16N 7°26E 173 D14
Schlichtingsheim = Szlichtyngowa Poland 51°42N 16°15E 185 G3
Schlochau = Człuchów Poland 53°41N 17°22E 184 E4
Schloppe = Człopa Poland 53°6N 16°6E 185 E3
Schlossgarten Germany 52°31N 13°18E 115 A2
Schlüchtern Germany 50°20N 9°32E 179 E5
Schmalkalden Germany 50°44N 10°26E 178 E6
Schmargendorf Germany 52°28N 13°17E 115 B2
Schmölln Germany 50°54N 12°19E 178 E8
Schneeberg Austria 47°47N 15°48E 180 D8
Schneeberg Sachsen, Germany 50°35N 12°38E 178 E8
Schneidemühl = Piła Poland 53°10N 16°48E 185 E3
Schneider U.S.A. 41°13N 87°28W 311 C9
Schneverdingen Germany 53°7N 9°48E 178 B5
Schœlcher Martinique 14°36N 61°7W 322 j
Schofield Barracks U.S.A. 21°29N 158°7W 302 K13
Schoharie U.S.A. 42°40N 74°19W 313 D10
Schoharie Cr. → U.S.A. 42°57N 74°18W 313 D10
Scholls U.S.A. 45°24N 122°56W 306 E4
Schönau = Swierzawa Poland 51°1N 15°54E 185 G2
Schönberg Mecklenburg-Vorpommern, Germany 53°52N 10°56E 178 B6
Schönberg Schleswig-Holstein, Germany 54°23N 10°21E 178 A6
Schönblick Germany 52°27N 13°43E 115 B5
Schönbrunn Austria 48°10N 16°19E 142 A1
Schönbuch ⌂ Germany 48°35N 9°2E 179 G5
Schönebeck Germany 52°1N 11°44E 178 C7
Schöneberg Germany 52°28N 13°20E 115 B3
Schönefeld Germany 52°22N 13°33E 115 B4
Schöneiche Germany 52°28N 13°41E 115 B5
Schöngau Germany 47°47N 10°53E 179 H6
Schöningen Germany 52°8N 10°56E 178 C6
Schönlanke = Trzcianka Poland 53°3N 16°25E 185 E3
Schönstein = Šoštanj Slovenia 46°23N 15°4E 199 B12
Schönwalde Germany 52°37N 13°7E 115 A1
Schoolcraft U.S.A. 42°7N 85°38W 311 B11
Schopfheim Germany 47°38N 7°50E 179 H3
Schorndorf Germany 48°47N 9°32E 179 G5
Schortens Germany 53°31N 7°56E 178 B3
Schotschekloof Cape Town, S. Africa 118 b1
Schottegat Neth. Ant. 12°7N 68°55W 322 g
Schouten I. Australia 42°20S 148°20E 281 G4
Schouten Is. = Supiori Indonesia 1°0S 136°0E 231 E9
Schouten Is. Papua N. G. 3°30S 144°30E 286 B3
Schouwen Neths. 51°43N 3°45E 170 C3
Schramberg Germany 48°13N 8°22E 179 G4
Schrankogel Austria 47°3N 11°7E 180 D4
Schreiber Canada 48°45N 87°20W 298 C2
Schrems Austria 48°47N 15°4E 180 C8
Schrobenhausen Germany 48°34N 11°16E 179 G7
Schroffenstein Namibia 27°11S 18°42E 270 C2
Schroon Lake U.S.A. 43°50N 73°46W 313 C11
Schröttersberg = Płock Poland 52°32N 19°40E 185 F6
Schruns Austria 47°5N 9°56E 180 D2
Schuchye = Shchūchīnsk Kazakhstan 52°56N 70°12E 217 B8
Schuler Canada 50°20N 110°6W 297 C6
Schulzendorf Germany 52°36N 13°16E 115 A2
Schumacher Canada 48°30N 81°16W 298 C3
Schurz U.S.A. 38°57N 118°49W 304 G4
Schuyler U.S.A. 41°27N 97°4W 308 E5
Schuylerville U.S.A. 43°6N 73°35W 313 C11
Schuylkill → U.S.A. 39°53N 75°12W 313 G9
Schuylkill Haven U.S.A. 40°37N 76°11W 313 F8
Schwabach Germany 49°19N 11°2E 179 F7
Schwaben □ Germany 48°15N 10°30E 179 G6
Schwabing Germany 48°9N 11°35E 131 B2
Schwäbisch-Fränkischer Wald ⌂ Germany 49°0N 9°30E 179 G5
Schwäbisch Gmünd Germany 48°48N 9°47E 179 G5
Schwäbisch Hall Germany 49°6N 9°44E 179 F5
Schwäbische Alb Germany 48°20N 9°30E 179 G5
Schwabmünchen Germany 48°10N 10°46E 179 G6
Schwalmstadt Germany 50°55N 9°10E 178 E5
Schwandorf Germany 49°20N 12°7E 179 F8
Schwanebeck Germany 52°37N 13°32E 115 A4
Schwanenwerder Germany 52°26N 13°10E 115 B2
Schwaner, Pegunungan Indonesia 1°0S 112°30E 235 C4
Schwanewede Germany 53°14N 8°35E 178 B4
Schwarmstedt Germany 52°39N 9°38E 178 C5
Schwarze Elster → Germany 51°48N 12°50E 178 D8
Schwarzenberg Germany 50°32N 12°47E 178 E8
Schwarzlackenau Austria 48°16N 16°23E 142 A2
Schwarzrand Namibia 25°37S 16°50E 270 C2
Schwarzwald Germany 48°30N 8°20E 179 G4
Schwatka Mts. U.S.A. 67°20N 156°30W 303 C8
Schwaz Austria 47°20N 11°44E 180 D4
Schwechat Austria 48°8N 16°28E 142 B2
Schwechat, Wien ✕ (VIE) Austria 48°7N 16°35E 142 B3
Schwedt Germany 53°3N 14°16E 178 B10
Schweidnitz = Świdnica Poland 50°50N 16°30E 185 H3
Schweinfurt Germany 50°3N 10°14E 179 E6
Schweiz = Switzerland ■ Europe 46°30N 8°0E 179 J4
Schweizer-Reneke S. Africa 27°11S 25°18E 270 C4
Schwenningen = Villingen-Schwenningen Germany 48°3N 8°26E 179 G4
Schwerin = Skwierzyna Poland 52°33N 15°30E 185 F2
Schwerin Germany 53°36N 11°22E 178 B7

Schweriner See *Germany* 53°43N 11°28E **178** B7
Schwetzingen *Germany* 49°23N 8°35E **179** F4
Schwiebus = Świebodzin
  Poland 52°15N 15°31E **185** F2
Schwyz *Switz.* 47°2N 8°39E **179** H4
Schwyz □ *Switz.* 47°2N 8°39E **179** H4
Sciacca *Italy* 37°31N 13°3E **200** E6
Sciar *Italy* 36°47N 14°42E **201** F7
Science and Industry, Museum of
  U.S.A. 41°47N 87°34W **119** C3
Sciliar △ *Italy* 46°28N 11°35E **198** B8
Scilla *Italy* 38°15N 15°43E **201** D8
Scilly, Isles of *U.K.* 49°56N 6°22W **169** H1
Scione *Greece* 39°57N 23°36E **202** G7
Scioto → *U.S.A.* 38°44N 83°1W **311** D13
Scitrek Museum *U.S.A.* 33°46N 84°23W **143** a1
Scituate *U.S.A.* 42°12N 70°44W **313** D14
Scobey *U.S.A.* 48°47N 105°25W **304** B11
Scone *N.S.W., Australia* 32°5S 150°52E **283** B9
Scone *Perth & Kinr., U.K.* 56°25N 3°24W **167** E5
Scopus, Mt. *West Bank* 31°48N 35°14E **123** D2
Scordia *Italy* 37°18N 14°51E **201** E7
Scoresby Sund *Greenland* 70°20N 21°46W **154** C8
Scoresbysund = Ittoqqortoormiit
  Greenland 70°20N 23°0W **154** C8
Scornicesti *Romania* 44°34N 24°33E **183** F9
Scotia *Calif., U.S.A.* 40°29N 124°6W **304** F1
Scotia *N.Y., U.S.A.* 42°50N 73°58W **313** D11
Scotia Sea *Antarctica* 56°5S 56°0W **151** B18
Scotland *Canada* 43°1N 80°22W **312** C4
Scotland □ *U.K.* 57°0N 4°0W **167** E5
Scott *Antarctica* 77°0S 165°0E **151** D11
Scott, C. *Australia* 13°30S 129°49E **278** B4
Scott Circle *Washington, D.C., U.S.A.* **143** a1
Scott City *U.S.A.* 38°29N 100°54W **308** F3
Scott Glacier *Antarctica* 66°15S 100°5E **151** C8
Scott I. *Antarctica* 67°0S 179°0E **151** C11
Scott Is. *Canada* 50°48N 128°40W **306** D2
Scott L. *Canada* 59°55N 106°18W **297** B7
Scott Monument *Edinburgh, U.K.* **121** b2
Scott Reef *Australia* 14°0S 121°50E **278** B3
Scottburgh *S. Africa* 30°15S 30°47E **271** D5
Scottdale *Georgia, U.S.A.* 33°47N 84°16W **113** B3
Scottdale *Pa., U.S.A.* 40°6N 79°35W **312** F5
Scottish Borders □ *U.K.* 55°35N 2°50W **167** F6
Scotts Head *N.S.W.,
  Australia* 30°45S 153°0E **283** A10
Scotts Head *Dominica* 15°13N 61°23W **323** k
Scotts Head Village
  Dominica 15°12N 61°22W **323** k
Scotts Valley *U.S.A.* 37°3N 122°1W **306** H4
Scottsbluff *U.S.A.* 41°52N 103°40W **308** E2
Scottsboro *U.S.A.* 34°40N 86°2W **315** D11
Scottsburg *U.S.A.* 38°41N 85°47W **311** F11
Scottsdale *Tas., Australia* 41°9S 147°31E **281** G4
Scottsdale *Ariz., U.S.A.* 33°40N 111°53W **305** K8
Scottsville *Ky., U.S.A.* 43°2N 77°47W **312** C7
Scottville *U.S.A.* 43°58N 86°17W **308** D10
Scranton *U.S.A.* 41°25N 75°40W **313** E9
Screven *U.S.A.* 31°29N 82°1W **316** D7
Scrub I. *Anguilla* 18°19N 62°55W **322** a
Scugog, L. *Canada* 44°10N 78°55W **312** B6
Sculeni *Moldova* 47°20N 27°37E **183** C12
Scunthorpe *U.K.* 53°36N 0°39W **168** D7
Scuol Schuls *Switz.* 46°48N 10°17E **179** J6
Scutari = Shkodër *Albania* 42°4N 19°32E **202** D3
Scutari = Üsküdar *Turkey* 41°1N 29°0E **122** D2
Sea Is. *U.S.A.* 31°30N 81°7W **315** F14
Sea Lake *Australia* 35°28S 142°55E **282** C5
Sea Point *S. Africa* 34°5S 18°23E **118** A1
Seabra = Tarauacá *Brazil* 12°25S 41°46W **333** D3
Seabra *Brazil* 38°58N 76°49W **143** B5
Seabrook, L. *Australia* 30°55S 119°40E **279** F2
Seacliff *U.S.A.* 37°47N 122°28W **136** B2
Seaford *E. Sussex, U.K.* 50°45N 0°7E **169** G8
Seaforth *N.S.W.,
  Australia* 33°48S 151°15E **139** A2
Seaforth *Queens., Australia* 20°55S 148°57E **280** b
Seaforth *Ont., Canada* 43°35N 81°25W **312** C3
Seaforth, L. *U.K.* 57°52N 6°36W **167** D2
Seagate *U.S.A.* 40°34N 74°0W **132** C1
Seagraves *U.S.A.* 32°57N 102°34W **314** E3
Seaham *U.S.A.* 54°50N 1°20W **168** C6
Seal → *Canada* 59°4N 94°48W **297** B10
Seal I. *Anguilla* 18°16N 63°9W **322** a
Seal L. *Canada* 54°20N 61°30W **299** B7
Seale *U.S.A.* 32°18N 85°10W **316** C4
Sealy *U.S.A.* 29°47N 96°9W **314** G6
Seaman *U.S.A.* 38°57N 83°34W **311** F13
Searchlight *U.S.A.* 35°28N 114°55W **307** K12
Searcy *U.S.A.* 35°15N 91°44W **314** D9
Searles L. *U.S.A.* 35°44N 117°21W **307** K9
Sears Tower *Chicago, U.S.A.* **119** c1
Seascale *U.S.A.* 54°24N 3°29W **168** C4
Seaside *Calif., U.S.A.* 36°37N 121°50W **306** J5
Seaside *Oreg., U.S.A.* 46°0N 123°56W **306** E3
Seaspray *Australia* 38°25S 147°15E **283** F7
Seat Pleasant *U.S.A.* 38°53N 76°53W **143** B4
Seattle *U.S.A.* 47°36N 122°19W **306** C4
Seattle-Tacoma Int. ✈ (SEA)
  U.S.A. 47°27N 122°18W **306** C4
Seaview *N.Z.* 41°15S 174°54E **143** B2
Seaward Kaikoura Ra.
  N.Z. 42°10S 173°44E **285** C8
SeaWorld *U.S.A.* 28°24N 81°28W **133** B2
Seba *Indonesia* 10°29S 121°50E **278** B3
Sebago L. *U.S.A.* 43°52N 70°34W **313** C14
Sebago Lake *U.S.A.* 43°51N 70°34W **313** C14
Sebangka *Indonesia* 0°7N 104°36E **234** B2
Sebastian *U.S.A.* 27°49N 80°28W **317** H9
Sebastián Vizcaíno, B.
  Mexico 28°0N 114°30W **318** B2
Sebastopol = Sevastopol
  Ukraine 44°35N 33°30E **189** K7
Sebastopol *U.S.A.* 38°24N 122°49W **306** G4
Sebatik *Asia* 4°10N 117°45E **235** B5
Sebba *Burkina Faso* 13°35N 0°32E **263** C5
Sebderat *Eritrea* 15°26N 36°42E **257** D4
Sebdou *Algeria* 34°38N 1°19W **261** B4
Sébé → *Gabon* 1°2S 13°56E **264** C2
Sébékoro *Mali* 12°58N 9°0W **262** C3
Seben *Turkey* 40°24N 31°34E **122** B4
Šebeş *Romania* 50°0N 14°30E **135** B3
Seberi *Romania* 45°58N 23°34E **183** E8
Sebeşului, Munţii
  Romania 45°36N 23°40E **183** E8
Sebewaing *U.S.A.* 43°44N 83°27W **309** D12
Sebezh *Russia* 56°14N 28°22E **188** C5
Sebha = Sabhā *Libya* 27°9N 14°29E **258** C2
Sébi *Mali* 15°0N 4°12W **262** B4
Şebinkarahisar *Turkey* 40°22N 38°28E **213** B8
Sebiş *Romania* 46°23N 22°13E **183** E8
Sebnitz *Germany* 51°0N 14°15E **178** E10
Sebou, Oued → *Morocco* 34°16N 6°40W **260** B3
Sebring *Fla., U.S.A.* 27°30N 81°27W **312** E3
Sebring *Ohio, U.S.A.* 40°55N 81°2W **312** F3
Sebringville *Canada* 43°24N 81°4W **312** C3
Sebta = Ceuta *N. Afr.* 35°52N 5°18W **260** A3
Sebuku *Indonesia* 3°30S 116°25E **235** E5
Sebuku, Teluk *Malaysia* 4°0N 118°10E **235** B5
Sečanj *Serbia* 45°25N 20°47E **182** E5

Secaucus *U.S.A.* 40°47N 74°3W **132** B1
Secchia → *Italy* 44°5N 11°0E **198** C8
Sechelt *Canada* 49°25N 123°42W **296** D4
Sechura *Peru* 5°35N 80°50W **330** B1
Sechura, Desierto de *Peru* 6°0S 80°30W **330** B1
Seclin *France* 50°33N 3°2E **173** B10
Second World War Memorial
  Washington, D.C., U.S.A. 46°37N 0°26W **172** F6
Secondigny *France* 46°37N 0°26W **172** F6
Sečovce *Slovak Rep.* 48°42N 21°40E **181** C14
Secretary I. *N.Z.* 45°15S 166°56E **285** F1
Secunderabad *India* 17°28N 78°30E **244** F4
Sécure → *Bolivia* 15°10S 64°52W **331** D5
Security *U.S.A.* 38°45N 104°45W **304** G11
Sedalia *U.S.A.* 38°42N 93°14W **310** F3
Sedam *India* 17°11N 77°17E **244** E3
Sedan *S. Austral.,
  Australia* 34°34S 139°19E **282** C3
Sedan *Ardennes, France* 49°43N 4°57E **173** C11
Sedan *Kans., U.S.A.* 37°8N 96°11W **308** G5
Sedano *Spain* 42°43N 3°49W **194** C7
Sedaw *Burma* 22°19N 96°19E **241** D6
Sedbergh *U.K.* 54°20N 2°31W **168** C5
Seddinsee *Germany* 52°23N 13°41E **115** B5
Seddon *N.Z.* 41°40S 174°7E **285** D5
Seddonville *N.Z.* 41°33S 172°1E **285** B7
Sedé Boqér *Israel* 30°52N 34°47E **251** H5
Sedeh *Fárs, Iran* 30°45N 52°11E **247** D7
Sedeh *Khorāsān, Iran* 33°20N 59°14E **247** C8
Séderon *France* 44°12N 5°32E **175** D9
Séderot *Israel* 31°32N 34°37E **251** D3
Sédhiou *Senegal* 12°44N 15°30W **262** C1
Sedico *Italy* 46°8N 12°6E **198** B9
Sedlčany *Czech Rep.* 49°40N 14°25E **180** B7
Sedley *Canada* 50°10N 104°0W **297** C8
Sedom *Israel* 31°5N 35°20E **251** G6
Sedona *U.S.A.* 34°52N 111°46W **305** J8
Sedova, Pik *Russia* 73°29N 54°58E **214** B6
Sedrata *Algeria* 36°7N 7°31E **261** A6
Sedro-Woolley *U.S.A.* 48°30N 122°14W **306** B4
Šeduva *Lithuania* 55°45N 23°45E **184** C10
Sędziszów *Poland* 50°35N 20°4E **185** H7
Sędziszów Małopolski
  Poland 50°5N 21°45E **185** H8
Seebad Ahlbeck
  Germany 53°56N 14°10E **178** B10
Seeberg *Germany* 52°33N 13°41E **115** A5
Seeburg = Jeziorany
  Poland 53°58N 20°46E **184** E7
Seefeld *Germany* 52°37N 13°40E **115** B5
Seefeld in Tirol *Austria* 47°19N 11°13E **180** D4
Seegefeld *Germany* 52°33N 13°5E **115** A1
Seehausen *Germany* 52°54N 11°45E **178** C7
Seeheim *Namibia* 26°50S 17°45E **270** C2
Seeheim-Jugenheim
  Germany 49°46N 8°40E **179** F4
Seehof *Germany* 52°24N 13°17E **115** B2
Seeis *Namibia* 22°29S 17°39E **270** B2
Seekoei → *S. Africa* 30°18S 25°1E **270** D4
Seeley's Bay *Canada* 44°29N 76°14W **313** B8
Seelow *Germany* 52°32N 14°23E **178** C10
Sées *France* 48°38N 0°10E **172** D7
Seesen *Germany* 51°54N 10°10E **178** D6
Seevetal *Germany* 53°26N 10°1E **178** B6
Seewinkel = Neusiedler See-
  Seewinkel △ *Austria* 47°50N 16°45E **181** D9
Şefaatli *Turkey* 39°30N 34°45E **212** C6
Seferihisar *Turkey* 38°10N 26°50E **205** D8
Séféto *Mali* 14°8N 9°49W **262** C3
Séfophe *Botswana* 22°11S 27°58E **271** B4
Sefrou *Morocco* 33°52N 4°52W **260** B4
Sefrou □ *Morocco* 33°49N 4°49W **260** B4
Sefton *N.Z.* 43°15S 172°41E **285** D7
Sefuri-San *Japan* 33°28N 130°18E **222** D2
Sefwi Bekwai *Ghana* 6°10N 2°25W **262** D4
Seg-ozero *Russia* 63°20N 33°46E **186** B5
Segag *Ethiopia* 7°39N 42°50E **267** C5
Segamat *Malaysia* 2°30N 102°50E **237** L4
Segarcea *Romania* 10°55N 3°42E **263** D4
Ségbana *Benin* 8°0N 11°0W **262** D2
Segbwema *S. Leone* 59°16N 17°50E **188** E3
Segeltorp *Sweden* 37°56N 12°50E **200** E5
Segesta *Italy* 1°24S 130°58E **231** E8
Seget *Indonesia* 31°55N 111°53W **305** L8
Segewold = Sigulda
  Latvia 57°10N 24°55E **186** B8
Segezha *Russia* 63°44N 34°19E **186** B5
Seggueur, O. → *Algeria* 32°14N 1°48E **261** B5
Seghe *Solomon Is.* 8°35S 157°54E **287** M9
Segonzac *France* 39°50N 0°30W **196** F4
Segorbe *Spain* 13°30N 6°16W **262** C3
Ségou *Mali* 13°30N 6°16W **262** C3
Ségou □ *Mali* 13°30N 6°16W **262** C3
Segovia = Coco →
  Cent. Amer. 15°0N 83°8W **320** D3
Segovia *Colombia* 7°7N 74°42W **328** B3
Segovia *Spain* 40°57N 4°10W **194** E6
Segovia □ *Spain* 40°55N 4°10W **194** E6
Segrate *Italy* 45°29N 9°17E **129** B2
Segré *France* 47°40N 0°52W **172** E6
Segre → *Spain* 41°40N 0°43E **196** D5
Seguam I. *U.S.A.* 52°19N 172°30W **303** K4
Seguam Pass *U.S.A.* 52°0N 172°30W **303** K4
Séguédine *Niger* 20°9N 12°55E **259** D2
Séguéla *Ivory C.* 7°55N 6°40W **262** D3
Séguélon *Ivory C.* 9°13N 7°7W **262** D3
Séguénéga *Burkina Faso* 13°25N 1°58W **263** C4
Seguin *U.S.A.* 29°34N 97°58W **314** G6
Segundo → *Argentina* 30°53S 62°44W **334** C3
Segundo *Spain* 38°3N 0°44W **197** G4
Segura, Sierra de *Spain* 38°5N 2°45W **197** G2
Seguro *Italy* 45°28N 9°3E **129** B1
Seh Konj, Küh-e *Iran* 30°6N 57°30E **247** D8
Seh Qal'eh *Iran* 33°40N 58°24E **247** C8
Sehithwa *Botswana* 20°30S 22°30E **270** B3
Sehlabathebe △ *Lesotho* 29°53S 29°7E **271** C4
Sehore *India* 23°10N 77°5E **242** H7
Sehulea *Papua N. G.* 9°58S 151°10E **286** E6
Sehwan *Pakistan* 26°28N 67°53E **242** F2
Şeica Mare *Romania* 46°1N 24°7E **183** D9
Seikan Tunnel *Japan* 41°20N 140°10E **220** D10
Seikpyu *Burma* 20°54N 94°48E **241** E5
Seil *U.K.* 56°18N 5°38W **167** E3
Seiland *Norway* 70°25N 23°15E **160** A20
Seilhac *France* 45°21N 1°41E **174** D5
Seiling *U.S.A.* 36°9N 98°56W **314** C5
Seille → *Moselle, France* 49°7N 6°11E **173** C13
Seille → *Saône-et-Loire,
  France* 46°31N 4°57E **173** F11
Sein, Î. de *France* 48°2N 4°52W **172** D2
Seinäjoki *Finland* 62°40N 22°51E **160** E20
Seine → *France* 49°26N 0°26E **172** C7
Seine, B. de la *France* 49°40N 0°40W **172** C6
Seine-et-Marne □ *France* 48°45N 3°0E **173** D10
Seine-Inférieure =
  Seine-Maritime □ *France* 49°40N 1°0E **172** C7
Seine-Maritime □ *France* 49°40N 1°0E **172** C7
Seine-St-Denis □ *France* 48°58N 2°24E **173** D9
Seini *Romania* 47°44N 23°21E **183** C8
Seirijai *Lithuania* 54°14N 23°49E **184** D10
Seis de Septiembre = Moron
  Argentina 34°39S 58°37W **334** C4
Seistan = Sīstān *Asia* 30°50N 61°0E **247** D9
Seistan, Daryācheh-ye = Sīstān,
  Daryācheh-ye *Iran* 31°0N 61°0E **247** D9

Seitler = Nyzhnohirskyy
  Ukraine 45°27N 34°38E **189** K8
Seixal *Portugal* 38°38N 9°5W **126** B2
Sejerø *Denmark* 55°54N 11°9E **163** J5
Sejerø Bugt *Denmark* 55°53N 11°15E **163** J5
Sejny *Poland* 54°6N 23°21E **184** D10
Seka *Ethiopia* 8°10N 36°52E **257** F4
Sekayu *Indonesia* 2°51S 103°51E **234** C2
Seke *Tanzania* 3°20S 33°31E **268** C3
Seke-Banza
  Dem. Rep. of the Congo 5°20S 13°16E **265** D2
Sekenke *Tanzania* 4°18S 34°11E **268** C3
Sekhira *Tunisia* 34°20N 10°5E **258** B2
Seki *Japan* 35°29N 136°55E **223** B8
Sekigahara *Japan* 35°48N 29°3E **205** E11
Sekiu *Japan* 35°22N 136°28E **223** B8
Sekondi-Takoradi *Ghana* 4°58N 1°45W **262** E4
Sekota *Ethiopia* 12°40N 39°2E **257** E4
Sekseũil *Kazakhstan* 47°5N 61°9E **216** C6
Seksna *Russia* 59°13N 38°30E **188** C10
Sekudai *Malaysia* 1°32N 103°39E **237** d
Sekuma *Botswana* 24°36S 23°50E **270** B3
Selah *U.S.A.* 46°39N 120°32W **304** C3
Selama *Malaysia* 5°12N 100°42E **237** K3
Selangor □ *Malaysia* 3°10N 101°30E **234** B2
Selárgius *Italy* 39°16N 9°10E **200** C2
Selaru *Indonesia* 8°9S 131°0E **231** F8
Selatan, Selat *Malaysia* 5°15N 100°20E **237** c
Selawik *U.S.A.* 66°36N 160°0W **303** C8
Selawik L. *U.S.A.* 66°30N 160°45W **303** C7
Selawik Nat. Wildlife Refuge △
  U.S.A. 66°35N 159°10W **303** C8
Selb *Germany* 50°10N 12°7E **179** E8
Selbjørnen *Norway* 63°15N 10°50E **164** A7
Selby *Gauteng, S. Africa* 26°12S 28°2E **123** B2
Selby *N. Yorks., U.K.* 53°47N 1°5W **168** D6
Selby *S. Dak., U.S.A.* 45°31N 100°2W **308** C3
Selca *Croatia* 43°20N 16°50E **199** E13
Selçuk *Turkey* 37°56N 27°22E **205** D8
Selden *U.S.A.* 39°33N 100°34W **308** F3
Sele → *Italy* 59°26N 151°43W **303** G10
Sele → *Italy* 40°29N 14°56E **201** B7
Selebi-Phikwe *Botswana* 21°58S 27°48E **274** B4
Selemdzha → *Russia* 51°42N 128°53E **215** D13
Selendi *Manisa, Turkey* 38°43N 28°50E **205** C10
Selendi *Manisa, Turkey* 38°46N 27°53E **205** C9
Selenga = Selenge Mörön →
  Asia 52°16N 106°16E **218** A5
Selenge
  Dem. Rep. of the Congo 1°58S 18°11E **264** C3
Selenge Mörön → *Asia* 52°16N 106°16E **218** A5
Selenicë *Albania* 40°33N 19°39E **202** F3
Selenter See *Germany* 54°18N 10°26E **178** A6
Sélestat *France* 48°16N 7°26E **173** D14
Seletan, Tanjung
  Indonesia 4°10S 114°40E **235** C4
Seletar, Pulau *Singapore* 1°26N 103°51E **138** A3
Seletar Hills *Singapore* 1°23N 103°52E **138** A3
Seletar Res. *Singapore* 1°24N 103°48E **138** A2
Selevac *Serbia* 44°28N 20°52E **202** B4
Selfoss *Iceland* 63°56N 21°0W **155** D6
Selhurst *U.K.* 51°23N 0°5W **125** B3
Sélibabi *Mauritania* 15°10N 12°15W **262** B2
Seliger, Ozero *Russia* 57°15N 33°0E **188** D7
Seligman *U.S.A.* 35°20N 112°53W **305** J7
Şelim *Turkey* 40°30N 42°46E **213** B10
Selima *Sudan* 21°22N 29°19E **256** C2
Selimiye *Turkey* 37°24N 27°40E **205** D9
Selinda Spillway →
  Botswana 18°35S 23°10E **270** A3
Sélingué, L. de *Mali* 11°37N 8°14W **262** C3
Selinsgrove *U.S.A.* 40°48N 76°52W **312** F8
Selizharovo *Russia* 56°51N 33°27E **188** D7
Selje *Norway* 62°3N 5°22E **164** B2
Seljord *Norway* 59°30N 8°40E **164** E5
Selkirk *Man., Canada* 50°10N 96°55W **297** C9
Selkirk *Ont., Canada* 42°49N 79°56W **312** D5
Selkirk *Borders, U.K.* 55°33N 2°50W **167** F6
Selkirk I. = Horse I.
  Canada 53°20N 99°6W **297** C9
Selkirk Mts. *Canada* 51°15N 117°40W **294** D8
Sellafield *U.K.* 54°25N 3°29W **168** C4
Sellama *Sudan* 12°51N 29°46E **257** E2
Sellia *Greece* 35°12N 24°23E **207** E5
Sellières *France* 46°50N 5°32E **173** F12
Sells *U.S.A.* 31°55N 111°53W **305** L8
Sellye *Hungary* 45°52N 17°51E **182** E2
Selma *Ala., U.S.A.* 32°25N 87°1W **315** C11
Selma *Calif., U.S.A.* 36°34N 119°37W **306** J7
Selma *N.C., U.S.A.* 35°32N 78°17W **315** D15
Selmer *U.S.A.* 35°10N 88°36W **315** D10
Selong *Indonesia* 8°39S 116°32E **235** D5
Selongey *France* 47°36N 5°11E **173** E12
Selouane *Morocco* 35°7N 2°57W **261** A4
Selous □ *Tanzania* 8°37S 37°42E **269** D4
Sélune → *France* 48°38N 1°22W **172** D5
Selva = La Selva del Camp
  Spain 41°13N 1°8E **196** D6
Selva *Argentina* 29°50S 62°0W **334** B3
Selva *Italy* 38°46N 2°54E **206** B3
Selva Lancandona = Montes
  Azules △ *Mexico* 16°21N 91°3W **319** D6
Selvagens, Ilhas *Madeira* 30°5N 16°0W **209** e
Selvas *Brazil* 6°30S 67°0W **330** B4
Selwyn L. *Canada* 60°0N 104°30W **297** B8
Selwyn Mts. *Canada* 63°0N 130°0W **294** C6
Selwyn Ra. *Papua New Guinea* 15°35S 168°12E **287** F6
Selwyn Ra. *Australia* 21°10S 140°0E **280** C2
Selyatyn *Ukraine* 47°52N 25°7E **183** C9
Sem *Norway* 59°14N 10°17E **164** E7
Sem Kolodezey = Lenino
  Ukraine 45°17N 35°46E **189** K8
Semadrek = Samothraki
  Greece 40°28N 25°28E **203** F8
Seman → *Albania* 40°47N 19°30E **202** F3
Semarang *Indonesia* 7°0S 110°26E **235** D4
Sematan *Malaysia* 1°48N 109°46E **235** B3
Sembabule *Uganda* 0°4S 31°25E **268** C3
Sembawang *Singapore* 1°39N 103°49E **138** A2
Sembé *Congo* 1°39N 14°36E **264** B2
Semdinli *Indonesia* 3°32N 117°58E **230** B5
Şemdinli *Turkey* 37°18N 44°35E **213** D11
Sémé *Senegal* 12°43N 30°31W **257** D3
Semeih *Sudan* 12°43N 30°53E **257** E3
Semenanjung Blambangan
  Indonesia 8°42S 114°29E **231** K17
Semendua
  Dem. Rep. of the Congo 3°10S 18°16E **264** C3
Semenov *Russia* 56°43N 44°30E **190** B7
Semenovka = Chernihiv,
  Ukraine 52°6N 31°40E **189** D7
Semenovka *Chernihiv,
  Ukraine* 52°6N 31°40E **189** D7
Semenovka *Kremenchuk,
  Ukraine* 49°37N 33°10E **189** H7
Semeru *Indonesia* 8°4S 112°55E **235** D4
Semey *Kazakhstan* 50°30N 80°10E **216** D9
Semichi Is. *U.S.A.* 52°42N 174°0E **303** K1
Semikarakorskiy *Russia* 47°30N 40°48E **191** G5
Semiluki *Russia* 51°41N 39°2E **189** G10
Seminoe Res. *U.S.A.* 42°9N 106°55W **304** E10

Seminole *Fla., U.S.A.* 27°50N 82°47W **317** H7
Seminole *Okla., U.S.A.* 35°14N 96°41W **314** D6
Seminole *Tex., U.S.A.* 32°43N 102°39W **314** E3
Seminole, L. *U.S.A.* 30°43N 84°52W **316** E5
Seminole Draw →
  U.S.A. 32°27N 102°20W **314** E3
Semipalatinsk = Semey
  Kazakhstan 50°30N 80°10E **217** B10
Semirara I. *Phil.* 12°4N 121°23E **232** E3
Semirara Is. *Phil.* 12°1N 121°20E **233** F3
Semisopochnoi I. *U.S.A.* 51°55N 179°36E **303** L2
Semitau *Indonesia* 0°29N 111°57E **235** B4
Semliki → *Uganda* 0°30N 30°4E **268** B3
Semlin = Zemun *Serbia* 44°51N 20°25E **202** B4
Semmelweis Museum
  Budapest, Hungary **117** c2
Semmering P. *Austria* 47°41N 15°45E **180** D8
Semnān *Iran* 35°40N 53°23E **247** C7
Semnān □ *Iran* 36°0N 54°0E **247** C7
Sempang Mengayau, Tanjong
  Malaysia 7°0N 116°40E **235** A5
Sempona *Malaysia* 4°30N 118°33E **235** B5
Semuda *Indonesia* 2°51S 112°58E **235** C4
Semur-en-Auxois *France* 47°30N 4°20E **173** E11
Semyonovka = Arsenev
  Russia 44°10N 133°15E **220** B6
Semyonovskoye = Bereznik
  Russia 62°51N 42°40E **186** B7
Sen → *Cambodia* 12°32N 104°28E **236** F5
Sena *Bolivia* 11°32S 67°11W **330** C4
Senā *Iran* 15°30N 129°0E **289** c
Sena *Mozam.* 17°25S 35°0E **269** F4
Sena → *Bolivia* 11°31S 67°11W **330** C4
Sena Madureira *Brazil* 9°5S 68°45W **330** B4
Senachwine L. *U.S.A.* 41°0N 89°18W **310** E7
Senador José Porfírio
  Brazil 2°35S 51°55W **329** D7
Senador Pompeu *Brazil* 5°40S 39°20W **332** C4
Senaga *Italy* 45°34N 9°7E **129** A2
Senaja *Malaysia* 6°45N 117°3E **235** A5
Senaki *Georgia* 42°15N 42°7E **191** J6
Senanga *Zambia* 16°7S 23°16E **265** F4
Senatobia *U.S.A.* 34°37N 89°58W **315** D10
Sencelles *Spain* 39°39N 2°54E **206** B9
Sendafa *Ethiopia* 9°11N 39°3E **257** F4
Sendai *Kagoshima, Japan* 31°50N 130°20E **222** F2
Sendai *Miyagi, Japan* 38°15N 140°53E **220** E10
Sendai-Wan *Japan* 38°15N 141°0E **220** E10
Senden *Bayern, Germany* 48°19N 10°4E **179** G6
Senden *Nordrhein-Westfalen,
  Germany* 51°52N 7°22E **178** D3
Sendhwa *India* 21°41N 75°6E **242** J6
Sendling *Germany* 48°7N 11°31E **131** B2
Sendlinger Tor Platz *Munich, Germany* **131** c1
Sendurjana *India* 21°32N 78°17E **244** D4
Sene → *Ghana* 7°30N 0°33W **263** D4
Senec *Slovak Rep.* 48°12N 17°23E **181** C10
Seneca *Ill., U.S.A.* 41°19N 88°37W **310** E7
Seneca *S.C., U.S.A.* 34°41N 82°57W **315** D13
Seneca Falls *U.S.A.* 42°55N 76°48W **313** D8
Seneca L. *U.S.A.* 42°40N 76°54W **312** D8
Senecaville L. *U.S.A.* 39°55N 81°25W **312** G3
Senegal ■ *W. Afr.* 14°30N 14°30W **262** C2
Senegal → *W. Afr.* 15°48N 16°32W **262** B1
Senegambia = Senegambia & Niger = Mali ■
  Africa 12°45N 12°0W **254** E2
Senegambia & Niger = Mali ■
  Africa 17°0N 3°0W **262** B4
Senekal *S. Africa* 28°20S 27°36E **271** C4
Senftenberg *Germany* 51°32N 14°0E **178** D10
Senga Hill *Zambia* 9°19S 31°11E **269** D3
Senge Khambab = Indus →
  Pakistan 24°20N 67°47E **242** G2
Sengerema *Tanzania* 2°42S 32°35E **268** C3
Sengiley *Russia* 53°58N 48°46E **190** D9
Sengua → *Zimbabwe* 17°7S 28°5E **269** F2
Senguerr → *Argentina* 45°35S 68°50W **336** C3
Senhor-do-Bonfim *Brazil* 10°30S 40°10W **332** D4
Senica *Slovak Rep.* 48°41N 17°25E **181** C10
Senigállia *Italy* 43°43N 13°13E **199** E10
Seniku *Burma* 25°32N 97°48E **241** C6
Senio → *Italy* 44°35N 12°15E **199** D9
Senirkent *Turkey* 38°7N 30°41E **205** C12
Senise *Italy* 40°9N 16°17E **201** B9
Senj *Croatia* 45°0N 14°58E **199** D11
Senja *Norway* 69°25N 17°30E **160** B17
Senju *Japan* 35°44N 139°48E **140** A3
Senkaku-Shotō
  E. China Sea 25°45N 123°30E **221** M1
Senkuang *Indonesia* 1°11N 104°2E **237** d
Senlis *France* 49°13N 2°35E **173** C9
Senmonorom *Cambodia* 12°27N 107°12E **236** F6
Sennâr □ *Sudan* 13°30N 33°35E **257** E3
Sennâr *Sudan* 13°0N 34°0E **257** E3
Senneterre *Canada* 48°25N 77°15W **298** C4
Senno *Belarus* 54°45N 29°43E **188** E6
Sênnori *Italy* 40°47N 8°35E **200** B1
Seno *Laos* 16°35N 104°50E **236** D5
Senoia *U.S.A.* 33°18N 84°33W **316** B5
Senonches *France* 48°34N 1°2E **172** D8
Senorbì *Italy* 39°32N 9°8E **200** C2
Senožeče *Slovenia* 45°43N 14°3E **199** C11
Senqu = Orange →
  S. Africa 28°41S 16°28E **270** C2
Senriyama *Japan* 34°47N 135°30E **133** A2
Sens *France* 48°11N 3°15E **173** D10
Senta *Serbia* 45°55N 20°3E **182** E5
Sentani *Indonesia* 2°36S 140°37E **231** E10
Sentery = Lubao
  Dem. Rep. of the Congo 5°17S 25°42E **265** D5
Sentinel *U.S.A.* 32°52N 113°13W **305** K7
Sentinel Peak *St.-Maarten* 18°2N 63°4W **322** a
Sentolo *Indonesia* 7°55S 110°13E **235** D4
Sentosa *Singapore* 1°16N 103°50E **138** B2
Sentry Hill *St.-Maarten* 23°17S 29°7E **271** B4
Senwabarana *S. Africa* 23°18S 29°31W **263** D4
Senya Beraku *Ghana* 5°28N 0°31W **263** D4
Seo de Urgel = La Seu d'Urgell
  Spain 42°22N 1°23E **196** C6
Seobinggo *S. Korea* 37°31N 126°58E **137** C1
Seocho *S. Korea* 37°28N 127°0E **137** C1
Seodaemun *S. Korea* 37°34N 126°55E **137** B1
Seogwipo *S. Korea* 33°13N 126°34E **224** a
Seohara *India* 29°15N 78°33E **242** E8
Seokkwan *S. Korea* 37°35N 127°1E **137** B2
Seonath → *India* 21°44N 82°28E **243** J9
Seondha *India* 26°9N 78°48E **243** G8
Seongdong *S. Korea* 37°33N 127°2E **137** C2
Seongnam *S. Korea* 37°26N 127°2E **137** C2
Seoni *India* 22°5N 79°30E **243** H8
Seoni Malwa *India* 22°27N 77°28E **242** H7
Seonsan *S. Korea* 36°14N 128°17E **224** G8
Seoul = Sŏul *S. Korea* 37°31N 126°58E **137** B2
Seoul Nat. Univ.
  S. Korea 37°28N 126°57E **137** C1
Seoul Tower *S. Korea* 37°33N 126°59E **137** B1
Separation Pt. *N.Z.* 40°47S 172°56E **285** A7
Sepatini → *Brazil* 7°36S 65°24W **330** B4

Sepi *Solomon Is.* 8°31S 159°52E **287** M10
Sepīdān *Iran* 30°20N 52°5E **247** D7
Sepik → *Papua N. G.* 3°49S 144°30E **286** B3
Sep'o *N. Korea* 38°57N 127°25E **224** C3
Sepolia *Greece* 38°1N 23°43E **112** A2
Sepólno Krajeńskie
  Poland 53°26N 17°30E **184** E4
Sepone *Laos* 16°45N 106°13E **236** D6
Sepopol *Poland* 54°16N 21°2E **184** D8
Sept-Îles *Canada* 50°13N 66°22W **299** B6
Septemvri *Bulgaria* 42°13N 24°6E **203** D8
Sepúlveda *Spain* 41°18N 3°45W **194** D7
Sepulveda Dam Rec. Area □
  U.S.A. 34°10N 118°28W **126** A2
Sequeros *Spain* 40°31N 6°2W **194** E4
Sertã *Portugal* 39°48N 8°6W **194** F2
Sertânia *Brazil* 8°5S 37°20W **332** C4
Sertãozinho *Brazil* 21°8S 48°5W **335** A6
Sêrtar *China* 32°20N 100°41E **248** B6
Serua *Indonesia* 6°18S 130°1E **231** F8
Serui *Indonesia* 1°53S 136°10E **231** E9
Serule *Botswana* 21°57S 27°20E **270** B4
Servia *Greece* 40°11N 22°2E **202** F6
Serzedelo *Portugal* 41°24N 8°14W **194** D2
Ses Salines *Spain* 39°21N 3°3E **206** B4
Sesayap → *Indonesia* 3°36N 117°15E **235** B5
Sese Is. *Uganda* 0°20S 32°20E **268** C3
Seseko-shima *Japan* 26°39N 127°52E **288** a
Sesepe *Indonesia* 1°30S 127°59E **231** E7
Sesfontein *Namibia* 19°7S 13°39E **270** A1
Sesheke *Zambia* 17°29S 24°13E **270** A3
Sésia → *Italy* 45°5N 8°37E **198** C5
Sésimbra *Portugal* 38°28N 9°6W **195** G1
Seskar *Russia* 60°5N 29°58E **188** B6
Sesori *India* 22°9N 78°31E **255** F4
Sessa Aurunca *Italy* 41°14N 13°56E **200** A6
Sesser *U.S.A.* 38°5N 89°1W **310** F7
S'Estanyol *Spain* 39°22N 2°54E **206** B3
Sestao *Spain* 43°18N 3°9W **192** A7
Sesto Calende *Italy* 45°44N 8°37E **129** A2
Sesto San Giovanni *Italy* 45°31N 9°13E **129** B2
Sesto Ulteriano *Italy* 45°24N 9°16E **129** B2
Sestri Levante *Italy* 44°16N 9°24E **198** D6
Sestriere *Italy* 44°57N 6°53E **198** D3
Sestroretsk *Russia* 60°5N 29°58E **188** B6
Sestrunj *Croatia* 44°10N 15°0E **199** D11
Sestu *Italy* 39°18N 9°6E **200** C2
Setagaya *Japan* 33°9N 130°28E **222** D2
Setaka *Japan* 42°26N 139°51E **220** C9
Setana *Japan* 43°25N 3°42E **174** E7
Sète *France* 43°25N 3°42E **174** E7
Sete Cidades △ *Brazil* 4°0S 41°37W **332** B3
Sete Lagoas *Brazil* 19°27S 44°16W **333** E3
Seter *Norway* 59°52N 10°19E **133** A3
Setesdalsheiene = Suldalsheiene
  Norway 59°28N 7°10E **164** E3
Setia Budi *Indonesia* 6°12S 106°49E **122** B1
Sétif *Algeria* 36°9N 5°26E **261** A6
Sétif □ *Algeria* 36°9N 5°26E **261** A6
Setit → *Sudan* 14°20N 35°50E **257** E4
Seto *Japan* 35°14N 137°6E **223** B8
Setonaikai *Japan* 34°20N 133°30E **222** C5
Setonaikai △ *Japan* 34°15N 133°15E **222** C5
Setsan *Burma* 16°3N 95°23E **241** G5
Settat *Morocco* 33°0N 7°40W **260** B3
Settat □ *Morocco* 33°5N 7°25W **260** B3
Setté-Cama *Gabon* 2°32S 9°45E **264** C1
Settebagni *Italy* 42°0N 12°31E **136** A2
Settecamini *Italy* 41°57N 12°38E **136** B4
Séttimo Milanese *Italy* 45°28N 9°3E **129** B1
Séttimo Torinese *Italy* 45°9N 7°46E **198** C4
Setting L. *Canada* 55°0N 98°38W **297** C9
Settle *U.K.* 54°5N 2°16W **168** C5
Settlement *Wake I.* 19°18N 166°38E **302** b
Settlement, The
  Br. Virgin Is. 18°43N 64°22W **321** b
Settlers *S. Africa* 25°2S 28°30E **271** C4
Setúbal *Portugal* 38°30N 8°58W **195** G2
Setúbal □ *Portugal* 38°25N 8°35W **195** G2
Setúbal, B. de *Portugal* 38°25N 8°35W **195** G2
Setuny → *Russia* 55°43N 37°21E **129** B2
Seugne → *France* 45°42N 0°32W **174** D3
Seul, Lac *Canada* 50°20N 92°30W **298** C1
Seulimeum *Indonesia* 5°27N 95°15E **234** A4
Seurre *France* 47°0N 5°7E **173** F12
Seutula *Finland* 60°20N 24°52E **121** A2
Sevan *Armenia* 40°33N 44°56E **191** K7
Sevan, Ozero = Sevana Lich
  Armenia 40°30N 45°20E **191** K7
Sevana Lich *Armenia* 40°30N 45°20E **191** K7
Sevastopol *Ukraine* 44°35N 33°30E **189** K7
Seven Corners *U.S.A.* 38°53N 77°9W **143** B3
Seven Islands = Sept-Îles
  Canada 50°13N 66°22W **299** B6
Seven Kings *U.K.* 51°33N 0°5E **125** A4
Seven Sisters *U.K.* 54°56N 120°10W **296** C3
Seventeenth Street Canal
  U.S.A. 30°3N 90°7W **131** A2
Sévérac-le-Château *France* 44°20N 3°5E **174** D7
Severn → *Ont., Canada* 56°2N 87°36W **298** A2
Severn → *U.K.* 51°35N 2°40W **169** F5
Severnaya Zemlya *Russia* 79°0N 100°0E **215** B11
Severnyye Uvaly *Russia* 60°0N 50°0E **186** C8
Severo-Kurilsk *Russia* 50°40N 156°8E **215** D16
Severo-Yeniseyskiy
  Russia 60°22N 93°1E **215** C10
Severo-Zapadnyy □ *Russia* 65°0N 40°0E **214** C4
Severobaykalsk *Russia* 55°39N 109°19E **215** D11
Severočeský □ *Czech Rep.* 50°30N 14°0E **180** A7
Severodonetsk = Syeverodonetsk
  Ukraine 48°58N 38°35E **189** H10
Severodvinsk *Russia* 64°27N 39°58E **186** B6
Severomoravský □
  Czech Rep. 49°38N 17°40E **181** B10
Severomorsk *Russia* 69°5N 33°27E **186** B25
Severouralsk *Russia* 60°9N 59°57E **186** B10
Seversk *Russia* 56°36N 84°49E **214** D9
Séveso → *Italy* 45°35N 9°9E **129** A1
Sevier → *U.S.A.* 39°4N 113°6W **304** G7
Sevier Desert *U.S.A.* 39°40N 112°45W **304** G7
Sevier L. *U.S.A.* 38°54N 113°9W **304** G7
Sevilla *Colombia* 4°16N 75°57W **328** C3
Sevilla *Spain* 37°23N 5°58W **195** H5
Sevilla = Seville □ *Spain* 37°25N 5°30W **195** H5
Seville *Spain* 37°23N 5°58W **195** H5
Seville *Fla., U.S.A.* 29°19N 81°30W **317** G8
Seville *Ohio, U.S.A.* 41°1N 81°45W **312** F3
Sevlievo *Bulgaria* 43°2N 25°6E **203** C9
Sevnica *Slovenia* 46°2N 15°19E **180** E8
Sevre-Nantaise → *France* 48°5N 6°31E **134** A4
Sèvre-Niortaise → *France* 46°28N 0°50W **174** B3
Sevsk *Russia* 52°10N 34°30E **189** F8
Sewa → *S. Leone* 7°20N 12°10W **262** D2
Sewani *India* 28°58N 75°39E **242** E6
Seward *Alaska, U.S.A.* 60°7N 149°27W **303** F10
Seward *Nebr., U.S.A.* 40°55N 97°6W **308** E5
Seward Peninsula *U.S.A.* 65°0N 164°0W **303** C7
Sewell *Chile* 34°10S 70°23W **334** C1
Sewer *Indonesia* 5°53S 134°40E **231** F8
Sewickley *U.S.A.* 40°32N 80°12W **312** F4
Sewri *India* 18°59N 72°50E **138** E2

Sexsmith Canada 55°21N 118°47W 296 B5
Seychelles ■ Ind. Oc. 5°0S 56°0E 272 c
Seyðisfjörður Iceland 65°16N 13°57W 155 B13
Seydişehir Turkey 37°25N 31°51E 212 D4
Seydvān Turkey 38°34N 45°2E 213 C11
Seyhan → Turkey 36°43N 34°53E 250 B5
Seyhan Barajı Turkey 37°2N 35°18E 212 D6
Seyitgazi Turkey 39°27N 30°43E 205 B12
Seyitömer Turkey 39°34N 29°52E 205 B11
Seym → Ukraine 51°27N 32°34E 189 G7
Seymchan Russia 62°54N 152°30E 211 C16
Seymour Vic., Australia 37°2S 145°10E 283 D6
Seymour Eastern Cape,
  S. Africa 32°33S 26°46E 271 D4
Seymour Conn., U.S.A. 41°24N 73°4W 313 E11
Seymour Ind., U.S.A. 38°58N 85°53W 311 F11
Seymour Tex., U.S.A. 33°35N 99°16W 314 E5
Seyne France 44°21N 6°22E 175 D10
Seyssel France 45°57N 5°50E 175 C9
Sežana Slovenia 45°43N 13°41E 199 C10
Sézanne France 48°40N 3°40E 173 D10
Sezze Italy 41°30N 13°3E 200 A6
Sfântu Gheorghe Covasna,
  Romania 45°52N 25°48E 183 E10
Sfântu Gheorghe Tulcea,
  Romania 44°53N 29°36E 183 F14
Sfântu Gheorghe, Brațul →
  Romania 44°51N 29°36E 183 F14
Sfax Tunisia 34°49N 10°48E 258 B2
Sfax □ Tunisia 34°40N 10°20E 261 B7
Sforzesco, Castello Italy 45°28N 9°10E 129 B2
Sha Kok Mei China 22°23N 114°16E 122 A2
Sha Tau Kok China 22°33N 114°13E 219 F11
Sha Tin China 22°23N 114°12E 122 A2
Sha Xi → China 26°35N 118°0E 229 D12
Sha Xian China 26°23N 117°45E 229 D11
Shaanxi □ China 35°0N 109°0E 226 G5
Sha'ar Binyamin
  West Bank 31°52N 35°16E 123 A2
Shaba = Katanga □
  Dem. Rep. of the Congo 8°0S 25°0E 268 D2
Shaba △ Kenya 0°38N 37°48E 268 B4
Shabeellaha Dhexe □
  Somali Rep. 3°0N 46°0E 267 D6
Shabeellaha Hoose □
  Somali Rep. 1°0N 44°0E 267 D5
Shabeelle → Somali Rep. 2°0N 44°0E 267 D5
Shabestar Iran 38°11N 45°41E 213 C11
Shabla Bulgaria 43°31N 28°32E 183 D12
Shabogamo L. Canada 53°15N 66°30W 299 B6
Shabrámant Egypt 29°56N 31°11E 117 B2
Shabunda
  Dem. Rep. of the Congo 2°40S 27°16E 268 C2
Shabwah Yemen 15°22N 47°1E 248 D4
Shache China 38°20N 77°10E 217 E9
Shackleton Fracture Zone
  S. Ocean 60°0S 60°0W 151 B18
Shackleton Ice Shelf
  Antarctica 66°0S 100°0E 151 C8
Shackleton Inlet
  Antarctica 83°0S 160°0E 151 E11
Shādegān Iran 30°40N 48°38E 247 D6
Shadi Jiangxi, China 26°7N 114°47E 229 D10
Shadi Jammu & Kashmir,
  India 33°24N 77°14E 243 C7
Shadrinsk Russia 56°5N 63°32E 214 D7
Shady Dale U.S.A. 33°24N 83°36W 316 B6
Shady Grove U.S.A. 30°17N 83°38W 316 E6
Shadyside U.S.A. 39°58N 80°45W 312 G4
Shafer, L. U.S.A. 40°46N 86°46W 311 D10
Shaffa Nigeria 10°30N 12°6E 263 G7
Shafter U.S.A. 35°30N 119°16W 307 K7
Shaftesbury U.K. 51°0N 2°11W 169 F5
Shaftsbury U.S.A. 43°0N 73°11W 313 D11
Shag Pt. N.Z. 45°29S 170°52E 285 F5
Shag Rocks Atl. Oc. 53°0S 41°0W 152 M7
Shagamu Nigeria 6°51N 3°39E 263 D5
Shageluk U.S.A. 62°41N 159°34W 303 B8
Shagram Pakistan 36°24N 72°20E 243 A5
Shah Alam Malaysia 3°5N 101°32E 237 L3
Shah Alizai Pakistan 29°25N 66°33E 242 E2
Shah Bunder Pakistan 24°13N 67°56E 242 G2
Shāh Jūy Afghan. 32°31N 67°25E 240 B2
Shah Mosque Iran 35°41N 51°25E 141 A2
Shahabad Karnataka,
  India 17°10N 76°54E 244 F3
Shahabad Punjab, India 30°10N 76°55E 242 D7
Shahabad Raj., India 25°15N 77°11E 242 G7
Shahabad Ut. P., India 27°36N 79°56E 243 F8
Shahada India 21°33N 74°30E 244 D2
Shahadpur Pakistan 25°55N 68°35E 242 G3
Shahapur India 15°50N 74°34E 245 G2
Shahbā' Syria 32°52N 36°38E 250 F7
Shahbazpur I. Bangla. 22°30N 90°45E 241 H17
Shahdād Iran 30°30N 57°40E 247 D8
Shahdād, Namakzār-e
  Iran 30°20N 58°20E 247 D8
Shahdādkot Pakistan 27°50N 67°55E 242 F2
Shahdara India 28°40N 77°18E 120 A2
Shahdol India 23°19N 81°26E 243 H9
Shahe Guangdong, China 37°0N 114°32E 226 F8
Shahe Hebei, China 37°0N 114°32E 226 F8
Shahganj India 26°3N 82°44E 243 F10
Shahgarh India 27°15N 69°50E 242 F3
Shahbāt Libya 32°48N 21°54E 258 B4
Shāhdān Afghan. 36°2N 67°40E 240 A2
Shahjahanpur India 27°54N 79°57E 243 F8
Shahpur = Salmās Iran 38°11N 44°47E 213 C11
Shahpur Karnataka, India 16°40N 76°48E 244 F3
Shahpur Mad. P., India 22°12N 77°58E 242 H7
Shahpur Baluchistan,
  Pakistan 28°46N 68°27E 242 E3
Shahpur Punjab, Pakistan 32°17N 72°26E 242 C5
Shahpur Chakar Pakistan 26°9N 68°38E 242 F3
Shahpura Mad. P., India 23°10N 80°45E 243 H9
Shahpura Raj., India 25°38N 74°56E 242 G6
Shahr-e Bābak Iran 30°7N 55°9E 247 D7
Shahr-e Kord Iran 32°15N 50°55E 247 C6
Shahr-e Rey Iran 35°35N 51°25E 141 B2
Shahrak-e Golshahr Iran 35°37N 51°18E 141 B1
Shahrak-e Qods Iran 35°41N 51°12E 141 B1
Shāhrakht Iran 33°38N 60°16E 247 C9
Shahrezā = Qomsheh
  Iran 32°0N 51°55E 247 C6
Shahrig Pakistan 30°15N 67°40E 242 D2
Shahrisabz Uzbekistan 39°3N 66°55E 217 F7
Shāhrud = Emāmrūd Iran 36°30N 55°0E 247 B7
Shahukou China 40°20N 112°18E 226 D7
Shaikh Aomar Iran 32°44N 48°28E 113 A2
Shaikhabad Afghan. 34°2N 68°45E 242 B3
Shajapur India 23°27N 76°21E 242 H6
Shajing China 22°44N 113°48E 219 F10
Shajuwan Taiwan 23°31N 121°22E 225 C3
Shakawe Botswana 18°28N 21°49E 270 A3
Shakenge
  Dem. Rep. of the Congo 6°14S 18°41E 265 D3
Shaker Heights U.S.A. 41°28N 81°32W 312 E3
Shakhtersk Russia 49°10N 142°8E 215 E15
Shakhtinsk Kazakhstan 49°40N 72°45E 217 E8
Shakhty Russia 47°40N 40°16E 191 G5
Shakhunya Russia 57°40N 46°46E 190 B8
Shaki Nigeria 8°41N 3°21E 263 D5
Shākir Egypt 27°30N 33°59E 256 B3

Shaksam Valley Asia 36°0N 76°20E 243 A7
Shaktoolik U.S.A. 64°20N 161°9W 303 D7
Shakurbasti India 28°41N 77°6E 120 A1
Shala, L. Ethiopia 7°30N 38°30E 257 F4
Shali Russia 43°9N 45°55E 191 J7
Shaliapin Lake Canada 44°36N 81°5W 312 B3
Shalkar Köli Kazakhstan 50°35N 51°47E 190 E10
Shalkiya India 28°16N 81°28E 124 B2
Shallow Lake Canada 44°36N 81°5W 312 B3
Shalqar Kazakhstan 47°48N 59°39E 216 C5
Shalqar Köli Kazakhstan 50°33N 51°40E 216 B4
Shalskiy Russia 61°48N 35°58E 188 B8
Shalu Taiwan 24°14N 120°34E 225 B2
Shaluli Shan China 30°40N 99°55E 228 B2
Shām Iran 26°39N 57°21E 247 E8
Shām, Bādiyat ash Asia 32°0N 40°0E 246 C3
Shām, J. ash Oman 23°10N 57°5E 249 B7
Sham Shui Po China 22°19N 114°9E 122 B1
Shamal Bahr el Ghazal □
  Sudan 8°0N 27°30E 257 F2
Shamâl Dârfûr □ Sudan 15°0N 25°0E 257 F2
Shamâl Kordofân □ Sudan 15°0N 30°0E 257 E3
Shamâl Sînî □ Egypt 30°30N 33°30E 251 H4
Shamanur India 28°44N 77°8E 120 A1
Shamattawa Canada 55°51N 92°5W 298 A1
Shamattawa → Canada 55°1N 85°23W 298 A2
Shambe Sudan 7°8N 30°46E 257 F3
Shambu △ Canada 6°57N 30°50E 257 F3
Shambu Ethiopia 9°32N 37°3E 257 F4
Shamgong Dzong
  Bhutan 27°13N 90°35E 241 B3
Shamian China 23°6N 113°13E 121 B2
Shamil Iran 27°30N 56°55E 247 E8
Shamkhor = Şämkir
  Azerbaijan 40°50N 46°0E 191 K8
Shamkhūh Iran 35°47N 57°50E 247 C8
Shamli India 29°32N 77°18E 242 E7
Shammar, Jabal Si. Arabia 27°40N 41°0E 246 E4
Shamo = Gobi Asia 44°0N 110°0E 226 C6
Shamo, L. Ethiopia 5°45N 37°30E 257 F4
Shamokin U.S.A. 40°47N 76°34W 313 F8
Shamrock Ont., Canada 45°23N 76°50W 313 A8
Shamrock Tex., U.S.A. 35°13N 100°15W 314 D4
Shamva Zimbabwe 17°20S 31°32E 269 F3
Shan □ Burma 21°30N 98°30E 241 E7
Shan Mei China 22°24N 114°10E 122 A2
Shan Shan China 42°52N 90°10E 217 D12
Shan Xian China 34°50N 116°5E 226 G9
Shana = Kurilsk
  Russia 45°14N 147°53E 215 E15
Shanan → Ethiopia 8°0N 40°20E 257 F5
Shanchengzhen China 42°20N 125°20E 224 A2
Shāndak Iran 28°28N 60°27E 247 D9
Shandon U.S.A. 35°39N 120°23W 306 K6
Shandong □ China 36°0N 118°0E 227 G10
Shandong Bandao China 37°0N 121°0E 227 F11
Shandur Pass Pakistan 36°4N 72°31E 243 A5
Shang Xian = Shangzhou
  China 33°50N 109°58E 226 H5
Shangalowe
  Dem. Rep. of the Congo 10°50S 26°30E 269 E2
Shangani Zimbabwe 19°41S 29°20E 271 A4
Shangani → Zimbabwe 18°41S 27°10E 269 F2
Shangbancheng China 40°50N 118°1E 227 D10
Shangcheng China 31°47N 115°26E 229 B10
Shangchuan Dao China 21°40N 112°50E 229 G9
Shangdu China 41°30N 113°30E 226 D7
Shanggao China 28°17N 114°55E 229 C10
Shanghai China 31°15N 121°26E 138 B2
Shanghai Hongqiao × (SHA)
  China 31°12N 121°20E 138 B1
Shanghai Pudong × (PVG)
  China 31°9N 121°47E 138 B2
Shanghai Shi □ China 31°0N 121°30E 229 B13
Shanghang China 25°2N 116°23E 229 E11
Shanghe China 37°20N 117°10E 227 F9
Shangjao = Shangrao
  China 28°25N 117°59E 229 C11
Shanglin China 23°27N 108°33E 228 F7
Shangnan China 33°32N 110°50E 226 H6
Shangqiu China 34°26N 115°36E 226 G8
Shangrao China 28°25N 117°59E 229 C11
Shangri-La = Zhongdian
  China 27°48N 99°42E 228 D2
Shangshui China 33°42N 114°35E 226 H8
Shangsi China 22°8N 107°58E 228 F6
Shangyou China 25°48N 114°32E 229 E10
Shangyu China 30°0N 120°35E 229 B13
Shangzhi China 45°22N 127°56E 227 B14
Shangzhou China 33°50N 109°58E 226 H5
Shanhetun China 44°33N 127°15E 227 B14
Shanhu Tan Taiwan 23°12N 120°23E 225 C2
Shanhua Taiwan 23°8N 120°17E 225 C2
Shani Nigeria 10°14N 12°2E 263 G7
Shānider Iraq 36°48N 44°14E 213 D11
Shankill Ireland 53°14N 6°7W 170 B3
Shanklin U.K. 50°38N 1°11W 169 G6
Shanlin Taiwan 22°57N 120°38E 225 C2
Shannon N.Z. 40°33S 175°25E 284 G4
Shannon → Ireland 52°35N 9°30W 166 D2
Shannon × (SNN) Ireland 52°42N 8°57W 166 D3
Shannon, Mouth of the
  Ireland 52°30N 9°55W 166 D2
Shannon Ø Greenland 75°10N 18°30W 154 B9
Shannonbridge Ireland 53°17N 8°3W 166 C3
Shannontown U.S.A. 33°53N 80°21W 316 B9
Shanshang Taiwan 23°6N 120°17E 225 C2
Shansi = Shanxi □ China 37°0N 112°0E 226 F7
Shantar, Ostrov Bolshoy
  Russia 55°9N 137°40E 215 D14
Shantipur India 23°17N 88°25E 243 H13
Shantou China 23°18N 116°40E 229 F11
Shantung = Shandong □
  China 36°0N 118°0E 227 G10
Shanwei China 22°48N 115°22E 229 F10
Shanxi □ China 37°0N 112°0E 226 F7
Shanyang China 33°31N 109°55E 226 H5
Shanyin China 39°25N 112°56E 226 E7
Shaodong China 27°15N 111°43E 229 D8
Shaoguan China 24°48N 113°35E 229 E9
Shaohing = Shaoxing
  China 30°0N 120°35E 229 B13
Shaoshan China 27°55N 112°32E 229 D9
Shaowu China 27°22N 117°28E 229 D11
Shaoxing China 30°0N 120°35E 229 B13
Shaoyang Hunan, China 27°14N 111°25E 229 D8
Shaoyang Hunan, China 26°59N 111°50E 229 D8
Shap U.K. 54°32N 2°40W 168 C5
Shapinsay U.K. 59°3N 2°51W 167 B6
Shaqlāwah Iraq 36°23N 44°27E 213 D11
Shaqq el Gi'eifer → Sudan 15°16N 26°0E 257 E2
Shaqrā' Si. Arabia 25°15N 45°16E 246 E5
Shaqrā' Yemen 13°22N 45°44E 248 D4
Shar Australia 30°30N 21°30E 261 C10
Sharafa Sudan 11°59N 27°5E 257 F2
Sharafkhāneh Iran 38°11N 45°23E 213 C11
Sharashova Belarus 52°34N 24°12E 185 F11
Sharavati → India 14°20N 74°25E 245 G2
Sharbaqty Kazakhstan 52°33N 78°7E 217 D9
Sharbatāt, Ra's ash
  Oman 17°56N 56°21E 249 C7
Sharbot Lake Canada 44°46N 76°41W 313 B8
Shardara, Step Kazakhstan 42°0N 68°0E 217 E7
Sharhorod Ukraine 48°45N 28°3E 185 D13
Shari Japan 43°55N 144°40E 220 C12
Shariff Kabunsuan □ Phil. 7°5N 124°5E 233 H5

Sharjah = Ash Shāriqah
  U.A.E. 25°23N 55°26E 247 E7
Shark B. Australia 25°30S 113°32E 279 E1
Shark Bay △ Australia 25°30S 113°30E 279 E1
Sharm el Sheikh Egypt 27°53N 34°18E 251 L5
Sharon Ont., Canada 44°6N 79°26W 312 B5
Sharon Mass., U.S.A. 42°7N 71°11W 313 D13
Sharon Pa., U.S.A. 41°14N 80°31W 312 E4
Sharon Wis., U.S.A. 42°30N 88°44W 310 D9
Sharon Springs Kans.,
  U.S.A. 38°54N 101°45W 308 F3
Sharon Springs N.Y.,
  U.S.A. 42°48N 74°37W 313 D10
Sharonville U.S.A. 39°16N 84°25W 311 E12
Sharp I. China 22°21N 114°17E 122 A2
Sharp Pk. Phil. 5°58N 125°31E 233 J5
Sharp Pt. Australia 10°58S 142°43E 286 F2
Sharpe L. Canada 54°24N 93°40W 298 B1
Sharpes U.S.A. 28°26N 80°46W 317 G8
Sharpsville U.S.A. 41°15N 80°29W 312 E4
Sharq al Istiwa'iya □ Sudan 5°0N 33°0E 257 G3
Sharqi, Al Jabal ash
  Lebanon 33°40N 36°10E 250 E7
Sharqīya □ Egypt 30°48N 31°48E 251 H2
Sharya Russia 58°22N 45°20E 190 A7
Shasha Ethiopia 6°29N 35°59E 257 F4
Shashemene Ethiopia 7°13N 38°33E 257 F4
Shashi Botswana 21°15S 27°27E 271 B4
Shashi Hubei, China 30°25N 112°14E 229 B9
Shashi → Africa 21°14S 29°20E 269 G2
Shasta, Mt. U.S.A. 41°25N 122°12W 304 F2
Shasta L. U.S.A. 40°43N 122°25W 304 F2
Shastrinagar India 28°40N 77°10E 120 A2
Shatawi Sudan 14°39N 32°57E 257 E3
Shāţi', Wādi ash → Libya 27°30N 15°0E 258 C3
Shatilki = Svyetlahorsk
  Belarus 52°38N 29°46E 177 B15
Shatsk Russia 54°5N 41°45E 190 C5
Shatsk Ukraine 51°29N 23°55E 185 G10
Shatsky Rise Pac. Oc. 33°0N 157°0E 288 D7
Shatskyi → Ukraine 51°30N 24°0E 185 G10
Shatt al Arab Asia 29°57N 48°34E 247 D6
Shatura Russia 55°33N 39°21E 188 E10
Shaturtof = Shatura
  Russia 55°33N 39°21E 188 E10
Shau Kei Wan China 22°16N 114°13E 122 B2
Shaumyani = Shulaveri
  Georgia 41°22N 44°45E 191 K7
Shaunavon Canada 49°35N 108°25W 297 D7
Shaver L. U.S.A. 37°9N 119°18W 306 H7
Shavli = Šiauliai
  Lithuania 55°56N 23°15E 184 C10
Shaw → Australia 20°21S 119°17E 278 D2
Shaw I. Australia 20°30S 149°2E 280 b
Shawanaga Canada 45°31N 80°17W 312 A4
Shawangunk Mts.
  U.S.A. 41°35N 74°30W 313 E10
Shawano U.S.A. 44°47N 88°36W 308 C9
Shawinigan Canada 46°35N 72°50W 293 B5
Shawmari, J. ash Jordan 30°35N 36°35E 251 H7
Shawnee Ga., U.S.A. 32°29N 81°25W 316 D8
Shawnee Kans., U.S.A. 39°1N 94°43W 310 E2
Shawnee Okla., U.S.A. 35°20N 96°55W 314 D6
Shawocun China 39°53N 116°13E 114 B1
Shay Gap Australia 20°30S 120°10E 278 D3
Shayang China 30°42N 112°29E 229 B9
Shaybārā Si. Arabia 25°26N 36°47E 246 E3
Shayib el Banat, Gebel
  Egypt 26°59N 33°29E 256 B3
Shaykh, J. ash Lebanon 33°25N 35°50E 250 E6
Shaykh Miskīn Syria 32°49N 36°9E 250 F7
Shaykh Sa'd Iraq 32°34N 46°17E 213 F12
Shaykh 'Uthmān Yemen 12°52N 44°59E 248 D4
Shaytanovo Zavod = Pervouralsk
  Russia 56°59N 59°59E 186 C10
Shayuan China 23°5N 113°15E 121 B2
Shāzand Iran 33°56N 49°24E 247 C6
Shazud Tajikistan 37°45N 72°24E 217 E8
Shcheglovo = Kemerovo
  Russia 55°20N 86°5E 214 D9
Shchekino Russia 54°1N 37°34E 188 E9
Shcherbakov = Rybinsk
  Russia 58°5N 38°50E 188 C10
Shchigry Russia 51°55N 36°58E 189 G9
Shchors Ukraine 51°48N 31°56E 189 G6
Shchuchīnsk Kazakhstan 52°56N 70°12E 217 B8
She Xian Anhui, China 29°50N 118°25E 229 C12
She Xian Hebei, China 36°30N 113°40E 226 F7
Shea Guyana 2°48N 59°4W 329 C6
Shebekino Russia 50°28N 36°54E 189 G10
Shebela → Ethiopia 7°32N 45°43E 267 D4
Shebele = Shabeelle →
  Somali Rep. 2°0N 44°0E 267 D5
Shebelē Ethiopia 8°8N 42°40E 257 F5
Sheberghān Afghan. 36°40N 65°45E 240 A2
Sheboygan U.S.A. 43°46N 87°45W 308 D10
Shebshi Mts. Nigeria 8°30N 12°0E 263 D7
Shedd Aquarium Chicago, U.S.A. 119 a3
Shediac Canada 46°14N 64°32W 299 C7
Sheelin, L. Ireland 53°48N 7°20W 170 A4
Sheen, L. Ireland 51°48N 9°31W 170 B2
Sheenjek → U.S.A. 66°45N 144°33W 303 C11
Sheep Haven Ireland 55°11N 7°52W 166 A4
Sheep Range U.S.A. 36°35N 115°15W 307 J11
Sheepshead Bay U.S.A. 40°35N 73°55W 122 C2
Sheerness U.K. 51°26N 0°47E 168 F8
Sheet Harbour Canada 44°56N 62°31W 299 D7
Sheffield N.Z. 43°23S 172°1E 285 D7
Sheffield S. Yorks., U.K. 53°23N 1°28W 168 D6
Sheffield Ala., U.S.A. 34°46N 87°41W 315 D11
Sheffield Ill., U.S.A. 41°21N 89°44W 310 D9
Sheffield Iowa, U.S.A. 42°54N 93°13W 310 B8
Sheffield Pa., U.S.A. 41°42N 79°3W 312 E5
Shegaon India 20°48N 76°47E 244 D3
Shehojele Ethiopia 10°40N 35°9E 257 E4
Shehong China 30°54N 105°18E 228 B5
Shehong = Argentina 49°35S 69°34W 336 C3
Shei-Pa △ Taiwan 24°36N 121°22E 225 B3
Shei Shan Taiwan 24°36N 121°22E 225 B3
Sheikh, W. el → Egypt 28°41N 33°41E 251 K4
Sheikh Zayed, Qana es
  Egypt 30°15N 30°56E 256 A4
Sheikh Zayed Canal = Sheikh
  Zayed, Qana es Egypt 30°15N 30°56E 256 A4
Shekhupura Pakistan 31°42N 73°58E 242 D5
Sheki = Şäki Azerbaijan 41°10N 47°5E 191 K8
Shekki = Zhongshan
  China 22°26N 113°20E 219 G10
Shekou China 22°29N 113°55E 219 G10
Shelbina U.S.A. 39°48N 92°2W 310 F7
Shelburne N.S., Canada 43°47N 65°20W 299 E6
Shelburne Ont., Canada 44°4N 80°15W 312 B4
Shelburne Vt., U.S.A. 44°23N 73°14W 313 B11
Shelburne B. Australia 11°55S 142°50E 286 F2
Shelburne Falls U.S.A. 42°36N 72°45W 313 D12

Shelbyville Ind., U.S.A. 39°31N 85°47W 311 E11
Shelbyville Ky., U.S.A. 38°13N 85°14W 311 F11
Shelbyville Mo., U.S.A. 39°48N 92°2W 310 F7
Shelbyville Tenn., U.S.A. 35°29N 86°28W 315 D11
Shelbyville, L. U.S.A. 39°26N 88°46W 311 E8
Sheldon Ill., U.S.A. 40°46N 87°34W 311 D9
Sheldon Iowa, U.S.A. 43°11N 95°51W 308 D6
Sheldon Mo., U.S.A. 37°40N 94°18W 310 G2
Sheldon S.C., U.S.A. 32°36N 80°48W 316 C9
Sheldon Point U.S.A. 62°32N 164°52W 303 C6
Sheldrake Canada 50°20N 64°51W 299 B7
Shelek Kazakhstan 43°33N 78°17E 217 D9
Shelengo, Khawr →
  Sudan 10°33N 28°40E 257 F2
Shelikhova, Zaliv
  Russia 59°30N 157°0E 215 D16
Shelikof Strait U.S.A. 57°30N 155°0W 303 D9
Shell Beach = Huntington Beach
  U.S.A. 33°40N 118°5W 307 M8
Shell Lakes Australia 29°20S 127°30E 279 E4
Shellbrook Canada 53°13N 106°24W 297 C7
Shellharbour Australia 34°31S 150°51E 283 C9
Shellman U.S.A. 31°46N 84°37W 316 D5
Shellsburg U.S.A. 42°6N 91°52W 310 B5
Shelon → Russia 58°13N 30°47E 188 C6
Shelter Bay = Port-Cartier
  Canada 50°2N 66°50W 299 B6
Shelter I. Hong Kong,
  China 22°19N 114°17E 122 B2
Shelter I. N.Y., U.S.A. 41°4N 72°20W 313 E12
Shelton Conn., U.S.A. 41°19N 73°5W 313 E11
Shelton Wash., U.S.A. 47°13N 123°6W 306 C3
Shemakha = Şamaxı
  Azerbaijan 40°38N 48°37E 191 K9
Shemonaïkha
  Kazakhstan 50°37N 81°54E 217 B10
Shēmri Albania 42°7N 20°13E 202 D4
Shemsi Sudan 19°2N 29°57E 256 D2
Shen Xian China 36°15N 115°40E 226 F8
Shenandoah Iowa,
  U.S.A. 40°46N 95°22W 308 E6
Shenandoah Pa., U.S.A. 40°49N 76°12W 313 F8
Shenandoah Va., U.S.A. 38°29N 78°37W 309 F14
Shenandoah → U.S.A. 39°19N 77°44W 309 F15
Shenandoah △ U.S.A. 38°35N 78°22W 309 F14
Shenchi China 39°8N 112°10E 226 E7
Shencottah India 8°59N 77°18E 245 K3
Shendam Nigeria 8°49N 9°30E 263 D6
Shendi Sudan 16°46N 33°22E 257 D3
Shendurni India 20°39N 75°36E 244 D2
Shenge S. Leone 7°54N 12°55W 262 D2
Shengfang China 39°3N 116°42E 226 E9
Shëngjergj Albania 41°17N 20°10E 202 E4
Shëngjin Albania 41°50N 19°35E 202 E3
Shengzhou China 29°35N 120°50E 229 C13
Shenjingzi China 44°40N 124°30E 227 B13
Shenkang Taiwan 24°9N 120°39E 226 E6
Shenmu China 38°50N 110°29E 226 E6
Shennongjia China 31°43N 110°44E 229 B8
Shenqiu China 33°25N 115°5E 226 H8
Shensi = Shaanxi □ China 35°0N 109°0E 226 G5
Shenyang China 41°48N 123°27E 224 B1
Sheo India 26°11N 71°15E 242 F4
Sheopur Kalan India 25°40N 76°40E 242 G7
Shepetivka Ukraine 50°10N 27°10E 177 C14
Shepherd Is. Vanuatu 16°55S 168°36E 287 F6
Shepherds Bush U.K. 51°30N 0°13W 125 A2
Shepherdsville U.S.A. 37°59N 85°43W 311 G11
Shepparton Australia 36°23S 145°26E 283 D6
Shepperton U.K. 51°23N 0°26W 125 B1
Sheppey, I. of U.K. 51°25N 0°48E 169 F8
Shepton Mallet U.K. 51°11N 2°33W 169 F5
Sheqi China 33°12N 112°57E 226 H7
Sher Khan Qala Afghan. 31°30N 66°13E 240 C2
Sher Qila Pakistan 36°7N 74°2E 243 A6
Sherab Uzbekistan 37°40N 66°17E 217 F7
Sherborne U.K. 50°57N 2°31W 169 G5
Sherbro I. S. Leone 7°45N 12°55W 262 D2
Sherbrooke N.S., Canada 45°8N 61°59W 299 C7
Sherbrooke Qué.,
  Canada 45°28N 71°57W 313 A13
Sherburne U.S.A. 42°41N 75°30W 313 D9
Sherburne Reef
  Papua N. G. 3°20S 148°0E 286 B5
Sherda Chad 20°7N 16°46E 259 D3
Shereik Sudan 18°44N 33°47E 257 D3
Shergarh India 27°7N 92°16E 241 B4
Shergarh India 26°20N 72°18E 242 F5
Sherghati India 24°34N 84°47E 243 G11
Sheridan Ark., U.S.A. 34°19N 92°24W 314 D8
Sheridan Ill., U.S.A. 41°32N 88°41W 311 C8
Sheridan Ind., U.S.A. 40°8N 86°13W 311 D10
Sheridan Wyo., U.S.A. 44°48N 106°58W 304 D10
Sheringham U.K. 52°56N 1°13E 168 E9
Sherkin I. Ireland 51°28N 9°26W 166 E2
Sherkot India 29°22N 78°35E 243 E8
Sherlovaya Gora
  Russia 50°34N 116°15E 215 D12
Sherman N.Y., U.S.A. 42°9N 79°35W 312 D5
Sherman Tex., U.S.A. 33°38N 96°36W 314 E6
Sherman Oaks U.S.A. 34°9N 118°28W 119 C2
Sherpur Bangla. 25°0N 90°0E 241 C3
Sherridon Canada 55°8N 101°5W 297 B8
Sherrills St. Kitts & Nevis 17°10N 62°32W 322 d
Shertallai India 9°42N 76°20E 245 K3
Sherwood N. Dak., U.S.A. 48°57N 101°38W 308 A3
Sherwood, L. U.S.A. 41°17N 94°3W 310 C3
Sherwood Forest U.K. 53°6N 1°7W 168 D6
Sherwood Park Canada 53°31N 113°19W 296 C6
Sheslay → Canada 58°48N 132°5W 296 B2
Shet Bandar India 18°57N 72°55E 142 B2
Shethanei L. Canada 58°48N 97°50W 297 B9
Shetland □ U.K. 60°30N 1°30W 167 A7
Shetland Is. U.K. 60°30N 1°30W 167 A7
Shetou Taiwan 23°53N 120°35E 225 C2
Shetpe Kazakhstan 44°10N 52°5E 216 D6
Shetrunji → India 21°13N 72°28E 244 D1
Sheung Fa Shan China 22°23N 114°5E 122 A1
Sheung Lau Wan China 22°12N 114°18E 122 B2
Sheung Shui China 22°31N 114°7E 219 F11
Sheung Wan China 22°17N 114°9E 122 B1
Sheva India 18°56N 72°55E 130 B2
Sheva Nhava India 18°56N 72°55E 130 B2
Shevaroy Hills India 11°58N 78°12E 245 H4
Shevchenko = Aktau
  Kazakhstan 43°50N 51°10E 216 E6
Shevchenkovo Ukraine 49°26N 32°46E 189 E14
Shevgaon India 19°21N 75°14E 244 E2
Shevihieh Iran 35°46N 40°8E 213 E12
Shewa Ethiopia 9°33N 38°51E 257 F4
Shey-Phoksundo △
  Nepal 29°17N 82°45E 243 E10
Sheyenne U.S.A. 47°50N 99°7W 308 B4
Sheyenne → U.S.A. 47°2N 96°50W 308 B5
Shiashkotan, Ostrov
  Russia 48°49N 154°6E 215 E16
Shibām Yemen 15°59N 48°36E 249 D5

Shiquan He = Indus →
  Pakistan 24°20N 67°47E 242 G2
Shīr Khān Afghan. 37°11N 68°36E 240 A3
Shīr Kūh Iran 31°39N 54°3E 247 D7
Shirabad = Sherabad
  Uzbekistan 37°40N 67°1E 217 E7
Shiragami-Misaki
  Japan 41°24N 140°12E 220 D10
Shirahama Japan 33°41N 135°20E 223 D7
Shirakawa Fukushima,
  Japan 37°7N 140°13E 221 F10
Shirakawa Gifu, Japan 36°17N 136°56E 223 A8
Shirane-San Gunma,
  Japan 36°48N 139°22E 223 A9
Shirane-San Yamanashi,
  Japan 35°42N 138°9E 223 B9
Shiraoi Japan 42°33N 141°21E 220 C10
Shiraz Iran 29°42N 52°30E 247 D7
Shirbin Egypt 31°11N 31°32E 256 H7
Shire → Africa 17°42S 35°19E 269 F4
Shiretoko-Misaki
  Japan 44°21N 145°20E 220 B12
Shiriya-Zaki Japan 41°25N 141°30E 220 D10
Shirley U.K. 52°25N 1°54W 167 E6
Shirogane Japan 35°37N 139°44E 140 B3
Shiroishi Japan 38°0N 140°37E 221 F10
Shirol India 16°47N 74°41E 244 F2
Shiroro Res. Nigeria 9°56N 6°54E 263 D6
Shirpur India 21°21N 74°57E 244 D2
Shirshov Ridge Pac. Oc. 58°0N 170°0E 288 B10
Shirvān Iran 37°30N 57°50E 247 B8
Shirwa, L. = Chilwa, L.
  Malawi 15°15S 35°40E 269 F4
Shishaldin Volcano
  U.S.A. 54°45N 163°58W 303 J7
Shishi China 24°44N 118°37E 229 E12
Shishmaref U.S.A. 66°15N 166°4W 303 C6
Shishou China 29°38N 112°22E 229 C9
Shitai China 30°12N 117°25E 229 B11
Shitennoji Temple Japan 34°39N 135°31E 133 B2
Shithāthah Iraq 32°34N 43°28E 213 G10
Shivamogga = Shimoga
  India 13°57N 75°32E 245 G2
Shively U.S.A. 38°12N 85°49W 311 F11
Shivpuri India 25°26N 77°42E 242 G7
Shiwei China 23°6N 113°12E 121 B2
Shixian China 43°5N 129°50E 227 C15
Shixing China 24°46N 114°5E 229 E10
Shiyan Guangdong,
  China 22°42N 113°56E 219 F10
Shiyan Hubei, China 32°35N 110°48E 229 A8
Shiyan Shuiku China 22°42N 113°54E 219 F10
Shiyata Egypt 29°25N 25°7E 256 B2
Shizhu China 29°58N 108°12E 228 C7
Shizuishan China 24°50N 104°0E 228 C5
Shizuoka Japan 34°57N 138°24E 223 B9
Shizuoka □ Japan 35°15N 138°40E 223 B9
Shklov = Shklow
  Belarus 54°16N 30°15E 177 A16
Shklow Belarus 54°16N 30°15E 177 A16
Shkodër Albania 42°4N 19°32E 202 D3
Shkodra = Shkodër
  Albania 42°4N 19°32E 202 D3
Shkumbini → Albania 41°2N 19°31E 202 E3
Shmidta, Ostrov Russia 81°0N 91°0E 215 A10
Shō-Gawa → Japan 36°47N 137°4E 223 A8
Shoal Cr. → U.S.A. 39°44N 93°32E 310 F7
Shoal L. Canada 49°33N 95°1W 297 D9
Shoal Lake Canada 50°30N 100°35W 297 C8
Shoalhaven →
  Australia 34°54S 150°42E 283 C9
Shoals U.S.A. 38°40N 86°47W 311 F10
Shōbara Japan 34°51N 133°1E 222 C5
Shōdo-Shima Japan 34°30N 134°15E 223 B8
Shogunle Nigeria 6°32N 3°22E 142 A2
Sholapur = Solapur India 17°43N 75°56E 244 F2
Sholomu Nigeria 6°32N 3°22E 142 A2
Shōmaro West Bank 32°15N 35°13E 251 F6
Shonian Harb. Palau 7°10N 134°23E 288 c
Shonzhy Kazakhstan 43°32N 79°28E 217 D9
Shooters Hill U.K. 51°28N 0°4E 125 B4
Shoranur India 10°46N 76°19E 245 J3
Shoranur U.K. 10°46N 76°19E 245 J3
Shoreditch London, U.K. 125 a5
Shoreham by Sea U.K. 50°50N 0°16W 169 G7
Shorewood U.S.A. 43°5N 87°53W 311 A9
Shori → Pakistan 28°29N 69°44E 242 E3
Shorkot Road Pakistan 30°50N 72°0E 242 D4
Shorter U.S.A. 32°24N 85°57W 316 C6
Shortland Is. Solomon Is. 7°0S 156°0E 287 L8
Shortlands I. Solomon Is. 7°0S 156°0E 287 L8
Shortt's I. India 20°47N 87°4E 244 D8
Shoshone Calif., U.S.A. 35°58N 116°16W 307 K10
Shoshone Idaho, U.S.A. 42°56N 114°25W 304 E6
Shoshone L. U.S.A. 44°22N 110°43W 304 D8
Shoshone Mts. U.S.A. 39°20N 117°25W 304 G5
Shoshone Botswana 22°56S 26°31E 270 C3
Shoshoni U.S.A. 43°14N 108°7W 304 E9
Shostka Ukraine 51°57N 33°32E 189 G7
Shot Iran 39°12N 44°49E 213 C11
Shotor Khūn Afghan. 34°48N 66°26E 240 B2
Shotover → N.Z. 44°59S 168°41E 285 E3
Shou Xian China 32°58N 116°48E 229 A11
Shouchang China 29°21N 119°12E 229 C12
Shouchia Taiwan 22°14N 120°50E 225 C3
Shoufeng Taiwan 23°52N 121°30E 225 C3
Shougang China 39°58N 116°10E 114 B1
Shouning China 27°27N 119°31E 229 D12
Shouyang China 37°54N 113°8E 226 F7
Show Low U.S.A. 34°15N 110°2W 305 J8
Showa Japan 35°36N 138°29E 223 B9
Showak Sudan 14°23N 35°52E 257 E4
Shpola Ukraine 49°1N 31°30E 185 C16
Shpykiv Ukraine 48°47N 28°34E 183 B13
Shqipëria = Albania ■
  Europe 41°0N 20°0E 202 E4
Shreveport U.S.A. 32°31N 93°45W 314 E8
Shri Mohangarh India 27°17N 71°18E 242 F4
Shrigonda India 18°37N 74°41E 244 E2
Shrinagar India 26°35N 74°43E 242 F6
Shropshire □ U.K. 52°36N 2°45W 169 E5
Shū Kazakhstan 43°36N 73°42E 217 D8
Shū → Kazakhstan 45°0N 67°44E 217 E7
Shu'ab, Ras Yemen 12°35N 53°25E 249 E8
Shuangbai China 24°39N 101°42E 228 E3
Shuangcheng China 45°20N 126°15E 227 B14
Shuangfeng China 27°26N 112°22E 229 D9
Shuanggou China 34°2N 117°30E 227 G9
Shuangjiang China 23°31N 99°46E 228 E2
Shuangliao China 43°29N 123°30E 227 C13
Shuangpai China 25°0N 111°30E 229 E8
Shuangshan China 44°42N 123°10E 227 B13
Shuangshipu = Fengxian
  China 33°56N 106°38E 226 H4
Shuangyang China 43°28N 125°40E 227 C13
Shuangyashan China 46°28N 131°5E 227 B16
Shuguri Falls Tanzania 8°33S 37°22E 268 D4
Shuiji China 27°30N 118°7E 229 D12
Shuiluo China 28°8N 100°30E 228 C3
Shujaabad Pakistan 29°50N 71°18E 242 E4
Shukpa Kunzang India 34°22N 78°22E 243 B8
Shūr → Fārs, Iran 28°30N 55°0E 247 D7

Shubrâ Egypt 30°5N 31°14E 117 A2
Shubrâ el Kheima Egypt 30°4N 31°14E 117 A2
Shubrâ Khit Egypt 31°2N 30°42E 256 H7
Shucheng China 31°28N 116°57E 229 B11
Shugozero Russia 59°54N 34°10E 188 C8
Shuguri Falls Tanzania 8°33S 37°22E 269 D4
Shuḩayr Yemen 14°41N 49°23E 249 E5
Shuiding = Huocheng China 44°0N 80°48E 217 D10
Shuiji China 27°13N 118°20E 229 D12
Shuikou China 23°10N 113°10E 121 A2
Shuili Taiwan 23°49N 120°51E 225 C2
Shuilien Taiwan 23°47N 121°34E 225 C3
Shuishang Taiwan 23°25N 120°23E 225 C2
Shuitiliao Taiwan 22°23N 120°35E 225 D2
Shuiye China 36°7N 114°8E 226 F8
Shujalpur India 23°18N 76°46E 242 H7
Shukpa Kunzang India 34°22N 78°22E 243 B8
Shulan China 44°28N 127°0E 227 B14
Shulaveri Georgia 41°22N 44°45E 191 K7
Shule China 39°25N 76°3E 217 E9
Shule He → China 40°20N 92°50E 218 B4
Shullsburg U.S.A. 42°35N 90°13W 310 B6
Shumagin Is. U.S.A. 55°7N 160°30W 303 J7
Shumanay Uzbekistan 42°38N 58°55E 216 D5
Shumen Bulgaria 43°18N 26°55E 203 C10
Shumerlya Russia 55°30N 46°25E 190 C8
Shumikha Russia 55°10N 63°15E 214 D7
Shûna, W. el → Egypt 29°38N 32°6E 251 J3
Shunayn, Sabkhat Libya 30°10N 21°0E 258 B4
Shunchang China 26°54N 117°48E 229 D11
Shunde China 22°42N 113°14E 229 F9
Shungay Kazakhstan 48°30N 46°45E 191 F8
Shungnak U.S.A. 66°52N 157°9W 303 C8
Shuo Xian = Shuozhou China 39°20N 112°33E 226 E7
Shuozhou China 39°20N 112°33E 226 E7
Shūr → Fārs, Iran 28°30N 55°0E 247 D7
Shūr → Kermān, Iran 30°52N 57°37E 247 D8
Shūr → Yazd, Iran 31°45N 55°15E 247 D7
Shūr Āb Iran 34°23N 51°11E 247 C6
Shūr Gaz Iran 29°10N 59°20E 247 D8
Shūrāb Iran 33°43N 56°29E 247 C8
Shuri Japan 26°13N 127°43E 288 a
Shūrjestān Iran 31°24N 52°25E 247 D7
Shurkhua Burma 22°15N 93°38E 241 D4
Shurugwi Zimbabwe 19°40S 30°0E 269 F3
Shūsf Iran 31°50N 60°5E 247 D9
Shūsh Iran 32°11N 48°15E 213 F13
Shushenskoye Russia 53°19N 91°56E 217 B12
Shūshtar Iran 32°0N 48°50E 247 D6
Shuswap L. Canada 50°55N 119°3W 296 C5
Shute Harbour △ Australia 20°17S 148°47E 280 b
Shuya Russia 56°50N 41°28E 190 B5
Shuyak I. U.S.A. 58°31N 152°30W 303 G9
Shuyang China 34°10N 118°42E 227 G10
Shuzenji Japan 34°58N 138°56E 223 C10
Shūzū Iran 29°52N 54°30E 247 D7
Shwangliao = Liaoyuan China 42°58N 125°2E 227 C13
Shwebo Burma 22°30N 95°45E 241 D5
Shwegu Burma 24°15N 96°26E 241 C6
Shwegun Burma 17°9N 97°39E 241 G6
Shwegyin Burma 17°55N 96°53E 241 G6
Shweli → Burma 23°45N 96°45E 241 D6
Shwenyaung Burma 20°46N 96°57E 241 E6
Shyamnagar India 13°21N 92°57E 245 H11
Shyghanaq Kazakhstan 45°6N 73°59E 217 C8
Shyghys Qazaqstan □ Kazakhstan 48°30N 82°0E 217 D10
Shymkent Kazakhstan 42°18N 69°36E 217 D7
Shyok India 34°13N 78°12E 243 B8
Shyok → Pakistan 35°13N 75°53E 243 B6
Shyroke Odesa, Ukraine 45°59N 30°5E 183 E15
Shyroke Ternopil, Ukraine 48°13N 23°6E 182 B8
Si Kiang = Xi Jiang → China 22°5N 113°20E 229 F9
Si Lanna △ Thailand 19°17N 99°12E 236 C2
Si Nakarin Res. Thailand 14°35N 99°0E 236 E2
Si-ngan = Xi'an China 34°15N 109°0E 226 G5
Si Prachan Thailand 14°37N 100°9E 236 E3
Si Racha Thailand 13°10N 100°48E 236 F3
Si Xian China 33°30N 117°50E 227 H9
Siachen Glacier Asia 35°20N 77°30E 243 B7
Sīah Chashmeh Iran 39°3N 44°25E 213 C11
Siahaf → Pakistan 29°3N 68°57E 242 E3
Siahan Range Pakistan 27°30N 64°40E 240 D2
Siak → Indonesia 1°13N 102°9E 234 B2
Siaksriindrapura Indonesia 0°51N 102°0E 234 B2
Sialkot Pakistan 32°32N 74°30E 242 C6
Sialsuk India 23°24N 92°45E 241 D4
Sialum Papua N. G. 6°5S 147°36E 286 D4
Siam = Thailand ■ Asia 16°0N 102°0E 236 E4
Sian = Xi'an China 34°15N 109°0E 226 G5
Sian Ka'an △ Mexico 19°35N 87°40W 319 D7
Siangtan = Xiangtan China 27°51N 112°54E 229 D9
Sianów Poland 54°13N 16°18E 184 D3
Siantan Indonesia 3°10N 106°15E 234 B3
Siàpo → Venezuela 2°7N 66°28W 328 C4
Sīāreh Iran 28°5N 60°14E 247 D9
Siargao I. Phil. 9°52N 126°3E 233 G6
Siari Pakistan 34°55N 76°40E 243 B7
Siasi Phil. 5°34N 120°50E 233 J3
Siasi I. Phil. 5°33N 120°51E 233 J3
Siassi Papua N. G. 5°40S 147°51E 286 C4
Siatista Greece 40°15N 21°33E 202 F5
Siaton Phil. 9°4N 123°2E 233 G4
Siau Indonesia 2°50N 125°25E 231 D7
Šiauliai Lithuania 55°56N 23°15E 184 C10
Šiauliai □ Lithuania 55°56N 23°19E 184 C10
Siavonga Zambia 16°33S 28°42E 271 A4
Siazan = Siyäzän Azerbaijan 41°3N 49°10E 191 K9
Sibâi, Gebel el Egypt 25°45N 34°10E 256 E2
Sibang Gabon 0°25N 9°31E 264 B1
Sibang Bali, Indonesia 8°34S 115°13E 231 K18
Sibay Russia 52°42N 58°39E 186 D10
Sibay I. Phil. 11°51N 121°29E 233 F3
Sibayi, L. S. Africa 27°20S 32°45E 271 C5
Sibdu Sudan 10°57N 26°17E 257 E2
Šibenik Croatia 43°48N 15°54E 199 E12
Siberia = Sibirskiy □ Russia 58°0N 90°0E 215 D10
Siberia Russia 60°0N 100°0E 150 D13
Siberië Neth. Ant. 12°14N 69°3W 322 g
Siberut Indonesia 0°42S 98°35E 234 C1
Siberut, Selat Indonesia 1°17S 98°45E 234 C1
Siberut △ Indonesia 1°36S 99°2E 234 C1
Sibi Pakistan 29°30N 67°54E 242 E2
Sibil = Oksibil Indonesia 4°59S 140°35E 231 E10
Sibiloi △ Kenya 4°0N 36°20E 268 B4
Sibirskiy □ Russia 58°0N 90°0E 215 D10
Sibirtsevo Russia 44°12N 132°26E 220 B5
Sibiti Congo 3°38S 13°19E 264 C2
Sibiu Romania 45°45N 24°9E 183 E9
Sibiu □ Romania 45°50N 24°15E 183 E9
Sibium Mts. Papua N. G. 9°19S 148°25E 286 E5
Sibley Ill., U.S.A. 40°35N 88°23W 311 D8
Sibley Iowa, U.S.A. 43°24N 95°45W 308 D6
Sibolga Indonesia 1°42N 98°45E 234 B1
Siborongborong Indonesia 2°13N 98°59E 237 L2
Sibsagar India 27°0N 94°36E 241 B5
Sibu Malaysia 2°18N 111°49E 235 B4
Sibuco Phil. 7°20N 122°10E 233 H4
Sibuguey B. Phil. 7°50N 122°45E 233 H4
Sibut C.A.R. 5°46N 19°10E 264 A3
Sibutu Phil. 4°45N 119°30E 235 B5
Sibutu Group Phil. 4°45N 119°20E 233 J2
Sibutu Passage E. Indies 4°50N 120°0E 233 J3
Sibuyan I. Phil. 12°25N 122°40E 232 E4
Sibuyan Sea Phil. 12°30N 122°20E 232 E4
Sic Romania 46°56N 23°53E 183 D8
Sicamous Canada 50°49N 119°0W 296 C5
Sicapoo, Mt. Phil. 18°1N 120°56E 232 B3
Sicasica Bolivia 17°22S 67°45W 330 D4
Siccus → Australia 31°55S 139°17E 282 A3
Sichelberg = Sierpc Poland 52°55N 19°43E 185 F6
Sichon Thailand 9°0N 99°54E 237 H2
Sichuan □ China 30°30N 103°0E 228 B5
Sichuan Pendi China 31°0N 105°0E 228 B5
Sicilia Italy 37°30N 14°30E 201 E7
Sicily = Sicilia Italy 37°30N 14°30E 201 E7
Sicily, Str. of Medit. S. 37°35N 11°56E 200 E4
Sico → Honduras 15°58N 84°58W 320 C3
Sicuani Peru 14°21S 71°10W 330 C3
Šid Serbia 45°8N 19°14E 182 E4
Sidamo Ethiopia 5°0N 37°50E 257 G4
Sidaouet Niger 18°34N 8°3E 259 E1
Sidari Greece 39°47N 19°41E 206 B9
Sidcup U.K. 51°25N 0°6E 125 B4
Siddapur India 14°20N 74°53E 245 G2
Siddhapur India 23°56N 72°25E 242 H5
Siddipet India 18°5N 78°51E 244 E4
Side Turkey 36°45N 31°23E 250 B2
Sidensjö Sweden 63°18N 18°17E 162 A12
Sidéradougou Burkina Faso 10°42N 4°12W 262 C4
Siderno Italy 38°16N 16°18E 201 D9
Sideros, Akra Greece 35°19N 26°19E 207 E7
Sidhauli India 27°17N 80°50E 243 F9
Sidhi India 24°25N 81°53E 243 G9
Sîdi Abd el Rahmân Egypt 30°55N 29°44E 256 A2
Sîdi Barrâni Egypt 31°38N 25°58E 256 A1
Sidi-bel-Abbès Algeria 35°13N 0°39W 261 A4
Sidi-bel-Abbès □ Algeria 34°50N 0°30W 261 B4
Sidi Bennour Morocco 32°40N 8°25W 260 B3
Sidi Bou Zid Tunisia 35°1N 9°16E 258 B1
Sidi Bou Zid □ Tunisia 35°0N 9°30E 258 B1
Sidi Boubekeur Algeria 35°1N 0°4E 261 A5
Sîdi Haneish Egypt 31°10N 27°35E 256 A2
Sidi Ifni Morocco 29°29N 10°12W 260 C2
Sidi Kacem Morocco 34°12N 5°42W 260 B3
Sîdi Omar Egypt 31°24N 24°57E 256 A1
Sidi Slimane Morocco 34°16N 5°56W 260 B3
Sidi Smaïl Morocco 32°50N 8°31W 260 B3
Sīdī 'Uzayz Libya 31°41N 24°55E 258 B4
Sidikalang Indonesia 2°45N 98°19E 237 L2
Sidimo Somali Rep. 2°27N 41°58E 267 D5
Siding No 14 = Ponoka Canada 52°42N 113°40W 296 C6
Sidirokastro Greece 41°13N 23°24E 202 E7
Sidlaw Hills U.K. 56°32N 3°2W 167 E5
Sidley, Mt. Antarctica 77°2S 126°2W 151 D14
Sidmouth U.K. 50°40N 3°15W 169 G4
Sidmouth, C. Australia 13°25S 143°36E 280 A3
Sidney B.C., Canada 48°39N 123°24W 306 B3
Sidney Mont., U.S.A. 47°43N 104°9W 304 C11
Sidney N.Y., U.S.A. 42°19N 75°24W 313 D9
Sidney Nebr., U.S.A. 41°8N 102°59W 308 E2
Sidney Ohio, U.S.A. 40°17N 84°9W 311 D12
Sidney Lanier, L. U.S.A. 34°10N 84°4W 316 A5
Sido Mali 11°37N 7°29W 262 C3
Sidoarjo Indonesia 7°27S 112°43E 235 D4
Sidoktaya Burma 20°27N 94°15E 241 E5
Sidon = Saydā Lebanon 33°35N 35°25E 250 E6
Sidra, G. of = Surt, Khalīj Libya 31°40N 18°30E 258 B3
Sidrolândia Brazil 20°55S 54°58W 331 E7
Siebenhirten Austria 48°8N 16°17E 142 B1
Siedlce Poland 52°10N 22°20E 185 F9
Siedlung Germany 52°35N 13°7E 115 A1
Sieg → Germany 50°46N 7°6E 178 E3
Siegburg Germany 50°47N 7°12E 178 E3
Siegen Germany 50°51N 8°0E 178 E4
Siekierki Poland 52°12N 21°4E 142 B2
Sielce Poland 52°12N 21°2E 142 B2
Siem Pang Cambodia 14°7N 106°23E 236 E6
Siem Reap = Siemreab Cambodia 13°20N 103°52E 236 F4
Siemensstadt Germany 52°32N 13°16E 115 A2
Siemiatycze Poland 52°27N 22°53E 185 F9
Siemreab Cambodia 13°20N 103°52E 236 F4
Siena Italy 43°19N 11°21E 199 E8
Sieniawa Poland 50°11N 22°38E 185 H9
Sienyang = Xianyang China 34°20N 108°40E 226 G5
Sieradz Poland 51°37N 18°41E 185 G5
Sieraków Poland 52°39N 16°2E 185 F3
Sierck-les-Bains France 49°26N 6°20E 173 C13
Sierning Austria 48°2N 14°18E 180 C7
Sierpc Poland 52°55N 19°43E 185 F6
Sierpe, Bocas de la Venezuela 10°0N 61°30W 329 G9
Sierra Blanca U.S.A. 31°11N 105°22W 314 F2
Sierra Blanca Peak U.S.A. 33°23N 105°49W 305 K11
Sierra City U.S.A. 39°34N 120°38W 306 F6
Sierra Colorada Argentina 40°35S 67°50W 336 B3
Sierra de Agalta △ Honduras 15°1N 85°48W 320 C2
Sierra de Aracena y Picas de Aroche △ Spain 37°53N 6°41W 195 H4
Sierra de Bahoruco △ Dom. Rep. 18°10N 71°25W 321 C5
Sierra de Baza △ Spain 37°20N 2°48W 197 H2
Sierra de Castril △ Spain 37°54N 2°50W 197 H2
Sierra de Espuña △ Spain 37°50N 1°31W 197 H3
Sierra de Grazalema △ Spain 36°31N 5°28W 195 J5
Sierra de Gredos △ Spain 40°17N 5°17W 194 E5
Sierra de Hornachuelos △ Spain 37°56N 5°14W 195 H5
Sierra de Huétor △ Spain 37°14N 3°30W 195 H7
Sierra de la Culata △ Venezuela 8°48N 70°56W 328 B3
Sierra de la Macarena △ Colombia 11°19N 74°1W 328 A3
Sierra de las Nieves △ Spain 36°42N 5°0W 195 J6
Sierra de las Quijadas △ Argentina 32°29S 67°5W 334 C2
Sierra de María-Los Vélez △ Spain 37°41N 2°10W 197 H2
Sierra de San Luis △ Venezuela 11°11N 69°33W 328 A4
Sierra de San Pedro Mártir △ Mexico 31°10N 115°30W 318 A1
Sierra de Yeguas Spain 37°7N 4°52W 195 H6
Sierra del São Mamede △ Portugal 39°17N 7°18W 195 F3
Sierra Gorda Chile 22°50S 69°15W 334 A2
Sierra Grande Argentina 41°36S 65°22W 336 B3
Sierra Leone ■ W. Afr. 9°0N 12°0W 262 D2
Sierra Leone Basin Atl. Oc. 5°0N 17°0W 152 F10
Sierra Leone Rise Atl. Oc. 7°0N 22°0W 152 F9
Sierra Madre Mexico 16°0N 93°0W 319 D6
Sierra Madre Calif., U.S.A. 34°9N 118°3W 126 B4
Sierra Madre Occidental Mexico 27°0N 107°0W 318 B3
Sierra Madre Oriental Mexico 25°0N 100°0W 318 C5
Sierra Mágina △ Spain 37°44N 3°28W 195 H7
Sierra Mojada Mexico 27°18N 103°41W 318 B4
Sierra Nevada Spain 37°3N 3°15W 195 H7
Sierra Nevada Calif., U.S.A. 39°0N 120°30W 306 H8
Sierra Nevada △ Spain 37°4N 3°7W 195 H7
Sierra Norte de Sevilla △ Spain 37°55N 5°46W 195 H5
Sierra Subbéticas △ Spain 37°26N 4°18W 195 H6
Sierra Vista U.S.A. 31°33N 110°18W 305 L8
Sierras de Cardeña y Montoro △ Spain 38°13N 4°15W 195 G6
Sierras de Cazorla, Segura y las Villas △ Spain 37°0N 2°45W 197 J2
Sierraville U.S.A. 39°36N 120°22W 306 F6
Sierre Switz. 46°17N 7°31E 179 J3
Sievering Austria 48°15N 16°20E 142 A2
Sifani Ethiopia 12°18N 40°19E 257 E5
Sifié Ivory C. 8°0N 7°5W 262 D3
Sifnos Greece 37°0N 24°45E 204 E6
Sifton Canada 51°21N 100°8W 297 C8
Sifton Pass Canada 57°52N 126°15W 296 B3
Sig Algeria 35°32N 0°12W 261 A4
Sigaboy = Governor Generoso Phil. 6°39N 126°5E 233 H6
Sigatoka Fiji 18°8S 177°32E 287 B1
Sigdal Norway 60°3N 9°38E 164 D6
Sigean France 43°2N 2°58E 174 E6
Siggiewi Malta 35°51N 14°26E 206 F7
Sighetu-Marmaţiei Romania 47°57N 23°52E 183 C8
Sighişoara Romania 46°12N 24°50E 183 D9
Sighthill U.K. 55°56N 3°17W 121 B2
Sigira Yemen 12°37N 54°20E 249 D6
Sigiriya Sri Lanka 7°57N 80°45E 245 L5
Sigli Indonesia 5°25N 96°0E 234 A1
Siglufjörður Iceland 66°12N 18°55W 155 A8
Siglunes Iceland 66°12N 18°50W 155 A8
Sigmaringen Germany 48°5N 9°12E 179 G5
Signa Italy 43°45N 11°10E 198 E8
Signakhi = Tsnori Georgia 41°40N 45°57E 191 K7
Signal de Botrang Belgium 50°29N 6°4E 170 D6
Signal Hill S. Africa 34°55S 18°24E 118 A1
Signal Pk. U.S.A. 33°20N 114°2W 307 M12
Signy I. Antarctica 60°43S 45°36W 151 C18
Signy-l'Abbaye France 49°40N 4°25E 173 C11
Sigourney U.S.A. 41°20N 92°12W 310 C4
Sigsbee U.S.A. 31°16N 83°52W 316 D6
Sigsbee Deep Caribbean 25°0N 92°0W 152 D1
Sigsig Ecuador 3°0S 78°50W 328 D2
Sigtuna Sweden 59°36N 17°44E 162 E11
Sigüenza Spain 41°3N 2°40W 196 D2
Siguiri Guinea 11°31N 9°10W 262 C3
Sigulda Latvia 57°10N 24°55E 188 D3
Sihanoukville = Kampong Saom Cambodia 10°38N 103°30E 237 G4
Sihawa India 20°19N 81°55E 244 D5
Siheung Gyeonggi-do, S. Korea 37°25N 126°47E 224 D3
Siheung Seoul, S. Korea 37°28N 126°54E 137 C1
Sihora India 23°29N 80°6E 243 H9
Sihuas Peru 8°40S 77°40W 330 B2
Sihui China 23°20N 112°40E 229 F9
Siikajoki → Finland 64°50N 24°43E 160 D21
Siilinjärvi Finland 63°4N 27°39E 160 E22
Siirt Turkey 37°57N 41°55E 213 D9
Siirt □ Turkey 37°55N 41°55E 213 D9
Sijarira Ra. = Chizarira Zimbabwe 17°36S 27°45E 269 F2
Sijunjung Indonesia 0°42S 100°58E 234 C2
Sika India 22°26N 69°47E 242 H3
Sikanni Chief → Canada 57°47N 122°15W 296 B4
Sikao Thailand 7°34N 99°21E 237 J2
Sikar India 27°33N 75°10E 242 F6
Sikasso Mali 11°18N 5°35W 262 C3
Sikasso □ Mali 10°55N 7°0W 262 C3
Sikátorpuszta Hungary 47°34N 19°10E 117 A3
Sikelenge Zambia 14°53S 24°14E 265 E4
Sikeston U.S.A. 36°53N 89°35W 308 G9
Sikhote Alin, Khrebet Russia 45°0N 136°0E 220 B8
Sikhote Alin Ra. = Sikhote Alin, Khrebet Russia 45°0N 136°0E 220 B8
Sikia Greece 40°2N 23°56E 202 F7
Sikinos Greece 36°40N 25°8E 205 E7
Sikkim □ India 27°50N 88°30E 241 B2
Siklós Hungary 45°50N 18°19E 182 E3
Sil → Spain 42°27N 7°43W 194 C3
Silacayoapan Mexico 17°30N 98°9W 319 D5
Silalė Lithuania 55°28N 22°12E 184 C9
Silampur India 28°39N 77°16E 120 B2
Silandro Italy 46°38N 10°46E 198 B7
Silang Phil. 14°14N 120°58E 232 D3
Silawad India 21°54N 74°54E 242 J6
Silay Phil. 10°47N 122°58E 233 F4
Silba Croatia 44°24N 14°41E 199 D11
Silchar India 24°49N 92°48E 241 C4
Sildegapet Norway 62°5N 5°0E 164 B2
Şile Turkey 41°10N 29°37E 203 E13
Silent Valley △ India 11°10N 76°20E 245 J3
Siler City U.S.A. 35°44N 79°28W 315 D15
Sileru → India 17°49N 81°24E 244 F5
Silesia = Śląsk Poland 51°0N 16°30E 176 C9
Silet Algeria 22°44N 4°37E 261 D5
Siletitengiz Köli Kazakhstan 53°20N 73°10E 217 B8
Silgarhi Doti Nepal 29°15N 81°0E 243 E9
Silghat India 26°35N 93°0E 241 B4
Silhouette Seychelles 4°29S 55°12E 272 c
Sili Burkina Faso 11°37N 2°30W 262 C4
Siliana Tunisia 36°5N 9°22E 261 A6
Siliana □ Tunisia 36°0N 9°20E 261 A6
Silifke Turkey 36°22N 33°58E 250 B4
Siliguri = Shiliguri India 26°45N 88°25E 241 B2
Silil Somali Rep. 11°0N 43°26E 267 B5
Siling Co China 31°50N 89°20E 218 D3
Silistea Nouă Romania 44°23N 25°1E 183 F10
Silistra Bulgaria 44°6N 27°19E 203 B11
Silivri Turkey 41°4N 28°14E 203 E12
Siljan Telemark, Norway 59°18N 9°42E 164 E6
Siljan Sweden 60°55N 14°45E 162 D8
Siljansnäs Sweden 60°47N 14°52E 162 D8
Silkeborg Denmark 56°10N 9°32E 163 H3
Silkwood Australia 17°45S 146°2E 280 B4
Silla Spain 39°22N 0°25W 197 F4
Sillajhuay, Cordillera Chile 19°46S 68°40W 330 D4
Sillamäe Estonia 59°24N 27°45E 188 C4
Sillé-le-Guillaume France 48°10N 0°8W 172 D6
Sillein = Žilina Slovak Rep. 49°12N 18°42E 181 B11
Sillim S. Korea 37°28N 126°56E 137 C1
Sillod India 20°18N 75°39E 244 D2
Silloth U.K. 54°52N 3°23W 168 C4
Sillustani Peru 15°50S 70°7W 330 D3
Silo Greece 41°10N 25°53E 203 E9
Siloam Springs U.S.A. 36°11N 94°32W 314 C7
Silopi Turkey 37°15N 42°27E 213 D10
Silsbee U.S.A. 30°21N 94°11W 314 F7
Siltou Chad 16°46N 15°33E 259 E3
Siluko Nigeria 6°35N 5°10E 263 D6
Šilutė Lithuania 55°21N 21°33E 184 C8
Silva Porto = Kuito Angola 12°22S 16°55E 265 E3
Silvan Turkey 38°7N 41°2E 213 C9
Silvani India 23°18N 78°25E 243 H8
Silvassa India 20°16N 73°1E 244 D1
Silver, L. U.S.A. 28°35N 81°23W 133 A2
Silver Bank W. Indies 20°30N 69°45W 321 B6
Silver Bank Passage W. Indies 20°0N 70°0W 321 B5
Silver City U.S.A. 32°46N 108°17W 305 K9
Silver Cr. → U.S.A. 43°16N 119°13W 304 E4
Silver Creek U.S.A. 42°33N 79°10W 312 D5
Silver Grove U.S.A. 39°2N 84°23W 311 E12
Silver Hill Montserrat 16°49N 62°11W 323 p
Silver Hill Md., U.S.A. 38°49N 76°55W 143 C4
Silver L. U.S.A. 38°39N 120°6W 306 G6
Silver Lake Calif., U.S.A. 34°5N 118°15W 126 B3
Silver Lake Calif., U.S.A. 35°21N 116°7W 307 K10
Silver Lake Ind., U.S.A. 41°4N 85°53W 311 C11
Silver Lake Oreg., U.S.A. 43°8N 121°3W 304 E3
Silver Lake Wis., U.S.A. 42°33N 88°13W 311 B8
Silver Spring U.S.A. 38°59N 77°2W 143 A3
Silver Springs U.S.A. 29°13N 82°3W 317 F7
Silverdalen Sweden 57°32N 15°45E 163 G9
Silvermine Mts. Ireland 52°47N 8°15W 166 D3
Silvermine Nature Reserve S. Africa 34°6S 18°27E 118 B1
Silverton N.S.W., Australia 31°52S 141°10E 282 A4
Silverton Colo., U.S.A. 37°49N 107°40W 305 H10
Silverton Tex., U.S.A. 34°28N 101°19W 314 D4
Silves Brazil 2°54S 58°27W 329 D6
Silves Portugal 37°11N 8°26W 195 H2
Silvi Marina Italy 42°34N 14°5E 199 F11
Silvia Colombia 2°37N 76°21W 328 C2
Silvies → U.S.A. 43°34N 119°2W 304 E4
Silvolantekojärvi Finland 60°17N 24°52E 121 B2
Silvrettahorn Switz. 46°50N 10°6E 198 B7
Silwa Bahari Egypt 24°45N 32°55E 256 C3
Silz Austria 47°16N 10°56E 180 D3
Sim, C. Morocco 31°26N 9°51W 260 B3
Simakumba Zambia 14°12S 23°16E 265 E4
Simaltala India 24°43N 86°33E 243 G12
Simaluguri India 26°55N 94°46E 241 B5
Sim'ān, J. Syria 36°20N 36°53E 250 B7
Simanggang = Sri Aman Malaysia 1°15N 111°32E 235 B4
Simao China 22°47N 101°5E 228 F3
Simão Dias Brazil 10°44S 37°49W 332 D4
Simara I. Phil. 12°48N 122°3E 232 E4
Simard, L. Canada 47°40N 78°40W 298 C4
Şīmareh → Iran 33°9N 47°41E 213 F12
Simav Turkey 39°4N 28°58E 205 B10
Simav → Turkey 40°23N 28°31E 203 F12
Simav Dağları Turkey 39°10N 28°30E 205 B10
Simba Dem. Rep. of the Congo 0°38N 22°59E 264 B4
Simba Tanzania 2°10S 37°36E 268 C4
Simbach Germany 48°16N 13°2E 179 G9
Simberi I. Papua N. G. 2°38S 152°0E 286 B7
Simbirsk = Ulyanovsk Russia 54°20N 48°25E 190 C9
Simbo Solomon Is. 8°16S 156°33E 287 M9
Simbo Tanzania 4°51S 29°41E 268 C2
Simcoe Canada 42°50N 80°23W 312 D4
Simcoe, L. Canada 44°25N 79°20W 312 B5
Simdega India 22°37N 84°31E 243 H11
Simei Singapore 1°20N 103°57E 138 A3
Simeonovgrad Bulgaria 42°1N 25°50E 203 D9
Simeria Romania 45°51N 23°1E 182 E8
Simeto → Italy 37°24N 15°6E 201 E8
Simeulue Indonesia 2°45N 95°45E 234 B1
Simferopol Ukraine 44°55N 34°3E 189 K8
Simi Greece 36°35N 27°50E 205 E9
Simi Valley U.S.A. 34°16N 118°47W 307 L8
Simien Mts. △ Ethiopia 13°19N 38°0E 257 E4
Simikot Nepal 30°0N 81°50E 243 E9
Similajau △ Malaysia 3°27N 113°15E 235 B4
Simineh → Iran 36°59N 45°54E 213 D11
Simiti Colombia 7°58N 73°57W 328 B3
Simitli Bulgaria 41°52N 23°7E 202 E7
Simla = Shimla India 31°2N 77°9E 242 D7
Simla India 22°35N 88°22E 124 B2
Simlångsdalen Sweden 56°43N 13°6E 163 H7
Şimleu-Silvaniei Romania 47°17N 22°50E 182 C7
Simlipal △ India 21°45N 86°30E 243 J12
Simmering Austria 48°10N 16°24E 142 A2
Simmering Heide Austria 48°10N 16°26E 142 A2
Simmern Germany 49°58N 7°30E 179 F3
Simmie Canada 49°56N 108°6W 297 D7
Simmler U.S.A. 35°21N 119°59W 307 K7
Simnas Lithuania 54°24N 23°39E 184 D10
Simo älv = Simojoki → Finland 65°35N 25°1E 160 D21
Simões Brazil 7°36S 40°49W 332 C3
Simojoki → Finland 65°35N 25°1E 160 D21
Simojovel Mexico 17°12N 92°38W 319 D6
Simonette → Canada 55°9N 118°15W 296 B5
Simonière, Plaine de la Guadeloupe 16°16N 61°19W 322 e
Simonkylä Finland 60°18N 25°1E 121 B3
Šimonovany = Partizánske Slovak Rep. 48°38N 18°23E 181 C11
Simonstown S. Africa 34°14S 18°26E 270 D2
Simontornya Hungary 46°45N 18°33E 182 D3
Simpang Empat Malaysia 5°27N 100°29E 237 c
Simpangkiri → Indonesia 2°50N 97°40E 234 B1
Simplicio Mendes Brazil 7°51S 41°54W 332 C3
Simplonpass Switz. 46°15N 8°3E 179 J4
Simplontunnel Switz. 46°15N 8°7E 179 J4
Simpson, Mt. Papua N. G. 10°2S 149°34E 286 F5
Simpson Bay Lagoon St.-Martin 18°3N 63°6W 322 a
Simpson Desert Australia 25°0S 137°0E 280 D2
Simpson Desert △ Australia 24°59S 138°21E 280 C2
Simpson Pen. Canada 68°34N 88°45W 295 D14
Simrishamn Sweden 55°33N 14°22E 163 J8
Simsbury U.S.A. 41°53N 72°48W 313 E12
Simsonbaai St.-Maarten 18°2N 63°7W 322 a
Simuk Indonesia 0°4S 97°52E 234 C1
Simunjan Malaysia 1°25N 110°45E 235 B4
Simunul Phil. 4°54N 119°51E 233 J2
Simushir, Ostrov Russia 46°50N 152°30E 215 E16
Sin Cowe I. S. China Sea 9°53N 114°19E 230 C4
Sin-do N. Korea 39°52N 124°14E 224 C2
Sina → India 17°30N 75°55E 244 F2
Sina Dhago Somali Rep. 5°50N 47°0E 267 C6
Sinabang Indonesia 2°30N 96°24E 234 B1
Sinai = Es Sînâ' Egypt 29°0N 34°0E 256 D2
Sinai, Mt. = Mûsa, Gebel Egypt 28°33N 33°59E 251 K4
Sinai, Mt. Grenada 12°4N 61°42W 323 q
Sinai Peninsula Egypt 29°30N 34°0E 251 J5
Sinaia Romania 45°21N 25°38E 183 E10
Sinait Phil. 17°52N 120°27E 232 C3
Sinako, Mt. Phil. 7°30N 125°17E 233 H5
Sinaloa □ Mexico 25°0N 107°30W 318 C3
Sinaloa de Leyva Mexico 25°50N 108°14W 318 B3
Sinalunga Italy 43°12N 11°44E 199 E8
Sinan China 27°56N 108°13E 228 D7
Sînandrei Romania 45°52N 21°13E 182 E6
Sinarades Greece 39°34N 19°51E 206 B9
Sīnāwan Libya 31°0N 10°37E 258 B2
Sinbaungwe Burma 19°43N 95°10E 241 F5
Sinbo Burma 24°46N 97°3E 241 C6
Sincan Turkey 40°0N 32°36E 212 B5
Sincanlı Turkey 38°45N 30°15E 205 C12
Sincé Colombia 9°15N 75°9W 328 B2
Sincelejo Colombia 9°18N 75°24W 328 B2
Sinch'ang N. Korea 40°7N 128°28E 224 B4
Sincheorwon S. Korea 38°8N 127°18E 224 C3
Sinch'ŏn N. Korea 38°17N 125°21E 224 C2
Sinchon Seoul, S. Korea 37°34N 126°57E 137 B1
Sinclair U.S.A. 41°47N 107°7W 304 F10
Sinclair, L. U.S.A. 33°8N 83°12W 316 B6
Sinclair Mills Canada 54°5N 121°40W 296 C4
Sinclair's B. U.K. 58°31N 3°5W 167 C5
Sinclairville U.S.A. 42°16N 79°16W 312 D5
Sind = Sindh □ Pakistan 26°0N 69°0E 242 G3
Sind → Jammu & Kashmir, India 34°18N 74°45E 243 B6
Sind → Mad. P., India 26°26N 79°13E 243 F8
Sind Sagar Doab Pakistan 32°0N 71°30E 242 D4
Sindal Denmark 57°28N 10°10E 163 G4
Sindang S. Korea 37°35N 127°2E 137 B2
Sindangan Phil. 8°10N 123°5E 233 G4
Sindangan Bay Phil. 8°11N 122°50E 233 G4
Sindangbarang Indonesia 7°27S 107°1E 235 D3
Sindara Gabon 1°7S 10°41E 264 C2
Sinde Zambia 17°28S 25°51E 269 F2
Sindelfingen Germany 48°42N 9°0E 179 G4
Sindewahi India 20°17N 79°39E 244 D4
Sindgi India 16°55N 76°14E 244 F3
Sindh = Indus → Pakistan 24°20N 67°47E 242 G2
Sindh □ Pakistan 26°0N 69°0E 242 G3
Sindhnur India 15°47N 76°46E 245 F3
Sindi India 20°48N 78°52E 244 D4
Sındırgı Turkey 39°13N 28°10E 205 B10
Sindou Burkina Faso 10°35N 5°4W 262 C3
Sindri India 23°45N 86°42E 243 H12
Sine → Senegal 14°10N 16°28W 262 C1
Sinegorskiy Russia 47°55N 40°52E 191 G5
Sinekli Turkey 41°14N 28°12E 203 E12
Sinelnikovo = Synelnykove Ukraine 48°25N 35°30E 189 H8
Sinendé Benin 10°20N 2°22E 263 C5
Sines Portugal 37°56N 8°51W 195 H2
Sines, C. de Portugal 37°58N 8°53W 195 H2
Sineu Spain 39°38N 3°1E 206 B4
Sinewit, Mt. Papua N. G. 4°44S 152°2E 286 C7
Sinfra Ivory C. 6°35N 5°56W 262 D3
Sing Buri Thailand 14°53N 100°25E 236 E3
Sing Sing = Ossining U.S.A. 41°10N 73°55W 313 E11
Singa Sudan 13°10N 33°57E 257 E3
Singako Chad 9°50N 19°29E 259 G3
Singalila △ India 27°10N 88°5E 241 B2
Singanallur India 11°2N 77°1E 245 J3
Singapore ■ Asia 1°17N 103°51E 138 B3
Singapore, Straits of Asia 1°15N 104°0E 237 d
Singapore, Univ. of Singapore 1°19N 103°49E 138 B2
Singapore Changi ✕ (SIN) Singapore 1°23N 103°59E 138 A3
Singaraja Indonesia 8°7S 115°6E 231 J18
Singatoka = Sigatoka Fiji 18°8S 177°32E 287 B1
Singen Germany 47°45N 8°50E 179 H4
Singida Tanzania 4°49S 34°48E 268 C3
Singida □ Tanzania 6°0S 34°30E 268 D3
Singkaling Hkamti Burma 26°0N 95°39E 241 C5
Singkang Indonesia 4°8S 120°1E 231 E6
Singkawang Indonesia 1°0N 108°57E 235 B3
Singkep Indonesia 0°30S 104°25E 234 C2
Singkil Indonesia 2°17N 97°49E 237 L1
Singleton Australia 32°33S 151°10E 283 B9
Singleton, Mt. N. Terr., Australia 22°0S 130°46E 278 D5
Singleton, Mt. W. Austral., Australia 29°27S 117°15E 279 E2
Singö Sweden 60°12N 18°45E 162 D12
Singoli India 25°0N 75°22E 242 G6
Singora = Songkhla Thailand 7°13N 100°37E 237 J3
Singri India 26°36N 92°29E 241 B4
Singsås Norway 62°56N 10°37E 164 B7
Singu Burma 22°33N 96°0E 241 D6
Singur India 18°22N 73°45E 244 E1
Sinhŭng Hamgyŏngnam-do, N. Korea 40°11N 127°34E 224 B3
Sinhŭng Hamgyŏngnam-do, N. Korea 41°8N 127°11E 224 B3
Sinicka → Russia 55°52N 37°18E 129 A1
Siniloan Phil. 14°25N 121°27E 232 D3
Sining = Xining China 36°34N 101°40E 218 C5
Siniscola Italy 40°34N 9°41E 200 B2
Sinj Croatia 43°42N 16°39E 199 E13
Sinjai Indonesia 5°7S 120°20E 231 F6
Sinjajevina Montenegro 42°57N 19°22E 202 D3
Sinjār Iraq 36°19N 41°52E 213 D9
Sinjār Syria 35°35N 37°7E 250 C8
Sinjār, Jabal Iraq 36°23N 41°47E 213 D9
Sinkat Sudan 18°55N 36°49E 256 D4
Sinki, Selat Singapore 1°15N 103°42E 138 B2
Sinkiang = Xinjiang Uygur Zizhiqu □ China 42°0N 86°0E 217 D11
Sinko Guinea 8°53N 8°16W 262 D3
Sinlumkaba Burma 24°16N 97°31E 241 C6
Sinmak N. Korea 38°25N 126°14E 224 C3
Sinmi-do N. Korea 39°33N 124°53E 224 C2
Sinnai Italy 39°18N 9°13E 200 C2
Sinnar India 19°48N 74°0E 244 E2
Sinni → Italy 40°8N 16°41E 201 B9
Sinnuris Egypt 29°26N 30°31E 256 J7
Sinoie, Lacul Romania 44°35N 28°50E 183 F13
Sinop Turkey 42°1N 35°11E 212 A6
Sinop □ Turkey 42°0N 35°0E 212 B6
Sinor India 21°55N 73°20E 242 J5
Sinp'o N. Korea 40°0N 128°13E 224 C4
Sinpa S. Korea 37°31N 127°0E 137 B2
Sinsang N. Korea 39°38N 127°24E 224 C3
Sinsheim Germany 49°15N 8°52E 179 F4
Sinsiang = Xinxiang China 35°18N 113°50E 226 G7
Sinsk Russia 61°8N 126°48E 215 C13
Sint Annabaai Neth. Ant. 12°6N 68°55W 322 g
Sint Christoffelberg Neth. Ant. 12°20N 69°8W 322 g
Sint-Genesius-Rode Belgium 50°45N 4°22E 116 B2
Sint Jorisbaai Neth. Ant. 12°7N 68°48W 322 g
Sint Marie, K. Neth. Ant. 12°11N 69°3W 322 g
Sint Marthabaai Neth. Ant. 12°11N 69°7W 322 g
Sint Michiel Neth. Ant. 12°8N 69°0W 322 g
Sint Nicolaas Aruba 12°27N 69°54W 322 f
Sint Nicolaas Neth. Ant. 12°17N 69°8W 322 g
Sint Willibrordus Neth. Ant. 12°17N 69°6W 322 g
Sintang Indonesia 0°5N 111°35E 235 B4
Sinton U.S.A. 28°2N 97°31W 314 G6
Sintra Portugal 38°47N 9°25W 195 G1
Sintra-Cascais △ Portugal 38°50N 9°25W 195 G1
Sinŭiju N. Korea 40°5N 124°24E 224 B2
Sinujif Somali Rep. 8°33N 48°59E 267 C6
Sinyukha → Ukraine 48°3N 30°51E 189 H6
Sinzig Germany 50°32N 7°14E 178 E3
Sio → Hungary 46°20N 18°53E 182 D3
Siocon Phil. 7°40N 122°10E 233 H4
Siófok Hungary 46°54N 18°3E 182 D3
Sioma Zambia 16°40S 23°36E 265 F4
Sioma Ngwezi △ Zambia 17°14S 23°26E 265 F4
Sion Maharashtra, India 19°3N 72°52E 130 A2
Sion Switz. 46°14N 7°20E 179 J3
Sion Mills U.K. 54°48N 7°29W 166 B4
Sionainn = Shannon → Ireland 52°35N 9°30W 166 D2
Sioux Center U.S.A. 43°5N 96°11W 308 D5
Sioux City U.S.A. 42°30N 96°24W 308 D5
Sioux Falls U.S.A. 43°33N 96°44W 308 D5
Sioux Lookout Canada 50°10N 91°50W 298 B1
Sioux Narrows Canada 49°25N 94°10W 297 D10
Sipadan Malaysia 4°6N 118°38E 235 B5
Sipalay Phil. 9°45N 122°24E 233 G4
Šipan Croatia 42°45N 17°52E 202 D1
Sipang, Tanjong Malaysia 1°48N 110°20E 235 B4
Siparia Trin. & Tob. 10°8N 61°31W 323 t
Sipil Dağı △ Turkey 38°35N 27°30E 205 C9
Siping China 43°8N 124°21E 227 C13
Sipiwesk L. Canada 55°5N 97°35W 297 B9
Siple Antarctica 75°0S 74°0W 151 D7
Sipocot Phil. 13°46N 122°58E 232 E4
Šipovo Bos.-H. 44°16N 17°6E 182 F2
Sipra → India 23°55N 75°28E 242 H6
Sipson U.K. 51°29N 0°26W 125 B1
Sipur India 21°11N 85°9E 244 D7
Sipura Indonesia 2°18S 99°40E 234 C1
Siqeil Egypt 30°7N 31°10E 117 A1
Siqueira Campos Brazil 23°42S 49°50W 333 F2
Siquia → Nic. 12°10N 84°20W 320 D3
Siquijor Phil. 9°12N 123°35E 233 G4
Siquijor □ Phil. 9°11N 123°35E 233 G4
Siquirres Costa Rica 10°6N 83°30W 320 D3
Siquisique Venezuela 10°34N 69°42W 328 A4
Şīr Abu Nu'ayr U.A.E. 25°20N 54°20E 247 E7
Şīr Banī Yās U.A.E. 24°19N 52°37E 247 E7
Sir Edward Pellew Group Australia 15°40S 137°10E 280 B2
Sir Graham Moore Is. Australia 13°53S 126°34E 278 B4
Sir James MacBrien, Mt. Canada 62°7N 127°41W 294 E6
Sira India 13°41N 76°49E 245 H3
Sira Vest-Agder, Norway 58°24N 6°40E 164 F3
Sira → Norway 58°23N 6°34E 164 F3
Siracusa Italy 37°4N 15°17E 201 E8
Sirajganj Bangla. 24°25N 89°47E 241 C2
Sirakoro Mali 12°41N 9°14W 262 C3
Şiran Turkey 40°11N 39°7E 213 B8
Sirasso Ivory C. 9°16N 6°6W 262 D3
Sirathu India 25°39N 81°19E 243 G9
Sirawai Phil. 7°34N 122°8E 233 H4
Sirdalsvatnet Norway 58°34N 6°43E 164 F3
Sīrdān Iran 36°39N 49°12E 213 D13
Sirdaryo □ Uzbekistan 40°30N 68°45E 217 D7
Sire Ethiopia 6°55N 35°36E 257 F4
Siren U.S.A. 45°47N 92°24W 308 C7
Sirente-Velino △ Italy 42°10N 13°32E 199 F10
Sirer Spain 38°56N 1°22E 206 D1
Siret Romania 47°55N 26°5E 183 C11
Siret → Romania 45°24N 28°1E 183 E12
Sirevåg Norway 58°30N 5°48E 164 F2
Sirghāyā Syria 33°51N 36°8E 250 E7
Şiria Romania 46°16N 21°38E 182 D6
Sirik, Tanjong Malaysia 2°47N 111°15E 235 B4
Sirinat △ Thailand 8°6N 98°17E 237 a
Sirino, Mte. Italy 40°7N 15°50E 201 B8
Sīrjān Iran 29°30N 55°45E 247 D7
Sirkali = Sirkazhi India 11°15N 79°41E 245 J4
Sirkazhi India 11°15N 79°41E 245 J4
Sirmans U.S.A. 30°21N 83°39W 316 E6
Sirmaur India 24°51N 81°23E 243 G9
Sirmilik △ Canada 72°50N 80°35W 295 C15
Sirna Greece 36°22N 26°42E 205 E8
Şirnak Turkey 37°32N 42°28E 213 D10
Sirohi India 24°52N 72°53E 242 G5
Sironj India 24°5N 77°39E 242 G7
Siros = Ermoupoli Greece 37°28N 24°57E 204 D6
Siroz = Serres Greece 41°5N 23°31E 202 E7
Sirpur India 19°29N 79°36E 244 E4
Sirr, Nafud as Si. Arabia 25°33N 44°35E 246 E5
Sirrayn Si. Arabia 19°38N 40°36E 248 C3
Sirretta Pk. U.S.A. 35°56N 118°19W 307 K8
Sīrrī Iran 25°55N 54°32E 247 E7
Sirsa India 29°33N 75°4E 242 E6
Sirsa → India 26°51N 79°4E 243 F8
Sirsi India 14°40N 74°49E 245 G2
Sirsilla India 18°23N 78°50E 244 E4
Siruela Spain 38°58N 5°3W 195 G5
Siruguppa India 15°38N 76°54E 245 F3
Sirur India 18°50N 74°23E 244 E2
Sirvān → Iran 35°4N 46°50E 213 E12
Širvintos Lithuania 55°3N 24°57E 184 C11
Sisak Croatia 45°30N 16°21E 199 C13
Sisaket Thailand 15°8N 104°23E 236 E5
Sisante Spain 39°25N 2°12W 197 F2
Sisargas, Is. Spain 43°21N 8°50W 194 B2
Sishen S. Africa 27°47S 22°59E 270 C3
Sishui Henan, China 34°48N 113°15E 226 G7
Sishui Shandong, China 35°42N 117°18E 227 G9
Sisian Armenia 39°31N 46°1E 213 C12
Sisiga Solomon Is. 7°54S 159°10E 287 L10
Sisimiut Greenland 66°40N 53°30W 154 D5
Sisipuk L. Canada 55°45N 101°50W 297 B8
Şişli Turkey 41°3N 28°58E 122 B1
Sisophon Cambodia 13°38N 102°59E 236 F4
Sissano Papua N. G. 3°0S 142°3E 286 B2
Sisseton U.S.A. 45°40N 97°3W 308 C5
Sisson = Mount Shasta U.S.A. 41°19N 122°19W 304 F2
Sissonne France 49°34N 3°51E 173 C10
Sīstān Asia 30°50N 61°0E 247 D9
Sīstān, Daryācheh-ye Iran 31°0N 61°0E 247 D9
Sīstān va Balūchestān □ Iran 27°0N 62°0E 247 E9
Sisteron France 44°12N 5°57E 175 D9
Sisters U.S.A. 44°18N 121°33W 304 D3
Sisters, The Grenada 12°18N 61°36W 323 q
Sisters, The Seychelles 4°16S 55°52E 272 c
Sisters Pk. Ascension I. 7°56S 14°22W 153 g
Sisters Rocks Trin. & Tob. 11°20N 60°39W 323 s
Siswa Bazar India 27°9N 83°46E 243 F10
Sitakili Mali 13°7N 11°14W 262 C2
Sitakunda Bangla. 22°37N 91°39E 241 D3
Sitamarhi India 26°37N 85°30E 243 F11
Sitampiky Madag. 16°41S 46°6E 272 B2
Sitangkai Phil. 4°40N 119°24E 233 J2
Sitapur India 27°38N 80°45E 243 F9
Siteki Swaziland 26°32S 31°58E 271 C5
Sitges Spain 41°17N 1°47E 196 D6
Sithonia Greece 40°0N 23°45E 202 F7
Sitia Greece 35°13N 26°6E 207 E7
Sitia ✕ (JSH) Greece 35°15N 26°5E 207 E7
Sítio da Abadia Brazil 14°48S 46°16W 333 D2
Sitito-Ozima Ridge Pac. Oc. 23°0N 143°0E 288 E6
Sitka U.S.A. 57°3N 135°20W 296 B1
Sitka △ U.S.A. 57°3N 135°19W 303 H14
Sitkinak I. U.S.A. 56°33N 154°10W 303 H9
Sitoti Botswana 23°15S 23°40E 270 B3
Sitra Egypt 28°40N 26°53E 256 B2
Sittang Myit → Burma 17°20N 96°45E 241 G6
Sittard Neths. 51°0N 5°52E 170 C5

Sittaung Burma 24°10N 94°35E 241 C5
Sittensen Germany 53°17N 9°32E 178 B5
Sittingbourne U.K. 51°21N 0°45E 169 F8
Sittona Eritrea 14°25N 37°23E 257 E4
Sittoung = Sittang Myit ➜
Burma 17°20N 96°45E 241 G6
Sittwe Burma 20°18N 92°45E 241 E4
Situbondo Indonesia 7°42S 114°0E 231 G16
Siufaalete Pt.
Amer. Samoa 14°17S 169°29W 302 f
Siulagi Pt. Amer. Samoa 14°13S 169°30W 302 g
Si'umu Samoa 14°1S 171°48W 287 W20
Siuna Nic. 13°37N 84°45W 320 D3
Siuri India 23°50N 87°34E 243 H12
Siutghiol, Lacul
Romania 44°15N 28°35E 183 F13
Sivaganga India 9°50N 78°28E 245 K4
Sivagiri India 9°16N 77°26E 245 K3
Sivakasi India 9°24N 77°47E 245 K3
Sīvand Iran 30°5N 52°55E 247 D7
Sivas Turkey 39°43N 36°58E 212 C7
Sivas ☐ Turkey 39°45N 37°0E 212 C7
Sivasamudram India 12°16N 77°10E 245 H3
Sivaslı Turkey 38°31N 29°42E 205 C11
Siverek Turkey 37°50N 39°19E 213 D8
Sivomaskinskiy Russia 66°40N 62°35E 186 A11
Sivota Greece 39°24N 20°13E 206 C10
Sivrihisar Turkey 39°30N 31°35E 212 C4
Sivros Greece 38°40N 20°39E 207 B2
Sīwa Egypt 29°11N 25°31E 256 B2
Sīwa, El Wâhât es Egypt 29°10N 25°30E 256 B2
Siwa Oasis = Sīwa, El Wâhât es
Egypt 29°10N 25°30E 256 B2
Siwalik Range Nepal 28°0N 83°0E 243 F10
Siwan India 26°13N 84°21E 243 F11
Siwana India 25°38N 72°25E 242 G5
Six Cross Roads Barbados 13°7N 59°28W 323 r
Sixmilebridge Ireland 52°44N 8°46W 166 D3
Sixth Cataract Sudan 16°20N 32°42E 257 D3
Siyabuswa S. Africa 25°7S 29°3E 271 C4
Siyah Kuh, Kavīr-e Iran 32°55N 53°55E 247 C7
Siyâl, Jazâ'ir Egypt 22°49N 36°12E 256 C4
Siyäzän Azerbaijan 41°3N 49°10E 191 K9
Siziwang Qi China 41°25N 111°40E 226 D6
Sjælland Denmark 55°30N 11°30E 163 J5
Sjælland ☐ Denmark 55°30N 11°30E 163 J5
Sjællands Odde Denmark 55°58N 11°24E 163 J5
Sjenica Serbia 43°16N 20°0E 202 C3
Sjoa Norway 61°41N 9°33E 164 C6
Sjöbo Sweden 55°37N 13°45E 163 J7
Sjøholt Norway 62°27N 6°52E 164 B3
Sjølisand Norway 61°29N 11°18E 164 C8
Sjötofta Sweden 57°22N 13°17E 163 G7
Sjötorp Sweden 58°50N 14°0E 163 F8
Sjumen = Shumen
Bulgaria 43°18N 26°55E 203 C10
Sjuntorp Sweden 58°12N 12°13E 163 F6
Skåbu Norway 61°32N 9°24E 164 C6
Skadarsko Jezero Europe 42°10N 19°20E 202 D3
Skadarsko Jezero △
Montenegro 42°10N 19°20E 202 D3
Skadovsk Ukraine 46°17N 32°52E 189 J7
Skælskør Denmark 55°15N 11°18E 163 J5
Skærbæk Denmark 55°9N 8°45E 163 J2
Skaftafell Iceland 64°1N 17°0W 155 C9
Skaftafell △ Iceland 64°9N 16°50W 160 D5
Skagafjarðarsýsla ☐
Iceland 65°30N 19°0W 155 B7
Skagafjörður Iceland 65°54N 19°35W 155 B7
Skagastølstindane
Norway 61°28N 7°52E 164 C4
Skagaströnd Iceland 65°50N 20°19W 155 B6
Skagatá Iceland 66°7N 20°6W 155 A6
Skagen Denmark 57°43N 10°35E 163 G4
Skagern Sweden 59°0N 14°20E 162 E8
Skagerrak Denmark 57°30N 9°0E 163 G2
Skagit ➜ U.S.A. 48°23N 122°22W 306 B4
Skagway U.S.A. 59°28N 135°19W 303 G14
Skala Greece 38°5N 20°47E 207 C2
Skala nad Zbruczem = Skala-Podilska Ukraine 48°50N 26°15E 183 B11
Skala-Podilska Ukraine 48°50N 26°15E 183 B11
Skalat Ukraine 49°23N 25°55E 177 D13
Skálavík Iceland 66°11N 23°29W 155 A3
Skalbmierz Poland 50°20N 20°25E 185 H7
Skälderviken Sweden 56°22N 12°30E 163 H6
Skålevik Norway 58°5N 8°1E 164 F5
Skalica Slovak Rep. 48°50N 17°15E 181 C10
Skallingen Denmark 55°32N 8°13E 163 J2
Skalni Dol = Kamenyak
Bulgaria 43°24N 26°57E 203 C10
Skanderborg Denmark 56°2N 9°55E 163 H3
Skåne Sweden 55°59N 13°30E 163 J7
Skåne län ☐ Sweden 56°15N 14°0E 163 H7
Skaneateles U.S.A. 42°57N 76°26W 313 D8
Skaneateles L. U.S.A. 42°51N 76°22W 313 D8
Skånevik Norway 59°43N 5°53E 164 E2
Skänninge Sweden 58°24N 15°5E 163 F9
Skanör med Falsterbo
Sweden 55°24N 12°50E 163 J6
Skansen Sweden 59°19N 18°7E 163 E2
Skantzoura Greece 39°5N 24°6E 204 B6
Skara Sweden 58°25N 13°30E 163 F7
Skärblacka Sweden 58°35N 15°54E 163 F9
Skardu Pakistan 35°20N 75°44E 243 B6
Skare Hordaland, Norway 59°55N 6°36E 164 E3
Skåre Sweden 59°26N 13°26E 162 E7
Skärhamn Sweden 57°59N 11°34E 163 G5
Skärholmen Sweden 59°16N 17°53E 139 B1
Skarnes Norway 60°15N 11°41E 164 D8
Skarpäng Sweden 59°26N 18°0E 139 A2
Skarpnäck Sweden 59°16N 18°7E 139 B2
Skarszewy Poland 54°4N 18°25E 184 D5
Skaryszew Poland 51°19N 21°15E 185 G8
Skaryszewski, Park
Poland 52°15N 21°3E 142 B2
Skarżysko-Kamienna
Poland 51°7N 20°52E 185 G7
Skattkärr Sweden 59°25N 13°40E 162 E7
Skattungbyn Sweden 61°10N 14°56E 162 C8
Skawina Poland 49°59N 19°50E 185 J6
Skebobruk Sweden 59°58N 18°36E 162 E12
Skeena ➜ Canada 54°9N 130°5W 296 C2
Skeena Mts. Canada 56°40N 128°30W 296 B3
Skegness U.K. 53°9N 0°20E 168 D8
Skei Norway 61°34N 6°28E 164 C3
Skeiðarársandur Iceland 63°54N 17°14W 155 D9
Skeiðflötur Iceland 63°26N 19°11W 155 D7
Skeldon = Corriverton
Guyana 5°55N 57°20W 329 B6
Skeleton Coast ⌓ Namibia 20°0S 13°20E 270 B1
Skellefteå Sweden 64°45N 20°50E 160 D19
Skellefteälven ➜
Sweden 64°45N 21°10E 160 D19
Skelleftehamn Sweden 64°40N 21°9E 160 D19
Skender Vakuf Bos.-H. 44°29N 17°22E 182 F2
Skeppsholmen Stockholm, Sweden 139 c3
Skerries, The U.K. 53°25N 4°36W 168 D3
Skhidnytsya Ukraine 49°13N 23°20E 185 J10
Skhiza Greece 36°41N 21°40E 204 E3
Ski Norway 59°43N 10°52E 164 E7
Skiathos Greece 39°12N 23°30E 204 B5
Skibbereen Ireland 51°33N 9°16W 166 E2
Skiddaw U.K. 54°39N 3°9W 168 C4
Skidegate Canada 53°15N 132°1W 296 C2
Skidra Greece 40°46N 22°10E 202 F6
Skien Norway 59°12N 9°35E 164 E6
Skierniewice Poland 51°58N 20°10E 185 G7
Skihist, Mt. Canada 50°12N 121°54W 296 C4
Skikda Algeria 36°50N 6°58E 261 A6
Skikda ☐ Algeria 36°45N 6°50E 261 A6
Skillet Fork ➜ U.S.A. 38°5N 88°5W 311 F8
Skillingaryd Sweden 57°27N 14°5E 163 G8
Skillinge Sweden 55°30N 14°16E 163 J8
Skilloura Cyprus 35°14N 33°10E 207 E9
Skinari, Akra Greece 37°56N 20°42E 207 D2
Skinnastaður Iceland 66°4N 16°27W 155 A10
Skinnskatteberg Sweden 59°50N 15°42E 162 E9
Skipton Vic., Australia 37°39S 143°40E 282 D5
Skipton N. Yorks., U.K. 53°58N 2°3W 168 D5
Skiptvet Norway 59°28N 11°11E 164 E8
Skiring, C. Senegal 12°26N 16°46W 262 C1
Skirmish Pt. Australia 11°59S 134°17E 280 A1
Skiropoula Greece 38°50N 24°21E 204 C6
Skiros Greece 38°55N 24°34E 204 C6
Skivarp Sweden 55°26N 13°34E 163 J7
Skive Denmark 56°33N 9°2E 163 H3
Skjærhalden Norway 59°2N 11°2E 164 E8
Skjálfandafljót ➜
Iceland 65°59N 17°25W 155 B9
Skjálfandi Iceland 66°5N 17°30W 155 A9
Skjeberg Norway 59°12N 11°12E 164 E8
Skjern Denmark 55°57N 8°30E 163 J2
Skjold Norway 59°31N 5°34E 164 E2
Skjolden Norway 61°29N 7°36E 164 C4
Skjöldólfsstaðir Iceland 65°19N 15°17W 155 B11
Skjønhaug Norway 59°39N 11°19E 164 E8
Skobelev = Farghona
Uzbekistan 40°23N 71°19E 217 D8
Skoczów Poland 49°49N 18°45E 185 J5
Skodje Norway 62°30N 6°43E 164 B3
Škofja Loka Slovenia 46°9N 14°19E 199 B11
Skógafoss Iceland 63°32N 19°28W 155 D7
Skógarnes Iceland 64°46N 22°34W 155 C4
Skoghall Sweden 59°20N 13°30E 162 E7
Skogstorp Sweden 59°19N 16°29E 162 E10
Skoki Poland 52°40N 17°11E 185 F4
Skokie U.S.A. 42°2N 87°43W 119 A2
Skokie ➜ U.S.A. 42°3N 87°46W 119 A2
Skokie Heritage Museum
U.S.A. 42°2N 87°44W 119 A2
Skoklefall Norway 59°50N 10°40E 133 A2
Skole Ukraine 49°3N 23°30E 177 D12
Skollenborg Norway 59°38N 9°43E 164 E6
Sköndal Sweden 59°15N 18°6E 139 B2
Skopelos Greece 39°9N 23°47E 204 B5
Skopí Greece 35°11N 26°2E 207 E7
Skopin Russia 53°55N 39°32E 188 D10
Skopje Macedonia 42°1N 21°26E 202 D5
Skopje ✈ (SKP)
Macedonia 41°59N 21°29E 202 E5
Skoppum Norway 59°23N 10°26E 164 E7
Skórcz Poland 53°47N 18°30E 184 E5
Skorping Denmark 56°50N 9°53E 163 H3
Skotfoss Norway 59°12N 9°30E 164 E6
Skotterud Norway 60°0N 12°7E 164 D9
Skövde Sweden 58°24N 13°50E 163 F7
Skovlunde Denmark 55°42N 12°25E 118 A2
Skovorodino Russia 54°0N 124°0E 215 D13
Skovshoved Denmark 55°45N 12°35E 118 A3
Skowhegan U.S.A. 44°46N 69°43W 309 C19
Skradin Croatia 43°52N 15°53E 199 E12
Skrea Sweden 56°53N 12°34E 163 H6
Skreia Norway 60°40N 10°56E 164 D7
Skrim Norway 59°31N 9°38E 164 E6
Skrunda Latvia 56°41N 22°1E 184 B9
Skrwa ➜ Poland 52°35N 19°32E 185 F6
Skudeneshavn Norway 59°10N 5°10E 164 E2
Skuleskogen △ Sweden 63°6N 18°30E 162 A12
Skull Ireland 51°32N 9°34W 166 E2
Skultorp Sweden 58°24N 13°51E 163 F7
Skultuna Sweden 59°43N 16°25E 162 E10
Skunk ➜ U.S.A. 40°42N 91°7W 310 D5
Skuodas Lithuania 56°16N 21°33E 184 B8
Skurup Sweden 55°28N 13°30E 163 J7
Skuru Sweden 59°18N 18°12E 139 B3
Skutskär Sweden 60°37N 17°25E 162 D11
Skútustaðir Iceland 65°34N 17°2W 155 B9
Skvyra Ukraine 49°44N 29°40E 177 D15
Skwierzyna Poland 52°33N 15°30E 185 F2
Sky Dome = Rogers Centre
Toronto, Canada 141 c1
Sky Lake U.S.A. 28°27N 81°23W 133 B2
Skye U.K. 57°15N 6°10W 167 D2
Skykomish U.S.A. 47°42N 121°22W 304 C3
Skyland U.S.A. 33°53N 84°19W 113 A3
Skyring, Seno Chile 52°35S 72°0W 336 D3
Skyros = Skiros Greece 38°55N 24°34E 204 C6
Skyttorp Sweden 60°5N 17°44E 162 D11
Slade Green U.K. 51°27N 0°11E 125 B5
Slade Point Australia 21°4S 149°13E 280 b
Slade Pt. Australia 21°5S 149°13E 280 b
Slættaratindur Færoe Is. 62°18N 7°1W 160 E9
Slagharen, Boca Neth. Ant. 12°16N 68°24W 322 h
Slagelse Denmark 55°23N 11°19E 163 J5
Slamet Indonesia 7°16S 109°8E 235 D3
Slane Ireland 53°42N 6°33W 166 C5
Slaney ➜ Ireland 52°26N 6°33W 166 D5
Slangberge S. Africa 31°32S 20°48E 270 D3
Slănic Romania 45°14N 25°58E 183 E10
Slano Croatia 42°48N 17°53E 202 D1
Slantsy Russia 59°7N 28°5E 188 C5
Slaný Czech Rep. 50°13N 14°6E 180 A7
Śląsk Poland 51°0N 16°30E 176 C9
Śląskie ☐ Poland 50°30N 19°0E 185 H6
Slåtbaken Sweden 58°25N 16°45E 163 F10
Slate Is. Canada 48°40N 87°0W 298 C2
Slater U.S.A. 39°13N 93°4W 310 E3
Slatina Croatia 45°42N 17°45E 182 E2
Slatina Romania 44°28N 24°22E 183 F9
Slatina Timiș Romania 45°15N 22°17E 182 E7
Slatington U.S.A. 40°45N 75°37W 313 F9
Slaton U.S.A. 33°26N 101°39W 314 E4
Slave ➜ Canada 61°18N 113°39W 296 A6
Slave Coast W. Afr. 6°0N 2°30E 263 D5
Slave Lake Canada 55°17N 114°43W 296 B6
Slave Pt. Canada 61°11N 115°56W 296 A5
Slavgorod Russia 53°1N 78°37E 217 B9
Slavinja Serbia 43°9N 22°50E 202 C6
Slavkov u Brna
Czech Rep. 49°10N 16°52E 181 B9
Slavkovský Les ⌓
Czech Rep. 50°5N 12°44E 180 A5
Slavonija Europe 45°20N 17°40E 182 E2
Slavonski Brod Croatia 45°11N 18°1E 182 E3
Slavsk Russia 55°3N 21°41E 184 C8
Slavska Ukraine 48°51N 23°27E 183 B8
Slavskoye Russia 54°30N 20°27E 184 D7
Slavuta Ukraine 50°15N 27°2E 177 C14
Slavyanka Russia 42°53N 131°21E 220 C5
Slavyanovo Bulgaria 43°28N 24°52E 203 C8
Slavyansk = Slovyansk
Ukraine 48°55N 37°36E 189 H9
Slavyansk-na-Kubani
Russia 45°15N 38°11E 189 K10
Sława Poland 51°52N 16°2E 185 G3
Slawharad Belarus 53°27N 31°0E 177 B16
Sławno Poland 54°20N 16°41E 184 D3
Sławoborze Poland 53°55N 15°42E 184 E2
Sleaford U.K. 53°0N 0°24W 168 D7
Sleaford B. Australia 34°55S 135°45E 281 E2
Sleat, Sd. of U.K. 57°5N 5°47W 167 D3
Sleðbrjótur Iceland 65°34N 14°30W 155 B12
Sleeper Is. Canada 58°30N 81°0W 295 F15
Sleeping Bear Dunes ⌓
U.S.A. 44°50N 86°5W 308 C10
Sleepy Eye U.S.A. 44°18N 94°43W 308 C6
Sleetmute U.S.A. 61°42N 157°10W 303 F8
Sleman Indonesia 7°40S 110°20E 235 D4
Slemon L. Canada 63°13N 116°4W 296 A5
Slependen Norway 59°52N 10°30E 133 A2
Ślesin Poland 52°22N 18°14E 185 F5
Slide Mt. U.S.A. 42°0N 74°25W 313 E10
Slidell U.S.A. 30°17N 89°47W 315 F10
Slidre Norway 61°5N 8°58E 164 C5
Sliema Malta 35°55N 14°30E 206 F8
Slieve Aughty Ireland 53°4N 8°30W 166 C3
Slieve Bloom Ireland 53°4N 7°40W 166 C4
Slieve Donard U.K. 54°11N 5°55W 166 B6
Slieve Gamph Ireland 54°6N 9°0W 166 B3
Slieve Gullion U.K. 54°7N 6°26W 166 B5
Slieve League Ireland 54°40N 8°42W 166 B3
Slieve Mish Ireland 52°12N 9°50W 166 D2
Slievenamon Ireland 52°25N 7°34W 166 D4
Sligeach = Sligo Ireland 54°16N 8°28W 166 B3
Sligo Ireland 54°16N 8°28W 166 B3
Sligo Pa., U.S.A. 41°6N 79°29W 312 E5
Sligo ☐ Ireland 54°8N 8°42W 166 B3
Sligo B. Ireland 54°18N 8°40W 166 B3
Slipi Indonesia 6°11S 106°47E 122 B1
Slippery Rock U.S.A. 41°4N 80°3W 312 E4
Slite Sweden 57°42N 18°48E 163 G12
Sliteres ⌓ Latvia 57°41N 22°1E 184 A9
Sliven Bulgaria 42°42N 26°19E 203 D10
Slivenec Czech Rep. 50°1N 14°21E 135 B2
Slivnitsa Bulgaria 42°50N 23°0E 202 D7
Sljeme Croatia 45°57N 15°58E 199 C12
Sloan U.S.A. 35°57N 115°13W 307 K11
Sloansville U.S.A. 42°45N 74°22W 313 D10
Slobidka Ukraine 47°54N 29°21E 183 C14
Slobodskoy Russia 58°40N 50°6E 186 C9
Slobozia Moldova 46°45N 29°42E 183 D14
Slobozia Argeș, Romania 44°30N 25°14E 183 F10
Slobozia Ialomița,
Romania 44°34N 27°23E 183 F12
Slocan Canada 49°48N 117°28W 296 D5
Slocomb U.S.A. 31°7N 85°36W 316 D4
Slomikhino = Zhalpaqtal
Kazakhstan 49°42N 49°25E 190 F9
Słomniki Poland 50°16N 20°4E 185 H7
Slonim Belarus 53°4N 25°19E 177 B13
Slot, The = New Georgia Sound
Solomon Is. 8°0S 158°20E 287 L9
Sloten Neths. 52°21N 4°48E 112 A1
Sloterdijk Neths. 52°23N 4°51E 112 A1
Sloterpark Neths. 52°22N 4°49E 112 A1
Slottet Oslo, Norway 133 a1
Slough U.K. 51°30N 0°36W 169 F7
Slough ☐ U.K. 51°30N 0°36W 169 F7
Sloughhouse U.S.A. 38°26N 121°12W 306 G5
Slovak Rep. ■ Europe 48°30N 20°0E 181 C13
Slovakia = Slovak Rep. ■
Europe 48°30N 20°0E 181 C13
Slovakian Ore Mts. = Slovenské Rudohorie Slovak Rep. 48°45N 20°0E 181 C12
Slovenia ■ Europe 45°58N 14°30E 199 C11
Slovenija = Slovenia ■
Europe 45°58N 14°30E 199 C11
Slovenj Gradec Slovenia 46°31N 15°5E 199 B12
Slovenska = Slovak Rep. ■
Europe 48°30N 20°0E 181 C13
Slovenska Bistrica
Slovenia 46°24N 15°35E 199 B12
Slovenské Konjice
Slovenia 46°20N 15°28E 199 B12
Slovenské Rudohorie
Slovak Rep. 48°45N 20°0E 181 C12
Slovenský Raj △
Slovak Rep. 48°53N 20°25E 181 C13
Slovyansk Ukraine 48°55N 37°36E 189 H9
Słowiński △ Poland 54°43N 17°26E 184 D4
Słubice Poland 52°22N 14°35E 185 F1
Sluch ➜ Ukraine 51°37N 26°38E 177 C14
Sluhy Czech Rep. 50°11N 14°33E 135 A3
Sluis Neths. 51°18N 3°23E 170 C3
Slŭnchev Bryag
Bulgaria 42°40N 27°41E 203 D11
Slunj Croatia 45°6N 15°33E 199 C12
Słupca Poland 52°15N 17°52E 185 F4
Słupia ➜ Poland 54°35N 16°51E 184 D3
Słupsk Poland 54°30N 17°3E 184 D4
Slurry S. Africa 25°49S 25°42E 270 C4
Slutsk = Pavlovsk Russia 50°26N 40°5E 190 E5
Slutsk Belarus 53°2N 27°31E 177 B14
Służew Poland 52°10N 21°1E 142 B2
Służewiec Poland 52°10N 21°2E 142 B2
Slyne Hd. Ireland 53°25N 10°10W 166 C1
Slyudyanka Russia 51°40N 103°40E 215 D11
Smaalenene = Østfold ☐
Norway 59°25N 11°25E 164 E8
Småland Sweden 57°15N 15°25E 163 G9
Smålandsfarvandet
Denmark 55°10N 11°20E 163 J5
Smålandsstenar Sweden 57°10N 13°25E 163 G7
Smalldeel = Theunissen
S. Africa 28°26S 26°43E 270 C4
Smalltree L. Canada 61°0N 105°0W 297 A8
Smallwood Res. Canada 54°5N 64°30W 299 B7
Smara W. Sahara 26°48N 11°41W 260 C2
Smarhon Belarus 54°20N 26°24E 177 A14
Šmarje Slovenia 46°15N 15°34E 199 B12
Smartt Syndicate Dam
S. Africa 30°45S 23°10E 270 D3
Smartville U.S.A. 39°13N 121°18W 306 F5
Smeaton Canada 53°30N 104°49W 297 C8
Smedby Sweden 56°41N 16°13E 163 H10
Smederevo Serbia 44°40N 20°57E 202 B4
Smederevska Palanka
Serbia 44°22N 20°58E 202 B4
Smedjebacken Sweden 60°8N 15°25E 162 D9
Smela = Smila Ukraine 49°15N 31°58E 189 H6
Smerwick Harbour
Ireland 52°12N 10°23W 166 D1
Smethport U.S.A. 41°49N 78°27W 312 E6
Smíchov Czech Rep. 50°4N 14°23E 135 B2
Smidovich Russia 48°36N 133°49E 215 E14
Śmigiel Poland 52°1N 16°32E 185 F3
Smila Ukraine 49°15N 31°58E 189 H6
Smilyan Bulgaria 41°29N 24°46E 203 E8
Smith Canada 55°10N 114°0W 296 B6
Smith B. U.S.A. 70°30N 154°20W 303 A9
Smith Center U.S.A. 39°47N 98°47W 308 F4
Smith Forest Preserve
U.S.A. 41°59N 87°45W 119 B2
Smith I. Nunavut,
Canada 60°45N 78°25W 295 E16
Smith I. India 13°20N 93°4E 245 H11
Smith Islands △ Australia 20°40S 149°9E 280 b
Smith River ⌓ U.S.A. 41°55N 124°0W 304 F1
Smith Sd. N. Amer. 78°25N 74°0W 154 B3
Smithburne ➜ Australia 17°3S 140°57E 280 B3
Smithers Canada 54°45N 127°10W 296 C3
Smithfield Free State,
S. Africa 30°9S 26°30E 271 D4
Smithfield N.C., U.S.A. 35°31N 78°21W 315 D15
Smithfield Utah, U.S.A. 41°50N 111°50W 304 F8
Smiths U.S.A. 32°32N 85°6W 316 C4
Smiths Falls Canada 44°55N 76°0W 313 B9
Smithsonian Institution
Washington, D.C., U.S.A. 143 b2
Smithton Australia 40°53S 145°6E 281 G4
Smithville Ont., Canada 43°6N 79°33W 312 C5
Smithville Ga., U.S.A. 31°54N 84°15W 316 D5
Smithville Mo., U.S.A. 39°23N 94°35W 310 E2
Smithville Tex., U.S.A. 30°1N 97°10W 314 F6
Smoke Creek Desert
U.S.A. 40°30N 119°40W 304 F4
Smoky ➜ Canada 56°10N 117°21W 296 B5
Smoky Bay Australia 32°22S 134°13E 281 E1
Smoky Hill ➜ U.S.A. 39°4N 96°48W 308 F5
Smoky Hills U.S.A. 39°15N 99°30W 308 F4
Smoky Lake Canada 54°10N 112°30W 296 C6
Smøla Norway 63°23N 8°3E 164 A5
Smolensk Russia 54°45N 32°5E 188 E7
Smolensk ☐ Russia 55°20N 33°0E 188 E7
Smolikas, Oros Greece 40°9N 20°58E 202 F4
Smolník Slovak Rep. 48°43N 20°44E 181 C13
Smolny Russia 59°56N 30°25E 137 B2
Smolny Cathedral Russia 59°56N 30°24E 137 B2
Smolyan Bulgaria 41°36N 24°38E 203 E8
Smooth Rock Falls
Canada 49°17N 81°37W 298 C3
Smoothstone L. Canada 54°40N 106°50W 297 C7
Smorgon = Smarhon
Belarus 54°20N 26°24E 177 A14
Smotrych Ukraine 48°57N 26°33E 183 B11
Smotrych ➜ Ukraine 48°34N 26°39E 183 B11
Smulți Romania 45°57N 27°44E 183 E12
Smyadovo Bulgaria 43°2N 27°1E 203 C11
Smygehamn Sweden 55°21N 13°22E 163 J7
Smyrna = İzmir Turkey 38°25N 27°8E 205 C9
Smyrna Del., U.S.A. 39°18N 75°36W 309 F16
Smyrna Ga., U.S.A. 33°53N 84°31W 316 B5
Snæfell Iceland 64°48N 15°34W 155 C11
Snaefell I. of Man 54°16N 4°27W 168 C3
Snæfellsjökull Iceland 64°49N 23°46W 155 C3
Snæfellsnessýsla ☐ Iceland 65°0N 23°0W 155 C3
Snake ➜ U.S.A. 46°12N 119°2W 304 C4
Snake Creek Canal
U.S.A. 25°57N 80°19W 128 A2
Snake I. Australia 38°47S 146°33E 283 E7
Snake Pt. Anguilla 18°17N 62°58W 322 a
Snake Range U.S.A. 39°0N 114°20W 304 G6
Snake River Plain U.S.A. 42°50N 114°0W 304 E7
Snakeden Branch ➜
U.S.A. 38°55N 77°18W 143 B1
Snarøya Norway 59°52N 10°33E 133 A2
Snasahögarna Sweden 63°13N 12°21E 162 A6
Snåsavatnet Norway 64°12N 12°0E 160 D15
Snättringe Sweden 59°15N 17°58E 139 B1
Snedsted Denmark 56°55N 8°32E 163 H2
Sneek Neths. 53°2N 5°40E 170 A5
Sneem Ireland 51°50N 9°54W 166 E2
Sneeuberge S. Africa 31°46S 24°20E 270 D3
Snegurovka = Tetiyev
Ukraine 49°22N 29°38E 177 D15
Snejbjerg Denmark 56°8N 8°54E 163 H2
Snelling Calif., U.S.A. 37°31N 120°26W 306 H6
Snelling S.C., U.S.A. 33°15N 81°27W 316 B8
Snells Beach N.Z. 36°25S 174°44E 284 C3
Snezhnoye Ukraine 48°0N 38°58E 189 J10
Sněžka Europe 50°41N 15°50E 185 A8
Snežnik Slovenia 45°36N 14°35E 199 C11
Śniadowo Poland 53°2N 22°0E 185 E8
Sniardwy, Jezioro Poland 53°48N 21°50E 184 E8
Śnieżka Europe 50°44N 15°44E 180 A8
Snigirevka = Snihurivka
Ukraine 47°2N 32°49E 189 J7
Snihurivka Ukraine 47°2N 32°49E 189 J7
Snillfjord Norway 63°24N 9°30E 164 A6
Snina Slovak Rep. 48°58N 22°9E 181 C15
Snizort, L. U.K. 57°33N 6°28W 167 D2
Snøhetta Norway 62°19N 9°16E 164 B6
Snohomish U.S.A. 47°55N 122°6W 306 C4
Snoqualmie Pass
U.S.A. 47°25N 121°25W 306 C5
Snoul Cambodia 12°4N 106°26E 237 F6
Snover U.S.A. 43°27N 82°58W 312 C2
Snovsk = Shchors
Ukraine 51°48N 31°56E 189 G6
Snow Hill U.S.A. 38°11N 75°24W 309 F16
Snow Lake Canada 54°52N 100°3W 297 C8
Snow Mt. Calif., U.S.A. 39°23N 122°45W 306 F4
Snow Mt. Maine, U.S.A. 45°18N 70°48W 313 A14
Snow Shoe U.S.A. 41°2N 77°57W 312 E7
Snowbird L. Canada 60°45N 103°0W 297 A8
Snowdon U.K. 53°4N 4°5W 168 D3
Snowdonia △ U.K. 53°7N 3°59W 168 D4
Snowdoun U.S.A. 32°15N 86°18W 316 C3
Snowdrift = Łutsel K'e
Canada 62°24N 110°44W 297 A6
Snowdrift ➜ Canada 62°24N 110°44W 297 A6
Snowflake U.S.A. 34°30N 110°5W 305 J8
Snowshoe Pk. U.S.A. 48°13N 115°41W 304 B6
Snowtown Australia 33°46S 138°14E 282 B3
Snowville U.S.A. 41°58N 112°43W 304 F7
Snowy ➜ Australia 37°46S 148°30E 283 D8
Snowy Mt. U.S.A. 43°42N 74°23W 313 C10
Snowy Mts. Australia 36°30S 148°20E 283 D8
Snowy River △
Australia 37°15S 147°29E 283 D7
Snug Corner Bahamas 22°33N 73°52W 321 B5
Snug Harbour Canada 45°22N 80°17W 312 A4
Snyatyn Ukraine 48°27N 25°38E 183 B10
Snyder Okla., U.S.A. 34°40N 98°57W 314 D5
Snyder Tex., U.S.A. 32°44N 100°55W 314 E4
Soacha Colombia 4°35N 74°13W 328 C3
Soahanina Madag. 18°42S 44°13E 272 B1
Soalala Madag. 16°6S 45°20E 272 B2
Soaloka Madag. 18°32S 45°15E 272 B2
Soamanonga Madag. 23°52S 44°47E 272 C1
Soan ➜ Pakistan 33°1N 71°44E 242 C4
Soanierana-Ivongo
Madag. 16°55S 49°35E 272 B2
Soanindraniny Madag. 19°54S 47°14E 272 B2
Șoarș Romania 45°56N 24°55E 183 E9
Soavina Madag. 20°23S 46°56E 272 C2
Soavinandriana Madag. 19°9S 46°45E 272 B2
Sob ➜ Ukraine 48°40N 29°15E 183 B14
Soba Nigeria 10°58N 8°4E 263 C6
Sobaeksan △ S. Korea 36°50N 128°25E 224 D4
Sobat, Nahr ➜ Sudan 9°22N 31°33E 257 F3
Soběslav Czech Rep. 49°16N 14°45E 180 B7
Sobhapur India 22°47N 78°17E 242 H8
Sobinka Russia 56°0N 40°0E 188 E11
Sobo-Yama Japan 32°51N 131°22E 222 E3
Søborg Denmark 55°43N 12°29E 118 A2
Sobótka Poland 50°54N 16°44E 185 H3
Sobra Croatia 42°44N 17°34E 199 F14
Sobradinho, Represa de
Brazil 9°30S 42°0W 332 C3
Sobral Brazil 3°50S 40°20W 332 B3
Sobrance Slovak Rep. 48°45N 22°11E 181 C15
Sobreda Portugal 38°39N 9°11W 126 B1
Sobreira Formosa
Portugal 39°46N 7°51W 194 F3
Soc Giang Vietnam 22°54N 106°1E 228 F6
Soc Trang Vietnam 9°37N 105°50E 237 H5
Soča ➜ Europe 46°20N 13°40E 180 E6
Socastee U.S.A. 33°41N 78°59W 315 E15
Sochaczew Poland 52°15N 20°13E 185 F7
Soch'e = Shache China 38°20N 77°10E 217 E9
Sochi Russia 43°35N 39°40E 191 J4
Sochos Greece 40°48N 23°22E 202 F7
Social Circle U.S.A. 33°39N 83°43W 316 B6
Société, Îs. de la
French Polynesia 17°0S 151°0W 289 f
Society Hill U.S.A. 32°26N 85°27W 316 C4
Society Is. = Société, Îs. de la
French Polynesia 17°0S 151°0W 289 f
Socompa, Portezuelo de
Chile 24°27S 68°18W 334 A2
Socorro = Fronteiras
Brazil 7°5S 40°37W 332 C3
Socorro Colombia 6°29N 73°16W 328 B3
Socorro Phil. 9°37N 125°58E 233 G5
Socorro N. Mex., U.S.A. 34°4N 106°54W 305 J10
Socorro Tex., U.S.A. 31°39N 106°18W 314 F1
Socorro, I. Mexico 18°45N 110°58W 318 D2
Socotra Yemen 12°30N 54°0E 249 D6
Socovos Spain 38°20N 1°58W 197 G3
Socuéllamos Spain 39°16N 2°47W 197 F2
Soda L. U.S.A. 35°10N 116°4W 305 J5
Soda Plains India 35°30N 79°0E 243 B8
Soda Springs U.S.A. 42°39N 111°36W 304 E8
Sodankylä Finland 67°29N 26°40E 160 C22
Soddy-Daisy U.S.A. 35°17N 85°10W 315 D12
Söderala Sweden 61°17N 16°55E 162 C10
Söderåsen △ Sweden 56°2N 13°13E 163 H7
Söderbärke Sweden 60°5N 15°33E 162 D9
Söderby Sweden 59°24N 18°12E 139 A3
Söderfors Sweden 60°23N 17°25E 162 D11
Söderhamn Sweden 61°18N 17°10E 162 C11
Söderköping Sweden 58°31N 16°20E 163 F10
Södermalm Sweden 59°18N 18°4E 139 B2
Södermanland Sweden 58°56N 16°55E 161 G17
Södermanlands län ☐
Sweden 59°10N 16°30E 162 E10
Södertälje Sweden 59°12N 17°39E 162 E11
Sodiri Sudan 14°27N 29°0E 257 E2
Sodo Ethiopia 7°0N 37°41E 257 F4
Sodpur India 22°42N 88°24E 124 A2
Södra Dellen Sweden 61°48N 16°43E 162 C10
Södra Finnskoga Sweden 60°42N 12°34E 162 D6
Södra Sandby Sweden 55°43N 13°21E 163 J7
Södra Ulvön Sweden 62°59N 18°38E 162 B12
Södra Vi Sweden 57°45N 15°45E 163 G9
Sodražica Slovenia 45°45N 14°39E 199 C11
Sodus U.S.A. 43°14N 77°4W 312 C7
Sodwana Bay △ S. Africa 27°35S 32°43E 271 C5
Soe Indonesia 9°52S 124°17E 278 A3
Soekmekaar = Morebeng
S. Africa 23°30S 29°55E 271 B4
Soest Nordrhein-Westfalen,
Germany 51°34N 8°7E 178 D4
Soest Neths. 52°9N 5°19E 170 B5
Soeurs, Î. des Canada 45°27N 73°32W 130 B2
Sofades Greece 39°20N 22°4E 204 B4
Sofaia Guadeloupe 16°17N 61°43W 322 e
Sofala ☐ Mozam. 19°30S 34°30E 271 A5
Sofara Mali 13°59N 4°9W 262 C4
Sofia = Sofiya Bulgaria 42°45N 23°20E 202 D7
Sofia ➜ Madag. 15°27S 47°23E 272 B2
Sofievka Ukraine 48°6N 33°55E 189 H7
Sofiko Greece 37°47N 23°3E 204 D5
Sofiya Bulgaria 42°45N 23°20E 202 D7
Sofiya ☐ Bulgaria 42°15N 23°20E 202 D7
Sofiya ✈ (SOF) Bulgaria 42°46N 23°28E 202 D7
Sofiyevka = Volnansk
Ukraine 48°2N 35°29E 189 H8
Sofrana Greece 36°5N 26°24E 205 E8
Sōfu-Gan Japan 29°49N 140°21E 221 K10
Sogakofe Ghana 6°2N 0°39E 263 D5
Sogamoso Colombia 5°43N 72°56W 328 B3
Sogār Iran 25°53N 58°6E 247 E8
Sögel Germany 52°50N 7°31E 178 C3
Sogeri Papua N. G. 9°26S 147°35E 286 E4
Sogn og Fjordane ☐
Norway 61°40N 6°45E 164 C3
Sogndalsfjøra Norway 61°14N 7°5E 164 C4
Søgne Norway 58°5N 7°48E 164 F4
Sognefjorden Norway 61°10N 5°50E 164 C2
Sognsvatn Norway 59°58N 10°43E 133 A3
Sogod Phil. 10°28N 124°59E 233 F5
Söğüt Bilecik, Turkey 40°2N 30°11E 205 A12
Söğüt Burdur, Turkey 37°2N 29°50E 205 D11
Söğüt Dağı Turkey 37°50N 29°55E 205 D11
Söğütköy Turkey 36°40N 28°8E 205 E10
Soh Iran 33°26N 51°27E 247 C6
Sohâg Egypt 26°33N 31°43E 256 B3
Sohagpur India 22°42N 78°12E 242 H8
Sohano Papua N. G. 5°22S 154°37E 286 C8
Sohela India 21°18N 83°24E 244 D6
Soheuksando S. Korea 34°4N 125°7E 224 E2
Sohm Abyssal Plain
Atl. Oc. 36°0N 55°0W 152 C6
Soho London, U.K. 125 b3
Soho New York, U.S.A. 132 e1
Soignes, Forêt de Belgium 50°47N 4°25E 116 B2
Soignies Belgium 50°35N 4°5E 170 D4
Soin Burkina Faso 12°47N 3°50W 262 C4
Soira Eritrea 14°45N 39°30E 257 E4
Soissons France 49°25N 3°19E 173 C10
Sōja Japan 34°40N 133°45E 222 C5
Sojat India 25°55N 73°45E 242 G5
Sok ➜ Russia 53°24N 50°8E 190 D10
Sok Kwu Wan China 22°12N 114°7E 122 B1
Sokal Ukraine 50°31N 24°15E 177 C13
Sokcho S. Korea 38°12N 128°36E 224 C4
Söke Turkey 37°48N 27°28E 205 D9
Sokelo
Dem. Rep. of the Congo 9°55S 24°36E 265 D4
Sokhumi Georgia 43°0N 41°0E 191 J5
Sokki, Oued In ➜ Algeria 29°30N 3°42E 261 C5
Sokna Norway 60°16N 9°58E 164 D6
Soknedal Norway 62°57N 10°13E 164 B7
Soko Banja Serbia 43°40N 21°51E 202 C5
Soko Is. China 22°10N 113°54E 219 G10
Sokodé Togo 9°0N 1°11E 263 D5
Sokol Russia 59°30N 40°5E 188 C11
Sokolac Bos.-H. 43°56N 18°48E 182 G3
Sokółka Poland 53°25N 23°30E 184 E10
Sokolniki Russia 55°47N 37°40E 129 B4
Sokolniki Park Russia 55°48N 37°40E 129 A4
Sokolo Ségou, Mali 14°53N 6°8W 262 C3
Sokolo Sikasso, Mali 10°52N 6°59W 262 C3
Sokolov Czech Rep. 50°12N 12°40E 180 A5
Sokołów Poland 52°9N 20°51E 142 C1
Sokołów Małpolski Poland 50°12N 22°7E 185 H9
Sokołów Podlaski Poland 52°25N 22°15E 185 F9
Sokoły Poland 52°59N 22°42E 185 F9
Sokoto Nigeria 13°2N 5°16E 263 C6
Sokoto ☐ Nigeria 12°30N 6°0E 263 C6
Sokoto ➜ Nigeria 11°20N 4°10E 263 C5
Sokyrnytsya Ukraine 48°27N 23°20E 183 B8
Sokyryany Ukraine 48°27N 27°25E 183 B12
Sol Iletsk Russia 51°10N 55°0E 186 D10
Sola Rogaland, Norway 58°53N 5°36E 164 F2
Sola Vanuatu 13°51S 167°33E 287 C6
Sola ➜ Poland 50°4N 19°15E 185 H6
Solai Kenya 0°2N 36°12E 268 B4
Solalinden Germany 48°5N 11°42E 131 B3
Solan India 30°55N 77°7E 242 D7
Solana Phil. 17°39N 121°41E 232 C3
Solana Beach U.S.A. 32°58N 117°16W 307 N9
Solander I. N.Z. 46°34S 166°54E 285 G1
Solano Phil. 16°31N 121°15E 232 C3
Solapur India 17°43N 75°56E 244 F2
Solca Romania 47°40N 25°50E 183 C10
Solda Gölü Turkey 37°33N 29°42E 205 D11
Soldănești Moldova 47°49N 28°48E 183 C13
Soldeu Andorra 42°35N 1°40E 196 C6
Soldier Field Chicago, U.S.A. 119 e3
Soldier Pt. Antigua & B. 17°2N 61°41W 322 b
Soldin = Myślibórz
Poland 52°55N 14°50E 185 F1
Soldotna U.S.A. 60°29N 151°3W 303 F10
Soléa Cyprus 35°5N 33°4E 207 E9
Solec Kujawski Poland 53°5N 18°14E 185 E5
Soledad Colombia 10°55N 74°46W 328 A3
Soledad Calif., U.S.A. 36°26N 121°20W 306 J5
Soledad Venezuela 8°10N 63°34W 329 B5
Solen Norway 61°53N 11°31E 164 C8
Solent, The U.K. 50°45N 1°25W 169 G6
Solenzara France 41°53N 9°23E 175 G13
Solesmes France 50°10N 3°30E 173 B10
Solfonntaggen Norway 60°2N 6°57E 164 D3
Solhan Turkey 38°57N 41°3E 213 C9
Solheim Norway 60°53N 5°27E 164 D2
Soligalich Russia 59°5N 42°10E 186 C7
Soligorsk = Salihorsk
Belarus 52°51N 27°27E 177 B14
Solihull U.K. 52°26N 1°47W 169 E6
Solikamsk Russia 59°38N 56°50E 186 C10
Solila Madag. 21°25S 46°37E 272 C2
Solimões = Amazonas ➜
S. Amer. 0°5S 50°0W 329 D8
Solin Croatia 43°33N 16°30E 199 E13
Solingen Germany 51°10N 7°5E 178 D3
Söll Austria 47°30N 12°11E 179 H8
Sollebrunn Sweden 58°8N 12°32E 163 F6
Sollefteå Sweden 63°12N 17°20E 162 A11
Sollentuna Sweden 59°25N 17°56E 139 A1
Sóller Spain 39°46N 2°43E 206 B3
Sollerön Sweden 60°55N 14°37E 162 D8
Solling Germany 51°42N 9°38E 178 D5
Solling-Vogler ⌓ Germany 51°45N 9°32E 178 D5
Solln Germany 48°4N 11°31E 131 B2
Sollsvika Norway 60°26N 4°58E 164 D1
Solna Sweden 59°21N 17°59E 139 A1
Solnechnogorsk Russia 56°10N 36°57E 188 D9
Solntsevo Russia 55°39N 37°24E 129 C2
Solo ➜ Indonesia 6°47S 112°22E 231 G15
Solofra Italy 40°50N 14°51E 201 B7
Sologne France 47°40N 1°45E 173 E8
Solok Indonesia 0°45S 100°40E 234 C2
Sololá Guatemala 14°49N 91°10W 320 D1
Sololo Kenya 3°33N 38°39E 268 B4
Solomon, N. Fork ➜
U.S.A. 39°29N 98°26W 308 F4
Solomon, S. Fork ➜
U.S.A. 39°25N 99°12W 308 F4
Solomon Is. Papua N. G. 6°0S 155°0E 286 D8
Solomon Is. ■ Pac. Oc. 6°0S 155°0E 287 L8
Solomon Rise Pac. Oc. 1°0N 157°0E 288 G7
Solomon Sea Papua N. G. 7°0S 150°0E 286 D6
Solon China 46°32N 121°10E 219 B7
Solon Springs U.S.A. 46°22N 91°49W 308 B8
Solonópole Brazil 5°44S 39°1W 332 C4
Solor Indonesia 8°27S 123°0E 231 F6
Solotcha Russia 54°48N 39°53E 188 E10
Solothurn Switz. 47°13N 7°32E 179 H3
Solothurn ☐ Switz. 47°18N 7°40E 179 H3
Solotvyn Ukraine 48°42N 24°25E 183 B9
Solsona Spain 42°0N 1°31E 196 C6
Solt Hungary 46°45N 19°1E 182 D4
Solta Croatia 43°24N 16°15E 199 E13
Soltānābād Khorāsān, Iran 34°13N 59°58E 247 C8
Soltānābād Khorāsān, Iran 36°29N 58°5E 247 B8
Soltau Germany 52°59N 9°50E 178 C5
Soltsy Russia 58°10N 30°30E 188 C6
Soltüstik Qazaqstan ☐
Kazakhstan 54°0N 70°0E 217 B8
Solund Norway 61°5N 4°50E 164 C1
Solunska Glava
Macedonia 41°44N 21°31E 202 E5
Solvang U.S.A. 34°36N 120°8W 307 L6
Solvay U.S.A. 43°3N 76°13W 313 C8
Sölvesborg Sweden 56°5N 14°35E 163 H8
Solvychegodsk Russia 61°21N 46°56E 186 B8
Solway Firth U.K. 54°49N 3°35W 168 C4
Solwezi Zambia 12°11S 26°21E 269 E2
Sōma Japan 37°40N 140°50E 220 F10
Soma Turkey 39°10N 27°35E 205 B9
Somabhula Zimbabwe 19°42S 29°40E 271 A4
Somali Pen. Africa 7°0N 46°0E 254 F8
Somali Rep. ■ Africa 7°0N 47°0E 267 C6
Somalia = Somali Rep. ■
Africa 7°0N 47°0E 267 C6
Somaliland ☐ Somali Rep. 9°0N 46°0E 267 C6
Sombe Dzong Bhutan 27°13N 89°8E 241 B2
Somberon France 47°20N 4°40E 173 E11
Sombo Angola 8°42S 20°59E 265 D4
Sombor Serbia 45°46N 19°9E 182 E4
Sombra Canada 42°43N 82°29W 312 D2
Sombrerete Mexico 23°38N 103°39W 318 C4
Sombrero Anguilla 18°37N 63°30W 321 C7
Sombrero Channel India 7°41N 93°35E 245 L11
Șomcuta Mare Romania 47°31N 23°28E 183 C8
Somdari India 25°47N 72°38E 242 G5
Someido ⌓ Spain 43°5N 6°11W 194 B4
Somers U.S.A. 48°5N 114°13W 304 B6
Somerset Bermuda 32°17N 64°52W 153 a
Somerset Ky., U.S.A. 37°5N 84°36W 309 G11
Somerset Mass., U.S.A. 41°47N 71°8W 313 E13
Somerset Md., U.S.A. 38°57N 77°5W 143 B3
Somerset Pa., U.S.A. 40°1N 79°5W 312 F5
Somerset ☐ U.K. 51°9N 3°0W 169 F5
Somerset East S. Africa 32°42S 25°35E 270 D4
Somerset I. Bermuda 32°17N 64°52W 153 a
Somerset I. Nunavut,
Canada 73°30N 93°0W 294 C13
Somerset West S. Africa 34°8S 18°50E 270 D2
Somersworth U.S.A. 43°16N 70°52W 313 C14
Somerton U.S.A. 32°36N 114°43W 305 K6
Somerville Mass., U.S.A. 42°22N 71°5W 116 A2
Somerville N.J., U.S.A. 40°35N 74°38W 313 F10
Someș ➜ Romania 47°49N 22°43E 182 C7
Somes I. N.Z. 41°15S 174°52E 143 B2
Someșul Mare ➜
Romania 47°9N 23°55E 183 C8
Somme ☐ France 49°57N 2°20E 173 C9
Somme ➜ France 50°11N 1°38E 173 B8
Somme, B. de la France 50°14N 1°33E 172 B8
Sommen Jönköping,
Sweden 58°12N 14°58E 163 F8
Sommen Östergötland,
Sweden 58°0N 15°15E 163 F9
Sommepy-Tahure France 49°15N 4°31E 173 C11
Sömmerda Germany 51°9N 11°7E 178 D7
Sommerfeld = Lubsko
Poland 51°45N 14°57E 185 G1
Sommesous France 48°44N 4°12E 173 D11
Sommières France 43°47N 4°6E 175 E8
Somnath India 20°53N 70°22E 242 J4
Somogy ☐ Hungary 46°19N 17°30E 182 D2
Somogyszob Hungary 46°18N 17°20E 182 D2
Somosomo Fiji 16°47S 179°58W 287 A3
Somosomo Str. Fiji 16°0S 180°0E 287 A3
Somoto Nic. 13°28N 86°37W 320 D2
Sompolno Poland 52°26N 18°30E 185 F5
Somport, Tunnel de Spain 42°48N 0°31W 196 C4
Somuncurá, Meseta de
Argentina 41°30S 67°0W 336 B3

Somvarpet *India* 12°36N 75°52E **245** H2
Son *Norway* 59°32N 10°42E **164** E7
Son ➔ *India* 25°42N 84°52E **243** G11
Son Ha *Vietnam* 15°3N 108°34E **236** E7
Son Hoa *Vietnam* 13°2N 108°58E **236** F7
Son La *Vietnam* 21°20N 103°50E **228** G4
Son Morrell *Spain* 39°44N 3°20E **206** B4
Son Rapinya *Spain* 39°35N 2°37E **206** B3
Son Sardina *Spain* 39°37N 2°40E **206** B3
Son Serra *Spain* 39°43N 3°13E **206** B4
Son Servera *Spain* 39°37N 3°21E **206** B4
Son Tay *Vietnam* 21°8N 105°30E **228** G5
Soná *Panama* 8°0N 81°20W **320** E3
Sonamarg *India* 34°18N 75°21E **243** B6
Sonamukhi *India* 23°18N 87°27E **243** H12
Sonamura *India* 23°29N 91°15E **241** D3
Sonar ➔ *India* 24°24N 79°56E **243** G8
Sonari *India* 18°54N 72°59E **130** B2
Sonch'ŏn *N. Korea* 39°48N 124°55E **224** C2
Sondags ➔ *S. Africa* 33°44S 25°51E **270** D4
Sóndalo *Italy* 46°20N 10°19E **198** B7
Sondar *India* 33°28N 75°56E **243** C6
Søndeled *Norway* 58°46N 9°3E **164** F6
Sønder Felding *Denmark* 55°57N 8°47E **163** J2
Sønder Omme *Denmark* 55°50N 8°54E **163** J2
Sønderborg *Denmark* 54°55N 9°49E **163** K3
Sondershausen *Germany* 51°22N 10°51E **178** D6
Sønderso *Denmark* 55°46N 12°21E **118** A2
Søndre Bergenhaus = Hordaland □ *Norway* 60°25N 6°15E **164** D3
Søndre Strømfjord = Kangerlussuaq *Greenland* 66°59N 50°40W **154** D5
Søndre Trøndhjem = Sør-Trøndelag □ *Norway* 63°0N 11°0E **164** A7
Sóndrio *Italy* 46°10N 9°52E **198** B6
Sondur ➔ *India* 20°40N 82°1E **244** D6
Sone *Mozam.* 17°23S 34°55E **269** F3
Sonepur *India* 20°55N 83°50E **244** D6
Sonfim *Brazil* 6°0S 67°52W **330** B4
Song *Nigeria* 9°49N 12°39E **263** D7
Song *Thailand* 18°28N 100°11E **236** C3
Song Cau *Vietnam* 13°27N 109°18E **236** F7
Song Hong ➔ *Vietnam* 22°0N 104°0E **228** F5
Song-Köl *Kyrgyzstan* 41°50N 75°12E **217** D9
Song Qingling, Former Residence of *Beijing, China* **114** a2
Song Xian *China* 34°12N 112°8E **226** G7
Songadh *India* 21°9N 73°33E **244** D1
Songan *Indonesia* 8°13S 115°24E **231** J18
Songavatnet *Norway* 59°52N 7°32E **164** E4
Songea *Tanzania* 10°40S 35°40E **269** E4
Songeons *France* 49°32N 1°50E **173** C8
Sŏnggan *N. Korea* 40°47N 126°34E **224** B3
Songgang *China* 22°46N 113°50E **219** F10
Songhua Hu *China* 43°35N 126°50E **227** C14
Songhua Jiang ➔ *China* 47°45N 132°30E **219** B8
Songimvelo ⌂ *S. Africa* 25°50S 31°2E **271** C5
Songjiang *Jilin, China* 42°34N 128°20E **224** A4
Songjiang *Shanghai, China* 31°1N 121°12E **229** B13
Songjianghe *China* 42°10N 127°29E **224** A3
Sŏngjin = Kimch'aek *N. Korea* 40°40N 129°10E **224** D4
Songkan *China* 28°35N 106°52E **228** C6
Songkhla *Thailand* 7°13N 100°37E **237** J3
Songming *China* 25°12N 103°2E **228** E4
Songnim *N. Korea* 38°45N 125°39E **224** C2
Songnisan ⌂ *S. Korea* 36°28N 127°45E **224** D3
Songo *Angola* 7°22S 14°51E **265** D2
Songo *Mozam.* 15°34S 32°38E **271** A5
Songo *Sudan* 9°47N 24°21E **259** G4
Songololo = Mbanza Ngungu *Dem. Rep. of the Congo* 5°12S 14°53E **265** D2
Songololo *Dem. Rep. of the Congo* 5°42S 14°2E **265** D2
Songpa *S. Korea* 37°30N 127°7E **137** B2
Songpan *China* 32°40N 103°30E **228** A4
Songtao *China* 28°11N 109°10E **228** C7
Songwe *Dem. Rep. of the Congo* 3°20S 26°16E **268** C2
Songwe ➔ *Africa* 9°44S 33°58E **269** D3
Songxi *China* 27°31N 118°44E **229** D12
Songzi *China* 30°12N 111°45E **229** B8
Sonhat *India* 23°29N 82°31E **243** H10
Sonid Youqi *China* 42°45N 112°48E **226** C7
Sonipat *India* 29°0N 77°5E **242** E7
Sonkach *India* 22°59N 76°21E **242** H7
Sonkovo *Russia* 57°50N 37°5E **188** D9
Sonmiani *Pakistan* 25°25N 66°40E **242** G2
Sonmiani B. *Pakistan* 25°15N 66°30E **242** G2
Sonnino *Italy* 41°25N 13°14E **200** A6
Sono ➔ *Minas Gerais, Brazil* 17°2S 45°32W **333** E2
Sono ➔ *Tocantins, Brazil* 9°58S 48°11W **332** C2
Sonobe *Japan* 35°6N 135°28E **223** B7
Sonoma *U.S.A.* 38°18N 122°28W **306** G4
Sonora *Calif., U.S.A.* 37°59N 120°23W **306** H6
Sonora *Tex., U.S.A.* 30°34N 100°39W **314** F4
Sonora □ *Mexico* 29°20N 110°40W **318** B2
Sonora ➔ *Mexico* 29°5N 110°55W **318** B2
Sonoran Desert *U.S.A.* 33°40N 113°30W **307** L12
Sonoyta *Mexico* 31°51N 112°50W **318** A2
Sonqor *Iran* 34°47N 47°36E **212** E12
Sonseca *Spain* 39°42N 3°57W **195** F7
Sonsón *Colombia* 5°43N 75°18W **328** B2
Sonsonate *El Salv.* 13°43N 89°44W **320** D2
Sonstorp *Sweden* 58°44N 15°38E **163** F9
Sonthofen *Germany* 47°30N 10°16E **179** H6
Sony Picture Studio *U.S.A.* 34°1N 118°4W **126** B2
Soochow = Suzhou *China* 31°19N 120°38E **229** B13
Sooke *Canada* 48°13N 123°43W **306** B3
Sool □ *Somali Rep.* 8°40N 47°30E **267** C6
Soomaaliya = Somali Rep. ■ *Africa* 7°0N 47°0E **267** C6
Sop Hao *Laos* 20°33N 104°27E **228** G5
Sop Prap *Thailand* 17°53N 99°20E **236** D2
Sopachuy *Bolivia* 19°29S 64°31W **331** D5
Sopchoppy *U.S.A.* 30°4N 84°29W **316** E5
Sopelana *Spain* 43°23N 2°58W **196** B2
Soperton *U.S.A.* 32°23N 82°35W **316** C7
Sopi *Indonesia* 2°34N 128°28E **231** D7
Sopo, Nahr ➔ *Sudan* 8°40N 26°30E **257** F2
Sopot *Bulgaria* 42°39N 24°45E **203** D8
Sopot *Poland* 54°27N 18°31E **184** D5
Sopot *Serbia* 44°29N 20°36E **202** B4
Sopotnica *Macedonia* 41°18N 21°13E **202** E5
Sopron *Hungary* 47°45N 16°32E **182** C1
Sopur *India* 34°18N 74°27E **243** B6
Sør-Rondane *Antarctica* 72°0S 25°0E **151** D4
Sør-Trøndelag □ *Norway* 63°0N 11°0E **164** A7
Sora *Italy* 41°43N 13°37E **199** G10
Sorab *India* 14°23N 75°6E **245** G2
Sorada *India* 19°45N 84°26E **244** E7
Sorah *Pakistan* 27°13N 68°56E **242** F3
Soråker *Sweden* 62°30N 17°32E **162** B11
Sorang *Kazakhstan* 49°46N 72°51E **217** C8
Sorano *Italy* 42°41N 11°43E **199** F8
Soraon *India* 25°37N 81°51E **243** G9
Sorata *Bolivia* 15°50S 68°40W **330** D4
Sorbas *Spain* 37°6N 2°7W **197** H2
Sörbygden *Sweden* 62°48N 16°12E **162** B10
Sord = Swords *Ireland* 53°28N 6°13W **120** A2
Sore *France* 44°18N 0°35W **174** D3
Søre Osa ➔ *Norway* 61°18N 11°46E **164** C8
Sorel-Tracy *Canada* 46°0N 73°10W **298** C5
Soresina *Italy* 45°17N 9°51E **198** C6
Sørfjorden *Norway* 60°20N 6°37E **164** D3
Sörforsa *Sweden* 61°43N 16°58E **162** C10
Sórgono *Italy* 40°1N 9°6E **200** B2
Sorgues *France* 44°1N 4°53E **175** D8
Sorgun *Turkey* 39°46N 35°11E **212** C6
Sorgun ➔ *Turkey* 36°36N 34°20E **250** B5
Sori *Papua N. G.* 1°58S 146°42E **286** A4
Soria *Spain* 41°43N 2°32W **196** D2
Soria □ *Spain* 41°46N 2°28W **196** D2
Soriano *Uruguay* 33°24S 58°19W **334** C4
Soriano nel Cimino *Italy* 42°25N 12°14E **199** F9
Sorkh, Kuh-e *Iran* 35°40N 58°30E **247** C8
Sorø *Denmark* 55°26N 11°32E **163** J5
Soro *Guinea* 10°9N 9°48W **262** C3
Soroca *Moldova* 48°8N 28°12E **183** B13
Sorocaba *Brazil* 23°31S 47°27W **335** A6
Sorochinsk *Russia* 52°26N 53°10E **186** D9
Soroka = Belomorsk *Russia* 64°35N 34°54E **186** B5
Soroki = Soroca *Moldova* 48°8N 28°12E **183** B13
Sorokino = Krasnodon *Ukraine* 48°17N 39°44E **189** H10
Soroksár *Hungary* 47°24N 19°7E **117** B2
Soroksari Duna ➔ *Hungary* 47°25N 19°5E **117** B2
Sorong *Indonesia* 0°55S 131°15E **231** E8
Soroni *Greece* 36°21N 28°1E **206** E12
Soroti *Uganda* 1°43N 33°35E **268** B3
Sørøya *Norway* 70°40N 22°30E **160** A20
Sørøyane *Norway* 62°25N 5°32E **164** B2
Sørøysundet *Norway* 70°25N 23°0E **160** A20
Sorraia ➔ *Portugal* 38°55N 8°53W **195** G2
Sorrell *Australia* 42°47S 147°34E **281** G4
Sorrento *Italy* 40°37N 14°22E **201** B7
Sorsele *Sweden* 65°31N 17°30E **160** D17
Sörsjön *Sweden* 61°24N 13°5E **162** C7
Sorso *Italy* 40°48N 8°34E **200** B1
Sorsogon *Phil.* 13°0N 124°0E **232** E5
Sorsogon □ *Phil.* 12°50N 123°55E **232** E4
Sortavala *Russia* 61°42N 30°41E **188** B6
Sortino *Italy* 37°9N 15°2E **201** E8
Sortland *Norway* 68°42N 15°25E **160** B16
Sortot *Sudan* 19°3N 30°28E **256** D3
Sørum *Norway* 60°30N 10°17E **164** D7
Sorvizhi *Russia* 57°52N 48°32E **190** B9
Sos del Rey Católico *Spain* 42°30N 1°13W **196** C3
Soscumica, L. *Canada* 50°15N 77°27W **298** B4
Sösdala *Sweden* 56°2N 13°41E **163** H7
Sosenka ➔ *Russia* 55°46N 37°42E **129** B4
Sosna ➔ *Russia* 52°42N 38°55E **189** F10
Sosnogorsk *Russia* 63°37N 53°51E **186** B9
Sosnovka *Kirov, Russia* 56°17N 51°17E **190** B10
Sosnovka *St. Petersburg, Russia* 60°0N 30°22E **137** B2
Sosnovka *Tambov, Russia* 53°13N 41°24E **190** D5
Sosnovyy Bor *Russia* 59°55N 29°6E **188** C5
Sosnowiec *Poland* 50°20N 19°10E **185** H6
Sosnowitz = Sosnowiec *Poland* 50°20N 19°10E **185** H6
Soso *C.A.R.* 3°55N 15°30E **264** B3
Sospel *France* 43°52N 7°27E **175** E11
Sossus Vlei *Namibia* 24°40S 15°23E **270** B2
Šoštanj *Slovenia* 46°23N 15°4E **199** B12
Sŏsura *N. Korea* 42°16N 130°36E **224** A5
Sot ➔ *India* 27°27N 79°37E **243** F8
Sotasæter *Norway* 61°49N 7°43E **164** C4
Sotavento *C. Verde Is.* 15°0N 25°0W **153** j
Sotik *Kenya* 0°41S 35°7E **268** C4
Sotkamo *Finland* 64°8N 28°23E **160** D23
Soto *Neth. Ant.* 12°16N 69°6W **322** g
Soto del Barco *Spain* 43°32N 6°4W **194** B4
Soto la Marina *Mexico* 23°46N 98°13W **319** C5
Soto la Marina ➔ *Mexico* 23°45N 97°45W **319** C5
Soto y Amío *Spain* 42°46N 5°53W **194** C5
Sotouboua *Togo* 8°34N 0°59E **263** D5
Sotrondio *Spain* 43°17N 5°36W **194** B5
Sotuf, Adrar *W. Sahara* 21°42N 15°36W **260** D1
Sotuta *Mexico* 20°36N 89°1W **319** C7
Souanké *Congo* 2°10N 14°3E **264** B2
Soubré *Ivory C.* 5°50N 6°35W **262** D3
Souda *Greece* 35°29N 24°4E **207** E5
Soudas, Ormos *Greece* 35°25N 24°10E **207** E5
Souderton *U.S.A.* 40°19N 75°19W **313** F9
Soufflay *Congo* 2°1N 14°54E **264** B2
Soufli *Greece* 41°12N 26°18E **203** E10
Soufrière *Dominica* 15°13N 61°22W **323** k
Soufrière *Guadeloupe* 16°5N 61°40W **322** e
Soufrière *St. Lucia* 13°51N 61°3W **323** m
Soufrière Bay *Dominica* 15°13N 61°22W **323** k
Soufrière Bay *St. Lucia* 13°51N 61°4W **323** m
Soufrière Hills Volcano *Montserrat* 16°43N 62°10W **323** p
Souillac *Lot, France* 44°53N 1°29E **174** D5
Souillac *Mauritius* 20°31S 57°31E **272** e
Souilly *France* 49°3N 5°17E **173** C12
Souk-Ahras *Algeria* 36°23N 7°57E **261** A6
Souk-Ahras □ *Algeria* 36°10N 7°55E **261** A6
Souk el Arba du Rharb *Morocco* 34°43N 5°59W **260** B3
Soukhouma *Laos* 14°38N 105°48E **236** E5
Sŏul = Seoul *S. Korea* 37°31N 126°58E **137** B2
Soulac-sur-Mer *France* 45°30N 1°7W **174** C2
Soulougou *Burkina Faso* 13°1N 0°25E **263** C5
Soultz-sous-Forêts *France* 48°57N 7°52E **173** D14
Sound, The = Øresund *Europe* 55°45N 12°40E **163** J6
Sound, The *U.K.* 50°20N 4°10W **169** G3
Sound I. *India* 12°58N 92°59E **245** H11
Soundview *U.S.A.* 40°49N 73°53W **132** B2
Sounio, Akra *Greece* 37°37N 24°1E **204** D6
Sour el Ghozlane *Algeria* 36°10N 3°45E **261** A5
Sources, Mt. aux *Lesotho* 28°45S 28°50E **271** C4
Soure *Brazil* 0°35S 48°30W **332** B2
Soure *Portugal* 40°4N 8°38W **194** E2
Souris *Man., Canada* 49°40N 100°20W **297** D8
Souris *P.E.I., Canada* 46°21N 62°15W **299** C7
Souris ➔ *N. Amer.* 49°40N 99°34W **308** A4
Sourou ➔ *Africa* 12°45N 3°25W **262** C4
Souripi *Greece* 39°6N 22°54E **204** B4
Sous, O. ➔ *Morocco* 30°27N 9°31W **260** B3
Sous le Vent, Is. *French Polynesia* 16°30S 155°30W **289** f
Sous le Vent, Région *Réunion* 21°12S 55°20E **272** f
Sous-Massa △ *Morocco* 31°26N 9°35W **260** B3
Sousa *Brazil* 6°45S 38°10W **332** C4
Sousel *Brazil* 2°38S 52°29W **332** B1
Sousel *Portugal* 38°57N 7°40W **195** G3
Sousse *Tunisia* 35°50N 10°38E **258** A2
Sousse □ *Tunisia* 35°40N 10°30E **261** A7
Soustons *France* 43°45N 1°19W **174** E2
Sout ➔ *S. Africa* 31°35S 18°24E **270** D2
South Africa ■ *Africa* 32°0S 23°0E **270** D3
South America 10°0S 60°0W **326** E5
South Andaman *India* 11°45N 92°10E **245** J11
South Atlantic Ocean 20°0S 10°0W **152** J10
South Aulatsivik I. *Canada* 56°45N 61°30W **299** A7
South Australia □ *Australia* 32°0S 139°0E **282** B3
South Australian Basin *Ind. Oc.* 38°0S 126°0E **288** L4
South Ayrshire □ *U.K.* 55°18N 4°41W **167** F4
South Baldy Pk. *U.S.A.* 34°6N 107°11W **305** J10
South Bass I. *U.S.A.* 41°39N 82°49W **312** E2
South Bay *U.S.A.* 26°40N 80°43W **317** J9
South Beach *Bahamas* 25°1N 77°20W **153** b
South Beach *N.Y., U.S.A.* 40°35N 74°4W **132** C1
South Beach Harbor *San Francisco, U.S.A.* **136** c3
South Beloit *U.S.A.* 42°29N 89°2W **310** B7
South Bend *Ind., U.S.A.* 41°41N 86°15W **311** C10
South Bend *Wash., U.S.A.* 46°40N 123°48W **306** D3
South Bend Park *U.S.A.* 33°42N 84°23W **113** B2
South Boston *Mass., U.S.A.* 42°20N 71°2W **116** A2
South Boston *Va., U.S.A.* 36°42N 78°54W **309** G14
South Branch *Canada* 47°55N 59°2W **299** C8
South Branch Chicago River ➔ *Chicago, U.S.A.* **119** d1
South Brook *Canada* 49°26N 56°5W **299** C8
South Brother I. *India* 10°56N 92°37E **245** J11
South Bruny I. *Australia* 43°20S 147°15E **281** G4
South C. = Kalae *U.S.A.* 18°55N 155°41W **302** E6
South Carolina □ *U.S.A.* 34°0N 81°0W **315** E14
South Charleston *U.S.A.* 38°22N 81°44W **309** F13
South China Sea *Asia* 10°0N 113°0E **230** C4
South Comino Channel *Malta* 36°0N 14°20E **206** F7
South Congaree *U.S.A.* 33°53N 81°9W **316** B8
South Cotabato □ *Phil.* 6°0N 125°0E **233** J5
South Cumberland Is. △ *Australia* 20°42S 149°11E **280** b
South Dakota □ *U.S.A.* 44°15N 100°0W **308** C4
South Dayton *U.S.A.* 42°21N 79°3W **312** D5
South Daytona *U.S.A.* 29°10N 81°0W **317** F8
South Decatur *U.S.A.* 33°44N 84°16W **113** B3
South Deerfield *U.S.A.* 42°29N 72°37W **313** D12
South Deering *U.S.A.* 41°42N 87°33W **119** C3
South Downs *U.K.* 50°52N 0°25W **169** G7
South East B. *Ascension I.* 7°57S 14°18W **153** g
South East C. *Australia* 43°40S 146°50E **281** G4
South East Forest △ *Australia* 37°0S 149°30E **283** D8
South East Is. *Australia* 34°17S 123°30E **279** F3
South El Monte *U.S.A.* 34°3N 118°2W **126** B4
South Elgin *U.S.A.* 42°0N 88°18W **311** C8
South Esk ➔ *U.K.* 56°43N 2°31W **167** E6
South Fiji Basin *Pac. Oc.* 26°0S 175°0E **288** K9
South Foreland *U.K.* 51°8N 1°24E **169** F9
South Fork American ➔ *U.S.A.* 38°57N 120°59W **306** G5
South Fork Edisto ➔ *U.S.A.* 33°16N 80°54W **316** B9
South Fork Feather ➔ *U.S.A.* 39°17N 121°36W **306** F5
South Fork Grand ➔ *U.S.A.* 45°43N 102°17W **308** C2
South Fork Licking ➔ *U.S.A.* 38°40N 84°18W **311** F12
South Fork Milk ➔ *U.S.A.* 48°4N 106°19W **304** B10
South Fork Republican ➔ *U.S.A.* 40°3N 101°31W **308** E3
South Gate *U.S.A.* 33°56N 118°12W **126** C3
South Georgia *Antarctica* 54°30S 37°0W **151** B1
South Gloucestershire □ *U.K.* 51°32N 2°28W **169** F5
South Grand ➔ *U.S.A.* 38°17N 93°25W **310** F3
South Hadley *U.S.A.* 42°16N 72°35W **313** D12
South Harbor *Phil.* 14°34N 120°58E **127** B1
South Harrow *U.K.* 51°33N 0°21W **125** A1
South Haven *U.S.A.* 42°24N 86°16W **311** B10
South Hd. *Australia* 33°50S 151°16E **139** B2
South Henik L. *Canada* 61°30N 97°20W **297** A9
South Hill Village *Anguilla* 18°11N 63°5W **322** a
South Hills *S. Africa* 26°14S 28°5E **123** B2
South Horr *Kenya* 2°12N 36°56E **268** B4
South I. *India* 10°3N 72°17E **245** J1
South I. *Eastern, Kenya* 2°35N 36°35E **268** B4
South I. *N.Z.* 44°0S 170°0E **285** E5
South Indian Lake *Canada* 56°47N 98°56W **297** B9
South Invercargill *N.Z.* 46°26S 168°23E **285** G3
South Island △ *Kenya* 2°39N 36°35E **268** B4
South Kensington *London, U.K.* **125** c2
South Kitui △ *Kenya* 1°48S 38°46E **268** C4
South Knife ➔ *Canada* 58°55N 94°37W **297** B10
South Koel ➔ *India* 22°32N 85°14E **243** H11
South Korea ■ *Asia* 36°0N 128°0E **227** G15
South Lake Tahoe *U.S.A.* 38°57N 119°59W **306** G6
South Lanarkshire □ *U.K.* 55°37N 3°53W **167** F5
South Lawn *U.S.A.* 38°47N 77°0W **143** C3
South Loop *Chicago, U.S.A.* **119** f2
South Loup ➔ *U.S.A.* 41°4N 98°39W **308** E4
South Luangwa △ *Zambia* 13°0S 31°20E **269** E3
South Lyon *U.S.A.* 42°28N 83°39W **311** B13
South Magnetic Pole *Antarctica* 64°8S 138°8E **151** C9
South Malé Atoll *Maldives* 4°0N 73°25E **272** d
South Malosmadulu Atoll *Maldives* 5°12N 73°0E **272** d
South Miami *U.S.A.* 25°42N 80°17W **128** B1
South Milwaukee *U.S.A.* 42°55N 87°52W **311** B9
South Molton *U.K.* 51°1N 3°51W **169** F4
South Monroe *U.S.A.* 41°54N 83°26W **311** C13
South Moose L. *Canada* 53°49N 100°1W **297** C8
South Nahanni ➔ *Canada* 61°3N 123°21W **296** A4
South Nation ➔ *Canada* 45°34N 75°6W **313** A9
South Natuna Is. = Natuna Selatan, Kepulauan *Indonesia* 2°45N 109°0E **235** B3
South Negril Pt. *Jamaica* 18°16N 78°22W **320** a
South New Hebrides Trench *Pac. Oc.* 22°30S 170°0E **277** E13
South Newport *U.S.A.* 31°38N 81°24W **316** D8
South Nilandu Atoll *Maldives* 2°52N 72°57E **272** d
South Norwood *U.K.* 51°23N 0°3W **125** B3
South of Market *San Francisco, U.S.A.* **136** c2
South Orkney Is. *Antarctica* 63°0S 45°0W **151** C18
South Ossetia □ *Georgia* 42°21N 44°2E **191** J7
South Otselic *U.S.A.* 42°38N 75°46W **313** D9
South Ozone Park *U.S.A.* 40°41N 73°49W **132** B3
South Pagai, I. = Pagai Selatan, Pulau *Indonesia* 3°0S 100°15E **234** C2
South Paris *U.S.A.* 44°14N 70°31W **313** B14
South Pasadena *U.S.A.* 34°7N 118°8W **126** B4
South Pekin *U.S.A.* 40°30N 89°39W **310** D7
South Pittsburg *U.S.A.* 35°1N 85°42W **315** D12
South Platte ➔ *U.S.A.* 41°7N 100°42W **308** E3
South Pole *Antarctica* 90°0S 0°0 **151** E
South Ponte Vedra Beach *U.S.A.* 30°3N 81°20W **316** E8
South Porcupine *Canada* 48°30N 81°12W **298** C3
South Portland *U.S.A.* 43°38N 70°15W **309** D18
South Pt. *Ascension I.* 8°0S 14°24W **153** g
South Pt. *Barbados* 13°2N 59°32W **323** r
South Pt. *Mich., U.S.A.* 44°52N 83°19W **312** B1
South Res. *U.S.A.* 42°26N 71°6W **116** A2
South River *Ont., Canada* 45°52N 79°23W **298** C4
South River *N.J., U.S.A.* 40°27N 74°23W **313** F10
South Ronaldsay *U.K.* 58°48N 2°58W **167** C6
South Ruislip *U.K.* 51°33N 0°24W **125** A1
South Rukuru *Malaysia* 10°44S 34°15E **269** E3
South San Francisco *U.S.A.* 37°38N 122°26W **136** C2
South San Gabriel *U.S.A.* 34°3N 118°6W **126** B4
South Sandwich Is. *Antarctica* 57°0S 27°0W **151** B1
South Sandwich Trench *Atl. Oc.* 56°0S 24°0W **151** B1
South Saskatchewan ➔ *Canada* 53°15N 105°5W **297** C7
South Seal ➔ *Canada* 58°48N 98°8W **297** B9
South Sentinel I. *India* 10°59N 92°14E **245** J11
South Shetland Is. *Antarctica* 62°0S 59°0W **151** C18
South Shields *U.K.* 55°0N 1°25W **168** C6
South Shore *U.S.A.* 41°45N 87°34W **119** C3
South Sioux City *U.S.A.* 42°28N 96°24W **308** D5
South Sister *U.S.A.* 44°4N 121°51W **304** D3
South Solomon Trench *Pac. Oc.* 11°0S 164°30E **277** C11
South Soufrière Hills *Montserrat* 16°41N 62°10W **323** p
South Street *Boston, U.S.A.* **116** c2
South Talpatti = New Moore I. *Ind. Oc.* 21°37N 89°10E **243** J13
South Taranaki Bight *N.Z.* 39°40S 174°5E **284** F3
South Tasman Rise *S. Ocean* 48°0S 146°0E **151** A10
South Thompson ➔ *Canada* 50°40N 120°20W **296** C4
South Twin I. *Canada* 53°7N 79°52W **298** B4
South Tyne ➔ *U.K.* 54°59N 2°8W **168** C5
South Ubian *Phil.* 5°11N 120°30E **233** J3
South Uist *U.K.* 57°20N 7°15W **167** D1
South Valley *U.S.A.* 35°1N 106°41W **305** J10
South Venice *U.S.A.* 27°3N 82°25W **317** H7
South Wayne *U.S.A.* 42°34N 89°53W **310** B7
South Wellesley Is. *Australia* 16°58S 139°17E **280** B2
South West Africa = Namibia ■ *Africa* 22°0S 18°9E **270** B2
South West B. *Ascension I.* 7°58S 14°25W **153** g
South West B. *Bahamas* 25°0N 77°32W **153** b
South West C. *Tas., Australia* 43°34S 146°3E **281** G4
South West C. *N.Z.* 47°17S 167°28E **285** H2
South West Pt. *Papua N. G.* 2°14S 146°34E **286** B4
South West Pt. *St. Helena* 15°59S 5°48W **153** h
South West Rocks *Australia* 30°52S 153°3E **283** A10
South Whitley *U.S.A.* 41°5N 85°38W **311** C11
South Williamsport *U.S.A.* 41°13N 77°0W **312** E8
South Yemen = Yemen ■ *Asia* 15°0N 44°0E **248** D4
South Yorkshire □ *U.K.* 53°27N 1°36W **168** D6
Southall *U.K.* 51°30N 0°22W **125** A1
Southampton *Ont., Canada* 44°30N 81°25W **312** B3
Southampton *Southampton, U.K.* 50°54N 1°23W **169** G6
Southampton *N.Y., U.S.A.* 40°53N 72°23W **313** F12
Southampton □ *U.K.* 50°54N 1°23W **169** G6
Southampton I. *Canada* 64°30N 84°0W **295** E15
Southaven *U.S.A.* 34°59N 90°0W **315** D9
Southbank *Canada* 54°2N 125°46W **296** C3
Southborough *U.K.* 51°23N 0°3E **125** B4
Southbridge *N.Z.* 43°48S 172°16E **285** D7
Southbridge *Mass., U.S.A.* 42°5N 72°2W **313** D12
Southeast C. *U.S.A.* 62°56N 169°39W **303** E5
Southeast Indian Ridge *Ind. Oc.* 43°0S 80°0E **273** J10
Southend *Sask., Canada* 56°19N 103°22W **297** B8
Southend *London, U.K.* 51°25N 0°0 **125** B3
Southend-on-Sea *U.K.* 51°32N 0°44E **169** F8
Southend-on-Sea □ *U.K.* 51°32N 0°44E **169** F8
Southern = Janub △ *Sudan* 6°50N 28°45E **257** F2
Southern = Yedebub Biheroch Bihereseboch na Hizboch □ *Ethiopia* 12°0N 36°0E **257** F4
Southern = Yuzhnyy □ *Russia* 44°0N 40°0E **191** H5
Southern □ *Malawi* 15°0S 35°0E **269** F4
Southern □ *S. Leone* 8°0N 12°30W **262** D2
Southern □ *Zambia* 16°20S 26°20E **269** F2
Southern Alps *N.Z.* 43°41S 170°11E **285** D5
Southern California, Univ. of *U.S.A.* 34°1N 118°17W **126** B3
Southern Cross *Australia* 31°12S 119°15E **279** F2
Southern Highlands □ *Papua N. G.* 6°15S 143°25E **286** D2
Southern Indian L. *Canada* 57°10N 98°30W **297** B9
Southern Lau Group *Fiji* 18°40S 178°40W **287** B3
Southern Leyte □ *Phil.* 10°30N 125°10E **233** F5
Southern Ocean *Antarctica* 62°0S 60°0E **151** C6
Southern Pines *U.S.A.* 35°11N 79°24W **315** D15
Southern Rhodesia = Zimbabwe ■ *Africa* 19°0S 30°0E **269** F3
Southern Uplands *U.K.* 55°28N 3°52W **167** F5
Southfield *U.S.A.* 42°28N 83°15W **311** B13
Southfields *U.K.* 51°26N 0°11W **125** B2
Southington *U.S.A.* 41°36N 72°53W **313** E12
Southland □ *N.Z.* 45°30S 168°0E **285** F3
Southold *U.S.A.* 41°4N 72°26W **313** E12
Southport *Queens., Australia* 27°58S 153°25E **281** D5
Southport *Mersey., U.K.* 53°39N 3°0W **168** D4
Southport *Fla., U.S.A.* 30°17N 85°38W **316** E4
Southport *La., U.S.A.* 29°57N 90°8W **131** B2
Southport *N.Y., U.S.A.* 42°3N 76°49W **312** D8
Southwark □ *U.K.* 51°29N 0°6W **125** B3
Southwest △ *Australia* 43°8S 146°5E **281** G4
Southwest Museum *U.S.A.* 34°6N 118°13W **126** B3
Southwest Pacific Basin *Pac. Oc.* 40°0S 140°0W **277** G17
Southwest Pt. *U.S. Virgin Is.* 17°40N 64°55W **321** b
Southwold *U.K.* 52°20N 1°41E **169** E9
Southwood △ *Australia* 27°48S 150°8E **281** D5
Soutpansberg *S. Africa* 23°0S 29°30E **271** B4
Souvigny *France* 46°33N 3°10E **173** F10
Søvang *Denmark* 55°34N 12°37E **118** B3
Sovata *Romania* 46°35N 25°3E **183** D10
Soverato *Italy* 38°41N 16°33E **201** D9
Sovetsk *Kaliningrad, Russia* 55°6N 21°50E **184** C8
Sovetsk *Kirov, Russia* 57°38N 48°53E **190** B9
Sovetskaya Gavan *Russia* 48°58N 140°18E **215** E15
Sovetskoye = Zelenokumsk *Russia* 44°24N 44°0E **191** H6
Sovicille *Italy* 43°17N 11°13E **199** E8
Søvik *Norway* 62°33N 6°17E **164** B3
Soweto *S. Africa* 26°14S 27°52E **123** B1
Sowhānak *Iran* 35°48N 51°31E **141** A3
Sowma'eh Sarā *Iran* 37°17N 49°18E **213** D13
Soya *Japan* 35°44N 139°55E **140** A4
Sōya-Kaikyō = La Perouse Str. *Asia* 45°40N 142°0E **220** B11
Sōya-Misaki *Japan* 45°30N 141°55E **220** B10
Soyangho *S. Korea* 37°57N 127°54E **224** D3
Soyaux *France* 45°39N 0°12E **174** C4
Søyland *Norway* 58°41N 5°36E **164** F2
Soyo *Angola* 6°13S 12°20E **265** D2
Sozaq *Kazakhstan* 44°8N 68°28E **217** D7
Sozh ➔ *Belarus* 51°57N 30°48E **177** B16
Sozopol *Bulgaria* 42°23N 27°42E **203** D11
Spa *Belgium* 50°29N 5°53E **170** D5
Spaans Lagoen *Aruba* 12°28N 69°58W **322** f
Spaanse Water *Neth. Ant.* 12°4N 68°51W **322** g
Spaccaforno = Íspica *Italy* 36°47N 14°55E **201** F7
Spain ■ *Europe* 39°0N 4°0W **192** D3
Spalato = Split *Croatia* 43°31N 16°26E **199** E13
Spalding *S. Austral., Australia* 33°30S 138°37E **282** B3
Spalding *Lincs., U.K.* 52°48N 0°9W **168** E7
Spanaway *U.S.A.* 47°6N 122°26W **306** C4
Spandau *Germany* 52°33N 13°9E **115** A1
Spånga *Sweden* 59°23N 17°53E **139** A1
Spangler *U.S.A.* 40°39N 78°48W **312** F6
Spanische Reitschule *Vienna, Austria* **142** b1
Spanish *Canada* 46°12N 82°20W **298** C3
Spanish Fork *U.S.A.* 40°7N 111°39W **304** F8
Spanish Monastery *U.S.A.* 25°55N 80°11W **128** A2
Spanish Pt. *Antigua & B.* 17°33N 61°44W **322** c
Spanish Pt. *Bermuda* 32°18N 64°49W **153** a
Spanish Riding School = Spanische Reitschule *Vienna, Austria* **142** b1
Spanish Town *Br. Virgin Is.* 17°43N 64°26W **321** b
Spanish Town *Jamaica* 18°0N 76°57W **320** a
Sparks *Ga., U.S.A.* 31°11N 83°26W **316** D6
Sparks *Nev., U.S.A.* 39°32N 119°45W **306** F7
Sparreholm *Sweden* 59°4N 16°49E **162** E10
Sparrow Bay *Grenada* 12°30N 61°27W **323** q
Sparta = Sparti *Greece* 37°5N 22°25E **204** D4
Sparta *Ga., U.S.A.* 33°17N 82°58W **316** B7
Sparta *Ill., U.S.A.* 38°8N 89°42W **310** F7
Sparta *Mich., U.S.A.* 43°10N 85°42W **311** A11
Sparta *N.J., U.S.A.* 41°2N 74°38W **313** E10
Sparta *Wis., U.S.A.* 43°56N 90°49W **308** D8
Spartanburg *U.S.A.* 34°56N 81°57W **315** D14
Spartel, C. *Morocco* 35°47N 5°56W **260** A3
Sparti *Greece* 37°5N 22°25E **204** D4
Spartivento, C. *Calabria, Italy* 37°55N 16°4E **201** E9
Spartivento, C. *Sard., Italy* 38°53N 8°50E **200** D1
Spartochori *Greece* 38°40N 20°46E **207** B2
Sparwood *Canada* 49°44N 114°53W **296** D6
Spas-Demensk *Russia* 54°20N 34°0E **188** E7
Spas-Klepiki *Russia* 55°10N 40°10E **188** E11
Spassk = Bednodemyanovsk *Russia* 53°55N 43°15E **190** D6
Spassk Dalniy *Russia* 44°40N 132°48E **220** B6
Spassk-Ryazanskiy *Russia* 54°24N 40°25E **188** E11
Spatha, Akra *Greece* 35°42N 23°43E **207** E4
Spatsizi ➔ *Canada* 57°42N 128°7W **296** B3
Spatsizi Plateau Wilderness ⌂ *Canada* 57°40N 128°0W **296** B3
Spean ➔ *U.K.* 56°55N 4°59W **167** E4
Spearfish *U.S.A.* 44°30N 103°52W **308** C2
Spearman *U.S.A.* 36°12N 101°12W **314** C4
Spectacle I. *U.S.A.* 42°19N 70°59W **116** A3
Speculator *U.S.A.* 43°30N 74°22W **313** C10
Speed *Australia* 35°21S 142°27E **282** C5
Speedway *U.S.A.* 39°48N 86°16W **311** E10
Speery I. *St. Helena* 16°1S 5°46W **153** h
Speia *Moldova* 46°59N 29°19E **183** D14
Speicher-See *Germany* 48°12N 11°42E **131** A3
Speightstown *Barbados* 13°15N 59°39W **323** r
Speising *Austria* 48°10N 16°17E **142** B1
Speke Gulf *Tanzania* 2°20S 32°50E **268** C3
Spello *Italy* 42°59N 12°40E **199** F9
Spence Bay = Taloyoak *Canada* 69°32N 93°32W **294** D13
Spencer *Idaho, U.S.A.* 44°22N 112°11W **304** D7
Spencer *Ind., U.S.A.* 39°17N 86°46W **311** E10
Spencer *Iowa, U.S.A.* 43°9N 95°9W **308** D6
Spencer *N.Y., U.S.A.* 42°13N 76°30W **313** D8
Spencer *Nebr., U.S.A.* 42°53N 98°42W **308** D4
Spencer, C. *Australia* 35°20S 136°53E **282** C2
Spencer B. *Namibia* 25°30S 14°47E **270** C1
Spencer G. *Australia* 34°0S 137°20E **282** C2
Spencerville *Ont., Canada* 44°51N 75°33W **313** B9
Spencerville *Ohio, U.S.A.* 40°43N 84°21W **311** D12
Spences Bridge *Canada* 50°25N 121°20W **296** C4
Spennymoor *U.K.* 54°42N 1°36W **168** C6
Spenser Mts. *N.Z.* 42°15S 172°45E **285** C7
Spentrup *Denmark* 56°33N 10°2E **163** H4
Sperchios ➔ *Greece* 38°57N 22°3E **204** C4
Sperillen *Norway* 60°28N 10°3E **164** D7
Sperrin Mts. *U.K.* 54°50N 7°0W **166** B5
Spessart *Germany* 49°56N 9°18E **179** F5
Spetalen *Norway* 59°18N 10°45E **164** E7
Spetses *Greece* 37°15N 23°10E **204** D5
Spey ➔ *U.K.* 57°40N 3°6W **167** D5
Speyer *Germany* 49°29N 8°25E **179** F4
Speyside *Trin. & Tob.* 11°17N 60°32W **323** s
Spezand *Pakistan* 29°59N 67°0E **242** E2
Spezzano Albanese *Italy* 39°40N 16°19E **201** C9
Sphinx *Egypt* 29°58N 31°8E **117** B1
Spickard *U.S.A.* 40°14N 93°36W **310** D3
Spiddle *Ireland* 53°15N 9°18W **166** C2
Spiekeroog *Germany* 53°46N 7°42E **178** B3
Spiez *Switz.* 46°40N 7°40E **179** J3
Spili *Greece* 35°13N 24°31E **207** E5
Spilimbergo *Italy* 46°7N 12°54E **199** B9
Spīn Būldak *Afghan.* 31°1N 66°25E **242** D2
Spinalonga *Greece* 35°18N 25°44E **207** E6
Spinazzola *Italy* 40°58N 16°5E **201** B9
Spineni *Romania* 44°43N 24°37E **183** F9
Spinifex ✪ *Australia* 28°30S 128°30E **279** E4
Spirding = Śniardwy, Jezioro *Poland* 53°48N 21°50E **184** E8
Spirit Lake *U.S.A.* 46°15N 122°9W **306** D4
Spirit River *Canada* 55°45N 118°50W **296** B5
Spiritwood *Canada* 53°24N 107°33W **297** C7
Spišská Nová Ves *Slovak Rep.* 48°58N 20°34E **181** C13
Spišské Podhradie *Slovak Rep.* 49°0N 20°48E **181** B13
Spit Junction *Australia* 33°49S 151°14E **139** A2
Spital *Austria* 47°42N 14°18E **180** D7
Spithead *U.K.* 50°45N 1°10W **169** G6
Spittal an der Drau *Austria* 46°48N 13°31E **180** E6
Spitzbergen = Svalbard *Arctic* 78°0N 17°0E **150** B8
Spjelkavik *Norway* 62°28N 6°22E **164** B3
Split *Croatia* 43°31N 16°26E **199** E13
Split ✕ (SPU) *Croatia* 43°33N 16°15E **199** E13
Split L. *Canada* 56°8N 96°15W **297** B9
Split Lake *Canada* 56°8N 96°15W **297** B9
Splitski Kanal *Croatia* 43°31N 16°20E **199** E13
Splügenpass *Switz.* 46°30N 9°20E **179** J5
Spofford *U.S.A.* 29°10N 100°25W **314** G4
Spokane *U.S.A.* 47°40N 117°24W **304** C5
Spoleto *Italy* 42°44N 12°44E **199** F9
Sponvika *Norway* 59°7N 11°15E **164** E8
Spoon ➔ *U.S.A.* 40°19N 90°4W **310** D6
Spooner *U.S.A.* 45°50N 91°53W **308** C8
Spořilov *Czech Rep.* 50°2N 14°29E **135** B3
Sporyy Navolok, Mys *Russia* 75°50N 68°40E **214** B7
Spot Pond *U.S.A.* 42°26N 71°4W **116** A2
Spotswood *Australia* 37°50S 144°52E **128** B1
Sprague *U.S.A.* 47°18N 117°59W **304** C5
Spratly I. *S. China Sea* 8°38N 111°55E **230** C4
Spratly Is. *S. China Sea* 8°20N 112°0E **230** C4
Spray *U.S.A.* 44°50N 119°48W **304** D4
Spreča ➔ *Bos.-H.* 44°44N 18°6E **182** F3
Spree ➔ *Germany* 52°32N 13°12E **178** C9
Spreewald *Germany* 51°58N 13°54E **178** D9
Spremberg *Germany* 51°34N 14°22E **178** D10
Sprengisandur *Iceland* 64°52N 18°7W **155** C8
Spring City *U.S.A.* 40°11N 75°33W **313** F9
Spring Cr. ➔ *U.S.A.* 30°54N 84°45W **316** E5
Spring Creek *U.S.A.* 40°44N 115°35W **304** F6
Spring Garden *Guyana* 6°59N 58°31W **329** B6
Spring Garden *Calif., U.S.A.* 39°52N 120°47W **306** F6
Spring Green *U.S.A.* 43°11N 90°4W **310** A6
Spring Hill *Ala., U.S.A.* 31°42N 85°58W **316** D4
Spring Hill *Fla., U.S.A.* 28°27N 82°41W **317** G7
Spring Mts. *U.S.A.* 36°0N 115°45W **307** J11
Spring Valley *Calif., U.S.A.* 32°44N 116°59W **307** N10
Spring Valley *Ill., U.S.A.* 41°20N 89°12W **310** C7
Spring Valley *Nev., U.S.A.* 36°6N 115°14W **124** B1
Springbok *S. Africa* 29°42S 17°54E **270** C2
Springboro *U.S.A.* 41°48N 80°22W **312** E4
Springdale *Nfld. & L., Canada* 49°30N 56°6W **299** C8
Springdale *Ark., U.S.A.* 36°11N 94°8W **314** C7
Springdale *Ohio, U.S.A.* 39°17N 84°29W **311** E12
Springe *Germany* 52°13N 9°33E **178** C5
Springeberg *Germany* 52°26N 13°43E **115** B5
Springer *U.S.A.* 36°22N 104°36W **305** H11
Springerville *U.S.A.* 34°8N 109°17W **305** J9
Springfield *Ont., Canada* 42°50N 80°56W **312** D4
Springfield *Dominica* 15°21N 61°23W **323** k
Springfield *N.Z.* 43°19S 171°56E **285** D6
Springfield *Colo., U.S.A.* 37°24N 102°37W **305** H12
Springfield *Fla., U.S.A.* 30°10N 85°37W **316** E4
Springfield *Ga., U.S.A.* 32°22N 81°18W **316** C8
Springfield *Ill., U.S.A.* 39°48N 89°39W **310** E7
Springfield *Ky., U.S.A.* 37°41N 85°13W **311** G11
Springfield *Mass., U.S.A.* 42°6N 72°35W **313** D12
Springfield *Mo., U.S.A.* 37°13N 93°17W **308** G7
Springfield *Ohio, U.S.A.* 39°55N 83°49W **311** E13
Springfield *Oreg., U.S.A.* 44°3N 123°1W **304** D2
Springfield *S.C., U.S.A.* 33°30N 81°17W **316** B8
Springfield *Tenn., U.S.A.* 36°31N 86°53W **315** C11
Springfield *Va., U.S.A.* 38°46N 77°10W **143** C2
Springfield *Vt., U.S.A.* 43°18N 72°29W **313** C12
Springfield, L. *U.S.A.* 39°46N 89°36W **310** E7
Springfontein *S. Africa* 30°15S 25°40E **270** D4
Springhill *Canada* 45°40N 64°4W **299** C7
Springhill *La., U.S.A.* 33°0N 93°28W **314** E8
Springhouse *Canada* 51°56N 122°7W **296** C4
Springs *S. Africa* 26°13S 28°25E **271** C4
Springsure *Australia* 24°8S 148°6E **280** C4
Springvale *Ga., U.S.A.* 31°50N 84°53W **316** D5
Springvale *Maine, U.S.A.* 43°28N 70°48W **313** C14
Springville *Calif., U.S.A.* 36°8N 118°49W **306** J8
Springville *Iowa, U.S.A.* 42°3N 91°27W **310** B5
Springville *N.Y., U.S.A.* 42°31N 78°40W **312** D6
Springville *Utah, U.S.A.* 40°10N 111°37W **304** F8
Springwater *U.S.A.* 42°38N 77°35W **312** D7
Sprottau = Szprotawa *Poland* 51°33N 15°35E **185** G2
Spruce-Creek *U.S.A.* 40°36N 78°9W **312** F6
Spruce Knob-Seneca Rocks ⌂ *U.S.A.* 38°50N 79°30W **309** F14
Spruce Mt. *U.S.A.* 44°12N 72°19W **313** B12
Sprucedale *Canada* 45°29N 79°28W **312** A5
Spur *U.S.A.* 33°28N 100°52W **314** E4
Spurn Hd. *U.K.* 53°35N 0°8E **168** D8
Spuž *Montenegro* 42°32N 19°10E **202** D3
Spuzzum *Canada* 49°37N 121°23W **296** D4
Spydeberg *Norway* 59°36N 11°5E **164** E8
Squam L. *U.S.A.* 43°45N 71°32W **313** C13
Squamish *Canada* 49°45N 123°10W **296** D4
Squantum *U.S.A.* 42°17N 71°0W **116** B2
Square Islands *Canada* 52°47N 55°47W **299** B8
Squillace, G. di *Italy* 38°45N 16°50E **201** D9
Squinzano *Italy* 40°26N 18°2E **201** B11
Squires, Mt. *Australia* 26°14S 127°28E **279** E4
Sragen *Indonesia* 7°26S 111°2E **235** D4
Srbac *Bos.-H.* 45°7N 17°30E **182** E2
Srbica *Kosovo* 42°45N 20°47E **202** D4
Srbija = Serbia ■ *Europe* 43°20N 20°0E **202** C4
Srbobran *Serbia* 45°32N 19°48E **182** E4
Sre Ambel *Cambodia* 11°8N 103°46E **237** G4
Sre Khtum *Cambodia* 12°10N 106°52E **237** F6
Sre Umbell = Sre Ambel *Cambodia* 11°8N 103°46E **237** G4
Srebrenica *Bos.-H.* 44°6N 19°18E **182** F4
Sredinny Ra. = Sredinnyy Khrebet *Russia* 57°0N 160°0E **215** D17
Sredinnyy Khrebet *Russia* 57°0N 160°0E **215** D17
Središće *Slovenia* 46°24N 16°17E **199** B13
Sredna Gora *Bulgaria* 42°40N 24°20E **203** D8
Srednaya Rogatka *Russia* 59°49N 30°22E **137** C2
Srednekolymsk *Russia* 67°27N 153°40E **215** C16
Sredni Rodopi *Bulgaria* 41°40N 24°45E **203** E8
Srednogorie *Bulgaria* 42°43N 24°10E **203** D8
Śrem *Poland* 52°6N 17°2E **185** F4
Sremska Mitrovica *Serbia* 44°59N 19°38E **182** F4
Sremski Karlovci *Serbia* 45°12N 19°56E **182** E4
Srepok ➔ *Cambodia* 13°33N 106°16E **236** F6
Sretensk *Russia* 52°10N 117°40E **215** D12
Sri Aman *Malaysia* 1°15N 111°32E **235** B4
Sri Kalahasti *India* 13°45N 79°44E **245** H4
Sri Lanka ■ *Asia* 7°30N 80°50E **245** L5
Sriharikota I. *India* 13°40N 80°20E **245** H5
Srikakulam *India* 18°14N 83°58E **244** E6
Srinagar *India* 34°5N 74°50E **243** B6
Sripur *Bangla.* 24°14N 90°30E **241** C3
Srivardhan *India* 18°4N 73°3E **244** E1
Srivilliputtur *India* 9°31N 77°40E **245** K3
Środa Śląska *Poland* 51°10N 16°36E **185** G3
Środa Wielkopolski *Poland* 52°15N 17°19E **185** F4
Śródmieście *Poland* 52°13N 21°0E **142** B2
Srono *Indonesia* 8°24S 114°16E **231** J17
Srpska Crnja *Serbia* 45°38N 20°44E **182** E5
Srpski Itebej *Serbia* 45°35N 20°44E **182** E5
Srungavarapukota *India* 18°7N 83°10E **244** E6
Ssese Is. = Sese Is. *Uganda* 0°20S 32°20E **268** C3
Ssuhu *Taiwan* 23°38N 120°13E **225** C2
Staaken *Germany* 52°31N 13°8E **115** A1
Staaten ➔ *Australia* 16°24S 141°17E **280** B3
Staaten River △ *Australia* 16°15S 142°40E **280** B3
Stabekk *Norway* 59°54N 10°36E **133** A2

Staberhuk Germany 54°23N 11°18E 178 A7
Stade Germany 53°35N 9°29E 178 B5
Staðarfell Iceland 65°7N 22°12W 155 B4
Staðarhólskirkja Iceland 65°23N 21°58W 155 B5
Staðastaður Iceland 64°49N 23°1W 155 C3
Stadhavet Norway 62°13N 5°0E 164 B2
Stadhiou Athens, Greece 112 c3
Stadhuis Amsterdam, Neths. 112 b3
Staður Húnavatnssýsla, Iceland 65°9N 21°3W 155 B5
Staður Ísafjarðarsýsla, Iceland 66°15N 22°50W 155 A4
Stadlandet Norway 62°10N 5°10E 164 B2
Stadlau Austria 48°13N 16°27E 142 A2
Stadshuset Stockholm, Sweden 139 b1
Stadskanaal Neths. 53°4N 6°55E 170 A6
Stadsschouwburg Amsterdam, Neths. 112 c1
Stadtallendorf Germany 50°48N 9°1E 178 E5
Stadthagen Germany 52°19N 9°13E 178 C5
Stadtlohn Germany 51°59N 6°55E 178 D2
Stadtroda Germany 50°52N 11°44E 178 E7
Stafafell Iceland 64°25N 14°52W 155 C12
Staffa U.K. 56°27N 6°21W 167 E2
Staffanstorp Sweden 55°39N 13°13E 163 J7
Stafford Staffs., U.K. 52°49N 2°7W 168 E5
Stafford Kans., U.S.A. 37°58N 98°36W 308 G4
Stafford, L. U.S.A. 29°20N 82°29W 317 F7
Stafford Springs U.S.A. 41°57N 72°18W 313 E12
Staffordshire □ U.K. 52°53N 2°10W 168 E5
Stagnone Italy 37°53N 12°26E 200 E5
Stagnone di Marsala ⌓ Italy 37°52N 12°26E 200 E5
Staines U.K. 51°26N 0°29W 169 F7
Stains France 48°57N 2°22E 134 A3
Stainz Austria 46°53N 15°17E 180 E8
Stakhanov Ukraine 48°35N 38°40E 189 H10
Stalać Serbia 43°43N 21°28E 202 C5
Stalin = Kuçovë Albania 40°47N 19°57E 202 F3
Stalin = Varna Bulgaria 43°13N 27°56E 203 C11
Stalin Pk. = Gerlachovský štit Slovak Rep. 49°11N 20°7E 181 B13
Stalin Pk. = imeni Ismail Samani, Pik Tajikistan 39°0N 72°2E 217 E8
Stalin Pk. = Musala Bulgaria 42°13N 23°37E 202 D7
Stalinabad = Dushanbe Tajikistan 38°33N 68°48E 217 E7
Stalingrad = Volgograd Russia 48°40N 44°25E 191 F7
Staliniri = Tskhinvali Georgia 42°14N 44°1E 191 J7
Stalinogorsk = Novomoskovsk Russia 54°5N 38°15E 188 E10
Stalinogrod = Katowice Poland 50°17N 19°5E 185 H6
Stalinsk = Novokuznetsk Russia 53°45N 87°10E 217 B11
Stalinstadt = Eisenhüttenstadt Germany 52°9N 14°38E 178 C10
Stallarholmen Sweden 59°22N 17°12E 162 E11
Ställdalen Sweden 59°56N 14°56E 162 E8
Stalowa Wola Poland 50°34N 22°3E 185 H9
Stalybridge U.K. 53°28N 2°3W 168 D5
Stamford Queens., Australia 21°15S 143°46E 280 C3
Stamford Lincs., U.K. 52°39N 0°29W 169 E7
Stamford Conn., U.S.A. 41°3N 73°32W 313 E11
Stamford N.Y., U.S.A. 42°25N 74°38W 313 D10
Stamford Tex., U.S.A. 32°57N 99°48W 314 E5
Stamford Hill U.K. 51°34N 0°4W 125 A3
Stammersdorf Austria 48°18N 16°24E 142 A2
Stamnes Norway 60°40N 5°45E 164 D2
Stamping Ground U.S.A. 38°16N 84°41W 311 F12
Stampriet Namibia 24°20S 18°28E 270 B2
Stamps U.S.A. 33°22N 93°30W 314 E8
Stanberry U.S.A. 40°13N 94°35W 310 D2
Stančevo = Kalipetrovo Bulgaria 44°5N 27°14E 203 B11
Standerton S. Africa 26°55S 29°7E 271 C4
Standish U.S.A. 43°59N 83°57W 309 D12
Stanford S. Africa 34°26S 19°29E 270 D2
Stanford Mont., U.S.A. 47°9N 110°13W 304 C8
Stånga Sweden 57°17N 18°29E 163 G12
Stange Norway 60°43N 11°5E 164 D8
Stanger S. Africa 29°27S 31°14E 271 C5
Stängselåsen = Salpausselkä Finland 61°3N 26°15E 188 B4
Stangvik Norway 62°55N 8°28E 164 B5
Stanhope Vic., Australia 36°27S 144°59E 283 D6
Stanhope Iowa, U.S.A. 42°17N 93°48W 310 B3
Stanimaka = Asenovgrad Bulgaria 42°1N 24°51E 203 D8
Stanišić Serbia 45°56N 19°10E 182 E4
Stanislaus ➝ U.S.A. 37°40N 121°14W 306 H5
Stanislav = Ivano-Frankivsk Ukraine 48°40N 24°40E 183 B9
Stanisławów = Ivano-Frankivsk Ukraine 48°40N 24°40E 183 B9
Stanisławów Poland 52°18N 21°33E 185 F8
Stanley Tas., Australia 40°46S 145°19E 281 G4
Stanley Hong Kong, China 22°13N 114°12E 122 B2
Stanley Falk. Is. 51°40S 59°51W 153 f
Stanley Durham, U.K. 54°53N 1°41W 168 C6
Stanley Idaho, U.S.A. 44°13N 114°56W 304 D6
Stanley N. Dak., U.S.A. 48°19N 102°23W 308 A2
Stanley N.Y., U.S.A. 42°48N 77°6W 312 D7
Stanley Falls = Boyoma, Chutes Dem. Rep. of the Congo 0°35N 25°23E 264 B5
Stanley Mission Canada 55°25N 104°33W 297 B8
Stanley Pen. China 22°12N 114°12E 122 B2
Stanley Pool = Malebo, Pool Africa 4°17S 15°20E 265 C3
Stanley Res. India 11°50N 77°40E 245 J3
Stanleyville = Kisangani Dem. Rep. of the Congo 0°35N 25°15E 268 B2
Stanmore U.K. 51°37N 0°18W 125 A2
Stannards U.S.A. 42°5N 77°55W 312 D7
Stanovoy Khrebet Russia 55°0N 130°0E 215 D14
Stanovoy Ra. = Stanovoy Khrebet Russia 55°0N 130°0E 215 D14
Stansmore Ra. Australia 21°23S 128°33E 278 D4
Stansted, London ✈ (STN) U.K. 51°54N 0°14E 169 F8
Stanthorpe Australia 28°36S 151°59E 281 D5
Stanton Ky., U.S.A. 37°54N 83°52W 311 G13
Stanton Tex., U.S.A. 32°8N 101°48W 314 E4
Stanwood U.S.A. 48°15N 122°23W 306 B4
Staples Ont., Canada 42°10N 82°35W 312 D2
Staples Minn., U.S.A. 46°21N 94°48W 308 B6
Stapleton N.Y., U.S.A. 40°36N 74°5W 132 C1
Stapleton Nebr., U.S.A. 41°29N 100°31W 308 E3
Stąporków Poland 51°9N 20°31E 185 G7
Star City Canada 52°50N 104°20W 297 C8
Star Ferry Hong Kong, China 122 a2
Star Harbour Solomon Is. 10°47S 162°19E 287 N12
Star Lake U.S.A. 44°10N 75°2W 313 B9
Stará Ďala = Hurbanovo Slovak Rep. 47°51N 18°11E 181 D11
Stará L'ubovňa Slovak Rep. 49°18N 20°42E 181 B13
Stara Moravica Serbia 45°50N 19°30E 182 E4
Stara Pazova Serbia 44°58N 20°10E 182 F5
Stara Planina Bulgaria 43°15N 23°0E 202 C7
Stara Sil Ukraine 49°29N 22°58E 185 J9
Stará Turá Slovak Rep. 48°47N 17°42E 181 C10
Stara Ushytsya Ukraine 48°35N 27°8E 183 B12
Stara Zagora Bulgaria 42°26N 25°39E 203 D9
Starachowice Poland 51°3N 21°2E 185 G8
Staraya Derevnya Russia 59°58N 30°15E 137 B1
Staraya Russa Russia 57°58N 31°23E 188 D6
Starbuck I. Kiribati 5°37S 155°55W 289 H12
Starchiojd Romania 45°19N 26°11E 183 E11
Starcke △ Australia 14°56S 145°2E 280 A4
Staré Město Czech Rep. 50°5N 14°25E 135 B2
Stare Miasto Warsaw, Poland 142 a2
Stargard in Pommern = Stargard Szczeciński Poland 53°20N 15°0E 184 E2
Stargard Szczeciński Poland 53°20N 15°0E 184 E2
Ståhreim Norway 61°56N 5°40E 164 C2
Stari Bar Montenegro 42°7N 19°10E 202 D3
Stari Bečej = Bečej Serbia 45°36N 20°3E 182 E5
Stari Trg Slovenia 45°29N 15°7E 199 C12
Staritsa Russia 56°33N 34°55E 188 D8
Starke U.S.A. 29°57N 82°7W 316 F7
Starke, L. U.S.A. 28°34N 81°32W 133 A1
Starkville U.S.A. 33°28N 88°49W 315 E10
Starnberg Germany 48°0N 11°21E 179 H7
Starnberger See Germany 47°54N 11°19E 179 H7
Starobilsk Ukraine 49°16N 39°0E 189 H10
Starodub Russia 52°30N 32°50E 189 F7
Starogard Gdański Poland 53°59N 18°30E 184 E5
Starokonstantinov = Starokonstyantyniv Ukraine 49°48N 27°10E 177 D14
Starokonstyantyniv Ukraine 49°48N 27°10E 177 D14
Starokozache Ukraine 46°20N 29°59E 183 D14
Starominskaya Russia 46°33N 39°0E 189 J10
Staroshcherbinovskaya Russia 46°40N 38°53E 189 J10
Starrs Mill U.S.A. 33°19N 84°31W 316 B5
Start Pt. U.K. 50°13N 3°39W 169 G4
Stary Sącz Poland 49°33N 20°35E 185 J7
Staryy Biryuzyak Russia 44°46N 46°50E 191 H8
Staryy Chartoriysk Ukraine 51°15N 25°54E 177 C13
Staryy Krym Ukraine 45°3N 35°8E 189 K8
Staryy Margilan = Marghilon Uzbekistan 40°27N 71°42E 217 D8
Staryy Oskol Russia 51°19N 37°55E 189 G9
Staryy Sambir Ukraine 49°27N 22°59E 185 J9
Stassfurt Germany 51°51N 11°35E 178 D7
Staszów Poland 50°33N 21°10E 185 H8
State Center U.S.A. 42°1N 93°10W 310 B3
State College U.S.A. 40°48N 77°52W 312 F7
Stateline U.S.A. 38°57N 119°56W 306 G7
Staten, I. = Estados, I. de Los Argentina 54°40S 64°30W 336 D4
Staten I. U.S.A. 40°35N 74°9W 313 F10
Staten Island Zoo U.S.A. 40°38N 74°6W 132 C1
Staten Islands Ferry Terminal U.S.A. 40°38N 74°4W 132 C1
Statenice Czech Rep. 50°9N 14°19E 135 B1
Statenville U.S.A. 30°42N 83°2W 316 E6
Statesboro U.S.A. 32°27N 81°47W 316 C8
Statesville U.S.A. 35°47N 80°53W 315 D14
Statham U.S.A. 33°58N 83°35W 316 B6
Stathelle Norway 59°3N 9°41E 164 E6
Statia = St. Eustatius W. Indies 17°20N 63°0W 322 a
Statue Square Hong Kong, China 122 c1
Stauffer U.S.A. 34°45N 119°3W 307 L7
Staunton Ill., U.S.A. 39°1N 89°47W 310 F7
Staunton Va., U.S.A. 38°9N 79°4W 309 F14
Stavanger = Rogaland □ Norway 59°12N 6°20E 164 E3
Stavanger Norway 58°57N 5°40E 164 F2
Stavelot Belgium 50°23N 5°55E 170 D5
Stavern Norway 59°0N 10°1E 164 F7
Stavoren Neths. 52°53N 5°22E 170 B5
Stavropol Russia 45°5N 42°0E 191 H6
Stavropol □ Russia 47°20N 42°50E 191 G6
Stavros Cyprus 35°1N 32°38E 207 E8
Stavros Ithaki, Greece 38°27N 20°39E 207 C2
Stavros Kriti, Greece 35°12N 24°45E 207 E5
Stavros Thessaloniki, Greece 40°39N 23°43E 202 F7
Stavros, Akra Greece 35°26N 24°58E 207 E5
Stavroupoli Greece 41°12N 24°45E 203 E8
Stawell Australia 37°5S 142°47E 282 D5
Stawell ➝ Australia 20°20S 142°55E 280 C3
Stawiski Poland 53°22N 22°9E 184 E9
Stawiszyn Poland 51°56N 18°4E 185 G5
Stayner Canada 44°25N 80°5W 312 B4
Stayton U.S.A. 44°48N 122°48W 304 D2
Steamboat Springs U.S.A. 40°29N 106°50W 304 F10
Stean Norway 59°16N 8°33E 164 E5
Stebbins U.S.A. 63°31N 162°17W 303 E7
Steblevë Albania 41°23N 20°33E 202 E4
Stedelijk Museum Neths. 52°21N 4°52E 112 A2
Steele Ala., U.S.A. 33°56N 86°12W 316 B3
Steele N. Dak., U.S.A. 46°51N 99°55W 308 B4
Steele Creek Australia 37°44S 144°52E 128 A1
Steelton U.S.A. 40°14N 76°50W 312 F8
Steelville U.S.A. 37°58N 91°22W 310 G5
Steen River Canada 59°40N 117°12W 296 B5
Steenkool = Bintuni Indonesia 2°7S 133°32E 231 E8
Steenokkerzeel Belgium 50°55N 4°31E 116 A2
Steens Mt. U.S.A. 42°35N 118°40W 304 E4
Steenstrup Gletscher Greenland 75°15N 57°0W 154 B5
Steenwijk Neths. 52°47N 6°7E 170 B6
Steep Pt. Australia 26°8S 113°8E 279 E1
Steep Rock Canada 51°30N 98°48W 297 C9
Steer, L. U.S.A. 28°31N 81°30W 133 A2
Ştefan Vodă Moldova 46°27N 29°42E 183 D14
Ştefăneşti Romania 47°44N 27°15E 183 C12
Stefanie L. = Chew Bahir Ethiopia 4°40N 36°50E 257 G4
Stefanie △ Ethiopia 4°55N 36°55E 257 G4
Stefansson Bay Antarctica 67°20S 59°8E 151 C5
Stefansson I. Canada 73°20N 105°45W 295 C10
Stege Denmark 54°59N 12°18E 163 K6
Stegi = Siteki Swaziland 26°32S 31°58E 271 C5
Steglitz Germany 52°27N 13°19E 115 B2
Stegman = Artesia U.S.A. 32°51N 104°24W 305 K11
Ştei Romania 46°32N 22°27E 182 D7
Steiermark □ Austria 47°26N 15°0E 180 D8
Steigerwald Germany 49°44N 10°26E 179 F6
Steigerwald ⌓ Germany 49°50N 10°30E 179 F6
Steilacoom U.S.A. 47°10N 122°36W 306 C4
Steilrandberge Namibia 17°45S 13°20E 270 A1
Stein = Kamnik Slovenia 46°14N 14°37E 199 B11
Steinbach Canada 49°32N 96°40W 297 D9
Steinfurt Germany 52°9N 7°20E 178 C3
Steinhatchee U.S.A. 29°40N 83°23W 316 F6
Steinhausen Namibia 21°49S 18°20E 270 B2
Steinheim Germany 51°51N 9°5E 178 D5
Steinhuder Meer Germany 52°29N 9°21E 178 C5
Steinhuder Meer ⌓ Germany 52°30N 9°16E 178 C5
Steinkjer Norway 64°1N 11°31E 160 D14
Steinkopf S. Africa 29°18S 17°43E 270 C2
Steinshamn Norway 62°47N 6°28E 164 B3
Steinwald ⌓ Germany 49°55N 12°8E 179 F8
Stellarton Canada 45°32N 62°30W 299 C7
Stellenbosch S. Africa 33°58S 18°50E 270 D2
Stelvio, Paso dello Italy 46°32N 10°27E 198 B7
Stenay France 49°29N 5°12E 173 C12
Stendal Germany 52°36N 11°53E 178 C7
Stende Latvia 57°11N 22°33E 184 A9
Stenen Koraal Neth. Ant. 12°10N 68°56W 322 g
Stenhamra Sweden 59°20N 17°41E 162 E11
Stenhousemuir U.K. 56°2N 3°48W 167 E5
Stenshuvud △ Sweden 55°39N 14°15E 163 J8
Stenstorp Sweden 58°17N 13°45E 163 F7
Stenungsund Sweden 58°6N 11°50E 163 F5
Steornabhaigh = Stornoway U.K. 58°13N 6°23W 167 C2
Stepanakert = Xankändi Azerbaijan 39°52N 46°49E 213 C12
Stepanavan Armenia 41°1N 44°23E 191 K7
Stepaside Ireland 53°15N 6°12W 120 B2
Stephansdom Vienna, Austria 142 b2
Stephens, C. N.Z. 40°42S 173°58E 285 A8
Stephens Creek Australia 31°50S 141°30E 282 A4
Stephens I. B.C., Canada 54°10N 130°45W 296 C2
Stephens I. N.Z. 40°40S 174°1E 285 A9
Stephens L. Canada 56°32N 95°0W 297 B9
Stephenville Nfld. & L., Canada 48°31N 58°35W 299 C8
Stephenville Tex., U.S.A. 32°13N 98°12W 314 E5
Stepney U.K. 51°30N 0°3W 125 A3
Stepnica Poland 53°38N 14°36E 184 E1
Stepnogorsk Kazakhstan 52°21N 71°53E 217 B8
Stepnoi = Elista Russia 46°16N 44°14E 191 G7
Steppe Asia 50°0N 50°0E 210 C7
Steps Pt. Amer. Samoa 14°23S 170°45W 302 f
Sterea Ellas □ Greece 38°50N 23°0E 204 C4
Sterkstroom S. Africa 31°32S 26°32E 270 D4
Sterling Alaska, U.S.A. 60°32N 150°46W 303 F10
Sterling Colo., U.S.A. 40°37N 103°13W 304 F12
Sterling Ga., U.S.A. 31°16N 81°34W 316 D8
Sterling Ill., U.S.A. 41°48N 89°42W 310 C7
Sterling Kans., U.S.A. 38°13N 98°12W 308 F4
Sterling City U.S.A. 31°51N 101°0W 314 F4
Sterling Heights U.S.A. 42°35N 83°2W 311 B13
Sterling Park U.S.A. 37°41N 122°27W 136 B2
Sterling Run U.S.A. 41°25N 78°12W 312 E6
Sterlitamak Russia 53°40N 56°0E 186 D10
Sternberg Germany 53°42N 11°50E 178 B7
Šternberk Czech Rep. 49°45N 17°15E 181 B10
Sternes Greece 35°30N 24°9E 207 E5
Sterzing = Vipiteno Italy 46°54N 11°26E 199 B8
Stettin = Szczecin Poland 53°27N 14°27E 184 E1
Stettiner Haff Germany 53°47N 14°15E 178 B10
Stettler Canada 52°19N 112°40W 296 C6
Steubenville U.S.A. 40°22N 80°37W 312 F4
Stevenage U.K. 51°55N 0°13W 169 F7
Stevens Point U.S.A. 44°31N 89°34W 308 C9
Stevens Pottery U.S.A. 32°57N 83°17W 316 C6
Stevens Village U.S.A. 66°1N 149°6W 303 C10
Stevenson U.S.A. 45°42N 121°53W 306 E5
Stevenson ➝ Australia 27°6S 135°33E 281 D2
Stevenson L. Canada 53°55N 96°0W 297 C9
Stevensville U.S.A. 46°30N 114°5W 304 C6
Stevns Klint Denmark 55°17N 12°28E 163 J6
Steward U.S.A. 41°51N 89°1W 310 C7
Stewardson U.S.A. 39°16N 88°38W 311 E8
Stewart B.C., Canada 55°56N 129°57W 296 B3
Stewart Ga., U.S.A. 33°25N 83°52W 316 B6
Stewart Nev., U.S.A. 39°5N 119°46W 306 F7
Stewart ➝ Canada 63°19N 139°26W 294 E4
Stewart, C. Australia 11°57S 134°56E 280 A1
Stewart, I. Chile 54°50S 71°15W 336 D2
Stewart I. N.Z. 46°58S 167°54E 285 G2
Stewarts Point U.S.A. 38°39N 123°24W 306 G3
Stewartsville U.S.A. 39°45N 94°30W 310 E2
Stewartville U.S.A. 43°51N 92°29W 308 D7
Stewiacke Canada 45°9N 63°22W 299 C7
Steynsburg S. Africa 31°15S 25°49E 270 D4
Steyr Austria 48°3N 14°25E 180 C7
Steyr ➝ Austria 48°3N 14°25E 180 C7
Steytlerville S. Africa 33°17S 24°19E 270 D3
Stia Italy 43°48N 11°42E 199 E8
Sticklinge udde Sweden 59°23N 18°6E 139 A2
Stickney U.S.A. 41°49N 87°46W 119 C2
Stigler U.S.A. 35°15N 95°8W 314 D7
Stigliano Italy 40°24N 16°14E 201 B9
Stigtomta Sweden 58°47N 16°48E 163 F10
Stikine ➝ Canada 56°40N 132°30W 296 B2
Stilfontein S. Africa 26°51S 26°50E 270 C4
Stilida Greece 38°55N 22°47E 204 C4
Stillmore U.S.A. 32°27N 82°13W 316 C7
Stillorgan Ireland 53°17N 6°11W 120 B2
Stillwater N.Y., U.S.A. 42°55N 73°41W 313 D11
Stillwater Okla., U.S.A. 36°7N 97°4W 314 C6
Stillwater Range U.S.A. 39°50N 118°5W 304 G4
Stillwater Res. U.S.A. 43°54N 75°3W 313 C9
Stilo, Pta. Italy 38°25N 16°35E 201 D9
Stilwell U.S.A. 35°49N 94°38W 314 D7
Stînga Nistrului □ Moldova 47°20N 29°15E 183 C14
Štip Macedonia 41°42N 22°10E 202 E6
Stira Greece 38°9N 24°14E 204 C6
Stirling Ont., Canada 44°18N 77°33W 312 B7
Stirling N.Z. 46°15S 169°49E 285 G4
Stirling Stirling, U.K. 56°8N 3°57W 167 E5
Stirling □ U.K. 56°12N 4°18W 167 E4
Stirling Ra. Australia 34°23S 118°0E 279 F2
Stirling Range △ Australia 34°26S 118°20E 279 F2
Stittsville Canada 45°15N 75°55W 313 A9
Stjernøya Norway 70°20N 22°40E 160 A20
Stjørdalshalsen Norway 63°29N 10°51E 164 A7
Stock Island U.S.A. 24°32N 81°34W 317 L8
Stockach Germany 47°50N 9°1E 179 H5
Stockaryd Sweden 57°19N 14°36E 163 G8
Stockbridge Ga., U.S.A. 33°33N 84°14W 316 B5
Stockbridge Mich., U.S.A. 42°27N 84°11W 311 B12
Stockerau Austria 48°24N 16°12E 181 C9
Stockholm Sweden 59°19N 18°4E 139 B2
Stockholm Arlanda ✈ (ARN) Sweden 59°41N 17°56E 139 A1
Stockholms län □ Sweden 59°30N 18°20E 162 E12
Stockport U.K. 53°25N 2°9W 168 D5
Stocksbridge U.K. 53°29N 1°35W 168 D6
Stocksund Sweden 59°23N 18°3E 139 A2
Stockton Calif., U.S.A. 37°58N 121°17W 306 H5
Stockton Ill., U.S.A. 42°21N 90°1W 310 B6
Stockton Kans., U.S.A. 39°26N 99°16W 308 F4
Stockton Mo., U.S.A. 37°42N 93°48W 310 G3
Stockton-on-Tees U.K. 54°35N 1°19W 168 C6
Stockton-on-Tees □ U.K. 54°35N 1°19W 168 C6
Stockton Plateau U.S.A. 30°30N 102°30W 314 F3
Stoczek Łukowski Poland 51°58N 21°58E 185 G8
Stöde Sweden 62°28N 16°35E 162 B10
Stöðvarfjörður Iceland 64°49N 13°52W 155 C13
Stodůlky Czech Rep. 50°3N 14°19E 135 B1
Stoeng Treng Cambodia 13°31N 105°58E 236 F5
Stoer, Pt. of U.K. 58°16N 5°23W 167 C3
Stogovo Macedonia 41°31N 20°38E 202 E4
Stoholm Denmark 56°30N 9°8E 163 H3
Stoke N.Z. 41°19S 173°14E 285 B8
Stoke Newington U.K. 51°33N 0°4W 125 A3
Stoke-on-Trent U.K. 53°1N 2°11W 168 D5
Stoke-on-Trent □ U.K. 53°1N 2°11W 168 D5
Stokes △ Australia 33°45S 121°11E 279 F3
Stokes Bay Canada 45°0N 81°28W 312 B3
Stokes Pt. Australia 40°10S 143°56E 281 G3
Stokes Ra. Australia 15°50S 130°50E 278 C5
Stokes Valley N.Z. 41°10S 174°59E 143 B2
Stokkseyri Iceland 63°50N 21°2W 155 D5
Stokksnes Iceland 64°14N 14°58W 155 C12
Stokmarknes Norway 68°34N 14°54E 160 B16
Stolac Bos.-H. 43°5N 17°59E 202 C1
Stolberg Germany 50°47N 6°13E 178 E2
Stolbovoy, Ostrov Russia 74°44N 135°14E 215 B14
Stolbtsy = Stowbtsy Belarus 53°30N 26°43E 177 B14
Stolin Belarus 51°53N 26°50E 177 C14
Stöllet Sweden 60°26N 13°15E 162 D7
Stolnici Romania 44°31N 24°48E 183 F9
Stolp = Słupsk Poland 54°30N 17°3E 184 D4
Stolpmünde = Ustka Poland 54°35N 16°55E 184 D3
Stomio Greece 35°21N 23°32E 207 E4
Ston Croatia 42°51N 17°43E 199 F14
Stone U.K. 52°55N 2°9W 168 E5
Stone Canyon Res. U.S.A. 34°6N 118°27W 126 B2
Stone Mountain U.S.A. 33°49N 84°10W 316 B5
Stone Park U.S.A. 41°53N 87°52W 119 B1
Stoneboro U.S.A. 41°20N 80°7W 312 E4
Stonebridge U.K. 51°32N 0°16W 125 A2
Stoneham U.S.A. 42°29N 71°5W 116 A2
Stonehaven U.K. 56°59N 2°12W 167 E6
Stonehenge Queens., Australia 24°22S 143°17E 280 C3
Stonehenge Wilts., U.K. 51°9N 1°45W 169 F6
Stonewall Canada 50°10N 97°19W 297 C9
Stongfjorden Norway 61°26N 5°10E 164 C2
Stonington U.S.A. 39°44N 89°12W 310 E7
Stony Brook Res. U.S.A. 42°15N 71°8W 116 B2
Stony Creek ➝ U.S.A. 41°38N 87°41W 119 C2
Stony Hill Jamaica 18°5N 76°48W 320 a
Stony I. U.S.A. 43°53N 76°19W 313 C8
Stony L. Man., Canada 58°51N 98°40W 297 B9
Stony L. Ont., Canada 44°30N 78°5W 312 B6
Stony Point U.S.A. 41°14N 73°59W 313 E11
Stony Pt. U.S.A. 43°50N 76°18W 313 C8
Stony Rapids Canada 59°16N 105°50W 297 B7
Stony River U.S.A. 61°47N 156°35W 303 F8
Stony Tunguska = Tunguska, Podkamennaya ➝ Russia 61°50N 90°13E 215 C10
Stonyford U.S.A. 39°23N 122°33W 306 F4
Stopnica Poland 50°27N 20°57E 185 H7
Storå Sweden 59°42N 15°6E 162 E9
Storå ➝ Denmark 56°20N 8°19E 163 H2
Stora Gla Sweden 59°30N 12°30E 162 E6
Stora Le Sweden 59°5N 11°55E 162 E5
Stora Lulevatten Sweden 67°10N 19°30E 160 C18
Stora Värtan Sweden 59°25N 18°7E 139 A2
Stóra-Vatnshorn Iceland 65°4N 21°33W 155 B5
Storavan Sweden 65°45N 18°10E 160 D18
Stord Norway 59°52N 5°23E 164 E2
Stordalen Norway 62°23N 7°0E 164 B4
Store Bælt Denmark 55°20N 11°0E 163 J4
Store Hareskov Denmark 55°46N 12°23E 118 A2
Store Heddinge Denmark 55°18N 12°23E 163 J6
Store Jukleggi = Høgeloft Norway 61°3N 8°12E 164 C5
Store Koldewey Greenland 76°30N 19°0W 154 B9
Store Magleby Denmark 55°35N 12°35E 118 B3
Store Mosse △ Sweden 57°18N 13°55E 163 G7
Store Sotra Norway 60°18N 5°4E 164 D1
Storebro Sweden 57°35N 15°52E 163 G9
Støren Norway 63°3N 10°18E 164 A7
Storerikvollen Norway 63°7N 11°58E 164 A8
Storfjellsætra Norway 61°40N 10°30E 164 C7
Storfjorden Norway 62°28N 6°35E 164 B3
Storfors Sweden 59°32N 14°17E 162 E8
Storholmen Sweden 59°23N 18°8E 139 A2
Stóridalur Iceland 63°38N 19°57W 155 D7
Stórinúpur Iceland 64°3N 20°10W 155 C6
Storkerson Pen. Canada 72°30N 106°30W 294 C10
Storkyrkan Stockholm, Sweden 139 c2
Storli Norway 62°42N 9°25E 164 B6
Storlien Sweden 63°19N 12°6E 162 A6
Storm B. Australia 43°10S 147°30E 281 G4
Storm Lake U.S.A. 42°39N 95°13W 308 D6
Stormberge S. Africa 31°16S 26°17E 270 D4
Stormsrivier S. Africa 33°59S 23°52E 270 D3
Stornoway U.K. 58°13N 6°23W 167 C2
Storo Italy 45°51N 10°35E 198 C7
Storozhinets = Storozhynets Ukraine 48°14N 25°45E 183 B10
Storozhynets Ukraine 48°14N 25°45E 183 B10
Storrs U.S.A. 41°49N 72°15W 313 E12
Storsjöen Hedmark, Norway 60°20N 11°40E 164 D8
Storsjöen Hedmark, Norway 61°30N 11°14E 164 C8
Storsjön Gävleborg, Sweden 60°35N 16°45E 162 D10
Storsjön Jämtland, Sweden 62°48N 13°12E 162 B7
Storsjön Jämtland, Sweden 63°9N 14°30E 162 A8
Storsølnkletten Norway 61°59N 10°16E 164 C7
Storstrømmen Greenland 76°17N 22°25W 154 B8
Storuman Sweden 65°5N 17°10E 160 D17
Storuman, L. Sweden 65°13N 16°50E 160 D17
Stóruvellir Iceland 65°30N 17°29W 155 B9
Storvätteshågna Sweden 62°6N 12°30E 162 B6
Storvigelen Norway 62°32N 12°2E 164 B9
Storvik Sweden 60°35N 16°33E 162 D10
Storvreta Sweden 59°58N 17°44E 162 E11
Story City U.S.A. 42°11N 93°36W 310 B3
Stouffville Canada 43°58N 79°15W 312 C5
Stoughton Sask., Canada 49°40N 103°0W 297 D8
Stoughton Wis., U.S.A. 42°55N 89°13W 310 B8
Stour ➝ Dorset, U.K. 50°43N 1°47W 169 G6
Stour ➝ Kent, U.K. 51°18N 1°22E 169 F9
Stour ➝ Suffolk, U.K. 51°57N 1°4E 169 F9
Stourbridge U.K. 52°28N 2°8W 169 E5
Stout L. Canada 52°0N 94°40W 297 C10
Stove Pipe Wells Village U.S.A. 36°35N 117°11W 307 J9
Støvring Denmark 56°54N 9°50E 163 H3
Stow U.S.A. 41°10N 81°27W 312 E3
Stowbtsy Belarus 53°30N 26°43E 177 B14
Stowmarket U.K. 52°12N 1°0E 169 E9
Stoyka Russia 59°57N 30°25E 137 B2
Strabane U.K. 54°50N 7°27W 166 B4
Stracin Macedonia 42°13N 22°2E 202 D6
Stradella Italy 45°5N 9°18E 198 C6
Strahan Australia 42°9S 145°20E 281 G4
Strakonice Czech Rep. 49°15N 13°53E 180 B6
Straldzha Bulgaria 42°35N 26°40E 203 D10
Stralsund Germany 54°18N 13°4E 178 A9
Strand Hedmark, Norway 61°17N 11°17E 164 C8
Strand Western Cape, S. Africa 34°9S 18°48E 270 D2
Strand London, U.K. 125 b4
Stranda Møre og Romsdal, Norway 62°19N 6°58E 164 B3
Stranda Nord-Trøndelag, Norway 63°33N 10°14E 160 E14
Strandasýsla □ Iceland 65°45N 21°45W 155 B5
Strandby Denmark 57°30N 10°29E 163 G4
Strandfontein S. Africa 34°4S 18°33E 118 B2
Strangford L. U.K. 54°30N 5°37W 166 B6
Strängnäs Sweden 59°23N 17°2E 162 E11
Stranorlar Ireland 54°48N 7°46W 166 B4
Stranraer U.K. 54°54N 5°1W 167 G3
Strasbourg Sask., Canada 51°4N 104°55W 297 C8
Strasbourg Bas-Rhin, France 48°35N 7°42E 173 D14
Strasburg Germany 53°30N 13°43E 178 B9
Strasburg Moldova 47°8N 28°36E 183 C13
Strašnice Czech Rep. 50°4N 14°28E 135 B2
Stråssa Sweden 59°45N 15°12E 162 E9
Strassburg = Aiud Romania 46°19N 23°44E 183 D8
Strasstrudering Germany 48°6N 11°41E 131 B3
Stratford N.S.W., Australia 32°7S 151°55E 283 B9
Stratford Vic., Australia 37°59S 147°7E 283 D7
Stratford Ont., Canada 43°23N 81°0W 312 C4
Stratford N.Z. 39°20S 174°19E 284 F3
Stratford London, U.K. 51°33N 0°0 125 A4
Stratford Calif., U.S.A. 36°11N 119°49W 306 J7
Stratford Conn., U.S.A. 41°12N 73°8W 313 E11
Stratford Tex., U.S.A. 36°20N 102°4W 314 C3
Stratford-upon-Avon U.K. 52°12N 1°42W 169 E6
Strath Spey U.K. 57°9N 3°49W 167 D5
Strathalbyn Australia 35°13S 138°53E 282 C3
Strathaven U.K. 55°40N 4°5W 167 F4
Strathcona ⌓ Canada 49°38N 125°40W 296 D3
Strathfield Australia 33°52S 151°5E 139 B1
Strathmore Alta., Canada 51°5N 113°18W 296 C6
Strathmore Angus, U.K. 56°37N 3°7W 167 E5
Strathmore Calif., U.S.A. 36°9N 119°4W 306 J7
Strathnaver Canada 53°20N 122°33W 296 C4
Strathpeffer U.K. 57°35N 4°32W 167 D4
Strathroy Canada 42°58N 81°38W 312 D3
Strathy Pt. U.K. 58°36N 4°1W 167 C4
Strattanville U.S.A. 41°12N 79°19W 312 E5
Stratton U.S.A. 45°8N 70°26W 313 A14
Stratton Mt. U.S.A. 43°4N 72°55W 313 C12
Straubing Germany 48°52N 12°34E 179 G8
Straumnes Iceland 66°26N 23°8W 155 A3
Strausberg Germany 52°35N 13°54E 178 C9
Strawberry ➝ U.S.A. 40°10N 110°24W 304 F8
Strawberry Point U.S.A. 42°41N 91°32W 310 B5
Strážnice Czech Rep. 48°54N 17°19E 181 C10
Streaky B. Australia 32°48S 134°13E 281 E1
Streaky Bay Australia 32°51S 134°18E 281 E1
Streatham U.K. 51°25N 0°7W 125 B3
Streatham Vale U.K. 51°24N 0°8W 125 B3
Streator U.S.A. 41°8N 88°50W 311 C8
Strebersdorf Austria 48°17N 16°23E 142 A2
Středočeský □ Czech Rep. 49°55N 14°30E 180 B7
Streetsboro U.S.A. 41°14N 81°21W 312 E3
Streetsville Canada 43°35N 79°42W 312 C5
Strehaia Romania 44°37N 23°10E 183 F8
Strehlen = Strzelin Poland 50°46N 17°2E 185 H4
Strelcha Bulgaria 42°25N 24°19E 203 D8
Strelka Russia 58°5N 93°3E 215 D10
Streng ➝ Cambodia 13°12N 103°37E 236 F4
Stresa Italy 45°52N 8°28E 198 C5
Střešovice Czech Rep. 50°5N 14°23E 135 B2
Streymoy Færoe Is. 62°8N 7°5W 160 E9
Strezhevoy Russia 60°42N 77°34E 214 C8
Stříbro Czech Rep. 49°44N 13°0E 180 A6
Strickland ➝ Papua N. G. 7°35S 141°36E 286 D1
Striegau = Strzegom Poland 50°58N 16°20E 185 H3
Strilky Ukraine 49°20N 22°59E 185 J9
Strimonas ➝ Greece 40°46N 23°51E 202 F7
Strip, The U.S.A. 36°7N 115°10W 124 B2
Střížkov Czech Rep. 50°7N 14°28E 135 B2
Stroeder Argentina 40°12S 62°37W 336 B4
Strofades Greece 37°15N 21°0E 204 D3
Strogino Russia 55°48N 37°24E 129 B2
Strokestown Ireland 53°46N 8°7W 166 C3
Stroma U.K. 58°41N 3°7W 167 C5
Strombeek-Bever Belgium 50°54N 4°21E 116 A2
Stromberg-Heuchelberg ⌓ Germany 49°2N 8°50E 179 F4
Strómboli Italy 38°47N 15°13E 201 D8
Stromeferry U.K. 57°21N 5°33W 167 D3
Strommen Norway 59°57N 11°0E 164 E7
Stromness U.K. 58°58N 3°17W 167 C5
Stromovka Czech Rep. 50°6N 14°25E 135 B2
Strömsbruk Sweden 61°52N 17°18E 162 C11
Stromsburg U.S.A. 41°7N 97°36W 308 E5
Strömsnäsbruk Sweden 56°35N 13°45E 163 H7
Strömstad Sweden 58°56N 11°10E 163 F5
Strömsund Sweden 63°51N 15°33E 160 E16
Stronghurst U.S.A. 40°45N 90°55W 310 D6
Strongili Greece 36°6N 29°42E 205 E11
Strongoli Italy 39°16N 17°3E 201 C10
Strongsville U.S.A. 41°19N 81°50W 312 E3
Stronie Śląskie Poland 50°18N 16°53E 185 H3
Stronsay U.K. 59°7N 2°35W 167 B6
Stropkov Slovak Rep. 49°13N 21°39E 181 B14
Stroud U.K. 51°45N 2°13W 169 F5
Stroud Road Australia 32°18S 151°57E 283 B9
Stroudsburg U.S.A. 40°59N 75°12W 313 F9
Stroumbi Cyprus 34°53N 32°29E 207 E8
Štrpce Kosovo 42°14N 21°1E 202 D5
Struer Denmark 56°30N 8°35E 163 H2
Struga Macedonia 41°11N 20°44E 202 E4
Strugi Krasnyye Russia 58°21N 29°1E 188 C5
Strumica Macedonia 41°28N 22°41E 202 E6
Strumica ➝ Europe 41°20N 23°22E 202 E7
Strumok Ukraine 45°43N 29°27E 183 E14
Struthers U.S.A. 41°4N 80°39W 312 E4
Stryama Bulgaria 42°16N 24°54E 203 D8
Stryker U.S.A. 48°41N 114°46W 304 B6
Stryków Poland 51°55N 19°33E 185 G6
Stryn Norway 61°54N 6°43E 164 C3
Stryy Ukraine 49°16N 23°48E 177 D12
Strzegom Poland 50°58N 16°20E 185 H3
Strzelce Krajeńskie Poland 52°52N 15°33E 185 F2
Strzelce Opolskie Poland 50°31N 18°18E 185 H5
Strzelecki Cr. ➝ Australia 29°37S 139°59E 281 D2
Strzelecki Desert Australia 29°30S 140°0E 281 D3
Strzelin Poland 50°46N 17°2E 185 H4
Strzelno Poland 52°35N 18°9E 185 F5
Strzybnica Poland 50°28N 18°48E 185 H5
Strzyżów Poland 49°52N 21°47E 185 J8
Stuart Fla., U.S.A. 27°12N 80°15W 317 H9
Stuart Iowa, U.S.A. 41°30N 94°19W 310 C2
Stuart Nebr., U.S.A. 42°36N 99°8W 308 D4
Stuart ➝ Canada 54°0N 123°35W 296 C4
Stuart Bluff Ra. Australia 22°50S 131°52E 278 D5
Stuart I. U.S.A. 63°35N 162°30W 303 E7
Stuart L. Canada 54°30N 124°30W 296 C4
Stuart Mts. N.Z. 45°2S 167°39E 285 F2
Stuart Ra. Australia 29°10S 134°56E 281 D1
Stubbekøbing Denmark 54°53N 12°9E 163 K6
Stubbs St. Vincent 13°7N 61°9W 323 n
Stuben Austria 47°10N 10°8E 180 D3
Štubnianske Teplice = Turčianske Teplice Slovak Rep. 48°52N 18°52E 181 C11
Studen Kladenets, Yazovir Bulgaria 41°37N 25°30E 203 E9
Studenka Czech Rep. 49°44N 18°5E 181 B11
Studholme N.Z. 44°42S 171°9E 285 E6
Studio City U.S.A. 34°8N 118°24W 126 B2
Studley Park Trin. & Tob. 11°11N 60°40W 323 s
Stugudalen Norway 62°53N 11°53E 164 B8
Stugun Sweden 63°10N 15°40E 162 A9
Stuhlweissenburg = Székesfehérvár Hungary 47°15N 18°25E 182 C3
Stuhm = Sztum Poland 53°55N 19°1E 184 E6
Stuhr Germany 53°5N 8°44E 178 B4
Stull L. Canada 54°24N 92°34W 298 B1
Stung Treng = Stoeng Treng Cambodia 13°31N 105°58E 236 F5
Stupart ➝ Canada 56°0N 93°25W 298 A1
Stupava Slovak Rep. 48°17N 17°2E 181 C10
Stupino Russia 54°57N 38°2E 188 E10
Stureby Sweden 59°15N 18°4E 139 B2
Sturge I. Antarctica 67°26S 164°47E 151 C11
Sturgeon B. Canada 52°0N 97°50W 297 C9
Sturgeon Bay U.S.A. 44°50N 87°23W 308 C10
Sturgeon Falls Canada 46°25N 79°57W 298 C4
Sturgeon L. Alta., Canada 55°6N 117°32W 296 B5
Sturgeon L. Ont., Canada 50°0N 90°45W 298 C1
Sturgeon L. Ont., Canada 44°28N 78°43W 312 B6
Sturgis Sask., Canada 51°56N 102°36W 297 C8
Sturgis Mich., U.S.A. 41°48N 85°25W 311 C11
Sturgis S. Dak., U.S.A. 44°25N 103°31W 308 C2
Sturkö Sweden 56°5N 15°42E 163 H9
Štúrovo Slovak Rep. 47°48N 18°41E 181 D11
Sturt △ Australia 27°17S 141°37E 281 D3
Sturt Cr. ➝ Australia 19°8S 127°50E 278 C4
Sturt Stony Desert Australia 28°30S 141°0E 281 D3
Sturts Meadows Australia 31°18S 141°42E 282 A4
Stutterheim S. Africa 32°33S 27°28E 270 D4
Stuttgart Baden-W., Germany 48°48N 9°11E 179 G5
Stuttgart Ark., U.S.A. 34°30N 91°33W 314 D9
Stuttgart Echterdingen ✈ (STR) Germany 48°42N 9°11E 179 G5
Stutthof = Sztutowo Poland 54°20N 19°15E 184 D6
Stuvsta Sweden 59°15N 18°0E 139 B2
Stuyvesant U.S.A. 42°23N 73°45W 313 D11
Stykkishólmur Iceland 65°2N 22°40W 155 B4
Styria = Steiermark □ Austria 47°26N 15°0E 180 D8
Styrsö Sweden 57°37N 11°46E 163 G5
Su-no-Saki Japan 34°58N 139°45E 223 C11
Su Xian = Suzhou China 33°41N 116°59E 226 H9
Suakin Sudan 19°8N 37°20E 256 D4
Suakin Archipelago Sudan 18°42N 38°30E 256 D4
Suan N. Korea 38°42N 126°22E 224 C3
Suanhwa = Xuanhua China 40°40N 115°2E 226 D8
Suao Taiwan 24°36N 121°51E 225 B3
Suapure ➝ Venezuela 6°48N 67°1W 328 B4
Suar India 29°2N 79°3E 243 E8
Suau Papua N. G. 10°37S 150°2E 286 F6
Suavanao Solomon Is. 7°35S 158°47E 287 L10
Şubā Si. Arabia 27°10N 35°40E 246 E2
Subang Indonesia 6°34S 107°45E 235 D3
Subankhata India 26°48N 91°25E 241 B4
Subansiri ➝ India 26°48N 93°50E 241 B4
Subarnagiri India 19°50N 83°51E 244 C6
Subarnarekha ➝ India 22°34N 87°24E 243 H12
Subay', Urūq Si. Arabia 22°15N 43°5E 256 C5
Subayhah Si. Arabia 30°2N 38°50E 246 D3
Subcetate Romania 45°36N 23°0E 182 E8
Subhepur India 28°44N 77°15E 120 A2
Subi Indonesia 2°58N 108°50E 235 B3
Subiaco Italy 41°56N 13°5E 199 G10
Subic B. Phil. 14°44N 120°12E 232 D3
Subotica Serbia 46°6N 19°39E 182 D4
Suburban Canal U.S.A. 30°2N 90°11W 131 B1
Suca Ethiopia 6°31N 39°14E 257 F4
Sucat Phil. 14°27N 121°2E 127 C2
Suceava Romania 47°38N 26°16E 183 C11
Suceava □ Romania 47°37N 25°40E 183 C10
Suceava ➝ Romania 47°32N 26°32E 183 C11
Sucha-Beskidzka Poland 49°44N 19°35E 185 J6
Suchan = Partizansk Russia 43°8N 133°9E 220 C6
Suchań Poland 53°18N 15°18E 185 E2
Suchdol Czech Rep. 50°8N 14°22E 135 B2
Suchedniów Poland 51°3N 20°49E 185 G7
Suchil Mexico 23°39N 103°54W 318 C4
Suchou = Suzhou China 31°19N 120°38E 229 B13
Süchow = Xuzhou China 34°18N 117°10E 227 G9
Suchowola Poland 53°33N 23°3E 184 E10
Sucio ➝ Colombia 7°27N 77°7W 328 B2
Suck ➝ Ireland 53°17N 8°3W 166 C3
Suckling, Mt. Papua N. G. 9°49S 148°53E 286 E5
Sucre Bolivia 19°0S 65°15W 331 D4
Sucre Colombia 8°49N 74°44W 328 B3
Sucre □ Colombia 8°50N 75°40W 328 B2
Sucre □ Venezuela 10°25N 63°30W 329 A5
Sucuaro Colombia 4°34N 68°50W 328 C4
Sucumbíos □ Ecuador 0°6S 76°52W 328 D2
Sućuraj Croatia 43°10N 17°8E 199 E14
Sucuriju Brazil 1°39N 49°57W 332 A2
Sucuriú ➝ Brazil 20°47S 51°38W 331 E7
Sucy-en-Brie France 48°46N 2°31E 134 B4
Sud □ Cameroon 2°30N 11°45E 263 E7
Sud, Pte. Comoros Is. 11°53S 43°29E 272 a
Sud. Pte. du Canada 49°3N 62°14W 299 C7
Sud-Kivu □ Dem. Rep. of the Congo 3°0S 28°30E 268 C2
Sud-Ouest □ Cameroon 5°25N 9°20E 263 D6
Sud-Ouest, Pte. Qué., Canada 49°23N 63°36W 299 C7
Sud Ouest, Pte. Mauritius 20°28S 57°18E 272 e
Suda ➝ Russia 59°0N 37°40E 188 C9
Sudak Ukraine 44°51N 34°57E 189 K8
Sudan U.S.A. 34°4N 102°32W 314 D3
Sudan ■ Africa 15°0N 30°0E 257 E3
Sudauen = Suwałki Poland 54°8N 22°59E 184 D9
Sudbury Ont., Canada 46°30N 81°0W 298 C3
Sudbury Suffolk, U.K. 52°2N 0°45E 169 E8
Sûdd Sudan 8°20N 30°0E 257 F3
Suddie Guyana 7°8N 58°29W 329 B6
Sudeifel = Deutsch-Luxemburgischer ⌓ Germany 49°58N 6°12E 179 F2
Süderbrarup Germany 54°38N 9°45E 178 A5
Süderlügum Germany 54°52N 8°54E 178 A4
Süderoogsand Germany 54°27N 8°28E 178 A4
Sudeten Mts. = Sudety Europe 50°20N 16°45E 181 A9
Sudety Europe 50°20N 16°45E 181 A9
Suðavík Iceland 66°2N 23°0W 155 A3
Südheide ⌓ Germany 52°46N 10°10E 178 C6
Suður-múlasýsla □ Iceland 65°0N 14°30W 155 C12
Suður-þingeyjarsýsla □ Iceland 65°30N 17°0W 155 B9
Suðureyri Iceland 66°7N 23°32W 155 A3
Suðuroy Færoe Is. 61°32N 6°50W 160 F9
Sudi Tanzania 10°11S 39°57E 269 E4
Sudirman, Pegunungan Indonesia 4°30S 137°0E 231 E9
Sudiţi Romania 44°35N 27°38E 183 F12
Sudogda Russia 55°55N 40°50E 190 C5
Sudong, Pulau Singapore 1°13N 103°44E 237 d
Sudostroy = Severodvinsk Russia 64°27N 39°58E 186 B6

Sudova Vyshnya
Ukraine 49°46N 23°22E 185 J10
Sudzha Russia 51°14N 35°17E 189 G8
Sue ➝ Sudan 7°41N 28°3E 257 F2
Sue, L. U.S.A. 28°34N 81°21W 133 A2
Sueca Spain 39°12N 0°21W 197 F4
Suedinenie Bulgaria 42°16N 24°33E 203 D8
Suemez I. U.S.A. 55°15N 133°20W 296 B2
Suez = El Suweis Egypt 29°58N 32°31E 256 J8
Suez, G. of = Suweis, Khalîg el
Egypt 28°40N 33°0E 256 J8
Suez Canal = Suweis, Qanâ es
Egypt 31°0N 32°20E 256 H8
Suffield Canada 50°12N 111°10W 296 C6
Suffolk U.S.A. 36°44N 76°35W 309 G15
Suffolk □ U.K. 52°16N 1°0E 169 E9
Şufīān Iran 38°16N 45°58E 213 C11
Suga-no-Sen Japan 35°25N 134°25E 222 B6
Şugag Romania 45°47N 23°37E 183 E8
Sugamo Japan 35°44N 139°43E 140 A3
Sugar ➝ U.S.A. 42°26N 89°12W 310 B7
Sugar Cr. ➝ Ill., U.S.A. 40°9N 89°38W 310 D7
Sugar Cr. ➝ Ind., U.S.A. 39°51N 87°21W 311 E9
Sugar Grove U.S.A. 41°59N 79°20W 312 E5
Sugar Hill U.S.A. 34°6N 84°2W 316 A5
Sugar Loaf Grenada 12°13N 61°36W 323 q
Sugar Loaf Mt. = Açúcar, Pão de
Brazil 22°56S 43°9W 135 B2
Sugar Loaf Pt. St. Helena 15°54S 5°42W 153 h
Sugarcreek U.S.A. 41°25N 79°52W 312 E5
Sugarive ➝ India 26°16N 86°24E 243 F12
Sugbai Passage Phil. 5°22N 120°33E 233 J3
Suge Japan 35°37N 139°32E 140 B2
Sughd □ Tajikistan 40°0N 69°0E 217 E7
Suginami Japan 35°41N 139°37E 140 A2
Suğla Gölü Turkey 37°20N 32°0E 212 D5
Suguk = Salluit Canada 62°14N 75°38W 295 E16
Sugō Japan 35°34N 139°33E 140 B2
Sugun China 39°53N 76°47E 217 E9
Suhaia, Lacul Romania 43°45N 25°15E 183 G10
Şuḩār Oman 24°20N 56°40E 247 E8
Sühbaatar Mongolia 50°17N 106°10E 218 A5
Sühbaatar □ Mongolia 45°30N 114°0E 226 B8
Suheli Par India 10°5N 72°17E 245 J1
Suhl Germany 50°36N 10°42E 178 E6
Şuhut Turkey 38°31N 30°32E 205 C12
Sui Pakistan 28°37N 69°19E 242 E3
Sui Sai Wan China 22°16N 114°14E 122 B1
Sui Xian China 34°25N 115°2E 226 G8
Suiá Missu ➝ Brazil 11°13S 53°15W 331 C7
Šuica Bos.-H. 43°52N 17°11E 182 G2
Suichang China 28°29N 119°15E 229 C12
Suichuan China 26°20N 114°32E 229 D10
Suide China 37°30N 110°12E 226 F6
Suifenhe China 44°25N 131°10E 227 B16
Suihua China 46°32N 126°55E 219 B7
Suijiang China 28°40N 103°59E 228 C4
Suining Hunan, China 26°35N 110°10E 229 D8
Suining Jiangsu, China 33°56N 117°58E 227 H9
Suining Sichuan, China 30°26N 105°35E 228 B5
Suiping China 33°10N 113°59E 226 H7
Suippes France 49°8N 4°30E 173 C11
Suir ➝ Ireland 52°16N 7°9W 166 D4
Suisse = Switzerland ■
Europe 46°30N 8°0E 179 J4
Suisun City U.S.A. 38°15N 122°2W 306 G4
Suita Japan 34°45N 135°30E 133 A2
Suitland U.S.A. 38°50N 76°55W 143 B4
Suixi China 21°19N 110°18E 229 G8
Suiyang Guizhou, China 27°58N 107°18E 228 D6
Suiyang Heilongjiang,
China 44°30N 130°56E 227 B16
Suizhong China 40°21N 120°20E 227 D11
Suizhou China 31°42N 113°24E 229 B9
Sujangarh India 27°42N 74°31E 242 F6
Sukabumi Indonesia 6°56S 106°50E 234 D3
Sukadana Kalimantan,
Indonesia 1°10S 110°0E 235 C4
Sukadana Sumatera,
Indonesia 5°5S 105°33E 234 D3
Sukagawa Japan 37°17N 140°23E 221 F10
Sukaraja Indonesia 2°28S 110°25E 235 C4
Sukarnapura = Jayapura
Indonesia 2°28S 140°38E 231 E10
Sukarno, Puntjak = Jaya, Puncak
Indonesia 3°57S 137°17E 231 E9
Sukawati Indonesia 8°35S 115°17E 231 K18
Sukchar India 22°42N 88°22E 124 A2
Sukch'ŏn N. Korea 39°22N 125°35E 224 C2
Sukhindol Bulgaria 43°11N 25°10E 203 C9
Sukhinichi Russia 54°8N 35°10E 188 E8
Sukhona ➝ Russia 61°15N 46°39E 186 C6
Sukhothai Thailand 17°1N 99°49E 236 D2
Sukhumi = Sokhumi
Georgia 43°0N 41°0E 191 J5
Sukkertoppen = Maniitsoq
Greenland 65°26N 52°55W 154 D5
Sukkur Pakistan 27°42N 68°54E 242 F3
Sukkur Barrage Pakistan 27°40N 68°50E 242 F3
Sukma India 18°24N 81°45E 244 E5
Sukovo Serbia 43°4N 22°37E 202 C6
Sukri ➝ India 25°4N 71°43E 242 G4
Sukumo Japan 32°56N 132°44E 222 E4
Sukunka ➝ Canada 55°45N 121°15W 296 B4
Sul, Canal do Brazil 0°10S 48°30W 332 B2
Sula Norway 61°7N 4°54E 164 C1
Sula ➝ Ukraine 49°40N 32°41E 189 H7
Sula, Kepulauan Indonesia 1°45S 125°0E 231 E7
Sulaco ➝ Honduras 15°2N 87°44W 320 C2
Sulaiman Range Pakistan 30°30N 69°50E 242 D3
Sulak ➝ Russia 43°20N 47°34E 191 J8
Sulakyurt Turkey 40°9N 33°43E 212 B5
Sūlār Iran 31°53N 51°54E 247 D6
Sulawesi Indonesia 2°0S 120°0E 231 E6
Sulawesi Barat □ Indonesia 3°0S 119°0E 231 E5
Sulawesi Sea = Celebes Sea
Indonesia 3°0N 123°0E 231 D6
Sulawesi Selatan □
Indonesia 2°30S 120°0E 231 E6
Sulawesi Tengah □
Indonesia 1°30S 121°0E 231 E6
Sulawesi Tenggara □
Indonesia 3°50S 122°0E 231 E6
Sulawesi Utara □ Indonesia 1°0N 124°0E 231 D6
Suldalsheiene Norway 59°28N 7°10E 164 E3
Suldalsosen Norway 59°29N 6°29E 164 E3
Sulechów Poland 52°5N 15°40E 185 F2
Sulęcin Poland 52°26N 15°10E 185 F2
Sulei Solomon Is. 8°3S 159°34E 287 M10
Suleja Nigeria 9°10N 7°10E 263 D6
Sulejów Poland 51°26N 19°53E 185 G6
Sulejówek Poland 52°13N 21°17E 185 F8
Süleymanlı Turkey 38°58N 27°47E 205 C9
Sulima S. Leone 6°58N 11°32W 262 D2
Sulina Romania 45°10N 29°40E 183 E14
Sulina, Braţul ➝
Romania 45°10N 29°20E 183 E13
Sulingen Germany 52°41N 8°48E 178 C4
Sulița Romania 47°39N 26°59E 183 C11
Sulitjelma Norway 67°9N 16°3E 160 C17
Sulkowice Poland 49°50N 19°49E 185 J6
Sullana Peru 4°52S 80°39W 330 A1
Süller Turkey 38°9N 29°29E 205 C11
Sullivan Ill., U.S.A. 39°36N 88°37W 311 E8
Sullivan Ind., U.S.A. 39°6N 87°24W 311 E9
Sullivan Mo., U.S.A. 38°13N 91°10W 310 F5
Sullivan Bay Canada 50°55N 126°50W 296 C3
Sullivan I. = Lanbi Kyun
Burma 10°50N 98°20E 237 G2
Sullom Voe U.K. 60°27N 1°20W 167 A7
Sullorsuaq Greenland 70°5N 53°0W 154 C5
Sully U.S.A. 41°34N 92°50W 310 C4
Sully-sur-Loire France 47°45N 2°20E 173 E9
Sulmierzyce Poland 51°37N 17°32E 185 G4
Sulmona Italy 42°3N 13°55E 199 F10
Sülöğlu Turkey 41°44N 26°53E 203 E10
Sulphur La., U.S.A. 30°14N 93°23W 314 F8
Sulphur Okla., U.S.A. 34°31N 96°58W 314 D6
Sulphur Pt. Canada 60°56N 114°48W 296 A6
Sulphur Springs U.S.A. 33°8N 95°36W 314 E7
Sulsul Ethiopia 5°5N 44°50E 267 C5
Sultan Ont., Canada 47°36N 82°47W 298 C3
Sultan Wash., U.S.A. 47°52N 121°49W 306 C5
Sultan Dağları Turkey 38°20N 31°20E 212 C4
Sultan Hamud Kenya 2°1S 37°22E 268 C4
Sultan Kudarat Phil. 7°16N 124°18E 233 H5
Sultan Kudarat □ Phil. 6°30N 124°10E 233 H5
Sultan Naga Dimaporo
Phil. 7°55N 123°44E 233 H4
Sultan sa Barongis Phil. 6°45N 124°35E 233 H5
Sultānābād = Arāk Iran 34°0N 49°40E 247 C6
Sultanahme Camil Turkey 41°0N 28°58E 122 B1
Sultanhisar Turkey 37°53N 28°9E 205 D10
Sultaniça Turkey 40°37N 26°8E 203 F10
Sultaniye Turkey 40°11N 28°12E 203 F12
Sultanpur Mad. P., India 23°9N 77°56E 242 H8
Sultanpur Punjab, India 31°13N 75°11E 242 D6
Sultanpur Ut. P., India 26°18N 82°4E 243 F10
Sulu □ Phil. 5°30N 120°30E 233 J3
Sulu Arch. Phil. 6°0N 121°0E 233 J3
Sulu Sea E. Indies 8°0N 120°0E 233 G3
Sülüklü Turkey 38°53N 32°20E 212 C5
Sululta Ethiopia 9°10N 38°43E 257 F4
Suluova Turkey 40°46N 35°32E 212 B6
Sulūq Libya 31°44N 20°14E 258 B4
Suluru India 13°42N 80°1E 245 H5
Sulzbach Germany 49°18N 7°3E 179 F3
Sulzbach-Rosenberg
Germany 49°30N 11°44E 179 F7
Sulzberger Ice Shelf
Antarctica 78°0S 150°0W 151 E13
Sumaco -Napo Galeras △
Ecuador 0°34S 77°38W 328 D2
Sumalata Indonesia 1°0N 122°31E 231 D6
Sumale □ Ethiopia 7°0N 45°0E 267 C6
Sumampa Argentina 29°25S 63°29W 334 B3
Sumapaz △ Colombia 3°49N 74°13W 328 C3
Sumaré Brazil 22°48S 47°17W 333 F2
Sumatera Indonesia 0°40N 100°20E 234 B2
Sumatera Barat □
Indonesia 1°0S 101°0E 234 B1
Sumatera Utara □
Indonesia 2°30N 98°0E 234 B1
Sumatra = Sumatera
Indonesia 0°40N 100°20E 234 B2
Sumatra U.S.A. 30°1N 84°59W 316 E5
Sumava △ Czech Rep. 49°0N 13°49E 180 C6
Sumba Angola 6°15S 12°38E 265 D2
Sumba Indonesia 9°45S 119°35E 231 F5
Sumba, Selat Indonesia 9°0S 118°40E 231 F5
Sumbawa Indonesia 8°26S 117°30E 235 D5
Sumbawa Besar Indonesia 8°30S 117°26E 235 D5
Sumbe Angola 11°10S 13°48E 265 E2
Sumbu △ Zambia 8°43S 30°22E 269 D3
Sumburgh Hd. U.K. 59°52N 1°17W 167 B7
Sumdeo India 31°26N 78°44E 243 D8
Sumdo China 35°6N 78°41E 243 B8
Sumé Brazil 7°39S 36°55W 332 C4
Sumedang Indonesia 6°52S 107°55E 235 D3
Sümeg Hungary 46°59N 17°20E 182 D2
Sumeih Sudan 9°50N 27°39E 257 F2
Šumen = Shumen
Bulgaria 43°18N 26°55E 203 C10
Sumenep Indonesia 7°1S 113°52E 235 D4
Sumgait = Sumqayıt
Azerbaijan 40°34N 49°38E 191 K9
Sumida Japan 35°42N 139°49E 140 A3
Sumida ➝ Japan 35°39N 139°45E 140 A3
Sumisu-Jima Japan 31°27N 140°3E 223 F12
Sumiyoshi Japan 34°36N 135°30E 133 B2
Sumiyoshi Shrine Japan 34°36N 135°30E 133 B1
Summer L. U.S.A. 42°50N 120°45W 304 E3
Summerland Canada 49°32N 119°41W 296 D5
Summerland Key U.S.A. 24°40N 81°27W 317 L8
Summerside Canada 46°24N 63°47W 299 C7
Summersville U.S.A. 38°17N 80°51W 309 F13
Summerton U.S.A. 33°36N 80°20W 316 B9
Summertown U.S.A. 32°45N 82°16W 316 C7
Summerville Ont.,
Canada 43°37N 79°33W 141 B1
Summerville Ga.,
U.S.A. 34°29N 85°21W 315 D12
Summerville S.C., U.S.A. 33°1N 80°11W 316 B9
Summit Alaska, U.S.A. 63°20N 149°7W 303 E10
Summit Ill., U.S.A. 41°47N 87°47W 119 C2
Summit Lake Canada 54°20N 122°40W 296 C4
Summit Peak U.S.A. 37°21N 106°42W 305 H10
Sumner N.Z. 43°35S 172°48E 285 D7
Sumner Ill., U.S.A. 38°42N 87°53W 311 F9
Sumner Iowa, U.S.A. 42°51N 92°6W 310 B4
Sumner Wash., U.S.A. 47°12N 122°14W 306 C4
Sumner, L. N.Z. 42°42S 172°15E 285 C7
Sumner Tunnel Boston, U.S.A. 116 a3
Sumoto Japan 34°21N 134°54E 222 C6
Šumperk Czech Rep. 49°59N 16°59E 181 B9
Sumprabum Burma 26°33N 97°34E 241 B6
Sumqayıt Azerbaijan 40°34N 49°38E 191 K9
Sumter U.S.A. 33°55N 80°21W 316 B9
Sumxi China 34°35N 80°22E 217 F10
Sumy Ukraine 50°57N 34°50E 189 G8
Sumy □ Ukraine 50°50N 33°50E 189 G7
Sun City North West,
S. Africa 25°17S 27°3E 270 C4
Sun City Ariz., U.S.A. 33°35N 112°16W 305 K7
Sun City Calif., U.S.A. 33°42N 117°11W 307 M9
Sun City Center U.S.A. 27°43N 82°21W 317 H7
Sun Lakes U.S.A. 33°10N 111°52W 305 K8
Sun Prairie U.S.A. 43°11N 89°13W 310 A7
Sun Valley U.S.A. 43°42N 114°21W 304 E6
Sunagawa Japan 43°29N 141°55E 220 C10
Sunamachi Japan 35°40N 139°50E 140 A4
Sunan N. Korea 39°15N 125°40E 224 C2
Sunart, L. U.K. 56°42N 5°43W 167 E3
Sunburst U.S.A. 48°53N 111°55W 304 B8
Sunbury Vic., Australia 37°35S 144°44E 283 D6
Sunbury Pa., U.S.A. 40°52N 76°48W 313 F8
Sunbury-on-Thames
U.K. 51°25N 0°26W 125 B1
Sunchales Argentina 30°58S 61°35W 334 C3
Suncheon S. Korea 34°52N 127°31E 224 E3
Suncho Corral Argentina 27°55S 63°27W 334 B3
Sunch'ŏn N. Korea 39°25N 125°56E 224 C2
Suncook U.S.A. 43°8N 71°27W 313 C13
Sunda, Selat Indonesia 6°20S 105°30E 234 D3
Sunda Is. Indonesia 5°0S 105°0E 288 H2
Sunda Str. = Sunda, Selat
Indonesia 6°20S 105°30E 234 D3
Sunda Trench = Java Trench
Ind. Oc. 9°0S 105°0E 234 D2
Sundance Man., Canada 56°32N 94°4W 297 B10
Sundance Wyo.,
U.S.A. 44°24N 104°23W 304 D11
Sundar Nagar India 31°32N 76°53E 242 D7
Sundarbans Asia 22°0N 89°0E 241 E2
Sundarbans △ India 22°0N 88°45E 241 E2
Sundargarh India 22°4N 84°5E 244 C7
Sundays = Sondags ➝
S. Africa 33°44S 25°51E 270 D4
Sundbyberg Sweden 59°22N 17°57E 139 A1
Sundbyerne Denmark 55°39N 12°36E 118 B3
Sunderland Ont., Canada 44°16N 79°4W 312 B5
Sunderland Tyne & W.,
U.K. 54°55N 1°23W 168 C6
Sundi Lutete
Dem. Rep. of the Congo 4°34S 14°14E 265 C2
Sundown △ Australia 28°49S 151°38E 281 D5
Sundre Canada 51°49N 114°38W 296 C6
Sunds Denmark 56°13N 9°1E 163 H3
Sundsvall Sweden 62°23N 17°17E 162 B11
Sundsvallsbukten
Sweden 62°21N 17°25E 162 B11
Sung Hei Vietnam 10°20N 106°2E 237 G6
Sung Kong China 22°11N 114°17E 122 B2
Sungai Acheh Malaysia 5°8N 100°30E 237 c
Sungai Kolok Thailand 6°2N 101°58E 237 J3
Sungai Lembing Malaysia 3°55N 103°3E 237 L4
Sungai Petani Malaysia 5°37N 100°30E 237 K3
Sungaigerong Indonesia 2°59S 104°52E 234 C2
Sungailiat Indonesia 1°51S 106°8E 234 C3
Sungaipenuh Indonesia 2°1S 101°20E 234 C2
Sungaitiram Indonesia 0°45S 117°8E 235 C5
Sungari = Songhua Jiang ➝
China 47°45N 132°30E 219 B8
Sungei Kadut Industrial Estate
Singapore 1°24N 103°44E 138 A2
Sungei Selatar Res.
Singapore 1°24N 103°51E 138 A3
Sunghua Chiang = Songhua
Jiang ➝ China 47°45N 132°30E 219 B8
Sungikai Sudan 12°20N 29°51E 257 E2
Sungu Dem. Rep. of the Congo 5°15S 17°21E 264 C3
Sungurlu Turkey 40°12N 34°21E 212 B6
Sunja Croatia 45°21N 16°35E 199 C13
Sunland Park U.S.A. 31°50N 106°40W 305 L10
Sunnansjö Sweden 60°13N 14°58E 162 D8
Sunndalsøra Norway 62°40N 8°33E 164 B5
Sunne Sweden 59°52N 13°5E 162 E7
Sunnemo Sweden 59°53N 13°44E 162 E7
Sunnfjord Norway 61°35N 5°45E 164 C2
Sunnmøre Norway 62°35N 6°30E 164 B3
Sunnyside U.S.A. 46°20N 120°0W 304 C4
Sunnyvale U.S.A. 37°23N 122°2W 306 H4
Sunrise U.S.A. 26°8N 80°14W 317 J9
Sunrise Manor U.S.A. 36°12N 115°4W 124 A2
Sunrise Mountain Natural Area
U.S.A. 36°12N 114°58W 124 A2
Sunset Beach U.S.A. 21°40N 158°3W 302 J13
Sunset Park N.Y., U.S.A. 40°38N 73°59W 132 C2
Sunset Park Nev., U.S.A. 36°3N 115°6W 124 B2
Sunshine Coast Australia 26°30S 153°0E 276 F9
Suntar Russia 62°15N 117°30E 215 C12
Sunter Indonesia 6°7S 106°51E 122 A2
Sunter, Kali ➝ Indonesia 6°10S 106°53E 122 B2
Suntrana U.S.A. 63°52N 148°51W 303 E10
Sunwi-do N. Korea 37°43N 125°16E 224 D2
Sunyani Ghana 7°21N 2°22W 262 D4
Suō-Nada Japan 33°50N 131°30E 222 D3
Suomenlinna Finland 60°9N 24°59E 121 C2
Suomenselkä Finland 62°52N 24°0E 160 E21
Suomi = Finland ■ Europe 63°0N 27°0E 160 E22
Suomussalmi Finland 64°54N 29°10E 160 D23
Suoyarvi Russia 62°3N 32°20E 188 A7
Supai U.S.A. 36°15N 112°41W 305 H7
Supamo ➝ Venezuela 6°48N 61°50W 329 B5
Supaul India 26°10N 86°40E 243 F12
Superagüi △ Brazil 25°6S 48°18W 333 G2
Superior Ariz., U.S.A. 33°18N 111°6W 305 K8
Superior Mont., U.S.A. 47°12N 114°53W 304 C6
Superior Nebr., U.S.A. 40°1N 98°4W 308 E4
Superior Wis., U.S.A. 46°44N 92°6W 308 B7
Superior, L. N. Amer. 47°0N 87°0W 298 C2
Supetar Croatia 43°25N 16°32E 199 E13
Suphan Buri Thailand 14°14N 100°10E 236 E3
Suphan Dağı Turkey 38°54N 42°48E 213 C10
Supiori Indonesia 1°0S 136°0E 231 E9
Supraśl Poland 53°13N 23°19E 185 E10
Supraśl ➝ Poland 53°11N 22°57E 185 E9
Supreme Court
Washington, D.C., U.S.A. 143 b3
Supung N. Korea 40°27N 124°54E 224 B2
Supung Shuiku China 40°35N 124°50E 224 B2
Sūq 'Abs Yemen 16°0N 43°12E 248 D3
Sūq ash Shuyūkh Iraq 30°53N 46°28E 246 D5
Sūq Suwayq Si. Arabia 24°23N 38°27E 246 E3
Şuqaylabīyah Syria 35°23N 36°23E 250 C7
Suqian China 33°54N 118°8E 227 H10
Suquţra = Socotra Yemen 12°30N 54°0E 249 D6
Şūr Lebanon 33°19N 35°16E 250 E6
Şūr Oman 22°34N 59°32E 249 B7
Sur, Pt. U.S.A. 36°18N 121°54W 306 J5
Sur Bahr West Bank 31°44N 35°13E 123 B2
Sura India 22°33N 88°24E 124 B2
Sura ➝ Russia 56°6N 46°0E 190 C8
Surab Pakistan 28°25N 66°15E 242 E2
Surabaja = Surabaya
Indonesia 7°17S 112°45E 235 D4
Surabaya Indonesia 7°17S 112°45E 235 D4
Surahammar Sweden 59°43N 16°13E 162 E10
Suraia Romania 45°40N 27°25E 183 E12
Surakarta Indonesia 7°35S 110°48E 235 D4
Suraksan S. Korea 37°40N 127°4E 137 A2
Šurany Slovak Rep. 48°6N 18°10E 181 C11
Surat Queens., Australia 27°10S 149°6E 281 D4
Surat India 21°12N 72°55E 244 D1
Surat Thani Thailand 9°6N 99°20E 237 H2
Suratgarh India 29°18N 73°55E 242 E5
Surathkal India 12°58N 74°46E 245 H2
Suraxanı Azerbaijan 40°25N 50°1E 191 K10
Şurayrnīā Si. Arabia 25°7N 46°7E 246 E5
Suraż Poland 52°57N 22°57E 185 F9
Surazh Belarus 55°25N 30°44E 188 E6
Surazh Russia 53°5N 32°27E 189 F7
Surbiton U.K. 51°23N 0°17W 125 B2
Surduc Romania 47°15N 23°25E 183 C8
Surduc Pasul Romania 45°21N 23°23E 183 E8
Surdulica Serbia 42°41N 22°11E 202 D6
Surendranagar India 22°45N 71°40E 242 H4
Suresnes France 48°52N 2°13E 134 A2
Surf U.S.A. 34°41N 120°36W 307 L6
Surfers Paradise Australia 28°0S 153°25E 281 D5
Surfside U.S.A. 25°52N 80°7W 142 B2
Surgana India 20°34N 73°37E 244 D1
Surgères France 46°7N 0°47W 174 B3
Surgut Russia 61°14N 73°20E 214 C8
Súria Spain 41°50N 1°45E 196 D6
Suriapet India 17°10N 79°40E 244 F4
Suribachi Yama Iwo Jima 24°45N 141°17E 288 b
Surigao Phil. 9°47N 125°29E 233 G5
Surigao del Norte □ Phil. 9°40N 125°40E 233 G5
Surigao del Sur □ Phil. 8°45N 126°0E 233 G6
Surigao Strait Phil. 10°15N 125°23E 233 F5
Surin Thailand 14°50N 103°34E 236 E4
Surin Nua, Ko Thailand 9°30N 97°55E 237 H1
Surinam = Suriname ■
S. Amer. 4°0N 56°0W 329 C6
Surinam Mauritius 20°30S 57°30E 272 e
Suriname ■ S. Amer. 4°0N 56°0W 329 C6
Suriname ➝ Suriname 5°50N 55°15W 329 B6
Surjagarh India 19°36N 80°25E 244 E5
Surma ➝ Bangla. 24°34N 91°14E 241 C3
Sürmaq Iran 31°3N 52°48E 247 D7
Sürmene Turkey 41°0N 40°1E 213 B9
Surna ➝ Norway 62°59N 8°40E 164 B5
Surnadalsøra Norway 62°58N 8°40E 164 B5
Surovikino Russia 48°32N 42°55E 191 F6
Surquillo Peru 12°6S 77°1W 124 B2
Surrency U.S.A. 31°44N 82°12W 316 D7
Surrey Canada 49°7N 122°45W 306 A4
Surrey □ Jamaica 18°5N 76°34W 320 a
Surrey □ U.K. 51°15N 0°31W 169 F7
Surrey Hills Australia 33°53S 151°13E 139 B2
Sursand India 26°39N 85°43E 243 F11
Sursar ➝ India 26°14N 87°3E 243 F12
Sursee Switz. 47°11N 8°6E 179 H4
Sursk Russia 53°3N 45°40E 190 D7
Surskoye Russia 54°30N 46°44E 190 C8
Surt Libya 31°11N 16°39E 258 B3
Surt □ Libya 30°0N 17°30E 258 B3
Surt, Al Hamādah al
Libya 30°0N 17°50E 258 C3
Surt, Khalīj Libya 31°40N 18°30E 258 B3
Surtanahu Pakistan 26°22N 70°0E 242 F4
Surte Sweden 57°50N 12°1E 163 G6
Surtsey Iceland 63°20N 20°30W 155 D6
Surubim Brazil 7°50S 35°45W 332 C4
Sürüç Turkey 36°58N 38°25E 213 D8
Surud, Ras Somali Rep. 11°10N 47°30E 267 B6
Surud Ad Somali Rep. 10°42N 47°9E 267 B6
Suruga-Wan Japan 34°45N 138°30E 223 C10
Surumu ➝ Brazil 3°22N 60°19W 329 C5
Surxondaryo □ Uzbekistan 38°0N 67°30E 217 E7
Susa = Sousse Tunisia 35°50N 10°38E 258 A2
Susa Italy 45°8N 7°3E 198 C4
Susa ➝ Denmark 55°12N 11°42E 163 J5
Sušac Croatia 42°46N 16°30E 199 F13
Susaek S. Korea 37°34N 126°54E 137 B1
Sūsah Libya 32°52N 21°59E 258 B4
Susak Croatia 44°30N 14°18E 199 D11
Susaki Japan 33°22N 133°17E 222 D5
Susam-Adasi = Samos
Greece 37°45N 26°50E 205 D8
Süsangerd Iran 31°35N 48°6E 213 G13
Susanville U.S.A. 40°25N 120°39W 304 F3
Susch Switz. 46°46N 10°5E 179 J6
Suşehri Turkey 40°10N 38°6E 213 B8
Sušice Czech Rep. 49°17N 13°30E 180 B6
Susleni Moldova 47°25N 28°59E 183 C13
Susner India 23°57N 76°5E 242 H7
Susong China 30°10N 116°5E 229 B11
Susquehanna U.S.A. 41°57N 75°36W 313 E9
Susquehanna ➝ U.S.A. 39°33N 76°5W 313 G8
Susques Argentina 23°35S 66°25W 334 A2
Süssenbrunn Austria 48°16N 16°29E 142 A2
Sussex N.B., Canada 45°45N 65°37W 299 C6
Sussex N.J., U.S.A. 41°13N 74°37W 313 E10
Sussex, E. □ U.K. 51°0N 0°20E 169 G8
Sussex, W. □ U.K. 51°0N 0°30W 169 G7
Sussex Inlet Australia 35°10S 150°36E 283 C9
Sustut ➝ Canada 56°20N 127°30W 296 B3
Susuman Russia 62°47N 148°10E 215 C15
Susunu Indonesia 3°7S 133°39E 231 E8
Susurluk Turkey 39°54N 28°8E 205 B10
Susuz Turkey 40°46N 43°8E 213 B10
Susz Poland 53°44N 19°20E 184 E6
Sutay Uul Asia 46°35N 93°38E 218 B4
Sütçüler Turkey 37°29N 30°57E 212 D4
Şuteşti Romania 45°13N 27°27E 183 E12
Sutherland N.S.W.,
Australia 34°2S 151°4E 283 C9
Sutherland Northern Cape,
S. Africa 32°24S 20°40E 270 D3
Sutherland Highl., U.K. 58°12N 4°50W 167 C4
Sutherland Nebr., U.S.A. 41°10N 101°8W 308 E3
Sutherland Falls N.Z. 44°48S 167°46E 285 E2
Sutherland Road Barbados 13°16N 59°39W 323 r
Sutherlin U.S.A. 43°23N 123°19W 304 E2
Suthri India 23°3N 68°55E 242 H3
Sutjeska △ Bos.-H. 43°50N 18°32E 182 G3
Sutlej ➝ Pakistan 29°23N 71°3E 242 E4
Sutter U.S.A. 39°10N 121°45W 306 F5
Sutter Buttes U.S.A. 39°12N 121°49W 306 F5
Sutter Creek U.S.A. 38°24N 120°48W 306 G6
Sutton Qué., Canada 45°6N 72°37W 313 A12
Sutton Dublin, Ireland 53°23N 6°7W 120 A3
Sutton N.Z. 45°34S 170°8E 285 F5
Sutton London, U.K. 51°21N 0°11W 125 B2
Sutton Nebr., U.S.A. 40°36N 97°52W 308 E5
Sutton W. Va., U.S.A. 38°40N 80°43W 309 F13
Sutton ➝ Canada 55°15N 83°45W 298 A3
Sutton Coldfield U.K. 52°35N 1°49W 169 E6
Sutton in Ashfield U.K. 53°8N 1°16W 168 D6
Sutton L. Canada 54°15N 84°42W 298 B3
Suttor ➝ Australia 21°36S 147°2E 280 C4
Suttsu Japan 42°48N 140°14E 220 C10
Sutwik I. U.S.A. 56°34N 157°12W 303 H8
Suva Fiji 18°6S 178°30E 287 B2
Suva Gora Macedonia 41°45N 21°3E 202 E5
Suva Planina Serbia 43°10N 22°5E 202 C6
Suva Reka Kosovo 42°21N 20°50E 202 D4
Suvorov Russia 54°7N 36°30E 188 E9
Suvorov Is. = Suwarrow Is.
Cook Is. 13°15S 163°5W 289 J11
Suvorove Ukraine 45°35N 28°59E 183 E13
Suvorovo Bulgaria 43°20N 27°35E 203 C11
Suwa Japan 36°2N 138°8E 223 A10
Suwa-Ko Japan 36°3N 138°5E 223 A10
Suwałki Poland 54°8N 22°59E 184 D9
Suwana Indonesia 8°44S 115°36E 231 K18
Suwanee U.S.A. 34°3N 84°4W 316 A5
Suwannaphum Thailand 15°33N 103°47E 236 E4
Suwannee U.S.A. 29°20N 83°9W 317 F6
Suwannee ➝ U.S.A. 29°17N 83°10W 317 F6
Suwannee Sd. U.S.A. 29°20N 83°15W 317 F6
Suwanose-Jima Japan 29°38N 129°43E 221 K4
Suwarrow Is. Cook Is. 13°15S 163°5W 289 J11
Suwayqīyah, Hawr as
Iraq 32°40N 46°3E 213 G12
Suweis, Khalîg el Egypt 28°40N 33°0E 256 J8
Suweis, Qanâ es Egypt 31°0N 32°20E 256 H8
Suwon S. Korea 37°17N 127°1E 224 D3
Suyu S. Korea 37°37N 127°0E 137 B2
Suzaka Japan 36°39N 138°19E 223 A10
Suzdal Russia 56°29N 40°26E 188 D11
Suzhou Anhui, China 33°41N 116°59E 226 H9
Suzhou Jiangsu, China 31°19N 120°38E 229 B13
Suzu Japan 37°25N 137°17E 221 F8
Suzu-Misaki Japan 37°31N 137°21E 221 F8
Suzuka Japan 34°55N 136°36E 223 C8
Suzuka-Sammyaku
Japan 35°5N 136°30E 223 B8
Suzukishinden Japan 35°43N 139°31E 140 A2
Suzun Russia 53°47N 82°18E 217 B10
Suzzara Italy 44°59N 10°45E 198 D7
Svalbard Arctic 78°0N 17°0E 150 B8
Svalbard Radio = Longyearbyen
Svalbard 78°13N 15°40E 150 B8
Svalbarð Iceland 66°12N 15°43W 155 A11
Svalbarðseyri Iceland 65°45N 18°5W 155 B8
Svalöv Sweden 55°57N 13°8E 163 J7
Svalyava Ukraine 48°33N 22°59E 182 B7
Svaneke Denmark 55°8N 15°8E 163 J9
Svanemøllen Denmark 55°43N 12°34E 118 A3
Svängsta Sweden 56°16N 14°47E 163 H8
Svanskog Sweden 59°11N 12°34E 162 E6
Svappavaara Sweden 67°40N 21°3E 160 C19
Svärdsjö Sweden 60°45N 15°54E 162 D9
Svarstad Norway 59°27N 9°56E 164 E6
Svartå Sweden 59°8N 14°32E 162 E8
Svartárkot Iceland 65°20N 17°15W 155 B9
Svartevatn Norway 59°10N 6°56E 164 E3
Svartisen Norway 66°40N 13°59E 160 C15
Svartvik Sweden 62°19N 17°24E 162 B11
Svatove Ukraine 49°22N 38°15E 189 H10
Svatovo = Svatove
Ukraine 49°22N 38°15E 189 H10
Svatsum Norway 61°20N 9°50E 164 C6
Svay Chek Cambodia 13°48N 102°58E 236 F4
Svay Rieng Cambodia 11°9N 105°45E 237 G5
Sveaborg = Suomenlinna
Finland 60°9N 24°59E 121 C2
Svealand □ Sweden 60°20N 15°0E 162 D9
Svedala Sweden 55°30N 13°15E 163 J7
Sveg Sweden 62°2N 14°21E 162 B8
Sveindal Norway 58°29N 7°30E 164 F4
Sveinseyri Iceland 65°38N 23°51W 155 B3
Sveio Norway 59°33N 5°23E 164 E2
Svelgen Norway 61°46N 5°17E 164 C2
Svelvik Norway 59°37N 10°24E 164 E7
Svendborg Denmark 55°4N 10°35E 163 J4
Svene Norway 59°45N 9°31E 164 E6
Svenljunga Sweden 57°29N 13°5E 163 G7
Svenstavik Sweden 62°45N 14°26E 162 B8
Svenstrup Denmark 56°58N 9°50E 163 H3
Sverdlov Russia 55°46N 37°36E 129 B3
Sverdlovsk = Yekaterinburg
Russia 56°50N 60°30E 214 D7
Sverdlovsk Ukraine 48°5N 39°47E 189 H10
Sverdrup Chan. Canada 79°56N 96°25W 295 B12
Sverdrup Is. Canada 79°0N 97°0W 292 B10
Sverige = Sweden ■
Europe 57°0N 15°0E 161 H16
Svestad Norway 59°46N 10°36E 133 B2
Svetac Croatia 43°3N 15°43E 199 E12
Sveti Ivan = Zelina
Croatia 45°57N 16°16E 199 C13
Sveti Nikola, Prokhad
Europe 43°27N 22°6E 202 C6
Sveti Nikole Macedonia 41°51N 21°56E 202 E5
Sveti Rok Croatia 44°22N 15°39E 199 D12
Sveti Vrach = Sandanski
Bulgaria 41°35N 23°16E 202 E7
Svetlaya Russia 46°33N 138°18E 220 A9
Svetlogorsk = Svyetlahorsk
Belarus 52°38N 29°46E 177 B15
Svetlogorsk Russia 54°56N 20°10E 184 D7
Svetlograd Russia 45°25N 42°58E 191 H6
Svetlovodsk = Svitlovodsk
Ukraine 49°2N 33°13E 189 H7
Svetlyy Kaliningrad, Russia 54°41N 20°8E 184 D7
Svetlyy Orenburg, Russia 50°48N 60°51E 216 B6
Svidník Slovak Rep. 49°20N 21°37E 181 B14
Svignaskarð Iceland 64°40N 21°42W 155 C5
Svilaja Planina Croatia 43°49N 16°31E 199 E13
Svilajnac Serbia 44°15N 21°11E 202 B5
Svilengrad Bulgaria 41°49N 26°12E 203 E10
Svinafell Iceland 63°59N 16°51W 155 D10
Svinö Finland 60°7N 24°44E 121 C1
Svir ➝ Russia 60°30N 32°48E 188 B7
Sviritsa Russia 60°29N 32°51E 188 B7
Svishtov Bulgaria 43°36N 25°23E 203 C9
Svislach Belarus 53°3N 24°2E 185 E11
Svitava ➝ Czech Rep. 49°11N 16°37E 181 B9
Svitavy Czech Rep. 49°47N 16°28E 181 B9
Svitlovodsk Ukraine 49°2N 33°13E 189 H7
Svizzera = Switzerland ■
Europe 46°30N 8°0E 179 J4
Svobodnyy Russia 51°20N 128°0E 215 D13
Svoge Bulgaria 42°59N 23°23E 202 D7
Svolvær Norway 68°15N 14°34E 160 B16
Svorkmo Norway 63°10N 9°46E 164 A6
Svoronata Greece 38°7N 20°31E 207 C2
Svratka ➝ Czech Rep. 49°11N 16°38E 181 B9
Svrljig Serbia 43°25N 22°6E 202 C6
Svullrya Norway 60°25N 12°23E 164 D9
Svyatogorovsky Rudnik =
Dobropole Ukraine 48°25N 37°2E 189 H9
Svyetlahorsk Belarus 52°38N 29°46E 177 B15
Swa Burma 19°15N 96°17E 241 F6
Swa Tende
Dem. Rep. of the Congo 7°9S 17°7E 265 D3
Swabian Alps = Schwäbische Alb
Germany 48°20N 9°30E 179 G5
Swaffham U.K. 52°39N 0°42E 169 E8
Swains I. Amer. Samoa 11°11S 171°4W 289 J11
Swainsboro U.S.A. 32°36N 82°20W 316 C7
Swakop ➝ Namibia 22°38S 14°36E 270 B2
Swakopmund Namibia 22°37S 14°30E 270 B1
Swale ➝ U.K. 54°5N 1°20W 168 C6
Swamihalli India 14°52N 76°38E 245 G3
Swan ➝ W. Austral.,
Australia 32°3S 115°45E 279 F2
Swan ➝ Man., Canada 52°30N 100°45W 297 C8
Swan Hill Australia 35°20S 143°33E 282 C5
Swan Hills Canada 54°43N 115°24W 296 C5
Swan Is. = Santanilla, Is.
Honduras 17°22N 83°57W 320 C3
Swan L. Man., Canada 52°30N 100°40W 297 C8
Swan L. Ont., Canada 54°16N 91°11W 298 B1
Swan Ra. U.S.A. 48°0N 113°45W 304 C7
Swan Reach Australia 34°35S 139°37E 282 C3
Swan River Canada 52°10N 101°16W 297 C8
Swanage U.K. 50°36N 1°58W 169 G6
Swanley U.K. 51°23N 0°11E 125 B4
Swansea N.S.W., Australia 33°3S 151°35E 283 B9
Swansea Tas., Australia 42°8S 148°4E 281 G4
Swansea Ont., Canada 43°38N 79°28W 141 B2
Swansea Swansea, U.K. 51°37N 3°57W 169 F4
Swansea S.C., U.S.A. 33°44N 81°6W 316 B8
Swansea □ U.K. 51°38N 4°3W 169 F3
Swanton U.S.A. 41°35N 83°53W 311 C13
Swartberge S. Africa 33°20S 22°0E 270 D3
Swartmodder S. Africa 28°1S 20°32E 270 C3
Swartnossob ➝ Namibia 23°8S 18°42E 270 B2
Swartruggens S. Africa 25°39S 26°42E 270 C4
Swarzędz Poland 52°25N 17°4E 185 F4
Swastika Canada 48°7N 80°6W 298 C3
Swat ➝ Pakistan 34°40N 72°5E 243 B5
Swatow = Shantou
China 23°18N 116°40E 229 F11
Swaziland ■ Africa 26°30S 31°30E 271 C5
Sweden ■ Europe 57°0N 15°0E 161 H16
Swedru Ghana 5°32N 0°41W 263 D4
Sweet Grass U.S.A. 48°59N 111°58W 304 B8
Sweet Home U.S.A. 44°24N 122°44W 304 D2
Sweet Springs U.S.A. 38°58N 93°25W 310 F3
Sweetwater Nev., U.S.A. 38°27N 119°9W 306 G7
Sweetwater Tenn.,
U.S.A. 35°36N 84°28W 315 D12
Sweetwater Tex., U.S.A. 32°28N 100°25W 314 E4
Sweetwater ➝ U.S.A. 42°31N 107°2W 304 E10
Swellendam S. Africa 34°1S 20°26E 270 D3
Swider ➝ Poland 52°6N 21°14E 185 F8
Świdnica Poland 50°50N 16°30E 185 H3
Świdnik Poland 51°13N 22°39E 185 G9
Świdwin Poland 53°47N 15°49E 184 E2
Świebodzice Poland 50°51N 16°20E 185 H3
Świebodzin Poland 52°15N 15°31E 185 F2
Świecie Poland 53°25N 18°30E 184 E5
Świerzawa Poland 51°1N 15°54E 185 G2
Świętokrzyski △ Poland 50°53N 20°59E 185 H7
Świętokrzyskie □ Poland 50°45N 20°45E 185 H7
Świętokrzyskie, Góry
Poland 51°0N 20°30E 185 H7
Swift Current Canada 50°20N 107°45W 297 C7
Swift Current ➝
Canada 50°38N 107°44W 297 C7
Swifts Creek Australia 37°17S 147°44E 283 D7
Swilly, L. Ireland 55°12N 7°33W 166 A4
Swinburne I. U.S.A. 40°33N 74°3W 132 C1
Swindon U.K. 51°34N 1°46W 169 F6
Swindon □ U.K. 51°34N 1°46W 169 F6
Swinemünde = Świnoujście
Poland 53°54N 14°16E 184 E1
Swinford Ireland 53°57N 8°58W 166 C3
Świnoujście Poland 53°54N 14°16E 184 E1
Switzerland ■ Europe 46°30N 8°0E 179 J4
Swords Ireland 53°28N 6°13W 120 A2
Swoyerville U.S.A. 41°18N 75°53W 313 E9
Syasstroy Russia 60°9N 32°33E 188 B7
Sycamore Ill., U.S.A. 41°59N 88°41W 311 C8
Sycamore Ohio, U.S.A. 40°57N 83°10W 311 D13
Sychevka Russia 55°59N 34°16E 188 E8
Syców Poland 51°19N 17°40E 185 G4
Syddanmark □ Denmark 55°30N 9°0E 163 J2
Sydenham S. Africa 26°9S 28°5E 123 A2
Sydenham ➝ Canada 42°33N 82°25W 312 D2
Sydney N.S.W., Australia 33°52S 151°12E 139 B2
Sydney N.S., Canada 46°7N 60°7W 299 C7
Sydney, Univ. of
Australia 33°54S 151°11E 139 B2
Sydney Harbour △
Australia 33°50S 151°14E 139 B2
Sydney Harbour Bridge
Australia 33°51S 151°12E 139 B2
Sydney Kingsford Smith ✈ (SYD)
Australia 33°57S 151°11E 139 B2
Sydney L. Canada 50°41N 94°25W 297 C10
Sydney Mines Canada 46°18N 60°15W 299 C7
Sydney Opera House Sydney, Australia 139 a2
Sydproven = Alluitsup Paa
Greenland 60°30N 45°35W 154 E6
Sydra, G. of = Surt, Khalīj
Libya 31°40N 18°30E 258 B3
Sydstranden Denmark 55°34N 12°38E 118 B3
Syeverodonetsk Ukraine 48°58N 38°35E 189 H10
Syfteland Norway 60°14N 5°27E 164 D2
Syke Germany 52°55N 8°50E 178 C4
Sykesville U.S.A. 41°3N 78°50W 312 E6
Sykkylven Norway 62°23N 6°35E 164 B3
Syktyvkar Russia 61°45N 50°40E 186 B9
Sylacauga U.S.A. 33°10N 86°15W 316 B3
Sylarna Sweden 63°2N 12°13E 164 A9
Sylhet Bangla. 24°54N 91°52E 241 C3
Sylhet □ Bangla. 24°50N 91°50E 241 C3
Sylt Germany 54°54N 8°22E 178 A4
Sylte Norway 62°18N 7°17E 164 B4
Sylvan Beach U.S.A. 43°12N 75°44W 313 C9
Sylvan Lake Canada 52°20N 114°3W 296 C6
Sylvania N.S.W., Australia 34°0S 151°7E 139 C1
Sylvania Ga., U.S.A. 32°45N 81°38W 316 C8
Sylvania Ohio, U.S.A. 41°43N 83°42W 311 C13
Sylvester U.S.A. 31°32N 83°50W 316 D6
Sym Russia 60°20N 88°18E 214 C9
Symphony Hall San Francisco, U.S.A. 136 c1
Synelnykove Ukraine 48°25N 35°30E 189 H8
Synevyr △ Ukraine 48°30N 23°40E 183 B8
Synevyrska Polyana
Ukraine 48°35N 23°41E 183 B8
Synnervika Norway 62°25N 11°54E 164 B8
Synnfjell Norway 61°5N 9°46E 164 C6
Synnot Ra. Australia 16°30S 125°20E 278 C4
Syntagma Square Athens, Greece 112 b2
Synyak Ukraine 48°35N 22°51E 182 B7
Syon Park U.K. 51°28N 0°18W 125 B2
Syowa Antarctica 68°50S 12°0E 151 C5
Syracuse = Siracusa Italy 37°4N 15°17E 201 E8
Syracuse Ind., U.S.A. 41°26N 85°45W 311 C11
Syracuse Kans., U.S.A. 37°59N 101°45W 308 G3
Syracuse N.Y., U.S.A. 43°3N 76°9W 313 C8
Syracuse Nebr., U.S.A. 40°39N 96°11W 308 E5
Syrdarya ➝ Kazakhstan 46°3N 61°0E 216 C6
Syria ■ Asia 35°0N 38°0E 213 E8
Syriam Burma 16°44N 96°19E 241 G6
Syrian Desert = Shām, Bādiyat ash
Asia 32°0N 40°0E 246 C3
Syros = Ermoupoli
Greece 37°28N 24°57E 204 D6
Sysslebäck Sweden 60°44N 12°52E 162 D6
Syvden Norway 62°5N 5°44E 164 B2
Syzran Russia 53°12N 48°30E 190 D9
Szabolcs-Szatmár-Bereg □
Hungary 48°2N 21°45E 182 B6
Szadek Poland 51°41N 18°59E 185 G5
Szamocin Poland 53°2N 17°7E 185 E4
Szamos ➝ Hungary 48°7N 22°20E 182 B7
Szamotuły Poland 52°37N 16°33E 185 F3
Száraz ➝ Hungary 46°10N 21°15E 182 D6
Szarvas Hungary 46°50N 20°38E 182 D5
Százhalombatta Hungary 47°20N 18°58E 182 C3
Szczawnica Poland 49°26N 20°30E 185 J7
Szczebrzeszyn Poland 50°42N 22°59E 185 H9
Szczecin Poland 53°27N 14°27E 184 E1
Szczecinek Poland 53°43N 16°41E 184 E3
Szczeciński, Zalew = Stettiner Haff
Germany 53°47N 14°15E 178 B10
Szczekociny Poland 50°38N 19°48E 185 H6
Szczęśliwice Poland 52°12N 20°57E 142 B1
Szczucin Poland 50°18N 21°4E 185 H8
Szczuczyn Poland 53°36N 22°19E 184 E9
Szczyrk Poland 49°43N 19°2E 185 J6
Szczytna Poland 50°25N 16°28E 185 H3
Szczytno Poland 53°33N 21°0E 184 E7
Széchenyi-hegy
Hungary 47°29N 18°57E 117 B1
Szechuan Basin = Sichuan Pendi
China 31°0N 105°0E 228 B5
Szechwan = Sichuan □
China 30°30N 103°0E 228 B5
Szécsény Hungary 48°7N 19°30E 182 B4
Szeged Hungary 46°16N 20°10E 182 D5
Szeghalom Hungary 47°1N 21°10E 182 C6
Székesfehérvár Hungary 47°15N 18°25E 182 C3
Szekszárd Hungary 46°22N 18°42E 182 D3
Szendrő Hungary 48°24N 20°41E 182 B5
Szentendre Hungary 47°39N 19°4E 182 C4
Szentes Hungary 46°39N 20°21E 182 D5
Szentgotthárd Hungary 46°58N 16°19E 182 D1
Szentlőrinc Hungary 46°3N 18°1E 182 D3
Szépahalom Hungary 47°33N 19°0E 117 A1
Szeping = Siping China 43°8N 124°21E 227 C13
Szerencs Hungary 48°10N 21°12E 182 B6
Szentszentmiklós
Hungary 47°21N 19°3E 182 C4
Szigetvár Hungary 46°3N 17°46E 182 D2
Szikszó Hungary 48°12N 20°56E 182 B5
Szklarska Poreba Poland 50°50N 15°33E 185 H2
Szkwa ➝ Poland 53°11N 21°43E 185 E8
Szlichtyngowa Poland 51°42N 16°15E 185 G3
Szob Hungary 47°48N 18°53E 182 C3
Szolnok Hungary 47°10N 20°15E 182 C5
Szombathely Hungary 47°14N 16°38E 182 C1

Szprotawa Poland 51°33N 15°35E 185 G2
Sztálinváros = Dunaújváros
Hungary 46°58N 18°57E 182 D3
Sztum Poland 53°55N 19°1E 184 E6
Sztutowo Poland 54°20N 19°15E 184 D6
Szubin Poland 53°1N 17°45E 185 E4
Szydłowiec Poland 51°15N 20°51E 185 G7
Szypliszki Poland 54°17N 23°2E 184 D10

T

Ta Khli Thailand 15°15N 100°21E 236 E3
Ta Khli Khok Thailand 15°18N 100°20E 236 E3
Ta Lai Vietnam 11°24N 107°23E 237 G6
Ta Pieh Shan = Dabie Shan
China 31°20N 115°20E 229 B10
Taakoka Cook Is. 21°15S 159°43W 289 h
Taan Taiwan 24°22N 120°35E 225 B2
Taastrup Denmark 55°39N 12°18E 118 B1
Tab Hungary 46°44N 18°2E 182 D3
Tabacal Argentina 23°15S 64°15W 334 A3
Tabaco Phil. 13°22N 123°44E 232 E4
Tabagné Ivory C. 7°59N 3°4W 262 D4
Ţābah Si. Arabia 26°55N 42°38E 246 E4
Tabajara Brazil 8°56S 62°8W 331 B5
Tabalo Papua N. G. 1°24S 149°40E 286 A5
Tabalos Peru 6°26S 76°37W 330 B2
Tabanan Indonesia 8°32S 115°8E 231 K18
Tabankort Niger 17°44N 0°20E 263 B5
Tabaquite Trin. & Tob. 10°23N 61°18W 323 t
Tabar I. Papua N. G. 2°56S 152°0E 286 B7
Tabar Is. Papua N. G. 2°50S 152°0E 286 B7
Tabarka Tunisia 36°56N 8°46E 258 A1
Ţabas Khorāsān, Iran 32°48N 60°12E 247 C9
Ţabas Yazd, Iran 33°35N 56°55E 247 C8
Tabasará, Serranía de
Panama 8°35N 81°40W 320 E3
Tabasco □ Mexico 18°0N 92°40W 319 D6
Tabāsīn Iran 31°12N 57°54E 247 D8
Tabata Japan 35°44N 139°46E 140 A3
Tabatinga Brazil 4°16S 69°56W 330 A4
Tabatinga, Serra da
Brazil 10°30S 44°0W 332 D3
Tabayin Burma 22°42N 95°20E 241 D5
Tabelbala Algeria 29°24N 3°15W 260 C4
Tabelbala, Kahal de
Algeria 28°47N 2°0W 261 C4
Tabelembila Algeria 24°43N 4°16E 261 D5
Taber Canada 49°47N 112°8W 296 D6
Taberg Sweden 57°40N 14°6E 163 G8
Tabernacle
St. Kitts & Nevis 17°23N 62°46W 322 d
Tabi Angola 8°10S 13°18E 265 D2
Tabira Brazil 7°35S 37°33W 332 C4
Tabiteuea Kiribati 1°25S 174°50E 277 A13
Tabla Niger 13°46N 3°1E 263 C5
Tablada Argentina 34°41S 58°32W 117 C1
Tablas Phil. 12°25N 122°2E 232 E4
Tablas de Daimiel △ Spain 39°9N 3°40W 195 F7
Tablas Strait Phil. 12°40N 121°48E 232 E3
Table, Pte. de la Réunion 21°14S 55°48E 272 f
Table B. Nfld. & L.,
Canada 53°40N 56°25W 299 B8
Table B. Western Cape,
S. Africa 33°35S 18°25E 118 A1
Table C. N.Z. 39°6S 178°0E 284 F7
Table Grove U.S.A. 40°20N 90°27W 310 D6
Table I. Burma 14°12N 93°22E 245 G11
Table Mountain △
S. Africa 34°20S 18°28E 118 A1
Table Mt. S. Africa 33°58S 18°26E 118 A1
Table Rock L. U.S.A. 36°36N 93°19W 308 G7
Tableland Trin. & Tob. 10°16N 61°16W 323 t
Tabletop, Mt. Australia 23°24S 147°11E 280 C4
Taboão da Serra Brazil 23°36S 46°45W 137 B1
Tabocal Brazil 2°42S 57°40W 329 D6
Tábor Czech Rep. 49°25N 14°39E 180 B7
Tabora Tanzania 5°2S 32°50E 268 D3
Tabora □ Tanzania 5°0S 33°0E 268 D3
Tabou Ivory C. 4°30N 7°20W 262 E3
Tabrīz Iran 38°7N 46°20E 213 C12
Tabuaeran Kiribati 3°51N 159°22W 289 G12
Tabubil Papua N. G. 5°20S 141°15E 286 C1
Tabuenca Spain 41°42N 1°33W 196 D3
Tabuk Phil. 17°24N 121°25E 232 C3
Tabūk Si. Arabia 28°23N 36°36E 251 K7
Tabūk □ Si. Arabia 27°40N 36°50E 246 E3
Tabunifi Micronesia 9°28N 138°4E 287 S16
Taburno-Camposauro ⌓
Italy 41°8N 14°37E 201 A7
Tabwemasana, Mt.
Vanuatu 15°20S 166°44E 287 E4
Täby Sweden 59°26N 18°2E 139 A2
Tacámbaro de Codallos
Mexico 19°14N 101°28W 318 D4
Tacarigua Trin. & Tob. 10°38N 61°22W 323 t
Tacarigua, Laguna de
Venezuela 10°15N 65°50W 328 A4
Tacheng Xinjiang Uygur,
China 46°40N 82°58E 217 C10
Tacheng Taiwan 23°51N 120°19E 225 C2
Tach'i Taiwan 24°53N 121°17E 225 B3
Tachia Taiwan 24°25N 120°28E 225 B2
Tachia Hsi → Taiwan 24°20N 120°33E 225 B3
Tachibana-Wan Japan 32°45N 130°7E 222 E2
Tachikawa Japan 35°42N 139°25E 223 B11
Tach'ing Shan = Daqing Shan
China 40°40N 111°0E 226 D6
Táchira □ Venezuela 8°7N 72°15W 328 B3
Tachiumet Libya 26°19N 10°3E 261 C7
Tachoshui Taiwan 24°20N 121°44E 225 B3
Tachov Czech Rep. 49°47N 12°39E 180 B5
Tácina → Italy 38°57N 16°55E 201 D9
Tacloban Phil. 11°15N 124°58E 233 F5
Tacna Peru 18°0S 70°20W 330 D3
Tacna □ Peru 17°40S 70°20W 330 D3
Tacoma U.S.A. 47°14N 122°26W 306 C4
Tacopaya = Zudañez
Bolivia 19°6S 64°44W 331 D5
Tacuarembó Uruguay 31°45S 56°0W 335 C4
Tacuba Mexico 19°26N 99°11W 128 B1
Tacubaya Mexico 19°24N 99°10W 128 B1
Tacurong Phil. 6°40N 124°41E 233 H5
Tada-u Burma 21°49N 95°58E 241 E5
Tadahadi Solomon Is. 10°18S 161°35E 287 N11
Tademaït, Plateau du
Algeria 28°30N 2°30E 261 C5
Tādepallegudem India 16°50N 81°30E 244 F5
Tadéra Niger 20°29N 8°18E 261 D6
Tadine N. Cal. 21°33S 167°52E 288 d
Tadio, L. Ivory C. 5°10N 5°15W 262 D3
Tadjerdjeri, O. → Algeria 26°0N 8°0E 261 D6
Tadjerouna Algeria 33°31N 2°3E 261 B5
Tadjettaret, O. → Algeria 21°20N 7°22E 261 D6
Tadjmout Laghouat, Algeria 33°52N 2°30E 261 B5
Tadjmout Saoura, Algeria 25°37N 3°48E 261 C5
Tadjoura Djibouti 11°50N 42°55E 257 E5
Tadjoura, Golfe de Djibouti 11°50N 43°0E 257 E5
Tadmor N.Z. 41°27S 172°45E 285 B7
Tadoba △ India 20°30N 78°20E 244 D4
Tadotsu Japan 34°16N 133°45E 222 C5
Tadoule L. Canada 58°36N 98°20W 297 B9
Tadoussac Canada 48°11N 69°42W 299 C6
Tadpatri India 14°55N 78°1E 245 G4
Tadrés ⌓ Niger 16°0N 7°10E 263 B6
Tadzhikistan = Tajikistan ■
Asia 38°30N 70°0E 217 E8
Tae-an S. Korea 36°45N 126°17E 224 D3
Tae-an Seashore Nat. Park △
S. Korea 36°40N 126°0E 224 D3
Taebaek S. Korea 37°10N 128°59E 224 D4
Taebaeksan S. Korea 37°5N 128°54E 224 D4
T'aebaeksanmaek
S. Korea 37°40N 128°50E 224 D4
Taedong-gang →
N. Korea 38°41N 125°15E 224 C2
Taedong-man N. Korea 38°4N 125°7E 224 C2
Taegu = Daegu S. Korea 35°50N 128°37E 224 E4
Taegwan N. Korea 40°13N 125°12E 224 B2
Taehung N. Korea 40°5N 126°56E 224 B3
Taehwa-do N. Korea 39°26N 124°36E 224 C2
Taejŏn = Daejeon
S. Korea 36°20N 127°28E 224 D3
Tælavåg Norway 60°15N 4°58E 164 D1
Taen, Ko Thailand 9°22N 99°57E 237 b
Tafalla Spain 42°30N 1°41W 196 C3
Tafar Sudan 6°52N 28°15E 257 F2
Tafassasset, O. → Algeria 22°0N 9°57E 261 D6
Tafelbaai = Table B.
S. Africa 33°35S 18°25E 118 A1
Tafelberg Neth. Ant. 12°4N 68°50W 322 g
Tafelney, C. Morocco 31°3N 9°51W 260 B3
Tafermaar Indonesia 6°47S 134°10E 231 F8
Taffermit Morocco 29°37N 9°15W 260 C3
Tafi Viejo Argentina 26°43S 65°17W 334 B2
Tafīhān Iran 29°25N 52°39E 247 D7
Tafilalet Morocco 31°20N 4°45W 260 B4
Tafiré Ivory C. 9°4N 5°4W 262 D3
Tafjord Norway 62°14N 7°24E 164 B4
Tafnidilt Morocco 28°47N 10°58W 260 C2
Tafo Ghana 6°15N 0°20W 263 D4
Tafraoute Morocco 29°50N 8°58W 260 C3
Tafresh Iran 34°45N 49°57E 247 C6
Taft Iran 31°45N 54°14E 247 D7
Taft Phil. 11°57N 125°30E 233 F5
Taft Calif., U.S.A. 35°8N 119°28W 307 K7
Taft Fla., U.S.A. 28°25N 81°21W 133 B2
Taftan Pakistan 29°0N 61°30E 240 C1
Taftān, Kūh-e Iran 28°40N 61°0E 247 D9
Tafu Taiwan 23°37N 121°23E 225 C3
Tafwap India 7°23N 93°43E 245 L11
Taga Samoa 13°46S 172°28W 287 V19
Taga Dzong Bhutan 27°5N 89°55E 241 B2
Tagana-an Phil. 9°42N 125°35E 233 G5
Taganrog Russia 47°12N 38°50E 189 J10
Taganrogskiy Zaliv
Russia 47°0N 38°30E 189 J10
Tagânt □ Mauritania 19°0N 10°0W 260 E3
Tagap Ga Burma 26°56N 96°13E 241 B6
Tagatay Phil. 14°6N 120°56E 232 D3
Tagauayan I. Phil. 10°58N 121°13E 233 F3
Tagaung Burma 23°30N 96°2E 241 D6
Tagawa Japan 33°38N 130°51E 222 D2
Tagbilaran Phil. 9°39N 123°51E 233 G4
Tagdempt = Tiaret Algeria 35°20N 1°21E 261 A5
Tage Papua N. G. 6°19S 143°20E 286 D2
Tageran Canal Micronesia 9°33N 138°8E 287 R16
Tàggia Italy 43°52N 7°51E 198 E4
Taghit Algeria 30°58N 2°0W 261 B4
Tagish Canada 60°19N 134°16W 296 A2
Tagish L. Canada 60°10N 134°20W 296 A2
Tagkawayan Phil. 13°58N 122°32E 232 E4
Tagliacozzo Italy 42°4N 13°14E 199 F10
Tagliamento → Italy 45°38N 13°6E 199 C10
Tàglio di Po Italy 45°0N 12°12E 199 D9
Tagna Colombia 2°24S 70°37W 328 D3
Tago Phil. 9°2N 126°13E 233 G6
Tago, Mt. Phil. 8°23N 125°5E 233 G5
Tagomago Spain 39°2N 1°39E 206 C2
Tagourâret Mauritania 17°45N 7°45W 262 B3
Tagpochau, Mt.
N. Marianas 15°11N 145°44E 302 a
Taguatinga Distrito Federal,
Brazil 16°12S 44°35W 333 E2
Taguatinga Tocantins,
Brazil 12°27S 46°22W 333 D2
Tagudin Phil. 16°56N 120°27E 232 C3
Taguenout Chagguéret
Mali 21°14N 0°48W 261 D4
Taguig Phil. 14°31N 121°4E 127 B2
Tagula Papua N. G. 11°22S 153°15E 286 F7
Tagula I. Papua N. G. 11°30S 153°30E 286 F7
Tagum Phil. 7°33N 125°53E 233 H5
Tagus = Tejo → Europe 38°40N 9°24W 195 F2
Tahakopa N.Z. 46°30S 169°23E 285 G4
Tahala Morocco 34°0N 4°28W 260 B4
Tahan, Gunung Malaysia 4°34N 102°17E 237 K4
Tahānah-ye sūr Gol
Afghan. 31°43N 67°53E 240 C2
Tahara Japan 34°40N 137°16E 223 C9
Tahat Algeria 23°18N 5°33E 261 D6
Tāherī Iran 27°43N 52°20E 247 E7
Tahgong Pt. N. Marianas 15°6N 145°39E 302 e
Tahifet Algeria 22°58N 6°0E 261 D6
Tahiti French Polynesia 17°37S 149°27W 289 e
Tahlab → Pakistan 28°9N 62°45E 240 C1
Tahlequah U.S.A. 35°55N 94°58W 314 D7
Tahoe, L. U.S.A. 39°6N 120°2W 306 G6
Tahoe City U.S.A. 39°10N 120°9W 306 F6
Tahoka U.S.A. 33°10N 101°48W 314 E4
Taholah U.S.A. 47°21N 124°17W 306 C2
Tahora N.Z. 39°2S 174°49E 284 F3
Tahoua Niger 14°57N 5°16E 263 C6
Tahrūd Iran 29°26N 57°49E 247 D8
Tahsis Canada 49°55N 126°40W 296 D3
Tahta Egypt 26°44N 31°32E 256 B3
Tahtaköprü Turkey 39°57N 29°39E 203 G13
Tahtalı Dağları Turkey 38°20N 36°0E 212 C7
Tahu Taiwan 24°26N 120°52E 225 B2
Tahuamanú → Bolivia 11°6S 67°36W 330 C4
Tahuata, I. French Polynesia 9°57S 139°5W 289 f
Tahulandang Indonesia 2°27N 125°23E 231 D7
Tahuna Indonesia 3°38N 125°30E 231 D7
Taï Ivory C. 5°55N 7°30W 262 D3
Taï △ Ivory C. 5°25N 7°5W 262 D3
Tai Au Mun China 22°18N 114°17E 219 G11
Tai Hu China 31°5N 120°10E 229 B12
Tai Lo Shan China 22°21N 114°13E 122 A2
Tai Mo Shan China 22°25N 114°7E 219 G11
Tai O China 22°15N 113°52E 219 G10
Tai Pang Wan China 22°33N 114°24E 219 F11
Tai Po China 22°27N 114°10E 219 G11
Tai Po Tsai China 22°20N 114°15E 122 A2
Tai Rom Yen △ Thailand 8°45N 99°30E 237 H2
Tai Seng Singapore 1°20N 103°53E 138 A3
Tai Shan China 36°25N 117°20E 227 F9
Tai Shui Hang China 22°24N 114°13E 122 A2
Tai Tam B. China 22°13N 114°13E 122 B2
Tai Tam Tuk Res. China 22°14N 114°13E 122 B2
Tai Wai China 22°22N 114°10E 122 A2
Tai Wan Tau China 22°17N 114°17E 122 B2
Tai Wo Hau China 22°21N 114°7E 122 A1
Tai Yue Shan = Lantau I.
China 22°15N 113°56E 219 G10
Tai'an China 36°12N 117°8E 227 F9
Taiarapu, Presqu'île de
Tahiti 17°47S 149°14W 289 e
Taibei = T'aipei Taiwan 25°4N 121°29E 225 A3
Taibique Canary Is. 27°42N 17°58W 153 e1
Taibus Qi China 41°54N 115°22E 226 D8
Taicang China 31°30N 121°5E 229 B13
Taichow = Taizhou
China 32°28N 119°55E 229 A12
T'aichung Taiwan 24°9N 120°37E 225 B2
Taieri → N.Z. 46°3S 170°12E 285 G5
Taigu China 37°28N 112°30E 226 F7
Taihang Shan China 36°0N 113°30E 226 G7
Taihape N.Z. 39°41S 175°48E 284 F4
Taihe Anhui, China 33°20N 115°42E 226 H8
Taihe Jiangxi, China 26°47N 114°52E 229 D10
Taihoku = T'aipei
Taiwan 25°4N 121°29E 225 A3
Taihsi Taiwan 23°51N 120°16E 225 C2
Taihu China 30°22N 116°20E 229 B11
Taijiang China 26°39N 108°21E 228 D7
Taikang China 34°5N 114°50E 226 G8
Taikkyi Burma 17°20N 96°0E 241 G6
Tailem Bend Australia 35°12S 139°29E 282 C3
Tailfingen Germany 48°15N 9°1E 179 G5
T'ailuko Taiwan 24°9N 121°37E 225 B3
T'aimali Taiwan 22°36N 121°0E 225 D2
Taimyr Peninsula = Taymyr,
Poluostrov Russia 75°0N 100°0E 215 B11
Tain U.K. 57°49N 4°4W 167 D4
Tainaka Japan 34°36N 135°33E 133 B2
T'ainan Taiwan 23°0N 120°10E 225 D2
T'ainan □ Taiwan 23°15N 120°20E 225 C2
Tainggyo Burma 17°49N 94°29E 241 G5
Taining China 26°54N 117°9E 229 D11
Taiobeiras Brazil 15°49S 42°14W 333 E3
Taipa China 22°10N 113°35E 219 G10
T'aipei Taiwan 25°4N 121°29E 225 A3
T'aipei □ Taiwan 24°50N 121°35E 225 B3
Taiping Anhui, China 30°15N 118°6E 229 B12
Taiping Malaysia 4°51N 100°44E 237 K3
Taipingzhen China 33°35N 111°42E 226 H6
Taipu Brazil 5°37S 35°36W 332 C4
Tairbeart = Tarbert U.K. 57°54N 6°49W 167 D2
Tairenpokpi India 24°39N 93°40E 241 C4
Tairua N.Z. 37°0S 175°51E 284 D4
Taisha Japan 35°24N 132°40E 222 B4
Taishan China 22°14N 112°41E 229 F9
Taishō Japan 34°38N 135°27E 133 B1
Taishun China 27°30N 119°42E 229 D12
Taita N.Z. 41°12S 174°57E 143 B2
Taita Hills Kenya 3°25S 38°15E 268 C4
Taitao, C. Chile 45°53S 75°5W 336 C1
Taitao, Pen. de Chile 46°30S 75°0W 336 C2
T'aitung Taiwan 22°43N 121°4E 225 D3
T'aitung □ Taiwan 23°0N 121°0E 225 D3
Taivalkoski Finland 65°33N 28°12E 160 D23
Taiwan ■ Asia 23°30N 121°0E 225 C3
Taiwan Strait Asia 24°40N 120°0E 229 E12
Taixing China 32°11N 120°0E 229 A13
Taiyara Sudan 13°12N 30°47E 257 E3
Taiyiba Israel 32°36N 35°27E 250 F6
Taiyuan China 37°52N 112°33E 226 F7
Taizhong = T'aichung
Taiwan 24°9N 120°37E 225 B2
Taizhou China 32°28N 119°55E 229 A12
Taizhou Liedao China 28°30N 121°55E 229 C13
Ta'izz Yemen 13°35N 44°2E 248 D3
Tājābād Iran 30°2N 54°24E 247 D7
Tajapuru, Furo do Brazil 1°50S 50°25W 332 B1
Tajarḥī Libya 24°21N 14°28E 258 D2
Tajen Taiwan 22°17N 120°53E 225 D2
Tajikistan ■ Asia 38°30N 70°0E 217 E8
Tajima Japan 37°12N 139°46E 221 F9
Tajimi Japan 35°19N 137°8E 223 B9
Tajo = Tejo → Europe 38°40N 9°24W 195 F2
Tajrish Iran 35°48N 51°25E 141 A2
Tajumulco, Vol.
Guatemala 15°2N 91°55W 320 C1
Tājūrā Libya 32°51N 13°21E 258 B2
Tak Thailand 16°52N 99°8E 236 D2
Takāb Iran 36°24N 47°7E 213 D12
Takabanare-shima Japan 26°22N 127°59E 288 a
Takabba Kenya 3°21N 40°13E 267 D5
Takachiho Japan 32°42N 131°18E 222 E3
Takachu Botswana 22°37S 21°58E 270 B3
Takada Japan 37°7N 138°15E 221 F9
Takahagi Japan 36°43N 140°45E 221 F10
Takahashi Japan 34°51N 133°39E 222 C5
Takaido Japan 35°40N 139°37E 140 A2
Takaishi Japan 35°36N 139°31E 140 B2
Takaka N.Z. 40°51S 172°50E 285 A7
Takaki = Yamato
Japan 35°27N 139°25E 223 B11
Takalous, O. → Algeria 22°36N 7°21E 261 D6
Takamaka Seychelles 4°50S 55°30E 272 c
Takamatsu Japan 34°20N 134°5E 222 C6
Takanabe Japan 32°8N 131°30E 222 E3
Takangkou Taiwan 23°28N 121°29E 225 C3
Takaoka Japan 36°47N 137°0E 223 A9
Takapau N.Z. 40°2S 176°21E 284 G5
Takapuna N.Z. 36°47S 174°47E 284 C3
Takarazuka Japan 34°47N 135°20E 133 A1
Takaroa French Polynesia 14°28S 144°58W 289 f
Takasago Japan 34°45N 134°48E 140 A4
Takasaki Japan 36°20N 139°0E 223 A11
Takatsu Japan 35°36N 139°37E 140 B2
Takatsuki Japan 34°51N 135°37E 223 C7
Takaungu Kenya 3°38S 39°52E 268 C4
Takayama Japan 36°18N 137°11E 223 A9
Takayama-Bonchi Japan 36°0N 137°18E 223 B9
Take-Shima Japan 30°49N 130°26E 221 J5
Takefu Japan 35°50N 136°10E 223 B8
Takehara Japan 34°21N 132°55E 222 C4
Takengon Indonesia 4°45N 96°50E 234 B1
Takeo Japan 33°12N 130°1E 222 D2
Tåkern Sweden 58°22N 14°45E 163 F8
Takeshima = Tokdo
Asia 37°15N 131°52E 221 F5
Takeshita Japan 35°33N 139°32E 140 B2
Tākestān Iran 36°0N 49°40E 247 C6
Taketa Japan 32°58N 131°24E 222 E3
Takev Cambodia 10°59N 104°47E 237 G5
Takh India 33°6N 77°32E 243 C7
Takhār □ Afghan. 36°40N 70°0E 240 A3
Takhiatash Uzbekistan 42°20N 59°33E 216 D5
Takhmau Cambodia 11°29N 104°57E 237 G5
Takht-Sulaiman Pakistan 31°40N 69°58E 242 D3
Taki Papua N. G. 6°29S 155°52E 286 D8
Takiéta Niger 13°41N 8°32E 263 C6
Takikawa Japan 43°33N 141°54E 220 C10
Takinegawa Japan 35°45N 139°44E 140 A3
Takla L. Canada 55°15N 125°45W 296 B3
Takla Landing Canada 55°30N 125°50W 296 B3
Takla Makan China 38°0N 83°0E 217 E10
Taklamakan Shamo = Takla
Makan China 38°0N 83°0E 217 E10
Takoma Park U.S.A. 38°58N 77°0W 143 B3
Takotna U.S.A. 62°59N 156°4W 303 E8
Taksim Turkey 41°2N 28°58E 122 B1
Taksimo Russia 56°20N 114°52E 215 D12
Taku Japan 33°18N 130°3E 222 D2
Taku → Canada 58°30N 133°50W 296 B2
Takua Pa Thailand 8°52N 98°21E 237 H2
Takua Thung Thailand 8°24N 98°27E 237 a
Takum Indonesia 27°47N 93°37E 241 B4
Takum Nigeria 7°18N 9°36E 263 D6
Takume French Polynesia 15°49S 142°12W 289 f
Takundi
Dem. Rep. of the Congo 4°45S 16°34E 265 C3
Takutu → Brazil 3°1N 60°29W 329 C5
Takutu → Guyana 3°1N 60°29W 329 C5
Tal Halāl Iran 28°54N 55°1E 247 D7
Tala Uruguay 34°21S 55°46W 335 C4
Talachyn Belarus 54°25N 29°42E 188 E5
Talacogan Phil. 8°32N 125°39E 233 G5
Talagang Pakistan 32°55N 72°25E 242 C5
Talagante Chile 33°40S 70°50W 334 C1
Talahouhait Algeria 24°52N 1°5E 261 D5
Talaide Portugal 38°44N 9°18W 126 A1
Talaimannar Sri Lanka 9°6N 79°43E 245 K4
Talaïnt Morocco 29°41N 9°40W 260 C3
Talak Niger 18°0N 5°0E 263 B6
Talakag Phil. 8°16N 124°37E 233 G5
Talamanca, Cordillera de
Cent. Amer. 9°20N 83°20W 320 E3
Talampaya △ Argentina 29°43S 67°42W 334 B2
Talant France 47°19N 4°58E 173 E11
Talara Peru 4°38S 81°18W 330 A1
Talas Kyrgyzstan 42°30N 72°13E 217 D8
Talas Turkey 38°41N 35°33E 212 C6
Talas □ Kyrgyzstan 42°20N 72°0E 217 D8
Talas → Kazakhstan 44°0N 70°20E 217 D8
Talas Ala Too Kyrgyzstan 42°15N 72°0E 217 D8
Talasea Papua N. G. 5°20S 150°2E 286 C6
Talasskiy Alatau = Talas Ala Too
Kyrgyzstan 42°15N 72°0E 217 D8
Talâta Egypt 30°36N 32°20E 251 H3
Talata Mafara Nigeria 12°38N 6°4E 263 C6
Talaud, Kepulauan
Indonesia 4°30N 126°50E 231 D7
Talaud Is. = Talaud, Kepulauan
Indonesia 4°30N 126°50E 231 D7
Talavera de la Reina
Spain 39°55N 4°46W 194 F6
Talavera la Real Spain 38°53N 6°46W 195 G4
Talawgyi Burma 25°4N 97°19E 241 C6
Talayan Phil. 6°52N 124°24E 233 H5
Talayuela Spain 39°59N 5°36W 194 F5
Talbandh India 22°3N 86°20E 243 H12
Talbert, Sillon de France 48°53N 3°5W 172 D3
Talbot, C. Australia 13°48S 126°43E 278 B4
Talbotton U.S.A. 32°41N 84°32W 316 C5
Talbragar → Australia 32°12S 148°37E 283 B8
Talca Chile 35°28S 71°40W 334 D1
Talcahuano Chile 36°40S 73°10W 334 D1
Talcher India 21°0N 85°18E 244 D7
Talcho Niger 14°44N 3°28E 263 C5
Taldy Kurgan = Taldyqorghan
Kazakhstan 45°10N 78°45E 217 C9
Taldyqorghan Kazakhstan 45°10N 78°45E 217 C9
Tālesh Iran 37°58N 48°58E 213 D13
Tālesh, Kūhhā-ye Iran 37°42N 48°55E 213 D13
Talgar = Talghar
Kazakhstan 43°19N 77°15E 217 D9
Talghar Kazakhstan 43°19N 77°15E 217 D9
Talguharai Sudan 18°19N 35°56E 256 D4
Talguppa India 14°13N 74°56E 245 G2
Tali Post Sudan 5°55N 30°44E 257 F3
Taliabu Indonesia 1°50S 125°0E 231 E6
Taliao Taiwan 22°36N 120°23E 225 D2
Talibon Phil. 10°9N 124°20E 233 F5
Talichien Taiwan 24°58N 121°55E 225 B3
Taliganga India 22°30N 88°22E 124 B2
Talihina U.S.A. 34°45N 95°3W 314 D7
Talikota India 16°29N 76°17E 245 F3
Talin Taiwan 23°36N 120°27E 225 C2
Talipao Phil. 5°59N 121°7E 233 J3
Talipapa Phil. 14°41N 121°1E 127 A2
Talipparamba India 12°3N 75°21E 245 H2
Talisay Phil. 10°44N 122°58E 233 F4
Talisayan Phil. 9°0N 124°55E 233 G5
Taliwang Indonesia 8°50S 116°55E 235 D5
Talkeetna U.S.A. 62°20N 150°6W 303 E10
Talkha Egypt 31°3N 31°22E 251 G2
Tálknafjörður Iceland 65°34N 24°0W 155 B2
Tall 'Afar Iraq 36°22N 42°27E 213 D10
Tall Kalakh Syria 34°41N 36°15E 250 D7
Tall Kayf Iraq 36°29N 43°7E 213 D10
Talla Egypt 28°5N 30°43E 256 B3
Talladega U.S.A. 33°26N 86°6W 316 B3
Tallaganda △ Australia 35°29S 149°37E 283 C8
Tallaght Ireland 53°17N 6°22W 120 B1
Tallahassee U.S.A. 30°27N 84°17W 316 E5
Tallangatta Australia 36°15S 147°19E 283 D7
Tallapoosa U.S.A. 33°45N 85°17W 316 B4
Tallapoosa → U.S.A. 32°30N 86°16W 316 C3
Tallard France 44°28N 6°3E 175 D10
Tallarook Australia 37°5S 145°6E 283 D6
Tallassee U.S.A. 32°32N 85°54W 316 C4
Tällberg Sweden 60°51N 15°2E 162 D9
Tallering Pk. Australia 28°6S 115°37E 279 E2
Talli Pakistan 29°32N 68°8E 242 E3
Tallinn Estonia 59°22N 24°48E 188 C3
Tallkrogen Sweden 59°16N 18°4E 139 B2
Tallmadge U.S.A. 41°6N 81°27W 312 E3
Tallulah U.S.A. 32°25N 91°11W 314 E9
Tălmaciu Romania 45°38N 24°19E 183 E9
Talmest Morocco 31°48N 9°21W 260 B3
Talmont-St-Hilaire
France 46°27N 1°37W 174 B2
Talnakh Russia 69°29N 88°22E 215 C9
Talne Ukraine 48°50N 30°44E 189 H6
Talnoye = Talne Ukraine 48°50N 30°44E 189 H6
Taloda India 21°34N 74°11E 244 D2
Talodi Sudan 10°35N 30°22E 257 E3
Talofofo Guam 13°21N 144°45E 302 d
Ţāloqān Afghan. 36°44N 69°33E 240 A3
Talovaya Russia 51°6N 40°45E 190 E5
Taloyoak Canada 69°32N 93°32W 294 D13
Talpa de Allende
Mexico 20°23N 104°51W 318 C4
Talparo Trin. & Tob. 10°30N 61°17W 323 t
Talparo → Trin. & Tob. 10°34N 61°17W 323 t
Talquin, L. U.S.A. 30°23N 84°39W 316 E5
Talsi Latvia 57°10N 22°30E 184 A9
Talsi □ Latvia 57°20N 22°40E 184 A9
Talsinnt Morocco 32°33N 3°27W 261 B4
Taltal Chile 25°23S 70°33W 334 B1
Taltson → Canada 61°24N 112°46W 296 A6
Talwood Australia 28°29S 149°29E 281 D4
Talyawalka Cr. →
Australia 32°28S 142°22E 282 B5
Tam Ky Vietnam 15°34N 108°29E 236 E7
Tam Quan Vietnam 14°35N 109°3E 236 E7
Tama Tōkyō, Japan 35°38N 139°26E 140 B1
Tama Iowa, U.S.A. 41°58N 92°35W 310 C4
Tama → Japan 35°32N 139°39E 140 B2
Tama ⌓ Ethiopia 5°55N 36°5E 257 F4
Tama Abu, Banjaran
Malaysia 3°10N 115°5E 235 B5
Tama Kyūryō Japan 35°34N 139°30E 140 B2
Tamada Algeria 21°34N 3°20E 261 D5
Tamaden Japan 35°39N 139°38E 140 B2
Tamagawa-josui →
Japan 35°41N 139°47E 140 A1
Tamakautoga Cook Is. 19°5S 169°55W 289 g
Tamalameque Colombia 8°52N 73°49W 328 B3
Tamale Ghana 9°22N 0°50W 263 D4
Taman Russia 45°14N 36°41E 189 K9
Taman Negara △
Malaysia 4°38N 102°26E 237 K4
Taman Sari Indonesia 6°8S 106°48E 122 A1
T'aman Shan Taiwan 24°42N 121°27E 225 B3
Tamana Japan 32°58N 130°32E 222 E2
Tamana Kiribati 2°30S 175°59E 277 A14
Tamana, Mt. Trin. & Tob. 10°28N 61°12W 323 t
Tamanar Morocco 31°1N 9°46W 260 B3
Tamanduateí → Brazil 23°37S 46°38W 137 B2
Tamanhint Libya 27°13N 14°37E 258 C2
Tamani Mali 13°20N 6°50W 262 C3
Tamano Japan 34°29N 133°59E 222 C5
Tamanrasset Algeria 22°50N 5°30E 261 D6
Tamanrasset □ Algeria 24°0N 4°45E 261 D5
Tamanrasset, O. → Algeria 22°0N 2°0E 261 D5
Tamanthi Burma 25°19N 95°17E 241 C5
Tamaqua U.S.A. 40°48N 75°58W 313 F9
Tamar → U.K. 50°27N 4°15W 169 G3
Támara Colombia 5°50N 72°10W 328 B3
Tamarac U.S.A. 26°12N 80°15W 317 J9
Tamarin Mauritius 20°19S 57°20E 272 e
Tamarinda Spain 39°55N 3°49E 206 B4
Tamarite de Litera Spain 41°52N 0°25E 196 D5
Tamaroa U.S.A. 38°8N 89°14W 310 F7
Tamashima Japan 34°32N 133°40E 221 G6
Tamási Hungary 46°40N 18°18E 182 D3
Tamaské Niger 14°49N 5°43E 263 C6
Tamatave = Toamasina
Madag. 18°10S 49°25E 272 B2
Tamaulipas □ Mexico 24°0N 98°45W 319 C5
Tamaulipas, Sierra de
Mexico 23°30N 98°20W 319 C5
Tamazula Mexico 24°57N 106°57W 318 C3
Tamazunchale Mexico 21°16N 98°47W 319 C5
Tamba-Dabatou Guinea 11°50N 10°40W 262 C2
Tambach Kenya 0°36N 35°31E 268 B4
Tambacounda Senegal 13°45N 13°40W 262 C2
Tambacounda □ Senegal 14°0N 13°0W 262 C2
Tambaram India 12°55N 80°7E 245 H5
Tambea Solomon Is. 9°16S 159°41E 287 M10
Tambelan, Kepulauan
Indonesia 1°0N 107°30E 234 B3
Tambellup Australia 34°4S 117°37E 279 F2
Tambo Queens., Australia 24°54S 146°14E 280 C4
Tambo Peru 12°57S 74°1W 330 C3
Tambo → Peru 10°42S 73°47W 330 C3
Tambo de Mora Peru 13°30S 76°8W 330 C2
Tambobamba Peru 13°54S 72°8W 330 C3
Tamboerskloof S. Africa 33°56S 18°25E 118 A1
Tambohorano Madag. 17°30S 43°58E 272 B1
Tambopata → Peru 13°21S 69°36W 330 C4
Tambora Jakarta, Indonesia 6°8S 106°47E 122 A1
Tambora Nusa Tenggara Barat,
Indonesia 8°12S 118°5E 235 D5
Tamboritha, Mt.
Australia 37°31S 146°40E 283 D7
Tamboura C.A.R. 5°10N 25°12E 264 A5
Tambov Russia 52°45N 41°28E 190 D5
Tambov □ Russia 52°50N 41°20E 190 D5
Tambre → Spain 42°49N 8°53W 194 C2
Tambuku Indonesia 7°8S 113°40E 235 D4
Tambul Papua N. G. 5°54S 143°54E 286 C2
Tamburâ Sudan 5°40N 27°25E 257 F2
Tambuyukan, Gunong
Malaysia 6°13N 116°39E 235 A5
Tâmchekket Mauritania 17°25N 10°40W 262 B2
Tame Colombia 6°28N 71°44W 328 B3
Tâmega → Portugal 41°5N 8°21W 194 D2
Tamegroute Morocco 30°15N 5°39W 260 B3
Tamelelt Morocco 31°50N 7°32W 260 B3
Tamenglong India 25°0N 93°35E 241 C4
Tamerza Tunisia 34°23N 7°58E 258 B1
Tamgak, Adrar Niger 19°12N 8°35E 259 E1
Tamgué, Massif du
Guinea 12°0N 12°18W 262 C2
Tami Is. Papua N. G. 6°46S 147°55E 286 D4
Tamiahua, L. de Mexico 21°35N 97°35W 319 C5
Tamiami Canal U.S.A. 25°50N 81°0W 317 K8
Tamil Nadu □ India 11°0N 77°0E 245 J3
Tamis → Serbia 44°51N 20°39E 182 F5
Tamiya Egypt 29°29N 30°58E 256 J7
Tamlelt, Plaine de
Morocco 32°30N 2°20W 261 B4
Tamluk India 22°18N 87°58E 243 H12
Tammerfors = Tampere
Finland 61°30N 23°50E 188 B2
Tammisaari Finland 60°0N 23°26E 188 B2
Tammisalo Finland 60°11N 25°5E 121 B3
Tammūn Egypt 29°55N 31°35E 117 B2
Tämnaren Sweden 60°10N 17°25E 162 D11
Tampa Angola 15°30S 13°27E 265 F2
Tampa Fla., U.S.A. 27°56N 82°27W 317 H7
Tampa, Tanjung
Indonesia 8°55S 116°12E 231 K19
Tampa B. U.S.A. 27°50N 82°30W 317 H7
Tampa Int. ✈ (TPA)
U.S.A. 27°59N 82°32W 317 H7
Tamparan Phil. 7°53N 124°20E 233 H5
Tampere Finland 61°30N 23°50E 188 B2
Tampico Tamaulipas,
Mexico 22°13N 97°51W 319 C5
Tampico Ill., U.S.A. 41°38N 89°47W 310 C7
Tampin Malaysia 2°28N 102°13E 237 L4
Tampines Singapore 1°21N 103°56E 138 A3
Tampoi Malaysia 1°30N 103°39E 237 d
Tamrah Si. Arabia 20°24N 45°25E 248 B4
Tamri Morocco 30°49N 9°50W 260 B3
Tamrida = Qādub Yemen 12°37N 53°57E 249 D6
Tamsweg Austria 47°7N 13°49E 180 D6
Tamu Burma 24°13N 94°12E 241 C5
Tamuja Spain 39°38N 6°29W 195 F4
Tamuning Guam 13°29N 144°47E 302 d
Tamworth N.S.W.,
Australia 31°7S 150°58E 283 A9
Tamworth Ont., Canada 44°29N 77°0W 312 B8
Tamworth Staffs., U.K. 52°39N 1°41W 169 E6
Tan An Vietnam 10°32N 106°25E 237 G6
Tan Chau Vietnam 10°48N 105°12E 237 G5
T'an-do N. Korea 39°30N 124°41E 224 C2
Tan Iddah Algeria 26°33N 9°42E 261 C6
Tan-Tan Morocco 28°29N 11°1W 260 C2
Tana → Coast, Kenya 2°32S 40°31E 268 C5
Tana → Finnmark,
Norway 70°30N 28°14E 160 A23
Tana, L. Ethiopia 13°5N 37°30E 257 E4
Tana River Primate ⌓
Kenya 1°55S 40°7E 268 C5
Tanabe Japan 33°44N 135°22E 223 D7
Tanabi Brazil 20°37S 49°37W 333 F2
Tanacross U.S.A. 63°23N 143°21W 303 E12
Tanafjorden Norway 70°45N 28°25E 160 A23
Tanaga I. U.S.A. 51°48N 177°53W 303 L3
Tanaga Volcano U.S.A. 51°53N 178°8W 303 L3
Tanah Abang Indonesia 6°12S 106°48E 122 B1
Tanah Kusir Indonesia 6°15S 106°46E 122 B1
Tanah Merah Malaysia 5°48N 102°9E 234 A2
Tanahbala Indonesia 0°30S 98°30E 234 C1
Tanahgrogot Indonesia 1°55S 116°15E 235 C5
Tanahjampea Indonesia 7°10S 120°35E 231 F6
Tanahmasa Indonesia 0°12S 98°39E 234 C1
Tanahmerah Indonesia 6°5S 140°16E 231 F10
Tanakpur India 29°5N 80°7E 243 E9
Tanakura Japan 37°10N 140°20E 221 F10
Tanamalwila Sri Lanka 6°26N 81°8E 245 L5
Tanami Desert Australia 18°50S 132°0E 278 C5
Tanana U.S.A. 65°10N 152°4W 303 D9
Tanana → U.S.A. 65°10N 151°58W 303 D10
Tananarive = Antananarivo
Madag. 18°55S 47°31E 272 B2
Tananger Norway 58°57N 5°37E 164 F2
Tanannt Morocco 31°54N 6°56W 260 B3
Tanapag N. Marianas 15°14N 145°45E 302 e
Tánaro → Italy 44°55N 8°40E 198 D5
Tanauan Phil. 14°5N 121°10E 232 D3
Tanay Phil. 14°30N 121°17E 232 D3
Tanba-Sanchi Japan 35°7N 135°48E 223 B7
Tancheng China 34°25N 118°20E 227 G10
Tanch'ŏn N. Korea 40°27N 128°54E 224 B4
Tanda Ut. P., India 26°33N 82°35E 243 F10
Tanda Ut. P., India 28°57N 78°56E 243 E8
Tanda Ivory C. 7°48N 3°10W 262 D4
Tandag Phil. 9°4N 126°9E 233 G6
Tandaia Tanzania 9°25S 34°15E 269 D3
Tăndărei Romania 44°39N 27°40E 183 F12
Tandaué Angola 16°58S 18°5E 265 F3
Tandil Argentina 37°15S 59°6W 334 D4
Tandil, Sa. del Argentina 37°30S 59°0W 334 D4
Tandin Burma 19°33N 93°58E 241 F4
Tandjilé □ Chad 9°30N 16°30E 259 G3
Tandjilé → Chad 9°45N 15°50E 259 G2
Tandlianwala Pakistan 31°3N 73°9E 242 D5
Tando Adam Pakistan 25°45N 68°40E 242 G3
Tando Allahyar Pakistan 25°28N 68°43E 242 G3
Tando Bago Pakistan 24°47N 68°58E 242 G3
Tando Mohommed Khan
Pakistan 25°8N 68°32E 242 G3
Tando-Zinze Angola 5°22S 12°30E 265 D2
Tandou-Bengou Congo 3°50S 11°44E 264 C2
Tandou L. Australia 32°40S 142°5E 282 B5
Tandoureh △ Iran 37°50N 59°0E 247 B8
Tandragee U.K. 54°21N 6°24W 166 B5
Tandsjöborg Sweden 61°42N 14°43E 162 C8
Tandubas Phil. 5°8N 120°20E 233 J3
Tandula → India 21°6N 81°14E 244 D5
Tandula Tank India 20°40N 81°12E 244 D5
Tandur Andhra Pradesh,
India 19°11N 79°30E 244 E4
Tandur Andhra Pradesh,
India 17°14N 77°35E 244 F3
Tane-ga-Shima Japan 30°30N 131°0E 221 J5
Taneatua N.Z. 38°4S 177°1E 284 E6
Tanen Tong Dan = Dawna Ra.
Burma 16°30N 98°30E 236 D2
Tanew → Poland 50°29N 22°16E 185 H9
Tanezrouft Algeria 23°9N 0°11E 261 D5
Tanezzuft, W. → Libya 25°51N 10°19E 258 C2
Tang, Koh Cambodia 10°16N 103°7E 237 G4
Tang, Ra's-e Iran 25°21N 59°52E 247 E8
Tang Krasang Cambodia 12°34N 105°3E 236 F5
Tanga Tanzania 5°5S 39°2E 268 D4
Tanga □ Tanzania 5°20S 38°0E 268 D4
Tanga Is. Papua N. G. 3°20S 153°15E 286 B7
Tanga Langua Grenada 12°14N 61°39W 323 q
Tangail Bangla. 24°15N 89°55E 241 C2
Tangalla Sri Lanka 6°1N 80°48E 245 L5
Tanganyika = Tanzania ■
Africa 6°0S 34°0E 268 D3
Tanganyika, L. Africa 6°40S 30°0E 268 D3
Tangará da Serra Brazil 14°50S 57°47W 331 C6
Tangarare Solomon Is. 9°36S 159°41E 287 M10
Tangasseri India 8°53N 76°35E 245 K3
Tangaza Nigeria 13°19N 4°55E 263 C5
Tangelo Park U.S.A. 28°27N 81°26W 133 B2
Tangen Norway 60°37N 11°15E 164 D8
Tanger Morocco 35°50N 5°49W 260 A3
Tanger □ Morocco 35°43N 5°50W 260 A3
Tangerang Indonesia 6°11S 106°37E 234 D3
Tangerhütte Germany 52°26N 11°48E 178 C7
Tangermünde Germany 52°33N 11°58E 178 C7
Tanggu China 39°2N 117°40E 227 E9
Tanggula Shan China 32°40N 92°10E 218 C4
Tanggula Shankou
China 32°42N 92°27E 218 C4
Tanghe China 32°47N 112°50E 226 H7
Tanghla Range = Tanggula Shan
China 32°40N 92°10E 218 C4
Tangi India 19°56N 85°24E 244 E7
Tangier = Tanger
Morocco 35°50N 5°49W 260 A3
Tangjia China 22°22N 113°35E 219 G10
Tangjia Wan China 22°21N 113°36E 219 G10
Tangorin Australia 21°47S 144°12E 280 C3
Tangorombohitr'i Makay
Madag. 21°0S 45°15E 272 C2
Tangra Yumco China 31°0N 86°38E 218 C3
Tangshan China 39°38N 118°10E 227 E10
Tangtou China 35°28N 118°30E 227 G10
Tangub Phil. 8°3N 123°44E 233 G4
Tanguen-Dassouri
Burkina Faso 12°16N 1°42W 263 C4
Tanguiéta Benin 10°35N 1°21E 263 C5
Tangxi China 29°3N 119°25E 229 C12
Tangyan He → China 28°54N 108°19E 228 C7
Taniao Taiwan 22°23N 120°53E 225 D2
Tanimbar, Kepulauan
Indonesia 7°30S 131°30E 231 F8
Tanimbar Is. = Tanimbar,
Kepulauan Indonesia 7°30S 131°30E 231 F8
Taninthari = Tenasserim
Burma 12°6N 99°3E 237 F2
Tanis Egypt 31°0N 31°54E 251 H2
Tanjay Phil. 9°30N 123°5E 233 G4
Tanjong Malim Malaysia 3°42N 101°31E 237 L3
Tanjong Pelepas Malaysia 1°21N 103°33E 237 d
Tanjore = Thanjavur
India 10°48N 79°12E 245 J4
Tanjung Bali, Indonesia 8°21S 116°9E 231 J19
Tanjung Kalimantan,
Indonesia 2°10S 115°25E 235 C5
Tanjung Datu △ Malaysia 2°13N 109°3E 235 B3
Tanjung Duren Indonesia 6°10S 106°46E 122 B1
Tanjung Priok Indonesia 6°6S 106°52E 122 A2
Tanjung Puting △
Indonesia 2°54S 111°59E 235 C4
Tanjung Tokong Malaysia 5°28N 100°18E 237 c
Tanjungbalai Indonesia 2°55N 99°44E 234 B1
Tanjungbatu Indonesia 2°23N 118°3E 235 B5
Tanjungkarang Telukbetung =
Bandar Lampung
Indonesia 5°20S 105°10E 234 D3
Tanjungpandan
Indonesia 2°43S 107°38E 235 C3
Tanjungpinang Indonesia 1°5N 104°30E 234 B2
Tanjungpriok Indonesia 6°8S 106°55E 234 D3
Tanjungredeb Indonesia 2°9N 117°29E 235 B5
Tanjungselor Indonesia 2°55N 117°25E 235 B5
Tank Pakistan 32°14N 70°25E 242 C4
Tankhala India 21°58N 73°47E 242 J5
Tankwa-Karoo △
S. Africa 32°14S 19°50E 270 D2
Tanlu Taiwan 22°12N 120°44E 225 C2
Tanna Vanuatu 19°30S 169°20E 287 J7
Tännäs Sweden 62°26N 12°42E 162 B6
Tannersville U.S.A. 41°3N 75°18W 313 E9
Tannis Bugt Denmark 57°40N 10°15E 163 G4
Tannu Ola Asia 51°0N 94°0E 217 B12
Tannum Sands Australia 23°57S 151°22E 280 C5
Tano → Ghana 5°7N 2°56W 262 D4
Tanombella Algeria 25°30N 5°49E 261 C6
Tanon Str. Phil. 10°20N 123°30E 233 F4
Tanout Niger 14°50N 8°55E 259 F1
Tanquinho Brazil 11°58S 39°6W 333 D4
Tanshui Taiwan 25°10N 121°28E 225 A3
Tanshui Kang →
Taiwan 25°10N 121°25E 225 A3
Tansilla Burkina Faso 12°25N 4°23W 262 C4
Tanta Egypt 30°45N 30°57E 256 H7
Tantabin Burma 17°1N 95°59E 241 G5
Tantoyuca Mexico 21°21N 98°14W 319 C5

Tantung = Dandong
China 40°10N 124°20E 224 B2
T'antzu Taiwan 24°13N 120°42E 225 B2
Tanuku India 16°45N 81°44E 244 F5
Tanum Norway 59°53N 10°28E 133 A1
Tanūmah Si. Arabia 18°58N 42°10E 248 C3
Tanumshede Sweden 58°42N 11°20E 163 F5
Tanunda Australia 34°30S 139°0E 282 C3
Tanur India 11°1N 75°52E 245 J2
Tanus France 44°8N 2°19E 174 D6
Tanzania ■ Africa 6°0S 34°0E 268 D3
Tanzawa-Sanchi Japan 35°27N 139°0E 223 B11
Tanzhou China 22°16N 113°28E 219 G9
Tanzilla ➤ Canada 58°8N 130°43W 296 B2
Tao, Ko Thailand 10°5N 99°52E 237 G2
Tao'an = Taonan
China 45°22N 122°40E 227 B12
Tao'er He ➤ China 45°45N 124°5E 227 B13
Taohua Dao China 29°50N 122°20E 229 C14
Taolanaro Madag. 25°2S 47°0E 272 D2
Taole China 38°48N 106°40E 226 E4
Taonan China 45°22N 122°40E 227 B12
Taora Solomon Is. 7°21S 157°30E 287 L9
Taormina Italy 37°51N 15°17E 201 E8
Taos U.S.A. 36°24N 105°35W 305 H11
Taoudenni Mali 22°40N 3°55W 260 D4
Taoudrart, Adrar Algeria 24°25N 2°24E 261 D5
Taounate Morocco 34°25N 4°41W 260 B4
Taounate □ Morocco 34°30N 4°50W 260 B4
Taourirt Algeria 26°37N 0°20E 261 C5
Taourirt Morocco 34°25N 2°53W 261 B4
Taouz Morocco 30°53N 4°0W 260 B4
Taoyuan Hunan, China 28°55N 111°16E 229 C8
T'aoyüan Kaohsung,
Taiwan 23°9N 120°46E 225 C2
T'aoyüan Yünlin, Taiwan 25°0N 121°4E 225 B3
T'aoyüan □ Taiwan 24°55N 121°15E 225 B3
Tapa Estonia 59°15N 25°50E 188 C3
Tapa Shan = Daba Shan
China 32°0N 109°0E 228 B7
Tapachula Mexico 14°54N 92°17W 319 E6
Tapada Portugal 38°49N 9°16W 126 A1
Tapah Malaysia 4°12N 101°15E 237 K3
Tapajós ➤ Brazil 2°24S 54°41W 329 D7
Tapaktuan Indonesia 3°15N 97°10E 234 B1
Tapanahoni ➤ Suriname 4°20N 54°25W 329 C7
Tapanila Finland 60°15N 25°2E 121 B3
Tapanui N.Z. 45°56S 169°18E 285 F4
Taparo Pt. Trin. & Tob. 10°3N 61°38W 323 t
Tapauá Brazil 5°40S 64°20W 331 B5
Tapauá ➤ Brazil 5°40S 64°21W 331 B5
Tapaz Phil. 11°16N 122°32E 233 F4
Tapes Brazil 30°40S 51°23W 335 C5
Tapeta Liberia 6°29N 8°52W 262 D3
Taphan Hin Thailand 16°13N 100°26E 236 D3
Tapia de Casariego Spain 43°34N 6°56W 194 B4
Tapiales Argentina 34°42S 58°30W 117 C1
Tapiantana Group Phil. 6°20N 122°0E 233 H4
Tapiau = Gvardeysk
Russia 54°39N 21°5E 184 D8
Tapilon = Daanbantayan
Phil. 11°17N 124°2E 233 F5
Taping Taiwan 24°6N 120°53E 225 B2
Tapini Papua N. G. 8°19S 147°0E 286 E4
Tapiola Finland 60°10N 24°48E 121 B1
Tapiraí Brazil 19°52S 46°1W 333 E2
Tapirapé ➤ Brazil 10°41S 50°38W 332 D1
Tapirapecó, Serra
Venezuela 1°10N 65°0W 329 C5
Taplan Australia 34°33S 140°52E 282 C4
Tapo-Capara △ Venezuela 7°55N 71°15W 328 B3
Tapoeripa Suriname 5°22N 56°34W 329 B6
Tapolca Hungary 46°53N 17°29E 182 D2
Tapsia India 22°32N 88°23E 124 B2
Tapti ➤ India 21°8N 72°41E 244 D1
Tapu Taiwan 23°18N 120°35E 225 C2
Tapuae-o-Uenuku N.Z. 42°0S 173°39E 285 C8
Tapul Phil. 5°42N 120°55E 233 J3
Tapul Group Phil. 5°35N 120°50E 233 J3
Tapul I. Phil. 5°43N 120°55E 233 J3
Tapun India 27°35N 96°22E 241 B6
Tapurucuará Brazil 0°24S 65°2W 329 D4
Taputapu, C.
Amer. Samoa 14°20S 170°51W 302 f
Taputimu Amer. Samoa 14°21S 170°46W 302 f
Taqtaq Iraq 35°53N 44°35E 213 E11
Taquara Brazil 29°36S 50°46W 335 B5
Taquari ➤ Brazil 19°15S 57°17W 331 D6
Taquaritinga Brazil 21°24S 48°30W 333 F2
Tara Queens., Australia 27°17S 150°31E 281 D5
Tara Ont., Canada 44°28N 81°9W 312 B3
Tara Maharashtra, India 19°5N 72°49E 130 A1
Tara Japan 33°2N 130°11E 222 D2
Tara Russia 56°55N 74°24E 214 D8
Tara Zambia 16°58S 26°45E 269 F2
Tara ➤ Montenegro 43°21N 18°51E 202 C2
Tara △ Serbia 43°55N 19°30E 202 C3
Tara-Dake Japan 32°58N 130°6E 222 E2
Taraba □ Nigeria 8°0N 10°30E 263 D7
Taraba ➤ Nigeria 8°30N 10°15E 263 D7
Tarabuco Bolivia 19°10S 64°57W 331 D5
Tarābulus Lebanon 34°31N 35°50E 250 D6
Tarābulus Libya 32°49N 13°7E 258 B2
Tarābulus N. Afr. 31°0N 13°0E 258 B2
Tarabulus □ Libya 32°53N 13°11E 261 B7
Tarabya Turkey 41°8N 29°3E 122 B2
Taraclia Taraclia,
Moldova 45°54N 28°40E 183 E13
Taraclia Tighina, Moldova 46°34N 29°7E 183 D14
Taradale N.Z. 39°33S 176°53E 284 F5
Taradehi India 23°18N 79°21E 243 H8
Tarāghin Libya 26°0N 14°30E 258 C2
Taragi Japan 32°16N 130°56E 222 E2
Tarahouahout Algeria 22°41N 5°59E 261 D6
Tarajalejo Canary Is. 28°12N 14°7W 153 e2
Tarakan Indonesia 3°20N 117°35E 235 B5
Tarakit, Mt. Kenya 2°2N 35°10E 268 B4
Taralga Australia 34°26S 149°52E 283 C8
Tarama-Jima Japan 24°39N 124°42E 221 M2
Taramakau ➤ N.Z. 42°34S 171°8E 285 C6
Taran, Mys Russia 54°56N 19°59E 184 D6
Taranagar India 28°43N 74°50E 242 E6
Taranaki □ N.Z. 39°25S 174°30E 284 F3
Taranaki, Mt. N.Z. 39°17S 174°5E 284 F3
Tarancón Spain 40°1N 3°1W 196 E1
Tarangire △ Tanzania 4°21S 36°7E 268 C4
Taransay U.K. 57°54N 7°0W 167 D1
Táranto Italy 40°28N 17°14E 201 B10
Táranto, G. di Italy 40°8N 17°20E 201 B10
Tarapacá Colombia 2°56S 69°46W 328 D4
Tarapacá □ Chile 20°45S 69°30W 334 A2
Tarapoto Peru 6°30S 76°20W 330 B2
Taraquá Brazil 0°6N 68°28W 328 C4
Tarare France 45°54N 4°26E 175 C8
Tararua Ra. N.Z. 40°45S 175°25E 284 G4
Tarasag Vanuatu 14°12S 167°36E 287 D5
Tarascon France 43°48N 4°39E 175 E8
Tarascon-sur-Ariège
France 42°50N 1°36E 174 F5
Tarashcha Ukraine 49°30N 30°31E 177 D16
Tarata Peru 17°27S 70°2W 330 D3
Tarauacá Brazil 8°6S 70°48W 330 B3
Tarauacá ➤ Brazil 6°42S 69°48W 330 B4
Taravao Tahiti 17°43S 149°18W 289 e
Taravao, Isthme de
Tahiti 17°43S 149°19W 289 e
Taravo ➤ France 41°42N 8°49E 175 G12
Tarawa Kiribati 1°30N 173°0E 288 G9
Tarawai I. Papua N. G. 3°13S 143°15E 286 B2
Tarawera N.Z. 39°2S 176°36E 284 F5
Tarawera, L. N.Z. 38°13S 176°27E 284 E5
Tarawera, Mt. N.Z. 38°14S 176°32E 284 E5
Taraz Kazakhstan 42°54N 71°22E 217 D8
Tarazona Spain 41°55N 1°43W 196 D3
Tarazona de la Mancha
Spain 39°16N 1°55W 197 F3
Tårbæk Denmark 55°46N 12°35E 118 A3
Tarbagatay, Khrebet
Kazakhstan 48°0N 83°0E 217 C10
Tarbaj Kenya 2°12N 40°8E 267 D5
Tarbat Ness U.K. 57°52N 3°47W 167 D5
Tarbela Dam Pakistan 34°8N 72°52E 242 B5
Tarbert Kerry, Ireland 52°34N 9°22W 166 D2
Tarbert Argyll & Bute, U.K. 55°52N 5°25W 167 F3
Tarbert W. Isles, U.K. 57°54N 6°49W 167 D2
Tarbes France 43°15N 0°3E 174 E4
Tarboro U.S.A. 35°54N 77°32W 315 D16
Tarbū Libya 26°0N 15°5E 258 C3
Tărcău, Munţii Romania 46°39N 26°7E 183 D11
Tarcento Italy 46°13N 13°13E 199 B10
Tarchomin Poland 52°19N 20°58E 142 B1
Tarcoola Australia 30°44S 134°36E 281 E1
Tarcoon Australia 30°15S 146°43E 281 E4
Tarcutta Australia 35°16S 147°44E 283 C7
Tardeo India 18°57N 72°48E 130 B1
Tardets-Sorholus France 43°8N 0°52W 174 E3
Tardoire ➤ France 45°52N 0°14E 174 C4
Taredjerdja Algeria 25°12N 2°32E 261 C5
Taree Australia 31°50S 152°30E 283 A10
Tarella Australia 31°2S 143°2E 282 A5
Tarf, Ras Morocco 35°40N 5°11W 260 A3
Tarf, Ra's aṭ Si. Arabia 17°2N 42°22E 248 C3
Tarfa, W. el ➤ Egypt 28°25N 30°50E 256 B3
Tarfaya Morocco 27°55N 12°55W 260 C2
Târgovişte Romania 44°55N 25°27E 183 F10
Targówek Poland 52°16N 21°3E 142 B2
Târgu Bujor Romania 45°52N 27°54E 183 E12
Târgu Cărbuneşti
Romania 44°57N 23°31E 183 F8
Târgu Frumos Romania 47°12N 27°2E 183 C12
Târgu Jiu Romania 45°5N 23°19E 183 E8
Târgu Lăpuş Romania 47°27N 23°52E 183 C8
Târgu Mureş Romania 46°31N 24°38E 183 D9
Târgu Neamţ Romania 47°12N 26°25E 183 C11
Târgu Ocna Romania 46°16N 26°39E 183 D11
Târgu Secuiesc Romania 46°0N 26°10E 183 E11
Targuist Morocco 34°59N 4°14W 260 B4
Târguşor Romania 44°27N 28°25E 183 F13
Tarhăus, Vf. Romania 46°40N 26°8E 183 D11
Tarhbalt Morocco 30°39N 5°20W 260 B3
Tarhūnah Libya 32°27N 13°36E 258 B2
Tari Papua N. G. 5°54S 142°59E 286 C2
Tariba Venezuela 7°49N 72°13W 328 B3
Tarif U.A.E. 24°3N 53°46E 247 E7
Tarifa Spain 36°1N 5°36W 195 J5
Tarija Bolivia 21°30S 64°40W 334 A3
Tarija □ Bolivia 21°30S 63°30W 334 A3
Tarik I. Micronesia 7°20N 151°46E 287 T18
Tariku ➤ Indonesia 2°55S 138°26E 231 E9
Tarīm Yemen 16°3N 49°0E 249 C5
Tarim Basin = Tarim Pendi
China 40°0N 84°0E 217 E10
Tarim He ➤ China 39°30N 88°30E 217 E11
Tarim Pendi China 40°0N 84°0E 217 E10
Tarime Tanzania 1°21S 34°22E 266 E3
Taritatu ➤ Indonesia 2°54S 138°27E 231 E9
Tarka ➤ S. Africa 32°10S 26°0E 270 D4
Tarka La Bhutan 27°12N 89°44E 243 F13
Tarkastad S. Africa 32°0S 26°16E 270 D4
Tarkhankut, Mys
Ukraine 45°25N 32°30E 189 K7
Tarko Sale Russia 64°55N 77°50E 214 C8
Tarkwa Ghana 5°20N 2°0W 262 D4
Tarlac Phil. 15°29N 120°35E 232 D3
Tarlac □ Phil. 15°30N 120°30E 232 D3
Tarm Denmark 55°56N 8°31E 163 J2
Tarma Peru 11°25S 75°45W 330 C2
Tarmiya Iraq 33°40N 44°23E 213 G11
Tarn □ France 43°49N 2°8E 174 E6
Tarn ➤ France 44°5N 1°6E 174 D5
Tarn-et-Garonne □ France 44°8N 1°20E 174 D5
Tarna ➤ Hungary 47°31N 19°59E 182 C4
Târnava Mare ➤
Romania 46°10N 23°43E 183 D8
Târnava Mică ➤
Romania 46°9N 23°55E 183 D8
Târnăveni Romania 46°19N 24°13E 183 D9
Tärnby Denmark 55°37N 12°35E 118 B3
Tarnica Poland 49°4N 22°44E 185 J9
Tarnobrzeg Poland 50°35N 21°41E 185 H8
Tarnogród Poland 50°22N 22°45E 185 H9
Tarnopol = Ternopil
Ukraine 49°30N 25°40E 177 D13
Tarnos France 43°32N 1°28W 174 E2
Tarnova Moldova 48°10N 27°40E 183 B12
Târnova Romania 45°23N 21°59E 182 E6
Tarnów Poland 50°3N 21°0E 185 H8
Tarnowitz = Tarnowskie Góry
Poland 50°27N 18°54E 185 H5
Tarnowskie Góry Poland 50°27N 18°54E 185 H5
Tärnsjö Sweden 60°9N 16°56E 162 D10
Taro ➤ Italy 45°2N 10°15E 198 C7
Taroko △ Taiwan 24°10N 121°33E 225 B3
Ţārom Iran 28°11N 55°46E 247 D7
Taroom Australia 25°36S 149°48E 281 D4
Taroudannt Morocco 30°30N 8°52W 260 B3
Taroudannt □ Morocco 30°30N 8°25W 260 B3
Taroume Cook Is. 21°15S 159°45W 289 h
Tarp Germany 54°39N 9°24E 178 A5
Tarpeena Australia 37°37S 140°47E 282 D4
Tarpon Springs U.S.A. 28°9N 82°45W 317 G7
Tarqua Bay Nigeria 6°24N 3°23E 124 B2
Tarquínia Italy 42°15N 11°45E 199 F8
Tarrafal C. Verde Is. 15°18N 23°39W 153 j
Tarragona Spain 41°5N 1°17E 196 D6
Tarragona □ Spain 41°5N 1°0E 196 D6
Tarraleah Australia 42°17S 146°26E 281 G4
Tarrasa = Terrassa Spain 41°34N 2°1E 196 D7
Tàrrega Spain 41°39N 1°9E 196 D6
Tarrytown Ga., U.S.A. 32°19N 82°34W 316 C7
Tarrytown N.Y., U.S.A. 41°4N 73°52W 313 E11
Tårs Denmark 57°23N 10°7E 163 G4
Tarshiha = Me'ona Israel 33°1N 35°15E 250 E6
Tarsus Turkey 36°58N 34°55E 250 B5
Tarsus ➤ Turkey 36°46N 34°52E 250 B5
Tartagal Argentina 22°30S 63°50W 334 A3
Tartane Martinique 14°45N 60°55W 322 j
Tärtär Azerbaijan 40°20N 46°58E 191 K8
Tärtär ➤ Azerbaijan 40°26N 47°20E 191 K8
Tartas France 43°50N 0°49W 174 E3
Tartu Estonia 58°20N 26°44E 188 C4
Ţarţūs Syria 34°55N 35°55E 250 D6
Ţarţūs □ Syria 35°0N 36°0E 250 D7
Tarumirim Brazil 19°16S 41°59W 333 E3
Tarumizu Japan 31°29N 130°42E 222 F2
Tarussa Russia 54°44N 37°10E 188 E9
Tarutao = Ko Tarutao △
Thailand 6°31N 99°26E 237 J2
Tarutao, Ko Thailand 6°33N 99°40E 237 J2
Tarutung Indonesia 2°0N 98°54E 234 B1
Tarutyne Ukraine 46°12N 29°9E 183 D14
Tarvísio Italy 46°30N 13°35E 199 B10
Tarxien Malta 35°52N 14°31E 206 F8
Taşağıl Turkey 36°55N 31°14E 250 B2
Tasahku Burma 27°33N 97°52E 241 B6
Tasaret, O. ➤ Algeria 26°25N 1°59E 261 C5
Tasāwah Libya 26°0N 13°30E 258 C2
Tasböğet Kazakhstan 44°46N 65°33E 217 D7
Taseko ➤ Canada 52°8N 123°45W 296 C4
Tasgaon India 17°2N 74°39E 244 F2
Tash-Kömür Kyrgyzstan 41°40N 72°10E 217 D8
Tash-Kumyr = Tash-Kömür
Kyrgyzstan 41°40N 72°10E 217 D8
Tashauz = Dashoguz
Turkmenistan 41°49N 59°58E 216 D5
Tashi Chho Dzong = Thimphu
Bhutan 27°31N 89°45E 241 B2
Tashino = Pervomaysk
Russia 54°56N 43°58E 190 C6
Ţashk, Daryācheh-ye
Iran 29°45N 53°35E 247 D7
Tashkent = Toshkent
Uzbekistan 41°20N 69°10E 217 D7
Tashtagol Russia 52°47N 87°53E 217 B11
Tashu Taiwan 22°41N 120°25E 225 D2
Tasiilaq Greenland 65°40N 37°20W 154 D7
Tasik Kenyir Malaysia 5°5N 102°45E 237 K4
Tasikmalaya Indonesia 7°18S 108°12E 235 D3
Tåsinge Denmark 55°0N 10°35E 163 J4
Tåsjön Sweden 64°15N 15°40E 160 D16
Task Niger 14°56N 10°46E 259 F2
Taskan Russia 62°59N 150°20E 215 C16
Taşkent Turkey 36°55N 32°29E 250 B3
Taşköprü Turkey 41°30N 34°15E 212 B6
Taskul Papua N. G. 2°32S 150°27E 286 B6
Taşlâc Moldova 47°4N 29°24E 183 C14
Taşliçay Turkey 39°38N 43°22E 213 C10
Tasman □ N.Z. 41°30S 172°40E 285 B7
Tasman ➤ N.Z. 43°48S 170°8E 285 D5
Tasman, Mt. N.Z. 43°34S 170°12E 285 D5
Tasman Abyssal Plain
Pac. Oc. 34°30S 153°15E 276 G9
Tasman B. N.Z. 40°59S 173°25E 285 A8
Tasman Basin Pac. Oc. 46°0S 158°0E 288 M7
Tasman Glacier N.Z. 43°37S 170°12E 285 D5
Tasman Mts. N.Z. 41°3S 172°25E 285 B7
Tasman Pen. Australia 43°10S 148°0E 281 G4
Tasman Sea Pac. Oc. 36°0S 160°0E 277 H10
Tasmania □ Australia 42°0S 146°30E 281 G4
Tasmanian Wilderness World
Heritage Area △
Australia 43°0S 146°0E 281 G4
Tăşnad Romania 47°30N 22°33E 182 C7
Taşova Turkey 40°45N 36°19E 212 B7
Tassili n'Ajjer Algeria 25°47N 8°1E 261 C6
Tassili n'Ajjer △ Algeria 26°5N 6°0E 258 C1
Tassili-Oua-n-Ahaggar
Algeria 20°41N 5°30E 261 D6
Tassili Tin-Rerhoh Algeria 20°5N 3°55E 261 D5
Taşucu Turkey 36°19N 33°52E 250 B4
Taşucu Körfezi Turkey 36°16N 33°56E 250 B4
Tasuj Iran 38°18N 45°23E 213 C11
Tat Ton △ Thailand 15°57N 102°2E 236 E4
Tata Hungary 47°37N 18°19E 182 C3
Tata Morocco 29°46N 7°56W 260 C3
Tatabánya Hungary 47°32N 18°25E 182 C3
Tatakoto French Polynesia 17°20S 138°23W 289 f
Tatamá △ Colombia 5°5N 76°9W 328 B2
Tatamba Solomon Is. 8°21S 159°51E 287 M10
Tataouine Tunisia 32°57N 10°29E 258 B2
Tataouine □ Tunisia 32°0N 10°0E 261 B7
Tatar-Pazardzhik = Pazardzhik
Bulgaria 42°12N 24°20E 203 D8
Tatar Republic = Tatarstan □
Russia 55°30N 51°30E 190 C10
Tatarbunary Ukraine 45°50N 29°39E 183 E14
Tatarovo Russia 55°45N 37°24E 129 B2
Tatarsk Russia 55°14N 76°0E 217 A9
Tatarskiy Proliv Russia 50°0N 141°0E 215 E15
Tatarstan □ Russia 55°30N 51°30E 190 C10
Tatatóváros = Tata
Hungary 47°37N 18°19E 182 C3
Tatatua, Pte. Tahiti 17°44S 149°8W 289 e
Tatau Malaysia 2°53N 112°51E 235 B4
Tatau I. Papua N. G. 2°48S 151°57E 286 B6
Tatebayashi Japan 36°15N 139°32E 223 A11
Tateshina-Yama Japan 36°8N 138°11E 223 A10
Tateyama Japan 35°0N 139°50E 223 C11
Tathlina L. Canada 60°33N 117°39W 296 A5
Tathlīth Si. Arabia 19°32N 43°30E 248 C3
Tathlīth, W. ➤ Si. Arabia 20°35N 44°20E 248 B4
Tathong Channel China 22°15N 114°16E 122 B2
Tathong Pt. China 22°14N 114°17E 122 B2
Tathra Australia 36°44S 149°59E 283 D8
Tatinnai L. Canada 60°55N 97°40W 297 A9
Tatitlek U.S.A. 60°52N 146°41W 303 F11
Tatkon Burma 20°7N 96°13E 241 E6
Tatla Lake Canada 52°0N 124°20W 296 C4
Tatlisu Turkey 40°24N 27°55E 203 F11
Tatnam, C. Canada 57°16N 91°0W 297 B10
Tatra = Tatry Slovak Rep. 49°20N 20°0E 181 B13
Tatranský △ Slovak Rep. 49°10N 20°0E 181 B13
Tatry Slovak Rep. 49°20N 20°0E 181 B13
Tatshenshini ➤
Canada 59°28N 137°45W 296 B1
Tatsuno Hyōgo, Japan 34°52N 134°33E 222 C6
Tatsuno Nagano, Japan 35°58N 138°0E 223 B10
Tatta Pakistan 24°42N 67°55E 242 G2
Tatuapé Brazil 23°31S 46°33W 137 B2
Tatuí Brazil 23°25S 47°53W 335 A6
Tatum U.S.A. 33°16N 103°19W 305 K12
Tat'ung = Datong China 40°6N 113°18E 226 D7
Tatura Australia 36°29S 145°16E 283 D6
Tatvan Turkey 38°31N 42°15E 213 C10
Ta'ū Amer. Samoa 14°15S 169°30W 302 g
Tau Rogaland, Norway 59°3N 5°55E 164 E2
Tauá Brazil 6°1S 40°26W 332 C3
Taubaté Brazil 23°0S 45°36W 335 A6
Tauberbischofsheim
Germany 49°37N 9°39E 179 F5
Taucha Germany 51°23N 12°29E 178 D8
Tauern Austria 47°15N 12°40E 176 E7
Tauern-tunnel Austria 47°0N 13°12E 180 D6
Taufikia Sudan 9°24N 31°37E 257 F3
Taufkirchen Germany 48°2N 11°36E 131 B2
Taulé France 48°37N 3°55W 172 D3
Taumarunui N.Z. 38°53S 175°15E 284 E4
Taumaturgo Brazil 8°54S 72°51W 330 B3
Taung S. Africa 27°33S 24°47E 270 C3
Taungdwingyi Burma 20°1N 95°40E 241 E5
Taunggyi Burma 20°50N 97°0E 241 E6
Taungtha Burma 21°12N 95°25E 241 E5
Taungup Burma 18°51N 94°14E 241 F5
Taungup Pass Burma 18°40N 94°45E 241 F5
Taunsa Pakistan 30°42N 70°39E 242 D4
Taunsa Barrage Pakistan 30°42N 70°50E 242 D4
Taunton Somst., U.K. 51°1N 3°5W 169 F4
Taunton Mass., U.S.A. 41°54N 71°6W 313 E13
Taunus Germany 50°13N 8°34E 179 E4
Taupo N.Z. 38°41S 176°7E 284 E5
Taupo, L. N.Z. 38°46S 175°55E 284 E4
Tauragė Lithuania 55°14N 22°16E 184 C9
Tauragė □ Lithuania 55°15N 22°17E 184 C9
Tauranga N.Z. 37°42S 176°11E 284 D5
Tauranga Harb. N.Z. 37°30S 176°5E 284 D5
Taureau, Rés. Canada 46°46N 73°50W 298 C5
Tauri ➤ Papua N. G. 8°8S 146°8E 286 E4
Taurianova Italy 38°21N 16°1E 201 D9
Tauroa Pt. N.Z. 35°10S 173°4E 284 B2
Taurus Mts. = Toros Dağları
Turkey 37°0N 32°30E 250 B3
Taus = Domažlice
Czech Rep. 49°28N 12°58E 180 B5
Tauste Spain 41°58N 1°18W 196 D3
Tautira Tahiti 17°44S 149°9W 289 e
Tauyskaya Guba
Russia 59°20N 150°20E 215 D16
Tauz = Tovuz Azerbaijan 41°0N 45°40E 191 K7
Tavan Bogd Uul
Mongolia 49°10N 87°49E 217 C11
Tavares U.S.A. 28°48N 81°44W 317 G8
Tavares, I. dos Brazil 22°49S 43°6W 135 A2
Tavas Turkey 37°34N 29°4E 205 D11
Tavastehus = Hämeenlinna
Finland 61°0N 24°28E 188 B3
Tavda Russia 58°7N 65°8E 214 D7
Tavda ➤ Russia 57°47N 67°18E 214 D7
Taverner B. Canada 67°12N 72°25W 295 D17
Tavernes de la Valldigna
Spain 39°5N 0°13W 197 F4
Tavernier U.S.A. 25°1N 80°31W 317 K9
Taveta Kenya 3°23S 37°37E 268 C4
Taveuni Fiji 16°51S 179°58W 287 A3
Taviano Italy 39°59N 18°5E 201 C11
Tavignano ➤ France 42°7N 9°33E 175 F13
Tavira Portugal 37°8N 7°40W 195 H3
Tavistock Ont., Canada 43°19N 80°50W 312 C4
Tavistock Devon, U.K. 50°33N 4°9W 169 G3
Tavolara Italy 40°54N 9°42E 200 B2
Távora ➤ Portugal 41°8N 7°35W 194 D3
Tavoy Burma 14°2N 98°12E 236 E2
Tavrichanka Russia 43°18N 131°59E 220 C5
Tavropos ➤ Greece 39°10N 21°45E 204 B3
Tavros Greece 37°57N 23°43E 112 B2
Tavşanlı Turkey 39°32N 29°30E 205 B11
Tavua Fiji 17°37S 177°5E 287 A1
Tavuki Fiji 19°7S 178°8E 287 B2
Taw ➤ U.K. 51°4N 4°4W 169 F3
Tawa N.Z. 41°10S 174°49E 143 A1
Tawa ➤ India 22°48N 77°48E 242 H8
Tawa Res. India 22°35N 78°5E 244 C4
Tawa Tawa Mal Reef
Papua N. G. 11°3S 152°55E 286 F7
Tawai India 27°48N 96°46E 241 B6
Tawas City U.S.A. 44°16N 83°31W 309 C12
Tawau Malaysia 4°20N 117°55E 235 B5
Tawau Hills △ Malaysia 4°20N 117°54E 235 B5
Taweisha Sudan 12°19N 26°40E 257 E2
Tawi-Tawi Phil. 5°10N 120°15E 233 J3
Tawi-tawi □ Phil. 5°0N 120°0E 233 J3
Tawngche Burma 26°34N 95°38E 241 B5
Tawu Taiwan 22°22N 120°54E 225 D2
Tāwūq Iraq 35°8N 44°26E 213 E11
Tāwurghā' Libya 32°1N 15°2E 258 B3
Tāwurghā', Sabkhat
Libya 31°51N 15°15E 258 B3
Taxco Mexico 18°33N 99°36W 319 D5
Taxila Pakistan 33°42N 72°52E 242 C5
Taxkorgan Tajik Zizhixian
China 37°49N 75°14E 217 E9
Tay ➤ U.K. 56°37N 3°38W 167 E5
Tay, Firth of U.K. 56°25N 3°8W 167 E5
Tay, L. W. Austral.,
Australia 32°55S 120°48E 279 F3
Tay, L. Perth & Kinr., U.K. 56°32N 4°8W 167 E4
Tay ⌂ U.K. 56°43N 3°59W 167 E5
Tay Ninh Vietnam 11°20N 106°5E 237 G6
Tayabamba Peru 8°15S 77°16W 330 B2
Tayabas = Quezon Phil. 9°15N 117°59E 233 G1
Tayabas Phil. 14°1N 121°35E 232 D3
Tayabas Bay Phil. 13°45N 121°45E 232 E3
Taygetos Oros Greece 37°0N 22°23E 204 D4
Taylakova Russia 59°13N 74°0E 214 D8
Taylor B.C., Canada 56°13N 120°40W 296 B4
Taylor Fla., U.S.A. 30°26N 82°18W 316 E7
Taylor Mich., U.S.A. 42°14N 83°16W 311 B13
Taylor Nebr., U.S.A. 41°46N 99°23W 308 E4
Taylor Pa., U.S.A. 41°23N 75°43W 313 E9
Taylor Tex., U.S.A. 30°34N 97°25W 314 F6
Taylor, Mt. N.Z. 43°30S 171°20E 285 D6
Taylor, Mt. N. Mex.,
U.S.A. 35°14N 107°37W 305 J10
Taylorsville U.S.A. 38°2N 85°21W 311 F11
Taylorsville L. U.S.A. 38°0N 85°15W 311 G11
Taylorville U.S.A. 39°33N 89°18W 310 E7
Taymā Si. Arabia 27°35N 38°45E 246 E3
Taymyr, Oz. Russia 74°20N 102°0E 215 B11
Taymyr, Poluostrov
Russia 75°0N 100°0E 215 B11
Taypaq Kazakhstan 49°0N 51°47E 187 E9
Tayport U.K. 56°27N 2°52W 167 E6
Tayrona △ Colombia 11°20N 74°2W 328 A3
Tayshet Russia 55°58N 98°1E 215 D10
Taytay Phil. 10°45N 119°30E 233 F2
Taytay Bay Phil. 10°55N 119°35E 233 F2
Tayuan Taiwan 25°3N 121°11E 225 A3
Tayug Phil. 16°2N 120°45E 232 C3
Tayüling Taiwan 24°11N 121°18E 225 B3
Tāybād Iran 34°45N 60°45E 247 C9
Tāybād □ Iran 34°44N 60°44E 247 C9
Tayynsha Kazakhstan 53°50N 69°45E 217 B7
Taz ➤ Russia 67°32N 78°40E 214 C8
Taza Morocco 34°16N 4°6W 260 B4
Taza □ Morocco 34°15N 3°45W 260 B4
Tāza Khurmātū Iraq 35°18N 44°20E 213 E11
Tazawa-Ko Japan 39°43N 140°40E 220 E10
Taze Burma 22°57N 95°24E 241 D5
Tazenakht Morocco 30°35N 7°12W 260 B3
Tazerbo Libya 25°45N 21°0E 258 C4
Tazin ➤ Canada 59°48N 109°55W 297 B7
Tazin L. Canada 59°44N 108°42W 297 B7
Tazlina U.S.A. 62°4N 146°27W 303 E11
Tazouikert Mali 21°27N 1°16W 261 D4
Tazoult Algeria 35°29N 6°11E 261 A6
Tazovskiy Russia 67°30N 78°44E 214 C8
Tazrouk Algeria 23°24N 6°15E 261 D6
Tbilisi Georgia 41°43N 44°50E 191 K7
Tchad = Chad ■ Africa 15°0N 17°15E 259 F3
Tchad, L. Chad 13°30N 14°30E 259 F2
Tchaourou Benin 8°58N 2°40E 263 D5
Tch'eng-tou = Chengdu
China 30°38N 104°2E 228 B5
Tchentlo L. Canada 55°15N 125°0W 296 B4
Tchetti Benin 7°50N 1°40E 263 D5
Tchibanga Gabon 2°45S 11°0E 264 C2
Tchien Liberia 5°59N 8°15W 262 D3
Tchin Tabaraden Niger 15°58N 5°56E 263 B6
Tcholliré Cameroon 8°24N 14°10E 264 A2
Tch'ong-k'ing = Chongqing
China 29°35N 106°25E 228 C6
Tchoupitoulas Street
New Orleans, U.S.A. 131 b2
Tczew Poland 54°8N 18°50E 184 D5
Te Anau N.Z. 45°25S 167°43E 285 F2
Te Anau, L. N.Z. 45°15S 167°45E 285 F2
Te Araroa N.Z. 37°39S 178°25E 284 D7
Te Aroha N.Z. 37°32S 175°44E 284 D4
Te Awamutu N.Z. 38°1S 175°20E 284 E4
Te Ika a Maui = North I.
N.Z. 38°0S 175°0E 284 E4
Te Kaha N.Z. 37°44S 177°52E 284 D6
Te Karaka N.Z. 38°26S 177°53E 284 E6
Te Kauwhata N.Z. 37°25S 175°9E 284 D4
Te Kopuru N.Z. 36°2S 173°56E 284 C2
Te Kou Cook Is. 21°14S 159°46W 289 h
Te Kuiti N.Z. 38°20S 175°11E 284 E4
Te Manga Cook Is. 21°14S 159°45W 289 h
Te-n-Dghâmcha, Sebkhet
Mauritania 18°30N 15°55W 262 B1
Te Papa Museum N.Z. 41°18S 174°47E 143 B1
Te Puke N.Z. 37°46S 176°22E 284 D5
Te Teko N.Z. 38°2S 176°48E 284 E5
Te Waewae B. N.Z. 46°13S 167°33E 285 G2
Te Wai Pounamu = South I.
N.Z. 44°0S 170°0E 285 E5
Tea ➤ Brazil 0°30S 65°9W 328 D4
Teaca Romania 46°55N 24°30E 183 D9
Teague U.S.A. 31°38N 96°17W 314 F6
Teahupoo Tahiti 17°50S 149°16W 289 e
Teaneck U.S.A. 40°53N 74°1W 132 A1
Teano Italy 41°15N 14°4E 201 A7
Teapa Mexico 17°33N 92°57W 319 D6
Teba Spain 36°59N 4°55W 195 J6
Tebakang Malaysia 1°6N 110°30E 235 B4
Tébarat Niger 14°49N 4°27E 263 C5
Teberda Russia 43°30N 41°46E 191 J5
Teberu Malaysia 1°30N 103°42E 237 d
Tébessa Algeria 35°22N 8°8E 261 A6
Tébessa □ Algeria 35°0N 7°50E 261 B6
Tebet Indonesia 6°14S 106°50E 122 B2
Tebicuary ➤ Paraguay 26°36S 58°16W 334 B4
Tebingtinggi Riau,
Indonesia 1°0N 102°45E 234 B2
Tebingtinggi Sumatera Utara,
Indonesia 3°20N 99°9E 234 B1
Tébourba Tunisia 36°49N 9°51E 258 A1
Téboursouk Tunisia 36°29N 9°10E 258 A1
Tebulos Georgia 42°36N 45°17E 191 J7
Tecamachalco Mexico 19°25N 99°14W 128 B1
Tecate Mexico 32°34N 116°38W 307 N10
Tecer Dağları Turkey 39°27N 37°27E 212 C7
Tech ➤ France 42°36N 3°3E 174 F7
Techiman Ghana 7°35N 1°58W 262 D4
Techirghiol Romania 44°4N 28°32E 183 F13
Techou = Dezhou China 37°26N 116°18E 226 F9
Tecka Argentina 43°29S 70°48W 336 B2
Tecomán Mexico 18°55N 103°53W 318 D4
Tecopa U.S.A. 35°51N 116°13W 307 K10
Tecoripa Mexico 28°37N 109°57W 318 B3
Tecuala Mexico 22°23N 105°27W 318 C3
Tecuci Romania 45°51N 27°27E 183 E12
Tecumseh Ont., Canada 42°19N 82°54W 312 D2
Tecumseh Mich., U.S.A. 42°0N 83°57W 311 B13
Tecumseh Okla., U.S.A. 35°15N 96°56W 314 D6
Ted Somali Rep. 4°24N 43°55E 267 D5
Ted Williams Tunnel
U.S.A. 42°21N 71°1W 116 A2
Teddington U.K. 51°25N 0°20W 125 B1
Tedjert Algeria 21°23N 6°25E 261 D6
Tedzhen = Tejen
Turkmenistan 37°23N 60°31E 216 E6
Tees ➤ U.K. 54°37N 1°10W 168 C6
Tees B. U.K. 54°40N 1°9W 168 C6
Teeswater Canada 43°59N 81°17W 312 C3
Tefé Brazil 3°25S 64°50W 329 D5
Tefé ➤ Brazil 3°35S 64°47W 329 D5
Tefenni Turkey 37°18N 29°45E 205 D11
Tegal Indonesia 6°52S 109°8E 235 D3
Tegallalang Indonesia 8°27S 115°17E 231 J18
Tegalsari Indonesia 8°25S 114°8E 231 J17
Tegel Germany 52°34N 13°16E 115 A2
Tegel, Berlin ✈ (TXL)
Germany 52°35N 13°14E 115 A2
Tegeler See Germany 52°34N 13°15E 115 A2
Tegelort Germany 52°34N 13°15E 115 A2
Tegernsee Germany 47°43N 11°46E 179 H7
Teggiano Italy 40°23N 15°32E 201 B8
Tegid, L. = Bala, L. U.K. 52°53N 3°37W 168 E4
Tegina Nigeria 10°5N 6°11E 263 C6
Tegua Vanuatu 13°15S 166°37E 287 C4
Tegucigalpa Honduras 14°5N 87°14W 320 D2
Teguidda i-n-Tessoum
Niger 17°25N 6°37E 263 B6
Teguise Canary Is. 29°3N 13°33W 153 e2
Tehachapi U.S.A. 35°8N 118°27W 307 K8
Tehachapi Mts. U.S.A. 35°0N 118°30W 307 L8
Tehamiyam Sudan 18°20N 36°32E 256 D4
Teheran = Tehrān Iran 35°41N 51°25E 141 A2
Tehilla Sudan 17°42N 36°6E 256 D4
Téhini Ivory C. 9°39N 3°40W 262 D4
Tehoru Indonesia 3°23S 129°30E 231 E7
Tehrān Iran 35°41N 51°25E 141 A2
Tehrān □ Iran 35°30N 51°30E 247 C6
Tehrān Mehrābād ✈ (THR)
Iran 35°41N 51°18E 141 A1
Tehrān Pārs Iran 35°44N 51°32E 141 A3
Tehri India 30°23N 78°29E 243 D8
Tehuacán Mexico 18°27N 97°23W 319 D5
Tehuantepec Mexico 16°21N 95°13W 319 D5
Tehuantepec, G. de
Mexico 15°50N 95°12W 319 D5
Tehuantepec, Istmo de
Mexico 17°15N 94°30W 319 D6
Tehuantepec Fracture Zone
Pac. Oc. 13°0N 97°0W 289 F18
Tei Tong Tsui China 22°16N 114°17E 122 B2
Teide, Pico de Canary Is. 28°15N 16°38W 153 e1
Teifi ➤ U.K. 52°5N 4°41W 169 E3
Teign ➤ U.K. 50°32N 3°32W 169 G4
Teignmouth U.K. 50°33N 3°31W 169 G4
Teiuş Romania 46°12N 23°40E 183 D8
Teixeira Brazil 7°13S 37°15W 332 C4
Teixeira Pinto Guinea-Biss. 12°3N 16°0W 262 C1
Tejakula Indonesia 8°8S 115°20E 231 J18
Tejam India 29°57N 80°11E 243 E9
Tejen Turkmenistan 37°23N 60°31E 216 E6
Tejen ➤ Turkmenistan 37°24N 60°38E 247 B9
Tejo ➤ Europe 38°40N 9°24W 195 F2
Tejo, Rio ➤ Portugal 38°45N 9°3W 126 A2
Tejon Pass U.S.A. 34°49N 118°53W 307 L8
Tekamah U.S.A. 41°47N 96°13W 308 E5
Tekapo ➤ N.Z. 44°13S 170°21E 285 E5
Tekapo, L. N.Z. 43°53S 170°33E 285 D5
Tekax Mexico 20°12N 89°17W 319 C7
Teke Turkey 41°4N 29°39E 203 E13
Tekeli Kazakhstan 44°50N 79°0E 217 D9
Tekeze ➤ Ethiopia 14°20N 35°50E 257 E4
Tekija Serbia 44°42N 22°26E 202 B6
Tekirdağ Turkey 40°58N 27°30E 203 F11
Tekirdağ □ Turkey 41°0N 27°0E 203 E11
Tekirova Turkey 36°30N 30°32E 205 E12
Tekkali India 18°37N 84°15E 244 E7
Tekke Turkey 40°42N 36°12E 212 B7
Tekman Turkey 39°38N 41°29E 213 C9
Teknaf Bangla. 20°52N 92°18E 241 E4
Tekoa U.S.A. 47°14N 117°4W 304 C5
Tekokota
French Polynesia 17°18S 142°34W 289 f
Tekong Besar, Pulau
Singapore 1°25N 104°3E 237 d
Tekouiât, O. ➤ Algeria 22°25N 2°35E 261 D5
Tékro Chad 19°32N 20°56E 259 E4
Tekstilyshchik Russia 55°42N 37°41E 129 B4
Tel ➤ India 20°50N 83°54E 244 D6
Tel Aviv-Yafo Israel 32°4N 34°48E 251 F5
Tel Lakhish Israel 31°34N 34°51E 251 G5
Tel Megiddo Israel 32°35N 35°11E 250 F6
Tela Honduras 15°40N 87°28W 320 C2
Télagh Algeria 34°51N 0°32W 261 B4
Telanaipura = Jambi
Indonesia 1°38S 103°30E 234 C2
Telašćica ⌂ Croatia 43°55N 15°10E 199 E12
Telavi Georgia 42°0N 45°30E 191 J7
Telč Czech Rep. 49°11N 15°28E 180 B8
Telciu Romania 47°25N 24°24E 183 C9
Telde Canary Is. 27°59N 15°25W 153 e1
Tele ➤
Dem. Rep. of the Congo 2°48N 23°54E 264 B4
Telefomin Papua N. G. 5°10S 141°31E 286 C1
Telegraph Creek Canada 58°0N 131°10W 296 B2
Telegraph Hill San Francisco, U.S.A. 136 a2
Telekhany = Tsyelyakhany
Belarus 52°30N 25°46E 177 B13
Telemark Norway 59°15N 7°40E 161 G12
Telemark □ Norway 59°25N 8°30E 164 E5
Télemsès Niger 15°37N 4°44E 263 B5
Telén Argentina 36°15S 65°31W 334 D2
Telen ➤ Indonesia 0°10S 117°20E 235 C5
Teleneşti Moldova 47°30N 28°22E 183 C13
Teleng Iran 25°47N 61°3E 247 E9
Teleño Spain 42°23N 6°22W 194 C4
Teleorman □ Romania 44°0N 25°0E 183 G10
Teleorman ➤ Romania 43°52N 25°26E 183 G10
Telerhteba, Djebel Algeria 24°10N 6°51E 261 D6
Teles Pires ➤ Brazil 7°21S 58°3W 331 B6
Telescope Pk. U.S.A. 36°10N 117°5W 307 J9
Telescope Pt. Grenada 12°7N 61°36W 323 q
Teletaye Mali 16°31N 1°30E 263 B5
Telford U.K. 52°40N 2°27W 169 E5
Telford and Wrekin □
U.K. 52°45N 2°27W 168 E5
Telfs Austria 47°19N 11°4E 180 D4
Telhal Portugal 38°48N 9°18W 126 A1
Telida U.S.A. 63°23N 153°16W 303 E9
Télimélé Guinea 10°54N 13°2W 262 C2
Teljo, J. Sudan 14°42N 25°26E 257 E2
Telkwa Canada 54°41N 127°5W 296 C3
Tell City U.S.A. 37°57N 86°46W 311 G10
Teller U.S.A. 65°16N 166°22W 303 D6
Tellicherry India 11°45N 75°30E 245 J2
Telluride U.S.A. 37°56N 107°49W 305 H10
Telok Blangah Singapore 1°17N 103°49E 138 B2
Telok Datok Malaysia 2°49N 101°31E 234 B2
Teloloapán Mexico 18°21N 99°51W 319 D5
Telpos Iz Russia 63°16N 59°13E 186 B10
Telsen Argentina 42°30S 66°50W 336 B3
Telšiai Lithuania 55°59N 22°14E 184 C9
Telšiai □ Lithuania 55°59N 22°15E 184 C9
Teltow Germany 52°23N 13°17E 115 B2
Teltow kanal Germany 52°26N 13°29E 115 B3
Teluk Anson = Teluk Intan
Malaysia 4°3N 101°0E 237 K3
Teluk Bahang Malaysia 5°28N 100°13E 237 c
Teluk Betung = Bandar Lampung
Indonesia 5°20S 105°10E 234 D3
Teluk Darvel Malaysia 4°45N 118°30E 233 J2
Teluk Intan Malaysia 4°3N 101°0E 237 K3
Teluk Kumbar Malaysia 5°18N 100°14E 237 c
Telukbutun Indonesia 4°13N 108°12E 235 B3
Telukdalem Indonesia 0°33N 97°50E 234 B1
Tema Ghana 5°41N 0°0 263 D5
Temagami, L. Canada 47°0N 80°10W 298 C3
Temanggung Indonesia 7°18S 110°10E 235 D4
Temasint Algeria 23°18N 7°40E 261 D6
Tematangi
French Polynesia 21°41S 140°40W 289 f
Temax Mexico 21°9N 88°56W 319 C7
Temba S. Africa 25°20S 28°17E 271 C4
Tembagapura Indonesia 4°20S 137°0E 231 E9
Tembe
Dem. Rep. of the Congo 0°16S 28°14E 268 C2
Tembe ⌂ S. Africa 26°51S 32°24E 271 C5
Tembesi Indonesia 1°43S 103°6E 234 C2
Tembilahan Indonesia 0°19S 103°9E 234 C2
Temblador Venezuela 8°59N 62°44W 329 B5
Tembleque Spain 39°41N 3°30W 194 F7
Temblor Range U.S.A. 35°20N 119°50W 307 K7
Tembo Aluma Angola 7°42S 17°17E 265 D3
Teme ➤ U.K. 52°11N 2°13W 169 E5
Temecula U.S.A. 33°30N 117°9W 307 M9
Temengor, Tasik
Malaysia 5°24N 101°18E 237 K3
Temerloh Malaysia 3°27N 102°25E 237 L4
Teminabuan Indonesia 1°26S 132°1E 231 E8
Temir Kazakhstan 49°1N 57°14E 187 E10
Temir-Khan-Shura = Buynaksk
Russia 42°48N 47°7E 191 J8
Temirtau Kazakhstan 50°5N 72°56E 217 B8
Temirtau Russia 53°10N 87°30E 217 B11
Témiscamie ➤ Canada 50°59N 73°5W 299 B5
Témiscaming Canada 46°44N 79°5W 298 C4
Témiscamingue, L.
Canada 47°10N 79°25W 298 C4
Temnikov Russia 54°40N 43°11E 190 C6
Temnikovo Russia 55°43N 38°1E 129 B6
Temo ➤ Italy 40°17N 8°28E 200 B1
Temora Australia 34°30S 147°30E 283 C7
Temosachic Mexico 28°57N 107°51W 318 B3
Tempe U.S.A. 33°24N 111°54W 305 K8
Tempelburg = Czaplinek
Poland 53°34N 16°14E 184 E3
Tempelhof Germany 52°27N 13°23E 115 B3
Temperance U.S.A. 41°47N 83°34W 311 C13
Témpio Pausânia Italy 40°54N 9°6E 200 B2
Tempiute U.S.A. 37°39N 115°38W 306 H11
Templar Bank S. China Sea 9°0N 117°30E 233 F1
Temple U.S.A. 31°6N 97°21W 314 F6
Temple B. Australia 12°15S 143°3E 286 G2
Temple City U.S.A. 34°6N 118°3W 126 B4
Temple Hills U.S.A. 38°48N 76°56W 143 C4
Temple Mount Jerusalem 123 b3
Temple of Heaven China 39°52N 116°23E 114 B2
Temple of the Dawn = Arun
Bangkok, Thailand 113 b1
Temple Terrace U.S.A. 28°2N 82°23W 317 G7
Templemore Ireland 52°47N 7°51W 166 D4
Templeogue Ireland 53°18N 6°18W 120 B2
Templeton U.S.A. 35°33N 120°42W 306 K6
Templeton ➤ Australia 21°0S 138°40E 280 C2
Templin Germany 53°7N 13°28E 178 B9
Templo Mayor Mexico City, Mexico 128 b3
Tempoal de Sánchez
Mexico 21°31N 98°23W 319 C5
Temppeliaukio Church
Finland 60°10N 24°56E 121 B2
Tempué Angola 13°27S 18°52E 265 G3
Temryuk Russia 45°15N 37°24E 189 K9
Temska ➤ Serbia 43°17N 22°33E 202 C6
Temuco Chile 38°45S 72°40W 336 A2
Temuka N.Z. 44°14S 171°17E 285 E6
Ten Degree Channel
India 10°0N 92°30E 245 K11
Ten Thousand Is. U.S.A. 25°55N 81°45W 317 K8
Tena Ecuador 0°59S 77°49W 328 D2
Tenabo Mexico 20°3N 90°14W 319 C6
Tenafly U.S.A. 40°54N 73°58W 132 A2
Tenaha U.S.A. 31°57N 94°15W 314 F7
Tenakee Springs U.S.A. 57°47N 135°13W 296 B1
Tenali India 16°15N 80°35E 245 F5
Tenancingo de Degollado
Mexico 18°58N 99°36W 319 D5
Tenango del Valle Mexico 19°7N 99°33W 319 D5
Tenaro, Akra Greece 36°22N 22°27E 204 E4
Tenasserim Burma 12°6N 99°3E 237 F2

Tenasserim □ *Burma* 14°0N 98°30E **236** F2
Tenayuca, Pirámide de *Mexico* 19°31N 99°10W **128** A1
Tenby *U.K.* 51°40N 4°42W **169** F3
Tenda, Colle di *France* 44°7N 7°36E **175** D11
Tendaho *Ethiopia* 11°48N 40°54E **257** E5
Tende *France* 44°5N 7°35E **175** D11
Tendelti *Sudan* 13°1N 31°55E **257** E3
Tendjedi, Adrar *Algeria* 23°41N 7°32E **261** D6
Tendrara *Morocco* 33°3N 1°58W **261** B4
Tendrovskaya Kosa *Ukraine* 46°16N 31°35E **189** J6
Tendukhera *India* 23°24N 79°33E **243** H8
Teneguía, Volcanes de *Canary Is.* 28°28N 17°51W **153** e1
Teneida *Egypt* 25°30N 29°19E **256** B2
Tenenkou *Mali* 14°28N 4°55W **262** C4
Tenente Marques → *Brazil* 11°10S 59°56W **331** C6
Ténéré *Niger* 19°0N 10°30E **259** E2
Ténéré, Erg du *Niger* 17°35N 10°55E **259** E2
Tenerife *Canary Is.* 28°15N 16°35W **153** e1
Tenerife, Pico *Canary Is.* 27°43N 18°1W **153** e1
Tenerife Norte ✕ (TFN) *Canary Is.* 28°28N 16°17W **153** e1
Tenerife Sur ✕ (TFS) *Canary Is.* 28°3N 16°33W **153** e1
Ténès *Algeria* 36°31N 1°14E **261** A5
Teng Xian *Guangxi Zhuangzu, China* 23°21N 110°56E **229** F8
Teng Xian *Shandong, China* 35°5N 117°10E **227** G9
Tengah → *Singapore* 1°23N 103°43E **138** A2
Tengah, Kepulauan *Indonesia* 7°5S 118°15E **235** D5
Tengchong *China* 25°0N 98°28E **228** E2
Tengchowfu = Penglai *China* 37°48N 120°42E **227** F11
Tenggarong *Indonesia* 0°24S 116°58E **235** C5
Tengger Feng *China* 43°12N 86°48E **217** D11
Tengger Shamo *China* 38°0N 104°0E **218** C5
Tenggol, Pulau *Malaysia* 4°48N 103°41E **237** K4
Tengiz Köli *Kazakhstan* 50°30N 69°0E **217** B7
Tenhult *Sweden* 57°41N 14°20E **163** G8
Teniente Enciso △ *Paraguay* 21°5S 61°8W **334** A3
Teniente Rodolfo Marsh *Antarctica* 62°30S 58°0W **151** C18
Tenille *U.S.A.* 29°46N 83°19W **316** F6
Tenino *U.S.A.* 46°51N 122°51W **306** D4
Tenkasi *India* 8°55N 77°20E **245** K3
Tenke *Katanga, Dem. Rep. of the Congo* 11°22S 26°40E **269** E2
Tenke *Katanga, Dem. Rep. of the Congo* 10°32S 26°7E **269** E2
Tenkodogo *Burkina Faso* 11°54N 0°19W **263** C4
Tenna → *Italy* 43°14N 13°47E **199** E10
Tennant Creek *Australia* 19°30S 134°15E **280** B1
Tennessee □ *U.S.A.* 36°0N 86°30W **315** D11
Tennessee → *U.S.A.* 37°4N 88°34W **315** C10
Tennille *U.S.A.* 32°56N 82°48W **316** C7
Tennoji *Japan* 34°39N 135°30E **223** B12
Teno, Pta. de *Canary Is.* 28°21N 16°55W **153** e1
Tenom *Malaysia* 5°4N 115°57E **235** A5
Tenosique *Mexico* 17°29N 91°26W **319** D6
Tenri *Japan* 34°39N 135°49E **223** C7
Tenryū *Japan* 34°52N 137°49E **223** C9
Tenryū-Gawa → *Japan* 35°39N 137°48E **223** B9
Tensift, Oued → *Morocco* 32°3N 9°28W **260** B3
Tenterden *U.K.* 51°4N 0°42E **169** F8
Tenterfield *Australia* 29°0S 152°0E **281** D5
Tenuaiur, Uad → *W. Sahara* 21°36N 16°0W **260** D1
Teo = A Ramallosa *Spain* 42°45N 8°30W **194** C2
Teófilo Otoni *Brazil* 17°50S 41°30W **333** E3
Tepa *Indonesia* 7°52S 129°31E **231** F7
Tepa Pt. *Cook Is.* 19°6S 169°55W **289** g
Tepalcatepec → *Mexico* 18°35N 101°59W **318** D4
Tepalcates *Mexico* 19°23N 99°3W **128** B2
Tepecik *Bursa, Turkey* 40°7N 28°25E **203** F12
Tepecik *Kütahya, Turkey* 39°32N 29°28E **205** B11
Tepehuanes *Mexico* 25°21N 105°44W **318** B3
Tepelenë *Albania* 40°17N 20°2E **202** F4
Tepequem, Serra *Brazil* 3°45N 61°45W **329** C5
Tepetongo *Mexico* 22°28N 103°9W **318** C4
Tepeyac △ *Mexico* 19°30N 99°7W **128** B2
Tepic = Nayarit □ *Mexico* 22°0N 105°0W **318** C4
Tepic *Mexico* 21°30N 104°54W **318** C4
Teplá *Czech Rep.* 49°59N 12°52E **180** B5
Teplice *Czech Rep.* 50°40N 13°48E **180** A6
Teplitz = Teplice *Czech Rep.* 50°40N 13°48E **180** A6
Teplyk *Ukraine* 48°40N 29°44E **183** B14
Tepoca, C. *Mexico* 30°20N 112°25W **318** A2
Tequila *Mexico* 20°54N 103°47W **318** C4
Ter → *Spain* 42°2N 3°12E **196** C8
Ter Apel *Neths.* 52°53N 7°5E **170** B7
Téra *Niger* 14°0N 0°45E **263** C5
Tera → *Spain* 41°54N 5°44W **194** D5
Tera Kora *Neth. Ant.* 12°11N 68°16W **322** h
Teraina *Kiribati* 4°43N 160°25W **289** G12
Terakeka *Sudan* 5°26N 31°45E **257** F3
Téramo *Italy* 42°39N 13°42E **199** F10
Terang *Australia* 38°15S 142°55E **282** E5
Terang, Teluk *Indonesia* 8°44S 116°0E **231** K19
Terawhiti, C. *N.Z.* 41°16S 174°38E **284** H3
Terazit, Massif de *Niger* 20°2N 8°30E **259** D1
Tercan *Turkey* 39°47N 40°23E **213** C9
Terceira *Azores* 38°43N 27°13W **153** d1
Tercero → *Argentina* 32°58S 61°47W **334** C3
Terdal *India* 16°33N 75°3E **244** F2
Terebovlya *Ukraine* 49°18N 25°44E **177** D13
Teregova *Romania* 45°10N 22°16E **182** E7
Tereida *Sudan* 10°35N 31°17E **257** E3
Terek → *Russia* 44°0N 47°30E **191** J8
Terengganu □ *Malaysia* 4°55N 103°0E **234** B2
Terenos *Brazil* 20°26S 54°50W **331** E7
Terepaima △ *Venezuela* 9°58N 69°17W **328** B4
Tereshka → *Russia* 51°48N 46°26E **190** E8
Teresina *Brazil* 5°9S 42°45W **332** C3
Teresinha *Brazil* 0°58N 52°2W **329** C7
Terespol *Poland* 52°5N 23°37E **185** F10
Teressa *India* 8°15N 93°10E **245** K11
Teresva *Ukraine* 48°0N 23°42E **183** B8
Terewah, L. *Australia* 29°52S 147°35E **281** D4
Terges → *Portugal* 37°49N 7°41W **195** H3
Tergnier *France* 49°40N 3°17E **173** C10
Terhazza *Mali* 23°38N 5°22W **260** D3
Teridgerie Cr. → *Australia* 30°25S 148°50E **283** A8
Terijoki = Zelenogorsk *Russia* 60°12N 29°43E **188** B5
Terlizzi *Italy* 41°8N 16°32E **201** A9
Termas de Río Hondo *Argentina* 27°29S 64°52W **334** B3
Terme *Turkey* 41°11N 37°0E **212** B7
Termez = Termiz *Uzbekistan* 37°15N 67°15E **217** E7
Términi Imerese *Italy* 37°59N 13°42E **200** E6
Términos, L. de *Mexico* 18°37N 91°33W **319** D6
Termit, Massif de *Niger* 16°2N 11°20E **259** E2
Termiz *Uzbekistan* 37°15N 67°15E **217** E7
Térmoli *Italy* 42°0N 15°0E **199** F12
Ternate *Indonesia* 0°45N 127°25E **231** D7
Terneuzen *Neths.* 51°20N 3°50E **170** C3
Terney *Russia* 45°3N 136°37E **220** B8
Terni *Italy* 42°34N 12°37E **199** F9
Ternitz *Austria* 47°43N 16°2E **180** D9
Ternivka *Ukraine* 48°32N 29°58E **183** B14
Ternopil *Ukraine* 49°30N 25°40E **177** D13
Ternopil □ *Ukraine* 48°10N 25°10E **189** H3
Ternopol = Ternopil *Ukraine* 49°30N 25°40E **177** D13
Terowie *Australia* 33°8S 138°55E **282** B3
Terpni *Greece* 40°55N 23°26E **202** F7
Terra Bella *U.S.A.* 35°58N 119°3W **307** K7
Terra Nova △ *Canada* 48°33N 53°55W **299** C9
Terrace *Canada* 54°30N 128°35W **296** C3
Terrace Bay *Canada* 48°47N 87°5W **298** C2
Terracina *Italy* 41°17N 13°15E **200** A6
Terralba *Italy* 39°43N 8°39E **200** C1
Terranova di Sicilia = Gela *Italy* 37°4N 14°15E **201** E7
Terranova Pausania = Ólbia *Italy* 40°55N 9°31E **200** B2
Terrasini *Italy* 38°10N 13°4E **200** D6
Terrassa *Spain* 41°34N 2°1E **196** D7
Terrasson-la-Villedieu *France* 45°8N 1°18E **174** C5
Terrazzano *Italy* 45°32N 9°4E **129** A1
Terre-de-Bas *Guadeloupe* 15°51N 61°38W **322** e
Terre-de-Bas *Guadeloupe* 16°10N 61°7W **322** e
Terre-de-Haut *Guadeloupe* 15°52N 61°34W **322** e
Terre des Hommes *Canada* 45°31N 73°32W **130** A2
Terre Haute *U.S.A.* 39°28N 87°25W **311** E9
Terre Rouge *Mauritius* 20°7S 57°31E **272** e
Terrebonne B. *U.S.A.* 29°5N 90°35W **315** G9
Terrecht *Mali* 19°35N 0°22E **261** D4
Terrell *U.S.A.* 32°44N 96°17W **314** E6
Terrenceville *Canada* 47°40N 54°44W **299** C9
Terrick Terrick △ *Australia* 36°8S 144°13E **282** D6
Terrugem *Portugal* 38°41N 9°17W **126** A1
Terry *U.S.A.* 46°47N 105°19W **304** C11
Terrytown *U.S.A.* 29°54N 90°1W **131** B2
Terryville *U.S.A.* 41°41N 73°3W **313** E11
Terschelling *Neths.* 53°25N 5°20E **170** A5
Tersko-Kumskiy Kanal *Russia* 44°32N 44°38E **191** H7
Tertenía *Italy* 39°42N 9°34E **200** C2
Terter = Tärtär → *Azerbaijan* 40°26N 47°20E **191** K8
Teruel *Spain* 40°22N 1°8W **196** E3
Teruel □ *Spain* 40°48N 1°0W **196** E4
Tervel *Bulgaria* 43°45N 27°28E **203** C11
Tervola *Finland* 66°6N 24°49E **160** C21
Tervuren *Belgium* 50°49N 4°31E **116** B3
Tervuren, Park van *Belgium* 50°49N 4°31E **116** B3
Teryaweynya L. *Australia* 32°18S 143°22E **282** B5
Tešanj *Bos.-H.* 44°38N 18°1E **182** F3
Teschen = Cieszyn *Poland* 49°45N 18°35E **185** J5
Teseney *Eritrea* 15°5N 36°42E **257** D4
Tesha → *Russia* 55°38N 42°9E **190** C6
Teshekpuk L. *U.S.A.* 70°35N 153°26W **303** A9
Teshio *Japan* 44°53N 141°44E **220** B10
Teshio-Gawa → *Japan* 44°53N 141°45E **220** B10
Tešica *Serbia* 43°27N 21°45E **202** C5
Tesiyn Gol → *Mongolia* 50°40N 93°20E **218** A4
Teslić *Bos.-H.* 44°37N 17°54E **182** F2
Teslin *Canada* 60°10N 132°43W **296** A2
Teslin → *Canada* 61°34N 134°35W **296** A2
Teslin L. *Canada* 60°15N 132°57W **296** A2
Tesouro *Brazil* 16°4S 53°34W **331** D7
Tessalit *Mali* 20°12N 1°0E **261** D5
Tessaoua *Niger* 13°47N 7°56E **259** F1
Tessin *Germany* 54°2N 12°28E **178** A8
Tessit *Mali* 15°13N 0°18E **263** B5
Tessounfat *Mali* 22°53N 0°32E **261** D5
Test → *U.K.* 50°56N 1°29W **169** G6
Testa del Gargano *Italy* 41°50N 16°10E **199** G13
Testigos, Is. Los *Venezuela* 11°23N 63°7W **321** D7
Tét *Hungary* 47°30N 17°33E **182** C2
Têt → *France* 42°44N 3°2E **174** F7
Tetachuck L. *Canada* 53°18N 125°55W **296** C3
Tetas, Pta. *Chile* 23°31S 70°38W **334** A1
Tete *Mozam.* 16°13S 33°33E **269** F3
Tete □ *Mozam.* 15°15S 32°40E **269** F3
Tetenga, Caleta *Chile* 27°9S 109°19W **330** b
Tetepare *Solomon Is.* 8°45S 157°35E **287** M9
Teterev → *Ukraine* 51°1N 30°5E **177** C16
Teterow *Germany* 53°46N 12°34E **178** B8
Teteven *Bulgaria* 42°58N 24°17E **203** D8
Tethul → *Canada* 60°35N 112°12W **296** A6
Tetiyev *Ukraine* 49°22N 29°38E **177** D15
Tetlin *U.S.A.* 63°8N 142°31W **303** E12
Tetlin Junction *U.S.A.* 63°19N 142°36W **303** E12
Tetlin Nat. Wildlife Refuge ⌂ *U.S.A.* 62°40N 141°50W **303** E12
Tetlit Zheh = Fort McPherson *Canada* 67°30N 134°55W **294** D5
Teton → *U.S.A.* 47°56N 110°31W **304** C8
Tétouan *Morocco* 35°35N 5°21W **260** A3
Tétouan □ *Morocco* 35°35N 5°30W **260** A3
Tetovo *Macedonia* 42°1N 20°59E **202** D4
Tetschen = Děčín *Czech Rep.* 50°47N 14°12E **180** A7
Tetuán *Spain* 40°27N 3°42W **127** B1
Tetufera, Mt. *Tahiti* 17°40S 149°26W **289** e
Tetyukhe = Dalnegorsk *Russia* 44°32N 135°33E **220** B7
Tetyushi *Russia* 54°55N 48°49E **190** C9
Teuco → *Argentina* 25°35S 60°11W **334** B3
Teufelsberg *Germany* 52°29N 13°14E **115** B2
Teulada *Italy* 38°58N 8°46E **200** D1
Teulon *Canada* 50°23N 97°16W **297** C9
Teun *Indonesia* 6°59S 129°8E **231** F7
Teuri-Tō *Japan* 44°26N 141°19E **220** B10
Teutoburger Wald *Germany* 52°5N 8°22E **178** C4
Teutopolis *U.S.A.* 39°8N 88°29W **311** E8
Tevere → *Italy* 41°44N 12°14E **199** G9
Tevere ⌂ *Italy* 42°46N 12°14E **199** F9
Teverya *Israel* 32°47N 35°32E **250** F6
Teviot → *U.K.* 55°29N 2°38W **167** F6
Tewantin *Australia* 26°27S 153°3E **281** D5
Tewkesbury *U.K.* 51°59N 2°9W **169** F5
Texada I. *Canada* 49°40N 124°25W **296** D4
Texarkana *Ark., U.S.A.* 33°26N 94°2W **314** E7
Texarkana *Tex., U.S.A.* 33°26N 94°3W **314** E7
Texas *Australia* 28°49S 151°9E **281** D5
Texas □ *U.S.A.* 31°40N 98°30W **314** F5
Texas City *U.S.A.* 29°24N 94°54W **314** G7
Texel *Neths.* 53°5N 4°50E **170** A4
Texline *U.S.A.* 36°23N 103°2W **314** C3
Texoma, L. *U.S.A.* 33°50N 96°34W **314** E6
Teykovo *Russia* 56°55N 40°30E **188** D11
Teyvareh *Afghan.* 33°30N 64°24E **240** B2
Teza → *Russia* 56°32N 41°53E **190** B5
Tezin *Afghan.* 34°24N 69°30E **242** B3
Teziutlán *Mexico* 19°49N 97°21W **319** D5
Tezpur *India* 26°40N 92°45E **241** B4
Tezu *India* 27°55N 96°10E **241** B6
Tezzeron L. *Canada* 54°43N 124°30W **296** C4
Tha-anne → *Canada* 60°31N 94°37W **297** A10
Tha Deua *Laos* 17°57N 102°53E **236** D4
Tha Deua *Laos* 19°26N 101°50E **236** C3
Tha Li *Thailand* 17°37N 101°25E **236** D3
Tha Pla *Thailand* 17°48N 100°32E **236** D3
Tha Rua *Thailand* 14°34N 100°44E **236** E3
Tha Sala *Thailand* 8°40N 99°56E **237** H2
Tha Song Yang *Thailand* 17°34N 97°55E **236** D1
Thaba Putsoa *Lesotho* 29°45S 28°0E **271** C4
Thaba-Tseka *Lesotho* 29°32S 28°36E **271** C4
Thabana Ntlenyana *Lesotho* 29°30S 29°16E **271** C4
Thabaung *Burma* 17°2N 94°48E **241** G5
Thabazimbi *S. Africa* 24°40S 27°21E **271** B4
Thabeikkyin *Burma* 22°53N 95°59E **241** D5
Thabt, G. el *Egypt* 28°17N 34°1E **251** K5
Thādiq *Si. Arabia* 25°18N 45°52E **246** E5
Thai Binh *Vietnam* 20°35N 106°1E **228** G6
Thai Muang *Thailand* 8°24N 98°16E **237** H2
Thai Nguyen *Vietnam* 21°35N 105°55E **228** G5
Thailand ■ *Asia* 16°0N 102°0E **236** E4
Thailand, G. of *Asia* 11°30N 101°0E **237** G3
Thakhek *Laos* 17°25N 104°45E **236** D5
Thakurgaon *Bangla.* 26°2N 88°34E **241** B2
Thal *Pakistan* 33°28N 70°33E **242** C4
Thal Desert *Pakistan* 31°10N 71°30E **242** D4
Thala *Tunisia* 35°35N 8°40E **258** A1
Thala La = Hkakabo Razi *Burma* 28°25N 97°23E **241** B6
Thalabarivat *Cambodia* 13°33N 105°57E **236** F5
Thalassery = Tellicherry *India* 11°45N 75°30E **245** J2
Thalkirchen *Germany* 48°6N 11°32E **131** B2
Thallon *Australia* 28°39S 148°49E **281** D4
Thalu, Ko *Thailand* 9°26N 99°54E **237** b
Thalwil *Switz.* 47°17N 8°35E **179** H4
Thamarīt *Oman* 17°39N 54°2E **249** C6
Thames *N.Z.* 37°7S 175°34E **284** D4
Thames → *Ont., Canada* 42°20N 82°25W **312** D2
Thames → *U.K.* 51°29N 0°34E **169** F8
Thames → *Conn., U.S.A.* 41°18N 72°5W **313** E12
Thames, Firth of *N.Z.* 37°0S 175°25E **284** D4
Thames Ditton *U.K.* 51°23N 0°20W **125** B1
Thames Estuary *U.K.* 51°29N 0°52E **169** F8
Thamesford *Canada* 43°4N 81°0W **312** C4
Thamesmead *U.K.* 51°30N 0°7E **125** A4
Thamesville *Canada* 42°33N 81°59W **312** D3
Thāmit, W. → *Libya* 31°11N 16°8E **258** B3
Thamūd *Yemen* 17°18N 49°55E **249** C5
Than *India* 22°34N 71°11E **242** H4
Than Uyen *Vietnam* 22°0N 103°54E **236** B4
Thana Cr. → *India* 19°4N 72°54E **130** A2
Thana Gazi *India* 27°25N 76°19E **242** F7
Thanbyuzayat *Burma* 15°58N 97°44E **241** G6
Thandaung *Burma* 19°4N 96°41E **241** F6
Thandla *India* 23°0N 74°34E **242** H6
Thandwe *Burma* 18°20N 94°30E **241** F5
Thane *India* 19°12N 72°59E **244** E1
Thanesar *India* 30°1N 76°52E **242** D7
Thanet, I. of *U.K.* 51°21N 1°20E **169** F9
Thangool *Australia* 24°38S 150°42E **280** C5
Thanh Hoa *Vietnam* 19°48N 105°46E **236** C5
Thanh Hung *Vietnam* 9°55N 105°43E **237** H5
Thanh Pho Ho Chi Minh *Vietnam* 10°58N 106°40E **237** G6
Thanh Thuy *Vietnam* 22°55N 104°51E **236** A5
Thanjavur *India* 10°48N 79°12E **245** J4
Thanlwin = Salween → *Burma* 16°31N 97°37E **241** G6
Thann *France* 47°48N 7°5E **173** E14
Thano Bula Khan *Pakistan* 25°22N 67°50E **242** G2
Thaoge → *Botswana* 20°27S 22°36E **270** B3
Thaolintoa L. *Canada* 61°30N 96°25W **297** A9
Thaon-les-Vosges *France* 48°15N 6°24E **173** D13
Thap Lan △ *Thailand* 14°15N 102°16E **236** E4
Thap Sakae *Thailand* 11°30N 99°37E **237** G2
Thap Than *Thailand* 15°27N 99°54E **236** E2
Thar Desert *India* 28°0N 72°0E **242** F5
Tharad *India* 24°30N 71°44E **242** G4
Thargomindah *Australia* 27°58S 143°46E **281** D3
Tharp Fracture Zone *S. Ocean* 54°0S 135°0W **151** B14
Tharrawaddy *Burma* 17°38N 95°48E **241** G5
Tharrawaw *Burma* 17°41N 95°28E **241** G5
Tharthār, Buḩayrat ath *Iraq* 34°0N 43°15E **213** E10
Tharthar, L. = Tharthār, Buḩayrat ath *Iraq* 34°0N 43°15E **213** E10
Tharthār, W. ath → *Iraq* 34°32N 43°4E **213** E10
Thasopoula *Greece* 40°49N 24°45E **203** F8
Thasos *Greece* 40°40N 24°40E **203** F8
That Khe *Vietnam* 22°16N 106°28E **228** F6
Thatcher *Ariz., U.S.A.* 32°51N 109°46W **305** K9
Thatcher *Colo., U.S.A.* 37°33N 104°7W **305** H11
Thaton *Burma* 16°55N 97°22E **241** G6
Thau, Bassin de *France* 43°23N 3°36E **174** E7
Thaungdut *Burma* 24°30N 94°40E **241** C5
Thawatti *Burma* 19°32N 96°16E **241** F6
Thayer *U.S.A.* 36°31N 91°33W **308** G8
Thayetmyo *Burma* 19°20N 95°10E **241** F5
Thazi *Magwe, Burma* 19°59N 95°3E **241** F5
Thazi *Mandalay, Burma* 21°0N 96°5E **241** E6
Thbeng Meanchey *Cambodia* 13°49N 104°58E **236** F5
The Broads *U.K.* 52°45N 1°30E **168** E9
The Everglades *U.S.A.* 25°50N 81°0W **317** K9
The Gulf = Persian Gulf *Asia* 27°0N 50°0E **247** E6
The Hague = 's-Gravenhage *Neths.* 52°7N 4°17E **170** B4
The Pas *Canada* 53°45N 101°15W **297** C8
The Wash *U.K.* 52°58N 0°20E **168** E8
The Weald *U.K.* 51°4N 0°20E **169** F8
Thebes = Thiva *Greece* 38°19N 23°19E **204** C5
Thebes *Egypt* 25°40N 32°35E **256** B3
Thedaw *Burma* 21°5N 96°4E **241** E6
Thedford *U.S.A.* 41°59N 100°35W **308** E3
Theebine *Australia* 25°57S 152°34E **281** D5
Thègon *Burma* 18°39N 95°25E **241** F5
Thekulthili L. *Canada* 61°3N 110°0W **297** A7
Thelon → *Canada* 62°35N 104°3W **297** A8
Thénezay *France* 46°44N 0°2W **172** F6
Thenon *France* 45°9N 1°4E **174** C5
Theodore *Queens., Australia* 24°55S 150°3E **280** C5
Theodore *Sask., Canada* 51°26N 102°55W **297** C8
Theodore *Ala., U.S.A.* 30°33N 88°10W **315** F10
Theodore Roosevelt △ *U.S.A.* 47°0N 103°25W **308** B2
Theodore Roosevelt L. *U.S.A.* 33°40N 111°10W **305** K8
Thepha *Thailand* 6°52N 100°58E **237** J3
Thérain → *France* 49°15N 2°27E **173** C9
Theresa *U.S.A.* 44°13N 75°48W **313** B9
Theressa *U.S.A.* 29°50N 82°4W **316** F7
Therma = Eagle Nest *U.S.A.* 36°33N 105°16W **305** H11
Thermopolis *U.S.A.* 43°39N 108°13W **304** E9
Thermopylae *Greece* 38°48N 22°35E **204** C4
Thesprotia □ *Greece* 39°27N 20°22E **204** B2
Thessalon *Canada* 46°20N 83°30W **298** C3
Thessalonica, Gulf of = Thessaloniki Kolpos *Greece* 40°15N 22°45E **202** F6
Thessaloniki *Greece* 40°38N 22°58E **202** F6
Thessaloniki □ *Greece* 40°45N 23°0E **202** F7
Thessaloniki ✕ (SKG) *Greece* 40°30N 23°0E **202** F7
Thessaloniki Kolpos *Greece* 40°15N 22°45E **202** F6
Thessaly □ *Greece* 39°25N 22°0E **204** B4
Thetford *U.K.* 52°25N 0°45E **169** E8
Thetford Mines *Canada* 46°8N 71°18W **299** C5
Theun → *Laos* 18°19N 104°0E **236** C5
Theunissen *S. Africa* 28°26S 26°43E **270** C4
Thevenard *Australia* 32°9S 133°38E **281** E1
Thiais *France* 48°46N 2°23E **134** B3
Thiamis → *Greece* 39°15N 20°6E **204** B2
Thibaud *Dominica* 15°36N 61°24W **323** k
Thiberville *France* 49°8N 0°27E **172** C7
Thibodaux *U.S.A.* 29°48N 90°49W **315** G9
Thicket Portage *Canada* 55°19N 97°42W **297** B9
Thief River Falls *U.S.A.* 48°7N 96°10W **308** A5
Thiel Mts. *Antarctica* 85°15S 91°0W **151** E16
Thiene *Italy* 45°42N 11°29E **199** C8
Thiérache *France* 49°51N 3°45E **173** C10
Thiers *France* 45°52N 3°33E **174** C7
Thiès *Senegal* 14°50N 16°51W **262** C1
Thiès □ *Senegal* 14°45N 16°50W **262** C1
Thiesi *Italy* 40°31N 8°43E **200** B1
Thika *Kenya* 1°1S 37°5E **268** C4
Thille-Boubacar *Senegal* 16°31N 15°5W **262** B1
Thimân, W. → *Egypt* 28°4N 33°45E **251** K4
Thimphu *Bhutan* 27°31N 89°45E **241** B2
Thinadhoo *Maldives* 0°32N 72°56E **272** d
Thingangyun *Burma* 16°49N 96°12E **241** G6
Þingeyjarsýsla □ *Iceland* 65°40N 16°30W **155** B10
Þingeyri *Iceland* 65°52N 23°30W **155** B3
Þingmúli *Iceland* 65°2N 14°37W **155** B12
Þingvallavatn *Iceland* 64°11N 21°9W **155** C5
Þingvellir *Iceland* 64°15N 21°7W **155** C5
Þingvellir △ *Iceland* 64°16N 21°5W **155** C5
Thio *N. Cal.* 21°37S 166°14E **288** d
Thionville *France* 49°20N 6°10E **173** C13
Thira = Santorini *Greece* 36°23N 25°27E **205** E7
Thirasia *Greece* 36°26N 25°21E **205** E7
Third Cataract *Sudan* 19°42N 30°20E **256** D3
Thirsk *U.K.* 54°14N 1°19W **168** C6
Thiruvananthapuram = Trivandrum *India* 8°41N 77°0E **245** K3
Thiruvarur *India* 10°46N 79°38E **245** J4
Thisio *Athens, Greece* **112** c1
Thisted *Denmark* 56°58N 8°40E **163** H2
Þistilfjörður *Iceland* 66°18N 15°24W **155** A11
Thistle I. *Australia* 35°0S 136°8E **282** C2
Thistletown *Canada* 43°44N 79°34W **141** A1
Thitgy *Burma* 18°15N 96°13E **241** F6
Thithia = Cicia *Fiji* 17°45S 179°18W **287** A3
Thitpokpin *Burma* 19°24N 95°58E **241** F5
Thiva *Greece* 38°19N 23°19E **204** C5
Thiviers *France* 45°25N 0°54E **174** C4
Thizy *France* 46°2N 4°18E **173** F11
Þjórsá → *Iceland* 63°47N 20°48W **155** D6
Thlewiaza → *Canada* 60°29N 94°40W **297** A10
Thmar Puok *Cambodia* 13°57N 103°4E **236** F4
Tho Vinh *Vietnam* 19°16N 105°42E **236** C5
Thoa → *Canada* 60°31N 109°47W **297** A7
Thoen *Thailand* 17°43N 99°12E **236** D2
Thoeng *Thailand* 19°41N 100°12E **236** C3
Tholdi *Pakistan* 35°5N 76°6E **243** B7
Thomas *U.S.A.* 35°45N 98°45W **314** D5
Thomas, L. *Australia* 26°4S 137°58E **281** D2
Thomas Circle *Washington, D.C., U.S.A.* **143** a1
Thomas Hill Res. *U.S.A.* 39°34N 92°39W **310** E4
Thomas Hubbard, C. *Canada* 82°0N 94°25W **295** A13
Thomaston *U.S.A.* 32°53N 84°20W **316** C5
Thomastown *Australia* 37°40S 145°2E **128** A2
Thomasville *Ala., U.S.A.* 31°55N 87°44W **315** F11
Thomasville *Ga., U.S.A.* 30°50N 83°59W **316** E6
Thomasville *N.C., U.S.A.* 35°53N 80°5W **315** D14
Thompson *Man., Canada* 55°45N 97°52W **297** B9
Thompson *Pa., U.S.A.* 41°52N 75°31W **313** E9
Thompson → *B.C., Canada* 50°15N 121°24W **296** C4
Thompson → *Mo., U.S.A.* 39°46N 93°37W **310** E3
Thompson Falls *U.S.A.* 47°36N 115°21W **304** C6
Thompson I. *U.S.A.* 42°19N 70°59W **116** B3
Thompson Pk. *U.S.A.* 41°0N 123°2W **304** F2
Thompson Sd. *N.Z.* 45°8S 166°46E **285** F1
Thompson Springs *U.S.A.* 38°58N 109°43W **304** G9
Thompsontown *U.S.A.* 40°33N 77°14W **312** F7
Thomson *Ga., U.S.A.* 33°28N 82°30W **316** B7
Thomson *Ill., U.S.A.* 41°58N 90°6W **310** C6
Thomson → *Australia* 25°11S 142°53E **280** C3
Thomson's Falls = Nyahururu *Kenya* 0°2N 36°27E **268** B4
Thon Buri *Thailand* 13°45N 100°29E **113** B1
Thônes *France* 45°54N 6°18E **175** C10
Thong Yang *Thailand* 9°28N 99°56E **237** b
Thongwa *Burma* 16°45N 96°33E **241** G6
Thonon-les-Bains *France* 46°22N 6°29E **173** F13
Thonze *Burma* 17°38N 95°47E **241** G5
Thoothukudi = Tuticorin *India* 8°50N 78°12E **245** K4
Thorez *Ukraine* 48°4N 38°34E **189** H10
Þórisjökull *Iceland* 64°32N 20°43W **155** C6
Þórisvatn *Iceland* 64°20N 18°55W **155** C8
Þorkötlustaðir *Iceland* 63°50N 22°24W **155** D4
Þorlákshöfn *Iceland* 63°51N 21°22W **155** D5
Thorn = Toruń *Poland* 53°2N 18°39E **185** E5
Thornaby on Tees *U.K.* 54°33N 1°18W **168** C6
Thornbury *Vic., Australia* 37°44S 145°1E **128** A2
Thornbury *Ont., Canada* 44°34N 80°26W **312** B4
Thornbury *N.Z.* 46°17S 168°9E **285** G3
Thorncliffe *Canada* 43°42N 79°20W **141** A2
Thorne *U.K.* 53°37N 0°57W **168** D7
Thornhill *Canada* 43°48N 79°25W **141** A2
Thornton *Ont., Canada* 44°16N 79°43W **312** B5
Thornton *Western Cape, S. Africa* 33°55S 18°32E **118** A2
Thornton *Colo., U.S.A.* 39°52N 104°58W **304** G11
Thornton *Iowa, U.S.A.* 42°57N 93°23W **310** B3
Thornton Heath *U.K.* 51°23N 0°6W **125** B3
Thorntown *U.S.A.* 40°8N 86°36W **311** D10
Thorold *Canada* 43°7N 79°12W **312** C5
Thorpes *Barbados* 13°9N 59°37W **323** r
Þórshöfn *Iceland* 66°12N 15°20W **155** A11
Thouarcé *France* 47°17N 0°30W **172** E6
Thouars *France* 47°0N 0°15W **172** F6
Thouet → *France* 47°17N 0°6W **172** E6
Thouin, C. *Australia* 20°20S 118°10E **278** D2
Thousand Islands *U.S.A.* 44°20N 76°0W **313** B9
Thousand Oaks *U.S.A.* 34°10N 118°50W **307** L8
Thrace *Turkey* 41°0N 27°0E **203** F10
Thrace, Sea of *Greece* 40°30N 25°0E **203** F8
Thredbo *Australia* 36°31S 148°20E **283** D8
Three Forks *U.S.A.* 45°54N 111°33W **304** D8
Three Gorges Dam *China* 30°45N 111°15E **229** B8
Three Gorges Res. = Sanxia Shuiku *China* 30°10N 108°0E **219** C5
Three Hills *Canada* 51°43N 113°15W **296** C6
Three Hummock I. *Australia* 40°25S 144°55E **281** G3
Three Oaks *U.S.A.* 41°48N 86°36W **311** C10
Three Pagodas Pass *Asia* 15°20N 98°30E **236** E2
Three Points, C. *Ghana* 4°42N 2°6W **262** E4
Three Rivers *Calif., U.S.A.* 36°26N 118°54W **306** J8
Three Rivers *Mich., U.S.A.* 41°57N 85°38W **311** C11
Three Rivers *Tex., U.S.A.* 28°28N 98°11W **314** G5
Three Sisters Is. *Solomon Is.* 10°10S 161°57E **287** N11
Three Springs *Australia* 29°32S 115°45E **279** E2
Threipmuir Res. *U.K.* 55°51N 3°19W **121** B2
Thrissur = Trichur *India* 10°30N 76°18E **245** J3
Throgs Neck *U.S.A.* 40°48N 73°49W **132** B3
Throssell, L. *Australia* 27°33S 124°10E **279** E3
Throssell Ra. *Australia* 22°3S 121°43E **278** D3
Thrumshing △ *Bhutan* 27°25N 90°50E **241** B3
Thrushton △ *Australia* 27°47S 147°40E **281** D4
Thua → *Kenya* 1°31S 39°30E **268** C4
Thuamal Rampur *India* 19°23N 82°56E **244** E6
Thuan Hoa *Vietnam* 8°58N 105°30E **237** H5
Thubun Lakes *Canada* 61°30N 112°0W **297** A6
Thueyts *France* 44°41N 4°9E **175** D8
Thuin *Belgium* 50°20N 4°17E **170** D4
Thuir *France* 42°38N 2°45E **174** F6
Thule = Qaanaaq *Greenland* 77°30N 69°10W **154** B4
Thule Air Base = Uummannaq *Greenland* 77°33N 68°52W **154** B4
Thun *Switz.* 46°45N 7°38E **179** J3
Thunder B. *U.S.A.* 45°0N 83°20W **312** B1
Thunder Bay *Canada* 48°20N 89°15W **298** C2
Thunderbolt *U.S.A.* 32°3N 81°4W **316** C8
Thunersee *Switz.* 46°43N 7°39E **179** J3
Thung Salaeng Luang △ *Thailand* 16°43N 100°50E **236** D3
Thung Song *Thailand* 8°10N 99°40E **237** H2
Thunkar *Bhutan* 27°55N 91°0E **241** B3
Thuong Tra *Vietnam* 16°2N 107°42E **236** D6
Thur → *Switz.* 47°32N 9°10E **179** H5
Thurgau □ *Switz.* 47°34N 9°10E **179** H5
Thüringen □ *Germany* 51°0N 11°0E **178** D6
Thüringer Wald *Germany* 50°35N 11°0E **178** E6
Thuringowa △ *Australia* 19°18S 146°43E **280** B4
Thurles *Ireland* 52°41N 7°49W **166** D4
Thurn P. *Austria* 47°20N 12°25E **180** D5
Thurrock □ *U.K.* 51°31N 0°23E **169** F8
Thursday I. *Australia* 10°30S 142°3E **280** F2
Thurso *Qué., Canada* 45°36N 75°15W **298** C4
Thurso *Highl., U.K.* 58°36N 3°32W **167** C5
Thurso → *U.K.* 58°36N 3°32W **167** C5
Thurston I. *Antarctica* 72°0S 100°0W **151** D16
Thury-Harcourt *France* 48°59N 0°30W **172** D6
Thutade L. *Canada* 57°0N 126°55W **296** B3
Thy *Denmark* 56°52N 8°25E **163** H2
Thyborøn *Denmark* 56°42N 8°12E **163** H2
Þykkvabæjarklaustur *Iceland* 63°30N 18°22W **155** D8
Þykkvibær *Iceland* 63°45N 20°37W **155** D6
Thyolo *Malawi* 16°7S 35°5E **269** F4
Thyssen-Bornemisza, Museo *Madrid, Spain* **127** b3
Ti-n-Amzi → *Niger* 18°20N 4°32E **263** B5
Ti-n-Barraouene, O. → *Africa* 18°40N 4°5E **261** E5
Ti-n-Rerhoh *Algeria* 20°44N 4°2E **261** D5
Ti-n-Tanetfirt *Algeria* 24°49N 3°48E **261** D5
Ti-n-Tarabine, O. → *Algeria* 21°16N 7°25E **261** D6
Ti-n-Toumma *Niger* 16°4N 12°40E **259** E2
Ti-n-Zaouatene *Algeria* 19°55N 2°55E **261** E5
Ti-Tree *Australia* 22°5S 133°22E **280** C1
Tiadiaye *Senegal* 14°25N 16°40W **262** C1
Tiahuanacu *Bolivia* 16°33S 68°42W **330** D4
Tian Shan *Asia* 40°30N 76°0E **217** D9
Tian'anmen Square *Beijing, China* **114** c2
Tianchang *China* 32°40N 119°0E **229** A12
Tiancun *China* 39°54N 116°12E **114** B1
Tiandeng *China* 23°6N 107°7E **228** F6
Tiandong *China* 23°36N 107°8E **228** F6
Tian'e *China* 25°1N 107°9E **228** E6
Tianguá *Brazil* 3°44S 40°59W **332** B3
Tianhe *Guangdong, China* 23°7N 113°21E **121** B3
Tianhe *Guangxi Zhuangzu, China* 24°48N 108°40E **228** E7
Tianjin *China* 39°7N 117°12E **227** E9
Tiankoura *Burkina Faso* 10°47N 3°17W **262** C4
Tianlin *China* 24°21N 106°12E **228** E6
Tianmen *China* 30°39N 113°9E **229** B9
Tianquan *China* 30°7N 102°43E **228** B4
Tianshifu *China* 41°17N 124°22E **224** B2
Tianshui *China* 34°32N 105°40E **226** G3
Tiantai *China* 29°10N 121°2E **229** C13
Tiantan Park *Beijing, China* **114** c3
Tianyang *China* 23°42N 106°53E **228** F6
Tianyar *Indonesia* 8°12S 115°30E **231** J18
Tianzhen *China* 40°24N 114°5E **226** D8
Tianzhu *China* 26°54N 109°11E **228** D7
Tianzhuangtai *China* 40°43N 122°5E **227** D12
Tiarei *Tahiti* 17°32S 149°20W **289** e
Tiaret *Algeria* 35°20N 1°21E **261** A5
Tiaret □ *Algeria* 34°30N 1°30E **261** B5
Tias *Canary Is.* 28°57N 13°39W **153** e2
Tiassalé *Ivory C.* 5°58N 4°57W **262** D4
Tibagi *Brazil* 24°30S 50°24W **335** A5
Tibagi → *Brazil* 22°47S 51°1W **335** A5
Tibastī, Sarīr *Libya* 22°50N 18°30E **258** D3
Tibati *Cameroon* 6°22N 12°30E **263** D7
Tibe *Ethiopia* 9°2N 37°12E **257** F4
Tiber = Tevere → *Italy* 41°44N 12°14E **199** G9
Tiber Res. *U.S.A.* 48°19N 111°6W **304** B8
Tiberias = Teverya *Israel* 32°47N 35°32E **250** F6
Tiberias, L. = Yam Kinneret *Israel* 32°45N 35°35E **250** F6
Tibesti *Chad* 21°0N 17°30E **258** D3
Tibet = Xizang Zizhiqu □ *China* 32°0N 88°0E **217** F11
Tibet, L. *U.S.A.* 28°27N 81°31W **133** B1
Tibet, Plateau of *Asia* 32°0N 86°0E **210** E10
Tibiao *Phil.* 11°17N 122°2E **233** F4
Tibidabo *Spain* 41°25N 2°6E **114** A1
Tibiri *Niger* 13°34N 7°4E **263** C6
Ţibleş, Vf. *Romania* 47°32N 24°15E **183** C9
Ţibleşului, Munţii *Romania* 47°38N 24°5E **183** C9
Tibnī *Syria* 35°36N 39°50E **213** E8
Tibooburra *Australia* 29°26S 142°1E **281** D3
Tibradden Mt. *Ireland* 53°15N 6°16W **120** B2
Tibro *Sweden* 58°28N 14°10E **163** F8
Tiburon *U.S.A.* 37°52N 122°27W **136** A2
Tiburón, I. *Mexico* 29°0N 112°25W **318** B2
Tiburtino *Italy* 41°53N 12°30E **136** B2
Ticao I. *Phil.* 12°31N 123°42E **232** E4
Tice *U.S.A.* 26°40N 81°49W **317** J8
Tîchît *Mauritania* 18°21N 9°29W **262** B3
Tichla *Mauritania* 21°36N 14°58W **260** D2
Ticho *Ethiopia* 7°50N 39°32E **257** F4
Ticino □ *Switz.* 46°20N 8°45E **179** J4
Ticino → *Italy* 45°9N 9°14E **179** J4
Ticleni *Romania* 44°53N 23°24E **183** F8
Ticomán *Mexico* 19°31N 99°8W **128** A2
Ticonderoga *U.S.A.* 43°51N 73°26W **313** C11
Ticul *Mexico* 20°24N 89°32W **319** C7
Tidaholm *Sweden* 58°12N 13°58E **163** F7
Tidal Basin *Washington, D.C., U.S.A.* **143** c1
Tidan *Sweden* 58°34N 14°1E **163** F8
Tiddim *Burma* 23°28N 93°45E **241** D4
Tiden *India* 7°15N 93°33E **245** L11
Tideridjaouine, Adrar *Algeria* 23°0N 2°15E **261** D5
Tidikelt *Algeria* 26°58N 1°30E **261** C5
Tidioute *U.S.A.* 41°41N 79°24W **312** E5
Tidjikja *Mauritania* 18°29N 11°35W **262** B2
Tidmore = Seminole *U.S.A.* 35°14N 96°41W **314** D6
Tidore *Indonesia* 0°40N 127°25E **231** D7
Tiébissou *Ivory C.* 7°9N 5°10W **262** D3
Tiéboro *Chad* 21°20N 17°7E **259** D3
Tiefa *China* 42°28N 123°26E **224** A1
Tiefersee *Germany* 52°24N 13°5E **115** B1
Tiegang Shuiku *China* 22°37N 113°53E **219** F10
Tiel *Neths.* 51°53N 5°26E **170** C5
Tiel *Senegal* 14°55N 15°5W **262** C1
Tieling *China* 42°20N 123°55E **224** A1
Tielt *Belgium* 51°0N 3°20E **170** C3
Tien Shan = Tian Shan *Asia* 40°30N 76°0E **217** D9
Tien-tsin = Tianjin *China* 39°7N 117°12E **227** E9
Tien Yen *Vietnam* 21°20N 107°24E **236** B6
T'ienching = Tianjin *China* 39°7N 117°12E **227** E9
T'ienchung *Taiwan* 23°52N 120°35E **225** C2
Tienen *Belgium* 50°48N 4°57E **170** D4
Tiéningbé *Ivory C.* 8°11N 5°43W **262** D3
Tientsin = Tianjin *China* 39°7N 117°12E **227** E9
Tiergarten *Germany* 52°31N 13°20E **115** A3
Tieri *Australia* 23°2S 148°21E **280** C4
Tieroko, Tarso *Chad* 20°45N 17°52E **259** D3
Tierp *Sweden* 60°20N 17°30E **162** D11
Tierra Amarilla *Chile* 27°28S 70°18W **334** B1
Tierra Amarilla *N. Mex., U.S.A.* 36°42N 106°33W **305** H10
Tierra Colorada *Mexico* 17°11N 99°32W **319** D5
Tierra de Barros *Spain* 38°40N 6°30W **195** G4
Tierra de Campos *Spain* 42°10N 4°50W **194** C6
Tierra del Fuego □ *Argentina* 54°0S 67°45W **336** D3
Tierra del Fuego, I. Grande de *Argentina* 54°0S 69°0W **336** D3
Tierra del Fuego △ *Argentina* 54°50S 68°23W **336** D3
Tierralta *Colombia* 8°11N 76°4W **328** B2
Tiétar → *Spain* 39°50N 6°1W **194** F4
Tieté → *Brazil* 20°40S 51°35W **335** A5
Tifarati *W. Sahara* 26°9N 10°33W **260** C2
Tiffin *U.S.A.* 41°7N 83°11W **311** C13
Tiffin → *U.S.A.* 41°17N 84°23W **311** C12
Tiflèt *Morocco* 33°54N 6°20W **260** B3
Tiflis = Tbilisi *Georgia* 41°43N 44°50E **191** K7
Tifton *U.S.A.* 31°27N 83°31W **316** D6
Tifu *Indonesia* 3°39S 126°24E **231** E7
Tiga, Î. *N. Cal.* 21°7S 167°49E **288** d
Tiga Res. *Nigeria* 11°35N 8°30E **263** C6
Tigalda I. *U.S.A.* 54°6N 165°5W **303** J6
Tigaon *Phil.* 13°38N 123°30E **232** E4
Tigbauan *Phil.* 10°41N 122°27E **233** F4
Tighina *Moldova* 46°50N 29°30E **183** D14
Tigil *Russia* 57°49N 158°40E **215** D16
Tigiria *India* 20°29N 85°31E **244** D7
Tignall *U.S.A.* 33°52N 82°44W **316** B7
Tignish *Canada* 46°58N 64°2W **299** C7
Tigray □ *Ethiopia* 13°35N 39°15E **257** E4
Tigre → *Peru* 4°30S 74°10W **328** D3
Tigre → *Venezuela* 9°20N 62°30W **329** B5
Tigris = Dijlah, Nahr → *Asia* 31°0N 47°25E **246** D5
Tiguentourine *Algeria* 27°52N 9°8E **261** C6
Tigveni *Romania* 45°10N 24°31E **183** E9
Tigyaing *Burma* 23°45N 96°10E **241** D6
Tigzerte, O. → *Morocco* 28°10N 9°37W **260** C3
Tih, Gebel el *Egypt* 29°32N 33°26E **256** B3
Tihodaine, Erg de *Algeria* 25°15N 7°15E **261** C6
Tihwa = Ürümqi *China* 43°45N 87°45E **217** D11
Tijara *India* 27°56N 76°31E **242** F7
Tijgerhof *S. Africa* 33°53S 18°30E **118** A2
Tījī *Libya* 32°0N 11°18E **258** B2
Tijuana *Mexico* 32°32N 117°1W **307** N9
Tijuca *Brazil* 22°56S 43°13W **135** B1
Tijuca, Pico da *Brazil* 22°56S 43°17W **135** B1
Tijuca △ *Brazil* 22°56S 43°14W **135** B1
Tikahau *French Polynesia* 15°0S 148°10W **289** f
Tikal *Guatemala* 17°13N 89°24W **320** C2
Tikamgarh *India* 24°44N 78°50E **243** G8
Tikaré *Burkina Faso* 13°15N 1°43W **263** C4
Tikchik Lakes *U.S.A.* 60°0N 159°0W **303** G8
Tikéi *French Polynesia* 14°58S 144°32W **289** f
Tikhonkaya = Birobidzhan *Russia* 48°50N 132°50E **215** E14
Tikhoretsk *Russia* 45°56N 40°5E **191** H5
Tikhvin *Russia* 59°35N 33°30E **188** C7
Tikirarjuaq = Whale Cove *Canada* 62°10N 92°34W **297** A10
Tikkadouine, Adrar *Algeria* 24°28N 1°30E **261** D5
Tikkurila *Finland* 60°17N 25°2E **121** B3
Tikmehdāsh *Iran* 37°16N 46°54E **213** D12
Tiko *Cameroon* 4°4N 9°20E **263** E6
Tikopia *Pac. Oc.* 12°19S 168°49E **277** C12
Tikrīt *Iraq* 34°35N 43°37E **213** E10
Tiksi *Russia* 71°40N 128°45E **215** B13
Tiladummati Atoll *Maldives* 7°0N 73°20E **272** d
Tilak Nagar *India* 28°38N 77°5E **120** B1
Tilamuta *Indonesia* 0°32N 122°23E **231** D6
Tilanqiao *China* 31°15N 121°29E **138** B1
Tilburg *Neths.* 51°31N 5°6E **170** C5
Tilbury *Ont., Canada* 42°17N 82°23W **312** D2
Tilbury *Essex, U.K.* 51°27N 0°22E **169** F8
Tilcara *Argentina* 23°36S 65°23W **334** A2
Tilden *U.S.A.* 42°3N 97°50W **308** D5
Tilemsi, Vallée du *Mali* 17°42N 0°15E **263** B5
Tilhar *India* 28°0N 79°45E **243** F8
Tilia, O. → *Algeria* 27°32N 0°55E **261** C5
Tilichiki *Russia* 60°27N 166°5E **215** C17
Tililane *Algeria* 27°49N 0°6W **261** C4
Tilin *Burma* 21°41N 94°6E **241** E5
Tilissos *Greece* 35°20N 25°1E **207** E6
Till → *U.K.* 55°41N 2°13W **168** B5
Tillabéri *Niger* 14°28N 1°28E **263** C5
Tillamook *U.S.A.* 45°27N 123°51W **304** D2
Tillanchong I. *India* 8°30N 93°37E **245** K11
Tillberga *Sweden* 59°40N 16°39E **162** E10
Tillia *Niger* 16°8N 4°47E **263** B5
Tillman *U.S.A.* 32°28N 81°6W **316** C8
Tillsonburg *Canada* 42°53N 80°44W **312** D4
Tillyeria *Cyprus* 35°6N 32°40E **207** E8
Tilogne *Senegal* 16°0N 13°40W **262** B2
Tilos *Greece* 36°27N 27°27E **205** E9
Tilpa *Australia* 30°57S 144°24E **282** A6
Tilrhemt *Algeria* 33°9N 3°22E **261** B5
Tilsit = Sovetsk *Russia* 55°6N 21°50E **184** C8
Tilt → *U.K.* 56°46N 3°51W **167** E5
Tilton *U.S.A.* 43°27N 71°36W **313** C13
Tiltonsville *U.S.A.* 40°10N 80°41W **312** F4
Tim *Denmark* 56°12N 8°19E **163** H2
Tima *Egypt* 26°54N 31°25E **256** B3
Timah, Bukit *Singapore* 1°21N 103°46E **138** A2
Timanah *Asia* 19°0N 41°0E **248** C3
Timanfaya △ *Canary Is.* 29°0N 13°46W **153** e2
Timanskiy Kryazh *Russia* 65°58N 50°5E **186** A9
Timaru *N.Z.* 44°23S 171°14E **285** E6
Timashevo *Russia* 53°22N 51°9E **190** D10
Timashevsk *Russia* 45°35N 39°0E **191** H4
Timau *Kenya* 0°4N 37°15E **268** B4
Timbaki *Greece* 35°4N 24°45E **207** E5
Timbaúba *Brazil* 7°31S 35°19W **332** C4
Timbedgha *Mauritania* 16°17N 8°16W **262** B3
Timber Creek *Australia* 15°40S 130°29E **278** C5
Timber Lake *U.S.A.* 45°26N 101°5W **308** C3
Timber Mt. *U.S.A.* 37°6N 116°28W **306** H10

Timbio Colombia 2°20N 76°40W 328 C2
Timbiquí Colombia 2°46N 77°42W 328 C2
Timbo Guinea 10°35N 11°50W 262 C2
Timbo Liberia 5°35N 9°45W 262 D3
Timboon Australia 38°30S 142°58E 282 E5
Timbué, Ponta Mozam. 18°47S 36°22E 269 F4
Timbuktu = Tombouctou Mali 16°50N 3°0W 262 B4
Timdjaouine Algeria 21°37N 4°30E 261 D5
Timeïaouine Algeria 20°27N 1°50E 261 D5
Timellouline Algeria 29°22N 8°55E 261 C6
Times Square New York, U.S.A. 132 c2
Timétrin Mali 19°19N 0°34W 263 B4
Timétrine, Mts. Mali 19°25N 1°0W 263 B4
Timfi Oros Greece 39°59N 20°45E 204 B2
Timfristos, Oros Greece 38°57N 21°50E 204 C3
Timgad Algeria 35°29N 6°28E 261 A6
Timhadit Morocco 33°15N 5°4W 260 B3
Timi Cyprus 34°44N 32°31E 207 F8
Timia Niger 18°4N 8°40E 259 E1
Timimoun Algeria 29°14N 0°16E 261 C5
Timimoun, Sebkha de Algeria 28°50N 0°46E 261 C5
Timiris, Râs Mauritania 19°21N 16°30W 262 B1
Timiryazev Park Russia 55°49N 37°33E 129 B3
Timiş = Tamis → Serbia 44°51N 20°39E 182 F5
Timiş □ Romania 45°40N 21°30E 182 E6
Timiskaming, L. = Témiscamingue, L. Canada 47°10N 79°25W 298 C4
Timişoara Romania 45°43N 21°15E 182 E6
Timmersdala Sweden 58°32N 13°46E 163 F7
Timmins Canada 48°28N 81°25W 298 C3
Timmonsville U.S.A. 34°8N 79°57W 316 A10
Timok → Serbia 44°10N 22°40E 202 B6
Timoleague Ireland 51°39N 8°46W 166 E3
Timon Brazil 5°8S 42°52W 332 C3
Timor Asia 9°0S 125°0E 231 F7
Timor Leste = East Timor ■ Asia 8°50S 126°0E 231 F7
Timor Sea Ind. Oc. 12°0S 127°0E 278 B4
Timrå Sweden 62°29N 17°18E 162 B11
Timucuan ⌂ U.S.A. 30°28N 81°27W 316 E8
Tin, Ra's at Libya 32°37N 23°8E 258 B4
Tin Alkoum Algeria 24°42N 10°17E 261 D7
Tin Amzi, O. → Algeria 18°20N 4°32E 261 D6
Tin Atanai Algeria 25°52N 1°37E 261 C5
Tin Can Bay Australia 25°56S 153°0E 281 D5
Tin Can I. Nigeria 6°26N 3°21E 124 B2
Tin Ethisane Mali 19°3N 0°52W 263 B4
Tin Gornai Mali 16°38N 0°38W 263 B4
Tin Mt. U.S.A. 36°50N 117°10W 306 J9
Tina = Thina → S. Africa 31°18S 29°13E 271 D4
Tîna, Khalîg el Egypt 31°10N 32°40E 251 G3
Tinaca Pt. Phil. 5°30N 125°25E 233 J5
Tinaco Venezuela 9°42N 68°26W 328 B4
Tinajo Canary Is. 29°4N 13°42W 153 e2
Tinca Romania 46°46N 21°58E 182 D6
Tindal Australia 14°31S 132°22E 278 B5
Tindivanam India 12°15N 79°41E 245 H4
Tindouf Algeria 27°42N 8°10W 260 C3
Tindouf □ Algeria 27°25N 5°50W 260 C3
Tinée → France 43°55N 7°11E 175 E11
Tineo Spain 43°21N 6°27W 194 B4
Tinerhir Morocco 31°29N 5°31W 260 B3
Tinfouchi Algeria 28°52N 5°49W 260 C3
Tinfunque △ Paraguay 23°55S 60°17W 334 A3
Ting Jiang → China 24°45N 116°35E 229 E11
Ting Kau China 22°22N 114°4E 122 A1
Tinggi, Pulau Malaysia 2°18N 104°7E 237 L5
Tinghert, Ḥamâdat Libya 29°0N 9°0E 258 C1
Tingi Mts. S. Leone 8°55N 10°47W 262 D2
Tingkan Taiwan 23°48N 120°52E 225 C2
Tingkawk Sakan Burma 26°4N 96°44E 241 B6
Tinglayan Phil. 17°15N 121°9E 232 C3
Tinglev Denmark 54°57N 9°13E 163 K3
Tingmerkpuk Mt. U.S.A. 68°34N 162°28W 303 B7
Tingo María Peru 9°10S 75°54W 330 B2
Tingrela Ivory C. 10°27N 6°25W 262 C3
Tingsryd Sweden 56°31N 15°0E 163 H9
Tingstäde Sweden 57°44N 18°37E 163 G12
Tingvoll Norway 62°55N 8°12E 164 B5
Tingwon Group Papua N. G. 2°37S 149°42E 286 B5
Tinh Bien Vietnam 10°36N 104°57E 237 G5
Tinharé, I. de Brazil 13°30S 38°58W 333 D4
Tinian N. Marianas 15°0N 145°38E 302 e
Tinian Channel N. Marianas 14°54N 145°36E 302 e
Tinigua △ Colombia 2°30N 74°8W 328 C3
Tiniguiban Phil. 11°22N 119°30E 233 F2
Tinjar → Malaysia 4°4N 114°18E 235 B4
Tinkisso → Guinea 11°21N 9°10W 262 C3
Tinn = Atrå Norway 59°59N 8°45E 164 E5
Tinnevelly = Tirunelveli India 8°45N 77°45E 245 K3
Tinnoset Norway 59°43N 9°3E 164 E6
Tinnsjå Norway 59°55N 8°54E 164 E5
Tinogasta Argentina 28°5S 67°32W 334 B2
Tinos Greece 37°33N 25°8E 205 D7
Tiñoso, C. Spain 37°32N 1°6W 197 H3
Tinpahar India 24°59N 87°44E 243 G12
Tinputz Papua N. G. 5°33S 155°0E 286 C8
Tinrhert, Plateau du Algeria 29°30N 9°0E 258 C1
Tinsukia India 27°29N 95°20E 241 B5
Tinta Peru 14°3S 71°20W 330 C3
Tintamarre, Île St.-Martin 18°7N 63°2W 322 a
Tintâne Mauritania 16°18N 10°10W 262 B2
Tintina Argentina 27°2S 62°45W 334 B3
Tintinara Australia 35°48S 140°2E 282 C4
Tintioulé Guinea 10°13N 9°12W 262 C3
Tinto → Spain 37°12N 6°55W 195 H4
Tinui N.Z. 40°52S 176°5E 284 G5
Tinwald N.Z. 43°55S 171°43E 285 D6
Tiobraid Árran = Tipperary Ireland 52°28N 8°10W 166 D3
Tioga N. Dak., U.S.A. 48°24N 102°56W 308 A2
Tioga Pa., U.S.A. 41°55N 77°8W 312 E7
Tioman, Pulau Malaysia 2°50N 104°10E 237 L5
Tione di Trento Italy 46°2N 10°43E 198 B7
Tionesta U.S.A. 41°30N 79°28W 312 E5
Tior Sudan 6°26N 31°11E 257 F3
Tiouliline Algeria 27°1N 0°2W 261 C4
Tipaza Algeria 36°35N 2°26E 261 A5
Tipaza □ Algeria 36°35N 2°25E 261 A5
Tipitapa Nic. 12°12N 86°5W 320 D2
Tipp City U.S.A. 39°58N 84°11W 311 E12
Tippecanoe → U.S.A. 40°30N 86°45W 311 D10
Tipperary Ireland 52°28N 8°10W 166 D3
Tipperary □ Ireland 52°37N 7°55W 166 D4
Tipton Calif., U.S.A. 36°4N 119°19W 306 J7
Tipton Ind., U.S.A. 40°17N 86°2W 311 D10
Tipton Iowa, U.S.A. 41°46N 91°8W 310 C5
Tipton Mo., U.S.A. 38°39N 92°47W 310 F4
Tipton Mt. U.S.A. 35°32N 114°12W 307 K12
Tiptonville U.S.A. 36°23N 89°29W 315 C10
Tiptur India 13°15N 76°26E 245 H3
Tiquié → Brazil 0°5N 68°25W 328 C4
Tiquina Bolivia 16°13S 68°50W 330 D4
Tira West Bank 31°52N 35°7E 123 A1
Tiracambu, Serra do Brazil 3°15S 46°30W 332 B2
Tirahart, O. → Algeria 23°45N 3°10E 261 D5
Tirān Iran 32°45N 51°8E 247 C6
Tirān Si. Arabia 27°57N 34°32E 251 L5
Tiranë Albania 41°18N 19°49E 202 E3
Tiranë ✕ (TIA) Albania 41°57N 19°42E 202 E3
Tirano Italy 46°13N 10°10E 198 B7
Tirari Desert Australia 28°22S 138°7E 281 D2
Tiraspol Moldova 46°55N 29°35E 183 D14
Tiratimine Algeria 25°56N 3°37E 261 C5
Tirau N.Z. 37°58S 175°46E 284 D4
Tirdout Mali 16°7N 1°5W 263 B4
Tire Turkey 38°5N 27°45E 205 C9
Tirebolu Turkey 40°58N 38°45E 213 B8
Tiree U.K. 56°31N 6°55W 167 E2
Tiree, Passage of U.K. 56°30N 6°30W 167 E2
Tîrgovişte = Târgovişte Romania 44°55N 25°27E 183 F10
Tîrgu Jiu = Târgu Jiu Romania 45°5N 23°19E 183 E8
Tîrgu Mureş = Târgu Mureş Romania 46°31N 24°38E 183 D9
Tirgua △ Venezuela 10°5N 68°48W 328 A4
Tirich Mir Pakistan 36°15N 71°55E 240 A3
Tiriolo Italy 38°57N 16°30E 201 D9
Tiririca, Serra da Brazil 17°6S 47°6W 333 E2
Tiriro Guinea 10°27N 8°40W 262 C3
Tiris Zemmour □ Mauritania 24°0N 9°0W 260 D3
Tiritiri o te Moana = Southern Alps N.Z. 43°41S 170°11E 285 E4
Tirna → India 18°4N 76°57E 244 E3
Tírnavos Greece 39°45N 22°18E 204 B4
Tirodi India 21°40N 79°44E 244 D4
Tirol □ Austria 47°3N 10°43E 180 D3
Tiros Brazil 19°0S 45°58W 333 E2
Tirrukkovil Sri Lanka 7°7N 81°51E 245 L5
Tirsa Egypt 29°57N 31°12E 117 B2
Tirschenreuth Germany 49°53N 12°19E 179 F8
Tirschtiegel = Trzciel Poland 52°23N 15°50E 185 F2
Tirso → Italy 39°53N 8°32E 200 C1
Tirstrup Denmark 56°18N 10°42E 163 H4
Tirthahalli India 13°42N 75°14E 245 H2
Tirua Pt. N.Z. 38°25S 174°40E 284 E3
Tiruchchendur India 8°30N 78°11E 245 K4
Tiruchchirappalli India 10°45N 78°45E 245 J4
Tirukkoyilur India 11°57N 79°12E 245 J4
Tirumangalam India 9°49N 77°58E 245 K3
Tirumayam India 10°14N 78°45E 245 J4
Tirunelveli India 8°45N 77°45E 245 K3
Tirupati India 13°39N 79°25E 245 H4
Tiruppattur Tamil Nadu, India 10°8N 78°37E 245 J4
Tiruppattur Tamil Nadu, India 12°30N 78°30E 245 H4
Tiruppur India 11°5N 77°22E 245 J3
Tirur India 10°54N 75°55E 245 J2
Tiruttani India 13°11N 79°58E 245 H4
Tirutturaippundi India 10°32N 79°41E 245 J4
Tiruvadaimarudur India 11°2N 79°27E 245 J4
Tiruvalla India 9°23N 76°34E 245 K3
Tiruvallur India 13°9N 79°57E 245 H4
Tiruvannamalai India 12°15N 79°5E 245 H4
Tiruvettipuram India 12°39N 79°33E 245 H4
Tiruvottiyur India 13°10N 80°22E 245 H5
Tisa India 32°50N 76°9E 242 C7
Tisa → Serbia 45°15N 20°17E 182 E5
Tisdale Canada 52°50N 104°0W 297 C8
Tishomingo U.S.A. 34°14N 96°41W 314 D6
Tishrīyaa Iraq 33°18N 44°24E 113 B2
Tisjön Sweden 60°56N 13°0E 162 D7
Tisnaren Sweden 58°58N 15°56E 163 F9
Tišnov Czech Rep. 49°21N 16°25E 181 B9
Tisovec Slovak Rep. 48°41N 19°56E 181 C12
Tissamaharama Sri Lanka 6°17N 81°17E 245 L5
Tissān, Ḥasy Libya 28°14N 12°26E 261 C7
Tissemsilt Algeria 35°35N 1°50E 261 A5
Tissemsilt □ Algeria 35°45N 1°45E 261 A5
Tissint Morocco 29°57N 7°16W 260 C3
Tista → India 25°23N 89°43E 241 C2
Tistedal Norway 59°8N 11°27E 164 E8
Tisza = Tisa → Serbia 45°15N 20°17E 182 E5
Tiszaföldvár Hungary 46°58N 20°14E 182 D5
Tiszafüred Hungary 47°38N 20°50E 182 C5
Tiszalök Hungary 48°1N 21°20E 182 B6
Tiszavasvári Hungary 47°58N 21°18E 182 C6
Tit Ahaggar, Algeria 23°0N 5°10E 261 D6
Tit Tademait, Algeria 27°0N 1°29E 261 C5
Tit-Ary Russia 71°55N 127°2E 215 B13
Titabar India 26°36N 94°12E 241 B5
Titaguas Spain 39°53N 1°6W 196 F3
Titao Burkina Faso 13°45N 2°5W 263 C4
Titel Serbia 45°10N 20°18E 182 E5
Tithwal Pakistan 34°21N 73°50E 243 B5
Titicaca, L. S. Amer. 15°30S 69°30W 330 D4
Titikaveka Cook Is. 21°16S 159°45W 289 h
Titisee Germany 47°54N 8°10E 179 H4
Tititira Hd. N.Z. 43°36S 169°25E 285 D4
Tititut Burma 18°54N 95°16E 241 F5
Titiwa Nigeria 12°14N 12°53E 263 C7
Titlagarh India 20°15N 83°11E 244 D6
Tito Italy 40°35N 15°40E 201 B8
Titograd = Podgorica Montenegro 42°30N 19°19E 202 D3
Titova Korenica Croatia 44°45N 15°41E 199 D12
Titu Romania 44°39N 25°32E 183 F10
Titule Dem. Rep. of the Congo 3°15N 25°31E 268 B2
Titusville Fla., U.S.A. 28°37N 80°49W 317 G9
Titusville Pa., U.S.A. 41°38N 79°41W 312 E5
Tiu Keng Leng China 22°18N 114°15E 122 B2
Tivaouane Senegal 14°56N 16°45W 262 C1
Tivat Montenegro 42°28N 18°43E 202 D2
Tivedens △ Sweden 58°45N 14°35E 163 F8
Tiverton Ont., Canada 44°16N 81°32W 312 B3
Tiverton Devon, U.K. 50°54N 3°29W 169 G4
Tivoli Grenada 12°10N 61°37W 323 q
Tivoli Italy 41°58N 12°45E 199 G9
Tiwi Oman 22°45N 59°12E 249 B7
Tiwi ✪ Australia 11°33S 130°42E 278 B5
Tiyo Eritrea 14°41N 40°15E 257 E5
Tizapán Mexico 19°19N 99°13W 128 C1
Tizga Morocco 32°1N 5°9W 260 B3
Ti'zi N'Isli Morocco 32°28N 5°47W 260 B3
Tizi-Ouzou Algeria 36°42N 4°3E 261 A5
Tizi-Ouzou □ Algeria 36°35N 4°5E 261 A5
Tizimín Mexico 21°9N 88°9W 319 C7
Tiznados → Venezuela 8°16N 67°47W 328 B4
Tiznap He → China 38°21N 77°26E 217 E9
Tiznit Morocco 29°48N 9°45W 260 C3
Tiznit □ Morocco 29°35N 9°30W 260 C3
Tjæreborg Denmark 55°28N 8°36E 163 J2
Tjällmo Sweden 58°43N 15°21E 163 F9
Tjeggelvas Sweden 66°37N 17°45E 160 C17
Tjieggelvas = Tjeggelvas Sweden 66°37N 17°45E 160 C17
Tjirebon = Cirebon Indonesia 6°45S 108°32E 235 D3
Tjirrkarli ✪ Australia 26°0S 125°28E 279 E4
Tjluring Indonesia 8°25S 114°13E 231 J17
Tjøme Norway 59°8N 10°26E 164 E7
Tjörn Sweden 58°0N 11°35E 163 F5
Tjukayirla Roadhouse Australia 27°9S 124°34E 279 E3
Tjurabalan ✪ Australia 19°50S 128°0E 278 C4
Tkibuli = Tqibuli Georgia 42°26N 43°0E 191 J6
Tkvarcheli = Tqvarcheli Georgia 42°47N 41°42E 191 J5
Tlacotalpan Mexico 18°37N 95°40W 319 D5
Tlahualilo de Zaragoza Mexico 26°7N 103°27W 318 B4
Tlalnepantla → Mexico 19°30N 99°18W 128 A1
Tlalpan Mexico 19°18N 99°10W 128 C2
Tlaquepaque Mexico 20°39N 103°19W 318 C4
Tlaxcala Mexico 19°19N 98°14W 319 D5
Tlaxcala □ Mexico 19°25N 98°10W 319 D5
Tlaxiaco Mexico 17°25N 97°35W 319 D5
Tlemcen Algeria 34°52N 1°21W 261 B4
Tlemcen □ Algeria 34°38N 1°30W 261 B4
Tleta Sidi Bouguedra Morocco 32°16N 9°59W 260 B3
Tlokweng Botswana 24°40S 25°58E 270 B4
Tlumach Ukraine 48°51N 25°0E 183 B10
Tłuszcz Poland 52°25N 21°25E 185 F8
Tlyarata Russia 42°9N 46°26E 191 J8
Tmassah Libya 26°19N 15°51E 258 C3
To Bong Vietnam 12°45N 109°16E 236 F7
To Kwai Wan China 22°18N 114°11E 122 B2
To-Shima Japan 34°31N 139°17E 223 C11
Toa Payoh Singapore 1°20N 103°51E 138 A3
Toad → Canada 59°25N 124°57W 296 B4
Toad River Canada 58°51N 125°14W 296 B3
Toamasina Madag. 18°10S 49°25E 272 B2
Toamasina □ Madag. 18°0S 49°0E 272 B2
Toay Argentina 36°43S 64°38W 334 D3
Toba China 31°19N 97°42E 228 B1
Toba Japan 34°30N 136°51E 223 C8
Toba, Danau Indonesia 2°30N 97°30E 234 B1
Toba Kakar Pakistan 31°30N 69°0E 242 D3
Toba Tek Singh Pakistan 30°55N 72°25E 242 D5
Tobago Trin. & Tob. 11°10N 60°30W 323 s
Tobarra Spain 38°37N 1°44W 197 G3
Tobelo Indonesia 1°45N 127°56E 231 D7
Tobermory Ont., Canada 45°12N 81°40W 312 A3
Tobermory Argyll & Bute, U.K. 56°38N 6°5W 167 E2
Tobi Pac. Oc. 2°40N 131°10E 231 D8
Tobi-Shima Japan 41°12N 139°34E 220 D9
Tobias Fornier Phil. 10°30N 121°57E 233 F3
Tobiishi Hana Iwo Jima 24°45N 141°17E 288 b
Tobin, L. Australia 21°45S 125°49E 278 D4
Tobin L. Canada 53°35N 103°30W 297 C8
Toblach = Dobbiaco Italy 46°44N 12°14E 199 B9
Toboali Indonesia 3°0S 106°25E 234 C3
Tobol → Russia 58°10N 68°12E 214 D7
Toboli Indonesia 0°38S 120°5E 231 E6
Tobolsk Russia 58°15N 68°10E 214 D7
Tobor Senegal 12°40N 16°15W 262 C1
Toboso Phil. 10°43N 123°31E 233 F4
Tobruk = Tubruq Libya 32°7N 23°55E 258 B4
Tobyhanna U.S.A. 41°11N 75°25W 313 E9
Tobyl = Tobol → Russia 58°10N 68°12E 214 D7
Tobyl Kazakhstan 52°41N 62°34E 216 B6
Tocache Nuevo Peru 8°9S 76°26W 330 B2
Tocantínia Brazil 9°33S 48°22W 332 C2
Tocantinópolis Brazil 6°20S 47°25W 332 C2
Tocantins □ Brazil 10°0S 48°0W 332 D2
Tocantins → Brazil 1°45S 49°10W 332 B2
Toccoa U.S.A. 34°35N 83°19W 315 D13
Toce → Italy 45°56N 8°29E 198 C5
Tochi → Pakistan 32°49N 70°41E 242 C4
Tochigi Japan 36°25N 139°45E 223 A11
Tochigi □ Japan 36°45N 139°45E 223 A11
Tocina Spain 37°37N 5°44W 195 H5
Töcksfors Sweden 59°31N 11°52E 162 E5
Točná Czech Rep. 49°58N 14°25E 135 C2
Toco Chile 22°5S 69°35W 330 E4
Toco Trin. & Tob. 10°49N 60°57W 323 t
Toco Hills U.S.A. 33°49N 84°20W 113 B2
Toconao Chile 23°11S 68°1W 334 A2
Tocopilla Chile 22°5S 70°10W 334 A1
Tocqueville = Râs el Oued Algeria 35°57N 5°2E 261 A6
Tocumwal Australia 35°51S 145°31E 283 C6
Tocuyo → Venezuela 11°3N 68°23W 328 A4
Tocuyo de la Costa Venezuela 11°2N 68°23W 328 A4
Todalen Norway 62°49N 8°44E 164 B5
Todd → Australia 24°52S 135°48E 280 C2
Todds Road Trin. & Tob. 10°28N 61°20W 323 t
Toddu Atoll Maldives 4°25N 72°57E 272 d
Todeli Indonesia 1°40S 124°29E 231 E6
Todenyang Kenya 4°35N 35°56E 268 B4
Todgarh India 25°42N 73°58E 242 G5
Todi Italy 42°47N 12°24E 199 F9
Todos os Santos, B. de Brazil 12°48S 38°38W 333 D4
Todos Santos Mexico 23°26N 110°13W 318 C2
Todt Hill U.S.A. 40°36N 74°6W 132 C1
Todtnau Germany 47°49N 7°56E 179 H3
Toe Hd. U.K. 57°50N 7°8W 167 D1
Toecé Burkina Faso 11°50N 1°16W 263 C4
Toekomstig Stuwmeer Suriname 4°45N 57°30W 329 C6
Toetoes B. N.Z. 46°42S 168°41E 285 G3
Tofield Canada 53°25N 112°40W 296 C6
Tofino Canada 49°11N 125°55W 296 D3
Töfsingdalens △ Sweden 62°10N 12°28E 162 B6
Tofte Norway 59°33N 10°34E 164 E7
Tofua Tonga 19°45S 175°5W 287 P13
Toga Vanuatu 13°26S 166°42E 287 C4
Tōgane Japan 35°33N 140°22E 223 B12
Togba Mauritania 17°26N 10°12W 262 B2
Togbo C.A.R. 6°0N 17°27E 264 A3
Togdheer □ Somali Rep. 9°20N 45°25E 267 C6
Togdheer → Somali Rep. 6°26N 48°39E 267 C6
Togiak U.S.A. 59°4N 160°24W 303 G7
Togiak Nat. Wildlife Refuge ⌂ U.S.A. 59°20N 160°15W 303 G7
Togian, Kepulauan Indonesia 0°20S 121°50E 231 E6
Togliatti Russia 53°32N 49°24E 190 D9
Togo ■ W. Afr. 8°30N 1°35E 263 D5
Togo Wichale Somali Rep. 9°22N 43°40E 267 C5
Tögrög Mongolia 47°25N 92°13E 217 C12
Togtoh China 40°15N 111°10E 226 D6
Tohiea, Mt. Moorea 17°33S 149°49W 289 e
Tohma → Turkey 38°29N 38°23E 212 C8
Tōhoku □ Japan 39°50N 141°45E 220 E10
Töhöm Mongolia 44°27N 108°2E 226 B5
Tohopekaliga, East L. U.S.A. 28°18N 81°15W 317 G8
Tohopekaliga, L. U.S.A. 28°12N 81°24W 317 G8
Toi Cook Is. 18°57S 169°51W 289 g
Toi Japan 34°54N 138°47E 223 C10
Toibalewe India 10°32N 92°30E 245 J11
Toiny St.-Martin 17°53N 62°47W 322 a
Toinya Sudan 6°17N 29°46E 257 F2
Toiyabe Range U.S.A. 39°30N 117°0W 304 G5
Tojikiston = Tajikistan ■ Asia 38°30N 70°0E 217 E8
Tojo Indonesia 1°20S 121°15E 231 E6
Tōjō Japan 34°53N 133°16E 222 C5
Tok U.S.A. 63°20N 142°59W 303 E12
Toka Guyana 3°58N 59°17W 329 C6
Tokaanu N.Z. 38°58S 175°46E 284 E4
Tokachi-Dake Japan 43°17N 142°5E 220 C11
Tokachi-Gawa → Japan 42°44N 143°42E 220 C11
Tōkagi Japan 35°42N 139°55E 140 A4
Tokai Japan 35°2N 136°55E 223 B8
Tokai Plantation S. Africa 34°3S 18°24E 118 B1
Tōkaichiba Japan 35°31N 139°30E 140 B2
Tokaj Hungary 48°8N 21°27E 182 B6
Tokala Indonesia 1°30S 121°40E 231 E6
Tōkamachi Japan 37°8N 138°43E 221 F9
Tokanui N.Z. 46°34S 168°56E 285 G3
Tokar Sudan 18°27N 37°56E 256 D4
Tokara-Rettō Japan 29°37N 129°43E 221 K4
Tokarahi N.Z. 44°56S 170°39E 285 E5
Tokarevo Russia 55°38N 37°54E 129 C5
Tokashiki-Shima Japan 26°11N 127°21E 221 L3
Tokat Turkey 40°22N 36°35E 212 B7
Tokat □ Turkey 40°15N 36°30E 212 B7
Tŏkch'ŏn N. Korea 39°45N 126°18E 224 C3
Tokdo Asia 37°15N 131°52E 221 F5
Tokeland U.S.A. 46°42N 123°59W 306 D3
Tokelau Is. Pac. Oc. 9°0S 171°45W 277 B16
Toki Japan 35°18N 137°8E 223 B9
Toki Pt. Wake I. 19°19N 166°35E 302 b
Tokmak Kyrgyzstan 42°49N 75°15E 217 D9
Tokmak Ukraine 47°16N 35°42E 189 J8
Toko Ra. Australia 23°5S 138°20E 280 C2
Tokomaru Bay N.Z. 38°8S 178°22E 284 E7
Tokoname Japan 34°53N 136°51E 223 C8
Tokoro-Gawa → Japan 44°7N 144°5E 220 B12
Tokoroa N.Z. 38°13S 175°50E 284 E4
Tokorozawa Japan 35°47N 139°28E 223 B11
Toksook Bay U.S.A. 60°32N 165°0W 303 F6
Toksun China 42°47N 88°38E 217 D11
Toktogul Kyrgyzstan 41°50N 72°50E 217 D8
Toku Tonga 18°10S 174°11W 287 P13
Tokuji Japan 34°11N 131°42E 222 C3
Tokuno-Shima Japan 27°56N 128°55E 221 L4
Tokushima Japan 34°4N 134°34E 222 C6
Tokushima □ Japan 33°55N 134°0E 222 D6
Tokuyama Japan 34°3N 131°50E 222 C3
Tōkyō Japan 35°43N 139°45E 140 B3
Tōkyō □ Japan 35°40N 139°30E 223 B11
Tōkyō B. = Tōkyō-Wan Japan 35°25N 139°50E 140 B4
Tōkyō Disneyland Japan 35°37N 139°53E 140 B4
Tōkyō Haneda ✕ (HND) Japan 35°33N 139°46E 140 B3
Tōkyō Harbour Japan 35°38N 139°46E 140 B3
Tōkyō Narita ✕ (NRT) Japan 35°45N 140°25E 223 B12
Tōkyō-Wan Japan 35°25N 139°50E 140 B4
Tokzār Afghan. 35°52N 66°26E 240 B2
Tol I. Micronesia 7°20N 151°37E 287 U17
Tolaga Bay N.Z. 38°21S 178°20E 284 E7
Tolageak U.S.A. 70°3N 162°27W 303 A7
Tolbo Mongolia 48°25N 90°17E 217 C12
Tolbukhin = Dobrich Bulgaria 43°37N 27°49E 203 C11
Tolé C.A.R. 6°34N 16°1E 264 A3
Tōle Bī Kazakhstan 43°42N 73°46E 217 D8
Toledo Brazil 24°44S 53°45W 335 A5
Toledo Phil. 10°23N 123°38E 233 F4
Toledo Spain 39°50N 4°2W 194 F6
Toledo Ill., U.S.A. 39°16N 88°15W 311 E8
Toledo Iowa, U.S.A. 42°0N 92°35W 310 C4
Toledo Ohio, U.S.A. 41°39N 83°33W 311 C13
Toledo Oreg., U.S.A. 44°37N 123°56W 304 D2
Toledo Wash., U.S.A. 46°26N 122°51W 304 C2
Toledo, Montes de Spain 39°33N 4°20W 195 F6
Toledo Bend Res. U.S.A. 31°11N 93°34W 314 F8
Tolentino Italy 43°12N 13°17E 199 E10
Tolfa Italy 42°9N 11°56E 199 F8
Tolga Algeria 34°40N 5°22E 261 B6
Tolga Queens., Australia 17°15S 145°29E 280 B4
Tolga Hedmark, Norway 62°26N 11°1E 164 B8
Tolhuaca △ Chile 38°15S 71°50W 336 A2
Toli China 45°57N 83°37E 217 C10
Toliara Madag. 23°21S 43°40E 272 C1
Toliara □ Madag. 21°0S 45°0E 272 C2
Tolima Colombia 4°40N 75°19W 328 C2
Tolima □ Colombia 3°45N 75°15W 328 C2
Tolitoli Indonesia 1°5N 120°50E 231 D6
Tolka → Ireland 53°21N 6°14W 120 A1
Tolkmicko Poland 54°19N 19°31E 184 D6
Tollarp Sweden 55°55N 13°58E 163 J7
Tollensesee Germany 53°30N 13°13E 178 B9
Tollhouse U.S.A. 37°1N 119°24W 306 H7
Tollygunge = Taliganga India 22°30N 88°22E 124 B2
Tolmachevo Russia 58°56N 29°51E 188 C5
Tolmezzo Italy 46°24N 13°1E 199 B10
Tolmin Slovenia 46°11N 13°45E 199 B10
Tolna Hungary 46°25N 18°48E 182 D3
Tolna □ Hungary 46°30N 18°30E 182 D3
Tolo Dem. Rep. of the Congo 2°55S 18°34E 264 C3
Tolo, Teluk Indonesia 2°20S 122°10E 231 E6
Tolo Harbour China 22°27N 114°12E 219 G11
Tolochin = Talachyn Belarus 54°25N 29°42E 188 E5
Tolokiwa I. Papua N. G. 5°19S 147°37E 286 C4
Tolong Bay Phil. 9°20N 122°49E 233 G4
Tolono U.S.A. 39°59N 88°16W 311 E8
Tolosa Spain 43°8N 2°5W 196 B2
Tolox Spain 36°41N 4°54W 195 J6
Toltén Chile 39°13S 74°14W 336 A2
Toluca México, Mexico 19°17N 99°40W 319 D5
Toluca Ill., U.S.A. 41°0N 89°8W 310 C7
Tolworth U.K. 51°22N 0°17W 125 B2
Tolyatti = Togliatti Russia 53°32N 49°24E 190 D9
Tom Burke S. Africa 23°5S 28°0E 271 B4
Tom Price Australia 22°40S 117°48E 278 D2
Toma Burkina Faso 12°45N 2°53W 262 C4
Tomah U.S.A. 43°59N 90°30W 308 D8
Tomahawk U.S.A. 45°28N 89°44W 308 C9
Tomai Moldova 46°34N 28°19E 183 D13
Tomakomai Japan 42°38N 141°36E 220 C10
Tomales U.S.A. 38°15N 122°53W 306 G4
Tomales B. U.S.A. 38°15N 123°58W 306 G3
Tomanivi Fiji 17°37S 178°1E 287 A2
Tomar Portugal 39°36N 8°25W 195 F2
Tómaros, Oros Greece 39°29N 20°48E 204 B2
Tomarza Turkey 38°27N 35°48E 212 C6
Tomás Barrón Bolivia 17°35S 67°31W 330 D4
Tomashevka Belarus 51°33N 23°36E 185 G10
Tomashpil Ukraine 48°32N 28°31E 183 B13
Tomaszów Lubelski Poland 50°27N 23°25E 185 H10
Tomaszów Mazowiecki Poland 51°30N 20°2E 185 G7
Tomatlán Mexico 19°56N 105°15W 318 D3
Tomb of the Kings Jerusalem 123 a2
Tomba di Nerone Italy 41°58N 12°26E 136 B1
Tombadonkéa Guinea 11°0N 14°25W 262 C2
Tombador, Serra do Brazil 12°0S 58°0W 331 C6
Tombe Sudan 5°53N 31°40E 257 F3
Tombeau Bay Mauritius 20°6S 57°30E 273 d
Tombel Cameroon 4°45N 9°40E 264 B1
Tombigbee → U.S.A. 31°8N 87°57W 315 F11
Tomboco Angola 6°48S 13°18E 265 D2
Tombouctou Mali 16°50N 3°0W 262 B4
Tombouctou □ Mali 20°0N 3°0W 262 B4
Tombstone U.S.A. 31°43N 110°4W 305 L8
Tombua Angola 15°55S 11°55E 265 F2
Tomé Chile 36°36S 72°57W 336 A2
Tomé-Açu Brazil 2°25S 48°9W 332 B2
Tomelilla Sweden 55°33N 13°58E 163 J7
Tomelloso Spain 39°10N 3°2W 195 F7
Tomil Micronesia 9°31N 138°9E 287 R16
Tomil Harbor Pac. Oc. 9°30N 138°10E 287 R16
Tomilino Russia 55°39N 37°57E 129 C5
Tomingley Australia 32°26S 148°16E 283 B8
Tomini Indonesia 0°30N 120°30E 231 D6
Tomini, Teluk Indonesia 0°10S 121°0E 231 E6
Tominian Mali 13°17N 4°35W 262 C4
Tomiño Spain 41°59N 8°46W 194 D2
Tomintoul U.K. 57°15N 3°23W 167 D5
Tomioka Japan 36°15N 138°54E 223 A10
Tomislavgrad Bos.-H. 43°42N 17°13E 182 G2
Tomkinson Ranges Australia 26°11S 129°5E 279 E4
Tommot Russia 59°4N 126°20E 215 D13
Tommy Thompson Park Canada 43°38N 79°20W 141 B3
Tomnop Ta Suos Cambodia 11°20N 104°15E 237 G5
Tomo Colombia 2°38N 67°32W 328 C4
Tomo → Colombia 5°20N 67°48W 328 B4
Tomobe Japan 36°20N 140°20E 223 A12
Tomra Norway 62°34N 6°56E 164 B3
Toms Place U.S.A. 37°34N 118°41W 306 H8
Toms River U.S.A. 39°58N 74°12W 313 G10
Tomsk Russia 56°30N 85°5E 214 D9
Tömük Turkey 36°42N 34°23E 250 B5
Tona Spain 41°51N 2°14E 196 D7
Tonalá Chiapas, Mexico 16°4N 93°45W 319 D6
Tonalá Jalisco, Mexico 20°37N 103°14W 318 C4
Tonale, Passo del Italy 46°16N 10°35E 198 B7
Tonami Japan 36°40N 136°58E 223 A8
Tonantins Brazil 2°45S 67°45W 328 D4
Tonasket U.S.A. 48°42N 119°26W 304 B4
Tonate Fr. Guiana 5°0N 52°28W 329 C7
Tonawanda U.S.A. 43°1N 78°53W 312 D6
Tonb Iran 26°15N 55°15E 247 E7
Tonbo Burma 18°31N 95°25E 241 F5
Tonbridge U.K. 51°11N 0°17E 169 F8
Tonda Papua N. G. 8°55S 141°34E 286 E1
Tondabayashi Japan 34°30N 135°36E 223 C7
Tondano Indonesia 1°35N 124°54E 231 D6
Tondela Portugal 40°31N 8°5W 194 E2
Tønder Denmark 54°58N 8°50E 163 K2
Tondern = Tønder Denmark 54°58N 8°50E 163 K2
Tondi India 9°45N 79°4E 245 K4
Tondi Kiwindi Niger 14°28N 2°2E 263 C5
Tondibi Mali 16°39N 0°14W 263 B4
Tondo Phil. 14°36N 120°57E 127 B1
Tondoro Namibia 17°45S 18°50E 270 A2
Tone → Australia 34°25S 116°25E 279 F2
Tone-Gawa → Japan 35°44N 140°51E 223 B12
Tonekābon Iran 36°45N 51°12E 247 B6
Tong I. Papua N. G. 2°2S 147°47E 286 B4
Tong Xian China 39°55N 116°35E 226 E9
Tong-Yeong S. Korea 34°50N 128°20E 224 E4
Tonga Cameroon 4°58N 10°42E 264 B2
Tonga Sudan 9°28N 31°3E 257 F3
Tonga ■ Pac. Oc. 19°50S 174°30W 287 P13
Tonga Trench Pac. Oc. 18°0S 173°0W 277 D16
Tongaat S. Africa 29°33S 31°9E 271 C5
Tongala Australia 36°14S 144°56E 283 D6
Tong'an China 24°37N 118°8E 229 E12
Tongareva = Penrhyn Cook Is. 9°0S 158°0W 289 H12
Tongariro, Mt. N.Z. 39°8S 175°33E 284 F4
Tongariro △ N.Z. 39°8S 175°33E 284 F4
Tongass Nat. Forest U.S.A. 54°45N 133°0W 303 J14
Tongatapu Tonga 21°10S 175°10W 287 Q13
Tongatapu Group Tonga 21°0S 175°0W 287 Q13
Tongbai China 32°20N 113°23E 229 A9
Tongbinggo S. Korea 37°31N 126°58E 137 B1
Tongcheng Anhui, China 31°4N 116°56E 229 B11
Tongcheng Hubei, China 29°15N 113°50E 229 C9
Tongchuan China 35°6N 109°3E 226 G5
Tongdao China 26°10N 109°42E 228 D7
Tongeren Belgium 50°47N 5°28E 170 D5
Tonggu China 28°31N 114°20E 229 C10
Tonggu Jiao China 22°22N 113°37E 219 G10
Tongguan China 34°40N 110°25E 226 G6
Tonghai China 24°10N 102°53E 228 E4
Tonghua China 41°42N 125°58E 224 B2
Tongi = Tungi Bangla. 23°53N 90°24E 241 D3
Tongjiang China 31°58N 107°11E 228 B6
Tongjosŏn Man N. Korea 39°30N 128°0E 224 C4
Tongkil Phil. 6°4N 121°48E 233 H3
Tongking, G. of = Tonkin, G. of Asia 20°0N 108°0E 236 C7
Tongliang China 29°50N 106°3E 228 C6
Tongliao China 43°38N 122°18E 227 C12
Tongling China 30°55N 117°48E 229 B11
Tonglu China 29°45N 119°37E 229 C12
Tongnan = Anyue China 30°9N 105°50E 228 B5
Tongoa Vanuatu 16°54S 168°34E 287 F6
Tongobory Madag. 23°32S 44°20E 272 C1
Tongoy Chile 30°16S 71°31W 334 C1
Tongqiao China 31°21N 121°22E 138 A1
Tongquil I. Phil. 6°2N 121°51E 233 H3
Tongren China 27°43N 109°11E 228 D7
Tongres = Tongeren Belgium 50°47N 5°28E 170 D5
Tongsa Dzong Bhutan 27°31N 90°31E 241 B3
Tongsha Tao Taiwan 26°12N 128°28E 225 b
Tongshi China 18°30N 109°20E 236 C7
Tongue U.K. 58°29N 4°25W 167 C4
Tongue → U.S.A. 46°25N 105°52W 304 C11
Tongwei China 35°0N 105°5E 226 G3
Tongxiang China 30°39N 120°34E 229 B13
Tongxin China 36°59N 105°58E 226 F3
Tongyang N. Korea 39°9N 126°53E 224 C3
Tongyu China 44°45N 123°4E 227 B12
Tongzi China 28°9N 106°49E 228 C6
Tonica U.S.A. 41°13N 89°4W 310 C7
Tonj Sudan 7°20N 28°44E 257 F2
Tonj → Sudan 7°31N 28°55E 257 F2
Tonk India 26°6N 75°54E 242 F6
Tonkawa U.S.A. 36°41N 97°18W 314 C6
Tonkin = Bac Phan Vietnam 22°0N 105°0E 228 G5
Tonkin, G. of Asia 20°0N 108°0E 236 C7
Tonle Sap Cambodia 13°0N 104°0E 236 F5
Tonnay-Charente France 45°56N 0°55W 174 C3
Tonneins France 44°23N 0°19E 174 D4
Tonnerre France 47°51N 3°59E 173 E10
Tönning Germany 54°19N 8°56E 178 A4
Tono Japan 39°19N 141°32E 220 E10
Tonoas I. Micronesia 7°22N 151°52E 287 T18
Tonopah U.S.A. 38°4N 117°14W 305 G5
Tonoshō Japan 34°29N 134°11E 222 C6
Tonosí Panama 7°20N 80°20W 320 E3
Tons → Haryana, India 30°30N 77°39E 242 D7
Tons → Ut. P., India 26°1N 83°33E 243 F10
Tønsberg Norway 59°19N 10°25E 164 E7
Tonsina U.S.A. 61°39N 145°11W 303 F11
Tonstad Norway 58°40N 6°45E 164 F3
Tonto △ U.S.A. 33°39N 111°7W 305 K8
Tonumea Tonga 20°30S 174°30W 287 Q13
Tonya Turkey 40°53N 39°16E 213 B8
Tonzang Burma 23°36N 93°42E 241 D4
Tonzi Burma 24°39N 94°57E 241 C5
Toobanna Australia 18°42S 146°9E 280 B4
Toodyay Australia 31°34S 116°28E 279 F2
Tooele U.S.A. 40°32N 112°18W 304 F7
Toompine Australia 27°15S 144°19E 281 D3
Toomsboro U.S.A. 32°50N 83°5W 316 C6
Toora Australia 38°39S 146°23E 283 E7
Toora-Khem Russia 52°28N 96°17E 217 B13
Toorak Australia 37°50S 145°1E 128 B2
Tootias Somali Rep. 3°57N 43°57E 267 D5
Toowoomba Australia 27°32S 151°56E 281 D5
Top Springs Australia 16°37S 131°51E 278 C5
Topalu Romania 44°31N 28°3E 183 F13
Topanga State Park ⌂ U.S.A. 34°7N 118°31W 126 B1
Topaz U.S.A. 38°41N 119°30W 306 G7
Topeka U.S.A. 39°3N 95°40W 308 F6
Topkapı Turkey 41°1N 28°55E 122 B1
Topkapı Palace Turkey 41°0N 28°59E 122 B1
Topl'a → Slovak Rep. 48°45N 21°45E 181 C14
Topley Canada 54°49N 126°18W 296 C3
Toplica → Serbia 43°15N 21°49E 202 C5
Topliţa Romania 46°55N 25°20E 183 D10
Topo Azores 38°33N 27°45W 153 d1
Topo, Pta. do Azores 38°33N 27°46W 153 d1
Topocalma, Pta. Chile 34°10S 72°2W 334 C1
Topock U.S.A. 34°46N 114°29W 307 L12
Topola Serbia 44°17N 20°41E 202 B4
Topolčani Macedonia 41°14N 21°25E 202 F5
Topoľčany Slovak Rep. 48°35N 18°12E 181 C11
Topolnitsa → Bulgaria 42°11N 24°18E 203 D8
Topolobampo Mexico 25°36N 109°3W 318 B3
Topoloveni Romania 44°49N 25°5E 183 F10
Topolovgrad Bulgaria 42°5N 26°20E 203 D10
Topolvăţu Mare Romania 45°46N 21°41E 182 E6
Topozero, Ozero Russia 65°35N 32°0E 160 D25
Toppenish U.S.A. 46°23N 120°19W 304 C3
Topraisar Romania 44°1N 28°27E 183 F13
Toprakkale Turkey 37°5N 36°8E 250 A7
Topusko Croatia 45°18N 15°59E 199 C12
Toquepala Peru 17°24S 70°25W 330 D3
Toqyraūyn → Kazakhstan 46°48N 75°24E 217 C9
Tor di Quinto Italy 41°56N 12°27E 136 B1
Tor Pignattara Italy 41°53N 12°31E 136 B2
Tor Sapienza Italy 41°53N 12°35E 136 B2
Torà Spain 41°49N 1°25E 196 D6
Tora Kit Sudan 11°2N 32°36E 257 E3
Toraka Vestale Madag. 16°20S 43°58E 272 B1
Toranomon Tokyo, Japan 140 c3
Torata Peru 17°23S 70°1W 330 D3
Torbalı Turkey 38°10N 27°21E 205 C9
Torbat-e Heydārīyeh Iran 35°15N 59°12E 247 C8
Torbat-e Jām Iran 35°16N 60°35E 247 C9
Torbay Canada 47°40N 52°42W 299 C9
Torbay □ U.K. 50°26N 3°31W 169 G4
Tørberget Norway 61°8N 12°7E 164 C9
Torbjörntorp Sweden 58°12N 13°36E 163 F7
Torcy France 48°51N 2°39E 134 A4
Tordesillas Spain 41°30N 5°0W 194 D6
Töreboda Sweden 58°41N 14°7E 163 F8
Torekov Sweden 56°26N 12°37E 163 H6
Torellò Spain 42°3N 2°16E 196 C7
Toreno Spain 42°42N 6°30W 194 C4
Torfaen □ U.K. 51°43N 3°3W 169 F4
Torfajökull Iceland 63°54N 19°0W 155 D7
Torgau Germany 51°34N 13°0E 178 D8
Torgelow Germany 53°37N 14°1E 178 B10
Torghay Kazakhstan 49°38N 63°29E 216 C6
Torghay → Kazakhstan 48°1N 62°45E 216 C6
Torghay Ustirti Asia 51°0N 63°0E 216 B6
Torghay Zhylghasy Kazakhstan 52°0N 64°30E 216 B6
Torgovaya = Salsk Russia 46°28N 41°30E 191 G5
Torhamn Sweden 56°6N 15°50E 163 H9
Torhout Belgium 51°5N 3°7E 170 C3
Torhovytsya Ukraine 48°36N 25°26E 183 B10
Tori Ethiopia 7°53N 33°35E 257 F3
Tori-Shima Japan 30°29N 140°19E 221 J10
Torigni-sur-Vire France 49°3N 0°58W 172 C6
Torija Spain 40°44N 3°2W 196 E1
Torilla Pen. Australia 22°29S 150°5E 280 C5
Torino Italy 45°3N 7°40E 198 C4
Torit Sudan 4°27N 32°31E 257 G3
Torkamān Iran 37°35N 47°23E 213 D12
Torkovichi Russia 58°51N 30°21E 188 C6
Tormac Romania 45°30N 21°30E 182 E6
Tormes → Spain 41°18N 6°29W 194 D4
Tornado Mt. Canada 49°55N 114°40W 296 D6
Tornal'a Slovak Rep. 48°25N 20°20E 181 C13
Torneå = Tornio Finland 65°50N 24°12E 160 D21
Torneälven → Europe 65°50N 24°12E 160 D21
Torneträsk Sweden 68°24N 19°15E 160 B18
Torngat Mts. Canada 59°0N 63°40W 295 F19
Tornio Finland 65°50N 24°12E 160 D21
Tornionjoki = Torneälven → Europe 65°50N 24°12E 160 D21
Tornquist Argentina 38°8S 62°15W 334 D3
Toro Baleares, Spain 39°59N 4°8E 206 B5
Toro Zamora, Spain 41°35N 5°24W 194 D5
Torö Sweden 58°48N 17°50E 163 F11
Toro, Cerro del Chile 29°10S 69°50W 334 B2
Toro ⌂ Uganda 1°5N 30°22E 268 B3
Toro Pk. U.S.A. 33°34N 116°24W 307 M10
Torodi Niger 13°7N 1°47E 263 C5
Torokina Papua N. G. 6°14S 155°3E 286 D8
Törökszentmiklós Hungary 47°11N 20°27E 182 C5
Toronto N.S.W., Australia 33°0S 151°30E 283 B9
Toronto Ont., Canada 43°39N 79°20W 141 B2
Toronto Ohio, U.S.A. 40°28N 80°36W 312 F4
Toronto, Univ. of Canada 43°39N 79°23W 141 B2
Toronto City Centre ✕ (YTZ) Canada 43°38N 79°24W 141 B2
Toronto Harbour Canada 43°38N 79°21W 141 B2
Toronto I. Canada 43°37N 79°23W 141 B2
Toronto Lester B. Pearson Int. ✕ (YYZ) Canada 43°46N 79°35W 141 A1
Toropets Russia 56°30N 31°40E 188 D6
Tororo Uganda 0°45N 34°12E 268 B3
Toros Dağları Turkey 37°0N 32°30E 250 B3
Toros Monumental, Templo de Barcelona, Spain 114 a3
Torotoro Bolivia 18°7S 65°46W 331 D4
Torotoro △ Bolivia 18°7S 65°46W 331 D4
Torpa India 22°57N 85°6E 243 H11
Torpo Norway 60°40N 8°43E 164 D5
Torquay Vic., Australia 38°20S 144°19E 282 E6
Torquay Torbay, U.K. 50°27N 3°32W 169 G4
Torquemada Spain 42°2N 4°19W 194 C6
Torrais, Pta. Azores 39°43N 31°7W 153 d2
Torrance U.S.A. 33°50N 118°20W 307 M8
Torrão Portugal 38°16N 8°11W 195 G2
Torre Annunziata Italy 40°45N 14°27E 201 B7
Torre de Moncorvo Portugal 41°12N 7°8W 194 D3
Torre del Campo Spain 37°46N 3°53W 195 H7
Torre del Greco Italy 40°47N 14°22E 201 B7
Torre del Mar Spain 36°44N 4°6W 195 J6
Torre Latino-americana Mexico City, Mexico 128 b2
Torre Lupara Italy 41°59N 12°39E 136 B2
Torre Nova Italy 41°53N 12°37E 136 B2
Torre-Pacheco Spain 37°44N 0°57W 197 H4
Torre Pêllice Italy 44°49N 7°13E 198 D4
Torreblanca Spain 40°14N 0°12E 196 E5
Torrecampo Spain 38°29N 4°41W 195 G6
Torrecilla en Cameros Spain 42°15N 2°38W 196 C2
Torredembarra Spain 41°9N 1°24E 196 D6
Torredonjimeno Spain 37°46N 3°57W 195 H7
Torrejón de Ardoz Spain 40°27N 3°29W 194 E7
Torrejoncillo Spain 39°54N 6°28W 194 F4

Torrelaguna *Spain* 40°50N 3°38W 194 E7
Torrelavega *Spain* 43°20N 4°5W 194 B6
Torrellas → *Spain* 41°23N 2°1E 114 A1
Torremaggiore *Italy* 41°41N 15°17E 199 G12
Torremolinos *Spain* 36°38N 4°30W 195 J6
Torrens, L. *Australia* 31°0S 137°50E 282 A2
Torrens Cr. → *Australia* 22°23S 145°9E 280 C4
Torrens Creek *Australia* 20°48S 145°3E 280 C4
Torrent *Spain* 39°27N 0°28W 197 F4
Torrenueva *Spain* 38°38N 3°22W 195 G7
Torreón *Mexico* 25°33N 103°26W 318 B4
Torreperogil *Spain* 38°2N 3°17W 195 G7
Torres *Brazil* 29°21S 49°44W 335 B5
Torres *Mexico* 28°46N 110°47W 318 B2
Torres, Is. *Vanuatu* 13°15S 166°37E 287 C4
Torres del Paine △ *Chile* 51°3S 72°58W 336 D2
Torres Novas *Portugal* 39°27N 8°33W 195 F2
Torres Strait *Australia* 9°50S 142°20E 280 a
Torres Vedras *Portugal* 39°5N 9°15W 195 F1
Torrevécchia *Italy* 41°55N 12°25E 136 B1
Torrevieja *Spain* 37°59N 0°42W 197 H4
Torrey *U.S.A.* 38°18N 111°25W 304 G8
Torricelli Mts. *Papua N. G.* 3°23S 142°15E 286 B2
Torridge → *U.K.* 51°0N 4°13W 169 G3
Torridon, L. *U.K.* 57°35N 5°50W 167 D3
Torrijos *Phil.* 13°19N 122°5E 232 E4
Torrijos *Spain* 39°59N 4°18W 194 F6
Tørring *Denmark* 55°52N 9°29E 163 J3
Torrington *Conn., U.S.A.* 41°48N 73°7W 313 E11
Torrington *Wyo., U.S.A.* 42°4N 104°11W 304 E11
Torroella de Montgrí *Spain* 42°2N 3°8E 196 C8
Torrox *Spain* 36°46N 3°57W 195 J7
Torsås *Sweden* 56°24N 16°0E 163 H9
Torsby *Sweden* 60°7N 13°0E 162 D6
Torshälla *Sweden* 59°25N 16°28E 162 E10
Tórshavn *Færoe Is.* 62°5N 6°56W 160 E9
Torslanda *Sweden* 57°44N 11°45E 163 G5
Torsö *Sweden* 58°48N 13°45E 163 F7
Tortola *Br. Virgin Is.* 18°19N 64°45W 321 C7
Tórtoles de Esgueva *Spain* 41°49N 4°2W 194 D6
Tortoli *Italy* 39°55N 9°39E 200 C2
Tortona *Italy* 44°54N 8°52E 198 D5
Tortorici *Italy* 38°2N 14°49E 201 D7
Tortosa *Spain* 40°49N 0°31E 196 E5
Tortosa, C. *Spain* 40°41N 0°52E 196 E5
Tortosendo *Portugal* 40°15N 7°31W 194 E3
Tortue, Î. de la *Haiti* 20°5N 72°57W 321 B5
Tortuga *Trin. & Tob.* 10°22N 61°24W 323 t
Tortuguero △ *Costa Rica* 10°31N 83°29W 320 D3
Tortum *Turkey* 40°19N 41°35E 213 B9
Ţorūd *Iran* 35°25N 55°5E 247 C7
Torul *Turkey* 40°34N 39°18E 213 B8
Toruń *Poland* 53°2N 18°39E 185 E5
Torun *Ukraine* 48°40N 23°34E 183 B8
Tory Hill *Canada* 44°58N 78°16W 312 B6
Tory I. *Ireland* 55°16N 8°14W 166 A3
Torysa → *Slovak Rep.* 48°39N 21°21E 181 C14
Torzhok *Russia* 57°5N 34°55E 188 D8
Torzym *Poland* 52°19N 15°5E 185 F2
Tosa *Japan* 33°24N 133°23E 222 D5
Tosa-Shimizu *Japan* 32°52N 132°58E 222 E4
Tosa-Wan *Japan* 33°15N 133°30E 222 D5
Tosa-Yamada *Japan* 33°36N 133°38E 222 D5
Toscana □ *Italy* 43°25N 11°0E 198 E8
Toscanella = Tuscánia
Italy 42°25N 11°52E 199 F8
Toscano, Arcipelago
Italy 42°30N 10°30E 198 F7
Toshima *Japan* 35°43N 139°43E 140 A3
Toshimaen *Japan* 35°43N 139°38E 140 A2
Toshka *Egypt* 22°30N 31°53E 256 C3
Toshka, Buheirat en
Egypt 22°50N 31°0E 256 C3
Toshka Lakes = Toshka, Buheirat
en *Egypt* 22°50N 31°0E 256 C3
Toshkent *Uzbekistan* 41°20N 69°10E 217 D7
Toshkent □ *Uzbekistan* 41°0N 69°40E 217 D7
Tosno *Russia* 59°38N 30°46E 188 C6
Tossa de Mar *Spain* 41°43N 2°56E 196 D7
Tösse *Sweden* 58°58N 12°39E 163 F6
Tostado *Argentina* 29°15S 61°50W 334 B3
Tostedt *Germany* 53°17N 9°42E 178 B5
Tostón, Pta. de *Canary Is.* 28°42N 14°2W 153 e2
Tosu *Japan* 33°22N 130°31E 222 D2
Tosya *Turkey* 41°1N 34°2E 212 B6
Toszek *Poland* 50°27N 18°32E 185 H5
Totak *Norway* 59°40N 8°0E 164 E5
Totana *Spain* 37°45N 1°30W 197 H3
Totebo *Sweden* 57°38N 16°12E 163 G10
Toteng *Botswana* 20°22S 22°58E 270 B3
Tôtes *France* 49°41N 1°2E 172 C8
Tótkomlós *Hungary* 46°24N 20°45E 182 D5
Totland *Norway* 61°56N 5°23E 164 C2
Totma *Russia* 60°0N 42°40E 186 C7
Totnes *U.K.* 50°26N 3°42W 169 G4
Totness *Suriname* 5°53N 56°19W 329 B6
Toto *Angola* 7°9S 14°16E 265 D2
Toto *Nigeria* 8°26N 7°5E 263 D6
Totonicapán *Guatemala* 14°58N 91°12W 320 D1
Totora *Bolivia* 17°42S 65°9W 331 D4
Totoya, I. *Fiji* 18°57S 179°50W 287 B3
Totten Glacier *Antarctica* 66°45S 116°10E 151 C8
Tottenham *N.S.W.,*
Australia 32°14S 147°21E 283 B7
Tottenham *Vic.,*
Australia 37°48S 144°51E 128 A1
Tottenham *Ont., Canada* 44°1N 79°49W 312 B5
Tottenham *London, U.K.* 51°35N 0°4W 125 A3
Tottori *Japan* 35°30N 134°15E 222 B6
Tottori □ *Japan* 35°30N 134°12E 222 B6
Touâret *Niger* 20°17N 7°8E 261 D6
Touat *Algeria* 27°27N 0°30E 261 C5
Touba *Ivory C.* 8°22N 7°40W 262 D3
Touba *Senegal* 14°50N 15°55W 262 C1
Toubkal, Djebel *Morocco* 31°0N 8°0W 260 B3
Toubkal △ *Morocco* 31°0N 8°2W 260 B3
Toubou *Cameroon* 7°47N 15°22E 264 A3
T'ouch'eng *Taiwan* 24°52N 121°49E 225 B3
Toucy *France* 47°44N 3°15E 173 E10
T'oufen *Taiwan* 24°41N 120°54E 225 B2
Tougan *Burkina Faso* 13°11N 2°58W 262 C4
Touggourt *Algeria* 33°6N 6°4E 261 B6
Tougouri *Burkina Faso* 13°20N 0°30W 263 C4
Tougué *Guinea* 11°25N 11°50W 262 C2
Toukoto *Mali* 13°27N 9°52W 262 C3
Toul *France* 48°40N 5°53E 173 D12
Toulepleu *Ivory C.* 6°32N 8°24W 262 D3
Touliu *Taiwan* 23°42N 120°31E 225 C2
Toulon *Var, France* 43°10N 5°55E 175 E9
Toulon *Ill., U.S.A.* 41°6N 89°52W 310 C7
Toulouse *France* 43°37N 1°27E 174 E5
Toulouse Blagnac ✈ (TLS)
France 43°37N 1°22E 174 E5
Toulouse Street *New Orleans, U.S.A.* 131 b2
Toummo *Niger* 22°45N 14°8E 258 D2
Toummo, Mts. de *Africa* 22°43N 14°12E 258 D2
Toumodi *Ivory C.* 6°32N 5°4W 262 D3
Tounan *Taiwan* 23°41N 120°28E 225 C2
Tounassine, Hamada
Algeria 28°48N 5°0W 260 C4
Toungo *Nigeria* 8°20N 12°3E 263 D7
Toungoo *Burma* 19°0N 96°30E 240 C2
Touques → *France* 49°22N 0°8E 172 C7
Touraine *France* 47°20N 0°30E 172 E7
Tourane = Da Nang
Vietnam 16°4N 108°13E 236 D7
Tourcoing *France* 50°42N 3°10E 173 B10
Touriñán, C. *Spain* 43°3N 9°18W 194 B1
Tourîne *Mauritania* 22°23N 11°50W 260 D2
Tournai *Belgium* 50°35N 3°25E 170 D3
Tournan-en-Brie *France* 48°44N 2°46E 173 D9
Tournay *France* 43°13N 0°13E 174 E4
Tournon-St-Martin *France* 46°45N 0°58E 172 F7
Tournon-sur-Rhône *France* 45°4N 4°50E 175 C8
Tournus *France* 46°35N 4°54E 173 F11
Touros *Brazil* 5°12S 35°28W 332 C4
Tours *France* 47°22N 0°40E 172 E7
Tousidé, Pic *Chad* 21°1N 16°29E 259 D3
Toussoro, Mt. *C.A.R.* 9°7N 23°14E 264 A4
Toussus-le-Noble *France* 48°44N 2°6E 134 B1
Toussus-le-Noble ✈ (TNF)
France 48°44N 2°6E 134 B1
Touws → *S. Africa* 33°45S 21°11E 270 D3
Touwsrivier *S. Africa* 33°20S 20°2E 270 D3
Tovar *Venezuela* 8°20N 71°46W 328 B3
Tovarkovskiy *Russia* 53°40N 38°14E 188 F10
Tovdal *Norway* 58°47N 8°10E 164 F5
Tovdalselva → *Norway* 58°11N 8°7E 164 F5
Tovste *Ukraine* 48°50N 25°44E 183 B10
Tovuz *Azerbaijan* 41°0N 45°40E 191 K7
Towada *Japan* 40°37N 141°13E 220 D10
Towada-Hachimantai △
Japan 40°20N 140°55E 220 D10
Towada-Ko *Japan* 40°28N 140°55E 220 D10
Towanda *Ill., U.S.A.* 40°36N 88°53W 311 D8
Towanda *Pa., U.S.A.* 41°46N 76°27W 313 E8
Towarri △ *Australia* 31°50S 150°37E 283 A9
Towchāl Cable Car *Iran* 35°49N 51°24E 141 A2
Tower *U.S.A.* 47°48N 92°17W 308 B7
Tower, I. = Genovesa, I.
Ecuador 0°20N 89°58W 330 a
Tower Bridge *London, U.K.* 125 b5
Tower Hamlets □ *U.K.* 51°32N 0°2W 125 A3
Tower of London *U.K.* 51°30N 0°4W 125 A3
Towerhill Cr. →
Australia 22°28S 144°35E 280 C3
Towner *U.S.A.* 48°21N 100°25W 308 A3
Townsend *Ga., U.S.A.* 31°33N 81°31W 316 D8
Townsend *Mont., U.S.A.* 46°19N 111°31W 304 C8
Townshend I. *Australia* 22°10S 150°31E 280 C5
Townsville *Australia* 19°15S 146°45E 280 B4
Towot *Sudan* 6°12N 34°25E 257 F3
Towra Pt. *Australia* 34°0S 151°10E 139 C2
Towraghondī *Afghan.* 35°13N 62°16E 240 B1
Towson *U.S.A.* 39°24N 76°36W 309 F15
Towuti, Danau *Indonesia* 2°45S 121°32E 231 E6
Toxkan He → *China* 41°8N 80°11E 217 D10
Toya-Ko *Japan* 42°35N 140°51E 220 C10
Toyama *Japan* 36°40N 137°15E 223 A9
Toyama □ *Japan* 36°45N 137°30E 223 A9
Toyama-Wan *Japan* 37°0N 137°30E 221 F8
Toyapakeh *Indonesia* 8°41S 115°29E 231 K18
Toyen *Norway* 59°55N 10°47E 133 A3
Tōyō *Ehime, Japan* 33°56N 133°5E 222 D5
Tōyō *Kōchi, Japan* 33°26N 134°16E 222 D6
Toyohara = Yuzhno-Sakhalinsk
Russia 46°58N 142°45E 215 E15
Toyohashi *Japan* 34°45N 137°25E 223 C9
Toyokawa *Japan* 34°48N 137°27E 223 C9
Toyonaka *Japan* 34°46N 135°28E 133 A1
Toyooka *Japan* 35°35N 134°48E 222 B6
Toyota *Japan* 35°3N 137°7E 223 B9
Toyoura *Japan* 34°6N 130°57E 222 C2
Tozeur *Tunisia* 33°56N 8°8E 258 B1
Tozeur □ *Tunisia* 34°0N 8°5E 261 B6
Tqibuli *Georgia* 42°26N 43°0E 191 J6
Tqvarcheli *Georgia* 42°47N 41°42E 191 J5
Trâ Li = Tralee *Ireland* 52°16N 9°42W 166 D2
Trá Mhór = Tramore
Ireland 52°10N 7°10W 166 D4
Tra On *Vietnam* 9°58N 105°55E 237 H5
Trabancos → *Spain* 41°36N 5°15W 194 D5
Traben-Trarbach *Germany* 49°57N 7°7E 179 F3
Trabzon *Turkey* 41°10N 39°45E 213 B8
Trabzon □ *Turkey* 41°10N 39°45E 213 B8
Tracadie *Canada* 47°30N 64°55W 299 C7
Trachenburg = Żmigród
Poland 51°28N 16°53E 185 G3
Tracy *Qué., Canada* 46°1N 73°9W 298 C5
Tracy *Calif., U.S.A.* 37°44N 121°26W 306 H5
Tracy *Minn., U.S.A.* 44°14N 95°37W 308 C6
Tradate *Italy* 45°43N 8°54E 198 C5
Trade Town *Liberia* 5°40N 9°50W 262 D3
Traer *U.S.A.* 42°12N 92°28W 310 B4
Trafalgar *Vic., Australia* 38°14S 146°12E 283 E7
Trafalgar *Dominica* 15°19N 61°21W 323 k
Trafalgar, C. *Spain* 36°10N 6°2W 195 J4
Trafalgar Square *London, U.K.* 125 b3
Trafaria *Portugal* 38°40N 9°13W 126 A1
Tragonhsi *Greece* 37°27N 25°29E 205 D7
Traian *Brăila, Romania* 45°11N 27°44E 183 E12
Traian *Tulcea, Romania* 45°2N 28°15E 183 E13
Traição, Cor. → *Brazil* 23°35S 46°41W 137 B2
Traiguén *Chile* 38°15S 72°41W 336 A2
Trail *Canada* 49°5N 117°40W 296 D5
Traill Ø *Greenland* 72°30N 23°0W 154 C8
Traimit *Bangkok, Thailand* 113 c2
Trainor L. *Canada* 60°24N 120°17W 296 A4
Traíra → *Brazil* 1°4S 69°26W 328 D4
Trakai △ *Lithuania* 54°30N 25°10E 161 J21
Trákhonas *Cyprus* 35°12N 33°21E 207 E9
Tralee *Ireland* 52°16N 9°42W 166 D2
Tralee B. *Ireland* 52°17N 9°55W 166 D2
Tramore *Ireland* 52°10N 7°10W 166 D4
Tramore B. *Ireland* 52°9N 7°10W 166 D4
Tramuntana, Serra de
Spain 39°48N 2°54E 206 B3
Tran Ninh, Cao Nguyen
Laos 19°30N 103°10E 236 C4
Tranås *Sweden* 58°3N 14°59E 163 F8
Tranbjerg *Denmark* 56°6N 10°9E 163 H4
Tranby *Norway* 59°49N 10°15E 164 E7
Trancas *Argentina* 26°11S 65°20W 334 B2
Trancoso *Portugal* 40°49N 7°21W 194 E3
Tranebjerg *Denmark* 55°51N 10°36E 163 J4
Tranegilde *Denmark* 55°37N 12°20E 118 B2
Tranemo *Sweden* 57°30N 13°20E 163 G7
Trang *Thailand* 7°33N 99°38E 237 J2
Trangahy *Madag.* 19°7S 44°31E 272 B1
Trangan *Indonesia* 6°40S 134°20E 231 F8
Trangie *Australia* 32°4S 148°0E 283 B8
Trångsund *Sweden* 59°13N 18°8E 139 B2
Trångsviken *Sweden* 63°19N 13°59E 162 A7
Trani *Italy* 41°17N 16°25E 201 A9
Tranoroa *Madag.* 24°42S 45°4E 272 C2
Tranqueras *Uruguay* 31°13S 55°45W 335 C4
Trans-Alaska Pipeline
U.S.A. 70°11N 148°27W 303 A10
Transamerica Pyramid
San Francisco, U.S.A. 136 b2
Transantarctic Mts.
Antarctica 85°0S 170°0W 151 E12
Transbay Terminal
San Francisco, U.S.A. 136 b3
Transcarpathia = Zakarpattya □
Ukraine 48°20N 23°20E 183 B8
Transilvania *Romania* 46°30N 24°0E 183 D9
Transilvanian Alps = Carpații
Meridionali *Romania* 45°30N 25°0E 183 E9
Transjordan = Jordan ■
Asia 31°0N 36°0E 251 H7
Transnistria = Stînga Nistrului □
Moldova 47°20N 29°15E 183 C14
Transtrand *Sweden* 61°6N 13°20E 162 C7
Transtrandsfjällen *Sweden* 61°8N 13°0E 162 C6
Transylvania = Transilvania
Romania 46°30N 24°0E 183 D9
Trants Bay *Montserrat* 16°46N 62°9W 323 p
Trápani *Italy* 38°1N 12°29E 200 D5
Trappenfelde *Germany* 52°34N 13°39E 115 A4
Trapper Pk. *U.S.A.* 45°54N 114°18W 304 D6
Traralgon *Australia* 38°12S 146°34E 283 F7
Trarza □ *Mauritania* 18°0N 15°0W 260 E2
Trás-os-Montes = Cucumbi
Angola 10°17S 19°5E 265 E3
Trasacco *Italy* 41°57N 13°32E 199 G10
Trăscău, Munții *Romania* 46°14N 23°14E 183 D8
Trasimeno, L. *Italy* 43°8N 12°6E 199 E9
Träslövsläge *Sweden* 57°4N 12°16E 163 G6
Trastévere *Italy* 41°53N 12°28E 136 B1
Trasvase Tajo-Segura, Canal de
Spain 40°15N 2°55W 196 E2
Trat *Thailand* 12°14N 102°33E 237 F4
Tratani → *Pakistan* 29°19N 68°20E 242 E3
Traun *Austria* 48°14N 14°15E 180 C7
Traunreut *Germany* 47°57N 12°36E 179 H8
Traunsee *Austria* 47°55N 13°50E 180 D6
Traunstein *Germany* 47°52N 12°37E 179 H8
Travellers L. *Australia* 33°20S 142°0E 282 B5
Travemünde *Germany* 53°57N 10°52E 178 B6
Travers, Mt. *N.Z.* 42°1S 172°45E 285 C7
Traverse City *U.S.A.* 44°46N 85°38W 309 C11
Travis, L. *U.S.A.* 30°24N 97°55W 314 F6
Travnik *Bos.-H.* 44°17N 17°39E 182 F2
Trawbreaga B. *Ireland* 55°20N 7°25W 166 A4
Trbovlje *Slovenia* 46°12N 15°5E 199 B12
Treasure I. *U.S.A.* 37°49N 122°22W 136 B2
Treasure Island *U.S.A.* 27°46N 82°46W 317 H7
Treasury Is. *Solomon Is.* 7°22S 155°37E 287 L8
Trébbia → *Italy* 45°4N 9°41E 198 C6
Trebel → *Germany* 53°54N 13°2E 178 B9
Trébeurden *France* 48°46N 3°35W 172 D3
Trebević △ *Bos.-H.* 43°20N 18°45E 182 G3
Třebíč *Czech Rep.* 49°14N 15°55E 180 B8
Trebinje *Bos.-H.* 42°44N 18°22E 202 D2
Trebisacce *Italy* 39°52N 16°32E 201 C9
Trebišnjica → *Bos.-H.* 42°47N 18°8E 202 D2
Trebišov *Slovak Rep.* 48°38N 21°41E 181 C14
Trebitsch = Třebíč
Czech Rep. 49°14N 15°55E 180 B8
Trebižat → *Bos.-H.* 43°15N 17°30E 199 E14
Trebnitz = Trzebnica
Poland 51°20N 17°1E 185 G4
Trebnje *Slovenia* 45°54N 15°1E 199 C12
Třeboň *Czech Rep.* 49°1N 14°48E 180 B7
Trebonne *Australia* 18°37S 146°5E 280 B4
Třeboňsko △ *Czech Rep.* 49°1N 14°49E 180 B7
Třeboradice *Czech Rep.* 50°9N 14°31E 135 B3
Třebotov *Czech Rep.* 49°58N 14°17E 135 C1
Trebujena *Spain* 36°52N 6°11W 195 J4
Trecate *Italy* 45°26N 8°44E 198 C5
Tregaron *U.K.* 52°14N 3°56W 169 E4
Tregnago *Italy* 45°31N 11°10E 199 C8
Tregrosse Is. *Australia* 17°41S 150°43E 280 B5
Tréguier *France* 48°47N 3°16W 172 D3
Trégunc *France* 47°51N 3°51W 172 E3
Treherne *Canada* 49°38N 98°42W 297 D9
Tréia *Italy* 43°19N 13°19E 199 E10
Treignac *France* 45°32N 1°48E 174 C5
Treinta y Tres *Uruguay* 33°16S 54°17W 335 C5
Treis-karden *Germany* 50°10N 7°18E 179 E3
Treklyano *Bulgaria* 42°33N 22°36E 202 D6
Trelawney *Zimbabwe* 17°30S 30°30E 271 A5
Trélazé *France* 47°26N 0°30W 172 E6
Trelew *Argentina* 43°10S 65°20W 336 B3
Trélissac *France* 45°11N 0°47E 174 C4
Trelleborg *Sweden* 55°20N 13°10E 163 J7
Tremadog Bay *U.K.* 52°51N 4°18W 168 E3
Tremblay-en-France
France 48°56N 2°35E 134 A4
Tremblet *Réunion* 21°17S 55°48E 272 f
Trembowla = Terebovlya
Ukraine 49°18N 25°44E 177 D13
Tremedal = Monte Azul
Brazil 15°9S 42°53W 333 E3
Tremembe → *Brazil* 23°27S 46°34W 137 A2
Tremiti *Italy* 42°8N 15°30E 199 F12
Tremont *U.S.A.* 40°50N 73°52W 132 A2
Tremonton *U.S.A.* 41°43N 112°10W 304 F7
Tremp *Spain* 42°10N 0°52E 196 C5
Trenche → *Canada* 47°46N 72°53W 298 C5
Trenčiansky □
Slovak Rep. 48°45N 18°20E 181 C11
Trenčín *Slovak Rep.* 48°52N 18°4E 181 C11
Trengereid *Norway* 60°26N 5°37E 164 D2
Trenggalek *Indonesia* 8°3S 111°43E 235 D4
Trenno *Italy* 45°29N 9°6E 129 B1
Trenque Lauquen
Argentina 36°5S 62°45W 334 D3
Trent → *Ont., Canada* 44°6N 77°34W 312 B7
Trent → *England, U.K.* 53°41N 0°42W 168 D7
Trentino-Alto Adige □
Italy 46°30N 11°20E 199 B8
Trento *Italy* 46°4N 11°8E 198 B8
Trento *Agusan del S., Phil.* 8°3N 126°2E 233 G6
Trenton *Ont., Canada* 44°10N 77°34W 312 B7
Trenton *Fla., U.S.A.* 29°37N 82°49W 317 F7
Trenton *Mich., U.S.A.* 42°8N 83°11W 311 B13
Trenton *Mo., U.S.A.* 40°5N 93°37W 310 D3
Trenton *N.J., U.S.A.* 40°14N 74°46W 313 F10
Trenton *Nebr., U.S.A.* 40°11N 101°1W 308 E3
Trenton *Ohio, U.S.A.* 39°29N 84°28W 311 E12
Trenton *S.C., U.S.A.* 33°45N 81°51W 316 B8
Trepassey *Canada* 46°43N 53°25W 299 C9
Treptow *Germany* 52°29N 13°27E 115 B3
Treptow an der Rega = Trzebiatów
Poland 54°3N 15°18E 184 D2
Trepuzzi *Italy* 40°24N 18°4E 201 B11
Tres Arroyos *Argentina* 38°26S 60°20W 334 D3
Três Casas *Brazil* 6°59S 62°41W 331 B5
Três Corações *Brazil* 21°44S 45°15W 333 F2
Tres Equinas *Colombia* 0°43N 75°16W 328 C2
Três Lagoas *Brazil* 20°50S 51°43W 333 F1
Tres Lagos *Argentina* 49°35S 71°25W 336 C2
Tres Lomas *Argentina* 36°27S 62°51W 334 D3
Três Marias, Represa
Brazil 18°12S 45°15W 333 E2
Tres Montes, C. *Chile* 46°50S 75°30W 336 C1
Tres Pinos *U.S.A.* 36°48N 121°19W 306 J5
Três Pontas *Brazil* 21°23S 45°29W 333 F2
Tres Puentes, C. das
Angola 10°28S 13°32E 265 E2
Tres Puentes *Chile* 27°50S 70°15W 334 B1
Tres Puntas, C. *Argentina* 47°0S 66°0W 336 C3
Três Rios *Brazil* 22°6S 43°15W 333 F3
Tres Ríos, Sa. dos *Brazil* 22°56S 43°17W 135 B1
Tres Valles *Mexico* 18°15N 96°8W 319 D5
Tresco *U.K.* 49°57N 6°20W 169 H1
Tresfjord *Norway* 62°31N 7°7E 164 B4
Treska → *Macedonia* 42°0N 21°20E 202 E5
Treskavica *Bos.-H.* 43°40N 18°20E 182 G3
Trespaderne *Spain* 42°47N 3°24W 194 C7
Tresticklan △ *Sweden* 59°0N 11°42E 163 F5
Trets *France* 43°27N 5°41E 175 E9
Treuburg = Olecko *Poland* 54°2N 22°31E 184 D9
Treuchtlingen *Germany* 48°58N 10°54E 179 G6
Treuenbrietzen *Germany* 52°5N 12°52E 178 C8
Treungen *Norway* 59°1N 8°31E 164 E5
Trèves = Trier *Germany* 49°45N 6°38E 179 F2
Trevi *Italy* 42°52N 12°45E 199 F9
Trevi, Fontana di *Rome, Italy* 136 b3
Treviglio *Italy* 45°31N 9°35E 198 C6
Trevinca, Peña *Spain* 42°15N 6°46W 194 C4
Treviso *Italy* 45°40N 12°15E 199 C9
Trévoux *France* 45°57N 4°47E 175 C8
Trezzano sul Naviglio *Italy* 45°24N 9°4E 129 B1
Trgovište *Serbia* 42°20N 22°10E 202 D6
Triabunna *Australia* 42°30S 147°55E 281 G4
Trianda = Ialissos
Greece 36°24N 28°10E 206 E12
Trianda *Greece* 36°25N 28°10E 206 E12
Triangle *Zimbabwe* 21°2S 31°28E 271 B5
Triaucourt-en-Argonne
France 48°59N 5°2E 173 D12
Tribal Areas □ *Pakistan* 33°0N 70°0E 242 C4
Tribsees *Germany* 54°5N 12°44E 178 A8
Tribugá, G. de *Colombia* 5°45N 77°20W 328 B2
Tribulation, C. *Australia* 16°5S 145°29E 280 B4
Tribune *U.S.A.* 38°28N 101°45W 308 F3
Tribune Tower *Chicago, U.S.A.* 119 b2
Tricárico *Italy* 40°37N 16°9E 201 B9
Tricase *Italy* 39°56N 18°22E 201 C11
Trichinopoly = Tiruchchirappalli
India 10°45N 78°45E 245 J4
Trichonida, L. *Greece* 38°34N 21°30E 204 C3
Trichur *India* 10°30N 76°18E 245 J3
Trichy = Tiruchchirappalli
India 10°45N 78°45E 245 J4
Trida *Australia* 33°1S 145°1E 283 B6
Trier *Germany* 49°45N 6°38E 179 F2
Trieste *Lazio, Italy* 41°55N 12°30E 136 B2
Trieste *Trieste, Italy* 45°40N 13°46E 199 C10
Trieste, G. di *Italy* 45°40N 13°35E 199 C10
Trieux → *France* 48°43N 3°9W 172 D3
Triggiano *Italy* 41°4N 16°55E 201 A9
Triglav *Slovenia* 46°21N 13°50E 199 B10
Triglavski △ *Slovenia* 46°20N 13°50E 199 B10
Trigno → *Italy* 42°4N 14°48E 199 F11
Trigo de Morais = Guijá
Mozam. 24°27S 33°0E 271 B5
Trigueros *Spain* 37°24N 6°50W 195 H4
Tríkala *Greece* 39°34N 21°47E 204 B3
Tríkala □ *Greece* 39°41N 21°30E 204 B3
Trikeri *Greece* 39°6N 23°5E 204 B5
Trikomo *Cyprus* 35°17N 33°52E 207 E9
Trikora, Puncak
Indonesia 4°15S 138°45E 231 E9
Trilby *U.S.A.* 28°28N 82°12W 317 G7
Trilj *Croatia* 43°38N 16°42E 199 E13
Trillo *Spain* 40°42N 2°35W 196 E2
Trim *Ireland* 53°33N 6°48W 166 C5
Trimbak *India* 19°56N 73°33E 244 E1
Trimmu Dam *Pakistan* 31°10N 72°8E 242 D5
Trincomalee *Sri Lanka* 8°38N 81°15E 245 K5
Trindade *Brazil* 16°40S 49°30W 333 E2
Trindade, I. *Atl. Oc.* 20°20S 29°50W 152 J9
Třinec *Czech Rep.* 49°41N 18°39E 181 B11
Trinidad = Jose Abad Santos
Phil. 5°55N 125°39E 233 J5
Trinidad *Bolivia* 14°46S 64°50W 331 C5
Trinidad *Colombia* 5°25N 71°40W 328 B3
Trinidad *Cuba* 21°48N 80°0W 320 B4
Trinidad *Trin. & Tob.* 10°30N 61°15W 323 t
Trinidad *Uruguay* 33°30S 56°50W 334 C4
Trinidad *Colo., U.S.A.* 37°10N 104°31W 305 H11
Trinidad *D.C., U.S.A.* 38°54N 76°59W 143 B4
Trinidad → *Mexico* 17°49N 95°9W 319 D5
Trinidad, G. *Chile* 49°55S 75°25W 336 C1
Trinidad, I. *Argentina* 39°10S 62°0W 336 A4
Trinidad & Tobago ■
W. Indies 10°30N 61°20W 323 t
Trinitápoli *Italy* 41°21N 16°5E 201 A9
Trinité, Havre de
Martinique 14°44N 60°58W 322 j
Trinity *Nfld. & L., Canada* 48°59N 53°55W 299 C9
Trinity *Edinburgh, U.K.* 55°58N 3°12W 121 B2
Trinity *Tex., U.S.A.* 30°57N 95°22W 314 F7
Trinity → *Calif., U.S.A.* 41°11N 123°42W 304 F2
Trinity → *Tex., U.S.A.* 29°45N 94°43W 314 G7
Trinity B. *Canada* 48°20N 53°10W 299 C9
Trinity Church *New York, U.S.A.* 132 f1
Trinity College *Dublin, Ireland* 120 c3
Trinity Hills *Trin. & Tob.* 10°7N 61°7W 323 t
Trinity Is. *U.S.A.* 56°33N 154°25W 303 H9
Trinity Range *U.S.A.* 40°10N 118°40W 304 F4
Trinkat *India* 8°5N 93°30E 245 K11
Trinkitat *Sudan* 18°45N 37°51E 256 D4
Trino *Italy* 45°12N 8°18E 198 C5
Trinway *U.S.A.* 40°9N 82°1W 312 F2
Triolet *Mauritius* 20°4S 57°32E 272 e
Trionfale *Italy* 41°54N 12°26E 136 B1
Trionto, C. *Italy* 39°37N 16°43E 201 C9
Triora *Italy* 44°1N 7°46E 198 D4
Tripoli = Tarābulus
Lebanon 34°31N 35°50E 250 D6
Tripoli = Tarābulus *Libya* 32°49N 13°7E 258 B2
Trípoli *Greece* 37°31N 22°25E 204 D4
Tripoli *Iowa, U.S.A.* 42°49N 92°16W 310 B4
Tripolitania = Tarābulus
N. Afr. 31°0N 13°0E 258 B2
Tripura □ *India* 24°0N 92°0E 241 H18
Tripylos *Cyprus* 34°59N 32°41E 207 F8
Trischen *Germany* 54°4N 8°40E 178 A4
Tristan da Cunha *Atl. Oc.* 37°6S 12°20W 255 K2
Trisul *India* 30°19N 79°47E 243 D8
Triulzo *Italy* 45°25N 9°16E 129 B2
Trivandrum *India* 8°41N 77°0E 245 K3
Trivento *Italy* 41°47N 14°33E 199 G11
Trizin *Greece* 37°25N 23°15E 204 D5
Trnava *Slovak Rep.* 48°23N 17°35E 181 C10
Trnavský □ *Slovak Rep.* 48°30N 17°45E 181 C10
Troarn *France* 49°11N 0°11W 172 C6
Trobriand Is. *Papua N. G.* 8°30S 151°0E 286 E6
Trocadero *Paris, France* 134 b1
Trochu *Canada* 51°50N 113°13W 296 C6
Trodely I. *Canada* 52°15N 79°26W 298 B4
Troebratskiy *Kazakhstan* 54°25N 66°4E 217 B7
Trogir *Croatia* 43°32N 16°15E 199 E13
Troglav *Croatia* 43°56N 16°36E 199 E13
Tróia *Italy* 41°22N 15°18E 201 A8
Troilus, L. *Canada* 50°50N 74°35W 298 B5
Troina *Italy* 37°47N 14°36E 201 E7
Trois Boutiques *Mauritius* 20°26S 57°38E 272 e
Trois Fourches, Cap des
Morocco 35°26N 2°58W 261 A4
Trois-Pistoles *Canada* 48°5N 69°10W 299 C6
Trois Pitons, Morne
Dominica 15°22N 61°20W 323 k
Trois-Rivières *Qué.,*
Canada 46°25N 72°34W 298 C5
Trois-Rivières *Guadeloupe* 15°57N 61°40W 322 e
Trois Rivières *Martinique* 14°28N 60°58W 322 j
Troisdorf *Germany* 50°48N 7°11E 178 E3
Troitse-Lykovo *Russia* 55°47N 37°23E 129 B2
Troitsk *Russia* 54°10N 61°35E 216 B6
Troitsko Pechorsk
Russia 62°40N 56°10E 186 B10
Troitskosavsk = Kyakhta
Russia 50°30N 106°25E 215 D11
Troitskoye *Russia* 46°26N 44°15E 191 G7
Troitsky = Troitsk *Russia* 54°10N 61°35E 216 B6
Troja *Czech Rep.* 50°7N 14°25E 135 B2
Trölladyngja *Iceland* 64°54N 17°16W 155 C9
Trollbäcken *Sweden* 59°14N 18°12E 139 B3
Trollhättan *Sweden* 58°17N 12°20E 163 F6
Trollheimen *Norway* 62°46N 9°1E 164 B6
Trombay *India* 19°2N 72°56E 130 A2
Trombetas → *Brazil* 1°55S 55°35W 329 D6
Tromelin I. *Ind. Oc.* 15°52S 54°25E 273 F4
Tromøy *Norway* 58°27N 8°51E 164 F5
Tromsø *Norway* 69°40N 18°56E 160 B18
Tron *Thailand* 17°28N 100°7E 236 D3
Trona *U.S.A.* 35°46N 117°23W 307 K9
Tronador, Mte.
Argentina 41°10S 71°50W 336 B2
Trøndelag *Norway* 64°17N 11°50E 160 D14
Trondheim *Norway* 63°36N 10°25E 164 A7
Trondheimsfjorden
Norway 63°35N 10°30E 160 E14
Trondheimsleia *Norway* 63°25N 8°30E 164 A5
Trondhjem = Trondheim
Norway 63°36N 10°25E 164 A7
Trönninge *Sweden* 56°37N 12°51E 163 H6
Tronto → *Italy* 42°54N 13°55E 199 F10
Troodos *Cyprus* 34°55N 32°52E 207 F8
Troon *U.K.* 55°33N 4°39W 167 F4
Troparevo *Russia* 55°39N 37°29E 129 C2
Tropea *Italy* 38°41N 15°54E 201 D8
Tropic *U.S.A.* 37°37N 112°5W 305 H7
Tropojë *Albania* 42°23N 20°10E 202 D4
Troppau = Opava
Czech Rep. 49°57N 17°58E 181 B10
Trosa *Sweden* 58°54N 17°33E 163 F11
Trostan *U.K.* 55°3N 6°10W 166 A5
Trostberg *Germany* 48°1N 12°33E 179 G8
Trostyanets *Sumy,*
Ukraine 50°33N 34°59E 189 G8
Trostyanets *Vinnyts'ka,*
Ukraine 48°31N 29°11E 183 B14
Trotsk = Chapayevsk
Russia 53°0N 49°40E 190 D9
Trotsk = Gatchina *Russia* 59°35N 30°9E 188 C6
Trou Gras Pt. *St. Lucia* 13°51N 60°53W 323 m
Troumaka *St. Vincent* 13°18N 61°17W 323 n
Trout → *Canada* 61°19N 119°51W 296 A5
Trout L. *N.W.T., Canada* 60°40N 121°14W 296 A4
Trout L. *Ont., Canada* 51°20N 93°15W 297 C10
Trout Lake *N.W.T.,*
Canada 56°30N 114°32W 296 B6
Trout Lake *Wash., U.S.A.* 46°0N 121°32W 306 E5
Trout River *Canada* 49°29N 58°8W 299 C8
Trout Run *U.S.A.* 41°23N 77°3W 312 E7
Trouville-sur-Mer *France* 49°21N 0°5E 172 C7
Trowbridge *U.K.* 51°18N 2°12W 169 F5
Troy *Turkey* 39°57N 26°12E 205 B8
Troy *Ala., U.S.A.* 31°48N 85°58W 316 D4
Troy *Ill., U.S.A.* 38°44N 89°54W 310 F7
Troy *Ind., U.S.A.* 37°59N 86°55W 311 G10
Troy *Kans., U.S.A.* 39°47N 95°5W 308 F6
Troy *Mich., U.S.A.* 42°37N 83°9W 311 B13
Troy *Mo., U.S.A.* 38°59N 90°59W 310 F6
Troy *Mont., U.S.A.* 48°28N 115°53W 304 B6
Troy *N.Y., U.S.A.* 42°44N 73°41W 313 D11
Troy *Ohio, U.S.A.* 40°2N 84°12W 311 D12
Troy *Pa., U.S.A.* 41°47N 76°47W 313 E8
Troyan *Bulgaria* 42°57N 24°43E 203 D8
Troyes *France* 48°19N 4°3E 173 D11
Trpanj *Croatia* 43°1N 17°15E 199 E14
Trstenik *Serbia* 43°36N 21°0E 202 C5
Trubchevsk *Russia* 52°33N 33°47E 189 F7
Truchas Pk. *U.S.A.* 35°58N 105°39W 305 J11
Trucial States = United Arab
Emirates ■ *Asia* 23°50N 54°0E 247 F7
Truckee *U.S.A.* 39°20N 120°11W 306 F6
Trudeau, Montréal ✈ (YUL)
Canada 45°28N 73°44W 130 B1
Trudfront *Russia* 45°56N 47°40E 191 H8
Trudovoye *Russia* 43°17N 132°5E 220 C6
Trudyashchikhsya, Ostrov
Russia 59°58N 30°18E 137 B1
Trujillo *Colombia* 4°10N 76°19W 328 C2
Trujillo *Honduras* 16°0N 86°0W 320 C2
Trujillo *Peru* 8°6S 79°0W 330 B2
Trujillo *Spain* 39°28N 5°55W 195 F5
Trujillo *N. Mex., U.S.A.* 35°32N 104°42W 305 J11
Trujillo *Venezuela* 9°22N 70°38W 328 B3
Trujillo □ *Venezuela* 9°25N 70°30W 328 B3
Trujillo, Mte. = Duarte, Pico
Dom. Rep. 19°2N 70°59W 321 C5
Trujillo Alto *Puerto Rico* 18°21N 66°1W 321 b
Truk *Micronesia* 7°25N 151°46E 287 T17
Trumann *U.S.A.* 35°41N 90°31W 315 D9
Trumansburg *U.S.A.* 42°33N 76°40W 313 D8
Trumbull, Mt. *U.S.A.* 36°25N 113°19W 305 H7
Trŭn *Bulgaria* 42°51N 22°38E 202 D6
Trun *Orne, France* 48°50N 0°2E 172 D7
Trundle *Australia* 32°53S 147°35E 283 B7
Trung-Phan = Annam
Vietnam 16°0N 108°0E 236 E7
Truro *S. Austral., Australia* 34°24S 139°9E 282 C3
Truro *N.S., Canada* 45°21N 63°14W 299 C7
Truro *Corn., U.K.* 50°16N 5°4W 169 G2
Truskavets *Ukraine* 49°17N 23°30E 177 D12
Trŭstenik *Bulgaria* 43°31N 24°28E 203 C8
Trustrup *Denmark* 56°20N 10°46E 163 H4
Trutch *Canada* 57°44N 122°57W 296 B4
Truth or Consequences
U.S.A. 33°8N 107°15W 305 K10
Trutnov *Czech Rep.* 50°37N 15°54E 180 A8
Truyère → *France* 44°38N 2°34E 174 D6
Tryavna *Bulgaria* 42°54N 25°25E 203 D9
Tryonville *U.S.A.* 41°42N 79°48W 312 E5
Tryphena *N.Z.* 36°18S 175°28E 284 C4
Trysilelva → *Norway* 61°2N 12°35E 164 C9
Tryvasshøgda *Norway* 59°59N 10°40E 133 A3
Trzcianka *Poland* 53°3N 16°25E 185 E3
Trzciel *Poland* 52°23N 15°50E 185 F2
Trzcińsko Zdrój *Poland* 52°58N 14°35E 185 F1
Trzebiatów *Poland* 54°3N 15°18E 184 D2
Trzebiez *Poland* 53°38N 14°31E 184 E1
Trzebnica *Poland* 51°20N 17°1E 185 G4
Trzemeszno *Poland* 52°33N 17°48E 185 F4
Tržič *Slovenia* 46°22N 14°18E 199 B11
Tsagaannuur *Mongolia* 49°32N 89°42E 217 C11
Tsagan Aman *Russia* 47°34N 46°43E 191 G8
Tsala Apopka L. *U.S.A.* 28°53N 82°19W 317 G7
Tsamandas *Greece* 39°46N 20°21E 204 B2
Tsamkong = Zhanjiang
China 21°15N 110°20E 229 G8
Tsandi *Namibia* 17°42S 14°50E 270 A1
Tsangpo = Brahmaputra →
Asia 23°40N 90°35E 241 D3
Tsaochiao *Taiwan* 24°39N 120°51E 225 B2
Ts'aot'un *Taiwan* 23°58N 120°41E 225 C2
Tsaratanana *Madag.* 16°47S 47°39E 272 B2
Tsaratanana, Mt. de =
Maromokotro *Madag.* 14°0S 49°0E 272 A2
Tsaratanana □ *Madag.* 13°57S 48°52E 272 A2
Tsarekonstantinovka =
Kuybyshevo *Ukraine* 47°25N 36°40E 189 J9
Tsarevo = Michurin
Bulgaria 42°9N 27°51E 203 D11
Tsarevo *Bulgaria* 42°28N 25°52E 203 D9
Tsaribrod = Dimitrovgrad
Serbia 43°2N 22°48E 202 C6
Tsaritsani *Greece* 39°53N 22°14E 204 B4
Tsarkasianos *Greece* 38°10N 20°40E 207 C2
Tsarskoye Selo = Pushkin
Russia 59°45N 30°25E 188 C6
Tsaryovokokshaysk = Yoshkar Ola
Russia 56°38N 47°55E 190 B8
Tsau *Botswana* 20°8S 22°22E 270 B3
Tsavo *Kenya* 2°59S 38°28E 268 C4
Tsavo East △ *Kenya* 2°44S 38°47E 268 C4
Tsavo West △ *Kenya* 3°19S 37°57E 268 C4
Tsebrykove *Ukraine* 47°9N 30°10E 189 J6
Tselinograd = Astana
Kazakhstan 51°10N 71°30E 217 B8
Tsementny = Fokino
Russia 53°30N 34°22E 188 F8
Tseng Lan Shue *China* 22°20N 114°14E 122 A2
Tsengwen Hsi → *Taiwan* 23°8N 120°19E 225 C2
Tsengwen Shuiku
Taiwan 23°16N 120°34E 225 C2
Tsentralnyy □ *Russia* 52°0N 40°0E 190 D4
Tses *Namibia* 25°58S 18°8E 270 C2
Tsetserleg *Mongolia* 47°36N 101°32E 218 B5
Tseung Kwan *China* 22°20N 114°15E 122 B2
Tsévié *Togo* 6°25N 1°20E 263 D5
Tshabong *Botswana* 26°2S 22°29E 270 C3
Tshabuta
Dem. Rep. of the Congo 7°42S 23°7E 265 D4
Tshane *Botswana* 24°5S 21°54E 270 B3
Tshela *Dem. Rep. of the Congo* 4°57S 13°4E 265 C2
Tshesebe *Botswana* 21°51S 27°32E 271 B4
Tshibeke
Dem. Rep. of the Congo 2°40S 28°35E 268 C2
Tshibinda
Dem. Rep. of the Congo 2°23S 28°43E 268 C2
Tshikapa
Dem. Rep. of the Congo 6°28S 20°48E 265 D4
Tshilenge
Dem. Rep. of the Congo 6°17S 23°48E 265 D4
Tshindjambo
Dem. Rep. of the Congo 10°52S 22°43E 265 E4
Tshinota
Dem. Rep. of the Congo 7°2S 20°58E 265 D4
Tshinsenda
Dem. Rep. of the Congo 12°20S 28°0E 269 E2
Tshitadi
Dem. Rep. of the Congo 6°46S 21°43E 265 D4
Tshofa
Dem. Rep. of the Congo 5°13S 25°16E 265 D5
Tshuapa →
Dem. Rep. of the Congo 0°14S 20°42E 264 C4
Tshumbiri
Dem. Rep. of the Congo 2°38S 16°18E 264 C3
Tshwane = Pretoria
S. Africa 25°44S 28°12E 271 C4
Tshwane *Botswana* 22°24S 22°1E 270 B3
Tsiaotso = Jiaozuo
China 35°16N 113°12E 226 G7
Tsibirihina → *Madag.* 19°42S 44°31E 272 B1
Tsigara *Botswana* 20°22S 25°54E 270 B4
Tsihombe *Madag.* 25°10S 45°41E 272 D2
Tsiigehtchic *Canada* 67°15N 134°0W 294 D5
Ts'il-os △ *Canada* 51°9N 123°59W 296 C4
Tsim Sha Tsui *China* 22°18N 114°10E 122 B2
Tsimlyansk *Russia* 47°40N 42°6E 191 G6
Tsimlyansk Res. = Tsimlyanskoye
Vdkhr. *Russia* 48°0N 43°0E 191 F6
Tsimlyanskoye Vdkhr.
Russia 48°0N 43°0E 191 F6
Tsinan = Jinan *China* 36°38N 117°1E 226 F9
Tsineng *S. Africa* 27°5S 23°5E 270 C3
Tsing Yi *China* 22°21N 114°6E 122 A1
Tsinghai = Qinghai □
China 36°0N 98°0E 218 C4
Tsingshih = Jinshi
China 29°40N 111°50E 229 C8
Tsingtao = Qingdao
China 36°5N 120°20E 227 F11
Tsingy de Bemaraha ⌂
Madag. 18°35S 45°25E 272 B2
Tsingy de Namoroka ⌂
Madag. 16°29S 45°25E 272 B2
Tsining = Jining *China* 35°22N 116°34E 226 G9
Tsinjoarivo *Madag.* 19°37S 47°40E 272 B2
Tsinjomitondraka *Madag.* 15°40S 47°8E 272 B2
Tsinling Shan = Qinling Shandi
China 33°50N 108°10E 226 H5
Tsirigo = Kythira *Greece* 36°8N 23°0E 204 E5
Tsiroanomandidy *Madag.* 18°46S 46°2E 272 B2
Tsis I. *Micronesia* 7°17N 151°49E 287 U18
Tsiteli-Tsqaro *Georgia* 41°33N 46°0E 191 K8
Tsitondroina *Madag.* 21°19S 46°0E 272 C2
Tsitsihar = Qiqihar *China* 47°26N 124°0E 219 B7
Tsitsikamma △ *S. Africa* 34°3S 23°40E 270 D3
Tsivilsk *Russia* 55°50N 47°25E 190 C8
Tsivory *Madag.* 24°4S 46°5E 272 C2
Tskhinvali *Georgia* 42°14N 44°1E 191 J7
Tsna → *Russia* 54°55N 41°58E 190 C6
Tsnori *Georgia* 41°40N 45°57E 191 K7
Tso Moriri, L. *India* 32°50N 78°20E 243 C8
Tsobis *Namibia* 19°27S 17°30E 270 A2
Tsodilo Hill *Botswana* 18°49S 21°43E 270 A3
Tsogni *Gabon* 2°48S 10°10E 264 C2
Tsogttsetsiy = Baruunsuu
Mongolia 43°43N 105°35E 226 C3
Tsolo *S. Africa* 31°18S 28°37E 271 D4
Tsomo *S. Africa* 32°0S 27°42E 271 D4
Tsoukalades *Greece* 38°41N 20°47E 207 B2
Tsova *West Bank* 31°47N 35°5E 123 B1
Tsoying *Taiwan* 22°41N 120°17E 225 D2
Tsu *Japan* 34°45N 136°25E 223 C8
Tsu L. *Canada* 60°40N 111°52W 296 A6
Tsubata *Japan* 36°40N 136°44E 223 A8
Tsuchiura *Japan* 36°5N 140°15E 223 A12
Tsuen Wan *China* 22°22N 114°6E 122 A1
Tsugaru-Kaikyō *Japan* 41°35N 141°0E 220 D10
Tsuken-jima *Japan* 26°15N 127°56E 288 a
Tsukiji *Tokyo, Japan* 140 c5
Tsukuba *Japan* 36°2N 140°4E 223 A12
Tsukumi *Japan* 33°4N 131°52E 222 D3
Tsukushi-Sanchi *Japan* 33°25N 130°30E 222 D2
Tsumeb *Namibia* 19°9S 17°44E 270 A2
Tsumis *Namibia* 23°39S 17°29E 270 B2
Tsuna *Japan* 34°28N 134°56E 222 C6
Tsuno-Shima *Japan* 34°21N 130°52E 222 C2
Tsur Hadassa *Israel* 31°43N 35°6E 123 B1
Tsuru *Japan* 35°31N 138°57E 223 B10
Tsuruga *Japan* 35°45N 136°2E 223 B8
Tsuruga-Wan *Japan* 35°50N 136°3E 223 B8
Tsurugi *Japan* 36°29N 136°37E 223 A8
Tsurugi-San *Japan* 33°51N 134°6E 222 D6
Tsurumi → *Japan* 35°32N 139°40E 140 B3
Tsurumi-Saki *Japan* 32°56N 132°5E 222 E4
Tsuruoka *Japan* 38°44N 139°50E 220 E9
Tsurusaki *Japan* 33°14N 131°41E 222 D3
Tsushima *Ehime, Japan* 33°7N 132°32E 222 D4
Tsushima *Gifu, Japan* 35°10N 136°43E 223 B8
Tsushima *Nagasaki,*
Japan 34°20N 129°20E 222 C1
Tsuyama *Japan* 35°3N 134°0E 222 B6
Tsvetkovo *Ukraine* 49°8N 31°33E 189 H6
Tsyelyakhany *Belarus* 52°30N 25°46E 177 B13
Tsz Wan Shan *China* 22°20N 114°11E 122 A2
Tu → *Burma* 21°50N 96°15E 241 E6
Tua *Dem. Rep. of the Congo* 3°38S 16°38E 264 C3
Tua → *Papua N. G.* 6°30S 144°28E 286 D3
Tua → *Portugal* 41°13N 7°26W 194 D3
Tuaheni Pt. *N.Z.* 38°43S 178°4E 284 E7
Tuai *N.Z.* 38°47S 177°10E 284 E6
Tuam *Ireland* 53°31N 8°51W 166 C3
Tuamotu Arch. = Tuamotu Is.
Tuakau *N.Z.* 37°16S 174°59E 284 D3
Tual *Indonesia* 5°38S 132°44E 231 F8
Tualatin *U.S.A.* 45°23N 122°45W 306 E4

Tuam Ireland 53°31N 8°51W 166 C3
Tuamarina N.Z. 41°25S 173°59E 285 B8
Tuamotu, Îs.
French Polynesia 17°0S 144°0W 289 f
Tuamotu Arch. = Tuamotu, Îs.
French Polynesia 17°0S 144°0W 289 f
Tuamotu Ridge Pac. Oc. 20°0S 138°0W 289 K14
Tuan Giao Vietnam 21°35N 103°25E 236 B4
Tuanfeng China 30°38N 114°52E 229 B10
Tuanxi China 27°28N 107°8E 228 D6
Tuao Phil. 17°55N 121°22E 232 C3
Tuapa Cook Is. 18°57S 169°54W 289 g
Tuapse Russia 44°5N 39°10E 191 H4
Tuas Singapore 1°19N 103°39E 138 B1
Tuatapere N.Z. 46°8S 167°41E 285 G2
Tuba City U.S.A. 36°8N 111°14W 305 H8
Tuban Indonesia 6°54S 112°3E 235 D4
Tubani Botswana 24°46S 24°18E 270 B3
Tubarão Brazil 28°30S 49°0W 335 B6
Ṭūbās West Bank 32°20N 35°22E 251 F6
Tubas → Namibia 22°54S 14°35E 270 B2
Tubau Malaysia 3°10N 113°40E 235 B4
Tubbataha Reefs △ Phil. 8°53N 119°53E 233 G2
Tubigon Phil. 9°57N 123°58E 233 G4
Tübingen Germany 48°31N 9°4E 179 G5
Tubod Phil. 8°3N 123°48E 233 G4
Tubou Fiji 18°13S 178°48W 287 B3
Tubruq Libya 32°7N 23°55E 258 B4
Tubuai French Polynesia 23°18S 149°30W 289 f
Tubuaï, Îs. French Polynesia 25°0S 150°0W 289 f
Tuburan Basilan, Phil. 6°39N 122°16E 233 H4
Tuburan Cebu, Phil. 10°44N 123°49E 233 F4
Tuc Trung Vietnam 11°1N 107°12E 237 G6
Tucacas Venezuela 10°48N 68°19W 328 A4
Tucano Brazil 10°58S 38°48W 332 D4
T'uch'ang Taiwan 24°35N 121°29E 225 B3
Tuchitua Canada 60°55N 129°13W 296 A3
Tuchodi → Canada 58°17N 123°42W 296 B4
Tuchola Poland 53°33N 17°52E 184 E4
Tuchoměřice Czech Rep. 50°7N 14°16E 135 B1
Tuchów Poland 49°54N 21°1E 185 J8
Tuckahoe U.S.A. 40°56N 73°49W 132 A3
Tuckanarra Australia 27°7S 118°5E 279 E2
Tucker U.S.A. 33°51N 84°13W 316 B5
Tuckers Town Bermuda 32°20N 64°42W 153 a
Tucson U.S.A. 32°13N 110°58W 305 K8
Tucumán □ Argentina 26°48S 66°2W 334 B2
Tucumcari U.S.A. 35°10N 103°44W 305 J12
Tucunaré Brazil 5°18S 55°51W 331 B6
Tucupido Venezuela 9°17N 65°47W 328 B4
Tucupita Venezuela 9°2N 62°3W 329 B5
Tucuruí Brazil 3°42S 49°44W 332 B2
Tucuruí, Represa de Brazil 4°0S 49°30W 332 B2
Tucuruvi Brazil 23°28S 46°35W 137 A2
Tuczno Poland 53°13N 16°10E 185 E3
Tuddal Norway 59°46N 8°49E 164 E5
Tudela Spain 42°4N 1°39W 196 C3
Tudmur Syria 34°36N 38°15E 213 E8
Tudor, L. Canada 55°50N 65°25W 299 A6
Tudora Romania 47°31N 26°45E 183 C11
Tuella → Portugal 41°30N 7°12W 194 D3
Tuen Mun China 22°24N 113°59E 219 G10
Tueré → Brazil 2°48S 50°59W 332 B1
Tufanbeyli Turkey 38°15N 36°13E 212 C7
Tufello Italy 41°56N 12°32E 136 B2
Tüffer = Laško Slovenia 46°10N 15°16E 199 B12
Tufi Papua N. G. 9°8S 149°19E 286 E5
Tufnell Park U.K. 51°33N 0°8W 125 A3
Tufsingdal Norway 62°18N 11°44E 164 B8
Tufts Abyssal Plain
Pac. Oc. 47°0N 140°0W 289 C14
Tufts Univ. U.S.A. 42°24N 71°7W 116 A2
Tufu Pt. Amer. Samoa 14°13S 169°30W 302 g
Tugela → S. Africa 29°14S 31°30E 271 C5
Tughlakabad India 28°30N 77°16E 120 B2
Tugidak I. U.S.A. 56°30N 154°40W 303 H9
Tuguegarao Phil. 17°35N 121°42E 232 C3
Tugur Russia 53°44N 136°45E 215 D14
Tui Spain 42°3N 8°39W 194 C2
Tuileries, Jardin des Paris, France 134 b3
Tuineje Canary Is. 28°19N 14°3W 153 e2
Tukangbesi, Kepulauan
Indonesia 6°0S 124°0E 231 F6
Tukarak I. Canada 56°15N 78°45W 298 A4
Tukayyid Iraq 29°47N 45°36E 246 D5
Tûkh Egypt 30°21N 31°12E 256 H7
Tukhlya Ukraine 48°55N 23°28E 183 B8
Tukituki → N.Z. 39°36S 176°56E 284 F5
Tukobo Ghana 5°1N 2°47W 262 D4
Ṭūkrah Libya 32°30N 20°37E 258 B4
Tuktoyaktuk Canada 69°27N 133°2W 294 D5
Tuktut Nogait △ Canada 69°15N 122°0W 294 D7
Tuku Taiwan 23°41N 120°23E 225 C2
Tukums Latvia 56°58N 23°10E 184 B10
Tukums □ Latvia 56°55N 23°10E 184 B10
Tukuran Phil. 7°51N 123°34E 233 H4
Tukuyu Tanzania 9°17S 33°35E 269 D3
Tula Amer. Samoa 14°15S 170°34W 302 f
Tula Hidalgo, Mexico 20°3N 99°21W 319 C5
Tula Tamaulipas, Mexico 23°0N 99°43W 319 C5
Tula Nigeria 9°51N 11°27E 263 D7
Tula Russia 54°13N 37°38E 188 E9
Tula □ Russia 53°45N 37°30E 188 F9
Tulach Mhór = Tullamore
Ireland 53°16N 7°31W 166 C4
Tulagi Solomon Is. 9°5S 160°10E 287 M11
Tulak Afghan. 33°55N 63°40E 240 B1
Tulan Taiwan 22°53N 121°13E 225 D3
Tulancingo Mexico 20°5N 98°22W 319 C5
Tulangbawang →
Indonesia 4°24S 105°52E 234 C3
Tulare Serbia 42°48N 21°28E 202 D5
Tulare Calif., U.S.A. 36°13N 119°21W 306 J7
Tulare Lake Bed U.S.A. 36°0N 119°48W 306 K7
Tularosa U.S.A. 33°5N 106°1W 305 K10
Tulbagh S. Africa 33°16S 19°6E 270 D2
Tulcán Ecuador 0°48N 77°43W 328 C2
Tulcea Romania 45°13N 28°46E 183 E13
Tulcea □ Romania 45°0N 28°30E 183 E13
Tulchyn Ukraine 48°41N 28°49E 183 B13
Tüledi Araldary
Kazakhstan 45°2N 50°16E 191 H10
Tūleh Iran 34°35N 52°33E 247 C7
Tulemalu L. Canada 62°58N 99°25W 297 A9
Tulgheş Romania 46°58N 25°45E 183 D10
Tuli Zimbabwe 21°58S 29°13E 269 G2
Tulia U.S.A. 34°32N 101°46W 314 D4
Tuliszków Poland 52°5N 18°18E 185 F5
Tulita Canada 64°57N 125°30W 294 E6
Tulkarm West Bank 32°19N 35°2E 251 F6
Tulla Ireland 52°53N 8°46W 166 D3
Tullahoma U.S.A. 35°22N 86°13W 315 D11
Tullamarine Australia 37°41S 144°50E 128 A1
Tullamore N.S.W.,
Australia 32°39S 147°36E 283 B7
Tullamore Offaly, Ireland 53°16N 7°31W 166 C4
Tulle France 45°16N 1°46E 174 C5
Tulln Austria 48°20N 16°4E 180 C9
Tullow Ireland 52°49N 6°45W 166 D5
Tullus Sudan 11°7N 24°31E 257 E1
Tully Queens., Australia 17°56S 145°55E 280 B4
Tully N.Y., U.S.A. 42°48N 76°7W 313 D8
Ṭulmaythah Libya 32°40N 20°55E 258 B4
Tulnici Romania 45°51N 26°38E 183 E11
Tulovo Bulgaria 42°33N 25°32E 203 D9
Tulsa U.S.A. 36°10N 95°55W 314 C7
Tulse Hill U.K. 51°26N 0°6W 125 B3
Tulsequah Canada 58°39N 133°35W 296 B2
Tulu Milki Ethiopia 9°55N 38°20E 257 F4
Tulu Welel Ethiopia 8°56N 34°47E 257 F3
Tuluá Colombia 4°6N 76°11W 328 C2
Tuluceşti Romania 45°34N 28°2E 183 E13
Tuluksak U.S.A. 61°6N 160°58W 303 F7
Tulun Russia 54°32N 100°35E 215 D11
Tulungagung Indonesia 8°5S 111°54E 235 D4
Tuma Russia 55°10N 40°30E 188 E11
Tuma → Nic. 13°6N 84°35W 320 D3
Tumacacori ⌂ U.S.A. 31°35N 111°6W 305 L8
Tumaco Colombia 1°50N 78°45W 328 C2
Tumaco, Ensenada
Colombia 1°55N 78°45W 328 C2
Tumakuru = Tumkur
India 13°18N 77°6E 245 H3
Tumatumari Guyana 5°20N 58°55W 329 B6
Tumauini Phil. 17°17N 121°49E 232 C3
Tumba
Dem. Rep. of the Congo 3°10S 23°36E 264 C4
Tumba Sweden 59°12N 17°48E 162 E11
Tumba, L.
Dem. Rep. of the Congo 0°50S 18°0E 264 C3
Tumbarumba Australia 35°44S 148°0E 283 C8
Tumbaya Argentina 23°50S 65°26W 334 A2
Tumbes Peru 3°37S 80°27W 330 A1
Tumbes □ Peru 3°50S 80°30W 330 A1
Tumbler Ridge Canada 55°8N 121°0W 296 B4
Tumbur Sudan 4°20N 31°34E 257 G3
Tumbwe
Dem. Rep. of the Congo 11°25S 27°15E 269 E2
Tumby Bay Australia 34°21S 136°8E 282 C2
Tumd Youqi China 40°30N 110°30E 226 D6
Tumen China 43°0N 129°50E 224 A4
Tumen Jiang → China 42°20N 130°35E 224 A5
Tumeremo Venezuela 7°18N 61°30W 329 B5
Tumiritinga Brazil 18°58S 41°38W 333 E3
Tumkur India 13°18N 77°6E 245 H3
Tumon B. Guam 13°31N 144°48E 302 d
Tump Pakistan 26°7N 62°16E 240 D1
Tumpat Malaysia 6°11N 102°10E 237 J4
Tumsar India 21°26N 79°45E 244 D4
Tumu Ghana 10°56N 1°56W 262 C4
Tumucumaque, Serra
Brazil 2°0N 55°0W 329 C7
Tumupasa Bolivia 14°9S 67°55W 330 C4
Tumut Australia 35°16S 148°13E 283 C8
Tumwater U.S.A. 47°1N 122°54W 306 C4
Tuna India 22°59N 70°5E 242 H4
Tunadal Sweden 62°26N 17°22E 162 B11
Tunapuna Trin. & Tob. 10°38N 61°24W 323 t
Tunas de Zaza Cuba 21°39N 79°34W 320 B4
Tunbridge Wells = Royal
Tunbridge Wells U.K. 51°7N 0°16E 169 F8
Tunçbilek Turkey 39°37N 29°29E 205 B11
Tunceli Turkey 39°6N 39°31E 213 C8
Tunceli □ Turkey 39°5N 39°35E 213 C8
Tuncurry Australia 32°17S 152°29E 283 B10
Tundla India 27°12N 78°17E 242 F8
Tundubai Sudan 18°36N 28°35E 256 D2
Tunduru Tanzania 11°8S 37°25E 269 E4
Tundzha → Bulgaria 41°40N 26°35E 203 E10
Tung Chung China 22°17N 113°57E 219 G10
Tung Lung Chau China 22°15N 114°17E 122 B2
Tung O China 22°11N 114°8E 122 B1
Tunga → India 15°0N 75°50E 245 G2
Tunga Pass India 29°0N 94°14E 241 A5
Tungabhadra → India 15°57N 78°15E 245 G4
Tungabhadra Dam India 15°0N 75°50E 245 G2
Tungao Taiwan 24°31N 121°50E 225 B3
Tungaru Sudan 10°9N 30°52E 257 E3
Tungawan Phil. 7°30N 122°20E 233 H4
Tungchi Yü Taiwan 23°15N 119°40E 225 C1
Tungch'uan = Dongchuan
China 26°8N 103°1E 228 D4
Tungho Taiwan 22°58N 121°18E 225 D3
T'unghsiao Taiwan 24°29N 120°40E 225 B2
Tunghwa = Tonghua
China 41°42N 125°58E 224 B2
Tungi Bangla. 23°53N 90°24E 241 D3
Tungkang Taiwan 22°27N 120°26E 225 D2
Tungla Nic. 13°24N 84°21W 320 D3
T'unglo Taiwan 24°30N 120°47E 225 B2
Tungnafellsjökull
Iceland 64°45N 17°55W 155 C9
Tungsha Tao = Dongsha Dao
S. China Sea 20°45N 116°43E 229 G11
Tungshan Taiwan 24°38N 121°47E 225 B3
Tungshih Changhua,
Taiwan 24°12N 120°43E 225 B2
Tungshih Chiai, Taiwan 23°27N 120°8E 225 C2
Tungsten Canada 61°57N 128°16W 296 A3
Tungufell Iceland 64°17N 20°10W 155 C6
Tungurahua □ Ecuador 1°15S 78°35W 328 D2
Tunguska, Nizhnyaya →
Russia 65°48N 88°4E 215 C9
Tunguska, Podkamennaya →
Russia 61°50N 90°13E 215 C10
Tungyin Tao Taiwan 26°22N 128°29E 225 b
Tuni India 17°22N 82°36E 244 F6
Tunia Colombia 2°41N 76°31W 328 C2
Tunica U.S.A. 34°41N 90°23W 315 D9
Tunis Baghdād, Iraq 33°23N 44°21E 113 A2
Tunis Tunisia 36°50N 10°11E 258 A2
Tunis □ Tunisia 36°46N 10°10E 261 A7
Tunis ✕ (TUN) Tunisia 36°52N 10°14E 200 F3
Tunis, Golfe de Tunisia 37°0N 10°30E 258 A2
Tunisia ■ Africa 33°30N 9°10E 258 B1
Tunja Colombia 5°33N 73°25W 328 B3
Tunkhannock U.S.A. 41°32N 75°57W 313 E9
Tunliu China 36°13N 112°52E 226 F7
Tunnel Creek △
Australia 17°41S 125°18E 278 C4
Tunnsjøen Norway 64°45N 13°25E 160 D15
Tunø Denmark 55°57N 10°27E 163 J4
Tunungayualok I. Canada 56°0N 61°0W 299 A7
Tunuyán Argentina 33°35S 69°0W 334 C2
Tunuyán → Argentina 33°33S 67°30W 334 C2
Tunxi = Huangshan
China 30°8N 118°9E 229 B12
Tuo Jiang → China 28°50N 105°35E 228 C5
Tuolumne U.S.A. 37°58N 120°15W 306 H6
Tuolumne → U.S.A. 37°36N 121°13W 306 H5
Tuomarila Finland 60°11N 24°41E 121 B1
Tüp Kyrgyzstan 42°45N 78°20E 217 D9
Tūp Āghāj Iran 36°3N 47°50E 213 D12
Tupã Brazil 21°57S 50°28W 335 A5
Tupaciguara Brazil 18°35S 48°42W 333 E2
Tupelo U.S.A. 34°16N 88°43W 315 D10
Tupik Russia 55°42N 33°22E 188 E7
Tupinambarana, I. Brazil 3°0S 58°0W 329 D6
Tupirama Brazil 8°58S 48°12W 332 C2
Tupiratins Brazil 8°23S 48°8W 332 C2
Tupiza Bolivia 21°30S 65°40W 334 A2
Tupižnica Serbia 43°43N 22°10E 202 C6
Tupman U.S.A. 35°18N 119°21W 307 K7
Tupper Canada 55°32N 120°1W 296 B4
Tupper L. U.S.A. 44°10N 74°32W 313 B10
Tupper Lake U.S.A. 44°14N 74°28W 313 B10
Tüpqarghan Muyis
Kazakhstan 44°40N 50°19E 191 H10
Tupungato, Cerro
S. Amer. 33°15S 69°50W 334 C2
Tuquan China 45°18N 121°38E 227 B11
Túquerres Colombia 1°5N 77°37W 328 C2
Tura India 25°30N 90°16E 241 C3
Tura Russia 64°20N 100°17E 215 C11
Turabah Ḥā'il, Si. Arabia 28°20N 43°15E 246 D4
Turabah Makkah,
Si. Arabia 21°15N 41°34E 248 B3
Turagua, Serranía
Venezuela 7°20N 64°35W 329 B5
Turakina N.Z. 40°3S 175°16E 284 G4
Turakina → N.Z. 40°5S 175°8E 284 G4
Turakirae Hd. N.Z. 41°26S 174°56E 284 H3
Turama → Papua N. G. 7°40S 143°50E 286 D2
Tūrān Iran 35°39N 56°42E 247 C8
Turan Russia 51°55N 94°0E 217 B12
Turan Lowland Asia 43°30N 62°0E 216 D6
Turangi N.Z. 38°59S 175°48E 284 E4
Ṭurayf Si. Arabia 31°41N 38°39E 246 D3
Turbaco Colombia 10°21N 75°25W 328 A2
Turbacz Poland 49°30N 20°8E 185 J7
Turbat Pakistan 25°59N 63°4E 240 D1
Turbe Bos.-H. 44°15N 17°35E 182 F2
Turbeville U.S.A. 33°54N 80°1W 316 B9
Turbo Colombia 8°6N 76°43W 328 B2
Turčianske Teplice
Slovak Rep. 48°52N 18°52E 181 C11
Turco Bolivia 18°10S 68°11W 330 D4
Turcoaia Romania 45°7N 28°11E 183 E13
Turda Romania 46°34N 23°47E 183 D8
Tureberg Sweden 59°25N 17°55E 139 A1
Turéia French Polynesia 20°50S 138°32W 289 f
Turek Poland 52°3N 18°30E 185 F5
Turfan = Turpan China 43°58N 89°10E 217 D11
Turfan Basin = Turpan Pendi
China 42°40N 89°25E 217 D11
Turfan Depression = Turpan Pendi
China 42°40N 89°25E 217 D11
Turffontein S. Africa 26°14S 28°2E 123 B2
Turgayskaya Stolovaya Strana =
Torghay Ustirti Asia 51°0N 63°0E 216 B6
Turgeon → Canada 50°0N 78°56W 298 C4
Turgovishte Bulgaria 43°17N 26°38E 203 C10
Turgut Turkey 37°22N 28°4E 205 D10
Turgutlu Turkey 38°30N 27°43E 205 C9
Turgwe → Zimbabwe 21°31S 32°15E 271 B5
Turhal Turkey 40°24N 36°5E 212 B7
Turia → Spain 39°27N 0°19W 197 F4
Turiaçu Brazil 1°40S 45°19W 332 B2
Turiaçu → Brazil 1°36S 45°19W 332 B2
Turiec → Slovak Rep. 49°7N 18°55E 181 B11
Turin = Torino Italy 45°3N 7°40E 198 C4
Turinskaya Kultbaza = Tura
Russia 64°20N 100°17E 215 C11
Turka Ukraine 49°10N 23°2E 185 J10
Turkana, L. Africa 3°30N 36°5E 268 B4
Turkayel Ethiopia 8°7N 45°21E 267 C6
Türkeli Turkey 40°30N 27°30E 203 F11
Turkestan = Türkistan
Kazakhstan 43°17N 68°16E 217 D7
Turkestan Range Asia 39°35N 69°0E 217 E7
Túrkeve Hungary 47°6N 20°44E 182 C5
Turkey ■ Eurasia 39°0N 36°0E 212 C7
Turkey → U.S.A. 42°43N 91°2W 310 B5
Turkey Creek = Warmun
Australia 17°2S 128°12E 278 C4
Turkey L. U.S.A. 28°30N 81°28W 133 A2
Turkey Lake Park
U.S.A. 28°30N 81°28W 133 A2
Turki Russia 52°0N 43°15E 190 D6
Türkistan Kazakhstan 43°17N 68°16E 217 D7
Türkmenabat
Turkmenistan 39°6N 63°34E 247 B9
Türkmenbashi
Turkmenistan 40°5N 53°5E 247 A7
Turkmenistan ■ Asia 39°0N 59°0E 216 E5
Türkmenli Turkey 39°45N 26°30E 205 B8
Türkoğlu Turkey 37°23N 36°50E 212 D7
Turks & Caicos Is. ☒
W. Indies 21°20N 71°20W 321 B5
Turks Island Passage
W. Indies 21°30N 71°30W 321 B5
Turku Finland 60°30N 22°19E 162 D14
Turkwel → Kenya 3°6N 36°6E 268 B4
Turlock U.S.A. 37°30N 120°51W 306 H6
Turnagain Australia 9°34S 142°17E 280 a
Turnagain → Canada 59°12N 127°35W 296 B3
Turnagain, C. N.Z. 40°28S 176°38E 284 G5
Turneffe Is. Belize 17°20N 87°50W 320 C2
Turner U.S.A. 48°51N 108°24W 304 B9
Turner Field U.S.A. 33°44N 84°23W 113 B2
Turner Pt. Australia 11°47S 133°32E 280 A1
Turner Valley Canada 50°40N 114°17W 296 C6
Turners Falls U.S.A. 42°36N 72°33W 313 D12
Turner's Pen. S. Leone 7°20N 12°40W 262 D2
Turnham Green U.K. 51°29N 0°16W 125 B2
Turnhout Belgium 51°19N 4°57E 170 C4
Türnitz Austria 47°55N 15°29E 180 D8
Turnor L. Canada 56°35N 108°35W 297 B7
Turnov Czech Rep. 50°34N 15°10E 180 A8
Tŭrnovo = Veliko Tŭrnovo
Bulgaria 43°5N 25°41E 203 C9
Turnu Măgurele
Romania 43°46N 24°56E 183 G9
Turnu Roşu, P. Romania 45°33N 24°17E 183 E9
Turobin Poland 50°50N 22°44E 185 H9
Tuross Head Australia 36°3S 150°8E 283 D9
Turpan China 43°58N 89°10E 217 D11
Turpan Pendi China 42°40N 89°25E 217 D11
Turrawan Australia 30°28S 149°53E 283 A8
Turrës, Kala e Albania 41°10N 19°28E 202 E3
Turriff U.K. 57°32N 2°27W 167 D6
Tursāq Iraq 33°27N 45°47E 213 F11
Tursi Italy 40°15N 16°28E 201 B9
Tursunzoda Tajikistan 38°30N 68°13E 217 E7
Turtle Head I. Australia 10°56S 142°37E 280 A3
Turtle Is. Phil. 6°7N 118°14E 233 H2
Turtle Is. S. Leone 7°40N 13°0W 262 D2
Turtle L. Canada 53°36N 108°38W 297 C7
Turtle Lake U.S.A. 47°31N 100°53W 308 B3
Turtleford Canada 53°23N 108°57W 297 C7
Turtucaia = Tutrakan
Bulgaria 44°2N 26°40E 203 B10
Turua N.Z. 37°14S 175°35E 284 D4
Turukhansk Russia 65°21N 88°5E 215 C9
Turyinskiye Rudniki =
Krasnoturinsk Russia 59°46N 60°12E 186 C11
Turzovka Slovak Rep. 49°25N 18°35E 181 B11
Tuscaloosa U.S.A. 33°12N 87°34W 315 E11
Tuscánia Italy 42°25N 11°52E 199 F8
Tuscany = Toscana □
Italy 43°25N 11°0E 198 E8
Tuscarawas → U.S.A. 40°24N 81°25W 312 F3
Tuscarora Mt. U.S.A. 40°55N 77°55W 312 F7
Tuscola Ill., U.S.A. 39°48N 88°17W 311 E8
Tuscola Tex., U.S.A. 32°12N 99°48W 314 E5
Tuscolana, Via Italy 41°52N 12°31E 136 B2
Tuscumbia Ala., U.S.A. 34°44N 87°42W 315 D11
Tuscumbia Mo., U.S.A. 38°14N 92°28W 310 F4
Tushino Russia 55°50N 37°24E 129 A2
Tuskegee U.S.A. 32°25N 85°42W 316 C4
Tusket Wedge = Wedgeport
Canada 43°44N 65°59W 299 D6
Tustna Norway 63°10N 8°5E 164 A5
Tuszyn Poland 51°36N 19°33E 185 G6
Tutak Turkey 39°31N 42°46E 213 C10
Tutayev Russia 57°53N 39°32E 188 D10
Tuticorin India 8°50N 78°12E 245 K4
Tutin Serbia 42°58N 20°20E 202 D4
Tutóia Brazil 2°45S 42°20W 332 B3
Tutong Brunei 4°47N 114°40E 235 B4
Tutova → Romania 46°7N 27°30E 183 D12
Tutrakan Bulgaria 44°2N 26°40E 203 B10
Tuttle Creek L. U.S.A. 39°15N 96°36W 308 F5
Tuttlingen Germany 47°58N 8°48E 179 H4
Tutuala E. Timor 8°25S 127°15E 231 F7
Tutuba Vanuatu 15°33S 167°16E 287 E5
Tutubeia Papua N. G. 9°34S 150°40E 286 E6
Tutuila Amer. Samoa 14°19S 170°50W 302 f
Tutuko, Mt. N.Z. 44°35S 168°1E 285 E3
Tutun Egypt 29°9N 30°46E 256 J7
Tütz = Tuczno Poland 53°13N 16°10E 185 E3
Tuul Gol → Mongolia 48°30N 104°25E 218 B5
Tuva □ Russia 51°30N 95°0E 217 B12
Tuvalu ■ Pac. Oc. 8°0S 178°0E 277 B14
Tuvuca Fiji 17°40S 178°48W 287 A3
Ṭuwal Si. Arabia 22°17N 39°6E 248 B2
Tuxer Alpen Austria 47°10N 11°45E 180 D4
Tuxpan Mexico 20°57N 97°24W 319 C5
Tuxtla Gutiérrez Mexico 16°45N 93°7W 319 D6
Tuy = Tui Spain 42°3N 8°39W 194 C2
Tuy An Vietnam 13°17N 109°16E 236 F7
Tuy Duc Vietnam 12°15N 107°27E 237 F6
Tuy Hoa Vietnam 13°5N 109°10E 236 F7
Tuy Phong Vietnam 11°14N 108°43E 237 G7
Tuya L. Canada 59°7N 130°35W 296 B2
Tuyen Hoa Vietnam 17°50N 106°10E 236 D6
Tuyen Quang Vietnam 21°50N 105°10E 228 G5
Tuymazy Russia 54°36N 53°42E 216 B4
Tūysarkān Iran 34°33N 48°27E 213 E13
Tuyün = Duyun China 26°18N 107°29E 228 D6
Tuz Gölü Turkey 38°42N 33°18E 212 C5
Ţūz Khurmātū Iraq 34°56N 44°38E 213 E11
Tuzi Montenegro 42°22N 19°20E 202 D3
Tuzigoot △ U.S.A. 34°46N 112°2W 305 J7
Tuzla Bos.-H. 44°34N 18°41E 182 F3
Tuzla Turkey 36°42N 35°6E 250 B6
Tuzlov → Russia 47°17N 39°57E 189 J10
Tuzluca Turkey 40°3N 43°39E 213 B10
Tuzly 45°54N 30°6E 183 E15
Tvååker Sweden 57°4N 12°25E 163 G6
Tvardiţa Moldova 46°9N 28°58E 183 D13
Tvedestrand Norway 58°38N 8°58E 164 F5
Tver Russia 56°55N 35°55E 188 D8
Tver □ Russia 56°50N 35°0E 188 D8
Tvrdošin Slovak Rep. 49°21N 19°35E 181 B12
Tvrdošovce Slovak Rep. 48°6N 18°4E 181 C11
Tvŭrditsa Bulgaria 42°42N 25°53E 203 D9
Twain U.S.A. 40°1N 121°3W 306 E5
Twain Harte U.S.A. 38°2N 120°14W 306 G6
Twardogóra Poland 51°23N 17°28E 185 G4
Twee River Namibia 25°27S 19°27E 270 C2
Tweed Canada 44°29N 77°19W 312 B7
Tweed → U.K. 55°45N 2°0W 167 F6
Tweed Heads Australia 28°10S 153°31E 281 D5
Tweedsmuir ⌂ Canada 53°0N 126°20W 296 C3
Twelve Apostles S. Africa 33°58S 18°23E 118 A1
Twentieth Century Fox Studios
U.S.A. 34°4N 118°25W 126 B2
Twentynine Palms
U.S.A. 34°8N 116°3W 307 L10
Tweya
Dem. Rep. of the Congo 0°54S 18°58E 264 C3
Twickenham U.K. 51°26N 0°20W 125 B1
Twickenham Rugby Ground
U.K. 51°27N 0°20W 125 B1
Twillingate Canada 49°42N 54°45W 299 C9
Twin Bridges U.S.A. 45°33N 112°20W 304 D7
Twin City U.S.A. 32°35N 82°10W 316 C7
Twin Falls Canada 53°30N 64°32W 299 B7
Twin Falls Idaho, U.S.A. 42°34N 114°28W 304 E6
Twin Hills U.S.A. 59°23N 159°58W 303 G8
Twin Lakes U.S.A. 30°43N 83°13W 316 E6
Twin Peaks U.S.A. 37°45N 122°26W 136 B2
Twin Valley U.S.A. 47°16N 96°16W 308 B5
Twinnge Burma 23°10N 96°2E 241 D6
Twinsburg U.S.A. 41°19N 81°26W 312 E3
Twistringen Germany 52°48N 8°37E 178 C4
Twitchell Res. U.S.A. 34°59N 120°19W 307 L6
Two Boats Village
Ascension I. 7°56S 14°22W 153 g
Two Harbors U.S.A. 47°2N 91°40W 308 B8
Two Hills Canada 53°43N 111°52W 296 C6
Two Rivers U.S.A. 44°9N 87°34W 308 C10
Two Rock Mt. Ireland 53°15N 6°14W 120 B2
Two Rocks Australia 31°30S 115°35E 279 F2
Two Thumb Ra. N.Z. 43°45S 170°44E 285 D5
Twofold B. Australia 37°8S 149°59E 283 D8
Twyfelfontein Namibia 20°34S 14°22E 270 B1
Ty Ty U.S.A. 31°28N 83°39W 316 D6
Tyachiv Ukraine 48°1N 23°35E 177 D12
Tybee Island U.S.A. 32°1N 80°51W 316 C9
Tychy Poland 50°9N 18°59E 185 H5
Tyczyn Poland 49°58N 22°2E 185 J9
Tydal Norway 63°4N 11°34E 164 A8
Tyin Norway 61°18N 8°15E 164 C5
Tykocin Poland 53°13N 22°46E 185 E9
Tyler Minn., U.S.A. 44°17N 96°8W 308 C5
Tyler Tex., U.S.A. 32°21N 95°18W 314 E7
Tyligul → Ukraine 47°4N 30°57E 189 J6
Tylldal Norway 62°8N 10°48E 164 B7
Tymanivka Ukraine 48°34N 28°50E 183 B13
Tymon North Ireland 53°18N 6°20W 120 B1
Týn nad Vltavou
Czech Rep. 49°13N 14°26E 180 B7
Tynda Russia 55°10N 124°43E 215 D13
Tyndall U.S.A. 43°0N 97°50W 308 D5
Tyndinsky = Tynda
Russia 55°10N 124°43E 215 D13
Tyne → U.K. 54°59N 1°32W 168 C6
Tyne & Wear □ U.K. 55°6N 1°17W 168 B6
Týnec nad Sázavou
Czech Rep. 49°50N 14°36E 180 B7
Tynemouth U.K. 55°1N 1°26W 168 B6
Tynset Norway 62°17N 10°47E 164 B7
Tyonek U.S.A. 61°4N 151°8W 303 F10
Tyre = Sūr Lebanon 33°19N 35°16E 250 E6
Tyresta △ Sweden 59°12N 18°14E 162 E12
Tyrifjorden Norway 60°2N 10°8E 164 D7
Tyringe Sweden 56°9N 13°35E 163 H7
Tyristrand Norway 60°4N 10°6E 164 D7
Tyrnyauz Russia 43°21N 42°45E 191 J6
Tyrol = Tirol □ Austria 47°3N 10°43E 180 D3
Tyrone U.S.A. 40°40N 78°14W 312 F6
Tyrone □ U.K. 54°38N 7°11W 166 B4
Tyrrel Bay Grenada 12°27N 61°28W 323 q
Tyrrell → Australia 35°26S 142°51E 282 C5
Tyrrell, L. Australia 35°20S 142°50E 282 C5
Tyrrell L. Canada 63°7N 105°27W 297 A7
Tyrrhenian Sea Medit. S. 40°0N 12°30E 192 D6
Tysfjorden Norway 68°7N 16°25E 160 B17
Tysmenytsya Ukraine 48°54N 24°51E 183 B9
Tysnes Norway 60°1N 5°30E 164 D2
Tysnesøya Norway 60°0N 5°35E 164 D2
Tysons Corner U.S.A. 38°55N 77°13W 143 B2
Tysse Norway 60°23N 5°47E 164 D2
Tyssedal Norway 60°7N 6°35E 164 D3
Tystberga Sweden 58°51N 17°15E 163 F11
Tytuvėnai Lithuania 55°36N 23°12E 184 C10
Tyub Karagan, Mys = Tüpqarghan
Muyis Kazakhstan 44°40N 50°19E 191 H10
Tyuleni, Ostrova = Tüledi Araldary
Kazakhstan 45°2N 50°16E 191 H10
Tyuleniy Russia 44°28N 47°30E 191 H8
Tyuleniy, Mys
Azerbaijan 40°12N 50°22E 191 K10
Tyulgan Russia 52°22N 56°12E 186 D10
Tyumen Russia 57°11N 65°29E 214 D7
Tyup = Tüp Kyrgyzstan 42°45N 78°20E 217 D9
Tywi → U.K. 51°48N 4°21W 169 F3
Tywyn U.K. 52°35N 4°5W 169 E3
Tzaneen S. Africa 23°47S 30°9E 271 B5
Tzermiado Greece 35°12N 25°29E 207 E6
Tzia = Kea Greece 37°35N 24°22E 204 D6
Tzoumérka, Óros = Athamanon
Oros Greece 39°30N 21°26E 204 B3
Tzukong = Zigong
China 29°15N 104°48E 228 C5
Tzukuan Taiwan 22°46N 120°16E 225 D2
Tzupo = Boshan China 36°28N 117°49E 227 F9
Tzutung Taiwan 23°45N 120°30E 225 C2

U

U.S.A. = United States of
America ■ N. Amer. 37°0N 96°0W 301 H20
U.S. Capitol Washington, D.C., U.S.A. 143 b3
U.S. Cellular Field U.S.A. 41°50N 87°37W 119 C3
U.S.S. Arizona ⌂
U.S.A. 21°22N 157°57W 302 K14
U.S.S. Constitution = Old Ironside
Boston, U.S.A. 116 a3
U.S. Virgin Is. ☒ W. Indies 18°20N 65°0W 321 C7
Ua Huka French Polynesia 8°55S 139°32W 289 f
Ua Pu French Polynesia 9°25S 140°0W 289 f
Uachadi, Sierra = Uasadi-jidi
Venezuela 4°54N 65°18W 329 C4
Uad Atui → W. Sahara 20°4N 15°59W 260 D2
Uad el Jat → W. Sahara 26°47N 13°3W 260 C2
Uainambi Colombia 1°43N 69°51W 328 C4
Uamba Angola 7°21S 16°10E 265 D3
Uanle Uen = Wanleweyne
Somali Rep. 2°37N 44°54E 267 D5
Uasadi-jidi Venezuela 4°54N 65°18W 329 C4
Uati-Paraná → Brazil 1°51S 65°37W 328 D4
Uatumã → Brazil 2°26S 57°37W 329 D6
Uauá Brazil 9°50S 39°28W 332 C4
Uaupés Brazil 0°8S 67°5W 328 D4
Uaupés → Brazil 0°2N 67°16W 328 C4
Uaxactún Guatemala 17°25N 89°29W 320 C2
Ub Serbia 44°28N 20°6E 202 B4
Ubá Brazil 21°8S 43°0W 333 F3
Uba Nigeria 10°29N 13°13E 263 C7
Ubai Papua N. G. 5°39S 150°38E 286 C6
Ubaitaba Brazil 14°18S 39°20W 333 D4
Ubajara △ Brazil 3°55S 40°50W 332 B3
Ubangi = Oubangi →
Dem. Rep. of the Congo 0°30S 17°50E 264 C3
Ubaté Colombia 5°19N 73°49W 328 B3
Ubauro Pakistan 28°15N 69°45E 242 E3
Ubay Phil. 10°3N 124°28E 233 F5
Ubaye → France 44°28N 6°18E 175 D10
Ubayyiḍ, W. al → Iraq 32°34N 43°48E 213 F10
Ube Japan 33°56N 131°15E 222 D3
Úbeda Spain 38°3N 3°23W 195 G7
Ubeidiya West Bank 31°43N 35°17E 123 B2
Uberaba Brazil 19°50S 47°55W 333 E2
Uberaba → Brazil 23°35S 46°41W 137 B2
Uberaba, L. Brazil 17°30S 57°50W 331 D6
Uberlândia Minas Gerais,
Brazil 19°0S 48°20W 333 E2
Uberlândia Roraima,
Brazil 0°48N 59°20W 329 C6
Überlingen Germany 47°46N 9°10E 179 H5
Ubiaja Nigeria 6°41N 6°22E 263 D6
Ubin, Pulau Singapore 1°24N 103°57E 138 A3
Ubly U.S.A. 43°42N 82°55W 312 C2
Ubolratna Res. Thailand 16°45N 102°30E 236 D4
Ubombo S. Africa 27°31S 32°4E 271 C5
Ubon Ratchathani
Thailand 15°15N 104°50E 236 E5
Ubondo
Dem. Rep. of the Congo 0°55S 25°42E 268 C2
Ubort → Belarus 52°6N 28°30E 177 B15
Ubrique Spain 36°41N 5°27W 195 J5
Ubud Indonesia 8°30S 115°16E 231 J18
Ubuna Solomon Is. 10°11S 161°24E 287 N11
Ubundu
Dem. Rep. of the Congo 0°22S 25°30E 264 C5
Ucar Azerbaijan 40°31N 47°39E 213 B12
Ucayali → Peru 4°30S 73°30W 328 D3
Uccle Belgium 50°48N 4°22E 116 B2
Uchab Namibia 19°47S 17°42E 270 A2
Uchiko Japan 33°33N 132°39E 222 D4
Uchiura-Wan Japan 42°25N 140°40E 220 C10
Uchiza Peru 8°25S 76°20W 330 B2
Uchquduq Uzbekistan 41°50N 62°50E 216 D6
Uchte Germany 52°30N 8°54E 178 C4
Uchur → Russia 58°48N 130°35E 215 D14
Uckermark Germany 53°5N 13°30E 178 B9
Ucluelet Canada 48°57N 125°32W 296 D3
Úcua Angola 8°43S 14°8E 265 D2
Uda → Russia 54°42N 135°14E 215 D14
Uda Walawe △ Sri Lanka 6°20N 81°0E 245 L5
Udachnyy Russia 66°25N 112°24E 215 C12
Udagamandalam India 11°30N 76°44E 245 J3
Udainagar India 22°33N 76°13E 242 H7
Udaipur Raj., India 24°36N 73°44E 242 G5
Udaipur Tripura, India 23°32N 91°30E 241 D3
Udaipur Garhi Nepal 27°0N 86°35E 243 F12
Udala India 21°35N 86°34E 243 J12
Udalguri India 26°46N 92°8E 241 B4
Udayagiri Andhra Pradesh,
India 14°52N 79°19E 245 G4
Udayagiri Orissa, India 20°8N 84°23E 244 D7
Udbina Croatia 44°31N 15°47E 199 D12
Uddeholm Sweden 60°1N 13°38E 162 D7
Uddevalla Sweden 58°21N 11°55E 163 F5
Uddjaure Sweden 65°56N 17°49E 160 D17
Udelnaya Russia 60°0N 30°21E 137 A2
Udelnoe Russia 59°58N 30°20E 137 B1
Uden Neths. 51°40N 5°37E 170 C5
Udgir India 18°25N 77°5E 244 E3
Udhampur India 33°0N 75°5E 243 C6
Udi Nigeria 6°17N 7°21E 263 D6
Údine Italy 46°3N 13°14E 199 B10
Udintsev Fracture Zone
S. Ocean 57°0S 145°0W 151 B13
Udlding Germany 48°15N 11°25E 131 A1
Udmurtia □ Russia 57°30N 52°30E 186 C9
Udon Thani Thailand 17°29N 102°46E 236 D4
Udong Cambodia 11°48N 104°45E 237 G5
Udot I. Micronesia 7°22N 151°42E 287 T17
Udskaya Guba Russia 54°50N 135°45E 215 D14
Udu Pt. Fiji 16°9S 179°57W 287 A3
Udumalaippettai India 10°35N 77°15E 245 J3
Udupi India 13°25N 74°42E 245 H2
Udva India 20°5N 73°0E 244 D1
Udvoy Balkan Bulgaria 42°50N 26°50E 203 D10
Udzungwa △ Tanzania 7°52S 36°35E 268 D4
Udzungwa Range
Tanzania 9°30S 35°10E 269 D4
Ueckermünde Germany 53°44N 14°1E 178 B10
Ueda Japan 36°24N 138°16E 223 A10
Uedineniya, Os. Russia 78°0N 85°0E 150 B12
Uele →
Dem. Rep. of the Congo 3°45N 24°45E 264 B4
Uelen Russia 66°10N 170°0W 215 C19
Uelzen Germany 52°57N 10°32E 178 C6
Ueno Mie, Japan 34°45N 136°8E 223 C8
Ueno Tōkyō, Japan 35°42N 139°46E 140 A3
Uetersen Germany 53°40N 9°40E 178 B5
Uetze Germany 52°28N 10°11E 178 C6
Ufa Russia 54°45N 55°55E 186 D10
Ufa → Russia 54°40N 56°0E 186 D10
Uffenheim Germany 49°33N 10°14E 179 F6
Ugab → Namibia 20°55S 13°30E 270 B1
Ugalla → Tanzania 5°8S 30°42E 268 D3
Ugalla River △ Tanzania 5°50S 31°54E 268 D3
Uganda ■ Africa 2°0N 32°0E 268 B3
Ugento Italy 39°56N 18°10E 201 C11
Ugep Nigeria 5°53N 8°2E 263 D6
Ughelli Nigeria 5°33N 6°0E 263 D6
Ugie S. Africa 31°10S 28°13E 271 D4
Ugíjar Spain 36°58N 3°7W 195 J7
Ugine France 45°45N 6°25E 175 C10
Uglegorsk Russia 49°5N 142°2E 215 E15
Uglich Russia 57°33N 38°20E 188 D10
Ugljan Croatia 44°12N 15°10E 199 D12
Ugljane Croatia 43°35N 16°46E 199 E13
Ugolny = Beringovskiy
Russia 63°3N 179°19E 215 C18
Ugolny = Karpinsk
Russia 59°45N 60°1E 186 C11
Ugolnyye Kopi Russia 64°44N 177°42E 215 C18
Ugolnyye Kopi = Kopeysk
Russia 55°7N 61°37E 216 A6
Ugoofaaru Maldives 5°40N 73°0E 272 d
Ugra → Russia 54°30N 36°7E 188 E9
Ugŭrchin Bulgaria 43°6N 24°26E 203 C8
Uh → Slovak Rep. 48°37N 22°0E 181 C15
Uherské Hradiště
Czech Rep. 49°4N 17°30E 181 B10
Uherský Brod Czech Rep. 49°1N 17°40E 181 B10
Úhlava → Czech Rep. 49°45N 13°24E 180 B6
Uhlenhorst Namibia 23°45S 17°55E 270 B2
Uhniv Ukraine 50°22N 23°45E 185 H10
Üholičky Czech Rep. 50°9N 14°19E 135 B1
Uhrichsville U.S.A. 40°24N 81°21W 312 F3
Uhříněves Czech Rep. 50°2N 14°35E 135 B3
Uibhist a Deas = South Uist
U.K. 57°20N 7°15W 167 D1
Uibhist a Tuath = North Uist
U.K. 57°40N 7°15W 167 D1
Uiche Angola 12°2S 20°51E 265 E4
Uido S. Korea 34°36N 125°50E 224 E2
Uig U.K. 57°35N 6°21W 167 D2
Uíge Angola 7°30S 14°40E 265 D2
Uíge □ Angola 7°0S 16°0E 265 D3
Uiha Tonga 19°54S 174°25W 287 P13
Uijeongbu S. Korea 37°44N 127°2E 224 D3
Ŭiju N. Korea 40°15N 124°35E 224 B2
Uinta Mts. U.S.A. 40°45N 110°30W 304 F8
Uiryeong S. Korea 35°19N 128°15E 224 E4
Uis Namibia 21°8S 14°49E 270 B1
Uiseong S. Korea 36°21N 128°45E 224 D4
Uitenhage S. Africa 33°40S 25°28E 270 D4
Uithoorn Neths. 52°14N 4°50E 112 B1
Uithuizen Neths. 53°24N 6°41E 170 A6
Ujazd Poland 50°23N 18°21E 185 H5
Ujazdów Poland 52°13N 21°1E 142 B2
Ujazdowski Castle Warsaw, Poland 142 c3
Újfehértó Hungary 47°49N 21°41E 182 C6
Ujh → India 32°10N 75°18E 242 C6
Ujhani India 28°0N 79°6E 243 F8
Uji Japan 34°53N 135°48E 223 C7
Uji-guntō Japan 31°15N 129°25E 221 J4
Ujiyamada = Ise Japan 34°25N 136°45E 223 C8
Ujjain India 23°9N 75°43E 242 H6
Újpalota Hungary 47°32N 19°8E 117 A2
Újpest Hungary 47°35N 19°6E 117 A2
Ujście Poland 53°3N 16°45E 185 E3
Újszász Hungary 47°19N 20°7E 182 C5
Ujung Kulon △ Indonesia 6°46S 105°19E 234 D3
Ujung Pandang Indonesia 5°10S 119°20E 231 F5
Uka Russia 57°50N 162°0E 215 D17
Ukai Sagar India 21°20N 73°43E 244 D1
Ukara I. Tanzania 1°50S 33°0E 268 C3
Uke-Shima Japan 28°2N 129°14E 221 K4
Ukerewe I. Tanzania 2°0S 33°0E 268 C3
Ukholovo Russia 53°47N 40°30E 190 D5
Ukhrul India 25°10N 94°25E 241 C5
Ukhta Russia 63°34N 53°41E 186 B9
Uki Ni Masi Solomon Is. 10°15S 161°47E 287 N11
Ukiah U.S.A. 39°9N 123°13W 306 F3
Ukita Japan 35°40N 139°51E 140 A4
Ukmergė Lithuania 55°15N 24°45E 188 E3
Ukraine ■ Europe 49°0N 32°0E 189 H7
Uku Angola 11°24S 14°22E 265 E2
Ukwi Botswana 23°29S 20°30E 270 B3
Ula Turkey 37°6N 28°25E 212 D3
Ulaan-Uul Mongolia 44°13N 111°10E 226 B6
Ulaanbaatar Mongolia 47°55N 106°53E 218 B5
Ulaangom Mongolia 50°5N 92°10E 217 B12
Ulaanjirem Mongolia 45°5N 105°30E 226 B3
Ulak I. U.S.A. 51°22N 178°57W 303 L3
Ulala = Gorno-Altaysk
Russia 51°50N 86°5E 217 B11
Ulalu I. Micronesia 7°23N 151°41E 287 T17
Ulamambri Australia 31°19S 149°23E 283 A8
Ulamba
Dem. Rep. of the Congo 9°3S 23°38E 265 D4
Ulamona Papua N. G. 5°0S 151°15E 286 C6
Ulan Bator = Ulaanbaatar
Mongolia 47°55N 106°53E 218 B5
Ulan Erge Russia 46°19N 44°53E 191 G7
Ulan Khol Russia 45°18N 47°4E 191 H8
Ulan Ude Russia 51°45N 107°40E 215 D11
Ulanhad = Chifeng
China 42°18N 118°58E 227 C10
Ulanów Poland 50°30N 22°16E 185 H9
Ulaş Sivas, Turkey 39°26N 37°2E 212 C7
Ulaş Tekirdağ, Turkey 41°14N 27°42E 203 E11
Ulawa Solomon Is. 9°46S 161°57E 287 M11
Ulaya Morogoro, Tanzania 7°3S 36°55E 268 D4
Ulaya Tabora, Tanzania 4°25S 33°30E 268 C3
Ulcinj Montenegro 41°58N 19°10E 202 E3
Ulco S. Africa 28°21S 24°15E 270 C3
Ule älv = Oulujoki →
Finland 65°1N 25°30E 160 D21
Ule träsk = Oulujärvi
Finland 64°25N 27°15E 160 D22
Uleåborg = Oulu Finland 65°1N 25°29E 160 D21
Ulefoss Norway 59°17N 9°16E 164 E6
Ulëz Albania 41°46N 19°54E 202 E3
Ulfborg Denmark 56°16N 8°20E 163 H2
Ulhasnagar India 19°15N 73°10E 244 E1
Uliastay Mongolia 47°56N 97°28E 218 B4
Uljin S. Korea 36°59N 129°24E 224 D4
Uljma Serbia 45°2N 21°10E 182 E6
Ülken Kazakhstan 45°12N 73°58E 217 C8
Ülken Borsyq Qumy
Kazakhstan 47°0N 59°11E 216 C5
Ulla → Spain 42°39N 8°44W 194 C2
Ulladulla Australia 35°21S 150°29E 283 C9
Ullal India 12°48N 74°51E 245 H2
Ullapool U.K. 57°54N 5°9W 167 D3
Ullared Sweden 57°8N 12°42E 163 G6
Ulldecona Spain 40°36N 0°20E 196 E5
Ullerup Denmark 55°34N 12°36E 118 B3
Ulleungdo S. Korea 37°30N 130°30E 224 D5
Ullevål Norway 59°56N 10°46E 133 A3
Ullswater Ont., Canada 45°12N 79°29W 312 A5
Ullswater Cumb., U.K. 54°34N 2°52W 168 C5

Ulm *Germany* 48°23N 9°58E **179** G5
Ulmarra *Australia* 29°37S 153°4E **281** D5
Ulmeni *Buzău, Romania* 45°4N 26°40E **183** E11
Ulmeni *Maramureş, Romania* 47°28N 23°18E **183** C8
Ulonguè *Mozam.* 14°37S 34°19E **269** E3
Ulricehamn *Sweden* 57°46N 13°26E **163** G7
Ulrika *Sweden* 58°5N 15°23E **163** F9
Ulriksdal *Sweden* 59°23N 17°59E **139** A1
Ulsan *S. Korea* 35°20N 129°15E **224** E4
Ulsberg *Norway* 62°45N 10°0E **164** B6
Ulsta *U.K.* 60°30N 1°9W **167** A7
Ulsteinvik *Norway* 62°21N 5°53E **164** B2
Ulster □ *U.K.* 54°35N 6°30W **166** B5
Ulstrem *Bulgaria* 42°1N 26°27E **203** D10
Ultima *Australia* 35°30S 143°18E **282** C5
Ulubat Gölü *Turkey* 40°9N 28°35E **203** F12
Ulubey *Turkey* 38°25N 29°18E **205** C11
Uluborlu *Turkey* 38°4N 30°28E **205** C12
Uluçinar *Turkey* 36°24N 35°53E **250** B6
Uludağ *Turkey* 40°4N 29°13E **203** F13
Uludağ △ *Turkey* 40°5N 29°12E **203** F13
Uludere *Turkey* 37°28N 42°42E **213** D10
Ulugqat *China* 39°48N 74°15E **217** E8
Uluguru Mts. *Tanzania* 7°15S 37°40E **268** D4
Ulukışla *Turkey* 37°33N 34°28E **212** D6
Ulundi *S. Africa* 28°20S 31°25E **271** C5
Ulungur He → *China* 47°1N 87°24E **217** C11
Ulungur Hu *China* 47°20N 87°10E **217** C11
Ulupalakua *U.S.A.* 20°39N 156°24W **302** C5
Uluru *Australia* 25°23S 131°5E **279** E5
Uluru-Kata Tjuta △ *Australia* 25°19S 131°1E **279** E5
Ulutau *Kazakhstan* 48°39N 67°1E **217** C7
Uluwatu *Indonesia* 8°50S 115°5E **231** K18
Ulva *U.K.* 56°29N 6°13W **167** E2
Ulverston *U.K.* 54°13N 3°5W **168** C4
Ulverstone *Australia* 41°11S 146°11E **281** G4
Ulvik *Norway* 60°35N 6°54E **164** D3
Ulya *Russia* 59°10N 142°0E **215** D15
Ulyanka *Russia* 59°50N 30°14E **137** B1
Ulyanovo *Russia* 54°50N 22°6E **184** D9
Ulyanovsk *Russia* 54°20N 48°25E **190** C9
Ulyanovsk □ *Russia* 54°5N 48°5E **190** C9
Ulyasutay = Uliastay *Mongolia* 47°56N 97°28E **218** B4
Ulysses *Kans., U.S.A.* 37°35N 101°22W **308** G3
Ulysses *Pa., U.S.A.* 41°54N 77°46W **312** E7
Ulysses, Mt. *Canada* 57°20N 124°5W **296** B4
Ulysses S. Grant Nat. Historic Site ⌓ *U.S.A.* 38°33N 90°28W **310** F6
Ulyzhylanshyq → *Kazakhstan* 48°51N 63°46E **216** C6
Um Al-Khanazir Island *Iraq* 33°17N 44°22E **113** B2
Umag *Croatia* 45°26N 13°31E **199** C10
Umala *Bolivia* 17°25S 68°5W **330** D4
'Umān = Oman ■ *Asia* 23°0N 58°0E **249** B7
Uman *Ukraine* 48°40N 30°12E **177** D16
Uman I. *Micronesia* 7°17N 151°52E **287** U18
Umaria *India* 23°35N 80°50E **243** H9
Umarkhed *India* 19°37N 77°46E **244** E3
Umarkot *Pakistan* 25°15N 69°40E **242** G3
Umarpada *India* 21°27N 73°30E **242** J5
Umatac *Guam* 13°18N 144°39E **302** d
Umatilla *U.S.A.* 45°55N 119°21W **304** D4
Umba *Russia* 66°42N 34°11E **186** A5
Umbagog L. *U.S.A.* 44°46N 71°3W **313** B13
Umbakumba *Australia* 13°47S 136°50E **280** A2
Umbértide *Italy* 43°18N 12°20E **199** E9
Umboi I. *Papua N. G.* 5°40S 148°0E **286** C5
Umbrella Mts. *N.Z.* 45°35S 169°5E **285** F4
Umbria □ *Italy* 42°53N 12°30E **199** F9
Umeå *Sweden* 63°45N 20°20E **160** E19
Umeälven → *Sweden* 63°45N 20°20E **160** E19
Umeda *Japan* 34°41N 135°29E **133** A1
Umera *Indonesia* 0°12S 129°37E **231** E7
Umerkhadi *Mumbai, India* **130** b2
Umfuli → *Zimbabwe* 17°30S 29°23E **269** F2
Umfurudzi ⌓ *Zimbabwe* 17°6S 31°40E **269** F3
Umgusa *Zimbabwe* 19°29S 27°52E **269** F2
Umgwenya → *Mozam.* 25°14S 32°18E **271** C5
Umiat *U.S.A.* 69°22N 152°8W **303** B9
Umiujaq *Canada* 56°33N 76°33W **298** A4
Umka *Serbia* 44°40N 20°19E **202** B4
Umkomaas *S. Africa* 30°13S 30°48E **271** D5
Umm ad Daraj, J. *Jordan* 32°18N 35°48E **251** F6
Umm al Arānib *Libya* 26°10N 14°43E **258** C2
Umm al Khashab *Si. Arabia* 17°23N 42°32E **256** D5
Umm al Qaywayn *U.A.E.* 25°30N 55°35E **247** E7
Umm al Qittayn *Jordan* 32°18N 36°40E **251** F7
Umm al'Abīd *Libya* 27°31N 15°2E **258** C3
Umm Arda *Sudan* 15°17N 32°31E **257** D3
Umm Bāb *Qatar* 25°12N 50°48E **247** E6
Umm Badr *Sudan* 14°13N 27°58E **257** E2
Umm Bel *Sudan* 13°35N 28°0E **257** E2
Umm Birkah *Si. Arabia* 27°44N 36°31E **256** B4
Umm Boim *Sudan* 11°43N 25°27E **257** E2
Umm Dam *Sudan* 13°45N 30°59E **257** E3
Umm Debi *Sudan* 14°37N 30°23E **257** E3
Umm Dubban *Sudan* 15°23N 32°52E **257** D3
Umm Durman = Omdurmân *Sudan* 15°40N 32°28E **257** D3
Umm el Fahm *Israel* 32°31N 35°9E **251** F6
Umm Gafala *Sudan* 13°22N 27°15E **257** E2
Umm Gimala *Sudan* 11°27N 28°12E **257** E2
Umm Inderaba *Sudan* 17°30N 33°13E **256** D3
Umm Isheirât, G. *Egypt* 28°21N 34°18E **251** K5
Umm Keddada *Sudan* 13°33N 26°35E **257** E2
Umm Koweika *Sudan* 13°10N 32°16E **257** E3
Umm Lajj *Si. Arabia* 25°0N 37°23E **246** E3
Umm Merwa *Sudan* 18°4N 32°30E **256** D3
Umm Qantur *Sudan* 14°17N 31°22E **257** E3
Umm Qasr *Iraq* 30°1N 47°58E **246** D5
Umm Qurein *Sudan* 9°58N 28°55E **257** F2
Umm Ruwaba *Sudan* 12°50N 31°20E **257** E3
Umm Saiyala *Sudan* 14°25N 31°10E **257** E3
Umm Shanqa *Sudan* 13°14N 27°14E **266** B2
Umm Shugeira *Sudan* 13°34N 29°37E **266** B2
Umm Shutur *Sudan* 7°17N 33°14E **257** F3
Umm Sidr *Sudan* 14°29N 25°10E **257** E2
Umm Tais △ *Qatar* 26°7N 51°15E **249** A5
Umm Urūmah *Si. Arabia* 25°43N 36°35E **256** B4
Umm Zehetir *Egypt* 28°48N 32°31E **256** J8
Umnak I. *U.S.A.* 53°15N 168°20W **303** K5
Umniati → *Zimbabwe* 16°49S 28°45E **269** F2
Umpqua → *U.S.A.* 43°40N 124°12W **304** E1
Umpulo *Angola* 12°38S 17°42E **265** E3
Ümraniye *Turkey* 41°1N 29°4E **122** B2
Umred *India* 20°51N 79°18E **244** D4
Umreth *India* 22°41N 73°4E **242** H5
Umri *India* 19°2N 77°39E **244** E3
Umtata = Mthatha *S. Africa* 31°36S 28°49E **271** D4
Umuahia *Nigeria* 5°31N 7°26E **263** D6
Umuarama *Brazil* 23°45S 53°20W **335** A5
Umuda I. *Papua N. G.* 8°29S 143°46E **286** E2
Umurbey *Turkey* 40°13N 26°36E **203** F10
Umvukwe Ra. *Zimbabwe* 16°45S 30°45E **269** F3
Umzimvubu *S. Africa* 31°38S 29°33E **271** D4
Umzingwane → *Zimbabwe* 22°12S 29°56E **269** G2
Umzinto = eMuziwezinto *S. Africa* 30°15S 30°45E **271** D5
Una *India* 20°46N 71°8E **242** J4
Una → *Bos.-H.* 45°0N 16°20E **199** D13
Unac → *Bos.-H.* 44°30N 16°9E **199** D13
Unaðsdalur *Iceland* 66°7N 22°36W **155** A4
Unadilla *Ga., U.S.A.* 32°16N 83°44W **316** C6
Unadilla *N.Y., U.S.A.* 42°20N 75°19W **313** D9
Unaí *Brazil* 16°23S 46°53W **333** E2
Unalakleet *U.S.A.* 63°52N 160°47W **303** E7
Unalaska *U.S.A.* 53°53N 166°32W **303** K6
Unalaska I. *U.S.A.* 53°35N 166°50W **303** K6
'Unayzah *Si. Arabia* 26°6N 43°58E **246** E4
'Unayzah, J. *Asia* 32°12N 39°18E **213** F8
Uncastillo *Spain* 42°21N 1°8W **196** C3
Uncía *Bolivia* 18°25S 66°40W **330** D4
Uncompahgre Peak *U.S.A.* 38°4N 107°28W **304** G10
Uncompahgre Plateau *U.S.A.* 38°20N 108°15W **304** G9
Undara Volcanic △ *Australia* 18°14S 144°41E **280** B3
Unden *Sweden* 58°45N 14°25E **163** F8
Underbool *Australia* 35°10S 141°51E **282** C4
Underground Atlanta *U.S.A.* 33°45N 84°24W **113** B2
Underhill, L. *U.S.A.* 28°32N 81°20W **133** A3
Undersaker *Sweden* 63°19N 13°21E **162** A7
Underwood *Canada* 44°18N 81°29W **312** B3
Undredal *Norway* 60°57N 7°6E **164** D4
Unea I. *Papua N. G.* 4°53S 149°9E **286** C5
Unecha *Russia* 52°50N 32°37E **189** F7
Uneiuxi → *Brazil* 0°37S 65°34W **328** D4
Unětický potok → *Czech Rep.* 50°9N 14°24E **135** B2
Unga I. *U.S.A.* 55°15N 160°40W **303** J7
Ungarie *Australia* 33°38S 146°56E **283** B7
Ungarisch-Hradisch = Uherské Hradiště *Czech Rep.* 49°4N 17°30E **181** B10
Ungarisch-Ostra = Uherský Brod *Czech Rep.* 49°1N 17°40E **181** B10
Ungarra *Australia* 34°12S 136°2E **282** C2
Ungat *Papua N. G.* 2°40S 150°15E **286** B6
Ungava, Pén. d' *Canada* 60°0N 74°0W **295** F17
Ungava B. *Canada* 59°30N 67°30W **295** F18
Ungeny = Ungheni *Moldova* 47°11N 27°51E **183** C12
Unggi *N. Korea* 42°16N 130°28E **224** A5
Ungheni *Moldova* 47°11N 27°51E **183** C12
Unguala → *Ethiopia* 8°6N 41°9E **257** F5
Ungvár = Uzhhorod *Ukraine* 48°36N 22°18E **182** B7
Ungwana B. *Kenya* 2°45S 40°20E **268** C5
Ungwatiri *Sudan* 16°52N 36°10E **257** D4
Unhos *Portugal* 38°49N 9°7W **126** A2
Uni *Russia* 57°46N 51°31E **190** B10
União *Brazil* 4°35S 42°52W **332** B3
União da Vitória *Brazil* 26°13S 51°5W **335** B5
União dos Palmares *Brazil* 9°10S 36°2W **332** C4
Uničov *Czech Rep.* 49°46N 17°8E **181** B10
Unidad Santa Fe *Mexico* 19°23N 99°13W **128** B1
Uniejów *Poland* 51°59N 18°46E **185** G5
Unije *Croatia* 44°40N 14°15E **199** D11
Unimak I. *U.S.A.* 54°45N 164°0W **303** J7
Unimak Pass. *U.S.A.* 54°15N 164°30W **303** J6
Unini → *Brazil* 1°41S 61°31W **329** D5
Union *Miss., U.S.A.* 32°34N 89°7W **315** E10
Union *Mo., U.S.A.* 38°27N 91°0W **310** F6
Union *Ohio, U.S.A.* 39°55N 84°12W **311** E12
Union *S.C., U.S.A.* 34°43N 81°37W **315** D14
Union City *Calif., U.S.A.* 37°36N 122°1W **306** H4
Union City *Ga., U.S.A.* 33°35N 84°33W **316** B5
Union City *New York, U.S.A.* **132** b1
Union City *Ohio, U.S.A.* 40°12N 84°48W **311** D12
Union City *Pa., U.S.A.* 41°54N 79°51W **312** E5
Union City *Tenn., U.S.A.* 36°26N 89°3W **315** C10
Union Dale *U.S.A.* 41°43N 75°29W **313** E9
Union Gap *U.S.A.* 46°33N 120°28W **304** C3
Union Grove *U.S.A.* 42°41N 88°3W **311** B8
Union I. *St. Vincent* 12°36N 61°26W **323** n
Union Park *U.S.A.* 28°34N 81°17W **317** G8
Union Point *U.S.A.* 33°37N 83°4W **316** B6
Union Port *U.S.A.* 40°48N 73°51W **132** B2
Union Springs *Ala., U.S.A.* 32°9N 85°43W **316** C4
Union Springs *N.Y., U.S.A.* 42°50N 76°41W **313** D8
Union Square *San Francisco, U.S.A.* **136** b2
Union Star *U.S.A.* 39°59N 94°36W **310** E2
Union Station *Toronto, Canada* **141** c2
Union Station *Chicago, U.S.A.* **119** c1
Union Station *Washington, D.C., U.S.A.* **143** b3
Union Station *Los Angeles, U.S.A.* **127** b3
Union Station *New Orleans, U.S.A.* **131** b1
Union Station Plaza *Washington, D.C., U.S.A.* **143** b3
Uniondale *S. Africa* 33°39S 23°7E **270** D3
Uniontown *Ky., U.S.A.* 37°47N 87°56W **311** G9
Uniontown *Pa., U.S.A.* 39°54N 79°44W **309** F14
Unionville *Ga., U.S.A.* 31°26N 83°30W **316** D6
Unionville *Mo., U.S.A.* 40°29N 93°1W **310** D3
Unirea *Romania* 44°15N 27°35E **183** F12
United Arab Emirates ■ *Asia* 23°50N 54°0E **247** F7
United Arab Republic = Egypt ■ *Africa* 28°0N 31°0E **256** B3
United Center *U.S.A.* 41°53N 87°41W **119** B2
United Kingdom ■ *Europe* 53°0N 2°0W **165** E6
United Nations Headquarters *New York, U.S.A.* **132** c3
United Provinces = Uttar Pradesh □ *India* 27°0N 80°0E **243** F9
United States of America ■ *N. Amer.* 37°0N 96°0W **301** H20
Unity *Canada* 52°30N 109°5W **297** C7
Universal Studios *Calif., U.S.A.* 34°9N 118°21W **126** B2
Universal Studios *Fla., U.S.A.* 28°29N 81°29W **133** B2
Universales, Mtes. *Spain* 40°18N 1°33W **196** E3
Universidad *Spain* 40°27N 3°44W **127** B1
University City *U.S.A.* 38°39N 90°18W **310** F6
University Park *Md., U.S.A.* 38°58N 76°56W **143** B4
University Park *N. Mex., U.S.A.* 32°17N 106°45W **305** K10
University Place *U.S.A.* 47°14N 122°33W **306** C4
Unjha *India* 23°46N 72°24E **242** H5
Unmet *Vanuatu* 16°8S 167°15E **287** F5
Unna *Germany* 51°32N 7°42E **178** D3
Unnao *India* 26°35N 80°30E **243** F9
Uno, Ilha *Guinea-Biss.* 11°15N 16°13W **262** C1
Unpongkor *Vanuatu* 18°50S 168°59E **287** H6
Unruhstadt = Kargowa *Poland* 52°5N 15°51E **185** F2
Unsan *N. Korea* 40°6N 125°54E **224** B2
Unsengedsi → *Zimbabwe* 15°43S 31°14E **269** F3
Unst *U.K.* 60°44N 0°53W **167** A8
Unstrut → *Germany* 51°10N 11°48E **178** D7
Unter den Linden *Berlin, Germany* **115** a4
Unterbiberg *Germany* 48°6N 11°38E **131** B2
Unterdrauburg = Dravograd *Slovenia* 46°36N 15°5E **199** B12
Unterföhring *Germany* 48°11N 11°38E **131** A3
Unterfranken □ *Germany* 50°0N 10°0E **179** F5
Unterhaching *Germany* 48°3N 11°37E **131** B2
Unterlaa *Austria* 48°8N 16°24E **142** B2
Untermenzing *Germany* 48°10N 11°28E **131** A1
Unterschleissheim *Germany* 48°17N 11°34E **179** G7
Unuk → *Canada* 56°5N 131°3W **296** B2
Ünye *Turkey* 41°5N 37°15E **212** B7
Unzen-Amakusa △ *Japan* 32°15N 130°10E **222** E2
Unzen-Dake *Japan* 32°45N 130°17E **222** E2
Unzha *Russia* 58°0N 44°0E **190** A7
Unzha → *Russia* 57°49N 43°47E **190** B6
Uozu *Japan* 36°48N 137°24E **223** A9
Upata *Venezuela* 8°1N 62°24W **329** B5
Upatoi Cr. → *U.S.A.* 32°22N 84°58W **316** C5
Upemba, L. *Dem. Rep. of the Congo* 8°30S 26°20E **269** D2
Upemba △ *Dem. Rep. of the Congo* 9°0S 26°35E **269** D2
Upernavik *Greenland* 72°49N 56°20W **154** C5
Upington *S. Africa* 28°25S 21°15E **270** C3
Upleta *India* 21°46N 70°16E **242** J4
'Upolu *Samoa* 13°58S 172°0W **287** V20
Upolu Pt. *U.S.A.* 20°16N 155°52W **302** C6
Upper □ *Ghana* 10°30N 1°30W **263** C4
Upper Alkali L. *U.S.A.* 41°47N 120°8W **304** F3
Upper Arlington *U.S.A.* 40°0N 83°4W **311** E13
Upper Arrow L. *Canada* 50°30N 117°50W **296** C5
Upper Austria = Oberösterreich □ *Austria* 48°10N 14°0E **180** C7
Upper B. *U.S.A.* 40°40N 74°3W **132** C1
Upper Daly ✪ *Australia* 14°26S 131°3E **278** B5
Upper Darby *U.S.A.* 39°55N 75°16W **309** F16
Upper East Side *New York, U.S.A.* **132** b3
Upper Elmers End *U.K.* 51°23N 0°1W **125** B3
Upper Foster L. *Canada* 56°47N 105°20W **297** B7
Upper Hutt *N.Z.* 41°8S 175°5E **284** H4
Upper Klamath L. *U.S.A.* 42°25N 121°55W **304** E3
Upper Lake *U.S.A.* 39°10N 122°54W **306** F4
Upper Liard *Canada* 60°3N 128°54W **296** A3
Upper Manilla *Australia* 30°38S 150°40E **283** A9
Upper Manzanilla *Trin. & Tob.* 10°31N 61°4W **323** t
Upper Missouri Breaks ⌓ *U.S.A.* 47°50N 109°55W **304** C9
Upper Musquodoboit *Canada* 45°10N 62°58W **299** C7
Upper New York B. = Upper B. *U.S.A.* 40°40N 74°3W **132** C1
Upper Norwood *U.K.* 51°24N 0°6W **125** B3
Upper Peirce Res. *Singapore* 1°22N 103°47E **138** A2
Upper Red L. *U.S.A.* 48°8N 94°45W **308** A6
Upper Sandusky *U.S.A.* 40°50N 83°17W **311** D13
Upper Senegal & Niger = Mali ■ *Africa* 17°0N 3°0W **262** B4
Upper Sydenham *U.K.* 51°26N 0°4W **125** B3
Upper Tooting *U.K.* 51°25N 0°9W **125** B3
Upper Volta = Burkina Faso ■ *Africa* 12°0N 1°0W **262** C4
Upper West Side *New York, U.S.A.* **132** a2
Upphärad *Sweden* 58°9N 12°19E **163** F6
Uppland *Sweden* 59°59N 17°48E **162** D12
Upplands-Väsby *Sweden* 59°31N 17°54E **162** E11
Uppsala *Sweden* 59°53N 17°38E **162** E11
Uppsala län □ *Sweden* 60°0N 17°30E **162** D11
Upshi *India* 33°48N 77°52E **243** C7
Upton *London, U.K.* 51°32N 0°1E **125** A4
Upton *Wyo., U.S.A.* 44°6N 104°38W **304** D11
Uptown *U.S.A.* 41°58N 87°40W **119** B2
Uqsuqtuuq = Gjoa Haven *Canada* 68°38N 95°53W **294** D12
Ur *Iraq* 30°55N 46°25E **246** D5
Ur Kut *Somali Rep.* 3°31N 42°47E **267** D5
Ura-Tyube = Uroteppa *Tajikistan* 39°55N 69°1E **217** E7
Urabá, G. de *Colombia* 8°25N 76°53W **328** B2
Urad Qianqi *China* 40°40N 108°30E **226** D5
Uraga-Suidō *Japan* 35°13N 139°45E **223** B11
Urakawa *Japan* 42°9N 142°47E **220** C11
Ural = Uralskiy □ *Russia* 64°0N 70°0E **214** C7
Ural = Zhayyq → *Kazakhstan* 47°0N 51°48E **187** E9
Ural *Australia* 33°21S 146°12E **283** B7
Ural Mts. = Uralskie Gory *Eurasia* 60°0N 59°0E **186** C10
Uralla *Australia* 30°37S 151°29E **283** A9
Uralmedstroy = Krasnouralsk *Russia* 58°21N 60°3E **186** C11
Uralsk = Oral *Kazakhstan* 51°20N 51°20E **190** E10
Uralskie Gory *Eurasia* 60°0N 59°0E **186** C10
Uralskiy □ *Russia* 64°0N 70°0E **214** C7
Urambo *Tanzania* 5°4S 32°0E **268** D3
Uran *India* 18°53N 72°56E **130** B2
Urana *Australia* 35°15S 146°21E **283** C7
Urana, L. *Australia* 35°16S 146°10E **283** C7
Urandangi *Australia* 21°32S 138°14E **280** C2
Uranga *Australia* 30°31S 153°1E **283** A10
Uranium City *Canada* 59°34N 108°37W **297** B7
Urapuntja = Utopia *Australia* 22°14S 134°33E **280** C1
Uraricaá → *Brazil* 3°20N 61°56W **329** C5
Uraricoera *Brazil* 3°27N 60°59W **329** C5
Uraricoera → *Brazil* 3°2N 60°30W **329** C5
Urasoe *Japan* 26°15N 127°43E **288** a
Uravakonda *India* 14°57N 77°12E **245** G3
Urawa = Saitama *Japan* 35°54N 139°38E **223** B11
Uray *Russia* 60°5N 65°15E **214** C7
Urayasu *Japan* 35°39N 139°53E **140** B4
'Uray'irah *Si. Arabia* 25°57N 48°53E **247** E6
Urbakh = Pushkino *Russia* 51°16N 47°0E **190** E8
Urbana *Ill., U.S.A.* 40°7N 88°12W **311** D8
Urbana *Ohio, U.S.A.* 40°7N 83°45W **311** D13
Urbandale *U.S.A.* 41°38N 93°43W **310** C3
Urbánia *Italy* 43°40N 12°31E **199** E9
Urbano Santos *Brazil* 3°12S 43°23W **332** B3
Urbe ✈ *Italy* 41°57N 12°30E **136** B2
Urbel → *Spain* 42°21N 3°40W **194** C7
Urbino *Italy* 43°43N 12°38E **199** E9
Urbión, Picos de *Spain* 42°1N 2°52W **196** C2
Urca *Brazil* 22°56S 43°9W **135** B2
Urcos *Peru* 13°40S 71°38W **330** C3
Urdaneta *Phil.* 15°59N 120°34E **232** D3
Urdinarrain *Argentina* 32°37S 58°52W **334** C4
Urdos *France* 42°51N 0°35W **174** F3
Ure → *U.K.* 54°5N 1°20W **168** C6
Uren *Russia* 57°35N 45°55E **190** B7
Urengoy *Russia* 65°58N 78°22E **214** C8
Ureparapara *Vanuatu* 13°32S 167°20E **287** C5
Ures *Mexico* 29°26N 110°24W **318** B2
Ureshino *Japan* 33°6N 129°59E **222** D1
Urewera △ *N.Z.* 38°29S 177°7E **284** E6
Urfa = Sanliurfa *Turkey* 37°12N 38°50E **213** D8
Urga = Ulaanbaatar *Mongolia* 47°55N 106°53E **218** B5
Urganch *Uzbekistan* 41°40N 60°41E **216** D6
Urgench = Urganch *Uzbekistan* 41°40N 60°41E **216** D6
Ürgüp *Turkey* 38°38N 34°56E **212** C6
Uri *India* 34°8N 74°2E **243** B6
Uri □ *Switz.* 46°43N 8°35E **179** J4
Uribante → *Venezuela* 7°25N 71°50W **328** B3
Uribe *Colombia* 3°13N 74°24W **328** C3
Uribia *Colombia* 11°43N 72°16W **328** A3
Uricani *Romania* 45°20N 23°9E **182** E8
Urimba *Angola* 10°56S 16°32E **265** E3
Uriondo *Bolivia* 21°41S 64°41W **334** A3
Urique *Mexico* 27°13N 107°55W **318** B3
Urique → *Mexico* 26°29N 107°58W **318** B3
Uritsk *Russia* 59°49N 30°10E **137** C1
Urk *Neths.* 52°39N 5°36E **170** B5
Urkiola ⌓ *Spain* 43°6N 1°2W **196** B3
Urla *Turkey* 38°20N 26°47E **205** C8
Urlaţi *Romania* 44°59N 26°15E **183** F11
Urmia = Orūmīyeh *Iran* 37°40N 45°0E **213** D11
Urmia, L. = Orūmīyeh, Daryācheh-ye *Iran* 37°50N 45°30E **213** D11
Üröm *Hungary* 47°35N 19°1E **117** A2
Uromi *Nigeria* 6°42N 6°20E **263** D6
Uroševac *Kosovo* 42°23N 21°10E **202** D5
Uroteppa *Tajikistan* 39°55N 69°1E **217** E7
Uroyan, Montanas de *Puerto Rico* 18°12N 67°0W **321** b
Urrampinyi Iltjiltarri ✪ *Australia* 24°20S 132°10E **278** D5
Urrao *Colombia* 6°20N 76°11W **328** B2
Urshult *Sweden* 56°31N 14°50E **163** H8
Ursus *Poland* 52°11N 20°52E **142** B1
Ursvik *Sweden* 59°23N 17°57E **139** A1
Uru Uru, L. *Bolivia* 18°6S 67°8W **330** D4
Uruaçu *Brazil* 14°30S 49°10W **333** D2
Uruanã *Brazil* 15°30S 49°41W **333** E2
Uruapan *Mexico* 19°24N 102°3W **318** D4
Uruará *Brazil* 3°42S 53°51W **329** D7
Uruará → *Brazil* 2°6S 53°38W **329** D7
Urubamba *Peru* 13°20S 72°10W **330** C3
Urubamba → *Peru* 10°43S 73°48W **330** C3
Urubaxi → *Brazil* 0°31S 64°50W **329** D5
Urubu → *Brazil* 2°55S 58°25W **329** D6
Urucará *Brazil* 2°32S 57°45W **329** D6
Uruçuí *Brazil* 7°20S 44°28W **332** C3
Uruçuí, Serra do *Brazil* 9°0S 44°45W **332** C3
Uruçuí Prêto → *Brazil* 7°20S 44°38W **332** C3
Urucuia → *Brazil* 16°8S 45°5W **333** E2
Uruguai → *Brazil* 26°0S 53°30W **335** B5
Uruguaiana *Brazil* 29°50S 57°0W **334** B4
Uruguay ■ *S. Amer.* 32°30S 56°30W **334** C4
Uruguay → *S. Amer.* 34°12S 58°18W **334** C4
Urukthapel I. *Palau* 7°17N 134°25E **288** c
Urumchi = Ürümqi *China* 43°45N 87°45E **217** D11
Ürümqi *China* 43°45N 87°45E **217** D11
Uruna ✪ *Australia* 24°3S 133°1E **278** D5
Urundi = Burundi ■ *Africa* 3°15S 30°0E **268** C3
Urup → *Russia* 45°0N 41°10E **191** H5
Urup, Ostrov *Russia* 46°0N 151°0E **215** E16
Urutaí *Brazil* 17°28S 48°12W **333** E2
Uryupinsk *Russia* 50°45N 41°58E **190** E5
Ürzhar *Kazakhstan* 47°5N 81°38E **217** C10
Urzhum *Russia* 57°10N 49°56E **190** B9
Urziceni *Romania* 44°40N 26°42E **183** F11
Usa *Japan* 33°31N 131°21E **222** D3
Usa → *Russia* 66°16N 59°49E **186** A10
Uşak *Turkey* 38°43N 29°28E **205** C11
Uşak □ *Turkey* 38°30N 29°0E **205** C11
Usakos *Namibia* 21°54S 15°31E **270** B2
Usborne, Mt. *Falk. Is.* 51°40S 59°55W **153** f
Ušće *Serbia* 43°30N 20°39E **202** C4
Usedom *Germany* 53°55N 14°2E **178** B10
Usedom ⌓ *Germany* 53°55N 14°0E **178** B10
Useless Loop *Australia* 26°8S 113°23E **279** E1
Usera *Spain* 40°22N 3°42W **127** B1
'Usfān *Si. Arabia* 21°58N 39°27E **248** B2
Ushakova, Ostrov *Russia* 82°0N 80°0E **215** A8
Ushakovo *Russia* 54°37N 20°16E **184** D7
Ushant = Ouessant, Î. d' *France* 48°28N 5°6W **172** D1
Üsharal *Kazakhstan* 46°10N 80°56E **217** C10
Ushashi *Tanzania* 1°59S 33°57E **268** C3
Ushat *Sudan* 7°59N 29°28E **257** F2
'Ushayrah *Ar Riyāḑ, Si. Arabia* 25°35N 45°47E **246** E5
'Ushayrah *Makkah, Si. Arabia* 21°46N 40°42E **256** C5
Ushibuka *Japan* 32°11N 130°1E **222** E2
Ushigome *Japan* 35°42N 139°44E **140** A3
Üshtöbe *Kazakhstan* 45°16N 78°0E **217** C9
Ushuaia *Argentina* 54°50S 68°23W **336** D3
Ushumun *Russia* 52°47N 126°32E **215** D13
Ushytsya → *Ukraine* 48°35N 27°8E **183** B12
Usina *Brazil* 22°57S 43°17W **135** B1
Usino *Papua N. G.* 5°32S 145°23E **286** C3
Usinsk *Russia* 65°57N 57°27E **186** A10
Usk *Canada* 54°38N 128°26W **296** C3
Usk → *U.K.* 51°33N 2°58W **169** F5
Uska *India* 27°12N 83°7E **243** F10
Uskedalen *Norway* 59°56N 5°53E **164** E2
Üsküb = Skopje *Macedonia* 42°1N 21°26E **202** D5
Üsküdar *Turkey* 41°1N 29°0E **122** B2
Uslar *Germany* 51°39N 9°38E **178** D5
Usman *Russia* 52°5N 39°48E **189** F10
Usoke *Tanzania* 5°8S 32°24E **268** D3
Usolye-Sibirskoye *Russia* 52°48N 103°40E **215** D11
Usolye-Solikamskoye = Berezniki *Russia* 59°24N 56°46E **186** C10
Usoro *Nigeria* 5°33N 6°11E **263** D6
Uspallata, P. de *Argentina* 32°37S 69°22W **334** C2
Uspenka = Kirovskiy *Russia* 45°7N 133°30E **220** B6
Ussel *France* 45°32N 2°18E **174** C6
Usson-du-Poitou *France* 46°16N 0°31E **174** B4
Ussuriysk *Russia* 43°48N 131°59E **220** C5
Ussurka *Russia* 45°12N 133°31E **220** B6
Ust-Aldan = Batamay *Russia* 63°30N 129°15E **215** C13
Ust-Amginskoye = Khandyga *Russia* 62°42N 135°35E **215** C14
Ust-Buzulukskaya *Russia* 50°8N 42°11E **190** E6
Ust-Chaun *Russia* 68°47N 170°30E **215** C18
Ust-Chorna *Ukraine* 48°19N 23°56E **183** B8
Ust-Donetskiy *Russia* 47°35N 40°55E **191** G5
Ust-Ilimpeya = Yukta *Russia* 63°26N 105°42E **215** C11
Ust-Ilimsk *Russia* 58°3N 102°39E **215** D11
Ust-Ishim *Russia* 57°45N 71°10E **214** D8
Ust-Kamchatsk *Russia* 56°10N 162°28E **215** D17
Ust-Kamenogorsk = Öskemen *Kazakhstan* 50°0N 82°36E **217** C10
Ust-Khayryuzovo *Russia* 57°15N 156°45E **215** D16
Ust-Kut *Russia* 56°50N 105°42E **215** D11
Ust-Kuyga *Russia* 70°1N 135°43E **215** B14
Ust-Labinsk *Russia* 45°15N 39°41E **191** H4
Ust-Luga *Russia* 59°35N 28°20E **188** C5
Ust-Maya *Russia* 60°30N 134°28E **215** C14
Ust-Medveditskaya = Serafimovich *Russia* 49°36N 42°43E **190** F6
Ust-Mil *Russia* 59°40N 133°11E **215** D14
Ust-Nera *Russia* 64°35N 143°15E **215** C15
Ust-Nyukzha *Russia* 56°34N 121°37E **215** D13
Ust-Olenek *Russia* 73°0N 120°5E **215** B12
Ust-Omchug *Russia* 61°9N 149°38E **215** C15
Ust-Port *Russia* 69°40N 84°26E **214** C9
Ust-Slavyanka *Russia* 59°51N 30°32E **137** C3
Ust-Sysolsk = Syktyvkar *Russia* 61°45N 50°40E **186** B9
Ust-Tsilma *Russia* 65°28N 52°11E **186** A9
Ust-Urt = Ustyurt Plateau *Asia* 44°0N 55°0E **216** D5
Ust-Usa *Russia* 66°2N 56°57E **186** A10
Ust-Vorkuta *Russia* 67°24N 64°0E **186** A11
Ust-Zhuya = Chara *Russia* 56°54N 118°20E **215** D12
Ustaoset *Norway* 60°30N 8°2E **164** D5
Ustaritz *France* 43°24N 1°27W **174** E2
Ustecký □ *Czech Rep.* 50°30N 14°0E **180** A7
Uster *Switz.* 47°22N 8°43E **179** H4
Ústí nad Labem *Czech Rep.* 50°41N 14°3E **180** A7
Ústí nad Orlicí *Czech Rep.* 49°58N 16°24E **181** B9
Ústica *Italy* 38°42N 13°11E **200** D6
Ustinov = Izhevsk *Russia* 56°51N 53°14E **186** C9
Ustka *Poland* 54°35N 16°55E **184** D3
Ustroń *Poland* 49°43N 18°48E **185** J5
Ustrzyki Dolne *Poland* 49°27N 22°40E **185** J9
Ustupo *Panama* 9°27N 78°34W **328** B2
Ustyluh *Ukraine* 50°51N 24°10E **185** H11
Ustyurt Plateau *Asia* 44°0N 55°0E **216** D5
Ustyuzhna *Russia* 58°50N 36°32E **188** C9
Usu *China* 44°27N 84°40E **217** D10
Usuki *Japan* 33°8N 131°49E **222** D3
Usulután *El Salv.* 13°25N 88°28W **320** D2
Usumacinta → *Mexico* 18°24N 92°38W **319** D6
Usumbura = Bujumbura *Burundi* 3°16S 29°18E **268** C2
Usure *Tanzania* 4°40S 34°22E **268** C3
Usutuo → *Mozam.* 26°48S 32°7E **271** C5
Uta *Indonesia* 4°33S 136°0E **231** E9
Utah □ *U.S.A.* 39°20N 111°30W **304** G8
Utah L. *U.S.A.* 40°12N 111°48W **304** F8
Utansjö *Sweden* 62°46N 17°55E **162** B11
Utara, Selat *Malaysia* 5°28N 100°20E **237** c
Utarni *India* 26°5N 71°58E **242** F4
Utatlan *Guatemala* 15°2N 91°11W **320** C1
Ute Creek → *U.S.A.* 35°21N 103°50W **305** J12
Utebo *Spain* 41°43N 1°0W **196** D3
Utegi *Tanzania* 1°19S 34°13E **266** E3
Uteke *Sweden* 59°24N 18°15E **139** A3
Utena *Lithuania* 55°27N 25°40E **188** E3
Utete *Tanzania* 8°0S 38°45E **268** D4
Uthai Thani *Thailand* 15°22N 100°3E **236** E3
Uthal *Pakistan* 25°44N 66°40E **242** G2
Utiariti *Brazil* 13°0S 58°10W **331** C6
Utica *N.Y., U.S.A.* 43°6N 75°14W **313** C9
Utica *Ohio, U.S.A.* 40°14N 82°27W **312** F2
Utiel *Spain* 39°37N 1°11W **197** F3
Utikuma L. *Canada* 55°50N 115°30W **296** B5
Utila *Honduras* 16°6N 86°56W **320** C2
Utinga *Brazil* 12°6S 41°5W **333** D3
Utkela *India* 20°6N 83°10E **244** D6
Utne *Norway* 60°25N 6°37E **164** D3
Utnur *India* 19°22N 78°46E **244** E4
Uto *Japan* 32°41N 130°40E **222** E2
Utö *Sweden* 58°56N 18°16E **162** F12
Utopia *Australia* 22°14S 134°33E **280** C1
Utrata *Poland* 52°15N 21°4E **142** B2
Utraula *India* 27°19N 82°25E **243** F10
Utrecht *Neths.* 52°5N 5°8E **170** B5
Utrecht *KwaZulu Natal, S. Africa* 27°38S 30°20E **271** C5
Utrecht □ *Neths.* 52°6N 5°7E **170** B5
Utrera *Spain* 37°12N 5°48W **195** H5
Utría △ *Colombia* 5°57N 77°21W **328** B2
Utsira *Norway* 59°19N 4°53E **164** E1
Utsjoki → *Finland* 69°51N 26°59E **160** B22
Utsunomiya *Japan* 36°30N 139°50E **223** A11
Uttar Pradesh □ *India* 27°0N 80°0E **243** F9
Uttaradit *Thailand* 17°36N 100°5E **236** D3
Uttarakhand □ *India* 30°0N 79°30E **243** D8
Uttaranchal = Uttarakhand □ *India* 30°0N 79°30E **243** D8
Uttarpara *India* 22°39N 88°21E **124** B1
Utterslev Mose *Denmark* 55°42N 12°29E **118** A2
Utterson *Canada* 45°12N 79°19W **312** A5
Uttoxeter *U.K.* 52°54N 1°52W **168** E6
Utuado *Puerto Rico* 18°16N 66°42W **321** b
Uummannaq *Avannaarsua, Greenland* 77°33N 68°52W **154** B4
Uummannaq *Kitaa, Greenland* 70°58N 52°17W **150** B5
Uummannarsuaq = Nunap Isua *Greenland* 59°48N 43°55W **154** F6
Uunartoq Qeqertoq *Greenland* 71°33N 21°47W **154** C8
Uusikaarlepyy *Finland* 63°32N 22°31E **160** E20
Uusikaupunki *Finland* 60°47N 21°25E **188** B1
Uva *Russia* 56°59N 52°13E **190** B11
Uvá → *Colombia* 3°41N 70°3W **328** C3
Uvac → *Serbia* 43°35N 19°30E **202** C3
Uvalda *U.S.A.* 32°2N 82°31W **316** C7
Uvalde *U.S.A.* 29°13N 99°47W **314** G5
Uvarovo *Russia* 51°59N 42°14E **190** E6
Uvat *Russia* 59°5N 68°50E **214** D7
Uvdal *Norway* 60°17N 8°48E **164** D5
Uvéa, I. *Wall. & F. Is.* 13°18S 176°10W **277** C15
Uvinza *Tanzania* 5°5S 30°24E **268** D3
Uvira *Dem. Rep. of the Congo* 3°22S 29°3E **268** C2
Uvs □ *Mongolia* 49°38N 93°0E **217** C12
Uvs Nuur *Mongolia* 50°20N 92°30E **217** B12
Uwa *Japan* 33°22N 132°31E **222** D4
'Uwairidh, Ḩarrat al *Si. Arabia* 26°50N 38°0E **246** E3
Uwajima *Japan* 33°10N 132°35E **222** D4
Uwanda ⌓ *Tanzania* 7°46S 32°0E **268** D3
Uweinat, Jebel *Sudan* 21°54N 24°58E **256** C1
Uxbridge *Canada* 44°6N 79°7W **312** B5
Uxin Qi *China* 38°50N 109°5E **226** E5
Uxmal *Mexico* 20°22N 89°46W **319** C7
Uyak *U.S.A.* 57°38N 154°0W **303** H9
Üydzin *Mongolia* 44°9N 107°0E **226** B4
Uyo *Nigeria* 5°1N 7°53E **263** D6
Uyu → *Burma* 24°51N 94°57E **241** C5
Üyüklü Tepe *Turkey* 37°5N 27°21E **205** D9
Uyûn Mûsa *Egypt* 29°53N 32°40E **251** J3
Uyuni *Bolivia* 20°28S 66°47W **330** E4
Uzbekistan ■ *Asia* 41°30N 65°0E **217** D7
Uzboy → *Turkmenistan* 39°30N 55°0E **247** B7
Uzen, Bolshoi = Uzen, Mal → *Kazakhstan* 49°4N 49°44E **191** F9
Uzen, Mal → *Kazakhstan* 49°4N 49°44E **191** F9
Uzerche *France* 45°25N 1°34E **174** C5
Uzès *France* 44°1N 4°26E **175** D8
Uzh → *Ukraine* 51°15N 30°12E **177** C16
Uzhgorod = Uzhhorod *Ukraine* 48°36N 22°18E **182** B7
Uzhhorod *Ukraine* 48°36N 22°18E **182** B7
Uzhok *Ukraine* 48°59N 22°52E **182** B7
Užice *Serbia* 43°55N 19°50E **202** C3
Uzlovaya *Russia* 54°0N 38°5E **188** F10
Üzümlü *Turkey* 36°44N 29°14E **205** E11
Uzuncaburç *Turkey* 36°35N 33°57E **250** B4
Uzunköprü *Turkey* 41°16N 26°43E **203** E10
Uzunkuyu *Turkey* 38°17N 26°33E **205** C8

V

V.C. Bird Int. ✈ **(ANU)** *Antigua & B.* 17°8N 61°47W **322** b
Vaal → *S. Africa* 29°4S 23°38E **270** C3
Vaal Dam *S. Africa* 27°0S 28°14E **271** C4
Vaalwater *S. Africa* 24°15S 28°8E **271** B4
Vaasa *Finland* 63°6N 21°38E **160** E19
Vabre *France* 43°42N 2°24E **174** E6
Vác *Hungary* 47°49N 19°10E **182** C4
Vacaos, Mare aux *Mauritius* 20°22S 57°30E **272** e
Vacaria *Brazil* 28°31S 50°52W **335** B5
Vacata *Fiji* 17°15S 179°31W **287** A3
Vacaville *U.S.A.* 38°21N 121°59W **306** G5
Vaccarès, Étang de *France* 43°32N 4°34E **175** E8
Vach = Vakh → *Russia* 60°45N 76°45E **214** C8
Vache, Î. à *Haiti* 18°2N 73°35W **321** C5
Väckelsång *Sweden* 56°37N 14°58E **163** H8
Vaclavské náměstí *Prague, Czech Rep.* **135** b2
Vacoas *Mauritius* 20°18S 57°29E **272** e
Vada *India* 19°39N 73°8E **244** E1
Vadakara = Badagara *India* 11°35N 75°40E **245** J2
Vadaul *India* 19°2N 72°55E **130** A2
Väddö *Sweden* 60°0N 18°50E **162** D12
Väderstad *Sweden* 58°19N 14°55E **163** F8
Vadheim *Norway* 61°13N 5°49E **164** C2
Vadnagar *India* 23°47N 72°40E **242** H5
Vado Lígure *Italy* 44°17N 8°26E **198** D5
Vadodara *India* 22°20N 73°10E **242** H5
Vadsø *Norway* 70°3N 29°50E **160** A23
Vadstena *Sweden* 58°28N 14°54E **163** F8
Vaduj *India* 17°36N 74°27E **244** F2
Vaduz *Liech.* 47°8N 9°31E **179** H5
Værlandet *Norway* 61°18N 4°44E **164** C1
Værøy *Norway* 67°40N 12°40E **160** C15
Vagalat *Albania* 39°44N 20°8E **206** B10
Vågåmo *Norway* 61°52N 9°6E **164** C6
Vágar *Færoe Is.* 62°5N 7°15W **160** E9
Vagarshapat = Yejmiadzin *Armenia* 40°12N 44°19E **191** K7
Vaggeryd *Sweden* 57°30N 14°10E **163** G8
Vaghena *Solomon Is.* 7°25S 157°45E **287** L9
Vaghia *Greece* 38°19N 23°11E **204** C5
Vagia, Akra *Greece* 36°15N 28°11E **206** E12
Vagney *France* 48°1N 6°43E **173** D13
Vagnhärad *Sweden* 58°57N 17°33E **163** F11
Vagos *Portugal* 40°33N 8°42W **194** E2
Vågsfjorden *Norway* 68°50N 16°50E **160** B17
Váh → *Slovak Rep.* 47°43N 18°7E **181** D11
Vahitahi *French Polynesia* 18°44S 138°52W **289** f
Vahsel B. *Antarctica* 75°0S 35°0W **151** D1
Váhtjer = Gällivare *Sweden* 67°9N 20°40E **160** C19
Vaï *Greece* 35°15N 26°18E **207** E7
Vaiea *Cook Is.* 19°6S 169°54W **289** g
Vaigai → *India* 9°15N 79°10E **245** K4
Vaiges *France* 48°2N 0°30W **172** D6
Vaihingen *Germany* 48°54N 8°57E **179** G4
Vaihiria, L. *Tahiti* 17°40S 149°25W **289** e
Vaijapur *India* 19°58N 74°45E **244** E2
Vaikam *India* 9°45N 76°25E **245** K3
Vail *U.S.A.* 39°40N 106°20W **301** H18
Vailala → *Papua N. G.* 7°57S 145°25E **286** D3
Vailhau, Récif *Comoros Is.* 11°48S 43°4E **272** a
Vailly-sur-Aisne *France* 49°24N 3°31E **173** C10
Vailoatai *Amer. Samoa* 14°21S 170°46W **302** f
Vaippar → *India* 9°0N 78°25E **245** K4
Vairaatea *French Polynesia* 19°19S 139°20W **289** f
Vairao *Tahiti* 17°47S 149°17W **289** e
Vaires-sur-Marne *France* 48°52N 2°38E **134** A4
Vaisali → *India* 26°28N 78°53E **243** F8
Vaison-la-Romaine *France* 44°14N 5°4E **175** D9
Vaitogi *Amer. Samoa* 14°24S 170°44W **302** f
Vaitupu *Pac. Oc.* 7°28S 178°41E **277** B14
Vajpur *India* 21°24N 73°17E **244** D1
Vakaga → *C.A.R.* 9°48N 21°32E **264** A4
Vakarai *Sri Lanka* 8°8N 81°26E **245** K5
Vakarel *Bulgaria* 42°35N 23°40E **202** D7
Vakfikebir *Turkey* 41°2N 39°17E **213** B8
Vakh → *Russia* 60°45N 76°45E **214** C8
Vakhtan *Russia* 57°53N 46°47E **190** B8
Vaksdal *Norway* 60°29N 5°45E **164** D2
Vakuta I. *Papua N. G.* 8°51S 151°10E **286** E6
Vál *Hungary* 47°22N 18°40E **182** C3
Val-de-Marne □ *France* 48°45N 2°28E **173** D9
Val-d'Isère *France* 45°27N 6°59E **175** C10
Val-d'Oise □ *France* 49°5N 2°10E **173** C9
Val-d'Or *Canada* 48°7N 77°47W **298** C4
Val Grande △ *Italy* 46°3N 8°25E **198** B5
Val Marie *Canada* 49°15N 107°45W **297** D7
Val Thorens *France* 45°20N 6°33E **175** C10
Valaam *Russia* 61°22N 30°57E **188** B6
Valadares *Portugal* 41°5N 8°38W **194** D2
Valahia *Romania* 44°35N 25°0E **183** F9
Valaichenai *Sri Lanka* 7°54N 81°32E **245** L5
Valais □ *Switz.* 46°12N 7°45E **179** J3
Valais, Alpes du *Switz.* 46°5N 7°35E **179** J3
Valandovo *Macedonia* 41°19N 22°34E **202** E6
Valašské Meziříčí *Czech Rep.* 49°29N 17°59E **181** B10
Valatie *U.S.A.* 42°24N 73°40W **313** D11
Valaxa *Greece* 38°50N 24°29E **204** C6
Vålberg *Sweden* 59°23N 13°11E **162** E7
Valbo *Sweden* 60°40N 17°0E **162** D10
Valbondione *Italy* 46°2N 10°1E **198** B7
Valby *Denmark* 55°39N 12°29E **118** B2
Vălcani *Romania* 46°0N 20°26E **182** D5
Valcannuta *Italy* 41°52N 12°25E **136** B1
Vâlcea □ *Romania* 45°0N 24°10E **183** F9
Valcheta *Argentina* 40°40S 66°8W **336** B3
Valdagno *Italy* 45°39N 11°18E **199** C8
Valdahon *France* 47°8N 6°21E **173** E13
Valdai Hills = Valdayskaya Vozvyshennost *Russia* 57°0N 33°30E **188** D7
Valday *Russia* 57°58N 33°9E **188** D7
Valdayskaya Vozvyshennost *Russia* 57°0N 33°30E **188** D7
Valdeazogues → *Spain* 38°45N 4°55W **195** G6
Valdecañas, Embalse de *Spain* 39°45N 5°25W **194** F5
Valdelatas *Spain* 40°31N 3°42W **127** A1
Valdemarsvik *Sweden* 58°14N 16°40E **163** F10
Valdemoro *Spain* 40°12N 3°40W **194** E7
Valdepeñas *Spain* 38°43N 3°25W **195** G7
Valderaduey → *Spain* 41°31N 5°42W **194** D5
Valdérice *Italy* 38°4N 12°37E **200** D5
Valderrobres *Spain* 40°53N 0°9E **196** E5
Valdés, Pen. *Argentina* 42°30S 63°45W **336** B4
Valdez *Ecuador* 1°15N 79°0W **328** C2
Valdez *Alaska, U.S.A.* 61°7N 146°16W **303** F11
Valdgeym = Dobropole *Ukraine* 48°25N 37°2E **189** H9
Valdivia *Chile* 39°50S 73°14W **336** A2
Valdivia *Colombia* 7°11N 75°27W **328** B2
Valdivia Abyssal Plain *S. Ocean* 62°30S 70°0E **151** C6
Valdobbiádene *Italy* 45°54N 12°0E **199** C8
Valdosta *U.S.A.* 30°50N 83°17W **316** E6
Valdoviño *Spain* 43°36N 8°8W **194** B2
Valdres *Norway* 61°5N 9°5E **164** C6
Vale *Georgia* 41°30N 42°58E **191** K6
Vale *Oreg., U.S.A.* 43°59N 117°15W **304** E5
Vale *Va., U.S.A.* 38°55N 77°20W **143** B1
Vale of Glamorgan □ *U.K.* 51°28N 3°25W **169** F4
Valea lui Mihai *Romania* 47°32N 22°11E **182** C7
Valea Mărului *Romania* 45°49N 27°42E **183** E12
Valemount *Canada* 52°50N 119°15W **296** C5
Valença = Valença do Piauí *Brazil* 6°20S 41°45W **332** C3
Valença *Brazil* 13°20S 39°5W **333** D4
Valença *Portugal* 42°1N 8°34W **194** C2
Valença do Piauí *Brazil* 6°20S 41°45W **332** C3
Valençay *France* 47°9N 1°34E **173** E8
Valence *France* 44°57N 4°54E **175** D8
Valence d'Agen *France* 44°6N 0°53E **174** D4

Valencia Phil. 7°57N 125°3E 233 H5
Valencia Spain 39°27N 0°23W 197 F4
Valencia Trin. & Tob. 10°39N 61°11W 323 t
Valencia N. Mex., U.S.A. 34°48N 106°43W 305 J10
Valencia Venezuela 10°11N 68°0W 328 A4
Valencia □ Spain 39°20N 0°40W 197 F4
Valencia ✈ (VLC) Spain 39°20N 0°26W 197 F4
Valencia, G. de Spain 39°30N 0°20E 197 F5
Valencia de Alcántara Spain 39°25N 7°14W 195 F3
Valencia de Don Juan Spain 42°17N 5°31W 194 C5
Valencia I. Ireland 51°54N 10°22W 166 E1
Valenciennes France 50°20N 3°34E 173 B10
Văleni Romania 44°15N 24°45E 183 F9
Vălenii de Munte Romania 45°11N 26°2E 183 E11
Valensole France 43°50N 5°59E 175 E9
Valentigney France 47°27N 6°51E 173 E13
Valentim, Sa. do Brazil 6°0S 43°30W 332 C3
Valentin Russia 43°8N 134°17E 220 C7
Valentine Nebr., U.S.A. 42°52N 100°33W 308 D3
Valentine Tex., U.S.A. 30°35N 104°30W 314 F2
Valenton France 48°44N 2°27E 134 B3
Valenza Italy 45°1N 8°38E 198 C5
Våler Hedmark, Norway 60°41N 11°50E 164 D8
Våler Østfold, Norway 59°29N 10°51E 164 E7
Valera Piemonte, Italy 45°33N 9°3E 129 A1
Valera Venezuela 9°19N 70°37W 328 B3
Valesdir Vanuatu 16°47S 168°10E 287 F6
Valestrand Norway 59°40N 5°26E 164 E2
Valga Estonia 57°47N 26°2E 188 D4
Valguarnera Caropepe Italy 37°30N 14°23E 201 E7
Valier U.S.A. 48°18N 112°16W 304 B7
Valinco, G. de France 41°40N 8°52E 175 G12
Valjevo Serbia 44°18N 19°53E 202 B3
Valka Latvia 57°46N 26°3E 188 D3
Valkeakoski Finland 61°16N 24°2E 188 B2
Valkenswaard Neths. 51°21N 5°29E 170 C5
Vall de Uxó = La Vall d'Uixó Spain 39°49N 0°15W 196 F4
Valla Sweden 59°2N 16°20E 162 E10
Valladolid Yucatán, Mexico 20°41N 88°12W 319 C7
Valladolid Spain 41°38N 4°43W 194 D6
Valladolid □ Spain 41°38N 4°43W 194 D6
Vallata Italy 41°2N 15°15E 201 A8
Vallcarca Spain 41°25N 2°9E 114 A1
Valldemossa Spain 39°43N 2°37E 206 B3
Valldoreix Spain 41°27N 2°3E 114 A1
Valle Norway 59°13N 7°33E 164 E4
Valle d'Aosta □ Italy 45°45N 7°15E 198 C4
Valle de Aran Spain 42°50N 0°55E 196 C5
Valle de la Pascua Venezuela 9°13N 66°0W 328 B4
Valle de las Palmas Mexico 32°20N 116°43W 307 N10
Valle de Santiago Mexico 20°23N 101°12W 318 C4
Valle de Zaragoza Mexico 27°25N 105°50W 318 B3
Valle del Cauca □ Colombia 3°45N 76°30W 328 C2
Valle del Ticino ⌓ Italy 45°22N 9°0E 198 C6
Valle Fértil, Sierra del Argentina 30°20S 68°0W 334 C2
Valle Gran Rey Canary Is. 28°5N 17°20W 153 e1
Valle Hermoso Mexico 25°35N 97°40W 319 B5
Valle Nacional Mexico 17°47N 96°18W 319 D5
Vallecas Spain 40°22N 3°37W 127 B2
Vallecas, Cumbres de Spain 40°20N 3°33W 127 B2
Valledupar Colombia 10°29N 73°15W 328 A3
Vallegrande Bolivia 18°30S 64°10W 331 D5
Vallehermoso Canary Is. 28°10N 17°15W 153 e1
Vallejo U.S.A. 38°7N 122°14W 306 G4
Vallenar Chile 28°30S 70°50W 334 B1
Vallensbæk Denmark 55°38N 12°21E 118 B2
Vallensbæk Strand Denmark 55°36N 12°23E 118 B2
Vallentuna Sweden 59°32N 18°5E 162 E12
Vallentunasjön Sweden 59°27N 18°1E 139 A2
Valleranello Italy 41°46N 12°29E 136 C1
Valleraugue France 44°6N 3°39E 174 D7
Vallet France 47°10N 1°15W 172 E5
Valletta Malta 35°54N 14°31E 206 F8
Valley, The Anguilla 18°13N 63°4W 322 a
Valley Center U.S.A. 33°13N 117°2W 307 M9
Valley City U.S.A. 46°55N 98°0W 308 B5
Valley Falls Oreg., U.S.A. 42°29N 120°17W 304 E3
Valley Falls R.I., U.S.A. 41°54N 71°24W 313 E13
Valley Junction = West Des Moines U.S.A. 41°35N 93°43W 310 C3
Valley of Flowers △ India 30°50N 79°40E 243 D8
Valley of the Kings Egypt 25°41N 32°34E 256 B3
Valley Springs U.S.A. 38°12N 120°50W 306 G6
Valley Station U.S.A. 38°6N 85°52W 311 F11
Valley View U.S.A. 40°39N 76°33W 313 F8
Valley Wells U.S.A. 35°27N 115°46W 307 K11
Valleyview Canada 55°5N 117°17W 296 B5
Valli di Comácchio Italy 44°40N 12°15E 199 D9
Vallimanca, Arroyo Argentina 35°40S 59°10W 334 D4
Vallisaari Finland 60°7N 25°0E 121 C3
Vallo della Lucánia Italy 40°14N 15°16E 201 B8
Vallon-Pont-d'Arc France 44°24N 4°24E 175 D8
Vallorbe Switz. 46°42N 6°20E 179 J2
Valls Spain 41°18N 1°15E 196 D6
Vallvidrera Spain 41°24N 2°6E 114 A1
Valmaseda = Balmaseda Spain 43°11N 3°12W 196 B1
Valmeyer U.S.A. 38°18N 90°19W 310 F6
Valmiera Latvia 57°37N 25°29E 188 D3
Valnera Spain 43°9N 3°40W 194 B7
Valognes France 49°30N 1°28W 172 C5
Valona = Vlorë Albania 40°32N 19°28E 202 F3
Valongo Portugal 41°8N 8°30W 194 D2
Valozhyn Belarus 54°3N 26°30E 177 A14
Valpaços Portugal 41°36N 7°17W 194 D3
Valparai India 10°22N 76°58E 245 J3
Valparaíso Chile 33°2S 71°40W 334 C1
Valparaíso Zacatecas, Mexico 22°46N 103°34W 318 C4
Valparaiso Fla., U.S.A. 30°29N 86°30W 317 E3
Valparaiso Ind., U.S.A. 41°28N 87°4W 311 C9
Valparaíso □ Chile 33°2S 71°40W 334 C1
Valpovo Croatia 45°39N 18°25E 182 E3
Valpoy India 15°32N 74°8E 245 G2
Valréas France 44°24N 5°0E 175 D9
Vals Switz. 46°39N 9°11E 179 J5
Vals → S. Africa 27°23S 26°30E 270 C4
Vals, Tanjung Indonesia 8°26S 137°25E 231 F9
Vals-les-Bains France 44°42N 4°24E 175 D8
Valsad India 20°40N 72°58E 244 D1
Valsamata Greece 38°10N 20°36E 207 C2
Valtellina Italy 46°11N 9°55E 198 B6
Valþjofsstaður Iceland 65°1N 14°59W 155 B12
Valti Greece 38°27N 21°7E 207 C3
Valuyki Russia 50°10N 38°5E 189 G10
Valverde Canary Is. 27°48N 17°55W 153 e1
Valverde del Camino Spain 37°35N 6°47W 195 H4
Valverde del Fresno Spain 40°15N 6°51W 194 E4
Valvidrera → Spain 41°25N 2°0E 114 A1
Vama Romania 47°34N 25°42E 183 C10
Vambori India 19°17N 74°44E 244 E2
Vamdrup Denmark 55°25N 9°17E 163 J3
Våmhus Sweden 61°7N 14°29E 162 C8
Vamizi, I. Mozam. 11°2S 40°40E 269 E5
Vammala Finland 61°20N 22°54E 188 B2
Vamos Greece 35°24N 24°13E 207 E5
Vamsadhara → India 18°21N 84°8E 244 E7
Van Turkey 38°30N 43°20E 213 C10
Van □ Turkey 38°30N 43°20E 213 C10
Van, L. = Van Gölü Turkey 38°30N 43°0E 213 C10
Van Alstyne U.S.A. 33°25N 96°35W 314 E6
Van Blommestein Meer Suriname 4°45N 55°5W 329 C6
Van Buren = Kettering U.S.A. 39°41N 84°10W 311 E12
Van Buren N.B., Canada 47°10N 67°55W 299 C6
Van Buren Ark., U.S.A. 35°26N 94°21W 314 D7
Van Buren Maine, U.S.A. 47°10N 67°58W 309 B20
Van Buren Mo., U.S.A. 37°0N 91°1W 308 G8
Van Canh Vietnam 13°37N 109°0E 236 F7
Van Diemen, C. N. Terr., Australia 11°9S 130°24E 278 B5
Van Diemen, C. Queens., Australia 16°30S 139°46E 280 B2
Van Diemen G. Australia 11°45S 132°0E 278 B5
Van Gogh Museum Amsterdam, Neths. 112 c1
Van Gölü Turkey 38°30N 43°0E 213 C10
Van Horn U.S.A. 31°3N 104°50W 314 F2
Van Horne U.S.A. 42°1N 92°5W 310 B4
Van Meter U.S.A. 41°32N 93°57W 310 C3
Van Ninh Vietnam 12°42N 109°14E 236 F7
Van Rees, Pegunungan Indonesia 2°35S 138°15E 231 E9
Van Tivu India 8°51N 78°15E 245 K4
Van Wert U.S.A. 40°52N 84°35W 311 D12
Van Yen Vietnam 21°4N 104°42E 228 G5
Van Zylsrus S. Africa 26°52S 22°4E 270 C3
Vanadzor Armenia 40°48N 44°30E 191 K7
Vanak Iran 35°45N 51°23E 141 A2
Vanavana French Polynesia 20°47S 139°9W 289 f
Vanavara Russia 60°22N 102°16E 215 C11
Vanceburg U.S.A. 38°36N 83°19W 311 F13
Vancouver B.C., Canada 49°15N 123°7W 306 A3
Vancouver Wash., U.S.A. 45°38N 122°40W 306 E4
Vancouver, C. Australia 35°2S 118°11E 279 G2
Vancouver, Mt. U.S.A. 60°20N 139°41W 303 F13
Vancouver I. Canada 49°50N 126°0W 306 B2
Vancouver Int. ✈ (YVR) Canada 49°10N 123°10W 306 A3
Vanda = Vantaa Finland 60°18N 24°56E 121 B2
Vandalia Ill., U.S.A. 38°58N 89°6W 310 F7
Vandalia Mo., U.S.A. 39°19N 91°29W 310 E5
Vandalia Ohio, U.S.A. 39°54N 84°12W 311 E12
Vandavasi India 12°30N 79°30E 245 H4
Vandeloos B. Sri Lanka 8°0N 81°45E 245 L5
Vandenberg Village U.S.A. 34°43N 120°28W 307 L6
Vandergrift U.S.A. 40°36N 79°34W 312 F5
Vanderhoof Canada 54°0N 124°0W 296 C4
Vanderkloof Dam S. Africa 30°4S 24°40E 270 D3
Vanderlin I. Australia 15°44S 137°2E 280 B2
Vänern Sweden 58°47N 13°30E 163 F7
Vänersborg Sweden 58°26N 12°19E 163 F6
Vang Norway 61°7N 8°34E 164 C5
Vang Vieng Laos 18°58N 102°32E 236 C4
Vanga Kenya 4°35S 39°12E 268 C4
Vangaindrano Madag. 23°21S 47°36E 272 C2
Vangede Denmark 55°45N 12°30E 118 A3
Vangsnes Norway 61°9N 6°39E 164 C3
Vanguard Canada 49°55N 107°20W 297 D7
Vangunu Solomon Is. 8°40S 158°5E 287 M10
Vanikoro Pac. Oc. 11°39S 166°54E 277 C12
Vaniköy Turkey 41°3N 29°3E 122 B2
Vanimo Papua N. G. 2°42S 141°21E 286 B1
Vanino Russia 48°50N 140°5E 215 E15
Vanivilasa Sagara India 13°45N 76°30E 245 H3
Vaniyambadi India 12°46N 78°44E 245 H4
Vânju Mare Romania 44°25N 22°52E 182 F7
Vankleek Hill Canada 45°32N 74°40W 313 A10
Vanløse Denmark 55°41N 12°28E 118 A2
Vännäs Sweden 63°58N 19°48E 160 E18
Vannes France 47°40N 2°47W 172 E4
Vannøya Norway 70°6N 19°50E 160 A18
Vanoise, Massif de la France 45°25N 6°40E 175 C10
Vanrhynsdorp S. Africa 31°36S 18°44E 270 D2
Vansada India 20°47N 73°25E 244 D1
Vansbro Sweden 60°32N 14°15E 162 D8
Vanse Norway 58°6N 6°41E 164 F3
Vansittart B. Australia 14°3S 126°17E 278 B4
Vansittart I. Canada 65°50N 84°0W 295 D15
Vantaa Finland 60°18N 24°56E 121 B2
Vantaankoski Finland 60°18N 24°50E 121 B2
Vantaanpuisto Finland 60°18N 24°53E 121 B2
Vanua Balavu Fiji 17°12S 178°55W 287 A3
Vanua Lava Vanuatu 13°50S 167°30E 287 C5
Vanua Levu Fiji 16°33S 179°15E 287 A2
Vanua Vatu Fiji 18°22S 179°15W 287 B3
Vanuatu ■ Pac. Oc. 15°0S 168°0E 287 E6
Vanves France 48°49N 2°17E 134 B2
Vanwyksvlei S. Africa 30°18S 21°49E 270 D3
Vao N. Cal. 22°39S 167°32E 288 d
Vapnyarka Ukraine 48°32N 28°45E 183 B13
Var □ France 43°27N 6°18E 175 E10
Var → France 43°39N 7°12E 175 E11
Vara Sweden 58°16N 12°55E 163 F6
Vara, Pico da Azores 37°48N 25°13W 153 d3
Varada → India 15°0N 75°40E 245 G2
Varades France 47°25N 1°1W 172 E5
Varáita → Italy 44°9N 7°53E 198 D4
Varaldsøy Norway 60°6N 5°59E 164 D2
Varalé Ivory C. 9°40N 3°17W 262 D4
Varallo Italy 45°49N 8°15E 198 C5
Varāmīn Iran 35°20N 51°39E 247 C6
Varāmīn □ Iran 35°18N 51°35E 247 B6
Varanasi India 25°22N 83°0E 243 G10
Varangerfjorden Norway 70°3N 29°25E 160 A23
Varangerhalvøya Norway 70°25N 29°30E 160 A23
Varano, Lago di Italy 41°53N 15°45E 199 G12
Varaždin Croatia 46°20N 16°20E 199 B13
Varazze Italy 44°22N 8°34E 198 D5
Varberg Sweden 57°6N 12°20E 163 G6
Varcar Vakuf = Mrkonjić Grad Bos.-H. 44°26N 17°4E 182 F2
Vardak □ Afghan. 34°0N 68°0E 240 B3
Vardar = Axios → Greece 40°57N 22°35E 202 F6
Varde Denmark 55°38N 8°29E 163 J2
Varde Å → Denmark 55°35N 8°19E 163 J2
Vardenis Armenia 40°10N 45°43E 191 K7
Vardø Norway 70°23N 31°5E 160 A24
Varedo Italy 45°35N 9°8E 129 A1
Varel Germany 53°23N 8°8E 178 B4
Varella, Mui Vietnam 12°54N 109°26E 236 F7
Varėna Lithuania 54°12N 24°30E 188 E3
Varennes-sur-Allier France 46°19N 3°24E 173 F10
Varennes-Vauzelles France 47°3N 3°9E 173 E10
Vareš Bos.-H. 44°12N 18°23E 182 F3
Varese Italy 45°48N 8°50E 198 C5
Vârfurile Romania 46°19N 22°31E 182 D7
Vårgårda Sweden 58°2N 12°49E 163 F6
Vargem Bonita Brazil 20°20S 46°22W 333 F2
Vargem Grande Brazil 3°33S 43°56W 332 B3
Varginha Brazil 21°33S 45°25W 335 A6
Vargön Sweden 58°22N 12°20E 163 F6
Varhaug Norway 58°37N 5°41E 164 F2
Vari Greece 38°24N 20°35E 207 C2
Varillas Chile 24°0S 70°10W 334 A1
Varkaus Finland 62°19N 27°50E 188 A4
Varkiza Greece 37°50N 23°49E 112 C2
Värmdölandet Sweden 59°20N 18°33E 162 E12
Värmeln Sweden 59°35N 12°54E 162 E6
Värmlands län □ Sweden 60°0N 13°20E 162 E6
Värmlandsbro Sweden 59°11N 13°0E 162 E7
Varna Bulgaria 43°13N 27°56E 203 C11
Varna □ Bulgaria 43°20N 27°30E 203 C11
Varna → India 16°48N 74°32E 244 F2
Värnamo Sweden 57°10N 14°3E 163 G8
Varnsdorf Czech Rep. 50°55N 14°35E 180 A7
Varnville U.S.A. 32°51N 81°5W 316 C8
Várpalota Hungary 47°12N 18°8E 182 C3
Vars Ont., Canada 45°21N 75°21W 313 A9
Vars Hautes-Alpes, France 44°37N 6°42E 175 D10
Vartdal Norway 62°20N 6°8E 164 B3
Vartiokylä Finland 60°13N 25°6E 121 B3
Vartiosaari Finland 60°11N 25°5E 121 B3
Varto Turkey 39°10N 41°27E 213 C9
Varvarin Serbia 43°43N 21°20E 202 C5
Varysburg U.S.A. 42°46N 78°19W 312 D6
Varzaneh Iran 32°25N 52°40E 247 C7
Varzaqān Iran 38°29N 46°40E 213 C12
Várzea Alegre Brazil 6°47S 39°17W 332 C4
Várzea da Palma Brazil 17°36S 44°44W 333 E3
Várzea Grande Brazil 15°39S 56°8W 331 D6
Varzi Italy 44°49N 9°12E 198 D6
Varzo Italy 46°12N 8°15E 198 B5
Varzy France 47°22N 3°20E 173 E10
Vas □ Hungary 47°10N 16°55E 182 C1
Vasa = Vaasa Finland 63°6N 21°38E 160 E19
Vasa Barris → Brazil 11°10S 37°10W 332 D4
Vasamuseet Stockholm, Sweden 139 b3
Vásárosnamény Hungary 48°9N 22°19E 182 B7
Vascâo → Portugal 37°31N 7°31W 195 H3
Vaşcău Romania 46°28N 22°30E 182 D7
Vasco S. Africa 33°54S 18°34E 118 A2
Vascongadas = País Vasco □ Spain 42°50N 2°45W 196 C2
Vasfanārd Iran 35°38N 51°20E 141 B2
Vashi India 19°4N 72°59E 130 A2
Vāshīr Afghan. 32°16N 63°51E 240 B1
Vashkivtsi Ukraine 48°23N 25°31E 183 B10
Vasht = Khāsh Iran 28°15N 61°15E 240 C1
Vasilevichi Belarus 52°15N 29°50E 177 B15
Vasiliki Greece 38°37N 20°36E 207 B2
Vasiliko = Michurin Bulgaria 42°9N 27°51E 203 D11
Vasiliko Greece 38°25N 23°40E 204 C5
Vasilikos Greece 37°43N 20°59E 207 D2
Vasilkov = Vasylkiv Ukraine 50°7N 30°15E 177 C16
Vasilyevskiy, Ostrov Russia 59°55N 30°16E 137 B1
Vasilyova Sloboda = Chkolovsk Russia 56°50N 43°10E 190 B6
Vasilyovo = Chkolovsk Russia 56°50N 43°10E 190 B6
Vaslui Romania 46°38N 27°42E 183 D12
Vaslui □ Romania 46°30N 27°45E 183 D12
Väsman Sweden 60°9N 15°5E 162 D9
Vassar Man., Canada 49°10N 95°55W 297 D9
Vassar Mich., U.S.A. 43°22N 83°35W 309 D12
Vassfaret Norway 60°38N 9°28E 164 D6
Västerås Sweden 59°37N 16°38E 162 E10
Västerbotten Sweden 64°36N 20°4E 160 D19
Västerdalälven → Sweden 60°30N 14°7E 162 D8
Västergötland Sweden 58°0N 13°10E 163 F7
Västerhaninge Sweden 59°7N 18°6E 162 E12
Västervik Sweden 57°43N 16°33E 163 G10
Västmanland Sweden 59°45N 16°20E 161 G17
Västmanlands län □ Sweden 59°45N 16°20E 162 E10
Vasto Italy 42°8N 14°40E 199 F11
Västra Götalands Län □ Sweden 58°0N 13°0E 163 F6
Vasvár Hungary 47°3N 16°47E 182 C1
Vasylivka Ukraine 45°38N 28°50E 183 E13
Vasylkiv Ukraine 50°7N 30°15E 177 C16
Vatan France 47°4N 1°50E 173 E8
Vaté = Efate, I. Vanuatu 17°40S 168°25E 287 G6
Vatersay U.K. 56°55N 7°32W 167 E1
Vathi Greece 38°41N 20°47E 207 B2
Vathia Greece 36°29N 22°29E 204 E4
Vati Greece 36°3N 27°53E 206 E11
Vatia Amer. Samoa 14°15S 170°40W 302 f
Vatican City ■ Europe 41°54N 12°27E 136 B1
Vaticano, C. Italy 38°37N 15°50E 201 D8
Vatili Cyprus 35°6N 33°40E 207 E9
Vatin Serbia 45°12N 21°20E 182 E6
Vatiu = Atiu Cook Is. 20°0S 158°10W 289 J12
Vatnajökull Iceland 64°30N 16°48W 155 C10
Vatnajökull △ Iceland 64°24N 16°48W 155 C10
Vatnås Norway 59°58N 9°37E 164 E6
Vatnsfjörður Iceland 65°56N 22°30W 155 B4
Vatolakkos Greece 35°27N 23°53E 207 E4
Vatoloha Madag. 17°52S 47°48E 272 B2
Vatomandry Madag. 19°20S 48°59E 272 B2
Vatra-Dornei Romania 47°22N 25°22E 183 C10
Vatrak → India 23°9N 73°2E 242 H5
Vattaru Atoll Maldives 3°16N 73°25E 272 d
Vättern Sweden 58°25N 14°30E 163 F8
Vatu Vara Fiji 17°26S 179°31W 287 A3
Vatulele Fiji 18°33S 177°37E 287 B1
Vauclin, Mt. du Martinique 14°33N 60°53W 322 j
Vauclin, Pte. de Martinique 14°34N 60°49W 322 j
Vaucluse Australia 33°51S 151°15E 139 B2
Vaucluse □ France 43°50N 5°20E 175 E9
Vaucluse House Australia 33°51S 151°15E 139 B2
Vaucouleurs France 48°37N 5°40E 173 D12
Vaucresson France 48°50N 2°9E 134 A1
Vaud □ Switz. 46°35N 6°30E 179 J2
Vaudreuil-Dorion Canada 45°23N 74°3W 313 A10
Vaughan Canada 43°50N 79°32W 141 A1
Vaughn Mont., U.S.A. 47°33N 111°33W 304 C8
Vaughn N. Mex., U.S.A. 34°36N 105°13W 305 J11
Vauhallan France 48°44N 2°12E 134 B2
Vaujours France 48°56N 2°34E 134 A4
Vaujours L. Canada 55°27N 74°15W 298 A5
Vaupés = Uaupés → Brazil 0°2N 67°16W 328 C4
Vaupés □ Colombia 1°0N 71°0W 328 C3
Vauvert France 43°42N 4°17E 175 E8
Vauxhall Alta., Canada 50°5N 112°9W 296 C6
Vauxhall London, U.K. 125 c4
Vav India 24°22N 71°31E 242 G4
Vavatenina Madag. 17°28S 49°12E 272 B2
Vava'u Tonga 18°36S 174°0W 287 P14
Vava'u Group Tonga 18°40S 174°0W 287 P14
Vavoua Ivory C. 7°23N 6°29W 262 D3
Vavuniya Sri Lanka 8°45N 80°30E 245 K5
Vawkavysk Belarus 53°9N 24°30E 177 B13
Vaxholm Sweden 59°25N 18°20E 162 E12
Växjö Sweden 56°52N 14°50E 163 H8
Våxtorp Sweden 56°25N 13°8E 163 H7
Vayalpad India 13°39N 78°38E 245 H4
Vayenga = Severomorsk Russia 69°5N 33°27E 160 B25
Vaygach, Ostrov Russia 70°0N 60°0E 214 C7
Veadeiros Brazil 14°7S 47°31W 333 D2
Veaikevárri = Svappavaara Sweden 67°40N 21°3E 160 C19
Vechelde Germany 52°16N 10°22E 178 C6
Vechta Germany 52°44N 8°17E 178 C4
Vechte → Neths. 52°34N 6°6E 170 B6
Vecsés Hungary 47°26N 19°19E 117 B3
Vedaranniyam India 10°25N 79°50E 245 J4
Vedavågen Norway 59°17N 5°12E 164 E2
Veddige Sweden 57°17N 12°20E 163 G6
Vedea → Romania 43°42N 25°41E 183 G10
Vedi Armenia 39°54N 44°43E 213 C11
Vedia Argentina 34°30S 61°31W 334 C3
Vedrette di Ries-Aurina ⌓ Italy 46°54N 12°5E 199 B9
Vedum Sweden 58°11N 13°0E 163 F7
Veedersburg U.S.A. 40°7N 87°16W 311 D9
Veendam Neths. 53°5N 6°52E 170 A6
Veenendaal Neths. 52°2N 5°34E 170 B5
Vefsna → Norway 65°48N 13°10E 160 D15
Vega Nordland, Norway 65°40N 11°55E 160 D14
Vega Tex., U.S.A. 35°15N 102°26W 314 D3
Vega Alta Puerto Rico 18°25N 66°20W 321 b
Vega Baja Puerto Rico 18°27N 66°23W 321 b
Vega de Ribadeo = Vegadeo Spain 43°27N 7°4W 194 B3
Vegadeo Spain 43°27N 7°4W 194 B3
Vegårshei Norway 58°44N 8°51E 164 F5
Vegas Verde = North Las Vegas U.S.A. 36°11N 115°7W 124 A1
Veggli Norway 60°3N 9°9E 164 D6
Veglia = Krk Croatia 45°8N 14°40E 199 C11
Vegoritida, L. Greece 40°45N 21°45E 202 F5
Vegreville Canada 53°30N 112°5W 296 C6
Veiholmen Norway 63°31N 7°58E 164 A4
Veimandu Channel Maldives 2°10N 73°20E 272 d
Veinge Sweden 56°33N 13°4E 163 H7
Veisiejai Lithuania 54°6N 23°42E 184 D10
Vejbystrand Sweden 56°19N 12°45E 163 H6
Vejen Denmark 55°30N 9°9E 163 J3
Vejer de la Frontera Spain 36°15N 5°59W 195 J5
Vejle Denmark 55°43N 9°30E 163 J3
Vejle Fjord Denmark 55°40N 9°50E 163 J3
Vela Luka Croatia 42°59N 16°44E 199 F13
Velachha India 21°26N 73°1E 244 D1
Velanai I. Sri Lanka 9°45N 79°45E 245 K4
Velas Azores 38°41N 28°13W 153 d1
Velas, C. Costa Rica 10°21N 85°52W 320 D2
Velasco, Sierra de Argentina 29°20S 67°10W 334 B2
Velay, Mts. du France 45°0N 3°40E 174 D7
Velbert Germany 51°20N 7°3E 178 D3
Velddrif S. Africa 32°42S 18°11E 270 D2
Velebit ⌓ Croatia 44°30N 15°15E 199 D12
Velebit Planina Croatia 44°50N 15°20E 199 D12
Velebitski Kanal Croatia 44°45N 14°55E 199 D11
Veleka → Bulgaria 42°4N 27°58E 203 D11
Veleň Czech Rep. 50°10N 14°33E 135 A3
Velencei-tó Hungary 47°13N 18°36E 182 C3
Velenje Slovenia 46°23N 15°8E 199 B12
Veles Macedonia 41°46N 21°47E 202 E5
Veleslavin Czech Rep. 50°5N 14°21E 135 B2
Velestino Greece 39°23N 22°43E 204 B4
Vélez Colombia 6°1N 73°41W 328 B3
Vélez-Málaga Spain 36°48N 4°5W 195 J6
Vélez Rubio Spain 37°41N 2°5W 197 H2
Velhas → Brazil 17°13S 44°49W 333 E3
Velika Croatia 45°27N 17°40E 182 E2
Velika Gorica Croatia 45°44N 16°5E 199 C13
Velika Kapela Croatia 45°10N 15°5E 199 C12
Velika Kikinda = Kikinda Serbia 45°50N 20°30E 182 E5
Velika Kladuša Bos.-H. 45°11N 15°48E 199 C12
Velika Kruša Kosovo 42°19N 20°39E 202 D4
Velika Morava → Serbia 44°43N 21°3E 202 B5
Velika Plana Serbia 44°20N 21°4E 202 B5
Velikaya → Russia 57°48N 28°10E 188 D5
Velikaya Kema Russia 45°30N 137°12E 220 B8
Velikaya Lepetikha Ukraine 47°2N 33°58E 189 J7
Veliké Kapušany Slovak Rep. 48°34N 22°5E 181 C15
Velike Lašče Slovenia 45°49N 14°45E 199 C11
Veliki Jastrebac Serbia 43°25N 21°30E 202 C5
Veliki Kanal Serbia 45°45N 19°15E 182 E4
Veliki Popović Serbia 44°8N 21°18E 202 B5
Veliki Ustyug Russia 60°47N 46°20E 186 B8
Velikiye Luki Russia 56°25N 30°32E 188 D6
Veliko Gradište Serbia 44°46N 21°29E 202 B5
Veliko Tŭrnovo Bulgaria 43°5N 25°41E 203 C9
Velikonda Range India 14°45N 79°10E 245 G4
Vélingara Kolda, Senegal 13°12N 14°5W 262 C2
Vélingara Louga, Senegal 15°0N 14°40W 262 B2
Velingrad Bulgaria 42°4N 23°58E 202 D7
Velino, Mte. Italy 42°9N 13°23E 199 F10
Velizh Russia 55°36N 31°11E 188 E6
Vélizy-Villacoublay France 48°47N 2°11E 134 B2
Velka-Chuchle Czech Rep. 50°0N 14°23E 135 B2
Velké Karlovice Czech Rep. 49°20N 18°17E 181 B11
Velké Meziříčí Czech Rep. 49°21N 16°1E 180 B9
Velké Přilepy Czech Rep. 50°9N 14°19E 135 B1
Veľký Javorník Slovak Rep. 49°19N 18°22E 181 B11
Veľký Krtíš Slovak Rep. 48°12N 19°21E 181 C12
Veľký Meder Slovak Rep. 47°52N 17°46E 181 D10
Veľký Tribeč Slovak Rep. 48°28N 18°15E 181 C11
Vella G. Solomon Is. 8°0S 156°50E 287 M9
Vella Lavella Solomon Is. 7°45S 156°40E 287 L9
Vellar → India 11°30N 79°36E 245 J4
Velletri Italy 41°41N 12°47E 200 A5
Vellinge Sweden 55°29N 13°2E 163 J6
Vellmar Germany 51°22N 9°28E 178 D5
Vellore India 12°57N 79°10E 245 H4
Velopoula Greece 36°55N 23°27E 204 E5
Velsk Russia 61°10N 42°5E 188 B11
Velten Germany 52°42N 13°10E 178 C9
Veluwezoom △ Neths. 52°5N 6°0E 170 B6
Velva U.S.A. 48°4N 100°56W 308 A3
Velvendos Greece 40°15N 22°6E 202 F6
Velyka Mykhaylivka Ukraine 47°4N 29°52E 183 C14
Velyki Luchky Ukraine 48°25N 22°34E 182 B7
Velykyy Bereznyy Ukraine 48°54N 22°28E 182 B7
Velykyy Bychkiv Ukraine 47°58N 24°1E 183 C9
Vemb Denmark 56°21N 8°21E 163 H2
Vembanad L. India 9°36N 76°15E 245 K3
Vemdalen Sweden 62°27N 13°51E 162 B7
Ven Sweden 55°55N 12°45E 163 J6
Venaco France 42°14N 9°11E 175 F13
Venado Mexico 22°56N 101°6W 318 C4
Venado Tuerto Argentina 33°50S 62°0W 334 C3
Venafro Italy 41°29N 14°2E 201 A7
Venarey-les-Laumes France 47°32N 4°26E 173 E11
Venaría Italy 45°8N 7°38E 198 C4
Venčane Serbia 44°24N 20°28E 202 B4
Vence France 43°43N 7°6E 175 E11
Venda Seca Portugal 38°46N 9°15W 126 A1
Vendas Novas Portugal 38°39N 8°27W 195 G2
Vendée □ France 46°50N 1°35W 172 F5
Vendée → France 46°20N 1°10W 172 F5
Vendéen, Bocage France 46°40N 1°20W 174 B2
Vendeuvre-sur-Barse France 48°14N 4°28E 173 D11
Vendôme France 47°47N 1°3E 172 E8
Vendrell = El Vendrell Spain 41°10N 1°30E 196 D6
Vendsyssel Denmark 57°22N 10°0E 163 G4
Vendychany Ukraine 48°38N 27°48E 183 B12
Venelles France 43°35N 5°28E 175 E9
Véneta, L. Italy 45°23N 12°25E 199 C9
Venetian Islands U.S.A. 25°47N 80°9W 128 B2
Venetie U.S.A. 67°1N 146°25W 303 C11
Véneto □ Italy 45°30N 12°0E 199 C9
Venev Russia 54°22N 38°17E 188 E10
Venézia Italy 45°27N 12°21E 199 C9
Venézia, G. di Italy 45°15N 13°0E 199 C10
Venézia, Palazzo Rome, Italy 136 c2
Venézia Tridentina = Trentino-Alto Adige □ Italy 46°30N 11°20E 199 B8
Venezuela ■ S. Amer. 8°0N 66°0W 328 B4
Venezuela, G. de Venezuela 11°30N 71°0W 328 A3
Venezuelan Basin Cent. Amer. 14°0N 68°0W 321 C6
Vengurla India 15°53N 73°45E 245 G1
Vengurla Rocks India 15°55N 73°22E 245 G1
Venice = Venézia Italy 45°27N 12°21E 199 C9
Venice Calif., U.S.A. 33°59N 118°27W 126 C2
Venice Fla., U.S.A. 27°6N 82°27W 317 H7
Vénissieux France 45°42N 4°53E 175 C8
Venjansjön Sweden 60°54N 14°0E 162 D8
Venkatagiri India 14°0N 79°35E 245 H4
Venkatapuram India 18°20N 80°30E 244 E5
Venlo Neths. 51°22N 6°11E 170 C6
Vennachar Junction Canada 45°5N 77°14W 312 A7
Vennesla Norway 58°15N 7°59E 164 F4
Venosa Italy 40°58N 15°49E 201 B8
Venray Neths. 51°31N 6°0E 170 C6
Vent, Îs. du French Polynesia 17°30S 149°30W 289 f
Venta Lithuania 56°12N 22°42E 184 B9
Venta → Latvia 57°24N 21°33E 184 A8
Venta de Baños Spain 41°55N 4°30W 194 D6
Venta de Cardeña = Cardeña Spain 38°16N 4°20W 195 G6
Ventana, Punta de la Mexico 24°4N 109°48W 318 C3
Ventana, Sa. de la Argentina 38°0S 62°30W 334 D3
Ventas Spain 40°26N 3°40W 127 B1
Ventersburg S. Africa 28°7S 27°9E 270 C4
Ventersburgweg = Hennenman S. Africa 27°59S 27°1E 270 C4
Venterstad S. Africa 30°47S 25°48E 270 D4
Ventimíglia Italy 43°47N 7°36E 198 E4
Ventnor U.K. 50°36N 1°12W 169 G6
Ventorro del Cano Spain 40°23N 3°49W 127 B1
Ventoténe Italy 40°47N 13°25E 200 B6
Ventoux, Mt. France 44°10N 5°17E 175 D9
Ventspils Latvia 57°25N 21°32E 184 A8
Ventspils □ Latvia 57°20N 21°50E 184 A8
Ventuarí → Venezuela 3°58N 67°2W 328 C4
Ventucopa U.S.A. 34°50N 119°29W 307 L7
Ventura U.S.A. 34°17N 119°18W 307 L7
Venus U.S.A. 27°4N 81°22W 317 H8
Vénus, Pte. Tahiti 17°29S 149°29W 289 e
Venus B. Australia 38°40S 145°42E 283 E6
Venustiano Carranza Baja Calif., Mexico 30°25N 115°53W 318 A1
Venustiano Carranza Distrito Federal, Mexico 19°25N 99°5W 128 B2
Vera Argentina 29°30S 60°20W 334 B3
Vera Spain 37°15N 1°51W 197 H3
Veracruz Mexico 19°11N 96°8W 319 D5
Veracruz □ Mexico 19°0N 96°15W 319 D5
Veraval India 20°53N 70°27E 242 J4
Verbánia Italy 45°56N 8°33E 198 C5
Verbicaro Italy 39°45N 15°55E 201 C8
Verbier Switz. 46°6N 7°13E 179 J3
Vercelli Italy 45°19N 8°25E 198 C5
Verchovchevo Ukraine 48°32N 34°10E 189 H8
Vercors ⌓ France 45°0N 5°25E 175 D9
Verdalsøra Norway 63°48N 11°30E 160 E14
Verde → Argentina 41°56S 65°5W 336 B3
Verde → Goiás, Brazil 19°11S 50°44W 333 E1
Verde → Goiás, Brazil 18°1S 50°14W 333 E1
Verde → Mato Grosso, Brazil 11°54S 55°48W 331 C6
Verde → Mato Grosso do Sul, Brazil 21°25S 52°20W 331 E7
Verde → São Paulo, Brazil 23°29S 46°27W 137 A1
Verde → Chihuahua, Mexico 26°29N 107°58W 318 B3
Verde → Oaxaca, Mexico 15°59N 97°50W 319 D5
Verde → Veracruz, Mexico 21°10N 102°50W 318 C4
Verde → Paraguay 23°9S 57°37W 334 A4
Verde → Ariz., U.S.A. 33°33N 111°40W 300 J17
Verde, Cay Bahamas 23°0N 75°5W 321 B4
Verde Grande → Brazil 16°13S 43°49W 333 E3
Verde I. Phil. 13°33N 121°5E 232 E3
Verde Island Pass Phil. 13°34N 120°51E 232 E3
Verde Pequeno → Brazil 14°48S 43°31W 333 D3
Verden Germany 52°55N 9°14E 178 C5
Verdi Athina, Greece 38°2N 23°40E 112 A2
Verdi Nev., U.S.A. 39°31N 119°59W 306 F7
Verdikoussa Greece 39°47N 21°59E 204 B3
Verdon → France 43°43N 5°46E 175 E9
Verdon ⌓ France 43°50N 6°5E 175 E10
Verdugo Mts. U.S.A. 34°10N 118°16W 126 A2
Verdun Qué., Canada 45°27N 73°35W 130 B2
Verdun Meuse, France 49°9N 5°24E 173 C12
Verdun-sur-le-Doubs France 46°54N 5°2E 173 F12
Vereeniging S. Africa 26°38S 27°57E 271 C4
Verga, C. Guinea 10°30N 14°10W 262 C2
Vergara Uruguay 32°56S 53°57W 335 C5
Vergato Italy 44°17N 11°7E 198 D8
Vergemont Cr. → Australia 24°16S 143°16E 280 C3
Vergennes U.S.A. 44°10N 73°15W 313 B11
Vergt France 45°2N 0°43E 174 C4
Vérhalom Hungary 47°31N 19°1E 117 A2
Veria Greece 40°34N 22°12E 202 F6
Verín Spain 41°57N 7°27W 194 D3
Verkhnedvinsk = Vyerkhnyadzvinsk Belarus 55°45N 27°58E 188 E4
Verkhnetulomskoye Vdkhr. Russia 68°36N 31°12E 160 B24
Verkhnevilyuysk Russia 63°27N 120°18E 215 C13
Verkhniy Baskunchak Russia 48°14N 46°44E 191 F8
Verkhovye Russia 52°55N 37°15E 189 F9
Verkhovyna Ukraine 48°9N 24°47E 183 B9
Verkhoyansk Russia 67°35N 133°25E 215 C14
Verkhoyansk Ra. = Verkhoyanskiy Khrebet Russia 66°0N 129°0E 215 C13
Verkhoyanskiy Khrebet Russia 66°0N 129°0E 215 C13
Verma Norway 62°21N 8°3E 164 B5
Vermelho → Brazil 23°30S 46°46W 137 B1
Vermenton France 47°40N 3°42E 173 E10
Vermilion Alta., Canada 53°20N 110°50W 297 C6
Vermilion Ohio, U.S.A. 41°25N 82°22W 312 E2
Vermilion → Alta., Canada 53°22N 110°51W 297 C6
Vermilion → Ill., U.S.A. 41°19N 89°4W 310 C7
Vermilion B. U.S.A. 29°42N 92°0W 314 G9
Vermilion Bay Canada 49°51N 93°34W 297 D10
Vermilion L. U.S.A. 47°53N 92°26W 308 B7
Vermillion U.S.A. 42°47N 96°56W 308 D5
Vermillion → Canada 47°38N 72°56W 298 C5
Vermont U.S.A. 40°18N 90°26W 310 D6
Vermont □ U.S.A. 44°0N 73°0W 313 C12
Vermont Knolls U.S.A. 33°57N 118°21W 126 C3
Vermosh Albania 42°35N 19°42E 202 D3
Verna U.S.A. 27°23N 82°16W 317 H7
Vernadsky Antarctica 65°0S 64°0W 151 C17
Vernal U.S.A. 40°27N 109°32W 304 F9
Vernalis U.S.A. 37°36N 121°17W 306 H5
Vernazza Italy 44°10N 9°45E 198 D6
Verner Canada 46°25N 80°8W 298 C3
Verneuil-sur-Avre France 48°45N 0°55E 172 D7
Verneukpan S. Africa 30°0S 21°0E 270 D3
Vernier Switz. 46°11N 6°12E 179 J2
Vérnio Italy 44°3N 11°9E 198 D8
Vernon B.C., Canada 50°20N 119°15W 296 C5
Vernon Eure, France 49°5N 1°30E 172 C8
Vernon Calif., U.S.A. 34°0N 118°13W 126 B3
Vernon Ill., U.S.A. 38°48N 89°5W 310 F7
Vernon Ind., U.S.A. 38°59N 85°36W 311 F11
Vernon Tex., U.S.A. 34°9N 99°17W 314 D5
Vernonia U.S.A. 45°52N 123°11W 306 E3
Vernou Guadeloupe 16°11N 61°39W 322 e
Verny = Almaty Kazakhstan 43°15N 76°57E 217 D9
Vero Beach U.S.A. 27°38N 80°24W 317 H9
Véroia = Veria Greece 40°34N 22°12E 202 F6
Véroli Italy 41°41N 13°25E 199 G10
Verona Ont., Canada 44°29N 76°42W 313 B8
Verona Italy 45°27N 10°59E 198 C7
Verona Wis., U.S.A. 42°59N 89°32W 310 B7
Verrès Italy 45°40N 7°42E 198 C4
Verrières-le-Buisson France 48°44N 2°16E 134 B2
Verron Ra. Papua N. G. 4°21S 152°46E 286 C7
Versailles B. Aires, Argentina 34°38S 58°31W 117 B1
Versailles Yvelines, France 48°48N 2°7E 134 B1
Versailles Ill., U.S.A. 39°53N 90°39W 310 E6
Versailles Ind., U.S.A. 39°4N 85°15W 311 E11
Versailles Ky., U.S.A. 38°3N 84°44W 311 F12
Versailles Mo., U.S.A. 38°26N 92°51W 310 F4
Versailles Ohio, U.S.A. 40°13N 84°29W 311 D12
Versalles Bolivia 12°44S 63°18W 331 C5
Versmold Germany 52°2N 8°9E 178 C4
Vert, C. Senegal 14°45N 17°30W 262 C1
Vertou France 47°10N 1°28W 172 E5
Vertus France 48°54N 4°2E 173 D11
Verulam S. Africa 29°38S 31°2E 271 C5
Verviers Belgium 50°37N 5°52E 170 D5
Vervins France 49°50N 3°53E 173 C10
Veržej Slovenia 46°34N 16°13E 199 B13
Verzy France 49°9N 4°10E 173 C11
Vescovato France 42°30N 9°27E 175 F13
Veselí nad Lužnicí Czech Rep. 49°12N 14°43E 180 B7
Veselie Bulgaria 42°18N 27°38E 203 D11
Veselovskoye Vdkhr. Russia 46°58N 41°25E 191 G5
Veshenskaya Russia 49°35N 41°44E 190 F5
Veshnyaki Russia 55°43N 37°48E 129 B4
Vesle → France 49°23N 3°28E 173 C10
Vesolyy Posolok Russia 59°53N 30°28E 137 B2
Vesoul France 47°40N 6°11E 173 E13
Vessigebro Sweden 56°58N 12°40E 163 H6
Vest-Agder □ Norway 58°30N 7°15E 164 F4
Vestbygd Norway 58°6N 6°34E 164 F3
Vesterålen Norway 68°45N 15°0E 160 B16
Vestfjorden Norway 67°55N 14°0E 160 C16
Vestfold □ Norway 59°15N 10°0E 164 E7
Vestfossen Norway 59°44N 9°52E 164 E6
Vestgrønland = Kitaa □ Greenland 70°0N 47°0W 154 C6
Vestmannaeyjar Iceland 63°27N 20°15W 155 D6
Vestnes Norway 62°39N 7°5E 164 B4
Vestra Finland 60°19N 24°46E 121 B1
Vestre Gausdal Norway 61°12N 10°8E 164 C7
Vestskoven Denmark 55°41N 12°23E 118 A2
Vestspitsbergen Svalbard 78°40N 17°0E 150 B8
Vestur-skaftafellssýsla □ Iceland 63°50N 18°30W 155 D8
Vestvågøya Norway 68°18N 13°50E 160 B15
Vesuvio Italy 40°49N 14°26E 201 B7
Vesuvius, Mt. = Vesuvio Italy 40°49N 14°26E 201 B7
Vesyegonsk Russia 58°40N 37°16E 188 C9
Veszprém Hungary 47°8N 17°57E 182 C2
Veszprém □ Hungary 47°5N 17°55E 182 C2
Vésztő Hungary 46°55N 21°16E 182 D6
Vetapalem India 15°47N 80°18E 245 G5
Vetlanda Sweden 57°24N 15°3E 163 G9
Vetluga Russia 57°53N 45°45E 190 B7
Vetlugu → Russia 56°36N 46°4E 190 B8
Vetluzhskiy Kostroma, Russia 58°23N 45°26E 190 A7
Vetluzhskiy Nizhniy Novgorod, Russia 57°17N 45°12E 190 B7
Vetovo Bulgaria 43°42N 26°16E 203 C10
Vetralla Italy 42°20N 12°2E 199 F9
Vetren Bulgaria 42°15N 24°3E 203 D8
Vettore, Mte. Italy 42°49N 13°16E 199 F10
Veurne Belgium 51°5N 2°40E 170 C2
Vevay U.S.A. 38°45N 85°4W 311 F11
Veveno → Sudan 6°40N 32°58E 257 F3
Vevey Switz. 46°28N 6°51E 179 J2
Vevi Greece 40°47N 21°38E 202 F5
Veynes France 44°32N 5°49E 175 D9
Veys Iran 31°30N 49°0E 247 D6
Vézelay France 47°27N 3°45E 173 E10
Vézelise France 48°30N 6°5E 173 D13
Vézère → France 44°53N 0°53E 174 D4
Vezhen Bulgaria 42°50N 24°20E 203 D8
Vezirköprü Turkey 41°8N 35°27E 212 B6
Vezzani France 42°10N 9°15E 175 F13
Vi Thanh Vietnam 9°42N 105°26E 237 H5
Viacha Bolivia 16°39S 68°18W 330 D4
Viadana Italy 44°56N 10°31E 198 D7
Vialar = Tissemsilt Algeria 35°35N 1°50E 261 A5
Viamão Brazil 30°5S 51°0W 335 C5
Viana Brazil 3°13S 44°55W 332 B3
Viana Spain 42°31N 2°22W 196 C2
Viana do Alentejo Portugal 38°17N 7°59W 195 G3
Viana do Bolo Spain 42°11N 7°6W 194 C3
Viana do Castelo Portugal 41°42N 8°50W 194 D2
Viana do Castelo □ Portugal 41°50N 8°30W 194 D2
Vianden Lux. 49°56N 6°12E 170 E6
Viangchan = Vientiane Laos 17°58N 102°36E 236 D4
Vianópolis Brazil 16°40S 48°35W 333 E2
Vianos Greece 35°2N 25°21E 207 E6
Viar → Spain 37°36N 5°50W 195 H5
Viaréggio Italy 43°52N 10°14E 198 E7

Viaur → *France* 44°8N 1°58E **174** D5
Vibble *Sweden* 57°37N 18°16E **163** G12
Vibo Valéntia *Italy* 38°40N 16°6E **201** D9
Viborg *Denmark* 56°27N 9°23E **163** H3
Vibraye *France* 48°3N 0°44E **172** D7
Vic *Spain* 41°58N 2°19E **196** D7
Vic, Étang de *France* 43°29N 3°50E **174** E7
Vic-en-Bigorre *France* 43°24N 0°3E **174** E4
Vic-Fezensac *France* 43°47N 0°19E **174** E4
Vic-le-Comte *France* 45°39N 3°14E **173** G10
Vic-sur-Cère *France* 44°59N 2°38E **174** D6
Vicálvaro *Spain* 40°24N 3°36W **127** B2
Vicar *Spain* 36°50N 2°38W **197** J2
Vicente Lopez *Argentina* 34°31S 58°30W **117** B2
Vicente Pérez Rosales △ *Chile* 41°11S 72°12W **336** B2
Vicenza *Italy* 45°33N 11°33E **199** C8
Vich = Vic *Spain* 41°58N 2°19E **196** D7
Vichada □ *Colombia* 5°0N 69°30W **328** C4
Vichada → *Colombia* 4°55N 67°50W **328** C4
Vichuga *Russia* 57°12N 41°55E **190** B5
Vichy *France* 46°9N 3°26E **173** F10
Vickan *Sweden* 57°25N 6°10E **164** G3
Vicksburg *Ariz., U.S.A.* 33°45N 113°45W **307** M13
Vicksburg *Mich., U.S.A.* 42°7N 85°32W **311** B11
Vicksburg *Miss., U.S.A.* 32°21N 90°53W **315** E9
Vico *France* 42°10N 8°49E **175** F12
Vico, L. di *Italy* 42°19N 12°10E **199** F9
Vico del Gargano *Italy* 41°54N 15°57E **199** G12
Viçosa *Brazil* 9°28S 36°14W **332** C4
Viçosa do Ceará *Brazil* 3°34S 41°5W **332** B3
Vicovu de Sus *Romania* 47°56N 25°41E **183** C10
Victor *India* 21°0N 71°30E **242** J4
Victor Emanuel Ra. *Papua N. G.* 5°20S 142°15E **286** C2
Victor Harbor *Australia* 35°30S 138°37E **282** C3
Victor Hugo = Hamadia *Algeria* 35°28N 1°57E **261** A5
Victoria = Labuan *Malaysia* 5°20N 115°14E **235** A5
Victoria *Argentina* 32°40S 60°10W **334** C3
Victoria *B.C., Canada* 48°30N 123°25W **306** B3
Victoria *Chile* 38°13S 72°20W **336** A2
Victoria *Hong Kong, China* 22°17N 114°9E **122** B2
Victoria *Grenada* 12°12N 61°42W **323** q
Victoria *Guinea* 10°50N 14°32W **262** C2
Victoria *Gozo, Malta* 36°3N 14°14E **206** E6
Victoria *Mind. Or., Phil.* 13°12N 121°12E **232** E3
Victoria *Tarlac, Phil.* 15°35N 120°41E **232** D3
Victoria *Romania* 45°44N 24°41E **183** E9
Victoria *Seychelles* 4°38S 55°28E **272** c
Victoria *London, U.K.* **125** c3
Victoria *Kans., U.S.A.* 38°52N 99°9W **308** F4
Victoria *Tex., U.S.A.* 28°48N 97°0W **314** G6
Victoria □ *Australia* 37°0S 144°0E **282** D6
Victoria □ *Trin. & Tob.* 10°15N 61°27W **323** t
Victoria → *Australia* 15°10S 129°40E **278** C4
Victoria, Grand L. *Canada* 47°31N 77°30W **298** C4
Victoria, L. *Africa* 1°0S 33°0E **268** C3
Victoria, L. *N.S.W., Australia* 33°57S 141°15E **282** B4
Victoria, Mt. = Tomanivi *Fiji* 17°37S 178°1E **287** A2
Victoria, Mt. *Burma* 21°14N 93°55E **241** E4
Victoria, Mt. *Wellington, N.Z.* 41°18S 174°48E **143** B1
Victoria, Mt. *Papua N. G.* 8°55S 147°32E **286** E4
Victoria, Pont *Canada* 45°29N 73°32W **130** B2
Victoria and Alfred Waterfront *Cape Town, S. Africa* **118** a1
Victoria Beach *Canada* 50°40N 96°35W **297** C9
Victoria de Durango = Durango *Mexico* 24°3N 104°39W **318** C4
Victoria de las Tunas = Las Tunas *Cuba* 20°58N 76°59W **320** B4
Victoria Falls *Zimbabwe* 17°58S 25°52E **269** F2
Victoria Fjord *Greenland* 82°10N 46°0W **154** A6
Victoria Gardens *India* 18°58N 72°50E **130** B2
Victoria Harbour *Ont., Canada* 44°45N 79°45W **312** B5
Victoria Harbour *Hong Kong, China* 22°17N 114°10E **122** B1
Victoria I. *Canada* 71°0N 111°0W **294** C9
Victoria Island *Nigeria* 6°25N 3°25E **124** B2
Victoria L. *Nfld. & L., Canada* 48°20N 57°27W **299** C8
Victoria L. *Gauteng, S. Africa* 26°13S 28°9E **123** B2
Victoria Lawn Tennis Courts *Australia* 37°50S 145°1E **128** B2
Victoria Ld. *Antarctica* 75°0S 160°0E **151** D11
Victoria Nile → *Uganda* 2°14N 31°26E **268** B3
Victoria Park *Singapore* 1°19N 103°49E **138** B2
Victoria Peak *China* 22°16N 114°8E **122** B1
Victoria Peaks *Phil.* 9°22N 118°20E **233** G2
Victoria Pk. *Belize* 16°48N 88°37W **319** D7
Victoria Ra. *N.Z.* 42°12S 172°7E **285** C7
Victoria River *Australia* 16°25S 131°0E **278** C5
Victoria Str. *Canada* 69°31N 100°30W **294** D11
Victoria West *S. Africa* 31°25S 23°4E **270** D3
Victoria Wharf *Cape Town, S. Africa* **118** a2
Victorias *Phil.* 10°54N 123°5E **233** F4
Victoriaville *Canada* 46°4N 71°56W **299** C5
Victorica *Argentina* 36°20S 65°30W **334** D2
Victorville *U.S.A.* 34°32N 117°18W **307** L9
Vicuña *Chile* 30°0S 70°50W **334** C1
Vicuña Mackenna *Argentina* 33°53S 64°25W **334** C3
Vidal *U.S.A.* 34°7N 114°31W **307** L12
Vidalia *U.S.A.* 32°13N 82°25W **316** C7
Vidamlya *Belarus* 52°19N 23°47E **185** F10
Vidauban *France* 43°25N 6°27E **175** E10
Videbæk *Denmark* 56°6N 8°38E **163** H2
Videle *Romania* 44°17N 25°31E **183** F10
Videsæter *Norway* 61°57N 7°14E **164** C4
Vidette *U.S.A.* 33°2N 82°15W **316** B7
Vidigueira *Portugal* 38°12N 7°48W **195** G3
Vidin *Bulgaria* 43°59N 22°50E **202** C6
Vidio, C. *Spain* 43°35N 6°14W **194** B4
Vidisha *India* 23°28N 77°53E **242** H7
Vidos *Greece* 39°38N 19°55E **206** B9
Vidra *Romania* 45°56N 26°55E **183** E11
Viduša *Bos.-H.* 42°55N 18°21E **202** D2
Vidzy *Belarus* 55°23N 26°37E **188** E4
Viechtach *Germany* 49°4N 12°53E **179** F8
Viedma *Argentina* 40°50S 63°0W **336** B4
Viedma, L. *Argentina* 49°30S 72°30W **336** C2
Vieille Case *Dominica* 15°36N 61°24W **323** k
Vieira do Minho *Portugal* 41°38N 8°8W **194** D2
Vielha *Spain* 42°43N 0°44E **196** C5
Viella = Vielha *Spain* 42°43N 0°44E **196** C5
Vielsalm *Belgium* 50°17N 5°54E **170** D5
Vienenburg *Germany* 51°57N 10°34E **178** D6
Vieng Pou Kha *Laos* 20°41N 101°4E **228** G3
Vienna = Wien *Austria* 48°12N 16°22E **142** A2
Vienna *Ont., Canada* 42°41N 80°48W **312** D4
Vienna *Ga., U.S.A.* 32°6N 83°47W **316** C6
Vienna *Ill., U.S.A.* 37°25N 88°54W **308** G9
Vienna *Mo., U.S.A.* 38°11N 91°57W **310** F5
Vienna *Va., U.S.A.* 38°54N 77°16W **143** B2
Vienne *France* 45°31N 4°53E **175** C8
Vienne □ *France* 46°30N 0°42E **174** B4
Vienne → *France* 47°13N 0°5E **172** E7
Vientiane *Laos* 17°58N 102°36E **236** D4
Vientos, Paso de los *Caribbean* 20°0N 74°0W **321** C5
Vieques *Puerto Rico* 18°8N 65°25W **321** b
Vierge Pt. *St. Lucia* 13°49N 60°53W **323** m
Vierkant Pt. *Neth. Ant.* 12°7N 68°17W **322** h
Viernheim *Germany* 49°31N 8°35E **179** F4
Viersen *Germany* 51°15N 6°23E **178** D2
Vierwaldstättersee *Switz.* 47°0N 8°30E **179** J4
Vierzon *France* 47°13N 2°5E **173** E9
Vieste *Italy* 41°53N 16°10E **199** G13
Viet Tri *Vietnam* 21°18N 105°25E **236** B5
Vietnam ■ *Asia* 19°0N 106°0E **236** C6
Vietnam Veterans Memorial *U.S.A.* 38°53N 77°2W **143** B3
Vietnam War Museum *U.S.A.* 41°58N 87°39W **119** B3
Vietz = Witnica *Poland* 52°40N 14°54E **185** F1
Vieux-Boucau-les-Bains *France* 43°48N 1°23W **174** E2
Vieux Bourg *Guadeloupe* 16°20N 61°36W **322** e
Vieux Carré = French Quarter *New Orleans, U.S.A.* **131** a2
Vieux Fort *Guadeloupe* 15°57N 61°41W **322** e
Vieux Fort *Marie-Galante, Guadeloupe* 15°59N 61°17W **322** e
Vieux Fort *St. Lucia* 13°46N 60°58W **323** m
Vieux Fort, Pte. du *Guadeloupe* 15°57N 61°42W **322** e
Vieux Fort, R. du → *Guadeloupe* 15°59N 61°17W **322** e
Vieux Grand Port *Mauritius* 20°22S 57°42E **272** e
Vieux-Habitants *Guadeloupe* 16°4N 61°46W **322** e
Vieux-Habitants, Rivière des → *Guadeloupe* 16°3N 61°46W **322** e
Vieux-Montréal *Montréal, Canada* **130** b3
View Park *U.S.A.* 34°0N 118°20W **126** B3
Vif *France* 45°5N 5°41E **175** C9
Viga *Phil.* 13°52N 124°18E **232** E5
Vigan *Phil.* 17°35N 120°28E **232** C3
Vigário Geral *Brazil* 22°48S 43°18W **135** A1
Vigeland *Norway* 58°5N 7°18E **164** F4
Vigentino *Italy* 45°26N 9°13E **129** B2
Vigévano *Italy* 45°19N 8°51E **198** C5
Viggbyholm *Sweden* 59°26N 18°7E **139** A2
Vighignolo *Italy* 45°29N 9°2E **129** B1
Vigia = Almenara *Brazil* 16°11S 40°42W **333** E3
Vigia *Brazil* 0°50S 48°5W **332** B2
Vigla *Greece* 39°7N 20°50E **207** A2
Viglas, Akra *Greece* 35°54N 27°51E **206** F11
Vignemalle *France* 42°47N 0°10W **174** F3
Vigneulles-lès-Hattonchâtel *France* 48°59N 5°43E **173** D12
Vignola *Italy* 44°29N 11°1E **198** D8
Vigo *Spain* 42°12N 8°41W **194** C2
Vigo, Ría de *Spain* 42°15N 8°45W **194** C2
Vigrestad *Norway* 58°34N 5°42E **164** F2
Vigsø Bugt *Denmark* 57°8N 8°47E **163** G2
Vihiers *France* 47°10N 0°30W **172** E6
Vihowa *Pakistan* 31°8N 70°30E **242** D4
Vihowa → *Pakistan* 31°8N 70°41E **242** D4
Viikki *Finland* 60°13N 25°1E **121** B3
Viipuri = Vyborg *Russia* 60°43N 28°47E **188** B5
Vijayadurg *India* 16°30N 73°25E **244** F1
Vijayawada *India* 16°31N 80°39E **244** F5
Vijosë → *Albania* 40°37N 19°24E **202** F3
Vik *Iceland* 63°25N 19°1W **155** D7
Vik *Sogn og Fjordane, Norway* 61°21N 6°6E **164** C3
Vika *Sweden* 60°57N 14°28E **162** D8
Vikarabad *India* 17°20N 77°54E **244** E3
Vikarbyn *Sweden* 60°55N 15°1E **162** D9
Vike *Norway* 60°42N 5°35E **164** D2
Vikedal *Norway* 59°30N 5°55E **164** E2
Vikeke = Viqueque *E. Timor* 8°52S 126°23E **231** F7
Vikeland = Vigeland *Norway* 58°5N 7°18E **164** F4
Viken *Skåne, Sweden* 56°9N 12°34E **163** H6
Viken *Västra Götaland, Sweden* 58°39N 14°20E **163** F8
Vikersund *Norway* 59°58N 9°59E **164** E6
Vikeså *Norway* 58°38N 6°3E **164** F3
Vikevåg *Norway* 59°5N 5°41E **164** E2
Vikhroli *India* 19°6N 72°55E **130** A2
Viking *Canada* 53°7N 111°50W **296** C6
Vikmanshyttan *Sweden* 60°18N 15°50E **162** D9
Vikna *Norway* 64°55N 10°58E **160** D14
Vikos-Aoos △ *Greece* 40°0N 20°45E **204** B2
Vikøyri *Norway* 61°4N 6°34E **164** C3
Vila Alferes Chamusca = Guijá *Mozam.* 24°27S 33°0E **271** B5
Vila António Enes = Angoche *Mozam.* 16°8S 39°55E **269** F4
Vila Baleira *Madeira* 33°4N 16°20W **260** B1
Vila Bela da Santissima Trindade *Brazil* 15°0S 59°57W **331** C6
Vila Cabral = Lichinga *Mozam.* 13°13S 35°11E **269** E4
Vila Cabral = Niassa □ *Mozam.* 13°30S 36°0E **269** E4
Vila da Maganja *Mozam.* 17°18S 37°30E **269** F4
Vila da Ribeira Brava *C. Verde Is.* 16°32N 24°25W **153** j
Vila de Rei *Portugal* 39°41N 8°9W **194** F2
Vila do Bispo *Portugal* 37°5N 8°53W **195** H2
Vila do Conde *Portugal* 41°21N 8°45W **194** D2
Vila do Porto *Azores* 36°56N 25°9W **153** d4
Vila Franca de Xira *Portugal* 38°57N 8°59W **195** G2
Vila Franca do Campo *Azores* 37°43N 25°26W **153** d3
Vila Gamito *Mozam.* 14°12S 33°0E **269** E3
Vila Gomes da Costa *Mozam.* 24°20S 33°37E **271** B5
Vila Guilherme *Brazil* 23°30S 46°38W **137** B2
Vila Isabel *Brazil* 22°54S 43°15W **135** B1
Vila Jaguára *Brazil* 23°30S 46°45W **137** B1
Vila Machado *Mozam.* 19°15S 34°14E **269** F3
Vila Madalena *Brazil* 23°32S 46°41W **137** B1
Vila Maria *Brazil* 23°31S 46°36W **137** B2
Vila Mariana *Brazil* 23°34S 46°36W **137** B2
Vila Mouzinho *Mozam.* 14°48S 34°25E **269** E3
Vila Nova de Famalicão *Portugal* 41°25N 8°32W **194** D2
Vila Nova de Fos Côa *Portugal* 41°5N 7°9W **194** D3
Vila Nova de Gaia *Portugal* 41°8N 8°37W **194** D2
Vila Nova de Gaza = Xai-Xai *Mozam.* 25°6S 33°31E **271** C5
Vila Nova de Ourém *Portugal* 39°40N 8°35W **194** F2
Vila Nova do Corvo *Azores* 39°40N 31°8W **153** d2
Vila Pereira de Eça = Ondjiva *Angola* 16°48S 15°50E **265** F3
Vila Pery = Manica *Mozam.* 18°58S 32°59E **271** A5
Vila Pouca de Aguiar *Portugal* 41°30N 7°38W **194** D3
Vila Prudente *Brazil* 23°35S 46°33W **137** B2
Vila Real *Portugal* 41°17N 7°48W **194** D3
Vila-Real *Spain* 39°55N 0°3W **196** F4
Vila Real □ *Portugal* 41°36N 7°35W **194** D3
Vila Real de Santo António *Portugal* 37°10N 7°28W **195** H3
Vila-seca *Spain* 41°7N 1°9E **196** D6
Vila Texeira da Silva = Luau *Angola* 10°40S 22°10E **265** E4
Vila Vasco da Gama *Mozam.* 14°54S 32°14E **269** E3
Vila Velha *Amapá, Brazil* 3°13N 51°13W **329** C7
Vila Velha *Espírito Santo, Brazil* 20°20S 40°17W **333** F3
Vila Velha *Sergipe, Brazil* 11°20S 38°9W **332** D4
Vila Viçosa *Portugal* 38°45N 7°27W **195** G3
Viladecans *Spain* 41°18N 2°1E **114** B1
Vilafranca del Maestrat *Spain* 40°26N 0°16W **196** E4
Vilafranca del Penedès *Spain* 41°21N 1°40E **196** D6
Vilagarcía de Arousa *Spain* 42°34N 8°46W **194** C2
Vilaine → *France* 47°30N 2°27W **172** E4
Vilakalaka *Vanuatu* 15°25S 167°42E **287** E5
Vilanandro, Tanjona *Madag.* 16°11S 44°27E **272** B1
Vilanculos *Mozam.* 22°1S 35°17E **271** B6
Vilanova i la Geltrú *Spain* 41°13N 1°40E **196** D6
Vilar Formosa *Portugal* 40°38N 6°45W **194** E4
Vilaseca-Salou = Vila-seca *Spain* 41°7N 1°9E **196** D6
Vilbjerg *Denmark* 56°12N 8°46E **163** H2
Vilcabamba, Cordillera *Peru* 13°0S 73°0W **330** C3
Vilcanchos *Peru* 13°40S 74°25W **330** C3
Vilcheka, Ostrov *Russia* 80°0N 58°31E **214** B6
Vilcheka, Zemlya *Russia* 80°30N 60°30E **150** A11
Vilches *Spain* 38°12N 3°30W **195** G7
Vile Parle *India* 19°6N 72°51E **130** A2
Vileyka *Belarus* 54°30N 26°53E **177** A14
Vilhelmina *Sweden* 64°35N 16°39E **160** D17
Vilhena *Brazil* 12°40S 60°5W **331** C5
Viliya = Neris → *Lithuania* 55°8N 24°16E **188** E3
Viljandi *Estonia* 58°28N 25°30E **188** C3
Viljoensdorp = Newcastle *S. Africa* 27°45S 29°58E **271** C4
Vilkaviškis *Lithuania* 54°39N 23°2E **184** D10
Vilkija *Lithuania* 55°3N 23°35E **184** C10
Vilkitskogo, Proliv *Russia* 78°0N 103°0E **215** B11
Vilkomir = Ukmergė *Lithuania* 55°15N 24°45E **188** E3
Vilkovo = Vylkove *Ukraine* 45°28N 29°32E **183** E14
Villa Abecia *Bolivia* 21°0S 68°18W **334** A2
Villa Adelina *Argentina* 34°31S 58°33W **117** B1
Villa Ana *Argentina* 28°28S 59°40W **334** B4
Villa Angela *Argentina* 27°34S 60°45W **334** B3
Villa Ballester *Argentina* 34°33S 58°33W **117** B1
Villa Barilari *Argentina* 34°42S 58°20W **117** C2
Villa Bella = Serra Talhada *Brazil* 7°59S 38°18W **332** C4
Villa Bella *Bolivia* 10°25S 65°22W **331** C4
Villa Borghese *Rome, Italy* **136** a3
Villa Bosch *Argentina* 34°35S 58°33W **117** B1
Villa Bruzual *Venezuela* 9°20N 69°6W **328** C4
Villa C. Colon *Argentina* 34°41S 58°21W **117** C2
Villa Cañás *Argentina* 34°0S 61°35W **334** C3
Villa Cecilia = Ciudad Madero *Mexico* 22°19N 97°50W **319** C5
Villa Cisneros = Dakhla *W. Sahara* 23°50N 15°53W **260** D1
Villa Ciudadela *Argentina* 34°38S 58°33W **117** B1
Villa Constitución *Argentina* 33°15S 60°20W **334** C3
Villa de Arriaga *Mexico* 21°56N 101°20W **318** C4
Villa de Cura *Venezuela* 10°2N 67°29W **328** A4
Villa de Guadalupe *Mexico* 19°29N 99°6W **128** B2
Villa de María *Argentina* 29°55S 63°43W **334** B3
Villa de Méndez *Mexico* 25°7N 98°34W **319** B5
Villa del Nevoso = Ilirska-Bistrica *Slovenia* 45°34N 14°14E **199** C11
Villa del Rio *Spain* 37°59N 4°17W **195** H6
Villa del Rosario *Venezuela* 10°19N 72°19W **328** A3
Villa Devoto *Argentina* 34°36S 58°31W **117** B1
Villa Diamante *Argentina* 34°41S 58°25W **117** C2
Villa Dolores *Argentina* 31°58S 65°15W **334** C2
Villa Dominico *Argentina* 34°41S 58°19W **117** C3
Villa Frontera *Mexico* 26°56N 101°27W **318** B4
Villa Gesell *Argentina* 37°15S 56°55W **334** D4
Villa Grove *U.S.A.* 39°52N 88°10W **311** E8
Villa Guillermina *Argentina* 28°15S 59°29W **334** B4
Villa Hayes *Paraguay* 25°5S 57°20W **334** B4
Villa Hidalgo *Mexico* 24°15N 99°26W **319** C5
Villa Iris *Argentina* 38°12S 63°12W **334** D3
Villa Lugano *Argentina* 34°41S 58°27W **117** C2
Villa Lynch *Argentina* 34°35S 58°31W **117** B1
Villa Madero *Argentina* 34°41S 58°30W **117** C1
Villa María *Argentina* 32°20S 63°10W **334** C3
Villa Mazán *Argentina* 28°40S 66°30W **334** B2
Villa Minozzo *Italy* 44°22N 10°28E **198** D7
Villa Montes *Bolivia* 21°10S 63°30W **334** A3
Villa Ocampo *Argentina* 28°30S 59°20W **334** B4
Villa Ocampo *Durango, Mexico* 26°27N 105°31W **318** B3
Villa Ojo de Agua *Argentina* 29°30S 63°44W **334** B3
Villa Regina *Argentina* 39°6S 67°4W **336** A3
Villa Rica *U.S.A.* 33°44N 84°55W **316** B5
Villa Sáenz Pena *Argentina* 34°37S 58°32W **117** B1
Villa San Giovanni *Italy* 38°13N 15°38E **201** D8
Villa San Martín *Argentina* 28°15S 64°9W **334** B3
Villa Sanjurjo = Al Hoceïma *Morocco* 35°8N 3°58W **261** A4
Villa Santina *Italy* 46°24N 12°55E **199** B9
Villa Unión *Mexico* 23°12N 106°14W **318** C3
Villa Urquiza *Argentina* 34°34S 58°28W **117** B2
Villaba *Phil.* 11°13N 124°24E **233** F5
Villablino *Spain* 42°57N 6°19W **194** C4
Villacarlos *Spain* 39°53N 4°17E **206** B5
Villacarriedo *Spain* 43°14N 3°48W **194** B7
Villacarrillo *Spain* 38°7N 3°3W **195** G7
Villacastín *Spain* 40°46N 4°25W **194** E6
Villach *Austria* 46°37N 13°51E **180** E6
Villacidro *Italy* 39°27N 8°44E **200** C1
Villada *Spain* 42°15N 4°59W **194** C6
Villadiego *Spain* 42°31N 4°1W **194** C6
Villadóssola *Italy* 46°4N 8°16E **198** B5
Villafeliche *Spain* 41°10N 1°30W **196** D3
Villafranca *Spain* 42°17N 1°46W **196** C3
Villafranca de los Barros *Spain* 38°35N 6°18W **195** G4
Villafranca de los Caballeros *Spain* 39°26N 3°21W **195** F7
Villafranca del Cid = Vilafranca del Maestrat *Spain* 40°26N 0°16W **196** E4
Villafranca del Panadés = Vilafranca del Penedès *Spain* 41°21N 1°40E **196** D6
Villafranca di Verona *Italy* 45°21N 10°50E **198** C7
Villafranca Tirrena *Italy* 38°20N 15°25E **201** D8
Villagio Mussolini = Arboréa *Italy* 39°46N 8°35E **200** C1
Villagrán *Mexico* 24°29N 99°29W **319** C5
Villaguay *Argentina* 32°0S 59°0W **334** C4
Villaharta *Spain* 38°9N 4°54W **195** G6
Villahermosa *Tabasco, Mexico* 17°59N 92°55W **319** D6
Villahermosa *Spain* 38°46N 2°52W **197** G2
Villaines-la-Juhel *France* 48°21N 0°20W **172** D6
Villajoyosa *Spain* 38°30N 0°12W **197** G4
Villalba *Puerto Rico* 18°8N 66°30W **321** b
Villalba *Spain* 43°26N 7°40W **194** B3
Villalba de Guardo *Spain* 42°42N 4°49W **194** C6
Villalón de Campos *Spain* 42°5N 5°4W **194** C5
Villalpando *Spain* 41°51N 5°25W **194** D5
Villaluenga de la Sagra *Spain* 40°2N 3°54W **194** E7
Villamanán *Spain* 42°19N 5°35W **194** C5
Villamartín *Spain* 36°52N 5°38W **195** J5
Villamayor de Santiago *Spain* 39°50N 2°59W **196** F2
Villamblard *France* 45°2N 0°32E **174** C4
Villanova Monteleone *Italy* 40°30N 8°28E **200** B1
Villanueva *Colombia* 10°37N 72°59W **328** A3
Villanueva *N. Mex., U.S.A.* 35°16N 105°22W **305** J11
Villanueva de Castellón *Spain* 39°5N 0°31W **197** F4
Villanueva de Córdoba *Spain* 38°20N 4°38W **195** G6
Villanueva de la Fuente *Spain* 38°42N 2°42W **197** G2
Villanueva de la Serena *Spain* 38°59N 5°50W **195** G5
Villanueva de la Sierra *Spain* 40°12N 6°24W **194** E4
Villanueva de los Castillejos *Spain* 37°30N 7°15W **195** H3
Villanueva de los Infantes *Spain* 38°43N 3°1W **195** G7
Villanueva del Arzobispo *Spain* 38°10N 3°0W **197** G2
Villanueva del Fresno *Spain* 38°23N 7°10W **195** G3
Villanueva y Geltrú = Vilanova i la Geltrú *Spain* 41°13N 1°40E **196** D6
Villaputzu *Italy* 39°26N 9°34E **200** C2
Villaquilambre *Spain* 42°39N 5°33W **194** C5
Villar del Arzobispo *Spain* 39°44N 0°50W **196** F4
Villar del Rey *Spain* 39°7N 6°50W **195** F4
Villard-de-Lans *France* 45°3N 5°33E **175** C9
Villarramiel *Spain* 42°2N 4°55W **194** C6
Villarreal = Vila-Real *Spain* 39°55N 0°3W **196** F4
Villarrica *Chile* 39°15S 72°15W **336** A2
Villarrica *Paraguay* 25°40S 56°30W **334** B4
Villarrica △ *Chile* 39°24S 71°46W **336** A2
Villarrobledo *Spain* 39°18N 2°36W **197** F2
Villarroya de la Sierra *Spain* 41°27N 1°46W **196** D3
Villarrubia de los Ojos *Spain* 39°14N 3°36W **195** F7
Villars-les-Dombes *France* 46°0N 5°3E **173** F12
Villasayas *Spain* 41°24N 2°39W **196** D2
Villaseco de los Gamitos *Spain* 41°2N 6°7W **194** D4
Villasimíus *Italy* 39°8N 9°31E **200** C2
Villastar *Spain* 40°17N 1°9W **196** E3
Villatobas *Spain* 39°54N 3°20W **194** F7
Villaverde *Spain* 40°21N 3°42W **127** B1
Villaverde Bajo *Spain* 40°20N 3°40W **127** B1
Villavicencio *Argentina* 32°28S 69°0W **334** C2
Villavicencio *Colombia* 4°9N 73°37W **328** C3
Villaviciosa *Spain* 43°32N 5°27W **194** B5
Villazón *Bolivia* 22°0S 65°35W **334** A2
Ville-d'Avray *France* 48°49N 2°11E **134** B2
Ville-Marie *Canada* 47°20N 79°30W **298** C4
Ville Platte *U.S.A.* 30°41N 92°17W **314** F8
Villecresnes *France* 48°43N 2°31E **134** B4
Villedieu-les-Poêles *France* 48°50N 1°13W **172** D5
Villefort *France* 44°28N 3°56E **174** D7
Villefranche-de-Lauragais *France* 43°25N 1°44E **174** E5
Villefranche-de-Rouergue *France* 44°21N 2°2E **174** D6
Villefranche-du-Périgord *France* 44°38N 1°5E **174** D5
Villefranche-sur-Saône *France* 45°59N 4°43E **175** C8
Villejuif *France* 48°47N 2°21E **134** B3
Villel *Spain* 40°14N 1°12W **196** E3
Villemomble *France* 48°52N 2°30E **134** A4
Villemur-sur-Tarn *France* 43°51N 1°31E **174** E5
Villena *Spain* 38°39N 0°52W **197** G4
Villenauxe-la-Grande *France* 48°35N 3°33E **173** D10
Villenave-d'Ornon *France* 44°46N 0°33W **174** D3
Villeneuve-d'Ascq *France* 50°38N 3°9E **173** B10
Villeneuve-la-Garenne *France* 48°56N 2°19E **134** A2
Villeneuve-l'Archevêque *France* 48°14N 3°32E **173** D10
Villeneuve-le-Roi *France* 48°43N 2°24E **134** B3
Villeneuve-lès-Avignon *France* 43°58N 4°49E **175** E8
Villeneuve-St-Georges *France* 48°43N 2°27E **134** B3
Villeneuve-sur-Allier *France* 46°40N 3°13E **173** F10
Villeneuve-sur-Lot *France* 44°24N 0°42E **174** D4
Villeneuve-sur-Yonne *France* 48°5N 3°18E **173** D10
Villeparisis *France* 48°56N 2°36E **134** A4
Villeréal *France* 44°38N 0°45E **174** D4
Villers-Bocage *France* 49°3N 0°40W **172** C6
Villers-Cotterêts *France* 49°15N 3°4E **173** C10
Villers-sur-Mer *France* 49°21N 0°2W **172** C6
Villersexel *France* 47°33N 6°26E **173** E13
Villerupt *France* 49°28N 5°55E **173** C12
Villeurbanne *France* 45°46N 4°55E **175** C8
Villevaudé *France* 48°55N 2°39E **134** A4
Villiers *S. Africa* 27°2S 28°36E **271** C4
Villiers-le-Bâcle *France* 48°44N 2°8E **134** B1
Villiers-sur-Marne *France* 48°49N 2°32E **134** B4
Villingen-Schwenningen *Germany* 48°3N 8°26E **179** G4
Villinki *Finland* 60°9N 25°6E **121** C3
Villisca *U.S.A.* 40°56N 94°59W **310** D2
Villmanstrand = Lappeenranta *Finland* 61°3N 28°12E **188** B5
Villoresi, Canale *Italy* 45°33N 8°59E **129** A1
Villupuram *India* 11°59N 79°31E **245** J4
Vilna = Vilnius *Lithuania* 54°38N 25°19E **188** E3
Vilna *Canada* 54°7N 111°55W **296** C6
Vilnius *Lithuania* 54°38N 25°19E **188** E3
Vils *Austria* 47°33N 10°38E **180** D3
Vils → *Bayern, Germany* 48°37N 13°11E **179** G9
Vils → *Bayern, Germany* 49°10N 11°57E **179** F7
Vilsbiburg *Germany* 48°26N 12°22E **179** G8
Vilshofen *Germany* 48°37N 13°11E **179** G9
Vilusi *Montenegro* 42°44N 18°34E **202** D2
Vilvoorde *Belgium* 50°56N 4°26E **116** A2
Vilyuchinsk *Russia* 52°55N 158°24E **215** D16
Vilyuy → *Russia* 64°24N 126°26E **215** C13
Vilyuysk *Russia* 63°40N 121°35E **215** C13
Vimianzo *Spain* 43°7N 9°2W **194** B1
Vimioso *Portugal* 41°35N 6°31W **194** D4
Vimmerby *Sweden* 57°40N 15°55E **163** G9
Vimodrone *Italy* 45°30N 9°16E **129** A2
Vimont *Canada* 45°36N 73°43W **130** A1
Vimoutiers *France* 48°57N 0°10E **172** D7
Vimperk *Czech Rep.* 49°3N 13°46E **180** B6
Vina → *Cameroon* 7°45N 15°36E **264** A3
Viña del Mar *Chile* 33°0S 71°30W **334** C1
Vinanmek Mansion *Bangkok, Thailand* **113** a2
Vinarós *Spain* 40°30N 0°27E **196** E5
Vincendo *Réunion* 21°21S 55°41E **272** f
Vincennes *Val-de-Marne, France* 48°51N 2°26E **134** A3
Vincennes *Ind., U.S.A.* 38°41N 87°32W **311** F9
Vincennes, Bois de *France* 48°49N 2°26E **134** B3
Vincennes Bay *S. Ocean* 66°0S 109°0E **151** C8
Vincent *U.S.A.* 34°33N 118°11W **307** L8
Vinces *Ecuador* 1°32S 79°45W **328** D2
Vinchina *Argentina* 28°45S 68°15W **334** B2
Vindava = Ventspils *Latvia* 57°25N 21°32E **184** A8
Vindelälven → *Sweden* 63°55N 19°50E **160** E18
Vindeln *Sweden* 64°12N 19°43E **160** D18
Vinderup *Denmark* 56°29N 8°45E **163** H2
Vindhya Ra. *India* 22°50N 77°0E **242** H7
Vine Grove *U.S.A.* 37°49N 85°59W **311** G11
Vineland *Fla., U.S.A.* 28°23N 81°30W **133** B1
Vineland *N.J., U.S.A.* 39°29N 75°2W **309** F16
Vineuil *France* 47°35N 1°22E **172** E8
Vinga *Romania* 46°1N 21°14E **182** D6
Vingåker *Sweden* 59°2N 15°52E **162** E9
Vingelen *Norway* 62°25N 10°52E **164** B7
Vingnes *Norway* 61°7N 10°26E **164** C7
Vinh *Vietnam* 18°45N 105°38E **236** C5
Vinh Linh *Vietnam* 17°4N 107°2E **236** D6
Vinh Loi = Bac Lieu *Vietnam* 9°17N 105°43E **237** H5
Vinh Long *Vietnam* 10°16N 105°57E **237** G5
Vinh Yen *Vietnam* 21°21N 105°35E **228** G5
Vinhais *Portugal* 41°50N 7°5W **194** D3
Vinica *Croatia* 46°20N 16°9E **199** B13
Vinica *Macedonia* 41°53N 22°30E **202** E6
Vinica *Slovenia* 45°28N 15°16E **199** C12
Vinings *U.S.A.* 33°53N 84°29W **113** A2
Vinita *U.S.A.* 36°39N 95°9W **314** C7
Vinje *Sør-Trøndelag, Norway* 63°12N 9°0E **164** A5
Vinje *Telemark, Norway* 59°37N 7°51E **164** E4
Vinjo *Norway* 60°48N 6°30E **164** D3
Vinkovci *Croatia* 45°19N 18°48E **182** E3
Vinnitsa = Vinnytsya *Ukraine* 49°15N 28°30E **177** D15
Vinnytsya *Ukraine* 49°15N 28°30E **177** D15
Vinnytsya □ *Ukraine* 49°20N 28°15E **189** H5
Vinodelnoye = Ipatovo *Russia* 45°45N 42°50E **191** H6
Vinohrady *Prague, Czech Rep.* **135** c3
Vinoř *Czech Rep.* 50°8N 14°34E **135** B3
Vinslöv *Sweden* 56°7N 13°55E **163** H7
Vinson Massif *Antarctica* 78°35S 85°25W **151** D16
Vinstra *Norway* 61°37N 9°44E **164** C6
Vinstra → *Norway* 61°37N 9°44E **164** C6
Vintar *Phil.* 18°14N 120°39E **232** B3
Vintjärn *Sweden* 60°50N 16°4E **162** D10
Vinton *Calif., U.S.A.* 39°48N 120°10W **306** F6
Vinton *Iowa, U.S.A.* 42°10N 92°1W **310** B4
Vinton *La., U.S.A.* 30°11N 93°35W **314** F8
Vințu de Jos *Romania* 46°0N 23°30E **183** D8
Vinukonda *India* 16°4N 79°45E **245** F4
Viöl *Germany* 54°34N 9°11E **178** A5
Viola *U.S.A.* 41°12N 90°35W **310** C6
Violet Hill *China* 22°15N 114°11E **122** B2
Violet Town *Australia* 36°38S 145°42E **283** D6
Violet Valley ☼ *Australia* 17°10S 127°55E **278** C4
Vioolsdrif *S. Africa* 28°46S 17°39E **270** C2
Viotia □ *Greece* 38°20N 23°0E **204** C5
Vipacco = Vipava *Slovenia* 45°51N 13°58E **199** C10
Vipava *Slovenia* 45°51N 13°58E **199** C10
Vipiteno *Italy* 46°54N 11°26E **199** B8
Viqueque *E. Timor* 8°52S 126°23E **231** F7
Vir *Croatia* 44°17N 15°3E **199** D12
Virac *Phil.* 13°30N 124°20E **232** E5
Virachey *Cambodia* 13°59N 106°49E **236** F6
Virachey △ *Cambodia* 14°14N 106°55E **236** E6
Virago Sd. *Canada* 54°0N 132°30W **296** C2
Virajpet = Virarajendrapet *India* 12°10N 75°50E **245** H2
Viramgam *India* 23°5N 72°0E **242** H5
Viranşehir *Turkey* 37°13N 39°45E **213** D8
Virányos *Hungary* 47°31N 18°59E **117** A1
Virarajendrapet *India* 12°10N 75°50E **245** H2
Virawah *Pakistan* 24°31N 70°46E **242** G4
Virbalis *Lithuania* 54°39N 22°49E **184** D9
Virden *Man., Canada* 49°50N 100°56W **297** D8
Virden *Ill., U.S.A.* 39°30N 89°46W **310** E7
Vire *France* 48°50N 0°53W **172** D6
Vire → *France* 49°20N 1°7W **172** C5
Virei *Angola* 15°43S 12°52E **265** F2
Virgem da Lapa *Brazil* 16°49S 42°21W **333** E3
Virgenes, C. *Argentina* 52°19S 68°21W **336** D3
Virgin → *U.S.A.* 36°28N 114°21W **305** H6
Virgin Gorda *Br. Virgin Is.* 18°30N 64°26W **321** C7
Virgin Is. (British) ☑ *W. Indies* 18°30N 64°30W **321** C7
Virgin Is. (U.S.) ☑ *W. Indies* 18°20N 65°0W **321** C7
Virgin Islands △ *U.S. Virgin Is.* 18°21N 64°43W **321** b
Virginia *Free State, S. Africa* 28°8S 26°55E **270** C4
Virginia *Ill., U.S.A.* 39°57N 90°13W **310** E6
Virginia *Minn., U.S.A.* 47°31N 92°32W **308** B7
Virginia □ *U.S.A.* 37°30N 78°45W **309** G14
Virginia, L. *U.S.A.* 28°35N 81°20W **133** A2
Virginia Beach *U.S.A.* 36°49N 76°9W **309** F16
Virginia City *Mont., U.S.A.* 45°18N 111°56W **304** D8
Virginia City *Nev., U.S.A.* 39°19N 119°39W **306** F7
Virginia Falls *Canada* 61°38N 125°42W **296** A3
Virginia Gardens *U.S.A.* 25°48N 80°18W **128** B1
Virginia Key *U.S.A.* 25°44N 80°9W **128** B2
Virginiatown *Canada* 48°9N 79°36W **298** C4
Virje *Croatia* 46°4N 16°59E **199** B13
Viroflay *France* 48°48N 2°10E **134** B2
Vironas *Greece* 37°55N 23°45E **128** C2
Viroqua *U.S.A.* 43°34N 90°53W **308** D8
Virovitica *Croatia* 45°51N 17°21E **182** E2
Virpazar *Montenegro* 42°14N 19°6E **202** D3
Virpur *India* 21°51N 70°42E **242** J4
Virserum *Sweden* 57°20N 15°35E **163** G9
Virton *Belgium* 49°35N 5°32E **170** E5
Virú *Peru* 8°25S 78°45W **330** B2
Virudunagar *India* 9°30N 77°58E **245** K3
Virum *Denmark* 55°47N 12°27E **118** A2
Virunga △ *Dem. Rep. of the Congo* 0°5N 29°38E **268** B2
Vis *Croatia* 43°4N 16°10E **199** E13
Visalia *U.S.A.* 36°20N 119°18W **306** J7
Visayan Sea *Phil.* 11°30N 123°30E **233** F4
Visby *Sweden* 57°37N 18°18E **163** G12
Viscount Melville Sd. *Canada* 74°10N 108°0W **295** C10
Visé *Belgium* 50°44N 5°41E **170** D5
Vise, Ostrov *Russia* 79°33N 76°50E **214** B8
Višegrad *Bos.-H.* 43°47N 19°17E **182** G4
Viseu *Brazil* 1°10S 46°5W **332** B2
Viseu *Portugal* 40°40N 7°55W **194** E3
Viseu □ *Portugal* 40°40N 7°55W **194** E3
Vişeu de Sus *Romania* 47°45N 24°25E **183** C9
Vishakhapatnam *India* 17°45N 83°20E **244** F6
Vishnyaki *Russia* 55°46N 37°53E **129** B5
Vişina *Romania* 43°52N 24°27E **183** G9
Vişineşti *Moldova* 46°20N 28°27E **183** D13
Visingsö *Sweden* 58°2N 14°20E **163** F8
Visitacion Valley *U.S.A.* 37°42N 122°23W **136** B2
Viskafors *Sweden* 57°37N 12°50E **163** G6
Viskan → *Sweden* 57°14N 12°12E **163** G6
Viški Kanal *Croatia* 43°4N 16°5E **199** E13
Vislanda *Sweden* 56°46N 14°30E **163** H8
Visnagar *India* 23°45N 72°32E **242** H5
Višnja Gora *Slovenia* 45°58N 14°45E **199** C11
Viso, Mte. *Italy* 44°38N 7°5E **198** D4
Viso del Marqués *Spain* 38°32N 3°34W **195** G7
Visoko *Bos.-H.* 43°58N 18°10E **182** G3
Visokoi I. *Antarctica* 56°43S 27°15W **151** B1
Visp *Switz.* 46°17N 7°52E **179** J3
Vissefjärda *Sweden* 56°32N 15°35E **163** H9
Visselhövede *Germany* 52°59N 9°34E **178** C5
Vissenbjerg *Denmark* 55°23N 10°7E **163** J4
Vista *U.S.A.* 33°12N 117°14W **307** M9
Vista Alegre *Santiago, Chile* 33°30S 70°43W **137** C1
Vista Alegre *Lima, Peru* 12°9S 76°59W **124** B3
Vista Bella *Trin. & Tob.* 10°17N 61°27W **323** t
Vista Grove *U.S.A.* 33°51N 84°16W **113** A3
Vistonida, L. *Greece* 41°0N 25°7E **203** E9
Vistonikos, Ormos = Vistonida, L. *Greece* 41°0N 25°7E **203** E9
Vistula = Wisła → *Poland* 54°22N 18°55E **184** D5
Vistula Lagoon = Zalew Wiślany *Poland* 54°20N 19°50E **184** D6
Vit → *Bulgaria* 43°30N 24°30E **203** C8
Vita *India* 17°17N 74°33E **244** F2
Vitacura *Chile* 33°23S 70°35W **137** B2
Vitanje *Slovenia* 46°25N 15°18E **199** B12
Vitebsk = Vitsyebsk *Belarus* 55°10N 30°15E **188** E6
Viterbo *Italy* 42°25N 12°6E **199** F9
Vitez *Bos.-H.* 44°10N 17°48E **182** F2
Viti Levu *Fiji* 17°30S 177°30E **287** A1
Vitiaz Str. *Papua N. G.* 5°40S 147°10E **286** C4
Vitiaz Trench *Pac. Oc.* 10°0S 170°0E **277** C13
Vitigudino *Spain* 41°1N 6°26W **194** D4
Vitim *Russia* 59°28N 112°35E **215** D12
Vitim → *Russia* 59°26N 112°34E **215** D12
Vitina *Bos.-H.* 43°17N 17°29E **199** E14
Vitina *Greece* 37°40N 22°10E **204** D4
Vitínia *Italy* 41°47N 12°24E **136** C1
Vítkov *Czech Rep.* 49°46N 17°45E **181** B10
Vitória = Vitória de Santo Antão *Brazil* 8°10S 35°20W **332** C4
Vitória *Espírito Santo, Brazil* 20°20S 40°22W **333** F3
Vitória *Pará, Brazil* 2°54S 52°1W **329** D7
Vitória da Conquista *Brazil* 14°51S 40°51W **333** D3
Vitória de Santo Antão *Brazil* 8°10S 35°20W **332** C4
Vitoria-Gasteiz *Spain* 42°50N 2°41W **196** C2
Vitória Seamount *Atl. Oc.* 20°0S 44°0W **152** J8
Vitorino Freire *Brazil* 4°4S 45°10W **332** B2
Vitosha △ *Bulgaria* 42°36N 23°18E **202** D7
Vitré *France* 48°8N 1°12W **172** D5
Vitry-le-François *France* 48°43N 4°33E **173** D11
Vitry-sur-Seine *France* 48°47N 2°23E **134** B3
Vitsand *Sweden* 60°20N 13°0E **162** D7
Vitsi, Oros *Greece* 40°40N 21°25E **202** F5
Vitsyebsk *Belarus* 55°10N 30°15E **188** E6
Vitsyebsk □ *Belarus* 55°10N 28°20E **188** E5
Vittaryd *Sweden* 56°58N 13°57E **163** H7
Vitteaux *France* 47°24N 4°30E **173** E11
Vittel *France* 48°12N 5°57E **173** D12
Vittória *Italy* 36°57N 14°32E **201** F7
Vittório = Vittório Véneto *Italy* 45°59N 12°18E **199** C9
Vittório Véneto *Italy* 45°59N 12°18E **199** C9
Vittoriosa *Malta* 35°54N 14°31E **206** F8
Vittsjö *Sweden* 56°20N 13°40E **163** H7
Viveiro *Spain* 43°39N 7°38W **194** B3
Vivian *U.S.A.* 32°53N 93°59W **314** E8
Viviers *France* 44°30N 4°40E **175** D8
Vivonne *S. Austral., Australia* 35°59S 137°9E **282** C2
Vivonne *Vienne, France* 46°25N 0°15E **174** B4
Vivonne B. *Australia* 35°59S 137°9E **282** C2
Viwa *Fiji* 17°10S 177°58E **287** A1
Vizagapatam = Vishakhapatnam *India* 17°45N 83°20E **244** F6
Vizandino, Moussio *Athens, Greece* **112** b3
Vizcaíno, Desierto de *Mexico* 27°30N 113°45W **318** B2
Vizcaíno, Sierra *Mexico* 27°30N 114°0W **318** B2
Vizcaya □ *Spain* 43°15N 2°45W **196** B2
Vizcaya Museum and Gardens *U.S.A.* 25°44N 80°13W **128** B2
Vize *Turkey* 41°34N 27°45E **203** E11
Vizianagaram *India* 18°6N 83°30E **244** E6
Vizille *France* 45°5N 5°46E **175** C9
Viziñada *Croatia* 45°20N 13°46E **199** C10
Viziru *Romania* 45°0N 27°43E **183** E12
Vizlinsky Zaliv = Zalew Wiślany *Poland* 54°20N 19°50E **184** D6
Vizzini *Italy* 37°10N 14°45E **201** E7
Vlaardingen *Neths.* 51°55N 4°21E **170** C4
Vlachiotis *Greece* 36°52N 22°42E **204** E4
Vlădeasa, Vf. *Romania* 46°47N 22°50E **182** D7
Vladičin Han *Serbia* 42°42N 22°1E **202** D6
Vladikavkaz *Russia* 43°0N 44°35E **191** J7
Vladimir *Russia* 56°15N 40°30E **188** D11
Vladimir □ *Russia* 56°5N 40°10E **190** B5
Vladimir Volynskiy = Volodymyr-Volynskyy *Ukraine* 50°50N 24°18E **177** C13
Vladimirci *Serbia* 44°36N 19°50E **202** B3
Vladimirovac *Serbia* 45°1N 20°53E **182** E5
Vladimirovka = Yuzhno-Sakhalinsk *Russia* 46°58N 142°45E **215** E15
Vladimirovka *Russia* 48°27N 46°10E **191** F8
Vladimirovo *Bulgaria* 43°32N 23°22E **202** C7
Vladislavovka *Ukraine* 45°12N 35°29E **189** K8
Vladivostok *Russia* 43°10N 131°53E **220** C5
Vladykino *Russia* 55°51N 37°35E **129** A3
Vlăhița *Romania* 46°21N 25°31E **183** D10
Vlasenica *Bos.-H.* 44°11N 18°59E **182** F3
Vlašić *Bos.-H.* 44°19N 17°37E **182** F2
Vlašim *Czech Rep.* 49°40N 14°53E **180** B7
Vlasinsko Jezero *Serbia* 42°44N 22°22E **202** D6
Vlasotince *Serbia* 42°59N 22°7E **202** D6
Vlieland *Neths.* 53°16N 4°55E **170** A4
Vlissingen *Neths.* 51°26N 3°34E **170** C3
Vlorë *Albania* 40°32N 19°28E **202** F3
Vlorës, Gjiri i *Albania* 40°29N 19°27E **202** F3
Vltava → *Czech Rep.* 50°21N 14°30E **180** A7
Vnukovo *Russia* 55°37N 37°17E **129** C1
Vo Dat *Vietnam* 11°9N 107°31E **237** G6
Vobarno *Italy* 45°39N 10°30E **198** C7
Vočin *Croatia* 45°37N 17°33E **182** E2
Vöcklabruck *Austria* 48°1N 13°39E **180** C6
Vodice *Croatia* 43°47N 15°47E **199** E12
Vodňany *Czech Rep.* 49°9N 14°11E **180** B7
Vodnjan *Croatia* 44°59N 13°52E **199** D10
Vodopyanovo = Donskoy *Russia* 53°55N 38°15E **188** F10

Voe U.K. 60°21N 1°16W 167 A7
Vogan Togo 6°23N 1°30E 263 D5
Vogar Iceland 63°58N 22°22W 155 D4
Vogel Pk. Nigeria 8°24N 11°47E 263 D7
Vogelkop = Doberai, Jazirah Indonesia 1°25S 133°0E 231 E8
Vogelsberg Germany 50°31N 9°12E 178 E5
Voghera Italy 44°59N 9°1E 198 D6
Voh N. Cal. 20°58S 164°42E 288 d
Vohibinany Madag. 18°49S 49°4E 272 B2
Vohilava Madag. 21°4S 48°0E 272 C2
Vohimarina = Iharana Madag. 13°25S 50°0E 272 A3
Vohimena, Tanjon' i Madag. 25°36S 45°8E 272 D2
Vohipeno Madag. 22°22S 47°51E 272 C2
Voi Kenya 3°25S 38°32E 268 C4
Void-Vacon France 48°40N 5°36E 173 D12
Voineşti Iaşi, Romania 47°5N 27°27E 183 C12
Voineşti Prahova, Romania 45°5N 25°14E 183 E10
Voinjama Liberia 8°25N 9°44W 262 D3
Voiron France 45°22N 5°35E 175 C9
Voisey B. Canada 56°15N 61°50W 299 A7
Voitsberg Austria 47°3N 15°9E 180 D8
Vojens Denmark 55°16N 9°18E 163 J3
Vojmsjön Sweden 65°0N 16°24E 160 D17
Vojnić Croatia 45°19N 15°43E 199 C12
Vojnik Italy 46°18N 15°19E 199 B12
Vojvodina □ Serbia 45°20N 20°0E 182 E5
Vokeo I. Papua N. G. 3°14S 144°2E 286 B3
Vokhtoga Russia 58°46N 41°8E 188 C11
Vokovice Czech Rep. 50°5N 14°21E 135 B2
Volary Czech Rep. 48°54N 13°52E 180 C6
Volborg U.S.A. 45°51N 105°41W 304 D11
Volcán de Colima △ Mexico 19°30N 103°40W 318 D4
Volcano U.S.A. 19°26N 155°14W 302 D6
Volcano Is. = Kazan-Rettō Pac. Oc. 25°0N 141°0E 288 E6
Volcans △ Rwanda 1°30S 29°26E 268 C2
Volcans d'Auvergne ⌂ France 45°20N 2°40E 174 C6
Volchansk = Vovchansk Ukraine 50°17N 36°58E 189 G9
Volchikha Russia 52°2N 80°23E 217 B10
Volchya → Ukraine 48°32N 36°0E 189 H8
Volda Norway 62°9N 6°5E 164 B3
Volga = Privolzhskiy □ Russia 56°0N 50°0E 190 B10
Volga Russia 57°58N 38°16E 188 C10
Volga → Russia 46°0N 48°30E 191 G9
Volga Hts. = Privolzhskaya Vozvyshennost Russia 51°0N 46°0E 190 E7
Volgelsdorf Germany 52°30N 13°44E 115 B5
Volgo-Baltiyskiy Kanal Russia 60°0N 38°0E 188 B9
Volgo-Donskoy Kanal Russia 48°40N 43°37E 191 F7
Volgodonsk Russia 47°33N 42°5E 191 G6
Volgograd Russia 48°40N 44°25E 191 F7
Volgograd □ Russia 49°40N 44°30E 190 F7
Volgogradskoye Vdkhr. Russia 50°0N 45°20E 190 E8
Volgorechensk Russia 57°28N 41°14E 190 B5
Volimes Greece 37°52N 20°39E 207 D2
Volintiri Moldova 46°26N 29°37E 183 D14
Volissos Greece 38°29N 25°54E 205 C7
Volkach Germany 49°52N 10°14E 179 F6
Völkermarkt Austria 46°39N 14°39E 180 E7
Volkhonka-Zil Russia 55°39N 37°37E 129 C3
Volkhov Russia 59°55N 32°15E 188 C7
Volkhov → Russia 60°8N 32°20E 188 B7
Volkhovstroy = Volkhov Russia 59°55N 32°15E 188 C7
Völklingen Germany 49°15N 6°50E 179 F2
Volkovysk = Vawkavysk Belarus 53°9N 24°30E 177 B13
Volksrust S. Africa 27°24S 29°53E 271 C4
Voll Norway 62°31N 7°27E 164 B4
Vollen Norway 59°48N 10°27E 131 B1
Volnansk Ukraine 48°2N 35°29E 189 H8
Volnovakha Ukraine 47°35N 37°30E 189 J9
Volochanka Russia 71°0N 94°28E 215 B10
Volodarsk Russia 56°12N 43°15E 190 B6
Volodarskoye Russia 59°54N 30°23E 137 B2
Volodymyr-Volynskyy Ukraine 50°50N 24°18E 177 C13
Vologda Russia 59°10N 39°45E 188 C10
Vologda □ Russia 60°15N 39°0E 188 B10
Volokolamsk Russia 56°5N 35°57E 188 D8
Volokonovka Russia 50°33N 37°52E 189 G9
Volos Greece 39°24N 22°59E 204 B4
Vološinovo = Novi Bečej Serbia 45°36N 20°10E 182 E5
Volosovo Russia 59°27N 29°32E 188 C5
Volovets Ukraine 48°43N 23°11E 183 B8
Volovo Russia 53°35N 38°1E 188 F10
Volozhin = Valozhyn Belarus 54°3N 26°30E 177 A14
Volsk Russia 52°5N 47°22E 190 D8
Volta □ Ghana 7°0N 0°30E 263 D5
Volta → Ghana 5°46N 0°41E 263 D5
Volta, L. Ghana 7°30N 0°0 263 D5
Volta Blanche = White Volta → Ghana 9°10N 1°15W 263 D4
Volta Redonda Brazil 22°31S 44°5W 333 F3
Voltaire, C. Australia 14°16S 125°35E 278 B4
Volterra Italy 43°24N 10°51E 198 E7
Voltri Italy 44°26N 8°45E 198 D5
Volturno → Italy 41°1N 13°55E 200 A6
Volubilis Morocco 34°2N 5°33W 260 B3
Volvi, L. Greece 40°40N 23°34E 202 F7
Volyn □ Ukraine 51°15N 24°30E 189 G3
Volyně Czech Rep. 49°10N 13°53E 180 B6
Volynkina-Derevnya Russia 59°53N 30°18E 137 B1
Volzhsk Russia 55°57N 48°23E 190 C9
Volzhskiy Russia 48°56N 44°46E 191 F7
Vomo Fiji 17°30S 177°15E 287 A1
Vonavona Solomon Is. 8°15S 157°5E 287 M9
Vondelpark Neths. 52°21N 4°52E 112 A2
Vondrozo Madag. 22°49S 47°20E 272 C2
Vonitsa Greece 38°55N 20°53E 207 B2
Vopnafjörður Iceland 65°45N 14°50W 155 B12
Vorarlberg □ Austria 47°20N 10°0E 180 D2
Voras Oros Greece 40°57N 21°45E 202 F5
Vorbasse Denmark 55°39N 9°6E 163 J3
Vorchdorf Austria 48°0N 13°55E 180 C6
Vorderrhein → Switz. 46°49N 9°25E 179 J5
Vordingborg Denmark 55°10N 11°54E 163 J5
Vorë Albania 41°23N 19°40E 202 E3
Voreio Aigaio □ Greece 38°50N 25°30E 205 C7
Voreppe France 45°18N 5°39E 175 C9
Vori Greece 35°4N 24°49E 207 E5
Vorios Evoikos Kolpos Greece 38°45N 23°15E 204 C5
Vorkuta Russia 67°48N 64°20E 186 A11
Vorma → Norway 60°9N 11°29E 164 D8
Vormsi Estonia 59°1N 23°13E 188 C2
Vorona → Russia 51°22N 42°3E 190 E6
Voronezh Russia 51°40N 39°10E 189 G10
Voronezh Ukraine 51°47N 33°28E 189 G7
Voronezh □ Russia 51°30N 39°30E 190 E4
Voronezh → Russia 51°32N 39°10E 189 G10
Vorontsovo-Aleksandrovskoye = Zelenokumsk Russia 44°24N 44°0E 191 H6
Voroshilov = Ussuriysk Russia 43°48N 131°59E 220 C5
Voroshilovgrad = Luhansk Ukraine 48°38N 39°15E 189 H10
Voroshilovsk = Alchevsk Ukraine 48°30N 38°45E 189 H10
Voroshilovsk = Stavropol Russia 45°5N 42°0E 191 H6
Vorpommersche Boddenlandschaft △ Germany 54°25N 12°32E 178 A8
Vorskla → Ukraine 48°50N 34°10E 189 H8
Võrts Järv Estonia 58°16N 26°3E 188 C4
Võru Estonia 57°48N 26°54E 188 D4
Vösendorf Austria 48°7N 16°20E 142 B2
Vosges France 48°20N 7°10E 173 D14
Vosges □ France 48°12N 6°20E 173 D13
Vosges du Nord ⌂ France 49°0N 7°30E 173 D14
Voskopojë Albania 40°35N 20°33E 202 F4
Voskresensk Russia 55°19N 38°43E 188 E10
Voskresenskoye Russia 56°51N 45°30E 190 B7
Voss Norway 60°38N 6°26E 164 D3
Vostochnyy Russia 55°49N 37°51E 129 B5
Vostok = Neftegorsk Russia 44°25N 39°45E 191 H4
Vostok Antarctica 78°30S 106°50E 151 D8
Vostok I. Kiribati 10°5S 152°23W 289 J12
Votice Czech Rep. 49°38N 14°39E 180 B7
Votkinsk Russia 57°0N 53°55E 186 C9
Votkinskoye Vdkhr. Russia 57°22N 55°12E 186 C10
Votsuri-Shima Japan 25°45N 123°29E 221 M1
Votuporanga Brazil 20°24S 49°59W 333 F2
Vouga → Portugal 40°41N 8°40W 194 E2
Vouillé France 46°38N 0°10E 172 F7
Voula Greece 37°49N 23°45E 112 C2
Vouliagmeni Greece 37°50N 23°46E 112 C2
Voulkaria, L. Greece 38°52N 20°50E 207 B2
Voulou C.A.R. 8°33N 22°36E 264 A4
Vouxa, Akra Greece 35°37N 23°32E 207 E4
Vouzela Portugal 40°43N 8°7W 194 E2
Vouziers France 49°22N 4°40E 173 C11
Vovchansk Ukraine 50°17N 36°58E 189 G9
Vovodo → C.A.R. 5°40N 24°21E 264 A4
Vowchyn Belarus 52°18N 23°18E 185 F10
Voyageurs △ U.S.A. 48°32N 93°0W 308 A7
Voynitsa Russia 65°10N 30°20E 160 D24
Voyvozh Russia 62°56N 54°56E 214 C6
Vozhe, Ozero Russia 60°45N 39°0E 188 B10
Vozhega Russia 60°29N 40°12E 188 B11
Voznesensk Ukraine 47°35N 31°21E 189 J6
Voznesenye Russia 61°0N 35°28E 188 B8
Vrå Denmark 57°21N 9°56E 163 G3
Vráble Slovak Rep. 48°15N 18°16E 181 C11
Vraćevšnica Serbia 44°2N 20°34E 202 B4
Vrachneika Greece 38°10N 21°40E 204 C3
Vrådal Norway 59°20N 8°25E 164 E5
Vrancea □ Romania 45°50N 26°45E 183 E11
Vrancei, Munţii Romania 46°0N 26°30E 183 D11
Vrangel Russia 42°43N 133°5E 220 C6
Vrangelya, Ostrov Russia 71°0N 180°0E 215 B18
Vranica Bos.-H. 43°55N 17°50E 182 G2
Vranje Serbia 42°34N 21°54E 202 D5
Vranjska Banja Serbia 42°34N 22°1E 202 D6
Vranov nad Topľou Slovak Rep. 48°53N 21°40E 181 C14
Vransko Slovenia 46°17N 14°58E 199 B11
Vransko Jezero Croatia 43°53N 15°34E 199 E12
Vrapčište Macedonia 41°50N 20°53E 202 E4
Vratsa Bulgaria 43°15N 23°30E 202 C7
Vråvatn Norway 59°20N 8°8E 164 E5
Vrbas Serbia 45°40N 19°40E 182 E4
Vrbas → Bos.-H. 45°8N 17°29E 182 E2
Vrbnik Croatia 45°4N 14°40E 199 C11
Vrbovec Croatia 45°53N 16°28E 199 C13
Vrbovsko Croatia 45°24N 15°5E 199 C12
Vrchlabí Czech Rep. 50°38N 15°37E 180 A8
Vrede S. Africa 27°24S 29°6E 271 C4
Vredefort S. Africa 27°0S 27°22E 270 C4
Vredehoek S. Africa 33°57S 18°25E 118 A1
Vreden Germany 52°2N 6°50E 178 C2
Vredenburg S. Africa 32°56S 18°0E 270 D2
Vredendal S. Africa 31°41S 18°35E 270 D2
Vretstorp Sweden 59°1N 14°53E 162 E8
Vrgorac Croatia 43°12N 17°20E 199 E14
Vrhnika Slovenia 45°58N 14°15E 199 C11
Vriddhachalam India 11°30N 79°20E 245 J4
Vrïdi Ivory C. 5°15N 4°3W 262 D4
Vrigstad Sweden 57°22N 14°28E 163 G8
Vrindavan India 27°37N 77°40E 242 F7
Vrisses Greece 35°23N 24°13E 207 E5
Vrnograč Bos.-H. 45°10N 15°57E 199 C12
Vrondados Greece 38°25N 26°7E 205 C8
Vrpolje Croatia 45°13N 18°24E 182 E3
Vršac Serbia 45°8N 21°20E 182 E6
Vrsacki Kanal Serbia 45°15N 21°0E 182 E5
Vršovice Czech Rep. 50°4N 14°28E 135 B2
Vrútky Slovak Rep. 49°7N 18°55E 181 B11
Vryburg S. Africa 26°55S 24°45E 270 C3
Vryheid S. Africa 27°45S 30°47E 271 C5
Vsetín Czech Rep. 49°20N 18°0E 181 B11
Vu Liet Vietnam 18°43N 105°23E 236 C5
Vŭcha → Bulgaria 42°10N 24°26E 203 D8
Vučitrn Kosovo 42°49N 20°59E 202 D4
Vukovar Croatia 45°21N 18°59E 182 E3
Vuktyl Russia 63°52N 57°20E 214 C6
Vulcan Alta., Canada 50°25N 113°15W 296 C6
Vulcan Romania 45°23N 23°17E 183 E8
Vulcaneşti Moldova 45°41N 28°18E 183 E13
Vulcano Italy 38°24N 14°58E 201 D7
Vŭlchedrma Bulgaria 43°42N 23°27E 202 C7
Vulkaneshty = Vulcaneşti Moldova 45°41N 28°18E 183 E13
Vunduzi → Mozam. 18°56S 34°1E 269 F3
Vung Tau Vietnam 10°21N 107°4E 237 G6
Vunidawa Fiji 17°50S 178°21E 287 A2
Vunisea Fiji 19°3S 178°10E 287 B2
Vuranggo Solomon Is. 6°39S 156°38E 287 L9
Vurbitsa Bulgaria 42°59N 26°40E 203 D10
Vurshets Bulgaria 43°13N 23°23E 202 C7
Vutcani Romania 46°26N 27°59E 183 D12
Vuya Sudan 5°21N 29°40E 257 F2
Vuzlove Ukraine 48°22N 22°24E 182 B7
Vwaza ⌂ Malawi 10°58S 33°25E 269 E3
Vyara India 21°8N 73°28E 244 D1
Vyartsilya Russia 62°8N 30°45E 188 A6
Vyatka = Kirov Russia 58°35N 49°40E 186 D8
Vyatka → Russia 55°37N 51°28E 190 C10
Vyatskiye Polyany Russia 56°14N 51°5E 190 B10
Vyazemskiy Russia 47°32N 134°45E 215 E14
Vyazma Russia 55°10N 34°15E 188 E8
Vyazniki Russia 56°10N 42°10E 190 B6
Vyborg Russia 60°43N 28°47E 188 B5
Vyborgskaya Storona Russia 59°57N 30°22E 137 B2
Vychegda → Russia 61°18N 46°36E 186 B8
Vychodné Beskydy Europe 49°20N 22°0E 181 B15
Vyerkhnyadzvinsk Belarus 55°45N 27°58E 188 E4
Vyg-ozero Russia 63°47N 34°29E 186 B5
Vyhoda Ukraine 48°56N 23°55E 183 B8
Vykhino Russia 55°42N 37°48E 129 B4
Vyksa Russia 55°19N 42°11E 190 C6
Vylkove Ukraine 45°28N 29°32E 183 E14
Vylok Ukraine 48°6N 22°50E 182 B7
Vynohradiv Ukraine 48°9N 23°2E 182 B8
Vypin India 10°10N 76°15E 245 J3
Vyrnwy, L. U.K. 52°48N 3°31W 168 E4
Vyšehrad Czech Rep. 50°3N 14°25E 135 B2
Vyshkiv Ukraine 48°44N 23°39E 183 B8
Vyshkove Ukraine 48°3N 23°25E 183 B8
Vyshniy Volochek Russia 57°30N 34°30E 188 D8
Vyshzha = imeni 26 Bakinskikh Komissarov Turkmenistan 39°22N 54°10E 247 B7
Vyškov Czech Rep. 49°17N 17°0E 181 B9
Vysokaye Belarus 52°22N 23°22E 185 F10
Vysoké Mýto Czech Rep. 49°58N 16°10E 181 B9
Vysokovsk Russia 56°22N 36°30E 188 D9
Vyšší Brod Czech Rep. 48°37N 14°19E 180 C7
Vytegra Russia 61°0N 36°27E 188 B9
Vyzhnytsya Ukraine 48°15N 25°11E 183 B10
Vyzhnytsya ⌂ Ukraine 48°7N 25°15E 183 B10

W

W du Benin △ Benin 11°57N 2°43E 263 C5
W du Burkina Faso △ Burkina Faso 11°52N 2°50W 263 C4
W du Niger △ Niger 13°31N 2°28E 263 C5
W.A.C. Bennett Dam Canada 56°2N 122°6W 296 B4
Wa Ghana 10°7N 2°25W 262 C4
Waag Amsterdam, Neths. 112 b3
Waal → Neths. 51°37N 5°0E 170 C5
Waalwijk Neths. 51°42N 5°4E 170 C5
Waanyi-Garawa ✪ Australia 18°2S 137°33E 280 B2
Waat Sudan 8°10N 32°7E 257 F3
Wabag Papua N. G. 5°32S 143°40E 286 C2
Wabakimi △ Canada 50°43N 89°29W 298 B2
Wabana Canada 47°40N 53°0W 299 C9
Wabasca → Canada 58°22N 115°20W 296 B5
Wabasca-Desmarais Canada 55°57N 113°56W 296 B6
Wabash U.S.A. 40°48N 85°49W 311 D11
Wabash → U.S.A. 37°48N 88°2W 311 G8
Wabasso U.S.A. 27°45N 80°26W 317 H9
Wabawng Burma 26°20N 97°26E 241 D6
Wabi → Ethiopia 7°45N 40°50E 257 F5
Wabigoon L. Canada 49°44N 92°44W 297 D10
Wabowden Canada 54°55N 98°38W 297 C9
Wąbrzeźno Poland 53°16N 18°57E 185 E5
Wabu Hu China 32°20N 116°50E 229 A11
Wabuda I. Papua N. G. 8°23S 143°37E 286 E2
Wabuk Pt. Canada 55°20N 85°5W 298 A2
Wabush Canada 52°55N 66°52W 299 B6
Waccasassa B. U.S.A. 29°10N 82°50W 317 F7
Wąchock Poland 51°4N 21°1E 185 G8
Wachterhof Germany 48°2N 11°42E 131 B3
Wächtersbach Germany 50°14N 9°17E 179 E5
Wacissa U.S.A. 30°22N 83°59W 316 E6
Waco U.S.A. 31°33N 97°9W 314 F6
Waconichi, L. Canada 50°8N 74°0W 298 B5
Wad Ban Naqa Sudan 16°32N 33°9E 257 D3
Wad Banda Sudan 13°10N 27°56E 257 E2
Wad el Haddad Sudan 13°50N 33°30E 257 E3
Wad en Nau Sudan 14°10N 33°34E 257 E3
Wad Hamid Sudan 16°30N 32°45E 257 D3
Wad Medanî Sudan 14°28N 33°30E 257 E3
Wad Thana Pakistan 27°22N 66°23E 242 F2
Wadai Africa 12°0N 19°0E 254 E5
Wadala India 19°1N 72°51E 130 a2
Wadayama Japan 35°19N 134°52E 222 B6
Wadbilliga △ Australia 36°25S 149°35E 283 D8
Waddān Libya 29°9N 16°10E 258 C3
Waddeneilanden Neths. 53°25N 5°10E 170 A5
Waddenzee Neths. 53°6N 5°10E 170 A5
Waddi, Chappal Nigeria 7°2N 11°43E 263 D7
Waddington U.S.A. 44°52N 75°12W 313 B9
Waddington, Mt. Canada 51°23N 125°15W 296 C3
Waddy Pt. Australia 24°58S 153°21E 281 C5
Wadebridge U.K. 50°31N 4°51W 169 G3
Wadena Sask., Canada 51°57N 103°47W 297 C8
Wadena Minn., U.S.A. 46°26N 95°8W 308 B6
Wädenswil Switz. 47°14N 8°40E 179 H4
Wadern Germany 49°32N 6°53E 179 F2
Wadestown N.Z. 41°16S 174°46E 143 B1
Wadeye Australia 14°28S 129°52E 278 B4
Wadgaon India 18°44N 73°39E 244 E1
Wadhams Canada 51°30N 127°30W 296 C3
Wadhwan = Surendranagar India 22°45N 71°40E 242 H4
Wadhwan India 22°42N 71°41E 242 H4
Wadi India 17°4N 76°59E 244 F3
Wadi al-Arayis West Bank 31°43N 35°15E 123 B2
Wādī Al Ḥayāt □ Libya 26°26N 12°30E 258 C2
Wādī as Sīr Jordan 31°56N 35°49E 251 G6
Wādī Ash Shāṭi □ Libya 27°27N 13°37E 258 C2
Wādī Feirân Egypt 28°42N 33°19E 251 K4
Wādī Fira □ Chad 15°0N 21°0E 259 F4
Wādī Fukin West Bank 31°42N 35°6E 123 B1
Wādī Gemâl, I. Egypt 24°35N 35°10E 256 C4
Wādī Halfa Sudan 21°53N 31°19E 256 C3
Wādī Mūsā Jordan 30°19N 35°29E 251 H6
Wadi Rum △ Jordan 29°30N 35°20E 251 J6
Wadian China 32°42N 112°29E 229 A9
Wadlew Poland 51°31N 19°23E 185 G6
Wadley Ala., U.S.A. 33°7N 85°34W 316 B4
Wadley Ga., U.S.A. 32°52N 82°24W 316 C7
Wadowice Poland 49°52N 19°30E 185 J6
Wadsworth Nev., U.S.A. 39°38N 119°17W 304 G4
Wadsworth Ohio, U.S.A. 41°2N 81°44W 312 E3
Waduk Pluit Indonesia 6°5S 106°46E 122 A1
Waegwan S. Korea 35°59N 128°23E 224 E4
Wafangdian China 39°38N 121°58E 227 E11
Wafania Dem. Rep. of the Congo 1°23S 20°22E 264 C4
Wafrah Kuwait 28°33N 47°56E 246 D5
Wagadugu = Ouagadougou Burkina Faso 12°25N 1°30W 263 C4
Wagait ✪ Australia 13°1S 130°5E 278 B5
Wagener U.S.A. 33°39N 81°22W 316 B8
Wageningen Neths. 51°58N 5°40E 170 C5
Wageningen Suriname 5°50N 56°50W 329 B6
Wager B. Canada 65°26N 88°40W 295 D14
Wagga Wagga Australia 35°7S 147°24E 283 C7
Waggaman U.S.A. 29°55N 90°12W 131 B1
Waghai India 20°46N 73°29E 244 D1
Waghete Indonesia 4°10S 135°50E 231 E9
Wagin Australia 33°17S 117°25E 279 F2
Wagner U.S.A. 43°5N 98°18W 308 D4
Wagon Mound U.S.A. 36°1N 104°42W 305 H11
Wagoner U.S.A. 35°58N 95°22W 314 D7
Wagrowiec Poland 52°48N 17°11E 185 F4
Wah Pakistan 33°45N 72°40E 242 C5
Wah Fu China 22°15N 114°8E 122 B1
Wahai Indonesia 2°48S 129°35E 231 E7
Waharoa N.Z. 37°46S 175°45E 284 D4
Wahda Iraq 33°18N 44°26E 113 B2
Wahiawā U.S.A. 21°30N 158°2W 302 K13
Wahiawā District U.S.A. 21°31N 157°58W 302 J14
Wahiawā Res. U.S.A. 21°30N 158°3W 302 K13
Wâhid Egypt 30°48N 32°21E 251 H3
Wahnai Afghan. 32°40N 65°50E 242 C1
Wahni Ethiopia 12°40N 36°39E 257 E4
Wahoo U.S.A. 41°13N 96°37W 308 E5
Wahpeton U.S.A. 46°16N 96°36W 308 B5
Währing Austria 48°14N 16°20E 142 A2
Wahx, Ras il- Malta 35°56N 14°20E 206 F7
Wai India 17°56N 73°57E 244 F1
Wai'ale'ale U.S.A. 22°4N 159°30W 302 a
Waiale'e U.S.A. 21°41N 158°1W 302 J13
Waialua U.S.A. 21°34N 158°8W 302 J13
Waialua B. U.S.A. 21°35N 158°5W 302 J13
Waialua District U.S.A. 21°35N 158°5W 302 J13
Wai'anae U.S.A. 21°27N 158°11W 302 K13
Wai'anae Coast U.S.A. 21°26N 158°11W 302 K13
Wai'anae District U.S.A. 21°28N 158°10W 302 K13
Wai'anae Range U.S.A. 21°30N 158°10W 302 K13
Waiao Taiwan 24°54N 121°51E 225 B3
Waiapu → N.Z. 37°47S 178°29E 284 D7
Waiau N.Z. 42°39S 173°5E 285 C8
Waiau → Canterbury, N.Z. 42°47S 173°22E 285 C8
Waiau → Southland, N.Z. 46°12S 167°38E 285 G2
Waiawa → U.S.A. 21°23N 157°59W 302 K14
Waiawe Ganga → Sri Lanka 6°15N 81°0E 245 L5
Waibeem Indonesia 0°30S 132°59E 231 E8
Waiblingen Germany 48°49N 9°18E 179 G5
Waidhofen an der Thaya Austria 48°49N 15°17E 180 C8
Waidhofen an der Ybbs Austria 47°57N 14°46E 180 D7
Waidmannslust Germany 52°36N 13°20E 115 A3
Waigeo Indonesia 0°20S 130°40E 231 E8
Waihao → N.Z. 44°47S 171°10E 285 E6
Waihao Downs N.Z. 44°48S 170°55E 285 E5
Waiheke I. N.Z. 36°48S 175°6E 284 C4
Waihi N.Z. 37°23S 175°52E 284 D4
Waihi Beach N.Z. 37°25S 175°57E 284 D4
Waihola N.Z. 46°1S 170°8E 285 G5
Waihola L. N.Z. 45°59S 170°8E 285 F5
Waihou → N.Z. 37°15S 175°40E 284 D4
Waika Dem. Rep. of the Congo 2°22S 25°42E 264 C5
Waikabubak Indonesia 9°45S 119°25E 231 F5
Waikaia N.Z. 45°44S 168°51E 285 F3
Waikaka N.Z. 45°55S 169°1E 285 F4
Waikane U.S.A. 21°30N 157°51W 302 J14
Waikare, L. N.Z. 37°26S 175°13E 284 D4
Waikareiti, L. N.Z. 38°43S 177°10E 284 E6
Waikaremoana N.Z. 38°42S 177°12E 284 E6
Waikaremoana, L. N.Z. 38°49S 177°9E 284 E6
Waikari N.Z. 42°58S 172°41E 285 C7
Waikato → N.Z. 37°23S 174°43E 284 D3
Waikelo Indonesia 9°24S 119°19E 278 A2
Waikerie Australia 34°9S 140°0E 282 C4
Waikiekie N.Z. 35°57S 174°16E 284 B3
Waikīkī U.S.A. 21°17N 157°50W 302 K14
Waikokopu N.Z. 39°3S 177°52E 284 F6
Waikoloa Village U.S.A. 19°55N 155°49W 302 D6
Waikouaiti N.Z. 45°36S 170°41E 285 F5
Waikouaiti Downs N.Z. 45°30S 170°30E 285 F5
Wailea-Makena U.S.A. 20°40N 156°27W 302 C5
Wailing Wall = Western Wall Jerusalem 123 b3
Wailingding Dao China 22°6N 114°2E 219 G11
Wailua U.S.A. 22°3N 159°20W 302 A2
Wailuku U.S.A. 20°53N 156°30W 302 C5
Waimakariri → N.Z. 43°24S 172°42E 285 D7
Waimalu U.S.A. 21°24N 157°57W 302 K14
Waimänalo U.S.A. 21°21N 157°43W 302 K14
Waimänalo B. U.S.A. 21°20N 157°40W 302 K14
Waimänalo Beach U.S.A. 21°21N 157°42W 302 K14
Waimangaroa N.Z. 41°43S 171°46E 285 B6
Waimano → U.S.A. 21°25N 157°58W 302 K14
Waimarie N.Z. 41°35S 171°58E 285 B6
Waimate N.Z. 44°45S 171°3E 285 E6
Waimea Hawai'i, U.S.A. 21°58N 159°40W 302 B2
Waimea Hawai'i, U.S.A. 21°39N 158°3W 302 J13
Waimea B. U.S.A. 21°40N 158°5W 302 J13
Waimea Plain N.Z. 45°55S 168°35E 285 F3
Wainganga → India 18°50N 79°55E 244 E4
Waingapu Indonesia 9°35S 120°11E 231 F6
Waingmaw Burma 25°21N 97°26E 241 C6
Waini → Guyana 8°20N 59°50W 329 B6
Wainuiomata N.Z. 41°17S 174°56E 143 B2
Wainuiomata → N.Z. 41°20S 174°55E 143 B2
Wainwright Alta., Canada 52°50N 110°50W 297 C6
Wainwright Alaska, U.S.A. 70°38N 160°2W 303 A7
Waiotapu N.Z. 38°21S 176°25E 284 E5
Waiouru N.Z. 39°28S 175°41E 284 F4
Waipa → N.Z. 38°16S 175°21E 284 E4
Waipahi N.Z. 46°6S 169°15E 285 G4
Waipahu U.S.A. 21°23N 158°1W 302 K13
Waipapa Pt. N.Z. 46°40S 168°51E 285 G3
Waipara N.Z. 43°3S 172°46E 285 D7
Waipawa N.Z. 39°56S 176°38E 284 F5
Waipi'o U.S.A. 21°25N 158°0W 302 K14
Waipi'o Acres U.S.A. 21°28N 158°1W 302 K13
Waipi'o Peninsula U.S.A. 21°20N 158°0W 302 K14
Waipiro N.Z. 38°2S 178°22E 284 E7
Waipiro Bay N.Z. 38°1S 178°21E 284 E7
Waipoua Forest N.Z. 35°39S 173°33E 284 B2
Waipu N.Z. 35°59S 174°29E 284 B3
Waipukurau N.Z. 40°1S 176°33E 284 G5
Wairakei N.Z. 38°37S 176°6E 284 E5
Wairarapa, L. N.Z. 41°14S 175°15E 284 H4
Wairau → N.Z. 41°32S 174°7E 285 B9
Wairio N.Z. 45°59S 168°3E 285 F3
Wairoa N.Z. 39°3S 177°25E 284 F6
Wairoa → Hawke's Bay, N.Z. 39°4S 177°25E 284 F6
Wairoa → Northland, N.Z. 36°5S 173°59E 284 C2
Waisantiang Taiwan 23°29N 120°1E 225 C2
Waïsisi Vanuatu 19°32S 169°22E 287 J7
Waitaki → N.Z. 44°56S 171°7E 285 E6
Waitaki Plains N.Z. 44°22S 170°0E 285 E5
Waitangi N.Z. 35°16S 174°5E 284 B3
Waitara N.Z. 38°59S 174°15E 284 E3
Waitara → N.Z. 38°59S 174°14E 284 E3
Waitiki Landing N.Z. 34°31S 172°50E 284 A1
Waitoa N.Z. 37°37S 175°35E 284 D4
Waitomo Caves N.Z. 38°16S 175°7E 284 E4
Waitotara N.Z. 39°49S 174°44E 284 F3
Waitotara → N.Z. 39°51S 174°41E 284 F3
Waitsburg U.S.A. 46°16N 118°9W 304 C4
Waitzen = Vác Hungary 47°49N 19°10E 182 C4
Waiuku N.Z. 37°15S 174°45E 284 D3
Wajima Japan 37°30N 137°0E 221 F8
Wajir Kenya 1°42N 40°5E 268 B5
Waka Dem. Rep. of the Congo 1°1N 20°13E 264 B4
Waka Ethiopia 7°2N 37°20E 257 F4
Waka-Kungo Angola 11°21S 15°7E 265 E3
Wakarusa U.S.A. 41°32N 86°1W 311 C10
Wakasa Japan 35°20N 134°24E 222 B6
Wakasa-Wan Japan 35°40N 135°30E 223 B7
Wakatipu, L. N.Z. 45°5S 168°33E 285 F3
Wakaw Canada 52°39N 105°44W 297 C7
Wakaya Fiji 17°37S 179°0E 287 A2
Wakayama Japan 34°15N 135°15E 223 C7
Wakayama □ Japan 33°50N 135°30E 223 D7
Wake Japan 34°48N 134°8E 222 C6
Wake Forest U.S.A. 35°59N 78°30W 315 D15
Wake I. Pac. Oc. 19°18N 166°36E 302 b
WaKeeney U.S.A. 39°1N 99°53W 308 F4
Wakefield Jamaica 18°26N 77°42W 320 a
Wakefield N.Z. 41°24S 173°5E 285 B8
Wakefield W. Yorks., U.K. 53°41N 1°29W 168 D6
Wakefield Mass., U.S.A. 42°30N 71°5W 116 A2
Wakefield Mich., U.S.A. 46°29N 89°56W 308 B9
Wakema Burma 16°30N 95°11E 241 G5
Wākhān Afghan. 37°8N 73°4E 240 A4
Waki Japan 34°4N 134°9E 222 C6
Wakkanai Japan 45°28N 141°35E 220 B10
Wakkerstroom S. Africa 27°24S 30°10E 271 C5
Wakool Australia 35°28S 144°23E 282 C6
Wakool → Australia 35°5S 143°33E 282 C5
Wakre Indonesia 0°19S 131°5E 231 E8
Waku Papua N. G. 6°5S 149°9E 286 D5
Wakuach, L. Canada 55°34N 67°32W 299 A6
Wakulla U.S.A. 30°14N 84°14W 316 E5
Wakunai Papua N. G. 5°52S 155°13E 286 C8
Walagunya ✪ Australia 23°10S 120°50E 278 D3
Walamba Zambia 13°30S 28°42E 269 E2
Wałbrzych Poland 50°45N 16°18E 185 H3
Walbury Hill U.K. 51°21N 1°28W 169 F6
Walcha Australia 30°55S 151°31E 283 A9
Walcheren Neths. 51°30N 3°35E 170 C3
Walcott U.S.A. 41°46N 106°51W 304 F10
Wałcz Poland 53°17N 16°27E 185 E3
Waldbröl Germany 50°52N 7°37E 178 E3
Waldburg Ra. Australia 24°40S 117°35E 279 D2
Waldeck Germany 51°12N 9°4E 178 D5
Walden Colo., U.S.A. 40°44N 106°17W 304 F10
Walden N.Y., U.S.A. 41°34N 74°11W 313 E10
Waldenberg = Wałbrzych Poland 50°45N 16°18E 185 H3
Waldesruh Germany 52°28N 13°37E 115 B4
Waldkirch Germany 48°5N 7°58E 179 G3
Waldkirchen Germany 48°43N 13°36E 179 G9
Waldkraiburg Germany 48°11N 12°24E 179 G8
Waldo U.S.A. 29°48N 82°10W 316 F7
Waldperlach Germany 48°4N 11°40E 131 B3
Waldport U.S.A. 44°26N 124°4W 304 D1
Waldron U.S.A. 34°54N 94°5W 314 D7
Waldtrudering Germany 48°6N 11°42E 131 B3
Waldviertel Austria 48°30N 15°30E 180 C8
Walebing Australia 30°41S 116°13E 279 F2
Walembele Ghana 10°30N 1°58W 262 C4
Walensee Switz. 47°7N 9°13E 179 H5
Wales U.S.A. 65°37N 168°5W 303 D5
Wales □ U.K. 52°19N 4°43W 169 E3
Wales I. Canada 68°1N 86°40W 295 D14
Walewale Ghana 10°21N 0°50W 263 C4
Walgett Australia 30°0S 148°5E 281 E4
Walgreen Coast Antarctica 75°15S 105°0W 151 D15
Walhalla Australia 37°56S 146°29E 283 D7
Walis I. Papua N. G. 3°14S 143°18E 286 B2
Walker Mich., U.S.A. 42°58N 85°46W 311 B11
Walker Minn., U.S.A. 47°6N 94°35W 308 B6
Walker, L. Canada 50°20N 67°11W 299 B6
Walker L. Man., Canada 54°42N 95°57W 297 C9
Walker L. Nev., U.S.A. 38°42N 118°43W 304 G4
Walkerston Australia 21°11S 149°8E 280 b
Walkerton Ont., Canada 44°10N 81°10W 312 B3
Walkerton Ind., U.S.A. 41°28N 86°29W 311 C10
Walkinstown Ireland 53°19N 6°20W 120 B1
Wall U.S.A. 44°0N 102°8W 308 C2
Wall Street New York, U.S.A. 132 f1
Walla Walla N.S.W., Australia 35°45S 146°54E 283 C7
Walla Walla Wash., U.S.A. 46°4N 118°20W 304 C4
Wallabout Bay New York, U.S.A. 132 f2
Wallace Idaho, U.S.A. 47°28N 115°56W 304 C6
Wallace N.C., U.S.A. 34°44N 77°59W 315 D16
Wallaceburg Canada 42°34N 82°23W 312 D2
Wallacetown N.Z. 46°21S 168°19E 285 G3
Wallachia = Valahia Romania 44°35N 25°0E 183 F9
Wallal Australia 26°32S 146°7E 281 D4
Wallam Cr. → Australia 28°40S 147°20E 281 D4
Wallambin, L. Australia 30°57S 117°35E 279 F2
Wallan Australia 37°26S 144°59E 283 D6
Wallangarra Australia 28°56S 151°58E 281 D5
Wallaroo Australia 33°56S 137°39E 282 B2
Walldürn Germany 49°34N 9°22E 179 F5
Wallenhorst Germany 52°21N 8°1E 178 C4
Wallenpaupack, L. U.S.A. 41°25N 75°15W 313 E9
Wallerawang Australia 33°25S 150°4E 283 B9
Wallingat △ Australia 32°14S 152°25E 283 B10
Wallingford Conn., U.S.A. 41°27N 72°50W 313 E12
Wallingford Vt., U.S.A. 43°28N 72°58W 313 C12
Wallis & Futuna, Is. Pac. Oc. 13°18S 176°10W 277 C15
Wallowa U.S.A. 45°34N 117°32W 304 D5
Wallowa Mts. U.S.A. 45°20N 117°30W 304 D5
Walls U.K. 60°14N 1°33W 167 A7
Walls of Jerusalem △ Australia 41°56S 146°15E 281 G4
Wallsend Australia 32°55S 151°40E 283 B9
Wallula U.S.A. 46°5N 118°54W 304 C4
Wallumbilla Australia 26°33S 149°9E 281 D4
Walmsley L. Canada 63°25N 108°36W 297 A7
Walney, I. of U.K. 54°6N 3°15W 168 C4
Walnut U.S.A. 41°33N 89°36W 310 C7
Walnut Canyon ⌂ U.S.A. 35°15N 111°20W 305 J8
Walnut Creek U.S.A. 37°54N 122°4W 306 H4
Walnut Grove U.S.A. 34°4N 86°18W 316 A3
Walnut Hill U.S.A. 30°53N 87°30W 317 E2
Walnut Ridge U.S.A. 36°4N 90°57W 315 C9
Walpeup Australia 35°7S 142°2E 282 C5
Walpole W. Austral., Australia 34°58S 116°44E 279 F2
Walpole Mass., U.S.A. 42°9N 71°15W 313 D13
Walpole-Nornalup △ Australia 35°0S 116°45E 279 G2
Wals Austria 47°47N 12°58E 180 D5
Walsall U.K. 52°35N 1°58W 169 E6
Walsenburg U.S.A. 37°38N 104°47W 305 H11
Walsh U.S.A. 37°23N 102°17W 305 H12
Walsh → Australia 16°31S 143°42E 280 B3
Walsingham Canada 42°40N 80°31W 312 D4
Walsrode Germany 52°51N 9°35E 178 C5
Walt Disney Concert Hall Los Angeles, U.S.A. 127 b1
Walt Disney World U.S.A. 28°22N 81°33W 133 B1
Waltair India 17°44N 83°23E 244 F6
Walter D. Stone Memorial Zoo U.S.A. 42°28N 71°6W 116 A2
Walter F. George Res. U.S.A. 31°38N 85°4W 316 D4
Walterboro U.S.A. 32°55N 80°40W 316 C9
Walters U.S.A. 34°22N 98°19W 314 D5
Waltershausen Germany 50°54N 10°33E 178 E6
Waltershausen Gletscher Greenland 73°54N 24°25W 154 C8
Waltham U.S.A. 42°23N 71°14W 116 A1
Waltham Forest □ U.K. 51°35N 0°0 125 A3
Walthamstow U.K. 51°34N 0°1W 125 A3
Waltman U.S.A. 43°4N 107°12W 304 E10
Walton Ky., U.S.A. 38°52N 84°37W 311 F12
Walton N.Y., U.S.A. 42°10N 75°8W 313 D9
Walton-on-Thames U.K. 51°23N 0°24W 125 B1
Walton-on-the-Naze U.K. 51°51N 1°17E 169 F9
Waltonville U.S.A. 38°13N 89°2W 310 F7
Walu Burma 26°28N 98°2E 241 B7
Walvis Bay Namibia 23°0S 14°28E 270 B1
Walvis Ridge Atl. Oc. 26°0S 5°0E 152 J12
Walvisbaai = Walvis Bay Namibia 23°0S 14°28E 270 B1
Walwa Australia 35°59S 147°44E 283 C7
Wamba Équateur, Dem. Rep. of the Congo 1°37S 22°30E 264 C4
Wamba Orientale, Dem. Rep. of the Congo 2°10N 27°57E 268 B2
Wamba Rift Valley, Kenya 0°58N 37°19E 268 B4
Wamba Nigeria 8°57N 8°42E 263 D6
Wamba → Dem. Rep. of the Congo 3°56S 17°12E 265 C3
Wambardi ✪ Australia 16°2S 130°55E 278 C5
Wambeek Belgium 50°55N 4°30E 116 A3
Wamego U.S.A. 39°12N 96°18W 308 F5
Wamena Indonesia 4°4S 138°57E 231 E9
Wampana Karlantijpa ✪ Australia 17°45S 132°10E 278 C5
Wampaya ✪ Australia 17°20S 135°0E 280 B2
Wampsville U.S.A. 43°4N 75°42W 313 C9
Wamsutter U.S.A. 41°40N 107°58W 304 F10
Wamulan Indonesia 3°27S 126°7E 231 E7
Wan Chai China 22°16N 114°10E 122 B2
Wan Chai Lanes Hong Kong, China 122 c2
Wan Hat Burma 20°14N 97°53E 241 E6
Wan Kinghao Burma 21°34N 98°17E 241 E7
Wan Lai-kam Burma 21°21N 98°22E 241 E7
Wan Tup Burma 21°13N 98°42E 241 E7
Wan Xian China 38°47N 115°7E 226 E8
Wana Pakistan 32°20N 69°32E 242 C3
Wanaaring Australia 29°38S 144°9E 281 D3
Wanaka N.Z. 44°42S 169°9E 285 E4
Wanaka, L. N.Z. 44°33S 169°7E 285 E4
Wan'an China 26°26N 114°49E 229 D10
Wanani Comoros Is. 12°20S 43°47E 272 a
Wanapa Neth. Ant. 12°7N 68°14W 322 h
Wanapitei L. Canada 46°45N 80°40W 298 C3
Wanbi Australia 34°46S 140°17E 282 C4
Wandaik Guyana 4°27N 59°35W 329 C6
Wandel Sea = McKinley Sea Arctic 82°0N 0°0 154 A11
Wandérama Ivory C. 8°37N 4°25W 262 D4
Wanderer Zimbabwe 19°36S 30°1E 269 F3
Wandhari Pakistan 27°42N 66°48E 242 F2
Wanding China 24°5N 98°4E 228 E2
Wandle → U.K. 51°27N 0°12W 125 B2
Wando S. Korea 34°21N 126°41E 224 E3
Wandoan Australia 26°5S 149°55E 281 D4
Wandsworth □ U.K. 51°27N 0°11W 125 B2
Wandur Marine △ India 11°30N 92°30E 245 J11
Wanfu China 40°8N 122°38E 224 B1
Wang → Thailand 17°8N 99°2E 236 D2
Wang Center, The Boston, U.S.A. 116 c2
Wang Kai Sudan 9°3N 29°23E 257 F2
Wang Noi Thailand 14°13N 100°44E 236 E3
Wang Saphung Thailand 17°18N 101°46E 236 D3
Wang Thong Thailand 16°50N 100°26E 236 D3
Wanga Dem. Rep. of the Congo 2°58N 29°12E 268 B2
Wangal Indonesia 6°8S 134°9E 231 F8
Wangan Taiwan 23°21N 119°29E 225 C1
Wanganella Australia 35°6S 144°49E 283 C6
Wanganui N.Z. 39°56S 175°3E 284 F4
Wanganui → W. Coast, N.Z. 43°3S 170°26E 285 D5
Wanganui → Wanganui-Manawatu, N.Z. 39°55S 175°4E 284 F4
Wangaratta Australia 36°21S 146°19E 283 D7
Wangary Australia 34°35S 135°29E 281 E2
Wangcang China 32°18N 106°20E 228 A6
Wangcheng China 28°22N 112°49E 229 C9
Wangdu China 38°40N 115°7E 226 E8
Wangdu Phodrang Bhutan 27°28N 89°54E 241 B2
Wangen Germany 47°41N 9°50E 179 H5
Wangerin = Węgorzyno Poland 53°32N 15°33E 184 E2
Wangerooge Germany 53°47N 7°54E 178 B3
Wangiwangi Indonesia 5°22S 123°37E 231 F6
Wangjiang China 30°10N 116°42E 229 B11
Wangjing China 40°0N 116°28E 114 B2
Wangkung Taiwan 23°57N 120°20E 225 C2
Wangmo China 25°11N 106°5E 228 E6
Wangolodougou Ivory C. 9°55N 5°10W 262 D3
Wangqing China 43°12N 129°42E 227 C15
Wani India 20°5N 78°55E 244 D4
Wanigela Papua N. G. 9°21S 149°9E 286 E5
Wanimiyn ✪ Australia 15°55S 130°49E 278 C5
Wanjina Wunggurr Wilinggin ✪ Australia 16°0S 127°0E 278 C4
Wanjung Taiwan 23°43N 121°25E 225 C3
Wankaner India 22°35N 71°0E 242 H4
Wankhede Stadium Mumbai, India 130 c2
Wanless Canada 54°11N 101°21W 297 C8
Wanleweyne Somali Rep. 2°37N 44°54E 267 D5
Wanli Taiwan 25°10N 121°41E 225 A3
Wanluan Taiwan 22°34N 120°34E 225 D2
Wanneroo Australia 31°42S 115°46E 279 F2
Wannian China 28°42N 117°4E 229 C11
Wanning China 18°48N 110°22E 236 C8
Wannoo Billabong Roadhouse Australia 27°25S 115°49E 279 E2
Wannsee Germany 52°25N 13°9E 115 B1
Wanon Niwat Thailand 17°38N 103°46E 236 D4
Wanqinsha China 22°43N 113°33E 219 F10
Wanquan China 40°50N 114°40E 226 D8
Wanrong China 35°25N 110°50E 226 G6
Wansdorf Germany 52°38N 13°5E 115 A1
Wansen = Wiązów Poland 50°50N 17°10E 185 H4
Wanshan China 27°30N 109°12E 228 D7
Wanshan Qundao China 21°57N 113°45E 219 G10
Wanshengchang China 28°57N 106°53E 228 C6
Wanstead N.Z. 40°8S 176°30E 284 G5
Wanstead London, U.K. 51°34N 0°1E 125 A4
Wantage U.K. 51°35N 1°25W 169 F6
Wantan Taiwan 22°35N 120°29E 225 D2
Wantouliu Taiwan 24°1N 120°41E 225 B2
Wanxian China 30°42N 108°20E 228 B7
Wanyin Burma 20°23N 97°15E 241 E6
Wanyuan China 32°4N 108°3E 228 A7
Wanzai Guangdong, China 22°12N 113°31E 219 G10
Wanzai Jiangxi, China 28°7N 114°30E 229 C10
Wapakoneta U.S.A. 40°34N 84°12W 311 D12
Wapato U.S.A. 46°27N 120°25W 304 C3
Wapawekka L. Canada 54°55N 104°40W 297 C8
Wapello U.S.A. 41°11N 91°11W 310 C5
Wapikopa L. Canada 52°56N 87°53W 298 B2
Wapinda Dem. Rep. of the Congo 3°41N 22°48E 264 B4
Wapiti → Canada 55°5N 118°18W 296 B5
Wapping U.K. 51°30N 0°3W 125 A3
Wappingers Falls U.S.A. 41°36N 73°55W 313 E11
Wapsipinicon → U.S.A. 41°44N 90°19W 310 C6
Wapusk △ Canada 57°46N 93°22W 297 B10

War Galoh Somali Rep. 6°17N 47°31E 267 C6
War in the Pacific Nat. Hist. Park △
Guam 13°24N 144°39E 302 d
Warab Sudan 8°8N 28°37E 257 F2
Warab □ Sudan 7°30N 28°30E 257 F2
Warabi Japan 35°49N 139°41E 223 B11
Warakurna Australia 24°59S 128°17E 279 D4
Warangal India 17°58N 79°35E 244 F4
Waraseoni India 21°45N 80°2E 243 J9
Waratah Australia 41°30S 145°30E 281 G4
Waratah B. Australia 38°54S 146°5E 283 E7
Warburg Germany 51°28N 9°11E 178 D5
Warburton Vic.,
Australia 37°47S 145°42E 283 D6
Warburton W. Austral.,
Australia 26°8S 126°35E 279 E4
Warburton ✪ Australia 26°7S 126°34E 279 E4
Warburton → Australia 28°4S 137°28E 281 D2
Warburton Groove
Australia 28°18S 137°8E 281 A2
Warburton Ra. Australia 25°55S 126°28E 279 E4
Ward N.Z. 41°49S 174°11E 285 B9
Ward → Australia 26°28S 146°6E 281 D4
Ward Hunt, C. Papua N. G. 8°2S 148°10E 286 E5
Ward Hunt Str.
Papua N. G. 9°30S 150°0E 286 E6
Ward I. N.Z. 41°18S 174°54E 143 B2
Ward Mt. U.S.A. 37°12N 118°54W 306 H8
Wardang I. Australia 34°30S 137°20E 282 C2
Warden S. Africa 27°50S 29°0E 271 C4
Wardha India 20°45N 78°39E 244 D4
Wardha → India 19°57N 79°11E 244 E4
Wardija Point Malta 36°2N 14°11E 206 E6
Wards I. U.S.A. 40°47N 73°55W 132 B2
Wardsville Canada 42°39N 81°45W 312 D3
Ware Herts., U.K. 51°49N 0°0 169 F8
Ware Mass., U.S.A. 42°16N 72°14W 313 D12
Waregem Belgium 50°53N 3°27E 170 D3
Wareham U.S.A. 41°46N 70°43W 313 E14
Waremme Belgium 50°43N 5°15E 170 D5
Waren Germany 53°31N 12°40E 178 B8
Warendorf Germany 51°57N 8°1E 178 D4
Waresboro U.S.A. 31°15N 82°29W 316 D7
Waria → Papua N. G. 7°49S 147°41E 286 D4
Warialda Australia 29°29S 150°33E 281 D5
Wariap Indonesia 1°30S 134°5E 231 E8
Warin Chamrap
Thailand 15°12N 104°53E 236 E5
Warka Poland 51°47N 21°12E 185 G8
Warkopi Indonesia 1°12S 134°9E 231 E8
Warkworth N.Z. 36°24S 174°41E 284 C3
Warm Baths = Bela Bela
S. Africa 24°51S 28°19E 271 B4
Warm Springs Ga.,
U.S.A. 32°53N 84°41W 316 C5
Warm Springs Nev.,
U.S.A. 38°10N 116°20W 305 G5
Warman Canada 52°19N 106°30W 297 C7
Warmbad = Bela Bela
S. Africa 24°51S 28°19E 271 B4
Warmbad Namibia 28°25S 18°42E 270 C2
Warming I. = Uunartoq Qeqertoq
Greenland 71°33N 21°47W 154 C8
Warmińsko-Mazurskie □
Poland 54°0N 21°0E 184 D8
Warminster Wilts., U.K. 51°12N 2°10W 169 F5
Warminster Pa., U.S.A. 40°12N 75°6W 313 F9
Warmun Australia 17°2S 128°12E 278 C4
Warnberg Germany 48°4N 11°31E 131 B2
Warnemünde Germany 54°10N 12°4E 178 A8
Warner Brothers Studios
U.S.A. 34°9N 118°20W 126 B2
Warner Mts. U.S.A. 41°40N 120°15W 304 F3
Warner Robins U.S.A. 32°37N 83°36W 316 C6
Warnes Bolivia 17°30S 63°10W 331 D5
Warnow → Germany 54°6N 12°9E 178 A8
Waroona Australia 32°50S 115°58E 279 F2
Warora India 20°14N 79°1E 244 D4
Warrabah △ Australia 30°31S 150°56E 283 A10
Warrabri ✪ Australia 21°1S 134°19E 280 C1
Warracknabeal Australia 36°9S 142°26E 282 D5
Warragul Australia 38°10S 145°58E 283 E6
Warrâq el 'Arab Egypt 30°4N 31°11E 117 A2
Warrego → Australia 30°24S 145°21E 281 E4
Warrego Ra. Australia 24°58S 146°0E 280 C4
Warren N.S.W., Australia 31°42S 147°51E 283 A7
Warren Ark., U.S.A. 33°37N 92°4W 314 E8
Warren Ill., U.S.A. 42°29N 90°0W 310 B7
Warren Ind., U.S.A. 40°41N 85°26W 311 D11
Warren Mich., U.S.A. 42°28N 83°1W 311 B13
Warren Minn., U.S.A. 48°12N 96°46W 308 A5
Warren Ohio, U.S.A. 41°14N 80°49W 312 E4
Warren Pa., U.S.A. 41°51N 79°9W 312 E5
Warrenpoint U.K. 54°6N 6°15W 166 B5
Warrensburg Ill., U.S.A. 39°56N 89°4W 310 E7
Warrensburg Mo.,
U.S.A. 38°46N 93°44W 310 F3
Warrensburg N.Y.,
U.S.A. 43°29N 73°46W 313 C11
Warrenton Northern Cape,
S. Africa 28°9S 24°47E 270 C3
Warrenton Ga., U.S.A. 33°24N 82°40W 316 B7
Warrenton Mo., U.S.A. 38°49N 91°9W 310 F5
Warrenton Oreg.,
U.S.A. 46°10N 123°56W 306 D3
Warrenville U.S.A. 33°33N 81°48W 316 B8
Warri Nigeria 5°30N 5°41E 263 D6
Warringal Park Australia 37°45S 145°4E 128 A2
Warrington N.Z. 45°43S 170°35E 285 F5
Warrington Warrington,
U.K. 53°24N 2°35W 168 D5
Warrington Fla., U.S.A. 30°23N 87°17W 317 E2
Warrington □ U.K. 53°24N 2°35W 168 D5
Warriston U.K. 55°58N 3°11W 121 B2
Warrnambool Australia 38°25S 142°30E 282 E5
Warroad U.S.A. 48°54N 95°19W 308 A6
Warrumbungle △
Australia 31°18S 149°1E 283 A8
Warruwi Australia 11°36S 133°20E 280 A1
Warsa Indonesia 0°47S 135°55E 231 E9
Warsak Dam Pakistan 34°11N 71°19E 242 B4
Warsaw = Warszawa
Poland 52°14N 21°0E 142 B2
Warsaw Ill., U.S.A. 40°22N 91°26W 310 D5
Warsaw Ind., U.S.A. 41°14N 85°51W 311 C11
Warsaw Ky., U.S.A. 38°47N 84°54W 311 F12
Warsaw Mo., U.S.A. 38°15N 93°23W 310 F3
Warsaw N.Y., U.S.A. 42°45N 78°8W 312 D6
Warsaw Ohio, U.S.A. 40°20N 82°0W 312 F3
Warshiikh Somali Rep. 2°28N 45°55E 267 D6
Warstein Germany 51°26N 8°22E 178 D4
Warszawa Poland 52°14N 21°0E 142 B2
Warszawa ✈ (WAW)
Poland 52°9N 20°59E 142 B1
Warta Poland 51°43N 18°38E 185 G5
Warta → Poland 52°35N 14°39E 185 F1
Wartenberg Germany 52°34N 13°31E 115 A4
Wartenburg = Barczewo
Poland 53°50N 20°42E 184 E7
Warthbrücken = Koło
Poland 52°14N 18°40E 185 F5
Warthe = Warta →
Poland 52°35N 14°39E 185 F1
Warthen U.S.A. 33°6N 82°48W 316 B7
Warthenau = Zawiercie
Poland 50°30N 19°24E 185 H6
Waru Indonesia 3°30S 130°36E 231 E8
Warud India 21°30N 78°16E 244 D4
Warumungu ✪
Australia 19°15S 134°44E 280 B1
Warwick Queens.,
Australia 28°10S 152°1E 281 D5
Warwick Warks., U.K. 52°18N 1°35W 169 E6
Warwick Ga., U.S.A. 31°50N 83°57W 316 D6
Warwick N.Y., U.S.A. 41°16N 74°22W 313 E10
Warwick R.I., U.S.A. 41°42N 71°28W 313 E13
Warwickshire □ U.K. 52°14N 1°38W 169 E6
Wasaga Beach Canada 44°31N 80°1W 312 B4
Wasagaming Canada 50°39N 99°58W 297 C9
Wasatch Ra. U.S.A. 40°0N 111°30W 304 F8
Wasbank S. Africa 28°15S 30°9E 271 C5
Wasco Calif., U.S.A. 35°36N 119°20W 307 K7
Wasco Oreg., U.S.A. 45°36N 120°42W 304 D3
Wase Nigeria 9°4N 9°54E 263 D6
Waseca U.S.A. 44°5N 93°30W 308 C7
Wasekamio L. Canada 56°45N 108°45W 297 B7
Wasgomuwa △ Sri Lanka 7°45N 81°0E 245 L5
Wash, The U.K. 52°58N 0°20E 168 E8
Washago Canada 44°45N 79°20W 312 B5
Washburn Ill., U.S.A. 40°55N 89°17W 310 D7
Washburn N. Dak.,
U.S.A. 47°17N 101°2W 308 B3
Washburn Wis., U.S.A. 46°40N 90°54W 308 B8
Washim India 20°3N 77°0E 244 D3
Washington Neth. Ant. 12°17N 68°23W 322 h
Washington Tyne & W.,
U.K. 54°55N 1°30W 168 C6
Washington D.C., U.S.A. 38°53N 77°2W 143 B3
Washington Ga., U.S.A. 33°44N 82°44W 316 B7
Washington Ill., U.S.A. 40°42N 89°24W 310 D7
Washington Ind., U.S.A. 38°40N 87°10W 311 F9
Washington Iowa, U.S.A. 41°18N 91°42W 310 C5
Washington Mo., U.S.A. 38°33N 91°1W 310 F5
Washington N.C., U.S.A. 35°33N 77°3W 315 D16
Washington N.J., U.S.A. 40°46N 74°59W 313 F10
Washington Pa., U.S.A. 40°10N 80°15W 312 F4
Washington Utah,
U.S.A. 37°8N 113°31W 305 H7
Washington □ U.S.A. 47°30N 120°30W 304 C3
Washington, Mt.
U.S.A. 44°16N 71°18W 313 B13
Washington Court House
U.S.A. 39°32N 83°26W 311 E13
Washington Dulles Int. ✈ (IAD)
U.S.A. 38°57N 77°27W 143 B1
Washington Heights
U.S.A. 40°51N 73°56W 132 A2
Washington I. U.S.A. 45°23N 86°54W 308 C10
Washington Land
Greenland 80°30N 66°0W 154 A4
Washington Monument
Washington, D.C., U.S.A. 143 b1
Washington Park
U.S.A. 41°47N 87°36W 119 C3
Washington Ronald Reagan Nat. ✈
(DCA) U.S.A. 38°51N 77°2W 143 B3
Washington Slagbaai Nat. Park △
Neth. Ant. 12°16N 68°23W 322 h
Washougal U.S.A. 45°35N 122°21W 306 E4
Washpool △ Australia 29°22S 152°20E 281 D5
Washuk Pakistan 27°42N 64°45E 240 D2
Wasian Indonesia 1°47S 133°19E 231 E8
Wasilków Poland 53°12N 23°13E 185 E10
Wasilla U.S.A. 61°35N 149°26W 303 F10
Wasini Marine ⌂ Kenya 4°33S 39°14E 268 C4
Wasior Indonesia 2°43S 134°30E 231 E8
Wāsiṭ □ Iraq 32°50N 45°50E 213 F11
Wasjabo Suriname 5°13N 57°11W 329 B6
Waskaganish Canada 51°30N 78°40W 298 B4
Waskaiowaka L. Canada 56°33N 96°23W 297 B9
Waskesiu Lake Canada 53°55N 106°5W 297 C7
Wassaw I. U.S.A. 31°53N 80°58W 316 D9
Wassaw Sd. U.S.A. 31°55N 80°55W 316 D9
Wasserburg Germany 48°3N 12°14E 179 G8
Wasserkuppe Germany 50°29N 9°55E 178 E5
Wassy France 48°30N 4°58E 173 D11
Wasu Papua N. G. 5°58S 147°12E 286 C4
Wasua Papua N. G. 8°18S 142°52E 286 E2
Waswanipi Canada 49°40N 76°29W 298 C4
Waswanipi, L. Canada 49°35N 76°40W 298 C4
Wat Pho Bangkok, Thailand 113 b1
Watagans △ Australia 33°0S 151°28E 283 B9
Watam Papua N. G. 3°55S 144°33E 286 B3
Watampone Indonesia 4°29S 120°25E 231 E6
Watamu Kenya 3°23S 40°0E 268 C5
Watarrka △ Australia 24°20S 131°30E 278 D5
Watee Solomon Is. 10°30S 162°2E 287 N12
Watenstadt-Salzgitter = Salzgitter
Germany 52°9N 10°19E 178 C6
Water of Leith → U.K. 55°59N 3°10W 121 B1
Water Park Pt. Australia 22°56S 150°47E 280 C5
Water Tower Place Chicago, U.S.A. 119 a2
Water Valley U.S.A. 34°10N 89°38W 315 D10
Waterberg Plateau ⌂
Namibia 20°25S 17°18E 270 B2
Waterberge S. Africa 24°10S 28°0E 271 B4
Waterbury Conn., U.S.A. 41°33N 73°3W 313 E11
Waterbury Vt., U.S.A. 44°20N 72°46W 313 B12
Waterbury L. Canada 58°10N 104°22W 297 B8
Waterdown Canada 43°20N 79°53W 312 C5
Wateree → U.S.A. 33°45N 80°37W 316 B9
Waterford Canada 42°56N 80°17W 312 D4
Waterford Waterford,
Ireland 52°15N 7°8W 166 D4
Waterford Calif., U.S.A. 37°38N 120°46W 306 H6
Waterford Mich., U.S.A. 42°45N 83°32W 311 B13
Waterford Pa., U.S.A. 41°57N 79°59W 312 E5
Waterford Wis., U.S.A. 42°46N 88°13W 311 B8
Waterford □ Ireland 52°10N 7°40W 166 D4
Waterford Harbour Ireland 52°8N 6°58W 166 D5
Watergraafsmeer Neths. 52°21N 4°56E 112 A2
Waterhen L. Canada 52°10N 99°40W 297 C9
Waterland Neths. 52°26N 4°58E 112 A2
Waterloo Belgium 50°43N 4°25E 116 B2
Waterloo Ont., Canada 43°30N 80°32W 312 C4
Waterloo Qué., Canada 45°22N 72°32W 313 A12
Waterloo Wellington,
N.Z. 41°13S 174°56E 143 B2
Waterloo S. Leone 8°26N 13°8W 262 D2
Waterloo Trin. & Tob. 10°28N 61°28W 323 t
Waterloo Ill., U.S.A. 38°20N 90°9W 310 F6
Waterloo Ind., U.S.A. 41°26N 85°1W 311 C11
Waterloo Iowa, U.S.A. 42°30N 92°21W 310 B4
Waterloo N.Y., U.S.A. 42°54N 76°52W 312 D8
Waterloo Wis., U.S.A. 43°11N 88°59W 310 A8
Waterloo International London, U.K. 125 b4
Waterman U.S.A. 41°46N 88°47W 311 C8
Watermael-Boitsfort
Belgium 50°48N 4°25E 116 B2
Watersmeet U.S.A. 46°16N 89°11W 308 B9
Waterton Lakes △
Canada 48°45N 115°0W 296 D6
Watertown Conn., U.S.A. 41°36N 73°7W 313 E11
Watertown Fla., U.S.A. 30°11N 82°36W 316 E7
Watertown Mass., U.S.A. 42°22N 71°10W 116 A1
Watertown N.Y., U.S.A. 43°59N 75°55W 313 C9
Watertown S. Dak., U.S.A. 44°54N 97°7W 308 C5
Watertown Wis., U.S.A. 43°12N 88°43W 311 A8
Waterval-Boven S. Africa 25°40S 30°18E 271 C5
Waterville Qué., Canada 45°16N 71°54W 313 A13
Waterville Maine,
U.S.A. 44°33N 69°38W 309 C19
Waterville N.Y., U.S.A. 42°56N 75°23W 313 D9
Waterville Pa., U.S.A. 41°19N 77°21W 312 E7
Waterville Wash., U.S.A. 47°39N 120°4W 304 C3
Watervliet Mich., U.S.A. 42°11N 86°18W 311 B10
Watervliet N.Y., U.S.A. 42°44N 73°42W 313 D11
Wates Indonesia 7°51S 110°10E 235 D4
Watford Ont., Canada 42°57N 81°53W 312 D3
Watford Herts., U.K. 51°40N 0°24W 169 F7
Watford City U.S.A. 47°48N 103°17W 308 B2
Wathaman → Canada 57°16N 102°59W 297 B8
Wathaman L. Canada 56°58N 103°44W 297 B8
Watheroo Australia 30°15S 116°5E 279 F2
Watheroo △ Australia 30°19S 115°48E 279 F2
Wating China 35°40N 106°38E 226 G4
Watir, W. → Egypt 29°0N 34°40E 251 K5
Watkins Glen U.S.A. 42°23N 76°52W 312 D8
Watkinsville U.S.A. 33°52N 83°25W 316 B6
Watling I. = San Salvador I.
Bahamas 24°0N 74°40W 321 B5
Watom I. Papua N. G. 4°7S 152°4E 286 C7
Watonga U.S.A. 35°51N 98°25W 314 D5
Watrous Sask., Canada 51°40N 105°25W 297 C7
Watrous N. Mex.,
U.S.A. 35°48N 104°59W 305 J11
Watsa Dem. Rep. of the Congo 3°4N 29°30E 268 B2
Watseka U.S.A. 40°47N 87°44W 311 D9
Watsi Kenga
Dem. Rep. of the Congo 0°49S 20°34E 264 C4
Watson Canada 52°10N 104°30W 297 C8
Watson Lake Canada 60°6N 128°49W 296 A3
Watsonia Australia 37°43S 145°5E 128 A2
Watsontown U.S.A. 41°5N 76°52W 312 E8
Watsonville U.S.A. 36°55N 121°45W 306 J5
Watt Mt. Dominica 15°19N 61°19W 323 k
Wattiwarriganna Cr. →
Australia 28°57S 136°10E 281 D2
Wattwil Switz. 47°18N 9°6E 179 H5
Watu Dem. Rep. of the Congo 3°18S 20°3E 264 C4
Watuata = Batuata
Indonesia 6°12S 122°42E 231 F6
Watubela, Kepulauan
Indonesia 4°28S 131°35E 231 E8
Watubela Is. = Watubela,
Kepulauan Indonesia 4°28S 131°35E 231 E8
Wau = Wâw Sudan 7°45N 28°1E 257 F2
Wau Papua N. G. 7°21S 146°47E 286 D4
Waubamik Canada 45°27N 80°1W 312 A4
Waubay U.S.A. 45°20N 97°18W 308 C5
Waubra Australia 37°21S 143°39E 282 D5
Wauchope N.S.W.,
Australia 31°28S 152°45E 283 A10
Wauchope N. Terr.,
Australia 20°36S 134°15E 280 C1
Wauchula U.S.A. 27°33N 81°49W 317 H8
Waukarlycarly, L.
Australia 21°18S 121°56E 278 D3
Waukeenah U.S.A. 30°25N 83°57W 316 E6
Waukegan U.S.A. 42°22N 87°50W 311 B9
Waukesha U.S.A. 43°1N 88°14W 311 B8
Waukon U.S.A. 43°16N 91°29W 308 D8
Waupaca U.S.A. 44°21N 89°5W 308 C9
Waupun U.S.A. 43°38N 88°44W 308 D9
Waurika U.S.A. 34°10N 98°0W 314 D6
Wausau Fla., U.S.A. 30°38N 85°35W 316 E4
Wausau Wis., U.S.A. 44°58N 89°38W 308 C9
Wauseon U.S.A. 41°33N 84°8W 311 C12
Wautoma U.S.A. 44°4N 89°18W 308 C9
Wauwatosa U.S.A. 43°2N 88°0W 311 A9
Wave Hill = Kalkarindji
Australia 17°30S 130°47E 278 C5
Wave Rock ⌂ Australia 32°26S 118°53E 279 F2
Waveland U.S.A. 39°53N 87°3W 311 E9
Waveney → U.K. 52°35N 1°39E 169 E9
Waverley N.S.W.,
Australia 33°53S 151°15E 139 B2
Waverley N.Z. 39°46S 174°37E 284 F3
Waverley Gauteng, S. Africa 26°7S 28°4E 123 A2
Waverley Mass., U.S.A. 42°23N 71°10W 116 A1
Waverley Station Edinburgh, U.K. 121 b3
Waverly Ala., U.S.A. 32°44N 85°35W 316 C4
Waverly Fla., U.S.A. 27°59N 81°37W 317 H8
Waverly Ga., U.S.A. 31°6N 81°43W 316 D8
Waverly Ill., U.S.A. 39°36N 89°57W 310 E7
Waverly Iowa, U.S.A. 42°44N 92°29W 310 B4
Waverly Mo., U.S.A. 39°13N 93°31W 310 E3
Waverly N.Y., U.S.A. 42°1N 76°32W 313 E8
Waverly Hall U.S.A. 32°41N 84°44W 316 C5
Wavre Belgium 50°43N 4°38E 170 D4
Waw Burma 17°28N 96°41E 241 G6
Wâw Sudan 7°45N 28°1E 257 F2
Wāw al Kabīr Libya 25°20N 16°43E 258 C3
Wāw an Nāmūs Libya 24°55N 17°46E 258 D3
Wawa Ont., Canada 47°59N 84°47W 298 C3
Wawa Nigeria 9°54N 4°27E 263 D5
Wawa Sudan 20°30N 30°22E 256 C3
Wawanesa Canada 49°36N 99°40W 297 D9
Wawasee, L. U.S.A. 41°24N 85°42W 311 C11
Wawer Poland 52°13N 21°8E 142 B2
Wawoi → Papua N. G. 7°48S 143°16E 286 D2
Wawona U.S.A. 37°32N 119°39W 306 H7
Wawrzyszew Poland 52°17N 20°53E 142 B1
Waxahachie U.S.A. 32°24N 96°51W 314 E6
Waxxari China 38°42N 87°19E 217 E11
Way, L. Australia 26°45S 120°16E 279 E3
Way Kambas △ Indonesia 4°54S 105°43E 234 C3
Waya Fiji 17°19S 177°10E 287 A1
Waycross U.S.A. 31°13N 82°21W 316 D7
Wayi Sudan 5°8N 30°10E 257 F3
Wayland Mich., U.S.A. 42°40N 85°39W 311 B11
Wayland N.Y., U.S.A. 42°34N 77°35W 312 D7
Wayne Nebr., U.S.A. 42°14N 97°1W 308 D5
Wayne W. Va., U.S.A. 38°13N 82°27W 309 F12
Wayne City U.S.A. 38°21N 88°35W 311 F8
Wayne County, Detroit ✈ (DTW)
U.S.A. 42°13N 83°21W 311 B13
Wayne Lakes U.S.A. 40°1N 84°40W 311 D12
Waynesboro Ga., U.S.A. 33°6N 82°1W 316 B7
Waynesboro Miss.,
U.S.A. 31°40N 88°39W 315 F10
Waynesboro Pa., U.S.A. 39°45N 77°35W 309 F15
Waynesboro Va., U.S.A. 38°4N 78°53W 309 F14
Waynesburg U.S.A. 39°54N 80°11W 309 F13
Waynesville Mo., U.S.A. 37°50N 92°12W 310 G4
Waynesville N.C.,
U.S.A. 35°28N 82°58W 315 D13
Waynesville Ohio, U.S.A. 39°32N 84°5W 311 E12
Waynoka U.S.A. 36°35N 98°53W 314 C5
Wayside U.S.A. 33°4N 83°37W 316 B6
Waza Afghan. 33°22N 69°26E 240 B3
Waza △ Cameroon 11°15N 14°38E 259 F2
Wazikhwah Afghan. 32°11N 68°21E 240 B3
Wāzin Libya 31°58N 10°40E 258 B2
Wazirabad Delhi, India 28°43N 77°13E 120 A2
Wazirabad Pakistan 32°30N 74°8E 242 C6
Wazīristan Pakistan 33°0N 70°0E 242 C4
Waẓīrīya Iraq 33°22N 44°23E 113 A2
Wazirpur India 28°41N 77°10E 120 A2
Wda → Poland 53°25N 18°29E 184 E5
Wdi Indonesia 5°51N 95°18E 234 A1
Wé N. Cal. 20°55S 167°16E 288 d
Weald, The U.K. 51°4N 0°20E 169 F8
Wealdstone U.K. 51°35N 0°17W 125 A1
Wear Papua N. G. 8°37S 141°8E 286 E1
Wear → U.K. 54°55N 1°23W 168 C6
Weatherford Okla.,
U.S.A. 35°32N 98°43W 314 D5
Weatherford Tex., U.S.A. 32°46N 97°48W 314 E6
Weaubleau U.S.A. 37°54N 93°32W 310 G3
Weaverville U.S.A. 40°44N 122°56W 304 F2
Webb City U.S.A. 37°9N 94°28W 308 G6
Webequie Canada 52°59N 87°21W 298 B2
Weber N.Z. 40°24S 176°20E 284 G5
Weber Basin Pac. Oc. 6°0S 131°0E 276 B5
Webo = Nyaake Liberia 4°52N 7°37W 262 E3
Webster Mass., U.S.A. 42°3N 71°53W 313 D13
Webster N.Y., U.S.A. 43°13N 77°26W 312 C7
Webster S. Dak., U.S.A. 45°20N 97°31W 308 C5
Webster City U.S.A. 42°28N 93°49W 310 B3
Webster Springs U.S.A. 38°29N 80°25W 309 F13
Webuye Kenya 0°37N 34°46E 268 B3
Weda Indonesia 0°21N 127°50E 231 D7
Weda, Teluk Indonesia 0°20N 128°0E 231 D7
Weddell Abyssal Plain
S. Ocean 65°0S 20°0W 151 C2
Weddell I. Falk. Is. 51°50S 61°0W 153 f
Weddell Sea Antarctica 72°30S 40°0W 151 D1
Wedderburn Australia 36°26S 143°33E 282 D5
Weddin Mts. △ Australia 33°59S 148°0E 283 C8
Wedding Germany 52°32N 13°21E 115 A3
Wedel Germany 53°34N 9°42E 178 B5
Wedemark Germany 52°32N 9°43E 178 C5
Wedgeport Canada 43°44N 65°59W 299 D6
Wednesday I. Australia 10°31S 142°16E 286 F2
Wedowee U.S.A. 33°19N 85°29W 316 B4
Wedza Zimbabwe 18°40S 31°33E 269 F3
Wee Waa Australia 30°11S 149°26E 281 E4
Weed U.S.A. 41°25N 122°23W 304 F2
Weed Heights U.S.A. 38°59N 119°13W 306 G7
Weedsport U.S.A. 43°2N 76°33W 313 C8
Weedville U.S.A. 41°17N 78°30W 312 E6
Weehawken New York, U.S.A. 132 b1
Weeki Wachee U.S.A. 28°32N 82°35W 317 G7
Weel Shimbirro
Somali Rep. 2°23N 44°14E 267 D5
Weenen S. Africa 28°48S 30°7E 271 C5
Weener Germany 53°9N 7°20E 178 B3
Weert Neths. 51°15N 5°43E 170 C5
Weesp Neths. 52°18N 5°2E 112 B3
Węgierska-Górka Poland 49°36N 19°7E 185 J6
Węgliniec Poland 51°18N 15°10E 185 G2
Węgorzewo Poland 54°13N 21°43E 184 D8
Węgorzyno Poland 53°32N 15°33E 184 E2
Węgrów Poland 52°24N 22°0E 185 F9
Wehda □ Sudan 8°30N 30°0E 257 F3
Wei He → Hebei, China 36°10N 115°45E 226 F8
Wei He → Shaanxi,
China 34°38N 110°15E 226 G6
Weichang China 41°58N 117°49E 227 D9
Weichuan China 34°20N 113°59E 226 G7
Weida Germany 50°46N 12°2E 178 E8
Weiden Germany 49°41N 12°10E 179 F8
Weidling Austria 48°17N 16°18E 142 A1
Weidlingbach Austria 48°16N 16°15E 142 A1
Weifang China 36°44N 119°7E 227 F10
Weihai China 37°30N 122°6E 227 F12
Weil Germany 47°35N 7°37E 179 H3
Weilburg Germany 50°28N 8°17E 178 E4
Weilheim Germany 47°50N 11°9E 179 H7
Weimar Germany 50°58N 11°19E 178 E7
Weinan China 34°31N 109°29E 226 G5
Weingarten Germany 49°3N 8°31E 179 F4
Weinheim Germany 49°32N 8°39E 179 F4
Weining China 26°50N 104°17E 228 D5
Weipa Australia 12°40S 141°50E 280 A3
Weir → Queens.,
Australia 28°20S 149°50E 281 D4
Weir → Man., Canada 56°54N 93°21W 297 B10
Weir, L. U.S.A. 29°0N 81°57W 317 F8
Weir River Canada 56°49N 94°6W 297 B10
Weirsdale U.S.A. 28°59N 81°55W 317 G8
Weirton U.S.A. 40°24N 80°35W 312 F4
Weiser U.S.A. 44°15N 116°58W 304 D5
Weishan Shandong, China 34°47N 117°5E 227 G9
Weishan Yunnan, China 25°12N 100°20E 228 E3
Weissenburg Germany 49°2N 10°58E 179 F6
Weissenfels Germany 51°11N 12°0E 178 D7
Weissensee Germany 52°33N 13°27E 115 A3
Weisskirchen = Hranice
Czech Rep. 49°34N 17°45E 181 B10
Weisswasser Germany 51°30N 14°36E 178 D10
Weistritz = Bystrzyca →
Dolnośląskie, Poland 51°12N 16°55E 185 G3
Weistritz = Bystrzyca → Lubelskie,
Poland 51°21N 22°46E 185 G9
Wéitra Austria 48°41N 14°54E 180 C7
Weixi China 27°10N 99°10E 228 D2
Weixin China 27°48N 105°3E 228 D5
Weiyuan China 35°7N 104°10E 226 G3
Weiz Austria 47°13N 15°39E 180 D8
Weizhou Dao China 21°0N 109°5E 228 G7
Wejherowo Poland 54°35N 18°12E 184 D5
Wekusko L. Canada 54°40N 99°50W 297 C9
Wekuwa Pt. Neth. Ant. 12°13N 68°24W 322 h
Welch U.S.A. 37°26N 81°35W 309 G13
Welchman Hall Barbados 13°11N 59°34W 323 r
Weldya Ethiopia 11°50N 39°34E 257 E4
Welega Ethiopia 9°25N 34°20E 257 F3
Welford △ Australia 25°5S 143°16E 280 D3
Weligama Sri Lanka 5°58N 80°25E 245 M5
Welkite Ethiopia 8°15N 37°42E 257 F4
Welkom S. Africa 28°0S 26°46E 270 C4
Welland Canada 43°0N 79°15W 312 D5
Welland → U.K. 52°51N 0°5W 169 E7
Wellawaya Sri Lanka 6°44N 81°6E 245 L5
Welles Harbor
Midway Is. 28°13N 177°25W 302 c
Wellesley Hills U.S.A. 42°18N 71°16W 116 B1
Wellesley Is. Australia 16°42S 139°30E 280 B2
Wellesley Islands ✪
Australia 16°32S 139°23E 280 B2
Welling U.K. 51°27N 0°6E 125 B4
Wellingborough U.K. 52°19N 0°41W 169 E7
Wellington N.S.W.,
Australia 32°35S 148°59E 283 B8
Wellington Ont., Canada 43°57N 77°20W 312 C7
Wellington N.Z. 41°19S 174°46E 143 B1
Wellington Western Cape,
S. Africa 33°38S 19°1E 270 D2
Wellington Somst., U.K. 50°58N 3°13W 169 G4
Wellington Telford & Wrekin,
U.K. 52°42N 2°30W 169 E5
Wellington Colo., U.S.A. 40°42N 105°0W 304 F11
Wellington Kans., U.S.A. 37°16N 97°24W 308 G5
Wellington Mass., U.S.A. 42°24N 71°5W 116 A2
Wellington Mo., U.S.A. 39°8N 93°59W 310 E3
Wellington Nev., U.S.A. 38°45N 119°23W 306 G7
Wellington Ohio, U.S.A. 41°10N 82°13W 312 E2
Wellington Tex., U.S.A. 34°51N 100°13W 314 D4
Wellington □ N.Z. 41°0S 175°30E 284 G4
Wellington, I. Chile 49°30S 75°0W 336 C2
Wellington, L. Australia 38°6S 147°20E 283 E7
Wellington Chan. Canada 75°0N 93°0W 295 C13
Wellington Int. ✈ (WLE)
N.Z. 41°20S 174°50E 143 B1
Wellman U.S.A. 41°28N 91°50W 310 C5
Wells Somst., U.K. 51°13N 2°39W 169 F5
Wells Maine, U.S.A. 43°20N 70°35W 313 C14
Wells N.Y., U.S.A. 43°24N 74°17W 313 C10
Wells Nev., U.S.A. 41°7N 114°58W 304 F6
Wells, L. Australia 26°44S 123°15E 279 E3
Wells, Mt. Australia 17°25S 127°8E 278 C4
Wells Fargo Center Los Angeles, U.S.A. 127 b1
Wells Gray ⌂ Canada 52°30N 120°15W 296 C4
Wells-next-the-Sea U.K. 52°57N 0°51E 168 E8
Wells River U.S.A. 44°9N 72°4W 313 B12
Wellsboro U.S.A. 41°45N 77°18W 312 E7
Wellsburg U.S.A. 40°16N 80°37W 312 F4
Wellsford N.Z. 36°16S 174°32E 284 C3
Wellston = Warner Robins
U.S.A. 32°37N 83°36W 316 C6
Wellsville Mo., U.S.A. 39°4N 91°34W 310 E5
Wellsville N.Y., U.S.A. 42°7N 77°57W 312 D7
Wellsville Ohio, U.S.A. 40°36N 80°39W 312 F4
Wellsville Utah, U.S.A. 41°38N 111°56W 304 F8
Wellton U.S.A. 32°40N 114°8W 305 K6
Welmel, Wabi → Ethiopia 5°38N 40°47E 257 F5
Welo Ethiopia 11°50N 39°48E 257 E4
Welo Somali Rep. 9°25N 48°55E 267 C6
Wels Austria 48°9N 14°1E 180 C7
Welshpool Vic., Australia 38°42S 146°26E 283 E7
Welshpool Powys, U.K. 52°39N 3°8W 169 E4
Weltevreden Park
S. Africa 26°7S 27°56E 123 A1
Welungen = Wieluń
Poland 51°15N 18°34E 185 G5
Welwitschia = Khorixas
Namibia 20°16S 14°59E 270 B1
Welwyn Garden City
U.K. 51°48N 0°12W 169 F7
Wem U.K. 52°52N 2°44W 168 E5
Wembere → Tanzania 4°10S 34°15E 268 C3
Wembley U.K. 51°33N 0°17W 125 A2
Wemindji Canada 53°0N 78°49W 298 B4
Wemmel Belgium 50°55N 4°18E 116 A1
Wemmer Pan S. Africa 26°13S 28°3E 123 B2
Wemyss Canada 44°52N 76°23W 313 B8
Wen Xian China 34°55N 113°5E 226 G7
Wenatchee U.S.A. 47°25N 120°19W 304 C3
Wenceslas Square = Vaclavské
náměstí Prague, Czech Rep. 135 b2
Wenchang China 19°38N 110°42E 236 C8
Wencheng China 27°46N 120°4E 229 D13
Wenchi Ghana 7°46N 2°8W 262 D4
Wenchow = Wenzhou
China 28°0N 120°38E 229 D13
Wenchuan China 31°22N 103°35E 228 B4
Wenden U.S.A. 33°49N 113°33W 307 M13
Wendeng China 37°15N 122°5E 227 F12
Wendenschloss Germany 52°24N 13°35E 115 B4
Wendesi Indonesia 2°30S 134°17E 231 E8
Wendo Ethiopia 6°40N 38°27E 257 F4
Wendover U.S.A. 40°44N 114°2W 304 F6
Weng'an China 27°5N 107°25E 228 D6
Wengcheng China 24°22N 113°50E 229 E9
Wengen Switz. 46°37N 7°55E 173 F14
Wengyuan China 24°20N 114°9E 229 E10
Wenjiang China 30°44N 103°55E 228 B4
Wenling China 28°21N 121°20E 229 C13
Wenlock → Australia 12°2S 141°55E 286 G1
Wennington U.K. 51°30N 0°12E 125 A5
Weno Pac. Oc. 7°27N 151°52E 287 T18
Wenona U.S.A. 41°3N 89°3W 310 C7
Wenshan China 23°20N 104°18E 228 F5
Wenshang China 35°45N 116°30E 226 G9
Wenshui China 37°26N 112°1E 226 F7
Wensleydale U.K. 54°17N 2°0W 168 C5
Wensu China 41°15N 80°10E 217 D10
Wensum → U.K. 52°40N 1°15E 168 E8
Wentworth Australia 34°2S 141°54E 282 C4
Wentzel L. Canada 59°2N 114°28W 296 B6
Wentzville U.S.A. 38°49N 90°51W 310 F6
Wenut Indonesia 3°11S 133°19E 231 E8
Wenxi China 35°20N 111°10E 226 G6
Wenxian China 32°43N 104°36E 226 H3
Wenzhou China 28°0N 120°38E 229 D13
Weott U.S.A. 40°20N 123°55W 304 F2
Wepener S. Africa 29°42S 27°3E 270 C4
Werda Botswana 25°24S 23°15E 270 C3
Werdau Germany 50°44N 12°22E 178 E8
Werder Ethiopia 6°58N 45°1E 267 C6
Werder Brandenburg,
Germany 52°23N 12°55E 178 C8
Werdohl Germany 51°15N 7°46E 178 D3
Wereilu Ethiopia 10°40N 39°28E 257 E4
Weri Indonesia 3°10S 132°38E 231 E8
Werneck Germany 49°58N 10°5E 179 F6
Werneuchen Germany 52°38N 13°44E 115 A5
Wernigerode Germany 51°50N 10°47E 178 D6
Werra → Germany 51°24N 9°39E 178 D5
Werribee Australia 37°54S 144°40E 282 D6
Werrikimbe △
Australia 31°11S 152°15E 283 A10
Werrimull Australia 34°25S 141°38E 282 C4
Werris Creek Australia 31°18S 150°38E 283 A9
Werschetz = Vršac Serbia 45°8N 21°20E 182 E6
Wertach → Germany 48°22N 10°54E 179 G6
Wertheim Germany 49°45N 9°32E 179 F5
Wertingen Germany 48°33N 10°41E 179 G6
Wesel Germany 51°39N 6°37E 178 D2
Weser → Germany 53°36N 8°28E 178 B4
Weser-Ems □ Germany 53°0N 7°30E 178 C3
Weserbergland Germany 52°12N 9°7E 178 C5
Weserbergland Schaumburg
Hameln ⌂ Germany 52°8N 9°20E 178 C5
Wesermünde = Bremerhaven
Germany 53°33N 8°36E 178 B4
Wesiri Indonesia 7°30S 126°30E 231 F7
Weslaco U.S.A. 26°10N 97°58W 314 H6
Weslemkoon L. Canada 45°2N 77°25W 312 A7
Wesley Dominica 15°33N 61°18W 323 k
Wesleyville Nfld. & L.,
Canada 49°9N 53°33W 299 C9
Wesleyville Pa., U.S.A. 42°9N 80°1W 312 D4
Wessel, C. Australia 10°59S 136°46E 280 A2
Wessel Is. Australia 11°10S 136°45E 280 A2
Wesselburen Germany 54°13N 8°54E 178 A4
Wessington Springs
U.S.A. 44°5N 98°34W 308 C4
West U.S.A. 31°48N 97°6W 314 F6
West → U.S.A. 42°52N 72°33W 313 D12
West Allis U.S.A. 43°1N 88°0W 311 B8
West Antarctica
Antarctica 80°0S 90°0W 151 D15
West Baines →
Australia 15°38S 129°59E 278 C4
West Bank ■ Asia 32°6N 35°13E 251 F6
West Bend U.S.A. 43°25N 88°11W 308 D9
West Bengal □ India 23°0N 88°0E 243 H13
West Berkshire □ U.K. 51°25N 1°17W 169 F6
West Beskids = Západné Beskydy
Europe 49°30N 19°0E 181 B12
West Branch U.S.A. 44°17N 84°14W 309 C11
West Branch Susquehanna →
U.S.A. 40°53N 76°48W 313 F8
West Bromwich U.K. 52°32N 1°59W 169 E6
West Burra U.K. 60°5N 1°21W 167 A7
West Canada Cr. →
U.S.A. 43°1N 74°58W 313 C10
West Caroline Basin
Pac. Oc. 4°0N 138°0E 288 G5
West Carrollton U.S.A. 39°40N 84°17W 311 E12
West Chazy U.S.A. 44°49N 73°28W 313 B11
West Chester U.S.A. 39°58N 75°36W 313 G9
West Chicago U.S.A. 41°53N 88°12W 311 C8
West Coast □ N.Z. 43°15S 170°30E 285 D5
West Coast Namibia 21°53S 14°14E 270 B1
West Coast △ S. Africa 33°13S 18°0E 270 D2
West Columbia S.C.,
U.S.A. 33°59N 81°4W 316 B8
West Columbia Tex.,
U.S.A. 29°9N 95°39W 314 G7
West Covina U.S.A. 34°4N 117°54W 307 L9
West Des Moines U.S.A. 41°35N 93°43W 310 C3
West Don → Canada 43°44N 79°24W 141 A2
West Drayton U.K. 51°30N 0°28W 125 A1
West Dunbartonshire □
U.K. 55°59N 4°30W 167 F4
West End Bahamas 26°41N 78°58W 320 A4
West End Boston, U.S.A. 116 b1
West End Village Anguilla 18°10N 63°10W 322 a
West Falkland Falk. Is. 51°40S 60°0W 153 f
West Fargo U.S.A. 46°52N 96°54W 308 B5
West Fiji Basin Pac. Oc. 17°0S 173°0E 288 J9
West Fjord = Vestfjorden
Norway 67°55N 14°0E 160 C16
West Fork Trinity →
U.S.A. 32°48N 96°54W 314 E6
West Frankfort U.S.A. 37°54N 88°55W 310 G8
West Grand L. U.S.A. 45°14N 67°51W 309 C20
West Green U.S.A. 31°37N 82°44W 316 D7
West Ham U.K. 51°31N 0°1E 125 A4
West Harrow U.K. 51°34N 0°21W 125 A1
West Hartford U.S.A. 41°45N 72°44W 313 E12
West Haven U.S.A. 41°17N 72°57W 313 E12
West Hazleton U.S.A. 40°58N 76°0W 313 F9
West Heath U.K. 51°29N 0°7E 125 B4
West Helena U.S.A. 34°33N 90°38W 315 D9
West Hill Canada 43°46N 79°10W 141 A3
West Hollywood U.S.A. 34°5N 118°21W 126 B2
West Hurley U.S.A. 41°59N 74°7W 313 E10
West I. India 13°35N 92°54E 245 H11
West Ice Shelf Antarctica 67°0S 85°0E 151 C7
West Indies Cent. Amer. 15°0N 65°0W 321 D7
West Jefferson U.S.A. 39°57N 83°17W 311 E13
West Jordan U.S.A. 40°36N 111°56W 304 F8
West Kensington London, U.K. 125 c1
West Kilburn London, U.K. 125 a1
West Lafayette U.S.A. 40°27N 86°55W 311 D10
West Lamma Channel
China 22°14N 114°4E 122 B1
West Liberty Iowa,
U.S.A. 41°34N 91°16W 310 C5
West Liberty Ky., U.S.A. 37°55N 83°16W 311 G13
West Liberty Ohio,
U.S.A. 40°15N 83°45W 311 D13
West Linn U.S.A. 45°21N 122°36W 306 E4
West Lorne Canada 42°36N 81°36W 312 D3
West Los Angeles, Univ. of
U.S.A. 34°7N 118°23W 126 C2
West Lothian □ U.K. 55°54N 3°36W 167 F5
West Lunga → Zambia 13°6S 24°39E 265 E4
West Lunga △ Zambia 12°49S 24°47E 265 E4
West MacDonnell △
Australia 23°38S 132°59E 278 D5
West Mariana Basin
Pac. Oc. 15°0N 137°0E 288 F5
West Medford U.S.A. 42°25N 71°7W 116 A2
West Memphis U.S.A. 35°8N 90°10W 315 D9
West Miami U.S.A. 25°45N 80°17W 128 B1
West Midlands □ U.K. 52°26N 2°0W 169 E6
West Mifflin U.S.A. 40°21N 79°52W 312 F5
West Milford U.S.A. 41°8N 74°22W 313 E10
West Milton Ohio,
U.S.A. 39°58N 84°20W 311 E12
West Milton Pa., U.S.A. 41°1N 76°50W 312 E8
West Molesey U.K. 51°24N 0°22W 125 B1
West Monroe U.S.A. 32°31N 92°9W 314 E8
West New Britain □
Papua N. G. 5°0S 149°30E 286 C5
West New York New York, U.S.A. 132 a1
West Newton U.S.A. 40°14N 79°46W 312 F5
West Nicholson Zimbabwe 21°2S 29°20E 269 G2
West Odessa U.S.A. 31°50N 102°30W 314 F3
West of Twin Peaks
U.S.A. 37°43N 122°27W 136 B2
West Palm Beach U.S.A. 26°43N 80°3W 317 J9
West Palm Beach Canal
U.S.A. 26°40N 80°15W 317 J9
West Park S. Africa 26°9S 27°59E 123 A1
West Pensacola U.S.A. 30°25N 87°16W 317 E2
West Plains U.S.A. 36°44N 91°51W 308 G8
West Point Ga., U.S.A. 32°53N 85°11W 316 C4
West Point Iowa, U.S.A. 40°43N 91°27W 310 D5
West Point Ky., U.S.A. 37°59N 85°57W 311 G11
West Point Miss., U.S.A. 33°36N 88°39W 315 E10
West Point N.Y., U.S.A. 41°24N 73°58W 313 E11
West Point Nebr., U.S.A. 41°51N 96°43W 308 E5
West Point Va., U.S.A. 37°32N 76°48W 309 G15
West Point I. U.S.A. 33°8N 85°0W 316 B4
West Pt. = Ouest, Pte. de l'
Canada 49°52N 64°40W 299 C7
West Pt. Australia 35°1S 135°56E 282 C1
West Ra. Papua N. G. 4°15S 141°30E 286 C1
West Road → Canada 53°18N 122°53W 296 C4
West Rouge Canada 43°48N 79°7W 141 A4
West Roxbury U.S.A. 42°16N 71°9W 116 B2
West Rutland U.S.A. 43°36N 73°3W 313 C11
West Salem U.S.A. 38°31N 88°1W 311 F8
West Schelde → Westerschelde →
Neths. 51°25N 3°25E 170 C3
West Seneca U.S.A. 42°51N 78°48W 312 D6
West Sepik □ Papua N. G. 3°30S 142°0E 286 B2
West Siberian Plain Russia 62°0N 75°0E 210 B9
West Springfield U.S.A. 38°47N 77°13W 143 C2
West Sussex □ U.K. 50°55N 0°30W 169 G7
West Terre Haute U.S.A. 39°28N 87°27W 311 E9
West-Terschelling Neths. 53°22N 5°13E 170 A5
West Town U.S.A. 41°53N 87°42W 119 B2
West Union Iowa, U.S.A. 42°57N 91°49W 310 B5
West Union Ohio, U.S.A. 38°48N 83°33W 311 F13
West Unity U.S.A. 41°35N 84°26W 311 C12
West Valley City U.S.A. 40°42N 111°57W 304 F8
West Virginia □ U.S.A. 38°45N 80°30W 309 F13
West-Vlaanderen □ Belgium 51°0N 3°0E 170 D2
West Walker → U.S.A. 38°54N 119°9W 306 G7
West Wharf Pakistan 24°49N 66°58E 123 B1
West Wyalong Australia 33°56S 147°10E 283 B7
West Yellowstone
U.S.A. 44°40N 111°6W 304 D8
West Yorkshire □ U.K. 53°45N 1°40W 168 D6
Westall, Pt. Australia 32°55S 134°4E 281 E1
Westbay U.S.A. 30°18N 85°52W 316 E4
Westbourne Green London, U.K. 125 a1
Westbrook U.S.A. 43°41N 70°22W 309 D18
Westbury Australia 41°30S 146°51E 281 G4
Westby U.S.A. 48°52N 104°3W 304 B11
Westchester Calif.,
U.S.A. 33°57N 118°23W 126 C2
Westchester Ill., U.S.A. 41°51N 87°53W 119 B1
Westchester N.Y., U.S.A. 40°51N 73°51W 132 A2
Westcliff S. Africa 26°10S 28°1E 123 B2
Westdene S. Africa 26°10S 27°59E 123 B1
Westend Helsinki, Finland 60°9N 24°48E 121 C1
Westend Calif., U.S.A. 35°42N 117°24W 307 K9
Wester Hailes U.K. 55°55N 3°16W 121 B2
Westerham Germany 48°3N 11°36E 131 B2
Westerland Germany 54°54N 8°17E 178 A4
Westerly U.S.A. 41°22N 71°50W 313 E13
Western □ Ghana 5°30N 2°30W 262 D4
Western □ Kenya 0°30N 34°30E 268 B3
Western □ Papua N. G. 7°30S 142°0E 286 D2
Western □ S. Leone 8°30N 13°20W 262 D2
Western □ Zambia 15°0S 24°4E 265 F4
Western Addition
U.S.A. 37°47N 122°25W 136 B2

Western Australia □ Australia 25°0S 118°0E 279 E2
Western Cape □ S. Africa 34°0S 20°0E 270 D3
Western Dvina = Daugava ➔ Latvia 57°4N 24°3E 188 D3
Western Ghats India 14°0N 75°0E 245 H2
Western Highlands □ Papua N. G. 5°45S 144°30E 286 C3
Western Isles □ U.K. 57°30N 7°10W 167 D1
Western Sahara ■ Africa 25°0N 13°0W 260 D2
Western Samoa = Samoa ■ Pac. Oc. 14°0S 172°0W 287 V20
Western Sierra Madre = Madre Occidental, Sierra Mexico 27°0N 107°0W 318 B3
Western Wall Jerusalem 123 b3
Westernport U.S.A. 39°29N 79°3W 309 F14
Westerschelde ➔ Neths. 51°25N 3°25E 170 C3
Westerstede Germany 53°15N 7°55E 178 B3
Westerwald Germany 50°38N 7°56E 178 E3
Westfield Ill., U.S.A. 39°27N 88°0W 311 E8
Westfield Ind., U.S.A. 40°2N 86°8W 311 D10
Westfield Mass., U.S.A. 42°7N 72°45W 313 D12
Westfield N.Y., U.S.A. 42°20N 79°35W 312 D5
Westfield Pa., U.S.A. 41°55N 77°32W 312 E7
Westgate La., U.S.A. 30°0N 90°13W 131 A1
Westgate Md., U.S.A. 38°57N 77°6W 143 B3
Westhill U.K. 57°9N 2°19W 167 D6
Westhope U.S.A. 48°55N 101°1W 308 A3
Westlake Western Cape, S. Africa 34°4S 18°26E 118 B1
Westlake Calif., U.S.A. 34°4N 118°15W 126 B3
Westlake Calif., U.S.A. 37°42N 122°29W 136 B2
Westland U.S.A. 42°15N 83°20W 311 B13
Westland △ N.Z. 43°16S 170°16E 285 D5
Westland Bight N.Z. 42°55S 170°5E 285 C5
Westlock Canada 54°9N 113°55W 296 C6
Westmar Australia 27°55S 149°44E 281 D4
Westmeath □ Ireland 53°33N 7°34W 166 C4
Westminster London, U.K. 51°30N 0°7W 125 A3
Westminster Calif., U.S.A. 33°45N 118°0W 307 M8
Westminster Colo., U.S.A. 39°50N 105°2W 304 G11
Westminster Md., U.S.A. 39°34N 76°59W 309 F15
Westmont U.S.A. 40°19N 78°58W 312 F6
Westmorland U.S.A. 33°2N 115°37W 307 M11
Westmount Canada 45°29N 73°35W 130 B2
Weston Ont., Canada 43°42N 79°30W 141 A1
Weston Malaysia 5°10N 115°35E 235 A5
Weston Ohio, U.S.A. 41°21N 83°47W 311 C13
Weston Oreg., U.S.A. 45°49N 118°26W 304 D4
Weston W. Va., U.S.A. 39°2N 80°28W 309 F13
Weston I. Canada 52°33N 79°36W 298 B4
Weston-super-Mare U.K. 51°21N 2°58W 169 F5
Westover U.S.A. 40°45N 78°40W 312 F6
Westphalia U.S.A. 38°26N 92°0W 310 F5
Westport Ont., Canada 44°40N 76°25W 313 B8
Westport Mayo, Ireland 53°48N 9°31W 166 C2
Westport N.Z. 41°46S 171°37E 285 B6
Westport Ind., U.S.A. 39°11N 85°34W 311 E11
Westport N.Y., U.S.A. 44°11N 73°26W 313 B11
Westport Oreg., U.S.A. 46°8N 123°23W 306 D3
Westport Wash., U.S.A. 46°53N 124°6W 306 D2
Westpunt Neth. Ant. 12°22N 69°10W 322 g
Westray Man., Canada 53°36N 101°24W 297 C8
Westray Orkney, U.K. 59°18N 3°0W 167 B5
Westree Canada 47°26N 81°34W 298 C3
Westville Calif., U.S.A. 39°8N 120°42W 306 F6
Westville Fla., U.S.A. 30°46N 85°51W 316 E4
Westville Ill., U.S.A. 40°2N 87°38W 311 D9
Westville Ind., U.S.A. 41°32N 86°54W 311 C10
Westwego U.S.A. 29°54N 90°8W 131 B2
Westwood U.S.A. 40°18N 121°0W 304 F3
Westwood Lake U.S.A. 25°44N 80°23W 317 K9
Westwood Village U.S.A. 34°3N 118°26W 126 B2
Westzaan Neths. 52°28N 4°46E 112 A1
Wetar Indonesia 7°48S 126°30E 231 F7
Wetaskiwin Canada 52°55N 113°24W 296 C6
Wetherby U.K. 53°56N 1°23W 168 D6
Wethersfield U.S.A. 41°42N 72°40W 313 E12
Wetlet Burma 22°20N 95°53E 241 D5
Wetteren Belgium 51°0N 3°53E 170 D3
Wetton S. Africa 34°0S 18°31E 118 B2
Wetumpka U.S.A. 32°32N 86°13W 316 C3
Wetzlar Germany 50°32N 8°31E 178 E4
Wevok U.S.A. 68°53N 166°13W 303 B6
Wewahitchka U.S.A. 30°7N 85°12W 316 E4
Wewak Papua N. G. 3°38S 143°41E 286 B2
Wewoka U.S.A. 35°9N 96°30W 314 D6
Wexford Ont., Canada 43°45N 79°18W 141 A3
Wexford Wexford, Ireland 52°20N 6°28W 166 D5
Wexford □ Ireland 52°20N 6°25W 166 D5
Wexford Harbour Ireland 52°20N 6°25W 166 D5
Weybridge U.K. 51°22N 0°27W 125 B1
Weyburn Canada 49°40N 103°50W 297 D8
Weyer Markt Austria 47°51N 14°40E 180 D7
Weyhe Germany 52°58N 8°49E 178 C4
Weyib ➔ Ethiopia 7°15N 40°15E 257 F5
Weymouth N.S., Canada 44°30N 66°1W 299 D6
Weymouth Dorset, U.K. 50°37N 2°28W 169 G5
Weymouth Mass., U.S.A. 42°13N 70°58W 313 D14
Weymouth, C. Australia 12°37S 143°27E 280 A3
Wezembeek-Oppem Belgium 50°51N 4°29E 116 A2
Wha Ti Canada 63°8N 117°16W 294 E8
Whakaari N.Z. 37°30S 177°13E 284 D6
Whakamaru N.Z. 38°23S 175°50E 284 E4
Whakatane N.Z. 37°57S 177°1E 284 D6
Whakatane ➔ N.Z. 37°57S 177°1E 284 D6
Whale = Baleine ➔ Canada 58°15N 67°40W 299 A6
Whale Cove Canada 62°10N 92°34W 297 A10
Whale Pt. Ascension I. 7°57S 14°18W 153 g
Whales, B. of Antarctica 78°0S 160°0W 151 D12
Whalsay U.K. 60°22N 0°59W 167 A8
Whangaehu ➔ N.Z. 40°3S 175°6E 284 G4
Whangamata N.Z. 37°12S 175°53E 284 D4
Whangamomona N.Z. 39°8S 174°44E 284 F3
Whanganui △ N.Z. 39°17S 174°53E 284 F3
Whangaparaoa Pen. N.Z. 36°40S 174°45E 284 C4
Whangarei N.Z. 35°43S 174°21E 284 B3
Whangarei Harb. N.Z. 35°45S 174°28E 284 B3
Whangaroa Harb. N.Z. 35°4S 173°46E 284 B2
Whangaruru Harb. N.Z. 35°24S 174°23E 284 B3
Wharanui N.Z. 41°55S 174°6E 285 B9
Wharekauri = Chatham Is. Pac. Oc. 44°0S 176°40W 285 a
Wharfe ➔ U.K. 53°51N 1°9W 168 D6
Wharfedale U.K. 54°6N 2°1W 168 C5
Wharton N.J., U.S.A. 40°54N 74°35W 313 F10
Wharton Pa., U.S.A. 41°31N 78°1W 312 E6
Wharton Tex., U.S.A. 29°19N 96°6W 314 G6
Wharton Basin Ind. Oc. 22°0S 92°0E 273 F8
Whataroa N.Z. 43°18S 170°24E 285 D5
Whataroa ➔ N.Z. 43°7S 170°16E 285 D5
Whatcom = Bellingham U.S.A. 48°46N 122°29W 306 B4
Wheatfield U.S.A. 41°13N 87°4W 311 C9
Wheatland Calif., U.S.A. 39°1N 121°25W 306 F5
Wheatland Ind., U.S.A. 38°40N 87°19W 311 F9
Wheatland Wyo., U.S.A. 42°3N 104°58W 304 E11
Wheatley Canada 42°6N 82°27W 312 D2
Wheaton Ill., U.S.A. 41°52N 88°6W 311 C8
Wheaton Md., U.S.A. 39°3N 77°3W 309 F15
Wheaton Minn., U.S.A. 45°48N 96°30W 308 C5
Wheelbarrow Pk. U.S.A. 37°26N 116°5W 306 H10
Wheeler Oreg., U.S.A. 45°41N 123°53W 304 D2
Wheeler Tex., U.S.A. 35°27N 100°16W 314 D4
Wheeler ➔ Canada 57°2N 67°13W 299 A6
Wheeler L. U.S.A. 34°48N 87°23W 315 D11
Wheeler Pk. N. Mex., U.S.A. 36°34N 105°25W 305 H11
Wheeler Pk. Nev., U.S.A. 38°57N 114°15W 304 G6
Wheeler Ridge U.S.A. 35°0N 118°57W 307 L8
Wheelersburg U.S.A. 38°44N 82°51W 309 F12
Wheeling U.S.A. 40°4N 80°43W 312 F4
Whernside U.K. 54°14N 2°24W 168 C5
Whiddy I. Ireland 51°41N 9°31W 166 E2
Whim Creek Australia 20°50S 117°49E 278 D2
Whirlwind Reef Papua N. G. 4°42S 148°16E 286 C5
Whiskey Jack L. Canada 58°23N 101°55W 297 B8
Whiskeytown-Shasta-Trinity ⌂ U.S.A. 40°45N 122°15W 304 F2
Whistleduck Cr. ➔ Australia 20°15S 135°18E 280 C2
Whistler Canada 50°7N 122°58W 296 C4
Whitby Ont., Canada 43°52N 78°56W 312 C6
Whitby N. Yorks., U.K. 54°29N 0°37W 168 C7
Whitcombe Pass N.Z. 43°13S 170°55E 285 D5
White ➔ Ark., U.S.A. 33°57N 91°5W 314 E9
White ➔ Ind., U.S.A. 38°25N 87°45W 311 F9
White ➔ S. Dak., U.S.A. 43°42N 99°27W 308 D4
White ➔ Tex., U.S.A. 33°14N 100°56W 314 E4
White ➔ Utah, U.S.A. 40°4N 109°41W 304 F9
White ➔ Vt., U.S.A. 43°37N 72°20W 313 C12
White ➔ Wash., U.S.A. 47°12N 122°15W 306 C4
White, L. Australia 21°9S 128°56E 278 D4
White B. Canada 50°0N 56°35W 299 C8
White Bird U.S.A. 45°46N 116°18W 304 D5
White Butte U.S.A. 46°23N 103°18W 308 B2
White City Fla., U.S.A. 29°53N 85°13W 316 F4
White City Oreg., U.S.A. 42°26N 122°51W 304 E2
White Cliffs Australia 30°50S 143°10E 282 A5
White Cloud Hill = Baiyun Hill China 23°8N 113°15E 121 B2
White Desert = Es Sahrâ al Beida Egypt 27°50N 28°45E 256 B2
White Hall U.S.A. 39°26N 90°24W 310 E6
White Haven U.S.A. 41°4N 75°47W 313 E9
White Horse, Vale of U.K. 51°37N 1°30W 169 F6
White House, The Washington, D.C., U.S.A. 143 b1
White I. = Whakaari N.Z. 37°30S 177°13E 284 D6
White I. Grenada 12°36N 61°28W 323 q
White L. Ont., Canada 45°18N 76°31W 313 A8
White L. La., U.S.A. 29°44N 92°30W 314 G8
White Lake Canada 45°21N 76°29W 313 A8
White Mountain U.S.A. 64°41N 163°24W 303 D7
White Mountain Peak U.S.A. 37°38N 118°15W 305 H4
White Mountains Nat. Recr. Area ⌂ U.S.A. 65°30N 147°40W 303 D11
White Mts. Alaska, U.S.A. 65°30N 146°30W 303 D11
White Mts. Calif., U.S.A. 37°30N 118°15W 306 H8
White Mts. N.H., U.S.A. 44°15N 71°15W 313 B13
White Mts. △ Australia 20°43S 145°12E 280 C4
White Nile = Nîl el Abyad ➔ Sudan 15°38N 32°31E 257 D3
White Nile Dam = Khazzān Jabal al Awliyā Sudan 15°24N 32°20E 257 D3
White Oak U.S.A. 31°2N 81°43W 316 D8
White Otter L. Canada 49°5N 91°55W 298 C1
White Pass U.S.A. 46°38N 121°24W 306 D5
White Pigeon U.S.A. 41°48N 85°39W 311 C11
White Plains Ga., U.S.A. 33°28N 83°1W 316 B6
White Plains N.Y., U.S.A. 41°2N 73°46W 313 E11
White River Ont., Canada 48°35N 85°20W 298 C2
White River S. Dak., U.S.A. 43°34N 100°45W 308 D3
White Rock B.C., Canada 49°2N 122°48W 306 A4
White Rock N. Mex., U.S.A. 35°50N 106°12W 305 J10
White Russia = Belarus ■ Europe 53°30N 27°0E 177 B14
White Sands ⌂ U.S.A. 32°46N 106°20W 305 K10
White Sea = Beloye More Russia 66°30N 38°0E 160 C25
White Springs U.S.A. 30°20N 82°45W 316 E7
White Sulphur Springs Mont., U.S.A. 46°33N 110°54W 304 C8
White Sulphur Springs W. Va., U.S.A. 37°48N 80°18W 309 G13
White Swan U.S.A. 46°23N 120°44W 306 D6
White Volta ➔ Ghana 9°10N 1°15W 263 D4
Whitechapel U.K. 51°31N 0°3W 125 A3
Whitecliffs N.Z. 43°26S 171°55E 285 D6
Whitecourt Canada 54°10N 115°45W 296 C5
Whiteface Mt. U.S.A. 44°22N 73°54W 313 B11
Whitefield U.S.A. 44°23N 71°37W 313 B13
Whitefish U.S.A. 48°25N 114°20W 304 B6
Whitefish B. U.S.A. 46°40N 84°55W 298 C3
Whitefish Bay U.S.A. 43°6N 87°54W 311 A9
Whitefish L. Canada 62°41N 106°48W 297 A7
Whitefish Pt. U.S.A. 46°45N 84°59W 309 B11
Whitegull, L. = Goélands, L. aux Canada 55°27N 64°17W 299 A7
Whitehall Dublin, Ireland 53°22N 6°16W 120 A2
Whitehall London, U.K. 125 b3
Whitehall Mich., U.S.A. 43°24N 86°21W 308 D10
Whitehall Mont., U.S.A. 45°52N 112°6W 304 D7
Whitehall N.Y., U.S.A. 43°33N 73°24W 313 C11
Whitehall Wis., U.S.A. 44°22N 91°19W 308 C8
Whitehaven U.K. 54°33N 3°35W 168 C4
Whitehorse Canada 60°43N 135°3W 296 A1
Whiteman Ra. Papua N. G. 5°55S 150°0E 286 C6
Whitemark Australia 40°7S 148°3E 281 G4
Whiteplains Liberia 6°28N 10°40W 262 D2
Whiteriver U.S.A. 33°50N 109°58W 305 K9
Whitesand ➔ Canada 60°9N 115°45W 296 A5
Whitesands S. Africa 34°23S 20°50E 270 D3
Whitesboro N.Y., U.S.A. 43°7N 75°18W 313 C9
Whitesboro Tex., U.S.A. 33°39N 96°54W 314 E6
Whiteshell △ Canada 50°0N 95°40W 297 D9
Whiteside, Canal Chile 53°55S 70°15W 336 D2
Whiteville U.S.A. 34°20N 78°42W 315 D15
Whitewater U.S.A. 42°50N 88°44W 311 B8
Whitewater B. U.S.A. 25°15N 81°0W 317 K8
Whitewater Baldy U.S.A. 33°20N 108°39W 305 K9
Whitewater L. Canada 50°50N 89°10W 298 B2
Whitewood Queens., Australia 21°28S 143°30E 280 C3
Whitewood Sask., Canada 50°20N 102°20W 297 C8
Whitfield Australia 36°42S 146°24E 283 D7
Whithorn U.K. 54°44N 4°26W 167 G4
Whitianga N.Z. 36°47S 175°41E 284 C4
Whiting U.S.A. 41°41N 87°30W 311 C9
Whitman U.S.A. 42°5N 70°56W 313 D14
Whitmore Village U.S.A. 21°31N 158°1W 302 J13
Whitney Ont., Canada 45°31N 78°14W 312 A6
Whitney Nev., U.S.A. 36°4N 115°5W 124 B2
Whitney, Mt. U.S.A. 36°35N 118°18W 306 J8
Whitney Point U.S.A. 42°20N 75°58W 313 D9
Whitstable U.K. 51°21N 1°3E 169 F9
Whitsunday I. Australia 20°15S 149°4E 280 b
Whitsunday Islands △ Australia 20°15S 149°0E 280 b
Whittemore U.S.A. 43°4N 94°26W 310 A2
Whittier Alaska, U.S.A. 60°47N 148°41W 303 F10
Whittier Calif., U.S.A. 33°58N 118°2W 126 C4
Whittlesea Australia 37°27S 145°9E 283 D6
Whitton U.K. 51°27N 0°21W 125 B1
Wholdaia L. Canada 60°43N 104°20W 297 A8
Whyalla Australia 33°2S 137°30E 282 B2
Wiang Kosai △ Thailand 17°54N 99°29E 236 D2
Wiang Sa Thailand 18°34N 100°45E 236 C3
Wiarton Canada 44°40N 81°10W 312 B3
Wiawso Ghana 6°10N 2°25W 262 D4
Wiay U.K. 57°24N 7°13W 167 D1
Wiązów Poland 50°50N 17°10E 185 H4
Wibaux U.S.A. 46°59N 104°11W 304 C11
Wichabai Guyana 2°57N 59°35W 329 C6
Wichian Buri Thailand 15°39N 101°7E 236 E3
Wichita U.S.A. 37°42N 97°20W 308 G5
Wichita Falls U.S.A. 33°54N 98°30W 314 E5
Wick U.K. 58°26N 3°5W 167 C5
Wickenburg U.S.A. 33°58N 112°44W 305 K7
Wickepin Australia 32°50S 117°30E 279 F2
Wickham Australia 20°42S 117°11E 278 D2
Wickham, C. Australia 39°35S 143°57E 281 F3
Wickliffe U.S.A. 41°36N 81°28W 312 E3
Wicklow Ireland 52°59N 6°3W 166 D5
Wicklow □ Ireland 52°57N 6°25W 166 D5
Wicklow Hd. Ireland 52°58N 6°0W 166 D6
Wicklow Mts. Ireland 52°58N 6°26W 166 C5
Wicklow Mts. △ Ireland 53°6N 6°21W 166 C5
Widawa Poland 51°27N 18°51E 185 G5
Widawka ➔ Poland 51°27N 18°52E 185 G5
Wide B. Papua N. G. 5°5S 152°5E 286 C7
Widgeegoara Cr. ➔ Australia 28°51S 146°34E 281 D4
Widgiemooltha Australia 31°30S 121°34E 279 F3
Widnes U.K. 53°23N 2°45W 168 D5
Wido S. Korea 35°35N 126°17E 224 E3
Wiecbork Poland 53°21N 17°30E 185 E4
Wieden Austria 48°11N 16°22E 142 A2
Wiehengebirge = Nördlicher Teutoburger Wald-Wiehengebirge ⌂ Germany 52°18N 8°10E 178 C4
Wiehl Germany 50°56N 7°34E 178 E3
Wiek Germany 54°37N 13°17E 178 A9
Wielbark Poland 53°24N 20°55E 184 E7
Wieleń Poland 52°53N 16°9E 185 F3
Wielichowo Poland 52°7N 16°22E 185 F3
Wieliczka Poland 50°0N 20°5E 185 J7
Wielkopolski △ Poland 52°18N 16°45E 185 F3
Wielkopolskie □ Poland 52°10N 17°30E 185 F4
Wieluń Poland 51°15N 18°34E 185 G5
Wien Austria 48°12N 16°22E 142 A2
Wien-Schwechat ✕ (VIE) Austria 48°7N 16°35E 142 B3
Wiener Neustadt Austria 47°49N 16°16E 181 D9
Wienerberg Austria 48°9N 16°21E 142 B2
Wieprz ➔ Poland 51°34N 21°49E 185 G8
Wieprza ➔ Poland 54°26N 16°25E 184 D3
Wieruszów Poland 51°19N 18°9E 185 G5
Wierzbno Poland 52°11N 21°1E 142 B2
Wiesbaden Germany 50°4N 8°14E 179 E4
Wiesental Germany 49°13N 8°31E 179 F4
Wiesloch Germany 49°18N 8°41E 179 F4
Wiesmoor Germany 53°24N 7°47E 178 B3
Wieżyca Poland 54°14N 18°8E 184 D5
Wigan U.K. 53°33N 2°38W 168 D5
Wiggins Colo., U.S.A. 40°14N 104°4W 304 F11
Wiggins Miss., U.S.A. 30°51N 89°8W 315 F10
Wight, I. of U.K. 50°41N 1°17W 169 G6
Wigierski △ Poland 54°5N 23°5E 184 D10
Wigry, Jezioro Poland 54°2N 23°8E 184 D10
Wigston U.K. 52°35N 1°6W 169 E6
Wigton U.K. 54°50N 3°10W 168 C4
Wigtown U.K. 54°53N 4°27W 167 G4
Wigtown B. U.K. 54°46N 4°15W 167 G4
Wijde Wormer Neths. 52°28N 4°52E 112 A2
Wik and Wikway People ♡ Australia 13°55S 142°28E 280 A3
Wil Switz. 47°28N 9°3E 179 H5
Wilamowice Poland 49°55N 19°9E 185 J6
Wilanów Poland 52°10N 21°4E 142 B2
Wilanówka ➔ Poland 52°13N 21°6E 142 C2
Wilber U.S.A. 40°29N 96°58W 308 E5
Wilberforce Canada 45°2N 78°13W 312 A6
Wilberforce, C. Australia 11°54S 136°35E 280 A2
Wilburton U.S.A. 34°55N 95°19W 314 D7
Wilcannia Australia 31°30S 143°26E 282 A5
Wilcox U.S.A. 41°35N 78°41W 312 E6
Wildbad Germany 48°44N 8°33E 179 G4
Wildcat Cr. ➔ U.S.A. 40°28N 86°52W 311 D10
Wildenschwert = Ústí nad Orlicí Czech Rep. 49°58N 16°24E 181 B9
Wildeshausen Germany 52°54N 8°27E 178 C4
Wildeshauser Geest ⌂ Germany 52°54N 8°30E 178 C4
Wildon Austria 46°52N 15°31E 180 E8
Wildrose U.S.A. 36°14N 117°11W 307 J9
Wilds, The S. Africa 26°10S 28°2E 123 B2
Wildspitze Austria 46°53N 10°53E 180 E3
Wildwood U.S.A. 28°52N 82°2W 317 G7
Wilga ➔ Poland 51°52N 21°18E 185 G8
Wilge ➔ S. Africa 27°3S 28°20E 271 C4
Wilhelm, Mt. Papua N. G. 5°50S 145°1E 286 C3
Wilhelm II Coast Antarctica 68°0S 90°0E 151 C7
Wilhelmina Geb. Suriname 3°50N 56°30W 329 C6
Wilhelmina Top = Trikora, Puncak Indonesia 4°15S 138°45E 231 E9
Wilhelmsburg Austria 48°6N 15°36E 180 C8
Wilhelmshagen Germany 52°26N 13°42E 115 B5
Wilhelmshaven Germany 53°31N 8°7E 178 B4
Wilhelmstal Namibia 21°58S 16°21E 270 B2
Wilkes-Barre U.S.A. 41°15N 75°53W 313 E9
Wilkes I. Wake I. 19°18N 166°34E 302 b
Wilkes Land Antarctica 69°0S 120°0E 151 D9
Wilket Creek Park Canada 43°43N 79°21W 141 A2
Wilkie Canada 52°27N 108°42W 297 C7
Wilkieston U.K. 55°54N 3°24W 121 B1
Wilkinsburg U.S.A. 40°26N 79°52W 312 F5
Wilkinson Lakes Australia 29°40S 132°39E 279 E5
Will Rogers State Historical Park ⌂ U.S.A. 34°2N 118°30W 126 B1
Willacoochee U.S.A. 31°20N 83°3W 316 D6
Willandra △ Australia 33°12S 145°0E 283 B6
Willandra Creek ➔ Australia 33°22S 145°52E 282 B6
Willapa B. U.S.A. 46°40N 124°0W 304 C1
Willapa Hills U.S.A. 46°35N 123°25W 306 D3
Willard U.S.A. 41°3N 82°44W 312 E2
Willare Bridge Roadhouse Australia 17°43S 123°38E 278 C3
Willaumez Pen. Papua N. G. 5°15S 150°2E 286 C6
Willbriggie Australia 34°28S 146°2E 283 C7
Willbrook Ireland 53°17N 6°16W 120 B2
Willcox U.S.A. 32°15N 109°50W 305 K9
Willemstad Neth. Ant. 12°5N 68°55W 322 g
Willenberg = Wielbark Poland 53°24N 20°55E 184 E7
Willesden U.K. 51°32N 0°15W 125 A2
Willesden Green U.K. 51°32N 0°13W 125 A2
Willi Willi △ Australia 30°57S 152°27E 283 A10
William ➔ Canada 59°8N 109°19W 297 B7
William, Mt. Australia 37°17S 142°35E 282 D5
William 'Bill' Dannelly Res. U.S.A. 32°6N 87°24W 315 E11
William Creek Australia 28°58S 136°22E 281 D2
Williams W. Austral., Australia 33°2S 116°52E 279 F2
Williams Ariz., U.S.A. 35°15N 112°11W 305 J7
Williams Calif., U.S.A. 39°9N 122°9W 306 F4
Williams Harbour Canada 52°33N 55°47W 299 B8
Williams Lake Canada 52°10N 122°10W 296 C4
Williamsbridge U.S.A. 40°52N 73°51W 132 A2
Williamsburg Fla., U.S.A. 28°24N 81°26W 133 B2
Williamsburg Iowa, U.S.A. 41°40N 92°1W 310 C4
Williamsburg Ky., U.S.A. 36°44N 84°10W 309 G11
Williamsburg New York, U.S.A. 132 f3
Williamsburg Pa., U.S.A. 40°28N 78°12W 312 F6
Williamsburg Va., U.S.A. 37°16N 76°43W 309 G15
Williamsburg Bridge New York, U.S.A. 132 e2
Williamsfield U.S.A. 40°55N 90°1W 310 D6
Williamson N.Y., U.S.A. 43°14N 77°11W 312 C7
Williamson W. Va., U.S.A. 37°41N 82°17W 309 G12
Williamsport Ind., U.S.A. 40°17N 87°17W 311 D9
Williamsport Pa., U.S.A. 41°15N 77°1W 312 E7
Williamston Mich., U.S.A. 42°41N 84°17W 311 B12
Williamston N.C., U.S.A. 35°51N 77°4W 315 D16
Williamstown Vic., Australia 37°51S 144°52E 128 B1
Williamstown Ky., U.S.A. 38°38N 84°34W 311 F12
Williamstown Mass., U.S.A. 42°43N 73°12W 313 D11
Williamstown N.Y., U.S.A. 43°26N 75°53W 313 C9
Williamsville U.S.A. 39°57N 89°33W 310 E7
Willikies Antigua & B. 17°3N 61°42W 322 b
Willimantic U.S.A. 41°43N 72°13W 313 E12
Willingboro U.S.A. 40°3N 74°54W 309 E16
Willis, L. U.S.A. 28°23N 81°28W 133 B2
Willisburg U.S.A. 37°49N 85°8W 311 G11
Williston Northern Cape, S. Africa 31°20S 20°53E 270 D3
Williston Fla., U.S.A. 29°23N 82°27W 317 F7
Williston N. Dak., U.S.A. 48°9N 103°37W 308 A2
Williston S.C., U.S.A. 33°24N 81°25W 316 B8
Williston L. Canada 56°0N 124°0W 296 B4
Willits U.S.A. 39°25N 123°21W 304 G2
Willmar U.S.A. 45°7N 95°3W 308 C6
Willmore Wilderness ⌂ Canada 53°45N 119°30W 296 C5
Willoughby N.S.W., Australia 33°48S 151°12E 139 A2
Willoughby Ohio, U.S.A. 41°39N 81°24W 312 E3
Willoughby B. Antigua & B. 17°2N 61°44W 322 b
Willow U.S.A. 61°45N 150°3W 303 F10
Willow Bunch Canada 49°20N 105°35W 297 D7
Willow L. Canada 62°10N 119°8W 296 A5
Willow Springs U.S.A. 41°44N 87°51W 119 C1
Willow Tree Australia 31°40S 150°45E 283 A9
Willow Wall, The China 42°10N 122°0E 227 C12
Willowdale Ont., Canada 43°46N 79°25W 141 A2
Willowdale La., U.S.A. 30°0N 90°12W 131 A1
Willowick U.S.A. 41°38N 81°28W 312 E3
Willowlake ➔ Canada 62°42N 123°8W 296 A4
Willowmore S. Africa 33°15S 23°30E 270 D3
Willows U.S.A. 39°31N 122°12W 306 F4
Willowvale = Gatyana S. Africa 32°16S 28°31E 271 D4
Wills, L. Australia 21°25S 128°51E 278 D4
Wills Cr. ➔ Australia 22°43S 140°2E 280 C3
Willsboro U.S.A. 44°21N 73°24W 313 B11
Willunga Australia 35°15S 138°30E 282 C3
Wilma U.S.A. 30°9N 84°58W 316 E5
Wilmersdorf Berlin, Germany 115 c1
Wilmette U.S.A. 42°4N 87°42W 119 A2
Wilmington S. Austral., Australia 32°39S 138°7E 282 B3
Wilmington Kent, U.K. 51°25N 0°12E 125 B5
Wilmington Del., U.S.A. 39°45N 75°33W 309 F16
Wilmington Ill., U.S.A. 41°18N 88°9W 311 C8
Wilmington N.C., U.S.A. 34°14N 77°55W 315 D16
Wilmington Ohio, U.S.A. 39°27N 83°50W 311 E13
Wilmington Vt., U.S.A. 42°52N 72°52W 313 D12
Wilmslow U.K. 53°19N 2°13W 168 D5
Wilna = Vilnius Lithuania 54°38N 25°19E 188 E3
Wilpattu △ Sri Lanka 8°20N 79°50E 245 K4
Wilpena Australia 31°31S 138°37E 282 A3
Wilpena Cr. ➔ Australia 31°25S 139°29E 282 A3
Wilsall U.S.A. 45°59N 110°38W 304 D8
Wilson N.C., U.S.A. 35°44N 77°55W 315 D16
Wilson N.Y., U.S.A. 43°19N 78°50W 312 C6
Wilson Pa., U.S.A. 40°41N 75°15W 313 F9
Wilson ➔ Australia 16°48S 128°16E 278 C4
Wilson Bluff Australia 31°41S 129°0E 279 F4
Wilson Inlet Australia 35°0S 117°22E 279 G2
Wilson Str. Solomon Is. 8°0S 156°39E 287 M9
Wilsons Promontory Australia 38°59S 146°23E 283 E7
Wilsons Promontory △ Australia 38°59S 146°23E 283 D7
Wilster Germany 53°55N 9°23E 178 B5
Wilton Iowa, U.S.A. 41°35N 91°1W 310 C5
Wilton N. Dak., U.S.A. 47°10N 100°47W 308 B3
Wilton ➔ Australia 14°45S 134°33E 280 A1
Wiltshire □ U.K. 51°18N 1°53W 169 F6
Wiltz Lux. 49°57N 5°55E 170 E5
Wiluna Australia 26°36S 120°14E 279 E3
Wimbledon U.K. 51°25N 0°13W 125 B2
Wimbledon Common U.K. 51°26N 0°14W 125 B2
Wimbledon Park U.K. 51°25N 0°11W 125 B2
Wimbledon Tennis Ground U.K. 51°25N 0°12W 125 B2
Wimborne Minster U.K. 50°48N 1°59W 169 G6
Wimereux France 50°45N 1°37E 173 B8
Wimmera ➔ Australia 36°8S 141°56E 282 D4
Winam G. Kenya 0°20S 34°15E 268 C3
Winamac U.S.A. 41°3N 86°36W 311 C10
Winburg S. Africa 28°30S 27°2E 270 C4
Winchelsea Australia 38°10S 144°1E 282 E6
Winchendon U.S.A. 42°41N 72°3W 313 D12
Winchester N.Z. 44°11S 171°17E 285 E6
Winchester Hants., U.K. 51°4N 1°18W 169 F6
Winchester Conn., U.S.A. 41°53N 73°9W 313 E11
Winchester Idaho, U.S.A. 46°14N 116°38W 304 C5
Winchester Ill., U.S.A. 39°38N 90°27W 310 E6
Winchester Ind., U.S.A. 40°10N 84°59W 311 D12
Winchester Ky., U.S.A. 37°59N 84°11W 311 G12
Winchester Mass., U.S.A. 42°26N 71°8W 116 A2
Winchester N.H., U.S.A. 42°46N 72°23W 313 D12
Winchester Nev., U.S.A. 36°7N 115°7W 124 B2
Winchester Ohio, U.S.A. 38°56N 83°39W 311 F13
Winchester Tenn., U.S.A. 35°11N 86°7W 315 D11
Winchester Va., U.S.A. 39°11N 78°10W 309 F14
Wind ➔ U.S.A. 43°12N 108°12W 304 E9
Wind Cave △ U.S.A. 43°32N 103°17W 308 D2
Wind Point U.S.A. 42°47N 87°46W 311 B9
Wind River Range U.S.A. 43°0N 109°30W 304 E9
Windamere, L. Australia 32°48S 149°51E 283 B8
Windau = Ventspils Latvia 57°25N 21°32E 184 A8
Windber U.S.A. 40°14N 78°50W 312 F6
Winder U.S.A. 34°0N 83°45W 316 A6
Windermere Western Cape, S. Africa 33°55S 18°30E 118 A2
Windermere Cumb., U.K. 54°23N 2°55W 168 C5
Windermere Fla., U.S.A. 28°29N 81°32W 133 B1
Windfall U.S.A. 40°22N 85°57W 311 D11
Windhoek Namibia 22°35S 17°4E 270 B2
Windidda ♡ Australia 26°23S 122°12E 279 E3
Windisch-Feistritz = Slovenska Bistrica Slovenia 46°24N 15°35E 199 B12
Windischgarsten Austria 47°42N 14°21E 180 D7
Windischgratz = Slovenj Gradec Slovenia 46°31N 15°5E 199 B12
Windjana Gorge △ Australia 17°51S 125°0E 278 C3
Windom U.S.A. 43°52N 95°7W 308 D6
Windorah Australia 25°24S 142°36E 280 D3
Window Rock U.S.A. 35°41N 109°3W 305 J9
Windrush ➔ U.K. 51°43N 1°24W 169 F6
Windsor N.S.W., Australia 33°37S 150°50E 283 B9
Windsor N.S., Canada 44°59N 64°5W 299 D7
Windsor Ont., Canada 42°18N 83°0W 312 D2
Windsor N.Z. 44°59S 170°49E 285 E5
Windsor Gauteng, S. Africa 26°7S 27°59E 123 A1
Windsor Windsor & Maidenhead, U.K. 51°29N 0°36W 169 F7
Windsor Calif., U.S.A. 38°33N 122°49W 304 G2
Windsor Colo., U.S.A. 40°29N 104°54W 304 F11
Windsor Conn., U.S.A. 41°50N 72°39W 313 E12
Windsor Ill., U.S.A. 39°26N 88°36W 311 E8
Windsor Mo., U.S.A. 38°32N 93°31W 310 F3
Windsor N.Y., U.S.A. 42°5N 75°37W 313 D9
Windsor Vt., U.S.A. 43°29N 72°24W 313 C12
Windsor, Gare Montréal, Canada 130 c2
Windsor & Maidenhead □ U.K. 51°29N 0°40W 169 F7
Windsor Caves Jamaica 18°21N 77°39W 320 a
Windsor Hills U.S.A. 33°59N 118°22W 126 C2
Windsorton S. Africa 28°16S 24°44E 270 C3
Windward Grenada 12°31N 61°26W 323 q
Windward Is. W. Indies 13°0N 61°0W 321 D7
Windward Passage = Vientos, Paso de los Caribbean 20°0N 74°0W 321 C5
Windward Side Neth. Ant. 17°38N 63°14W 322 a
Windy Arbour Ireland 53°18N 6°14W 120 B2
Winefred L. Canada 55°30N 110°30W 297 B6
Winejok Sudan 9°1N 27°30E 257 F2
Winfield Iowa, U.S.A. 41°7N 91°26W 310 C5
Winfield Kans., U.S.A. 37°15N 96°59W 308 G5
Winfield Mo., U.S.A. 39°0N 90°44W 310 F6
Wingate Mts. Australia 14°25S 130°40E 278 B5
Wingellina = Irrunytju Australia 26°3S 128°56E 279 E4
Wingham N.S.W., Australia 31°48S 152°22E 283 A10
Wingham Ont., Canada 43°55N 81°20W 312 C3
Winisk Canada 55°17N 85°5W 298 A2
Winisk ➔ Canada 55°17N 85°5W 298 A2
Winisk L. Canada 52°55N 87°22W 298 B2
Wink U.S.A. 31°45N 103°9W 314 F3
Winkler Canada 49°10N 97°56W 297 D9
Winklern Austria 46°52N 12°52E 180 E5
Winlock U.S.A. 46°30N 122°56W 306 D4
Winneba Ghana 5°25N 0°36W 263 D4
Winnebago U.S.A. 42°16N 89°15W 310 B7
Winnebago, L. U.S.A. 44°0N 88°26W 308 D9
Winnecke Cr. ➔ Australia 18°35S 131°34E 278 C5
Winnemucca U.S.A. 40°58N 117°44W 304 F5
Winnemucca L. U.S.A. 40°7N 119°21W 304 F4
Winner U.S.A. 43°22N 99°52W 308 D4
Winnett U.S.A. 47°0N 108°21W 304 C9
Winnfield U.S.A. 31°56N 92°38W 314 F8
Winnibigoshish, L. U.S.A. 47°27N 94°13W 308 B6
Winning Germany 48°2N 11°37E 131 B2
Winnipeg Canada 49°54N 97°9W 297 D9
Winnipeg ➔ Canada 50°38N 96°19W 297 C9
Winnipeg, L. Canada 52°0N 97°0W 297 C9
Winnipeg Beach Canada 50°30N 96°58W 297 C9
Winnipegosis Canada 51°39N 99°55W 297 C9
Winnipegosis L. Canada 52°30N 100°0W 297 C9
Winnipesaukee, L. U.S.A. 43°38N 71°21W 313 C13
Winnisquam L. U.S.A. 43°33N 71°31W 313 C13
Winnsboro La., U.S.A. 32°10N 91°43W 314 E9
Winnsboro S.C., U.S.A. 34°23N 81°5W 315 D14
Winnsboro Tex., U.S.A. 32°58N 95°17W 314 E7
Winokapau, L. Canada 53°15N 62°50W 299 B7
Winona Minn., U.S.A. 44°3N 91°39W 308 C8
Winona Miss., U.S.A. 33°29N 89°44W 315 E10
Winooski U.S.A. 44°29N 73°11W 313 B11
Winooski ➔ U.S.A. 44°32N 73°17W 313 B11
Winschoten Neths. 53°9N 7°3E 170 A7
Winsen Germany 53°22N 10°13E 178 B6
Winsford U.K. 53°12N 2°31W 168 D5
Winslow = Bainbridge Island U.S.A. 47°38N 122°32W 306 C4
Winslow Ariz., U.S.A. 35°2N 110°42W 305 J8
Winslow Ind., U.S.A. 38°23N 87°13W 311 F9
Winslow Reef Kiribati 1°36S 174°57W 277 A16
Winsted U.S.A. 41°55N 73°4W 313 E11
Winston-Salem U.S.A. 36°6N 80°15W 315 C14
Winter Garden U.S.A. 28°34N 81°35W 317 G8
Winter Haven U.S.A. 28°1N 81°44W 317 G8
Winter Park U.S.A. 28°36N 81°20W 317 G8
Winterberg Germany 51°11N 8°33E 178 D4
Winterhaven U.S.A. 32°44N 114°38W 307 N12
Winters U.S.A. 38°32N 121°58W 306 G5
Winterset U.S.A. 41°20N 94°1W 310 C3
Wintersville U.S.A. 40°23N 80°42W 312 F4
Winterswijk Neths. 51°58N 6°43E 170 C6
Winterthur Switz. 47°30N 8°44E 179 H4
Winthrop U.S.A. 48°28N 120°10W 304 B3
Winton Queens., Australia 22°24S 143°3E 280 C3
Winton N.Z. 46°8S 168°20E 285 G3
Winton U.S.A. 36°24N 76°56W 315 C16
Wintua Vanuatu 16°30S 167°26E 287 F5
Wipper ➔ Germany 51°16N 11°12E 178 D7
Wirlyajarrayi ♡ Australia 21°45S 132°35E 278 D5
Wirraminna Australia 31°12S 136°13E 282 A2
Wirrulla Australia 32°24S 134°31E 281 E1
Wisbech U.K. 52°41N 0°9E 169 E8
Wisconsin □ U.S.A. 44°45N 89°30W 310 B7
Wisconsin ➔ U.S.A. 43°0N 91°15W 310 B5
Wisconsin Rapids U.S.A. 44°23N 89°49W 308 C9
Wisdom U.S.A. 45°37N 113°27W 304 D7
Wiseman U.S.A. 67°25N 150°6W 303 C10
Wishaw U.K. 55°46N 3°54W 167 F5
Wishek U.S.A. 46°16N 99°33W 308 B4
Wisła Poland 49°38N 18°53E 185 J5
Wisła ➔ Poland 54°22N 18°55E 184 D5
Wisłok ➔ Poland 50°13N 22°32E 185 H9
Wisłoka ➔ Poland 50°27N 21°23E 185 H8
Wismar Mecklenburg-Vorpommern, Germany 53°54N 11°29E 178 B7
Wismar Guyana 5°59N 58°18W 329 B6
Wisner U.S.A. 41°59N 96°55W 308 E5
Wissant France 50°52N 1°40E 173 B8
Wissembourg France 49°2N 7°57E 173 C14
Wissous France 48°44N 2°19E 134 B2
Wisznice Poland 51°48N 23°13E 185 G10
Witbank = eMalahleni S. Africa 25°51S 29°14E 271 C4
Witdraai S. Africa 26°58S 20°48E 270 C3
Witham U.K. 51°48N 0°40E 169 F8
Witham ➔ U.K. 52°59N 0°2W 168 E7
Withernsea U.K. 53°44N 0°1E 168 D8
Withlacoochee ➔ Fla., U.S.A. 30°24N 83°10W 316 E6
Withlacoochee ➔ Fla., U.S.A. 29°0N 82°45W 317 G7
Witjira △ Australia 26°22S 135°37E 281 D2
Witkowo Poland 52°26N 17°45E 185 F4
Witless Bay Canada 47°17N 52°50W 299 C9
Witney U.K. 51°48N 1°28W 169 F6
Witnica Poland 52°40N 14°54E 185 F1
Witnossob ➔ Namibia 23°55S 18°45E 270 C3
Witrivier S. Africa 25°20S 31°0E 271 C5
Wittdün Germany 54°38N 8°23E 178 A4
Witte Pan Neth. Ant. 12°3N 68°17W 322 h
Witten Germany 51°26N 7°20E 178 D3
Wittenau Germany 52°35N 13°19E 115 A2
Wittenberge Germany 53°0N 11°45E 178 B7
Wittenburg Germany 53°31N 11°4E 178 B7
Wittenheim France 47°44N 7°20E 173 E14
Wittenoom Australia 22°15S 118°20E 278 D2
Witti, Banjaran Malaysia 5°11N 116°29E 235 A5
Wittingau = Třeboň Czech Rep. 49°1N 14°48E 180 B7
Wittingen Germany 52°44N 10°44E 178 C6
Wittlich Germany 49°59N 6°53E 179 F2
Wittmund Germany 53°34N 7°46E 178 B3
Wittow Germany 54°38N 13°20E 178 A9
Wittstock Germany 53°10N 12°28E 178 B8
Witu Kenya 2°23S 40°26E 268 C5
Witu Is. Papua N. G. 4°50S 149°25E 286 C5
Witvlei Namibia 22°23S 18°32E 270 B2
Witwatersrand, Univ. of S. Africa 26°11S 28°1E 123 B2
Witzenhausen Germany 51°20N 9°51E 178 D5
Wiwon N. Korea 40°54N 126°3E 224 B3
Wixom U.S.A. 42°32N 83°32W 311 B13
Wkra ➔ Poland 52°27N 20°44E 185 F7
Władysławowo Poland 54°48N 18°25E 184 D5
Wleń Poland 51°2N 15°39E 185 G2
Wlingi Indonesia 8°5S 112°25E 235 D4
Włochy Poland 52°12N 20°54E 142 B1
Włocławek Poland 52°40N 19°3E 185 F6
Włodawa Poland 51°33N 23°31E 185 G10
Włoszczowa Poland 50°50N 19°55E 185 H6
Wo Mei China 22°21N 114°15E 122 A2
Wo Yi Hop China 22°23N 114°8E 122 A1
Woburn Ont., Canada 43°46N 79°12W 141 A3
Woburn Mass., U.S.A. 42°29N 71°9W 116 A2
Wodian China 32°50N 112°35E 226 H7
Wodonga Australia 36°5S 146°50E 283 D7
Wodzisław Śląski Poland 50°1N 18°26E 185 H5
Wœrth France 48°57N 7°45E 173 D14
Wohlau = Wołów Poland 51°20N 16°38E 185 G3
Woinbogoin China 32°51N 98°39E 228 A2
Woippy France 49°10N 6°8E 173 C13
Wotape Papua N. G. 8°33S 147°15E 286 E4
Wojcieszów Poland 50°58N 15°55E 185 H2
Wokam Indonesia 5°45S 134°28E 231 F8
Wokha India 26°6N 94°16E 241 B5
Woking U.K. 51°19N 0°34W 169 F7
Wokingham U.K. 51°24N 0°49W 169 F7
Wokingham □ U.K. 51°25N 0°51W 169 F7
Woko △ Australia 31°46S 151°49E 283 A9
Wola Poland 52°14N 20°57E 142 B1
Wolbrom Poland 50°24N 19°45E 185 H6
Wolcottville U.S.A. 41°32N 85°22W 311 C11
Wołczyn Poland 51°1N 18°3E 185 G5
Woldegk Germany 53°27N 13°34E 178 B9
Woldenberg = Dobiegniew Poland 52°59N 15°45E 185 F2
Woldenberg Park New Orleans, U.S.A. 131 b3
Wolf ➔ Canada 60°17N 132°33W 296 A2
Wolf, Volcán Ecuador 0°2N 91°20W 330 a
Wolf Creek U.S.A. 47°0N 112°4W 304 C7
Wolf L. Canada 60°24N 131°40W 296 A2
Wolf Point U.S.A. 48°5N 105°39W 304 B11
Wolf Trap Farm Park U.S.A. 38°56N 77°17W 143 B2
Wolfe Creek Crater △ Australia 19°10S 127°47E 278 C4
Wolfe I. Canada 44°7N 76°20W 313 B8
Wolfeboro U.S.A. 43°35N 71°13W 313 C13
Wolfen Germany 51°39N 12°15E 178 D8
Wolfenbüttel Germany 52°10N 10°33E 178 C6
Wolfratshausen Germany 47°54N 11°24E 179 H7
Wolfsberg Austria 46°50N 14°52E 180 E7
Wolfsburg Germany 52°25N 10°48E 178 C6
Wolgast Germany 54°3N 13°44E 178 A9
Wolgok S. Korea 37°35N 127°1E 237 B2
Wolhusen Switz. 47°4N 8°4E 179 H4
Wolica Warszawa, Poland 52°9N 21°3E 142 C2
Wolica Warszawa, Poland 52°7N 20°51E 142 C1
Wolin Poland 53°50N 14°37E 184 E1
Woliński △ Poland 53°57N 14°28E 184 E1
Wollaston Is. Chile 55°40S 67°30W 336 E3
Wollaston Forland Greenland 74°25N 19°40W 154 C9
Wollaston L. Canada 58°7N 103°10W 297 B8
Wollaston Lake Canada 58°3N 103°33W 297 B8
Wollaston Pen. Canada 69°30N 115°0W 294 D9
Wollemi △ Australia 33°0S 150°30E 283 B9
Wollongong Australia 34°25S 150°54E 283 C9
Wolmar = Valmiera Latvia 57°37N 25°29E 188 D3
Wolmaransstad S. Africa 27°12S 25°59E 270 C4
Wolmirstedt Germany 52°14N 11°37E 178 C7
Wolomin Poland 52°19N 21°15E 185 F8
Wołów Poland 51°20N 16°38E 185 G3
Wolseley S. Austral., Australia 36°23S 140°54E 282 D4
Wolseley Western Cape, S. Africa 33°26S 19°7E 270 D2
Wolsey U.S.A. 44°25N 98°28W 308 C4
Wolstenholme, C. Canada 62°35N 77°30W 292 C12
Wolsztyn Poland 52°8N 16°5E 185 F3
Woltersdorf Germany 52°27N 13°44E 115 B6
Woluwe-St-Lambert Belgium 50°50N 4°24E 116 A2
Woluwe-St-Pierre Belgium 50°50N 4°25E 116 A2
Wolvega Neths. 52°52N 6°0E 170 B6
Wolverhampton U.K. 52°35N 2°7W 169 E5
Wondai Australia 26°20S 151°49E 281 D5
Wonenara Papua N. G. 6°48S 145°53E 286 D3
Wong Chuk Hang China 22°15N 114°10E 122 B2
Wong Chuk Wan China 22°23N 114°17E 122 A2

Wong Chuk Yeung China 22°24N 114°15E 122 A2
Wonga Wongué △ Gabon 0°29S 9°25E 264 C1
Wongalarroo L. Australia 31°32S 144°0E 282 A6
Wongan Hills Australia 30°51S 116°37E 279 F2
Wonju S. Korea 37°22N 127°58E 224 D3
Wonosari Indonesia 7°58S 110°36E 235 D4
Wonosobo Indonesia 7°22S 109°54E 235 D3
Wonowon Canada 56°44N 121°48W 296 B4
Wŏnsan N. Korea 39°11N 127°27E 224 C3
Wonthaggi Australia 38°37S 145°37E 283 E6
Wood Buffalo △ Canada 59°0N 113°41W 296 B6
Wood Green U.K. 51°36N 0°6W 125 A3
Wood Is. Australia 16°24S 123°19E 278 C3
Wood L. Canada 55°17N 103°17W 297 B8
Wood Ridge U.S.A. 40°50N 74°4W 132 A1
Wood River U.S.A. 38°52N 90°5W 310 F6
Woodah, I. Australia 13°27S 136°10E 280 A2
Woodbine U.S.A. 30°58N 81°44W 316 F8
Woodbine Race Track Canada 43°43N 79°36W 141 A1
Woodbourne U.S.A. 41°46N 74°36W 313 E10
Woodbridge Ont., Canada 43°47N 79°36W 141 A1
Woodbridge Suffolk, U.K. 52°6N 1°20E 169 E9
Woodbridge B. Dominica 15°19N 61°25W 323 k
Woodburn N.S.W., Australia 29°6S 153°23E 281 A5
Woodburn Oreg., U.S.A. 45°9N 122°51W 304 D2
Woodbury U.S.A. 32°59N 84°35W 316 C5
Woodenbong Australia 28°24S 152°39E 281 D5
Woodend Australia 37°20S 144°33E 282 D6
Woodford Queens., Australia 26°58S 152°47E 281 D5
Woodford London, U.K. 51°36N 0°1E 125 A4
Woodford Bridge U.K. 51°36N 0°3E 125 A4
Woodford Green U.K. 51°36N 0°2E 125 A4
Woodfords U.S.A. 38°47N 119°50W 306 G7
Woodhaven U.S.A. 40°41N 73°51W 132 B2
Woodhouselee U.K. 55°52N 3°13W 121 B2
Woodlake U.S.A. 36°25N 119°6W 306 J7
Woodland Calif., U.S.A. 38°41N 121°46W 306 G5
Woodland Maine, U.S.A. 45°9N 67°25W 309 C20
Woodland Pa., U.S.A. 41°0N 78°21W 312 F6
Woodland Wash., U.S.A. 45°54N 122°45W 306 E4
Woodland Caribou ⌂ Canada 51°0N 94°45W 297 C10
Woodlands Singapore 1°26N 103°46E 138 A2
Woodlands, The U.S.A. 30°9N 95°29W 314 F7
Woodlark I. Papua N. G. 9°10S 152°50E 286 E7
Woodmont U.S.A. 38°59N 77°5W 143 B3
Woodonga Australia 36°10S 146°50E 281 F4
Woodridge Canada 49°20N 96°9W 297 D9
Woodroffe, Mt. Australia 26°20S 131°45E 279 E5
Woods, L. Australia 17°50S 133°30E 280 B1
Woods, L. of the N. Amer. 49°15N 94°45W 297 D10
Woods Bay Canada 45°8N 79°59W 312 A5
Woodside S. Austral., Australia 34°58S 138°52E 282 C3
Woodside Vic., Australia 38°31S 146°52E 283 E7
Woodside London, U.K. 51°23N 0°4W 125 B3
Woodside N.Y., U.S.A. 40°44N 73°54W 132 B2
Woodson U.S.A. 39°37N 90°14W 310 E6
Woodstock N.S.W., Australia 33°45S 148°53E 283 B8
Woodstock Queens., Australia 19°35S 146°50E 280 B4
Woodstock N.B., Canada 46°11N 67°37W 299 C6
Woodstock Ont., Canada 43°10N 80°45W 312 C4
Woodstock Western Cape, S. Africa 33°55S 18°27E 118 A1
Woodstock Oxon., U.K. 51°51N 1°20W 169 F6
Woodstock Ga., U.S.A. 34°6N 84°31W 316 A5
Woodstock Ill., U.S.A. 42°19N 88°27W 311 B8
Woodstock N.Y., U.S.A. 42°2N 74°7W 313 D10
Woodstock Vt., U.S.A. 43°37N 72°31W 313 C12
Woodsville U.S.A. 44°9N 72°2W 313 B13
Woodview Canada 44°35N 78°8W 312 B6
Woodville N.Z. 40°20S 175°53E 284 G4
Woodville Fla., U.S.A. 30°19N 84°15W 316 E5
Woodville Ga., U.S.A. 33°40N 83°7W 316 B6
Woodville Miss., U.S.A. 31°6N 91°18W 314 F9
Woodville Ohio, U.S.A. 41°27N 83°22W 311 C13
Woodville Tex., U.S.A. 30°47N 94°25W 314 F7
Woodward U.S.A. 36°26N 99°24W 314 C5
Woody U.S.A. 35°42N 118°50W 307 K8
Woody → Canada 52°31N 100°51W 297 C8
Woolacombe U.K. 51°10N 4°13W 169 F3
Woolamai, C. Australia 38°30S 145°23E 283 E6
Woolbrook Australia 30°56S 151°25E 283 A9
Wooler U.K. 55°33N 2°1W 168 B5
Woolgoolga Australia 30°6S 153°11E 281 E5
Woollahra Australia 33°53S 151°15E 139 B2
Woolloomooloo Sydney, Australia 139 b2
Woolooware B. Australia 34°15S 151°8E 139 C1
Woolwich U.K. 51°29N 0°4E 125 B4
Woolworth Building New York, U.S.A. 132 e1
Woomargama △ Australia 35°50S 147°15E 283 C7
Woomera Australia 31°5S 136°50E 282 A2
Woonsocket R.I., U.S.A. 42°0N 71°31W 313 E13
Woonsocket S. Dak., U.S.A. 44°3N 98°17W 308 C4
Wooramel → Australia 25°47S 114°10E 279 E1
Wooramel Roadhouse Australia 25°45S 114°17E 279 E1
Wooroonooran △ Australia 16°25S 146°1E 280 B4
Wooster U.S.A. 40°48N 81°56W 312 F3
Woqooyi Galbeed □ Somali Rep. 10°0N 44°30E 267 C5
Woraksan △ S. Korea 36°50N 128°5E 224 D4
Worcester Western Cape, S. Africa 33°39S 19°27E 270 D2
Worcester Worcs., U.K. 52°11N 2°12W 169 E5
Worcester Mass., U.S.A. 42°16N 71°48W 313 D13
Worcester N.Y., U.S.A. 42°36N 74°45W 313 D10
Worcestershire □ U.K. 52°13N 2°10W 169 E5
Worden U.S.A. 38°56N 89°50W 310 F7
Wörgl Austria 47°29N 12°3E 180 D5
Worker's Stadium China 39°55N 116°25E 114 B2
Workington U.K. 54°39N 3°33W 168 C4
Worksop U.K. 53°18N 1°7W 168 D6
Workum Neths. 52°59N 5°26E 170 B5
Worland U.S.A. 44°1N 107°57W 304 D10
World Bank Washington, D.C., U.S.A. 143 b1
World Financial Center New York, U.S.A. 132 e1
World Trade Center, Site of former = Ground Zero New York, U.S.A. 132 e1
World War Two Memorial Washington, D.C., U.S.A. 143 b1
Worli India 19°1N 72°49E 130 A1
Wormhout France 50°52N 2°28E 173 B9
Worms Germany 49°37N 8°21E 179 F4
Worsley Canada 56°31N 119°8W 296 B5
Wörth Bayern, Germany 49°1N 12°24E 179 F8
Worth Ill., U.S.A. 41°41N 87°47W 119 C2
Wortham U.S.A. 31°47N 96°28W 314 F6
Wörther See Austria 46°37N 14°10E 180 E7
Worthing U.K. 50°49N 0°21W 169 G7
Worthington Ind., U.S.A. 39°7N 86°59W 311 E10
Worthington Minn., U.S.A. 43°37N 95°36W 308 D6
Worthington Ohio, U.S.A. 40°5N 83°1W 311 D13
Worthington Pa., U.S.A. 40°50N 79°38W 312 F5
Wosi Indonesia 0°15S 128°0E 231 E7
Wote Kenya 1°47S 37°38E 268 C4
Wotjalum ✪ Australia 16°30S 123°45E 278 C3
Wotjobaluk ✪ Australia 37°0S 142°0E 281 C3
Wou-han = Wuhan China 30°31N 114°18E 229 B10
Wour Chad 21°14N 16°0E 259 D3
Wousi = Wuxi China 31°33N 120°18E 229 B13
Wowoni Indonesia 4°5S 123°5E 231 E6
Woy Woy Australia 33°30S 151°19E 283 B9
Wrangel I. = Vrangelya, Ostrov Russia 71°0N 180°0E 215 B18
Wrangell U.S.A. 56°28N 132°23W 296 B2
Wrangell Mts. U.S.A. 61°30N 142°0W 303 F12
Wrangell-St. Elias △ U.S.A. 61°0N 142°0W 303 F12
Wrath, C. U.K. 58°38N 5°1W 167 C3
Wray U.S.A. 40°5N 102°13W 304 F12
Wrekin, The U.K. 52°41N 2°32W 169 E5
Wrens U.S.A. 33°12N 82°23W 316 B7
Wren's Nest U.S.A. 33°44N 84°25W 113 B2
Wrexham U.K. 53°3N 3°0W 168 D4
Wrexham □ U.K. 53°1N 2°58W 168 D5
Wriezen Germany 52°42N 14°7E 178 C10
Wright = Paranas Phil. 11°42N 125°2E 233 F5
Wright Fla., U.S.A. 30°27N 86°38W 317 E3
Wright Wyo., U.S.A. 43°45N 105°28W 304 E11
Wright Pt. Canada 43°48N 81°44W 312 C3
Wrightmyo India 11°47N 92°43E 245 J11
Wrightson, Mt. U.S.A. 31°42N 110°51W 305 L8
Wrightsville U.S.A. 32°44N 82°43W 316 C7
Wrightwood U.S.A. 34°22N 117°38W 307 L9
Wrigley Canada 63°16N 123°37W 294 E7
Wrigley Building Chicago, U.S.A. 119 b2
Wrigley Field U.S.A. 41°56N 87°39W 119 B3
Wrocław Poland 51°5N 17°5E 185 G4
Wronki Poland 52°41N 16°21E 185 F3
Września Poland 52°21N 17°36E 185 F4
Wschowa Poland 51°48N 16°20E 185 G3
Wu He → Taiwan 24°9N 120°31E 225 B2
Wu Jiang → China 29°40N 107°20E 228 C6
Wu Kau Tang China 22°30N 114°14E 219 F11
Wu'an China 36°40N 114°15E 226 F8
Wubalawun ✪ Australia 15°28S 133°1E 278 C5
Wubin Australia 30°6S 116°37E 279 F2
Wubu China 37°28N 110°42E 226 F6
Wuchang China 44°55N 127°5E 227 B14
Wucheng China 37°12N 116°20E 226 F9
Wuch'i Taiwan 24°16N 120°31E 225 B2
Wuchieh Taiwan 24°41N 121°47E 225 B3
Wuchow = Wuzhou China 23°30N 111°18E 229 F8
Wuchuan Guangdong, China 21°33N 110°43E 229 G8
Wuchuan Guizhou, China 28°25N 108°3E 228 C7
Wuchuan Nei Monggol Zizhiqu, China 41°5N 111°28E 226 D6
Wuday'ah Si. Arabia 17°2N 47°7E 248 C4
Wudi China 37°40N 117°35E 227 F9
Wuding China 25°24N 102°21E 228 E4
Wuding He → China 37°2N 110°23E 226 F6
Wudinna Australia 33°0S 135°22E 281 E2
Wudu China 33°22N 104°54E 226 H3
Wufeng Henan, China 30°12N 110°42E 229 B8
Wufeng Taiwan 24°4N 120°42E 225 B2
Wugang China 26°44N 110°35E 229 D8
Wugong Shan China 27°30N 114°0E 229 D9
Wuguishan China 22°25N 113°25E 219 G9
Wugullar = Beswick Australia 14°34S 132°53E 278 B5
Wuhai China 39°47N 106°52E 218 C5
Wuhan China 30°31N 114°18E 229 B10
Wuhe China 33°10N 117°50E 227 H9
Wuhlgarten Germany 52°31N 13°34E 115 A4
Wuhsi = Wuxi China 31°33N 120°18E 229 B13
Wuhu China 31°22N 118°21E 229 B12
Wujiang China 31°10N 120°38E 229 B13
Wujiaochang China 31°18N 121°31E 138 B2
Wujih Taiwan 24°6N 120°38E 225 B2
Wukari Nigeria 7°51N 9°42E 263 D6
Wulai Taiwan 24°52N 121°33E 225 B3
Wulajie China 44°6N 126°33E 227 B14
Wulanbulang China 41°5N 110°55E 226 D6
Wular L. India 34°20N 74°30E 243 B6
Wulehe Ghana 8°39N 0°0 263 D5
Wulff Land Greenland 82°0N 49°0W 154 A6
Wulian China 35°40N 119°12E 227 G10
Wuliang Shan China 24°30N 100°40E 228 E3
Wuliaru Indonesia 7°27S 131°0E 231 F8
Wulicheng Taiwan 23°47N 121°0E 225 C3
Wuling Shan China 30°0N 110°0E 228 C7
Wulong China 29°22N 107°43E 228 C6
Wulu Taiwan 23°10N 121°2E 225 C3
Wulumuchi = Ürümqi China 43°45N 87°45E 217 D11
Wum Cameroon 6°24N 10°2E 263 D7
Wuming China 23°12N 108°18E 228 F7
Wun Rog Sudan 9°0N 28°20E 257 F2
Wundanyi Kenya 3°24S 38°22E 268 C4
Wuning China 29°17N 115°5E 229 C10
Wunna → India 20°18N 78°48E 244 D4
Wunnummin L. Canada 52°55N 89°10W 298 B2
Wunsiedel Germany 50°2N 12°0E 179 E8
Wunstorf Germany 52°25N 9°26E 178 C5
Wuntho Burma 23°55N 95°45E 241 D5
Wupatki △ U.S.A. 35°35N 111°20W 305 J8
Wuping China 25°5N 116°5E 229 E11
Wuppertal Nordrhein-Westfalen, Germany 51°16N 7°12E 178 D3
Wuppertal Western Cape, S. Africa 32°13S 19°12E 270 D2
Wuqia China 39°40N 75°7E 217 E9
Wuqing China 39°23N 117°4E 227 E9
Würm → Germany 48°8N 11°27E 131 B1
Würm-kanal Germany 48°13N 11°29E 131 A1
Wurralibi ✪ Australia 15°43S 137°1E 280 B2
Wurtsboro U.S.A. 41°35N 74°29W 313 E10
Würzburg Germany 49°46N 9°55E 179 F5
Wurzen Germany 51°22N 12°44E 178 D8
Wushan China 34°43N 104°53E 226 G3
Wushi China 41°9N 79°13E 217 D9
Wushishi Nigeria 9°46N 6°7E 263 D6
Wusi Vanuatu 15°21S 166°40E 287 E4
Wusih = Wuxi China 31°33N 120°18E 229 B13
Wusong China 31°22N 121°29E 138 A1
Wutach → Germany 47°37N 8°15E 179 H4
Wutai China 38°40N 113°12E 226 E7
Wuting = Huimin China 37°27N 117°28E 227 F9
Wutong China 25°24N 110°4E 229 E8
Wutonghaolai China 42°50N 120°5E 227 C11
Wutongqiao China 29°22N 103°50E 228 C4
Wutung Papua N. G. 2°34S 141°1E 286 B1
Wuwei Anhui, China 31°18N 117°54E 229 B11
Wuwei Gansu, China 37°57N 102°34E 218 C5
Wuxi Jiangsu, China 31°33N 120°18E 229 B13
Wuxi Sichuan, China 31°23N 109°35E 228 B7
Wuxiang China 36°49N 112°50E 226 F7
Wuxuan China 23°34N 109°38E 228 F7
Wuxue China 29°52N 115°30E 229 C10
Wuyang China 33°25N 113°35E 226 H7
Wuyi Hebei, China 37°46N 115°56E 226 F8
Wuyi Zhejiang, China 28°52N 119°50E 229 C12
Wuyi Shan China 27°0N 117°0E 229 D11
Wuyishan China 27°45N 118°0E 229 D12
Wuyo Nigeria 10°23N 11°50E 263 C7
Wuyuan Jiangxi, China 29°15N 117°50E 229 C11
Wuyuan Nei Monggol Zizhiqu, China 41°2N 108°20E 226 D5
Wuzhai China 38°54N 111°48E 226 E6
Wuzhi Shan China 18°45N 109°45E 236 C7
Wuzhong China 38°2N 106°12E 226 E4
Wuzhou China 23°30N 111°18E 229 F8
Wyaaba Cr. → Australia 16°27S 141°35E 280 B3
Wyalkatchem Australia 31°8S 117°22E 279 F2
Wyalusing U.S.A. 41°40N 76°16W 313 E8
Wyandotte U.S.A. 42°12N 83°9W 311 B13
Wyandra Australia 27°12S 145°56E 281 D4
Wyangala, L. Australia 33°54S 149°0E 283 B8
Wyara, L. Australia 28°42S 144°14E 281 D3
Wycheproof Australia 36°5S 143°17E 282 D5
Wycliffe Well Australia 20°48S 134°14E 280 C1
Wyczółki Poland 52°9N 20°59E 142 C1
Wye → U.K. 51°38N 2°40W 169 F5
Wyemandoo Australia 28°28S 118°29E 279 E2
Wygoda Poland 52°15N 21°7E 142 B2
Wyk Germany 54°41N 8°33E 178 A4
Wymondham U.K. 52°35N 1°7E 169 E9
Wymore U.S.A. 40°7N 96°40W 308 E5
Wynberg S. Africa 34°2S 18°28E 118 B1
Wyndham W. Austral., Australia 15°33S 128°3E 278 C4
Wyndham N.Z. 46°20S 168°51E 285 G3
Wynne U.S.A. 35°14N 90°47W 315 D9
Wynyard Tas., Australia 41°5S 145°44E 281 G4
Wynyard Sask., Canada 51°45N 104°10W 297 C8
Wyola L. Australia 29°8S 130°17E 279 E5
Wyoming Ont., Canada 42°57N 82°7W 312 D2
Wyoming Ill., U.S.A. 41°4N 89°47W 310 C7
Wyoming Iowa, U.S.A. 42°4N 91°0W 310 B6
Wyoming Mich., U.S.A. 42°54N 85°42W 311 B11
Wyoming □ U.S.A. 43°0N 107°30W 304 E10
Wyomissing U.S.A. 40°20N 75°59W 313 F9
Wyong Australia 33°14S 151°24E 283 B9
Wyperfeld △ Australia 35°35S 141°42E 282 C4
Wyrzysk Poland 53°10N 17°17E 185 E4
Wyśmierzyce Poland 51°37N 20°50E 185 G7
Wysoka Poland 53°13N 17°2E 185 E4
Wysokie Poland 50°55N 22°40E 185 H9
Wysokie Mazowieckie Poland 52°55N 22°30E 185 F9
Wyszków Poland 52°36N 21°25E 185 F8
Wyszogród Poland 52°23N 20°9E 185 F7
Wytheville U.S.A. 36°57N 81°5W 309 G13
Wyżyna Małopolska Poland 50°45N 20°0E 185 H7

X

Xa-Cassau Angola 9°5S 20°15E 265 D4
Xa-Muteba Angola 9°34S 17°50E 265 D3
Xaafuun Somali Rep. 10°25N 51°16E 267 B7
Xaafuun, Ras Somali Rep. 10°27N 51°24E 267 B7
Xabregas Portugal 38°43N 9°6W 126 A2
Xaçmaz Azerbaijan 41°31N 48°42E 191 K9
Xaghra Malta 36°3N 14°16E 206 E7
Xai-Xai Mozam. 25°6S 33°31E 271 C5
Xaidulla China 36°28N 77°59E 217 E9
Xainza China 30°58N 88°35E 218 C3
Xalapa Mexico 19°32N 96°55W 319 D5
Xalin Somali Rep. 9°6N 48°37E 267 C6
Xallas → Spain 42°54N 9°8W 194 C1
Xambioá Brazil 6°25S 48°40W 332 C2
Xangongo Angola 16°45S 15°5E 265 F3
Xankändi Azerbaijan 39°52N 46°49E 213 C12
Xanlar Azerbaijan 40°37N 46°12E 191 K8
Xanten Germany 51°39N 6°26E 178 D2
Xanthi Greece 41°10N 24°58E 203 E8
Xanthi □ Greece 41°10N 24°58E 203 E8
Xanthos Turkey 36°19N 29°18E 205 E11
Xanxerê Brazil 26°53S 52°23W 335 B5
Xapuri Brazil 10°35S 68°35W 330 C4
Xar Moron He → China 43°25N 120°35E 227 C11
Xarardheere Somali Rep. 4°33N 47°38E 267 D6
Xarrë Albania 39°44N 20°3E 206 B10
Xàtiva Spain 38°59N 0°32W 197 G4
Xau, L. Botswana 21°15S 24°44E 270 B3
Xavantina Brazil 21°15S 52°48W 335 A5
Xayar China 41°13N 82°48E 217 D10
Xenia U.S.A. 39°41N 83°56W 311 E13
Xeropotamos → Cyprus 34°42N 32°33E 207 F8
Xertigny France 48°3N 6°24E 173 D13
Xewkija Malta 36°2N 14°15E 206 E7
Xhora S. Africa 31°55S 28°38E 271 D4
Xhumo Botswana 21°7S 24°35E 270 B3
Xi Jiang → China 22°5N 113°20E 229 F9
Xi Xian Henan, China 32°20N 114°43E 229 A10
Xi Xian Shanxi, China 36°41N 110°58E 226 F6
Xia Xian China 35°8N 111°12E 226 G6
Xiachengzi China 44°40N 130°18E 227 B16
Xiachuan Dao China 21°40N 112°40E 229 G9
Xiaguan China 25°32N 100°16E 218 D5
Xiajiang China 27°30N 115°10E 229 D10
Xiajin China 36°56N 116°0E 226 F9
Xiamen China 24°25N 118°4E 229 E12
Xi'an China 34°15N 109°0E 226 G5
Xian Xian China 38°12N 116°6E 226 E9
Xianfeng China 29°40N 109°8E 228 C7
Xiang Jiang → China 28°55N 112°50E 229 C9
Xiangcheng Henan, China 33°29N 114°52E 226 H8
Xiangcheng Henan, China 33°50N 113°27E 226 H7
Xiangcheng Sichuan, China 28°53N 99°47E 228 C2
Xiangdu China 23°13N 106°58E 228 F6
Xiangfan China 32°2N 112°8E 229 A9
Xianggang = Hong Kong China 22°11N 114°14E 122 B1
Xianggang = Hong Kong □ China 22°11N 114°14E 219 G11
Xianghuang Qi China 42°2N 113°50E 226 C7
Xiangning China 35°58N 110°50E 226 G6
Xiangquan China 36°30N 113°1E 226 F7
Xiangquan He = Sutlej → Pakistan 29°23N 71°3E 242 E4
Xiangshan China 29°29N 121°51E 229 C13
Xiangshui China 34°12N 119°33E 227 G10
Xiangtan China 27°51N 112°54E 229 D9
Xiangxiang China 27°43N 112°28E 229 D9
Xiangyin China 28°38N 112°54E 229 C9
Xiangyun China 25°34N 100°35E 228 E3
Xiangzhou China 23°58N 109°40E 228 F7
Xianju China 28°51N 120°44E 229 C13
Xianning China 29°51N 114°16E 229 C10
Xianshui He → China 30°10N 100°59E 228 B3
Xiantao China 30°25N 113°25E 229 B9
Xianyang China 34°20N 108°40E 226 G5
Xianyou China 25°22N 118°38E 229 E12
Xiao Hinggan Ling China 49°0N 127°0E 219 B7
Xiao Xian China 34°15N 116°55E 226 G9
Xiaofeng China 30°35N 119°32E 229 B12
Xiaogan China 30°52N 113°55E 229 B9
Xiaogang Park China 23°6N 113°16E 121 B2
Xiaojin China 30°59N 102°21E 228 B4
Xiaolan China 22°38N 113°13E 229 F9
Xiaoping China 23°12N 113°19E 121 A2
Xiaoshan China 30°12N 120°18E 229 B13
Xiaoyi China 37°8N 111°48E 226 F6
Xiapu China 26°54N 119°59E 229 D12
Xiasha chong China 23°8N 113°9E 121 B1
Xiawa China 42°35N 120°38E 227 C11
Xiayi China 34°15N 116°10E 226 G9
Xichang Guangdong, China 23°9N 113°13E 121 B2
Xichang Sichuan, China 27°51N 102°19E 228 D4
Xicheng Beijing, China 114 b1
Xichong China 30°57N 105°54E 228 B5
Xichou China 23°25N 104°42E 228 F5
Xichuan China 33°0N 111°30E 226 H6
Xidan China 39°52N 116°20E 114 B2
Xide China 28°8N 102°19E 228 C4
Xiemahe China 31°38N 111°12E 229 B8
Xieng Khouang Laos 19°17N 103°25E 236 C4
Xifei He → China 32°45N 116°40E 226 H9
Xifeng Gansu, China 35°40N 107°40E 226 G4
Xifeng Guizhou, China 27°7N 106°42E 228 D6
Xifeng Liaoning, China 42°42N 124°45E 227 C13
Xifengzhen = Xifeng China 35°40N 107°40E 226 G4
Xigazê China 29°5N 88°45E 218 D3
Xihe China 34°2N 105°20E 226 G3
Xihua China 33°45N 114°30E 226 H8
Xilagani Greece 40°58N 25°28E 203 F9
Xili Shuiku China 22°36N 113°57E 219 F10
Xiliao He → China 43°32N 123°35E 227 C12
Xilin China 24°30N 105°6E 228 E5
Xilinhot China 43°52N 116°2E 226 C9
Xilokastro Greece 38°5N 22°38E 204 C4
Ximana Mozam. 19°24S 33°58E 269 F3
Xime Guinea-Biss. 11°59N 14°57W 262 C2
Ximeng China 22°50N 99°27E 228 F2
Xin Jiang → China 28°45N 116°35E 229 C11
Xin Xian = Xinzhou China 38°22N 112°46E 226 E7
Xinavane Mozam. 25°2S 32°47E 271 C5
Xinbin China 41°40N 125°2E 224 B2
Xincai China 32°43N 114°58E 229 A10
Xinchang China 29°28N 120°52E 229 C13
Xincheng Guangxi Zhuangzu, China 24°5N 108°39E 228 E7
Xincheng Jiangxi, China 26°48N 114°6E 229 D10
Xinchengzi China 42°2N 123°0E 224 A1
Xincun China 38°15N 117°45E 227 E9
Xindu China 30°50N 104°10E 228 B5
Xinfeng Guangdong, China 24°5N 114°16E 229 E10
Xinfeng Jiangxi, China 27°7N 116°11E 229 D11
Xinfeng Jiangxi, China 25°27N 114°58E 229 E10
Xinfengjiang Shuiku China 23°52N 114°30E 229 F10
Xing Xian China 38°27N 111°7E 226 E6
Xing'an Guangxi Zhuangzu, China 25°38N 110°40E 229 E8
Xingan Jiangxi, China 27°46N 115°20E 229 D10
Xingcheng China 40°40N 120°45E 227 D11
Xingguo China 26°21N 115°21E 229 D10
Xinghe China 40°55N 113°55E 226 D7
Xinghua China 32°58N 119°48E 227 H10
Xinghua Wan China 25°15N 119°20E 229 E12
Xinglong China 40°25N 117°30E 227 D9
Xingning China 24°3N 115°42E 229 E10
Xingping China 34°20N 108°28E 226 G5
Xingren China 25°24N 105°11E 228 E5
Xingshan China 31°15N 110°45E 229 B8
Xingtai China 37°3N 114°32E 226 F8
Xingu → Brazil 1°30S 51°53W 329 D7
Xingwen China 28°22N 104°50E 228 C5
Xingyang China 34°45N 112°52E 226 G7
Xingyi China 25°3N 104°59E 219 D5
Xinhe Hebei, China 37°30N 115°15E 226 F8
Xinhe Xinjiang Uygur, China 41°33N 82°37E 217 D10
Xinhua China 27°42N 111°13E 229 D8
Xinhuang China 27°21N 109°12E 228 D7
Xinhui China 22°25N 113°0E 229 F9
Xining China 36°34N 101°40E 218 C5
Xinjian China 28°37N 115°46E 229 C10
Xinjiang China 35°34N 111°11E 226 G6
Xinjiang Uygur Zizhiqu □ China 42°0N 86°0E 217 D11
Xinjie China 26°48N 101°55E 228 D3
Xinjin = Pulandian China 39°25N 121°58E 227 E11
Xinjin China 30°24N 103°47E 228 B4
Xinkai He → China 43°32N 123°35E 227 C12
Xinken China 22°39N 113°36E 219 F10
Xinle China 38°25N 114°40E 226 E8
Xinlitun China 42°0N 122°8E 227 D12
Xinlong China 30°57N 100°12E 228 B3
Xinmin China 41°59N 122°50E 224 B1
Xinning China 26°28N 110°50E 229 D8
Xinping China 24°5N 101°59E 228 E3
Xinshao China 27°21N 111°26E 229 D8
Xintai China 35°55N 117°45E 227 G9
Xintian China 25°55N 112°13E 229 E9
Xinwan China 22°47N 113°40E 219 F10
Xinxiang China 35°18N 113°50E 226 G7
Xinxing China 22°35N 112°15E 229 F9
Xinyang China 32°6N 114°3E 229 A10
Xinye China 32°30N 112°21E 229 A9
Xinyi China 22°25N 111°0E 229 F8
Xinyu China 27°49N 114°58E 229 D10
Xinzhan China 43°50N 127°18E 227 C14
Xinzheng China 34°20N 113°45E 226 G7
Xinzhou Hainan, China 19°43N 109°17E 236 C7
Xinzhou Hubei, China 30°50N 114°48E 229 B10
Xinzhou Shanxi, China 38°22N 112°46E 226 E7
Xinzo de Limia Spain 42°3N 7°47W 194 C3
Xiongyuecheng China 40°12N 122°5E 227 D12
Xiping Henan, China 33°22N 114°5E 226 H8
Xiping Henan, China 33°25N 111°8E 226 H6
Xiping Zhejiang, China 28°16N 119°29E 229 C12
Xique-Xique Brazil 10°50S 42°40W 332 D3
Xiruá → Brazil 6°3S 67°50W 330 B4
Xisha Qundao = Paracel Is. S. China Sea 15°50N 112°0E 230 A4
Xishui Guizhou, China 28°19N 106°9E 228 C6
Xishui Hubei, China 30°30N 115°15E 229 B10
Xitole Guinea-Biss. 11°43N 14°50W 262 C2
Xiu Shui → China 29°13N 116°0E 229 C10
Xiuning China 29°45N 118°10E 229 C12
Xiuren China 24°27N 110°12E 229 E8
Xiushan China 28°25N 108°57E 228 C7
Xiushui China 29°2N 114°33E 229 C10
Xiuwen China 26°49N 106°32E 228 D6
Xiuyan China 40°18N 123°11E 224 B1
Xixabangma Feng China 28°20N 85°40E 243 E11
Xixia China 33°25N 111°29E 226 H6
Xixiang China 33°0N 107°44E 219 F10
Xixón = Gijón Spain 43°32N 5°42W 194 B5
Xiyang China 37°38N 113°38E 226 F7
Xizang Zizhiqu □ China 32°0N 88°0E 217 F11
Xizhimen China 39°55N 116°19E 114 B1
Xlendi Malta 36°1N 14°12E 206 E6
Xochimilco, Parque Ecológico Mexico 19°18N 99°5W 128 C2
Xochob Mexico 19°21N 89°48W 319 D7
Xojayli = Khojayli Uzbekistan 42°29N 59°31E 216 D5
Xorazm □ Uzbekistan 43°0N 60°0E 216 D6
Xu Beihong Memorial Hall Beijing, China 114 a2
Xu Jiang → China 28°0N 116°25E 229 D11
Xuan Loc Vietnam 10°56N 107°14E 237 G6
Xuan'en China 30°0N 109°30E 228 C7
Xuanhan China 31°18N 107°38E 228 B6
Xuanhua China 40°40N 115°2E 226 D8
Xuanwei China 26°15N 103°59E 228 D5
Xuanwu Beijing, China 114 c1
Xuanzhou China 30°56N 118°43E 229 B12
Xuchang China 34°2N 113°48E 226 G7
Xudat Azerbaijan 41°38N 48°41E 191 K9
Xuddur Somali Rep. 4°11N 43°52E 267 D5
Xuefeng Shan China 27°5N 110°35E 229 D8
Xuejiaping China 31°39N 110°16E 229 B8
Xuhui China 31°11N 121°26E 138 B1
Xun Jiang → China 23°35N 111°30E 229 F8
Xun Xian China 35°42N 114°33E 226 G8
Xundian China 25°36N 103°15E 228 E4
Xunwu China 24°54N 115°37E 229 E10
Xunyang China 32°48N 109°22E 226 H5
Xunyi China 35°8N 108°20E 226 G5
Xupu China 27°53N 110°32E 229 D8
Xúquer → Spain 39°5N 0°10W 197 F4
Xushui China 39°2N 115°40E 226 E8
Xuwen China 20°20N 110°10E 229 G8
Xuyen Moc Vietnam 10°34N 107°25E 237 G6
Xuyong China 28°10N 105°22E 228 C5
Xuzhou China 34°18N 117°10E 227 G9
Xylophagou Cyprus 34°54N 33°51E 207 F9

Y

Y.S. Falls Jamaica 18°9N 77°49W 320 a
Ya Xian = Sanya China 18°14N 109°29E 236 C7
Yaamba Australia 23°8S 150°22E 280 C5
Ya'an China 29°58N 103°5E 228 C4
Yaapeet Australia 35°45S 142°3E 282 C5
Yaba Nigeria 6°30N 3°22E 124 A2
Yabassi Cameroon 4°30N 9°57E 263 E6
Yabayo Ivory C. 5°56N 6°36W 262 D3
Yabelo Ethiopia 4°50N 38°8E 257 G4
Yabelo ⌂ Ethiopia 6°0N 37°50E 257 F4
Yablanitsa Bulgaria 43°2N 24°5E 203 C8
Yablonovyy Khrebet Russia 53°0N 114°0E 215 D12
Yablonovyy Ra. = Yablonovyy Khrebet Russia 53°0N 114°0E 215 D12
Yabluniv Ukraine 48°24N 24°57E 183 B9
Yablunytsya Ukraine 48°19N 24°29E 183 B9
Yabrai Shan China 39°40N 103°0E 226 E2
Yabrūd Syria 33°58N 36°39E 250 E7
Yabucoa Puerto Rico 18°3N 65°53W 321 b
Yacambú △ Venezuela 9°42N 69°27W 328 B4
Yacheng China 18°22N 109°6E 236 C7
Yackandandah Australia 36°18S 146°52E 283 D7
Yacuiba Bolivia 22°0S 63°43W 334 A3
Yacuma → Bolivia 13°38S 65°23W 331 C4
Yadgir India 16°45N 77°5E 244 F3
Yadkin → U.S.A. 35°23N 80°4W 315 D14
Yadong China 27°26N 88°56E 241 B2
Yadrin Russia 55°57N 46°12E 190 C8
Yadua Fiji 16°49S 178°18E 287 A2
Yaeyama-Rettō Japan 24°30N 123°40E 221 M1
Yafran Libya 32°4N 12°31E 258 B2
Yafran □ Libya 32°0N 12°20E 258 B2
Yaftābād Iran 35°37N 51°17E 141 B1
Yagaba Ghana 10°14N 1°20W 263 C4
Yagaji-shima Japan 26°39N 128°0E 288 a
Yagasa Cluster Fiji 18°57S 178°28W 287 B3
Yağcılar Turkey 39°25N 28°23E 205 B10
Yagodnoye Russia 62°33N 149°40E 215 C15
Yagoua Cameroon 10°20N 15°13E 259 F3
Yaguas → Peru 2°45S 70°10W 328 D3
Yahara Japan 35°44N 139°37E 140 A2
Yahila Orientale, Dem. Rep. of the Congo 0°13N 24°28E 264 B4
Yahila Orientale, Dem. Rep. of the Congo 1°48N 23°37E 264 B4
Yahk Canada 49°6N 116°10W 296 D5
Yaho Japan 35°40N 139°26E 140 A1
Yahotyn Ukraine 50°17N 31°46E 189 G6
Yahuma Dem. Rep. of the Congo 1°0N 23°10E 264 B4
Yahyalı Turkey 38°5N 35°2E 212 C6
Yaita Japan 36°48N 139°56E 221 F9
Yaiza Canary Is. 28°57N 13°46W 153 e2
Yaizu Japan 34°52N 138°20E 223 C10
Yajiang China 30°2N 100°57E 228 B3
Yajua Nigeria 11°27N 12°49E 263 C7
Yakacık Turkey 36°46N 36°11E 250 B7
Yakage Japan 34°37N 133°35E 222 C5
Yakamba Dem. Rep. of the Congo 2°42N 19°38E 264 B3
Yakapınar Turkey 36°57N 35°36E 250 B6
Yakima U.S.A. 46°36N 120°31W 304 C3
Yakima → U.S.A. 46°15N 119°14W 304 C4
Yakire Japan 35°45N 139°54E 140 A4
Yakishiri-Jima Japan 44°26N 141°25E 220 B10
Yako Burkina Faso 12°59N 2°15W 262 C4
Yakobi I. U.S.A. 58°0N 136°30W 296 B1
Yakoma Dem. Rep. of the Congo 4°5N 22°27E 264 B4
Yakoruda Bulgaria 42°1N 23°39E 202 D7
Yakossi C.A.R. 5°37N 23°19E 264 A4
Yakovlevka Russia 44°26N 133°28E 220 B6
Yakovlevskoye = Privolzhsk Russia 57°23N 41°16E 190 B5
Yaku-Shima Japan 30°20N 130°30E 221 J5
Yakumo Japan 42°15N 140°16E 220 C10
Yakutat U.S.A. 59°33N 139°44W 303 G13
Yakutat B. U.S.A. 59°45N 140°45W 303 G12
Yakutia = Sakha □ Russia 66°0N 130°0E 215 C14
Yakutsk Russia 62°5N 129°50E 215 C13
Yala Thailand 6°33N 101°18E 237 J3
Yala △ Sri Lanka 6°20N 81°30E 245 L5
Yalata Australia 31°59S 132°26E 279 F5
Yalata ✪ Australia 31°35S 132°7E 279 F5
Yalboroo Australia 20°50S 148°40E 280 b
Yale U.S.A. 43°8N 82°48W 312 C2
Yalgorup △ Australia 32°39S 115°38E 279 F2
Yali Dem. Rep. of the Congo 0°4N 21°3E 264 B4
Yaligimba Dem. Rep. of the Congo 2°13N 22°56E 264 B4
Yalikanda Dem. Rep. of the Congo 0°23N 24°47E 264 B4
Yalinga C.A.R. 6°33N 23°10E 264 A4
Yalkabul, Pta. Mexico 21°32N 88°37W 319 C7
Yallahs Jamaica 17°53N 76°35W 320 a
Yallahs Hill Jamaica 17°54N 76°30W 320 a
Yalleroi Australia 24°3S 145°42E 280 C4
Yalobusha → U.S.A. 33°33N 90°10W 315 E9
Yaloké C.A.R. 5°19N 17°5E 264 A3
Yalong Jiang → China 26°40N 101°55E 228 D3
Yalova Turkey 40°41N 29°15E 203 F13
Yalpirakinu ✪ Australia 22°24S 132°15E 278 D5
Yalpuh, Ozero Ukraine 45°30N 28°41E 183 E13
Yalta Ukraine 44°30N 34°10E 189 K8
Yalu Jiang → China 39°55N 124°19E 224 C2
Yalvaç Turkey 38°17N 31°10E 212 C4
Yam Australia 9°54S 142°46E 280 a
Yam Ha Melaḥ = Dead Sea Asia 31°30N 35°30E 251 G6
Yam Kinneret Israel 32°45N 35°35E 250 C6
Yamada Fukuoka, Japan 33°33N 130°49E 222 D2
Yamada Kanagawa, Japan 35°33N 139°37E 140 B2
Yamada Ōsaka, Japan 34°47N 135°32E 133 A2
Yamaga Japan 33°1N 130°41E 222 D2
Yamagata Japan 38°15N 140°15E 220 E10
Yamagata □ Japan 38°30N 140°0E 220 E10
Yamagawa Japan 31°12N 130°39E 222 F2
Yamaguchi Japan 34°10N 131°32E 222 C3
Yamaguchi □ Japan 34°20N 131°40E 222 C3
Yamal, Poluostrov Russia 71°0N 70°0E 214 B8
Yamal Pen. = Yamal, Poluostrov Russia 71°0N 70°0E 214 B8
Yamanaka Japan 36°15N 136°22E 223 A8
Yamanashi Japan 35°41N 138°40E 223 B10
Yamanashi □ Japan 35°40N 138°40E 223 B10
Yamantau, Gora Russia 54°15N 58°6E 186 D10
Yamasaki Japan 35°0N 134°32E 222 C6
Yamato Japan 35°27N 139°25E 223 B11
Yamato → Japan 34°36N 135°26E 133 B1
Yamato Ridge Sea of Japan 39°20N 135°0E 220 E7
Yamatotakada Japan 34°31N 135°45E 223 C7
Yamba Australia 29°26S 153°23E 281 D5
Yambarran Ra. Australia 15°10S 130°25E 278 C5
Yambata Dem. Rep. of the Congo 2°26N 21°58E 264 B4
Yambéring Guinea 11°50N 12°18E 262 C2
Yâmbiô Sudan 4°35N 28°16E 257 G2
Yambol Bulgaria 42°30N 26°30E 203 D10
Yamboyo Dem. Rep. of the Congo 0°40N 22°18E 264 B4
Yamburg Russia 68°21N 77°8E 214 C8
Yambuya Dem. Rep. of the Congo 1°17N 24°34E 264 B4
Yamdena Indonesia 7°45S 131°20E 231 F8
Yame Japan 33°13N 130°35E 222 D2
Yamethin Burma 20°29N 96°18E 241 E6
Y'Ami Phil. 21°6N 121°57E 232 A3
Yamma Yamma, L. Australia 26°16S 141°20E 281 D3
Yamoussoukro Ivory C. 6°49N 5°17W 262 D3
Yampa → U.S.A. 40°32N 108°59W 304 F9
Yampi Sd. Australia 16°8S 123°38E 278 C3
Yampil Moldova 48°15N 28°15E 177 D15
Yampol = Yampil Moldova 48°15N 28°15E 177 D15
Yamrat Nigeria 10°11N 9°55E 263 C6
Yamrukchal = Botev Bulgaria 42°44N 24°52E 203 D8
Yamuna → India 25°30N 81°53E 243 G9
Yamunanagar India 30°7N 77°17E 242 D7
Yamzho Yumco China 28°48N 90°35E 218 D4
Yan Nigeria 10°5N 12°11E 263 C7
Yan Kit Singapore 1°21N 103°58E 138 A3
Yan Oya → Sri Lanka 9°0N 81°10E 245 K5
Yana → Russia 71°30N 136°0E 215 B14
Yanagawa Japan 33°10N 130°24E 222 D2
Yanahara Japan 34°58N 134°2E 222 C6
Yanai Japan 33°58N 132°7E 222 D4
Yan'an China 36°35N 109°26E 226 F5
Yanaul Russia 56°25N 55°0E 186 C10
Yanbian China 26°47N 101°31E 228 D3
Yanbu 'al Baḥr Si. Arabia 24°0N 38°5E 246 F3
Yanchang China 36°43N 110°1E 226 F6
Yancheng Henan, China 33°35N 114°0E 226 H8
Yancheng Jiangsu, China 33°23N 120°8E 227 H11
Yanchep Australia 31°33S 115°37E 279 F2
Yanchi China 37°48N 107°20E 226 F4
Yanchuan China 36°51N 110°10E 226 F6
Yanco Australia 34°38S 146°27E 283 C7
Yanco Cr. → Australia 35°14S 145°35E 283 C6
Yandeyarra ✪ Australia 21°17S 118°24E 278 D2
Yandicoogina Australia 22°49S 119°12E 278 D2
Yandina Solomon Is. 9°7S 159°13E 287 M10
Yandja Dem. Rep. of the Congo 1°41S 17°43E 264 C3
Yandongi Dem. Rep. of the Congo 2°51N 22°16E 264 B4
Yandoon Burma 17°0N 95°40E 241 G5
Yanfeng China 25°52N 101°8E 228 E3
Yanfolila Mali 11°11N 8°9W 262 C3
Yang Xian China 33°15N 107°30E 226 H4
Yang-yang S. Korea 38°4N 128°38E 224 C4
Yang-Yang Senegal 15°30N 15°20W 262 B1
Yangambi Dem. Rep. of the Congo 0°47N 24°24E 264 B4
Yangbi China 25°41N 99°58E 228 E2
Yangcheng China 35°28N 112°22E 226 G7
Yangcheon S. Korea 37°30N 126°51E 137 B1
Yangchow = Yangzhou China 32°21N 119°26E 229 A12
Yangch'ü = Taiyuan China 37°52N 112°33E 226 F7
Yangchüan = Yangquan China 37°58N 113°31E 226 F7
Yangchun China 22°11N 111°48E 229 F8
Yangdok N. Korea 39°13N 126°38E 224 C3
Yanggang-do □ N. Korea 41°15N 128°0E 224 B4
Yanggao China 40°21N 113°55E 226 D7
Yanggu China 36°8N 115°43E 226 F8
Yanghuayuan China 39°49N 116°18E 114 C1
Yangiyul Uzbekistan 41°0N 69°3E 217 D7
Yangjae S. Korea 37°29N 127°2E 137 C2
Yangjiang China 21°50N 111°59E 229 G8
Yangjiazhuang China 31°22N 121°25E 138 A1
Yangjing China 31°15N 121°32E 138 B2
Yangju S. Korea 37°47N 127°7E 224 D3
Yangliuqing China 39°2N 117°5E 227 E9
Yangmei Taiwan 24°55N 121°8E 225 B3
Yangmingshan △ Taiwan 25°9N 121°32E 225 A3
Yangon = Rangoon Burma 16°45N 96°20E 241 G6
Yangonde Dem. Rep. of the Congo 0°3N 22°43E 264 B4
Yangping China 31°12N 111°25E 229 B8
Yangpingguan China 32°58N 106°5E 226 H4
Yangpu China 31°16N 121°32E 138 B2
Yangpu Park China 31°17N 121°31E 138 B2
Yangquan China 37°58N 113°31E 226 F7
Yangsan S. Korea 35°20N 129°2E 224 E4
Yangshan China 24°30N 112°40E 229 E9
Yangshuo China 24°48N 110°29E 229 E8
Yangtse = Chang Jiang → China 31°48N 121°10E 229 B13
Yangtze Kiang = Chang Jiang → China 31°48N 121°10E 229 B13
Yangudi Rassa △ Ethiopia 10°50N 40°42E 257 E5
Yangxin China 29°50N 115°12E 229 C10
Yangyuan China 40°1N 114°10E 226 D8
Yangzhong China 32°22N 119°22E 229 A12
Yangzhou China 32°21N 119°26E 229 A12
Yanhe China 28°31N 108°29E 228 C7
Yanji China 42°59N 129°30E 227 C15
Yanjin China 28°5N 104°18E 228 C5
Yanjing China 29°7N 98°33E 228 C2
Yankari △ Nigeria 9°50N 10°28E 259 G2
Yankton U.S.A. 42°53N 97°23W 308 D5
Yankunytjatjara-Antakirinja ✪ Australia 27°20S 134°30E 281 A1
Yannawa Thailand 13°43N 100°32E 113 B2
Yanonge Dem. Rep. of the Congo 0°35N 24°38E 264 B4
Yanov = Ivanava Belarus 52°7N 25°29E 177 B13
Yanqi China 42°5N 86°35E 217 D11

Yanqing China 40°30N 115°58E 226 D8
Yanshan Hebei, China 38°4N 117°22E 227 E9
Yanshan Jiangxi, China 28°15N 117°41E 229 C11
Yanshan Yunnan, China 23°35N 104°20E 228 F5
Yanshou China 45°28N 128°22E 227 B15
Yantabulla Australia 29°21S 145°0E 281 D4
Yantai China 37°34N 121°22E 227 F11
Yantarnyy Russia 54°52N 19°57E 184 D6
Yantian China 22°35N 114°16E 219 F11
Yanting China 31°11N 105°24E 228 B5
Yantra → Bulgaria 43°40N 25°37E 203 C9
Yanuca Fiji 18°24S 178°0E 287 B1
Yanununbeyan △ Australia 35°29S 149°24E 283 C8
Yanwa China 27°35N 98°55E 228 D2
Yanyuan China 27°25N 101°30E 228 D3
Yanzhou China 35°35N 116°49E 226 G9
Yao Chad 12°56N 17°33E 259 F3
Yao Japan 34°37N 135°36E 223 C7
Yao Noi, Ko Thailand 8°7N 98°37E 237 a
Yao Xian China 34°55N 108°59E 226 G5
Yao Yai, Ko Thailand 8°0N 98°35E 237 a
Yao'an China 25°31N 101°18E 228 E3
Yaodu China 32°45N 105°22E 228 A5
Yaoundé Cameroon 3°50N 11°35E 263 E7
Yaowan China 34°15N 118°3E 227 G10
Yap Pac. Oc. 9°30N 138°10E 287 R16
Yapacana △ Venezuela 3°49N 66°44W 328 C4
Yapehe Dem. Rep. of the Congo 0°13S 24°28E 264 C4
Yapei Ghana 9°10N 1°10W 263 D4
Yapen Indonesia 1°50S 136°0E 231 E9
Yapen, Selat Indonesia 1°20S 136°10E 231 E9
Yapero Indonesia 4°59S 137°11E 231 E9
Yappar → Australia 18°22S 141°16E 280 B3
Yapuparra ✪ Australia 27°15S 126°20E 279 E4
Yaqaga Fiji 16°35S 178°36E 287 A2
Yaqui → Mexico 27°37N 110°39W 318 B2
Yar-Sale Russia 66°50N 70°50E 214 C8
Yaracuy □ Venezuela 10°20N 68°45W 328 A4
Yaracuy → Venezuela 10°33N 68°15W 328 A4
Yaraka Australia 24°53S 144°3E 280 C3
Yaransk Russia 57°22N 47°49E 190 B8
Yarbasan Turkey 38°59N 28°49E 205 C10
Yardımcı Burnu Turkey 36°13N 30°25E 205 E12
Yare → U.K. 52°35N 1°38E 169 E9
Yaremcha Ukraine 48°27N 24°33E 183 B9
Yaren Nauru 0°33S 166°55E 288 H8
Yarensk Russia 62°11N 49°15E 186 B8
Yarfa Si. Arabia 24°37N 38°35E 256 C4
Yarí → Colombia 0°20S 72°20W 328 D3
Yarīm Yemen 14°20N 44°22E 248 D4
Yaritagua Venezuela 10°5N 69°8W 328 A4
Yarkand = Shache China 38°20N 77°10E 217 E9
Yarkant He → China 40°26N 80°59E 217 D10
Yarker Canada 44°23N 76°46W 313 B8
Yarkhun → Pakistan 36°17N 72°30E 243 A5
Yarlung Ziangbo Jiang = Brahmaputra → Asia 23°40N 90°35E 241 D3
Yarmouth Canada 43°50N 66°7W 299 D6
Yarmūk Iraq 33°18N 44°19E 113 B1
Yarmūk → Syria 32°42N 35°40E 250 F6
Yaroslavl Russia 57°35N 39°55E 188 D10
Yaroslavl □ Russia 59°20N 38°50E 188 C10
Yarra → Trin. & Tob. 10°48N 61°21W 323 t
Yarra Bend Park Australia 37°47S 145°0E 128 A2
Yarra Ranges △ Australia 37°40S 146°3E 283 D7
Yarra Yarra Lakes Australia 29°40S 115°45E 279 E2
Yarram Australia 38°29S 146°39E 283 E7
Yarraman Australia 26°50S 152°0E 281 D5
Yarras Australia 31°25S 152°20E 283 A10
Yarraville Australia 37°48S 144°53E 128 A1
Yarrawonga Australia 36°0S 146°0E 283 D7
Yarrie Australia 20°40S 120°12E 278 D3
Yartsevo Sib., Russia 60°20N 90°0E 215 C10
Yartsevo Smolensk, Russia 55°6N 32°43E 188 E7
Yarumal Colombia 6°58N 75°24W 328 B2
Yasa Dem. Rep. of the Congo 3°50S 21°25E 264 C4
Yasawa Fiji 16°47S 177°31E 287 A1
Yasawa Group Fiji 17°0S 177°23E 287 A1
Yaselda Belarus 52°7N 26°28E 177 B14
Yasen Ukraine 48°45N 24°10E 183 B9
Yashbum Yemen 14°19N 46°56E 248 D4
Yashi Nigeria 12°23N 7°54E 263 C6
Yashikera Nigeria 9°44N 3°29E 263 D5
Yashiro-Jima Japan 33°55N 132°15E 222 D4
Yashkul Russia 46°11N 45°21E 191 G7
Yasin Pakistan 36°24N 73°23E 243 A5
Yasinovataya Ukraine 48°7N 37°57E 189 H9
Yasinski, L. Canada 53°16N 77°35W 298 B4
Yasinya Ukraine 48°16N 24°21E 183 B9
Yasnyy Russia 51°1N 59°58E 216 B5
Yasothon Thailand 15°50N 104°10E 236 E5
Yass Australia 34°49S 148°54E 283 C8
Yasugi Japan 35°26N 133°15E 222 B5
Yāsūj Iran 30°31N 51°31E 247 D6
Yasuní △ Ecuador 1°19S 76°3W 328 D2
Yat Niger 20°28N 13°27E 259 D2
Yata → Bolivia 10°29S 65°26W 331 C4
Yata → C.A.R. 10°23N 22°45E 264 A4
Yata-Ngaya ⌓ C.A.R. 9°15N 23°25E 264 A4
Yatağan Turkey 37°20N 28°10E 205 D10
Yatakala Niger 14°50N 0°22E 263 C5
Yaté N. Cal. 22°9S 166°57E 288 d
Yates Center U.S.A. 37°53N 95°44W 308 G6
Yates Pt. N.Z. 44°29S 167°49E 285 E2
Yathkyed L. Canada 62°40N 98°0W 297 A9
Yathong Australia 32°37S 145°33E 283 B6
Yatolemu Dem. Rep. of the Congo 0°25N 24°35E 264 B4
Yatsuo Japan 36°34N 137°8E 223 A9
Yatsushiro Japan 32°30N 130°40E 222 E2
Yatsushiro-Kai Japan 32°30N 130°25E 222 E2
Yatta Plateau Kenya 2°0S 38°0E 268 C4
Yatua → Venezuela 1°30N 66°30W 328 C4
Yauca Peru 15°39S 74°35W 330 D3
Yauco Puerto Rico 18°2N 66°51W 321 b
Yauri Peru 14°47S 71°25W 330 C3
Yauya Peru 8°59S 77°17W 330 B2
Yauyos Peru 12°19S 75°50W 330 C2
Yauza → Russia 55°54N 37°43E 129 B4
Yaval India 21°10N 75°42E 244 D2
Yavarí → Peru 4°21S 70°2W 330 A3
Yávaros Mexico 26°42N 109°31W 318 B3
Yavatmal India 20°20N 78°15E 244 D4
Yavero → Peru 12°6S 72°57W 330 C3
Yavne Israel 31°52N 34°45E 251 G5
Yavoriv Ukraine 49°55N 23°20E 185 J10
Yavorov = Yavoriv Ukraine 49°55N 23°20E 185 J10
Yavuzeli Turkey 37°18N 37°24E 212 D7
Yawatahama Japan 33°27N 132°24E 222 D4
Yawnghwe Burma 20°39N 96°56E 241 E6
Yawri B. S. Leone 8°22N 13°0W 262 D2
Yaxi China 27°33N 106°41E 228 D6
Yaxian = Sanya China 18°14N 109°29E 236 C7
Yayama Dem. Rep. of the Congo 1°16S 23°7E 264 C4
Yayladağı Turkey 35°54N 36°3E 250 C7
Yazagyo Burma 23°30N 94°6E 241 D5
Yazd Iran 31°55N 54°27E 247 D7
Yazd □ Iran 32°0N 55°0E 247 D7
Yazd-e Khvāst Iran 31°31N 52°7E 247 D7
Yazdān Iran 33°30N 60°50E 240 B1
Yazıköy Turkey 36°40N 27°20E 205 E9
Yazman Pakistan 29°8N 71°45E 242 E4
Yazoo → U.S.A. 32°22N 90°54W 315 E9
Yazoo City U.S.A. 32°51N 90°25W 315 E9
Ybbs Austria 48°12N 15°4E 180 C8
Ybycuí △ Paraguay 26°5S 56°46W 334 B4
Ybytyruzú △ Paraguay 25°51S 56°11W 335 B4
Ye Burma 15°15N 97°15E 236 E1
Ye-ngan Burma 21°9N 96°27E 241 E6
Ye-u Burma 22°46N 95°26E 241 D5
Ye Xian = Laizhou China 37°8N 119°57E 227 F10
Ye Xian China 33°35N 113°25E 226 H7
Yea Australia 37°14S 145°26E 283 D6
Yeading U.K. 51°31N 0°23W 125 A1
Yebawmi Burma 25°15N 95°45E 241 C5
Yebbi-Souma Chad 21°7N 17°54E 259 D3
Yebyu Burma 14°15N 98°13E 236 E2
Yecheng China 37°54N 77°26E 217 E9
Yecheon S. Korea 36°39N 128°27E 224 D4
Yecla Spain 38°35N 1°5W 197 G3
Yécora Mexico 28°20N 108°58W 318 B3
Yedashe Burma 19°10N 96°20E 241 F6
Yedebub Biheroch Bihereseboch na Hizboch □ Ethiopia 12°0N 36°0E 257 F4
Yedigöller △ Turkey 40°55N 31°55E 212 B4
Yedikule Turkey 40°59N 28°55E 122 C1
Yedintsy = Edineţ Moldova 48°9N 27°18E 183 B12
Yedri Chad 22°25N 17°30E 259 D3
Yedseram → Nigeria 12°30N 14°5E 263 C7
Yeed Somali Rep. 4°33N 43°2E 267 D5
Yefremov Russia 53°8N 38°3E 188 F10
Yegguéba Niger 19°59N 12°52E 259 E2
Yeghegnadzor Armenia 39°44N 45°19E 213 C11
Yegorlyk → Russia 46°35N 41°57E 191 G5
Yegorlykskaya Russia 46°35N 40°35E 191 G5
Yegoryevsk Russia 55°27N 38°55E 188 E10
Yegri-Dere = Ardino Bulgaria 41°34N 25°9E 203 E9
Yegros Paraguay 26°20S 56°25W 334 B4
Yehbuah Indonesia 8°23S 114°45E 231 J17
Yehuda, Midbar Israel 31°35N 35°15E 251 G6
Yei Sudan 4°9N 30°40E 257 G3
Yei, Nahr → Sudan 6°15N 30°13E 257 F3
Yeji Ghana 8°13N 0°39W 263 D4
Yejmiadzin Armenia 40°12N 44°19E 191 K7
Yekaterinburg Russia 56°50N 60°30E 214 D7
Yekaterinenshtadt = Marks Russia 51°45N 46°50E 190 E8
Yekaterinodar = Krasnodar Russia 45°5N 39°0E 191 H4
Yekumbe Dem. Rep. of the Congo 1°2S 23°27E 264 C4
Yelabuga Russia 55°45N 52°4E 190 C11
Yelan Russia 50°55N 43°43E 190 E6
Yelandur India 12°6N 77°0E 245 H3
Yelarbon Australia 28°33S 150°38E 281 D5
Yelatma Russia 55°0N 41°45E 190 C5
Yelcho, L. Chile 43°18S 72°18W 336 B2
Yelenovka = Sevan Armenia 40°33N 44°56E 191 K7
Yelenovskiye Karyery = Dokuchayevsk Ukraine 47°44N 37°40E 189 J9
Yelets Russia 52°40N 38°30E 189 F10
Yélimané Mali 15°9N 10°34W 262 B2
Yelizavetgrad = Kirovohrad Ukraine 48°35N 32°20E 189 H7
Yelizovo Russia 53°11N 158°23E 215 D16
Yell U.K. 60°35N 1°5W 167 A7
Yell Sd. U.K. 60°33N 1°15W 167 A7
Yellamanchilli = Elamanchili India 17°33N 82°50E 244 F6
Yellandu India 17°39N 80°23E 244 F5
Yellapur India 14°58N 74°43E 245 G2
Yellareddi India 18°12N 78°2E 244 E4
Yellow = Huang He → China 37°55N 118°50E 227 F10
Yellow → U.S.A. 30°30N 87°0W 317 E3
Yellow Sea China 35°0N 123°0E 227 G12
Yellowhead Pass Canada 52°53N 118°25W 296 C5
Yellowknife Canada 62°27N 114°29W 296 A6
Yellowknife → Canada 62°31N 114°19W 296 A6
Yellowstone → U.S.A. 47°59N 103°59W 304 C12
Yellowstone △ U.S.A. 44°40N 110°30W 304 D8
Yellowstone L. U.S.A. 44°27N 110°22W 304 D8
Yelnya Russia 54°35N 33°15E 188 E7
Yelsk Belarus 51°50N 29°10E 177 C15
Yelwa Nigeria 10°49N 4°41E 263 C5
Yemanzhelinsk Russia 54°58N 61°18E 216 B6
Yemassee U.S.A. 32°41N 80°51W 316 C9
Yembongo Dem. Rep. of the Congo 3°12N 19°2E 264 B3
Yemen ■ Asia 15°0N 44°0E 248 D4
Yemin Moshe Jerusalem 123 b2
Yemmiganur India 15°44N 77°29E 245 G3
Yen Bai Vietnam 21°42N 104°52E 228 G5
Yenagoa Nigeria 4°58N 6°16E 263 E6
Yenakiyeve Ukraine 48°15N 38°15E 189 H10
Yenakiyevo = Yenakiyeve Ukraine 48°15N 38°15E 189 H10
Yenangyat Burma 21°6N 94°48E 241 E5
Yenangyaung Burma 20°30N 95°0E 241 E5
Yenanma Burma 19°46N 94°49E 241 F5
Yenbo = Yanbu 'al Baḥr Si. Arabia 24°0N 38°5E 246 F3
Yenchao Taiwan 22°46N 120°21E 225 D2
Yenda Australia 34°13S 146°14E 283 C7
Yende Millimou Guinea 8°55N 10°10W 262 D2
Yendéré Burkina Faso 10°12N 4°59W 262 C4
Yendi Ghana 9°29N 0°1W 263 D4
Yengisar China 38°56N 76°9E 217 E9
Yengo Congo 0°22N 15°29E 264 B3
Yengo △ Australia 33°0S 150°55E 283 B9
Yéni Niger 13°30N 3°1E 263 C5
Yeni Erenköy = Yialousa Cyprus 35°32N 34°10E 207 E10
Yeni-Pazar = Novi Pazar Serbia 43°12N 20°28E 202 C4
Yenice Ankara, Turkey 39°14N 32°42E 212 C5
Yenice Aydın, Turkey 37°49N 28°35E 205 D10
Yenice Çanakkale, Turkey 39°55N 27°17E 205 B9
Yenice Edirne, Turkey 40°42N 26°9E 203 F10
Yenice Kahramanmaraş, Turkey 37°0N 35°4E 250 B6
Yenice → Turkey 37°37N 35°33E 212 D6
Yenifoça Turkey 38°44N 26°51E 205 C8
Yenihisar Turkey 37°22N 27°16E 205 D9
Yenikapı Turkey 41°0N 28°56E 122 B1
Yeniköy Bursa, Turkey 40°31N 29°22E 203 F13
Yeniköy Çanakkale, Turkey 39°55N 26°10E 205 B8
Yeniköy İstanbul, Turkey 41°6N 29°3E 122 B2
Yeniköy Kütahya, Turkey 38°52N 29°17E 205 C11
Yenipazar Turkey 37°49N 28°11E 205 D10
Yenişehir Turkey 40°16N 29°38E 203 F13
Yenisey → Russia 71°50N 82°40E 214 B9
Yeniseysk Russia 58°27N 92°13E 215 D10
Yeniseyskiy Zaliv Russia 72°20N 81°0E 214 B9
Yenki = Yanji China 42°59N 129°30E 227 C15
Yenne France 45°43N 5°44E 175 C9
Yenotayevka Russia 47°15N 47°0E 191 G8
Yenpu Taiwan 22°45N 120°35E 225 D2
Yenshui Taiwan 23°19N 120°16E 225 C2
Yenyuka Russia 57°57N 121°15E 215 D13
Yeo → U.K. 51°2N 2°49W 169 G5
Yeo, L. Australia 28°0S 124°30E 279 E3
Yeo I. Canada 45°24N 81°48W 312 A3
Yeoju S. Korea 37°20N 127°35E 224 D3
Yeola India 20°2N 74°30E 244 D2
Yeon-gi S. Korea 36°35N 127°15E 224 D3
Yeoncheon S. Korea 38°5N 127°4E 224 C3
Yeong-am S. Korea 34°47N 126°42E 224 E3
Yeong-ilman S. Korea 36°4N 129°28E 224 D4
Yeong-wol S. Korea 37°11N 128°28E 224 D4
Yeong-yang S. Korea 36°39N 129°7E 224 D4
Yeongcheon S. Korea 35°58N 128°56E 224 E4
Yeongdeok S. Korea 36°24N 129°22E 224 D4
Yeongdeungpo S. Korea 37°31N 126°54E 137 B1
Yeongdong Chungcheongbuk-do, S. Korea 36°10N 127°46E 224 D3
Yeongdong Seoul, S. Korea 37°30N 127°1E 137 B2
Yeonggwang S. Korea 35°16N 126°30E 224 E3
Yeongheungdo S. Korea 37°15N 126°27E 224 D3
Yeongju S. Korea 36°50N 128°40E 224 D4
Yeongju △ S. Korea 35°45N 129°20E 224 D4
Yeosu S. Korea 34°47N 127°45E 224 E3
Yeotmal = Yavatmal India 20°20N 78°15E 244 D4
Yeouido S. Korea 37°31N 126°55E 137 B1
Yeovil U.K. 50°57N 2°38W 169 G5
Yepes Spain 39°55N 3°39W 194 F7
Yeppoon Australia 23°5S 150°47E 280 C5
Yerba Buena I. U.S.A. 37°48N 122°21W 136 B2
Yerbent Turkmenistan 39°30N 58°50E 216 E5
Yerbogachen Russia 61°16N 108°0E 215 C11
Yerevan Armenia 40°10N 44°31E 191 K7
Yerington U.S.A. 38°59N 119°10W 304 G4
Yerkesik Turkey 37°7N 28°19E 205 D10
Yerköy Turkey 39°38N 34°28E 212 C6
Yerla → India 16°50N 74°30E 244 F2
Yermak Kazakhstan 52°2N 76°55E 214 D8
Yermo U.S.A. 34°54N 116°50W 307 L10
Yerólakkos Cyprus 35°11N 33°15E 207 E9
Yeropol Russia 65°15N 168°40E 215 C17
Yeroskipos Cyprus 34°46N 32°28E 207 F8
Yerres France 48°43N 2°30E 134 B4
Yershov Russia 51°23N 48°27E 190 E9
Yerupajá, Cerro Peru 10°16S 76°55W 330 C2
Yerushalayim = Jerusalem Israel/West Bank 31°47N 35°10E 123 B2
Yerville France 49°40N 0°53E 172 C7
Yes Tor U.K. 50°41N 4°0W 169 G4
Yesagyo Burma 21°38N 95°14E 241 E5
Yesan S. Korea 36°41N 126°51E 224 D3
Yeshin Burma 23°43N 95°6E 241 D5
Yeşikent = Erzin Turkey 36°57N 36°11E 250 B7
Yeşil → Turkey 37°20N 33°16E 250 A4
Yeşildere Turkey 37°9N 33°31E 250 A4
Yeşilhisar Turkey 38°20N 35°5E 212 C6
Yeşilırmak → Turkey 41°22N 36°37E 212 B7
Yeşilkent Turkey 36°57N 36°12E 212 D7
Yeşilköy Turkey 40°57N 28°49E 203 F12
Yeşilova Turkey 37°31N 29°46E 205 D11
Yeşilyurt Manisa, Turkey 38°22N 28°40E 205 C10
Yeşilyurt Muğla, Turkey 37°10N 28°20E 205 D10
Yeski Dzhumaya = Târgovişte Romania 44°55N 25°27E 183 F10
Yesnogorsk Russia 54°32N 37°38E 188 E9
Yeso U.S.A. 34°26N 104°37W 305 J11
Yessentuki Russia 44°5N 42°53E 191 H6
Yessey Russia 68°29N 102°10E 215 C11
Yeste Spain 38°22N 2°19W 197 G2
Yetman Australia 28°56S 150°48E 281 D5
Yetti Mauritania 26°10N 7°50W 260 C3
Yeu, Î. d' France 46°42N 2°20W 172 F4
Yevdokimovskoye = Krasnogvardeyskoye Russia 45°52N 41°33E 191 H5
Yevlakh = Yevlax Azerbaijan 40°39N 47°7E 191 K8
Yevlax Azerbaijan 40°39N 47°7E 191 K8
Yevpatoriya Ukraine 45°15N 33°20E 189 K7
Yeya → Russia 46°40N 38°40E 189 J10
Yeysk Russia 46°40N 38°12E 189 J10
Yezd = Yazd Iran 31°55N 54°27E 247 D7
Yezerishche Belarus 55°50N 29°59E 188 E5
Ygatimi Paraguay 24°5S 55°40W 335 A4
Yhati Paraguay 25°45S 56°35W 334 B4
Yhú Paraguay 25°0S 56°0W 335 B4
Yí → Uruguay 33°7S 57°8W 334 C4
Yi 'Allaq, G. Egypt 30°21N 33°31E 251 H4
Yi He → China 34°10N 118°8E 227 G10
Yi Xian Anhui, China 29°55N 117°57E 229 C11
Yi Xian Hebei, China 39°20N 115°30E 226 E8
Yi Xian Liaoning, China 41°30N 121°22E 227 D11
Yialiás → Cyprus 35°9N 33°44E 207 E9
Yialousa Cyprus 35°32N 34°10E 207 E10
Yibin China 28°45N 104°32E 228 C5
Yichang China 30°40N 111°20E 229 B8
Yicheng Henan, China 31°41N 112°12E 229 B9
Yicheng Shanxi, China 35°42N 111°40E 226 G6
Yichuan China 36°2N 110°10E 226 F6
Yichun Heilongjiang, China 47°44N 128°52E 219 B7
Yichun Jiangxi, China 27°48N 114°22E 229 D10
Yidu China 36°43N 118°28E 227 F10
Yidun China 30°22N 99°21E 228 B2
Yiexiu China 23°8N 113°16E 121 B2
Yifag Ethiopia 12°4N 37°46E 257 E4
Yifeng China 28°22N 114°45E 229 C10
Yigo Guam 13°32N 144°53E 302 d
Yiheyuan China 39°59N 116°15E 114 B1
Yihuang China 27°30N 116°12E 229 D11
Yijun China 35°28N 109°8E 226 G5
Yılanlıkale Turkey 36°59N 35°47E 250 B6
Yıldız Dağları Turkey 41°48N 27°36E 203 E11
Yıldız Park Turkey 41°2N 29°1E 122 B2
Yıldızeli Turkey 39°51N 36°36E 212 C7
Yilehuli Shan China 51°20N 124°20E 219 A7
Yiliang Yunnan, China 27°38N 104°2E 228 D5
Yiliang Yunnan, China 24°56N 103°11E 228 E4
Yilong China 31°34N 106°23E 228 B6
Yimen China 24°40N 102°10E 228 E4
Yimianpo China 45°7N 128°2E 227 B15
Yinchuan China 38°30N 106°15E 226 E4
Yindaik Burma 23°35N 95°22E 241 D5
Yindarlgooda, L. Australia 30°40S 121°52E 279 F3
Yindjibarndi ✪ Australia 22°0S 118°35E 278 D2
Ying He → China 32°30N 116°30E 226 H9
Ying Xian China 39°32N 113°10E 226 E7
Yingcheng China 30°56N 113°35E 229 B9
Yingde China 24°10N 113°25E 229 E9
Yingjiang China 24°41N 97°55E 228 E1
Yingjing China 29°41N 102°52E 228 C4
Yingkou China 40°37N 122°18E 224 B1
Yingkow = Yingkou China 40°37N 122°18E 224 B1
Yingshan Henan, China 31°35N 113°50E 229 B9
Yingshan Hubei, China 30°41N 115°32E 229 B10
Yingshan Sichuan, China 31°4N 106°35E 228 B6
Yingshang China 32°38N 116°12E 229 A11
Yingtan China 28°12N 117°0E 229 C11
Yingualyalya ✪ Australia 18°49S 129°12E 278 C4
Yinhangzhen China 31°20N 121°31E 138 A2
Yining China 43°58N 81°10E 217 D10
Yiningarra ✪ Australia 20°53S 129°27E 278 D4
Yinjiang China 28°1N 108°21E 228 C7
Yinmabin Burma 22°10N 94°55E 241 D5
Yioúra = Giaros Greece 37°32N 24°40E 204 D6
Yipinglang China 25°10N 101°52E 228 E3
Yirba Muda Ethiopia 6°12N 38°42E 257 F4
Yirga Alem Ethiopia 6°48N 38°22E 257 F4
Yirol Sudan 6°33N 30°30E 257 F3
Yirrkala Australia 12°14S 136°56E 280 A2
Yishan China 24°28N 108°38E 228 E7
Yishui China 35°47N 118°30E 227 G10
Yishun Singapore 1°26N 103°51E 138 A3
Yitong China 43°13N 125°20E 227 C13
Yiwu China 29°20N 120°3E 229 C13
Yixing China 31°21N 119°48E 229 B12
Yiyang Henan, China 34°27N 112°10E 226 G7
Yiyang Hunan, China 28°35N 112°18E 229 C9
Yiyang Jiangxi, China 28°22N 117°20E 229 C11
Yizhang China 25°27N 112°57E 229 E9
Yizheng China 32°18N 119°10E 229 A12
Ylästö Finland 60°17N 24°54E 121 B2
Yli-Kitka Finland 66°8N 28°30E 160 C23
Yliki, L. Greece 38°24N 23°15E 204 C5
Ylitornio Finland 66°19N 23°39E 160 C20
Ylivieska Finland 64°4N 24°28E 160 D21
Ymer Ø Greenland 73°9N 24°20W 154 C8
Yngaren Sweden 58°50N 16°35E 163 F10
Yoakum U.S.A. 29°17N 97°9W 314 G6
Yob ⌓ Eritrea 17°15N 37°50E 257 D4
Yobe □ Nigeria 12°0N 11°30E 263 C7
Yoboki Djibouti 11°30N 42°6E 267 B5
Yobuko Japan 33°32N 129°54E 222 D1
Yodo → Japan 34°45N 135°35E 133 A2
Yog Pt. Phil. 14°6N 124°12E 232 D5
Yoğuntaş Turkey 41°50N 27°4E 203 E11
Yogyakarta Indonesia 7°49S 110°22E 235 D4
Yogyakarta □ Indonesia 7°48S 110°22E 235 D4
Yoho △ Canada 51°25N 116°30W 296 C5
Yojoa, L. de Honduras 14°53N 88°0W 320 D2
Yok Don △ Vietnam 12°50N 107°40E 236 F6
Yokadouma Cameroon 3°26N 14°55E 264 B2
Yōkaichi Japan 35°6N 136°12E 223 B8
Yōkaichiba Japan 35°42N 140°33E 223 B12
Yokkaichi Japan 34°55N 136°38E 223 C8
Yoko Cameroon 5°32N 12°20E 263 D7
Yokohama Japan 35°27N 139°28E 223 B11
Yokosuka Japan 35°20N 139°40E 223 B11
Yokote Japan 39°20N 140°30E 220 E10
Yola Nigeria 9°10N 12°29E 263 D7
Yolaina, Cordillera de Nic. 11°30N 84°0W 320 D3
Yolombo Dem. Rep. of the Congo 1°36S 23°12E 264 C4
Ýolöten Turkmenistan 37°18N 62°21E 247 B9
Yom → Thailand 15°35N 100°1E 236 E3
Yombi Gabon 1°26S 10°37E 264 C2
Yona Guam 13°25N 144°46E 302 d
Yonago Japan 35°25N 133°19E 222 B5
Yonaguni-Jima Japan 24°27N 123°0E 221 M1
Yonaha-Dake Japan 26°43N 128°13E 288 a
Yŏnan N. Korea 37°55N 126°11E 224 D3
Yonezawa Japan 37°57N 140°4E 220 F10
Yong-in S. Korea 37°14N 127°12E 224 D3
Yong Peng Malaysia 2°0N 103°3E 237 M4
Yong Sata Thailand 7°8N 99°41E 237 J2
Yongama Dem. Rep. of the Congo 0°2N 24°35E 264 B4
Yongamp'o N. Korea 39°56N 124°23E 224 C2
Yong'an China 25°59N 117°25E 229 E11
Yongcheng China 33°55N 116°20E 226 H9
Yongchuan China 29°17N 105°55E 228 C5
Yongchun China 25°16N 118°20E 229 E12
Yongde China 24°5N 99°25E 228 E2
Yongdeng China 36°38N 103°25E 226 F2
Yongding China 24°43N 116°45E 229 E11
Yongdingman China 39°50N 116°20E 114 B2
Yonge Street Toronto, Canada 141 b3
Yongfeng China 27°20N 115°22E 229 D10
Yongfu China 24°59N 109°59E 228 E7
Yongfucun China 23°8N 113°17E 121 B2
Yonggyap Pass India 29°17N 95°37E 241 A5
Yonghe China 36°46N 110°38E 226 F6
Yonghong India 26°28N 94°58E 241 B5
Yŏnghŭng N. Korea 39°31N 127°18E 224 C3
Yŏnghŭng-man N. Korea 39°14N 127°30E 224 C3
Yongji China 34°52N 110°28E 226 G6
Yongjia China 28°10N 120°45E 229 C13
Yongkang Yunnan, China 24°9N 99°20E 228 E2
Yongkang Zhejiang, China 28°55N 120°2E 229 C13
Yongnian China 36°47N 114°29E 226 F8
Yongning Guangxi Zhuangzu, China 22°44N 108°28E 228 F7
Yongning Ningxia Huizu, China 38°15N 106°14E 226 E4
Yongping China 25°27N 99°38E 228 E2
Yongqing China 39°25N 116°28E 226 E9
Yongren China 26°4N 101°40E 228 D3
Yongsan S. Korea 37°32N 126°58E 137 B1
Yongshan China 28°11N 103°35E 228 C4
Yongsheng China 26°38N 100°46E 228 D3
Yongshun China 29°2N 109°51E 228 C7
Yongtai China 25°49N 118°58E 229 E12
Yongxin = Jinggangshan China 26°58N 114°15E 229 D10
Yongxing China 26°9N 113°8E 229 D9
Yongxiu China 29°2N 115°42E 229 C10
Yongzhou China 26°17N 111°37E 229 D8
Yonibana S. Leone 8°30N 12°19W 262 D2
Yonkers U.S.A. 40°56N 73°52W 132 A2
Yonne □ France 47°50N 3°40E 173 E10
Yonne → France 48°23N 2°58E 173 D9
Yopal Colombia 5°21N 72°23W 328 B3
York W. Austral., Australia 31°52S 116°47E 279 F2
York Ont., Canada 43°40N 79°26W 141 A2
York York, U.K. 53°58N 1°6W 168 D6
York Ala., U.S.A. 32°29N 88°18W 315 E10
York Nebr., U.S.A. 40°52N 97°36W 308 E5
York Pa., U.S.A. 39°58N 76°44W 309 F15
York, C. Australia 10°42S 142°31E 286 F2
York, City of □ U.K. 53°58N 1°6W 168 D6
York, Kap Greenland 75°55N 66°25W 154 B4
York, Vale of U.K. 54°15N 1°25W 168 C6
York I. Antigua & B. 17°2N 61°40W 322 b
York Mills Canada 43°45N 79°22W 141 A2
York Sd. Australia 15°0S 125°5E 278 C4
York Univ. Canada 43°43N 79°22W 141 A1
Yorke Pen. Australia 34°50S 137°40E 282 C2
Yorketown Australia 35°2S 137°33E 282 C2
Yorkshire Dales △ U.K. 54°12N 2°10W 168 C5
Yorkshire Wolds U.K. 54°8N 0°31W 168 C7
Yorkton Canada 51°11N 102°28W 297 C8
Yorkville Calif., U.S.A. 38°52N 123°13W 306 G3
Yorkville Ga., U.S.A. 33°55N 84°58W 316 B5
Yorkville Ill., U.S.A. 41°38N 88°27W 311 C8
Yoro Honduras 15°9N 87°7W 320 C2
Yoron-Jima Japan 27°2N 128°26E 221 L4
Yorosso Mali 12°17N 4°55W 262 C4
Yos Sudarso, Pulau = Dolak, Pulau Indonesia 8°0S 138°30E 231 F9
Yosemite △ U.S.A. 37°45N 119°40W 306 H7
Yosemite Village U.S.A. 37°45N 119°35W 306 H7
Yoshida Japan 34°40N 132°42E 222 C4
Yoshimatsu Japan 32°0N 130°47E 222 F2
Yoshino-Kumano △ Japan 34°12N 135°55E 223 C7
Yoshkar Ola Russia 56°38N 47°55E 190 B8
Yotala Bolivia 19°10S 65°17W 331 D4
Yotsuya Tokyo, Japan 140 a2
Yotvata Israel 29°55N 35°2E 251 J6
You Jiang → China 22°50N 108°6E 228 F6
You Xian China 27°1N 113°17E 229 D9
You'anmen China 39°51N 116°19E 114 B1
Youbou Canada 48°53N 124°13W 306 B2
Youghal Ireland 51°56N 7°52W 166 E4
Youghal B. Ireland 51°55N 7°49W 166 E4
Youkounkoun Guinea 12°35N 13°11W 262 C2
Young N.S.W., Australia 34°19S 148°18E 283 C8
Young Sask., Canada 51°47N 105°45W 297 C7
Young Uruguay 32°44S 57°36W 334 C4
Young I. Antarctica 66°25S 162°24E 151 C11
Young Ra. N.Z. 44°10S 169°30E 285 E4
Younghusband, L. Australia 30°50S 136°5E 282 A2
Younghusband Pen. Australia 36°0S 139°25E 282 D3
Youngsfield S. Africa 34°0S 18°30E 118 B1
Youngstown Alta., Canada 51°35N 111°10W 297 C6
Youngstown Fla., U.S.A. 30°22N 85°26W 316 E4
Youngstown N.Y., U.S.A. 43°15N 79°3W 312 C5
Youngstown Ohio, U.S.A. 41°6N 80°39W 312 E4
Youngsville U.S.A. 41°51N 79°19W 312 E5
Youngwood U.S.A. 40°14N 79°34W 312 F5
Youssoufia Morocco 32°16N 8°31W 260 B3
Youxi China 26°10N 118°13E 229 D12
Youyang China 28°47N 108°42E 228 C7
Youyu China 40°10N 112°20E 226 D7
Yozgat Turkey 39°51N 34°47E 212 C6
Yozgat □ Turkey 39°30N 35°0E 212 C6
Ypacaraí △ Paraguay 25°18S 57°19W 334 B4
Ypané → Paraguay 23°29S 57°19W 334 A4
Yport France 49°45N 0°15E 172 C7
Ypres = Ieper Belgium 50°51N 2°53E 170 D2
Ypsilanti U.S.A. 42°14N 83°37W 311 B13
Yreka U.S.A. 41°44N 122°38W 304 F2
Yrghyz Kazakhstan 48°37N 61°16E 216 C6
Yrghyz → Kazakhstan 48°6N 62°30E 216 C6
Ysabel Chan. Papua N. G. 2°0S 150°0E 286 B6
Yssingeaux France 45°9N 4°8E 175 C8
Ystabøhamn Norway 59°3N 5°23E 164 E2
Ystad Sweden 55°26N 13°50E 163 J7
Ysyk-Köl = Balykchy Kyrgyzstan 42°26N 76°12E 217 D9
Ysyk-Köl Kyrgyzstan 42°25N 77°15E 217 D9
Ysyk-Köl □ Kyrgyzstan 42°0N 78°0E 217 D9
Ythan → U.K. 57°19N 1°59W 167 D7
Ytre Arna Norway 60°27N 5°25E 164 D2
Ytre Enebakk Norway 59°44N 11°0E 164 E8
Ytre Rendal Norway 61°46N 11°8E 164 C8
Ytterhogdal Sweden 62°12N 14°56E 162 B8
Ytyk-Kyuyel Russia 62°30N 133°45E 215 C14
Yu Jiang → China 23°22N 110°3E 228 F7
Yü Shan Taiwan 23°25N 120°52E 225 C2
Yü Shan △ Taiwan 24°45N 121°12E 225 C3
Yu Xian = Yuzhou China 34°10N 113°28E 226 G7
Yu Xian Hebei, China 39°50N 114°35E 226 E8
Yu Xian Shanxi, China 38°5N 113°20E 226 E7
Yuan Jiang → Hunan, China 28°55N 111°50E 229 C8
Yuan Jiang → Yunnan, China 22°20N 103°59E 228 F4
Yuan'an China 31°3N 111°34E 229 B8
Yüanch'ang Taiwan 23°39N 120°18E 225 C2
Yuanjiang Hunan, China 28°47N 112°21E 229 C9
Yuanjiang Yunnan, China 23°32N 102°0E 228 F4
Yüanli Taiwan 24°27N 120°39E 225 B2
Yüanlin Taiwan 23°58N 120°30E 225 C2
Yuanling China 28°29N 110°22E 229 C8
Yuanmingyuan Park China 40°0N 116°17E 114 A1
Yuanmou China 25°42N 101°53E 228 E3
Yuanqu China 35°18N 111°40E 226 G6
Yuanshan Taiwan 24°45N 121°43E 225 B3
Yuanxiatian China 23°12N 113°17E 121 A2
Yuanyang Henan, China 35°3N 113°58E 226 G7
Yuanyang Yunnan, China 23°10N 102°43E 228 F4
Yuat → Papua N. G. 4°10S 143°52E 286 C2
Yuba → U.S.A. 39°8N 121°36W 306 F5
Yuba City U.S.A. 39°8N 121°37W 306 F5
Yūbari Japan 43°4N 141°59E 220 C10
Yubdo Ethiopia 8°58N 35°24E 257 F4
Yūbetsu Japan 44°13N 143°50E 220 B11
Yubo Sudan 5°23N 27°25E 257 F2
Yucatán □ Mexico 20°50N 89°0W 319 C7
Yucatán, Canal de Caribbean 22°0N 86°30W 320 B2
Yucatán, Península de Mexico 19°30N 89°0W 292 H11
Yucatan Basin Cent. Amer. 19°0N 86°0W 320 C3
Yucatan Channel = Yucatán, Canal de Caribbean 22°0N 86°30W 320 B2
Yucca U.S.A. 34°52N 114°9W 307 L12
Yucca Valley U.S.A. 34°8N 116°27W 307 L10
Yucheng China 36°55N 116°32E 226 F9
Yüch'ih Taiwan 23°54N 120°56E 225 C2
Yuching Taiwan 23°7N 120°27E 225 C2
Yuci = Jinzhong China 37°42N 112°46E 226 F7
Yudu China 25°59N 115°30E 229 E10
Yuechi China 30°34N 106°25E 228 B6
Yuen Long China 22°26N 114°2E 219 G11
Yuendumu Australia 22°16S 131°49E 278 D5
Yuendumu ✪ Australia 22°21S 131°40E 278 D5
Yueqing China 28°9N 120°59E 229 C13
Yueqing Wan China 28°5N 121°20E 229 D13
Yuexi Anhui, China 30°50N 116°20E 229 B11
Yuexi Sichuan, China 28°37N 102°26E 228 C4
Yuexiu Park China 23°8N 113°16E 121 B2
Yueyang China 29°21N 113°5E 229 C9
Yufu-Dake Japan 33°17N 131°33E 222 D3
Yugan China 28°43N 116°37E 229 C11
Yuğluk Dağı Turkey 36°59N 33°50E 250 B4
Yugo-Zarad Russia 55°40N 37°30E 129 B3
Yugorenok Russia 59°47N 137°40E 215 D14
Yuhalixqui, Volcan Mexico 19°19N 99°4W 128 C2
Yuhuan China 28°9N 121°12E 229 C13
Yühuan Dao China 28°5N 121°15E 229 C13
Yujiang China 28°10N 116°43E 229 C11
Yukhnov Russia 54°44N 35°15E 188 E8
Yūki Japan 36°18N 139°53E 223 A11
Yukon U.S.A. 35°31N 97°45W 314 D6
Yukon → U.S.A. 62°32N 163°54W 303 E7
Yukon-Charley Rivers ⌓ U.S.A. 65°15N 144°0W 303 D12
Yukon Delta Nat. Wildlife Refuge ⌓ U.S.A. 61°0N 163°0W 303 F7
Yukon Flats U.S.A. 66°40N 145°45W 303 C11
Yukon Territory □ Canada 63°0N 135°0W 294 E5
Yüksekova Turkey 37°34N 44°16E 213 D11
Yukta Russia 63°26N 105°42E 215 C11
Yukuhashi Japan 33°44N 130°59E 222 D2
Yulara Australia 25°10S 130°55E 279 E5
Yule → Australia 20°41S 118°17E 278 D2
Yuleba Australia 26°37S 149°24E 281 D4
Yulee U.S.A. 30°38N 81°36W 316 E8
Yuli China 41°19N 86°15E 217 D11
Yuli Nigeria 9°44N 10°12E 263 D7
Yüli Taiwan 23°20N 121°18E 225 C3
Yulin Guangxi Zhuangzu, China 22°40N 110°8E 229 F8
Yulin Hainan, China 18°10N 109°31E 236 C7
Yulin Shaanxi, China 38°20N 109°30E 226 E5
Yuma Ariz., U.S.A. 32°43N 114°37W 307 N12
Yuma Colo., U.S.A. 40°8N 102°43W 304 F12
Yuma, B. de Dom. Rep. 18°20N 68°35W 321 C6
Yumali Australia 35°32S 139°45E 282 C3
Yumbe Uganda 3°28N 31°15E 268 B3
Yumbi Équateur, Dem. Rep. of the Congo 1°53S 16°34E 264 C3
Yumbi Maniema, Dem. Rep. of the Congo 1°12S 26°15E 268 C2
Yumbo Colombia 3°35N 76°28W 328 C2
Yumen China 39°50N 97°30E 218 C4
Yumurtalık Turkey 36°45N 35°48E 250 B6
Yun Gui Gaoyuan China 26°0N 104°0E 228 E3
Yun Ling China 27°0N 99°20E 228 D2
Yun Xian Hubei, China 32°50N 110°46E 229 A8
Yun Xian Yunnan, China 24°27N 100°8E 228 E3
Yuna Australia 28°20S 115°0E 279 E2
Yunak Turkey 38°49N 31°43E 212 C4
Yunan China 23°12N 111°30E 229 F8
Yunaska I. U.S.A. 52°38N 170°40W 303 K5
Yuncheng Henan, China 35°36N 115°57E 226 G8
Yuncheng Shanxi, China 35°2N 111°0E 226 G6
Yunfu China 22°50N 112°5E 229 F9
Yung Shue Wan China 22°13N 114°6E 122 B1
Yungan Taiwan 22°49N 120°12E 225 D2
Yungas Bolivia 17°0S 66°0W 331 D4
Yungay Chile 37°10S 72°5W 334 D1
Yungay Peru 9°2S 77°45W 330 B2
Yungk'ang Taiwan 23°2N 120°15E 225 C2
Yungki = Jilin China 43°44N 126°30E 227 C14
Yungning = Nanning China 22°48N 108°20E 228 F7
Yunhe China 28°8N 119°33E 229 C12
Yunkai Dashan China 22°30N 111°0E 229 F8
Yunkanjini ✪ Australia 22°33S 131°6E 278 D5
Yünlin □ Taiwan 23°40N 120°20E 225 C2
Yunlong China 25°57N 99°13E 228 E2
Yunmeng China 31°2N 113°43E 229 B9
Yunnan □ China 25°0N 102°0E 228 E4
Yunotsu Japan 35°5N 132°21E 222 B4
Yunquera de Henares Spain 40°47N 3°11W 196 E1
Yunshui Taiwan 23°23N 120°31E 225 C2
Yunt Dağı Turkey 38°56N 27°13E 205 C9
Yunta Australia 32°34S 139°36E 281 E2
Yunxi China 33°0N 110°22E 226 H6
Yunxiao China 23°59N 117°18E 229 F11
Yupanqui Basin Pac. Oc. 19°0S 101°0W 289 J17
Yuping China 27°13N 108°56E 228 D7
Yupukarri Guyana 3°45N 59°20W 329 C6
Yuqing China 27°13N 107°53E 228 D6
Yuraygir △ Australia 29°45S 153°15E 281 D5
Yurga Russia 55°42N 84°51E 214 D9
Yurimaguas Peru 5°55S 76°7W 330 B2
Yurkiyka Ukraine 48°42N 28°35E 183 B13
Yurungkax He → China 38°5N 80°34E 217 E10
Yuryev = Tartu Estonia 58°20N 26°44E 188 C4
Yuryev-Polskiy Russia 56°30N 39°40E 188 D10
Yuryevets Russia 57°25N 43°2E 190 B6
Yuscarán Honduras 13°58N 86°45W 320 D2
Yûsef, Bahr → Egypt 28°25N 30°35E 256 B3
Yushan China 28°42N 118°10E 229 C12
Yushanzhen China 29°28N 108°22E 228 C7
Yushe China 37°4N 112°58E 226 F7
Yushu Jilin, China 44°43N 126°38E 227 B14
Yushu Qinghai, China 33°5N 96°55E 218 C4
Yūsofābād Iran 35°43N 51°24E 141 A2
Yusufeli Turkey 40°50N 41°33E 213 B9
Yutai China 35°0N 116°45E 226 G9
Yutian Hebei, China 39°53N 117°45E 227 E9
Yutian Sinkiang-Uigur, China 36°52N 81°42E 217 E10
Yütze = Jinzhong China 37°42N 112°46E 226 F7
Yüweng Tao Taiwan 23°36N 119°30E 225 C1
Yuxarı Qarabağ = Nagorno-Karabakh □ Azerbaijan 39°55N 46°45E 213 C12
Yuxi China 24°30N 102°35E 228 E4
Yuyao China 30°3N 121°10E 229 B13
Yuzawa Japan 39°10N 140°30E 220 E10
Yuzha Russia 56°34N 42°1E 190 B6
Yuzhno-Kurilsk Russia 44°1N 145°51E 215 E15
Yuzhno-Sakhalinsk Russia 46°58N 142°45E 215 E15
Yuzhno-Sukhokumsk Russia 44°40N 45°35E 191 H7
Yuzhnouralsk Russia 54°26N 61°15E 216 B6
Yuzhnyy □ Russia 44°0N 40°0E 191 H5
Yuzhou China 34°10N 113°28E 226 G7
Yuzovka = Donetsk Ukraine 48°0N 37°45E 189 J9
Yvelines □ France 48°40N 1°45E 173 D8
Yverdon-les-Bains Switz. 46°47N 6°39E 179 J2
Yvetot France 49°37N 0°44E 172 C7
Yzeure France 46°33N 3°22E 173 F10

Z

Zaandam Neths. 52°26N 4°49E 112 A1
Zaandijk Neths. 52°28N 4°49E 112 A1
Zaanstad Neths. 52°27N 4°50E 112 A1
Zab, Monts du Algeria 34°55N 5°0E 261 B6
Zāb al Kabīr → Iraq 36°1N 43°24E 213 D10
Zāb aş Şaghīr → Iraq 35°17N 43°29E 213 E10
Žabalj Serbia 45°21N 20°5E 182 E5
Žabari Serbia 44°22N 21°15E 202 B5
Zabarjad Egypt 23°40N 36°12E 256 C4
Zabaykalsk Russia 49°40N 117°25E 215 E12
Zabbar Malta 35°53N 14°32E 206 F8
Záběhlice Czech Rep. 50°3N 14°29E 135 B2
Zabīd Yemen 14°0N 43°10E 248 D3
Zabīd, W. → Yemen 14°7N 43°6E 248 D3
Zabki Poland 52°17N 21°6E 142 B2
Ząbkowice Śląskie Poland 50°35N 16°50E 185 H3
Žabljak Montenegro 43°18N 19°5E 202 C3
Zabłudów Poland 53°0N 23°19E 185 F9
Żabno Poland 50°9N 20°53E 185 H7
Zabol Iran 31°0N 61°32E 247 D9
Zābol □ Afghan. 32°0N 67°0E 240 C2
Zābolī Iran 27°10N 61°35E 247 E9
Zabolotiv Ukraine 48°28N 25°18E 183 B10
Zabolottya Ukraine 51°38N 24°16E 185 G11
Zabré Burkina Faso 11°12N 0°36W 263 C4
Zábřeh Czech Rep. 49°53N 16°52E 181 B9
Zabrze Poland 50°18N 18°50E 185 H5
Zabuzhzhya Ukraine 51°21N 23°42E 185 G10
Zabzuga Ghana 9°20N 0°30E 263 D5
Zacapa Guatemala 14°59N 89°31W 320 D2
Zacapu Mexico 19°50N 101°43W 318 D4
Zacatecas Mexico 22°47N 102°35W 318 C4
Zacatecas □ Mexico 23°0N 103°0W 318 C4
Zacatecoluca El Salv. 13°29N 88°51W 320 D2
Zacharo Greece 37°30N 21°39E 204 D3
Zachary U.S.A. 30°39N 91°9W 314 F9
Zachodnio-Pomorskie □ Poland 53°40N 15°50E 184 E2
Żacisze Poland 52°17N 21°4E 142 B2
Zacoalco de Torres Mexico 20°14N 103°35W 318 C4
Zacualtipán Mexico 20°39N 98°36W 319 C5

Zadar Croatia 44°8N 15°14E 199 D12
Zadawa Nigeria 11°33N 10°19E 263 C7
Zadetkyi Kyun Burma 10°0N 98°25E 237 G2
Zadonsk Russia 52°25N 38°56E 189 F10
Zafarqand Iran 33°11N 52°29E 247 C7
Zafra Spain 38°26N 6°30W 195 G4
Żagań Poland 51°39N 15°22E 185 G2
Zagaoua Chad 16°0N 21°10E 259 E4
Žagarė Lithuania 56°21N 23°15E 184 B10
Zagazig Egypt 30°40N 31°30E 256 H7
Zāgheh Iran 33°30N 48°42E 247 C6
Zaghouan Tunisia 36°23N 10°10E 258 A2
Zaghouan □ Tunisia 36°20N 10°0E 261 A7
Zaglou Algeria 27°17N 0°3W 261 C4
Zagnanado Benin 7°18N 2°28E 263 D5
Zagora Greece 39°27N 23°6E 204 B5
Zagora Morocco 30°22N 5°51W 260 B3
Zagorje Slovenia 46°8N 15°0E 199 B11
Zagórów Poland 52°10N 17°54E 185 F4
Zagorsk = Sergiyev Posad Russia 56°20N 38°10E 188 D10
Zagorsky = Krasnozavodsk Russia 56°27N 38°25E 188 D10
Zagórz Poland 49°30N 22°14E 185 J9
Zagreb Croatia 45°50N 15°58E 199 C12
Zagreb ✕ (ZAG) Croatia 45°45N 16°4E 199 C13
Zāgros, Kūhhā-ye Iran 33°45N 48°5E 247 C6
Zāgros Mts. = Zāgros, Kūhhā-ye Iran 33°45N 48°5E 247 C6
Žagubica Serbia 44°15N 21°47E 202 B5
Zaguinaso Ivory C. 10°1N 6°14W 262 C3
Zagyva → Hungary 47°5N 20°4E 182 C5
Zahamena △ Madag. 17°37S 48°49E 272 B4
Zāhedān Fārs, Iran 28°46N 53°52E 247 D7
Zāhedān Sīstān va Balūchestān, Iran 29°30N 60°50E 247 D9
Zahirabad India 17°43N 77°37E 244 F3
Zahlah Lebanon 33°52N 35°50E 250 E6
Zahna Germany 51°55N 12°49E 178 D8
Záhony Hungary 48°25N 22°11E 182 B7
Zahrā Iraq 33°22N 44°19E 113 A1
Ẓahrān Si. Arabia 17°40N 43°30E 248 C3
Zainsk Russia 55°18N 52°4E 190 C11
Zaïre = Congo → Africa 6°4S 12°24E 265 D2
Zaïre = Congo, Dem. Rep. of the ■ Africa 3°0S 23°0E 265 C4
Zaire □ Angola 7°0S 14°0E 265 D2
Zaječar Serbia 43°53N 22°18E 202 C6
Zaka Zimbabwe 20°20S 31°29E 271 B5
Zakamensk Russia 50°23N 103°17E 215 D11
Zakani Dem. Rep. of the Congo 2°33N 23°16E 264 B4
Zakarpattya □ Ukraine 48°20N 23°20E 183 B8
Zakataly = Zaqatala Azerbaijan 41°38N 46°35E 191 K8
Zakbayemé Cameroon 4°2N 10°34E 264 B2
Zakharkovo Russia 55°46N 37°18E 129 B1
Zakhodnaya Dzvina = Daugava → Latvia 57°4N 24°3E 188 D3
Zākhū Iraq 37°10N 42°50E 213 D10
Zakinthos = Zakynthos Greece 37°47N 20°54E 207 D2
Zakinthos, Diavlos Greece 37°50N 21°0E 207 D2
Zakopane Poland 49°18N 19°57E 185 J6
Zakouma Chad 10°54N 19°49E 259 F3
Zakouma △ Chad 10°52N 19°45E 259 F3
Zakroczym Poland 52°26N 20°38E 185 F7
Zakros Greece 35°6N 26°10E 207 E7
Zakynthos Greece 37°47N 20°54E 207 D2
Zakynthos □ Greece 37°47N 20°57E 204 D2
Zakynthos ✕ (ZTH) Greece 37°45N 20°50E 207 D2
Zala Angola 7°52S 13°42E 265 D2
Zala Ethiopia 6°28N 37°13E 257 F4
Zala □ Hungary 46°42N 16°50E 182 D1
Zala → Hungary 46°43N 17°16E 182 D2
Zalaegerszeg Hungary 46°53N 16°47E 182 D1
Zalakomár Hungary 46°33N 17°10E 182 D2
Zalalövő Hungary 46°51N 16°35E 182 D1
Zalamea de la Serena Spain 38°40N 5°38W 195 G5
Zalamea la Real Spain 37°41N 6°38W 195 H4
Zalari Russia 53°33N 102°30E 215 D11
Zalău Romania 47°12N 23°3E 182 C8
Žalec Slovenia 46°16N 15°10E 199 B12
Zaleshchiki = Zalishchyky Ukraine 48°45N 25°45E 183 B10
Zalesye Russia 54°50N 21°31E 184 D8
Zalew Wiślany Poland 54°20N 19°50E 184 D6
Zalewo Poland 53°50N 19°41E 184 E6
Ẓalim Si. Arabia 22°43N 42°10E 248 B3
Zalingei Sudan 12°51N 23°29E 259 F4
Zalishchyky Ukraine 48°45N 25°45E 183 B10
Zalmah, J. az Libya 25°30N 24°40E 258 C4
Žalov Czech Rep. 50°10N 14°22E 135 A2
Zalṭan Ajdābiyā, Libya 28°51N 19°52E 258 C3
Zalṭan Zuwārah, Libya 32°57N 11°52E 258 B2
Zalṭan, Jabal Libya 28°46N 19°45E 258 C3
Zalun Burma 17°29N 95°34E 241 G5
Załuski Poland 52°9N 20°55E 142 C1
Zama L. Canada 58°45N 119°5W 296 B5
Zambales □ Phil. 15°20N 120°10E 232 D3
Zambales Mts. Phil. 15°45N 120°5E 232 D3
Zambeke Dem. Rep. of the Congo 2°8N 25°17E 268 B2
Zambeze → Africa 18°35S 36°20E 269 F4
Zambezi = Zambeze → Africa 18°35S 36°20E 269 F4
Zambezi Zambia 13°30S 23°15E 265 E4
Zambezi △ Zimbabwe 17°54S 25°41E 269 F2
Zambezia □ Mozam. 16°15S 37°30E 269 F4
Zambia ■ Africa 15°0S 28°0E 269 F2
Zamboanga Phil. 6°59N 122°3E 233 H4
Zamboanga del Norte □ Phil. 8°0N 123°0E 233 H4
Zamboanga del Sur □ Phil. 7°40N 123°0E 233 H4
Zambrano Colombia 9°45N 74°49W 328 B3
Zambrów Poland 52°59N 22°14E 185 F9
Zamdorf Germany 48°8N 11°35E 131 B2
Zametchino Russia 53°30N 42°30E 190 D6
Zamfara □ Nigeria 12°10N 6°0E 263 C6
Zamfara → Nigeria 12°5N 4°2E 263 C5
Zamora Ecuador 4°4S 78°58W 328 D2
Zamora Michoacan, Mexico 19°59N 102°16W 318 D4
Zamora Spain 41°30N 5°45W 194 D5
Zamora □ Spain 41°30N 5°46W 194 D5
Zamora → Ecuador 2°59S 78°15W 328 D2
Zamora-Chinchipe □ Ecuador 4°15S 78°50W 328 D2
Zamość Poland 50°43N 23°15E 185 H10
Zamtang China 32°26N 101°6E 228 A3
Zamuro, Sierra del Venezuela 4°0N 62°30W 329 C5
Zamzam, W. → Libya 30°58N 14°48E 258 B2
Zan Ghana 9°26N 0°17W 263 D4
Zanaga Congo 2°48S 13°48E 264 C2
Záncara → Spain 39°18N 3°18W 197 F1
Zanda China 31°32N 79°50E 218 C2
Zanderij Suriname 5°20N 55°16W 329 B6
Zandu Dem. Rep. of the Congo 5°11S 18°16E 265 D3
Zandvoort Neths. 52°22N 4°32E 170 B4
Zanesville U.S.A. 39°56N 82°1W 312 G2
Zanevka Russia 59°55N 30°31E 137 B3
Zangābād Iran 38°26N 46°44E 246 B5
Zangliveri Greece 40°36N 23°15E 202 F7
Zangoza = Sangüesa Spain 42°37N 1°17W 196 C3
Zangue → Mozam. 17°50S 35°21E 269 F4
Zanjān Iran 36°40N 48°35E 213 D13
Zanjān □ Iran 37°20N 49°30E 247 B6
Zanjān → Iran 37°8N 47°47E 247 B6
Zannone Italy 40°58N 13°3E 200 B6
Zanow = Sianów Poland 54°13N 16°18E 184 D3
Zante = Zakynthos Greece 37°47N 20°54E 207 D2
Zanthus Australia 31°2S 123°34E 279 F3
Zanzibar Tanzania 6°12S 39°12E 268 D4
Zanzūr Libya 32°55N 13°1E 258 B2
Zaouatallaz Algeria 24°52N 8°30E 261 D6
Zaouiet El-Kala = Bordj Omar Driss Algeria 28°10N 6°40E 261 C6
Zaouiet Reggâne Algeria 26°32N 0°3E 261 C5
Zaoyang China 32°10N 112°45E 229 A9
Zaozernyy Kazakhstan 53°6N 71°9E 217 B8
Zaozhuang China 34°50N 117°35E 227 G9
Zap Suyu = Zāb al Kabīr → Iraq 36°1N 43°24E 213 D10
Zapadna Morava → Serbia 43°38N 21°30E 202 C5
Zapadnaya Dvina = Daugava → Latvia 57°4N 24°3E 188 D3
Zapadnaya Dvina Russia 56°15N 32°3E 188 D7
Západné Beskydy Europe 49°30N 19°0E 181 B12
Zapadni Rodopi Bulgaria 41°50N 24°0E 202 E7
Západočeský □ Czech Rep. 49°35N 13°0E 180 B6
Zapala Argentina 39°0S 70°5W 336 A2
Zapaleri, Cerro Bolivia 22°49S 67°11W 334 A2
Zapata U.S.A. 26°55N 99°16W 314 H5
Zapatón → Spain 39°0N 6°49W 195 F4
Zapiga Chile 19°40S 69°55W 330 D4
Zapolyarnyy Russia 69°26N 30°51E 160 B24
Zapopán Mexico 20°43N 103°24W 318 C4
Zaporizhzhya Ukraine 47°50N 35°10E 189 J8
Zaporizhzhya □ Ukraine 46°55N 35°50E 189 J8
Zaporozhye = Zaporizhzhya Ukraine 47°50N 35°10E 189 J8
Zapote Phil. 14°27N 120°56E 127 C1
Zappeion Athens, Greece 112 c2
Zaqatala Azerbaijan 41°38N 46°35E 191 K8
Zara Turkey 39°58N 37°43E 212 C7
Zarafshon Uzbekistan 41°34N 64°12E 216 D6
Zaragoza Colombia 7°30N 74°52W 328 B3
Zaragoza Coahuila, Mexico 28°29N 100°55W 318 B4
Zaragoza Nuevo León, Mexico 23°58N 99°46W 319 C5
Zaragoza Spain 41°39N 0°53W 196 D4
Zaragoza □ Spain 41°35N 1°0W 196 D4
Zarand Kermān, Iran 30°46N 56°34E 247 D8
Zarand Markazī, Iran 35°18N 50°25E 247 C6
Zărandului, Munții Romania 46°14N 22°7E 182 D7
Zaranj Afghan. 30°55N 61°55E 240 C1
Zarasai Lithuania 55°40N 26°20E 188 E4
Zárate Argentina 34°7S 59°0W 334 C4
Zarautz Spain 43°17N 2°10W 196 B2
Zaraysk Russia 54°48N 38°53E 188 E10
Zaraza Venezuela 9°21N 65°19W 329 B4
Zard, Kūh-e Iran 32°22N 50°4E 247 C6
Zarechye Russia 55°41N 37°22E 129 B2
Zāreh Iran 35°7N 49°9E 247 C6
Zari Nigeria 13°4N 12°45E 263 C7
Zaria Nigeria 11°0N 7°40E 263 C6
Zarineh → Iran 36°17N 46°26E 213 D12
Zarinsk Russia 53°43N 84°55E 217 B10
Żarki Poland 50°38N 19°23E 185 H6
Zarko Greece 39°38N 22°6E 204 B4
Zarneh Iran 33°55N 46°10E 246 C5
Zărneşti Romania 45°33N 25°18E 183 E10
Zaros Greece 35°8N 24°54E 207 E5
Żarów Poland 50°56N 16°29E 185 H3
Zarqā', Nahr az → Jordan 32°10N 35°37E 251 F6
Zarrīn Iran 32°46N 54°37E 247 C7
Zarrīnābād Iran 36°25N 48°17E 213 D13
Zaruma Ecuador 3°40S 79°38W 328 D2
Żary Poland 51°37N 15°10E 185 G2
Zarza de Granadilla Spain 40°14N 6°3W 194 E4
Zarzaïtine Algeria 28°15N 9°34E 261 C6
Zarzal Colombia 4°24N 76°4W 328 C2
Zarzis Tunisia 33°31N 11°2E 258 B2
Zas Spain 43°4N 8°53W 194 B2
Zashaghan Kazakhstan 51°11N 51°20E 216 B4
Zaskar → India 34°13N 77°20E 243 B7
Zaskar Mts. India 33°15N 77°30E 243 C7
Zastavna Ukraine 48°31N 25°51E 183 B10
Zastron S. Africa 30°18S 27°7E 270 D4
Žatec Czech Rep. 50°20N 13°32E 180 A6
Zaterechnyy Russia 44°48N 45°11E 191 H7
Zatishye = Elektrostal Russia 55°41N 38°32E 188 E10
Zator Poland 49°59N 19°28E 185 J6
Zatyshshya Ukraine 47°20N 29°51E 183 C14
Zavala Bos.-H. 42°50N 17°59E 202 D1
Zavāreh Iran 33°29N 52°28E 247 C7
Zave Zimbabwe 17°6S 30°1E 271 A5
Zaventem Belgium 50°53N 4°28E 116 A2
Zavetnoye Russia 47°13N 43°50E 191 G6
Zavidovići Bos.-H. 44°27N 18°10E 182 F3
Zavitaya = Zavitinsk Russia 50°10N 129°20E 215 D13
Zavitinsk Russia 50°10N 129°20E 215 D13
Zavodovski, I. Antarctica 56°0S 27°45W 151 B1
Zavodskoy = Komsomolskiy Russia 54°27N 45°33E 190 C7
Zavolzhsk Russia 57°30N 42°0E 190 B6
Zavolzhye = Zavolzhsk Russia 57°30N 42°0E 190 B6
Zavolzhye Russia 56°37N 43°26E 190 B6
Zawady Poland 52°10N 21°6E 142 B2
Zawadzkie Poland 50°37N 18°28E 185 H5
Zawichost Poland 50°48N 21°51E 185 H8
Zawidów Poland 51°1N 15°1E 185 G2
Zawiercie Poland 50°30N 19°24E 185 H6
Zāwiyah, J. az Syria 35°45N 36°35E 250 C7
Zāwiyat al Bayḍā = Al Bayḍā Libya 32°50N 21°44E 258 B4
Zāwiyat Masūs Libya 31°35N 21°1E 258 B4
Zâwiyet Abû Musallam Egypt 29°56N 31°9E 117 B1
Zawrā' Park Iraq 33°18N 44°23E 113 B2
Zâwyet Shammas Egypt 31°30N 26°37E 256 A2
Zâwyet Um el Rakham Egypt 31°18N 27°1E 256 A2
Zâwyet Ungeîla Egypt 31°23N 26°42E 256 A2
Zāyā Iraq 33°33N 44°13E 246 C5
Zāyandeh → Iran 32°35N 52°0E 247 C7
Zaymah Si. Arabia 21°37N 40°6E 248 B3
Zaysan Kazakhstan 47°28N 84°52E 217 C10
Zaysan Köli Kazakhstan 48°0N 83°0E 217 C10
Zayü China 28°48N 97°27E 228 C1
Zazafotsy Madag. 21°11S 46°21E 272 C2
Zāzamt, W. → Libya 30°29N 14°30E 258 B2
Zāzir, O. → Algeria 22°0N 5°40E 261 D6
Zázrivá Slovak Rep. 49°16N 19°7E 181 B12
Zbarazh Ukraine 49°43N 25°44E 177 D13
Zbąszyń Poland 52°14N 15°56E 185 F2
Zbąszynek Poland 52°16N 15°51E 185 F2
Zblewo Poland 53°56N 18°19E 184 E5
Zbraslav Czech Rep. 49°58N 14°23E 135 C2
Zbruch → Ukraine 48°32N 26°27E 183 B11
Zbuzany Czech Rep. 50°1N 14°17E 135 B1
Žďár nad Sázavou Czech Rep. 49°34N 15°57E 180 B8
Zdiby Czech Rep. 50°9N 14°27E 135 B2
Zdolbuniv Ukraine 50°30N 26°15E 177 C14
Ždrelo Serbia 44°16N 21°28E 202 B5
Zduńska Wola Poland 51°37N 18°59E 185 G5
Zduny Poland 51°39N 17°21E 185 G4
Zearing U.S.A. 42°10N 93°18W 310 B3
Zeballos Canada 49°59N 126°50W 296 D3
Zebbug Malta 35°52N 14°26E 206 F7
Zebbug Gozo, Malta 36°4N 14°14E 206 E6
Zebediela S. Africa 24°20S 29°17E 271 B4
Zebila Ghana 10°55N 0°30W 263 C4
Zebulon U.S.A. 33°6N 84°21W 316 B5
Zeebrugge Belgium 51°19N 3°12E 170 C3
Zeehan Australia 41°52S 145°25E 281 G4
Zeekoevlei S. Africa 34°4S 18°31E 118 B2
Zeeland U.S.A. 42°49N 86°1W 311 B10
Zeeland □ Neths. 51°30N 3°50E 170 C3
Zeelandia Neth. Ant. 17°30N 62°59W 322 a
Zeerust S. Africa 25°31S 26°4E 270 C4
Ẓefat Israel 32°58N 35°29E 250 F6
Zegdou Algeria 29°51N 4°45W 260 C4
Zege Ethiopia 11°43N 37°18E 257 E4
Zeggerene, Iracher Mali 16°49N 2°16E 263 B5
Zégoua Mali 10°32N 5°35W 262 C3
Zehak Iran 30°53N 61°42E 247 D9
Zehden = Cedynia Poland 52°53N 14°12E 185 F1
Zehdenick Germany 52°58N 13°20E 178 C9
Zehlendorf Germany 52°26N 13°16E 115 B2
Zeigler U.S.A. 37°54N 89°3W 310 G7
Zeil, Mt. Australia 23°30S 132°23E 278 D5
Zeila = Saylac Somali Rep. 11°21N 43°30E 267 B5
Zeist Neths. 52°5N 5°15E 170 B5
Zeitz Germany 51°2N 12°7E 178 D8
Zejtun Malta 35°51N 14°32E 206 F8
Żelechów Poland 51°49N 21°54E 185 G8
Zelena Ukraine 48°3N 24°45E 183 B9
Zelengora Bos.-H. 43°22N 18°30E 202 C2
Zelenodolsk Russia 55°55N 48°30E 190 C9
Zelenogorsk Russia 60°12N 29°43E 188 B5
Zelenograd Russia 56°1N 37°12E 188 D9
Zelenogradsk Russia 54°53N 20°29E 184 D7
Zelenokumsk Russia 44°24N 44°0E 191 H6
Zeleqa, W. → Egypt 29°7N 34°31E 251 J5
Železná Ruda Czech Rep. 49°8N 13°15E 180 B6
Železnik Serbia 44°43N 20°23E 202 B4
Zelfana Algeria 32°27N 4°15E 261 B5
Zelienople U.S.A. 40°48N 80°8W 312 F4
Želiezovce Slovak Rep. 48°3N 18°40E 181 C11
Zelina Croatia 45°57N 16°16E 199 C13
Zell Baden-W., Germany 47°42N 7°52E 179 H3
Zell Rhld-Pfz., Germany 50°1N 7°10E 179 E3
Zell am See Austria 47°19N 12°47E 180 D5
Zella-Mehlis Germany 50°39N 10°40E 178 E6
Zelmen = Rovnoye Russia 50°52N 46°3E 190 E8
Zelów Poland 51°28N 19°14E 185 G6
Zeltweg Austria 47°11N 14°45E 180 D7
Zelyony Dol = Zelenodolsk Russia 55°55N 48°30E 190 C9
Žemaitijos △ Lithuania 56°2N 21°55E 184 B8
Zembra, I. Tunisia 37°5N 10°56E 258 A2
Zemgale = Jelgava Latvia 56°41N 23°49E 184 B10
Zémio C.A.R. 5°2N 25°5E 264 A5
Zemlya Imperatora Nikolaya II = Severnaya Zemlya Russia 79°0N 100°0E 215 B11
Zemmora Algeria 35°44N 0°51E 261 A5
Zemmur W. Sahara 25°5N 12°0W 260 C2
Zemongo △ C.A.R. 6°45N 25°5E 264 A5
Zemoul, O. → Algeria 29°15N 7°0W 260 C3
Zempelburg = Sępólno Krajeńskie Poland 53°26N 17°30E 184 E4
Zempléni-hegység Hungary 48°25N 21°25E 182 B6
Zemplinska šírava Slovak Rep. 48°48N 22°0E 181 C15
Zempoala Mexico 19°27N 96°23W 319 D5
Zemun Serbia 44°51N 20°25E 202 B4
Zendeh Jān Afghan. 34°21N 61°45E 240 B1
Zengbé Cameroon 5°46N 13°4E 263 D7
Zengcheng China 23°13N 113°52E 229 F9
Zenica Bos.-H. 44°10N 17°57E 182 F2
Zenne → Belgium 51°4N 4°26E 116 A2
Zentsūji Japan 34°14N 133°47E 222 C5
Zenza → Angola 8°45S 13°24E 265 D2
Zenza do Itombe Angola 9°16S 14°13E 265 D2
Žepče Bos.-H. 44°28N 18°2E 182 F3
Zephyr Field U.S.A. 30°1N 90°5W 131 B1
Zephyrhills U.S.A. 28°14N 82°11W 317 G7
Zepu China 38°11N 77°16E 217 E9
Zeraf, Bahr ez → Sudan 9°42N 30°52E 257 F3
Żerań Poland 52°18N 20°58E 142 B1
Zerbst Germany 51°58N 12°5E 178 D8
Zerhamra Algeria 29°58N 2°30W 260 C4
Żerków Poland 52°4N 17°32E 185 F4
Zermatt Switz. 46°2N 7°46E 179 J3
Zernez Switz. 46°42N 10°7E 179 J6
Zernograd Russia 46°52N 40°19E 191 G5
Zernovoy = Zernograd Russia 46°52N 40°19E 191 G5
Zero Milestone Washington, D.C., U.S.A. 143 b1
Zerqan Albania 41°27N 20°20E 202 E4
Zerzeń Poland 52°12N 21°7E 142 B2
Zestaponi Georgia 42°6N 43°0E 191 J6
Zetel Germany 53°25N 7°58E 178 B3
Zetland = Shetland □ U.K. 60°30N 1°30W 167 A7
Zeulenroda Germany 50°39N 11°59E 178 E7
Zévallos Guadeloupe 16°18N 61°17W 322 e
Zeven Germany 53°17N 9°16E 178 B5
Zevenaar Neths. 51°56N 6°5E 170 C6
Zévio Italy 45°22N 11°8E 198 C8
Zeya Russia 53°48N 127°14E 215 D13
Zeya → Russia 51°42N 128°53E 215 D13
Zeyne Turkey 36°25N 33°31E 250 B4
Zeytinbağı Turkey 40°24N 28°47E 203 F12
Zeytinburnu Turkey 40°58N 28°53E 122 C1
Zeytindağ Turkey 38°58N 27°4E 205 C9
Zghartā Lebanon 34°21N 35°53E 250 D6
Zgierz Poland 51°50N 19°27E 185 G6
Zgorzelec Poland 51°10N 15°0E 185 G2
Zgurița Moldova 48°8N 28°1E 183 B13
Zhabei China 31°16N 121°26E 138 B1
Zhabinka Belarus 52°13N 24°2E 185 F11
Zhabokrych Ukraine 48°23N 28°59E 183 B13
Zhalagash Kazakhstan 45°5N 64°40E 216 C6
Zhalpaqtal Kazakhstan 49°42N 49°25E 190 F9
Zhaltyr Kazakhstan 51°37N 69°49E 217 B7
Zhambyl = Taraz Kazakhstan 42°54N 71°22E 217 D8
Zhambyl □ Kazakhstan 44°0N 72°0E 217 D8
Zhanatas Kazakhstan 43°35N 69°35E 217 D7
Zhangaly Kazakhstan 47°1N 50°37E 191 G10
Zhangaözen Kazakhstan 43°18N 52°48E 187 F9
Zhangaqala Kazakhstan 48°56N 49°36E 191 F9
Zhangaqazaly Kazakhstan 45°48N 62°6E 216 C6
Zhangatas = Zhanatas Kazakhstan 43°35N 69°35E 217 D7
Zhangbei China 41°10N 114°45E 226 D8
Zhangguangcai Ling China 45°0N 129°0E 227 B15
Zhangjiabian China 22°33N 113°28E 219 F9
Zhangjiagang China 31°55N 120°30E 229 B13
Zhangjiakou China 40°48N 114°55E 226 D8
Zhangping China 25°17N 117°23E 229 E11
Zhangpu China 24°8N 117°35E 229 E11
Zhangshu China 28°4N 115°29E 229 C10
Zhangwu China 42°43N 123°52E 227 C12
Zhangye China 38°50N 100°23E 218 C5
Zhangzhou China 24°30N 117°35E 229 E11
Zhanhua China 37°40N 118°8E 227 F10
Zhänibek Kazakhstan 49°25N 46°50E 190 F8
Zhanjiang China 21°15N 110°20E 229 G8
Zhannetty, Ostrov Russia 76°43N 158°0E 215 B16
Zhanyi China 25°38N 103°48E 228 E4
Zhanyu China 44°30N 122°30E 227 B12
Zhao Xian China 37°43N 114°45E 226 F8
Zhao'an China 23°41N 117°10E 229 F11
Zhaocheng China 36°22N 111°38E 226 F6
Zhaojue China 28°1N 102°49E 228 C4
Zhaoping China 24°11N 110°48E 229 E8
Zhaoqing China 23°0N 112°20E 229 F9
Zhaotong China 27°20N 103°44E 228 D4
Zhaoyuan Heilongjiang, China 45°27N 125°0E 227 B13
Zhaoyuan Shandong, China 37°20N 120°23E 227 F11
Zhari Namco China 31°6N 85°36E 218 C3
Zharkent Kazakhstan 44°10N 80°0E 217 D10
Zharkovskiy Russia 55°56N 32°19E 188 E7
Zhashkiv Ukraine 49°15N 30°5E 177 D16
Zhashui China 33°40N 109°8E 226 H5
Zhaslyk Uzbekistan 43°58N 57°10E 216 D5
Zhayrang Kazakhstan 48°20N 70°10E 217 C8
Zhayylma Kazakhstan 51°37N 61°33E 216 B6
Zhayyq → Kazakhstan 47°0N 51°48E 187 E9
Zhdanov = Mariupol Ukraine 47°5N 37°31E 189 J9
Zhdanov Russia 55°44N 37°41E 129 B2
Zhecheng China 34°7N 115°20E 226 G8
Zhegao China 31°46N 117°45E 229 B11
Zhejiang □ China 29°0N 120°0E 229 C13
Zheleznodorozhnyy = Qŭnghirot Uzbekistan 43°2N 58°50E 216 D5
Zheleznodorozhnyy Kaliningrad, Russia 54°22N 21°19E 184 D8
Zheleznodorozhnyy Komi, Russia 62°35N 50°55E 186 B9
Zheleznodorozhnyy Moskva, Russia 55°45N 38°0E 129 B6
Zheleznogorsk Russia 52°22N 35°23E 189 F8
Zheleznogorsk-Ilimskiy Russia 56°34N 104°8E 215 D11
Zheltyye Vody = Zhovti Vody Ukraine 48°21N 33°31E 189 H7
Zhen'an China 33°27N 109°9E 226 H5
Zhenba China 32°34N 107°58E 228 A6
Zhenfeng China 25°22N 105°40E 228 E5
Zheng'an China 28°32N 107°27E 228 C6
Zhengding China 38°8N 114°32E 226 E8
Zhenghe China 27°20N 118°50E 229 D12
Zhengyang China 32°37N 114°22E 229 A10
Zhengyangguan China 32°30N 116°29E 229 A11
Zhengzhou China 34°45N 113°34E 226 G7
Zhenhai China 29°59N 121°42E 229 C13
Zhenjiang China 32°11N 119°26E 229 A12
Zhenkang China 23°58N 99°0E 228 F2
Zhenlai China 45°50N 123°5E 227 B12
Zhenning China 26°4N 105°45E 228 D5
Zhenping Henan, China 33°10N 112°16E 226 H7
Zhenping Shaanxi, China 31°59N 109°31E 228 B7
Zhenru China 31°16N 121°22E 138 B1
Zhenxiong China 27°27N 104°50E 228 D5
Zhenyuan Gansu, China 35°35N 107°30E 226 G4
Zhenyuan Guizhou, China 27°4N 108°21E 228 D7
Zherdevka Russia 51°56N 41°29E 190 E5
Zherebkove Ukraine 47°50N 29°52E 183 C14
Zhernovka Russia 59°56N 30°30E 137 B2
Zherong China 27°15N 119°52E 229 D12
Zhetiqara Kazakhstan 52°11N 61°12E 216 B6
Zhezdi Kazakhstan 48°3N 67°3E 217 C7
Zhezqazghan Kazakhstan 47°44N 67°40E 217 C7
Zhicheng China 30°25N 111°27E 229 B8
Zhicun China 23°0N 113°18E 121 B2
Zhidan China 36°48N 108°48E 226 F5
Zhigansk Russia 66°48N 123°27E 215 C13
Zhigulevsk Russia 53°28N 49°30E 190 D9
Zhijiang Hubei, China 30°28N 111°45E 229 B8
Zhijiang Hunan, China 27°27N 109°42E 228 D7
Zhijin China 26°37N 105°45E 228 D5
Zhilinda Russia 70°0N 114°20E 215 C12
Zhilino Russia 54°54N 21°54E 184 D8
Zhirnovsk Russia 50°57N 44°49E 190 E7
Zhirnovsky = Zhirnovsk Russia 50°57N 44°49E 190 E7
Zhirnoye = Zhirnovsk Russia 50°57N 44°49E 190 E7
Zhitomir = Zhytomyr Ukraine 50°20N 28°40E 177 C15
Zhizdra Russia 53°45N 34°40E 188 F8
Zhlobin Belarus 52°55N 30°0E 177 B16
Zhmerynka Ukraine 49°2N 28°2E 177 D15
Zhob Pakistan 31°20N 69°31E 242 D3
Zhob → Pakistan 32°4N 69°50E 242 C3
Zhodzina Belarus 54°5N 28°17E 177 A15
Zhokhova, Ostrov Russia 76°4N 152°40E 215 B16
Zholkev = Nesterov Ukraine 50°4N 23°58E 177 C12
Zholkva = Nesterov Ukraine 50°4N 23°58E 177 C12
Zhongdian China 27°48N 99°42E 228 D2
Zhongdong China 22°48N 107°47E 228 F6
Zhongdu China 24°40N 109°40E 228 E7
Zhongguancun China 39°59N 116°18E 114 B1
Zhongning China 37°29N 105°40E 226 F3
Zhongshan Antarctica 69°0S 39°50E 151 C6
Zhongshan Guangdong, China 22°26N 113°20E 219 G9
Zhongshan Guangxi Zhuangzu, China 24°29N 111°18E 229 E8
Zhongshan Park Beijing, China 114 c3
Zhongshan Park Shanghai, China 31°13N 121°24E 138 B1
Zhongshankong China 22°35N 113°29E 219 F9
Zhongtiao Shan China 35°0N 111°10E 226 G6
Zhongwei China 37°30N 105°12E 226 F3
Zhongxiang China 31°12N 112°34E 229 B9
Zhongyang China 37°20N 111°11E 226 F6
Zhorany Ukraine 51°19N 23°58E 185 G10
Zhosaly Kazakhstan 45°29N 64°4E 216 C6
Zhoucun Guangdong, China 23°11N 113°11E 121 A2
Zhoucun Shandong, China 36°47N 117°48E 227 F9
Zhoujiadu China 31°11N 121°29E 138 B1
Zhoujiazhen China 31°16N 121°33E 138 B2
Zhouning China 27°12N 119°20E 229 D12
Zhoushan China 30°1N 122°6E 229 B14
Zhoushan Dao China 30°5N 122°10E 229 C14
Zhouzhi China 34°10N 108°12E 226 G5
Zhouzhuangzi China 39°51N 116°16E 114 B1
Zhovti Vody Ukraine 48°21N 33°31E 189 H7
Zhovtneve Lubelskie, Ukraine 50°42N 24°12E 185 H11
Zhovtneve Mykolayiv, Ukraine 46°54N 32°3E 189 J7
Zhu Jiang → China 22°45N 113°37E 229 F9
Zhuanghe China 39°40N 123°0E 224 C1
Zhucheng China 36°0N 119°27E 227 G10
Zhugqu China 33°40N 104°30E 226 H3
Zhuhai China 22°17N 113°34E 219 G10
Zhuji China 29°40N 120°10E 229 C13
Zhujiang Kou China 22°20N 113°45E 219 G10
Zhukovka Russia 53°35N 33°50E 188 F7
Zhulebino Russia 55°42N 37°50E 129 B5
Zhumadian China 32°59N 114°2E 226 H8
Zhuo Xian = Zhuozhou China 39°28N 115°58E 226 E8
Zhuolu China 40°20N 115°12E 226 D8
Zhuozhou China 39°28N 115°58E 226 E8
Zhuozi China 41°0N 112°25E 226 D7
Zhushadi China 23°11N 113°22E 121 A3
Zhushan China 32°15N 110°13E 229 A8
Zhuxi China 32°25N 109°40E 228 A7
Zhuzhou China 27°49N 113°12E 229 D9
Zhvanets Ukraine 48°33N 26°30E 183 B11
Zhympity Kazakhstan 50°16N 52°35E 216 B4
Zhytomyr Ukraine 50°20N 28°40E 177 C15
Zhytomyr □ Ukraine 50°50N 28°10E 189 G5
Zi Shui → China 28°40N 112°40E 229 C9
Žiar nad Hronom Slovak Rep. 48°35N 18°53E 181 C11
Ziarat Pakistan 30°25N 67°49E 242 D2
Zibo China 36°47N 118°3E 227 F10
Zichang China 37°18N 109°40E 226 F5
Zidarovo Bulgaria 42°20N 27°24E 203 D11
Zidi = Wandhari Pakistan 27°42N 66°48E 242 F2
Ziębice Poland 50°37N 17°2E 185 H4
Ziebingen = Cybinka Poland 52°12N 14°46E 185 F1
Ziegenhals = Głuchołazy Poland 50°19N 17°24E 185 H4
Zielenzig = Sulęcin Poland 52°26N 15°10E 185 F2
Zielona Poland 52°14N 21°11E 142 B3
Zielona Góra Poland 51°57N 15°31E 185 G2
Zielonka Poland 52°18N 21°9E 142 B2
Zierikzee Neths. 51°40N 3°55E 170 C3
Ziesar Germany 52°16N 12°17E 178 C8
Zifta Egypt 30°43N 31°14E 256 H7
Zighan Libya 25°29N 22°8E 258 C4
Zigon Burma 18°20N 95°37E 241 F5
Zigong China 29°15N 104°48E 228 C5
Ziguéy Chad 14°43N 15°50E 259 F3
Ziguinchor Senegal 12°35N 16°20W 262 C1
Ziguinchor □ Senegal 12°45N 16°20W 262 C1
Zihuatanejo Mexico 17°39N 101°33W 318 D4
Zijin China 23°33N 115°8E 229 F10
Zile Turkey 40°15N 35°52E 212 B6
Žilina Slovak Rep. 49°12N 18°42E 181 B11
Žilinský □ Slovak Rep. 49°10N 19°0E 181 B12
Zillah Libya 28°30N 17°33E 258 C3
Zillertaler Alpen Austria 47°6N 11°45E 180 D4
Zima Russia 54°0N 102°5E 215 D11
Zimapán Mexico 20°45N 99°21W 319 C5
Zimba Zambia 17°20S 26°11E 269 F2
Zimbabwe Zimbabwe 20°16S 30°54E 269 G3
Zimbabwe ■ Africa 19°0S 30°0E 269 F3
Zimmi S. Leone 7°20N 11°20W 262 D2
Zimnicea Romania 43°40N 25°22E 183 G10
Zimovniki Russia 47°10N 42°25E 191 G6
Zina Cameroon 11°19N 14°54E 259 F2
Zinave △ Mozam. 21°35S 33°40E 271 B5
Zinder Niger 13°48N 9°0E 259 F1
Zinder □ Niger 15°0N 10°30E 263 C7
Zinga C.A.R. 3°49N 18°34E 264 B3
Zinga Tanzania 9°16S 38°49E 269 D4
Zingaro △ Italy 38°6N 12°53E 200 D5
Zingst Germany 54°26N 12°39E 178 A8
Ziniaré Burkina Faso 12°35N 1°18W 263 C4
Zinnowitz Germany 54°4N 13°54E 178 A9
Zinovyevsk = Kirovohrad Ukraine 48°35N 32°20E 189 H7
Zion St. Kitts & Nevis 17°8N 62°33W 322 d
Zion Ill., U.S.A. 42°27N 87°50W 311 B9
Zion △ U.S.A. 37°15N 113°5W 305 H7
Zionsville U.S.A. 39°57N 86°16W 311 E10
Zipaquirá Colombia 5°0N 74°0W 328 C3
Zirbitzkogel Austria 47°4N 14°34E 180 D7
Zirc Hungary 47°17N 17°52E 182 C2
Žiri Slovenia 46°5N 14°5E 199 B11
Žirje Croatia 43°39N 15°42E 199 E12
Zirke = Sieraków Poland 52°39N 16°2E 185 F3
Zirl Austria 47°17N 11°14E 180 D4
Zirndorf Germany 49°27N 10°57E 179 F6
Ziros Greece 35°5N 26°8E 207 E7
Zirreh, Gowd-e Afghan. 29°45N 62°0E 240 C1
Zisterdorf Austria 48°33N 16°45E 181 C9
Zitácuaro Mexico 19°24N 100°22W 318 D4
Žitava → Slovak Rep. 48°14N 18°21E 181 C11
Žitište Serbia 45°30N 20°32E 182 E5
Zitong China 31°37N 105°10E 228 B5
Zitsa Greece 39°47N 20°40E 204 B2
Zittau Germany 50°53N 14°48E 178 E10
Zitundo Mozam. 26°48S 32°47E 271 C5
Živinice Bos.-H. 44°27N 18°36E 182 F3
Ziwa Maghariba = Kagera □ Tanzania 2°0S 31°30E 268 C3
Ziway Ethiopia 7°56N 38°43E 266 C4
Ziway, L. Ethiopia 8°0N 38°50E 257 F4
Zixi China 27°45N 117°4E 229 D11
Zixing China 25°59N 113°21E 229 E9
Ziyang Shaanxi, China 32°32N 108°31E 226 H5
Ziyang Sichuan, China 30°6N 104°40E 228 B5
Ziyuan China 26°2N 110°40E 229 D8
Ziyun China 25°45N 106°5E 228 E6
Ziz, Oued → Morocco 31°40N 4°15W 260 B4
Zizhong China 29°48N 104°47E 228 C5
Zizhuyuan Park China 39°54N 116°18E 114 B1
Žižkov Czech Rep. 50°5N 14°28E 135 B2
Zizur Mayor Spain 42°47N 1°41W 196 C3
Zlarin Croatia 43°42N 15°49E 199 E12
Zlatar Croatia 46°5N 16°3E 199 B13
Zlatar Serbia 43°25N 19°47E 202 C3
Zlataritsa Bulgaria 43°2N 25°55E 203 C9
Zlaté Moravce Slovak Rep. 48°23N 18°24E 181 C11
Zlatibor Serbia 43°45N 19°43E 202 C3
Zlatitsa Bulgaria 42°41N 24°7E 203 D8
Zlatna Romania 46°8N 23°11E 183 D8
Zlatna Panega Bulgaria 43°5N 24°9E 203 C8
Zlatni Pyasŭtsi Bulgaria 43°18N 28°3E 203 C12
Zlatograd Bulgaria 41°22N 25°7E 203 E9
Zlatoust Russia 55°10N 59°40E 186 D10
Zletovo Macedonia 41°59N 22°17E 202 E6
Zličín Czech Rep. 50°3N 14°17E 135 B1
Zlín Czech Rep. 49°14N 17°40E 181 B10
Zlínský □ Czech Rep. 49°20N 17°40E 181 B10
Zliṭan Libya 32°32N 14°35E 258 B2
Złocieniec Poland 53°30N 16°1E 184 E3
Złoczew Poland 51°24N 18°35E 185 G5
Zlot Serbia 44°1N 21°58E 202 B5
Złotoryja Poland 51°8N 15°55E 185 G2
Złotów Poland 53°22N 17°2E 184 E4
Zmeinogorsk Kazakhstan 51°10N 82°13E 217 B10
Żmigród Poland 51°28N 16°53E 185 G3
Zmiyev Ukraine 49°39N 36°27E 189 H9
Znamenka = Znamyanka Ukraine 48°45N 32°30E 189 H7
Znamensk Russia 54°36N 21°16E 184 D8
Znamyanka Ukraine 48°45N 32°30E 189 H7
Żnin Poland 52°51N 17°44E 185 F4
Znojmo Czech Rep. 48°50N 16°2E 180 C9
Zobeyrī Iran 34°10N 46°40E 246 C5
Zobia Dem. Rep. of the Congo 3°0N 25°59E 268 B2
Zobten = Sobótka Poland 50°54N 16°44E 185 H3
Zócalo Mexico City, Mexico 128 b3
Zoetermeer Neths. 52°3N 4°30E 170 B4
Zogang China 29°55N 97°42E 228 C1
Zogno Italy 45°48N 9°40E 198 C6
Zogqên China 32°13N 98°47E 228 A2
Zografou Greece 37°58N 23°47E 112 B2
Zohreh → Iran 30°16N 51°15E 247 D6
Zolfo Springs U.S.A. 27°30N 81°48W 317 H8
Żoliborz Poland 52°16N 20°57E 142 B1
Zolochiv Ukraine 49°45N 24°51E 177 D13
Zolotonosha Ukraine 49°39N 32°5E 189 H7
Zolotyy Potik Ukraine 48°54N 25°20E 183 B10
Zomba Malawi 15°22S 35°19E 269 F4
Zongo Dem. Rep. of the Congo 4°20N 18°35E 264 B3
Zonguldak Turkey 41°28N 31°50E 212 B4
Zonguldak □ Turkey 41°20N 31°45E 212 B4
Zongyang China 30°42N 117°12E 229 B11
Zonnebloem S. Africa 33°56S 18°26E 118 A1
Zonqor Pt. Malta 35°52N 14°34E 206 F8
Zonza France 41°45N 9°11E 175 G13
Zoo Baba Niger 18°13N 13°2E 259 E2
Zorgo Burkina Faso 12°15N 0°35W 263 C4
Zorita Spain 39°17N 5°39W 195 F5
Zorleni Romania 46°14N 27°44E 183 D12
Zornitsa Bulgaria 42°23N 26°58E 203 D10
Zorritos Peru 3°43S 80°40W 330 A1
Żory Poland 50°3N 18°44E 185 H5
Zorzor Liberia 7°46N 9°28W 262 D3
Zossen Germany 52°13N 13°27E 178 C9
Zou Xiang China 35°30N 116°58E 226 G9
Zouan-Hounien Ivory C. 6°55N 8°15W 262 D3
Zouar Chad 20°30N 16°32E 259 D3
Zouérate = Zouîrât Mauritania 22°44N 12°21W 260 D2
Zouîrât Mauritania 22°44N 12°21W 260 D2
Zouri Gabon 1°1S 8°53E 264 C1
Zourika Niger 19°16N 7°52E 259 E1
Zourma Burkina Faso 11°20N 0°50W 263 C4
Zousfana, O. → Algeria 31°28N 2°17W 261 B4
Zoutkamp Neths. 53°20N 6°18E 170 A6
Zrenjanin Serbia 45°22N 20°23E 182 E5
Zuarungu Ghana 10°49N 0°46W 263 C4
Zuatá → Venezuela 7°52N 65°22W 329 B4
Zuba Nigeria 9°11N 7°12E 263 D6
Zubayr Yemen 15°3N 42°10E 248 D3
Zubin Potok Kosovo 42°54N 20°41E 202 D4
Zubtsov Russia 56°10N 34°34E 188 D8
Zudañez Bolivia 19°6S 64°44W 331 D5
Zuénoula Ivory C. 7°34N 6°3W 262 D3
Zuera Spain 41°51N 0°49W 196 D4
Zuetina = Az Zuwaytīnah Libya 30°58N 20°7E 258 B4
Ẓufār Oman 17°40N 54°0E 249 C6
Zug Switz. 47°10N 8°31E 179 H4
Zug W. Sahara 21°36N 14°9W 260 D2
Zugdidi Georgia 42°30N 41°55E 191 J5
Zugersee Switz. 47°7N 8°35E 179 H4
Zugliget Hungary 47°30N 18°59E 117 B1
Zugló Hungary 47°31N 19°8E 117 A2
Zugspitze Germany 47°25N 10°59E 179 H6
Zuhd, J. az Si. Arabia 28°20N 35°17E 251 K6
Zuid-Holland □ Neths. 52°0N 4°35E 170 C4
Zuidbeveland Neths. 51°30N 3°50E 170 C3
Zuiderwoude Neths. 52°26N 5°2E 112 A3
Zuidhorn Neths. 53°15N 6°23E 170 A6
Zújar Spain 37°34N 2°50W 195 H8
Zújar → Spain 39°1N 5°47W 195 G5
Żukowo Poland 54°21N 18°22E 184 D5
Zula Eritrea 15°17N 39°40E 257 D4
Zulia □ Venezuela 10°0N 72°10W 328 B3
Züllichau = Sulechów Poland 52°5N 15°40E 185 F2
Zülpich Germany 50°41N 6°39E 178 E2
Zülz = Biała Poland 50°24N 17°40E 185 H4
Zumaia Spain 43°19N 2°15W 196 B2
Zumárraga Spain 43°5N 2°19W 196 B2
Zumbi Brazil 22°49S 43°10W 135 A1
Zumbo Mozam. 15°35S 30°26E 269 F3
Zummo Nigeria 9°51N 12°59E 263 D7
Zumpango Mexico 19°48N 99°6W 319 D5
Zunderdorp Neths. 52°24N 4°58E 112 A2
Zundi Angola 10°28S 16°8E 265 E3
Zungeru Nigeria 9°48N 6°8E 263 D6
Zunhua China 40°18N 117°58E 227 D9
Zuni Pueblo U.S.A. 35°4N 108°51W 305 J9
Zunyi China 27°42N 106°53E 228 D6
Zuo Jiang → China 22°50N 108°6E 228 F6
Zuozhou China 22°42N 107°27E 228 F6
Županja Croatia 45°4N 18°43E 182 E3
Žur Kosovo 42°13N 20°34E 202 D4
Zurbātīyah Iraq 33°9N 46°3E 213 F12
Zürich Switz. 47°22N 8°32E 179 H4
Zürich □ Switz. 47°26N 8°40E 179 H4
Zürichsee Switz. 47°18N 8°40E 179 H4
Żuromin Poland 53°4N 19°51E 185 E6
Zurrieq Malta 35°50N 14°28E 206 F7
Žut Croatia 43°52N 15°17E 199 E12
Zutphen Neths. 52°9N 6°12E 170 B6
Zuurberg △ S. Africa 33°12S 25°32E 270 D4
Zuvuvu → Brazil 23°40S 46°42W 137 C1
Zuwārah Libya 32°58N 12°1E 258 B2
Zūzan Iran 34°22N 59°53E 247 C8
Žužemberk Slovenia 45°52N 14°56E 199 C11
Zvanka = Volkhov Russia 59°55N 32°15E 188 C7
Zvečan Kosovo 42°54N 20°50E 202 D4
Zvenigorodka = Zvenyhorodka Ukraine 49°4N 30°56E 189 H6
Zvenyhorodka Ukraine 49°4N 30°56E 189 H6
Zvezdets Bulgaria 42°6N 27°26E 203 D11
Zvishavane Zimbabwe 20°17S 30°2E 269 G3
Zvolen Slovak Rep. 48°33N 19°10E 181 C12
Zvonce Serbia 42°57N 22°34E 202 D6
Zvornik Bos.-H. 44°26N 19°5E 182 F4
Zwanenburg Neths. 52°23N 4°45E 112 A1
Zwedru = Tchien Liberia 5°59N 8°15W 262 D3
Zweibrücken Germany 49°15N 7°21E 179 F3
Zwenkau Germany 51°13N 12°20E 178 D8
Zwettl Austria 48°35N 15°9E 180 C8
Zwickau Germany 50°44N 12°30E 178 E8
Zwierzyniec Poland 50°36N 22°58E 185 H9
Zwiesel Germany 49°1N 13°13E 179 F9
Zwittau = Svitavy Czech Rep. 49°47N 16°28E 181 B9
Zwoleń Poland 51°21N 21°35E 185 G8
Zwölfaxing Austria 48°6N 16°28E 142 B2
Zwolle Neths. 52°31N 6°6E 170 B6
Zwolle La., U.S.A. 31°38N 93°39W 314 F8
Żychlin Poland 52°15N 19°37E 185 F6
Żyrardów Poland 52°3N 20°28E 185 F7
Zyryan Kazakhstan 49°43N 84°20E 217 C10
Zyryanka Russia 65°45N 150°51E 215 C16
Zyryanovsk = Zyryan Kazakhstan 49°43N 84°20E 217 C10
Zyuzino Russia 55°39N 37°34E 129 C3
Żywiec Poland 49°42N 19°10E 185 J6

KEY TO EUROPEAN MAP PAGES

▨	Large scale maps (>1:3 900 000)
■	Medium scale maps (1:4 000 000 – 1:7 900 000)
■	Small scale maps (<1:8 000 000)
● Paris p134	City maps

155 ICELAND

WORLD COUNTRY INDEX

Country	Page
Afghanistan	240
Albania	202
Algeria	260–261
Angola	265
Argentina	334, 336
Armenia	213
Australia	278–283
Austria	180–181
Azerbaijan	213
Azores	153
Bahamas	320–321
Bahrain	249
Bangladesh	241
Barbados	322
Belarus	188–189
Belgium	170
Belize	320
Benin	263
Bhutan	241
Bolivia	330–331
Bosnia-Herzegovina	198, 202
Botswana	270
Brazil	328–335
Brunei	235
Bulgaria	202–203
Burkina Faso	262–263
Burma (Myanmar)	236–237, 241
Burundi	268
Cambodia	236–237
Canary Is.	153
Cameroon	259, 264
Canada	294–299
Cape Verde Is.	153
Central African Republic	264
Chad	259
Chile	330, 334, 336
China	218–219, 226–229
Colombia	328
Comoros	272
Congo	264–265
Congo, Dem. Rep. of the	264–265, 268–269
Costa Rica	320
Croatia	182, 199
Cuba	320–321
Cyprus	207
Czech Republic	180–181
Denmark	163
Djibouti	267
Dominican Republic	321
Ecuador	328
Egypt	256
El Salvador	320
England	168–169
Equatorial Guinea	264
Eritrea	266–267
Estonia	188
Ethiopia	266–267
Fiji	287
Finland	160–161
France	172–175
French Guiana	329
Gabon	264
Gambia	262
Georgia	213

Country	Page
Germany	178–179
Ghana	262–263
Greece	202–205
Greenland	154
Guadeloupe	322
Guatemala	320
Guinea	262
Guinea-Bissau	262
Guyana	329
Haiti	321
Honduras	320
Hungary	182
Iceland	155
India	241, 242–245
Indonesia	230–231, 234–235
Iran	246–247
Iraq	246–247
Irish Republic	166
Israel	250–251
Italy	198–201
Ivory Coast	262
Jamaica	320
Japan	220–223
Jordan	251
Kazakhstan	216–217
Kenya	268
Korea, North	224
Korea, South	224
Kosovo	202
Kuwait	246–247
Kyrgyzstan	217
Laos	236
Latvia	188
Lebanon	250
Lesotho	271
Liberia	262
Libya	258
Lithuania	188
Luxembourg	170
Macedonia	202
Madagascar	272
Malawi	269
Malaysia	234–235
Mali	260–263
Malta	206
Martinique	322
Mauritania	260, 262
Mauritius	272
Mexico	318–319
Moldova	183
Mongolia	218–219
Montenegro	202
Morocco	260–261
Mozambique	269, 271
Namibia	270
Nepal	243
Netherlands	170
New Zealand	284–285
Nicaragua	320
Niger	259, 263
Nigeria	263
Northern Ireland	166
Norway	160–161, 164

Country	Page
Oman	249
Pakistan	240
Panama	320
Papua New Guinea	286
Paraguay	334–335
Peru	328, 330
Philippines	232–233
Poland	184–185
Portugal	194–195
Puerto Rico	321
Qatar	249
Réunion	272
Romania	182–183
Russia	186–191, 214–215
Rwanda	268
St. Lucia	322
Samoa	287
Saudi Arabia	246–249
Scotland	167
Senegal	262
Serbia	182, 202
Seychelles	272
Sierra Leone	262
Singapore	237
Slovak Republic	181
Slovenia	199
Solomon Is.	287
Somali Republic	267
South Africa	270–271
Spain	194–197
Sri Lanka	245
Sudan	256–257
Suriname	329
Swaziland	271
Sweden	160–163
Switzerland	179
Syria	212–213
Taiwan	225
Tajikistan	217
Tanzania	268–269
Thailand	236–237
Togo	263
Tonga	287
Trinidad and Tobago	323
Tunisia	261
Turkey	212–213
Turkmenistan	216–217
Uganda	268
Ukraine	189
United Arab Emirates	249
United Kingdom	166–169
USA	300–317
Uruguay	334–335
Uzbekistan	216–217
Vanuatu	287
Venezuela	328–329
Vietnam	236–237
Wales	168–169
Yemen	248–249
Zambia	265, 269
Zimbabwe	269

Arctic Circle

160 Færoe Is.

165

167 Shetland Is.

167 Orkney Is.

168 Edinburgh p121

166

UNITED KINGDOM

176

170

Dublin p120

IRELAND

Am

NE

192

171 London p125

172

○ Paris

174 FRANC

194

196

ANDORRA

Barcelona p114

PORTUGAL

SPAIN

Madrid p127

Lisbon p126

206 Balearic

ALGE